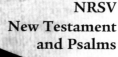
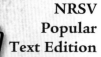

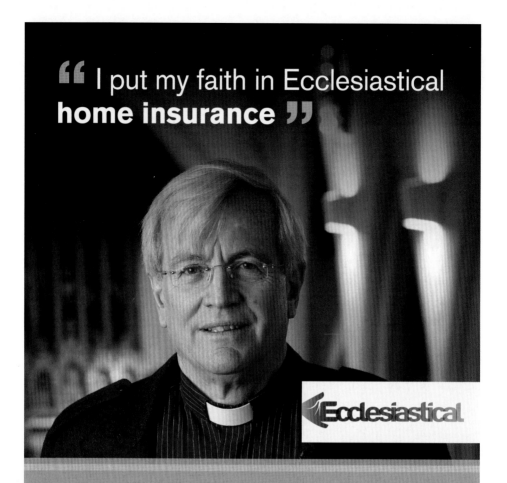

LOVE T~~HY~~ every NEIGHBOUR

Jesus calls us to love our neighbour – and not just the ones next door. We're all made in God's image, which means the whole world is our neighbourhood, and every person in it is precious. But sadly, many of our global neighbours go without the basics of life.

Christian Aid Week unites more than 20,000 churches across Britain and Ireland to challenge this injustice. We'll be knocking on our neighbours' doors to collect envelopes, organising church collections, inviting our community round for fundraising breakfasts and doing a whole host of other fun things to demonstrate God's love for the poor.

Will you join us?

caweek.org

christian **aid** week

We believe in life before death

English Clergy Association

Founded 1938
www.clergyassoc.co.uk

Patron: The Rt. Rev'd and Rt. Hon. The Lord Bishop of London;
President: Professor Sir Anthony Milnes Coates, Bt., B.Sc., M.D,. F.R.C.P.
Parliamentary Vice-Presidents: The Rt. Hon. The Lord Cormack, F.S.A.

**The Association seeks to be a Church of England
mutual resource and support for clergy (with
Freehold or on Common Tenure) patrons and
churchwardens requiring information or insight.
Donations to the *Benefit Fund* provide Clergy Holidays:
Gifts, Legacies, Church Collections much appreciated.
Registered Charity No. 258559**

Tuesday 17th May 2016 2p.m.
Bishop Josiah Idowu-Fearon
Secretary General of the Anglican Communion
who will also preside at the service of Holy Communion at 12.45pm

St. Giles-in-the-Fields, London
(St. Giles High St. Tottenham Court Road tube)

p.m.smith@exeter.ac.uk for Membership enquiries
4 St John's Road, Windsor, SL4 3QN

Buffet lunch upon reservation

Annual Address usually printed in the
Members' journal *Parson & Parish*.

THE PRAYER BOOK SOCIETY exists to promote the use of the Book of Common Prayer and to defend the worship and doctrine contained therein. Diocesan branches provide members with regular meetings, Prayer Book services and advice on church matters. PBS also runs the yearly Cranmer Awards for young people.

It has a popular mail order book company stocking a wide range of religious books and Christmas cards.

Donations are needed and appreciated. Please contact the office on 0118 984 2582 or via the website www.pbs.org.uk for a membership form.

Patron: The Prince of Wales
Ecclesiastical Patron: The Bishop of London
Chairman: Prudence Dailey

Co limited by guarantee no. 4786973 & Charity no. 1099295.
Isle of Man Co Registration 4369F & Charity no. 952

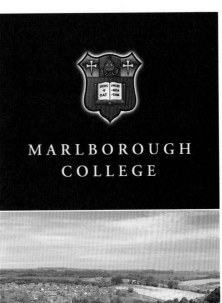

MARLBOROUGH COLLEGE

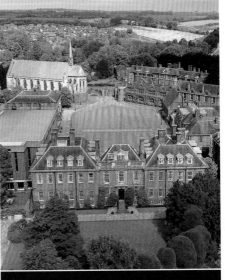

A coeducational, full boarding environment for 13-18 year olds.

CLERGY BURSARIES AVAILABLE

www.marlboroughcollege.org

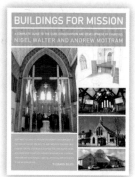

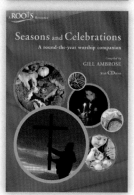

  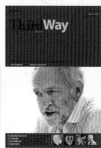 

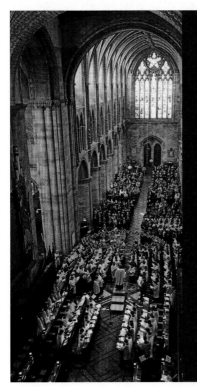

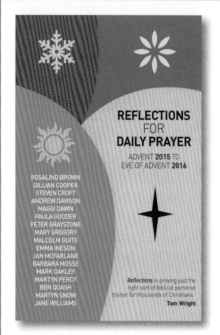

cpas
Making Mission Possible

PCC Tonight

A GUIDE TO LEADING A PCC

SIX SESSIONS FOR YOUR PCC TO USE

INCLUDES OVER 30 DOWNLOADABLE RESOURCES

VISIT **WWW.CPAS.ORG.UK /PCCTONIGHT** TO DISCOVER MORE

PRACTICAL IDEAS ON HOW TO CREATE A DYNAMIC, FUN AND FAITH-FILLED PCC.

TACKLING POVERTY TOGETHER
CHURCH URBAN FUND

TOGETHER
WE CAN TACKLE
POVERTY IN ENGLAND

Together, churches are transforming the lives of the poorest and most marginalised.

Join in www.cuf.org.uk

Could you be their Chaplain?

Since the formation of the Royal Air Force Chaplains' Branch in 1918, chaplains have been an integral part of the RAF 'story' and have taken the Church to where it's needed most. As an RAF Chaplain you'll be involved in the lives of our personnel, regardless of their rank or religious background. Your personal sacrifice may be considerable as you'll serve with our people wherever they go, providing vital spiritual, pastoral and ethical support in places of conflict, including on the front-line. Your home-based duties will be equally important in support of personnel and their families on RAF stations. While exploring innovative ways of engaging with your community, you can also expect to fulfill the more traditional roles of leading worship and officiating at weddings, baptisms and funerals.
A whole new congregation awaits you. **Be part of the story. Contact us now.**

www.raf.mod.uk/chaplains

The Royal Air Force values every individual's unique contribution, irrespective of race, ethnic origin, religion, gender, sexual orientation or social background.

Produced by Air Media Centre, HQ Air Command. 0357_11RD © UK MOD Crown Copyright, 2011

CROCKFORD'S
CLERICAL DIRECTORY

2016–2017

CROCKFORD'S
CLERICAL DIRECTORY
104TH EDITION

2016–2017

A directory of the clergy
of the Church of England
the Church in Wales
the Scottish Episcopal Church
the Church of Ireland

SINCE 1858

CHURCH HOUSE PUBLISHING

Crockford's Clerical Directory published December 2015 for The Archbishops' Council by:

Church House Publishing
Church House
Great Smith Street
London SW1P 3AZ

104th edition (2016–2017) © The Archbishops' Council 2015.

Please send any corrections to the Compiler, Crockford (address as above), Tel (020) 7898 1012
E-mail crockford@churchofengland.org

ISBN 978 0 7151 1097 3 (hardback)
        978 0 7151 1098 0 (paperback)

Jacket and cover design by Aubrey Design

Typeset by   Printed by
RefineCatch Ltd,   William Clowes Ltd,
Bungay, Suffolk   Beccles, Suffolk

CONTENTS

INDEX TO ADVERTISEMENTS

Advertisements can be found on the following pages

The inclusion of an advertisement is for the purposes of information and is not to be taken as implying acceptance of the objects of the advertiser by the publisher.

"A wonderful place for a wonderful retirement"

The College of St Barnabas is a residential community of retired Anglican clergy, set in beautiful Surrey countryside. Married couples are very welcome, as are those who have been widowed. Admission is open to licensed Church Workers and Readers; there are facilities for visitors and guests. Occasional quiet days and private retreats can be accommodated.

Residents are encouraged to lead active, independent lives. There is a Nursing Wing, to which both internal and direct admission are possible, providing domiciliary, residential and full nursing care for those who need it. This enables most residents to remain members of the College for the rest of their lives. It is sometimes possible to offer respite care here.

Sheltered 'Cloister flats' all have separate sitting rooms, bedrooms and *en suite* facilities. There are two Chapels; Mass and Evensong are celebrated daily. We have three Libraries and a well equipped Common Room. Meals are served in the Refectory or may be taken privately when necessary.

For further details or to arrange a preliminary visit, please see our website or contact the Warden, Fr Howard Such, at:

**The College of St Barnabas,
Blackberry Lane, Lingfield, Surrey, RH7 6NJ**

**Tel. 01342 870260   Fax. 01342 871672
Email: warden@collegeofstbarnabas.com
Website: www.st-barnabas.org.uk**

INTRODUCTION

This, the one hundred and fourth edition of *Crockford's Clerical Directory*, provides details as at 7 August 2015 of more than 27,000 clergy and deaconesses in the Church of England (including the Diocese in Europe), the Church in Wales, the Scottish Episcopal Church, and the Church of Ireland. It also includes in the main biographical section those Michaelmas ordinands of whom we were notified in advance.

First published in 1858, the publication of *Crockford* now spans over one-and-a-half centuries. The Oxford University Press purchased the copyright for *Crockford* in 1921, publishing thirty-six editions before transferring ownership to the Church Commissioners and the Central Board of Finance, on economic grounds, sixty years later. This is the seventh edition under the sole ownership of the Archbishops' Council.

The publishing, design, advertising, selling and distribution of the directory are carried out by Church House Publishing in partnership with the *Crockford* Department, who are responsible for maintaining the data published here and *via* the *Crockford* on-line subscription service (www.crockford.org.uk), first launched in 2004 and relaunched with a completely new website and supporting database in June 2015. The information that generates the biographical entries is stored on a database, which is updated daily. The new website is also updated after each working day. Much of the information is obtained indirectly from the Church Commissioners' central clergy pay-roll. However, some 9,000 (about one-third) of the clergy are not on the central pay-roll. These are principally non-stipendiary ministers, those engaged in some form of ministry outside the parochial system (such as hospital, university, prison or service chaplains) and those serving in Wales, Scotland and Ireland. In maintaining the records of these clergy, we continue to rely greatly on the assistance of bishops' secretaries and diocesan offices, and information contained in diocesan directories, year books and the Church Press. We are also grateful for the help provided by the central authorities of the Church in Wales, the Scottish Episcopal Church, the Church of Ireland, the Ministry of Defence, the Hospital Chaplaincies Council, and our various overseas contacts.

A tremendous amount of help has come from the clergy themselves. We are enormously grateful to all those who have provided us with information, and have helped to minimize omissions and errors. For reasons of time, space and consistency, we are unable to include all the information clergy request us to publish, and we apologise that it has not always been possible to respond to each letter individually. We are also grateful to Richard Christmas, Angela Florence, Abigail Clausen and Sally Hughes, who have been responsible for most of the work in compiling this directory.

We are always glad to be informed of amendments to entries, and we particularly appreciate any information about clergy whose addresses are not currently known to us (see list on p. 1310). Information relating to omissions or amendments should be sent to the *Crockford* Department; requests for archival information from earlier editions should be addressed in writing to Lambeth Palace Library; for other information, please consult the Church of England's website at www.churchofengland.org.

Crockford Department	*The Librarian*
Church House	*Lambeth Palace Library*
Great Smith Street	*Lambeth Palace*
London SW1P 3AZ	*London SE1 7JU*
Telephone (020) 7898 1012	Telephone (020) 7898 1400
E-mail: crockford@churchofengland.org	E-mail: archives@churchofengland.org

JOHN CROCKFORD

John Crockford was the eldest child of a Somerset schoolmaster and his wife, John and Hannah Crockford; and by 1841 he was working as an attorney's clerk in Taunton, Somerset. John Crockford Sr was described in 1869 as Gentleman, of Rowbarton near Taunton. By his early twenties he was in business as a printer and publisher at 29 Essex Street, Strand; and it was from that address that *Crockford* was first published in 1858. On 6 December of the same year, John Crockford moved to new business premises at 346 Strand and 19 Wellington Street North.

His private address at that time was 16 Oakley Square, Hampstead Road; though by 1865 he had moved to 10 Park Road, Haverstock Hill.

Crockford's business association of more than two decades with Edward William Cox (1809–1879) had begun in 1843, when the *Law Times* first appeared. Both men are claimed as publisher – Crockford by Boase in *Modern English Biography*; Cox by the *Athenaeum* and by *Notes and Queries*. There is similar lack of agreement over other publications, such as the ill-fated *Critic*. "[Crockford] tried to establish a literary paper, the *Critic*. To this he brought all his great ability, but after fifteen years he gave it up in despair" (*Notes and Queries*): whereas the *Dictionary of National Biography* has it that Cox became "proprietor of . . . two other papers called respectively 'The Critic' and 'The Royal Exchange'."

The truth appears to be that the two men, who shared the same business address in Essex Street, were joint founders of a number of projects. Cox – the elder, more established and richer man – was often the financier and named publisher, with Crockford as the manager of the undertaking. Each had his own specialities: Cox, called to the bar in 1843, and successively Recorder of Helston & Falmouth (1857–1868) and of Portsmouth (1868–1879), was no doubt the leader in the establishment of the *Law Times*, to which, in *DNB*'s words, he "thenceforth devoted . . . the larger portion of his time and attention." But the legend which has arisen that Cox, restrained by professional ethics from using his own name, chose, almost at random, the name of one of his clerks to bear the title of his new clerical directory in 1858 – thus, in the words of the first postwar editor (probably Newman) bestowing "a more than tomb-stone meed of remembrance" – cannot be substantiated. As the jubilee account of the *Field* notes, Crockford was an equal partner in the success of the joint enterprises: "It was John Crockford who purchased the paper for Mr Cox. He obtained it from Mr Benjamin Webster for a trifling sum . . . In a short time the net profits amounted to 20,000*l*. a year. The management was placed under Crockford's control. He was a splendid man of business" (*Notes and Queries*).

The first *Clerical Directory* (1858), "A Biographical and Statistical Book of Reference for facts relating to the clergy and the Church", seems to have been assembled in a very haphazard fashion, with names added "as fast as they could be obtained", out of alphabetical order and with an unreliable index. By 1860 the *Directory* had become a very much more useful work of reference; and by 1917, with the absorption of its only serious rival, the *Clergy List*, reigned supreme.

No more than glimpses survive of Crockford's personality, and those mostly from the account of him given by John C. Francis, in the *Field* jubilee article already referred to. "I had occasion to call upon him a short time before his death, when we joined in a hearty laugh over his former furious attacks upon the *Athenaeum*. 'Dilke's Drag' he used to call it, and would accuse it of 'vulgar insolence and coxcombry' and 'the coarsest vulgarity'. As we parted he said, 'You have the *Athenaeum* to be proud of, and we have the *Field*.'"

John Crockford died suddenly at his home on 13 January 1865, at the age of 41. He left a widow, Annie (née Ellam) whom he married on 24 December 1847 at St Pancras Old Church. A daughter, Florence Annie, was born in St Pancras in 1852. (Florence married Arthur Brownlow in 1875 and had a son called Frederick.) His very brief will, proved 6 February 1865 at the Principal Probate Registry, left everything to his widow. His personal effects were valued at less than £1,000, but the family must have lived in some style, since one of the witnesses to the will was the resident coachman. Crockford's widow moved to 4 Upper Eton Place, Tavistock Hill, and died there on 26 July 1868.

BRENDA HOUGH

A request from the *Dictionary of National Biography* for a notice of the life of John Crockford led to the preparation of this article, a shorter version of which appeared in *The Dictionary of National Biography: Missing Persons*, 1993. For the information from the 1841 Census, and the record of Crockford's daughter Florence, we are indebted to Mr Ken Rhoades, of Kent.

Who is included in *Crockford*?

Crockford includes details of over 27,000 clergy and deaconesses of the Church of England, the Church in Wales, the Scottish Episcopal Church and the Church of Ireland. Clergy currently serving overseas qualify for inclusion if they have trained or have been licensed in this country (see **Overseas clergy**). Clergy who have died since the last edition are listed on p. 1312. Generally, clergy who have resigned their offices (but not their orders) are included unless they are known to have been received into another Church. A small number of clergy are excluded at their own request.

Readers and lay workers are not included: please consult diocesan directories. The *Who's Who* section of *The Church of England Year Book* (published annually by Church House Publishing and covering most aspects of the life and institutions of the Church of England) lists members of General Synod and principal members of staff of the Church's central organizations.

Addresses and telephone numbers

Where more than one land line telephone number is given, the first will normally relate to the address shown.

Addressing the clergy

See p. *1277*.

Appointment details in the *Biographies* section

These reflect the legal pastoral situation prevailing at 7 August 2015, the date of the compilation of this edition of *Crockford*. Conventional districts, proprietary chapels and local ecumenical projects are also recorded. Benefice names are only recorded once in a biographical entry when they apply to successive appointments.

Crockford does not record group ministries, informal local arrangements, areas of special responsibility, emeritus appointments (except as reflected in the style of address), licence or permission to officiate when held in conjunction with another appointment from the same diocese, commissary appointments, examining chaplaincies, or secular appointments (except for educational or charitable posts).

Appointments held before ordination are not included (apart from service as a deaconess) unless they straddle the date of ordination.

Archbishops overseas

The presiding (arch-)bishop or metropolitan of each of the provinces of the Anglican Communion is listed in the main *Biographies* section, cross-referenced as appropriate, together with the Moderator of each of the united churches.

Archdeaconries

See *Archdeaconries, deaneries and rural/area deans* on p. 1060.

Archdeacons

Look up the place name in *Biographies*: this is cross-referenced to a personal name.

Bishops (diocesan, area, suffragan, and provincial episcopal visitors)

Look up the place name in *Biographies*: this is cross-referenced to a personal name. See also p. 1012, which lists the diocesan, area, suffragan and assistant bishops by diocese, as well as provincial episcopal visitors.

Bishops (assistant)

See *Bishops in England, Wales, Scotland and Ireland* on p. 1012.

Bishops in the House of Lords

See p. 1015.

Bishops overseas
See *Bishops of Anglican dioceses overseas* on p. 1279, and *Bishops of united churches* on p. 1303. Further information about the Anglican Communion can be found in *The Church of England Year Book*.

Bishops and archbishops, former
A list of former archbishops and bishops (diocesan and suffragan) will be found on p. 1016.

Boundaries, provincial and diocesan
Maps of England and Wales, Scotland and Ireland, showing provincial and diocesan boundaries and cathedral cities, will be found on pp. 1318–1321.

Cathedral clergy
See *Cathedrals* on p. 1053 for full-time cathedral clergy. The list does not include honorary appointments.

Chapel Royal
See *Royal Peculiars* on p. 1055.

Christian names
The name by which a person prefers to be known, if not the first Christian name, is underlined (for example, SMITH, David John prefers to be called John). Names 'in religion' or names not part of a person's legal name are shown in parentheses.

Church: how to find the names of clergy responsible for a particular church
Look up the place name in the appropriate *Benefices and churches* section, see p. 1068: if the entry is in bold type, the names of all clergy are listed and can be cross-referenced in the *Biographies* section; if the place name is not in bold type, the name of the benefice is given where the names of all clergy will be found.

Church: how to find the names of clergy responsible for a particular church when there is a vacancy
If the benefice is vacant, the telephone number of the clergy house is usually given in the appropriate *Benefices and churches* section to enable contact to be made with a new incumbent or priest-in-charge. The deanery reference (e.g. *Guildf 2*) following the benefice name cross-refers to *Archdeaconries, deaneries and rural deans* on p. 1060 by means of which the name of the rural dean responsible for the vacant benefice can be found.

College chaplains
See p. 1274 for chaplains at universities, colleges of further education, colleges of higher education, sixth-form colleges, and schools.

Corrections
Please send notice of any corrections to:
Crockford Compiler, Church House, Great Smith Street, London SW1P 3AZ
T: (020) 7898 1012 E: crockford@churchofengland.org

Crockford
The full title is *Crockford's Clerical Directory*. *Crockford* (not *Crockford's*) is an accepted abbreviation. See also the biography of John Crockford on p. *1265*.

Deaconesses
See separate section on p. 1011.

Deacons
See *Biographies* section.

Deaneries
See rural or area deans below.

Deans
Look up the place name in *Biographies*: this is cross-referenced to a personal name. See also *Cathedrals* on p. 1053, and *Royal Peculiars* on p. 1055.

Diocesan offices
Details of the diocesan offices in England, Wales, Scotland and Ireland can be found on p. 1056.

E-mail addresses
These are provided where known. See after the telephone and/or fax number.

Europe, chaplains in
See *Diocese in Europe* on p. 1262.

Fax numbers
The exchange number is only given if different from that of the preceding telephone number.

Hospital chaplains
Whole-time and part-time hospital chaplains are listed under their NHS trusts on p. 1269. Cross-references have been inserted for individual hospitals.

Lay workers
Lay workers are not included in *Crockford*: please consult diocesan directories.

London churches
See *English benefices and churches* on p. 1068. City and Guild churches are listed under LONDON CITY CHURCHES and LONDON GUILD CHURCHES. In other cases, see under church name (e.g. LANGHAM PLACE (All Souls), WESTMINSTER (St Matthew)).

Married or single?
Crockford does not provide information on marital status. However, we have included the form of address Miss, Mrs or Ms where requested. Where there has been a change of surname, a cross-reference may be found from the previous name.

Non-stipendiary clergy
Non-stipendiary clergy are listed in the main *Biographies* section.

Ordination courses
See *Theological colleges and courses* on p. 1277.

Overseas clergy
Clergy who are on the *Crockford* database and who are currently serving overseas qualify for inclusion. Service overseas has in the past been recorded simply by country, though higher office (e.g. as bishop or archdeacon) has also been noted. Other eligible appointments are now being added on request.

Overseas addresses and telephone numbers are given as required by a user in the UK, and include the international access and country codes, as well as the area code. If dialling from within the country concerned, the user will need to omit the international access and country codes, and dial zero immediately before the area code.

Patronage
The patron of each benefice is listed under the benefice name in *English benefices and churches* on p. 1068.

Prison chaplains
See p. 1267.

Proprietary chapels
See *English benefices and churches* on p. 1068.

Provincial episcopal visitors
Look up the place name in *Biographies*: this is cross-referenced to a personal name. See also p. 1012, which lists the diocesan, area, suffragan and assistant bishops and provincial episcopal visitors.

Provosts
Look up the place name in *Biographies*: this is cross-referenced to a personal name. See also *Cathedrals* on p. 1053.

Queen's Chaplains
See *Royal Peculiars* on p. 1055.

Readers
Readers are not included in *Crockford*: please consult diocesan directories.

Religious orders
For members of religious orders where the Christian name alone is commonly used (e.g. Brother Aidan) a cross-reference is provided to the surname. Names 'in religion' not forming part of a person's legal name will be shown in parentheses. Details of religious communities are provided in *The Church of England Year Book*.

Retired clergy
The description 'rtd' does not imply that ministry has ceased, only that clergy so described are now in receipt of a pension. All eligible appointments are now recorded.

Rural or area deans
See *Archdeaconries, deaneries and rural/area deans* on p. 1060. To find who is the rural dean of a particular church, look up the place or benefice name in the appropriate *Benefices* section: the deanery reference (e.g. *Guildf 2*) following the benefice name cross-refers to *Archdeaconries, deaneries and rural deans* on p. 1060 where the name of the rural dean responsible can be found.

School chaplains
See p. 1274 for chaplains in schools.

Service chaplains
See p. 1265.

Sixth-form colleges
See p. 1274.

Theological colleges and courses
See p. 1277.

University chaplains
See p. 1274.

HOW TO ADDRESS THE CLERGY

In offering the advice below, we do not intend to imply that other practices are necessarily to be discouraged (for example, the use of Father as in 'Father Smith' or 'Father Alan'). A good deal depends on circumstances, and, where a personal preference is known, it is usually good practice to follow it.

The following notes show acceptable current usage

   (a) on an envelope or formal listing
   (b) in starting a social letter or in speech, and
   (c) when referring to a member of the clergy

Category (a) is not open to much variation, owing to the formality of the context, but categories (b) and (c) will often vary according to circumstances. It is always acceptable to use the appropriate Christian name in place of initials (for example, the Revd Alice Smith). In the absence of any style or title conferred by a post, all deacons and priests are styled 'The Reverend', and all who have been consecrated bishop are styled 'The Right Reverend'.

For abbreviations, see paragraph 13 below.

1 Deacons and Priests
   (a) The Reverend A B Smith
   (b) Mr/Mrs/Miss/Ms Smith (unless it is known that some other style is preferred—the title Vicar or Rector is acceptable only if the person so addressed really is the incumbent of the parish where you live or worship)
   (c) The Reverend A B Smith at the first mention, and Mr/Mrs/Miss/Ms Smith thereafter

> *Notes* 1 The form 'Reverend Smith' or 'The Reverend Smith' should *never* be used this side of the Atlantic. If the Christian name or initials are not known, the correct forms are
>   (a) The Reverend — Smith, *or* The Reverend Mr/Mrs/Miss/Ms Smith
>   (b) Mr/Mrs/Miss/Ms Smith
>   (c) The Reverend Mr/Mrs/Miss/Ms Smith at the first mention, and Mr/Mrs/Miss/Ms Smith thereafter
>
> 2 There is no universally accepted way of addressing an envelope to a married couple of whom both are in holy orders. We recommend the style 'The Reverend A B and the Reverend C D Smith'.
> 3 Where the husband is in holy orders and the wife is not, the customary style is 'The Reverend A B and Mrs Smith'.
> 4 Where the wife is in holy orders and the husband is not, we recommend the style 'Mr A B Smith and the Reverend Mrs Smith'.

2 Prebendaries
   (a) The Reverend Prebendary A B Smith
   (b) Prebendary Smith
   (c) Prebendary Smith

3 Canons (both Residentiary and Honorary)
   (a) The Reverend Canon A B Smith
   (b) Canon Smith
   (c) Canon Smith

4 Archdeacons
   (a) The Venerable the Archdeacon of X
   (b) Archdeacon, *or more formally* Mr/Madam Archdeacon
   (c) The Archdeacon of X at the first mention, and the Archdeacon thereafter

> *Notes* 1 In the case of an archdeacon (or dean/provost, bishop, or archbishop) in office, the style above is to be preferred. The personal name should be used only for the purpose of identification.
> 2 For an archdeacon emeritus, the correct forms are
>   (a) The Venerable A B Smith
>   (b) Archdeacon
>   (c) Archdeacon Smith

5 Deans and Provosts
(a) The Very Reverend the Dean/Provost of X
(b) Dean/Provost, *or more formally* Mr/Madam Dean/Provost
(c) The Dean/Provost of X at the first mention, and the Dean thereafter (see also note 1 to paragraph 4 above)

6 Bishops, Diocesan and Suffragan
(a) The Right Reverend the Bishop of X, *or* The Right Reverend the Lord/Lady Bishop of X
(b) Bishop, *or more formally* My Lord/Lady
(c) The Bishop of X at the first mention, and the Bishop thereafter (see also note 1 to paragraph 4 above)

Notes 1 It is a matter of individual preference whether the title 'Lord/Lady' should be used.
2 The Bishop of London is a Privy Councillor, and has the style 'The Right Reverend and Right Honourable the Lord Bishop of London'.
3 The Bishop of Meath and Kildare is styled 'The Most Reverend'.

7 Assistant and Retired Bishops
(a) The Right Reverend A B Smith
(b) Bishop
(c) Bishop Smith

8 Archbishops
(a) The Most Reverend the Lord Archbishop of X
(b) Archbishop, *or more formally* Your Grace
(c) (His Grace) the Archbishop of X at the first mention, and the Archbishop thereafter (see also note 1 to paragraph 4 above)

Notes 1 The Archbishops of Canterbury and York, being Privy Councillors, also have 'Right Honourable' included in their style (for example, The Most Reverend and Right Honourable the Lord Archbishop of Canterbury).
2 The presiding bishop of the Scottish Episcopal Church is the Primus, and the correct forms are
    (a) The Most Reverend the Primus
    (b) Primus
    (c) Primus

3 A retired archbishop properly reverts to the status of bishop, but may be given as a courtesy the style of an archbishop.

9 Chaplains to the Armed Services
(a) The Reverend A B Smith RN (*or* CF *or* RAF)
(b) Padre, *or* Padre Smith
(c) The Padre, *or* Padre Smith

10 Titled Clerics
Where a member of the clergy also holds a temporal title, this is always preceded in writing by the ecclesiastical one.

Barons (other than retired archbishops)
(a) The Reverend the Lord Smith of X
(b) Lord Smith
(c) The Reverend the Lord Smith at the first mention, and Lord Smith thereafter

Baronets
(a) The Reverend Sir Alan Smith Bt
(b) Sir Alan Smith or Sir Alan
(c) The Reverend Sir Alan Smith at the first mention, and Sir Alan thereafter

Knights
An ordained priest may be appointed to an order of knighthood, but will not normally receive the accolade or title. The appropriate designation will follow the name or ecclesiastical title, e.g. The Right Reverend the Bishop of X, KCVO. If he was knighted *before* he was ordained, he will retain his title, and will be addressed in much the same manner as a baronet.

Dames
(a) The Reverend Dame Alice Smith
(b) Dame Alice Smith or Dame Alice
(c) The Reverend Dame Alice Smith at the first mention, and Dame Alice thereafter

Wives of Barons, Baronets and Knights
(a) The Reverend Lady Smith (of X)
(b) Lady Smith
(c) The Reverend Lady Smith at the first mention, and Lady Smith thereafter

Sons and daughters of peers
(a) The Reverend the Honourable Jocelyn Smith, *or* The Reverend Lord/Lady Jocelyn Smith (as appropriate)
(b) Mr/Mrs/Miss/Ms Smith, *or* Lord/Lady Jocelyn Smith
(c) The Reverend J K Smith at the first mention, and Mr/Mrs/Miss/Ms Smith thereafter; *or* the Reverend Lord/Lady Jocelyn Smith at the first mention, and Lord/Lady Jocelyn thereafter.

11 Ordained Members of Religious Orders
(a) The Reverend Alan/Alice Smith XYZ; The Reverend Brother Alan/Sister Alice XYZ
(b) Father, Father Smith, *or* Father Alan; Mother, Mother Smith, *or* Mother Alice; Brother Alan/Sister Alice
(c) The Reverend Alan/Alice Smith; Father Alan Smith; Mother Alice Smith; Father Smith; Brother Alan/Sister Alice

Notes 1 A name 'in religion', shown in parentheses in the biographical entry, should be used in preference to the baptismal name or initials. Sometimes the surname is not used. In this Directory, however, the entry will be found under the surname, whether it is normally used or not, and, if appropriate, a cross-reference is given under the Christian name.
2 Some orders use 'Brother' and 'Sister' for lay and ordained members without distinction, along with Christian names.
3 It is customary to specify the religious order by giving the appropriate letters after the name.

12 Academics
When a member of the clergy holds more than one title, the ecclesiastical one is normally used.

Professor also Canon	(a) The Reverend Canon A B Smith
	(b) Canon Smith, *or* Professor Smith, according to context
	(c) Canon Smith, *or* Professor Smith, according to context
Canon also Doctor	(a) The Reverend Canon A B Smith (degree)
	(b) Canon Smith, *or* Dr Smith, according to context
	(c) Canon Smith, *or* Dr Smith, according to context

13 Abbreviations
The following abbreviations are in common use

Reverend:	Revd *or* Rev
Father:	Fr
Right Reverend:	Rt Revd *or* Rt Rev
Prebendary:	Preb
Venerable:	Ven

Reverend, Right Reverend, Very Reverend, Most Reverend and Venerable, whether abbreviated or not, should always be preceded by the definite article.

ABBREVIATIONS USED IN
CROCKFORD'S CLERICAL DIRECTORY

A

AAAI .... Associate, Institute of Administrative Accountants
AB...................... Bachelor of Arts (USA)
Ab...................... (Diocese of) Aberdeen and Orkney
ABEng................. Associate Member of the Association of Building Engineers
Aber................... Aberdeen
ABIA .... Associate, Bankers' Institute of Australasia
ABIPP .... Associate, British Institute of Professional Photography
ABIST.................. Associate, British Institute of Surgical Technology
ABM .... Advisory Board of Ministry (now Ministry Division)
Abp .... Archbishop
ABPsS .... Associate, British Psychological Society (now see AFBPsS)
ABSM .... Associate, Birmingham and Midland Institute School of Music
Abth .... Aberystwyth
ACA.................... Associate, Institute of Chartered Accountants
ACABE................. Associate, Chartered Association of Building Engineers (formerly ABEng)
ACC.................... Anglican Consultative Council
ACCA.................. Associate, Chartered Association of Certified Accountants (formerly AACCA)
ACCM .... Advisory Council for the Church's Ministry (now Ministry Division)
ACCS.................. Associate, Corporation of Secretaries
ACCTS............... Association for Christian Conferences, Teaching, and Service
ACE .... Associateship of the College of Education
.... Member, Association of Conference Executives
ACF .... Army Cadet Force
ACIArb................ Associate, Chartered Institute of Arbitrators
ACIB .... Associate, Chartered Institute of Bankers (formerly AIB)
ACIBS.................. Associate, Chartered Institute of Bankers in Scotland
ACII .... Associate, Chartered Insurance Institute
ACIOB .... Associate, Chartered Institute of Building
ACIPA .... Associate, Chartered Institute of Patent Agents
ACIPD................. Associate, Chartered Institute of Personnel and Development
ACIS .... Associate, Institute of Chartered Secretaries and Administrators
ACIT .... Associate, Chartered Institute of Transport
ACMA................. Associate, Chartered Institute of Management Accountants (formerly ACWA)
ACMI .... Associate, Chartered Management Institute (formerly AIMgt)
ACORA .... Archbishops' Commission on Rural Areas
ACP .... Associate, College of Preceptors
ACS .... Additional Curates Society
ACSM .... Associate, Camborne School of Mines
ACT .... Australian Capital Territory
.... Australian College of Theology

ACUPA................ Archbishops' Commission on Urban Priority Areas
AD .... Area Dean
Ad...................... Advanced
AdDipEd .... Advanced Diploma in Education
Admin .... Administration
.... Administrative
.... Administrator
Adn .... Archdeacon
Adnry .... Archdeaconry
Adv.................... Advisory
.... Adviser
AEdRD .... Associateship in Educational Research and Development
AFAIM................ Associate Fellow, Australian Institute of Management
AFBPsS.............. Associate Fellow, British Psychological Society (formerly ABPsS)
AFC .... Air Force Cross
AFIMA .... Associate Fellow, Institute of Mathematics and its Applications
AFOM................. Associate, Faculty of Occupational Medicine
Agric................... Agricultural
.... Agriculture
AGSM................. Associate, Guildhall School of Music and Drama
AHSM or AHA .... Associate, Institute of Health Service Management (formerly Administrators)
AIA..................... Associate, Institute of Actuaries
AIAS................... Associate, Incorporated Association of Architects and Surveyors
AIAT................... Associate, Institute of Animal Technicians
Aid..................... Aidan
.... Aidan's
AIDS .... Acquired Immunity Deficiency Syndrome
AIFST .... Associate, Institute of Food Science and Technology
AIGCM .... Associate, Incorporated Guild of Church Musicians
AIIM .... Associate, Institute of Investment Management
AIL..................... Associate, Institute of Linguists
AIMgt................. Associate, Institute of Management (now see ACMI)
AIMLS................. Associate, Institute of Medical Laboratory Sciences
AIMSW............... Associate, Institute of Medical Social Work
AIPM .... Associate, Institute of Personnel Management (now see ACIPD)
AITI.................... Associate, Institute of Taxation in Ireland
AKC .... Associate, King's College London
ALA..................... Associate, Library Association
ALAM .... Associate, London Academy of Music
ALBC .... Associate, London Bible College
ALCD.................. Associate, London College of Divinity
ALCM .... Associate, London College of Music
ALSM.................. Associate, Lancashire School of Music
alt...................... alternate
AM .... Albert Medal
.... Master of Arts (USA)
AMA .... Associate, Museums Association
AMASI .... Associate Member of the Architects and Surveyors Institute

AMCST .... Associate, Manchester College of Science and Technology
AMCT .... Associate, Manchester College of Technology
AMIBF................. Associate Member, Institute of British Foundrymen
AMIC .... Associate Member, Institute of Counselling
AMICME............. Associate Member, Institute of Cast Metal Engineers
AMIDHE .... Associate Member, Institute of Domestic Heating Engineers
AMIEHO .... Associate Member, Institution of Environmental Health Officers
AMIM .... Associate Member, Institute of Metals
AMIMMM .... Associate Member, Institute of Materials, Minerals and Mining
AMInstT.............. Associate Member, Institute of Transport
AMInstTA........... Associate Member, Institute of Transport Administration
AMITD................ Associate Member, Institute of Training and Development (now see ACIPD)
AMIW.................. Associate Member, Institute of Welfare (formerly AMIWO)
AMRSH.............. Associate Member, Royal Society of Health
AMSIA .... Associate Member, Society of Investment Analysts
AMusLCM .... Associate in Music, London College of Music
AMusTCL............ Associate in Music, Trinity College of Music London
ANC .... African National Congress
Andr .... Andrew
.... Andrew's
.... Andrews
Angl................... Anglican
.... Anglicans
Ant .... Anthony
.... Anthony's
AO...................... Officer, Order of Australia
APhS................... Associate, Philosophical Society of England
Appt .... Appointment
ARAM .... Associate, Royal Academy of Music
ARCA.................. Associate, Royal College of Art
ARCIC................. Anglican–Roman Catholic International Commission
ARCM .... Associate, Royal College of Music
ARCO .... Associate, Royal College of Organists
ARCO(CHM) .... Associate, Royal College of Organists with Diploma in Choir Training
ARCS .... Associate, Royal College of Science
ARCST .... Associate, Royal College of Science and Technology (Glasgow)
ARCT .... Associate, Royal Conservatory of Music Toronto
ARCUK............... Architects' Registration Council of the United Kingdom
Arg .... (Diocese of) Argyll and The Isles
ARHistS.............. Associate, Royal Historical Society
ARIAM .... Associate, Royal Irish Academy of Music
Arm .... (Diocese of) Armagh
ARMCM .... Associate, Royal Manchester College of Music

ARPS .... Associate, Royal Photographic Society
ARSCM .... Associate, Royal School of Church Music
ARSM .... Associate, Royal School of Mines
AS .... Associate in Science (USA)
ASCA .... Associate, Society of Company and Commercial Accountants
Assn .... Association
Assoc .... Associate
ASSP .... Society of All Saints Sisters of the Poor
Asst. .... Assistant
ASVA .... Associate, Incorporated Society of Valuers and Auctioneers
ATC .... Air Training Corps
ATCL .... Associate, Trinity College of Music London
ATD .... Art Teacher's Diploma
ATh(SA) .... Associate in Theology (South Africa)
ATI .... Associate, Textile Institute
ATII .... Associate Member, Institute of Taxation
ATL .... Association of Teachers and Lecturers
ATV .... Associated Television
Aug .... Augustine
.... Augustine's
Aus .... Australian
Aux .... Auxiliaries
.... Auxiliary
AVCM .... Associate, Victoria College of Music

B

b........................ Born
B & W................ (Diocese of) Bath and Wells
B or Bapt .... Baptist
.... Baptist's
BA...................... Bachelor of Arts
BA(Econ) .... Bachelor of Arts in Economics
BA(Ed) .... Bachelor of Arts in Education
BA(QTS) .... Bachelor of Arts (Qualified Teacher Status)
BA(Theol) .... Bachelor of Arts in Theology
BA(ThM)............ Bachelor of Arts in Theology in Ministry
BAdmin .... Bachelor of Administration
BAgr .... Bachelor of Agriculture
BAgrSc............... Bachelor of Agricultural Science
BAI..................... Bachelor of Engineering (also see BE and BEng)
Ball .... Balliol
Ban .... (Diocese of) Bangor
BAO.................... Bachelor of Obstetrics
BAppSc............... Bachelor of Applied Science
BAppSc(Agric) .... Bachelor of Applied Science (Agriculture)
BAppSc(OT) .... Bachelor of Applied Science (Occupational Therapy)
BArch................. Bachelor of Architecture
Barn................... Barnabas
.... Barnabas's
Bart.................... Bartholomew
.... Bartholomew's
BASc .... Bachelor of Applied Science
BATM .... Bachelor of Arts in Theology and Ministry
BBA.................... Bachelor of Business Administration
BBC .... British Broadcasting Corporation
BBS .... Bachelor of Business Studies
BC .... British Columbia (Canada)
BCA .... Bachelor of Commerce and Administration
BCC.................... British Council of Churches (now CTBI)
BCE.................... Bachelor of Civil Engineering
BCh or BChir...... Bachelor of Surgery (also see BS and ChB)
BChD.................. Bachelor of Dental Surgery
BCL..................... Bachelor of Civil Law
BCMS .... Bible Churchmen's Missionary Society (now Crosslinks)
BCom or
BComm .... Bachelor of Commerce
BCombStuds ...... Bachelor of Combined Studies

BCommWelf....... Bachelor of Community Welfare
BD .... Bachelor of Divinity
Bd....................... Board
BDA.................... Bachelor of Dramatic Art
BDiv................... Bachelor of Divinity
BDQ.................... Bachelor of Divinity Qualifying Examination
BDS .... Bachelor of Dental Surgery
BDSc................... Bachelor of Dental Science
BE .... Bachelor of Engineering (also see BAI and BEng)
BEc .... Bachelor of Economics (Australia)
BEcon .... Bachelor of Economics (USA)
BEd..................... Bachelor of Education
Bedf................... Bedford
BEdSt................. Bachelor of Educational Studies
Belf .... Belfast
BEM.................... British Empire Medal
BEng................... Bachelor of Engineering (also see BAI and BE)
BèsL................... Bachelier ès lettres
BFA .... Bachelor of Fine Arts
BFBS .... British and Foreign Bible Society
BHSc................... Bachelor of Health Sciences
Bibl .... Biblical
BIE .... Bachelor of Industrial Engineering (USA)
Birm................... (Diocese of) Birmingham
BL .... Bachelor of Law
Blackb................ (Diocese of) Blackburn
BLib.................... Bachelor of Librarianship
BLitt................... Bachelor of Letters
BM .... Bachelor of Medicine (also see MB)
BM, BCh............. Conjoint degree of Bachelor of Medicine, Bachelor of Surgery
BMedSci .... Bachelor of Medical Science
BMet .... Bachelor of Metallurgy
BMin................... Bachelor of Ministry
BMMF .... Bible and Medical Missionary Fellowship (now Interserve)
BMU.................... Board for Mission and Unity
BMus .... Bachelor of Music (also see MusB and MusBac)
BMusEd .... Bachelor of Music Education
BN .... Bachelor of Nursing
BNC.................... Brasenose College
Bp....................... Bishop
BPaed .... Bachelor of Paediatrics
BPh or BPhil ...... Bachelor of Philosophy
BPharm .... Bachelor of Pharmacy
BPhil(Ed)............ Bachelor of Philosophy (Education)
BPI .... Bachelor of Planning
BPR&TM............. Bachelor of Parks, Recreation and Tourism Management
BProfStud .... Bachelor of Professional Studies
Br........................ British
Bradf.................. (Diocese of) Bradford
Bre..................... (Diocese of) Brechin
BRE .... Bachelor of Religious Education (USA)
BRF .... Bible Reading Fellowship
Brig..................... Brigadier
Bris .... (Diocese of) Bristol
BS .... Bachelor of Science (also see BSc)
.... Bachelor of Surgery (also see BCh, BChir and ChB)
BSB .... Brotherhood of St Barnabas
BSc .... Bachelor of Science (also see BS)
BSc(Econ) .... Bachelor of Science in Economics
BSc(Soc) .... Bachelor of Science (Sociology)
BScAgr................ Bachelor of Science in Agriculture
BScEcon............. Bachelor of Science in Economics
BScEng............... Bachelor of Science in Engineering (also see BSE)
BScFor .... Bachelor of Science in Forestry
BScTech.............. Bachelor of Technical Science
BSE .... Bachelor of Science in Engineering (also see BScEng)
BSEd .... Bachelor of Science in Education (USA)

BSocAdmin......... Bachelor of Social Administration
BSocSc................ Bachelor of Social Science (also see BSSc)
BSP .... Brotherhood of St Paul
BSS .... Bachelor of Social Studies
BSSc .... Bachelor of Social Science (also see BSocSc)
BST .... Bachelor of Sacred Theology
BSW.................... Bachelor of Social Work
BT....................... Bachelor of Teaching
Bt........................ Baronet
BTech .... Bachelor of Technology
BTh or BTheol..... Bachelor of Theology (also see STB)
BTS .... Bachelor of Theological Studies
BUniv.................. Bachelor of the University
BVetMed............. Bachelor of Veterinary Medicine (also see VetMB)
BVM&S .... Bachelor of Veterinary Medicine and Surgery
BVSc .... Bachelor of Veterinary Science

C

C .... Curate
c.......................... Consecrated
C & O................. (Diocese of) Cashel and Ossory (united dioceses of Cashel, Waterford, Lismore, Ossory, Ferns and Leighlin)
C of E................. Church of England
C of S .... Church of Scotland
C&G.................... City and Guilds
C, C & R............. (Diocese of) Cork, Cloyne and Ross
c/o...................... Care of
CA .... Church Army
.... Member, Institute of Chartered Accountants of Scotland
CA(Z).................. Member, Institute of Chartered Accountants of Zimbabwe
CACTM .... Central Advisory Council for the Ministry (now Ministry Division)
Cam .... Cambridge
Can...................... Canon
Cand .... Candidate
.... Candidate's
.... Candidates'
CANDL .... Church and Neighbourhood Development in London
Cant .... (Diocese of) Canterbury
Capt .... Captain
CARA .... Care and Resources for people affected by AIDS/HIV
CARE .... Christian Action Research and Education
Carl..................... (Diocese of) Carlisle
CASA .... Anglican Church of the Southern Cone of America
Cath .... Catharine/Catherine
.... Catharine's/Catherine's
Cathl .... Cathedral
CB .... Companion, Order of the Bath
CBDTI................. Carlisle and Blackburn Diocesan Training Institute
CBE.................... Commander, Order of the British Empire
CBIM .... Companion, British Institute of Management
CBiol................... Chartered Biologist
CCBI................... Council of Churches for Britain and Ireland (now see CTBI)
CCC .... Corpus Christi College
.... Council for the Care of Churches
CCCS.................. Commonwealth and Continental Church Society
CChem................ Chartered Chemist
CCWA .... Churches Community Work Alliance
CD....................... Canadian Forces Decoration
.... Conventional District (also see ED)
CDir..................... Chartered Director
Cdre .... Commodore
CECD .... Church of England Council for the Deaf

CECS — Church of England Children's Society (now known as the Children's Society)

CEMS — Church of England Men's Society

Cen — Centre

— Center

— Central

CEng — Chartered Engineer

CEnv — Chartered Environmentalist

Cert — Certificate(e)

CertEd — Certificate of Education

CertFE — Certificate of Further Education

CertHE — Certificate in Higher Education

CETD — Certificate in the Education of the Deaf

CF — Chaplain to the Forces

CGA — Community of the Glorious Ascension

CGeol — Chartered Geologist

CH — Companion of Honour

Ch — Christ

— Christ's

— Church

Ch Ch — Christ Church

Chan — Chancellor

Chapl — Chaplain

— Chaplaincies

— Chaplaincy

— Chaplains

Chas — Charles

— Charles's

ChB — Bachelor of Surgery (also see BCh, BChir and BS)

Chelmsf — (Diocese of) Chelmsford

Chelt — Cheltenham

Ches — (Diocese of) Chester

Chich — (Diocese of) Chichester

Chmn — Chairman

— Chairwoman

Chpl — Chapel

Chr — Christian

— Christians

Chris — Christopher

— Christopher's

Chrys — Chrysostom

— Chrysostom's

Chu — Churchill

C-in-c — Curate-in-charge

CIO — Church Information Office

CIPFA — Chartered Institute of Public Finance and Accountancy

CITC — Church of Ireland Theological College

CITP — Chartered Information Technology Professional

CJGS — Community of the Companions of Jesus the Good Shepherd

Clem — Clement

— Clement's

Cl-in-c — Cleric-in-charge

Cllr — Councillor/Counsellor

Clogh — (Diocese of) Clogher

CMath — Chartered Mathematician

CMD — Cambridge Mission to Delhi (now see USPG)

— Continuing Ministerial Development

CME — Continuing Ministerial Education

CMG — Companion, Order of St Michael and St George

CMJ — Church's Ministry among Jewish People

CMP — Company of Mission Priests

CMS — Church Mission Society (formerly Church Missionary Society)

CNZM — Companion, New Zealand Order of Merit

Co — Company

— County

— Counties

Col — Colonel

Coll — College

Colleg — Collegiate

Comdr — Commander

Comdr OM (Italy) — Commander, Order of Merit of the Italian Republic

Commn — Commission

Commr — Commissioner

Comp — Comprehensive

Conf — Confederation

— Conference

Conn — (Diocese of) Connor

Co-ord — Co-ordinator

— Co-ordinating

COPEC — Conference on Politics, Economics and Community

CORAT — Christian Organizations Research and Advisory Trust

CORE — City Outreach through Renewal Evangelism

Corp — Corporation

Coun — Council

Cov — (Diocese of) Coventry

CP — Community Priest

CPA — Chartered Patent Agent (formerly FCIPA)

CPAS — Church Pastoral Aid Society

CPEng — Chartered Professional Engineer (of Institution of Engineers of Australia)

CPFA — Member Chartered Institute of Public Finance and Accountancy (formerly IPFA)

CPhys — Chartered Physicist of the Institute of Physics

CPM — Colonial Police Medal

CPsychol — Chartered Member, British Psychological Society

CQSW — Certificate of Qualification in Social Work

CR — Community of the Resurrection (Mirfield)

CSA — Community of St Andrew

CSC — Community of the Sisters of the Church

CSci — Chartered Scientist

CSD — Community of St Denys

CSF — Community of St Francis

CSG — Company of the Servants of God

CSMV — Community of St Mary the Virgin

CSocSc — Certificate in Social Science

CSP — Community of St Peter

CSS — Certificate in Social Work

CSSM — Children's Special Service Mission

CStat — Chartered Statistician

CSWG — Community of the Servants of the Will of God

CTA — Chartered Tax Adviser

CTABRSM — Certificate of Teaching, Associated Board of the Royal Schools of Music

CTBI — Churches Together in Britain and Ireland (formerly CCBI)

Cttee — Committee

CUF — Church Urban Fund

Cust — Custodian

— Custody

Cuth — Cuthbert

— Cuthbert's

CVO — Commander, Royal Victorian Order

CWME — Commission on World Mission and Evangelism

CY — Church and Youth

CYCW — Certificate in Youth and Community Work

CYFA — Church Youth Fellowships Association

Cypr — Cyprian

— Cyprian's

D

d — Ordained Deacon

D & D — (Diocese of) Down and Dromore

D & G — (Diocese of) Dublin and Glendalough

D & R — (Diocese of) Derry and Raphoe

D&C — Dean and Chapter

DACE — Diploma in Adult and Continuing Education

DAES — Diploma in Advanced Educational Studies

DAPC — Diploma in Advanced Psychological Counselling

DArch — Doctor of Architecture

Darw — Darwin

DASAE — Diploma of Advanced Study in Adult Education

DASE — Diploma in the Advanced Study of Education

DASHE — Diploma in Advanced Studies in Higher Education

DASS — Diploma in Applied Social Studies

DASSc — Diploma in Applied Social Science

Dav — David

— David's

DB — Bachelor of Divinity (USA)

DBE — Dame Commander, Order of the British Empire

DBF — Diocesan Board of Finance

DBP — Diocesan Board of Patronage

DC — District of Columbia (USA)

DCC — Diploma in Crisis Counselling of the Institute of Counselling

DCE — Diploma of a College of Education

DCL — Doctor of Civil Law

DCnL — Doctor of Canon Law

DCR(R) — Diploma of the College of Radiographers

DCYW — Diploma in Community and Youth Work

DD — Doctor of Divinity

DDS — Doctor of Dental Surgery

DEd — Doctor of Education (also see EdD)

DEHC — Diploma in the Education of Handicapped Children

DEng — Doctor of Engineering

Dep — Deputy

Dept — Department

DèS — Docteur ès sciences

DèsL — Docteur ès lettres

Det — Detention

DFC — Distinguished Flying Cross

DFM — Distinguished Flying Medal (Canada)

DHA — District Health Authority

DHL — Doctor of Humane Letters

DHSc — Doctor of Health Science

DHumLit — Doctor of Humane Letters

Dio — Diocese

Dioc — Diocesan

Dip — Diploma

DipAdEd — Diploma in Advanced Education

DipAE — Diploma in Adult Education

DipCOT — Diploma of the College of Occupational Therapists

DipEd — Diploma in Education

DipHE — Diploma in Higher Education

DipOT — Diploma in Occupational Therapy

DipSW — Diploma in Social Work

Dir — Director

Distr — District

Div — Divinity

Div Test — Divinity Testimonium

DL — Deputy Lieutenant

DLC — Diploma of Loughborough College

DLitt — Doctor of Letters (also see LittD)

DLitt et Phil — Doctor of Letters and Philosophy

DLSc — Doctor of Legal Science

DM — Doctor of Medicine

DMin — Doctor of Ministry

DMinTh — Doctor of Ministry and Theology

DMus — Doctor of Music

Dn — Deacon

Dn-in-c — Deacon-in-charge

DOE — Department of the Environment

Dom — Domestic

Down — Downing

DPhil — Doctor of Philosophy (also see PhD)

DProf — Doctor in Professional Studies

Dr — Doctor

Dr rer nat — Doctor of Natural Science

Dr Théol — Doctor of Theology (France)

DRCOG — Diploma of the Royal College of Obstetricians and Gynaecologists

DrThéol — Doctor of Theology (Germany)

DSc — Doctor of Science (also see ScD)

DSC — Distinguished Service Cross

DSc(Eng) .... Doctor of Science in Engineering
DSM .... Distinguished Service Medal
DSO .... Companion, Distinguished Service Order
DSocSc .... Doctor of Social Science
Dss .... Deaconess
dss .... Admitted Deaconess
DST .... Doctor of Sacred Theology (also see STD)
DTech .... Doctor of Technology
DTh *or* DTheol ... Doctor of Theology (also see ThD)
DThM *or* .... Doctor of Theology and
DThMin .... Ministry
DTI .... Department of Trade and Industry
Dub .... Dublin
DUniv .... Doctor of the University
DUP .... Docteur de l'Université de Paris
Dur .... (Diocese of) Durham

E

E .... East
.... Eastern
EAMTC .... East Anglian Ministerial Training Course
EC .... Emergency Commission
Ecum .... Ecumenical
.... Ecumenics
.... Ecumenism
Ed .... Editor
.... Editorial
ED .... Ecclesiastical District (also see CD)
.... Efficiency Decoration
EdD .... Doctor of Education (also see DEd)
Edin .... (Diocese of) Edinburgh
Edm .... Edmund
.... Edmund's
EdM .... Master of Education (USA) (also see MEd)
Educn .... Education
.... Educational
Edw .... Edward
.... Edward's
Eliz .... Elizabeth
.... Elizabeth's
Em .... Emanuel
.... Emmanuel
Emb .... Embassy
EMMTC .... East Midlands Ministry Training Course
EN(G) .... Enrolled Nurse (General)
EN(M) .... Enrolled Nurse (Mental)
EngD .... Doctor of Engineering
EngTech .... Engineering Technician
Episc .... Episcopal
.... Episcopalian
ERD .... Emergency Reserve Decoration
ERMC .... Eastern Region Ministry Course
ESC .... École Supérieure de Commerce
ESMI .... Elderly, Sick and Mentally Infirm
Eur .... (Diocese in) Europe (formerly Diocese of Gibraltar in Europe)
.... European
EurIng .... European Engineer
Ev .... Evangelist
.... Evangelist's
.... Evangelists
Evang .... Evangelical
.... Evangelism
Ex .... (Diocese of) Exeter
Exam .... Examining
Exec .... Executive
Exor .... Executor
Ext .... Extension

F

F&HE .... Further and Higher Education
FAA .... Fellow, Institution of Administrative Accountants
FACOG .... Fellow, American College of Obstetricians and Gynaecologists
FADO .... Fellow, Association of Dispensing Opticians

FAEB .... Fellow, Academy of Environmental Biology (India)
FAIM .... Fellow, Australian Institute of Management
FAIWCW .... Fellow, Australian Institute of Welfare and Community Workers
FASI .... Fellow, Architects' and Surveyors' Institute
FBA .... Fellow, British Academy
FBCartS .... Fellow, British Cartographic Society
FBCO .... Fellow, British College of Ophthalmic Opticians (Optometrists)
FBCS .... Fellow, British Computer Society
FBDO .... Fellow, Association of British Dispensing Opticians
FBEng .... Fellow, Association of Building Engineers
FBIM .... Fellow, British Institute of Management (formerly MBIM)
FBIS .... Fellow, British Interplanetary Society
FBIST .... Fellow, British Institute of Surgical Technologists
FBOA .... Fellow, British Optical Association
FBPICS .... Fellow, British Production and Inventory Control Society
FBPsS .... Fellow, British Psychological Society
FBS .... Fellow, Burgon Society
FCA .... Fellow, Institute of Chartered Accountants
FCCA .... Fellow, Chartered Association of Certified Accountants (formerly FACCA)
FCFI .... Fellow, Clothing and Footwear Institute
FCIArb .... Fellow, Chartered Institute of Arbitrators
FCIB .... Fellow, Chartered Institute of Bankers
FCIB .... Fellow, Corporation of Insurance Brokers
FCIE .... Fellow, Association of Charity Independent Examiners
FCIH .... Fellow, Chartered Institute of Housing
FCII .... Fellow, Chartered Insurance Institute
FCILA .... Fellow, Chartered Institute of Loss Adjusters
FCIM .... Fellow, Chartered Institute of Marketing (formerly FInstM)
FCIOB .... Fellow, Chartered Institute of Building
FCIPD .... Fellow, Chartered Institute of Personnel and Development
FCIS .... Fellow, Institute of Chartered Secretaries and Administrators
FCIT .... Fellow, Chartered Institute of Transport
FCMA .... Fellow, Chartered Institute of Management Accountants
FCMI .... Fellow, Chartered Management Institute (formerly FIMgt)
FCO .... Foreign and Commonwealth Office
FCollP .... Ordinary Fellow, College of Preceptors
FCOptom .... Fellow, College of Optometrists
FCP .... Fellow, College of Preceptors
FCT .... Fellow, Association of Corporate Treasurers
FDS .... Fellow in Dental Surgery
FDSRCPSGlas ...... Fellow in Dental Surgery, Royal College of Physicians and Surgeons of Glasgow
FDSRCS .... Fellow in Dental Surgery, Royal College of Surgeons of England
FE .... Further Education
FEI .... Fellow, Energy Institute
Fell .... Fellow

FEPA .... Fellow, Evangelical Preachers' Association
FETC .... Further Education Teacher's Certificate
FFA .... Fellow, Institute of Financial Accountants
FFAEM .... Fellow, Faculty of Accident and Emergency Medicine
FFARCS .... Fellow, Faculty of Anaesthetists, Royal College of Surgeons of England
FFChM .... Fellow, Faculty of Church Music
FFDRCSI .... Fellow, Faculty of Dentistry, Royal College of Surgeons in Ireland
FFHom .... Fellow, the Faculty of Homoeopathy
FFOM .... Fellow, Faculty of Occupational Medicine
FFPH .... Fellow, Faculty of Public Health (formerly FFPHM)
FFPHM .... Fellow, Faculty of Public Health Medicine (now see FFPH)
FFPM .... Fellow, Faculty of Pharmaceutical Medicine
FGA .... Fellow, Gemmalogical Association
FGCM .... Fellow, Guild of Church Musicians
FGMS .... Fellow, Guild of Musicians and Singers
FGS .... Fellow, Geological Society of London
FHA .... Fellow, Institute of Hospital Administrators (now see FHSM)
FHCIMA .... Fellow, Hotel Catering and Institutional Management Association
FHEA .... Fellow, Higher Education Academy
FHSM .... Fellow, Institute of Health Services Management
FIA .... Fellow, Institute of Actuaries
FIBiol .... Fellow, Institute of Biology
FIBMS .... Fellow, Institute of Biomedical Sciences
FICE .... Fellow, Institution of Civil Engineers
FIChemE .... Fellow, Institution of Chemical Engineers
FICM .... Fellow, Institution of Commercial Managers
FICS .... Fellow, International College of Surgeons
FIDiagE .... Fellow, Institution of Diagnostic Engineers
FIED .... Fellow, Institution of Engineering Designers
FIEE .... Fellow, Institution of Electrical Engineers (formerly FIERE)
FIEEE .... Fellow, Institute of Electrical and Electronics Engineers (NY)
FIERE .... Fellow, Institution of Electronic and Radio Engineers (now see FIEE)
FIET .... Fellow, Institution of Engineering and Technology
FIFireE .... Fellow, Institution of Fire Engineers
FIHospE .... Fellow, Institute of Hospital Engineering
FIHT .... Fellow of the Institution of Highways and Transportation
FIIM .... Fellow, Institution of Industrial Managers (formerly FIPlantE)
FIL .... Fellow, Institute of Linguists
FIMA .... Fellow, Institute of Mathematics and its Applications
FIMarEST .... Fellow, Institute of Marine Engineering, Science and Technology
FIMechE .... Fellow, Institution of Mechanical Engineers
FIMI .... Fellow, Institute of the Motor Industry
FIMLS .... Fellow, Institute of Medical Laboratory Sciences

FIMM .... Fellow, Institution of Mining and Metallurgy (now see FIMMM)

FIMMM .... Fellow, Institute of Materials, Minerals and Mining

FIMS .... Fellow, Institute of Management Specialists

FInstAM .... Fellow, Institute of Administrative Management

FInstD .... Fellow, Institute of Directors

FInstE .... Fellow, Institute of Energy

FInstLEx .... Fellow, Institute of Legal Executives

FInstLM .... Fellow, Institute of Leadership and Management

FInstMC .... Fellow, Institute of Measurement and Control

FInstP .... Fellow, Institute of Physics

FInstSMM .... Fellow, Institute of Sales and Marketing Management

FInstTT .... Fellow, Institute of Travel and Tourism

FINucE .... Fellow, Institution of Nuclear Engineers (now see FNucI)

FIOSH .... Fellow, Institute of Occupational Safety and Health

FIPD .... Fellow, Institute of Personnel Development

FIPEM .... Fellow, Institute of Physics and Engineering in Medicine

FIQA .... Fellow, Institute of Quality Assurance

FISM .... Fellow, Institute of Supervisory Management

FIST .... Fellow, Institute of Science and Technology

FIStructE .... Fellow, Institution of Structural Engineers

Fitzw .... Fitzwilliam

FKC .... Fellow, King's College London

FLA .... Fellow, Library Association

FLAME .... Family Life and Marriage Education

FLCM .... Fellow, London College of Music

FLIA .... Fellow, Life Insurance Association

FLS .... Fellow, Linnean Society

FMA .... Fellow, Museums Association

FNI .... Fellow, Nautical Institute

FNMSM .... Fellow, North and Midlands School of Music

FNucI .... Fellow, Nuclear Institute (formerly FINucE)

Foundn .... Foundation

FPhS .... Fellow, Philosophical Society of England

FPS .... Fellow, Pharmaceutical Society of Great Britain

FRACI .... Fellow, Royal Australian Chemical Institute

FRAeS .... Fellow, Royal Aeronautical Society

FRAI .... Fellow, Royal Anthropological Institute

FRAM .... Fellow, Royal Academy of Music

Fran .... Francis

.... Francis's

FRAS .... Fellow, Royal Asiatic Society

.... Fellow, Royal Astronomical Society

FRCA .... Fellow, Royal College of Anaesthetists

FRCGP .... Fellow, Royal College of General Practitioners

FRCM .... Fellow, Royal College of Music

FRCO .... Fellow, Royal College of Organists

FRCOG .... Fellow, Royal College of Obstetricians and Gynaecologists

FRCOphth .... Fellow, Royal College of Ophthalmologists

FRCP .... Fellow, Royal College of Physicians

FRCP(C) .... Fellow, Royal College of Physicians of Canada

FRCPath .... Fellow, Royal College of Pathologists

FRCPCH .... Fellow, Royal College of Paediatrics and Child Health

FRCPEd .... Fellow, Royal College of Physicians Edinburgh

FRCPGlas .... Fellow, Royal College of Physicians and Surgeons, Glasgow (also see FRCSGlas)

FRCPsych .... Fellow, Royal College of Psychiatrists

FRCR .... Fellow, Royal College of Radiologists

FRCS .... Fellow, Royal College of Physicians and Surgeons of England

FRCSE or FRCSEd Fellow, Royal College of Surgeons of Edinburgh

FRCSGlas .... Fellow, Royal College of Physicians and Surgeons, Glasgow (also see FRCPGlas)

FRCSI .... Fellow, Royal College of Surgeons in Ireland

FRCVS .... Fellow, Royal College of Veterinary Surgeons

FREng .... Fellow, Royal Academy of Engineering

FRGS .... Fellow, Royal Geographical Society

FRHistS .... Fellow, Royal Historical Society

FRHS .... Fellow, Royal Horticultural Society

FRIAS .... Fellow, Royal Incorporation of Architects of Scotland

FRIBA .... Fellow, Royal Institute of British Architects

FRICS .... Fellow, Royal Institution of Chartered Surveyors (formerly FLAS and FSI)

FRIN .... Fellow, Royal Institute of Navigation

FRINA .... Fellow, Royal Institution of Naval Architects

FRIPH .... Fellow, Royal Institute of Public Health

FRMetS .... Fellow, Royal Meteorological Society

FRPharmS .... Fellow, Royal Pharmaceutical Society

FRS .... Fellow, Royal Society

FRSA .... Fellow, Royal Society of Arts

FRSAI .... Fellow, Royal Society of Antiquaries of Ireland

FRSC .... Fellow, Royal Society of Canada

.... Fellow, Royal Society of Chemistry (formerly FRIC)

FRSCM .... Honorary Fellow, Royal School of Church Music

FRSE .... Fellow, Royal Society of Edinburgh

FRSH .... Fellow, Royal Society for Public Health

FRSL .... Fellow, Royal Society of Literature

FRSM or FRSocMed Fellow, Royal Society of Medicine

FRTPI .... Fellow, Royal Town Planning Institute

FSA .... Fellow, Society of Antiquaries

FSAScot .... Fellow, Royal Society of Antiquaries of Scotland

FSCA .... Fellow, Royal Society of Company and Commercial Accountants

FSJ .... Fellowship of St John the Evangelist

FSR .... Fellowship Diploma of the Society of Radiographers

FSS .... Fellow, Royal Statistical Society

FTC .... Flying Training Command

FTCL .... Fellow, Trinity College of Music London

FTII .... Fellow, Institute of Taxation

FVCM .... Fellow, Victoria College of Music

FWeldI .... Fellow, Institute of Welding

G

G&C .... Gonville and Caius

Gabr .... Gabriel

.... Gabriel's

GB .... Great Britain

GBSM .... Graduate of the Birmingham School of Music

GCMG .... Knight Grand Cross, Order of St Michael and St George

GCVO .... Knight Grand Cross, Royal Victorian Order

Gd .... Good

Gen .... General

Geo .... George

.... George's

GFS .... Girls' Friendly Society

GGSM .... Graduate Diploma of the Guildhall School of Music and Drama

Gib .... Gibraltar

GIBiol .... Graduate of the Institute of Biology

GIFireE .... Graduate of the Institute of Fire Engineers

GIMechE .... Graduate of the Institution of Mechanical Engineers

GInstP .... Graduate of the Institute of Physics

GIPE .... Graduate of the Institution of Production Engineers

Glam .... Glamorgan

Glas .... (Diocese of) Glasgow and Galloway

.... Glasgow

GLCM .... Graduate Diploma of the London College of Music

Glos .... Gloucestershire

Glouc .... (Diocese of) Gloucester

GM .... George Medal

GMus .... Graduate Diploma in Music

GMusRNCM .... Graduate in Music of the Royal Northern College of Music

GNSM .... Graduate of the Northern School of Music

Gov .... Governor

Gp .... Group

Gr .... Grammar

GradCIPD .... Graduate of the Chartered Institute of Personnel and Development

GradICSA .... Graduate of the Institute of Chartered Secretaries and Administrators

GradIPM .... Graduate of the Institute of Personnel Management

Greg .... Gregory

.... Gregory's

GRIC .... Graduate Membership, Royal Institute of Chemistry

GRNCM .... Graduate of the Royal Northern College of Music

GRSC .... Graduate of the Royal School of Chemistry

GRSM .... Graduate of the Royal Schools of Music

GSM .... (Member of) Guildhall School of Music and Drama

Gt .... Great

GTCL .... Graduate Diploma of Trinity College of Music, London

Gtr .... Greater

Guildf .... (Diocese of) Guildford

H

H .... Holy

H&FE .... Higher and Further Education

HA .... Health Authority

Hatf .... Hatfield

HCIMA .... Hotel and Catering International Management Association

Hd .... Head

HDipEd .... Higher Diploma in Education

HE .... Higher Education

Heref .... (Diocese of) Hereford

Hertf .... Hertford

Hist .... Historic

.... Historical

.... History

HIV .... Human Immunodeficiency Virus

HM .... Her (or His) Majesty

HMI .... Her (or His) Majesty's Inspector (or Inspectorate)

HMS .... Her (or His) Majesty's Ship

Ho .... House

Hon .... Honorary

Hon .... Honourable

Hon GCM .... Honorary Member, Guild of Church Musicians

HonDLaws...........	Honorary Doctor of Laws
HonFChS..............	Honorary Fellow, Society of Chiropodists
HonRCM	Honorary Member, Royal College of Music
Hosp.....................	Hospital
HQ	Headquarters
HTV	Harlech Television
HVCert	Health Visitor's Certificate

I

I............................	Incumbent
IAAP.....................	International Association for Analytical Psychology
IBA.......................	Independent Broadcasting Authority
ICF.......................	Industry Churches Forum (formerly Industrial Christian Fellowship)
ICM	Irish Church Missions
ICS.......................	Intercontinental Church Society
IDC.......................	Inter-Diocesan Certificate
IDWAL	Inter-Diocesan West Africa Link
IEAB.....................	Igreja Episcopal Anglicana do Brasil
IEng.....................	Incorporated Engineer (formerly TEng(CEI))
IFES......................	International Fellowship of Evangelical Students
ILEA	Inner London Education Authority
IME.......................	Initial Ministerial Education
IMMM.................	Institute of Materials, Minerals and Mining
Imp.......................	Imperial
Inc	Incorporated
Ind.......................	Industrial
....	Industry
Info......................	Information
INSEAD...............	Institut Europen d'Administration des Affaires
Insp	Inspector
Inst	Institut
....	Institute
....	Institution
Intercon..............	Intercontinental
Internat	International
Interpr	Interpretation
IPFA	Member, Chartered Institute of Public Finance and Accountancy
Is..........................	Island
....	Islands
....	Isle
....	Isles
ISO	Imperial Service Order
IT	Information Technology
ITV	Independent Television
IVF	Inter-Varsity Fellowship of Evangelical Unions (now see UCCF)
IVS	International Voluntary Service

J

Jas........................	James
....	James's
JCD......................	Doctor of Canon Law
JCL.......................	Licentiate in Canon Law
JD	Doctor of Jurisprudence
JEM......................	Jerusalem and the East Mission (now see JMECA)
Jes........................	Jesus
JMECA	Jerusalem and Middle East Church Association (formerly JEM)
Jo.........................	John
....	John's
Jos.......................	Joseph
....	Joseph's
JP	Justice of the Peace
Jt..........................	Joint
Jun......................	Junior

K

K...........................	King
....	King's
K, E & A...............	(Diocese of) Kilmore, Elphin and Ardagh
KA........................	Knight of St Andrew, Order of Barbados

Kath.....................	Katharine/Katherine
....	Katharine's/Katherine's
KBE......................	Knight Commander, Order of the British Empire
KCB......................	Knight Commander, Order of the Bath
KCMG...................	Knight Commander, Order of St Michael and St George
KCVO....................	Knight Commander, Royal Victorian Order
KPM	King's Police Medal
Kt.........................	Knight

L

L & K	(Diocese of) Limerick and Killaloe (united dioceses of Limerick, Ardfert, Aghadoe, Killaloe, Kilfenora, Clonfert, Kilmacduagh and Emly)
Lamp..................	Lampeter
Lanc.....................	Lancaster
LASI	Licentiate, Ambulance Service Institute
Laur.....................	Laurence
....	Laurence's
Lawr.....................	Lawrence
....	Lawrence's
LBIPP	Licentiate, British Institute of Professional Photography
LCC	London County Council
LCL......................	Licentiate in Canon Law
LCP......................	Licentiate, College of Preceptors
LCST....................	Licentiate, College of Speech Therapists
LCTP....................	Lancashire and Cumbria Theological Partnership
Ld	Lord
LDiv.....................	Licentiate in Divinity
Ldr.......................	Leader
LDS......................	Licentiate in Dental Surgery
LEA	Local Education Authority
Lect	Lecturer
Leic......................	(Diocese of) Leicester
Leon	Leonard
....	Leonard's
LEP	Local Ecumenical Partnership
Lèsl......................	Licencié ès lettres
LGCM...................	Lesbian and Gay Christian Movement
LGSM...................	Licentiate, Guildhall School of Music and Drama
Lib	Librarian
....	Library
Lic.......................	Licence
....	Licensed
....	Licentiate
LICeram..............	Licentiate, Institute of Ceramics
Lich.....................	(Diocese of) Lichfield
LicTh...................	Licence in Theology
LIMA....................	Licentiate, Institute of Mathematics and its Applications
Linc.....................	(Diocese of) Lincoln
Lit	Literature
LittD....................	Doctor of Letters (also see DLitt)
Liturg.................	Liturgical
Liv.......................	(Diocese of) Liverpool
LLA	Lady Literate in Arts
LLAM....................	Licentiate, London Academy of Music and Dramatic Art
Llan	(Diocese of) Llandaff
LLB	Bachelor of Laws
LLCM...................	Licentiate, London College of Music
LLCM(TD)	Licentiate, London College of Music (Teachers' Diploma)
LLD......................	Doctor of Laws
LLM	Master of Laws
LMH	Lady Margaret Hall
LMPA...................	Licentiate Master, Photographers' Association
LNSM	Local Non-stipendiary Minister (or Ministry)
Lon	(Diocese of) London
LOROS.................	Leicestershire Organization for the Relief of Suffering
Loughb................	Loughborough
LRAM...................	Licentiate, Royal Academy of Music
LRCP....................	Licentiate, Royal College of Physicians

LRCPI	Licentiate, Royal College of Physicians of Ireland
LRCSEng.............	Licentiate of the Royal College of Surgeons in England
LRCSI	Licentiate, Royal College of Surgeons in Ireland
LRPS	Licentiate, Royal Photographic Society
LRSC	Licentiate, Royal Society of Chemistry
LRSM	Licentiate Diploma of the Royal Schools of Music
LSE.......................	London School of Economics and Political Science
LSHTM.................	London School of Hygiene and Tropical Medicine
LSIAD...................	Licentiate, Society of Industrial Artists and Designers
LSocEth................	Licence en Sociologie-Ethnologie
Lt.........................	Lieutenant
Lt.........................	Little
LTCL....................	Licentiate, Trinity College of Music London
Ltd......................	Limited
LTh......................	Licentiate in Theology (also see LST)
LVCM	Licentiate, Victoria College of Music
LVO......................	Lieutenant, Royal Victorian Order
LWCMD	Licentiate, Welsh College of Music and Drama

M

M & K	(Diocese of) Meath and Kildare
MA	Master of Arts
MA(Ed)................	Master of Arts in Education
MA(MM)...............	Master of Arts in Mission and Ministry
MA(Theol)...........	Master of Arts in Theology
MA(TS)................	Master of Arts in Theological Studies
MAAIS..................	Member, Association of Archaeological Illustrators and Surveyors
MAAT	Member, Association of Accounting Technicians
MACC	Member, Australian College of Chaplains
MACE	Member, Australian College of Educators
MACT	Member, Association of Corporate Treasurers
MAE......................	Member, Academy of Experts
Magd	Magdalen/Magdalene
....	Magdalen's/Magdalene's
MAgrSc................	Master of Agricultural Science
MAJA....................	Member, Association of Jungian Analysts
MAMIT	Member, Associate of Meat Inspectors Trust
Man......................	(Diocese of) Manchester
Man Dir...............	Managing Director
Mansf	Mansfield
MAPM...................	Member, Association for Project Management
MAPsS	Member, Australian Psychological Society
MArAd.................	Master of Archive Administration
MArch	Master of Architecture
Marg	Margaret
....	Margaret's
MASI.....................	Member, Architects and Surveyors Institute
MAT......................	Master of Arts and Teaching (USA)
MATA....................	Member, Animal Technicians' Association
MATCA.................	Member, Air Traffic Control Association
MATM	Master of Arts in Theology and Ministry
Matt	Matthew
....	Matthew's
MB	Bachelor of Medicine (also see BM)

MB,BS *or* MB,ChB	Conjoint degree of Bachelor of Medicine, Bachelor of Surgery
MBA	Master of Business Administration
MBACP	Member, British Association for Counselling and Psychotherapy
MBAOT	Member, British Association of Occupational Therapists (formerly MAOT)
MBAP	Member, British Association of Psychotherapists
MBASW	Member, British Association of Social Workers
MBATOD	Member, British Association of Teachers of the Deaf
MBC	Metropolitan (or Municipal) Borough Council
MBChA	Member, British Chiropody Association
MBCS	Member, British Computer Society
MBE	Member, Order of the British Empire
MBEng	Member, Association of Building Engineers
MBES	Member, Biological Engineering Society
MBIM	Member, British Institute of Management (later MIMgt)
MBKSTS	Member, British Kinematograph, Sound and Television Society
MBM	Master of Business Management
MBPsS	Member, British Psychological Society
MC	Military Cross
MCA	Member, Institute of Chartered Accountants
MCB	Master in Clinical Biochemistry
MCCDRCS	Member in Clinical Community Dentistry, Royal College of Surgeons
MCD	Master of Civic Design
MCE	Master of Civil Engineering
MCGI	Member, City and Guilds of London Institute
MChem	Master of Chemistry
MChemA	Master in Chemical Analysis
MChOrth	Master of Orthopaedic Surgery
MChS	Member, Society of Chiropodists
MCIArb	Member, Chartered Institute of Arbitrators
MCIBS	Member, Chartered Institute of Bankers in Scotland
MCIBSE	Member, Chartered Institute of Building Service Engineers
MCIEH	Member, Chartered Institute of Environmental Health (formerly MIEH)
MCIH	Member, Chartered Institute of Housing (formerly MIH)
MCIJ	Member, Chartered Institute of Journalists
MCIL	Member, Chartered Institute of Linguists
MCIM	Member, Chartered Institute of Marketing (formerly MInstM)
MCIMA	Member, Chartered Institute of Management Accountants
MCIOB	Member, Chartered Institute of Building
MCIPD	Member, Chartered Institute of Personnel and Development
MCIPS	Member, Chartered Institute of Purchasing and Supply
MCIT	Member, Chartered Institute of Transport
MCIWEM	Member, Chartered Institution of Water and Environmental Management
MCL	Master of Canon Law
MCLIP	Member, Chartered Institute of Library and Information Professionals
MCMI	Member, Chartered Management Institute (formerly MBIM and MIMgt)

MCollP	Member, College of Preceptors
MCom	Master of Commerce
MCommH	Master of Community Health
MCS	Member of Christian Spirituality
	Master of Christian Studies
MCSD	Member, Chartered Society of Designers
MCSP	Member, Chartered Society of Physiotherapy
MCST	Member, College of Speech Therapists
MCT	Member, Association of Corporate Treasurers
MD	Doctor of Medicine
MDA	Master of Defence Administration
MDefStud	Master of Defence Studies
MDiv	Master of Divinity
ME	Master of Engineering (also see MEng)
MEd	Master of Education
MEHS	Member, Ecclesiastical History Society
MEng	Master of Engineering
Mert	Merton
MèsL	Maîtrise ès Lettres Modernes
Metrop	Metropolitan
MFA	Master of Fine Art
MFHom	Member, Faculty of Homeopathy
MFOM	Member, Faculty of Occupational Medicine
MGDSRCS	Membership in General Dental Surgery, Royal College of Surgeons of England
Mgt	Management
MHCIMA	Member, Hotel Catering and Institutional Management Association
MHort (RHS)	Master of Horticulture, Royal Horticultural Society
MHSc	Master of Health Science
MHSM	Member, Institute of Health Services Management
MHums	Master of Humanities
MIA	Malawi Institute of Architects
MIAAP	Member, International Association for Analytical Psychology
MIAAS	Member, Incorporated Association of Architects and Surveyors
MIAM	Member, Institute of Administrative Management
MIAP	Member, Institution of Analysts and Programmers
MIAT	Member, Institute of Asphalt Technology
MIBC	Member, Institute of Business Counsellors
MIBCO	Member, Institution of Building Control Officers
MIBF	Member, Institute of British Foundrymen
MIBiol	Member, Institute of Biology
MICA	Member, International Cartographic Association
MICAS	Member, Institute of Chartered Accountants of Scotland
MICE	Member, Institution of Civil Engineers (formerly AMICE)
MICFM	Member, Institute of Charity Fundraising Managers
MICFor	Member, Institute of Chartered Foresters
Mich	Michael
	Michael's
	Michael and All Angels
MIChemE	Member, Institution of Chemical Engineers
MICM	Member, Institute of Credit Management
MICorrST	Member, Institution of Corrosion Science and Technology
MICS	Member, Institute of Chartered Shipbrokers
Midl	Midlands
MIE	Member, Institute of Engineers and Technicians

MIEAust	Member, Institute of Engineers and Technicians Australia
MIED	Member, Institute of Engineering Designers
MIEE	Member, Institution of Electrical Engineers (formerly AMIEE & MIERE)
MIEEE	Member, Institute of Electrical and Electronics Engineers (NY)
MIEEM	Member, Institute of Ecology and Environmental Management
MIEIecIE	Corporate Member, Institution of Electrical and Electronics
MIEIecIE	Incorporated Engineers
MIET	Member, Institution of Engineering and Technology
MIEx	Member, Institute of Export
MIGasE	Member, Institution of Gas Engineers
MIHEEM	Member, Institute of Healthcare Engineering and Estate Management
MIHM	Member, Institute of Healthcare Management
MIHT	Member, Institution of Highways and Transportation
MIIExE	Member, Institute of Incorporated Executive Engineers
MIIM	Member, Institution of Industrial Managers
MIInfSc	Member, Institute of Information Scientists
MIL	Member, Institute of Linguists
Mil	Military
MILT	Member, Institute of Logistics and Transport
MIM	Member, Institute of Metals (formerly Institution of Metallurgists)
	Member, Institute of Management Accountants
MIMA	Member, Institute of Mathematics and its Applications
MIMarEST	Member, Institute of Marine Engineering, Science and Technology
MIMC	Member, Institute of Management Consultants
MIMechE	Member, Institution of Mechanical Engineers (formerly AMIMechE)
MIMI	Member, Institute of the Motor Industry
MIMunE	Member, Institution of Municipal Engineers
Min	Minister
	Ministers
	Ministries
	Ministry
	Minor
MinI	Ministerial
MInstC(Glas)	Member, Institute of Counselling (Glasgow)
MInstD	Member, Institute of Directors
MInstE	Member, Institute of Energy
MInstGA	Member, Institute of Group Analysis
MInstP	Member, Institute of Physics
MInstPI	Member, Institute of Patentees and Inventors
MInstPkg	Member, Institute of Packaging
MInstPS	Corporate Member, Institute of Purchasing and Supply
MInstTA	Member, Institute of Transport Administration
MINucE	Member, Institute of Nuclear Engineers
MIOSH	Member, Institution of Occupational Safety and Health
MIOT	Member, Institute of Operating Theatre Technicians
MIPI	Member, Institute of Private Investigators

MIPR.................. Member, Institute of Public Relations
MIProdE.............. Member, Institution of Production Engineers
MIQA .... Member, Institute of Quality Assurance
MIRSE................ Member, Institution of Railway Signal Engineers
MISE................. Member, Institute of Sales Engineers
MISM .... Member, Institute of Supervisory Management
Miss.................. Mission
.... Missions
.... Missionary
Missr................. Missioner
MIStructE .... Member, Institute of Structural Engineers
MISW .... Member, Institute of Social Welfare
MITI................. Member, Institute of Translation and Interpreting
MITMA.............. Member, Institute of Trade Mark Agents
MITPA.............. Member, International Tax Planning Association
MIW .... Member, Institute of Welfare (formerly MIWO)
ML.................... Master of Leadership
MLI.................. Member, Landscape Institute
MLib................. Master of Librarianship
MLitt................ Master of Letters
MLL.................. Master of Laws
MLS .... Master of Library Studies
MM .... Military Medal
MMath .... Master of Mathematics
MMCET............. Martyrs' Memorial and Church of England Trust
MMedSc............. Master of Medical Science
MMet................ Master of Metallurgy
MMin .... Master of Ministry
MMinTheol .... Master in Ministry and Theology
MMS .... Member, Institute of Management Services
MMus................ Master of Music (also see MusM)
MN................... Master of Nursing
MNI.................. Member, Nautical Institute
MOD................. Ministry of Defence
Mon .... (Diocese of) Monmouth
Mor .... (Diocese of) Moray, Ross and Caithness
MPA.................. Master of Public Administration
MPH .... Master of Public Health
MPhil................ Master of Philosophy
MPhilF .... Master of Philosophical Foundations
MPhys .... Master of Physics
MPS.................. Master of Professional Studies
MPsychSc .... Master of Psychological Science
MRAC............... Member, Royal Agricultural College
MRAeS.............. Member, Royal Aeronautical Society
MRCGP .... Member, Royal College of General Practitioners
MRCO .... Member, Royal College of Organists
MRCOG .... Member, Royal College of Obstetricians and Gynaecologists
MRCP .... Member, Royal College of Physicians
MRCPath .... Member, Royal College of Pathologists
MRCPsych .... Member, Royal College of Psychiatrists
MRCS .... Member, Royal College of Surgeons
MRCSE.............. Member, Royal College of Surgeons of Edinburgh
MRCVS.............. Member, Royal College of Veterinary Surgeons
MRelSc.............. Master of Religious Science
MRes .... Master of Research
MRIA .... Member, Royal Irish Academy
MRICS .... Member, Royal Institution of Chartered Surveyors
MRIN................ Member, Royal Institute of Navigation
MRINA.............. Member, Royal Institution of Naval Architects

MRIPHH............. Member, Royal Institute of Public Health and Hygiene
MRPharmS .... Member, Royal Pharmaceutical Society (formerly MPS)
MRSC .... Member, Royal Society of Chemistry (formerly MRIC)
MRSL................ Member, Order of the Republic of Sierra Leone
MRSPH .... Member, Royal Society for the Promotion of Health
MRST................ Member, Royal Society of Teachers
MRTPI............... Member, Royal Town Planning Institute
MRTvS .... Member, Royal Television Society
MS.................... Master of Science (USA)
.... Master of Surgery
MSacMus .... Master of Sacred Music
MSAICE .... Member, South African Institution of Civil Engineers
MSc .... Master of Science
MSc(Econ).......... Master of Science in Economics
MSci .... Master of Natural Sciences
MScRel .... Maîtrise ès Sciences Religieuses
MSE.................. Master of Science in Engineering (USA)
.... Minister (or Ministers) in Secular Employment
MSERT .... Member, Society of Electronic and Radio Technicians
MSHAA............. Member, Society of Hearing Aid Audiologists
MSI................... Member, Securities Institute
MSIAD............... Member, Society of Industrial Artists and Designers
MSoc................. Maîtrise en Sociologie
MSocSc .... Master of Social Sciences (also see MSSc)
MSocWork.......... Master of Social Work (USA)
MSOSc .... Member, Society of Ordained Scientists
MSOTS.............. Member, Society for Old Testament Study
MSR................. Member, Society of Radiographers
MSSc .... Master of Social Science (also see MSocSc)
MSSCh .... Member, School of Surgical Chiropody
MSSTh............... Member, Society for the Study of Theology
MSt .... Master of Studies
MSTSD .... Member, Society of Teachers of Speech and Drama
MSW .... Master of Social Work
Mt .... Mount
MTD.................. Master of Transport Design
MTech .... Master of Technology
MTh or MTheol.. Master of Theology (also see STM and ThM)
MThSt or MTS.... Master of Theological Studies
MU .... Mothers' Union
MusB or MusBac Bachelor of Music (also see BMus)
MusD or MusDoc Doctor of Music
MusM................ Master of Music (also see MMus)
MVO .... Member, Royal Victorian Order

N

N .... North
.... Northern
NACRO .... National Association for the Care and Rehabilitation of Offenders
NASA................. National Aeronautics and Space Administration (USA)
Nat .... National
Nath .... Nathanael/Nathaniel
.... Nathanael's/Nathaniel's
NCEC .... National Christian Education Council
NE .... North East
NEITE................ North East Institute for Theological Education
NEOC .... North East Oecumenical Course (formerly North East Ordination Course)
Newc.................. (Diocese of) Newcastle

NHS................... National Health Service
Nic..................... Nicholas/Nicolas
.... Nicholas's/Nicolas's
NIDA .... National Institute of Dramatic Art
NJ .... New Jersey
NOC.................. Northern Ordination Course
Nor.................... (Diocese of) Norwich
Northn .... Northampton
Nottm .... Nottingham
NS .... Nova Scotia (Canada)
NSM.................. Non-stipendiary Minister (or Ministry)
NSPCC .... National Society for the Prevention of Cruelty to Children
NSW.................. New South Wales (Australia)
NT .... New Testament
NTMTC .... North Thames Ministerial Training Course
Nuff................... Nuffield
NUI.................... National University of Ireland
NUU.................. New University of Ulster
NW..................... North West/Northwestern
NWT.................. North West Territories (Canada)
NY .... New York (USA)
NZ .... New Zealand

O

OAM .... Medal of the Order of Australia
OBE .... Officer, Order of the British Empire
OBI .... Order of British India
OCF .... Officiating Chaplain to the Forces
OCM .... Officiating Chaplain to the Military
Offg................... Officiating
Offic.................. Officiate
OGS .... Oratory of the Good Shepherd
OH .... Ohio
OHP.................. Order of the Holy Paraclete
OLM .... Ordained Local Minister (or Ministry)
OM.................... Order of Merit
OM(Ger)............ Order of Merit of Germany
OMF.................. Overseas Missionary Fellowship
ONZ .... Order of New Zealand
Ord.................... Ordained
.... Ordinands
.... Ordination
Org.................... Organization
.... Organizer
.... Organizing
OSB .... Order of St Benedict
OSP .... Order of St Paul
OT .... Old Testament
Ox .... (Diocese of) Oxford

P

P .... Patron(s)
.... Priest
p .... Ordained Priest
P in O .... Priest in Ordinary
Par.................... Parish
.... Parishes
Paroch .... Parochial
Past................... Pastoral
Patr................... Patrick
.... Patrick's
.... Patronage
PBS .... Pengeran Bintang Sarawak (Companion of the Order of the Star, Sarawak)
PC .... Perpetual Curate
.... Privy Counsellor
PCC .... Parochial Church Council
Pemb................. Pembroke
Penn.................. Pennsylvania (USA)
Perm.................. Permission
Pet.................... (Diocese of) Peterborough
.... Peter
.... Peter's
Peterho.............. Peterhouse
PEV .... Provincial Episcopal Visitor
PGCE .... Postgraduate Certificate in Education

PGDE.................. Postgraduate Diploma in Education
PGTC.................. Postgraduate Teaching Certificate
PhB..................... Bachelor of Philosophy
PhC..................... Pharmaceutical Chemist
PhD..................... Doctor of Philosophy (also see DPhil)
PhD(Educ).......... Doctor of Philosophy in Education
Phil .... Philip
.... Philip's
PhL..................... Licentiate of Philosophy
P-in-c .... Priest-in-charge
plc .... public limited company
PM...................... Priest Missioner
PO .... Post Office
Poly .... Polytechnic
Portsm................ (Diocese of) Portsmouth
PQCSW .... Post-Qualifying Certificate in Social Work
Preb.................... Prebendary
Prec .... Precentor
Prep.................... Preparatory
Pres.................... President
Prin..................... Principal
Pris..................... Prison
.... Prisons
Prof..................... Professor
.... Professorial
Progr .... Program
.... Programme
.... Programmes
Prop.................... Proprietary
Prov .... Province
.... Provincial
PsychD .... Professional Doctor of Counselling Psychology
Pt........................ Point
PV....................... Priest Vicar

Q

QC...................... Queen's Counsel
QGM.................. Queen's Gallantry Medal
QHC.................. Honorary Chaplain to The Queen
Qld..................... Queensland
QN .... Queen's Nurse
QPM................... Queen's Police Medal
QSM................... Queen's Service Medal
QSO .... Queen's Service Order of New Zealand
QTS.................... Qualified Teacher Status
Qu .... Queen
.... Queen's
.... Queens'
QUB .... The Queen's University of Belfast
QVRM................ Queen's Volunteer Reserve Medal

R

R......................... Rector
.... Royal
R and D .... Research and Development
R of O .... Reserve of Officers
R&SChTrust....... Rochester and Southwark Church Trust
RAAChD .... Royal Australian Army Chaplains' Department
RAAF.................. Royal Australian Air Force
RAChD .... Royal Army Chaplains' Department
RAD or RADD .... Royal Association in Aid of Deaf People (formerly Deaf and Dumb)
RADA.................. Royal Academy of Dramatic Art
RADICLE .... Residential and Drop-in Centre London Enterprises
RAEC .... Royal Army Educational Corps
RAF .... Royal Air Force
RAFVR................ Royal Air Force Volunteer Reserve
RAM .... (Member) Royal Academy of Music
RAN.................... Royal Australian Navy
RANSR................ Royal Australian Naval Strategic Reserve
RAuxAF.............. Royal Auxiliary Air Force
RC .... Roman Catholic
RCA .... Royal College of Art
RCAF .... Royal Canadian Air Force
RCM.................... Royal College of Music

RCN.................... Royal Canadian Navy
.... Royal College of Nursing
RCNT.................. Registered Clinical Nurse Teacher
RCPS.................. Royal College of Physicians and Surgeons
RCS..................... Royal College of Surgeons of England
RCSE................... Royal College of Surgeons of Edinburgh
RD .... Royal Navy Reserve Decoration
.... Rural Dean
RE....................... Religious Education
Reg...................... Registered
Rehab .... Rehabilitation
Relig .... Religion(s)
.... Religious
Relns................... Relations
Rem..................... Remand
Rep...................... Representative
Res...................... Residence
.... Resident
.... Residential
.... Residentiary
Resp.................... Responsibility
Resurr .... Resurrection
Revd................... Reverend
RFN .... Registered Fever Nurse
RGN .... Registered General Nurse
RHV .... Registered Health Visitor
RIA...................... Royal Irish Academy
RIBA................... (Member) Royal Institute of British Architects (formerly ARIBA)
Rich .... Richard
.... Richard's
Ripon.................. Ripon and Leeds
RLSMD............... Royal London School of Medicine and Dentistry
RM...................... Registered Midwife
RMA or RMC ...... Royal Military Academy (formerly College), Sandhurst
RMCM................ Royal Manchester College of Music
RMCS .... Royal Military College of Science, Shrivenham
RMHN .... Registered Mental Health Nurse
RMN.................... Registered Mental Nurse
RN....................... Registered Nurse (Canada)
.... Royal Navy
RN(MH).............. Registered Nurse (for the mentally handicapped)
RNCM................. Royal Northern College of Music
RNIB................... Royal National Institute for the Blind
RNLI .... Royal National Lifeboat Institution
RNMH .... Registered Nurse for the Mentally Handicapped
RNR..................... Royal Naval Reserve
RNT .... Registered Nurse Tutor
RNVR.................. Royal Naval Volunteer Reserve
RNZN .... Royal New Zealand Navy
Rob...................... Robinson
Roch .... (Diocese of) Rochester
RS .... Religious Studies
RSAMD............... Royal Scottish Academy of Music and Drama
RSCM .... (Member) Royal School of Church Music
RSCN .... Registered Sick Children's Nurse
Rt........................ Right
RTCert .... Certified Reality Therapist
Rtd or rtd .... Retired
RTE .... Radio Telefís Éireann
RVC .... Royal Veterinary College
RVO .... Royal Victorian Order

S

S......................... South
.... Southern
S & B .... (Diocese of) Swansea and Brecon
S & M .... (Diocese of) Sodor and Man
SA....................... Salvation Army
Sacr .... Sacrist
.... Sacristan
SAMS.................. South American Mission Society (now see CMS)

SAOMC .... St Albans and Oxford Ministry Course
SAP .... (Member) Society of Analytical Psychologists
Sarum................. (Diocese of) Salisbury
Sav .... Saviour
.... Saviour's
ScD...................... Doctor of Science (also see DSc)
Sch .... School
SCM .... State Certified Midwife
.... Student Christian Movement
SE .... South East
Sec...................... Secretary
SEITE.................. South East Institute for Theological Education
Selw.................... Selwyn
Sem..................... Seminary
Sen .... Senior
SEN .... State Enrolled Nurse
SHARE .... Shelter Housing and Renewal Experiment
Sheff................... (Diocese of) Sheffield
Shep................... Shepherd
SM....................... Master of Science (USA)
SMF .... Society for the Maintenance of the Faith
SNTS .... Society for New Testament Studies
SNWTP............... Southern North West Training Partnership
So .... Souls
.... Souls'
SOAS .... School of Oriental and African Studies
Soc .... Social
.... Society
SOMA................. Sharing of Ministries Abroad
SOSc................... Society of Ordained Scientists
Southn .... Southampton
SPCK .... Society for Promoting Christian Knowledge
SPG .... Society for the Propagation of the Gospel (now see USPG)
Sqn Ldr.............. Squadron Leader
SRCh .... State Registered Chiropodist
SRD .... State Registered Dietician
SRN .... State Registered Nurse
SROT .... State Registered Occupational Therapist
SRP .... State Registered Physiotherapist
SS .... Saints
.... Saints'
.... Sidney Sussex
SSB .... Society of the Sisters of Bethany
SSC .... Solicitor before the Supreme Court (Scotland)
SSEES.................. School of Slavonic and East European Studies
SSF .... Society of St Francis
SSJ .... Society of St John of Jerusalem
SSJE .... Society of St John the Evangelist
SSM.................... Self-supporting Minister (or Ministry)
.... Society of the Sacred Mission
St........................ Saint
St Alb .... (Diocese of) St Albans
.... St Alban
.... St Alban's
St And .... (Diocese of) St Andrews, Dunkeld and Dunblane
St As .... (Diocese of) St Asaph
St D .... (Diocese of) St Davids
St E .... (Diocese of) St Edmundsbury and Ipswich
STB .... Bachelor of Theology (also see BTh)
STD .... Doctor of Sacred Theology (also see DST)
Ste .... Sainte
Steph.................. Stephen
.... Stephen's
STETS .... Southern Theological Education and Training Scheme
STh...................... Scholar in Theology (also see ThSchol)
.... Student in Theology
STL .... Reader (or Professor) of Sacred Theology

STM	Master of Theology (also see MTh or MTheol and ThM)
STV	Scottish Television
Sub	Substitute
Succ	Succentor
Suff	Suffragan
Supt	Superintendent
SW	South West
S'wark	(Diocese of) Southwark
S'well	(Diocese of) Southwell and Nottingham
	Southwell
SWJ	Servants with Jesus
SWMTC	South West Ministry Training Course
Syn	Synod

T

T, K & A	(Diocese of) Tuam, Killala and Achonry
TA	Territorial Army
Tas	Tasmania
TAVR	Territorial and Army Volunteer Reserve
TC	Technician Certificate
TCD	Trinity College, Dublin
TCert	Teacher's Certificate
TD	Team Deacon
	Territorial Efficiency Decoration
TDip	Teacher's Diploma
TEAR	The Evangelical Alliance Relief
Tech	Technical
	Technological
	Technology
TEM	Territorial Efficiency Medal
temp	temporarily
TEng	Senior Technician Engineer
Th	Theologian
	Theological
	Theology
ThA	Associate of Theology
ThB	Bachelor of Theology (USA)
ThD	Doctorate in Theology (also see DTh)
ThL	Theological Licentiate
ThM	Master of Theology (also see MTh or MTheol and STM)
Thos	Thomas
	Thomas's
ThSchol	Scholar in Theology (also see STh)

Tim	Timothy
	Timothy's
TISEC	Theological Institute of the Scottish Episcopal Church
TM	Team Minister (or Ministry)
TP	Team Priest
TR	Team Rector
Tr	Trainer
	Training
Treas	Treasurer
	Treasurer's
Trin	Trinity
TS	Training Ship
TSB	Trustee Savings Bank
TV	Team Vicar
	Television
TVS	Television South

U

UAE	United Arab Emirates
UCCF	Universities and Colleges Christian Fellowship of Evangelical Unions (formerly IVF)
UCD	University College, Dublin
UEA	University of East Anglia
UED	University Education Diploma
UK	United Kingdom
UKRC	United Kingdom Register of Counsellors
UMCA	Universities' Mission to Central Africa (now see USPG)
UMIST	University of Manchester Institute of Science and Technology
UNISA	University of South Africa
Univ	University
UPA	Urban Priority Area (or Areas)
URC	United Reformed Church
US or USA	United States (of America)
USCL	United Society for Christian Literature
USPG	United Society for the Propagation of the Gospel (formerly SPG, UMCA, and CMD)
UWE	University of the West of England
UWIC	University of Wales Institute, Cardiff

UWIST	University of Wales Institute of Science and Technology

V

V	Vicar
	Virgin
	Virgin's
Ven	Venerable
VetMB	Bachelor of Veterinary Medicine (also see BVetMed)
Vic	Victoria (Australia)
Vin	Vincent
	Vincent's
Voc	Vocation(s)
	Vocational
VRD	Royal Naval Volunteer Reserve Officers' Decoration
VRSM	Volunteer Reserves Service Medal

W

W	West
	Western
w	with
W/Cdr	Wing Commander
Wadh	Wadham
Wakef	(Diocese of) Wakefield
WCC	World Council of Churches
WEC	Worldwide Evangelism Crusade
WEMTC	West of England Ministerial Training Course
Westf	Westfield
Westmr	Westminster
Wilts	Wiltshire
Win	(Diocese of) Winchester
Wm	William
WMMTC	West Midlands Ministerial Training Course
Wolfs	Wolfson
Wolv	Wolverhampton
Worc	(Diocese of) Worcester
WRAF	Women's Royal Air Force

Y

YMCA	Young Men's Christian Association
YOI	Young Offender Institution
YWAM	Youth with a Mission

AAGAARD, Canon Angus Robert. b 64. Moray Ho Coll of Educn CQSW 86. Ripon Coll Cuddesdon BTh 93. **d** 93 **p** 94. C Taunton St Andr *B & W* 93-97; TV Southampton (City Cen) *Win* 97-01; TR N Lambeth *S'wark* from 01; Hon Can Asante and Mampong Ghana from 15. *St Anselm's Vicarage, 286 Kennington Road, London SE11 5DU* T: (020) 7735 3415 F: 7735 3403 M: 07810-646644
E: angus.aagaard@googlemail.com

ABAYOMI-COLE, Bimbisara Alfred (Bimbi). b 58. CCC Ox BA 80 MA 85. Trin Coll Bris BA 94. **d** 94 **p** 95. C Deptford St Pet *S'wark* 94-98; V Crofton St Paul *Roch* from 98. *St Paul's Vicarage, 2 Oakwood Road, Orpington BR6 8JH* T: (01689) 852939 *or* 850697
E: bimbiabayomi_cole@hotmail.com

ABBOTT, Barry Joseph. b 59. Sunderland Univ BA 98 MCIEH. NEOC 89. **d** 92 **p** 93. NSM Bishopwearmouth Ch Ch *Dur* 92-98; NSM Silksworth 98-00; P-in-c Lumley 00-04; AD Chester-le-Street 02-04; P-in-c Whickham 04-08; R from 08. *The Rectory, Church Chare, Whickham, Newcastle upon Tyne NE16 4SH* T: 0191-488 7397 M: 07801-074909

ABBOTT, Christopher Ralph. b 38. Univ of Wales (Lamp) BA 59. Wells Th Coll 59. **d** 61 **p** 62. C Camberwell St Giles *S'wark* 61-67; C Portsea St Mary *Portsm* 67-70; V Portsea St Cuth 70-87; P-in-c Gt Milton *Ox* 87-88; P-in-c Lt Milton 87-88; R Gt w Lt Milton and Gt Haseley 88-93; R Chailey *Chich* 93-00; Chapl Chailey Heritage Hosp Lewes 95-00; rtd 00; PtO *Chich* from 01; Hon C Purbrook *Portsm* 03-05. *6 Winchfield Crescent, Havant PO9 3SP* T: (023) 9247 7376
E: christopherabbott@jonty.fsnet.co.uk

ABBOTT, Craig Andrew. b 75. St Martin's Coll Lanc BA 96. LCTP 10. **d** 12 **p** 13. C Lancaster St Thos *Blackb* from 12. *97 Barton Road, Lancaster LA1 4EN* T: (01524) 844172 M: 07813-903420 E: craigandalison@sky.com

ABBOTT, Canon David John. b 52. CertEd. St Jo Coll Nottm. **d** 87 **p** 88. C Biddulph *Lich* 87-90; C Tunbridge Wells St Jas *Roch* 90-92; TV Tunbridge Wells St Jas w St Phil 92-98; V Sunnyside w Bourne End *St Alb* from 98; RD Berkhamsted 04-09; Hon Can St Alb from 15. *The Vicarage, Ivy House Lane, Berkhamsted HP4 2PP* T: (01442) 865100
E: ssvicarage@yahoo.co.uk

ABBOTT, David Robert. b 49. Edin Univ BD 72. Qu Coll Birm 72. **d** 74 **p** 75. C Kirkby *Liv* 74-78; C Ditton St Mich 78-80; R Ashton-in-Makerfield H Trin 80-14; rtd 14. *65 Meadow Brook, Wigan WN5 8ED*

ABBOTT (née BUSH), Esther Rachma Hartley. b 66. LMH Ox BA 88 St Jo Coll Dur BA 04. Cranmer Hall Dur 02. **d** 04 **p** 05. C Bethnal Green St Matt w St Jas the Gt *Lon* 04-07; C Staines 07-10; P-in-c Westfield *B & W* 10-15; Chapl Norton Radstock Coll of FE 10-14; P-in-c Woodhill *Sarum* from 15; C Lyneham w Bradenstoke from 15. *The Vicarage, Clyffe Pypard, Swindon SN4 7PY* M: 07854-852806 T: (01793) 731134
E: reverendrachma@gmail.com

ABBOTT, Miss Geraldine Mary. b 33. SRN 55 SCM 58 Open Univ BA 77 Lon Univ MTh 85. Oak Hill Th Coll BA 82. **dss** 86 **d** 87 **p** 94. Tutor Oak Hill Th Coll 86-96; St Alb St Paul *St Alb* 86-94; Hon Par Dn 87-94; Hon C from 94. *2 Wheatleys, St Albans AL4 9UE* T: (01727) 860869

ABBOTT (née ROBERTS), Ms Judith. b 55. Collingwood Coll Dur BA 76 Goldsmiths' Coll Lon PGCE 77. SWMTC 00. **d** 03 **p** 04. C Burrington, Chawleigh, Cheldon, Chulmleigh etc *Ex* 03-06; C Axminster, Chardstock, All Saints etc 06-12; PtO *B & W* 13-14; NSM Chaffcombe, Cricket Malherbie etc from 14. *Braytons, Wreath Green, Tatworth, Chard TA20 2SN* T: (01460) 220689 E: judith754@btinternet.com

ABBOTT, Mrs Kathleen Frances. b 60. STETS 96. **d** 99 **p** 00. NSM St Helens and Sea View *Portsm* 99-02; P-in-c Wootton 02-14; AD W Wight 12-14; rtd 15. *48 Fairfield Gardens, Sandown PO36 9EZ* E: abbott.kath@gmail.com

ABBOTT, Canon Nigel Douglas Blayney. b 37. Open Univ BA 87. Bps' Coll Cheshunt 58. **d** 61 **p** 62. C Northampton St Mich *Pet* 61-64; C Wanstead St Mary *Chelmsf* 64-66; Chapl St Jo Sch Tiffield 66-69; V Earls Barton *Pet* 69-73; V Cov H Trin 73-80; Provost St Jo Cathl Oban 80-86; R Oban St Jo 80-86; TR Hemel Hempstead *St Alb* 86-96; RD 94-96; R Much

Hadham 96-02; Hon Can St Alb 96-02; rtd 02; PtO *Ely* from 03. *1 Cambridge Road, Ely CB7 4HJ* T: (01353) 662256
E: ndba75@icloud.com

ABBOTT, Peter John. b 48. CQSW 86. St Mich Coll Llan 94. **d** 96 **p** 97. C Neath w Llantwit *Llan* 96-98; C Merthyr Tydfil Ch Ch 98-00; P-in-c Llangeinor w Nantymoel and Wyndham 00-02; V Cwm Ogwr 02-03; TV Ebbw Vale *Mon* 03-13; TV Upper Ebbw Valleys 13-14; rtd 14. *19 Pantglas, Llanbradach, Caerphilly CF83 3PD* T: (029) 2086 6434

ABBOTT, Richard. b 43. **d** 07 **p** 08. OLM Bisley and W End *Guildf* 07-13. *241 Arethusa Way, Bisley, Woking GU24 9BU* T: (01483) 481165 M: 07810-800114
E: richard_abbott@hotmail.co.uk

ABBOTT, Stephen Anthony. b 43. K Coll Cam BA 65 MA 69 Edin Univ BD 68 Harvard Univ ThM 69. Edin Th Coll 66. **d** 69 **p** 70. C Deal St Leon *Cant* 69-72; Chapl K Coll Cam 72-75; C Cambridge St Matt *Ely* 75-76; Asst Chapl Bris Univ and Hon C Clifton St Paul 77-80; PtO *Bris* 81-04; P-in-c Mangotsfield 04-10; rtd 10; PtO *Bris* from 10; *Glouc* from 11. *24 Melrose Close, Yate, Bristol BS37 7AY* T: (01454) 315073
E: abbott.steve@btinternet.com

ABBOTT, Stephen John. b 62. Qu Mary Coll Lon LLB 83. Linc Th Coll BTh 92. **d** 92 **p** 93. C E Dereham and Scarning *Nor* 92-95; TV Penistone and Thurlstone *Wakef* 95-97; R Brandon and Santon Downham w Elveden *St E* 97-00; P-in-c Gt Barton 00-04; PtO 04-08; R Bansfield 08-12; rtd 12. *12 Skylark Close, Bury St Edmunds IP32 7GH* M: 07742-396523
E: sj.abbott@lineone.net

ABBOTT, Mrs Valerie Ann. b 45. Keele Univ BA 68. Trin Coll Bris MLitt 00. **d** 00 **p** 01. NSM Knowle St Martin *Bris* 00-01; NSM Brislington St Chris and St Cuth 01-04; NSM Mangotsfield 04-10; rtd 10; PtO *Bris* from 10; *Glouc* from 11. *24 Melrose Close, Yate, Bristol BS37 7AY* T: (01454) 315073 M: 07979-997968 E: val.abbott@btinternet.com

ABECASSIS, Joanna Margaret. b 54. Girton Coll Cam BA 75 MA 79 PhD 81. WEMTC 99. **d** 02 **p** 03. C Tavistock and Gulworthy *Ex* 02-07; TV Totnes w Bridgetown, Berry Pomeroy etc 07-10; P-in-c Bradford-on-Avon H Trin *Sarum* 10-13; R Bradford on Avon H Trin, Westwood and Wingfield from 13. *Holy Trinity Vicarage, 18A Woolley Street, Bradford-on-Avon BA15 1AF* T: (01225) 864444
E: joanna@abecassis.freeserve.co.uk

ABEL, David John. b 31. S'wark Ord Course 71. **d** 74 **p** 75. NSM Crowhurst *S'wark* 74-85; NSM Lingfield and Crowhurst 85-92; PtO 92-98; *Chich* 98-07; *St E* from 03. *13 Church Street, Boxford, Sudbury CO10 5DU* T: (01787) 211765

ABELL, Canon Brian. b 37. Nottm Univ BA 61 DipEd Leeds Univ MA 95. Cuddesdon Coll 61. **d** 63 **p** 64. C Lightcliffe *Wakef* 63-66; C-in-c Mixenden CD 66-68; Lect Linc Coll of Tech 68-69; Chapl Trent Coll Nottm 70-74; V Thorner *Ripon* 74-82; V Far Headingley St Chad 82-86; Deputation Appeals Org CECS 86-89; V Masham and Healey *Ripon* 89-00; Hon Can Ripon Cathl 99-00; rtd 00; PtO *Leeds* from 00. *Manor Garth, 1 Manor Road, Harrogate HG2 0HP* T/F: (01423) 526112
E: b.abell@btinternet.com

ABELL, George Derek. b 31. Selw Coll Cam BA 54 MA 68. Qu Coll Birm 54. **d** 56 **p** 57. C Stoke upon Trent *Lich* 56-60; C Wolverhampton 60-64; R Bridgnorth St Mary *Heref* 64-70; P-in-c Oldbury 64-70; R Atherton N Australia 70-73; R Withington w Westhide and Weston Beggard *Heref* 73-81; R Withington w Westhide 81-83; P-in-c Sutton St Nicholas w Sutton St Michael 76-81; R 81-83; Preb Heref Cathl 82-83; V Basing *Win* 83-88; rtd 88; PtO *Heref* 88-04. *25 Eastfield Court, Church Street, Faringdon SN7 8SL* T: (01367) 240731

ABELL, Peter John. b 45. Chich Th Coll 67. **d** 70 **p** 71. C Churchdown St Jo *Glouc* 70-74; Chapl RAF 74-98; R Kilkhampton w Morwenstow *Truro* 98-09; rtd 09; PtO *York* from 11. *66 Minster Avenue, Beverley HU17 0ND* T: (01482) 862816 E: 66minster@66minster.karoo.co.uk

ABERDEEN AND ORKNEY, Bishop of. See GILLIES, The Rt Revd Robert Arthur

ABERDEEN AND ORKNEY, Dean of. See NIMMO, The Very Revd Alexander Emsley

ABERDEEN, Provost of. *Vacant*

✠**ABERNETHY, The Rt Revd Alan Francis.** b 57. QUB BA 78 BD 89. CITC. **d** 81 **p** 82 **c** 07. C Dundonald *D & D* 81-84; C Lecale Gp 84-86; I Helen's Bay 86-90; I Ballyholme 90-07; Preb Down Cathl 00-07; Cen Dir of Ords 04-07; Bp Conn from 07. *Bishop's House, 3 Upper Malone Road, Belfast BT9 6TD* T: (028) 9066 1942 *or* 9082 8870
E: bishop@connor.anglican.org

ABINGTON, David John Barringer. b 48. EAMTC 91. **d** 94 **p** 95. C Newport w Longford and Chetwynd *Lich* 94-96; C Newport w Longford, Chetwynd and Forton 96-98; R Adderley, Ash, Calverhall, Ightfield etc 98-02; R Brading w Yaverland *Portsm* 02-11; rtd 11; PtO *Portsm* from 11. *26 Lincoln Way, Bembridge PO35 5QJ* T: (01983) 874690 M: 07855-086978
E: david.abington@btinternet.com

ABLETT, Edwin John. b 37. Clifton Th Coll 64. **d** 67 **p** 68. C Sneinton St Chris w St Phil *S'well* 67-70; R High and Gd Easter w Margaret Roding *Chelmsf* 70-73; SAMS Chile 73-75; C Gt Baddow *Chelmsf* 75-78; V Newchapel *Lich* 78-82; V S Westoe *Dur* 82-86; V Tibshelf *Derby* 86-00; rtd 00; PtO St D 00-09; Win from 10. *Copihue, 18 Sherley Green, Bursledon, Southampton SO31 8FL* T: (023) 8040 6413
E: john.copihue@btinternet.com

ABLETT, Mrs Jennifer Vera. b 46. **d** 00 **p** 01. OLM Claydon and Barham *St E* 00-13; NSM from 13. *10 Phillipps Road, Barham, Ipswich IP6 0AZ* T: (01473) 830205

ABLEWHITE, Stanley Edward. b 30. Birm Univ BSocSc 59 LSE CASS 60. Tyndale Hall Bris 64 Wycliffe Hall Ox 73. **d** 73 **p** 74. C Much Woolton *Liv* 73-77; V Brough w Stainmore *Carl* 77-84; Ecum Min Aldridge *Lich* 84-90; P-in-c Swindon 90-96; P-in-c Himley 90-96; rtd 96; PtO *Lich* from 04. *33 Paddock Lane, Aldridge, Walsall WS9 0BP* T: (01922) 658710

ABRAHAM, Brian. b 42. **d** 00 **p** 01. OLM Burscough Bridge *Liv* 00-12; rtd 12. *4 Mere Court, Burscough, Ormskirk L40 0TQ* T: (01704) 892547

ABRAHAM, Canon David Alexander. b 37. AKC 61. **d** 62 **p** 63. C Oswestry St Oswald *Lich* 62-63; C Gt Wyrley 63-65; C Sprowston *Nor* 65-67; V Ormesby w Scratby 67-81; R Oxborough w Foulden and Caldecote 81-87; R Cockley Cley w Gooderstone 81-87; V Didlington 81-87; R Gt and Lt Cressingham w Threxton 81-87; R Hilborough w Bodney 81-87; P-in-c Nor St Giles 87-96; Chapl Asst Norfolk and Nor Hosp 87-91; V Thorpe St Matt *Nor* 96-00; Hon Can Nor Cathl 95-00; rtd 00; PtO *Nor* from 00; Hon PV Nor Cathl from 14. *170 Desmond Drive, Old Catton, Norwich NR6 7JW* T: (01603) 402797 E: dalyn170@yahoo.co.uk

ABRAHAM, Canon John Callis Harford. b 31. Univ of W Aus BA 52. Westcott Ho Cam 53. **d** 55 **p** 56. C Wigan St Anne *Liv* 55-57; C Northam Perth Australia 57-60; R Wongan Hills 60-62; Vice-Warden Wollaston Th Coll& R Graylands 63-67; P-in-c City Beach 66-67; LtO *Birm* 67-68; R Applecross Perth Australia 68-76; Can Perth 71-84; R Leeming Australia 76-79; Chapl Home Miss 79-81; R Wembley 81-89; R Albany 90-94; Can Bunbury 92-94; rtd 94. *10 Royston Park, Pioneer Road, Albany WA 6330, Australia* T: (0061) (8) 9841 1809

ABRAHAM, Richard James. b 42. Liv Univ BA 63. Ridley Hall Cam 64. **d** 66 **p** 67. C Warrington St Ann *Liv* 66-70; C Golborne 70-73; V Bickershaw 73-78; V Ewerby w Evedon *Linc* 78-82; R Kirkby Laythorpe w Asgarby 78-82; R Kirkby Laythorpe 82-03; rtd 03. *23 Londesborough Way, Metheringham, Lincoln LN4 3HW*

ABRAHAMS, Peter William. b 42. Southn Univ BA 77. Sarum Th Coll 77. **d** 78 **p** 79. C Bitterne Park *Win* 78-82; C Old Brumby *Linc* 82-84; V Mitcham Ascension *S'wark* 84-91; TV Riverside *Ox* 91-06; rtd 06; PtO *Ox* 06-12. *17 Snowberry Close, Wokingham RG41 4AQ* T: 0118-989 3072
E: frapeter@aol.com

ABRAM, Paul Robert Carrington. b 36. MVO 07. Keble Coll Ox BA 62 MA 65. Chich Th Coll 60. **d** 62 **p** 63. C Redcar *York* 62-65; CF 65-89; V Salcombe *Ex* 89-96; Miss to Seafarers from 89; rtd 96; Chapl to The Queen 96-06; Chapl St Pet-ad-Vincula at HM Tower of Lon 96-06; Dep P in O 96-06; PtO *Win* from 09. *Paddock End, Kimpton, Andover SP11 8PG* T: (01264) 772349 E: paul.jo@virgin.net

ABRAM, Steven James. b 50. Lon Univ BD 76. Oak Hill Th Coll 71. **d** 76 **p** 77. C Biddulph *Lich* 76-79; C Heatherlands St Jo *Sarum* 79-83; Libya 83-84; C Stratford-on-Avon w Bishopton *Cov* 84; V Alderholt *Sarum* 84-90; V Daubhill *Man* 90-04; TV Mid Trent *Lich* from 07. *St Peter's House, 2 Vicarage Way, Hixon, Stafford ST18 0FT* T: (01889) 270418
E: sj@abram.org.uk

ABRAMS, Leonard. **d** 14 **p** 15. NSM Purley St Mark *S'wark* from 14. *Address temp unknown*

ABREY, Mrs Barbara May. b 52. Trin Coll Bris 09. **d** 11 **p** 12. OLM Wroughton *Bris* from 11. *17 Edgar Row Close, Wroughton, Swindon SN4 9LR* T: (01793) 633024
E: barbaraabrey@hotmail.com

ABREY, Mark Evans John. b 66. Ripon Coll Cuddesdon BTh 93. **d** 93 **p** 94. C W Derby St Mary *Liv* 93-97; P-in-c Anfield St Marg 97-01; Chapl R Liverpool Children's NHS Trust 95-99; R Chase *Ox* from 01; P-in-c Chadlington and Spelsbury, Ascott under Wychwood 01-05; P-in-c Ascott under Wychwood 05-07. *The Vicarage, Church Road, Chadlington, Chipping Norton OX7 3LY* T: (01608) 676572 E: mark@abreys.com *or* rector@thechasebenefice.org.uk

ABREY, Canon Philip James. b 51. NOC 82. **d** 85 **p** 86. NSM Hindley All SS *Liv* 85-90; C Caversham St Pet and Mapledurham etc *Ox* 90-00; Min Caversham Park LEP 90-00; Co Ecum Officer (Berks) 96-00; PtO *Cov* 01-07; Chapl HM Pris The Mount from 02; Hon Can St Alb *St Alb* from 13. *HM Prison, The Mount, Molyneux Avenue, Bovingdon, Hemel Hempstead HP3 0NZ* T: (01442) 834363
E: philip.abrey@hmps.gsi.gov.uk

ABSALOM, Alexander James David Edward. b 69. St Jo Coll Dur BA 91. Cranmer Hall Dur 92. **d** 94 **p** 95. C Cranham Park *Chelmsf* 94-98; PtO *Sheff* 98-05; Miss P Philadelphia St Thos 05-07; USA from 07. *5907 Pecan Grove Place, Edmond OK 73034, USA* T: (001) (405) 749 8044 E: alex@theabsaloms.net

ABULEMOI, Joseph Oriho. *See* CHOUFAR, Joseph Oriho Abulemoi

ACARNLEY, Rita Kay. b 57. Girton Coll Cam BA 79 MA 83 Newc Univ MA 94 St Jo Coll Dur BA 98. Cranmer Hall Dur 96. **d** 99 **p** 00. NSM Humshaugh w Simonburn and Wark Newc 99-00; Tutor TISEC and Prov Local Collaborative Min Officer 00-03; R Stonehaven and Catterline *Bre* 03-07; P-in-c Muchalls 03-07. *13 Midtown, Poolewe, Achnasheen IV22 2LW* T: (01445) 781315 E: ritaacarnley@dunelm.org.uk

ACHESON, Canon Denise Mary. BTh. **d** 05 **p** 06. C Ballyholme *D & D* 05-08; I Dunmurry *Conn* 08-13; Treas Belf Cathl from 13. *Belfast Cathedral, Donegall Street, Belfast BT1 2HB* F: (028) 9023 8332 E: canondenise@belfastcathedral.org

ACHESON, James Malcolm. b 48. BNC Ox BA 70 MA 73. Sarum & Wells Th Coll 83. **d** 85 **p** 86. C Highgate St Mich *Lon* 85-88; TV Tisbury *Sarum* 88-94; R Storrington *Chich* 94-14; rtd 14. *Address temp unknown*

ACHONRY, Dean of. *See* GRIMASON, The Very Revd Alistair John

ACHURCH, Peter William Hammond. b 37. Ridley Coll Melbourne 82. **d** 82 **p** 84. C Port Lincoln Australia 82-84; P-in-c Elliston w Lock and Wuddina 86; R 87-89; Par P Leigh Creek 89-93; TV Madeley *Heref* 00-05; rtd 05. *34 Birchall Road, Goolwa Beach SA 5214, Australia* T: (0061) (08) 8555 3279

ACKERLEY, Glyn James. b 57. Kent Univ MA 04 K Coll Lon PhD 13. Cranmer Hall Dur 84. **d** 87 **p** 88. C Tonbridge SS Pet and Paul *Roch* 87-90; R Willingham *Ely* 90-94; R Rampton 90-94; V Chatham St Phil and St Jas *Roch* 94-09; P-in-c Shorne 09-12; V from 12; Dioc Dir of Ords from 09. *The Vicarage, Butcher's Hill, Shorne, Gravesend DA12 3EB* T: (01474) 822239 M: 07595-171748 E: g.ackerley@btconnect.com

ACKERMAN, David Michael. b 71. Westmr Coll Ox BTh 95 Brighton Univ PGCE 98 Cardiff Univ LLM 11. Pontificium Institutum Internationale Angelicum Rome STB 01 MA 02. **d** 01 **p** 02. In RC Ch 01-04; C Fairford and Kempsford w Whelford *Glouc* 05-08; P-in-c Sherborne, Windrush, the Barringtons etc 08-12; Dioc Ecum Officer 08-12; V Kensal Green St Jo *Lon* from 13. *St John's Vicarage, Kilburn Lane, London W10 4AA* T: (020) 8969 2615 M: 07826-931399
E: dmackerman@hotmail.com

ACKFORD, Christopher Mark. b 60. Univ Coll Lon BDS 83 K Coll Lon MSc 89. Ripon Coll Cuddesdon 02. **d** 04 **p** 05. C Bracknell *Ox* 04-07; TV Aylesbury 07-14; V Bierton and Hulcott from 15. *The Vicarage, St James Way, Bierton, Aylesbury HP22 5ED* T: (01296) 424466 M: 07780-554032
E: mark@ackford.wanadoo.co.uk

ACKLAM, Leslie Charles. b 46. Birm Univ BEd 71. Ripon Coll Cuddesdon 78. **d** 80 **p** 81. C Chingford St Anne *Chelmsf* 80-83; C Spalding St Mary and St Nic *Linc* 83-85; V Spalding St Paul 85-93; P-in-c Linc St Faith and St Martin w St Pet 93-06; Chapl Linc Univ 06-11; rtd 12; PtO *S'wark* from 13. *25 Ravensroost, 27 Beulah Hill, London SE19 3LN* M: 07742-324680 E: lesacklam@gmail.com

ACKLAND, Canon John Robert Warwick. b 47. **d** 82 **p** 83. NSM Shooters Hill Ch Ch *S'wark* 82-88; NSM Mottingham St Andr w St Alban 82-94; NSM Woolwich St Thos 94-96; NSM Bellingham St Dunstan 96-03; Hon Chapl S'wark Cathl 98-03; P-in-c Perry Hill St Geo w Ch Ch and St Paul 03-04; V 04-12; TR Forest Hill w Lower Sydenham from 12; Hon Can S'wark Cathl from 05. *The Vicarage, Vancouver Road, London SE23 2AF* T: (020) 8699 7676 *or* 8699 7202 M: 07831-516662
E: johnackland1@aol.com

ACKROYD, David Andrew. b 66. Coll of Ripon & York St Jo BA 90 St Jo Coll Dur BA 97. Cranmer Hall Dur 94. **d** 97 **p** 98. C Lilleshall and Sheriffhales *Lich* 97-01; Asst Chapl R Wolv

Hosps NHS Trust 01-02; C Ogley Hay *Lich* 02-03; PtO 10-11; TR Cheswardine, Childs Ercall, Hales, Hinstock etc from 11. *The Vicarage, High Street, Cheswardine, Market Drayton TF9 2RS* T: (01630) 661204 E: revandy320@btopenworld.com

ACKROYD, Dennis. b 36. Cranmer Hall Dur 67. **d** 70 **p** 71. C Newcastle w Butterton *Lich* 70-73; C Horsell *Guildf* 73-77; P-in-c Moreton and Woodsford w Tincleton *Sarum* 77-82; R 82-86; RD Dorchester 79-85; R Ewhurst *Guildf* 86-94; V Cleckheaton St Luke and Whitechapel *Wakef* 94-02; rtd 02; PtO *Sarum* from 03. *17 Charles Street, Weymouth DT4 7JG* T: (01305) 778122 E: rev.dennis@virgin.net

ACKROYD, Eric. b 29. Leeds Univ BA 51 Liv Univ MA 71 Leic Univ MA(Ed) 86. Cranmer Hall Dur 53. **d** 55 **p** 56. C Newland St Jo *York* 55-58; Succ Birm Cathl 58-60; Chapl K Sch Bruton 61-66; Lect Kirkby Fields Coll of Educn Liv 67-72; Sen Lect Nene Coll of HE Northn 72-85; rtd 85. *14 Phippsville Court, St Matthew's Parade, Northampton NN2 7JW* T: (01604) 713328

ACKROYD, Canon Peter Michael. b 60. Jes Coll Cam BA 82 MA 86 Fontainebleau MBA 87 Edin Univ PhD 02. Wycliffe Hall Ox BA 93 MA 00. **d** 94 **p** 95. C Denton Holme *Carl* 94-97; Sec Proclamation Trust 97-00; V Wootton *St Alb* from 02; Hon Can St Alb from 15. *The Vicarage, Church Road, Wootton, Bedford MK43 9HF* T: (01234) 768391 E: ackroyds@lineone.net

ACKROYD, Prof Ruth. b 49. St Aid Coll Dur BA 70 Man Univ MPhil 87 Sheff Univ DMinTh 03. **d** 04 **p** 05. NSM Hoole *Ches* 04-15; V Thornton-le-Moors w Ince and Elton from 15. *The Vicarage, Ince Lane, Elton, Chester CH2 4QB* E: r.ackroyd@chester.ac.uk

ACLAND, Mrs Sophia Caroline Annabel. b 61. Somerville Coll Ox BA 11 MA 11. Ripon Coll Cuddesdon 08. **d** 11 **p** 12. NSM Cam w Stinchcombe *Glouc* from 11; NSM All Hallows by the Tower etc *Lon* from 14. *The Mount House, Alderley, Wotonunder-Edge GL12 7QT* T: (01453) 842233 or (020) 7481 2928 E: sophia@acland.force9.co.uk

ACONLEY, Carole Ann. b 51. Hull Univ BTh 01. NEOC 99. **d** 02 **p** 03. NSM Langtoft w Foxholes, Butterwick, Cottam etc *York* 02-12; PtO from 13. *Hawthorn Farm, Langtoft, Driffield YO25 3BT* T: (01377) 267219 E: caroleaconley@gmail.com

ACREMAN, John. b 53. Oak Hill Th Coll 86. **d** 88 **p** 89. C Iver *Ox* 88-92; R Hook Norton w Gt Rollright, Swerford etc from 92. *The Rectory, Hook Norton, Banbury OX15 5QQ* T: (01608) 737223 E: acreman@xalt.co.uk

ACWORTH, The Ven Richard Foote. b 36. SS Coll Cam BA 62 MA 65. Cuddesdon Coll 61. **d** 63 **p** 64. C Fulham St Etheldreda *Lon* 63-64; C Langley All SS and Martyrs *Man* 64-66; C Bridgwater St Mary w Chilton Trinity *B & W* 66-69; V Yatton 69-81; V Yatton Moor 81; P-in-c Taunton St Jo 81-84; P-in-c Taunton St Mary 81-85; V 85-93; Preb Wells Cathl 87-93; Adn Wells, Can Res and Preb Wells Cathl 93-03; rtd 03; PtO *B & W* from 04. *Corvedale Cottage, Ganes Terrace, Croscombe, Wells BA5 3QJ* T: (01749) 342242 E: vendick@talktalk.net

ACWORTH, Richard John Philip. b 30. Ch Ch Ox BA 52 MA 56 Paris Univ DèsL 70. **d** 63 **p** 63. C Walthamstow St Mary w St Steph *Chelmsf* 68-70; P-in-c Lt Sampford 70-76; P-in-c Gt Sampford w Hempstead 74-76; Lect Bath Coll of HE 76-77; Lect Th Derby Lonsdale Coll 77-82; Derbyshire Coll of HE 83-88; P-in-c Newton Tracey, Alverdiscott, Huntshaw etc *Ex* 88-96; TR Newton Tracey, Horwood, Alverdiscott etc 96-98; RD Torrington 94-97; rtd 98; PtO *Portsm* from 98. *91 Oaklands Road, Havant PO9 2RL* T: (023) 9245 0567

ADAIR, Raymond. b 33. Ripon Hall Ox 70. **d** 72 **p** 73. C Knottingley *Wakef* 72-75; C Sandal St Helen 75-77; V Sandal St Cath 77-87; V Brownhill 87-97; rtd 97; PtO *Leeds* from 99. *15 Chestnut Fold, Upper Lane, Netherton, Wakefield WF4 4NG* T: (01924) 274640

ADAIR, Canon William Matthew. b 52. Open Univ BA. CITC 77. **d** 77 **p** 78. C Portadown St Mark *Arm* 77-78; Asst Chapl Miss to Seamen 78-80; C Lisburn Ch Ch Cathl 80-84; I Kildress w Altedesert *Arm* 84-92; I Portadown St Columba from 92; Dioc Sec Min of Healing 95-99; Can Arm Cathl from 08. *St Columba's Rectory, 81 Loughgall Road, Portadown, Craigavon BT62 4EG* T: (028) 3833 2746

ADAM, Andrew Keith Malcolm. b 57. Bowdoin Coll USA BA 79 Duke Univ (USA) PhD 91. Yale Div Sch MDiv 86 STM 87. **d** 86 **p** 86. Chapl St Thos Day Sch & C New Haven Ch Ch USA 86-87; Chapl Assoc Duke Univ 97-90; Asst Prof Eckerd Coll 90-94; P-in-c Tampa St Jas 91-92; Asst Prof Princeton Th Sem 94-99; Prof Seabury-Western Th Sem 99-08; P-in-c Evanston St Luke 01-02; Lect Glas Univ 09-13; NSM St Mary's Cathl 10-13; Sen Tutor St Steph Ho Ox from 13. *St Stephen's House, 16 Marston Street, Oxford OX4 1JX* T: (01865) 613500 M: 07514-800612 E: akm.adam@gmail.com

ADAM, Canon David. b 36. Kelham Th Coll 54. **d** 59 **p** 60. C Auckland St Helen *Dur* 59-63; C Owton Manor CD 63-67; V Danby *York* 67-90; Can and Preb York Minster 89-90; V Holy Is *Newc* 90-03; rtd 03; PtO *Newc* from 03. *The Old Granary, Warren Mill, Belford NE70 7EE* T: (01668) 214770

ADAM, Lawrence. b 38. NOC 82. **d** 82 **p** 83. C Thornton-le-Fylde *Blackb* 82-86; Dioc Video Production Co-ord 85-97; P-in-c Scorton 86-91; C W Burnley All SS 91-97; P-in-c Ashton St Jas *Man* 97-99; TV Ashton 00-03; rtd 03; PtO *Ches* from 03. *23 Dryden Avenue, Cheadle SK8 2AW*

ADAM, Lindsay Anne. *See* YATES, Lindsay Anne

ADAM, Canon Peter James Hedderwick. b 46. Lon Univ BD 73 MTh 76 Dur Univ PhD 81. Ridley Coll Melbourne ThL 69. **d** 70 **p** 71. C Ivanhoe St Jas Australia 70-72; C Rosanna 72; Hon C Holborn St Geo w H Trin and St Bart *Lon* 72-73; C Essendon St Thos Australia 73-74; Tutor Ridley Coll 73-74; Tutor St Jo Coll Dur 75-82; Hon C Dur St Cuth 75-82; P-in-c Carlton St Jude Australia 82-88; V 88-01; Adn Melbourne 88-91; Chapl Melbourne Univ 95-01; Prin Ridley Coll 01-12; rtd 12; Can Melbourne from 96. *PO Box 603, North Carlton VIC 3054, Australia* E: pjhadam@gmail.com

ADAM, William Jonathan. b 69. Man Univ BA 91 Univ of Wales (Cardiff) LLM 03 PhD 09 FRHistS 11. Westcott Ho Cam 92 Bossey Ecum Inst Geneva. **d** 94 **p** 95. C Beaconsfield *Ox* 94-97; C Witney 97-98; TV 98-02; P-in-c Girton *Ely* 02-07; R 07-10; Dioc Ecum Officer 02-10; V Winchmore Hill St Paul *Lon* from 10. *St Paul's Vicarage, Church Hill, London N21 1JA* T: (020) 8886 3545 E: wja@luxmundi.co.uk

ADAMOLEKUN, Bola. b 72. St Jo Coll Nottm. **d** 14 **p** 15. *Unit 6, D D I House, 1-21 Elkstone Road, London W10 5NT* M: 07701-032297 E: bola_adamolekun@yahoo.co.uk

ADAMS, Canon Alison Mary. b 51. Girton Coll Cam MA 73 Birm Univ BMus 76 CertEd 77 Sheff Univ MPhil 93. EMMTC 94. **d** 97 **p** 98. NSM Burbage w Aston Flamville *Leic* 97-05; Dir Bloxham Project 00-05; Chapl HM YOI Glen Parva 06-13; Dioc and Cathl Soc Resp Enabler from 13; Hon Can Leic Cathl from 15. *29 Leicester Lane, Desford, Leicester LE9 9JJ* T: (01455) 823674

ADAMS, Amanda Elaine. QUB BSc BTh. **d** 06 **p** 07. C Ballymena w Ballyclug *Conn* 06-09; I Ballyrashane w Kildollagh from 09. *The Rectory, 9 Sandelwood Avenue, Coleraine BT52 1JW* T: (028) 7034 3061 E: aeadams@hotmail.co.uk

ADAMS, Anthony Paul. b 41. SAOMC 95. **d** 98 **p** 99. NSM Banbury St Hugh *Ox* 98-01; P-in-c Wootton w Glympton and Kiddington 01-04; P-in-c Broughton and Duddon *Carl* 04-10; rtd 10; PtO *Ox* from 11. *10 Quarry Road, Witney OX28 1JS* T: (01993) 775859 E: adamsfamily2@btinternet.com

ADAMS, Brian Hugh. b 32. Pemb Coll Ox BA 54 MA 57. Sarum & Wells Th Coll 77. **d** 79 **p** 80. Hon C Crediton *Ex* 79-81; Chapl St Brandon's Sch Clevedon 81-85; C Street w Walton *B & W* 86-88; RD Glastonbury 86-92 and 93-97; V Baltonsborough w Butleigh and W Bradley 88-97; rtd 97; PtO *B & W* from 97. *Manor Cottage, Weir Lane, Yeovilton, Yeovil BA22 8EU* T: (01935) 840462 M: 07980-605284 E: adamsbj@btinternet.com

ADAMS, Canon Brian Peter. b 47. FInstD FRSA Avery Hill Coll CertEd 70. S'wark Ord Course 90. **d** 93 **p** 94. NSM Tonbridge SS Pet and Paul *Roch* 93-99; P-in-c Chatham St Mary w St Jo 99-14; Hon Can Roch Cathl 09-14; rtd 14. *3 St Davids Gate, Maidstone ME16 9EP* T: (01622) 728032 M: 07778-777824 E: bpadams@btinternet.com

ADAMS, Mrs Celia. b 39. R Holloway Coll Lon BSc 60 Cam Univ CertEd 61. Sarum & Wells Th Coll 86. **d** 88 **p** 94. NSM Canley *Cov* 88-91; NSM Cov N Deanery 91-92; C Coventry Caludon *Cov* 92-97; Asst to Dioc Dir of Educn 92-93; Asst Chapl Geo Eliot Hosp NHS Trust Nuneaton 97-01; rtd 01; PtO *Ban* from 01; *Cov* from 01. *Cefn-y-Mor, 102 Plas Edwards, Tywyn LL36 0AS* T: (01654) 711604 E: nigeladams864@btinternet.com

ADAMS, The Ven Charles Alexander. b 29. JP MBE 73 CBE 82. AKC 59. **d** 60 **p** 61. C Bishopwearmouth St Mich w St Hilda *Dur* 60-63; C Ox SS Phil and Jas 63-66; C Tunbridge Wells St Barn *Roch* 66-68; Miss to Seafarers St Vincent from 68; Can Kingstown Cathl from 73; Adn St Vincent & The Grenadines 76-98; rtd 98. *Bequia Rectory, Port Elizabeth, Bequia, St Vincent and the Grenadines* T: (001784) 458 3234 F: 457 3532 E: caadams@caribsurf.com

ADAMS, Christine Frances. *See* BULL, Christine Frances

ADAMS, Christopher John. b 40. **d** 98 **p** 99. C Luton St Fran *St Alb* 98-05; rtd 06; PtO *St Alb* from 06. *91 Byron Road, Luton LU4 0HX* T: (01582) 529373 E: chrisandsallyadams@ntlworld.com

ADAMS, David. *See* ADAMS, John David Andrew

ADAMS, David James. b 58. Trin Coll Bris 95. **d** 97 **p** 98. C Wirksworth *Derby* 97-00; P-in-c Seale and Lullington 00-02; R Seale and Lullington w Coton in the Elms 02-05; CF from 05. *c/o MOD Chaplains (Army)* F: 381824 T: (01264) 383430

3

ADAMS, Canon David John Anthony. b 46. QUB BSc 70. Bris Sch of Min 81. **d** 84 **p** 85. NSM Sea Mills *Bris* 84-97; C Henbury 97-00; V Longwell Green 00-13; AD Kingswood and S Glos 06-11; Hon Can Bris Cathl 10-13; rtd 13. *31 Elberton Road, Bristol BS9 2PZ* T: 0117-968 4625 M: 07803-330727
E: djaadams@virginmedia.com

ADAMS, Donald John. b 46. St Jo Coll Nottm 86. **d** 88 **p** 89. C Byfleet *Guildf* 88-93; P-in-c E Molesey St Mary 93-03; PtO *S'wark* 96-03; rtd 03. *4 Boxbush Close, South Cerney, Cirencester GL7 5XS* T: (01285) 852009
E: cada.adams@virgin.net

ADAMS, Douglas George. b 39. St Luke's Coll Ex CertEd 69 MEd 87 ALBC 65. SWMTC 86. **d** 89 **p** 90. NSM Bude Haven and Marhamchurch *Truro* 89-93; P-in-c St Mewan 93-04; P-in-c Mevagissey and St Ewe 00-04; Chapl Mt Edgcumbe Hospice *Truro* rtd 04; PtO *Truro* from 05. *9 Arundel Terrace, Bude EX23 8LS* T: (01288) 353842
E: douglasadams@tiscali.co.uk

ADAMS, Gillian Linda. *See* WILTON, Gillian Linda

ADAMS, Godfrey Bernard. b 47. **d** 93 **p** 94. OLM Saddleworth *Man* 93-09; PtO from 09. *Shawfields House, Shaws, Uppermill, Oldham OL3 6JX* T: (01457) 875126

ADAMS, Hubert Theodore. b 28. FCA. **d** 98 **p** 99. OLM Blurton *Lich* 98-11; OLM Blurton and Dresden 11-13; PtO from 14. *12 Wakefield Road, Stoke-on-Trent ST4 5PT* T: (01782) 415364
E: theoadams@live.co.uk

ADAMS, Ian Robert. b 57. R Holloway Coll Lon BA 79. Ridley Hall Cam 95. **d** 97 **p** 98. C Thame *Ox* 97-04; Ldr mayBe 04-09; Missional Community Developer CMS 09-15; Miss Spirituality Adv from 15. *Old Walls, Fore Street, Aveton Gifford, Kingsbridge TQ7 4LL* T: (01548) 550388 M: 07889-906983
E: ian@thestillpoint.org.uk

ADAMS, Canon James Michael. b 49. Man Univ LLB 71 Lon Univ PGCE 79. St Jo Coll Nottm 80. **d** 82 **p** 83. C Luton St Mary *St Alb* 82-85; TV Cove St Jo *Guildf* 85-92; V Chislehurst Ch Ch *Roch* 92-14; Hon Can Roch Cathl 09-14; rtd 14. *15 Beck Yeat, Coniston LA21 8HT* T: (01539) 441758
E: michaeladamsccc@gmail.com

ADAMS, Mrs Jayne Maxine. b 57. Westhill Coll Birm CertEd 78. WMMTC 94. **d** 97 **p** 98. NSM Cotteridge *Birm* 97-99; NSM Nechells 99-05; NSM Bournville 05-07; Asst Chapl Dudley Gp NHS Foundn Trust 07-13; NSM Selly Oak St Mary *Birm* from 14. *95 Mavis Road, Birmingham B31 2SB* T: 0121-574 0436
E: jaynevicar@aol.com

ADAMS, John. b 82. Univ Coll Ox BA 05. Wycliffe Hall Ox BA 12. **d** 13 **p** 14. C Wimbledon Em Ridgway Prop Chpl *S'wark* from 13. *25 Richmond Road, London SW20 0PG* M: 07863-544228 E: johnfredadams@gmail.com

ADAMS, John David Andrew. b 37. TCD BA 60 MA 64 BD 69 Div Test 61 Reading Univ MEd 74. **d** 62 **p** 63. C Belfast St Steph *Conn* 62-65; Asst Master Lacunza Academy Spain 65-67; Asst Master Tower Ramparts Sch Ipswich 67-70; Asst Master Robert Haining Sch Surrey 70-74; Hd Master St Paul's Secondary Sch Addlestone 74-82; Hd Master Weydon Secondary Sch Farnham 82-98; NSM Bourne *Guildf* 88-99; NSM The Bourne and Tilford 99-07; Chapl to The Queen 94-07; Consultant to Secondary Schs 98-07; PtO *Guildf* from 08. *Brookside Farm, Oast House Crescent, Farnham GU9 0NP* T: (01252) 726888 E: j.david_adams@ntworld.com

ADAMS, Canon John Mark Arthur. b 67. Reading Univ BSc 89. St Jo Coll Nottm MA 98 MPhil 07. **d** 99 **p** 00. C Skegby *S'well* 99-02; C Bletchley *Ox* 02-07; P-in-c Mansfield St Jo *S'well* 07-10; P-in-c Ladybrook 09-10; V Mansfield St Jo w St Mary from 10; AD Mansfield from 10; Hon Can S'well Minster from 15. *The Vicarage, St John Street, Mansfield NG18 1QH* T: (01623) 660822 *or* 625999

ADAMS, John Peter. b 42. Lon Univ BD 69. Oak Hill Th Coll 65. **d** 70 **p** 71. C Whitnash *Cov* 70-73; Hon Asst Chapl Basle *Eur* 73-74; Chapl Davos 74-75; Chapl Düsseldorf 75-76; C Gt Baddow *Chelmsf* 77-80; Miss Eur Chr Miss 80-91; PtO *Chelmsf* 80-91; Hon Asst Vienna w Prague *Eur* 90-91; Asst Chapl Zürich 91-95; P-in-c Harmondsworth *Lon* 95-99; TV Shebbear, Buckland Filleigh, Sheepwash etc *Ex* 99-02; rtd 02; PtO *Ex* from 02. *The Leas, Kingscott, Torrington EX38 7JW* T: (01805) 622161
E: john@adams1100.freeserve.co.uk

ADAMS, John Richard. b 38. St D Coll Lamp BA 62 Lich Th Coll 62. **d** 64 **p** 65. C Falmouth K Chas *Truro* 64-68; C Bath Twerton-on-Avon *B & W* 68-72; C Milton *Win* 72-79; P-in-c Weymouth St Edm *Sarum* 79-90; V 90-95; Chapl Westhaven Hosp Weymouth 79-94; P-in-c The Winterbournes and Compton Valence *Sarum* 95-03; rtd 03. *1 Manor Barn, Bothenhampton, Bridport DT6 4BJ* T: (01308) 422808

ADAMS, Jonathan Henry. b 48. St Andr Univ MA 73. Cranmer Hall Dur 73. **d** 76 **p** 77. C Upperby St Jo *Carl* 76-78; C Sunderland St Chad *Dur* 78-82; Soc Resp Officer 83-91; TV

Willington *Newc* 91-96; Local Min Development Officer 91-96; P-in-c Byker St Silas *Newc* 96-01; PtO from 01; rtd 13. *5A Tunstall Vale, Sunderland SR2 7HP* T: 0191-525 1881
E: jonathan@openroad.fsnet.co.uk

ADAMS, Mark. *See* ADAMS, John Mark Arthur

ADAMS, Martin Philip. b 57. Open Univ BA 99 K Coll Lon MA 13. Sarum & Wells Th Coll 88. **d** 90 **p** 91. C Sandringham w W Newton *Nor* 90-93; P-in-c Docking w The Birchams and Stanhoe w Barwick 93-95; V Docking, the Birchams, Stanhoe and Sedgeford 95-97; V Orrell *Liv* 97-03; R Aughton St Mich 03-08; Dir Dioc OLM Scheme 03-11; Dir Studies SNWTP 08-11; Dean of Studies 11-14; Ed ROOTS for Churches Ltd from 15. *The Vicarage, Intake Lane, Bickerstaffe, Ormskirk L39 0HW* T: (01695) 727607 M: 07939-396934
E: martin.adams@rootsontheweb.com

ADAMS, Michael. *See* ADAMS, James Michael

ADAMS, Canon Michael John. b 48. St Jo Coll Dur BA 77. Ripon Coll Cuddesdon 77. **d** 79 **p** 80. C Falmouth K Chas *Truro* 79-81; C St Buryan, St Levan and Sennen 81-83; P-in-c Lanlivery w Luxulyan 83-84; V 84-88; V St Agnes 88-99; V Newquay 99-14; RD Powder 90-96; rtd 14; Hon Can Truro Cathl from 03; PtO *Ex* from 94. *5 Trevemper Road, Newquay TR7 2HR* T: (01637) 853930 E: m.j.adams20@gmail.com

ADAMS, Nicholas Stephen. b 68. K Coll Lon BA 04. Westcott Ho Cam 06. **d** 09 **p** 10. Partnership P E Bris 09-11; C Soundwell 11-13; NSM 13-15. *15 Bexley Road, Bristol BS16 3SS* T: 0117-965 9792 M: 07952-005137
E: nickadams100@hotmail.com

ADAMS, Nigel Charles. b 60. St Jo Coll Dur BA 81 Greenwich Univ PGCE 92. Oak Hill Th Coll MA 14. **d** 14 **p** 15. C Barton Seagrave w Warkton *Pet* from 14. *5 Lavendon Court, Barton Seagrave, Kettering NN15 6QH* E: revnigeladams3@gmail.com

ADAMS, Nigel David. b 40. Sarum & Wells Th Coll 86. **d** 88 **p** 89. C Tile Hill *Cov* 88-91; C Coventry Caludon 91-92; TV 92-97; Asst Chapl HM YOI Onley 92-95; Sub Chapl HM Pris Birm 95-01; P-in-c Nuneaton St Mary *Cov* 97-01; rtd 01; PtO *St As* from 01; *Cov* from 01; AD Ystumaner *Ban* 05-09 and from 13. *Cefn-y-Mor, 102 Plas Edwards, Tywyn LL36 0AS* T: (01654) 711604 E: nigeladams864@btinternet.com

ADAMS, Olugboyega Adeoye. b 55. Univ of Illinois BSc 81 Univ of Kansas MSc 82 Lon Univ PhD 93 Nottm Univ MA 08. EMMTC 99. **d** 02 **p** 03. C Glenfield *Leic* 02-05; V Peckham St Mary Magd *S'wark* from 05. *St Mary's Vicarage, 22 St Mary's Road, London SE15 2DW* T: (020) 7639 4596
E: oadams.smm@gmail.com

ADAMS, Peter. b 62. Bris Univ CertEd 52 Lon Univ AdDipEd 72. Oak Hill Th Coll 91. **d** 91 **p** 92. NSM Towcester w Easton Neston *Pet* 91-95; PtO *Ex* from 94. *Longmeads, Bovey Tracey, Newton Abbot TQ13 9LZ* T: (01626) 832518

ADAMS, Canon Peter. b 37. K Coll Lon AKC 65 Trin Coll Cam MA 70. St Boniface Warminster 65. **d** 66 **p** 67. C Clapham H Trin *S'wark* 66-70; Chapl Trin Coll Cam 70-75; Warden Trin Coll Cen Camberwell 75-83; V Camberwell St Geo *S'wark* 75-83; RD Camberwell 80-83; P-in-c W Dulwich All SS and Em 83-85; V 85-92; V Addington 92-02; Hon Can S'wark Cathl 99-02; rtd 03; PtO *S'wark* from 04. *26 Mansfield Road, South Croydon CR2 6HN* T: (020) 8680 3191
E: canon.adams@talk21.com

ADAMS, Peter Anthony. b 48. K Coll Lon BD 70 AKC 70 MTh 72. **d** 72 **p** 74. LtO *Eur* 72-73; C Ashford *Cant* 73-79; P-in-c Ramsgate H Trin 79-86; P-in-c Ramsgate St Geo 84-86; R Ramsgate H Trin and St Geo from 86. *Address temp unknown*

ADAMS, Peter Harrison. b 41. Tyndale Hall Bris 63. **d** 68 **p** 69. C Kendal St Thos *Carl* 68-71; C W Bromwich Gd Shep w St Jo *Lich* 71-75; R Aldham *Chelmsf* 76-81; R Marks Tey 76-81; R Marks Tey w Aldham and Lt Tey 81-85; Dioc Missr 85-06; rtd 06; Through Faith Miss Ev from 06; Hon C Colchester St Jo *Chelmsf* from 85. *4 St Jude Gardens, Colchester CO4 0QJ* T: (01206) 854041 E: peter@through-faith-missions.org

ADAMS, Canon Raymond William. b 58. Reading Univ BA 79. Oak Hill Th Coll BA 85. **d** 85 **p** 86. C Blackpool St Thos *Blackb* 85-88; C Padiham 88-90; TV Rodbourne Cheney *Bris* 90-02; RD Cricklade 97-99; V Haydon Wick from 02; Hon Can Bris Cathl from 09. *The Vicarage, 54 Furlong Close, Swindon SN25 1QP* T: (01793) 634258 E: r.adams4@ntlworld.com

ADAMS, Richard. *See* ADAMS, John Richard

ADAMS, Richard John. b 48. Leeds Univ BA 70. SAOMC 94. **d** 97 **p** 98. C N Hinksey and Wytham *Ox* 97-01; V Fence-in-Pendle and Higham *Blackb* 01-11; rtd 11. *Tros y Mor, LLangoed, Beaumaris LL58 8SB* T: (01248) 490770
E: richard@gwyneth.net

ADAMS, Roger Charles. b 36. Em Coll Cam BA 60 MA 64. Tyndale Hall Bris 60. **d** 62 **p** 63. C Longfleet *Sarum* 62-65; C Uphill *B & W* 66-71; R Ramsden Crays w Ramsden Bellhouse *Chelmsf* 71-78; SW Area Sec BFBS 78-84; P-in-c Plymouth

St Aug *Ex* 84-85; TV Plymouth Em w Efford 85-90; V Paignton Ch Ch 90-01; rtd 01; PtO *Ex* from 01. *171 Elburton Road, Plymouth PL9 8HY* T: (01752) 407287

ADAMS, Ruth. *See* OATES, Ruth

ADAMS, Ms Ruth Helen. b 73. St Jo Coll Dur BA 94 TCD BTh 97. CITC 94. **d** 97 **p** 98. C Drumragh w Mountfield *D & R* 97-99; Chapl Trin Coll Cam 00-06; P-in-c Bar Hill *Ely* 06-11; V Chesterton St Geo from 12. *St George's Vicarage, 8 Chesterfield Road, Cambridge CB4 1LN* T: (01223) 423374 E: vicar@stgeorgeschesterton.org.uk *or* rev.r.h.adams@gmail.com

ADAMS, Stephen Paul. b 56. Ex Univ BSc 78. Sarum & Wells Th Coll 85. **d** 87 **p** 88. C Swansea St Nic *S & B* 87-88; C Llwynderw 88-91; R Badby w Newham and Charwelton w Fawsley etc *Pet* 91-97; R Abington 97-06; RD Northn 01-06; Dean Min Development St Mich Coll Llan from 06. *St Michael and All Angels' College, 54 Cardiff Road, Llandaff, Cardiff CF5 2YJ* T: (029) 2056 3379 F: 2083 8008

ADAMS (née DABIN), Susan. b 51. NTMTC 96. **d** 00 **p** 01. NSM Hullbridge *Chelmsf* 00-03 and 07-10; NSM Rawreth w Rettendon 07-10; NSM Ashingdon w S Fambridge 03-07; NSM Rettendon and Hullbridge from 10. *49 Crouch Avenue, Hullbridge, Hockley SS5 6BS* T: (01702) 231825 E: susansecretarybird@btinternet.com

ADAMS, Theo. *See* ADAMS, Hubert Theodore

ADAMS, William Thomas. b 47. Ches Coll of HE CertEd 69 Open Univ BA 74 Leic Univ MA 91. EAMTC 97. **d** 00 **p** 01. NSM Helmdon w Stuchbury and Radstone etc *Pet* 00-03; NSM Astwell Gp 03-05; R 05-12; rtd 12; PtO *Pet* from 12. *Brookdale, Mill Road, Whitfield, Brackley NN13 5TQ* T: (01280) 850683 E: will@adamsbrookdale.com

ADAMSON, Anthony Scott. b 49. Newc Univ BA 70. Cranmer Hall Dur 75. **d** 78 **p** 79. C High Elswick St Paul *Newc* 78-86; C Benwell 86-92; V Tweedmouth 92-05; P-in-c Scremerston and Spittal 02-05; AD Norham 00-05; I Stranorlar w Meenglas and Kilteevogue *D & R* 06-13; rtd 14. *67 Quinton Road, Coventry CV3 5FE* E: tkadamson@eircom.net

ADAMSON, Arthur John. b 38. Keble Coll Ox BA 61 MA 65. Tyndale Hall Bris 61. **d** 63 **p** 64. C Redhill H Trin *S'wark* 63-66; Chapl Trent Park Coll of Educn 66-69; C Enfield Ch Ch Trent Park *Lon* 66-70; Ind Chapl and V Battersea St Geo w St Andr *S'wark* 70-74; R Reedham *Nor* 74-80; Min Beighton and Moulton 75-80; P-in-c Cantley w Limpenhoe and Southwood 77-80; R Oulton St Mich 80-90; Chapl Lothingland Hosp 80-90; R Laceby *Linc* 90-98; R Laceby and Ravendale Gp 98-03; rtd 03; PtO *Pet* from 03. *24 Mill Lane, Cottesmore, Oakham LE15 7DL* T: (01572) 812816 E: ajaca@compuserve.com *or* ajohnadamson@aol.com

ADAMSON, Graham William. b 76. Robert Gordon Univ Aber BA 98. Trin Coll Bris 12. **d** 14 **p** 15. C Bushey *St Alb* from 14. *73 Little Bushey Lane, Bushey WD23 4RA* M: 07979-963707 E: grahad1@hotmail.co.uk

ADAN, Howard Keith. b 62. **d** 01 **p** 02. C Amsterdam w Den Helder and Heiloo *Eur* 01-04; Asst Chapl 04-07; Angl Development Ostend and Bruges 08; Old Catholic Ch The Netherlands 08-09; Asst Chapl The Hague *Eur* 09-11; R Cedar St Phil Canada from 11. *St Philip's Cedar, 1797 Cedar Road, Nanaimo BC V9X 1L6, Canada*

ADDENBROOKE, Keith Paul. b 67. Warwick Univ BSc 90 MA 05 Lanc Univ MA 03. Qu Coll Birm BA 07. **d** 07 **p** 08. C Upton (Overchurch) *Ches* 07-10; V Tranmere St Paul w St Luke from 10. *St Paul's Vicarage, 306 Old Chester Road, Birkenhead CH42 3XD* T: 0151-645 4258 E: k.addenbrooke32@btinternet.com

ADDENBROOKE, Peter Homfray. b 38. Trin Coll Cam BA 59 MA 68. Ex Univ PGCE 60. Lich Th Coll 61. **d** 63 **p** 64. C Bakewell *Derby* 63-67; C Horsham *Chich* 67-73; P-in-c Colgate 73-98; Adv for Past Care and Counselling 73-93; rtd 98; PtO *Chich* from 99. *Oaks, Forest Road, Colgate, Horsham RH12 4SZ* T: (01293) 851362

ADDINGTON, David John. b 47. FInstLEx 72 FCIArb 96. St Jo Coll Nottm 98. **d** 01 **p** 03. Asst P Warwick St Mary Bermuda 03-08; Hon C St George St Pet from 08; Chapl Miss to Seafarers from 05; Hon C March St Jo *Ely* 08-11; PtO from 11. *Eben-Ezer Cottage, 79 New Park, March PE15 8RT* T/F: (01354) 650139 M: 07775-796543 E: fradders@btinternet.com

ADDIS, Rosemary Anne. **d** 14 **p** 15. C Edin Gd Shep from 14. *Flat 2F1, 8 Marlborough Street, Edinburgh EH15 2BG* T: 0131-669 9231 E: rosieaddis@yahoo.co.uk

ADDISON, David John Frederick. b 37. K Coll Dur BA 60 DipEd 62 Birm Univ MA 79 Bris Univ MLitt 93. Wells Th Coll 64. **d** 66 **p** 71. C Rastrick St Matt *Wakef* 66-67; PtO *Bradf* 67-71; Hon C Manningham St Luke 71-73; PtO *Glouc* 77-79; Hon C Bisley w Oakridge 79-81; V Newland and Redbrook w Clearwell 81-02; Chapl R Forest of Dean Coll 89-02;

PtO *Glouc* 02-08; *Mon* 04-08; TV Langtree *Ox* from 08. *The Vicarage, Crabtree Corner, Ipsden, Wallingford OX10 6BN* T: (01491) 682832 M: 07815-806313 E: davidaddison10@btinternet.com

ADDISON, Ms Joyce Heather. b 56. Goldsmiths' Coll Lon BA 81 PGCE 91. Regent Coll Vancouver MDiv 09. **d** 11 **p** 12. C Maidstone St Martin *Cant* 11-15; P-in-c from 15. *85 Loose Road, Maidstone ME15 7DA* M: 07854-481259 T: (01622) 669351

ADDY, William Henry. b 54. SNWTP 09. **d** 12 **p** 13. NSM Fazakerley Em *Liv* 12-14; NSM Mossley Hill from 14. *7 Broadacre Close, Liverpool L18 2JW* T: 0151-722 3417 M: 07836-225709 E: bill@addyfamily.com

ADEKANYE, The Ven Joseph (Kehinde). b 47. Oak Hill Th Coll BA 84 Liv Inst of Educn MA 98. Immanuel Coll Ibadan. **d** 72 **p** 73. Nigeria 72-80, 84-97 and from 00; Lect Abp Vining Coll of Th Akure from 94; PtO *Liv* 97-00. *Archbishop Vining College, PO Box 3, Akure, Nigeria* T: (00234) (34) 233031

ADEKUNLE, Elizabeth. **d** 07 **p** 08. C Homerton St Luke *Lon* 07-11; Dioc Discretion 11; Chapl St Jo Coll Cam from 11. *St John's College, Cambridge CB2 1TP* T: (01223) 338600 *or* 338617 E: lizadeola@yahoo.co.uk *or* ea287@cam.ac.uk

ADELOYE, The Ven Emmanuel Olufemi. b 60. Ilorin Univ Nigeria BA 85 Ibadan Univ Nigeria MA 95. Immanuel Coll Ibadan 89. **d** 91 **p** 92. Chapl to Bp Egba Nigeria 91-92; C Egba Cathl 92-95; V Emta All SS 95-99; Personal Asst to Bp Ibadan S 99-00; Adn Odo-Ona and V Odo-Ona St Paul 00-06; PtO *S'wark* 07; C Lewisham St Mary 07-08; C Lagos Pentecost Nigeria 09-10; P-in-c 10; V Iju St Jo and Iju-Ishaga from 10. *PO Box 3616, Agege, Lagos, Nigeria* E: kehindevenadeloye@yahoo.com

ADEMOLA, Canon Ade. b 62. Goldsmiths' Coll Lon BA 91 N Lon Univ MA 94. NTMTC 95. **d** 98 **p** 99. NSM Lt Ilford St Barn *Chelmsf* 98-02; V Leyton Em from 02; Can Ibadan from 03. *Emmanuel Vicarage, 149 Hitcham Road, London E17 8HL* T: (020) 8539 2200 M: 07941-029084 E: orison@ademola.eu

ADESANYA, The Ven Stephen Adedotun. b 57. Ogun State Univ MEd 97 Ado-Ekiti State Univ PhD 03. Evang Th Faculty Osijek Croatia BTh 91. **d** 91 **p** 92. Nigeria 91-07; Adn Iwade and V Italupe Em 03-07; PtO *S'wark* 07-09; P-in-c Romaldkirk w Laithkirk *Ripon* 09-13; P-in-c Startforth and Bowes and Rokeby w Brignall 09-13; V Burnley St Cuth *Blackb* from 13; V Brierfield from 13. *St Cuthbert's Vicarage, Barbon Street, Burnley BB10 1TS* M: 07950-713797 E: dtndsny@yahoo.com

ADETAYO, Mrs Abigail Olufunke. b 47. SRN 74 SCM 75 Greenwich Univ PGCE 07. SEITE 06. **d** 09 **p** 10. NSM Peckham St Mary Magd *S'wark* from 09. *158 Torridon Road, London SE6 1RD* T/F: (020) 8695 1713 M: 07746-035727 E: jadetayo@aol.com

ADEY, John Douglas. b 33. Man Univ BSc 54. Coll of Resurr Mirfield 56. **d** 58 **p** 59. C Forton *Portsm* 58-64; C Northolt St Mary *Lon* 64-67; V Snibston *Leic* 67-72; V Outwood *Wakef* 72-78; V Clifton 78; V Upton Priory *Ches* 79-81; V Hyde St Thos 81-82; V Newton in Mottram 82-89; R Roos and Garton w Tunstall, Grimston and Hilston *York* 89-92; C Woodchurch *Ches* 92-95; C Coppenhall 95-98; rtd 98; PtO *Portsm* 98-09. *1 Dulverton Hall, Esplanade, Scarborough YO11 2AR*

ADEY HUISH, Helen Louise. b 59. Bris Univ BA 81 Qu Coll Cam PhD 87. SAOMC 01. **d** 04 **p** 05. NSM Banbury *Ox* 04-07; Chapl Ox Radcliffe Hosps NHS Trust 07-12; Chapl Ox Univ Hosps NHS Trust 12-13; PtO *Ox* from 09. *Timberhurst, The Green, Shenington, Banbury OX15 6NE* T: (01295) 670285 E: adey.huish@onetel.com

ADEY-WILLIAMS, Thelma Naomi. b 53. Portsm Univ CertEd 98. STETS 03. **d** 06 **p** 07. NSM Pembrook *Portsm* 06-07; C Carew *St D* 07-08; TV 08-12; P-in-c Llansteffan and Llan-y-bri etc 12-14; Dioc Officer for Soc Resp 12-14; rtd 14; PtO *St D* from 15. *4 Bishop's Lane, Pembroke SA71 5JN* E: thelmabarber@btinternet.com

ADFIELD, Richard Ernest. b 31. Oak Hill Th Coll 62. **d** 64 **p** 65. C Bedworth *Cov* 64-67; V Whitehall Park St Andr Hornsey Lane *Lon* 67-77; V Kensington St Helen w H Trin 77-86; V Turnham Green Ch Ch 86-92; rtd 92; PtO *Chich* from 92; Chapl Brighton and Sussex Univ Hosps NHS Trust 02-03; Chapl Whittington Coll Felbridge 03-11. *363 Hangleton Road, Hove BN3 7LQ* T: (01273) 732538

✠**ADIE, The Rt Revd Michael Edgar.** b 29. CBE 94. St Jo Coll Ox BA 52 MA 56 Surrey Univ DUniv 95. Westcott Ho Cam 52. **d** 54 **p** 55 **c** 83. C Pallion *Dur* 54-57; Abp's Dom Chapl *Cant* 57-60; V Sheff St Mark Broomhall 60-69; RD Hallam 66-69; R Louth w Welton-le-Wold *Linc* 69-75; P-in-c N w S Elkington 69-75; TR Louth 75-76; V Morton w Hacconby 76-83; Adn Linc 77-83; Can and Preb Linc Cathl 77-83; Bp Guildf 83-94; rtd 95; PtO *Portsm* from 95; Hon Asst Bp Portsm 95-14; Hon Asst Bp Chich from 96. *4 Lochnagar Way, Ballater AB35 5PB* T: (013397) 53709

ADLAM, David John. b 47. d 06 p 07. OLM Dickleburgh and The Pulhams *Nor* from 06. *Weggs Farm, Common Road, Dickleburgh, Diss IP21 4PJ* T: (01379) 741200 F: 741800 M: 07860-417158 E: john@adlams.net

ADLAM, Keith Richard. b 44. STETS 00. d 03 p 04. NSM Binstead and Havenstreet St Pet *Portsm* 03-07; NSM Northwood 07-11; NSM Gurnard 07-11; NSM Cowes St Faith 07-11; P-in-c Wroxall from 11. *The Vicarage, 55 Clarence Road, Wroxall, Ventnor PO28 3BY* T: (01983) 854325 M: 07552-793366 E: revkeith@kjr-group.co.uk

ADLEY, Ernest George. b 38. Leeds Univ BA 61. Wells Th Coll 62. d 64 p 65. C Bideford *Ex* 64-67; C Yeovil St Mich *B & W* 67-70; V Taunton Lyngford 70-79; R Skegness and Winthorpe *Linc* 79-91; R Wantage Downs *Ox* 91-03; rtd 03; PtO *Ox* from 04. *13 Pixton Close, Didcot OX11 0BX* T: (01235) 210395

ADLINGTON, David John. b 51. AKC 73. K Coll Lon 70 St Aug Coll Cant 73. d 74 p 75. C Clapham St Paul *S'wark* 74-77; C Bethnal Green St Matt *Lon* 77-80; P-in-c Stepney St Pet w St Benet 80-84; PV and Succ S'wark Cathl 84-87; PV and Succ Llan Cathl 88-91; Dioc Dir of Educn 91-00; V St Hilary 91-94; TV Cowbridge 94-95; C Whitchurch 95-00; P-in-c Folkestone St Mary and St Eanswythe *Cant* 00-02; V 02-09; P-in-c Elham w Denton and Wootton 09-13; Hon Min Can Cant Cathl 01-13; P-in-c Folkestone St Pet 13-15; V from 13; C Folkestone St Mary, St Eanswythe and St Sav 13-15; V from 15; AD Elham from 14. *St Peter's Vicarage, North Street, Folkestone CT19 6AL* T: (01303) 254472 E: david.adlington@btinternet.com

ADMAN, Fayaz. b 63. Pakistan Adventist Sem Sheikhupura BA 94. St Thos Th Coll Karachi 97. d 98 p 99. Dn St Jo Cathl Peshawar Pakistan 98-99; P 00-03; Presbyter Peshawar City All SS 99-00; Bp's Chapl 01-03; V Charsada, Shabqadar and Ghalana 00-04; C S Rochdale *Man* 04-07; P-in-c Bolton St Paul w Em 07-11; P-in-c Daubhill 07-11; TV W Bolton from 11. *Emmanuel Vicarage, Edward Street, Bolton BL3 5LQ* T: (01204) 393282 E: revfadman_bpchp_dop@hotmail.com

ADOYO, Miss Eugeniah Ombwayo. b 54. Lon Bible Coll 84 Westmr Coll Ox BA 86 MPhil 90. dss 82 d 91 p 91. Kenya 82-94; Internat Sec Crosslinks 94-97; Hon C Hatcham St Jas *S'wark* 94-97; C S'wark Ch Ch and Chapl S Lon Ind Miss 97-02; TV Plaistow and N Canning Town *Chelmsf* 02-09; TV Harwich Peninsula 10-14; R Longsight St Luke *Man* from 14; P-in-c Birch-in-Rusholme St Agnes w Longsight St Jo etc from 14. *St Agnes's Rectory, Slade Lane, Manchester M13 0GN* T: 0161-224 2596 M: 07765-278787 E: eugeniah@fsmail.net

ADSETTS, Ms Marilyn Ann. b 47. St Jo Coll York CertEd 69 Leeds Univ BEd 70 Spurgeon's Coll Lon MTh 00. EAMTC 98. d 00 p 01. C Rushmere *St E* 00-03; V Rhymney *Mon* 03-07; rtd 07; PtO *Mon* from 07. *Grace House, 15 Weston Park, Weston under Penyard, Ross-on-Wye HR9 7FR* E: mbygrace@aol.com

ADSHEAD, Adele Elizabeth. b 64. BEd. St Jo Coll Nottm. d 14 p 15. NSM Ashby-de-la-Zouch and Breedon on the Hill *Leic* from 14. *Address temp unknown* E: adele.adshead@gmail.com

ADU-BOACHIE, Francis. b 60. Oak Hill Th Coll. d 95 p 96. C Stonebridge St Mich *Lon* 95-01; V Wembley St Jo from 01. *The Vicarage, 3 Crawford Avenue, Wembley HA0 2HX* T: (020) 8902 0273 E: francis@adu-boachie.freeserve.co.uk

ADYERI, James Joloba. b 58. Redcliffe Coll 96 Chelt & Glouc Coll of HE BA 09. United Th Coll Bangalore 91. d 84 p 85. Uganda 85-88, 89-91, 92-96 and from 99; India 88-89 and 91-92; PtO *Glouc* 96-99. *PO Box 84, Mityana, Uganda* T: (0256) (46) 23 36

ÆLRED, Brother. *See* ARNESEN, Raymond Halfdan

AFFLECK, Stuart John. b 47. AKC 69. St Aug Coll Cant. d 70 p 71. C Prittlewell St Mary *Chelmsf* 70-75; Asst Chapl Charterhouse Sch Godalming 75-78; Chapl 78-80; Warden Pilsdon Community 80-94; PtO *S'wark* from 03; rtd 07. *3 Chislehurst Road, Richmond TW10 6PW*

AGAR, George. b 40. Edin Univ BSc 63 Ox Univ PGCE 64. NOC 92. d 94 p 95. Hd Biddulph High Sch Stoke-on-Trent 94-96; NSM Sandbach *Ches* 94-99; NSM Hartford from 99. *128 Middlewich Road, Sandbach CW11 1FH* T: (01270) 760191 E: georgea@stjohnshartford.org

AGASSIZ, David John Lawrence. b 42. St Pet Hall Ox BA 64 MA 67 Imp Coll Lon PhD 94. Ripon Hall Ox 64. d 66 p 67. C Southampton St Mary w H Trin *Win* 66-71; V Enfield St Jas *Lon* 71-80; P-in-c Grays Thurrock *Chelmsf* 80-83; P-in-c Grays All SS 81-84; P-in-c Lt Thurrock St Mary 81-84; P-in-c W Thurrock 81-83; P-in-c Grays SS Pet and Paul, S Stifford and W Thurrock 83-84; TR Grays Thurrock 84-90; Hon Can Chelmsf Cathl 90-93; Dioc Development Rep 90-93; PtO 93-94; Kenya 98-00; PtO *S'wark* 02-07; *B & W* from 08. *The Garden House, Stafford Place, Weston-super-Mare BS23 2QZ* T: (01934) 620486 M: 07813-566957 E: david.agassiz@gmail.com

AGBELUSI, Canon Dele Omotayo. b 51. Ahmadu Bello Univ Zaria MSc 81 Oak Hill Th Coll BA 99 Spurgeon's Coll MTh 09.

Immanuel Coll Ibadan. d 86 p 87. Nigeria 86-96; C Edmonton All SS w St Mich *Lon* 97-99; V Hornsey Ch Ch from 99; Hon Can Akure Nigeria from 08. *Christ Church Vicarage, 32 Crescent Road, London N8 8AX* T: (020) 8340 1656 *or* 8340 1566 E: agbelusi@aol.com

AGER, Mrs Christabel Ruth. b 51. Bedf Coll Lon BA 73 Gipsy Hill Coll of Educn PGCE 74 MCLIP 98. STETS BA 10. d 10 p 11. NSM Beercrocombe w Curry Mallet, Hatch Beauchamp etc *B & W* from 10. *14 Morgans Rise, Bishops Hull, Taunton TA1 5HW* T: (01823) 335424 E: ager@talk21.com

AGER, David George. b 52. Lon Univ BA 73 Solicitor 77. SWMTC 01. d 04 p 05. NSM Deane Vale *B & W* 04-09; NSM Taunton St Jas 09-12; NSM Blackdown from 12; Bp's Officer for Ord NSM (Taunton Adnry) from 09. *14 Morgans Rise, Bishops Hull, Taunton TA1 5HW* T: (01823) 335424 M: 07887-893918 E: ager@talk21.com

AGGETT, Miss Vivienne Cecilia. b 33. Sarum & Wells Th Coll 86. d 88 p 94. C Binley *Cov* 88-91; C Hednesford *Lich* 91-96; rtd 96; PtO *Cov* from 98; *Lich* from 04; Asst Chapl Gtr Athens *Eur* 01-08. *Batsi, 845 03 Andros, Greece* T: (0030) (2282) 041102 M: 6936-295647 E: aggett@otenet.gr

AGGREY, Solomon Samuel. b 49. BSc 76. Immanuel Coll Ibadan MA 84. d 80 p 82. Nigeria 80-88; Miss Partner CMS from 88; C Gorton Em and Gorton St Jas *Man* 93-95. *68 Booth Street, Denton, Manchester M34 3HY*

AGNEW, Kevin Raymond Christopher. b 59. Chich Th Coll. d 94 p 95. C Eastbourne St Mary *Chich* 94-98; V Roughey 98-14; P-in-c Willingdon from 14. *35A Church Street, Willingdon, Eastbourne BN20 9HR* T: (01323) 502079

AGNEW, Stephen Mark. b 54. Univ of Wales (Ban) BSc 76 Southn Univ BTh 81. Sarum & Wells Th Coll 76. d 79 p 80. C Wilmslow *Ches* 79-84; V Crewe St Jo 84-90; Chapl Bromsgrove Sch 90-99; V Claines St Jo *Worc* 99-12; P-in-c Old Swinford Stourbridge from 12. *The Rectory, Rectory Road, Stourbridge DY8 2HA* M: 07762-250749 E: revsmagnew@yahoo.com

A'HERNE-SMITH, Mrs Mary Catriona. b 65. Bris Univ BA 86 PGCE 88. Coll of Resurr Mirfield 13. d 14 p 15. C Sutton in Ashfield St Mary *S'well* from 14. *10 Huthwaite Road, Sutton-in-Ashfield NG17 2GW* M: 07948-272669 E: mezcat@icloud.com

AHMADINIA, Ebrahim Esmael. d 00 p 15. Hon C Ankara *Eur* from 15. *Address temp unknown*

AHON, Ahon Bol Nyuar. b 62. Birm Chr Coll MA 06. Tyndale Th Sem Amsterdam. d 01 p 03. C St Mark's Cathl Luwero Uganda 01-03; Chapl Kiwoko Hosp 01-03; Hon Chapl Birm Cathl 03-05; P-in-c Ostend *Eur* 06-07; Sudan 08-09. *Flat 3, 45 Avenue Road, London N15 5JG* M: 07956-165426 E: de_nyuar@yahoo.com

AHRENS, Irene Karla Elisabeth. b 40. Berlin Univ Bonn Univ PhD 69 Lon Bible Coll BA 92 K Coll Lon MTh 93. SEITE 93. d 95 p 96. NSM Kew St Phil and All SS w St Luke *S'wark* 95-99; Asst Chapl Berlin *Eur* from 00. *Wildpfad 26, 14193 Berlin, Germany* T: (0049) (30) 8972 8552 E: irene.ahrens@epost.de

AIDLEY, Jessica-Jil Stapleton. b 42. Westf Coll Lon BSc 67 UEA PhD 73 PGCE 84. d 99 p 00. OLM High Oak, Hingham and Scoulton w Wood Rising *Nor* 99-04; PtO *Mon* 04-05; NSM Rockfield and Dingestow Gp 05-09; PtO *Chich* 09; NSM Brighton St Nic from 09. *21 Crown Street, Brighton BN1 3EH* T: (01273) 723298 E: j.aidley@btopenworld.com

AIKEN, Canon Nicholas John. b 58. Sheff Univ BA. Wycliffe Hall Ox 80. d 82 p 83. C Ashtead *Guildf* 82-86; Dioc Youth Officer 86-93; R Wisley w Pyrford from 93; RD Woking 03-08; Hon Can Guildf Cathl from 10. *The Rectory, Aviary Road, Woking GU22 8TH* T: (01932) 352914 E: rector@wisleywithpyrford.org

AIKEN, The Very Revd Simon Mark. b 62. St Andr Univ MTheol 85. Ripon Coll Cuddesdon 86. d 88 p 89. C Burnley St Matt w H Trin *Blackb* 88-91; C Heyhouses on Sea 91-94; V Musbury 94-99; V Longridge 99-06; Sub Dean Bloemfontein 06-10; Chapl Free State Univ S Africa 06-10; Adn Maluti 07-09; Dean Kimberley from 10; Adn Karoo S Africa from 11. *The Deanery, 4 Park Road, Belgravia, Kimberley 8301 South Africa* T: (0027) (53) 833 3437 E: kkdiocese.dean@telkomsa.net

AIKENHEAD, Mary. *See* CANTACUZENE, Mary

AINGE, Canon David Stanley. b 47. Ian Ramsey Coll Brasted 68 Oak Hill Th Coll 70. d 73 p 74. C Bitterne *Win* 73-77; C Castle Church *Lich* 77-79; P-in-c Becontree St Alb *Chelmsf* 79-89; P-in-c Becontree St Jo 85-89; TR Becontree S 89-91; RD Barking and Dagenham 86-91; V Leyton St Mary w St Edw 91-96; P-in-c Leyton St Luke 91-96; V Leyton St Mary w St Edw and St Luke 96-03; RD Waltham Forest 94-00; R Gt Dunmow and Barnston 03-13; Hon Can Chelmsf Cathl 97-13; rtd 13; PtO *Chelmsf* from 15. *42 Abels Road, Church End, Halstead CO9 1EW* E: davidainge@aol.com

AINSCOUGH, Malcolm Ralph. b 52. Liv Univ BEd 76. St Mich Coll Llan 85. **d** 87 **p** 88. C Fleur-de-Lis *Mon* 87-90; C Chepstow 90-91; TV Cwmbran 91-95; V Newport St Steph and H Trin 95-03; R Hasland *Derby* from 03; V Temple Normanton from 03. *The Rectory, 49 Churchside, Hasland, Chesterfield S41 0JX* T: (01246) 232486 E: malcolmainscough@yahoo.com

AINSWORTH, Mrs Janina Helen Margaret. b 50. Ripon Coll Cuddesdon. **d** 05 **p** 06. NSM E Farnworth and Kearsley *Man* 05-07; Chief Educn Officer Abps' Coun 07-14; PtO *Lon* 07-12; Hon C St Geo-in-the-East w St Paul 12-14; rtd 14; NSM Turton Moorland *Man* from 14. *St Maxentius Rectory, Bolton Road, Bolton BL2 3EU* T: (01204) 304240

AINSWORTH, Mark John. b 64. Lon Univ MTh 92. Wycliffe Hall Ox 86. **d** 89 **p** 90. C Chipping Barnet w Arkley *St Alb* 89-93; USA from 93. *270 Bent Road, Wyncote PA 19095-1503, USA* T: (001) (215) 517 8568 E: mjaec@earthlink.net

AINSWORTH, Canon Michael Ronald. b 50. K Coll Lon LLB 71 LLM 72 Trin Hall Cam BA 74 MA 79. Westcott Ho Cam 72. **d** 75 **p** 76. C Scotforth *Blackb* 75-78; Chapl St Martin's Coll of Educn 78-82; Chapl NOC 82-89; R Withington St Chris *Man* 89-94; TR Worsley 94-07; AD Eccles 00-05; Hon Can *Man* Cathl from 04; R St Geo-in-the-East w St Paul *Lon* 07-14; rtd 14; PtO *Man* from 15; *Blackb* from 15. *St Maxentius Rectory, Bolton Road, Bolton BL2 3EU* T: (01204) 304240 E: michael@ainsworths.org.uk *or* rector.stgile@gmail.com

AINSWORTH, Paul Henry. b 46. JP. Man Poly BA 81. NOC 85. **d** 88 **p** 89. NSM Salterhebble All SS *Wakef* 88-92; C Golcar 92-96; TV Moor Allerton *Ripon* 96-09; TV Moor Allerton and Shadwell 09-11; rtd 11. *21 Oak Drive, Leeds LS10 4GQ* T: 0113-271 6176 E: batandball1@btopenworld.com

AINSWORTH, Peter. b 34. Lon Univ BD 57. Coll of Resurr Mirfield 69. **d** 70 **p** 71. C Leeds St Wilfrid *Ripon* 70-74; TV Tong *Bradf* 74-77; V Fairweather Green 77-94; rtd 94; PtO *Wakef* 94-02; *York* from 03. *34 Dulverton Hall, Esplanade, Scarborough YO11 2AR* T: (01723) 340134

AINSWORTH-SMITH, Canon Ian Martin. b 41. MBE 06. Selw Coll Cam BA 64 MA 68. Westcott Ho Cam 64. **d** 66 **p** 67. C Mill Hill Jo Keble Ch *Lon* 66-69; USA 69-71; C Purley St Mark *S'wark* 71-73; Chapl St Geo Hosp Lon 73-94; Chapl St Geo Healthcare NHS Trust Lon 94-06; Hon Can S'wark Cathl 95-06; rtd 06; PtO *B & W* from 06; Dioc Adv Hosp Chapl from 07. *Knutsford Cottage, North Street, Milverton, Taunton TA4 1LG* T: (01823) 400365 M: 07732-324568 E: jeanianas@btinternet.com

AIRD, Robert Malcolm. b 31. Lon Univ BSc 54. Westcott Ho Cam 75. **d** 77 **p** 78. C Burnham *B & W* 77-79; P-in-c Taunton Lyngford 79-84; V 84-87; R Dulverton and Brushford 87-94; rtd 94. *Arran Cottage, East Street, Chulmleigh EX18 7DD* T: (01769) 581042

AIRD, Wendy Elizabeth. b 41. SEITE. **d** 00 **p** 01. NSM Streatham Immanuel and St Andr *S'wark* 00-05; NSM Chevington and Shilbottle *Newc* 05-08; P-in-c Chevington 08-11; rtd 11. *12 Middle Park, Alston CA9 3AR* M: 07711-301813 E: chevvic@btinternet.com

AIREY, Robert William. b 54. **d** 99 **p** 00. OLM Holcombe *Man* 99-08; OLM Holcombe and Hawkshaw from 09. *4 Pine Street, Haslingden, Rossendale BB4 5ND* T: (01706) 224743

AIREY, Simon Christopher. b 60. Trin Coll Bris BA 87. **d** 87 **p** 88. C Wilton *B & W* 87-90; Chapl Scargill Ho 90-93; TV Kingswood *Bris* 93-96; Asst P Nether Springs Northumbria Community 96-98 and 02-03; C Bath Abbey w St Jas *B & W* 98-02; C Nailsea Ch Ch w Tickenham 03-09; Chapl Grey Coll Dur 09-11; P-in-c Criftins w Dudleston and Welsh Frankton *Lich* from 11. *The Vicarage, Criftins, Ellesmere SY12 9LN* T: (01691) 690212 M: 07740-799191 E: getthevicar@yahoo.com

AISBITT, Joanne. *See* LISTER, Joanne

AISBITT, Michael. b 60. St Pet Coll Ox BA 81 MA 84. Westcott Ho Cam 81. **d** 84 **p** 85. C Norton St Mary *Dur* 84-87; C Kirkleatham *York* 87-90; V S Bank 90-96; R Whitby 96-97; TR Whitby w Aislaby and Ruswarp 97-00; R Attleborough w Besthorpe *Nor* 00-09; RD Thetford and Rockland 03-09. *16 The Acres, Stokesley, Middlesbrough TS9 5QA* E: m_aisbitt@hotmail.com

AISBITT, Osmond John. b 35. St Chad's Coll Dur BA 57. **d** 61 **p** 62. C Ashington *Newc* 61-64; C Blyth St Mary 64-68; V Cleckheaton St Jo *Wakef* 68-75; V Horbury 75-78; V Horbury w Horbury Bridge 78-97; rtd 97; PtO *Carl* 97-00 and from 02; P-in-c Nerja and Almuñécar *Eur* 00-02. *8 Stonecross Gardens, Ulverston LA12 7HA* T: (01229) 585622

AITCHISON, Charles Baillie. b 45. New Coll Dur BEd 85 Bede Coll Dur TCert 67 Newc Univ DAES 74 ACP 69. LNSM course 85. **d** 93 **p** 98. NSM Peebles *Edin* from 93; NSM Innerleithen from 93. *45 Whitehaugh Park, Peebles EH45 9DB* T: (01721) 729750 *or* T/F: 724008

AITKEN, Christopher William <u>Mark</u>. b 53. Dur Univ BA 75. Westcott Ho Cam 76. **d** 79 **p** 80. C Finchley St Mary *Lon* 79-82; C Radlett *St Alb* 82-85; V Sprowston *Nor* 85-90; R Beeston St Andr 85-90; R Sprowston w Beeston 90-93; Chapl Sherborne Sch 93-04; Hd Master St Lawr Coll Ramsgate 04-12; Master R Foundn of St Kath in Ratcliffe from 13. *The Royal Foundation of St Katharine, 2 Butcher Row, London E14 8DS* T: (020) 7790 3540 F: 7702 7603 E: enquiries@stkatharine.org.uk

AITKEN, Leslie St John Robert. b 41. Open Univ BA 75. Cranmer Hall Dur 62. **d** 65 **p** 66. C Worc St Barn w Ch Ch 65-69; C Halesowen 69-73; P-in-c Wyche 73-80; R Blackley St Pet *Man* 80-99; Chapl Booth Hall Hosp Man 80-89; R Sutton, Huttoft and Anderby *Linc* 99-06; rtd 06. *17 Old School Mews, Spilsby PE23 5QU*

AITKEN, Valerie Anne. b 46. STETS 01. **d** 04 **p** 05. NSM Perivale *Lon* from 04; P-in-c from 14. *22 Woodfield Road, London W5 1SH* T: (020) 8997 6819 M: 07968-345992 E: valerie.aitken2@btinternet.com

AITKEN, William <u>Stuart</u>. b 35. FCFI MSIAD CertEd. Cant Sch of Min 79. **d** 82 **p** 83. NSM Roch 82-86; C Orpington All SS 86-88; R Burham and Wouldham 88-96; Dioc Communications Officer 88-96; rtd 96; PtO *Roch* from 96. *18 Commissioners Road, Rochester ME2 4EB* T: (01634) 715892

AITON, Janice Haran. MA 79 Jordanhill Coll Glas PGCE 80. TISEC 98. **d** 01 **p** 02. C St Andrews St Andr *St And* 01-04; I Dunboyne and Rathmolyon *M & K* from 04. *1 The Close, Plunkett Hall, Dunboyne, Co Meath, Republic of Ireland* T/F: (00353) (1) 825 3288 E: janice_aiton@lineone.net

AITON, Canon Robert Neilson. b 36. Univ of Wales BA 59 DipEd 60. Chich Th Coll 74. **d** 76 **p** 77. C E Grinstead St Swithun *Chich* 76-83; R Lavant 83-90; Chapl St Barn Hospice Worthing 90-95; V Durrington *Chich* 90-01; Can and Preb Chich Cathl from 99; rtd 01; LtO *Chich* from 01. *Fieldings, Joys Croft, Chichester PO19 4NJ* T: (01243) 781728 E: maiton@talk21.com

AJAEFOBI, Joseph Obichukwu. b 63. Anambra State Univ of Tech Nigeria BEng 88 Loughb Univ PhD 04. Trin Coll Umuahia 90. **d** 92 **p** 93. Chapl Nkpor H Innocents Nigeria 92-00; PtO *Leic* from 01; Asst Chapl Loughb Univ from 05. *15 Stirling Avenue, Loughborough LE11 4LJ* M: 07796-672212 E: joeajaefobi@yahoo.co.uk

✠**AJETUNMOBI, The Rt Revd Jacob Ademola.** b 48. Middx Univ BA 93. Igbaja Sem Nigeria BTh 73 Lon Bible Coll BA 80. **d** 83 **p** 83 **c** 99. Bp's Chapl and V Ilesa St Marg Nigeria 83-88; Chapl to Nigerian Students in UK (CMS) 88-99; Miss Partner CMS 88-99; Bp Ibadan S from 99. *59 Milton Avenue, London NW10 8PL* or *c/o Bishopscourt, PO Box 166, Ibadan, Nigeria* T: (020) 8969 2379 *or* (00234) (22) 316464 E: jacajet@aol.com

AJIBADE, Ms Ijeoma. b 65. Univ of Nigeria LLB 87 S Bank Univ MA 96 Heythrop Coll Lon MA 09. SEITE BA 10. **d** 10 **p** 11. NSM Kensington St Mary Abbots w Ch Ch and St Phil *Lon* from 10; Hon Min Can S'wark Cathl from 11. *25 Duffield Drive, London N15 4UH* M: 07876-783360 T: (020) 8376 0598 E: revdije@gmail.com

AJOKU, Canon Nelson Iheanacho. b 46. Trin Coll Umuahia 03. **d** 99 **p** 00. PtO Dio Egbu Nigeria 99-07; PtO *Lon* 08-13; Can Egbu Nigeria from 06. *187 Kneller Court, Academy Gardens, Northolt UB5 5PL* T: (020) 8842 3840 M: 07946-654713 E: rev.nelsonajoku@yahoo.co.uk

AJUKA, Sampson Chikwere. b 72. Qu Coll Birm BA 08. **d** 08 **p** 09. C Venice w Trieste *Eur* 08-11; Dioc C and P-in-c Devenish w Boho *Clogh* from 12; Chapl to Bp Clogh from 12. *The Rectory, 10 Castletown Road, Monea, Enniskillen BT74 8GG* T: (028) 6634 1672 M: 07908-856207 E: sampressindeed@yahoo.com

AKERS, Miss Rachel Leanne. b 81. Ches Univ BA 13 MA 15. St Jo Coll Nottm 13. **d** 15. C Kidderminster E *Worc* from 15. *107 Shakespeare Drive, Kidderminster DY10 3QX* M: 07578-340464 E: rachelakers1@aol.com

✠**AKINOLA, The Rt Revd Peter Jasper.** b 44. Virginia Th Sem MTS 81 Hon DD 93. **d** 78 **p** 79 **c** 89. V Abuja St Jas Nigeria 78-79; V Suleja St Jas 81-84; Prov Missr 84-89; Bp Abuja 89-10; Abp Prov III Nigeria 97-10; Primate All Nigeria 00-10; rtd 10. *PO Box 212, ADCP, Abuja, Nigeria* T: (00234) (9) 523 6928 *or* 523 0989 F: 523 0986 M: 90-805853

AKKER, Derek Alexander. b 46. Bradf Univ MA 83. NOC 85. **d** 88 **p** 89. C Mossley *Man* 88-90; C Bury St Mary 90-92; V Lever Bridge 92-97; TV Wolstanton *Lich* 97-99; V Hattersley *Ches* 99-09; rtd 09; PtO *Man* from 09; *Ches* from 10. *54 Purbeck Drive, Bury BL8 1JQ* T: 0161-797 0105 E: derekakker111@btinternet.com

AKRILL, Dean. b 71. York Univ BA 97. Ripon Coll Cuddesdon BTh 00. **d** 00 **p** 01. C Swinton *Sheff* 00-01; C Wath-upon-Dearne 01-04; V Mosbrough 04-08; C Sprowston w Beeston *Nor* from 08. *The Newlands, 15 Blue Bear Lane, Norwich NR7 8RX* E: dean@sprowston.org.uk

ALAN MICHAEL, Brother. *See* PATERSON, Alan Michael

ALASAUKKO-OJA, Tuomas. *See* MÄKIPÄÄ, Tuomas

ALBAN JONES, Canon Timothy Morris. b 64. MBE 03. Warwick Univ BA 85. Ripon Coll Cuddesdon 85. **d** 88 **p** 89. C Tupsley *Heref* 88-93; TV Ross 93-00; P-in-c Soham *Ely* 00-01; P-in-c Wicken 00-01; V Soham and Wicken 02-15; RD Fordham and Quy 10-15; Warden of Readers 12-15; Hon Can Ely Cathl 12-15; Bp's Chapl *Pet* from 15; Can Res Pet Cathl from 15. *The Bishops' Office, The Palace, Minster Precincts, Peterborough PE1 1YA* T: (01733) 562492
E: tim.albanjones@peterborough-diocese.org.uk

ALBERS, Johannes Reynoud (Joop). b 47. Hogeschool Holland BTh 92 Amsterdam Univ MTh 98. EAMTC 99. **d** 00 **p** 01. C Voorschoten *Eur* 00-02; C Amsterdam w Den Helder and Heiloo 02-04; Asst Chapl 04-12; P-in-c Haarlem from 12; Angl Chapl Amsterdam Airport Schiphol from 07. *Dorpsweg 134, 1697 KH Schellinkhout, The Netherlands* T: (0031) (22) 950 1611 *or* (61) 009 8239 E: joopalbers@quicknet.nl

ALBINSON, Thomas Roy. b 79. Ripon Coll Cuddesdon 09. **d** 12 **p** 13. C Littlemore *Ox* from 12. *20 Vicarage Close, Oxford OX4 4PL* T: (01865) 771345 E: tomalbinson@gmail.com

ALBON, Lionel Frederick Shapland. b 31. CEng MIMechE 60. St Alb Minl Tr Scheme 80. **d** 83 **p** 84. NSM Bromham w Oakley *St Alb* 83-88; NSM Bromham w Oakley and Stagsden 88-89; Ind Chapl 89-96; rtd 96; LtO *St Alb* 96-09; PtO from 09. *38 Glebe Rise, Sharnbrook, Bedford MK44 1JB* T: (01234) 781560 E: lionel@albon.fsnet.co.uk

ALBY, Harold Oriel. b 45. Witwatersrand Univ BA 68 MA 77. Sarum Th Coll 68. **d** 71 **p** 72. C Germiston St Boniface S Africa 71-74; C Johannesburg Cathl 74-75; R Ermelow w Pet Relief 75-78; R Potchefstroom 78-82; R Boksburg 82-89; P-in-c Forton *Portsm* 89-96; V Milton 96-10; rtd 11; PtO and Dioc Archivist George S Africa from 11. *7 Plover Road, Heatherlands, George, 6529 South Africa* T: (0027) (44) 873 0797
E: orielalby@hotmail.com

ALCOCK (née TOYNBEE), Mrs Claire Louise. b 65. Reading Univ BA 86 Goldsmiths' Coll Lon PGTC 87. Ox Min Course 07. **d** 10 **p** 11. NSM Langtree *Ox* from 10. *St Mary's House, High Street, Whitchurch on Thames, Reading RG8 7DF* T: 0118-984 3435 M: 07519-861040 E: claire_alcock@hotmail.com

ALCOCK, Donald. b 52. McGill Univ Montreal BA 74 MA 76 Univ of S California PhD 85. Huron Coll Ontario MDiv 00. **d** 00 **p** 00. Canada 00-10; NSM Gt Amwell w St Margaret's and Stanstead Abbots *St Alb* 10-12; P-in-c Woore and Norton in Hales *Lich* from 12. *The Vicarage, Nantwich Road, Woore, Crewe CW3 9SA* T: (01630) 647911 E: dga952@hotmail.com

ALCOCK, Edwin James. b 31. AKC 57. **d** 58 **p** 59. C Old St Pancras w Bedford New Town St Matt *Lon* 58-62; C Hillingdon St Andr 62-81; V N Acton St Gabr 81-01; rtd 01; PtO *Lon* from 01. *17 Westfields Road, London W3 0AX* T: (020) 8896 2748

ALCOCK, Mrs Lynda Mary. b 45. St Gabr Coll Lon TCert 67. SAOMC 96. **d** 99 **p** 00. OLM Shires' Edge *Ox* from 99. *Copperfields, Swan Lane, Great Bourton, Banbury OX17 1QR* T: (01295) 750744 E: lynalcock@btinternet.com

ALCOCK, Terry. b 08 **p** 09. NSM Narraghmore and Timolin w Castledermot etc *D & G* from 08; Asst Chapl Adelaide and Meath Hosp Dublin from 10. *Lacken, Blessington, Co Wicklow, Republic of Ireland* T: (00353) (45) 865896 M: 87-054 8544

ALDCROFT, Malcolm Charles. b 44. Leeds Univ MA 94. NOC 79. **d** 82 **p** 83. NSM Alverthorpe *Wakef* 82-85; NSM Horbury Junction 85-93; Sub Chapl HM Pris and YOI New Hall 94-97; Sub Chapl HM Pris Wakef 96-97; R Cupar and Ladybank *St And* 97-05; Chapl Stratheden Hosp Fife 97-05; Dioc Miss Officer and Min Development Co-ord *Mor* 05-07; Hon C Arpafeelie 05-07; Warden of Readers 06-07; Hon C St Andrews All SS *St And* from 08; TV Edin St Mich and All SS 08-11; LtO from 11. *14 Cherry Lane, Cupar KY15 5DA* T: (01334) 650264 E: m33aldcroft@tiscali.co.uk

ALDEN, Andrew Michael. b 65. Bris Univ BA 88 Ex Univ PGCE 89 Lon Univ MA 98. Wycliffe Hall Ox 01. **d** 03 **p** 04. C Weston-super-Mare St Paul *B & W* 03-07; V from 07. *Somerset House, 20 Addiscombe Road, Weston-super-Mare BS23 4LT* T: (01934) 621120 E: revandrewalden@btinternet.com

ALDEN, Mrs Pamela Ann (Pat). b 42. St Gabr Coll Lon TCert 67. **d** 02 **p** 03. OLM Camberwell St Giles w St Matt *S'wark* 02-07; NSM Camberwell St Phil and St Mark 07-12; PtO from 12. *189 Upland Road, London SE22 0DG* T: (020) 8693 5207 F: 8693 6408 M: 07710-281374 E: pat@looksouth.net

ALDER, Mrs Anne-Louise. b 63. STETS 99. **d** 02 **p** 03. C Cowes H Trin and St Mary *Portsm* 02-05; C Cowes St Faith 05-06; C Newport St Thos 06-07; P-in-c Shipdham w Bradenham *Nor* 07-14; P-in-c Barnham Broom and Upper Yare 10-12; Dioc Fresh Expressions Asst 13-14; V Hellesdon from 14. *The Vicarage, Broom Avenue, Hellesdon, Norwich NR6 6LG* E: louise.alder@lineone.net

ALDERMAN, Canon John David. b 49. Man Univ BA 71 Selw Coll Cam BA 79 MA 80 Lon Inst of Educn PGCE 72. Ridley Hall Cam 77. **d** 80 **p** 81. C Hartley Wintney, Elvetham, Winchfield etc *Win* 80-83; V Bursledon 83-92; R Dibden 92-05; AD Lyndhurst 04-05; Hon Can Win Cathl 01-05; Patr Sec CPAS 05-11; rtd 11. *32 Stuart Close, Warwick CV34 6AQ* T: (01926) 400743
E: jandgalderman@btinternet.com

ALDERSLEY, Ian. b 42. FIBMS 68. Wycliffe Hall Ox 89. **d** 91 **p** 92. C Allestree *Derby* 91-94; R Brailsford w Shirley and Osmaston w Edlaston 94-06; P-in-c Yeaveley 05-06; P-in-c Ruishton w Thornfalcon *B & W* 06-10; P-in-c Creech St Michael 08-10; rtd 10; Retirement Chapl *Derby* from 12. *Tite Cottage, Main Street, Winster, Matlock DE4 2DH* T: (01629) 650413 E: aldersley_ian@yahoo.co.uk

ALDERSON, Gary. b 38. ERMC. **d** 08 **p** 09. NSM Wellingborough St Mark *Pet* 08-13; NSM Wellingborough All SS from 13; NSM Wellingborough All Hallows from 13. *75 Chatsworth Drive, Wellingborough NN8 5FD* T: (01933) 402770
E: garymalderson@yahoo.co.uk

ALDERSON, Mrs Hannah Samantha Joy. b 86. Ex Univ BA 08. Ripon Coll Cuddesdon MTh 13. **d** 13 **p** 14. C Bridgwater H Trin and Durleigh *B & W* from 13. *11 Alexandra Road, Bridgwater TA6 3HE* M: 07546-397981
E: hannahsjalderson@gmail.com

ALDERSON, Mrs Maureen. b 40. WMMTC 90. **d** 93 **p** 94. NSM Yardley St Cypr Hay Mill *Birm* 93-96; P-in-c 96-00; V 00-02; P-in-c Gainford and Winston *Dur* 02-07. *5 St Michaels Court, Northallerton DL7 8YX* T: (01609) 779265

ALDERSON, Major Robin Edward Richard. b 44. **d** 04 **p** 05. OLM Alde River *St E* 04-07; NSM Brandeston w Kettleburgh and Easton 07-13; rtd 13; PtO *St E* from 13. *The Cloisters, Sandy Lane, Snape, Saxmundham IP17 1SD* T/F: (01728) 688255 M: 07790-242002 E: robin.alderson@virgin.net

ALDERSON, Roger James Ambrose. b 47. Lon Univ BD 70 AKC 71 Man Univ 76 Liv Inst of Educn PGCE 93. St Aug Coll Cant. **d** 71 **p** 72. C Lawton Moor *Man* 71-75; C Barton w Peel Green 75-76; R Heaton Norris St Thos 76-85; V Bedford Leigh 85-92; V Cleadon Park *Dur* 99-07; rtd 07. *73 West Drive, Sunderland SR6 7SL* T: 0191-536 1236 M: 07710-722817

ALDERTON, Mrs Jill Alvina. b 59. SEITE 12. **d** 15. NSM Crawley Down All SS *Chich* from 15. *20 Hylands Close, Crawley RH10 6RX* T: (01293) 418692 E: jill@aldertonhome.plus.com

ALDERTON, Mary Louise. *See* PRICE, Mary Louise

ALDERTON-FORD, Canon Jonathan Laurence. b 57. St Jo Coll Nottm BTh 85. **d** 85 **p** 86. C Gaywood, Bawsey and Mintlyn *Nor* 85-87; C Herne Bay Ch Ch *Cant* 87-90; Min Bury St Edmunds St Mary *St E* 90-91; Min Moreton Hall Estate CD 91-94; V Bury St Edmunds Ch Ch from 94; Hon Can St E Cathl from 08. *18 Heldhaw Road, Bury St Edmunds IP32 7ER* T: (01284) 769956 *or* T/F: 725391 E: worship@ccmh.org.uk *or* revdjonathanford@gmail.com

ALDIS, John Arnold. b 43. Univ of Wales (Cardiff) BA 65 Lon Univ BD 67. Clifton Th Coll 65. **d** 69 **p** 70. C Tonbridge SS Pet and Paul *Roch* 69-72; C St Marylebone All So w SS Pet and Jo *Lon* 72-77; Overseas Service Adv CMS 77-80; C Welling *Roch* 77-80; V Leic H Trin w St Jo 80-89; Hon Can Leic Cathl 88-89; V W Kowloon St Andr Hong Kong 89-99; Sen Chapl Protestant Ch Oman 00-01; V Whitton St Alb 02-08; rtd 08. *146 Arrowsmith Drive, Stonehouse GL10 2QR* E: john.aldis@btinternet.com

ALDIS, John Philip. b 83. Keble Coll Ox BA 05 Fitzw Coll Cam BA 11 Peterho Cam MPhil 12. Ridley Hall Cam 09. **d** 12 **p** 13. C Newbury St Nic and Speen *Ox* 12-15. *24 Victoria Avenue, Worcester WR5 1ED* M: 07815-503485
E: johnaldis@gmail.com

ALDIS, Miss Rosemary Helen. b 40. Southn Univ BSc 62 Ox Univ Inst of Educn DipEd 63 Keele Univ MSc 67. All Nations Chr Coll MA 99. **d** 05 **p** 05. NSM Gabalfa *Llan* 05-10; PtO from 11; Hon Tutor St Mich Coll Llan 05-10; Hon Chapl from 11. *94 Glendower Court, Velindre Road, Cardiff CF14 2TZ* T: (029) 2062 6337 E: aldisrosemary@gmail.com

ALDOUS, Alexander Charles Victor. b 56. Southn Univ BA 81 K Alfred's Coll Win PGCE 83. S Dios Minl Tr Scheme 91. **d** 94 **p** 95. Chapl Oundle Sch 94-97; Chapl Benenden Sch 98-01; Chapl Oakham Sch from 02. *Oakham School, Chapel Close, Market Place, Oakham LE15 6DT* T: (01572) 758591 *or* 723941 E: aa@oakham.rutland.sch.uk

ALDOUS, John Herbert. b 37. CQSW 83. Bp Otter Coll 94. **d** 96 **p** 00. NSM Gosport Ch Ch *Portsm* 96-00; NSM Rowner 00-02; R Sabie St Pet S Africa 02-05; PtO Dio Natal from 05; rtd 05. *PO Box 522, Munster, 4278 South Africa* T: (0027) (39) 312 0415

ALDRIDGE, Mrs Anne Louise. b 59. Nottm Univ BEd 80. EAMTC 96. **d** 99 **p** 00. NSM Milton *Ely* 99-03; Chapl Milton Children's Hospice 99-03; Deputy Chapl Team Ldr Cam Univ

Hosps NHS Foundn Trust 03-11; Tutor Ridley Hall Cam from 10. *Ridley Hall, Ridley Hall Road, Cambridge CB3 9HG* T: (01223) 741072 E: ala290@cam.ac.uk

ALDRIDGE, Christopher John. b 35. Trin Hall Cam BA 57 MA 61. Ripon Hall Ox 59. **d** 60 **p** 61. C Coalville *Leic* 60-64; P-in-c Clifton St Fran *S'well* 64-71; P-in-c Clifton 71-72; V Gospel Lane St Mich *Birm* 72-90; V Selly Oak St Mary 90-00; rtd 00; PtO *Birm* 00-14. *4 Paradise Lane, Birmingham B28 0DS* T: 0121-777 0446 E: chris@paradiselane.co.uk

ALDRIDGE, Canon Harold John. b 42. Oak Hill Th Coll 65. **d** 69 **p** 70. C Rawtenstall St Mary *Man* 69-72; CMJ 72-76; C Woodford Wells *Chelmsf* 76-79; TV Washfield, Stoodleigh, Withleigh etc *Ex* 79-86; V Burton *Ches* 86-90; P-in-c Shotwick 90; V Burton and Shotwick 91-07; Dioc Clergy Widows and Retirement Officer 91-07; RD Wirral S 96-06; Hon Can Ches Cathl 98-07; Chapl Clatterbridge Hosp Wirral 86-91; Chapl Wirral Hosp NHS Trust 91-97; Chapl Wirral and W Cheshire Community NHS Trust 97-03; Chapl Cheshire and Wirral Partnerships NHS Trust 03-07; rtd 07; PtO *Ches* from 08. *Tedda Junction, 9 Moorhouse Close, Chester CH2 2HU* T: (01244) 371628

ALDRIDGE, Mark Richard. b 58. Oak Hill Th Coll BA 89. **d** 89 **p** 90. C Combe Down w Monkton Combe and S Stoke *B & W* 89-90; C Woodside Park St Barn *Lon* 90-94; P-in-c Cricklewood St Gabr and St Mich 94-99; V 99-04; Min Oak Tree Angl Fellowship 04-15; Dir New Wine Internat Min from 15; LtO from 15. *100 Creffield Road, London W3 9PX* T: (020) 8992 9343 E: marka@oaktree.org.uk

ALDRIDGE-COLLINS, Murray Allan Leonard. b 73. Bris Univ BSc 09. St Steph Ho Ox 13. **d** 15. C Ilfracombe, Lee, Woolacombe, Bittadon etc *Ex* from 15. *St Peter's House, Highfield Road, Ilfracombe EX34 9LH* M: 07985-734119 E: murrayaldridge-collins@hotmail.co.uk

ALDWINCKLE, Jonathan Frederick. b 62. ERMC 12. **d** 15. C Kettering Ch the King *Pet* from 15. *9 Churchill Way, Kettering NN15 5DP* E: jon-wend_aldwinckle@lineone.net *or* jonaldwinckle@ctk.org.uk

ALESSI, John. b 55. **d** 10 **p** 11. C Longton Hall *Lich* 10-13; P-in-c from 13. *The Vicarage, 131 Longton Hall Road, Blurton, Stoke-on-Trent ST3 2EL* T: (01782) 598366 M: 07766-952836 E: johnalessi2000@hotmail.com

ALEXANDER, Ann Maria. b 58. Surrey Univ BA 01. Cuddesdon Coll 07. **d** 09 **p** 10. C Chiswick St Nic w St Mary *Lon* 09-13; TV Ifield *Chich* from 13. *St Alban's Vicarage, Gossops Drive, Crawley RH11 8LD* M: 07961-853343 E: anejmi@virginmedia.com

ALEXANDER, David Graham. b 61. Ridley Hall Cam 87. **d** 89 **p** 90. C New Barnet St Jas *St Alb* 89-93; C Northwood H Trin *Lon* 93-95; V Stopsley *St Alb* from 95. *The Vicarage, 702 Hitchin Road, Luton LU2 7UJ* T: (01582) 729194 F: 450375 E: stopsley@aol.com

ALEXANDER, Prof Freda. b 41. Girton Coll Cam BA 62 MMath 11 Edin Univ PhD 67 Lon Univ MSc 81. TISEC 06. **d** 08. NSM Edin St Jo from 08. *79 Great King Street, Edinburgh EH3 6RN* T: 0131-557 4474 E: freda.alexander1@btinternet.com

ALEXANDER, James Crighton. b 43. Qu Coll Cam BA 65 MA 69. Cuddesdon Coll 68. **d** 68 **p** 69. C Much Wenlock w Bourton *Heref* 68-72; V Oakington *Ely* from 72; P-in-c Dry Drayton 85-95. *The Vicarage, 99 Water Lane, Oakington, Cambridge CB24 3AL* T: (01223) 232396 E: free2live@btinternet.com

ALEXANDER, Canon James Douglas. b 27. Linc Th Coll 57. **d** 58 **p** 59. C Frodingham *Linc* 58-61; V Alvingham w N and S Cockerington 61-65; V Keddington 61-65; R Gunhouse w Burringham 65-70; R Peterhead *Ab* 70-76; R Aberdeen St Mary 76-95; Miss to Seafarers 78-06; Can St Andr Cathl from 79; Chapl HM Pris Aber 82-06; P-in-c Cove Bay *Ab* 85-90; rtd 95; Dioc Supernumerary *Ab* from 95. *21 Whitehall Road, Aberdeen AB25 2PP* T: (01224) 643202

ALEXANDER, Jane Louise. *See* MacLAREN, Jane Louise

ALEXANDER, Mrs Jean Ann. b 44. Southn Univ BTh 00 SRN 65 SCM 67. Ripon Coll Cuddesdon 06. **d** 07 **p** 08. NSM Lytchett Minster *Sarum* 07-10; NSM The Lytchetts and Upton from 10. *1 Palmers Orchard, Lytchett Matravers, Poole BH16 6HG* T: (01202) 631033 E: jalexanderlmpc@btinternet.com

ALEXANDER, Julius Erik Louis. b 66. Wycliffe Hall Ox 89. **d** 92 **p** 93. C Hoole *Ches* 92-94; C Offerton 94-98; TV Upper Holloway *Lon* 98-03; Asst Chapl Southn Univ Hosps NHS Trust 03-06; Chapl Oakhaven Hospice Trust from 06. *Oakhaven Hospice Trust, Lower Pennington Lane, Lymington SO41 8ZZ* T: (01590) 677773 F: 677582 E: jalexander@blueyonder.co.uk

ALEXANDER, Canon Loveday Constance Anne. b 47. Somerville Coll Ox BA 69 MA 78 DPhil 78. NOC 98. **d** 99 **p** 00. NSM Alderley Edge *Ches* from 99; Can Th Ches Cathl

03-14; PtO *Sheff* from 00. *5 Nevill Road, Bramhall, Stockport SK7 3ET* T: 0161-439 7946 E: l.c.alexander@sheffield.ac.uk

ALEXANDER, Canon Michael George. b 47. Open Univ BA 90 DipEd 91. Sarum & Wells Th Coll 74. **d** 77 **p** 78. C Wednesfield *Lich* 77-80; C Tettenhall Wood 80-83; Distr Min 83-85; Dioc Adv in Adult and Youth Educn *Derby* 85-89; V Hazlewood 85-89; V Turnditch 85-89; Par Educn Adv (Laity Development) 89-96; Dioc Laity Development Adv 96-00; Dioc Dir Studies Bp's Centres of Learning 96-00; P-in-c Ticknall, Smisby and Stanton-by-Bridge 00-01; P-in-c Barrow-on-Trent w Twyford and Swarkestone 00-01; V Ticknall, Smisby and Stanton by Bridge etc 01-07; RD Melbourne 02-07; P-in-c Loscoe 07-12; C Morley w Smalley and Horsley Woodhouse 07-12; RD Heanor 09-11; Hon Can Derby Cathl 09-12; rtd 12. *79 Allerburn Lea, Alnwick NE66 2NQ* T: (01665) 510684 E: mike.alexander@ticvic.fsnet.co.uk

ALEXANDER, Nancy Joan. *See* WALLACE, Nancy Joan

ALEXANDER, Nicholas Edward. b 68. Leic Poly BSc 90. Oak Hill Th Coll BA 06. **d** 06 **p** 07. C Linc Minster Gp 06-12; C Linc St Pet in Eastgate 12-15; C Bury St Edmunds St Mary *St E* from 15. *c/o The Parish Office, St Mary's Church, Honey Hill, Bury St Edmunds IP33 1RT* T: (01284) 754680 E: nickalexander110@hotmail.com

ALEXANDER, Pamela Mary. b 50. **d** 13. NSM Roch from 13. *10 College Road, Chatham ME4 4QX* T: (01634) 817500

ALEXANDER, Peter John. b 36. CQSW 73. Oak Hill Th Coll 92. **d** 95 **p** 96. NSM Aspenden, Buntingford and Westmill *St Alb* 95-02; rtd 02; PtO *Nor* from 02. *Dell Gate, 4 The Dell, Bodham, Holt NR25 6NG* T: (01263) 588126 E: peter.brenda2@tiscali.co.uk

ALEXANDER, Mrs Rachel Clare. b 57. EAMTC 96. **d** 99 **p** 00. NSM Mattishall w Mattishall Burgh, Welborne etc *Nor* 99-02; PtO 02-03 and 11; NSM Rugby St Matt *Cov* 03-04; NSM Thorpe Acre w Dishley *Leic* 11-15. *2 Mount Grace Road, Loughborough LE11 4FR* T: (01509) 843083 E: rachel.alexander@virgin.net

ALEXANDER, Robert. b 37. Lon Univ LLB 60 St Cath Coll Ox BA 62. St Steph Ho Ox 60. **d** 63 **p** 64. C Kensington St Mary Abbots w St Geo *Lon* 63-68; C Notting Hill 71-74; TV 74-79; Australia from 79; rtd 02. *302/27 Neutral Street, North Sydney NSW 2060, Australia* T/F: (0061) (2) 9954 0543 E: robalexand@bigpond.com

ALEXANDER, Sarah Louise. b 72. Wycliffe Hall Ox 02. **d** 04 **p** 05. C Enfield Ch Ch Trent Park *Lon* 04-08; C Newbury *Ox* 08-14; C Redhill H Trin *S'wark* from 14. *3 Ringwood Avenue, Redhill RH1 2DY* M: 07889-146141 E: sarah-alex1@yahoo.co.uk

ALEXANDER, Wilfred Robert Donald. b 35. TCD BA 58 MA 80. **d** 63 **p** 63. C Raheny w Coolock *D & G* 63-67; Min Can St Patr Cathl Dublin 65-67; Hon C Herne Hill St Paul *S'wark* 68-70; Asst Master Gosforth Gr Sch 71-76; Hon C Long Benton St Mary *Newc* 74-76; Chapl St Mary and St Anne's Sch Abbots Bromley 76-80; V Cauldon *Lich* 80-83; V Waterfall 80-83; P-in-c Calton 80-83; P-in-c Grindon 80-83; V Blackb St Luke w St Phil 83-89; V Rainhill *Liv* 89-92; R Croft w Southworth 92-99; C Croft w Southworth and Newchurch 99-01; rtd 01. *16 Hawkshaw Close, Birchwood, Warrington WA3 7NF* T: (01925) 851472

ALEXANDER-WATTS, Tristan Nathaniel. b 66. SEITE 99. **d** 03 **p** 04. NSM Eltham H Trin *S'wark* 03-10; Chapl Qu Eliz Hosp NHS Trust 04-11; Chapl Bromley Hosps NHS Trust 05-09; Chapl Oxleas NHS Foundn Trust 05-09; Chapl S Lon Healthcare NHS Trust 09-10; Chapl Newham Univ Hosp NHS Trust from 12; Chapl Richard Ho Children's Hospice from 12. *Newham General Hospital, Glen Road, London E13 8SL* T: (020) 7363 8053 M: 07970-016009 E: tristanshout@live.co.uk *or* tristan.alexander-watts@nhs.net

ALFORD, John. b 35. Nottm Univ BSc 58 DipEd 76. Qu Coll Birm 74. **d** 77 **p** 78. NSM Edmond *Lich* 77-87; C Cheadle 87-88; C Cheadle w Freehay 88-89; P-in-c Wootton Wawen *Cov* 89-95; P-in-c Grafham *Ely* 95-00; P-in-c Ellington 95-00; P-in-c Easton 95-00; P-in-c Spaldwick w Barham and Woolley 95-00; V 00-01; rtd 01; PtO *Ely* from 01. *4 Armstrong Close, Perry, Huntingdon PE28 0DF* T: (01480) 812075 E: johnalford@talktalk.net

ALGEO, Nicholas Arthur. b 81. Wycliffe Hall Ox BA 14. **d** 14 **p** 15. C Leyton Ch Ch *Chelmsf* from 14. *87 Bulwer Road, London E11 1BY* M: 07739-344625 E: arthuralgeo@gmail.com

ALIDINA (née LINGARD), Jennifer Mary. b 59. Ox Min Course 05. **d** 07 **p** 08. C Chipping Norton *Ox* 07-10; Asst Chapl HM Pris Bullingdon 10-11; P-in-c Ellingham and Harbridge and Hyde w Ibsley *Win* 11-14; PtO *Sarum* from 14; Win from 14. *Iris Hollow, New Road, Stoborough, Wareham BH20 5BB* T: (01929) 505007 E: revjennyalidina@gmail.com *or* jennyalidina@irishollow.co.uk

ALISON, Sister. *See* FRY, Alison Jacquelyn

ALKER, Canon Adrian. b 49. Wadh Coll Ox BA 70 Lanc Univ MA 71. Ripon Coll Cuddesdon 77. **d** 79 **p** 80. C W Derby St Mary *Liv* 79-83; Dioc Youth Officer *Carl* 83-88; V Sheff St Mark Broomhill 88-08; Dioc Dir of In-Service Tr 90-08; Hon Can Sheff Cathl 05-08; Dir Miss Resourcing *Leeds* 08-15; rtd 15. *Address temp unknown*

ALKIRE, Sabina Marie. b 69. Univ of Illinois BA 89 Magd Coll Ox MPhil 94 MSc 95 DPhil 99. **d** 00 **p** 02. NSM Washington St Alb and St Phil USA 00-03; NSM Boston St Steph 03-07; Chapl Assoc Magd Coll Ox from 06; NSM Cowley St Jo *Ox* from 08. *3 Mansfield Road, Oxford OX1 3TB* T: (01865) 271529 F: 281801 M: 07792-505847 E: sabina.alkire@qeh.ox.ac.uk

ALLABY, Miss Mary Dorothea. b 60. Bedf Coll Lon BA 82 W Sussex Inst of HE PGCE 83. Trin Coll Bris 88. **d** 92 **p** 94. Par Dn Ipsley *Worc* 92-94; C 94-96; TV Bloxwich *Lich* 96-02; V Trent Vale 02-03. *Address withheld by request* E: mary@allaby.freeserve.co.uk

ALLABY, Simon Arnold Kenworthy. b 65. St Chad's Coll Dur BA 88. Trin Coll Bris 88. **d** 90 **p** 91. C Preston on Tees *Dur* 90-93; C Chester le Street 93-99; R Ardingly *Chich* 99-05. *Fenners, Top Street, Bolney, Haywards Heath RH17 5PP* M: 07837-637113 E: simon@sixnineteen.co.uk

ALLAIN CHAPMAN, The Ven Justine Penelope Heathcote. b 67. K Coll Lon BA 88 AKC 88 PGCE 89 DThMin 11 Nottm Univ MDiv 93. Linc Th Coll 91. **d** 93 **p** 94. C Forest Hill *S'wark* 93-96; TV Clapham Team 96-01; V Clapham St Paul 02-04; Dir Miss and Past Studies SEITE 04-13; Vice Prin 07-13; Adn Boston *Linc* from 13. *Archdeacon's House, Castle Hill, Welbourn, Lincoln LN5 0NF* T: (01400) 273335 M: 07715-077993 E: justine.allainchapman@lincoln.anglican.org

ALLAN, Andrew John. b 47. Westcott Ho Cam 76. **d** 79 **p** 80. C Whitstable All SS w St Pet *Cant* 79-84; C Whitstable 84-86; P-in-c Littlebourne 86-87; P-in-c Ickham w Wickhambreaux and Stodmarsh 86-87; R Littlebourne and Ickham w Wickhambreaux etc 87-10; rtd 10. *The Moorings, Old Road, Liskeard PL14 6DL* T: (01579) 349074

ALLAN, Canon Archibald Blackie. b 35. Edin Th Coll 57. **d** 60 **p** 61. C Aberdeen St Jo *Ab* 60-63; R 82-00; Chapl St Paul's Cathl Dundee 63-68; P-in-c Aberdeen St Clem *Ab* 68-76; Vice-Provost St Andr Cathl 76-82; Can St Andr Cathl 80-00; Hon Can from 01; rtd 00; LtO *Ab* from 01. *32 Craigiebuckler Terrace, Aberdeen AB15 8SX* T: (01224) 316636 E: canonarchiea@aol.com

ALLAN, Donald James. b 35. Sarum & Wells Th Coll 63. **d** 65 **p** 66. C Royton St Paul *Man* 65-71; V Middleton Junction 71-78; P-in-c Finmere w Mixbury *Ox* 78-83; R Finmere w Mixbury, Cottisford, Hardwick etc 83; Chapl Westcliff Hosp 83-87; V Westcliff St Andr *Chelmsf* 83-87; R Goldhanger w Lt Totham 87-01; rtd 01; P-in-c St Goran w Caerhays *Truro* 01-06. *23 Stirrup Close, Wimborne BH21 2UQ* T: (01202) 880645 E: donald.allan2@btinternet.com

ALLAN, Janet Ross. b 57. St Mellitus Coll BA 13. **d** 13 **p** 14. C Thorpe Bay *Chelmsf* from 13. *20 Wansfell Gardens, Southend-on-Sea SS1 3SW* T: (01702) 873944 M: 07958-534465 E: janetrallan@hotmail.com

ALLAN, Jeanette Winifred. b 40. ALA 63. St And Dioc Tr Course 79. **dss** 81 **d** 86 **p** 94. NSM Hillfoot's TM *St And* 81-86; NSM Bridge of Allan *St And* 86-88; NSM Dunblane 88-98; R Glenrothes 98-06; rtd 06; LtO *St And* from 07. *Pernettya, Sinclairs Street, Dunblane FK15 0AH* T: (01786) 821151 E: pernettya@googlemail.com

ALLAN, John. *See* ALLAN, Andrew John

ALLAN, Preb John William. b 58. St Olaf Coll Minnesota BA 80 Birm Univ 86. Trin Lutheran Sem Ohio MDiv 84 Qu Coll Birm 90. **d** 91 **p** 92. In Lutheran Ch (USA) 84-86; C Newport w Longford and Chetwynd *Lich* 91-94; P-in-c Longdon 94-01; Local Min Adv (Wolverhampton) 94-01; V Alrewas from 01; V Wychnor from 01; RD Lich 04-14; Preb Lich Cathl from 11. *The Vicarage, Church Road, Alrewas, Burton-on-Trent DE13 7BT* T: (01283) 790486 E: revdjohnallan@revdjohnallan.plus.com

ALLAN, Peter Burnaby. b 52. Clare Coll Cam BA 74 MA 78 St Jo Coll Dur BA 82. Cranmer Hall Dur 80. **d** 83 **p** 84. C Chaddesden St Mary *Derby* 83-86; C Brampton St Thos 86-89; TV Halesworth w Linstead, Chediston, Holton etc *St E* 89-94; TR Trunch *Nor* 94-03; R Ansley and Arley *Cov* from 03; RD Nuneaton 06-12. *The Vicarage, 60 Birmingham Road, Ansley, Nuneaton CV10 9PS* T: (024) 7639 9070 E: peter@allan49.fsworld.co.uk

ALLAN, Peter George. b 50. Wadh Coll Ox BA 72 MA 76. Coll of Resurr Mirfield 72. **d** 75 **p** 76. C Stevenage St Geo *St Alb* 75-78; Chapl Wadh Coll and C Ox St Mary V w St Cross and St Pet 78-82; CR from 85; Prin Coll of Resurr Mirfield from 11. *House of the Resurrection, Stocks Bank Road, Mirfield WF14 0BN* T: (01924) 494318

ALLARD, John Ambrose. b 30. Bps' Coll Cheshunt 63. **d** 65 **p** 66. C Leigh-on-Sea St Marg *Chelmsf* 65-69; P-in-c Rawreth w Rettendon 69-70; R 70-72; V Barkingside St Fran 73-84; V E Ham St Geo 84-86; V St Osyth 86-95; rtd 95; PtO *Nor* 97-02; *St E* 97-02; Hon C Stonehaven *Bre* 03-07. *23 St Nicholas Drive, Banchory AB31 5YG* T: (01330) 822761

ALLARD, Roderick George. b 44. Lon Univ BA 77 Sheff Poly MSc 88 Loughb Coll of Educn CertEd 96. NOC 97. **d** 99 **p** 00. NSM Charlesworth and Dinting Vale *Derby* 99-13; NSM Glossop and Hadfield 11-13; PtO *Leic* from 14. *37 Sutton Lane, Sutton in the Elms, Broughton Astley, Leicester LE9 6QF* T: (01455) 289356 M: 07976-435160 E: r.allard@sky.com

ALLARDICE, Alexander Edwin. b 49. SRN. Chich Th Coll 73. **d** 76 **p** 77. C Rugeley *Lich* 76-79; C Felixstowe St Jo *St E* 79-81; TV Ipswich St Fran 81-87; C Lostwithiel *Truro* 87-90; C Boconnoc w Bradoc 87-90; C St Veep 87-90; C St Winnow 87-90; R Lostwithiel, St Winnow w St Nectan's Chpl etc 90-97; R Mevagissey and St Ewe 97-99; rtd 99; PtO *Truro* 99-13; *Portsm* from 13. *20 Garstons Road, Fareham PO14 4EG* T: (01329) 609558 E: alex.allardice@classicfm.net

ALLBERRY, Samuel. b 75. Wycliffe Hall Ox BTh 03. **d** 05 **p** 06. NSM Ox St Ebbe w H Trin and St Pet 05-08; C Maidenhead St Andr and St Mary from 08. *St Mary's Close, 14 High Street, Maidenhead SL6 1YY* T: (01628) 638866 E: sam_allberry@yahoo.co.uk

ALLBERRY, William Alan John. b 49. Ch Coll Cam BA 70 MA 71. Ripon Coll Cuddesdon 84. **d** 86 **p** 87. C Brixton St Matt *S'wark* 86-90; V Wandsworth St Paul 90-98; R Esher *Guildf* 98-12; RD Emly 01-06; rtd 12; Lect Tamilnadu Th Sem Madurai India from 12; PtO *Guildf* from 12; *S'wark* from 12. *48 Ditton Road, Surbiton KT6 6RB* T: (020) 8390 2019 E: william@allberry.org

ALLBUTT, Mavis Miriam. b 51. **d** 98 **p** 99. OLM Meir *Lich* 98-08; P-in-c 08-13; rtd 13; PtO *Lich* from 13. *Hayloft Cottage, Lockwood Road, Kingsley Holt, Stoke-on-Trent ST10 2DH* E: mavis.allbutt@btinternet.com

ALLCHIN, Miss Maureen Ann. b 50. Edge Hill Coll of HE CertEd 71 Sussex Univ MA 93. S Dios Minl Tr Scheme 88. **d** 91 **p** 94. Hd Past Faculty Steyning Gr Sch 79-92; NSM Southwick St Mich *Chich* 91-93; C Storrington 93-95; TV Bridport *Sarum* 95-05; LtO 05-06; P-in-c Canalside Benefice 06-08; LtO 08-09 and 10-15; P-in-c Trowbridge H Trin 09-10; rtd 10; P-in-c Seend, Bulkington and Poulshot *Sarum* from 15. *4 Northfields, Bulkington, Devizes SN10 1SE* T: (01380) 828931 E: maureen@mallchin.co.uk

ALLCOCK, Jeremy Robert. b 63. Trin Coll Bris BA 92. **d** 92 **p** 93. C Walthamstow St Luke *Chelmsf* 92-96; V E Ham St Paul 96-05; V Paddington St Steph w St Luke *Lon* from 05; V Bayswater from 12; AD Westmr Paddington from 11. *St Stephen's Vicarage, 25 Talbot Road, London W2 5JF* T: (020) 7792 2283 E: jeme6@aol.com

ALLCOCK, Peter Michael. b 37. Oak Hill Th Coll 65. **d** 68 **p** 69. C Upper Tulse Hill St Matthias *S'wark* 68-71; C Dunkeswell and Dunkeswell Abbey *Ex* 71-72; P-in-c Luppitt and Monkton 72-75; V Okehampton w Inwardleigh 75-80; TV Solihull *Birm* 80-85; V Highbury New Park St Aug *Lon* 85-89; V E and W Horndon w Lt Warley and Childerditch *Chelmsf* 89-02; rtd 02; PtO *Birm* 03-05; *Cov* 03-05; NSM Shepshed and Oaks in Charnwood *Leic* 05-07. *10 Arden Close, Balsall Common, Coventry CV7 7NY* T: (01676) 532346 E: pma946078@aol.com

ALLDRED, Barbara. b 45. SNWTP. **d** 10 **p** 11. OLM Newchurch w Croft *Liv* from 10. *20 Glebelands, Culcheth, Warrington WA3 4DX* T: (01925) 763603

ALLDRIT, Nicolas Sebastian Fitz-Ansculf. b 41. St Edm Hall Ox BA 63 MA 69 DPhil 69. Cuddesdon Coll 72. **d** 72 **p** 73. C Limpsfield and Titsey *S'wark* 72-81; Tutor Linc Th Coll 81-96; Sub-Warden 88-96; R Witham Gp *Linc* 97-07; rtd 07; PtO *Pet* 07-12. *104 Orchard Hill, Little Billing, Northampton NN3 9AG* T: (01604) 407115

ALLDRITT, Richard James Lee. b 79. Somerville Coll Ox MEng 01. Oak Hill Th Coll 10. **d** 13 **p** 14. C Cambridge H Sepulchre *Ely* from 13. *9 Victoria Street, Cambridge CB1 1JP* M: 07788-952137 E: rich.alldritt@stag.org *or* rich.alldritt@gmail.com

ALLEN, Andrew Michael. b 84. Ripon Coll Cuddesdon BA 09. **d** 10 **p** 11. C Aston Clinton w Buckland and Drayton Beauchamp *Ox* 10-13; Chapl and Fell Ex Coll Ox from 13. *Exeter College, Turl Street, Oxford OX1 3DP* T: (01865) 279600 E: andrew.curate@gmail.com

ALLEN, Andrew Stephen. b 55. Nottm Univ BPharm 77 MPS. St Steph Ho Ox 78. **d** 81 **p** 82. C Gt Ilford St Mary *Chelmsf* 81-83; C Luton All SS w St Pet *St Alb* 83-86; TV Chambersbury 86-91; TV Brixham w Churston Ferrers and Kingswear *Ex* 91-01; TR 01-06; P-in-c Upton cum Chalvey *Ox* 06-08; TR from 08. *St Mary's Rectory, 34 Upton Park, Slough SL1 2DE* T/F: (01753) 529988 E: andrewallen@fastmail.com

ALLEN, Beverley Carole. *See* PINNELL, Beverley Carole

ALLEN, Brian. *See* ALLEN, Frank Brian

ALLEN, Brian. b 58. Oak Hill NSM Course 90. **d** 93 **p** 94. NSM W Norwood St Luke *S'wark* 93-02; NSM Gipsy Hill Ch Ch 02-08. *76 Bradley Road, London SE19 3NS* T: (020) 8771 4282 *or* 8686 8282

ALLEN, Brian Stanley. b 24. Roch Th Coll 65. **d** 67 **p** 68. C Roch 67-74; P-in-c Drypool St Jo *York* 74-80; TV Drypool 80; V Marlpool *Derby* 80-87; rtd 87; PtO *York* from 90. *22 Sycamore Terrace, York YO30 7DN* T: (01904) 653418

ALLEN, Mrs Caroline Anne. b 59. ERMC 08. **d** 11 **p** 12. C Kesgrave *St E* 11-14; P-in-c Walton and Trimley from 14. *1 Parsonage Close, Felixstowe IP11 2QR* M: 07970-737639 T: (01394) 279290 E: carolineallen121@gmail.com

ALLEN, Miss Charlotte. b 79. St Jo Coll Dur BA 00 Anglia Poly Univ MA 03. Westcott Ho Cam 00. **d** 03 **p** 04. C Southwick *Chich* 03-07; V Portchester *Portsm* 07-12; Co-ord of IME *Sarum* from 12; Dioc Dir of Ords from 13; NSM Salisbury St Thos and St Edm from 13. *25 Lime Kiln Way, Salisbury SP2 8RN* T: (01722) 438661 M: 07540-058125 E: charlie.allen@salisbury.anglican.org

ALLEN, Christopher Dennis. b 50. Fitzw Coll Cam BA 73 MA 77. Cuddesdon Coll 74. **d** 76 **p** 77. C Kettering St Andr *Pet* 76-79; C Pet H Spirit Bretton 79-82; R Bardney *Linc* 82-87; V Knighton St Mary Magd *Leic* 87-11; V Cosby and Whetstone from 11. *The Vicarage, Church Lane, Whetstone, Leicester LE8 6BA* T: 0116-286 6329 E: rev.c.allen@googlemail.com

ALLEN, Christopher Leslie. b 56. Leeds Univ BA 78. St Jo Coll Nottm 79. **d** 80 **p** 81. C Birm St Martin 80-85; Tr and Ed Pathfinders 85-89; Hd 89-92; Midl Youth Dept Co-ord CPAS 85-89; Hon C Selly Park St Steph and St Wulstan *Birm* 86-92; V Hamstead St Bernard 92-95; NSM Kidderminster St Mary and All SS w Trimpley etc *Worc* 03-11; NSM Ribbesford w Bewdley and Dowles and Wribbenhall from 11. *The Brambles, Dowles Road, Bewdley DY12 2RD* T: (01299) 409057 M: 07956-303037 E: chris.allen@compass.uk.net

ALLEN, David. b 38. Llan Dioc Tr Scheme. **d** 76 **p** 77. C Fairwater *Llan* 76-84; Chapl Bp of Llan High Sch 84-97; LtO *Llan* from 84. *1 Kenley Close, Llandaff, Cardiff CF5 2PA* T: (029) 2056 0252

ALLEN, David Edward. b 70. Van Mildert Coll Dur BSc 91. Ripon Coll Cuddesdon BA 94 MA 11. **d** 95 **p** 96. C Grantham *Linc* 95-99; C W Hampstead St Jas *Lon* 99-01; C Kilburn St Mary w All So and W Hampstead St Jas 01-02; V Finsbury St Clem w St Barn and St Matt from 02; Chapl Moorfields Eye Hosp NHS Trust from 04. *St Clement's Vicarage, King Square, London EC1V 8DA* T: (020) 7251 0706 E: davideallen@blueyonder.co.uk

ALLEN, Derek. b 57. MCIOB 89. **d** 99 **p** 00. OLM Bacup Ch Ch *Man* 99-04; OLM Bacup and Stacksteads from 04. *180 New Line, Bacup OL13 9RU* T: (01706) 875960 E: allen.newline@cwcom.net

ALLEN, Canon Francis Arthur Patrick. b 26. Em Coll Saskatoon Div Test 52. **d** 51 **p** 52. Miss Nipawin Canada 51-52; Miss Meadow Lake 52-54; Miss Medstead 54-57; C Bishopwearmouth St Nic *Dur* 57-59; Chapl Miss to Seamen Kobe Japan 59-63; Hon Can Kobe from 63; V Kingston upon Hull St Matt *York* 63-67; P-in-c Oberon Australia 67; R 68-73; P-in-c Cobar 73-75; Chapl Torres Strait 76-78; R Waikerie 78-82; R Willunga 82-89; R Bamaga 89-91; rtd 91. *Unit 12, 133 Macquarie Road, Springwood NSW 2777, Australia* T: (0061) (2) 4751 9778

ALLEN, Frank Brian. b 47. K Coll Lon BD AKC 71. **d** 71 **p** 72. C Leam Lane *Dur* 71-74; C Tynemouth Ch Ch *Newc* 74-78; Chapl Preston Hosp N Shields 74-78; Chapl Newc Poly 78-84; V Newc St Hilda 84-88; Chapl Nottm Mental Illness and Psychiatric Unit 88-89; Chapl for Mental Health Newc Mental Health Unit 89-94; Chapl Newc City Health NHS Trust 94-96; Chapl Team Leader 96-06; Chapl Team Leader Northumberland, Tyne and Wear NHS Foundn Trust 06-12; rtd 12; Visiting Fell Newc Univ from 96. *43 Cherryburn Gardens, Newcastle upon Tyne NE4 9UQ* T: 0191-274 9335 E: brian_allen63@hotmail.com

ALLEN, Canon Geoffrey Gordon. b 39. Sarum Th Coll 64. **d** 66 **p** 67. C Langley Marish *Ox* 66-70; Miss to Seamen 70-82; Chapl Rotterdam w Schiedam *Eur* 78-82; Asst Chapl The Hague 84-93; Chapl Voorschoten 84-93; Can Brussels Cathl 89-04; Adn NW Eur 93-04; Chapl E Netherlands 93-04; P-in-c Haarlem 95-02; rtd 04. *Hans Brandts Buyslaan 22, 6952 BK Dieren, The Netherlands* T: (0031) (313) 412533 E: g.g.allen@zonnet.nl

ALLEN, Giles David. b 70. RCM BMus 91 Leeds Univ MA 05. Coll of Resurr Mirfield 92. **d** 95 **p** 96. C Palmers Green St Jo *Lon* 95-99; V Lund *Blackb* 99-12; CF from 12. *c/o MOD Chaplains (Army)* F: 381824 T: (01264) 383430 E: giles.lund@tiscali.co.uk

ALLEN, Gordon Richard. b 29. St Jo Coll Dur BA 54 MA 58. **d** 55 **p** 56. C N Meols *Liv* 55-58; Uganda 58-63; V Lathom *Liv* 64-68; USA from 68; rtd 94. *237 Emerys Bridge Road, South Berwick ME 03908-1935, USA*

ALLEN, Hugh Edward. b 47. Bp Otter Coll Chich CertEd 68. Sarum & Wells Th Coll 79. **d** 81 **p** 82. C Frome St Jo *B & W* 81-85; R Old Cleeve, Leighland and Treborough 85-97; RD Exmoor 92-97; P-in-c The Stanleys *Glouc* 97-99; PtO *B & W* 99-05; P-in-c Charlton Musgrove, Cucklington and Stoke Trister 05-10; RD Bruton and Cary 06-10; rtd 10; PtO *B & W* from 11; RD Tone from 12. *Woodpeckers, Langley Marsh, Wiveliscombe, Taunton TA4 2UL* T: (01984) 624166 E: hallenarkwood@yahoo.co.uk

ALLEN, Jacqueline Lesley. *See* McKENNA, Jacqueline Lesley

ALLEN, Jamie. *See* ALLEN, Timothy James

ALLEN, Mrs Jane Rosemary. b 39. Cartrefle Coll of Educn BA 83 PGCE 84. St As & Ban Minl Tr Course 99. **d** 00 **p** 01. C Llandudno *Ban* 00-05; TV 05-09; rtd 09; PtO *St As* from 09. *29 Manor Park, Gloddaeth Avenue, Llandudno LL30 2SE* E: revmil@hotmail.com

ALLEN, Johan. b 49. Lanc Univ CertEd 75 Roehampton Inst BEd 88. S'wark Ord Course 05. **d** 08 **p** 09. NSM W Streatham St Jas *S'wark* 08-12; NSM Furzedown from 12. *54 Leigham Vale, London SW16 2JQ* T: (020) 7564 8588 M: 07743-156786 E: johanallen@btinternet.com

ALLEN, John Clement. b 32. K Coll Lon 54. **d** 58 **p** 59. C Middlesbrough St Martin *York* 58-60; C Northallerton w Kirby Sigston 60-64; V Larkfield *Roch* 64-70; R Ash 70-79; R Ridley 70-79; RD Cobham 76-79; R Chislehurst St Nic 79-97; rtd 97; PtO *Sarum* from 97. *The Peppergarth, 9 Lane Fox Terrace, Penny Street, Sturminster Newton DT10 1DE* T: (01258) 473754

ALLEN, The Very Revd John Edward. b 32. Univ Coll Ox BA 56 MA 63 Fitzw Coll Cam BA 68. Westcott Ho Cam 66. **d** 68 **p** 69. C Deal St Leon *Cant* 68-71; P-in-c Clifton St Paul *Bris* 71-78; Chapl Bris Univ 71-78; P-in-c Chippenham St Andr w Tytherton Lucas 78-82; Provost Wakef 82-97; rtd 97; PtO *York* from 98. *The Glebe Barn, Main Street, Sawdon, Scarborough YO13 9DY* T: (01723) 859854 E: jeallen70@btinternet.com

ALLEN, Mrs Kathleen. b 46. Westmr Coll Ox MTh 02. NOC 88. **d** 91 **p** 94. NSM Colne H Trin *Blackb* 91-94; NSM Colne Ch Ch 94-98; NSM Colne and Villages 98-06; rtd 06; PtO *B & W* from 09. *80 Stoddens Road, Burnham-on-Sea TA8 2DB* T: (01278) 793627 E: krabos@tiscali.co.uk

ALLEN, Malcolm. b 60. Open Th Coll BA 00. Trin Coll Bris 94. **d** 96 **p** 97. C Skirbeck H Trin *Linc* 96-00; TV Cheltenham St Mark *Glouc* 00-09; TR Bishop's Cleeve and Woolstone w Gotherington etc from 09. *The Rectory, 4 Church Approach, Bishops Cleeve, Cheltenham GL52 8NG* T: (01242) 677851 E: malcallen147@btinternet.com

ALLEN, Matthew Frederick James. b 82. Univ of Wales (Cardiff) BSc 03 St Jo Coll Dur BA 09 Dur Univ MA 11. Cranmer Hall Dur 07. **d** 10 **p** 11. C Kendal St Thos *Carl* 10-14; P-in-c Accrington Ch Ch *Blackb* from 14. *3 Bentcliffe Gardens, Accrington BB5 2NX* T: (01254) 235089 M: 07739-465073 E: revmattallen@gmail.com

ALLEN, Michael Stephen. b 37. Nottm Univ BA 60. Cranmer Hall Dur 60. **d** 62 **p** 63. C Sandal St Helen *Wakef* 62-66; Hon C Tile Cross *Birm* 66-70; V 72-84; Hon C Bletchley *Ox* 70-72; Vice-Prin Aston Tr Scheme 84-91; Hon C Boldmere *Birm* 85-91; P-in-c Easton w Colton and Marlingford *Nor* 91-93; Local Min Officer 91-93; Dioc Adv in Adult Educn *S'well* 93-02; rtd 02; PtO *S'well* from 02. *8 Grenville Rise, Arnold, Nottingham NG5 8EW* T: 0115-967 9515 E: msa@amd.fsnet.co.uk

ALLEN, Patricia. *See* LEWER ALLEN, Patricia

ALLEN, Peter Henry. b 34. Nottm Univ BA 66. Kelham Th Coll 58. **d** 66 **p** 67. C Salisbury St Martin *Sarum* 66-70; C Melksham 70-73; C Paignton Ch Ch *Ex* 73-76; P-in-c W Holloway St Dav *Lon* 76-77; V Barnsbury St Dav w St Clem 77-84; P-in-c Brentford St Faith 84-87; TV Brentford 87-91; TV Catford (Southend) and Downham *S'wark* 91-01; rtd 01; PtO *Roch* 01-13; *S'wark* from 14. *72 Westmount Road, London SE9 1JE* M: 07939-580266 E: peterbeth46@gmail.com

ALLEN, Peter John. b 34. Leic Coll of Educn CertEd 74 Leic Univ BEd 75 MA 79. EAMTC 89. **d** 92 **p** 93. NSM Ketton w Tinwell *Pet* 92-94; NSM Easton on the Hill, Collyweston w Duddington etc 94-96; Chapl St Pet Viña del Mar Chile 96-99; NSM Culworth w Sulgrave and Thorpe Mandeville etc *Pet* 00-04; rtd 04; PtO *Pet* from 04. *24 Holm Close, Weedon, Northampton NN7 4TJ* T: (01327) 349292 E: peterjallen@tinyworld.co.uk

ALLEN, Canon Peter John Douglas. b 35. Jes Coll Cam BA 61 MA 64 PGCE 67. Westcott Ho Cam 60. **d** 62 **p** 63. C Wyken *Cov* 62-65; C Boston Ch of Advent USA 65-66; Chapl Jes Coll Cam 66-72; Chapl K Sch Cant 72-87; Hon Min Can Cant Cathl 73-87; Second Master and Sen Chapl Sedbergh Sch 87-93; P-in-c Edin St Ninian 93-06; Tutor Edin Th Coll 94;

Tutor TISEC 95-01; Prec and Can St Mary's Cathl 94-06; rtd 06; Chapl Edin Academy 99-07; Chapl Fettes Coll Edin 02-07. *12A Grosvenor Crescent, Edinburgh EH12 5EL* T: 0131-337 0027 E: pa@dioceseofedinburgh.org

ALLEN, Peter Richard. b 62. Qu Coll Birm BA 04. **d** 04 **p** 05. C Hackenthorpe *Sheff* 04-07; TV Gleadless 07-08; Chapl for Sport 07-13; TV Halstead Area *Chelmsf* from 13. *St Andrew's Rectory, 5 Shut Lane, Earls Colne, Colchester CO6 2RE* T: (01787) 220347 M: 07772-926278 E: prallen1962@gmail.com

ALLEN, Philip Gerald. b 48. Trin Coll Bris 71. **d** 73 **p** 74. C Portsea St Luke *Portsm* 73-75; C-in-c 75-79; C Southsea St Jude 75-79; P-in-c Gatten St Paul 79-85; V from 85. *St Paul's Vicarage, St Paul's Crescent, Shanklin PO37 7AW* T: (01983) 862027

ALLEN, Mrs Rebecca Susan. b 71. Qu Coll Birm 12. **d** 15. C Springfield *Birm* from 15. *63 Grove Road, Sparkhill, Birmingham B11 4DB* T: 0121-325 5331 E: beccysallen@gmail.com

ALLEN, Richard. b 57. BA PGCE. SWMTC. **d** 06 **p** 07. NSM Ottery St Mary, Alfington, W Hill, Tipton etc *Ex* from 06; PtO *B & W* from 09. *23 Salisbury Road, Exmouth EX8 1SL* M: 07973-463783 E: rja@millfieldprep.com

ALLEN, Richard James. b 46. Wells Th Coll 69. **d** 71 **p** 72. C Upholland *Liv* 71-75; TV 76-79; TV Padgate 79-85; V Weston-super-Mare St Andr Bournville *B & W* 85-93; V Williton 93-10; P-in-c St Decumans 08-10; Chapl Somerset Primary Care Trust 93-10; rtd 10; PtO *B & W* from 10. *26 Causeway Terrace, Watchet TA23 0HP* T: (01984) 248119 M: 07789-242245 E: richzakers@uwclub.net

ALLEN, Richard John. b 55. City Univ BSc 76 FCOptom 80. ERMC 04. **d** 07 **p** 08. NSM Lexden *Chelmsf* 07-14; PtO from 14. *22 Fitzwilliam Road, Colchester CO3 3RZ* T: (01206) 578051 M: 07969-435951 E: richard.allen@zen.co.uk

ALLEN, Richard John Slaney. b 54. **d** 00 **p** 01. NSM Tooting All SS *S'wark* 00-04; NSM Streatham Ch Ch w St Marg 05-08; Chapl SW Lon and St George's Mental Health NHS Trust 03-13; PtO *S'wark* 10-14; *St Alb* from 15; Chapl Herts Partnership NHS Foundn Trust from 15. *Hertfordshire Partnership NHS Trust, 99 Waverley Road, St Albans AL3 5TL* E: richard.allen@hpft.nhs.uk

ALLEN, Richard Lee. b 41. Liv Inst of Educn TCert 67. NOC 80. **d** 83 **p** 84. NSM Colne Ch Ch *Blackb* 83-90; P-in-c Trawden 91-98; NSM Colne and Villages 98-06; Chapl Burnley Health Care NHS Trust 99-03; Chapl E Lancs Hosps NHS Trust 03-06; rtd 06; PtO *B & W* from 09. *80 Stoddens Road, Burnham-on-Sea TA8 2DB* T: (01278) 793627 M: 07971-023095

ALLEN, Roger Charles Brews. b 44. Loughb Univ BTech 66 Solicitor 77. **d** 92 **p** 93. OLM S Elmham and Ilketshall *St E* 92-95; OLM Bungay H Trin w St Mary 95-13; NSM Bungay 13-14; rtd 14; PtO *St E* from 14. *33A Earsham Street, Bungay NR35 1AF* T: (01986) 896927 E: ra@acg-solicitors.co.uk

ALLEN, Roy Vernon. b 43. Open Univ BA 81 Birm Univ MA 84. Sarum Th Coll 67. **d** 70 **p** 71. C Hall Green Ascension *Birm* 70-74; V Temple Balsall 74-78; P-in-c Smethwick St Steph 78-81; V Smethwick St Mich 78-81; V Smethwick SS Steph and Mich 81-86; V Marston Green 86-13; rtd 13; PtO *Birm* from 13. *16 Orchard Close, Curdworth, Sutton Coldfield B76 9DX* T: (01675) 470629 E: roy_v_allen@hotmail.com

ALLEN, Canon Steven. b 49. Nottm Univ BA 73. St Jo Coll Nottm 73. **d** 75 **p** 76. C Gt Horton *Bradf* 75-80; V 89-02; V Upper Armley *Ripon* 80-89; RD Bowling and Horton *Bradf* 98-02; Dioc Tr Officer *Leeds* 02-14; Hon Can Bradf Cathl 00-14; rtd 14. *1 Hawkstone Avenue, Guiseley, Leeds LS20 8ET* T: (01943) 510653 E: steve.allen@bradford.anglican.org

ALLEN, Stuart Philip. b 73. St Cath Coll Ox BA 95. Oak Hill Th Coll BA 02. **d** 02 **p** 03. C Burford w Fulbrook, Taynton, Asthall etc *Ox* 02-06; Lect Proclamation Trust and Hon C Tooting Graveney St Nic *S'wark* 06-10; R S Warks Seven Gp *Cov* from 10. *The Vicarage, Broad Street, Long Compton, Shipston-on-Stour CV36 5JH* T: (01608) 684207 E: rectorsw7@gmail.com

ALLEN, Canon Susan Rosemary. b 47. Warwick Univ BSc 68 Trevelyan Coll Dur PGCE 69. Sarum Th Coll 93. **d** 96 **p** 97. C Goldsworth Park *Guildf* 96-01; TV Hemel Hempstead *St Alb* 01-09; TR 09-13; Hon Can St Alb 11-13; rtd 13. *33 Swansfield Park Road, Alnwick NE66 1AT* E: revsue33@googlemail.com

ALLEN, Mrs Suzanna Claire. b 75. St Jo Coll Nottm 09. **d** 11 **p** 12. C Wareham *Sarum* 11-15; C Horton, Chalbury, Hinton Martel and Holt St Jas from 15; C Witchampton, Stanbridge and Long Crichel etc from 15; C Wimborne Minster from 15. *The Rectory, Hinton Martel, Wimborne BH21 7HD* E: suzannacallen@hotmail.co.uk

ALLEN, Thomas Davidson. b 49. QUB BA. CITC 81. **d** 84 **p** 85. C Magheralin w Dollingstown *D & D* 84-86; I Kilwarlin Upper w Kilwarlin Lower 86-91; I Maghera w Killelagh *D & R* 91-03; I Donaghcloney w Waringstown *D & D* 03-09; rtd 09;

P-in-c Gweedore, Carrickfin and Templecrone *D & R* from 10. *1 Parker Gardens, Castledawson, Magherafelt BT45 8AS* T: (028) 7946 9045 M: 07858-045272 E: tallen@talk21.com

ALLEN, Thomas Henry. b 42. NOC 87. **d** 90 **p** 91. C Upholland *Liv* 90-93; TV Walton-on-the-Hill 93-07; rtd 07. *13 Crosgrove Road, Liverpool L4 8TE* T: 0151-476 9705

ALLEN, The Very Revd Timothy James. b 71. Warwick Univ BA 93. Ripon Coll Cuddesdon BTh 99. **d** 99 **p** 00. C Nuneaton St Mary *Cov* 99-02; V Seend, Bulkington and Poulshot *Sarum* 02-03; Hon C Winslow w Gt Horwood and Addington *Ox* 03-05; V Gt Cornard *St E* 05-09; V New Plymouth St Mary New Zealand 09-10; Dean Taranaki from 10. *37 Vivian Street, New Plymouth 4310, New Zealand* T: (0064) (6) 758 3111 E: dean@taranakicathedral.org.nz

ALLEN, Zachary Edward. b 52. Warwick Univ BA 74. Ripon Coll Cuddesdon 78. **d** 81 **p** 82. C Bognor *Chich* 81-84; C Rusper and Roughey 84-86; TV Carl H Trin and St Barn 86-90; Chapl Strathclyde Ho Hosp Carl 86-90; V Findon w Clapham and Patching *Chich* 90-01; V Rustington from 01. *The Vicarage, Claigmar Road, Rustington, Littlehampton BN16 2NL* T: (01903) 784749

ALLERTON, Patrick. b 78. NTMTC. **d** 10 **p** 11. C Onslow Square and S Kensington St Aug *Lon* 10-14; C Fulham St Dionis from 14. *23 Pooles Lane, London SW10 0RH* E: patallerton@hotmail.com

ALLEYNE, Sir John Olpherts Campbell Bt. b 28. Jes Coll Cam BA 50 MA 55. **d** 55 **p** 56. C Southampton St Mary w H Trin *Win* 55-58; Chapl Cov Cathl 58-62; Chapl Clare Hall Cam 62-66; Chapl Bris Cathl 66-68; Area Sec (SW England) Toc H 68-71; V Speke All SS *Liv* 71-73; TR Speke St Aid 73-76; R Win St Matt 76-93; rtd 93; PtO *Guildf* from 93. *2 Ash Grove, Guildford GU2 8UT* T: (01483) 573824

ALLFORD, Judith Mary. b 55. Sheff Univ BA Lon Univ BD. Trin Coll Bris 77. dss 86 **d** 87 **p** 94. Par Dn Deptford St Jo w H Trin *S'wark* 87-91; Asst Chapl Dulwich Hosp 91-93; Asst Chapl K Coll Hosp Lon 91-95; Asst Chapl King's Healthcare NHS Trust 93-95; Chapl N Surrey Primary Care Trust from 95. *St Peter's Hospital, Guildford Road, Chertsey KT16 0PZ* T: (01932) 872000 ext 3324 E: judith.allford@asph.nhs.uk

ALLIES, Lorna Gillian. b 46. UEA BSc 93 Sheff Univ EdD 01. **d** 05 **p** 06. OLM Thurton *Nor* 05-07; NSM Bunwell, Carleton Rode, Tibenham, Gt Moulton etc 07-09; P-in-c Rackheath and Salhouse 09-14; Dioc Rural Adv 06-09; rtd 14; PtO *Nor* 14-15; Hon C Acle and Bure to Yare from 15. *The Rectory, Church Road, Reedham, Norwich NR13 3TZ* M: 07706-482284 E: l.allies@sky.com

ALLIN, Philip Ronald. b 43. Reading Univ MA 96 Birm Univ CQSW. Lich Th Coll 71. **d** 71 **p** 72. C Sutton in Ashfield St Mary *S'well* 71-74; Chapl to Sutton Cen 74-76; LtO *S'well* 74-76; P-in-c Grove 76-77; R Ordsall 76-80; V Mansfield St Mark 81-83; TR Hermitage and Hampstead Norreys, Cold Ash etc *Ox* 83-96; OCM 83-96; Chapl Nine o'clock Service *Sheff* 96-03; rtd 03; Bp's Adv in Past Care and Counselling *Sheff* 03-08; Warden of Spiritual Direction *Dur* from 08; PtO from 14. *Hareholme House, New Brancepeth, Durham DH7 7HH* T: 0191-373 9743

ALLINGTON, Andrew William. b 57. ACA 81 Sheff Univ BA 78. Cranmer Hall Dur BA 95. **d** 95 **p** 96. C Clifton *York* 95-99; P-in-c Stainforth *Sheff* 99-02; V 02-13; V Filey *York* from 13. *The Vicarage, 5 Belle Vue Crescent, Filey YO14 9AD* T: (01723) 512645 M: 07799-077871 E: allingtonandrew@hotmail.com

ALLINSON, Capt Paul Timothy. b 63. CA Tr Coll 82 Edin Th Coll 89. **d** 91 **p** 92. C Peterlee *Dur* 91-94; C Shadforth and Sherburn w Pittington 94-97; P-in-c Byers Green 97-04; P-in-c Seaton Carew from 04; P-in-c Greatham from 09; Dioc Children's Adv from 94. *6 Front Street, Greatham, Hartlepool TS25 2ER* T: (01429) 872626 M: 07888-726535 E: revdpaul@lineone.net

ALLISON, Elliott Desmond. b 36. UNISA BA 64 K Coll Lon MTh 74. S Africa Federal Th Coll. **d** 69 **p** 70. *Flat 1, 20 Southview Gardens, Worthing BN11 5JA*

ALLISON, Canon James Timothy. b 61. Man Univ BSc 83. Oak Hill Th Coll BA 89. **d** 89 **p** 90. C Walkden Moor *Man* 89-93; Chapl Huddersfield Univ *Wakef* 93-98; V Erringden 98-12; RD Calder Valley 06-12; P-in-c Coley *Leeds* from 12; Hon Can Wakef Cathl from 10; Bp's Rural Adv from 14; C Northowram *Wakef* from 14. *Coley Vicarage, 41 Ing Head Terrace, Halifax HX3 7LB* T: (01422) 202292 E: erringden@aol.com

ALLISON, Keith. b 34. Dur Univ BA 59. Ely Th Coll 59. **d** 61 **p** 62. C Sculcoates *York* 61-64; C Stainton-in-Cleveland 64-65; C Leeds St Pet *Ripon* 65-70; V Micklefield *York* 70-74; V Appleton-le-Street w Amotherby 74-78; P-in-c Barton-le-Street 77-78; P-in-c Salton 77-80; R Amotherby w Appleton and Barton-le-Street 78-82; Chapl Lister Hosp Stevenage 82-90; P-in-c St Ippolyts *St Alb* 82-85; V 85-90; Chapl Hitchin

Hosp 86-90; Chapl Shotley Bridge Gen Hosp 90-94; Chapl NW Dur HA 90-94; Sen Chapl N Dur Healthcare NHS Trust 94-98 and 98-00; rtd 00; PtO *Dur* from 00. *2 Middlewood Road, Lanchester, Durham DH7 0HL*   T: (01207) 529046

ALLISON, Michael John. b 33. Leeds Univ BSc 97 ATI 58. Wilson Carlile Coll 05. **d** 05 **p** 06. NSM Windhill *Bradf* 05-08; PtO *Leeds* from 08. *33 Busy Lane, Shipley BD18 1DX* T: (01274) 587194   E: m.john.allison@talktalk.net

ALLISON, Rosemary Jean. *See* WHITLEY, Rosemary Jean

ALLISON, Susan Ann. b 61. EMMTC 06. **d** 06 **p** 07. C Gt and Lt Coates w Bradley *Linc* 06-09; P-in-c Fotherby 09-14; R from 14; P-in-c Somercotes and Grainthorpe w Conisholme 09-14; R from 14; RD Louthesk from 11. *The Rectory, Peppin Lane, Fotherby, Louth LN11 0UW*   T: (01507) 602312 M: 07920-133329   E: susan.333allison@btinternet.com

✠**ALLISTER, The Rt Revd Donald Spargo.** b 52. Peterho Cam BA 74 MA 77 Ches Univ Hon DTh 11. Trin Coll Bris 74. **d** 76 **p** 77 **c** 10. C Hyde St Geo *Ches* 76-79; C Sevenoaks St Nic *Roch* 79-83; V Birkenhead Ch Ch *Ches* 83-89; R Cheadle 89-02; RD 99-02; Adn *Ches* 02-10; Bp Pet from 10. *Bishops Lodging, The Palace, Minster Precincts, Peterborough PE1 1YA*   T: (01733) 562492   F: 890077   E: bishop@peterborough-diocese.org.uk

ALLISTER, John Charles. b 77. Ch Coll Cam BA 00 MA 03 MSci 00 St Anne's Coll Ox PGCE 01. Wycliffe Hall Ox BA 08. **d** 09 **p** 10. C Hurdsfield *Ches* 09-12; V Nottingham St Jude S'well from 12. *403 Woodborough Road, Nottingham NG3 5HE* T: 0115-960 4102   M: 07981-556253 E: john.allister@cantab.net *or* revjohnallister@gmail.com

ALLMAN, Mrs Susan. b 56. Bris Univ BA 77. WEMTC 93. **d** 96 **p** 97. NSM Henleaze *Bris* 96-99; C Southmead 99-02; V Two Mile Hill St Mich 02-08; Partnership P E Bris 08-10; P-in-c Titchfield *Portsm* from 10; AD Fareham from 13. *The Vicarage, 24 Frog Lane, Titchfield, Fareham PO14 4DU*   T: (01329) 842324 M: 07775-977298   E: susanrev@hotmail.co.uk

ALLMARK, Leslie. b 48. Open Univ BA 90. **d** 01 **p** 02. OLM Halliwell St Luke *Man* 01-08; rtd 08; PtO *Man* from 08. *75 Crosby Road, Bolton BL1 4EJ*   T: (01204) 845795 E: leslie@allmark.freeserve.co.uk

ALLON-SMITH, Roderick David. b 51. Leic Univ BA PhD Cam Univ MA. Ridley Hall Cam 79. **d** 82 **p** 83. C Kinson *Sarum* 82-86; V Westwood *Cov* 86-96; RD Cov S 92-96; P-in-c Radford Semele 96-04; Dioc Dir Par Development and Evang 01-03; Dioc Missr *Dur* 04-10; AD Dur 08-10; R Lanercost, Walton, Gilsland and Nether Denton *Carl* from 10; RD Brampton 12-15. *The Vicarage, Lanercost, Brampton CA8 2HQ*   T: (01697) 72478   E: lanercostrod@btinternet.com

ALLPORT, David Jack. b 55. Ox Univ BA MEd. Qu Coll Birm 78. **d** 80 **p** 81. C Abingdon w Shippon *Ox* 80-83; C-in-c Woodgate Valley CD *Birm* 83-91; PtO *Lich* from 91. *122 Cherry Tree Avenue, Walsall WS5 4JL*   T: (01922) 640059

ALLRED, Frank. b 23. Tyndale Hall Bris 62. **d** 64 **p** 65. C Halliwell St Pet *Man* 64-67; V Ravenhead *Liv* 67-75; R Chadwell *Chelmsf* 75-82; TV Heworth H Trin *York* 82-86; rtd 87; PtO *York* from 87. *12 Viking Road, Bridlington YO16 6TW*   T: (01262) 677321

ALLS, Mrs Anna Kate. b 78. St Jo Coll Nottm BA 12. **d** 12 **p** 13. C Bestwood Em w St Mark *S'well* 12-14; C Brinsley w Underwood from 14; C Eastwood from 14. *The Vicarage, 102A Church Lane, Brinsley, Nottingham NG16 5AB* E: john_anna_alls@hotmail.co.uk

ALLSO, Michael Neal. b 48. FRICS 72 MCIArb 73 MAE 00. SWMTC 95. **d** 98 **p** 99. NSM Ex St Thos and Em 98-01; NSM Colyton, Southleigh, Offwell, Widworthy etc 01-03; NSM Colyton, Musbury, Southleigh and Branscombe 03-04; C Widecombe-in-the-Moor, Leusdon, Princetown etc 04-07; C Ashburton, Bickington, Buckland in the Moor etc 07-08; NSM Dunster, Carhampton, Withycombe w Rodhuish etc *B & W* 08-11; rtd 11. *3 Croft House, Widecroft Road, Iver SL0 9QH*   E: revm.allso@btinternet.com

ALLSOP, Anthony James. b 37. AKC 62. **d** 63 **p** 64. C Leytonstone St Marg w St Columba *Chelmsf* 63-68; V Gt Ilford St Alb 68-80; V Gainsborough St Jo *Linc* 80-85; V Hockerill *St Alb* 85-02; Chapl Essex and Herts Community NHS Trust 85-95 and 95-01; Chapl N Essex Mental Health Partnership NHS Trust 01-02; rtd 02; PtO *Ches* from 03. *63 Longdown Road, Congleton CW12 4QH*   T: (01260) 280628 E: anthonyallsop@aol.com

ALLSOP, Mrs Beryl Anne. b 45. EMMTC 94. **d** 97 **p** 98. NSM Clipstone *S'well* 97-00; NSM Blidworth w Rainworth 00-10; rtd 10; PtO *S'well* from 11. *The Old Post Office, Bottom Row, Pleasley Vale, Mansfield NG19 8RS*   T: (01623) 811095 E: beryl@faithfulfish.co.uk

ALLSOP, David. b 50. **d** 10 **p** 11. NSM Musbury *Blackb* from 10; NSM Haslingden w Grane and Stonefold from 10; NSM Laneside from 10. *7 Elizabeth Drive, Haslingden, Rossendale BB4 4JB*   T: (01706) 224663   M: 07986-004401 E: davidallsop@hotmail.com

ALLSOP, David George. b 48. Wycliffe Hall Ox. **d** 99 **p** 00. C Chenies and Lt Chalfont, Latimer and Flaunden *Ox* 99-02; P-in-c 02-08; R from 08. *The Rectory, Chenies, Rickmansworth WD3 6ER*   T: (01923) 284433   M: 07818-441431 E: cheniesrectory@aol.com

ALLSOP, Patrick Leslie Fewtrell. b 52. Fitzw Coll Cam BA 74 MA 78. Ripon Coll Cuddesdon BA 78 MA 83. **d** 79 **p** 80. C Barrow St Matt *Carl* 79-82; Chapl Eton Coll 82-88; Chapl K Sch Roch 89-02; Hon PV Roch Cathl 89-97; Chapl St Paul's Sch Barnes from 02. *St Paul's School, Lonsdale Road, London SW13 9JT*   T: (020) 8746 5434

ALLSOP, Peter William. b 33. Kelham Th Coll 58. **d** 58 **p** 59. C Woodford St Barn *Chelmsf* 58-61; C Upholland *Liv* 61-65; V Wigan St Geo 65-71; P-in-c Marham *Ely* 71-72; TV Fincham 72-76; V Trawden *Blackb* 76-90; C Marton 90-92; C S Shore H Trin 92-98; rtd 98; PtO *Blackb* from 98. *31 Lomond Avenue, Blackpool FY3 9QL*   T: (01253) 696624 E: peter.w.allsop@talktalk.net

ALLSOP, The Ven Christine. b 47. Aston Univ BSc 68. S Dios Minl Tr Scheme 86. **d** 89 **p** 94. C Caversham St Pet and Mapledurham etc *Ox* 89-94; C Bracknell 94; TV 94-98; P-in-c Bourne Valley *Sarum* 98-00; TR 00-05; RD Alderbury 99-05; Can and Preb Sarum Cathl 02-05; Adn Northn *Pet* 05-13; Can Pet Cathl 05-13; rtd 13. *Mellor Cottage, 2 Walkers Lane, Lambourn, Hungerford RG17 8YE*   T: (01488) 674108

ALLSOPP, Mark Dennis. b 66. Cuddesdon Coll 93. **d** 96 **p** 97. C Hedworth *Dur* 96-98; C Gt Aycliffe 98-00; TV Gt Aycliffe and Chilton 00-04; P-in-c Kirklevington and High and Low Worsall *York* 04-08; Chapl HM Pris Kirklevington Grange 04-08; Chapl RN from 08. *Royal Naval Chaplaincy Service, Mail Point 1-2, Leach Building, Whale Island, Portsmouth PO2 8BY* T: (023) 9262 5055   F: 9262 5134

ALLSOPP, Mrs Patricia Ann. b 48. St Mary's Coll Chelt CertEd 69. Qu Coll Birm. **d** 00 **p** 01. C Upton-on-Severn, Ripple, Earls Croome etc *Worc* 00-04; P-in-c Finstall 04-05; V 05-08; RD Bromsgrove 06-08; rtd 08. *22 Byron Close, Enderby, Leicester LE19 4QB*   E: rev.tricia@ukonline.co.uk

ALLSOPP, Stephen Robert. b 50. BSc 71 MSc 72 PhD 75. Mon Dioc Tr Scheme 81. **d** 84 **p** 85. NSM Trevethin *Mon* 84-88; Asst Chapl K Sch Roch 88-07; Chapl K Prep Sch Roch 99-07; rtd 07; Hon PV Roch Cathl from 89. *117 Prince's Street, Rochester ME1 2EA*   T: (01634) 409878 E: stephen.allsopp@diocese-rochester.org

ALLSWORTH, Peter Thomas. b 44. St Mich Coll Llan 93. **d** 93 **p** 94. C Prestatyn *St As* 93-96; V Esclusham 96-06; C Rhyl w St Ann 06-10; P-in-c Bodelwyddan 10; P-in-c Rhuddlan and Bodelwyddan 10-11; rtd 11; PtO *St As* from 11. *Subiaco, 10 Tirionfa, Rhuddlan, Rhyl LL18 6LT*   T: (01745) 590683 E: peterallsworth@btinternet.com

ALLTON, Canon Paul Irving. b 38. Man Univ BA 60. **d** 63 **p** 64. C Kibworth Beauchamp *Leic* 63-66; C Reading St Mary V *Ox* 66-70; R Caston and V Griston *Nor* 70-75; P-in-c Sturston w Thompson and Tottington 70-75; V Hunstanton St Mary w Lt Ringstead 75-80; V Holme-next-the-Sea 75-80; V Hunstanton St Mary w Ringstead Parva, Holme etc 80-85; RD Heacham and Rising 81-85; Hon Can Nor Cathl 85-93; TR Lowestoft and Kirkley 85-93; TR Keynsham *B & W* 93-96; TR Gaywood *Nor* 96-01; rtd 01; PtO *Nor* from 01. *Rustic Lodge, 29 Hall Lane, West Winch, King's Lynn PE33 0PJ*   T: (01553) 840355 E: paulallton@btinternet.com

ALLUM, Jeremy Warner. b 32. Wycliffe Hall Ox 60. **d** 62 **p** 63. C Hornchurch St Andr *Chelmsf* 62-67; P-in-c W Derby St Luke *Liv* 67-69; V 69-75; P-in-c Boulton *Derby* 75-90; RD Melbourne 86-90; V Hathersage 90-98; rtd 98; PtO *Derby* from 98. *32 Sandown Avenue, Mickleover, Derby DE3 0QQ* T: (01332) 231253

ALLWOOD, Linda Angela Fredrika. b 76. Newc Univ BA 00. Cranmer Hall Dur 01. **d** 03 **p** 04. C Northampton St Giles *Pet* 03-06; PtO *St E* 06-07. *Address temp unknown* E: linda_allwood@hotmail.com

ALLWOOD, Martin Eardley. b 71. Natal Univ BSc 92. Ripon Coll Cuddesdon 08. **d** 10 **p** 11. C Hundred River *St E* 10-14; R The Street Par *York* from 14. *The Rectory, Church Street, Amotherby, Malton YO17 6TN*   T: (01653) 690913 M: 07891-478269   E: meallwood110@googlemail.com

ALLWRIGHT, Mrs Janet Margaret. b 40. Oak Hill Th Coll 87. **d** 90 **p** 94. NSM Galleywood Common *Chelmsf* 90-93; NSM Downham w S Hanningfield 93-99; Chapl HM Pris Bullwood Hall 98-03; TV Canvey Is *Chelmsf* 03-06; rtd 06; PtO *Chelmsf* from 06. *13 Burnside Close, Chelmsford CM1 4EH* T: (01245) 349452   E: jmallwright@btinternet.com

ALMOND, Kenneth Alfred. b 36. EMMTC 76 Linc Th Coll 78. **d** 79 **p** 80. C Boston *Linc* 79-82; V Surfleet 82-87; RD Elloe W 86-96; V Spalding St Jo w Deeping St Nicholas 87-98; rtd 98; PtO *Linc* from 99. *1 Buckingham Close, Fishtoft, Boston PE21 9QB*   T/F: (01205) 352805 E: ken.hilary@btopenworld.com

ALP, Mrs Elaine Alison. b 54. Oak Hill Th Coll 87. d 00. Dn-in-c Blackb St Mich w St Jo and H Trin 00-02; Par Dn Fleetwood St Nic 02-06; PtO 06-07; NSM Ribbleton 07-14. *7 Queen Victoria Road, Burnley BB10 3DH* T: (01282) 788516 E: deaconalison@hotmail.com

ALSBURY, Colin. b 56. Ch Ch Ox BA 77 MA 81. Ripon Coll Cuddesdon 77. **d** 80 **p** 81. C Oxton *Ches* 80-84; V Crewe All SS and St Paul 84-92; Ind Chapl 92-95; V Kettering St Andr *Pet* 95-02; V Frome St Jo *B & W* from 02; V Woodlands from 02; RD Frome from 10. *St John's Vicarage, Vicarage Close, Frome BA11 1QL* T: (01373) 472853 E: colin.alsbury@zetnet.co.uk

ALSOP, Barbara Lynn. b 48. **d** 11 **p** 12. NSM Epsom St Martin *Guildf* from 11. *15 Meadow Way, Bookham, Leatherhead KT23 3NY* T: (01372) 458492 E: revlynnalsop@talktalk.net

ALTHAM, Donald. b 40. Liv Univ BA 62. NOC 87. **d** 90 **p** 91. NSM Ramsbottom St Jo and St Paul *Man* 90-96; NSM Holcombe 99-04; NSM Walmersley Road, Bury 04-12; Chapl Asst Burnley Health Care NHS Trust 93-03; Chapl Asst E Lancs Hosps NHS Trust 03-05; rtd 12; PtO *Man* from 12. *850 Burnley Road, Bury BL9 5JT* T: 0161-761 1603

✠**ALVAREZ-VELAZQUEZ, The Rt Revd David Andres.** b 41. Inter American Univ Puerto Rico BA 62 Caribbean Cen of Advanced Studies MS 82. NY Th Sem MDiv 65. **d** 65 **p** 65 **c** 87. C St Mich Puerto Rico 65; Chapl Episc Cathl Sch 65-67; R St Mark 67-70; R St Jo Cathl 70-79; R Trujillo Alto St Hilda 79-87; Bp from 87. *PO Box 902, Saint Just Station, Saint Just, 00978, Puerto Rico* T: (001) (787) 761 9800 M: 376 4125 F: 761 0320 E: iep@spiderlinkpr.net

ALVEY, Martyn Clifford. b 53. EMMTC 96. **d** 99 **p** 00. NSM Burton Joyce w Bulcote and Stoke Bardolph *S'well* 99-02; C Worksop St Jo 02-06; P-in-c Worksop Ch Ch 06-11; V 11-15; P-in-c Shireoaks 13-15; V Worksop Ch Ch and Shireoaks from 15; AD Worksop 04-06. *34 Boscombe Road, Worksop S81 7SB* T: (01909) 473998 E: martynalvey@btinternet.com

AMAT-TORREGROSA, Gabriel José. b 42. R Superior Coll of Music Madrid MA 63. Bapt Th Sem Ruschlikon Zürich 64. **d** 71 **p** 72. Spain 71-98; Asst Chapl Zürich *Eur* 98-07; P-in-c Marseille w Aix-en-Provence 08-13. *Alcalde Crispí 14, 5è2a, 08207 Sabadell, Spain* E: gjamat@hotmail.com

AMBANI, Stephen Frederick. b 45. Univ of Wales (Lamp) BA 90. St Jo Coll Nottm 86 CA Tr Coll Nairobi 70. **d** 83 **p** 83. Kenya 83-93; C Glan Ely *Llan* 93-95; C Whitchurch 95-97; V Nantymoel w Wyndham 97-99; V Tonyrefail w Gilfach Goch and Llandyfodwg 99-03; V Tonyrefail w Gilfach Goch 04; rtd 05. *68 St Winifred's Road, Bridgend CF31 4PN* T: (01656) 653589

AMBROSE, James Field. b 51. Newc Univ BA 73. Cranmer Hall Dur. **d** 80 **p** 81. C Barrow St Geo w St Luke *Carl* 80-83; C Workington St Jo 83-85; R Montford w Shrawardine and Fitz *Lich* 85-88; Ch Radio Officer BBC Radio Shropshire 85-88; Chapl RAF 88-92; Voc and Min Adv CPAS 92-99; TV Syston *Leic* 99-06; C Leic Martyrs 06-07; V Heald Green St Cath *Ches* from 07; Chapl St Ann's Hospice Manchester from 07. *The Vicarage, 217 Outwood Road, Heald Green, Cheadle SK8 3JS* T: 0161-437 4614 or 437 3685 E: jfambrose@btinternet.com

AMBROSE, John George. b 30. Lon Univ BD Ox Univ PGCE. **d** 74 **p** 75. C Rayleigh *Chelmsf* 74-79; V Hadleigh St Barn 79-95; rtd 95; PtO *Chelmsf* from 95. *9 Fairview Gardens, Leigh-on-Sea SS9 3PD* T: (01702) 474632

AMBROSE, Thomas. b 47. Sheff Univ BSc 69 PhD 73 Em Coll Cam BA 77 MA 84. Westcott Ho Cam 75. **d** 78 **p** 79. C Morpeth *Newc* 78-81; C N Gosforth 81-84; R March St Jo *Ely* 84-93; RD March 89-93; P-in-c Witchford w Wentworth 93-99; Dioc Dir of Communications 93-99; Chapl K Sch Ely 94-96; V Trumpington *Ely* 99-08; PtO from 14. *229 Arbury Road, Cambridge CB4 2JJ* M: 07711-263083 E: tom.ambrose@ely.anglican.org

AMELIA, Alison. b 67. Hull Univ BA 03 St Jo Coll Dur BA 05. Cranmer Hall Dur 03. **d** 05 **p** 06. C Nunthorpe *York* 05-06; C Hessle 06-09; Chapl United Lincs Hosps NHS Trust from 09. *62 Glengarry Way, Greylees, Sleaford NG34 8XU* E: alison.amelia@ulh.nhs.uk

AMES, Jeremy Peter. b 49. K Coll Lon BD 71 AKC 71. **d** 72 **p** 73. C Kennington St Jo *S'wark* 72-75; Chapl RN 75-04; Chapl RN Engineering Coll 86-89; USA 91-93; Dir of Ords RN 00-04; QHC 02-04; Master St Nic Hosp Salisbury 04-11; PtO *Sarum* from 11. *Springfield, Stratford Road, Stratford sub Castle, Salisbury SP1 3LQ* T: (01722) 322542

AMES, Reginald John. b 27. Bps' Coll Cheshunt 51. **d** 54 **p** 55. C Edmonton St Alphege *Lon* 54-58; C Mill Hill Jo Keble Ch 58-60; P-in-c Northwood Hills St Edm 61-64; V 64-92; rtd 92; Hon C Moffat *Glas* 92-01; LtO from 92. *Oakbank, Lochwood, Beattock, Moffat DG10 9PS* T: (01683) 300381

AMES-LEWIS, Richard. b 45. Em Coll Cam BA 66 MA 70. Westcott Ho Cam 76. **d** 78 **p** 79. C Bromley St Mark *Roch* 78-81; C Edenbridge 81-84; V 84-91; P-in-c Crockham Hill H Trin 84-91; P-in-c Barnes St Mary *S'wark* 91-97; TR Barnes 97-00; RD Richmond and Barnes 94-00; TR E Dereham and Scarning *Nor* 00-06; P-in-c Swanton Morley w Beetley w E Bilney and Hoe 02-06; TR Dereham and Distr 06-09; RD Dereham in Mitford 03-08; Hon Can Nor Cathl 06-09; rtd 09; PtO *Ely* from 09. *21 Victoria Street, Cambridge CB1 1JP* T: (01223) 300615 E: ameslewis@btinternet.com

AMEY, Graham George. b 44. Lon Univ BD 70. Tyndale Hall Bris 67. **d** 71 **p** 72. C Hornsey Rise St Mary *Lon* 71-74; C St Helens St Helen *Liv* 74-79; V Liv All So Springwood 79-91; V Whiston 91-02; V Aigburth 02-12; rtd 12. *213 Rose Lane, Liverpool L18 5EA* T: 0151-378 4687

AMEY, John Mark. b 59. Ripon Coll Cuddesdon 98. **d** 00 **p** 01. C Winchmore Hill St Paul *Lon* 00-04; V Sutton *Ely* 04-11; R Witcham w Mepal 04-11; V St Ives from 11; Chapl ATC from 03. *The Vicarage, Westwood Road, St Ives PE27 6DH* T: (01480) 384334 M: 07905-122090 E: vicar@stivesparishchurch.org.uk or vicar.stives@gmail.com

AMEY, Phillip Mark. b 73. Win Univ BA 11. STETS 03. **d** 06 **p** 07. C Southsea H Spirit *Portsm* 06-09; P-in-c Purbrook 09-12; P-in-c Southsea H Spirit from 12; C Milton from 12. *The Vicarage, 26 Victoria Grove, Southsea PO5 1NE* T: (023) 9311 7159 E: phillip.amey@sky.com

AMIS, Ronald. b 37. Linc Th Coll 74. **d** 76 **p** 77. C Grantham w Manthorpe *Linc* 76-78; C Grantham 78-79; P-in-c Holbeach Hurn 79-81; V Long Bennington w Foston 81-91; V Corby Glen 91-93; RD Grantham 90-92; rtd 93; PtO *Pet* 93-03 and from 09; *Ches* 06-08. *9 Cotton End, Bretton, Peterborough PE3 9TF* T: (01733) 261152 M: 07739-307865 E: ron_amis@hotmail.com

AMOS, Alan John. b 44. OBE 79. K Coll Lon BD 66 MTh 67 AKC 67. St Steph Ho Ox 68. **d** 69 **p** 70. C Hoxton H Trin w St Mary *Lon* 69-72; Lebanon 73-82; Lect Liturg Studies Westcott Ho Cam 82-85; Vice-Prin 85-89; Prin Cant Sch of Min 89-94; Co-Prin SEITE 94-96; Chapl Medway NHS Foundn Trust 96-09; Hon PV Roch Cathl 95-04; Hon Can Roch Cathl 04-09; P-in-c Newington w Hartlip and Stockbury *Cant* 09-13; P-in-c Upchurch w Lower Halstow 09-13; P-in-c Iwade 09-13; V The Six 13; rtd 13; PtO *Cant* 14; *Sarum* from 15. *11 The Glebe, Shroton, Blandford Forum DT11 8PX* T: (01258) 860897 E: alanmedway@btinternet.com

AMOS, Brother. See YONGE, James Mohun

AMOS, Colin James. b 62. Univ of Wales (Lamp) BA 83 CQSW 85. Ridley Hall Cam 93. **d** 93 **p** 94. C Aberdare *Llan* 93-96; V Port Talbot St Theodore 96-12; AD Margam 08-12; V Kilburn St Aug w St Jo *Lon* from 12. *St Augustine's Vicarage, Kilburn Park Road, London NW6 5XB* T: (020) 7624 1637 E: fr.amos@sky.com

AMYES, Emma Charlotte. b 65. Redcliffe Coll BA 01. Ridley Hall Cam. **d** 04 **p** 05. C Hucclecote *Glouc* 04-10; TV Worle *B & W* from 10. *15 Woodpecker Drive, Weston-super-Mare BS22 8SR* T: (01934) 517442 M: 07866-808635 E: emma.amyes@virgin.net

AMYES, Geoffrey Edmund. b 74. Bris Univ BSc 96 Cam Univ BTh 04. Ridley Hall Cam 01. **d** 04 **p** 05. C Hucclecote *Glouc* 04-09; PtO 09-10. *15 Woodpecker Drive, Weston-super-Mare BS22 8SR* T: (01934) 517442 M: 07792-519910 E: g.amyes@btinternet.com

AMYS, Richard James Rutherford. b 58. Trin Coll Bris BA 90. **d** 90 **p** 91. C Whitnash *Cov* 90-93; P-in-c Gravesend H Family w Ifield *Roch* 93-95; R 95-99; R Eastington, Frocester, Haresfield etc *Glouc* 99-15; rtd 15. *Address temp unknown* M: 07796-956050 E: richardjramys@aol.com

ANAN, Gabriel Jaja. b 48. Regents Th Coll BA 92 Univ of E Lon MA 96 PhD 08 Middx Univ BA 03 MCIT 92. NTMTC 00. **d** 03 **p** 04. NSM Victoria Docks St Luke *Chelmsf* 03-07; NSM Forest Gate St Sav w W Ham St Matt 07-09; NSM N Woolwich w Silvertown 09-10; NSM E Ham St Geo from 10. *67 Bedale Road, Romford RM3 9TU* T: (01708) 349564 M: 07734-707887 E: gabriel58@hotmail.com

ANAND, Jessie Nesam Nallammal. b 54. Madurai Univ BSc 75 BEd 76 Annamalai Univ MA 84. Tamilnadu Th Sem BD 91 New Coll Edin MTh 94 EMMTC 02. **d** 03 **p** 04. NSM Birstall and Wanlip *Leic* 03-05; NSM Emmaus Par Team 05-07; PtO *S'wark* 07-11; C Bermondsey St Hugh CD 11-14. *All Saints' Vicarage, 100 Prince of Wales Drive, London SW11 4BD* T: (020) 7622 3809 M: 07811-189358 E: jessieanand@yahoo.co.uk

ANAND, The Very Revd Sekar Anand Asir. b 53. Madurai Univ BSc 75 Serampore Univ BD 79 New Coll Edin MTh 93 Annamalai Univ MA 99. **d** 80 **p** 81. C Nayaith St Jo India 80-82; R Tuticorin St Paul 82-84; Sec Tirunelveli Children's Miss 84-91; C Edin St Pet 91-92; Hon C Burmantofts St Steph and St Agnes *Ripon* 92-93; C Edin St Mark 93-95; Provost

Palayamcottai Cathl India 95-00; C Leic Resurr 00-07; C Battersea Fields *S'wark* from 07. *All Saints' Vicarage, 100 Prince of Wales Drive, London SW11 4BD* T: (020) 7622 3809 M: 07711-492946 E: anandjessie@yahoo.co.uk

ANCRUM, John. b 28. Clifton Th Coll 55. **d** 58 **p** 59. C Branksome St Clem *Sarum* 58-61; C Sparkhill St Jo *Birm* 61-63; V Tibshelf *Derby* 63-70; Canada 70-74; P-in-c Salwarpe *Worc* 74-75; P-in-c Tibberton w Bredicot and Warndon 75-76; P-in-c Hadzor w Oddingley 76; P-in-c Hadzor w Oddingley and Tibberton w Bredicot 76-78; LtO *Chelmsf* 78-81; Chapl HM Pris Stafford 81-82; Chapl HM Pris Dartmoor 82-89; LtO *Ex* 88-89; rtd 89; PtO *Ex* from 89. *14 Merrivale View Road, Dousland, Yelverton PL20 6NS*

ANDAYI, Elphas Ombuna. b 57. St Phil Th Coll Maseno 78. **d** 79 **p** 81. Kenya 79-98 and from 99; Provost Butere 92-97; C Sparkhill w Greet and Sparkbrook *Birm* 98-99. *PO Box 199, Bukura, Kenya* T: (00254) (333) 20038 F: 20412

ANDERS, Mrs Erika Gertrud. b 45. ACT 88 St Jo Coll Nottm 99. **d** 92 **p** 02. C Proserpine St Paul Australia 92; C Hamburg *Eur* 99-07; Asst Chapl from 07. *Niendorfer Kirchenweg 5C, 22459 Hamburg, Germany* T: (0049) (40) 582850 F: 582841 M: 162-700 0404 E: erika.anders@fco.gov.uk

ANDERS, Jonathan Cyril. b 36. Wycliffe Hall Ox 69. **d** 71 **p** 72. C Prescot *Liv* 71-74; C-in-c 74-76; R Wavertree St Mary 76-81; V Aigburth 81-01; rtd 01; PtO *Liv* from 03. *3 Silverleigh, Liverpool L17 5BL* T: 0151-728 9997

ANDERS, Roger John. b 38. Man Univ LLB 61. NOC 91. **d** 94 **p** 95. NSM New Mills *Derby* 94-97; NSM Buxton w Burbage and King Sterndale 97-98; NSM Adderley, Ash, Calverhall, Ightfield etc *Lich* 98-03; R 03-10; rtd 10. *11 Mount Crescent, Whitchurch SY13 1GW* T: (01948) 664088 E: anders@u.genie.co.uk

ANDERSEN, Paul John. b 49. Univ of Alabama BA. Protestant Th Sem Virginia MDiv 77. **d** 77 **p** 83. USA 77-82; Belize 82-84; Chapl Zagreb *Eur* 84-85; Chapl Belgrade 85-86; USA 86-89; India 89-91; Sierra Leone 92-93; Chapl Valletta *Eur* 94-96; Chapl Skopje 96-98; NSM Worcester St Luke USA 98-00; NSM S Barre Ch 00-02; R Milford Trin Ch 02-06. *Christ Church Parish (Episcopal), PO Box 15, Christchurch VA 23031, USA* T: (001) (804) 758 2006 E: paulandersen@earthlink.net

ANDERSON, Albert Geoffrey (Geoff). b 42. Ex Univ BA 65 MA 67. Qu Coll Birm. **d** 75 **p** 76. C Helsby and Ince *Ches* 75-77; C Helsby and Dunham-on-the-Hill 77-78; TV Gleadless *Sheff* 78-85; V Thorpe Hesley 85-92; R Ribbesford w Bewdley and Dowles *Worc* 92-03; rtd 03. *2 Waterworks Road, Worcester WR1 3EX* T: (01905) 612634 E: ga@priest.com

ANDERSON, Alice Calder. b 50. Moray Ho Coll of Educn DipEd 76. Local Minl Tr Course 90. **d** 93 **p** 95. NSM Edin St Barn from 93. *20 Pentland Road, Bonnyrigg EH19 2LG* T: 0131-654 0506

ANDERSON, Mrs Ann. b 57. Cranmer Hall Dur 01. **d** 03 **p** 04. C Chester le Street *Dur* 03-07; P-in-c Hetton-Lyons w Eppleton 07; R from 07. *The Rectory, Houghton Road, Hetton-le-Hole, Houghton le Spring DH5 9PH* T: 0191-517 3102

ANDERSON, Preb Brian Arthur. b 42. Sarum Th Coll 75. **d** 78 **p** 79. C Plymouth St Jas Ham *Ex* 78-80; Org Sec CECS B & W, Ex and Truro 80-89; TV Saltash *Truro* 89-94; RD E Wivelshire 91-94; P-in-c St Breoke and Egloshayle 94-96; R 96-02; RD Trigg Minor and Bodmin 95-02; P-in-c Torpoint 02-09; P-in-c Antony w Sheviock 02-09; Preb St Endellion 99-09; rtd 09. *44 Essa Road, Saltash PL12 4EE* T: (01752) 511271 M: 07710-231219

ANDERSON, Brian Glaister. b 35. K Coll Lon 57. **d** 79 **p** 79. Chapl St Fran Sch Hooke 79; C Croydon St Jo *Cant* 80-83; Dep Chapl HM Youth Cust Cen Glen Parva 83-84; Chapl HM YOI Hewell Grange 84-89; Chapl HM Rem Cen Brockhill 84-89; Chapl HM Pris Parkhurst 89-96; rtd 96; PtO *Portsm* 12-14; *S'wark* from 14. *Flat W11, The College of St Barnabas, Blackberry Lane, Lingfield RH7 6NJ* T: (01342) 872843 M: 07900-272006 E: brianders78@gmail.com

ANDERSON, Mrs Christine. b 42. **d** 09. OLM Skegness Gp *Linc* from 09. *14 Revesby Drive, Skegness PE25 2HT* T: (01754) 767678

ANDERSON, David Graham. b 33. MICE MIStructE. St Mich Coll Llan 85. **d** 88 **p** 89. C Llanishen and Lisvane *Llan* 88-90; C Fazeley *Lich* 90-94; PtO *Heref* 96-01; *Llan* 01-08 and from 11. *7 Rowan Close, Penarth CF64 5BU* T: (029) 2071 1013

ANDERSON, David Lee. b 75. Westmr Coll Ox BTh 96. Ripon Coll Cuddesdon MTh 98. **d** 98 **p** 99. C Balderton *S'well* 98-02; V Haworth 02-07; P-in-c Longridge *Blackb* 07-12; V from 12. *The Vicarage, Church Street, Longridge, Preston PR3 3WA* T: (01772) 783281 E: vicaroflongridge@aol.com

ANDERSON, David Richard. b 58. Lanc Univ BEd 79. EAMTC 96. **d** 99 **p** 00. C N Walsham w Antingham *Nor* 99-02; R Stalham, E Ruston, Brunstead, Sutton and Ingham 02-06;

P-in-c Smallburgh w Dilham w Honing and Crostwight 05-06; TV Wrexham *St As* 06-11; Chapl St Jos High Sch Wrexham 06-11; V Romford St Edw *Chelmsf* 11-14; P-in-c Yeovil St Mich *B & W* from 14. *The Vicarage, 137 St Michael's Avenue, Yeovil BA21 4LW* M: 07956-267265 T: (01935) 474898 E: fr.anderson.yeovil@gmail.com

ANDERSON, Digby Carter. b 44. Reading Univ BA Brunel Univ MPhil 73 PhD 77. **d** 85 **p** 86. NSM Luton St Sav *St Alb* from 85. *17 Hardwick Place, Woburn Sands, Milton Keynes MK17 8QQ* T: (01908) 584526

ANDERSON, Donald Whimbey. b 31. Trin Coll Toronto BA 54 MA 58 LTh 57 STB 57 ThD 71. **d** 56 **p** 57. Canada 57-59 and 75-88; and from 96; Japan 59-74; Philippines 74-75; Dir Ecum Affairs ACC 88-96; rtd 96. *Conference on the Religious Life, PO Box 99, Little Britain ON K0M 2C0, Canada* T/F: (001) (705) 786 3330 E: dwa@nexicom.net

ANDERSON, Geoff. *See* ANDERSON, Albert Geoffrey

ANDERSON, Mrs Gillian Ann. b 52. NTMTC 05. **d** 08 **p** 09. NSM Lambourne w Abridge and Stapleford Abbotts *Chelmsf* 08-09; NSM Loughton St Jo 09-11; P-in-c High Laver w Magdalen Laver and Lt Laver etc from 11. *The Lavers Rectory, Magdalen Laver, Ongar CM5 0ES* T: (01279) 426774 M: 07954-429153 E: gillanderson@ntlworld.com *or* revgillanderson@gmail.com

ANDERSON, Gordon Stuart. b 49. St Jo Coll Nottm. **d** 82 **p** 83. C Hattersley *Ches* 82-86; C Dagenham *Chelmsf* 86-91; TV Mildenhall *St E* 91-01; V Southminster *Chelmsf* 01-11; P-in-c Steeple 08-11; V Southminster and Steeple 11-14; RD Maldon and Dengie 06-11; rtd 14; PtO *St E* from 14. *11 Yew Tree Close, Mildenhall, Bury St Edmunds IP28 7SJ* T: (01638) 711260 M: 07549-539174 E: gandr42@btinternet.com

ANDERSON, Graeme Edgar. b 59. Poly of Wales BSc 82. St Jo Coll Nottm MTh 02. **d** 02 **p** 03. C Brislington St Luke *Bris* 02-05; C Galleywood Common *Chelmsf* 05-09; P-in-c Radcliffe-on-Trent and Shelford *S'well* 09-11; V from 11. *The Vicarage, 2 Vicarage Lane, Radcliffe-on-Trent, Nottingham NG12 2FB* T: 0115-923 9643 M: 07840-926736 E: graemeandjudy@gmail.com

ANDERSON, Hugh Richard Oswald. b 35. Roch Th Coll 68. **d** 70 **p** 71. C Minehead *B & W* 70-76; C Darley w S Darley *Derby* 76-80; R Hasland 80-94; V Temple Normanton 80-94; rtd 94; PtO *Derby* from 94. *32 Barry Road, Brimington, Chesterfield S43 1PX* T: (01246) 551020

ANDERSON, Ivo Borisov. BA 03. **d** 15. OLM Stratford St Paul and St Jas *Chelmsf* from 15. *52 Fortis Green, London N2 9EL*

ANDERSON, James. b 36. Magd Coll Ox BA 59 MA 64 Leeds Univ MA 00. **d** 02 **p** 03. NSM Holme and Seaton Ross Gp *York* 02-08; P-in-c The Beacon from 08. *61 Moor Lane, Carnaby, Bridlington YO16 4UT* T: (01262) 401688

ANDERSON, James Frederick Wale. b 34. G&C Coll Cam BA 58 MA 62. Cuddesdon Coll 60. **d** 62 **p** 63. C Leagrave *St Alb* 62-65; C Eastleigh *Win* 65-70; R Sherfield-on-Loddon 70-86; P-in-c Stratfield Saye w Hartley Wespall 75-86; R Sherfield-on-Loddon and Stratfield Saye etc 86-87; R Newton Valence, Selborne and E Tisted w Colemore 87-99; rtd 99; Chapl Surrey Hants Borders NHS Trust 01-04; Hon C Farnham *Guildf* 01-04; PtO from 07; *Win* from 11. *1 Potter's Gate, Farnham GU9 7EJ* T: (01252) 710728

ANDERSON, Canon James Raffan. b 33. Edin Univ MA 54 FRSA 90. Edin Th Coll 56. **d** 58 **p** 59. Chapl St Andr Cathl 58-59; Prec St Andr Cathl 59-62; CF (TA) 59-67; Chapl Aber Univ *Ab* 60-62; Chapl Glas Univ 62-69; Chapl Lucton Sch 69-71; Chapl Barnard Castle Sch 71-74; Asst Dir of Educn *Blackb* 74-78; P-in-c Whitechapel 74-78; Bp's Officer for Min *Cov* 78-87; Hon Can Cov Cathl 83-87; Miss Sec Gen Syn Bd for Miss and Unity 87-92; rtd 92; PtO *Blackb* 98-13. *Bramble Cottage, Lower Quinton, Stratford-upon-Avon CV37 8SG* T: (01789) 721779 E: jamesanders@onetel.com

ANDERSON, Jane Alison. **d** 14 **p** 15. NSM Woodhorn w Newbiggin *Newc* from 14. *52 Castle Way, Pegswood, Morpeth NE61 6XH*

ANDERSON (née FLAHERTY), Mrs Jane Venitia. b 68. Oak Hill Th Coll BA 92. **d** 93 **p** 94. C Timperley *Ches* 93-97; C Cheshunt *St Alb* 97-99; P-in-c N Springfield *Chelmsf* from 99. *The Vicarage, St Augustine's Way, Beardsley Drive, Springfield, Chelmsford CM1 6GX* T: (01245) 466160 E: revjaney@talktalk.net

ANDERSON, Jeffrey. b 56. Cranmer Hall Dur. **d** 07 **p** 08. C Chester le Street *Dur* 07-11; PtO from 14. *The Rectory, Houghton Road, Hetton-le-Hole, Houghton le Spring DH5 9PH* T: 0191-517 3102

ANDERSON, Jeremy. *See* ANDERSON, Brian Glaister

ANDERSON, Jeremy Dudgeon. b 41. Edin Univ BSc 63. Trin Coll Bris 75. **d** 77 **p** 78. C Bitterne *Win* 77-81; TV Wexcombe *Sarum* 81-91; Evang Enabler (Reading Deanery) *Ox* 91-96; V

Epsom Common Ch Ch *Guildf* 96-00; C Kinson *Sarum* 00-06; rtd 06. *The Croft, Church Road, Crowborough TN6 1ED* T: (01892) 655825

ANDERSON, Mrs Joanna Elisabeth. b 53. St Andr Univ MTheol 75. EMMTC 85. **d** 88 **p** 95. Par Dn Crosby *Linc* 88-92; Warden Iona Community *Arg* 92-95; R S Trin Broads *Nor* 95-02; Dir Body, Mind, Spirit Project 02-05; R Stiffkey and Bale *Nor* 05-09; C Hexham *Newc* 09-12; Is Cen Dir Iona Community *Arg* from 12. *Iona Community, Abbey and MacLeod Centres, Isle of Iona PA76 6SN* T: (01681) 700404 F: 700460 E: ionacomm@iona.org.uk

ANDERSON, John Robert. b 75. QUB BD 96 TCD MPhil 98. CITC 96. **d** 98 **p** 99. C Magherafelt *Arm* 98-02; C Ballymena w Ballyclug *Conn* 02-05; I Billy w Derrykeighan from 05; Bp's Dom Chapl from 08. *The New Rectory, 231 Castlecat Road, Dervock, Ballymoney BT53 8BP* T: (028) 2074 1241 E: j.e.anderson231@gmail.com

ANDERSON, Julie. b 60. St Jo Coll Nottm 09. **d** 11 **p** 12. C Liv Ch Ch Norris Green 11-14; P-in-c Long Stanton w St Mich *Ely* from 14; P-in-c Over from 14. *The Vicarage, Horseware, Over, Cambridge CB24 5NX* M: 07540-613068 E: julie_anderson51@yahoo.co.uk

ANDERSON, Canon Keith Bernard. b 36. Qu Coll Cam BA 60 MA 64. Tyndale Hall Bris 60. **d** 62 **p** 63. C Bootle St Leon *Liv* 62-65; Lect Can Warner Mem Coll Buye Burundi 66-73; Dir Th Educn by Ext Studies Dio Nakuru Kenya 74-77; Dir Th by Ext Studies Mt Kenya E 78-82; Hon Can Mt Kenya E from 82; P-in-c Newnham and Doddington w Wychling *Cant* 83-88; Chapl Cannes w Grasse *Eur* 88-94; Dir and Chapl Mulberry Ho High Ongar 94-95; TV Horley *S'wark* 96-01; rtd 01; PtO *S'wark* 01-05; *Chich* from 01. *93 Rusper Road, Horsham RH12 4BJ* T: (01403) 262185 E: kb.anderson@virgin.net

ANDERSON, Canon Keith Edward. b 42. Fitzw Coll Cam BA 77 MA 83 MRCS 83. Ridley Hall Cam 74. **d** 77 **p** 78. C Goodmayes All SS *Chelmsf* 77-80; Chapl Coll of SS Mark and Jo Plymouth *Ex* 80-87; RD Plymouth Moorside 83-86; V Northampton H Sepulchre w St Andr and St Lawr *Pet* 87-98; RD Northn 92-98; Adv for Min Willesden *Lon* 98-03; Can Res Win Cathl and Adv for Ord Min Development *Win* 03-08; rtd 08; PtO *Win* from 08. *49 Chaundler Road, Winchester SO23 7HW* T: (01962) 853429 E: keith.anderson20@btinternet.com

ANDERSON, Kenneth. b 38. G&C Coll Cam BA 62 MA 66. Westcott Ho Cam 63. **d** 65 **p** 66. C Nor St Steph 65-68; Chapl Norfolk and Nor Hosp 65-68; C Wareham w Arne *Sarum* 68-71; Chapl Sherborne Sch 71-83; Zimbabwe 83-94; Chapl Trevelyan and Van Mildert Coll *Dur* 95-04; Dioc Voc Adv 95-04; rtd 04. *39 Hallgarth Street, Durham DH1 3AT* T: 0191-383 0628 *or* 374 3770

ANDERSON, Martin Edward. b 73. Humberside Univ BA 95 St Jo Coll Dur BA 02. Cranmer Hall Dur 99. **d** 02 **p** 03. C Gt Aycliffe and Chilton *Dur* 02-05; TV Sunderland 05-07; Chapl Sunderland Minster 07-13; P-in-c Norton St Mary from 13; P-in-c Norton St Mich from 13. *2 Brambling Close, Norton, Stockton-on-Tees TS20 1TX* E: revmartin@outlook.com

ANDERSON, Michael. b 38. **d** 06 **p** 07. NSM Dungeon Hill and The Caundles w Folke and Holwell *Sarum* 06-07; NSM Vale of White Hart 07-09; Lic to RD Sherborne 09-10; NSM Gifle Valley *Sarum* 10-13; NSM Three Valleys from 13. *Tiley House, Middlemarsh, Sherborne DT9 5QL* T: (01300) 345375 M: 07966-664319 E: michael@tileyhouse.freeserve.co.uk

ANDERSON, Canon Michael Garland. b 42. Clifton Th Coll 62. **d** 66 **p** 67. C Fareham St Jo *Portsm* 66-69; C Worting *Win* 69-74; V Hordle 74-07; RD Lyndhurst 82-00; Hon Can Win Cathl 92-07; rtd 07; PtO *Win* from 07. *20 Forestlake Avenue, Ringwood BH24 1QU* T: (01425) 471490 E: canon.m.g.anderson@ukgateway.net

ANDERSON, Canon Michael John Austen. b 35. AKC 60. **d** 66 **p** 67. C Southall Ch Redeemer *Lon* 66-69; C Hampstead Garden Suburb 69-73; V S Mimms St Giles 73-80; V The Brents and Davington w Oare and Luddenham *Cant* 80-86; V Margate All SS 86-00; Hon Can Cant Cathl 97-00; rtd 00; PtO *Cant* from 01. *Camwa Ash, Bull Lane, Boughton-under-Blean, Faversham ME13 9AH* T: (01227) 752352 M: 07885-211863

ANDERSON, Nicholas Patrick. b 53. Lanc Univ BA 87. Allen Hall 79. **d** 81 **p** 82. In RC Ch 81-89; C Gt Crosby St Faith *Liv* 89-92; C Walton-on-the-Hill 92-95; V Pemberton St Fran Kitt Green 95-04; V Rainhill 04-14; Hon Can Liv Cathl 10-14; V Harpenden St Jo *St Alb* from 14. *St John's Vicarage, 5 St John's Road, Harpenden AL5 1DJ* T: (01582) 467168 E: frnicholasanderson@yahoo.co.uk

ANDERSON, Mrs Pearl Ann. b 46. St Andr Univ MA 68 MCIPD 74. Cant Sch of Min 90. **d** 93 **p** 00. Par Dn Epping St Jo *Chelmsf* 93-95; Adv to Coun for Soc Resp Roch and Cant 95-02; Asst Chief Exec Ch in Soc Roch and Cant 02-06; PtO

Roch from 95; Hon C Biddenden and Smarden *Cant* 00-06; rtd 06; PtO *Cant* from 06. *1 Gibbs Hill, Headcorn, Ashford TN27 9UD* T: (01622) 890043 M: 07811-209448 E: pearlanderson@btinternet.com

ANDERSON, Peter John. b 44. Nottm Univ BA 65 BA 73 Ex Univ CertEd 66. St Jo Coll Nottm. **d** 74 **p** 75. C Otley *Bradf* 74-77; TV Marfleet *York* 77-84; V Greasbrough *Sheff* 84-95; I Clonmel Union *C, C & R* 95-02; I Rathcooney Union 95-02; Chapl Cannes *Eur* 02-09; rtd 09. *100 route de la Colle, 06140 Tourrettes-sur-Loup, France* T: (0033) 9 50 41 68 40 E: pjhmander@yahoo.com

ANDERSON, Peter Scott. b 49. Nottm Univ BTh 72 CertEd. Kelham Th Coll 68. **d** 74 **p** 75. C Sheff St Cecilia Parson Cross 74-77; C Leytonstone St Marg w St Columba *Chelmsf* 77-81; P-in-c Forest Gate St Edm 81-89; V 89-90; P-in-c Plaistow 90-94; V Willesden Green St Andr and St Fran *Lon* 94-08; V Lewisham St Mary *S'wark* 08-11; rtd 12. *2A Wilton Crescent, London SW19 3FF* T: (020) 8542 8243 E: psanderson@hotmail.co.uk

ANDERSON, Philip Gregory. b 80. Keble Coll Ox BA 01. Ripon Coll Cuddesdon BA 04. **d** 05 **p** 06. C Prescot *Liv* 05-09; Chapl Liv Hope Univ 09-12; P-in-c Pemberton St Jo *Liv* 12-15; V from 15. *St John's Vicarage, 2 Shelley Drive, Orrell, Wigan WN5 8HW* T: (01942) 375209 E: vicarstjohnpemberton@gmail.com

ANDERSON, Canon Roderick Stephen. b 43. Cant Univ (NZ) BSc 63 PhD 67 New Coll Ox BA 72. Wycliffe Hall Ox 70. **d** 73 **p** 74. C Bradf Cathl 73-75; C Allerton 76-78; V Cottingley 78-94; V Heaton St Barn 94-09; C 09-11; RD Airedale 88-95; Chapl Bradf Univ and Bradf Coll 04-11; Hon Can Bradf Cathl 94-11; rtd 11; PtO *Leeds* from 11. *40 Low Wood, Wilsden, Bradford BD15 0JS* M: 07900-675350 E: rod.anderson@bradford.anglican.org

ANDERSON, Canon Rosemary Ann. b 36. Ex Univ BA 59. NOC 83. **dss** 86 **d** 87 **p** 94. Oldham St Paul *Man* 86-87; Hon Par Dn 87-89; Bp's Adv for Women's Min 88-99; Par Dn Roughtown 93-94; P-in-c 94-99; Hon Can Man Cathl 96-99; rtd 99; PtO *Man* 99-11. *11E Rhodes Hill, Lees, Oldham OL4 5EA* T: 0161-620 1549

ANDERSON, Scott. *See* ANDERSON, Peter Scott

ANDERSON, Stephen George. b 54. Liv Univ BA 75 ACIB. NOC 05. **d** 08 **p** 09. NSM Gt Shelford *Ely* 08-12; PtO 12-14; NSM Cambridge St Clem from 14. *3 Dukes Meadow, Stapleford, Cambridge CB22 5BH* T: (01223) 843859 M: 07889-003588 E: fr.stephen.anderson@googlemail.com

ANDERSON, Timothy George. b 59. Ealing Coll of HE BA 82. Wycliffe Hall Ox 83. **d** 86 **p** 87. C Harold Wood *Chelmsf* 86-90; C Whitfield *Derby* 90-95; P-in-c Wolverhampton St Luke *Lich* 95-98; V 98-01; I Dundonald *D & D* from 01. *St Elizabeth's Rectory, 26 Ballyregan Road, Dundonald, Belfast BT16 1HY* T: (028) 9048 3153 *or* 9048 2644 E: t.j.anderson@btinternet.com

ANDERSON, Timothy James Lane. b 59. Pemb Coll Ox BA 80 MA 90. St Jo Coll Nottm 89. **d** 93 **p** 94. C Reigate St Mary *S'wark* 93-95; PtO *S'well* from 95. *3 Dale Lane, Beeston, Nottingham NG9 4EA* T: 0115-922 4773

ANDERSON, William. CITC. **d** 09 **p** 10. NSM Killyman *Arm* 09-10; C Tullaniskin w Clonoe from 10. *215 Brackaville Road, Dungannon BT71 4EJ* M: 07901-852565 T: (028) 8774 1297 E: william@apple37.plus.com

ANDERSON-MacKENZIE, Janet Melanie. b 70. Edin Univ BSc 93 PhD 97 Trin Coll Bris MA 07. WEMTC 01. **d** 04 **p** 05. C Woolavington w Cossington and Bawdrip *B & W* 04-05; C Wellington and Distr 05-08; P-in-c Box w Hazlebury and Ditteridge *Bris* from 08; C Colerne w N Wraxall from 11. *The Vicarage, Church Lane, Box, Corsham SN13 8NR* T/F: (01225) 744458 E: janet@anderson-mackenzie.co.uk

ANDERTON, David. b 15. C Tettenhall Regis *Lich* from 15. *Address temp unknown*

ANDERTON, David Edward. b 60. Leeds Poly BSc 92. St Jo Coll Nottm 02. **d** 04 **p** 05. C Daybrook *S'well* 04-06; C Hucknall Torkard 06-09; TV Newark w Coddington from 09. *3 Swinderby Close, Newark NG24 2SY* T: (01636) 610485 M: 07751-269412 E: d.anderton1@btinternet.com

ANDERTON, David Ernest. b 36. CEng 68 MIMechE 68. **d** 00 **p** 01. OLM Eccleston Ch Ch *Liv* 00-06; rtd 06. *16 Croxteth Drive, Rainford, St Helens WA11 8JZ* T: (01744) 637600 M: 07751-038014

ANDERTON, Mrs Elaine Irene. b 73. Sussex Univ BA 96. WMMTC 06. **d** 09 **p** 10. C Smestow Vale *Lich* 09-13; C Tettenhall Wood and Perton 13; Chapl Compton Hospice from 13. *Compton Hospice Ltd, Compton Hall, 4 Compton Road West, Wolverhampton WV3 9DH* T: (01902) 774554 E: elaineanderton@compton-hospice.org.uk

ANDERTON, Frederic Michael. b 31. Pemb Coll Cam MA 57 IAAP. Westcott Ho Cam 64. **d** 66 **p** 67. C St John's Wood *Lon*

66-69; C All Hallows by the Tower etc 70-77; C St Giles Cripplegate w St Bart Moor Lane etc 77-82; C Zürich *Eur* 82-86; PtO *Lon* 94-00; rtd 96. *61 Brassey Road, Winchester SO22 6SB* T: (01962) 856326　F: 852851　E: robin.anderton@lineone.net

ANDERTON, Peter. b 45. Sarum & Wells Th Coll 80. **d** 82 **p** 83. C Adel *Ripon* 82-86; P-in-c Dacre w Hartwith 86-90; P-in-c Thornthwaite w Thruscross and Darley 88-90; V Dacre w Hartwith and Darley w Thornthwaite 90-91; V Owton Manor *Dur* 91-02; V Torrisholme *Blackb* 02-03; P-in-c Hunslet St Mary *Ripon* 03; V Hunslet w Cross Green 03-07; rtd 07; PtO *Dur* from 09. *133 Westbourne Avenue, Hartlepool TS25 5HZ* E: fr.peter@ntlworld.com

ANDREW, Brian. b 31. Oak Hill Th Coll 75. **d** 77 **p** 78. C Broadwater St Mary *Chich* 77-81; R Nettlebed w Bix and Highmore *Ox* 81-87; V Shenstone *Lich* 87-96; rtd 96; PtO *Ex* 97-01; *Derby* 01-11. *1 Redcotts, St Botolphs Road, Worthing BN11 4JW*

ANDREW, David Neil. b 62. Down Coll Cam BA 83 MA 87 PhD 88. Ridley Hall Cam 93. **d** 93 **p** 94. C Heatherlands St Jo *Sarum* 93-98; P-in-c White Waltham w Shottesbrooke *Ox* from 98; P-in-c Waltham St Lawrence 07-11. *The Vicarage, Waltham Road, White Waltham, Maidenhead SL6 3JD* T: (01628) 822000

ANDREW, David Shore. b 39. Liv Univ BA 61 CertEd 62. OLM course 97. **d** 99 **p** 00. NSM Birkenshaw w Hunsworth *Leeds* from 99. *448 Oxford Road, Gomersal, Cleckheaton BD19 4LD* T: (01274) 873339

ANDREW, Donald. b 35. Tyndale Hall Bris 63. **d** 66 **p** 67. C Croydon Ch Ch Broad Green *Cant* 66-69; C Ravenhead *Liv* 69-72; Scripture Union 72-77; V Rushen *S & M* 77-82; TR Heworth H Trin *York* 82-00; rtd 00; PtO *York* from 05. *60 Viking Road, Bridlington YO16 6TW* T: (01262) 601273

ANDREW, Jeremy Charles Edward. b 68. St Jo Coll Dur BA 01. Cranmer Hall Dur 98. **d** 01. C Newquay *Truro* 01-04; P-in-c Perranzabuloe 04-10; P-in-c Crantock 05-06; C Crantock w Cubert 06-07; P-in-c 07-10; V Perranzabuloe and Crantock w Cubert 10-14; Dioc Dir of Ords 12-14; P-in-c Warmley, Syston and Bitton *Bris* 14-15; R from 15. *The Vicarage, Church Avenue, Warmley, Bristol BS30 5JJ* E: j.andrew.102@btinternet.com

ANDREW, John. b 60. St Mich Coll Llan 98. **d** 00 **p** 01. C Oystermouth *S & B* 00-06; V Upper Wye 06-07; P-in-c Swansea St Nic 07-08; rtd 09. *13 Park Street, Mumbles, Swansea SA3 4DA* T: (01792) 360408

ANDREW, Jonathan William. b 50. Univ Coll Ox MA 78 FCA 80. Ripon Coll Cuddesdon 02. **d** 04 **p** 05. NSM Hersham *Guildf* from 04. *Orchard, 6 Westacres, Esher KT10 9JE* T: (01372) 479776　M: 07968-765188 E: jonathanandrew@stpetershersham.com

ANDREW, Paul Roland. b 70. Oak Hill Th Coll BA 06. **d** 06 **p** 07. C Plymouth Em, St Paul Efford and St Aug *Ex* 06-09; Chapl RN from 09. *Royal Naval Chaplaincy Service, Mail Point 1-2, Leach Building, Whale Island, Portsmouth PO2 8BY* T: (023) 9262 5055　F: 9262 5134　E: paulosandrews@blueyonder.co.uk

ANDREW, Philip John. b 62. Nottm Univ BSc 84. St Jo Coll Nottm MTh 02. **d** 02 **p** 03. C Reading Greyfriars *Ox* 02-06; V Reigate St Mary *S'wark* from 06. *St Mary's Vicarage, 76 Church Street, Reigate RH2 0SP* T: (01737) 242973 E: phil.andrew@stmaryreigate.org

ANDREW, Sydney William. b 55. Cranmer Hall Dur 82. **d** 85 **p** 86. C Horncastle w Low Toynton *Linc* 85-88; V Worlaby 88-93; V Bonby 88-93; V Elsham 88-93; rtd 93; LtO *Linc* 93-95; Hon C Brocklesby Park 95-04; Hon C Croxton 96-04; Hon C Caistor Gp from 04. *10 Bentley Lane, Grasby, Barnetby DN38 6AW* T: (01652) 628586　E: bridget.revdoc@clara.co.uk

ANDREW, Canon William Hugh. b 32. Selw Coll Cam BA 56 MA 60. Ridley Hall Cam 56. **d** 58 **p** 59. C Woking St Mary *Guildf* 58-61; C Farnborough 61-64; V Gatten St Paul *Portsm* 64-71; R Weymouth St Mary *Sarum* 71-76; V Heatherlands St Jo 76-82; Can and Preb Sarum Cathl 81-86; R Alderbury and W Grimstead 82-86; PtO *Bris* 86-88; Communications Dir Bible Soc 86-94; Communications Consultant 94-97; Hon C The Lydiards *Bris* 88-94; C W Swindon and the Lydiards 94-96; Hon C 96-98; rtd 96; PtO *Win* from 98. *31 Charnock Close, Hordle, Lymington SO41 0GU* T: (01425) 627220

ANDREWES, Nicholas John. b 64. Southn Univ BA 87 La Sainte Union Coll PGCE 88. Cranmer Hall Dur BTh 93. **d** 96 **p** 97. C Dovecot *Liv* 96-00; TV Pendleton *Man* 00-03; P-in-c Lower Crumpsall w Cheetham St Mark 03-10; P-in-c Oldham St Paul 10-14; V Oldham St Paul and Werneth from 14. *St Paul's Vicarage, 55 Belgrave Road, Oldham OL8 1LU* T: 0161-624 1068 E: nick.andrewes@phonecoop.coop

ANDREWS, Anthony Brian. b 33. Lon Univ BA 54 AKC 58. Coll of Resurr Mirfield 56. **d** 58 **p** 59. C Haggerston St Columba *Lon* 58-60; C N Hammersmith St Kath 60-63; V Goldthorpe *Sheff* 63-74; V Notting Hill St Mich and Ch Ch *Lon* from 74. *St Michael's Vicarage, 35 St Lawrence Terrace, London W10 5SR* T: (020) 8969 0776　F: 8969 0805　E: a.b.a@btinternet.com *or* archangel@supanet.com

ANDREWS, Anthony John. b 35. S'wark Ord Course 75. **d** 80 **p** 81. NSM Cheam *S'wark* 80-83; C Epsom St Martin *Guildf* 83-86; V Barton *Portsm* 86-89; Chapl Northwick Park and St Mark's NHS Trust Harrow 90-98; C Regent's Park St Mark *Lon* 98-00; rtd 00; PtO *Lon* from 00. *112 Albury Drive, Pinner HA5 3RG*

ANDREWS, Benjamin. b 75. St Steph Ho Ox 97. **d** 00 **p** 01. C Whitchurch *Llan* 00-03; C Newton Nottage 03-05; C Cardiff St Mary and St Steph w St Dyfrig etc 05-12; R Cadoxton-juxta-Barry from 12. *The Rectory, 21 Rectory Road, Barry CF63 3QB* T: (01446) 406690　E: frbenandrews@aol.com

ANDREWS, Canon Brian Keith. b 39. Keble Coll Ox BA 62 MA 69. Coll of Resurr Mirfield 62. **d** 64 **p** 65. C Is of Dogs Ch Ch and St Jo w St Luke *Lon* 64-68; C Hemel Hempstead *St Alb* 68-71; TV 71-79; V Abbots Langley 79-05; RD Watford 88-94; Hon Can St Alb 94-05; rtd 05; PtO *Glouc* from 06. *High Pleck, Littleworth, Amberley, Stroud GL5 5AG* T: (01453) 873068

ANDREWS, Canon Christopher Paul. b 47. Fitzw Coll Cam BA 70 MA 73. Westcott Ho Cam 69. **d** 72 **p** 73. C Croydon St Jo *Cant* 72-75; C Gosforth All SS *Newc* 75-79; TV Newc Epiphany 80-87; RD Newc Cen 82-87; V Alnwick and Chapl Alnwick Infirmary 87-96; R Grantham *Linc* 96-13; P-in-c Grantham, Manthorpe 11-13; RD Grantham 09-11; Can and Preb Linc Cathl 04-13; Chapl United Lincs Hosps NHS Trust 99-01; rtd 13; Chapl to The Queen from 09; PtO *St E* from 14. *74 Daisy Avenue, Bury St Edmunds IP32 7PH* T: (01284) 723785　E: candrews3007@gmail.com

ANDREWS, Clive Frederick. b 43. St Jo Coll Nottm 81. **d** 83 **p** 84. C Leic St Jas 83-86; Ind Chapl 86-90; Hon TV Melton Gt Framland 89-90; TV Clifton *S'well* 90-92; P-in-c Gamston w Eaton and W Drayton 92-94; R 94-08; P-in-c Elkesley w Bothamsall 92-08; Chapl Bramcote Sch Notts 92-08; rtd 08. *15 Oakwood Grove, Edwinstowe, Mansfield NG21 9JT* E: cliveand@waitrose.com

ANDREWS, Edward Robert. b 33. Brasted Th Coll 60 St Mich Coll Llan 62. **d** 64 **p** 65. C Kingswinford St Mary *Lich* 64-69; Chapl RAF 69-88; R St Just-in-Roseland w Philleigh *Truro* 88-99; rtd 99; PtO *Ex* from 00. *2 Ingleside, Gunsdown Villas, Station Road, South Molton EX36 3EA* T: (01769) 572386

ANDREWS, Mrs Jean. b 48. Leic Univ BSc 70. NTMTC. **d** 10 **p** 11. NSM Downham w S Hanningfield *Chelmsf* 10-11; NSM Downham w S Hanningfield and Ramsden Bellhouse from 11. *3 Sewards End, Wickford SS12 9PB* T: (01268) 733817 E: jean@rjandrews.me.uk

ANDREWS, Preb John Colin. b 47. Open Univ BA 93. Sarum & Wells Th Coll 78. **d** 80 **p** 81. C Burnham *B & W* 80-84; V Williton 84-92; P-in-c Ashwick w Oakhill and Binegar 92-02; Dioc Communications Officer 92-12; TV Yatton Moor 02-12; Preb Wells Cathl 04-12; rtd 12. *Cherry Tree House, Kenn Street, Kenn, Clevedon BS21 6TN* T: (01275) 877806 M: 07971-484061　E: john.andrews150@btinternet.com

ANDREWS, John Elfric. b 35. Ex Coll Ox BA 59 MA 63. Wycliffe Hall Ox 59. **d** 61 **p** 62. C Pittville All SS *Glouc* 61-66; Cand Sec Lon City Miss 66-92; LtO *S'wark* 66-92; R Kingham w Churchill, Daylesford and Sarsden *Ox* 92-99; rtd 99; PtO *St E* from 01. *4 St George's Road, Felixstowe IP11 9PL* T: (01394) 283557　E: john.andrew@care4free.net

ANDREWS, John Francis. b 34. Jes Coll Cam BA 58 MA 62. S'wark Ord Course 78. **d** 81 **p** 82. NSM Upper Norwood All SS *S'wark* 81-87; NSM Dulwich St Barn 89-92; NSM S Dulwich St Steph 92-95; PtO 95-01; *Sarum* from 01. *1 Kennington Square, Wareham BH20 4JR* T: (01929) 555311 E: jecajfa@btinternet.com

ANDREWS, John George William. b 42. Qu Coll Birm 65. **d** 68 **p** 69. C Smethwick St Matt w St Chad *Birm* 68-71; CF 71-97; P-in-c Lyme Regis *Sarum* 97-98; TV Golden Cap Team 98-03; rtd 03. *North Gate House, Stapledon Lane, Ashburton, Newton Abbot TQ13 7AE*

ANDREWS, John Robert. b 42. Nottm Coll of Educn CertEd 63 FRSA 92 FCMI 92. **d** 04 **p** 05. OLM Farewell *Lich* 04-10; rtd 10. *1 Chaseley Gardens, Burntwood WS7 9DJ* T: (01543) 674354 M: 07711-246656　E: johnrobert.andrews@btinternet.com

ANDREWS, Judith Marie. b 47. Avery Hill Coll CertEd 68. **d** 00 **p** 01. OLM Wilford Peninsula *St E* 00-08; TV from 08. *Hillside, Tower Hill, Hollesley, Woodbridge IP12 3QX* T: (01394) 411642 E: judith.andrews@btopenworld.com

ANDREWS, Keith. b 47. St Mich Coll Llan 79. **d** 81 **p** 82. C Penarth w Lavernock *Llan* 81-85; V Nantymoel w Wyndham 85-91; RD Bridgend 89-93; R Coychurch w Llangan and St Mary Hill 91-98; V Caerau St Cynfelin 98-12; rtd 12; PtO *Llan* from 14. *Graig Fryn, 18 Vale View Villas, Ogmore Vale, Bridgend CF32 7DP* T: (01656) 713901

ANDREWS, Morey Alisdair Christopher. b 66. Leic Poly BSc 91 MRICS 91. St Jo Coll Nottm MA 99. **d** 99 **p** 00. C Yate New

Town *Bris* 99-02; C Downend 02-06; V Eynsham and
Cassington *Ox* from 06. *The Vicarage, 45 Acre End Street,
Eynsham, Witney OX29 4PF* T: (01865) 881323 *or* 881450
E: moreyandrews@btinternet.com

ANDREWS, Mrs Natalie Janis. b 78. Univ of Cen England in
Birm BSc 00. Ridley Hall Cam 10. **d** 12 **p** 13. C Loughborough
All SS w H Trin *Leic* 12-13; C Loughborough Em and St Mary in
Charnwood 13-14; C Loughborough Em from 15. *60 Brush
Drive, Loughborough LE11 1LT* M: 07710-426744
E: natalieandrews@talktalk.net

ANDREWS, Paul Douglas. b 54. Univ of Wales (Abth) BLib 76
PhD 99. SAOMC. **d** 00 **p** 01. NSM Kempston and Biddenham
St Alb 00-03; C Leighton Buzzard w Eggington, Hockliffe etc
03-05; TV Billington, Egginton, Hockliffe etc 06-08; P-in-c
St Neots *Ely* from 08; C Eynesbury from 12. *The Vicarage,
Church Street, St Neots PE19 2BU* T: (01480) 472297
E: p.d.andrews@btinternet.com

ANDREWS, Penny. *See* MAGINN, Penny

ANDREWS, Peter Douglas. b 52. SEN 72 SRN 78. St Steph Ho
Ox 86. **d** 88 **p** 89. C Perry Barr *Birm* 88-92; TV Swindon New
Town *Bris* 92-98; V Streatham St Pet *S'wark* from 98. *St Peter's
Vicarage, 113 Leigham Court Road, London SW16 2NS* T: (020)
8769 2922 E: frpeterandrews@aol.com

ANDREWS, Raymond Cyril. b 50. SEITE 00. **d** 03 **p** 04. C E
Dulwich St Jo *S'wark* 03-07; P-in-c S'wark St Geo w St Alphege
and St Jude 07-13; rtd 13; PtO *S'wark* from 13. *21 Trinity
Court, Charlton Lane, London SE7 8LR* T: (020) 3643 4211
M: 07930-695571 E: revrayandrews@aol.com

ANDREWS, Richard John. b 57. Bris Univ BA 78 CertEd 79.
Ripon Coll Cuddesdon 82. **d** 84 **p** 85. C Kidderminster
St Mary and All SS, Trimpley etc *Worc* 84-87; Chapl Derbyshire
Coll of HE 87-89; Hon C Derby Cathl 87-89; V Chellaston
89-93; V Spondon 93-05; TR Dunstable *St Alb* from 05; RD
09-14. *The Rectory, 8 Furness Avenue, Dunstable LU6 3BN*
T: (01582) 703271 E: rector@dunstableparish.org.uk

ANDREWS, Robert. *See* ANDREWS, Edward Robert

ANDREWS, Stephen. b 69. **d** 11 **p** 12. OLM Gt Yarmouth *Nor*
from 11. *19 Forth Close, Caister-on-Sea, Great Yarmouth
NR30 5UW* T: (01493) 377897 M: 07973-468411
E: revdstephen@btinternet.com

ANDREYEV, Michael. b 62. Hatf Coll Dur BA 85. Wycliffe Hall
Ox BA 93 MA 03. **d** 96 **p** 97. C Surbiton Hill Ch Ch *S'wark*
96-01; NSM Stapenhill w Cauldwell *Derby* 02-03; P-in-c 03-06;
V from 06. *3 Stapenhill Road, Burton-on-Trent DE15 9AF*
T: (01283) 530320 E: office@stpetersstapenhill.org.uk *or*
andreyevs07@talktalk.net

ANETTS, Roy. b 55. Qu Coll Birm 06. **d** 09 **p** 10. NSM Acocks
Green *Birm* 09-12; NSM Yardley St Cypr Hay Mill 12-13; P-in-c
from 13; P-in-c S Yardley St Mich from 14. *The Vicarage,
7 Fordrough, Yardley, Birmingham B25 8DL* T: 0121-753 1542
E: revroy@hotmail.com

ANGEL, Andrew Richard. b 67. St Pet Coll Ox BA 89 Lon
Inst of Educn PGCE 90 Surrey Univ MA 94 Cant Ch Ch
Univ MA 06. St Jo Coll Nottm PhD 04. **d** 02 **p** 03. C Dartford
Ch Ch *Roch* 02-05; Tutor SEITE 05-10; Tutor St Jo Coll
Nottm from 10. *St John's College, Chilwell Lane, Bramcote,
Nottingham NG9 3DS* T: 0115-925 1114
E: a.angel@stjohns-nottm.ac.uk

ANGEL, Gervais Thomas David. b 36. Ch Ch Ox BA 59 MA 62
Bris Univ MEd 78 Lon Univ PGCE 72. Wycliffe Hall Ox 57.
d 61 **p** 62. C Aberystwyth St Mich *St D* 61-65; Tutor Clifton
Th Coll 65-71; Dean of Studies Trin Coll Bris 71-81; Dir of
Studies 81-90; Area Sec (W and SW) SAMS 90-02; NSM Stoke
Gifford *Bris* 92-02; rtd 02; PtO *Bris* from 02. *82 Oak Close, Little
Stoke, Bristol BS34 6RD* T: (01454) 618081 M: 07967-441426
F: 0117-904 8588 E: gervais.angel@blueyonder.co.uk

ANGELICI, Ruben. b 80. S Nazarene Univ (USA) BSc 02 Man
Univ BA 05 MA 06 Jes Coll Cam PhD 15 Edge Hill Univ
PGCE 09. Westcott Ho Cam 11. **d** 15. C Sleaford *Linc* from 15.
11 Covel Road, Sleaford NG34 8BP M: 07741-453080
E: fr.ruben@outlook.com

ANGELL, Miss Elizabeth Patricia. b 54. Univ of Wales (Ban)
BA 72. Trin Coll Bris BA 08. **d** 08 **p** 09. C Fosse *Leic* 08-11; TV
Bridgnorth, Tasley, Astley Abbotts, etc *Heref* from 11.
32 Goodwood Avenue, Bridgnorth WV15 5BD T: (01746)
767187 E: elizabethangell49@btinternet.com

ANGELL, Geoffrey. b 63. St Jo Coll Nottm. **d** 01 **p** 02. C
Daventry, Ashby St Ledgers, Braunston etc *Pet* 01-04; C
Oakham, Hambleton, Egleton, Braunston and Brooke 04-07;
P-in-c Barrowden and Wakerley w S Luffenham etc 07-13;
Chapl Univ Hosps Leic NHS Trust from 13. *Leicester General
Hospital, Gwendolen Road, Leicester LE5 4PW* T: 03003-031573
E: rector@artangells.com

ANGELO, Brother. *See* DEACON, Donald

ANGIER, Patrick John Mark. b 61. Leic Univ BSc 83. Trin Coll
Bris. **d** 03 **p** 04. C Stratford-upon-Avon, Luddington etc 03-06;

V Prestbury *Ches* from 06. *Meadowside, New Road, Prestbury,
Macclesfield SK10 4HP* T: (01625) 829288 *or* 827625
M: 07971-923668 E: patrick.angier@btinternet.com

ANGLE, John Edwin George. b 42. Lon Bible Coll BD 65 Liv
Univ AdDipEd 73 Univ of Wales MEd 75. WEMTC 92. **d** 94
p 95. NSM Clevedon St Andr and Ch Ch *B & W* 94-97; NSM
Worle 97-98; P-in-c Camelot Par 98-01; R 01-06; Warden
of Readers Wells Adnry 02-05; rtd 06; PtO *B & W* from 06.
14 Farthing Combe, Axbridge BS26 2DR T: (01934) 733695
M: 07970-968652 E: johnangle@btinternet.com

ANGOVE, Ms Helen Teresa. b 71. Bath Univ BEng 93. Ripon
Coll Cuddesdon BTh 97. **d** 97 **p** 98. C Bridgwater St Mary,
Chilton Trinity and Durleigh *B & W* 97-01; P-in-c Elstree
St Alb 01-03; USA from 03. *150 N San Marino Avenue, Pasadena
CA 91107, USA* T: (001) (626) 793 7386
E: htangove@yahoo.com

ANGUS, Canon Edward. b 39. Man Univ BA 60. Qu Coll Birm.
d 62 **p** 63. C Chorley St Geo *Blackb* 62-65; C S Shore H Trin
65-68; R Bretherton 68-76; V Altham w Clayton le Moors
76-90; V Preesall 90-04; RD Garstang 96-01; Hon Can Blackb
Cathl 98-04; rtd 04; PtO *Blackb* from 04. *14 Lazenby
Avenue, Fleetwood FY7 8QH* T: (01253) 686817

ANI, Joel Osita. b 72. Qu Coll Birm BA 08. **d** 08 **p** 10. C Telford
Park *S'wark* 08-09; C Clapham Park All SS 09-12. *6 Blenheim
Gardens, London SW2 5DB* T: (020) 8674 1889
M: 07903-234444 E: joel_ani123@yahoo.com

ANITA, Sister. *See* COOK, Anita Isabel

ANKER, Malcolm. b 39. Univ of Wales BA 61. Bps' Coll
Cheshunt 61. **d** 63 **p** 64. C Marfleet *York* 63-66; C Cottingham
66-69; V Skirlaugh w Long Riston 69-74; V Bilsdale and
Brough w Brantingham 74-84; V Tadcaster 84-86; V Tadcaster
w Newton Kyme 86-91; V Oatlands *Guildf* 91-05; rtd 05;
PtO *Guildf* 05-13; *Sheff* from 15. *27 Ringstead Avenue, Sheffield
S10 5SL* T: 0114-453 4858
E: malcolm.anker@googlemail.com

ANKER-PETERSEN, Robert Brian. b 52. Aber Univ MTh 88.
Wycliffe Hall Ox BA 79 MA 88. **d** 93 **p** 94. C Perth St Ninian
St And 93-96; Bp's Researcher on Ch's Min of Healing from 93;
Dir Bield Retreat and Healing Cen from 93; Dioc Dir of
Healing *St And* from 97. *Blackruthven House, Tibbermore, Perth
PH1 1PY* T: (01738) 583238
E: robin@bieldatblackruthven.org.uk

ANKERS, Canon Charles William (Bill). b 42. FIMI. NEOC 89.
d 93 **p** 95. NSM York St Luke 93-95; C Kexby w Wilberfoss
95-98; Asst Chapl HM Pris Full Sutton 95-98; V Norton juxta
Malton *York* 98-11; Can and Preb York Minster from 10;
rtd 11; PtO *York* from 11. *10 Beechwood Road, Norton,
Malton YO17 9EJ* T: (01653) 693930
E: canonbill-norton@hotmail.co.uk

ANKETELL, Jeyarajan. b 41. Lon Univ BSc 62 PhD 67 MInstP.
Coll of Resurr Mirfield 69. **d** 73 **p** 74. Asst Chapl Newc Univ
73-75; Asst Chapl Lon Univ 75-77; Teacher 78-05; LtO *S'wark*
81-83; Chasetown High Sch 85-05; NSM Lich St Mary w
St Mich 86-96; NSM Lich St Mich w St Mary and Wall 96-15;
PtO from 15. *7 Wissage Lane, Lichfield WS13 6DQ* T: (01543)
268897 E: jeyan.anketell@ntlworld.com

ANNANCY, Felix. b 62. **d** 87 **p** 88. C Fenton *Lich* 87-88; Ghana
88-98 and from 00; C Stalybridge St Paul *Ches* 98-00. *PO Box
329, Aksombo, Eastern Region, Ghana*

✠**ANNAS, The Rt Revd Geoffrey Peter.** b 53. Sarum & Wells
Th Coll. **d** 83 **p** 84 **c** 10. C S'wark H Trin w St Matt 83-87;
TV Walworth 87-94; Warden Pemb Coll Miss Walworth
87-94; V Southampton Thornhill St Chris *Win* 94-10; Hon
Can Win Cathl 07-10; Area Bp Stafford *Lich* from 10. *Ash
Garth, Broughton Crescent, Barlaston, Stoke-on-Trent ST12 9DD*
T: (01782) 373308 F: 373705
E: bishop.stafford@lichfield.anglican.org

ANNE, Sister. *See* PROUDLEY, Anne

ANNESLEY-GAMESTER, The Hon Colette Louise Anselm. b 67.
R Holloway Coll Lon BA 89 MA 08 Lucy Cavendish Coll Cam
BTh 12 Bulmershe Coll of HE PGCE 91. **d** 12 **p** 13. Spire Hill
Sarum 12; C from 12. *Snowdon House, 7 Gold Street, Stalbridge,
Sturminster Newton DT10 2LX* T: (01963) 364675
E: colette.gamester@btinternet.com

ANNIS, Herman North. b 28. Lich Th Coll 62. **d** 64 **p** 65.
C Kilburn St Aug *Lon* 64-67; C Toxteth Park St Agnes *Liv*
67-70; V 70-82; V Hempton and Pudding Norton *Nor*
82-84; P-in-c Sculthorpe w Dunton and Doughton 82-84;
V Northampton H Trin *Pet* 84-95; rtd 95; Hon C Brighton
St Bart *Chich* 95-99. *13 rue des Ormeaux, 53500 Montenay,
France* T: (0033) 2 43 13 09 54

ANNIS, Jennifer Mary. b 49. Middx Univ BA 95. Oak Hill Th
Coll 92. **d** 95 **p** 97. NSM Digswell and Panshanger *St Alb*
95-97; NSM Codicote 97-98 and 99-00; Tanzania 98-99; Chapl
ATC from 99; NSM Fishguard w Llanychar and Pontfaen w

Morfil etc *St D* from 10. *Glanafon, Trecwn, Haverfordwest SA62 5XT* T: (01348) 840689
E: jennie.annis@btinternet.com

ANNIS, Rodney James. b 43. Ex Univ BA 75 MA 79 PhD 86. Ripon Coll Cuddesdon 75. **d** 76 **p** 77. C Brixham *Ex* 76-77; Asst Chapl Ex Univ 77-80; Chapl Ex Sch 77-80; C Boston *Linc* 80-84; Chapl Trin Hall Cam 84-87; Chapl St Edw K and Martyr Cam *Ely* 84-87; V Bush Hill Park St Steph *Lon* 87-13; rtd 13. *The Vicarage, 43A Village Road, Enfield EN1 2ET*

ANN-MARIE, Sister. *See* STUART, Ann-Marie Lindsay

ANNON, Jacqueline. b 62. **d** 01 **p** 02. OLM Tooting All SS *S'wark* 01-04. *31 Hamilton Road, London SE27 9RZ* T: (020) 8670 7441

ANNS, Pauline Mary. *See* HIGHAM, Pauline Mary

ANSAH, Canon Kwesi Gyebi Ababio (George). b 54. Oak Hill Th Coll BTh 97. Simon of Cyrene Th Inst 90. **d** 93 **p** 94. C Peckham St Mary Magd *S'wark* 93-96; V W Dulwich Em from 96; Hon Can Kumasi from 04. *Emmanuel Vicarage, 94 Clive Road, London SE21 8BU* T: (020) 8670 2793 M: 07771-783693 E: gkansa@aol.com

ANSCOMBE, John Thomas. b 51. Ex Univ BA 72. Cranmer Hall Dur. **d** 74 **p** 75. C Upper Armley *Ripon* 74-77; C Leeds St Geo 78-81; Exec Producer Scripture Union 81-96; Hon C Beckenham Ch Ch *Roch* from 82. *22 Hawthornedene Road, Bromley BR2 7DY* T/F: (020) 8462 4831 M: 07736-070160 E: john.anscombe@diocese-rochester.org

ANSELL, Antony Michael. b 40. St Jo Coll Nottm 78. **d** 80 **p** 81. C Harrow Weald St Mich *Lon* 80-84; Hon C Ches Square St Mich w St Phil 86-88; Hon C Mayfair Ch Ch 88-02; PtO *Win* 02-15. *Fullerton Mill, Fullerton, Andover SP11 7LA* T: (01264) 861076 M: 07855-943615 E: a.ansell@andover.co.uk

ANSELL, John Christopher. b 49. Sarum & Wells Th Coll 79. **d** 81 **p** 82. C Dartford St Alb *Roch* 81-84; C Leybourne and Larkfield 84-88; TV Mortlake w E Sheen *S'wark* 88-98; V Mitcham SS Pet and Paul 98-14; rtd 14. *Tankards Spring, High Street, Chalford, Stroud GL6 8DJ* M: 07974-432562 E: jsansell@hotmail.com

ANSELL, Mrs Mandy. b 47. **d** 04 **p** 05. OLM Rockland St Mary w Hellington, Bramerton etc *Nor* from 04. *44 The Street, Rockland St Mary, Norwich NR14 7AH* T: (01508) 538654 E: mandy.ansell44@gmail.com

ANSELL, Mark Stephen. b 68. Univ of Wales (Abth) BLib 89 Abth Univ PGCE 98. St Mich Coll Llan 12. **d** 14 **p** 15. C Henfynyw w Aberaeron and Llanddewi Aberarth etc *St D* from 14. *Dyffryn, Lampeter Road, Aberaeron SA46 0ED* T: (01545) 570094 E: revmarkansell@btinternet.com

ANSELL, Philip Harding. b 67. LMH Ox BA 89 Rob Coll Cam BA 92. Ridley Hall Cam. **d** 93 **p** 94. C Rainham w Wennington *Chelmsf* 93-97; C Rodbourne Cheney *Bris* 97-01; V Moseley St Agnes *Birm* from 01. *St Agnes' Vicarage, 5 Colmore Crescent, Birmingham B13 9SJ* T/F: 0121-449 0368

ANSELM, Brother. *See* SMYTH, Robert Andrew Laine

ANSLOW, Mrs Patricia Margaret. b 49. Yorks Min Course 08. **d** 11 **p** 12. NSM Bramham *York* from 11. *4 Pine Tree Avenue, Boston Spa, Wetherby LS23 6HA* T: (01937) 844789 M: 07903-262880 E: t.anslow@hotmail.co.uk

ANSON (née DRAX), Mrs Elizabeth Margaret. b 57. St Jo Coll Nottm 91. **d** 94 **p** 95. C Kimberworth *Sheff* 94-95; C Doncaster St Mary 95-97; rtd 97; PtO *Sheff* from 10. *62 School Green Lane, Sheffield S10 4GR* T: 0114-229 5478

ANSON, Harry. b 35. FInstFF 79. St Jo Coll Nottm 83. **d** 88 **p** 03. NSM Ayr *Glas* 88-93; Hon Chapl Miss to Seamen 91-93; rtd 94. *Fairview, Balbinny, Aberlemno, Forfar DD8 3PF* T/F: (01307) 830446 M: 07790-470660 E: h2avro@hotmail.com

ANSTEY, Nigel John. b 55. Cranmer Hall Dur 84. **d** 87 **p** 88. C Plumstead St Jo w St Jas and St Paul *S'wark* 87-91; TV Ipswich St Fran *St E* 91-97; TV Walthamstow *Chelmsf* from 97. *St Luke's Vicarage, 17A Greenleaf Road, London E17 6QQ* T: (020) 8520 2885 E: nigel.anstey@btinternet.com

ANSTICE, John Neville. b 39. Lon Univ BSc 63. Cuddesdon Coll 69. **d** 71 **p** 72. C Stonebridge St Mich *Lon* 71-74; Chapl Woodbridge Sch 74-76; TV Droitwich *Worc* 76-80; P-in-c Salwarpe 76-79; PtO *Chich* from 80; rtd 99. *10 Selham Close, Crawley RH11 0EH* T: (01293) 535654

ANTELL, Roger Howard. b 47. Lon Univ BD 71 Warwick Univ MSc 79 Ox Univ MTh 99. Ripon Coll Cuddesdon 97. **d** 99 **p** 00. C Ashchurch *Glouc* 99-03; R Stoke Prior, Wychbold and Upton Warren *Worc* 03-11; rtd 11. *Hafodwen, Dinas Cross, Newport SA42 0SG* T: (01348) 811391 E: roger.antell@btinternet.com

ANTHONY, Canon Ian Charles. b 47. NW Ord Course 76. **d** 79 **p** 80. NSM Lt Lever *Man* from 79; Hon Can Man Cathl from 12. *36 Meadow Close, Little Lever, Bolton BL3 1LG* T: (01204) 791437

ANTHONY, John Thomas. **d** 15. NSM Cen Swansea *S & B* from 15. *11 Church Close, Neath SA10 7TF* T: (01639) 638434 E: johnanthony1@tiscali.com

ANTHONY, Peter Benedict. b 79. Magd Coll Ox BA 02 MA 05 St Steph Ho Ox MSt 10 DPhil 15. St Steph Ho Ox 03 Ven English Coll Rome 05. **d** 06 **p** 07. C Hendon St Mary and Ch Ch *Lon* 06-09; Jun Dean St Steph Ho Ox 09-13; Jun Chapl Mert Coll Ox 10-13; P-in-c Kentish Town *Lon* from 13. *The Church House, Ospringe Road, London NW5 2JB* T: (020) 7284 3728 M: 07949-005550 E: peterbanthony@hotmail.com

ANTHONY, Miss Sheila Margaret. b 52. Wycliffe Hall Ox BTh 04. **d** 04 **p** 05. C Bideford, Northam, Westward Ho!, Appledore etc *Ex* 04-08; P-in-c Bluntisham cum Earith w Colne and Woodhurst *Ely* 08-10; P-in-c Holywell w Needingworth 08-10; V Bluntisham cum Earith w Colne and Holywell etc from 10. *The Rectory, 6 Rectory Road, Bluntisham, Huntingdon PE28 3LN* T: (01487) 740456 E: sheila@saintintraining.co.uk

ANTHONY MARY, Father. *See* HIRST, Anthony Melville

ANTOINE, Emma Louise. b 72. Newc Univ BA 96. Westcott Ho Cam 02. **d** 05 **p** 06. C High Wycombe *Ox* 05-06; C Wokingham All SS 06-09; P-in-c Chorlton-cum-Hardy St Werburgh *Man* 12-14; PtO from 14. *The Rectory, 6 Edge Lane, Manchester M21 9JF* T: 0161-881 3063 E: revemma@hotmail.co.uk

AOKO, Mrs Olushola Ibiwunmi. b 55. SEITE 03. **d** 06 **p** 07. C Bermondsey St Mary w St Olave, St Jo etc *S'wark* 06-10; TV St Laur in Thanet *Cant* from 10. *St Christopher's House, Kimberley Road, Ramsgate CT12 6HH* T: (01843) 594160 M: 07896-337578 E: shol1012@yahoo.co.uk

AOTEAROA, Bishop of. *See* TUREI, The Most Revd William Brown

ap GWILYM, Canon Gwynn. b 50. Univ of Wales (Ban) BA 71 MA 76. Wycliffe Hall Ox BA 84 MA 89 MPhil 00. **d** 84 **p** 85. C Ynyscynhaearn w Penmorfa and Porthmadog *Ban* 84-86; R Penegoes and Darowen w Llanbryn-Mair 86-97; R Mallwyd w Cemais, Llanymawddwy, Darowen etc 97-02; P-in-c Penyfai *Llan* 02-05; P-in-c Cardiff Dewi Sant 05-07; Language Officer Ch in Wales from 07; Metrop Can Llan Cathl from 14. *The Rectory, Llandough Hill, Llandough, Penarth CF64 2NA* T: (029) 2071 0890

ap IORWERTH, Geraint. b 50. Univ of Wales (Cardiff) MPhil 90 Open Univ BA 78. Burgess Hall Lamp 69 Westmr Past Foundn 73 St Mich Coll Llan 73. **d** 74 **p** 75. C Holyhead w Rhoscolyn w Llanfair-yn-Neubwll *Ban* 74-78; R Pennal w Corris and Esgairgeiliog 78-12; rtd 12. *Oak Tree House, Dranllwyn Lane, Machen, Caerphilly CF83 8QS* E: apennal@ouvip.com

ap ROBERT, Rhun Gwynedd. **d** 14 **p** 15. C Aberavon *Llan* from 14. *62 Mariners Point, Port Talbot SA12 6DN* T: (01639) 415651 E: rhunaprobert@parishofaberavon.org.uk

ap SION, Tania. **d** 15. NSM Bro Tysilio *Ban* from 15. *Address temp unknown*

APARANGA, Herbert Okidi. b 59. Kingston Univ BA 97. Cranmer Hall Dur 10. **d** 12 **p** 13. C Blackheath St Jo *S'wark* from 12. *Flat B, 15 St Johns Park, London SE3 7TD* M: 07808-300795 E: aparanga@hotmail.co.uk

APOKIS, Konstantinos Fotios. b 61. Monash Univ BA 82. Ridley Coll Melbourne BTh 87 ACT MTh 96. **d** 88 **p** 88. C Greythorn Australia 88-90; C Port Melbourne 90-91; P-in-c 91-10; Res Asst World Vision 93-95; Chapl Incolink Support Services Unit 96-99; Manager 96-99; Clergy Tr Officer *S'well* 10-12; Dir Educn and Tr CA 12; PtO *Sheff* 12-13; *Roch* from 13; *Cant* from 14. *18 Kings Avenue, Rochester ME1 3DS* M: 07500-795477 T: (01634) 924803 E: kapokis@diocant.org *or* capokis@sky.com

APOKIS, Canon Sally-Ann. b 62. Dip Teaching. Ridley Coll Melbourne BMin 96. **d** 97. Chapl Camberwell Girls's Gr Sch Australia 97-00; Chapl Shelford Gr Sch 01-07; Chapl Melbourne Girls' Gr Morris Hall 08; Chapl Galilee Regional Catholic Sch 09; Asst Dn Port Melbourne H Trin 97-09; Hon C Crosspool *Sheff* 12-13; Chapl Sheff Univ 12-13; Chapl Kent Univ *Cant* from 13; Chapl Cant Ch Ch Univ from 13; Chapl Greenwich Univ *S'wark* from 13; Hon Can Cant Cathl from 13. *18 Kings Avenue, Rochester ME1 3DS* T: (01634) 924803 *or* 883203 M: 07850-763368 E: sally-medwaychaplain@gre.ac.uk

APPELBE, Canon Frederick Charles. b 52. CITC 87. **d** 87 **p** 88. C Waterford w Killea, Drumcannon and Dunhill *C & O* 87-90; C Taney *D & G* 90-92; I Rathmichael from 92; Can Ch Ch Cathl Dublin from 02. *Rathmichael Rectory, Shankill, Co Dublin, Republic of Ireland* T: (00353) (1) 282 2803 F: 258 6080 M: 87-248 2410 E: rathmichael@dublin.anglican.org

APPLEBY, Anthony Robert Nightingale. b 40. K Coll Lon AKC 62. St Boniface Warminster 62. **d** 63 **p** 64. C Cov St Mark 63-67; CF 67-95; R Dulverton and Brushford *B & W* 95-02; rtd 02. *9 Ashleigh Park, Bampton, Tiverton EX16 9LF* T: (01398) 331122

APPLEBY, David. b 60. St Jo Coll Dur BA 04. Cranmer Hall Dur 02. **d** 04 **p** 05. C W Acklam *York* 04-08; R Aylestone

St Andr w St Jas *Leic* 08-14; TV Plymstock and Hooe *Ex* from 14. *5 Cobb Lane, Plymouth PL9 9BQ*
E: applebydave@btinternet.com

APPLEBY, Janet Elizabeth. b 58. Bris Univ BSc 80 MSc 81 Newc Poly BA 90. Cranmer Hall Dur 01. **d** 03 **p** 04. C Newc H Cross 03-06; TV Willington 06-15; Dioc Ecum Officer from 12. *282 Wingrove Road North, Newcastle upon Tyne NE4 9EE* T: 0191-275 0211 E: janeteappleby@yahoo.com

APPLEBY, Ms Jennie. b 58. Southlands Coll Lon CertEd 81. Cranmer Hall Dur 01. **d** 03 **p** 04. C Marton-in-Cleveland *York* 03-05; C Coatham and Dormanstown 05-08; R Emmaus Par Team *Leic* 08-14; TV Plymstock and Hooe *Ex* from 14. *5 Cobb Lane, Plymouth PL9 9BQ*

APPLEBY, Mrs Melanie Jayne. b 65. RGN 86. Ripon Coll Cuddesdon 01. **d** 03 **p** 04. C Reddish *Man* 03-06; TV Wythenshawe from 06. *St Richard's Vicarage, 42 Lomond Road, Manchester M22 5JD* M: 07876-191572 E: melanieappleby@hotmail.com

APPLEFORD, Kenneth Henry. b 30. Portsm Dioc Tr Course 91. **d** 92. NSM Portsea St Mary *Portsm* 92-00; rtd 00. *124 Stride Avenue, Portsmouth PO3 6HN* T: (023) 9281 4685

APPLEFORD, Canon Patrick Robert Norman. b 25. Trin Coll Cam BA 49 MA 54. Chich Th Coll 50. **d** 52 **p** 53. C Poplar All SS w St Frideswide *Lon* 52-58; Chapl Bps' Coll Cheshunt 58-61; Educn Sec USPG 61-66; Dean Lusaka 66-72; P-in-c Sutton St Nicholas w Sutton St Michael *Heref* 73-75; Dir of Educn *Chelmsf* 75-90; Can Chelmsf Cathl 78-90; rtd 90; PtO *Chelmsf* from 90. *35 Sowerberry Close, Chelmsford CM1 4YB* T: (01245) 443508

APPLEGATE, The Ven John. b 56. Bris Univ BSc 78. Trin Coll Bris PhD 85. **d** 84 **p** 85. C Collyhurst *Man* 84-87; Asst Chapl Monsall Hosp 84-87; C Broughton St Jas w St Clem and St Matthias *Man* 87-94; R Broughton St Jo 94-96; TR Broughton 96-02; AD Salford 97-02; Research Fell and Lect Man Univ from 00; Bp's Adv Hosp Chapl 02-08; Adn Bolton 02-08; Dir SNWTP from 08. *University of Chester, Crab Lane, Warrington WA2 0DB* T: (01925) 534373
E: snwtpprincipal@chester.ac.uk

APPLETON, Mrs Bonita. b 55. Man Univ MA 08. St Jo Coll Nottm 91. **d** 93 **p** 94. C Camberley St Paul *Guildf* 93-96; Chapl Elmhurst Ballet Sch 95-96; TV Cove St Jo *Guildf* 96-03; Chapl Farnborough Sixth Form Coll 97-00; Dioc Par Resources Officer *Guildf* 03-10; NSM Knaphill w Brookwood 05-10; TR S Gillingham *Roch* 10-15; RD Gillingham 11-15. *Egerton House, Egerton House Road, Egerton, Ashford TN27 9BD* T: (01233) 756354 E: appletonbonnie@gmail.com

APPLETON, John Bearby. b 42. Linc Th Coll 74. **d** 76 **p** 77. C Selby Abbey *York* 76-79; C Epsom St Barn *Guildf* 79-82; V Linc All SS 82-94; rtd 02. *33 South End, Osmotherley, Northallerton DL6 3BN*

APPLETON, Ruth Elizabeth. *See* WALKER, Ruth Elizabeth

APPLIN, David Edward. b 39. Oak Hill Th Coll 63. **d** 65 **p** 66. C Ox St Clem 65-69; C Felixstowe SS Pet and Paul *St E* 69-71; LtO *Win* 71-91; Travelling Sec Ruanda Miss 71-74; Home Sec 74-77; Gen Sec 77-81; Dir Overseas Personnel Dept TEAR Fund 82-87; Overseas Dir 87-92; Hon C Kempshott *Win* 91-92; R Awbridge w Sherfield English 92-97; Exec Dir Samaritan's Purse Internat from 95. *Flat 4, 25 Christchurch Road, St Cross, Winchester SO23 9SU* T: (01962) 865678

APPS, Bryan Gerald. b 37. Univ of Wales (Lamp) BA 59 St Cath Coll Ox BA 61 MA 65. Wycliffe Hall Ox 59. **d** 61 **p** 62. C Southampton St Alb *Win* 61-65; C Andover w Foxcott 65-69; P-in-c Freemantle 69-72; R 73-78; V Pokesdown All SS 78-03; rtd 03; PtO *Win* from 03. *14 Bartlett Drive, Bournemouth BH7 7JT* T: (01202) 418360 E: bryanapps@talk21.com

APPS, David Ronald. b 34. Univ of Wales (Lamp) BA 57. Sarum Th Coll 57. **d** 59 **p** 60. C Southbourne St Chris *Win* 59-62; C Weeke 62-67; V Alton All SS 67-80; V Charlestown *Truro* 80-97; Miss to Seamen 80-97; rtd 99. *12 Walnut Close, Exminster, Exeter EX6 8SZ* T: (01392) 823672

APPS-HUGGINS, Mrs Lorraine Georgina. b 63. Cant Ch Ch Univ BA 13. Local Minr Tr Course 07. **d** 10 **p** 11. OLM Deal St Geo *Cant* 10-14; NSM Downsfoot 14; V from 14. *The Vicarage, Vicarage Lane, Selling, Faversham ME13 9RD* T: (01227) 752027 E: appshuggins@aol.com

AQUILON-ELMQVIST, Mrs Gunilla. **p** 91. Sweden 91-05; C Wexford w Ardcolm and Killurin *C & O* 05-09; I Norra Asum Sweden from 10. *Kustvägen 54, 294 74 Sölvesborg, Sweden* E: gunilla.aquilon-elmqvist@svenskakyrkan.se

ARANZULLA, John Paul. b 71. G&C Coll Cam BA 94 Oak Hill Th Coll BA 01. K Coll Lon 01. **d** 04 **p** 05. C Muswell Hill St Jas w St Matt *Lon* 04-08; Crosslinks Italy from 08. *via Guibotti 14, 40134 Bologna, Italy*

ARBER, Gerald Kenneth Walter. b 37. Open Univ BA 87. Oak Hill NSM Course 81. **d** 84 **p** 85. NSM Romford St Edw *Chelmsf* 84-95; NSM Cranham from 95; PtO *Cant* from 13. *5 Hill Grove, Romford RM1 4JP* T: (01708) 750070

ARBUTHNOT, Paul Ian. b 81. TCD BA 03 MA 06 MLitt 07. CITC BTh 10. **d** 10 **p** 11. C Glenageary *D & G* 10-12; Chan V St Patr Cathl Dublin 11-12; PV Ch Ch Cathl Dublin 11-12; Prec and Min Can St Alb Abbey *St Alb* from 12. *1 The Deanery, Sumpter Yard, Holywell Hill, St Albans AL1 1BY* T: (01727) 890207 M: 07780-460439 E: paul.arbuthnot@gmail.com

ARCH, Ian Michael. b 75. Univ Coll Dur MSc 97 Peterho Cam BA 02. Westcott Ho Cam 00. **d** 03 **p** 04. C Bromborough *Ches* 03-05; Chapl Ches Univ 05-11; Dean of Chpl 10-11; V Marton, Siddington w Capesthorne, and Eaton etc from 11. *The Vicarage, School Lane, Marton, Macclesfield SK11 9HD* T: (01260) 224447 E: revd.arch@gmail.com

ARCHER, Alan Robert. b 38. AKC 56. Lich Th Coll 65. **d** 68 **p** 69. C Lower Mitton *Worc* 68-71; C Foley Park 71-74; V Warndon 74-79; P-in-c Clifton upon Teme 79-81; P-in-c Lower Sapey 79-81; P-in-c The Shelsleys 79-81; V Malvern Wells and Wyche 81-83; TV Braunstone *Leic* 83-91; P-in-c Bemerton *Sarum* 91-03; Dioc Link Officer for ACUPA 92-94; rtd 03. *15 Summerfield Road, Stourport-on-Severn DY13 9BE* T: (01299) 822983

ARCHER, David John. b 69. Reading Univ BSc 91 PhD 95 Cam Univ BTh 05. Ridley Hall Cam 02. **d** 05 **p** 06. C Abingdon *Ox* 05-09; R Purley from 09. *The Rectory, 1 Westridge Avenue, Purley on Thames, Reading RG8 8DE* T: 0118-326 0839 E: david.archer@stmaryspurley.org.uk

ARCHER, Graham John. b 58. Lanc Univ BSc 79. St Jo Coll Nottm 82. **d** 85 **p** 86. C Ipswich St Matt *St E* 85-89; C Walton 89-95; P-in-c 95-99; Chapl Local Health Partnerships NHS Trust 96-99; P-in-c Portswood Ch Ch *Win* 99-05; V 05-12; P-in-c Portswood St Denys 00-02; Hon Can Win Cathl 11-12; Dir Min CPAS from 12; PtO *Cov* 13-15. *CPAS, Unit 3, Sir William Lyons Road, University of Warwick Science Park, Coventry CV4 7EZ* T: 03001-230780

ARCHER, John Thomas. b 28. GIMechE 68 CQSW 83. EMMTC 79. **d** 80 **p** 81. NSM Derby St Thos 80-86; V Edlington Sheff 87-98; rtd 98; PtO *Lich* 04-10. *Little Croft, 20 Adderley, Cheadle, Stoke-on-Trent ST10 2NJ* T: (01538) 751541

ARCHER, Keith Malcolm. b 40. Man Univ BA 61 MA 80 Magd Coll Cam BA 67 MA 72. Ridley Hall Cam 66. **d** 68 **p** 69. C Newland St Jo *York* 68-72; Hon C Kersal Moor *Man* 72-79; Ind Chapl 72-93; V Weaste 93-09; TV Pendleton 08-09; TV Salford All SS 09-10; rtd 10; PtO *Man* from 11. *Flat 2, 86-88 Wellington Road, Eccles, Manchester M30 9GW* M: 07943-366502 E: keitharcher@hotmail.com

ARCHER, Michael James. b 67. St Jo Coll Dur BA 90 St Edm Coll Cam PhD 95. Ridley Hall Cam 92. **d** 94 **p** 95. C Littleover *Derby* 94-97; C Edgware *Lon* 97-98; TV 98-01; P-in-c Bletchley *Ox* 01-08; R 08-13; P-in-c Portswood Ch Ch *Win* from 13. *Highfield Vicarage, 36 Brookvale Road, Southampton SO17 1QR* E: mikearcher101@sky.com

ARCHER, Michael John. b 37. Trin Coll Bris 76. **d** 78 **p** 79. C Kinson *Sarum* 78-81; C Harpenden St Nic *St Alb* 81-88; P-in-c Rashcliffe and Lockwood *Wakef* 88-00; rtd 00; PtO *Truro* from 02. *Seaview Cottage, Porthallow, Helston TR12 6PW* T: (01326) 280502

ARCHER, Neill Ian. b 61. UEA BA 82. NTMTC 96. **d** 99 **p** 00. C Ripley *Derby* 99-02; C Forster Tuncurry Australia 02-03; PtO *Lon* 03-04; P-in-c Malmesbury w Westport and Brokenborough *Bris* from 04; C St Somerford, Lt Somerford, Seagry, Corston etc from 09; AD N Wilts from 09. *The Vicarage, Holloway, Malmesbury SN16 9BA* T: (01666) 823126 M: 07946-540720 E: neilljarcher@tiscali.co.uk

ARCHER, Sarah Elizabeth. *See* HARTLEY, Sarah Elizabeth

ARCHER, Simon Antony. b 65. Staffs Poly BA 90. Ripon Coll Cuddesdon 10. **d** 12 **p** 13. C Glouc St Paul and St Steph from 12. *29 Seymour Road, Gloucester GL1 5PN* M: 07815-164991 E: tigerssi@talktalk.net

ARCHIBALD, Peter Ben. b 83. Robert Gordon Univ Aber BSc 04. St Steph Ho Ox BTh 08. **d** 08 **p** 09. C Middlesbrough All SS *York* 08-11; Lead Chapl Middlesbrough Coll 09-11; P-in-c Kettering St Mary *Pet* 11-13; CF from 13. *c/o MOD Chaplains (Army)* T: (01264) 383430 F: 381824 M: 07793-535628 E: peter.archibald100@mod.uk *or* frbenarchibald@gmail.com

ARCUS, Jeffrey. b 40. NW Ord Course 72. **d** 75 **p** 76. C Halliwell St Thos *Man* 75-78; C Walmsley 78-81; P-in-c Bury Ch King 81-82; TV Bury Ch King w H Trin 82-93; V Ramsbottom St Jo and St Paul 93-05; C Edenfield and Stubbins 04-05; TV Ramsbottom and Edenfield 05-08; rtd 08; PtO *Man* from 08. *44 Clarendon Gardens, Bromley Cross, Bolton BL7 9GX*

ARDAGH-WALTER, Christopher Richard. b 35. Univ of Wales (Lamp) BA 58. Chich Th Coll 58. **d** 60 **p** 61. C Heavitree *Ex* 60-64; C Redcar *York* 64-67; C King's Worthy *Win* 67-69; C-in-c Four Marks 70-73; V 73-76; P-in-c Eling, Testwood and Marchwood 76-78; TR Totton 76-84; R The Sherbornes w Pamber 84-88; V Froyle and Holybourne 88-95; C Verwood *Sarum* 95-97; rtd 97; PtO *Win* from 98; Ox 01-14; *Birm* from 14. *1 Ashfield Gardens, Ashfield Road, Birmingham B14 7AS* T: 0121-449 9663 E: crawalter@btinternet.com

ARDERN, Geoffrey. b 47. Cliff Coll MA 04. SNWTP 09. **d** 11 **p** 12. NSM Maghull and Melling *Liv* from 11. *22 Waltho Avenue, Liverpool L31 6BE* T: 0151-527 1383 E: ardernhouse@aol.com

ARDILL, Robert William Brian. b 40. QUB BSc 63 PhD 67 SOSc. Ox NSM Course 80 St Jo Coll Nottm 84. **d** 83 **p** 85. NSM Sunninghill *Ox* 83-84; Hon Chapl R Holloway Coll *Lon* 83-84; C Lenton *S'well* 85-87; PtO *Leic* 92-95; C Harpenden St Nic *St Alb* 95-00; R N Tawton, Bondleigh, Sampford Courtenay etc *Ex* 00-10; rtd 10. *8 Hanover Gardens, Cullompton EX15 1XA* T: (01884) 798386 E: brian.ardill@googlemail.com

ARDING, Richard. b 52. ACIB 84. Oak Hill Th Coll 90. **d** 92 **p** 93. C Bromley Common St Aug *Roch* 92-96; V Wilmington from 96; RD Dartford 07-13. *The Vicarage, 1 Curate's Walk, Dartford DA2 7BJ* T: (01322) 220561 M: 07773-104767 E: richard.arding@diocese-rochester.org

ARDIS, Canon Edward George. b 54. Dur Univ BA 76. CITC 76. **d** 78 **p** 79. C Dublin Drumcondra w N Strand and St Barn *D & G* 78-81; C Dublin St Bart w Leeson Park 81-84; I Ardamine w Kiltennel, Glascarrig etc *C & O* 84-89; Can Tuam Cathl 89-03; Dean Killala 89-03; I Killala w Dunfeeny, Crossmolina etc 89-93; I Killala w Dunfeeny, Crossmolina, Kilmoremoy etc 94-03; Dir of Ords 95-03; I Dublin Irishtown w Donnybrook *D & G* 03-13; Dean's V Cork Cathl from 13; Can Ch Ch Cathl Dublin from 08. *9 Dean Street, Cork, Republic of Ireland* T: (00353) (21) 241 6081 M: 87-637 6241 E: tedardis@eircom.net *or* deansvicar@cork.anglican.org *or* tedardis@yahoo.ie

ARDIS, John Kevin. **d** 06 **p** 07. C Dublin Ch Ch Cathl Gp 06-08; Dean's V Crick St Fin Barre's Union *C, C & R* 08-11; Chapl Univ Coll Cork 11-13; I Abbeystrewry Union from 13; Bp's Dom Chapl from 14. *The Rectory, Coronea Drive, Skibbereen, Co Cork, Republic of Ireland* T: (00353) (28) 21234 M: 87-680 7289 E: john_ardis@yahoo.com

ARDLEY, Annette Susan. *See* ROSE, Annette Susan

ARDOUIN, Timothy David Peter. Univ of Wales (Lamp) BA 94 Univ of Wales (Cardiff) MTh 08. St Mich Coll Llan. **d** 08 **p** 09. C Gorseinon *S & B* 08-11; P-in-c Llanrhidian w Llanyrnewydd from 11. *The Vicarage, Llanrhidian, Swansea SA3 1EH* T: (01792) 391353 M: 07871-420089 E: frtimardouin@btinternet.com

ARENS, Canon Johannes. b 69. Heythrop Coll Lon MTh 97. **d** 96 **p** 97. Old Catholic Ch Germany 96-04; TV Harrogate St Wilfrid *Ripon* 04-06; V Manston 06-11; Can Res Leic Cathl from 11. *The Precentor's House, 23 St Martins, Leicester LE1 5DE* T: 0116-261 5364 E: johannes.arens@leccofe.org

ARGENTINA, Bishop of. *See* VENABLES, Gregory James

ARGLES, Mrs Christine. b 57. Bris Univ BA 00. Trin Coll Bris 00. **d** 02 **p** 03. C Nailsea Ch Ch w Tickenham *B & W* 02-05; Chapl Weston Area Health NHS Trust 05-07; Chapl Cardiff and Vale NHS Trust from 07. *Cardiff and Vale NHS Trust, Cardigan House, Heath Park, Cardiff CF14 4XW* T: (029) 2074 7747 M: 07763-476127 E: chrisargles@aol.com

ARGUILE, Canon Roger Henry William. b 43. Dur Univ LLB 64 Keble Coll Ox BA 70 MA 75. St Steph Ho Ox 69 Ripon Hall Ox 70. **d** 71 **p** 72. C Walsall *Lich* 71-76; TV Blakenall Heath 76-83; TV Stafford 83-95; P-in-c St Neots *Ely* 95-97; V 97-07; Hon Can Ely Cathl 01-07; RD St Neots 02-07; rtd 07; PtO *Nor* from 07. *10 Marsh Lane, Wells-next-the-Sea NR23 1EG* T: (01328) 711788 E: arguile@btinternet.com

ARGYLE, Edward Charles. b 55. Edith Cowan Univ (Aus) BSocSc 99. St Barn Coll Adelaide 77. **d** 80 **p** 80. C Whitford Australia 80-82; C Gt Yarmouth *Nor* 83-85; I Kilcooley w Littleon, Crohane and Fertagh *C & O* 85-94; Can Ossory and Leighlin Cathls 90-94; USA 92; Min Cranbrook w Mt Barker Australia 95-05; R Albany 02-05; P-in-c Jerramungup 05-07; P-in-c Williams 07-11; P-in-c Albany from 11. *PO Box 5520, Albany WA 6332, Australia* T: (0061) (8) 9841 3360 M: 428-514119 E: edwardandjudy@bigpond.com

ARGYLL AND THE ISLES, Bishop of. *See* PEARSON, The Rt Revd Kevin

ARGYLL AND THE ISLES, Dean of. *See* SWIFT, The Very Revd Andrew Christopher

ARKELL, Kevin Paul. b 53. Preston Poly BTh 86 Leeds Univ MA 95. Sarum & Wells Th Coll 84. **d** 86 **p** 87. C S Petherton w The Seavingtons *B & W* 86-88; P-in-c Gt Harwood St Bart *Blackb* 88-90; V 90-95; TR Darwen St Pet w Hoddlesden 95-03; Acting RD Darwen 97-98; AD Blackb and Darwen 98-03; P-in-c Pokesdown All SS *Win* 03-11; P-in-c Bournemouth St Clem 08-11; V Newport St Thos *Portsm* from 11; V Newport St Jo from 11. *The Vicarage, 72A Medina Avenue, Newport PO30 1HF* T: (01983) 539580 M: 07971-800083 E: kevin@thearkells.co.uk

ARLIDGE, Lucille Monica. b 56. WMMTC 04. **d** 07 **p** 08. NSM Birchfield *Birm* 07-11; PtO *Lich* 11-14; P-in-c Smethwick St Matt w St Chad *Birm* from 14. *23 Willow Road, Great Barr, Birmingham B43 6LB* T: 0121-358 3321 E: lucyarlidge@yahoo.com

ARMAGH, Archbishop of. *See* CLARKE, The Most Revd Richard Lionel

ARMAGH, Archdeacon of. *See* SCOTT, The Ven Terence

ARMAGH, Dean of. *See* DUNSTAN, The Very Revd Gregory John Orchard

ARMAN, Canon Brian Robert. b 54. St Jo Coll Dur BA 77. Cranmer Hall Dur 74. **d** 78 **p** 79. C Lawrence Weston *Bris* 78-82; C Bishopston 82-88; R Filton 88-15; P-in-c Horfield St Greg 03-05; Hon Can Bris Cathl 01-15; rtd 15. *59 Kenmore Crescent, Bristol BS7 0TP*

✠**ARMES, The Rt Revd John Andrew.** b 55. SS Coll Cam BA 77 MA 81 Man Univ PhD 96. Sarum & Wells Th Coll 77. **d** 79 **p** 80 **c** 12. C Walney Is *Carl* 79-82; Chapl to Agric 82-86; TV Greystoke, Matterdale and Mungrisdale 82-86; TV Watermillock 82-86; TV Man Whitworth 86-88; TR 88-94; Chapl Man Univ 86-94; P-in-c Goodshaw and Crawshawbooth 94-98; AD Rossendale 94-98; R Edin St Jo 98-12; Dean Edin 10-12; Bp Edin from 12. *Bishop's Office, 21A Grosvenor Crescent, Edinburgh EH12 5EL* T: 0131-538 7044 E: bishop@edinburgh.anglican.org

ARMITAGE, Richard Norris. b 51. Birm Univ PhD 10 AKC. St Aug Coll Cant 73. **d** 74 **p** 75. C Chapelthorpe *Wakef* 74-77; C W Bromwich All SS *Lich* 77-82; P-in-c Ketley 82-83; V Oakengates 82-83; V Ketley and Oakengates 83-89; V Evesham *Worc* 89-96; V Evesham w Norton and Lenchwick 96-05; RD Evesham 00-05; Chapl Wilts Constabulary *Bris* from 05. *The Rectory, Churchway, Blunsdon, Swindon SN26 7DG* T: (01793) 729592 E: richard.armitage@wiltshire.pnn.police.uk

ARMITAGE, Susan. b 46. Th Ext Educn Coll 91. **d** 92 **p** 95. Pretoria Corpus Christi S Africa 92-97; C Fawley *Win* 97-00; C Chandler's Ford 00-04; TV Wylye and Till Valley *Sarum* 04-11; rtd 11. *36 St Margaret's Mead, Marlborough SN8 4BA* T: (01672) 513678 E: suearmitage@savernake.com

ARMITSTEAD, Margaretha Catharina Maria. b 65. Free Univ of Amsterdam MA 89. SAOMC 00. **d** 03 **p** 04. C Littlemore *Ox* 03-06; P-in-c from 06. *The Vicarage, St Nicholas Road, Littlemore, Oxford OX4 4PP* T: (01865) 748003 *or* 779885 E: margreetarmitstead@btinternet.com

ARMITT, Andy John. b 68. Moorlands Bible Coll 88 Trin Coll Bris BA 00. **d** 00 **p** 01. C Millhouses H Trin *Sheff* 00-03; R Bisley and W End *Guildf* from 03. *The Rectory, Clews Lane, Bisley, Woking GU24 9DY* T/F: (01483) 473377 M: 07811-909782 E: office@bweparish.org

ARMSON, Canon John Moss. b 39. Selw Coll Cam BA 61 MA 64 St Andr Univ PhD 65. Coll of Resurr Mirfield 64. **d** 66 **p** 67. C Notting Hill St Jo *Lon* 66-69; Chapl and Fell Down Coll Cam 69-73; Chapl Westcott Ho Cam 73-76; Vice-Prin 76-82; Prin Edin Th Coll 82-89; Can St Mary's Cathl 82-89; Can Res Roch Cathl 89-01; rtd 01; Member Hengrave Ecum Community 01-03; PtO *Heref* 03-14; *Leic* from 14. *4 Stuart Court, High Street, Kibworth, Leicester LE8 0LR* E: j.armson@virgin.net

ARMSTEAD, Paul Richard. b 63. Ox Poly BA 85 ACA 89 FCA 99. St Steph Ho Ox BTh 11. **d** 08 **p** 09. C Northampton St Matt *Pet* 08-12; P-in-c Milton *Portsm* from 12; C Southsea H Spirit from 12. *St James's Vicarage, 287 Milton Road, Southsea PO4 8PG* T: (023) 9273 2786 E: paularmstead@btinternet.com

ARMSTRONG, Adrian Christopher. b 48. LSE BSc 70 K Coll Lon PhD 80. EAMTC 84. **d** 87 **p** 88. NSM Linton *Ely* 87-95; P-in-c N and S Muskham *S'well* 95-00; P-in-c Averham w Kelham 95-00; PtO *B & W* 01-02; Hon C Wiveliscombe w Chipstable, Huish Champflower etc 02-06; Hon C Lydeard St Lawrence w Brompton Ralph etc 06-09; rtd 10. *Cridlands Barn, Brompton Ralph, Taunton TA4 2RU* T: (01984) 632191 E: drmudpie@btinternet.com

ARMSTRONG, Alexander Milford. b 57. Local MinI Tr Course. **d** 95 **p** 95. NSM Livingston LEP *Edin* 95-97; C Cleator Moor w Cleator *Carl* 97-98; C Frizington and Arledcon 97-98; C Crosslacon 98-99; V Westfield St Mary 99-10; P-in-c Aldingham, Dendron, Rampside and Urswick from 10. *The Vicarage, Church Road, Great Urswick, Ulverston LA12 0TA* T: (01229) 581383 E: amvarmstrong@hotmail.com

ARMSTRONG, The Very Revd Christopher John. b 47. Nottm Univ BTh 75. Kelham Th Coll 72. **d** 75 **p** 76. C Maidstone All SS w St Phil and H Trin *Cant* 76-79; Chapl St Hild and St Bede Coll *Dur* 79-84; Abp's Dom Chapl and Dir of Ords *York* 85-91; V Scarborough St Martin 91-01; Dean Blackb from 01. *The Deanery, Preston New Road, Blackburn BB2 6PS* T: (01254) 52502 *or* 51491 F: 689666 E: dean@blackburncathedral.co.uk

ARMSTRONG, Christopher John Richard. b 35. Fribourg Univ LTh 60 Ch Coll Cam BA 64 MA 68 PhD 79. Edin Th Coll 74.

d 59 **p** 59. In RC Ch 59-71; Lect Aber Univ *Ab* 68-74; C Ledbury *Heref* 74-76; P-in-c Bredenbury and Wacton w Grendon Bishop 76-79; P-in-c Edwyn Ralph and Collington w Thornbury 76-79; P-in-c Pencombe w Marston Stannett and Lt Cowarne 76-79; R Cherry Burton *York* 79-80; Tutor Westcott Ho Cam 80-85; V Bottisham *Ely* 85-89; P-in-c Lode and Longmeadow 85-89; P-in-c Cropthorne w Charlton *Worc* 89-93; Dioc Local Min Sec 89-93; R Aberdaron w Rhiw and Llanfaelrhys etc *Ban* 93-99; rtd 99; PtO *Heref* 99-06; *Ban* 99-06; *Leeds* from 06. *52 Bradford Road, Burley in Wharfedale, Ilkley LS29 7PU* T: (01943) 864761

ARMSTRONG, David Thomas. b 62. St Mellitus Coll BA 14. **d** 14 **p** 15. C Lexden *Chelmsf* from 14. *2 Garden Drive, Colchester CO3 9GS* T: (01206) 710414
E: david@davidtarmstrong.com

ARMSTRONG, Eileen. **d** 95 **p** 96. NSM *M & K* from 95. *Hennigan, Nobber, Co Meath, Republic of Ireland* T: (00353) (46) 905 2314

ARMSTRONG, Fiona Heather. See HAWORTH, Fiona Heather

ARMSTRONG, John Edwin. b 51. Leic Univ CertEd 73 BEd 74. Ridley Hall Cam 91. **d** 93 **p** 94. C Gt Wilbraham *Ely* 93-96; P-in-c Bassingbourn 96-02; V 02-04; P-in-c Whaddon 96-02; V 02-04; P-in-c Southam *Cov* from 04; P-in-c Ufton from 04; RD Southam 08-11. *The Rectory, Park Lane, Southam, Leamington Spa CV47 0JA* T: (01926) 812413
E: revarmstrong@yahoo.com

ARMSTRONG, John Gordon. b 64. Man Poly BSc 86 MSc 91 Man Univ MA 03. Wycliffe Hall Ox 95. **d** 97 **p** 98. C Pennington *Man* 97-01; P-in-c Holcombe and Hawkshaw Lane 01-07; TV Deane from 07. *St Andrew's Vicarage, Crescent Avenue, Over Hulton, Bolton BL5 1EN* T: (01204) 651851
E: armstrongfamily@ntlworld.com

ARMSTRONG, Mrs Margaret Betty. b 48. SRN 70 RSCN 71. Westcott Ho Cam 89. **d** 92 **p** 94. NSM Linton *Ely* 92-95; NSM Shudy Camps 92-95; NSM Castle Camps 92-95; NSM Bartlow 92-95; NSM N and S Muskham and Averham w Kelham *S'well* 95-00; P-in-c Lydeard St Lawrence w Brompton Ralph etc *B & W* 01-09; rtd 10. *Cridlands Barn, Brompton Ralph, Taunton TA4 2RU* T: (01984) 623191
E: mpidge@btinternet.com

ARMSTRONG, Canon Maurice Alexander. b 62. Ulster Poly BA 84. CITC 84. **d** 87 **p** 88. C Portadown St Mark *Arm* 87-90; I Sixmilecross w Termonmaguirke 90-95; I Richhill 95-01; I Tempo and Clabby *Clogh* from 01; Can Clogh Cathl from 12. *St Margaret's Rectory, 177 Clabby Road, Clabby, Fivemiletown BT75 0RD* T: (028) 8952 1697
E: jeanarmstrong@yahoo.co.uk

ARMSTRONG, Preb Nicholas Paul. b 58. Bris Univ BSc 79. Trin Coll Bris 91. **d** 93 **p** 94. C Filey *York* 93-97; P-in-c Alveley and Quatt *Heref* 97-98; R from 98; RD Bridgnorth 13-15; Preb Heref Cathl from 12. *The Rectory, Alveley, Bridgnorth WV15 6ND* T/F: (01746) 780326 E: nicka@inbox.com

ARMSTRONG, Rosemary. See WYNN, Rosemary

ARMSTRONG, Samuel David. b 48. BD MTh. **d** 86 **p** 87. C Cambridge H Trin w St Andr Gt *Ely* 86-89; V Cambridge St Martin 89-00; I Carrigaline Union *C, C & R* 00-11; rtd 11; PtO *Ely* from 12. *11 Castlerocklands, Carrickfergus BT38 8FY*

ARMSTRONG, Samuel George. b 39. Ox Univ Inst of Educn TCert 65 Open Univ BA 72 Reading Univ MSc 89. S Dios Minl Tr Scheme 90. **d** 93 **p** 94. NSM N Tadley St Mary *Win* 93-08; PtO from 08. *The Cedars, Blakes Lane, Tadley, Basingstoke RG26 3PU* T: 0118-981 6593
E: sammie@armstrongsg.freeserve.co.uk

ARMSTRONG, Mrs Susan Elizabeth. b 45. **d** 05 **p** 06. OLM Tilstock, Edstaston and Whixall *Lich* 05-09; OLM Edstaston, Fauls, Prees, Tilstock and Whixall from 09; OLM Whitchurch from 13. *Tarragon Cottage, Shrewsbury Street, Prees, Whitchurch SY13 2DH* T: (01948) 840039
E: s.armstrong01@btinternet.com

ARMSTRONG, Mrs Valri. b 50. Man Univ BA 73. **d** 04 **p** 05. OLM Stoke by Nayland w Leavenheath and Polstead *St E* 04-13; NSM from 13. *Orchid House, 38 Bramble Way, Leavenheath, Colchester CO6 4UN* T: (01206) 262814
E: mrsvarmstrong@hotmail.co.uk

ARMSTRONG, William. b 29. Sarum Th Coll 52. **d** 54 **p** 55. C Hebburn St Cuth *Dur* 54-55; C Ferryhill 55-57; C Gateshead H Trin 57-60; V Cassop cum Quarrington 60-66; Australia 66-81; Asst Dir of Educn *Liv* 81-90; V Aintree St Pet 81-88; TV Speke St Aid 88-90; rtd 90. *3 Downing Court, Grenville Street, London WC1N 1LX* T: (020) 7713 7847

ARMSTRONG-MacDONNELL, Mrs Vivienne Christine. b 42. Open Univ BA 89 Ex Univ MEd 01 Lambeth MA 05. Ripon Coll Cuddesdon 88. **d** 90 **p** 94. C Crediton and Shobrooke *Ex* 90-93; Dioc Adv in Adult Tr 93-00; rtd 00; PtO *Ex* 00-07; Bp's Adv for Spirituality 07-09. *Strand House, Woodbury, Exeter EX5 1LZ* T/F: (01395) 232790
E: spiritualityadviser@exeter.anglican.org

ARNALL-CULLIFORD, Jane Margaret. See CULLIFORD, Jane Margaret

ARNESEN, Christopher Paul. b 48. Lon Univ BA 70. Sarum & Wells Th Coll 78. **d** 80 **p** 81. C Dalton-in-Furness *Carl* 80-83; C Ranmoor *Sheff* 83-86; R Distington *Carl* 86-93; TV Sheff Manor 93-97; Mental Health Chapl Sheff Care Trust 98-04; PtO *Sheff* from 04; Bp's Adv in Past Care and Counselling 08-13; rtd 13. *39 Greystones Crescent, Sheffield S11 7JN* T: 0114-266 8836 E: paul.arnesen@arnies.org.uk

ARNESEN, Raymond Halfdan (Brother Ælred). b 25. Qu Coll Cam BA 49 MA 54. Linc Th Coll 50. **d** 52 **p** 53. C Newc St Fran 52-55; SSF 55-66; Cistercian Monk from 66; Ewell Monastery 66-04; rtd 95. *2 Brentmead Close, London W7 3EW* T: (020) 8579 2074

ARNOLD, Adrian Paul. b 69. St Steph Ho Ox. **d** 01 **p** 02. C Staincliffe and Carlinghow *Wakef* 01-04; V New Cantley *Sheff* 04-08; C Hesketh w Becconsall *Blackb* 09-12; V Middleton Junction *Man* 12-15; TV Staveley and Barrow Hill *Derby* from 15. *St Francis's Vicarage, 30 Cedar Street, Hollingwood, Chesterfield S43 2LE* M: 07951-873597
E: frarnold@btinternet.com

ARNOLD, Miss Briony Alice (Bee). b 79. Univ of E Lon BA 01. BA 14. **d** 14 **p** 15. C Cov St Fran N Radford from 14. *21 Tulliver Street, Coventry CV6 3BY* T: (024) 7659 1448 M: 07872-326008 E: bee.arnold@gmail.com

ARNOLD, Christine Sabina. b 60. **d** 12 **p** 13. NSM Broadstairs *Cant* from 12. *6 East Northdown Close, Margate CT9 3YA* T: (01843) 224449 E: chris.arnold06@btinternet.com

ARNOLD, David Alun. b 78. St Andr Univ MTheol 00. Coll of Resurr Mirfield 01. **d** 03 **p** 04. C Ribbleton *Blackb* 03-05; C Hawes Side and Marton Moss 05-07; Bp's Dom Chapl 07-12; V Adlington from 12; Asst Dir of Ords from 06. *St Paul's Vicarage, Railway Road, Adlington, Chorley PR6 9QZ* T: (01257) 480253 M: 07786-168261

ARNOLD, Derek John. b 59. Wycliffe Hall Ox 01. **d** 03 **p** 04. C St Jo in Bedwardine *Worc* 03-06; TV Kidderminster St Jo and H Innocents 06-09; TR 09-14; P-in-c Ombersley w Doverdale from 14; P-in-c Elmley Lovett w Hampton Lovett and Elmbridge etc from 14; P-in-c Hartlebury from 14. *The Rectory, Main Road, Ombersley, Droitwich WR9 0EW* M: 07789-631346
E: rector.kwtm@virginmedia.com

ARNOLD, Elisabeth Anne Truyens. b 44. TCert 66. **d** 91 **p** 94. OLM Ipswich St Thos *St E* 91-00; Chapl Dioc Min Course 00-01; OLM Tutor 01-06; rtd 06; PtO *St E* from 06. *66 Bromeswell Road, Ipswich IP4 3AT* T: (01473) 257406

ARNOLD, Ernest Stephen. b 27. **d** 64 **p** 65. C Aberavon *Llan* 64-68; V Ferndale 68-74; Cyprus 81-85; rtd 94; PtO *Portsm* from 94. *Barn Cottage, Apse Manor Road, Shanklin PO37 7PN* T: (01983) 866324

ARNOLD, Frances Mary. b 64. R Holloway Coll Lon BA 86 Anglia Ruskin Univ MA 07 Dur Univ PGCE 90. Westcott Ho Cam 01. **d** 04 **p** 05. C Biggleswade *St Alb* 04-07; Exec Officer Abps' Coun 07-13; PtO *Lon* 08-13; V Sawbridgeworth *St Alb* from 13. *The Vicarage, Sheering Mill Lane, Sawbridgeworth CM21 9ND* T: (01279) 722073
E: francesmarnold@btinternet.com

ARNOLD, Geoff. See ARNOLD, Michael John

ARNOLD, Jane Elizabeth. b 50. **d** 11. NSM Kingswinford St Mary *Worc* from 11. *59 Buckingham Grove, Kingswinford DY6 9BT* E: jane.arnold128@btinternet.com

ARNOLD, Mrs Janet Rachel. b 64. **d** 14 **p** 15. C Woodchurch from 14. *Charis, 17 Thurstaston Road, Irby, Wirral CH61 0HA* T: 0151-648 7768

ARNOLD, Jennifer Anne. b 54. Univ Coll Lon BSc 75 MB, BS 78 FRCR 85. Qu Coll Birm 00. **d** 02 **p** 03. C Aston SS Pet and Paul *Birm* 02-08; C Aston St Jas and Nechells 05-08; C Aston and Nechells 08-12; R The Quinton from 12. *The Rectory, 773 Hagley Road West, Quinton, Birmingham B32 1AJ* T: 0121-422 2031 M: 07754-449266
E: arnolds68@btopenworld.com

ARNOLD, The Very Revd John Robert. b 33. OBE 02. SS Coll Cam BA 57 MA 61 Lambeth DD 99. Westcott Ho Cam 58. **d** 60 **p** 61. C Millhouses H Trin *Sheff* 60-63; Chapl and Lect Southn Univ 63-72; Gen Sec Gen Syn Bd for Miss and Unity 72-78; Hon Can Win Cathl 74-78; Dean Roch 78-89; Dean Dur 89-02; rtd 03; PtO *Cant* from 02. *26 Hawks Lane, Canterbury CT1 2NU* T: (01227) 764703

ARNOLD, Jonathan Allen. b 69. St Pet Coll Ox BA 92 MA 99 K Coll Lon PhD 04 LTCL 89 LRAM 94. Ripon Coll Cuddesdon 03. **d** 05 **p** 06. NSM Chalgrove w Berrick Salome *Ox* 05-08; Chapl Worc Coll Ox from 08. *Worcester College, Oxford OX1 2HB or Garsington Rectory, 17 Southend, Garsington, Oxford OX44 9DH* T: (01865) 278371 M: 07939-093085
E: jonathan.arnold@worc.ox.ac.uk

✠**ARNOLD, The Rt Revd Keith Appleby.** b 26. Trin Coll Cam BA 50 MA 55. Westcott Ho Cam 50. **d** 52 **p** 53 **c** 80. C

Haltwhistle *Newc* 52-55; C Edin St Jo 55-61; R 61-69; CF (TA) 58-62; V Kirkby Lonsdale w Mansergh *Carl* 69-73; RD Berkhamsted *St Alb* 73-80; TR Hemel Hempstead 73-80; Suff Bp Warw *Cov* 80-90; Hon Can Cov Cathl 80-90; rtd 90; Hon Asst Bp Ox from 97. *9 Dinglederry, Olney MK46 5ES* T: (01234) 713044

ARNOLD, Michael John (Geoff). b 44. Rhodes Univ BA 68 St Edm Hall Ox BA 72 MA 77. St Jo Coll Nottm 93. **d** 98 **p** 98. Chapl Clayesmore Sch Blandford 98-01; Chapl St Jo Coll Johannesburg S Africa 01-09; rtd 09. *26 Gerard Street, Observatory, 2198 South Africa* T: (0027) (11) 648 9932 M: 72-372 3080 E: arnoldmj@hotmail.com

ARNOLD, Monica. b 64. **d** 11 **p** 12. NSM Bloxwich *Lich* 11-15; C Walsall St Matt from 15. *21 Tudor Close, Burntwood WS7 0BW* T: (01543) 305199 E: revd.monica@mail.com

ARNOLD, Mrs Norma. b 48. SNWTP 09. **d** 11 **p** 12. NSM Grassendale *Liv* from 11. *28 Ambergate Road, Liverpool L19 9AU* T: 0151-427 2320 E: norma.arnold@tesco.net

ARNOLD, Norman. *See* ARNOLD, Victor Norman

ARNOLD, Philip Robert. b 75. Qld Univ of Tech BN 96. St Jo Coll Nottm 07. **d** 09 **p** 10. C Pudsey St Lawr and St Paul *Bradf* 09-13; C Farsley 09-13; V Calverley *Leeds* from 13. *The Vicarage, Town Gate, Calverley, Pudsey LS28 5NF* T: (01132) 577968 M: 07758-266922 E: phil@psarnold.plus.com

ARNOLD, Canon Roy. b 36. St D Coll Lamp BA 62. **d** 63 **p** 64. C Brislington St Luke *Bris* 63-66; C Ches St Mary 67-70; V Brinnington w Portwood 71-75; V Sale St Paul 75-82; R Dodleston 82-84; V Sheff St Oswald 84-90; Dioc Communications Officer 84-97; Chapl w the Deaf 90-97; Hon Can Sheff Cathl 95-97; rtd 97; PtO *Ches* from 97. *49 Crossfield Road, Bollington, Macclesfield SK10 5EA* T: (01625) 575472

ARNOLD, Ms Sonja Marie. b 63. Wycliffe Hall Ox BTh 98. **d** 98 **p** 99. Assoc V Hammersmith St Simon *Lon* 98-06; Dean of Women's Min Kensington Area 02-06; Network Miss P *Bris* 07-12; Tutor Trin Coll Bris 09-12; C E Twickenham St Steph *Lon* from 12. *308 Richmond Road, Twickenham TW1 2PD* M: 07809-636419 T: (020) 8892 5258 E: sonjaarnold@yahoo.com

ARNOLD, Victor Norman. b 45. Oak Hill Th Coll 91. **d** 94 **p** 95. NSM Chigwell and Chigwell Row *Chelmsf* 94-98; C W Ham 98-04; C Hornchurch St Andr 04-10; rtd 10; PtO *Chelmsf* from 10. *Spring Cottage, 6 Spring Grove, Loughton IG10 4QA* T: (020) 8508 6572 E: stanrews@me.com

ARNOTT, Preb David. b 44. Em Coll Cam BA 66. Qu Coll Birm 68. **d** 69 **p** 70. C Charlton St Luke w St Paul *S'wark* 69-73; C S Beddington St Mich 73-78; Chapl Liv Poly 78-82; V Bridgwater St Fran *B & W* 86-02; Preb Wells Cathl 00-02; V Yealmpton and Brixton *Ex* 02-09; P-in-c 09-11; RD Ivybridge 03-11; rtd 09. *14 Woodlands Avenue, Exmouth EX8 4QP* E: revdavid.arnott@virgin.net

ARORA, Arun. b 71. Birm Univ LLB 93 St Jo Coll Dur BA 06 Solicitor 96. Cranmer Hall Dur 04. **d** 07 **p** 08. C Harrogate St Mark *Ripon* 07-10; Abp's Dir of Communications *York* 06-09; Pioneer Min Wolv City Cen *Lich* 10-12; Dir Communications Abps' Coun from 12; Public Preacher *St Alb* from 13. *Church House, Great Smith Street, London SW1P 3AZ* T: (020) 7898 1462 E: arun.arora@churchofengland.org *or* arunarora1@yahoo.co.uk

ARRAND, The Ven Geoffrey William. b 44. K Coll Lon BD 66 AKC 66. **d** 67 **p** 68. C Washington *Dur* 67-70; C S Ormsby w Ketsby, Calceby and Driby *Linc* 70-73; TV Gt Grimsby St Mary and St Jas 73-79; TR Halesworth w Linstead and Chediston *St E* 79-80; TR Halesworth w Linstead, Chediston, Holton etc 80-85; R Hadleigh w Layham and Shelley 85-94; Dean Bocking 85-94; RD Hadleigh 86-94; Adn Suffolk 94-09; Hon Can St E Cathl 91-09; rtd 09; PtO *St E* from 09. *8 Elm Close, Saxilby, Lincoln LN1 2QH* T: (01522) 826967

ARTHUR, Graeme Richard. b 52. Univ of NSW BCom 78 Heythrop Coll Lon MA 09. Linc Th Coll 93. **d** 93 **p** 94. C Witney *Ox* 93-97; R Westcote Barton w Steeple Barton, Duns Tew and Sandford St Martin and Over w Nether Worton from 97. *The Rectory, 29 Enstone Road, Westcote Barton, Chipping Norton OX7 7AA* T: (01869) 340510 E: graeme@arfa.clara.net

ARTHUR, Canon Ian Willoughby. b 40. Lon Univ BA 63 BA 66 PGCE 64 Lambeth STh 94 Kent Univ MA 98. Ripon Coll Cuddesdon 78. **d** 80 **p** 81. C Kempston Transfiguration *St Alb* 80-83; R Potton w Sutton and Cockayne Hatley 83-96; P-in-c Sharnbrook and Knotting w Souldrop 96-98; R 98-04; RD Sharnbrook 97-04; Hon Can St Alb 99-04; rtd 04; PtO *St Alb* from 04; *Ox* from 05; *Cov* from 09. *35 London Road, Chipping Norton OX7 5AX* T: (01608) 646839 E: iwarthur@btinternet.com

ARTHUR, Canon Kenneth Paul. b 64. Univ of Wales (Cardiff) BScEcon 86 Roehampton Inst PGCE 87 Cardiff Univ LLM 08. St Steph Ho Ox BTh 05. **d** 00 **p** 01. C Bodmin w Lanhydrock

and Lanivet *Truro* 00-02; P-in-c Treverbyn and Boscoppa 02-06; P-in-c St Dennis from 06; RD St Austell 05-10; Warden of Readers 05-10; Deputy Warden of Readers from 10; Dir Minl Formation and Development from 06; Hon Can Truro Cathl from 13. *The Rectory, 16 Trelavour Road, St Dennis, St Austell PL26 8AH* T: (01726) 822317

ARTHY, Canon Nicola Mary. b 64. St Jo Coll Ox BA 85 MA 93. SEITE. **d** 00 **p** 01. C Guildf H Trin w St Mary 00-01; C Farncombe 01-04; P-in-c Toddington, Stanton, Didbrook w Hailes etc *Glouc* 04-05; TV Winchcombe 05-09; AD Tewkesbury and Winchcombe 07-09; P-in-c Glouc St Mary de Lode and St Mary de Crypt etc 09-10; R Glouc City and Hempsted from 10; Can Res Glouc Cathl from 09. *The Rectory, Rectory Lane, Hempsted, Gloucester GL2 5LW* T: (01452) 523808 M: 07944-721835 E: nikkiarthy@btinternet.com

ARTLEY, Clive Mansell. b 30. St Jo Coll Dur BA 56 Leeds Univ MA(Theol) 01. Cranmer Hall Dur. **d** 58 **p** 59. C Eston *York* 58-61; R Burythorpe w E Acklam and Leavening 61-64; CF 64-73; Teacher 73-93; PtO *York* from 73; rtd 93. *56 High Street, Castleton, Whitby YO21 2DA* T: (01287) 660470

ARTLEY, Miss Pamela Jean. b 47. Worc Coll of Educn CertEd 68 Hull Univ MEd 91 ALCM 73. NEOC 99. **d** 02 **p** 03. NSM Bridlington Priory *York* 02-05; P-in-c Nafferton w Wansford 05-14; rtd 14. *11 Bempton Drive, Bridlington YO16 7HG* E: revdjeanartley@btinternet.com

ARTUS, Stephen James. b 60. Man Poly BA 82 W Midl Coll of Educn PGCE 84. St Jo Coll Nottm MA 95. **d** 95 **p** 96. C Altrincham St Geo *Ches* 95-99; P-in-c Norton 99-05; V 05-07; C Wybunbury and Audlem w Doddington 10-12; PtO from 12. *Address withheld by request*

ARUNDEL, Canon Michael. b 36. Qu Coll Ox BA 60 MA 64. Linc Th Coll 60. **d** 62 **p** 63. C Hollinwood *Man* 62-65; C Leesfield 65-69; R Newton Heath All SS 69-80; RD N Man 75-80; P-in-c Eccles St Mary 80-81; TR Eccles 81-91; R Man St Ann 91-01; Hon Can Man Cathl 82-01; rtd 01; PtO *Man* from 01. *20 Kiln Brow, Bromley Cross, Bolton BL7 9NR* T: (01204) 591156

ARVIDSSON, Canon Carl Fredrik. b 66. Regents Th Coll 88 Chich Th Coll 92. **d** 92 **p** 93. C Southsea H Spirit *Portsm* 92-94; C Botley, Curdridge and Durley 94-96; P-in-c Ringwould w Kingsdown *Cant* 96-97; R 97-01; Sen Chapl K Sch Cant from 01; Hon Min Can Cant Cathl from 01; Hon C Deal St Andr 13-15; Hon Can Antsiranana from 13. *1 The Mint Yard, The Precincts, Canterbury CT1 2EZ* T: (01227) 595631 *or* 595613 E: cfa@kings-school.co.uk

ASBRIDGE, Preb John Hawell. b 26. Dur Univ BA 47. Bps' Coll Cheshunt 47. **d** 49 **p** 50. C Barrow St Geo *Carl* 49-52; C Fort William *Arg* 52-54; C Lon Docks St Pet w Wapping St Jo 54-55; C Kilburn St Aug 55-59; V Northolt Park St Barn 59-66; V Shepherd's Bush St Steph w St Thos 66-96; Preb St Paul's Cathl 89-96; rtd 96; PtO *B & W* from 05. *Crystal Glen, The Old Mineral Line, Roadwater, Watchet TA23 0RL* T: (01984) 640211

ASBRIDGE, Nigel Henry. b 58. Bris Univ BA 80. Chich Th Coll 87. **d** 89 **p** 90. C Tottenham St Paul *Lon* 89; C W Hampstead St Jas 89-94; P-in-c Hornsey H Innocents 94-04; P-in-c Stroud Green H Trin 02-04; Nat Chapl-Missr Children's Soc 04-09; NSM Edmonton St Alphege and Ponders End St Matt *Lon* 06-10; P-in-c Edmonton St Mary w St Jo 10-13; V from 13; P-in-c Gt Cambridge Road St Jo and St Jas from 13. *St John's Vicarage, Dysons Road, London N18 2DS* T: (020) 8807 2767 M: 07905-499323 E: nigelasbridge@hotmail.com

ASH, Arthur Edwin. b 44. St Jo Coll Nottm 85. **d** 87 **p** 88. C Attleborough *Cov* 87-91; V Garretts Green *Birm* 91-02; rtd 02; PtO *Birm* 02-12; *Cov* from 04. *1 Margetts Close, Kenilworth CV8 1EN* T: (01926) 853547 E: aash@tinyworld.co.uk

ASH, Brian John. b 32. ALCD 62. **d** 62 **p** 63. C Plymouth St Andr *Ex* 62-66; Area Sec CMS Cant and Roch 66-73; V Bromley Common St Aug *Roch* 73-97; rtd 97; PtO *Chelmsf* 97-00. *The Vines, 95 Green Lane, Leigh-on-Sea SS9 5QU* T: (01702) 523644 E: brianash2@googlemail.com

ASH, Christopher Brian Garton. b 53. Trin Hall Cam MA 76. Wycliffe Hall Ox BA 92. **d** 93 **p** 94. C Cambridge H Sepulchre *Ely* 93-97; P-in-c Lt Shelford 97-02; R 02-04; Dir Cornhill Tr Course from 04. *The Cornhill Training Course, 140-148 Borough High Street, London SE1 1LB* T: (020) 7407 0562 E: cbga@proctrust.org.uk

ASH, David Nicholas. b 61. Southlands Coll Lon BA 82. Wycliffe Hall Ox BTh 03. **d** 03 **p** 04. C Walsall *Lich* 03-06; P-in-c Petton w Cockshutt, Welshampton and Lyneal etc 06-12; C Wellington All SS w Eyton from 12; Local Par Development Adv Shrewsbury Area from 10. *1 Stile Rise, Shawbirch, Telford TF5 0LR* T: (01952) 641229

ASH, John Christopher Garton. b 84. St Cuth Soc Dur BA 06. Wycliffe Hall Ox BA 13. **d** 13 **p** 14. C Ches Square St Mich w St Phil *Lon* from 13. *24 Sullivan Road, London SE11 4UH* M: 07886-892995 T: (020) 7730 2170
E: john.ash06@gmail.com

ASH, Canon Nicholas John. b 59. Bath Univ BSc 81 Nottm Univ BTh 88. Linc Th Coll 85. **d** 88 **p** 89. C Hersham *Guildf* 88-93; P-in-c Flookburgh *Carl* 93-97; Dioc Officer for Stewardship 94-97; TV Cartmel Peninsula 97-98; Dir of Ords 97-03; P-in-c Dalston 98-00; P-in-c Wreay 98-00; P-in-c Raughton Head w Gatesgill 98-00; V Dalston w Cumdivock, Raughton Head and Wreay 01-03; Can Res Portsm Cathl 03-09; TR Cartmel Peninsula *Carl* from 09. *The Rectory, Hampsfell Road, Grange-over-Sands LA11 6BE* T: (01539) 532757
E: nickash405@hotmail.com *or* cptmrrector@gmail.com

ASH, Nicholas Martin. b 62. Ch Ch Coll Cant BEd 86. SEITE 06. **d** 09 **p** 10. NSM Faversham *Cant* 09-13; Chapl Medway Secure Tr Cen from 13. *Medway Secure Training Centre, Sir Evelyn Road, Rochester ME1 3YB* T: (01634) 823300 M: 07896-006282
E: revnickash@gmail.com

ASHBRIDGE, Clare Patricia Esther. *See* KAKURU, Clare Patricia Esther

ASHBRIDGE, Miss Kathleen Mary. b 30. Alnwick Tr Coll CertEd 51. **d** 03 **p** 04. NSM Caldbeck, Castle Sowerby and Sebergham *Carl* 03-08; PtO from 08. *Sharpe House, Caldbeck, Wigton CA7 8EX* T: (016974) 78205

ASHBURNER, David Barrington. b 26. Ch Coll Cam BA 51 MA 55. Wycliffe Hall Ox 51. **d** 53 **p** 54. C Coalville *Leic* 53-56; C Leic H Apostles 56-58; V Bucklebury w Marlston *Ox* 58-70; V Belton *Leic* 70-75; P-in-c Osgathorpe 73-75; R Belton and Osgathorpe 75-79; V Frisby-on-the-Wreake w Kirby Bellars 79-82; V Uffington w Woolstone and Baulking *Ox* 82-91; P-in-c Shellingford 83-91; RD Vale of White Horse 87-91; rtd 91; PtO *Glouc* 91-13; *Ox* from 91. *7 Stonefern Court, Stow Road, Moreton-in-Marsh GL56 0DW* T: (01608) 650347

✠**ASHBY, The Rt Revd Godfrey William Ernest Candler.** b 30. Lon Univ AKC 54 BD 54 PhD 69. **d** 55 **p** 56 **c** 80. C St Helier *S'wark* 55-57; P-in-c St Mark's Miss Cape Town S Africa 58-60; Sub-Warden St Paul's Th Coll Grahamstown 60-66; R Alice 66-68; Sen Lect Rhodes Univ 68-75; Can Grahamstown Cathl 69-75; Dean and Adn Grahamstown 75-80; Bp St John's 80-85; Prof Div Witwatersrand Univ S Africa 85-88; Asst Bp Johannesburg 85-88; Asst Bp Leic 88-95; P-in-c Newtown Linford 92-95; Hon Can Leic Cathl 93-95; rtd 95; Asst Bp George S Africa 95-08; Hon Asst Bp Portsm 08-11; Hon Asst Bp Ex from 11. *11 Gracey Court, Woodland Road, Broadclyst, Exeter EX5 3GA* M: 07968-396195 E: godfreyashby@gmail.com

ASHBY, Mrs Judith Anne Stuart. b 53. Man Univ BSc 74 MSc 76 Ox Brookes Univ PGCE 99. STETS 96. **d** 99 **p** 00. NSM Swindon Ch Ch *Bris* 99-05; P-in-c Cricklade w Latton 05-12; C Ashton Keynes, Leigh and Minety 07-12; rtd 12; Dean Women's Min *Bris* from 13. *57 Greywethers Avenue, Swindon SN3 1QG* T: (01793) 978528 E: judith.ashby@tiscali.co.uk

ASHBY, Kevin Patrick. b 53. Jes Coll Ox BA 76 MA 80. Wycliffe Hall Ox 76. **d** 78 **p** 79. C Market Harborough *Leic* 78-82; C Horwich H Trin Man 82-84; C Horwich 84; TV 84-90; R Billing *Pet* 90-01; RD Northn 98-01; R Buckingham *Ox* 01-09; AD 04-09; TR Melton Mowbray *Leic* from 09; AD Framland 11-15. *57 Burton Road, Melton Mowbray LE13 1DL* T: (01664) 410393 E: kevinp.ashby@virgin.net

ASHBY, Mrs Linda. b 48. Dartford Coll of Educn CertEd 70. **d** 03 **p** 04. OLM N w S Wootton *Nor* from 03. *4 Melford Close, South Wootton, King's Lynn PE30 3XH* T: (01553) 672893
E: linda_ashby@tiscali.co.uk

ASHBY, Pauline. b 53. **d** 13 **p** 14. NSM Hugglescote w Donington, Ellistown and Snibston *Leic* from 13. *58 Leicester Road, Groby, Leicester LE6 0DJ* T: 0116-231 3061

ASHBY, Peter George. b 49. Univ of Wales (Cardiff) BSc(Econ) 70. Linc Th Coll 70. **d** 73 **p** 74. C Bengeo *St Alb* 73-75; Chapl Hatf Poly 76-79; C Apsley End 80; TV Chambersbury 80-82; Adn N Harare Zimbabwe 82-87; V Eskdale, Irton, Muncaster and Waberthwaite *Carl* 87-93; TR Sedgley All SS *Worc* 93-99; TV Tettenhall Regis *Lich* 99-04; V W Bromwich St Jas w St Paul 04-06; R Bradeley, Church Eaton, Derrington and Haughton 06-11; rtd 11; PtO *B & W* from 12. *24 Bryant Gardens, Clevedon BS21 5HE* T: (01275) 542677 M: 07756-897547 E: peterg.ashby@gmail.com

ASHBY, Philip Charles. b 52. Birm Univ BSc 73 Lon Univ MSc 74 PhD 93. WEMTC 05. **d** 08 **p** 09. NSM Stratton St Margaret w S Marston etc *Bris* 08-11; NSM Garsdon, Lea and Cleverton and Charlton 11-12; NSM N Swindon St Andr from 14. *57 Greywethers Avenue, Swindon SN3 1QG* T: (01793) 978528 E: phil.ashby@tiscali.co.uk

ASHCROFT, Canon Ann Christine. b 46. Cov Coll of Educn TCert 68. NOC 82. **d** 87 **p** 94. Chapl Trin C of E High Sch Man 86-91; Burnage St Nic Man 86-95; Hon Par Dn 87-95; Dio Adv

Man Coun for Educn 91-95; TV Wareham and Chapl Purbeck Sec Sch *Sarum* 95-02; TR By Brook *Bris* 02-10; P-in-c Colerne w N Wraxall 06-10; Hon Can Bris Cathl 08-10; rtd 10. *Beckside, Baslow Road, Ashford-in-the-Water, Bakewell DE45 1QA* E: annashcroft@bybrook.org.uk *or* ann.ashcroft664@btinternet.com

ASHCROFT, The Ven Mark David. b 54. Worc Coll Ox BA 77 MA 82 Fitzw Coll Cam BA 81. Ridley Hall Cam 79. **d** 82 **p** 83. C Burnage St Marg *Man* 82-85; Tutor St Paul's Sch of Div Kapsabet Kenya 86-89; Prin St Paul's Th Coll Kapsabet 90-96; R Harpurhey *Man* 96-09; R Harpurhey St Steph 96-06; AD N Man 00-06; Adn Man from 09; Hon Can Man Cathl from 04. *14 Moorgate Avenue, Manchester M20 1HE* T/F: 0161-448 1976 E: archdeaconman@manchester.anglican.org

ASHDOWN, Andrew William Harvey. b 64. K Coll Lon BD 88 AKC 88. Sarum & Wells Th Coll 88. **d** 90 **p** 91. C Cranleigh *Guildf* 90-94; V Ryhill *Wakef* 94-98; P-in-c Denmead *Portsm* 98-99; V 99-05; S Asia Regional Officer USPG 05-06; Hon C Tadley S and Silchester *Win* 05-06; P-in-c Knight's Enham and Smannell w Enham Alamein 06-09; TR 09-14; V Knight's Enham 14-15. *The Vicarage, 33 Crescent Rd, North Baddesley, Southampton SO52 9HU* E: andrewashdown@talktalk.net

ASHDOWN, Anthony Hughes. b 37. AKC 63. **d** 64 **p** 65. C Tettenhall Regis *Lich* 64-67; P-in-c Bassaleg *Mon* 67-70; P-in-c Gatooma Rhodesia 70-77; P-in-c Longton St Jas *Lich* 77-78; P-in-c Longton St Jo 77-78; R Longton 78-80; TR Cove St Jo *Guildf* 80-87; Chapl Lisbon *Eur* 87-90; V Wanstead H Trin Hermon Hill *Chelmsf* 90-00; rtd 02; PtO *Chich* from 00. *88 Shippam Street, Chichester PO19 1AY* T: (01243) 532405

ASHDOWN, Ms Lucyann. b 64. LSE BSc 95 RGN 86 RM 88. NTMTC BA 08. **d** 08 **p** 09. C Stoke Newington St Mary and Brownswood Park *Lon* 08-11; P-in-c Blaenau Irfon *S & B* 11-14; P-in-c Irfon Valley 11-14; Chapl Farleigh Hospice from 14; PtO *St E* from 15. *Farleigh Hospice, North Court Road, Broomfield, Chelmsford CM1 7FH* T: (01245) 457311
E: lucyann.ashdown@gmail.com

ASHDOWN, Philip David. b 57. Imp Coll Lon BSc 79 NW Univ Chicago MS 80 Cranfield Inst of Tech PhD 85 ARCS 79. Ripon Coll Cuddesdon 91. **d** 93 **p** 94. C Houghton le Spring *Dur* 93-96; V Stockton and Chapl Stockton Campus Dur Univ 96-02; V Stockton St Pet *Dur* from 02; P-in-c Elton from 09. *St Peter's Vicarage, 11 Lorne Court, Stockton-on-Tees TS18 3UB* T: (01642) 670981 E: philip.ashdown@durham.anglican.org

ASHDOWN, Victoria Louisa. b 69. Ripon Coll Cuddesdon 09. **d** 12 **p** 13. NSM Whitchurch w Tufton and Litchfield *Win* 12-15. *The Vicarage, 33 Crescent Rd, North Baddesley, Southampton SO52 9HU* E: revdvictoria@gmail.com

ASHE, The Ven Francis John. b 53. Sheff Univ BMet 74. Ridley Hall Cam 77. **d** 79 **p** 80. C Ashtead *Guildf* 79-82; S Africa 82-87; R Wisley w Pyrford *Guildf* 87-93; V Godalming 93-01; TR 01-09; RD 96-02; Hon Can Guildf Cathl 03-09; Adn Lynn *Nor* from 09. *Holly Tree House, Whitwell Road, Sparham, Norwich NR9 5PN* T: (01362) 688032
E: archdeacon.lynn@norwich.anglican.org

ASHENDEN, Canon Gavin Roy Pelham. b 54. Bris Univ LLB 76 Oak Hill Th Coll BA 80 Heythrop Coll Lon MTh 89 Sussex Univ DPhil 98. **d** 80 **p** 81. C Bermondsey St Jas w Ch Ch *S'wark* 80-83; TV Sanderstead All SS 83-89; Chapl and Sen Lect Sussex Univ *Chich* 89-12; V Jersey Gouray St Martin *Win* from 12; Can and Preb Chich Cathl 03-05; Wiccamical Preb from 05; Chapl to The Queen from 08. *The Vicarage, Le Grande Route de Faldouet, St Martin, Jersey JE3 6UA* T: (01534) 853255 M: 07797-828454 E: gavin@ashenden.org

ASHFORD-OKAI, Fred. b 57. NUI BA 90 Lanc Univ MA 92 TCD HDipEd 93. St Pet Sem Ghana 79 NTMTC 06. **d** 84 **p** 85. NSM E Ham w Upton Park and Forest Gate *Chelmsf* 07-09; PtO from 14. *8 Bream Gardens, London E6 6HX* M: 07940-984883 E: fashfordokai@googlemail.com

ASHFORD, Archdeacon of. *See* DOWN, The Ven Philip Roy

ASHFORTH, David Edward. b 37. Lon Univ BSc ARCS 59. Qu Coll Birm 60. **d** 61 **p** 62. C Scarborough St Columba *York* 61-65; C Northallerton w Kirby Sigston 65-67; V Keyingham 67-73; Chapl Imp Coll *Lon* 73-89; V Balderstone *Blackb* 89-01; Dir Post-Ord Tr 89-01; rtd 01; PtO *Leeds* from 02. *Sunnyholme Cottage, Preston under Scar, Leyburn DL8 4AH* T: (01969) 622438 E: d.ashforth@btinternet.com

ASHLEY, Brian. b 36. S'wark Ord Course 75. **d** 77 **p** 78. NSM Horsell *Guildf* 77-07; PtO 07-12. *5 Birtley House, 38 Claremont Avenue, Woking GU22 7QB* T: (01483) 761232
E: brianthebusiness@onetel.com

ASHLEY, Clive Ashley. b 54. Croydon Coll of Art and Design LSIAD 75 Lon Hosp SRN 80 E Ham Coll of Tech TCert 82. Aston Tr Scheme 81 Cranmer Hall Dur 84. **d** 86 **p** 87. C Withington St Paul *Man* 86-89; Asst Chapl Freeman Hosp Newc 89-92; Chapl St Rich and Graylingwell Hosps *Chich* 92-98; Chapl Sussex Weald and Downs NHS Trust 95-98;

Chapl and Bereavement Cllr R W Sussex Trust 98-01; R New Fishbourne *Chich* 01-10; P-in-c Appledram 01-10; P-in-c Lt Baddow *Chelmsf* 10-13; P-in-c Danbury from 13. *St John's Rectory, 55 Main Road, Danbury, Chelmsford CM3 4NG* T: (01245) 223140 M: 07747-155119 E: cliveashley@btinternet.com

ASHLEY, Jane Isobel. *See* HULME, Jane Isobel

ASHLEY, Ms Rosemary Clare. b 60. Dur Univ BA 82 Birkbeck Coll Lon MSc 01 Brunel Univ MPhil 05. Wycliffe Hall Ox 02. d 05 p 06. C Leyton St Cath and St Paul *Chelmsf* 05-09; NSM 09-12. *114 Hainault Road, London E11 1EL* T: (020) 8923 4782 M: 07984-618534 E: rosyashley@hotmail.com

ASHLEY, Miss Victoria Lesley. St Mich Coll Llan. d 08 p 09. C Tredegar *Mon* 08-12; P-in-c Pontnewydd from 12. *Holy Trinity Vicarage, 44 Church Road, Pontnewydd, Cwmbran NP44 1AT* T: (01633) 482300 E: revvla@btinternet.com

ASHLEY-ROBERTS, James. b 53. Lon Univ BD 77. Oak Hill Th Coll 75 Wycliffe Hall Ox 79. d 80 p 81. C Gt Warley Ch Ch *Chelmsf* 80-83; C E Ham St Paul 83-85; TV Holyhead w Rhoscolyn w Llanfair-yn-Neubwll *Ban* 85-88; TR 88-91; V Penrhyndeudraeth w Llanfrothen w Beddgelert 91-97; R Ffestiniog w Blaenau Ffestiniog 97-01; PtO 01-12; P-in-c Llangefni w Tregaean w Llanddyfnan 12-13. *26 Garrabost, Isle of Lewis HS2 0PW* M: 07881-770437 E: revjamesashleyroberts@sky.com

ASHMAN, Paul Andrew. b 70. Wycliffe Hall Ox 05. d 07 p 08. C Portswood Ch Ch *Win* 07-11; New Zealand from 11. *27 Searle Street, Auckland 1072, New Zealand* T: (0064) (9) 574 6537 *or* 373 3268 M: 21-550104 E: ashmanpaul@gmail.com *or* paul@stpauls.org.nz

ASHMAN, Peter Michael. b 61. Ex Univ LLB 83 LLM 84 BTh(Min) 12 Called to the Bar (Inner Temple) 85. SWMTC 07. d 10 p 11. C Ex St Jas 10-13; P-in-c Ipplepen, Torbryan and Denbury 13-14; R Ipplepen w Torbryan, Denbury and Broadhempston w Woodland from 14. *The Rectory, Paternoster Lane, Ipplepen, Newton Abbot TQ12 5RY* T: (01803) 813847 E: peter@ashman61.info

ASHMAN, Peter Nicholas. b 52. CSS 81 SEN 73. Sarum & Wells Th Coll 87. d 89 p 90. C Stafford *Lich* 89-93; R Dymchurch w Burmarsh and Newchurch *Cant* 93-99; R Lyminge w Paddlesworth, Stanford w Postling etc from 99. *The Rectory, Rectory Lane, Lyminge, Folkestone CT18 8EG* T: (01303) 862432 *or* T/F: 862345 E: p.ashman@btinternet.com

ASHMAN, Mrs Vanessa Mary. b 53. Cant Ch Ch Univ BA 07. d 03 p 04. NSM Lyminge w Paddlesworth, Stanford w Postling etc *Cant* 03-13; C Bewsborough from 13. *The Rectory, Barfrestone Road, Eythorne, Dover CT15 4AH* T: (01304) 831124 E: vanessa.ashman@btinternet.com

ASHTON, Anthony Joseph. b 37. Oak Hill Th Coll 62. d 65 p 66. C Crookes St Thos *Sheff* 65-68; C Heeley 68-73; V Bowling St Steph *Bradf* 73-78; R Chesterfield H Trin *Derby* 78-92; rtd 93; PtO *Derby* 93-00. *19 High Park, Stafford ST16 1BL* T: (01785) 223943

✠**ASHTON, The Rt Revd Cyril Guy.** b 42. Lanc Univ MA 86. Oak Hill Th Coll 64. d 67 p 68 c 00. C Blackpool St Thos *Blackb* 67-70; Voc Sec CPAS 70-74; V Lancaster St Thos *Blackb* 74-91; Lanc Almshouses 76-90; Dioc Dir of Tr *Blackb* 91-00; Hon Can Blackb Cathl 91-00; Suff Bp Doncaster *Sheff* 00-11; rtd 11; Hon Asst Bp Blackb and Liv from 11. *Charis, 17C Quernmore Road, Lancaster LA1 3EB* T: (01524) 848684 M: 07968-371596 E: bpcg.ashton@btinternet.com

ASHTON, David. b 52. Sarum Th Coll 93. d 96 p 97. NSM St Leonards Ch Ch and St Mary *Chich* 96-98; NSM Upper St Leonards St Jo 98-99; C Uckfield 99-02; V Langney 02-14; rtd 14. *3 Streatfield Road, Uckfield TN22 2BG* T: (01825) 768643 E: frdavidashton@aol.com

ASHTON, David William. b 51. Reading Univ BA 74 Lanc Univ PGCE 75. Wycliffe Hall Ox 79. d 82 p 83. C Shipley St Pet *Bradf* 82-85; C Tadley St Pet *Win* 85-88; V Sinfin *Derby* 88-91; Chapl Sophia Antipolis *Eur* 91-94; P-in-c Swanwick and Pentrich *Derby* 95-00; V 00-02; RD Alfreton 95-02; Dioc Dir of Ords 99-02; Chapl Derby Hosps NHS Foundn Trust from 02. *Chaplaincy Services, Derby City General Hospital, Uttoxeter Road, Derby DE22 3NE* T: (01332) 340131 E: david.ashton@derbyhospitals.nhs.uk *or* david.ashton1@nhs.net

ASHTON, Eleanor Jane. *See* RANCE, Eleanor Jane

ASHTON, Grant. *See* ASHTON, William Grant

ASHTON, Hubert Samuel. b 86. Trin Coll Ox BA 08. Oak Hill Th Coll 12. d 15. C Chelsea St Jo w St Andr *Lon* from 15. *St Andrew's Church, 43 Park Walk, London SW10 0AU* M: 07789-870962 E: sam.ashton86@gmail.com

ASHTON, James Paul. b 75. UWE BA 97. Wycliffe Hall Ox BTh 06. d 06 p 07. C Horley *S'wark* 06-09; C S Merstham 09-10; TV Merstham, S Merstham and Gatton 10-14. *2 Castle Way, Worthing BN13 1DD* T: (01903) 693550 E: rev.jp.ashton@gmail.com

ASHTON, Janet Heather Hephzibah. b 52. Westcott Ho Cam. d 07 p 08. C Wenlock *Heref* 07-11; TV Kidderminster St Mary and All SS w Trimpley etc *Worc* 11-15; TV Kidderminster Ismere from 15. *50 Nursery Grove, Kidderminster DY11 5BG* T: (01562) 741381 M: 07737-916499 E: jan@janashton.co.uk

✠**ASHTON, The Rt Revd Jeremy Claude.** b 30. Trin Coll Cam BA 53 MA 57. Westcott Ho Cam 53. d 55 p 56 c 76. C Bury St Mary *Man* 55-60; CF (TA) 57-60; CF (TA - R of O) 60-70; Papua New Guinea 60-86; Asst Bp Papua 76-77; Bp Aipo Rongo 77-86; rtd 86; Australia from 86. *38 Urquhart Street, Castlemaine Vic 3540, Australia* T/F: (0061) (3) 5472 1074

ASHTON, Miss Joan Elizabeth. b 54. Sheff Hallam Univ BA 10 Eaton Hall Coll of Educn CertEd 76. Cranmer Hall Dur 91. d 93 p 94. Par Dn Darnall-cum-Attercliffe *Sheff* 93-94; C Hillsborough and Wadsley Bridge 94-96; P-in-c Stainforth 96-98; P-in-c Arksey 98-03; Asst Chapl Doncaster R Infirmary and Montagu Hosp NHS Trust 98-01; Asst Chapl Doncaster and Bassetlaw Hosps NHS Foundn Trust 01-04; Co-ord Chapl Services Rotherham Gen Hosps NHS Trust from 04. *Rotherham District General Hospital, Moorgate Road, Rotherham S60 2UD* T: (01709) 820000 E: joan.ashton@rothgen.nhs.uk

ASHTON, Kenneth. b 61. Ridley Hall Cam. d 08 p 09. C Walthamstow *Chelmsf* 08-11; P-in-c Hainault from 11. *St Paul's Vicarage, 143 Arrowsmith Road, Chigwell IG7 4NZ* T: (020) 8500 3366 M: 07932-071715 E: ashtonken@gmail.com *or* kena@stpauls-hainault.org.uk

ASHTON, Lesley June. b 49. York Univ BA 89. NEOC 00. d 04 p 05. C Roundhay St Edm *Ripon* 04-08; P-in-c Hawksworth Wood 08-11; TV Abbeylands 11-13; rtd 13; Hon C Fountains Gp *Leeds* from 13; Asst Dir of Ords *Ripon* 10-14; Assoc Dioc Dir of Ords *Leeds* from 14. *1 Hazel Close, Grewelthorpe, Ripon HG4 3BL* M: 07813-354772 E: lesley.ashton1@ntlworld.com

ASHTON, Mrs Margaret Lucie. b 40. St Jo Coll Nottm 79. dss 83 d 87 p 94. Billericay and Lt Burstead *Chelmsf* 83-99; NSM 87-99; rtd 99; Hon C Fordingbridge and Breamore and Hale etc *Win* 01-05; PtO from 05. *3 Stephen Martin Gardens, Fordingbridge SP6 1RF* T: (01425) 656205 E: peterdashton@onetel.com

ASHTON, Mrs Mary Isabel. b 57. Robert Gordon Inst of Tech Aber BSc 78 Open Univ PGCE 96. St Steph Ho Ox 07. d 09 p 10. C Whitewater *Win* 09-13; V Guildf All SS 13-14. *The Vicarage, Wigan Road, Euxton, Chorley PR7 6JH* T: (01257) 262102 E: mary.ashton@mac.com

ASHTON, Neville Anthony. b 45. Sarum & Wells Th Coll 78. d 80 p 81. C Hattersley *Ches* 80-82; C Lancaster Ch Ch w St Jo and St Anne *Blackb* 82-84; R Church Kirk 84-15; rtd 15. *Address temp unknown*

ASHTON, Canon Peter Donald. b 34. Lon Univ BD 62. ALCD 61. d 62 p 63. C Walthamstow St Mary *Chelmsf* 62-68; V Girlington *Bradf* 68-73; Dir Past Studies St Jo Coll Nottm 73-80; TR Billericay and Lt Burstead *Chelmsf* 80-99; Chapl Mayflower Hosp Billericay 80-99; Chapl Thameside Community Healthcare NHS Trust 80-99; RD Basildon *Chelmsf* 89-99; Hon Can Chelmsf Cathl 92-99; rtd 99; Hon C Fordingbridge and Breamore and Hale etc *Win* 01-10; PtO from 10. *3 Stephen Martin Gardens, Fordingbridge SP6 1RF* T: (01425) 656205 E: peterdashton@onetel.com

ASHTON, Preb Samuel Rupert. b 42. Sarum & Wells Th Coll. d 83 p 84. C Ledbury w Eastnor *Heref* 83-86; R St Weonards w Orcop, Garway, Tretire etc 86-98; RD Ross and Archenfield 91-95 and 96-98; P-in-c Cradley w Mathon and Storridge 98-99; R 99-07; Preb Heref Cathl 97-07; rtd 07; PtO *Heref* from 08. *The Old Greyhound, Longtown, Hereford HR2 0LD* T: (01873) 860492

ASHTON, Samuel. *See* ASHTON, Hubert Samuel

ASHTON (née JONES), Mrs Susan Catherine. b 48. Qu Coll Birm 09. d 11 p 12. NSM Knowle *Birm* from 11. *1467 Warwick Road, Knowle, Solihull B93 9LU* T: (01564) 776895 E: sueashton2003@yahoo.co.uk

ASHTON, William Grant. b 57. St Chad's Coll Dur BA 79. Oak Hill Th Coll BA 85. d 85 p 86. C Lancaster St Thos *Blackb* 85-89; CF 89-14; Chapl R Memorial Chpl Sandhurst 06-07; QHC 11-14; V Euxton *Blackb* from 14. *The Vicarage, Wigan Road, Euxton, Chorley PR7 6JH* T: (01257) 262102 E: wgashton@mac.com

ASHURST, Mrs Judith Anne. b 57. St Aid Coll Dur BA 80 St Jo Coll Dur BA 08 ACIB 83. Cranmer Hall Dur 06. d 08 p 09. C Belmont and Pittington *Dur* 08-11; C Chester le Street from 11. *16 Park Road North, Chester-le-Street DH3 3SD* E: judith.ashurst@btinternet.com

ASHWELL, Anthony John. b 42. St Andr Univ BSc 65. Sarum & Wells Th Coll 86. d 88 p 89. C Plymstock *Ex* 88-91; C Axminster, Chardstock, Combe Pyne and Rousdon 91-92; TV 92-95; C Crediton and Shobrooke 95-97; TV Bride Valley

Sarum 97-07; P-in-c Symondsbury 05-07; RD Lyme Bay 03-06; rtd 07; PtO *Sarum* 07-11. *7 Hill Lane, Hathersage, Hope Valley S32 1AY* T: (01433) 650719 E: anthony@vencot.plus.com

ASHWIN, Canon Vincent George. b 42. Worc Coll Ox BA 65. Coll of Resurr Mirfield 65. **d** 67 **p** 68. C Shildon *Dur* 67-70; C Newc St Fran 70-72; R Mhlosheni Swaziland 72-75; R Manzini 75-79; V Shildon *Dur* 79-85; V Fenham St Jas and St Basil *Newc* 85-97; RD Newc W 89-97; V Haydon Bridge and Beltingham w Henshaw 97-04; RD Hexham 97-02; Hon Can Newc Cathl 00-04; rtd 04; PtO *S'well* from 04. *83 Westgate, Southwell NG25 0LS* T: (01636) 813975
E: vincentashwin@tiscali.co.uk

ASHWIN-SIEJKOWSKI, Piotr Jan. b 64. Warsaw Univ PhD 97. Coll of Resurr Mirfield 98. **d** 91 **p** 92. Poland 92-98; C Tile Hill *Cov* 99-01; Chapl and Lect Univ Coll Chich 01-04; TV Richmond St Mary w St Matthias and St Jo *S'wark* 04-13; C Twickenham St Mary *Lon* from 13. *27 Strafford Road, Twickenham TW1 3AD* T: (020) 8891 5753
E: piotrashwin@btinternet.com

ASHWORTH, Canon David. b 40. Nottm Univ BPharm 62. Linc Th Coll 63. **d** 65 **p** 66. C Halliwell St Thos *Man* 65-69; C Heywood St Jas 69-72; C-in-c Heywood St Marg CD 72-78; V Hale *Ches* 78-87; V Hale and Ashley 87-96; V Prestbury 96-05; RD Bowdon 87-95; RD Macclesfield 98-03; Hon Can Ches Cathl 94-05; rtd 05; PtO *Ches* from 05. *12 Lime Close, Sandbach CW11 1BZ* T: (01270) 529187
E: david@ashworth39.freeserve.co.uk

ASHWORTH, Graham Ernest. b 52. LCTP 07. **d** 10 **p** 11. NSM Leyland St Ambrose *Blackb* from 10. *39 Lowther Drive, Leyland PR26 6QB* T: (01772) 495422 M: 07541-988288
E: mrgraham.ashworth@blueyonder.co.uk

ASHWORTH, James Nigel. b 55. York Univ BA 77. Cranmer Hall Dur 93. **d** 93 **p** 94. C Rothwell *Ripon* 93-96; Chapl Campsfield Ho Oxon 96-99; Hon C Akeman *Ox* 96-99; V Kemsing w Woodlands *Roch* 99-08; R Man St Ann from 08. *St Anne's Rectory, 98 Rigby Street, Salford M7 4BQ* T: 0161-792 1123
E: rectorofstanns@btinternet.com

ASHWORTH, John Russell. b 33. Lich Th Coll 57. **d** 60 **p** 61. C Castleford All SS *Wakef* 60-62; C Luton St Sav *St Alb* 63-67; V Clipstone *S'well* 67-70; V Bolton-upon-Dearne *Sheff* 70-82; V Thornhill Lees *Wakef* 82-98; rtd 98; PtO *Leeds* from 99. *Walsingham, 2 Vicarage Road, Savile Town, Dewsbury WF12 9PD* T: (01924) 461269

ASHWORTH, Keith Benjamin. b 33. NW Ord Course 76. **d** 79 **p** 80. C Pennington *Man* 79-83; P-in-c Bolton St Bede 83-88; V 88-95; V Hillock 95-01; rtd 01; PtO *Man* 01-06; *Blackb* from 06. *3 Sandpiper Place, Thornton-Cleveleys FY5 3FE* T: (01253) 855793

ASHWORTH, Mark Stephen. b 71. Birm Univ BSocSc 91 Goldsmiths' Coll Lon PGCE 96. Oak Hill Th Coll BA 14. **d** 14 **p** 15. C Crowborough *Chich* from 14. *1 Croft Cottages, Church Road, Crowborough TN6 1ED* M: 07708-491289
E: mashworth71@gmail.com

ASHWORTH, Martin. b 41. AKC 63. **d** 64 **p** 65. C Wythenshawe Wm Temple Ch CD *Man* 64-71; R Haughton St Anne 71-83; V Prestwich St Marg 83-06; rtd 06; PtO *Man* 06-08. *17 Plane Tree Nest Lane, Halifax HX2 7PL*

ASHWORTH, Nigel. *See* ASHWORTH, James Nigel

ASHWORTH, Timothy. b 52. Worc Coll of Educn CertEd 74. Oak Hill Th Coll BA 81. **d** 82 **p** 83. C Tonbridge St Steph *Roch* 82-85; C-in-c Whittle-le-Woods *Blackb* 85-90; Chapl Scargill Ho 90-96; V Ingleton w Chapel le Dale *Bradf* 96-03; TV Yate New Town *Bris* 03-08; NSM Lostock St Thos and St Jo and Bolton St Bede *Man* 09-13; Chapl HM Pris Forest Bank 12-15. *27 Water Lane, West Malling ME19 6HH* T: (01732) 870279
E: timashworth52@tiscali.co.uk

ASHWORTH, Mrs Vivien. b 52. Worc Coll of Educn CertEd 73. Trin Coll Bris 79 Oak Hill Th Coll BA 82. **d** 82 **p** 94. Tonbridge St Steph *Roch* 82-85; Whittle-le-Woods *Blackb* 85-90; Hon Par Dn 87-90; Chapl Scargill Ho 90-96; Hon C Ingleton w Chapel le Dale *Bradf* 96-03; Dioc Youth Adv 96-01; Hon C Yate New Town *Bris* 03-07; TV 07-08; Sub Chapl HM Pris Ashfield 04-09; P-in-c Lostock St Thos and St Jo *Man* 09-15; P-in-c Bolton St Bede 09-15; Guardian Pilsdon at Malling Community from 15. *27 Water Lane, West Malling ME19 6HH* T: (01732) 870279
E: viv.ashworth01@tiscali.co.uk

ASINUGO, Mrs Christiana Chidinma. b 56. NTMTC. **d** 09 **p** 10. C Becontree St Mary *Chelmsf* 09-13; C W Ham St Matt from 13. *St Matthew's Vicarage, 38 Dyson Road, London E15 4JX* T: (020) 8221 0902 E: ccasinugo@yahoo.co.uk

ASIR, Jebamani Sekar Anand. *See* ANAND, Sekar Anand Asir

ASKEW, Miss Alison Jane. b 57. Dur Univ BA 78 PGCE 79. S Dios Minl Tr Scheme 93. **d** 95 **p** 96. NSM Kingsclere *Win* 95-96; Asst Chapl N Hants Hosps NHS Trust 95-99; Chapl 99-04; Sen Chapl Basingstoke and N Hants NHS Foundn Trust

04-10; P-in-c Kirby-on-the-Moor, Cundall w Norton-le-Clay etc *Leeds* from 10. *The Vicarage, 13 The Croft, Kirby Hill, Boroughbridge, York YO51 9YA* T: (01423) 326585

ASKEW, Benjamin Paul. b 79. Sheff Univ BA 01 PGCE 03. St Mellitus Coll BA 13. **d** 13 **p** 14. Pioneer Min *Leeds* from 13. *156 Pannal Ash Road, Harrogate HG2 9AJ* T: (01423) 560558
E: askewben@gmail.com

ASKEW, Ms Catherine Clasen. b 75. Princeton Th Sem MDiv 01. Cranmer Hall Dur 08. **d** 10 **p** 11. NSM Amble *Newc* 10-12; NSM Bothal and Pegswood w Longhirst 12-15; NSM Chevington from 15. *Address temp unknown*
T: (01289) 388235 E: catherineaskew@gmail.com

ASKEW, Peter Timothy. b 68. Ridley Hall Cam 00. **d** 02 **p** 03. C Bilton *Ripon* 02-06; C Harrogate St Mark and Chapl St Aid Sch Harrogate 06-09; PtO *Newc* 10-11; NSM Felton from 11. *Croft Cottage, Acton Home Farm, Felton, Morpeth NE65 9NU* M: 07754-046029 E: pete.askew2@ntlworld.com

ASKEW, Preb Richard George. b 35. BNC Ox BA 59 MA 63. Ridley Hall Cam 62. **d** 64 **p** 65. C Chesham St Mary *Ox* 64-66; C Mossley Hill St Matt and St Jas *Liv* 66-67; Chapl Ox Pastorate 67-72; Asst Chapl BNC Ox 67-71; R Ashtead *Guildf* 72-83; RD Leatherhead 80-83; Can Res and Treas Sarum Cathl 83-90; Dioc Adv on Miss and Min *B & W* 83-90; R Bath Abbey w St Jas 90-00; Preb Wells Cathl 92-00; PtO *Sarum* 00-01; TV Cley Hill Warminster 01-04; rtd 04. *Shepherd's Lea, 46 The Pastures, Westwood, Bradford-on-Avon BA15 2BH* T: (01985) 844587 E: askew.easter@btinternet.com

ASKEY, Gary Simon. b 64. K Coll Lon LLB 99 Univ Coll Lon LLM 00 Univ of S Qld MEd 04. St Steph Ho Ox 88. **d** 91 **p** 92. SSM 87-99; Prior SSM Priory Kennington 96-98; C Middlesbrough All SS *York* 91-94; Sub-Chapl HM Pris Holme Ho 92-94; C Whitby *York* 94-96; Missr Whitby Miss and Seafarer's Trust 94-96; LtO *S'wark* 96-03; Hon C Angell Town St Jo 98-03; PtO 05-07; Hon C Walworth St Jo from 07. *St John's Cottage, 16 Larcom Street, London SE17 1NQ* T: (020) 7450 1530 E: simon@askey.gs

ASKEY, John Stuart. b 39. Chich Th Coll 63. **d** 66 **p** 67. C Feltham *Lon* 66-69; C Epsom Common Ch Ch *Guildf* 69-72; C Chesterton Gd Shep *Ely* 72-74; R Stretham w Thetford 74-93; Dioc Spirituality Officer 75-98; Dioc Youth Officer 80-99; P-in-c Brinkley, Burrough Green and Carlton 93-97; P-in-c Westley Waterless 93-97; P-in-c Dullingham 93-97; P-in-c Stetchworth 93-97; R Raddesley Gp 97-99; Chapl Gothenburg w Halmstad, Jönköping etc *Eur* 99-04; rtd 04. *165A Lewes Road, Brighton BN2 3LD* T: (01273) 604789

ASKEY, Matthew. b 74. Loughb Coll BA 96 Bretton Hall Coll MA 99 Leeds Univ BA 09 Huddersfield Univ PGCE 06. Coll of Resurr Mirfield 07. **d** 09 **p** 10. C Elland *Wakef* 09-13; Chapl Minster Sch *S'well* from 13. *5 Vicar's Court, Church Street, Southwell NG25 0HP* T: (01636) 817298 M: 07814-502034
E: frmaskey@btinternet.com

ASKEY, Mrs Susan Mary. b 44. Leeds Univ MA 00. NOC 99. **d** 99 **p** 00. C Golcar *Wakef* 99-02; P-in-c Drighlington 02-12; rtd 12. *26 Handel Street, Golcar, Huddersfield HD7 4AB* E: smaskey@aol.com

ASKEY, Thomas Cyril. b 29. Sheff Univ BSc 50 Man Univ MA(Theol) 81 ACIPA 58 MITMA 76. NW Ord Course 70. **d** 73 **p** 74. NSM Gawsworth *Ches* 73-76; PtO 76-80; rtd 81; PtO *Derby* 99-05. *Address temp unknown*

ASKWITH, Mrs Helen Mary. b 57. Thames Valley Univ BSc 00. ERMC 04. **d** 07 **p** 08. NSM Wembley St Jo *Lon* 07-10; NSM Northolt Park St Barn 10-12; V Wembley Park from 12. *St Augustine's Vicarage, 13 Forty Avenue, Wembley HA9 8JL* T: (020) 8908 5995 M: 07711-643220 E: hdaskwith@aol.com

ASMELASH, Berhane Tesfamariam. b 56. Addis Ababa Univ MD 89 Lon Bible Coll MPhil 04. SEITE BA 08. **d** 08 **p** 09. C Upper Holloway *Lon* 08-12; NSM Dalston H Trin w St Phil and Haggerston All SS 12-13; C Plumstead Common *S'wark* from 13. *The Vicarage, Thornhill Avenue, London SE18 2HS* M: 07838-167198 E: berhanea@fastmail.fm

ASPINALL, Philip Norman. b 51. Cam Univ MA ATI. WMMTC 86. **d** 89 **p** 90. NSM Cov E 89-98. *139 Wiltshire Court, Nod Rise, Mount Nod, Coventry CV5 7JP* T: (024) 7646 7509

✠**ASPINALL, The Most Revd Phillip John.** b 59. Univ of Tasmania BSc 80 Trin Coll Melbourne BD 88 Monash Univ PhD 89 Deakin Univ MBA 98. Melbourne Coll of Div. **d** 88 **p** 89 **c** 98. C S Launceston Australia 88-89; Asst P Brighton 89-91; P-in-c Bridgwater w Gagebrook 91-94; Dir Anglicare Tas 94-98; Adn for Ch and Soc 97-98; Asst Bp Adelaide 98-02; Abp Brisbane from 02; Primate of Australia from 05. *Bishopsbourne, GPO Box 421, Brisbane QLD 4001, Australia* T: (0061) (7) 3835 2222 F: 3832 5030 E: archbishops@anglicanbrisbane.org.au

ASQUITH, Barbara Rosemary. b 37. **d** 03 **p** 04. OLM S Ossett *Wakef* 03-06; OLM Batley All SS and Purlwell *Leeds* from 06. *115 Teall Street, Ossett WF5 0HS* T: (01924) 271302 M: 07754-859247

ASQUITH (née SHIPLEY), June Patricia. b 54. Liv Hope BA 00 PGCE 01. SNWTP 08. **d** 10 **p** 11. NSM Walton Breck *Liv* 10-12; C Bootle 12-14; R Wavertree St Mary from 14. *St Mary's Rectory, 1 South Drive, Wavertree, Liverpool L15 8JJ*
E: june150@btinternet.com

ASQUITH, Michael John. b 60. St D Coll Lamp BA 82 MPhil 91 Ch Ch Coll Cant PGCE 83. Cant Sch of Min 91. **d** 94 **p** 95. C S Ashford Ch Ch Cant 94-98; P-in-c Weldon w Deene *Pet* 98-00; P-in-c Corby Epiphany w St Jo 98-06; Dep Dioc Dir of Educn *Leic* 06-10; R Lowestoft St Marg *Nor* from 11. *St Margaret's Rectory, 147 Hollingsworth Road, Lowestoft NR32 4BW* T: (01502) 573046 M: 07503-377360 E: mikeasq@aol.com

ASQUITH, Rosemary. *See* ASQUITH, Barbara Rosemary

ASSON, Geoffrey Ormrod. b 34. Univ of Wales (Ban) BA 54 St Cath Coll Ox BA 56 MA 61. St Steph Ho Ox 54. **d** 57 **p** 58. C Aberdare *Llan* 57-59; C Roath 59-61; R Hagworthingham w Asgarby and Lusby *Linc* 61-65; P-in-c Mavis Enderby w Raithby 62-65; V Friskney 65-69; R S Ormsby w Ketsby, Calceby and Driby 69-74; R Harrington w Brinkhill 69-74; R Oxcombe 69-74; R Ruckland w Farforth and Maidenwell 69-74; R Somersby w Bag Enderby 69-74; R Tetford and Salmonby 69-74; P-in-c Belchford 71-74; P-in-c W Ashby 71-74; V Riverhead w Dunton Green *Roch* 75-80; R Kington w Huntington *Heref* 80-82; RD Kington and Weobley 80-86; P-in-c Almeley 81-82; P-in-c Knill 81-82; P-in-c Old Radnor 81-82; R Kington w Huntington, Old Radnor, Kinnerton etc 82-86; V Mathry w St Edren's and Grandston etc *St D* 86-97; Bp's Rural Adv and Tourist Officer 91-95; rtd 96. *Sincerity, St Dogmaels, Cardigan SA43 3JZ* T: (01239) 615591

ASTBURY, Susan. b 61. St Hugh's Coll Ox BA 82 MA 85 DPhil 85. SWMTC 05. **d** 08 **p** 09. C Teignmouth, Ideford w Luton, Ashcombe etc *Ex* 08-12; PtO from 12. *3 The Strand, Shaldon, Teignmouth TQ14 0DL* T: (01626) 873807
E: sue.ast@btinternet.com

ASTIN, Howard Keith. b 51. Warwick Univ LLB. Trin Coll Bris 83. **d** 83 **p** 84. C Kirkheaton *Wakef* 83-88; V Bowling St Jo *Leeds* from 88. *St John's Vicarage, 96 Lister Avenue, Bradford BD4 7QS* T: (01274) 727355
E: howard.astin@bradford.anglican.org *or* h.astin@virgin.net

ASTIN, Canon Moira Anne Elizabeth. b 65. Clare Coll Cam BA 86 MA 90. Wycliffe Hall Ox BA 96. **d** 95 **p** 96. C Newbury *Ox* 95-99; C Thatcham 99-01; TV 01-05; TV Woodley 05-09; V Southlake 09-11; Angl Ecum Officer (Berks) 03-11; Dioc Ecum Officer 10-11; P-in-c Frodingham and New Brumby *Linc* from 11; Can and Preb Linc Cathl from 12. *The Vicarage, Vicarage Gardens, Scunthorpe DN15 7AZ* T: (01724) 334873
E: moira.astin@btinternet.com

ASTIN, Timothy Robin. b 58. St Edm Hall Ox BA 79 Darw Coll Cam PhD 82 FGS. Ox Min Course 90. **d** 93 **p** 94. NSM Reading St Jo *Ox* 93-95; NSM Newbury 95-99; NSM Beedon and Peasemore w W Ilsley and Farnborough 99-05; NSM Woodley 05-11; NSM Frodingham and New Brumby *Linc* 11-13; P-in-c Bottesford w Ashby from 13. *The Vicarage, 10 Old School Lane, Bottesford, Scunthorpe DN16 3RD* T: (01724) 334873
E: t.r.astin@reading.ac.uk

ASTLEY, Prof Jeffrey. b 47. Down Coll Cam BA 68 MA 72 Dur Univ PhD 79. Qu Coll Birm 68. **d** 70 **p** 71. C Cannock *Lich* 70-73; Lect and Chapl St Hild Coll Dur 73-75; Sen Lect and Chapl SS Hild and Bede Coll Dur 75-77; Prin Lect and Hd RS Bp Grosseteste Coll Linc 77-81; Dir N of England Inst for Chr Educn 81-13; PtO *Dur* from 81. *8 Vicarage Court, Heighington Village, Newton Aycliffe DL5 6SD* E: jeff.astley@durham.ac.uk *or* jagdaa71@aol.com

ASTON, Glyn. b 29. Univ of Wales (Abth) BA 54 TCert 55. Sarum & Wells Th Coll 84. **d** 79 **p** 80. Hon C Maindee Newport *Mon* 79-85; C 85-86; V Llangwm Uchaf and Llangwm Isaf w Gwernesney etc 86-99; rtd 99; LtO *Mon* from 99. *Flat 4, 47 Caerau Road, Newport NP20 4HH*

ASTON, Heather Jane. b 54. Cen Lancs Univ MBA 02. SWMTC 10. **d** 13 **p** 14. C Meneage *Truro* from 13. *38 Bosnoweth, Helston TR13 8FR* T: (01326) 564162 M: 07960-965787 E: heather_solo@msn.com

ASTON, John Bernard. b 34. Leeds Univ BA 55 PGCE 56. Qu Coll Birm 72. **d** 75 **p** 76. NSM Shenstone *Lich* 75-05; NSM Stonnall 00-05; Chapl HM YOI Swinfen Hall 90-99; PtO *Lich* from 05. *4 Footherley Road, Shenstone, Lichfield WS14 0NJ* T: (01543) 480388

ASTON, John Leslie. b 47. Open Univ BSc 99 Win Univ MA 07. Oak Hill Th Coll BA 80. **d** 80 **p** 81. C Trentham *Lich* 80-83; C Meir Heath 83-85; V Upper Tean 85-91; CF 91-02; C Andover w Foxcott *Win* 02-05; P-in-c Felixstowe SS Pet and Paul *St E* 05-11; V from 11. *The Vicarage, 14 Picketts Road, Felixstowe IP11 7JT* T: (01394) 284049
E: johnaston@oldfelixstoweparish.org

ASTON, Mrs Kim Elizabeth. b 57. Colchester Inst of Educn BA 78 LRAM 78. SEITE 00. **d** 03 **p** 04. C Croydon St Jo *S'wark*

03-10; V Welling from 10. *St Mary's Vicarage, Sandringham Drive, Welling DA16 3QU* T: (020) 8856 3247
E: astonkim@hotmail.com

ASTON, Michael James. b 48. Loughb Univ BSc 70 MBCS 85. NTMTC 98. **d** 01 **p** 02. NSM Writtle w Highwood *Chelmsf* 01-07; P-in-c W Hanningfield 07-11; rtd 11; PtO *Chelmsf* from 11. *15 Weller Grove, Chelmsford CM1 4YJ* T: (01245) 442547 M: 07940-417418 E: mikaston@globalnet.co.uk

ASTON, Roger. b 52. Ox Poly BEd 83. SAOMC 96. **d** 99 **p** 00. OLM Eynsham and Cassington *Ox* from 99. *9 Bell Close, Cassington, Witney OX29 4EP* T: (01865) 880757
E: rogera52@aol.com

ASTON, Ms Sheelagh Mary. NEOC 02. **d** 05 **p** 06. C Windy Nook St Alb *Dur* 05-10; P-in-c Oxclose from 10; Dioc Ecum Officer from 10. *37 Brancepeth Road, Washington NE38 0LA* T: 0191-415 9468

ASTON SMITH, Anthony. b 29. Trin Coll Cam BA 52 MA 56 PhD 56 CEng MIM FIDiagE MICorrST AMIMechE. Ox NSM Course 86. **d** 93 **p** 94. NSM Ox St Giles and SS Phil and Jas w St Marg 93-99; rtd 99; PtO *Ox* from 99. *32 Chalfont Road, Oxford OX2 6TH* T: (01865) 557090
E: a.j.astonsmith@btinternet.com

ASTON, Archdeacon of. *See* HEATHFIELD, The Ven Simon David

ASTON, Suffragan Bishop of. *See* WATSON, The Rt Revd Andrew John

ATACK, Elaine. b 57. Man Univ BA 78. St Mich Coll Llan 09. **d** 12 **p** 13. C St As and Chapl St As Cathl 12-14; R Bala from 14. *The Rectory, Castle Street, Bala LL23 7YA* T: (01678) 521047
E: atacks@hush.com

ATACK, John Philip. b 49. Lanc Univ MA 91. Linc Th Coll 86. **d** 88 **p** 89. C Cleveleys *Blackb* 88-92; V Appley Bridge 92-96; P-in-c Mostyn w Ffynnongroyw *St As* 99-03; P-in-c Colwyn 03-08; R Colwyn and Llanelian 08-14; AD Rhos 09-12; AD Llanrwst and Rhos 12-14; Chapl Conwy and Denbighshire NHS Trust 05-10; Hon Chapl Miss to Seafarers 01-03; rtd 14; PtO *St As* from 15. *The Rectory, Castle Street, Bala LL23 7YA* T: (01678) 521047 E: atacks@hush.com

ATALLAH, David Alexander. b 74. Ox Univ MPhys 97 Ex Univ MSc 99 PhD 03. Wycliffe Hall Ox 09. **d** 11 **p** 12. C Okehampton, Inwardleigh, Belstone, Sourton etc *Ex* 11-15; C Maidenhead St Andr and St Mary *Ox* from 15. *1 Hemsdale, Maidenhead SL6 6SL* E: vicar@atallahfamily.co.uk

ATFIELD, Gladys. b 39. Univ Coll Lon BSc 53. Gilmore Course. **dss** 79 **d** 87 **p** 94. Bexley St Mary *Roch* 79-01; Hon C 87-01; rtd 01; PtO *Roch* from 01. *6 Clarendon Mews, High Street, Bexley DA5 1JS* T: (01322) 551741

ATFIELD, Graham Roy. b 60. Kent Univ BA 82. SEITE 08. **d** 11 **p** 12. NSM Rye *Chich* from 11. *104 Elphinstone Road, Hastings TN34 2BS* T: (01424) 717382 M: 07810-554268
E: grahamatfield@hotmail.co.uk

ATFIELD, Tom David. b 80. Bris Univ BA 02 MPhil 10 Inst for Chr Studies Toronto MPhilF 06 Birm Univ ThD 11 PGCE 06. Qu Coll Birm 08. **d** 11 **p** 12. C Bromsgrove *Worc* 11-15; TV Dudley from 15. *St Barnabas' Vicarage, Middlepark Road, Dudley DY1 2LD* M: 07855-021509 E: rev@eml.cc

ATHA, Gareth William. b 83. Leeds Univ BSc 05 York St Jo Univ MA 10 Selw Coll Cam BTh 14. Westcott Ho Cam 11. **d** 14 **p** 15. C Beverley Minster *York* from 14. *23 Outer Trinities, Beverley HU17 0HN* M: 07779-697383
E: gareth.atha@googlemail.com

ATHERFOLD, Mrs Evelyne Sara. b 43. Leeds Inst of Educn CertEd 64. NOC 82. **dss** 85 **d** 92 **p** 94. Kirk Sandall and Edenthorpe *Sheff* 85-87; NSM Fishlake w Sykehouse and Kirk Bramwith etc 87-00; P-in-c 00-03; R 03-11; P-in-c 11-14; Hon C 14-15; Chapl HM YOI Hatfield 96-03. *Runswick House, Hay Green, Fishlake, Doncaster DN7 5JY* T: (01302) 841396 M: 07980-282270 E: eve.atherfold@virgin.net

ATHERLEY, Keith Philip. b 56. St Steph Ho Ox 77. **d** 80 **p** 81. C Armley w New Wortley *Ripon* 80-82; C Harrogate St Wilfrid and St Luke 82-85; V Forcett and Stanwick w Aldbrough 85-89; CF 89-03; PtO *St Alb* 05-08; *York* from 11. *Address temp unknown* M: 07946-758951

ATHERSTONE, Andrew Castell. b 74. Ch Coll Cam BA 95 MA 98 Wycliffe Hall Ox MSt 99 DPhil 01 FRHistS 08. **d** 01 **p** 02. C Abingdon *Ox* 01-05; NSM Eynsham and Cassington from 05; Research Fell Latimer Trust from 05; Tutor Wycliffe Hall Ox from 07. *44 Shakespeare Road, Eynsham, Witney OX29 4PY* T: (01865) 731239
E: andrew.atherstone@wycliffe.ox.ac.uk

ATHERSTONE, Canon Castell Hugh. b 45. Natal Univ BA 67. St Chad's Coll Dur MA 79. **d** 70 **p** 70. C Pietermaritzburg St Alphege S Africa 70-72; C Berea St Thos 72-74; C Kloor 74-77; R Hillcrest 77-80; R Newcastle 80-83; Dioc Stewardship Adv *Ely* 83-87; P-in-c Doddington w Benwick 83-87; R Frant w Eridge *Chich* 87-95; P-in-c Rotherfield w Mark Cross 94-95;

RD Rotherfield 90-94; V Seaford w Sutton 95-10; RD Lewes and Seaford 97-07; Can and Preb Chich Cathl 02-10; rtd 10; PtO *Ox* from 10. *9 The Tennis, Cassington, Witney OX29 4EL* T: (01865) 880475 E: hugh@atherstone.net

ATHERTON, Graham Bryson. b 47. FTCL 68 GRSM 69 ARMCM 69 Man Univ CertEd 70. Edin Th Coll 77. **d** 79 **p** 80. C Orford St Marg *Liv* 79-82; V Warrington St Barn 82-88; V Leeds Halton St Wilfrid *Ripon* 88-95; BD Whitkirk 92-95; TR Guiseley w Esholt *Bradf* 95-13; rtd 13. *113A Stocks Bank Road, Mirfield WF14 0EU* T: (01924) 650225

ATHERTON, Henry Anthony. b 44. Univ of Wales BSc 67 DipEd 68 Fitzw Coll Cam BA 72 MA 75 Heythrop Coll Lon MTh 00 FGS 68. Westcott Ho Cam 70. **d** 72 **p** 73. C Leamington Priors All SS *Cov* 72-75; C Orpington All SS *Roch* 75-78; V Gravesend St Mary 78-87; Chapl St Jas Hosp Gravesend 82-87; V Bromley St Andr *Roch* 87-10; rtd 10; PtO *Roch* from 10; S'wark from 12. *20 Laleham Road, London SE6 2HT* T: (020) 8695 0212
E: anthony6atherton@btinternet.com

ATHERTON, Canon John Robert. b 39. Lon Univ BA 60 Man Univ MA 74 PhD 79. Coll of Resurr Mirfield 60. **d** 62 **p** 63. C Aberdeen St Marg *Ab* 62-64; C Bury St Mark *Man* 64-67; P-in-c Glas St Marg 67-68; R Hulme St Geo *Man* 68-74; Ind Chapl 68-74; Asst Dir Wm Temple Foundn 74-79; Dir from 79; LtO *Man* 74-84; Can Res Man Cathl 84-04; rtd 04; PtO *Man* from 04. *102 Fairview Drive, Adlington, Chorley PR6 9SB* T: (01257) 474882 M: 07989-969567

ATHERTON, Lionel Thomas. b 45. Univ of Wales (Ban) BA 74 St Luke's Coll Ex. St Steph Ho Ox 74. **d** 76 **p** 77. C Chenies and Lt Chalfont *Ox* 76-79; C Fleet *Guildf* 79-84; V S Farnborough 84-89; TR Alston Team *Newc* 89-96; V Chorley St Pet *Blackb* 96-10; Bp's Adv on New Relig Movements 02-10; rtd 10; PtO *Derby* from 14. *36 Windsor Park Road, Buxton SK17 7NP* T: (01298) 74204 E: lionel.atherton@sky.com

ATHERTON, Paul Christopher. b 56. Chich Th Coll. **d** 82 **p** 83. C Orford St Marg *Liv* 82-86; CR 86-88; Chapl Univ of Wales (Cardiff) *Llan* 88-89; TV Walton St Mary *Liv* 89-92; C Westmr St Matt *Lon* 92-96; C Somers Town 96-97; V Bush Hill Park St Mark from 97; P-in-c Bush Hill Park St Steph from 13; Chapl N Middx Hosp NHS Trust from 97. *The Vicarage, St Mark's Road, Enfield EN1 1BE* T: (020) 8363 2780
E: paul.atherton@blueyonder.co.uk

ATHERTON, Philip Andrew. b 51. Wycliffe Hall Ox. **d** 84 **p** 85. C Ox St Clem 84-87; Lic Preacher *Man* 87-99; Ind Missr 87-99; PtO 00-03; *Carl* from 04. *68 Harrot Hill, Cockermouth CA13 0BL* T: (01900) 827431

ATHERTON, Philip Gordon. b 47. NTMTC BA 07. **d** 07 **p** 08. NSM Hornsey H Innocents *Lon* from 07; NSM Stroud Green H Trin from 07; NSM Harringay St Paul from 10. *4 Pensilver Close, Barnet EN4 9DJ* T: (020) 8441 5524 M: 07901-355235
E: philipatherton@tiscali.co.uk

ATKIN, Arthur Courtney Qu'appelle. b 19. Dur Univ BA 44. Lich Th Coll 59. **d** 59 **p** 60. Chapl Bromsgrove Jun Sch 59-64; C Kidderminster St Geo *Worc* 59-60; C Bromsgrove All SS 60-64; Chapl RN 64-69; Chapl R Hosp Sch Holbrook 69-72; P-in-c Brixham *Ex* 72-74; Chapl Colston's Sch Bris 74-79; P-in-c Pitcombe w Shepton Montague and Bratton St Maur *B & W* 79-85; rtd 86; PtO *B & W* 86-93; *Heref* from 93. *6 Leadon Bank, Orchard Lane, Ledbury HR8 1BY*

ATKINS, Andrew John. b 72. St Jo Coll Nottm 09. **d** 11 **p** 12. C Ex St Dav 11-14; P-in-c Milton Abbot, Dunterton, Lamerton etc from 14. *The Vicarage, The Parade, Milton Abbot, Tavistock PL19 0NZ* M: 07599-058129 E: andya4jc@gmail.com

ATKINS, Austen Shaun. b 55. St Pet Coll Ox MA 82 Selw Coll Cam MA 85. Ridley Hall Cam 79. **d** 82 **p** 83. C S Mimms Ch Ch *Lon* 82-86; C Fulham St Matt 86-91; P-in-c Fulham St Dionis 91-03; V 03-04; C Ox St Andr 05-09; Chapl Bedford Sch from 09. *The Chaplaincy, Bedford School, De Parys Avenue, Bedford MK40 2TU* T: (01234) 362239
E: chaplain@bedfordschool.org.uk

ATKINS, Canon David John. b 43. Kelham Th Coll 64. **d** 68 **p** 69. C Lewisham St Mary S'wark 68-72; Min Motspur Park 72-77; P-in-c Mitcham Ascension 77-82; V 82-83; P-in-c Downham w S Hanningfield *Chelmsf* 83-88; R 88-01; P-in-c w Hanningfield 90-93; RD Chelmsf S 93-01; V Maldon All SS w St Pet 01-09; Hon Can Chelmsf Cathl 00-09; rtd 09; PtO *Chelmsf* from 09. *19 The Green, Hadleigh, Ipswich IP7 6AE* T: (01473) 822535 E: atkins.d@btinternet.com

ATKINS, Dean John. b 70. Univ of Wales (Cardiff) BD 93. St Steph Ho Ox 93. **d** 95 **p** 96. C Merthyr Dyfan *Llan* 95-99; V Aberaman and Abercwmboi w Cwmaman 99-01; Dioc Youth Officer from 01; P-in-c Roath St Sav 08-12; V Cardiff St German w St Sav from 12. *St Anne's, 1 North Church Street, Cardiff CF10 5HB* T: (029) 2049 9867

ATKINS, Forrest William (Bill). b 59. Ch Coll Cam MA 85 Lon Univ BD 84. Ridley Hall Cam 83. **d** 86 **p** 87. C Normanton

Derby 86-90; C Stratford St Jo and Ch Ch w Forest Gate St Jas *Chelmsf* 90-97; Asst Chapl Dubai and Sharjah w N Emirates 97-03; I Mohill w Farnaught, Aughavas, Oughteragh etc *K, E & A* 03-13; Preb Elphin Cathl 08-13; I Eglish w Killylea *Arm* from 13. *154 Killylea Road, Armagh BT60 4LN* T: (028) 3756 8874 E: fwatkins@eircom.net

ATKINS, Jane Elizabeth. b 51. EMMTC 98. **d** 01 **p** 02. NSM Fenn Lanes Gp *Leic* 01-05; Sub Chapl HM Pris Leic 03-05; P-in-c Ashill w Saham Toney *Nor* 05-07; V Ashill, Carbrooke, Ovington and Saham Toney from 07. *The Rectory, Swaffham Road, Ashill, Thetford IP25 7BT* T: (01760) 441191

ATKINS, Joy Katherine. b 75. Lon Sch of Th BTh 97 Dur Univ PGCE 98. St Jo Coll Nottm MTh 09. **d** 09 **p** 10. C Uxbridge *Lon* 09-12; Chapl Twyford C of E High Sch Acton and Wm Perkin C of E High Sch 12-13; C Reading Greyfriars *Ox* from 13. *93 York Road, Reading RG1 8DU* E: joyatkins@hotmail.com

ATKINS (née HARDING), Ms Lesley Anne. b 58. Westcott Ho Cam 98 SEITE 99. **d** 01 **p** 02. C Walmer *Cant* 01-03; C Broadstairs 03-04; PtO 05-07; NSM Barkston and Hough Gp *Linc* 07-10; P-in-c Hattersley *Ches* from 10. *St Barnabas' Vicarage, Hattersley Road East, Hyde SK14 3EQ* T: 0161-368 2795 E: lesley@revlesleyanne.plus.com

ATKINS, Nicholas Steven. b 60. Oak Hill Th Coll BA 88. **d** 88 **p** 89. C Shepton Mallet w Doulting *B & W* 88-91; C Combe Down w Monkton Combe and S Stoke 91-93; TV N Wingfield, Clay Cross and Pilsley *Derby* 93-98; V Essington *Lich* 98-05; P-in-c Ipswich St Matt *St E* 05-06; R Triangle, St Matt and All SS from 06. *St Matthew's Rectory, 3 Portman Road, Ipswich IP1 2ES* T: (01473) 251630

ATKINS, Canon Paul Henry. b 38. St Mich Coll Llan 62. **d** 65 **p** 66. C Sheringham *Nor* 65-68; V Southtown 68-84; RD Flegg (Gt Yarmouth) 78-84; R Aylmerton w Runton 84-99; P-in-c Beeston Regis 98-99; P-in-c Gresham 98-99; R Aylmerton, Runton, Beeston Regis and Gresham 99-03; RD Repps 86-95; Hon Can Nor Cathl 88-03; rtd 03; PtO *Nor* from 03. *34 Regis Avenue, Beeston Regis, Sheringham NR26 8SW* T: (01263) 820147 E: paulatkins07@btinternet.com

ATKINS, Robert Brian. b 49. Open Univ BA 94 CIPFA 78. SAOMC 94. **d** 97 **p** 98. NSM Bicester w Bucknell, Caversfield and Launton *Ox* from 97. *8 Tubb Close, Bicester OX26 2BN* T: (01869) 327415 M: 07832-573938

ATKINS, Roger Francis. b 30. AKC 54. **d** 55 **p** 56. C Bromley All Hallows *Lon* 55-58; C Eastleigh *Win* 58-62; Missr The Murray Australia 62-65; R Mossman 65-69; Adn Carpentaria 69-71; V Wolverley *Worc* 71-76; V S Hackney St Mich w Haggerston St Paul *Lon* 76-85; TV Gleadless *Sheff* 85-93; rtd 93; PtO *Sheff* from 93. *27 Stannington Glen, Sheffield S6 6NA* T: 0114-234 0543

ATKINS, Mrs Sarah Christine. b 83. Magd Coll Cam MA 09. Ridley Hall Cam 12. **d** 14. C Trumpington *Ely* from 14. *18 Beech Drive, Trumpington, Cambridge CB2 9PR* T: (01223) 847608 M: 07906-659655 E: sarah.atkins@cantab.net

ATKINS, Shaun. *See* ATKINS, Austen Shaun

ATKINS, Timothy David. b 45. Ridley Hall Cam 71. **d** 74 **p** 75. C Stoughton *Guildf* 74-79; C Chilwell *S'well* 79-84; R Eastwood 84-91; V Finchley Ch Ch *Lon* 91-10; Chapl Barnet Healthcare NHS Trust 92-01; Chapl Enfield Primary Care Trust 01-10; rtd 10; PtO *Lon* 10-12; Hon C Uxbridge from 12. *75 Belmont Road, Uxbridge UB8 1QU* T: (01895) 231801 M: 07875-747760
E: ta.atkins@hotmail.co.uk

ATKINS, Timothy James. b 38. Worc Coll Ox BA 62. Cuddesdon Coll 62. **d** 64 **p** 65. C Stafford St Mary *Lich* 64-67; C Loughborough St Pet *Leic* 67-69; C Usworth *Dur* 69-71; LtO *Newc* 71-76; P-in-c Slaley 76-87; P-in-c Shotley 87-05; Dioc Child Protection Adv 98-06; PtO *Dur* from 06. *5 Railway Terrace, Witton le Wear, Bishop Auckland DL14 0AL* T: (01388) 488626

ATKINS, William. *See* ATKINS, Forrest William

ATKINSON, Adam. b 67. Birm Univ BA 89. Wycliffe Hall Ox 05. **d** 07 **p** 08. C Shadwell St Paul w Ratcliffe St Jas *Lon* 07-11; V Bethnal Green St Pet w St Thos from 11. *St Peter's Vicarage, St Peter's Close, London E2 7AE* T: (020) 7229 0550 M: 07780-992112 E: adam@spbg.info

ATKINSON, Ms Audrey. b 54. Univ of Wales (Lamp) BA 97 Trin Coll Carmarthen PGCE 98. Coll of Resurr Mirfield 06. **d** 08 **p** 09. C Beadnell and N Sunderland *Newc* 08-11; Dep Warden Launde Abbey *Leic* 11; TV Oakham, Ashwell, Braunston, Brooke, Egleton etc *Pet* 11-14; Chapl HM Pris Full Sutton from 14. *HM Prison, Full Sutton, York YO41 1PS* M: 07833-198968 T: (01759) 475100 E: audreyatkinson@hotmail.co.uk

ATKINSON, Brian Colin. b 49. Sarum & Wells Th Coll 85. **d** 87 **p** 88. C Up Hatherley *Glouc* 87-90; R Upper Stour *Sarum* 90-95; TR Trowbridge H Trin 95-04; P-in-c Fairford and Kempsford w Whelford *Glouc* 04-08; TR S Cotswolds 09-11; AP Fairford 04-11; rtd 14; Hon C Minchinhampton w Box and Amberley *Glouc* from 14. *The Vicarage, The Croft, Fairford GL7 4BB* T: (01285) 712467 E: katki01225@aol.com

ATKINSON, Christopher John. b 57. Man Univ BA 80. Qu Coll Birm 82. **d** 85 **p** 86. C Stalybridge *Man* 85-88; P-in-c Westhall w Brampton and Stoven *St E* 88-89; P-in-c Sotterley, Willingham, Shadingfield, Ellough etc 88-89; P-in-c Hundred River Gp of Par 90-92; R Hundred River 92-97; P-in-c Eye w Braiseworth and Yaxley 97-00; P-in-c Occold 97-00; P-in-c Bedingfield 97-00; R Eye 00-03; RD Hartismere 97-03; V Bourne *Linc* from 03; RD Beltisloe from 13. *The Vicarage, Church Walk, Bourne PE10 9UQ* T: (01778) 422412 E: chris_atk@yahoo.com

ATKINSON, Canon Christopher Lionel Varley. b 39. K Coll Lon 63. Chich Th Coll 65. **d** 67 **p** 68. C Sowerby Bridge w Norland *Wakef* 67-70; P-in-c Flushing *Truro* 70-73; Dioc Adv in RE 70-73; PtO *Worc* 74-78; TR Halesowen 78-88; RD Dudley 79-87; Hon Can Worc Cathl 83-88; V Cartmel *Carl* 88-97; TV Cartmel Peninsula 97-98; RD Windermere 94-98; Hon Can Carl Cathl 94-98; TR Bensham *Dur* 98-03; AD Gateshead 99-03; rtd 03; Bp's Adv Spiritual Development *Dur* 03-08; Hon Can Dur Cathl from 01; PtO from 11. *4 Attwood Place, Tow Law, Bishop Auckland DL13 4ER* T: (01388) 731749

ATKINSON, Clive James. b 68. QUB BSc 90. CITC 90. **d** 93 **p** 94. C Belfast H Trin and Ardoyne *Conn* 93-95; C Belfast H Trin and St Silas 96-97; I Belfast Upper Falls 97-02; Chapl Vevey w Château d'Oex *Eur* from 02. *The Parsonage, chemin de Champsavaux 1, 1807 Blonay, Vaud, Switzerland* T: (0041) (21) 943 2239 E: info@allsaints.ch

ATKINSON, David. b 64. St Cuth Soc Dur BA 02. Cranmer Hall Dur 02. **d** 04 **p** 05. C Dunston *Dur* 04-07; C Pelton and W Pelton 07-10; P-in-c Dunston 10-11; V from 11. *St Nicholas' Vicarage, Willow Avenue, Dunston, Gateshead NE11 9UN* T: 0191-460 9327 E: revd.atkinson@btinternet.com

ATKINSON, Prof David. b 44. Hull Univ BSc 66 Newc Univ PhD 69 CBiol FIBiol FRSA MIEEM. TISEC 03. **d** 05 **p** 06. C Aberdeen St Andr *Ab* 05-07; NSM Bieldside 07-09; NSM Auchindoin from 09; NSM Inverurie from 09; NSM Kemnay from 09. *33 Norman Gray Park, Blackburn, Aberdeen AB21 0ZR* T: (01224) 791163 E: atkinson390@btinternet.com

ATKINSON, Canon David James. b 41. K Coll Lon BD 63 AKC 63 Selw Coll Cam BA 65 MA 72. Linc Th Coll 65. **d** 66 **p** 67. C Linc St Giles 66-70; Asst Chapl Newc Univ 70-73; P-in-c Adbaston *Lich* 73-80; Adult Educn Officer 73-75; Dioc Dir of Educn 75-82; Preb Lich Cathl 79-82; Chapl Hull Univ *York* 82-87; Dioc Dir of Educn *Linc* 87-94; P-in-c Bishop Norton, Waddingham and Snitterby 94-01; PtO from 01; Can and Preb Linc Cathl 89-06; rtd 06. *4 The Orchards, Middle Rasen, Market Rasen LN8 3TL* T: (01673) 849979

✠**ATKINSON, The Rt Revd David John.** b 43. K Coll Lon BSc 65 AKC 65 PhD 69 Bris Univ MLitt 73 Ox Univ MA 85 MSOSc. Trin Coll Bris and Tyndale Hall Bris 69. **d** 72 **p** 73 **c** 01. C Halliwell St Pet *Man* 72-74; C Harborne Heath *Birm* 74-77; Lib Latimer Ho *Ox* 77-80; Chapl CCC *Ox* 80-93; Fell 84-93; Visiting Lect Wycliffe Hall *Ox* 84-93; Can Res and Chan S'wark Cathl 93-96; Adn Lewisham 96-01; Suff Bp Thetford *Nor* 01-09; rtd 09; Asst Bp S'wark from 09. *6 Bynes Road, South Croydon CR2 0PR* T: (020) 8406 0895 E: davidatkinson43@virginmedia.com

ATKINSON, Derek Arthur. b 31. K Coll Lon BD 59 AKC 59. **d** 60 **p** 61. C Ashford *Cant* 60-64; C Deal St Leon 64-68; R E w W Ogwell *Ex* 68-81; Asst Dir of RE 68-78; Dep Dir and Children's Adv 78-88; R Ogwell and Denbury *Ex* 81-84; R Kenton w Mamhead and Powderham 84-88; rtd 88; PtO *Ex* 88-98. *High Trees, Fulford Road, Fulford, Stoke-on-Trent ST11 9QT* T: (01782) 397156 E: derek-atkinson@lineone.net

ATKINSON, Mrs Heather Dawn. b 69. Leeds Univ BA 02. NOC 03. **d** 05 **p** 06. C Morley *Wakef* 05-08; P-in-c Moldgreen and Rawthorpe *Leeds* from 08. *The Vicarage, 35 Church Street, Huddersfield HD5 9DL* T: (01484) 424432 M: 07766-575371 E: heatherwood19@yahoo.com

ATKINSON, Mrs Heather Mary Ann. b 66. St Mellitus Coll 12. **d** 15. NSM S Hackney St Mich w Haggerston St Paul *Lon* from 15. *Address unknown*

ATKINSON, Ian. b 33. BNC Ox BA 58 MA 63. Coll of Resurr Mirfield 56. **d** 58 **p** 59. C Welling *S'wark* 58-62; C Camberwell St Giles 62-63; V Wandsworth Common St Mary 63-67; C Pretoria Cathl S Africa 67-68; C Oxted *S'wark* 68-69; Asst Chapl Ch Hosp Horsham 70-85; NSM Dalmahoy *Edin* 85-91; Asst Master Clifton Hall Sch 85-91; NSM Dunkeld *St And* from 92; rtd 98. *2 Pinel Lodge, Druids Park, Murthly, Perth PH1 4ES* T: (01738) 710561

ATKINSON, Jane Louise. b 66. **d** 13 **p** 14. NSM Kirkham *Blackb* from 13. *35 Bispham Road, Poulton-le-Fylde FY6 7PE* T: (01253) 893383 E: janemell@sky.com

ATKINSON, Ms Judith Angela. b 70. Leeds Univ BA 92 Fitzw Coll Cam BA 95 MA 02. Ridley Hall Cam 93. **d** 96 **p** 97. C Chester le Street *Dur* 96-00; Community Employment Development Worker 00-01; NSM Dunston *Dur* 01-02;

Ch Partnership Co-ord N Tyneside 00-02; LtO *Birm* 03-06; Regional Manager KeyRing Living Support Networks 03-05; Dir (Research and Projects) 05-07; PtO Canberra & Goulburn Australia from 07. *United Theological College, 16 Masons Drive, North Parramatta, NSW 2151, Australia* T: (0061) (2) 8838 8921 E: juditha_stephenb@hotmail.com

ATKINSON, Mrs Kate Bigwood. b 56. Cranmer Hall Dur 94. **d** 96 **p** 97. C Woking St Jo *Guildf* 96-00; NSM Haslemere and Grayswood 00-03; Assoc P Incline Village USA from 03. *818 Barbara Street, Incline Village NV 89451-8514, USA*

ATKINSON, Canon Lewis Malcolm. b 34. Cranmer Hall Dur. **d** 82 **p** 83. C Chapeltown *Sheff* 82-85; V Sheff St Paul 85-93; Ind Chapl 85-99; RD Ecclesfield 90-93; V Oughtibridge 93-99; RD Tankersley 96-99; Hon Can Sheff Cathl 98-99; rtd 99; PtO *Sheff* from 99. *14 Rowan Close, Chapeltown, Sheffield S35 1QE*

ATKINSON, Margaret Ann. b 50. **d** 07 **p** 08. OLM Fawdon *Newc* from 07. *48 Brotherlee Road, Newcastle upon Tyne NE3 2SL*

ATKINSON, Marianne Rose. b 39. Girton Coll Cam BA 61 CertEd 62 MA 64. Linc Th Coll 86. **d** 88 **p** 94. C S w N Hayling *Portsm* 88-91; C Rainham *Roch* 91-92; Asst Chapl Salford R Hosps NHS Trust 92-97; Hon C Prestwich St Marg *Man* 94-97; Chapl R United Hosp Bath NHS Trust 97-00; rtd 00; PtO *B & W* 00-03; *St E* from 03. *68 Barons Road, Bury St Edmunds IP33 2LW* T: (01284) 752075 E: torrensatkinson@aol.com

ATKINSON, Megan Annice. b 37. SRN 58. STETS 95. **d** 98 **p** 01. NSM Bridgemary *Portsm* 98-02; NSM Locks Heath 02-04; rtd 04; PtO *Portsm* from 05. *23 Home Rule Road, Locks Heath, Southampton SO31 6LH* T: (01489) 575331 E: meganatkinson1@msn.com

ATKINSON, Michael Hubert. b 33. Qu Coll Ox BA 57 MA 60. Ripon Hall Ox 56. **d** 58 **p** 59. C Attercliffe w Carbrook *Sheff* 58-60; Ind Chapl 60-66; C Sharrow St Andr 60-66; Ind Chapl *Pet* 66-71; Sen Ind Chapl *Cant* 71-79; Research Officer Gen Syn Bd for Soc Resp 79-87; Representation Sec USPG 88-92; TV High Wycombe *Ox* 92-97; Chapl Bucks Coll of HE 94-97; rtd 97. *7 Birch Court, Old Bridge Rise, Ilkley LS29 9HH* T: (01943) 609891

ATKINSON, Nigel Terence. b 60. Sheff Univ BA 82 St Jo Coll Dur MA 96. Westmr Th Sem (USA) MDiv 87 Cranmer Hall Dur 87. **d** 89 **p** 90. C Oakwood St Thos *Lon* 89-92; P-in-c Dolton *Ex* 92-95; P-in-c Iddesleigh w Dowland 92-95; P-in-c Monkokehampton 92-95; Warden Latimer Ho *Ox* 95-98; V Knutsford St Jo and Toft *Ches* from 98. *The Vicarage, 11 Gough's Lane, Knutsford WA16 8QL* T: (01565) 632834 F: 755160 E: nigelatk@me.com

ATKINSON, Canon Patricia Anne. b 47. EAMTC 86. **d** 89 **p** 01. NSM Nor St Steph 89-94; LtO from 94; Chapl Norfolk Primary Care Trust from 00; Chapl Norwich and Nor Univ Hosp NHS Trust 01-11; NSM Brundall w Braydeston and Postwick *Nor* 01-02; Hon Can Nor Cathl from 06. *32 Berryfields, Brundall, Norwich NR13 5QE* T: (01603) 714720 E: revpat@live.co.uk

ATKINSON, Paul William. b 64. St Steph Ho Ox 07. **d** 09 **p** 10. C Castleford *Wakef* 09-13; C Smawthorpe 11-12; P-in-c Ravensthorpe and Thornhill Lees w Savile Town *Leeds* from 13. *St Saviour's Vicarage, Church Street, Ravensthorpe, Dewsbury WF13 3LA* T: (01924) 672103 E: fr.paul.atkinson@live.co.uk

ATKINSON, Peter Duncan. b 41. Univ Coll Dur BA 62. Linc Th Coll 63. **d** 65 **p** 66. C Beckenham St Geo *Roch* 65-69; C Caversham *Ox* 69-75; P-in-c Millfield St Mark *Dur* 76-86; V Dedworth *Ox* 86-93; TV Aylesbury 93-05; rtd 05. *24 Grimbald Road, Knaresborough HG5 8HD* T: (01423) 866593

ATKINSON, The Very Revd Peter Gordon. b 52. St Jo Coll Ox BA 74 MA 78 Worc Univ Hon DLitt 14 FRSA 06. Westcott Ho Cam 77. **d** 79 **p** 80. C Clapham Old Town *S'wark* 79-83; P-in-c Tatsfield 83-90; R Bath H Trin *B & W* 90-91; Prin Chich Th Coll 91-94; Can and Preb Chich Cathl 91-97; R Lavant 94-97; Can Res and Chan Chich Cathl 94-97; Dean Worc from 07. *The Deanery, 10 College Green, Worcester WR1 2LH* T: (01905) 732939 *or* 732909 F: 732906 E: peteratkinson@worcestercathedral.org.uk

ATKINSON, Philip Charles. b 50. Hull Univ BA 71 PhD 76 Chorley Coll of Educn CertEd 77. NOC 81. **d** 84 **p** 85. NSM Bolton SS Simon and Jude *Man* 84-87; Chapl R Wolv Sch 87-05; rtd 05. *9 Musbury Avenue, Cheadle Hulme, Cheadle SK8 7AT* T: 0161-486 9761 E: philipandann4177@tiscali.co.uk

ATKINSON, Philip John. b 69. Birkbeck Coll Lon PhD 04. Ridley Hall Cam 08. **d** 10 **p** 11. C Ox St Aldate from 10. *St Aldate's Parish Office, 40 Pembroke Street, Oxford OX1 1BP* T: (01865) 254800 E: phil.atkinson@staldates.org.uk

ATKINSON, Philip Stephen. b 58. K Coll Lon BD 80 AKC 80 Dur Univ MA 97. Ridley Hall Cam 81. **d** 83 **p** 84. C Barrow St Matt *Carl* 83-86; C Kirkby Lonsdale 86-89; R Redmarshall *Dur* 89-95; V Bishopton w Gt Stainton 89-95; C Kirkby Lonsdale *Carl* 95-97; Chapl Casterton Sch Lancs 95-09; NSM

Kirkby Lonsdale *Carl* 97-09; Chapl Taunton Sch 09-11; R Odd Rode *Ches* from 11. *Odd Rode Rectory, Church Lane, Scholar Green, Stoke-on-Trent ST7 3QN* T: (01270) 882195
E: rector.oddrode@gmail.com

✠**ATKINSON, The Rt Revd Richard William Bryant.** b 58. OBE 02. Magd Coll Cam MA. Ripon Coll Cuddesdon. **d** 84 **p** 85 **c** 12. C Abingdon w Shippon *Ox* 84-87; TV Sheff Manor 87-91; TR 91-96; Hon Tutor Ripon Coll Cuddesdon 87-92; V Rotherham *Sheff* 96-02; Hon Can Sheff Cathl 98-02; Adn Leic 02-12; Suff Bp Bedford *St Alb* from 12. *Bishop's Lodge, Bedford Road, Cardington, Bedford MK44 3SS* T: (01234) 831432
F: 831484 E: bishopbedford@stalbans.anglican.org

ATKINSON, Miss Ruth Irene. b 58. Worc Coll of Educn BEd 80 Cant Ch Ch Univ MA 08. Qu Coll Birm 06. **d** 09 **p** 10. C Old Swinford Stourbridge *Worc* 09-14; V Bartley Green *Birm* from 14. *96 Romsley Road, Birmingham B32 3PS*
M: 07432-660538 T: 0121-476 5287
E: revruthvicarbg@gmail.com

ATKINSON, Canon Samuel Charles Donald. b 30. TCD BA 54. **d** 55 **p** 56. C Belfast St Simon *Conn* 55-62; I Ballynaclough *L & K* 62-68; I Cloughjordan w Modreeny 68-87; Dioc Youth Adv (Killaloe) 75-83; Dioc Info Officer 76-88; Can Killaloe Cathl 76-82; Chan Killaloe Cathl 82-96; I Cloughjordan w Borrisokane etc 87-96; rtd 96. *Dromore Lodge, Rockcorry, Co Monaghan, Republic of Ireland* T: (00353) (42) 42356

ATKINSON, Simon James. b 71. St Chad's Coll Dur BA 93 Ustinov Coll Dur PGCE 04 PGDE 08. St Steph Ho Ox 93. **d** 95 **p** 96. C Norton St Mary *Dur* 95-96; C Hartlepool H Trin 96-99; TV Jarrow 99-01; V Chich St Wilfrid 01-03; PtO *Dur* 03-09; Lon 09-10; NSM Old St Pancras from 10; Headteacher Hampstead Paroch C of E Primary Sch from 10; CMP from 98. *Hampstead Parochial Primary School, Holly Bush Vale, London NW3 6TX* T: (020) 7435 4135 E: head@hampsteadprim.camden.sch.uk

ATKINSON, Terence Harry. b 52. Coll of Resurr Mirfield 88. **d** 90 **p** 91. C Bottesford w Ashby *Linc* 90-93; TV Cleethorpes 93-98; C-in-c Cleethorpes St Fran CD 98-01; V Chapel St Leonards w Hogsthorpe 01-03; P-in-c Gt Grimsby St Andr w St Luke and All SS 03-13. *Address temp unknown*

ATKINSON, Mrs Valerie. b 50. **d** 12. NSM Teignmouth, Ideford w Luton, Ashcombe etc *Ex* from 12. *9 Oakley Close, Teignmouth TQ14 8RX* T: (01626) 776771 E: valian09@btinternet.com

ATKINSON, Wendy Sybil. b 53. Man Univ BA 95. NOC 95. **d** 97 **p** 98. NSM Brinnington w Portwood *Ches* 97-99; C 99-01; NSM Werneth from 01. *8 Freshfield Close, Marple Bridge, Stockport SK6 5ES* T: 0161-427 5612

ATKINSON-JONES, Mrs Susan Florence. b 64. Univ of Wales (Cardiff) BD 93. St Mich Coll Llan 96. **d** 98 **p** 99. C Bargoed and Deri w Brithdir *Llan* 98-05; TV Sanderstead *S'wark* from 05. *35 Audley Drive, Warlingham CR6 9AH* T: (020) 8657 5505 E: susan@sanderstead-parish.org.uk

ATLING, Canon Edwood Brian. b 46. ACIB FCMI. Westcott Ho Cam 00. **d** 02 **p** 03. NSM Godmanchester *Ely* 02-04; P-in-c Abbots Ripton w Wood Walton 04-12; P-in-c Kings Ripton 04-12; P-in-c Houghton w Wyton 04-13; R Hartford and Houghton w Wyton from 13; RD Huntingdon from 06; Hon Can Ely Cathl from 10. *Blue Cedars, 70 Common Lane, Hemingford Abbots, Huntingdon PE28 9AW* T: (01480) 493975 F: 496240 M: 07775-544679 E: atling@btopenworld.com

ATTA-BAFFOE, Victor Reginald. b 59. Trin Coll Toronto BTh 88 Episc Div Sch Cambridge (USA) MA 92 Yale Univ STM 93. St Nic Th Coll Ghana LTh 87. **d** 88 **p** 89. Ghana 88-90 and 93-98; USA 90-93; Lect St Nic Th Coll 88-90 and 93-98; NSM Finsbury Park St Thos *Lon* from 99. *20 Great Peter Street, London SW1P 2BU* T: (020) 7222 3704 F: 7233 0255

ATTAWAY, Mrs Elizabeth Ann. b 36. Herts Coll CertEd 56. Cant Sch of Min 93 Bp Otter Coll 57. **d** 96 **p** 97. NSM Maidstone St Paul *Cant* 96-02; NSM Boxley w Detling from 02. *1 Staplers Court, Penenden Heath, Maidstone ME14 2XB* T: (01622) 762656 E: glattaway@btinternet.com

ATTEW, Richard John. b 82. Wolv Univ BA 04 Univ of Wales (Abth) PGCE 05. Ridley Hall Cam 12. **d** 15. C Tye Green w Netteswell *Chelmsf* from 15. *4 Willowfield, Harlow CM18 6RR* M: 07958-481215 E: richardattew@hotmail.co.uk

ATTFIELD, David George. b 31. Magd Coll Ox BA 54 MA 58 BD 61 K Coll Lon MPhil 72 Dur Univ MA 81. Westcott Ho Cam 57. **d** 58 **p** 59. C Edgbaston St Aug *Birm* 58-61; C Ward End 61-62; Lect Div St Kath Coll Tottenham 62-64; All SS Coll Tottenham 64-68; Sen Lect St Bede Coll Dur 68-75; St Hild and St Bede Coll 75-80; TV Drypool *York* 80-86; R Newton Heath All SS *Man* 86-96; rtd 97; PtO *Dur* from 97. *19 Laburnum Avenue, Durham DH1 4HA* T: 0191-383 0509

ATTLEY, Ronald. b 46. Open Univ BA 87. Brasted Th Coll 66 Chich Th Coll 68. **d** 70 **p** 71. C Heworth St Mary *Dur* 70-73; C Hulme Ascension *Man* 73-75; R Corozal and Orange Walk Belize 76-79; V Leadgate *Dur* 79-84; Chapl HM Rem Cen Ashford 84-87; Chapl HM Pris Ashwell 87-89; Chapl HM Pris Stocken 87-89; Chapl HM Pris Frankland 89-92; Chapl HM

YOI Deerbolt 92-96; V Bath St Barn w Englishcombe *B & W* 96-00; Belize 00; V Brinnington w Portwood *Ches* 01-06; P Narrogin Australia 06-12; rtd 12. *103 Clayton Road, Narrogin WA 6312, Australia*

ATTWATER, Mrs Sallyanne. b 48. Westmr Coll Ox MTh 98. S Dios Minl Tr Scheme 86. **d** 94 **p** 95. Chapl Asst Eastbourne Distr Gen Hosp 94-95; Asst Chapl Princess Alice Hospice Esher 94-95; Asst Chapl All SS Eastbourne 94-95; C E Grinstead St Swithun *Chich* 95-98; P-in-c Bishop's Cannings, All Cannings etc *Sarum* 98-10; RD Devizes 07-10; rtd 10. *51 St Kitts Drive, Eastbourne BN23 5TL* T: (01323) 472266 E: sally.attwater@gmail.com

ATTWATER, Canon Stephen Philip. b 47. ALCM 67. Linc Th Coll 85. **d** 87 **p** 88. C Warrington St Elphin *Liv* 87-90; P-in-c Eccleston St Thos 90-94; V 94-99; V Padgate 99-13; AD Warrington 05-12; Hon Can Liv Cathl 05-12; rtd 13. *The Vicarage, 1 Briers Close, Fearnhead, Warrington WA2 0DN* T: (01925) 823108 E: stephen@attwater1.freeserve.co.uk

ATTWOOD, Andrew Michael. b 66. Derby Coll of Educn BEd 91. Trin Coll Bris BA 02. **d** 02 **p** 03. C Leamington Priors St Mary *Cov* 02-10; V Kenilworth St Jo from 10. *St John's Vicarage, Clarke's Avenue, Kenilworth CV8 1HX* T: (01936) 853203 E: andrew@stjohnschurchkenilworth.org.uk

ATTWOOD, Preb Carl Norman Harry. b 53. Bris Univ BA 74. Cuddesdon Coll BA 76 MA 80. **d** 77 **p** 78. C Tupsley *Heref* 77-82; R Colwall w Upper Colwall and Coddington 82-08; Bp's Voc Officer 83-89; RD Ledbury 90-96; Chapl St Jas Sch Malvern 86-08; Preb Heref Cathl 97-08; rtd 08; PtO *Worc* from 82; *Heref* from 08. *The Lodge, Old Colwall, Malvern WR13 6HF* T: (01604) 540788 E: carl@attwoods.org

ATTWOOD, David John Edwin. b 51. Dur Univ BA 76 Em Coll Cam BA 73 MA 77. Cranmer Hall Dur 74. **d** 77 **p** 78. C Rodbourne Cheney *Bris* 77-79; C Lydiard Millicent w Lydiard Tregoz 79-85; Dir and Lect Trin Coll Bris 85-97; V Prenton *Ches* 97-02; R Sundridge w Ide Hill and Toys Hill *Roch* 02-13; rtd 13. *65 The Ridge, Hastings TN34 2AB* E: david@attwood27.freeserve.co.uk

ATTWOOD, Mrs Jennifer. b 71. **d** 08 **p** 09. NSM Lingfield and Crowhurst *S'wark* 08-15; NSM Lingfield and Dormansland from 15. *28 Headland Way, Lingfield RH7 6BP* T: (01342) 833100 E: jennyattwood@aol.com

ATTWOOD, Leslie Thomas. b 42. UWE MA 94 Cranfield Univ MBA MCIPD 76. St Steph Ho Ox. **d** 83 **p** 84. C Ascot Heath *Ox* 83-86; Dioc Tr Officer Truro 86-88; C Wallasey St Hilary *Ches* 98-00; C Devizes St Pet *Sarum* 00-02; TV Godrevy *Truro* 02-07; TR 07-09; rtd 09. *Chyrempter, Perranuthnoe, Penzance TR20 9NQ* T: (01736) 710449 E: attwood99@lineone.net

ATTWOOD, Peter John. b 44. ACIB 68. SEITE 00. **d** 03 **p** 04. NSM Langton Green *Roch* 03-06; C S Molton w Nymet St George, High Bray etc *Ex* 06-12; RD S Molton 09-12; rtd 12. *Brome Cottage, 86 Castle Hill, Nether Stowey, Bridgwater TA5 1NB* T: (01278) 734588 M: 07714-026402 E: rev@podlea.co.uk

ATTY, Norman Hughes. b 40. Dur Univ BA 62. Cranmer Hall Dur 62. **d** 65 **p** 66. C Blackb St Gabr 65-67; Asst Master Billinge Sch Blackb 67-71; City of Leic Boys' Sch 71-73; P-in-c Elmley Lovett w Hampton Lovett *Worc* 73-78; P-in-c Elmbridge w Rushock 74-78; R Elmley Lovett w Hampton Lovett and Elmbridge etc 78-85; Hon Can Worc Cathl 81-85; rtd 05; PtO *Blackb* from 05. *The Dog Inn, King Street, Whalley, Clitheroe BB7 9SP* T: (01254) 823009

ATWELL, The Very Revd James Edgar. b 46. Ex Coll Ox BA 68 MA 73 BD 94 Harvard Univ ThM 70. Cuddesdon Coll 68. **d** 70 **p** 71. C E Dulwich St Jo *S'wark* 70-74; C Cambridge Gt St Mary w St Mich *Ely* 74-77; Chapl Jes Coll Cam 77-81; V Towcester w Easton Neston *Pet* 81-95; RD Towcester 83-91; Provost St E 95-00; Dean St E 00-04; Dean Win from 06. *The Deanery, The Close, Winchester SO23 9LS* T: (01962) 857203 E: the.dean@winchester-cathedral.org.uk

✠**ATWELL, The Rt Revd Robert Ronald.** b 54. St Jo Coll Dur BA 75 Dur Univ MLitt 79. Westcott Ho Cam 76. **d** 78 **p** 79 **c** 08. C Mill Hill Jo Keble Ch *Lon* 78-81; Chapl Trin Coll Cam 81-87; OSB 87-98; LtO *Ox* 87-97; PtO *Ely* 97-98; V Primrose Hill St Mary w Avenue Road St Paul *Lon* 98-08; Suff Bp Stockport *Ches* 08-14; Bp Ex from 14. *The Palace, Exeter EX1 1HY* T: (01392) 272362 F: 430923 E: bishop.of.exeter@exeter.anglican.org

AUBREY-JONES, Adrian Frederick. b 51. ERMC 04. **d** 07 **p** 08. NSM Dersingham w Anmer and Shernborne *Nor* 07-10; TV Dereham and Distr from 10; RD Dereham in Mitford from 15. *The Vicarage, Woodgate Lane, Swanton Morley, Dereham NR20 4NS* T: (01362) 638378 M: 07775-514567 E: a3351adrian@aol.com

AUCHMUTY, John Robert. b 67. ACCA. CITC 89. **d** 92 **p** 93. C Dundela St Mark *D & D* 92-96; I Eglish w Killylea *Arm*

96-01; I Killaney w Carryduff *D & D* 01-07; I Knock from 07. *St Columba's Rectory, 29 King's Road, Knock, Belfast BT5 6JG* T: (028) 9047 1514 E: johnauchmuty@btinternet.com

AUCKLAND, Mrs Susan Frances. b 49. **d** 12 **p** 13. OLM Scole, Brockdish, Billingford, Thorpe Abbots etc *Nor* 12-14; OLM Redenhall w Scole from 14. *Greenbanks, 8 Karen Close, Scole, Diss IP21 4DL* T: (01379) 740325 M: 07825-838403 E: susanauckland@btinternet.com

AUCKLAND, Archdeacon of. *See* BARKER, The Ven Nicholas John Willoughby

AUDEN, Lawson Philip. b 45. DL 06. Qu Coll Birm 73. **d** 78 **p** 81. C Spalding St Mary and St Nic *Linc* 78-81; TV Wordsley *Lich* 81-82; TV Kidderminster St Mary and All SS, Trimpley etc *Worc* 82-87; Ind Chapl 82-87; PtO 87-97; *Cov* 87-01; *Birm* 90-97; *Lich* 90-97; *Glouc* 94-97; Chapl Worcs Community Healthcare NHS Trust 91-97; P-in-c Pebworth w Dorsington and Honeybourne *Glouc* 97-99; Chapl Miss to Seafarers 99-10; Millennium Officer *Glouc* 99-01; PtO from 01; *B & W* 00-04; rtd 10; PtO *B & W* from 11. *351 Nore Road, Portishead, Bristol BS20 8EX* T: (01275) 390305 M: 07715-553174 E: philipauden@gmail.com

AUDIBERT, Mrs Janice Elizabeth. b 56. **d** 99 **p** 00. OLM Oakdale *Sarum* 99-02; C N Poole Ecum Team 02-06; TV from 06. *24 Blackbird Close, Poole BH17 7YA* T/F: (01202) 389751 E: janice.audibert@tesco.net

AULD, The Very Revd Jeremy Rodger. b 66. Edin Univ LLB 87 Solicitor 89 Barrister 97. TISEC BD 04. **d** 04 **p** 05. C Edin St Pet 04-06; Hon Chapl Edin Univ 04-06; R Dollar *St And* 06-10; Provost St Paul's Cathl Dundee from 10. *4 Richmond Terrace, Dundee DD2 1BQ* T: (01382) 646296 *or* 224486 M: 07828-568002 E: jeremy.auld@btinternet.com

AULD, Mrs Sheila Edith. b 38. Newc Poly BA 87 Univ of Northumbria at Newc MA 99. NEOC 91. **d** 94 **p** 95. Project Worker Cedarwood Trust 88-02; NSM Newc St Gabr 94-02; rtd 02; PtO *Newc* from 02. *5 Gibson Fields, Hexham NE46 1AS* T: (01434) 602297

AUSSANT, Mrs Jill Amaryllis. b 53. Ripon Coll Cuddesdon. **d** 07 **p** 08. NSM Crawley and Littleton and Sparsholt w Lainston *Win* 07-08; NSM The Downs from 08. *121 Hocombe Road, Chandler's Ford, Eastleigh SO53 5QD* T: (023) 8026 9799

AUSTEN, Glyn Benedict. b 54. UEA BA 77 MPhil 80. Ripon Coll Cuddesdon BA 81 MA 85. **d** 82 **p** 83. C Newport w Longford and Chetwynd *Lich* 82-85; C Hawley H Trin *Guildf* 85-87; R Barnack w Ufford and Bainton *Pet* 87-03; Asst Master Stamford High Sch from 03. *31 Hill View Road, South Witham, Grantham NG33 5QW* T: (01572) 767944 *or* (01780) 484200 F: 484201 E: g.b.austen@ukf.net

AUSTEN, Canon John. b 46. St Cath Coll Cam BA 69 MA 72. Qu Coll Birm. **d** 71 **p** 72. C Thornaby on Tees *York* 71-74; C Aston St Jas *Birm* 74-82; Chapl Aston Univ 82-88; C Handsworth St Andr 88-11; Hon Can Birm Cathl 06-11; rtd 11; PtO *Birm* from 11. *151 Church Lane, Handsworth, Birmingham B20 2RU* T: 0121-554 8882 E: john@jausten.freeserve.co.uk

AUSTEN, Simon Neil. b 67. Warwick Univ BSc 88. Wycliffe Hall Ox BA 93 MA 97. **d** 94 **p** 95. C Gt Chesham *Ox* 94-98; Chapl Stowe Sch 98-02; V Houghton *Carl* 02-13; R Ex St Leon w H Trin from 13. *St Leonard's Rectory, 27 St Leonard's Road, Exeter EX2 4LA* T: (01392) 286993 E: simon@hkchurch.org.uk

AUSTERBERRY, Preb David Naylor. b 35. Birm Univ BA 58. Wells Th Coll 58. **d** 60 **p** 61. C Leek St Edw *Lich* 60-63; Iran 64-70; Chapl CMS Foxbury 70-73; V Walsall Pleck and Bescot *Lich* 73-82; R Brierley Hill 82-88; R Kinnerley w Melverley and Knockin w Maesbrook 88-99; RD Oswestry 92-95; Preb Lich Cathl 96-00; rtd 00; PtO *Heref* from 00; *Lich* from 00. *Chad Cottage, Dovaston, Kinnerley, Oswestry SY10 8DT* T: (01691) 682039

AUSTERBERRY, John Maurice. b 62. Birm Univ BA 83. Sarum & Wells Th Coll 84. **d** 86 **p** 87. C Clayton *Lich* 86-89; Asst Chapl Withington Hosp Man 89-95; Chapl Tameside and Glossop NHS Trust 95-99; Chapl Univ Hosp of N Staffs NHS Trust from 99; Bp's Adv on Healthcare Chapl *Lich* from 11. *University Hospital of North Staffordshire, Newcastle Road, Stoke-on-Trent ST4 6QG* T: (01782) 715444 *or* 676400 F: 552017 E: john.austerberry@uhns.nhs.uk

AUSTIN, Canon Alfred George. b 36. Ridley Coll Melbourne ThL 61. **d** 61 **p** 62. C Bendigo All SS Australia 63-64; R W End 64-70; R Eaglehawk and Bp's Dom Chapl 70-77; C Dartford St Alb *Roch* 77-79; R Tatura Australia 79-84; R W Bendigo 84-90; R Kyneton 90-93; Can Bendigo Cathl 83-97; I Essendon Ch Ch 97-00; rtd 01. *Brooklyn, 3 Alpina Place, Kangaroo Flat Vic 3555, Australia* T: (0061) (3) 5447 0174

AUSTIN (née JONES), Mrs Angela Mary. b 51. Man Univ BSc 00. WEMTC 10. **d** 13 **p** 14. NSM S Cerney w Cerney Wick, Siddington and Preston *Glouc* from 13. *April Cottage, Somerford Keynes, Cirencester GL7 6DT* T: (01285) 860692 M: 07776-101253 E: z3phariah317@gmail.com

AUSTIN, Mrs Catherine Brenda. b 57. **d** 00 **p** 01. OLM Coddenham w Gosbeck and Hemingstone w Henley *St E* 00-13; NSM from 13. *Fait Accompli, 7 Freeman Avenue, Henley, Ipswich IP6 0RZ* T: (01473) 830100

AUSTIN, David Robert Ernest. b 47. **d** 13 **p** 14. NSM Kemble, Poole Keynes, Somerford Keynes etc *Glouc* from 13. *April Cottage, Somerford Keynes, Cirencester GL7 6DT* T: (01285) 860692 M: 07504-295822 E: davidreaustin@hotmail.com

AUSTIN, David Samuel John. b 63. St Jo Coll Dur BATM 11. Cranmer Hall Dur 09. **d** 11 **p** 12. C Addingham *Leeds* 11-15; V New Catton St Luke *Nor* from 15. *St Luke's Vicarage, 61 Aylsham Road, Norwich NR3 2HF* M: 07740-922468 E: dsj.austin@gmail.com

AUSTIN, The Ven George Bernard. b 31. St D Coll Lamp BA 53. Chich Th Coll 53. **d** 55 **p** 56. C Chorley St Pet *Blackb* 55-57; C Notting Hill St Clem *Lon* 57-60; Asst Chapl Lon Univ 60-61; C Dunstable St Alb 61-64; V Eaton Bray 64-70; V Bushey Heath 70-88; Hon Can St Alb 78-88; Adn York 88-99; Can and Preb York Minster 88-99; rtd 99; PtO *York* from 99; *St Alb* from 10. *1 Priory Court, 169 Sparrows Herne, Bushey WD23 1EF* T: (020) 8420 4116 E: george.austin@virgin.net

AUSTIN, Miss Jane. b 43. SRN 64 SCM 66. dss 81 **d** 87 **p** 94. Tonbridge SS Pet and Paul *Roch* 81-98; C 87-98; Hon Can Roch Cathl 96-98; P-in-c Meltham *Wakef* 98-01; V 01-07; P-in-c Helme 00-01; RD Almondbury 01-06; rtd 07; PtO *Leeds* from 08. *177 Bourne View Road, Netherton, Huddersfield HD4 7JS* T: (01484) 664212 E: j.austin.meltham@care4free.net

AUSTIN, Leslie Ernest. b 46. Trin Coll Bris 72. **d** 74 **p** 75. C Paddock Wood *Roch* 74-79; C Upper Armley *Ripon* 79-81; V Horton *Bradf* 81-85; V Long Preston w Tosside 85-97; TR Shirwell, Loxhore, Kentisbury, Arlington, etc *Ex* 97-12; rtd 12. *7 Kennedy Close, Chester CH2 2PL* T: (01244) 314723 E: les@austin85.freeserve.co.uk

AUSTIN, Lucie. b 48. Th Ext Educn Coll. **d** 08 **p** 09. C Sunninghill St Steph S Africa 08-10; PtO *Ox* 11-12; NSM Icknield from 12. *20 Raven Road, Stokenchurch, High Wycombe HP14 3QP* T: (01494) 483729 M: 07906-684987 E: luciea48@gmail.com

AUSTIN, Margaret Rose. b 41. Qu Coll Birm 01. **d** 03 **p** 04. NSM Farewell *Lich* 03-09; NSM Gentleshaw 03-09; NSM Hammerwich 03-09; rtd 09; PtO *Lich* from 13. *137 Highfields Road, Chasetown, Burntwood WS7 4QT* T: (01543) 686883

AUSTIN, Canon Michael Ridgwell. b 33. Lon Univ BD 57 PhD 69 Birm Univ MA 66 FRHistS. Lon Coll of Div ALCD 56. **d** 57 **p** 58. C Ward End *Birm* 57-60; PC Derby St Andr 60-66; Lect Th Derbyshire Coll of HE 66-73; Prin Lect 73-85; Chapl Derby Cathl 66-81; Can Res Derby Cathl 81-85; Bp's Adv on Tr *S'well* 85-88; Dir Post-Ord Tr 86-94; Can Res S'well Minster 88-94; Dioc Dir of Tr 88-94; Abps' Adv for Bps' Min 94-98; rtd 98; PtO *S'well* from 04. *7 Dudley Doy Road, Southwell NG25 0NJ* T: (01636) 812604

AUSTIN, Mrs Rosemary Elizabeth. b 68. K Alfred's Coll Win BEd 91 Ex Univ BTh 14. SWMTC 08. **d** 11 **p** 12. C Fremington, Instow and Westleigh *Ex* 11-15; TR Shirwell, Loxhore, Kentisbury, Arlington, etc from 15. *The Parsonage, 1 The Glebe, Bratton Fleming, Barnstaple EX31 4RE* T: (01598) 711962 E: rosieaustin@live.co.uk

AUSTIN, Mrs Susan Frances. b 47. Open Univ BA 81. Cant Sch of Min 87. **d** 92 **p** 94. Ashford *Cant* 90-92; Chapl Ch Ch High Sch Ashford 90-94; C Gt Chart *Cant* 92-94; C Ashford 92-94; C Estover *Ex* 94-96; V Stevenage All SS Pin Green *St Alb* 96-98; P-in-c Bredgar w Bicknor and Frinsted w Wormshill etc *Cant* 00-04; rtd 04; PtO *Cant* 04-13. *Stepping Stones, Park Lane, Carhampton, Minehead TA24 6NL* T: (01643) 822550 M: 07443-948306 E: susanandralphaustin@hotmail.com

AUSTRALIA, Primate of. *See* ASPINALL, The Most Revd Phillip John

AVANN, Canon Penelope Joyce. b 46. dss 83 **d** 87 **p** 98. Southborough St Pet w Ch Ch and St Matt *Roch* 83-89; Par Dn 87-89; Warden Past Assts 89-10; Par Dn Beckenham St Jo *Roch* 89-94; C 94-02; C Green Street Green and Pratts Bottom from 02; Hon Can Roch Cathl from 94. *9 Ringwood Avenue, Orpington BR6 7SY* T/F: (01689) 861742 M: 07710-418839 E: penny.avann@rochester.anglican.org

AVENT, Raymond John. b 28. St D Coll Lamp BA 55 Coll of Resurr Mirfield 55. **d** 57 **p** 58. C Bury H Trin *Man* 57-60; C Holborn St Alb w Saffron Hill St Pet *Lon* 60-66; C Munster Square St Mary Magd 66-67; V Tottenham St Paul 67-77; RD E Haringey 73-77; V Kilburn St Aug w St Jo 77-87; AD Westmr Paddington 79-84; R St Vedast w St Mich-le-Querne etc 87-94; rtd 94; PtO *Lon* 94-00; *Glouc* from 00. *Maryvale House, Catbrook, Chipping Campden GL55 6DE* T: (01386) 841323 E: avent@campadene.fsnet.co.uk

AVERAY, Philip Roger. b 75. **d** 14 **p** 15. C Drybrook, Lydbrook and Ruardean *Glouc* from 14. *The Rectory, High Street, Ruardean GL17 9US* T: (01594) 546711 E: philipaveray@gmail.com

AVERY, Andrew James. b 58. Open Univ BA 81 Dudley Coll of Educn CertEd 79. St Jo Coll Nottm 06. **d** 08 **p** 09. C Brundall w Braydeston and Postwick *Nor* 08-11; TV Gt Yarmouth 11-13; P-in-c Greenhithe St Mary *Roch* from 13. *The Rectory, 131 Mounts Road, Greenhithe DA9 9ND* T: (01322) 385289 M: 07976-523554 E: revavery@hotmail.co.uk

AVERY, Mrs Jane Frances. b 44. Univ of Wales (Newport) BA 94. **d** 14 **p** 15. OLM Llandogo w Whitebrook Chpl and Tintern Parva *Mon* from 14. *Woodside, Parkend Walk, Coalway, Gloucester GL16 7JR* T: (01594) 837013 E: janeavery@live.co.uk

AVERY, Mrs Lydia Dorothy Ann. b 57. Sheff Univ MA 03 Bath Spa Univ Coll PGCE 97. STETS BA 08. **d** 08 **p** 09. C Pilton w Croscombe, N Wootton and Dinder *B & W* 08-11; P-in-c Winscombe and Sandford from 11. *The Vicarage, Winscombe Hill, Winscombe BS25 1DE* T: (01934) 843164 E: ldavery@btinternet.com

AVERY, Richard Julian. b 52. Keble Coll Ox BA 73. St Jo Coll Nottm 74. **d** 77 **p** 78. C Macclesfield St Mich *Ches* 77-80; Asst P Prince Albert St Dav Canada 82-83; C Becontree St Mary *Chelmsf* 84-87; R Hudson Bay Canada 87-90; R Duncan 90-97; TV Cheltenham St Mark *Glouc* 97-03; PtO 03-06; P-in-c Berkeley w Wick, Breadstone, Newport, Stone etc 06-11; V from 11. *The Vicarage, Church Lane, Berkeley GL13 9BN* T: (01453) 810294 E: averyfamily@yahoo.com

AVERY, Robert Edward. b 69. Magd Coll Cam BA 90. Ripon Coll Cuddesdon 90. **d** 93 **p** 94. C Cen Telford *Lich* 93-96; C Cambridge Gt St Mary w St Mich *Ely* 96-99; V Tamerton Foliot *Ex* 99-03; V Tunbridge Wells K Chas *Roch* 03-15; R Nor St Pet Mancroft w St Jo Maddermarket from 15. *The Vicarage, 5D Frant Road, Tunbridge Wells TN2 5SB* T: (01892) 525455 E: robert.avery@diocese-rochester.org

AVERY, Canon Russel Harrold. b 46. JP 74. Moore Th Coll Sydney 66. **d** 77 **p** 77. C Curtin Australia 77; C S Queanbeyan 77-78; C Prenton *Ches* 78-79; Chapl Tunis St Geo Tunisia 79-82; Chapl Maisons-Laffitte *Eur* 82-88; R Lane Cove Australia 88-98; Chapl Nord Pas de Calais *Eur* 98-00; Chapl Lille 00-02; Ind Chapl Australia 02-06; Chapl RAAF 04-09; Sen State Chapl NSW Police from 09; Hon Can Goulburn Cathl from 09. *1A Alliedale Close, Hornsby NSW 2077, Australia* T: (0061) (2) 9487 5580 E: rhavery@cia.com.au

AVESON, Ian Henry. b 55. Jes Coll Ox BA 77 MA 81 Univ Coll Dur PGCE 78 Birkbeck Coll Lon MSc 85. St Mich Coll Llan BD 97. **d** 97 **p** 98. C Penarth All SS *Llan* 97-99; TV Aberystwyth *St D* 99-07; V Llandingat w Myddfai from 07. *The Vicarage, 42 Broad Street, Llandovery SA20 0AY* T: (01550) 720524 E: ianaveson@hotmail.com

AVEYARD, Ian. b 46. Liv Univ BSc 68 Sheff Univ MEd 00. ALCD 72 St Jo Coll Nottm 71. **d** 71 **p** 72. C Bradley *Wakef* 71-74; C Knowle *Birm* 74-79; P-in-c Cofton Hackett 79; P-in-c Barnt Green 79; V Cofton Hackett w Barnt Green 80-94; Dioc Dir of Reader Tr 85-94; Warden of Readers 91-94; Course Leader St Jo Coll Nottm 96-99; P-in-c Thanington and Dioc Dir of Ords *Cant* 99-09; rtd 09. *19 The Damsells, Tetbury GL8 8JA* T: (01666) 502278 E: ian.aveyard1@btinternet.com

AVIS, Elizabeth Mary. *See* BAXTER, Elizabeth Mary

AVIS, Canon Paul David Loup. b 47. Lon Univ BD 70 PhD 76. Westcott Ho Cam 73. **d** 75 **p** 76. C S Molton, Nymet St George, High Bray etc *Ex* 75-80; V Stoke Canon, Poltimore w Huxham and Rewe etc 80-98; Preb Ex Cathl 93-08; Sub Dean Ex Cathl 97-08; Can Th Ex Cathl from 08; Hon Prof Ex Univ from 09; Gen Sec Coun for Chr Unity 98-11; Th Consultant Angl Communion Office 11-12; Chapl to The Queen from 08; Ed *Ecclesiology* from 04. *Lea Hill, Membury, Axminster EX13 7AQ* T: (01404) 881881 E: reception@leahill.co.uk

AVISON, Sara Jane. *See* CALDERIN, Sara Jane

AWRE, Canon Richard William Esgar. b 56. Univ of Wales BA 78. Wycliffe Hall Ox 78. **d** 81 **p** 82. C Blackpool St Jo *Blackb* 81-84; Asst Dir of Ords and Voc Adv 84-89; C Altham w Clayton le Moors 84-89; V Longridge 89-99; V Kenilworth St Nic *Cov* 99-15; RD Kenilworth 01-09; Hon Can Cov Cathl 11-15; rtd 15. *The Vicarage, 7 Elmbank Road, Kenilworth CV8 1AL* T: (01926) 854367 or 857509 E: stnicholasken@aol.com

AXE, Terence Arthur. b 46. **d** 14 **p** 15. NSM Constantine *Truro* from 14. *Trebarvah Woon, Trebarvah Woon, Constantine, Falmouth TR11 5QJ* T: (01326) 340140 E: tvaxe123@gmail.com

AXFORD, Mrs Christine Ruth. b 53. Glam Coll of Educn BEd 75. STETS BTh 00. **d** 00 **p** 02. NSM Yeovil w Kingston Pitney *B & W* 00-01; NSM N Hartismere *St E* 02-08; NSM Tyndale *Glouc* from 08. *The Vicarage, Culverhay, Wotton-under-Edge GL12 7LS* T: (01453) 842175 E: chris.axford@metronet.co.uk

AXFORD, Canon Robert Henry. b 50. Univ of Wales BEng 72 CEng 85. Sarum & Wells Th Coll 89. **d** 91 **p** 92. C Castle Cary w Ansford *B & W* 91-95; P-in-c Queen Camel w W Camel,

Corton Denham etc 95-01; R 01-02; R N Hartismere *St E* 02-08; RD Hartismere 04-08; P-in-c Wotton-under-Edge w Ozleworth, N Nibley etc *Glouc* 08-11; V Tyndale from 11; AD Wotton 09-13; Hon Can Glouc Cathl from 13. *The Vicarage, Culverhay, Wotton-under-Edge GL12 7LS* T: (01453) 842175 E: rob@robaxford.plus.com

AXON, Andrew John. b 76. Univ of Wales (Lamp) BTh 97 Univ of Wales (Ban) MTh 09. Trin Coll Bris 99. **d** 01 **p** 02. C Sevenhampton w Charlton Abbots, Hawling etc *Glouc* 01-05; V Ruddington *S'well* 05-10; P-in-c Hucclecote *Glouc* from 10. *12 Royal Lane, Gloucester GL1 3QW* E: ajaxon@mail.com

AXTELL, Stephen Geoffrey. b 57. Open Univ BSc 96. St Jo Coll Nottm 00. **d** 02 **p** 03. C Coseley Ch Ch *Worc* 02-06; Chapl Rotterdam *Eur* 06-12; Chapl Rotterdam w Schiedam Miss to Seafarers 06-12; V Westfield St Mary *Carl* from 12. *St Mary's Vicarage, Salisbury Street, Workington CA14 3TA*

AYERS, Canon John. b 40. FCollP Bris Univ BEd 75 Newton Park Coll Bath MEd 89 FRSA 94. **d** 77 **p** 78. NSM Corsham *Bris* 77-79; NSM Gtr Corsham 79-88; NSM Ditteridge 88-92; NSM Box w Hazlebury and Ditteridge 93-10; Hon Can Bris Cathl 94-10; rtd 10. *Toad Hall, Middlehill, Box, Corsham SN13 8QP* T: (01225) 742123 E: johnayers@middlehill.netlineuk.net

AYERS, Martin John. b 79. Trin Hall Cam MA 03 Solicitor 04. Oak Hill Th Coll 08. **d** 11 **p** 12. C Preston All SS *Blackb* from 11. *226 Tag Lane, Ingol, Preston PR2 3TX* M: 07976-170916 E: martin.ayers@talk21.com

AYERS, Paul Nicholas. b 61. St Pet Coll Ox BA 82 MA 86. Trin Coll Bris 83. **d** 85 **p** 86. C Clayton *Bradf* 85-88; C Keighley St Andr 88-91; V Wrose 91-97; V Pudsey St Lawr and St Paul *Leeds* from 97. *The Vicarage, Vicarage Drive, Pudsey LS28 7RL* T: 0113-256 4197 or 257 7843 E: paul.ayers@bradford.anglican.org

AYERS-HARRIS, Mrs Rebecca Theresa. b 70. Nottm Univ BA 91 Birm Univ PGCE 92. WEMTC 01. **d** 04 **p** 05. NSM Leominster *Heref* 04-08; Chapl Sherborne Sch for Girls from 08. *Sherwell, Bradford Road, Sherborne DT9 3QL* T: (01935) 812245 E: rah@sherborne.com

AYERST, Gabrielle Mary. b 52. St Luke's Coll Ex BEd 74. SEITE 97. **d** 00 **p** 01. NSM Surbiton St Andr and St Mark *S'wark* 00-08. *6 Bell Tower Park, Berwick-upon-Tweed TD15 1ND* T: (01289) 302680 E: gadrillea@paff.nsf.org.uk

AYLETT, Miss Barbara Celia. b 46. Open Univ BA 91 SRN 73 SCM 74 Surrey Univ PGCE 83. **d** 14 **p** 15. OLM Harlow Town Cen w Lt Parndon *Chelmsf* from 14. *105 Hare Street Springs, Harlow CM19 4AT* T: (01279) 413749 E: b.aylett@btinternet.com

AYLETT, Graham Peter. b 59. Qu Coll Cam BA 81 MA 84 PhD 85 St Jo Coll Dur BA 88. Cranmer Hall Dur 86 All Nations Chr Coll 96. **d** 90 **p** 91. C Wilton *B & W* 90-94; C Runcorn All SS *Ches* 94-96; C Thetford *Nor* 97-98; Mongolia from 98. *c/o JCS, PO Box 49/532, Ulaanbaatar 210349, Mongolia*

AYLETT, Mrs Nicola Jane. b 63. St Anne's Coll Ox BA 84 St Jo Coll Dur BA 89. Cranmer Hall Dur 87 All Nations Chr Coll 96. **d** 90 **p** 94. C Wilton *B & W* 90-94; NSM Runcorn All SS *Ches* 94-96; PtO *Nor* 97-98; Mongolia from 98. *c/o JCS, PO Box 49/532, Ulaanbaatar 210349, Mongolia*

AYLING, Mrs Ann Margaret. b 39. Edge Hill Coll of HE TCert 59. STETS 07. **d** 10 **p** 11. NSM Bridport *Sarum* from 10. *4 Manor Farm Court, Walditch, Bridport DT6 4LQ* T: (01308) 424896 E: ann@bridport-team-ministry.org

AYLING, Miss Dallas Jane. b 53. Trin Coll Bris BA 94. **d** 98 **p** 99. C Ellesmere Port *Ches* 98-02; TV Birkenhead Priory 02-06; TR 06-07; R from 07; RD Birkenhead from 11. *10 Cavendish Road, Birkenhead CH41 8AX* T: 0151-653 6092 E: revddallasayling@yahoo.co.uk

AYLING, Canon John Michael. b 37. St Cath Coll Cam BA 60 MA 64. Linc Th Coll 60. **d** 62 **p** 63. C Stoke upon Trent *Lich* 62-66; C Codsall 66-67; Australia 67-71; Solomon Is 71-72; LtO *St Alb* 72-91; TR Boscastle w Davidstow *Truro* 91-98; R 98-02; RD Stratton 98-02; Hon Can Truro Cathl 01-02; rtd 02; PtO *Heref* from 03. *Woodstock House, Church Street, Leominster HR6 8ED* T: (01568) 611523 E: john.ayling@virgin.net

AYLING, Mrs Susan Pamela. b 48. OBE 03. SEITE 95. **d** 98 **p** 99. NSM Oxshott *Guildf* 98-02; NSM Cuddington 02-10; NSM Long Ditton 10-12; NSM Ewell from 12. *114 Edenfield Gardens, Worcester Park KT4 7DY* T: (020) 8337 6347 or 7438 6589 E: sue.ayling@btinternet.com

AYLWARD, James Gareth. b 45. St Cath Coll Cam BA 68 MA 72. St As Minl Tr Course 94. **d** 97 **p** 98. NSM Wrexham *St As* 97-00; V Broughton 00-05; V Broughton and Berse Drelincourt 05-14; V Broughton w Berse and Southsea from 14. *The Vicarage, Bryn-y-Gaer Road, Pentre Broughton, Wrexham LL11 6AT* T: (01978) 721511

AYO, Ms Margaret Florence Aceng. b 55. St Mellitus Coll 12. **d** 15. NSM Notting Dale St Clem w St Mark and St Jas *Lon* from 15. *Address temp unknown*

AYODEJI, Olakunle. b 66. Obafemi Awolowo Univ BSc 86. Westcott Ho Cam 12. **d** 14 **p** 15. C Pinner *Lon* from 14. *37 Eastcote Road, Pinner HA5 1EL* M: 07790-504812 E: kunleayodeji@yahoo.co.uk

AYOK-LOEWENBERG, Joseph. b 60. DipEd 91. Trin Coll Bris 85. **d** 88 **p** 89. C Swanage and Studland *Sarum* 88-90; Cam Univ Miss Bermondsey 90; Crowther Hall CMS Tr Coll Selly Oak 90-91; C Barnes St Mary *S'wark* 91-92; C Earlsfield St Jo 92; CMS Uganda 92-95; P-in-c Symondsbury and Chideock *Sarum* 96-98; TV Golden Cap Team 98-01; CMS Egypt 02-06; Hon C Barnes *S'wark* 06-09; TV Kidderminster St Geo *Worc* 09-12. *Address temp unknown*

✠**AYONG, The Most Revd James Simon.** b 44. Newton Th Coll Martin Luther Sem BTh. **d** 82 **p** 84 **c** 96. Papua New Guinea from 82; Asst P Popondetta Resurr 85-86; Lect Newton Th Coll 87-88; Prin 89-93; Par P Gerehu 94-95; Bp Aipo Rongo 95-09; Abp Papua New Guinea 96-09; rtd 09. *Kumbun Village, PO Box 806, Kimbe, West New Britain, Papua New Guinea*

AYRES, Anthony Lawrence. b 47. Trin Coll Bris 69. **d** 73 **p** 74. C Plumstead All SS *S'wark* 73-77; Hon C 77-00; CA Counselling Team from 83; rtd 12. *37 Donaldson Road, London SE18 3JZ* T: (020) 8856 1542

AYRES, Dean Matthew. b 68. Bris Univ BSc 89. Ridley Hall Cam 00. **d** 02 **p** 03. C Epsom Common Ch Ch *Guildf* 02-06; Chapl W Lon Univ from 06. *The Chaplaincy, University of West London, St Mary's Road, London W5 5RF* T: (020) 8231 2365 E: ayresnograces@yahoo.co.uk

AZER, Ms Helen. b 77. Ch Ch Ox BA 00 MA 03. Wycliffe Hall Ox BTh 04. **d** 04 **p** 05. C Ox St Aldate 04-07; C Cumnor from 07. *St Michael's Church Office, 1 Abingdon Road, Cumnor, Oxford OX2 9QN* T: (01865) 861541 E: gryphius2000@hotmail.com

B

BABB, Ann Elizabeth. b 38. Battersea Coll of Educn TDip 59. Qu Coll Newfoundland 96 St Steph Ho Ox 05. **d** 06. C Antwerp St Boniface *Eur* 06-11; rtd 11. *Leo van Hullebuschstraat 37, 2900 Schoten, Belgium* T: (0032) (3) 685 3420 E: ann.babb@skynet.be

BABB, Canon Geoffrey. b 42. Man Univ BSc 64 MA(Theol) 74 Linacre Coll Ox BA 67. Ripon Hall Ox 65. **d** 68 **p** 69. C Heywood St Luke *Man* 68-71; C-in-c Loundsley Green Ascension CD *Derby* 71-76; TV Old Brampton and Loundsley Green 76-77; TV Stafford and Dioc Soc Resp Officer *Lich* 77-88; Preb Lich Cathl 87-88; P-in-c Salford Sacred Trin *Man* 88-99; Dir CME 88-99; TR Wythenshawe 99-06; TV 06-07; Hon Can Man Cathl 89-07; rtd 07; PtO *Man* 07-08 and from 13; *Newc* 07-10; *Derby* 10-12. *24 Bottomley Side, Manchester M9 8EP* E: gandjbabb@btinternet.com

BABB, Mrs Julia Bebbington. b 69. Man Univ BA 98 St Jo Coll Dur MA 00. Cranmer Hall Dur. **d** 00 **p** 01. C Langley and Parkfield *Man* 00-04; V Cowgate *Newc* 04-10; P-in-c Whittington *Derby* 10-11; R 12; Tr Officer CMD and IME 4-7 *Man* from 12. *Discipleship and Ministry Training, Church House, 90 Deansgate, Manchester M3 2GH* T: 0161-828 1448 E: juliababb@manchester.anglican.org

BABBAGE, Canon Stuart Barton. b 16. Man Univ AM 95. St Jo Coll Auckland 35 Univ of NZ BA 35 MA 36 K Coll Lon PhD 42. Tyndale Hall Bris 37 ACT ThD 50. **d** 39 **p** 40. C Havering-atte-Bower *Chelmsf* 39-41; Tutor and Lect Oak Hill Th Coll 39-41; Chapl-in-Chief RAF 42-46; Australia 46-63; Dean Sydney 47-53; Dean Melbourne 53-62; Prin Ridley Coll Melbourne 53-63; V Atlanta and Austell USA 63-65; Visiting Prof Columbia Th Sem 63-67; Pres Conwell Th Sch Philadelphia 67-69; Vice-Pres and Dean Gordon-Conwell Th Sem 69-73; Master New Coll Univ of NSW Australia 73-82; Registrar ACT 77-92; rtd 83; Hon Can Sydney from 83. *46 St Thomas Street, Waverley NSW 2024, Australia* T: (0061) (2) 9665 1882

BABER, Helen Charlotte. b 67. STETS 10. **d** 13 **p** 14. C Stratton St Margaret w S Marston etc *Bris* from 13. *The Vicarage, South Marston, Swindon SN3 4SR* T: (01793) 821412 M: 07767-310773 E: helenbaber@me.com

BABBINGTON, David Paul Simon. b 66. Qu Coll Birm BA 15. **d** 15. C Pelsall *Lich* from 15. *9 Sanstone Road, Walsall WS3 3SJ* E: davidbabbington@me.com

BABINGTON, Canon Gervase Hamilton. b 30. Keble Coll Ox BA 57 MA 57. Wells Th Coll 55. **d** 57 **p** 58. C Sheff St Geo and St Steph 57-60; P-in-c Manor Park CD 60-65; R Waddington *Linc* 65-81; RD Graffoe 74-81; Can and Preb Linc Cathl 77-95; V Gainsborough All SS 81-90; RD Corringham 82-87; R Walesby 90-95; rtd 95; PtO *Linc* 95-98. *15 Highfields, Nettleham, Lincoln LN2 2ST* T: (01522) 595702

BABINGTON, Canon Peter Gervase. b 69. Aston Univ BSc 91 Birm Univ MPhil 03. Cuddesdon Coll BTh 98. **d** 98 **p** 99. C Salter Street and Shirley *Birm* 98-02; V Bournville from 02; AD Moseley 07-13; Hon Can Birm Cathl from 15. *The Vicarage, 61 Linden Road, Birmingham B30 1JT* T: 0121-472 1209 or 472 7215 E: vicar@bournvilleparishchurch.org.uk or pgbabington@gmail.com

BACH, Mrs Frances Mary. b 48. Open Univ BA AIL. CITC BTh. **d** 94 **p** 95. NSM Ballynure and Ballyeaston *Conn* 94-96; C Larne and Inver 96-99; C Glynn w Raloo 96-99; I Armoy w Loughguile and Drumtullagh 99-12; rtd 13. *141A Ballinlea Road, Stranocum, Ballymoney BT53 8PX* T: (028) 2075 1081 E: frances.bach@btinternet.com

BACH, John Edward Goulden. b 40. JP. Dur Univ BA 66. Cranmer Hall Dur 66. **d** 69 **p** 70. C Bradf Cathl 69-72; Chapl and Lect NUU 73-84; Chapl and Lect Ulster Univ from 84. *The Anglican Chaplaincy, 70 Hopefield Avenue, Portrush BT56 8HE* T: (028) 2082 3348 or 2032 4549 or 7032 4652 F: 7032 4604 E: revjegbach@hotmail.com or jeg.bach@ulst.ac.uk

BACHE, Richard Andrew Foley. b 64. **d** 12. C Okehampton, Inwardleigh, Belstone, Sourton etc *Ex* from 12. *Priory Cottage, 27 Priory Close, Tavistock PL19 9DJ* T: (01822) 820536 E: rich.foley@btinternet.com

BACHELL, Kenneth George. b 22. Lon Univ BD 49. K Coll Lon 55. **d** 56 **p** 57. C Bitterne Park *Win* 56-60; C-in-c Andover St Mich CD 60-64; V Andover St Mich 64-68; V Southampton St Alb 68-76; Warden Dioc Conf Ho Crawshawbooth *Man* 76-79; P-in-c Crawshawbooth 76-79; V Holdenhurst *Win* 79-83; V Froyle and Holybourne 83-87; rtd 87; PtO *Blackb* 88-98; *St And* from 88. *18 Cherrylea, Auchterarder PH3 1QG* T: (01764) 663824

BACK, Esther Elaine. See McCAFFERTY, Esther Elaine

BACKHOUSE, Alan Eric. b 37. Keble Coll Ox BA 61 MA 67. Tyndale Hall Bris 61. **d** 64 **p** 65. C Burnage St Marg *Man* 64-67; C Cheadle Hulme St Andr *Ches* 67-70; V Buglawton 70-80; V New Ferry 80-87; V Tarvin 87-93; V Knypersley *Lich* 93-99; Patr Sec Ch Soc Trust 99-00; C Watford *St Alb* 99-02; rtd 02; PtO *St As* from 09. *Perelandra, Church Pitch, Llandyssil, Montgomery SY16 6LQ* T: (01686) 669963

BACKHOUSE, Colin. b 41. Birm Coll of Art & Design BA 67 MCSD 82. Oak Hill Th Coll 85. **d** 87 **p** 88. C Branksome St Clem *Sarum* 87-91; P-in-c Bluntisham cum Earith w Colne and Woodhurst *Ely* 91-92; R 92-07; rtd 07; PtO Cyprus and the Gulf from 09. *13 Hillside View, Midsomer Norton, Bath BA3 2TB* M: 07811-960048 E: colin.backhouse@googlemail.com

BACKHOUSE, John. b 30. Univ Coll Southn BA 50. Wycliffe Hall Ox 51. **d** 53 **p** 54. C Eccleston St Luke *Liv* 53-55; C Maghull 55-58; V Lathom 58-64; Area Sec CMS *Linc* and *Ely* 64-71; PtO *Leic* 72-78; *Cov* 75-78; V Thorpe Acre w Dishley *Leic* 78-83; R Ab Kettleby Gp 83-89; P-in-c Bitteswell 89-94; RD Guthlaxton II 90-94; rtd 94; PtO *Leic* from 94. *29 Peashill Close, Sileby, Loughborough LE12 7PT* T: (01509) 812016

BACKHOUSE, Jonathan Roland. b 60. Jes Coll Cam BA 82 MA 85. Trin Coll Bris 01. **d** 03 **p** 04. C Nailsea H Trin *B & W* 03-07; Chapl RN 07-15; Chapl Naples w Sorrento, Capri and Bari *Eur* from 15. *Christ Church, via S Pasquale a Chiaia 15B, 80121 Naples, Italy* T: (0039) (081) 411842 E: jcbackhouse@bigfoot.com or vicar@christchurchnaples.org

BACKHOUSE, Robert. b 45. ALCD 70. **d** 70 **p** 71. C Harold Wood *Chelmsf* 70-74; Publicity Sec CPAS 74-78; rtd 00; PtO *Sarum* 01-05. *10 Eccleston Square, London SW1V 1NP*

BACON, David Gary. b 62. Leic Univ BA 83 Southn Univ BTh 88. Sarum & Wells Th Coll 85. **d** 88 **p** 89. C Bromley St Mark *Roch* 88-92; C Lynton, Brendon, Countisbury, Lynmouth etc *Ex* 92; TV 92-95; P-in-c Lapford, Nymet Rowland and Coldridge 95-99; P-in-c Dartford St Alb *Roch* 99-05; P-in-c Bramshaw and Landford w Plaitford *Sarum* 05-06; TV Forest and Avon from 06; RD Alderbury from 14. *The Rectory, Bramshaw, Lyndhurst SO43 7JF* T: (01794) 390256 E: davidbramrec@aol.com

BACON, Derek Robert Alexander. b 44. Birkbeck Coll Lon BA 92 MSc 94 Ulster Univ PhD 04. TCD Div Sch 69. **d** 71 **p** 72. C Templemore *D & R* 71-73; V Choral Derry Cathl 72-73;

C Heeley *Sheff* 74-76; V Sheff St Pet Abbeydale 76-82; Chapl Gt Ormond Street Hosp for Children NHS Trust 82-95; Visiting Fell Ulster Univ 95-97; PtO *Conn* from 04; rtd 09. *19 Ballycairn Road, Coleraine BT51 3HX*

BACON, Eric Arthur. b 23. Qu Coll Birm 68. **d** 69 **p** 70. C Linc St Pet-at-Gowts and St Andr 69-71; C Asterby Gp 71-74; V Anwick 74-78; V S Kyme 74-78; P-in-c Kirkby Laythorpe w Asgarby 76-78; P-in-c Ewerby w Evedon 76-78; P-in-c Burton Pedwardine 76-78; V Messingham 78-89; rtd 89; PtO *Linc* 89-01. *2 Curtois Close, Branston, Lincoln LN4 1LJ* T: (01522) 794265

BACON, Janet Ann. b 57. Man Univ LLB 78. NTMTC 95. **d** 98 **p** 99. NSM Stifford *Chelmsf* 98-01; P-in-c Sandbach Heath w Wheelock *Ches* 01-03; V 03-12; V Cheadle Hulme All SS from 12. *All Saints' Vicarage, 27 Church Road, Cheadle Hulme, Cheadle SK8 7JL* T: 0161-485 3455 E: j.bacon@virgin.net

BACON, John Martindale. b 22. St Aid Birkenhead 54. **d** 57 **p** 58. C Bury St Paul *Man* 57-59; C-in-c Clifton Green St Thos CD 59-71; V Astley Bridge 71-87; rtd 87; PtO *Man* 87-00; *Blackb* 87-11. *21 Lichen Close, Charnock Richard, Chorley PR7 5TT* T: (01257) 792535 E: johnandcon.bacon@tiscali.co.uk

BACON, Mrs Julie. b 65. Solicitor . Yorks Min Course. **d** 14 **p** 15. C Shipley St Pet *Leeds* from 14. *2B Nab Lane, Shipley BD18 4HB*

BADDELEY, The Ven Martin James. b 36. Keble Coll Ox BA 60 MA 64. Linc Th Coll 60. **d** 62 **p** 63. C Stretford St Matt *Man* 62-64; Lect Linc Th Coll 65-66; Tutor 66-69; Chapl 68-69; Chapl Fitzw Coll and New Hall Cam 69-74; Can Res Roch Cathl 74-80; Hon Can Roch Cathl 80-96; Prin S'wark Ord Course 80-94; Co-Prin SEITE 94-96; Adn Reigate S'wark 96-00; rtd 00; PtO *Heref* from 00; *Worc* from 01. *3 Abbeyfield House, 12 Green Hill, London Road, Worcester WR5 2AA* T: (01905) 764833

BADEN, Peter Michael. b 35. CCC Cam BA 59 MA 62. Cuddesdon Coll 58. **d** 60 **p** 61. C Hunslet St Mary and Stourton *Ripon* 60-63; LtO *Wakef* 63-64; C E Grinstead St Swithun *Chich* 65-68; V Brighton St Martin 68-74; TR Brighton Resurr 74-76; R Westbourne and V Stansted 76-84; V Copthorne 84-91; V Clifton and R Dean *Carl* 91-00; P-in-c Mosser 99-00; rtd 00; PtO *Pet* from 00; *Carl* from 01. *62 Springfield Avenue, Thrapston, Kettering NN14 4TN* T: (01832) 733186 E: pmbaden@gmail.com

BADGER, Mark. b 65. Qu Coll Birm BTh 96. **d** 96 **p** 97. C Barbourne *Worc* 96-01; P-in-c Worc St Geo w St Mary Magd 01-05; Chapl R Gr Sch Worc 02-05; Chapl Thames Valley Police *Ox* 05-07; Man Dir Motov8 04-12; R Kempsey and Severn Stoke w Croome d'Abitot *Worc* from 12. *Appletree Cottage, 31 Napleton Lane, Kempsey, Worcester WR5 3PX* T: (01905) 820057 E: motov8@supanet.com

BADGER-WATTS, Mrs Lorraine Gwyneth. b 76. De Montfort Univ BSc 99. St Mich Coll Llan BTh 13. **d** 13 **p** 14. C Petryal and Betws yn Rhos *St As* from 13. *Capel Garnedd, Llangernyw, Abergele LL22 8RR* T: (01745) 860411 M: 07402-429991 E: revbadger.watts@hotmail.co.uk

BADHAM, Prof Paul Brian Leslie. b 42. Jes Coll Ox BA 65 MA 69 Jes Coll Cam BA 68 MA 72 Birm Univ PhD 73. Westcott Ho Cam 66. **d** 68 **p** 69. C Edgbaston St Bart *Birm* 68-69; C Rubery 69-73; LtO *St D* from 73; Lect Th Univ of Wales (Lamp) 73-83; Sen Lect 83-88; Reader 88-91; Prof Th 91-07; rtd 07; Dir Alister Hardy Relig Experience Research Cen from 02. *4 Coed y Bryn, Aberaeron SA46 0DW* T: (01545) 571244 M: 07968-626902 E: pblbadham@hotmail.com

BAGE, Damon John. b 71. Teesside Univ BA 95. St Steph Ho Ox 01. **d** 03 **p** 04. C Stockton St Jo *Dur* 03-07; P-in-c Norton St Mich 07-13; Chapl John Snow Coll Dur 06-13; V Cockerton from 13. *St Mary's Vicarage, 17 Newton Lane, Darlington DL3 9EX* E: frdamon.bage@stmaryscockerton.org

BAGG, Marcus Christopher. b 75. Bath Univ BSc 96. Trin Coll Bris BA 07. **d** 07 **p** 08. C Stanmore *Win* 07-11; P-in-c Gatcombe *Portsm* 11-14; R from 14; P-in-c Carisbrooke St Nic 11-14; V from 14; P-in-c Carisbrooke St Mary 11-14; V from 14. *The Vicarage, 56 Castle Road, Carisbrooke, Newport PO30 1DP* T: (01983) 718908 E: marcus.carisbrooke@yahoo.co.uk

BAGGALEY, Mrs Patricia Anne. b 45. Open Univ BSc 96 RGN 68. ERMC 05. **d** 07 **p** 08. NSM Trunch *Nor* 07-11; C 11-15; P-in-c Trunch Group from 15. *Anglesea, Rosebery Road, West Runton, Cromer NR27 9QW* T: (01263) 837490 E: baggaley157@btinternet.com

BAGGS, Steven. b 70. **d** 09 **p** 10. NSM White Horse *Sarum* 09-12; V Frome Valley *Heref* from 12. *The Vicarage, Bishop's Frome, Worcester WR6 5AP*

BAGNALL, Katherine Janet. b 67. Sunderland Univ BEd 92. NEOC 02. **d** 05 **p** 06. NSM Monkwearmouth *Dur* 05-06; C Darlington St Mark w St Paul 06-10; P-in-c Sunderland

St Mary and St Pet from 10. *The Clergy House, Springwell Road, Sunderland SR3 4DY* T: 0191-528 3754 E: katherine.bagnall@ntlworld.com

BAGOTT, Paul Andrew. b 61. Leeds Univ BA 85. Westcott Ho Cam 86. **d** 88 **p** 89. C Chingford SS Pet and Paul *Chelmsf* 88-91; C Pimlico St Sav *Lon* 91-95; P-in-c Clerkenwell H Redeemer and St Mark 95-01; V Clerkenwell H Redeemer 02-13; V Clerkenwell St Mark 02-13; P-in-c Earl's Court St Cuth w St Matthias from 13; PV Westmr Abbey from 08. *St Cuthbert's Clergy House, 50 Philbeach Gardens, London SW5 9EB* T: (020) 7370 3263

BAGSHAW, Paul Stanley. b 55. Selw Coll Cam BA 78 MA 81 CQSW 80. NOC 85. **d** 88 **p** 89. Ind Missr *Sheff* 86-90; C Handsworth Woodhouse 88-90; NSM 91-93; C Newark S'well 93-96; P-in-c Ordsall 96-08; C Byker St Ant *Newc* 12-14; V Billy Mill from 14; V Marden w Preston Grange from 14. *St Aidan's Vicarage, 29 Billy Mill Lane, North Shields NE29 8BZ* T: 0191-908 4474 E: st.hildamarden@gmail.com *or* st.aidanbilllymill@gmail.com

BAGSHAWE, John Allen. b 45. St Jo Coll Dur BA 70. Cranmer Hall Dur 67. **d** 71 **p** 72. C Bridlington Priory *York* 71-75; C N Ferriby 75-79; V Kingston upon Hull St Matt w St Barn 79-10; AD W Hull 00-10; rtd 10. *334 Southcoates Lane, Hull HU9 3TR* T: (01482) 702220 E: allen@bagshawe.karoo.co.uk

BAGULEY, Andrew James. b 72. Glas Univ BSc 94 Jordanhill Coll Glas PGCE 97. Ridley Hall Cam 13. **d** 15. C Belper *Derby* from 15. *7 Ashdene Gardens, Belper DE56 1TG* E: andrew.baguley@which.net

BAGULEY, David Mark. b 61. Man Univ BSc 83 MSc 86 Open Univ MBA 94 Wolfs Coll Cam PhD 05. ERMC 09. **d** 11 **p** 12. Visiting Prof Anglia Ruskin Univ *Chelmsf* from 10; NSM Milton *Ely* from 11; NSM Waterbeach from 11; NSM Landbeach from 11. *272 Cherry Hinton Road, Cambridge CB1 7AU* E: dmb29@cam.ac.uk

BAGULEY, Paul. b 36. NTMTC 94. **d** 98 **p** 99. NSM N Harrow St Alb *Lon* 98-13; PtO 13. *86 Central Avenue, Pinner HA5 5BP* T: (020) 8866 3454 E: paulbaguley@waitrose.com

BAILES, Kenneth. b 35. Dur Univ BA 69 DPhil. **d** 71 **p** 72. C Redcar *York* 71-73; TV Redcar w Kirkleatham 73-74; P-in-c Appleton Roebuck w Acaster Selby 74-80; C Sutton on the Forest 80-82; R Stamford Bridge Gp 82-90; V Healaugh w Wighill, Bilbrough and Askham Richard 90-95; rtd 95; PtO *York* 98-11. *Lawnith House, Stuton Grove, Tadcaster LS24 9BD* T: (01937) 831245 M: 07764-614139 E: kb13@btinternet.com

BAILES, Mrs Rachel Jocelyn. b 60. Huddersfield Sch of Music BA 81 Kingston Poly PGCE 83 Leeds Univ MEd 96 BA 07. NOC 04. **d** 07 **p** 08. C Thornes and Lupset *Wakef* 07-11; Chapl Mid Yorks Hosps NHS Trust from 11. *Trust HQ and Education Centre, Pinderfields Hospital, Aberford Road, Wakefield WF1 4DG* T: 08448-118110 E: rjbailes@tiscali.co.uk

BAILEY, Preb Adrian Richard. b 57. Cranmer Hall Dur 89. **d** 91 **p** 92. C Oswestry St Oswald *Lich* 91-94; C Oswestry 94; C Shobnall 94-99; C Burton 94-99; Town Cen Chapl 94-99; P-in-c Shobnall 99-01; P-in-c Hengoed w Gobowen 01-08; C Weston Rhyn and Selattyn 05-07; P-in-c Selattyn 07-08; P-in-c Selattyn and Hengoed w Gobowen from 08; Chapl Robert Jones/Agnes Hunt Orthopaedic NHS Trust from 01; RD Oswestry *Lich* from 09; Preb Lich Cathl from 13. *The Vicarage, Old Chirk Road, Gobowen, Oswestry SY11 3LL* T/F: (01691) 661226 E: arb2@totalise.co.uk

BAILEY, Alan George. b 40. Open Univ BA 93. Ripon Hall Ox 62. **d** 64 **p** 65. C Formby H Trin *Liv* 64-67; C Upholland 67-70; P-in-c Edgehill St Dunstan 70-74; V 74-81; RD Toxteth 78-81; PtO 81-83; Asst Chapl Liv Cathl 83-85; C Liv Our Lady and St Nic w St Anne 85-89; V Waddington *Bradf* 89-03; rtd 03. *66 Woone Lane, Clitheroe BB7 1BJ* T: (01200) 425699

BAILEY, Andrew Henley. b 57. AKC 78. Sarum & Wells Th Coll 79. **d** 80 **p** 81. C Romsey *Win* 80-83; V Bournemouth St Alb 83-93; R Milton from 93. *The Rectory, Church Lane, New Milton BH25 6QN* T/F: (01425) 615150 E: andrew@miltonrectory.freeserve.co.uk

BAILEY, Andrew John. b 37. Trin Coll Cam BA 61 MA. Ridley Hall Cam 60. **d** 63 **p** 64. C Drypool *York* 63-66; C Melton Mowbray w Thorpe Arnold *Leic* 66-69; C-in-c Skelmersdale Ecum Cen *Liv* 69-79; V Langley Mill *Derby* 79-90; V Gt Faringdon w Lt Coxwell *Ox* 90-02; AD Vale of White Horse 97-01; rtd 02; PtO *Ches* from 02. *58 Manor Road, Sandbach CW11 2ND* T: (01270) 764076 E: baileyaj@talk21.com

BAILEY, Canon Angela. b 61. Kent Univ BA 82. Qu Coll Birm 83. **dss** 85 **d** 87 **p** 94. Reculver and Herne Bay St Bart *Cant* 85-88; Par Dn 87-88; Asst Chapl Hull Univ *York* 88-92; Sen Chapl 94-98; PtO *Dur* 94-98; P-in-c Rowley w Skidby 98-09; R 10-14; V Walkington 10-14; P-in-c Bishop Burton 10-14; RD Beverley 07-12; Chapl E Riding Community Health Trust 98-04; Can and Preb York Minster from 03; Dioc

Ecum Officer 07-09; Dioc Adv for Lay Development from 14. *Diocesan House, Aviator Court, Clifton Moor, York YO30 4WJ* T: (01904) 699500 E: angela@petermichael.karoo.co.uk

BAILEY, Bertram Arthur. b 20. Tyndale Hall Bris 65. **d** 67 **p** 68. C Bath St Luke *B & W* 67-72; C Bickenhill w Elmdon *Birm* 72-73; R N Tawton *Ex* 73-79; R N Tawton and Bondleigh 79-87; rtd 87; PtO *B & W* from 87; Clergy Retirement and Widows' Officer 89-06. *4 Uphill Road South, Weston-super-Mare BS23 4SD* T: (01934) 633552

BAILEY, Canon Bethan. b 54. Univ of Wales CertEd 93 BTh 07 MCSP 75. St Jo Coll Nottm 04. **d** 06 **p** 07. C Dolgellau w Llanfachreth and Brithdir etc *Ban* 06-10; C Ardudwy Deanery 10; P-in-c Penrhyndeudraeth and Llanfrothen w Maentwrog etc *Ban* 11-13; Dioc Children's Officer 10-13; R Bro Ardudwy from 13. *Corsygedol Farm, Dyffryn Ardudwy LL44 2RJ* T: (01341) 247231 E: bethbaileydol@tiscali.co.uk

BAILEY, Brendan John. b 61. Strathclyde Univ BSc 83 K Coll Lon MA 99. Ripon Coll Cuddesdon BTh 93. **d** 94 **p** 95. C Purley *Ox* 94-99; R Nettlebed w Bix, Highmoor, Pishill etc from 99; P-in-c Nuffield from 06. *The Rectory, High Street, Nettlebed, Henley-on-Thames RG9 5DD* T: (01491) 641575 E: baileybj@ndo.co.uk

BAILEY, Canon Brian Constable. b 36. K Coll Lon AKC 62. **d** 63 **p** 64. C Mill Hill Jo Keble Ch *Lon* 63-66; C Gt Stanmore 66-69; C Gt Marlow *Ox* 69-72; R Burghfield 72-81; R Wokingham All SS 81-96; Hon Can Ch Ch 94-96; TV Pinhoe and Broadclyst *Ex* 96-00; rtd 00; V of Close Sarum Cathl 00-01. *2 Rose Cottages, Maudlin Road, Totnes TQ9 5TG* T: (01803) 865992 E: brianbailey579@btinternet.com

BAILEY, Mrs Carolyn. b 64. Ox Min Course 07. **d** 10 **p** 11. NSM Gt Missenden w Ballinger and Lt Hampden *Ox* from 10. *Mill House, 81 Aylesbury Road, Wendover, Aylesbury HP22 6JJ* T: (01296) 624814 M: 07841-583303 E: carolyn.bailey1@virgin.net

BAILEY, Mrs Christine Ann. b 55. All SS Cen for Miss & Min 11. **d** 14 **p** 15. OLM Urmston *Man* from 14. *16 Westmorland Road, Urmston, Manchester M41 9HJ* T: 0161-747 5123 E: christine.bailey70@ntlworld.com

BAILEY, The Ven David Charles. b 52. Linc Coll Ox BA 75 MA 78 MSc 77. St Jo Coll Nottm BA 79. **d** 80 **p** 81. C Worksop St Jo *S'well* 80-83; C Edgware *Lon* 83-87; V S Cave and Ellerker w Broomfleet *York* 87-97; RD Howden 91-97; V Beverley Minster 97-08; P-in-c Routh 97-08; Can and Preb York Minster 98-08; Adn Bolton *Man* from 08. *14 Springside Road, Bury BL9 5JE* T: 0161-761 6117 F: 763 7973 E: archdeaconbolton@manchester.anglican.org

BAILEY, David Ross. b 58. UNISA BTh 82. St Bede's Coll Umtata 80. **d** 82 **p** 82. C Somerset West S Africa 82-85; C Elgin 85-87; R Atlantis 87-95; R Salt River 95-08; P-in-c Honicknowle *Ex* 08-14; C Ernesettle 08-14; C Whitleigh 08-14; V Ernesettle, Whitleigh and Honicknowle from 14. *St Francis's Presbytery, 53 Little Dock Lane, Plymouth PL5 2LP* T/F: (01752) 773874 M: 07864-059302

BAILEY, Dennis. b 53. Man Univ BEd 74 BMus 74 TCD MA 06 PhD 11. St Jo Coll Nottm BTh 79. **d** 79 **p** 80. C Netherley Ch Ch CD *Liv* 79-83; S Africa from 83. *PO Box 625, Hilton, 3245 South Africa* T: (0027) 82-275 3641 *or* 33-343 1093 E: dbaileysa@gmail.com

BAILEY, Derek Gilbert. b 42. Div Hostel Dub 65. **d** 68 **p** 69. C Cork St Luke w St Ann *C, C & R* 68-72; CF 72-06; Rtd Officer Chapl RAChD from 06; PtO *York* from 98; *Sheff* 97-01 and from 03. *c/o MOD Chaplains (Army)* T: (01980) 615804 F: 615800

BAILEY, Derek William. b 39. Man Univ BA 96. Cranmer Hall Dur 64. **d** 67 **p** 68. C Sutton *Liv* 67-69; C Chapel-en-le-Frith *Derby* 69-73; V Hadfield 73-90; R Collyhurst *Man* 90-95; V Chaddesden St Mary *Derby* 95-02; rtd 02; PtO *York* from 03. *187 Bishopthorpe Road, York YO23 1PD* T: (01904) 628080

BAILEY, Edward Peter. b 35. Nottm Univ MA 93. Qu Coll Birm. **d** 62 **p** 63. C Ordsall *S'well* 62-66; C Clifton w Glapton 66-71; V Lady Bay 71-83; Relig Affairs Adv to Radio Trent 83-85; C Gedling 86-89; C Bilborough St Jo 89-00; rtd 00; PtO *York* from 00. *Cragside Cottage, 18 Egton Road, Aislaby, Whitby YO21 1SU*

BAILEY, Elizabeth. b 47. **d** 03 **p** 04. OLM Bishop's Cannings, All Cannings etc *Sarum* 03-09; rtd 09. *Lynden, The Street, Bishop's Cannings, Devizes SN10 2LD* T: (01380) 860400 E: liz@iftco.com

BAILEY, Mrs Elizabeth Carmen. b 45. EAMTC 89. **d** 93 **p** 94. NSM Roughton and Felbrigg, Metton, Sustead etc *Nor* 93-95 and 99-02; P-in-c 02-06; NSM Cromer and Gresham 95-99; C Buxton w Oxnead, Lammas and Brampton 06-07; C Bure Valley 07-10; rtd 10; PtO *Nor* from 12. *5 Warren Road, Southrepps, Norwich NR11 8UN* T: (01263) 833785 E: elizabeth.bailey2@btopenworld.com

BAILEY, Ms Helen Margaret. b 69. Hull Univ BA 92 PGCE 99 SS Coll Cam BA 09. Westcott Ho Cam 07. **d** 10 **p** 11. C High Harrogate Ch Ch *Ripon* 10-14; R Minchinhampton w Box and Amberley *Glouc* from 14. *The Rectory, Butt Street, Minchinhampton, Stroud GL6 9JP* T: (01453) 882289 E: helen@minchchurch.org.uk

BAILEY, Ian Arthur. b 53. York Univ BA 74 DPhil 78. WEMTC. **d** 01 **p** 02. NSM Clifton H Trin, St Andr and St Pet *Bris* 01-02; NSM Henleaze 02-14; NSM Shirehampton from 14. *5 Queens Gate, Stoke Bishop, Bristol BS9 1TZ* T: 0117-968 6251 E: iandfbailey@blueyonder.co.uk

BAILEY, Canon Ivan John. b 33. Keble Coll Ox BA 57 MA 65. St Steph Ho Ox 57. **d** 59 **p** 60. C Ipswich All Hallows *St E* 59-62; Clerical Sec CEMS 62-66; V Cringleford *Nor* 66-81; RD Humbleyard 73-81; R Colney 80-81; Relig Adv Anglia TV 81-91; P-in-c Kirby Bedon w Bixley and Whitlingham *Nor* 81-92; Hon Can Nor Cathl 84-98; Chapl St Andr Hosp Norwich 92-94; Chapl Mental Health Unit Nor HA 92-94; Chapl Norfolk Mental Health Care NHS Trust 94-98; rtd 98; PtO *Nor* from 98. *21 Cranleigh Rise, Norwich NR4 6PQ* T: (01603) 453565 E: ivan@bailey1966.freeserve.co.uk

BAILEY, Ms Jane Rome. b 50. Univ of Wales (Ban) BA 99 BTh 03. Ban Ord Course 00. **d** 03 **p** 04. C Llifon and Talybolion Deanery *Ban* 03-06; P-in-c Trefdraeth w Aberffraw, Llangadwaladr etc 06-10; TV Holyhead 10-13; C Bro Cybi from 13. *St Seiriol's House, 25 Gors Avenue, Holyhead LL65 1PB* T: (01407) 764780 E: jane.r.bailey@btinternet.com

BAILEY, Joshua John. b 85. Wycliffe Hall Ox 12. **d** 15. C Rothley *Leic* from 15. *11 Oldfield Lane, Rothley, Leicester LE7 7QD* E: joshjbailey@gmail.com

BAILEY, Joyce Mary Josephine. See OUTEN, Joyce Mary Josephine

BAILEY, Judith Elizabeth Anne. See MILLER, Judith Elizabeth Anne

BAILEY, Justin Mark. b 55. Birm Univ BA 77 Southn Univ MTh 97 Wolv Poly PGCE 78. Ripon Coll Cuddesdon 90. **d** 92 **p** 93. C Oakdale *Sarum* 92-96; P-in-c Milton Abbas, Hilton w Cheselbourne etc 96-05; P-in-c Piddletrenthide w Plush, Alton Pancras etc 02-05; V Piddle Valley, Hilton, Cheselbourne etc 05-06; P-in-c Bruton and Distr *B & W* from 06. *The Rectory, Plox, Bruton BA10 0EF* T: (01749) 812616 E: frjustin@btinternet.com

BAILEY, Mark David. b 62. Ripon Coll Cuddesdon 87. **d** 90 **p** 91. C Leigh Park *Portsm* 90-93; C Fleet *Guildf* 93-95; TV Basingstoke *Win* 95-00; P-in-c Twyford and Owslebury and Morestead 00-08; R Lower Dever from 08. *The Rectory, 6 Green Close, South Wonston, Winchester SO21 3EE* T: (01962) 886883 E: mark-bailey@talktalk.net

BAILEY, Canon Mark Robert. b 60. St Paul's Coll Chelt BA 81. Trin Coll Bris BA 89. **d** 89 **p** 90. C Heigham H Trin *Nor* 89-94; Chapl UEA 92-93; TV Cheltenham St Mary, St Matt, St Paul and H Trin *Glouc* 94-07; TR Cheltenham H Trin and St Paul from 07; Hon Can Glouc Cathl from 04. *100 Hewlett Road, Cheltenham GL52 6AR* T: (01242) 582398 *or* 808750 E: mark.bailey@trinitycheltenham.com

BAILEY, Martin Tristram. b 57. Oak Hill Th Coll 89. **d** 91 **p** 92. C Brundall w Braydeston and Postwick *Nor* 91-95; TV Plymouth St Andr and Stonehouse *Ex* 95-06; Chapl St Dunstan's Abbey Sch Plymouth 02-05; V Riseley w Bletsoe *St Alb* from 06. *The Vicarage, 16 Church Lane, Riseley, Bedford MK44 1ER* T: (01234) 708234 E: martin@7baileys.freeserve.co.uk

BAILEY, Michael Joseph. b 78. Open Univ BSc 02 City Univ MSc 05 RN 96. St Steph Ho Ox BTh 11. **d** 10 **p** 11. C Holbrooks *Cov* 10-13; Pioneer P *Lon* 13-14; P-in-c Sidley Chich from 14. *All Saints' Vicarage, All Saints' Lane, Bexhill-on-Sea TN39 5HA* M: 07713-258429 E: frmichaelbailey@gmail.com

BAILEY, Nicholas Andrew. b 55. Open Univ BA 84 Nottm Univ CertEd 80. Ripon Coll Cuddesdon 88. **d** 90 **p** 91. C Guisborough *York* 90-92; Chapl Repton Prep Sch from 92. *Repton Preparatory School, Foremarke Hall, Milton, Derby DE65 6EJ* T: (01283) 703269 E: twonickleby@aol.com

BAILEY, Miss Patricia Laura. b 49. Wall Hall Coll Aldenham CertEd 72. NTMTC 95. **d** 98 **p** 99. NSM Hackney Marsh *Lon* 98-01; NSM S Hackney St Jo w Ch Ch 01-04; NSM Cosby and Whetstone *Leic* 04-11; P-in-c Ibstock w Heather from 11. *The Rectory, 2 Hinckley Road, Ibstock LE67 6PB* T: (01530) 263729

BAILEY, Peter. See BAILEY, Edward Peter

BAILEY, Canon Peter Robin. b 43. St Jo Coll Dur BA 64. Trin Coll Bris 72. **d** 74 **p** 75. C Corby St Columba *Pet* 74-77; C Bishopsworth *Bris* 77-82; V Sea Mills 82-97; RD Westbury and Severnside 91-97; P-in-c Bishopston 97-98; P-in-c Bris St Andr w St Bart 97-98; TR Bishopston and St Andrews

98-09; Hon Can Bris Cathl 97-09; rtd 09; PtO *B & W* from 10. *4 The Croft, Backwell, Bristol BS48 3LY* T: (01275) 790611 M: 07970-180460 E: peterandheather@blueyonder.co.uk

BAILEY, Richard William. b 47. Oak Hill Th Coll BA 84. **d** 84 **p** 85. C Huyton St Geo *Liv* 84-87; V Wombridge *Lich* 87-97; P-in-c Shenstone and Stonnall 97-06; Chapl HM Pris Dovegate 06-12; PtO *Lich* from 14. *28 Rosliston Road, Walton-on-Trent, Swadlincote DE12 8NQ* T: (01283) 711785
E: ricthevicmadasafish@btinternet.com

BAILEY, Richard William. b 38. Man Univ BSc 59. Ripon Hall Ox 63. **d** 65 **p** 66. C Tonge *Man* 65-68; C Stretford St Matt 68-71; R Abbey Hey 71-80; V E Crompton 80-86; V Chadderton St Matt 86-98; R Stand 98-04; rtd 04; PtO *Leeds* from 07. *41 Ley Top Lane, Allerton, Bradford BD15 7LT* T: (01274) 483344 E: jean_richard@btinternet.com

BAILEY, Robert Henry. b 45. FCA 69. NOC 99. **d** 02 **p** 03. NSM Dewsbury *Wakef* 02-05; Sub Chapl HM Pris Leeds 02-05; NSM Felkirk *Wakef* 05-13; rtd 12. *Address temp unknown* E: robertbailey.minster@btinternet.com

BAILEY, Canon Robert William. b 49. Open Univ BA 91. Bernard Gilpin Soc Dur 68 Lich Th Coll 69. **d** 72 **p** 73. C Stoke *Cov* 72-75; Chapl RAF 75-99; RD Calne *Sarum* 97-98; TV Cartmel Peninsula *Carl* 99-11; Hon Can Carl Cathl 05-11; rtd 11; PtO *Sarum* 11-12; Asst Chapl Dorothy House Hospice Winsley 12-13; TV The Cannings and Redhorn *Sarum* 13-15; PtO from 15. *Longmead, The Cartway, Wedhampton, Devizes SN10 3QD* T: (01380) 840587
E: robertandsue2011@yahoo.com

BAILEY, Simon. b 56. Man Univ MusB Nottm Univ BCombStuds. Linc Th Coll. **d** 83 **p** 84. C Armley w New Wortley *Ripon* 83-86; C Harrogate St Wilfrid and St Luke 86-90; R Harby, Long Clawson and Hose *Leic* 90-94; V Woodhall *Bradf* 94-03; RD Calverley 98-01; R N Adelaide Ch Ch Australia 03-07; R Glen Osmond from 07. *2 Pridmore Road, Glen Osmond SA 5064, Australia* T: (0061) (8) 8379 1494 *or* 8379 4114 F: 8338 3442 E: rector@stsavioursgo.net

BAILEY, Stella. b 76. Westhill Coll Birm BTheol 98. Ripon Coll Cuddesdon 07. **d** 09 **p** 10. C Walsgrave on Sowe *Cov* 09-13; V Cov St Mary from 13. *63 Broad Lane, Coventry CV5 7AH* T: (024) 7667 3138 E: chacethedog@sky.com

BAILEY, Stephen. b 39. Leic Univ BA 61. Clifton Th Coll 61. **d** 62 **p** 63. C Wellington w Eyton *Lich* 62-66; C Rainham *Chelmsf* 66-69; V Ercall Magna *Lich* 69-75; V Rowton 69-75; RD Wrockwardine 72-75; V W Bromwich Gd Shep w St Jo 75-83; P-in-c W Bromwich St Phil 80-81; V 81-83; R Chadwell *Chelmsf* 83-96; RD Thurrock 92-96; V Galleywood Common 96-04; rtd 04; PtO *Chelmsf* from 04. *64 Bridport Way, Braintree CM7 9FJ* T: (01376) 550859

BAILEY, Stephen Andrew. b 75. St Jo Coll Nottm 05. **d** 07 **p** 08. C Walton-on-Thames *Guildf* 07-11; TV Oadby *Leic* from 11; Warden of Readers from 13. *St Paul's House, Hamble Road, Oadby, Leicester LE2 4NX*
E: steveandangiebailey@tiscali.co.uk

BAILEY, Stephen John. b 57. Sarum & Wells Th Coll 88. **d** 90 **p** 91. C Redhill H Trin *S'wark* 90-95; Chapl E Surrey Coll 91-93; P-in-c Betchworth *S'wark* 95-00; V 00-06; P-in-c Buckland 95-00; R 00-06; R Hamilton H Trin Bermuda 06-13; R Guernsey Ste Marie du Castel *Win* from 13; V Guernsey St Matt from 13. *The Rectory, Rue de la Lande, Castel, Guernsey GY5 7EJ* T: (01481) 256793
E: steveandgillbailey@hotmail.com

BAILEY, Mrs Susan Mary. b 40. F L Calder Coll Liv CertEd 61. EAMTC 89. **d** 92 **p** 94. NSM Chelmsf Cathl 92-93; NSM Needham Market w Badley *St E* 93-95; NSM Belper *Derby* 96-00; NSM Allestree St Nic and Quarndon 00-05; Chapl Morley Retreat and Conf Ho Derby 00-05; rtd 05. *28 Burleigh Way, Wickwar, Wotton-under-Edge GL12 8LR* T: (01454) 294112 E: susan.m.bailey@gmail.com

BAILEY, Yvonne Mary. *See* HOBSON, Yvonne Mary

BAILIE, Alison Margaret. b 62. Leeds Univ LLB 83. Trin Coll Bris BA 98. **d** 98 **p** 99. C Halliwell St Pet *Man* 98-05; P-in-c Droylsden St Mary 05-09; R from 09. *St Mary's Rectory, Dunkirk Street, Droylsden, Manchester M43 7FB* T: 0161-370 1569 E: alison@bailie.free-online.co.uk

BAILLIE, Frederick Alexander. b 21. FRGS Open Univ BA 75 QUB MA 86 PhD 87. CITC 53. **d** 55 **p** 56. C Belfast St Paul *Conn* 55-59; C Dunmurry 59-61; RAChD 57-84; I Eglantine *Conn* 61-69; I Belfast Whiterock 69-74; Hd of S Ch Miss Ballymacarrett 74-79; I Magheraculmoney *Clogh* 79-87; Dioc Communications Officer 80-86; Hon CF from 84; Can Clogh Cathl 85-87; rtd 87. *Home Farm Care Centre, Home Farm Road, Portree IV51 9LX* T: (01478) 613760
E: fabaillie@btinternet.com

BAILLIE, Terence John. b 46. New Coll Ox BA 69 MA 78 Man Univ MSc 72. St Jo Coll Nottm 74. **d** 77 **p** 78. C Chadwell *Chelmsf* 77-80; C Bickenhill w Elmdon *Birm* 80-84;

V Bedminster St Mich *Bris* 84-96; V Clevedon St Andr and Ch *Ch B & W* 96-12; rtd 12. *33 Belgrave Road, Weston-super-Mare BS22 8AJ* T: (01934) 643429
E: tandam.baillie@btinternet.com

BAILY, Linda Rosemary. **d** 06 **p** 07. NSM Llanaber w Caerdeon *Ban* from 06. *Llwyn Gloddaeth, Abermaw, Barmouth LL42 1DX* T: (01341) 280524

BAILY, Canon Robert Spencer Canning. b 21. G&C Coll Cam BA 42 MA 46. Westcott Ho Cam 42. **d** 44 **p** 45. C Sherborne w Castleton and Lillington *Sarum* 44-46; C Heacham *Nor* 46-47; C Bedford All SS *St Alb* 48-50; C-in-c Hayes St Edm CD *Lon* 50-56; R Blofield w Hemblington *Nor* 56-69; P-in-c Perlethorpe *S'well* 69-87; Dir of Educn 69-87; Hon Can S'well Minster 80-87; rtd 87; PtO *Linc* 87-02; *S'well* 87-00. *17 Ravendale Close, Grantham NG31 8BS* T: (01476) 568614

BAILY, Mrs Sally. b 65. Kingston Univ MBA 97. Trin Coll Bris MA 14. **d** 13 **p** 14. C Gt Chesham *Ox* from 13. *31 Chapmans Crescent, Chesham HP5 2QT* T: (01494) 775184 M: 07826-251432 E: curate@cheshamchurch.co.uk

BAIN, Alan. b 48. Thames Poly BSc 72. St Jo Coll Nottm. **d** 77 **p** 78. C Wakef St Andr and St Mary 77-81; V Bath Odd Down *B & W* 81-82; P-in-c Combe Hay 81-82; V Bath Odd Down w Combe Hay from 82. *The Vicarage, 39 Frome Road, Bath BA2 2QF* T: (01225) 832838 *or* T/F: 835228
E: alanbain@stphilipstjames.org

BAIN, Andrew John. b 55. Newc Poly BA 77 Edin Univ MTh 89. Edin Th Coll 86. **d** 88 **p** 89. Chapl St Mary's Cathl 88-91; C Edin St Mary 88-91; R Edin St Jas 91-98; P-in-c Edin St Marg 93-98; R Haddington 98-06; P-in-c Edin St Ninian 06-10; Dioc Dir of Ords 95-98 and 06-07; Chapl Emmaus Ho 10-13; R Dunbar *Edin* from 13. *Emmaus House, 14 Gilmore Place, Edinburgh EH3 9NQ* E: andrewbain99@hotmail.com

BAIN, David Roualeyn Findlater (Roly). b 54. Bris Univ BA 75. Ripon Coll Cuddesdon 76. **d** 78 **p** 79. C Perry Hill St Geo *S'wark* 78-81; Chapl Asst Guy's Hosp Lon 81-84; Succ S'wark Cathl 81-84; V Streatham St Paul 84-90; PtO *Bris* 90-08; Hon C Almondsbury and Olveston from 08. *The Vicarage, The Street, Olveston, Bristol BS35 4DA* T/F: (01454) 616593
E: roly@rolybain.co.uk

BAIN, The Ven John Stuart. b 55. Van Mildert Coll Dur BA 77. Westcott Ho Cam 78. **d** 80 **p** 81. C Washington *Dur* 80-84; C Dunston 84-86; V Shiney Row 86-92; V Herrington 86-92; P-in-c Whitworth w Spennymoor 92-97; P-in-c Merrington 94-97; AD Auckland 96-02; V Spennymoor, Whitworth and Merrington 97-02; Hon Can Dur Cathl 98-02; Adn Sunderland from 02; P-in-c Hedworth 02-13; P-in-c E Boldon 09-13; P-in-c Boldon 10-13; C The Boldons from 13. *St Nicholas' Vicarage, Hedworth Lane, Boldon Colliery NE35 9JA* T: 0191-536 2300 F: 519 3369
E: archdeacon.of.sunderland@durham.anglican.org

BAIN, Lawrence John Weir. b 60. NTMTC BA 05. **d** 05 **p** 06. C Stoughton *Guildf* 05-09; P-in-c Camberley Heatherside from 09. *30 Yockley Close, Camberley GU15 1QH* T: (01276) 691127 F: 678015 E: revlarrybain@aol.com

BAIN-DOODU, Canon Joseph Justice. b 56. Cape Coast Univ Ghana MEd 09. St Nic Th Coll Ghana LTh 86. **d** 86 **p** 86. Ghana 86-97 and 99-08; Hon C Sheldon *Birm* 97-98; PtO *Portsm* 09-12. *Address temp unknown* M: 07532-104795 E: josephbaindoodu@gmail.com

BAINBRIDGE, Mrs Christine Susan. b 48. St Aid Coll Dur BA 70 K Coll Lon MA 99. SEITE 93. **d** 96 **p** 97. C S'wark H Trin w St Matt 96-99; Asst to Bp Woolwich (Greenwich Area) 99-03; C Lee Gd Shep w St Pet 99-03; P-in-c Deptford St Jo w H Trin 03-06; TR Deptford St Jo w H Trin and Ascension 06-13; rtd 13; PtO *S'wark* 13-14. *16 The Mount, Reading RG1 5HL* T: 0118-931 1587 M: 07939-662980
E: bainbridgerev@gmail.com

BAINBRIDGE, David George. b 42. Wadh Coll Ox BA 63 MA 67 Lon Inst of Educn PGCE 67. Ridley Hall Cam 84. **d** 86 **p** 87. C Downend *Bris* 86-90; TV Yate New Town 90-01; Warden Lee Abbey Internat Students' Club Kensington 01-07; rtd 07; PtO *Glouc* from 08. *2 Kingsmead, Lechlade GL7 3BW* T: (01367) 250347 E: bainbridge1973@yahoo.co.uk

BAINBRIDGE, John Richard. b 35. Pemb Coll Cam BA 59 MA 63. Clifton Th Coll 65. **d** 67 **p** 68. C Ex St Leon w H Trin 67-70; P-in-c Penge St Paul *Roch* 70-73; Chapl Uppingham Sch 73-87; V Stevenage St Nic and Graveley *St Alb* 87-98; rtd 98; PtO *Pet* from 99. *Willowdown Cottage, 8 Laxton, Corby NN17 3AT* T: (01780) 450308

BAINBRIDGE, Mrs Phyllis Marion. b 49. Aber Univ BSc 81. St Jo Coll Nottm 10. **d** 11 **p** 12. NSM Littleover *Derby* 11-12; NSM Mickleover All SS 12-14; NSM Mickleover St Jo 12-14; NSM Mickleover from 14. *357 Duffield Road, Allestree, Derby DE22 2DG* T: (01332) 554700 M: 07776-434792
E: revdphyllisbainbridge@gmail.com

BAINBRIDGE, Richard Densham. b 49. Ch Coll Cam BA 71 MA 75 Edge Hill Coll of HE PGCE 72. S'wark Ord Course 91. **d** 94 **p** 95. C Bermondsey St Jas w Ch Ch S'wark 94-99; V Lee Gd Shep w St Pet 99-14; AD E Lewisham 06-13; rtd 14. *16 The Mount, Reading RG1 5HL* T: 0118-931 1587
E: revrdb@yahoo.com

BAINES, Alan William. b 50. S Bank Poly BSc 72. Trin Coll Bris 92. **d** 94 **p** 95. C Chenies and Lt Chalfont, Latimer and Flaunden Ox 94-98; V Eye Pet 98-05; Post Ord Tr Co-ord 00-05; TV Duston 05-15; rtd 15. *14 Bittern Avenue, Abbeydale, Gloucester GL4 4WA* E: a.baines93@ntlworld.com

BAINES, Derek Alfred. b 53. MCSP 75. CBDTI 99. **d** 02 **p** 03. NSM Lostock Hall Blackb 02-09; NSM Lostock Hall and Farington Moss 09-11; R Hoole from 11. *16 Middlefield, Leyland PR26 7AE* T/F: (01772) 641521 M: 07774-200885
E: baines5253@btinternet.com

BAINES, Edward. See BAINES, Noel Edward

BAINES, John Charles. b 68. Ripon Coll Cuddesdon 00. **d** 02 **p** 03. C Morton and Stonebroom w Shirland Derby 02-06; P-in-c New Mills 06-12; V from 12; RD Glossop 10-13. *St George's Vicarage, Church Lane, New Mills, High Peak SK22 4NP* T: (01663) 743225 E: vicar@newmillschurch.co.uk

BAINES, Keith. b 46. **d** 99 **p** 00. OLM Atherton and Hindsford Man 99-02; OLM Atherton and Hindsford w Howe Bridge 02-05; TV 05-11; rtd 11. *17 The Cedars, Chorley PR7 3RH* E: baines1s@btinternet.com

✠**BAINES, The Rt Revd Nicholas.** b 57. Bradf Univ BA 80. Trin Coll Bris BA 87. **d** 87 **p** 88 **c** 03. C Kendal St Thos Carl 87-91; C Leic H Trin w St Jo 91-92; V Rothley 92-00; RD Goscote 96-00; Adn Lambeth S'wark 00-03; Area Bp Croydon 03-11; Bp Bradf 11-14; Bp Leeds from 14. *Hollin House, Weetwood Avenue, Leeds LS16 5NG* T: 0113-284 4300
E: bishop.nick@westyorkshiredales.anglican.org

BAINES, Noel Edward (Ted). b 29. St Jo Coll Dur BSc 52 MA 62. **d** 54 **p** 55. C Rainham Chelmsf 54-58; C Surbiton Hill Ch Ch S'wark 58-61; V Southborough St Matt Roch 61-67; V Beckenham St Jo 67-74; Hd RE Taunton Manor High Sch Caterham 74-83; Keston Inst 85-91; Hon C Bromley Ch Ch Roch 91-98; Hon C New Beckenham St Paul from 98; rtd 94. *10 Bromley Avenue, Bromley BR1 4BQ* T/F: (020) 8460 8256 E: ted.baines@diocese-rochester.org

BAINES, Mrs Sharon June. b 52. Sheff Hallam Univ MSc 05 MCSP 74. LCTP 06. **d** 09 **p** 10. NSM Penwortham St Leon Blackb from 09. *16 Middlefield, Leyland PR26 7AE* T/F: (01772) 641521 E: baines5253@btinternet.com

BAIRD, Agnes Murry (Nancy). b 35. Man Univ CertEd 70. EAMTC 93. **d** 96 **p** 97. NSM Bramford St E 96-98; NSM Haughley w Wetherden and Stowupland 98-09; rtd 09; PtO St E from 09. *1 Burls Yard, Crown Street, Needham Market, Ipswich IP6 8AJ* T: (01449) 720567
E: nancy@ctlconnect.co.uk

BAIRD, Paul Drummond. b 48. N Co Coll Newc CertEd 71 Open Univ BA 85. Ripon Coll Cuddesdon 88. **d** 90 **p** 91. C Chandler's Ford Win 90-93; V Hythe 93-03; P-in-c Compton and Otterbourne 03-06; rtd 08. *5 Kensington Close, Eastleigh SO50 6NS* T: (023) 8064 7536 M: 07802-431012
E: paulbaird@aol.com

BAIRD, Mrs Sally. b 53. St As Minl Tr Course 04. **d** 06. NSM Bistre St As from 06. *100 Park Avenue, Bryn-y-Baal, Mold CH7 6TP* T: (01352) 758831 E: sally.baird@btinternet.com

BAIRD, Canon William Stanley. b 33. TCD BA 54 Div Test. **d** 56 **p** 57. C Carlow w Urglin and Staplestown C & O 56-59; I Dunganstown D & G 59-64; C Knock D & D 64-69; P-in-c Kilwarlin Upper w Kilwarlin Lower 69-71; I 71-72; Warden Ch Min of Healing (Ireland) 72-79; I Dublin Drumcondra w N Strand D & G 79-91; Dir of Ords (Dub) 84-99; Can Ch Ch Cathl Dublin 88-99; I Swords w Donabate and Kilsallaghan 91-99; rtd 99. *5 Weavers Way, Wheaton Hall, Dublin Road, Drogheda, Co Louth, Republic of Ireland* T: (00353) (41) 984 6645 E: hmbaird@icloud.com

BAISLEY, George. b 45. Sarum & Wells Th Coll 78. **d** 80 **p** 81. C Glouc St Geo w Whaddon 80-83; R Welford w Weston and Clifford Chambers 83-87; Chapl Myton Hamlet Hospice 87-91; Chapl Warw Univ Cov 87-91; R Berkswell 91-03; RD Kenilworth 96-01; Chapl Bromley Coll 03-04; P-in-c Doddington, Newnham and Wychling Cant 04-07; P-in-c Teynham w Lynsted and Kingsdown 04-07; P-in-c Norton 04-07; rtd 07; PtO Chelmsf 07-08; P-in-c N Ockendon 08-12; PtO Roch from 13. *25 Bromley College, London Road, Bromley BR1 1PE* T: 07974-151056
E: george@baisley45.co.uk

BAKER, Alan. b 42. Liv Univ BA 64. Carl Dioc Tr Inst 93. **d** 96 **p** 97. NSM Flookburgh Carl 96-97; NSM Cartmel Peninsula 97-07; PtO Blackb from 98; Carl from 08. *1 Church View, Priest Lane, Cartmel, Grange-over-Sands LA11 6PU* T: (015395) 36551

BAKER, Albert George. b 30. Qu Coll Birm. **d** 61 **p** 62. C Merton St Mary S'wark 61-64; C Limpsfield and Titsey 64-65; C Chapel-en-le-Frith Derby 65-68; R Odd Rode Ches 68-76; V Holme Cultram St Mary Carl 76-78; R Blofield w Hemblington Nor 78-94; rtd 94. *240 Raedwald Drive, Bury St Edmunds IP32 7DN* T: (01284) 701802

BAKER, Alexander David Laing. b 74. **d** 11 **p** 12. C Edin Ch Ch 11-12; NSM Burnley St Matt w H Trin Blackb 12-14; PtO from 14. *Little Dudlands Farm, Rimington Lane, Rimington, Clitheroe BB7 4EA* T: (01200) 415968 E: alexbaker@priests.uk.net

BAKER, Alicia Mary. b 63. Cliff Coll MA 11. Trin Coll Bris BA 03. **d** 03 **p** 04. C E Ham St Paul Chelmsf 03-07; P-in-c Abercarn and Cwmcarn Mon 07-12; V Dudley Wood and Cradley Heath Worc from 12. *St Luke's Vicarage, 29A Upper High Street, Cradley Heath B64 5HX* T: (01384) 591096
E: aliciabakeruk@btinternet.com

BAKER, Andrew James. b 81. St Mellitus Coll 12. **d** 15. C Maghull and Melling Liv from 15. *53 Calder Drive, Maghull L31 9DR* M: 07972-921587 E: andyjimbaker@gmail.com

BAKER, Angela Mary. b 42. **d** 91. Par Dn Battersea St Sav and St Geo w St Andr S'wark 91-94; C 94-96; C Battersea Fields 96-02; rtd 02; PtO Roch from 03. *Finches, Ide Hill, Sevenoaks TN14 6JW* T: (01732) 750470

BAKER, Mrs Ann Christine. b 49. Edin Univ BEd 71. CBDTI 98. **d** 01 **p** 02. NSM St Bees Carl 01-04; P-in-c Eskdale, Irton, Muncaster and Waberthwaite 04-09; V 09-12; rtd 12; PtO Carl from 13. *Heatherside, Abbey Road, St Bees CA27 0EG* T: (01946) 822498 E: j.h.baker@btinternet.com

BAKER, Anne-Marie Clare. See BIRD, Anne-Marie Clare

BAKER, Anthony Peter. b 38. Hertf Coll Ox BA 59 MA 63. Clifton Th Coll 60. **d** 63 **p** 64. C Ox St Ebbe w St Pet 63-66; C Welling Roch 66-70; V Redland Bris 70-79; Lect Tyndale Hall Bris 70-71; Lect Trin Coll Bris 71-77; V Beckenham Ch Ch Roch 79-94; Chapl Beckenham Hosp 79-94; V Hove Bp Hannington Memorial Ch Chich 94-03; rtd 03; PtO Chich from 04. *12 Paradise Close, Eastbourne BN20 8BT* T: (01323) 438783

BAKER, Miss Barbara Ann. b 36. Linc Th Coll 85. **d** 87 **p** 94. Par Dn Hornchurch St Andr Chelmsf 87-94; C 94-97; rtd 97; PtO Chelmsf from 97. *120 Devonshire Road, Hornchurch RM12 4LN* T: (01708) 477759

BAKER, Canon Bernard George Coleman. b 36. Lon Univ BD 61. Oak Hill Th Coll 61. **d** 63 **p** 64. C Broadwater St Mary Chich 63-66; BCMS Miss P and Chapl Morogoro Cen Ch Tanzania 66-79; V Moshi St Marg 79-84; Hon Can Morogoro from 77; Hon Can Mt Kilimanjaro from 82; C-in-c Ryde St Jas Prop Chpl Portsm 84-96; Crosslinks 96-01; Asst P Ruaha Cathl Tanzania 96-01; Teacher Amani Chr Tr Cen 96-01; rtd 01; PtO Ex from 02. *70 Sedgefield Drive, Thurnby, Leicester LE7 9PS* T: 0116-241 9181

BAKER (formerly BARTON), Mrs Caroline Janet. b 61. Ex Univ BA 83. Westcott Ho Cam 93. **d** 96 **p** 97. C Ivybridge w Harford Ex 96-02; P-in-c Torquay St Luke 02-05; Dioc Adv in Adult Tr 02-05; rtd 05. *11 Arundel Close, Exeter EX2 8UG* T: (01392) 426781

BAKER, Charles Edward. b 47. **d** 87 **p** 88. NSM Dublin Clontarf D & G 87-90; NSM Delgany 90-94; NSM Dublin Sandford w Milltown 94-97; NSM Dublin St Patr Cathl Gp 97-12; NSM Dublin St Cath and St Jas w St Audoen from 12; Treas V St Patr Cathl Dublin 01-05. *12 Aranleigh Vale, Rathfarnham, Dublin 14, Republic of Ireland* T: (00353) (1) 494 6465

BAKER, Prof Christopher James. b 54. St Cath Coll Cam BA 75 MA 78 PhD 78 CEng 83 FICE 96 FIHT 95. EMMTC 85. **d** 88 **p** 89. NSM Matlock Bath Derby 88-95; NSM Matlock Bath and Cromford 95; NSM Beeston S'well 95-98; PtO Lich 98-00; NSM Lich St Mich w St Mary and Wall 00-10; NSM Lich Ch Ch 10-13; PtO from 13. *28 Grosvenor Close, Lichfield WS14 9SR* T: (01543) 256320 or 262211 E: cjsmbaker@btinternet.com

BAKER, Christopher Peter. b 64. St Cuth Soc Dur BA 95 Greenwich Univ PGCE 96. SEITE 99. **d** 02 **p** 03. C Kennington St Mark S'wark 02-06; Chapl Greenwich Univ 07-13. *Holy Trinity Vicarage, 241 High Street, Sheerness ME12 1UR*

BAKER, Christopher Richard. b 61. Man Univ BA 83 PhD 02 Southn Univ BTh 90 Heythrop Coll Lon MTh 92. Sarum & Wells Th Coll 86. **d** 89 **p** 93. C Dulwich St Barn S'wark 89-92; Tutor Sarum & Wells Th Coll 92-94; Dir Chr Tr Milton Keynes Ox 94-98; Dir Tr OLM 98-99; Development Officer Wm Temple Foundn 01-04; Research Dir from 04. *Luther King House, Brighton Grove, Rusholme, Manchester M14 5JP* T: 0161-249 2502 M: 07779-000021
E: temple@wtf.org.uk

BAKER, David Ayshford. b 66. St Aid Coll Dur BA 88. Wycliffe Hall Ox BTh 97. **d** 97 **p** 98. C Chadwell Heath Chelmsf 97-01; C Surbiton Hill Ch Ch S'wark 01-09; R E Dean w Friston and Jevington Chich from 09. *The Rectory, Gilberts Drive, East Dean, Eastbourne BN20 0DL* T: (01323) 423266

BAKER, David Clive. b 47. Sarum & Wells Th Coll 76. **d** 78 **p** 79. C Shirley *Birm* 78-82; R Wainfleet All SS w St Thos *Linc* 82-83; P-in-c Wainfleet St Mary 82-83; P-in-c Croft 82-83; R The Wainfleets and Croft 83-86; V Stirchley *Birm* 86-96; PtO 97-98; V Handsworth St Mich 98-02; Chapl Aston Univ 99-02; C Codsall *Lich* 02-05; P-in-c Coven 04-05; V Bilbrook and Coven 05-12; rtd 12; PtO *Heref* 12-14; P-in-c Rickerscote *Lich* from 14. *St Peter's Vicarage, 16 Chestnut Drive, Stafford ST17 9WE* M: 07958-468819

BAKER, David Frederick. b 32. Clifton Th Coll 67. **d** 69 **p** 70. C Bilton *Ripon* 69-71; C Heworth w Peasholme St Cuth *York* 71-75; V Sand Hutton w Gate and Upper Helmsley 75-77; P-in-c Sand Hutton 75-77; V 77-80; R Preston in Holderness 80; P-in-c Sproatley 80; R Preston and Sproatley in Holderness 80-89; C Topcliffe 89; V Baldersby w Dalton, Dishforth etc 89-96; rtd 96; PtO *York* 96-08; *Ripon* 96-08. *6 Mains Court, Westhill AB32 6QZ* T: (01224) 743070

BAKER, David John. b 27. LRAM 50 GRSM 51. Ely Th Coll 53. **d** 55 **p** 56. C Swanley St Mary *Roch* 55-58; C Guildf St Nic 58-63; Prec St Alb Abbey *St Alb* 63-67; P-in-c Colney St Pet 67-68; V 68-73; R Tattenham Corner and Burgh Heath *Guildf* 73-84; R Fetcham 84-96; rtd 96; PtO *Guildf* from 96. *1 Terra Cotta Court, Quennels Hill, Wrecclesham, Farnham GU10 4SL* T: (01252) 734202

BAKER, David Jordan. b 35. Univ of Wales (Lamp) BA 59. Ely Th Coll 59. **d** 61 **p** 62. C Spalding St Mary and St Nic *Linc* 61-66; C Gainsborough All SS 66-69; V Wrawby 69-78; V Melton Ross w New Barnetby 70-78; V Linc St Pet-at-Gowts and St Andr 78-94; rtd 98; PtO *Linc* from 01. *Fartherwell, The Paddock, Canwick, Lincoln LN4 2RX* T: (01522) 526903

BAKER, Dilly. *See* BAKER, Hilary Mary

BAKER, Mrs Elizabeth May Janet Margaret. b 51. Bretton Hall Coll CertEd 73. Ox Min Course 04. **d** 07 **p** 08. NSM Watling Valley *Ox* 07-10; NSM Stantonbury and Willen 10-15; R Pitlochry *St And* from 15; R Strathtay from 15; R Kilmaveonaig from 15; R Kinloch Rannoch from 15. *3 Knockard Place, Pitlochry PH16 5JF* T: (01796) 472005 E: beth@willenbakers.co.uk

BAKER, Frank Thomas. b 36. Selw Coll Cam BA 61. Coll of Resurr Mirfield. **d** 63 **p** 64. C Mackworth St Fran *Derby* 63-66; C Leeds St Pet *Ripon* 66-73; P-in-c Stanley *Dur* 73-74; R Crook 73-74; Chapl Bucharest *Eur* 74-75; C Tewkesbury w Walton Cardiff *Glouc* 75-81; Min Can Windsor 81-86; rtd 86. *15 Hartford Court, 33 Filey Road, Scarborough YO11 2TP* T: (01723) 352466

BAKER, Frederick Peter. b 24. Bps' Coll Cheshunt 58. **d** 60 **p** 61. C Peckham St Jude *S'wark* 60; C Peckham St Jo 60-63; C Mitcham St Mark 63-66; C Northampton St Pet w Upton 66-69; P-in-c Northampton St Lawr 69-71; V Northampton St Edm 71-78; V Spratton 78-83; R Walgrave w Hannington and Wold 83-89; rtd 89; PtO *Win* 89-98; *Ely* 00-08. *73 Five Arches, Orton Wistow, Peterborough PE2 6FQ* T: (01733) 371349

BAKER, Gillian Devonald. b 40. S Dios Minl Tr Scheme 88. **d** 91 **p** 94. NSM Redhorn *Sarum* 91-07; TV 02-07; Chapl HM Pris Erlestoke 94-01. *Address temp unknown* E: gillie@riskman.plus.com

BAKER, The Very Revd Graham Brinkworth. b 26. AKC 54. **d** 55 **p** 56. C Wandsworth St Anne *S'wark* 55-58; Canada from 58. *1280 Tracksell Avenue, Victoria BC V8P 2C9, Canada*

BAKER, Mrs Heather Elizabeth. b 48. WEMTC 94. **d** 97 **p** 98. NSM Ewyas Harold w Dulas, Kenderchurch etc *Heref* 97-98; C 98-00; C Burghill and Stretton Sugwas 00-01; P-in-c Glasbury and Llowes w Clyro and Betws *S & B* 02-08; rtd 08; PtO *Heref* 09-15. *Park Lodge, Pontrilas, Hereford HR2 0HE* E: heather@parklodge.org.uk

BAKER, Hugh Crispin. b 58. Open Univ BA 92. Linc Th Coll 95. **d** 95 **p** 96. C Birstall and Wanlip *Leic* 95-99; V Middlestown *Wakef* 99-09; P-in-c Mirfield 09-14; V Leeds from 14; Dioc Rural Officer *Wakef* 04-14. *The Vicarage, 3 Vicarage Meadow, Mirfield WF14 9JL* T: (01924) 505790 E: hughcbaker@googlemail.com

BAKER, Hugh John. b 46. Birm Univ BSocSc 68. Cuddesdon Coll 69. **d** 71 **p** 72. C Binley *Cov* 71-74; C Pemberton St Mark Newtown *Liv* 74-78; TV Sutton 78-90; V Hints *Lich* 90-05; V Fazeley 90-13; V Canwell 05-13; R Drayton Bassett 05-13; rtd 13; PtO *Lich* from 13; Chapl S Staffs Healthcare NHS

Trust 00-10; Chapl Burton Hosps NHS Foundn Trust from 10. *21 Reedmace, Tamworth B77 1BH* E: hughbaker@hughbaker.plus.com

BAKER, Iain. b 70. St D Coll Lamp BA 91. Oak Hill Th Coll BA 99. **d** 99 **p** 00. C Gt Clacton *Chelmsf* 99-03; V Kidsgrove *Lich* from 03. *St Thomas's Vicarage, The Avenue, Kidsgrove, Stoke-on-Trent ST7 1AG* T: (01782) 772895 or 771727 E: ib.ib@virgin.net

BAKER, Canon James Henry. b 39. MBE 02. Kelham Th Coll 62. **d** 67 **p** 68. C Sheff Arbourthorne 67-70; C Pemberton St Jo *Liv* 70-71; Chapl and Prec St Mary's Cathl 71-74; R Lochgelly *St And* 74-84; P-in-c Rosyth and Inverkeithing 76-84; Can St Ninian's Cathl Perth 83-84; TR Whitehaven *Carl* 84-04; RD Calder 96-01; rtd 04; Hon C Eskdale, Irton, Muncaster and Waberthwaite *Carl* 05-12; Hon Can Carl Cathl 96-12; PtO from 13. *Heatherside, Abbey Road, St Bees CA27 0EG* T: (01946) 822498 E: j.h.baker@btinternet.com

BAKER, Jean Margaret. b 47. Sheff Univ BSc 69 DipEd 70 Lon Univ BD 78. All Nations Chr Coll 75 Gilmore Course 81. **dss** 82 **d** 87 **p** 97. Liv Our Lady and St Nic w St Anne 82-87; Chapl Huyton Coll 87; Chapl St Mary and St Anne's Sch Abbots Bromley 87-91; Chapl Howell's Sch Denbigh 91-98; C Denbigh *St As* 97-08; rtd 08; PtO *St As* from 09. *Lle Braf, 28 Abrams Lane, Denbigh LL16 3SS* T: (01745) 812262 E: margaret@smallrev.demon.co.uk

BAKER, Jenifer Marlene. b 44. Bris Univ BSc 65 Univ of Wales (Swansea) PhD 71 York St Jo Coll BA 05. **d** 05 **p** 06. OLM Ruyton XI Towns w Gt and Lt Ness *Lich* from 05. *Clock Cottage, Church Street, Ruyton XI Towns, Shrewsbury SY4 1LA* T: (01939) 260910

BAKER (formerly ROBINSON), Jennifer Elizabeth. b 53. Sheff Hallam Univ BA 96. NOC 01. **d** 04 **p** 06. NSM Fishlake w Sykehouse and Kirk Bramwith etc *Sheff* 04-08; PtO 08-11; Chapl Rotherham, Doncaster and S Humber NHS Trust from 13. *8 Kirkham Mews, Wistow, Selby YO8 3PN* T: (01757) 268056 E: jennifer-baker@hotmail.co.uk

BAKER, John Alfred. b 41. **d** 02 **p** 03. OLM Herne *Cant* 02-05; OLM St Nicholas at Wade w Sarre and Chislet w Hoath 05-11; OLM Minster w Monkton 05-11; PtO from 11. *Oakfield, 219 Canterbury Road, Herne Bay CT6 7HB* T: (01227) 362519 M: 07960-107169 E: john-baker@kent35.fslife.co.uk

BAKER, John Carl. b 55. Chich Th Coll 77. **d** 80 **p** 81. C Wigan St Andr *Liv* 80-83; V Hollinfare 83-85; TV Seacroft *Ripon* 85-89; TV Bottesford w Ashby *Linc* 89-94; V Liv St Paul Stoneycroft 94-02; V Altcar and Hightown 02-09; rtd 09. *49 Moor Lane, Southport PR8 3NY* T: (01704) 570639 E: revjcb@btopenworld.com

BAKER, John Reginald. b 62. Hatf Coll Dur BSc 83. Wycliffe Hall Ox 86. **d** 89 **p** 90. C Amersham *Ox* 89-92; C Greenford H Cross *Lon* 92-97. *11A Lakeside Road, London W14 0DX* T: (020) 8574 3762

✠**BAKER, The Rt Revd Jonathan Mark Richard.** b 66. St Jo Coll Ox BA 88 MPhil 90. St Steph Ho Ox BA 92. **d** 93 **p** 94 **c** 11. C Ascot Heath *Ox* 93-96; C Reading St Mark 96; P-in-c Reading H Trin 96-99; V 99-02; P-in-c Reading H Trin 96-99; V 99-02; Prin Pusey Ho 03-13; Hon C Ox St Thos 08-13; Suff Bp Ebbsfleet (PEV) *Cant* 11-13; Hon Asst Bp Ox 11-13; Asst Bp B & W 11-13; Suff Bp Fulham *Lon* from 13. *The Old Deanery, Dean's Court, London EC4V 5AA* T: (020) 7932 1130 E: bishop.fulham@london.anglican.org

BAKER, Canon Jonathan William. b 61. SS Coll Cam MA 85. Wycliffe Hall Ox BA 91. **d** 92 **p** 93. C Sanderstead All SS *S'wark* 92-96; P-in-c Scalby w Ravenscar and Staintondale *York* 96-97; V Scalby 97-04; P-in-c Hackness w Harwood Dale 96-97; V 97-04; P-in-c Scarborough St Luke 03-04; Can Res Pet Cathl from 04. *Canonry House, 14 Minster Precincts, Peterborough PE1 1XX* T: (01733) 897335 or 355310 F: 355316 E: jonathan.baker@peterborough-cathedral.org.uk

BAKER, Mrs Julie Ann Louise. b 77. Univ of Wales (Lamp) BA 98. St Mich Coll Llan BTh 06. **d** 06 **p** 07. C Barry All SS *Llan* 06-09; PtO Llan Cathl 09-13. *Address temp unknown* E: julie@treeherder.co.uk

BAKER, Canon Kenneth William. b 38. EMMTC 92. **d** 96 **p** 97. NSM Welford w Sibbertoft and Marston Trussell *Pet* 96-99; P-in-c 98-01; P-in-c N w S Kilworth and Misterton *Leic* 01-03; P-in-c Swinford w Catthorpe, Shawell and Stanford 01-03; TR Gilmorton, Peatling Parva, Kimcote etc 03-11; RD Guthlaxton 05-11; Hon Can Leic Cathl 06-11; rtd 11; PtO *Pet* from 11; *Leic* 11-12; C Ascension TM 12-14; PtO from 15. *2 Reynolds Close, Rugby CV21 4DD* T: (01788) 575621 E: kw.baker@btinternet.com

BAKER, Miss Laura Mary. b 89. St Jo Coll Dur BA 10. Westcott Ho Cam 11. **d** 14 **p** 15. C King's Lynn St Marg w St Nic *Nor* from 14. *The Pilot Hoy, 10 Pilot Street, King's Lynn PE30 1QL* E: laurabaker27@tiscali.co.uk or curate@stmargaretskingslynn.org.uk

BAKER, Marc Crispin. b 75. Westmr Coll Ox BTh 96. Oak Hill Th Coll 00. **d** 02 **p** 03. C Upton (Overchurch) *Ches* 02-06; TV Cheltenham St Mary, St Matt, St Paul and H Trin *Glouc* 06-07; C Cheltenham St Mary w St Matt 07-12; C Cheltenham St Mary w St Matt and St Luke 12-13; P-in-c Kea *Truro* from 13. *St Kea House, Killiow, Truro TR3 6AE* T: (01872) 260134 E: vicar@stkea.org.uk

BAKER, Margaret. b 55. **d** 08 **p** 09. C Herringthorpe *Sheff* 08-10; C Rivers Team 10-12; TV from 12. *The Vicarage, 24 Highgate, Sheffield S9 1WL* T: 0114-242 1724 E: margaret.baker@sheffield.anglican.org

BAKER, Michael William. b 38. Roch Th Coll 68. **d** 70 **p** 71. C Woodmansterne *S'wark* 70-75; TV Danbury *Chelmsf* 75-78; P-in-c Barrington *Ely* 78-90; V 90-97; P-in-c Shepreth 78-90; V 90-97; rtd 97; PtO *Nor* from 98. *The White House, Church Street, Elsing, Dereham NR20 3EB* T: (01362) 637370 E: hmb@waitrose.com

BAKER, Canon Miles Anthony. b 71. Brunel Univ BA 92. Ridley Hall Cam 99. **d** 02 **p** 03. C Paignton Ch Ch and Preston St Paul *Ex* 02-05; P-in-c Upton 05-08; Dioc Miss Enabl 08-14; Dir Miss *Pet* from 14; Can Pet Cathl from 15. *The Rectory, 32 West Street, Ecton, Northampton NN6 0QF* T: (01604) 407899 E: miles.baker@peterborough-diocese.org.uk

BAKER, Canon Neville Duff. b 35. St Aid Birkenhead 60. **d** 63 **p** 64. C Stranton *Dur* 63-66; C Houghton le Spring 66-68; V Tudhoe Grange 68-07; P-in-c Merrington 91-94; RD Auckland 83-94; Hon Can Dur Cathl 90-07; rtd 07; PtO *Dur* from 09. *2 The Bents, Sunderland SR6 7NX*

BAKER, Noel Edward Lloyd. b 37. Sarum & Wells Th Coll 73. **d** 75 **p** 76. C Charlton Kings St Mary *Glouc* 75-79; V Clearwell 79-81; R Eastington and Frocester 81-97; RD Stonehouse 90-94; P-in-c Eastington and Frocester 97-98; P-in-c Standish w Haresfield and Moreton Valence etc 97-98; rtd 98; PtO *Glouc* from 00. *46 Dozule Close, Leonard Stanley, Stonehouse GL10 3NL* T: (01453) 823569 E: noelbaker@greenbee.net

BAKER, Mrs Pamela Daphne. b 73. Ox Min Course. **d** 08. NSM Blackbird Leys *Ox* 08-14. *Address temp unknown* M: 07717-377516 E: pamelabaker53@gmail.com

BAKER, Paul Anthony. b 64. St Chad's Coll Dur BA 85. St Steph Ho Ox BA 88 MA 98. **d** 89 **p** 90. C Hartlepool St Aid *Dur* 89-93; TV Jarrow 93-98; V Sunderland Pennywell St Thos 98-04; V Darlington St Mark w St Paul from 04. *St Mark's Vicarage, 394 North Road, Darlington DL1 3BH* T: (01325) 382400

BAKER, Peter Colin. b 43. Sarum & Wells Th Coll. **d** 82 **p** 83. C Bridgemary *Portsm* 82-86; V Ash Vale *Guildf* 86-99; P-in-c Earlham St Anne *Nor* 99-08; P-in-c Earlham St Mary 99-08; rtd 08. *15 Linden Close, Laverstock, Salisbury SP1 1PN* M: 07710-844243 E: peter.baker854@ntlworld.com

BAKER, Peter Graham. b 55. MA PhD. St Stephen Ho Ox. **d** 82 **p** 83. C Ches H Trin 82-86; C Holborn St Alb w Saffron Hill St Pet *Lon* 86-91; V Golders Green 91-01; AD W Barnet 95-00; V Regent's Park St Mark 01-11; rtd 11. *Glebe House, Church Road, Spexhall, Halesworth IP19 0RQ* E: petergbaker@freeuk.com

BAKER, Robert James. b 80. Oriel Coll Ox BA 04 MA 08. Wycliffe Hall Ox BA 07. **d** 08 **p** 09. C Chesham Bois *Ox* 08-12; R Stoke H Cross w Dunston, Arminghall etc *Nor* from 12. *Holy Cross Vicarage, Mill Road, Stoke Holy Cross, Norwich NR14 8PA* M: 07855-774384 E: baker_robertj@hotmail.com

BAKER, Canon Robert John Kenneth. b 50. Southn Univ BSc 71 MICE 79. Oak Hill Th Coll 88. **d** 90 **p** 91. C Cromer *Nor* 90-94; R Pakefield from 94; Hon Can Nor Cathl from 07. *The Rectory, The Causeway, Pakefield, Lowestoft NR33 0JZ* T: (01502) 574040 E: bcbaker@sky.com

BAKER, Canon Robert Mark. b 50. Bris Univ BA 73. St Jo Coll Nottm 74. **d** 76 **p** 77. C Portswood Ch Ch *Win* 76-80; R Witton w Brundall and Braydeston *Nor* 80-89; P-in-c Buckenham w Hassingham and Strumpshaw 80-86; R Brundall w Braydeston and Postwick 89-05; RD Blofield 89-94; TR Thetford from 05; Hon Can Nor Cathl from 93. *The Rectory, 6 Redcastle Road, Thetford IP24 3NF* T: (01842) 762291 E: bob-baker@hotmail.com

BAKER, Ronald Kenneth. b 43. Open Univ BA 80. St Jo Coll Nottm LTh 87. **d** 87 **p** 88. C Paddock Wood *Roch* 87-90; V Ramsgate St Mark *Cant* 90-95; P-in-c Ewhurst and Bodiam *Chich* 95-98; V 98-03; rtd 03; PtO *Chich* from 03. *49 Coneyburrow Gardens, St Leonards-on-Sea TN38 9RZ* T: (01424) 851870 E: revronbaker@talktalk.net

BAKER, Roy David. b 36. St Aid Birkenhead 59. **d** 62 **p** 63. C Garston *Liv* 62-64; C N Meols 64-68; V Newton-le-Willows 68-73; V Crossens 73-82; V Blundellsands St Nic 82-01; rtd 01; PtO *Liv* from 03. *18 Ennerdale Road, Formby, Liverpool L37 2EA* T: (01704) 830622

BAKER, Sarah Jane. b 59. Lon Univ MB, BS 82 Sheff Univ MPhil 00 Coll of Ripon & York St Jo MA 02. NOC 99. **d** 02 **p** 03. NSM Kinsley w Wragby *Wakef* 02-04; NSM Sandal St Cath 04-07; PtO 07-11; NSM Westbrook St Jas *Liv* 11-14; TR Warrington W from 14. *20 Michigan Place, Great Sankey, Warrington WA5 8DT* T: (01925) 657954 M: 07885-376182 E: sarah.baker17@btinternet.com *or* sarahbakercouk@gmail.com

BAKER, The Ven Simon Nicholas Hartland. b 57. K Coll Lon BD 78. Qu Coll Birm 79. **d** 81 **p** 82. C Tupsley *Heref* 81-85; V Shinfield *Ox* 85-98; Prin Berks Chr Tr Scheme 93-98; Lay Min Adv and Warden of Readers *Win* 98-02; Dir of Min Development 02-07; Dir of Min and Past Planning 07-13; Hon Can Win Cathl 08-13; Adn Lich from 13; R Lich St Mich w St Mary and Wall from 13. *10 Mawgan Drive, Lichfield WS14 9SD*

BAKER, Stuart. b 44. MATA 63 AIAT 65. Ripon Coll Cuddesdon 92. **d** 93 **p** 94. C Whitchurch *Bris* 93-97; R Brightling, Dallington, Mountfield etc *Chich* 97-10; rtd 10. *8 Ayscue Close, Eastbourne BN23 6HE* T: (01323) 720168

BAKER, Canon William John. b 45. FCII 80. Cranmer Hall Dur 87. **d** 89 **p** 90. C Sale St Anne *Ches* 89-93; V Crewe St Andr w St Jo 93-15; P-in-c Crewe Ch Ch 03-13; RD Nantwich 06-13; Hon Can Ches Cathl 08-15; rtd 15. *17 Lyceum Way, Crewe CW1 3YF* T: (01270) 488063 M: 07768-843654 E: revbaker@aol.com

BAKERE, The Very Revd Ronald Duncan. b 35. TCD BA 58 MA 61 BD 62 Ch Ch Ox MA 66 FRSA 68 FBIM 79. Div Test 59. **d** 59 **p** 60. C Knockbreda *D & D* 59-61; C Dublin Zion Ch *D & G* 61-63; Min Can St Patr Cathl Dublin 62-64; CF (TA) 65-67; Lect Th Ex Univ Inst Educn 67-72; Prin Kuka Teachers' Coll Nigeria 73-77; Cen Org Red Cross Ex 78-81; PtO *Ex* 82-85; P-in-c Chew Magna w Dundry *B & W* 86-87; Hd RS Sir John Cass Foundn *Lon* 88-93; Dean Port Moresby Papua New Guinea 93-96; Visiting Prof H Spirit RC Sem 94-96; Hospitaller and Sen Chapl St Barts Hosp Lon 96-97; rtd 97; PtO *Lon* 96-04. *11B Sussex Heights, St Margarets Place, Brighton BN1 2FQ* M: 07958-061962

BAKEWELL, Jeremy Edgar. b 44. **d** 12 **p** 13. OLM Aldridge *Lich* from 12. *37 St Mary's Way, Walsall WS9 0AB* T: (01922) 459345 E: bakewell1@btinternet.com

BAKKER, Gregory Kendall. b 66. California State Univ BA 89. Trin Episc Sch for Min Penn MDiv 92 Trin Coll Bris 99. **d** 92 **p** 93. C Tariffville USA 92-96; Lect St Phil Coll Kongwa Tanzania 96-99; C Wroughton *Bris* 00-02; TV Stratton St Margaret w S Marston etc 02-08; V Sholing *Win* from 08. *The Vicarage, 41 Station Road, Southampton SO19 8FN* T: (023) 8044 8337 E: gbakker@tiscali.co.uk *or* sholingvicarage@googlemail.com

BAKKER (née CAMPBELL), Mrs Jane Judith. b 68. Trin Coll Bris BA 01. **d** 01 **p** 02. NSM Lyddington and Wanborough and Bishopstone etc *Bris* 01-03; NSM Stratton St Margaret w S Marston etc 03-08; NSM Sholing *Win* from 08; AD Southampton from 13. *The Vicarage, 41 Station Road, Southampton SO19 8FN* T: (023) 8044 8337 E: jjbakker@tiscali.co.uk *or* jane@sholingchurch.com

BALCHIN, Michael John. b 38. Selw Coll Cam BA 60 MA 64. Wells Th Coll 60. **d** 62 **p** 63. C Bournemouth H Epiphany *Win* 62-65; C Bris St Mary Redcliffe w Temple etc 65-69; R Norton sub Hamdon *B & W* 69-70; P-in-c Chiselborough w W Chinnock 69-70; R Norton sub Hamdon w Chiselborough 70-77; P-in-c Chipstable w Huish Champflower and Clatworthy 77-82; R 82-88; PtO *Ban* from 88; rtd 03. *The Barn, Middle Penygelly, Kerry, Newtown SY16 4LX* T: (01686) 670710

BALDOCK, Andrew Robert. b 67. St Jo Coll Dur BA 00. Cranmer Hall Dur 98. **d** 00 **p** 02. C Peterlee *Dur* 00-01; C Felling 01-03; C Dur St Nic 03-05; V Cheadle All Hallows *Ches* 05-08; PtO *Ox* 12-14; R Ayr *Glas* from 14; R Girvan from 14; R Maybole from 14. *Address temp unknown* M: 07854-491981 E: baldock67@btinternet.com

BALDOCK, Charles William Martin. b 52. Nottm Univ BPharm 73 York St Jo Coll MA 07. St Jo Coll Nottm LTh. **d** 85 **p** 86. C Nailsea Ch Ch *B & W* 85-89; V Brampton Bierlow *Sheff* 89-00; RD Wath 95-00; Hon Can Sheff Cathl 98-00; V Dringhouses *York* from 00; RD City of York 04-12; Chapl St Leon Hospice York from 02. *St Edward's Vicarage, Tadcaster Road, Dringhouses, York YO24 1QG* T: (01904) 706120 *or* T/F: 709111 E: ms@msbaldock.plus.com *or* parishoffice@care4free.net

BALDOCK, Canon Norman. b 29. K Coll Lon BD 52 AKC 52. **d** 53 **p** 54. C Cant St Pet w H Cross 53-54; C Thornton Heath St Jude 54-58; V Ash w W Marsh 58-67; V Sheerness H Trin w St Paul 67-75; V Margate St Jo 75-94; RD Thanet 80-86; Hon Can Cant Cathl 82-94; Chapl Margate Gen Hosp 82-94; rtd 94; PtO *Cant* 94-14. *9 Beach Avenue, Birchington CT7 9VS* T: (01843) 841173

BALDOCK, Reginald David. b 48. Oak Hill Th Coll 72. **d** 75 **p** 76. C Plymouth St Jude *Ex* 75-79; C Ardsley *Sheff* 79-85; V Rawthorpe *Wakef* 85-96; C Salterhebble All SS 96-98; P-in-c Bournemouth St Jo w St Mich *Win* from 98. *The Vicarage, 13 Durley Chine Road South, Bournemouth BH2 5JT* T: (01202) 761962 E: r.baldock1@ntlworld.com

BALDRY, John Netherway. b 19. Lon Univ BA 53. **d** 79 **p** 80. NSM Brighton St Paul *Chich* 79-11; NSM Brighton St Mich and St Paul from 11. *81 Windsor Court, Tongdean Lane, Brighton BN1 5JS* T: (01273) 501268

BALDWICK, Frank Eric. b 24. Ripon Hall Ox 54. **d** 55 **p** 56. C Newark Ch Ch and Hawton *S'well* 55-58; C W Bridgford 58-60; V Oldham St Barn *Man* 60-65; R Gt Lever 65-78; V Hindsford 78-81; TV Clifton *S'well* 81-89; rtd 89; PtO *S'well* 89-10. *35 Lady Bay Road, West Bridgford, Nottingham NG2 5BJ* T: 0115-982 1273

BALDWIN, Colin Steven. b 61. Brighton Poly BA 85. St Jo Coll Nottm MTh 01. **d** 01 **p** 02. C Billericay and Lt Burstead *Chelmsf* 01-05; P-in-c Prittlewell St Steph from 05. *26 Ashingdon Grove, Westcliff-on-Sea SS0 0QF* T: (01702) 352448 M: 07714-048450 *or* 305953 E: csbald@aol.com *or* colin@ststephens.org.uk

BALDWIN, David Frederick Beresford. b 57. Ripon Coll Cuddesdon 93. **d** 95 **p** 96. C Uttoxeter w Bramshall *Lich* 95-97; C Uttoxeter Area 97-98; V Tilstock, Edstaston and Whixall 98-08; P-in-c Prees 03-08; P-in-c Fauls 03-08; Rural Chapl (Salop Adnry) 00-08; RD Wem and Whitchurch 06-08; P-in-c The Lulworths, Winfrith Newburgh and Chaldon *Sarum* 08-10; C Wool and E Stoke 09-10; TR Beaminster Area from 10. *The Rectory, 3 Clay Lane, Beaminster DT8 3BU* T: (01308) 862150 E: revddavidbaldwin@yahoo.co.uk

BALDWIN, Derek Wilfred Walter. b 23. Lon Univ LTh 74. ALCD 56. **d** 52 **p** 53. C Sharrow St Andr *Sheff* 52-54; C Woodlands 54-56; V Shepley *Wakef* 56-59; V Earl's Heaton 59-66; Org Sec CECS B & W, Ex and Truro 66-72; R Morchard Bishop *Ex* 72-73; Org Sec CECS St Alb and Ox 73-77; C Portishead *B & W* 77-79; R Wymondham w Edmondthorpe *Leic* 79-80; P-in-c St Mewan *Truro* 80-81; V Crowan w Godolphin 81-83; C Cockington *Ex* 83-87; rtd 87; PtO *Ex* 90-09. *1 Case Gardens, Seaton EX12 2AP*

BALDWIN, Mrs Frances Mary. b 49. SRN 71. SEITE 99. **d** 02 **p** 03. NSM Caterham *S'wark* 02-10; Asst Chapl E Sussex Healthcare NHS Trust from 11. *46 Hawkhurst Way, Bexhill-on-Sea TN39 3SN* T: (01424) 842864
E: francesb3@btinternet.com

BALDWIN, John Charles. b 39. Bris Univ BSc 61 Sussex Univ DPhil 65 FBCS CEng. St Steph Ho Ox 82. **d** 83 **p** 84. C Llandaff w Capel Llanilltern *Llan* 83-90; V Ewenny w St Brides Major 90-92; LtO from 92; Hon Chapl Llan Cathl from 96; rtd 04. *60 Llantrisant Road, Llandaff, Cardiff CF5 2PX* T: (029) 2055 4457 F: 2038 7835
E: dovemaster@gmail.com

BALDWIN, Canon Jonathan Michael. b 58. Chich Th Coll 92. **d** 94 **p** 95. C Crawley *Chich* 94-96; C New Shoreham 96-02; C Old Shoreham 96-02; Chapl Gatwick Airport from 02; C Crawley from 02; Can and Preb Chich Cathl from 12. *18 Alingbourne Close, Ifield, Crawley RH11 0QJ* T: (01293) 406001 E: jonathan@theairport.wanadoo.co.uk

BALDWIN, Julia Clare. *See* PICKLES, Julia Clare

BALDWIN, Peter Alan. b 48. Bede Coll Dur BA 70. Qu Coll Birm 72. **d** 73 **p** 74. C Hartlepool St Oswald *Dur* 73-75; C Darlington H Trin 75-78; OGS from 77; C-in-c Bishop Auckland Woodhouse Close CD *Dur* 78-82; V Ferryhill 82-88; V Pendleton St Thos *Man* 88-89; P-in-c Charlestown 88-89; TR Pendleton St Thos w Charlestown 89-90; TR Newton Aycliffe *Dur* 90-96; TR Gt Aycliffe 96-97; V The Trimdons 97-99; AD Sedgefield 96-99; P-in-c Bramley *Ripon* 99-00; TR 00-02; Hon C Harrogate St Wilfrid 02-03; Hon C Methley w Mickletown 03-04; Dom Chapl to Bp Horsham *Chich* 04-06; P-in-c Ashington, Washington and Wiston w Buncton 05-06; P-in-c Brightlingsea *Chelmsf* 06-11; rtd 11; Hon C Halifax *Wakef* 11-13; Hon C Todmorden w Cornholme and Walsden *Leeds* 13-15; PtO *Dur* from 15. *61 Hutton Way, Durham DH1 5BW* T: 0191-375 7364 E: peter.baldwin21@yahoo.co.uk

BALDWIN, Shaun. b 64. Man Univ BA 04. Ushaw Coll Dur 82. **d** 89 **p** 90. In RC Ch 89-00; NSM Hawes Side and Marton Moss *Blackb* 11-12; P-in-c Waterside Par 12-13; V 13-14; C Stalmine w Pilling 12-13; V 13-14; V Broughton from 14. *The Vicarage, 410 Garstang Road, Broughton, Preston PR3 5JB* T: (01772) 862330 M: 07720-722263 E: shaunbaldwin64@hotmail.com

BALDWIN, Mrs Vivien Lindsay. b 50. SAOMC 97. **d** 98 **p** 99. NSM Westbury w Turweston, Shalstone and Biddlesden *Ox* 98-00; C W Buckingham 00-02; P-in-c Stoneleigh w Ashow *Cov* 02-07; Rural Life Officer 02-06; Chapl W Midl Police *Birm* 07-09; PtO *Pet* 07-12; Chapl Northants Police from 12.

20 Castle Road, Woodford Halse, Daventry NN11 3RS T: (01327) 264722 M: 07720-811477
E: vivien.baldwin@northants.pnn.police.uk

BALDWIN, William. b 48. RMN 73 FRSH 83. NW Ord Course 75. **d** 78 **p** 79. C Royton St Anne *Man* 78-82; V Halliwell St Thos 82-87; TR Atherton 87-99; TR Atherton and Hindsford 99-02; TV Atherton and Hindsford w Howe Bridge 02-08; AD Leigh 01-08; TV Turton Moorland 08-13; rtd 13; PtO *Man* from 13. *Address temp unknown*
E: frbill@fsmail.net

BALE, Edward William Carre. b 22. AKC 55. **d** 55 **p** 56. C Mansfield SS Pet and Paul *S'well* 55-59; C Corby St Jo *Pet* 59-61; R Corby SS Pet and Andr 61-69; V Wollaston and Strixton 69-87; rtd 88; PtO *Ox* from 88; *Pet* 89-94. *27 The Crescent, Haversham, Milton Keynes MK19 7AN* T: (01234) 391443 E: tedcarrebale@lineone.net

BALE, Kenneth John. b 34. Univ of Wales (Lamp) BA 58. Qu Coll Birm. **d** 60 **p** 61. C Mitcham St Olave *S'wark* 60-63; C Warlingham w Chelsham and Farleigh 63-67; V Battersea Rise St Mark 67-85; PtO 85-88; Hon C Balham St Mary and St Jo 88-90; V S Wimbledon All SS 90-01; Dioc Adv Min of Healing 91-01; rtd 01; PtO *Sheff* from 01. *23 Selhurst Crescent, Bessacarr, Doncaster DN4 6EF* M: 07710-212263 F: (01302) 371850

BALE, Mrs Sandra Jane. b 62. SEITE 12. **d** 15. NSM Forest Row *Chich* from 15. *Borders, Herons Lea, Copthorne, Crawley RH10 3HE* T: (01342) 718303 E: sandra.bale@tesco.net

BALE, Simon John. b 62. Univ of Wales (Cardiff) BSc 84 PhD 88. STETS 10. **d** 13 **p** 14. C Highbridge *B & W* from 13; Dioc Inter Faith Adv from 15. *3 Brunels Way, Highbridge TA9 3LF* T: (01278) 792701 M: 07970-936325 E: sj_bale@icloud.com

BALE, Susannah. b 67. Univ of Wales (Cardiff) BA 90 BTh 06. St Mich Coll Llan 03. **d** 06 **p** 07. C Betws w Ammanford *St D* 06-08; C Bro Teifi Sarn Helen 08-10; P-in-c Llanybydder and Llanwenog w Llanllwni etc from 10. *The Vicarage, Llanllwni, Pencader SA39 9DR* T: (01559) 395413
E: suzybale@hotmail.com

BALFOUR, Andrew Crispin Roxburgh. b 49. Coll of Resurr Mirfield 93. **d** 95 **p** 96. C S Lafford *Linc* 95-99; P-in-c St Neot and Warleggan *Truro* 99-00; P-in-c Cardynham 99-00; R St Neot and Warleggan w Cardynham 00-14; P-in-c Altarnon w Bolventor, Laneast and St Clether 10-14; rtd 14. *Tredarras Barn, Altarnun, Launceston PL15 7SF*

BALFOUR, David Ian Bailey. b 33. **d** 63 **p** 63. C Ashburton New Zealand 63-66; P-in-c Aranui-Wainoni 66-71; Asst P Christchurch 66-71; V Lyttelton 72-75; V Symonds Street 75-84; P-in-c Kaitaia 85; P-in-c Henderson 85-86; V Rangiora 90-93; V Timaru 93-98; Adn S Canterbury and V Marchwell 94-98; NSM Dumfries *Glas* 08; LtO from 08; *Mor* from 08; NSM Keith 09-13. *1 Balleigh Wood, Edderton IV19 1LF* T: (01862) 821645 M: 07527-445156
E: david.loma@baileybalfour.com

BALFOUR, Hugh Rowlatt. b 54. SS Coll Cam BA 76. Ridley Hall Cam 78. **d** 81 **p** 82. C Bedford Ch Ch *St Alb* 81-86; P-in-c Camberwell Ch Ch *S'wark* 86-90; V from 90. *Christ Church Vicarage, 79 Asylum Road, London SE15 2RJ* T: (020) 7639 5662 E: hrbalfours@btinternet.com

BALFOUR, Mrs Loloma Jill. b 40. RN 61. **d** 80 **p** 81. Chapl Symonds Street New Zealand 80-83; Chapl Carrington and Oakley Hosps 85-87; V Campbells Bay 87-90; V Rangiora 90-93; Chapl Timaru Hosp 94-00; NSM Dumfries *Glas* 05-08; LtO 08-09; *Mor* 08-09; NSM Keith 10-13. *1 Balleigh Wood, Edderton IV19 1LF* T: (01862) 821645 M: 07527-445156
E: david.loma@baileybalfour.com

BALFOUR, Mark Andrew. b 66. York Univ BA 88 R Holloway Coll Lon PhD 98. Trin Coll Bris BA 01. **d** 02 **p** 03. C Churchdown *Glouc* 02-06; V Furze Platt *Ox* from 06. *The Vicarage, 259 Courthouse Road, Maidenhead SL6 6HF* T: (01628) 621961 E: thebalfours@btinternet.com

BALFOUR, Mrs Penelope Mary. b 47. St Andr Univ MA 69 St Jo Coll York DipEd 72. Coates Hall Edin 89 St Jo Coll Nottm 84. **d** 88 **p** 95. C Dundee St Marg *Bre* 88-94; Dioc AIDS Officer 90-94; NSM Invergowrie 94-96; C 00-07; Chapl Abertay Univ 94-97; C Dundee St Marg 96-00; PtO from 08. *10 Strathaird Place, Dundee DD2 4TN* T: (01382) 643114
E: pennybalfour@btinternet.com

BALKWELL, Judith Alison. b 59. **d** 10 **p** 11. NSM Musbury *Blackb* from 10. *15 Hyacinth Close, Haslingden, Rossendale BB4 6JU* T: (01706) 223652 E: judithbalkwell@nhs.net

BALKWILL, Canon Michael Robert. b 67. Univ of Wales (Lamp) BD 89 Univ of Wales (Cardiff) MTh 92. St Mich Coll Llan 89 Bp Tucker Coll Mukono 91. **d** 91 **p** 92. C Llanrhos *St As* 91-97; Bp's Visitor from 94; R Llanfyllin and Bwlchycibau 97-11; AD Llanfyllin 05-11; Bp's Chapl and Press Officer from 11; Can Cursal and Can Res St As Cathl from 11. *The Vicarage, 1 Llys Trewithan, St Asaph LL17 0DJ* T: (01745) 583503
E: michaelbalkwill@churchinwales.org.uk

BALKWILL, Roger Bruce. b 41. St Mich Coll Llan 61. **d** 64 **p** 65. C Llantrisant *Llan* 64-68; C Caerphilly 68-73; Youth Chapl Dio Matabeleland Rhodesia 73-76; P-in-c Ilam w Blore Ray and Okeover *Lich* 76-81; P-in-c Albrighton 81-82; V 82-08; P-in-c Beckbury 89-90; P-in-c Badger 89-90; P-in-c Ryton 89-90; P-in-c Kemberton, Sutton Maddock and Stockton 89-90; RD Shifnal 89-98; P-in-c Donington 00-08; P-in-c Boningale 97-08; V Albrighton, Boningale and Donington 08-10; RD Edgmond and Shifnal 08-10; rtd 10; PtO *Lich* 10-13; Hon C Priors Lee and St Georges' from 13. *3 Ainsdale Drive, Priorslee, Telford TF2 9QJ* T: (01952) 274713

BALL, Alan. b 26. Qu Coll Birm 72. **d** 75 **p** 75. NSM Hamstead St Paul *Birm* 75-93; rtd 93; PtO *Portsm* from 93. *25 Tebourba Drive, Alverstoke, Gosport PO12 2NT* T: (023) 9260 1694

BALL, Alison Margaret. b 63. **d** 13 **p** 14. OLM Loddon, Sisland, Chedgrave, Hardley and Langley *Nor* from 13. *Burlingham House, 11 Langley Road, Chedgrave, Norwich NR14 6HD* T: (01508) 528126 E: ball880am@btinternet.com

BALL, Andrew Thomas. b 54. K Coll Lon BD 75 AKC 75. Sarum & Wells Th Coll 76. **d** 77 **p** 78. C Ribbleton *Blackb* 77-80; C Sedgley All SS *Lich* 80-84; V Pheasey 84-90; Chapl Gd Hope Distr Gen Hosp Sutton Coldfield 90-94; Chapl Gd Hope Hosp NHS Trust Sutton Coldfield from 94. *Chaplain's Office, Good Hope Hospital, Rectory Road, Sutton Coldfield B75 7RR* T: 0121-243 1948 *or* 378 2211 ext 2676

BALL, Anthony Charles. b 46. Lon Univ BD 71. Chich Th Coll 72. **d** 73 **p** 74. C Heref St Martin 73-76; C Ealing St Pet Mt Park *Lon* 76-82; V Ruislip Manor St Paul 82-11; rtd 11. *44 Ashdown, Eaton Road, Hove BN3 3AQ*

BALL, Canon Anthony James. b 68. St Chad's Coll Dur BA 89 Heythrop Coll Lon MA 10. NTMTC 97. **d** 00 **p** 01. NSM Madrid *Eur* 00-03; Chapl Damascus 03-05; Abp's Sec for Internat and Inter-Relig Relns *Cant* 05-09; Abp's Chapl 09-11; Lic Preacher *Lon* 07-11; Public Preacher *S'wark* 10-11; R Worth, Pound Hill and Maidenbower *Chich* from 11; Chapl Worth Sch from 12; Hon Can All SS Cathl Cairo from 07; Hon Can Madrid Cathl from 07. *The Rectory, Church Road, Worth, Crawley RH10 7RT* T: (01293) 882229 E: rector@worthparish.org.uk

BALL, Anthony Michael. b 46. Kelham Th Coll 66. **d** 70 **p** 71. C Kingswinford St Mary *Lich* 70-74; C W Bromwich All SS 74-76; P-in-c Priorslee 76-80; V 80-82; Asst Chapl HM Pris Liv 82-83; Chapl 88-95; Chapl HM Pris Lewes 83-88; Featherstone 95-00; The Verne 00-06; rtd 11. *La Providence, 21 Portland Road, Weymouth DT4 9ES* T: (01305) 787027 E: tonyball2008@hotmail.co.uk

BALL, Mrs Carol Maureen. b 58. NTMTC BA 08. **d** 08 **p** 09. C Danbury *Chelmsf* 08-12; V S Woodham Ferrers from 12; P-in-c Woodham Ferrers and Bicknacre from 13. *The Vicarage, 18 Victoria Road, South Woodham Ferrers, Chelmsf CM3 5LR* T: (01245) 322134 M: 07860-894139 E: revcarolball@gmail.com

BALL, Christopher Jonathan. b 61. Ripon Coll Cuddesdon. **d** 07 **p** 08. C Bedford St Andr *St Alb* 07-11; P-in-c Ashwell w Hinxworth and Newnham 11-14; V Ripponden *Leeds* from 14; V Barkisland w W Scammonden from 14. *The Vicarage, Ripponden, Sowerby Bridge HX6 4DF* T: (01462) 742277 E: c.j.ball@mac.com

BALL, Christopher Rowland. b 40. Wycliffe Hall Ox. **d** 82 **p** 83. C Heysham *Blackb* 82-86; TV Swanborough *Sarum* 86-90; R Llanyblodwel and Trefonen *Lich* 90-99; rtd 99; PtO *Lich* 01-03. *27 Wallace Lane, Forton, Preston PR3 0BA* T: (01524) 791619

BALL, Geoffrey Ernest. b 49. Ox Min Course 00. **d** 03. NSM Winslow w Gt Horwood and Addington *Ox* 03-14; rtd 14; PtO *Ox* from 14. *4 Fledgelings Walk, Winslow, Buckingham MK18 3QU* E: geoffball3@btinternet.com

BALL, Ian Raymond. b 45. CertEd Univ of Wales MPhil. Glouc Th Course 81. **d** 85 **p** 87. NSM Churchstoke w Hyssington and Sarn *Heref* from 85; Lic to Bp Ludlow from 87; LtO *St As* from 93. *Bachaethlon Cottage, Sarn, Newtown SY16 4HH* T: (01686) 670505 M: 07966-022404 E: ian@pathways-development.com

BALL, Mrs Jane. b 68. Charlotte Mason Coll of Educn BEd 91. St Steph Ho Ox 01. **d** 03 **p** 04. C Bedale and Leeming *Ripon* 03-05; Hon C Devizes St Jo w St Mary *Sarum* 05-07; Chapl Godolphin Sch 07-14; V E Meon *Portsm* 14-07; V Langrish from 14; C W Meon and Warnford from 14. *The Vicarage, Church Street, East Meon, Petersfield GU32 1NH* T: (01730) 823618 M: 07771-804324 E: jandjball@btinternet.com

BALL, Mrs Jema Mary. b 83. Man Univ BSc 04. Trin Coll Bris BA 12. **d** 12 **p** 13. C Countesthorpe w Foston *Leic* 12-15; C Oundle w Ashton and Benefield w Glapthorn *Pet* from 15. *41 Hillfield Road, Oundle, Peterborough PE8 4QR* M: 07966-733836

BALL, John Kenneth. b 42. Lon Univ BSc 64 AKC 64. Linc Th Coll 69. **d** 71 **p** 72. C Garston *Liv* 71-74; C Eastham *Ches* 74-75; C Barnston 75-77; V Over St Jo 77-82; V Helsby and Dunham-on-the-Hill 82-94; RD Frodsham 88-94; P-in-c Alvanley 92-94; V Hoylake 94-98; rtd 98; P-in-c Downholme and Marske *Ripon* 00-05; C Richmond w Hudswell and Downholme and Marske 05-07; PtO *Blackb* from 06. *2 King Street, Longridge, Preston PR3 3RQ* T: (01772) 783172

⛪**BALL, The Rt Revd John Martin.** b 34. Univ of Wales BA 55. Tyndale Hall Bris. **d** 59 **p** 60 **c** 95. C Blackb St Jude 59-63; C Eldoret Kenya 69-71; C Nakuru Cathl 71-75; V Nairobi St Fran 75-79; Dep Gen Sec BCMS 79-81; Gen Sec Crosslinks 81-95; Hon C Sidcup Ch Ch *Roch* 81-95; Hon Can Karamoja from 88; Asst Bp Tanzania 95-00; rtd 00; Hon Asst Bp Chelmsf from 00. *5 Hill View Road, Chelmsford CM1 7RS* T: (01245) 268296 E: ball_john@onetel.com

BALL, John Roy. b 47. Fitzw Coll Cam MA 71. Wycliffe Hall Ox 83. **d** 85 **p** 86. C Stockport St Mary *Ches* 85-88; C Fazeley *Lich* 88-94; Res Min Drayton Bassett 89-94; Chapl Grenoble *Eur* 94-00; P-in-c Lithuania 00-05; Asst Chapl Amsterdam w Den Helder and Heiloo 05-12; rtd 12; PtO *Lich* from 13. *20 Robin Close, Uttoxeter ST14 8TP* T: (01889) 567459 E: royball77@gmail.com

BALL, Jonathan. b 63. BNC Ox BA 85 MA 01 Leeds Univ BA 87 Cardiff Univ MTh 06. Coll of Resurr Mirfield 85. **d** 88 **p** 89. C Blakenall Heath *Lich* 88-92; V Rugeley 92-96; CF 96-08; Bp's Chapl *Sarum* 08-12; Chief Exec R Marines Charitable Trust Fund from 13. *Building 32, HMS Excellent, Whale Island, Portsmouth PO2 8ER* M: 07500-872081 T: (023) 9254 7201

BALL, Mrs Judith Anne. b 48. Nottm Univ BA 70 Liv Univ PGCE 71. NOC 98. **d** 01 **p** 02. C Upholland *Liv* 01-12; rtd 12. *31 Ryder Crescent, Aughton, Ormskirk L39 5EY* T: (01695) 421579

BALL, Kevin Harry. b 55. Linc Th Coll 92. **d** 94 **p** 95. C New Mills *Derby* 94-96; C Walthamstow St Sav *Chelmsf* 96-98; V Stocksbridge *Sheff* 98-00; C Barnsley St Mary *Wakef* 00-01; Chapl Barnsley Coll 00-01; P-in-c Sneinton St Cypr *S'well* 01-05; Chapl Notts Fire and Rescue Service 04-05; Sen Chapl Man Airport 05-11; R Calow and Sutton cum Duckmanton *Derby* from 11; Jt Dioc Ecum Officer from 12. *The Rectory, Top Road, Calow, Chesterfield S44 5AF* T: (01246) 462192 E: k.h.ball@tinyworld.co.uk

BALL, Mrs Marion Elaine. b 68. Hertf Coll Ox BA 90 St Jo Coll Dur BA 99. Cranmer Hall Dur 97. **d** 02 **p** 03. C Kingston upon Hull H Trin *York* 02-11; PtO *Sheff* from 12. *12 Church Lane, Hook, Goole DN14 5PN* T: (01405) 767721 E: marion.ball001@btinternet.com

BALL, Mark Francis. b 72. St Jo Coll Dur BA 94. St Steph Ho Ox BA 00. **d** 01 **p** 02. C Poulton-le-Fylde *Blackb* 01-04; TV Loughton St Jo *Chelmsf* 04-08; P-in-c Cant St Pet w St Alpege and St Marg etc from 08; P-in-c Cant St Dunstan w H Cross from 10; Asst Dir of Ords from 09; Jt AD Cant 11-14. *83 St Peter's Lane, Canterbury CT1 2BO* T: (01227) 472557 E: mark@canterburycityparish.org.uk

BALL, Martin Francis. b 62. Wycliffe Hall Ox 06. **d** 08 **p** 09. C Woking Ch Ch *Guildf* 08-11; V Knutton *Lich* 11-13; V Newcastle St Geo from 11. *St George's Vicarage, 28 Hempstalls Lane, Newcastle ST5 0SS* M: 07816-398459 E: martball@gmail.com

⛪**BALL, The Rt Revd Michael Thomas.** b 32. Qu Coll Cam BA 55 MA 59. **d** 71 **p** 71 **c** 80. CGA from 60; Prior Stroud Priory 64-76; C Whiteshill *Glouc* 71-76; LtO 76; P-in-c Stanmer w Falmer *Chich* 76-80; Chapl Sussex Univ 76-80; Suff Bp Jarrow *Dur* 80-90; Angl Adv Tyne Tees TV 84-90; Bp Truro 90-97; rtd 97; PtO *B & W* 01-10. *The Coach House, The Manor, Aller, Langport TA10 0RA* T: (01458) 250495 E: aller.ball@tiscali.co.uk

BALL, Nicholas Edward. b 54. Man Univ BA 75 Ox Univ MA 85. Ripon Coll Cuddesdon 79. **d** 80 **p** 81. C Yardley Wood *Birm* 80-83; C Moseley St Mary 83-86; Chapl Cen 13 83-85; V Bartley Green *Birm* 86-95; P-in-c Hall Green St Pet 95-97; PtO 00-03; Chapl Birm Children's Hosp NHS Trust and Birm Heartlands and Solihull NHS Trust 03-09; rtd 09; Chapl Birm Children's Hosp NHS Trust from 13. *5 Princethorpe Close, Shirley, Solihull B90 2LP* T: 0121-243 1336 E: nicholaseball@hotmail.com

BALL, Norman. b 41. Liv Univ BA 63 Ch Coll Liv CertEd 72. Cuddesdon Coll 65. **d** 68 **p** 69. C Broseley w Benthall *Heref* 68-72; Hd RS Christleton High Sch 72-75; V Plemstall w Guilden Sutton *Ches* 75-79; Hd RS Neston Co High Sch 79-94; NSM Dodleston *Ches* 86-91; NSM Buckley *St As* 91-94; TV Hawarden 94-00; rtd 00; PtO *St As* from 00. *White Cottage, Lower Mountain Road, Penyffordd, Chester CH4 0EX* T: (01244) 661132

BALL, Peter Edwin. b 44. Lon Univ BD 65 DipEd. Wycliffe Hall Ox 75. **d** 77 **p** 78. C Prescot *Liv* 77-80; R Lawford *Chelmsf*

80-99; RD Harwich 91-96; P-in-c Broomfield 99-04; V 04-10; rtd 10; PtO *Chelmsf* from 10; *St E* from 11. *14 Merriam Close, Brantham, Manningtree CO11 1RY* T: (01206) 393316 E: pebblej@btinternet.com

✠**BALL, The Rt Revd Peter John.** b 32. Qu Coll Cam BA 54 MA 58. Wells Th Coll 54. **d** 56 **p** 57 **c** 77. C Rottingdean *Chich* 56-58; Novice SSM 58-60; CGA from 60; Prior CGA 60-77; LtO *Birm* 65-66; P-in-c Hoar Cross *Lich* 66-69; LtO *B & W* 69-77; Suff Bp Lewes *Chich* 77-84; Area Bp Lewes 84-92; Can and Preb Chich Cathl 78-92; Bp Glouc 92-93; rtd 93; PtO *B & W* 01-10. *The Coach House, The Manor, Aller, Langport TA10 0RA* T: (01458) 250495

BALL, Peter Terence. b 49. **d** 07 **p** 08. OLM Hanborough and Freeland *Ox* from 07. *137 Wroslyn Road, Freeland, Witney OX29 8HP* T: (01993) 882859 E: ptb49@yahoo.co.uk

BALL, Canon Peter William. b 30. Worc Coll Ox BA 53 MA 57. Cuddesdon Coll 53. **d** 55 **p** 56. C Poplar All SS w St Frideswide *Lon* 55-61; V Preston Ascension 61-68; R Shepperton 68-84; RD Staines 72-74; RD Spelthorne 74-83; Preb St Paul's Cathl 76-84; Can Res and Chan St Paul's Cathl 84-90; PtO *Sarum* from 90; rtd 95. *Whittonedge, Whittonditch Road, Ramsbury, Marlborough SN8 2PX* T: (01672) 520259 E: peterball@whittonedge.org.uk

BALL, Philip John. b 63. Coll of Ripon & York St Jo BA 91. Cranmer Hall Dur 97. **d** 99 **p** 00. C Linthorpe *York* 99-02; C Kingston upon Hull H Trin 02-07; N Humberside Ind Chapl 08-11; V Airmyn, Hook and Rawcliffe *Sheff* from 11. *The Vicarage, 12 Church Lane, Hook, Goole DN14 5PN* T: (01405) 767721 E: philip.ball001@btinternet.com

BALL, Philip John. b 52. Bris Univ BEd 75 Ox Univ MTh 98. Ripon Coll Cuddesdon 79. **d** 82 **p** 83. C Norton St Mich *Dur* 82-84; C Greenford H Cross *Lon* 84-88; V Hayes St Edm 88-97; AD Hillingdon 94-97; TR Bicester w Bucknell, Caversfield and Launton *Ox* 97-07; AD Bicester and Islip 00-05; R Abington *Pet* from 07; Asst Dir Ords from 14. *The Rectory, 5 Abington Park Crescent, Northampton NN3 3AD* T: (01604) 631041 E: philipjball@btinternet.com

BALL, Phillip Eric. b 53. Open Univ BA 91. Qu Coll Birm 07. **d** 09 **p** 10. NSM Walsall St Matt *Lich* 09-11; NSM Walsall St Martin from 11. *Dinglebank, 13 Bodmin Rise, Walsall WS5 3HY* M: 07775-518879 E: phillipball53@hotmail.com

BALL, Canon Rita Enid. b 49. Sheff Univ LLB 69. SAOMC 94. **d** 97 **p** 98. NSM Newbury *Ox* 97-03; R Wantage Downs 03-09; TR Hermitage from 09; AD Newbury 10-15; Hon Can Ch Ch from 12. *The Rectory, High Street, Hermitage, Thatcham RG18 9ST* T: (01635) 202967 E: rita.e.ball@btinternet.com

BALL, Roy. See BALL, John Roy

BALL, Stephen Andrew. b 54. Wycliffe Hall Ox. **d** 05 **p** 06. C Hilperton w Whaddon and Staverton etc *Sarum* 05-07; C Canalside Benefice 07-08; P-in-c 08-12; R from 12. *22 Warren Road, Staverton, Trowbridge BA14 8UZ* T: (01225) 774903 E: sb54rev@gmail.com

BALL, Stephen James. b 62. SWMTC 09. **d** 12. NSM Salcombe and Malborough w S Huish *Ex* from 12. *4 Veales Road, Kingsbridge TQ7 1EX* T: (01548) 856509 E: stephenjamesball@gmail.com

BALL, Timothy William. b 60. Trin Coll Bris 96. **d** 96 **p** 97. C Harlow St Mary and St Hugh w St Jo the Bapt *Chelmsf* 96-99; V Springfield H Trin 99-11; Ind Chapl 00-11; TR Loughrigg *Carl* 11-15; TV St Baddow *Chelmsf* from 15. *62 Longmead Avenue, Chelmsford CM2 7EY* T: (01245) 901612 E: timmyball@tesco.net

BALL, Vernon. b 34. Ox Min Course 87. **d** 90 **p** 91. NSM Banbury *Ox* 90-99. *20 Springfield Avenue, Banbury OX16 9HT* T: (01295) 265740

BALLANTINE, Canon Peter Sinclair. b 46. Nottm Univ MTh 85. K Coll Lon BA 68 AKC 68 St Jo Coll Nottm 70 Lon Coll of Div ALCD 71 BD 73 LTh 74. **d** 73 **p** 74. C Rainham *Chelmsf* 73-77; C Wennington 73-77; TV Barton Mills *St E* 77-79; TV Barton Mills, Beck Row w Kenny Hill etc 80-82; Chapl Liv Poly 83-86; Tr Officer Rugby Deanery *Cov* 86-97; P-in-c Churchover w Willey 86-97; P-in-c Clifton upon Dunsmore and Newton 86-97; Dir Buckingham Adnry Chr Tr Progr *Ox* 97-02; TV Stantonbury and Willen 02-15; Hon Can Ch Ch 12-15; rtd 15. *2 Carroll Close, Newport Pagnell MK16 8QQ* M: 07984-902641 E: pballarev@yahoo.com

BALLANTINE, Roderic Keith. b 44. Chich Th Coll 66. **d** 69 **p** 70. C Nunhead St Antony *S'wark* 69-72; C S Hackney St Jo w Ch Ch *Lon* 72-75; P-in-c Kensal Town St Thos w St Andr and St Phil 75-79; V Stoke Newington St Andr 79-05; rtd 05; PtO *Lon* from 06. *67 Savernake Road, London NW3 2LA* T: (020) 7267 2744

BALLANTYNE, Jane Elizabeth. See KENCHINGTON, Jane Elizabeth Ballantyne

BALLARD, The Ven Andrew Edgar. b 44. Dur Univ BA 66. Westcott Ho Cam 66. **d** 68 **p** 69. C St Marylebone St Mary *Lon*

68-72; C Portsea St Mary *Portsm* 72-76; V Haslingden w Haslingden Grane *Blackb* 76-82; V Walkden Moor *Man* 82-93; TR Walkden Moor w Lt Hulton 93-98; AD Farnworth 90-98; Chapl Salford Coll 82-92; P-in-c Rochdale *Man* 98-99; TR 00; Adn Rochdale 00-05; Adn Man 05-09; Hon Can Man Cathl 98-09; rtd 09. *30 Swift Drive, Scawby Brook, Brigg DN20 9FL* T: (01652) 659560 E: ae.ballard@btinternet.com

BALLARD, Ann. See BALLARD, Elsie Ann

BALLARD, Miss Anne Christina. b 54. LRAM 76 HonRCM 93 ARAM 94. Wycliffe Hall Ox 82. dss 85 **d** 87 **p** 94. Hove Bp Hannington Memorial Ch *Chich* 85-87; Chapl St Mich Sch Burton Park 87-89; Chapl RCM and Imp Coll *Lon* 89-93; Prec Ch Ch *Ox* 93-98; P-in-c Ivinghoe w Pitstone and Slapton 98-03; P-in-c Llanbadarn Fawr, Llandegley and Llanfihangel etc *S & B* 03-08; V Alstonfield, Butterton, Ilam etc *Lich* from 08. *The Vicarage, Alstonefield, Ashbourne DE6 2FX* T: (01335) 310216 M: 07773-734201 E: annieballard@supanet.com

BALLARD, Charles Martin. b 29. Jes Coll Cam BA 52 MA 56. **d** 58 **p** 59. C Doncaster St Geo *Sheff* 58-61; V Balne 61-62; r-d 94; PtO *Ely* 95-00. *35 Abbey Road, Cambridge CB5 8HH* T: (01223) 562737

BALLARD, Duncan Charles John. b 65. Sheff Univ BSc 87. St Mich Coll Llan 00. **d** 02 **p** 03. C Worc St Barn w Ch Ch 02-06; TV Worc SE 06-11; P-in-c Hampton in Arden *Birm* 11-12; P-in-c Bickenhill 11-12; R Hampton-in-Arden w Bickenhill from 12; Chapl Birm Airport from 11; P-in-c Barston from 15; AD Solihull from 13. *The Vicarage, 1 High Street, Hampton-in-Arden, Solihull B92 0AE* T: (01675) 442339 E: duncan.ballard@me.com

BALLARD, Elsie Ann. b 60. **d** 09 **p** 10. NSM Norton in the Moors *Lich* 09-14; rtd 14. *94 Chatterley Drive, Kidsgrove, Stoke-on-Trent ST7 4LL* T: (01782) 785586

BALLARD, Canon Michael Arthur. b 44. Lon Univ BA 66. Westcott Ho Cam 68. **d** 70 **p** 71. C Harrow Weald All SS *Lon* 70-73; C Aylesbury *Ox* 73-78; V Eastwood *Chelmsf* 78-90; RD Hadleigh 83-90; R Southchurch H Trin 90-13; RD Southend 94-00; Hon Can Chelmsf Cathl 89-13; rtd 13; PtO *Chelmsf* from 14. *159 Kensington Road, Southend-on-Sea SS1 2SZ* T: (01702) 616950 E: michael.ballard473@btinternet.com

BALLARD, Nigel Humphrey. b 48. Linc Th Coll 92. **d** 94 **p** 95. C Old Brumby *Linc* 94; C Bottesford w Ashby 94-97; P-in-c Helpringham w Hale 97-01; rtd 02; PtO *St E* from 14. *Chestnut Lodge, Mellis Road, Wortham, Diss IP22 1PY* T: (01379) 788081

BALLARD, Steven Peter. b 52. Man Univ BA 73 MA 74 Philipps Univ Marburg DrTheol 98. St Steph Ho Ox 76. **d** 78 **p** 79. C Lancaster St Mary *Blackb* 78-81; C Blackpool St Mich 81-84; V Brierfield 84-94; PtO *Carl* 95-07; Hon C Dumfries *Glas* from 09. *Avalon, Bankend, Dumfries DG1 4RN* T: (01387) 770438 M: 07799-350798 E: revsteven@stjohnsdumfries.org

BALLARD-TREMEER, Mrs Margaret Eileen. b 39. K Alfred's Coll Win TDip 62. Th Ext Educn Coll 86. **d** 90 **p** 94. C St Mary's Cathl Johannesburg S Africa 90-03; C Bramley 03-05; PtO *Roch* from 05. *313 Pickhurst Lane, West Wickham BR4 0HW* T: (020) 8777 5694 E: margaret@ecoharmony.org

BALLENTINE, Ian Clarke. b 46. Aston Univ BSc 71 CEng. BTh. **d** 91 **p** 92. C Lurgan St Jo *D & D* 91-95; I Mallusk *Conn* 95-07; Nat Dir (Ireland) SOMA UK from 07. *12 Gordonville, Coleraine BT52 1EF* T: (028) 7035 8328 E: iancballentine@gmail.com

BALLENTYNE, Mrs Fiona Virginia Grace. b 61. ALAM 80 R Holloway Coll Lon BA 83 Dur Univ PGCE 90. EAMTC 95. **d** 97 **p** 98. NSM Halesworth w Linstead, Chediston, Holton etc *St E* 97-98; C Sole Bay 98-00; Chapl St Felix Sch Southwold 99-00; Chapl HM YOI Castington 00-05; Chapl Northumbria Healthcare NHS Trust 00-05; Chapl HM Pris Sudbury 05-12; Chapl HM Pris Foston Hall 11-12; C Walton-on-Trent w Croxall, Rosliston etc *Derby* 13-14; C Stapenhill Immanuel 13-14; Chapl HM Pris Drake Hall from 15. *HM Prison Drake Hall, Eccleshall, Stafford ST21 6LQ* T: (01785) 774100 E: fionaballentyne@live.com

BALLINGER, Miss Charlotte Emily. b 85. Pemb Coll Ox BA 07 Em Coll Cam MPhil 09. Westcott Ho Cam 07. **d** 10 **p** 11. C Chipping Barnet *St Alb* 10-13; Chapl Univ Coll *Lon* from 13. *11 Ormonde Mansions, 106A Southampton Row, London WC1B 4BP* M: 07890-038722 E: ceballinger@gmail.com

BALLINGER, Francis James. b 43. AKC 70. **d** 71 **p** 85. C Weston-super-Mare St Sav *B & W* 71-72; Dir Bd Soc Resp *Leic* 85-88; Hon C Bringhurst w Gt Easton 85-88; TV Melksham *Sarum* 88-93; P-in-c Coughton and Spernall, Morton Bagot and Oldberrow *Cov* 93-98; Dioc Rural Adv 93-98; R Kingstone w Clehonger, Eaton Bishop etc *Heref* 98-03; rtd 04. *4 Broxurn Road, Warminster BA12 8EX* T: (01985) 300316 E: f.ballinger@midnet.com

BALLISTON THICKE, James. See THICKE, James Balliston

BALMER, Walter Owen. b 30. NOC 83. **d** 86 **p** 87. NSM Gateacre *Liv* 86-91; NSM Hale 91-00; PtO from 00. *38 Grangemeadow Road, Liverpool L25 4SU* T: 0151-421 1189

BALOGUN, Olusegun Joseph. b 69. Ogun State Univ BSc 91 Lagos Univ MSc 96. Immanuel Coll Ibadan 96. **d** 98 **p** 99. Nigeria 98-02; C Mansfield St Jo *S'well* 04-06; V Beckton St Mark *Chelmsf* 06-15; Chapl RN from 15. *Royal Navy Chaplaincy Service, Mail Point 1.2, Leach Building, Whale Island, Portsmouth PO2 8BY* M: 07960-050923 T: (023) 9262 5055 F: 9262 5134

BAMBER, Jeremy John. b 56. St Jo Coll Cam MA 82. STETS 06. **d** 09 **p** 10. NSM Southover *Chich* from 09. *29 Montacute Road, Lewes BN7 1EN* T: (01273) 474923 E: jjbj@bambers.net

BAMBER, Canon Patrick Herbert. b 71. Dundee Univ MA 93. Wycliffe Hall Ox BTh 02. **d** 02 **p** 03. C St Austell *Truro* 02-09; I Calry *K, E & A* from 09; Can Elphin Cathl from 12. *Calry Rectory, The Mall, Sligo, Co Sligo, Republic of Ireland* T: (00353) (71) 914 6513 E: patrick.bamber@talktalk.net

BAMBER, Canon Sheila Jane. b 54. Univ of Wales (Lamp) BA 75 Sheff Univ MA 77 Open Univ MBA 94. Ripon Coll Cuddesdon 96. **d** 98 **p** 99. C Dur St Cuth 98-01; C Sacriston and Kimblesworth 01-02; TV Dur N 02-09; Hon C Lanchester 09-10; Dioc Dir of Educn 04-10; Adv for Women's Min 09-10; Hon Can Dur Cathl 06-10; Can Res Newc Cathl 10-12; Can Provost Sunderland Minster *Dur* from 12; AD Wearmouth from 15. *177 Queen Alexandra Road, Sunderland SR3 1XN* T: 0191-520 2304 *or* 565 4066 M: 07989-542565 E: canonprovost@sunderlandminster.org

BAMBERG, Robert William. b 43. Chu Coll Cam BA 65 PGCE 68. SWMTC 98. **d** 01 **p** 02. NSM Kingsteignton and Teigngrace *Ex* 01-08; PtO 08-10. *Tynyffordd, Ystrad Meurig SY25 6AX* T: (01974) 831725

BAMFORD, Geoffrey Belk. b 35. Lon Univ BA 57 Leic Coll of Educn PGCE 58. **d** 99 **p** 00. OLM Upper Holme Valley *Leeds* from 99. *11 Flushouse, Holmbridge, Holmfirth HD9 2QY* T: (01484) 682532 E: jmgbbamford@tiscali.co.uk

BAMFORTH, Canon Marvin John. b 48. NOC 78. **d** 81 **p** 82. C Barnoldswick w Bracewell *Bradf* 81-84; V Cullingworth 84-88; V Mornington New Zealand 88-89; V Thornton in Lonsdale w Burton in Lonsdale *Bradf* 89-98; P-in-c Bentham St Jo 93-98; Dioc Chapl MU 91-94; Chapl Paphos Cyprus 98-05; rtd 06; Chapl Miss to Seafarers Limassol Cyprus 06-14; Hon Can Kinkizi from 08. *27 Coopers Holt Close, Skellingthorpe, Lincoln LN6 5SY* E: marvinandsue@cytanet.com.cy

BAMFORTH, Stuart Michael. b 35. Hertf Coll Ox BA 58 MA 61. Sarum Th Coll 60. **d** 62 **p** 63. C Adel *Ripon* 62-67; V Hempton and Pudding Norton *Nor* 67-71; V Toftrees w Shereford 67-71; P-in-c Pensthorpe 67-71; P-in-c Colkirk 69-70; LtO *Derby* 72-77; *Leeds* from 77; rtd 95; PtO *York* from 01. *52 Beverley Road, Market Weighton, York YO43 3JP* T: (01430) 874105

BAMPING, Mrs Susan Janet. b 49. LCTP 08. **d** 11 **p** 12. NSM Cross Fell Gp *Carl* from 11. *Croft House Barn, Kirkland Road, Skirwith, Penrith CA10 1RL* T: (01768) 879085 E: alan.sue.bamping@btinternet.com

BAMPTON, Edward Thomas William. b 74. Pemb Coll Ox MBiochem 97 Wolfs Coll Ox MSc 98 DPhil 02. Qu Coll Birm 12. **d** 14 **p** 15. C Shepshed and Oaks in Charnwood *Leic* from 14. *12 Smithy Way, Shepshed, Loughborough LE12 9TQ* E: etwb19@gmail.com

BANBURY, David Paul. b 62. Coll of Ripon & York St Jo BA 84. Ridley Hall Cam 85. **d** 88 **p** 89. C Blackb St Jas 88-90; C Preston St Cuth 90-95; P-in-c Bradf St Clem 95-00; V 00; CPAS Evang 01-08; Dir Miss and Faith Stratford-upon-Avon, Luddington etc *Cov* 08-11; Ldr Par Miss Support *Blackb* from 11. *171 Dunkirk Lane, Leyland PR26 7SP* T: (01772) 432069 E: banbury.family@btinternet.com

BANCROFT, Mrs Patricia Ann. b 64. STETS. **d** 10 **p** 11. C Kingsclere and Ashford Hill w Headley *Win* 10-14; R Lynch w Iping Marsh and Milland *Chich* from 14. *St Luke's Rectory, Fernhurst Road, Milland, Liphook GU30 7LU* E: trishbancroft@aol.com

BANDAWE, Mrs Christine. b 57. Liv Univ BTh 06. NOC 01. **d** 04 **p** 05. C Middleton St Mary *Ripon* 04-08; TV Seacroft *Leeds* from 08. *30 Fearnville Road, Leeds LS8 3EA*

BANDS, Canon Leonard Michael. b 40. Rhodes Univ BA 64. St Paul's Coll Grahamstown. **d** 69 **p** 70. C Uitenhage S Africa 69-72; R Alexandria 72-75; Chapl Rhodes Univ 75-80; Chapl Dioc Sch for Girls Grahamstown 80-86; Chapl Dioc Coll Cape Town 87-94; Dean Bloemfontein 94-02; C Lockerbie *Glas* 03-11; C Moffat 03-11; rtd 11. *Montagu Cottage, 20 Princes Street, Lochmaben, Lockerbie DG11 1PQ* T: (01387) 811149 M: 07766-341094 E: michael.bands@btinternet.com

BANFIELD, Andrew Henry. b 48. AKC 71. St Aug Coll Cant 72. **d** 73 **p** 74. C Crayford *Roch* 73-76; Youth Chapl *Glouc* 77-89; Soc Services Development Officer Glos Co Coun from 89. *49 Cleevelands Drive, Cheltenham GL50 4QD*

BANGAY, Edward Newman. b 37. CQSW 75. New Coll Lon BD 60. **d** 98 **p** 98. NSM Yeovil w Kingston Pitney *B & W* 98-02; Chapl E Somerset NHS Trust 98-02; PtO *B & W* from 02. *Castle Cottage, Main Street, Mudford, Yeovil BA21 5TE* T: (01935) 850452 E: edward@bangay.com

BANGAY (formerly REAST), Mrs Eileen Joan. b 40. Open Univ BA 93. EMMTC 81. **dss** 84 **d** 87 **p** 94. Linc St Mary-le-Wigford w St Benedict etc 80-90; C 87-90; C Stamford All SS w St Jo 90-93; NSM Walesby 93-95; P-in-c Sutton Bridge 95-00; V 00; RD Elloe E 99-00; rtd 01; PtO *Linc* from 01. *35 Welland Mews, Stamford PE9 2LW* T: (01780) 765115

BANGAY, Miss Ellouise Claire. b 91. Leeds Univ BA 12. Cranmer Hall Dur 13. **d** 15. C York Minster from 15. *2 College Street, York YO1 7JF* M: 07792-166001 E: ellie.bangay@gmail.com

BANGOR, Archdeacon of. *See* DAVIES, The Ven Richard Paul

BANGOR, Bishop of. *See* JOHN, The Rt Revd Andrew Thomas Griffith

BANGOR, Dean of. *Vacant*

BANHAM, Richard Mark. b 69. Sheff City Poly BSc 92. Trin Coll Bris 04. **d** 06 **p** 07. C Wroughton *Bris* 06-10; P-in-c Wheathampstead *St Alb* 10-12; R from 12. *The Rectory, Old Rectory Gardens, Wheathampstead, St Albans AL4 8AD* T: (01582) 833144 E: richard@banham.org

BANISTER, Desmond Peter. b 52. K Coll Lon BA 75 AKC 75. SAOMC 02. **d** 05 **p** 06. Hd Master Quainton Hall Sch Harrow 98-09; NSM Hatch End St Anselm *Lon* 05-08; NSM Hillingdon All SS 09; V from 09; AD Hillingdon from 13; PtO *Ox* from 05. *All Saints' Vicarage, Ryefield Avenue, Uxbridge UB10 9BT* T: (01895) 239457 E: ppash@uk2.net

BANISTER, Jane Catherine. b 67. Man Univ BA 90 Em Coll Cam BA 96. Westcott Ho Cam 94. **d** 97 **p** 98. C Addington *S'wark* 97-00; C Wisley w Pyrford *Guildf* 00-02; PtO *St Alb* 03-08; NSM Tring from 08. *The Rectory, 2 The Limes, Station Road, Tring HP23 5NW* T: (01442) 822170

BANISTER, Canon Martin John. b 39. Worc Coll Ox BA 62 MA 68. Chich Th Coll 62. **d** 64 **p** 65. C Wellingborough All Hallows *Pet* 64-67; C Heene *Chich* 67-70; V Denford w Ringstead *Pet* 70-78; P-in-c Wilshamstead *St Alb* 78-80; P-in-c Houghton Conquest 78-80; V Wilshamstead and Houghton Conquest 80-89; RD Elstow 86-89; V Waltham Cross 89-04; RD Cheshunt 00-04; Hon Can St Alb 03-04; rtd 04; PtO *St Alb* from 04. *35 Cottonmill Lane, St Albans AL1 2BT* T: (01727) 847082

BANKS, Allen James. b 48. CBDTI 98. **d** 01 **p** 02. OLM Kells *Carl* 01-05; NSM from 05; RD Calder from 14. *36 Basket Road, Whitehaven CA28 9AH* T: (01946) 61470 E: allenbanks@btinternet.com

BANKS, Brian William Eric. b 35. Lon Univ BD 69 Open Univ BA 94. Wycliffe Hall Ox 63. **d** 65 **p** 66. C Swindon Ch Ch *Bris* 65-68; C Halesowen *Worc* 68-71; R Wychbold and Upton Warren 71-77; V Bengeworth 77-87; RD Evesham 81-87; R Freshwater *Portsm* 87-00; R Yarmouth 95-00; rtd 00; PtO *Sarum* 01-09. *12 St Davids Road, Leyland PR25 4XX* T: (01772) 435707

BANKS, Mrs Dawn. b 56. CBDTI 01. **d** 04 **p** 05. OLM Preesall *Blackb* 04-05; OLM Waterside Par 05-07; NSM from 07. *Squires Gate Farm, Head Dyke Lane, Pilling, Preston PR3 6SD* T: (01253) 790250

BANKS, Geoffrey Alan. b 43. St Andr Univ MA 66. NOC 84. **d** 87 **p** 88. NSM Shelley and Shepley *Wakef* 87-89; C Halifax 89-91; V Holmfield 91-98; TV Upper Holme Valley 98-09; rtd 09; PtO *Leeds* from 09. *3 Brookside Fold, Oxenhope, Keighley BD22 9HQ* T: (01535) 244876 E: revgeoffbanks@gmail.com

BANKS, Helen. b 52. Yorks Min Course. **d** 09 **p** 10. NSM Garforth *Ripon* 09-13; PtO *Leeds* from 13. *Westfield Cottage, Carr Lane, Thorner, Leeds LS14 3HD* T: 0113-289 2668 E: helen.banks@yahoo.co.uk

BANKS, John Alan. b 32. Hertf Coll Ox BA 54 MA 58. Westcott Ho Cam 56. **d** 58 **p** 59. C Warsop *S'well* 58-61; C Ox St Aldate w H Trin 61-64; V Ollerton *S'well* 64-75; V Boughton 64-75; R Wollaton 75-83; RD Beeston 77-81; LtO 83-85; C Bramcote 85-86; C Arnold 86-95; rtd 95; PtO *S'well* from 95. *247 Oxclose Lane, Nottingham NG5 6FB* T: 0115-926 6814

BANKS, Matthew Clayton. b 79. **d** 13 **p** 14. C St Helen Bishopsgate w St Andr Undershaft etc *Lon* from 13. *Christ Church Mayfair, Down Street, London W1J 7AN* M: 07886-382569 E: matthewclaytonbanks@gmail.com

BANKS, Michael Lawrence. b 40. Open Univ BA 72 Brunel Univ MA 82. Westcott Ho Cam 84. **d** 86 **p** 87. C Cheshunt *St Alb* 86-89; Chapl HM Pris Blundeston 89-90; V Leagrave *St Alb* 90-94; V Hatfield Hyde 95-01; rtd 01; PtO *Nor* 01-03 and 05-11; P-in-c Barningham w Matlaske w Baconsthorpe etc 03-05; Chapl Beeston Sch from 11. *Quarndon, Post Office Lane, Saxthorpe, Norwich NR11 7BL* T: (01263) 587319 E: mbanks@tiscali.co.uk

BANKS, Canon Michael Thomas Harvey. b 35. Ushaw Coll Dur 58 Open Univ BA 75. **d** 63 **p** 64. C Winlaton *Dur* 69-71; P-in-c Bishopwearmouth Gd Shep 71-75; TV Melton Mowbray w Thorpe Arnold *Leic* 75-80; TR Loughborough Em 80-88; Dir of Ords 83-97; Hon Can Leic Cathl 83-87; Can Res and Chan Leic Cathl 87-03; Assoc P Christianity S 93-95; Hon C Leic H Spirit 01-03; rtd 03; PtO *Glouc* from 04. *Harvard House, 7 Harvard Close, Moreton-in-Marsh GL56 0JT*
T: (01608) 650706

✠**BANKS, The Rt Revd Norman.** b 54. Oriel Coll Ox BA 76 MA 80. St Steph Ho Ox 79. **d** 82 **p** 83 **c** 11. C Newc Ch Ch w St Ann 82-87; P-in-c 87-90; V Tynemouth Cullercoats St Paul 90-00; V Walsingham, Houghton and Barsham *Nor* 00-11; P-in-c 11-12; RD Burnham and Walsingham 08-11; Chapl to The Queen 09-11; Suff Bp Richborough (PEV) *Cant* from 11; Hon Asst Bp Guildf from 12; Hon Asst Bp Nor from 12; Hon Asst Bp St E from 12; Hon Asst Bp Ely from 12; Hon Asst Bp St Alb *St Alb* from 13. *Parkside House, Abbey Mill Lane, St Albans AL3 4HE* T: (01727) 836358 E: bishop@richborough.org.uk

BANKS, Canon Philip Charles. b 61. NE Lon Poly BSc 85 Nottm Univ BTh 93 MRICS 87. Linc Th Coll 90. **d** 93 **p** 94. C Chelmsf Ascension 93-94; C Brentwood St Thos 94-98; P-in-c Elmstead 98-03; V Coggeshall w Markshall 03-12; Bp's Press Officer 97-05; Bp's Dom Chapl 01-04; RD Dedham and Tey 08-11; Can Res St E Cathl from 12. *1 Abbey Precinct, The Great Churchyard, Bury St Edmunds IP33 1RS* T: (01284) 748720 *or* 761982 M: 07798-61886
E: precentor@stedscathedral.org

BANKS, Stephen John. b 65. Newc Univ BSc 87. St Jo Coll Nottm MA 96. **d** 97 **p** 98. C Sheldon *Birm* 97-00; P-in-c Austrey and Warton 00-07; P-in-c Newton Regis w Seckington and Shuttington 06-07; R N Warks from 07; AD Polesworth 02-07; Bp's Rural Adv from 12. *The Vicarage, 132 Main Road, Austrey, Atherstone CV9 3EB* T: (01827) 839022

BANKS, Susan Angela. *See* GRIFFITHS, Susan Angela

BANKS, Mrs Susan June. b 60. NOC 03. **d** 06 **p** 07. C Medlock Head *Man* 06-09; TV Heywood 09-10; P-in-c Heywood St Marg and Heap Bridge from 10. *St Margaret's Vicarage, 27 Heys Lane, Heywood OL10 3RD* T: (01706) 368053 E: sbanks4@sky.com

BANKS, Vivienne Philippa. *See* BRIDGES, Vivienne Philippa

BANNER, John William. b 36. Open Univ BA 78. Tyndale Hall Bris 61. **d** 64 **p** 65. C Bootle St Leon *Liv* 64-66; C Wigan St Jas 66-69; C Stapleton *Bris* 69-70; Gen Sec Scripture Union Australia 70-72; V Liv Ch Ch Norris Green 72-82; V Tunbridge Wells H Trin w Ch Ch *Roch* 82-05; rtd 05. *Kingsmead, Burwash Common, Etchingham TN19 7NA* T: (01435) 882977
E: john@secondremake.plus.com

BANNER, Michael Charles. b 61. Ball Coll Ox BA 83 MA 86 DPhil 87. **d** 86 **p** 87. Fell St Pet Coll Ox 85-88; Dean Peterho Cam 88-94; Prof Moral and Soc Th K Coll Lon 94-04; NSM Balsham, Weston Colville, W Wickham etc *Ely* 01-04; Prof Edin Univ 04-06; Dean Trin Coll Cam from 06. *Trinity College, Cambridge CB2 1TQ* T: (01223) 338563 F: 338564

BANNISTER, Preb Anthony Peter. b 40. Ex Univ BA 62. Clifton Th Coll 63. **d** 65 **p** 66. C Uphill *B & W* 65-69; C Hove Bp Hannington Memorial Ch *Chich* 69-74; V Wembdon *B & W* 74-91; Youth Chapl 80-83; RD Bridgwater 80-89; V Taunton St Jas 91-05; Preb Wells Cathl 97-05; rtd 05; PtO *B & W* from 05. *12 Mitre Court, Taunton TA1 3ER* T: (01823) 259110 M: 07576-697889 E: apbannister@talktalk.net

BANNISTER, Clifford John. b 53. Hatf Coll Dur BA 76. Ripon Coll Cuddesdon 84. **d** 86 **p** 87. C Weymouth H Trin *Sarum* 86-89; TV Basingstoke *Win* 89-94; V Hedge End St Jo 94-09; AD Eastleigh 07-09; P-in-c Win St Bart 09-10; R Win St Bart and St Lawr w St Swithun from 10. *St Lawrence Rectory, Colebrook Street, Winchester SO23 9LH* T: (01962) 852032 E: cliffbannister@hotmail.co.uk

BANNISTER, Gregory Simon. b 80. **d** 14 **p** 15. C Enfield Ch Ch Trent Park *Lon* from 14. *13 Wilton Road, Cockfosters, Barnet EN4 9DX* M: 07738-670221 E: gsbannister@gmail.com

BANNISTER, John Leslie. b 55. Lanc Univ MA 99. CBDTI 95. **d** 98 **p** 99. C Flimby and Netherton *Carl* 98-00; C Whitehaven 00-02; TV 02-04; TR 04-13; PtO 13-14; *Blackb* 13-14; V Lund from 14. *Lund Vicarage, Church Lane, Clifton, Preston PR4 0ZE* T: (01772) 683617 M: 07788-562488
E: johnlbannister@tiscali.co.uk

BANNISTER, Lesley. b 30. **d** 99 **p** 00. OLM Gt Cornard *St E* 99-07; PtO from 07. *58 Broom Street, Great Cornard, Sudbury CO10 0JT* T: (01787) 372889

BANNISTER, Peter. *See* BANNISTER, Anthony Peter

BANNISTER, Peter Edward. b 38. Leeds Univ BSc 60. Linc Th Coll 72. **d** 74 **p** 75. C Norbury St Steph *Cant* 74-77; C Allington and Maidstone St Pet 77-80; R Temple Ewell w Lydden 80-86; TV Bracknell *Ox* 86-93; P-in-c Swallowfield 93-03; rtd 03; PtO *Leeds* from 04. *15 Ryeland Street, Cross Hills, Keighley BD20 8SR* T: (01535) 636036
E: peterandlesleyb@btinternet.com

BANNISTER-PARKER, Mrs Charlotte. b 63. Trevelyan Coll Dur BA 84 Dur Univ MA 92 Middx Univ BA 05. Westmr Past Foundn 00. **d** 05 **p** 06. NSM Ox St Mary V w St Cross and St Pet 05-13; NSM Summertown from 13. *8 Belbroughton Road, Oxford OX2 6UZ* T: (01865) 512252 M: 07745-347395
E: charlotte@the6gbps.co.uk

BANNON, Lyndon Russell. b 73. Ches Coll of HE BA 95 Univ Coll Ches PGCE 96 Leeds Univ MA 06. NOC 04. **d** 06 **p** 07. NSM Leasowe *Ches* 06-10; NSM Willaston from 10. *7 Nelson's Croft, Wirral CH63 3DU* T: 0151-334 9931
E: lyndonbannon123@btinternet.com

BANTING, Canon David Percy. b 51. Magd Coll Cam MA 74. Wycliffe Hall Ox MA 79. **d** 80 **p** 81. C Ox St Ebbe w H Trin and St Pet 80-83; Min St Jos Merry Hill CD *Lich* 83-90; V Chadderton Ch Ch *Man* 90-98; V Harold Wood *Chelmsf* from 98; Hon Can Chelmsf Cathl from 09. *The Vicarage, 15 Athelstan Road, Harold Wood, Romford RM3 0QB* T: (01708) 376400 *or* 342080 E: david.banting@stpetersharoldwood.org

BANTING, Dawn Ann. b 70. STETS. **d** 13 **p** 14. NSM Portsm Cathl from 13. *3 Bramley Close, Waterlooville PO7 7SU* T: (023) 9226 8840 M: 07980-489658

BANTING, The Ven Kenneth Mervyn Lancelot Hadfield. b 37. Pemb Coll Cam BA 61 MA 65. Cuddesdon Coll 64. **d** 65 **p** 66. Asst Chapl Win Coll 65-70; C Leigh Park *Portsm* 70-72; TV Hemel Hempstead *St Alb* 73-79; V Goldington 79-88; P-in-c Renhold 80-82; RD Bedford 84-87; V Portsea St Cuth *Portsm* 88-96; RD Portsm 94-96; Adn Is of Wight 96-03; Hon Can Portsm Cathl 95-96; rtd 03; PtO *Portsm* from 03; *Chich* from 04; RD Westbourne 09-11. *Furzend, 38A Bosham Hoe, Bosham PO18 8ET* T: (01243) 572340
E: furzend@merlinbanting.plus.com

BANYARD, Douglas Edward. b 21. S'wark Ord Course 69. **d** 71 **p** 72. NSM Selsdon St Jo w St Fran *Cant* 71-77; PtO *Portsm* from 77; *Chich* 77-08. *22 Lower Wardown, Petersfield GU31 4NY* T: (01730) 261004

BANYARD, Michael George. b 47. Ch Ch Coll Cant CertEd 69 Birm Univ BPhil 79 Open Univ MA 92. Westcott Ho Cam 01. **d** 03 **p** 04. NSM Chippenham *Ely* 03-08; NSM Fordham St Pet 07-08; NSM Isleham 07-08; NSM Kennett 07-08; NSM Snailwell 07-08; R Three Rivers Gp from 08; Dioc Spirituality Officer from 10; RD Fordham and Quy from 15. *The Vicarage, 24 Mildenhall Road, Fordham, Ely CB7 5NR* T: (01638) 720807 E: banyardmg1@yahoo.co.uk

BANYARD, Peter Vernon. b 35. Sarum Th Coll 57. **d** 59 **p** 60. C Southampton Maybush St Pet *Win* 59-63; C Tilbury Docks *Chelmsf* 63-65; Miss to Seamen 63-65; Namibia 65-68; V Chesterfield SS Aug *Derby* 68-74; TV Grantham w Manthorpe *Linc* 74-78; TV Grantham 78-79; Chapl Warminster Sch 79-85; V Hykeham *Linc* 85-88; rtd 88; PtO *Linc* 88-12; *St Alb* from 13. *53 Beken Court, First Avenue, Watford WD25 9PG* E: ppbanyard@hotmail.com

BANYARD, Canon Sheila Kathryn. b 53. Univ of Wales (Ban) BA 75 K Coll Lon MA 83 Ox Univ MTh 99. Cranmer Hall Dur 76. **dss** 82 **d** 92 **p** 94. Sunbury *Lon* 82-85; Asst Chapl Ch Hosp Horsham 85-90; Chapl Malvern Girls' Coll 90-95; TV Droitwich Spa *Worc* 95-00; TR 00-10; RD Droitwich 99-02; RD Droitwich from 10; Hon Can Worc Cathl from 03. *The Rectory, 205 Worcester Road, Droitwich WR9 8AS* T/F: (01905) 773134 T: 794952 E: sk.banyard@virgin.net *or* droitwich.parish@virgin.net

✠**BARAHONA, The Most Revd Martin de Jesus.** c 92. Bp El Salvador from 92; Primate Cen America 02-10. *47 Avenida Sur, 723 Col Flor Blanca, Apt Postal (01), 274 San Salvador, El Salvador* T: (00503) 223 2252 *or* 224 6136 F: 223 7952 E: anglican@saltel.net

BARBARA JUNE, Sister. *See* KIRBY, Barbara Anne June

BARBER, Ann. *See* BARBER, Margaret Ann

BARBER, Ms Annabel Ruth. b 58. Leeds Univ BSc 80 Anglia Ruskin Univ MA 10. NEOC 01. **d** 04 **p** 05. C Scawby, Redbourne and Hibaldstow *Linc* 04-07; Chapl N Lincs and Goole Hosps NHS Trust 07-12; Lic Preacher *Linc* 12-14; R Waddington from 14; Discipleship Development Adv from 14. *The Rectory, 1 Viking Close, Waddington, Lincoln LN5 9RA* T: (01522) 721306 E: annabel.barber@advancedit.org.uk

BARBER, Anne Louise. *See* STEWART, Anne Louise

BARBER, Canon Christopher Albert. b 33. Ch Coll Cam BA 53 MA 57. Coll of Resurr Mirfield 56. **d** 58 **p** 59. C Cov St Pet 58-61; C Stokenchurch and Cadmore End *Ox* 61-64; V Royton St Paul *Man* 64-70; V Stapleford *Ely* 70-80; RD Shelford 76-80; V Cherry Hinton St Andr 80-88; Hon Can Ely Cathl 88-98; R Cottenham 88-92; RD N Stowe 90-92; V Terrington St John 92-98; V Tilney All Saints 92-98; rtd 98; PtO *Ely* from 98; Asst Rtd Clergy and Clergy Widow(er)s' Officer 00-07; Retired Clergy Officer from 07; PV Ely Cathl from 03. *20 King Edgar Close, Ely CB6 1DP* T: (01353) 612338
E: chrisbarber2@ntlworld.com

BARBER, Craig John Francis. b 71. STETS 98. **d** 02 **p** 03. NSM Brighton St Bart *Chich* 02-03; C Brighton St Geo w St Anne and St Mark 03-06; TV Worth 06-08; C Worth, Pound Hill and Maidenbower 08-10; Chapl Lon Metrop Univ from 10. *St Luke's House, 21 Roscoe Street, London EC1Y 8PT* T: (020) 7320 2384

BARBER, Garth Antony. b 48. Southn Univ BSc 69 Lon Univ MSc 79 FRAS MSOSc. St Jo Coll Nottm. **d** 76 **p** 77. C Hounslow H Trin *Lon* 76-79; Chapl City of Lon Poly 79-86; P-in-c Twickenham All Hallows 86-97; Chapl Richmond Coll 87-97; Chapl UEA *Nor* 97-02; P-in-c Kingswood *S'wark* 02-11; V 11-13; AD Reigate 06-12; rtd 13. *11 Jasmine Close, Chartham, Canterbury CT4 7TF* T: (01737) 507293
E: garth.barber@sky.com

BARBER, Canon Hilary John. b 65. Aston Tr Scheme 92 Sarum Th Coll 94. **d** 96 **p** 97. C Moston St Jo *Man* 96-00; R Chorlton-cum-Hardy St Clem 00-07; P-in-c Chorlton-cum-Hardy St Werburgh 05-07; Dioc Music Adv 03-07; V Halifax *Leeds* from 07; P-in-c Siddal from 13; Hon Can Wakef Cathl from 11. *The Vicarage, Kensington Road, Halifax HX3 0HN* T: (01422) 365477 E: h.barber@halifaxminster.org.uk

BARBER, John Eric Michael. b 30. Wycliffe Hall Ox 63. **d** 65 **p** 66. C Lupset *Wakef* 65-68; C Halifax St Jo Bapt 68-70; V Dewsbury St Matt and St Jo 70-80; V Perry Common *Birm* 80-95; rtd 95; PtO *Sarum* from 95. *21A Westhill Road, Weymouth DT4 9NB* T: (01305) 786553

BARBER, Mrs Margaret Ann. b 31. GTCL 52. Dalton Ho Bris 55 Sarum & Wells Th Coll 82. **dss** 83 **d** 87 **p** 94. Wimborne Minster and Holt *Sarum* 83-90; Par Dn 87-90; rtd 90; Hon Par Dn Hampreston *Sarum* 90-94; Hon C 94-02; PtO from 02. *1 Highbrow Place, 2 St Mary's Road, Ferndown BH22 9HB* T: (01202) 873626

BARBER, Miss Marion. b 50. Birkbeck Coll Lon BSc 97 K Coll Lon MSc 03. **d** 07 **p** 08. NSM Lee St Mildred *S'wark* from 07. *12B Beechfield Road, London SE6 4NE* T: (020) 8690 6035

BARBER, Martin John. b 35. Univ Coll Lon BA 61. Linc Th Coll 61. **d** 63 **p** 64. C Stepney St Dunstan and All SS *Lon* 63-67; Chapl K Sch Bruton 67-93; rtd 93; PtO *B & W* from 93. *1 Plox Green, Bruton BA10 0EY* T: (01749) 812290

BARBER, Michael. *See* BARBER, John Eric Michael

BARBER, Neil Andrew Austin. b 63. Ealing Coll of Educn BA 85. NTMTC 94. **d** 98 **p** 98. St Mary's Chr Workers' Trust 95-01; NSM Eastrop *Win* 98-01; V Normanton *Derby* from 01. *St Giles's Vicarage, 16 Browning Street, Derby DE23 8DN* T: (01332) 767483 E: neil.barber@stgiles-derby.org.uk

✠**BARBER, The Rt Revd Paul Everard.** b 35. St Jo Coll Cam BA 58 MA 66. Wells Th Coll 58. **d** 60 **p** 61 **c** 89. C Westborough *Guildf* 60-66; V York Town St Mich 66-73; V Bourne 73-80; RD Farnham 74-79; Hon Can Guildf Cathl 80-89; Adn Surrey 80-89; Suff Bp Brixworth *Pet* 89-01; Can Pet Cathl 89-01; rtd 01; Hon Asst Bp *B & W* from 01. *Hillside, 41 Somerton Road, Street BA16 0DR* T: (01458) 442916

BARBER, Philip Kenneth. b 43. St Jo Coll Dur BA 65 Sheff Univ DipEd 66. N Ord Course 74. **d** 76 **p** 77. NSM Burscough Bridge *Liv* 76-84; Asst Master Ormskirk Gr Sch 76-84; P-in-c Brigham *Carl* 84-85; V 85-89; P-in-c Mosser 84-85; V 85-89; P-in-c Borrowdale 89-94; Chapl Keswick Sch 89-94; P-in-c Beetham and Educn Adv *Carl* 94-99; P-in-c Brampton and Farlam and Castle Carrock w Cumrew 99-02; P-in-c Irthington, Crosby-on-Eden and Scaleby 99-02; P-in-c Hayton w Cumwhitton 99-02; TR Eden, Gelt and Irthing 02-04; rtd 04; PtO *Carl* from 04; *Blackb* from 05. *18 Holbeck Avenue, Morecambe LA4 6NP* T: (01524) 401695
E: philipbarber326@btinternet.com

BARBER, Ralph Warwick. b 72. Lon Guildhall Univ BA 94. Ripon Coll Cuddesdon 03. **d** 05 **p** 06. C Newquay *Truro* 05-08; Chapl RN from 08. *Royal Naval Chaplaincy Service, Mail Point 1-2, Leach Building, Whale Island, Portsmouth PO2 8BY* T: (023) 9262 5055 F: 9262 5134
E: ralphwbarber@aol.com

BARBER, Royston Henry. b 38. Univ of Wales (Abth) BD 86. United Th Coll Abth 83. **d** 86 **p** 87. NSM Tywyn w Aberdyfi *Ban* 86-92; NSM Cannington, Otterhampton, Combwich and Stockland *B & W* 93-98; PtO from 98; *Ex* from 00. *30 Carlton Court, Blenheim Road, Minehead TA24 5PL* T: (01643) 708783

BARBER, Sheila. b 50. NOC 96. **d** 99 **p** 00. C Dinnington *Sheff* 99-02; V Woodhouse St Jas 02-09; rtd 09. *5 Gannow Close, Killamarsh, Sheffield S21 2BB* T: 0114-247 6537
E: sheilab@uwclub.net

BARBER, Thelma Naomi. *See* ADEY-WILLIAMS, Thelma Naomi

BARBOUR, Mrs Jennifer Louise. b 32. JP 67. St Hugh's Coll Ox BA 54 MA 57 Barrister-at-Law 55. Gilmore Course 80. **dss** 81 **d** 87 **p** 94. Bray and Braywood *Ox* 81-84; Hermitage and Hampstead Norreys, Cold Ash etc 84-87; Chapl Leeds Poly *Ripon* 87-92; Chapl Leeds Metrop Univ 92-95; rtd 95;

NSM Shipton Moyne w Westonbirt and Lasborough *Glouc* 95-99; PtO *Bris* from 95; *Glouc* from 99; *Cov* from 00; *Worc* from 00. *1 Newlands Court, Stow on the Wold, Cheltenham GL54 1HN* T: (01451) 798165

BARBOUR, Walter Iain. b 28. Pemb Coll Cam BA 48 MA 53 FICE 65. Ox NSM Course 78. **d** 81 **p** 82. NSM Bray and Braywood *Ox* 81-84; NSM Thatcham 84-87; TV Moor Allerton *Ripon* 87-95; rtd 95; NSM Shipton Moyne w Westonbirt and Lasborough *Glouc* 95-98; PtO *Bris* from 95; *Glouc* 98-01; *Cov* 00-06; *Worc* from 00. *1 Newlands Court, Stow on the Wold, Cheltenham GL54 1HN* T: (01451) 798165

BARBY, Canon Sheana Braidwood. b 38. Bedf Coll Lon BA 59. EMMTC 81. **dss** 84 **d** 87 **p** 94. Derby St Paul 84-87; NSM Derby Cathl 87-03; Dioc Dir of Ords 90-97; Par Educn Adv 93-01; rtd 03; Hon Can Derby Cathl from 96; RD Derby N 00-05; PtO from 05. *2 Margaret Street, Derby DE1 3FE* T: (01332) 383301 E: sheana@talktalk.net

BARCLAY, Mrs Christine Ann. b 54. TISEC. **d** 07 **p** 08. C St Andrews All SS *St And* 07-10; R Tayport 10-12; R Bathgate *Edin* from 12; R Linlithgow from 12. *The Rectory, 85 Acredales, Linlithgow EH49 6JA* T: (01506) 846069
E: christine.barclay1@btopenworld.com

BARCLAY, Ian Newton. b 33. Clifton Th Coll 58. **d** 61 **p** 62. C Cullompton *Ex* 61-63; C Ashill w Broadway *B & W* 63-66; V Chatham St Phil and St Jas *Roch* 66-69; C St Helen Bishopsgate w St Martin Outwich *Lon* 70-73; V Prestonville St Luke *Chich* 73-81; LtO 82-93; rtd 93; P-in-c Cannes *Eur* 98-02. *35 Marine Avenue, Hove BN3 4LH*
E: ibarclay692@btinternet.com

BARCLAY, Mrs Susan Molly. b 47. Wycliffe Hall Ox. **d** 87 **p** 99. Hon Par Dn March St Wendreda *Ely* 87-96; Tutor Past Studies Ridley Hall Cam 96-05; PtO *Ely* from 05. *42 Greystoke Road, Cambridge CB1 8DS* T: (01223) 246877
E: sigb2@medschl.cam.ac.uk

BARCROFT, The Very Revd Ian David. b 60. UMIST BSc 83 Edin Univ BD 88 Glas Univ MTh 01. Edin Th Coll 85. **d** 88 **p** 89. Prec St Ninian's Cathl Perth 88-92; Min Perth St Ninian 88-92; P-in-c Aberdeen St Clem *Ab* 92-97; R Hamilton *Glas* from 97; Dean Glas from 10. *The Rectory, 4C Auchingramont Road, Hamilton ML3 6JT* T/F: (01698) 429895
E: dean@glasgow.anglican.org

BARDELL, Alan George. b 44. City Univ BSc. **d** 92 **p** 93. OLM Addlestone *Guildf* 92-06; rtd 06; PtO *Guildf* from 07. *14 Dickens Drive, Addlestone KT15 1AW* T: (01932) 847574
E: alanbardell@aol.com

BARDELL, Terence Richard. b 51. EMMTC 04. **d** 01 **p** 02. OLM Coningsby w Tattershall *Linc* 01-05; C Gt Grimsby St Mary and St Jas 05-06; TV 06-09; P-in-c Chapel St Leonards w Hogsthorpe from 09. *The Vicarage, Church Lane, Chapel St Leonards, Skegness PE24 5UJ* T: (01754) 871176

BARDSLEY, Warren Nigel Antony. b 52. AKC 74. St Aug Coll Cant 74. **d** 75 **p** 76. C Leeds St Aid *Ripon* 75-78; C Cov St Jo 78-80; P-in-c Stoke Golding w Dadlington *Leic* 80-89; TV Swinton and Pendlebury *Man* 90-94. *Orchard House, 22 Upper Olland Street, Bungay NR35 1BH* T: (01986) 895760

BARDWELL, Mrs Elaine Barbara. b 60. K Coll Lon BA 81 AKC 81. St Steph Ho Ox BA 85 MA 90. **dss** 86 **d** 87 **p** 95. Hornsey H Trin 86-89; C 87-89; Dir Past Studies St Steph Ho Ox 89-96; V New Marston *Ox* from 96; AD Cowley 02-07. *The Vicarage, 8 Jack Straws Lane, Headington, Oxford OX3 0DL* T: (01865) 434340 M: 07779-086231 E: elaine.bardwell@ntlworld.com

BARDWELL, John Edward. b 53. Jes Coll Cam BA 75 MA 79 Ox Univ BA 85 MA 90. St Steph Ho Ox 83. **d** 86 **p** 87. C Heref H Trin 86-89; PtO *Ox* 90-96. *The Vicarage, 8 Jack Straws Lane, Headington, Oxford OX3 0DL* T: (01865) 434340

BAREHAM, Miss Sylvia Alice. b 36. Hockerill Coll Cam CertEd 59 Open Univ BA 83 Ox Univ DipEd 84. Ox Min Course 86. **d** 89 **p** 94. NSM N Leigh *Ox* 89-93; NSM Bampton w Clanfield 93-95; NSM Kedington *St E* 95-97; NSM Hundon w Barnardiston 95-97; NSM Haverhill w Withersfield, the Wrattings etc 95-97; NSM Stourhead 97-05; NSM Lark Valley 05-07; rtd 07; PtO *Chelmsf* from 05; *St E* from 07. *Davaar, Old Hall Lane, Fornham St Martin, Bury St Edmunds IP31 1SS* T: (01284) 724899

BARFOOT, John Henry. b 38. **d** 08 **p** 09. NSM Tintagel *Truro* 08-13; rtd 13. *32 Trehannick Close, St Teath, Bodmin PL30 3LF* T: (01208) 851450 E: revbarfoot@talktalk.net

BARFORD, Patricia Ann. b 47. Univ of Wales (Cardiff) BSc 68 PhD 73. WMMTC 95. **d** 98 **p** 99. NSM Stoke Prior, Wychbold and Upton Warren *Worc* 98-05; C Redditch H Trin 05-08; TV 08-09; rtd 09; PtO *Worc* from 09. *Greenfields, Church Road, Dodford, Bromsgrove B61 9BY* T: (01527) 871614
E: thebarfords@hotmail.com

BARGE, Preb Ann Marina. b 42. S'wark Ord Course 89. **d** 96 **p** 97. C Ludlow *Heref* 96-12; Preb Heref Cathl 11-12;

rtd 12; PtO *Heref* from 12. *8 Old Street, Ludlow SY8 1NP*
T: (01584) 877307 E: ann.barge@googlemail.com

BARGE, David Robert. b 45. S Dios Minl Tr Scheme 92. **d** 95
p 96. NSM Westfield *B & W* 95-00; C Frome St Jo and St Mary
00; V Frome St Mary 01-10; RD Frome 08-10; rtd 10;
PtO *B & W* from 10. *26 Charolais Drive, Bridgwater TA6 6EX*
T: (01278) 431655 M: 07772-559721
E: dbarge@btinternet.com

BARGE, Marian Elizabeth. Trin Coll Bris. **d** 00. NSM
Mynyddislwyn *Mon* 00-14; rtd 14; PtO *Mon* from 14.
8 Pinewood Court, Pontllanfraith, Blackwood NP12 2PA
T: (01495) 227208

BARGH, George Edward Norman. b 25. St Jo Coll Cam BA 48
MA 53 Leeds Univ LLB 51. Carl Dioc Tr Course 80. **d** 83 **p** 84.
NSM Ulverston St Mary w H Trin *Carl* 83-86; P-in-c Egton
w Newland 86-87; P-in-c Blawith w Lowick 86-87;
P-in-c Egton-cum-Newland and Lowick 87-89; rtd 90; PtO
Carl from 90. *8 Highfield Road, Grange-over-Sands LA11 7JA*
T: (015395) 35755

BARHAM, Ian Harold. b 40. Clifton Th Coll 64. **d** 66 **p** 67.
C Broadwater St Mary *Chich* 66-69 and 72-76; Burundi 71-72;
R Beyton and Hessett *St E* 76-79; PtO 79-81; Hon C Bury
St Edmunds St Mary 81-84; Chapl St Aubyn's Sch Tiverton
84-96; Chapl Lee Abbey 96-99; rtd 00; PtO *Ex* from 00.
53 Sylvan Road, Exeter EX4 6EY T: (01392) 251643

BARHAM, Mrs Jennifer Mary. b 43. RN 65. Oak Hill Th Coll 92.
d 95 **p** 96. NSM Leigh-on-Sea St Aid *Chelmsf* 95-02; NSM Gt
Burstead 02-07; Chapl Basildon and Thurrock Gen Hosps NHS
Trust 01-03; PtO *Chelmsf* 07-08; NSM Canvey Is from 08.
47 Walker Drive, Leigh-on-Sea SS9 3QT T: (01702) 558766
E: jen-john@barham47.freeserve.co.uk

✠**BARHAM, The Rt Revd Kenneth Lawrence.** b 36. OBE 01.
Clifton Th Coll BD 63. **d** 63 **p** 64 **c** 93. C Worthing St Geo
Chich 63-65; C Sevenoaks St Nic *Roch* 65-67; C Cheltenham
St Mark *Glouc* 67-70; V Maidstone St Luke *Cant* 70-79; S Area
Sec Rwanda Miss 79-84; P-in-c Ashburnham w Penhurst
Chich 84-01; Asst Bp Cyangugu (Rwanda) 93-96; Bp 96-01;
rtd 01; Hon Asst Bp Chich from 05. *Rosewood, Canadia Road,
Battle TN33 0LR* T/F: (01424) 773073
E: bishopken@btinternet.com

BARHAM, Peter. b 62. Selw Coll Cam MA 83. Linc Th Coll
BTh 94. **d** 94 **p** 95. C Fornham All SS and Fornham St Martin
w Timworth *St E* 94-97; P-in-c Cockfield w Bradfield St Clare,
Felsham etc 97-01; Min Can St E Cathl 98-03; Chapl 01-03;
Can Res St E Cathl 03-08; V Ponteland *Newc* from 08. *The
Vicarage, Thornhill Road, Ponteland, Newcastle upon Tyne
NE20 9PZ* T: (01661) 822140 E: revpeterbarham@aol.com

BARKER, Cameron Timothy. b 62. Rhodes Univ BA 83 Nottm
Univ MA(TS) 96. St Jo Coll Nottm 94. **d** 96 **p** 97. C W
Streatham St Jas *S'wark* 96-00; V Herne Hill from 00. *The
Vicarage, 1 Finsen Road, London SE5 9AX* T: (020) 7771 0381
E: vicar@hernehillparish.org.uk

BARKER, Prof Charles Philip Geoffrey. b 50. Lon Univ
MB, BS 75 MS 91 FRCS 79 FICS 92. S Dios Minl Tr Scheme 95.
d 98 **p** 99. NSM Alverstoke *Portsm* 98-02; NSM The Lickey
Birm 02-06; NSM Empangeni H Cross S Africa 06-10; NSM
Maple Ridge St Jo Canada from 10. *36198 Cascade Ridge Drive,
Mission BC V2V 7G9, Canada* T/F: (001) (604) 814 2072
E: barkerphilip30@gmail.com

✠**BARKER, The Rt Revd Clifford Conder.** b 26. TD 71. Oriel Coll
Ox BA 50 MA 55. St Chad's Coll Dur. **d** 52 **p** 53 **c** 76.
C Falsgrave *York* 52-55; C Redcar 55-57; V Sculcoates 57-63; CF
(TA) 58-74; P-in-c Sculcoates St Silas *York* 59-61; V Rudby in
Cleveland w Middleton 63-70; RD Stokesley 65-70; V York
St Olave w St Giles 70-76; RD City of York 71-75; Can and Preb
York Minster 73-76; Suff Bp Whitby 76-83; Suff Bp Selby
83-91; rtd 91; Hon Asst Bp York from 95. *13 Dulverton
Hall, The Esplanade, Scarborough YO11 2AR* T: (01723) 340113

BARKER, David Robert. b 45. Worc Coll Ox BA 67 MA 70.
Virginia Th Sem BD 72. **d** 72 **p** 73. C Roehampton H Trin
S'wark 72-75; Chapl Goldsmiths' Coll Lon 75-79; Min Tr
Officer *Cov* 79-85; Selection Sec and Sec for Continuing Minl
Educn ACCM 85-90; V Sutton Valence w E Sutton and Chart
Sutton *Cant* 90-08; rtd 08. *1 Colletts Close, Corfe Castle,
Wareham BH20 5HG* T: (01929) 481477
E: david_pennybarker@hotmail.com

BARKER, Gordon Frank. b 43. Heriot-Watt Univ MSc 75 Sheff
Univ MA 98. S & M Dioc Tr Inst 91. **d** 94 **p** 95. NSM Malew
S & M 94-00; V Grain w Stoke *Roch* 00-04; Through Faith Miss
Ev 00-04; P-in-c Andreas and Jurby *S & M* 04-08; P-in-c Lezayre
04-05; rtd 08; PtO *S & M* from 10. *The Harp Inn, Cross
Four Ways, Ballasalla, Isle of Man IM9 3DH* T: (01624) 824116

BARKER, Howard. *See* BARKER, John Howard

BARKER, John. **d** 13 **p** 14. Asst Chapl Vienna *Eur* from 13.
3 Aygedzor First Alley, Yerevan, Armenia M: (00374) 9-530 4012
E: revjohnwbarker@gmail.com

BARKER, Canon John Howard. b 36. Southn Univ BA 58. Ripon
Coll Cuddesdon 80. **d** 82 **p** 83. C W Leigh *Portsm* 82-84;
V Cosham 84-88; Bp's Dom Chapl 88-96; Hon Can Portsm
Cathl 93-02; V St Helens and Sea View 96-02; rtd 02;
PtO *Portsm* from 02. *Coniston Lodge, 3 Coniston Drive, Ryde
PO33 3AE* T: (01983) 618674 M: 07802-281797
E: jhbarker@netcomuk.co.uk

BARKER, John Stuart. b 30. Keele Univ BA 55. Wells Th Coll 55.
d 57 **p** 58. C Oswestry St Oswald *Lich* 57-60; C Portishead
B & W 60-63; V Englishcombe 63-69; R Priston 63-69; V Chew
Magna w Dundry 70-85; rtd 94. *9 West Street, Axbridge
BS26 2AA* T: (01934) 732740

BARKER, Jonathan. b 55. Hull Univ BA 79. Westcott Ho
Cam 79. **d** 83 **p** 84. C Sketty *S & B* 83-86; Chapl Sport and
Leisure 83-86; C Swansea St Mary w H Trin *S & B* 85-86;
Bermuda 86-90; TV Liv Our Lady and St Nic w St Anne 90-93;
P-in-c S Shore St Pet *Blackb* 93-98; Chapl Blackpool Victoria
Hosp NHS Trust 93-98; V Cleckheaton St Jo *Wakef* 98-08;
Chapl St Pancras Internat and K Cross Stations *Lon* 08-14;
P-in-c Romaldkirk w Laithkirk *Leeds* from 14; P-in-c Startforth
and Bowes and Rokeby w Brignall from 14; P-in-c Eggleston
Dur from 14; P-in-c Middleton-in-Teesdale w Forest and Frith
from 14. *Ashbourne, Cotherstone, Barnard Castle DL12 9PR*
M: 07896-934881 T: (01833) 650761
E: jonathanbarker19.jb@gmail.com

BARKER, Ms Joyce. b 46. Nottm Univ BPharm 68. Yorks Min
Course 09. **d** 11 **p** 12. NSM Barnby Dun *Sheff* 11-13; NSM
Hatfield from 13. *52A Harpenden Drive, Dunscroft, Doncaster
DN7 4HN* T: (01302) 844970 E: joycebarkertwin@gmail.com

BARKER, Julian Roland Palgrave. b 37. Magd Coll Cam BA 61
MA 65. Westcott Ho Cam 61. **d** 63 **p** 64. C Stafford St Mary
Lich 63-66; Chapl Clare Hall Cam 66-69; Chapl Clare Coll
Cam 66-70; Tutor St Aug Coll Cant 70-71; TV Raveningham
Nor 71-78; TR 78-82; V Foremark *Derby* 82-02; V Repton 82-02;
C Bretby w Newton Solney 01-02; V Foremark and Repton w
Newton Solney 02-03; RD Repton 91-95; rtd 03; PtO *St E* from
06. *Old Bank House, 12 Market Hill, Framlingham, Woodbridge
IP13 9AN* T: (01728) 621057

BARKER, Mark. b 62. ACIB 90. St Jo Coll Nottm BTh 95. **d** 95
p 96. C Barking St Marg w St Patr *Chelmsf* 95-98; C Cranham
Park 98-04; V Tonbridge St Steph *Roch* from 04. *St Stephen's
Vicarage, 6 Brook Street, Tonbridge TN9 2PJ* T: (01732) 353079
E: mark.barker@diocese-rochester.org

BARKER, Miriam Sarah Anne. b 62. Lon Univ MB, BS 86.
SEITE 08. **d** 11 **p** 12. C Southborough St Pet w Ch Ch and
St Matt etc *Roch* from 11. *St Stephen's Vicarage, 6 Brook Street,
Tonbridge TN9 2PJ* T: (01732) 353079 M: 07783-228275
E: miriambarker@live.co.uk

BARKER, Neil Anthony. b 52. St Andr Univ BSc 73. Ridley Hall
Cam 74. **d** 77 **p** 78. C Leic H Apostles 77-81; C Camberley
St Paul *Guildf* 81-86; R Bradfield *Ox* 86-88; R Bradfield and
Stanford Dingley 88-92; R Woodmansterne *S'wark* 92-05;
AD Reigate 05; Chapl MU 96-02; TR Modbury, Bigbury,
Ringmore, Kingston etc *Ex* from 05; RD Woodleigh 07-12. *The
Vicarage, Church Lane, Modbury, Ivybridge PL21 0QN* T: (01548)
830260 E: revneil@i.am

BARKER, The Ven Nicholas John Willoughby. b 49. Oriel
Coll Ox BA 73 BA 75 MA 77. Trin Coll Bris 75. **d** 77 **p** 78.
C Watford *St Alb* 77-80; TV Didsbury St Jas and Em *Man*
80-86; TR Kidderminster St Geo *Worc* 86-07; RD Kidderminster
01-07; Hon Can Worc Cathl 03-07; Adn Auckland and
Can Dur Cathl from 07; P-in-c Darlington H Trin from 07.
Holy Trinity Vicarage, 45 Milbank Road, Darlington DL3 9NL
T: (01325) 480444 F: 354027
E: archdeacon.of.auckland@durham.anglican.org

BARKER, Philip. *See* BARKER, Charles Philip Geoffrey

BARKER, Robert Gardiner. b 59. **d** 14 **p** 15. NSM Ellesmere
Port *Ches* from 14. *The Vicarage, Seymour Drive, Ellesmere Port
CH66 1LZ* T: 0151-356 0040

BARKER, The Ven Timothy Reed. b 56. Qu Coll Cam BA 79
MA 82. Westcott Ho Cam 78. **d** 80 **p** 81. C Nantwich *Ches*
80-83; V Norton 83-88; V Runcorn All SS 88-94; Urban Officer
88-90; Dioc Communications Officer 91-98; Bp's Chapl 94-98;
Hon P Asst Ches Cathl 94-98; V Spalding St Mary and St Nic
Linc 98-09; P-in-c Spalding St Paul 07-09; RD Elloe W 00-09;
RD Elloe E 08-09; Adn Linc from 09; Can and Preb Linc
Cathl from 03. *5 Manor Court, Nettleham, Lincoln LN2 2XQ*
M: 07590-950041 T: (01522) 504095
E: archdeacon.lincoln@lincoln.anglican.org

BARKING, Area Bishop of. *See* HILL, The Rt Revd Peter

BARKS, Jeffrey Stephen. b 45. Cranmer Hall Dur 66. **d** 71 **p** 72.
C Wootton *St Alb* 71-74; C Boscombe St Jo *Win* 74-76;
C Ringwood 76-80; P-in-c Spaxton w Charlynch *B & W* 80;
P-in-c Enmore w Goathurst 80; P-in-c Spaxton w Goathurst,
Enmore and Charlynch 80-81; R 81-92; RD Bridgwater 89-94;
V Wembdon 92-07; rtd 07. *77 Alfoxton Road, Bridgwater
TA6 7NW* T: (01278) 423647 E: stephenbarks@dsl.pipex.com

BARLEY, Ann Christine. b 47. **d** 93 **p** 94. OLM Walton *St E* 93-00; OLM Walton and Trimley 00-08; rtd 08; PtO *St E* from 08. *Carmel, 13 New Road, Trimley St Mary, Felixstowe IP11 0TQ* T: (01394) 283752 E: ann.carmel@lineone.net

BARLEY, Canon Christopher James. b 56. St Steph Ho Ox 91. **d** 93 **p** 94. C Upton cum Chalvey *Ox* 93-96; TV High Wycombe 96-01; V Swinton *Sheff* from 01; Dioc Chapl MU from 08; Hon Can Sheff Cathl from 10. *The Vicarage, 50 Golden Smithies Lane, Swinton, Mexborough S64 8DL* T: (01709) 582259 E: chris.barley@sheffield.anglican.org

BARLEY, Gordon Malcolm. b 59. Aston Tr Scheme 94 Oak Hill Th Coll 96. **d** 98 **p** 99. C Walthamstow St Jo *Chelmsf* 98-02; TV Barking St Marg w St Patr 02-12; V Ovenden *Leeds* from 12. *St George's Vicarage, 2 Bracewell Drive, Halifax HX3 5HY* T: (01422) 354153 E: gordon_barley@ntlworld.com

BARLEY, Ivan William. b 48. Loughb Univ MA 01 CEng 74 MIET 74. **d** 93 **p** 94. OLM Walton *St E* 93-00; OLM Walton and Trimley 00-13; NSM 13-14; Dioc NSM/OLM Officer 02-10; rtd 14; PtO *St E* from 14. *Carmel, 13 New Road, Trimley St Mary, Felixstowe IP11 0TQ* T: (01394) 283752 E: iwbarley@gmail.com

BARLEY, Canon Lynda Mary. b 53. York Univ BA 74 PGCE 75 Lon Univ MSc 76 Anglia Ruskin Univ DProf 14 FSS 77. S'wark Ord Course 93. **d** 96 **p** 97. NSM Lower Nutfield *S'wark* 96-97; NSM Littleham w Exmouth *Ex* 97-98; NSM Tedburn St Mary, Whitestone, Oldridge etc 98-00; Hd Research and Statistics Abps' Coun 00-11; NSM Cullompton, Willand, Uffculme, Kentisbeare etc *Ex* 03-11; Preb Ex Cathl 09-11; Can Res and Pastor Truro Cathl from 11; C Truro St Mary from 12; P-in-c Tresillian and Lamorran w Merther from 12; P-in-c St Michael Penkevil from 12. *Truro Cathedral, 14 St Mary's Street, Truro TR1 2AF* T: (01872) 245016 F: 277788 E: canonpastor@trurocathedral.org.uk

BARLEY, Victor Laurence. b 41. St Jo Coll Cam MA 66 Ch Ch Ox DPhil 72 FRCSEd 75 FRCR 76. **d** 02 **p** 03. NSM Flax Bourton and Barrow Gurney *B & W* 02-06; NSM Clevedon St Jo 06-09; NSM Chew Stoke w Nempnett Thrubwell from 09. *1 Home Orchard, Chew Stoke, Bristol BS40 8UZ* T: (01275) 332914 E: victor.barley@tiscali.co.uk

BARLING, Michael Keith. b 38. Oak Hill Th Coll 63. **d** 66 **p** 67. C Portman Square St Paul *Lon* 66-70; C Enfield Ch Ch Trent Park 70-74; V Sidcup St Andr *Roch* 74-78; Dir Fountain Trust 78-81; Chapl Bethany Fellowship and Roffey Place 81-88; Hon C Kennington St Mark *S'wark* 88-89; rtd 03. *Candleford, The Street, Slinfold, Horsham RH13 0RR* M: 07855-231755 E: michael.barling1@homecall.co.uk

BARLOW, Alan David. b 36. Worc Coll Ox BA 59 MA 65. Wycliffe Hall Ox 59. **d** 61 **p** 62. C Wealdstone H Trin *Lon* 61-67; V Neasden cum Kingsbury St Cath 67-73; Chapl Cranleigh Sch Surrey 73-81; Chapl Cheltenham Ladies' Coll 82-01; rtd 01; PtO *Glouc* from 02. *22 Moorend Road, Leckhampton, Cheltenham GL53 0EU* T/F: (01242) 584668 E: revdavid@globalnet.co.uk

BARLOW, Clive Christopher. b 42. Linc Th Coll 67. **d** 70 **p** 71. C Surbiton St Mark *S'wark* 70-74; C Spring Park *Cant* 74-77; V Ash w Westmarsh 77-92; R Chartham 92-08; RD E Bridge 86-92; RD W Bridge 95-01; rtd 08; PtO *Cant* from 08. *5 Barton Road, Canterbury CT1 1YG* T: (01227) 784779 E: c.barlow@btinternet.com

BARLOW, Darren. b 65. Ridley Hall Cam 96. **d** 98 **p** 99. C Rayleigh *Chelmsf* 98-01; TV Billericay and Lt Burstead 01-06; TR Grays Thurrock from 06; RD Thurrock from 11. *The Rectory, 10 High View Avenue, Grays RM17 6RU* T: (01375) 377379 E: revbarlow@talktalk.net

BARLOW, David. See BARLOW, Alan David

BARLOW, David. b 50. Leeds Univ BA 71 MA 99. Wycliffe Hall Ox 71. **d** 73 **p** 74. C Horninglow *Lich* 73-75; C Wednesfield St Thos 75-77; C Bloxwich 77-78; Chapl RN 78-08; Prin Armed Forces Chapl Cen Amport Ho 05-08; P-in-c Baughurst, Ramsdell, Wolverton w Ewhurst etc *Win* 08-14; QHC from 04; R Baughurst, Ramsdell, Wolverton w Ewhurst etc *Win* from 14. *The Rectory, Crabs Hill, Wolverton, Tadley RG26 5RU* T: (01635) 297543 E: barlow857@btinternet.com

BARLOW, Canon Edward Burnley. b 29. St Aid Birkenhead 56. **d** 58 **p** 59. C Lenton Abbey *S'well* 58-61; C Ipswich All SS *St E* 61-63; R Fishtoft *Linc* 63-76; V Linc St Giles 76-96; Can and Preb Linc Cathl 92-05; rtd 96; PtO *Linc* 96-99. *8 Pynder Close, Washingborough, Lincoln LN4 1EX* T: (01522) 793762

BARLOW, James Derek. b 64. Ex Univ BA 87. Ripon Coll Cuddesdon 09. **d** 11 **p** 12. C Burnham *Ox* from 11. *12 Hatchgate Gardens, Burnham, Slough SL1 8DD*

BARLOW, Paul Andrew. b 59. Imp Coll Lon BSc 80 UMIST PhD 84 Bolton Inst of HE PGCE 85. Aston Tr Scheme 89 Chich Th Coll 91. **d** 93 **p** 94. C Hale *Guildf* 93-97; C Christchurch *Win* 97-01; P-in-c Alton All SS 01-09; C Alton 10-11; Chapl Dublin Sandymount *D & G* from 11. *Gealán, Durham Road,*

Sandymount, Dublin 4, Republic of Ireland T: (00353) (1) 516 3457 M: 85-284 9564 E: paul.barlow@upcmail.ie

BARLOW, Paul Benson. b 31. Fitzw Coll Cam BA 73 MA 77 FRSA 94. **d** 64 **p** 65. C Bath Abbey w St Jas *B & W* 64-74; Dep Hd Master Leys High Sch Redditch 74-81; Hd Master Jo Kyrle High Sch Ross-on-Wye 82-96; PtO *Heref* 82-85; LtO 85-92; NSM Walford and St John w Bishopswood, Goodrich etc 92-97; PtO 97-08. *The Coach House, Hentland, Ross-on-Wye HR9 6LP*

BARLOW, Robert Mark. b 53. St Jo Coll Nottm 84. **d** 86 **p** 87. C Colwich w Gt Haywood *Lich* 86-91; R Crick and Yelvertoft w Clay Coton and Lilbourne *Pet* 91-04; Bp's Rural Officer 98-04; Chapl to Agric and Rural Life *Worc* 04-10; C Worcs W 05-10; P-in-c Teme Valley S from 10. *The Rectory, Broadheath, Tenbury Wells WR15 8QW* T: (01886) 853286 M: 07947-600627 E: temevalleyvicar@gmail.com

BARLOW, Canon Timothy David. b 46. Univ Coll Ox BA 67 MA 71 Lon Univ BD 71. Oak Hill Th Coll 71. **d** 71 **p** 72. C Marple All SS *Ches* 71-74; C Northwood Em *Lon* 74-78; Chapl Vevey w Château d'Oex and Villars *Eur* 78-84; Switzerland 84-89; V Romiley *Ches* 89-11; Hon Can Ches Cathl 08-11; rtd 11; PtO *Ches* from 11. *Bryn Araul, Winllan Road, Llansanffraid SY22 6TS* E: timdbarlow@gmail.com

BARLOW, William George. b 40. Liv Univ BSc 62 Univ of Wales BD 65. St Mich Coll Llan 76. **d** 76 **p** 77. C Roath *Llan* 76-79; TV Cyncoed *Mon* 79-83; R Radyr *Llan* 83-05; RD Llan 95-04; rtd 05. *15 Cae Tymawr, Whitchurch, Cardiff CF14 2HB* T: (029) 2065 2519

BARNARD, Canon Anthony Nevin. b 36. St Jo Coll Cam BA 60 MA 64. Wells Th Coll 61. **d** 63 **p** 64. C Cheshunt *St Alb* 63-65; Tutor Wells Th Coll 65-66; Chapl 66-69; Vice-Prin 69-71; Dep Prin Sarum & Wells Th Coll 71-77; Dir S Dios Minl Tr Scheme 74-77; Can Res and Chan Lich Cathl 77-06; Warden of Readers 77-91; Dir of Tr 86-91; rtd 06; PtO *Lich* from 06. *1 The Stables, The Knoll, Barton under Needwood, Burton-on-Trent DE13 8AB* T: (01283) 711505

BARNARD, Catherine Elizabeth. b 54. York Univ BA 76 Dur Univ BA 79. Cranmer Hall Dur 77. **dss** 80 **d** 87 **p** 94. Mexborough *Sheff* 80-83; Sheff Manor 83-90; Hon Par Dn 87-90; Hon Par Dn Bolsterstone 90-94; C 94-08; P-in-c Stocksbridge 08-13; V Northowram *Wakef* from 14. *King Cross Vicarage, West Royd Avenue, Halifax HX1 3NU* T: (01422) 352933

BARNARD, Jonathan Dixon. b 46. St Cath Coll Cam BA 68. Cuddesdon Coll 69. **d** 71 **p** 72. C Silksworth *Dur* 71-74; C Hatfield Hyde *St Alb* 74-78; TV Hitchin 78-86; TR Penrith w Newton Reigny and Plumpton Wall *Carl* 86-91; rtd 91. *4 Hallin Croft, Penrith CA11 8AA* T: (01768) 63000

BARNARD, Kevin James. b 52. Keble Coll Ox BA 77 MA 79 Sheff Univ PhD 14. Cranmer Hall Dur 77. **d** 79 **p** 80. C Swinton *Sheff* 79-83; TV Sheff Manor 83-90; V Bolsterstone 90-13; Bp's Adv on Issues Relating to Ageing 94-13; V King Cross *Leeds* from 13. *King Cross Vicarage, West Royd Avenue, Halifax HX1 3NU* T: (01422) 352933

BARNARD, Kevin Paul. b 64. Hull Univ BSc 85. Ridley Hall Cam 10. **d** 12 **p** 13. C Warwick *Cov* 12-15; V Westerham *Roch* from 15. *The Vicarage, Borde Hill, Vicarage Hill, Westerham TN16 1TL* M: 07795-314121 T: (01959) 563127 E: kevin.p.barnard@googlemail.com or rev.kevinbarnard@gmail.com

BARNARD, Timothy John William. b 53. Magd Coll Cam BA 75 MA 78. **d** 13 **p** 14. OLM Amersham *Ox* from 13. *2A Stanley Hill Avenue, Amersham HP7 9BD* T: (01494) 728478 M: 07971-871667 E: timbar_uk@yahoo.co.uk

BARNDEN, Saskia Gail. b 50. Waterloo Univ (Canada) BA 70 Victoria Univ (BC) MA 71 Indiana Univ PhD 88 Westmr Coll Ox CertEd 75. SAOMC 97. **d** 00 **p** 01. Asst Chapl Wycombe Abbey Sch 00-01; Chapl Haberdashers' Monmouth Sch for Girls 01-12; Chapl St Mary's Hospice from 13. *47 Elvetham Road, Birmingham B15 2LY* T: 0121-440 5677 or 472 1191 M: 07813-616574

BARNES, Alan Duff. b 42. St Steph Ho Ox 75. **d** 77 **p** 78. C Wanstead H Trin Hermon Hill *Chelmsf* 77-80; C Clacton St Jas 80-82; R Cranham 82-89; V Calcot *Ox* 89-07; rtd 07; PtO *Ox* from 07; *Win* from 10. *18 Hartleys, Silchester, Reading RG7 2QE*

BARNES, Brian. b 49. St Mich Coll Llan 93. **d** 93 **p** 94. C Betws w Ammanford *St D* 93-96; V Llanwnda, Goodwick w Manorowen and Llanstinan 96-15; rtd 15. *Glan y Don, Penbanc, Fishguard SA65 9BJ* E: revb@hotmail.com

BARNES, Canon Brian. b 42. Sussex Univ MA 82. Cant Sch of Min 79. **d** 82 **p** 83. NSM Maidstone All SS and St Phil w Tovil *Cant* 82-89; C 89-92; FE Adv Gen Syn Bd of Educn 86-92; R Staplehurst *Cant* 92-02; V Hythe 02-08; RD W Charing 95-99; AD Cranbrook 99-01; Hon Can Cant Cathl 01-08; rtd 08. *9 Egerton Road, Lincoln LN2 4PJ* T: (01522) 569508 E: brian.barnes@virgin.net

BARNES, Christopher. b 57. d 06 p 07. NSM Bowling St Jo *Leeds* from 06. *257 Bowling Hall Road, Bradford BD4 7TJ* T: (01274) 306230 E: chrisbarnes257@hotmail.co.uk

BARNES, Christopher Charles. b 51. Victoria Univ Wellington BA 79 TDip 79. Trin Coll Bris. d 00 p 01. C Langport Area *B & W* 00-03; P-in-c Burton and Rosemarket *St D* 03-07; Chapl Miss to Seafarers Milford Haven 03-07; Port Chapl Kobe Japan 07-09; Port Chapl Auckland New Zealand 09-12. *28 Dorset Street, Opunake, Taranaki, New Zealand* M: 27-724 4759

BARNES, Colin. b 33. St Jo Coll York CertEd 58. St Aid Birkenhead 61. d 64 p 65. C Eccles St Mary *Man* 64-66; C Barrow St Geo w St Luke *Carl* 66-68; V Goodshaw *Man* 68-80; P-in-c Wythenshawe St Martin 80-83; New Zealand 83-98; rtd 98; PtO *Man* 98-10; *Blackb* 08-10. *7 Louis Street, Trentham, Upper Hutt 5018, New Zealand*

BARNES, David Keith. b 53. Linc Th Coll. d 89 p 90. C E Crompton *Man* 89-93; V Belfield 93-99; V Honley *Wakef* 99-12; P-in-c Bude Haven and Marhamchurch *Truro* from 12; P-in-c Stratton and Launcells from 12. *The Rectory, 8 Falcon Terrace, Bude EX23 8LJ* T: (01288) 352254 E: d.barnes645@btinternet.com

BARNES, Derek Ian. b 44. Leeds Univ BA 66. Westcott Ho Cam 66. d 68 p 69. C Far Headingley St Chad *Ripon* 68-71; Chapl Qu Eliz Coll *Lon* 72-77; Warden Lee Abbey Internat Students' Club Kensington 77-81; Hon C Willesden Green St Gabr *Lon* 81-83; P-in-c Southall H Trin 84-98; P-in-c Southall St Geo 89-92; PtO 99-02; Chapl W Lon Mental Health NHS Trust 02-11; rtd 11; PtO *Lon* from 12. *19 Wimborne Avenue, Hayes UB4 0HG* T: (020) 8354 8974 E: derekibarnes@gmail.com

BARNES, Duncan Christopher. b 64. Warwick Univ BA 90. Trin Coll Bris BA 93. d 93 p 94. C Hornchurch St Andr *Chelmsf* 93-98; V Bicker *Linc* 98-00; V Donington 98-00; TV Woughton *Ox* 00-08. *61 Green Lane, Wolverton, Milton Keynes MK12 5HW* T: (01908) 226886 E: dbgreenleys@gmail.com

BARNES, Mrs Enid Mabel. b 68. Homerton Coll Cam Dip Teaching 58. WMMTC 87. d 90 p 94. Par Dn Walsall St Paul *Lich* 90-94; C 94-96; TV Chell 96-02; rtd 02; PtO *Lich* 02-04. *10 Hind Avenue, Breaston, Derby DE72 3DG* T: (01332) 873665 E: enidbarnes@hotmail.com

BARNES, Harvey Thomas. b 61. SWMTC 02. d 05 p 06. C Plympton St Mary *Ex* 05-08; P-in-c Whitchurch 08-09. *9 Dawlish Walk, Plymouth PL6 8PZ*

BARNES, Miss Heather Dawn. b 75. Liv Hope BA 96 PGCE 97. Ridley Hall Cam 03. d 05 p 06. C Luton Lewsey St Hugh *St Alb* 05-09; P-in-c Hartshill and Galley Common *Cov* from 09. *The New Vicarage, Church Road, Hartshill, Nuneaton CV10 0LY* T: (024) 7639 2266

BARNES, Mrs Helen Clark. b 61. Worc Coll of Educn BA 82. Ox Min Course 07. d 10 p 11. NSM Haddenham w Cuddington, Kingsey etc *Ox* 10-14; TV Cottesloe from 14. *The Vicarage, 27B Aylesbury Road, Wing, Leighton Buzzard LU7 0PD* E: helen.barnes1503@gmail.com

BARNES, Jennifer. b 45. Leeds Univ MA 96. NOC 94. d 96 p 97. C Thorne *Sheff* 96-99; C Clifton St Jas 99-01; Chapl HM Pris Featherstone 01-04; Chapl HM YOI Swinfen Hall 04-05; P-in-c Barnsley St Edw *Wakef* 05-07; Chapl HM Pris and YOI New Hall 07-08; rtd 08; PtO *Wakef* 07-09; NSM Lundwood 09-11; PtO *Sheff* from 14. *Carlton House, 71 Woodhead Road, Honley, Holmfirth HD9 6PP* T: (01484) 660876 E: jbjcb@tiscali.co.uk

BARNES, Jeremy Paul Blissard. b 70. Southn Univ BSc 92. Wycliffe Hall Ox BTh 99. d 99 p 00. C Brompton H Trin w Onslow Square St Paul *Lon* 99-05; C Shadwell St Paul w Ratcliffe St Jas 05-09; V E Twickenham St Steph from 09. *17 Claremont Road, Twickenham TW1 2QX*

BARNES, Canon John Barwick. b 32. AKC 58. d 59 p 60. C Brentwood St Thos *Chelmsf* 59-65; R Arkesden w Wicken Bonhunt 65-71; V Gt Ilford St Mary 71-99; Hon Can Chelmsf Cathl 95-99; rtd 99; PtO *Chelmsf* from 99. *352 Henley Road, Ilford IG1 2TJ* T: (020) 8478 1954

BARNES, John Christopher. b 43. MA ATI. Linc Th Coll 78. d 80 p 81. C Guiseley *Bradf* 80-83; TV Guiseley w Esholt 83-86; V Rawdon 86-92; R Armthorpe *Sheff* 92-98; TR Maltby 98-01; RD Doncaster 96-98; Hon Can Sheff Cathl 00-01; TR Blakenall Heath *Lich* 01-05; P-in-c Gomersal *Wakef* 05-09; P-in-c Cleckheaton St Jo 08-09; rtd 09; P-in-c Lundwood *Wakef* 09-11; P-in-c Wentworth *Sheff* from 14. *Carlton House, 71 Woodhead Road, Honley, Holmfirth HD9 6PP* T: (01485) 660876 E: jbjcb@tiscali.co.uk

BARNES, John Seymour. b 30. Qu Coll Birm 58. d 61 p 62. C Bromsgrove St Jo *Worc* 61-64; C Kingsthorpe *Pet* 64-66; C Styvechale *Cov* 66-69; P-in-c Avon Dassett w Farnborough 69-75; P-in-c Cov St Alb 75-84; R Weddington and Caldecote 84-89; P-in-c Wilnecote *Lich* 89-90; V Bentley 90-96; rtd 96;

PtO *Lich* 96-04. *10 Hind Avenue, Breaston, Derby DE72 3DG* T: (01332) 873665

BARNES, Josephine Ella. b 39. d 12 p 13. OLM Hope, Castleton and Bradwell *Derby* from 12. *2 Cavedale Cottage, Market Place, Castleton, Hope Valley S33 8WQ* T: (01433) 621443 E: josephine.barnes1@btinternet.com

BARNES, Jules Ann. b 60. St Mary's Coll Dur BA 83 Dur Univ MSc 84 RGN 95. Ripon Coll Cuddesdon 08. d 10 p 11. C Wilton w Netherhampton and Fugglestone *Sarum* 10-14; Bp's Chapl *Bris* from 14; Min Can Bris Cathl from 15. *Bishop's Office, 58A High Street, Winterbourne, Bristol BS36 1JQ* T: (01454) 777728 E: barnesjules@hotmail.com

BARNES, Canon Katrina Crawford. b 52. K Coll Lon BA 98 AKC 98. Oak Hill Th Coll 90. d 93 p 94. NSM Bromley H Trin *Roch* 93-98; C Meopham w Nurstead 98-00; Assoc Staff Tutor SEITE 99-03; R Longfield *Roch* 01-06; V Bromley Common St Aug from 06; Bp's Adv for Ord Women's Min 05-11; AD Bromley 11-15; Hon Can Roch Cathl from 05. *St Augustine's Vicarage, Southborough Lane, Bromley BR2 8AT* T: (020) 8467 1351 E: katrina_barnes@talk21.com

BARNES, Lee. b 74. Trin Coll Bris BA 03 MA 09. d 09 p 10. C Malmesbury w Westport and Brokenborough *Bris* 09-12; C Gt Somerford, Lt Somerford, Seagry, Corston etc 09-12; PtO 12-13; LtO 13-14; P-in-c Bris St Steph w St Jas and St Jo w St Mich etc from 14; P-in-c Clifton H Trin, St Andr and St Pet from 14. *Holy Trinity Church, Hotwell Road, Bristol BS8 4ST* T: 0117-907 0804 E: lee@saint-stephens.com

BARNES, Margaret Anne. b 56. d 13 p 14. OLM Oulton Broad *Nor* from 13. *53 Dell Road East, Lowestoft NR33 9LA* T: (01502) 538122 E: mooskieanddave09@hotmail.co.uk

BARNES, Mrs Mary Jane. b 48. St Jo Coll Nottm 97. d 99 p 00. C Harefield *Lon* 99-02; TV New Windsor *Ox* 02-10; C 10-15; P-in-c Old Windsor 10-14; V 14-15; rtd 15. *The Vicarage, Church Road, Old Windsor, Windsor SL4 2PQ* T: (01753) 865778 M: 07930-337407 E: mary@harefield9.fsnet.co.uk

BARNES, Canon Matthew John. b 68. Leeds Univ MA 99. St Jo Coll Nottm BA 93. d 96 p 97. C Stanley *Wakef* 96-99; TV N Wingfield, Clay Cross and Pilsley *Derby* 99-08; R Brampton St Thos from 08; RD Chesterfield 11-15; Hon Can Derby Cathl from 13. *The Rectory, 674 Chatsworth Road, Chesterfield S40 3NU* T: (01246) 567634 M: 07977-976348 E: rector@st-thomas-brampton.org

BARNES, Canon Neal Duncan. b 63. Leeds Univ BSc 84 Cranfield Inst of Tech PhD 92. Oak Hill Th Coll 93. d 95 p 96. C Biggleswade *St Alb* 95-99; V Anlaby St Pet *York* 99-10; P-in-c Kingston upon Hull H Trin 10-11; V from 11; Hon Chapl Ambulance Service Hull from 99; Can and Preb York Minster from 13. *Holy Trinity Vicarage, 66 Pearson Park, Hull HU5 2TQ* T: (01482) 342292 M: 07581-280785 E: neal@anvic.karoo.co.uk *or* vicar@holy-trinity.org.uk

BARNES, Canon Neil. b 42. Kelham Th Coll 61 Bps' Coll Cheshunt 65. d 68 p 69. C Poulton-le-Fylde *Blackb* 68-72; C Ribbleton 72-75; V Knuzden 75-81; Chapl Prestwich Hosp *Man* 81-88; Chapl Salford Mental Health Services NHS Trust 88-04; Manager Chapl Services 94-04; Hon Can Man Cathl 96-04; rtd 04; PtO *Blackb* from 04; *Man* from 04. *Leads Cottage, Bacup Road, Cliviger, Burnley BB11 3QZ* T: (01282) 451533 E: neilbarnes@bigfoot.com

BARNES, Paul. *See* BYLLAM-BARNES, Paul William Marshall

BARNES, Paul Nicholas. b 58. Qu Coll Birm 89. d 91 p 92. C Weymouth H Trin *Sarum* 91-95; P-in-c Studley 95-07; P-in-c Mere w W Knoyle and Maiden Bradley 07-12. *18 Innox Road, Trowbridge BA14 9AT* T: (01225) 781662

BARNES, Peter Frank. b 52. St Jo Coll Nottm LTh 81. d 81 p 82. C Colne St Bart *Blackb* 81-83; C Melton Mowbray w Thorpe Arnold *Leic* 83-86; P-in-c Barlestone 86-89; V Broughton and Duddon *Carl* 89-98; V Shrewsbury St Geo w Greenfields *Lich* 98-08; P-in-c Bicton, Montford w Shrawardine and Fitz 98-00; P-in-c Myddle 08-11; P-in-c Broughton 08-11; P-in-c Loppington w Newtown 08-11; R St John's-in-the-Vale, Threlkeld and Wythburn *Carl* from 11. *The Rectory, Threlkeld, Keswick CA12 4RT* T: (017687) 79714 E: peterbarnes52@tiscali.co.uk

BARNES, Philip John. b 52. Cant Ch Ch Univ BA 08. SEITE 01. d 04 p 05. NSM Gravesend St Mary *Roch* 04-06; C Gravesend St Aid 06-09; TV S Gillingham from 09. *58 Parkwood Green, Gillingham ME8 9PP* T: (01634) 306806 M: 07764-151833 E: philip.barnes@diocese-rochester.org

BARNES, Philip Richard. b 73. Westmr Coll Ox BTh 94 Heythrop Coll Lon MA 99. St Steph Ho Ox 98. d 00 p 01. C Ruislip St Martin *Lon* 00-03; Shrine P Shrine of Our Lady of Walsingham 03-08; V Northwood Hills St Edm *Lon* from 08; AD Harrow from 13. *St Edmund's Vicarage, 2 Pinner Road, Northwood HA6 1QS* T: (020) 8866 9230 E: frphilipbarnes@btinternet.com

BARNES, Robin James. b 52. d 05 p 06. OLM Debenham and Helmingham *St E* 05-13; NSM from 13. *119 Gardeners Road, Debenham, Stowmarket IP14 6RZ* T: (01728) 861498
E: robin@rbarnes.fsnet.co.uk

BARNES, Roland Peter. b 59. Ban Ord Course 01. d 03 p 04. NSM Bro Ddyfi Uchaf *Ban* 03-05; P-in-c 05-14; P-in-c Bro Cyfeiliog a Mawddwy from 14; AD Cyfeiliog and Mawddwy from 12. *Y Rheithordy, Mallwyd, Machynlleth SY20 9HJ* T: (01650) 531650

BARNES, Sally. *See* BARNES, Sylvia Frances

BARNES, Stephen. b 46. Hull Univ BA 69. Clifton Th Coll 69. d 72 p 73. C Girlington *Bradf* 72-74; TV Glyncorrwg w Afan Vale and Cymmer Afan *Llan* 74-79; R 79-86; V Aberavon 86-01; V Dulais Valley 01-13; rtd 13. *43 Heol Maes y Dre, Ystradgynlais, Swansea SA9 1HA* T: (01639) 841882
E: stephen.barnes41@btinternet.com

BARNES, Stephen John. b 59. Univ of Wales (Cardiff) BSc 80. Chich Th Coll 83. d 86 p 87. C Neath w Llantwit *Llan* 86-89; C Coity w Nolton 89-95; V Troedyrhiw w Merthyr Vale from 95. *The Vicarage, Nixonville, Merthyr Vale, Merthyr Tydfil CF48 4RF* T: (01443) 690249 E: light2house@btinternet.com

BARNES, Stephen William. b 53. Man Univ BSc. St Jo Coll Nottm. d 83 p 84. C Chadwell Heath *Chelmsf* 83-87; C Becontree St Alb 88-89; Deanery Youth Chapl 88-91; C Becontree S 89-91; TV Worth *Chich* 91-98; Chapl Willen Hospice Milton Keynes from 99. *90 Bradwell Road, Bradville, Milton Keynes MK13 7AD*
E: chaplain@willen-hospice.org.uk

BARNES, Mrs Sylvia Frances (Sally). b 43. Shoreditch Coll Lon CertEd 75. S Tr Scheme 92. d 96 p 97. NSM Cusop w Blakemere, Bredwardine w Brobury etc *Heref* 96-07; PtO 07-13; rtd 13; PtO *Heref* from 15. *Pwll Cwm, Arthur's Stone Lane, Dorstone, Hereford HR3 6AY* T: (01981) 500252

BARNES, Thomas. *See* BARNES, William Thomas

BARNES, Timothy. b 56. Birm Univ BSc 78. Westcott Ho Cam 96 Lon Bible Coll 82. d 98 p 99. C Shrub End *Chelmsf* 98-02; V Leigh-on-Sea St Aid 02-11; P-in-c Bocking St Pet from 11. *St Peter's Vicarage, 6 St Peters in the Fields, Braintree CM7 9AR* T: (01376) 349267 E: timbarnes1@btinternet.com

BARNES, William Joseph Athanasius. b 57. St Andr Univ MTheol 84 Newc Univ MA 02 RGN 89. Westcott Ho Cam 91. d 92 p 93. C S Bank *York* 92-95; C Northallerton w Kirby Sigston 95-97; V Dormanstown 97-01; P-in-c Netherton St Andr *Worc* 01-06; P-in-c Darby End 03-06; PtO *York* from 15. *20 Cropton Close, Redcar TS10 4HU* T: (01642) 471772
E: bja.barnes@btopenworld.com

BARNES, Canon William Thomas. b 39. Dur Univ BA 60. Wycliffe Hall Ox 60. d 62 p 63. C Scotforth *Blackb* 62-66; C Cleveleys 66-67; V Colne Ch Ch 67-74; V Bamber Bridge St Sav 74-01; Hon Can Blackb Cathl 00-04; rtd 04; PtO *Blackb* from 04. *12 Little Close, Farington Moss, Leyland PR26 6QU* T: (01772) 457646 E: tom.beryl.barnes@hotmail.co.uk

BARNES-CLAY, Peter John Granger. b 43. Cam Univ CertEd 69 MCollP. Chich Th Coll 72. d 75 p 82. C Earlham St Anne *Nor* 75-76; Asst Master Hewett Sch Nor 76-83; Chapl Nor Cathl from 80; Hon C Eaton 81-83; C 83-87; R Winterton w E and W Somerton and Horsey 87-92; R Weybourne Gp 92-03; RD Holt 95-02; rtd 03; PtO *Nor* 03-05; C Smallburgh w Dilham w Honing and Crostwight 05-06; P-in-c 06-08; PtO from 08; *St E* from 14. *Hunters End, 1 Danby Close, Eaton Rise, Norwich NR4 6RH* T: (01603) 501199
E: becketsthree1@aol.com

BARNETT, Alec James Leon. b 44. Em Coll Cam BA 66 MA 70 PGCE 71. Cuddesdon Coll 66. d 69 p 70. C Preston St Jo *Blackb* 69-72; Asst Master Hutton Grammar Sch 70-72; Asst Chapl Uppingham Sch 72-80; Hd of RE 73-80; Dir Farmington/Ampleforth Project 79-83; C Witney Ox 80-84; P-in-c Lt Compton w Chastleton, Cornwell etc 84-88; Prin Ox Chr Tr Scheme 84-88; P-in-c St Michael Penkevil *Truro* 88-95; P-in-c Lamorran and Merther 88-95; Dioc Tr Officer 88-95; Chapl Strasbourg *Eur* 95-01; Abp Cant's Rep at Eur Inst from 95; PtO *Truro* from 95; rtd 01. *7 rue des Magnolias, La Croix, 17800 St Léger, France* T: (0033) (5) 46 94 99 25 F: 46 94 95 01
E: james.barnett@wanadoo.fr

BARNETT, Ann. *See* BARNETT, Patricia Ann

BARNETT, David John. b 33. Magd Coll Ox BA 56 MA 61. St Steph Ho Ox BA 58. d 59 p 60. C Styvechale *Cov* 59-62; Chapl Rohes Univ S Africa 62-68; P-in-c Grahamstown St Bart 62-68; LtO Cape Town 68-69; Chapl and Lect Univ of Rhodesia 70-76; V Colindale St Matthias *Lon* 77-90; R Finchley St Mary 90-98; rtd 98; PtO *Ex* 98-08. *2 Curlew Way, Exeter EX4 4EW* T: (01392) 431486

BARNETT, Dudley Graham. b 36. Ch Ch Ox BA 62 MA 65. St Steph Ho Ox 62. d 64 p 65. C Abbey Hey *Man* 64-68; V Swinton H Rood 68-90; R Old Trafford St Hilda 90-01;

R Firswood and Gorse Hill 01-02; rtd 02; PtO *Man* from 02. *6A Gilda Crescent Road, Eccles, Manchester M30 9AG* T: 0161-707 9767

BARNETT, Mrs Gillian. b 62. All SS Cen for Miss & Min 12. d 15. C Walmersley Road, Bury *Man* from 15. *27 Birley Street, Bury BL9 5DT* M: 07955-411893 E: barnettgill@hotmail.co.uk

BARNETT, James. *See* BARNETT, Alec James Leon

BARNETT, James Andrew McWilliam. b 76. Leeds Univ BA 99. Trin Coll Bris BA 01. d 02 p 03. C Bolton St Paul w Em *Man* 02-05; TV Leeds St Geo *Ripon* 05-10; Pioneer Min to New Communities *Leeds* from 10. *14 Parkside Green, Leeds LS6 4NY* T: 0113-243 8498 M: 07747-892192

BARNETT, John. *See* BARNETT, David John

BARNETT, Canon John Raymond. b 51. Lon Univ LLB 74 BD 86 Birm Univ MA 98 De Montfort Univ MA 11. Westcott Ho Cam 74. d 77 p 78. C Northfield *Birm* 77-81; V Hamstead St Bernard 81-91; R The Quinton 91-03; AD Edgbaston 98-03; P-in-c Oldbury 03-07; P-in-c Langley St Jo 03-07; P-in-c Langley St Mich 03-07; P-in-c Londonderry 04-07; V Oldbury, Langley and Londonderry 07-09; Hon Can Birm Cathl 01-09; P-in-c Darlaston All SS *Lich* 09-13; C Moxley 09-13; C Darlaston St Lawr 09-13; P-in-c Pheasey from 13; Interfaith Officer Wolverhampton Area from 09. *88 Hillingford Avenue, Birmingham B43 7HN* M: 07967-166931
E: john.barnett@lichfield.anglican.org

BARNETT (née JACKSON), Mrs Lisa Helen. b 79. Reading Univ BA(Ed) 01 Cam Univ BA 06. Ridley Hall Cam 04. d 07 p 08. C Patcham *Chich* 07-11; P-in-c Scaynes Hill 11-15; V from 15. *The Vicarage, Vicarage Lane, Scaynes Hill, Haywards Heath RH17 7PB* T: (01444) 831827 M: 07989-761575
E: revlisa@btinternet.com

BARNETT, Michael. *See* BARNETT, Raymond Michael

BARNETT, Miss Patricia Ann. b 38. Whitelands Coll Lon CertEd. Cranmer Hall Dur 75. dss 78 d 87 p 94. Gateacre *Liv* 78-82; Litherland St Paul Hatton Hill 82-88; Par Dn 87-88; Par Dn Platt Bridge 88-94; C 94-95; V Skelmersdale Ch at Cen 95-98; rtd 98; PtO *Liv* from 00. *Address temp unknown*

BARNETT, Peter Geoffrey. b 46. AKC 71. St Aug Coll Cant 71. d 72 p 73. C Wolverhampton *Lich* 72-77; P-in-c Caldmore 77-83; TR Bris St Agnes and St Simon w St Werburgh 83-87; P-in-c Bris St Paul w St Barn 83-87; TR Bris St Paul's 87-94; Warden Pilsdon Community 94-04; PtO *Roch* from 04; *S & B* from 13. *Catchpool Cottage, Llanmadoc, Swansea SA3 1DE* T: (01792) 386767 E: thebarnettfamily@talktalk.net

BARNETT, Preb Raymond Michael. b 31. Man Univ BA 54. Wells Th Coll 54. d 56 p 57. C Fallowfield *Man* 56-59; Madagascar 59-60; V Blackrod *Man* 60-67; V Woolavington *B & W* 67-76; RD Bridgwater 72-76; V St Decumans 76-96; RD Quantock 78-86 and 93-95; Preb Wells Cathl 89-96; rtd 96; PtO *B & W* 96-08. *22 Fosbrooke House, Clifton Drive, Lytham St Annes FY8 5RQ*

BARNETT-COWAN, Bruce Edgar. b 52. BA MDiv. d 78 p 78. R Schefferville Canada 78-83; Co-president Henry Budd Coll for Min 83-91; P-in-c Runnymede St Paul 92-02; Interim P Toronto St Clem w St Matt 03-07; Interim P Coldwater-Medonte 08-09; NSM Ealing All SS *Lon* 10-14; NSM W Acton St Martin 10-14; Canada from 14. *729 Annette Street, Toronto ON M6S 2E3, Canada* T: (001) (416) 766 7403
E: bruce_barnett_cowan@hotmail.com

BARNFATHER, Thomas Fenwick. b 52. Cant Ch Ch Univ BSc 09. Linc Th Coll 86. d 88 p 89. C Sedgefield *Dur* 88-91; TV E Darlington 91-92; CF 92-96; V Heybridge w Langford *Chelmsf* 96-98; Chapl HM YOI Dover 98-00; Chapl HM Pris Swaleside 00-01; P-in-c Aylesham w Adisham *Cant* 01-04; Asst Dir of Ords 02-05; PtO 04-09; P-in-c Westgate St Sav 09-12; P-in-c Lanzarote *Eur* 12-14; PtO *Leic* from 15. *31 Alexandra Street, Thurmaston, Leicester LE4 8FD* M: 07513-060519 T: 0116-212 1277
E: tombarnfather@gmail.com

BARNSHAW, Anthony James. b 72. Man Univ BA 97. St Jo Coll Nottm 03. d 05 p 06. C Kersal Moor *Man* 05-08; TV Ramsbottom and Edenfield 08-15; C Cheadle Hulme St Andr *Ches* from 15. *198 Bruntwood Lane, Cheadle Hulme, Cheadle SK8 6BE* E: a.barnshaw@btopenworld.com

BARNSLEY, David Edward. b 75. Ox Brookes Univ BSc 97. Oak Hill Th Coll BA 03. d 03 p 04. C Kilnhurst *Sheff* 03-06; C Duffield and Lt Eaton *Derby* from 06. *138 Alfreton Road, Little Eaton, Derby DE21 5DE* T: (01332) 585190
E: davidb@rnsley.freeserve.co.uk *or* vicar@littleeatonchurch.co.uk

BARNSLEY, Canon Melvyn. b 46. Dur Univ BA 67 Lon Univ CertEd. St Chad's Coll Dur 64. d 71 p 72. C Cov St Thos 71-74; C Cov St Jo 71-75; V New Bilton 75-82; R Stevenage St Andr and St Geo *St Alb* 82-14; Hon Steavenage 89-99; Hon Can St Alb 00-14; rtd 14; PtO *St Alb* from 14; *Ely* from 14. *48 Hogsden Leys, St Neots PE19 6AD* T: (01480) 474498
E: melvynbarnsley@gmail.com

BARNSTAPLE, Archdeacon of. *See* BUTCHERS, The Ven Mark Andrew

BARNSTAPLE, Archdeacon of. *See* GUNN JOHNSON, The Ven David Allan

BAROI, The Rt Revd Michael.. Bp Dhaka and Moderator Ch of Bangladesh 03-08. *St Thomas's Church, 54 Johnson Road, Dhaka-1, Bangladesh* T/F: (00880) (2) 238218
E: cob@citechco.net *or* cbdacdio@bangla.net

BARON, Thomas Michael. b 63. St Steph Ho Ox 85. **d** 88 **p** 89. C Hartlepool St Paul *Dur* 88-92; Chapl Asst Hartlepool Gen Hosp 89-92; Asst Chapl Whittington Hosp NHS Trust 92-95; Chapl Enfield Community Care NHS Trust 95-01; Chapl Chase Farm Hosps NHS Trust 95-99; Chapl Barnet and Chase Farm Hosps NHS Trust from 99; Chapl Barnet, Enfield and Haringey Mental Health Trust from 01; Chapl Enfield Primary Care Trust from 01. *The Chaplaincy, Chase Farm Hospital, The Ridgeway, Enfield EN2 8JL* T: (020) 8375 1078 *or* 8882 1195
E: frtom.baron@btinternet.com

BARON, Mrs Vanessa Lillian. b 57. City Univ BSc 79 Fitzw Coll Cam BA 84 MA 85 Birkbeck Coll Lon MA 06 SRN 79. Ridley Hall Cam 83. **dss** 86 **d** 87 **p** 94. Roxbourne St Andr *Lon* 86-89; Par Dn 87-89; NSM Roxeth 92-95; Lic Preacher from 95; Asst Chapl Harrow Sch 95-04; Chapl St Paul's Girls' Sch Hammersmith from 04. *2 Kennet House, Harrow Park, Harrow HA1 3JE* T: (020) 8872 8182 *or* 7603 2288 E: vbaron@spgs.org

BARR, Alan. b 59. TCD BTh 07. **d** 07 **p** 08. C Bray *D & G* 07-09; I Sixmilecross w Termonmaguirke *Arm* from 09. *St Michael's Rectory, 104 Cooley Road, Sixmilecross, Omagh BT79 9DH* T: (028) 8075 7097 M: 87-948 4408 E: alnbarr@gmail.com *or* sixmilecross@armagh.anglican.org

BARR, John. *See* BARR, Michael John Alexander

BARR (née HAYTER), Mary Elizabeth. b 58. Jes Coll Ox BA 80 CertEd 81 MA 84 Qu Coll Ox DPhil 85. Ridley Hall Cam 84. **dss** 86 **d** 87 **p** 94. Chapl Cam Univ Pastorate 86-91; Cambridge H Trin w St Andr Gt *Ely* 86-87; Par Dn 87-91; PtO 91-92; *Ex* 92-94; NSM Torquay St Luke 94-97; NSM St Malvern St Mary *Worc* from 97; Chapl Worcs Community Healthcare NHS Trust 99-01; Chapl Worcs Community and Mental Health Trust from 01. *Priory Vicarage, Clarence Road, Malvern WR14 3EN* T: (01684) 563707 *or* 561020
E: office@greatmalvernpriory.org.uk *or* revdoc@mehb4.plus.com

BARR, Michael John Alexander. b 60. Qu Coll Ox BA 82 MA 86 Pemb Coll Cam BA 86 MA 90. Ridley Hall Cam 84. **d** 87 **p** 88. C Earley St Pet *Ox* 87-89; C Cambridge Gt St Mary w St Mich Ely 89-92; Chapl Girton Coll Cam 90-92; P-in-c Torquay St Luke *Ex* 92-97; Dioc Communications Officer 92-97; P-in-c Gt Malvern St Mary *Worc* 97-99; V from 99; RD Malvern 01-07; Hon Can Worc Cathl from 15. *Priory Vicarage, Clarence Road, Malvern WR14 3EN* T: (01684) 563707 *or* 561020
E: jmbarr@ukonline.co.uk *or* office@greatmalvernpriory.org.uk

BARR, Norma Margaret. b 41. Trin Coll Bris BA 99. **d** 00 **p** 01. C Aberdour *St And* 01-03; P-in-c Pontiac Grace Ch USA 03-05. *3300 W Kinnickinnic River Parkway, Apartment 2, Milwaukee WI 53215, USA* E: normabarr@gmail.com

BARR-HAMILTON, Nicholas James. b 74. Rob Coll Cam MA 96. Oak Hill Th Coll BA 08. **d** 08 **p** 09. C Linthorpe *York* 08-12; V Fatfield *Dur* from 12. *Fatfield Vicarage, 14 Ewesley, Washington NE38 9JG* E: nickbarr-hamilton@o2.co.uk

BARR JOHNSTON, Charles Walter. b 38. BSc 61. Oak Hill Th Coll 62. **d** 64 **p** 65. C Tollington Park St Mark w St Anne *Lon* 64-68; SAMS 68-95; Argentina 68-95; PtO *Cov* 95-96. *Casilla de Correo 187, Salta, Argentina*

BARRACLOUGH, Mrs Barbara Amanda Juliet. b 61. Stirling Univ BA 83 Ches Coll of HE MA 00. NOC 97. **d** 00 **p** 01. C Lupset *Wakef* 00-04; V W Ardsley *Leeds* 04-15; R Sprotbrough *Sheff* from 15; AD Adwick from 15. *The Rectory, 42A Spring Lane, Sprotbrough, Doncaster DN5 7QG* M: 07890-614579 E: amanda.barraclough1@btinternet.com

BARRACLOUGH, Mrs Naomi Hannah Shrine. b 88. Lanc Univ BSc 10. Cranmer Hall Dur 12. **d** 15. C Wirksworth *Derby* from 15. *7 Meadow Place, Matlock DE4 3SE* M: 07872-056471
E: nhsbarraclough@gmail.com

BARRACLOUGH, Canon Owen Conrad. b 32. Pemb Coll Cam BA 55 MA 59. Westcott Ho Cam 56. **d** 57 **p** 58. C Chippenham St Andr w Tytherton Lucas *Bris* 57-62; V Harringay St Paul *Lon* 62-70; Bp's Chapl for Community Relns *Cov* 70-77; P-in-c Baginton 72-77; V Swindon Ch Ch *Bris* 77-97; Chapl Princess Marg Hosp Swindon 77-89; Hon Can Bris Cathl 87-97; rtd 98; PtO *Bris* from 98; *Glouc* 98-01; Jt P-in-c Staverton w Boddington and Tredington etc 01-04; Hon C Twigworth, Down Hatherley, Norton, The Leigh etc 04-06; Hon C Leckhampton SS Phil and Jas w Cheltenham St Jas 06-09; Hon C S Cheltenham 10-11. *Robin Hollow, 10A Church*

Road, St Marks, Cheltenham GL51 7AN T: (01242) 230855
E: obarraclough@btinternet.com

BARRAND, George William (Bill). b 33. Lon Coll of Div 59. **d** 62 **p** 63. C Bucknall and Bagnall *Lich* 62-65; C Parr *Liv* 65-69; Australia from 70; rtd 98. *2/20 Riversdale Road, Yarra Junction Vic 3797, Australia* T: (0061) (3) 5967 2592

BARRAS, June. b 58. **d** 10 **p** 11. OLM Warkworth and Acklington Newc 10-13; rtd 13. *8 St Omer Road, Acklington, Morpeth NE65 9DA* T: (01670) 760650

BARRATT, Mrs Elizabeth June. b 32. ACP 65. Trin Coll Bris 75. **dss** 78 **d** 87 **p** 94. Par Dn W Kilburn St Luke w St Simon and St Jude *Lon* 87-94; C 94-98; rtd 98; Hon C Kensal Rise St Mark and St Martin *Lon* 99-11; Hon C Kensal Rise St Martin from 11. *68A Bathhurst Gardens, London NW10 5HY* T: (020) 8968 5951 M: 07763-474602
E: ejbarratt@hotmail.co.uk

BARRATT, Julie Anne. b 60. SNWTP. **d** 13 **p** 14. NSM Constable Lee *Man* from 13. *9 Crawshaw Grange, Crawshawbooth, Rossendale BB4 8LY* T: (01706) 217141 M: 07941-294296
E: jabarratt@ntlworld.com

BARRATT, Canon Philip Norman. b 62. Aston Tr Scheme 87 St Steph Ho Ox 89 Coll of Resurr Mirfield 90. **d** 92 **p** 93. C Heywood St Luke w All So *Man* 92-96; V Thornham St Jas 96-12; Can Res Man Cathl from 12. *2 Booth Clibborn Court, Park Lane, Salford M7 4PJ* T: (01706) 645256
E: canon.precentor@manchester.cathedral.org

BARRELL, Adrian Edward. b 36. Keble Coll Ox BA 59. Ely Th Coll 59. **d** 62 **p** 63. C Plymouth St Jas Ham *Ex* 62-66; C Bideford 66-70; V Walkhampton 70-80; rtd 01. *Cartref, Dousland, Yelverton PL20 6PA* T: (01822) 852612

BARRETT, Alan. b 48. Southn Univ BA 69. Wycliffe Hall Ox 74. **d** 77 **p** 78. C Conisbrough *Sheff* 77-80; C Lower Homerton St Paul *Lon* 80-81; C-in-c Hounslow Gd Shep Beavers Lane CD 81-87; R Langdon Hills *Chelmsf* 87-97; P-in-c Tamworth *Lich* 97-03; V 03-13; RD 99-04; rtd 13. *Neale House, Neale's Row, Great Urswick, Ulverston LA13 0SX* T: (01229) 582179
E: alan.barrett@breathemail.net

BARRETT, Alastair David. b 75. Fitzw Coll Cam BA 97 MA 01 Birm Univ BD 00. Qu Coll Birm MA 01. **d** 01 **p** 02. C Sutton Coldfield St Chad *Birm* 01-04; C Oldbury, Langley and Londonderry 04-10; P-in-c Hodge Hill 10-13; TR from 13. *8 Dreghorn Road, Hodge Hill, Birmingham B36 8LJ* T: 0121-747 6982 E: hodgehillvicar@hotmail.co.uk

BARRETT, Mrs Alexandra Mary. b 75. Clare Coll Cam BA 96 MA 99. Westcott Ho Cam 00. **d** 03 **p** 04. C Godmanchester *Ely* 03-07; R Buckden w the Offords 07-14; USA from 14. *Address temp unknown* E: reverendally@gmail.com

BARRETT, Arthur. *See* BARRETT, Kenneth Arthur Lambart

BARRETT, Mrs Brigid. b 44. RN 90. STETS MA 11. **d** 11 **p** 12. NSM Parkstone St Pet and St Osmund w Branksea *Sarum* 11-15; NSM Wareham from 15. *1 Wyatts Lane, Wareham BH20 4NH* T: (01929) 553460 E: brigid4946@tiscali.co.uk

BARRETT, Christopher Paul. b 49. AKC 71 St Aug Coll Cant 71. **d** 72 **p** 73. C Tupsley *Heref* 72-75; C Ex St Thos 75-79; R Atherington and High Bickington 79-83; V Burrington 79-83; Asst Dir of Educn 79-87; P-in-c Sticklepath 83-84; P-in-c Barnstaple 83-85; TV 85-90; V Whipton 90-99; TV Ex St Thos and Em 99-05; Chapl Burton Hosps NHS Foundn Trust 05-14; rtd 14. *18 Cheadle Close, Littleover, Derby DE23 3SH* T: (01332) 516345 E: revcbarrett@aol.com

BARRETT, Clive. b 55. Ox Univ BA 76 MA 80 CertEd 77 Leeds Univ PhD 98. St Steph Ho Ox 80. **d** 83 **p** 84. C Wakef Cathl 83-87; Asst Chapl Leeds Univ *Ripon* 87-97; Dioc Development Rep 89-92; P-in-c Middleton St Cross 98-07; Co Ecum Development Officer W Yorks *Leeds* from 07; Hon C Headingley from 08. *West Yorkshire Ecumenical Council, Hinsley Hall, 62 Headingley Lane, Leeds LS6 2BX* T: 0113-261 8053 M: 07966-540699 E: clivebarrett@wyec.co.uk

BARRETT, Canon Derek Leonard. b 25. St Fran Coll Brisbane ThL 57. **d** 57 **p** 58. Australia 57-63; C Ramsgate St Geo *Cant* 64-65; C Putney St Mary *S'wark* 65-67; V Kidderminster St Jo *Worc* 67-77; V Stourbridge St Thos 77-90; RD Stourbridge 83-89; Hon Can Worc Cathl 87-90; rtd 90; PtO *Glouc* 90-02; *Worc* 90-02. *Lotty Leven, Crystal Waters, M/S 16, Maleny QLD 4552, Australia* T: (0061) (7) 5494 4710

BARRETT, Mrs Diane Joan. b 46. **d** 10 **p** 12. OLM Bolton St Bede and Lostock St Thos and St Jo *Man* 10-15; rtd 15. *6 Whitland Avenue, Bolton BL1 5FB* T: (01204) 847870
E: dianejoanbarrett@sky.com

BARRETT, John Joseph James. b 38. Lon Univ BD 65. Sarum & Wells Th Coll. **d** 78 **p** 78. C Danbury *Chelmsf* 78-80; Ind Chapl 80-83; C Dovercourt 80-83; TV Dovercourt and Parkeston 83-89; V Rubery *Birm* 89-04; rtd 04; PtO *Sheff* from 04. *4 Arran Hill, Thrybergh, Rotherham S65 4BH* T: (01709) 850288 E: rev.barrett@btinternet.com

BARRETT, Jonathan Murray. b 68. Oak Hill Th Coll BA 98. **d** 98 **p** 99. C Pennycross *Ex* 98-02; TV Plymouth Em, St Paul Efford and St Aug 02-08; V Thurnby w Stoughton *Leic* 08-13; P-in-c Houghton-on-the-Hill, Keyham and Hungarton 11-13; TR Cornerstone Team from 13. *The Vicarage, Thurnby, Leicester LE7 9PN* T: 0116-241 2263

BARRETT, Canon Kenneth. b 42. Univ of Wales (Lamp) BA 64. St Steph Ho Ox 65. **d** 67 **p** 68. C Poulton-le-Fylde *Blackb* 67-69; C S Shore H Trin 69-72; V Brierfield 72-83; V Chorley St Geo 83-07; Hon Can Blackb Cathl 03-07; rtd 07; PtO *Blackb* from 07. *24 Astley Road, Chorley PR7 1RR* T: (01257) 233421

BARRETT, The Very Revd Kenneth Arthur Lambart. b 60. CITC BTh 94. **d** 97 **p** 98. C Seagoe *D & D* 97-00; I Dublin Booterstown *D & G* 00-04; I Dublin Mt Merrion 00-04; I Boyle and Elphin w Aghanagh, Kilbryan etc *K, E & A* 04-08; I Taunagh w Kilmactranny, Ballysumaghan etc 04-08; I Rossorry *Clogh* 08-14; Dir of Ords 11-14; Can Clogh Cathl 12-14; Dean Raphoe *D & R* from 14; I Raphoe w Raymochy and Clonleigh from 14. *The Deanery, Raphoe, Co Donegal, F93 KT21, Republic of Ireland* T: (00353) (74) 914 5226 E: deanarthur@raphoe.anglican.org

BARRETT, Canon Kenneth Sydney. b 26. Roch Th Coll 60. **d** 62 **p** 63. C Wollaton *S'well* 62-65; C Hucknall Torkard 65-67; R Collie Australia 67-73; R Mandurah 73-92; Can Bunbury 76-92; rtd 92. *PO Box 818, 2 Loxton Street, Mandurah WA 6210, Australia* T/F: (0061) (8) 9581 2519 E: joykenb@westnet.com.au

BARRETT, Canon Marion Lily. b 54. Ex Univ BA 01 SRN 75. SWMTC 91. **d** 94 **p** 95. C St Mawgan w St Ervan and St Eval *Truro* 94-97; C St Breoke and Egloshayle 97-98; Asst Chapl R Cornwall Hosps Trust 98-99; Chapl 00-05; R St Mewan w Mevagissey and St Ewe *Truro* from 05; RD St Austell from 10; Convenor Bp's Gp for Min of Healing from 11; Hon Can Truro Cathl from 13. *The Rectory, St Mewan Lane, St Mewan, St Austell PL26 7DP* T: (01726) 72679 E: marionstmewan@btinternet.com

BARRETT, Mark Hugh. b 75. Natal Univ BArch 00. Trin Coll Bris 10. **d** 12. C Sidmouth, Woolbrook, Salcombe Regis, Sidbury etc *Ex* from 12. *25 Lymebourne Park, Sidmouth EX10 9HZ* T: (01395) 512645 M: 07739-432013 E: markbandhelenb@hotmail.com *or* mark.barrett@sidvalley.org.uk

BARRETT, Matthew Edward John. b 73. Ripon Coll Cuddesdon 11. **d** 13 **p** 14. C Guernsey St Michel du Valle *Win* from 13. *St Michael's House, 54 Rue des Fleurs, Les Barras Lane, Vale, Guernsey GY6 8HB* T: (01481) 251842 E: revmatthewbarrett@gmail.com

BARRETT, Paul. *See* BARRETT, Christopher Paul

BARRETT, Mrs Rachel Jeanne Alexandra. b 56. Ex Univ BA 78 PGCE 79. SWMTC 92. **d** 95 **p** 96. NSM Ex St Mark 95-96; NSM Ex St Mark, St Sidwell and St Matt 96-00; Chapl St Margaret's Sch Ex 00-05; Chapl Derby High Sch from 05. *Derby High School, Hillsway, Littleover, Derby DE23 3DT* T: (01332) 514267 F: 516085 E: rbarret@derbyhigh.derby.sch.uk

BARRETT, Robert David. b 48. **d** 11 **p** 12. OLM Alford w Rigsby *Linc* from 11. *14 East Street, Alford LN13 9EQ* T: (01507) 462135 E: frbob@btinternet.com

BARRETT, Ronald Reginald. b 30. Roch Th Coll 61. **d** 64 **p** 65. C Spring Park *Cant* 64-66; C Thornton Heath St Jude 66-68; V Greengates *Bradf* 68-73; V Shelf 73-79; V Embsay w Eastby 79-87; V Farndon and Coddington *Ches* 87-92; rtd 92; PtO *Bradf* 92-10; *Man* 10-13; *Sheff* from 13. *10 James Smith House, 11 Marlborough Road, Sheffield S10 1DA* T: 0114-266 7206 E: revrb30@gmail.com

BARRETT, Stephen David Norman. b 54. Aber Univ BSc 75 Edin Univ BD 78. Edin Th Coll 75. **d** 78 **p** 79. C Ardrossan *Glas* 78-80; R Peterhead *Ab* 80-81; Chapl HM Pris Peterhead 80-81; R Renfrew *Glas* 81-87; R Bishopbriggs 87-94; Chapl HM Pris Glas (Barlinnie) 87-94; Chapl Stobhill NHS Trust 87-94; P-in-c Port Glas 94-99; R 99-08; rtd 08; PtO *Glas* from 09. *9 Birnock Avenue, Renfrew PA4 0YW* T: 0141-886 6796

BARRETT, Mrs Susan Lesley. b 56. E Sussex Coll of HE CertEd 77 BEd 78. WMMTC 03. **d** 06. NSM Bowbrook N *Worc* 06-07; NSM Droitwich Spa 07-10; NSM Ombersley w Doverdale 10-14; NSM Hartlebury 10-14; NSM Elmley Lovett w Hampton Lovett and Elmbridge etc 10-14. *55-57 High Street, Feckenham, Redditch B96 6HU* T/F: (01527) 893866 M: 07717-412441 E: sue@artmetal.co.uk

BARRETT FORD, Carol Mary. *See* FORD, Carol Mary

BARRIBAL, Richard James Pitt. b 45. Trin Coll Bris. **d** 80 **p** 81. C Northampton St Giles *Pet* 80-82; V Long Buckby w Watford 82-86; PtO 86-00; *Leic* 00-08; P-in-c Welham, Glooston and Cranoe and Stonton Wyville 08-10; PtO from 14. *The Thatched House, 6 Church Bank, Great Easton, Market Harborough LE16 8SN* T: (01536) 772127 E: richard.barribal@btinternet.com

BARRIE, John Arthur. b 38. K Coll Lon 58 Bps' Coll Cheshunt 59. **d** 63 **p** 64. C Southgate St Mich *Lon* 63-66; CF 66-88; Sen CF 88-93; Chapl Guards Chpl Lon 88-92; QHC 91-93; P-in-c Heref H Trin 93-96; P-in-c Breinton 95-96; V St Marylebone St Mark Hamilton Terrace *Lon* 96-10; Ecum Adv Two Cities Area 99-10; rtd 10; PtO *Lon* from 10. *The Vicarage, 4 Beaudesert Mews, West Drayton UB7 7PE* T: (01895) 442194 E: rosybarrie1@btinternet.com

BARRIE (née HEITZMANN), Mrs Pamela. b 58. Open Univ BA 90 Kingston Univ MA 05. STETS 09. **d** 12 **p** 13. NSM Shepperton and Littleton *Lon* from 12. *131A Laleham Road, Staines TW18 2EG* M: 07806-762745 E: pamelabarrie3284@hotmail.co.uk

BARRIE, Mrs Rosemary Joan. b 62. Bris Univ BA 83 PGCE 84. Qu Coll Birm 87 Perkins Sch of Th (USA) 89. **d** 07 **p** 08. NSM W Kilburn St Luke and Kilburn St Mary w All So and W Hampstead St Jas *Lon* 07-08; NSM St Marylebone St Mark Hamilton Terrace 08-10; C Twickenham St Mary 10-13; Chapl St Mary's Sch Twickenham 10-13; V W Drayton *Lon* from 13. *The Vicarage, 4 Beaudesert Mews, West Drayton UB7 7PE* T: (01895) 442194 E: rosybarrie1@btinternet.com

BARRINGER, Philip Leslie. b 65. **d** 13 **p** 14. NSM Rivers Team *Sheff* from 13. *59 Cramfit Crescent, Dinnington, Sheffield S25 2XT* T: (01909) 518194 E: philbarringer@aol.com

BARRINGTON, The Very Revd Dominic Matthew Jesse. b 62. Hatf Coll Dur BA 84 MSc 85 LTCL. Ripon Coll Cuddesdon BA 94 MA 98 Ch Div Sch of Pacific MTS 95. **d** 95 **p** 96. C Mortlake w E Sheen *S'wark* 95-98; Chapl St Chad's Coll Dur 98-03; P-in-c Kettering SS Pet and Paul 03-10; R 10-15; Dean Chicago USA from 15. *Address temp unknown*

✠**BARRINGTON-WARD, The Rt Revd Simon.** b 30. KCMG 01. Magd Coll Cam BA 53 MA 57. Wycliffe Coll Toronto Hon DD Westcott Ho Cam 54. **d** 56 **p** 57 **c** 85. Chapl Magd Coll Cam 56-60; Nigeria 60-63; Fell and Dean of Chpl Magd Coll Cam 63-69; Prin Crowther Hall CMS Tr Coll Selly Oak 69-74; Gen Sec CMS 75-85; Hon Can Derby Cathl 75-85; Chapl to The Queen 84-85; Bp Cov 85-97; rtd 97; Hon Fell Magd Coll Cam from 87; Hon Asst Chapl from 98; Hon Asst Bp Ely from 97. *4 Searle Street, Cambridge CB4 3DB* T: (01223) 740460 E: sb292@cam.ac.uk

BARRON, Arthur Henry. b 45. Solicitor 72. SEITE 99. **d** 02 **p** 03. NSM Addiscombe St Mary Magd w St Martin *S'wark* 02-06; Chapl Asst St Mary's NHS Trust Paddington 05-09; Chapl Guy's and St Thos' NHS Foundn Trust 09-12; rtd 12; PtO *S'wark* 06-07; NSM Woodmansterne from 07; Chapl S'wark Cathl from 13. *23 Little Woodcote Lane, Purley CR8 3PZ* T: (020) 8660 1921 M: 07710-275977 E: art_barron@hotmail.com

BARRON, John William. b 66. Imp Coll Lon BSc 88. Cranmer Hall Dur 06. **d** 08 **p** 09. C Whickham *Dur* 08-11; V High Spen and Rowlands Gill from 11. *2 Beechwood, High Spen, Rowlands Gill NE39 2BL* T: (01207) 542815 E: john.barron@ntlworld.com

BARRON, Leslie Gill. b 44. ACII 69. Lich Th Coll 67. **d** 70 **p** 71. C Bishopwearmouth Ch Ch *Dur* 70-72; C Bishopwearmouth St Mary V w St Pet CD 72-75; C Harton 75-77; V Lumley 77-88; P-in-c Hendon and Sunderland 89-90; R Hendon 90-94; P-in-c Ushaw Moor 94-95; V Bearpark and Ushaw Moor 95-04; PtO from 04; rtd 08. *34 Breconsgill Close, Hartlepool TS24 8PH* T: (01429) 291197 E: l.barron@ntlworld.com

BARRON, Richard Davidson. b 51. Lon Univ BSc 74. Trin Coll Bris 75. **d** 78 **p** 79. C Bradley *Wakef* 78-81; C Heworth H Trin *York* 81-82; TV 82-89; Chapl York Distr Hosp 82-86; R Greenhithe St Mary *Roch* 89-12; R Fairlight and Pett Chich from 12. *The Rectory, 15C Battery Hill, Fairlight, Hastings TN35 4AP* T: (01424) 812799 E: rbarron100@yahoo.co.uk

BARRON, Mrs Sonia Patricia. b 55. Lon Univ BEd 80 Nottm Univ MA 00. St Mellitus Coll 08. **d** 11 **p** 12. C Chilwell *S'well* 11-14; R Claypole *Linc* from 14; RD Loveden from 14. *The New Rectory, 6 Rectory Lane, Claypole, Newark NG23 5BH* T: (01636) 626720 E: sbarron55@gmail.com *or* rectorclaypole5@gmail.com

BARRON, Ms Sylvia. b 50. Maria Grey Coll Lon CertEd 72. All SS Cen for Miss & Min 11. **d** 14 **p** 15. NSM Spotland and Oakenrod *Man* from 14. *35 Holstein Avenue, Rochdale OL12 6DL* T: (01706) 658766 E: barronsylvia@yahoo.co.uk

BARRON, Canon Victor Robert. b 45. St Luke's Coll Ex CertEd 70. Trin Coll Bris 76. **d** 78 **p** 79. C Rainham *Chelmsf* 78-81; V Easton H Trin w St Gabr and St Lawr and St Jude *Bris* 81-89; TR Kinson *Sarum* 89-00; RD Poole 94-00; Can and Preb Sarum Cathl 99-00; rtd 00; PtO *Sarum* 00-05; Hon C Witchampton, Stanbridge and Long Crichel etc 05-07. *159 Middlehill Road, Wimborne BH21 2HJ* T: (01202) 885434 E: vicbarron@onetel.com

BARROW, Christine. *See* BARROW, Margaret Christine

BARROW, Mrs Evelyne. b 68. Yorks Min Course 12. **d** 15. NSM Upper Holme Valley *Leeds* from 15. *17 Windmill Hill Lane, Emley Moor, Huddersfield HD8 9TP* T: (01924) 848070
E: esb44@icloud.com

BARROW, Gillian Stephanie. *See* BARROW-JONES, Gillian Stephanie

BARROW, Jack Alexander. b 81. St Andr Univ BSc 03 MLitt 07. Ripon Coll Cuddesdon BA 12. **d** 13 **p** 14. C Frodingham and New Brumby *Linc* 13-14; C Gt and Lt Coates w Bradley from 14. *26 Meadowbank, Great Coates, Grimsby DN37 9PG* T: (01472) 884399 M: 07971-669587
E: alexbarrow1@gmail.com

BARROW (née DONSON), Mrs Margaret Christine. b 44. Homerton Coll Cam CertEd 65. Westcott Ho Cam 08. **d** 09 **p** 10. NSM Girton *Ely* 09-14; NSM Madingley 12-14; PtO from 14. *2 Cockerton Road, Girton, Cambridge CB3 0QW* T: (01223) 277674 E: mcbarrow@mac.com

BARROW, Paul Beynon. b 48. Liv Univ LLB 69 Man Univ MA 01. St Steph Ho Ox 02. **d** 04 **p** 05. NSM Ches H Trin 04-05; P-in-c Hargrave 05-11; V 11-13; rtd 13. *Dullah House, Eyton, Wrexham LL13 0SN* M: 07792-154388
E: paul.barrow6@btopenworld.com

BARROW-JONES, Mrs Gillian Stephanie. b 77. Regent's Park Coll Ox BA 98. Westcott Ho Cam 08. **d** 10 **p** 11. C Gainsborough and Morton *Linc* 10-13; R Wolverton *Ox* from 13. *Holy Trinity House, 28 Harvester Close, Greenleys, Milton Keynes MK12 6LE*

BARRY, Colin Lionel. b 49. Open Univ BSc 94. Bp Attwell Tr Inst 85. **d** 96 **p** 97. NSM Arbory *S & M* 96-13; NSM Arbory and Castletown from 13. *80 Ballanorris Crescent, Ballabeg, Castletown, Isle of Man IM9 4ER* T: (01624) 823080

BARRY, Ms Jacqueline Françoise. Univ of Bordeaux II LSocEth 86 MSoc 87 York Univ PGCE 91. Ridley Hall Cam. **d** 99 **p** 00. C Sydenham H Trin *S'wark* 99-03; C W Kilburn St Luke w St Simon and St Jude *Lon* 03-13; C Paddington Em Harrow Road 03-13; C W Kilburn St Luke and Harrow Road Em from 13. *Emmanuel Vicarage, 44C Fermoy Road, London W9 3NH* T: (020) 8969 0438 E: jackie.barry@lineone.net

BARRY, Canon Jonathan Peter Oulton. b 47. TCD BA 70 MA 73 Hull Univ BA 73 QUB PhD 84. Ripon Hall Ox 73. **d** 74 **p** 75. C Dundela St Mark *D & D* 74-79; I Ballyphilip w Ardquin 79-85; Dioc Info Officer 80-90; I Comber from 85; Preb St Audoen St Patr Cathl Dublin from 01. *The Rectory, 12 Windmill Hill, Comber, Newtownards BT23 5WH* T: (028) 9187 2283 E: comber@down.anglican.org

BARRY, Keith Gordon. b 67. TCD BA 92. CITC 92. **d** 94 **p** 95. C Templemore *D & R* 94-97; V Choral Derry Cathl 94-95; Dean's V 95-97; P-in-c 97; CF 97-07; Sen CF from 07; Chapl R Memorial Chpl Sandhurst from 14. *c/o MOD Chaplains (Army)* T: (01264) 383430 F: 381824

BARRY, Nicholas Brian Paul. b 61. Leic Univ BA 83. St Steph Ho Ox 84. **d** 87 **p** 88. C St John's Wood *Lon* 87-90; Chapl RAF 90-15; Dep Chapl-in-Chief 09-15; QHC from 09; V Jersey St Luke w St Jas *Win* from 15. *Address temp unknown*

BARSLEY, Canon Margaret Ann. b 39. Totley Hall Coll CertEd 60. EMMTC 79. **dss** 83 **d** 87 **p** 94. Kirton in Holland *Linc* 83-89; NSM 87-89; NSM Skirbeck Quarter 89-96; P-in-c Swineshead 96-99; V 99-04; RD Holland W 97-04; Can and Preb Linc Cathl from 00; rtd 04. *44 Sentance Crescent, Kirton, Boston PE20 1XF* T: (01205) 723824
E: margaret@churchlane8539.freeserve.co.uk

BARTER, Christopher Stuart. b 49. Chich Th Coll. **d** 84 **p** 85. C Margate St Jo *Cant* 84-88; V Whitwood and Chapl Castleford, Normanton and Distr Hosp 88-95; P-in-c Ravensthorpe *Wakef* 95-98; AIDS Cllr W Yorks HA 95-98; TV Gt Yarmouth *Nor* 98-02; R Somersham w Pidley and Oldhurst *Ely* 02-10; V Somersham w Pidley and Oldhurst and Woodhurst 10-13; P-in-c Holywell w Needingworth 07-08; RD St Ives 06-10; rtd 13; PtO *Ely* from 14. *11 Rye Close, Littleport, Ely CB6 1GH*
E: christopher.barter@btopenworld.com

BARTER, The Very Revd Donald. b 34. St Fran Coll Brisbane ThL 69 ACT ThSchool 74. **d** 69 **p** 70. C Townsville Australia 69-72; R Mareeba 72-76; R Ingham 76-81; Adn of the W and R Mt Isa 81-86; Dean Townsville 86-90; Chapl Miss to Seamen 86-90; Appeals Dir SPCK 90-93; LtO *Leic* 90-93; Australia from 93; Asst to Dean St Jas Cathl 94-00. *49 Macrossan Street, South Townsville Qld 4810, Australia* T/F: (0061) (7) 4772 7036 M: 414-989593 E: dba18613@bigpond.net.au

BARTER, Geoffrey Roger. b 41. Bris Univ BSc 63. Clifton Th Coll 65. **d** 67 **p** 68. C Normanton *Derby* 67-70; C Rainham *Chelmsf* 70-75; V Plumstead St Jo w St Jas and St Paul *S'wark* 75-82; V Frogmore *St Alb* 82-01; rtd 01; PtO *Chich* from 02. *45 West Front Road, Pagham, Bognor Regis PO21 4SZ* T: (01243) 262522

BARTER, Leonard Reginald Treseder. b 38. **d** 95 **p** 96. OLM St Stythians w Perranarworthal and Gwennap *Truro* 95-08; PtO from 08. *Vellandrucia Foundry, Stithians, Truro TR3 7BU* T: (01209) 860341

BARTER, Michael Christopher Charles. b 74. Coll of Resurr Mirfield 07. **d** 09 **p** 10. C Hangleton *Chich* 09-13; P-in-c Graffham w Woolavington from 13; Chapl Seaford Coll Petworth from 13. *The Rectory, Graffham, Petworth GU28 0NL* E: mikeccbarter@hotmail.co.uk

BARTER, Susan Kathleen. b 53. Open Univ MBA 97 Anglia Ruskin Univ MA 09. Ridley Hall Cam 01. **d** 03 **p** 04. C Happisburgh, Walcott, Hempstead w Eccles etc *Nor* 03-06; C Bacton w Edingthorpe w Witton and Ridlington 04-06; C Ward End w Bordesley Green *Birm* from 06. *St Paul's Vicarage, 405 Belchers Lane, Birmingham B9 5SY* T: 0121-772 0418 M: 07778-063644 E: susan@stpaulscrossover.org.uk

BARTHOLOMEW, Craig Gerald. b 61. UNISA BTh 82 Potchefstroom Univ MA 92 Bris Univ PhD 97. Wycliffe Hall Ox BA 84 MA 88. **d** 86 **p** 87. C Pinetown Ch Ch S Africa 87-89; Lect Geo Whitefield Coll Cape Town 89-92; Research Fell Glos Univ 97-04; PtO *Glouc* 98-04; Canada from 04. *Redeemer University College, 777 Garner Road, Ancaster ON L9K 1J4, Canada* T: (001) (905) 648 2139 ext 4270
E: cbartho@redeemer.ca

BARTHOLOMEW, David Grant. b 50. Univ of Wales (Lamp) BA 77. Chich Th Coll 91. **d** 93 **p** 94. C Petersfield *Portsm* 93-96; R Etton w Helpston and Maxey *Pet* 96-98; R Burghclere w Newtown and Ecchinswell w Sydmonton *Win* from 98. *The Rectory, Well Street, Burghclere, Newbury RG20 9HS* T: (01635) 278470 E: davidrectory@aol.com

BARTLAM, Alan Thomas. b 51. Bris Univ BEd 74. Linc Th Coll 88. **d** 90 **p** 91. C Longdon-upon-Tern, Rodington, Uppington etc *Lich* 90-92; C Tilstock and Whixall 92-95; V Tilstock, Edstaston and Whixall 95-98; R Bewcastle, Stapleton and Kirklinton etc *Carl* 98-06; V Streetly *Lich* 06-11; rtd 11. *45-47 Main Street, New Deer, Turriff AB53 6TA*

BARTLE, Canon David Colin. b 29. Em Coll Cam BA 53 MA 57. Ridley Hall Cam 53. **d** 55 **p** 56. C Birm St Martin 55-57; C Boscombe St Jo *Win* 57-60; V Lowestoft St Jo *Nor* 60-70; P-in-c Thetford St Cuth w H Trin 70-72; P-in-c Thetford St Mary 70-72; P-in-c Thetford St Pet w St Nic 70-72; TR Thetford 72-75; P-in-c Kilverstone 70-75; P-in-c Croxton 70-75; Teacher Bournemouth Sch 75-83; R Brantham w Stutton *St E* 83-90; RD Samford 86-90; P-in-c Roxwell *Chelmsf* 90-93; Dioc Dir of Ords 90-93; Dioc Lay Min Adv 90-93; Hon Can Chelmsf Cathl 91-93; rtd 93; PtO *Win* 93-98; Chapl R Bournemouth and Christchurch Hosps NHS Trust 98-00. *26 Gracey Court, Woodland Road, Broadclyst, Exeter EX5 3GA* E: dbartle8@aol.com

BARTLE-JENKINS, Paul. b 43. Bris & Glouc Tr Course. **d** 84 **p** 86. NSM Bris St Agnes and St Simon w St Werburgh 84-87; NSM Bris St Paul's 87-09; P-in-c 07-09. *188A Henleaze Road, Westbury-on-Trym, Bristol BS9 4NE* T: 0117-962 0286
E: fatherpaul00@hotmail.com

BARTLEM, Gregory John. b 68. Ox Brookes Univ BA 05. Qu Coll Birm 07. **d** 09 **p** 10. NSM Cheylesmore *Cov* 09-11; C Cov Cathl from 11. *17 Courtleet Road, Coventry CV3 5GS* T: (024) 7650 5524 M: 07967-662184 E: greg.bartlem@covcofe.org

BARTLETT, Alan Bennett. b 58. G&C Coll Cam BA 81 MA 85 Birm Univ PhD 87 St Jo Coll Dur BA 90. Cranmer Hall Dur 88. **d** 91 **p** 92. C Newc H Cross 91-94; C Newburn 94-96; Tutor Cranmer Hall Dur 96-08; V Dur St Giles from 08; P-in-c Shadforth and Sherburn from 08. *St Giles's Vicarage, Gilesgate, Durham DH1 1QQ* T: 0191-384 2452
E: vicarsgss@live.co.uk

BARTLETT, Anthony Martin. b 43. Cranmer Hall Dur 74. **d** 77 **p** 78. C Heworth St Mary *Dur* 77-80; V Cleadon 80-84; CF (TA) 81-90; Prec Dur Cathl 85-87; V Harton 87-95; P-in-c Hendon 95-96; R 96-97; V Greenlands *Blackb* 01-12; rtd 12; PtO *Blackb* from 12. *3 Keats Close, Thornton-Cleveleys FY5 2SA* T: (01253) 273471 E: bcressell@aol.com

BARTLETT, David John. b 36. Pemb Coll Ox BA 61. Linc Th Coll 63. **d** 65 **p** 66. C Wollaton *S'well* 65-70; V Woodthorpe 70-83; V Farnsfield 83-01; P-in-c Kirklington w Hockerton 83-01; RD S'well 83-93; Chapl Rodney Sch Kirklington 83-01; rtd 01; PtO *S'well* from 01. *6 De Havilland Way, Farndon Road, Newark NG24 4RF* T: (01636) 651582

BARTLETT, David William. b 59. Trin Coll Bris 89. **d** 91 **p** 92. C Frinton *Chelmsf* 91-95; TV Eston w Normanby *York* 95-96; Assoc P Worksop St Jo *S'well* 96-01; TV Trunch *Nor* 01-14; P-in-c Overstrand, Northrepps, Sidestrand etc 12-14; R Bardney *Linc* from 14. *10 Church Lane, Bardney, Lincoln LN3 5TZ* T: (01526) 397363 E: revdb@btinternet.com

BARTLETT, George Frederick. b 34. Clifton Th Coll 61. **d** 64 **p** 65. C Branksome St Clem *Sarum* 64-71; V Gt Baddow

Chelmsf 71-72; PtO *Win* 81-87; rtd 99. *8 Glencarron Way, Southampton SO16 7EF* T: (023) 8032 5162
E: george.bartlett@cwcom.net

BARTLETT, Prof John Raymond. b 37. BNC Ox BA 59 MA 62 BLitt 62 TCD MA 70 LittD 94. Linc Th Coll 61. **d** 63 **p** 64. C W Bridgford *S'well* 63-66; Lect Div TCD 66-86; Assoc Prof Bibl Studies 86-92; Fell 75-92; Prof Past Th 90-01; Prin CITC 89-01; Treas Ch Ch Cathl Dublin 86-88; Prec 88-01; rtd 01. *102 Sorrento Road, Dalkey, Co Dublin, Republic of Ireland* T: (00353) (1) 284 7786 E: jrbartlett@eircom.net

BARTLETT, Kenneth Vincent John. b 36. OBE 93. Oriel Coll Ox BA 61 BTh 63. Ripon Hall Ox 61. **d** 63 **p** 64. C Paddington St Jas *Lon* 63-67; LtO from 67; rtd 01. *25 Tudor Road, Kingston-upon-Thames KT2 6AS* T: (020) 8541 0378
E: shaa4949@aol.com

BARTLETT, Canon Maurice Edward. b 33. G&C Coll Cam BA 59 MA 63. Wells Th Coll 59. **d** 60 **p** 61. C Batley All SS *Wakef* 60-64; Bp's Dom Chapl 64-66; Dir of Ords 64-66; Asst Chapl HM Pris Wakef 64-66; V Allerton *Liv* 66-81; V Lancaster St Mary *Blackb* 81-97; Chapl HM Pris Lanc Castle 81-97; Hon Can Blackb Cathl 87-97; rtd 97. *Waverley House, Bowness-on-Solway, Wigton CA7 5AG*

BARTLETT, Michael Fredrick. b 52. Ex Univ BA 74 Liv Univ BPhil 75. Van English Coll Rome 74 Ripon Coll Cuddesdon BA 79 MA. **d** 79 **p** 80. C Kirkby *Liv* 79-82; C Wordsley *Lich* 82-83; TV 83-88; Chapl Wordsley Hosp 82-88; TV Redditch, The Ridge *Worc* 88-05; TR Redditch Ch the K from 05. *St Peter's House, Littlewoods, Redditch B97 5LB* T: (01527) 545709

✠**BARTLETT, The Rt Revd Peter.** b 54. **d** 96 **p** 97 **c** 08. SAMS Bolivia 96-05; TV Parr *Liv* 05-08; Bp Paraguay from 08. *Iglesia Anglicana Paraguya, Casilla de Correo 1124, Asunción, Paraguay* T: (00595) (21) 200933 *or* 214795 E: iapar@sce.cnc.una.py

BARTLETT, Canon Richard Charles. b 68. St Kath Coll Liv BA 90 Surrey Univ MA 01. Westcott Ho Cam 91. **d** 94 **p** 95. C Wareham *Sarum* 94-98; Assoc V Ealing All SS *Lon* 98-02; Chapl Twyford C of E High Sch Acton 98-02; USPG Brazil 02-05; Hon Can Brasilia Cathl from 05; V Northwood H Trin *Lon* from 05; AD Harrow 07-13. *Holy Trinity Vicarage, Gateway Close, Northwood HA6 2RP* T: (01923) 825732
E: richard.bartlett@london.anglican.org

BARTLETT, Allan Benjamin. b 77. Univ Coll Lon BA 98 York Univ MA 99 PhD 04. Ripon Coll Cuddesdon 05. **d** 08 **p** 09. C Louth *Linc* 08-09; C Saxilby Gp 09-11; P-in-c Aylmerton, Runton, Beeston Regis and Gresham *Nor* 11-13; PtO 14-15; Chapl Univ of Wales (Trin St Dav) *St D* from 15. *The Chaplaincy, Forest Road, Lampeter SA48 8AN* T: (01570) 424759
E: vitrearum@googlemail.com

BARTON, Andrew Edward. b 53. St Jo Coll Ox MA 77 DPhil 80 Idaho Univ MTh 06 MRSC. Ridley Hall Cam 87. **d** 90 **p** 91. C Ringwood *Win* 90-94; R Baughurst, Ramsdell, Wolverton w Ewhurst etc 95-07; R Auchterarder and Muthill *St And* 07-14; Chapl N Police Convalescent Homes 07-14; P-in-c Headley All SS *Guildf* from 14; LtO Adelaide Australia from 09. *All Saints' Rectory, High Street, Headley, Bordon GU35 8PP* M: 07778-771651
E: james.kessog@gmail.com *or* priest@allsaintsheadley.plus.com

BARTON, Andrew Peter. b 70. Loughb Univ BEng 92 Cam Univ BTh 12. Westcott Ho Cam 10. **d** 12 **p** 14. C Yelverton, Meavy, Sheepstor and Walkhampton *Ex* 12-14; C Bere Ferrers from 14. *The Vicarage, 1 Manor Farm, Dousland, Yelverton PL20 6NR* M: 07977-400179 E: apbarton@sky.com *or* apbarton@me.com

BARTON, Canon Arthur Michael. b 33. CCC Cam BA 57 MA 61. Wycliffe Hall Ox 57. **d** 59 **p** 60. Min Can Bradf Cathl 59-61; C Maltby *Sheff* 61-63; V Silsden *Bradf* 63-70; V Moor Allerton *Ripon* 70-81; TR 81-82; V Wetherby 82-98; Chapl HM YOI Wetherby 82-89; RD Harrogate *Ripon* 88-95; Hon Can Ripon Cathl 89-98; rtd 98; PtO *Leeds* from 98. *42 Church Square Mansions, Church Square, Harrogate HG1 4SS* T: (01423) 520105 E: teambarton@aol.com

BARTON, Caroline Janet. *See* BAKER, Caroline Janet

BARTON, The Ven Charles John Greenwood. b 36. ALCD 63. **d** 63 **p** 64. C Cant St Mary Bredin 63-66; V Whitfield w W Langdon 66-75; V S Kensington St Luke *Lon* 75-83; AD Chelsea 80-83; Chief Broadcasting Officer for C of E 83-90; Adn Aston *Birm* 90-03; Can Res Birm Cathl 90-02; P-in-c Bickenhill 02-03; rtd 03; PtO *Cant* from 03; Abp's Communications Adv *York* 05-06; Acting Hon Adv to Abp York 07; Abp's Chapl and Researcher 08. *7 The Spires, Canterbury CT2 8SD* M: 07743-118544 E: johnbarton@waitrose.com

BARTON, Dale. b 49. Selw Coll Cam BA 71 MA 76. Linc Th Coll 71. **d** 73 **p** 74. C Gosforth All SS *Newc* 73-77; Lesotho 77-81; Dep Warden CA Hostel Cam 82-83; C Shepton Mallet w Doulting *B & W* 83-88; TV Preston St Steph *Blackb* 88-96;

V 96-99; Bp's Adv on Inter-Faith Relns 99-07; P-in-c Bradf St Clem *Leeds* from 07; P-in-c Bradf St Aug Undercliffe from 07. *The Vicarage, 294A Barkerend Road, Bradford BD3 9DF* T: (01274) 665109 E: dale.barton720@gmail.com

BARTON, David Gerald Story. b 38. Selw Coll Cam BA 62 MA 66. Cuddesdon Coll 63. **d** 65 **p** 66. C Cowley St Jas *Ox* 65-67; C Hambleden 67-70; Hon C Hammersmith St Jo *Lon* 72-77; Hon C Paddington St Jas 77-81; Hd Master Soho Par Sch 81-88; Hon C Westmr St Jas *Lon* 81-92; RE Project Officer Lon Dioc Bd for Schs 88-92; Dioc Schs Adv *Ox* 93-99; rtd 00; Hon C Iffley *Ox* 93-06; PtO from 06. *254 Iffley Road, Oxford OX4 1SE* T: (01865) 240059 E: daviebarton@aol.com

BARTON, Edward. b 23. **d** 75 **p** 76. C Budock *Truro* 75-79; P-in-c St Stithians w Perranarworthal 79-80; V St Stythians w Perranarworthal and Gwennap 80-82; rtd 88; PtO *Truro* from 98. *Riversmeet, 5 Riviera Estate, Malpas, Truro TR1 1SR* T: (01872) 271686

BARTON, Canon Geoffrey. b 27. Oriel Coll Ox BA 48 MA 52. Chich Th Coll 49. **d** 51 **p** 52. C Arnold *S'well* 51-53; C E Retford 53-54; V Mirfield Eastthorpe St Paul *Wakef* 54-60; V Boroughbridge w Roecliffe *Ripon* 60-73; V Aldborough w Boroughbridge and Roecliffe 73; P-in-c Farnham w Scotton and Staveley and Copgrove 73-74; R 74-77; Chapl Roundway Hosp Devizes 77-92; Can and Preb Sarum Cathl 86-92; rtd 92; PtO *Sarum* from 01. *4B Willow House, Downlands Road, Devizes SN10 5EA* T: (01380) 725311

BARTON (née CRABB), Helen Maria. b 56. Lon Bible Coll BA 83 St Jo Coll Dur MA 04 St Mary's Coll Strawberry Hill PGCE 98. Cranmer Hall Dur 01. **d** 03 **p** 04. C Wisley w Pyrford *Guildf* 03-04; C Lanchester *Dur* 04-06; C Hexham *Newc* 06-08; V Widdrington 08-15; P-in-c Barlaston *Lich* from 15. *The Vicarage, 2 Longton Road, Barlaston, Stoke-on-Trent ST12 9AA* E: helen@the-bartons.com

BARTON, John. *See* BARTON, Charles John Greenwood

BARTON, Canon John. b 25. MBE 91. Keble Coll Ox BA 48 MA 50. Ely Th Coll 48. **d** 50 **p** 51. C Worksop St Anne *S'well* 50-53; C Harrogate St Wilfrid *Ripon* 53-56; V Beeston Hill H Spirit 56-60; Chapl Pinderfields and Stanley Royd Hosp Wakef 60-72; RD Wakef 68-72; Chapl Jo Radcliffe Hosp and Radcliffe Infirmary 72-90; Chapl Chu Hosp Ox 72-89; Hon Can Ch Ch *Ox* 77-94; RD Cowley 89-94; rtd 90; PtO *Ox* 94-01; *Roch* from 01. *150A Longlands Road, Sidcup DA15 7LF* T: (020) 8300 7073

BARTON, Prof John. b 48. Keble Coll Ox BA 69 MA 73 Mert Coll Ox DPhil 74 St Cross Coll Ox DLitt 88. **d** 73 **p** 73. Jun Research Fell Mert Coll Ox 73-74; Lect St Cross Coll Ox 74-89; Fell 74-91; Chapl 79-91; Lect Th Ox Univ 74-89; Reader 89-91; Oriel and Laing Prof of Interpr of H Scrip from 91; Fell Oriel Coll Ox from 91; Can Th Win Cathl 91-03. *11 Withington Court, Abingdon OX14 3QA* T: (01235) 525925
E: johnbarton@oriel.ox.ac.uk

BARTON, John Michael. b 40. TCD BA 62 Div Test. **d** 63 **p** 64. C Coleraine *Conn* 63-68; C Portadown St Mark *Arm* 68-71; I Carnteel and Crilly 71-83; I Derryloran 83-97; Bp's C Acton and Drumbanagher 97-09; Can Arm Cathl 94-09; Treas 98-01; Chan Arm Cathl 01-09; rtd 09. *23 Strand Cottages, Sheskburn Avenue, Ballycastle BT54 6HR* T: (028) 2076 9673
E: jm7mabarton@talktalk.net

BARTON, Mrs Margaret Ann Edith. b 48. Newc Univ BA 71. EMMTC 95. **d** 98 **p** 99. NSM Castle Bytham w Creeton *Linc* 98-04; P-in-c Corby Glen 04-12; rtd 12; PtO *Linc* from 13. *Blanchland House, 15 Swinstead Road, Corby Glen, Grantham NG33 4NU* T: (01476) 550763

BARTON, Michael. *See* BARTON, Arthur Michael

BARTON, Michael James. b 78. Sheff Univ MEng 01 Man Univ BSc 06. Wycliffe Hall Ox 11. **d** 13 **p** 14. C Claygate *Guildf* from 13. *4 Ashton Place, Claygate, Esher KT10 0BN* M: 07866-508697 E: mikebarton@holytrinityclaygate.org.uk

BARTON, Patrick Michael. Huddersfield Univ BA. BTh. **d** 05 **p** 06. C Arm St Mark 05-08; I Ballintoy w Rathlin and Dunseverick *Conn* from 08. *The Rectory, 2 Ballinlea Road, Ballintoy, Ballycastle BT54 6NQ* T: (028) 2076 8155
E: patribart@aol.com

BARTON, Paul. **d** 14. NSM Torquay St Matthias, St Mark and H Trin *Ex* from 14. *Rowdale, Ridge Road, Maidencombe, Torquay TQ1 4TD* T: (01803) 327504

BARTON (née McVEIGH), Mrs Sandra. b 58. Reading Univ BA 80. Cranmer Hall Dur 93. **d** 95 **p** 96. C Stranton *Dur* 95-98; P-in-c Blackhall, Castle Eden and Monkhesleden 98-99; R 99-02; PtO *Blackb* 02-06; *Ely* 06-10; *St E* 08-11; C Mildenhall

from 11. *The Old Village Stores, 6 The Street, Freckenham, Bury St Edmunds IP28 8HZ* T: (01638) 720770
E: revsandiebarton@gmail.com

BARTON, Stephen Christian. b 52. Macquarie Univ (NSW) BA 75 DipEd 75 Lanc Univ MA 78 K Coll Lon PhD 92. Cranmer Hall Dur 91. **d** 93 **p** 94. NSM Neville's Cross St Jo CD *Dur* 93-00; NSM Dur St Marg and Neville's Cross St Jo 00-06; PtO *Newc* 06-15; *Lich* from 15. *The Vicarage, 2 Longton Road, Barlaston, Stoke-on-Trent ST12 9AA*
E: s.c.barton@durham.ac.uk

BARTON, Stephen William. b 50. St Jo Coll Cam BA 73 Leeds Univ MPhil 81. Coll of Resurr Mirfield 75. **d** 77 **p** 78. C Horton *Bradf* 77-80; USPG 80-92; Presbyter Dhaka St Thos Bangladesh 81-88; St Andr Th Coll Dhaka 88-92; TV Southampton (City Cen) *Win* 92-98; Chapl Manager Birm Women's Healthcare NHS Trust 99-06; rtd 06; PtO *Birm* from 09. *290 City Road, Birmingham B16 0NE* T: 0121-429 2176
E: notrabnehpets@yahoo.co.uk

BARTON, Timothy Charles. b 47. Sarum & Wells Th Coll 73. **d** 76 **p** 77. C Upholland *Liv* 76-80; V Dalton 80-15; rtd 15. *Address temp unknown*

BARTON, Trevor James. b 50. St Alb Minl Tr Scheme 79. **d** 87 **p** 88. NSM Hemel Hempstead *St Alb* from 87. *46 Crossfell Road, Hemel Hempstead HP3 8RQ* T/F: (01442) 251537
E: trevorbarton@hotmail.com

BARWELL, Brian Bernard Beale. b 30. Preston Poly CertEd 79. AKC 59 St Boniface Warminster 59. **d** 60 **p** 61. C Heywood St Jas *Man* 60-63; V Smallbridge 63-69; V Farington *Blackb* 69-72; C-in-c Blackb St Luke w St Phil 72-75; C Standish 75-76; LtO 76-92; rtd 92; PtO *Blackb* 92-11. *70 Claytongate, Coppull, Chorley PR7 4PS* T: (01257) 794251

BARZEY, Ms Michele Alison Lesley. b 63. Trin Coll Bris BA 94. **d** 94. C Gravelly Hill *Birm* 94-96; PtO 00-06. *6 Topcliffe House, Yatesbury Avenue, Birmingham B35 6DU* T: 0121-730 3094

BASAVARAJ, Mrs Patricia Margaret. b 37. SRN 61 SCM 62. **d** 00. OLM Verwood *Sarum* 00-07; PtO 07-08. *Hope Cottage, Church Hill, Verwood BH31 6HT* T: (01202) 822920

BASFORD HOLBROOK, Colin Eric. b 42. St Steph Ho Ox 73. **d** 75 **p** 76. C Dovecot *Liv* 75-78; V Hollinfare 79-83; CMS 83-88; Cyprus 83-91; Chapl Athens w Kifissia, Patras, Thessaloniki etc *Eur* 91-93; Chapl Athens w Patras, Thessaloniki and Voula 93-94; rtd 02. *31 Church Street, Uttoxeter ST14 8AG*

BASH, Anthony. b 52. Bris Univ LLB 73 LLM 76 Glas Univ BD 88 Clare Hall Cam PhD 96. Westcott Ho Cam 94. **d** 96 **p** 97. C Kingston upon Hull H Trin *York* 96-99; V N Ferriby 99-04; Chapl to Legal Profession 97-04; Hon Fell Hull Univ 97-04; Chapl and Fell Univ Coll Dur 05-06; TR Dur N 06-08; Chapl and Tutor Hatf Coll Dur from 08; Hon Research Fell Univ Coll Dur from 08. *Hatfield College, North Bailey, Durham DH1 3RQ* T: 0191-334 2636
E: anthony.bash@durham.ac.uk

BASHFORD, Richard Frederick. b 36. Clifton Th Coll. **d** 68 **p** 69. C Bedworth *Cov* 68-71; C Lower Homerton St Paul *Lon* 71-75; V Bordesley Green *Birm* 75-81; R Birm Bp Latimer w All SS 81-06; rtd 06. *244 Adams Hill, Birmingham B32 3PD* T: 0121-421 1807 E: domusmariae@blueyonder.co.uk

BASHFORD, Robert Thomas. b 49. Ch Coll Cam BA 70 CertEd 72 MA 74 Lon Univ BD 84 MPhil 89. Oak Hill Th Coll 86. **d** 88 **p** 89. C Frinton *Chelmsf* 88-91; C Galleywood Common 91-96; V Clapham *St Alb* 96-02; P-in-c Westgate St Jas *Cant* 02-06; V 06-12; rtd 12; PtO *Pet* from 13. *66 Grosvenor Way, Barton Seagrave, Kettering NN15 6TZ* T: (01536) 723056 E: randbbashford@hotmail.com

BASHFORTH, Canon Alan George. b 64. Ex Univ MA. Ripon Coll Cuddesdon BTh 96. **d** 96 **p** 97. C Calstock *Truro* 96-98; C St Ives 98-01; V St Agnes and Mount Hawke w Mithian 01-14; P-in-c St Clement 12-14; RD Powder 04-12; Hon Can Truro Cathl 13-14; Can Res and Chan Truro Cathl from 14; Hon C Truro St Mary from 15. *The Cathedral Office, 14 St Mary's Street, Truro TR1 2AF* T: (01872) 245012
E: alanbashforth@trurocathedral.org.uk

BASINGSTOKE, Suffragan Bishop of. *See* WILLIAMS, The Rt Revd David Grant

BASKERVILLE, John. b 45. Open Univ BA 78. Sarum & Wells Th Coll 92. **d** 93 **p** 94. C Wanstead St Mary w Ch Ch *Chelmsf* 93-96; C Chingford SS Pet and Paul 96-98; V Felkirk w Brierley *Wakef* 98-04; rtd 04. *131 Howard Road, Upminster RM14 2UQ* T: (01708) 641242 M: 07710-209469

BASON, Mrs Carol. b 44. De Montfort Univ BSc 96. **d** 09 **p** 10. OLM S Lawres Gp *Linc* from 09. *Walnut Tree Cottage, 15 Church Lane, Reepham, Lincoln LN3 4DQ* T: (01522) 753282 M: 07749-211397 E: cbason@tiscali.co.uk

BASS, Colin Graham. b 41. Liv Univ BSc 62 Fitzw Ho Cam BA 64 MA 68. Ox NSM Course 84. **d** 87 **p** 88. Dir of Studies Leighton Park Sch Reading 87-97; NSM Earley St Pet *Ox* 87-92;

NSM Reading Deanery 92-11; PtO from 11. *9 Bramley Close, Reading RG6 7PL* T: 0118-966 3732 E: colin.bass@lineone.net

BASS, George Michael. b 39. Ely Th Coll 62. **d** 65 **p** 66. C Romaldkirk *Ripon* 65-68; C Kenton Ascension *Newc* 68-71; CF 71-94; Chapl Northumbria Healthcare NHS Trust 95-02; rtd 02; PtO *Newc* from 02. *35 Kelso Drive, North Shields NE29 9NS* T: 0191-258 2514

BASS, Mrs Marguerite Rowena. b 61. MA BD ARCM. St Jo Coll Nottm. **d** 05 **p** 06. C Wellingborough All SS *Pet* 05-08; PtO 08-11; Chapl HM Pris Rye Hill 08; Chapl St Andr Hosp Northn 08-10; Chapl Cambs and Pet NHS Foundn Trust 10-12; P-in-c High Framland Par *Leic* from 12. *High Framland Rectory, 5 Croxton Lane, Harston, Grantham NG32 1PP* T: (01933) 460213 E: bassrowena@btopenworld.com

BASS, Mrs Rosemary Jane. b 38. Linc Th Coll 76. **dss** 79 **d** 87 **p** 94. Bedford All SS *St Alb* 79-84; Leavesden 84-94; Par Dn 87-94; C 94-95; V Luton St Andr 95-01; rtd 01; PtO *St Alb* from 01. *3 Highfield Road, Oakley, Bedford MK43 7TA* T: (01234) 822126 E: roanj@btinternet.com

BASSETT, Mrs Rosemary Louise. b 42. STETS. **d** 00 **p** 01. NSM The Winterbournes and Compton Valence *Sarum* 00-08; P-in-c 03-08; NSM Dorchester 08-14; PtO from 14. *12 Lime Close, Dorchester DT1 2HQ* T: (01305) 262615
E: trl@bassett-online.com

BASSFORD, Toby Paul. b 79. Sheff Univ BA 00 MA 13. **d** 13 **p** 14. C Philadelphia St Thos *Sheff* from 13. *17 Shirley Road, Sheffield S3 9AH* T: 0114-241 9560 M: 07740-363970
E: toby@citybase.org

BASTABLE, Richard Michael. b 83. Ex Univ BA 04 St Edm Coll Cam MPhil 08. Westcott Ho Cam 06. **d** 08 **p** 09. C Ruislip St Martin *Lon* 08-10; C St Andr Holborn 10-13; V Hammersmith St Luke from 13. *St Luke's Vicarage, 450 Uxbridge Road, London W12 0NS* T: (020) 8749 7523 M: 07816-074597 E: rbastable@gmail.com

BASTEN, Richard Henry. b 40. Codrington Coll Barbados 60. **d** 63 **p** 64. Br Honduras 63-67; Barbados 68-72; C Hartlepool H Trin *Dur* 72-73; Chapl Bedstone Coll 73-88; C Clun w Chapel Lawn *Heref* 73-77; P-in-c Clungunford 77-78; R Clungunford w Clunbury and Clunton, Bedstone etc 78-88; R Rowde and Poulshot *Sarum* 88-95; rtd 95; PtO *Glouc* from 95. *41 Bewley Way, Churchdown, Gloucester GL3 2DU* T: (01452) 859738

BASTIDE, Derek. b 44. Dur Univ BA 65 Reading Univ DipEd 66 Sussex Univ MA 77. Chich Th Coll 76. **d** 77 **p** 78. Hon C Lewes All SS, St Anne, St Mich and St Thos *Chich* 77-84; Prin Lect Brighton Poly 80-92; Prin Lect Brighton Univ from 92; P-in-c Hamsey *Chich* from 84. *The Rectory, Offham, Lewes BN7 3PX* T: (01273) 474356
E: dandj@bastide8.wanadoo.co.uk

BASTON, Caroline Jane. b 56. Birm Univ BSc 78 CertEd 79. Ripon Coll Cuddesdon 87. **d** 89 **p** 94. Par Dn Southampton Thornhill St Chris *Win* 89-94; C 94-95; R Win All SS w Chilcomb and Chesil 95-06; Dioc Communications Officer 95-98; Dioc Dir of Ords 99-06; Hon Can Win Cathl 00-06; Adn Is of Wight *Portsm* 06-11; P-in-c N Swindon St Andr *Bris* from 11; Warden CSMV from 13. *8 Figsbury Close, Swindon SN25 1UA* T: (01793) 702715
E: cjbaston17@gmail.com

BATCHELOR, Alan Harold. b 30. Bris Univ BA 54 Hull Univ MA 63. Linc Th Coll 54. **d** 56 **p** 57. C Kingston upon Hull St Alb *York* 56-60; C Attercliffe w Carbrook *Sheff* 60-62; India 63-87; Ind Chapl *Ripon* 87-95; C Kirkstall 92-95; rtd 95; PtO *Leeds* from 01. *16 Moor Grange Rise, Leeds LS16 5BP* T: 0113-226 9671

BATCHELOR, Andrew George. b 59. St Jo Coll Nottm 07. **d** 09 **p** 10. C Ulverston St Mary w H Trin *Carl* 09-13; V Walney Is from 13. *St Mary's Vicarage, Promenade, Walney, Barrow-in-Furness LA14 3QU* M: 07934-483439 T: (01229) 227976
E: rev.andyb@gmail.com

BATCHELOR, John Millar. CITC 76. **d** 78 **p** 79. C Belfast All SS *Conn* 78-80; I Eglish w Killylea *Arm* 80-96; I Ballyhalbert w Ardkeen *D & D* 96-01; rtd 01. *Rhone Brae, 102 Eglish Road, Dungannon BT70 1LB* T: (028) 8775 0177
E: jm-batchelor@outlook.com

BATCHELOR, Martin John. b 60. Plymouth Poly BSc 91. St Jo Coll Nottm MA 95. **d** 95 **p** 96. C Brecon St Mary and Battle w Llanddew *S & B* 95-97; Min Can Brecon Cathl 95-97; C Sketty 97-00; TV Hawarden *St As* 00-05; V Bistre from 05; AD Hawarden from 10. *Bistre Vicarage, Mold Road, Buckley CH7 2NH* T: (01244) 550947 E: martinbtchlr@gmail.com

BATCHELOR, Michael Patrick. b 55. Qu Coll Birm 11. **d** 13 **p** 14. OLM Willenhall St Steph *Lich* from 13. *24 Rockland Gardens, Willenhall WV13 3HP* T: (01902) 606615
E: m.batchelor922@btinternet.com

BATCHELOR, Veronica. b 47. **d** 10 **p** 11. NSM Forest and Avon *Sarum* from 10. *Evergreen, Hale Purlieu, Fordingbridge SP6 2NN* T: (01725) 513878 E: batchelor446@btinternet.com

BATCHFORD, Philip John. b 71. Sheff Univ BA 99. Ridley Hall Cam 00. **d** 02 **p** 03. C Sheff St Mary Bramall Lane 02-05; V Netherthorpe St Steph 05-13; P-in-c Sheff St Bart 11-13; V Sheffield Vine from 13; AD Hallam from 13. *The Vicarage, 115 Upperthorpe Road, Sheffield S6 3EA* T: 0114-276 7130
E: phil.batchford@sheffield.anglican.org

BATCOCK, Neil Gair. b 53. UEA BA 74. Westcott Ho Cam 94. **d** 96 **p** 97. C Barton upon Humber *Linc* 96-99; TV Totnes w Bridgetown, Berry Pomeroy etc *Ex* 99-06; P-in-c Blakeney w Cley, Wiveton, Glandford etc *Nor* 06-10; R 10-13; P-in-c Walpole St Peter w Walpole St Andrew *Ely* 13-15; P-in-c W Walton 13-15; rtd 15; PtO *Nor* from 15. *104 London Road, King's Lynn PE30 5ES* T: (01553) 768547 M: 07584-070123
E: gair2@aol.com

BATE, Dylan Griffin. b 48. Mon Dioc Tr Scheme 91. **d** 94 **p** 95. NSM Fleur-de-Lis *Mon* 94-96; NSM Bedwellty 96-97; C Pontypool 97-99; C Tenby *St D* 99-02; R Begelly w Ludchurch and Crunwere 02-05; C Risca *Mon* 05-13; rtd 13; NSM Lower Islwyn *Mon* from 13. *The Vicarage, Twyn Road, Abercarn, Newport NP11 5GU* T: (01495) 246553

BATE, Miss Jennifer Anne. b 50. Ches Univ BA 15. St Jo Coll Nottm 10. **d** 12 **p** 13. C Allonby, Cross Canonby and Dearham *Carl* from 12. *Solway Bungalow, Pow Hill, Kirkbride, Wigton CA7 5LF* T: (016973) 51873
E: jennybate@btinternet.com

BATE, Preb Lawrence Mark. b 40. Univ Coll Ox BA 63. Coll of Resurr Mirfield 65. **d** 67 **p** 68. C Benwell St Jas *Newc* 67-69; C Monkseaton St Pet 69-72; TV Withycombe Raleigh *Ex* 72-84; RD Aylesbeare 81-84; R Alphington 84-00; RD Christianity 95-99; TV Heavitree w Ex St Paul 00-02; TV Heavitree and St Mary Steps 02-05; Preb Ex Cathl 02-10; rtd 05. *Chapple Court, Kenn, Exeter EX6 7UR* T: (01392) 833485 E: morleybate@freeuk.com

BATE, Michael Keith. b 42. Lich Th Coll 67. **d** 69 **p** 70. C W Bromwich St Jas *Lich* 69-73; C Thornhill *Wakef* 73-76; V Wrenthorpe 76-82; V Upper Gornal *Lich* 82-93; V Worc 93-05; TV Gornal and Sedgley 05-08; Chapl Burton Road Hosp Dudley 82-94; Chapl Dudley Gp of Hosps NHS Trust 94-00; rtd 08; PtO *Lich* from 09. *44 Wentworth Road, Wolverhampton WV10 8EF* E: michael.bate@tesco.net

BATE, Stephen Donald. b 58. Sheff Univ BSc 79 Cov Univ PhD 92 CEng 97 MIET 97. **d** 05 **p** 06. OLM Whitnash *Cov* 05-12; C Stratford-upon-Avon, Luddington etc from 12. *3 Coopers Close, Stratford-upon-Avon CV37 0RS* T: (01789) 299195 M: 07773-583356 E: sbate@aol.com

BATEMAN, James Edward. b 44. Univ Coll Lon BSc 65. Trin Coll Bris 71. **d** 74 **p** 75. C Woodlands *Sheff* 74-77; C Rushden w Newton Bromswold *Pet* 77-84; R Vange *Chelmsf* 84-94; V Southminster 94-01; P-in-c Nazeing and Roydon 01-03; Warden Stacklands Retreat Ho W Kingsdown 03-05; C Rainham *Roch* 05-09; rtd 09; PtO *Pet* 11-14. *11 Ryeburn Way, Wellingborough NN8 3AH* T: (01933) 440106
E: jimbateman@talktalk.net

BATEMAN, Leslie Adrian. b 61. **d** 14 **p** 15. C Goole *Sheff* from 14. *9 Sundrew Avenue, Goole DN14 6FD* T: (01405) 720315 M: 07735-536046 E: curateatgoole@outlook.com *or* adrian.bateman@sheffield.anglican.org

BATEMAN, Nest Wynne. Univ of Wales (Cardiff) BA 71 CQSW 73. Westcott Ho Cam 08. **d** 09 **p** 10. NSM Lich Cathl from 09. *21 Christchurch Lane, Lichfield WS13 8BA* T: (01543) 257681 M: 07729-256364 E: nestbateman@aol.com

BATEMAN, Patrick John. b 64. Ches Univ BA 14. St Jo Coll Nottm 99. **d** 01 **p** 02. C Wallington *S'wark* 01-05; P-in-c Chipstead 05-11; R 11-12; V Ilkley All SS *Leeds* from 12. *58 Curly Hill, Ilkley LS29 0DA* T: (01943) 431126 M: 07764-171400 E: vicar@ilkleyallsaints.org.uk

BATES, David Frederick. b 61. St Mellitus Coll BA 15. **d** 15. NSM Mardyke *Chelmsf* from 15. *22 Nordmann Place, South Ockendon RM15 6XA*

BATES, Elaine Austwick. b 57. Newc Univ BSc 79 MSc 80 Lanc Univ PGCE 00. LCTP 06. **d** 10 **p** 11. NSM Barrow St Paul *Carl* from 10. *17 Harrel Lane, Barrow-in-Furness LA13 9LN* T: (01229) 822149 E: elaine@stpaulsbarrow.org.uk *or* ebates@live.co.uk

✠**BATES, The Rt Revd Gordon.** b 34. Kelham Th Coll 54. **d** 58 **p** 59 **c** 83. C New Eltham All SS *S'wark* 58-62; Asst Youth Chapl *Glouc* 62-64; Youth Chapl Liv 65-69; Chapl Liv Cathl 65-69; V Huyton St Mich 69-73; Can Res and Prec Liv Cathl 73-83; Dir of Ords 73-83; Suff Bp Whitby *York* 83-99; rtd 99; Hon Asst Bp Carl and Blackb 99-09; NSM Kirkby Lonsdale *Carl* 03-09; Hon Asst Bp York from 12. *19 Fernwood Close, Brompton, Northallerton DL6 2UX* T: (01609) 761586

BATES, James. b 46. Linc Th Coll 73. **d** 75 **p** 76. C Ewell *Guildf* 75-77; C Farncombe 77-80; V Pet St Mary Boongate 80-92; V Kingston All SS w St Jo *S'wark* 92-05; P-in-c Win St Cross w St Faith and Master St Cross Hosp 05-07; V Offerton *Ches*

07-12; rtd 12. *166 Donaghadee Road, Bangor BT20 4PB* T: (028) 9147 3068

BATES, James Paul. b 64. QUB BSc PGCE Cranfield Univ MSc MPhil. **d** 06. NSM Bangor Abbey *D & D* 06-07. *16 Craigowen Road, Holywood BT18 0DL* T: (028) 9042 2077
E: paul_tssf@hotmail.com

BATES, Mrs Nichola Jane. b 63. Trin Coll Bris 09. **d** 11 **p** 12. C Freiston, Butterwick w Bennington, and Leverton *Linc* 11-14; C Old Leake w Wrangle 11-14; C Friskney 11-14; C Stamford Ch 14-15; C Stamford St Geo w St Paul 14-15; V Stamford Ch Ch from 15. *28 Little Casterton Road, Stamford PE9 1BE* M: 07760-484793 T: (01780) 766026

BATES, Robert John. b 50. FRICS 81. EAMTC 99. **d** 02 **p** 03. NSM Pet St Mary Boongate 02-05; C Ketton, Collyweston, Easton-on-the-Hill etc 05-09; Chapl Algarve *Eur* 09-14; Chapl Oporto from 14. *St James, Largo de Matermidade Júlio Dinis, 4050 Porto, Portugal* T: (00351) (22) 609 1006
E: rev.bobbates@virgin.net

BATES, Mrs Rosemary Eileen Hamilton. b 45. Ripon Coll Cuddesdon 87. **d** 89 **p** 94. Par Dn Brackley St Pet w St Jas 89-94; C 94-95; P-in-c N Hinksey and Wytham *Ox* 95-04; rtd 04; PtO *Ely* 04-08. *12 rue Hugo Derville, 56110 Gourin, France* T: (0033) 2 97 23 57 18 E: revrosie@rosiebates.com

BATES, Stuart Geoffrey. b 61. Univ of Wales (Lamp) BA 82. St Steph Ho Ox 83. **d** 85 **p** 86. C Bromley St Mark *Roch* 85-88; C Westmr St Matt *Lon* 88-89; C Gt Ilford St Mary *Chelmsf* 89-95; V Crofton Park St Hilda w St Cypr *S'wark* from 95. *St Hilda's Vicarage, 35 Buckthorne Road, London SE4 2DG* T: (020) 8699 1277

BATES, Mrs Susan Rita. b 65. ERMC 12. **d** 15. C Yoxmere *St E* from 15. *The Vicarage, 1 Oakwood Park, Yoxford, Saxmundham IP17 3JU* T: (01728) 667095 M: 07944-159606
E: soobeedoo@hotmail.com

BATES, Thomas Henry Robert St John. b 83. Univ of Wales BMus 07 Cardiff Univ BTh 15. St Mich Coll Llan 11. **d** 14 **p** 15. C Merthyr Tydfil St Dav and Abercanaid *Llan* from 14. *4 Lancaster Terrace, Merthyr Tydfil CF47 8SL* T: (01685) 386072 E: frtombates@hotmail.com

BATES, William Frederic. b 49. St Jo Coll Dur BSc 72 BA 74 MA 97. Cranmer Hall Dur. **d** 75 **p** 76. C Knutsford St Jo and Toft *Ches* 75-78; C Ripley *Derby* 78-80; R Nether and Over Seale 81-93; V Lullington 81-93; V Allestree St Nic from 93; Bp's Adv on New Relig Movements from 99; P-in-c Quarndon from 00; RD Duffield 09-10. *The Vicarage, 4 Lawn Avenue, Allestree, Derby DE22 2PE* T: (01332) 550224
E: williambates@btconnect.com

BATES, William Hugh. b 33. Keble Coll Ox BA 56 MA 59. Westcott Ho Cam 59. **d** 60 **p** 61. C Horsforth *Ripon* 60-63; Tutor St Chad's Coll Dur 63-70; V Bishop Wilton *York* 70-76; RD Pocklington 74-76; V Pickering 76-82; Prin NEOC 79-94; P-in-c Crayke w Brandsby and Yearsley *York* 82-94; P-in-c Stillington and Marton w Moxby 82-94; rtd 94; PtO *York* from 94. *2 The Bungalows, Main Street, Bugthorpe, York YO41 1QG* T: (01759) 368402

BATESON, Canon Geoffrey Frederick. b 27. K Coll Lon BD 51 AKC 51. **d** 52 **p** 53. C Tynemouth Cullercoats St Paul *Newc* 52-56; C Gosforth All SS 56-60; V Monkseaton St Pet 60-68; V Newc St Geo 68-77; RD Newc 75-77; R Morpeth 77-89; Chapl St Geo and Cottage Hosp Morpeth 77-89; Hon Can Newc Cathl 80-89; rtd 89; PtO *York* from 91. *1 Netherby Close, Sleights, Whitby YO22 5HD* T: (01947) 810997

BATESON, Canon James Howard. b 36. Qu Mary Coll Lon BSc 57 MSOSc 88. EMMTC 85. **d** 87 **p** 88. NSM W Bridgford *S'well* 87-88; NSM Wilford Hill 88-95; Dioc Officer for NSMs 94-04; P-in-c Kilvington and Staunton w Flawborough 96-04; Hon Can S'well Minster 99-04; rtd 04; PtO *S'well* from 04. *45 Stamford Road, West Bridgford, Nottingham NG2 6GD* T/F: 0115-923 1820 E: h_bateson@primeuk.net

BATESON, Keith Nigel. b 43. **d** 00 **p** 01. OLM Wonersh w Blackheath *Guildf* from 00. *Advent Cottage, Blackheath Lane, Wonersh, Guildford GU5 0PN* T: (01483) 892753
E: keith@batesonfamily.net

BATESON, Mrs Tracey Jane. b 74. St Mark & St Jo Coll Lon BEd 96. Trin Coll Bris BA 03 MPhil 04. **d** 04 **p** 05. C Holdenhurst and Iford *Win* 04-07; CF 07-13; C The Brents and Davington *Cant* from 13; C Ospringe from 13; C Faversham from 14. *The Vicarage, Brent Hill, Faversham ME13 7EF* T: (01795) 533272 E: rev.bateson@gmail.com

BATEY, Caroline Elizabeth. b 52. **d** 08 **p** 09. OLM Warrington H Trin *Liv* 08-14; OLM Warrington H Trin and St Ann from 14. *22 Fairclough Avenue, Warrington WA1 2JS*
E: cabethbatey@hotmail.com

BATH, David James William. b 43. Oak Hill NSM Course 87. **d** 89 **p** 90. NSM Henley *Ox* 89-90; Gen Manager Humberside Gd News Trust 90-96; NSM Anlaby St Pet *York* 96-04; P-in-c Anlaby Common St Mark 04-10; rtd 10. *24 Lawnswood, Hessle HU13 0PT* E: davidjwbath@hotmail.com

BATH AND WELLS, Bishop of. *See* HANCOCK, The Rt Revd Peter
BATH, Archdeacon of. *See* PIGGOTT, The Ven Andrew John
BATHURST, Bishop of. *See* HURFORD, Richard Warwick
BATLEY-GLADDEN, Dane Christopher. b 68. St Steph Ho Ox 96. d 99 p 00. C Hendon St Alphage *Lon* 99-01; C-in-c Grahame Park St Aug CD 01-14; V Swanley St Mary *Roch* from 14. *St Mary's Vicarage, London Road, Swanley BR8 7AQ* T: (01322) 662201 E: vicar@swanleyparish.org.uk
BATSON, Lee Paul. b 77. R Holloway Coll Lon BA 99 MA 00 Selw Coll Cam BA 03. Westcott Ho Cam 01. d 04 p 05. C Saffron Walden w Wendens Ambo, Littlebury etc *Chelmsf* 04-08; P-in-c Boreham from 08; Co Ecum Officer from 08; C N Springfield from 14; P-in-c E Hanningfield from 15. *The Vicarage, Church Road, Boreham, Chelmsford CM3 3EG* T: (01245) 451087 M: 07526-915645 E: lbatson@chelmsford.anglican.org
BATSON, Paul Leonard. b 47. Southn Univ BTh 79. Sarum & Wells Th Coll 73. d 75 p 76. C Chesham St Mary *Ox* 75-79; Dioc Youth Adv *Newc* 79-85; V Earley St Pet *Ox* 85-93; PtO *Sarum* 01-08; Hon C N Bradford on Avon and Villages 10-15; PtO from 15. *Maple Cottage, 78 Murhill, Limpley Stoke, Bath BA2 7FB* T: (01225) 722721 E: plbatson@gmail.com
BATSON, William Francis Robert. b 43. St Jo Coll Dur BA 72. Cranmer Hall Dur. d 73 p 74. C Eastwood *S'well* 73-77; R Long Marton w Dufton and w Milburn *Carl* 77-79; V Flimby 79-85; TR Raveningham *Nor* 85-91; R Kinver and Enville *Lich* 91-00; V Ledsham w Fairburn *York* 00-08; rtd 08; PtO *Carl* from 09. *8 Langdale Avenue, Carlisle CA2 5QG* T: (01228) 537798 E: bob.batson@btinternet.com
BATSTONE, Bruce. b 70. Bris Univ BA 92. St Steph Ho Ox 98. d 00 p 01. C Leigh-on-Sea St Marg *Chelmsf* 00-03; C Old St Pancras *Lon* 03-07; TV 07-11; Chapl Camden and Islington NHS Foundn Trust 03-11; R Hornsey St Mary w St Geo *Lon* from 11. *Hornsey Rectory, 140 Cranley Gardens, London N10 3AH* T: (020) 8883 6486 E: frbrucehornseyparishchurch@gmail.com
BATT, Canon Joseph William. b 39. Keele Univ BA 62. Ripon Hall Ox 63. d 64 p 65. C Bushbury *Lich* 64-68; C Walsall 68-71; Tr Officer and Youth Chapl Dio Ibadan Nigeria 71-75; Hon Can Oke-Osun from 94; Area Sec CMS Guildf and Chich 75-84; V Ottershaw *Guildf* 84-04; rtd 04; PtO *Leeds* from 07. *8 Parkwood Road, Shipley BD18 4SS* T: (01274) 589775 E: joe@jbatt.force9.co.uk
BATT, Canon Kenneth Victor. b 41. Wycliffe Hall Ox 68. d 71 p 72. C Yateley *Win* 71-76; R The Candover Valley 76-82; R Durrington *Sarum* 82-89; V Kempshott *Win* 89-00; P-in-c Bournemouth H Epiphany 00-05; V 05-08; rtd 08; Hon Can Win Cathl from 07; Hon C Tadley w Pamber Heath and Silchester from 08. *St Mary's House, 10 Romans Field, Silchester, Reading RG7 2QH* T: 0118-970 2353
BATT, Mrs Linda. d 14 p 15. NSM Magor *Mon* from 14. *44 Goossens Close, Newport NP19 9JN*
BATTE, Mrs Kathleen. b 47. Homerton Coll Cam TCert 68. NEOC 91. d 94 p 95. NSM Newc St Gabr 94-96; NSM Wilford Hill *S'well* 96-99; P-in-c Cinderhill 99-05; Bp's Adv for Self-Supporting Min 05-07; Chapl Crowhurst Chr Healing Cen 07-10; Sen Chapl 10-12; rtd 12. *10 Bracey Rise, West Bridgford, Nottingham NG2 7AX* T: 0115-923 4503 E: kath.batte@talk21.com
BATTEN, Stuart William. b 73. Univ of Wales (Abth) BD 94 MTh 96. Trin Coll Bris 96. d 98 p 99. C Northolt St Jos *Lon* 98-01; TV Hucknall Torkard *S'well* 01-06; P-in-c Wickham Bishops w Lt Braxted *Chelmsf* 06-14; P-in-c Barkingside H Trin from 14; P-in-c Barkingside St Fran from 15; Asst Dir of Ords from 06. *Holy Trinity Vicarage, 36 Mossford Green, Ilford IG6 2BJ* T: (020) 8550 2669 E: stuart.batten@btinternet.com
BATTERSBY, David George Sellers. b 32. AKC 57. St Boniface Warminster 57 Lambeth STh 80. d 58 p 59. C Glas St Marg 58-60; C Burnley St Pet *Blackb* 60-62; V Warton St Paul 62-71; Chapl K Wm's Coll Is of Man 71-91; C Ashchurch *Glouc* 91-97; rtd 97; PtO *Glouc* from 97; *Worc* from 97; *Ox* from 03. *Shill Brook Cottage, Buckland Road, Bampton OX18 2AA* T: (01993) 851414 E: dgsb@fan.com
BATTERSBY, Richard David. b 69. Sheff Univ BA 13 FCCA. Yorks Min Course 10. d 13 p 14. NSM Brayton *York* from 13. *8 Orchard End, Hemingbrough, Selby YO8 6RJ* T: (01757) 630641 M: 07795-302119 E: revrichardb@gmail.com
BATTERSBY, Simon Charles. b 64. Wycliffe Hall Ox BTh 01. d 01 p 02. C Askern *Sheff* 01-03; Chapl Bethany Sch Goudhurst 03-07; Chapl Culford Sch Bury St Edmunds from 08. *Culford School, Bury St Edmunds IP28 6TX* T: (01284) 728615 M: 07900-242757 E: chaplain@culford.co.uk
BATTERSHELL, Mrs Anne Marie. b 33. Ox Poly BEd 83. SAOMC 95. d 98 p 99. NSM Goring w S Stoke *Ox* 98-01;

NSM Brafferton w Pilmoor, Myton-on-Swale etc *York* 01-03; rtd 03; PtO *Leeds* from 04; *Man* from 07. *26 Winterbutlee Grove, Todmorden OL14 7QU* T: (01706) 839848 E: rev.anne@hotmail.co.uk
BATTERSHELL, Rachel Damaris. b 65. RN 88. SNWTP 08. d 11 p 12. C Coldhurst and Oldham St Steph *Man* 11-14; TV Ashton from 14. *2A Hutton Avenue, Ashton-under-Lyne OL6 6QY* M: 07563-630594 E: rev.rachel@hotmail.co.uk
BATTEY, Alexander Robert Fenwick. b 77. St Andr Univ MA 99. Ripon Coll Cuddesdon BA 04 MA 08. d 05 p 06. C Whitby w Aislaby and Ruswarp *York* 05-08; CF 08-12; V Old Basing and Lychpit *Win* from 12. *The Vicarage, Church Lane, Old Basing, Basingstoke RG24 7DJ* T: (01256) 354707 E: vicar@stmarysoldbasing.org
BATTIN (née WEBB), Mrs Frances Mary. b 52. WEMTC 92. d 95 p 96. NSM Inkberrow w Cookhill and Kington w Dormston *Worc* 95-98; Asst Chapl HM Pris Brockhill 98-03; PtO *Worc* 03-07; NSM Church Lench w Rous Lench and Abbots Morton etc from 07. *2 The Rowans, Harvington, Evesham WR11 8SX* T: (01386) 870159 E: franbattin@btinternet.com
BATTISON, David John. b 62. ACIB 93. St Jo Coll Nottm 07. d 09 p 10. C Matlock Bath and Cromford *Derby* 09-11; C Matlock Bank and Tansley from 11. *Blossom House, 4 Ashtree Close, Matlock DE4 3SJ* T: (01629) 581940 M: 07971-506088 E: davidbattison@btinternet.com
BATTISON, Mark Richard. b 62. EMMTC 01. d 04 p 05. NSM Leic St Jas 04-07; NSM Oadby 07-09; NSM Guilsborough and Hollowell and Cold Ashby etc *Pet* 09-11; R 11-14; P-in-c Barrowden and Wakerley w S Luffenham etc from 14. *The Rectory, 11 Church Lane, Barrowden, Oakham LE15 8ED* T: (01572) 747192 M: 07717-200777 E: markbattison@btinternet.com
BATTLE, Dean of. *See* EDMONDSON, The Very Revd John James William
BATTMAN, John Brian. b 37. ALCD 61. d 61 p 62. C Fulham Ch Ch *Lon* 61-64; SAMS Argentina 64-69; Paraguay 69-76; Adn Paraguay 70-76; Ext Sec SAMS 77-80; V Romford Gd Shep *Chelmsf* 80-92; V Werrington *Pet* 92-02; rtd 02; PtO *St E* from 02. *57 Glencoe Road, Ipswich IP4 3PP* T: (01473) 717902 E: john.battman@ntlworld.com
BATTY, John Ivan. b 35. Clifton Th Coll 59. d 62 p 63. C Clayton *Bradf* 62-67; V Toxteth Park St Clem *Liv* 67-73; R Darfield *Sheff* 73-90; Chapl Düsseldorf *Eur* 90-95; V The Marshland *Sheff* 95-00; rtd 00; PtO *Sheff* from 00; *Linc* from 00. *4 St Lawrence Way, Tallington, Stamford PE9 4RH* T/F: (01780) 740151
BATTY, Leslie. b 48. d 14 p 15. OLM Ringstone in Aveland Gp *Linc* from 14. *4 Waverley Close, Morton, Bourne PE10 0PN* T: (01778) 571267 M: 07890-010735 E: batty527@btinternet.com
BATTY, Mark Alan. b 56. BSc. Ripon Coll Cuddesdon. d 82 p 83. C Bottesford w Ashby *Linc* 82-86; V Scunthorpe All SS 86-95; P-in-c N Wolds Gp 95-97; V 97-12; rtd 12. *43 Grantham Road, Bracebridge Heath, Lincoln LN4 2LE*
BATTY, Canon Stephen Roy. b 58. Chich Th Coll 88. d 90 p 91. C Wimborne Minster and Holt *Sarum* 90-94; P-in-c Yetminster w Ryme Intrinseca and High Stoy 94-02; V Branksome St Aldhelm 02-15; R Bride Valley from 15; PtO *Win* 02-14; Can and Preb Sarum Cathl from 10. *The Rectory, Church Street, Burton Bradstock, Bridport DT6 4QS* T: (01308) 898799 E: stephen.batty@talktalk.net
BATTYE, John Noel. b 42. TCD BA 64 MA 73. CITC 66. d 66 p 67. C Drumglass *Arm* 66-69; C Ballynafeigh St Jude *D & D* 70-73; Chapl Pemb Coll Cam 73-78; Bp's C Knocknagoney *D & D* 78-80; I Cregagh 80-08; Preb Castleknock St Patr Cathl Dublin 94-08; rtd 08. *18 Enniscrone Park, Portadown, Craigavon BT63 5DQ* T: (028) 3833 1161 M: 07707-540052
BATTYE, Ms Lisa Katherine. b 55. Man Univ BN 78 MA(Theol) 96 Liv Univ MTh 00 RM 79. NOC 96. d 99 p 00. C Clifton *Man* 99-02; R Kersal Moor from 02; AD Salford from 13. *St Paul's Rectory, 1 Moorside Road, Salford M7 3PJ* T: 0161-792 5362 E: lisabattye@stpaulsparish.org.uk
BAUDAINS, Mrs Geraldine Louise. b 58. Ex Univ BTh 07. SWMTC 02. d 05 p 06. NSM Jersey All SS and Jersey St Simon *Win* 05-12; R Jersey St Martin from 12. *Le Chataignier, La Rue du Flicquet, St Martin, Jersey JE3 6BP* T: (01534) 855556 E: baudains@jerseymail.co.uk
✠**BAUERSCHMIDT, The Rt Revd John Crawford.** b 59. Kenyon Coll Ohio BA 81. Gen Th Sem (NY) MDiv 84. d 84 p 85 c 07. C Worcester All SS USA 84-87; Lib Pusey Ho 87-91; R Albermarle Ch Ch USA 92-97; R Covington Ch Ch 97-07; Bp Tennessee from 07. *50 Vantage Way, Suite 107, Nashville TN 37228-1524, USA* T: (001) (615) 251 3322 F: 251 8010 E: info@episcopaldiocese-tn.org
BAUGHAN, Emma Louise Langley. *See* LANGLEY, Emma Louise
BAUGHEN, Andrew Jonathan. b 64. Lon Guildhall Univ BA 87. Wycliffe Hall Ox BTh 94. d 94 p 95. C Battersea Rise St Mark

S'wark 94-97; P-in-c Clerkenwell St Jas and St Jo w St Pet *Lon* 97-00; V from 00. *St James's Church, Clerkenwell Close, London EC1R 0EA*   T: (020) 7251 1190   E: vicar@jc-church.org

✠**BAUGHEN, The Rt Revd Michael Alfred.** b 30. Lon Univ BD 55. Oak Hill Th Coll 51. **d** 56 **p** 57 **c** 82. C Hyson Green *S'well* 56-59; C Reigate St Mary *S'wark* 59-61; Ord Cand Sec CPAS 61-64; R Rusholme H Trin *Man* 64-70; TV St Marylebone All So w SS Pet and Jo *Lon* 70-75; R 75-82; AD Westmr St Marylebone 78-82; Preb St Paul's Cathl 79-82; Bp Ches 82-96; rtd 96; Hon Asst Bp Lon 96-06; Hon Asst Bp Guildf from 06; PtO *S'wark* 97-02. *23 The Atrium, Woolsack Way, Godalming GU7 1EN*   T: (01483) 808151   M: 07990-275563   E: mandmbaughen@gmail.com

BAULCOMB, Canon Geoffrey Gordon. b 46. K Coll Lon BD 86. AKC 68. **d** 69 **p** 70. C Crofton Park St Hilda w St Cypr *S'wark* 69-74; TV Padgate *Liv* 74-79; R Whitton and Thurleston w Akenham *St E* 79-03; Hon Can St E Cathl 03; rtd 03; PtO *St E* from 03; *Chich* from 04. *Greenlands, 39 Filching Road, Eastbourne BN20 8SE*   T: (01323) 641746   M: 07880-731232   E: geoffreybaulcomb@hotmail.com

BAUN, Jane Ralls. b 60. **d** 10 **p** 11. NSM Abingdon *Ox* from 10; Lect Ripon Coll Cuddesdon from 13. *68 Vicarage Road, Oxford OX1 4RE*   T: (01865) 244559   E: jane.baun@theology.ox.ac.uk

BAVERSTOCK, David John. b 76. K Coll Lon BA 00 MA 01. Westcott Ho Cam 07. **d** 09 **p** 11. C Mill End and Heronsgate w W Hyde *St Alb* 09-10; C Cheshunt 10-13; C Liv Our Lady and St Nic from 13. *Liverpool Parish Church, Old Churchyard, Liverpool L2 8TZ*   T: 0151-236 5287 *or* 227 5118   M: 07921-887513   E: frdavid@livpc.co.uk

✠**BAVIN, The Rt Revd Timothy John.** b 35. Worc Coll Ox BA 59 MA 61 FRSCM 91. Cuddesdon Coll 59. **d** 61 **p** 62 **c** 74. C Pretoria Cathl S Africa 61-64; Chapl 65-69; C Uckfield *Chich* 69-71; V Brighton Gd Shep Preston 71-73; Dean and Adn Johannesburg 73-74; Bp Johannesburg 74-85; Bp Portsm 85-95; OGS 87-97; OSB from 96; PtO *Win* 96-14; Hon Asst Bp Portsm from 12; Hon Asst Bp Win from 13. *Abbey of Our Lady and St John, Abbey Road, Beech, Alton GU34 4AP*   T: (01420) 562145 *or* 563575   F: 561691

BAVINGTON, John Eduard. b 68. Loughb Univ BEng 91. Trin Coll Bris BA 99. **d** 99 **p** 00. C W Ealing St Jo w St Jas *Lon* 99-02; V Bradf St Clem 02-06; Chapl Giggleswick Sch 06-13; V Gt Horton *Leeds* from 13. *30 Bartle Close, Bradford BD7 4QH*   T: (01274) 283058   M: 07704-854978   E: john.bavington@bradford.anglican.org

BAWDEN, Sheila Irene. b 55. **d** 11 **p** 12. NSM Bodmin w Lanhydrock and Lanivet *Truro* from 11. *Chimes, 8 Church Lane, Lostwithiel PL22 0EQ*   M: 07879-551046   E: sheila.stevens55@btinternet.com

BAWTREE, Andrew James. b 66. Univ of Wales BD 91 Ch Ch Coll Cant PGCE 92. St Jo Coll Nottm MA 95. **d** 96 **p** 97. C Hoddesdon *St Alb* 96-99; R S Boston Trin Ch USA 00-07; P-in-c River *Cant* from 07. *The Vicarage, 23 Lewisham Road, Dover CT17 0QG*   T: (01304) 822037   E: rockabillyrev@hotmail.com

BAWTREE, Canon Robert John. b 39. Oak Hill Th Coll 62. **d** 67 **p** 68. C Folkestone St Jo *Cant* 67-70; C Boscombe St Jo *Win* 70-73; C Kinson *Sarum* 73-75; TV Bramerton w Surlingham *Nor* 76-82; R Arborfield w Barkham *Ox* 82-91; V Hildenborough *Roch* 91-04; RD Tonbridge 95-01; Hon Can Roch Cathl 02-04; rtd 04; Hon C Camelot Par *B & W* 04-08. *47 Mount Pleasant Road, Weald, Sevenoaks TN14 6QB*   T: (01732) 464427   E: robert.bawtree@virgin.net

BAXANDALL, Canon Peter. b 45. Tyndale Hall Bris 67. **d** 70 **p** 72. C Kidsgrove *Lich* 70-71; C St Helens St Mark *Liv* 71-75; C Ardsley *Sheff* 75-77; Rep Leprosy Miss E Anglia 77-86; P-in-c March St Wendreda *Ely* 86-87; R 87-11; P-in-c March St Jo 09-11; RD March 93-09; Hon Can Ely Cathl 07-11; rtd 12; PtO *Nor* from 11. *22 Westland Road, Lowestoft NR33 9AB*   T: (01502) 583228   E: peter.baxandall840@btinternet.com

BAXENDALE, John Richard. b 48. Cranmer Hall Dur 89. **d** 91 **p** 92. C Carl St Jo 91-94; C Dalston 94-95; P-in-c Monton *Man* 95-96; TV Eccles 96-04; V Clifton 04-13; rtd 13. *34 Oxford Street, Ulverston LA12 0AZ*   E: baxendale901@btinternet.com

BAXENDALE, Rodney Douglas. b 45. Ex Univ BA 66 Cardiff Univ MTh 10 Leeds Univ PGCE 68. Linc Th Coll 78. **d** 80 **p** 81. C Maidstone All SS and St Phil w Tovil *Cant* 80-83; Chapl RN 83-03; Chapl Plymouth Hosps NHS Trust 06-08; Sen Chapl 08-13; rtd 13; PtO *Ex* from 13. *17 Valletort Road, Plymouth PL1 5PH*   T: (01752) 500573   E: thebaxendale@blueyonder.co.uk

BAXTER, Alexander. b 74. Westcott Ho Cam 10. **d** 13 **p** 14. *St Philip's Place, 10 St Philip's Way, Eastbourne BN22 8LW*   M: 07957-848378   T: (01323) 370638   E: alexbaxter66@yahoo.co.uk

BAXTER, Anthony. b 54. SEITE 99. **d** 02 **p** 08. NSM Romford Ascension Collier Row *Chelmsf* 02-07; NSM Hutton from 07.

44 Prower Close, Billericay CM11 2BU   T: (01277) 655514   M: 07909-984675   E: tony@tonybaxter.co.uk

BAXTER, Carlton Edwin. **d** 07 **p** 08. NSM Lurgan Ch the Redeemer *D & D* 07-10; NSM Maghaberry from 10. *33 Charnwood Grange, Portadown, Craigavon BT63 5TU*

BAXTER, David. *See* BAXTER, Richard David

BAXTER, David Norman. b 39. Open Univ BA 87. Kelham Th Coll 59. **d** 64 **p** 65. C Tonge Moor *Man* 64-68; Chapl RN 68-84; P-in-c Becontree St Pet *Chelmsf* 84-85; TV Becontree W 85-86; TR 86-94; Spain from 94; rtd 99. *C/ Vidal i Barraquer, 10, Escalera B, 1-2, 08870 Sitges (Barcelona), Spain*   T: (0034) 938 946 151   F: 938 943 800   E: dnbaxter@teleline.es

BAXTER, Dennis Alexander. b 56. Sheff Univ BA 96. St Mich Coll Llan 03. **d** 05 **p** 06. C Tenby *St D* 05-09; P-in-c Llanedi w Tycroes and Saron 09-14. *33 Thetford Road, Dagenham RM9 6AP*   M: 07963-467702   E: aarowkosky2@aol.com

BAXTER (*née* AVIS), Elizabeth Mary. b 49. Leeds Metrop Univ BA 93 Win Univ MPhil 13 CYCW 77. NOC 81. **dss** 84 **d** 87 **p** 94. Leeds St Marg and All Hallows *Ripon* 84-93; Par Dn 87-93; Chapl Abbey Grange High Sch 85-93; Par Dn Topcliffe *York* 93-94; C 94-96; C Thirsk 96-07; Jt Dir H Rood Ho Cen for Health and Past Care 93-07; Exec Dir from 07; PtO *Leeds* from 93; *Dur* from 94; *Newc* from 94; *Sheff* from 95; *Bradf* 95-04; *York* from 08. *5 Glendale Road, Wooler NE71 6DN*   T: (01668) 283125 *or* (01845) 522580   E: elizabethbaxter@gmx.co.uk

BAXTER, Jane Elizabeth. b 51. EAMTC 98. **d** 01 **p** 02. C Clare w Poslingford, Cavendish etc *St E* 01-04; P-in-c Lyddington w Stoke Dry and Seaton etc *Pet* 04-10; C Bulwick, Blatherwycke w Harringworth and Laxton 04-10; V Lyddington, Bisbrooke, Caldecott, Glaston etc from 10. *The Rectory, 4 Windmill Way, Lyddington, Oakham LE15 9LY*   T: (01572) 822717   E: revjanebaxter@gmail.com

BAXTER, John Richard. b 44. ACII 66. STETS 96. **d** 99 **p** 00. NSM Banstead *Guildf* 99-03; TV Surrey Weald 03-11; rtd 11. *11 Arundel Avenue, Epsom KT17 2RF*   T: (020) 8393 6767   M: 07974-692334   E: revdjohn@virginmedia.com

BAXTER, Canon Richard David. b 33. Kelham Th Coll 53. **d** 57 **p** 58. C Carl St Barn 57-59; C Barrow St Matt 59-64; V Drighlington *Wakef* 64-73; V Penistone 73-80; V Carl St Aid and Ch 80-86; Can Res Wakef Cathl 86-97; Prec from 86; Vice-Provost 92-97; rtd 97; PtO *Carl* from 97; Hon V Choral Carl Cathl 04-14; PtO *York* from 14. *4 Dulverton Hall, Esplanade, Scarborough YO11 2AR*   T: (01723) 374106   E: canondavidbaxter@btinternet.com

BAXTER, Stanley Robert. b 31. Leeds Univ MA 90 FRSA 96 MICM 96 MInstD 97 FRSH 99 FRSocMed 02 FCIM 07 FRSPH 04. Chich Th Coll 79. **d** 80 **p** 81. In Lutheran Ch 71-79; C Far Headingley St Chad *Ripon* 80-82; P-in-c Leeds St Marg 82-87; P-in-c Leeds All Hallows w Wrangthorn 85-87; P-in-c Topcliffe *York* 93-95; NSM 95-96; NSM Thirsk 96-07; Dir Leeds Cen for Urban Th Studies 88-93; Assoc Chapl Leeds Univ *Ripon* 91-93; Jt Dir H Rood Ho Cen for Health and Past Care 93-07; Dir Miss from 07; PtO *Leeds* from 93; *Dur* from 94; *Newc* from 94; *Sheff* from 95; *York* from 07; Chapl N Yorks and York Primary Care Trust 03-07. *5 Glendale Road, Wooler NE71 6DN*   T: (01668) 283125 *or* (01845) 522580   E: stanleybaxter@gmx.com

BAXTER, Stephen. **d** 14 **p** 15. NSM St Olave Hart Street w All Hallows Staining etc *Lon* from 14. *Address temp unknown*

BAXTER, Stuart. b 43. Liv Univ BA 65 Nottm Univ PGCE 66. Cuddesdon Coll 66. **d** 70 **p** 71. C Kirkby *Liv* 70-73; C Ainsdale 73-76; CMS 76-77 and 83-84; Sierra Leone 77-83; V Nelson in Lt Marsden *Blackb* 84-92; V Lostock Hall 92-99; P-in-c Hatton *Derby* 99-04; Asst Chapl HM Pris Sudbury 99-03; Asst Chapl HM Pris Foston Hall 03-06; rtd 06; PtO *Derby* from 06. *11 Pingle Crescent, Belper DE56 1DY*   T: (01773) 827309

BAXTER, Terence Hugh. b 48. Leeds Poly BSc 74. NOC 89. **d** 92 **p** 93. NSM Guiseley w Esholt *Bradf* 92-04; NSM Weston w Denton 04-08; NSM Leathley w Farnley, Fewston and Blubberhouses 04-08; NSM Washburn and Mid-Wharfe 08-09. *Address temp unknown*   M: 07985-391298   E: terry.baxter@tesco.net

BAYCOCK, Philip Louis. b 33. Wells Th Coll 64. **d** 66 **p** 67. C Kettering SS Pet and Paul 66-68; C St Peter-in-Thanet *Cant* 68-72; V Bobbing w Iwade 72-73; PtO 73-76; V Thanington w Milton 77-84; R Chagford w Gidleigh and Throwleigh *Ex* 84-01; rtd 01; PtO *Ex* from 01. *7 Grove Meadow, Sticklepath, Okehampton EX20 2NE*   T: (01837) 840617   E: louisb@care4free.net

BAYES, Frederick Alan. b 60. Imp Coll Lon BSc 81 St Jo Coll Dur BA 92. BA 92 Cranmer Hall Dur 92. **d** 93 **p** 94. C Talbot Village *Sarum* 93-97; Chapl St Hild and St Bede Coll *Dur* 97-03; Bp's Adv in Interfaith Matters 02-03; V Penllergaer *S & B* from 03. *The Vicarage, 16 Swansea Road, Penllergaer, Swansea SA4 9AQ*   T: (01792) 892603

✠**BAYES, The Rt Revd Paul.** b 53. Birm Univ BA 75. Qu Coll Birm 76. **d** 79 **p** 80 **c** 10. C Tynemouth Cullercoats St Paul *Newc* 79-82; Chapl Qu Eliz Coll *Lon* 82-87; Chapl Chelsea Coll 85-87; TV High Wycombe *Ox* 87-90; TR 90-94; TR Totton *Win* 95-04; AD Lyndhurst 00-04; Nat Miss and Evang Adv Abps' Coun 04-10; Hon Can Worc Cathl 07-10; Suff Bp Hertford *St Alb* 10-14; Bp Liv from 14. *Bishop's Lodge, Woolton Park, Liverpool L25 6DT* T: 0151-421 0831 F: 428 3055
E: bishopslodge@liverpool.anglican.org

BAYFORD, Terence Michael. b 48. Westmr Coll Ox MTh 96. Wilson Carlile Coll 70 NOC 97. **d** 99 **p** 00. Dep Chapl HM Pris Wakef 99-01; NSM Alverthorpe *Wakef* 99-01; Chapl HM Pris Moorland 01-05; Chapl HM Pris Wealstun 05-15; rtd 15. *Address temp unknown*

BAYLDON, Roger. b 38. MBE 74 TD 99. **d** 04 **p** 05. OLM Parkstone St Pet and St Osmund w Branksea *Sarum* 04-08. *58 Britannia Road, Poole BH14 8BB* M: 07831-272773 T: (01202) 467670 E: r.bayldon@btinternet.com *or* roger@bayldon.com

BAYLEY, Anne Christine. b 34. OBE 86. Girton Coll Cam BA 55 MB, ChB 58 FRCS 66 FRCSEd 86. St Steph Ho Ox 90. **d** 91 **p** 94. NSM Wembley Park St Aug *Lon* 91-97; PtO *York* 97-05; Heref 05-08. *52 Frome Court, Bartestree, Hereford HR1 4DX* T: (01432) 850220

BAYLEY, Michael John. b 36. CCC Cam BA 60 MA 64 Sheff Univ PhD 73. Linc Th Coll 60. **d** 62 **p** 63. C Leeds Gipton Epiphany *Ripon* 62-66; NSM Sheff St Mark Broomhill 67-93; C Sheff St Mary w Highfield Trin 93-95; C Sheff St Mary Bramall Lane 95-00; rtd 00. *27 Meadowbank Avenue, Sheffield S7 1PB* T: 0114-258 5248

BAYLEY, Oliver James Drummond. b 49. Mansf Coll Ox MA PGCE. St Jo Coll Nottm 81. **d** 83 **p** 84. C Bath Weston St Jo w Kelston *B & W* 83-88; P-in-c Bathampton 88-93; P-in-c Claverton 92-93; R Bathampton w Claverton 93-96; Chapl Dauntsey's Sch Devizes 96-02; rtd 02; PtO *Win* from 01. *19 Treeside Road, Southampton SO15 5FY* T: (023) 8078 6498 E: ojdb80@hotmail.com

BAYLEY, Canon Raymond. b 46. Keble Coll Ox BA 68 MA 72 Ex Univ PhD 86. St Chad's Coll Dur 68. **d** 69 **p** 70. C Mold *St As* 69-74; Lay Tr Officer 71-74; C Llandaff w Capel Llanilltern *Llan* 74; PV Llan Cathl and Lay Tr Officer 74-77; V Cwmbach 77-80; Dir Past Studies St Mich Coll Llan 80-84; Lect Univ of Wales (Cardiff) *Llan* 80-84; V Ynysddu *Mon* 84-86; V Griffithstown 86-92; Tutor Dioc Minl Tr Course 84-92; V Rhosymedre *St As* 92-96; Warden and R Ruthin w Llanrhydd 96-09; Tutor Dioc Minl Tr Course 92-06; Dir CME 94-01; Warden of Readers 02-09; Hon Can St As Cathl 04-09; rtd 09; PtO *St As* from 09; *S'wark* from 15. *11 Maes Glanrafon, Brook Street, Mold CH7 1RJ* T: (01352) 752345
E: raymond.bayley537@btinternet.com

BAYLIS (née LOFTS), Mrs Sally Anne. b 55. Kent Univ BA 78 K Coll Lon MA 80 Nottm Univ PGCE 93. St Jo Coll Nottm 01. **d** 03 **p** 04. C Gedling *S'well* 03-07; Chapl HM Pris w Daybrook 07-11; V from 11. *St Paul's Vicarage, 241 Oxclose Lane, Nottingham NG5 6FB* T: 0115-926 2686 E: k.baylis@ntlworld.com

BAYLISS, Geoffrey Brian Tudor. b 60. R Holloway Coll Lon BSc 83 Univ of Wales (Swansea) PGCE 85 Univ of Wales (Ban) MA 11. EAMTC 96. **d** 99 **p** 00. NSM Panfield and Rayne *Chelmsf* 99-04; TV Halstead Area 04-10; RD Hinckford 08-10; P-in-c Tolleshunt D'Arcy and Tolleshunt Major 10-11; P-in-c Tollesbury w Salcot Virley 10-11; V N Blackwater from 11; RD Witham from 11. *The Vicarage, 37 Church Street, Tolleshunt D'Arcy, Maldon CM9 8TS* T: (01621) 869895
E: g.bayliss41@btinternet.com

BAYLISS, Grant David. b 75. Ex Univ BA 96 Wolfs Coll Ox DPhil 05 Ox Univ MA 05. Ripon Coll Cuddesdon BA 99. **d** 03 **p** 04. C Prestbury and All SS *Glouc* 03-07; Chapl St Jo Coll Cam 07-11; Lect Ripon Coll Cuddesdon from 11. *Ripon College, Cuddesdon, Oxford OX44 9EX* T: (01895) 874404
E: grant.bayliss@ripon-cuddesdon.ac.uk

BAYLOR, Canon Nigel Peter. b 58. NUI BA 80 TCD MPhil 88. **d** 84 **p** 86. C Carrickfergus *Conn* 84-87; C Dundela St Mark *D & D* 87-89; I Galloon w Drummully *Clogh* 89-94; Adult Educn Adv 91-94; I Carnmoney *Conn* 94-03; I Jordanstown from 03; Can Belf Cathl from 12. *The Rectory, 120A Circular Road, Jordanstown, Newtownabbey BT37 0RH* T: (028) 9086 2119 E: revbaylor_munster@hotmail.co.uk

BAYLY, Mrs Janet. b 43. **d** 08. OLM Schorne *Ox* from 08. *Crandon Farm, North Marston, Buckingham MK18 3PQ* T: (01296) 670225 E: crancon@dial.pipex.com

BAYMAN, Ann Bernette. b 45. **d** 04 **p** 05. OLM Yoxmere *St E* 04-10; rtd 10; PtO *St E* from 10. *Dove Cottage, 4 South Road, Beccles NR34 9NN* T: (01502) 471709 M: 07884-072944 E: annie@dovecottage.orangehome.co.uk

BAYMAN, Brynn Alton. b 66. Witwatersrand Univ BA 87 PGCE 88. Ripon Coll Cuddesdon 09. **d** 11 **p** 12. OLM

Finchampstead and California *Ox* from 11. *Bevirs, Mordaunt Drive, Wellington College, Crowthorne RG45 7QQ* T: (01344) 779327 E: brynnbayman@hotmail.com

BAYNE, Canon David William. b 52. St Andr Univ MA 75. Edin Th Coll 88. **d** 90 **p** 91. C Dumfries *Glas* 90-92; P-in-c 92-93; R 93-99; Chapl Dumfries and Galloway Primary Care NHS Trust 92-99; Chapl Crichton R Hosp Dumfries 92-99; Chapl HM Pris Dumfries 96-99; R Castle Douglas *Glas* from 99; Can St Mary's Cathl from 99. *The Rectory, 68 St Andrew Street, Castle Douglas DG7 1EN* T/F: (01556) 503818 E: dwbayne@aol.com

BAYNE, Mrs Felicity Meriel. b 47. WEMTC 91. **d** 94 **p** 95. NSM Cheltenham Ch Ch *Glouc* 94-98; NSM Leckhampton St Pet 98-09; Chapl Glenfall Ho 09-13; rtd 13. *Hamfield House, Ham Road, Charlton Kings, Cheltenham GL52 6NG* T: (01242) 237074 E: felicity.bayne@btinternet.com

BAYNE-JARDINE, Anthea Mary. *See* GRIGGS, Anthea Mary

BAYNES, Mrs Clare. b 57. Reading Univ BA 79. SAOMC 01. **d** 04 **p** 05. NSM Chambersbury *St Alb* 04-08; NSM St Alb St Steph from 08. *4 Pilgrim Close, Park Street, St Albans AL2 2JD* T: (01727) 875524 E: clare@simonbaynes.fsnet.co.uk

BAYNES, Canon Matthew Thomas Crispin. b 62. UEA BA 83 Qu Coll Cam BA 86 MA 91. Westcott Ho Cam 85. **d** 87 **p** 88. C Southgate Ch Ch *Lon* 87-90; C Gt Berkhamsted *St Alb* 90-95; V Coseley Ch Ch *Worc* 95-99; R Bredon w Bredon's Norton from 99; P-in-c Overbury w Teddington, Alstone etc from 09; RD Pershore 05-11; Hon Can Worc Cathl from 10. *The Rectory, Bredon, Tewkesbury GL20 7LT* T: (01684) 772237
E: matthew@tcbaynes.fsnet.co.uk

BAYNES, Simon Hamilton. b 33. New Coll Ox BA 57 MA 62. Wycliffe Hall Ox 57. **d** 59 **p** 60. C Rodbourne Cheney *Bris* 59-62; Japan 63-80; C Keynsham *B & W* 80-84; P-in-c Winkfield *Ox* 84-85; V Winkfield and Cranbourne 85-99; rtd 99; LtO *Ox* 99-02; Hon C Thame from 02. *23 Moorend Lane, Thame OX9 3BQ* T: (01844) 213673
E: baynes@psa-online.com

BAYNES, Timothy Francis de Brissac. b 29. Ely Th Coll 59. **d** 61 **p** 62. C Hockerill *St Alb* 61-65; C Mansfield Woodhouse *S'well* 65-67; Ind Chapl *Man* 67-94; P-in-c Miles Platting St Jo 67-72; rtd 94; PtO *Man* 94-97. *46 Kirkbie Green, Kendal LA9 7AJ* T: (01539) 740605

BAYNES, William Hendrie. b 39. Adelaide Univ BA 60. S'wark Ord Course 77. **d** 79 **p** 80. C Notting Hill All SS w St Columb *Lon* 79-85; PtO 86-87 and 99-00; Hon C Paddington St Sav 88-98; Asst Chapl St Mary's NHS Trust Paddington 94-99; Hon C Paddington St Jas *Lon* 00-10; PtO from 10. *39E Westbourne Gardens, London W2 5NR* T: (020) 7727 9530
E: will.baynes@london.anglican.org

BAYNHAM, Matthew Fred. b 57. BNC Ox BA 78 Birm Univ MPhil 00. Wycliffe Hall Ox 80. **d** 83 **p** 84. C Yardley St Edburgha *Birm* 83-87; TV Bath Twerton-on-Avon *B & W* 87-93; V Reddal Hill St Luke *Worc* 93-00; RD Dudley 98-00; Chapl Bp Grosseteste Coll Linc 00-05; Assoc Chapl Liv Univ 05-07; Sen Res Tutor from 07; P-in-c Llanllwchaearn and Llanina *St D* from 11. *Y Ficerdy, Penrhiwgaled Lane, Cross Inn, Llandysul SA44 6NS* T: (01545) 561878
E: matthewbaynham@hotmail.com

BAYS, Mrs Helen Margaret. b 48. Kent Univ BA 69 RGN 71 RHV 73. STETS 97. **d** 00 **p** 01. NSM Calne and Blackland *Sarum* 00-02; NSM Dawlish *Ex* 02-12; rtd 12. *14 Stockton Hill, Dawlish EX7 9LP* T: (01626) 862860 E: hbays@talktalk.net

BAZELY, Stephen William. b 80. Ox Brookes Univ BSc 05. Oak Hill Th Coll BA 11. **d** 11 **p** 12. C Deane *Man* 11-14; PtO 14-15; P-in-c Willaston *Ches* from 15. *12 Broadlake, Willaston, Neston CH64 2XB* T: 0151-327 3639 E: cc.willaston@gmail.com

BAZELY, William Francis. b 53. Sheff Univ BEng 75. St Jo Coll Nottm 78. **d** 81 **p** 82. C Huyton St Geo *Liv* 81-84; TV Netherthorpe *Sheff* 84-92; Chapl Lambeth Healthcare NHS Trust 92-98; Chapl Guy's and St Thos' Hosps NHS Trust Lon 98-01; C Rotherham *Sheff* 01-03; Chapl Rotherham Gen Hosps NHS Trust 01-03; Chapl Doncaster and S Humber Healthcare NHS Trust 01-03; Sen Chapl Norfolk and Suffolk NHS Foundn Trust 03-14; rtd 14; Hon C Brampton St Thos *Derby* from 15. *8 Pennywell Drive, Holymoorside, Chesterfield S42 7EY* M: 07702-974680 E: wbazely@gmail.com

✠**BAZLEY, The Rt Revd Colin Frederick.** b 35. St Pet Coll Ox BA 57 MA 61. Tyndale Hall Bris 57. **d** 59 **p** 60 **c** 69. C Bootle St Leon *Liv* 59-62; SAMS Miss Chile 62-00; Adn Cautin and Malleco 67-69; Asst Bp Cautin and Malleco 69-75; Asst Bp Santiago 75-77; Bp Chile 77-00; Primate CASA Chile 77-83; Primate Inglesia Anglicana del Cono Sur 89-95; rtd 00; Hon Asst Bp Ches from 00; Warden of Readers 00-05; RD Wallasey 09-11. *121 Brackenwood Road, Higher Bebington, Wirral CH63 2LU* T: 0151-608 1193 M: 07866-391333
E: cbazley@gmail.com

BAZLINTON, Stephen Cecil. b 46. Lon Univ BDS RCS LDS. Ridley Hall Cam 78. **d** 85 **p** 86. NSM Stebbing w Lindsell

Chelmsf 85-04; NSM Stebbing and Lindsell w Gt and Lt Saling 04-08; PtO from 08. *St Helens, High Street, Stebbing, Dunmow CM6 3SE* T: (01371) 856495 E: revbaz@care4free.co.uk

BEACH, Jonathan Mark. b 67. Essex Univ BSc 89. Trin Coll Bris BA 94. d 94 p 95. C Oulton Broad *Nor* 94-97; Chapl RAF 97-13; Chapl St Mary's Sch Calne from 13. *St Mary's School, 63 Curzon Street, Calne SN11 0DF* T: (01249) 857200 E: jbeach@stmaryscalne.org

BEACH, Mark Howard Francis. b 62. Kent Univ BA 83 Nottm Univ MA 95 K Coll Lon DMin 11. St Steph Ho Ox 85. d 87 p 88. C Beeston *S'well* 87-90; C Hucknall Torkard 90-93; R Gedling 93-01; R Netherfield 96-01; Bp's Chapl *Wakef* 01-03; TR Rugby *Cov* 03-12; Dean Roch 12-15; Dir Blackfriars Settlement from 15. *Blackfriars Settlement, 1 Rushworth Street, London SE1 0RB* M: 07957-584856 E: mark.beach62@gmail.com

BEACH, Stephen John. b 58. Man Univ BA 81 BD 88 Didsbury Coll of Educn PGCE 82. NOC 92. d 93 p 94. C Harwood *Man* 93-97; TV Westhoughton and Wingates 97-01; P-in-c Devonport St Budeaux *Ex* 01-02; V from 02. *St Budeaux Vicarage, Agaton Road, Plymouth PL5 2EW* T: (01752) 361019 *or* 351087 E: steph.beach@xalt.co.uk

BEACHAM, Peter Martyn. b 44. OBE 08. Ex Coll Ox BA 65 MA 70 Lon Univ MPhil 67 FSA 92 MRTPI 69. Sarum Th Coll 70. d 73 p 74. C Ex St Martin, St Steph, St Laur etc 73-74; NSM Cen Ex 74-90; PtO from 99. *Bellever, Barrack Road, Exeter EX2 6AB* T: (01392) 435074 E: peter-beacham1@live.co.uk

BEACON, Canon Ralph Anthony. b 44. St Mich Coll Llan 70. d 71 p 72. C Neath w Llantwit *Llan* 71-74; TV Holyhead w Rhoscolyn w Llanfair-yn-Neubwll *Ban* 74-78; R Llanenddwyn w Llanddwywe, Llanbedr w Llandanwg 78-99; V Harlech and Llanfair-juxta-Harlech etc 99-11; RD Ardudwy 89-02; AD 02-12; Hon Can Ban Cathl 91-97; Can Cursal Ban Cathl 97-11; Can and Preb Ban Cathl 03-11; rtd 11. *Hen Tyrpeg, Harlech LL46 2UU* M: 07713-421858 T: (01766) 780031

BEACON, Canon Stephanie Kathleen Nora. b 49. Univ of Wales (Ban) BA 70 PGCE 71. NW Ord Course 94. d 96 p 97. NSM Llanenddwyn w Llanddwywe, Llanbedr w Llandanwg *Ban* 96-98; C Ardudwy 98-99; P-in-c Llanenddwyn w Llanddwywe, Llanbedr w Llandanwg 99-01; R 01-11; R Bro Ardudwy Uchaf 11-13; Can Cursal Ban Cathl 11-13; rtd 13. *Hen Tyrpeg, Harlech LL46 2UU* M: 07713-421858 T: (01766) 780031

BEADLE, David Alexander. b 37. St And Dioc Tr Course. d 88 p 89. NSM St Andrews St Andr *St And* from 88. *48 Clayton Caravan Park, St Andrews KY16 9YB* T: (01334) 870001 E: dabeadle@lineone.net

BEADLE, Canon Janet Mary. b 52. Philippa Fawcett Coll CertEd 74. EAMTC 91. d 94 p 95. C Kingston upon Hull H Trin *York* 94-98; V Ness Gp *Linc* from 98; Bp's Adv in Women's Min 00-08; Can and Preb Linc Cathl from 03. *The Vicarage, 10 Church Street, Thurlby, Bourne PE10 0EH* T: (01778) 422475 E: reverendcanonjanetbeadle@gmail.com

BEADLE, Liam Paul. b 84. St Pet Coll Ox BA 07 MA 11 St Jo Coll Dur MA 10. Cranmer Hall Dur 07. d 09 p 10. C Enfield St Andr *Lon* 09-13; V Honley *Leeds* from 13. *The Vicarage, St Mary's Road, Honley, Holmfirth HD9 6AZ* E: liam.beadle@gmail.com

BEADLE, Mrs Lorna. b 40. NEOC 92. d 95 p 96. NSM Ashington *Newc* from 95; Chapl MU from 02. *9 Arundel Square, Ashington NE63 8AW* T: (01670) 816467

BEAHAN, Alan. b 46. Birm Univ BA 87 York Univ PGCE 89 St Jo Coll Dur BA 07. Cranmer Hall Dur 05. d 07 p 08. C Warrington St Elphin *Liv* 07-10; P-in-c Hindley All SS from 10; P-in-c Hindley St Pet 13-15. *The Vicarage, 192 Atherton Road, Hindley, Wigan WN2 3XA* T: (01942) 255175 E: alanbeahan@yahoo.co.uk

✠**BEAK, The Rt Revd Robert Michael Cawthorn.** b 25. OBE 90. Lon Bible Coll. d 53 p 54 c 84. C Tunbridge Wells St Jo *Roch* 53-55; BCMS 55-56 and 84-89; Kenya 56-69 and 84-89; R Heanton Punchardon *Ex* 70-79; R Heanton Punchardon w Marwood 79-84; OCM 70-80; RD Barnstaple *Ex* 77-81; Preb Ex Cathl 82-84; Asst Bp Mt Kenya E 84-89; rtd 90; Hon Asst Bp Derby from 91. *Ashcroft Cottage, Butts Road, Ashover, Chesterfield S45 0AX* T: (01246) 590048

BEAK, Stephen Robert. b 64. City Univ BSc 86. Wycliffe Hall Ox BTh 94. d 94 p 95. C Lache cum Saltney *Ches* 94-97; C Howell Hill *Guildf* 97-01; NSM Woking St Mary 01-05; V from 05. *St Mary's Vicarage, Bethany House, West Hill Road, Woking GU22 7UJ* T: (01483) 761269 E: vicar@stmaryofbethany.org.uk

BEAKE, The Ven Stuart Alexander. b 49. Em Coll Cam BA 72 MA 76. Cuddesdon Coll 72. d 74 p 75. C Hitchin St Mary *St Alb* 74-76; C Hitchin 77-79; TV Hemel Hempstead 79-85; Bp's Dom Chapl *S'well* 85-87; V Shottery St Andr *Cov* 87-00;

RD Fosse 93-99; Dioc Dir of Ords 96-00; Hon Can Cov Cathl 98-00; Can Res and Sub-Dean Cov Cathl 00-05; Adn Surrey *Guildf* from 05; Hon Can Guildf Cathl 05-10; Can Res Guildf Cathl from 10; Warden CSP from 08. *Archdeacon's House, Lime Grove, West Clandon, Guildford GU4 7UT* T: (01483) 211924 *or* 790352 F: 790333 E: stuart.beake@cofeguildford.org.uk *or* sabeake@msn.com

BEAKEN, Robert William Frederick. b 62. SS Paul & Mary Coll Cheltenham BA 83 Lambeth STh 90 MA 01 K Coll Lon PhD 09 FSAScot 01 FRHistS 12. Ripon Coll Cuddesdon 85 Ven English Coll & Pontifical Gregorian Univ Rome 87. d 88 p 89. C Forton *Portsm* 88-92; C Shepshed *Leic* 92-94; V Colchester St Barn *Chelmsf* 94-02; P-in-c Gt and Lt Bardfield from 02. *The Vicarage, Braintree Road, Great Bardfield, Braintree CM7 4RN* T: (01371) 810267 E: robert@webform.com

BEAL, David Michael. b 61. St Jo Coll Nottm BTh 89. d 89 p 90. C Marton *Blackb* 89-92; C Darwen St Pet w Hoddlesden 92-93; TV 93-97; R Itchingfield w Slinfold *Chich* 97-09; R W Chiltington from 09; RD Storrington from 11. *The Rectory, East Street, West Chiltington, Pulborough RH20 2JY* E: beals@tesco.net

BEALES, Christopher Leader Day. b 51. St Jo Coll Dur BA 72. Cranmer Hall Dur 72. d 76 p 77. C Upper Armley and Ind Chapl *Ripon* 76-79; *Dur* 79-84; Sen Chapl 82-84; Sec Ind Cttee of Gen Syn Bd for Soc Resp 85-91; Sec Inner Cities Relig Coun (DOE) 92-94; Dir Churches' Regional Commn in the NE Newc and *Dur* 94-98; Consultant Dir 98; Chief Exec Employment Focus 99-07; C Thamesmead *S'wark* 99-01; PtO 01-10; Chief Exec Afghan Action from 05; P-in-c Woburn Sands *St Alb* 08-12; V from 12. *St Michael's Vicarage, 30 Church Road, Woburn Sands, Milton Keynes MK17 8TR* T: (01908) 582581 E: chrisbeales@afghanaction.com

BEALES, John David. b 55. SS Hild & Bede Coll Dur BA 77 Univ of W Aus DipEd 79. St Jo Coll Nottm 81. d 83 p 84. C Scarborough Australia 83-86; Dioc Youth Chapl Perth 86-89; Dir Educn and Tr Philo Trust 89-90; NSM Nottingham St Nic *S'well* 89-95; Dir Evang Melbourne Australia 95-00; PtO *Chelmsf* 99-01; Pioneer Min from 14. *DNA Networks, Abbeygate Two, 9 Whitewell Road, Colchester CO2 7DE* T: (01206) 616737 E: dna.networks@ntlworld.com *or* davidbeales@icloud.com

BEALING, Mrs Patricia Ramsey. b 39. Lightfoot Ho Dur IDC 63. dss 63 d 87 p 94. Rekendyke *Dur* 85-06; Par Dn 87-94; C 94-06; Chapl S Tyneside Healthcare Trust from 88; PtO *Dur* from 13. *31 Cedar Drive, Jarrow NE32 4BF* T: 0191-519 2588

BEAMENT, Canon Owen John. b 41. MBE 01. Bps' Coll Cheshunt 61. d 64 p 65. C Deptford St Paul *S'wark* 64-68; C Peckham St Jo 69-73; C Vauxhall St Pet 73-74; V Hatcham Park All SS from 74; Hon Can S'wark Cathl from 97. *All Saints' Vicarage, 22 Erlanger Road, London SE14 5TG* T: (020) 7639 3497 E: owenbeament@aol.com

BEAMER, Neville David. b 40. Univ of Wales (Lamp) BA 62 Jes Coll Ox BA 65 MA 70. Wycliffe Hall Ox 64. d 65 p 66. C Hornchurch St Andr *Chelmsf* 65-68; C Warwick St Mary *Cov* 68-72; V Holton-le-Clay *Linc* 72-75; P-in-c Stoneleigh w Ashow *Cov* 75-79; P-in-c Baginton 77-79; V Fletchamstead 79-86; Warden Whatcombe Ho Blandford Forum 86-90; R Jersey St Lawr and V Jersey Millbrook St Matt *Win* 90-95; V Yateley 95-03; P-in-c Eversley 98-03; R Yateley and Eversley 03-05; RD Odiham 95-04; rtd 05; PtO *Cov* from 05. *8 Aintree Road, Stratford-upon-Avon CV37 9FL* T: (01789) 263435 E: nbeamer@hotmail.com

BEAN, Douglas Jeyes Lendrum. b 25. Worc Coll Ox BA 50 MA 53. Ely Th Coll 50. d 51 p 52. C Croydon Woodside *Cant* 51-54; Min Can Windsor 54-59; V Reading St Laur *Ox* 59-68; Chapl HM Borstal Reading 61-68; RD Reading *Ox* 65-68; Min Can St Paul's Cathl 68-72; Hon Min Can from 72; V St Pancras w St Jas and Ch Ch 72-93; PV Westmr Abbey 75-80; rtd 93; PtO *Lon* from 99. *3 Bishop Street, London N1 8PH* T: (020) 7226 8340

BEAN, James Corey. b 35. Centenary Coll New Jersey BA 58 Long Is Univ MS 74. Seabury-Western Th Sem LTh 61. d 61 p 62. USA 61-79 and from 90; Chapl Wiesbaden *Eur* 79-90. *PO Box 490, Pomeroy WA 99347-0490, USA* T: (001) (509) 843 1871

BEAN, Canon John Victor. b 25. Down Coll Cam BA 47 MA 51. Sarum Th Coll 48. d 50 p 51. C Milton *Portsm* 50-55; C Fareham SS Pet and Paul 55-59; V St Helens 59-66; V Cowes St Mary 66-91; RD W Wight 68-72; Hon Can Portsm Cathl 70-91; P-in-c Cowes St Faith 77-80; C-in-c Gurnard All SS CD 78-91; Chapl to The Queen 80-95; rtd 91; PtO *Portsm* from 91. *23 Queens Road, Ryde PO33 3BG* T: (01983) 562856

BEANE, Canon Andrew Mark. b 72. St Jo Coll Nottm BA 02. d 02 p 03. C Thorpe St Matt *Nor* 02-05; P-in-c Horsham St Faith, Spixworth and Crostwick 05-06; R 06-12; P-in-c Aylsham from 12; P-in-c Cawston w Booton and Brandiston etc from 12; P-in-c Oulton St Mich from 15; RD Ingworth from 13; Hon Can Nor Cathl from 15. *The Vicarage, Cawston Road, Aylsham, Norwich NR11 6NB* T: (01263) 732686 M: 07898-932654 E: andrew.beane@btinternet.com

BEANEY, Canon John. b 47. Trin Coll Bris 77. **d** 79 **p** 80. C Bromley Ch Ch *Roch* 79-84; V Broadheath *Ches* 84-08; Chapl Altrincham Gen Hosp 91-94; Chapl Trafford Healthcare NHS Trust 94-98; P-in-c Norton *Ches* 08-14; Ecum Officer (Gtr Man) 02-14; Hon Can Ches Cathl 10-14; rtd 14. *5 Wivern Place, Runcorn WA7 1RZ* E: j.beaney@virginmedia.com

BEARCROFT, Bramwell Arthur. b 52. Homerton Coll Cam BEd 82. EAMTC 87. **d** 90 **p** 91. Chapl and Hd RS Kimbolton Sch Cambs 88-94; NSM Tilbrook *Ely* 90-94; NSM Covington 90-94; NSM Catworth Magna 90-94; NSM Keyston and Bythorn 90-94; NSM Cary Deanery *B & W* 94-02; Hd Master Hazlegrove Sch 94-02; Asst Chapl Aquitaine *Eur* from 10. *Clé de Tève, Devillac, 47210 Lot et Garonne, France* T: (0033) 5 53 71 46 24 E: jenniferbearcroft@hotmail.com

BEARD, Christopher Robert. b 47. Chich Th Coll 81. **d** 83 **p** 84. C Chich St Paul and St Pet 83-86; TV Ifield 86-91; V Haywards Heath St Rich 91-99; P-in-c Donnington 99-12; Chapl St Wilfrid's Hospice Eastbourne 99-12; rtd 12. *70 Victoria Road, Chichester PO19 7JA* T: (01243) 696034 M: 07845-482779

BEARD, Laurence Philip. b 45. Lon Univ BA 68. Trin Coll Bris 88. **d** 90 **p** 91. C Trentham *Lich* 90-94; V Wolverhampton St Matt 94-01; P-in-c Hartshill *Cov* 01-08; rtd 08. *14 Beechcroft Avenue, Croxley Green, Rickmansworth WD3 3EQ* T: (01923) 222312 E: lpbeard@talk21.com

BEARD, Robert John Hansley. b 61. St Andr Univ BD 85. Ripon Coll Cuddesdon 86 Ch Div Sch of the Pacific (USA) 87. **d** 88 **p** 89. C Sheff Manor 88-91; C Rotherham 91-94; V Sheff St Pet Abbeydale 94-02; Assoc Chapl Sheff Hallam Univ 95-98; Bp's Adv on Interfaith Issues 96-02; Intercultural Regeneration Development Worker Simunye from 02. *18 Arnside Road, Sheffield S8 0UX* T: 0114-255 6335 E: arjay61@hotmail.com

BEARDALL, Raymond. b 32. St Jo Coll Nottm 70. **d** 72 **p** 73. C Ilkley All SS *Bradf* 72-74; C Seasalter *Cant* 74-79; V Farndon *S'well* 79-84; R Thorpe 79-84; V Blidworth 84-97; rtd 97; PtO *S'well* from 03. *102 Arun Dale, Mansfield Woodhouse, Mansfield NG19 9RF* E: ray@beardallhome.fsnet.co.uk

BEARDMORE, John Keith. b 42. FCP 85 Bris Univ BEd 74 K Coll Lon MA 90. **d** 77 **p** 78. NSM Maindee Newport *Mon* from 77. *16 Hove Avenue, Newport NP19 7QP* T: (01633) 263272

BEARDSHAW, David. b 37. JP . Wells Th Coll 65. **d** 67 **p** 68. C Wood End *Cov* 67-69; C Stoke 70-73; V Whitley 73-77; Dioc Educn Officer 77-87; P-in-c Offchurch and Warden Offa Retreat Ho 87-93; rtd 93. *188 Ashington Grove, Coventry CV3 4DB*

BEARDSLEY, Christina. b 51. Sussex Univ BA 73 St Jo Coll Cam PhD 99 Leeds Univ MA 07. Westcott Ho Cam 76. **d** 78 **p** 79. C Portsea N End St Mark *Portsm* 78-85; V Catherington and Clanfield 85-00; Chapl Worthing and Southlands Hosps NHS Trust 00-01; Asst Chapl Chelsea and Westmr Hosp NHS Found Trust 01-04; Chapl 04-08; Hd Multi-Faith Chapl from 08; Visiting Lect St Mary's Univ Twickenham *Lon* from 10. *Chaplains' Office, Chelsea and Westminster Hospital, 369 Fulham Road, London SW10 9NH* T: (020) 8746 8083 E: christina.beardsley@chelwest.nhs.uk

BEARDSLEY, Nigel Andrew. b 61. Sheff Hallam Univ BSc 88 Nottm Univ MA 00. EMMTC 97. **d** 00 **p** 01. C Bath Bathwick *B & W* 00-05; Chapl RN from 05. *Royal Naval Chaplaincy Service, Mail Point 1-2, Leach Building, Whale Island, Portsmouth PO2 8BY* T: (023) 9262 5055 F: 9262 5134

BEARE, William. b 33. TCD BA 58. **d** 59 **p** 60. C Waterford St Patr *C & O* 59-62; C Cork H Trin w Shandon St Mary *C, C & R* 62-64; I Rathcormac 64-68; I Marmullane w Monkstown 68-76; Dioc C 76-82; I Stradbally w Ballintubbert, Coraclone etc *C & O* 82-99; Can Ossory and Leighlin Cathls 88-90; Chan Ossory and Leighlin Cathls 90-92; Prec Ossory and Leighlin Cathls 92-99; Dean Lismore and I Lismore w Cappoquin, Kilwatermoy, Dungarvan etc 99-08; Preb Stagonil St Patr Cathl Dublin 95-08; rtd 09. *24 Lapp's Court, Hartland's Avenue, Glasheen, Cork, Republic of Ireland* T: (00353) (21) 497 5980 M: 87-233 1508

BEARN, Hugh William. b 62. Man Univ BA 84 MA 98. Cranmer Hall Dur 86. **d** 89 **p** 90. C Heaton Ch Ch *Man* 89-92; Chapl RAF 92-96; V Tottington *Man* from 96; CF (TA) 96-02; Chapl Bury Hospice 99-03; CF (ACF) from 06; Chapl to The Queen from 06. *St Ann's Vicarage, Chapel Street, Tottington, Bury BL8 4AP* T: (01204) 883713 E: hughbearn@aol.com

BEARPARK, Canon John Michael. b 36. Ex Coll Ox BA 59 MA 63. Linc Th Coll 59. **d** 61 **p** 62. C Bingley H Trin *Bradf* 61-64; C Baildon 64-67; V Fairweather Green 67-77; Chapl Airedale NHS Trust 77-94; V Steeton *Bradf* 77-94; Hon Can Bradf Cathl 89-01; V Bentham St Marg 94-01; P-in-c Bentham St Jo 99-01; RD Ewecross 94-00; rtd 01; PtO *Leeds* from 01. *31 Northfields Crescent, Settle BD24 9JP* T: (01729) 822712 E: johnbearpark@yahoo.co.uk

BEASLEY, Canon Elizabeth Parish. b 58. Wake Forest Univ USA BA 79 Univ of the S STM 04 STM 04. Harvard Div Sch MDiv 89. **d** 98 **p** 99. V Honolulu St Geo USA 98-01; P-in-c Kapaa All SS 02-05; V Kaneohe St Jo 05-07; Can for Min Development Dio Hawaii 07-11; Can to the Ordinary 11-14; I Adare and Kilmallock w Kilpeacon, Croom etc *L & K* from 14. *The Rectory, Adare, Co Limerick, Republic of Ireland* T: (00353) (61) 396227 E: revlizadare@gmail.com

✣**BEASLEY, The Rt Revd Noel Michael Roy.** b 68. Imp Coll Lon BSc 91 Oriel Coll Ox DPhil 95 St Jo Coll Dur BA 98. Cranmer Hall Dur 96. **d** 99 **p** 00 **c** 15. C Newport w Longford, Chetwynd and Forton *Lich* 99-03; Chapl Westcott Ho Cam 03-07; Vice Prin 07-10; Dioc Dir of Miss *Ox* 10-15; Hon Can Ch Ch 14-15; Suff Bp Hertford *St Alb* from 15. *Bishopswood, 3 Stobarts Close, Knebworth SG3 6ND* T: (01438) 817260 E: bishophertford@stalbans.anglican.org

BEATER, David MacPherson. b 44. Chich Th Coll 66. **d** 69 **p** 70. C Withington St Crispin *Man* 69-72; C Lightbowne 72-74; V Prestwich St Hilda 74-81; V Northfleet *Roch* 81-85; C Bickley 86-90; TV Stanley *Dur* 90-97; CMP from 91; SSF 97-01; C Seaton Hirst *Newc* 01-05; rtd 05; PtO *Cant* 07-10. *7 Ferndown, 146 Minnis Road, Birchington CT7 9QE* T: (01843) 842166

BEATON, Mark Timothy. b 61. Univ of Wales (Ban) BA 83. Trin Coll Bris 03. **d** 05 **p** 06. C Swindon St Jo and St Andr *Bris* 05-08; P-in-c New Radnor and Llanfihangel Nantmelan etc *S & B* 08-11; R from 11; AD Maelienydd from 14. *The Rectory, School Lane, New Radnor, Presteigne LD8 2SS* T: (01544) 350342 E: mark.beaton@tesco.net

BEATTIE, David George. b 42. MIMechE 76. CITC 01. **d** 04 **p** 05. NSM Belfast H Trin and St Silas *Conn* 04-09; NSM Whitehouse 09-10; Chapl Belfast Health and Soc Care Trust from 10; NSM Ematris w Rockcorry, Aghabog and Aughnamullan *Clogh* from 11. *Tircooney, Stonebridge, Clones, Co Monaghan, Republic of Ireland* T: (00353) (47) 57752 E: beattie5@eircom.net

BEATTIE, Ian David. b 36. Univ of NZ BA 58. St Jo Coll Auckland LTh 60. **d** 60 **p** 61. C Epsom St Andr New Zealand 60-64; C Shirley St Jo *Cant* 64-65; V S Wimbledon St Andr *S'wark* 65-71; C Napier St Aug New Zealand 71-73; V Onehunga 73-96; rtd 96. *1/148A Tasman Street, Nelson 7010, New Zealand* T: (0064) (3) 546 7507

BEATTIE, Margaret. *See* BREWSTER, Margaret

BEATTIE, Canon Noel Christopher. b 41. TCD BTh 65 Cranfield Inst of Tech MSc 86. **d** 68 **p** 69. C Belfast H Trin *Conn* 68-70; C Belfast St Bart 70-73; C Doncaster St Mary *Sheff* 73-77; TV Northampton Em *Pet* 77-88; Ind Chapl 85-88; *Linc* 88-92; *Roch* 92-04; Hon Can Roch Cathl 00-04; rtd 04; PtO *Heref* from 05. *6 Oaks Road, Church Stretton SY6 7AX* T: (01694) 725530 E: noelbt@globalnet.co.uk

BEATTIE, Pamela. b 61. **d** 12. OLM Linc St Jo 12-14. *The Nightingales, 38 Brinkhall Way, Welton, Lincoln LN2 3NS* T: (01673) 863408

BEAUCHAMP, Anthony Hazlerigg Proctor. b 40. Trin Coll Cam BA 62 MA 66 MICE 68. St Jo Coll Nottm 73. **d** 75 **p** 76. C New Humberstone *Leic* 75-77; C-in-c Polegate *Chich* 77-80; Chapl Bethany Sch Goudhurst 80-86; Chapl Luckley-Oakfield Sch Wokingham 86-88; Chapl Clayesmore Sch Blandford 89-93; R Kirby-le-Soken w Gt Holland *Chelmsf* 93-00; Asst P Wetheral w Warwick *Carl* 00-01; rtd 01; PtO *Carl* 00-01; *Chich* from 01. *2 Stelvio Cottages, 17 Beachy Head Road, Eastbourne BN20 7QP* T: (01323) 732743

BEAUCHAMP, Gerald Charles. b 55. Hull Univ BA 78 K Coll Lon MA 96. Coll of Resurr Mirfield 78. **d** 80 **p** 81. C Hatcham St Cath *S'wark* 80-83; S Africa 83-86; C Ealing St Steph Castle Hill *Lon* 86-88; P-in-c Brondesbury St Anne w Kilburn H Trin 88-89; V 89-93; Chapl Kilburn Coll 88-93; C Chelsea St Luke and Ch Ch *Lon* 93-96; V W Brompton St Mary w St Pet 96-04; AD Chelsea 02-04; SSJE 04-07; C St Marylebone All SS *Lon* 07-10; P-in-c St Marylebone St Cypr from 10; P-in-c St Marylebone Annunciation Bryanston Street from 10. *16 Clarence Gate Gardens, Glentworth Street, London NW1 6AY* T: (020) 7258 0031 or 7258 0724 E: gerald.beauch@btconnect.com

BEAUCHAMP, John Nicholas. b 57. Wycliffe Hall Ox 92. **d** 94 **p** 95. C Ipswich St Jo *St E* 94-97; TV Beccles St Mich 97-05; P-in-c Beccles St Mich and St Luke 05-08; R 08-15; V Canonbury St Steph *Lon* from 15. *St Stephen's Vicarage, 9 River Place, London N1 2DE* T: (020) 7226 7526 E: reverendjohnbeauchamp@gmail.com

BEAUCHAMP, Julian Thomas Proctor. b 68. Ex Univ BA 91. Oak Hill Th Coll BA 05. **d** 05 **p** 06. C Cheadle *Ches* 05-08; R Waverton w Aldford and Bruera from 08. *The Rectory, Village Road, Waverton, Chester CH3 7QN* T: (01244) 336668 M: 07974-397022 E: jules@stpeterswaverton.org.uk

BEAUMONT, Adam John. b 75. Bris Univ BSc 97 PGCE 01. Trin Coll Bris MA 12. **d** 12 **p** 13. C Westbury-on-Trym H Trin *Bris*

12-15; TV Gtr Corsham and Lacock from 15. *The Vicarage, Folly Lane, Lacock, Chippenham SN15 2LL* M: 07903-672067 E: adamjbeaumont@gmail.com

BEAUMONT, Canon Brian Maxwell. b 34. Nottm Univ BA 56. Wells Th Coll 58. **d** 59 **p** 60. C Clifton *S'well* 59-62; C E Stoke w Syerston 62; C Edgbaston St Geo *Birm* 62-65; V Smethwick St Alb 65-70; V Blackb H Trin 70-77; Asst Dir RE 70-73; Dir RE 73-92; Hon Can Blackb Cathl 73-77 and 92-99; Can Res Blackb Cathl 77-92; V Goosnargh w Whittingham 92-99; Bp's Adv for Rural Areas 92-99; rtd 99; PtO *Blackb* from 00. *14 Green Drive, Barton, Preston PR3 5AT* T: (01772) 861131

BEAUMONT, Mrs Catherine Grace La Touche. b 60. SS Coll Cam MA 83 Darw Coll Cam PGCE 83 Solicitor 87. **d** 09 **p** 10. OLM Clopton w Otley, Swilland and Ashbocking *St E* 09-13; OLM Carlford from 13. *Otley Hall, Hall Lane, Otley, Ipswich IP6 9PA* T: (01473) 890264 M: 07801-3423 36 E: catherine.beaumont@otleyhall.co.uk

BEAUMONT, Christopher Siward. b 78. Ridley Hall Cam 13. **d** 15. C Bradley Stoke N CD *Bris* from 15. *The Vicarage, Mautravers Close, Bradley Stoke, Bristol BS32 8ED* T: 0117-969 7441 M: 07743-407365 E: chris@chrisandcat.net

BEAUMONT, Mrs Jane. b 56. Ches Coll of HE BTh. NOC 01. **d** 04 **p** 05. NSM Chadkirk *Ches* 04-08; C Ashton-upon-Mersey St Mary Magd from 08. *23 Rydal Avenue, Sale M33 6WN* T: 0161-282 2207 E: janebeaumont@live.co.uk

BEAUMONT, Canon John Philip. b 32. Leeds Univ BA 55. Coll of Resurr Mirfield 55. **d** 57 **p** 58. C Leeds St Marg *Ripon* 57-60; C Wellingborough All Hallows *Pet* 60-64; V Wellingborough St Andr 64-70; Chapl HM Borstal Wellingborough 64-70; V Finedon *Pet* 70-96; Can Pet Cathl 80-96; RD Higham 83-87; rtd 96; PtO *Pet* from 96. *9 Warren Bridge, Oundle, Peterborough PE8 4DQ* T: (01832) 273863 E: john@beaumont.plus.com

BEAUMONT, Stephen Martin. b 51. K Coll Lon BD 73 AKC 74. St Aug Coll Cant 73. **d** 74 **p** 75. C Benwell St Jas *Newc* 74-77; Asst Chapl Marlborough Coll 77-81; R Ideford, Luton and Ashcombe *Ex* 81-84; Bp's Dom Chapl 81-84; Chapl Taunton Sch 85-91; Chapl Haileybury Coll 92-00; Second Chapl and Hd Div Tonbridge Sch 00-04; Sen Chapl 04-11; P-in-c Chiddingstone w Chiddingstone Causeway *Roch* 11-12; R from 12. *The Rectory, Chiddingstone, Edenbridge TN8 7AH* T: (01892) 870478

BEAUMONT, Canon Terence Mayes. b 41. Lon Univ BA 63. Linc Th Coll 68. **d** 71 **p** 72. C Hitchin St Mary *St Alb* 71-74; C Harpenden St Nic 75-79; V Stevenage St Pet Broadwater 79-87; V St Alb St Mich 87-06; Hon Can St Alb 05-06; rtd 06. *65 Weatherby, Dunstable LU6 1TP* T: (01582) 661333 E: y.beaumont123@btinternet.com

BEAUMONT, Mrs Veronica Jean. b 38. Ox Min Course 90. **d** 93 **p** 94. NSM High Wycombe *Ox* 93-03; NSM W Wycombe w Bledlow Ridge, Bradenham and Radnage from 03; Fundraising Manager (Oxon) Children's Soc from 95. *Edgehill, Upper Stanley Road, High Wycombe HP12 4DB* T: (01494) 523697 E: veronica.beaumont@virgin.net

BEAVAN, Canon Edward Hugh. b 43. Ex Coll Ox BA 70 MA 74 Solicitor 66. Cuddesdon Coll 69. **d** 71 **p** 72. C Ashford St Hilda *Lon* 71-74; C Newington St Mary *S'wark* 74-76; R Sandon *Chelmsf* 76-86; V Thorpe Bay 86-98; P-in-c Bradwell on Sea 98-05; P-in-c St Lawrence 98-05; V Burnham 05-09; Ind Chapl 98-05; RD Maldon and Dengie 00-05; Hon Can Chelmsf Cathl 02-09; rtd 09; PtO *Chelmsf* from 09. *19 Wordsworth Road, Colchester CO3 4HR* T: (01206) 564577 E: hugh@beavan.go-plus.net

BEAVER, William Carpenter. b 45. Colorado Coll BA Wolfs Coll Ox DPhil 76. Ox NSM Course 79. **d** 82 **p** 83. NSM Kennington St Jo w St Jas *S'wark* 82-95; NSM Avonmouth St Andr *Bris* 96-97; NSM Bris St Mary Redcliffe w Temple etc 95-08; NSM St Andr Holborn *Lon* 01-04; Dir Communications for C of E 97-02; Dir Communications for Br Red Cross 02-04; Speech Writer to the Ld Mayor of Lon 04-10; NSM Iffley *Ox* from 10; OCM from 09. *50 Church Way, Iffley, Oxford OX4 4EF* T: (01865) 778061 E: william.beaver@btinternet.com

BEAVIS, Adrian Neill. b 74. Worc Coll Ox BA 97. Wycliffe Hall Ox MTh 00. **d** 00 **p** 01. C E Twickenham St Steph *Lon* 00-08; V S Kensington St Luke from 08. *12 Wharfedale Street, London SW10 9AL* T: (020) 7370 0338 E: adrian@stlukeschurch.co.uk

BEAVIS, Sandra Kathleen. b 51. Univ Coll Chich BA 01. **d** 98 **p** 07. C Southbourne w W Thorney *Chich* 98-05; C Bedhampton *Portsm* 05-09; PtO 09-10; P-in-c Soberton w Newtown from 10; OCM from 02. *The Vicarage, Webbs Green, Soberton, Southampton SO32 3PY* T: (01489) 877400 E: sandrabeavis@btinternet.com

BEAZLEY, Prof John Milner. b 32. Man Univ MB, ChB 57 MRCOG 62 FRCOG 73 FACOG 89 MD 64. St Deiniol's Hawarden 83. **d** 86 **p** 87. NSM W Kirby St Bridget *Ches* 86-89;

NSM Newton 89-92; NSM Hayton w Cumwhitton *Carl* 92-98; rtd 99; PtO *Carl* from 99. *High Rigg, Faugh, Heads Nook, Carlisle CA8 9EA* T: (01228) 70353

BEAZLEY-LONG, Clive. b 77. Greenwich Univ BSc 99. Trin Coll Bris 08. **d** 10 **p** 11. C Chertsey, Lyne and Longcross *Guildf* 10-14; V Erith St Paul *Roch* from 14. *The Vicarage, 44A Colyers Lane, Erith DA8 3NP* E: revclive@hotmail.co.uk

BEBB, Erica Charlotte. b 61. STETS. **d** 09 **p** 10. NSM Sea Mills *Bris* 09-13; NSM Clifton Ch Ch w Em from 13. *21 Bramble Drive, Bristol BS9 1RE* T: 0117-968 2153 E: info@3inone.co.uk

BEBBINGTON, Julia. *See* BABB, Julia Bebbington

BECHTOLD, Bryant Coffin. b 51. Georgia Inst of Tech BCE 73 MCE 75 Univ of Utah PhD 78 Univ of the S (USA) MDiv 86. **d** 86 **p** 87. C Atlanta St Luke USA 86-87; C Deltona 87-89; V Price and E Carbon 90-97; V Fort Worth Ch the King 97-00; R 00-06; PtO *St Alb* 06-07; P-in-c The Wainfleet Gp *Linc* 07-13; rtd 13. *301 Cedar Ridge Drive, Cave Junction OR 97523, USA*

BECK, Alan. b 28. AKC 50. **d** 53 **p** 54. C N Harrow St Alb *Lon* 53-56; C Northolt St Mary 56-59; C Loughborough All SS *Leic* 59-61; V Crookham *Guildf* 61-69; V Puriton *B & W* 69-78; P-in-c Pawlett 74-78; V Puriton and Pawlett 78-79; P-in-c Staplegrove 79-84; R 84-88; rtd 88; PtO *B & W* 88-97 and 04-07. *Redwing, Creech Heathfield, Taunton TA3 5EG* T: (01823) 443030

BECK, Amanda Ruth. b 68. Liv Univ BA 91 Birm Univ BD 93. Qu Coll Birm 91. **d** 94 **p** 95. C W Derby Gd Shep *Liv* 94-99; Asst Chapl Voorschoten *Eur* 99-02; P-in-c Kingston Vale St Jo *S'wark* 03-12; TV Kingston from 12; Chapl SW Lon and St George's Mental Health NHS Trust from 13. *St John's Vicarage, Robin Hood Lane, London SW15 3PY* T: (020) 8546 4079 E: mandy.beck@alty.org

BECK, Mrs Gillian Margaret. b 50. Sheff Univ CertEd 71 Nottm Univ BTh 78. Linc Th Coll 74. **dss** 78 **d** 87. Gt Grimsby St Mary and St Jas *Linc* 78-83; St Paul's Cathl 84-87; Hon Par Dn St Botolph Aldgate w H Trin Minories 87-88; Par Dn Monkwearmouth St Andr *Dur* 88-94; C 94-96; NSM Eppleton and Hetton le Hole 97-04; NSM E Rainton 04-11; NSM W Rainton 04-11; PtO from 13. *The Rectory, South Street, West Rainton, Houghton le Spring DH4 6PA* T: 0191-584 7595

BECK, John Edward. b 28. ARCM 52 FRCO 59 St Jo Coll Ox BA 56 MA 59. Wells Th Coll 56. **d** 58 **p** 59. C Dursley *Glouc* 58-61; C Glouc St Paul 61-63; S Rhodesia 63-65; Rhodesia 65-70; C Cheltenham Ch Ch *Glouc* 70-77; C Cirencester 77-93; rtd 93; PtO *Glouc* from 93. *25 Bowling Green Road, Cirencester GL7 2HD* T: (01285) 653778

BECK, Ms Karen Maureen. b 53. R Holloway Coll Lon BA 74. St Alb Minl Tr Scheme 88. **d** 92 **p** 94. Par Dn Royston *St Alb* 92-94; C 94-96; TV Chipping Barnet w Arkley 96-02; P-in-c Heddon-on-the-Wall *Newc* 02-07; Chapl Northumbria Police 02-07; P-in-c Didcot All SS *Ox* from 07. *The Rectory, 140 Lydalls Road, Didcot OX11 7EA* T: (01235) 813244 E: karen.beck140@gmail.com

BECK, Michael Leonard. b 50. K Coll Lon BD 77 AKC 77. Linc Th Coll 77. **d** 78 **p** 79. C Gt Grimsby St Mary and St Jas *Linc* 78-83; Min Can and Succ St Paul's Cathl 83-88; V Monkwearmouth St Andr *Dur* 88-96; TR Monkwearmouth 97; R Eppleton and Hetton le Hole 97-04; AD Houghton 97-04; P-in-c Lyons 00-04; P-in-c W Rainton from 04; P-in-c E Rainton from 04; Dir Reader Min 04-09; Tutor Lindisfarne Regional Tr Partnership from 09. *The Rectory, South Street, West Rainton, Houghton le Spring DH4 6PA* T: 0191-584 7595

BECK, The Very Revd Peter John. b 48. Mert Coll Ox BA 69 MA 73. Sarum Th Coll 69. **d** 72 **p** 73. C Banbury *Ox* 72-75; TV 75-78; Dioc Youth and Community Officer 75-78; P-in-c St Mary-le-Wigford w St Benedict etc 78-81; Chapl Linc City Cen 78-81; TV Glenfield New Zealand 81-85; V Mt Albert St Luke 86-93; Adn Waitemata 87-93; V Auckland St Matt 93-00; Adn Auckland 98-00; Hon Asst P Wellington Cathl 00-02; Dir Vaughan Park Retreat Cen 02; Dean Christchurch 02-13; V Gen Christchurch 03-13; rtd 13. *11 Draper Street, Richmond, Christchurch 8013, New Zealand* M: 21-654445 E: peterbeck@xtra.co.nz

BECK, Roger William. b 48. Chich Th Coll 79. **d** 81 **p** 82. C St Marychurch *Ex* 81-85; TV Torre 85-88; V Torquay St Jo and Ellacombe 88-94; C Plympton St Mary from 94. *27 Pinewood Close, Plympton, Plymouth PL7 2DW* T: (01752) 336393

BECK, Mrs Sandra Veronica. b 52. St Jo Coll Nottm 97. **d** 00 **p** 01. NSM Digswell and Panshanger *St Alb* 00-04; NSM Codicote 04-08; PtO 08-09; Chapl E and N Herts NHS Trust 09-13; PtO *St Alb* from 13. *4 Grange Rise, Codicote, Hitchin SG4 8YR* T: (01438) 820191 E: csbeck@btinternet.com

BECK, Stephen Andrew. b 70. K Coll Lon BSc 93 Liv Univ PGCE 97. Trin Coll Bris 11. **d** 13 **p** 14. C Woodlands *Sheff* from 13. *11 Crabgate Lane, Skellow, Doncaster DN6 8LE* M: 07739-509967 T: (01302) 953091 E: revstevebeck@gmail.com

BECKERLEG, Barzillai. b 20. Selw Coll Cam BA 43 MA 46. Westcott Ho Cam 42. **d** 44 **p** 45. C Golders Green St Alb *Lon* 44-48; Chapl St Jo Coll Dur 48-52; LtO *Dur* 49-52; V Battersea St Mary *S'wark* 52-58; V Wentworth *Sheff* 58-59; Hd Master Newc Cathl Choir Sch 59-62; Prec Newc Cathl 59-62; R Duncton *Chich* 62-64; R Burton w Coates 62-64; V Kippington *Roch* 64-75; R E Bergholt *St E* 75-79; Chapl St Mary's Sch Wantage 79-85; rtd 85; PtO *Truro* from 85; *Roch* 86-93; *Chich* from 93; *Roch* from 00; *S'wark* from 00. *17 Ramsay Hall, 9-13 Byron Road, Worthing BN11 3HN* T: (01903) 200376

BECKETT, Bonnie. *See* BECKETT, Yvonne Janine

BECKETT, Glynis. b 58. **d** 10 **p** 11. OLM Radley and Sunningwell *Ox* 10-15; OLM Radley, Sunningwell and Kennington from 15. *18 Sadlers Court, Abingdon OX14 2PA* T: (01235) 529505 E: glynis.beckett@lmh.ox.ac.uk

BECKETT, Graham. b 49. St As Minl Tr Course 95. **d** 99 **p** 00. NSM Hawarden *St As* 99-01; C 01-07; V Gorsedd w Brynford, Ysgeifiog and Whitford 07-14; P-in-c Mostyn 13-14; AD Holywell 11-14; rtd 14. *Hillview, Church Lane, Aston Hill, Ewloe, Deeside CH5 3BF* T: (01244) 535269

BECKETT, John Adrian. b 61. Bris Univ BVSc 85. Trin Coll Bris. **d** 00 **p** 01. C Harrogate St Mark *Ripon* 00-04; P-in-c Sevenhampton w Charlton Abbots, Hawling etc *Glouc* 04-14; P-in-c Torquay St Matthias, St Mark and H Trin *Ex* from 14. *The Rectory, Wellswood Avenue, Torquay TQ1 2QE* T: (01803) 293119 M: 07513-346521 E: jandrbeckett@btinternet.com

BECKETT, Michael Shaun. b 55. ACA 79. Oak Hill Th Coll BA 88. **d** 88 **p** 89. C Cambridge St Barn *Ely* 88-93; P-in-c Cambridge St Paul 93-94; V from 94. *St Paul's Vicarage, 15 St Paul's Road, Cambridge CB1 2EZ* T: (01223) 354186 *or* 315832 F: 471792 E: church@centrestpauls.org.uk

BECKETT, Mrs Patricia Anne. b 44. **d** 00 **p** 01. NSM Cheddleton *Lich* 00-06; NSM Upper Tean 06-12; PtO from 13. *10 Wallis Way, Stoke-on-Trent ST2 7JQ* T: (01782) 769718

BECKETT, Mrs Yvonne Janine (Bonnie). b 50. Qu Coll Birm 13. **d** 15. C Walsall Pleck and Bescot *Lich* from 15. *1 Newhall Crescent, Cannock WS11 7ZD* T: (01543) 270011 E: bonniebeckett@talktalk.net

BECKHAM, John Francis. b 25. Bps' Coll Cheshunt 65. **d** 67 **p** 68. C Leytonstone St Jo *Chelmsf* 67-70; C Colchester St Mary V 70-73; R Lawford 73-80; V Gt w Lt Chesterford 80-90; rtd 90; PtO *St E* from 91. *North Barn, Reckford Road, Westleton, Saxmundham IP17 3BE* T: (01728) 648969

BECKINSALE, Mrs Pamela Rachel. b 46. Man Univ BSc 69. Cant Sch of Min 88. **d** 91 **p** 94. NSM Sittingbourne St Mich *Cant* 91-96; Hon Chapl Thames Gateway NHS Trust 96-98; Chapl from 98. *8 Glovers Crescent, Bell Road, Sittingbourne ME10 4DU* T: (01795) 471632 *or* 418300

BECKLEY, Peter William (Pedr). b 52. Lon Univ BSc 73 CertEd. Trin Coll Bris 76. **d** 79 **p** 80. C Plymouth St Jude *Ex* 79-83; C Ecclesall *Sheff* 83-88; V Greystones from 88; P-in-c Endcliffe from 11. *The Vicarage, 1 Cliffe Farm Drive, Sheffield S11 7JW* T: 0114-266 7686 E: pedr@talktalk.net

BECKLEY, Simon Richard. b 38. Lon Univ BA 61. Oak Hill Th Coll 58. **d** 63 **p** 64. C Watford St Luke *St Alb* 63-67; C New Ferry *Ches* 67-70; C Chadderton Ch Ch *Man* 70-73; V Friarmere 73-80; V Tranmere St Cath *Ches* 80-03; Chapl Wirral Community Healthcare NHS Trust 80-97; Chapl Wirral and W Cheshire Community NHS Trust 97-03; rtd 03; PtO *Ches* from 04. *162 Heathbank Avenue, Wirral CH61 4YG* T: 0151-648 7767

BECKWITH, Ian Stanley. b 36. Nottm Univ BA 58 Selw Coll Cam CertEd 59 Westmr Coll Ox MTh 96. Linc Th Coll 78. **d** 79 **p** 80. NSM Linc Cathl 79-85; Sen Lect Bp Grosseteste Coll Linc 80-86; NSM Wallingford w Crowmarsh Gifford etc *Ox* 91-97; OLM Tr Officer (Berks) 96-02; P-in-c Gt Coxwell w Buscot, Coleshill etc 97-02; rtd 02; PtO *Heref* from 02; *Lich* 02-11. *2 Affcot Mill, Affcot, Church Stretton SY6 6RL* T: (01694) 781667

BECKWITH, Canon John Douglas. b 33. AKC 57. **d** 58 **p** 65. C Streatham St Leon *S'wark* 58-59; LtO *Ripon* 59-60; Tutor Ijebu-Igbo Gr Sch and Molusi Coll Nigeria 60-62; C Bedale *Ripon* 62-63; C Mottingham St Andr w St Alban *S'wark* 64-69; Chapl Gothenburg w Halmstad and Jönköping *Eur* 69-70; Chapl to Suff Bp Edmonton 70-77; Dir of Ords *Lon* 70-77; V Brookfield St Anne, Highgate Rise 77-88; Can Gib Cathl 84-88; Hon Can Gib Cathl 88-05; P-in-c Bladon w Woodstock *Ox* 88-93; P-in-c Wootton and Kiddington w Asterleigh 88; C Kidlington w Hampton Poyle 93-94; PtO *Lon* from 94; rtd 98; PtO *Eur* from 98. *4 St James's Close, Bishop Street, London N1 8PH* T: (020) 7226 6672 M: 07710-277124 E: malbis@dircon.co.uk

BECKWITH, John James. b 53. UMIST BSc 74 Newc Univ PGCE 88. **d** 02 **p** 03. OLM Bothal and Pegswood w Longhirst *Newc* 02-04; C Morpeth 04-07; V Belford and Lucker from 07.

The Vicarage, North Bank, Belford NE70 7LY T: (01668) 213545 E: johnange@ne61yg.wanadoo.co.uk

BECKWITH, Roger Thomas. b 29. St Edm Hall Ox BA 52 MA 56 BD 85 Lambeth DD 92. Ripon Hall Ox 51 Tyndale Hall Bris 52 Cuddesdon Coll 54. **d** 54 **p** 55. C Harold Wood *Chelmsf* 54-57; C Bedminster St Luke w St Silas *Bris* 57-59; Tutor Tyndale Hall Bris 59-63; Lib Latimer Ho Ox 63-73 and from 94; Warden 73-94; Lect Wycliffe Hall Ox 71-94; Hon C Wytham Ox 88-89; Hon C N Hinksey and Wytham 90-96; rtd 94; Hon C Ox St Mich w St Martin and All SS 97-03; PtO from 03. *310 Woodstock Road, Oxford OX2 7NR* T: (01865) 557340

BEDEAU (*née* MILLS), Mrs Melina. b 40. Local Minl Tr Course. **d** 00 **p** 04. NSM W Bromwich St Phil *Lich* 00-03; NSM W Bromwich Gd Shep w St Jo 03-13; PtO from 13. *4 Jervoise Street, West Bromwich B70 9LY* T: 0121-553 6833

BEDELL, Anthony Charles John. b 59. Worc Coll Ox BA 81 Univ Coll Chich PGCE 05 ACA 84. Linc Th Coll BTh 90. **d** 90 **p** 91. C Newbold w Dunston *Derby* 90-94; C Bedford Leigh *Man* 94-98; V Blackb St Luke w St Phil 98-03; Min Partnership Development Officer *Pet* 03; L'Arche Bognor Community 03-04; PtO *Chich* 03-04; LtO from 04; Teacher Bognor Regis Community Coll from 05. *22 Armada Way, Littlehampton BN17 6QY* T: (01903) 717719 E: abedell@wsgfl.org.uk

BEDFORD, Christopher John. b 40. CEng 68 MIStructE 68. **d** 05 **p** 06. OLM Chobham w Valley End *Guildf* from 05. *23 Swallow Rise, Knaphill, Woking GU21 2LG* T: (01483) 480127 E: ahbedford@hotmail.com

BEDFORD, Mrs Linda. b 43. **d** 07. NSM Hanley Castle, Hanley Swan and Welland *Worc* from 06. *Address temp unknown* E: lbedford_uk@yahoo.co.uk

BEDFORD, Michael Anthony. b 38. Reading Univ BSc 59 Heythrop Coll Lon MA 00. **d** 01 **p** 02. NSM Ruislip St Martin *Lon* from 01. *7 Chandos Road, Eastcote, Pinner HA5 1PR* T: (020) 8866 4332 E: mabedford7cr@waitrose.com

BEDFORD, Archdeacon of. *See* HUGHES, The Ven Paul Vernon

BEDFORD, Suffragan Bishop of. *See* ATKINSON, The Rt Revd Richard William Bryant

BEE, Mrs Judith Mary. b 52. STETS 03. **d** 06 **p** 07. NSM Hambledon *Portsm* 06-10; NSM Buriton from 10. *St Mary's House, 41 North Lane, Buriton, Petersfield GU31 4RS* T: (01730) 269390 E: judith.bee@clara.co.uk

BEEBEE, Meyrick Richard Legge. b 43. SAOMC 99. **d** 02 **p** 03. NSM Gerrards Cross and Fulmer *Ox* from 02. *Lychgate House, 34 Austenway, Chalfont St Peter, Gerrards Cross SL9 8NW* E: meyrick.beebee@saintjames.org.uk

BEEBY, Matthew. b 57. Oak Hill Th Coll. **d** 11 **p** 12. NSM Mayfair Ch Ch *Lon* from 11. *16 Abbott Avenue, London SW20 8SQ*

BEECH, Miss Ailsa. b 44. N Co Coll Newc TDip 65. Trin Coll Bris 78. **dss** 80 **d** 87 **p** 94. Pudsey St Lawr and St Paul *Bradf* 80-88; Par Dn 87-88; C Attleborough *Cov* 88-89; Par Dn Cumnor *Ox* 89-92; Asst Chapl Walsgrave Hosp Cov 92-94; Asst Chapl Walsgrave Hosps NHS Trust 94-96; Chapl 96-00; Chapl Univ Hosps Cov and Warks NHS Trust 00-04; rtd 04; PtO *York* from 04. *Oxenby, Whitby Road, Pickering YO18 7HL* T: (01751) 472689 E: ailsab@talktalk.net

BEECH, Preb Charmian Patricia. b 45. RGN 66 RHV 70 TCert 74. St As Minl Tr Course 99. **d** 02 **p** 03. C Connah's Quay *St As* 02-04; P-in-c Hodnet *Lich* 04-14; Dioc Child Protection Officer 04-14; RD Hodnet 11-14; Preb Lich Cathl 13-14; rtd 14; PtO *Heref* from 15; *Lich* from 15. *3 Railway Mews, Minsterly Road, Pontesbury, Shrewsbury SY5 0QH* E: salop@charmianbeech14.plus.com

BEECH, Frank Thomas. b 36. Tyndale Hall Bris 64. **d** 66 **p** 67. C Penn Fields *Lich* 66-70; C Attenborough w Chilwell *S'well* 70-74; P-in-c 74-75; P-in-c Attenborough 75-76; V 76-84; V Worksop St Anne 84-03; Chapl Welbeck Coll 84-03; rtd 04; PtO *S'well* from 04. *43 Bescar Lane, Ollerton, Newark NG22 9BS* M: 07743-592012 E: frank.beech@lineone.net

BEECH, John. b 41. St Jo Coll Nottm. **d** 83 **p** 83. C York St Paul 83-84; P-in-c Bubwith w Ellerton and Aughton 84-85; P-in-c Thorganby w Skipwith and N Duffield 84-85; V Bubwith w Skipwith 85-87; V Acomb H Redeemer 87-00; P-in-c Westleigh St Pet *Man* 00-01; rtd 01; PtO *York* from 04. *6 Water Ark Cottages, Goathland, Whitby YO22 5JZ* E: jobe69@btinternet.com

BEECH, John Thomas. b 38. St Aid Birkenhead 64. **d** 67 **p** 68. C Burton St Paul *Lich* 67-70; Chapl RN 70-85; V Ellingham and Harbridge and Ibsley *Win* 85-94; Chapl Whiteley Village *Guildf* 94-03; rtd 03. *10 Friars Walk, Barton-on-Sea, New Milton BH25 7DA*

BEECH, Mrs Linda. b 59. **d** 06 **p** 07. NSM Blymhill w Weston-under-Lizard *Lich* 06-09; NSM Watershed 09-14; rtd 14; PtO *Lich* from 15. *The New Rectory, School Lane, Blymhill, Shifnal TF11 8LH* T: (01952) 850149 E: beeches7@tiscali.co.uk

BEECH, Peter John. b 34. Bps' Coll Cheshunt 58. **d** 61 **p** 62. C Fulham All SS *Lon* 61-64; S Africa 64-67; V S Hackney St Mich *Lon* 68-71; P-in-c Haggerston St Paul 68-71; V S Hackney St Mich w Haggerston St Paul 71-75; V Wanstead H Trin Hermon Hill *Chelmsf* 75-89; P-in-c St Mary-at-Latton 89-90; V 90-99; rtd 99; PtO *Ely* from 99. *9 Fitzgerald Close, Ely CB7 4QB* T: (01353) 666269

BEECH-GRÜNEBERG, Keith Nigel. b 72. CCC Ox BA 93 MA 96 St Jo Coll Dur BA 97 PhD 02. Cranmer Hall Dur 95. **d** 01 **p** 02. C Pangbourne w Tidmarsh and Sulham *Ox* 01-04; Dir Studies Dioc Bd Stewardship 04-11; Dir Local Min Tr from 11. *3 Gall Close, Abingdon OX14 3XY* M: 07731-894344 E: keith.beech-gruneberg@oxford.anglican.org

BEECHAM, Clarence Ralph. b 35. S'wark Ord Course. **d** 83 **p** 84. NSM Leigh-on-Sea St Jas *Chelmsf* 83-86. *27 Scarborough Drive, Leigh-on-Sea SS9 3ED* T: (01702) 574923

BEECROFT, Benjamin Harold. b 77. Trin Coll Bris BA 98. **d** 00 **p** 01. C Stapleford *S'well* 00-04; C Warfield *Ox* 04-07; V Addlestone *Guildf* from 07. *The Vicarage, 140 Church Road, Addlestone KT15 1SJ* T: (01932) 842879 E: ben.beecroft@btinternet.com

BEECROFT, Mrs Christine Mary. b 62. RGN 85. Trin Coll Bris BA 97 MA 99. **d** 98 **p** 99. C Roxeth *Lon* 98-00; PtO *S'well* 00-02; C Stapleford 02-04; NSM Warfield *Ox* 04-07; C Addlestone *Guildf* from 09. *The Vicarage, 140 Church Road, Addlestone KT15 1SJ* T: (01932) 842879 E: chrisbeecroft@btinternet.com

BEECROFT, Miriam Joanna. **d** 15. C Bro Ardudwy *Ban* from 15. *The Rectory, Mon Dirion, Old Llanfair Road, Harlech LL46 2SS* T: (01766) 781553 E: miriam@esgobaethbangor.net

BEEDELL, Trevor Francis. b 31. ALCD 65. **d** 65 **p** 66. C Walton St E 65-68; R Hartshorne *Derby* 68-79; RD Repton 74-79; V Overedge 79-86; Chapl HM Det Cen Foston Hall 79-80; Dioc Dir of Chr Stewardship *Derby* 79-97; rtd 97; PtO *Derby* from 97. *185 High Lane West, West Hallam, Ilkeston DE7 6HP* T: 0115-932 5589

BEEDON, David Kirk. b 59. Birm Univ BA 89 MPhil 93. Qu Coll Birm 86. **d** 89 **p** 90. C Cannock *Lich* 89-92; V Wednesbury St Bart 92-99; R Lich St Mich w St Mary and Wall 99-12; P-in-c Lich Ch CH 07-09; Chapl HM Pris Ranby from 12. *HM Prison, Ranby, Retford DN22 8EU* T: (01777) 862325 E: dkbeedon@btinternet.com

BEER, Anthony Mark. St Mich Coll Llan. **d** 09 **p** 10. NSM Caerau w Ely *Llan* 09-11; C Llantwit Major 11-13; TV from 13. *The New Rectory, Trepit Road, Wick, Cowbridge CF71 7QL* T: (01656) 895068 E: wickvic004@icloud.com

BEER, Ms Deborah Marion. b 57. SEITE 12. **d** 15. NSM Hurstpierpoint *Chich* from 15. *11 Welbeck Drive, Burgess Hill RH15 0BB* M: 07530-039299 E: revdebbiebeer@gmail.com

BEER, Mrs Janet Margaret. b 43. Goldsmiths' Coll Lon CertEd 64. Oak Hill Th Coll 83. **dss** 86 **d** 87 **p** 94. London Colney St Pet *St Alb* 86-97; Hon C 87-97; Chapl St Alb High Sch for Girls 87-89; Chapl Middx Univ *Lon* 94-97; NSM Northaw and Cuffley *St Alb* 97-09; rtd 09; PtO *Portsm* from 09. *L'Auberge, 15 Seymour Road, Lee-on-the-Solent PO13 9EG* T: (023) 9255 0264 E: j.m.beer@btinternet.com

BEER, The Ven John Stuart. b 44. Pemb Coll Ox BA 65 MA 70 Fitzw Coll Cam MA 78. Westcott Ho Cam 69. **d** 71 **p** 72. C Knaresborough St Jo *Ripon* 71-74; Chapl Fitzw Coll and New Hall Cam 74-80; Fell Fitzw Coll 77-80; Bye-Fell from 01; P-in-c Toft w Caldecote and Childerley *Ely* 80-83; R 83-87; P-in-c Hardwick 80-83; R 83-87; V Grantchester 87-97; Dir of Ords, Post-Ord Tr and Student Readers from 88; Hon Can Ely Cathl from 89; Adn Huntingdon 97-04; Acting Adn Wisbech 02-04; Adn Cam 04-14; rtd 14. *19 St Mark's Court, Cambridge CB3 9LE* E: johnbeer1@btinternet.com

BEER, Kevin Lionel Charles. b 74. SWMTC 09. **d** 12 **p** 13. C Parkham, Alwington, Buckland Brewer etc *Ex* 12-14; NSM from 12. *The Rectory, Parkham, Bideford EX39 5PL* T: (01237) 451661 E: mrkevinlcbeer@btinternet.com

BEER, Kevin Vincent. b 65. Ox Min Course 09. **d** 12. C Beaconsfield *Ox* from 12. *27 Crossways, Beaconsfield HP9 2HX* T: (01494) 673021 M: 07740-869501 E: kvbeer@gmail.com

BEER, Michael Trevor. b 44. Chich Th Coll 66. **d** 69 **p** 70. C Leagrave *St Alb* 69-73; C St Geo Cathl Kingstown St Vincent 73-74; C Thorley w Bishop's Stortford H Trin *St Alb* 74-80; V London Colney St Pet 80-97; V Northaw and Cuffley 97-09; rtd 09; PtO *Portsm* from 09. *L'Auberge, 15 Seymour Road, Lee-on-the-Solent PO13 9EG* T: (023) 9255 0264 E: j.m.beer@btinternet.com

BEER, Nigel David. b 62. Portsm Poly BSc 84. St Jo Coll Nottm MA 93. **d** 93 **p** 94. C Rastrick St Matt *Wakef* 93-96; C Bilton *Ripon* 96-98; TV Moor Allerton 98-09; TV Moor Allerton and Shadwell 09-13; Asst Dir of Ords 05-13; V Stanwix *Carl*

from 13. *The Vicarage, Dykes Terrace, Carlisle CA3 9AS* T: (01228) 514600 E: rev.beer@hotmail.co.uk

BEER, William Barclay. b 43. ACT ThA 68 St Steph Ho Ox. **d** 71 **p** 72. C St Marychurch *Ex* 71-76; V Pattishall w Cold Higham *Pet* 76-82; V Northampton St Benedict 82-85; V Chislehurst Annunciation *Roch* 85-12; rtd 12. *St Mary's Vicarage, Lansdowne Road, London N17 9XE* T: (020) 8808 6644 E: williambbeer@tiscali.co.uk

BEESLEY, Aran Paul. b 71. Linc Sch of Th and Min 11 Westcott Ho Cam 14. **d** 15. C Stamford All SS w St Jo *Linc* from 15. *2 Highgrove Gardens, Stamford PE9 2GR* M: 07490-055905 E: aran.beesley@gmail.com

BEESLEY, Daniel Edward. b 76. Man Univ BA 01. Wycliffe Hall Ox 13. **d** 15. C Risborough *Ox* from 15. *26 Summerleys Road, Princes Risborough HP27 9DT* M: 07590-123603 T: (01844) 344654 E: revdbeesley@gmail.com

BEESLEY, John Stanley. b 70. St Martin's Coll Lanc BSc 92. WEMTC 06. **d** 09 **p** 10. C Ludlow *Heref* 09-12; R Diddlebury w Munslow, Holdgate and Tugford from 12. *St Michael's Rectory, Park Lane, Munslow, Craven Arms SY7 9EU* T: (01584) 841488 E: revjbeesley@gmail.com

BEESLEY, Michael Frederick. b 37. K Coll Cam BA 59. Westcott Ho Cam 60. **d** 61 **p** 64. C Eastleigh *Win* 61-69; rtd 02. *24 Charmouth Grove, Poole BH14 0LP* T: (01202) 773471 E: michaelbeesley@ntlworld.com

BEESLEY, Ramon John. b 27. Magd Coll Ox BA 51 MA 55. Wycliffe Hall Ox 51. **d** 53 **p** 56. C Gerrards Cross *Ox* 53-54; Asst Chapl Embley Park Sch Romsey 54-58; PtO *Win* 54-58; Asst Master Farnham Sch 58-62; PtO *Guildf* 58-62; *Win* from 63; Hd Science Gore Sch New Milton 63-69; Dep Hd Applemore Sch Dibden Purlieu 69-74; Hd Master Bellemoor Sch Southn 74-84; rtd 84. *3 Cranwell Close, Bransgore, Christchurch BH23 8HY* T: (01425) 672040

BEESON, Christopher George. b 48. Man Univ BSc 70. Qu Coll Birm 72. **d** 75 **p** 76. C Flixton St Mich *Man* 75-78; C Newton Heath All SS 78-80; R Gorton St Jas 80-90; Dioc Communications Officer *Blackb* 91-92; C Ribbleton 92-93; rtd 93; PtO *Blackb* from 93. *24 Arnold Close, Ribbleton, Preston PR2 6DX* T: (01772) 702675 E: cbeeson@cix.co.uk

BEESON, The Very Revd Trevor Randall. b 26. OBE 97. K Coll Lon MA 76 FKC 87 Southn Univ Hon DLitt 99. **d** 51 **p** 52. C Leadgate *Dur* 51-54; C Norton St Mary 54-56; C-in-c Stockton St Chad CD 56-60; V Stockton St Chad 60-65; C St Martin-in-the-Fields *Lon* 65-71; V Ware St Mary *St Alb* 71-76; Can Westmr Abbey 76-87; Treas Westmr Abbey 78-82; I Westmr St Marg 82-87; Chapl to Speaker of Ho of Commons 82-87; Dean Win 87-96; rtd 96; PtO *Win* from 96. *69 Greatbridge Road, Romsey SO51 8FE* T: (01794) 514627

BEESTON, Andrew Bernard. b 41. RMN 64 RGN 67. NEOC 99. **d** 01 **p** 02. NSM Cullercoats St Geo *Newc* 01-06; NSM Long Benton 06-09; NSM Earsdon and Backworth from 09. *21 Deepdale Road, Cullercoats, North Shields NE30 3AN* T: 0191-259 0431 E: abeeston@ukf.net

BEET, Duncan Clive. b 65. LLB. Ridley Hall Cam 98. **d** 01 **p** 02. C Northampton Em *Pet* 01-04; P-in-c Mears Ashby and Hardwick and Sywell from 04. *The Vicarage, 46 Wellingborough Road, Mears Ashby, Northampton NN6 0DZ* T: (01604) 812907 E: beet805@btinternet.com

BEETHAM, Anthony. b 32. Lon Univ BSc 53. Ox NSM Course. **d** 75 **p** 76. Dir Chr Enquiry Agency 88-97; NSM Ox St Clem 75-02; rtd 02; PtO *Ox* from 03. *44 Rose Hill, Oxford OX4 4HS* T: (01865) 770923

BEETON, David Ambrose Moore. b 39. Chich Th Coll 62. **d** 65 **p** 66. C Forest Gate St Edm *Chelmsf* 65-71; V Rush Green 71-81; V Coggeshall w Markshall 81-02; rtd 02; PtO *Nor* from 03. *Le Strange Cottages, 2 Hunstanton Road, Heacham, King's Lynn PE31 7HH* T: (01485) 572150

BEEVER, Miss Alison Rosemary. b 59. Man Univ BA 80. Linc Th Coll 88. **d** 90 **p** 94. Par Dn Watford Ch Ch *St Alb* 90-94; C 94-96; V Tilehurst St Cath *Ox* 96-01; P-in-c Cen Ex and Dioc Dir of Ords Ex 01-04; rtd 04. *7 Langridge Road, Paignton TQ3 3PT* T: (01803) 553645

BEEVERS, Preb Colin Lionel. b 40. K Coll Lon BSc 62 PhD 66 CEng 70 MIET 70 MBIM 73. Sarum & Wells Th Coll 87. **d** 89 **p** 90. C Ledbury w Eastnor *Heref* 89-93; C Lt Marcle 89-93; Asst Dir of Tr 92-96; P-in-c Kimbolton w Hamnish and Middleton-on-the-Hill 93-96; P-in-c Bockleton w Leysters 93-96; P-in-c Ledbury w Eastnor 96-98; P-in-c Much Marcle 96-98; TR Ledbury 98-05; RD 96-02; Preb Heref Cathl 02-05; Chapl Herefordshire Primary Care Trust 96-05; rtd 05; PtO *Worc* from 06. *55 Lion Court, Worcester WR1 1UT* T: (01905) 24132 E: annandcolin.beevers@virgin.net

BEGBIE, Jeremy Sutherland. b 57. Edin Univ BA 77 Aber Univ BD 80 PhD 87 LRAM 80 ARCM 77 MSSTh. Ridley Hall Cam 80. **d** 82 **p** 83. C Egham *Guildf* 82-85; Chapl Ridley

Hall Cam 85-87; Dir Studies 87-92; Vice-Prin 93-00; Assoc Prin 00-09; Hon Reader St Andr Univ 00-09; Research Prof Th Duke Div Sch USA from 09. *Duke University Divinity School, Box 90968, Durham NC 27708, USA* T: (001) (919) 660 3591 E: jeremy.begbie@duke.edu

BEGGS, Norman Lindell. b 32. N Lon Poly CQSW 77. S Dios Minl Tr Scheme 86. **d** 89 **p** 90. NSM Milborne St Andrew w Dewlish *Sarum* 89-92; C 92-95; C Piddletrenthide w Plush, Alton Pancras etc 92-95; C Puddletown and Tolpuddle 92-95; rtd 95; PtO *Sarum* from 95. *Wallingford House, Dewlish, Dorchester DT2 7LX* T: (01258) 837320

BEGLEY, Mrs Helen. b 59. Kingston Poly BA 81. NOC 87. **d** 89 **p** 94. Par Dn Leeds H Trin *Ripon* 89-90; Chapl to the Deaf 89-96; Par Dn Leeds City 91-94; C 94-96; Chapl to the Deaf (Wilts) *Sarum* 96-06; NSM Upper Wylye Valley 03-11; NSM Melksham from 11. *71 The Common, Broughton Gifford, Melksham SN12 8NE* T: (01225) 782649 E: begleyhelen4@gmail.com

BEGLEY, Peter Ernest Charles. b 55. St Mellitus Coll BA 10. **d** 10 **p** 11. C New Thundersley *Chelmsf* 10-15; P-in-c Southminster and Steeple from 15. *The Vicarage, Burnham Road, Southminster CM0 7ES* T: (01621) 772300 E: pf.begley@btinternet.com

BEHENNA, Preb Gillian Eve. b 57. CertEd 78. St Alb Minl Tr Scheme 82. **dss** 85 **d** 87 **p** 94. Chapl to the Deaf *Sarum* 85-90; Chapl w Deaf People *Ex* 90-04; Preb Ex Cathl 02-04; Chapl w Deaf Community *Bris* from 05; Nat Deaf Min Adv Abps' Coun from 13; Hon Can Bris Cathl from 11. *1 Saxon Way, Bradley Stoke, Bristol BS32 9AR* T: (01454) 202483 M: 07715-707135 E: gillbehenna@me.com

BEHREND, Michael Christopher. b 60. St Jo Coll Cam BA 82 MA 86 PGCE 83. Oak Hill Th Coll 93. **d** 97 **p** 98. C Hensingham *Carl* 97-02; TV Horwich and Rivington *Man* from 02; C Blackrod from 11. *St Catherine's House, Richmond Street, Horwich, Bolton BL6 5QT* T: (01204) 697162

BELCADE, Joshua. BNC Ox BA. S'wark Ord Course 10. **d** 13. NSM S Wimbledon All SS *S'wark* from 13; Hon Chapl Epsom Racecourse from 13. *5 Edge Hill, London SW19 4LR* T: (020) 7898 1610 E: jbelcade@gmail.com

BELCHER, Mrs Catherine Jane Allington. b 53. Charlotte Mason Coll of Educn CertEd 75. EAMTC 02. **d** 05 **p** 06. NSM Nor St Mary Magd w St Jas 05-11; NSM Nor Lakenham St Jo and All SS and Tuckswood from 13. *70 Mill Hill Road, Norwich NR2 3DS* M: 07708-650897 E: revkatebelcher@yahoo.co.uk

BELCHER, David John. b 44. Ch Ch Ox BA 65 MA 69. Cuddesdon Coll 68. **d** 70 **p** 71. C Gateshead St Mary *Dur* 70-72; C Stockton St Pet 73-76; LtO *Lich* 76-81; P-in-c W Bromwich Ch Ch 81-85; P-in-c W Bromwich Gd Shep w St Jo 85-89; V 89-95; RD W Bromwich 90-94; R Bratton, Edington and Imber, Edington etc *Sarum* 95-03; rtd 03; Hon C Smestow Vale *Lich* 03-07; PtO 09-14. *81 The Lindens, Newbridge Crescent, Wolverhampton WV6 0LS* T: (01902) 750903

BELCHER, Canon Derek George. b 50. Univ of Wales (Cardiff) MEd 86 LLM 04 Lon Univ PGCE 82 MRSPH 73 MBIM 82 FRSH 00. Chich Th Coll 74. **d** 77 **p** 78. C Newton Nottage *Llan* 77-81; PV Llan Cathl 81-87; V Margam 87-01; RD 99-01; TR Cowbridge 01-15; AD Vale of Glam 08-11; rtd 15; P-in-c Penmark w Llancarfan w Llantrithyd *Llan* from 15; Can Llan Cathl from 97. *The Rectory, Llancarfan, Barry CF62 3AJ* M: 07796-170671 T: (01446) 751786 E: dgbelc@gmail.com

BELFAST, Archdeacon of. *See* DAVISON, The Ven George Thomas William

BELFAST, Dean of. *See* MANN, The Very Revd John Owen

BELHAM, John Edward. b 42. K Coll Lon BSc 65 AKC 65 PhD 70. Oak Hill Th Coll 69. **d** 72 **p** 73. C Cheadle Hulme St Andr *Ches* 72-75; C Cheadle 75-83; R Gressenhall w Longham w Wendling etc *Nor* 83-08; P-in-c Mileham 07-08; rtd 08; PtO *Nor* from 08. *6 Brentwood, Norwich NR4 6PW* T: (01603) 456925 E: johnbelham@lords-prayer.co.uk

BELHAM, Michael. b 23. Lon Univ BScEng 50. **d** 67 **p** 68. C Northwood Hills St Edm *Lon* 67-69; C Hendon St Mary 69-73; V Tottenham H Trin 73-78; V Hillingdon St Jo 78-85; P-in-c Broughton *Ox* 85; R Broughton w N Newington and Shutford 85-90; Chapl Horton Gen Hosp 85-90; rtd 90; PtO *Pet* 90-01; *Ox* 90-01; Sec DBP 95-01; PtO *B & W* from 01. *24 Carlton Court, Wells BA5 1SF* T: (01749) 675236 E: michael-belham@blueyonder.co.uk

BELING, David Gibson. b 30. Fitzw Ho Cam BA 54 MA 58. **d** 56 **p** 57. C Radipole *Sarum* 56-59; C Broadwater St Mary *Chich* 59-61; R W Knighton w Broadmayne *Sarum* 61-73; V Paignton St Paul Preston *Ex* 73-91; rtd 91; PtO *Ex* 91-09. *51 Manor Road, Paignton TQ3 2HZ*

BELITHER, John Roland. b 36. Oak Hill Th Coll 83. **d** 86 **p** 87. NSM Bushey Heath *St Alb* 86-91; V Marsh Farm 91-06; rtd 06; PtO *St Alb* from 06. *43 Mallard Road, Abbots Langley WD5 0GE* T: (01923) 494399

BELL, Adrian Christopher. b 48. AKC 70. St Aug Coll Cant 70. **d** 71 **p** 72. C Sheff St Aid w St Luke 71-74; C Willesborough w Hinxhill *Cant* 74-78; P-in-c Bredgar w Bicknor and Frinsted w Wormshill etc 78; P-in-c Hollingbourne w Hucking 78-82; P-in-c Leeds w Broomfield 79-82; V Hollingbourne and Hucking w Leeds and Broomfield 82-84; V Herne Bay Ch Ch 84-91; R Washingborough w Heighington and Canwick *Linc* 91-01; R Fakenham w Alethorpe *Nor* 01-14; rtd 14; PtO *Nor* from 14. *Orchard House, 19 Whitsands Road, Swaffham PE37 7BJ* T: (01760) 627039 M: 07706-480489 E: adrian.bell4@uwclub.net

BELL, Canon Alan John. b 47. Liv Univ BA 68. Ridley Hall Cam 69. **d** 72 **p** 73. C Speke St Aid *Liv* 72-77; P-in-c Halewood 77-81; R Wavertree St Mary 81-88; Chapl Mabel Fletcher Tech Coll and Olive Mt Hosp 81-88; R Fakenham w Alethorpe *Nor* 88-00; RD Burnham and Walsingham 92-00; TR Stockport SW *Ches* 00-07; V Stockport St Geo 07-12; RD Stockport 05-12; Hon Can Ches Cathl 08-12; rtd 12; PtO *Ely* from 13; *Nor* from 14. *24 Hall Road, Clenchwarton, King's Lynn PE34 4AT* T: (01480) 435488 *or* 278106 E: vicaralanbell@aol.com

BELL, Allan McRae. b 49. Moray Ho Teacher Tr Coll Edin CertEd 80 E Lon Univ BA 90. S'wark Ord Course 86. **d** 92 **p** 95. NSM Bow H Trin and All Hallows *Lon* 91-93; NSM R Foundn of St Kath in Ratcliffe 93-95; Chapl Univ of California USA 95-96; P-in-c Bolinas St Aidan 96-97. *177 Well Street, London E9 6QU* T: (020) 8985 1978

BELL, Anne Elizabeth. b 38. RGN 60. SAOMC 98. **d** 08 **p** 08. NSM Shrivenham and Ashbury *Ox* 08-12; PtO from 12. *Whitcot, Shotover Corner, Uffington, Faringdon SN7 7RH* T: (01367) 820091 E: anne@shotover.fsnet.co.uk

BELL, Anthony Lawson. b 47. AKC 72. St Aug Coll Cant 71. **d** 72 **p** 73. C Peterlee *Dur* 72-77; C-in-c Stockton St Jas CD 82-89; P-in-c Byers Green 89-96; Ind Chapl Teesside 89-96; P-in-c Ault Hucknall *Derby* 96-99; V Ault Hucknall and Scarcliffe 99-12; rtd 12; PtO *Roch* from 13. *4 Godfrey Close, Rochester ME2 3QS* T: (01634) 711445

BELL, Antony Fancourt. b 28. Magd Coll Ox BA 51 MA 58. Wells Th Coll 54. **d** 56 **p** 57. C Clapham H Trin *S'wark* 56-59; C Gillingham *Sarum* 59-61; R Stanway *Chelmsf* 61-94; RD Dedham and Tey 81-91; rtd 94. *7 Postern Close, Portchester, Fareham PO16 9NB* T: (023) 9237 8272

BELL, Arthur James. b 33. Ch Coll Cam BA 57 MA 60. Coll of Resurr Mirfield 57. **d** 59 **p** 60. C New Cleethorpes *Linc* 59-63; C Upperby St Jo *Carl* 63-66; P-in-c Wabasca Canada 67-72; 77-83; PtO *Ely* 73-75; LtO *Carl* 75-76; Warden Retreat of the Visitation Rhandirmwyn 83-99; PtO *Dur* from 00. *Burnside, 22 Rose Terrace, Stanhope, Bishop Auckland DL13 2PE* T: (01388) 526514

BELL, Barnaby. *See* BELL, Simon Barnaby

BELL, Bede. *See* BELL, William Wealands

BELL, Brian Thomas Benedict. b 64. Newc Poly BA 87 Newc Univ PGCE 88 Univ of Northumbria at Newc MA 93 Leeds Univ BA 97. Coll of Resurr Mirfield. **d** 97 **p** 98. C Tynemouth Cullercoats St Paul *Newc* 97-01; V Horton 01-08; V Horbury w Horbury Bridge *Leeds* from 08. *2 Elm Grove, Horbury, Wakefield WF4 5EP* T: (01924) 273671 E: fatherbrian@virginmedia.com

BELL, Catherine Ann. *See* MOSS, Catherine Ann

BELL, Charles William. b 43. TCD Div Test 66 BA 66 MA 69. CITC 64. **d** 67 **p** 68. C Newtownards *D & D* 67-70; C Larne and Inver *Conn* 70-74; C Ballymena w Ballyclug 74-80; Bp's C Belfast Ardoyne 80-87; Bp's C Belfast Ardoyne w H Redeemer 88; I Eglantine 89-11; S Conn Dioc Info Officer 89-11; Preb Conn Cathl 04-11; rtd 11. *2 Beechwood Crescent, Moira, Craigavon BT67 0LA* T: (028) 9261 9834 E: williambell@btinternet.com

BELL, Colin Douglas. b 65. QUB BTh 94 TCD MPhil 96. CITC 94. **d** 96 **p** 97. C Dundonald *D & D* 96-98; C Knock 98-00; I Lack *Clogh* 00-02; I Rathcoole *Conn* 02-05; CF 05-07 and from 08; I Aghadrumsee w Clogh and Drumsnatt 07-08; PtO *York* from 11. *c/o MOD Chaplains (Army)* F: 381824 T: (01264) 383430

BELL, Cyril John. b 22. Lon Univ BA 48. Wycliffe Hall Ox 52. **d** 53 **p** 54. C Monkwearmouth St Pet *Dur* 53-56; Asst Master Bede Gr Sch Sunderland 53-56; Lect and Chapl Union Chr Coll Alwaye S India 56-60; LtO *Ches* 62-87; Hon C Westlands St Andr *Lich* 66-71; Hd RE Marple Comp Sch 71-87; rtd 87; PtO *Lich* 87-96. *49 Delamere Road, Nantwich CW5 7DF* T: (01270) 628910

BELL, David. b 52. **d** 12 **p** 13. NSM Hampton Hill *Lon* 12-15; NSM Kingston *S'wark* from 15. *20 Vicarage Road, Hampton Wick, Kingston upon Thames KT1 4ED* T: (020) 8977 2482 E: davidbell@stjames-hamptonhill.org.uk

BELL, David Bain. b 57. Bp Otter Coll BEd 82. Ox Min Course 04. **d** 07 **p** 08. NSM Stantonbury and Willen *Ox* 07-10; TV Watling Valley 10-15; V Silsoe, Pulloxhill and

Flitton *St Alb* from 15. *The Vicarage, Fir Tree Road, Silsoe, Bedford MK45 4EA* T: (01525) 861163
E: fivebells2007@hotmail.co.uk

BELL, David James. b 62. QUB BSc 84 BTh. **d** 91 **p** 92. C Ballyholme *D & D* 91-94; C Coleraine *Conn* 94-00; I Ardtrea w Desertcreat *Arm* from 00. *Tullyhogue Rectory, 50 Lower Grange Road, Cookstown BT80 8SL* T/F: (028) 8676 1163
E: rev.davidjbell@gmail.com

BELL, Canon David Owain. b 49. Dur Univ BA 69 Fitzw Coll Cam BA 72 MA 80. Westcott Ho Cam 70. **d** 72 **p** 73. C Houghton le Spring *Dur* 72-76; C Norton St Mary 76-78; P-in-c Worc St Clem 78-84; R 84-85; R Old Swinford Stourbridge 85-97; TR Kidderminster St Mary and All SS w Trimpley etc 97-13; RD Stourbridge 90-96; Hon Can Worc Cathl 96-13; rtd 14. *60A Main Road, Kempsey WR5 3JF* T: (01905) 820209 E: dowainbell@yahoo.co.uk

BELL, Canon Donald Jon. b 50. DL 12. Sarum & Wells Th Coll 73. **d** 76 **p** 77. C Jarrow *Dur* 76-80; C Darlington St Cuth w St Hilda 80-83; V Wingate Grange 83-89; V Sherburn w Pittington 89-95; R Shadforth 94-95; P-in-c Dur St Cuth 95-97; V 97-02; R Witton Gilbert 97-02; TR Dur N 02-05; AD Dur 93-05; Chapl Dur and Darlington Fire and Rescue Brigade 95-05; Bp's Sen Chapl and Exec Officer 05-12; P-in-c Kelloe and Coxhoe from 12; P-in-c Chilton from 12; Hon Can Dur Cathl from 01. *20 St Phillips Close, Auckland Park, Bishop Auckland DL14 8BD* E: jonb22@btinternet.com

BELL, Dorothy Jane. b 53. Teesside Univ BSc 93. Cranmer Hall Dur 01. **d** 03 **p** 04. C Washington *Dur* 03-07; P-in-c Stockton St Jo from 07; P-in-c Stockton St Jas from 07. *St John the Baptist Vicarage, 190 Durham Road, Stockton-on-Tees TS19 0PS* T: (01642) 674119

BELL, Duncan John. b 83. Sheff Univ MEng 06 PhD 11. Oak Hill Th Coll BA 14. **d** 14 **p** 15. C Woodseats St Chad *Sheff* from 14. *15 Booker Road, Sheffield S8 0GH* T: 0114-274 5233 M: 07833-448014 E: duncan.j.bell@gmail.com *or* duncan.bell@sheffield.anglican.org

BELL, Evelyn Ruth. b 52. Univ of Wales (Cardiff) BSc(Econ). SAOMC 97. **d** 00 **p** 01. C Waltham Cross *St Alb* 00-03; Chapl HM Pris Highpoint from 03. *HM Prison Edmunds Hill, Stradishall, Newmarket CB8 9YN* T: (01440) 743595
E: eve.bell@hmps.gsi.gov.uk

BELL, Canon Francis William Albert. b 28. TCD BA 52 MA 57 BD 57. **d** 53 **p** 54. C Belfast St Mich *Conn* 53-55; C Belfast All SS 55-61; C Ballynafeigh St Jude *D & D* 61-63; P-in-c Ballyhalbert 63-71; P-in-c Ardkeen 67-71; I Ballyhalbert w Ardkeen 71-95; Miss to Seamen 71-95; Can Belf Cathl 89-95; rtd 95. *Stationbanks, 18 Kilmore Road, Crossgar, Downpatrick BT30 9HJ* T: (028) 4483 1665

BELL, Mrs Glynis Mary. b 44. Leeds Univ BA 66. SAOMC 99. **d** 02 **p** 03. OLM Newport Pagnell w Lathbury and Moulsoe *Ox* from 02. *6 Kipling Drive, Newport Pagnell MK16 8EB* T: (01908) 612971

BELL, Godfrey Bryan. b 44. TD 00. Oak Hill Th Coll 72. **d** 75 **p** 76. C Penn Fields *Lich* 75-79; R Dolton *Ex* 79-89; R Iddesleigh w Dowland 79-89; R Monkokehampton 79-89; R Tollard Royal w Farnham, Gussage St Michael etc *Sarum* 89-96; TV Washfield, Stoodleigh, Withleigh etc *Ex* 96-06; TR 06-09; CF (ACF) 09-87; CF (TA) 87-99; rtd 09. *Bethany, 3 Alstone Road, Tiverton EX16 4JL* T: (01884) 252874
E: bells.bethany@btinternet.com

BELL, Graham Dennis Robert. b 42. K Coll Lon BSc 63 AKC 63 Nottm Univ MTh 73 ALCM 74 Lambeth STh 01. Tyndale Hall Bris 65. **d** 68 **p** 69. C Stapleford *S'well* 68-71; C Barton Seagrave *Pet* 71-73; C Barton Seagrave w Warkton 73-76; PtO *Nor* 76-82; V Wickham Market *St E* 82-86; V Wickham Market w Pettistree and Easton 86-98; R Thrapston *Pet* 98-07; rtd 07; PtO *Pet* from 11. *22 Cottesmore Avenue, Barton Seagrave, Kettering NN15 6QX* T: (01536) 725924
E: grahambellgood@talktalk.net

BELL, Canon Jack Gorman. b 23. Lon Univ BSc 48. Oak Hill Th Coll 51. **d** 53 **p** 54. C Blackpool Ch Ch *Blackb* 53-55; C Chadderton Ch Ch *Man* 55-59; R Man St Jerome w Ardwick St Silas 59-69; V Mosley Common 69-89; Hon Can Man Cathl 87-89; rtd 89; PtO *Carl* 89-11. *39 The Moorings, Stafford Street, Stone ST15 8QZ* T: (01785) 286126

✠**BELL, The Rt Revd James Harold.** b 50. St Jo Coll Dur BA 72 St Pet Hall Ox BA 74 MA 78. Wycliffe Hall Ox 72. **d** 75 **p** 76 **c** 04. Hon C St Mich w St Martin and All SS 75-76; Chapl and Lect BNC Ox 76-82; R Northolt St Mary *Lon* 82-93; AD Ealing 91-93; Adv for Min Willesden 93-97; Dioc Dir of Min and Tr *Ripon* 97-99; Dioc Dir of Miss 99-04; Can Res Ripon Cathl 97-99; Hon Can from 99; Suff Bp Knaresborough *Ripon* 04-15; Suff Bp Ripon Leeds from 15. *Thistledown, Main Street, Exelby, Bedale DL8 2HD* T/F: (01677) 423525
E: bishop.james@westyorkshiredales.anglican.org

BELL, James Samuel. b 40. MBE 71. RMA 59 St Chad's Coll Dur BA 69. Coll of Resurr Mirfield 71. **d** 72 **p** 73. C Lambeth St Phil *S'wark* 72-73; C N Lambeth 74; P-in-c Invergordon St Ninian *Mor* 74-77; P-in-c Dornoch 74-77; P-in-c Brora 74-77; V Pet H Spirit Bretton 77-83; P-in-c Marholm 82-83; Sen Chapl Tonbridge Sch 83-00; rtd 00. *Clocktower House, Edderton, Tain IV19 1LJ* T: (01862) 821305

BELL, Jane. *See* BELL, Dorothy Jane

BELL, Canon Jeffrey William. b 37. Buckingham Univ MA 94. Sarum Th Coll 60. **d** 63 **p** 64. C Northampton St Matt *Pet* 63-66; C Portishead *B & W* 66-68; C Digswell *St Alb* 68-72; V Pet St Jude 72-79; V Buckingham *Ox* 79-93; RD 84-88 and 89-90; V Portsea N End St Mark *Portsm* 93-03; Hon Can Portsm Cathl 00-03; rtd 03; Hon C The Bourne and Tilford *Guildf* 03-13; PtO *Portsm* from 13. *164 Northern Parade, Portsmouth PO2 9LT* T: (023) 9265 0033

BELL, Jennifer Kathryn. *See* McWHIRTER, Jennifer Kathryn

BELL, John. *See* BELL, Cyril John

BELL, John. *See* BELL, Donald Jon

BELL, John Christopher. b 33. TCD BA 56 MA 66. TCD Div Sch Div Test. **d** 56 **p** 57. C Newtownards *D & D* 56-59; C Willowfield 59-62; I Carrowdore 62-70; I Drumbo 70-98; Chapl Young Offender Cen Belf 79-98; Can Down Cathl 87-98; Treas Down Cathl 91-98; rtd 98. *Ashwell House, 6 Ballywillin Road, Crossgar, Downpatrick BT30 9LE* T: (028) 4483 1907

BELL, John Edward. b 34. Cranmer Hall Dur. **d** 67 **p** 68. C Harraby *Carl* 67-70; C Dalton-in-Furness 70-72; V Pennington 72-75; V Carl St Herbert w St Steph 75-84; V Wreay 84-85; rtd 99; PtO *Carl* from 01. *189 Brampton Road, Carlisle CA3 9AX* T: (01228) 522746

BELL, John Holmes. b 50. Sheff City Coll of Educn CertEd 71. Oak Hill Th Coll BA 80. **d** 80 **p** 81. C Leic St Phil 80-83; C Portswood Ch Ch *Win* 83-86; TV S Molton w Nymet St George, High Bray etc *Ex* 86-01; V Stoke Fleming, Blackawton and Strete 01-15; rtd 15. *Address temp unknown*
E: john@ding-dong.fsnet.co.uk

BELL, Jonathan Robert. b 84. Nottm Univ BA 06. Oak Hill Th Coll BA 14. **d** 14 **p** 15. C Stanton-by-Dale w Dale Abbey and Risley *Derby* from 14. *10 Brecon Close, Long Eaton, Nottingham NG10 4JW* T: 0115-998 9566 M: 07736-286861
E: jonathan@srdachurches.org

BELL, Julie. **d** 14. Glenavy w Tunny and Crumlin *Conn* 14-15; C Lisburn Ch Ch from 15. *1 Windermere Avenue, Belfast BT8 6SZ* T: (028) 9070 2375 M: 07973-840628 E: bellju@tcd.ie

BELL, Karl Edwin. b 33. Minnesota Univ BA 56. Seabury-Western Th Sem MDiv 61. **d** 61 **p** 62. USA 61-71 and 76-92; Venezuela 71-76; Chapl Wiesbaden *Eur* from 92. *St Augustine of Canterbury, Frankfurterstrasse 3, 65189 Wiesbaden, Germany* T: (0049) (611) 306674 F: 372270
E: bell@wiesbaden.netsurf.de

BELL, Kenneth Murray. b 30. Sarum & Wells Th Coll 75. **d** 74 **p** 76. PtO *Guildf* 74-76; C Hartley Wintney and Elvetham *Win* 76-77; C Hartley Wintney, Elvetham, Winchfield etc 77-80; V Fair Oak 80-95; rtd 96; PtO *Win* from 96. *12 Hill Meadow, Overton, Basingstoke RG25 3JD* T: (01256) 770890
E: keny12@talk21.com

BELL, Kevin David. b 58. Newc Univ MA 93 Univ of Wales (Lamp) MA 06 FRSA 11 FRSA 11. Aston Tr Scheme 78 Sarum & Wells Th Coll 80. **d** 83 **p** 84. C Weoley Castle *Birm* 83-87; C Acocks Green 87-89; CF 89-07; Asst Chapl Gen 07-15; Chapl Guards Chpl Lon 12-14; Dir of Ords 07-11; V Twickenham All Hallows *Lon* from 15. *All Hallows' Vicarage, 138 Chertsey Road, Twickenham TW1 1EW* M: 07512-079257
E: bellscmkd@yahoo.co.uk

BELL, Canon Nicholas Philip Johnson. b 46. St Jo Coll Dur BSc 69. St Jo Coll Nottm 70. **d** 73 **p** 74. C Chadderton Ch Ch *Man* 73-77; C Frogmore *St Alb* 77-81; V Bricket Wood 81-91; RD Aldenham 87-91; V Luton St Mary 91-12; Hon Can St Alb 01-12; rtd 12; PtO *St Alb* from 12; *Nor* from 14. *6B North Street, Sheringham NR26 8LW* E: revnickbell@gmail.com

BELL, Owain. *See* BELL, David Owain

BELL, Paul Joseph. b 35. Dur Univ BA 56 DipEd 57. Trin Coll Bris 77. **d** 77 **p** 78. Burundi 77-81; C Highbury Ch Ch w St Jo and St Sav *Lon* 82-85; V Middleton w E Winch *Nor* 85-95; P-in-c Barningham w Matlaske w Baconsthorpe etc 95-99; R 99-02; rtd 02; PtO *Portsm* from 02. *21 Hurst Point View, Totland Bay PO39 0AQ* T: (01983) 756180

BELL, Mrs Rebecca Mary. b 79. UWE BSc 00. Trin Coll Bris 10. **d** 13 **p** 14. C Charlton Kings H Apostles *Glouc* from 13. *16 Sydenham Road South, Cheltenham GL52 6EF* M: 07793-021121

BELL, Prof Richard Herbert. b 54. Univ Coll Lon BSc 75 PhD 79 Tubingen Univ DrTheol 91. Wycliffe Hall Ox BA 82 MA 87. **d** 83 **p** 84. C Edgware *Lon* 83-86; Germany 86-90; Lect Th

Nottm Univ 90-97; Sen Lect 97-05; Reader 05-08; Prof from 08. *Department of Theology and Religious Studies, University Park, Nottingham NG7 2RD* T: 0115-951 5858 F: 951 5887 E: richard.bell@nottingham.ac.uk

BELL, Robert Clarke. b 30. Roch Th Coll 63. **d** 65 **p** 66. C Leeds All SS *Ripon* 65-67; C Claxby w Normanby-le-Wold *Linc* 67-69; R Newark St Leon *S'well* 69-71; V Gosberton Clough *Linc* 71-74; P-in-c Quadring 73-74; Chapl to the Deaf 74-85; V Harmston and Coleby 85-94; RD Graffoe 92-94; rtd 94; PtO *Blackb* 94-05; *Carl* 94-98. *8 Brookfield Avenue, Nettleham, Lincoln LN2 2TB* T: (01522) 753732

BELL, Robert Mason. b 35. Lon Coll of Div 66. **d** 68 **p** 69. C Burgess Hill St Andr *Chich* 68-78; R Lewes St Jo sub Castro 78-00; rtd 00. *10 Rufus Close, Lewes BN7 1BG* T: (01273) 470561

BELL, Ross Kinninmonth. b 64. Bradf and Ilkley Coll BA 87. Aston Tr Scheme 89 Westcott Ho Cam 91. **d** 94 **p** 95. C W Bromwich All SS *Lich* 94-98; TV Cen Wolverhampton 98-02; Chapl Bilston Street Police Station 04-06; PtO *Edin* from 06. *Address temp unknown* T: 0131-552 3060 M: 07976-157022 E: ro.bell@btinternet.com

BELL, Mrs Shena Margaret. b 49. EAMTC. **d** 00 **p** 01. C Earls Barton *Pet* 00-04; P-in-c Raunds 04-07; P-in-c Ringstead and Stanwick w Hargrave 04-07; R Raunds, Hargrave, Ringstead and Stanwick from 07. *The Vicarage, High Street, Raunds, Wellingborough NN9 6HS* T: (01933) 461509 E: shena.m.bell@gmail.com

BELL, Simon Barnaby. b 48. Bris Univ CertEd 70. Sarum & Wells Th Coll 87. **d** 89 **p** 90. C Ewyas Harold w Dulas, Kenderchurch etc *Heref* 89-93; P-in-c Clungunford w Clunbury and Clunton, Bedstone etc 93-01; R 01-11; P-in-c Hopesay 02-11; rtd 11. *49 Warden Close, Presteigne LD8 2DH*

BELL, Stephen Andrew. b 53. SCRTP 13. **d** 15. NSM Chiddingfold *Guildf* from 15. *11 Yewens, Chiddingfold, Godalming GU8 4SD* T: (01428) 683795

BELL, Canon Stuart Rodney. b 46. Ex Univ BA 67. Tyndale Hall Bris 69. **d** 71 **p** 72. C Henfynyw w Aberaeron and Llanddewi Aberarth *St D* 71-74; V 81-88; V Llangeler 74-80; TR Aberystwyth 88-13; Chapl Aberystwyth Univ from 94; Ev St Teilo Trust from 95; AD Llanbadarn Fawr 12-14; Can St D Cathl 01-13; rtd 13; PtO *St D* from 13. *Gwel Enlli, Borth SY24 5NS* E: stuart@prudence45.plus.com

BELL, Mrs Susan. b 62. Lindisfarne Regional Tr Partnership 13. **d** 15. NSM Darlington St Hilda and St Columba *Dur* from 15. *52 Tyne Crescent, Darlington DL1 5AS* M: 07850-675877 T: (01325) 257618 E: suebell158@hotmail.co.uk

BELL (née STEWART), Mrs Susan Catherine. b 57. St Martin's Coll Lanc BEd 80. LCTP 08. **d** 10 **p** 11. C Longridge *Blackb* 10-14; I Ballywalter w Inishargie *D & D* from 14. *15 Westland Drive, Ballywalter, Newtownards BT22 2TH* M: 07738-305129 T: (028) 4275 7579 E: bellsue9@gmail.com *or* vicarofballywalter@gmail.com

BELL, Terrance James. b 63. Toronto Univ BA 92. Trin Coll Toronto MDiv 97. **d** 97 **p** 98. C Wedmore w Theale and Blackford *B & W* 97-01; C Hampstead St Jo *Lon* 01-06; Chapl Eden Hall Marie Curie Hospice 01-06; P-in-c King's Walden and Offley w Lilley *St Alb* 06-11; V from 11. *Millstone Corner, Salusbury Lane, Offley, Hitchin SG5 3EG* T: (01462) 768123 E: kwol@btinternet.com

BELL, Timothy John Keeton. b 59. Trin Coll Bris BA 02. **d** 02 **p** 03. C Saltford w Corston and Newton St Loe *B & W* 02-06; Chapl Bath Spa Univ 04-06; P-in-c Wick w Doynton and Dyrham *Bris* from 06. *The Vicarage, 57 High Street, Wick, Bristol BS30 5QQ* T: 0117-937 3581 E: tim.vicar@gmail.com

BELL, William. *See* BELL, Charles William

BELL, William Wealands. b 63. York Univ MA 86 Dur Univ PGCE 87 Leeds Univ BA 99. Coll of Resurr Mirfield 97. **d** 99 **p** 00. C Jarrow *Dur* 99-02; Novice CR 02-04; Chapl Aldenham Sch Herts 04-07; Can Res Lich Cathl 07-14; P-in-c Croydon St Andr *S'wark* 14-15; V from 15; Chapl St Andr C of E High Sch Croydon from 14. *St Andrew's Vicarage, 6 St Peter's Road, Croydon CR0 1HD* T: (020) 8406 5622 E: wealandsbell@gmail.com

BELLAMY, Canon David Quentin. b 62. Univ of Wales (Cardiff) BMus 84 Univ of Wales (Ban) MA 93. Ripon Coll Cuddesdon 87 Ch Div Sch of the Pacific (USA). **d** 90 **p** 91. C Rhyl w St Ann *St As* 90-94; V Llay 94-04; V Prestatyn 04-15; AD St As 10-15; Can Cursal St As Cathl from 14; R Colwyn and Llanelian from 15. *The Vicarage, 28 Bodelwyddan Avenue, Old Colwyn, Colwyn Bay LL29 9NP* T: (01492) 478659 E: dqbellamy@yahoo.co.uk

BELLAMY, Mrs Dorothy Kathleen. b 33. Gilmore Course 74. **dss** 82 **d** 87 **p** 94. Par Dn Hampton Wick *Lon* 87-88; Par Dn Teddington St Mark and Hampton Wick 88-90; Par Dn Westbury *Sarum* 90-94; C 94-96; rtd 97; NSM Freshwater

and Yarmouth *Portsm* 97-09. *9 Strathwell Crescent, Whitwell, Ventnor PO38 2QZ* T: (01983) 731545

BELLAMY, Mrs Janet Mary. b 45. Westf Coll Lon BA 66 Birm Univ BLitt 98 MEd 93 Cam Univ PGCE 67. **d** 09 **p** 10. NSM Hope Bowdler w Eaton-under-Heywood *Heref* 09-13; NSM Apedale Gp from 13. *Orchard House, Diddlebury, Craven Arms SY7 9DH* T: (01584) 841511 E: janetmbellamy@googlemail.com

BELLAMY, John Stephen. b 55. Jes Coll Ox BA 77 MA 81 Liv Univ PhD 06. St Jo Coll Nottm. **d** 84 **p** 85. C Allerton *Liv* 84-87; C Southport Ch Ch 87-89; Bp's Dom Chapl 89-91; V Birkdale St Jas 91-08; V Dur St Nic from 08. *11 Beechways, Durham DH1 4LG* T: 0191-384 6066 E: vicar@stnics.org.uk

BELLAMY, Canon Mervyn Roger Hunter. b 47. Sussex Univ CertEd Heythrop Coll Lon MA 04. St Mich Coll Llan 81. **d** 81 **p** 82. C Frecheville and Hackenthorpe *Sheff* 81-85; V Shiregreen St Hilda 85-94; RD Ecclesfield 93-94; R Rawmarsh w Parkgate 94-01; P-in-c King's Sutton and Newbottle and Charlton *Pet* 01-09; V from 09; RD Brackley 05-13; Can Pet Cathl from 09. *The Vicarage, Church Avenue, King's Sutton, Banbury OX17 3RJ* T: (01295) 811364 E: rogerbellamy@hotmail.co.uk

BELLAMY, Mrs Norma Edna. b 44. Birm Univ CertEd 75 Open Univ BA 83. **d** 10 **p** 11. OLM Shareshill *Lich* from 10. *10 Meadowlark Close, Hednesford, Cannock WS12 1UE* T: (01543) 876809 M: 07866-431211 E: robert.jbellamy@virgin.net

BELLAMY, Peter Charles William. b 38. Birm Univ MA 70 PhD 79 AKC 61. **d** 62 **p** 63. C Allestree *Derby* 62-65; Chapl All SS Hosp Birm 65-73; Chapl St Pet Coll of Educn Saltley 73-78; Chapl and Lect Qu Eliz Hosp Birm 78-90; Lect Past Psychology Birm Univ 79-92; Manager HIV Services Birm Cen HA 90-92; Commr for Public Health Cen and S Birm HA 92-96; Research Fell Birm Univ 97-02; Local Min Development Adv *Heref* 01-06; Dioc Co-ord for Min of Deliverance from 06. *Orchard House, Diddlebury, Craven Arms SY7 9DH* T: (01584) 841511 E: petercbellamy@googlemail.com

BELLAMY, Quentin. *See* BELLAMY, David Quentin

BELLAMY, Richard William. b 62. SEITE 07. **d** 10 **p** 11. NSM Cheriton St Martin *Cant* 10-11; NSM Cheriton w Newington 11-12; NSM Folkestone Trin from 12. *37 Pine Way, Folkestone CT19 4QL* T: (01303) 271059 M: 07952-928427 E: r.w.bellamy@btinternet.com

BELLAMY, Roger. *See* BELLAMY, Mervyn Roger Hunter

BELLAMY, Stephen. *See* BELLAMY, John Stephen

BELLAMY-KNIGHTS, Peter George. b 41. Leic Univ BSc 63 Man Univ MSc 67 PhD 70 Lon Univ BD 03 CMath 91 FIMA 91 CEng 94 FRaeS 98. Man OLM Scheme 03. **d** 04 **p** 05. NSM Man Cathl 04-11; rtd 11; PtO *Man* from 11. *113 Old Hall Lane, Manchester M14 6HL* T: 0161-224 2702

BELLENES, Peter Charles. b 49. Thurrock Coll Essex CQSW 72. Linc Th Coll 79. **d** 81 **p** 90. C Penistone *Wakef* 81-82; Hon C Liskeard, St Keyne, St Pinnock, Morval etc *Truro* 91; Hon C Menheniot 91-99; P-in-c Marldon *Ex* 99-03; TV Totnes w Bridgetown, Berry Pomeroy etc 03-09; rtd 09; C Duloe, Herodsfoot, Morval and St Pinnock *Truro* from 15. *Little Grove, Harrow Barrow, Callington PL17 8JN* T: (01822) 833508 E: pbellenes@aol.com

BELLENGER, Peter John Russell. b 74. New Coll Ox BA 96 MA 02 St Jo Coll Dur BA 03 St Andr Univ MPhil 09. Cranmer Hall Dur 01. **d** 04 **p** 05. C Tollington *Lon* 04-07; P-in-c 10-12. *20 Collingham Road, London SW5 0LX*

BELLINGER, Canon Denys Gordon. b 29. Sheff Univ BA 49. Westcott Ho Cam 51. **d** 53 **p** 54. C Ribbleton *Blackb* 53-56; C Lancaster St Mary 56-58; V Colne H Trin 58-68; V Scotforth 68-93; RD Lancaster 82-89; Hon Can Blackb Cathl 86-93; rtd 93; PtO *Blackb* from 93. *40 Yewlands Drive, Garstang, Preston PR3 1JP* T: (01995) 601539

BELLINGER, Richard George. b 47. Univ of Wales (Abth) BSc(Econ) 69. S Dios Minl Tr Scheme 91. **d** 94 **p** 95. NSM Guernsey St Steph *Win* 94-96; NSM Guernsey St Martin 96-09; PtO 09-14. *La Maison des Vinaires, Rue des Vinaires, St Pierre du Bois, Guernsey GY7 9EZ* T: (01481) 63203 F: 66989

BELLIS, Huw. b 72. Univ of Wales (Lamp) BA 94. Westcott Ho Cam 96. **d** 98 **p** 99. C Merrow *Guildf* 98-02; TV Tring *St Alb* 02-08; TR from 08. *The Rectory, 2 The Limes, Station Road, Tring HP23 5NW* T: (01442) 822170 E: huwbellis@btinternet.com

BELOE, Mrs Jane. b 46. STETS. **d** 04 **p** 05. NSM Shedfield *Portsm* 04-06; NSM Bishop's Waltham from 06; NSM Upham from 06. *Roughay Cottage, Popes Lane, Upham, Southampton SO32 1JB* T: (01489) 860452 E: janebeloe@btinternet.com

BELOE, Robert Francis. b 39. Sarum Th Coll. **d** 65 **p** 71. C Nor Heartsease St Fran 65-66; C Edmonton St Mary w St Jo *Lon* 68-70; C St Marylebone Ch Ch w St Paul 70-74; P-in-c Wicken *Ely* 74-76; V 76-00; rtd 00; PtO *Ely* 00-08; *Carl* from 08. *20 Lakehead Court, Keswick CA12 5EU* T: (017687) 74796

BELSHAW, Patricia Anne. b 47. **d** 05 **p** 06. OLM Leyland St Jas *Blackb* 05-07; NSM 07-10; NSM Darwen St Pet 10-13; rtd 13; PtO *Blackb* from 13. *9 The Laund, Leyland PR26 7XX* T: (01772) 453624 E: patriciabelshaw@yahoo.co.uk

BEMENT, Peter James. b 43. Univ of Wales (Cardiff) BA 64 PhD 69. Wycliffe Hall Ox 92. **d** 94 **p** 95. C Hubberston *St D* 94-97; V Llandeilo Fawr and Taliaris 97-08; rtd 08. *21 Chandler's Yard, Burry Port SA16 0FE* T: (01554) 833905

BENCE, Helen Mary. b 44. Leic Univ BA 65 PGCE 66. EMMTC 93. **d** 97 **p** 98. NSM Humberstone *Leic* 97-02; NSM Thurnby Lodge 01-02; TV Oadby 03-08; NSM Thurnby w Stoughton 08-13; NSM Cornerstone Team from 13. *The Grange, 126 Shanklin Drive, Leicester LE2 3QB* T: 0116-270 7820 E: helenbence@leicester.freeserve.co.uk

BENDALL, Robin Andrew. b 64. Qu Mary Coll Lon BA 86. SEITE 08. **d** 11 **p** 13. NSM Sandwich and Worth *Cant* from 11. *24 Delfside, Sandwich CT13 9RL* T: (01304) 617458 E: robinbendall@hotmail.com

BENDELL, David James. b 38. ACIB 74. S'wark Ord Course 84. **d** 87 **p** 88. NSM Surbiton Hill Ch Ch *S'wark* 87-03; PtO 10-14. *3 Pine Walk, Surbiton KT5 8NJ* T: (020) 8399 7143 E: bendell@talktalk.net

BENDING, Richard Clement. b 47. Southn Univ BSc 68. Ridley Hall Cam 87. **d** 89 **p** 90. Par Dn St Neots *Ely* 89-92; V Buckden 92-99; P-in-c Hail Weston 97-99; P-in-c Terrington St John 99-02; P-in-c Tilney All Saints 99-02; P-in-c Wiggenhall St Germans and Islington 99-02; P-in-c Wiggenhall St Mary Magd 99-02; V E Marshland 02-05; rtd 05; PtO *Nor* from 05. *Dawn Cottage, Newgate Green, Cley, Holt NR25 7TT* T: (01263) 741603 E: richard.bending@o2.co.uk

BENDOR-SAMUEL, David Carey. b 57. Ox Min Course 13. **d** 15. C Beckley, Forest Hill, Horton-cum-Studley and Stanton St John *Ox* from 15. *Address temp unknown*

BENDREY (née BRIGNALL), Elizabeth Jane. b 69. St Mary's Coll Twickenham BA 91 Heythrop Coll Lon MA 02 Cam Univ BTh 06. Westcott Ho Cam 04. **d** 06 **p** 07. C Witham *Chelmsf* 06-09; P-in-c Black Notley 09-12; R from 12; RD Braintree from 13. *The Rectory, 265C London Road, Black Notley, Braintree CM77 8QQ* T: (01376) 567971 M: 07940-516741 E: bethbendrey@hotmail.co.uk

BENDREY, Iain Robert. b 73. Bp Grosseteste Coll BA 96 Birm Univ MEd 03. ERMC 06. **d** 08 **p** 09. NSM Wickham Bishops w Lt Braxted *Chelmsf* 08-12; NSM Bocking St Pet from 12. *The Rectory, 265C London Road, Black Notley, Braintree CM77 8QQ* T: (01376) 567971 M: 07960-810687 E: curate@churchinwickhambishops.org.uk

BENEDICT, Brother. *See* WINSPER, Arthur William

BENFIELD, Paul John. b 56. Newc Univ LLB 77 Southn Univ BTh 89 Barrister-at-Law (Lincoln's Inn) 78. Chich Th Coll 86. **d** 89 **p** 90. C Shiremoor *Newc* 89-92; C Hexham 92-93; TV Lewes All SS, St Anne, St Mich and St Thos *Chich* 93-97; R Pulborough 97-00; V Fleetwood St Nic *Blackb* from 00. *St Nicholas' Vicarage, Highbury Avenue, Fleetwood FY7 7DJ* T/F: (01253) 874402 E: benfield@btinternet.com

BENFORD, Steven Charles. b 61. Leic Univ MB, ChB 86. NEOC 97. **d** 00 **p** 01. NSM Northallerton w Kirby Sigston *York* 00-04; P-in-c York St Luke 04-14; V Northolt St Jos *Lon* from 14. *St Joseph's Vicarage, 430 Yeading Lane, Northolt UB5 6JS* M: 07739-201523 T: (020) 8841 1547 E: frstevebenford@me.com

BENGE, Charles David. b 40. Cranmer Hall Dur 63. **d** 68 **p** 69. C Millfield St Mark *Dur* 68-72; C Hensingham *Carl* 72-75; TV Maghull *Liv* 75-82; V Bootle St Leon 82-97; NSM Ormskirk 97-01; rtd 01; PtO *Liv* from 03. *26 Drummersdale Lane, Scarisbrick, Ormskirk L40 9RB* T: (01704) 880956

BENHAM, Ms Sandra Rhys. b 59. Westcott Ho Cam 04. **d** 06 **p** 07. C Gainsborough and Morton *Linc* 06-09; P-in-c Quarrington w Old Sleaford 09-15; P-in-c Silk Willoughby 09-15; P-in-c Cranwell 09-11; V Baildon *Bradf* from 15. *The Vicarage, Church Hill, Baildon, Shipley BD17 6NE* T: (01274) 589005 E: sandrabenham@btinternet.com

BENISON, Canon Brian. b 41. K Coll Lon 61. Bps' Coll Cheshunt 63. **d** 66 **p** 67. C Tynemouth Ch Ch *Newc* 66-70; C Gosforth All SS 70-72; TV Cullercoats St Geo 73-81; V Denton 81-93; V Blyth St Mary 93-04; RD Bedlington 98-03; Chapl Cheviot and Wansbeck NHS Trust 93-98; Chapl Northumbria Healthcare NHS Trust 98-04; Hon Can Newc Cathl from 01; rtd 04. *64 Monks Wood, North Shields NE30 2UA* T: 0191-257 1631 E: brian.benison@btinternet.com

BENJAMIN, Adrian Victor. b 42. Wadh Coll Ox BA 66 MA 68. Cuddesdon Coll 66. **d** 68 **p** 69. C Gosforth All SS *Newc* 68-71; C Stepney St Dunstan and All SS *Lon* 71-75; V Friern Barnet All SS 75-12; Relig Ed ITV Oracle 83-92; rtd 12. *Carlton Cottage, 75 Church Lane, Sutton-on-Sea, Mablethorpe LN12 2JA*

✠**BENN, The Rt Revd Wallace Parke.** b 47. UCD BA 69. Trin Coll Bris 69. **d** 72 **p** 73 **c** 97. C New Ferry *Ches* 72-76; C Cheadle 76-82; V Audley *Lich* 82-87; V Harold Wood *Chelmsf* 87-97; Chapl Harold Wood Hosp Chelmsf 87-96; Area Bp Lewes *Chich* 97-12; Can and Preb Chich Cathl 97-12; rtd 12; PtO *Pet* from 13. *10 Glade Close, Burton Latimer, Kettering NN15 5YG* E: twobenns@gmail.com

BENNET, Hadley Jane. b 66. **d** 09 **p** 10. NSM Grayshott *Guildf* 09-13; Chapl Alton Coll from 13. *Landfall, Three Gates Lane, Haslemere GU27 2ET* T: (01428) 658166 E: hadleybennet@yahoo.co.uk

BENNET, Mark David. b 62. SS Coll Cam BA 84 MA 92 Anglia Poly Univ MA 04 ACA 89. Westcott Ho Cam 98. **d** 01 **p** 02. C Chapel Allerton *Ripon* 01-05; TV Gt Parndon *Chelmsf* 05-07; P-in-c 07-09; TR 09-11; TR Thatcham *Ox* from 11; AD Newbury from 15. *The Rectory, 17 Church Gate, Thatcham RG19 3PN* T: (01635) 867342 E: markbennet@btinternet.com

BENNETT, Alan Robert. b 31. Roch Th Coll 62. **d** 64 **p** 65. C Asterby w Goulceby *Linc* 64-67; C St Alb St Pet *St Alb* 67-70; R Banham *Nor* 70-72; CF 72-77; P-in-c Colchester St Mary Magd *Chelmsf* 77; TV Colchester St Leon, St Mary Magd and St Steph 77-81; R Colne Engaine 81-88; P-in-c Stoke Ferry w Wretton *Ely* 88-89; V 89-96; V Whittington 88-96; rtd 96; Hon C Wimbotsham w Stow Bardolph and Stow Bridge etc *Ely* 96-00; PtO from 00. *34 West Way, Wimbotsham, King's Lynn PE34 3PZ* T: (01366) 385958

BENNETT, Canon Alan William. b 42. Sarum Th Coll 65. **d** 68 **p** 69. C Fareham H Trin *Portsm* 68-71; C Brighton St Matthias *Chich* 71-73; C Stanmer w Falmer and Moulsecoomb 73-75; C Moulsecoomb 76; V Lower Sandown St Jo *Portsm* 76-80; V Soberton w Newtown 80-87; R Aston Clinton w Buckland and Drayton Beauchamp *Ox* 87-07; RD Wendover 94-04; Hon Can Ch Ch 03-07; rtd 07; Asst Chapl Costa Almeria and Costa Calida *Eur* from 10. *2 Chapman Close, Aylesbury HP21 8FY* E: canonbennett@hotmail.co.uk

BENNETT, Alexander Steven Frederick. b 69. Hull Univ BA 91. Westcott Ho Cam 93. **d** 95 **p** 96. C Whitton and Thurleston w Akenham *St E* 95-99; OGS from 99; C Oswestry *Lich* 99-01; V Oswestry H Trin 01-04; CF from 04. *c/o MOD Chaplains (Army)* F: 381824 T: (01264) 383430 E: armypadre@hotmail.com

BENNETT, Mrs Alison. b 63. Open Univ BSc 03 DipSW 99. STETS 05. **d** 08 **p** 09. C Bramshott and Liphook *Portsm* 08-12; TV Basingstoke *Win* from 12. *75 Cumberland Avenue, Basingstoke RG22 4BQ*

BENNETT, Ms Anne Yvonne. b 62. Open Univ MSc 95 Imp Coll Lon MBA 00. Cranmer Hall Dur 06. **d** 08 **p** 09. C Harton *Dur* 08-12; C Cleadon Park 09-12; V Borstal *Roch* from 12; Chapl HM Pris Cookham Wood from 12. *The Vicarage, 76 Borstal Street, Rochester ME1 3HL* T: (01634) 324960 E: timeshift@btinternet.com

BENNETT, Anton Wayne. b 69. SW Poly Plymouth BSc 90. Westcott Ho Cam 00. **d** 02 **p** 03. C Pendleton *Man* 02-05; R Abberton, The Flyfords, Naunton Beauchamp etc *Worc* 05-07; rtd 07. *18 Victoria Street, Settle BD24 9HD* T: (01729) 822349 E: father.anton@virgin.net

BENNETT, Arnold Ernest. b 29. K Coll Lon BD 59 AKC 53. **d** 54 **p** 55. C S w N Hayling *Portsm* 54-59; C Stevenage *St Alb* 59-64; R N w S Wootton *Nor* 64-74; V Hykeham *Linc* 74-85; V Heckfield w Mattingley and Rotherwick *Win* 85-99; rtd 99; PtO *Win* from 99. *24 Cricket Green, Hartley Wintney, Hook RG27 8PP* T: (01252) 843147

BENNETT, Avril Elizabeth Jean. b 63. BEd. **d** 00 **p** 01. NSM Dublin Crumlin w Chapelizod *D & G* 00-03; NSM Tallaght from 03. *17 Ardeevin Court, Lucan, Co Dublin, Republic of Ireland* T: (00353) (1) 628 2353

BENNETT, Ben. *See* BENNETT, Stuart

BENNETT, Charles William. b 38. LTh. St Jo Coll Auckland 60. **d** 63 **p** 64. C Tauranga New Zealand 63-68; V Clive 68-71; C St Jo Cathl Napier 71-74; V Waipaoa 74-79; C N Walsham w Antingham *Nor* 80-81; V Waipaoa New Zealand 81-82; V Te Puke 82-87; V Dannevirke and P-in-c Woodville 87-91; V Westshore 91-93; Min Enabler 94-03; V Waipawa from 05. *59 McGrath Street, Napier South, Napier 4110, New Zealand* T: (0064) (6) 835 9924 F: 835 9920 E: bwbennett@inspire.net.nz

BENNETT, Mrs Christina Mary. b 45. **d** 07 **p** 08. NSM Henfield w Shermanbury and Woodmancote *Chich* from 07. *17 Gresham Place, Henfield BN5 9QJ* T: (01273) 492222 E: christina@cmb45.wanadoo.co.uk

BENNETT, Christopher Ian. b 75. TCD BA 98 BTh 00. CITC 97. **d** 00 **p** 01. C Larne and Inver *Conn* 00-03; C Holywood *D & D* 03-09; Bp's C Belfast Titanic Quarter from 09; P-in-c Belfast St Clem 12-15. *29 Loughview Terrace, Greenisland, Carrickfergus BT38 8RE* T: (028) 9085 2895 M: 07980-885991 E: cands2000@hotmail.com

BENNETT, Clifford Orford. b 32. St Mich Coll Llan 73. **d** 75 **p** 76. C Holywell *St As* 75-79; V Pontblyddyn 79-99; rtd 99. *4 Bryn Teg, Brynford, Holywell CH8 8AP* T: (01352) 719028

BENNETT, David Edward. b 35. Fitzw Ho Cam BA 56 MA 60 Lon Univ PGCE. Wells Th Coll 58. **d** 60 **p** 61. C Lightcliffe *Wakef* 60-62; NE Area Sec Chr Educn Movement 62-68; Gen Insp RE Nottm Co Coun 68-00; Hon C Holme Pierrepont w Adbolton *S'well* 71-85; NSM Radcliffe-on-Trent and Shelford etc 85-00; rtd 00; PtO *S'well* from 04. *The Old Farmhouse, 65 Main Street, Gunthorpe, Nottingham NG14 7EY* T: 0115-966 3451

BENNETT, Donovan Harry. b 27. Qu Mary Coll Lon BScEng 52 FGS 61 AMICE 61 CEng 61 FICE 72. Moray Ord Course 88. **d** 92 **p** 93. Hon C Dingwall *Mor* 92-93; Hon C Strathpeffer 92-93; Hon C Inverness St Mich 93-95; Assoc Chapl Raigmore Hosp NHS Trust Inverness 94-96; P-in-c Grantown-on-Spey *Mor* 96-99; Can St Andr Cathl Inverness 98-00; PtO from 99. *8 Brewster Drive, Forres IV36 2JW* T: (01309) 671478 E: donovan.bennett@btinternet.com

BENNETT, Elizabeth Mary. b 47. **d** 10 **p** 11. NSM Broughton Gifford, Gt Chalfield and Holt *Sarum* 10-14; NSM Hordle *Win* from 14. *Church Cottage, Sway Road, Tiptoe, SO41 6FR* T: (01425) 627771 E: revelizabeth1@gmail.com

BENNETT, Garry Raymond. b 46. K Coll Lon 66 St Aug Coll Cant 69. **d** 70 **p** 71. C Mitcham St Mark *S'wark* 70-73; C Mortlake w E Sheen 73-75; TV 76-78; V Herne Hill St Paul 78-88; P-in-c Ruskin Park St Sav and St Matt 82-88; V Herne Hill 89; Sen Dioc Stewardship Adv *Chelmsf* 89-94; TR Southend 94-98; Dir and Chapl Herne Hill Sch *S'wark* 98-04; PtO *St D* from 00. *Hendre House, Llandeloy, Haverfordwest SA62 6LW* T: (01348) 831160 E: phyll.bennett@btinternet.com

BENNETT, Canon Geoffrey Kenneth. b 56. Ex Univ MA 01. Oak Hill Th Coll. **d** 89 **p** 90. C Ipswich St Matt *St E* 89-92; R St Ruan w St Grade and Landewednack *Truro* 92-98; V Budock from 98; P-in-c Mawnan 03-13; RD Carnmarth S from 12; Hon Can Truro Cathl from 14. *The Vicarage, Merry Mit Meadow, Budock Water, Falmouth TR11 5DW* T: (01326) 376422 E: g.k.bennett@amserve.net

BENNETT, Canon George Edward. b 51. Univ of Wales (Abth) BA 72. St Steph Ho Ox 73. **d** 76 **p** 77. C Clifton All SS w Tyndalls Park *Bris* 76-78; C Clifton All SS w St Jo 78-82; Chapl Newbury and Sandleford Hosps 82-93; TV Newbury *Ox* 82-93; V Llwynderw *S & B* 93-06; V Newton St Pet from 06; AD Clyne 98-12; Hon Can Brecon Cathl 00-02; Can Res Brecon Cathl from 02. *The Vicarage, Mary Twill Lane, Mumbles, Swansea SA3 4RB* T: (01792) 368348 E: bennettgandr@phonecoop.coop

BENNETT, Graham Eric Thomas. b 53. Sarum & Wells Th Coll 88. **d** 90 **p** 91. C Baswich *Lich* 90-94; C Codsall 94-00; P-in-c Willenhall St Steph 00-05; V from 05; AD Wolverhampton 05-11. *St Stephen's Vicarage, 27 Wolverhampton Street, Willenhall WV13 2PS* T: (01902) 605239 E: grahambennett.69@btinternet.com

BENNETT, Handel Henry Cecil. b 33. MCIM. Cant Sch of Min 79. **d** 82 **p** 83. NSM St Margarets-at-Cliffe w Westcliffe etc *Cant* 82-85; Dir Holy Land Chr Tours 85-94; Holy Land Consultant F T Tours 95-96; Sen Travel Consultant Raymond Cook Chr Tours from 96; PtO *St Alb* 85-99; *Ex* from 99. *Camps Bay, 2 Victoria Road, Sidmouth EX10 8TZ* T: (01395) 514211

BENNETT, Helen Anne. See EDWARDS, Helen Anne

BENNETT, Canon Ian Frederick. b 30. Ch Coll Cam BA 54 MA 62. Westcott Ho Cam 61. **d** 63 **p** 64. C Hemel Hempstead *St Alb* 63-68; Asst Chapl Man Univ 69-73; Sen Chapl 73-79; C Chorlton w Medlock 69-73; P-in-c 73-79; TR Man Whitworth 79; Dioc Tr Officer *Birm* 79-88; Hon Can Birm Cathl 86-88; Can Res Newc Cathl 88-98; Dioc Dir of Min and Tr 90-98; Dir Post-Ord Tr 97-98; rtd 98; PtO *Newc* from 98. *21 Otterburn Avenue, Gosforth, Newcastle upon Tyne NE3 4RR* T: 0191-285 1967

BENNETT, John David. b 58. Ox Univ BA 79 MA 83. Westcott Ho Cam 81. **d** 83 **p** 84. C Taunton St Andr *B & W* 83-86; Chapl Trowbridge Coll *Sarum* 86-90; Asst P Studley 86-90; V Yeovil H Trin *B & W* 90-95; R Yeovil H Trin w Barwick 95-02; R Sprowston w Beeston *Nor* 02-10; RD Nor N 05-10; V Spalding St Mary and St Nic *Linc* from 10; P-in-c Spalding St Paul from 10. *The Parsonage, 1 Halmer Gate, Spalding PE11 2DR* T: (01775) 719668 E: jdbennett@gmail.com

BENNETT, John Dudley. b 44. Open Univ BA 87 Lanc Univ MA 92 Huddersfield Univ PGCE 04. Coll of Resurr Mirfield 08. **d** 09 **p** 09. NSM Bolton Abbey *Bradf* 09-14; rtd 14; PtO *Leeds* from 15. *Honeysuckle Cottage, The Green, Linton, Skipton BD23 5HJ* T: (01756) 753763 E: brj.linton@virgin.net

BENNETT, John Seccombe. b 59. Wye Coll Lon BSc 81 Leic Poly CertEd 84. Trin Coll Bris. **d** 00 **p** 01. C Llanrhian w Llanhywel

and Carnhedryn etc *St D* 00-01; C Dewisland 01-02; TV 02-11; V Cardigan w Mwnt and Y Ferwig w Llangoedmor from 11; Min Can St D Cathl from 00; AD Cemais and Sub-Aeron from 14. *The Vicarage, Maesydderwen, Cardigan SA43 1PE* T: (01239) 615466 E: jsbkbennett@btinternet.com

BENNETT, Marian Joyce. b 53. BEd. EMMTC. **d** 06 **p** 07. NSM Castle Donington and Lockington cum Hemington *Leic* 06-10; NSM Mountsorrel Ch Ch and St Pet 10-13; PtO 13; NSM Castle Donington and Lockington cum Hemington from 13. *174 Leicester Road, Loughborough LE11 2AH* T: (01509) 263601 E: mbloughborough@hotmail.co.uk

BENNETT, Mark Ian. b 61. K Coll Cam BA 83 MA 86. Trin Coll Bris BA 94. **d** 94 **p** 95. C Selly Park St Steph and St Wulstan *Birm* 94-97; C Harrow Trin St Mich *Lon* 97-99; Hon C Redland *Bris* 99-00; TV Drypool *York* 00-06; V Gee Cross *Ches* from 06. *16 Higham Lane, Hyde SK14 5LX* T: 0161-368 2337 E: mark@holytrinitychurch-gx.org.uk

BENNETT, Mark Stephen. b 66. Cant Univ (NZ) MusB 89 Cant Ch Ch Univ BA 14. SEITE 07. **d** 10 **p** 11. NSM Staplehurst *Cant* 10-12; Chapl Dulwich Prep Sch Cranbrook 10-12; Chapl St Edm Sch Cant from 13; Hon Min Can Cant Cathl 11-12; Min Can from 13. *2 St Edmund's Cottages, Giles Lane, Canterbury CT2 7LR* M: 07709-376668 E: chaplain@stedmunds.org.uk

BENNETT, Michael John. b 43. AKC 66. St Boniface Warminster 66. **d** 67 **p** 68. C Chester le Street *Dur* 67-71; C Portland All SS w St Pet *Sarum* 71-74; V Portland St Jo 74-85; Chapl Portland Hosp Weymouth 74-85; R Alveley and Quatt *Heref* 85-92; Dep Chapl HM YOI Glen Parva 93-95; TV Wrexham *St As* 95-99; V Llansantffraid-ym-Mechain and Llanfechain 99-05; C Rhyl w St Ann 05-09; rtd 09; Hon C Redmarley D'Abitot, Bromesberrow, Pauntley etc *Glouc* 09-12; PtO from 15. *65 Robert Raikes Avenue, Tuffley, Gloucester GL4 0HL* T: (01452) 301337 E: sheilabennett123btinternet.com

BENNETT, Milen George Penev. Bulgarian Evang Th Inst BA 03. OLM Stratford St Paul and SS Jas *Chelmsf* from 15. *65 Falkland Park Avenue, London SE25 6SQ*

BENNETT, Nigel John. b 47. Oak Hill Th Coll 66. **d** 71 **p** 72. C Tonbridge St Steph *Roch* 71-75; C Heatherlands St Jo *Sarum* 75-79; P-in-c Kingham w Churchill, Daylesford and Sarsden *Ox* 79; R 80-85; Chapl Blue Coat Sch Reading 85-08; rtd 08; PtO *Ox* 08-09; Hon C Southsea St Jude *Portsm* 09-14; PtO from 14. *19 Ashburton Road, Southsea PO5 3JS* T: (023) 9242 1463 E: nigelbennett@virginmedia.com

BENNETT, Osmond Shirley. b 36. Oriel Coll Ox BA 67. Ripon Hall Ox 64. **d** 68 **p** 69. C Stocking Farm *Leic* 68-71; C Thurcaston 71-72; V Leic St Marg 72-82; V Leic St Marg and All SS 83-89; R Houghton-on-the-Hill, Keyham and Hungarton 89-00; rtd 00. *48 Wide Lane, Hathern, Loughborough LE12 5LN* T: (01509) 553644

BENNETT, Paul. b 55. Southn Univ BTh 94. St Steph Ho Ox 95. **d** 97 **p** 98. C Willingdon *Chich* 97-00; C Hangleton 00-04; R Letchworth *St Alb* from 04. *St Michael's Rectory, 39 South View, Letchworth Garden City SG6 3JJ* T: (01462) 684822 F: 643592 E: revpaulbennett@ntlworld.com

BENNETT, Paul William. b 61. Linc Th Coll 95. **d** 95 **p** 96. C Thornton-le-Fylde *Blackb* 95-00; V Wesham 00-03; P-in-c Treales 00-03; V Wesham and Treales 03-08; Chapl Dunkirk Miss to Seafarers *Eur* 08-14; P-in-c Meir *Lich* from 14; P-in-c Longton from 14. *The Rectory, Rutland Road, Stoke-on-Trent ST3 1EH* T: (01782) 595098 E: mowbreck@aol.com

BENNETT, Miss Rachel Elizabeth. b 56. W Sussex Inst of HE CertEd 79. **d** 04. NSM Littlehampton and Wick *Chich* 04-05; C Durrington 05-07; Chapl Worthing and Southlands Hosps NHS Trust 08-09; Chapl W Sussex Hosps NHS Foundn Trust from 09. *Worthing Hospital, Lyndhurst Road, Worthing BN11 2DH* T: (01903) 205111 M: 07810-350098 E: rachel.bennett3@tesco.net

BENNETT, Robert Geoffrey. b 43. FCA. **d** 05 **p** 06. OLM Woking St Jo *Guildf* from 05. *10 Barricane, Woking GU21 7RB* T: (01483) 722832 E: robgbennett@tiscali.co.uk

BENNETT, Roger Sherwood. b 35. Nottm Univ BA 56. Wells Th Coll 58. **d** 59 **p** 60. C Mansfield Woodhouse *S'well* 59-60; C Spalding St Mary and St Nic *Linc* 60-63; V Gedney 63-69; Chapl RNR 65-68; Chapl RN 69-90; V Amport, Grateley, Monxton and Quarley *Win* 90-95; rtd 96; PtO *Win* 96-12. *Le Reduit, School Lane, Nether Wallop, Stockbridge SO20 8EH* T: (01264) 782336

BENNETT, Roy Donald. b 40. Nottm Univ MA 97. St Jo Coll Nottm 78. **d** 80 **p** 81. C Fletchamstead *Cov* 80-83; C Bedworth 83-87; P-in-c Studley 87-93; Chapl Univ Hosp Nottm 93-96; Chapl Qu Medical Cen Nottm 94-96; Chapl Bassetlaw Hosp and Community Services NHS Trust 96-01; Chapl Doncaster and Bassetlaw Hosps NHS Trust 01-02; rtd 02; PtO *Sarum* 03-08. *21 High Street, Puddletown, Dorchester DT2 8RT* T: (01305) 848144 E: roy@revroy.com

BENNETT, Shirley. See BENNETT, Osmond Shirley

BENNETT (née FORD), Ms Simone Louise. b 70. Warwick Univ BA 92. Westcott Ho Cam 00. **d** 02 **p** 03. C Stockingford *Cov* 02-03; C Didsbury Ch Ch and Withington St Chris *Man* 03-05; Hon C Abberton, The Flyfords, Naunton Beauchamp etc *Worc* 06-09. *18 Victoria Street, Settle BD24 9HD* T: (01729) 822349 M: 07946-548366 E: simone.bennett@virgin.net

BENNETT, Stephen. See BENNETT, Mark Stephen

BENNETT, Stuart (Ben). b 61. St Jo Coll Nottm BA 02. **d** 02 **p** 03. C Consett *Dur* 02-06; P-in-c Castleside 06-11; rtd 11. *Address withheld by request* E: ysdben@btinternet.com

BENNETT, Ms Toni Elizabeth. b 56. Worc Coll of Educn BA 81 Sheff Poly 87. St Jo Coll Nottm MA 94. **d** 96 **p** 97. C Heanor *Derby* 96-00; TV Bedworth *Cov* 00-08; R Montgomery and Forden and Llandyssil *St As* from 08; AD Pool from 10. *The Rectory, Lions Bank, Montgomery SY15 6PT* T: (01686) 668243 E: toni.rev@btinternet.com

BENNETT, William Leslie. b 52. TCD Div Sch. **d** 90 **p** 91. C Carrickfergus *Conn* 90-93; I Lisnaskea *Clogh* 93-00; I Newcastle w Newtownmountkennedy and Calary *D & G* from 00. *The Rectory, Church Lane, Newcastle, Greystones, Co Wicklow, Republic of Ireland* T: (00353) (1) 281 9300 M: 87-948 0317 E: bennettwilliam1@gmail.com

BENNETT-SHAW, Miss Anne Elizabeth. b 38. **d** 02 **p** 03. OLM Upper Wylye Valley *Sarum* from 02. *5 Hospital of St John, Heytesbury, Warminster BA12 0HW* T: (01985) 840339 E: revannebennettshaw@btinternet.com

BENNETT-REES, Catherine Mary. See MEAKIN, Catherine Mary

BENNETTS, Ms Rachel Mary. b 69. Homerton Coll Cam BEd 91. Trin Coll Bris BA 01. **d** 02 **p** 03. C Wroughton *Bris* 02-06; TV N Farnborough *Guildf* from 06; Chapl Farnborough Sixth Form Coll from 07. *The Vicarage, 45 Sand Hill, Farnborough GU14 8ER* T: (01252) 543789 M: 07749-045449 E: racheagle@yahoo.co.uk

BENNIE, Stanley James Gordon. b 43. Edin Univ MA 65. Coll of Resurr Mirfield 66. **d** 68 **p** 69. C Ashington *Newc* 68-70; Prec St Andr Cathl Inverness 70-74; Itinerant Priest 74-81; R Portsoy *Ab* 81-84; R Buckie 81-84; R Stornoway *Arg* 84-10; R Eorropaidh 84-95; rtd 10. *St Lennan, 13A Scotland Street, Stornoway HS1 2JN* T: (01851) 703259 M: 07768-660612 E: gm4ptq@btinternet.com

BENNISON, Philip Owen. b 42. Dur Univ BA 64. Coll of Resurr Mirfield 64. **d** 66 **p** 67. C Guisborough *York* 66-67; C S Bank 67-71; C Thornaby on Tees St Paul 71-72; TV Thornaby on Tees 72-74; R Skelton in Cleveland 74-78; R Upleatham 75-78; Chapl Freeman Hosp Newc 78-84; V Ashington *Newc* 84-93; Chapl N Tees Health NHS Trust Stockton-on-Tees 93-98; Chapl N Tees and Hartlepool NHS Trust 99-02; P-in-c Newton Flowery Field *Ches* 02-10; P-in-c Hyde St Thos 02-10; rtd 10; PtO *York* from 10; *Dur* from 12. *62 Glaisdale Road, Yarm TS15 9RP* T: (01653) 646624 E: philip_bennison@hotmail.com

BENNISON, Timothy Paul. b 63. Aber Univ BD 94. Edin Th Coll 95. **d** 97 **p** 98. C St Andr Cathl 97-00; Asst Chapl Aberdeen Univ 97-00; P-in-c Aberdeen St Jas *Ab* 00-03; Dioc Miss 21 Co-ord 00-03; P-in-c Glencarse *Bre* 05-08; R Dunfermline *St And* 08-12. *Address temp unknown* M: 07411-616163

BENOY, Canon Stephen Michael. b 66. Clare Coll Cam BA 87 MA 90. Trin Coll Bris BA 93. **d** 96 **p** 97. C New Malden and Coombe *S'wark* 96-02; Kingston Borough Youth Project 00-02; V Kettering Ch the King *Pet* 02-11; Dir of Ords and Voc from 11; Can Pet Cathl from 13. *Diocese of Peterborough, Bouverie Court, 6 The Lakes, Bedford Road, Northampton NN4 7YD* T: (01604) 887047 E: steve.benoy@peterborough-diocese.org.uk

BENSKIN, David Peter. b 53. Qu Coll Birm 11. **d** 13 **p** 14. C Heart of England *Cov* from 13; Asst Chapl Rainsbrook Secure Tr Cen from 13. *Rainsbrook Secure Training Centre, Onley Park, Willoughby, Rugby CV23 8SY* T: (01788) 528800 M: 07811-295775 E: david@dbenskin.wanadoo.co.uk

BENSON, Ashley Dawn. See ROSS, Ashley Dawn

BENSON, Christopher Hugh. b 53. Bath Academy of Art BA 75 Keble Coll Ox BA 78 MA 87. Chich Th Coll 78. **d** 80 **p** 81. C Heavitree w Ex St Paul 80-83; P-in-c Broadclyst 83-85; TV Pinhoe and Broadclyst 85-90; V Kingsteignton and Teigngrace 90-08; Chapl Plymouth Univ 92-95; RD Newton Abbot and Ipplepen 01-07; C Baslow w Curbar and Stoney Middleton *Derby* 08-11; C Ashford w Sheldon and Longstone 08-11; V Longstone, Curbar and Stony Middleton 11-14; rtd 14. *1 Leighon Cottages, Manaton, Newton Abbot TQ13 9UP* T: (01629) 640257 E: christopher4cbenson8.wanadoo.co.uk

BENSON, David. See BENSON, John David

BENSON, Gareth Neil. b 47. Jordan Hill Coll Glas TCert 80. St And NSM Tr Scheme 77. **d** 81 **p** 82. NSM Glenrothes *St And*

81-88; NSM Kirkcaldy 88-04; P-in-c 04-12; NSM Kinghorn 88-04; P-in-c 04-12; rtd 12. *Address temp unknown* E: fathergareth@btinternet.com

BENSON, The Ven George Patrick. b 49. Ch Ch Ox BA 70 Lon Univ BD 77 Open Univ MPhil 94. All Nations Chr Coll 78 St Jo Coll Nottm 89. **d** 91 **p** 92. C Upton (Overchurch) *Ches* 91-95; V Barnston 95-11; RD Wirral N 98-08; Hon Can Ches Cathl 09-11; Adn Heref from 11. *3 Hatterall Close, Hereford HR1 1GA* T: (01432) 265659 E: archdeacon@hereford.anglican.org

BENSON, Mrs Hilary Christine. b 51. Man Univ BA 72 Hughes Hall Cam PGCE 73. Trin Coll Bris 81. **dss** 84 **d** 87 **p** 94. Starbeck *Ripon* 84-86; Birm St Martin w Bordesley St Andr 86-91; NSM 87-91; NSM Brandwood 91-97; Chapl Birm Univ 92-97; Chapl St Edw Sch Ox 97-00; Chapl Qu Anne's Sch Caversham 00-13; rtd 14; PtO *Derby* from 14. *31 Dale Road, Buxton SK17 6LN* T: (01298) 213519 E: hcbenson@ntlworld.com

BENSON, John David. b 36. St Aid Birkenhead 58. **d** 61 **p** 62. C Kingston upon Hull St Martin *York* 61-65; C Marfleet 65-68; V Ingleby Greenhow 68-72; P-in-c Kildale 68-72; Asst Youth Chapl 68-72; Dioc Youth Chapl *Sheff* 72-78; V Thorne 78-91; V Totley 91-98; rtd 98; PtO *Sheff* from 98. *14 Ash Hill Crescent, Hatfield, Doncaster DN7 6HY* T: (01302) 846359

BENSON, Canon John Patrick. b 52. Ch Coll Cam BA 73 MA 76 PhD 76. Trin Coll Bris 78. **d** 81 **p** 82. C Walmley *Birm* 81-84; C Chadkirk *Ches* 84-86; V St Geo Singapore 87-95; Dir of Tr 95-01; V Chpl of Resurr 01-07; Hon Can Singapore 96-07; Dean Cambodia 93-05; Dean Laos 98-00; rtd 07; PtO *Ches* from 09. *Cherry Trees, Queens Park Road, Chester CH4 7AD* T: (01244) 671170 E: johnpbenson@gmail.com

BENSON, John Patrick. b 51. Univ of Wales (Ban) BSc 72. Trin Coll Bris 83. **d** 85 **p** 86. C Stoke Damerel *Ex* 85-88; P-in-c Petrockstowe, Petersmarland, Merton and Huish 88; TV Shebbear, Buckland Filleigh, Sheepwash etc 89-94; RD Torrington 93-94; P-in-c Newport, Bishops Tawton and Tawstock 94-97; TV Barnstaple 97-07; R Knockholt w Halstead *Roch* from 07. *The Rectory, Church Road, Halstead, Sevenoaks TN14 7HQ* T: (01959) 532133 E: john.benson3@btinternet.com

BENSON, Nicholas Henry. b 53. Man Univ BSc 75 Leeds Univ MSc 77. Trin Coll Bris 81. **d** 84 **p** 85. C Starbeck *Ripon* 84-86; C Birm St Martin w Bordesley St Andr 86-91; Chapl to the Markets 86-91; V Brandwood 91-97; PtO *Ox* 99-01; NSM Reading St Jo 01-14; PtO *Derby* from 14. *31 Dale Road, Buxton SK17 6LN* T: (01298) 213519 E: saintbede@ntlworld.com

BENSON, Paddy. See BENSON, George Patrick

BENSON, Philip Richard. b 85. QUB BTh 06 MTh 09. **d** 14 **p** 15. Finaghy *Conn* 14-15; C Larne and Inver from 15. *23 Glenburn Avenue, Glynn, Larne BT40 3DJ* M: 07850-345156 E: revphilipbenson@gmail.com

BENSON, Philip Steven. b 59. Ulster Univ BSc 81 LLCM 80. S Dios Minl Tr Scheme 88. **d** 92 **p** 93. Producer Relig Broadcasting Dept BBC 91-94; NSM W Ealing St Jo w St Jas *Lon* 92-94; Relig Progr Producer BBC Man from 94. *4 Cranford Avenue, Knutsford WA16 0EB* T: (01565) 652513 F: 641695

BENSON, Mrs Rachel Candia. b 43. JP 76. TCD MA 66 Lon Univ PGCE 67. S'wark Ord Course 84. **d** 87 **p** 94. NSM Putney St Marg *S'wark* 87-97; NSM Sand Hutton and Whitwell w Crambe, Flaxton and Foston *York* 97-07; PtO from 07. *Grange Farm, Westow, York YO60 7NJ* T: (01653) 658296 F: 658456 E: rachel.benson4@btopenworld.com

BENSON, Richard John. b 55. Birm Coll of Educn CertEd 78. Ripon Coll Cuddesdon 92. **d** 94 **p** 95. C Alford w Rigsby *Linc* 94-97; R Partney Gp 97-12; V Taddington, Chelmorton and Monyash etc *Derby* from 12. *The Vicarage, Church Street, Monyash, Bakewell DE45 1JH* T: (01629) 812234 E: parson_benson@yahoo.co.uk

BENSON, Steven. See BENSON, Philip Steven

BENSON, Thomas Henry Frank. b 66. SWMTC 06. **d** 09 **p** 10. C Bideford, Northam, Westward Ho!, Appledore etc *Ex* 09-12; P-in-c Buckfastleigh w Dean Prior 12-14; R Staverton w Landscove, Littlehempston, Buckfastleigh and Dean Prior from 14. *The Vicarage, Glebelands, Buckfastleigh TQ11 0BH* T: (01364) 644875

BENT, David Michael. b 55. Leeds Univ BSc 77. Trin Coll Bris BA 94. **d** 96 **p** 97. C Gorleston St Andr *Nor* 96-00; TR Brinsworth w Catcliffe and Treeton *Sheff* 00-03; TR Rivers Team from 03. *The Vicarage, 61 Whitehill Lane, Brinsworth, Rotherham S60 5JR* T: (01709) 363850 E: davidbent99@btinternet.com

BENT, Mrs Helen Margaret. b 56. Sheff Univ BMus 77 Trent Poly PGCE 78 Suffolk Poly BA 00. EAMTC 97. **d** 98 **p** 99. C Gorleston St Mary *Nor* 98-00; C Brightside w Wincobank *Sheff* 00-04; Bp's Adv in Music and Worship 05-15; Hd Minl Tr RSCM from 15; C Rivers Team *Sheff* from 15. *The*

Vicarage, 61 Whitehill Lane, Brinsworth, Rotherham S60 5JR T: (01709) 363850 E: helen@thebents.co.uk *or* helen.bent@sheffield.anglican.org

BENT, The Very Revd Michael Charles. b 31. Kelham Th Coll 51. **d** 55 **p** 56. C Wellingborough St Mary *Pet* 55-60; New Zealand 60-85; Adn Taranaki 76-85; Dean H Trin Cathl Suva Fiji 85-89; Can St Pet Cathl Hamilton New Zealand 90-94; Papua New Guinea 94-96; New Zealand from 96. *34 Brooklands Road, New Plymouth 4601, New Zealand* T: (0064) (6) 753 5507 E: miro@clear.net.nz

BENTALL, Canon Jill Margaret. b 44. MCSP 66. S Dios Minl Tr Scheme 91. **d** 94 **p** 95. NSM Knights Enham *Win* 94-02; C Andover w Foxcott 02-09; P-in-c Pastrow 09-14; RD Andover 06-10; Hon Can Win Cathl 11-14; rtd 14; PtO *Win* from 14. *Address temp unknown* E: jill.bentall@btinternet.com

BENTHAM, Canon John William. b 58. Loughb Univ BSc 80 Nottm Univ LTh 85. St Jo Coll Nottm 82. **d** 85 **p** 86. C Burmantofts St Steph and St Agnes *Ripon* 85-88; C Horsforth 88-90; P-in-c Nottingham St Sav *S'well* 90-92; V 92-98; Chapl Nottm Univ from 98; AD Nottingham W 06-08; AD W Bingham from 08; Hon Can S'well Minster from 10. *51 Chaworth Road, West Bridgford, Nottingham NG2 7AE* T: 0115-846 1054 *or* 846 6037 E: john.bentham@nottingham.ac.uk

BENTHAM, Philip John (Ben). b 55. Hull Univ BA 83 PGCE 85. Trin Coll Bris MA 96. **d** 96 **p** 97. C Wrockwardine Deanery *Lich* 96-00; P-in-c Chipinge and Chimanimani Zimbabwe 00-03; Chapl Viña del Mar St Pet Chile 03-07; Chapl Bethany Sch Goudhurst 08-13; Chapl Dur Sch from 13. *Durham School, Durham DH1 4SZ* T: 0191-386 4783 E: benbentham@yahoo.co.uk

✠**BENTLEY, The Rt Revd David Edward.** b 35. Leeds Univ BA 56. Westcott Ho Cam 58. **d** 60 **p** 61 **c** 86. C Bris St Ambrose Whitehall 60-62; C Guildf H Trin w St Mary 62-66; R Headley All SS 66-73; R Esher 73-86; RD Emly 77-82; Hon Can Guildf Cathl 80-86; Chmn Dioc Coun Soc Resp 80-86; Suff Bp Lynn *Nor* 86-93; Chmn Cand Cttee ACCM 87-91; ABM 91-93; Bp Glouc 93-03; rtd 04; Hon Asst Bp Lich from 04; PtO *Cov* from 04. *19 Gable Croft, Lichfield WS14 9RY* T: (01543) 419376

BENTLEY, Frances Rymer. *See* COCKER, Frances Rymer

BENTLEY, Frank Richard. b 41. K Coll Lon BD 67 AKC 67. **d** 68 **p** 69. C Feltham *Lon* 68-72; P-in-c Bethnal Green St Bart 72-77; R Bow w Bromley St Leon 77-88; P-in-c Mile End Old Town H Trin 77-88; P-in-c Bromley All Hallows 77-88; AD Tower Hamlets 83-88; TR E Ham w Upton Park and Forest Gate *Chelmsf* 88-97; P-in-c Petersham *S'wark* 97-07; Chapl HM Pris Latchmere Ho 97-07; rtd 07; PtO *St E* from 08. *104 Cannon Street, Bury St Edmunds IP33 1JU* T: (01284) 766063 E: richard.bentley32@btinternet.com

BENTLEY, The Ven Frank William Henry. b 34. AKC 57. **d** 58 **p** 59. C Shepton Mallet *B & W* 58-62; R Kingsdon w Podymore-Milton 62-66; P-in-c Yeovilton 62-66; P-in-c Babcary 64-66; V Wiveliscombe 66-76; RD Tone 73-76; V St Jo in Bedwardine *Worc* 76-84; P-in-c Worc St Mich 82-84; RD Martley and Worc W 80-84; Hon Can Worc Cathl 81-84; Adn Worc and Can Res Worc Cathl 84-99; rtd 99; PtO *Worc* from 04; Chapl to The Queen 94-04. *Willow Cottage, Station Road, Fladbury, Pershore WR10 2QW* T: (01386) 861847 E: f.bentley123@btinternet.com

BENTLEY, Graham John. b 29. S'wark Ord Course 77. **d** 80 **p** 81. NSM Merton St Mary *S'wark* 80-83; C Balham St Mary 83-84; C Wimbledon 85-86; V Raynes Park St Sav 86-95; rtd 95; PtO *Guildf* from 95. *61 Clarence Road, Fleet, Aldershot GU51 3RY* T: (01252) 682464

BENTLEY, Canon Ian Robert. b 55. Sheff Univ BA 76 Sheff City Poly PGCE 78. Cranmer Hall Dur 93. **d** 95 **p** 96. C Mattishall w Mattishall Burgh, Welborne etc *Nor* 95-98; R Ditchingham, Hedenham, Broome, Earsham etc 98-06; V Oulton Broad from 06; RD Lothingland 10-14; Hon Can Nor Cathl from 10. *St Mark's Vicarage, 212 Bridge Road, Lowestoft NR33 9JX* T: (01502) 572563 E: canonbentley@stmarksob.org

BENTLEY, Ian Ronald. b 51. BA 79. Oak Hill Th Coll 76. **d** 79 **p** 80. C Northwood Em *Lon* 79-85; C St Marylebone All So w SS Pet and Jo 85-88; C Langham Place All So 88-91; V Eynsham and Cassington *Ox* 91-05; V Chineham *Win* from 05. *The Vicarage, 1 Hartswood, Chineham, Basingstoke RG24 8SJ* T: (01256) 474980 E: ibentley4@googlemail.com

BENTLEY, Lesley. b 55. Univ of Wales (Lamp) BA 76 RMN 80. St Jo Coll Nottm MTh 82. **dss** 82 **d** 87 **p** 94. Mickleover St Jo *Derby* 82-84; Thornton Liv 84-89; Par Dn 87-89; Dir Diaconal Mins 89-92; Par Dn Farnworth 92-94; C 94-95; V Westbrook St Phil 95-01; Hon Can Liv Cathl 99-01; V Bilton *Ripon* 01-03; TR 03-09; Initial Minl Educn Officer 03-09; Dir Min Development *Lich* 09-10; Dir Min from 10. *The Vicarage, Salt Lane, Salt, Stafford ST18 0BW* T: (01889) 508066 E: lesley_bentley@btinternet.com

BENTLEY, Canon Paul. b 48. Sarum & Wells Th Coll. **d** 93 **p** 94. C Ex St Dav 93-96; P-in-c Marlpool *Derby* 96-01; V 01-02; Chapl Derbyshire Community Health Services 96-00; Chapl Amber Valley Primary Care Trust 00-02; Chapl Mansfield Distr Primary Care Trust 02-13; P-in-c Mansfield St Lawr *S'well* from 13; Hon Can S'well Minster from 11. *3 Shaw Street, Mansfield NG18 2NP* T: (01623) 662898 E: revpaulb@aol.com

BENTLEY, Paul Nicholas. b 80. Man Univ BA 03. St Jo Coll Nottm MTh 14. **d** 14 **p** 15. C Frankby w Greasby *Ches* from 14. *2 Summertrees Avenue, Wirral CH49 2QD* M: 07967-672778 E: paulnbentley@gmail.com

BENTLEY, Richard. *See* BENTLEY, Frank Richard

BENTON-EVANS, Martin James William. b 69. K Coll Lon BA 90 Anglia Poly Univ PGCE 97. Ripon Coll Cuddesdon BTh 03. **d** 03 **p** 04. C Ivybridge w Harford *Ex* 03-06; P-in-c St Teath *Truro* 06-12; P-in-c Lanteglos by Camelford w Advent 06-12; Chapl Sir Jas Smith's Community Sch Camelford 10-12; R Peebles *Edin* from 12; R Innerleithen from 12. *Tweeddale Rectory, 45 Edderston Road, Peebles EH45 9DT* M: 07915-650434 E: jim@benton-evans1.demon.co.uk

BENWELL, John Desmond. Jes Coll Cam BA 54 MA 58. St Jo Coll Nottm. **d** 89 **p** 89. Somalia 89-90; Chapl Fontainebleau *Eur* 91-93; Hon C Portswood Ch Ch *Win* 93-99; rtd 99; PtO *Win* from 04. *14 Furzedown Road, Southampton SO17 1PN* T: (023) 8055 7622

BENWELL, Michael Patrick. b 55. Jes Coll Cam BA 77 Glas Univ PhD 80. Sarum & Wells Th Coll BTh 92. **d** 92 **p** 93. C Eastleigh *Win* 92-95; Chapl Leeds Metrop Univ *Ripon* 95-99; TV Seacroft 99-06; TR Leeds from 06; AD Whitkirk from 09. *St Luke's Vicarage, Stanks Lane North, Leeds LS14 5AS* T: 0113-273 1302 E: benwell@ndirect.co.uk

BENYON, Oliver William Yates. b 80. Ox Brookes Univ BA 02. Wycliffe Hall Ox 13. **d** 15. C Cambridge H Trin *Ely* from 15. *39 Eland Way, Cherry Hinton, Cambridge CB2 9XQ* M: 07739-710947 E: olibenyon@me.com

BENYON, Thomas Yates. b 74. Edin Univ MA 98 Lon Inst of Educn PGCE 99. Trin Coll Bris. **d** 15. C Peasedown St John w Wellow and Foxcote etc *B & W* from 15. *1 French Close, Peasedown St John, Bath BA2 8SN* M: 07725-037435 E: tybenyon@mac.com

BENZIES, Neil Graham. b 44. Bede Coll Dur. Cranmer Hall Dur 93. **d** 95 **p** 96. NSM Stockton St Pet *Dur* 95-08; PtO from 15. *62 Fairwell Road, Stockton-on-Tees TS19 7HX* T: (01642) 582322

BERDINNER, Clifford. b 24. SS Mark & Jo Univ Coll Plymouth BA 88 Ex Univ MPhil 95. **d** 64 **p** 65. C Leic St Pet 64-67; R Heather 67-72; NSM Totnes and Berry Pomeroy *Ex* 86-91; NSM Totnes, Bridgetown and Berry Pomeroy 91-94; rtd 89; PtO *Ex* from 89. *Little Croft, 30 Droridge, Dartington, Totnes TQ9 6JQ* T: (01803) 732518

BERESFORD, Charles Edward. b 45. St Jo Coll Nottm. **d** 86 **p** 87. C Bushbury *Lich* 86-90; TV Glascote and Stonydelph 90-98; TR N Wingfield, Clay Cross and Pilsley *Derby* 98-11; rtd 11. *8 Spring Close, Belper DE56 2TY* T: (01773) 826519 E: charles.belper@uwclub.net

BERESFORD, David Charles. b 56. Leeds Univ BA 09 ACIB 93. Coll of Resurr Mirfield 07. **d** 09 **p** 10. C Lancing w Coombes *Chich* 09-11; C Bury w Houghton and Coldwaltham and Hardham 11-13; P-in-c Marsh Farm *St Alb* from 13. *The Vicarage, 40 Purway Close, Luton LU3 3RT* T: (01582) 260157 E: davidberesford@gmail.com

BERESFORD, Canon Eric Brian. b 57. Liv Univ BSc 78 Univ of K Coll Halifax NS Hon DD. Wycliffe Hall Ox BA 82 MA 86. **d** 82 **p** 83. C Upton (Overchurch) *Ches* 82-85; Canada from 85; Asst Prof Ethics McGill Univ Montreal 88-96; Consultant Ethics and Interfaith Relns Gen Syn 96-04; President Atlantic Sch of Th Halifax NS from 05; Consultant Ethics ACC 99-05; Hon Can Montreal from 99. *Atlantic School of Theology, 660 Francklyn Street, Halifax NS B3H 3B5, Canada* T: (001) (902) 423 6801 E: eberesford@astheology.ns.ca

BERESFORD, Mrs Florence. b 33. Cranmer Hall Dur 75. **dss** 78 **d** 87 **p** 94. Eighton Banks *Dur* 78-86; Lobley Hill 86-87; Par Dn 87-90; Par Dn Chester le Street 90-91; rtd 91; PtO *Dur* from 04. *Gilead, 39 Picktree Lodge, Chester-le-Street DH3 4DH* T: 0191-388 7425

BERESFORD, Patrick Larner. b 53. Lon Bible Coll BA 77. **d** 10 **p** 11. NSM Weston super Mare St Jo *B & W* 10-12; TV Horsham *Chich* from 12. *St John's House, Church Road, Broadbridge Heath, Horsham RH12 3LD* T: (01403) 265238 E: paddyjfj04@btinternet.com

BERESFORD, Peter Marcus de la Poer. b 49. Cranmer Hall Dur 74. **d** 77 **p** 78. C Walney Is *Carl* 77-80; C Netherton 80-83; TV Wednesfield *Lich* 83-88; TV Rugby *Cov* 88-97; Chapl Rugby Hosps 88-97; R Barby w Kilsby *Pet* 97-14; rtd 14. *Address temp unknown* E: petermberesford@hotmail.co.uk

BERESFORD JONES, Gareth Martin. b 70. Ex Univ BA 93 Fitzw Coll Cam BTh 01. Westcott Ho Cam 98. **d** 01 **p** 02. C Sidcup St Jo *Roch* 01-05; Chapl Ealing Hosp NHS Trust 05-06; PtO *Ely* 08-09; *Carl* 09-11; NSM Beetham 11-13; rtd 13; PtO *Carl* from 13. *6 Leighton Beck Road, Slack Head, Milnthorpe LA7 7AX* T: (015395) 62912 M: 07810-272076 E: gmbj27@mac.com

BERESFORD-PEIRSE, Mark de la Poer. b 45. Qu Coll Birm 73. **d** 76 **p** 77. C Garforth *Ripon* 76-79; C Beeston 79-83; V Barton and Manfield w Cleasby 83-90; V Pannal w Beckwithshaw 90-01; Dioc Chapl MU 91-98; R W Tanfield and Well w Snape and N Stainley 01-09; rtd 09. *15 Eastfield Avenue, Richmond DL10 4NH* T: (01748) 826649

BERESFORD-WEBB, Miss Petra May Elizabeth Broomé. b 66. Cardiff Univ BTh 14 NE Wales Inst of HE CertEd 01. St Mich Coll Llan 09. **d** 12 **p** 13. C E Radnor *S & B* 12-14; C Blaenau Irfon from 14; C Irfon Valley from 14; Bp's Officer for Min to Children and Families from 14. *9 Cae Nant, Newbridge-on-Wye, Llandrindod Wells LD1 6LQ* M: 07966-799546 T: (01597) 860842 E: petra.beresfordwebb@yahoo.com

BERG, John Russell. b 36. MBE 78. Sarum Th Coll 57. **d** 60 **p** 61. C Ipswich St Aug *St E* 60-64; C Whitton and Thurleston w Akenham 64-65; Miss to Seafarers 65-04; Hong Kong 65-68; Japan 68-04; rtd 01; PtO *St E* from 04. *23 Old Maltings Court, Old Maltings Approach, Melton, Woodbridge IP12 1AE* T: (01394) 383748 E: jrberg@tiscali.co.uk

BERGQUIST, Anders Karim. b 58. Peterho Cam BA 79 MA 83 PhD 90. St Steph Ho Ox BA 85 MA 90. **d** 86 **p** 87. C Abbots Langley *St Alb* 86-89; Hon C Cambridge St Mary Less *Ely* 89-97; Tutor Westcott Ho Cam 89-95; Vice-Prin 95-97; Can Res St Alb *St Alb* 97-02; Minl Development Officer 97-02; V St John's Wood Lon from 02. *St John's House, St John's Wood High Street, London NW8 7NE* T: (020) 7722 4378 *or* 7586 3864 E: vicar.stjohnswood@london.anglican.org

BERKSHIRE, Archdeacon of. See GRAHAM, The Ven Olivia Josephine

BERMUDA, Archdeacon of. See DOUGHTY, The Ven Andrew William

BERMUDA, Bishop of. See WHITE, The Rt Revd Patrick George Hilliard

BERNARD, Miss Moina Suzanne. b 56. Cranmer Hall Dur 07. **d** 09 **p** 10. NSM Tong *Bradf* 09-13; NSM Shipley St Pet *Leeds* from 13. *21 Roundwood, Shipley BD18 4JP* M: 07967-709444 E: moinah@googlemail.com

BERNARDI, Frederick John. b 33. JP 75. Chich Th Coll 55. **d** 58 **p** 59. C Blackb St Luke 58-60; C Ribbleton 60-63; V Brinsley w Underwood *S'well* 63-66; V St Leon Barbados 67-71; V Sparkbrook St Agatha *Birm* 71-77; P-in-c Sparkbrook Ch 73-75; V Haywards Heath St Wilfrid *Chich* 77-80; TR 80-87; Chapl Madrid *Eur* 87-90; NSM Tooting All SS *S'wark* 90-91; V Hanger Hill Ascension and W Twyford St Mary *Lon* 91-95; rtd 95; PtO *Chich* from 95. *42 Woodlands Way, Southwater, Horsham RH13 9HZ* T: (01403) 733335 E: stella@knights-templar.org.uk *or* john@bernardi.co.uk

BERNERS-WILSON, Preb Angela Veronica Isabel. b 54. St Andr Univ MTheol 76. Cranmer Hall Dur 77. **dss** 79 **d** 87 **p** 94. Southgate Ch Ch *Lon* 79-82; St Marylebone Ch Ch 82-84; Ind Chapl 82-84; Chapl Thames Poly *S'wark* 84-91; Chapl Bris Univ 91-95; C Bris St Mich and St Paul 94-95; P-in-c Colerne w N Wraxall 95-01; R 01-04; Chapl Bath Univ *B & W* from 04; Preb Wells Cathl from 09. *Chaplain's House, The Avenue, Claverton Down, Bath BA2 7AX* T: (01225) 386193 E: a.berners-wilson@bath.ac.uk *or* abw@colrec.freeserve.co.uk

BERNHARD, Peter James. b 55. Magd Coll Ox BA 76 MA 80. SAOMC 03. **d** 06 **p** 07. NSM Homerton St Luke *Lon* 06-08; Hon Chapl Homerton Univ Hosp NHS Trust Lon 07-08; PtO *Ox* 08-10; *Lon* 09-13. *16 Doves Yard, London N1 0HQ* M: 07970-855354 E: souldernspring@aol.com

BERRETT, Michael Vincent. b 56. St Chad's Coll Dur BA 78. Ox Min Course 06. **d** 09 **p** 10. NSM Wantage *Ox* from 09. *Old Stock Cottage, Farnborough, Wantage OX12 8NT* T: (01488) 639635 E: mvberrett@gmail.com

BERRIDGE, Grahame Richard. b 38. S'wark Ord Course 71. **d** 72 **p** 73. NSM S Beddington St Mich *S'wark* 72-75; NSM Merton St Jas 75-81; PtO from 81. *11 Cedar Walk, Kingswood, Tadworth KT20 6HW* T: (01737) 358882

BERRIMAN, Brinley John. b 50. Univ Coll Lon BSc 71. SWMTC 95. **d** 98 **p** 99. NSM St Ives and Halsetown *Truro* 98-00; P-in-c Lanteglos by Camelford w Advent 00-05; P-in-c St Buryan, St Levan and Sennen 05-12; rtd 12. *Bosorne House, Bosorne, St Just, Penzance TR19 7NR* T: (01736) 787322 E: brin@dreckly.net

BERRIMAN, Gavin Anthony. b 60. S'wark Ord Course 87. **d** 90 **p** 91. C Greenwich St Alfege w St Pet and St Paul *S'wark* 90-94; V Lee St Aug from 94. *St Augustine's Vicarage, 336 Baring Road, London SE12 0DU* T: (020) 8857 4941

BERRY, Canon Adrian Charles. b 50. Mert Coll Ox BA 71 MA 78. Cuddesdon Coll 72. **d** 75 **p** 76. C Prestbury *Glouc* 75-79; C Cirencester 79-83; V Cam w Stinchcombe 83-88; Dioc Ecum Officer 83-95; P-in-c Twyning 88-95; R Leckhampton St Pet 95-02; Dioc Min Development Officer *Llan* 02-14; P-in-c Wenvoe and St Lythans 02-09; R Barry All SS 09-14; Can Llan Cathl 02-14; rtd 14. *70 Meek Road, Newent GL18 1DX* T: (01531) 820981

BERRY, Alan Peter. b 36. NW Ord Course 74. **d** 77 **p** 78. NSM Headingley *Ripon* 77-78; NSM Chapel Allerton 78-91; PtO *Leeds* from 91. *17 High Street, Spofforth, Harrogate HG3 1BQ* T: (01937) 590503 E: apeterberry@btinternet.com

BERRY, Anthony Nigel. b 53. Lon Bible Coll BA 80. Sarum & Wells Th Coll 84. **d** 87 **p** 88. NSM Howell Hill *Guildf* 87-90; C 90; C Farnham 90-93; R Abinger cum Coldharbour 93-14; R Abinger and Coldharbour and Wotton and Holmbury St Mary from 15; Tr Officer for Past Assts from 94. *The Rectory, Abinger Lane, Abinger Common, Dorking RH5 6HZ* T: (01306) 730746 E: revanberry@aol.com

BERRY, David Llewellyn Edward. b 39. St Jo Coll Cam BA 61 MA 65. Wells Th Coll 64. **d** 66 **p** 67. C Poplar All SS w St Frideswide *Lon* 66-69; C Ellesmere Port *Ches* 69-73; V Brafferton w Pilmoor and Myton-on-Swale *York* 73-79; P-in-c Thormanby 78-79; R Skelton w Upleatham 79-87; Chapl Barrow St Aid *Carl* 87-97; Rotterdam *Eur* 97-99; rtd 99; PtO *Carl* from 04. *2 The Croft, Warcop, Appleby-in-Westmorland CA16 6PH* T: (01768) 342175

BERRY, David Nicholas. b 77. York Univ BA 00 St Jo Coll Dur BA 10. Cranmer Hall Dur 08. **d** 10 **p** 11. C Mansfield St Jo w St Mary *S'well* 10-14; V Bentley *Sheff* from 14. *The Vicarage, 3A High Street, Bentley, Doncaster DN5 0AA* M: 07733-127698 T: (01302) 876272 E: dave.b@stpetersbentley.org

BERRY, Mrs Eleanor Shields. b 48. Derby Univ BEd 95. EMMTC 01. **d** 04 **p** 05. NSM Morley w Smalley and Horsley Woodhouse *Derby* 04-09; NSM Spondon from 09. *5 Gilbert Close, Spondon, Derby DE21 7GP* T: (01332) 675265 E: es.berry@ukonline.co.uk *or* e.berry80@ntlworld.com

BERRY, Prof Frank John. b 47. Lon Univ BSc 72 PhD 75 DSc 88 FRSC 84. Qu Coll Birm 96. **d** 99 **p** 00. Prof Inorganic Chemistry Open Univ from 91; Hon Prof Chemistry Birm Univ from 07; NSM Rednal 99-04; NSM Birm St Martin w Bordesley St Andr 04-07; NSM Moseley St Mary and St Anne from 07. *44 Middle Park Road, Selly Oak, Birmingham B29 4BJ* T: 0121-475 2718 E: frank@berry44.fsworld.co.uk

BERRY, Miss Heather Evelyn. b 45. Lon Univ BA 67 Ex Univ PGCE 68. **d** 00 **p** 01. OLM Gaywood *Nor* 00-14; C Gt w Lt Massingham, Harpley, Rougham etc 14-15; R Rougham, Weasenham and Wellingham from 15. *12 Kent Road, King's Lynn PE30 4AF* T: (01553) 764098 E: heberry@talktalk.net

BERRY, Canon Ian Thomas Henry. b 73. QUB BSc 94. CITC BTh 98. **d** 98 **p** 99. C Bangor Abbey *D & D* 98-02; I Monaghan w Tydavnet and Kilmore *Clogh* from 02; Preb Clogh Cathl from 11. *The Rectory, Clones Road, Monaghan, Republic of Ireland* T: (00353) (47) 81136 E: monaghan@clogher.anglican.org

BERRY, John. b 41. Dur Univ BA 62. Oak Hill Th Coll 63. **d** 65 **p** 66. C Burnage St Marg *Man* 65-68; C Middleton 68-70; Travelling Sec IVF 70-73; V Derby St Pet 73-76; P-in-c Derby St Pet and Ch Ch w H Trin 73-76; V 76-81; Bp's Officer for Evang *Carl* 81-86; P-in-c Bampton w Mardale 81-86; Evang Sec N Wingfield, Pilsley and Tupton *Derby* 86-89; Evang Alliance 89-92; V Guernsey H Trin *Win* 92-98; TR Broadwater *Chich* 98-07; rtd 07. *27 Blythe Close, Newport Pagnell MK16 9DN* T: (01908) 217631 E: reverendjohn@sky.com

BERRY, Paul Edward. b 56. NOC 91. **d** 94 **p** 95. C Halliwell St Luke *Man* 94-98; TV Horwich and Rivington 98-08; TV Edgware *Lon* from 08. *1 Beulah Close, Edgware HA8 8SP* T: (020) 8958 9730

BERRY, The Very Revd Peter Austin. b 35. Keble Coll Ox BA 59 BTh 61 MA 63 Birm Univ Hon DD 97. St Steph Ho Ox 59. **d** 62 **p** 63. C Cov St Mark 62-66; Dioc Community Relns Officer 64-70; C Cov Cathl 66-73; Can Res Cov Cathl 73-86; Vice-Provost Cov Cathl 77-86; Bp's Adv for Community Relns 77-86; Provost Birm 86-99; rtd 99; PtO *Cov* from 99; *Birm* 00-12. *High Ridge, Well Lane, High Offley, Stafford ST20 0NY*

BERRY, Mrs Philippa Raines. b 51. Man Univ BA 72 Univ of Wales (Cardiff) CertEd 73. St Jo Coll Nottm 82. **d** 95 **p** 96. NSM Leic H Apostles 95-04; P-in-c from 04. *The Vicarage, 281 Fosse Road South, Leicester LE3 1AE* T: 0116-282 4336 E: pipberry@hotmail.com

BERRY, Sister Susan Patricia (Sister Sue). b 49. Bris Univ BA 70 Hughes Hall Cam PGCE 72. Qu Coll Birm 77. **dss** 86 **d** 87 **p** 94. Chapl Barn Fellowship Whatcombe Ho 86-89; Chapl Lee Abbey 89-91; NSM Thatcham *Ox* 93-95; CSF from 95; PtO *B & W* 96-97 and 98-10; Chapl Guy's and St Thos' Hosps NHS Trust Lon 97-98; PtO *S'wark* 97-98 and from 10. *St Alphege Clergy House, Pocock Street, London SE1 0BJ* T: (020) 7928 8910 E: suecsf@franciscans.org.uk

BERRY, Timothy Hugh. b 50. Reading Univ BA 72. Oak Hill NSM Course 81. **d** 84 **p** 85. NSM Swanley St Paul *Roch* 84-88; C Gorleston St Andr *Nor* 88-93; V Grain w Stoke *Roch* 93-95; rtd 95; PtO *Roch* 01-15. *2 De Lacy Road, Northallerton DL7 8WD* M: 07932-182981 E: timberry@bigfoot.com

BERRY-DAVIES, Charles William Keith. b 48. MIOT 71. Linc Th Coll. **d** 83 **p** 84. C Hythe *Cant* 83-86; Chapl RAF 86-09; rtd 09; PtO *B & W* from 09. *11 Stafford Place, Weston-super-Mare BS23 2QZ* T: (01934) 621344

BERSON, Alan Charles. b 31. Univ of Michigan BA 52 MA 53 Lon Univ PhD 62. St Steph Ho Ox 63. **d** 65 **p** 66. C Leeds St Pet *Ripon* 65-68; C St Giles-in-the-Fields *Lon* 68; LtO 69-80; PtO 80-88. *32 Bath Hill Court, Bath Road, Bournemouth BH1 2HP* T: (01202) 319122

BERSWEDEN, Judith Anne. b 63. St Jo Coll Dur BA 84. Ripon Coll Cuddesdon BA 91. **d** 92 **p** 94. Par Dn Mirfield *Wakef* 92-94; NSM Robert Town 94-97; NSM Roberttown w Hartshead 97-00; NSM Alderbury Deanery *Sarum* from 00; Chapl Bp Wordsworth Sch Salisbury from 01. *The Rectory, Winterslow, Salisbury SP5 1RE* T: (01980) 862231
E: judith.bersweden@dsl.pipex.com

BERSWEDEN, Nils Herry Stephen. b 57. Newc Univ BSc 78. Ripon Coll Cuddesdon 88. **d** 90 **p** 91. C Mirfield *Wakef* 90-93; P-in-c Purlwell 93-94; P-in-c Robert Town 94-97; V Roberttown w Hartshead 97-00; P-in-c Winterslow *Sarum* 00-01; TV Clarendon 01-08; TR from 08. *The Rectory, Winterslow, Salisbury SP5 1RE* T: (01980) 862231
E: nils.bersweden@clarendonteam.org

BERTRAM, Canon Richard Henry. b 27. TCD BA 50 MA 64. CITC 50. **d** 53 **p** 54. C Sligo Cathl 53-56; C Dublin Booterstown *D & G* 56-58; I Stranorlar w Meenglas and Kilteevogue *D & R* 58-65; I Dublin St Cath w St Jas *D & G* 65-73; I Dublin Irishtown 73-74; I Dublin Irishtown w Donnybrook 74-02; Can Ch Ch Cathl Dublin 86-02; Treas Ch Ch Cathl Dublin 95-02; rtd 02. *Glencoe, The Harbour, North Beach, Greystones, Co Wicklow, Republic of Ireland* T: (00353) (1) 287 5320

BESSANT, Brian Keith. b 32. Roch Th Coll 65. **d** 67 **p** 68. C Chatham St Wm *Roch* 67-70; C Cove St Jo *Guildf* 71-74; V Frimley Green 74-97; rtd 97; PtO *Guildf* from 97. *14 Tay Close, Farnborough GU14 9NB* T: (01252) 376530

BESSANT, Christopher Dixon. b 69. Nottm Univ MA 14. Ridley Hall Cam 07. **d** 09 **p** 10. C Gt Bookham *Guildf* 09-13; V Chobham w Valley End from 13; Tutor Local Min Progr from 14. *Chobham Vicarage, Bagshot Road, Chobham, Woking GU24 8BY* T: (01276) 858197 M: 07800-719405
E: c_bessant@hotmail.com

BESSANT, Canon Idwal Brian. b 39. Cardiff Coll of Art ATD 62. St Mich Coll Llan 65. **d** 68 **p** 69. C Llantwit Major and St Donat's *Llan* 68-73; R Llangammarch w Garth, Llanlleonfel etc *S & B* 73-77; V Crickhowell 77-78; CMS Miss 78-83; Cyprus 80-83; V Crickhowell w Cwmdu and Tretower *S & B* 83-91; RD Crickhowell 86-91; V Llanwrtyd w Llanddulas in Tir Abad etc 91-04; Can Res Brecon Cathl 98-04; RD Builth 02-04; rtd 04. *10 Bronant, Bronllys Road, Talgarth, Brecon LD3 0HF* T: (01874) 712380

BESSANT, Canon Simon David. b 56. Sheff Univ BMus 77 MA 00. St Jo Coll Nottm. **d** 81 **p** 82. C Litherland St Jo and St Jas *Liv* 81-84; C Holloway Em w Hornsey Road St Barn *Lon* 84-86; C Holloway St Mark w Em 86-91; V Blackb Redeemer 91-98; Acting RD Blackb 97-98; Dir Miss and Evang 98-07; Dir CME 02-07; Hon Can Blackb Cathl 06-07; V Ecclesall *Sheff* 07-12; V Mortomley St Sav High Green from 12; P-in-c Grenoside from 14. *The Vicarage, 25A Mortomley Lane, High Green, Sheffield S35 3HS* T: 0114-418 2036
E: simon.bessant@stsaviours.info

BESSANT, Stephen Michael. b 53. St Seiriol Cen 13. **d** 14 **p** 15. NSM Llanstadwel *St D* from 14. *28 Greenhall Park, Johnston, Haverfordwest SA62 3PT* T: (01437) 890701
E: smbessant@btinternet.com

BESSANT, Preb Stephen Lyn. b 53. Bris Univ BA 75. Wycliffe Hall Ox 75. **d** 77 **p** 78. C Patchway *Bris* 77-80; TV Swindon St Jo and St Andr 80-83; TV Eston w Normanby *York* 83-90; V Cogges Ox 90-94; P-in-c S Leigh 90-94; V Cogges and S Leigh 94-01; P-in-c Alphington, Shillingford St George and Ide *Ex* 01-12; R from 12; RD Christianity from 06; Preb Ex Cathl from 09. *The Rectory, 6 Lovelace Gardens, Exeter EX2 8XQ* T: (01392) 437662 E: rectory6ssmgi@btinternet.com

BEST, Karen Belinda. See LUND, Karen Belinda

BEST, Canon Raymond. b 42. Sarum & Wells Th Coll 71. **d** 74 **p** 75. C Whorlton *Newc* 74-78; C Seaton Hirst 78-83; C Benwell St Jas 83-85; TV Benwell 85-89; V Walker 89-00; P-in-c Byker St Martin 96-99; V Haltwhistle and Greenhead 00-10; Hon Can Newc Cathl 97-10; AD Hexham 02-06; rtd 10. *The Annexe, 3 Admiral Close, Swarland, Morpeth NE65 9GZ* T: (01670) 783434 E: canonbest@aol.com

BEST, Mrs Ruth Helen. b 54. **d** 05 **p** 06. OLM Triangle, St Matt and All SS *St E* 05-13; NSM from 13. *2 Newson Street, Ipswich IP1 3NY* T: (01473) 424121

BESTELINK, Canon William Meindert Croft. b 48. Hull Univ BA 70 FRSA 78. Cuddesdon Coll 71. **d** 73 **p** 74. C Holt *Nor* 73-74; C E Dereham w Hoe 74-76; C Thorpe St Andr 76-80; R Colby w Banningham and Tuttington 80-90; R Felmingham 80-90; R Suffield 80-90; P-in-c Roydon St Remigius 90-04; P-in-c Scole, Brockdish, Billingford, Thorpe Abbots etc 02-04; P-in-c Gillingham w Geldeston, Stockton, Ellingham etc 04-09; RD Redenhall 00-03; Dioc Rural Officer 99-09; Hon Can Nor Cathl 02-09; rtd 09; PtO *Nor* from 09. *3 Linkside, 26 Park Road, Cromer NR27 0EA* T: (01263) 511278 M: 07909-690073 E: wmcbestelink@hotmail.co.uk

BESTLEY, Peter Mark. b 60. Qu Coll Cam MA Univ of Wales (Cardiff) MPhil 92. St Mich Coll Llan 89. **d** 92 **p** 93. C Hampton All SS *Lon* 92-95; Chapl W Middx Univ Hosp NHS Trust 95-99; Hon C Bracknell *Ox* 04-06; C Easthampstead from 06. *4 Qualitas, Bracknell RG12 7QG* T: (01344) 426741
E: peter.bestley@lineone.net

BESWETHERICK, Andrew Michael. b 55. Ex Univ BEd 80. S'wark Ord Course 87. **d** 90 **p** 91. Dep Hd Maze Hill Sch Greenwich 88-98; NSM Blackheath St Jo *S'wark* from 90; Hd Sixth Form Rosemary Sch Islington from 98. *112 Charlton Road, London SE7 7EY* T: (020) 8853 0853
E: aj@4bes.eclipse.co.uk

BESWICK, Canon Gary Lancelot. b 38. ALCD 63. **d** 63 **p** 64. C Walthamstow St Mary *Chelmsf* 63-67; C Laisterdyke *Bradf* 67-70; V Idle 70-78; Area Sec (NW England) SAMS 78-92; Area Sec (N Thames) 92-97; Hon Can N Argentina from 87; R Gt Smeaton w Appleton Wiske and Birkby etc *Ripon* 97-03; rtd 03. *17 Gustory Road, Crantock, Newquay TR8 5RG* T: (01637) 831361

BESWICK, Jane. See VOST, Jane

BETSON, Christopher James. b 81. Writtle Agric Coll BSc 03 St Jo Coll Dur BA 09. Cranmer Hall Dur 06. St Jo Coll Dur BA 09. **d** 09 **p** 10. C Anston *Sheff* 09-12; V Tickhill w Stainton from 12. *The Vicarage, 2 Sunderland Street, Tickhill, Doncaster DN11 9QJ* T: (01302) 742224 E: chrisbetson@hotmail.com

BETSON (née BIDDINGTON), Mrs Laura Claire. b 84. Trin Coll Cam BA 05 St Jo Coll Dur MA 08. Cranmer Hall Dur 06. **d** 08 **p** 09. C Aston cum Aughton w Swallownest and Ulley *Sheff* 08-12; PtO from 12. *The Vicarage, 2 Sunderland Street, Tickhill, Doncaster DN11 9QJ* T: (01302) 742224 M: 07984-960749
E: laura_biddington@yahoo.co.uk

BETSON, Mark John. b 77. Univ Coll Lon BSc 99 Birkbeck Coll Lon PhD Cam Univ BA 06. Westcott Ho Cam 04. **d** 07 **p** 08. C Southwick *Chich* 07-10; P-in-c Lower Beeding 10-15; V from 15. *The Vicarage, Handcross Road, Plummers Plain, Horsham RH13 6NU* T: (01403) 891367 M: 07801-273074
E: m.betson@hotmail.co.uk

BETSON, Stephen. b 53. Sarum & Wells Th Coll 89. **d** 91 **p** 92. C Sittingbourne St Mich *Cant* 91-95; V Fairweather Green *Bradf* 95-01; R Hockwold w Wilton *Ely* 01-06; R Weeting 01-06; P-in-c Stanground 06-12; P-in-c St Mary Cray and St Paul's Cray *Roch* 12-14; rtd 14. *1 Purbeck Close, Eastbourne BN23 8EX* E: stephenbetson@hotmail.co.uk

BETTELEY, John Richard. b 46. Sarum & Wells Th Coll 81. **d** 83 **p** 84. C Auchterarder *St And* 83-85; C Dunblane 83-85; Chapl RAF 85-89; R Callander *St And* 89-94; P-in-c Aberfoyle 89-94; P-in-c Doune 89-94; R Ballachulish *Arg* 94-04; R Glencoe 94-04; R Onich 94-04; Dioc Youth Officer 94-01; Syn Clerk 99-04; Can St Jo Cathl Oban 99-04; Can Cumbrae 99-04; R Aboyne 04-06; R Ballater 04-06; R Braemar 04-06. *3 School Street, Fearn, Tain IV20 1SX* T: (01862) 832774 M: 07713-914602 E: johnrbetteley@aol.com

BETTERIDGE, Kelly Anne. b 69. Roehampton Inst BA 92. Qu Coll Birm 08. **d** 10 **p** 11. C Nuneaton St Nic *Cov* 10-14; V from 14; P-in-c Weddington and Caldecote from 14. *61 Ambleside Way, Nuneaton CV11 6AU* T: (024) 7634 6900
E: kells612@yahoo.co.uk

BETTERIDGE, Simon Frank. b 66. St Jo Coll Nottm. **d** 00 **p** 01. C Studley *Cov* 00-02; C Leamington Priors St Paul 02-04; Chapl Univ Hosps Cov and Warks NHS Trust from 04. *61 Ambleside Way, Nuneaton CV11 6AU* M: 07743-870601 E: simon.betty@yahoo.com or simon.betteridge@uhcw.nhs.uk

BETTINSON, Philip Keith. b 79. Univ of Wales (Abth) BEng 01. St Mich Coll Llan BTh 11. **d** 11 **p** 12. C Cilcain, Gwernaffield, Llanferres etc *St As* 11-14; C Wrexham from 14. *The Vicarage, 37 Acton Gate, Wrexham LL11 2PW* T: (01978) 264584
E: rev@jara23.co.uk

BETTIS, Canon Margaret Jean. b 42. Gilmore Ho 72. **dss** 77 **d** 87 **p** 94. Kenya 77-79; Tutor Crowther Hall CMS Tr Coll Selly Oak 79-82; Hodge Hill *Birm* 82-87; Par Dn 87; Par Dn Flitwick *St Alb* 87-93; P-in-c Westoning w Tingrith 93-94; V 94-04;

Hon Can St Alb 97-04; rtd 04; PtO *St Alb* 04-05; *Glouc* 05-06; Hon C Cirencester from 06. *19 Bathurst Road, Cirencester GL7 1SA* T: (01285) 658695

BETTRIDGE, Canon Graham Winston. b 39. Kelham Th Coll 60. **d** 65 **p** 66. C Burley in Wharfedale *Bradf* 65-67; C Baildon 67-70; V Harden and Wilsden 70-81; TR Kirkby Lonsdale *Carl* 81-06; Hon Can Carl Cathl 89-06; rtd 06; Chapl Cumbria Constabulary *Carl* 96-09; PtO *Leeds* from 06; *Carl* from 09. *Moorgate Cottage, Maypole Green, Long Preston, Skipton BD23 4PJ* T: (01729) 841113
E: canongraham@mintegrity.co.uk

BETTS, Alan John. b 55. Portsm Poly BSc 77 St Martin's Coll Lanc PGCE 81. St Jo Coll Nottm 93. **d** 93 **p** 94. C Cannock *Lich* 93-01; P-in-c Endon w Stanley 01-04; V Bagnall w Endon from 04; P-in-c Brown Edge from 15. *St Luke's Vicarage, Leek Road, Endon, Stoke-on-Trent ST9 9BH* T: (01782) 502166

BETTS, Canon Anthony Clive. b 40. Wells Th Coll 63. **d** 65 **p** 66. C Leeds All Hallows w St Simon *Ripon* 65-67; C Wetherby 67-70; C Adel 70-73; V Leeds All SS 73-79; V Leeds Richmond Hill 79-84; R Knaresborough 84-03; TR 03-05; RD Harrogate 95-98; Hon Can Ripon Cathl 04-05; rtd 05; PtO *York* from 06. *Thistle Hill Care Centre, Thistle Hill, Knaresborough HG5 8LS* T: (01423) 869200
E: tonybetts@bettst.freeserve.co.uk

BETTS, David John. b 38. Lon Univ BSc 61. Oak Hill Th Coll 63. **d** 65 **p** 66. C Slough *Ox* 65-70; C Welling *Roch* 70-75; V Swanley St Paul 75-93; R Nottingham St Nic *S'well* 93-98; TV Canford Magna *Sarum* 98-04; rtd 04. *290 Rempstone Road, Wimborne BH21 1SZ* T: (01202) 840537
E: davidbetts@tesco.net

BETTS, Edmund John. b 51. St Chad's Coll Dur BA 72 Lanc Univ MA 81 Ches Univ DProf 15. Qu Coll Birm 73. **d** 76 **p** 77. C Leagrave *St Alb* 76-79; Asst Chapl R Albert Hosp Lanc 79-81; Chapl Lea Castle Hosp Kidderminster 81-86; Chapl Kidderminster Gen Hosp 81-86; Prov Officer Educn for Min Ch in Wales 86-88; Exec Sec for Min 88-90; TR Haverhill w Withersfield, the Wrattings etc *St E* 90-97; V Haverhill w Withersfield 97-06; RD Clare 91-06; Hon Can St E Cathl 02-06; CUF Link Officer 02-06; V Altrincham St Geo *Ches* from 06; P-in-c Altrincham St Jo from 07. *St George's Vicarage, Townfield Road, Altrincham WA14 4DS* T: 0161-928 1279
E: edmund.betts1@btinternet.com

BETTS, Ivan Ringland. b 38. TCD BA 61 MA 67. **d** 62 **p** 63. C Ballyholme *D & D* 62-65; C Dundela St Mark 65-69; Miss to Seamen 69-73; Sudan 69-71; Trinidad and Tobago 71-73; C Drumglass *Arm* 73-81; I Augher w Newtownsaville and Eskrahoole *Clogh* 81-86; Bp's C Ballymacarrett St Martin *D & D* 86-02; rtd 02. *56 Norwood Drive, Belfast BT4 2EB* T: (028) 9065 0723 E: ivanbetts@btinternet.com

BETTS, Mrs Patricia Joyce. b 43. St Kath Coll Lon CertEd 64 FRSA 96. S Dios Minl Tr Scheme 90. **d** 96 **p** 97. NSM Bath Widcombe *B & W* 96-00; P-in-c 00-05; PtO from 05. *Hunter's Lodge, North Road, Bath BA2 6HP* T: (01225) 464918 M: 07545-350565 E: candpbetts@talktalk.net

BETTS, Paul Robert. b 31. Lon Univ BSc 51. Oak Hill Th Coll 53. **d** 56 **p** 57. C Plymouth St Jude *Ex* 56-59; C Cheltenham St Mark *Glouc* 59-63; V Finchley St Paul Long Lane *Lon* 63-76; Warden St Columba Cen Cam 76-79; R Datchworth w Tewin *St Alb* 79-96; rtd 96; PtO *Ex* from 96. *20 Gracey Court, Woodland Road, Broadclyst, Exeter EX5 3GA* T: (01392) 468838 M: 07855-715382 E: paul.betts303@btinternet.com

BETTS, Richard Alan. b 56. ACA 83 UEA BA 77. Sarum & Wells Th Coll 93. **d** 93 **p** 94. C Mile Cross *Nor* 93-97; TV Dorchester *Sarum* 97-12; Asst Chapl Dorset Co Hosp NHS Foundn Trust from 12; Sub Chapl HM Pris Dorchester from 12. *30 Scholl Drive, Crossways, Dorchester DT2 8WR* T: (01305) 262394 E: richardbetts42@aol.com

BETTS, The Ven Steven James. b 64. York Univ BSc 86. Ripon Coll Cuddesdon 87. **d** 90 **p** 91. C Bearsted w Thurnham *Cant* 90-94; Bp's Chapl *Nor* 94-97; V Old Catton 97-05; RD Nor N 01-05; Bp's Officer for Ord and Initial Tr 05-12; Adn Norfolk from 12; Hon Can Nor Cathl from 08. *8 Boulton Road, Thorpe St Andrew, Norwich NR7 0DF* T: (01603) 559199
E: archdeacon.norfolk@norwich.anglican.org

BEURKLIAN-CARTER, Mrs Santou. b 70. McMaster Univ Ontario BA 92 Toronto Univ MDiv 02. St Mellitus Coll 10. **d** 12 **p** 13. C Gt Ilford St Jo *Chelmsf* 12-14; C Woodford St Mary w St Phil and St Jas from 14. *116 Blythswood Road, Ilford IG3 8SG* T: (020) 8599 0399 M: 07939-876045
E: sbcarter@btinternet.com

BEVAN, Mrs Angela Ruth. b 54. Qu Coll Birm. **d** 07 **p** 08. NSM Shenley Green *Birm* 07-14; PtO from 14. *204 Shenley Fields Road, Birmingham B29 5BL* T: 0121-477 9924
E: abevan54@yahoo.co.uk

BEVAN, Christopher Jeremy. Lon Inst BA 89 Lon Guildhall Univ MA 97 Cardiff Univ BA 11. **d** 11 **p** 12. C Llanelli *S & B*

from 11. *Llanelly Rectory, Abergavenny Road, Gilwern, Abergavenny NP7 0AD* T: (01873) 830280
E: christopher.bevan@btinternet.com

BEVAN, David Graham. b 34. Univ of Wales (Lamp) BA 54 LTh 56. Gen Th Sem (NY) MDiv 57. **d** 57 **p** 58. C Llanelli *St D* 57-60; CF 60-76; rtd 99. *148 Bromley Heath Road, Bristol BS16 6JJ* T: 0117-956 0946

BEVAN, Gareth Edward. b 58. **d** 10 **p** 11. NSM Wembley Park *Lon* 10-12; NSM Preston from 12. *57 Oakington Avenue, Wembley HA9 8HX* T: (020) 8908 3719 M: 07876-133314
E: gbevan76@googlemail.com

BEVAN, Janet Mary. See MOORE, Janet Mary

BEVAN, Judith Anne. See EGAR, Judith Anne

BEVAN, Paul John. b 49. Bris Sch of Min 84. **d** 87. NSM Bishopsworth *Bris* 87-96. *10 Brookdale Road, Headley Park, Bristol BS13 7PZ* T: 0117-964 6330

BEVAN, Peter John. b 54. K Coll Lon BA 76 AKC 76 MA 86. St Steph Ho Ox BA 79. **d** 80 **p** 81. C Brighouse *Wakef* 80-83; C Chapelthorpe 83-86; V Scholes 86-95; V Potters Bar *St Alb* from 95. *The Vicarage, 15 The Walk, Potters Bar EN6 1QQ* T: (01707) 644539 or 645080

BEVAN, Philip Frank. b 41. Brasted Th Coll 63 Chich Th Coll 65. **d** 67 **p** 68. C Walton St Mary *Liv* 67-71; P-in-c Long Is SS Pet and Paul Bahamas 71-73; R Nassau St Matt 73-78; PtO *S'wark* from 00. *5 Dunstable Road, Richmond TW9 1UH* T: (020) 8940 3622 M: 07970-961539
E: fr.philip@btinternet.com

BEVAN, Mrs Rebecca Anne. b 64. Reading Univ BA 86. Ox Min Course 04. **d** 07 **p** 08. NSM Thatcham *Ox* 07-10; R Aldermaston and Woolhampton from 10. *The Rectory, Wasing Lane, Aldermaston, Reading RG7 4LX* T: 0118-971 2281
E: beckywinterbevan@aol.com

BEVAN, Canon Richard Justin William. b 22. LTh 42 St Chad's Coll Dur BA 45 DTh 72 PhD 80. St Aug Coll Cant 39. **d** 45 **p** 46. C Stoke upon Trent *Lich* 45-49; Chapl Aberlour Orphanage 49-51; LtO *Mor* 49-51; *Blackb* 51-52; C Church Kirk 52-56; C Whalley 56-61; R Dur St Mary le Bow w St Mary the Less 61-64; Chapl Dur Univ 61-74; V Dur St Oswald 64-74; P-in-c Dur St Mary le Bow w St Mary the Less 64-67; R 67-74; R Grasmere *Carl* 74-82; Can Res, Lib and Treas Carl Cathl 82-89; Vice-Dean Carl 86-89; Chapl to The Queen 86-93; rtd 89; PtO *Carl* from 89. *15 Solway Park, Carlisle CA2 6TH* T: (01228) 631428

BEVAN, Rodney. b 57. Leeds Univ BA 80 Keele Univ PGCE 81 Open Univ MA 99. Cranmer Hall Dur 97. **d** 99 **p** 00. C Ogley Hay *Lich* 99-03; TV Rossendale Middle Valley *Man* 03-04; TR from 04. *St Anne's Vicarage, Ashworth Road, Rossendale BB4 9JE* T: (01706) 221889 E: revrodbev@hotmail.com

BEVER, Canon Michael Charles Stephen. b 44. Selw Coll Cam BA 66 MA 70. Cuddesdon Coll 67. **d** 69 **p** 70. C Steeton *Bradf* 69-72; C Northampton St Mary *Pet* 72-74; Niger 75-79; P-in-c Elmstead *Chelmsf* 80-83; V 83-85; V Bocking St Pet 85-96; P-in-c Odiham *Win* 96-07; rtd 07; Hon Can Awka from 93; PtO *Portsm* from 08; *Win* 07-14. *68A Drift Road, Waterlooville PO8 0NX* T/F: (023) 9259 6895 E: mcsb@ozala.plus.com

BEVERIDGE, Mrs Freda Joy. b 38. Qu Mary Coll Lon BA 59 Lon Inst of Educn PGCE 60. Ripon Coll Cuddesdon 83. **dss** 85 **d** 87 **p** 94. Ox St Giles and SS Phil and Jas w St Marg 85-88; Par Dn 87-88; Par Dn Woughton 88-94; C 94-95; TR 95-97; C Woodham *Guildf* 97-00; rtd 00; PtO *Sarum* from 01. *Moonraker Cottage, 27 New Road, Chiseldon, Swindon SN4 0LY* T: (01793) 741064 E: freda.27@btinternet.com

BEVERIDGE, Simon Alexander Ronald. b 61. Nottm Univ BA 84. Chich Th Coll 84. **d** 87 **p** 88. C Braunton *Ex* 87-90; TV N Creedy 90-93; Chapl RN from 93. *Royal Naval Chaplaincy Service, Mail Point 1-2, Leach Building, Whale Island, Portsmouth PO2 8BY* T: (023) 9262 5055 F: 9262 5134

BEVERLEY, Anne Ruth. b 76. Cen Lancs Univ BA 97 Cumbria Univ BA 14. LCTP 11. **d** 14 **p** 15. NSM S Shore H Trin *Blackb* from 14; NSM S Shore St Pet from 14. *2 Tudor Gate, Lytham St Annes FY8 3US* M: 07841-742022
E: anne.beverley@btinternet.com

BEVERLEY, David John. b 46. Univ of Wales (Lamp) BA 68. Linc Th Coll 71. **d** 73 **p** 74. C Cov E 73-76; C Immingham *Linc* 76-84; V Bracebridge Heath 84-86; Ind Chapl 86-97; P-in-c Scunthorpe Resurr 97-01; V 01-02; R Trentside E 02-11; rtd 11. *73 Peveril Avenue, Scunthorpe DN17 1BG* T: (01724) 279914 E: davejbev@aol.com

BEVERLEY, Sister. See DAVIES, Beverley

BEVERLEY, Suffragan Bishop of (Provincial Episcopal Visitor). See WEBSTER, The Rt Revd Glyn Hamilton

BEVERLY, Mrs Sue. b 53. Cardiff Univ BTh 08. St Mich Coll Llan 05. **d** 07 **p** 08. NSM Coity, Nolton and Brackla *Llan* 07-12; Asst Dir of Min 10; AD Bridgend 11-12; R Broseley w Benthall, Jackfield, Linley etc *Heref* from 12. *3 Blakeway Close, Broseley TF12 5SS* T: (01952) 882647
E: rector@broseleyparishes.org.uk

BEVINGTON, Canon Colin Reginald. b 36. ALCD 63. **d** 63 **p** 64. C Devonport St Budeaux *Ex* 63-65; C Attenborough w Chilwell *S'well* 65-68; R Benhall w Sternfield *St E* 68-74; P-in-c Snape w Friston 73-74; V Selly Hill St Steph *Birm* 74-81; P-in-c Selly Oak St Wulstan 80-81; V Selly Park St Steph and St Wulstan 81-88; Dioc Adv on Miss *St E* 88-95; Dioc and Co Ecum Officer 88-99; Hon Can St E Cathl 93-00; Bp's Dom Chapl and Personal Asst 95-99; R Holbrook, Freston, Woolverstone and Wherstead 99-00; RD Samford 99-00; rtd 01; PtO *St E* 01-05; *Blackb* from 07. *4 Highgrove Road, Lancaster LA1 5FS* T: (01524) 64851
E: bevington@capel19.freeserve.co.uk

BEVINGTON, David John. b 51. Ch Coll Cam BA 72 MA 76. Trin Coll Bris 73. **d** 76 **p** 77. C Tulse Hill H Trin *S'wark* 76-79; C Galleywood Common *Chelmsf* 79-82; TV Hanley H Ev *Lich* 82-90; TV Hemel Hempstead *St Alb* 90-99; V Calbourne w Newtown *Portsm* from 99; V Shalfleet from 99. *The Vicarage, 4 Manor Green, Shalfleet, Newport PO30 4QT* T: (01983) 531238 E: dbevington@lineone.net

BEVIS, Anthony Richard. b 34. Chich Th Coll 87. **d** 87 **p** 89. NSM Hamble le Rice *Win* 87-94; NSM Woolston 94-08; Chapl Southn Community Services NHS Trust 90-01; Chapl Southn City Primary Care Trust 01-08; PtO *Win* 08-14. *Lynwood, High Street, Hamble, Southampton SO31 4HA* T: (023) 8045 3102 or 8047 2258

BEVIS-KNOWLES, Julia. **d** 14 **p** 15. NSM Ruislip Manor St Paul *Lon* from 14. *Address temp unknown*

BEWES, Anthony Charles Neill. b 71. Birm Univ BA 93. Wycliffe Hall Ox 96. **d** 99 **p** 00. C Sevenoaks St Nic *Roch* 99-05; Team Ldr Titus Trust from 05. *45 Lonsdale Road, Oxford OX2 7ES* T: (01865) 553625 E: anthony@bewes.com

BEWES, Helen Catherine. See SCAMMAN, Helen Catherine

BEWES, Preb Richard Thomas. b 34. OBE 05. Em Coll Cam BA 58 MA 61. Ridley Hall Cam 57. **d** 59 **p** 60. C Beckenham Ch Ch *Roch* 59-65; V Harold Wood *Chelmsf* 65-74; V Northwood Em *Lon* 74-83; R St Marylebone All So w SS Pet and Jo 83-88; P-in-c Portman Square St Paul 87-88; R Langham Place All So 88-04; Preb St Paul's Cathl 88-04; rtd 04; PtO *Lon* from 05; *Guildf* from 14. *Montreat, 2 Home Close, Virginia Water GU25 4DH* T: (01344) 841341 E: richard.bewes@talk21.com

BEWLEY, Robin John. b 63. St Jo Coll Ox BA 86 MA 95 Fitzw Coll Cam BA 99 PhD 05. Ridley Hall Cam. **d** 00 **p** 01. NSM Histon and Impington *Ely* 00-04; C Harborne Heath *Birm* 04-11; V Kettering Ch the King *Pet* from 11. *The Vicarage, Deeble Road, Kettering NN15 7AA* T: (01536) 512828 M: 07733-346631 E: rob@thebewleys.co.uk *or* vicar@ctk.org.uk

BEXON, Mrs Valerie Joan. b 60. Chelt & Glouc Coll of HE BA 96. Wycliffe Hall Ox 07. **d** 09 **p** 10. C Wotton-under-Edge w Ozleworth, N Nibley etc *Glouc* 09-10; C Sodbury Vale 10-12; R Brimpsfield w Birdlip, Syde, Daglingworth etc from 12. *The Rectory, Duntisbourne Leer, Cirencester GL7 7AS* T: (01285) 821040 M: 07882-882796 E: valeriebexon@btinternet.com

BEYNON, Malcolm. b 36. Univ of Wales (Lamp) BA 56 Univ of Wales (Cardiff) PGCE 71. St Mich Coll Llan 56. **d** 59 **p** 60. C Aberavon *Llan* 59-62; C Whitchurch 63-68; V Llanwynno 68-73; Chapl Old Hall Sch Wellington Shropshire 74-75; Chapl Nevill Holt Sch Market Harborough 75-82; Chapl Denstone Coll Prep Sch Uttoxeter 82-93; V Dale and St Brides w Marloes *St D* 93-01; rtd 01. *22 Ostrey Bank, St Clears, Carmarthen SA33 4AH* T: (01994) 231872

BEYNON, Nigel David. b 68. Collingwood Coll Dur BSc 90 Fitzw Coll Cam BA 94. Ridley Hall Cam 92. **d** 95 **p** 96. C Fulham St Matt *Lon* 95-98; Assoc V St Helen Bishopsgate w St Andr Undershaft etc 98-07; Student Team Ldr 01-07. *78 Aubert Park, London N5 1TS*

BEYNON, Paul John. b 66. SWMTC 09. **d** 12 **p** 13. C Boscastle w Davidstow *Truro* 12-15; C Boscastle and Tintagel Gp from 15. *38 Clover Lane Close, Boscastle PL35 0AL* M: 07730-037113 E: p-beynon@sky.com

BEYNON, Vincent Wyn. b 54. Anglia Poly Univ MA 04 Hockerill Coll Cam CertEd 76 Lambeth STh 97. St Mich Coll Llan 78. **d** 81 **p** 82. C Llantrisant *Llan* 81-83; C Caerphilly 84-85; R Gelligaer 85-88; TV Gtr Corsham *Bris* 88-97; R Potton w Sutton and Cockayne Hatley *St Alb* 97-08; RD Biggleswade 01-06; P-in-c Stoke Prior, Wychbold and Upton Warren *Worc* from 12; NSM Bowbrook N from 14; NSM Bowbrook S from 14. *The Rectory, Fish House Lane, Stoke Prior, Bromsgrove B60 4JT* T: (01527) 832501 E: wynbeynon@gmail.com

BHATTI, Kamran. b 67. **d** 14 **p** 15. C Preston Risen Lord *Blackb* from 14. *33 Bairstow Street, Preston PR1 3TN*

BHUTTA, Mrs Patricia Frances Mary. b 52. Kent Univ BA 74. Ox Min Course 08. **d** 10 **p** 11. NSM Cumnor *Ox* 10-13; NSM Aldermaston and Woolhampton from 13. *The Vicarage,*

Bird's Lane, Midgham, Reading RG7 5UL T: 0118-971 0124 M: 07968-089566 E: pat@patbhutta.co.uk

BIANCHI, Mrs Margaret Ruth. b 56. St Mary's Coll Dur BA 77. Cranmer Hall Dur 78. **dss** 80 **d** 91 **p** 94. Chester le Street *Dur* 80-83; W Pelton 83-91; NSM 91-95; PtO from 95. *8 Lindisfarne, Washington NE38 7JR* T: 0191-417 0852

BIANCHI, Robert Frederick. b 56. St Jo Coll Dur BA 77. Cranmer Hall Dur 78. **d** 80 **p** 81. C Chester le Street *Dur* 80-83; C W Pelton 83-86; P-in-c 86-95; PtO from 95. *8 Lindisfarne, Washington NE38 7JR* T: 0191-417 0852

BIBBY, Paul Benington. b 27. Magd Coll Cam BA 51 MA 56. Westcott Ho Cam 55. **d** 57 **p** 58. C Flixton St Mich *Man* 57-60; C Woolwich St Mary w H Trin *S'wark* 60-62; V Hurst *Man* 62-69; Hd of Cam Ho Camberwell 69-76; R Shepton Mallet *B & W* 76-81; P-in-c Doulting w E and W Cranmore and Downhead 78-81; R Shepton Mallet w Doulting 81-82; Sen Chapl Eton Coll 82-87; R Hambleden Valley *Ox* 87-93; rtd 93; PtO *Nor* from 94. *Vine Cottage, Cross Lane, Stanhoe, King's Lynn PE31 8PS* T: (01485) 518291

BICK, David Jim. b 33. ALCD 59 LTh 74. **d** 59 **p** 60. C Glouc St Cath 59-61; C Coleford w Staunton 61-63; R Blaisdon w Flaxley 63-72; V Coaley 72-83; P-in-c Arlingham 80-83; P-in-c Frampton on Severn 80-83; Hon C Saul w Fretherne and Framilode 83-84; PtO from 84; rtd 98. *St Joseph's, Prinknash Park, Cranham, Gloucester GL4 8EU* T: (01452) 812973

BICK (née GRIFFITHS), Mrs Sarah. b 75. Ex Univ BA 96 Homerton Coll Cam PGCE 99. Qu Coll Birm 07. **d** 09 **p** 10. C Coleford, Staunton, Newland, Redbrook etc *Glouc* 09-13; V from 13. *40 Boxbush Road, Coleford GL16 8DN* T: (01594) 835476 M: 07773-651893 E: sarah@thebickerage.org.uk

BICKERSTETH, David Craufurd. b 50. Wycliffe Hall Ox 71. **d** 75 **p** 76. C Beverley Minster *York* 75-79; C Farnborough *Guildf* 79-81; P-in-c Dearham *Carl* 81-85; V 85-86; R Gosforth w Nether Wasdale and Wasdale Head 86-93; P-in-c Harraby 93-97; V Maryport 98-04; TR Maryport, Netherton and Flimby 04-06; Dioc Chapl MU 94-97; R Draycott-le-Moors w Forsbrook *Lich* 06-15; P-in-c Upper Tean 08-14; rtd 15. *Sunnybrae, Greenodd, Ulverston LA12 7RG* T: (01229) 861184 E: david.bickersteth@btinternet.com

BICKERSTETH, Edward Piers. b 56. MRICS 80. Wycliffe Hall Ox 89. **d** 91 **p** 92. NSM Bebington *Ches* 91-92; C 92-94; Proclamation Trust 94-98; P-in-c Arborfield w Barkham *Ox* 98-02; R from 02. *The Rectory, Church Lane, Arborfield, Reading RG2 9HZ* T: 0118-976 0285

✠**BICKERSTETH, The Rt Revd John Monier.** b 21. KCVO 89. Ch Ch Ox BA 49 MA 53 Open Univ BA 97. Wells Th Coll 48. **d** 50 **p** 51 **c** 70. C Moorfields *Bris* 50-54; C-in-c Hurst Green CD *S'wark* 54-62; V Chatham St Steph *Roch* 62-70; Hon Can Roch Cathl 68-70; Suff Bp Warrington *Liv* 70-75; Bp B & W 75-87; ChStJ and Sub-Prelate from 77; Clerk of the Closet 79-89; rtd 87. *10 Elizabeth Court, Crane Bridge Road, Salisbury SP2 7UX* T: (01722) 238804

BICKERSTETH, Simon Craufurd. b 77. St Jo Coll Dur BA 98. Wycliffe Hall Ox 99. **d** 01 **p** 02. C Windermere *Carl* 01-05; TV Walsall St Matt *Lich* 05-11; V Walsall St Martin from 11. *St Martin's House, 17 Daffodil Road, Walsall WS5 3DQ* T: (01922) 611909 M: 07752-853148 E: simon.bickersteth@tiscali.co.uk

BICKLEY, Mrs Alice Elizabeth Ann. b 60. Qu Coll Birm 06. **d** 09 **p** 10. C Leagrave *St Alb* 09-13; P-in-c Hexagon *Leic* from 13. *The Rectory, Honeypot Lane, Husbands Bosworth, Lutterworth LE17 6LY* T: (01858) 880351 M: 07977-601437 E: lizbickley@btinternet.com

BICKLEY, Mrs Pamela. b 59. Birm Univ BPhil 99. WEMTC 06. **d** 09 **p** 10. NSM Minsterley, Habberley and Hope w Shelve *Heref* 09-12; Dioc Voc Adv from 12. *High Ridge, Gorsty Bank, Snailbeach, Shrewsbury SY5 0LX* T: (01743) 792824 E: shepherdstock@aol.com

BICKNELL, Carl Royston. b 62. Wycliffe Hall Ox. **d** 10 **p** 10. NSM Stapenhill w Cauldwell *Derby* 10-13. *Bungalow 2, Drakelow House, Walton Road, Burton-on-Trent DE15 9UA* T: (01283) 534288

BICKNELL, Jonathan Richard. b 62. Wycliffe Hall Ox. **d** 00 **p** 01. C Chesham Bois *Ox* 00-02. *210 High Street, Berkhamsted HP4 1AG* T: (01442) 872447

BICKNELL (née RIDING), Mrs Pauline Alison. b 61. SEN 82. Oak Hill Th Coll BA 90. **d** 90 **p** 96. Par Dn Moor Allerton *Ripon* 90-93; Par Dn Leeds St Aid 93-94; C 94-96; C Rothwell 96-99; TV Drypool *York* 99-05; P-in-c Slyne w Hest *Blackb* 05-06; R Slyne w Hest and Halton w Aughton from 06. *The Vicarage, Summerfield Drive, Slyne, Lancaster LA2 6AQ* T: (01524) 822128 E: pauline@thebicknells.org

BIDDELL, Canon Christopher David. b 27. Ch Coll Cam BA 48 MA 52. Ridley Hall Cam 51. **d** 51 **p** 52. C Hornchurch St Andr

Chelmsf 51-54; Succ S'wark Cathl 54-56; P-in-c Wroxall *Portsm* 56-61; R Bishop's Waltham 62-75; RD 69-74; V Stockport St Geo *Ches* 75-86; Hon Can Ches Cathl 81-86; Can Res Ches Cathl 86-93; RD Stockport 85-86; Vice-Dean Ches 91-93; rtd 93; P-in-c Duncton *Chich* 95-98; P-in-c Tillington 95-98; P-in-c Upwaltham 95-98; PtO from 98. *3 Park Terrace, Tillington, Petworth GU28 9AE* T: (01798) 342008

BIDDINGTON, Laura Claire. *See* BETSON, Laura Claire

BIDDINGTON, Terence Eric. b 56. Hull Univ BA 77 Trin & All SS Coll Leeds PGCE 78 Leeds Univ PhD 86 Nottm Univ BTh 88 Man Univ MA(Theol) 96 MCollP 83. Linc Th Coll 85. **d** 88 **p** 89. C Harpenden St Jo *St Alb* 88-90; Chapl Keele Univ *Lich* 90-93; Freelance Th Educator and Asst Lect Keele Univ 94-99; Assoc Min Betley and Keele *Lich* 90-93; Asst Dir Cornerstone St Aug *Man* 95-96; Mental Health Advocate Stockport 96-98; Dir and Sen Advocate Stockport MIND from 99; PtO *Man* 99-01; P-in-c Heaton Norris Ch w All SS 01-02; C Heatons 02-03; Asst Chapl Man Mental Health Partnership 01-03; Chapl Man Univ from 03; Chapl Man Metrop Univ from 03; Chapl RNCM from 03. *St Peter's House, Oxford Road, Manchester M13 9GH* T: 0161-275 2894
E: terry.biddington@manchester.ac.uk

BIDDINGTON, Mrs Wendy Elizabeth. b 51. Cov Univ BSc 93 SRN 73 SCM 74. Qu Coll Birm 07. **d** 09 **p** 10. OLM Wellesbourne *Cov* 09-12; NSM from 12. *72 Mountford Close, Wellesbourne, Warwick CV35 9QQ* T: (01789) 840953
E: nlb@biddington.spacomputers.com

BIDDLE, Joanna Elizabeth. *See* JEPSON, Joanna Elizabeth

BIDDLE, Nicholas Lawrence. *See* JEPSON-BIDDLE, Nicholas Lawrence

BIDDLE, Miss Rosemary. b 44. CertEd 67. Cranmer Hall Dur 76. **dss** 79 **d** 87 **p** 94. Sheldon *Birm* 79-83; Burntwood *Lich* 83-87; Par Dn 87-89; Par Dn Gt Wyrley 89-94; C 94-99; rtd 99; PtO *Lich* from 00. *8 Brook Lane, Great Wyrley, Walsall WS6 6BQ* T: (01922) 419032

BIDDLECOMBE, Francis William. b 30. St Mich Coll Llan 57. **d** 59 **p** 60. C Llangynwyd w Maesteg *Llan* 59-62; C Roath 62-65; V Llanddewi Rhondda w Bryn Eirw 65-71; V Berse and Southsea *St As* 71-79; P-in-c Teme Valley S *Worc* 79-85; rtd 92; PtO *Heref* 92-13; *Worc* from 92. *Four Winds, New Road, Highley, Bridgnorth WV16 6NN* T: (01746) 861746
E: francis@sagainternet.co.uk

BIDE, Mary Elizabeth. b 53. St Anne's Coll Ox BA 74 MA 78. S Dios Minl Tr Scheme 91. **d** 94 **p** 95. C Gt Bookham *Guildf* 94-98; Year Tutor Dioc Min Course 96-03; P-in-c Frimley Green 98-01; V Frimley Green and Mytchett 02-03; Prec Ch Ch *Ox* 03-07; TR Wimbledon *S'wark* from 07; Chapl to The Queen from 13. *The Rectory, 14 Arthur Road, London SW19 7DZ* T: (020) 8946 2830 or 8946 2605 F: 8946 6293
E: rector.wimbledon@stmaryswimbledon.org

BIDEN, Neville Douglas. b 31. S'wark Ord Course 76. **d** 79 **p** 80. C Ash *Guildf* 79-82; NSM Surbiton St Andr and St Mark *S'wark* 87-91; Chapl Asst Long Grove Hosp Epsom 90-91; PtO *Guildf* 90-91 and 97-06; C Coulsdon St Jo *S'wark* 91-96; rtd 96; PtO *Heref* 95-97; *Win* from 01. *5 Taylor Drive, Bramley, Tadley RG26 5XB* T: (01256) 880459 E: rev.nev@virgin.net

BIDGOOD, Julian Paul. b 71. Sussex Univ BA 92. Oak Hill Th Coll BA 03. **d** 03 **p** 04. C Ox St Ebbe w H Trin and St Pet 03-08; C Arborfield w Barkham from 08. *5 Somerville Close, Wokingham RG41 4SW* M: 07779-296511
E: julian@abch.org.uk

BIELBY, Canon Elaine Elizabeth. b 57. Surrey Univ MSc 83. Ripon Coll Cuddesdon 96. **d** 98 **p** 99. C Marton-in-Cleveland *York* 98-01; P-in-c Welton w Melton 01-12; V from 12; Tr Officer E Riding from 01; Dean of Women's Min from 08; Can and Preb York Minster from 10. *St Helen's Vicarage, Cowgate, Welton, Brough HU15 1ND* T: (01482) 666677
E: ebielby@ebielby.karoo.co.uk

BIENFAIT, Alexander. b 61. Hatf Poly BSc 86. Sarum & Wells Th Coll BTh 94. **d** 94 **p** 95. C Battersea St Luke *S'wark* 94-96; C Clapham Team 96-99; TV Whitstable *Cant* 99-07; P-in-c Biddenden and Smarden from 07. *The Rectory, High Street, Biddenden, Ashford TN27 8AH* T: (01580) 291454
E: alexander.bienfait@gmail.com

BIERBAUM, Ms Ruth Anne. b 67. RN 89. Trin Coll Bris BA 98. **d** 99 **p** 00. C Filey *York* 99-02; C Coxheath, E Farleigh, Hunton, Linton etc *Roch* 02-08; Lead Mental Health Chapl Kent & Medway NHS and Soc Care Partnership Trust from 08; PtO *Roch* from 08; *Cant* from 08. *52 Stag Road, Chatham ME5 8LG* T: (01634) 670715 or 838944 M: 017954-227184
E: ruth@bierbaumfreeserve.co.uk or ruth.bierbaum@kmpt.nhs.uk

BIGG, Andrew John. b 82. Jes Coll Ox MPhys 05 Leeds Univ BA 10 Sheff Univ MA 11. Coll of Resurr Mirfield. **d** 11 **p** 12. C Cottingham *York* 11-14; Asst Chapl Paris St Geo *Eur* from 14.

St George, 7 rue Auguste-Vacquerie, 75116 Paris, France T: (0033) 1 47 20 22 51 E: bigg.andrew@gmail.com

BIGG, Howard Clive. b 40. Fitzw Coll Cam BA 68 MA 72. Ridley Hall Cam 73. **d** 74 **p** 75. C Worksop St Jo *S'well* 74-76; Min Can St Alb *St Alb* 76-77; PtO *Ches* 78-82; *Ely* 82-99; Vice-Prin Romsey Ho Cam 86-89; NSM Cambridge St Benedict *Ely* 99-01; rtd 05; PtO *Ely* 08-13. *4 Pershore Road, Hardwick, Cambridge CB23 7XQ* T: (01954) 211673
E: hcb29@cam.ac.uk

BIGGAR, Prof Nigel John. b 55. Worc Coll Ox BA 76 MA 88 Chicago Univ AM 80 PhD 86 Regent Coll Vancouver MCS 81. **d** 90 **p** 91. Lib Latimer Ho Ox 85-91; Asst Lect Chr Ethics Wycliffe Hall Ox 87-94; Chapl Oriel Coll Ox 90-99; Prof Th Leeds Univ *Ripon* 99-04; Prof Th TCD 04-07; Can Ch Ch Cathl Dublin 05-07; Regius Prof Moral and Past Th Ox Univ from 07; Can Res Ch Ch *Ox* from 07. *Christ Church, Oxford OX1 1DP* T: (01865) 276219
E: nigel.biggar@chch.ox.ac.uk

BIGGIN, Ronald. b 20. NW Ord Course 70. **d** 73 **p** 74. C Thelwall *Ches* 73-79; V 79-87; rtd 87; NSM Lt Leigh and Lower Whitley *Ches* 90-93; PtO from 93. *12 Wilmslow Crescent, Thelwall, Warrington WA4 2JE* T: (01925) 261531

BIGGS, David James. b 55. St Jo Coll Auckland LTh 82. **d** 81 **p** 82. New Zealand 81-86; C Stevenage St Andr and St Geo *St Alb* 86-89; TV Moulsecoomb *Chich* 89-99; C Brighton St Pet w Chpl Royal 99-02; P-in-c Brighton Chpl Royal from 09; Chapl St Mary's Hall Brighton from 03. *4 Parochial Mews, Princes Street, Brighton BN2 1WF* T: (01273) 774492
E: david@crbtn.freeserve.co.uk

BIGGS, George Ramsay. b 45. Liv Univ BA 67 Qu Coll Cam BA 73. Westcott Ho Cam 72. **d** 74 **p** 75. C Lee St Aug *S'wark* 74-78; TV Eling, Testwood and Marchwood *Win* 78; TV Totton 78-93; V E and W Wellow 93-98; V E w W Wellow and Sherfield English 98-11; Hosp Chapl Adv (Bournemouth Adnry) 02-11; rtd 11. *10 Bowerhill Road, Salisbury SP1 3DN* T: (01722) 329215

BIGGS, Laurence John. b 60. Leeds Univ BSc 81. Trin Coll Bris 92. **d** 94 **p** 95. C St Alb St Paul *St Alb* 94-99; V Codicote 99-14; P-in-c Nunthorpe *York* from 14. *114 Gypsy Lane, Nunthorpe, Middlesbrough TS7 0DR*
E: laurencebiggs@gmail.com

BIGGS, Philip John. b 51. Ripon Hall Ox 74. **d** 77 **p** 78. C Maidstone All SS w St Phil and H Trin *Cant* 77-80; Dioc Youth Officer Truro 80-84; Chapl St Hilda's Angl Sch Australia 84-87; R Bicton 87-91; R Mosman Park 92-10; 98-04; Hon Chapl Miss to Seafarers 84-10; Can Res and Chan Blackb Cathl 10-11; Poland 11-12; P-in-c Lytham St Cuth *Blackb* 12-15; Hon C St Neot and Warleggan w Cardynham *Truro* from 15. *The Vicarage, St Neot, Liskeard PL14 6NG* M: 07521-282876 T: (01579) 320472 E: perectoruk@yahoo.co.uk

BIGGS, Stewart Richard. b 58. SEITE. **d** 01 **p** 02. C Tunbridge Wells St Jas w St Phil *Roch* 01-04; C Tunbridge Wells St Jas 04-05; V St Mary Cray and St Paul's Cray 05-06. *Address temp unknown* M: 07967-979559 E: revstewb@xalt.co.uk

BIGMORE, Graeme Paul. b 57. Univ of Wales (Cardiff) BTh 95. St Mich Coll Llan 89. **d** 92 **p** 93. C Cardiff St Jo *Llan* 92-96; City Cen Chapl Cardiff 94-96; C Rhondda 96-98; V Tylorstown w Ynyshir 98-05; V Ynyshir from 05. *The Vicarage, Graig Road, Porth CF39 0NS* T: (01443) 684148

BIGNELL, Alan Guy. b 39. Lon Univ BA 64. Ox NSM Course 78. **d** 81 **p** 82. NSM Upton cum Chalvey *Ox* 81-90; NSM Burnham and Slough Deanery 90-10; PtO from 10. *Little Gidding, 2 Turners Road, Slough SL3 7AN* T: (01753) 523005
E: abignell@waitrose.com

BIGNELL, David Charles. b 41. EMMTC 76. **d** 79 **p** 80. C Porchester *S'well* 79-82; V Awsworth w Cossall 82-86; V Edwalton 86-06; Bp's Ecum Officer 84-06; rtd 06; C Nottingham All SS, St Mary and St Pet *S'well* 08-09; C Attenborough 13-14. *6 Allendale Avenue, Beeston, Nottingham NG9 6AN* T: 0115-925 0060

BIGWOOD, Kate Elizabeth. *See* ATKINSON, Kate Bigwood

BILES, David George. b 35. AKC 58 Open Univ BA 75 Lambeth STh 91 Leeds Univ MA 96. **d** 59 **p** 60. C Cockerton *Dur* 59-62; C Winlaton 62-67; P-in-c Dipton 67-74; R Wolviston 74-89; P-in-c Thirkleby w Kilburn and Bagby *York* 89-90; V 90-00; RD Thirsk 90-91; RD Mowbray 91-00; rtd 00; PtO *York* from 00; *Sheff* from 11. *10 King Rudding Close, Riccall, York YO19 6RY* T/F: (01757) 248829

BILES, Mrs Kathleen Anne. b 52. Bradf Univ BA 74. St Jo Coll Nottm 98. **d** 04 **p** 06. C Ch Ch Cathl Stanley Falkland Is from 04. *PO Box 166, 14 Kent Road, Stanley FIQQ 1ZZ, Falkland Islands* T/F: (00500) 21897
E: kbiles@horizon.co.fk

BILES, Canon Timothy Mark Frowde. b 35. St Mich Coll Llan 60. **d** 64 **p** 66. C Middleton St Cross *Ripon* 64-66; Chapl St Fran Sch Hooke 66-72; P-in-c Toller Porcorum w

Hooke *Sarum* 72-79; P-in-c Melplash w Mapperton 74-79; P-in-c Beaminster 77-79; TR Beaminster Area 79-00; Can and Preb Sarum Cathl 83-00; RD Beaminster 84-89; rtd 00; PtO *Sarum* from 01. *36 Hound Street, Sherborne DT9 3AA* T: (01935) 816247 E: tim@tjbiles.freeserve.co.uk

BILINDA, Mrs Lesley Anne. b 59. Aber Univ MA 81 All Nations Chr Coll BA 98. Ripon Coll Cuddesdon MA 13. **d** 13 **p** 14. C Fulham St Andr *Lon* from 13. *Basement Flat, 15 Palliser Road, London W14 9EB* M: 07956-587176
E: lesleybilinda@gmail.com

BILL, Alan. b 29. K Coll Lon BD 66 AKC 66. **d** 67 **p** 68. C Gt Burstead *Chelmsf* 67-70; TV Thornaby on Tees *York* 71-76; R E Gilling 76-81; V Ormesby 81-91; rtd 91; PtO *Newc* from 91. *13 Wilmington Close, Tudor Grange, Newcastle upon Tyne NE3 2SF* T: 0191-242 4467

BILL, Canon Thomas Andrew Graham. b 47. Dur Univ BA 76. Cranmer Hall Dur. **d** 77 **p** 78. C Penwortham St Mary *Blackb* 77-80; C Torrisholme 80-82; P-in-c Accrington St Pet 82-89; P-in-c Haslingden St Jo Stonefold 82-89; V Skerton St Chad 89-03; R Burnley St Pet 03-11; P-in-c Burnley St Steph 08-11; R Burnley St Pet and St Steph 11-13; Hon Can Blackb Cathl 03-13; rtd 13; PtO *Blackb* from 13. *26 Thornton Road, Morecambe LA4 5PE* T: (01524) 417117
E: tom@tombill.entadsl.com

BILLETT, Canon Anthony Charles. b 56. Bris Univ BEd. Wycliffe Hall Ox 82. **d** 85 **p** 86. C Waltham Abbey *Chelmsf* 85-88; C Nor St Pet Mancroft w St Jo Maddermarket 88-91; V Stalham and E Ruston w Brunstead 91-00; R Stalham, E Ruston, Brunstead, Sutton and Ingham 00-01; R Diss 01-14; TR from 14; RD Redenhall 06-15; Hon Can Nor Cathl from 10. *The Rectory, 26 Mount Street, Diss IP22 4QG* T: (01379) 642072
E: disschurch2@btconnect.com

BILLETT (née RANDALL), Mrs Elizabeth Nicola. b 55. RGN 75 SCM 81. EAMTC 94. **d** 97 **p** 98. C Loddon, Sisland w Hales and Heckingham *Nor* 97-98; C Loddon, Sisland, Chedgrave, Hardley and Langley 98-01; TV Hempnall from 02. *The Flat, George's House, The Street, Woodton, Bungay NR35 1LZ* T: (01508) 482366

BILLETT, Mrs Justine Elizabeth Stearman. b 82. Reading Univ BSc 08. Ripon Coll Cuddesdon BA 15. **d** 15. C Banwell *B & W* from 15; C Congresbury w Puxton and Hewish St Ann from 15. *7 Weetwood Road, Congresbury, Bristol BS49 5BN* M: 07778-049265 E: justine.billett@gmail.com

BILLIN, David Robert. b 55. S Bank Poly BSc 77 CEng 82 MIET 82 MIRSE 86 EurIng 89. **d** 06 **p** 07. NSM Carshalton *S'wark* from 06. *33 Beeches Avenue, Carshalton SM5 3LJ* T: (020) 8647 5046 M: 07946-609387
E: davidbillin1955@btinternet.com

BILLIN, Mrs Susan Lynn. b 59. S Bank Univ BSc 99 Greenwich Univ CertEd 96 RGN 82. SEITE 02. **d** 05 **p** 06. NSM S Beddington and Roundshaw *S'wark* from 05. *33 Beeches Avenue, Carshalton SM5 3LJ* T: (020) 8647 5046
E: lynn_billin@lineone.net

BILLINGHURST, Richard George. b 48. St Jo Coll Cam BA 70 MA 74 FIA 76. Ridley Hall Cam 76. **d** 79 **p** 80. C Caversham *Lich* 79-81; C Cullompton *Ex* 81-84; R Redgrave cum Botesdale w Rickinghall *St E* 84-92; R Skellingthorpe w Doddington *Linc* from 92; RD Graffoe 94-02 and from 14. *The Rectory, 50 Lincoln Road, Skellingthorpe, Lincoln LN6 5UY* T: (01522) 682520 F: 693330 M: 07971-590378
E: acorns@clara.co.uk

BILLINGS, Canon Alan Roy. b 42. Em Coll Cam BA 65 MA 69 Bris Univ PGCE 66 Leic Univ MEd 75 NY Th Sem DMin 87. Linc Th Coll. **d** 68 **p** 69. C Knighton St Mary Magd *Leic* 68-72; P-in-c Sheff Gillcar St Silas 72-76; V Beighton 76-77; Hd RE Broadway Sch Barnsley 77-81; PtO *Sheff* 77-81; V Walkley 81-86; Dir Ox Inst for Ch and Soc 86-92; PtO *Ox* 86-92; Vice-Prin Ripon Coll Cuddesdon 88-92; Prin WMMTC 92-94; V Kendal St Geo *Carl* 94-07; C Grayrigg 06-07; Warden of Readers 96-03; Dir Cen for Ethics and Relig Lanc Univ 00-07; Hon Can Carl Cathl 05-07; rtd 07. *43 Northfield Court, Sheffield S10 1QR* T: 0114-267 6549
E: alanbillingsuk@yahoo.com

BILLINGS, Derek Donald. b 30. Fitzw Ho Cam BA 54 MA 59. Tyndale Hall Bris 55. **d** 56 **p** 57. C Attenborough w Bramcote and Chilwell *S'well* 56-58; R Ashley w Silverley *Ely* 59-66; V Bottisham 66-80; R Houghton w Wyton 80-97; rtd 97; PtO *Ely* from 97. *The Limes, 59 Cambridge Street, Godmanchester, Huntingdon PE29 2AY* T: (01480) 414244

BILLINGS, Roger Key. b 41. ACIB. Oak Hill Th Coll BA 80. **d** 80 **p** 81. C Tunbridge Wells St Jas *Roch* 80-84; V Chatham St Paul w All SS 84-95; V Carterton *Ox* 95-03; TR Brize Norton and Carterton 03-07; AD Witney 03-07; rtd 07; PtO *Nor* from 07. *Maudville, Norwich Road, Cromer NR27 9JU* T: (01263) 519055 E: rogerbillings@btinternet.com

BILLINGS, Mrs Valerie Ann. b 52. Nottm Trent Univ CertEd 02. EMMTC 07. **d** 09 **p** 10. NSM Ockbrook *Derby* 09-14; PtO from

15. *14 Conway Avenue, Borrowash, Derby DE72 3GT* T: (01332) 726285 E: valbillings1@gmail.com

BILLINGSLEY, Raymond Philip. b 48. Open Univ BA 98 DASS 98 FCMA 80. Qu Coll Birm 87. **d** 89 **p** 90. C Yardley St Edburgha *Birm* 89-92; V Ward End 92-96; V Brymbo *St As* 96-04; V Northop 04-13; rtd 13; PtO *St As* from 14. *14 Ffordd y Fran, Flint CH6 5UP* T: (01352) 375156
E: revraybillingsley@gmail.com

BILLINGTON, George. b 45. St Jo Coll Nottm 92. **d** 94 **p** 95. C Accrington St Jo w Huncoat *Blackb* 94-98; C Whittle-le-Woods 98-00; V Stalmine w Pilling 00-10; rtd 10. *Brookvale, Sterridge Valley, Berrynarnor, Ilfracombe EX34 9TB* T: (01271) 883546 E: g.billington@btconnect.com

BILLINGTON, Miss Shelley Louise. b 82. St Martin's Coll Lanc BA 03. Trin Coll Bris 10. **d** 14 **p** 15. C Hanley H Ev *Lich* from 14. *301 Ruxley Road, Bucknall, Stoke-on-Trent ST2 9BG* T: (01782) 885013 M: 07411-992565
E: shelley_india@yahoo.co.uk

BILLOWES, David. b 20. Chich Th Coll. **d** 76 **p** 77. NSM Cowes St Mary *Portsm* 76-91; Chapl St Mary's Hosp Newport 82-91; rtd 91; PtO *Portsm* 91-06. *3 Greenfields, Gosfield, Halstead CO9 1TR* T: (01787) 472823

BILLSON, Kevin Michael. b 58. Lon Univ BD 81. Qu Coll Birm 10. **d** 11 **p** 12. C Brereton and Rugeley *Lich* 11-15; R Blofield *Nor* from 15. *The Rectory, 10 Oak Wood, Blofield, Norwich NR13 4JQ* M: 07941-341911
E: kevin.billson@eraith.net

BILSTON, Canon Barbara Bradley. b 35. Man Univ BA 58 Essex Univ MA 75. EAMTC 96. **d** 97 **p** 98. NSM Bacton w Wyverstone and Cotton *St E* 97-00; NSM Bacton w Wyverstone, Cotton and Old Newton etc 00-04; Asst to RD Stowmarket 04-05; RD from 05; Hon Can St E Cathl from 12. *Boy's Hall, Ward Green, Old Newton, Stowmarket IP14 4EY* T/F: (01449) 781253 M: 07889-516674
E: b.b.bilston@open.ac.uk

BILTON, Canon Paul Michael. b 52. AKC 74. St Aug Coll Cant 74. **d** 75 **p** 76. C Skipton Ch Ch *Bradf* 75-79; Ind Chapl *Worc* 79-81; V Greetland and W Vale *Wakef* 81-88; R Mablethorpe w Trusthorpe *Linc* 88-91; V Bradf St Wilfrid Lidget Green 91-04; P-in-c Bradf St Columba w St Andr 00-04; V Bradf St Wilfrid w St Columba *Leeds* from 04; RD Bowling and Horton *Bradf* 02-14; AD *Leeds* 14; Hon Can Bradf Cathl from 04. *St Wilfrid's Vicarage, St Wilfrid's Road, Bradford BD7 2LU* T: (01274) 572504
E: paul.bilton@bradford.anglican.org

BIMSON, Sara Margaret. b 56. St Jo Coll Nottm BA. **d** 03 **p** 04. C Maidstone St Martin *Cant* 03-08; rtd 08; Voc Officer *Cant* 08-10; PtO from 08; Hon Min Can Cant Cathl from 12. *39 Ivy Lane, Canterbury CT1 1TU* T: (01227) 760655
E: sara-mary@hotmail.com

BINDING, Ms Frances Mary. b 59. York Univ BA 81 Newc Poly PGCE 82. WEMTC 98. **d** 02 **p** 03. C Bromyard *Heref* 02-07; TV Worc SE 07-13; P-in-c Wraxall *B & W* from 13. *41 Vowles Close, Wraxall, Bristol BS48 1PP* E: franmbinding@gmail.com

BINDOFF, Ms Anna. b 70. Leeds Univ BA 94. Ripon Coll Cuddesdon BA 97. **d** 98 **p** 99. Asst Chapl New Coll Ox 98-01; Hon C Blackbird Leys *Ox* 98-01; C 01-04. *23 Brook Street, Watlington OX49 5JH* T: (01491) 613327

BING, Canon Alan Charles. b 56. St Edm Hall Ox BA 78 MA 91 Ex Univ MA 96. Oak Hill Th Coll 89. **d** 91 **p** 92. C Fremington *Ex* 91-94; C-in-c Roundswell CD 94-97; TV Barnstaple 97-99; Chapl N Devon Coll Barnstaple 96-99; P-in-c Ulverston St Mary w H Trin *Carl* 99-04; R from 04; RD Furness from 10; Hon Can Carl Cathl from 09. *The Rectory, 15 Ford Park Crescent, Ulverston LA12 7JR* T/F: (01229) 584331
E: alanbing@live.co.uk

BINGHAM, Mrs Marie Joyce Phyllis. b 27. Glouc Sch of Min 80. dss 84 **d** 87 **p** 94. Glouc St Mary de Crypt w St Jo and Ch Ch 84-85; Glouc St Mary de Lode and St Nic 85-87; Hon C 87-95; Hon C Glouc St Mary de Crypt w St Jo and Ch Ch 94-95; Hon C Glouc St Mary de Crypt w St Jo, Ch Ch etc 95-98; PtO from 98. *Clematis Cottage, 1 Queenwood Grove, Prestbury, Cheltenham GL52 3NG* T: (01452) 242252

BINGHAM, Norman James Frederick. b 26. Lon Univ BSc 51. Tyndale Hall Bris 61. **d** 63 **p** 64. C Chell *Lich* 63-67; C Macclesfield St Mich *Ches* 67-71; P-in-c Macclesfield St Pet 71-73; V Leyton St Mary w St Edw *Chelmsf* 73-91; RD Waltham Forest 81-86; P-in-c Leyton St Luke 82-91; rtd 91; PtO *St Alb* from 91. *97 Monks Walk, Buntingford SG9 9DP* T: (01763) 272275

BINKS, Andrew John. b 49. Open Univ BA Leeds Univ MA 06. NOC 03. **d** 06 **p** 07. NSM Haslingden w Grane and Stonefold *Blackb* 06-09; NSM Accrington St Jo w Huncoat 09-13; rtd 14; PtO *Blackb* from 14; *Man* from 14. *18 Sandown Road, Haslingden, Rossendale BB4 6PL* T: (01706) 229285
E: jmbinks@tiscali.co.uk

BINKS, Canon Edmund Vardy. b 36. K Coll Lon BD 61 AKC 61 Liv Univ Hon LLD 98 FRSA 89. **d** 62 **p** 63. C Selby Abbey *York* 62-65; Asst Chapl Univ Coll of Ripon and York St Jo 65-83; Hd St Kath Coll Liv 83-87; Prin Ches Coll of HE 87-98; Hon Can Ches Cathl 95-98; PtO *Chich* from 98; rtd 01. *2 Lodge Close, Lewes BN7 1AR* T: (01273) 487136

BINKS, Robert Peter. b 73. Trin Coll Bris 08. **d** 10 **p** 11. C Basildon St Andr w H Cross *Chelmsf* 10-14; P-in-c Warley Ch Ch and Gt Warley St Mary from 14. *Christ Church Vicarage, 79 Mount Crescent, Warley, Brentwood CM14 5DD* T: (01277) 220428 E: rob.binks@me.com

BINKS, Mrs Susan Jane. b 59. Yorks Min Course 13. **d** 15. NSM Kirkdale w Harome, Nunnington and Pockley *York* from 15. *Helleborous Cottage, Main Street, Harome, York YO62 5JF* T: (01439) 770523 E: binksharome@btinternet.com

BINLEY, Miss Teresa Mary. b 37. Dalton Ho Bris 61. **d** 87 **p** 94. Par Dn Ashton upon Mersey St Mary Magd *Ches* 87-92; Bp's Officer for Women in Min 87-92; C Chaddesden St Mary *Derby* 92-98; rtd 98; PtO *Derby* from 98. *27 Hindscarth Crescent, Mickleover, Derby DE3 9NN* T: (01332) 511146

BINNEY, Mark James Gurney. b 58. K Coll Lon BD 80. Qu Coll Birm 84. **d** 86 **p** 87. C Hornchurch St Andr *Chelmsf* 86-89; C Hutton 89-91; V Pheasey *Lich* 91-96; TV Wombourne w Trysull and Bobbington 96-99; V Wilnecote 99-08; P-in-c Hampton w Sedgeberrow and Hinton-on-the-Green *Worc* from 08; P-in-c Bengeworth from 14. *St Andrew's Vicarage, 54 Pershore Road, Evesham WR11 2PQ* T: (01386) 446381 E: reverend-mark-binney@hotmail.co.uk

BINNS, Miss Catherine Dorothy. b 70. Univ of Cen England in Birm BSc 04 Leeds Univ BA 07 RN 99. NOC 04. **d** 07 **p** 08. NSM Stand *Man* from 07; NSM Hillock and Unsworth from 15; Chapl Bolton Hosps NHS Trust from 15. *23 Scott Street, Radcliffe, Manchester M26 1EX* T: (01204) 707922 E: cath@chazfrog.fsnet.co.uk

BINNS, David John. b 39. Moore Th Coll Sydney ThL 64. **d** 64 **p** 65. Australia 64-67; C Norbiton *S'wark* 67-69; Australia from 70; R Adelaide St Luke 80-98; Assoc Min 98-00; rtd 00. *Unit 4/2 Spence Avenue, Myrtle Bank SA 5064, Australia* T: (0061) (8) 8338 5779 M: 0417-860560 E: djb29@ozemail.com.au

BINNS, Miss Elizabeth Ann. b 55. MBE 06. Man Metrop Univ BA 87 RGN 77. **d** 05 **p** 06. OLM Bury St Jo w St Mark *Man* 05-10; OLM Walmersley Road, Bury 10-14; NSM Radcliffe from 14. *36 Raymond Avenue, Bury BL9 6NN* T: 0161-764 5071 M: 07976-818157 E: elizabethbinns@aol.com

BINNS, Mrs Janet Victoria. b 57. ACIB 96. Ox Min Course 04. **d** 07 **p** 08. C Slough *Ox* 07-10; C Eton w Eton Wick, Boveney and Dorney 10-11; Olympics Co-ord 11-12; PtO 13; R Hedsor and Bourne End from 13. *34 Fieldhead Gardens, Bourne End SL8 5RN* T: (01628) 523046 E: revjanetbinns@btinternet.com

BINNS, Canon John Richard Elliott. b 51. St Jo Coll Cam MA 76 K Coll Lon PhD 89. Coll of Resurr Mirfield 74. **d** 76 **p** 77. C Clapham Old Town *S'wark* 76-80; TV Mortlake w E Sheen 80-87; V Upper Tooting H Trin 87-94; V Cambridge Gt St Mary w St Mich *Ely* from 94; RD Cambridge N 07-11; Hon Can Ely Cathl from 07. *Great St Mary's Vicarage, 39 Madingley Road, Cambridge CB3 0EL* T: (01223) 355285 *or* 741716 F: 462914 E: jb344@cam.ac.uk

BINNS, Peter Rodney. b 44. St Andr Univ MA 66. Ox NSM Course 72. **d** 75 **p** 76. NSM Amersham on the Hill *Ox* 75-90; NSM Wingrave w Rowsham, Aston Abbotts and Cublington 90-97; NSM Hawridge w Cholesbury and St Leonard 90-97; NSM Amersham on the Hill from 97. *16 Turnfurlong Row, Turnfurlong Lane, Aylesbury HP21 7FF* T: (01296) 330836 F: 337965 E: peter.binns166@btinternet.com

BINNY, John Wallace. b 46. Univ of Wales (Lamp) BA 70. St Mich Coll Llan 69. **d** 71 **p** 72. C Llantrisant *Llan* 71-77; V Troedyrhiw w Merthyr Vale 77-82; R Eglwysbrewis w St Athan, Flemingston, Gileston 82-95; R Eglwysbrewis w St Athan w Gileston 95-03; V Pentyrch w Capel Llanillterne 03-11; rtd 11; PtO *Llan* from 11. *Oakdene, 27 Porthamal Road, Cardiff CF14 6AQ* T: (029) 2062 0360

BINSLEY, Michael. b 60. **d** 09 **p** 10. OLM Yoxall *Lich* from 09. *83 Lightwood Road, Yoxall, Burton-on-Trent DE13 8QE* T: (01543) 472761

BIRCHAM, Anthony Leng. b 33. MBE 90. Linc Coll Ox BA 59 MA 61. Linc Th Coll 58. **d** 60 **p** 61. C Redcar *York* 60-73; C Redcar w Kirkleatham 73-74; Chapl Teesside Ind Miss 62-74; Can Res and Treas Wells Cathl 74-78; NSM Wells St Thos w Horrington 89-98; rtd 98; PtO *B & W* from 98; RD Shepton Mallet 07-11. *Beeches, Cannards Grave Road, Shepton Mallet BA4 4LX* T: (01749) 330382 M: 07802-725024 E: tonybirbeck@hotmail.co.uk

BIRBECK, John Trevor. b 49. ACIB 77. St Jo Coll Nottm 86. **d** 88 **p** 89. C Eccleshill *Bradf* 88-92; V Hurst Green and Mitton 92-03; R Rawmarsh w Parkgate *Sheff* from 03; C Greasbrough from 10; C Kimberworth and Kimberworth Park from 10. *The Rectory, 2 High Street, Rawmarsh, Rotherham S62 6NE* T: (01709) 527160 E: john.birbeck@ntlworld.com

BIRCH, Barry. b 46. Sheff Univ CertEd 69 Lon Univ BA 74 MIL 84 MCollP 85. **d** 06 **p** 07. NSM Cantley *Sheff* 06-08; P-in-c Eastchurch w Leysdown and Harty *Cant* 08-12; Hon C W Sheppey 12; rtd 12; PtO *Eur* from 13. *Richard Holstraat 133, 2551 HR Gravenhage, The Netherlands* T: (0031) (70) 213 4042 E: barrybirch@hotmail.com

BIRCH, Derek. b 31. Univ of Wales (Lamp) BA 58. Coll of Resurr Mirfield 58. **d** 60 **p** 61. C S Elmsall *Wakef* 60-62; C Penistone w Midhope 62-66; V Silkstone 66-89; Chapl Stainborough 76-89; P-in-c Hoyland Swaine *Wakef* 85-89; V Hoylandswaine and Silkstone w Stainborough 89-97; rtd 98; PtO *Leeds* from 98. *46 Pengeston Road, Penistone, Sheffield S36 6GW* T: (01226) 761523

BIRCH, Mrs Elizabeth Ann Marie. b 65. Ball Coll Ox BA 88 MA 05. NTMTC BA 06. **d** 06 **p** 07. NSM Pinner *Lon* 06-09; R Wantage Downs *Ox* from 09. *The Rectory, Church Street, East Hendred, Wantage OX12 8LA* T: (01235) 833235

BIRCH, Graham James. b 62. NOC BTh 94. **d** 97 **p** 98. C Southport St Phil and St Paul *Liv* 97-01; P-in-c Wigan St Cath 01-07; V Ainsdale from 07. *The Vicarage, 708 Liverpool Road, Southport PR8 3QE* T: (01704) 577760 E: madrebgra@aol.com

BIRCH, Mark Russell. b 70. Bris Univ BVSc 93 Em Coll Cam BA 99. Westcott Ho Cam 97. **d** 00 **p** 01. C Cirencester *Glouc* 00-03; Chapl and Fell Ex Coll Ox 03-06; Chapl Helen and Douglas Ho Ox 06-10; Chapl Treloar Coll Alton 10-12; P-in-c Win St Cross w St Faith 12-14; Chapl St Cross Hosp 12-14. *10 Cripstead Lane, Winchester SO23 9SE* T: (01962) 622006 E: mark.birch@me.com

BIRCH, Richard Arthur. b 51. Brighton Poly BSc 73 Chelsea Coll Lon MSc 76. SEITE 98. **d** 01 **p** 02. NSM Folkestone St Jo *Cant* 01-04; NSM Hawkinge w Acrise and Swingfield 04-07; NSM Hythe 07-08; NSM Doddington, Newnham and Wychling 08-14; NSM Kingsdown and Creekside from 14. *The Vicarage, The Street, Doddington, Sittingbourne ME9 0BH* T: (01795) 886265 E: richarda.birch@btinternet.com

BIRCH, Thomas David Keith. b 81. Glas Univ MA 03 Edin Univ MSc 06. Ripon Coll Cuddesdon BA 14. **d** 14 **p** 15. C Gosforth St Nic *Newc* from 14. *59 Sturdee Gardens, Newcastle upon Tyne NE2 3QU* M: 07976-047707 E: tdkbirch@hotmail.com

BIRCH, Thomas Reginald. b 33. AKC 57. St Boniface Warminster 67. **d** 68. C Basildon St Andr CD *Chelmsf* 68-69; Ind Chapl 69-88; rtd 88. *29 Muspole Street, Norwich NR3 1DJ* T: (01603) 631446

BIRCHALL, John Dearman. b 70. St Andr Univ MA 93. Wycliffe Hall Ox BTh 99. **d** 99 **p** 00. C Purley Ch Ch *S'wark* 99-02; C Fisherton Anger *Sarum* 02-08; V Surbiton Hill Ch Ch *S'wark* from 08. *Christ Church Vicarage, 7 Christ Church Road, Surbiton KT5 8JJ* T: (020) 8399 3733 *or* 8390 7215 E: john.birchall@ccsurbiton.org

BIRCHALL, Robert Gary. b 59. Sheff Univ BA 81. St Jo Coll Nottm 85. **d** 88 **p** 89. C Manston *Ripon* 88-91; C Leic Martyrs 91-94; C New Humberstone 94-95; V Burnopfield *Dur* 95-14; V Burnopfield and Dipton 14; AD Lanchester 06-14; V Boldmere *Birm* from 14. *209 Station Road, Sutton Coldfield B73 5LE* T: 0121-354 4501 E: garybirchall1@gmail.com

BIRCHARD, Canon Thaddeus Jude. b 45. Louisiana State Univ BA 66. Kelham Th Coll 66. **d** 70 **p** 71. C Devonport St Mark Ford *Ex* 70-73; C Southend St Jo w St Mark, All SS w St Fran etc *Chelmsf* 73-76; TV Poplar *Lon* 76-80; V Paddington St Jo w St Mich 80-01; Hon Can Louisiana from 90; rtd 01; PtO *Lon* from 02. *12 Dibdin House, Maida Vale, London W9 1QG* T: (020) 7328 2380 E: thaddeus@birchard.co.uk

BIRD, Mrs Ann Maud. b 39. **d** 00 **p** 01. OLM W Bromwich All SS *Lich* 00-13; PtO from 13. *16 Caldwell Street, West Bromwich B71 2DN* T: 0121-588 4335

BIRD (née BAKER), Mrs Anne-Marie Clare. b 56. Wye Coll Lon BSc 78 Glas Univ MSc 80. St Jo Coll Nottm 88. **d** 90 **p** 94. Par Dn Levenshulme St Pet *Man* 90-94; C 94-95; P-in-c Crumpsall 95-03; TV Keynsham *B & W* 03-05; rtd 05; PtO *B & W* from 05. *26 Culvers Road, Keynsham, Bristol BS31 2DW* T: 0117-904 8585 M: 07753-424913 E: annemarie.motherbird@googlemail.com

BIRD, Anthony Peter. b 31. St Jo Coll Ox BA 54 BTh 55 MA 57 Birm Univ MB, ChB 70. Cuddesdon Coll 55. **d** 57 **p** 58. C Stafford St Mary *Lich* 57-60; Chapl Cuddesdon Coll 60-61; Vice-Prin 61-64; C Selly Oak St Wulstan *Birm* 64-68; LtO 68-79; Prin Qu Coll Birm 74-79; PtO *Birm* from 85. *93 Bournbrook Road, Birmingham B29 7BX*

BIRD, Brian Edward. b 37. Rhodes Univ BA. **d** 75. S Africa 75-99 and from 08; Bp's C Mt Merrion *D & D* 99-05; rtd 05. *58 Sutherland Road, Hunters Village, Knysna, 6571 South Africa* T: (0027) (143) 841921 E: brian_bird23@hotmail.com

BIRD, The Very Revd David John. b 46. St D Coll Lamp BA 70 Duquesne Univ PhD 87. Gen Th Sem (NY) STM 74. **d** 70 **p** 71. C Kidderminster St Geo *Worc* 70-72; Chapl Trin Sch New York USA 72-78; V Rochdale Ch Ch 78-79; R New Kensington St Andr 79-89; R Washington Grace Ch 89-03; Dean Trin Cathl San Jose from 03. *Trinity Cathedral, 81 North 2nd Street, San Jose, CA 95113-1205, USA* T: (001) (408) 293 7953 F: 293 4993 E: david3933@aol.com

BIRD, Canon David Ronald. b 55. York Univ BA 76. St Jo Coll Nottm 83. **d** 86 **p** 87. C Kinson *Sarum* 86-90; R Thrapston *Pet* 90-97; P-in-c Islip 94-95; RD Higham 94-97; V Northampton St Giles 97-12; Can Pet Cathl 01-12; P-in-c Tollington *Lon* 12-14; TR from 14. *St Mark's Vicarage, 1 Moray Road, London N4 3LD* E: drbirdis@gmail.com

BIRD, Douglas Norman. b 38. **d** 92 **p** 93. OLM New Bury *Man* 92-06; PtO *Blackb* from 06; *Man* from 06. *Address temp unknown*

BIRD, Canon Frederick Hinton. b 38. St Edm Hall Ox BA 62 MA 66 Univ of Wales MEd 81 PhD 86. St D Coll Lamp BD 65. **d** 65 **p** 66. C Mynyddislwyn *Mon* 65-67; Min Can St Woolos Cathl 67-70; Chapl Anglo-American Coll Farringdon 70-71; PtO *Ox* 70-78; *Cant* 72-78; *Mon* 76-82; V Rushen *S & M* 82-03; Can St German's Cathl 93-03; rtd 03; PtO *S & M* from 04. *Conrhenny, 56 Selborne Drive, Douglas, Isle of Man IM2 3NL* T: (01624) 621624

BIRD, Geoffrey. b 44. Dioc OLM tr scheme 97. **d** 99 **p** 00. Asst Chapl HM YOI and Remand Cen Brinsford 99; Sen Chapl 99-04; Chapl HM Pris Shepton Mallet 04-09; rtd 09. *2 Hosey Road, Sturminster Newton DT10 1QP* T: (01258) 472904

BIRD, Henry John Joseph. b 37. ARCO 58 Qu Coll Cam BA 59 MA 63. Linc Th Coll 62. **d** 64 **p** 65. C Harbledown *Cant* 64-68; C Skipton H Trin *Bradf* 68-70; V Oakworth 70-81; Chapl Abingdon Sch 81-82; P-in-c Doncaster St Geo *Sheff* 82-85; V 85-02; rtd 02; PtO *Sheff* from 05; *Leeds* from 14. *332 Thorne Road, Doncaster DN2 5AL* T: (01302) 365589

BIRD, Hinton. *See* BIRD, Frederick Hinton

BIRD, Hugh Claud Handley. b 24. FRCGP SS Coll Cam MA MB BCh. Ridley Hall Cam. **d** 86 **p** 86. NSM Coxheath w E Farleigh, Hunton and Linton *Roch* 86-95; PtO *Cant* 95-14. *The Slate Barn, Seamark Road, Brooksend, Birchington CT7 0JL* T: (01843) 846619

BIRD, Ian Nicholas. b 62. Qu Eliz Coll Lon BSc 83 Newc Univ PhD 87 Heythrop Coll Lon MA 10. SAOMC 03. **d** 06 **p** 07. C Chandler's Ford *Win* 06-10; V from 10. *The Vicarage, 30 Hursley Road, Chandler's Ford, Eastleigh SO53 2FT* T: (023) 8025 4739 M: 07733-213535 E: ianbird@parishofchandlersford.org.uk

BIRD, Jeffrey David. b 54. Nottm Univ BCombStuds 85. Linc Th Coll 82. **d** 85 **p** 86. C Frome St Jo *B & W* 85-88; Asst Chapl HM Pris Pentonville 88-89; Chapl HM Pris Dartmoor 89-95; Chapl HM Pris Albany 95-03; Chapl HM Pris Linc 03-07; Chapl HM Pris Stafford from 07. *HM Prison, 54 Gaol Road, Stafford ST16 3AW* T: (01785) 773000 F: 773001

BIRD, Jeremy Paul. b 56. Ex Univ BSc 77 Hull Univ MA 88. Sarum Th Coll 78. **d** 80 **p** 81. C Tavistock and Gulworthy *Ex* 80-83; Chapl Teesside Poly *York* 83-88; R Chipstable w Huish Champflower and Clatworthy *B & W* 88-93; Rural Affairs Officer 88-93; V Uffculme *Ex* 93-01; P-in-c Dawlish 01-09; P-in-c Exwick from 09. *The Vicarage, Exwick Hill, Exeter EX4 2AQ* T: (01392) 255500 E: jerry@credamus.freeserve.co.uk

BIRD, John. *See* BIRD, Henry John Joseph

BIRD, John Anthony. b 45. EMMTC 00. **d** 03 **p** 04. NSM Thringstone St Andr *Leic* 03-09; NSM Whitwick and Swannington 07-09; NSM Whitwick, Thringstone and Swannington 09-11; NSM Shepshed and Oaks in Charnwood from 11. *8 Buckingham Drive, Loughborough LE11 4TE* T: (01509) 234962 E: curate.thringstone@tiscali.co.uk

BIRD, Mrs Margaret Kathleen. b 48. SAOMC 04. **d** 06 **p** 07. NSM Cox Green *Ox* 06-10; NSM New Windsor from 10; AD Maidenhead and Windsor from 14. *73 Alma Road, Windsor SL4 3HD* T: (01753) 315397 M: 07881-712611 E: margaret.bird@talktalk.net

BIRD, Nicholas William Randle. b 70. Univ of Cen England in Birm BSc 99 RGN 92. NEOC 02. **d** 05 **p** 06. C Thirsk *York* 05-09; P-in-c Dunnington 09-12; P-in-c Stockton-on-the-Forest w Holtby and Warthill 09-12; R Rural E York from 12. *The Rectory, 30 Church Street, Dunnington, York YO19 5PW* T: (01904) 489349 E: frnick.bird@btinternet.com

BIRD, Norman David. b 32. CQSW 73. Coll of Resurr Mirfield 87. **d** 89 **p** 90. NSM Willesden Green St Andr and

St Fran *Lon* 89-92; NSM Preston Ascension 93-98; r-d 98; PtO *Lon* 99-13. *5 Oldfield Road, London NW10 9UD* T: (020) 8451 4160

BIRD, Canon Peter Andrew. b 40. Wadh Coll Ox BA 62 MA 68. Ridley Hall Cam 63. **d** 65 **p** 66. C Keynsham w Queen Charlton *B & W* 65-68; C Strood St Nic *Roch* 68-72; TV Strood 72-79; V S Gillingham 79-89; V Westerham 89-02; Hon Can Roch Cathl 01-02; PtO 02-05; *Derby* from 05. *Iona, Prospect Terrace, Stanedge Road, Bakewell DE45 1DG* T: (01629) 813087 E: pabird@googlemail.com

BIRD, Roger Alfred. b 49. AKC 72. St Aug Coll Cant 72. **d** 73 **p** 74. C Prestatyn *St As* 73-78; R Llandysilio and Penrhos and Llandrinio etc 78-92; Dioc RE Adv 84-14; Dioc Dir of Educn 89-14; R Guilsfield 92-97; R Guilsfield w Pool Quay 97-02; V Guilsfield w Buttington 02-14; Hon Can St As Cathl 93-13; RD Pool 96-01; and AD 07-10; rtd 14. *15 Maes y Celyn, Guilsfield, Welshpool SY21 9BL* T/F: (01938) 554245 E: rogerb_800@fsmail.net

BIRD, Miss Sarah Ann. b 74. Trin Coll Bris 13. **d** 15. C Linc St Geo Swallowbeck from 15. *120A Station Road, Waddington, Lincoln LN5 9QS* M: 07834-069959 E: sarahbird777@gmail.com

BIRDSALL, Sandra. **d** 15. C Penarth All SS *Llan* from 15. *84 Coleridge Avenue, Penarth CF64 2SR* E: sandra.birdsall@btinternet.com

BIRDSEYE, Miss Jacqueline Ann. b 55. Sussex Univ BEd 78 Southn Univ BTh 88 K Coll Lon MTh 93. Sarum & Wells Th Coll 85. **d** 88 **p** 94. C Egham Hythe *Guildf* 88-91; C Fleet 91-92; C Shottermill 92-95; C Leavesden *St Alb* 95-98; R Ashwell w Hinxworth and Newnham 98-05; R Moreton, Woodsford and Crossways w Tincleton *Sarum* from 05. *The Rectory, 17 Warmwell Road, Crossways, Dorchester DT2 8BS* T: (01305) 854046 E: j.birdseye@btinternet.com

BIRDWOOD, William Halhed. b 51. St Jo Coll Dur BA 73. Sarum & Wells Th Coll 76. **d** 78 **p** 79. C Royston *St Alb* 78-82; C Thorley w Bishop's Stortford H Trin 82-89; Chapl HM Pris Ex 89-96; Chapl HM Pris Dartmoor from 96; LtO *Ex* from 89. *HM Prison Dartmoor, Princetown, Yelverton PL20 6RR* T: (01822) 890261 F: 890679

BIRKENHEAD, Suffragan Bishop of. *See* SINCLAIR, The Rt Revd Gordon Keith

BIRKETT, Christine Joy. b 53. Univ of Wales (Cardiff) BTheol 99 PGCE 01. Trin Coll Bris 07. **d** 08 **p** 09. NSM Berkeley w Wick, Breadstone, Newport, Stone etc *Glouc* 08-10; NSM Cainscross w Selsley 10-12; NSM Rodborough and The Stanleys w Selsley 12-13; P-in-c Upton St Leonards from 13. *The Rectory, 12 Bondend Road, Upton St Leonards, Gloucester GL4 8AG* T: (01452) 627828 E: cjoyb1953@yahoo.co.uk

BIRKETT, Mrs Joyce. b 38. WMMTC 84. **d** 87 **p** 94. Par Dn Hill Birm 87-91; Asst Chapl Highcroft Hosp Birm 87-91; Par Dn Rowley Regis *Birm* 91-94; C 94-96; V Londonderry 96-01; rtd 01; PtO *Birm* from 01. *83 Callowbrook Lane, Rubery, Rednal, Birmingham B45 9HP* T: 0121-457 9759

BIRKETT, Mrs Julie Anne. b 56. SWMTC. **d** 10 **p** 11. NSM Hutton and Locking *B & W* 10-13; NSM Weston super Mare St Jo from 13. *19 Stanhope Road, Weston-super-Mare BS23 4LP* T: (01934) 625587 E: rebelrevd@gmail.com

BIRKETT, Kirsten. BSc PhD. **d** 15. Lect Oak Hill Th Coll from 15. *Oak Hill College, Chase Side, London N14 4PS* T: (020) 8449 0467

BIRKETT, Neil Warren. b 45. Lanc Univ BEd 74 Southn Univ MA 84. Kelham Th Coll 65. **d** 77 **p** 77. NSM Win St Matt from 77. *Corrymeela, 132 Teg Down Meads, Winchester SO22 5NS* T: (01962) 864910

BIRKIN, Mrs Elspeth Joyce (Joy). b 36. CertEd 58. WMMTC 95. **d** 96 **p** 97. NSM Hanley Castle, Hanley Swan and Welland *Worc* 96-01; NSM Berrow w Pendock, Eldersfield, Hollybush etc 01-04; PtO 04-13; *Llan* from 13. *11 Spitzkop, Llantwit Major CF61 1RD*

BIRKINSHAW, Ian George. b 58. Pemb Coll Ox BA 81 Leeds Univ MA 97 Sheff Univ PGCE 82. NOC 93. **d** 96 **p** 97. NSM Chapeltown *Sheff* 96-97; C Normanton *Wakef* 98-01; C York St Mich-le-Belfrey 01-08; TR Huntington 08-10; R from 10. *The Rectory, Chestnut Court, Huntington, York YO32 9RD* T: (01904) 766550 or 768006 E: ian.birkinshaw@huntingtonparish.org.uk

BIRMINGHAM, Archdeacon of. *See* OSBORNE, The Ven Hayward John

BIRMINGHAM, Bishop of. *See* URQUHART, The Rt Revd David Andrew

BIRMINGHAM, Dean of. *See* OGLE, The Very Revd Catherine

BIRNIE, Ms Ruth Burdett. b 41. Glas Univ MA 64 Jordanhill Coll Glas PGCE 65 Leeds Univ MA 73. NEOC 02. **d** 04 **p** 05. NSM Gosforth All SS *Newc* from 04. *27 Delaval Terrace, Newcastle upon Tyne NE3 4RT* T: 0191-284 1393 E: ruth@birnie27.fsnet.co.uk

BIRT, David Edward. b 26. St Steph Ho Ox 86. **d** 86 **p** 87. NSM Ealing Ch the Sav *Lon* 86-99; PtO from 99. *10 Manor Court Road, London W7 3EL* T: (020) 8579 4871

BIRT, Richard Arthur. b 43. Ch Ch Ox BA 66 MA 69. Cuddesdon Coll 67. **d** 69 **p** 70. C Sutton St Mich *York* 69-71; C Wollaton *S'well* 71-75; R Kirkby in Ashfield 75-80; P-in-c Duxford *Ely* 80-87; R 87-88; P-in-c Hinxton 80-87; V 87-88; P-in-c Ickleton 80-87; V 87-88; V Weobley w Sarnesfield and Norton Canon *Heref* 88-00; P-in-c Letton w Staunton, Byford, Mansel Gamage etc 88-00; rtd 00; PtO *Heref* from 00. *7 Great Western Court, Canonmoor Street, Hereford HR4 9YA* T: (01432) 360804

BIRTWISTLE, Canon James. b 33. FCA 66. Ely Th Coll 57. **d** 59 **p** 60. C Southport St Luke *Liv* 59-63; V Cleator Moor w Cleator *Carl* 63-70; R Letchworth *St Alb* 70-73; P-in-c Wareside 73-80; Dep Dir of Educn 77-80; Dioc Dir of Educn 80-98; Hon Can St Alb 85-98; P-in-c Hertingfordbury 88-98; rtd 98; PtO *Ex* from 99. *9 Stoneborough Lane, Budleigh Salterton EX9 6HL* T: (01395) 442517

BIRTWISTLE, Lesley Sutherland. b 44. LLB. EMMTC 00. **d** 00 **p** 01. NSM Appleby Gp *Leic* 00-07; NSM Measham 07-08; NSM Packington w Normanton-le-Heath 07-08; NSM Donisthorpe and Moira w Stretton-en-le-Field 07-08; NSM Woodfield from 08. *14 Nethercroft Drive, Packington, Ashby-de-la-Zouch LE65 1WT* T: (01530) 413309 E: lesley@bwistle.f9.co.uk

BISCOE, Mrs Erika Jayne. b 66. Ox Min Course 12. **d** 15. C Bicester w Bucknell, Caversfield and Launton *Ox* from 15. *Address temp unknown*

BISCOE, Ian Rowland. b 68. Ox Min Course 06. **d** 07 **p** 08. C Cherwell Valley *Ox* 07-12; TV Bicester w Bucknell, Caversfield and Launton from 12. *4 Orpine Close, Bicester OX26 3ZJ* T: (01869) 232439 M: 07971-519234 E: ian.biscoe@googlemail.com

BISH, Donald. b 26. Ripon Hall Ox. **d** 75 **p** 75. C S Gillingham *Roch* 75-79; R Wateringbury w Teston and W Farleigh 79-92; rtd 92; PtO *Cant* 92-09; *Roch* 92-98 and 00-04. *5 Eynesford Road, Allington, Maidstone ME16 0TD* T: (01622) 661847

BISH, Jonathan James Peter. b 88. Ball Coll Ox BA 09 Peterho Cam BA 12. Westcott Ho Cam 10. **d** 13 **p** 14. C Halifax *Leeds* from 13. *12 Phoenix Court, Todmorden OL14 5SJ* M: 07535-495956 E: j.bish@halifaxminster.org.uk

BISHOP, Mrs Alice Margaret Marion. b 67. Newnham Coll Cam BA 89 MA 93 Lon Univ MTh 92. St Steph Ho Ox 92. **d** 94. C Stepney St Dunstan and All SS *Lon* 94-99. *6 Cathedral Close, Guildford GU2 7TL*

BISHOP, Canon Andrew Scott. b 70. Leeds Univ BA 93 Heythrop Coll Lon MTh 02 K Coll Lon DThMin 14. St Steph Ho Ox BTh 93. **d** 96 **p** 97. C Westmr St Steph w St Jo *Lon* 96-99; C Kensington St Mary Abbots w St Geo 99-03; V Old Basing and Lychpit *Win* 03-11; AD Basingstoke 08-11; Can Res Guildf Cathl from 11; Chapl Surrey Univ from 11. *6 Cathedral Close, Guildford GU2 7TL* T: (01483) 573805 E: as.bishop@tiscali.co.uk *or* a.bishop@surrey.ac.uk

BISHOP, Canon Anthony John. b 43. G&C Coll Cam BA 66 MA 69 Lon Univ MTh 69. ALCD 67. **d** 68 **p** 70. C Eccleston St Luke *Liv* 69-73; C Gt Baddow *Chelmsf* 73-77; CMS Nigeria 77-84; Lect Lon Bible Coll 84-85; TV Chigwell *Chelmsf* 85-93; P-in-c Walthamstow St Jo 93-98; V 98-09; rtd 09; Hon Can Kano from 00; PtO *Chelmsf* from 12. *7 High Meadows, Chigwell IG7 5JY* T: (020) 8501 4998 E: tony_bishop@talktalk.net

BISHOP, The Ven Anthony Peter. b 46. CB 01. Nottm Univ MPhil 84 ALCD 71 FRSA 87. St Jo Coll Nottm 71. **d** 71 **p** 72. C Beckenham St Geo *Roch* 71-75; Chapl RAF 75-91; Command Chapl RAF 91-98; Chapl-in-Chief RAF 98-01; Can and Preb Linc Cathl 98-01; Hon C Tewkesbury w Walton Cardiff and Twyning *Glouc* 01-03; C 03-06; rtd 06. *La Croix Blanche, 50810 St Germain d'Elle, France*

BISHOP, Canon Christopher. b 48. St Aug Coll Cant 71. **d** 72 **p** 73. C Gt Ilford St Mary *Chelmsf* 72-75; C Upminster 75-78; Adn's Youth Chapl 77-80; Dioc Youth Officer 80-86; Chapl Stansted Airport 86-13; P-in-c Manuden w Berden 86-03; P-in-c Manuden w Berden and Quendon w Rickling 03-13; RD Newport and Stansted 89-05; Hon Can Chelmsf Cathl 99-13; rtd 13; PtO *Chelmsf* from 14. *2 St Mary's View, Saffron Walden CB10 2GF* E: chrismitre@hotmail.com

BISHOP, Craig. See BISHOP, Stephen Craig

BISHOP, David. b 65. St Jo Coll Nottm 01. **d** 03 **p** 04. C Boulton *Derby* 03-07; V Ogley Hay *Lich* from 07. *St James's Vicarage, 37 New Road, Brownhills, Walsall WS8 6AT* T: (01543) 372187 *or* 373251

BISHOP, David Henry Ryder. b 27. MRAC 50. Tyndale Hall Bris 54. **d** 57 **p** 58. C Sevenoaks St Nic *Roch* 57-59; C Branksome St Clem *Sarum* 59-63; Chapl Jinja Uganda 64-67; Dep Sec CCCS 68; R Ox St Clem 69-91; Zimbabwe 91-93; rtd 93; PtO *Ox* from 99. *40 Old High Street, Headington, Oxford OX3 9HN* T: (01865) 760099 E: david.bishop@uwclub.net

BISHOP, Donald. b 22. Lon Univ BSc 48. Qu Coll Birm 56. **d** 57 **p** 58. C Trowbridge H Trin *Sarum* 57-60; CF (TA) 58-68; V Bodicote *Ox* 60-87; P-in-c Broughton 71-85; rtd 87; PtO *Cov* 87-01; *Leeds* from 01. *17 Westminster Road, Halifax HX3 8DH* T: (01422) 200844

BISHOP, Mrs Evelyn Joy. b 43. **d** 01 **p** 02. NSM Penkridge *Lich* 01-04; NSM Baswich from 04. *21 Farmdown Road, Stafford ST17 0AP* T: (01785) 603074

BISHOP, Huw Daniel. b 49. Univ of Wales (Lamp) BA 71. Bp Burgess Hall Lamp 71. **d** 73 **p** 74. C Carmarthen St Pet *St D* 73-77; Prov Youth Chapl Wales 77-79; V Llanybydder and Llanwnnen w Llanwnnen *St D* 79-80; Youth and Community Officer 80-81; Hd RS Carre's Gr Sch Sleaford 81-85; Hd RS K Sch Pet 85-91; Assoc Hd Teacher St Pet Colleg Sch Wolv 91-98; Hd Teacher St Teilo's High Sch Cardiff 98-01; Prin St Pet Colleg Sch Wolv 01-10; Asst Dioc Dir of Educn *Lich* 10-13; PtO from 11; *St D* 13-14; CF (TA) from 85. *Ger y Bryn, 217 Waterloo Road, Penygroes, Llanelli SA14 7RB*

BISHOP, The Ven Ian Gregory. b 62. Portsm Poly BSc 84 MRICS 87. Oak Hill Th Coll BA 91. **d** 91 **p** 92. C Purley Ch Ch *S'wark* 91-95; P-in-c Saxlingham Nethergate and Shotesham *Nor* 95-97; TR Newton Flotman, Swainsthorpe, Tasburgh, etc 98-01; V Middlewich w Byley *Ches* 01-11; RD Middlewich 05-10; Adn Macclesfield from 11. *57A Sandbach Road, Congleton CW12 4LH* T: (01260) 272875 M: 07715-102519 E: ian.bishop@chester.anglican.org

BISHOP, Jeffrey Paul. b 67. Texas A&M Univ BA 88 MD 93 Dallas Univ MTh 00. **d** 99 **p** 00. C Dallas Incarnation USA 99-05; PtO *Ex* 05-06; PV Ex Cathl 06-07; USA from 07. *1106 Lawrence Avenue, Nashville TN 37204, USA* T: (001) (615) 942 7074

BISHOP, Jeremy Simon. b 54. Nottm Univ BSc 75 Yonsei Univ S Korea 84. All Nations Chr Coll 82 Wycliffe Hall Ox 89. **d** 91 **p** 92. C Macclesfield Team *Ches* 91-98; R Carlton Colville w Mutford and Rushmere *Nor* 98-99; V Carlton Colville and Mutford from 99; RD Lothingland from 14. *The Rectory, Rectory Road, Carlton Colville, Lowestoft NR33 8BB* T: (01502) 565217 E: jbishop771@aol.com

BISHOP, John Charles Simeon. b 46. Chich Th Coll 77. **d** 79 **p** 79. SSF 66-86; P-in-c Edin St Dav 82-86; Chapl to the Deaf *Birm* 86-99; C Portsea N End St Mark *Portsm* 99-01; Chapl to the Deaf *Linc* 01-11; rtd 11; PtO *Dur* from 11. *7 Rowley Drive, Ushaw Moor, Durham DH7 7QR* T: 0191-373 0205 E: jcsbishop@btinternet.com

BISHOP, Kathleen Rachel. b 51. Open Univ BA 88 Saffron Walden Coll CertEd 76. ERMC 05. **d** 08 **p** 09. NSM Raddesley Gp *Ely* 08-12; NSM Balsham, Weston Colville, W Wickham etc from 12; NSM Gt w Lt Abington from 12; NSM Hildersham from 12. *4 The Woodlands, Linton, Cambridge CB21 4UF* T: (01223) 892288 E: revkathy@hotmail.co.uk *or* michael.bishop@virgin.net

BISHOP, Keith William. b 45. SEITE 00. **d** 03 **p** 04. NSM Balham St Mary and St Jo *S'wark* 03-07; NSM Clapham Common St Barn 07-12; rtd 12; PtO *Birm* from 12. *Address temp unknown* T: 0121-243 1020 E: keithwilliambishop@hotmail.com

BISHOP, Mandy Louise. b 61. Univ of E Lon BA 00. NTMTC BA 09. **d** 09 **p** 10. C Moulsham St Luke *Chelmsf* 09-13; V Ormesby St Marg w Scratby, Ormesby St Mich etc *Nor* from 13. *The Rectory, Church View, Ormesby, Great Yarmouth NR29 3PZ* T: (01493) 731917 M: 07854-790234 E: revdmandy@btinternet.com

BISHOP, Mark Andrew. b 58. Down Coll Cam BA 80 MA 83 Barrister 81. EAMTC 99. **d** 02 **p** 03. Dep Chan *Roch* from 01; NSM Cambridge St Mary Less *Ely* from 02. *10 Wordsworth Grove, Cambridge CB3 9HH* T: (01223) 362281 E: mark.bishop@btinternet.com

BISHOP, Mark Christopher. b 81. Sheff Hallam Univ BA 03. **d** 08 **p** 09. Roxeth *Lon* 06-08; C Oak Tree Angl Fellowship 08-11; LtO 11-14; Pioneer Min from 14. *19 Larch Avenue, London W3 7LH* M: 07779-585105 E: revmarkbishop@gmail.com

BISHOP, Philip Michael. b 47. Lon Univ BD 69 AKC 69. St Aug Coll Cant 70. **d** 71 **p** 72. C Mansfield Woodhouse *S'well* 71-76; C Liscard St Mary w St Columba *Ches* 76-78; V Thornton-le-Moors w Ince and Elton 78-90; V Sutton w Carlton and Normanton upon Trent etc *S'well* 90-96; P-in-c Ch Broughton w Barton Blount, Boylestone etc *Derby* 96-98; P-in-c Longford, Long Lane, Dalbury and Radbourne 96-98; R Boylestone, Church Broughton, Dalbury, etc from 98. *The Vicarage, Chapel Lane, Church Broughton, Derby DE65 5BB* T: (01283) 585296 E: rev@michaelbishop.name

BISHOP, Phillip Leslie. b 44. K Coll Lon BD 66 AKC 66. **d** 67 **p** 68. C Albrighton *Lich* 67-70; C St Geo-in-the-East St Mary *Lon* 70-71; C Middlesbrough Ascension *York* 71-73; P-in-c

Withernwick 73-77; Ind Chapl 73-82; V Gt Ayton w Easby and Newton-in-Cleveland 82-89; RD Stokesley 85-89; R Guisborough 89-08; Chapl S Tees Community and Mental NHS Trust 90-99; Chapl Tees and NE Yorks NHS Trust 99-08; Chapl Langbaurgh Primary Care Trust 02-08; rtd 08; PtO *York* from 08; *Dur* from 13. *2 Sunny Side Grove, Stockton-on-Tees TS18 5DH* T: (01642) 582281

BISHOP, Roger John. b 49. SEITE 06. **d** 09 **p** 10. NSM Lamberhurst and Matfield *Roch* from 09. *Brambletye, Maidstone Road, Five Oak Green, Tonbridge TN12 6QR* T: (01892) 833232 E: rogerjbishop@hotmail.com

BISHOP, Simeon. *See* BISHOP, John Charles Simeon

BISHOP, Stephen Craig. b 68. Wye Coll Lon BSc 90 Man Univ MA 92 Ex Univ MPhil 97 Glos Univ PGCE 98. Wycliffe Hall Ox 03. **d** 05 **p** 06. C Thornbury and Oldbury-on-Severn w Shepperdine *Glouc* 05-09; TV S Cotswolds 09-14; V Chipping Campden w Ebrington from 14. *The Vicarage, Church Street, Chipping Campden GL55 6JG* T: (01386) 840677 E: scraigbishop@hotmail.com

BISHOP, Stephen John. b 62. Hull Univ BA 84 PGCE 86. Ripon Coll Cuddesdon 90 Ch Div Sch of the Pacific (USA) 90. **d** 92 **p** 93. C Syston *Leic* 92-95; C Market Harborough 95-97; TV Market Harborough and The Transfiguration etc 97-00; R Six Saints circa Holt from 00; Rural Officer (Leic Adnry) from 01. *The Rectory, Rectory Lane, Medbourne, Market Harborough LE16 8DZ* T: (01858) 565933 E: stephenjbishop@openworld.com

BISHOP, Stephen Patrick. b 60. Dioc OLM tr scheme 99. **d** 02 **p** 03. OLM Purley Ch Ch S'wark from 02. *Elmwood, 117 Mitchley Avenue, South Croydon CR2 9HP* T: (020) 8651 2840 E: bishopelmwood@aol.com

BISHOP, Mrs Susan Linda. b 66. Trin Coll Bris 12. **d** 15. NSM Filton *Bris* from 15. *Address temp unknown*

BISHOP, Miss Waveney Joyce. b 38. Westf Coll Lon BSc 60. Cranmer Hall Dur. **dss** 82 **d** 87 **p** 94. Hon Par Dn Bishopsworth *Bris* 87-94; Hon C 94-96; rtd 96; PtO *Bris* 96-99; B & W from 98. *14 Saxby Close, Clevedon BS21 7YF* T: (01275) 343533

BISIG (*née* BOULNOIS), Linda Dianne. b 59. Trin Coll Bris 92. **d** 96 **p** 97. C Brampton Bierlow *Sheff* 96-99; Asst Chapl Berne w Neuchâtel *Eur* from 00. *Jubiläumsplatz 2, CH-3066 Berne, Switzerland* T: (0041) (31) 352 8567 F: 351 0548

BISSET, Michael Davidson. b 55. NTMTC 96. **d** 99 **p** 00. C Ickenham *Lon* 99-03; P-in-c Penn *Ox* 03-04; P-in-c Tyler's Green 03-04; V Penn and Tylers Green from 04. *The Vicarage, Church Road, Penn, High Wycombe HP10 8NU* T: (01895) 676092 E: mike.bisset@talk21.com

BISSEX, Mrs Janet Christine Margaret. b 50. Westhill Coll Birm CertEd 72. Trin Coll Bris 76. **dss** 86 **d** 87 **p** 94. Netherton *Liv* 78-83; Toxteth Park St Bede 86-93; Par Dn 87-93; Dn-in-c Kirkdale St Mary and St Athanasius 93-94; P-in-c 94-03; C Litherland St Andr 03; TV Bootle 04-12; rtd 12. *4 Garth Court, Haigh Road, Liverpool L22 3XL* T: 0151-538 4767 E: revjanetb@yahoo.co.uk

BISSON, Joyce Elaine. b 52. Liv Univ BTh 98 Nottm Coll of Educn TCert 73. NOC 06. **d** 08 **p** 09. NSM Gt Meols *Ches* 08-11; NSM Bromborough from 11. *14 Howbeck Drive, Prenton CH43 6UY* T: 0151-652 7888 E: elainebisson@yahoo.co.uk

BLACK, Canon Alexander Stevenson. b 28. Glas Univ MA 53. Edin Th Coll 53. **d** 55 **p** 56. C Dumfries *Glas* 55-58; Chapl Glas Univ 58-61; C Glas St Mary 58-61; P-in-c E Kilbride 61-69; R Edin St Columba 69-79; TV Edin St Jo 79-83; R Haddington 83-93; R Dunbar 83-93; rtd 93; Can St Mary's Cathl 88-00; Hon Can St Mary's Cathl from 00. *3 Bass Rock View, Canty Bay, North Berwick EH39 5PJ* T: (01620) 894771 E: alexander3black@btinternet.com

BLACK, David Roger. b 46. **d** 12 **p** 13. NSM Tattenhall w Burwardsley and Handley *Ches* 12-14; NSM Tilston and Shocklach from 14. *Woodcroft, Church Road, Tilston, Malpas SY14 7HB* T: (01829) 250615

BLACK, Dominic Paul. b 70. S Bank Univ BSc 95 St Jo Coll Dur BA 98 MA 11. Cranmer Hall Dur 95. **d** 98 **p** 99. C N Hull St Mich *York* 98-04; V N Ormesby from 04; RD Middlesbrough from 11. *The Vicarage, James Street, North Ormesby, Middlesbrough TS3 6LD* T: (01642) 271814 *or* 961898 M: 07445-395806 E: dominic.black@trinitycentre.org

BLACK, Douglas John. b 58. Middx Poly BA 80. Ridley Hall Cam 89. **d** 91 **p** 92. C Wrexham *St As* 91-01; Chapl NE Wales Inst of HE 93-01; V Thelwall *Ches* from 02. *All Saints' Vicarage, Bell Lane, Thelwall, Warrington WA4 2SX* T: (01925) 261166 E: revdouglasblack@aol.com

BLACK, Canon Ian Christopher. b 62. Kent Univ BA 85 Nottm Univ MDiv 93. Linc Th Coll 91. **d** 93 **p** 94. C Maidstone All SS and St Phil w Tovil *Cant* 93-96; P-in-c The Brents and Davington w Oare and Luddenham 96-02; Hon Min Can Cant

Cathl 97-02; Asst Dir Post-Ord Tr 98-02; V Whitkirk *Ripon* 02-12; Capitular Can *Ripon* Cathl 08-12; Can Res Pet Cathl from 12; V Pet St Jo from 12; RD Pet from 15. *26 Minster Precincts, Peterborough PE1 1XZ* T: (01733) 873064 E: canonianblack@btinternet.com

BLACK, Ian Forbes. b 29. St Aid Birkenhead 55. **d** 58 **p** 59. C Bramhall *Ches* 58-61; C Witton 61-63; P-in-c Prestonpans *Edin* 63-68; R Edin Ch Ch-St Jas 68-71; Asst Chapl HM Pris Liv 71-72; Chapl HM Pris Haverigg 72-73; R Bootle w Corney *Carl* 73-75; P-in-c Whicham w Whitbeck 73-75; R Bootle, Corney, Whicham and Whitbeck 75-86; P-in-c Orton St Giles 86-89; R 89-94; P-in-c Aikton 86-89; R 89-94; rtd 94; PtO *Carl* from 98. *Solwayside, Port Carlisle, Wigton CA7 5BU* T: (016973) 51964

BLACK, Miss Imogen Nadine Laura. b 79. Trin Coll Ox BA 02 MA 05 MSt 03. St Steph Ho Ox 08. **d** 11 **p** 12. C Belper Ch Ch w Turnditch *Derby* from 11. *26 Leighton Way, Belper DE56 1SX* T: (01773) 880918 E: imogen.black@trinity-oxford.com *or* curate@christchurchbelper.org.uk

BLACK (formerly NAPIER), Jennifer Beryl. b 39. S Dios Minl Tr Scheme 89. **d** 93 **p** 96. NSM Itchen Valley *Win* 93-01; PtO from 02; Hon C Cupar *St And* from 05. *Forresters Cottage, Edenwood, Cupar KY15 5NX* T: (01334) 653159 *or* (01962) 771702 E: jenniblackedenwood@yahoo.co.uk

BLACK, Canon Neville. b 36. MBE 97. Oak Hill Th Coll 61. **d** 64 **p** 65. C Everton St Ambrose w St Tim *Liv* 64-69; P-in-c Everton St Geo 69-71; V 71-81; P-in-c Everton St Benedict 70-72; P-in-c Everton St Chad w Ch Ch 70-72; Nat Project Officer Evang Urban Tr Project 74-81; TR St Luke in the City *Liv* 81-04; Chapl Liv Women's Hosp NHS Trust 82-04; Tutor NOC 82-89; Dir Gp for Urban Min and Leadership *Liv* 84-95; Hon Can Liv Cathl 87-04; P-in-c Edgehill St Dunstan 98-02; rtd 05. *19 Montfort Drive, Liverpool L19 3RJ* T: 07699-727640 (pager) E: neville.black@btinternet.com

BLACK, Canon Robert John Edward Francis Butler. b 41. TCD BA 65 HDipEd 70 MA 85. CITC 66. **d** 66 **p** 67. C Jordanstown *Conn* 66-68; C Dublin St Steph and St Ann *D & G* 68-73; C Stillorgan w Blackrock 73-85; Hd Master Dundalk Gr Sch *Arm* 85-96; LtO from 85; Hd Master Kilkenny Coll *C & O* from 96; Can Ossory Cathl from 96. *10 Carysfort Wood, Blackrock, Co. Dublin, Republic of Ireland* T/F: (00353) (01) 2780300 E: robertblack05@eircom.net

BLACK, Samuel James. b 38. CITC. **d** 68 **p** 69. C Cloughfern *Conn* 68-72; C Lisburn St Paul 72-78; I Rasharkin w Finvoy 78-82; I Belfast Upper Malone (Epiphany) 82-95; I Ballymore *Arm* 95-05; rtd 05. *Toberhewny Hall, 22 Toberhewny Lane, Lurgan, Craigavon BT66 8JZ* T: (028) 3834 3267

BLACK, William Henry. St Deiniol's Hawarden. **d** 88 **p** 89. NSM Malahide w Balgriffin *D & G* 88-89; NSM Dublin St Ann and St Steph 89-94; C 94-00; Hon Asst Chapl Miss to Seamen 89-00; I Dublin Drumcondra w N Strand *D & G* 00-07; rtd 07. *27 Greendale Avenue, Dublin 5, Republic of Ireland* T: (00353) (1) 832 3141 M: 86-150 3747 E: willieblack@eircom.net

BLACKALL, Mrs Margaret Ivy. b 38. St Kath Coll Lon CertEd 58. EAMTC 82. **dss** 86 **d** 87 **p** 94. NSM Wickham Market w Pettistree and Easton *St E* 86-88; Par Dn Leiston 88-92; Par Dn Gt and Lt Glemham, Blaxhall etc 92-94; P-in-c 94-96; R 96-02; P-in-c Sternfield w Benhall and Snape 98-02; rtd 03; PtO *St E* from 03. *6 Orchard Place, Wickham Market, Woodbridge IP13 0RU* T: (01728) 747326 M: 07850-632900 E: mgtblack@globalnet.co.uk

BLACKALL, Robin Jeremy McRae. b 35. Ridley Hall Cam 67. **d** 69 **p** 70. C Stowmarket *St E* 69-72; R Stanstead w Shimplingthorne and Alpheton 72-77; R Bradwell on Sea *Chelmsf* 77-79; R St Lawrence 77-79; Warden Bede Ho Staplehurst 79-81; Chapl HM Det Cen Blantyre Ho 81-82; R Edith Weston w N Luffenham and Lyndon w Manton *Pet* 86-95; P-in-c Upwell St Pet *Ely* 95-99; P-in-c Outwell 95-99; Dioc Rural Miss Officer 95-01; P-in-c Barton Bendish w Beachamwell and Shingham 99-01; P-in-c Boughton 99-01; P-in-c Wereham 99-01; rtd 01; PtO *Ely* from 01; *Nor* from 02. *The Pightle House, Eastmoor Road, Eastmoor, King's Lynn PE33 9PZ* T: (01366) 328663 F: 328163 E: rjmb@globalnet.co.uk

BLACKALL, Susan Elizabeth. b 52. Qu Univ Kingston Ontario BA 74 MA 75 CCC Ox DPhil 82. SEITE 00. **d** 03 **p** 04. NSM Eltham St Barn S'wark 03-12; NSM Greenwich St Alfege from 12; Asst Chapl Greenwich Univ from 12; Asst Chapl RN Coll Greenwich from 12; Dir Ords Woolwich Area S'wark from 13. *8 Park Place House, Park Vista, London SE10 9ND* T: (020) 8853 3302 *or* 7916 5000 E: s.blackall@research-int.com

BLACKBURN, Anne Dorothy. *See* WOOD, Anne Dorothy

BLACKBURN, David James. b 45. Hull Univ BA 67. Trin Coll Bris 85. **d** 87 **p** 88. C Bromsgrove St John *Worc* 87-90; V Cradley 90-01; R Kinver and Enville *Lich* 01-12; rtd 12. *39 Milestone Drive, Hagley, Stourbridge DY9 0LW* T: (01562) 720389 E: blackburn337@btinternet.com

BLACKBURN, Helen Claire. b 55. Leeds Univ BA 76 MA 99 PGCE 78 ARCM 75. NOC 96. **d** 99 **p** 00. C Sheff Cathl 99-01; Asst Chapl Cen Sheff Univ Hosps NHS Trust 01-04; Chapl Sheff Teaching Hosps NHS Trust 04-06; C Ranmoor *Sheff* 06-07; P-in-c Abbeydale St Jo 07-09; Lead Chapl Willowbrook Hospice 10-13; TR E Widnes *Liv* from 13. *Bishop's House, 34 Central Avenue, Eccleston Park, Prescot L34 2QP* T: 0151-426 1897 M: 07714-329638 E: helen_blackburn@hotmail.co.uk

BLACKBURN, Jane Elizabeth. *See* PROUDFOOT, Jane Elizabeth

BLACKBURN, The Ven John. b 47. CB 04. Open Univ BA 88. St Mich Coll Llan 66. **d** 71 **p** 72. C Risca *Mon* 71-76; CF (TA) 73-76; CF 76-99; Dep Chapl Gen 99-00; Chapl Gen 00-04; Adn for the Army 99-04; QHC from 96; Hon Can Ripon Cathl 01-04; V Risca *Mon* 04-13; V Lower Islwyn 13; rtd 13; PtO *S & B* from 14. *St Hilary, 11 Gelli Avenue, Risca, Newport NP11 6QF* E: northmanor@btinternet.com

BLACKBURN, Sister Judith Elizabeth. b 58. SEITE 99. **d** 02 **p** 03. NSM Old Ford St Paul and St Mark *Lon* 02-05; P-in-c Bethnal Green St Pet w St Thos 05-11; NSM Bethnal Green St Matt w St Jas the Gt from 11. *St Saviour's Priory, 18 Queensbridge Road, London E2 8NX* T: (020) 7739 9976 M: 07855-510393 E: judithblackburn@aol.com

BLACKBURN, Keith Christopher. b 39. K Coll Lon BD 63 AKC 63. St Boniface Warminster 63. **d** 64 **p** 65. C Surbiton St Andr *S'wark* 64-66; C Battersea St Mary 67-70; Teacher Sir Walter St John Sch Battersea 67-70; Hon C Eltham H Trin *S'wark* 70-76; Hd of Ho Crown Woods Sch Eltham 70-76; Dep Hd Master Altwood C of E Sch 76-82; Chapl and Hd Master St Geo Sch Gravesend 83-93; Hon C Fawkham and Hartley *Roch* 83-93; V Seal SS Pet and Paul 93-05; rtd 05; PtO *Heref* from 05. *7 Riverview Court, Bridge Street, Hereford HR4 9BQ* T: (01432) 278399 E: revkcb@aol.com

BLACKBURN, Peter James Whittaker. b 47. Sydney Univ BA 69. Coll of Resurr Mirfield. **d** 72 **p** 73. C Felixstowe St Jo *St E* 72-76; C Bournemouth St Pet w St Swithun, H Trin etc *Win* 76-79; R Burythorpe, Acklam and Leavening w Westow *York* 79-85; Chapl Naples Ch Ch *Eur* 85-91; Chapl Algarve 91-97; PtO *Lon* 07-09; Hon C Hampstead Ch Ch from 09. *8 Hampstead Square, London NW3 1AB* T: (020) 7435 5818 E: peter.blackburn@virgilio.it

✠**BLACKBURN, The Rt Revd Richard Finn.** b 52. St Jo Coll Dur BA 74 Hull Univ MA 97. Westcott Ho Cam 81. **d** 83 **p** 84 **c** 09. C Stepney St Dunstan and All SS *Lon* 83-87; P-in-c Isleworth St Jo 87-92; V Mosbrough *Sheff* 92-99; RD Attercliffe 96-99; Hon Can Sheff Cathl 98-99; Adn Sheff and Rotherham 99-09; Can Res Sheff Cathl 99-05; Suff Bp Warrington *Liv* from 09. *Bishop's House, 34 Central Avenue, Eccleston Park, Prescot L34 2QP* T: 0151-705 2140 F: 709 2885 E: bishopofwarrington@liverpool.anglican.org

BLACKBURN, Archdeacon of. *See* HAWLEY, The Ven John Andrew

BLACKBURN, Bishop of. *See* HENDERSON, The Rt Revd Julian Tudor

BLACKBURN, Dean of. *See* ARMSTRONG, The Very Revd Christopher John

BLACKDEN, Mrs Diane Janice. b 40. **d** 06. NSM Buxted and Hadlow Down *Chich* from 06. *Oak Hill, Five Ashes, Mayfield TN20 6HL* T: (01435) 872082

BLACKER, Herbert John. b 36. Bris Univ BSc 59. Cranmer Hall Dur. **d** 61 **p** 62. C Wednesbury St Bart *Lich* 61-63; C Chasetown 63-65; C Chigwell *Chelmsf* 65-69; TV Barnham Broom w Kimberley, Bixton etc *Nor* 69-76; R Burgh Parva w Briston 76-92; P-in-c Melton Constable w Swanton Novers 86-92; R Briston w Burgh Parva and Melton Constable 92-01; rtd 01; PtO *Nor* from 01; *St E* from 04. *8 Lloyds Avenue, Kessingland, Lowestoft NR33 7TP* T: (01502) 742232

BLACKETT, James Gilbert. b 27. Tyndale Hall Bris 52. **d** 55 **p** 56. C Heworth H Trin *York* 55-57; C Newburn *Newc* 57-58; C Newc St Barn and St Jude 58-61; V Broomfleet *York* 61-67; V Ledsham 67-74; V Burton All SS *Lich* 74-82; V Burton All SS w Ch Ch 82-92; rtd 92; PtO *Ox* 92-11; *Pet* from 92. *103 Milford Avenue, Stony Stratford, Milton Keynes MK11 1EZ* T: (01908) 265149

BLACKETT, Robert Peter. b 63. Dur Univ BSc 85 Open Univ BSc 07. Ripon Coll Cuddesdon BTh 95. **d** 95 **p** 96. C Wigton *Carl* 95-00; R Bowness-on-Solway, Kirkbride and Newton Arlosh from 00. *The Rectory, Church Road, Kirkbride, Carlisle CA7 5HY* T: (01697) 351256

BLACKFORD, Barry Douglas. b 52. Southn Inst BSc 96 MCMI 00 MBCS 04. STETS 05. **d** 08 **p** 09. C N Poole Ecum Team *Sarum* 08-12; TV Melksham 12-14; TR from 14. *The Rectory, Canon Square, Melksham SN12 6LX* T: (01225) 709083 M: 07866-430428 E: revbar@hotmail.com

BLACKIE, Richard Footner (Brother Edmund). b 37. St Cath Coll Cam BA 59 MA 63 Worc Coll Ox BA 59 BSc 61. Ely Th Coll 60. **d** 62 **p** 63. C Saffron Walden *Chelmsf* 62-65; SSF from

66. *Society of St Francis, 42 Balaam Street, London E13 8AQ* T: (020) 7476 5189

BLACKLEDGE, David John. b 51. Oak Hill Th Coll 89. **d** 92 **p** 93. NSM Woodford Wells *Chelmsf* from 92. *Hornbeam, 143 Monkhams Lane, Woodford Green IG8 0NW* T: (020) 8262 7690 E: davidjblackledge@aol.com

BLACKLEDGE, Philip Vincent Patrick. b 74. Edin Univ BMus 92 BD 02. TISEC 99. **d** 02 **p** 03. C Edin St Mary 02-06; Chapl St Mary's Cathl 03-06; P-in-c Linlithgow 06-11; P-in-c Bathgate 06-11; C Edin Ch Ch 12-13; R Melrose from 13. *Holy Trinity Rectory, 20 High Cross Avenue, Melrose TD6 9SU* E: philipblackledge@aol.com

BLACKLEY, Miles. b 69. Wycliffe Hall Ox. **d** 05 **p** 06. C Ches Square St Mich w St Phil *Lon* 05-08; C St Olave Hart Street w All Hallows Staining etc 08-10; C St Kath Cree 08-10; PtO *S'wark* from 11. *22 Assembly Apartments, 24 York Grove, London SE15 2NZ* E: milesblackley@hotmail.com

BLACKMAN, Brian David Eric. b 38. Ox NSM Course 82. **d** 85 **p** 86. NSM Reading St Luke *Ox* 85-86; NSM Reading St Luke w St Bart 86-08; PtO from 08. *13 Avebury Square, Reading RG1 5JH* T: 0118-926 0345

BLACKMAN (née PRATT), Christine Fiona. b 60. Reading Univ BSc 81. Ox Min Course 88. **d** 91 **p** 94. NSM Reading St Luke w St Bart *Ox* 91-94 and from 95; NSM Earley St Pet 94-95. *13 Avebury Square, Reading RG1 5JH* T: 0118-926 0345

BLACKMAN, Clive John. b 51. Hull Univ BSc 73 MSc 74. Qu Coll Birm 75. **d** 78 **p** 79. C Folkestone St Sav *Cant* 78-81; Chapl Birm Univ 81-86; V Thorpe St Matt *Nor* 86-94; R Cringleford w Colney and Bawburgh 94-98; Asst Dir Lay and Reader Tr 98-03; Dir Reader Tr 03-11; Chapl Nor City Coll of F&HE 03-15; rtd 15. *13 Norvic Drive, Norwich NR4 7NN* T: (01603) 505776 or 773538 E: cblackman@ccn.ac.uk

BLACKMAN, Michael Orville. b 46. Univ of W Ontario BMin 80. Codrington Coll Barbados 67. **d** 71 **p** 71. C St Jo Cathl Antigua 71-73; R H Innocents w St Sav Barbados 73-78; Hon C Westminster St Jas Canada 78-80; P-in-c St Patr Barbados 80-86; TV E Ham w Upton Park and Forest Gate *Chelmsf* 86-91; R St Pet Barbados 91-97; V Dalton *Sheff* 97-03; P-in-c Raynes Park St Sav *S'wark* 03-10; P-in-c S Wimbledon All SS 03-10; V Raynes Park St Sav and S Wimbledon All SS from 10. *St Saviour's Vicarage, Church Walk, London SW20 9DG* T: (020) 8542 2787 E: michael.blackman1@btopenworld.com

BLACKMAN, Peter Richard. b 28. Sarum Th Coll 52. **d** 55 **p** 56. C Aylestone *Leic* 55-60; V Ratby cum Groby 60-84; TR 84-93; rtd 93; PtO *Chich* from 93. *25 Turnbull Road, Chichester PO19 7LY* T: (01243) 787299

BLACKMORE, Frank Ellis. b 43. Univ of Wales (Lamp) BA 66. Wells Th Coll 65. **d** 67 **p** 68. C S'wark St Geo 67-70; Hon C Camberwell St Giles 70-79; NSM Paddington St Sav *Lon* 79-01. *35 Leith Mansions, Grantully Road, London W9 1LH* T: (020) 7289 3020 E: ellisblackmore@btinternet.com

BLACKMORE, Robert Ivor. b 37. Univ of Wales (Lamp) 59 Open Univ BA 78 Univ of Wales MTh 94. **d** 62 **p** 63. C Llangynwyd w Maesteg *Llan* 62-65; C Dowlais 65-67; C Neath w Llantwit 67-71; V Fochriw w Deri 71-73; V Troedrhiwgarth 73-80; V Seven Sisters 80-00; rtd 02. *28 Hen Parc Lane, Upper Killay, Swansea SA2 7EY*

BLACKMORE, Vernon John. b 50. Southn Univ BSc Man Univ MSc K Coll Lon MTh. Oak Hill Th Coll. **d** 82 **p** 83. C Ecclesall *Sheff* 82-87; Bp's Adv on Youth 87-90; Ed Lion Publishing 87-90; Dir Publications, Tr and Sales CPAS 90-99. *6 Guy Street, Warwick CV34 4LN* T: (01926) 498351

BLACKSHAW, Brian Martin. b 43. Lanc Univ MA 74 Ch Ch Ox BA 95 MA 96. Ox NSM Course 87. **d** 90 **p** 91. NSM Amersham *Ox* 90-93; C Hatch End St Anselm *Lon* 93-95; V Cheshunt St Alb 96-07; rtd 07; PtO *St Alb* from 13; *Lon* from 13. *Holly Bush, Flaunden Lane, Flaunden, Hemel Hempstead HP3 0PQ* T: (01442) 832254 E: brianblackshaw@f2s.com

BLACKSHAW, Trevor Roland. b 36. GIMechE 59. Lon Coll of Div 67. **d** 69 **p** 70. C New Catton St Luke *Nor* 69-73; C Luton Lewsey St Hugh *St Alb* 73-78; V Llandinam w Trefeglwys w Penstrowed *Ban* 78-85; Dioc Dir of Adult Educn 83-85; Consultant Dir Wholeness Through Ch Min 86-92; Midl Regional Co-ord Crosslinks 92-97; Dir and Warden Divine Healing Miss Crowhurst 97-02; rtd 02; PtO *Lich* 04-06 and from 07; P-in-c Weston Rhyn and Selattyn 06-07. *28 Regent Court, Roft Street, Oswestry SY11 2BU* T: (01691) 659645 E: trevor@blackshawt.freeserve.co.uk

BLACKSTONE, James Christopher. b 75. Peterho Cam BA 97. Westcott Ho Cam 06. **d** 10 **p** 11. C Eltham H Trin *S'wark* 10-14; PtO from 14. *St Paul's School, 80 Lonsdale Road, London SW13 9JT* T: (020) 8748 9162 E: jim.blackstone47@gmail.com

BLACKTOP, Graham Leonard. b 33. St Alb Minl Tr Scheme 82. **d** 85 **p** 86. NSM Rickmansworth *St Alb* 85-92; PtO *Sarum* 92-15. *Dairy House, Wolfeton, Dorchester DT2 9QN* T/F: (01305) 262184

BLACKWALL, David d'Arcy Russell. b 35. Southn Univ BSc 60. Wycliffe Hall Ox 63. **d** 65 **p** 66. C Southampton Thornhill St Chris *Win* 65-68; V Long Sutton 69-72; Chapl Lord Wandsworth Coll Hook 69-74; Hon C Odiham w S Warnborough *Win* 72-75; Chapl St Lawr Coll Ramsgate 75-95; Hd Jun Sch 95-97; rtd 97; PtO *Sarum* from 98. *3 Constable Way, Salisbury SP2 8LN* T: (01722) 335695

BLACKWELL, Geoffrey Albert. b 27. Lon Coll of Div 62. **d** 65 **p** 66. C Clifton *York* 65-69; Chapl RN 69-73; Warden St Mich Home of Healing Cleadon 73-75; V S Hetton *Dur* 75-82; CSWG 83-94; P-in-c Burpham *Chich* 95-96; rtd 96; PtO *Chich* 96-05. *1 Highfield Gardens, Rustington, Littlehampton BN16 2PZ* T: (01903) 782219

BLACKWELL, Nicholas Alfred John. b 54. Warwick Univ MA 97. St Jo Coll Nottm BTh 85. **d** 85 **p** 86. C Birkenhead Priory *Ches* 85-88; C Stratford-on-Avon w Bishopton *Cov* 88-91; TV Cov E 91-98. *74 Brays Lane, Coventry CV2 4DW* T: (024) 7626 1161 E: nblackwell54@gmail.com

BLACKWELL-SMYTH, Charles Peter Bernard. b 42. TCD BA 64 MA 71 MB 73. Gen Th Sem (NY) MDiv 65. **d** 65 **p** 66. C Bangor Abbey *D & D* 65-67; C Dublin Ch Ch Leeson Park *D & G* 67-69; P-in-c Carbury *M & K* 73-75; Hon C St Stephen in Brannel *Truro* 87-94; PtO from 94. *Parcgwyn, Rectory Road, St Stephen, St Austell PL26 7RL* T: (01726) 822465

BLACOE, Brian Thomas. b 36. Open Univ BA. Oak Hill Th Coll 63. **d** 66 **p** 67. C Dundonald *D & D* 66-69; C Drumcree *Arm* 69-74; I Ardtrea w Desertcreat 74-78; I Annalong *D & D* 78-95; I Knocknamuckley 95-08; Can Dromore Cathl 93-08; Prec 02-08; rtd 08. *91 Richmond Drive, Tandragee, Craigavon BT62 2GW* T: (028) 3884 2029 M: 07745-564056 E: elizabeth.blacoe@gmail.com

BLADE, Brian Alan. b 24. ACCS 55 ASCA 66. Roch Th Coll 67. **d** 69 **p** 70. C Barnehurst *Roch* 69-71; C Crayford 71-76; V Buttershaw St Aid *Bradf* 76-80; R Etton w Helpston *Pet* 80-86; V Hardingstone and Horton and Piddington 86-90; rtd 90; PtO *Cant* 90-12; *Roch* from 90. *25 Dan Drive, Faversham ME13 7SW* T: (01795) 531842 E: revbrianblade@tesco.net

BLADE, Mrs Susan Joan. b 58. SEITE 97. **d** 00 **p** 01. NSM Wateringbury and Teston *Roch* 00-02; Asst Chapl Maidstone and Tunbridge Wells NHS Trust 00-02; Sen Chapl 02-06; Chapl Cant Ch Ch Univ 07-10; P-in-c Sampford Peverell, Uplowman, Holcombe Rogus etc *Ex* 10-11; TR from 11. *The Rectory, Blackdown View, Sampford Peverell, Tiverton EX16 7BE* T: (01884) 829461 E: sue.blade@gmail.com

BLADEN, Mrs Catherine Robin. b 64. ERMC 12. **d** 15. C Sancroft *St E* from 15. *4 Samuel Vince Road, Fressingfield, Eye IP21 5SP* M: 07939-469805 E: cathybladen@hotmail.com

BLAGDEN, Ms Susan. b 64. Ox Min Course 89 Ripon Coll Cuddesdon 97. **d** 99 **p** 00. C Grantham *Linc* 99-03; Asst Chapl Stoke Mandeville Hosp NHS Trust 03-10; R Bangor Monachorum, Worthenbury and Marchwiel *St As* 10-12; R Bro Enlli *Ban* 12-14; Dir of Ords from 14; C Dwylan from 14. *The Rectory, Llanllechid, Bangor LL57 3SD* E: blagdensm@gmail.com

BLAGG, Colin. b 31. Leeds Univ BA 57. Coll of Resurr Mirfield 57. **d** 59 **p** 60. C Edin Old St Paul 59-63; R Gourock *Glas* 63-68; Chapl to the Deaf RADD Lon 68-74; Hon C Stoke Newington St Olave *Lon* 73-74; Chapl to the Deaf *Chich* 74-80; V Shoreham Beach 80-96; rtd 97; PtO *Chich* from 97. *5 Broomfield Way, Felpham, Bognor Regis PO22 8AQ* T: (01243) 582742

BLAIN, Anne Sharon. b 46. RGN 89. Dioc OLM tr scheme 98. **d** 01 **p** 02. OLM Tadworth *S'wark* from 01. *Watts Cottage, Watts Lane, Tadworth KT20 5RW* T: (01737) 355347 F: 351546 M: 07811-267238 E: breusis@aol.com

BLAINE, Alastair John Park. b 79. Westmr Coll of Educn BEd 03. Ripon Coll Cuddesdon 11. **d** 13 **p** 14. C Witney *Ox* from 13. *14 Rissington Drive, Witney OX28 5FG* T: (01993) 359756 M: 07855-797477 E: rev.alastair.blaine@gmail.com

BLAIR, Mrs Catherine Jill. b 62. Nottm Univ BA 84 BArch 87 RIBA 88. St Jo Coll Nottm MA 02. **d** 02 **p** 03. C Goldsworth Park *Guildf* 02-06; C Woking St Paul from 06; RD Woking from 10. *St Paul's Vicarage, Pembroke Road, Woking GU22 7ED* T: (01483) 850489 E: cathy@stpaulswoking.org.uk

BLAIR, Henry. *See* BLAIR, William Henry

BLAIR, Canon John Wallace. b 48. Lon Univ BSc 70. Qu Coll Birm 79. **d** 81 **p** 82. C Chorlton-cum-Hardy St Werburgh *Man* 81-83; CF 83-97; I Faughanvale *D & R* 97-13; Can Derry Cathl 09-13; rtd 13; Chapl Madeira *Eur* from 14. *The Parsonage, Holy Trinity, 18 rua do Quebra Costas, 9000 Funchal, Madeira* T: (00351) (291) 220674

BLAIR, Jonathan Lewis. b 62. Nottm Univ BA 84 ACA 88. St Jo Coll Nottm. **d** 02 **p** 03. C Goldsworth Park *Guildf* 02-06; P-in-c Woking St Paul from 06. *St Paul's Vicarage, Pembroke Road, Woking GU22 7ED* T: (01483) 850489 *or* 888611 E: jonny.blair@tiscali.co.uk *or* jonny@stpaulswoking.org.uk

BLAIR, Philip Hugh. b 39. St Edm Hall Ox BA 62 MA 67 Ex Univ DipEd 75 PhD 84. Ridley Hall Cam 62. **d** 64 **p** 65. C Camborne *Truro* 64-68; C Kenwyn 68-70; Sudan 70-73; P-in-c Probus *Truro* 73-74; P-in-c St Enoder 74-75; PtO Cyprus and the Gulf 90-94; rtd 04. *St Martin's, 121 Newland, Sherborne DT9 3DU* T/F: (01935) 816022 E: philip@philipblair.net

BLAIR, Canon William Henry. b 66. QUB BAgr 89 TCD BTh 04. CITC 01. **d** 04 **p** 05. C Monaghan w Tydavnet and Kilmore Clogh 04-06; C Magheraculmoney 06-11; I from 11; Can Clogh Cathl from 15. *The Rectory, 47 Main Street, Kesh, Enniskillen BT93 1TF* T: (028) 6863 1820 E: henry@ardess.org

BLAIR-CHAPPELL, Mrs Elcineide. b 47. Sao Paulo Univ Brazil 74 Birm Poly PGCE 88. WMMTC 00. **d** 03 **p** 04. NSM Erdington *Birm* from 03; NSM Birm St Martin w Bordesley St Andr from 08; Hon Chapl Birm Children's Hosp NHS Trust from 07. *18 Kempson Avenue, Sutton Coldfield B72 1HJ* T: 0121-682 5340

BLAKE, Colin David. b 52. Rolle Coll CertEd Ex Univ BEd Lon Univ BD. Trin Coll Bris 81. **d** 84 **p** 85. C Hucclecote *Glouc* 84-88; C Patchway and Min Bradley Stoke N CD *Bris* 88-00; TV Worle *B & W* 00-09; Miss P Bradf Adnry *Leeds* 09-14; Adv in Fresh Expressions Min 09-14; V Wrose *Bradf* from 14. *The Vicarage, Wrose Road, Bradford BD2 1LN* E: colinblake1@gmail.com

BLAKE, Ian Martyn. b 57. Oak Hill Th Coll BA 79. **d** 80 **p** 81. C Widford *Chelmsf* 80-84; C Barton Seagrave w Warkton *Pet* 84-90; V Sneinton St Chris w St Phil *S'well* 90-01; C Howell Hill w Burgh Heath *Guildf* 01-06; PtO 06-12; *S'wark* 08-12; P-in-c Thornton Heath St Paul from 12. *St Paul's Church, St Paul's Road, Thornton Heath CR7 8NB* T: (020) 8643 2817 M: 07904-340783 E: revdimblake@gmail.com

BLAKE, Ms Katharine Naomi. b 67. Southn Univ BA 89. Westcott Ho Cam 09. **d** 11 **p** 12. C Pinner Lon 11-14; V Queensbury All SS from 14. *The Vicarage, 24 Waltham Drive, Edgware HA8 5PQ* T: (020) 8952 4536 E: kate@kateandtony.org.uk

BLAKE, Mrs Margaret. b 48. Open Univ BA 87. S'wark Ord Course 92. **d** 95 **p** 96. C Farnham *Guildf* 95-01; P-in-c Farncombe 01-05; R 05-09; rtd 09. *Tan-y-Llan, Llanfihangel-Nant-Bran, Brecon LD3 9NA* T: (01874) 636390 E: revmargaretblake@aol.com

BLAKE, Max. *See* BLAKE, Steven Robert

BLAKE, Peta Ruth. b 44. Lambeth STh 89 Episc Div Sch Cam Mass MA 89 DMin 90. Trin Coll Bris 82. **dss** 83 **d** 87. New Swindon St Barn Gorse Hill *Bris* 83-88; Par Dn 87-88; PtO 88-93. *303 Beckett Condo, 220 Beckett Street, Arcadia, Pretoria, 0083 South Africa*

BLAKE, Philip Charles. b 29. Mitchell Coll of Adv Educn (NSW) BA 80 Macquarie Univ (NSW) MA 86 FAIWCW 88 MACC 88. Oak Hill Th Coll 54. **d** 57 **p** 58. C Slough *Ox* 57-60; C Uphill *B & W* 60-62; V Branston *Lich* 62-69; C-in-c Marshwiel Australia 69-72; R Denistone E w Marsfield 72-75; Chapl Long Bay Pris 75-80; Chapl W Metrop Pris 81-83; Sen Chapl Dept Corrective Services 81-85; Chapl Parramatta Hosp 86-91; Chapl Tas Univ 91-94; rtd 94. *127 Rose Court, Hopetoun Village, Castle Hill NSW 2153, Australia*

BLAKE, Stephen. b 59. Ch Coll Cam MA 85 Wadh Coll Ox BM, BCh 84 MRCGP 88. Ox Min Course 07. **d** 10 **p** 11. NSM Burford w Fulbrook, Taynton, Asthall etc *Ox* 10-13; NSM Chipping Norton from 13. *Morecroft, Hastings Hill, Churchill, Chipping Norton OX7 6NA* T: (01608) 658545 E: stephenblake@burfordchurch.org

BLAKE, Steven Robert (Max). b 53. Furzedown Coll of Educn CertEd 74 Brentwood Coll of Educn BEd 91. NTMTC 98. **d** 01 **p** 02. NSM Orsett and Bulphan and Horndon on the Hill *Chelmsf* from 01. *Oakfield, Victoria Road, Horndon-on-the-Hill, Stanford-le-Hope SS17 8ND* T: (01375) 360522 E: max@hobnob.org.uk

BLAKELEY, Julian Graham. b 60. Oak Hill Th Coll BA 88. **d** 88 **p** 89. C Bedworth *Cov* 88-91; C Harlow St Mary and St Hugh w St Jo the Bapt *Chelmsf* 91-95; R Darfield *Sheff* 95-03; TR Eston w Normanby *York* from 03. *429 Normanby Road, Middlesbrough TS6 0ED* T: (01642) 206264 E: julianblakeley@hotmail.co.uk

BLAKELY, Denise Irene. *See* CADDOO, Denise Irene

BLAKELY, Mark Francis James. b 75. Wolv Univ LLB 98 Lon Metrop Univ MA 09 Solicitor 01. St Mellitus Coll BA 15. **d** 15. C Becontree S *Chelmsf* from 15. *3 Barnard Close, Chislehurst BR7 6PQ* T: (020) 8467 7679 M: 07979-863409 E: mfjblakely@gmail.com

BLAKEMAN, Mrs Janet Mary. b 36. Man Univ BA 57 CertEd 58. Carl Dioc Tr Course 87. **d** 90 **p** 97. NSM Wetheral w Warwick *Carl* 90-97; NSM Thornthwaite cum Braithwaite, Newlands etc 97-01; PtO from 01. *1 The Coach House, Romaldkirk, Barnard Castle DL12 9ED* T: (01833) 650143

BLAKESLEY, John. b 50. Keble Coll Ox BA 72 MA 76. St Steph Ho Ox 72. **d** 74 **p** 75. C Egremont *Carl* 74-77; C Doncaster Ch Ch *Sheff* 77-79; V Auckland St Helen *Dur* 79-94; Chapl Tindale Crescent Hosp *Dur* 90-94; Tutor St Chad's Coll *Dur* 95-00; C Ch the King *Newc* 00-03; V Cambois and Sleekburn 03-12; rtd 12; PtO *York* from 12; Lect Th Dur Univ from 91. *11 Clarence Road, Nunthorpe, Middlesbrough TS7 0DA*
T: (01642) 319549 E: jblakesley@btinternet.com

BLAKEY, Canon Cedric Lambert. b 54. Fitzw Coll Cam BA 76 MA 80. St Jo Coll Nottm 77. **d** 79 **p** 80. C Cotmanhay *Derby* 79-83; C-in-c Blagreaves St Andr CD 83-89; P-in-c Sinfin Moor 84-89; V Heanor 89-97; RD 94-97; Bp's Dom Chapl 97-05; NSM Derby Cathl 05-11; Hon Can Derby Cathl 02-11; Vice Provost St Mary's Cathl from 11. *St Mary's Cathedral, 300 Great Western Road, Glasgow G4 9JB* T: 0141-339 6691 F: 334 5669
E: cedric.blakey@googlemail.com *or* viceprovost@thecathedral.org

BLAKEY, William George. b 51. Southn Univ BSc 72 PGCE 73. Oak Hill Th Coll BA 82. **d** 82 **p** 83. C Cheltenham St Mark *Glouc* 82-85; P-in-c Parkham, Alwington, Buckland Brewer etc *Ex* 85-86; R 86-94; TR 94-01; P-in-c Lundy Is 92-01; RD Hartland 89-96; TR Wareham *Sarum* 01-07; TR Brize Norton and Carterton *Ox* from 07; AD Witney 08-13. *St John's Vicarage, 6 Burford Road, Carterton OX18 3AA*
T: (01993) 846996 E: rector@theblakeys.co.uk

BLAMEY, Mark Kendall. b 62. Bris Poly BSc 84 MRICS 86. Ripon Coll Cuddesdon 99. **d** 01 **p** 02. C Cowley St Jo *Ox* 01-04; P-in-c Goring w S Stoke 04-07; V Goring and Streatley w S Stoke 07-13; PtO *Win* from 14. *6 Gros Puits, Fountain Lane, St Saviour, Jersey JE2 7RL* T: (01534) 631875
E: mkblamey@gmail.com

BLAMIRE, Jean. *See* PROSSER, Jean

BLAMIRE, Philip Gray. b 50. St Pet Coll Birm CertEd 71 Wall Hall Coll Aldenham BEd 76 UEA MA 91. EAMTC 00. **d** 03 **p** 04. C Swaffham *Nor* 03-07; P-in-c Weybourne Gp 07-10; R from 10. *The Rectory, The Street, Weybourne, Holt NR25 7SY*
T: (01263) 588268 E: philgb@lineone.net

BLAMIRE-BROWN, Charles Richard. b 21. St Cath Soc Ox BA 49 MA 53. Cuddesdon Coll 49. **d** 51 **p** 52. C Bedale *Ripon* 51-53; C Welwyn *St Alb* 53-58; P-in-c Tewin 58-67; R 67-75; RD Hatfield 71-75; V Chipperfield St Paul 75-86; rtd 86. *7 Willoughby Avenue, Kenilworth CV8 1DG* T: (01926) 850808

BLANCH, Michael Dennis. b 46. TD and Bar 88. Birm Univ BSocSc 69 PGCE 70 PhD 75. NOC 07. **d** 09 **p** 10. NSM Askrigg w Stallingbusk *Ripon* 09-12; NSM Hawes and Hardraw 09-12; NSM Eastbourne St Mich *Chich* 12-13; P-in-c Hampden Park and The Hydnye from 13. *4 Ashburnham Road, Eastbourne BN21 2HU* T: (01323) 747944 M: 07792-240684
E: mike@blanch.org

BLANCH, Paul Frederick. b 56. St Cuth Soc Dur BA 97. Chich Th Coll 83. **d** 86 **p** 87. C Chaddesden St Phil *Derby* 86-88; C Auckland St Andr and St Anne *Dur* 88-91; P-in-c Hunwick 91-94; Chapl HM Pris Edin 98-02; P-in-c Edin St Salvador 98-00; R 00-02; P-in-c Wester Hailes St Luke 00-02; P-in-c Melton *St E* 02-03; P-in-c Ufford w Bredfield and Hasketon 02-03; R Melton and Ufford 03-05; V Meir Heath and Normacot *Lich* 05-09; R Schenectady St Geo USA from 09. *St George's Rectory, 23 Front Street, Schenectady NY 12305-1301, USA* T: (001) (518) 374 3163
E: frpaul@meltuff.freeserve.co.uk

BLANCHARD, Canon Christopher John. b 46. Univ of Wales (Lamp) BA 70. St Mich Coll Llan 86. **d** 79 **p** 80. NSM Chepstow *Mon* 79-81; NSM Itton and St Arvans w Penterry and Kilgwrrwg etc 81-86; TV Ebbw Vale 87-89; R Llangenni and Llanbedr Ystrad Yw w Patricio *S & B* 89-98; V Chepstow *Mon* from 98; Hon Can St Woolos Cathl from 14. *The Vicarage, 25 Mount Way, Chepstow NP16 5NF* T: (01291) 620980
E: frchris2@icloud.com

BLANCHARD, Frank Hugh. b 30. St Jo Coll Dur BA 54 MA 62. **d** 55 **p** 56. C Bottesford *Linc* 55-58; CMS 58-65; C Kirby Grindalythe *York* 65-67; V 67-71; C N Grimston w Wharram Percy and Wharram-le-Street 65-67; V 67-71; P-in-c Thorpe Bassett 67-71; P-in-c Settrington 67-68; V Scarborough St Jas 71-79; P-in-c Scarborough H Trin 78-79; V Scarborough St Jas and H Trin 79-86; R Stockton-on-the-Forest w Holtby and Warthill 87-94; rtd 94; P-in-c Rothesay *Arg* 94-96; PtO *York* from 00. *23 Front Street, Sowerby, Thirsk YO7 1JG*
T: (01845) 574446

BLANCHARD, Mrs Jean Ann. b 43. St Alb Minl Tr Scheme 79. dss 85 **d** 87 **p** 94. Mill End and Heronsgate w W Hyde *St Alb* 85-92; Hon Par Dn 87-92; Par Dn Luton All SS w St Pet 92-94; C 94-95; P-in-c Skirbeck Quarter *Linc* 96-97; V 97-01; P-in-c Digby Gp 01-08; rtd 08. *92 High Street, Billingborough, Sleaford NG34 0QD* T: (01529) 240536
E: jean.blanchard@btinternet.com

BLANCHARD, Canon Lawrence Gordon. b 36. Edin Univ MA 60. Linc Th Coll 63. **d** 65 **p** 66. C Woodhouse *Wakef* 65-67; C Cannock *Lich* 67-70; Chapl Waterford Sch Mbabane Swaziland 70-72; R Mbabane All SS 72-75; LtO 75-76; TV Raveningham *Nor* 76-80; V Ancaster *Linc* 80-87; Dir LNSM 80-87; Can and Preb Linc Cathl 85-88; Dir of Tr CA 88-93; V Roxton w Gt Barford *St Alb* 93-98; rtd 98; PtO *St E* 99-09; *Ely* from 09. *7A Barton Road, Ely CB7 4HZ*
T: (01353) 654133 E: sonialaurie3@hotmail.com

BLANCHARDE, Hilary Mary. b 61. STETS. **d** 09 **p** 10. NSM Horfield H Trin *Bris* from 09. *149 Abbey Road, Bristol BS9 3QH*

BLANCHFLOWER, Mrs Rachel Elizabeth. b 80. ERMC 12. **d** 15. C Chesterton Gd Shep *Ely* from 15. *Address temp unknown*

BLAND, Caroline Anne. b 61. Glos Univ BEd 04. WEMTC 12. **d** 15. C Wotton St Mary *Glouc* from 15. *30 Simon Road, Longlevens, Gloucester GL2 0TP* M: 07858-032222
T: (01452) 883779

BLAND, Mrs Elizabeth Anne. b 63. Collingwood Coll Dur BA 85. SAOMC 01. **d** 04 **p** 05. C N Shields *Newc* 04-08; V Ashington 08-15; TV Gt Aycliffe *Dur* from 15. *St Francis's Vicarage, Burnhope, Newton Aycliffe DL5 7ER* T: (01325) 324622 E: elizabeth.a.bland@googlemail.com

BLAND, Jean Elspeth. b 42. K Coll Lon BA 63. Glouc Sch of Min 87. **d** 90 **p** 94. Par Dn Cen Telford *Lich* 90-94; Asst Chapl HM Pris Shrewsbury 92-94; Chapl HM Pris and YOI Doncaster 94-98; C Goole *Sheff* 99; P-in-c Purleigh, Cold Norton and Stow Maries *Chelmsf* 99-08; rtd 08. *33 Seagers, Great Totham, Maldon CM9 8PB* T: (01621) 829646
E: ebland@prowselyan.plus.com

BLAND, Mrs Lesley Nicole. b 57. Ch Ch Coll Cant BEd 78. ERMC 10. **d** 13 **p** 14. NSM Kym Valley *Ely* from 13; Chapl Kimbolton Sch from 13. *The Spinney, 2 Rose Lane, Pinchbeck, Spalding PE11 3RN* T: (01775) 719123 M: 07805-078992
E: lnb@kimbolton.cambs.sch.uk

BLANDFORD-BAKER, Neil James. b 64. Dundee Univ BSc 86. St Jo Coll Nottm BTh 92. **d** 93 **p** 94. C The Quinton *Birm* 93-96; V E Acton St Dunstan w St Thos Lon 96-06; Dir of Ords Willesden Area 02-06; V Histon *Ely* from 06; P-in-c Impington from 06; RD N Stowe from 07. *The Vicarage, 9A Church Street, Histon, Cambridge CB24 9EP* T: (01223) 233456 or 232255
E: jamesbb@btinternet.com

BLANEY, Laurence. b 41. Open Univ BA 85 Essex Univ MA 88 PhD 95. Oak Hill Th Coll 66. **d** 69 **p** 70. C Leyton St Mary w St Edw *Chelmsf* 69-73; P-in-c Wimbish w Thunderley 73-77; P-in-c Mayland 77-82; P-in-c Steeple 77-82; R Pitsea 82-95; R Pitsea w Nevendon 95-96; P-in-c Mayland 96-06; P-in-c Steeple 96-06; rtd 06; PtO *Chelmsf* 06-12; P-in-c Purleigh 12-15. *14 Piercys, Basildon SS13 3HN* T: (01268) 552254
E: laurie@blaney.info

BLANKENSHIP, Charles Everett. b 42. Santa Clara Univ BA 64. Cuddesdon Coll 71. **d** 74 **p** 75. C Catford (Southend) and Downham *S'wark* 74-78; P-in-c Battersea St Phil w St Bart 78-83; V 83-85; TV Wimbledon 85-91; P-in-c Welling 91-92; V 92-99; P-in-c S Norwood St Alb 99-06; RD Croydon N 02-06; rtd 06; PtO *S'wark* from 06. *16 Bromley College, London Road, Bromley BR1 1PE* T: (020) 8464 2443 M: 07816-154407 E: charles.blankenship@btinternet.com

BLANKLEY, Roger Henry. b 32. MRICS 60. Clifton Th Coll 62. **d** 66 **p** 67. C Peckham St Mary Magd *S'wark* 66-69; SAMS 70-74; Brazil 74-80; R Gillingham w Geldeston, Stockton, Ellingham etc *Nor* 80-91; P-in-c Charmouth and Catherston Leweston *Sarum* 91-97; rtd 97; PtO *Glouc* from 97; *Cov* 98-00 and 02-06; Asst Area Sec SAMS 98-00. *12 Hubbard Close, Buckingham MK18 1YS* T: (01280) 814710
E: mblankley@rblankley.freeserve.co.uk

BLATCHLEY, Ms Elizabeth. b 62. Wycliffe Hall Ox 01. **d** 03 **p** 04. C Northolt St Jos *Lon* 03-06; C Telford Park *S'wark* 06-11; V Homerton St Luke *Lon* from 11. *St Luke's Vicarage, 23 Cassland Road, London E9 7AL* T: (020) 8985 2263
E: betsy.blatchley@london.anglican.org

BLATCHLY, Owen Ronald Maxwell. b 30. Bps' Coll Cheshunt 62. **d** 64 **p** 65. C Boxmoor St Jo *St Alb* 64-67; C Boreham Wood All SS 67-69; C Frimley *Guildf* 69-77; V Manaccan w St Anthony-in-Meneage *Truro* 77-82; R Binfield *Ox* 82-97; rtd 97; PtO *Truro* from 97. *1 Rose Cottages, East Road, Stithians, Truro TR3 7BD* T: (01209) 860845

BLATHERWICK, Mrs Jane Lesley. b 63. St Jo Coll Nottm. **d** 05 **p** 06. C Arnold *S'well* 05-09; P-in-c Carlton-in-Lindrick and Langold w Oldcotes 09-11; R from 11. *The Rectory, 21 Grange Close, Carlton-in-Lindrick, Worksop S81 9DX* T: (01909) 732498
E: janeblatherwick@aol.com

BLAY, Ian. b 65. Man Univ BA 88. Westcott Ho Cam 89. **d** 91 **p** 92. C Withington St Paul *Man* 91-94; C Elton All SS 94-96; R Droylsden St Andr 96-05; Dioc Ecum Officer 98-05; R Mobberley *Ches* from 05. *The Rectory, Church Lane, Mobberley, Knutsford WA16 7RA* T: (01565) 873218 M: 07879-004033 E: ianblay@btinternet.com

BLAY, Kenneth Neil. b 72. Leeds Univ BA 07. Coll of Resurr Mirfield 05. **d** 07 **p** 08. C E Crompton *Man* 07-08; C Dearnley 08-10; P-in-c Morley w Noranda Australia 10-15. *Address temp unknown* E: nkblay@btinternet.com

BLEAKLEY, Melvyn Thomas. b 43. K Coll Lon BD 66 AKC 66 Reading Univ TCert 78. **d** 67 **p** 68. C Cross Heath *Lich* 67-70; TV High Wycombe *Ox* 70-77; PtO 77-00; NSM Chalfont St Giles 00-15; NSM Chalfont St Giles, Seer Green and Jordans from 15. *294 Hughenden Road, High Wycombe HP13 5PE* T: (01494) 529315 E: melvyn_bleakley@hotmail.com

BLEAZARD, John George. b 57. Univ of Wales (Abth) BA 79 Qu Coll Birm MA 06. Ripon Coll Cuddesdon 06. **d** 08 **p** 09. C Gt Cornard *St E* 08-11; R W Kirby St Bridget *Ches* from 11. *40 Village Road, West Kirby, Wirral CH48 7HE* T: 0151-625 1052 E: johnbleazard@hotmail.com

BLEE, Peter Michael. b 64. St Jo Coll Cam BA 86. St Steph Ho Ox BTh 94. **d** 94 **p** 95. C Guildf St Nic 94-97; C Whipton *Ex* 97-03; P-in-c Berwick w Selmeston and Alciston *Chich* 03-07; R 07-10; R Arlington, Berwick, Selmeston w Alciston etc from 10. *The Parsonage, Berwick, Polegate BN26 6SR* T: (01323) 870512 E: peter.blee@berwickchurch.org.uk

BLEWETT, Martin Arthur. b 60. Keele Univ BA 82 Glos Univ MA 04. Trin Coll Bris 07. **d** 09 **p** 10. C Seaford w Sutton *Chich* 09-13; P-in-c Timsbury w Priston, Camerton and Dunkerton *B & W* from 13. *The Rectory, South Road, Timsbury, Bath BA2 0EJ* T: (01761) 472448 M: 07854-273489 E: martinblewett@gmail.com

BLEWETT, Roy. b 32. K Coll Lon BSc 54 MPhil 74. Edin Th Coll 81. **d** 82 **p** 83. C Newc St Fran 82-85; P-in-c Branxton and Cornhill w Carham 85-91; rtd 92; PtO *Truro* 92-08. *37 Summerland Park, Upper Killay, Swansea SA2 7HU* T: (01792) 201561

BLEWETT, Timothy John. b 67. Surrey Univ BA 88 Cam Univ BA 92 MA 92 Coll of Ripon & York St Jo MA 96 Buckingham Univ MA 11. Westcott Ho Cam 89. **d** 92 **p** 93. C Knaresborough *Ripon* 92-95; V Hanmer, Bronington, Bettisfield, Tallarn Green *St As* 95-98; Can Res and Can Cursal St As Cathl 98-03; Asst Dioc Dir of Ords 98-00; 00-03; Dioc Officer for Min and Adv for CME 98-03; CF 03-04; P-in-c Loddington *Leic* 04-12; Warden Launde Abbey 04-12; Dir and Chapl Ark Trust from 12. *Sycamore House, New Road, Burton Lazars, Melton Mowbray LE14 2UU* M: 07971-528915 E: tim@ark-trust.org.uk

BLICK, John Harold Leslie. b 36. Univ of Wales (Lamp) BA 61. Bps' Coll Cheshunt 61. **d** 63 **p** 64. C Radlett *St Alb* 63-66; Min St Cem Miss Labrador Canada 66-71; Min Marsh Farm CD *St Alb* 71-76; R Shaw cum Donnington *Ox* 76-89; rtd 96; PtO *Mon* from 96. *Springwood, Cleddon, Trelleck NP25 4PN* T: (01600) 860094 F: 869045 E: revdjblick@aol.com

BLIGH, Francis Charles. b 71. Newc Univ BA 94. Oak Hill Th Coll BA 08. **d** 08 **p** 09. C Virginia Water *Guildf* 08-12; Asst Chapl Amsterdam w Den Helder and Heiloo *Eur* from 12. *De Kuilenaar 60, 1851 RZ Heiloo, The Netherlands* T: (0031) (72) 531 5023 E: francisblight@christchurch.nl

BLIGHT, Philip Hamilton. b 36. Lon Univ BSc 57 PhD 61 MEd 79 St Cath Coll Ox BA 63 MInstP 75. S'wark Ord Course 86. **d** 88 **p** 89. C Abington *Pet* 88-90; V Bozeat w Easton Maudit 90-99; R Hackett Australia 99-01; rtd 01; PtO *Nor* from 02. *49 Norwich Road, Cromer NR27 0EX* T: (01263) 511385 E: philipbligh752@btinternet.com

BLISS, Allan Ernest Newport. b 29. K Coll Lon AKC 50. St Boniface Warminster 54. **d** 54 **p** 57. C Wooburn Ox 54-56; C Whitley Ch Ch 56-58; C Hatcham Park All SS *S'wark* 63-68; C Sundon w Streatley *St Alb* 68-73; P-in-c Caldecote All SS 74-78; V 78-91; V Old Warden 81-91; PtO 91-05; rtd 94. *6 Jubilee Gardens, Biggleswade SG18 0JW* T: (01767) 313797

BLISS, Canon David Charles. b 52. Aston Univ BSc 75 Cranfield Inst of Tech MSc 82. St Jo Coll Nottm 87. **d** 89 **p** 90. C Burntwood *Lich* 89-93; Chapl St Matt Hosp Burntwood 89-93; TV Aston cum Aughton w Swallownest, Todwick etc *Sheff* 93-02; R Todwick 02-08; AD Laughton 03-08; Chapl among Deaf People 97-08; V Rotherham from 08; AD 08-11; Hon Can Sheff Cathl from 06. *51 Hallam Road, Rotherham S60 3ED* T: (01709) 364341 E: david.bliss@sheffield.anglican.org

BLISS, John Derek Clegg. b 40. Sarum Th Coll. **d** 68 **p** 69. C Wymondham *Nor* 68-73; V Easton 73-80; R Colton 73-80; R Madera H Trin USA 80-89; Human Outreach Agency Hayward 92-96; rtd 01; C Coconut Grove St Steph USA from 01. *4 Edgewater Hillside, Westport CT 06880-6101, USA* T: (001) (203) 222 1879 E: jb106600@aol.com

BLISS, Mrs Lyn Elizabeth. b 54. SS Mark & Jo Univ Coll Plymouth CertEd 76. Ox Min Course 06. **d** 09 **p** 10. NSM Bradfield and Stanford Dingley *Ox* from 09; NSM Bucklebury

w Marlston from 09. *Holly Hedges, 2 Broad Lane, Upper Bucklebury, Reading RG7 6QJ* T: (01635) 862281 M: 07824-741225 E: lyn.bliss@virgin.net

BLISSARD-BARNES, Christopher John. b 36. ARCO 55 Linc Coll Ox BA 61 MA 64. Ridley Hall Cam 61. **d** 63 **p** 64. C Woking St Paul *Guildf* 63-67; C Orpington Ch Ch *Roch* 67-71; P-in-c Heref St Jas 71-78; Chapl Heref Gen Hosp 71-78; R Hampreston *Sarum* 78-88; TR 88-89; RD Wimborne 80-85; P-in-c Hambledon *Guildf* 89-94; R Newdigate 94-01; Warden of Readers 93-99; rtd 01; PtO *Win* from 02. *148 Olivers Battery Road South, Winchester SO22 4LF* T/F: (01962) 862082 E: chrisandfreda@virginmedia.com

BLOCKLEY, Christopher John Hamilton. b 72. UWE LLB 96 Rob Coll Cam BTh 04 Barrister-at-Law (Gray's Inn) 98. Ridley Hall Cam 01. **d** 04 **p** 05. C Kingswood *Bris* 04-07; Chapl Bps' Coll Glouc from 07. *29 Wellesley Street, Gloucester GL1 4QP* T: (01452) 539956 or 524879 ext 137 M: 07795-266674 E: chris_blockley@hotmail.com

BLODWELL, Ms Christine Maria. b 46. Open Univ BA Jo Dalton Coll Man CertEd 71. NOC 04. **d** 05 **p** 06. NSM Marple All SS *Ches* from 05. *12 Ventura Court, Ollersett Avenue, New Mills, High Peak SK22 4LL* T: (01663) 746523 M: 07931-714130 E: cmblodwell@aol.com

BLOFELD, Thomas Guest. *See* GUEST-BLOFELD, Thomas

BLOGG, Kevin Derek. b 55. Ch Ch Coll Cant BSc 82 PGCE 87. Franciscan Ho of Studies. **d** 84 **p** 85. NSM Eythorne and Elvington w Waldershare etc *Cant* 89-92; Orchard Sch Cant 89-90; Harbour Sch Dover 92-93; NSM Colkirk w Oxwick w Pattesley, Whissonsett etc *Nor* 95-02; NSM Gressenhall w Longham w Wendling etc from 02; Sidestrand Hall Sch Nor from 94. *The Rectory Barn, Rectory Road, Gressenhall, Dereham NR19 2QG* T: (01362) 861084 E: bloggbarn@aol.com

BLOKLAND, Jantje Hendrika. b 82. Radboud Univ Nijmegen MSc 06 PhD 10 Utrecht Univ BA 12 Westcott Ho Cam MA 14. Westcott Ho Cam 12. **d** 14 **p** 15. C Marlborough *Sarum* from 14. *10 Alexandra Terrace, Blowhorn Street, Marlborough SN8 1DA* T: (01672) 515970 M: 07554-486575 E: jblokland@gmail.com

BLOOD, David John. b 36. G&C Coll Cam BA 60 MA 64. Westcott Ho Cam 60. **d** 62 **p** 63. C Rushmere *St E* 62-66; C Harringay St Paul *Lon* 66-70; LtO 71-81; rtd 01. *42 Churston Gardens, London N11 2NL*

BLOOD, Canon Michael William. b 44. AKC 67. **d** 69 **p** 70. C Moseley St Agnes *Birm* 69-75; V Cotteridge 75-09; Relig Progr Producer BBC Radio W Midl 76-06; Hon Can Birm Cathl 97-09; rtd 09; PtO *Birm* from 09. *19 Nursery Drive, Birmingham B30 1DR* T: 0121-458 2815 E: michaelblood@blueyonder.co.uk

BLOOD, Stephen John. b 28. Keble Coll Ox BA 53 MA 58. Coll of Resurr Mirfield 53. **d** 55 **p** 56. C Greenford H Cross *Lon* 55-58; C Forest Gate St Edm *Chelmsf* 58-61; C-in-c Ashford St Hilda CD *Lon* 61-73; V Ashford St Hilda 73-00; rtd 00; PtO *St Alb* from 00. *69 Hampstead Road, Kings Langley WD4 8BS* T: (01923) 268453

BLOOM, Mrs Lara Susan. b 67. Ripon Coll Cuddesdon 13. **d** 15. C Redmarley D'Abitot, Bromesberrow, Pauntley etc *Glouc* from 15. *The Vicarage, St Mary's Close, Dymock GL18 2AX* M: 07901-003575 E: larabloom@outlook.com

BLOOMER, Ms Sherry Lesley. b 50. TD 91. Liv Jo Moores Univ BA 91 Wolv Poly CertEd 83 RN 73 RM 74 RHV 78. Westcott Ho Cam 95. **d** 97 **p** 98. C Llangollen w Trevor and Llantysilio *St As* 97-00; R Cilcain and Nannerch and Rhydymwyn 00-04; V Worc St Clem and Lower Broadheath 04-12; Chapl Worc Univ 04-12; rtd 12; PtO *St As* from 14. *13 Tudor Avenue, Prestatyn LL19 9HN* T: (01745) 850141 E: sherry@sbloomer.freeserve.co.uk

BLOOMFIELD, Mrs Brenda Elizabeth. b 41. Gipsy Hill Coll of Educn TCert 63. **d** 07 **p** 08. NSM Upper Weardale *Dur* 07-11; rtd 11; PtO *Dur* from 11. *1 Broadwood View, Frosterley, Bishop Auckland DL13 2RT* T: (01388) 527980

BLOOMFIELD, Mrs Christine Louise. b 52. ERMC 05. **d** 08 **p** 09. C Strasbourg *Eur* 08-13; NSM Lausanne 14. *Address temp unknown* E: bloomfieldhilaire@wanadoo.fr

BLOOMFIELD, John Michael. b 35. Univ of Wales (Lamp) BA 57. Sarum Th Coll 59. **d** 61 **p** 62. C Fordington *Sarum* 61-64; C Branksome St Aldhelm 64-66; Youth Chapl *Win* 66-69; R Win All SS w Chilcomb and Chesil 71-79; P-in-c Corsley *Sarum* 79-81; P-in-c Swanage and Studland 83-86; Chapl HM Pris Dorchester 87-89; C Dorchester *Sarum* 87-89; Chapl HM Pris The Verne 89-00; rtd 00; PtO *Sarum* from 01. *15 Provost Street, Fordingbridge SP6 1AY* T: (01425) 837735 E: swanbeck3@gmail.com

BLOOMFIELD, John Stephen. b 56. Chich Th Coll 83. **d** 86 **p** 87. C Chich St Paul and St Pet 86-89; TV Littlehampton and Wick 89-98; V Hunstanton St Edm w Ringstead *Nor* from 98. *St Edmund's Vicarage, 53 Northgate, Hunstanton PE36 6DS* T: (01485) 532531 E: bloomfield545@btinternet.com

BLOOMFIELD, Sister Susan Marie. b 65. **d** 13 **p** 14. Dioc Chapl amongst Deaf People *S'well* from 13. *5 Blake Close, Arnold, Nottingham NG5 6NB* E: smbloomfield@gmail.com

BLOOR, Amanda Elaine. b 62. Leic Univ BA 83 York Univ MA 02 K Coll Lon PhD 12 Open Univ PGCE 96. Ripon Coll Cuddesdon 02. **d** 04 **p** 05. C Hambleden Valley *Ox* 04-07; Bp's Dom Chapl 07-13; Dioc Adv for Women's Min and Dir of Ords (Berks) from 13. *Diocesan Church House, North Hinksey, Oxford OX2 0NB* T: (01865) 208221 E: amanda.bloor@oxford.anglican.org

BLOOR, Preb Terence Bernard. b 62. Liv Univ BTh 02. NOC 99. **d** 02 **p** 03. C Hadley *Lich* 02-06; P-in-c Basford from 06; RD Newcastle from 11; Chapl N Staffs Combined Healthcare NHS Trust 06-13; Preb Lich Cathl from 15. *211 Basford Park Road, Newcastle ST5 0PG* T: (01782) 619045 M: 07890-980749 E: terry.bloor@btinternet.com

BLORE, Canon John Francis. b 49. Jes Coll Ox BA 72 MA 76. Wycliffe Hall Ox 73. **d** 75 **p** 76. C Waltham Abbey *Chelmsf* 75-78; C E Ham St Geo 78-81; R Colchester St Mich Myland 81-00; Chapl Oxley Parker Sch Colchester 81-00; P-in-c Halstead St Andr w H Trin and Greenstead Green *Chelmsf* 00-04; TR Halstead Area 04-15; RD Hinckford 03-08; Hon Can Chelmsf Cathl 09-15; rtd 15; PtO *Nor* from 15. *Alden Cottage, Lexham Road, Litcham, King's Lynn PE32 2QQ* T: (01328) 701242 E: jf.blore@btinternet.com

BLOUNT, Robin George. b 38. Lon Coll of Div 61 Wycliffe Hall Ox 67. **d** 68 **p** 69. C Bletchley *Ox* 68-71; C Washington *Dur* 71-74; TV Chelmsley Wood *Birm* 74-76; Ind Chapl *Worc* 76-89; Asst P Dudley St Jo 76-88; Asst P Dudley St Thos and St Luke 88-89; Ind Chapl (Eurotunnel Development) *Cant* 89-03; rtd 03; PtO *Cant* from 03. *82 Mabledon Avenue, Ashford TN24 8BN* E: robin.blount38@gmail.com

BLOXAM-ROSE, Canon Simon Franklyn. b 61. Southn Univ BTh MA 92 PhD 99 HonFLCM 88. Chich Th Coll 85. **d** 88 **p** 89. C Bassaleg *Mon* 88-89; Chapl Aldenham Sch Herts 89-94; Sen Chapl Millfield Sch Somerset 94-06; CF from 06; Can St Jo Pro-Cathl Katakwa from 95. *c/o MOD Chaplains (Army)* F: 381824 T: (01264) 383433

BLOXHAM, Oliver. b 27. Ely Th Coll 60. **d** 62 **p** 63. C Newc H Cross 62-65; C Ponteland 65-69; V Dudley 69-79; P-in-c Balkwell 79-81; V 81-92; rtd 92; PtO *Newc* from 92. *182 Eastern Way, Ponteland, Newcastle upon Tyne NE20 9RH*

BLUNDELL, Catherine. b 62. SAOMC 96. **d** 99 **p** 00. C Furze Platt *Ox* 99-03; TV Bracknell 03-09; V Winkfield and Cranbourne 09-15; TR Chalke Valley *Sarum* from 15. *The Rectory, Newtown, Broad Chalke, Salisbury SP5 5DS* T: (01722) 780134 E: catherine.blundell@btinternet.com

BLUNDELL, Peter Grahame. b 61. Ealing Coll of Educn BA 83. Oak Hill NSM Course 91. **d** 94 **p** 95. NSM Kensington St Barn *Lon* 94-97; Zimbabwe 97-99; Assoc Min Romford Gd Shep *Chelmsf* 99-04; I Richmond Hill St Jo Canada from 04. *19 Waldron Crescent, Richmond Hill ON L4E 4A3, Canada* T: (001) (289) 809 1450 E: peter@ecclesiact.com

BLUNDEN, Jacqueline Ann. *See* MILLER, Jacqueline Ann

BLUNDEN, Jeremy Augustine. b 61. BSc CEng 88 MIStructE 88. SEITE 99. **d** 99 **p** 00. NSM Sydenham St Bart *S'wark* 99-01; C 01-03; V Clapham H Spirit 03-12; TR Warlingham w Chelsham and Farleigh from 12. *The Rectory, 35 Dane Road, Warlingham CR6 9NP* T: (01883) 624125 E: jeremy.blunden@btopenworld.com

BLUNSUM, Charles Michael. b 28. ACIB 51 MBIM 86. **d** 74 **p** 75. C Stoke Bishop *Bris* 74-79; Chapl Brunel Manor Chr Cen Torquay 79-94; rtd 94; PtO *Ex* from 94. *16A Hollywater Close, Torquay TQ1 3TN* T: (01803) 214371

BLUNT, Christopher John Scanen. b 73. Rob Coll Cam MA 97 MEng 97. St Jo Coll Nottm MTh 13. **d** 13 **p** 14. C Ches St Paul from 13; C Huntington from 13. *St Luke's Vicarage, 14 Celandine Close, Huntington, Chester CH3 6DT* M: 07503-706906 E: chrisblunt.jas@gmail.com

BLUNT, Jeremy William. b 49. Birm Univ MEd 85 GRNCM 73. **d** 07 **p** 08. OLM Streetly *Lich* from 07. *63 Lindrosa Road, Sutton Coldfield B74 3LB* T: 0121-353 9712 M: 07849-689180 E: jeremy.blunt@virgin.net

BLYDE, Ian Hay. b 52. Liv Univ BSc 74 Edin Univ BD 80. Edin Th Coll 77. **d** 80 **p** 81. C Ainsdale *Liv* 80-83; Chapl Birkenhead Sch Merseyside 83-90; V Over St Chad *Ches* 90-93; Chapl Ex Sch and St Marg Sch 93-98; NSM Littleham w Exmouth *Ex* 03-06; TV Brixham w Churston Ferrers and Kingswear 06-13; TR from 13. *The Rectory, 16 Holwell Road, Brixham TQ5 9NE* T: (01803) 851340

BLYTH, Canon Andrew Kenneth Eric. b 63. Roehampton Inst BA 86 Middx Univ PGCE 87. Ridley Hall Cam 98. **d** 00 **p** 01. C Luton St Mary *St Alb* 00-04; P-in-c Walton H Trin *Ox* 04-09; V from 09; AD Aylesbury from 10; Hon Can Ch Ch

from 13. *The Rectory, 42 Redwood Drive, Aylesbury HP21 7TN* T: (01296) 394906 M: 07905-181002 E: andrew.blyth@htaylesbury.org

BLYTH, Bryan Edward Perceval. b 22. Linc Coll Ox BA 49 MA 52. Wells Th Coll 48. **d** 50 **p** 51. C Timperley *Ches* 50-52; C Talbot Village *Sarum* 52-55; C-in-c Weymouth St Edm 55; P-in-c 56-63; Asst Dir of Educn *Chelmsf* 64-67; Hon C Mountnessing 67-68; Hon C Ingatestone w Buttsbury 67-68; Teacher Ingatestone Sec Modern Sch 67-68; Teacher Westwood Co Jun Sch 68-72; Dep Hd 72-87; Hon C Thundersley *Chelmsf* 80-84; rtd 87; PtO *Sarum* from 98; Win 98-13. *Greenways, 19 Chiltern Drive, New Milton BH25 7JY* T: (01425) 611140

BLYTH, Mrs Geraldine Anne. b 50. Llan Dioc Tr Scheme 90. **d** 94 **p** 97. C Llantrisant *Llan* 94-01; P-in-c Llanharry 01-06; Chapl Pontypridd and Rhondda NHS Trust 01-06; V Llangynwyd w Maesteg *Llan* from 06. *18 Llynfi Court, Maesteg CF34 9NJ* T: (01656) 716020

BLYTH, Graham. *See* BLYTH, Michael Graham

BLYTH, Ian John. b 40. Rhodes Univ BA 66 Natal Univ BEd 81 MEd 96. **d** 82 **p** 83. Dioc Educn Officer Natal S Africa 83-85; R Pietermaritzburg St Luke 85-87; LtO 88-01; NSM W Woodhay w Enborne, Hampstead Marshall etc *Ox* 02-09; NSM Kintbury w Avington 05-09; rtd 09; Hon C Burstwick w Thorngumbald *York* 09-12; Hon C Burstwick, Burton Pidsea etc 12-14. *The Rectory, Ottringham Road, Keyingham, Hull HU12 9RX* T: (01964) 622907 M: 07900-857096 E: ianblyth0801@btinternet.com

BLYTH, John Reddie. b 25. Wadh Coll Ox BA 48 MA 50. Ridley Hall Cam 48. **d** 50 **p** 51. C Southport Ch Ch *Liv* 50-52; C Enfield Ch Ch Trent Park *Lon* 52-55; V Plymouth St Jude *Ex* 55-63; E Midl Area Sec CPAS 63-70; V Parkstone St Luke *Sarum* 70-90; Chapl Uplands Sch Parkstone 70-73; rtd 90; PtO *Chich* from 90. *5 Powell Road, Newick, Lewes BN8 4LS* T: (01825) 722011

BLYTH, Kenneth Henry. b 35. Oak Hill Th Coll 58. **d** 61 **p** 62. C St Alb St Paul *St Alb* 61-65; P-in-c Aspenden and Layston w Buntingford 65-66; R 66-72; R Washfield, Stoodleigh, Withleigh etc *Ex* 72-82; P-in-c Cruwys Morchard 72-74; RD Tiverton 76-82; V Eastbourne H Trin *Chich* 82-00; rtd 00; PtO *Ex* from 00. *Hamslade House, Bampton, Tiverton EX16 9JA* T: (01398) 351461

BLYTH, Canon Michael Graham. b 53. Jes Coll Ox BA 75 MA 78 Dur Univ PhD 79. Qu Coll Birm 82. **d** 84 **p** 85. C Nantwich *Ches* 84-86; C Coppenhall 86-88; TV Stoneleigh *Chelmsf* 88-95; P-in-c Danbury 95-11; R 11-12; RD Chelmsf S 01-07; Hon Can Chelmsf Cathl 07-12; rtd 12; PtO *Chelmsf* from 14. *Selkirk House, 8 Rennie Walk, Heybridge, Maldon CM9 4QH* T: (01621) 854068 E: michaelg@canongate.org.uk

BOAG, David. b 46. Edin Th Coll 69. **d** 72 **p** 73. C Edin Old St Paul 72-75; P-in-c Edin St Andr and St Aid 75-88; LtO from 88. *13 Fleming Place, Fountainhall, Galashiels TD1 2TA* T: (01578) 760606

BOAG, Michael John. b 61. Leeds Univ BA 00. Coll of Resurr Mirfield 98. **d** 00 **p** 01. C Howden *York* 00-03; Min Can and Succ Windsor 03-11; Chapl St Geo Sch Windsor 03-06; Dean's V 06-11; R Upper Coquetdale *Newc* from 11. *The Rectory, Rothbury, Morpeth NE65 7TL* T: (01669) 620482

BOAK, Canon Donald Kenneth. b 30. MBAOT 53. S'wark Ord Course 82. **d** 85 **p** 86. C Tulse Hill H Trin and St Matthias *S'wark* 85-88; C Surbiton St Matt 88-91; Intercon Ch Soc, SAMS and Miss to Seamen 91-95; Peru 91-95; Dean Lima 93-95; rtd 95; Hon Can Peru from 95; Hon C Bournemouth St Andr *Win* 96-99; PtO *Sarum* 98-01; Win 99-14. *3 Hymans Way, Totton, Southampton SO40 3DL* T: (023) 8086 8265

BOAKES, Canon Norman. b 50. Univ of Wales (Swansea) BA 71 Univ of Wales (Lamp) LTh 73 Ox Univ MTh 96. Dioc Bangor Hall Lamp 71. **d** 73 **p** 74. C Swansea St Mary w H Trin *S & B* 73-78; Chapl Univ of Wales (Swansea) 76-78; Chapl K Alfred Coll *Win* 78-82; V Colbury 82-91; Chapl Ashurst Hosp 82-91; Chapl Mental Handicap Services Unit 82-91; V Southampton Maybush St Pet *Win* 91-06; P-in-c Southampton St Jude 04-06; V Maybush and Southampton St Jude 06-07; Bp's Adv for Hosp Chapl 87-00; AD Southampton 02-07; CMD Officer 08-14; Hon Can Win Cathl 11-14; PtO from 14; Archdeacons' Nat Exec Officer from 14. *21 Redcourt, Chetwynd Road, Southampton SO16 3TX* T: (023) 8076 7735 E: norman.boakes@churchofengland.org

BOARDMAN, Frederick Henry. b 25. Liv Univ BSc 46 St Cath Soc Ox BA 49 MA 54 Birm Univ MEd 71 PhD 77 Lon Univ PGCE 68. Wycliffe Hall Ox 47. **d** 50 **p** 51. C Bootle Ch Ch *Liv* 50-52; C-in-c Netherton CD 52-57; V Stechford *Birm* 57-63; LtO 63-69; *Liv* 71-89; Hon C Sutton 76-89; Hon C Burtonwood 89-02; rtd 90; PtO *Liv* from 92. *Woodside, Burtonwood Road, Great Sankey, Warrington WA5 3AN* T: (01925) 635079

BOARDMAN, The Ven Jonathan. b 63. Magd Coll Cam BA 89 Magd Coll Ox MA 90. Westcott Ho Cam 87. **d** 90 **p** 91. C W Derby St Mary *Liv* 90-93; Prec St Alb Abbey *St Alb* 93-96; TR Catford (Southend) and Downham *S'wark* 96-99; RD E Lewisham 99; Chapl Rome *Eur* from 99; Sen Tutor Angl Cen Rome from 00; Can Gib Cathl from 07; Adn Italy and Malta from 09; P-in-c Padova from 12. *All Saints, via del Babuino 153, 00187 Rome, Italy* T: (0039) (06) 3600 2171 *or* T/F: 3600 1881 E: j.boardman@allsaintsrome.org *or* office@allsaintsrome.org

BOARDMAN, Miss Kathryn Louise. b 72. Hull Univ BA 94 MA 95 Cam Univ BTh 12 FHEA 07. Westcott Ho Cam 10. **d** 12 **p** 13. C Heworth St Mary *Dur* from 12. *28 Rectory Road East, Gateshead NE10 9DN* M: 07990-645948 E: kate@kateboardman.me.uk

BOARDMAN, Canon Philippa Jane. b 63. MBE 11. Jes Coll Cam BA 85 MA 89. Ridley Hall Cam 87. **d** 90 **p** 94. Par Dn Walthamstow St Mary w St Steph *Chelmsf* 90-93; C Hackney Wick St Mary of Eton w St Aug *Lon* 93-96; P-in-c Old Ford St Paul and St Mark 96-03; V 03-13; Dean of Women's Min Stepney Area 94-02; Preb St Paul's Cathl 02-13; Can Res and Treas St Paul's Cathl from 13. *3 Amen Court, London EC4M 7BU* T: (020) 7246 8378 E: canonspa@stpaulscathedral.org.uk

BOARDMAN, Shona Ross. b 66. DipSW 00. Trin Coll Toronto MDiv 09. **d** 09 **p** 10. C Edin St Jo 09-11; P-in-c Stornoway *Arg* 12-14; P-in-c Dunkeld *St And* from 14; P-in-c Stanley from 14. *Address temp unknown*

BOCKING (Suffolk), Dean of. *See* THROWER, The Very Revd Martin Charles

BODDAM-WHETHAM, Paul Nathaniel. b 52. Em Coll Cam BA 73. ERMC 09. **d** 12 **p** 13. NSM St Alb Ch Ch from 12. *32 Upper Hall Park, Berkhamsted HP4 2NP* T: (01442) 865281 M: 07713-069876 E: paulbw.cc@virginmedia.com

BODDAM-WHETHAM, Tudor Alexander. b 76. St Aid Coll Dur BA 97. Wycliffe Hall Ox 06. **d** 08 **p** 09. C Houghton *Carl* 08-11; P-in-c Barony of Burgh from 11. *The Rectory, Burgh-by-Sands, Carlisle CA5 6AW* T: (01228) 576324 E: vicartudor@gmail.com

BODDINGTON, Canon Alan Charles Peter. b 37. Oak Hill Th Coll 63. **d** 66 **p** 67. C Bedworth *Cov* 66-69; Bp's Officer for Min 69-75; Bp's Chapl for Miss 69-73; P-in-c Wroxall and Honiley 72-75; V Westwood 75-85; Asst Chapl Warw Univ 78-85; TR N Farnborough *Guildf* 85-02; RD Aldershot 88-93; Hon Can Guildf Cathl 92-02; rtd 02; PtO *Cov* from 02. *Tremar, Hathaway Lane, Stratford-upon-Avon CV37 9BJ* T: (01789) 263643 M: 07866-909092 E: bodds4@btinternet.com

BODDY, Alan Richard. b 47. Ripon Coll Cuddesdon. **d** 84 **p** 85. C Eastcote St Lawr *Lon* 84-87; C Kensington St Mary Abbots w St Geo 87-90; Chapl HM Pris Brixton 90-91; Chapl HM Pris Send 91-92; Chapl HM Pris Downview 91-92; Chapl HM Pris High Down 92-98; Chapl HM Pris Wormwood Scrubs 98-02; rtd 02; PtO *Lon* from 02; *Ox* 02-04; *S'wark* 02-13; PV Westmr Abbey from 02. *105 Valiant House, Vicarage Crescent, London SW11 3LX* E: alanboddy@dsl.pipex.com

BODDY, David. b 57. Linc Th Coll 92. **d** 92 **p** 93. C Peterlee *Dur* 92-95; C Penshaw 95-97; P-in-c Shiney Row 95-98; P-in-c Herrington 95-98; TV S Shields All SS 98-04; V Haswell, Shotton and Thornley 04-13; P-in-c Somerleyton, Ashby, Fritton, Herringfleet etc *Nor* from 13. *The Rectory, The Street, Somerleyton, Lowestoft NR32 5PT* T: (01502) 733374 M: 07971-304622 E: davidboddy1@gmail.com

BODEKER, Brian Mark. b 60. Cant Univ (NZ) BCom 82. Ox Min Course 09. **d** 12 **p** 13. NSM Didcot All SS *Ox* 12-14; C from 14. *1 Holly Lane, Harwell, Didcot OX11 6DA* M: 07970-111110 E: markbodeker@btinternet.com

BODLE, Richard Talbot. b 70. Southn Univ LLB 91. Wycliffe Hall Ox BTh 98. **d** 98 **p** 99. C S Mimms Ch Ch *Lon* 98-02; TV Edgware 02-08; V Churt and Hindhead *Guildf* from 08. *St Alban's Vicarage, Wood Road, Hindhead GU26 6PX* T: (01428) 605305 E: richard@bodle.plus.com *or* vicar@stalbanshindhead.org.uk

BODMIN, Archdeacon of. *See* ELKINGTON, The Ven Audrey Anne

BODY, Andrew. b 46. Pemb Coll Cam BA 68 MA 71. Ridley Hall Cam 68. **d** 70 **p** 71. C New Bury *Man* 70-73; TV Droylsden St Mary 73-78; V Low Harrogate St Mary *Ripon* 78-92; TR Redhorn *Sarum* 92-97; V Chobham w Valley End *Guildf* 97-12; RD Surrey Heath 06-11; rtd 12; PtO *Heref* from 12. *Holyrood, 17 Temeside Estate, Ludlow SY8 1LD* T: (01584) 877465 E: corpora12@btinternet.com

BODY, Mrs Shuna Jane. b 67. MBE 14. SEITE 98. **d** 01 **p** 02. NSM Brookland, Fairfield, Brenzett w Snargate etc *Cant* from 01. *Hope Farm, Snargate, Romney Marsh TN29 9UQ* T: (01797) 343977 M: 07977-981990 E: shunabody@hotmail.com

BODYCOMBE, Stephen John. b 58. Lanchester Poly Cov BA. St Mich Coll Llan. **d** 83 **p** 84. C Cardiff St Jo *Llan* 83-86; V Dinas and Penygraig w Williamstown 86-00; V Dyffryn from 00. *The Vicarage, Dyffryn, Neath SA10 7AZ* T: (01792) 814237

BOFFEY, Ian. b 40. Glas Univ MA 63. Glas NSM Course 75. **d** 75 **p** 78. NSM Dalry *Glas* 75-78; P-in-c 78-97; N Ayrshire TM from 97. *2 Kinloch Avenue, Stewarton, Kilmarnock KA3 3HF* T: (01560) 482586 E: ian.boffey2@btinternet.com

BOGA, Bishop of. *See* NJOJO, The Rt Revd Patrice Byankya

BOGGUST, Mrs Patricia Anne. b 42. Portsm Dioc Tr Course. **d** 90 **p** 98. NSM Hook w Warsash *Portsm* 90-94; NSM Locks Heath 94-09; Chapl Univ Hosp Southn NHS Foundn Trust from 01. *21 Beverley Close, Park Gate, Southampton SO31 6QU* T: (01489) 573586

BOGLE, Ms Elizabeth. b 47. York Univ BA 68 Leeds Univ PGCE 69. S'wark Ord Course 93. **d** 96 **p** 97. NSM E Greenwich *S'wark* 96-00; NSM Hatcham St Jas 00-06; NSM Newington St Paul 06-14; PtO from 14. *96 Grierson Road, London SE23 1NX* T: (020) 8699 9996 E: elizabethbogle@hotmail.com

BOGLE, James Main Lindam Linton. b 33. Peterho Cam BA 56 MA 60. Wells Th Coll 59. **d** 61 **p** 62. C Bermondsey St Anne *S'wark* 61-65; Chapl S'wark Univ 65-72; V Brayton 72-76; V Forest Hill St Aug *S'wark* 76-83; C Hatcham St Cath 83-85; Hon C 91-03; C Herne Hill St Paul 86-87; rtd 87; PtO *S'wark* from 04. *96 Grierson Road, London SE23 1NX* T: (020) 8699 9996 E: jamesmllbogle@hotmail.com

BOGLE, The Very Revd Paul David. b 57. CITC BTh 10. **d** 10 **p** 11. C Dunboyne and Rathmolyon *M & K* 10-13; I Trim and Athboy Gp from 13; Dean Clonmacnoise from 14. *St Patrick's Deanery, St Loman's Street, Trim, Co Meath, Republic of Ireland* T: (00353) (46) 943 6698 E: pdbogle@gmail.com

BOHAN, Kimberly Anne. b 72. St Andr Univ MA 93 Smith Coll (USA) MAT 94 St Andr Univ BD 99 Edin Univ MTh 03. **d** 03 **p** 04. C Glas St Ninian 03-06; R Dunoon *Arg* 06-09; P-in-c Rothesay 06-09; P-in-c Tighnabruaich 06-09; R Dunblane *St And* 09-12; P-in-c Waltham *Linc* 13-14; P-in-c Barnoldby le Beck 13-14; P-in-c New Waltham 13-14; P-in-c Laceby and Ravendale Gp 13-14; R Waltham Gp from 14. *The Rectory, 95 High Street, Waltham, Grimsby DN37 0PN* E: kbohan@btinternet.com

BOLAND, Christopher Paul. b 75. Hertf Coll Ox MPhys 97. Ridley Hall Cam BTh 01. **d** 01 **p** 02. C Skirbeck H Trin *Linc* 01-05; P-in-c Grantham, Harrowby w Londonthorpe from 05; RD Grantham from 12. *The Vicarage, Edinburgh Road, Grantham NG31 9QZ* T: (01476) 564781 M: 07791-702537 E: cpboland@btinternet.com

BOLAND, Geoffrey. b 56. Open Univ BA 03. Oak Hill Th Coll 87. **d** 89 **p** 90. C Ormskirk *Liv* 89-94; C Woodside Park St Barn *Lon* 94-99; TV Canford Magna *Sarum* from 99. *11 Plantagenet Crescent, Bournemouth BH11 9PL* T: (01220) 573872 E: brevgeoff@ntlworld.com

BOLD, Peter Edward. b 64. Sheff Univ BEng 86 PhD 90. Cranmer Hall Dur BA 94. **d** 95 **p** 96. C Grenoside *Sheff* 95-97; C Rotherham and Dioc Communications Officer 97-01; P-in-c Brampton Bierlow 01-05; V 05-11; TR Dronfield w Holmesfield *Derby* from 11. *The Rectory, 24 Church Street, Dronfield S18 1QB* T: (01246) 411531 E: pebold@talk21.com

BOLDING, Alan Frederick. b 40. NTMTC. **d** 07 **p** 07. NSM Woodford Bridge *Chelmsf* 07-13; PtO from 13. *21 Portman Drive, Woodford Green IG8 8QN* T: (020) 8550 2070 M: 07932-797983 E: apbolding@onetel.com

BOLE, Malcolm Dennis. b 30. Oak Hill Th Coll 65. **d** 67 **p** 68. C Bridlington Priory *York* 67-70; Lect Stanley Smith Th Coll Gahini Rwanda 71; Prin 71-72; Lect École de Théologie Butare 72-73; P-in-c Combe Hay *B & W* 74-81; V Bath Odd Down 74-81; P-in-c Taunton St Jas 81-84; V 84-90; R Bicknoller w Crowcombe and Sampford Brett 90-98; rtd 98; PtO *B & W* from 01. *7 Putsham Mead, Kilve, Bridgwater TA5 1DZ* T: (01278) 741297 E: mjbole@btinternet.com

BOLEN, Mrs Susan Melanie. b 63. INSEAD MBA 91 K Coll Lon MA 11. ERMC 12. **d** 15. C Frimley *Guildf* from 15. *4 Warren Rise, Frimley, Camberley GU16 8SH* M: 07799-656615 T: (01276) 785869 E: susan@frimley.org.uk *or* s.bolen@mac.com

BOLLARD, Canon Richard George. b 39. Fitzw Ho Cam BA 61 MA 65 K Coll Lon BD 63 AKC 63. **d** 64 **p** 65. C Southampton Maybush St Pet *Win* 64-68; Chapl Aston Univ *Birm* 68-74; TR Chelmsley Wood 74-82; V Coleshill and Maxstoke 82-04; RD Coleshill 82-92; Hon Can Birm Cathl 85-04; Dioc Ecum Officer 97-02; rtd 04; PtO *Heref* from 05. *Moreton Cottage, 12 Prince Edward Road, Hereford HR4 0LG* T: (01432) 267414

BOLLEY, Michael Francis. b 55. St Cath Coll Ox BA 76 MSc 77 MA 92. Ripon Coll Cuddesdon 90. **d** 92 **p** 93. C Pinner *Lon*

92-95; C Eastcote St Lawr 95-99; P-in-c Southall H Trin 99-06; V from 06. *Holy Trinity Vicarage, Park View Road, Southall UB1 3HJ* T: (020) 8571 7329
E: michael@bolley.freeserve.co.uk

BOLSTER, Christopher David. b 77. St Mary's Coll Twickenham BA 99. STETS MA 11. **d** 11 **p** 12. C Stanwix *Carl* 11-15; V Clifton *Man* from 15. *St Anne's Vicarage, 237 Manchester Road, Clifton, Swinton, Manchester M27 6PP* T: (01228) 524436 M: 07970-943244
E: cdbolster2000@tiscali.co.uk

BOLSTER, David Richard. b 50. BA. St Jo Coll Nottm. **d** 84 **p** 85. C Luton Lewsey St Hugh *St Alb* 84-87; V Woodside w E Hyde 87-01; V Edmonton St Aldhelm *Lon* 01-10; PtO *Blackb* from 15. *3 Arnside Crescent, Morecambe LA4 5PP* T: (01524) 923861
E: dandmbolster@psmail.net

BOLSTER, Mrs Lucy Clare. b 74. St Jo Coll Nottm 12. **d** 15. NSM Sheffield Vine *Sheff* from 15. *20 Westmoreland Street, Sheffield S6 3JA* M: 07948-403155 E: lucy_bolster@hotmail.com

BOLT, George Henry. b 34. MInstP 75 CPhys 75 Lon Univ BSc 60 Bath Univ MSc 75. S Dios Minl Tr Scheme 85. **d** 88 **p** 89. NSM Oldbury *Sarum* 88-89; Chapl Chippenham Tech Coll 89-90; C Kington St Michael *Bris* 90-92; P-in-c Aldenham *St Alb* 92-98; rtd 98; PtO *Ban* from 98. *Ty Capel Ffrwd, Llanfachreth, Dolgellau LL40 2NR* T: (01341) 422006

BOLT, Mrs Mary Veronica. b 36. S Dios Minl Tr Scheme 90. **d** 93 **p** 94. NSM Aldenham *St Alb* 93-98; Sub-Chapl HM Pris The Mount 93-98; rtd 98; PtO *Ban* 98-99; P-in-c Maentwrog w Trawsfynydd 99-03. *Ty Capel Ffrwd, Llanfachreth, Dolgellau LL40 2NR* T: (01341) 422006 E: mary.bolt@care4free.net

BOLTON, Canon Christopher Leonard. b 60. St Mich Coll Llan. **d** 83 **p** 84. C Lampeter *St D* 83-86; P-in-c Llanarth and Capel Cynon w Talgarreg etc 86-87; V from 87; AD Glyn Aeron from 02; Hon Can St D Cathl from 09. *The Vicarage, Llanarth SA47 0NJ* T: (01545) 580745

BOLTON, Canon Jane Elizabeth. b 53. Leic Univ BA 75. Ripon Coll Cuddesdon 95. **d** 97 **p** 98. C Sheff St Mark Broomhill 97-02; P-in-c Dinnington 02-04; P-in-c Laughton w Throapham 03-04; P-in-c Dinnington w Laughton and Throapham 04-05; R 05-11; AD Laughton 08-11; P-in-c Ravenfield, Hooton Roberts and Braithwell from 11; SSM Officer from 11; Hon Can Sheff Cathl from 10. *The Rectory, Micklebring Lane, Braithwell, Rotherham S66 7AS* T: (01709) 812665 E: mail@janebolton.co.uk *or* jane.bolton@sheffield.anglican.org

BOLTON, John. b 43. SS Paul & Mary Coll Cheltenham DipEd 64. Trin Coll Bris 83. **d** 85 **p** 86. C Minehead *B & W* 85-89; R Winford w Felton Common Hill 89-98; C-in-c Locking Castle CD 98-06; rtd 06; PtO *B & W* from 06. *The Poppies, 13 Cornlands, Sampford Peverell, Tiverton EX16 7UA* T: (01884) 821445 E: johnbolton455@btinternet.com

BOLTON, Mrs Judith Ann. b 48. ERMC 12. **d** 13 **p** 14. NSM Hemingford Abbots *Ely* from 13; NSM Hemingford Grey from 13. *10 Westmeare, Hemingford Grey, Huntingdon PE28 9BZ* T: (01480) 370036 E: judithbolton10@gmail.com

BOLTON, Kelvin. b 53. Wilson Carlile Coll 88 Trin Coll Bris BA 98. **d** 98 **p** 99. C Walton Breck Ch Ch *Liv* 98-01; V Goose Green 01-08; P-in-c Walton Breck from 08. *Christ Church Vicarage, 157 Hartnup Street, Liverpool L5 1UWp* T: 0151-263 2518 E: kelvb@uwclub.net

BOLTON, Paul Edward. b 71. St Jo Coll *Ox* BA 94 MA 98 Peterho Cam BA 97. Ridley Hall Cam 95. **d** 98 **p** 99. C Lowestoft Ch Ch *Nor* 98-01; Titus Trust from 01. *33 Wharton Road, Headington, Oxford OX3 8AL* T: (01865) 756334
E: paul_bolton@lineone.net

BOLTON, Peter Richard Shawcross. b 58. Warwick Univ BA 79. Sarum & Wells Th Coll 80. **d** 83 **p** 84. C Beckenham St Jas *Roch* 83-86; C Bedford Leigh *Man* 86-88; V Royton St Paul 88-94; AD Tandle 93-94; P-in-c Lower Broughton Ascension 95-01; P-in-c Salford Ordsall St Clem 98-01; P-in-c Ardwick St Benedict 99-01; V Leavesden *St Alb* 01-07; V Weston super Mare All SS and St Sav *B & W* 07-10; rtd 10; PtO *Ches* 12-14; Hon C Ilkeston H Trin *Derby* 14-15; Hon C Long Eaton St Laur 14-15; CMP 99-10 and from 13. *Holy Trinity Vicarage, 1 Cotmanhay Road, Ilkeston DE7 8HR* M: 07988-891440
E: prsb58@gmail.com

BOLTON, Richard David Edward. b 52. MA. St Steph Ho Ox 79. **d** 81 **p** 82. C Rawmarsh w Parkgate *Sheff* 81-84; Chapl Wellingborough Sch 85-92; Chapl Merchant Taylors' Sch Northwood 91-11; P-in-c Winchmore Hill H Trin *Lon* from 12; P in O from 96. *Holy Trinity Vicarage, 6 King's Avenue, London N21 3NA* T: (020) 8364 1583
E: rdeb2010@btinternet.com

BOLTON-DEBBAGE, Grant William Vivian. b 86. St Aid Coll Dur BA 08. Ripon Coll Cuddesdon 12. **d** 14 **p** 15. C Gt Yarmouth *Nor* from 14. *18 Royal Avenue, Great Yarmouth NR30 4EB* T: (01493) 301758 E: gboltondebbage@gmail.com

BOLTON, Archdeacon of. See BAILEY, The Ven David Charles

BOLTON, Suffragan Bishop of. See EDMONDSON, The Rt Revd Christopher Paul

BOMFORD, Canon Rodney William George. b 43. BNC Ox BA 64 MA 68. Coll of Resurr Mirfield 67 Union Th Sem (NY) STM 69. **d** 69 **p** 70. C Deptford St Paul *S'wark* 69-77; V Camberwell St Giles w St Matt 77-01; RD Camberwell 87-97; Hon Can S'wark Cathl 93-01; rtd 01. *The Manor House, Modbury, Ivybridge PL21 0RA* T: (01548) 831277

BOMYER, Julian Richard Nicholas Jeffrey. b 55. AKC 78 Sarum & Wells Th Coll 78. **d** 79 **p** 80. C Rugby *Cov* 79-84; TV 85-88; P-in-c Clifton upon Dunsmore w Brownsover 84-85; Prec Ch Ch *Ox* 88-93; V Hampton *Worc* 93-01; P-in-c Sedgeberrow w Hinton-on-the-Green 00-01; R Hampton w Sedgeberrow and Hinton-on-the-Green 01-06; rtd 06. *52 Elmside, Evesham WR11 3DZ* T: (01386) 421559
E: julian@bomyer.co.uk

BOND, Andrew James Douglas. b 81. Ridley Hall Cam 11. **d** 14. C Penge Lane H Trin *Roch* from 14. *St John's Vicarage, St John's Road, London SE20 7EQ* M: 07939-051990
E: bondboy81@hotmail.com

BOND, Andrew Thomas. b 50. Leeds Univ BA 74 Solicitor 79. Ox Min Course 09. **d** 12 **p** 13. NSM Pangbourne w Tidmarsh and Sulham *Ox* from 12. *Heron Lodge, 32 The Moors, Pangbourne, Reading RG8 7LP* T: 0118-984 5297 M: 07917-623444 E: at.bond@btinternet.com

BOND, Anne. See BOND, Sybilla Anne

✠**BOND, The Rt Revd Charles Derek.** b 27. AKC 51. **d** 52 **p** 53 **c** 76. C Friern Barnet St Jas *Lon* 52-56; LtO *Birm* 56-58; Midl Sch Sec SCM 56-58; V Harringay St Paul *Lon* 58-62; V Harrow Weald All SS 62-72; P-in-c Pebmarsh *Chelmsf* 72-73; Adn Colchester 72-76; Area Bp Bradwell 76-92; rtd 92; Hon Asst Bp Glouc and Worc 92-06; PtO *Chelmsf* 06-12; Hon Asst Bp Chelmsf from 07. *52 Horn Book, Saffron Walden CB11 3JW* T: (01799) 521308 E: derekbond@greenbee.net

BOND, Daniel Michael. b 75. Bp Grosseteste Coll BA 97 Cam Univ BTh 02. Ridley Hall Cam 99. **d** 02 **p** 03. C Ranworth w Panxworth, Woodbastwick etc *Nor* 02-05; R Acle w Fishley, N Burlingham, Beighton w Moulton 05-07; Chapl Aldenham Sch Herts 07-11; Chapl Merchant Taylors' Sch Northwood from 12; PtO *Lon* from 12. *3 East Drive, Sandy Lodge Lane, Northwood HA6 2HT* T: (01923) 820644
E: dbond@mtsn.org.uk

BOND, David. b 36. Oak Hill Th Coll 72. **d** 74 **p** 75. C Leyton St Mary w St Edw *Chelmsf* 74-78; C Slough *Ox* 78-80; V Selby St Jas *York* 80-93; P-in-c Wistow 80-82; V 82-93; RD Selby 89-93; P-in-c Northiam *Chich* 93-94; R 94-99; rtd 99; PtO *Chich* from 00. *32 Reginald Road, Bexhill-on-Sea TN39 3PH* T: (01424) 731845

BOND, David Hugh Tremayne. b 64. Ripon Coll Cuddesdon 13. **d** 15. C Kingsbridge, Dodbrooke, and W Alvington *Ex* from 15. *The Vicarage, Townsend Close, West Alvington, Kingsbridge TQ7 3QA* M: 07875-781709
E: dhtb@btinternet.com

BOND, David Matthew. b 38. Leic Univ BA 59 Leeds Univ PGCE 67 Nottm Univ MA 85. Sarum Th Coll 59. **d** 61 **p** 62. C Leic St Anne 61-64; E England Sec SCM 64-66; Hon C Nor St Pet Mancroft 64-67; Lect and Hd of Section Pet Regional Coll 67-96; Lect Pet Coll of Adult Educn from 96; Hon C N Stamford All SS w St Pet *Linc* 74-81; Hon C Stamford All SS w St Jo from 81; PtO *Pet* 85-07 and from 12. *2 The Courtyard, Cotterstock, Peterborough PE8 5HD* T: (01832) 226255

BOND, David Warner. b 32. MA BSc(Econ). Cant Sch of Min 79. **d** 82 **p** 83. NSM Otham w Langley *Cant* 82-10; PtO from 11. *6 Denton Close, Maidstone ME15 8ER* T: (01622) 202239 F: 205149 E: dwbond@blueyonder.co.uk *or* dwbond@bigfoot.com

BOND, Derek. See BOND, Charles Derek

BOND, Elizabeth Ruth. b 58. Anglia Ruskin Univ MA 13 SRN 79 SCM 81. Westcott Ho Cam 10. **d** 12 **p** 13. C Irthlingborough, Gt Addington, Lt Addington etc *Pet* from 13. *The Rectory, Church Street, Woodford, Kettering NN14 4EX* T: (01832) 735522 E: revdruth@gmail.com

BOND, Mrs Gita Devi. b 57. N Lon Poly BSc 80 Chelsea Coll Lon PGCE 81. Ridley Hall Cam 06. **d** 08 **p** 09. C The Ramseys and Upwood *Ely* 08-12. *23 Signal Road, Ramsey, Huntingdon PE26 1NG* T: (01487) 821105 M: 07977-555895
E: gita.bond@hotmail.com

BOND, Gordon. b 44. Chich Th Coll 68. **d** 71 **p** 72. C Wisbech St Aug *Ely* 71-74; C Wembley Park St Aug *Lon* 74-77; C York Town St Mich *Guildf* 77-80; TV Haywards Heath St Wilfrid *Chich* 80-82; V Lower Beeding 82-86; V E Grinstead St Mary 86-06; RD E Grinstead 98-04; rtd 06. *6 St Andrew's Close, Reigate RH2 7JF*

BOND, Mrs Jill Margaret. b 45. Newton Park Coll Bath TCert 67. WEMTC 04. **d** 06 **p** 07. OLM Redmarley D'Abitot,

Bromesberrow, Pauntley etc *Glouc* 06-11; NSM from 11. *Southfield, Hawcross, Redmarley, Gloucester GL19 3JQ* T: (01452) 840202 E: rev.jbond@googlemail.com

BOND, Canon John Albert. b 35. LRAM 55 GGSM 56 St Cath Soc Ox BA 61 MA 65 MPhil 77 Seabury-Western Th Sem BD 62. Wycliffe Hall Ox 58. **d** 62 **p** 63. C Chelmsf Cathl 62-63; Succ Chelmsf Cathl 63-64; Prec Chelmsf Cathl 64-66; LtO 66-69; Lect Ch Ch Coll Cant 69-73; Sen Lect Ch Ch Coll Cant 73-85; Prin Lect and Hd RS Cant Ch Ch Univ Coll 85-00; Hon Min Can Cant Cathl 70-85; Hon Can Cant Cathl 85-00; rtd 00; PtO *Cant* from 03. *1 St Lawrence Forstal, Canterbury CT1 3PA* T: (01227) 765575

BOND, The Very Revd John Frederick Augustus. b 45. Open Univ BA 75. CITC 64. **d** 67 **p** 69. C Lisburn St Paul *Conn* 67-70; C Finaghy 70-77; I Ballynure and Ballyeaston 77-99; I Skerry w Rathcavan and Newtowncrommelin from 99; Can Conn Cathl 96-98; Prec 98-01; Dean Conn from 01. *The Rectory, 49 Rectory Gardens, Broughshane, Ballymena BT42 4LF* T/F: (028) 2586 1215 M: 07711-285728 E: jfa.bond@btinternet.com *or* dean@connor.anglican.org

BOND, Kim Mary. *See* BURGESS, Kim Mary

BOND, Lawrence. b 53. ACIB 77. Sarum & Wells Th Coll 92. **d** 92 **p** 93. C Saffron Walden w Wendens Ambo and Littlebury *Chelmsf* 92-95; TV 96-00; P-in-c Takeley w Lt Canfield 00-04; R 04-09; RD Dunmow and Stansted 02-09; P-in-c Sible Hedingham w Castle Hedingham 09-15; RD Hinckford 10-15; rtd 15. *34 Cedar Close, Walton on the Naze CO14 8NJ* T: (01255) 484741 E: revlbond@hotmail.com

BOND, Linda. b 52. Nottm Univ BEd 80 Lon Inst of Educn MA 89. EAMTC 96. **d** 99 **p** 00. C Brackley St Pet w St Jas 99-03; C Skegness Gp *Linc* 03-09; P-in-c Bromham w Oakley and Stagsden *St Alb* from 09. *The Vicarage, 47 Stagsden Road, Bromham, Bedford MK43 8PY* T: (01234) 823268 E: revdlinda@talktalk.net

BOND, Mrs Marian Nancy Hamlyn. b 49. Univ of Wales (Cardiff) BSc(Econ) 71 Westmr Coll Ox PGCE 72 Ex Univ MEd 77. SEITE BA 06. **d** 06 **p** 07. NSM Marden *Cant* 06-09; NSM Len Valley 09-11; NSM Tunstall and Bredgar from 11; Asst Dir of Ords from 09. *The Vicarage, Parsonage Lane, Bredgar, Sittingbourne ME9 8HA* M: 07966-442181 T: (01622) 884387 E: mnhbond@googlemail.com

BOND, Mark Francis Wilson. b 53. Sarum & Wells Th Coll 89. **d** 91 **p** 92. C Taunton Lyngford *B & W* 91-95; V Highbridge 95-02; R Jersey St Brelade *Win* from 02. *The Rectory, La Marquanderie Hill, St Brelade, Jersey JE3 8EP* T: (01534) 742302 F: 490878 E: rector@stbreladeschurch.com

BOND, Norman. b 23. Wycliffe Hall Ox. **d** 70 **p** 71. C Warrington St Ann *Liv* 70-73; P-in-c 73-77; P-in-c Warrington St Pet 73-77; V Wigan St Cath 77-88; rtd 88; PtO *Carl* 88-01; *Liv* 88-98; *S & M* 01-09. *Longs Croft, Gate Lane, Freshwater PO40 9QD* T: (01983) 760799

BOND, Paul Maxwell. b 36. TD 73. Glos Univ BA 00 ACIB 56. Oak Hill Th Coll 76. **d** 79 **p** 80. NSM Wisley w Pyrford *Guildf* 79-91; Org Children's Soc SW Lon 88-91; C Egham *Guildf* 91-93; C Horsell 93-94; V Rockfield and St Maughen's w Llangattock etc *Mon* 94-99; rtd 99; Hon C Islip w Charlton on Otmoor, Oddington, Noke etc *Ox* 99-01; Hon C Ray Valley 01-04; Nat Liaison Officer Ch Tourism Assn 99-04; PtO *Guildf* 08-13. *Fosters, Pyrford Heath, Pyrford, Woking GU22 8SS* T: (01932) 351137 E: paul_bond@bigfoot.com

BOND, Ruth. *See* BOND, Elizabeth Ruth

BOND, Mrs Susan Fraser. b 55. SS Hild & Bede Coll Dur BEd 78 Leeds Univ MA 00. NOC 96. **d** 99 **p** 00. C Tickhill w Stainton *Sheff* 99-02; R Warmsworth 02-10; AD W Doncaster 06-07; V Ampleforth w Oswaldkirk, Gilling E etc *York* from 10. *The Vicarage, West End, Ampleforth, York YO62 4DU* T: (01439) 788867 E: sue@bond007.fslife.co.uk

BOND, Mrs Sybilla Anne. b 44. **d** 12 **p** 13. NSM Swanage and Studland *Sarum* from 12. *51 West Street, Corfe Castle, Wareham BH20 5HA* T: (01929) 480249 E: furzemans@go-plus.net

BONE, David Hugh. b 39. Worc Coll Ox BA 63 MA 67. OLM Almondsbury and Olveston *Bris* from 06. *3 Hardy Lane, Tockington, Bristol BS32 4LJ* T: (01454) 614601 M: 07958-414729 E: david.bone10@btinternet.com

BONE, Mrs Evelyn Mary. b 48. WEMTC 05. **d** 08 **p** 09. NSM Draycot *Bris* from 08. *Somerford House, 2 Fairleigh Rise, Kington Langley, Chippenham SN15 5QF* T: (01249) 750519 E: langley@gebone.mail1.co.uk

BONE, Janet. b 05 **p** 06. NSM Trellech and Penallt *Mon* 05-09; NSM Monmouth w Overmonnow etc from 09. *Ty Ffynnon, The Narth, Monmouth NP25 4QJ* T: (01600) 860466

BONE, Simon Adrian. b 78. Ripon Coll Cuddesdon BA 09. **d** 09 **p** 10. C Newquay *Truro* 09-11; C Chacewater w St Day and Carharrack 11-14; P-in-c from 14; C Devoran 11-14; P-in-c from 14; C Feock 11-14; P-in-c from 14; C St Stythians w

Perranarworthal and Gwennap 11-14; P-in-c from 14; Asst Rural Link Officer from 13. *The Rectory, Church Street, St Day, Redruth TR16 5LD* T: (01209) 822862 M: 07971-270615 E: fathersimon@btinternet.com

BONHAM, Mrs Valerie. b 47. ALA 94. SAOMC 94. **d** 97 **p** 98. NSM Newbury *Ox* 97-98; C Cookham 98-02; P-in-c Coleford w Holcombe *B & W* 02-14; rtd 14. *89 Balch Road, Wells BA5 2BX* T: (01749) 676326 E: valerie.bonham@zen.co.uk

BONHAM-CARTER, Gerard Edmund David. b 31. Lon Univ BSc 53. S'wark Ord Course 84. **d** 87 **p** 88. NSM Wandsworth St Paul *S'wark* 87-04; Chapl R Hosp for Neuro-Disability 92-04; PtO *St E* from 87; *S'wark* from 04. *7 Fleur Gates, Princes Way, London SW19 6QQ* T: (020) 8788 1230 *or* 8780 5075 E: gerard.bonham-carter@ukgateway.net

BONIFACE, Lionel Ernest George. b 36. Lon Coll of Div BD 64 ALCD 63. **d** 64 **p** 65. C Attenborough w Chilwell *S'well* 64-69; C Farndon 69-71; C Thorpe 69-71; P-in-c Mansfield St Aug 71-77; V Oughtibridge *Sheff* 77-92; Ind Chapl 79-81; P-in-c Treeton 92-93; TV Brinsworth w Catcliffe and Treeton 93-98; rtd 98; PtO *Sheff* 99-13. *1 Green Oak Grove, Sheffield S17 4GG* T: 0114-235 0415

BONIWELL, Timothy Richard. b 51. AKC 73. St Aug Coll Cant 74. **d** 75 **p** 76. C Walthamstow St Mich *Chelmsf* 75-78; C Wigmore Abbey *Heref* 78-83; C Studley and Chapl Trowbridge Coll *Sarum* 83-86; V Bath St Barn w Englishcombe *B & W* 86-95; R Tintinhull w Chilthorne Domer, Yeovil Marsh etc 95-02; V Enfield St Geo *Lon* 02-05; Chapl Convent of St Mary at the Cross Edgware 05-10; Chapl Barnet and Chase Farm Hosps NHS Trust from 10. *Chase Farm Hospital, The Ridgeway, Enfield EN2 8JL* T: 08451-114000 E: boniwell@btinternet.com

BONNER, David Robert. b 28. ASCA 66 FCIS 72 FCIB 74. S'wark Ord Course 74. **d** 77 **p** 78. NSM Hampton All SS *Lon* 77-84; P-in-c Twickenham All SS 84-91; rtd 91; PtO *Lon* 91-05. *17 St James's Road, Hampton Hill, Hampton TW12 1DH* T: (020) 8979 1565

BONNER, James Maxwell Campbell. b 28. Sydney Univ BSc 48 DipEd 49. Oak Hill Th Coll BD 59. **d** 60 **p** 61. C Walthamstow St Mary *Chelmsf* 60-63; C Morden *S'wark* 63-65; Australia from 65; rtd 98. *1206/5 Albert Road, Strathfield NSW 2135, Australia* T: (0061) (2) 9763 7535

BONNET, Tom. b 51. Univ of Wales (Cardiff) BTh 90. St Mich Coll Llan 90. **d** 90 **p** 91. C Criccieth w Treflys *Ban* 90-91; C Denio w Abererch 91-93; R Llanfachraeth 93-94; R Valley w Llanfachraeth 94-97; R Valley w Llechylched and Caergeiliog 98-07; AD Llifon and Talybolion 04-07; V Caerhun and Llangelynnin and Llanbedr-y-Cennin from 07. *Caerhun Vicarage, Tyn-y-Groes, Conwy LL32 8UG* T: (01492) 650250 M: 07713-548941 E: revtbonnet@btinternet.com

BONNEY, The Very Revd Mark Philip John. b 57. St Cath Coll Cam BA 78 MA 82. St Steph Ho Ox BA 84 MA 89. **d** 85 **p** 86. C Stockton St Pet *Dur* 85-88; Chapl St Alb Abbey 88-90; Prec 90-92; V Eaton Bray w Edlesborough 92-96; R Gt Berkhamsted 96-04; RD Berkhamsted 02-04; Can Res and Treas Sarum Cathl 04-12; Dean Ely from 12. *The Deanery, The College, Ely CB7 4DN* T: (01353) 660316 E: m.bonney@elycathedral.org

BONNEY, Prof Richard John. b 47. Ox Univ DPhil 73. **d** 96 **p** 97. NSM Knighton St Mary Magd *Leic* 96-11; C-in-c Knighton St Guthlac CD from 11. *7 Carisbrooke Park, Leicester LE2 3PQ* T: 0116-212 5677 E: bon@leicester.anglican.org

BONNEY, Stuart Campbell. b 51. Edin Univ BD 83. Edin Th Coll 81. **d** 83 **p** 84. C Edin St Luke and Edin St Martin 83-86; P-in-c Auchterarder and Muthill *St And* 86-90; Dep Chapl HM Pris Leeds 90-91; Chapl HM Pris Moorland 91-96; Chapl HM YOI Polmont from 96; P-in-c Bathgate and Linlithgow *Edin* 96-01. *HM Young Offenders Institution, Redding Road, Brightons, Falkirk FK2 0AB* T: (01324) 711558

BONNEYWELL, Miss Christine Mary. b 57. Univ of Wales (Lamp) BA 78 LTh 80. Sarum & Wells Th Coll 80. **d** 81 **p** 94. C Swansea St Pet *S & B* 81-84; C Llangyfelach 84-86; Chapl Univ of Wales (Lamp) *St D* 86-90; Educn Officer Wells Cathl 90-95; C Yeovil H Trin w Barwick 95-97; Chapl Yeovil Distr Hosp 95-97; Chapl Pilgrim Health NHS Trust Boston 97-01; Chapl United Lincs Hosps NHS Trust from 01. *The Chaplaincy, Pilgrim Hospital, Sibsey Road, Boston PE21 9QT* or *4 Hospital Lane, Boston PE21 9BY* T: (01205) 355151 F: 354395 T: (01205) 364801 ext 2243

BONSALL, Charles Henry Brash. b 42. Ex Univ BA 66. Ridley Hall Cam 66. **d** 68 **p** 69. C Cheltenham St Mary *Glouc* 68-72; Sudan 72-77 and 79-83; PtO *Nor* 78; Development and Miss Sec Intercon Ch Soc 83-93; rtd 93; PtO *Birm* from 91. *3 Pakenham Road, Birmingham B15 2NE* T: 0121-440 6143

BONSEY, Hugh Richmond Lowry. b 49. Sarum & Wells Th Coll 74. **d** 76 **p** 77. C Bris St Mary Redcliffe w Temple etc

76-80; TV Sutton *Liv* 80-88; P-in-c Yatton Keynell *Bris* 88-89; P-in-c Biddestone w Slaughterford 88-89; P-in-c Castle Combe 88-89; P-in-c W Kington 88-89; P-in-c Nettleton w Littleton Drew 88-89; C Westbury-on-Trym H Trin 89-90; V Peasedown St John w Wellow *B & W* 90-04; TV Lower Wylye and Till Valley *Sarum* from 04. *The Rectory, West Street, Great Wishford, Salisbury SP2 0PQ* T: (01722) 790363
E: hughbonsey@gmail.com

BONTING, Prof Sjoerd Lieuwe. b 24. Amsterdam Univ BSc 44 MSc 50 PhD 52 Lon Univ BD 58 SOSc. Washington Dioc Course 63. **d** 63 **p** 64. C Bethesda St Luke USA 63-65; Prof Biochemistry Nijmegen Univ 65-85; Chapl Nijmegen, Eindhoven, Arnhem and Twenthe *Eur* 80-85; Asst Sunnyvale St Thos USA 85-90; Asst Palo Alto St Mark 90-93; PtO *Eur* from 93. *Specreyse 12, 7471 TH Goor, The Netherlands* T: (0031) (547) 260947 E: s.l.bonting@wxs.nl

BOOKER, Ms Alison Susan Wray. b 74. Worc Coll of Educn BA 95 York St Jo Coll MA 04. Westcott Ho Cam 06. **d** 08 **p** 09. C Countesthorpe w Foston *Leic* 08-11; C Church Langton cum Tur Langton etc 11-13; C Houghton-on-the-Hill, Keyham and Hungarton 11-13; V Coplow from 13; Warden Past Assts from 14. *The Vicarage, Gaulby Road, Billesdon, Leicester LE7 9AG* T: 0116-259 6321
E: abooker@leicester.anglican.org

BOOKER, Gerald Dennis. b 30. St Pet Coll Ox BA 52 MA 56. Ridley Hall Cam 53 Oak Hill Th Coll 80. **d** 81 **p** 82. Hon C Hertford All SS *St Alb* 81-83; R Bramfield w Stapleford and Waterford 83-96; Chapl Herts Univ 90-96; rtd 96; PtO *St Alb* from 96. *The Garden House, Churchfields, Hertford SG13 8AE*

BOOKER, Michael Charles. b 36. LLCM 57 ARCO 58. Lon Coll of Div LTh 63. **d** 63 **p** 64. C Royston *St Alb* 63-66; C Mildenhall *St E* 66-68; Min Can St E Cathl 68-83; Prec 70-83; Chapl Framlingham Coll 84-99; rtd 99; PtO *St E* from 99. *29 The Mowbrays, Framlingham, Woodbridge IP13 9DL* T: (01728) 723122

BOOKER, Michael Paul Montague. b 57. Jes Coll Ox BA 79 Bris Univ PGCE 80. Trin Coll Bris BA 87. **d** 87 **p** 88. C Cant St Mary Bredin 87-91; V Leamington Priors St Mary *Cov* 91-96; Dir Miss and Past Studies Ridley Hall Cam 96-05; P-in-c Comberton *Ely* 05-10; P-in-c Toft w Caldecote and Childerley 05-10; TR Lordsbridge from 10; RD Bourn from 13. *The Vicarage, 92 Swaynes Lane, Comberton, Cambridge CB3 7EF* T: (01223) 260095 E: mpmb2@yahoo.co.uk *or* mikebooker@lordsbridge.org

BOOKLESS, Andrew Pitcairn. b 63. Sheff Univ BA 85. St Jo Coll Nottm 90. **d** 92 **p** 93. C Llantrisant *Llan* 92-95; C Llangynwyd w Maesteg 95-97; V Bargoed and Deri w Brithdir 97-12; R Hubberston *St D* 12-14; I Hubberston and Herbrandston from 15. *The Rectory, 35 Westaway Drive, Hakin, Milford Haven SA73 3EQ* T: (01646) 696914 E: ahbookless@googlemail.com

BOOKLESS, David John Charles. b 62. Jes Coll Cam MA 83 PGCE. Trin Coll Bris MA 91. **d** 91 **p** 92. C Southall Green St Jo *Lon* 91-99; P-in-c Southall St Geo 99-01; Nat Dir A Rocha UK 01-11; Adv for Th and Chs A Rocha Internat from 11; Hon C Southall Green St Jo *Lon* from 03. *13 Avenue Road, Southall UB1 3BL* T: (020) 8571 0981 M: 07974-212713
E: dave.bookless@arocha.org

BOOKLESS, Mrs Rosemary. b 26. Westf Coll Lon BA 47 DipEd 49 Serampore Univ BD 72. St Mich Ho Ox 56. **dss** 80 **d** 91 **p** 94. Willoughby-on-the-Wolds w Wysall and Widmerpool *S'well* 80-85; rtd 85; PtO *Leic* 85-89; Loughborough Em 89-91; NSM 91-95; NSM Loughborough Em and St Mary in Charnwood 95-97; PtO 97-03. *19 Capel Court, The Burgage, Prestbury, Cheltenham GL52 3EL* T: (01242) 236937
E: rosemary.bookless926@btinternet.co.uk

BOON, Miss Hilary Joy. b 44. Bath Coll of HE TCert 65 Birm Univ BPhil 83. Yorks Min Course 08. **d** 10 **p** 11. NSM Hutton Cranswick w Skerne, Watton and Beswick *York* from 10. *Homefield, 1 Laburnum Avenue, Cranswick, Driffield YO25 9QH* T: (01377) 202084 M: 07970-370913
E: hilaryboon@hilaryboon.karoo.co.uk

BOON, Mrs Linda Margaret Claire. b 57. Buckingham Univ BA 79 Birm Univ PGCE 80 MEd 91. Yorks Min Course 09. **d** 12 **p** 13. NSM Ripon Cathl from 12. *Cowgate Manor Barn, Shaw Mills, Harrogate HG3 3HP* T: (01423) 779179 M: 07961-893163 E: lindaboon@dsl.pipex.com

BOON, Marion. *See* SIMMONS, Marion

BOON, Nigel Francis. b 39. St Jo Coll Nottm. **d** 83 **p** 84. C St Helens St Helen *Liv* 83-86; V Kirkdale St Lawr 86-92; V Huyton Quarry 92-99; rtd 11. *13/81 Lake Road, Devenport, North Shore, Auckland 0624, New Zealand*
E: nigelfboon@hotmail.com

BOON, Stephen David. b 81. Em Coll Cam MA 04. Wycliffe Hall Ox BA 10. **d** 12 **p** 13. NSM Tunbridge Wells St Jo *Roch* from 12. *11 The Nightingales, Queens Road, Tunbridge Wells TN4 9LU* T: (01892) 548424 E: stephen.boon@cantab.net

BOON, William John. b 54. Glouc Sch of Min 84. **d** 88 **p** 89. NSM Matson *Glouc* 88-91; C Gt Witcombe 91-95; C Brockworth 91-96; P-in-c Sharpness w Purton and Brookend 96-99; P-in-c Slimbridge 97-99; R Sharpness, Purton, Brookend and Slimbridge from 00; AD Dursley 02-07. *The Vicarage, Sanigar Lane, Newtown, Berkeley GL13 9NF* T: (01453) 811360 E: bill.boon@btinternet.com

BOORMAN, Hugh Ronald. b 58. Ox Min Course 07. **d** 08 **p** 08. C Didcot All SS *Ox* from 08. *Barnabas House, 12 Trent Road, Didcot OX11 7RB* T: (01235) 819036 M: 07980-046162 E: hugh.boorman1@btinternet.com

BOOT, Felicity Olivia. b 43. TCert 64. STETS 94. **d** 97 **p** 98. NSM Lyndhurst and Emery Down and Minstead *Win* 97-04; Chapl Southn Univ Hosps NHS Trust 04-09; rtd 09; PtO *Win* from 09. *The Firs, Pikes Hill, Lyndhurst SO43 7AY* T: (023) 8028 2616
E: felicityboot@hotmail.com

BOOTH, Charles. *See* BOOTH, Ewart Charles

BOOTH, Charles Robert. b 48. Leeds Univ CertEd 75. NOC 79. **d** 82 **p** 83. C Eccleshill *Bradf* 82-84; C Jersey St Brelade *Win* 84-88; C Newman Australia 88-90; V Blurton *Lich* 90-93; Chapl Frederick Irwin Angl Communion Sch Mandurah Australia 94-98; R Spearwood Australia 99-03; rtd 03; PtO Perth from 03. *PO Box 174, Toodyay WA 6566, Australia* T: (0061) (8) 9574 2175 M: 40-149 0738
E: boothimages@westnet.com.au

BOOTH, David. b 44. Coll of Resurr Mirfield 72. **d** 74 **p** 75. C Osmondthorpe St Phil *Ripon* 74-77; C Armley w New Wortley 77-79; V Leeds St Wilfrid 79-95; V Royton St Paul *Man* 95-09; rtd 09. *13 Lyon Street, Shaw, Oldham OL2 7RU* T: (01706) 661172

BOOTH, David John. b 55. Leeds Univ BA 76 Leeds Poly PGCE 77. St Mellitus Coll 13. **d** 14 **p** 15. OLM Southend Chelmsf from 14. *13 Guildford Road, Southend-on-Sea SS2 5AR* T: (01702) 612038 M: 07984-160203
E: davidbooth@blueyonder.co.uk

BOOTH, Derek. b 36. LTCL ALCM AKC 61. **d** 62 **p** 63. C Woodchurch *Ches* 62-65; C Penrith St Andr *Carl* 65-67; C Tranmere St Paul *Ches* 67-70; C Wilmslow 70-72; V Micklehurst 73-97; C Staveley and Barrow Hill *Derby* 97-01; rtd 01; PtO *Derby* from 01. *9 Ilam Close, Inkersall, Chesterfield S43 3EW* T: (01246) 475421
E: delbooth@talktalk.net

BOOTH, Eric James. b 43. Open Univ BA 84. NOC 86. **d** 89 **p** 90. NSM Nelson St Phil *Blackb* 89-93; NSM Fence and Newchurch-in-Pendle 93-97; NSM Padiham w Hapton and Padiham Green 97-03; rtd 03; PtO *Blackb* from 04. *5 Round Hill Place, Cliviger, Burnley BB10 4UA* T: (01282) 450708

BOOTH, Ewart Charles. b 67. LTCL 85 K Coll Lon LLB 88. Sarum & Wells Th Coll BTh 93. **d** 93 **p** 95. NSM Tadley St Pet *Win* 93-95; C Highcliffe w Hinton Admiral 95-00; R W Parley *Sarum* from 00. *The Rectory, 250 New Road, West Parley, Ferndown BH22 8EW* T: (01202) 873561
E: elizabethbooth872@btinternet.com

BOOTH, Graham Richard. b 55. Birm Univ BSocSc 75. St Jo Coll Nottm 89. **d** 91 **p** 92. C Woodthorpe *S'well* 91-96; P-in-c Trowell 96-02; P-in-c Awsworth w Cossall 00-02; R Trowell, Awsworth and Cossall 02-05; Community of Aid and Hilda from 05. *The Lifeboat House, Holy Island, Berwick-upon-Tweed TD15 2SQ* T/F: (01289) 389110
E: g.r.booth@ntlworld.com

BOOTH, Ian George. b 64. Chich Th Coll 85 Linc Th Coll 87. **d** 88 **p** 89. C Pet St Mary Boongate 88-90; C Hawley H Trin *Guildf* 90-94; V Willesden St Mary *Lon* 94-03; P-in-c Gosport H Trin *Portsm* 03-05; V 05-06; V Gosport Ch Ch 05-06; RD Gosport 03-06; V Leigh-on-Sea St Marg *Chelmsf* from 09. *St Margaret's Vicarage, 1465 London Road, Leigh-on-Sea SS9 2SB* T: (01702) 471773 E: frianbooth@hotmail.com

BOOTH, Jon Alfred. b 42. Nottm Univ BA 64 Lon Univ MPhil 72. Coll of Resurr Mirfield 78. **d** 80 **p** 81. C Elland *Wakef* 80-84; C Royston and Carlton 84-09; rtd 09; PtO *Leeds* from 09; *York* from 10. *Millbank Cottage, Thorpe Bassett, Malton YO17 8LU* T: (01944) 758518

BOOTH, Kenneth Neville. b 41. Otago Univ BA 62 MA 63 BD 66 MTh 69 St Andr Univ PhD 74. St Jo Coll Auckland 63. **d** 65 **p** 66. C St Paul's Cathl Dunedin New Zealand 65-69; PtO *St And* 70-71; Lect St Andr Univ 70-71; Lect St Jo Coll Auckland New Zealand 72-80; Asst P Tamaki St Thos 73-80; Warden Selwyn Coll Dunedin 81-85; Lect 85-97; V Roslyn 85-97; Adn Dunedin 86-95; V Gen 92-97; Dir Th Ho 97-06. *30 Church Lane, Merivale, Christchurch 8014, New Zealand* T: (0064) (3) 355 9145 F: 355 6140

BOOTH, Martin Allison. b 54. K Coll Lon MA 06. SEITE. **d** 09 **p** 10. C Wimbledon *S'wark* 09-12; V Riverhead w Dunton Green *Roch* from 12. *St Mary's Vicarage, The Glebe Field, Shoreham Lane, Sevenoaks TN13 3DR* T: (01732) 455736
E: mmejbooth@msn.com

BOOTH, Michael Kevin. b 47. Louvain Univ Belgium BA. St Jo Coll Nottm 88 Oscott Coll (RC) 65. **d** 71 **p** 72. In RC Ch 71-87; C N Reddish *Man* 88-89; R Heaton Norris Ch w All SS 89-99; rtd 99; PtO *Man* 00-08; *Derby* from 06. *3 Potter Road, Hadfield, Glossop SK13 2RA* T: (01457) 853963

BOOTH, Paul Harris. b 49. St Jo Coll Nottm. **d** 79 **p** 80. C Thorpe Edge *Bradf* 79-82; P-in-c Frizinghall 82-83; TV Shipley St Paul and Frizinghall 83-97; rtd 97; PtO *Leeds* from 97; Hon Chapl Bradf Cathl from 11. *11 Derwent Avenue, Wilsden, Bradford BD15 0LY* T: (01535) 958939
E: paul.booth@bradford.anglican.org

BOOTH, Terrence Richard. b 44. Edith Cowan Univ (Aus) BA 98. St Jo Coll Morpeth. **d** 69 **p** 70. C Corowa Australia 69-71; Asst Broken Hill 72-74; P-in-c Urana/Jerilderie 74-79; C Chesterfield St Mary and All SS *Derby* 79-81; Chapl Chesterfield R Hosp 79-81; R Coolamon/Ganmain Australia 82; RD Murrumbridge 83-84; Chapl Bunbury Cathl Gr Sch 85-93; Chapl Edith Cowan Univ 86-92; R Casino 94-98; R Ithaca-Ashgrove 98-01; AD from 01. *286 Waterworks Road, PO Box 31, Ashgrove Qld 4060, Australia* T: (0061) (7) 3366 2320 F: 3366 9793 E: stpaulsash@iprimus.com.au

BOOTHBY, Frank. b 29. St D Coll Lamp 56. **d** 58 **p** 59. C Maghull *Liv* 58-61; C N Meols 61-64; Miss to Seamen 64; rtd 94. *7 Belsfield Drive, Hesketh Bank, Preston PR4 6YB*

BOOTHBY, Mrs Julia. b 64. St Andr Univ MTheol 87. SAOMC 02. **d** 04 **p** 05. C Welwyn *St Alb* 04-08; TV Ouzel Valley 08-11; TV Bp's Hatfield, Lemsford and N Mymms from 11. *The Vicarage, North Mymms Park, North Mymms, Hatfield AL9 7TN* T: (01727) 822887 M: 07952-514228
E: juliabby@sky.com

BOOTHMAN, Ms Olive. b 31. TCD BA. **d** 94 **p** 95. NSM Clondalkin w Rathcoole *D & G* from 94. *Miley Hall, Blessington, Co Wicklow, Republic of Ireland* T: (00353) (45) 865119

BOOTHROYD, Richard. b 78. Northumbria Univ BSc 01. Wycliffe Hall Ox BTh 12. **d** 12 **p** 13. C Wandsworth St Mich w St Steph *S'wark* from 12. *50 Combemartin Road, London SW18 5PR* T: (020) 8877 3003 M: 07976-450087
E: rich@stmikes-ststeves.org.uk

BOOTS, Claude Donald Roy. b 26. Roch Th Coll 67. **d** 69 **p** 70. C Midsomer Norton *B & W* 69-73; V Westfield 73-80; R Ilton w Hambridge, Earnshill, Isle Brewers etc 80-91; rtd 91; PtO *B & W* from 91. *41 Furlong Close, Midsomer Norton, Bath BA3 2PR* T: (01761) 419263 E: pairofboots@uwclub.net

BOOYS, Canon Susan Elizabeth. b 56. Bris Univ BA 78 LMH Ox PGCE 79. SAOMC 92. **d** 95 **p** 96. C Kidlington w Hampton Poyle *Ox* 95-99; TV Dorchester 99-05; TR from 05; TV Warborough 99-05; TR from 05; AD Aston and Cuddesdon 07-12; Hon Can Ch Ch from 08. *The Rectory, Manor Farm Road, Dorchester-on-Thames, Wallingford OX10 7HZ* T/F: (01865) 340007 E: rector@dorchester-abbey.org.uk

BOREHAM, Harold Leslie. b 37. S'wark Ord Course. **d** 72 **p** 73. C Whitton and Thurleston w Akenham *St E* 72-77; R Saxmundham 77-85; V Felixstowe SS Pet and Paul 85-96; Chapl Felixstowe Hosp 85-96; Chapl Bartlet Hosp Felixstowe 95-96; P-in-c Ramsgate St Mark *Cant* 96-01; V 01-03; Chapl E Kent NHS and Soc Care Partnership Trust 98-03; rtd 03; PtO *St E* from 03. *313 St John's Road, Colchester CO4 0JR* T: (01206) 853769 E: harrylboreham@googlemail.com

BORLEY, Mark Letchford. b 61. Lon Univ BSc 83 PhD 87. St Jo Coll Nottm MTh 03. **d** 04 **p** 05. C W Swindon and the Lydiards *Bris* 04-05; C Swindon St Aug and Swindon All SS w St Barn 05-07; C Cricklade w Latton 07-09; P-in-c Allington and Maidstone St Pet *Cant* 09-12; PtO 12-14; C W Sheppey 14-15; V Ewell St Fran *Guildf* from 15. *The Minister's House, 71 Ruxley Lane, Epsom KT19 9FF* M: 07811-124237

BORROWDALE, Geoffrey Nigel. b 61. Southn Univ BSc 83 W Sussex Inst of HE PGCE 94. Chich Th Coll 87. **d** 90 **p** 99. C Tilehurst St Mich *Ox* 90-91; PtO *Chich* 93-97; NSM Sunninghill *Ox* 98-99; C Bracknell 99-01; P-in-c Theale and Englefield 01-11; C The Churn 11-13; V Hayes St Anselm *Lon* from 13. *St Anselm's Vicarage, 101 Nield Road, Hayes UB3 1SQ* T: (020) 8561 7058 E: fathergeoffrey@waitrose.com

BORTHWICK, Alexander Heywood. b 36. Open Univ BA 80 Surrey Univ MSc 89 MBPsS 90. Lich Th Coll 57. **d** 60 **p** 61. C Glas Ch Ch 60-62; C Landore *S & B* 62-64; C Swansea St Thos and Kilvey 64-65; Br Guiana 65-66; Guyana 66-70; C Oystermouth *S & B* 70-71; USPG 71-83; Area Sec Man and Liv 71-76; Area Sec Blackb and S & M 73-76; Sch and Children's Work Sec 76-83; Chapl Tooting Bec Hosp Lon 83-91; Chapl Charing Cross Hosp Lon 92-94; Chapl Hammersmith Hosps NHS Trust 94-00; TR Catford (Southend) and Downham *S'wark* 00-04; rtd 04. *Le Roc de Brolange, 5 Brolange, 17150 Soubran, France* T: (0033) 5 46 48 46 23

BORTHWICK, Anne Christine. See ROWLEY, Anne Christine

BOSHER, Philip Ross. b 61. Sarum & Wells Th Coll 84. **d** 87 **p** 88. C Warminster St Denys *Sarum* 87-88; C Warminster St Denys, Upton Scudamore etc 88-90; P-in-c Farley w Pitton and W Dean w E Grimstead 90-91; TV Alderbury Team 91-96; CF from 96. *c/o MOD Chaplains (Army)* F: 381824 T: (01264) 383430

BOSS, Mrs Ann. b 42. Cen Lancs Univ BA 93. CBDTI 99. **d** 02 **p** 03. NSM Scorton and Barnacre and Calder Vale *Blackb* 02-05; P-in-c Hanmer Springs New Zealand 05-10; PtO *Blackb* from 10. *School House Barn, Inglewhite Road, Inglewhite, Preston PR3 2LD* T: (01995) 643146 E: ann.boss227@btinternet.com

BOSSCHAERT, Anthony John. b 34. St Fran Coll Brisbane 65 ACT ThL 69. **d** 68 **p** 69. C Maryborough Australia 68-72; C Roath *Llan* 72-73; C Leckhampton SS Phil and Jas w Cheltenham St Jas *Glouc* 73-76; R Skipton Australia 76-80; C Westmr St Steph w St Jo *Lon* 80-82; TV Wood Green St Mich w Bounds Green St Gabr etc 82-89; In URC 89-03; rtd 03. *55 Willow Way, Potters Bar EN6 2PR* T: (01707) 665445
E: anton4.bosschaert@gmail.com

BOSSWARD, Eric Paul. b 63. CQSW 90. Trin Coll Bris BA 99. **d** 99 **p** 00. C Ecclesall *Sheff* 99-01; C Netherthorpe St Steph 01-04; Co-ord Chapl HM YOI Castington 04-12; V Preston St Cuth *Blackb* from 12. *St Cuthbert's Vicarage, 20 Black Bull Lane, Fulwood, Preston PR2 3PX* T: (01772) 717346
E: eric.bossward@talktalk.net

BOSTOCK, Peter Anthony. b 64. Nottm Univ BA 85 Fitzw Coll Cam BA 89. Westcott Ho Cam 87. **d** 90 **p** 91. C Brighton St Matthias *Chich* 90-94; C Leytonstone St Marg w St Columba *Chelmsf* 94-98; P-in-c Bishopwearmouth Gd Shep *Dur* 98-02; V Monk Bretton *Wakef* 02-03; P-in-c Ryhill 03-12; P-in-c Sharlston 03-12; V Grangetown *Dur* from 12; CMP from 99. *St Aidan's Vicarage, Ryhope Road, Sunderland SR2 9RS* T: 0191-514 3485 M: 07969-407767
E: pbostock@tiscali.co.uk

BOSTON, Jonathan Bertram. b 40. Ely Th Coll 61. **d** 64 **p** 65. C Eaton *Nor* 64-70; Sen Chapl ACF Norfolk 66-05; Chapl Norfolk Constabulary *Nor* from 94; V Horsham St Faith w Newton St Faith 70-90; V Horsford 71-90; V Horsford and Horsham w Newton St Faith 90-97; P-in-c Litcham w Kempston, E and W Lexham, Mileham etc 97-06; rtd 06; PtO *Nor* from 06. *Bevan House, Front Street, Litcham, King's Lynn PE32 2QG* T: (01328) 701200

BOSTON, Archdeacon of. See ALLAIN CHAPMAN, The Ven Justine Penelope Heathcote

BOSWELL, Canon Colin John Luke. b 47. Sarum & Wells Th Coll 72. **d** 74 **p** 75. C Upper Tooting H Trin *S'wark* 74-78; C Sydenham St Phil 78-79; C St Helier 80-83; P-in-c Caterham 83-95; P-in-c Chaldon 85-95; RD Caterham 85-95; V Croydon St Jo from 95; RD Croydon Cen 00-06; Hon Can S'wark Cathl from 99. *Croydon Vicarage, 20A Haling Park Road, South Croydon CR2 6NE* T: (020) 8688 1387 or 8688 8104 F: 8688 5877 M: 07931-850905

BOTHAM, Arthur. b 53. St Jo Coll Nottm. **d** 00 **p** 01. C Hartley Wintney, Elvetham, Winchfield etc *Win* 00-04; TV Basingstoke 04-14; V Popley w Limes Park and Rooksdown from 14; AD Basingstoke 11-15. *The Vicarage, 25 Tewkesbury Close, Popley, Basingstoke RG24 9DU* T: (01256) 324734
E: arthur.botham@btinternet.com

BOTT, Graham Paul. b 49. Staffs Univ MBA 95. NOC 00. **d** 03 **p** 04. NSM Rickerscote *Lich* 03-13; P-in-c Hoar Cross w Newchurch from 13; Chapl Abbots Bromley Sch from 14. *Church Cottage, Maker Lane, Hoar Cross, Burton-on-Trent DE13 8QR* T: (01283) 576058
E: graham.pbott@btopenworld.com

BOTT, Theodore Reginald. b 27. MBE 03. Birm Univ BSc 52 PhD 68 DSc 84 CEng 58 FIChemE 68. WMMTC 85. **d** 86 **p** 87. NSM Harborne St Faith and St Laur *Birm* 86-97; PtO from 97. *17 Springavon Croft, Birmingham B17 9BJ* T: 0121-427 4209

BOTTERILL, David Darrell. b 45. Open Univ BA. Sarum & Wells Th Coll. **d** 83 **p** 84. C Blandford Forum and Langton Long etc *Sarum* 83-86; TV Shaston 86-00; Chapl HM YOI Guys Marsh 89-91; P-in-c Portland St Jo *Sarum* 00-09; Asst Chapl N Dorset Primary Care Trust 01-09; rtd 09; Hon Chapl Miss to Seafarers from 02. *41 Hawthorn Avenue, Gillingham SP8 4ST* T: (01747) 821601 E: david.botterill45@btinternet.com

BOTTING, Canon Michael Hugh. b 25. K Coll Lon BSc 51 AKC K Coll Lon PGCE 52. Ridley Hall Cam 54. **d** 56 **p** 57. C Onslow Square St Paul *Lon* 56-61; V Fulham St Matt 61-72; RD Hammersmith 67; V Leeds St Geo *Ripon* 72-84; RD Headingley 81-84; Hon Can Ripon Cathl 82-84; R Aldford and Bruera *Ches* 84-90; rtd 90; Jt Dir Lay Tr *Ches* 90-95; PtO 95-07. *c/o D Botting Esq, 181 Willow Avenue, Birmingham B17 8HJ* E: michael.botting@btinternet.com

BOTTING, Paul Lloyd. b 43. Brasted Th Coll 67 St Mich Coll Llan 69. **d** 71 **p** 72. C Hucknall Torkard *S'well* 71-74; C Cen Torquay *Ex* 74-76; P-in-c Sutton in Ashfield St Mich *S'well* 76;

V 77-88; Chapl King's Mill Hosp Sutton-in-Ashfield 85-88; NSM Vale of Belvoir *Leic* 95-97; C High Framland Par 97-01; C Waltham on the Wolds, Stonesby, Saxby etc 97-01; C Wymondham w Edmondthorpe, Buckminster etc 97-01; P-in-c High Framland Par 01-10; rtd 10; PtO *Leic* from 10; S'well from 11. *9 Orchard Close, Radcliffe-on-Trent, Nottingham NG12 2BN* T: 0115-933 2591 M: 07770-853762
E: plb@pixie-cat.fslife.co.uk

BOTTLEY, Mrs Kate. b 75. Trin & All SS Coll Leeds BA 97 Open Univ MTh 08. St Jo Coll Nottm LTh 08. **d** 08 **p** 09. C Skegby w Teversal *S'well* 08-11; P-in-c Blyth and Scrooby w Ranskill 11-13; V from 13; Chapl N Notts Coll of FE from 11. *The Vicarage, St Martin's Close, Blyth, Worksop S81 8DW* T: (01909) 591857 M: 07910-242404

BOTTOMER, Sally. b 68. **d** 14 **p** 15. C Aston Clinton w Buckland and Drayton Beauchamp *Ox* from 14. *33 Bishops Field, Aston Clinton, Aylesbury HP22 5BB* T: (01296) 631929 M: 07967-208181 E: sallybottomer@btinternet.com

BOTTOMLEY, Gordon. b 31. Oak Hill Th Coll 51. **d** 55 **p** 56. C Kinson *Sarum* 55-58; LtO *Man* 58-63; N Area Sec BCMS 58-63; V Hemswell w Harpswell *Linc* 63-72; V Glentworth 63-72; Chapl RAF 63-71; R Bucknall and Bagnall *Lich* 72-80; TR 80-82; P-in-c Worthing H Trin *Chich* 82-88; V Camelsdale 88-96; rtd 96; PtO *Portsm* 98-12. *6 Jay Close, Fareham PO14 3TA*

BOTWRIGHT, Adrian Paul. b 55. St Jo Coll Ox MA PGCE. Westcott Ho Cam 80. **d** 82 **p** 83. C Chapel Allerton *Ripon* 82-85; Chapl Chapel Allerton Hosp 82-85; C Bourne *Guildf* 85-88; V Weston 88-94; R Skipton H Trin *Bradf* 94-13; P-in-c Embsay w Eastby 05-13; Hon Can Bradf Cathl 02-13; PtO *York* from 14. *24 Ripon Way, Carlton Miniott, Thirsk YO7 4LR* T: (01845) 523491 E: adrianbotwright@gmail.com

BOUCHER, Brian Albert. b 39. Univ of Wales (Lamp) BA 61. Chich Th Coll 61. **d** 63 **p** 64. C Hoxton H Trin w St Mary *Lon* 63-67; Chapl RN 67-68; Asst Chapl Harrow Sch 68-73; Chapl 73-86; P-in-c Clerkenwell H Redeemer w St Phil *Lon* 86-91; P-in-c Myddleton Square St Mark 86-91; Chapl Hurstpierpoint Coll 92-96; rtd 96; PtO *Chich* from 01. *20 Summervale Road, Tunbridge Wells TN4 8JB* T: (01892) 530342

BOUCHER, Geoffrey John. b 61. Warwick Univ BA 82 K Coll Lon 94. Ridley Hall Cam 94. **d** 96 **p** 97. C Tavistock and Gulworthy *Ex* 96-01; P-in-c W Monkton *B & W* 01-11; R W Monkton w Kingston St Mary, Broomfield etc 11-15; RD Taunton 10-15. *Address temp unknown*
E: geoffboucher@btinternet.com

BOUDIER, Rosemary. *See* TALLOWIN, Rosemary

BOUGHEY, Richard Keith. b 26. Man Univ MEd 71. Qu Coll Birm 77. **d** 80 **p** 82. NSM Upper Tean *Lich* 80-81; NSM Stoke-upon-Trent 80-81; NSM Uttoxeter w Bramshall 82-88; rtd 88; PtO *Lich* 88-11 and from 11. *Kontokali, The Old Lane, Deadman's Green, Checkley, Stoke-on-Trent ST10 4NQ* T: (01538) 722013

BOUGHTON, Mrs Elisabeth Mary Victoria. b 66. St Anne's Coll Ox BA 87 MA 93. Ridley Hall Cam 89. **d** 91 **p** 94. C Guildf Ch Ch 91-95; Chapl St Cath Sch Bramley 92-97; NSM Fetcham *Guildf* 97-14; Chapl Guildf YMCA 04-14; Tutor CME *Guildf* 08-14; PtO *Ox* from 14. *The Vicarage, Manor Road, Goring, Reading RG8 9DR*

BOUGHTON, Canon Michael John. b 37. Kelham Th Coll 57. **d** 62 **p** 63. C Grantham St Wulfram *Linc* 62-66; C Kingsthorpe *Pet* 66-68; C Linc St Nic w St Jo Newport 68-72; V Scunthorpe All SS 72-79; V Crowle 79-89; TR Bottesford w Ashby 89-02; Can and Preb Linc Cathl from 00; rtd 02; PtO *Linc* from 02. *45 Albion Crescent, Lincoln LN1 1EB* T: (01552) 569653
E: mboughton@aol.com

BOUGHTON, Paul Henry. b 55. Imp Coll Lon BScEng 77 ARSM 77 ACA 80. Ridley Hall Cam 89. **d** 91 **p** 92. C Guildf Ch Ch 91-96; R Fetcham 96-14; V Goring and Streatley w S Stoke *Ox* from 14. *The Vicarage, Manor Road, Goring, Reading RG8 9DR* E: boughtonfamily@yahoo.com

BOUGHTON, Miss Ruth Frances. b 52. Ox Brookes Univ BA 10. Birm Bible Inst 71. **d** 07 **p** 08. OLM Chenies and Lt Chalfont, Latimer and Flaunden *Ox* 07-10; NSM from 10. *17 Bell Lane, Amersham HP7 9PF* T: (01494) 764221
E: revboughton@live.co.uk

BOULCOTT, Thomas William. b 16. Bps' Coll Cheshunt 47. **d** 49 **p** 50. C Hitchin St Mary *St Alb* 49-51; C Kempston All SS 51-54; Chapl Bedf Gen Hosp 52-54; V Newfoundpool *Leic* 54-61; V N Evington 61-73; Chapl Leic Gen Hosp 62-73; V Loppington w Newtown *Lich* 73-85; RD Wem and Whitchurch 83-85; rtd 85; PtO *Lich* from 85. *Silver Birch, Tilley Road, Wem, Shrewsbury SY4 5HA* T: (01939) 233602

BOULD, Preb Arthur Roger. b 32. Selw Coll Cam BA 54 MA 58 Wadh Coll Ox BA 55 DipEd 57 MA 58. St Steph Ho Ox 54. **d** 57 **p** 58. C Wednesfield St Thos *Lich* 57-64; V Wellington Ch

Ch 64-71; R Cheadle 71-88; P-in-c Freehay 84-88; R Cheadle w Freehay 88-91; Chapl Cheadle R Hosp 71-91; Chapl HM Pris Moorcourt 72-82; RD Cheadle *Lich* 72-91; Preb Lich Cathl 83-99; Asst to Bp Wolv 91-97; Bp Lich's Past Aux 97-99; C Stafford 97-99; rtd 99; PtO *Lich* 00-10. *The College of St Barnabas, Blackberry Lane, Lingfield RH7 6NJ*

BOULLIER, Canon Kenneth John. b 51. Trin Coll Bris 82. **d** 84 **p** 85. C Heref St Pet w St Owen and St Jas 84-87; V Nutley *Chich* 88-93; R Maresfield 88-93; New Zealand 93-97; R Nailsea H Trin *B & W* 97-08; P-in-c St Just-in-Roseland and St Mawes *Truro* from 08; RD Powder from 13; Hon Can Truro Cathl from 15. *16 Waterloo Close, St Mawes, Truro TR2 5BD* T: (01326) 270248 E: revkjb@hotmail.co.uk

BOULNOIS, Linda Dianne. *See* BISIG, Linda Dianne

BOULT, David Ronald. b 51. Bris Univ BSc 73. St Mich Coll Llan 04. **d** 07 **p** 08. NSM Llantwit Major *Llan* 07-10; NSM Cowbridge from 11. *52 The Verlands, Cowbridge CF71 7BY* T/F: (01446) 772166 M: 07767-818257
E: daveboult@hotmail.co.uk

BOULT, Geoffrey Michael. b 56. Southn Univ BTh 88 Bris Univ MA 92 Birm Univ MSc 96 PGCE 98. Sarum & Wells Th Coll 77. **d** 80 **p** 81. C Newark w Hawton, Cotham and Shelton *S'well* 80-83; TV Melksham *Sarum* 83-90; P-in-c Charminster and Stinsford 90-95; PtO *Birm* 95-96; *Sarum* 95-98; Hon C Bradford Peverell, Stratton, Frampton etc 09-14; P-in-c Arlesey w Astwick *St Alb* from 14. *The Rectory, 77 Church Lane, Arlesey SG15 6UX* T: (01462) 731227 M: 07970-371757
E: vicar@arlesey.org.uk

BOULTBEE, John Michael Godolphin. b 22. Oak Hill Th Coll 66. **d** 68 **p** 69. C Hawkwell *Chelmsf* 68-71; C St Keverne *Truro* 71-73; V Constantine 74-79; P-in-c St Merryn 79-81; V 81-87; rtd 87; PtO *Ex* from 87. *July Cottage, 8 Williams Close, Dawlish EX7 9SP* T: (01626) 865761

BOULTER, Adam Charles. b 71. Bath Coll of HE BA 93 Kingston Univ MA 04 Fitzw Coll Cam BA 07 MA 11. Westcott Ho Cam 05. **d** 08 **p** 09. C Battersea St Mary *S'wark* 08-12; Port Chapl Aqaba Jordan from 12. *Church of St Peter and St Paul, PO Box 568, Aqaba 77110, Jordan* T: (00962) (3) 201 8630
E: adamboulter@cantab.net

BOULTER, Michael Geoffrey. b 32. Lon Univ BD 56. Tyndale Hall Bris 53. **d** 57 **p** 58. C Tranmere St Cath *Ches* 57-60; R Cheetham Hill *Man* 60-65; V Tollard Royal w Farnham *Sarum* 65-66; Chapl Alderney Hosp Poole 66-96; V Branksome St Clem *Sarum* 66-96; rtd 96. *7 Temple Trees, 13 Portarlington Road, Bournemouth BH4 8BU* T: (01202) 768718

BOULTER, Paul Roger. b 81. St Jo Coll Dur BA 03. Ridley Hall Cam 12. **d** 15. C Bedford Ch Ch *St Alb* from 15. *161 Dudley Street, Bedford MK40 3SY* T: (01234) 301708
E: curate@ccbedford.org

BOULTER, Robert George. b 49. Man Univ BA 90. St Aug Coll Cant 72. **d** 75 **p** 76. C Langley All SS and Martyrs *Man* 75-80; V Lower Kersal 80-84; Oman 84-86; Slough Community Chapl *Ox* 86-87; R Whalley Range St Marg *Man* 87-99; P-in-c from 99; Chapl Trin and All SS Coll Leeds from 07. *St Margaret's Rectory, Rufford Road, Manchester M16 8AE* T: 0161-226 1289

BOULTON, Christopher David. b 50. Keble Coll Ox BA 71 MA 80. Cuddesdon Coll 71. **d** 74 **p** 75. C St Mary-at-Latton *Chelmsf* 74-77; C Shrub End 77-80; P-in-c Gt Bentley 80-83; V 83-89; V Cherry Hinton St Andr *Ely* 89-04; P-in-c Teversham 90-04; P-in-c Much Hadham *St Alb* 04-05; TR Albury, Braughing, Furneux Pelham, Lt Hadham etc 06-12; RD Bishop's Stortford 07-12; Chapl Bromley Coll from 12. *Chaplain's House, Bromley College, London Road, Bromley BR1 1PE* T: (020) 8460 4712
E: bromleysheppardscolleges@btconnect.com

BOULTON, Ms Louise Jane. b 72. Goldsmiths' Coll Lon BA 93 Heythrop Coll Lon MA 98. SEITE 02. **d** 05 **p** 06. NSM Wandsworth St Anne *S'wark* 05-08; NSM Wandsworth St Anne w St Faith 08-10; PtO from 12. *17 Somers Road, London SW2 2AE* T: (020) 7096 1646 M: 07989-333016
E: louise@trespassersw.net

BOULTON, Wallace Dawson. b 31. MCIJ 86. Lon Coll of Div 65. **d** 67 **p** 68. C Bramcote *S'well* 67-71; Dioc Public Relns Officer 69-71; Hon C St Bride Fleet Street w Bridewell etc *Lon* 71-86; Guild Chapl from 86; Publicity Sec CMS 71-79; Media Sec 79-86; Ed C of E Newspaper 86-88; LtO *Chich* 84-94; PtO 94-96; rtd 96; Hon C St Leonards St Leon *Chich* 96-01 and 04-09; P-in-c 01-03; Hon C St Leonards St Ethelburga and St Leon from 09. *44 Winterbourne Close, Hastings TN34 1XQ* T: (01424) 713743 E: revw.boulton@talktalk.net

BOULTON-LEA, Peter John. b 46. St Jo Coll Dur BA 68. Westcott Ho Cam 69. **d** 71 **p** 72. C Farlington *Portsm* 72-75; C Darlington St Jo *Dur* 75-77; R E and W Horndon w Lt Warley *Chelmsf* 77-82; V Hersham *Guildf* 82-91; R Kirk Sandall and Edenthorpe *Sheff* 91-96; RD Doncaster 95-96; V Campsall

96-97; R Burghwallis and Campsall 97-98; V Tattenham Corner and Burgh Heath *Guildf* 98-03; V Thorne *Sheff* 03-08; rtd 08; PtO *Ox* from 08. *25 Larkfields, Headington, Oxford OX3 8PF* T: (01865) 744302

BOULTON-REYNOLDS, Mrs Jean. b 49. Sarum Th Coll 93. **d** 96 **p** 97. C Harnham *Sarum* 96-99; C Salisbury St Mark 99-01; TV Westborough *Guildf* 01-05; TV Barnes *S'wark* 05-11; rtd 11; PtO *Sarum* from 12. *17 Springfield Crescent, Royal Wootton Bassett, Swindon SN4 7AP* E: revjbr@sarum26.freeserve.co.uk

BOUMENJEL, Nejib. b 73. St Jo Coll Nottm. **d** 14 **p** 15. C Birm St Geo from 14. *98 Bridge Street West, Birmingham B19 2YX* M: 07769-624598 E: b_nejib2002@yahoo.co.uk

BOUNDY, David. b 34. Kelham Th Coll 55. **d** 59 **p** 60. C Stirchley *Birm* 59-64; Chapl E Birm Hosp 64-74; V Bordesley St Oswald *Birm* 64-70; V S Yardley St Mich 70-74; R Bideford *Ex* 74-82; RD Hartland 80-82; R Northfield *Birm* 82-88; P-in-c Penzance St Mary w St Paul *Truro* 88-90; V 90-94; rtd 94; Chapl Convent of St Mary at the Cross Edgware 94-99; PtO *Ex* 00-05. *34 Milford Hill, Salisbury SP1 2QX* T: (01722) 410341 E: retreat5@btopenworld.com

BOUNDY, Canon Gerald Neville. b 36. BA. Linc Th Coll. **d** 65 **p** 66. C Bris St Mary Redcliffe w Temple etc 65-70; P-in-c Southmead 70-72; V 72-81; V Clutham St Sav w St Mary 81-99; Hon Can Bris Cathl 96-99; rtd 99; PtO *Bris* from 99. *10 Morley Road, Southville, Bristol BS3 1DT* T: 0117-966 3337

BOURDEAUX, Canon Michael Alan. b 34. St Edm Hall Ox BA 57 MA 61 Lambeth DD 96. Wycliffe Hall Ox BA 59. **d** 60 **p** 61. C Enfield St Andr *Lon* 60-64; P-in-c Charlton St Luke w St Paul *S'wark* 64-65; LtO *Roch* 65-92; Visiting Prof St Bernard's Sem Rochester USA 69; Gen Dir Keston Inst 69-99; Hon Can Roch Cathl 90-99; rtd 99; PtO *Ox* from 04. *101 Church Way, Iffley, Oxford OX4 4EG* T: (01865) 777276 E: mbourdeaux@freenet.co.uk

✠**BOURKE, The Rt Revd Michael Gay.** b 41. CCC Cam BA 63 MA 67. Cuddesdon Coll 65. **d** 67 **p** 68 **c** 93. C Gt Grimsby St Jas *Linc* 67-71; C Digswell *St Alb* 71-73; C-in-c Panshanger CD 73-78; Course Dir St Alb Minl Tr Scheme 75-87; V Southill *St Alb* 78-86; Adn Bedford 86-93; Area Bp Wolverhampton *Lich* 93-06; rtd 07; PtO *Heref* from 07. *The Maltings, Little Stretton, Church Stretton SY6 6AP* T: (01694) 722910

BOURKE, Peter Charles. b 80. Union Th Coll Belf BTh 02. Oak Hill Th Coll 07. **d** 09 **p** 10. C Moreton *Ches* 09-12; C Dundonald *D & D* from 12. *8 Meadowbank Park, Dundonald, Belfast BT16 2BN* T: (028) 9508 9369 E: peter_bourke@hotmail.com

BOURKE, Canon Ronald Samuel James. b 50. MA HDipEd. **d** 79 **p** 80. C Portadown St Mark *Arm* 79-83; I Carnteel and Crilly 83-90; I Mountmellick w Coolbanagher, Rosenallis etc *M & K* 90-97; I Kingscourt w Syddan 97-09; Chan Kildare Cathl 00-09; Can Meath 00-09; I Boyle and Elphin w Aghanagh, Kilbryan etc *K, E & A* from 09; Preb Tipper St Patr Cathl Dublin from 00; Can Elphin Cathl from 12. *The Rectory, Riverstown, Co Sligo, Republic of Ireland* T: (00353) (71) 916 5368 E: rsjbourke@hotmail.com

BOURKE, Stanley Gordon. b 48. CITC 78. **d** 78 **p** 79. C Dundonald *D & D* 78-80; C Lurgan Ch the Redeemer 81-82; I Dungiven w Bovevagh *D & R* 82-89; I Lurgan St Jo *D & D* 89-03; I Inishmacsaint *Clogh* 03-14; Preb Clogh Cathl 06-14; Chan Clogh Cathl 11-14; rtd 14. *63 Church Avenue, Bangor BT20 3EG* M: 07975-993213 E: sgbourke@hotmail.co.uk

BOURNE, Anne Clare. b 63. Univ of Wales (Cardiff) BEd 85. SEITE 08. **d** 11 **p** 12. NSM Sevenoaks St Luke *Roch* from 11. *Charein, 27 St James's Road, Sevenoaks TN13 3NQ* T: (01732) 456788 M: 07512-734224 E: rev.annebourne@talktalk.net

BOURNE, Mrs Carole Sylvia. b 47. York Univ BA 68 LSE MSc 79 PhD 85. SEITE 99. **d** 02 **p** 03. C Epsom St Martin *Guildf* 02-05; NSM E Molesey 05-12; RD Emly 10-12; PtO *S'wark* from 14. *13 Corkran Road, Surbiton KT6 6PL* T: (020) 8390 8611 M: 07957-295864 E: cbeezles@me.com

BOURNE, Colin Douglas. b 56. Culham Coll of Educn CertEd 77. Oak Hill Th Coll BA 04. **d** 04 **p** 05. C Wellington All SS w Eyton *Lich* 04-08; P-in-c Toton *S'well* 08-11; V from 11. *95 Stapleford Lane, Beeston, Nottingham NG9 6FZ* T: 0115-973 1138 M: 07862-967879 E: colin@bournesenf.supanet.com

BOURNE, David James. b 54. Reading Univ BA 76. Trin Coll Bris 77. **d** 79 **p** 80. C W Bromwich Gd Shep w St Jo *Lich* 79-84; V Riseley w Bletsoe *St Alb* 84-05; V Hailsham *Chich* from 05. *St Mary's Vicarage, Vicarage Road, Hailsham BN27 1BL* T: (01323) 842381 E: davidjbourne@googlemail.com

BOURNE, Canon Dennis John. b 32. Ridley Hall Cam 58. **d** 60 **p** 61. C Gorleston St Andr *Nor* 60-64; Min Gorleston St Mary CD 64-79; V Costessey 79-86; R Hingham w Wood Rising w Scoulton 86-97; RD Hingham and Mitford 90-95; Hon Can Nor Cathl 93-97; rtd 97; PtO *Nor* 97-06. *Amron, Star Lane, Long Stratton, Norwich NR15 2XH* T: (01508) 530863 E: johnbourne@onetel.com

BOURNE, Mrs Diana Mary. b 46. St Jo Coll York BEd 68. S Dios Minl Tr Scheme 92. **d** 95 **p** 96. C Pinner *Lon* 95-00; V Lamberhurst and Matfield *Roch* 00-06; rtd 07; PtO *Roch* from 07; *Cant* from 07. *The Pump House, Angley Road, Cranbrook TN17 2PN* T: (01580) 712005 E: revdbourne@hotmail.com

BOURNE, Henry. b 34. Spurgeon's Coll 55. **d** 64 **p** 65. C Handsworth St Mary *Birm* 64-67; Chapl RAF 67-85; Asst Chapl-in-Chief RAF 85-87; P-in-c Bourn *Ely* 87-88; V 88-89; P-in-c Kingston 87-88; R 88-89; V Caxton 88-89; R Bourn and Kingston w Caxton and Longstowe 89-91; rtd 91; PtO *Truro* 95-00 and from 01; Hon C Sampford Peverell, Uplowman, Holcombe Rogus etc *Ex* 00-01. *16 Gracey Court, Woodland Road, Broadclyst, Exeter EX5 3GA* T: (01392) 757843

BOURNE, Hugh Edward. b 86. Sussex Univ BSc 08. Oak Hill Th Coll BA 15. **d** 15. C Lindfield *Chich* from 15. *2 Church Close, Francis Road, Lindfield, Haywards Heath RH16 2JB* M: 07879-620322 T: (01444) 483945 E: revhughbo@gmail.com

BOURNE, The Ven Ian Grant. b 32. Univ of NZ BA 55 Otago Univ BD 75. **d** 56 **p** 57. New Zealand 56-65 and from 67; Adn Wellington 78-86 and 90-95; C Epsom St Martin *Guildf* 65-67. *26 Annan Grove, Papakowhai, Porirua 5024, New Zealand* T: (0064) (4) 233 0466 E: ian.mary@bourne.co.nz

BOURNE, John. *See* BOURNE, Dennis John

BOURNE, John Mark. b 49. Cant Sch of Min 88. **d** 91 **p** 92. C Allington and Maidstone St Pet *Cant* 91-94; V Marden 94-03; Chapl HM Pris Blantyre Ho 94-02; rtd 03. *9 Eylesden Court, Bearsted, Maidstone ME14 4BF* T: (01622) 734420 E: revjohnbourne@classicnet.net

BOURNE, Nigel Irvine. b 60. St Jo Coll Ox BA 82 MA 86 Open Univ MBA 09. Trin Coll Bris BA 92. **d** 92 **p** 93. C Bedhampton *Portsm* 92-94; C Newport St Jo 94-98; V Chalk *Roch* from 98. *The Vicarage, 2A Vicarage Lane, Gravesend DA12 4TF* T: (01474) 567906 F: 745147 E: vicarofchalk@hotmail.com

BOURNE, Canon Philip John. b 61. Sussex Univ BEd 83 Aber Univ MLitt 86 Ex Univ MEd 96 FRSA 97. Cranmer Hall Dur 85. **d** 87 **p** 88. C Gildersome *Wakef* 87-89; Chapl Ex Univ 89-93; Assoc Chapl The Hague and Voorschoten *Eur* 94 and 95; Chapl Voorschoten 96-06; Can Brussels Cathl 04-06; Dir of Ords *Chich* 07-14; TR Sidmouth, Woolbrook, Salcombe Regis, Sidbury etc *Ex* from 14. *The Rectory, Glen Road, Sidmouth EX10 8RW* T: (01395) 512595 E: philipbourne@btinternet.com

BOURNE, Mrs Sarah. b 15. C Shipston-on-Stour w Honington and Idlicote *Cov* from 15. *Address temp unknown*

BOURNEMOUTH, Archdeacon of. *See* ROUCH, The Ven Peter Bradford

BOURNER, Paul. b 48. CA Tr Coll. **d** 90 **p** 91. C Ipswich St Mary at Stoke w St Pet *St E* 90-93; R Ufford w Bredfield and Hasketon 93-01; V Ipswich St Thos 01-14; rtd 14; PtO *St E* from 15. *62 Dereham Avenue, Ipswich IP3 0QF* E: paul.bourner@ntlworld.com

BOUSFIELD, Andrew Michael. b 70. Middx Univ BA 92. Oak Hill Th Coll BA 00. **d** 00 **p** 01. C Beckenham Ch Ch *Roch* 00-03; C Surbiton Hill Ch Ch *S'wark* 03-07; C Patcham *Chich* from 07. *32 Fairview Rise, Brighton BN1 5GL* T: (01273) 503926 M: 07866-434117 E: andybousfield@yahoo.co.uk

BOUSKILL, David Walter. b 72. Westcott Ho Cam 95. **d** 98 **p** 99. C Henley w Remenham *Ox* 98-02; TV Bicester w Bucknell, Caversfield and Launton 02-08; TV Horsham *Chich* from 08. *Holy Trinity House, Blunts Way, Horsham RH12 2BL* T: (01403) 265401 E: fr.david@bouskill.co.uk

BOUTAN, Marc Robert. b 53. Univ of Iowa BA 74. Fuller Th Sem California MD 87 Virginia Th Sem 90. **d** 91 **p** 92. USA 91-96 and from 99; Asst Chapl Brussels *Eur* 96-99. *St James Episcopal Church, 1872 Camp Road, Charleston, SC 29412, USA*

BOUTLE, David Francis. b 44. Leeds Univ BSc 67. Cuddesdon Coll 69. **d** 72 **p** 73. C Boston *Linc* 72-77; C Waltham 77-80; P-in-c Morton 80-81; V 81-94; Chapl W Lindsey NHS Trust 80-94; Local Mental Health Chapl 88-94; P-in-c Heckington Gp *Linc* 94-10; rtd 10. *3 Hengist Close, Quarrington, Sleaford NG34 8WU* T: (01529) 415384 E: boutle.heck@btinternet.com

BOVEY, Denis Philip. b 29. Ely Th Coll 50. **d** 53 **p** 54. C Southwick St Columba *Dur* 53-57; PtO *Ox* 57-59; LtO *Chich* 62-64; C W Hartlepool St Aid *Dur* 64-66; R Aberdeen St Jas *Ab* 66-74; R Old Deer 74-89; R Longside 74-89; R Strichen 74-89; Can St Andr Cathl 75-88; Syn Clerk 78-83; Dean Ab 83-88; R Alford 89-94; R Auchindoir 89-94; R Inverurie 89-94; P-in-c Dufftown 89-94; P-in-c Kemnay 89-94; rtd 94. *15 Loskin Drive, Glasgow G22 7QW* T: 0141-574 3603

BOVILL, Francis William. b 34. St Aid Birkenhead 55. **d** 58 **p** 59. C Bispham *Blackb* 58-61; C Crosthwaite Keswick *Carl* 61-64;

V Radcliffe St Andr *Man* 64-68; P-in-c Woodside St Steph *Glouc* 68; V 69-73; V Scotby *Carl* 73-96; P-in-c Cotehill and Cumwhinton 94-96; rtd 96; PtO *Carl* from 96. *Crosthwaite, West Road, Wigton CA7 9RG* T: (016973) 43410

BOWDEN, Andrew. *See* BOWDEN, Robert Andrew

BOWDEN, Andrew David. b 59. Newc Univ BA 80 BArch 83. Cranmer Hall Dur 95. **d** 97 **p** 98. C Monkseaton St Pet *Newc* 97-01; V Whorlton 01-09; PtO *York* 10-11; P-in-c Weaverthorpe w Helperthorpe, Luttons Ambo etc from 11; C Old Malton 11-13; C New Malton 11-13; C Malton and Old Malton from 13. *Chapel House, Back Lane, West Lutton, Malton YO17 8TF* M: 07544-705064 E: andy@woldsvalley.plus.com

BOWDEN, Andrew John. b 77. Nottm Trent Univ BSc 99. Wycliffe Hall Ox 09. **d** 11 **p** 12. C Laleham *Lon* from 11. *169 Elizabeth Avenue, Staines TW18 1JN* T: (01784) 880271 E: andrew.bowden@allsaintslaleham.org.uk

BOWDEN, John-Henry David. b 47. Magd Coll Cam BA 69 MA 73 MIL 78. S Dios Minl Tr Scheme 81. **d** 84 **p** 85. NSM Redlynch and Morgan's Vale *Sarum* 84-88; NSM Cuckfield *Chich* 88-92; NSM St Mary le Bow w St Pancras Soper Lane etc *Lon* 92-98; NSM Chailey *Chich* 98-04; P-in-c Venice w Trieste *Eur* 04-09; rtd 09; P-in-c Málaga *Eur* 11-13; PtO from 13. *Dene House, South Chailey, Lewes BN8 4AB* T: (01273) 401464

BOWDEN, Lynne. b 53. Bris Univ BA 77 PGCE 78. **d** 06 **p** 07. OLM Oatlands *Guildf* from 06; NSM 06-15. *Ulverstone House, Broom Way, Weybridge KT13 9TG* T: (01932) 842216 F: 842238 M: 07931-599045 E: a.curate@btinternet.com *or* lynne@bowden.freeserve.co.uk

BOWDEN, Mrs Mary Eiluned. **d** 07 **p** 08. NSM Gipsy Hill Ch Ch *S'wark* 07-09; C W Dulwich All SS 09-11; P-in-c Haslemere and Grayswood *Guildf* from 11. *Church Hill Gate, Tanners Lane, Haslemere GU27 1BS* T: (01428) 658107 M: 07921-315894 E: revmarybowden@btconnect.com

BOWDEN, Philip William. b 76. Ripon Coll Cuddesdon 08. **d** 10 **p** 11. C Portsea St Mary *Portsm* 10-14; P-in-c Dallington *Pet* from 14. *St James's Vicarage, Vicarage Lane, Northampton NN5 7AX* T: (01604) 461780 E: frphillbowden@gmail.com

BOWDEN, Canon Robert Andrew. b 38. Worc Coll Ox BA 62 MA 67 BDQ 68. Cuddesdon Coll 63. **d** 65 **p** 66. C Wolverhampton St Geo *Lich* 65-69; C Duston *Pet* 69-72; R Byfield 72-79; Chapl R Agric Coll Cirencester 79-82; R Coates, Rodmarton and Sapperton etc *Glouc* 79-04; Bp's Adv on Rural Soc 81-93; Local Min Officer 93-04; rtd 04; Hon C Kemble, Poole Keynes, Somerford Keynes etc *Glouc* 04-08; Chapl to The Queen 92-08; Hon Can Glouc Cathl 90-08; PtO from 08. *Washbrook Cottage, Caudle Green, Cheltenham GL53 9PW* T: (01285) 821067 E: bowdencoates@btinternet.com

BOWDEN-PICKSTOCK, Mrs Susan Mary. b 63. Bp Otter Coll BA 85 RGN 88. Ridley Hall Cam 09. **d** 11 **p** 12. C Bluntisham cum Earith w Colne and Holywell etc *Ely* 11-14; P-in-c Hunstanton St Mary w Ringstead Parva etc *Nor* from 14. *The Rectory, Broad Lane, Brancaster, King's Lynn PE31 8AU* M: 07912-293905 E: revroses@gmail.com

BOWEN, Canon Colin Wynford. b 48. St D Coll Lamp. **d** 71 **p** 72. C Hubberston *St D* 71-75; R Cosheston w Nash and Upton 75-77; V Carew and Cosheston w Nash and Upton 77-84; V Pembroke St Mary w St Mich 85-01; V Haverfordwest St Martin w Lambston 01-09; P-in-c Camrose 04-09; Can St D Cathl 01-09; R Llangenni and Llanbedr Ystrad Yw w Patricio *S & B* 09-13; rtd 13; PtO *S & B* from 14. *4 Clywedog Drive, Llandrindod Wells LD1 5BZ* T: (01597) 823325 M: 07770-572464 E: colin710bowen@btinternet.com

BOWEN, Daniel Joseph George. b 51. St Mich Coll Llan 96. **d** 98 **p** 99. C Gorseinon *S & B* 98-00; C Cen Swansea 00-01; TV 01-02; V Birchfield *Birm* 02-07; rtd 07. *Dryslwyn, 41 Station Road, Ystradgynlais, Swansea SA9 1NX* T: (01639) 843020 E: daniel@bowen4515.freeserve.co.uk

BOWEN, David Gregory. b 47. Lanchester Poly Cov BSc 69. Cuddesdon Coll 69. **d** 74 **p** 75. C Rugby St Andr *Cov* 74-77; C Charlton St Luke w H Trin *S'wark* 78-80; TV Stantonbury *Ox* 80-82; PtO *B & W* 82-07; *Ab* from 08. *Erraid Station House, Stronsay, Orkney KW17 2AS* T: (01857) 616435 M: 07762-569920 E: dbowenuk@btinternet.com

BOWEN, David John. b 46. Glouc Th Course 83. **d** 86 **p** 88. NSM Ross w Brampton Abbotts, Bridstow and Peterstow *Heref* 86-88; C Kingstone w Clehonger, Eaton Bishop etc 88-93; P-in-c Lugwardine w Bartestree and Weston Beggard 93; P-in-c Lugwardine w Bartestree, Weston Beggard etc 93-94; V S 01-10; P-in-c Withington w Westhide 04-10; RD Heref Rural 99-05; rtd 10. *2 Tavern Meadow, Hope-under-Dinmore, Leominster HR6 0NP* T: (01568) 614906 E: david@djbowen.demon.co.uk

BOWEN, Ms Delyth. b 54. St D Coll Lamp BA 90. St Mich Coll Llan. **d** 91 **p** 97. C Llandybie *St D* 91-95; Dn-in-c Llanllwni 95-97; V Llanybydder and Llanwenog w Llanllwni 97-02;

V Betws w Ammanford 02-11; V Cynwyl Gaeo w Llansawel and Talley etc 11-12; rtd 12. *6 Roderick Close, Townhill, Swansea SA1 6AJ* T: (01792) 920081 E: delyth.amman@btopenworld.com

BOWEN, Gareth James. b 60. Lon Guildhall Univ BA 99 ARPS 00. NTMTC 99. **d** 02 **p** 04. C Leyton St Cath and St Paul *Chelmsf* 02-05; C Upminster 05-07; V Barnehurst *Roch* from 07. *St Martin's Vicarage, 93 Pelham Road, Bexleyheath DA7 4LY* T: (01322) 523344 M: 07775-674504 E: gareth@bowen.to

BOWEN, Canon Jennifer Ethel. b 46. Liv Univ BSc 68 CertEd 69. NOC 80. **dss** 83 **d** 87 **p** 94. Blundellsands St Nic *Liv* 83-86; W Derby St Mary 86-94; Par Dn 87-94; C 94-08; AD W Derby 01-08; Hon Can Liv Cathl 03-08; rtd 08. *6 Springhill Court, Liverpool L15 9EJ* T: 0151-291 0845 E: jenny@happyserver.w.uk

BOWEN, John. b 39. **d** 68 **p** 69. C Aberavon *Llan* 68-73; Australia from 73. *3 Sculptor Street, Giralang ACT 2617, Australia* T: (0061) (2) 6241 5317 *or* 6234 2252 F: 6234 2263 E: john.bowen@radford.com.au

BOWEN, John Roger. b 34. St Jo Coll Ox BA 59 MA 62. Tyndale Hall Bris 59. **d** 61 **p** 62. C Cambridge St Paul *Ely* 61-65; Tanzania 65-76; Kenya 76-80; Dir Past Studies St Jo Coll Nottm 80-85; Tutor 85-95; Gen Sec Crosslinks 96-00; rtd 99; PtO *Ely* from 01; Asst Retired Clergy Officer from 09. *26 Lingholme Close, Cambridge CB4 3HW* T: (01223) 352592 E: bowenrw@onetel.com

BOWEN, Julie Elizabeth. b 64. S Glam Inst HE BEd 86. SEITE 09. **d** 12 **p** 13. C Bexley *Roch* from 12. *St Martin's Vicarage, 93 Pelham Road, Bexleyheath DA7 4LY* T: (01322) 523344 M: 07775-674503 E: julie@bowen.to

BOWEN, Mark Franklin. b 61. Coll of H Cross (USA) BA 79 Univ of S Florida MA 89. **d** 93. Asst Chapl Univ of S Florida USA 93-96; C Tampa St Andr 96-97; PtO *S'wark* 07-09; Co-ord Inclusive Ch *Eur* from 09; Teacher Internat Sch of Basel from 09. *309 Guterstrasse, Basel 4053, Switzerland* T: (0041) (61) 331 0961 E: markfbowen@hotmail.com

BOWEN, Canon Roger William. b 47. Magd Coll Cam BA 69 MA 73 Heythrop Coll Lon MA 01 ALCD 72. St Jo Coll Nottm 69. **d** 72 **p** 73. C Rusholme H Trin *Man* 72-75; Rwanda Miss (CMS) Burundi 75-84; Tutor and Lect All Nations Chr Coll Ware 85-91; Hon C Ware Ch Ch *St Alb* 86-91; Gen Sec Mid-Africa Min (CMS) 91-97; V Lt Amwell *St Alb* 97-04; RD Hertford and Ware 99-04; CMS Burundi 04-07; rtd 07. *The Outlook, Porteynon, Swansea SA3 1NL* T: (01792) 391591

BOWEN, Canon Stephen Allan. b 51. Leic Univ BA 72. Glouc Sch of Min 88. **d** 91 **p** 92. NSM Bream *Glouc* 91-92; NSM Tidenham w Beachley and Lancaut 91-94; C Glouc St Jas and All SS 94-97; P-in-c Woodchester and Brimscombe 97-00; R 00-11; AD Stonehouse 07-08; AD Stroud 08-11; TR Cheltenham St Mark from 11; Hon Can Glouc Cathl from 09. *St Mark's Rectory, Fairmount Road, Cheltenham GL51 7AQ* T: (01242) 695732 E: sabowen75@googlemail.com

BOWEN, Stephen Guy. b 47. Qu Coll Cam BA 68 MA 72 Bris Univ MA 72. Clifton Th Coll 69. **d** 71 **p** 72. C Chelsea St Jo *Lon* 71-73; C Guildf St Sav 73-76; C Guildf St Sav w Stoke-next-Guildford 76-77; C Wallington *S'wark* 77-79; V Felbridge 79-12; rtd 13; PtO *S'wark* from 15. *3 The Courtyard, East Grinstead RH19 3XU* T: (01342) 321135 E: sg@bowenfelbridge.idps.co.uk

BOWER, Allen Cleeve. b 71. Trin Coll Bris 10. **d** 12 **p** 13. C Kensal Rise St Mark *Lon* 12-15; V Tipton St Matt *Lich* from 15. *St Matthew's Vicarage, 107A Dudley Road, Tipton DY4 8DJ* T: 0121-522 2555 E: revallenb@gmail.com

BOWER, Brian Mark. b 60. QUB BA. **d** 85 **p** 86. C Orangefield w Moneyreagh *D & D* 85-87; I Inver w Mountcharles, Killaghtee and Killybegs *D & R* 87-93; Miss to Seafarers from 87; I Augher w Newtownsaville and Eskrahoole *Clogh* 93-03. *48 Campsie Road, Omagh BT79 0AG* M: 07816-449399

BOWERMAN, Andrew Mark. b 67. Southn Univ BSc 88 Brunel Univ MSW 91. Wycliffe Hall Ox 00. **d** 02 **p** 03. C Bradf St Aug Underclife 02-05; Miss P Bradf Adnry 05-09; P-in-c Wareham *Sarum* 09-12; TR 12-14; Co-Dir Angl Alliance from 14; Hon C Hardington Vale *B & W* from 15. *The Rectory, 38 Church Lane, Rode, Frome BA11 6PN* M: 07720-398659 E: andy.bowerman@aco.org

BOWERMAN, Mrs Lynn Joan. b 56. STETS 12. **d** 15. C Branksome St Clem *Sarum* from 15. *Address temp unknown*

BOWERS, Dale Arthur. b 69. MBE 12. St Steph Ho Ox BTh 04. **d** 04 **p** 07. C St Paul's St Helena 04-10; V from 10. *China Lane, Jamestown STHL 122, St Helena* T: (00290) 2960 E: dale.penny@cwimail.sh

BOWERS, Canon David. b 56. Man Univ BA 79. Wycliffe Hall Ox 82. **d** 84 **p** 85. C Lawton Moor *Man* 84-87; C Walmsley 87-93; V Milnrow 93-98; P-in-c Deerhurst and Apperley w Forthampton etc *Glouc* 98-04; V 04-08; Assoc Dir of Ords 98-08; V S Cerney w Cerney Wick, Siddington and Preston

Glouc from 08; Hon Can Glouc Cathl from 12. *The Vicarage, Silver Street, South Cerney, Cirencester GL7 5TP*   T: (01285) 860221   E: dbowers@btinternet.com *or* vicar@churnside-parishes.org.uk

BOWERS, Canon Francis <u>Malcolm</u>. b 44. Chan Sch Truro 79. **d** 82 **p** 83. NSM Penzance St Mary w St Paul *Truro* 82-83; C 86-88; NSM Madron 83-86; TV Redruth w Lanner and Treleigh 88-91; V St Blazey 91-15; P-in-c Lanlivery w Luxulyan 01-08; P-in-c Luxulyan 08-15; P-in-c Tywardreath w Tregaminion 02-15; RD St Austell 96-05; Hon Can Truro Cathl 01-15; rtd 15. *Address temp unknown*   M: 07974-818631   E: fathermalcolmrightee@tiscali.co.uk

BOWERS, Gary David. b 70. Trin Coll Bris 13. **d** 15. C Heacham *Nor* from 15; C Snettisham w Ingoldisthorpe and Fring from 15. *The Rectory, 18 Park Lane, Snettisham, King's Lynn PE31 7NW*   T: (01485) 554387   M: 07568-584030   E: revgary.hsbenefice@gmail.com

BOWERS, Canon John Edward. b 23. TD 68. AKC 50. **d** 51 **p** 52. C Leic St Pet 51-55; Sacr S'wark Cathl 55-57; CF (TA) 56-67; V Loughborough St Pet *Leic* 57-63; V Ashby-de-la-Zouch St Helen w Coleorton 63-88; CF (R of O) 67-78; RD Akeley W *Leic* 76-88; Hon Can Leic Cathl 78-88; rtd 88; PtO *Derby* 88-94; *Leic* 88-94; *Ely* 94-00. *19 Curtis Drive, Heighington, Lincoln LN4 1GF*   T: (01522) 791330

BOWERS, Canon John Edward William. b 32. St Aid Birkenhead 60. **d** 63 **p** 64. C Bromborough *Ches* 63-68; Ind Chapl 68-74; P-in-c Crewe St Pet 69-71; V Crewe St Mich 71-74; TR Ellesmere Port 74-79; V Hattersley 79-91; Hon Can Ches Cathl 80-02; RD Mottram 88-91; V Bunbury and Tilstone Fearnall 91-98; P-in-c Leasowe 98-02; rtd 02; PtO *Ches* from 02. *2 Shalford Grove, Wirral CH48 9XY*   T: 0151-625 4831

BOWERS, Canon Julian Michael. b 48. Middx Univ BA 97 Goldsmiths' Coll Lon MA 00. Edin Th Coll 69. **d** 72 **p** 73. C Chippenham St Andr w Tytherton Lucas *Bris* 72-74; C Henbury 74-77; Chapl Kandy H Trin Sri Lanka 77-82; P-in-c Evercreech w Chesterblade and Milton Clevedon *B & W* 82-83; V 83-89; V Enfield St Jas *Lon* 89-04; Chapl St Andr Hosp Northn 04-12; Can Pet Cathl 10-12; rtd 12; Past Care and Counselling Adv *Pet* from 13; Hon C Brigstock w Stanion and Lowick and Sudborough from 13. *41 Kipling Road, Kettering NN16 9JZ*   T: (01536) 525520   E: revjbowers@gmail.com

BOWERS, Michael Charles. b 52. Sarum & Wells Th Coll 89. **d** 91 **p** 92. C St Peter-in-Thanet *Cant* 91-95; V Reculver and Herne Bay St Bart 95-02; P-in-c Fen Ditton and Horningsea *Ely* 02-15; P-in-c Teversham 04-15; rtd 15. *Address temp unknown*   E: michael@mcbvic.demon.co.uk

BOWERS, Preb Peter. b 47. Linc Th Coll 72. **d** 76 **p** 77. C Mackworth St Fran *Derby* 76-78; C Maidstone St Martin *Cant* 78-83; V Elmton *Derby* 83-89; R Swimbridge w W Buckland and Landkey *Ex* 89-10; RD Shirwell 01-10; Preb Ex Cathl 07-10; rtd 10; PtO *York* from 11. *Endellion, 30 Kingsgate, Bridlington YO15 3PU*   T: (01262) 676096   E: pbowers62@btinternet.com *or* pebo@live.co.uk

BOWERS, Mrs Rosemary Christine. b 49. Ripon Coll Cuddesdon 99. **d** 01 **p** 02. C Rossendale Middle Valley *Man* 01-04; P-in-c Micklehurst *Ches* 04-09; P-in-c Kinnerley w Melverley and Knockin w Maesbrook *Lich* 09-12; P-in-c Maesbury 11-12; rtd 12; Hon C Ripponden and Barkisland w W Scammonden *Wakef* 12-14; TV Rossendale Middle Valley *Man* 14-15. *7 Bowler Way, Greenfield, Oldham OL3 7FQ*   T: (01457) 514172   E: revrosie86@sky.com

BOWES, Mrs Beryl Sylvia. b 48. Hull Univ BTh 89 Leeds Univ MA 06 SRN 70 RSCN 71. NEOC 89. **d** 91 **p** 94. NSM Kirk Ella *York* 91-99; Chapl R Hull Hosps NHS Trust 93-99; P-in-c Kexby w Wilberfoss *York* 99-04; R The Street Par 04-12; rtd 12; PtO *York* from 12. *17 Uppleby, Easingwold, York YO61 3BQ*   T: (01347) 822258   E: bsbowes@gmail.com

BOWES, Canon John Anthony Hugh. b 39. Ch Ch Ox BA 62 MA 65. Westcott Ho Cam 63. **d** 65 **p** 66. C Langley All SS and Martyrs *Man* 65-68; Asst Chapl Bris Univ 68-73; TV Cramlington *Newc* 73-76; P-in-c Oldland *Bris* 76-80; TR 80-84; V Westbury-on-Trym St Alb 84-05; Hon Can Bris Cathl 02-05; rtd 05. *4 Royal Albert Road, Bristol BS6 7NY*   T: 0117-973 5844

BOWES, Peter Hugh. b 48. Hull Univ LLB 69 Dur Univ MA 05 DThM 12 Solicitor 72. Cranmer Hall Dur 02. **d** 03 **p** 04. NSM Pocklington and Owsthorpe and Kilnwick Percy etc *York* 03-04; NSM The Street Par 04-07; NSM New Malton 06-07; P-in-c 07-13; C Old Malton 10-13; C Weaverthorpe w Helperthorpe, Luttons Ambo etc 11-13; Assoc Dir of Ords 05-10; RD S Ryedale 11-13; rtd 13; PtO *York* from 13. *17 Uppleby, Easingwold, York YO61 3BQ*   T: (01347) 822258   M: 07775-757723

BOWES-SMITH, Edward Michael Crispin. b 67. K Coll Lon LLB 89 AKC 89 Solicitor 90 Selw Coll Cam BA 96. Ridley Hall Cam 94. **d** 97 **p** 98. C Combe Down w Monkton Combe and

S Stoke *B & W* 97-00; C Enfield Ch Ch Trent Park *Lon* 00-03; P-in-c Linc Minster Gp 03-12; V Linc St Pet in Eastgate from 12. *St Peter's Vicarage, Lee Road, Lincoln LN2 4BH*   T: (01522) 568529   E: bowessmith@waitrose.com

BOWETT, Canon Richard Julnes. b 45. EAMTC 86. **d** 89 **p** 90. C Hunstanton St Mary w Ringstead Parva, Holme etc *Nor* 89-93; C King's Lynn St Marg w St Nic 93-95; V Watton w Carbrooke and Ovington 95-02; RD Breckland 99-02; P-in-c Ashill w Saham Toney 00-01; Dioc Sec 02-09; rtd 09; Hon Can Nor Cathl 05-13; PtO from 13. *29 Low Road, Hellesdon, Norwich NR6 5AE*   T: (01603) 406256   E: richard.bowett@sky.com

BOWIE, Michael Nicholas Roderick. b 59. Sydney Univ BA 78 CCC Ox DPhil 90. St Steph Ho Ox MA 90. **d** 91 **p** 92. C Swanley St Mary *Roch* 91-93; C Penarth w Lavernock *Llan* 93-96; Australia 96-00; R Norton *Sheff* 00-05; TR Gt Berkhamsted, Gt and Lt Gaddesden etc *St Alb* 05-14; RD Berkhamsted 09-14; C St Marylebone All SS *Lon* from 14. *6 Margaret Street, London W1W 8RQ*   T: (020) 7636 1788   E: mnrbowie@hotmail.com

BOWIE, Sara. b 53. Open Univ BA 83 Surrey Univ BA 02. STETS 99. **d** 02 **p** 03. NSM Camberley St Mich Yorktown *Guildf* 02-07; C Coity, Nolton and Brackla *Llan* 07-10; P-in-c Essington *Lich* from 10; P-in-c Shareshill from 10. *The Vicarage, 11 Brookhouse Lane, Featherstone, Wolverhampton WV10 7AW*   T: (01902) 727579

BOWKER, Prof John Westerdale. b 35. Worc Coll Ox BA 58. Ripon Hall Ox. **d** 61 **p** 62. C Endcliffe *Sheff* 61-62; Fell Lect and Dir of Studies CCC Cam 62-74; Lect Div Cam Univ 70-74; Prof RS Lanc Univ 74-86; Hon Prov Can Cant Cathl 85-03; Dean of Chpl Trin Coll Cam 86-91; rtd 91; LtO *Cant* 91-94; PtO *Ely* 94-00. *14 Bowers Croft, Cambridge CB1 8RP*

BOWKETT, Graham Philip. b 67. Open Univ BSc 99. NEOC 06. **d** 09 **p** 10. C Thirsk *York* 09-12; P-in-c Upper Itchen *Win* 12-15; R from 15. *The Rectory, The Goodens, Cheriton, Alresford SO24 0QH*   T: (01962) 771226   E: bowkett520@hotmail.co.uk *or* rector@upperitchen.plus.com

✠**BOWLBY, The Rt Revd Ronald Oliver.** b 26. Trin Coll Ox BA 50 MA 54. Westcott Ho Cam 50. **d** 52 **p** 53 **c** 73. C Pallion *Dur* 52-56; C Billingham St Cuth 56-57; C-in-c Billingham St Aid CD 57-60; V Billingham St Aid 60-66; V Croydon St Jo *Cant* 66-73; Hon Can Cant Cathl 70-73; Bp Newc 73-80; Bp S'wark 80-91; rtd 91; Hon Asst Bp Lich 91-10; PtO 10-14. *Swan Hill House, 6 Swan Hill, Shrewsbury SY1 1NQ*   E: rbowlby@phonecoop.coop

BOWLER, Christopher Peter. **d** 12 **p** 13. NSM Upper Ithon Valley *S & B* 12-14; C Vale of Gwrynne from 14; Bp's Officer for Min to Children and Families from 14. *The Rectory, Llangenny, Crickhowell NP8 1HD*   T: (01873) 810591   E: revchrisbowler@gmail.com

BOWLER, Christopher William. See JAGE-BOWLER, Christopher William

BOWLER, David Edward. b 53. Northumbria Univ BA 04 RMN 80. NEOC 05. **d** 08 **p** 09. NSM Cramlington *Newc* 08-13; Chapl Northgate and Prudhoe NHS Trust 10-13; Chapl Northumberland, Tyne and Wear NHS Foundn Trust 10-13; V Delaval *Newc* from 13. *The Vicarage, The Avenue, Seaton Sluice, Whitley Bay NE26 4QW*   T: 0191-237 1982   E: djbowler@sky.com

BOWLER, David Henderson. b 54. Kent Univ BA 75. St Jo Coll Nottm 75. **d** 78 **p** 79. C Bramcote *S'well* 78-82; TV Kirby Muxloe *Leic* 82-88; V Quorndon from 88. *27 Mansfield Avenue, Quorn, Loughborough LE12 8BD*   E: dhb300154@aol.com

BOWLER, Preb Kenneth Neville. b 37. K Coll Lon 57. **d** 61 **p** 62. C Buxton *Derby* 61-67; R Sandiacre 67-75; V E Bedfont *Lon* 75-87; AD Hounslow 82-87; V Fulham All SS 87-02; Preb St Paul's Cathl 85-02; rtd 02; PtO *St Alb* from 03. *The Coach House, 22 Brincliffe Crescent, Sheffield S11 9AW*   T: 0114-250 0043

BOWLER, Neil. b 70. Nottm Trent Univ LLB 92 Leeds Univ BA 05 Solicitor 93. Coll of Resurr Mirfield 03. **d** 05 **p** 06. C Doncaster St Jude *Sheff* 05-08; R Whiston 09-13; AD Rotherham 11-13; V Ranmoor from 13. *Ranmoor Vicarage, 389A Fulwood Road, Sheffield S10 3GA*   T: 0114-230 1671   E: nbowler34@yahoo.co.uk *or* neil.bowler@sheffield.anglican.org

BOWLES, Arthur William. b 36. **d** 96 **p** 97. OLM Gt Yarmouth *Nor* 96-06; PtO from 06. *4 Onslow Avenue, Great Yarmouth NR30 4DT*   T: (01493) 842360   E: revawb@talktalk.net

BOWLES, David Gordon Desmond. **d** 13. Taney *D & G* 13-15; C Douglas Union w Frankfield *C, C & R* from 15. *64 Willowbank, Church Road, Blackrock, Cork, Republic of Ireland*   M: 86-817 8306   E: dgd_bowles@yahoo.co.uk

BOWLES, Peter John. b 39. Lon Univ BA 60. Linc Th Coll 71. **d** 73 **p** 74. C Clay Cross *Derby* 73-76; C Boulton 76-79; R Brailsford w Shirley 79-85; P-in-c Osmaston w Edlaston

81-85; R Brailsford w Shirley and Osmaston w Edlaston 85-89; TR Old Brampton and Loundsley Green 89-98; V Hope, Castleton and Bradwell 98-04; rtd 04; PtO *Nor* from 04. *3 Blackhorse Yard, Wells-next-the-Sea NR23 1BN* T: (01328) 711119 E: panda8@mypostoffice.co.uk

BOWLEY, Canon John Richard Lyon. b 46. MRTPI 76 Dur Univ BA 68 QUB MSc 72. CITC. **d** 79 **p** 80. C Knock *D & D* 79-81; Bp's C Knocknagoney 81-90; I Ballywalter w Inishargie 90-11; Can Down Cathl 03-11; rtd 12. *18 Enniscrone Park, Portadown, Craigavon BT63 5DQ* M: 07925-075841

BOWMAN, Miss Alison Valentine. b 57. St Andr Univ MA 79. St Steph Ho Ox 86. **d** 89 **p** 94. Par Dn Peacehaven *Chich* 89-94; C 94-95; Chapl to Bp Lewes 93-95; TV Rye 95-03; P-in-c Preston St Jo w Brighton St Aug and St Sav 03-09; V from 09. *33 Preston Drove, Brighton BN1 6LA* T: (01273) 555033

BOWMAN, Clifford William. b 57. St Jo Coll Dur BA 78 Nottm Univ MA 96. Ridley Hall Cam 80. **d** 82 **p** 83. C Sawley *Derby* 82-85; C Hucknall Torkard *S'well* 85-89; R Warsop 89-00; Dioc Chapl amongst Deaf People 00-06; TV Uxbridge *Lon* from 06. *St Andrew's Vicarage, Nursery Waye, Uxbridge UB8 2BJ* T: (01895) 239055 E: c.bowman@dunelm.org.uk

BOWMAN, Canon Ivelaw Alexander. b 46. **d** 97 **p** 98. OLM Stockwell Green St Andr *S'wark* 97-03; OLM Stockwell St Andr and St Mich from 03; Chapl S Lon and Maudsley NHS Foundn Trust 03-07; Hon Can S'wark Cathl from 05. *16 Horsford Road, London SW2 5DN* T: (020) 7733 2309

BOWMAN, Prof John. b 16. Glas Univ MA 38 BD 41 Ch Ch Ox DPhil 45. **d** 50 **p** 54. Hon C Leeds St Geo *Ripon* 51-53; Hon C Kirkstall 53-54; PtO *York* 54-59; Australia from 59; rtd 73. *15 Haines Street, North Melbourne Vic 3051, Australia* T/F: (0061) (3) 9329 0794 E: mbowman@vicnet.net.au

BOWMAN-EADIE, Preb Russell Ian. b 45. K Coll Lon BD 71 AKC 71 ACP 68 FCP. St Aug Coll Cant 71. **d** 72 **p** 73. C Hammersmith St Pet *Lon* 72-74; V Leic St Nic 74-81; Chapl Leic Univ 74-81; Adult Educn Adv *Dur* 81-84; Dir of Tr *B & W* 84-09; Preb Wells Cathl 90-09; Can Res and Treas Wells Cathl 02-09; rtd 10. *8 Shaftesbury Place, Rustington, Littlehampton BN16 2GA* T: (01903) 774580 E: russell.bowmaneadie@googlemail.com

BOWN, Mrs Marcia Helen. b 52. EMMTC. **d** 10 **p** 11. C N Wingfield, Clay Cross and Pilsley *Derby* from 10. *43 Rupert Street, Lower Pilsley, Chesterfield S45 8DB* T: (01773) 872550 E: marciabown@hotmail.co.uk

BOWNASS (née FRYER), Alison Jane. b 56. Univ Coll of Swansea BSc 78 Birm Poly PGCE 90. Qu Coll Birm 05. **d** 07 **p** 08. C The Quinton *Birm* 07-10; PtO 10-11; C Hill 11-14; PtO from 14. *41 Silvermead Road, Sutton Coldfield B73 5SR* T: 0121-321 1600 M: 07958-911378 E: alison@bownass.co.uk

BOWNESS, William Gary. b 48. Warwick Univ BSc 69 Chicago State Univ DMin 98. Ripon Coll Cuddesdon 80. **d** 82 **p** 83. C Lancaster St Mary *Blackb* 82-86; V Lostock Hall 86-91; V Whittington w Arkholme and Gressingham 91-02; RD Tunstall 93-99; Dir Post-Ord Tr 00-02; R Alderley w Birtles *Ches* 02-07; P-in-c Henbury 07-13; rtd 13; PtO *Ches* from 13. *18 Jasmine Avenue, Macclesfield SK10 3GH* T: (01625) 424113 E: garybowness@btinternet.com

BOWRING, Stephen John. b 55. R Holloway Coll Lon BMus 77 St Mary's Coll Twickenham PGCE 78. EMMTC 89. **d** 92 **p** 93. C Thurmaston *Leic* 92-95; V Shepshed 95-02; R River *Cant* 02-06; P-in-c Charlton-in-Dover 05-06; AD Dover 03-06; Hon Min Can Cant Cathl 04-06; V Chesterton St Geo *Ely* 06-11; R Kym Valley from 11; C E Leightonstone from 14. *The Rectory, Church Lane, Tilbrook, Huntingdon PE28 0JS* E: kymvicar@gmail.com or stephenbowring@btinternet.com

BOWRON, Hugh Mark. b 52. Cant Univ (NZ) BA 74 MA 76. Coll of Resurr Mirfield 76. **d** 79 **p** 80. C Northampton St Mary *Pet* 79-82; V Ellesmere New Zealand 82-86; V Addington St Mary 86-95; V Wellington St Pet 95-05; V Avonside H Trin from 05. *2/142 Avonside Drive, Christchurch, New Zealand* T: (0064) (3) 389 3024 E: office@holytrinityavonside.co.nz

BOWSER, Alan. b 35. Univ of Wales (Lamp) BA 60. **d** 63 **p** 64. C Gateshead St Chad Bensham *Dur* 63-67; C Owton Manor CD 67-72; V Horden 72-02; rtd 02. *Kengarth House, Coast Road, Blackhall Colliery, Hartlepool TS27 4HF* T: 0191-586 1753

BOWSHER, Andrew Peter. b 59. Reading Univ BA 81. St Jo Coll Nottm 83. **d** 86 **p** 87. C Grenoside *Sheff* 86-89; C Darfield 89-91; P-in-c Haley Hill *Wakef* 91-96; V Bradf St Aug Undercliffe 96-99; Chapl Bradf Univ and Bradf Coll 99-04; PtO *Dur* from 04; Tutor St Jo Coll Nottm 07-11; Chapl Northumbria Univ *Newc* from 11. *The Team Rectory, Rotherham Road, Dinnington S25 2RR* T: 07876-401339 E: andii.bowsher@northumbria.ac.uk

BOWSKILL, Mrs Amanda. b 49. STETS 96. **d** 99 **p** 00. NSM Winklebury *Win* 99-03; NSM Tadley S and Silchester 03-04;

NSM Kempshott 05-10; PtO from 10. *10 Portway Place, Basingstoke RG23 8DT* T: (01256) 327301 E: mandy.bowskill@cwcom.net

BOWSKILL, Robert Preston. b 48. S Dios Minl Tr Scheme 88. **d** 91 **p** 92. NSM Eastrop *Win* 91-94; NSM Winklebury 94-05; NSM Kempshott 05-10; PtO from 10. *10 Portway Place, Basingstoke RG23 8DT* T: (01256) 327301 E: bob.bowskill@cwcom.net

BOWTELL, Paul William. b 47. Lon Univ BSc 68. St Jo Coll Nottm 80. **d** 82 **p** 83. C Gorleston St Andr *Nor* 82-85; TV Forest Gate St Sav w W Ham St Matt *Chelmsf* 85-91; R Spitalfields Ch Ch w All SS *Lon* 91-02; Co-ord Transform Newham 02-06; Chapl to Bp Barking *Chelmsf* 06-14; C Leyton St Cath and St Paul 07-14; rtd 14. *14 Chapel Street, Rowhedge, Colchester CO5 7JS*

BOWYER, Arthur Gustavus Frederick. b 36. **d** 00 **p** 01. NSM Kingswood *S'wark* from 00. *41 Tattenham Grove, Epsom KT18 5QT* T: (01737) 357913 M: 07939-533506 E: arthurbowyer578@btinternet.com

BOWYER, Geoffrey Charles. b 54. ACA 79 ATII 82 Lanc Univ BA 76. St Jo Coll Nottm 85. **d** 87 **p** 88. C Walton *St E* 87-89; C Macclesfield Team *Ches* 89-91; V Cinderford St Steph w Littledean *Glouc* 91-95; V Brockenhurst *Win* 95-98; Hon C Trull w Angersleigh *B & W* from 00. *36 Bakers Close, Bishops Hull, Taunton TA1 5HD* T: (01823) 335289 E: us4bowyers@aol.com

BOWYER, Gerry. b 60. Cliff Th Coll MA 10. **d** 10 **p** 10. C Aberdeen St Ninian *Ab* 10; Bp's Ev for Fresh Expressions and Ch Planting from 11. *2 Buckie Road, Bridge of Don, Aberdeen AB22 8DG* T: (01224) 706916 M: 07956-098566 E: gerry.bowyer@live.com

BOX, Mrs Patricia Jane. b 54. ERMC 12. **d** 15. NSM Bures w Assington and Lt Cornard *St E* from 15. *Water House, 4 Croftside, Bures CO8 5LL* T: (01787) 227528 E: valleyfarmboxes@btopenworld.com

BOX, Reginald Gilbert (Brother Reginald). b 20. Lon Univ BD 41 AKC 41 Em Coll Cam BA 52 MA 57 Lambeth STh 91 Hon RSCM 81. Westcott Ho Cam 41. **d** 43 **p** 44. C Chingford SS Pet and Paul *Chelmsf* 43-47; Chapl Bps' Coll Cheshunt 47-50; SSF from 51; LtO *Ely* 51-55; *Sarum* 55-61; C Cambridge St Benedict *Ely* 61-67; Chapl Coll of SS Mark and Jo Chelsea 67-69; New Zealand 69-84; Australia 69-84; Melanesia 69-84; PtO *Sarum* from 84; *Ely* 85-97; Chapl Chich Th Coll 90-93; PtO *Cant* 05-13; *Newc* from 13. *Society of St Francis, The Friary, Alnmouth, Alnwick NE66 3NJ* T: (01665) 830213 E: reginaldssf@franciscans.org.uk

BOXALL, David John. b 41. Dur Univ BA 63. Sarum Th Coll 65. **d** 66 **p** 67. C Ipswich St Aug *St E* 66-69; C Bourne *Linc* 69-71; C Woodside Park St Barn *Lon* 71-72; C Thundersley *Chelmsf* 72-76; P-in-c Farcet *Ely* 76-77; TV Stanground and Farcet 77-85; V Guyhirn w Ring's End 85-90; V Southea w Murrow and Parson Drove 85-90; P-in-c Fletton 90-94; PtO 94-00 and 05-08; rtd 99. *11 Plover Drive, March PE15 9HY* T: (01354) 659905

BOXALL, Keith Michael. b 37. Trin Coll Bris. **d** 82 **p** 83. C Staines St Pet *Lon* 82-83; C Staines St Mary and St Pet 83-85; C Lydiard Millicent w Lydiard Tregoz *Bris* 85-86; TV The Lydiards 86-93; V Mangotsfield 93-03; rtd 03; PtO *Bris* from 03; *Llan* 03-15. *7 Burnham Road, Knaphill, Woking GU21 2AE* M: 07745-016038 T: (01483) 497613 E: keith.boxall1@btinternet.com

BOXALL, Canon Martin Alleyne. b 37. Wells Th Coll 65. **d** 67 **p** 68. C Crowthorne *Ox* 67-70; C Tilehurst St Mich 70-76; V Tilehurst St Cath 76-78; V Padstow *Truro* 78-00; Miss to Seafarers from 78; RD Pydar *Truro* 93; Hon Can Truro Cathl from 93; rtd 01; Dioc Officer for Unity *Truro* from 01. *Goonhilland Farmhouse, Burnthouse, St Gluvias, Penryn TR10 9AS* T: (01872) 863241 E: martinboxall@aol.com

BOXALL, Simon Roger. b 55. St Jo Coll Cam BA 76 MA 80. Ridley Hall Cam 77. **d** 79 **p** 80. C Eaton *Nor* 79-82; SAMS Brazil 82-04; P-in-c Belo Horizonte St Pet 84-88; P-in-c Santiago St Tim 88-91; P-in-c Horizontina H Spirit 88-91; C Bagé Crucifixion 93-94; R Jaguarao Ch Ch 94-98; English Chapl Rio de Janeiro 99-04; TV Thamesmead *S'wark* 05-14; V Chesterton *Lich* from 14. *The Vicarage, Church Street, Chesterton, Newcastle ST5 7HJ* T: (01782) 562479

BOXER, Caroline Victoria. *See* SKELTON, Caroline Victoria

BOXLEY, Christopher. b 45. K Coll Lon BD 68 AKC 68 Southn Univ CertEd 73 Reading Univ MA 84. **d** 69 **p** 70. C Bitterne Park *Win* 69-73; Hd RS Midhurst Gr Sch from 73; Dir Midhurst and Petworth RS Cen from 78; PtO *Chich* 73-78; P-in-c Heyshott 78-15. *1 Pinewood Court, Church Road, West Lavington, Midhurst GU29 0EH* E: boxley@talktalk.net

BOYCE, Christopher Allan. b 44. ARIBA 69. S Dios Minl Tr Scheme 84. **d** 87 **p** 88. NSM Eastbourne All SS *Chich* 87-93; C Upton (Overchurch) *Ches* 93-96; V New Brighton St Jas w Em 96-02; P-in-c New Brighton All SS 98-02; TV Bicester w

Bucknell, Caversfield and Launton *Ox* 02-11; rtd 11. *4 Freshwaters, 92/94 Sturgeon Street, Ormiston QLD 4160, Australia* E: christopher.boyce468@gmail.com

BOYCE, John Frederick. b 33. ALCD 57. **d** 57 **p** 58. C Earlsfield St Andr *S'wark* 57-60; C Westerham *Roch* 60-63; C Farnborough 63-66; V Sutton at Hone 66-73; P-in-c Chiddingstone 73-74; R Chiddingstone w Chiddingstone Causeway 74-84; V Brenchley 84-98; rtd 98; PtO *Chich* from 99. *3 Orchard Rise, Groombridge, Tunbridge Wells TN3 9RU* T: (01892) 864633

BOYCE, Joy. b 46. **d** 05 **p** 06. NSM Streatham Ch Ch w St Marg *S'wark* 05-09; NSM Southfields St Barn from 09. *60 Westover Road, London SW18 2RH*   T: (020) 8874 1905 M: 07867-830273 E: joy.boyce@fujitsu.com

BOYCE, Canon Kenneth Albert. b 51. St Edm Hall Ox BA 72 MA 76 Selw Coll Cam BA 75 MA 79. Westcott Ho Cam 73. **d** 75 **p** 76. C Evington *Leic* 75-78; P-in-c Gt Bowden w Welham 78-81; Dioc Stewardship Adv 78-81; Chapl Leic Poly 81-86; TV Leic H Spirit 82-86; P-in-c Astwood Bank and Chapl to the Deaf *Worc* 86-93; R Fladbury, Wyre Piddle and Moor 93-98; P-in-c Cropthorne w Charlton 94-98; R Fladbury w Wyre Piddle and Moor etc 98-00; RD Pershore 97-00; TR Worc SE from 00; RD Worc E from 05; Hon Can Worc Cathl from 07. *The Rectory, 6 St Catherine's Hill, Worcester WR5 2EA*   T: (01905) 355119 E: ken.boyce76@googlemail.com

BOYCE, Ms Susan. b 59. Ch Ch Coll Cant MA 00 Birm Univ BPhil 06. Ripon Coll Cuddesdon 05. **d** 06 **p** 07. NSM Rushall *Lich* 06-11; PtO from 11. *c/o the Lord Bishop of Lichfield, 22 The Close, Lichfield WS13 7LG*   M: 07941-927245 E: sueboyceca@hotmail.com

BOYCE, William Alexander. **d** 03 **p** 04. C Willowfield *D & D* 03-04; C Bangor Abbey 04-07; I Mallusk *Conn* from 07. *The Rectory, 6 Carwood Drive, Newtownabbey BT36 5LP*   T/F: (028) 9087 9029 E: weebill@hotmail.com

BOYCE-TILLMAN, Prof June Barbara. b 43. MBE . St Hugh's Coll Ox BA 65 Lon Inst of Educn PGCE 66 PhD 87 LRAM 74. Dioc OLM tr scheme. **d** 06 **p** 07. NSM Streatham St Paul *S'wark* 06-10; PtO from 10; *Win* from 10. *108 Nimrod Road, London SW16 6TQ*   M: 07850-208721 : F: (020) 8677 8752 E: junebt@globalnet.co.uk

BOYD, Alan McLean. b 50. St Jo Coll Nottm 84. **d** 79 **p** 80. C Bishop's Waltham *Portsm* 79-83; Chapl Reading Univ *Ox* 83-88; Chapl E Birm Hosp 88-94; Chapl Birm Heartlands and Solihull NHS Trust 94-14; rtd 14. *38 Rodborough Road, Dorridge, Solihull B93 8EF*   T: (01564) 730115

BOYD, Canon Alexander Jamieson. b 46. St Chad's Coll Dur BSc 68 Nottm Univ PGCE 69 MSB FSAScot. Coll of Resurr Mirfield 69. **d** 79 **p** 80. NSM Musselburgh *Edin* 79-83; CF 83-00; P-in-c Loddington *Leic* 00-03; Warden Launde Abbey 00-03; P-in-c Mareham-le-Fen and Revesby *Linc* 03-06; P-in-c Hameringham w Scrafield and Winceby 03-06; P-in-c Mareham on the Hill 03-06; R Fen and Hill Gp 06-14; P-in-c Bain Valley Gp 12-14; RD Horncastle 06-11; Can and Preb Linc Cathl 09-14; rtd 14. *Springfield, 14B Bute Terrace, Millport, Isle of Cumbrae KA28 0BA*   T: (01475) 530151 E: alec@ajboyd.wanadoo.co.uk

BOYD, Allan Gray. b 41. St Jo Coll Nottm 84. **d** 87 **p** 88. Hon Chapl Miss to Seafarers from 87; NSM Glas St Gabr 87-93; NSM Greenock 93-96; NSM Paisley St Barn 96-00; NSM Paisley H Trin 96-00; NSM Alexandria 00-01; NSM Clydebank 02-08; rtd 09; LtO *Glas* from 09. *47 Holms Crescent, Erskine PA8 6DJ*   T: 0141-812 2754

BOYD, Canon David Anthony. b 42. Sarum & Wells Th Coll 72. **d** 75 **p** 76. C Ches H Trin 75-79; R 85-93; V Congleton St Jas 79-85; V Farndon and Coddington 93-07; RD Malpas 97-04; Hon Can Ches Cathl 02-07; rtd 07; PtO *Ches* from 08. *68 St James Avenue, Upton, Chester CH2 1NL*   T: (01244) 348800 E: tony.boyd42@googlemail.com

BOYD, James. *See* BOYD, William James

BOYD, Mrs Julie Marie. b 67. Ox Poly BSc 89. ERMC 09. **d** 12 **p** 13. C Dersingham w Anmer and Shernborne *Nor* from 12. *6 Paiges Close, Dersingham, King's Lynn PE31 6UF*   T: (01485) 540055 M: 07923-473103 E: boydjulie@aol.com

BOYD, Canon Samuel Robert Thomas. b 62. **d** 90 **p** 91. NSM Derryloran *Arm* 90-95; C 95-97; I Woodschapel w Gracefield 97-05; I Killyman from 05; Can Arm Cathl from 13. *St Andrew's Rectory, 85 Dungorman Road, Dungannon BT71 6SE* T/F: (028) 8772 2500 E: killyman@armagh.anglican.org

BOYD, Canon Stephen William. b 71. Aston Tr Scheme 95 Ripon Coll Cuddesdon BTh 00. **d** 00 **p** 01. C Walton-on-the-Hill *Liv* 00-04; V Westbrook St Jas 04-09; P-in-c Orford St Marg 09-13; V from 13; AD Warrington from 12; Hon Can Liv Cathl from 12. *St Margaret's Vicarage, 2 St Margaret's Avenue, Warrington WA2 8DT*   T: (01925) 631937

BOYD, Stuart Adrian. b 51. Open Univ BA 99 UWE MA 02. STETS 02. **d** 05 **p** 07. NSM Brent Knoll, E Brent and Lympsham *B & W* 05-06; NSM Knowle H Nativity *Bris* 06-09; PtO *B & W* 09-14; NSM Weston super Mare All SS and St Sav from 14. *29 Stafford Road, Weston-super-Mare BS23 3BN* T: (01934) 627897 M: 07749-223473 E: sboyd@homecall.co.uk

BOYD, William James. **d** 07 **p** 08. C Magheralin w Dollingstown *D & D* 07-11; I Dromore *Clogh* from 11. *The Rectory, 19 Galbally Road, Dromore, Omagh BT78 3EE* T: (028) 8289 8246 E: jamesthegrey@hotmail.com

BOYD, Canon William John Peter. b 28. Lon Univ BA 48 BD 53 PhD 77 Birm Univ MA 60. **d** 57 **p** 58. C Aston SS Pet and Paul *Birm* 57-60; V W Smethwick 60-63; V St Breward *Truro* 63-68; Adult Educn Chapl 64-85; Dioc Ecum Officer 65-83; R St Ewe 68-73; Preb St Endellion 73-85; V St Kew 73-77; R Falmouth K Chas 77-85; RD Carnmarth S 84-85; Dir of Tr 85-93; Prin SWMTC 85-93; Can Res and Chan Truro Cathl 85-93; rtd 93; PtO *Truro* from 93. *7 Chapel Crescent, Zelah, Truro TR4 9HN*

BOYD-WILLIAMS, Anthony Robert. b 46. St Mich Coll Llan 86. **d** 88 **p** 89. C Tonyrefail w Gilfach Goch *Llan* 88-91; V Treharris w Bedlinog 91-96; V Ocker Hill *Lich* 96-05; RD Wednesbury 03-05; rtd 05; PtO *Cov* from 05. *36 Kendall Avenue, Stratford-upon-Avon CV37 6SQ*   T: (01789) 290488 E: stratters@btinternet.com

BOYDEN, Peter Frederick. b 41. Lon Univ BSc 62 AKC 62 Em Coll Cam BA 64 MA 68 MLitt 69. Ridley Hall Cam 63. **d** 66 **p** 67. C Chesterton St Andr *Ely* 66-68; C Wimbledon St Mark 68-72; Chapl K Sch Cant 72-89; Asst Chapl Radley Coll 89-02; rtd 02; PtO *Derby* from 02. *30 Chesterfield Road, Shirland, Alfreton DE55 6BN*   T: (01773) 830552 E: pandjboyden@aol.com

BOYES, Canon David Arthur Stiles. b 30. Lon Coll of Div 62. **d** 63 **p** 64. C Islington St Mary *Lon* 63-71; V Canonbury St Steph 71-75; V St Paul's Cray St Barn *Roch* 75-85; P-in-c Earl Soham w Cretingham and Ashfield *St E* 85-96; Dioc Development Officer 86-92; RD Loes 91-95; Hon Can St E Cathl 95-96; rtd 96; PtO *St E* from 96. *13 Magdalen Drive, Woodbridge IP12 4EF*   T: (01394) 383389

BOYES, Matthew John. b 70. Roehampton Inst BA 91. Wycliffe Hall Ox BTh 99. **d** 99 **p** 00. C Bury St Edmunds Ch Ch *St E* 99-02; P-in-c Penn Street *Ox* 02-06; V Turnham Green Ch Ch *Lon* 06-11; Chapl HM YOI Feltham from 11. *HM Young Offender Institution, Bedfont Road, Feltham TW13 4ND*   T: (020) 8844 5000 F: 8844 5001 E: matt_boyez@dsl.pipex.com

BOYES, Michael Charles. b 27. Lon Univ BA 53 BD 58. Wells Th Coll 53. **d** 55 **p** 56. C Heavitree *Ex* 55-61; C Exwick 61-68; V Broadclyst 68-83; RD Aylesbeare 77-81; TV Sampford Peverell, Uplowman, Holcombe Rogus etc 83-85; TR 85-92; rtd 92; PtO *Ex* from 92. *Old Brewery Cottage, 1 East Street, Uffculme, Cullompton EX15 3AL*   T: (01884) 840492

BOYLAND, Alice Teresa. b 41. **d** 99 **p** 05. NSM Llangybi and Coedypaen w Llanbadoc *Mon* 99-04; NSM Chard and Distr *B & W* 05-06; NSM Chaffcombe, Cricket Malherbie etc 06-11; rtd 11; PtO *B & W* from 11. *62 Linkhay Orchard, South Chard, Chard TA20 2QS*   T: (01460) 221010 E: daveterri@waitrose.com

BOYLAND, David Henry. b 58. TCD BA 79 BAI 79. TCD Div Sch BTh 91. **d** 91 **p** 92. C Seapatrick *D & D* 91-94; I Celbridge w Straffan and Newcastle-Lyons *D & G* 94-98; I Kilmakee *Conn* from 98. *Kilmakee Rectory, 60 Killeaton Park, Dunmurry, Belfast BT17 9HE*   T: (028) 9061 0505 *or* 9061 1024

BOYLAND, Henry Hubert. b 23. CITC. **d** 84 **p** 85. NSM Dunboyne Union *M & K* 84-87; Bp's C Carrickmacross w Magheracloone *Clogh* 87-90; I 90-93; rtd 93. *2 Spring View, Wheaton Hall, Dublin Road, Drogheda, Co Louth, Republic of Ireland*   T: (00353) (41) 984 4724

BOYLAND, Peter James. b 68. TCD BA 92 MA 07. St Steph Ho Ox 07. **d** 09 **p** 10. C Towcester w Caldecote and Easton Neston etc *Pet* 09-11; R Claremont Australia from 11. *The Rectory, 2 Queenslea Drive, Claremont WA 6010, Australia* T: (0061) (8) 9384 9244 M: 40-680 3152 E: frboyland@gmail.com

BOYLE, Andrew McKenzie. b 45. Down Coll Cam BA 67 MA 71 CEng 72 MICE 72. WMMTC 82. **d** 85 **p** 86. NSM Woodthorpe *S'well* 85-87; PtO *Roch* 88-90 and 91-96; Hon C Sevenoaks St Luke CD 90-91; NSM Sundridge w Ide Hill and Toys Hill from 96. *Greenridge, 35 Garth Road, Sevenoaks TN13 1RU* T: (01732) 456546 F: 450060 E: andrew.boyle@diocese-rochester.org

BOYLE, Charles Robert. b 69. Edin Univ MA 92. Ridley Hall Cam 08. **d** 10 **p** 11. C Kea *Truro* 10-13; V Branksome Park All SS *Sarum* from 13. *The Vicarage, 28 Western Road, Poole BH13 7BP*   T: (01202) 041147 M: 07979-857200 E: vicarallsaints@gmail.com

✠**BOYLE, The Rt Revd Christopher John.** b 51. AKC 75. St Aug Coll Cant 75. **d** 76 **p** 77 **c** 01. C Wylde Green *Birm* 76-80; Bp's Dom Chapl 80-83; R Castle Bromwich SS Mary and Marg 83-01; AD Coleshill 92-99; P-in-c Shard End 96-97; Hon Can Birm Cathl 96-01; Bp N Malawi 01-09; Asst Bp Leic from 09. *5 The Pastures, Anstey, Leicester LE7 7QR* E: bishopboyle@googlemail.com *or* bishop.boyle@leccofe.org

BOYLE, Mrs Lynn. b 58. Leeds Univ BEd 79 BA 07. NOC 04. **d** 07 **p** 08. NSM Stockport St Sav *Ches* 07-11; V Werneth from 11. *St Paul's Vicarage, Compstall Brow, Compstall, Stockport SK6 5HU* T: 0161-427 1259　M: 07971-390019 E: lynnboyle1@aol.com

BOYLE, Paul. d 01 **p** 02. C Cen Cardiff *Llan* 01-03; C Barry All SS 03-05; P-in-c Pontypridd St Matt and Cilfynydd w Llanwynno 05-08; P-in-c Burton and Rosemarket *St D* 08-11; P-in-c Camrose 11-15; Asst Dioc Officer for Soc Resp 11-12; Safeguarding Officer 13; Chapl Pembrokeshire Coll 13-15; P-in-c Jeffreyston w Reynoldston and Loveston etc *St D* from 15. *The Vicarage, 7 Churchill Park, Jeffreyston, Kilgetty SA68 0SD* T: (01646) 651598

BOYLE, Robert Leslie. b 52. EMMTC 97. **d** 00 **p** 01. NSM Derby St Anne and St Jo 00-08; C Paignton St Jo *Ex* 08-13; P-in-c Douglas St Matt *S & M* 13-14; V from 14. *St Matthew's Vicarage, 62 Ballabrooie Way, Douglas, Isle of Man IM1 4HB* T: (01624) 676310 E: robert.boyle7@btinternet.com

BOYLES, Peter John. b 59. Univ of Wales (Lamp) BA 84. Sarum & Wells Th Coll 86. **d** 88 **p** 89. C Ches St Mary 88-91; C Neston 91-95; R Lavendon w Cold Brayfield, Clifton Reynes etc *Ox* 95-99; V Dent w Cowgill *Bradf* 99-12; V *Carl* from 12. *The Vicarage, Flintergill, Dent, Sedbergh LA10 5QR* T: (015396) 25226

BOYLING, Canon Denis Hudson. b 16. Keble Coll Ox BA 38 MA 42. Cuddesdon Coll 39. **d** 40 **p** 41. C Sheff St Cuth 40-46; Chapl K Coll Hosp Lon 46-49; Chapl United Sheff Hosps 49-57; V Endcliffe *Sheff* 57-68; Hon Can Sheff Cathl 58-68; V Almondbury *Wakef* 68-75; RD 68-75; Hon Can Wakef Cathl 72-75; Can Res Wakef Cathl 75-82; rtd 82; PtO *Heref* 82-13. *The Old Coach House, Bargates, Leominster HR6 8QT*

BOYLING, The Very Revd Mark Christopher. b 52. Keble Coll Ox BA 74 MA 78. Cuddesdon Coll BA 76. **d** 77 **p** 78. C Kirkby *Liv* 77-79; P-in-c 79-80; TV 80-85; Bp's Dom Chapl 85-89; V Formby St Pet 89-94; Can Res and Prec Liv Cathl 94-04; Dean Carl from 04. *The Deanery, The Abbey, Carlisle CA3 8TZ* T: (01228) 523335　F: 548151 E: dean@carlislecathedral.org.uk

BOYNS, Martin Laurence Harley. b 26. St Jo Coll Cam BA 49 MA 51. Ridley Hall Cam 50. **d** 52 **p** 53. C Woodmansterne *S'wark* 52-55; C Folkestone H Trin w Ch Ch *Cant* 55-58; V Duffield *Derby* 58-71; V Rawdon *Bradf* 71-76; Chapl Woodlands Hosp Rawdon 71-76; R Melton *St E* 76-85; R Gerrans w St Anthony in Roseland *Truro* 85-92; Miss to Seamen 85-92; rtd 92; PtO *Truro* from 92. *Bojunda, Boscaswell Village, Pendeen, Penzance TR19 7EP* T: (01736) 788390

BOYNS, Timothy Martin Harley. b 58. Warwick Univ BA 80 Nottm Univ BCombStuds 84. Linc Th Coll 81. **d** 84 **p** 85. C Oxhey St Matt *St Alb* 84-87; TV Solihull *Birm* 87-94; V Lillington *Cov* 94-06; RD Warwick and Leamington 99-06; V Hessle *York* from 06; AD W Hull from 10; RD Hull from 11. *All Saints' Vicarage, 4 Chestnut Avenue, Hessle HU13 0RH* T: (01482) 648555 E: timboyns@timboyns.karoo.co.uk

BOYSE, Felix Vivian Allan. b 17. LVO 78. CCC Cam BA 39 MA 42. Cuddesdon Coll 39. **d** 40 **p** 41. C New Mills *Derby* 40-43; P-in-c 43-45; Vice-Prin Cuddesdon Coll 46-51; V Kingswood *S'wark* 51-58; V St Mary Abchurch *Lon* 58-61; Prin St Geo Coll Jerusalem 61-64; Chapl Chpl Royal Hampton Court Palace 65-82; Preacher Lincoln's Inn 82-93; rtd 93; PtO *Chich* from 83. *Rose Cottage, Rookwood Road, West Wittering, Chichester PO20 8LT* T: (01243) 514320

BRABIN-SMITH, Ms Lorna Daphne. b 54. Leeds Univ BSc 75. Westcott Ho Cam 03. **d** 05 **p** 06. C Emmaus Par Team *Leic* 05-08; TV Fosse from 08. *The Parsonage, 20 Hoby Road, Thrussington, Leicester LE7 4TH* T: (01664) 424962

BRABY (née QUINTON), Rosemary Ruth. b 53. Univ Coll Lon BA 75 Lon Inst of Educn PGCE 79. **d** 06 **p** 07. OLM Old Catton *Nor* 06-09; PtO 09-10; NSM Trowse from 10. *49 Woodland Drive, Norwich NR6 7AZ* T: (01603) 427165 F: 479556 E: rosemary.braby@ntlworld.com

BRACE, Alistair Andrew. b 53. Newc Univ MB, BS 76. WMMTC 90. **d** 94. NSM Broseley w Benthall, Jackfield, Linley etc *Heref* 94-98. *58 Spout Lane, Benthall, Broseley TF12 1QY* T: (01952) 884031

BRACEGIRDLE, Canon Christopher Andrew. b 56. Dur Univ BEd 79 St Edm Ho Cam BA 84 MA 89 Cov Univ PhD 05. Ridley Hall Cam 82. **d** 85 **p** 86. C Livesey *Blackb* 85-88; TV E

Farnworth and Kearsley *Man* 88-92; V Astley w Chapl Wigan and Leigh Health Services NHS Trust 92-98; P-in-c Walkden Moor w Lt Hulton *Man* 98-99; TR Walkden and Lt Hulton 99-03; V Heaton Ch Ch 03-10; Tutor Dioc OLM and Reader Course 97-06; AD Bolton 05-10; Bp's Sen Chapl 10-14; TR Daisy Hill, Westhoughton and Wingates from 14; Warden of Readers from 08; Hon Can Man Cathl from 07. *The Rectory, Market Street, Westhoughton, Bolton BL5 3AZ* T: (01942) 859251 E: rectordhww@gmail.com

BRACEGIRDLE, Canon Cynthia Wendy Mary. b 52. LMH Ox BA 73 MA 77 Liv Univ DipAE 82. NOC. **d** 87 **p** 94. Chapl Asst Man R Infirmary 85-88; Dir Dioc OLM Scheme *Man* 89-02; Hon Can Man Cathl 98-02; rtd 03; PtO *Carl* from 03. *Drigg Hall, Drigg, Holmrook CA19 1XG* E: ignatius@globalnet.co.uk

BRACEGIRDLE, Robert Kevin Stewart. b 47. Univ Cath Ox BA 69 MA 73. St Steph Ho Ox 70. **d** 73 **p** 74. C Dorchester *Sarum* 73-75; C Woodchurch *Ches* 75-78; V Bidston 78-82; P-in-c Salford St Ignatius *Man* 82-86; R Salford St Ignatius and Stowell Memorial 86-02; P-in-c Salford Ordsall St Clem 99-02; P-in-c Millom *Carl* 02-06; V 06-13; rtd 13. *Drigg Hall, Drigg, Holmrook CA19 1XG* E: robert.bracegirdle@btinternet.com

BRACEWELL, Canon David John. b 44. Leeds Univ BA 66 Man Univ MA 82. Tyndale Hall Bris 67. **d** 69 **p** 70. C Tonbridge St Steph *Roch* 69-72; C Shipley St Pet *Bradf* 72-75; V Halliwell St Paul *Man* 75-84; R Guildf St Sav 84-10; Hon Can Guildf Cathl 05-10; rtd 10. *53 Fairlands Road, Fairlands, Guildford GU3 3HZ* E: djbracewell@gmail.com

BRACEWELL, Howard Waring. b 35. FRGS 73. Tyndale Hall Bris. **d** 63 **p** 63. Canada 63-72; Travel Miss't World Radio Miss Fellowship 72-77; P-in-c Ashill *Nor* 72-74; Hon C Bris St Phil and St Jacob w Em 77-84; PtO *St Alb* 84-86; R Odell 86-88; V Pavenham 86-88; LtO *Man* 88-93; Assoc Min St Andrew's Street Bapt Ch Cambridge 94-99; Assoc Min Halliwell St Luke *Man* 99-01; rtd 01; PtO *Man* 01-14. *16 Avon Road, Melksham SN12 8AY* E: howard@igloovut.fsnet.co.uk

BRACEWELL, Mrs Norma Lesley. b 47. SEITE 08. **d** 10 **p** 11. OLM Cant All SS 10-12; NSM 12-13. *Address temp unknown* E: norma@bracewell.org

BRACEY, David Harold. b 36. AKC 63. **d** 64 **p** 65. C Westleigh St Pet *Man* 64-67; C Dunstable *St Alb* 67-70; V Benchill *Man* 70-76; V Elton St Steph 76-87; V Howe Bridge 87-00; rtd 00; PtO *Ban* from 06. *Rhiw Awel, Sarn, Pwllheli LL53 8EY* T: (01758) 730381

BRACEY, Dexter Lee. b 70. Lanc Univ BA 92. St Steph Ho Ox BTh 11. **d** 09 **p** 10. C St Marychurch *Ex* 09-13; P-in-c Swindon New Town *Bris* from 13. *St Mark's Rectory, 18 Park Lane, Swindon SN1 5EL* T: (01803) 326203 E: dexter_bracey@yahoo.co.uk *or* swindonnewtown@btinternet.com

BRACHER, Paul Martin. b 59. Solicitor 84 Ex Univ LLB 80. Trin Coll Bris BA 90. **d** 90 **p** 91. C Sparkhill w Greet and Sparkbrook *Birm* 90-93; Chapl Birm Women's Hosp 92-93; P-in-c Lea Hall *Birm* 93-98; V from 98. *St Richard's Vicarage, Hallmoor Road, Birmingham B33 9QY* T: 0121-783 2319 E: richard1552@aol.com

BRACKENBURY, The Ven Michael Palmer. b 30. Linc Th Coll 64. **d** 66 **p** 67. C S Ormsby w Ketsby, Calceby and Driby *Linc* 66-69; V Scothern w Sudbrooke 69-77; RD Lawres 73-78; Bp's Personal Asst 77-88; Dioc Dir of Ords 77-87; Can and Preb Linc Cathl 79-95; Dioc Lay Min Adv 86-87; Adn Linc 88-95; rtd 95. *18 Lea View, Ryhall, Stamford PE9 4HZ* T: (01780) 752415

✠**BRACKLEY, The Rt Revd Ian James.** b 47. Keble Coll Ox BA 69 MA 73. Cuddesdon Coll 69. **d** 71 **p** 72 **c** 96. C Bris Lockleaze St Mary Magd w St Fran 71-74; Asst Chapl Bryanston Sch 74-77; Chapl 77-80; V E Preston w Kingston *Chich* 80-88; RD Arundel and Bognor 82-87; TR Haywards Heath St Wilfrid 88-96; RD Cuckfield 89-95; Suff Bp Dorking *Guildf* from 96; Hon Can Guildf Cathl from 96. *13 Pilgrim's Way, Guildford GU4 8AD* T: (01483) 570829　F: 567268 E: bishop.ian@cofeguildford.org.uk

BRACKLEY, Mark Ozanne. b 53. Boro Road Teacher Tr Coll CertEd 75. S'wark Ord Course 90. **d** 93 **p** 94. C Hampstead St Steph w All Hallows *Lon* 93-97; V W Green Ch Ch w St Pet 97-04; Chapl Univ Coll Lon Hosps NHS Foundn Trust 04-08; Chapl Bolton Hospice from 08; PtO *Man* from 13. *Bolton Hospice, Queens Park Street, Bolton BL1 4QT* T: (01204) 663066 F: 663060

BRACKNALL, Richard David Guy. b 43. Ian Ramsey Coll Brasted 71 Ripon Hall Ox 73. **d** 75 **p** 76. C Pocklington w Yapham-cum-Meltonby, Owsthorpe etc *York* 75-78; TV Thornaby on Tees 78-84; V New Marske 84-90; P-in-c Wilton 84-90; Ind Chapl 90-95; PtO from 05. *34 Margrove Park, Boosbeck, Saltburn-by-the-Sea TS12 3BX* T: (01287) 653417

BRADBERRY, Canon John Stephen. b 47. Hull Univ BSc 70 Leeds Univ CertEd 71 MEd 86 Bradf Univ PhD 91. NW Ord Course 76. **d** 79 **p** 80. NSM Warley *Leeds* from 79; Chapl H Trin Sch Holmfield 91-06; Chapl Rishworth Sch Ripponden from 06; Bp's Officer for NSMs *Wakef* 95-04; RD Halifax 07-14; AD *Leeds* from 14; Hon Can Wakef Cathl from 13. *129 Paddock Lane, Halifax HX2 0NT*   T: (01422) 358282
E: sbradberry@tiscali.co.uk

BRADBROOK, Mrs Averyl. b 46. Girton Coll Cam BA 67 MA 88 Man Univ PGCE 69 MA(Theol) 96. NOC 90. **d** 93 **p** 94. C Heaton Ch Ch *Man* 93-96; P-in-c Elton St Steph 96-02; Bp's Adv on Women in Min 01-02; V Moseley St Mary *Birm* 02-05; P-in-c Moseley St Anne 04-05; TR Eden, Gelt and Irthing *Carl* 05-10; rtd 10; PtO *Carl* from 11. *2 Ellerbank, Cowan Head, Burneside, Kendal LA8 9HX*   T: (01539) 724262 M: 07808-290817 E: abradbrook@btinternet.com

BRADBROOK, Peter David. b 33. Kelham Th Coll 54. **d** 60 **p** 61. C Ches St Oswald St Thos 60-63; C Fulham St Etheldreda *Lon* 64-65; V Congleton St Jas *Ches* 65-79; V Wheelock 79-92; V Crewe All SS and St Paul 92-98; rtd 98; PtO *Ches* from 00. *20 Magdelen Court, College Fields, Dane Bank Avenue, Crewe CW2 8FF*   T: (01270) 669420

BRADBURY, George Graham. b 35. AKC 58. **d** 59 **p** 60. C Portsea St Mary *Portsm* 59-62; C Melksham *Sarum* 62-64; R Winfrith Newburgh w Chaldon Herring 64-68; CF 68-71; rtd 96. *Wayside, Brook Street, Shipton Gorge, Bridport DT6 4NA* T: (01308) 897714

BRADBURY, Mrs Jane. b 58. Liv Univ BA 80 Wolfs Coll Cam BTh 13. Westcott Ho Cam 11. **d** 13 **p** 14. C Helston and Wendron *Truro* from 13. *The Vicarage, Wendron, Helston TR13 0NA* E: janebradbury1@gmail.com

BRADBURY, Julian Nicholas Anstey. b 49. BNC Ox BA 71 MA 75 Birm Univ MA 84 Cardiff Univ PhD 07. Cuddesdon Coll 71. **d** 73 **p** 74. C S'wark H Trin 73-74; C S'wark H Trin w St Matt 74-76; USA 76-79; V Tottenham H Trin *Lon* 79-85; Dir Past Th Sarum & Wells Th Coll 85-90; P-in-c Yatton Keynell *Bris* 90-97; P-in-c Biddestone w Slaughterford 90-97; P-in-c Castle Combe 90-97; P-in-c W Kington 90-97; P-in-c Nettleton w Littleton Drew 90-97; Fell Horfield H Trin 97-02; Sen Fell K Fund 02-07; 07-12; Dir Nursing and Cross-Sector Leadership Development NHS Leadership Academy from 13; PtO *Ox* 02-09; Hon C Ox St Giles and SS Phil and Jas w St Marg from 09. *8 Osberton Road, Oxford OX2 7NU*   T: (01865) 580823 M: 07900-607099 E: nicholas@nicholasbradbury.co.uk

BRADBURY, Justin Robert Grant. b 66. St Andr Univ MA 92. Wycliffe Hall Ox 06. **d** 08 **p** 09. C Southbroom *Sarum* 08-12; CF from 12. *c/o MOD Chaplains (Army)*   F: 381824 T: (01264) 383430 E: justinrgbradbury@hotmail.co.uk

BRADBURY, Canon Matthew Laurence. b 58. Kent Univ BA 79 Solicitor 83. EAMTC 00. **d** 03 **p** 04. NSM Sutton and Witcham w Mepal *Ely* 03-06; NSM Haddenham and Wilburton 06-08; V Wisbech St Mary and Guyhirn w Ring's End etc from 08; RD Wisbech Lynn Marshland from 11; Hon Can Ely Cathl from 12. *The Vicarage, Church Road, Wisbech St Mary, Wisbech PE13 4RN*   T: (01945) 410814 M: 07704-139898 E: matthew.bradbury@ely.anglican.org

BRADBURY, Nicholas. *See* BRADBURY, Julian Nicholas Anstey

BRADBURY, Paul. b 72. St Cath Coll Cam BA 93 N Lon Univ MA 99. Trin Coll Bris BA 04. **d** 04 **p** 05. C Bitterne Park *Win* 04-08; C Pioneer Min Poole Old Town *Sarum* from 08. *43 Green Road, Poole BH1 1QH* E: bradsare@btinternet.com

BRADBURY, Robert Douglas. b 50. Ripon Coll Cuddesdon 75. **d** 76 **p** 77. C Harlescott *Lich* 76-81; V Ruyton 81-88; P-in-c Gt w Lt Ness 84-88; V Ruyton XI Towns w Gt and Lt Ness 88-99. *Fairview, Holyhead Road, Froncysyllte, Llangollen LL20 7PU* T: (01691) 777898

BRADDICK-SOUTHGATE, Charles Anthony Michael. b 70. K Coll Lon BD 92 MA 08. Chich Th Coll 92. **d** 94 **p** 95. C Catford St Laur *S'wark* 94-97; V Nunhead St Antony w St Silas 97-09; PtO 11-13 and from 15; Hon C Crofton Park St Hilda w St Cypr 13-15. *25 Parrock Road, Gravesend DA12 1QE*

BRADDOCK, Canon Andrew Jonathan. b 71. SS Coll Cam BA 92 MA 96 PhD 12. Ridley Hall Cam 95. **d** 98 **p** 99. C Ranworth w Panxworth, Woodbastwick etc *Nor* 98-01; R Cringleford and Colney 01-08; RD Humbleyard 04-08; Miss and Evang Officer *Glouc* 08-13; Hon Can Glouc Cathl 11-13; Dir Miss and Min from 13; Can Res Glouc Cathl from 13. *Church House, College Green, Gloucester GL1 2LY*   T: (01452) 610346 E: abraddock@glosdioc.org.uk

BRADDY, Andrew (Richard). b 67. Birm Univ BA 88 City Univ MA 89 Goldsmiths' Coll Lon PhD 99 ABSM 88. SEITE BA 10. **d** 10 **p** 11. C Whitstable *Cant* 10-14; V Wantsum Gp from 14. *The Vicarage, St Mildred's Road, Minster, Ramsgate CT12 4DE* M: 07813-384972   T: (01843) 821250 E: arichard.braddy@gmail.com

BRADFORD, Alan. b 57. Southn Univ BSc 79 Warwick Univ PGCE 80. St Jo Coll Nottm MTh 04. **d** 04 **p** 05. C Countesthorpe w Foston *Leic* 04-08; C Warfield *Ox* 08-15; C Bracknell 15. *2 Dorset Vale, Warfield, Bracknell RG42 3JL* T: (01344) 425000   M: 07546-219581
E: abradford@hotmail.co.uk

BRADFORD, John. b 34. Lon Univ BA 60 Birm Univ MEd 81 FRSA FRGS. Oak Hill Th Coll 55. **d** 60 **p** 61. C Walcot B & W 60-64; Asst Master Wendover C of E Primary Sch 64-65; Hd RE Dr Challoner's High Sch Lt Chalfont 65-69; PtO *Ox* 66-70; Lect St Pet Coll of Educn Saltley 70-77; PtO *Birm* 70-71 and from 05; LtO 71-03; PtO *Cov* from 77; Nat Chapl-Missr Children's Soc 77-99; PtO Ch in Wales from 89; rtd 99. *27 Marsh Lane, Solihull B91 2PG*   T: 0121-704 9895
E: revjohnbradford@aol.com

BRADFORD, Mark James. b 78. York Univ BA 00. St Jo Coll Nottm 10. **d** 13 **p** 14. C Ripon H Trin *Leeds* from 13. *14 Filey Avenue, Ripon HG4 2DH*   M: 07967-740536
E: markjamesbradford@googlemail.com

BRADFORD, Peter. b 38. Sarum Th Coll 69. **d** 70 **p** 71. C Holdenhurst *Win* 70-73; C Stanmore 73-77; P-in-c Eling, Testwood and Marchwood 77-78; R Marchwood 78-86; C Christchurch 86-90; C Andover w Foxcott 90-92; V E and W Worldham, Hartley Mauditt w Kingsley etc 92-04; rtd 04. *Old Forge House, 22 Church Street, Helston TR13 8TQ* T: (01326) 560574

BRADFORD, Phillip James. b 81. York Univ BA 02 MA 04 PhD 08. Westcott Ho Cam 07. **d** 10 **p** 11. C Worc SE 10-13; C St Jo in Bedwardine 13-15; P-in-c Worc Dines Green St Mich and Crown E, Rushwick from 15. *99 Sebright Avenue, Worcester WR5 2HJ*   T: (01905) 350098 E: phillipbradford@yahoo.com

BRADFORD, Simon. b 77. **d** 12 **p** 13. NSM Milton *Ely* 12; NSM Waterbeach from 12; NSM Landbeach from 12. *22 Heron Walk, Waterbeach, Cambridge CB25 9BZ*
E: sd_bradford@hotmail.com

BRADFORD, Steven John. b 59. Open Univ MBA 01. St Jo Coll Nottm 06. **d** 08 **p** 09. C Bearsted w Thurnham *Cant* 08-11; V Gorleston St Andr *Nor* 11-15; P-in-c Folkestone St Jo *Cant* from 15. *4 Cornwallis Avenue, Folkestone CT19 5JA*
E: stevejbradford@btinternet.com

BRADFORD, Archdeacon of. *See* LEE, The Ven David John
BRADFORD, Dean of. *See* LEPINE, The Very Revd Jeremy John
BRADFORD, Suffragan Bishop of. *See* HOWARTH, The Rt Revd Toby Matthew

BRADING, Christopher. b 58. St Steph Ho Ox 12. **d** 14 **p** 15. C Swinton *Sheff* from 14. *19 Low Golden Smithies, Swinton, Mexborough S64 8DF* E: chris@brading.net *or* chris.brading@sheffield.anglican.org

BRADING, Jeremy Clive. b 74. Birm Univ BA 95 MPhil 98. Westcott Ho Cam 00. **d** 02 **p** 03. C Man Clayton St Cross w St Paul 02-05; TV Pendleton 05-07; P-in-c Daisy Hill 07-12; C Westhoughton and Wingates 11-12; R Chickerell w Fleet *Sarum* from 12; P-in-c Abbotsbury, Portesham and Langton Herring from 12. *The Rectory, East Street, Chickerell, Weymouth DT3 4DS*   T: (01305) 784915   M: 07786-567140 E: jeremybrading@gmail.com

BRADISH, Paul Edward. b 61. Reading Univ LLB 83. Ripon Coll Cuddesdon MA 07. **d** 07 **p** 08. C Wokingham St Sebastian *Ox* 07-08; C Upper Kennet *Sarum* 08-10; R Shiplake w Dunsden and Harpsden *Ox* from 10. *The Rectory, Church Lane, Shiplake, Henley-on-Thames RG9 4BS*   T: 0118-940 1549 M: 07766-831661 E: revpaulbradish@gmail.com

BRADLEY, Andrew Robert. b 65. Clare Coll Cam BA 88. St Jo Coll Nottm MA 94. **d** 94 **p** 95. C Burnage St Marg *Man* 94-98; TV Didsbury St Jas and Em 98-04; Nat Co-ord Acorn Chr Foundn 04-11; Chapl Christie Hosp NHS Trust Man from 11. *The Christie NHS Foundation Trust, Wilmslow Road, Manchester M20 4BX*   T: 0161-446 3000

BRADLEY, Anthony David. b 56. Wye Coll Lon BSc 76. St Jo Coll Nottm 86. **d** 88 **p** 89. C Southchurch Ch Ch *Chelmsf* 88-91; C Cov H Trin 91-97; P-in-c Budbrooke 97-06; Dioc Lay Tr Adv 93-06; Development Dir Forward Vision 06-07; rtd 07; PtO *Carl* from 06. *12 St George's Road, Millom LA18 5BA*   T: (01229) 770535
E: tony.bradley@dial.pipex.com

BRADLEY, Anthony Edward. b 39. Perth Bible Coll 93. **d** 89 **p** 96. Dn-in-c Ravensthorpe Australia 95-96; P-in-c 96-99; C Wotton St Mary *Glouc* 00-04; rtd 04. *PO Box 1083, Bridgetown WA 6255, Australia*   T: (0061) (8) 9761 2917 E: tonychris@westnet.com.au

BRADLEY, Brian Hugh Granville. b 32. Univ Coll Ox 51. Lon Coll of Div 59. **d** 62 **p** 63. C E Twickenham St Steph *Lon* 62-65; C Herne Bay Ch Ch *Cant* 65-69; Miss to Seamen Teesside 69-71; Ceylon 71-72; Sri Lanka 72-74; Chapl Amsterdam w Haarlem and Den Helder *Eur* 75-79; Chapl Lyon w Grenoble and Aix-les-Bains 79-85; TV Bucknall and Bagnall

Lich 87-93; Assoc Chapl Dubai and Sharjah w N Emirates 93-97; rtd 97; PtO *Win* 97-03. *19 Gracey Court, Woodland Road, Broadclyst, Exeter EX5 3GA*

BRADLEY, Clifford David. b 36. Lon Univ BA 60. St Aid Birkenhead 60. **d** 62 **p** 63. C Stoneycroft All SS *Liv* 62-65; C Chipping Sodbury and Old Sodbury *Glouc* 65-68; Br Honduras 68-70; C Leckhampton SS Phil and Jas *Glouc* 70-71; V Badgeworth w Shurdington 71-79; Dioc Missr *S & M* 79-84; V Santan 79-84; V Braddan 79-84; Bp's Dom Chapl 81-84; V Stroud and Uplands w Slad *Glouc* 84-89; C Shepshed *Leic* 90-92; R Leire w Ashby Parva and Dunton Bassett 92-99; rtd 99; P-in-c Renhold *St Alb* 99-06; PtO from 06. *47 Paddock Close, Clapham, Bedford MK41 6BD* T: (01234) 305981

BRADLEY, Colin John. b 46. Edin Univ MA 69. Sarum & Wells Th Coll 72. **d** 75 **p** 76. C Easthampstead *Ox* 75-79; V Shawbury *Lich* 79-90; R Moreton Corbet 80-90; P-in-c Stanton on Hine Heath 81-90; Can Res Portsm Cathl and Dir of Ords *Portsm* 90-98; C Chich 98-00; C Chich St Paul and Westhampnett 00-01; P-in-c Cocking, Bepton and W Lavington 01-14; rtd 14. *9 Manor Villas, Fareham Road, Wickham, Fareham PO17 5DB* E: zen101842@zen.co.uk

BRADLEY (née DRAPER), Mrs Elizabeth Ann. b 38. Nottm Univ BTh 75. Linc Th Coll 71. **dss** 84 **d** 87 **p** 94. Ind Chapl *Linc* 84-91; Bracebridge 84-91; Hon C 87-91; GFS Ind Chapl *Lon* 91-96; Hon Chapl GFS 96-98; Riverside Chapl *S'wark* 96; C Leighton Buzzard w Eggington, Hockliffe etc *St Alb* 98-01; PtO 01-02; Chapl Luton and Dunstable Hosp NHS Foundn Trust from 02. *14 Wren Terrace, Wixams, Bedford MK42 6BP* E: elizabeth.bradley@ldh-tr.anglox.nhs.uk

BRADLEY, Gary Scott. b 53. Lon Univ LLB 75. Ripon Coll Cuddesdon 75. **d** 78 **p** 79. C St John's Wood *Lon* 78-83; V Paddington St Sav 83-11; P-in-c Paddington St Mary 95-11; P-in-c Paddington St Mary Magd 98-03; V Lt Venice from 11. *6 Park Place Villas, London W2 1SP* T: (020) 7723 1968 F: 7724 5332 M: 07957-140371 T: (020) 7262 3787 E: vicar@parishoflittlevenice.com

BRADLEY, Joy Elizabeth. *See* COUSANS, Joy Elizabeth

BRADLEY, Mrs Julie Caroline. b 59. Ex Univ BSc 80. WEMTC 00. **d** 03 **p** 04. NSM Stoke Gifford *Bris* from 03. *113 North Road, Stoke Gifford, Bristol BS34 8PE* T: 0117-979 3418 E: cjcbradley@deltats.co.uk

BRADLEY, Mrs Karen Tracey. b 64. St Jo Coll Nottm 10. **d** 12 **p** 13. C Walton St Jo *Derby* 12-15; TV E Scarsdale from 15. *The Vicarage, Main Street, Shirebrook, Mansfield NG20 8DN* M: 07823-440513 T: (01623) 748577 E: rev.karen@yahoo.co.uk

BRADLEY, Mrs Mary. **d** 12 **p** 13. NSM Meanwood *Leeds* from 12. *3 Dale Park Close, Leeds LS16 7PR*

BRADLEY, Canon Michael Frederick John. b 44. Qu Coll Birm 76. **d** 77 **p** 78. C Sheff St Cuth 77-78; C Alford w Rigsby *Linc* 78-83; V Bracebridge 83-90; V Flitwick *St Alb* 90-14; RD Ampthill and Shefford 08-13; Hon Can *St Alb* 10-14; rtd 14; PtO *St Alb* from 14. *14 Wren Terrace, Wixams, Bedford MK42 6BP* E: revmichael@virginmedia.com

BRADLEY, Michael Louis. b 54. Dartington Coll of Arts BA 77 K Coll Lon MMus 84. ERMC. **d** 11 **p** 12. NSM Loughton St Jo *Chelmsf* 11-15; C Barkingside St Fran from 15. *144 Fencepiece Road, Ilford IG6 2LA* T: (020) 8500 2970 E: mikebradley03@yahoo.co.uk

BRADLEY, The Ven Peter David Douglas. b 49. Nottm Univ BTh 79. Ian Ramsey Coll Brasted 74 Linc Th Coll 75. **d** 79 **p** 80. C Upholland *Liv* 79-83; TR 94-01; V Dovecot 83-94; Dir CME 89-02; Hon Can Liv Cathl from 00; Adn Warrington from 01; TR Upholland 01-11. *30 Sandbrook Road, Orrell, Wigan WN5 8UD* T: (01695) 624131 *or* 0151-705 2154 E: peter.bradley@liverpool.anglican.org

BRADLEY, The Very Revd Peter Edward. b 64. Trin Hall Cam BA 86 MA 90 FRSA 02. Ripon Coll Cuddesdon 86. **d** 88 **p** 89. C Northampton St Mich w St Edm *Pet* 88-91; Chapl G&C Coll Cam 91-95; TV Abingdon *Ox* 95-98; TV High Wycombe 98-03; TR 03; Dean Sheff from 03. *Sheffield Cathedral, Church Street, Sheffield S1 1HA* T: 0114-263 6063 F: 263 6075 E: dean@sheffield-cathedral.org.uk

BRADLEY, Philip John Paul. b 64. Birm Univ BSc 85. Trin Coll Bris 09. **d** 11 **p** 12. C Oldland *Bris* 11-14; C Longwell Green 13-14; P-in-c Cricklade w Latton from 14. *14 Bath Road, Cricklade, Swindon SN6 6EY* M: 07947-030808 T: 0117-329 1404 E: fivebradleys@yahoo.co.uk

BRADLEY, Ronald Percival. b 25. ACP 51 FRSA 52 TCert 49. Ex & Truro NSM Scheme 80. **d** 83 **p** 84. C Honiton, Gittisham, Combe Raleigh, Monkton etc *Ex* 83-86; P-in-c Halberton 86-87; rtd 90. *Thornbury Villas Care Home, 128 Peverell Park Road, Plymouth PL3 4NE* T: (01752) 263572

BRADLEY, Susan Frances. b 59. Wolv Univ BSc 92 Liv Univ MSc 96 RGN 81 RSCN 81. Trin Coll Bris BA 10. **d** 10 **p** 11. C Glenfield *Leic* 10-13; TV Woodfield from 13. *The Rectory, 17*

Rectory Lane, Appleby Magna, Swadlincote DE12 7BQ T: (01530) 271327 M: 07855-095060 E: suebradley@onetel.com

BRADLEY, Mrs Susan Kathleen. b 47. Hull Coll of Educn TCert 68 Open Univ BA 84 MA 96. **d** 05 **p** 06. OLM S Lawres Gp *Linc* from 05. *17 Holly Close, Cherry Willingham, Lincoln LN3 4BH* T: (01522) 750292 E: rev.s.bradley@gmail.com

BRADLEY (née NAYLOR), Ms Vivien Frances Damaris. b 55. New Hall Cam BA 78 MA 82 RGN 86. Ripon Coll Cuddesdon. **d** 93 **p** 94. C Northampton St Jas *Pet* 93-95; Chapl Asst Southn Univ Hosps NHS Trust 95-98; Chapl 98-00; Chapl Addenbrooke's NHS Trust 00-03; PtO *Nor* from 03. *7 Station Road, Kimberley, Wymondham NR18 9HB* T: (01603) 757807 E: vivien@wolistic.co.uk

BRADLEY, Miss Wendy Jayne. b 66. All SS Cen for Miss & Min 12. **d** 15. NSM Aspley *S'well* from 15. *10 Norwood Road, Nottingham NG7 3FJ* M: 07971-770836 E: wendyjayne.bradley@gmail.com

BRADNUM, Canon Ella Margaret. b 41. CertEd 64 St Hugh's Coll Ox MA 65. **dss** 69 **d** 87 **p** 94. Illingworth *Wakef* 69-72; Batley All SS 72-73; Lay Tr Officer 77-82; Min Tr Officer 82-88; Sec Dioc Bd of Min *Wakef* 88-06; Warden of Readers 88-02; Co-ord Lay Tr 88-02; Hon Can Wakef Cathl 94-06; Prin Wakef Min Scheme 97-06; rtd 06. *4 Southlands Drive, Huddersfield HD2 2LT* T: (01484) 420721

BRADNUM, Richard James. b 39. Pemb Coll Ox BA 62 MA 67. Ridley Hall Cam 62. **d** 64 **p** 65. C Birm St Martin 64-68; C Sutton St Jas *York* 68-69; PtO *Wakef* 71-72; C Batley All SS 72-74; V Gawthorpe and Chickenley Heath 74-86; V Mixenden 86-97; rtd 97; PtO *Wakef* 97-99; Hon Retirement Officer *Leeds* from 99. *4 Southlands Drive, Huddersfield HD2 2LT* T: (01484) 420721

BRADSHAW, Benjamin James. b 86. Sheff Univ BA 12. Coll of Resurr Mirfield 09. **d** 13. Braunton *Ex* 12-13; C from 13. *11 Hazel Avenue, Braunton EX33 2EZ* T: (01271) 815664 M: 07521-286641 E: brother_ben@btinternet.com

BRADSHAW, Charles Anthony. b 44. Qu Coll Birm MA 76. **d** 75 **p** 76. C Whickham *Dur* 75-78; C Bilton *Cov* 78-81; TV Coventry Caludon 81-89; V Birstall and Wanlip *Leic* 89-99; TR Vale of Belvoir 00-04; TV Caterham *S'wark* 04-12; rtd 12; PtO *S'wark* from 13. *39 Mill Lane, Hurst Green, Oxted RH8 9DF* T: (01883) 724742 E: cab@paxchristi.wanadoo.co.uk

BRADSHAW, Denis Matthew. b 52. Chich Th Coll 77. **d** 80 **p** 81. C Ruislip St Martin *Lon* 80-84; C Northolt Park St Barn 84-86; V Northolt St Jos 86-01; P-in-c Hayes St Nic CD 94-00; V Kennington St Jo w St Jas *S'wark* 01-09; V Burgess Hill St Edw *Chich* from 09. *St Edward's Vicarage, 7 Bramble Gardens, Burgess Hill RH15 8UQ* T: (01444) 241300 E: denis.bradshaw1@btinternet.com

BRADSHAW, Graham. b 58. Edin Univ BD 86. Edin Th Coll 83. **d** 86 **p** 87. C Thornton-le-Fylde *Blackb* 86-89; C Kirkby Lonsdale *Carl* 89-91; V Langford *St Alb* 91-97; Papua New Guinea 97-99; R Aspley Guise w Husborne Crawley and Ridgmont *St Alb* from 00. *The Rectory, Church Street, Aspley Guise, Milton Keynes MK17 8HN* T: (01908) 583169 E: gbradshaw@tinyworld.co.uk

BRADSHAW, Miss Jennie McNeille. b 47. UEA BA 69. Cranmer Hall Dur 85. **d** 90 **p** 94. Par Dn Herne *Cant* 90-94; C 94-95; P-in-c Claybrooke cum Wibtoft and Frolesworth *Leic* 95-96; R 96-06; P-in-c Burham and Wouldham *Roch* 06-11; rtd 12; PtO *Cant* from 13. *Amberville, Tunstall Road, Tunstall, Sittingbourne ME10 1YQ* T: (01795) 423307 E: jenniebradshaw@mypostoffice.co.uk

BRADSHAW (née DAY), Mrs Jennifer Ann. b 67. Aber Univ BSc 89. Wycliffe Hall Ox BTh 95. **d** 95 **p** 96. C Whitburn *Dur* 95-98; C Monkwearmouth 98-99; TV 99-01; NSM Silksworth 02-12; TV N Wearside from 12. *The Rectory, 2A Park Avenue, Sunderland SR6 9PU* T: 0191-548 6607 E: jenniferabradshaw@btinternet.com

BRADSHAW, Canon Malcolm McNeille. b 45. Kelham Th Coll 65. **d** 70 **p** 71. C New Addington *Cant* 70-76; Chapl Milan w Cadenabbia, Varese and Lugano *Eur* 77-82; V Boxley w Detling *Cant* 82-99; Sen Chapl Gtr Athens *Eur* from 99; Hon Can Malta Cathl from 01. *c/o the British Embassy, Plutarchou 1, 106-75 Athens, Greece* T/F: (0030) (210) 721 4906 E: anglican@otenet.gr

BRADSHAW, Canon Paul Frederick. b 45. Clare Coll Cam BA 66 MA 70 K Coll Lon PhD 71 Ox Univ DD 94 FRHistS 91. Westcott Ho Cam 67. **d** 69 **p** 70. C W Wickham St Jo *Cant* 69-71; C Cant St Martin and St Paul 71-73; Tutor Chich Th Coll 73-78; V Flamstead *St Alb* 78-82; Dir of Minl Tr Scheme 78-82; Vice-Prin Ripon Coll Cuddesdon 83-85; USA 85-95; Prof Th Notre Dame Univ 85-13; Hon Can N Indiana from 90; PV Westmr Abbey 95-13; PtO *Guildf* from 95; Dioc Liturg Officer *Eur* from 07; rtd 10. *367 Pine Valley Drive, Fairview TX 75069, USA* T: (001) (214) 856 0799 E: bradshaw.1@nd.edu

BRADSHAW, Philip Hugh. b 39. Qu Coll Ox BA 64 MA 67. S'wark Ord Course 88. **d** 91 **p** 92. NSM Bletchingley *S'wark*

91-98; Ldr Community of Celebration 91-98; NSM Redhill St Jo *S'wark* 98-10; PtO from 10. *35 Cavendish Road, Redhill RH1 4AL* T: (01737) 778760 E: bradshaws@ccct.co.uk

BRADSHAW, Richard Gordon Edward. b 66. Southn Univ LLB 90. Wycliffe Hall Ox BTh 94. d 97 p 98. C Bishopwearmouth St Gabr *Dur* 97-00; C Silksworth 00-01; P-in-c 01-03; V 03-12; TR Monkwearmouth from 12; AD Wearmouth 08-15. *The Rectory, 2A Park Avenue, Sunderland SR6 9PU* T: 0191-548 6607

BRADSHAW, Roy John. b 49. Sarum & Wells Th Coll 85. d 87 p 88. C Gainsborough All SS *Linc* 87-90; V New Waltham 90-94; R Killamarsh *Derby* 94-06; C Barlborough and Renishaw 05-06; rtd 06; PtO *Derby* from 07. *22 St Peter's Close, Duckmanton, Chesterfield S44 5JJ* T: (01246) 822280 E: rbradshaw@hotmail.co.uk

BRADSHAW, Timothy. b 50. Keble Coll Ox BA 72 MA 78 PhD. St Jo Coll Nottm BA 75. d 76 p 77. C Clapton Park All So *Lon* 76-79; Lect Trin Coll Bris 80-91; Hon C Sea Mills *Bris* 83-91; Tutor Regent's Park Coll Ox from 91; NSM Ox St Aldate w St Matt 91-94; NSM Ox St Matt 95-07. *54 St Giles, Oxford OX1 3LU* T: (01865) 288147 E: timothy.bradshaw@regents.ox.ac.uk

BRADSHAW, Veronica. *See* CAROLAN, Veronica

BRADWELL, Area Bishop of. *See* WRAW, The Rt Revd John Michael

BRADY, Frederick Herbert James. b 33. Sydney Univ BSc 55 DipEd 56 Lon Univ BD 65. Moore Th Coll Sydney ThL 59. d 60 p 60. Australia 60-63 and from 69; LtO *Lon* 63-69; rtd 00. *18 Capel Street, West Melbourne Vic 3003, Australia* T: (0061) (3) 9328 8487 *or* 9650 3791 F: 9650 4718 E: brady@ioville.net.au

BRADY, Canon Ian. b 59. Ridley Hall Cam. d 01 p 02. C Cromer *Nor* 01-04; V Belmont *Lon* 04-09; P-in-c Douglas St Thos *S & M* 09-14; V from 14; Can St German's Cathl from 14. *St Thomas's Vicarage, Marathon Avenue, Douglas, Isle of Man IM2 4JA* T: (01624) 611503 E: i.bradybunch@btopenworld.com

BRADY, Mrs Lynda. b 60. SRN 83. SA Internat Tr Coll 87 Oak Hill Th Coll 07. d 07 p 08. NSM Belmont *Lon* 07-09; NSM Douglas St Thos *S & M* from 09; Chapl Hospice Is of Man from 09. *St Thomas's Vicarage, Marathon Avenue, Douglas, Isle of Man IM2 4JA* T: (01624) 611503 M: 07974-995561 E: revbrady@btopenworld.com

BRADY, Canon Madalaine Margaret. b 45. Univ of Wales (Ban) BD 88 CertEd 91 MA 92. d 89 p 97. Asst Chapl Univ of Wales (Ban) 89-96; Dioc Communications Officer 94-12; Dioc Lay Min Officer 95-10; C Archllechwedd 96-97; P-in-c Llanfaelog 97-02; R Llanfaelog and Llangwyfan 02-12; AD Llifon and Talybolion 07-12; Can Cursal Ban Cathl 03-09; Can and Treas Ban Cathl 09-12; rtd 12; PtO *Ban* from 14. *4 Salem Place, Llanllechid, Bangor LL57 3ES* T: (01248) 605299 E: dmbrady@btinternet.com

BRAE, David. b 80. Trin Coll Bris BA 09. d 10 p 11. C Bishop's Cleeve and Woolstone w Gotherington etc *Glouc* 10-13; C Cheltenham Ch Ch 13; TV Bacup and Stacksteads *Man* from 13. *Christ Church Vicarage, Greensnook Lane, Bacup OL13 9DQ* M: 07793-714882 E: wonderfulworld@me.com

BRAE, Mrs Yvonne Rosetta. b 45. WEMTC 05. d 08 p 09. NSM Cheltenham St Luke and St Jo and Cheltenham St Mich *Glouc* 08-12; NSM Charlton Kings H Apostles 12-13; NSM Sodbury Vale from 13. *86 Arle Road, Cheltenham GL51 8LB* T: (01242) 519780 M: 07940-452211 E: jmyr@blueyonder.co.uk

BRAGG, Annette Frances. *See* STICKLEY, Annette Frances

BRAGG, Marie-Elsa Beatrice Roche. b 65. Ripon Coll Cuddesdon. d 07 p 09. NSM St Marylebone St Paul *Lon* 07-09; NSM Kilburn St Mary w All So and W Hampstead St Jas from 09. *12 Woodside, London NW11 6HH* E: meboxford@hotmail.com

BRAGG, Mrs Rosemary Eileen. b 41. MRPharmS 64. St Steph Ho Ox 99. d 00 p 01. NSM Boyne Hill *Ox* 00-06; NSM Golden Cap Team *Sarum* 06-11; rtd 11. *Dove Inn Cottage, 48 Silver Street, Lyme Regis DT7 3HR* T: (01297) 442403 E: rosie@bragg.eu

BRAID, Simon. b 54. SS Coll Cam MA 76 FCA 79. SEITE 06. d 08 p 10. NSM Hildenborough *Roch* from 09. *Petresfield, Fordcombe Road, Penshurst, Tonbridge TN11 8DL* T: (01892) 871453 M: 07802-809849 E: simonbraid@uwclub.net

BRAILSFORD, Matthew Charles. b 64. Newc Univ BSc 86 St Jo Coll Dur BA 95. Cranmer Hall Dur 92. d 95 p 96. C Hull St Jo Newland *York* 95-06; P-in-c N Ferriby 06-14; V from 14. *The Vicarage, 20 Aston Hall Drive, North Ferriby HU14 3EB* T: (01482) 633195 E: matthew.brailsford@ukgateway.net

BRAIN, Mrs Marina. b 52. d 01 p 02. OLM Wokingham St Sebastian *Ox* 01-05; Chapl HM Pris Reading 05-06; Chapl HM Pris Grendon and Spring Hill 05-06; Chapl HM Pris High

Down 06-10; Chapl HM Pris Coldingley 10-13; Sen Chapl HM Pris Win from 13. *HM Prison Winchester, Romsey Road, Winchester SO22 5DF* T: (01962) 723000 E: suburbanday@aol.com

BRAIN, Michael Charles. b 39. Culham Coll Ox TCert 61 ACP 65. Lich Th Coll 68. d 70 p 71. C Stone St Mich *Lich* 70-73; C Harlescott 73-76; C Longton St Jas 76-77; P-in-c Dudley St Edm *Worc* 77-79; V 79-04; Chapl Dudley Coll of Tech 77-04; rtd 04; PtO *Worc* from 04. *33 Dibdale Road, Dudley DY1 2RX* T: (01384) 232774

BRAISBY, Rosemary Frances. b 47. d 13 p 14. OLM Gt Waltham w Ford End *Chelmsf* from 13; OLM The Chignals w Mashbury from 13; OLM Gt and Lt Leighs and Lt Waltham from 15. *Oak House, Littley Green, Chelmsford CM3 1BU* T: (01245) 361927

BRAITHWAITE, Albert Alfred. b 24. Clifton Th Coll. d 59 p 60. C Bestwood St Matt *S'well* 59-62; Chapl RN 62-81; QHC from 77; C Southsea St Jude *Portsm* 82-90; rtd 90; PtO *Portsm* from 90. *16 Charminster, 46 Craneswater Park, Southsea PO4 0NU* T: (023) 9273 8753

BRAITHWAITE, Mrs Catherine Anne. b 58. Lanc Univ BEd 79. LCTP 10. d 12 p 13. NSM Colne and Villages *Blackb* 12-14; NSM Colne from 14. *10 Sykes Close, Salterforth, Barnoldswick BB18 5SZ* T: (01282) 814237 E: cathbraithwaite@googlemail.com

BRAITHWAITE, Canon Michael Royce. b 34. Linc Th Coll 71. d 73 p 74. C Barrow St Geo w St Luke *Carl* 73-77; V Kells 77-88; RD Calder 84-88; V Lorton and Loweswater w Buttermere 88-99; Ldr Rural Life and Agric Team 93-96; Member Rural Life and Agric Team 96-99; RD Derwent 94-98; Hon Can Carl Cathl 94-99; rtd 99; PtO *Carl* from 00. *High Green Farm, Bothel, Carlisle CA7 2JA* T: (016973) 23429

BRAITHWAITE, Canon Roy. b 34. Dur Univ BA 56. Ridley Hall Cam 58. d 60 p 61. C Blackb St Gabr 60-63; C Burnley St Pet 63-66; V Accrington St Andr 66-74; V Blackb St Jas 74-95; RD Blackb 86-91; Hon Can Blackb Cathl 93-98; V Garstang St Helen Churchtown 95-98; Dioc Ecum Officer 95-98; rtd 98; PtO *Blackb* from 98. *9 Barker Lane, Mellor, Blackburn BB2 7ED* T: (01254) 240724

BRALESFORD, Nicholas Robert. b 53. St Jo Coll Nottm LTh 79 BTh 79. d 79 p 80. C Leic St Chris 79-82; C Heeley *Sheff* 82-85; TV Kings Norton *Birm* 85-90; V Chapel-en-le-Frith *Derby* 90-13; rtd 13; PtO *Blackb* from 13. *Flat 4, Anselm Court, Pembroke Avenue, Blackpool FY2 9QD* T: (01253) 500474 M: 07505-338853 E: nrb24601@hotmail.co.uk

BRALEY, Robert James. *See* RILEY-BRALEY, Robert James

BRAMHALL, Eric. b 39. St Cath Coll Cam BA 61 MA 65. Tyndale Hall Bris 61. d 63 p 64. C Eccleston St Luke *Liv* 63-66; C Bolton Em *Man* 66-69; PtO *Ches* 70-74; V Aughton Ch Ch *Liv* 75-92; Chapl Ormskirk Children's Hosp 75-92; V Childwall All SS *Liv* 92-04; rtd 04; PtO *St As* from 09. *Henfaes, Prior Street, Ruthin LL15 1LT* T: (01824) 702757

BRAMHALL, John. b 49. d 08. NSM Greenham *Ox* from 08. *56 Greyberry Copse Road, Thatcham RG19 8XB* T: (01635) 42348 E: johnbramuk@yahoo.co.uk

BRAMLEY, Elizabeth. d 15. C Llandeilo Tal-y-bont *S & B* from 15. *Weatheroak, Llanhamlach, Brecon LD3 7YB* T: (01874) 665267 E: liz.bramley@icloud.com

BRAMLEY, Thomas Antony. b 44. BSc PhD. TISEC 95. d 96 p 97. NSM Penicuik *Edin* from 96; NSM W Linton from 96. *44 Bavelaw Crescent, Penicuik EH26 9AT*

BRAMMER, David John. b 62. d 99 p 00. C Acton St Mary *Lon* 99-02; C Ealing All SS and Chapl Twyford C of E High Sch Acton 02-09; R Acton St Mary *Lon* 09-14. *30 Northbank Road, London E17 4JZ* E: rev.d.brammer@btinternet.com

BRAMPTON, Canon Fiona Elizabeth Gordon. b 56. St Jo Coll Dur BA 78 BA 83. Cranmer Hall Dur 81. dss 84 d 87 p 94. Bris St Andr Hartcliffe 84-90; Par Dn 87-90; C Orton Waterville *Ely* 90-96; C-in-c Orton Goldhay CD 90-96; TV The Ortons, Alwalton and Chesterton 96-00; V Haddenham from 00; V Wilburton from 00; P-in-c Witchford w Wentworth from 08; RD Ely 03-09; Hon Can Ely Cathl from 05. *The Vicarage, Church Lane, Haddenham, Ely CB6 3TB* T: (01353) 740309 E: fiona.brampton@ely.anglican.org

BRAMPTON, Timothy John Gordon. b 59. Coll of SS Mark and Jo Plymouth BA 01 Sheff Univ BA 12. Coll of Resurr Mirfield 10. d 12 p 13. C Standish *Blackb* from 12. *St Wilfrid's House, 7 Rectory Lane, Standish, Wigan WN6 0XA* M: 07962-277664 E: timbrampton@btinternet.com

BRANCHE, Caren Teresa. *See* TOPLEY, Caren Teresa

BRAND, Peter John. b 32. Lon Univ BSc 54. Edin Dioc NSM Course 75. d 83 p 84. NSM Edin St Hilda from 83. *24 Drum Brae Park, Edinburgh EH12 8TF* T: 0131-339 4406

BRAND, Canon Richard Harold Guthrie. b 65. Dur Univ BA 87. Ripon Coll Cuddesdon 87. d 89 p 90. C N Lynn w St Marg

and St Nic *Nor* 89-92; C King's Lynn St Marg w St Nic 92-93; C Croydon St Jo *S'wark* 93-96; TV Fendalton New Zealand 96-98; P-in-c Hambledon *Portsm* 98-06; Dir of Ords 98-06; P-in-c Market Harborough and The Transfiguration etc *Leic* 06-08; TR from 08; AD Gartree I from 13; AD Gartree II from 13; Hon Can Leic Cathl from 16. *The Rectory, Rectory Lane, Market Harborough LE16 8AS* T: (01858) 462926
E: richard.brand@virgin.net

BRAND, Stuart William. b 30. Leeds Univ BSc 53. Coll of Resurr Mirfield 53. **d** 55 **p** 56. C Stepney St Dunstan and All SS *Lon* 55-59; C Acton Green St Pet 59-60; C-in-c Godshill CD *Portsm* 60-63; Malawi 63-67; V Widley w Wymering *Portsm* 67-72; Chapl Fieldhead Hosp Wakef 72-80; Chapl Pinderfields Gen Hosp Wakef 72-80; Chapl Stanley Royd Hosp Wakef 72-80; Chapl Brook Gen Hosp Lon 80-95; Chapl Greenwich Distr Hosp Lon 80-95; rtd 95; PtO *Ox* from 96. *17 Hayfield Road, Oxford OX2 6TX* T: (01865) 316456

BRANDES, Simon Frank. b 62. Univ of Wales (Ban) BA 83. Edin Th Coll 83. **d** 85 **p** 86. C Barton w Peel Green *Man* 85-88; C Longsight St Jo w St Cypr 88-90; R 90-94; Asst Dioc Youth Officer 88-94; V Lt Lever 94-02; P-in-c Lydgate w Friezland 02-03; TR Saddleworth 03-07; V Chiswick St Nic w St Mary *Lon* from 07. *Chiswick Vicarage, Chiswick Mall, London W4 2PJ* T: (020) 8995 4717 M: 07775-526285

BRANDIE, Canon Beaumont Lauder. b 40. MBE 07. K Coll Lon AKC 64 BD 66. **d** 65 **p** 66. C Whitton St Aug *Lon* 65-71; C Portsea St Mary *Portsm* 71-77; TR Brighton Resurr *Chich* 77-09; V Brighton St Martin w St Wilfrid and St Alban 09-11; RD Brighton 97; Can and Preb Chich Cathl 87-11; rtd 11. *48 A'Becket Gardens, Worthing BN13 2BN* T: (01903) 264471 M: 07789-044476
E: beaumont.brandie@btinternet.com

BRANDON, Mrs Helen Beatrice. b 55. Heythrop Coll Lon MA 02. SAOMC 03. **d** 06 **p** 07. NSM Burton Latimer *Pet* 06-07; NSM Earls Barton 07-09; Abps' Adv for Healing Min from 07; PtO *Lon* from 07; Pet from 09. *Clopton Manor, Clopton, Kettering NN14 3DZ* T: (01832) 720346 F: 720446
E: beatrice@healingministry.org.uk

BRANDON, Milesius. b 69. Heythrop Coll Lon BA 92 MA 07 City Univ MSc 04 RMN 97 PGCE 98. St Steph Ho Ox MTh 09. **d** 09 **p** 10. C Clerkenwell H Redeemer *Lon* 09-12; C Croydon St Jo *S'wark* from 13. *37 Alton Road, Croydon CR0 4LZ*
E: mbrandon51@hotmail.com

BRANDRETH, Mrs Jacqueline. b 59. **d** 07 **p** 08. OLM Pendlebury St Jo *Man* from 07. *36 Asten Fold, Salford M6 7JH*

BRANDSMA, Michael John. b 55. Trin Coll Bris 12. **d** 14 **p** 15. C Hartshill and Galley Common *Cov* from 14. *40 Holte Road, Atherstone CV9 1HN* M: 07979-680213
E: visionhope@live.co.uk

BRANSCOMBE, Michael Peter. b 65. St Jo Coll Cur BA 95 Trin Episc Sch for Min DMin 08. Cranmer Hall Dur 92. **d** 95 **p** 96. C Ogley Hay *Lich* 95-01; Dioc Voc Officer 98-01; Asst R Palm Harbor USA 01-03; Assoc R Clearwater Ascension 03-15; C Birm St Martin from 15. *102 Ridgacre Lane, Quinton, Birmingham B32 1PT* T: 0121-246 6539 M: 07481-726762
E: mike@branscombe.us

BRANSON, Robert David. b 46. Linc Th Coll 74. **d** 77 **p** 78. C Kempston Transfiguration *St Alb* 77-80; C Goldington 80-82; V Marsh Farm 82-91; V Aylsham *Nor* 91-11; RD Ingworth 00-10; Chapl Norfolk Primary Care Trust 99-11; rtd 11; PtO *Nor* from 11. *28 Alford Grove, Norwich NR7 8XB* T: (01603) 418177 E: rdlbransons@btinternet.com

BRANSTON, Ms Anna Louise. b 63. WEMTC 12. **d** 15. C Heref S Wye from 15. *26 St Clare's Court, Lower Bullingham, Hereford HR2 6PX* T: (01584) 876958 M: 07777-692458
E: abranston2002@gmail.com

BRANT, Jonathan David. b 70. K Coll Lon MA 02 Trin Coll Ox MPhil 06 DPhil 09. St Mellitus Coll 09. **d** 11 **p** 12. Chapl Ox Pastorate from 11; NSM Ox St Clem 11-15; PtO from 15. *33 Jack Straw's Lane, Headington, Oxford OX3 0DL* M: 07854-771041 T: (01865) 426778
E: jonathan.brant@oxfordpastorate.org

BRANT, Ms Karlyn Lee. b 72. Birm Univ. BA 99 MA 01. Ripon Coll Cuddesdon 01. **d** 03 **p** 04. C Gaywood *Nor* 03-07; R Dunster, Carhampton, Withycombe w Rodhuish etc *B & W* 07-13. *River Breeze, Orchard Close, Colyford, Colyton EX24 6QH* E: revd.lee@btinternet.com

BRASCHI, Lawrence. b 77. Bris Univ BSc 98 SOAS Lon MA 04. Wycliffe Hall Ox 12. **d** 14. C Plymouth St Andr and Stonehouse *Ex* from 14. *18 Glenhurst Road, Plymouth PL3 5LT* M: 07773-429467 E: lawbraschi@hotmail.com

BRASIER, Ralph Henry (Jim). b 30. Cant Sch of Min 82. **d** 85 **p** 86. C S Ashford Ch Ch *Cant* 85-89; V Pembury *Roch* 89-95; rtd 95; PtO *Win* 95-14; *Portsm* from 95. *72 Jenkyns Close, Botley, Southampton SO30 2UU* T: (01489) 788332

BRASSIL, Seán Adrian. b 56. Westf Coll Lon BSc 79. STETS 97. **d** 00 **p** 01. NSM Westborough *Guildf* 00-04; NSM Woking St Jo 04-05; C Addlestone 05-10; P-in-c Whitchurch *Ex* from 10. *The Vicarage, 204 Whitchurch Road, Tavistock PL19 9DQ* T: (01822) 612936 E: priest.incharge@standrewandjames.org

BRASSIL, Thomas James. b 83. Ex Univ BSc 05. Wycliffe Hall Ox 11. **d** 14. C Elburton *Ex* from 14. *19 Long Park Close, Plymouth PL9 9JQ* T: (01752) 547492 M: 07729-466942
E: tom.brassil@gmail.com

BRATLEY, David Frederick. b 42. Linc Th Coll 80. **d** 82 **p** 83. C Holbeach *Linc* 82-85; R Fleet w Gedney 85-07; RD Elloe E 01-05; rtd 07. *1 Setts Green, Bourne PE10 0FZ* T: (01778) 392567

BRATTON, Mark Quinn. b 62. Lon Univ BA 84 K Coll Lon MA 98 Warwick Univ PhD 12 Barrister-at-Law (Middle Temple) 87. Pontifical Gregorian Univ 93 Wycliffe Hall Ox BA 94. **d** 94 **p** 95. C W Ealing St Jo w St Jas *Lon* 94-98; Chapl Warw Univ *Cov* 98-09; AD Cov S 02-09; P-in-c Berkswell 09-14; R from 14; AD Kenilworth from 13. *The Rectory, Meriden Road, Berkswell, Coventry CV7 7BE* T: (01676) 533766 or 533605 M: 07540-604225
E: markbratton@berkswellchurch.org

BRAUN, Thomas Anthony. b 53. St Jo Coll Ox BA 76 MA 76 Univ Coll Lon PhD 80. S'wark Ord Course 89. **d** 92 **p** 93. NSM Surbiton St Andr and St Mark *S'wark* 92-05. *8 Kings Drive, Surbiton KT5 8NG* T: (020) 8399 6898

BRAVERY, Christine Louise. *See* WILSON, Christine Louise

BRAVINER, William Edward. b 66. Leic Poly BSc 88 St Jo Coll Dur BA 94 ACA 91. Cranmer Hall Dur 92. **d** 95 **p** 96. C Royton St Anne *Man* 95-99; R Lansallos and V Talland *Truro* 99-03; P-in-c Duloe, Herodsfoot, Morval and St Pinnock 01-03; TR Jarrow *Dur* 03-14; P-in-c S Shields St Simon 09-13; AD Jarrow 05-13; TV Billingham from 14. *The Vicarage, 12A Tintern Avenue, Billingham TS23 2DE* T: (01642) 801357 M: 07875-385982 E: bill@braviner.com

BRAVINGTON, Timothy Frederick Desmond. b 34. Trin Coll Cam BA 56 MA 70. Cuddesdon Coll 56. **d** 58 **p** 59. C Caledon S Africa 58-61; Asst Chapl St Andr Coll Grahamstown 61-64; R Namaqualand 64-71; R Bellville Transfiguration 71-76; R Durban N St Martin-in-the-Fields 76-83; R Stellenbosch St Mary 84-88; R Elgin St Mich 88-98; rtd 98; PtO *Eur* 06-09; *Ox* from 08. *63 Cutteslowe House, Park Close, Oxford OX2 8NP* T: (01865) 511416 E: timbrav@gmail.com

BRAY, Christopher Laurence. b 53. Leeds Univ BSc 74 Qu Univ Kingston Ontario MSc 76. St Jo Coll Nottm 78. **d** 81 **p** 82. C Aughton Ch Ch *Liv* 81-84; Hon C Scarborough St Mary w Ch Ch and H Apostles *York* 84-88; Chapl Scarborough Coll 84-88; V St Helens St Matt Thatto Heath *Liv* 88-98; V Southport All SS and All So 98-02; rtd 02; PtO *Liv* from 03. *12 Ulverscroft, 25 Bidston Road, Prenton CH43 2JY* T: 0151-653 8797 E: chrislbray@aol.com

BRAY, Gerald Lewis. b 48. McGill Univ Montreal BA 69 Sorbonne Univ Paris LittD 73. Ridley Hall Cam 76. **d** 78 **p** 79. C Canning Town St Cedd *Chelmsf* 78-80; Tutor Oak Hill Th Coll 80-92; Ed *Churchman* from 83; Angl Prof Div Beeson Div Sch Samford Univ Alabama from 93. *16 Manor Court, Cambridge CB3 9BE* T: (01223) 311804 or (001) (205) 726 2585 F: (01223) 566608 or (001) (205) 726 2234
E: glbray@samford.edu

BRAY, Jason Stephen. b 69. SS Hild & Bede Coll Dur BA 90 MA 91 Fitzw Coll Cam PhD 96 MSOTS 97. Westcott Ho Cam 95. **d** 97 **p** 98. C Abergavenny St Mary w Llanwenarth Citra *Mon* 97-99; Min Can St Woolos Cathl 99-02; V Blaenavon w Capel Newydd from 02; P-in-c Abersychan and Garndiffaith 09-11. *The Rectory, 7 Westminster Drive, Wrexham LL12 7AT* T: (01978) 350971 E: jasonbray@aol.com

BRAY, Jeremy Grainger. b 40. Man Univ BA 62. Wells Th Coll 62. **d** 64 **p** 65. C Bris St Andr w St Bart 64-67; C Bris H Cross Inns Court 67-71; C-in-c Stockwood CD 71-73; V Bris Ch the Servant Stockwood 73-83; RD Brislington 79-83; P-in-c Chippenham St Pet 83-88; V 88-93; V Fishponds St Jo 93-04; rtd 04. *46 Charter Road, Chippenham SN15 2RA* T: (01249) 655661 E: jg.bray@btinternet.com

BRAY, Joyce. b 32. CA Tr Coll. **dss** 80 **d** 87 **p** 94. Par Dn Derringham Bank *York* 87-94; Hon C 94-03; rtd 94; PtO *York* from 03. *413 Willerby Road, Hull HU5 5JD* T: (01482) 502193

BRAY, Kenneth John. b 31. St Mich Coll Llan 65. **d** 67 **p** 72. C Killay *S & B* 67-68; C S Harrow St Paul *Lon* 71-73; C Hillingdon St Jo 73-76; C Chipping Sodbury and Old Sodbury *Glouc* 76-79; C Worle *B & W* 79-80; LtO *Ches* 80-83; TV Wrexham *St As* 83-85; V Llay 85-94; rtd 94. *c/o M Bray Esq, 18 Springfield Road, Poole BH14 0LQ* T: (01202) 741206

BRAY, Mrs Madeline. b 54. **d** 13 **p** 14. NSM Bideford, Northam, Westward Ho!, Appledore etc *Ex* from 13. *16 Hanson Park, Northam, Bideford EX39 3SA* T: (01237) 477488
E: maddybray@care4free.net

BRAY, Richard Antony. b 77. CCC Ox MA 05. Oak Hill Th Coll BA 09. **d** 09 **p** 10. C St Botolph without Aldersgate *Lon* 09-14; R Limehouse from 14. *Limehouse Rectory, 5 Newell Street, London E14 7HP* M: 07798-940554 T: (020) 7987 1502 E: brayra2001@yahoo.co.uk

BRAY, Simon Lee. b 77. Birm Univ BMus 00 St Jo Coll Dur BA 15. Cranmer Hall Dur 13. **d** 15. C Beverley St Nic *York* from 15. *7 St Nicholas Drive, Beverley HU17 0QY* M: 07816-448030 E: slbray77@gmail.com

BRAY, Mrs Wendy Elizabeth. b 60. UEA BEd 83. Trin Coll Bris 12. **d** 14. C Pennycross *Ex* from 14. *17 Thornhill Road, Plymouth PL3 5NF* T: (01752) 661340 M: 07887-987159 E: wendyebray@hotmail.co.uk

BRAYBROOKE, Marcus Christopher Rossi. b 38. Magd Coll Cam BA 62 MA 65 Lon Univ MPhil 68 Lambeth DD 04. Wells Th Coll 63. **d** 64 **p** 65. C Highgate St Mich *Lon* 64-67; C Frindsbury w Upnor *Roch* 67-72; TV 72-73; P-in-c Swainswick w Langridge and Woolley *B & W* 73-76; R 76-79; Dir of Tr 79-84; Hon C Bath Ch Ch Prop Chpl 84-91; Exec Dir Coun of Chrs and Jews 84-87; rtd 88; PtO *Bris* 88-93; Preb Wells Cathl 90-93; Chapl Bath St Mary Magd Holloway 92-93; Hon C Dorchester *Ox* 93-05. *17 Courtiers Green, Clifton Hampden, Abingdon OX14 3EN* T: (01865) 407566 E: marcusbray@aol.com

BRAYBROOKS, Bridget Ann. *See* MACAULAY, Bridget Ann

BRAZELL, Denis Illtyd Anthony. b 42. Trin Coll Cam BA 64 MA 68. Wycliffe Hall Ox 78. **d** 80 **p** 81. C Cheltenham Ch Ch *Glouc* 80-84; V Reading St Agnes w St Paul *Ox* 84-96; PtO *Guildf* 96-97; Warden and Chapl Acorn Chr Healing Trust 97-99; rtd 99; Co-Dir Word for Life Trust from 99; PtO *Glouc* 02-09; Lead Chapl St Andr Healthcare 09-15. *129 Balden Road, Harborne, Birmingham B32 2EL* T: 0121-427 2934 M: 07980-813159 E: denisbrazell@mac.com

BRAZIER, Annette Michaela. *See* HAWKINS, Annette Michaela

BRAZIER, Catharine Honor. b 67. ERMC 09. **d** 12 **p** 13. NSM Thrapston, Denford and Islip *Pet* 12-13; NSM Aldwincle, Clopton, Pilton, Stoke Doyle etc from 13. *21 Mill Road, Islip, Kettering NN14 3LB* T: (01832) 735491 E: pure.brasspot@btopenworld.com

BRAZIER, Eric James Arthur. b 37. Qu Coll Birm 84. **d** 86 **p** 87. C Lighthorne *Cov* 86-89; P-in-c 89-92; P-in-c Chesterton 89-92; P-in-c Newbold Pacey w Moreton Morrell 89-92; R Astbury and Smallwood *Ches* 92-99; rtd 99; PtO *Ches* from 99; *Lich* 00-11; *Heref* from 00. *Wolf's Head Cottage, Chirbury, Montgomery SY15 6BP* T: (01938) 561450

BRAZIER, Canon Raymond Venner. b 40. Wells Th Coll 68. **d** 71 **p** 72. C Horfield St Greg *Bris* 71-75; P-in-c Bris St Matt and St Nath 75-79; V 79-05; RD Horfield 85-91; P-in-c Bishopston 93-97; Hon Can Bris Cathl 94-05; rtd 05; PtO *Bris* from 05; Chapl to The Queen 98-10. *51 Chalks Road, Bristol BS5 9EP* T: 0117-952 3209 E: rayvb@tiscali.co.uk

BRAZIER, Thomas Ian. b 72. Natal Univ BSc 95 MSc 97. Cranmer Hall Dur 10. **d** 12 **p** 13. C Washington *Dur* from 12. *38 Brancepeth Road, Washington NE38 0LA* M: 07799-217775 E: tom_coe@firstsolo.net

BRAZIER-GIBBS, Samantha Elizabeth. b 78. Ridley Hall Cam 03. **d** 06 **p** 08. C Grays Thurrock *Chelmsf* 06-09; NSM Harlow St Mary and St Hugh w St Jo the Bapt 10-12; NSM Church Langley 10-12; NSM Fyfield, Moreton w Bobbingworth etc from 12; NSM Chipping Ongar w Shelley from 12. *The Vicarage, Broomfields, Hatfield Heath, Bishop's Stortford CM22 7EH* T: (01279) 730288 M: 07876-301307 E: revsbg@mac.com

BREADEN, Robert William. b 37. Edin Th Coll 58. **d** 61 **p** 62. C Broughty Ferry *Bre* 61-65; R 72-07; R Carnoustie 65-72; Can St Paul's Cathl Dundee 77-07; Dean Bre 84-07; rtd 07; P-in-c Portree *Arg* 07-12. *6 Chapel Road, Evanton, Dingwall IV16 9XT* E: ateallach@aol.com

BREADMORE, Martin Christopher. b 67. Lon Univ LLB 89. Wycliffe Hall Ox BTh 93. **d** 93 **p** 94. C Herne Bay Ch Ch *Cant* 93-97; C Camberley St Paul *Guildf* 97-01; Chapl Elmhurst Ballet Sch 97-98; C Wallington S'wark 01-10; Dir Lic Min Kensington Area *Lon* from 10. *207 London Road, Twickenham TW1 1EJ* T: (020) 8891 0324 E: martin.breadmore@london.anglican.org

BREADON, John Desmond. b 73. St Andr Univ BD 96 Birm Univ PhD 02. Westcott Ho Cam 99. **d** 01 **p** 02. C W Bromwich All SS *Lich* 01-05; Chapl St Geo Post 16 Cen *Birm* 05-08; Nat Adv for FE/Chapl Abps' Coun 08-10; PtO *Birm* 11-12. *Address temp unknown*

BREAR, Alvin Douglas. b 43. **d** 87 **p** 96. NSM Leic H Spirit 87-88; NSM Leic Ch Sav 88-96; NSM Leic Presentation 96-10; PtO *Blackb* from 10; Finland 98. *Sahurintie 44, SF28800 Pori, Finland* T: (00358) (2) 648 2060 E: douglas.brear@tse.fi

BREBNER, Martin James. b 47. OBE 02. Imp Coll Lon BSc 68 ARCS 68. St Alb Minl Tr Scheme 87. **d** 90 **p** 91. Hon C Letchworth St Paul w Willian *St Alb* 90-94; Hon C St Ippolyts

95-01; PtO 01-02; *Linc* from 02. *Willowcroft, Greatford, Stamford PE9 4QA* T: (01778) 561145 F: 561157 E: martinbrebner@yahoo.com

BRECH, Miss Suzy Zelda. b 73. Man Univ BSc 95 Roehampton Inst PGCE 97. SEITE 06. **d** 09 **p** 10. NSM Battersea St Mich *S'wark* 09-12. *Address temp unknown*

BRECHIN, Bishop of. *See* PEYTON, The Rt Revd Nigel

BRECHIN, Dean of. *See* BRIDGER, The Very Revd Francis William

BRECKLES, Robert Wynford. b 48. St Edm Hall Ox BA 72 MA 74. CertEd. Cranmer Hall Dur. **d** 79 **p** 80. C Bulwell St Mary *S'well* 79-84; V Lady Bay 84-05; V Lady Bay w Holme Pierrepont and Adbolton 06-12; rtd 12. *25 Goodwood Road, Nottingham NG8 2FT* T: 0115-854 3795

BRECKNELL, David Jackson. b 32. Keble Coll Ox BA 53 MA 57. St Steph Ho Ox 56. **d** 58 **p** 59. C Streatham St Pet *S'wark* 58-62; C Sneinton St Steph w St Alb *S'well* 62-64; C Solihull *Birm* 64-68; V Streatham St Paul *S'wark* 68-75; R Rumboldswyke *Chich* 75-81; P-in-c Portfield 79-81; R Whyke w Rumboldswhyke and Portfield 81-95; rtd 95; PtO *Chich* from 95; P-in-c Boxgrove 98-99. *8 Priory Close, Boxgrove, Chichester PO18 0EA* T: (01243) 784841 E: david.brecknell@tesco.net

BRECKWOLDT, Peter Hans. b 57. Man Poly BA 79. Oak Hill Th Coll BA 88. **d** 88 **p** 89. C Knutsford St Jo and Toft *Ches* 88-92; V Moulton *Pet* 92-11; V New Borough and Leigh *Sarum* from 11. *The Vicarage, 15 St John's Hill, Wimborne BH21 1BX* T: (01202) 886551 E: pjbreckwoldt@o2.co.uk

BRECON, Archdeacon of. *See* JEVONS, The Ven Alan Neil

BRECON, Dean of. *See* SHACKERLEY, The Very Revd Albert Paul

BREED, Mrs Verena. b 69. **d** 02 **p** 02. NSM Prestbury *Ches* 02-04; V Bosley and N Rode w Wincle and Wildboarclough 04-14; RD Macclesfield 12-14; TR Bicester w Bucknell, Caversfield and Launton *Ox* from 14. *The Rectory, 6 Tinkers Lane, Bicester OX26 6ES* T: (01869) 240744 E: verenabreed@talktalk.net

BREEDS, Christopher Roger. b 51. Lon Univ CertEd 73 LGSM 83. Chich Th Coll 84. **d** 87 **p** 88. C E Grinstead St Swithun *Chich* 87-90; TV Aldrington 90-92; P-in-c Hove St Andr Old Ch 92-93; TV Hove 93-99; V Wivelsfield from 99; RD Cuckfield 06-11. *New Vicarage, Church Lane, Wivelsfield, Haywards Heath RH17 7RD* T: (01444) 471783 E: christopher.breeds@virgin.net

BREEN, Alan Terence. **d** 14. Greystones *D & G* 14-15; C from 15. *Address temp unknown*

BREENE, Timothy Patrick Brownell. b 59. Kent Univ BA 81 CCC Cam BA 89 MA 90. Ridley Hall Cam 87. **d** 90 **p** 93. C Hadleigh w Layham and Shelley *St E* 90-95; C Martlesham w Brightwell 95-03; rtd 03. *85 Cliff Road, Felixstowe IP11 9SQ* T: (01394) 283718

BREFFITT, Geoffrey Michael. b 46. CChem MRIC 72 Trent Poly CertEd 77. Qu Coll Birm 87. **d** 89 **p** 90. C Prenton *Ches* 89-92; V Frankby w Greasby 92-01; Dioc Ecum Officer 00-01; V German St Jo *S & M* 01-08; V Foxdale 01-08; V Patrick 01-08; RD Castletown and Peel 04-08; P-in-c Weston *Ches* 08-13; rtd 13. *181 Marion Road, Prestatyn LL19 7DG* E: geoff.breffitt@sky.com

BRENDON-COOK, John Lyndon. b 37. FRICS. SWMTC. **d** 81 **p** 82. NSM Bodmin *Truro* 81-82; NSM St Breoke and Egloshayle 82-90; NSM Helland 90-94; P-in-c 94-98; NSM Cardynham 90-94; rtd 98; PtO *Truro* from 98. *Address temp unknown*

BRENNAN, John Lester. b 20. MRCP 51 FRCPath 77 Barrister-at-Law (Middle Temple) 71 Lon Univ MB, BS 44 MD 52 LLM 86. St Aug Coll Cant 54. **d** 55 **p** 56. India 55-65; Hon C Woodside Park St Barn *Lon* 65-69; LtO *Lich* 69-88; P-in-c Chrishall *Chelmsf* 88-89; Hon C 89-91; Hon C Heydon, Gt and Lt Chishill, Chrishall etc 91-93; PtO *St Alb* from 93. *16 Butterfield Road, Wheathampstead AL4 8PU* T: (01582) 832230

BRENNAND (née PUNSHON), Ms Carol Mary. b 59. Liv Inst of Educn BEd 83. Ridley Hall Cam 92. **d** 94 **p** 95. C Bushey *St Alb* 94-97; C Watford Ch Ch 97-00; P-in-c Ash Vale *Guildf* 00-06; V 06-07; P-in-c Claybrooke cum Wibtoft and Frolesworth *Leic* 07-08; P-in-c Leire w Ashby Parva and Dunton Bassett 07-08; C Upper Soar 08-09; R from 09. *The Vicarage, Main Road, Claybrooke Parva, Lutterworth LE17 5AE* T: (01455) 208878 E: carolbrennand@btinternet.com

BRENNAND, Ian Peter. b 55. Univ of Wales (Trin St Dav) BA 12. STETS 01. **d** 04 **p** 05. C Frimley *Guildf* 04-07; Chapl Univ Hosps Leic NHS Trust from 08. *The Vicarage, Main Road, Claybrooke Parva, Lutterworth LE17 5AE* T: (01455) 202262 E: ianbrennand@btinternet.com

BRENT, Philip. b 68. K Coll Lon BD 89. Cuddesdon Coll 94. **d** 96 **p** 97. C Sawbridgeworth *St Alb* 96-99; C Skegness and Winthorpe *Linc* 99-03; Chapl United Lincs Hosps NHS Trust 00-03; R Market Deeping *Linc* from 03; RD Elloe W from 13. *The Rectory, 13 Church Street, Market Deeping, Peterborough PE6 8DA* T: (01778) 342237 E: philip@candace.fsnet.co.uk

BRERETON, Catherine Louise. *See* WILLIAMS, Catherine Louise

BRETEL, Keith Michael. b 51. St Mich Coll Llan 79. **d** 81 **p** 82. C Thundersley *Chelmsf* 81-84; CF 84-06; Chapl Guards Chpl Lon 03-05; P-in-c St Raphaël *Eur* from 11. *St John the Evangelist, avenue Paul Doumer, 83700 St Raphaël, France* T: (0033) (4) 94 95 45 78

BRETHERTON, Canon Anthony Atkinson. b 51. Cant Univ (NZ) BA 74 Waikato Univ (NZ) MMS 97. St Jo Th Coll (NZ) LTh 74 STh 76. **d** 75 **p** 76. Asst C Ashburton New Zealand 75-78; Asst P St Geo-in-the-East w St Paul *Lon* 79-80; V Te Kauwhata New Zealand 80-85; V Cam 85-91; Can St Pet Cathl Waikato 88-90; Offg Min Waikato 91-01; LtO *L & K* 02-07; PtO *B & W* from 07. *18 Vicars Close, Wells BA5 2UJ* M: 07738-993809 E: tonybretherton@hotmail.com

BRETHERTON, Donald John. b 18. Lon Univ BD 57. Handsworth Coll Birm 38 Headingley Coll Leeds 38 St Aug Coll Cant 59. **d** 60 **p** 61. In Methodist Ch 42-59; C Cant St Martin w St Paul 60-62; V Thornton Heath St Jude 62-70; V Herne 70-82; RD Reculver 74-80; rtd 82; PtO *Cant* from 84. *Martin's, The Green, Chartham, Canterbury CT4 7JW* T: (01227) 730255

BRETT, Dennis Roy Anthony. b 46. Sarum & Wells Th Coll 86. **d** 88 **p** 89. C Bradford-on-Avon H Trin *Sarum* 88-92; P-in-c Bishopstrow and Boreham 92-01; R from 01; Chapl Warminster Hosp 92-14. *50 Gypsy Lane, Warminster BA12 9LR* T: (01985) 213000 E: thebretts8@yahoo.co.uk

BRETT, John. b 65. G&C Coll Cam BA 88 SOAS Lon MA 96. St Mellitus Coll BA 13. **d** 13 **p** 14. C Rusholme H Trin *Man* from 13. *158 Platt Lane, Manchester M14 7PY* T: 0161-478 8122 M: 07941-342916 E: jandjbrett@yahoo.fr

BRETT, Canon Paul Gadsby. b 41. St Edm Hall Ox BA 62 MA 66. Wycliffe Hall Ox 64. **d** 65 **p** 66. C Bury St Pet *Man* 65-68; Asst Ind Chapl 68-72; Ind Chapl *Worc* 72-76; Sec Ind Cttee of Gen Syn Bd for Soc Resp 76-84; Dir Soc Resp *Chelmsf* 85-94; Can Res Chelmsf Cathl 85-94; R Shenfield 94-08; rtd 08. *Ore Cottage, Mill Road, Friston, Saxmundham IP17 1PH* T: (01728) 687767 E: paul.brett@btinternet.com

BRETT, Canon Peter Graham Cecil. b 35. Em Coll Cam BA 59 MA 63. Cuddesdon Coll 59. **d** 61 **p** 62. C Tewkesbury w Walton Cardiff *Glouc* 61-64; C Bournemouth St Pet *Win* 64-66; Chapl Dur Univ 66-72; R Houghton le Spring 72-83; RD Houghton 80-83; Can Res Cant Cathl 83-01; rtd 01; PtO *Cant* from 01. *3 Appledore Road, Tenterden TN30 7AY* T: (01580) 761794 E: pandgbrett@btinternet.com

BREUILLY, Mrs Elizabeth Linda. b 48. York Univ BA 70. WMMTC 02. **d** 05 **p** 06. NSM Bournville *Birm* 05-10; NSM Water Eaton *Ox* from 10. *18 Bradwell Road, Loughton, Milton Keynes MK5 8AJ* T: (01908) 606983 E: lizbreuilly@btinternet.com

BREUSS, Mrs Kristin Lynn. b 68. Univ of N Carolina BA 90 Columbia Univ MBA 98. St Mellitus Coll BA 14. **d** 14 **p** 15. C W Hampstead Trin *Lon* from 14. *29 Netherhall Gardens, London NW3 5RL* T: (020) 7435 0083 M: 07932-770239 E: kristinbreuss@gmail.com

BREW, William Kevin Maddock. b 49. **d** 78 **p** 79. C Raheny w Coolock *D & G* 78-80; Bp's C Dublin Finglas 80-83; I Mountmellick w Coolbanagher, Rosenallis etc *M & K* 83-89; I Ahoghill w Portglenone *Conn* 89-05; I Howth *D & G* from 05. *The Rectory, 94 Howth Road, Howth, Co Dublin, Republic of Ireland* T: (00353) (1) 832 3019 E: howth@dublin.anglican.org

BREW, William Philip. b 43. Derby Coll of Educn CertEd 64 FCollP 84. NOC 84. **d** 87 **p** 88. In Independent Methodist Ch 70-83; Hd Master Birtenshaw Sch 78-90; NSM Holcombe *Man* 87-90; TV Horwich 91-93; TV Horwich and Rivington 93-97; V Lostock St Thos and St Jo 97-08; P-in-c Bolton St Bede 04-08; AD Deane 98-05; rtd 08; PtO *Leeds* from 08; *Eur* from 12. *22 Deganwy Drive, Kirkheaton, Huddersfield HD5 0NG* T: (01484) 301295 E: brewsp@gmail.com

BREWER, Barry James. b 44. Oak Hill Th Coll 72. **d** 75 **p** 76. C Hove Bp Hannington Memorial Ch *Chich* 75-78; C Church Stretton *Heref* 78-81; TV Bishopsnympton, Rose Ash, Mariansleigh etc *Ex* 81-87; R Swynnerton and Tittensor *Lich* 87-07; RD Stone 07; rtd 07; PtO *Lich* 14-15. *2 Hazel Close, Seaton EX12 2UG* E: barrybrewer@btinternet.com

BREWER, Ms Christina Anne. b 51. SEITE BA 11. **d** 11 **p** 12. C Crofton St Paul *Roch* 11-15; C Canonry *Cant* from 15. *55 Place Farm Avenue, Orpington BR6 8DG* E: ca.brewer@tesco.net

BREWER, Mrs Susan Comport. b 55. LMH Ox MA 76 Cant Ch Ch Univ MA 10. SEITE 99. **d** 02 **p** 03. C Dartford St Edm *Roch* C 02-07; V Milton next Gravesend Ch Ch from 07; RD Gravesend from 13. *The Vicarage, 48 Old Road East, Gravesend DA12 1NR* T: (01474) 352643 M: 07930-492323 E: suec@brewer86.plus.com

BREWERTON, Andrew Robert. b 70. Oak Hill Th Coll BA 05. **d** 05 **p** 06. C Gt Clacton *Chelmsf* 05-09; V Kilnhurst *Sheff* from

09; AD Wath from 12. *The Vicarage, Highthorn Road, Kilnhurst, Mexborough S64 5TX* T: (01709) 589674 E: andy@brewerton.org

BREWIN, David Frederick. b 39. Leic Poly BSc PhD. Lich Th Coll 63. **d** 66 **p** 67. C Shrewsbury H Cross *Lich* 66-69; C Birstall *Leic* 69-73; V Eyres Monsell 73-79; V E Goscote 79-82; V E Goscote w Ratcliffe and Rearsby 82-90; R Thurcaston 90-91; R Thurcaston w Cropston 92-05; rtd 05; PtO *Leic* from 05; *Pet* from 06. *28 Welland Way, Oakham LE15 6SL* T: (01572) 720073

BREWIN, Donald Stewart. b 41. Ch Coll Cam BA 62 MA 66. Ridley Hall Cam 68. **d** 71 **p** 72. C Ecclesall *Sheff* 71-75; V Anston 75-81; V Walton H Trin *Ox* 81-89; TR 89-94; RD Aylesbury 90-94; Nat Dir SOMA UK 94-07; PtO *St Alb* from 94; rtd 07. *Wickham Cottage, Gaddesden Turn, Great Billington, Leighton Buzzard LU7 9BW* T: (01525) 373644 M: 07816-362797 E: donsbrewin@gmail.com

BREWIN, Karan Rosemary. b 42. CA Tr Coll 77 Glas NSM Course 80. **dss** 84 **d** 85 **p** 15. Clarkston *Glas* 84-89; Hon C 86-89 and 91-97; OHP 89 and 98-02; PtO *York* 01-02 and from 13; PtO Johannesburg S Africa 03-05; PtO Swaziland 06-11. *St Hilda's Priory, Sneaton Castle, Whitby YO21 3QN* T: (01947) 602079

BREWIN, Wilfred Michael. b 45. Nottm Univ BA 69. Cuddesdon Coll 69. **d** 70 **p** 71. C Walker *Newc* 70-73; C Alnwick St Paul 73-74; C Alnwick w Edlingham and Bolton Chpl 74-77; Fell Shelf Univ 77-79; C Greenhill *Sheff* 79; P-in-c Eggleston *Dur* 79-81; V Norton St Mich 81-87; V Headington *Ox* 87-10; rtd 10. *Rose Cottage, New Road, Chatton, Alnwick NE66 5PU* T: (01668) 215319 E: michael.brewin@hotmail.com

BREWIS, Robert David. b 81. Lanc Univ BSc 03. Oak Hill Th Coll MTh 11. **d** 11 **p** 12. C Washfield, Stoodleigh, Withleigh etc *Ex* 11-14; NSM Chadderton Ch Ch *Man* from 14. *58 Oakbank Avenue, Chadderton, Oldham OL9 0PP* E: rbrewis02@hotmail.com

BREWSTER, Christine Elaine. b 45. Newc Univ BA 67 CertEd 68 Lon Univ MA 84 DipEd 82 Univ of Wales (Ban) PhD 07 ALCM 76 LTCL 78. SAOMC 95. **d** 98 **p** 99. NSM Aylesbury *Ox* 98-00; NSM Dacre w Hartwith and Darley w Thornthwaite *Ripon* 00-01; C Wetherby 01-04; PtO 04-08; P-in-c Llanwnnog and Caersws w Carno *Ban* 08-12; rtd 12; PtO *Ban* from 12. *Michaelmas Cottage, Lingen, Bucknell SY7 0DY* T: (01544) 267338 E: cbmichaelmas@yahoo.co.uk

BREWSTER, David Thomas. b 68. GLCM 90 ALCM 89. Cranmer Hall Dur BA 99. **d** 99 **p** 00. C Bidston *Ches* 99-03; TV Stockport SW 03-07; V Edgeley and Cheadle Heath from 07. *St Mark's Vicarage, 66 Berlin Road, Stockport SK3 9QF* T: 0161-480 5896 E: dtbrewster@talktalk.net

BREWSTER, Jonathan David. b 67. Bucks Coll of Educn BA 89 Bris Univ BA 94 K Coll Lon MA 01. Trin Coll Bris 91. **d** 94 **p** 95. C Gt Horton *Bradf* 94-98; Chapl Univ of Westmr *Lon* 98-03; V Highbury Ch Ch w St Jo and St Sav from 03; AD Islington from 14. *Christ Church Vicarage, 155 Highbury Grove, London N5 1SA* T: (020) 7226 4544 M: 07977-127244 E: vicar@christchurchhighbury.com

BREWSTER (née BEATTIE), Margaret. b 43. S'wark Ord Course 90. **d** 93 **p** 94. NSM S'wark H Trin w St Matt 93-97; NSM Newington St Paul 97-04; NSM Dunstable *St Alb* 04-07; rtd 07; PtO *Linc* from 07. *39 Glen Drive, Boston PE21 7QB* T: (01205) 351298 E: m.brewster789@btinternet.com

BREWSTER, Samuel Paul William. b 86. Selw Coll Cam MA 11. Wycliffe Hall Ox MTh 13. **d** 13 **p** 14. C Maidenhead St Andr and St Mary *Ox* from 13. *107 Grenfell Road, Maidenhead SL6 1EX* M: 07899-843461 T: (01628) 311353 E: sam@thebrewsters.org.uk

BRIAN, Brother. *See* HARLEY, Brian Mortimer

BRIAN, Stephen Frederick. b 54. Sussex Univ BEd 77 Open Univ MA 90 Lanc Univ MPhil 97 Surrey Univ PhD 03. Qu Coll Birm 82. **d** 85 **p** 86. C Scotforth *Blackb* 85-88; V Freckleton 88-97; V Bagshot *Guildf* 97-06; Chapl Heathfield St Mary's Sch Wantage 06-07; P-in-c Mid Loes *St E* 07-08; R from 08; RD Loes 13-14. *The Rectory, Church Lane, Earl Soham, Woodbridge IP13 7SD* T: (01728) 685308 E: sfb4510@aol.com

BRICE, Christopher John. b 48. St Edm Ho Cam MA 80. Wycliffe Hall Ox 82. **d** 82 **p** 83. C N Hinksey *Ox* 82-86; Chapl Nuff Coll Ox 84-86; V S Hackney St Mich w Haggerston St Paul *Lon* 86-93; Adv for Soc Justice 93-08; Hon C De Beauvoir Town St Pet 93-08; P-in-c Kentish Town St Martin w St Andr 08-13; V from 13. *9 Beresford Road, London N5 2HS* T: (020) 7226 3834 *or* 7932 1121 E: chris.brice@london.anglican.org

BRICE, Derek William Fred. b 39. Poly Cen Lon MA 87 MCIM 89 FCMI 82. **d** 02 **p** 03. OLM Cheam *S'wark* from 02;

PtO from 09. *Mallow, Parkside, Cheam, Sutton SM3 8BS* T: (020) 8642 0241 *or* 8693 4324 E: derekbrice@blueyonder.co.uk

BRICE, Jonathan Andrew William. b 61. **d** 92 **p** 93. C Buckhurst Hill *Chelmsf* 92-96; C Victoria Docks Ascension 96; P-in-c 96-98; V 98-06; Chapl Felsted Sch 06-11; R Aspen Ch Ch USA from 11. *536 West North Street, Aspen CO 81611-1253, USA* T: (001) (970) 987 1524
E: rev@christchurchaspen.org

BRICE, Neil Alan. b 59. Man Univ BA 81 Hughes Hall Cam CertEd 87. Westcott Ho Cam 82. **d** 84 **p** 85. C Longton *Lich* 84-86; Hd of Relig Studies Coleridge Community Coll Cam 87-89; NSM Cherry Hinton St Andr *Ely* 88-89; C Fulbourn 89-92; C Gt Wilbraham 89-92; C Lt Wilbraham 89-92; V Arrington 92-00; R Orwell 92-00; R Wimpole 92-00; R Croydon w Clopton 92-00; P-in-c Barrington 98-00; R Orwell Gp 00-09; R Lerwick *Ab* from 10. *St Magnus' Rectory, Greenfield Place, Lerwick, Shetland ZE1 0AQ* T: (01595) 693862 M: 07713-259262 E: revnab@btinternet.com

BRICE, Paul Earl Philip. b 54. Bath Univ BSc 77. Wycliffe Hall Ox 83. **d** 86 **p** 87. C Gt Baddow *Chelmsf* 86-89; Chapl Imp Coll Lon and St Mary's Hosp Med Sch 89-95; Chapl R Coll of Art 90-95; Sec HE/Chapl C of E Bd of Educn 95-02; Hon C S Kensington St Jude *Lon* 95-02; R Hartfield w Coleman's Hatch *Chich* 02-12; Chapl SS Coll Cam from 12. *Sidney Sussex College, Cambridge CB2 3HU* T: (01223) 338800

BRICKMAN, Mark. b 60. Jes Coll Cam MA 81. Trin Coll Bris 10. **d** 12 **p** 13. C Ox St Aldate from 12. *25 Norreys Avenue, Oxford OX1 4ST* T: (01865) 254800
E: mark.brickman@staldates.org.uk

BRIDEWELL, Mrs Alison Clare. b 66. Win Univ BA 11. STETS 11. **d** 14 **p** 15. C Bemerton *Sarum* from 14. *27 Paul's Dene Crescent, Salisbury SP1 3QU* T: (01722) 504289 M: 07847-952868 E: alison.bridewell@ntlworld.com

BRIDGE, John Jeremy. b 74. Ripon Coll Cuddesdon 07. **d** 09 **p** 10. C Four Oaks *Birm* 09-13; C Wylde Green from 13. *17 Greenhill Road, Sutton Coldfield B72 1DS* M: 07868-308351 E: johnjbridge@sky.com

BRIDGE, Martin. b 45. Lon Univ BA 66 Linacre Coll Ox BA 71 MA 73. St Steph Ho Ox 69. **d** 72 **p** 73. C St Peter-in-Thanet *Cant* 72-77; New Zealand from 77. *PO Box 87-145, Meadowbank, Auckland, New Zealand* T: (0064) (9) 521 5013 *or* 521 0636 E: martin.bridge@xtra.co.nz

BRIDGE, Mrs Sheila Margaret. b 62. St Jo Coll Nottm. **d** 11 **p** 12. C Rugby W *Cov* 11-13; Min Rugby St Pet and St Jo CD from 13. *St Peter's Vicarage, 63A Lower Hillmorton Road, Rugby CV21 3TQ*

BRIDGEN, Andrew Grahame. b 57. Aston Univ BSc 81 Surrey Univ BA 03 FCCA 95. STETS 00. **d** 03 **p** 04. NSM Portchester *Portsm* 03-04; C Portsea St Luke 05-07; PtO from 08. *9 Campbell Road, Southsea PO5 1RH* T: (023) 9234 8617

BRIDGEN, John William. b 40. K Coll Cam BA 62 MA 66. Ripon Hall Ox 66. **d** 70 **p** 72. C Headstone St Geo *Lon* 70-71; C Hanwell St Mary 71-75; C Tolladine *Worc* 75; TV Worc St Barn w Ch Ch 76; R Barrow *St E* 76-83; V Denham St Mary 76-83; PtO *Ely* 84-88 and from 91; rtd 88; PtO *Glas* 89-91. *57 St Philip's Road, Cambridge CB1 3DA* T: (01223) 571748 E: j.bridgen@ntlworld.com

BRIDGEN, Mark Stephen. b 63. K Coll Lon BD 85. Cranmer Hall Dur 86. **d** 88 **p** 89. C Kidderminster St Jo and St Innocents *Worc* 88-92; C Nor St Pet Mancroft w St Jo Maddermarket 92-94; V Longbridge *Birm* 94-00; V Wednesbury St Bart *Lich* 00-07; P-in-c Gnosall and Moreton 08-10; R Adbaston, High Offley, Knightley, Norbury etc 10-15; R Paston *Pet* from 15. *The Rectory, 236 Fulbridge Road, Peterborough PE4 6SN* T: mark.bridgen@btinternet.com

BRIDGER, The Very Revd Francis William. b 51. Pemb Coll Ox BA 73 MA 78 Bris Univ PhD 81. Trin Coll Bris 74. **d** 78 **p** 79. C Islington St Jude Mildmay Park *Lon* 78-82; Lect St Jo Coll Nottm 82-90; V Woodthorpe *S'well* 90-99; Prin Trin Coll Bris 99-05; Prof Fuller Th Sem USA 05-08; PtO *Nor* 11-12; R Broughty Ferry *Bre* from 12; Dean Bre from 13. *3 Wyvis Place, Broughty Ferry, Dundee DD5 3SX* M: 07507-885476 E: fbridger@yahoo.ie

BRIDGER, Canon Gordon Frederick. b 32. Selw Coll Cam BA 53 MA 58. Ridley Hall Cam 54. **d** 56 **p** 57. C Islington St Mary *Lon* 56-60; C Cambridge St Sepulchre *Ely* 60-62; V Fulham St Mary N End *Lon* 62-69; C Edin St Thos 69-76; R Heigham H Trin *Nor* 76-87; RD Nor S 79-86; Hon Can Nor Cathl 84-87; Prin Oak Hill Th Coll 87-96; rtd 96; PtO *Nor* from 96. *The Elms, 4 Common Lane, Sheringham NR26 8PL* T: (01263) 823522 E: gebridger@lineone.net

BRIDGER, Mrs Helen Ruth. b 68. Bradf Univ BA 91. Trin Coll Bris BA 06. **d** 05 **p** 06. C Altadena USA 05-06; C Arcadia Transfiguration 06-08; C Nuthall and Kimberley *S'well* 08-10; Chapl Qu Eliz Hosp King's Lynn NHS Foundn Trust 10-12;

C Broughty Ferry *Bre* from 12. *3 Wyvis Place, Broughty Ferry, Dundee DD5 3SX* E: helenbridger@yahoo.com

BRIDGES, Mrs Gillian Mary. b 43. EAMTC 85. **d** 88 **p** 94. NSM Hellesdon *Nor* 88-96; NSM Lakenham St Jo 96-97; Assoc V Lakenham St Alb 97-99; Assoc V Sprowston w Beeston 99-08; rtd 08; PtO *Nor* from 08. *2 Vera Road, Norwich NR6 5HU* T: (01603) 789634 E: sgbridges63v@talktalk.net

BRIDGES, John Malham. b 57. TD . Goldsmiths' Coll Lon BSc 80. Ridley Hall Cam 03. **d** 05 **p** 06. C Cranleigh *Guildf* 05-08; Chapl RN from 08. *Royal Naval Chaplaincy Service, Mail Point 1-2, Leach Building, Whale Island, Portsmouth PO2 8BY* T: (023) 9262 5055 F: 9262 5134 E: jmbridges@cantab.net

BRIDGES, Simon Patrick (Sid). b 73. Ox Brookes Univ BA 04. Ridley Hall Cam 12. **d** 14 **p** 15. C Orton Longueville w Bottlebridge *Ely* 14; C The Ortons from 14. *The Rectory, 67 Church Drive, Orton Waterville, Peterborough PE2 5HE* T: (01733) 233402 M: 07851-609020 E: sidbridges@live.co.uk

BRIDGES (née BANKS), Mrs Vivienne Philippa. b 46. Somerville Coll Ox BA 69. SAOMC 02. **d** 05 **p** 06. NSM Wolvercote *Ox* 05-10; NSM Wolvercote and Wytham from 10. *6 Haslemere Gardens, Oxford OX2 8EL* T: (01865) 558705 E: vivpbridges@btinternet.com

BRIDGEWATER, Guy Stevenson. b 60. Ch Ch Ox BA 83. Trin Coll Bris BA 87. **d** 87 **p** 88. C Radipole and Melcombe Regis *Sarum* 87-90; Chapl Lee Abbey 90-93; V Cranbrook *Cant* 93-98; Dioc Officer for Par Resources (Miss and Lay Tr) *Glouc* 98-07; Dioc Can Res Glouc Cathl 02-07; TR Horsham *Chich* from 07; RD from 09. *The Vicarage, Causeway, Horsham RH12 1HE* T: (01403) 272919 *or* 253762

BRIDGEWATER, Robert. b 69. Sheff Hallam Univ BEd 92 MSc 97. Oak Hill Th Coll BA 15. **d** 15. C Chapeltown *Sheff* from 15. *32 Mafeking Place, Chapeltown, Sheffield S35 2UT* M: 07595-938138 E: rob@bridgewaterfamily.me.uk

BRIDGEWOOD, Bruce William. b 41. K Coll Lon BA 02 Heythrop Coll Lon MA 06. St Paul's Coll Grahamstown LTh 67. **d** 67 **p** 68. C Plumstead S Africa 67-69; C Somerset W 70-71; Hon C Stanmer w Falmer *Chich* 81-86; Hon C Westmr St Matt *Lon* 90-93; Hon C Alexandra Park 93-04; P-in-c Friern Barnet St Pet le Poer 04-13; rtd 13; PtO *Ox* from 13. *15 Temple Orchard, Amersham Hill, High Wycombe HP13 6PH* E: brucebridgewood@gmail.com

BRIDGMAN, Canon Gerald Bernard. b 22. St Cath Coll Cam BA 50 MA 55. Bible Churchmen's Coll Bris 46 Wycliffe Hall Ox 50. **d** 51 **p** 52. C Broadwater St Mary *Chich* 51-54; C Ox St Aldate 54-56; C-in-c Southgate CD *Chich* 56-59; V Southgate 59-67; V Kingston upon Hull H Trin *York* 67-87; Chapl Hull R Infirmary 67-87; AD Cen and N Hull *York* 81-86; Can and Preb York Minster 83-87; rtd 87; PtO *Chich* from 87. *129 The Welkin, Lindfield, Haywards Heath RH16 2PL* T: (01444) 484563

BRIDGMAN, James William. b 85. Man Univ BA 06. Trin Coll Bris BA 09 MA 10. **d** 10 **p** 11. C Heswall *Ches* 10-13; V Timperley from 13. *The Vicarage, 12 Thorley Lane, Timperley, Altrincham WA15 7AZ* T: 0161-980 4330 E: revjimb1017@gmail.com

BRIDGMAN (née JOYCE), Mrs Jennifer Claire. b 84. Man Univ BA 06. Trin Coll Bris BA 08 MPhil 10. **d** 10 **p** 11. C Heswall *Ches* 10-13; Young Voc Adv 11-13; C Broadheath 13-14; C Timperley from 14. *The Vicarage, 12 Thorley Lane, Timperley, Altrincham WA15 7AZ* T: 0161-980 4330 M: 07709-471494 E: revjb99@gmail.com

BRIDGWATER, Philip Dudley. b 31. St Alb Minl Tr Scheme 88. **d** 91 **p** 92. NSM Buxton w Burbage and King Sterndale *Derby* 91-94 and 98-01; NSM Fairfield 94-98; PtO from 01. *Millstone, 9 College Road, Buxton SK17 9DZ* T: (01298) 72876

BRIDLE, Canon Geoffrey Peter. b 52. CITC 87. **d** 87 **p** 88. C Lurgan Ch the Redeemer *D & D* 87-91; I Carnteel and Crilly *Arm* 91-99; I Cleenish w Mullaghdun *Clogh* from 99; Can Clogh Cathl from 15. *Cleenish Rectory, Bellanaleck, Enniskillen BT92 2BA* T: (028) 6634 8259 F: 6634 8620 E: geoffreypbridle@mail.com

BRIDSON, Paula Rosalia Antonia. b 56. **d** 14 **p** 15. OLM Toxteth St Philemon w St Gabr and St Cleopas *Liv* from 14. *40 Garswood Street, Liverpool L8 9TB* T: 0151-283 6281 E: paula_bridson@yahoo.com

BRIDSON, Canon Raymond Stephen. b 58. Southn Univ BTh 82. Chich Th Coll. **d** 82 **p** 83. C St Luke in the City *Liv* 82-86; TV Ditton St Mich 86-98; V Anfield St Columba from 98; AD Walton 02-13; Hon Can Liv Cathl from 03. *St Columba's Vicarage, Pinehurst Avenue, Liverpool L4 2TZ* T: 0151-474 7231 E: frray@blueyonder.co.uk

BRIDSTRUP, Juergen Walter. b 44. St Alb Minl Tr Scheme 84. **d** 87 **p** 88. C Leagrave *St Alb* 87-90; V Goff's Oak St Jas 90-08; TV Cheshunt 08-09; rtd 09. *4 The Vineyard, Lower Broad Street, Ludlow SY8 1PH* T: (01584) 876992 E: juergen.bridstrup@btinternet.com

BRIEN, John Richard. b 57. Kingston Poly BSc 80. EAMTC 98. **d** 01 **p** 02. NSM Mistley w Manningtree and Bradfield *Chelmsf* from 01. *1 East View, Crown Street, Dedham, Colchester CO7 6AN* T: (01206) 322706 E: brienfamily@tiscali.co.uk

BRIERLEY, Charles Ian. b 46. MIMI 69. S Dios Minl Tr Scheme 90. **d** 93 **p** 94. NSM Wellington and Distr *B & W* 93-11; rtd 11. *Shady Oak, 19 Immenstadt Drive, Wellington TA21 9PT* T: (01823) 666101 E: brierley@aol.com

BRIERLEY, John Michael. b 32. Lon Univ BD 71. Lich Th Coll 57. **d** 60 **p** 61. C Lower Mitton *Worc* 60-62; C-in-c Dines Green St Mich CD 62-68; V Worc St Mich 69-71; R Eastham w Rochford 71-79; P-in-c Knighton-on-Teme 76-79; P-in-c Teme Valley N 79; P-in-c Reddal Hill St Luke 79-81; V 81-92; rtd 92; PtO *Worc* from 92. *10 Woodhouse Way, Cradley Heath, Warley B64 5EL* T: (01384) 633527

BRIERLEY, Canon Michael William. b 73. CCC Cam BA 94 MA 98 Birm Univ PhD 07. Ripon Coll Cuddesdon BA 98. **d** 98 **p** 99. C Marnhull *Sarum* 98-01; C Okeford 98-01; Bp's Dom Chapl *Ox* 01-07; P-in-c Tavistock and Gulworthy *Ex* 07-14; Can Res and Prec Worc Cathl from 14. *15A College Green, Worcester WR1 2LH* T: (01905) 732940 E: michaelbrierley@worcestercathedral.org.uk

BRIERLEY, Philip. b 49. Salford Univ BSc 74. **d** 92 **p** 93. OLM Stalybridge *Man* 92-13; P-in-c from 13. *30 Cranworth Street, Stalybridge SK15 2NW* T: 0161-338 2368 E: philip.brierley@yahoo.co.uk

BRIERLEY, William David. b 64. Kent Univ BA 87 New Coll Ox DPhil 93. Ripon Coll Cuddesdon. **d** 93 **p** 94. C Amersham *Ox* 93-97; TV Wheatley 97-05. *37 Chessbury Road, Chesham HP5 1JT* E: william.brierley@tesco.net

BRIGGS, Christopher Ronald. b 58. K Coll Lon BD 79 AKC 79 PGCE 80. Sarum & Wells Th Coll 87. **d** 89 **p** 90. C Horsell *Guildf* 89-93; Hong Kong 93-97; V Norton St Alb 97-00; Sen Chapl Haileybury Coll from 00. *Lawrence Cottage, 2 Hailey Lane, Hertford Heath, Hertford SG13 7NX* T/F: (01992) 462922 T: 706314 E: chrisbriggs@freenet.co.uk

BRIGGS, Enid. b 50. CBDTI 03. **d** 06 **p** 07. NSM Walton-le-Dale St Leon w Samlesbury St Leon *Blackb* 06-13; NSM Walton-le-Dale St Leon 12-14; NSM Bamber Bridge St Aid 11-14; LtO from 14. *209 Chorley Road, Walton-le-Dale, Preston PR5 4JS* T: (01772) 879264 E: enid_briggs@hotmail.com

BRIGGS, George William. b 76. Wadh Coll Ox BA 98 Fitzw Coll Cam BA 02. Ridley Hall Cam 00. **d** 03 **p** 04. C Old Trafford St Bride *Man* 03-06; P-in-c Clapham Park All SS *S'wark* 06-11; V 11-14; P-in-c Kendal St Thos *Carl* from 14; P-in-c Crook from 14. *St Thomas's Vicarage, South View Lane, Kendal LA9 4QN* T: (015395) 83058 E: georgebriggs.work@gmail.com

BRIGGS, Gordon John. b 39. CIPFA. SAOMC 95. **d** 98 **p** 99. OLM Farnham Royal w Hedgerley *Ox* 98-11; PtO from 11. *52 Freemans Close, Stoke Poges, Slough SL2 4ER* T: (01753) 662536

BRIGGS, Canon John. b 39. Edin Univ MA 61. Ridley Hall Cam 61. **d** 63 **p** 64. C Jesmond Clayton Memorial *Newc* 63-66; Schs Sec Scripture Union 66-79; Tutor St Jo Coll Dur 67-74; LtO *Dur* 67-74; *Edin* 74-79; V Chadkirk *Ches* 79-88; RD 85-88; TR Macclesfield Team 88-04; Hon Can Ches Cathl 96-04; Chapl W Park Hosp Macclesfield 90-99; rtd 04; PtO *Ches* from 04. *16 Lostock Hall Road, Poynton, Stockport SK12 1DP* T: (01625) 267228 E: john.briggs20@ntlworld.com

BRIGGS, Michael Weston. b 40. Edin Th Coll 61. **d** 64 **p** 65. C Sneinton St Steph w St Alb *S'well* 64-67; C Beeston 67-70; P-in-c Kirkby Woodhouse 70-74; V Harworth 74-81; R Harby w Thorney and N and S Clifton 81-94; R N Wheatley, W Burton, Bole, Saundby, Sturton etc 94-05; P-in-c Clarborough w Hayton 03-05; CF (ACF) 74-97; rtd 05; PtO *S'well* from 06. *3 Monkwood Close, Collingham, Newark NG23 7SY* T: (01636) 893344 E: m_w_briggs@lineone.net

BRIGGS, Richard Stephen. b 66. **d** 15. NSM Dur St Giles from 15; NSM Shadforth and Sherburn from 15. *St Catherine's House, Front Street, Broompark, Durham DH7 7QX* T: 0191-386 9506 M: 07810-880133 E: richard.briggs@durham.ac.uk

BRIGGS, The Very Revd Roger Edward. b 36. ALCD 61. **d** 61 **p** 61. Canada 61-71; C Upper Armley *Ripon* 71-72; Canada 72-99; Dean Arctic 96-99; rtd 99. *Apartment 1207, 415 Greenview Avenue, Ottawa ON K2B 8G5, Canada*

BRIGGS, William James. b 75. Univ of Tasmania BE 97. Ridley Coll Melbourne BMin 03. **d** 02 **p** 03. C Burnie Australia 02-08; P-in-c 10-11; P-in-c Wynyard 05-07; Project P Somerset Project 09-13; C Hobart Cathl 11-15; C Newbury St Nic and Speen *Ox* from 15. *14 Strawberry Hill, Newbury RG14 1XJ* T: (01635) 285712 E: will.briggs@gmail.com

BRIGHOUSE, George Alexander (Alex). b 46. NOC 87. **d** 90 **p** 91. NSM Ingrow w Hainworth *Bradf* 90-91; NSM Keighley All SS 92; NSM Bradf St Wilfrid Lidget Green 92-04; NSM Bradf St Wilfrid w St Columba *Leeds* from 04. *Address temp unknown* M: 07428-360446 E: alexanderbrighouse@googlemail.com

BRIGHT, George Frank. b 50. Peterho Cam BA 71 MA 75 LSE MSc 83 SAP 99. Coll of Resurr Mirfield 71. **d** 74 **p** 75. C Notting Hill *Lon* 74-77; PtO 77-84; P-in-c Kentish Town St Benet and All SS 84-89; P-in-c Kensington St Jo 89-93; V 93-06. *The Vicarage, 176 Holland Road, London W14 8AH* T: (020) 7602 4655 E: gfb@dircon.co.uk

BRIGHT, Reginald. b 26. Tyndale Hall Bris 57. **d** 60 **p** 61. C Toxteth Park St Philemon w St Silas *Liv* 60-63; P-in-c Everton St Polycarp 63-65; R Orton St Giles *Carl* 65-72; V Holme 72-79; P-in-c W Newton 79-81; V Bromfield w Waverton 79-81; R Bowness 81-93; rtd 93; PtO *Carl* from 93. *Spinney House, Cannon Field, Roadhead, Carlisle CA6 6NB* T: (016977) 48645

BRIGHTMAN, Peter Arthur. b 30. ALCD 61 LTh 74. **d** 64 **p** 65. C Westgate St Jas *Cant* 64-67; C Lydd 67-70; C Lt Coates *Linc* 70; C Heaton Ch Ch *Man* 71-72; V Bolton SS Simon and Jude 72-77; R Bath St Sav *B & W* 77-85; R Farmborough, Marksbury and Stanton Prior 85-90; C Coney Hill *Glouc* 90-93; C Hardwicke, Quedgeley and Elmore w Longney 93-95; rtd 95; PtO *B & W* from 95. *2 Westmead Cottages, Weston, Bath BA1 4DT* T: (01225) 315076 M: 07528-891148

BRIGHTON, Margaret Elizabeth. b 53. Qu Coll Birm BA 07. WMMTC 04. **d** 07 **p** 08. C Boldmere *Birm* 07-10; V The Lickey from 10. *The Vicarage, 30 Lickey Square, Lickey, Birmingham B45 8HB* T: 0121-445 6781 E: margaret.brighton@ntlworld.com

BRIGHTON, Terrence William. b 43. SWMTC 85. **d** 88 **p** 89. C Dawlish *Ex* 88-92; P-in-c Newton Poppleford w Harpford 92-94; V Newton Poppleford, Harpford and Colaton Raleigh 94-98; RD Ottery 96-98; P-in-c W Lavington and the Cheverells *Sarum* 98-02; Rural Officer (Ramsbury Area) 98-02; P-in-c Charleton w Buckland Tout Saints etc *Ex* 02-05; R 05-08; RD Woodleigh 03-07; rtd 08. *30 Millway, Chudleigh, Newton Abbot TQ13 0JN* M: 07974-294044 E: twb@madasafish.com

BRIGHTWELL, Miss Elaine. b 57. STETS 09. **d** 12 **p** 13. NSM Pilton w Croscombe, N Wootton and Dinder *B & W* from 12. *57 Whitstone Rise, Shepton Mallet BA4 5QA* M: 07986-639230 E: elainbri@talktalk.net

BRIGHTWELL, Johanna Clare. See CLARE, Johanna Howard

BRIGNALL, Elizabeth Jane. See BENDREY, Elizabeth Jane

BRIGNALL, Simon Francis Lyon. b 54. St Jo Coll Dur BA 78. Wycliffe Hall Ox 80. **d** 83 **p** 84. C Colne St Bart *Blackb* 83-86; SAMS Peru 86-96; P-in-c Tetsworth, Adwell w S Weston, Lewknor etc *Ox* 96-98; TV Thame 98-09; P-in-c Wriggle Valley *Sarum* 09-13; TV Three Valleys from 13. *The Rectory, Church Street, Yetminster, Sherborne DT9 6LG* T: (01935) 872237 M: 07718-627674 E: brignall97as@btinternet.com

BRIMACOMBE, Keith John. b 59. Open Univ BA 92 Westmr Coll Ox MTh 00. SWMTC 99. **d** 01 **p** 03. NSM Ottery St Mary, Alfington, W Hill, Tipton etc *Ex* 01-07; Trinidad and Tobago 07-09; PtO Cyprus and the Gulf 09-10; Chapl Ahmadi St Paul Kuwait 11-13; C Fremington, Instow and Westleigh *Ex* from 13. *61 Hanson Park, Northam, Bideford EX39 3SB* E: brimacombe.keith@gmail.com

BRIMICOMBE, Mark. b 44. Nottm Univ BA 66 CertEd. SWMTC 83. **d** 85 **p** 86. NSM Plympton St Mary *Ex* from 85. *4 David Close, Stoggy Lane, Plympton, Plymouth PL7 3BQ* T: (01752) 338454 E: mark@thebrambles.eclipse.co.uk

BRIMSON, Mrs Dawn Diana. b 44. Ex Univ BTh 08. SWMTC 02. **d** 05 **p** 06. NSM Quantoxhead *B & W* 05-07; NSM Quantock Coast 07-14; PtO from 14. *Ridges, Holford, Bridgwater TA5 1DU* T: (01278) 741413 E: ddbrimson70@btinternet.com

BRINDLE, Keith Joseph. b 69. Middx Univ BSc 93 Wolv Univ MSc 95 Cranfield Univ PhD 98. Trin Coll Bris 10. **d** 12 **p** 13. C Deane Vale *B & W* from 12. *3 Manning Road, Cotford St Luke, Taunton TA4 1NY* T: (01823) 430038 E: keithbrindle@hotmail.co.uk

BRINDLE, Peter John. b 47. MIStructE 72 FLS 05. NOC 78. **d** 81 **p** 82. NSM Bingley All SS *Bradf* 81-84; NSM Bingley H Trin 84-86; V Keighley All SS 86-91; V Kirkstall *Ripon* 91-96; V Beeston 96-02; TR 02-04; TR Leic Presentation 04-07; P-in-c N Evington 07-09; rtd 09; PtO *York* from 14. *5 Showfield Close, Sherburn in Elmet, Leeds LS25 6LW* T: (01977) 680026 M: 07860-157363 E: peter.brindle23@gmail.com

BRINDLEY, Angela Mary. See SPEEDY, Angela Mary

BRINDLEY, The Very Revd David Charles. b 53. K Coll Lon BD 75 AKC 75 MTh 76 MPhil 81. St Aug Coll Cant 75. **d** 76 **p** 77. C Epping St Jo *Chelmsf* 76-79; Lect Coll of SS Paul and Mary Cheltenham 79-82; Dioc Dir of Tr *Leic* 82-86; V Quorndon 82-86; Prin WEMTC *Glouc* 87-94; Dir of Minl Tr 87-94; Dioc Officer for NSM 88-94; Hon Can Glouc Cathl 92-94; TR Warwick *Cov* 94-02; Dean Portsm

from 02. *The Deanery, 13 Pembroke Road, Portsmouth PO1 2NS*
T: (023) 9282 4400 *or* 9289 2963
E: david.brindley@portsmouthcathedral.org.uk

BRINDLEY, Canon Stuart Geoffrey Noel. b 30. St Jo Coll Dur BA 53. **d** 55 **p** 56. C Newc St Anne 55-58; C Tynemouth Cullercoats St Paul 58-60; C Killingworth 60-63; V Newsham 63-69; W Germany 69-76; Asst Master Wyvern Sch Weston-super-Mare 76-80; V Stocksbridge *Sheff* 80-88; RD Tankersley 85-88; V Rotherham 88-96; Hon Can Sheff Cathl 95-96; rtd 96; PtO *Newc* from 96. *Hambury, Backcrofts, Rothbury, Morpeth NE65 7XY* T: (01669) 621472

BRINKWORTH, Canon Christopher Michael Gibbs. b 41. Lanc Univ BA 70. Kelham Th Coll 62. **d** 67 **p** 68. C Lancaster St Mary *Blackb* 67-70; C Milton *Portsm* 70-74; V Ault Hucknall *Derby* 74-84; V Derby St Anne and St Jo 84-06; Hon Can Derby Cathl 00-06; rtd 06; PtO *Derby* from 06. *3 Westfield Grove, Derby DE22 3SG* T: (01332) 208478
E: michaelbrinkworth@btinternet.com

BRION, Martin Philip. b 33. Ex Univ BA 55. Ridley Hall Cam 57. **d** 59 **p** 60. C Balderstone *Man* 59-62; C Morden *S'wark* 62-66; V Low Elswick *Newc* 66-73; P-in-c Giggleswick *Bradf* 73-77; V 77-80; V Camerton H Trin W Seaton *Carl* 80-86; V Dearham 86-95; rtd 95; PtO *Carl* from 95. *7 Falcon Place, Moresby Parks, Whitehaven CA28 8YF* T: (01946) 691912

BRISBANE, Archbishop of. *See* ASPINALL, Phillip John

BRISCOE, Allen. b 42. Liv Univ BSc 64 CertEd 65. Coll of Resurr Mirfield 90. **d** 92 **p** 93. C Shiremoor *Newc* 92-95; V Barnsley St Pet and St Jo *Wakef* 95-10; Asst Dioc Ecum Officer 01-03; Bp's Adv for Ecum Affairs 03-06; RD Barnsley 04-09; rtd 10; Hon C Goldthorpe w Hickleton *Sheff* from 11. *37 Holly Grove, Goldthorpe, Rotherham S63 9LA* T: (01709) 896739
E: abriscoe@talk21.com

BRISCOE, Canon Frances Amelia. b 35. Univ of Wales CertEd 55 Man Univ BA 71 MA 74. Gilmore Course 74. **dss** 77 **d** 87 **p** 94. Gt Crosby St Luke *Liv* 76-81; Dioc Lay Min Adv 81-87; Chapl Liv Cathl 81-89; Dir Diaconal Mins 87-89; Lect St Deiniol's Minl Tr Scheme 88-00; Hon Can Liv Cathl 88-00; AD Sefton 89-00; Dir of Reader Studies 89-00; Dn-in-c Hightown *Liv* 92-94; P-in-c 94-00; rtd 00; PtO *Liv* from 01. *5 Derwent Avenue, Formby, Liverpool L37 2JT*
T: (01704) 830075

BRISCOE, Mark. b 71. Coll of Ripon & York St Jo BA 95. Ripon Coll Cuddesdon 05. **d** 07 **p** 08. C Saxilby Gp *Linc* 07-10; P-in-c Corringham and Blyton Gp 10-14; P-in-c Glentworth Gp 10-14; V Trentcliffe Gp from 14. *The Vicarage, Church Lane, Blyton, Gainsborough DN21 3JZ* T: (01427) 629105

BRISON, The Ven William Stanley. b 29. Alfred Univ NY BSc 51 Connecticut Univ MDiv 57 STM 71. Berkeley Div Sch. **d** 57 **p** 57. USA 57-72; V Davyhulme Ch Ch *Man* 72-81; R Newton Heath All SS 81-85; AD N Man 81-85; Hon Can Man Cathl 82-85; Adn Bolton 85-92; TV E Farnworth and Kearsley 85-89; C Bolton St Thos 89-92; CMS 92-94; Nigeria 92-94; P-in-c Pendleton St Thos w Charlestown *Man* 94-95; TR Pendleton 95-98; rtd 98; PtO *Man* from 99. *2 Scott Avenue, Bury BL9 9RS* T: 0161-764 3998

BRISTOL, Archdeacon of. *See* FROUDE, The Ven Christine Ann

BRISTOL, Bishop of. *See* HILL, The Rt Revd Michael Arthur

BRISTOL, Dean of. *See* HOYLE, The Very Revd David Michael

BRISTOW, Keith Raymond Martin. b 56. Ex Univ BA 78. Chich Th Coll 87. **d** 89 **p** 90. C Kirkby *Liv* 89-93; C Portsea St Mary *Portsm* 93-03; R Ash *Guildf* from 03. *The Rectory, Ash Church Road, Ash, Aldershot GU12 6LU* T: (01252) 321517
E: frkeithbristow@ntlworld.com

BRISTOW, Malcolm William. b 49. JP 94. SNWTP 11. **d** 12 **p** 13. OLM Bolton St Bede *Man* from 12. *8 Winton Grove, Bolton BL3 4UX* T: (01204) 659816 M: 07702-519007
E: malcolm.bristow@ntlworld.com

BRISTOW, Canon Peter Edmund. b 49. Pontificium Institutum Internationale Angelicum Rome JCL 77 St Jos Coll Upholland 67. **d** 72 **p** 73. In RC Ch 72-87; C Poplar *Lon* 89-92; Lay Tr Officer 89-90; TV Droitwich Spa *Worc* 92-94; TR 94-00; V Boston Spa *York* 00-11; P-in-c Bramham 09-11; P-in-c Thorp Arch w Walton 00-11; V Bramham from 11; RD New Ainsty 06-11; Ghana from 14. *The Vicarage, 86 High Street, Boston Spa, Wetherby LS23 6EA* T: (01937) 842454
E: pebristow49@gmail.com

BRISTOW, Roger. b 60. Aston Tr Scheme 81 Ridley Hall Cam 83. **d** 86 **p** 87. C Leyton St Mary w St Edw *Chelmsf* 86-90; TV Kings Norton *Birm* 90-98; V Bromley H Trin *Roch* from 98. *Holy Trinity Vicarage, Church Lane, Bromley BR2 8LB* T/F: (020) 8462 1280 M: 07778-397224
E: roger.bristow@diocese-rochester.org

BRITT, Eric Stanley. b 47. St Jo Coll Nottm BTh 75. **d** 74 **p** 75. C Chorleywood Ch Ch *St Alb* 74-78; C Frimley *Guildf* 78-80; P-in-c Alresford *Chelmsf* 80-88; R Takeley w Lt Canfield 88-93; Asst Chapl R Free Hosp Lon 93-96; Chapl Mid-Essex Hosp

Services NHS Trust 96-00; Chapl Algarve *Eur* 01-06; rtd 06. *5 De Lisle Close, Papworth Everard, Cambridge CB23 3UT*
E: e.britt@btinternet.com

BRITT, Sister Mary Stephen. b 44. Stockwell Coll of Educn TCert 65 Open Univ BA 76. SAOMC 02. **d** 05 **p** 06. CSJB from 96; NSM Hanborough and Freeland *Ox* 05-13; PtO from 13; Asst Chapl Ripon Coll Cuddesdon from 14. *Harriet Monsell House, Ripon College Cuddesdon, Oxford OX44 9EX*
E: marycsjb@csjb.org.uk

BRITT, William Thomas. b 60. Westmr Coll Fulton (USA) BA 82. St Mellitus Coll BA 11. **d** 11 **p** 12. C Kempston Transfiguration *St Alb* 11-15; V Stotfold and Radwell from 14. *The Vicarage, 61 Church Road, Stotfold, Hitchin SG5 4NE*
E: revd.bill.britt@gmail.com

BRITTAIN, John. b 23. St Aug Coll Cant 59. **d** 60 **p** 61. C Heref St Martin 60-62; V Highley 62-88; rtd 88. *26 Stuart Court, High Street, Kibworth, Leicester LE8 0LR*

BRITTEN, Mrs Diana. b 39. **d** 07 **p** 08. OLM Cley Hill Villages *Sarum* 07-11; NSM from 11. *69 Lane End, Corsley, Warminster BA12 7PG* T: (01373) 832515
E: diana.britten@btinternet.com

BRITTLE, Miss Janice Lilian. b 50. Man Poly BA 74 Open Univ BA 84 Sheff Univ MMedSc 00 RGN 76. **d** 04 **p** 05. OLM Rugeley *Lich* 04-06; OLM Brereton and Rugeley 06-14; PtO from 14. *3 Norwood House, Peakes Road, Rugeley WS15 2ND* T: (01889) 586138 E: janice.brittle@btinternet.com

BRITTON, Christine Mary. *See* BEECROFT, Christine Mary

BRITTON, David Robert. b 80. Leeds Univ BA 03 Fitzw Coll Cam BA 09. Ridley Hall Cam 07. **d** 10 **p** 11. C W Streatham St Jas *S'wark* 10-12; C Furzedown 12-14; V Leytonstone St Jo *Chelmsf* from 14. *St John's Vicarage, 44 Hartley Road, London E11 3BL* T: (020) 8279 7738 M: 07732-135178
E: rev.britton@gmail.com

BRITTON, Mrs Jennifer Mary. **d** 14 **p** 15. NSM Carmarthen St Pet and Abergwili etc *St D* from 14; NSM Abergwili w Capel y Groes from 14. *1 Heol Penllain, Peniel, Carmarthen SA32 7AT* T: (01267) 238463 E: david@penllain.wanadoo.co.uk

BRITTON, John Timothy Hugh. b 50. Dundee Univ BSc 73. Trin Coll Bris 73. **d** 76 **p** 77. C Cromer *Nor* 76-79; P-in-c Freethorpe w Wickhampton 79-82; P-in-c Beighton and Moulton 79-82; P-in-c Halvergate w Tunstall 79-82; CMS 82-89; Uganda 83-89; R Allesley *Cov* 89-02; P-in-c Offchurch 02-15; P-in-c Long Itchington and Marton 02-15; P-in-c Wappenbury w Weston under Wetherley 02-15; P-in-c Hunningham 02-15; rtd 15. *Address temp unknown* E: timbritton@myrealbox.com

BRITTON, Neil Bryan. b 35. Em Coll Cam BA 59 MA 63. Clifton Th Coll 61. **d** 63 **p** 64. C Eastbourne All SS *Chich* 63-67; C Ashtead *Guildf* 67-70; Chapl Scargill Ho 70-74; Chapl Aiglon Coll and Asst Chapl Villars *Eur* 74-78; In Reformed Ch of Switzerland 78-98; rtd 00; USA 01-05; PtO *Win* from 10. *Rose Cottage, 7 Newbury Road, Kingsclere, Newbury RG20 5SP* T: (01635) 297687 M: 07903-120368
E: britton.neil@googlemail.com

BRITTON, Canon Paul Anthony. b 29. SS Coll Cam BA 52 MA 57. Linc Th Coll 52. **d** 54 **p** 55. C Upper Norwood St Jo *Cant* 54-57; C Wantage *Ox* 57-61; V Stanmore *Win* 61-70; V Bitterne Park 70-80; Can Res Win Cathl 80-94; Lib Win Cathl 81-85; Can Res and Treas Win Cathl 85-94; rtd 94; PtO *Sarum* from 94. *Pemberton, High Street, Hindon, Salisbury SP3 6DR* T: (01747) 820406

BRITTON, Robert. b 37. Oak Hill Th Coll 78. **d** 79 **p** 80. C St Helens St Helen *Liv* 79-83; V Lowton St Mary 83-02; AD Winwick 89-01; rtd 02; PtO *Man* 03-14; *Liv* from 03. *15 Balmoral Avenue, Lowton, Warrington WA3 2ER* T: (01942) 711135

BRITTON, Ronald George Adrian Michael (Robert). b 24. Univ of State of NY BSc 78 Lambeth STh 82. St D Coll Lamp 63. **d** 82 **p** 82. Arabia 82-85; Chapl Alassio *Eur* 85-90; 92-93; Chapl San Remo 86; Hon C Southbourne St Kath *Win* 90-92; rtd 96; PtO *Bris* from 97. *2 Cherry Tree Road, Bristol BS16 4EY* T: 0117-965 5734 E: robert@britton320.fsnet.co.uk

BRITTON, Stephen Paul. b 55. Trin Coll Bris. **d** 12 **p** 13. OLM Longwell Green *Bris* from 12. *15 Central Avenue, Bristol BS15 3PG* T: 0117-961 4796 E: s.britton@btinternet.com

BRITTON, Timothy. *See* BRITTON, John Timothy Hugh

BRIXTON, Miss Corinne Jayne. b 63. Ex Univ BSc 84. Wycliffe Hall Ox BTh 95. **d** 95. C Leytonstone St Jo *Chelmsf* 95-00; C Buckhurst Hill 00-15. *2A Camfield Close, Basingstoke RG21 3AQ* E: cbrixton@aol.com

BRIXWORTH, Suffragan Bishop of. *See* HOLBROOK, The Rt Revd John Edward

BROAD, Mrs Christine Jane. b 63. Leeds Univ BSc 86 BA 06. NOC 03. **d** 06 **p** 07. C Newchapel *Lich* 06-09; TV Hanley H Ev 09-13; TR from 13. *19 Widecombe Road, Birches Head, Stoke-on-Trent ST1 6SL* T: (01782) 852280
E: christine@broad1959.freeserve.co.uk

BROAD, David Nicholas Andrew. b 59. Man Univ BA. Edin Th Coll. **d** 87 **p** 88. C Fulham All SS *Lon* 87-90; TV Clare w Poslingford, Cavendish etc *St E* 90-93; TV Totton *Win* 93-99; R Abbotts Ann and Upper and Goodworth Clatford 99-15; Hon C Lewes St Anne and St Mich and St Thos etc *Chich* from 15. *St Michael's Rectory, St Andrew's Lane, Lewes BN7 1UW* E: dna.broad@virgin.net

BROAD, Canon Hugh Duncan. b 37. Lich Th Coll 64. **d** 67 **p** 68. C Heref H Trin 67-72; Asst Master Bp's Sch Heref 72-73; C Fareham SS Pet and Paul *Portsm* 74-76; V Heref All SS 76-90; R Matson *Glouc* 90-97; V Glouc St Geo w Whaddon 97-03; Hon Can Glouc Cathl 02-03; rtd 03; P-in-c Costa Almeria and Costa Calida *Eur* 03-13; Hon Can Gib Cathl 13. *44 Vensfield Road, Quedgeley, Gloucester GL2 4FX* E: hugh.broad@yahoo.co.uk

BROAD, Hugh Robert. b 49. St Mich Coll Llan 67. **d** 72 **p** 73. C Tenby w Gumfreston *St D* 72-75; C Caerau w Ely *Llan* 75-79; V Llanharan w Peterston-super-Montem 79-89; RD Bridgend 88-89; Ex-Paroch Officer 90; V Whatborough Gp *Leic* 90-08; rtd 08. *12 Cooke Close, Thorpe Astley, Braunstone, Leicester LE3 3RG* E: hugh_broad@hotmail.com

BROAD, Canon William Ernest Lionel. b 40. Ridley Hall Cam 64. **d** 66 **p** 67. C Ecclesfield *Sheff* 66-69; Chapl HM Pris Wormwood Scrubs 69; Chapl HM Pris Albany 70-74; Chapl HM Rem Cen Risley 74-76; V Ditton St Mich *Liv* 76-81; TR 82-83; P-in-c Mayland and Steeple *Chelmsf* 83-91; V Blackhall *Dur* 91-97; TR Gt Aycliffe 97-03; P-in-c Chilton 03; TV Gt Aycliffe and Chilton 03-04; Hon Can Dur Cathl 02-04; rtd 04; PtO *Dur* from 04. *Moorcote, Thornley, Tow Law, Bishop Auckland DL13 4NU* T: (01388) 731350 E: bill@deagol.fsnet.co.uk

BROADBENT, Mrs Doreen. b 36. **d** 94 **p** 95. OLM Stalybridge *Man* 94-02; PtO 02-14. *37 Ladysmith Road, Ashton-under-Lyne OL6 9DJ* T: 0161-330 9085

BROADBENT, Hugh Patrick Colin. b 53. Selw Coll Cam BA 75 MA. **d** 78 **p** 79. C Chatham St Steph *Roch* 78-82; C Shortlands 82-84; C Edenbridge 84-87; C Crockham Hill H Trin 84-87; V Bromley H Trin 87-97; V Bromley St Jo 97-09; Chapl St Olave's Gr Sch Orpington 95-09; R Snodland All SS w Ch *Roch* from 09; RD Cobham from 11. *The Vicarage, 11 St Katherine's Lane, Snodland ME6 5EH* T: (01634) 240232 E: hugh.broadbent@diocese-rochester.org

BROADBENT, Neil Seton. b 53. Qu Coll Birm. **d** 81 **p** 82. C Knaresborough *Ripon* 81-84; C Leeds Gipton Epiphany 84-87; LtO 87-89; Chapl Minstead Community *Derby* 89; PtO from 89; Dir Sozein from 93. *The Old Vicarage, Church Lane, Horsley Woodhouse, Ilkeston DE7 6BB* T: (01332) 780598 E: neil.broadbent@sozein.org.uk

BROADBENT, Paul John. b 41. Oak Hill Th Coll 83. **d** 85 **p** 86. C Duston *Pet* 85-88; TV Ross w Brampton Abbotts, Bridstow and Peterstow *Heref* 88-91; R Pattishall w Cold Higham and Gayton w Tiffield *Pet* 91-10; rtd 10; P-in-c Fairwarp *Chich* from 10. *The Vicarage, Fairwarp, Uckfield TN22 3BL* T: (01825) 712277 M: 07786-865015 E: pj.broadbent1@btinternet.com

✠**BROADBENT, The Rt Revd Peter Alan.** b 52. Jes Coll Cam BA 74 MA 78. St Jo Coll Nottm 74. **d** 77 **p** 78 **c** 01. C Dur St Nic 77-80; C Holloway Em w Hornsey Road St Barn *Lon* 80-83; Chapl N Lon Poly 83-89; Hon C Islington St Mary 83-89; V Harrow Trin St Mich 89-94; AD Harrow 94; Adn Northolt 95-01; P-in-c Southall H Trin 98-99; Area Bp Willesden from 01. *173 Willesden Lane, London NW6 7YN* T: (020) 8451 0189 F: 8451 4606 M: 07957-144674 E: bishop.willesden@btinternet.com

BROADBENT, Ralph Andrew. b 55. K Coll Lon BD 76 AKC 76 Birm Univ PhD 04. Chich Th Coll 77. **d** 78 **p** 79. C Prestwich St Mary *Man* 78-82; R Man Miles Platting 82-84; CF 84-87; TV Wordsley *Lich* 88-93; Chapl Wordsley Hosp 88-93; Chapl Ridge Hill Hosp 88-93; V Wollescote *Worc* 93-15; rtd 15. *70 Harry Davis Court, Armstrong Drive, Worcester WR1 2AJ* T: (01905) 769893 E: ralphbroadbent@btinternet.com

BROADBENT, Thomas William. b 45. Chu Coll Cam BA 66 MA 70 PhD 70. Ridley Hall Cam 75. **d** 78 **p** 79. C Allington and Maidstone St Pet *Cant* 78-82; Chapl Mid Kent Coll of H&FE 80-82; C Kings Heath *Birm* 82-84; Hon C Pendleton St Thos *Man* 84-89; TV Pendleton St Thos w Charlestown 89-92; Chapl Salford Univ 84-92; P-in-c Claydon and Barham *St E* 92-08; P-in-c Coddenham w Gosbeck and Hemingstone w Henley 99-08; P-in-c Gt and Lt Blakenham w Baylham and Nettlestead 02-08; Chapl Suffolk Coll 92-00; P-in-c Witham Gp *Linc* 08-14; rtd 14. *8 Abbey Road, Bardney, Lincoln LN3 5XA* T: (01526) 397101

BROADBERRY, Canon Richard St Lawrence. b 31. TCD BA 53 BD 59 MLitt 66. **d** 54 **p** 55. C Dublin St Thos *D & G* 54-56; C Dublin Grangegorman 56-62; Min Can St Patr Cathl Dublin 58-62; Hon Clerical V Ch Ch Cathl Dublin 62-64;

C Dublin Clontarf 62-64; C Thornton Heath St Jude *Cant* 64-66; V Norwood All SS 66-82; V Upper Norwood All SS w St Marg 82-84; RD Croydon N 81-84; Hon Can Cant Cathl 82-84; V Merton St Mary *S'wark* 85-92; RD Croydon N 85; Hon Can S'wark Cathl 85-01; V Riddlesdown 92-01; rtd 01; PtO *S'wark* from 01. *73 Court Avenue, Coulsdon CR5 1HG* T: (01737) 551109 E: rm.broadberry@gmail.com

BROADHEAD, Mrs Lynn. b 59. Yorks Min Course 08. **d** 11 **p** 12. NSM Thorpe Hesley *Sheff* 11-13; NSM Greasbrough 13-15; V Thorpe Hesley from 15. *The Vicarage, 30 Barnsley Road, Thorpe Hesley, Rotherham S61 2RR* T: 0114-246 3487 M: 07811-336183 E: revd.lynn.broadhead@sky.com

BROADHURST, Jonathan Robin. b 58. Univ Coll Ox BA 81 MA 86. Wycliffe Hall Ox 85. **d** 88 **p** 89. C Hull St Jo Newland *York* 88-91; P-in-c Burton Fleming w Fordon, Grindale etc 91-92; V 92-98; C Kingston upon Hull H Trin 98-01; P-in-c Rastrick St Jo *Wakef* 01-06; rtd 06. *1 Moravian Terrace, Halifax HX3 8AL* T: (01422) 209549 M: 07790-899195 E: jonathan@broadhurst-jr.freeserve.co.uk

BROADIE, Stephen Kim. b 76. Leeds Univ BA 99 Bris Univ PGCE 03. Ridley Hall Cam 10. **d** 12 **p** 13. C Welling *Roch* from 12. *52 Clifton Road, Welling DA16 1QD* T: (020) 8306 1829 M: 07763-105092 E: stephenbroadie@gmail.com

BROADLEY, Michael John. b 66. Roehampton Inst BA 87. Trin Coll Bris 93. **d** 96 **p** 97. C Egham *Guildf* 96-01; TV Horsham *Chich* 01-10; P-in-c Loughborough Em and St Mary in Charnwood *Leic* 10-14; P-in-c Loughborough Em from 15. *Emmanuel Rectory, 47 Forest Road, Loughborough LE11 3NW* T: (01509) 263264 E: broadley@bigfoot.com

BROCK, Michael John. b 52. Birm Univ BSc 74. St Jo Coll Nottm BA 77. **d** 78 **p** 79. C Stapleford *S'well* 78-82; C Bestwood St Matt 82-86; TV Bestwood 86-90; R Epperstone 90-05; R Gonalston 90-05; V Oxton 90-05; P-in-c Woodborough 02-05; RD S'well 93-96; Dioc Adv in Rural Affairs 97-02; R Dersingham w Anmer and Shernborne *Nor* 05-15; RD Heacham and Rising 07-11; C Snettisham w Ingoldisthorpe and Fring 14-15; P-in-c Ingoldisthorpe 14-15; rtd 15; P-in-c Sutton Bonington w Normanton-on-Soar *S'well* from 15. *19A Park Lane, Sutton Bonington, Loughborough LE12 5NQ* E: mjb65@btinternet.com *or* revmjb@gmail.com

BROCKBANK, Arthur Ross. b 51. NOC 87. **d** 90 **p** 91. C Haughton St Mary *Man* 90-93; V Bircle 93-12; P-in-c Walmersley 04; Chapl Bury Healthcare NHS Trust 93-02; Chapl Co-ord Pennine Acute Hosps NHS Trust 02-03; rtd 12. *12 Dickinson Road, Liverpool L37 4BX* T: (01704) 461346

BROCKBANK, Donald Philip. b 56. Univ of Wales (Ban) BD 78. Sarum & Wells Th Coll 79. **d** 81 **p** 82. C Prenton *Ches* 81-85; TV Birkenhead Priory 85-91; V Altrincham St Jo 91-96; Urban Officer 91-96; Dioc Ecum Officer *Lich* 96-98; C Lich St Mich w St Mary and Wall 96-98; V Acton and Worleston, Church Minshull etc *Ches* 98-06; rtd 07; Dioc Adv in Spirituality *Ches* 07-12. *1 Plover Avenue, Winsford CW7 1LA* T: (01606) 593651 E: donald@brockbankrev.freeserve.co.uk

BROCKBANK, John Keith. b 44. Dur Univ BA 65. Wells Th Coll 66. **d** 68 **p** 69. C Preston St Matt *Blackb* 68-71; C Lancaster St Mary 71-73; V Habergham All SS 73-83; P-in-c Gannow 81-83; V W Burnley All SS 83-86; Dioc Stewardship Adv 86-92; P-in-c Shireshead 86-92; V Kirkham 92-09; rtd 09; PtO *Blackb* from 09. *44 Esthwaite Gardens, Lancaster LA1 3RG* T: (01524) 847520 E: revjkb@talktalk.net

BROCKBANK, John Stanley. b 41. CBDTI 97. **d** 00 **p** 01. OLM Arnside Carl 00-11; rtd 11; PtO *Carl* from 11. *Hough Close, 5 Ash Meadow Road, Arnside, Carnforth LA5 0AE* T: (01524) 761634

BROCKHOUSE, Canon Grant Lindley. b 47. Adelaide Univ BA 71 Ex Univ MA 81. St Barn Coll Adelaide 70. **d** 73 **p** 74. C Edwardstown w Ascot Park Australia 73-74; Tutor St Barn Coll Belair 74-78; C Ex St Jas 78-80; Asst Chapl Ex Univ 80-83; V Marldon 83-98; Dep PV Ex Cathl 81-98; RD Torbay 95-98; V Higham Ferrers w Chelveston *Pet* 98-13; RD Higham 03-11; Can Pet Cathl 07-13; rtd 13; PtO *Pet* from 14. *71 Bishops Road, Peterborough PE1 5AS* T: (01733) 753339 E: grantbrockhouse@gmail.com

BROCKIE, Canon William James Thomson. b 36. Pemb Coll Ox BA 58 MA 62. Linc Th Coll 58. **d** 60 **p** 61. C Lin St Jo Bapt CD *Linc* 60-63; V Gt Staughton *Ely* 63-68; Chapl HM Borstal Gaynes Hall 63-68; TV Edin St Jo 68-76; Chapl Edin Univ 71-76; USA 76; R Edin St Martin 76-01; P-in-c Wester Hailes St Luke 79-90; Hon Can St Mary's Cathl from 98; rtd 00; Hon C Edin St Hilda and Edin St Fillan 02-03. *31 Holly Bank Terrace, Edinburgh EH11 1SP* T: 0131-337 6482 E: billjennybrockie@hotmail.com

BROCKLEBANK, John. b 32. NOC 83. **d** 86 **p** 87. NSM Warrington St Barn *Liv* 86-93; NSM Orford St Marg 93-97; PtO from 97. *53 St Mary's Road, Penketh, Warrington WA5 2DT* T: (01925) 722063

BROCKLEHURST, Ian Christopher. b 62. All SS Cen for Miss & Min 12. d 15. NSM Coldhurst and Oldham St Steph *Man* from 15. *4 Higher Lydgate Park, Grasscroft, Oldham OL4 4EF* T: (01457) 877731 E: iancb53@btinternet.com

BROCKLEHURST, John Richard. b 51. Univ Coll Ox BA 72 Lon Univ CertEd 74. Oak Hill Th Coll BA 81. d 81 p 82. C Harwood *Man* 81-85; V Hopwood 85-97; P-in-c Friarmere 97-03; TV Saddleworth 03-08; P-in-c Waddington *Bradf* 08-14; V 14; Hon C Hurst Green and Mitton 08-14; Hon C Bolton by Bowland w Grindleton 08-14; V Waddington *Blackb* from 14. *The Vicarage, Slaidburn Road, Waddington, Clitheroe BB7 3JQ* T/F: (01200) 422481 E: waddowvicar@talktalk.net

BROCKLEHURST, Simon. b 63. Cranmer Hall Dur 86. d 89 p 90. C Clifton *S'well* 89-93; TV 93-96; P-in-c Mabe *Truro* 96-99; Miss to Seamen 96-99; V Ham St Andr *S'wark* from 99; Inland Hon Chapl Miss to Seafarers from 00. *St Andrew's Vicarage, Church Road, Ham, Richmond TW10 5HG* T/F: (020) 8940 9017 E: revsimonb@btinternet.com

BRODDLE, Christopher Stephen Thomas. b 57. d 87 p 88. C Lisburn St Paul *Conn* 87-90; CF 90-07; Sen CF from 07. *c/o MOD Chaplains (Army)* T: (01264) 383430 F: 381824

BRODIE, Miss Ann. b 55. Ex Univ BA 76 PGCE 77. St Jo Coll Nottm 03. d 05 p 06. C Putney St Marg *S'wark* 05-09; P-in-c 09-12; V from 12. *St Margaret's Vicarage, 46 Luttrell Avenue, London SW15 6PE* T: (020) 8788 5522 E: vicar@stmargaretsputney.org.uk

BRODIE, Frederick. b 40. Leic Teacher Tr Coll TCert 61. St Jo Coll Nottm 90. d 92 p 93. C Lutterworth w Cotesbach *Leic* 92-95; P-in-c Mountsorrel Ch Ch and St Pet 95-97; V 97-03; rtd 03; PtO *Leic* from 03. *11 Cooper Lane, Ratby, Leicester LE6 0QG* T: 0116-238 7959

BRODY, Paul. b 40. NOC 85. d 88 p 89. C Leigh St Mary *Man* 88-90; C Peel 90-91; TR 91-97; TV Worsley 97-07; rtd 07; PtO *Man* from 07. *29 Parkfield Avenue, Tyldesley, Manchester M29 7BE* T: (01942) 700102 E: brendabrody@blueyonder.co.uk

BROGGIO, Bernice Muriel Croager. b 35. Bedf Coll Lon BA 57 K Coll Lon BD 66 Glas Univ DASS 72. dss 84 d 87 p 94. Bris St Paul w St Barn 84-87; Hon Par Dn Bris St Paul's 87-88; C Charlton St Luke w H Trin *S'wark* 88-95; V Upper Tooting H Trin 95-03; Hon Can S'wark Cathl 95-03; RD Tooting 96-02; TV Bensham *Dur* 03-05; PtO from 05; Hon C Bensham 06-07; Hon C Birtley from 07; PtO *Eur* from 10; rtd 06. *86 Woodburn, Gateshead NE10 8LY* T: 0191-495 0959 M: 07900-327316 E: b.broggio@btinternet.com

BROMAGE, Kenneth Charles. b 51. EAMTC. d 90 p 91. NSM Woolpit w Drinkstone *St E* 90-92; Chapl RN 92-11; rtd 11. *Address temp unknown*

BROMFIELD, Michael. b 32. Kelham Th Coll 54 Lich Th Coll 59. d 62 p 63. C Sedgley All SS *Lich* 62-64; C Tunstall Ch Ch 64-67; P-in-c Grindon 67-70; R 70-80; P-in-c Butterton 67-70; V 70-80; R Hope Bowdler w Eaton-under-Heywood *Heref* 80-97; R Rushbury 80-97; V Cardington 80-97; rtd 98; PtO *Lich* from 98. *11 Walklate Avenue, Newcastle ST5 0PR* T: (01782) 630716 E: bromfield@stoke54.freeserve.co.uk

BROMFIELD, Nicholas Robert. b 60. St Jo Coll Cam MA 82. WEMTC 98. d 02 p 03. C Tidenham w Beachley and Lancaut *Glouc* 02-07; C St Briavels w Hewelsfield 05-07; R Drybrook, Lydbrook and Ruardean from 07. *The Rectory, Oakland Road, Harrow Hill, Drybrook GL17 9JX* T: (01594) 542232 E: bromfields@email.msn.com

BROMFIELD, Richard Allan. b 47. Sussex Univ MA 96 LVCM 85. Chich Th Coll 86. d 88 p 89. C Durrington *Chich* 88-95; V Woodingdean 95-12; Chapl Nuffield Hosp Brighton 96-12; rtd 12. *34 Rowan Way, Angmering, Littlehampton BN16 4FW* E: r.a.bromfield@btinternet.com

BROMILEY, Paul Nigel. b 49. Univ of Wales (Cardiff) BSc 71. Oak Hill Th Coll 88. d 90 p 91. C Gee Cross *Ches* 90-94; P-in-c Millbrook 94-03; Master Wyggeston's Hosp Leic 03-14; rtd 14; PtO *Leic* from 14. *6 Russett Close, Barwell, Leicester LE9 8HZ* E: paul.bromiley@zen.co.uk

BROMILEY, Philip Arthur. b 73. Westmr Coll Ox BTh 94 St Jo Coll Dur MA 98. Cranmer Hall Dur 95. d 98 p 99. C Marton *Blackb* 98-01; Assoc P Calne and Blackland *Sarum* 01-06; P-in-c Oldbury 06-08; R from 08. *The Rectory, The Street, Cherhill, Calne SN11 8XR* T: (01249) 820062 E: philbromiley@gmail.com

BROMLEY, Deborah Joan. *See* SCOTT-BROMLEY, Deborah Joan

BROMLEY, Mrs Janet Catherine Gay. b 45. Surrey Univ BSc 68 Bradf Univ MSc 72 Brunel Tech Coll Bris FE TCert 86. S Dios Minl Tr Scheme 91. d 94 p 96. C Westbury-on-Trym H Trin *Bris* 94-96; C Wroughton 96-00; Dean Women's Min 98-00; R Dursley *Glouc* 00-13; AD 07-09; rtd 13. *40 Kings Fee, Monmouth NP25 5BW* T: (01600) 713847 E: revdjanet@googlemail.com

BROMLEY, Richard. b 60. Birm Chr Coll MA 02. d 08 p 09. NSM Binley *Cov* 08-11; PtO from 11. *22 Chaceley Close, Coventry CV2 2SF* T: (024) 7660 4152 M: 07772-496029 E: rbromley@ics-uk.org

BROMLEY AND BEXLEY, Archdeacon of. *See* WRIGHT, The Ven Paul

BRONNERT, Preb David Llewellyn Edward. b 36. Ch Coll Cam BA 57 MA 61 PhD 61 Lon Univ BD 62. Tyndale Hall Bris 60. d 63 p 64. C Cheadle Hulme St Andr *Ches* 63-67; C Islington St Mary *Lon* 67-69; Chapl N Lon Poly 69-75; V Southall Green St Jo 75-01; Preb St Paul's Cathl 89-01; P-in-c Southall St Geo 92-99; AD Ealing W 84-90; rtd 01; PtO *Ox* from 04. *101 Walton Way, Aylesbury HP21 7JP* T: (01296) 484048 E: david.bronnert@talk21.com

BRONNERT, John. b 33. Man Univ MA(Theol) 84 Univ of Wales (Lamp) PhD 98 ACA 57 FCA 68. Tyndale Hall Bris 65. d 68 p 69. C Hoole *Ches* 68-71; P-in-c Parr *Liv* 71-73; TV 73-85; V Runcorn St Jo Weston *Ches* 85-98; rtd 98; PtO *Liv* 85-04; *Man* 98-14. *Tyndale, 15 Craig Avenue, Flixton, Urmston, Manchester M41 5RS* T: 0161-748 7061 E: revddrjohn.bronnert@tiscali.co.uk

BROOK, Adrian John. b 60. STETS 08. d 11 p 12. C Pimperne, Stourpaine, Durweston and Bryanston *Sarum* 11-14; Chapl to Travelling People 12-14; TV Okehampton, Inwardleigh, Belstone, Sourton etc *Ex* from 14. *St Bridget's House, Bridestowe, Okehampton EX20 4ER* M: 07932-546510 E: abrook1@live.co.uk

BROOK, David Thomas. b 46. d 11 p 12. OLM Lt Aston *Lich* from 11. *35 Kensington Drive, Sutton Coldfield B74 4UD* T: 0121-353 6106 E: d_brook@sky.com

BROOK, John Brendan Paul. b 79. CCC Ox MEng 01. Oak Hill Th Coll BA 06. d 06 p 07. C Hailsham *Chich* 06-10; Min The Haven CD from 10. *1 Columbus Drive, Eastbourne BN22 6RR* T: (01323) 325989 E: jbrook@gmail.com

BROOK, Jonathan Roger Wilson. b 67. St Jo Coll Nottm 05. d 07 p 08. C Ripley *Derby* 07-10; TV N Wingfield, Clay Cross and Pilsley 10-13. *Address temp unknown* M: 07939-472799 E: jonathan-susie.brook@tiscali.co.uk

BROOK, Neville. *See* BROOK, William Neville

BROOK, Peter Geoffrey (Brother Simon). b 47. NOC 91. d 94 p 95. CGA from 71; NSM Heywood and Middleton Deanery 94-96; PtO *Ex* from 96. *The Priory, Lamacraft Farm, Start Point, Chivelstone, Kingsbridge TQ7 2NG* T: (01548) 511474 E: ascensioncga@fsmail.net

BROOK, Priestly. b 42. CBDTI 04. d 07 p 08. NSM Colne and Villages *Blackb* 07-12; rtd 12; PtO *Leeds* from 13. *The Coach House, Foulds Road, Trawden, Colne BB8 8NT* T: (01282) 869876 E: priestlybrook1@btinternet.com

BROOK, Stephen Edward. b 44. Univ of Wales (Abth) BSc 65 DipEd 66. Wycliffe Hall Ox 71 All Nations Chr Coll 85. d 74 p 75. C Heworth H Trin *York* 74-77; C Linthorpe 77-80; TV Deane *Man* 80-85; Crosslinks 86-96; Portugal 88-96; P-in-c Bacup St Sav *Man* 96-03; P-in-c Tunstead 99-03; V Blackpool St Mark *Blackb* 03-12; P-in-c Blackpool St Mich 10-12; V Layton and Staining 12; rtd 12; PtO *Leic* from 13. *35 Oakham Grove, Ashby-de-la-Zouche LE65 2QP* E: revstephenbrook@gmail.com

BROOK, William Neville. b 31. S'wark Ord Course 66. d 69 p 70. C Maidstone St Martin *Cant* 69-75; V Hartlip w Stockbury 75-80; R Willesborough w Hinxhill 80-87; R Willesborough 87-89; V Gt Staughton and Hail Weston *Ely* 89-96; rtd 96; PtO *Chich* from 96. *27 Middleton Drive, Eastbourne BN23 6HD* T: (01323) 731243

BROOKE, Ailsa Rosanne. b 47. Yorks Min Course 10. d 12 p 13. NSM Upper Holme Valley *Leeds* from 12. *20 Fulstone Hall Lane, New Mill, Holmfirth HD9 7DW* T: (01484) 681155 E: ailsabrooke@tinyworld.co.uk

BROOKE, Miss Bridget Cecilia. b 31. Coll of Resurr Mirfield 88. d 89 p 94. Hon Par Dn Ranmoor *Sheff* 89-94; Hon C 94-04; Bp's Adv for NSMs 94-01; PtO from 04. *3 Magnolia Court, Storth Lane, Sheffield S10 3HN* T: 0114-230 2147

BROOKE, David Fewsdale. b 43. St Paul's Coll Grahamstown 80. d 90 p 90. Asst Chapl Dioc Coll Cape Town S Africa 90-92; NSM Crawford St Jo 93-97; NSM Sea Point St Jas 98-99; PtO *Newc* 00; C Norham and Duddo 01-04; C Cornhill w Carham 01-04; C Branxton 01-04; R Dunkeld *St And* from 04; R Strathtay from 04. *Spoutside, Snaigow, Dunkeld PH8 0RD* T: (01738) 710726 M: 07840-183707 E: stmarys.birnam@btinternet.com

BROOKE, David Martin. b 58. Selw Coll Cam BA 80 MA 83 Lon Inst of Educn PGCE 81. SAOMC 96. d 99 p 00. C Luton Lewsey St Hugh *St Alb* 99-00; NSM Sunnyside w Bourne End 00-02; C 02-04; V Bishopton w Gt Stainton *Dur* 04-13; R Redmarshall 04-13; R Grindon and Stillington 04-13; R Stockton Country Par from 14; P-in-c Billingham St Mary 10-13; AD Stockton from 07. *The Rectory, 22 Church Lane,*

Redmarshall, Stockton-on-Tees TS21 1ES   T: (01740) 630810 M: 07967-326085 E: revdbrooke@stocktonsix.org.uk *or* david@revd.co.uk

BROOKE, Katherine Margaret. b 58. GRSM 79 LRAM 80 ARCM 80. SAOMC 01. **d** 04 **p** 05. C Auckland St Andr and St Anne *Dur* 04-07; C Stranton 07-11; Chapl HM Pris Holme Ho from 11. *HM Prison Holme House, Holme House Road, Stockton-on-Tees TS18 2QU*   T: (01642) 744115 M: 07973-539729 E: katherine.brooke@hmps.gsi.gov.uk

BROOKE, Canon Robert. b 44. Qu Coll Birm 70. **d** 73 **p** 74. C Man Resurr 73-76; C Bournville *Birm* 76-77; Chapl Qu Eliz Coll *Lon* 77-82; C Bramley *Ripon* 82-85; TV 85-86; V Hunslet Moor St Pet and St Cuth 86-93; Chapl People w Learning Disabilities *Leeds* from 86; TV Seacroft *Ripon* 93-03; TV Beeston 03-10; Chapl Leeds Mental Health Teaching NHS Trust 94-03; Hon Can Ripon Cathl 01-10; rtd 10. *103 Crossgates Road, Leeds LS15 7PA*   E: bob.brooke@another.com

BROOKE, Canon Rosemary Jane. b 53. Cam Univ BEd 75 Open Univ BA 83. NOC 86. **d** 89 **p** 94. NSM Poynton *Ches* 89-05; Bp's Adv for Women in Min 96-05; P-in-c Werneth 05-10; Can Res Ches Cathl from 10. *3 Bridge Place, Chester CH1 1SA*   T: (01244) 351432 E: scrolls2@btinternet.com

BROOKE, Timothy Cyril. b 38. Les Coll Cam BA 60 MA 70 Middx Poly CQSW 76. Ripon Coll Cuddesdon 84. **d** 86 **p** 87. C Hillmorton *Cov* 86-90; V Earlsdon 90-98; V Cov St Fran N Radford 98-05; rtd 05; PtO *Cov* from 05. *80 Broadway, Coventry CV5 6NU*   T: (024) 7667 9126 E: brooke@care4free.net

BROOKE, Vernon. b 41. St Aid Birkenhead 62. **d** 65 **p** 66. C Crofton Park St Hilda w St Cypr *S'wark* 65-68; C Eccleshill *Bradf* 68-70; Ind Chapl *Linc* 70-84; *Derby* 84-97; *Chich* 97-06; rtd 06; PtO *Pet* from 06. *5 Blakesley Close, Northampton NN2 8PA*   T: (01604) 845585 E: vernonbrooke@yahoo.co.uk

BROOKE-TAYLOR, John Drury Arthur. b 48. Cam Univ BA 69 MA 73 Solomon Is Coll of HE Solicitor 72. Trin Coll Bris 11. **d** 13 **p** 14. OLM Clifton H Trin, St Andr and St Pet *Bris* from 13; OLM Bris St Steph w St Jas and St Jo w St Mich etc from 14. *2 Oldfield Road, Bristol BS8 4QQ*   T: 0117-926 5517 E: dru@brooke-taylor.freeserve.co.uk

BROOKER, Mrs Anna Lesley. b 56. York Univ BA 78 MA 79 Homerton Coll Cam PGCE 80. Ridley Hall Cam 01. **d** 03 **p** 04. C Brentford *Lon* 03-06; P-in-c Isleworth All SS 06-11; V 11-15; Dean of Women's Min Kensington Area 12-15; P-in-c Haswell, Shotton and Thornley *Dur* from 14. *The Vicarage, Shotton Colliery, Durham DH6 2JW*   E: albrooker@email.com

BROOKER, Ruth Muriel. b 53. Wycliffe Hall Ox 96. **d** 98 **p** 99. C Beverley Minster *York* 98-02; R Haddlesey w Hambleton and Birkin 02-03; PtO *S'well* 03-04; *Lich* from 05. *13 West Park Court, Connaught Road, Wolverhampton WV1 4SQ*   T: (01902) 711782 *or* (01384) 233511 E: ruth@christianvocations.org

BROOKER, Mrs Wendy Ann. b 41. St Alb Minl Tr Scheme 82. dss 85 **d** 87 **p** 94. Pinner *Lon* 85-87; Par Dn Greenhill St Jo 87-88; Ind Chapl 89-94; C Hayes St Edm 95-99; Chapl R Nat Orthopaedic Hosp NHS Trust from 99. *16 Rosecroft Walk, Pinner HA5 1LL*   T: (020) 8866 0795 E: wd.brooker@ukf.net

BROOKES, Colin Stuart. b 70. Lon Bible Coll BA 93. Ridley Hall Cam 00. **d** 02 **p** 03. C Cambridge St Barn *Ely* 02-06; C Woodside Park St Barn *Lon* from 06. *St Barnabas' Vicarage, 68 Westbury Road, London N12 7PD*   M: 07973-840340 E: colinbrookes@stbarnabas.co.uk

BROOKES, David Charles. b 45. St Mich Coll Llan 84. **d** 86 **p** 87. C Llanishen and Lisvane *Llan* 86-88; TV Brighouse St Martin *Wakef* 89-92; TV Brighouse and Clifton 92-94; V Hollingbourne and Hucking w Leeds and Broomfield *Cant* 94-03; rtd 03. *19 Orchards Rise, Richards Castle, Ludlow SY8 4EZ*   T: (01584) 831276 E: david@dcbrookes.freeserve.co.uk

BROOKES, Edwin William. b 39. St Mark & St Jo Coll Lon TCert 63 Birm Univ BPhil(Ed) 85 Open Univ BA 73 BA 93. OLM course 95. **d** 98 **p** 99. OLM Cen Wolverhampton *Lich* from 98. *23 Chetwynd Road, Blakenhall, Wolverhampton WV2 4NZ*   T: (01902) 654979 F: 562616 E: ed.brookes@blueyonder.co.uk

BROOKES, Geoffrey John Denis. b 24. CMS Tr Coll Crowther Hall 78 Ridley Hall Cam 84. **d** 85 **p** 86. Bahrain 85-88; Project Officer Ch Action w the Unemployed 88-91; Hon C Hastings All So *Chich* 88-91; Asst Chapl Milan w Genoa and Varese *Eur* 91-94; Canada 94-97; PtO *Chich* 97-99 and 01-02; *Guildf* 03-12. *50 Chapel Court, Church Street, Dorking RH4 1BT*   T: (01306) 884287

BROOKES, Keith Roy. b 37. JP 74. Leeds Univ DipEd 72 MHCIMA MRSPH. St Aid Birkenhead 64. **d** 80 **p** 81. Hon C Stockport St Thos *Ches* 80-85; Hon C Stockport St Thos w St Pet 86-91; C 91-98; Hon C 99-10. *42 Derby Road, Stockport SK4 4NE*   T: 0161-442 0301

BROOKES, Laurence. b 33. **d** 02 **p** 03. OLM Flockton cum Denby Grange *Wakef* 02-06; OLM Emley 02-06; PtO *Leeds*

from 06. *Treetops, 6 Chessington Drive, Flockton, Wakefield WF4 4TJ*   T: (01924) 848238 E: lauriemarybrookes@supanet.com

BROOKES, Mrs Marian. d 15. OLM Ripley *Derby* from 15. *12 Birch Close, Ripley DE5 3QA*   T: (01773) 745259 M: 07792-052150 E: marijimb@aol.com

BROOKES, Robin Keenan. b 47. Trin Coll Bris 72. **d** 75 **p** 76. C Livesey *Blackb* 75-78; C Burnley St Pet 78-80; P-in-c Bawdeswell w Foxley *Nor* 80-83; I Donagh w Tyholland and Errigal Truagh *Clogh* 83-91; Dioc Communications Officer 90-91; I Dublin Drumcondra w N Strand *D & G* 91-99; Chapl Ayia Napa Cyprus 99-06; Chapl Famagusta 06-10; PtO *Nor* from 11. *69 Beresford Road, Lowestoft NR32 2NQ*   T: (01502) 446301 *or* 583283 E: rkbc1947@gmail.com

BROOKES, Steven David. b 60. Lanc Univ BA 81. Ripon Coll Cuddesdon 82. **d** 85 **p** 86. C Stanley *Liv* 85-88; C W Derby St Mary 88-90; Chapl RN 90-94; R Weybridge *Guildf* 94-03; P-in-c Liv Our Lady and St Nic w St Anne 03-07; R Liv Our Lady and St Nic 07-13; Chapl R Hosp Chelsea from 13. *15 College Court, Royal Hospital Chelsea, Royal Hospital Road, London SW3 4SR*   T: (020) 7881 5238 *or* 7881 5234 M: 07930-855146 E: chaplain@chelsea-pensioners.org.uk

BROOKFIELD, Alun John. b 50. Lon Univ BMus 72 Spurgeon's Coll Lon BA 82. **d** 00 **p** 01. NSM Stratton St Margaret w S Marston etc *Bris* 00-02; P-in-c Cwmtawe Uchaf *S & B* 03-15; rtd 15. *Bryntirion, Capel Gwynfe, Llangadog SA19 9RE*   T: (01550) 740228 E: a.brookfield@ntlworld.com

BROOKFIELD, Patricia Anne. *See* HARDACRE, Patricia Anne

BROOKS, Alan Leslie. b 43. Nor City Coll TCert 65. Dioc OLM tr scheme 98. **d** 01 **p** 02. OLM Waterloo Ch Ch and St Jo *Liv* 01-13; rtd 13. *6 Kingsway, Waterloo, Liverpool L22 4RQ*   T: 0151-920 8770 E: alanbrooks@blueyonder.co.uk

BROOKS, Mrs Alison Margaret. b 46. EMMTC. **d** 03 **p** 04. Asst Chapl Qu Medical Cen Nottm Univ Hosp NHS Trust from 03. *12 Russell Avenue, Wollaton, Nottingham NG8 2BL*   T: 0115-928 6269 E: aandp.brooks@sb-computers.co.uk

BROOKS, Catherine Elizabeth. b 57. LCTP. **d** 08 **p** 09. C Blackb St Jas 08-12; C Blackb St Steph and St Jas 12-13; P-in-c Blackb St Fran and St Aid 13-10; P-in-c Blackb Christ the King 13-14; V Blackb St Aid, St Luke, St Mark and St Phil from 14. *St Aidan's Vicarage, 170 St Aidan's Avenue, Blackburn BB2 4EA*   T: (01254) 664093

BROOKS, Mrs Christine Anne. b 62. STETS. **d** 09 **p** 10. C N Poole Ecum Team *Sarum* 09-13; C Kinson and W Howe 13-14; TV from 14. *41 Moore Avenue, Bournemouth BH11 8AT*   T: (01202) 581135 *or* 911962 E: christine.brooks3@uwclub.net

BROOKS, Mrs Christine Ellen. b 43. Sheff Univ BA 65 Lon Univ BD 81 Lambeth STh 81. EAMTC 86. **d** 88 **p** 94. NSM Palgrave w Wortham and Burgate *St E* 88-89; Par Dn Thorndon w Rishangles, Stoke Ash, Thwaite etc 89-94; P-in-c Aldringham w Thorpe, Knodishall w Buxlow etc 94-04; R Whinlands 04-13; Asst P Sternfield w Benhall and Snape 98-03; P-in-c Alde River 03-06; rtd 13; PtO *St E* from 13. *Far End Cottage, Low Road, Friston, Saxmundham IP17 1PW*   T: (01728) 688972 M: 07752-652833 E: cebwhinlands@btinternet.com

BROOKS, David Edward. b 73. **d** 09 **p** 10. OLM Middleton and Thornham *Man* from 09. *The Vicarage, Boardman Lane, Middleton, Manchester M24 4TU*   M: 07904-520906 E: dave@thelaunch.org.uk

BROOKS, Dorothy Anne. *See* MOORE BROOKS, Dorothy Anne

BROOKS, Canon Francis Leslie. b 35. Kelham Th Coll 55. **d** 59 **p** 60. C Woodlands *Sheff* 59-61; Ind Missr S Yorkshire Coalfields 61-66; V Moorends *Sheff* 66-72; Chapl HM Borstal Hatfield 67-72; Chapl HM Pris Acklington 72-75; Chapl HM Borstal Wellingborough 75-79; Chapl HM Pris Wakef 79-83; Area Sec USPG Wakef and Bradf 83-88; V Carleton and E Hardwick *Wakef* 88-96; Can Mara (Tanzania) from 88; rtd 96; PtO *Wakef* 03-04; Hon C Chevington *Newc* 04-11. *5 Newfield Green Road, Sheffield S2 2BQ*

BROOKS, Glen. b 62. Ripon Coll Cuddesdon 12. **d** 14 **p** 15. C Northampton H Trin and St Paul *Pet* from 14. *104 Semilong Road, Northampton NN2 6EX*   T: (01604) 461232 M: 07967-672939 E: glen.brooks@virgin.net

BROOKS, Hannah Victoria. *See* HIGGINSON, Hannah Victoria

BROOKS, Ian George. b 47. Selw Coll Cam BA 68 MA 72. Chich Th Coll 68. **d** 70 **p** 71. C Stoke Newington St Mary *Lon* 70-74; C Hoxton St Anne w St Sav and St Andr 74-75; C Hoxton St Anne w St Columba 75-80; P-in-c Croxteth St Paul *CD Liv* 80-81; V Croxteth from 81. *St Paul's Vicarage, Delabole Road, Liverpool L11 6LG*   T/F: 0151-548 9009 E: frigb@blueyonder.co.uk

BROOKS, Jeremy Paul. b 67. Leic Univ LLB 88 Clare Coll Cam BA 96 MA 01 K Coll Lon MA 00. Ridley Hall Cam 94. **d** 97 **p** 98. C Highgate St Mich *Lon* 97-01; P-in-c Hoddesdon *St Alb*

01-07; V 07-10; TR Beaconsfield *Ox* from 10. *The Rectory, Wycombe End, Beaconsfield HP9 1NB* T: (01494) 730876 E: brooks.jeremy@sky.com

BROOKS, Jonathan Thorburn. b 53. Solicitor 76 G&C Coll Cam BA 75. Trin Coll Bris 84. **d** 86 **p** 87. C Dagenham *Chelmsf* 86-88; PtO *Glouc* 03; NSM Thornbury and Oldbury-on-Severn w Shepperdine 03-05. *12 Hyde Avenue, Thornbury, Bristol BS35 1JA* T: (01454) 411853

BROOKS, Malcolm David. b 45. **d** 71 **p** 72. C Pontlottyn w Fochriw *Llan* 71-72; C Caerphilly 72-78; V Ferndale w Maerdy 78-81; C Port Talbot St Theodore 82-84; V Ystrad Mynach 84-85; V Ystrad Mynach w Llanbradach 85-06. *33 Heol y Gors, Whitchurch, Cardiff CF14 1HF*

BROOKS (*née* LEWIS), Mrs Marjorie Ann. b 47. Liv Univ BA 68 Man Univ CertEd 69. WEMTC 07. **d** 13 **p** 14. OLM Bridgnorth, Tasley, Astley Abbotts, etc *Heref* from 13. *2 The Hawthorns, Bridgnorth WV16 5JG* T: (01746) 761942 M: 07751-553736 E: marjorie.brooks47@googlemail.com

BROOKS, Patrick John. b 27. Man Univ BA 49 DipEd. Oak Hill Th Coll 78. **d** 77 **p** 79. Burundi 77-80; PtO *Ex* 80-83; P-in-c Phillack w Gwithian and Gwinear *Truro* 83-88; R 88-93; rtd 93; PtO *Chich* from 93. *Abbots, Claigmar Road, Rustington, Littlehampton BN16 2NL*

BROOKS, Paul John. b 59. Loughb Univ BSc 81. St Jo Coll Nottm 87. **d** 90 **p** 91. C Long Eaton St Jo *Derby* 90-94; Min Jersey St Paul Prop Chpl *Win* from 94. *5 Claremont Avenue, St Saviour, Jersey JE2 7SF* T: (01534) 880393 E: pjbvic@aol.com

BROOKS, Peter. b 55. St Mich Coll Llan 97. **d** 99 **p** 00. C Morriston *S & B* 99-01; P-in-c Rhayader and Nantmel 01-02; P-in-c Cwmdauddwr w St Harmon and Llanwrthwl 02-05; P-in-c Llanwrthwl w St Harmon, Rhayader, Nantmel etc 05-08; P-in-c Gwastedyn 08-11; V Three Cliffs from 11. *The Vicarage, 88 Pennard Road, Pennard, Swansea SA3 2AD* T: (01792) 232928 E: peter.brooks256@btinternet.com

BROOKS, Philip. b 82. Reading Univ BA 03 MA 04 K Coll Lon MA 10. Ridley Hall Cam 10. **d** 13 **p** 14. C Oxted and Tandridge *S'wark* 13-14; C Oxted from 14. *3 Ravensbrook, 12 Snatts Hill, Oxted RH8 0BN* M: 07969-066906 E: phil_brooks1982@hotmail.com

BROOKS, Philip David. b 52. MA Cam Univ MTh. St Jo Coll Nottm 80. **d** 83 **p** 84. C Ipsley *Worc* 83-87; V Fulford w Hilderstone *Lich* 87-95; Chapl Stallington Hosp 87-95; P-in-c Crich *Derby* 95-01; V Crich and S Wingfield from 01; Dioc Adv Past Care and Counselling from 03; RD Alfreton from 09. *The Vicarage, 19 Coasthill, Crich, Matlock DE4 5DS* T: (01773) 852449 E: philipdbro@aol.com

BROOKS, Mrs Susan Margaret. b 50. Philippa Fawcett Coll CertEd 71 Open Univ BA 95. SEITE 00. **d** 03 **p** 11. NSM Chatham St Paul w All SS *Roch* 03-05; NSM Snodland All SS w Ch Ch from 11. *189 Malling Road, Snodland ME6 5EE* T: (01634) 241350 E: suebrooks@talk21.com

BROOKS, Mrs Susan Vera. b 51. NOC 87. **d** 90 **p** 94. Par Dn Carleton and E Hardwick *Wakef* 90-93; TV Almondbury w Farnley Tyas 93-98; Chapl Huddersfield NHS Trust 98-01; Chapl Calderdale and Huddersfield NHS Trust 01-03; Lead Chapl 03-12; NSM Crosland Moor and Linthwaite *Leeds* from 12. *44 Heaton Gardens, Huddersfield HD1 4JA* T: (01484) 538778

BROOKS, Mrs Vivien June. b 47. Univ of Wales (Ban) BA 68 Southn Univ MA 70. Ridley Hall Cam 87. **d** 89 **p** 95. C Exning St Martin w Landwade *St E* 89-92; Par Dn Hermitage and Hampstead Norreys, Cold Ash etc *Ox* 92-94; C 94-95; P-in-c Cox Green 95-03; Co Ecum Officer (Berks) 00-03; P-in-c Earls Colne w White Colne and Colne Engaine *Chelmsf* 03-04; TV Halstead Area 04-12; rtd 12; PtO *St E* from 13; *Chelmsf* from 14. *28 Normandie Way, Bures CO8 5BE* T: (01787) 227120 E: vivienbrooks@googlemail.com

BROOKS, Vivienne Christine. See ARMSTRONG-MacDONNELL, Vivienne Christine

BROOKSBANK, Alan Watson. b 43. Univ of Wales (Lamp) BA 64 Edin Univ MEd 76. Edin Th Coll 64. **d** 66 **p** 67. C Cleator Moor w Cleator *Carl* 66-70; V Dalston 70-80; P-in-c Greystoke, Matterdale and Mungrisdale 80-81; R 81-83; R Watermillock 81-83; R Hagley *Worc* 83-95; Bp's Officer for NSM 88-95; V Claines St Jo 95-98; rtd 98. *169 Northfields Lane, Brixham TQ5 8RD*

BROOKSHAW, Miss Janice Chitty. b 48. Anglia Ruskin Univ MA 12 MCIPD 90. Ripon Coll Cuddesdon 96. **d** 98 **p** 99. C Beaconsfield *Ox* 98-02; P-in-c The Stodden Churches *St Alb* 02-03; R 03-14; rtd 14. *3 The Old Dairy, Easton, Winchester SO21 1EU* T: (01962) 779988 E: revjanbrookshaw@btinternet.com

BROOM, The Ven Andrew Clifford. b 65. Keele Univ BSocSc 86. Trin Coll Bris BA 92. **d** 92 **p** 93. C Wellington All SS w Eyton *Lich* 92-96; C Brampton St Thos *Derby* 96-00; V Walton St Jo

00-09; Dir of Miss and Min 09-14; Hon Can Derby Cathl 11-14; Adn E Riding *York* from 14. *Brimley Lodge, 27 Molescroft Road, Beverley HU17 7DX* E: ader@yorkdiocese.org

BROOME, Mildred Dorothy. b 43. **d** 00 **p** 01. NSM Malden St Jo *S'wark* 00-13; PtO from 13. *124 The Manor Drive, Worcester Park KT4 7LW* T: (020) 8337 1572 E: m.broome@hotmail.co.uk

BROOMFIELD, Iain Jonathan. b 57. Univ Coll Ox MA 87. Wycliffe Hall Ox 80. **d** 83 **p** 84. C Beckenham Ch Ch *Roch* 83-87; Sen Schs Worker Titus Trust 87-00; V Bromley Ch Ch *Roch* from 00. *Christ Church Vicarage, 18 Highland Road, Bromley BR1 4AD* T: (020) 8313 9882 *or* 8464 1898 F: 8464 5846 E: iain.broomfield@christchurchbromley.org

BROOMHEAD, Mark Roger. b 71. Nottm Univ BSc 00. St Jo Coll Nottm 06. **d** 08 **p** 09. C N Wingfield, Clay Cross and Pilsley *Derby* 08-10; C Brampton St Thos from 10; C Chesterfield St Mary and All SS from 11; C Chesterfield SS Aug from 11; C Chesterfield H Trin and Ch from 11. *35 Whitecotes Park, Chesterfield S40 3RT* T: (01246) 555988 E: mark@theorderoftheblacksheep.com

BROSNAN, Mark. b 61. St Martin's Coll Lanc BA 83 RMN 88 Otley Agric Coll. EAMTC 92. **d** 95 **p** 96. C Rushmere *St E* 95-98; PtO *Chelmsf* 01-05; Hon C W w E Mersea 05-08; Hon C Peldon w Gt and Lt Wigborough 05-08; P-in-c Hadleigh St Barn 08-12; P-in-c Kirkbymoorside w Gillamoor, Farndale etc *York* 12; V from 12; C Kirby Misperton w Normanby and Salton from 12. *The Vicarage, Church Street, Kirkbymoorside, York YO62 6AZ* T: (01751) 431452 E: gohiking@hotmail.co.uk

BROSTER, Godfrey David. b 52. Ealing Tech Coll BA 75. Ripon Coll Cuddesdon 78. **d** 81 **p** 82. C Crayford *Roch* 81-82; C Brighton Resurr *Chich* 82-86; C-in-c The Hydneye CD 86-91; R Plumpton w E Chiltington 91-93; R Plumpton w E Chiltington cum Novington from 93. *The Rectory, Station Road, Plumpton Green, Lewes BN7 3BU* T: (01273) 890570

BROTHERSTON, Miss Isabel Mary. b 42. Cranmer Hall Dur 81. **dss** 83 **d** 87 **p** 94. Coleshill *Birm* 83-87; Par Dn Duddeston w Nechells 87-92; Par Dn Harlescott *Lich* 92-94; C 94-04; R Llanddulas and Llysfaen *St As* 04-08; rtd 08. *3 Marlow Terrace, Mold CH7 1HH* T: (01352) 756011 E: mbrother@live.co.uk

BROTHERTON, The Ven John Michael. b 35. St Jo Coll Cam BA 59 MA 63. Cuddesdon Coll 59. **d** 61 **p** 62. C Chiswick St Nic w St Mary *Lon* 61-65; Chapl Trin Coll Port of Spain Trinidad and Tobago 65-69; R Diego Martin 69-75; V Cowley St Jo *Ox* 76-81; Chapl St Hilda's Coll Ox 76-81; RD Cowley *Ox* 78-81; V Portsea St Mary *Portsm* 81-91; Hon Can Kobe Japan from 86; Adn Chich 91-02; rtd 02; PtO *Lon* from 03; *Chich* from 03. *Flat 2, 23 Gledhow Gardens, London SW5 0AZ* T: (020) 7373 5147 E: jmbrotherton@yahoo.co.uk

BROTHERTON, Michael. b 56. MBE 93. Univ of Wales (Abth) BD 80. Wycliffe Hall Ox 80. **d** 81 **p** 82. Hon Chapl Miss to Seamen 81-84; C Pembroke Dock *St D* 81-84; Chapl RN 84-11; rtd 11. *Address temp unknown*

BROTHERWOOD, Nicholas Peter. b 50. Oak Hill Th Coll BA 83. **d** 83 **p** 84. C Nottingham St Nic *S'well* 83-86; Canada from 86; Dir Quebec Lodge 86-89; Angl Chapl McGill Univ 89-91; Assoc R Westmount St Steph from 91. *3498 Harvard Avenue, Montreal QC H4A 2W3, Canada* T: (001) (514) 489 4158 F: 932 0550 E: st.stephens@qc.aira.com

BROTHWELL, Paul David. b 37. Lich Th Coll 62. **d** 65 **p** 66. C Honley *Wakef* 65-68; Min Can Wakef Cathl 68-71; V Whittington St Giles *Lich* 71-83; P-in-c Weeford 78-83; V Whittington w Weeford 83-92; Chapl Kidderminster Gen Hosp 92-94; Chapl Kidderminster Health Care NHS Trust 94-99; Chapl Worcs Acute Hosps NHS Trust 00-01; Chapl Worcs Community and Mental Health Trust 01-02; Hon Can Antananarivo 02; rtd 02; PtO *Worc* from 02. *8 Hillside Close, Stourport-on-Severn DY13 0JW* T: (01299) 823495 *or* (01562) 823424 ext 3306 E: paul.brothwell@btopenworld.com

BROTHWELL, Ruth. b 60. **d** 10 **p** 12. NSM Merrow *Guildf* 10-13; NSM Worplesdon 13-15; PtO from 15. *Foxgrove, Burnt Common Lane, Ripley, Woking GU23 6HD* T: (01483) 223571 E: ruthbrothwell@yahoo.com

BROTHWOOD, Ian Sidney. b 56. K Coll Lon BD 84. Linc Th Coll 87. **d** 89 **p** 90. C Selsdon St Jo w St Fran *S'wark* 89-97; P-in-c S Norwood St Alb 93-97; V 97-99; V Reigate St Mark 99-04; P-in-c Selsdon St Jo w St Fran 04-06; R 06-12; V Croydon St Mich w St Jas from 12. *St Michael's Vicarage, 39 Oakfield Road, Croydon CR0 2UX* T: (020) 8686 9343 E: fr.ian@btinternet.com

BROTHWOOD, John. b 31. Peterho Cam MA 55 MB, BChir 55. S'wark Ord Course 89. **d** 91 **p** 92. NSM Dulwich St Barn S'wark 91-04. *98 Woodwarde Road, London SE22 8UT* T: (020) 8693 8273

BROUGH, Gerald William. b 32. Trin Coll Cam BA 55 MA 59. Ridley Hall Cam 55. **d** 57 **p** 58. C Westgate St Jas *Cant* 57-60; C New Addington 60-62; V Mancetter *Cov* 62-73; P-in-c

Bourton w Frankton and Stretton on Dunsmore etc 73-74; R 74-93; rtd 93; PtO *Cov* from 93. *17 Brookhurst Court, Beverley Road, Leamington Spa CV32 6PB* T: (01926) 430759 E: gwbrls@aol.com

BROUGH (née CROWLE), Mrs Sarah Ann. b 65. Ripon Coll Cuddesdon BTh 99. **d** 99 **p** 00. C Godalming *Guildf* 99-03; Chapl Godalming Coll 01-03; R Chiddingfold *Guildf* from 03. *The Rectory, Coxcombe Lane, Chiddingfold, Godalming GU8 4QA* T: (01428) 682008 M: 07747-031524 E: sarahbrough@btinternet.com

BROUGHALL, Rodney John. b 32. **d** 96 **p** 97. OLM Watton w Carbrooke and Ovington *Nor* 96-02; rtd 02; PtO *Nor* from 02. *15 Garden Close, Watton, Thetford IP25 6DP* T: (01953) 881989 E: rodbroughall@hotmail.com

BROUGHTON, James Roger. b 48. Leeds Univ BA 71 Nottm Univ CertEd 72 Liv Univ MEd 00. Wycliffe Hall Ox 87. **d** 89 **p** 90. C Stoneycroft All SS *Liv* 89-92; P-in-c Carr Mill 92-94; V 94-96; Chapl Duke of York's R Mil Sch Dover 96-08; rtd 08; PtO *Cant* from 08. *Woodstock, St Vincent Road, St Margarets-at-Cliffe, Dover CT15 6ET* T: (01304) 853840

BROUGHTON, Lynne Mary. b 46. Melbourne Univ BA 67 PhD 79. EAMTC 99. **d** 00 **p** 01. NSM Wood Ditton w Saxon Street *Ely* 00-07; NSM Kirtling 00-07; NSM Cheveley 00-07; NSM Ashley w Silverley 00-07; PtO from 07. *85 Richmond Road, Cambridge CB4 3PS* T: (01223) 322014 E: lmb27@hermes.cam.ac.uk

BROUGHTON, Canon Stuart Roger. b 36. Wilson Carlile Coll 59 St Mich Coll Llan 61. **d** 64 **p** 65. C Bromley Ch Ch *Roch* 64-67; SAMS 67-79 and 86-95; Miss Paraguayan Chaco Paraguay 67-70; R Salvador Gd Shep Brazil 70-79; V Stoke sub Hamdon *B & W* 79-83; Hon CF 82-86; V Blackb Ch Ch w St Matt 83-86; R Alcacer do Sal Portugal 86-91; Chapl Rio de Janeiro Brazil 91-95; rtd 96; Chapl Agia Napa Cyprus 96; Chapl Ch Ch Cathl Falkland Is 97-98; P-in-c Corfu *Eur* 98-01; Hon C Jersey St Paul Prop Chpl *Win* 01-03; Chapl to Abp Congo 03-05; Hon Can Bukavu from 04; LtO Sydney Australia 06-11; PtO *St Alb* 12-13. *45 West Street, Southport PR8 1QS* E: stuartrbroughtonsouthport@gmail.com

BROUN, Canon Claud Michael. b 30. BNC Ox BA 55. Edin Th Coll 56. **d** 58 **p** 59. Chapl St Mary's Cathl 58-62; Can St Mary's Cathl 84-95; Hon Can St Mary's Cathl from 95; P-in-c Cambuslang 62-70; R 70-75; R Hamilton 75-88; R Gatehouse of Fleet 88-95; R Kirkcudbright 88-95; rtd 95. *Martin Lodge, Ardross Place, Alness IV17 0PX* T: (01349) 882442

BROWELL (née SHILLINGTON), Mrs Maureen Lesley. b 57. MIH 89. NEOC 02. **d** 05 **p** 06. Soc Resp Officer *Ripon* 99-08; NSM Hoylandswaine and Silkstone w Stainborough *Wakef* 05-08; TV Almondbury w Farnley Tyas 08-12; Dioc Co-ord for Soc Resp 08-10; V Hoylandswaine and Silkstone w Stainborough *Leeds* from 12. *The Vicarage, 12 High Street, Silkstone, Barnsley S75 4JN* T: (01226) 492294 M: 07930-194421 E: maureenbrowell@talktalk.net

BROWN, Mrs Ailsa Elizabeth. b 64. Hull Univ BA 94 Nottm Univ MA 10. EMMTC 07. **d** 10 **p** 11. NSM Barton upon Humber *Linc* from 10. *21 Ferriby Road, Barton-upon-Humber DN18 5LE* T: (01652) 634855 E: brown5le@btinternet.com

BROWN, Canon Alan. b 37. Tyndale Hall Bris 59. **d** 63 **p** 64. C Braintree *Chelmsf* 63-66; C Tooting Graveney St Nic *S'wark* 66-68; C Chesham St Mary *Ox* 68-70; V Hornsey Rise St Mary *Lon* 70-75; V Sidcup Ch Ch *Roch* 75-88; V Newport St Jo *Portsm* 88-01; P-in-c Newport St Thos 96-99; V 99-01; RD W Wight 91-96; Hon Can Portsm Cathl 95-01; rtd 01. *65 Sherbourne Avenue, Ryde PO33 3PW* T: (01983) 566956

BROWN, Alan George. b 51. Bradf Univ BSc 84 Leeds Univ CertEd 81 MBA 92 SRN 72 RMN 75 RNT 81. NOC 92. **d** 95 **p** 96. NSM Ilkley St Marg *Bradf* 95-10; Hd of Division Applied Health Studies Leeds Univ 98-07; Bp's Adv for Hosp Chapl *Bradf* 03-14; LtO 10-14; Bp's Inspector for Minl Tr *Leeds* from 10; PtO *York* from 14. *Argyll Lodge, High Street, Scalby, Scarborough YO13 0PT* T: (01723) 503122 E: brown.alan.george@gmail.com

BROWN, Alan Michael Ernest. b 52. St Chad's Coll Dur BA 74. St Jo Coll Nottm 81. **d** 83 **p** 84. C Bridlington Priory *York* 83-86; V Morton St Luke *Bradf* 86-02; PtO *Leeds* from 04; Mental Health Worker Bradf City Primary Care Trust 02-07. *6 South View Terrace, Bingley BD16 3EJ* T: (01274) 511970

BROWN, Alec George. b 53. Univ of Zimbabwe DipSW 80 Univ of Wales (Cardiff) MSc(Econ) 87. St Deiniol's Hawarden 88 NOC 90. **d** 93 **p** 94. C Stockton Heath *Ches* 93-96; C Thelwall 96-97; V 97-01; V Gt Budworth from 01; P-in-c Antrobus from 13; RD Gt Budworth from 10. *The Vicarage, High Street, Great Budworth, Northwich CW9 6HF* T: (01606) 891324 E: alec-brown@tiscali.co.uk

BROWN, Mrs Alison Louise. b 60. RGN 83. STETS 05. **d** 08 **p** 09. C Horsell *Guildf* 08-12; C N Hants Downs *Win* from 12. *The Vicarage, The Bury, Odiham, Hook RG29 1ND* T: (01256) 704154 E: alison@slbalb.co.uk

BROWN, Allan James. b 47. K Coll Lon BD 69 AKC 69 MTh 70. St Aug Coll Cant 69. **d** 73 **p** 74. Chapl St Geo Sch Jerusalem 73-74; Chapl St Marg Sch Nazareth 74-75; C Clifton *S'well* 75-77; CF 77-99; Asst Chapl Gen 99-00; V Ilkeston St Mary *Derby* 00-10; P-in-c Ilkeston St Jo 05-10; rtd 10; PtO *S'well* from 10. *63 Highfield Road, Nottingham NG2 6DR* E: brown@lorisallan.freeserve.co.uk

BROWN, Andrew. b 65. **d** 95 **p** 96. OLM Heywood *Man* 95-05. *24 Honiton Close, Heywood OL10 2PF* T: (01706) 623091

BROWN, Andrew (Bod). b 66. Man Univ BSc 87. Oak Hill Th Coll BA 02. **d** 03 **p** 04. C Hyde St Geo *Ches* 03-06; V Weaverham from 06. *The Vicarage, Church Street, Weaverham, Northwich CW8 3NJ* T: (01606) 852110 E: weaverhamvicar@dsl.pipex.com

BROWN, The Ven Andrew. b 55. St Pet Coll Ox BA 80 MA 82. Ridley Hall Cam 79. **d** 80 **p** 81. C Burnley St Pet *Blackb* 80-82; C Elton All SS *Man* 82-86; P-in-c Ashton St Pet 86-93; V 94-96; V Halliwell St Luke 96-03; Can Th Derby Cathl and Dioc CME Adv *Derby* 03-11; Adn of Man *S & M* from 11; V Douglas St Geo 11-14; V Douglas St Geo and All SS from 15. *St George's Vicarage, 16 Devonshire Road, Douglas, Isle of Man IM2 3RB* T: (01624) 675430 E: archdeacon@sodorandman.im

BROWN, Andrew James. b 71. **d** 11 **p** 12. C Walton Breck *Liv* 11-15; TR Fazakerley Em from 15. *St Paul's Vicarage, Formosa Drive, Liverpool L10 7LB*

BROWN, Andrew James. b 60. Univ of Wales (Ban) BA 81. Ripon Coll Cuddesdon 07. **d** 09 **p** 10. C Castle Bromwich SS Mary and Marg *Birm* 09-13; P-in-c Eccleston *Blackb* from 13; P-in-c Charnock Richard from 13. *The Rectory, 30 Lawrence Lane, Eccleston, Chorley PR7 5SJ* T: (01257) 452777 E: father.andrew@btinternet.com

BROWN, Mrs Angela. b 58. SWMTC 11. **d** 14 **p** 15. C Redruth w Lanner and Treleigh *Truro* from 14. *11 Park Road, Redruth TR15 2JF* T: (01209) 210980 M: 07729-118696 E: angela@soulspark.org.uk

BROWN, Canon Anne Elizabeth. b 61. SWMTC 06. **d** 09 **p** 10. C Probus, Ladock and Grampound w Creed and St Erme *Truro* 09-12; P-in-c Three Rivers from 12; Hon Can Truro Cathl from 15. *52 Trelinnoe Gardens, South Petherwin, Launceston PL15 7TH* T: (01566) 770649

BROWN, Anthony Frank Palmer. b 31. Fitzw Ho Cam BA 56 Fitzw Coll Cam MA 84. Cuddesdon Coll 56. **d** 58 **p** 59. C Aldershot St Mich *Guildf* 58-61; C Chiswick St Nic w St Mary *Lon* 61-66; Asst Chapl Lon Univ 65-70; LtO 70-72; C-in-c Hammersmith SS Mich and Geo White City Estate CD 72-74; P-in-c Upper Sunbury St Sav 74-80; V 80-01; rtd 01; PtO *Chich* from 02. *6 Church Lane, Ditchling, Hassocks BN6 8TB* T: (01273) 843847

BROWN, Preb Anthony Paul. b 55. Reading Univ BSc 75 MRICS 87. Qu Coll Birm 77. **d** 80 **p** 81. C Pelsall *Lich* 80-83; C Leighton Buzzard w Eggington, Hockliffe etc *St Alb* 83-87; TV Langley Marish *Ox* 87-93; V Pet St Mary Boongate 93-98; TR Wombourne w Trysull and Bobbington *Lich* 98-02; TR Smestow Vale from 02; Preb Lich Cathl from 09. *The Vicarage, School Road, Wombourne, Wolverhampton WV5 9ED* T: (01902) 892234 *or* 897700 E: revpbrown@aol.com

BROWN, Antony William Keith. b 26. RN Coll Dartmouth 43. Trin Coll Bris 86. **d** 87 **p** 88. NSM Lawrence Weston *Bris* 87-89; Chapl Casablanca *Eur* 89-93; Asst Chapl Paris St Mich 94-00; rtd 00; PtO *Bris* from 01. *50 Oatley House, Cote Lane, Bristol BS9 3TN* T: 0117-962 8067 E: brownantony26@gmail.com

BROWN, Arthur William Stawell. b 26. St Jo Coll Ox BA 50 MA 51. Cuddesdon Coll 63. **d** 65 **p** 66. C Edin St Jo 65-66; C Petersfield w Sheet *Portsm* 67-75; V Portsea St Alb 75-79; R Smithfield St Bart Gt *Lon* 79-91; R St Sepulchre w Ch Ch Greyfriars etc 81-91; Chapl Madeira *Eur* 90-93; rtd 91; PtO *Ex* 93-09. *Clare Park, Crondall, Farnham GU10 5DT* T: (01252) 851200

BROWN, Barry Ronald. b 48. Ridley Coll Melbourne ThL 72. **d** 73 **p** 74. Australia 73-77 and 85-95; C Richmond St Mary *S'wark* 78-79; C Richmond St Mary w St Matthias and St Jo 79; C Edin Old St Paul 79-80; Chapl Belgrade w Zagreb *Eur* 81-82; Canada from 95. *52 Queen Street, Belleville ON K8N 1T7, Canada* T: (001) (613) 968 9873 E: bbrownhome@hotmail.com

BROWN, Benjamin Brumas Martin. b 71. Goldsmiths' Coll Lon BA 99 Jes Coll Cam BA 11. Westcott Ho Cam 09. **d** 12 **p** 13. C Cheam *S'wark* from 12. *4 Tudor Close, Sutton SM3 8QS* T: (020) 8641 2183 M: 07890-858121 E: brownoctopus@yahoo.com

BROWN, Canon Bernard Herbert Vincent. b 26. Mert Coll Ox BA 50 MA 52. Westcott Ho Cam 50. **d** 52 **p** 53. C Rugby

St Andr *Cov* 52-56; C Stoke Bishop *Bris* 56-59; Youth Chapl 56-62; Ind Chapl *Roch* 62-73; Bp's Dom Chapl 66-73; R Crawley *Chich* 73-79; TR 79-83; Ind Chapl *Bris* 83-92; Bp's Soc and Ind Adv 84-92; Hon Can Bris Cathl 85-92; RD Bris City 85-91; rtd 92; PtO *Sarum* from 92. *33B London Road, Dorchester DT1 1NF* T: (01305) 260806
E: jcullenbrown@btinternet.com

BROWN, Bill Charles Balfour. b 44. Linc Th Coll 87. **d** 89 **p** 90. C Moulsham St Luke *Chelmsf* 89-91; C Prittlewell 91-94; V Worksop St Paul *S'well* 95-12; rtd 12. *46 Holding, Worksop S81 0TD* E: fatherbill@btopenworld.com

BROWN, Bod. *See* BROWN, Andrew

BROWN (née BRYCE), Mrs Brenda Dorothy. b 48. **d** 11 **p** 13. NSM Trowell, Awsworth and Cossall *S'well* from 11. *41 Park Hill, Awsworth, Nottingham NG16 2RD* T: 0115-932 9328

BROWN, Brian Ernest. b 36. ALA 64. Oak Hill NSM Course 82. **d** 85 **p** 86. NSM Wallington *S'wark* 85-91; C 91-00; rtd 00; PtO *Nor* from 00. *6 Burnside, Necton, Swaffham PE37 8ER* T: (01760) 721292 E: briansylviabrown@aol.com

BROWN, Mrs Caroline Jane. b 59. Sussex Univ BA 80. Westcott Ho Cam 05. **d** 09 **p** 10. C Prittlewell *Chelmsf* 09-10; C Hadleigh St Jas 10-13; P-in-c Gt Waltham w Ford End from 13; P-in-c The Chignals w Mashbury from 13; P-in-c Gt and Lt Leighs and Lt Waltham from 15. *The Vicarage, 1 Glebe Meadow, Great Waltham, Chelmsford CM3 1EX* T: (01245) 364081 M: 07511-632903 E: cj.brown42@hotmail.co.uk

BROWN, Caryll Diane. b 50. **d** 13 **p** 14. OLM E w W Harling, Bridgham w Roudham, Larling etc *Nor* from 13. *Carrick House, 7 West Harling Road, East Harling, Norwich NR16 2SL* T: (01953) 717451 E: c@rrickhouse.com

BROWN, Charles Henry. b 48. Tulane Univ (USA) BA 70 Ch Coll Cam 75 MA 81. Westcott Ho Cam. **d** 00 **p** 01. C Boston *Linc* 00-03; Lect 03-05; Lic Preacher 05-06; P-in-c Crowland from 06. *The Abbey Rectory, East Street, Crowland, Peterborough PE6 0EN* T: (01733) 211763

BROWN, Mrs Christine Ann. b 42. Keele Univ CertEd 72. LCTP 10. **d** 11 **p** 12. NSM Dent w Cowgill *Bradf* 11-12; NSM Carl from 12. *Dale View, Laning, Dent, Sedbergh LA10 5QJ* T: (015396) 25418 E: christinelucy2014@gmail.com

BROWN, Mrs Christine Lilian. b 54. Ex Univ BA 75 Newc Univ MA 93. NEOC 01. **d** 04 **p** 05. NSM Ponteland *Newc* from 04; Chapl St Oswald's Hospice Newc from 08. *4 Woodlands, Ponteland, Newcastle upon Tyne NE20 9EU* T: (01661) 824196

BROWN, Christopher. *See* BROWN, Paul David Christopher

BROWN, Christopher. b 38. AKC 62 CQSW 68. St Boniface Warminster 62. **d** 63 **p** 64. C Crofton Park St Hilda w St Cypr *S'wark* 63-64; C S Beddington St Mich 64-67; C Herne Hill St Paul 67-68; LtO 68-72; *Lich* 72-76; *Worc* 77-79; *Ox* 79-86; PtO *Birm* 74-76; *Worc* 76-79; *Ox* 79-86; *Chelmsf* from 86; Dir and Chief Exec NSPCC 89-95. *7 Baronia Croft, Colchester CO4 9EE* T: (01206) 852904 E: chribrow@yahoo.co.uk

BROWN, Christopher. b 43. Linc Th Coll 79. **d** 81 **p** 82. C Stafford St Jo *Lich* 81-85; V Alton w Bradley-le-Moors and Oakamoor w Cotton 85-94; Chapl Asst Nottm City Hosp NHS Trust 94-05; Sen Chapl 05-06; rtd 06. *3 Kingsbury Drive, Nottingham NG8 3EP* T: 0115-929 4821
E: revbrowncj@aol.com

BROWN, Christopher Charles. b 58. Univ of Wales (Cardiff) LLB 79 Solicitor 82. Westcott Ho Cam 87. **d** 90 **p** 91. C Taunton St Mary *B & W* 90-94; R Timsbury and Priston 94-00; P-in-c Urmston *Man* 00-10; AD Stretford 05-10; TR Radcliffe 10-14; V Fishguard w Llanychar and Pontfaen w Morfil etc *St D* from 14. *The Vicarage, High Street, Fishguard SA65 9AU* T: (01348) 875536 E: revchrisbrown4@gmail.com

BROWN, Christopher David. b 49. Birm Univ BEd 72. St Mich Coll Llan 92. **d** 94 **p** 95. C Swansea St Thos and Kilvey *S & B* 94-96; C Swansea St Jas 96-98; St Helena 99-01; Chapl and Hd RS Epsom Coll 01-03; Chapl Ellesmere Coll 03-05. *Flat 1, 13 Worcester Road, Malvern WR14 4QY*
E: kristophdavid@hotmail.com

BROWN, Christopher Edgar Newall. b 31. Oak Hill Th Coll 51. **d** 55 **p** 56. C Surbiton Hill Ch Ch *S'wark* 55-57; C Gipsy Hill Ch Ch 57-61; V Plumstead All SS 61-70; V Sissinghurst *Cant* 70-73; P-in-c Frittenden 72-73; R Sissinghurst w Frittenden 73-76; PtO *S & M* 84-91 and from 96; Bp's Dom Chapl 91-95; rtd 96. *21 College Green, Castletown, Isle of Man IM9 1BE* T: (01624) 822364

BROWN, Christopher Howard. b 49. **d** 03 **p** 04. OLM Uttoxeter Area *Lich* from 03. *21 Carter Street, Uttoxeter ST14 8EY* T: (01889) 567492 E: revchrishbrown@aol.co.uk

BROWN, Christopher James. b 50. Open Univ MA 92. Trin Coll Bris 91. **d** 93 **p** 94. C Skelmersdale St Paul *Liv* 93-97; Chapl Asst Salford R Hosps NHS Trust 97-03; Chapl Trafford Healthcare NHS Trust from 03. *Trafford Healthcare NHS Trust, Moorside Road, Davyhulme, Manchester M41 5SL* T: 0161-748 4022 *or* 746 2624

BROWN, Clive Lindsey. b 33. Southn Univ BA 55. Oak Hill Th Coll 57. **d** 59 **p** 60. C Becontree St Mary *Chelmsf* 59-62; P-in-c Balgowlah w Manly Vale Australia 62-69; P-in-c Balgowlah Heights 66-69; R 69-72; R Roseville E 72-98; rtd 98. *14/11 Addison Road, Manly NSW 2095, Australia*

BROWN, Prof Colin. b 32. Liv Univ BA 53 Lon Univ BD 58 Nottm Univ MA 61 DD 94 Bris Univ PhD 70. Tyndale Hall Bris 55. **d** 58 **p** 59. C Chilwell *S'well* 58-61; Lect Tyndale Hall Bris 61-78; Vice Prin 67-70; Dean Studies 70-71; Prof Systematic Th Fuller Th Sem California USA from 78; Assoc R Altadena St Mark from 80; Assoc Dean Adv Th Studies 88-97; rtd 00. *1024 Beverly Way, Altadena CA 91001-2516, USA* T: (001) (626) 798 7180 E: colbrn@fuller.edu

BROWN, Daniel James. b 83. Sheff Univ BA 06 MA 13. Yorks Min Course 10. **d** 13 **p** 14. C Philadelphia St Thos *Sheff* from 13. *6 Gilpin Street, Sheffield S6 3RG* T: 0114-241 9560 E: dan.brown@stthomaschurch.org.uk

BROWN, David. **d** 15 **p** 15. C Woodside Park St Barn *Lon* from 15. *St Barnabas' Church, Holden Road, London N12 7DN* T: (020) 8343 5770 E: davidbrown@stbarnabas.co.uk

BROWN, David Andrew. b 72. York Univ BA 93. Wycliffe Hall Ox BTh 04. **d** 04 **p** 05. C Rugby St Matt *Cov* 04-07; C Rugby W 08; P-in-c Budbrooke 08-14; V from 14. *23 Robins Grove, Warwick CV34 6RF* T: (01926) 497298

BROWN, David Charles Girdlestone. b 42. Solicitor 67. S'wark Ord Course 87. **d** 90 **p** 91. NSM Milford *Guildf* 90-92; NSM Haslemere 92-01; PtO *Chich* 02-04 and from 14; LtO 04-08; P-in-c Barlavington, Burton w Coates, Sutton and Bignor 08-14; rtd 14. *The Orchard, Rogate, Petersfield GU31 5HU* T: (01730) 821867 E: dbrown501@btinternet.com

BROWN, David Frederick. b 38. Univ of Illinois BA 60. Seabury-Western Th Sem MDiv 67. **d** 67 **p** 67. C Evanston St Mark USA 67-68; C Camarillo St Columba 68-69; P-in-c 69-70; C San Francisco H Innocents 70-75; C Grace Cathl 70-75; Hon C Battersea Ch Ch and St Steph *S'wark* 78-83; Sen Chapl R Marsden NHS Trust 83-00; rtd 00; PtO *Lon* from 02. *12 Caversham House, 21-25 Caversham Street, London SW3 4AE* T: (020) 7352 3457

BROWN, Canon David Lloyd. b 44. TCD BTh 90. **d** 86 **p** 87. C Cregagh *D & D* 86-91; Bp's C Knocknagoney 91-12; I from 12; Can Down Cathl from 07. *The Aslan Centre, 13A Knocknagoney Road, Belfast BT4 2NF* T/F: (028) 9076 3343 T: 9076 0420 E: davidlloydbrown@googlemail.com

BROWN, David Mark. b 67. Bp Grosseteste Coll BSc 93. Oak Hill Th Coll 05. **d** 07. C Sidmouth, Woolbrook, Salcombe Regis, Sidbury etc *Ex* 07-11; P-in-c Stevenage St Nic and Graveley *St Alb* from 11. *St Nicholas' House, 2A North Road, Stevenage SG1 4AF* T: (01438) 354355 M: 07814-911937 E: revdmb@aol.com

BROWN, David Victor Arthur. b 44. Em Coll Cam BA 66 MA 70 CertEd. Linc Th Coll 72. **d** 74 **p** 75. C Bourne *Linc* 74-77; Chapl St Steph Coll Broadstairs 77-79; Chapl Asst N Gen Hosp Sheff 81-84; C Sheff St Cuth 81-84; Chapl Ridge Lea Hosp Lanc 84-92; Chapl Lanc Moor Hosp 84-92; Chapl Lanc R Infirmary 87-92; Chapl Lanc Priority Services NHS Trust and Lanc Acute Hosps NHS Trust 92-98; Chapl Morecambe Bay Hosps NHS Trust and Morecambe Bay Primary Care Trust 98-09; Hon C Scorton and Barnacre and Calder Vale *Blackb* 06-09; P-in-c 09-12; V 12-14; P-in-c Warsaw *Eur* from 14. *ul Dorotowska 7/5, Warsaw 02-347, Poland* E: dlgbrown@aol.com

BROWN, Prof David William. b 48. Edin Univ MA 70 Oriel Coll Ox BA 72 Clare Coll Cam PhD 76 FBA 02. Westcott Ho Cam 75. **d** 76 **p** 77. Chapl, Fell and Tutor Oriel Coll Ox 76-90; Van Mildert Prof Div Dur Univ 90-07; Can Res Dur Cathl 90-07; Wardlaw Prof St Andr Univ *St And* from 07. *St Mary's College, University of St Andrews, St Andrews KY16 9JU* E: dwb21@st-andrews.ac.uk

BROWN (née BOWERS), Lady (Denise Frances). b 50. City Univ BSc 72. SAOMC 99. **d** 02 **p** 03. NSM Beedon and Peasemore w W Ilsley and Farnborough *Ox* 02-10; NSM Brightwalton w Catmore, Leckhampstead etc 05-10; NSM E Downland from 10. *Bridleway Cottage, Stanmore, Beedon, Newbury RG20 8SR* T/F: (01635) 281825 M: 07901-914975

BROWN, Derek. *See* BROWN, John Derek

BROWN, Derek. b 42. Lindisfarne Regional Tr Partnership 10. **d** 10 **p** 11. NSM Gateshead St Helen *Dur* from 10; PtO from 15. *29 Heathfield Road, Gateshead NE9 5HH* T: 0191-487 5922 M: 07985-512766 E: derekderekb@aol.com

BROWN, Canon Henry Pridgeon. b 46. Cam Coll of Art and Tech BA 67 Leeds Univ PGCE 71. St Steph Ho Ox 90. **d** 92 **p** 93. C Finchley St Mary *Lon* 92-95; C W Hampstead St Jas 95-99; V Eyres Monsell *Leic* 99-08; TV Leic Presentation 08-09; Min Leic St Barn CD 09-13; rtd 13; PtO *Leic* from 13. *38 Gainsborough Road, Leicester LE2 3DE* T: 0116-270 9750 E: dbrown@leicester.anglican.org

BROWN

BROWN, Canon Donald Fryer. b 31. St Jo Coll Dur BA 56. Cranmer Hall Dur 60. **d** 61 **p** 62. Min Can Bradf Cathl 61-64; C Bingley All SS 64-66; V Low Moor H Trin 66-97; Hon Can Bradf Cathl 85-97; RD Bowling and Horton 87-95; rtd 97; PtO *Leeds* from 97. *3 Northfield Gardens, Wibsey, Bradford BD6 1LQ* T: (01274) 671869 E: donaldandiris@hotmail.co.uk

BROWN, Mrs Doreen Marion. b 39. Cam Univ CertEd 67. NOC 85. **d** 88 **p** 94. Par Dn Axminster, Chardstock, Combe Pyne and Rousdon *Ex* 88-92; Ind Chapl *Linc* 92-98; TV Brumby 98-05; rtd 05. *7 Thorngarth Lane, Barrow-upon-Humber DN19 7AW* T: (01469) 532102 E: doreen.bn@lineone.net

BROWN, Douglas Adrian Spencer. b 29. Univ of W Aus BA 50 MA 71 K Coll Lon MTh 90. St Mich Th Coll Crafers 50. **d** 53 **p** 54. SSM 54-00; Chapl St Mich Th Coll Crafers Australia 54-60; Chapl Kelham Th Coll 60-66; Chapl Univ of W Aus Australia 66-71; P-in-c Canberra St Alb 71-75; Warden St Mich Th Coll Crafers 75-82; P-in-c Adelaide St Jo 78-82; Academic Dean Adelaide Coll of Div 79-81; Visiting Scholar Union Th Sem NY 82; President Adelaide Coll of Div 88; PtO *Lon* 88-90; Chapl Bucharest w Sofia *Eur* 90-91; Dir Angl Cen Rome 91-95; Chapl Palermo w Taormina *Eur* 95-96; Lect Newton Th Coll Papua New Guinea 97; PtO *Dur* 97-00; S'wark 99-00; Dir Nor Cathl Inst 00-02; Hon PV Nor Cathl 00-02; PtO 01-02. *6 Gilmour Road, Roleystone WA 6111, Australia* E: brown.douglas75@gmail.com

BROWN, Mrs Elizabeth Alexandra Mary Gordon. b 67. Westcott Ho Cam 06. **d** 08 **p** 09. C Merrow *Guildf* 08-11; NSM Bedlington *Newc* from 12. *68 Shields Road, Morpeth NE61 2RZ* T: (01670) 515556 M: 07768-075803

BROWN, Ms Elizabeth Ann. b 43. **d** 00 **p** 01. OLM W Bromwich All SS *Lich* 01-08; OLM Wednesbury St Paul Wood Green 08-10; rtd 10; PtO *Lich* from 11. *307 Beaconview Road, West Bromwich B71 3PS* T: 0121-588 7530 E: e.a.brown@talktalk.net

BROWN, Miss Elizabeth Charlotte. b 54. Bris Univ BSc 74 PGCE 77. Trin Coll Bris 93. **d** 95 **p** 96. C Taunton Lyngford *B & W* 95-99; TV Bath Twerton-on-Avon 99-06; C N Swindon St Andr *Bris* 06-11; C Swindon Dorcan 11-14; rtd 14; Hon C The Cannings and Redhorn *Sarum* from 15. *The Vicarage, The Street, Bishop's Cannings, Devizes SN10 2LD* M: 07504-316960 E: beth@revbethbrown.org.uk

BROWN, Mrs Elizabeth Mary Godwin. b 48. St Matthias Coll Bris CertEd 69. WEMTC 07. **d** 10 **p** 11. NSM Leominster *Heref* from 10. *Fairleigh House, Hereford Terrace, Leominster HR6 8JP* T: (01568) 613634 M: 07971-917141 E: elizabethmgbrown@hotmail.com

BROWN, Eric. b 28. Leeds Univ BA 98. NW Ord Course 73. **d** 76 **p** 77. NSM S Kirkby *Wakef* 76-83; NSM Knottingley 83-94; NSM Kellington w Whitley 89-94; Sub Chapl HM Pris Lindholme 90-94; PtO *Leeds* from 94. *Wynberg, Barnsley Road, South Kirby, Pontefract WF9 3BG* T: (01977) 643683

BROWN, Ernest Harry. b 32. St Mich Coll Llan. **d** 59 **p** 60. C Swansea St Pet *S & B* 59-62; C Gowerton w Waunarlwydd 62-68; CF (TA) 62-68; Chapl to the Deaf *S & B* 68-98; rtd 98. *Montreaux, 30 Lon Cedwyn, Sketty, Swansea SA2 0TH* T: (01792) 207628

BROWN, Geoffrey Alan. b 34. **d** 99 **p** 00. OLM Bury St Edmunds St Mary *St E* 99-07; rtd 07; PtO *St E* from 07. *Rodenkirchen, 12 Sharp Road, Bury St Edmunds IP33 2NB* T: (01284) 769725

BROWN, Geoffrey Gilbert. b 38. Dur Univ BA 62 DipEd 63 Fitzw Coll Cam BA 69 MA 73 FBIS. Westcott Ho Cam 67. **d** 70 **p** 71. C Gosforth All SS *Newc* 70-73; Chapl Dauntsey's Sch Devizes 73-76; Chapl St Paul's Colleg Sch Hamilton New Zealand 76-78; V Barrow St Aid *Carl* 79-86; Chapl Ch Coll Canterbury New Zealand 86-90; C Digswell and Panshanger *St Alb* 91-93; Chapl E Herts Hospice Care 94-07; rtd 07. *32 Uplands, Welwyn Garden City AL8 7EW* T: (01707) 327565

BROWN, Graham Stanley. See REAPER-BROWN, Graham Stanley

BROWN, Mrs Harriet Nina. b 37. Open Univ BA 77 Lon Univ CertEd 57. Gilmore Course 50 Oak Hill Th Coll 83. **dss** 83 **d** 87 **p** 94. Greenstead *Chelmsf* 83-90; Par Dn 87-90; Asst Chapl R Hosp Sch Holbrook 90-93; PtO *Chelmsf* from 93; *St E* 93-96; P-in-c Gt and Lt Blakenham w Baylham and Nettlestead 96-01; rtd 01. *22 Gainsborough Road, Colchester CO3 4QN* T: (01206) 523072

BROWN, Ian Barry. See KING-BROWN, Ian Barry

BROWN, Ian David. b 53. UEA BA 76. Wycliffe Hall Ox BA 80. **d** 81 **p** 82. C Southsea St Jude *Portsm* 84-89; Chapl Coll of SS Paul and Mary Cheltenham 84-89; V Lt Heath *St Alb* 89-05; V Frindsbury w Upnor and Chattenden *Roch* 05-14; P-in-c Chalfont St Giles *Ox* 14-15; P-in-c Seer Green and Jordans 14-15; R Chalfont St Giles, Seer Green and Jordans from 15. *The Rectory, 2 Deanway, Chalfont St Giles HP8 4JH* T: (01494) 872097 E: ianandjuliebrown@gmail.com

BROWN, Canon Jack Robin. b 44. Linc Th Coll 67. **d** 69 **p** 70. C Canning Town St Cedd *Chelmsf* 69-72; C Dunstable *St Alb* 72-78; V Luton St Andr 78-85; V Kempston Transfiguration 85-00; RD Bedford 92-98; Hon Can St Alb 97-09; Dioc Officer for Local Min 00-09; rtd 10; P-in-c Mill End and Heronsgate w W Hyde *St Alb* 10-11; Asst Dir of Ords from 11. *9 Westmead, Princes Risborough HP27 9HP* T: (01844) 347178 E: randvbrown@btinternet.com

BROWN, Mrs Jacqueline Kay. b 43. Saffron Walden Coll CertEd 65. **d** 08 **p** 09. OLM Newton Longville, Mursley, Swanbourne etc *Ox* from 08. *5 Berry Way, Newton Longville, Milton Keynes MK17 0AS* T: (01908) 270159

BROWN, James Douglas. b 52. S'wark Ord Course 93. **d** 96 **p** 97. NSM Shooters Hill Ch Ch *S'wark* 96-01; P-in-c E Malling *Roch* 02-07; P-in-c Wateringbury and Teston 02-07; V E Malling, Wateringbury and Teston 07-15; RD Malling 07-14; rtd 15. *The Vicarage, 2 The Grange, East Malling, West Malling ME19 6AH* T/F: (01732) 843282 M: 07957-906297 E: james.brown@diocese-rochester.org

BROWN, Canon James Philip. b 30. Ex Coll Ox BA 54 MA 55. Westcott Ho Cam 54. **d** 56 **p** 57. C Hemel Hempstead *St Alb* 56-63; V Hellesdon *Nor* 63-71; P-in-c Kirkley w Lowestoft St Jo 71-78; TV Lowestoft St Marg 76-78; TV Lowestoft and Kirkley 79-81; P-in-c Northleach w Hampnett and Farmington *Glouc* 81-95; RD Northleach 83-92; P-in-c Cold Aston w Notgrove and Turkdean 86-95; Hon Can Glouc Cathl 91-95; rtd 95; PtO *Ex* from 95. *The Priest's House, 1 St Scholastica's Abbey, Teignmouth TQ14 8FF* T: (01626) 773623

BROWN, Mrs Jane Catherine Deborah. b 65. York Univ BA 89. Cranmer Hall Dur 13. **d** 15. C Bramham *York* from 15. *The Vicarage, Church Causeway, Thorp Arch, Wetherby LS23 7AE* T: (01937) 849148 M: 07981-310373 E: janebrown160@live.com

BROWN, Jane Madeline. See SHARP, Jane Madeline

BROWN, Mrs Janice Elizabeth. b 65. Univ of Wales (Ban) BTh 04. **d** 04 **p** 05. C Botwnnog w Bryncroes w Llangwnnadl w Penllech *Ban* 04-05; C Llyn and Eifionydd 05-07; P-in-c Denio w Abererch 07-09; V 09-12; V Dwylan from 12. *The Vicarage, Church Road, Penmaenmawr LL34 6BN* T: (01492) 339781 M: 07969-655497

BROWN, Mrs Jean Louise. b 49. WEMTC 05. **d** 08 **p** 09. NSM Lechlade *Glouc* 08; NSM S Cotswolds from 09; TV from 11. *Orchard House, High Street, Meysey Hampton, Cirencester GL7 5JT* M: 07957-657935 E: jeanbrown50@mail.com

BROWN, Jennifer. b 44. Guy's Hosp Medical Sch MSc 91 Southn Univ BDS 67 Open Univ BA 81. Ripon Coll Cuddesdon 08. **d** 09 **p** 10. NSM The Downs *Win* 09-13; NSM Lower Dever from 13. *Address temp unknown* M: 07870-772905 E: jenniferandjosie@hotmail.com

BROWN, Mrs Jennifer Elizabeth. b 70. Geo Mason Univ Virginia BSc 91. SAOMC 02. **d** 05 **p** 06. C Ox St Clem 05-08; Chapl Jes Coll Ox 09. *49 Laburnum Road, Oxford OX2 9EN* T: (01865) 279757 E: chaplain@jesus.ox.ac.uk *or* chaplain@jenbrown.org.uk

BROWN, Jenny. b 78. St Martin's Coll Lanc BA 99. Oak Hill Th Coll BA 03. **d** 03 **p** 04. C Hyde St Geo *Ches* 03-06; C Weaverham from 06. *The Vicarage, Church Street, Weaverham, Northwich CW8 3NJ* T: (01606) 852110 E: revjennybrown@yahoo.com

BROWN, Mrs Joan Leslie. b 31. SS Hild & Bede Coll Dur CertEd 55. Oak Hill Th Coll BA 85. **dss** 85 **d** 87 **p** 94. Fulwood *Sheff* 85-88; Par Dn 87-88; Team Dn Netherthorpe 88-93; NSM Ellesmere St Pet 93-99; rtd 99; PtO *Sheff* from 00. *15 Dover Gardens, Sheffield S3 7LB* T: 0114-273 1364

BROWN, John. b 64. Kent Univ BA 86. Westcott Ho Cam 87. **d** 90 **p** 91. C Lt Ilford St Mich *Chelmsf* 90-94; C E Ham w Upton Park and Forest Gate 94; TV 94-01; P-in-c Gt Ilford St Luke 01-14; V from 14. *St Luke's Vicarage, Baxter Road, Ilford IG1 2HN* T: (020) 8478 1248 *or* 8553 7606 E: livingfaith@stluke-ilford.org.uk

BROWN, Canon John Bruce. b 42. Nottm Univ BA 64 MA 68. Cuddesdon Coll 64. **d** 66 **p** 67. C Warwick St Nic *Cov* 66-71; C Bp's Hatfield *St Alb* 71-78; V Watford St Mich 78-08; RD Watford 94-99; Hon Can St Alb 02-08; rtd 08; PtO *Ox* from 09. *Broomfield Cottage, Poffley End, Hailey, Witney OX29 9US* T: (01993) 703029 E: patandjohnb@yahoo.co.uk

BROWN, John Derek. b 41. Linc Th Coll 71. **d** 73 **p** 74. C Rotherham *Sheff* 73-76; P-in-c W Pinchbeck *Linc* 76-78; V Surfleet 76-82; R Boultham 83-94; RD Christianity 85-92; P-in-c Epworth and Wroot 94-97; R Epworth Gp 97-05; RD Is of Axholme 96-05; Can and Preb Linc Cathl 88-05; rtd 05. *1A St John's Avenue, Kidderminster DY11 6AT* T: (01562) 510524 E: jbrown@wanadoo.fr

BROWN, Canon John Duncan. b 43. St Pet Coll Ox BA 64 BA 66 MA 68. Lon Univ BSc. Wycliffe Hall Ox 65. **d** 67 **p** 68. C Kingston upon Hull H Trin *York* 67-69; C St Leonards

St Leon *Chich* 69-72; Hon C Norbiton *S'wark* 72-75; C Kirkcaldy *St And* 75-78; Prec and Chapl Chelmsf Cathl 78-86; P-in-c Kelvedon Hatch 86-92; P-in-c Navestock 86-92; P-in-c Fryerning w Margaretting 92-99; Bp's ACORA Officer 92-99; Hon Can Chelmsf Cathl 93-03; rtd 99. *556 Galleywood Road, Chelmsford CM2 8BX* T: (01245) 358185
E: canonjbrown@mac.com

BROWN, Canon John Roger. b 37. AKC 60. **d** 61 **p** 62. C New Eltham All SS *S'wark* 61-64; C Bexhill St Pet *Chich* 64-68; V Eastbourne St Elisabeth 68-75; V E Grinstead St Swithun 75-97; Chapl Qu Victoria Hosp NHS Trust East Grinstead 75-97; PtO *Chich* 97-99; RD E Grinstead 82-93; Can and Preb Chich Cathl 89-98; TV Worth 00-04; rtd 05. *120 Malthouse Road, Crawley RH10 6BH* T: (01293) 520454
E: jroger.brown@tesco.net

BROWN, Jonathan. b 60. Univ Coll Dur BA 83 MA 85 Ex Univ CertEd 86. Ripon Coll Cuddesdon 86 Ch Div Sch of the Pacific (USA) 88. **d** 89 **p** 90. C Esher *Guildf* 89-97; TV Crawley *Chich* 97-04; Chapl St Cath Hospice Crawley 97-04; V Earlsfield St Andr *S'wark* from 04. *22 St Andrew's Court, Waynflete Street, London SW18 3QF* T: (020) 8946 4214

BROWN, Prof Judith Margaret. b 44. Girton Coll Cam MA 69 PhD 68 Natal Univ Hon DSocSc 01. Ripon Coll Cuddesdon 09. **d** 09 **p** 10. NSM Osney *Ox* from 09; Past Assoc to Chapl Ball Coll Ox from 09. *97 Victoria Road, Oxford OX2 7QG* T: (01865) 514486 or 277736
E: judith.brown@history.ox.ac.uk

BROWN, Mrs Kathleen Margaret. b 40. MBE 07. QUB BD BTh. **d** 88 **p** 90. C Carrickfergus *Conn* 88-92; I Belfast St Paul w St Barn 92-07; Can Belf Cathl 00-07; rtd 07. *3 The Avenue, Carrickfergus BT38 8LT* T: (028) 9336 6787
E: kbrown117@btinternet.com

BROWN, Keith Michael. b 42. **d** 07 **p** 08. OLM Earlham *Nor* 07-12; rtd 12; PtO *Nor* from 12. *115 Colman Road, Norwich NR4 7HF* T: (01603) 464707
E: keith.brown93@ntlworld.com

BROWN, Kenneth Arthur Charles. b 27. ACP 65. **d** 84 **p** 85. OLM Ingoldsby *Linc* 84-97. *Address temp unknown*

BROWN, Kenneth Roger. b 48. St Chad's Coll Dur BA 69. Liturg Inst Trier 72. **d** 73 **p** 74. C Patchway *Bris* 73-77; C Fishponds St Jo 77-79; Chapl RAF 79-95; Chapl HM Pris Pentonville 95-96; Chapl HM Pris Wellingborough 96-98; PtO *B & W* 99-00; P-in-c Crook Peak 00-11; R 11-14; rtd 14. *7 Peelers Court, Moorland Street, Axbridge BS26 2BB* T: (01934) 733805
E: kenandyvonne@hotmail.co.uk

BROWN, Miss Louise Margaret. b 53. MBE 05. Trin Coll Bris 80. dss 83 **d** 87 **p** 94. Woodley St Jo the Ev *Ox* 84-87; Par Dn Woodley 87-92; Asst Chapl Reading Hosps 92-94; C Shinfield *Ox* 93-94; P-in-c Dedworth 94-96; V from 96; P-in-c Clewer St Andr 04-13. *3 Convent Court, Hatch Lane, Windsor SL4 3QR* T: (01753) 864591

BROWN, Canon Malcolm Arthur. b 54. Oriel Coll Ox BA 76 MA 82 Man Univ PhD 00. Westcott Ho Cam 77. **d** 79 **p** 80. C Riverhead w Dunton Green *Roch* 79-83; TV Southampton (City Cen) *Win* 83-91; Assoc Dir Wm Temple Foundn 91-93; Exec Sec 93-00; Hon C Heaton Moor *Man* 95-00; Prin EAMTC *Ely* 00-05; Prin ERMC 05-07; Dir Miss and Public Affairs Abps' Coun from 07; Hon Can Ely Cathl from 14; Hon Can Man Cathl from 15. *Church House, Great Smith Street, London SW1P 3AZ* T: (020) 7898 1000
E: malcolm.brown@churchofengland.org

BROWN, Mandy Kathleen. b 57. SEITE. **d** 10 **p** 11. C Bp's Hatfield, Lemsford and N Mymms *St Alb* 10-13; V Bishop's Stortford from 13. *Holy Trinity Vicarage, 69 Havers Lane, Bishop's Stortford CM23 3PA* T: (01707) 691601
M: 07772-121277 E: brownm05@hotmail.co.uk

BROWN, Marcus Clement. b 51. SEITE 08. **d** 10 **p** 11. NSM Iford w Kingston and Rodmell *Chich* 10-13; NSM Iford w Kingston and Rodmell and Southease from 13. *Abergavenny House, Mill Lane, Rodmell, Lewes BN7 3HS* T: (01273) 473939
M: 07815-157756 E: marcusandjennyrodmell@gmail.com

BROWN (née PATTERSON), Mrs Marjorie Jean. b 54. Wooster Coll USA BA 76 K Coll Lon MA 04. S Dios Minl Tr Scheme 92. **d** 95 **p** 96. C Poplar *Lon* 95-99; P-in-c Stamford Hill St Thos 99-02; V 02-09; P-in-c Upper Clapton St Matt 06-08; Dean of Women's Min Stepney Area 02-07; V Primrose Hill St Mary w Avenue Road St Paul from 09; Asst Dir of Ords Edmonton Area from 14. *St Mary's Vicarage, 44 King Henry's Road, London NW3 3RP* T: (020) 7722 3062 E: revmarjorie@gmail.com

BROWN, Mark Edward. b 61. Southn Univ BSc 83 Cam Univ PGCE 84 Brunel Univ MTh 98. Trin Coll Bris BA 88. **d** 88 **p** 89. C Egham *Guildf* 88-92; C Northwood Em *Lon* 92-96; Assoc V 96-02; Bp's Officer for Evang 96-02; Can Missr *S'well* 02-07; Hon Can S'well Minster 02-07; P-in-c Tonbridge SS Pet and Paul *Roch* 07-10; V from 10; RD Tonbridge from 10. *The Vicarage, Church Street, Tonbridge TN9 1HD* T: (01732) 770962
E: mark@tonbridgeparishchurch.org.uk

BROWN, Martin Warwick. b 65. BSc MA. ERMC. **d** 07 **p** 08. NSM St Alb St Mary Marshalswick *St Alb* 07-09; NSM Leavesden 09-13. *Apartment 2206, Sunshine Residence, Qais Bin Al Hosain Street, Al Khobar, Saudi Arabia*

BROWN, Michael Brian. b 56. Trin Coll Bris BA 97 Coll of Resurr Mirfield 98. **d** 99 **p** 00. C Trowbridge St Jas *Sarum* 99-02; C Bruton and Distr *B & W* 02-09; C Bickleigh and Shaugh Prior *Ex* 09-12; Chapl Plymouth Hosps NHS Trust 09-12; P-in-c St John w Millbrook *Truro* from 12; P-in-c Maker w Rame from 12; C Torpoint 12-15. *The Vicarage, Newport Street, Millbrook, Torpoint PL10 1BW* T: (01752) 822264
E: fr.michaelbrown@btopenworld.com

BROWN, Murray. *See* BROWN, Phillip Murray

BROWN, Nicholas Francis Palgrave. b 23. Fitzw Ho Cam BA 51 MA 54. **d** 53 **p** 54. C Warwick St Nic *Cov* 53-55; C Birm St Paul 55-60; V Temple Balsall 60-66; Gen Sec Ind Chr Fellowship 66-76; V St Kath Cree *Lon* 66-71; Chapl and Dir of Studies Holland Ho Cropthorne 76-88; P-in-c Cropthorne w Charlton *Worc* 76-88; Adult Educn Officer 80-85; rtd 88; PtO *Worc* from 88. *Bredon View, 40 Bridge Street, Pershore WR10 1AT* T: (01386) 556816

BROWN, Nicholas James Watson. b 76. R Holloway Coll Lon BMus 98 Lon Inst of Educn PGCE 99. Ripon Coll Cuddesdon 08. **d** 09 **p** 10. C Warminster St Denys and Upton Scudamore *Sarum* 09-13; P-in-c Louth *Linc* from 13. *The Rectory, Westgate, Louth LN11 9YE* T: (01507) 605360
M: 07901-852198 E: njwbrown@btinternet.com

BROWN, Nina. *See* BROWN, Harriet Nina

BROWN, Canon Norman Charles Harry. b 27. Univ of Wales BSc 46. St Mich Coll Llan 48. **d** 50 **p** 51. C Canton St Jo *Llan* 50-57; C Llanishen and Lisvane 58-63; V Miskin 63-97; RD Aberdare 82-97; Can Llan Cathl 86-97; rtd 97; PtO *Llan* from 04. *33 Bron y Deri, Mountain Ash CF45 4LL* T: (01443) 476631

BROWN, Canon Norman John. b 34. Thames Poly MA 90. Ripon Hall Ox 72. **d** 74 **p** 75. C High Wycombe *Ox* 74-78; V Tilehurst St Cath 78-82; V Boyne Hill 82-04; Chapl Windsor and Maidenhead Coll 87-89; Hon Can Ch Ch *Ox* 03-04; rtd 04; PtO *Ox* from 04. *Bosbury, 1 St James Close, Pangbourne, Reading RG8 7AP* T: 0118-984 5823 E: revbrown@waitrose.com

BROWN, Patricia Valerie. b 37. CertEd 58. STETS BTh 95. **d** 98 **p** 99. NSM Tadley St Pet *Win* 98-02; NSM Tadley S and Silchester 02-07; rtd 07; PtO *Win* from 10. *58 Bowmonts Road, Tadley, Basingstoke RG26 3SB* T: 0118-981 4860
E: pvbrown@tinyonline.co.uk

BROWN, Paul. *See* BROWN, Anthony Paul

BROWN, Paul David Christopher. b 50. Lon Univ LLB 71. EMMTC 81. **d** 84 **p** 85. NSM Wollaton *S'well* 84-13; PtO *Chelmsf* 13-14; NSM Thaxted from 14. *6 Bellrope Meadow, Sampford Road, Thaxted, Dunmow CM6 2FE* T: (01371) 831515
M: 07734-605921 E: pdchrisbrown@gmail.com

BROWN, Canon Penelope Jane. b 57. St Steph Ho Ox 94. **d** 96 **p** 97. C Croydon St Jo *S'wark* 96-99; V Croydon St Matt 99-09; AD Croydon Cen 07-09; P-in-c Limpsfield and Titsey 09-10; TR Limpsfield and Tatsfield 10-12; Hon Can S'wark Cathl 08-12; PtO from 12; *St E* 12-13 and from 14; Hon C Woodbridge St Mary 13-14. *2 The Orangery, Nacton, Ipswich IP10 0ET* T: (01473) 655153 M: 07710-883787
E: canpennyb@btinternet.com

BROWN, Canon Peter. b 47. RMN 69. Kelham Th Coll 69. **d** 74 **p** 75. CMP from 75; C Hendon *Dur* 74-80; C Byker St Ant *Newc* 80-90; C Brandon and Ushaw Moor *Dur* 90-05; V 05-12; Hon Can Dur Cathl 01-12; rtd 12; PtO *Dur* from 12. *29 Willow Green, Sunderland SR2 7NL* T: 0191-903 1863
M: 07719-545522 E: 47peterbrown@gmail.com

BROWN, Peter. b 53. St Chad's Coll Dur BA 75. Sarum & Wells Th Coll 75. **d** 77 **p** 78. C Tunstall Ch Ch *Lich* 77-79; C Tunstall 79-80; C Willenhall H Trin 80-83; V Weston Rhyn 83-88; Australia 88-90; R Hubberston *St D* 90-01; V Chilvers Coton w Astley *Cov* 01-10; rtd 10; PtO *St D* from 12; *Leic* from 14. *43C Albany Street, Loughborough LE11 5NB* T: (01509) 214185
E: petelaine@btinternet.com

BROWN, Peter. b 38. Leeds Univ BSc 62 PhD 65. Nashotah Ho 85. **d** 87 **p** 88. R Minneapolis St Andr USA 87-89; C Sprowston w Beeston *Nor* 89-92; P-in-c W Winch w Setchey and N Runcton 92-98; P-in-c Middleton w E Winch 96-98; P-in-c Nor St Andr and Nor St Geo Colegate 98-99; Chapl Norfolk and Nor Health Care NHS Trust 98-99; rtd 00; PtO *Leic* 00-12. *41 Main Street, Cosby, Leicester LE9 1UW* T: 0116-286 6184 E: peterbrown@tesco.net

BROWN, Peter Russell. b 43. Oak Hill Th Coll. **d** 71 **p** 72. C Gt Faringdon w Lt Coxwell *Ox* 71-73; C Reading Greyfriars 73-74; V Forty Hill Jes Ch *Lon* 74-81; V Laleham 81-09; rtd 09; PtO *Cant* from 10. *42A Tothill Street, Minster, Ramsgate CT12 4AJ* T: (01843) 822294 E: revprb43@yahoo.com

BROWN, Peter Thomas. b 43. Leic Univ BSc 64. WEMTC 00. d 03 p 04. OLM Prestbury and All SS *Glouc* 03-08; NSM N Cheltenham 08-13; rtd 13. *32 Gallops Lane, Prestbury, Cheltenham GL52 5SD* T: (01242) 529774
E: pete.brown@northchelt.org.uk

BROWN, Philip. *See* BROWN, James Philip

BROWN, Philip Anthony. b 54. Oak Hill Th Coll BA 91. d 91 p 92. C Rock Ferry *Ches* 91-95; V Hattersley 95-98; V Harold Hill St Geo *Chelmsf* 98-09; P-in-c Chartham *Cant* 09-14; P-in-c Stone Street Gp 11-14; V Chartham and Upper Hardres w Stelling from 14; Asst Dir of Ords from 09. *The Rectory, The Green, Chartham, Canterbury CT4 7JW* T: (01227) 738256
E: filbrown@btinternet.com

BROWN, Canon Philip Roy. b 41. St Steph Ho Ox 78. d 80 p 81. C Highters Heath *Birm* 80-83; P-in-c Washwood Heath 83-87; V Tysoe w Oxhill and Whatcote *Cov* 87-93; R Harbury and Ladbroke 93-07; RD Southam 95-97 and 99-02; Hon Can Cov Cathl 00-07; rtd 07; PtO *Cov* 07-11; Hon C Aston Cantlow and Wilmcote w Billesley from 11. *3 Margetts Close, Kenilworth CV8 1EN* T: (01926) 850638 E: brownphilip5@sky.com

BROWN, Phillip John. b 75. Univ of Wales (Lamp) BTh 10 Nottm Univ MA 14. WEMTC 05. d 08 p 09. C Heref S Wye 08-13; TV from 13. *1 Holme Lacy Road, Hereford HR2 6DD* T: (01432) 353275 E: pbrown777@aol.com

BROWN, Phillip Murray. b 59. Keele Univ BSc 80. Trin Coll Bris. d 87 p 88. C Greasbrough *Sheff* 87-91; Ind Chapl 87-93; V Thorne 91-99; V Norton Lees St Paul from 99. *St Paul's Vicarage, 6 Angerford Avenue, Sheffield S8 9BG* T: 0114-255 1945 E: murray.stpauls@btinternet.com

BROWN, Raymond John. b 49. Ox Univ BEd 71. Wycliffe Hall Ox 72. d 75 p 76. C Barking St Marg w St Patr *Chelmsf* 75-78; C Walton H Trin *Ox* 78-82; V Enfield St Mich *Lon* 82-91; Chapl St Mich Hosp Enfield 82-91; R Springfield All SS *Chelmsf* 91-14; rtd 14. *33 Ebsay Drive, York YO30 4XR*
E: raymondjohnbrown@talktalk.net

BROWN, Richard Alexander. b 74. d 13 p 14. NSM N Thornaby *York* 13-14; NSM Middlesbrough Ascension from 14. *Glebe House Cottage, Ingleby Arncliffe, Northallerton DL6 3JX* T: (01609) 882842 E: richard.brown@yorksj.ac.uk

BROWN, Richard George. b 38. Dur Univ BSc 63. Wells Th Coll 63. d 65 p 66. C Norton St Mary *Dur* 65-69; C N Gosforth *Newc* 69-71; Chapl Wells Cathl Sch 71-81; P-in-c Dulverton and Brushford *B & W* 81-83; R 83-86; Chapl Millfield Jun Sch Somerset 86-89; Chapl Brighton Coll 89-92; Chapl Benenden Sch 92-94; PtO *Chich* 94-97; P-in-c Poynings w Edburton, Newtimber and Pyecombe 97-04; rtd 04. *4 Standean Farm Cottages, Standean Farm, Brighton BN1 8ZA* T: (01273) 501469 E: richardgb@ukgateway.net

BROWN, Robert. b 47. Man Univ BSc 72 Open Univ BA 86 Dur Univ MA 87. NEOC 95. d 98 p 99. C Yarm *York* 98-01; V Ormesby 01-12; rtd 12. *7 Whinflower Drive, Stockton-on-Tees TS20 1TQ*

BROWN, Robert Peter Cameron. b 63. K Coll Lon BSc 84 Imp Coll Lon MSc 87 Lon Bible Coll BA 97 Dur Univ PhD 13. Cranmer Hall Dur 01. d 03 p 04. C Upper Weardale *Dur* 03-08; PtO *Carl* 09-13; NSM Bewcastle, Stapleton and Kirklinton etc from 13. *Greenholme, Bewcastle, Carlisle CA6 6PW* T: (016977) 48438 E: rob@bewcastlehouseofprayer.org.uk

BROWN, Robin. *See* BROWN, Jack Robin

BROWN, Robin. b 38. Leeds Univ BA 60 MPhil 69. Qu Coll Birm 89. d 91 p 92. C Far Headingley St Chad *Ripon* 91-94; V Hawksworth Wood 94-00; rtd 00; PtO *Leeds* from 00. *Dale Edge, 2A Harbour View, Bedale DL8 2DQ* T/F: (01677) 425483 M: 07960-277495 E: robin.stel1@btinternet.com

BROWN, Roger. *See* BROWN, John Roger

BROWN, Capt Roger George. b 37. CQSW. CA Tr Coll SEITE 92. d 95 p 96. C Maidstone St Martin *Cant* 95-97; C Oakham, Hambleton, Egleton, Braunston and Brooke *Pet* 97-04; Chapl Leics and Rutland Healthcare NHS Trust 97-04; rtd 04; Asst Chapl Kettering Gen Hosp NHS Trust 04-12; Chapl from 12. *5 Valley Walk, Kettering NN16 0LY* T: (01536) 524954 E: chaplaincy@kgh.nhs.uk

BROWN, Canon Roger Lee. b 42. Univ of Wales (Lamp) BA 63 Univ Coll Lon MA 73 Univ of Wales (Ban) DLitt 08 FSA 01. Wycliffe Hall Ox 66. d 68 p 69. C Dinas and Penygraig w Williamstown *Llan* 68-70; C Bargoed and Deri w Brithdir 70-72; TV Glyncorrwg w Afan Vale and Cymmer Afan 72-74; R 74-79; V Tongwynlais 79-93; R Welshpool w Castle Caereinion *St As* 93-07; AD Pool 01-07; Can Cursal St As Cathl 02-07; rtd 07; PtO *St As* from 09. *14 Berriew Road, Welshpool SY21 7SS* T: (01938) 552161

✠**BROWN, The Rt Revd Ronald.** b 26. St Jo Coll Dur BA 50. d 52 p 53 c 74. C Chorley St Laur *Blackb* 52-56; V Whittle-le-Woods 56-61; V Halliwell St Thos *Man* 61-69; R Ashton St Mich 69-74; RD Ashton-under-Lyne 69-74; Suff Bp Birkenhead *Ches* 74-92; rtd 92; PtO *Ches* 92-00. *16 Andrew Crescent, Chester CH4 7BQ* T: (01244) 629955

BROWN, Canon Rosalind. b 53. Lon Univ BA 74. Yale Div Sch MDiv 97. d 97 p 97. V Canonsburg St Thos USA 97-99; Vice-Prin OLM Scheme *Sarum* 99-05; Tutor STETS 99-05; Can Res Dur Cathl from 05. *6A The College, Durham DH1 3EQ* T: 0191-384 2415 F: 386 4267
E: rosalind.brown@durhamcathedral.co.uk

BROWN, Preb Rosémia. b 53. Ripon Coll Cuddesdon 97. d 99 p 00. C Shoreditch St Leon and Hoxton St Jo *Lon* 99-00; C Shoreditch St Leon w St Mich 00-02; TV Hackney 02-03; V Clapton St Jas from 03; Preb St Paul's Cathl from 13. *134 Rushmore Road, London E5 0EY* T: (020) 8985 1750

BROWN, Roy. *See* BROWN, Philip Roy

BROWN, Sandra Ann. b 51. d 04 p 05. NSM Linc St Geo Swallowbeck 04-14. *10 Station Road, North Hykeham, Lincoln LN6 9AQ* T: (01522) 870065
E: sandra.brown77@ntlworld.com

BROWN, Canon Sarah Romilly Denner. b 65. Nottm Univ BA 86. ERMC 05. d 08 p 09. NSM Welford w Sibbertoft and Marston Trussell *Pet* 08-11; TV Daventry, Ashby St Ledgers, Braunston etc from 11; RD Daventry from 13; Can Pet Cathl from 15. *The Rectory, 71 High Street, Braunston, Daventry NN11 7HS* T: (01788) 890298 M: 07803-902864
E: sarah@talkingdirect.co.uk

BROWN, Sharon Lesley. b 63. Leeds Univ BA 86 Sheff Univ BA 14 Bretton Hall Coll PGCE 88. Yorks Min Course 11. d 14 p 15. C Abbeylands *Leeds* from 14. *Kirkstall Vicarage, Vicarage View, Leeds LS5 3HF* M: 07951-708937
E: sharondrums@sky.com

BROWN, Canon Simon Nicolas Danton. b 37. Clare Coll Cam BA 61 MA 65. S'wark Ord Course 61 Linc Th Coll 63. d 64 p 65. C Lambeth St Mary the Less *S'wark* 64-66; Chapl and Warden LMH Settlement 66-72; P-in-c Southampton St Mary w H Trin *Win* 72-73; TV Southampton (City Cen) 73-79; R Gt Brickhill w Bow Brickhill and Lt Brickhill *Ox* 79-84; TR Burnham w Dropmore, Hitcham and Taplow 84-04; RD Burnham and Slough 87-02; Hon Can Ch Ch 94-04; Dioc Consultant for Deanery Development 97-04; Sen Exec Asst to Bp Buckingham 02-04; rtd 04; PtO *St E* from 04. *Seagulls, Pin Mill Road, Chelmondiston, Ipswich IP9 1JN* T: (01473) 780051 E: simon.brown1@orange.net

BROWN, Sonya Helen Joan. *See* WRATTEN, Sonya Helen Joan

BROWN, Stephen Charles. b 60. Leeds Univ BA 83 BA 89 Reading Univ PGCE 89. Coll of Resurr Mirfield 87. d 90 p 91. C Whitkirk *Ripon* 90-93; Asst Youth Chapl 92-95; C Chapel Allerton 93-95; R Stanningley St Thos 95-01; Chapl MU 98-01; V Laneside *Blackb* from 01; Hon Chapl ATC 03-07. *St Peter's Vicarage, Helmshore Road, Haslingden, Rossendale BB4 4BG* T: (01706) 213838 E: highlow@talktalk.net

BROWN, Stephen George. b 54. STETS 13. d 15. NSM Kilburn St Aug w St Jo *Lon* from 15. *Address temp unknown*

BROWN, Stephen James. b 44. Bradf Univ BSc 69. Westcott Ho Cam 71. d 72 p 73. C Seaton Hirst *Newc* 72-75; C Marton-in-Cleveland *York* 75-77; Dioc Youth Adv *Dur* 77-82; V Thorner *Ripon* 82-92; Dioc Officer for Local Min 90-01; P-in-c Ripley w Burnt Yates 92-09; Chapl Yorkshire TV 89-09; rtd 09; PtO *York* from 10. *88 Prince Rupert Drive, Tockwith, York YO26 7QS* T: (01423) 359142 M: 07521-705350
E: stephenbrown83@hotmail.co.uk

BROWN, Susan Gertrude. b 48. Univ of Wales (Swansea) BA 71 Roehampton Inst PGCE 72. St Mich Coll Llan 98. d 02 p 03. NSM Gelligaer *Llan* 02-04; NSM Eglwysilan 04-07; LtO 07-08; NSM Caerphilly 08-13; Dioc Adv for NSM 10-13; rtd 14; PtO *Llan* from 14. *2 Caerleon Court, Caerphilly CF83 2UF* T: (029) 2140 3773
E: suebrown27_uk@yahoo.com

BROWN, Terence George Albert. b 49. SS Mark & Jo Univ Coll Plymouth BEd 75. ERMC 04. d 06 p 09. NSM Langdon Hills *Chelmsf* 06-09; NSM Gt Wakering w Foulness 09-13; NSM Barling w Lt Wakering 09-13; P-in-c Sandon from 13. *The Vicarage, 1 Glebe Meadow, Great Waltham, Chelmsford CM3 1EX* T: (01245) 364081 M: 07944-444675
E: tgabrown@hotmail.com

✠**BROWN, The Rt Revd Thomas John.** b 43. San Francisco Th Sem DMin 84. St Jo Coll Auckland. d 72 p 73 c 91. C Christchurch St Alb New Zealand 72-74; C Leic St Jas 74-76; V Upper Clutha New Zealand 76-79; V Roslyn 79-85; V Lower Hutt St Jas 85-91; Adn Belmont 87-91; Asst Bp Wellington 91-97; Bp Wellington 97-12; rtd 12. *PO Box 24 040, Manners Street, Wellington 6142, New Zealand*
M: (0064)21-444875 E: tommitre10@gmail.com

BROWN, Mrs Verity Joy. b 68. Qu Mary Coll Lon BA 89. Ripon Coll Cuddesdon BTh 93. d 93 p 94. C Barnard Castle w Whorlton *Dur* 93-95; C Bensham 95-97; PtO from 97. *75 Eamont Gardens, Hartlepool TS26 9JE* T: (01429) 423186

BROWN, Mrs Veronica Mary. b 60. Rowan Univ (USA) BA 83 St Jos Univ (USA) MBA 94. STETS 09. d 12 p 13.

C Newport St Thos *Portsm* 12-14; C Newport St Jo 12-14; C Whippingham w E Cowes from 14. *2 St Faith's Road, Cowes PO31 7HH* M: 07921-514906
E: vbrown@brownassociates.mailstreet.com

BROWN, Victor Charles. b 31. S'wark Ord Course 67. **d** 71 **p** 72. C Pinhoe *Ex* 71-73; C Egg Buckland 73-74; C Oakdale St Geo *Sarum* 74-77; R Old Trafford St Hilda *Man* 77-83; R Chigwell Row *Chelmsf* 83-92; R Fenny Bentley, Kniveton, Thorpe and Tissington *Derby* 92-96; rtd 96; PtO *Sarum* 96-08. *5 Gracey Court, Woodland Road, Broadclyst, Exeter EX5 3GA*
T: (01392) 462799

BROWN, Wallace. b 44. Oak Hill Th Coll 77. **d** 79 **p** 80. C Oadby *Leic* 79-85; V Quinton Road W St Boniface *Birm* 85-03; Hon Can Birm Cathl 01-03; TR Ipsley *Worc* 03-09; rtd 09. *2 Coppice Close, Withington, Hereford HR1 3PP*
E: wallace@rncb.ac.uk

BROWN, Wendy Anne. *See* WALE, Wendy Anne

BROWNBRIDGE, Bernard Alan. b 19. NW Ord Course 74. **d** 77 **p** 78. NSM Huntington *York* 77-80; V Sand Hutton 80-86; rtd 87; Hon C Birdsall w Langton *York* 87-92; PtO 92-11. *2 Duncombe Close, Malton YO17 7YY* T: (01653) 697626

BROWNE, Arnold Samuel. b 52. St Jo Coll Ox BA 73 MA 77 SS Coll Cam PhD 87 Surrey Univ MSc 89 MBPsS 92. Westcott Ho Cam 76. **d** 78 **p** 79. C Esher *Guildf* 78-81; C Worplesdon 81-86; Chapl R Holloway and Bedf New Coll 86-92; Fell and Dean of Chpl Trin Coll Cam 92-06; PtO *Nor* from 06. *18 Riverside Road, Norwich NR1 1SN* T: (01603) 629362
E: arnoldbrowne@btinternet.com

BROWNE, Aubrey Robert Caulfeild. b 31. Moore Th Coll Sydney 54. **d** 55 **p** 56. Australia 55-71; Producer of Relig Radio Progr USPG 72-84; Hon C S Kensington St Steph *Lon* 78-88; Hd of Area Sec Dept USPG 84-87; P-in-c Nunhead St Antony S'wark 88-90; V Nunhead St Antony w St Silas 90-96; rtd 97; Australia from 97. *15 Caroma Avenue, Kyeemagh NSW 2216, Australia* T: (0061) (2) 9567 5371

BROWNE, Miss Christine Mary. b 53. Nottm Univ BEd 75. EMMTC 87. **d** 90 **p** 94. C Bulwell St Mary *S'well* 90-95; TV Hucknall Torkard 95-00; Dep Chapl HM Pris Nor 00-01; Chapl HM YOI Swinfen Hall 01-03; PtO *Derby* 03-05; P-in-c Dudley St Aug Holly Hall *Worc* 05-09; TV Dudley 09-14; Chapl Merry Hill Shopping Cen 05-14; P-in-c Laugharne and Llansadwrnen and Pendine and Llanmiloe *St D* from 14. *The Vicarage, Broadway, Laugharne, Carmarthen SA33 4NU* T: (01994) 427488

BROWNE, Herman Beseah. b 65. Cuttington Univ Coll BTh 86 K Coll Lon BD 90 AKC 90 Heythrop Coll Lon PhD 94. **d** 87 **p** 97. C N Lambeth *S'wark* 90-91; Tutor Simon of Cyrene Th Inst 90-96; Abp's Asst Sec for Ecum and Angl Affairs *Cant* 96-01; Abp's Officer for Angl Communion 01-05; PtO *S'wark* 96-04; Hon Prov Can Cant Cathl 01-04; Liberia from 05. *Trinity Cathedral, PO Box 10-0277, 1000 Monrovia 10, Liberia* T: (00231) 224760 F: 227519

BROWNE, Ian Cameron. b 51. St Cath Coll Ox BA 74 MA 78 Fitzw Coll Cam BA 76 MA 80. Ridley Hall Cam 74. **d** 77 **p** 78. C Cheltenham Ch Ch *Glouc* 77-80; Hon C Shrewsbury St Chad *Lich* 80-83; Asst Chapl Shrewsbury Sch 80-83; Chapl Bedford Sch 83-96; Sen Chapl Oundle Sch 97-11; rtd 11; PtO *Pet* from 12. *46C North Street, Oundle, Peterborough PE8 4AL* T: (01832) 273541 E: the.revb@virgin.net

BROWNE, Mrs Karen. b 64. Ox Min Course 06. **d** 09 **p** 10. NSM Newport Pagnell w Lathbury and Moulsoe *Ox* from 09. *94 Lakes Lane, Newport Pagnell MK16 8HR* T: (01908) 217703
E: karen_browne@btopenworld.com

BROWNE, Leonard Joseph. b 58. St Cath Coll Cam BA 81 MA 84. Trin Coll Bris 87. **d** 89 **p** 90. C Reading Greyfriars *Ox* 89-92; V Cambridge St Barn *Ely* 92-00; Sen Chapl and Hd Div Dean Close Sch Cheltenham 00-03; Hd Master Dean Close Prep Sch from 03. *Dean Close Preparatory School, Lansdown Road, Cheltenham GL51 6QS* T: (01242) 512217
E: hmdcps@deanclose.org.uk *or* lj-browne@supanet.com

BROWNE, Peter Clifford. b 59. Bris Univ BA 80 SRN 82. Ripon Coll Cuddesdon 88. **d** 90 **p** 91. C Southgate Ch Ch *Lon* 90-92; NSM Kemp Town St Mary *Chich* 93-95; Chapl United Bris Healthcare NHS Trust 96-98; NSM Southmead *Bris* 98-02; Chapl HM Pris Preston 02-10; Chapl HM Pris Shepton Mallet 10-13; Chapl HM Pris and YOI Guys Marsh from 13. *HM Prison Guys Marsh, Shaftesbury SP7 0AH* T: (01747) 856400

BROWNE, Robert. *See* BROWNE, Aubrey Robert Caulfeild

BROWNHILL, Mrs Diane. b 56. Dioc OLM tr scheme 03. **d** 06 **p** 07. C Man Apostles w Miles Platting 06-09; TV Heatons from 09. *St Thomas' Rectory, 6 Heaton Moor Road, Stockport SK4 4NS* T: 0161-432 1912 M: 07505-781530
E: gldbrownhill@aol.com

BROWNING, Derek. *See* BROWNING, Robert Derek

BROWNING, Edward Barrington Lee (Barry). b 42. St Pet Coll Saltley TCert 65. Ripon Coll Cuddesdon 90. **d** 92 **p** 93. C Falmouth K Chas *Truro* 92-96; R Roche and Withiel 96-01; P-in-c Manaccan w St Anthony-in-Meneage and St Martin 01-06; P-in-c Cury and Gunwalloe w Mawgan 01-06; rtd 06; PtO *Truro* 06-10; P-in-c St Goran w Caerhays 10-13. *73 Park Way, St Austell PL25 4HR* T: (01726) 65194
E: barry.browningbtinternet.com

✥**BROWNING, The Rt Revd George Victor.** b 42. Chas Sturt Univ NSW DLitt 07. St Jo Coll Morpeth ThL 66. **d** 66 **p** 67 **c** 85. C Inverell Australia 66-68; C Armidale 68-69; V Warialda 69-73; Vice Prin St Jo Coll Morpeth 73-76; R Singleton and Adn Upper Hunter 76-84; R Woy Woy and Adn Cen Coast 84-85; Asst Bp Brisbane 85-93; Prin St Fran Th Coll 88-91; Bp Canberra and Goulburn 93-08; Dir Aus Cen Christianity and Culture 96-08; P-in-c Wriggle Valley *Sarum* 08-09; rtd 09. *24 Henry Place, Long Beach NSW 2536, Australia*
T: (0061) (2) 4472 7470 E: gandmbrowning@bigpond.com

BROWNING, Canon Jacqueline Ann. b 44. Sarum Th Coll 93. **d** 96 **p** 97. NSM New Alresford w Ovington and Itchen Stoke Win 96-02; Past Asst Win Cathl 02-12; Min Can Win Cathl 06-09; Hon Can Win Cathl 09-12; rtd 13. *1 Paddock Way, Alresford SO24 9PN* T: (01962) 734372 *or* 857237
E: jackie.browning@winchester-cathedral.org.uk

BROWNING, Canon John William. b 36. Keele Univ BA 61. Ripon Hall Ox 61. **d** 63 **p** 64. C Baswich *Lich* 63-66; Chapl Monyhull Hosp Birm 67-72; Chapl Wharncliffe Hosp Sheff 72-78; Chapl Middlewood Hosp Sheff 72-94; Hon Can Sheff Cathl 84-97; Chapl Sheff Mental Health Unit 85-94; Chapl Community Health Sheff NHS Trust 94-97; Chapl Sheff (South) Mental Health Centres 94-97; rtd 97; PtO *Sheff* from 97. *1 Anvil Close, Sheffield S6 5JN* T: 0114-234 3740
E: johnpatbrowning@hotmail.com

BROWNING, Julian. b 51. St Jo Coll Cam BA 72 MA 76. Ripon Coll Cuddesdon 77. **d** 80 **p** 81. C Notting Hill *Lon* 80-81; C W Brompton St Mary w St Pet 81-84; PtO 84-91; NSM Paddington St Sav 99-06; NSM St Marylebone St Cypr from 06. *82 Ashworth Mansions, Grantully Road, London W9 1LN* T: (020) 7286 6034 E: julian.browing@yahoo.co.uk

BROWNING, Kevin John. b 56. Ridley Hall Cam 96. **d** 98 **p** 99. C Northampton Em *Pet* 98-01; P-in-c Hardwick *Ely* 01-09; C Cranham Park *Chelmsf* from 10. *226 Moor Lane, Upminster RM14 1HN* T: (01708) 702241
E: kevinbrowningatstlukes@gmail.com

BROWNING, Miss Rachel. b 69. Oak Hill Th Coll BA 08. **d** 09. NSM Hastings Em and St Mary in the Castle *Chich* from 09. *11A Emmanuel Road, Hastings TN34 3LB* T: (01424) 430980 M: 07939-126955 E: rach.browning@gmail.com *or* rach@emmanuelhastings.org.uk

BROWNING, Robert Derek. b 42. Guildf Dioc Min Course 98. **d** 01 **p** 02. OLM Lightwater *Guildf* from 01. *16 Guildford Road, Lightwater GU18 5SN* T: (01276) 474345
E: derekandcarol.b@tiscali.co.uk

BROWNING, Mrs Rosheen Elizabeth. b 76. Middx Univ BA 98 Cant Ch Ch Univ Coll PGCE 03. Ridley Hall Cam 13. **d** 15. C Paddock Wood *Roch* from 15. *3 Ashcroft Close, Paddock Wood, Tonbridge TN12 6LG* M: 07984-454340
E: rosheen@standrewspw.org.uk

BROWNING, Canon Wilfrid Robert Francis. b 18. Ch Ch Ox BA 40 MA 44 BD 49. Cuddesdon Coll 40. **d** 41 **p** 42. C Towcester w Easton Neston *Pet* 41-44; C Woburn Square Ch Ch *Lon* 44-46; Chapl St Deiniol's Lib Hawarden 46-48; Chapl Heswall Nautical Sch 46-48; C-in-c Hove St Rich CD *Chich* 48-51; Lect Cuddesdon Coll 51-59; R Gt Haseley *Ox* 51-59; Warden Whalley Abbey *Blackb* 59-63; Can Res Blackb Cathl 59-65; Dir Post-Ord Tr 62-65; Lect Cuddesdon Coll 65-70; Can Res Ch Ch *Ox* 65-87; Hon Can Ch Ch 87-89; Dir Post-Ord Tr 65-85; Dir of Ords 65-85; Dir Ox NSM Course 72-89; rtd 87; Hon C N Hinksey and Wytham *Ox* 89-09; Tutor Westmr Coll Ox 93-99. *The College of St Barnabas, Blackberry Lane, Lingfield RH7 6NJ* T: (01342) 872853

BROWNLIE, Miss Caroline Heddon. b 47. CQSW 75. Qu Coll Birm IDC 81. **d** 87 **p** 94. Asst Chapl Fairfield Hosp Hitchin 87-91; NSM Ashwell w Hinxworth and Newnham *St Alb* 92-98; Chapl HM Rem Cen Low Newton 99-01; PtO *St Alb* 04-05; P-in-c Gilling and Kirkby Ravensworth *Ripon* 05-07; rtd 07; PtO *Ely* from 07. *9 Mount Pleasant, Cambridge CB3 0BL* T: (01223) 350663
E: carolineatno9@talktalk.net

BROWNRIDGE, David Leonard Robert. b 76. Univ of Wales (Lamp) BA 97. Trin Coll Bris 98. **d** 00 **p** 01. C Henfynyw w Aberaeron and Llanddewi Aberarth *St D* 00-04; V Laugharne w Llansadwrnen and Llanddowror etc *St D* 04-12; P-in-c Llanffestiniog w Blaenau Ffestiniog etc *Ban* 12-13; R Bro Moelwyn from 13. *The Rectory, The Square, Blaenau Ffestiniog LL41 3UW* T: (01766) 831871 E: dlrbrownridge@gmail.com

BROWNSELL, Preb John Kenneth. b 48. Hertf Coll Ox BA 69 BA 72 MA 89. Cuddesdon Coll 70. **d** 73 **p** 74. C Notting Hill All SS w St Columb *Lon* 73-74; C Notting Hill 74-76; TV 76-82; V Notting Hill All SS w St Columb from 82; AD Kensington 84-92; Preb St Paul's Cathl from 92; Dir of Ords 95-12. *The Vicarage, Powis Gardens, London W11 1JG* T: (020) 7727 5919 E: jkb@allsaintsnottinghill.org.uk

BROXHAM, Ms Ann. b 47. York St Jo Coll BA 03. Westcott Ho Cam 10. **d** 10. NSM Littleport *Ely* 10-13; NSM Crosland Moor and Linthwaite *Leeds* from 13. *The Vicarage, Church Lane, Linthwaite, Huddersfield HD7 5TA* T: (01484) 842621 E: annbroxham@yahoo.co.uk

BRUCE, Miss Amanda Jane. b 67. Liv Univ BSc 87 Southn Univ PGCE 89 Chelt & Glouc Coll of HE AdDipEd 01. Wycliffe Hall Ox 06. **d** 08 **p** 09. C Haydock St Mark *Liv* 08-12; TR Sutton from 12. *Sutton Rectory, 225 Gartons Lane, Clock Face, St Helens WA9 4RB* T: (01744) 608027 E: revamandabruce@bluebottle.com

BRUCE, David Crosby. b 72. SS Coll Cam MA 94 PGCE 95 Bris Univ MEd 05. Trin Coll Bris 10. **d** 12 **p** 13. C Meole Brace *Lich* from 12. *7 Dargate Close, Shrewsbury SY3 9QE* T: (01743) 369322 E: davecbruce@gmail.com

BRUCE, David Ian. b 47. St Mich Coll Llan 70. **d** 73 **p** 74. C Bordesley St Benedict *Birm* 73-74; C Llanishen and Lisvane *Llan* 74-81; V Canley *Cov* 81-90; V Longford 90-97; rtd 97; PtO *Cov* from 97. *122 Hugh Road, Coventry CV3 1AF* T: (024) 7644 5789

BRUCE, Francis Bernard. b 30. Trin Coll Ox BA 52 MA 56. Westcott Ho Cam 52. **d** 54 **p** 55. C Bury St Mary *Man* 54-59; C Sherborne w Castleton and Lillington *Sarum* 59-61; R Croston *Blackb* 61-86; V Bibury w Winson and Barnsley *Glouc* 86-95; rtd 95; PtO *Glouc* from 95. *6 Gloucester Street, Cirencester GL7 2DG* T: (01285) 641954

BRUCE, James Hamilton. b 57. Dur Univ BSc 78 Newc Univ MSc 79 St Andr Univ PhD 99. Trin Coll Bris 81. **d** 84 **p** 85. C Walmley *Birm* 84-86; PtO *Carl* 87-95; W Cumbria Sch Worker N Schs Chr Union 87-93; Nat Development Officer Wales Scripture Union 93-94; Chapl Turi St Andr Kenya 95-96; NSM St Andrews St Andr *St And* 96-99; R Penicuik and W Linton *Edin* 99-03; PtO *Win* 03-06; V Lyndhurst and Emery Down and Minstead from 06. *The Vicarage, 5 Forest Gardens, Lyndhurst SO43 7AF* T: (023) 8028 2154 E: bruces@talktalk.net

BRUCE, John Cyril. b 41. EMMTC 95. **d** 98 **p** 99. NSM Spalding St Mary and St Nic *Linc* 98-05; P-in-c Grantham, Manthorpe 05-08; rtd 09. *5 Welwyn Close, Grantham NG31 7JU* T: (01476) 561546　M: 07947-156933 E: john@john-bruce.co.uk

BRUCE, Kathrine Sarah. b 68. Leeds Univ BA 89 St Jo Coll Dur BA 01 MATM 07 Dur Univ PhD 14 Trin & All SS Coll Leeds PGCE 91. Cranmer Hall Dur 98. **d** 01 **p** 02. C Ripon H Trin 01-04; Chapl Trevelyan Coll *Dur* 04-08; Chapl Van Mildert Coll 04-08; NSM Dur St Oswald 04-06; NSM Dur St Oswald and Shincliffe 06-08; Chapl St Jo Coll Dur 08-13; Dep Warden and Tutor from 13. *St John's College, 3 South Bailey, Durham DH1 3RJ* T: 0191-334 3500

BRUCE, Leslie Barton. b 23. Liv Univ MB, ChB 48. **d** 71 **p** 72. NSM Wavertree H Trin *Liv* 71-05. *3 Childwall Park Avenue, Liverpool L16 0JE* T: 0151-722 7664

BRUCE, Rosemary. b 47. **d** 09 **p** 10. NSM Drayton St Pet (Abingdon) *Ox* from 09. *4 Greenacres, Drayton, Abingdon OX14 4JU* T: (01235) 525284　E: rosie-bruce@hotmail.co.uk

BRUCE, Mrs Susan Elizabeth. b 52. **d** 08 **p** 09. OLM Haughton le Skerne *Dur* 08-14; NSM Middleton St George from 14. *14 Haughton Green, Darlington DL1 2DF* T: (01325) 281567 M: 07810-720490　E: s.bruce178@ntlworld.com

BRUECK, Ms Jutta. b 61. LSE MSc 89 Heythrop Coll Lon MA 92 Fitzw Coll Cam BA 96 MA 00. Westcott Ho Cam 94. **d** 97 **p** 98. C Is of Dogs Ch Ch and St Jo w St Luke *Lon* 97-01; Chapl Guildhall Sch of Music and Drama 01-06; Chapl Fitzw Coll Cam 06-08; P-in-c Cambridge St Jas *Ely* 08-15; P-in-c Ipswich St Thos *St E* from 15. *St Thomas's Vicarage, 102 Cromer Road, Ipswich IP1 5EP* M: 07958-360564 E: jutta.brueck@cofesuffolk.org

BRUNN, Steven. b 67. Ridley Hall Cam. **d** 05 **p** 06. C Chertsey, Lyne and Longcross *Guildf* 05-09; V Oatlands from 10. *The Vicarage, 5 Beechwood Avenue, Weybridge KT13 9TE* T: (01932) 429937　E: steve.brunn@ntlworld.com

BRUNNING, Canon David George. b 32. St D Coll Lamp BA 53. St Mich Coll Llan 53. **d** 55 **p** 56. C Llantwit Major and St Donat's *Llan* 55-59; C Usk and Monkswood w Glascoed Chpl and Gwehelog *Mon* 59-62; V Abercarn 62-71; V Pontnewydd 71-89; RD Pontypool 89-97; R Panteg 90-98; Can St Woolos Cathl from 94; rtd 98; LtO *Mon* from 98; PtO *Llan* from 98. *6 Spitzkop, Llantwit Major CF61 1RD* T: (01446) 792124

BRUNNING, Neil. b 29. NW Ord Course 73. **d** 76 **p** 77. C Cheadle Hulme All SS *Ches* 76-79; V 79-88; V Glentworth *Linc* 88-93; P-in-c Hemswell w Harpswell 88-93; V Glentworth Gp 93-94; rtd 94; PtO *Linc* from 94. *11 Cavendish Drive, Lea, Gainsborough DN21 5HU* T/F: (01427) 617938 E: neilbrun@aol.com

BRUNO, Canon Allan David. b 34. AKC 59. St Boniface Warminster 59. **d** 60 **p** 61. C Darlington H Trin *Dur* 60-64; C Kimberley Cathl and Chapl Bp's Hostel S Africa 64-65; Asst Chapl Peterhouse Dioc Boys' Sch Rhodesia 65-70; Overseas Chapl Scottish Episc Ch 70-75; C Edin Old St Paul 75-76; Dir of Miss Prov of S Africa 76-80; Namibia 80-86; Dean Windhoek 81-86; R Falkirk *Edin* 86-95; Hon Can Kinkizi from 95; Bp's Dom Chapl *Bradf* 96-99; Bp's Past Asst 99-01; rtd 01; PtO *Leeds* from 01; *Blackb* from 02; Bp's Officer for Rtd Clergy and Widows Craven Adnry *Leeds* from 10. *Pond House, 5 Twine Walk, Burton in Lonsdale, Carnforth LA6 3LR* T: (015242) 61616　E: david@bruno81.freeserve.co.uk

BRUNSKILL, Mrs Sheila Kathryn. *See* BANYARD, Sheila Kathryn

BRUNSWICK, Canon Robert John. b 38. TD 86. St Aid Birkenhead 60. **d** 63 **p** 64. C Neston *Ches* 63-66; CF (TA - R of O) 65-96; C Warrington St Paul *Liv* 66-68; V Liv St Paul Stoneycroft 68-78; V Southport St Luke 78-87; R Croston *Blackb* 87-01; R Croston and Bretherton 01-05; Chapl Bp Rawstorne Sch Preston 88-05; Hon Can Koforidua from 94; rtd 05. *60 St Clements Avenue, Farington, Leyland PR25 4QU* T: (01772) 426094

BRUNT, Alison. b 60. Nottm Univ BSc 82 K Coll Lon MA 01 SS Coll Cam BTh 12. Westcott Ho Cam 10. **d** 12 **p** 13. C S Croydon St Pet and St Aug *S'wark* 12-15; V Norbury St Oswald from 15. *The Vicarage, 2B St Oswald's Road, London SW16 3SB* T: (020) 8764 2853　E: rev.alison@outlook.com

BRUNT, Prof Peter William. b 36. OBE 94 CVO 01. Liv Univ MB 59 MD 67 Lon Univ FRCP 74 FRCPEd. Ab Dioc Tr Course. **d** 96 **p** 97. NSM Bieldside *Ab* 96-07; PtO *Carl* from 08; *Ab* from 11. Flat 4, 1 Hillpark Rise, Edinburgh EH4 7BB T: 0131-312 6687　E: peterbrunt123@btinternet.com

BRUNT, Canon Philippa Ann. b 53. Leeds Univ BA 74 Leeds and Carnegie Coll PGCE 75. WEMTC 95. **d** 98 **p** 99. C Cinderford St Steph w Littledean *Glouc* 98-01; V Parkend and Viney Hill from 01; AD Forest S from 09; Hon Can Glouc Cathl from 10. *The Vicarage, Lower Road, Yorkley, Lydney GL15 4TN* T: (01594) 562828　E: pabrunt@btinternet.com

BRUNYEE, Miss Hilary. b 46. Linc Th Coll 76. dss 81 **d** 87 **p** 94. Par Dn Peel *Man* 87-94; TV 94-99; TV Walkden and Lt Hulton 99-00; rtd 00; PtO *Man* from 00. *38 Holly Avenue, Worsley, Manchester M28 3DW* T: 0161-790 7761

BRUSH, Canon Sally. b 47. Lon Univ BD 75 Univ of Wales MPhil 96. Trin Coll Bris 73. dss 76 **d** 80 **p** 97. Flint *St As* 76-83; C 80-83; C Cefn 83-87; C St As and Tremeirchion 83-87; Chapl St As Cathl 83-87; Dn-in-c Cerrigydrudion w Llanfihangel Glyn Myfyr etc 87-97; V 97-07; RD Edeirnion 98-04; Hon Can St As Cathl 01-07; rtd 07; PtO *St As* from 09; *Ban* from 10. *Persondy, 1 Tyddyn Terrace, Cerrigydrudion, Corwen LL21 9TN* T: (01490) 420048

BRUSH (née HAMILTON), Sarah Louise. b 74. Reading Univ BA 97 MA 98 PhD 01. Qu Coll Birm MA 14. **d** 14 **p** 15. C Halas *Worc* from 14. *89 Stourbridge Road, Halesowen B63 3UA* E: sarahbrush@hotmail.co.uk

BRYAN, Angela Edwina. b 82. York Univ BA 03 York St Jo Coll PGCE 04. St Jo Coll Nottm 07. **d** 10 **p** 11. C Tipton St Matt *Lich* 10-14; P-in-c Kirkholt *Man* from 14. *St Thomas's Vicarage, Cavendish Road, Rochdale OL11 2QX* T: (01706) 649373 E: kirkholtrev@outlook.com

BRYAN, Cecil William. b 43. TCD BA 66 MA 73. CITC 66. **d** 68 **p** 69. C Dublin Zion Ch *D & G* 68-72; Chapl RAF 72-75; Dioc Info Officer *D & G* 75-90; I Castleknock w Mulhuddart, Clonsilla etc 75-89; Chapl K Hosp Sch Dub 89-99; I Tullow *D & G* 99-07; Can Ch Ch Cathl Dublin 03-07; rtd 07. *2 Grange Heights, Green Road, Newbridge, Co Kildare, Republic of Ireland* T: (00353) (45) 435572　M: 87-221 2004 E: c.bryan@iol.ie

BRYAN, Christopher Paul. b 75. Univ Coll Ox BA 96 St Jo Coll Dur BA 99. Cranmer Hall Dur 97. **d** 00 **p** 01. C Old Swinford Stourbridge *Worc* 00-04; P-in-c Lechlade *Glouc* 04-08; TV Fairford Deanery 09-10; P-in-c Sherston Magna, Easton Grey, Luckington etc *Bris* from 10; P-in-c Hullavington, Norton and Stanton St Quintin from 10. *The Rectory, 1 Rectory Close, Stanton St Quintin, Chippenham SN14 6DT* T: (01666) 837522　M: 07906-175331 E: christopher.bryan123@btinternet.com

BRYAN, David John. b 56. Liv Univ BSc 77 Hull Univ BTh 85 Qu Coll Ox DPhil 89. Ox Min Course 89. **d** 90 **p** 91. C Abingdon *Ox* 90-93; Tutor Qu Coll Birm 93-01; Dean of Studies 95-01; R Haughton le Skerne *Dur* 01-11; Dir Studies Lindisfarne Reg

Tr Partnership from 11. *2 Kingfisher Close, Esh Winning, Durham DH7 9AN* T: 0191-373 9698

BRYAN, Helen Ann. b 68. NTMTC BA 07. **d** 07 **p** 08. NSM Laindon w Dunton *Chelmsf* 07-13; P-in-c E and W Horndon w Lt Warley and Childerditch from 13. *The Rectory, 147 Thorndon Avenue, West Horndon, Brentwood CM13 3TR* M: 07747-397973 E: hbryan@talktalk.net

BRYAN, Judith Claire. See STEPHENSON, Judith Claire

BRYAN, Michael John Christopher. b 35. Wadh Coll Ox BA 58 BTh 59 MA 63 Ex Univ PhD 83. Ripon Hall Ox 59. **d** 60 **p** 61. C Reigate St Mark *S'wark* 60-64; Tutor Sarum & Wells Th Coll 64-69; Vice-Prin 69-71; USA 71-74; Sen Officer Educn and Community Dept *Lon* 74-79; Chapl Ex Univ 79-83; USA from 83; rtd 95; PtO *Ex* from 95. *148 Proctors Hall Road, Sewanee TN 37375-0860, USA* T: (001) (931) 598 0860

BRYAN, Patrick Joseph. b 41. St Jo Coll Cam BA 63 MA 67. St Steph Ho Ox 73. **d** 75 **p** 76. C Rushall *Lich* 75-78; C Brierley Hill 78-80; P-in-c Walsall St Mary and All SS Palfrey 80-87; PtO from 13. *12 Derwent Road, Wolverhampton WV6 9ES* T: (01902) 689550 E: pjjmbryan@blueyonder.co.uk

BRYAN, Canon Sherry Lee. b 49. Open Univ BA 12. WMMTC 88. **d** 91 **p** 94. Par Dn St Columb Minor and St Colan *Truro* 91-94; C 94-96; P-in-c St Teath 96-05; P-in-c Blisland w St Breward 05-15; P-in-c Helland 05-15; R Blisland w Temple, St Breward and Helland from 15; Chapl Cornwall Healthcare NHS Trust 99-02; RD Trigg Minor and Bodmin *Truro* 02-13; Hon Can Truro Cathl from 03. *The Rectory, Green Briar, Coombe Lane, St Breward, Bodmin PL30 4DX* T: (01208) 851829

BRYAN, Canon Timothy Andrew. b 56. St Edm Hall Ox MA 80. S'wark Ord Course 93. **d** 96 **p** 97. NSM Morden *S'wark* 96-99; NSM Carshalton Beeches 99-05; NSM Sutton 05-08; Resettlement Chapl HM Pris Wandsworth 07-08; Co-ord Chapl from 08; Hon Can S'wark Cathl from 15. *HM Prison Wandsworth, PO Box 757, Heathfield Road, London SW18 3HS* T: (020) 8588 4000 E: timbryan7@aol.com

BRYAN, William Terence. b 38. Dudley Coll of Educn CertEd 68. Chich Th Coll 73. **d** 75 **p** 76. C Shrewsbury St Giles *Lich* 75-79; V Churchstoke w Hyssington and Sarn *Heref* 79-03; rtd 04; P-in-c Betws Cedewain and Tregynon and Llanwyddelan *St As* 07-15; PtO from 15. *29 Llys Melyn, Tregynon, Newtown SY16 3EE* T: (01686) 650899

BRYANT, Canon Andrew Watts. b 57. St Jo Coll Dur BA 78 Birm Univ MA 81. Qu Coll Birm 80. **d** 83 **p** 84. C Pelsall *Lich* 83-87; NSM 91-94; PtO 87-92; NSM Streetly 94-96; NSM Beckbury, Badger, Kemberton, Ryton, Stockton etc 96-99; R Worplesdon *Guildf* 99-09; Chapl Merrist Wood Coll of Agric and Horticulture 01-09; TR Portishead *B & W* 09-15; Can Res Nor Cathl from 15; P-in-c Nor St Mary in the Marsh from 15. *52 The Close, Norwich NR1 4EG* T: (01603) 218331 E: canon.missionandpastoral@cathedral.org.uk

BRYANT, Canon Christopher. b 32. K Coll Lon AKC 60. **d** 61 **p** 62. C Fareham H Trin *Portsm* 61-65; C Yatton Keynell *Bris* 65-71; C Biddestone w Slaughterford 65-71; C Castle Combe 65-71; V Chirton, Marden and Patney *Sarum* 71-76; V Chirton, Marden, Patney, Charlton and Wilsford 76-78; P-in-c Devizes St Jo w St Mary 78-79; R 79-97; RD Devizes 83-93; Can and Preb Sarum Cathl 87-04; rtd 97; Master St Nic Hosp Salisbury 97-04. *34 Mill Road, Salisbury SP2 7RZ* T: (01722) 502336 E: rukit@btopenworld.com

BRYANT, David Henderson. b 37. K Coll Lon BD 60 AKC 60. **d** 61 **p** 62. C Trowbridge H Trin *Sarum* 61-63; C Ewell *Guildf* 63-67; V Leiston *St E* 67-73; Chapl RN 73; C Northam *Ex* 74-75; P-in-c Clavering w Langley *Chelmsf* 76-77; Teacher Mountview High Sch Harrow 77-85; P-in-c Boosbeck w Moorsholm *York* 85-89; V 89-90; V Sowerby 90-95; P-in-c Sessay 90-95; V Lastingham w Appleton-le-Moors, Rosedale etc 95-99; rtd 99. *35 West End, Kirkbymoorside, York YO62 6AD* T: (01751) 430269

BRYANT, Donald Thomas. b 29. SE Essex Coll BSc 56 Birkbeck Coll Lon BSc 58 FSS 59. S'wark Ord Course 85. **d** 88 **p** 89. NSM Redhill St Matt *S'wark* 88-99; PtO 99-04 and from 05; NSM Salfords 04-05. *3 Mulberry Walk, Ditchling Common, Burgess Hill RH15 0SZ* T: (01444) 254167

BRYANT, Canon Edward Francis Paterson. b 43. S'wark Ord Course 75. **d** 78 **p** 79. NSM Hadlow *Roch* 78-84; C Dartford St Alb 84-87; R Hollington St Leon *Chich* 87-93; V Bexhill St Aug 93-99; TR Bexhill St Pet 99-12; P-in-c Sedlescombe w Whatlington 02-05; rtd 12; RD Battle and Bexhill *Chich* 98-04 and 10-13; Can and Preb Chich Cathl from 00. *14 Highwater View, St Leonards-on-Sea TN38 8EL* T: (01424) 853687 F: 07970-991268 M: 07824-859044 E: invenietis@gmx.com

BRYANT, Graham Trevor. b 41. Keble Coll Ox BA 63 MA 67. Chich Th Coll 64. **d** 66 **p** 67. C Leeds St Wilfrid *Ripon* 66-69;

C Haywards Heath St Wilfrid *Chich* 69-74; V Crawley Down All SS 74-79; V Bexhill St Aug 79-85; V Charlton Kings St Mary *Glouc* 85-02; rtd 02; PtO *Glouc* from 03. *6 The Close, Cheltenham GL53 0PQ* T: (01242) 520313

BRYANT, Huw Adrian. b 82. St Mich Coll Llan BTh 13. **d** 13 **p** 14. C Bro'r Holl Saint *Ban* 13-15; C Bro Enlli from 15. *The Vicarage, Ala Road, Pwllheli LL53 5BL* E: huwtree@hotmail.com

✠**BRYANT, The Rt Revd Mark Watts.** b 49. St Jo Coll Dur BA 72. Cuddesdon Coll 72. **d** 75 **p** 76 **c** 07. C Addlestone *Guildf* 75-79; C Studley *Sarum* 79-83; V 83-88; Chapl Trowbridge Coll 79-83; Voc Development Adv and Dioc Dir of Ords *Cov* 88-96; Hon Can Cov Cathl 93-01; TR Coventry Caludon 96-01; AD Cov E 99-01; Adn Cov 01-07; Can Res Cov Cathl 06-07; Suff Bp Jarrow *Dur* from 07. *Bishop's House, Ivy Lane, Gateshead NE9 6QD* T: 0191-491 0917 F: 491 5116 E: bishop.of.jarrow@durham.anglican.org

BRYANT, Patricia Ann. b 36. Qu Mary Coll Lon BA 58. St Mich Coll Llan 94. **d** 91 **p** 97. NSM Llanbadoc *Mon* 91-93; NSM Llangybi and Coedypaen w Llanbadoc 93-94; C 94-98; Asst Chapl Gwent Tertiary Coll 94-98; V Merthyr Cynog and Dyffryn Honddu etc *S & B* 98-02; rtd 03. *5 Trebarried Court, Llandefalle, Brecon LD3 0NB* T: (01874) 754087 E: bryants@surfaid.org

BRYANT, Peter James. b 35. Jes Coll Cam BA 58 MA 64 UWIST 59 FInstM. St Deiniol's Hawarden 86 St Mich Coll Llan 96. **d** 97 **p** 98. NSM Raglan-Usk *Mon* 97-98; NSM Merthyr Cynog and Dyffryn Honddu etc *S & B* 98-02. *5 Trebarried Court, Llandefalle, Brecon LD3 0NB* T: (01874) 754087 E: bryants@surfaid.org

BRYANT, Canon Richard Kirk. b 47. Ch Coll Cam BA 68 MA 72. Cuddesdon Coll 70. **d** 72 **p** 73. C Newc St Gabr 72-75; C Morpeth 75-78; C Benwell St Jas 78-82; V Earsdon and Backworth 82-93; V Wylam 93-97; Prin Local Min Scheme 97-11; Prin Reader Tr 97-11; Hon Can Newc Cathl 97-11; rtd 11. *10 Highworth Drive, Newcastle upon Tyne NE7 7FB* T: 0191-240 1510 E: rk.bryant@virginmedia.com

BRYANT, Richard Maurice. b 46. MAAIS 80. WMMTC 90. **d** 93 **p** 94. NSM The Stanleys *Glouc* 93-98; NSM Glouc St Geo w Whaddon 98-04; NSM Twigworth, Down Hatherley, Norton, The Leigh etc 04-08; NSM Bisley, Chalford, France Lynch, and Oakridge 08-11; rtd 11; PtO *Glouc* from 11. *6 Church Street, Kings Stanley, Stonehouse GL10 3HW* T: (01453) 823172

BRYANT, Sarah Elizabeth. See WOOD-ROE, Sarah Elizabeth

BRYARS, Peter John. b 54. BA MEd PhD. St Jo Coll Nottm. **d** 84 **p** 85. C Hull St Martin w Transfiguration *York* 84-87; TV Drypool 87-90; TV Glendale Gp *Newc* 90-94; P-in-c Heddon-on-the-Wall 94-01; Adult Educn Adv 94-01; V Delaval 01-11; AD Bedlington 03-09; Dioc Chapl MU 02-07; rtd 12; Bp's Adv for Healing Min *Newc* from 06. *36 Newlands Road, Blyth NE24 2QJ* E: pjbryars@btinternet.com

BRYCE, Brenda Dorothy. See BROWN, Brenda Dorothy

BRYCE, Michael Adrian Gilpin. b 47. TCD BA 71 MA 95. CITC 74. **d** 77 **p** 78. C Clondalkin w Tallaght *D & G* 77-79; C Ch Ch Cathl and Chapl Univ Coll Dub 79-82; I Ardamine w Kiltennel, Glascarrig etc *C & O* 82-84; CF 84-00; I Lisbellaw *Clogh* 00-05; R Bolam w Whalton and Hartburn w Meldon *Newc* from 05; V Nether Witton from 05; Chapl Kirkley Hall Coll from 05. *The Rectory, Whalton, Morpeth NE61 3UX* T: (01670) 775360

BRYCE, Paul Russell. b 79. SS Mark & Jo Univ Coll Plymouth BA 00. Wycliffe Hall Ox MTh. **d** 06 **p** 07. C Paignton Ch Ch and Preston St Paul *Ex* 06-10; P-in-c Charles w Plymouth St Matthias from 10. *The Vicarage, 6 St Lawrence Road, Plymouth PL4 6HN* T: (01752) 225516

BRYDON, Michael Andrew. b 73. St Chad's Coll Dur BA 95 MA 96 PhD 00. St Steph Ho Ox BA 01. **d** 02 **p** 03. C Bexhill St Pet *Chich* 02-06; C Brighton St Paul 06-08; C Brighton St Mich 06-08; Dioc Adv for Educn and Tr of Adults 06-08; R Catsfield and Crowhurst from 08. *The Rectory, Church Lane, Catsfield, Battle TN33 9DR* T: (01424) 892988

BRYER, Anthony Colin. b 51. Qu Eliz Coll Lon BSc 72. Trin Coll Bris 72. **d** 75 **p** 76. C Preston St Cuth *Blackb* 75-78; C Becontree St Mary *Chelmsf* 78-81; TV Loughton St Mary and St Mich 81-88; C Clifton St Paul *Bris* 88-91; P-in-c 91-94; R Bris St Mich and St Paul 94-96; In C of S and LtO *Edin* 96-04; P-in-c Towcester w Caldecote and Easton Neston *Pet* 04-07; C Greens Norton w Bradden and Lichborough 06-07; V Towcester w Caldecote and Easton Neston etc 07-11; Ind Chapl *Edin* from 11. *4 Yewlands Gardens, Edinburgh EH16 6TA* T: 0131-672 2232 M: 07814-832004 E: tony.bryer51@gmail.com

BRYER, The Ven Paul Donald. b 58. Sussex Univ BEd 80 Nottm Univ MA 96. St Jo Coll Nottm. **d** 90 **p** 91. C Tonbridge St Steph *Roch* 90-94; TV Camberley St Paul *Guildf* 94-99; V Camberley St Mary 99-01; V Dorking St Paul 01-14; RD

Dorking 09-14; Adn Dorking from 14; Hon Can Guildf Cathl from 14. *The Old Cricketers, Portsmouth Road, Ripley, Woking GU23 6ER* T: (01483) 479300 *or* 790352
E: paul.bryer@cofeguildford.org.uk

BRYSON, James Ferguson. b 55. NE Lon Poly BSc 79 RIBA 93. SEITE 04. **d** 07 **p** 08. C Old Ford St Paul and St Mark *Lon* 07-10; P-in-c Eltham St Jo *S'wark* from 11. *The Vicarage, Sowerby Close, London SE9 6HB*
E: fergusonbryson@btinternet.com

BRYSON, Neil Dominic. b 50. Open Univ BA 76 Lon Inst of Educn MA 84 St Matthias Coll Bris CertEd 71. Ox Min Course 10. **d** 12 **p** 13. NSM Boyne Hill *Ox* from 12. *5 Chatsworth Close, Maidenhead SL6 4RD* T: (01628) 713498
M: 07553-091225 E: frneil@ymail.com

BRYSON, Philip Neil William. b 82. Man Metrop Univ BA 05. St Jo Coll Nottm 12. **d** 15. C Bedford St Paul *St Alb* from 15. *55 Crown Quay, Prebend Street, Bedford MK40 1BN* T: (01234) 344058 E: fr.phil.bryson@outlook.com

BUBBERS, Richard David. b 55. Keble Coll Ox BA 78 MA 93 Solicitor 81. St Jo Coll Nottm 10. **d** 12 **p** 13. C Ipsley *Worc* 12-15; P-in-c Alvechurch from 15; Ind Chapl from 15. *The Rectory, School Lane, Alvechurch, Birmingham B48 7SB* M: 07968-507878 E: rdb9999@hotmail.com

BUCHAN, Geoffrey Herbert. b 38. CEng MIMechE. NOC 91. **d** 94 **p** 95. NSM Barnton *Ches* 94-96; NSM Goostrey 96-99; C Stretton and Appleton Thorn 99-12; rtd 12. *12 Hough Lane, Anderton, Northwich CW9 6AB* T: (01606) 74512
E: gbuchan@tiscali.co.uk

BUCHAN, Ms Janet Elizabeth Forbes. b 56. Ex Univ BA 79 K Coll Lon MSc 90 Surrey Univ PGCE 93. SEITE 08. **d** 11 **p** 12. C W Hackney *Lon* 11-14; P-in-c Goodmayes St Paul *Chelmsf* from 14. *St Paul's Vicarage, 20 Eastwood Road, Ilford IG3 8XA* M: 07749-104870 T: (020) 8597 8141
E: janetbuchan@gmail.com

BUCHAN, Mrs Kirstine Dilys. b 60. St Jo Coll Nottm 13. **d** 15. NSM Radford All So and St Pet *S'well* from 15. *50 Barrydale Avenue, Beeston, Nottingham NG9 1GN* M: 07871-162672
E: kirstine@gmx.co.uk

BUCHAN, Matthew Alexander John. b 69. St Andr Univ MA 92. Wycliffe Hall Ox BTh 95. **d** 98 **p** 99. C Horninglow *Lich* 98-01; TV Moulsecoomb *Chich* 01-04; Bp's Chapl *Glouc* 04-06; P-in-c Leybourne *Roch* 06-14; R from 14; RD Malling from 14; Chapl RAuxAF from 11. *The Rectory, 73 Rectory Lane North, Leybourne, West Malling ME19 5HD* T: (01732) 842187
E: frbuchan@frbuchan.force9.co.uk

BUCHANAN, Andrew Derek. b 64. Stirling Univ BA 90. Wycliffe Hall Ox 98. **d** 01 **p** 02. C Plas Newton *Ches* 01-03; C Ches Ch Ch 03-06; C Plas Newton w Ches Ch Ch 07-11; Asst Chapl Ches Univ 03-11; V Ruddington *S'well* from 11. *The Vicarage, Wilford Road, Ruddington, Nottingham NG11 6EL* T: 0115-921 4522 E: rev_buchanan@hotmail.com

✠**BUCHANAN, The Rt Revd Colin Ogilvie.** b 34. Linc Coll Ox BA MA Lambeth DD 93. Tyndale Hall Bris 59. **d** 61 **p** 62 **c** 85. C Cheadle *Ches* 61-64; Tutor St Jo Coll Nottm 64-85; Lib 64-69; Registrar 69-74; Dir of Studies 74-75; Vice-Prin 75-78; Prin 79-85; Hon Can S'well Minster 81-85; Suff Bp Aston *Birm* 85-89; Asst Bp Roch 89-96; Asst Bp S'wark 90-91; V Gillingham St Mark *Roch* 91-96; Area Bp Woolwich *S'wark* 96-04; rtd 04; Hon Asst Bp Bradf 04-14; Hon Asst Bp Ripon and Leeds 05-14. *21 The Drive, Alwoodley, Leeds LS17 7QB* T: 0113-267 7721 E: cobdleeds@btinternet.com

BUCHANAN, Eoin George. b 59. Glyndwr Univ MA 11. Qu Coll Birm 98. **d** 00 **p** 01. C Dovercourt and Parkeston w Harwich *Chelmsf* 00-04; C Ramsey w Lt Oakley 02-04; TR N Hinckford 04-12; R Flegg Coastal Benefice *Nor* 12-13. *Address temp unknown* M: 07740-051812 E: okyan12@icloud.com

BUCHANAN, James Kenyon. b 79. Qu Coll Cam BA 02 MA 06. Oak Hill Th Coll MTh 10. **d** 10 **p** 11. C Clerkenwell St Mark *Lon* 10-13; Sen Min Melville Union Ch Johannesburg S Africa from 13. *56 Richmond Avenue, Auckland Park, Johannesburg, 2092 South Africa*
E: jameskbuchanan@googlemail.com

BUCHANAN, John Fraser Walter. b 32. Em Coll Cam BA 55. **d** 93 **p** 94. OLM Wainford *St E* 93-07; rtd 07; PtO *St E* from 07. *The Hermitage, Bridge Street, Beccles NR34 9BA* T: (01502) 712154

BUCHANAN, Stephanie Joan. b 65. Linc Coll Ox BA 88 MA 02 Selw Coll Cam BA 01 Goldsmiths' Coll Lon PGCE 93. Ridley Hall Cam 99. **d** 02 **p** 03. C Mirfield *Wakef* 02-06; TV Em TM 06-12; V Wakef St Jo *Leeds* from 12. *St John's Vicarage, 65 Bradford Road, Wakefield WF1 2AA* T: (01924) 371029
E: stephanie.buchanan@btinternet.com

BUCHANAN, Thomas. b 67. **d** 13 **p** 14. NSM St Marg Lothbury and St Steph Coleman Street etc *Lon* from 13; PtO *Ely* from 14. *St Margaret's Church, Lothbury, London EC2R 7HH* T: (020) 7726 4878 E: buchanantom@hotmail.co.uk

BUCK, Ashley. *See* BUCK, William Ashley

BUCK, David Andrew. b 64. GMusRNCM 88. Ripon Coll Cuddesdon 97. **d** 99 **p** 00. C Poulton-le-Sands w Morecambe St Laur *Blackb* 99-03; V Hednesford *Lich* 03-10; Chapl Wheatfields Hospice from 12. *The Vicarage, Wakefield Road, Lightcliffe, Halifax HX3 8TH* T: (01422) 202424

BUCK, Mrs Jacqueline Rosemary. b 66. ERMC 06. **d** 09 **p** 10. NSM Cople, Moggerhanger and Willington *St Alb* 09-12; NSM Goldington from 12. *54 Henderson Way, Kempston, Bedford MK42 8NP* T: (01234) 407020 E: jackiebuck@hotmail.co.uk

BUCK (née JONES), Kathryn Mary. b 59. Birm Univ BA 81 MEd 91 Sheff Univ PGCE 82. Ripon Coll Cuddesdon. **d** 99 **p** 00. C Uttoxeter Area *Lich* 99-00; C Scotforth *Blackb* 00-03; TV Cannock *Lich* 03-09; TV Cannock and Huntington 09-10; C Hednesford 05-10; V Lightcliffe and Hove Edge *Leeds* from 11. *The Vicarage, Wakefield Road, Lightcliffe, Halifax HX3 8TH* T: (01422) 202424

BUCK, Canon Nicholas John. b 57. Leic Univ BScEng 79. Ridley Hall Cam 81. **d** 84 **p** 85. C Oakwood St Thos *Lon* 84-87; C Darnall and Attercliffe *Sheff* 87-90; V Kimberworth 90-96; Chapl Scargill Ho 96-01; P-in-c Bassingham Gp *Linc* 01-06; R 06-15; P-in-c Branston w Nocton and Potterhanworth 12-15; P-in-c Metheringham w Blankney and Dunston 12-15; RD Graffoe 09-14; V Linc St Giles from 15; Can and Preb Linc Cathl from 10. *The Vicarage, 25 Shelley Drive, Lincoln LN2 4BY* E: nick_buck@tiscali.co.uk

BUCK, Canon Richard Peter Holdron. b 37. AKC 64. Lambeth Hon MA 93. **d** 65 **p** 66. C Mill Hill Jo Keble Ch *Lon* 65-68; C St Marylebone All SS 68-74; Can Res and Treas Truro Cathl 74-76; V Primrose Hill St Mary w Avenue Road St Paul *Lon* 76-84; Bp's Ecum Adv *S'wark* 84-91; P-in-c Dulwich Common St Pet 84-86; Hon Can S'wark Cathl 90-98; C Rotherhithe St Kath w St Barn 91-92; C Bermondsey St Kath w St Bart 92-94; C Greenwich St Alfege w St Pet and St Paul 94-98; rtd 98. *50 Viceroy Lodge, 143 Kingsway, Hove BN3 4RB* T: (01273) 710155

BUCK, William Ashley. b 61. Man Univ BA 82 Ox Univ BA 86 MA 91. Ripon Coll Cuddesdon 84. **d** 87 **p** 88. C Addington *S'wark* 87-91; C Pimlico St Pet w Westmr Ch Ch *Lon* 91-94; TV Wenlock *Heref* 94-03; RD Condover 00-03; R Cleobury Mortimer w Hopton Wafers etc from 03. *The Rectory, The Hurst, Cleobury Mortimer, Kidderminster DY14 8EG* T: (01299) 270264

BUCKINGHAM, The Ven Hugh Fletcher. b 32. Hertf Coll Ox BA 57 MA 60. Westcott Ho Cam 55. **d** 57 **p** 58. C Halliwell St Thos *Man* 57-60; C Sheff Gillcar St Silas 60-65; V Hindolveston *Nor* 65-70; V Guestwick 65-70; R Fakenham w Alethorpe 70-88; Chmn Dioc Bd Soc Resp 81-88; RD Burnham and Walsingham *Nor* 81-87; Hon Can Nor Cathl 85-88; Adn E Riding *York* 88-98; Can and Preb York Minster 88-01; rtd 98; PtO *York* from 01. *2 Rectory Corner, Brandsby, York YO61 4RJ* T: (01347) 888202

BUCKINGHAM, Paul John. b 63. Bris Univ BVSc 87. WMMTC 94. **d** 98. NSM Kington w Huntington, Old Radnor, Kinnerton etc *Heref* from 98. *The Cottage, Prospect Lane, Kington HR5 3BE* T: (01544) 231357

BUCKINGHAM, Richard Arthur John. b 49. Univ of Wales (Cardiff) BA 71 PGCE 72. Chich Th Coll 73. **d** 76 **p** 77. C Llantwit Major *Llan* 76-80; C Leigh-on-Sea St Marg *Chelmsf* 80-84; C Westmr St Matt *Lon* 84-87; R Stock Harvard *Chelmsf* 87-02; PtO *Lon* from 02. *3 Priory Close, London N3 1BB* T: (020) 8371 0178 E: rbuckingham@waitrose.com

BUCKINGHAM, Terence John. b 52. Aston Univ BSc 73 MSc 75 PhD 78 FCOptom 74. Coll of Resurr Mirfield 01. **d** 03 **p** 04. NSM Harrogate St Wilfrid *Ripon* 03-09; P-in-c Nidd 09-10; NSM Leeds St Wilfrid from 10. *29 Dalesway, Guiseley, Leeds LS20 8JN* T: (01943) 876066 M: 07815-994017
E: terry.j.buckingham@btopenworld.com

BUCKINGHAM, Archdeacon of. *See* GORHAM, The Ven Karen Marisa

BUCKINGHAM, Area Bishop of. *See* WILSON, The Rt Revd Alan Thomas Lawrence

BUCKLE, Graham Charles. b 59. ERMC 08. **d** 11 **p** 12. NSM Silverstone and Abthorpe w Slapton etc *Pet* from 11. *10 Waits Yard, Litchborough, Towcester NN12 8LX* M: 07901-660593
E: gdjlg@tiscali.co.uk

BUCKLE, Graham Martin. b 62. Southn Univ BTh 89 Sheff Univ MMinTheol 04. Sarum & Wells Th Coll 85. **d** 89 **p** 90. C Paddington St Jas *Lon* 89-94; P-in-c Paddington St Pet 94-00; R St Marylebone St Paul 00-14; Dir of Ords Two Cities Area 99-08; V Westmr St Matt from 14. *21 Vincent Square, London SW1P 2NA* T: (020) 7834 1300 E: vicar@ssswsj.com

BUCKLER, Andrew Jonathan Heslington. b 68. Trin Coll Ox BA 89 MA 96. Wycliffe Hall Ox BTh 93. **d** 96 **p** 97. C Ox St Aldate 96-00; Crosslinks France from 00. *12 rue de Gassicourt, 78200 Mantes la Jolie, France* T: (0033) 1 30 33 07 95 E: bucklers@clara.net

BUCKLER, George Anthony (Tony). b 35. Open Univ BA 74. Lich Th Coll 58. **d** 61 **p** 62. C Old Swinford *Worc* 61-65; C Droitwich St Nic w St Pet 65-67; C Droitwich St Andr w St Mary 65-67; Chapl Claybury Hosp Woodford Bridge 67-78; Chapl Co Hosp Linc and St Geo Hosp Linc 78-87; Chapl The Lawn Hosp Linc 78-81; Chapl Wexham Park Hosp Slough 87-90; Chapl Mapperley Hosp Nottm 90-94; Chapl Nottm Mental Illness and Psychiatric Unit 90-93; Chapl Notts Healthcare NHS Trust 94-96; Chapl Wells Rd Cen Nottm 94-96; Chapl Qu Medical Cen Nottm 94-96; Chapl Highbury Hosp Nottm 94-96; rtd 96. *73 Westfield Drive, Lincoln LN2 4RE*

BUCKLER, Canon Guy Ernest Warr. b 46. ACA 69 FCA 79. Linc Th Coll 71. **d** 74 **p** 75. C Dunstable *St Alb* 74-77; C Houghton Regis 77-86; TV Willington *Newc* 86-88; TR 88-95; Chapl N Tyneside Coll of FE 88-95; R Bedford St Pet w St Cuth *St Alb* 95-05; R Bushey 05-11; RD Aldenham 08-11; Hon Can St Alb 10-11; rtd 11. *18 Deans Close, Abbots Langley WD5 0HL* T: (01923) 269975 E: gbuckler@hotmail.com

BUCKLER, Kenneth Arthur. b 50. S Bank Univ MSc 94. NTMTC 95. **d** 98 **p** 99. C Welwyn w Ayot St Peter *St Alb* 98-01; P-in-c Kimpton w Ayot St Lawrence 01-05; Asst Chapl E Herts NHS Trust 99-00; Asst Chapl E and N Herts NHS Trust 00-04; Chapl Team Ldr 04-05; V Hounslow W Gd Shep *Lon* 05-12; rtd 12; PtO *Lon* from 12. *104 Royal Lane, Uxbridge UB8 3QY* M: 07909-970545 E: kenbuckler@ymail.com

BUCKLER, The Very Revd Philip John Warr. b 49. St Pet Coll Ox BA 70 MA 74. Cuddesdon Coll 70. **d** 72 **p** 73. C Bushey Heath *St Alb* 72-75; Chapl Trin Coll Cam 75-81; Min Can and Sacr St Paul's Cathl 81-87; V Hampstead St Jo 87-99; AD N Camden 93-98; Can Res St Paul's Cathl 99-07; Can Res and Treas St Paul's Cathl 00-07; Dean Linc from 07. *The Deanery, 11 Minster Yard, Lincoln LN2 1PJ* T: (01522) 561611 E: dean@lincolncathedral.com

BUCKLES, Ms Jayne Elizabeth. b 53. **d** 07 **p** 08. NSM Penrhyndeudraeth and Llanfrothen w Maentwrog etc *Ban* 07-10; R St Edm Way *St E* from 10. *The Rectory, Harrow Green, Lawshall, Bury St Edmunds IP29 4PB* T: (01284) 830513 E: jaynebuckles@btinternet.com

BUCKLEY, Alexander Christopher Nolan. b 67. Univ of Wales (Abth) BD 89 Man Univ MA 06. St Mich Coll Llan. **d** 91 **p** 94. C Llandudno *Ban* 91-92; C Ynyscynhaearn w Penmorfa and Porthmadog 92-93 and 94-96; Jesuit Volunteer Community Manchester 93-94; C Caerau w Ely *Llan* 96-01; V Trowbridge Mawr *Mon* 01-03; Chapl ATC 96-03; PtO *Mon* 03-09; *Man* 04-09; R Llanllyfni *Ban* from 12; P-in-c Leeds Belle Is St Jo and St Barn from 12; C Hunslet w Cross Green from 12; CMP from 02. *The Vicarage, 30 Low Grange View, Leeds LS10 3DT*

BUCKLEY, Anthony Graham. b 63. Keble Coll Ox BA 84 MA 90 PGCE 85. Wycliffe Hall Ox 96. **d** 98 **p** 99. C Folkestone St Jo *Cant* 98-00; V 00-08; AD Elham 05-08; Hon Can Cant Cathl 08; Chapl Alleyn's Sch Dulwich from 08; Hon C Dulwich St Barn *S'wark* from 08; Dir of IME Woolwich Area from 09. *53 Gilkes Crescent, London SE21 7PB* E: antmon64@hotmail.com

BUCKLEY, Christine Judith. d 15. NSM Poynton *Ches* from 15. *The Vicarage, Spuley Lane, Pott Shrigley, Macclesfield SK10 5RS* T: (01625) 573316 M: 07709-032435 E: bcklyc@aol.com

BUCKLEY, Christopher Ivor. b 48. Chich Th Coll 84. **d** 86 **p** 87. C Felpham w Middleton *Chich* 86-89; C Jersey St Brelade *Win* 89-93; V Jersey St Mark 93-06; Chapl Jersey Airport 00-06; V E Radnor *S & B* 06-10; rtd 11; PtO *Win* from 10. *1 Les Petites Champs, La Rue du Flicquet, St Martin, Jersey JE3 6BP* T: (01534) 738265 M: 07797-714595 E: christopher.buckley@jerseymail.co.uk

BUCKLEY, David Rex. b 47. Ripon Coll Cuddesdon 75. **d** 77 **p** 78. C Witton Ches 77-81; V Backford 81-85; Youth Chapl 81-85; V Barnton 85-93; P-in-c Bickerton w Bickley 93-97; P-in-c Harthill and Burwardsley 93-97; C Bickerton, Bickley, Harthill and Burwardsley 97-01; P-in-c Sandbach 01-03; V 03-07; rtd 08; Chapl Cheshire Constabulary *Ches* 08-12. *308 Swanlow Lane, Winsford CW7 4BN* T: (01606) 559437 M: 07810-791417 E: rex@chazandrex.freeserve.co.uk

BUCKLEY, Ms Debra. b 59. Birm Poly BA 81. Qu Coll Birm 08. **d** 10 **p** 11. C Balsall Heath and Edgbaston SS Mary and Ambrose *Birm* 10-14; V Smethwick from 14. *The Vicarage, 93A Church Road, Smethwick B67 6EE* T: 0121-558 1763 E: debbuckley@phonecoop.coop

BUCKLEY, Ernest Fairbank. b 25. Jes Coll Cam BA 49 MA 50 Jes Coll Ox BLitt 53. Westcott Ho Cam 55. **d** 55 **p** 56. C Rochdale *Man* 55-58; V Hey 58-64; V Baguley 64-79; V Clun w Chapel Lawn, Bettws-y-Crwyn and Newcastle *Heref* 79-87; RD Clun Forest 82-87; rtd 88. *The Old Barn, Brassington, Matlock DE4 4HL* T: (01629) 540821 E: buckley@w3z.co.uk

BUCKLEY, Heather Eileen. b 52. BEd. **d** 11 **p** 12. C Prenton *Ches* from 11. *57 Field Road, Wallasey CH45 5BG* T: 0151-639 4326 E: rainbowheatherhuggins@hotmail.com

BUCKLEY, John. b 42. **d** 95 **p** 96. C Macclesfield Team *Ches* 95-01; P-in-c Pott Shrigley 01-15; Chapl E Cheshire NHS Trust from 01; rtd 15. *Address temp unknown*

BUCKLEY, Michael. b 49. St Jo Coll Dur Cranmer Hall Dur 77. **d** 79 **p** 80. C Birkdale St Jo *Liv* 79-82; TV Maghull 82-88; V Earlestown 88-98; V Gt Sankey 98-14; TR Warrington W 14; rtd 14; PtO *Blackb* from 14. *7 College Close, Longridge, Preston PR3 3AX* T: (01772) 386634 E: m3uckley@gmail.com

BUCKLEY, Rex. *See* BUCKLEY, David Rex

BUCKLEY, Richard Francis. b 44. Ripon Hall Ox 69. **d** 72 **p** 73. C Portsea St Cuth *Portsm* 72-75; C Portsea All SS w St Jo Rudmore 75-79; Chapl RN 79-00; PtO *B & W* from 00. *Ste Croix, Coryate Close, Higher Odcombe, Yeovil BA22 8UJ* T/F: (01935) 864039 M: 07766-711944 E: r.j.buckley@greenbee.net

BUCKLEY, Richard John. b 43. Hull Univ BSc(Econ) 64 PhD 87 Strathclyde Univ MSc 69. Sarum Th Coll 64. **d** 66 **p** 67. C Huddersfield St Jo *Wakef* 66-68; C Sutton St Jas *York* 69-71; TV Sutton St Jas and Wawne 71-75; V Handsworth Woodhouse *Sheff* 75-85; R Adwick-le-Street 85-91; V Went-worth and Area Co-ord (S Yorks) Chr Aid 91-97; Area Co-ord (S and E Yorkshire) Chr Aid 97-07; rtd 07; PtO *York* 97-07; *Sheff* from 97. *2 Kirkstead Abbey Mews, Thorpe Hesley, Rotherham S61 2UZ* T: 0114-246 5064 E: richard@buckjley.wanadoo.co.uk

BUCKLEY, Richard Simon Fildes. b 63. WMMTC 97. **d** 00 **p** 01. NSM Moseley St Mary *Birm* 00-04; NSM Soho St Anne w St Thos and St Pet *Lon* 05-09 and 12-13; P-in-c from 13; PtO 09-12. *St Anne's Rectory, 55 Dean Street, London W1D 6AF* T: (020) 7437 1012 M: 07976-290351 E: simon@simonbuckley.co.uk

BUCKLEY, Stephen Richard. b 45. Cranmer Hall Dur 82. **d** 84 **p** 85. C Iffley *Ox* 84-88; TV Halesowen *Worc* 88-00; TR Sedgley All SS 00-05; TR Gornal and Sedgley from 05; P-in-c Sedgley St Mary from 10. *All Saints' Vicarage, Vicar Street, Sedgley, Dudley DY3 3SD* T: (01902) 883255 E: srb55@talktalk.net

BUCKLEY, Timothy Denys. b 57. BA. St Jo Coll Nottm. **d** 83 **p** 84. C S Westoe *Dur* 83-85; C Paddington Em Harrow Road *Lon* 85-88; C Binley *Cov* 88-98; Min Binley Woods LEP 88-98; V Belton Gp *Linc* 98-13; P-in-c Crowle Gp 09-12. *34 Outerwyke Road, Bognor Regis PO22 8HX* T: (01243) 278731 E: timothybuckley@breathe.com

BUCKLEY, Timothy John. b 67. Jes Coll Cam BA 90 MA 94 Lambeth MA 11. Wycliffe Hall Ox BTh 99. **d** 99 **p** 00. C Langdon Hills *Chelmsf* 99-02; P-in-c Devonport St Mich and St Barn *Ex* 02-15; V from 15. *St Barnabas' Vicarage, 10 De la Hay Avenue, Plymouth PL3 4HU* T: (01752) 666544 E: rev.tim@virgin.net

BUCKLEY, Timothy Simon. b 72. St Mellitus Coll. **d** 11 **p** 12. C Combe Down w Monkton Combe and S Stoke *B & W* 11-14; C Bath Widcombe 11-14; P-in-c from 14. *The Orchard, Forefield Rise, Bath BA2 4PL* E: tim@timbuck2.co.uk

BUCKMAN, Rossly David. b 36. TCD BA 64 MA 67 St Pet Coll Ox BA 65 MA 98. Moore Th Coll Sydney. **d** 59 **p** 60. C Eastwood Australia 59-60; C Port Kembla 60-61; C Dublin Harold's Cross *D & G* 61-64; C S St Mich 64-65; Lect Clifton Th Coll 65-69; CF 69-76; Tutor Canberra Coll of Min Australia 77-80; P-in-c Mid Marsh Gp *Linc* 81-82; R 82-89; P-in-c Blakehurst Australia 89-91; R 91-00; Chapl Düsseldorf *Eur* 00-05; rtd 05. *1/40 Bundoran Parade, Mont Albert North VIC 3129, Australia* T: (0061) (3) 9890 4340 F: 9899 9849 E: buckmen@bigpond.com

BUCKMAN, Stephen Leslie. b 55. **d** 12 **p** 13. NSM Roughey *Chich* from 12. *Wendy's Cottage, Five Oaks Road, Slinfold, Horsham RH13 0RQ* T: (01403) 783263

BUCKNALL, Ms Alison Mary. b 55. Leeds Univ BA 76 Trin Coll Bris MA 94. Qu Coll Birm 94. **d** 96 **p** 97. C The Quinton *Birm* 96-00; C Sutton Coldfield H Trin 00-01; Asst Chapl N Bris NHS Trust from 01. *North Bristol NHS Trust, Beckspool Road, Frenchay, Bristol BS16 1LE* T: 0117-970 1070

BUCKNALL, Allan. b 35. St Matthias Coll Bris CertEd 73. ALCD 62. **d** 62 **p** 63. C Harlow New Town w Lt Parndon *Chelmsf* 62-69; Chapl W Somerset Miss to Deaf 69-71; PtO *Bris* 71-77; P-in-c Wisborough Green *Chich* 77-79; R Tillington 78-86; R Duncton 82-86; R Upwaltham 82-86; C Henfield w Shermanbury and Woodmancote 88-89; Asst Chapl Princess Marg Hosp Swindon 89-96; Angl Chapl Swindon and Marlborough NHS Trust 96-00; rtd 00; PtO *Bris* from 00. *5 The Willows, Highworth, Swindon SN6 7PG* T: (01793) 762721

BUCKNALL, Miss Ann Gordon. b 32. K Coll Lon BSc 53 Hughes Hall Cam DipEd 54. Qu Coll Birm 80. **dss** 81 **d** 87 **p** 94. Birm St Aid Small Heath 81-85; Balsall Heath St Paul 85-92; Par Dn 87-92; C Handsworth St Jas 92-95; rtd 95; PtO *Lich* from 95. *20 St Margaret's Road, Lichfield WS13 7RA* T: (01543) 257382

BUDD, Canon John Christopher. b 51. QUB BA 73. CITC. **d** 82 **p** 83. C Ballymena w Ballyclug *Conn* 82-85; C Jordanstown w Monkstown 85-88; I Craigs w Dunaghy and Killagan 88-97; Dioc Info Officer 89-97; Bp's Dom Chapl from 94; I Derriaghy w Colin from 97; Can Conn Cathl from 11. *Derriaghy Rectory, 20 Derriaghy Road, Magheralave, Lisburn BT28 3SH* T: (028) 9061 0859

BUDD, Philip John. b 40. St Jo Coll Dur BA 63 MLitt 71 Bris Univ PhD 78. Cranmer Hall Dur. **d** 66 **p** 67. C Attenborough w Chilwell *S'well* 66-69; Lect Clifton Th Coll 69-71; Lect Trin Coll Bris 72-80; Tutor Ripon Coll Cuddesdon 80-88; Asst Chapl and Tutor Westmr Coll Ox 80-00; Lect 88-00; Asst Chapl and Tutor Ox Brookes Univ 00-03; Lect 00-03; Hon C N Hinksey and Wytham 03-06; PtO from 06. *4 Clover Close, Oxford OX2 9JH* T: (01865) 863682
E: budds@talk21.com

BUDD, Rob. b 77. Nottm Univ BA 99 Warwick Univ PGCE 05. Trin Coll Bris 11. **d** 13 **p** 14. C Cov H Trin from 13. *85 Stoney Road, Coventry CV3 6HH* T: (024) 7650 3729
M: 07811-945647 E: rob.budd@talk21.com

BUDDEN, Alexander Mark. b 60. UEA BA 84. SEITE 01. **d** 04 **p** 05. NSM Mitcham St Barn *S'wark* 04-08; PtO 09-11; NSM Wimbledon from 11. *29 Dane Road, London SW19 2NB* T: (020) 8542 0622 M: 07738-290534
E: markbudden@sky.com

BUDDLE, William Robert. b 61. Nottm Univ BSc 83. Trin Coll Bris 11. **d** 13 **p** 14. C Combe Down w Monkton Combe and S Stoke *B & W* from 13. *13A Fox Hill, Bath BA2 5QL* E: sally.buddle@gmail.com

BUDGELL, Mrs Anne Margaret. b 44. RGN 66. STETS 07. **d** 10 **p** 11. NSM Vale of White Hart *Sarum* 10-13; NSM Three Valleys from 13. *7 Fox's Close, Holwell, Sherborne DT9 5LH* T: (01963) 23428 E: budgells@hotmail.co.uk

BUDGELL, Peter Charles. b 50. Lon Univ BD 74. **d** 83 **p** 84. C Goodmayes All SS *Chelmsf* 83-86; C Chipping Barnet w Arkley *St Alb* 86-88; V Luton St Anne 88-06; V Luton St Anne w St Chris from 06. *The Vicarage, 7 Blaydon Road, Luton LU2 0RP* T/F: (01582) 720052 E: pcbudgell@aol.com

BUDGETT, Preb Anthony Thomas. b 26. TD 60. Oriel Coll Ox BA 50 MA 57. Wells Th Coll 57. **d** 59 **p** 60. C Hendford *B & W* 59-63; PC Lopen 63-68; R Seavington St Mich w St Mary 63-68; V Somerton 68-80; RD Ilchester 72-81; P-in-c Compton Dundon 76-80; R Somerton w Compton Dundon 80-81; R Somerton w Compton Dundon, the Charltons etc 81-84; Preb Wells Cathl 83-90; P-in-c Bruton w Lamyatt, Wyke and Redlynch 84-85; P-in-c Batcombe w Upton Noble 84-85; P-in-c S w N Brewham 84-85; TR Bruton and Distr 85-90; rtd 90; PtO *Ex* 90-09; *B & W* from 04. *Cornerways, White Ball, Wellington TA21 0LS* T: (01823) 672321

BUFTON (née FORSHAW), Mrs Janet Elisabeth. b 41. Redland Coll of Educn CertEd 61. **d** 99 **p** 00. OLM Debenham w Aspall and Kenton *St E* 99-04; OLM Helmingham w Framsden and Pettaugh w Winston 99-04; OLM Debenham and Helmingham 04-07; rtd 07; PtO *St E* from 09. *Harkaway Cottage, 9 Fenn Street, Winston, Stowmarket IP14 6LD* T: (01728) 860535

BUGG, Canon Peter Richard. b 33. Univ of BC BA 62. Wells Th Coll 63. **d** 64 **p** 64. C Whitley Ch Ch *Ox* 64-67; C Ludlow *Heref* 67-69; LtO Zambia 69-72; P-in-c Brill w Boarstall *Ox* 72-78; P-in-c Chilton w Dorton 77-78; V Brill, Boarstall, Chilton and Dorton 78-97; Hon Can Ch Ch 92-97; rtd 97; LtO Kimberley and Kuruman S Africa 95-98; PtO *Ox* 04-12; *Worc* from 09. *6 Woodward Parks, Fladbury, Pershore WR10 2RB* T: (01386) 860531
E: pjbugg@btinternet.com

BUGLER, Canon Derek Leslie. b 25. Gen Th Sem NY 62. **d** 64 **p** 64. USA 64-90 and from 04; rtd 90; LtO *Win* 90-04. *51 Raymond Road, Brunswick ME 04011, USA*
E: dbugler@gwi.net

BUIK, Canon Allan David. b 39. St Andr Univ BSc 61. Coll of Resurr Mirfield 66. **d** 68 **p** 69. PtO *Win* 68-69; CMP from 69; C Eastleigh *Win* 69-72; C Brighton St Bart *Chich* 72-74; C Lavender Hill Ascension *S'wark* 74-78; V Kingstanding St Mark *Birm* 78-86; Guyana 86-91; V Tunstall *Lich* 91-07; rtd 07; P-in-c Hempton and Pudding Norton *Nor* 07-12; Chantry P Shrine of Our Lady of Walsingham 06-12; Hon Can Georgetown Guyana from 10; PtO *Roch* from 12. *17 Hermitage Road, Higham, Rochester ME3 7DB* T: (01474) 823824 M: 07703-479715 E: allanbuik@gmail.com

BUIKE, Desmond Mainwaring. b 32. Ex Coll Ox BA 55 MA 69 Leeds Univ CertEd 72. **d** 57 **p** 58. C Man St Aid 57-60; C Ox SS Phil and Jas 60-63; V Queensbury *Bradf* 63-71; PtO 71-85; V Glaisdale *York* 85-93; rtd 93; PtO *York* from 93. *Wayside, 3 White Bridge Road, Whitby YO21 3JQ* T: (01947) 821440

BULCOCK, Andrew Marcus. b 62. **d** 03 **p** 04. OLM Elton St Steph *Man* 03-06; PtO 06-08; OLM Turton Moorland from 08. *5 Fieldhead Avenue, Bury BL8 2LX* T: 0161-761 6347

BULL, Andrew David. b 70. Hull Univ BSc 91 Sheff Univ PGCE 92. Regents Th Coll BA 99. **d** 07 **p** 08. C Macclesfield Team *Ches* 07-10; P-in-c Bredbury St Mark from 10. *St Mark's Vicarage, 61 George Lane, Bredbury, Stockport SK6 1AT* T: 0161-406 6552 E: ukbulls@aol.com

BULL, Mrs Christine. b 45. Bedf Coll Lon BA 67. NOC 91. **d** 94 **p** 95. NSM High Lane *Ches* 94-98; NSM Stockport SW 98-99; PtO *Derby* 98-04; *Ches* 99-04; *Man* from 00; C Hale and Ashley *Ches* 04-07; NSM Wormhill, Peak Forest w Peak Dale and Dove Holes *Derby* 07-08; P Pastor Ches Cathl 08-13; rtd 13. *Well Cottage, 28 Mellor Road, New Mills, High Peak SK22 4DP* T: (01244) 699044 E: revchristinebull@yahoo.co.uk

BULL (née ADAMS), Canon Christine Frances. b 53. Cam Inst of Educn CertEd 74. NEOC 97. **d** 00 **p** 01. NSM St Oswald in Lee w Bingfield *Newc* from 00; P-in-c from 07; Hon Can Newc Cathl from 14. *East Side Lodge, Bingfield, Newcastle upon Tyne NE19 2LE* T: (01434) 672303
E: pc.bull@ukonline.co.uk

BULL, Christopher Bertram. b 45. Lon Bible Coll BA 87. Wycliffe Hall Ox 88. **d** 90 **p** 91. C Leominster *Heref* 90-95; P-in-c Westbury 95-02; R 02-10; P-in-c Yockleton 95-02; R 02-10; P-in-c Gt Wollaston 95-02; V 02-10; P-in-c Worthen 07-10; rtd 10; PtO *Lich* from 12. *12 Aldersley Way, Ruyton XI Towns, Shrewsbury SY4 1NE* T: (01939) 260059
E: cbbull@live.co.uk

BULL, Christopher David. b 59. Univ of Wales MA 08. St Jo Coll Nottm 89. **d** 91 **p** 92. C Bowbrook S *Worc* 91-95; P-in-c Flackwell Heath *Ox* 95-00; V from 00; RD Wycombe 97-05. *The Vicarage, 9 Chapel Road, Flackwell Heath, High Wycombe HP10 9AA* T: (01628) 522795 or 533004 E: vicar@ccfh.org.uk

BULL, David. b 72. Worc Coll Ox BA 94. Wycliffe Hall Ox BA 07. **d** 08 **p** 09. C Reigate St Mary *S'wark* 08-12; TR Gt Marlow w Marlow Bottom, Lt Marlow and Bisham *Ox* from 12. *The Rectory, The Causeway, Marlow SL7 2AA* T: (01628) 471650 E: davebull@marlowanglican.org

BULL, George. *See* BULL, William George

BULL, John. *See* BULL, Michael John

BULL, Malcolm George. b 35. Portsm Dioc Tr Course 87. **d** 87 **p** 98. NSM Farlington *Portsm* 87-90; NSM Widley w Wymering 92-93; NSM S Hayling 93-97; NSM Hayling Is St Andr 97-00; Bp's Adv for Cults and New Relig Movements 99-00; rtd 00; PtO *Portsm* 00-01 and from 04; P-in-c Greatworth and Marston St Lawrence etc *Pet* 01-04. *20 Charleston Close, Hayling Island PO11 0JY* T: (023) 9246 2025 E: bullmg@bushinternet.com

BULL, Marcus. b 69. **d** 15. NSM Erringden Leeds from 15. *23 Adelaide Street, Hebden Bridge HX7 6BT* M: 07970-017112

BULL, Martin Wells. b 37. Worc Coll Ox BA 61 MA 68. Ripon Hall Ox 61. **d** 63 **p** 64. C Blackley St Andr *Man* 63-67; C Horton *Bradf* 67-68; V Ingrow w Hainworth 68-78; RD S Craven 74-77; V Bingley All SS 78-80; TR 80-92; P-in-c Gargrave 92-02; rtd 02; PtO *Leeds* from 03. *21 Magdalen's Close, Ripon HG4 1HH* T: (01765) 601422 M: 07870-138386

BULL, Michael John. b 35. Roch Th Coll 65. **d** 67 **p** 68. C N Wingfield *Derby* 67-69; C Skegness *Linc* 69-72; R Ingoldmells w Addlethorpe 72-79; Area Sec USPG *S'wark* 79-85; Area Org RNLI (Lon) 86-88; C Croydon St Jo *S'wark* 89-93; P-in-c Mitcham Ch Ch 93-97; V Colliers Wood Ch Ch 97-00; rtd 00; PtO *Nor* 00-04; Hon C Guiltcross 04-08; P-in-c 08-13. *The Rectory, Back Street, Garboldisham, Diss IP22 2SD* T: (01953) 688347 E: mjbull@waitrose.com

BULL, Canon Robert David. b 51. Westmr Coll Ox MTh 03. Ripon Coll Cuddesdon 74. **d** 77 **p** 78. C Worsley *Man* 77-80; C Peel 80-81; TV 81-86; P-in-c Wisbech St Aug *Ely* 86-88; V 88-02; RD Wisbech 92-02; R Lich St Chad 02-11; P-in-c Longdon 08-10; Can Res Bris Cathl from 11. *41 Salisbury Road, Bristol BS6 7AR* T: 0117-926 4879
E: canon.pastor@bristol-cathedral.co.uk

BULL, Mrs Ruth Lois Clare. b 54. Univ of Wales (Lamp) BA 76 W Midl Coll of Educn PGCE 77. Qu Coll Birm 08. **d** 11 **p** 12. NSM Burntwood *Lich* 11-12; NSM Lich St Mich w St Mary and Wall from 12. *36 Broadlands Rise, Lichfield WS14 9SF* T: (01543) 319296 E: dkbrlcb@hotmail.com

BULL, Stephen Andrew. b 58. St Jo Coll Nottm 91. **d** 93 **p** 94. C Wroughton *Bris* 93-96; P-in-c Eyemouth *Edin* 96-98; LtO from 98. *12 Craigs Court, Torphichen, Bathgate EH48 4NU* T: (01506) 650070 E: stvbull@btinternet.com

BULL, Miss Susan Helen. b 58. Qu Mary Coll Lon BSc 79 All Hallows Coll Dublin MA 11 ACIS 84. STETS BTh 98. **d** 98 **p** 99. NSM Epsom St Barn *Guildf* 98-04; Chapl Surrey and Borders Partnership NHS Trust from 04; PtO *S'wark* from 06. *41 Stamford Green Road, Epsom KT18 7SR* T: (01372) 742703
E: shbull@btinternet.com

BULL, Canon Timothy Martin. b 65. Worc Coll Ox BA 87 MA 93 Dur Univ PhD 94 Fitzw Coll Cam BA 98 MA 07 K Coll Lon PhD 11 FRSA 96 CEng 96 MBCS 96. Ridley Hall Cam 96. **d** 99 **p** 00. C Bath Walcot *B & W* 99-03; P-in-c Langham w Boxted *Chelmsf* 03-13; Colchester Area CME Adv 03-13; Dir Min and Min Development Officer *St Alb* from 13; Can Res St Alb from 13. *43 Holywell Hill, St Albans AL1 1HD* T: (01727) 854532 E: dom@stalbans.anglican.org *or* canondrtim@gmail.com

BULL, Mrs Wendy Jane. b 63. Birm Chr Coll MA 08. Ripon Coll Cuddesdon 11. **d** 13 **p** 14. C Gt Marlow w Marlow Bottom, Lt Marlow and Bisham *Ox* from 13. *9 Chapel Road, Flackwell Heath, High Wycombe HP10 9AA* T: (01628) 522795 E: wendy@revbull.co.uk

BULL, William George. b 28. Sarum Th Coll 65. **d** 66 **p** 67. C Salisbury St Mich *Sarum* 66-69; V Swallowcliffe w Ansty 69-75; Dioc Youth Officer 69-71; P-in-c Laverstock 75-81; V 81-93; rtd 94; PtO *Sarum* from 94. *Bungalow 1, Boreham Field, Warminster BA12 9EB* T: (01985) 847830 E: geobull@talktalk.net

BULLAMORE, John Richard. b 41. Linc Coll Ox BA 69 MA 69. Wycliffe Hall Ox 74. **d** 95 **p** 95. NSM Eorropaidh *Arg* 95-98; NSM Bath St Sav w Swainswick and Woolley *B & W* 98-08; NSM Knaresborough *Ripon* 08-12; rtd 12; PtO *Leeds* from 12. *21 Hornbeam Way, Leeds LS14 2HP* T: 0113-318 9756 E: john.bullamore@homecall.co.uk

BULLEN, Mrs Jacqueline. b 61. Westcott Ho Cam 11. **d** 13 **p** 14. C Fosse *Leic* from 13. *The Vicarage, 25 Ling Dale, East Goscote, Leicester LE7 3XW* M: 07729-706157 T: 0116-264 0051 E: jacqbullen@aol.com

BULLEN, Marilyn Patricia. *See* MARTIN, Marilyn Patricia

BULLEN, Neil Geoffrey Osbourne. b 64. Qu Coll Birm 13. **d** 15. C Knighton St Mary Magd *Leic* from 15. *25 Ling Dale, East Goscote, Leicester LE7 3XW* T: 0116-264 0051 M: 07729-004642 E: revdneil@yahoo.com

BULLIMORE, Canon Christine Elizabeth. b 46. Nottm Univ BA 67. St Jo Coll Nottm 96. **d** 96 **p** 97. Bp's Adv Past Care and Counselling *Wakef* 92-99; *Leeds* from 01; NSM S Ossett *Wakef* 96-99; P-in-c Emley and Flockton cum Denby Grange 99-11; RD Kirkburton 05-11; Hon Can Wakef Cathl 08-11; r-d 11. *5 Snowgate Head, New Mill, Holmfirth, Huddersfield HD9 7DH* T: (01484) 521025 M: 07921-588276 E: chrisbullimore@sky.com

BULLIMORE, Matthew James. b 77. Em Coll Cam BA 99 MA 03 PhD 07 Man Univ MPhil 02. Harvard Div Sch 99 Westcott Ho Cam 01. **d** 05 **p** 06. C Roberttown w Hartshead *Wakef* 05-07; Bp's Dom Chapl 07-11; V Royston *Leeds* from 11; P-in-c Felkirk from 13. *The Clergy House, Church Street, Royston, Barnsley S71 4QZ* T: (01226) 722410 E: mjb56@cantab.net

BULLIVANT, Ronald. b 32. CertEd. St Mich Coll Llan. **d** 59 **p** 60. C Roath St German *Llan* 59-61; P-in-c Bradf H Trin 61-66; V Horbury *Wakef* 66-69; LtO *Ripon* 70-78; PtO *Nor* 78-81; LtO 81-98; PtO *Man* 99-11. *15 Dulverton Hall, Esplanade, Scarborough YO11 2AR*

BULLOCH, William Gillespie. b 68. St Steph Ho Ox. **d** 01 **p** 02. C Bognor *Chich* 01-05; V Leigh-on-Sea St Jas *Chelmsf* from 05. *St James's Vicarage, 103 Blenheim Chase, Leigh-on-Sea SS9 3BY* T: (01702) 471786 E: frbill.bulloch@gmail.com

BULLOCK, Andrew Belfrage. b 50. Univ of Wales (Ban) BSc 73 MEd 81 Westmr Coll Ox PGCE 79. Wycliffe Hall Ox 94. **d** 97 **p** 98. C Sandhurst *Ox* 97-02; P-in-c Alfrick, Lulsley, Suckley, Leigh and Bransford *Worc* 02-08; TV Worcs W 09-14. *Address temp unknown* M: 07958-654331 E: abullock@waitrose.com

BULLOCK, Andrew Timothy. b 56. Southn Univ BTh 91. Sarum & Wells Th Coll 89. **d** 91 **p** 92. C Erdington St Barn *Birm* 91-94; TV Solihull 94-03; P-in-c Acocks Green 03-08; V from 08; AD Yardley and Bordesley from 12. *The Vicarage, 34 Dudley Park Road, Acocks Green, Birmingham B27 6QR* T/F: 0121-706 9764 E: andrewbullock2@blueyonder.co.uk

BULLOCK, Ian. b 44. Cranmer Hall Dur. **d** 08 **p** 09. C Pontefract St Giles *Wakef* 08-11; P-in-c Heckmondwike 11-12; P-in-c Liversedge w Hightown 11-12; V Heckmondwike (w Norristhorpe) and Liversedge *Leeds* from 12. *The Vicarage, 25 Church Street, Heckmondwike WF16 0AX* T: (01924) 401275 E: ianb@mailshack.com

BULLOCK, Jude Ross. b 58. Heythrop Coll Lon BD 89. Allen Hall 84. **d** 89 **p** 90. In RC Ch 89-97; C Lt Ilford St Mich *Chelmsf* 01-05; V Chingford St Anne from 05. *St Anne's Vicarage, 200A Larkshall Road, London E4 6NP* T: (020) 8529 4740 M: 07976-395732 E: juderbullock1@yahoo.co.uk

BULLOCK, Kenneth Poyser. b 27. Down Coll Cam BA 50 MA 55. Ridley Hall Cam 50. **d** 52 **p** 53. C Aston SS Pet and Paul *Birm* 52-56; R Openshaw *Man* 56-63; V Ainsworth 63-91; rtd 91; PtO *St As* from 09. *26 Plas Penrhyn, Penrhyn Bay, Llandudno LL30 3EU* T: (01492) 543333

BULLOCK, Canon Michael. b 49. Hatf Coll Dur BA 71. Coll of Resurr Mirfield 72. **d** 75 **p** 76. C Pet St Jo 75-79; Zambia 79-86; V Longthorpe *Pet* 86-91; Chapl Naples w Sorrento, Capri and Bari *Eur* 91-99; OGS from 93; P-in-c Liguria *Eur* 99-00; Chapl Gtr Lisbon 00-12; Can Malta Cathl 98-12; rtd 12. *22 Georgian Court, Spalding PE11 2QT* T: (01775) 714454

BULLOCK, Philip Mark. b 59. Qu Coll Birm 05. **d** 08 **p** 09. C Cov E 08-10; TV 10-13; P-in-c S Shields St Aid and St Steph *Dur* from 13; P-in-c Rekendyke from 13. *St Cuthbert's Vicarage, 218 Sunderland Road, South Shields NE34 6AT* M: 07831-147822 E: rev.philip@virgin.media.com

BULLOCK, Miss Rosemary Joy. b 59. Portsm Poly BA 81 Southn Univ BTh 94. Sarum & Wells Th Coll 89. **d** 91 **p** 94. Par Dn Warblington w Emsworth *Portsm* 91-94; C 94-95; C Gt Parndon *Chelmsf* 95-98; TV Beaminster Area *Sarum* 98-03; P-in-c Ridgeway 03-04. *82 Green Lane, Shanklin PO37 7HD* T: (01983) 863345

BULLOCK (née WHEALE), The Ven Sarah Ruth. b 64. Surrey Univ BA 86 St Jo Coll Dur BA 93. Cranmer Hall Dur 90. **d** 93 **p** 94. C Kersal Moor *Man* 93-98; P-in-c Whalley Range St Edm 98-04; P-in-c Moss Side St Jas w St Clem 99-04; R Whalley Range St Edm and Moss Side etc 04-13; Dioc Voc Adv 98-05; Chapl MU 00-06; Bp's Adv for Women's Min *Man* 09-13; Borough Dean Man 10-12; AD Hulme 12-13; Hon Can Man Cathl 07-13; Adn York from 13. *1 New Lane, Huntington, York YO32 9NU* T: (01904) 758241 E: adyk@yorkdiocese.org

BULLOCK, Stephanie Clair. b 46. St Mary's Hosp Medical Sch Lon MB, BS 70. Ripon Coll Cuddesdon 90. **d** 92 **p** 94. Par Dn Cuddesdon *Ox* 92-94; Tutor Ripon Coll Cuddesdon 92-94; Asst Chapl Ox Radcliffe Hosp NHS Trust 94-97; Chapl Ox Radcliffe Hosps NHS Trust 97-02; Hon C Headington St Mary *Ox* 03-09; PtO from 09. *Church Farm, Church Lane, Old Marston, Oxford OX3 0PT* T: (01865) 722926 E: stephaniebullock9@gmail.com

BULLOCK, Victor James Allen. b 67. Southn Univ BTh 90 St Mary's Coll Twickenham PGCE 91. St Steph Ho Ox 92. **d** 94 **p** 95. C Cowley St Jas *Ox* 94-95; C Reading St Giles 95-99; V Fenny Stratford from 99. *The Vicarage, Manor Road, Milton Keynes MK2 2HW* T: (01908) 372825 E: saintmartinschurch@hotmail.com

BULLWORTHY, Rita Irene. b 48. Glos Univ BA 09. SWMTC 09. **d** 11. NSM N Tawton, Bondleigh, Sampford Courtenay etc *Ex* 11-13; NSM Chagford, Gidleigh, Throwleigh etc from 13. *Rivendell House, Sampford Courtenay, Okehampton EX20 2TF* T: (01837) 89168 E: ritabullworthy@yahoo.co.uk

BULMAN, Madeline Judith. *See* STRONG, Madeline Judith

BUNCE, Christopher Edward. b 82. Westcott Ho Cam. **d** 12 **p** 13. C Hammersmith St Pet *Lon* 12-15; P-in-c Stevenage St Andr and St Geo *St Alb* from 15. *The Rectory, Cuttys Lane, Stevenage SG1 1UP* E: cebunce@gmail.com

BUNCE (née HOW), Gillian Carol. b 53. K Coll Lon MB, BS 77 MRCGP 82 MFHom 96. STETS 04. **d** 07 **p** 08. NSM Worle *B & W* from 07. *85 Clevedon Road, Tickenham, Clevedon BS21 6RD* T: (01275) 810610 E: gill.how@blueyonder.co.uk

BUNCE, Michael John. b 49. Westcott Ho Cam. **d** 80 **p** 81. C Grantham *Linc* 80-83; TV 83-85; R Tarfside *Bre* 85-92; R Brechin 85-92; R Auchmithie 91-92; Provost St Paul's Cathl Dundee 92-97; Chapl Menorca *Eur* 00-12; PtO *Nor* from 14. *Water Mill Cottage, Low Road, Tasburgh, Norwich NR15 1AR*

BUNCE, Raymond Frederick. b 28. Ely Th Coll 54. **d** 57 **p** 58. C Hillingdon St Andr *Lon* 57-62; C Greenford H Cross 62-67; V Ealing All SS 67-89; Chapl Ascot Priory 89-90; rtd 90; PtO *Portsm* from 91; *Chich* from 99. *45 Guillards Oak, Midhurst GU29 9JZ* T: (01730) 816282

BUNCH, Canon Andrew William Havard. b 53. Selw Coll Cam BA 74 MA 78 PhD 79. Ox NSM Course 84. **d** 87 **p** 88. NSM Wantage *Ox* 87-91; C New Windsor 91-93; TV 93-97; V Ox St Giles and SS Phil and Jas w St Marg from 97; Hon Can Ch Ch from 09. *The Vicarage, Church Walk, Oxford OX2 6LY* T: (01865) 510460 E: vicar@churchwalk.eclipse.co.uk

BUNDAY, Mrs Janet Lesley. b 56. Nottm Univ BA 78 Univ of Wales (Lamp) MA 08 Lon Inst of Educn PGCE 79 Anglia Ruskin Univ MA 12. Ridley Hall Cam 08. **d** 10 **p** 11. NSM Potton w Sutton and Cockayne Hatley *St Alb* 10-12; C Blyth Valley *St E* 12-13; TV from 13. *79 Dukes Drive, Halesworth IP19 8TJ* T: (01986) 873766 E: jan@bunday.co.uk

BUNDAY, Canon Paul. b 30. Wadh Coll Ox BA 54 MA 58. ALCD 56. **d** 56 **p** 57. C Woking St Jo *Guildf* 56-60; Chapl Reed's Sch Cobham 60-66; R Landford w Plaitford *Sarum* 66-77; RD Alderbury 73-77; TR Radipole and Melcombe Regis 77-86; RD Weymouth 82-85; Can and Preb Sarum Cathl 83-95; TV Whitton 86-91; TR 91-95; Chapl Duchess of Somerset Hosp Froxfield 86-94; rtd 95; PtO *Sarum* from 95. *4 Springfield Park, Tisbury, Salisbury SP3 6QN* T: (01747) 871530

BUNDAY, Richard William. b 76. Lanc Univ BA 98 MA 04. Cranmer Hall Dur 98. **d** 00 **p** 01. C Redcar *York* 00-01; C Marton *Blackb* 01-04; P-in-c Ashton-on-Ribble St Mich w Preston St Mark 04-06; TR W Preston 06-10; P-in-c Kirkham 10-11;

V from 11; AD from 15. *The Vicarage, Church Street, Kirkham, Preston PR4 2SE* E: richard.bunday@virginmedia.com

BUNDOCK, Canon Anthony Francis. b 49. Qu Coll Birm 81. **d** 83 **p** 84. C Stansted Mountfitchet *Chelmsf* 83-86; TV Borehamwood *St Alb* 86-94; TR Seacroft *Ripon* 94-05; AD Whitkirk 00-05; TR Leeds City 05-14; Hon Can Ripon Cathl 05-14; rtd 14; TV Risborough *Ox* from 14. *The Vicarage, 1 Church Lane, Lacey Green, Princes Risborough HP27 0QX* T: 0113-278 6237 E: tony.pat.bundock@virgin.net

BUNDOCK, Edward Leigh. b 52. Keble Coll Ox BA 73 Open Univ PhD 94 MAAT. St Steph Ho Ox 74. **d** 76 **p** 77. C Malvern Link w Cowleigh *Worc* 76-80; C-in-c Portslade Gd Shep CD *Chich* 80-88; V Wisborough Green 88-94; PtO *Guildf* 96-97; P-in-c E and W Rudham, Houghton-next-Harpley etc *Nor* 97-99; R E w W Rudham, Helhoughton etc from 99. *The Rectory, South Raynham Road, West Raynham, Fakenham NR21 7HH* T: (01328) 838385

BUNDOCK, Canon John Nicholas Edward. b 45. Wells Th Coll 66. **d** 70 **p** 71. C Chingford SS Pet and Paul *Chelmsf* 70-74; P-in-c Gt Grimsby St Matt Fairfield CD *Linc* 74-81; V Hindhead *Guildf* 81-99; RD Farnham 91-96; V Bramley and Grafham 99-15; RD Cranleigh 04-12; Chapl Gosden Ho Sch 99-15; Hon Can Guildf Cathl 09-15; rtd 15; PtO *Guildf* from 15. *Address temp unknown* E: jnebundock@tiscali.co.uk

BUNDOCK, Nicholas John. b 73. Sheff Univ BSc 94 PhD 98 Fitzw Coll Cam BA 01. Ridley Hall Cam 99. **d** 02 **p** 03. C Mortomley St Sav High Green *Sheff* 02-05; TV Didsbury St Jas and Em *Man* 05-10; TR from 10. *St James's Rectory, 9 Didsbury Park, Manchester M20 5LH* T: 0161-434 6518 *or* 446 4150 E: nickbundock@stjamesandemmanuel.org

BUNDOCK, Ronald Michael. b 44. Leeds Univ BSc 65. Ox NSM Course 87. **d** 90 **p** 91. NSM Buckingham *Ox* 90-98; NSM Stowe 98-14; P-in-c 03-14; PtO from 14; AD Buckingham from 11. *1 Holton Road, Buckingham MK18 1PQ* T: (01280) 813887 E: ron_judith_bun@btinternet.com

BUNGARD, Mrs Rosemary. d 15. C Portree *Arg* from 15. *Ceol na Mara, West Suisnish, Isle of Raasay, Kyle IV40 8NX* E: ceolnamara@waitrose.com

BUNKER (née HARDING), Mrs Elizabeth. b 47. Chelsea Coll Lon BSc 67 MSc 69. SAOMC 04. **d** 06 **p** 07. NSM Baldock w Bygrave and Weston *St Alb* 06-10; NSM St Paul's Walden from 10. *Arana, 6 Hitchin Road, Letchworth Garden City SG6 3LL* T: (01462) 686808 F: 679276 M: 07850-413724 E: elizabethbunker@hotmail.com

BUNKER, Janet Constance. b 59. Qu Mary Coll Lon BSc 81 R Holloway & Bedf New Coll Lon PhD 85 Open Univ MA(Ed). Westcott Ho Cam 05. **d** 07 **p** 08. C Cambridge Ascension *Ely* 07-10; TV from 10. *Ascension Rectory, 95 Richmond Road, Cambridge CB4 3PS* T: (01223) 229976 M: 07811-357564 E: janet_ascension@yahoo.com

BUNKER, The Very Revd Michael. b 37. Oak Hill Th Coll 59. **d** 63 **p** 64. C Alperton *Lon* 63-66; C St Helens St Helen *Liv* 66-70; V Muswell Hill St Matt *Lon* 70-79; V Muswell Hill St Jas 78-79; V Muswell Hill St Jas w St Matt 79-92; AD W Haringey 85-90; Preb St Paul's Cathl 90-92; Dean Pet 92-06; rtd 06; PtO *Pet* from 10. *21 Black Pot Lane, Oundle, Peterborough PE8 4AT* T: (01832) 273032 E: mandmbbythesea@btinternet.com

BUNN, Mrs Rosemary Joan. b 60. EAMTC 94. **d** 97 **p** 98. NSM Sprowston w Beeston *Nor* 97-01; R Stoke H Cross w Dunston, Arminghall etc 01-11; R Belton and Burgh Castle from 11. *The Rectory, Beccles Road, Belton, Great Yarmouth NR31 9JQ* T: (01493) 780210

BUNNELL, Adrian. b 49. Univ of Wales (Abth) BSc 72. St Mich Coll Llan 74. **d** 75 **p** 76. C Wrexham *St As* 75-78; C Rhyl w St Ann 78-79; CF 79-95; R Aberfoyle and Callander *St And* 95-03; R Newport-on-Tay 03-06; rtd 06. *Gauger Hall Cottage, Forneth, Blairgowrie PH10 6SP* T: (01350) 724317 E: adrian.bunnell@tesco.net

BUNTING, Edward Garth. b 70. TCD BTh 99. CITC 96. **d** 99 **p** 00. C Clooney w Strathfoyle *D & R* 99-02; I Leckpatrick w Dunnalong 02-06; I Belfast Upper Malone (Epiphany) *Conn* 06-10; I Finaghy 06-10; PV Ch Ch Cathl Dublin from 10. *1 Ulster Street, Phibsborough, Dublin 7, Republic of Ireland* T: (00353) (1) 868 4675 E: garth@christchurch.ie

BUNTING, Canon Ian David. b 33. Ex Coll Ox BA 58 MA 61. Tyndale Hall Bris 57 Princeton Th Sem ThM 60. **d** 60 **p** 61. C Bootle St Leon *Liv* 60-63; V Waterloo St Jo 64-71; Dir Past Studies St Jo Coll Dur 71-78; R Chester le Street *Dur* 78-87; RD Chester-le-Street 84-88; Kingham Hill Fellow 87-89; Dioc Dir of Ords *S'well* 90-99; C Lenton 90-97; Hon Can S'well Minster 93-99; Bp's Research Officer 97-00; rtd 00; PtO *S'well* from 00. *8 Crafts Way, Southwell NG25 0BL* T: (01636) 813868 E: ibunting@waitrose.com

BUNTING (née BYRNE), Mrs Lynda. b 47. STETS 06. **d** 08 **p** 09. NSM Chandler's Ford *Win* 08-14. *18 Queen's Road, Chandler's Ford, Eastleigh SO53 5AH* T: (023) 8026 9418 E: lyndabunting@aol.com

BUNTING, Steven Leo. b 81. **d** 12 **p** 13. C Oystermouth *S & B* 12-14; P-in-c Swansea St Thos and Kilvey from 14; Bp's Officer for Min to Children and Families from 14. *St Thomas Vicarage, Lewis Street, St Thomas, Swansea SA1 8BP* T: (01792) 652891 E: stevenbunting@hotmail.co.uk

BUNYAN, David Richard. b 48. Edin Th Coll 93. **d** 96 **p** 97. NSM Musselburgh *Edin* 96-98; NSM Prestonpans 96-98; C Edin St Dav 98-00; R Grangemouth 00-13; P-in-c Bo'ness 00-13; rtd 13. *14 Clerwood Bank, Edinburgh EH12 8PZ* T: (01314) 766586 E: drbdoe@blueyonder.co.uk *or* bunyandr@gmail.com

BUNYAN, Richard Charles. b 43. Oak Hill Th Coll 63 Ridley Hall Cam 69. **d** 71 **p** 72. C Luton Ch Ch *Roch* 71-74; C Bexleyheath Ch Ch 74-76; C Bexley St Jo 76-79; TV Northampton Em *Pet* 79-81; V Erith St Jo *Roch* 81-86; V S Woodham Ferrers *Chelmsf* 86-89; Chapl Scargill Ho 89-90; Sub Chapl HM Pris Swaleside 91-94; Dep Chapl HM Pris Belmarsh 94-96; Chapl HM Pris Littlehey 96-08; rtd 08; PtO *Ely* from 08; Dioc Spirituality Officer 07-10. *6 Swan End, Buckden, St Neots PE19 5SW* T: (01480) 812950 E: rbunyan@btinternet.com

BUQUÉ, Mrs Helena Margareta. b 55. Chich Inst of HE BEd 95. SEITE 09. **d** 12 **p** 13. NSM Findon w Clapham and Patching *Chich* 12-15; P-in-c from 15. *The Rectory, School Hill, Findon, Worthing BN14 0TR* M: 07504-333853 T: (01903) 873601 E: findon.rectory@btinternet.com

BUR, Patricia Margaret. *See* CAPRIELLO, Patricia Margaret

BURBERRY, Miss Frances Sheila. b 60. ACII 83. TISEC 03. **d** 06 **p** 07. C Edin St Pet 06-11; R Edin St Ninian from 11; Chapl Edin Univ from 06. *163 Craigleith Road, Edinburgh EH4 2EB* E: frances.burberry@tiscali.co.uk *or* frances.burberry@ed.ac.uk

BURBIDGE, Barry Desmond. b 52. STETS 94. **d** 97 **p** 98. NSM Fleet *Guildf* 97-03; NSM Crondall and Ewshot 03-11; Chapl Frimley Park Hosp NHS Foundn Trust from 06. *1 Sydney Loader Place, Blackwater, Camberley GU17 0AF* T: (01252) 875394 E: b.burbidge@ntlworld.com *or* barry.burbidge@fph-tr.nhs.uk

BURBIDGE, Richard John. b 77. Lon Guildhall Univ BSc 00. Oak Hill Th Coll BTh 11. **d** 11 **p** 12. C Lowestoft Ch Ch *Nor* 11-14; C Moulton *Pet* from 14. *8 Cubleigh Close, Moulton, Northampton NN3 7BG* M: 07973-801254 E: richburbidge@googlemail.com

BURBRIDGE, The Very Revd John Paul. b 32. K Coll Cam BA 54 MA 58 New Coll Ox BA 54 MA 58 FSA 89. Wells Th Coll 58. **d** 59 **p** 60. C Eastbourne St Mary *Chich* 59-62; V Choral York Minster 62-66; Can Res and Prec York Minster 66-76; Adn Richmond *Ripon* 76-83; Can Res Ripon Cathl 76-83; Dean Nor 83-95; rtd 95; PtO *Ripon* 95-06; LtO *Glas* from 08. *The Clachan Bothy, Newtonairds, Dumfries DG2 0JL* T: (01387) 820403 E: fremington124@yahoo.co.uk *or* revpaul@stjohnsdumfries.org

BURBRIDGE, Richard James. b 47. Univ of Wales (Ban) BSc 68. Oak Hill Th Coll 68. **d** 72 **p** 73. C Rodbourne Cheney *Bris* 72-75; C Downend 75-78; P-in-c Bris H Cross Inns Court 78-83; C Fishponds All SS 83-86; V 86-97; RD Stapleton 89-95; C Bishopston 97-98; C Bris St Andr w St Bart 97-98; TV Bishopston and St Andrews 98-12; rtd 12. *10 Scandrett Close, Bristol BS10 7SS* T: 0117-950 4945 E: burbridge466@btinternet.com

BURBURY, Janet. b 56. Sunderland Univ CertEd 02. Cranmer Hall Dur 05. **d** 07 **p** 08. C Hart w Elwick Hall *Dur* 07-11; P-in-c from 11; AD Hartlepool from 13. *The Vicarage, Hart, Hartlepool TS27 3AP* T: (01429) 262340 M: 07958-131271 E: janetb_231@hotmail.co.uk

BURCH, Charles Edward. b 57. Trin Coll Cam MA 80 Lon Business Sch MBA 87. ERMC 05. **d** 07 **p** 08. NSM Harpenden St Jo *St Alb* 07-11; V Bovingdon from 11; Dioc Voc Officer from 11. *10 Church Street, Bovingdon, Hemel Hempstead HP3 0LU* E: charlesburch57@hotmail.com

BURCH, Canon John Christopher. b 50. Trin Coll Cam BA 71 MA 76 Leeds Univ MPhil 95. St Jo Coll Nottm 73. **d** 76 **p** 77. C Sheff St Jo 76-79; C Holbeck Ripon 79-82; V Burmantofts St Steph and St Agnes 82-95; Can Res and Prec Cov Cathl 95-02; Chapl to Clergy of UPA 99-02; C-in-c Braunstone Park CD *Leic* 02-08; V Braunstone Park 08-15; RD Christianity S 04-08; AD City of Leic 08-09; rtd 15; PtO *Leic* from 15. *11 Marsden Lane, Leicester LE2 8LS* E: chris@burches.co.uk

BURCH, Canon Peter John. b 36. ACA 60 FCA 71. Ripon Hall Ox 62. **d** 64 **p** 65. C Brixton St Matt *S'wark* 64-67; Chapl Freetown St Aug Sierra Leone 68-72; P-in-c Chich St Pet 72-76; V Broadwater Down 76-85; V Steyning 85-94; R Ashurst 85-94; Hon Can Bauchi from 93; V Broadway *Worc* 94-96; V Broadway w Wickhamford 96-02; rtd 02; PtO *Glouc* from 03; *Worc* from 04. *6 Jordan's Close, Willersey, Broadway WR12 7QD* T: (01386) 853837 E: pj_pjburch@hotmail.com

BURCH, Stephen Roy. b 59. St Jo Coll Nottm 82. **d** 85 **p** 86. C Ipswich St Aug *St E* 85-89; Youth Chapl *Cov* 89-94; P-in-c

Kinwarton w Gt Alne and Haselor 89-99; R 99-04; P-in-c Coughton 02-04; RD Alcester 99-04; V Fletchamstead from 04; AD Cov S from 10; AD Kenilworth 10-13. *St James's Vicarage, 395 Tile Hill Lane, Coventry CV4 9DP* T: (024) 7646 6262 E: vicar@stjamesfletch.org.uk

BURCHELL, Mrs Elizabeth Susan. b 53. Sheff Univ BSc 74. SAOMC 04. **d** 07 **p** 08. NSM Banbury St Leon *Ox* 07-10; P-in-c 10-13; V from 13. *St Leonard's Vicarage, 46A Middleton Road, Banbury OX16 4RG* T: (01295) 271008 M: 07709-754914 E: revsueb@btinternet.com

BURDEN, Miss Anne Margaret. b 47. Ex Univ BSc 69 CQSW 72. Linc Th Coll 89. **d** 91 **p** 94. Par Dn Mill Hill Jo Keble Ch *Lon* 91-94; C 94; TV Basingstoke *Win* 94-02; Dioc Adv for Women's Min 00-02; TV Brixham w Churston Ferrers and Kingswear *Ex* 02-10; rtd 10. *Ainsdale, Dornafield Road, Ipplepen, Newton Abbot TQ12 5SJ* T: (01803) 813520 E: anne-burden@virgin.com

BURDEN, Derek Ronald. b 37. Sarum Th Coll 59. **d** 62 **p** 63. C Cuddington *Guildf* 62-64; C Leamington Priors All SS *Cov* 64-66; C Stamford All SS w St Pet *Linc* 66-74; C-in-c Stamford Ch Ch 71-74; P-in-c Ashbury w Compton Beauchamp *Ox* 74-77; V 77-81; V Ashbury, Compton Beauchamp and Longcot w Fernham 81-84; V Wokingham St Sebastian 84-97; P-in-c Wooburn 97-02; rtd 02; PtO *Sarum* 03-05; *Win* from 06. *5 Cranford Park Drive, Yateley GU46 6JR* T: (01252) 890657

BURDEN, Michael Henry. b 36. Selw Coll Cam BA 59 MA 62 Hull Univ MEd 79. Ridley Hall Cam 59. **d** 61 **p** 62. C Ashton-upon-Mersey St Mary Magd *Ches* 62-65; Chapl St Pet Sch York 65-70; Asst Master Beverley Gr Sch 70-74; R Walkington *York* 74-77; Chapl Asst Berwick R Infirmary 82-94; P-in-c Berwick H Trin *Newc* 82-87; V 87-89; P-in-c Berwick St Mary 82-87; V Berwick H Trin and St Mary 89-94; P-in-c Skirwith, Ousby and Melmerby w Kirkland *Carl* 94-98; Sec Guild of St Raphael 94-98; rtd 99; PtO *Newc* 99-09. *The College of St Barnabas, Blackberry Lane, Lingfield RH7 6NJ* T: (01342) 872849

BURDEN, Paul. b 62. Rob Coll Cam BA 84 MA 88 AMIMechE 87. Wycliffe Hall Ox BA 91. **d** 92 **p** 93. C Clevedon St Andr and Ch Ch *B & W* 92-96; R Bathampton w Claverton 96-14; Warden of Readers Bath Adnry 06-14; Tutor STETS from 14. *STETS, 19 The Close, Salisbury SP1 2EE* T: (01722) 424820 E: p.burden@tiscali.co.uk

BURDEN, Robert John. b 55. Imp Coll Lon BSc 76 ARCS 76. ERMC 11. **d** 13 **p** 14. OLM Cressing w Stisted and Bradwell etc *Chelmsf* from 13. *254 Coggeshall Road, Marks Tey, Colchester CO6 1HT* T: (01206) 211890 M: 07808-516349 E: e_burden@hotmail.com

BURDETT, John Fergusson. b 25. Pemb Coll Cam BA 47 MA 79. **d** 79 **p** 80. C Edin St Jo 79-87 and 90-95; Cyprus 87-90; rtd 95; Hon C Edin St Jo 95-00; LtO from 00. *80/1 Barnton Park View, Edinburgh EH4 6HJ* T: 0131-339 7226 F: 317 1179 E: revjb@blueyonder.co.uk

BURDETT, Canon Stephen Martin. b 49. AKC 72. St Aug Coll Cant 73. **d** 74 **p** 75. C Walworth St Pet *S'wark* 74-75; C Walworth 75-77; C Benhilton 77-80; P-in-c Earlsfield St Jo 80-83; V 83-89; V N Dulwich St Faith 89-99; Ldr Post Ord Tr Woolwich Area 96-99; TR Southend *Chelmsf* 99-15; Hon Can Chelmsf Cathl 09-15; RD Southend 10-15; rtd 15. *144 Alexandra Road, Southend-on-Sea SS1 1HB* T: (01702) 342687 E: stephen@burdett436.orangehome.co.uk

BURDON, Anthony James. b 46. Ex Univ LLB 67 Lon Univ BD 73. Oak Hill Th Coll 71. **d** 73 **p** 74. C Ox St Ebbe w St Pet 73-76; C Church Stretton *Heref* 76-78; Voc Sec CPAS and Hon C Bromley Ch Ch *Roch* 78-81; V Filkins w Broadwell, Broughton, Kelmscot etc *Ox* 81-84; R Broughton Poggs w Filkins, Broadwell etc 84-85; V Reading St Jo 85-96; C California and Adv for Spirituality (Berks) 96-98; Warden and P-in-c Cumbrae (or Millport) *Arg* 98-04; V Burstwick w Thorngumbald *York* 04-11; P-in-c Roos and Garton w Tunstall, Grimston and Hilston 08-11; RD S Holderness 06-09; rtd 11; PtO *York* from 11. *22 Wheatlands Close, Pocklington, York YO42 2UT* T: (01759) 304290 E: pamandtonyburdon@btinternet.com

BURDON, Canon Christopher John. b 48. Jes Coll Cam BA 70 MA 74 Glas Univ PhD 95. Coll of Resurr Mirfield 71. **d** 74 **p** 75. C Chelmsf All SS 74-78; TV High Wycombe *Ox* 78-84; P-in-c Olney w Emberton 84-90; R 90-92; LtO *Glas* 92-94; Lay Tr Officer *Chelmsf* 94-99; Prin NOC 00-07; Can Th and CME Adv *St E* 07-13; rtd 13; PtO *Chelmsf* from 14. *9 Boswells Drive, Chelmsford CM2 6LD* T: (01245) 492706 E: cjburdon@btinternet.com

BURDON, Mrs Pamela Muriel. b 46. Ex Univ BA 68 Reading Univ DipEd 69. Wycliffe Hall Ox 88. **d** 90 **p** 94. Par Dn Reading St Jo *Ox* 90-94; C 94-96; P-in-c California 96-98; NSM Cumbrae (or Millport) *Arg* 98-04; NSM Burstwick w Thorngumbald *York* 04-11; C Preston and Sproatley in Holderness 05-06; P-in-c 06-11; C Roos and Garton w Tunstall,

Grimston and Hilston 08-11; rtd 11; PtO *York* from 12. *22 Wheatlands Close, Pocklington, York YO42 2UT* T: (01759) 304290 E: pamandtonyburdon@btinternet.com

BURFITT, Edward Ronald. b 42. MIMA 64. Cranmer Hall Dur 91. **d** 93 **p** 94. C Monkseaton St Mary *Newc* 93-97; rtd 97. *Cragston Court, Cragston Close, Blakelaw, Newcastle upon Tyne NE5 3SR* T: 0191-286 4443 M: 07870-762522 E: revburf@aol.com

BURFITT, Mrs Natalie May. b 70. Liv Univ BA 92 Reading Univ PGCE 96. Qu Coll Birm 12. **d** 15. C S Cheltenham *Glouc* from 15. *58 Hall Road, Cheltenham GL53 0HE* T: (01242) 527021 M: 07793-493473 E: burfittnatalie@gmail.com

BURFORD, Anthony Francis. b 55. Oak Hill Th Coll BA 98. **d** 98 **p** 99. C Cov H Trin 98-02; P-in-c Rye Park St Cuth *St Alb* 02-07; V 07-11; V S Hornchurch St Jo and St Matt *Chelmsf* from 11. *St John's Vicarage, South End Road, Rainham RM13 7XT* T: (01708) 555260 M: 07500-007479 E: revdtonyburford@googlemail.com

BURGE, Edward Charles Richard. b 70. Liv Univ BA 92. Ridley Hall Cam 93. **d** 96 **p** 97. C Cayton w Eastfield *York* 96-99; P-in-c Lythe w Ugthorpe 99-03; Children's Officer (Cleveland Adnry) 99-03; Hon Chapl Miss to Seafarers 02-03; Dioc Youth and Children's Work Co-ord *Wakef* 04-10; P-in-c Roberttown w Hartshead 10-12; P-in-c Scholes 10-12; V Hartshead, Hightown, Roberttown and Scholes *Leeds* from 12. *The Vicarage, Scholes Lane, Scholes, Cleckheaton BD19 6PA* T: (01924) 873024 E: richard.burge@talktalk.net

BURGE-THOMAS, Mrs Ruth Anne. b 66. **d** 04 **p** 05. C Clapham H Spirit *S'wark* 04-14; V from 14; Chapl St Mark's C of E Academy Mitcham from 10. *The Vicarage, 15 Elms Road, London SW4 9ER* E: ruth@burgethomas.com

BURGER, David Joseph Cave. b 31. Selw Coll Cam BA 58 MA 62 Leic Univ 68. Coll of Resurr Mirfield 58. **d** 60 **p** 61. C Chiswick St Paul Grove Park *Lon* 60-63; C Charlton St Luke w H Trin *S'wark* 63-65; Warden St Luke Tr Ho Charlton 63-65; Chapl Moor Park Coll Farnham 66; Teacher Ysgol y Gader Dolgellau 68-85; Resettlement Officer Ches Aid to the Homeless 88-93; rtd 92; PtO *Ban* from 96. *Pwllygele Mawr, Llanfachreth, Dolgellau LL40 2DP* T: (01341) 450350

BURGESS, Alan James. b 51. Ridley Hall Cam 87. **d** 89 **p** 90. C Glenfield *Leic* 89-92; V Donisthorpe and Moira w Stretton-en-le-Field 92-06; RD Akeley W 00-06; C Ravenstone and Swannington 06-09; P-in-c Thringstone St Andr 06-09; P-in-c Whitwick St Jo the Bapt 07-09; R Whitwick, Thringstone and Swannington from 09. *The Vicarage, 37 North Street, Whitwick, Coalville LE67 5HB* T: (01530) 223481 E: sunergos@bigfoot.com

BURGESS, Mrs Anne. b 52. STETS 04. **d** 07 **p** 08. NSM Isleworth St Fran *Lon* 07-13; PtO 13-14; Chapl R Marsden NHS Foundn Trust from 14. *24 Penwerris Avenue, Isleworth TW7 4QX* T: (020) 8570 4238 E: anne@ivanburgess.co.uk

BURGESS, Charles Anthony Robert. b 53. STETS. **d** 11 **p** 12. NSM Bath Weston All SS w N Stoke and Langridge *B & W* 11-15; NSM Bathford from 15. *The Vicarage, 27 Church Street, Bathford, Bath BA1 7RS* E: cj.burgess@lineone.net

BURGESS, Canon Clive Brian. b 63. Trin Coll Bris BA 00. **d** 00 **p** 01. C Oxton *Ches* 00-03; V Brewood *Lich* 03-08; V Bishopswood 03-08; R Bentham *Bradf* 08-11; Rural Miss Adv 08-11; P-in-c Onchan *S & M* 11-14; TR Onchan, Lonan and Laxey from 14; Hon Can St German's Cathl from 15. *St Peter's Vicarage, Church Road, Onchan, Isle of Man IM3 1BF* T: (01624) 675797 E: cliveburgess@me.com

BURGESS, David James. b 58. Southn Univ BSc 80. St Jo Coll Nottm. **d** 89 **p** 90. C S Mimms Ch Ch *Lon* 89-93; C Hanwell St Mary w St Chris 93-97; P-in-c Hawridge w Cholesbury and St Leonard *Ox* 97-08; R from 08; P-in-c The Lee 97-08; V from 08. *The Vicarage, The Lee, Great Missenden HP16 9LZ* T: (01494) 837315 E: d.burgess@clara.net

BURGESS, Preb David John. b 39. Trin Hall Cam BA 62 MA 66 Univ Coll Ox MA 66 FRSA 91. Cuddesdon Coll 62. **d** 65 **p** 66. C Maidstone All SS w St Phil *Cant* 65; Asst Chapl Univ Coll Ox 66-70; Chapl 70-78; Can and Treas Windsor 78-87; V St Lawr Jewry *Lon* 87-08; Preb St Paul's Cathl 02-08; Chapl to The Queen 87-09; rtd 08. *62 Orbel Street, London SW11 3NZ* T: (020) 7585 1572

BURGESS, Mrs Denise. b 49. **d** 00 **p** 01. OLM Glascote and Stonydelph *Lich* 00-06; NSM 06-07; NSM Elford 07-15; NSM Mease Valley from 15. *23 Croft Close, Elford, Tamworth B79 9BU* M: 07818-890184 E: burgess.denise@virgin.net

BURGESS, Canon Edwin Michael. b 47. Lon Coll Bible BA 69 MA 73. Coll of Resurr Mirfield 70. **d** 72 **p** 73. C Beamish *Dur* 72-77; C Par *Truro* 77-80; P-in-c Duloe w Herodsfoot 80-83; R 83-86; Jt Dir SWMTC 80-86; Subwarden St Deiniol's Lib Hawarden 86-91; R Oughtrington *Ches* 91-05; P-in-c Warburton 93-05; R Oughtrington and Warburton from 05; CME Officer 99-03; Asst Chapl (Warrington) Ches Univ from

03; Dioc Chapl MU from 02; Hon Can Ches Cathl from 10. *The Rectory, Stage Lane, Lymm WA13 9JB* T: (01925) 752388 E: m.e.burgess@tesco.net

BURGESS, Mrs Geraldine Mary. b 54. Ox Univ BA 75 Southn Univ PGCE 76. SEITE 12. **d** 15. NSM Ifield *Chich* from 15. *Greenways, Newlands, Balcombe RH17 6JA* T: (01444) 811628 E: stevegerryburgess@gmail.com

BURGESS, Canon Henry Percival. b 21. Leeds Univ BA 48. Coll of Resurr Mirfield 48. **d** 50 **p** 51. C Northfield *Birm* 50-54; V Shaw Hill 54-62; V Wylde Green 62-89; Hon Can Birm Cathl 75-90; RD Sutton Coldfield 76-88; rtd 90; PtO *Birm* from 90. *39 Chestnut Drive, Birmingham B36 9BH* T: 0121-747 9926

BURGESS, Hugh Nigel. b 55. Edin Univ BSc 76 Aber Univ MA 79. St As Minl Tr Course. **d** 06 **p** 07. NSM Halkyn w Caerfallwch w Rhesycae *St As* from 06; P-in-c from 07. *The Chimneys, 7 Leete Park, Rhydymwyn, Mold CH7 5JJ* T: (01352) 741646 E: hugh@halkynparish.wanadoo.co.uk

BURGESS, Jane Ellen. b 63. STETS BA 10. **d** 07 **p** 08. C Frome H Trin *B & W* 07-10; P-in-c Bathford from 10. *The Vicarage, 27 Church Street, Bathford, Bath BA1 7RS* T: (01225) 858325 E: jane@stswithunsbathford.co.uk

BURGESS, Mrs Jean Ann. b 62. Nottm Univ MA 03. EMMTC 00. **d** 03 **p** 04. C Gresley *Derby* 03-09; C Derby St Alkmund and St Werburgh 09-13; P-in-c from 13. *200 Duffield Road, Derby DE22 1BL* T: (01332) 332681 E: jean@stalkmunds.org.uk

BURGESS, John David. b 51. Ex Univ BSc 73 Sussex Univ PGCE 94. Trin Coll Bris 07. **d** 08 **p** 09. NSM Westfield and Guestling *Chich* 08-15; NSM Brede w Udimore and Beckley and Peasmarsh from 15. *Bethel, Eight Acre Lane, Three Oaks, Hastings TN35 4NL* T: (01424) 751779 E: revd.john.burgess@gmail.com

BURGESS, The Ven John Edward. b 30. Lon Univ BD 57. ALCD 56. **d** 57 **p** 58. C Bermondsey St Mary w St Olave and St Jo *S'wark* 57-60; C Southampton St Mary w H Trin *Win* 60-62; V Dunston w Coppenhall *Lich* 62-67; Chapl Stafford Coll of Tech 63-67; V Keynsham w Queen Charlton *B & W* 67-75; R Burnett 67-75; RD Keynsham 72-75; Adn Bath and Preb Wells Cathl 75-95; rtd 96; PtO *B & W* from 96; *Sarum* from 96. *12 Berryfield Road, Bradford-on-Avon BA15 1SX* T: (01225) 868905

BURGESS, John Henry William. b 35. Wells Th Coll 65. **d** 67 **p** 68. C Teddington St Alb *Lon* 67-72; C Northolt St Jos 72-74; PtO *B & W* 93-99 and 00-06; rtd 95; C Bruton and Distr *B & W* 99-00; PtO *Nor* from 04. *9 Fairview Drive, Colkirk, Fakenham NR21 7NT* T: (01328) 863410 E: burgess9@btinternet.com

BURGESS, John Michael. b 36. ALCD 61. **d** 61 **p** 62. C Eccleston St Luke *Liv* 61-64; C Avondale St Mary Magd Rhodesia 64-68; R Marlborough 68-74; V Nottingham St Andr *S'well* 74-79; Bp's Adv on Community Relns 77-79; V Earlestown *Liv* 79-87; RD Warrington 82-87; TR Halewood 87-94; V Southport St Phil and St Paul 94-01; AD N Meols 95-00; rtd 01; PtO *Liv* from 03. *3 Glencoyne Drive, Southport PR9 9TS* T: (01704) 506843

BURGESS, John Mulholland. b 32. Cranmer Hall Dur 58. **d** 61 **p** 62. C Frimley *Guildf* 61-67; C Cheltenham St Luke and St Jo *Glouc* 67-69; P-in-c Withington w Compton Abdale 69-74; R Woolstone w Gotherington and Oxenton 74-75; Chapl Rotterdam w Schiedam etc *Eur* 75-78; Chapl Sliema 78-80; C Nottingham All SS *S'well* 80; C Rolleston w Morton 80-83; C Rolleston w Fiskerton, Morton and Upton 83-84; V Mansfield St Aug 84-99; Asst RD Mansfield 88-92; RD 92-98; rtd 99; PtO *S'well* from 03. *278 Westfield Lane, Mansfield NG19 6NQ* T: (01623) 421163

BURGESS, Kate Lamorna. b 64. Man Poly BA 86 Leeds Univ MA 97. NEOC 99. **d** 02 **p** 03. OHP 92-03; C Hessle *York* 02-06; TV Howden 06-10; P-in-c Stretford St Matt *Man* from 10. *St Matthew's Rectory, 39 Sandy Lane, Stretford, Manchester M32 9DB* T: 0161-865 2535 E: kburgess1@tiscali.co.uk

BURGESS (née BOND), Mrs Kim Mary. b 58. SRN 79. Trin Coll Bris 84. **d** 87 **p** 94. Par Dn Cullompton *Ex* 87-91; Asst Chapl N Staffs R Infirmary Stoke-on-Trent 91-95; NSM Audley *Lich* 95-00. *38 Birch Avenue, Alsager, Stoke-on-Trent ST7 2QY*

BURGESS, Laura Jane. See JØRGENSEN, Laura Jane

BURGESS, Michael. See BURGESS, Edwin Michael

BURGESS, Michael Anglin. b 34. St Deiniol's Hawarden 81. **d** 83 **p** 84. C Habergham Eaves St Matt *Blackb* 83-85; C Burnley St Matt w H Trin 85-86; V Preston St Matt 86-93; V Nelson St Bede 93-99; rtd 99; PtO *Blackb* from 99. *39 Reedley Road, Reedley, Burnley BB10 2LU* T: (01282) 449727 E: revmab1@ntlworld.com

BURGESS, Canon Michael James. b 42. Coll of Resurr Mirfield 74. **d** 76 **p** 77. C Leigh-on-Sea St Marg *Chelmsf* 76-79; C St Peter-in-Thanet *Cant* 79-82; Chapl Royal St Geo Coll Toronto Canada 82-89; R Toronto Epiphany and St Mark

89-04; R Toronto Transfiguration from 04; Can Toronto from 01. *318W-118 Montgomery Avenue, Toronto ON M4R 1E3, Canada* T: (001) (416) 482 2462 *or* 489 7798 F: 489 3272 E: michaelburgess@sympatico.ca

BURGESS, Neil. b 53. Univ of Wales (Lamp) BA 75 Nottm Univ MTh 87 PhD 93. St Mich Coll Llan 75. **d** 77 **p** 78. C Cheadle *Lich* 77-79; C Longton 79-82; TV Hanley H Ev 82-86; C Uttoxeter w Bramshall 86-87; Lect Linc Th Coll 87-95; Hon C Linc Minster Gp 88-95; Dioc Dir of Clergy Tr *S'well* 95-00; C Newark 97-00; PtO *Linc* 00-06; Hon C Linc St Pet-at-Gowts and St Andr from 06; Hon C Linc St Botolph from 06; Hon C Linc St Mary-le-Wigford w St Benedict etc from 06; Hon C Linc St Faith and St Martin w St Pet from 06; Hon C Linc St Swithin from 06. *23 Drury Lane, Lincoln LN1 3BN* T: (01522) 539408 E: ann.burgess@btinternet.com

BURGESS, Prof Paul Christopher James. b 41. Qu Coll Cam BA 63 MA 67. Lon Coll of Div 66. **d** 68 **p** 69. C Islington St Mary *Lon* 68-72; C Church Stretton *Heref* 73-74; Lect Gujranwala Th Sem Pakistan 74-83; Warden Carberry Tower (Ch of Scotland) 84-86; Progr Co-ord 86-88; TV Livingston LEP *Edin* 88-92; Prof and Lib Gujranwala Th Sem 94-08; rtd 08. *Springvale, Halket Road, Lugton, Kilmarnock KA3 4EE* T: (01505) 850254 E: paulandcathie@gmail.com

BURGESS, Peter Alan. b 40. St Edm Ho Cam BA 86 MA 89 MPhil 86 St Jo Coll York MA 99. Cranmer Hall Dur 02. **d** 03 **p** 04. NSM Wheldrake w Thorganby *York* 03-08; NSM Derwent Ings 08-14; PtO from 14. *2 Derwent Drive, Wheldrake, York YO19 6AL* T: (01904) 448309 E: burgesspr@btinternet.com

BURGESS, Roy. b 32. S Dios Minl Tr Scheme 80. **d** 83 **p** 84. NSM Bentworth and Shalden and Lasham *Win* 83-89; R Ingoldsby *Linc* 89-97; RD Beltisloe 93-97; rtd 97; PtO *Nor* from 98. *28 Stuart Court, High Street, Kibworth, Leicester LE8 0LR*

BURGESS, Roy Graham. b 47. Birm Univ CertCYW 72. Ox Min Course 91. **d** 94 **p** 95. C Easthampstead *Ox* 94-99; C Wokingham St Paul 99-04; P-in-c Owlsmoor 04-09; V 09-14; rtd 15; PtO *Ox* from 15. *Strathpeffer, 4 Appletree Place, Bracknell RG42 1YN* T: (01344) 780110 E: revroy@btinternet.com

BURGHALL, Kenneth Miles. b 34. Selw Coll Cam BA 57 MA 61. Qu Coll Birm 57. **d** 59 **p** 60. C Macclesfield St Mich *Ches* 59-63; CF 63-67; P-in-c Birkenhead Priory *Ches* 71-87; V Macclesfield St Paul 71-87; V Lower Peover 87-04; P-in-c Over Peover 92-04; rtd 04; PtO *Ches* from 04. *45 Ullswater Road, Congleton CW12 4JE* T: (01260) 289727

BURGON, Canon George Irvine. b 41. Open Univ BA 92. Edin Th Coll 62. **d** 65 **p** 66. C Dundee St Mary Magd *Bre* 65-68; C Wellingborough All Hallows *Pet* 68-71; P-in-c Norton 71-73; TV Daventry w Norton 73-75; V Northampton St Mary 75-98; R Rothwell w Orton, Rushton w Glendon and Pipewell 98-08; Can Pet Cathl 95-08; rtd 08; PtO *Pet* from 08. *47 Woodlands Avenue, Barton Seagrave, Kettering NN15 6QS* T: (01536) 722193 E: georgeburgon@yahoo.co.uk

BURGON, Mrs Lynne. b 58. RGN 80 RM 83. SWMTC 03. **d** 06 **p** 07. NSM Fremington *Ex* 06-07; C Okehampton w Inwardleigh, Bratton Clovelly etc 07-11; V Bampton, Morebath, Clayhanger, Petton etc 11-14; PtO from 14. *2 Barton Cottages, Monkleigh, Bideford EX39 5JX* E: l.burgon@btinternet.com

BURKE, Canon Christopher Mark. b 65. Cov Poly LLB 87 Heythrop Coll Lon MA 06. Ripon Coll Cuddesdon 89. **d** 92 **p** 93. C Nunthorpe *York* 92-96; V S Bank 96-02; R Stepney St Dunstan and All SS *Lon* 02-10; Can Res Sheff Cathl 10-13; Can Res and Prec Sheff Cathl from 13; Vice Dean from 13. *49 Broomgrove Road, Sheffield S10 2NA* T: 0114-263 6066 F: 279 7412 M: 07950-434333 E: christopher.burke@sheffield-cathedral.org.uk

BURKE, Colin Douglas. b 41. Bp Otter Coll CertEd 64. **d** 92 **p** 93. OLM Fressingfield, Mendham, Metfield, Weybread etc *St E* 92-99; P-in-c Oare w Culbone *B & W* from 99. *The Rectory, Oare, Lynton EX35 6NX* T: (01598) 741270

BURKE, Elisabeth Ann. b 44. St Matthias Coll Bris CertEd 66. **d** 05 **p** 06. OLM E Horsley and Ockham w Hatchford and Downside *Guildf* 05-14; PtO from 14. *39 Copse Road, Cobham KT11 2TW* T: (01932) 863886 E: elisabethb@ntlworld.com

BURKE, Mrs Elizabeth Mary Ann. b 72. Liv Univ BA 95 Surrey Univ MBA 06. Westcott Ho Cam 12. **d** 13 **p** 14. C Bickleigh and Shaugh Prior *Ex* 13-14; C Plymouth Crownhill Ascension from 14. *172 Aberdeen Avenue, Plymouth PL5 3UW* M: 07990-978485 E: eaburke@btinternet.com

BURKE, Eric John. b 44. Llan Dioc Tr Scheme 81. **d** 85 **p** 86. NSM Cardiff St Jo *Llan* 85-95; Chapl Asst Univ Hosp of Wales and Llandough NHS Trust 95-00; Chapl Asst Cardiff and Vale NHS Trust from 00. *Chaplaincy Department, University Hospital of Wales, Heath Park, Cardiff CF4 4XW* T: (029) 2074 3230 *or* 2079 8147

BURKE, Jonathan. b 53. Lon Univ BEd. Westcott Ho Cam 79. d 82 p 83. C Weymouth H Trin *Sarum* 82-85; R Bere Regis and Affpuddle w Turnerspuddle 85-92; NSM Talbot Village 04-08; TR White Horse 08-15; RD Heytesbury 13-15; rtd 15; PtO *Sarum* from 15. *10 Graycot Close, Bournemouth BH10 7BU*
E: jonathan_burke2003@yahoo.co.uk

BURKE, Kelvin Stephen. b 56. Man Univ BA 77 FCA 81. Cranmer Hall Dur. d 99 p 00. C Stanley *Wakef* 99-02; P-in-c Wakef St Andr and St Mary 02-06; Asst Chapl Leeds Teaching Hosps NHS Trust 06-10; PtO *Portsm* from 11; Chapl Isle of Wight Primary Care Trust from 12. *7 Steephill Court Road, Ventnor PO38 1UH* T: (01983) 854261
M: 07793-979907

BURKE, Mary. *See* BURKE, Elizabeth Mary Ann

BURKE, Michael Robert. b 61. Leeds Univ BA 83. Trin Coll Bris BA 89. d 89 p 90. C Anston *Sheff* 89-92; V Crosspool 92-00; V Hucclecote *Glouc* 00-09; PtO 09-15; TV Keynsham *B & W* from 15. *9 Chelmer Grove, Keynsham, Bristol BS31 1QA*
M: 07432-530153 E: mikburke@blueyonder.co.uk

BURKE, Patrick. CITC. d 09 p 10. C Douglas Union w Frankfield *C, C & R* 09-12; I Castlecomer w Colliery Ch, Mothel and Bilboa *C & O* from 12. *The Rectory, Castlecomer, Co Kilkenny, Republic of Ireland* T: (00353) (56) 444 1677 M: 87-630 9421
E: pathos@eircom.net

BURKE, Wayne Jackson. b 51. San Francisco State Univ BA 76 MA 78 Univ of Wales (Cardiff) PhD 91. St Steph Ho Ox 01. d 02 p 03. Hon C Gtr Athens *Eur* 02-12. *1 Iridos, Amarousion, 151-22 Athens, Greece* T/F: (0030) (210) 614 8198
E: paterw@hol.gr

BURKE, Canon William Spencer Dwerryhouse. b 46. Ripon Coll Cuddesdon 90. d 92 p 93. C Watford St Mich *St Alb* 92-95; R Castor w Sutton and Upton w Marholm *Pet* 95-15; Can Pet Cathl 07-15; rtd 15; PtO *Ely* from 15; *Pet* from 15. *26 Well Lane, Shaftesbury SP7 8LW* T: (01747) 853295
E: wburke@btinternet.com *or* wsdburke@outlook.com

BURKETT, Canon Christopher Paul. b 52. Warwick Univ BA 75 Westmr Coll Ox MTh 93 Liv Univ PhD 10. Qu Coll Birm 75. d 78 p 79. C Streetly *Lich* 78-81; C Harlescott 81-83; TV Leek and Meerbrook 83-89; Chapl Leek Morlands Hosp 83-89; Area Sec USPG Ches 89-92; V Whitegate w Lt Budworth *Ches* 92-00; Asst CME Officer 93-00; Can Res Ches Cathl 00-10; Hon Can Ches Cathl from 11; Bp's Chapl 00-10; Dioc Dir of Min from 10; C Ches H Trin from 10. *36 Abbots Park, Chester CH1 4AN* T: (01244) 399941 M: 07921-040153 *or* 681973 ext 256
E: christopher.burkett@chester.anglican.org

BURKILL, Mark Edward. b 56. MA PhD. Trin Coll Bris. d 84 p 85. C Cheadle *Ches* 84-88; C Harold Wood *Chelmsf* 88-91; V Leyton Ch Ch from 91. *The Vicarage, 52 Elm Road, London E11 4DW* T: (020) 8539 4980
E: m.burkill@ntlworld.com

BURKITT, Paul Adrian. b 49. RMN 75 SRN 77. St Steph Ho Ox 84. d 86 p 87. C Whitby *York* 86-90; V Egton w Grosmont 90-93; V Newington w Dairycoates 93-96; P-in-c Kingston upon Hull St Mary 96-07; P-in-c Sculcoates 04-07; rtd 07; PtO *York* 07-14; P-in-c Kingston upon Hull St Mary from 14. *75 Denaby Court, Barnsley Street, Hull HU8 7SS*
T: (01482) 218879 E: paul@angela75.karoo.co.uk

BURKITT, Richard Francis. b 49. Leeds Univ BA 71 CertEd 72. Sarum & Wells Th Coll 82. d 90 p 90. R Fraserburgh w New Pitsligo *Ab* 90-95; R Fortrose, Cromarty and Arpafeelie *Mor* 95-08; C Inverness St Mich 08-09; LtO 09-13; rtd 13; P-in-c Strathnairn St Paul *Mor* from 13. *60 Grant Street, Inverness IV3 8BS* M: 07717-457247 E: burkitt@supanet.com

BURKITT-GRAY, Mrs Joan Katherine. b 47. Portsm Poly BSc 68 Southn Univ MPhil 74. SEITE 00. d 04 p 05. NSM Lee St Marg *S'wark* from 04; Hon Asst Chapl St Chris Hospice Lon 08-09. *7 Foxes Dale, London SE3 9BD* T: (020) 8463 0365 *or* 8768 4500 E: joanburkittgray@gmail.com

BURLAND, Clive Beresford. b 37. Sarum & Wells Th Coll 81. d 85 p 86. C Warblington w Emsworth *Portsm* 85-87; C Cowes St Mary 87-92; V Gurnard 92-98; R Northwood 93-98; rtd 98; PtO *Portsm* from 98. *5A Orchard Close, Freshwater PO40 9BQ* T: (01983) 753949

BURLEIGH, David John. b 42. FCII 69. St Deiniol's Hawarden 84. d 87 p 88. NSM Lache cum Saltney *Ches* 87-88; NSM Eastham 89-92; C Birkenhead Priory 92-95; P-in-c Duloe w Herodsfoot *Truro* 95-99; TV Liskeard, St Keyne, St Pinnock, Morval etc 95-99; R Duloe, Herodsfoot, Morval and St Pinnock 99-01; V Bath St Barn w Englishcombe *B & W* 01-10; rtd 10; PtO *B & W* from 11. *1 Vine Gardens, Frome BA11 2LX* T: (01373) 300820
E: david.burleigh@hotmail.co.uk

BURLEIGH, Walter Coleridge. b 41. WMMTC 89. d 89 p 90. NSM N Evington *Leic* 90-96; PtO from 96. *20 Border Drive, Leicester LE4 2JH* T: 0116-235 9230

BURLES, Robert John. b 54. Bris Univ BSc 75. St Jo Coll Nottm LTh 86. d 88 p 89. C Mansfield SS Pet and Paul *S'well* 88-91; C The Lydiards *Bris* 91-92; TV W Swindon and the Lydiards 92-97; TR Swindon St Jo and St Andr 97-11; AD Swindon 06-11; Hon Can Bris Cathl 04-11; P-in-c Takeley w Lt Canfield *Chelmsf* from 11. *The Rectory, Parsonage Road, Takeley, Bishop's Stortford CM22 6QX* T: (01279) 870214
M: 07946-496418 E: rob@burles.org.uk

BURLEY, John Roland James. b 46. St Jo Coll Cam BA 67 MA 70. Trin Episc Sch for Min Ambridge Penn MDiv 88. d 81 p 82. SAMS Chile 81-90; TV Southgate *Chich* 90-99; R Alfold and Loxwood *Guildf* 99-07; P-in-c 08-11; rtd 11; PtO *Heref* from 11. *72 Dahn Drive, Ludlow SY8 1XZ* T: (01584) 873155
E: john@burleys.co.uk

BURLEY, Michael. b 58. Ridley Hall Cam 86. d 89 p 90. C Scarborough St Mary w Ch Ch and H Apostles *York* 89-92; C Drypool 93; TV 93-97; V Sutton St Mich 97-03; V Burley in Wharfedale *Bradf* 03-13; Assoc Dioc Dir of Ords 07-13; P-in-c Staines *Lon* from 13. *St Peter's Vicarage, 14 Thames Side, Staines-upon-Thames TW18 2HA* T: (01784) 453039
E: michael.burley@btinternet.com

BURLEY, Richard Alexander. b 80. Warwick Univ BA 01 Fitzw Coll Cam BA 07. Ridley Hall Cam 05. d 08 p 09. C Bilton *Cov* 08-12; V Wythall *Birm* from 12. *15 Hawthorn Drive, Hollywood, Birmingham B47 5QT* T: 0121-430 2775 M: 07777-665117
E: rich@burley.biz *or* churchoffice@wythallchurch.net

BURLTON, Aelred Harry. b 49. Sarum & Wells Th Coll 75. d 78 p 79. C Feltham *Lon* 78-82; Chapl Heathrow Airport 83-94; P-in-c Harmondsworth 92-94; R St Buryan, St Levan and Sennen *Truro* 94-05; rtd 05. *Farway Barn, Hellangove Farm, Gulval, Penzance TR20 8XD* T: (01736) 330426

BURMAN, Philip Harvey. b 47. Kelham Th Coll 66. d 70 p 71. C Huyton St Mich *Liv* 70-75; C Farnworth 75-77; TV Kirkby 77-83; V Hindley All SS 83-93; V Middlesbrough St Martin *York* 93-97; V Middlesbrough St Martin w St Cuth 97-99; P-in-c Eccleston St Thos *Liv* 99-08; V Liv St Chris Norris Green from 08. *St Christopher's Vicarage, Lorenzo Drive, Liverpool L11 1BQ* T: 0151-226 1637
E: philip.h.burman@googlemail.com

BURMAN, William Guest. b 26. St Cath Coll Cam MA 55 Worc Coll Ox MA 63. St Steph Ho Ox 81. d 83 p 84. C Weymouth H Trin *Sarum* 83-86; R Exton and Winsford and Cutcombe w Luxborough *B & W* 86-89; TV Langport Area 89-91; rtd 91; PtO *B & W* 91-98 and from 02; Master Bath St Mary Magd Holloway 94-11. *The College of St Barnabas, Blackberry Lane, Lingfield RH7 6NJ*

BURMESTER, Stephen John. b 66. Leeds Univ BSc 87. Wycliffe Hall Ox 96. d 98 p 99. C Lenton *S'well* 98-02; C Bebington *Ches* 02-08; V Handforth from 08. *The Vicarage, 36 Sagars Road, Handforth, Wilmslow SK9 3EE* T: (01625) 250559 *or* 532145 E: steve.burmester@gmail.com

BURN, Geoffrey Livingston. b 60. Sydney Univ BSc 83 Imp Coll Lon PhD 87 St Jo Coll Dur BA 95. Cranmer Hall Dur 93. d 96 p 97. C St Austell *Truro* 96-03; PtO *Cant* 03-06; P Forest S Deanery *Glouc* 06-11; Hon C Cinderford St Jo 06-10; Hon C Cinderford w Littledean 10-11; Chapl Glos Primary Care Trust 06-11; Chapl HM YOI Roch from 11. *HM Young Offender Institution, 1 Fort Road, Rochester ME1 3QS* T: (01634) 803100
E: geoffrey@burn.eclipse.co.uk

BURN, Mrs Helen Mary. b 64. Down Coll Cam BA 86 New Coll Ox PGCE 88 Ex Univ MA 02 PhD 11. SWMTC 00. d 03 p 04. C Eythorne and Elvington w Waldershare etc *Cant* 03-06; Dir of Studies Local Min Tr Scheme 03-06; Dir Reader Tr *Glouc* 06-11; Tutor WEMTC 06-12; Dir of Studies Ripon Coll Cuddesdon 11-12; Sen Lect Glos Univ *Glouc* 09-12; V Roch St Justus from 12. *St Justus's Vicarage, 1 Binnacle Road, Rochester ME1 2XR* T: (01634) 841183 M: 07818-492553
E: helenmburn@gmail.com

BURN, Leonard Louis. b 44. K Coll Lon BD 67 AKC 67. d 68 p 69. C Kingswinford St Mary *Lich* 68-70; C S Ascot *Ox* 70-72; C Caversham 72-76; Chapl Selly Oak Hosp Birm 76-81; Chapl Bris City Hosp 81-82; P-in-c Bris St Mich 81-83; R Peopleton and White Ladies Aston w Churchill etc *Worc* 83-88; V Bengeworth 88-97; Chapl St Richard's Hospice Worc 88-97; Chapl Evesham Coll 90-97; rtd 97; PtO *Glouc* from 97; *Worc* 97-98; Chapl Worcs Community and Mental Health Trust from 98. *Beckford Rise, Beckford, Tewkesbury GL20 7AN* T/F: (01386) 881160 M: 07734-505663
E: leonard.burn@btinternet.com

BURN, Michael Campbell. b 46. JP 01. City of Leeds Coll of Educn CertEd 68 Open Univ MA 88 Univ of Wales (Trin St Dav) LTh 12. Yorks Min Course 12. d 12 p 13. NSM Rotherham *Sheff* 12-14; NSM Wath-upon-Dearne from 14. *The Vicarage, Church Street, Wath-upon-Dearne, Rotherham S63 7RD* T: (01709) 872299 M: 07712-620303
E: michaelcburn@btinternet.com

BURN, Richard James Southerden. b 34. Pemb Coll Cam BA 56. Wells Th Coll 56. **d** 58 **p** 59. C Cheshunt *St Alb* 58-62; C Leighton Buzzard 65-66; C Glastonbury St Jo *B & W* 66-68; P-in-c Prestonpans *Edin* 68-71; P-in-c Stokesay *Heref* 71-75; P-in-c Dorrington 75-81; P-in-c Stapleton 75-81; P-in-c Leebotwood w Longnor 75-81; P-in-c Smethcott w Woolstaston 81; TR Melbury *Sarum* 81-87; P-in-c Quendon w Rickling and Wicken Bonhunt *Chelmsf* 87-92; R Quendon w Rickling and Wicken Bonhunt etc 92-95; rtd 95; V Isleworth St Fran *Lon* 95-00; Hon C S Warks Seven Gp *Cov* 06-09; PtO *Heref* from 12. *The Old School House, 29 Lydbury North, Craven Arms SY7 8AU* T: (01588) 680465
E: richard.burn58@yahoo.co.uk

BURN, Robert Pemberton. b 34. Peterho Cam BA 56 MA 60 Lon Univ PhD 68. CMS Tr Coll Chislehurst 60. **d** 63 **p** 81. India 63-71; PtO *Ely* 71-81; P-in-c Foxton 81-88; PtO *Ex* from 89. *Sunnyside, Barrack Road, Exeter EX2 6AB* T: (01392) 430028

BURN-MURDOCH, Aidan Michael. b 35. Trin Coll Cam BA 60 MA 63. Ridley Hall Cam 59. **d** 61 **p** 62. C Bishopwearmouth St Gabr *Dur* 61-63; Tutor Ridley Hall Cam 63-67; CMS Miss 67-70; India 68-70; R Hawick *Edin* 70-77; Bp's Co-ord of Evang *S & B* 77-81; R Reynoldston w Penrice and Llangennith 77-83; R Port Eynon w Rhosili and Llanddewi and Knelston 83-89; R Uddingston and Cambuslang *Glas* 89-97; rtd 97; P-in-c Eyemouth *Edin* 98-00; PtO *Glas* from 09. *19 Blairston Avenue, Bothwell, Glasgow G71 8RZ* T: (01698) 853377

BURNAGE, Arthur Gavin. b 63. Ulster Univ BA 85 Cam Univ MA 05. Wycliffe Hall Ox 05. **d** 07 **p** 08. C Aldridge *Lich* 07-12; C Walsall St Pet 12-13; P-in-c from 13. *9 Stonebeech Court, 20 Bloxwich Road, Walsall WS2 8BF*
E: gav.burnage@googlemail.com

BURNE, Sambrooke Roger. b 47. Lon Univ MB, BS 70 MRCGP 74. SAOMC 03. **d** 06 **p** 07. NSM Blackbird Leys *Ox* 06-14; PtO *Pet* from 14. *43 Glebe Rise, Kings Sutton, Banbury OX17 3PH* T: (01295) 811936 M: 07901-882957
E: rogerburne@gmail.com *or* roger.burne@ntlworld.com

BURNET, Norman Andrew Gray. b 32. Aber Univ BEd 77 Cam Univ MLitt 92. Edin Th Coll 53. **d** 55 **p** 56. C Ayr *Glas* 55-58; C St Jo Cathl Umtata S Africa 58-63; R Mt Frere 63-69; R Leven *St And* 72; PtO *Ab* 73-81; *Bre* 73-81; *Ely* 73-81; P-in-c Brinkley, Burrough Green and Carlton 82-83; P-in-c Westley Waterless 82-83; Australia 83-84; R Fraserburgh w New Pitsligo *Ab* 85-89; P-in-c Bicker *Linc* 89; V Bicker and Wigtoft 89-97; rtd 97; PtO *Nor* 97-99; *Linc* 97-00. *61 Westlode Street, Spalding PE11 2AE* T/F: (01775) 767429

BURNETT (formerly DRURY), Mrs Caroline Nora. b 60. SAOMC 00. **d** 03 **p** 04. C Leavesden *St Alb* 03-09; C Bushey 09-13; P-in-c Compton w Shackleford and Peper Harow *Guildf* from 13. *Handpost Cottage, The Street, Compton, Guildford GU3 1ED* E: caroline_burnett@btinternet.com

BURNETT, Gemma Claire. b 82. CCC Cam MA 07 MPhil 05 PhD 11. Westcott Ho Cam 07. **d** 11 **p** 12. C Plaistow St Mary *Roch* 11-14; Chapl Trin Coll Cam from 14. *Trinity College, Cambridge CB2 1TQ* M: 07584-689879 T: (01223) 338400
E: gemmaburnettchetwynd@gmail.com

BURNETT, Canon John Capenhurst. b 19. AKC 49. **d** 49 **p** 50. C Shirehampton *Bris* 49-53; C Stoke Bishop 53-56; V Wroughton 56-76; RD Cricklade 70-76; Hon Can Bris Cathl 74-85; V Bris St Andr w St Bart 76-85; rtd 85; PtO *Bris* from 85. *57 Upper Cranbrook Road, Bristol BS6 7UR* T: 0117-924 5284

BURNETT, Mrs Patricia Kay. b 38. Newnham Coll Cam MA 60. Sarum Th Coll 94. **d** 97 **p** 98. NSM Jarvis Brook *Chich* 97-08; rtd 08. *20 St Richards Road, Crowborough TN6 3AT* T: (01892) 655668

BURNETT, Susan Mary. b 50. Lon Univ BEd 73. Cranmer Hall Dur 76. **dss** 78 **d** 87 **p** 94. Welling *S'wark* 78-83; E Greenwich Ch Ch w St Andr and St Mich 83-91; Par Dn 87-91; Par Dn Sydenham All SS 91-94; C 94-95; C Lower Sydenham St Mich 91-95; V 95-09; rtd 09. *9 Grove Park, Chichester PO19 3HY* T: (01243) 532748

BURNETT-HALL, Mrs Karen. b 46. Bp Grosseteste Coll CertEd 68 Lon Univ BD 82. Oak Hill Th Coll 86. **d** 89 **p** 94. Par Dn Norbury *Ches* 89-92; NSM York St Paul 93-95; NSM York St Barn 95-99; P-in-c 00-09; P-in-c Wimbotsham w Stow Bardolph and Stow Bridge etc *Ely* from 11. *The Rectory, Church Road, Wimbotsham, King's Lynn PE34 3QG* T: (01366) 384342 E: karen.bh@btinternet.com

BURNHAM, Stephen Patrick James. b 75. Ch Ch Ox BA 97. Westcott Ho Cam 00. **d** 02 **p** 03. C Vale of Belvoir *Leic* 02-05; TV Leic Resurr 05-12; V Leic St Anne, St Paul w St Aug from 12. *St Anne's Vicarage, 76 Letchworth Road, Leicester LE3 6FH* M: 07905-882805

BURNIE, Judith. *See* SWEETMAN, Judith

BURNINGHAM, Frederick George. b 34. ALCD 60. **d** 60 **p** 61. C New Beckenham St Paul *Roch* 60-63; Canada 63-68 and 89-95; C Wisley w Pyrford *Guildf* 68-69; P-in-c Sydenham H Trin *S'wark* 69-71; C Broadwater St Mary *Chich* 72-77; R Sotterley, Willingham, Shadingfield, Ellough etc *St E* 77-82; R Ipswich St Clem w H Trin 82-89; P-in-c Thorndon w Rishangles, Stoke Ash, Thwaite etc 95-99; rtd 99; PtO *Leeds* from 99. *8 Meadow Rise, Skipton BD23 1BT* T: (01756) 794440
E: f.burningham@btopenworld.com

BURNINGHAM, Richard Anthony. b 47. Keele Univ BA 70 Aber Univ CQSW 77 Roehampton Inst PGCE 85. All Nations Chr Coll 82 Oak Hill Th Coll 94. **d** 96 **p** 97. C Reigate St Mary *S'wark* 96-00; V Weston *Win* 00-12; rtd 12; PtO *Win* from 12. *30 Earle House, Winnall Manor Road, Winchester SO23 0NA* T: (01962) 808213 E: burningham@btinternet.com

BURNISTON, Aubrey John. b 53. St Jo Coll Dur BA 92 Leeds Univ MA 03. Cranmer Hall Dur 79. **d** 83 **p** 84. C Owton Manor *Dur* 83-86; TV Rugby *Cov* 86-93; V Heaton St Martin *Bradf* 93-09; Bp's Adv in Liturgy 00-09; V Islington St Jas w St Pet *Lon* from 09. *St James's Vicarage, 1A Arlington Square, London N1 7DS* T: (020) 7226 4108
E: vicar@stjamesislington.com

BURNLEY, Suffragan Bishop of. *See* NORTH, The Rt Revd Philip John

BURNS, Arthur. *See* BURNS, Williams Arthur

BURNS, Dane. b 51. **d** 85 **p** 86. C Enniskillen *Clogh* 85-87; I Augher w Newtownsaville and Eskrahoole 87-92; Dioc Communications Officer 91-92; I Camus-juxta-Bann *D & R* 92-96. *86 Donneybrewer Road, Eglinton, Londonderry BT47 3PD*

BURNS, Canon Edward Joseph. b 38. Liv Univ BSc 58 St Cath Soc Ox BA 61 MA 64. Wycliffe Hall Ox 58. **d** 61 **p** 62. C Leyland St Andr *Blackb* 61-64; C Burnley St Pet 64-67; V Chorley St Jas 67-75; V Fulwood Ch Ch 75-03; RD Preston 79-86; Chapl Sharoe Green Hosp Preston 81-94; Hon Can Blackb Cathl 86-03; Bp's Adv on Hosp Chapls 89-94; rtd 03; PtO *Blackb* from 03. *17 Greenacres, Fulwood, Preston PR2 7DA* T: (01772) 864741 E: eddieandsheila@ejburns.freeserve.co.uk

BURNS, Canon James Denis. b 43. Lich Th Coll 69. **d** 72 **p** 73. C Gt Wyrley *Lich* 72-75; C Atherton *Man* 75-76; Asst Chapl Sheff Ind Miss 76-79; C-in-c Masborough St Paul w St Jo 76-78; C-in-c Northfield St Mich 76-78; V Rotherham St Paul, St Mich and St Jo Ferham Park 78-79; V Lancaster Ch Ch *Blackb* 79-81; V Lancaster Ch Ch w St Jo and St Anne 81-86; V Chorley St Pet 86-96; R Rufford 96-07; Warden Past Assts 96-06; C Croston and Bretherton 06-07; rtd 07; Hon C Hesketh w Becconsall *Blackb* 07-09; Hon Can Blackb Cathl 99-09; PtO from 09; *Man* from 09. *7 Devon Drive, Diggle, Oldham OL3 5PP* T: (01457) 810074

BURNS, John Macdonald. *See* ODA-BURNS, John Macdonald

BURNS, Mrs Lucinda Roberte. b 56. Qu Coll Birm BA 11. **d** 11 **p** 12. NSM Gt Hanwood and Longden and Annscroft etc *Heref* 11-14; Chapl Adcote Sch from 14; C Ruyton XI Towns w Gt and Lt Ness *Lich* 14-15; P-in-c 15. *The Vicarage, Little Ness Road, Ruyton XI Towns, Shrewsbury SY4 1LQ* T: (01939) 261234 M: 07913-944095 E: lucinda.burns@virgin.net

BURNS, Matthew. Leeds Univ BA. Coll of Resurr Mirfield. **d** 05 **p** 06. C Wrexham *St As* 05-08; V Towyn 08-10; P-in-c 10-11; TV Wrexham from 11. *55 Princess Street, Wrexham LL13 7US* T: (01978) 264834
E: matthew.burns@wrexhamparish.org.uk

BURNS, Canon Michael John. b 53. AKC 76. Chich Th Coll 76. **d** 77 **p** 78. C Broseley w Benthall *Heref* 77-81; C Stevenage All SS Pin Green *St Alb* 81-84; V Tattenham Corner and Burgh Heath *Guildf* 84-92; C and Chapl Younger People Milton Keynes *Ox* 92-00; P-in-c Potters Bar K Chas *St Alb* 00-12; V from 12; AD Barnet from 11; Hon Can St Alb from 13. *The Vicarage, 8 Dugdale Hill Lane, Potters Bar EN6 2DW* T: (01707) 661266

BURNS, Robert Joseph. b 34. Wycliffe Hall Ox 67. **d** 71 **p** 72. C Portswood Ch Ch *Win* 71-73; C Woking St Jo *Guildf* 73-77; C Glas St Mary 77; Bp's Dom Chapl 77-78; R Glas Gd Shep and Ascension 78-92; rtd 92. *Laverton Cottage, Paragon Place, Lansdowne, Bourton-on-the-Water GL54 2FJ*

BURNS, Stephen. b 70. Grey Coll Dur BA 92 MA 94 Clare Coll Cam MLitt 96 Dur Univ PhD 03. Ridley Hall Cam 93. **d** 96 **p** 97. C Houghton le Spring *Dur* 96-99; TV Gateshead 99-02; Dir Urban Miss Cen Cranmer Hall 99-02; Tutor Qu Coll Birm 03-06; Chapl and Lect St Jo Coll Dur 06-07; Fell Chas Sturt Univ Australia from 07. *United Theological College, 16 Masons Drive, North Parramatta, NSW 2151, Australia* T: (0061) (2) 8838 8921 F: 9683 6617
E: stephenb@nsw.uca.org.au *or* sburns@csu.edu.au

BURNS, Stuart Keith. b 66. Bp Grosseteste Coll BEd 88 Lon Univ BD 94 Leeds Univ MA 95 PhD 99. St Jo Coll Nottm. **d** 03 **p** 04. C St Bowden w Welham, Glooston and Cranoe etc *Leic* 03-06; Hd Sch for Min from 06. *The Rectory, 3 Stonton Road, Church Langton, Market Harborough LE16 7SZ* T: (01858) 540202 E: stuart.burns@leccofe.org

BURNS, The Rt Revd Stuart Maitland. b 46. Leeds Univ BA 67. Coll of Resurr Mirfield 67. **d** 69 **p** 70. C Wyther *Ripon* 69-73; Asst Chapl Leeds Univ and Leeds Poly 73-77; P-in-c Thornthwaite w Thruscross and Darley 77-84; V Leeds Gipton Epiphany 84-89; OSB from 89; Prior Burford Priory 96-01; Abbot from 01; LtO *Ox* 89-08; PtO *Worc* from 10. *Mucknell Abbey, Mucknell Farm Lane, Stoulton, Worcester WR7 4RB* T: (01905) 345900 E: abbot@mucknellabbey.org.uk

BURNS, Stuart Sandeman. b 62. Natal Univ BA 85 Ball Coll Ox BA 89 MA 94. St Paul's Coll Grahamstown. **d** 89 **p** 90. C Stanger S Africa 90-91; Dir Scripture Union Ind Schs 92-94; R Drankensberg 95-97; Chapl W Prov Prep Sch 98-99; I Kinneigh Union *C, C & R* 99-02; TV Bourne Valley *Sarum* 02-08; I Down H Trin w Hollymount *D & D* from 08; Min Can Down Cathl from 10. *The Rectory, 12 The Meadows, Strangford Road, Downpatrick BT30 6LN* T: (028) 4461 2286 E: stuart.burns01@gmail.com

BURNS, Williams Arthur. b 51. CITC 08. **d** 11 **p** 12. NSM Glendermott *D & R* from 11. *33 Sevenoaks, Londonderry BT47 6AL* T: (028) 7134 4354 M: 07917-358317 E: arthurburns33@hotmail.co.uk

BURR, Mrs Ann Pamela. b 39. S Dios Minl Tr Scheme 83. **dss** 86 **d** 87 **p** 94. Fareham H Trin *Portsm* 86-06; Hon C 87-06; Hon Asst Chapl Knowle Hosp Fareham 86-90; Asst Chapl Qu Alexandra Hosp Portsm 90-92; Chapl Portsm Hosps NHS Trust 92-00; rtd 06; PtO *Portsm* from 06. *3 Bruce Close, Fareham PO16 7QJ* T: (01329) 281375 E: ann.burr@hotmail.co.uk

BURR, Mrs Anna Victoria. b 58. Southn Univ BA 80 Leeds Univ MA 07. NOC 04. **d** 07 **p** 08. NSM Fulford *York* 07-11; P-in-c Haddlesey w Hambleton and Birkin from 11. *The Rectory, Millfield Road, Chapel Haddlesey, Selby YO8 8QF* T: (01757) 270325 E: avburr@btinternet.com

BURR, Christopher Edward. b 68. Univ of Wales (Cardiff) BTh 01. St Mich Coll Llan 98. **d** 01 **p** 02. C Llantrisant *Llan* 01-04; P-in-c Pwllgwaun and Llanddewi Rhondda 04-10; V Lisvane from 10. *The Vicarage, Green Gables, 2 Llwyn y Pia Road, Lisvane, Cardiff CF14 0SY* T: (029) 2075 3338 E: chris.burr1@ntlworld.com

BURR, Paul David. b 62. Birm Univ LLB 83. St Jo Coll Nottm MA 99. **d** 99 **p** 00. C Newark *S'well* 99-02; C Eaton *Nor* 02-05; P-in-c Swardeston w E Carleton, Intwood, Keswick etc 05-09; R from 09. *The Vicarage, The Common, Swardeston, Norwich NR14 8EB* T: (01508) 570550 E: paul.burr@tiscali.co.uk

BURR, Raymond Leslie. b 43. NEOC 82 Edin Th Coll 84. **d** 85 **p** 86. C Hartlepool St Paul *Dur* 85-87; C Sherburn w Pittington 87-89; R Lyons 89-95; RD Houghton 94-96; V S Shields St Hilda w St Thos 95-08; rtd 08. *57 Pierremont Road, Darlington DL3 6DN* T: (01325) 463666 E: ray@burr.org.uk

BURRELL, David Philip. b 56. Southn Univ BTh 90. Sarum & Wells Th Coll 85. **d** 88 **p** 89. C Ixworth and Bardwell *St E* 88-91; P-in-c Haughley w Wetherden 91-96; P-in-c Culford, W Stow and Wordwell w Flempton etc 96-98; R Lark Valley 98-14; R Four Rivers from 14. *The Vicarage, 15 Noyes Avenue, Laxfield, Woodbridge IP13 8EB* T: (01986) 798136 E: theparsnips@googlemail.com

BURRELL, Martin John. b 51. Cant Ch Ch Univ Coll MA 00 ARCM 71. Trin Coll Bris BA 95. **d** 95 **p** 96. C Cant St Mary Bredin 95-99; V Cranbrook 99-09; Asst Dir of Ords 06-09; P-in-c Bushmead *St Alb* 09-14; V from 14. *Church House, 73 Hawkfields, Luton LU2 7NW* T: (01582) 487327 M: 07791-536713 E: mburrell51@googlemail.com

BURRELL, Timothy Graham. b 43. JP 83. St Steph Ho Ox 69. **d** 72 **p** 07. C Haltwhistle *Newc* 72-73; NSM Harrogate St Wilfrid *Ripon* 06-13; rtd 13; PtO *Leeds* from 13; Chapl to Suff Bp Beverley (PEV) *York* from 10. *8 St Hilda's Road, Harrogate HG2 8JY* T: (01423) 883832 M: 07885-681379 E: tim.burrell@virgin.net

BURRETT, Miss Gaynor Elizabeth. b 59. St Jo Coll Nottm 04. **d** 06 **p** 07. C Branksome St Clem *Sarum* 06; C 06-10; P-in-c Kingston, Langton Matravers and Worth Matravers from 11. *The Rectory, St George's Close, Langton Matravers, Swanage BH19 3HZ* T: (01929) 421179 E: gaynorburrett@btinternet.com

BURRIDGE, Matthew Guy. b 73. Univ Coll Lon BSc 94 MB, BS 97. NTMTC BA 08. **d** 08 **p** 09. NSM Kentish Town St Silas and H Trin w St Barn *Lon* 08-14; NSM Tottenham St Benet Fink from 14; NSM Tottenham St Phil from 14. *Health E1 Homeless Medical Centre, 9-11 Brick Lane, London E1 6PU* T: (020) 7247 0090 E: fr.matthewburridge@googlemail.com

BURRIDGE, Canon Richard Alan. b 55. Univ Coll Ox BA 77 MA 81 Nottm Univ CertEd 78 PhD 89. St Jo Coll Nottm 82. **d** 85 **p** 86. C Bromley SS Pet and Paul *Roch* 85-87; Chapl Ex Univ 87-94; Dean K Coll Lon from 94; Lay Preacher *Lon* from 94; PtO *S'wark* from 98; *Chelmsf* from 05; Can Th Sarum Cathl from 13. *King's College, Strand, London WC2R 2LS* T: (020) 7848 2333 F: 7848 2344 E: dean@kcl.ac.uk

BURRIDGE-BUTLER, Paul David. *See* BUTLER, Paul David

BURROW, Miss Alison Sarah. b 59. Homerton Coll Cam BEd 82. Westcott Ho Cam 84. **d** 87 **p** 03. Par Dn Hebden Bridge *Wakef* 87-88; Par Dn Prestwood and Gt Hampden *Ox* 88-90; Par Dn Olney w Emberton 90-92; rtd 92; Hon C Bedford St Pet w St Cuth *St Alb* 02-07; P-in-c Renhold from 07. *The Vicarage, Church Road, Renhold, Bedford MK41 0LU* T: (01234) 771317 E: as.burrow@ntlworld.com

BURROW, Canon Margaret Anne. b 46. Open Univ BA 82 Leeds Univ MSc 85 Lon Univ TCert 68. Coll of Resurr Mirfield 06. **d** 07 **p** 08. NSM Douglas St Ninian *S & M* 07-08; NSM St German's Cathl 08-13; Bp's Chapl from 14; Can St German's Cathl from 14. *Thie yn Aspick, 4 The Falls, Douglas, Isle of Man IM4 4PZ* T: (01624) 622108 M: 07624-235711 E: chaplain@sodormanand.im

BURROW, Ronald. b 31. Univ Coll Dur BA 55. St Steph Ho Ox 83. **d** 85 **p** 86. C Dawlish *Ex* 85-87; TV Ottery St Mary, Alfington, W Hill, Tipton etc 87-91; P-in-c Pyworthy, Pancrasweek and Bridgerule 91-95; rtd 95; PtO *Ex* from 95. *3 Riverside, Dolphin Street, Colyton EX24 6LU* T/F: (01297) 553882

BURROW, Stephen Paul. b 62. Univ Coll Dur BA 84. Trin Coll Bris 09. **d** 11 **p** 12. C Chilcompton w Downside and Stratton on the Fosse *B & W* 11-15; R Heyford w Stowe Nine Churches and Flore etc *Pet* from 15. *The Rectory, Church Lane, Nether Heyford, Northampton NN7 3LQ* M: 07511-544375 E: s_p_burrow@yahoo.co.uk

BURROWS, Canon Brian Albert. b 34. Atlantic Sch of Th BTh 83. St Aid Birkenhead 56. **d** 59 **p** 60. C Sutton St Geo *Ches* 59-62; Canada 62-69 and from 74; V Stratton St Margaret *Bris* 70-74; Hon Can Frobisher Bay 78-80; rtd 99. *334 Mary Street, Niagara on the Lake ON L0S 1J0, Canada*

BURROWS, Christopher Mark. b 75. St Mellitus Coll 08. **d** 11 **p** 12. C W Hampstead Trin *Lon* 11-14; P-in-c Barkingside St Laur *Chelmsf* from 14. *St Laurence's Vicarage, Donington Avenue, Ilford IG6 1AJ* M: 07939-130151 T: (020) 8554 3456 E: revchrisburrows@icloud.com

BURROWS, Prof Clifford Robert. b 37. OBE 05. Univ of Wales BSc 62 Lon Univ PhD 69 DSc(Eng) 89 Aston Univ Hon DSc 01 MIMechE 68 FIMechE 82 FIEE 98 FREng 98. Chich Th Coll 75. **d** 76 **p** 77. NSM Brighton St Pet *Chich* 76-78; NSM Brighton St Pet w Chpl Royal 78-80; NSM Brighton St Pet w Chpl Royal and St Jo 80-82; PtO *Glas* 82-85 and 86-89; NSM Clarkston 85-86; NSM Bath Ch Ch Prop Chpl *B & W* 90-10; rtd 10; PtO *B & W* from 11. *Stonecroft, Entry Hill Drive, Bath BA2 5NL* T: (01225) 334743 F: 429990 E: c.r.burrows@bath.ac.uk

BURROWS, Clive Robert. b 60. Bath Coll of HE BEd 82 Ches Coll of HE BA 04. NOC 01. **d** 04 **p** 05. C N Wingfield, Clay Cross and Pilsley *Derby* 04-09; P-in-c Hyson Green and Forest Fields *S'well* 09-11; V from 11. *St Stephen's Vicarage, 18 Russell Road, Nottingham NG7 6HB* T: 0115-978 4480 E: clive@revburrows.plus.com

BURROWS, Canon David. b 62. Leeds Univ BA 85 MA 03. Linc Th Coll 86. **d** 88 **p** 89. C Kippax w Allerton Bywater *Ripon* 88-91; C Manston 91-95; Chapl Killingbeck Hosp 94; V Halifax St Anne Southowram *Wakef* 95-00; P-in-c Charlestown 95-00; V Southowram and Claremount 00-02; TV Halifax 02-05; TR 05-12; R *Leeds* from 12; C Stainland w Outlane from 06; C Greetland and W Vale from 08; RD Brighouse and Elland *Wakef* 08-14; AD *Leeds* from 14; Chapl Overgate Hospice from 02; Hon Can Wakef Cathl from 13. *All Saints' Vicarage, Charles Street, Elland HX5 0JF* T: (01422) 373184 M: 07932-694555 E: rectorofelland@btinternet.com

BURROWS, David MacPherson. b 43. NOC. **d** 82 **p** 83. NSM Newburgh *Liv* 82-93; NSM Newburgh w Westhead 93-12; Dioc Adv NSM 03-11; rtd 12. *34 Woodrow Drive, Newburgh, Wigan WN8 7LB* T: (01257) 462948 E: davidmacburrows@msn.com

BURROWS, Diane. b 48. **d** 05 **p** 06. NSM Saltash *Truro* from 05. *20 Andrews Way, Hatt, Saltash PL12 6PE* T: (01752) 842540 E: di.burrows@connells.co.uk

BURROWS, Graham Charles. b 47. Leeds Univ CertEd 69 Open Univ BA 81. NOC 87. **d** 90 **p** 91. C Chorlton-cum-Hardy St Clem *Man* 90-93; TV Horwich 93; TV Horwich and Rivington 93-94. *20 Glazebury Drive, Westhoughton, Bolton BL5 3JZ* T: (01942) 550404

BURROWS, Graham John. b 63. Jes Coll Cam BA 84 MA 88 Goldsmiths' Coll Lon PGCE 94. Oak Hill Th Coll 07. **d** 09 **p** 10. C Polegate *Chich* 09-13; P-in-c Burton and Holme *Carl* from 13. *The Vicarage, Glebe Close, Burton, Carnforth LA6 1PL* M: 07740-622962 T: (01524) 781210 E: vicarburtonholme@btinternet.com

BURROWS, Jean. b 54. CertEd 75. Trin Coll Bris 89. **d** 91 **p** 94. C Allesley *Cov* 91-95; C Thorley *St Alb* 95-99; P-in-c Harrold and Carlton w Chellington 99-06; R 06-07; P-in-c Boughton under Blean w Dunkirk and Hernhill *Cant* from 07; P-in-c

Goodnestone w Graveney from 15. *The Vicarage, 101 The Street, Boughton-under-Blean, Faversham ME13 9BG* T: (01227) 751410 E: jeanburrows@jeanius.me.uk

BURROWS, Canon John Edward. b 36. Leeds Univ BA 60 PGCE 63. Coll of Resurr Mirfield. d 63 p 65. C Much Hadham *St Alb* 63-65; Hon C Haggerston St Mary w St Chad *Lon* 65-73; P-in-c Finsbury St Clem w St Barn and St Matt 73-76; Chapl Woodbridge Sch 76-83; V Ipswich St Bart *St E* 83-03; Hon Can St E Cathl 01-03; rtd 03; PtO *St E* from 03; *Chelmsf* from 14. *55 Berners Street, Ipswich IP1 3LN* T: (01473) 216629
E: burrows@freenetname.co.uk

BURROWS, Joseph Atkinson. b 32. St Aid Birkenhead 58. d 61 p 62. C Hoole *Ches* 61-67; Jamaica 67-68; C Ayr *Glas* 68-74; R Prestwick 74-78; Hon Chapl RAF 74-78; Hon Chapl RN 74-78; C Cronulla Australia 78-81; R Naremburn and Cammeray 81-87; Asst Min St Ives 87-02; Sen Asst Min from 02. *1/23 Ayres Road, St Ives NSW 2075, Australia* T: (0061) (2) 0144 3019

✣**BURROWS, The Rt Revd Michael Andrew James.** b 61. TCD BA 82 MA 85 MLitt 86. d 87 p 88 c 06. C Douglas Union w Frankfield *C, C & R* 87-91; Dean of Res TCD 91-94; Min Can St Patr Cathl Dublin 91-94; I Bandon Union *C, C & R* 94-02; Can Cork and Cloyne Cathls 96-02; Dean Cork and I Cork St Fin Barre's Union 02-06; Bp C & O from 06. *Bishop's House, Troysgate, Kilkenny, Republic of Ireland* T: (00353) (56) 778 6633 E: cfobishop@gmail.com

BURROWS, Canon Paul Anthony. b 55. Nottm Univ BA 77 Gen Th Sem NY STM 88. St Steph Ho Ox 77. d 79 p 80. C Camberwell St Giles *S'wark* 79-81; C St Helier 81-83; C Fareham SS Pet and Paul *Portsm* 83-85; V Union St Luke and All SS New Jersey USA 85-90; R Temple Hills St Barn Maryland 90-95; P-in-c Des Moines St Mark Iowa 95-01; Can Des Moines Cathl 98-01; R San Francisco Advent of Ch the K from 01. *162 Hickory Street, San Francisco CA 94102, USA* E: rector@advent-sf.org

✣**BURROWS, The Rt Revd Peter.** b 55. BTh. Sarum & Wells Th Coll 80. d 83 p 84 c 12. C Baildon *Bradf* 83-87; R Broughton Astley *Leic* 87-95; TR Broughton Astley and Croft w Stoney Stanton 95-00; RD Guthlaxton I 94-00; Dir of Ords 97-03; Par Development Officer 00-03; Dir Min, Tr and Par Development 03-05; Hon Can Leic Cathl 98-05; Adn Leeds *Ripon* 05-12; Suff Bp Doncaster *Sheff* from 12. *Doncaster House, Church Lane, Fishlake, Doncaster DN7 5JW* T: (01302) 846610
E: bishoppeter@bishopofdoncaster.org.uk

BURROWS, Philip Geoffrey. b 59. Birm Univ BSc 80. Oak Hill Th Coll 90. d 92 p 93. C Poynton *Ches* 92-96; Min Cheadle Hulme Em Ch 96-03; V Mottram in Longdendale 03-11; CF from 11. *c/o MOD Chaplains (Army)* T: (01264) 383430 F: 381824 M: 07817-314979
E: philipburrows@man4god.co.uk

BURROWS, Samuel Reginald. b 30. AKC 57. d 58 p 59. C Shildon *Dur* 58-62; C Heworth St Mary 62-67; C-in-c Leam Lane CD 67-72; C-in-c Bishopwearmouth St Mary V w St Pet CD 72-77; R Bewcastle and Stapleton *Carl* 77-82; R Harrington 82-90; P-in-c Millom 90; V 90-95; rtd 95. *40 Lindisfarne Road, Durham DH1 5YQ*

BURROWS, Victoria Elizabeth. b 61. STETS 01. d 04 p 05. C The Bourne and Tilford *Guildf* 04-07; R Long Ditton 07-14; P-in-c R Wootton Bassett *Sarum* 14-15; V from 15; RD Calne from 14. *The Vicarage, Glebe Road, Royal Wootton Bassett, Swindon SN4 7DU* T: (01793) 854302
E: vicki.burrows@me.com

BURSELL, Michael Hingston McLaughlin. b 70. K Coll Cam MA 96 Open Univ MBA 02. ERMC 05. d 08 p 09. NSM Halstead Area *Chelmsf* from 08. *Bowyer's, North Road, Great Yeldham, Halstead CO9 4QD* T: (01787) 237486 M: 07971-926937 F: 08700-517360
E: mike.bursell@anglicanpriest.org

BURSELL, Canon Rupert David Hingston. b 42. QC 86. Ex Univ LLB 63 St Edm Hall Ox BA 67 MA 72 DPhil 72. St Steph Ho Ox 67. d 68 p 69. NSM St Marylebone w H Trin *Lon* 68-69; NSM Almondsbury *Bris* 69-71; NSM Bedminster St Fran 71-75; NSM Bedminster 75-82; NSM Bris Ch Ch w St Ewen and All SS 83-88; NSM City of Bris 83-88; LtO 88-95; *B & W* 72-92; Chan *Dur* from 89; *B & W* 92; *St Alb* 92-02; Hon Can St Alb 96-02; NSM Cheddar *B & W* 93-11; Dep Chan *York* 94-02; Hon CF 96-01; Chan *Ox* 02-13; Hon Can Ch Ch from 11. *Diocesan Registry, 16 Beaumont Street, Oxford OX1 2LZ*

BURSLEM, Christopher David Jeremy Grant. b 35. AKC 85. d 59 p 60. C Bocking St Mary *Chelmsf* 59-63; C Glouc All SS 64-67; R Amberley 67-87; P-in-c Withington and Compton Abdale w Haselton 87-98; rtd 98; PtO *Derby* from 98. *44 Vestry Road, Oakwood, Derby DE21 2BL* T: (01332) 830146 E: jeremy_burslem@hotmail.com

BURSON-THOMAS, Canon Michael Edwin. b 52. Sarum & Wells Th Coll 84. d 86 p 87. C Bitterne Park *Win*

86-89; V Lockerley and E Dean w E and W Tytherley 89-95; P-in-c Fotherby *Linc* 95-99; Asst Local Min Officer 95-99; V Horncastle w Low Toynton 99-06; R Greetham w Ashby Puerorum 99-06; V High Toynton 99-06; R Horncastle Gp 06-07; RD Horncastle 01-06; P-in-c Scotter w E Ferry 07-14; P-in-c Scotton w Northorpe 07-14; RD Manlake and Is of Axholme 11; rtd 14; Gen Preacher *Linc* from 14; Can and Preb Linc Cathl from 12. *The Rectory, Church Road, Waddington, Gainsborough DN21 4ST* T: (01673) 818974
E: mbursonthomas@btinternet.com

BURSTON, Richard John. b 46. MRICS 70 MRTPI 73. S Dios Minl Tr Scheme 89. d 93 p 94. NSM Stratton St Margaret w S Marston etc *Bris* 93-13. *17 Crawley Avenue, Swindon SN3 4LB* T: (01793) 822403

BURSTON, Canon Robert Benjamin Stuart. b 45. St Chad's Coll Dur BA 68. d 70 p 71. C Whorlton *Newc* 70-77; V Alwinton w Holystone and Alnham 77-83; TR Glendale Gp from 83; Hon Can Newc Cathl from 95. *The Rectory, 5 Fenton Drive, Wooler NE71 6DT* T/F: (01668) 281551

BURSTON, Stephen. b 70. Southn Univ BA 92. Ridley Hall Cam 12. d 14 p 15. C Worth, Pound Hill and Maidenbower *Chich* from 14. *11 Gregory Close, Maidenbower, Crawley RH10 7LB* M: 07988-395468
E: steve.burston@worthparish.org.uk

BURT, David Alan. b 44. Southn Univ BTh 98. STETS 95. d 98 p 99. C Goring-by-Sea *Chich* 98-06; P-in-c Lyminster 06-10; rtd 10. *15 Fernhurst Drive, Goring-by-Sea, Worthing BN12 5AH*

BURT, Paul Andrew. b 52. Leeds Univ BA 74 K Coll Lon MA 02 Univ of Wales (Ban) PhD 09. Ridley Hall Cam 82. d 84 p 85. C Edin St Thos 84-88; CMS Bahrain 88-90; R Melrose *Edin* 91-00; Chapl Borders Gen Hosp NHS Trust 93-98; Ho Master Win Coll 00-04; Hd RS Pilgrims' Sch 00-04; Chapl and Hd RE K Coll Sch Cam 04-06; Sen Chapl Win Coll 06-12; Sen Chapl Miss to Seafarers Dubai from 12; Regional Dir Gulf and S Asia Miss to Seafarers from 14. *The Angel Appeal, The Mission to Seafarers, Dubai, United Arab Emirates* M: 50-552 6044
E: paul.burt.mts@gmail.com

BURT, Roger Malcolm. b 45. MBE 91. St Jo Coll Auckland. d 73 p 74. V Tinui New Zealand 73-80; P-in-c Colton *Nor* 80; P-in-c Easton 80; V Easton w Colton and Marlingford 80-88; CF 88-01; P-in-c E Coker w Sutton Bingham and Closworth *B & W* 01-10; rtd 10. *3 Barwick House, Barwick, Yeovil BA22 9TB* T: (01935) 414061 M: 07778-427784
E: rogermburt@gmail.com

BURTON, Andrew John. b 63. St Kath Coll Liv BA 84. Cranmer Hall Dur 86. d 88 p 89. C Harlescott *Lich* 88-91; C Ches H Trin 91-94; P-in-c Congleton St Jas 94-01; R Calton, Cauldon, Grindon, Waterfall etc *Lich* 01-08; RD Alstonfield 03-08; V Bushey Heath *St Alb* from 08. *St Peter's Vicarage, 19 High Road, Bushey Heath, Bushey WD23 1EA* T: (020) 8950 1424
E: fr.burton@btinternet.com

BURTON, Antony William James. b 29. Ch Coll Cam BA 52 MA 56. Cuddesdon Coll 52. d 54 p 55. C Linc St Nic w St Jo Newport 54-57; C Croydon St Jo *Cant* 57-62; V Winterton *Linc* 62-82; V Roxby w Risby 70-82; RD Manlake 76-82; V Nettleham 82-94; rtd 94; PtO *Linc* 94-02. *28 Eastfield Road, Messingham, Scunthorpe DN17 3PG* T: (01724) 763916

BURTON, Miss Barbara Louise. b 57. Leic Univ LLB 81 Solicitor 84. ERMC 03. d 06 p 07. NSM March St Jo *Ely* 06-10; P-in-c Barton Bendish w Beachamwell and Shingham from 10; P-in-c Wereham from 10; P-in-c Fincham from 10; P-in-c Shouldham from 10; P-in-c Shouldham Thorpe from 10; P-in-c Boughton from 10; P-in-c Marham from 10; P-in-c Watlington from 14; P-in-c Holme Runcton w S Runcton and Wallington from 14; P-in-c Tottenhill w Wormegay from 14; RD Fincham and Feltwell from 12. *The Rectory, High Street, Fincham, King's Lynn PE33 9EL* T: (01366) 347321 *or* 348079
E: barbaraburton@btinternet.com

BURTON, Christopher Paul. b 38. FCA 75 Bris Univ PhD 00. Clifton Th Coll 67. d 69 p 70. C Wandsworth All SS *S'wark* 69-72; C York St Paul 72-75; V Castle Vale *Birm* 75-82; R Gt Parndon *Chelmsf* 82-99; TR 99-03; rtd 03; PtO *St E* 04-07. *Damson Cottage, 69B London Road North, Poynton, Stockport SK12 1AG* T: (01625) 875266

BURTON, Canon Daniel John Ashworth. b 63. Regent's Park Coll Ox BA 88 MA 93 Heythrop Coll Lon MTh 93. St Mich Coll Llan 93. d 94 p 95. C Mountain Ash *Llan* 94-97; R St Brides Minor w Bettws 97-02; R St Brides Minor w Bettws w Aberkenfig 02-03; P-in-c Cheetham *Man* 03-12; AD N Man 10-12; TR Salford All SS from 12; Hon Can Man Cathl from 13. *The Rectory, 92 Fitzwarren Street, Salford M6 5RS* T: 0161-745 7608 E: ashworthburton@gmail.com

BURTON, David Alan. b 53. St Jo Coll Dur BA 75. Westcott Ho Cam 81. d 84 p 85. C Bedford St Andr *St Alb* 84-87; C Leighton Buzzard w Eggington, Hockliffe etc 87-91;

V Kingsbury Episcopi w E Lambrook *B & W* 91-94; V Kingsbury Episcopi w E Lambrook, Hambridge etc 94-95; R Bishops Lydeard w Bagborough and Cothelstone 95-03; rtd 04; C Dawlish and Kenton, Mamhead, Powderham, Cofton and Starcross *Ex* 06-11; P-in-c Hemyock w Culm Davy, Clayhidon and Culmstock from 11. *The Rectory, Hemyock, Cullompton EX15 3RQ* T: (01823) 681029
E: david_burton@dsl.pipex.com

BURTON, Desmond Jack. b 49. Sarum & Wells Th Coll 70. **d** 73 **p** 74. C Lakenham St Jo *Nor* 73-77; C Gt Yarmouth 77-80; R Tidworth *Sarum* 80-83; Chapl HM Pris Pentonville 83-84; Chapl HM Pris Standford Hill 84-88; Chapl HM Pris Swaleside 88-93; Chapl HM Pris Roch 93-99; Chapl HM Pris Whitemoor 99-05; Chapl HM Pris Whatton 05-09; P-in-c Balcombe *Chich* from 09. *The Rectory, Haywards Heath Road, Balcombe, Haywards Heath RH17 6PA* T: (01444) 811249

BURTON, Graham John. b 45. Bris Univ BA 69. Tyndale Hall Bris 69. **d** 71 **p** 72. C Leic St Chris 71-75; C Southall Green St Jo *Lon* 75-79; CMS Pakistan 80-92; P-in-c Basford w Hyson Green *S'well* 92-98; P-in-c Hyson Green and Forest Fields 98-01; Assoc P 01-07; Dir Rainbow Project 01-07; rtd 07; PtO *S'well* from 07. *6 Meadow Brown Road, Nottingham NG7 5PH*

BURTON, Hugh Anthony. b 56. Edin Univ BD 79. Cranmer Hall Dur 81. **d** 83 **p** 84. C Coalville and Bardon Hill *Leic* 83-87; P-in-c Packington w Normanton-le-Heath 87-92; V 92-96; TV Kidderminster St Geo *Worc* 96-08; P-in-c 08-12; TR Kidderminster E from 12; RD Kidderminster from 13. *The Rectory, 30 Leswell Street, Kidderminster DY10 1RP* T: (01562) 824490 E: hugh.burton@kidderminstereast.org.uk

BURTON, Michael John. b 55. Leeds Univ BSc 76 Leeds Poly BSc 80. St Jo Coll Nottm 86. **d** 88 **p** 89. C Charles w Plymouth St Matthias *Ex* 88-92; V Paignton St Paul Preston 92-99; TV Almondbury w Farnley Tyas *Wakef* 99-02; V Roade and Ashton w Hartwell *Pet* 02-11; C Collingtree w Courteenhall and Milton Malsor 09-11; V Salcey from 11; RD Towcester 03-09. *The Vicarage, 18 Hartwell Road, Roade, Northampton NN7 2NT* T: (01604) 862284
E: michaelburton5@aol.com

BURTON, Nicholas Guy. b 69. Bris Univ BSc 91 ACCA 00. Ridley Hall Cam 03. **d** 05 **p** 06. C Ore St Helen and St Barn *Chich* 05-09; C Bexhill St Steph 09-11. *Address temp unknown* M: 07851-742049 E: ngb.cofe@tiscali.co.uk

BURTON, Nicholas John. b 52. St Steph Ho Ox 77. **d** 80 **p** 81. C Leic St Matt and St Geo 80-82; C Leic Resurr 82-83; TV 83-88; C Narborough and Huncote 88-90; R 90-10; rtd 10. *Address withheld by request* E: mrnjb@talktalk.net

BURTON, Norman George. b 30. NOC. **d** 83 **p** 84. C Rothwell w Lofthouse *Ripon* 83-86; C Rothwell 86-87; V Lofthouse 87-96; rtd 96; PtO *Leeds* from 96. *28 Temple Row Close, Leeds LS15 9HR* T: 0113-260 1129

BURTON, Mrs Sarah Elizabeth. b 55. St As Minl Tr Course 00. **d** 03 **p** 04. C Llanrhos 03-08; C Colwyn Bay w Brynymaen 08-12; P-in-c Towyn 12-15; C Llanddulas and Llysfaen 12-15; C Abergele and St George 12-15; rtd 15; Hon C Llanrwst, Llanddoged w Capel Garmon etc St As from 15. *The Rectory, 16 Y Bryn, Glan Conwy, Colwyn Bay LL28 5NJ* T: (01492) 593123

BURTON, Mrs Zoe. b 66. Open Univ BSc 99 Nottm Univ MA 11. EMMTC 07. **d** 10 **p** 11. NSM Ravenshead *S'well* 10-13; P-in-c Ollerton w Boughton from 13. *The Vicarage, 65 Larch Road, Ollerton, Newark NG22 9SX* T: (01623) 682818
E: revzoe@live.co.uk

BURTON EVANS, David. *See* EVANS, David Burton

BURTON-JONES, The Ven Simon David. b 62. Em Coll Cam BA 84 MA 88. St Jo Coll Nottm BTh 92 MA 93. **d** 93 **p** 94. C Darwen St Pet w Hoddlesden *Blackb* 93-96; C Biggin Hill *Roch* 96-98; P-in-c Plaistow St Mary 98-00; V 00-05; R Chislehurst St Nic 05-10; AD Bromley 01-06; Adn Roch from 10; Can Res Roch Cathl from 10. *The Archdeaconry, King's Orchard, Rochester ME1 1TG* T: (01634) 813533 *or* 560000
E: archdeacon.rochester@rochester.anglican.org

BURTT, Andrew Keith. b 50. Massey Univ (NZ) BA 72 MA 74 DipEd 76. St Jo Coll (NZ) LTh 82. **d** 81 **p** 82. New Zealand 81-83; CF 84-92; Sen Chapl Brighton Coll 93-03; Chapl Portsm Gr Sch from 03. *8 Penny Street, Portsmouth PO1 2NH* T: (023) 9268 1395

BURTWELL, Stanley Peter. b 32. Leeds Univ BA 55. Coll of Resurr Mirfield 55. **d** 57 **p** 58. C Leeds St Hilda *Ripon* 57-61; S Africa 61-72; P-in-c Gt Hanwood *Heref* 72-78; R 78-83; RD Pontesbury 80-83; V Upper Norwood St Jo *Cant* 83-84;

V *S'wark* 85-90; RD Croydon N 85-90; TR Bourne Valley *Sarum* 90-97; rtd 97; PtO *Sarum* from 97. *Splinters, 116 High Street, Swanage BN19 2NY* T: (01929) 421785
E: pburtwell@yahoo.co.uk

BURUNDI, Archbishop of. *See* NTAHOTURI, The Most Revd Bernard

BURY, Miss Dorothy Jane. b 53. Lanc Univ BA 96 MA 98 St Hild Coll Dur CertEd 75. Ripon Coll Cuddesdon 00. **d** 02 **p** 03. C Thornton-le-Fylde *Blackb* 02-06; P-in-c Wigan St Anne *Liv* 06-12; Chapl Deanery C of E High Sch Wigan 06-12; V Fence-in-Pendle and Higham *Blackb* from 12. *The Vicarage, 12 Wheatcroft Avenue, Fence, Burnley BB12 9QL* T: (01282) 617316 M: 07715-560031 E: tillybury@hotmail.co.uk

BURY, The Very Revd Nicholas Ayles Stillingfleet. b 43. Qu Coll Cam BA 65 MA 69 Ch Ch Ox MA 71. Cuddesdon Coll. **d** 69. C Liv Our Lady and St Nic 68-71; Chapl Ch Ch Ox 71-75; V Stevenage St Mary Shephall *St Alb* 75-84; V St Peter-in-Thanet *Cant* 84-97; RD Thanet 93-97; Hon Can Cant Cathl 94-97; Dean Glouc 97-10; rtd 10. *122 The Homend, Ledbury HR8 1BZ* T: (01531) 636075

BUSBY, Ian Frederick Newman. b 32. Roch Th Coll 61. **d** 64 **p** 65. C Bedale *Ripon* 64-67; C Stevenage St Geo *St Alb* 67-71; V Stevenage St Mary Shephall 71-75; V Kildwick *Bradf* 75-92; rtd 93; PtO *Leeds* from 93. *12 Currergate Mews, Skipton Road, Steeton, Keighley BD20 6PE* T: (01535) 652099

BUSBY, John. b 38. St Cath Coll Cam MA 60 CEng. **d** 93 **p** 94. OLM Worplesdon *Guildf* 93-02; OLM Pirbright 02-04; PtO from 06. *Iona, Fox Corner, Worplesdon, Guildford GU3 3PP* T: (01483) 234562 E: john.busby@ionaforcorner.plus.com

BUSFIELD, Miss Lynn Maria. b 60. Trin Coll Bris BA 99. **d** 99 **p** 00. C Scartho *Linc* 99-03; TV Marlborough *Sarum* 03-05; Chapl Mt Edgcumbe Hospice 05-08; P-in-c Fladbury, Hill and Moor, Wyre Piddle etc *Worc* 09-11; P-in-c Peopleton and White Ladies Aston w Churchill etc 11-13; C Fladbury, Hill and Moor etc and Abberton, The Flyfords, Naunton Beauchamp etc 11-13; Chapl Heart of England NHS Foundn Trust from 13. *60 Horrell Road, Birmingham B26 2PD* T: 0121-742 2895 E: lynnbusfield@btinternet.com

BUSH, Mrs Ann Kathleen. b 47. MATCA 65. Ox Min Course 90. **d** 93 **p** 94. NSM Warfield *Ox* 93-96; Dep Chapl HM Pris Wormwood Scrubs 96-97; Chapl HM Pris Reading 97-99; Sen Chapl HM Pris Feltham 99-01; R Fort Smith Canada from 01. *PO Box 64, Fort Smith NT X0E 0P0, Canada* T: (001) (867) 872 3438 E: abush@auroranet.nt.ca

BUSH, Caspar James Barnard. b 68. Newc Univ BSc 90. SWMTC 09. **d** 12 **p** 13. C Perranzabuloe and Crantock w Cubert *Truro* from 12. *Arrallas Farm, Ladock, Truro TR2 4NP* T: (01872) 510044 E: casparbush@gmail.com

BUSH, David. b 25. FRIBA 47 Liv Univ BArch 47. S'wark Ord Course 73. **d** 77 **p** 77. C Douglas St Geo and St Barn *S & M* 77-80; Chapl Ballamona Hosp and Cronk Grianagh 80-86; V Marown *S & M* 80-87; R The Rissingtons *Glouc* 87-92; PtO *Glouc* 92-98; *S & M* 97-99; *Ely* from 99. *23 Ash Grove, Burwell, Cambridge CB25 0DR* T: (01638) 741839
E: dandac.bush@care4free.net

BUSH, George Raymond. b 57. St Jo Coll Cam BA 81 MA 84 Univ of Wales LLM 95. Ripon Coll Cuddesdon BA 84 MA 88. **d** 85 **p** 86. C Leeds St Aid *Ripon* 85-89; Chapl St Jo Coll Cam 89-94; V Hoxton St Anne w St Columba *Lon* 94-02; R St Mary le Bow w St Pancras Soper Lane etc from 02. *The Rector's Lodgings, Cheapside, London EC2V 6AU* T: (020) 7248 5139 F: 7248 0509 E: grbush@london.anglican.org

BUSH, Mrs Glenda. b 41. NOC 92. **d** 95 **p** 96. NSM Bolton St Phil *Man* 95-99; C 99-02; C Bolton SS Simon and Jude 99-02; P-in-c 02-06; rtd 06; PtO *Man* from 06. *46 Mary Street West, Horwich, Bolton BL6 7JU* T: (01204) 691539

BUSH, Mrs Kathryn Ann. b 60. OLM course 95. **d** 99 **p** 00. OLM Mareham-le-Fen and Revesby *Linc* 99-06; OLM Mareham on the Hill 99-06; OLM Hameringham w Scrafield and Winceby 99-06; OLM Fen and Hill Gp from 06. *Wheatsheaf Farm, Chapel Lane, New Bolingbroke, Boston PE22 7LF* T: (01205) 480631 M: 07775-736344

BUSH, Kieran John Christopher. b 80. Ch Coll Cam BA 01 MA 05. Oak Hill Th Coll MTh 11. **d** 11 **p** 12. C Dagenham *Chelmsf* 11-15; V Walthamstow St Jo from 15. *The Vicarage, 18 Brookscroft Road, London E17 4LH* M: 07709-119325
E: kieranbush@hotmail.com

BUSH, Rachma. *See* ABBOTT, Esther Rachma Hartley

BUSH, The Very Revd Roger Charles. b 56. K Coll Lon BA 78 Leeds Univ BA 85. Coll of Resurr Mirfield 83. **d** 86 **p** 87. C Newbold w Dunston *Derby* 86-90; TV Leic Resurr 90-94; TR Redruth w Lanner and Treleigh *Truro* 94-04; RD Carnmarth N 96-03; Hon Can Truro Cathl 03-04; Can Res Truro Cathl 04-12; Adn Cornwall 06-12; Dean Truro from 12. *Westwood House, Tremorvah Crescent, Truro TR1 1NL* T: (01872) 225630
E: roger@truro.anglican.org

BUSH, Lt Col Walter Patrick Anthony. b 39. **d** 07 **p** 08. OLM Watercombe *Sarum* 07-11; NSM from 11. *Holworth Farmhouse, Holworth, Dorchester DT2 8NH* T: (01305) 852242
E: bushinarcadia@yahoo.co.uk

BUSHAU, Reginald Francis. b 49. Shimer Coll Illinois AB 71. St Steph Ho Ox BA 73 MA 98. **d** 74 **p** 75. C Deptford St Paul *S'wark* 74-77; C Willesden St Andr and Gladstone Park St Fran *Lon* 77-82; P-in-c Brondesbury St Anne w Kilburn H Trin 83-88; V Paddington St Mary Magd 88-97; AD Westmr Paddington 92-97; P-in-c S Kensington St Steph 96-98; V from 98. *9 Eldon Road, London W8 5PU* T: (020) 7937 5083 *or* 7370 3418 E: bushrf@aol.com

BUSHBY, Michael Reginald. b 42. LSE BSc 70 Leeds Univ MA 97. **d** 02 **p** 03. NSM S Cave and Ellerker w Broomfleet *York* 02-05; P-in-c Newbald from 05. *The Vicarage, 7 Dot Hill Close, North Newbald, York YO43 4TS* T: (01430) 801068 M: 07976-493359 E: michaelbushby@btinternet.com

BUSHELL, Anthony Colin. b 59. Pemb Coll Ox MA 82 Barrister 83. S'wark Ord Course 93. **d** 96 **p** 97. NSM Felsted and Lt Dunmow *Chelmsf* 96-98; NSM Stanway 98-06; NSM Greenstead w Colchester St Anne 06-14; P-in-c Stanway from 14. *Pump Hall, Middle Green, Wakes Colne, Colchester CO6 2BJ* T: (01787) 222487 E: vicartone@aol.com

BUSHELL, Mrs Linda Mary. b 52. Bradf and Ilkley Coll BEd 91. STETS 06. **d** 09 **p** 10. NSM Bembridge *Portsm* from 09. *2 Rowborough Cottages, Rowborough Lane, Brading, Sandown PO36 0AY* T: (01983) 400261
E: linda.bushell1@btinternet.com

BUSHELL, Stephen Lionel. b 60. K Coll Lon BA 84. Ripon Coll Cuddesdon 92. **d** 94 **p** 95. C Exhall *Cov* 94-97; Asst P Shelswell *Ox* 97-05; Asst Chapl Aylesbury Vale Community Healthcare NHS Trust 97-05; Chapl Oxon & Bucks Mental Health Partnership NHS Trust from 05. *6 Aris Way, Buckingham MK18 1FX* T: (01280) 823772
E: tostephenbushell@hotmail.com *or* stephen.bushell@obmh.nhs.uk

BUSHYAGER, Ronald Robert. b 77. Belmont Univ Nashville BSc 00. Wycliffe Hall Ox BTh 04. **d** 04 **p** 05. C Gamston and Bridgford *S'well* 04-07; C Abingdon *Ox* 07-10; Chapl to Bp Kensington *Lon* 10-12; C E Twickenham St Steph 12-14; PtO *Guildf* from 15. *St Paul's Vicarage, 7 South Terrace, Dorking RH4 2AB* T: (01306) 881998 E: ronbushyager@ntlworld.com

BUSHYAGER (née TWITCHEN), Mrs Ruth Kathleen Frances. b 77. Bris Univ MSci 99. Wycliffe Hall Ox BA 04. **d** 05 **p** 06. C Wilford *S'well* 05-07; NSM Abingdon *Ox* 08; Asst Chapl St Edw Sch Ox 08-10; Area Missr Kensington Area *Lon* 10-14; V Dorking St Paul *Guildf* from 14. *St Paul's Vicarage, 7 South Terrace, Dorking RH4 2AB* T: (01306) 881998

BUSK, David Westly. b 60. Magd Coll Cam BA 83 St Jo Coll Dur BA 88. Cranmer Hall Dur 86. **d** 89 **p** 90. C Old Swinford Stourbridge *Worc* 89-93; USPG Japan 94-95; C Fukuoka Cathl 95-96; P-in-c Nagasaki H Trin 96-06; P-in-c Godmanchester *Ely* 06-13; P-in-c Hilton 11-13; V Godmanchester and Hilton from 13. *The Vicarage, 59 Post Street, Godmanchester, Huntingdon PE29 2AQ* T: (01480) 436400 *or* T/F: 453354 M: 07765-851757 E: dwbusk@hotmail.com

BUSK, Horace. b 34. Clifton Th Coll 56. **d** 60 **p** 61. C Burton All SS *Lich* 60-63; Paraguay 63-66; C Silverhill St Matt *Chich* 66-67; LtO *Sarum* 67-69; C W Kilburn St Luke w St Simon and St Jude *Lon* 69-74; TV Ashwellthorpe w Wreningham *Nor* 74-81; P-in-c Meysey Hampton w Marston Meysey and Castle Eaton *Glouc* 81-82; R 82-04; rtd 04; PtO *Glouc* from 04. *23 Eastcote Road, Cirencester GL7 2DB* T: (01285) 650884

BUSS, Gerald Vere Austen. b 36. CCC Cam PhD 87. St Steph Ho Ox 59. **d** 63 **p** 64. C Petersham *S'wark* 63-66; C Brompton H Trin *Lon* 66-69; Asst Chapl Hurstpierpoint Coll 70-73; Chapl 74-90; Ho Master 90-94; History teacher 94-96; r-d 96. *Souches, The Street, Albourne, Hassocks BN6 9DJ* T/F: (01273) 832465

BUSS, Philip Hodnett. b 37. Ch Coll Cam BA 59 MA 63. Tyndale Hall Bris 61. **d** 63 **p** 64. Tutor Lon Coll of Div 62-66; Chapl 66-69; Hon C Northwood Em *Lon* 63-70; V Handsworth Woodhouse *Sheff* 70-74; V Fulham Ch Ch *Lon* 74-82; V Woking St Pet *Guildf* 82-88; Hon C Ham St Rich *S'wark* 94-98; rtd 02; PtO *Cant* from 14. *27 Coleman Drive, Kemsley, Sittingbourne ME10 2EA* T: (01795) 430589

BUSSELL, Ian Paul. b 62. Reading Univ BA 84 Kingston Poly PGCE 85. Qu Coll Birm MA 98. **d** 98 **p** 99. C Twickenham St Mary *Lon* 98-01; TV Godalming *Guildf* 01-07; P-in-c Leckhampton SS Phil and Jas w Cheltenham St Jas *Glouc* 07-09; TV S Cheltenham 10-11; Dioc Dir of Ords from 11. *56 Leckhampton Road, Cheltenham GL53 0BG* T: (01242) 256104 E: ianbussell@googlemail.com

BUSSELL, Ronald William. b 34. CA Tr Coll 57 St Deiniol's Hawarden 81. **d** 83 **p** 84. Hatcham St Jas *S'wark* 01-75; Claughton cum Grange *Ches* C 83-85; P-in-c Preston

St Oswald *Blackb* 85-87; V Fleetwood St Nic 87-93; Dioc Chapl MU 91-95; R Tarleton 93-95; rtd 95; PtO *Blackb* from 95. *4 Willoughby Avenue, Thornton-Cleveleys FY5 2BW* T: (01253) 820067 E: ron.bussell@talk21.com

BUSSEY, Diane Jean. b 57. **d** 07 **p** 08. OLM Clifton w Newton and Brownsover *Cov* from 07; Chapl Rainsbrook Secure Tr Cen from 09. *2 Teasel Close, Rugby CV23 0TJ* T: (01788) 339278 E: diane.bussey1@ntlworld.com

BUSSEY, Norman. b 22. Clifton Th Coll 63. **d** 65 **p** 66. C Upton (Overchurch) *Ches* 65-69; V Bradley *Wakef* 69-88; rtd 88; PtO *Glouc* from 88. *43 Crispin Road, Winchcombe, Cheltenham GL54 5JX* T: (01242) 602754

BUSSEY, Rachel Anne. b 36. STETS 00. **d** 03 **p** 04. NSM Durrington *Sarum* 03-11; NSM Avon Valley 08-11; TV Avon River from 11; Dioc Safeguarding Adv from 11. *3 Birchwood Drive, Durrington, Salisbury SP4 8ER* T: (01980) 594335 M: 07899-926034 E: rachel.bussey@ntlworld.com

BUSSMANN, Mrs Mary Elizabeth. b 52. Leeds Univ MA 06. Trin Coll Bris. **d** 06 **p** 07. C Otham w Langley *Cant* 06-10; R E Horsley and Ockham w Hatchford and Downside *Guildf* 10-14; Asst Chapl Vevey w Château d'Oex *Eur* from 14. *All Saints, avenue de la Prairie 40, 1800 Vevey, Switzerland* E: ebussmann@btinternet.com

BUSTARD, Guy Nicholas. b 51. K Coll Lon BD 77 AKC 77. St Steph Ho Ox 77. **d** 78 **p** 79. C Hythe *Cant* 78-81; Chapl RN 81-85; V Haddenham and Wilburton *Ely* 85-89; Chapl Qu Eliz Hosp Welwyn Garden City 89-92; Chapl E Herts NHS Trust 92-00; Chapl E and N Herts NHS Trust 00-02; PtO *St Alb* from 02. *2 Copper Beeches, Welwyn AL6 0SS* T: (01438) 717916

BUSTIN, Canon Peter Ernest. b 32. Qu Coll Cam BA 56 MA 60. Tyndale Hall Bris 56. **d** 57 **p** 58. C Welling *Roch* 57-60; C Farnborough *Guildf* 60-62; V Hornsey Rise St Mary *Lon* 62-70; R Barnwell *Pet* 70-78; RD Oundle 76-84; P-in-c Luddington w Hemington and Thurning 77-78; R Barnwell w Thurning and Luddington 78-84; V Southwold *St E* 84-97; RD Halesworth 90-95; Hon Can St E Cathl 91-97; rtd 97; PtO *St E* from 97. *55 College Street, Bury St Edmunds IP33 1NH* T: (01284) 767708 E: bustin@saintedmunds.vispa.com

BUSTIN, Peter Laurence. b 54. St Steph Ho Ox. **d** 83 **p** 84. C Northolt St Mary *Lon* 83-86; C Pimlico St Pet w Westmr Ch Ch 86-88; C Heston 88-91; P-in-c Twickenham All SS 91-98; V 98-11; rtd 11; P-in-c Beaulieu-sur-Mer *Eur* 11-13. *54 Keats Way, Greenford UB6 9HE* E: peter@padova.fsnet.co.uk

BUSTIN, Timothy Mark. b 75. UWE BA 98. Wycliffe Hall Ox 05. **d** 07 **p** 08. C Bletchley *Ox* 07-10; C Waikanae New Zealand from 10. *2 Pemi Kupa Street, Waikanae 5036, New Zealand* E: tim.busters@freeserve.co.uk

BUTCHER, Andrew John. b 43. Trin Coll Cam BA 66 MA 69. Cuddesdon Coll 66. **d** 68 **p** 69. C Sheff St Mark Broomhall 68-70; P-in-c Louth H Trin *Linc* 70-72; Chapl RAF 72-87; LtO *Ox* 85-87; TR Cove St Jo *Guildf* 87-91; V Egham Hythe 91-98; V Docking, the Birchams, Stanhoe and Sedgeford *Nor* 98-08; rtd 08; PtO *Nor* from 08. *67 The Street, Hindringham, Fakenham NR21 0PR* T: (01328) 878526 M: 07887-506876 E: andrewj.butcher2@btinternet.com

BUTCHER, Miss Ann Lesley. b 46. Lon Coll of Printing BA 67 Ex Univ BTh 09. SWMTC 06. **d** 09 **p** 10. NSM St Michael Penkevil *Truro* 09-12; NSM Tregony w St Cuby and Cornelly 09-12; NSM Tresillian and Lamorran w Merther 09-12; NSM St Stythians w Perranarworthal and Gwennap from 12; NSM Chacewater w St Day and Carharrack from 12; NSM Feock from 12. *Burnwithian House, Burnwithian, St Day, Redruth TR16 5LG* T: (01209) 820788
E: mail@annbutcher.demon.co.uk

BUTCHER, Edwin William. b 39. Portsm Dioc Tr Course 91 STETS 04. **d** 92 **p** 05. NSM Ryde All SS *Portsm* 92-09; PtO 09-11. *23 Quarry Road, Ryde PO33 2TX* T: (01983) 616889

BUTCHER (née POTTS), Canon Heather Dawn. b 52. **d** 98 **p** 99. C Attleborough w Besthorpe *Nor* 98-01; R Bunwell, Carleton Rode, Tibenham, Gt Moulton etc 01-09; RD Depwade 03-09; R Cringleford and Colney from 09; Bp's Adv for Women's Min from 11; Hon Can Nor Cathl from 13. *The Vicarage, 7A Newmarket Road, Cringleford, Norwich NR4 6UE* T: (01603) 458467 E: vicarage.cringleford@btinternet.com

BUTCHER, Philip Ian Christopher. b 77. Seale-Hayne Agric Coll BSc 01. Ripon Coll Cuddesdon 11. **d** 13 **p** 14. C Honiton, Gittisham, Combe Raleigh, Monkton etc *Ex* from 13. *5 Glen Farm Crescent, Honiton EX14 2GX* T: (01404) 45484 M: 07775-762376 E: philip@pbutcher1.oranghome.co.uk

BUTCHER, Philip Warren. b 46. Trin Coll Cam BA 68 MA 70. Cuddesdon Coll 68. **d** 70 **p** 71. C Bris St Mary Redcliffe w Temple etc 70-73; Hon C W Wickham St Fran *Cant* 73-78; Chapl Abingdon Sch 78-85; Chapl Nor Sch 85-98; V Horsford and Horsham w Newton St Faith *Nor* 98-04; rtd 04; P-in-c Barningham w Matlaske w Baconsthorpe etc *Nor* 05-09; PtO from 09. *The Vicarage, 7A Newmarket Road, Cringleford, Norwich NR4 6UE* T: (01603) 458467 E: pw.butcher@btinternet.com

BUTCHER, Richard Peter. b 50. St Chad's Coll Dur BA 71. Chich Th Coll 73. **d** 74 **p** 75. C Yeovil St Mich *B & W* 74-77; Chapl Wellingborough Sch 77-83; R Gt w Lt Billing *Pet* 83-88; Chapl Bp Stopford Sch Kettering 88-90; PtO *Pet* 90-01. *55 Field Street, Kettering NN16 8EN*

BUTCHER, Roger John. b 71. St Steph Ho Ox 10. **d** 12 **p** 13. C Wyke Regis *Sarum* from 12. *13 Clarence Road, Weymouth DT4 9EE* M: 07502-118210 T: (01305) 787954
E: roger_butcher@hotmail.com

BUTCHERS, The Ven Mark Andrew. b 59. Trin Coll Cam BA 81 K Coll Lon MTh 90 PhD 06. Chich Th Coll BTh 87. **d** 87 **p** 88. C Chelsea St Luke and Ch Ch *Lon* 87-90; C Mitcham SS Pet and Paul *S'wark* 90-93; R N Tawton, Bondleigh, Sampford Courtenay etc *Ex* 93-99; Chapl and Fell Keble Coll Ox 99-05; C Wolvercote w Summertown *Ox* 05-07; P-in-c Wolvercote 07-10; V Wolvercote and Wytham 10-15; AD Ox 12-15; Adn Barnstaple *Ex* from 15. *Stage Cross, Sanders Lane, Bishops Tawton, Barnstaple EX32 0BE* T: (01271) 375475
E: archdeacon.of.barnstaple@exeter.anglican.org

BUTLAND, Canon Cameron James. b 58. Open Univ MA 12. Ripon Coll Cuddesdon 81. **d** 84 **p** 85. C Tettenhall Regis *Lich* 84-88; V Bodicote *Ox* 88-95; TR Witney 95-04; RD 97-02; R Grasmere *Carl* from 04; V Rydal from 04; Chapl Rydal Hall from 04; Dioc Ecum Officer 11-14; Hon Can Carl Cathl from 14. *The Rectory, Grasmere, Ambleside LA22 9SW* T/F: (015394) 35326 E: cdsa03@gmail.com

BUTLAND, Godfrey John. b 51. Grey Coll Dur BA 72. Wycliffe Hall Ox 73. **d** 75 **p** 76. C Much Woolton *Liv* 75-78; Bp's Dom Chapl 78-81; V Everton St Geo 81-94; AD Liv N 89-94; V Allerton 94-05; P-in-c Mossley Hill St Barn 04-05; TV Mossley Hill 05-06; TR 06-15; AD Liv S 00-06; Hon Can Liv Cathl 03-06; TR Cockermouth Area *Carl* from 15. *The Vicarage, Little Broughton, Cockermouth CA13 0YG* T: (01900) 825763

BUTLER, Canon Alan. b 53. Cant Dioc Tr Inst 89. **d** 89 **p** 90. NSM Flookburgh *Carl* 89-93; C Maryport 93-96; C Flimby 93-96; P-in-c 96-98; TV Saltash *Truro* 98-09; TR from 09; P-in-c Landrake w St Erney and Botus Fleming from 12; C St Germans from 12; Hon Can Truro Cathl from 10. *The Rectory, St Stephens, Saltash PL12 4AP* T: (01752) 842323

BUTLER, Canon Alan. b 57. Leic Univ BA 78. Coll of Resurr Mirfield 80. **d** 83 **p** 84. C Skerton St Luke *Blackb* 83-87; C Birch w Fallowfield *Man* 87-90; V Claremont H Angels 90-95; Chapl Pendleton Coll 95-99; TV Pendleton *Man* 95-99; P-in-c High Crompton 99-15; V High Crompton and Thornham from 15; AD Oldham E 09-14; Hon Can Man Cathl from 11. *St Mary's Vicarage, 18 Rushcroft Road, Shaw, Oldham OL2 7PR* T/F: (01706) 847455
E: alanbutler@freenetname.co.uk

BUTLER, Angela Madeline. b 47. Oak Hill NSM Course 87. **d** 90 **p** 94. Hon Par Dn Chipperfield St Paul *St Alb* 90-93; Dn-in-c 93-94; P-in-c 94-01; Staff Oak Hill Th Coll 93-97; Springboard Missr 97-01; P-in-c Hempsted and Dioc Springboard Missr *Glouc* 01-07; rtd 07. *22 Esplanade Road, Newquay TR7 1QB* T: (01637) 859238
E: angelambutler@btinternet.com

BUTLER, Catherine Elizabeth. b 46. **d** 06 **p** 07. NSM Waltham Gp *Linc* from 06. *8 Danesfield Avenue, Waltham, Grimsby DN37 0QE* T: (01472) 587692 E: elsiebutlerdane@msn.com

BUTLER, Cecil Anthony. b 37. Sarum Th Coll 65. **d** 68 **p** 69. C Gillingham *Sarum* 68-70; CF 70-74; R Whittington St Jo *Lich* 74-83; rtd 02; PtO S & M from 10. *The Mines House, The Mines Yard, Laxey, Isle of Man IM4 7NJ* T: (01624) 860085 M: 07967-497721

BUTLER, Christine Jane. b 66. Cranmer Hall Dur. **d** 10 **p** 11. C Cheddar, Draycott and Rodney Stoke *B & W* 10-14; P-in-c Pilton w Croscombe, N Wootton and Dinder from 14. *The Rectory, Pilton, Shepton Mallet BA4 4DX* M: 07910-479145
E: butlerchristine19@gmail.com

BUTLER, Christopher. b 67. St Jo Coll Nottm 99. **d** 01 **p** 02. C Retford *S'well* 01-05; P-in-c Holbeck *Ripon* 05-12; C Beeston Hill and Hunslet Moor 11-12; V Ripon H Trin *Leeds* from 12. *Holy Trinity Vicarage, 3 College Road, Ripon HG4 2AE* T: (01765) 605865 E: crbutler@bigfoot.com

BUTLER, Christopher John. b 25. Leeds Univ BA 50. Chich Th Coll 50. **d** 52 **p** 53. C Kensington St Mary Abbots w St Geo *Lon* 52-57; Australia 57-59; V Blackmoor *Portsm* 60-70; V Wellingborough St Andr *Pet* 70-79; P-in-c Garsington *Ox* 79-83; R Garsington and Horspath 83-95; rtd 95; PtO *Portsm* from 95; *Chich* from 95; *Guildf* from 95; *Win* from 95. *33 Oak Tree Road, Whitehill, Bordon GU35 9DF* T: (01420) 475311

BUTLER, Colin Sydney. b 59. Bradf Univ BSc 81. Wycliffe Hall Ox 81. **d** 84 **p** 85. C Farsley *Bradf* 84-87; C Bradf St Aug Undercliffe 87-89; P-in-c Darlaston All SS *Lich* 89-95; Ind Missr 89-95; TR Chell 95-99; CF 99-15; rtd 15. *33 Cotton Lane, Birmingham B13 9SB* M: 07724-674365
E: revcsb@btopenworld.com

BUTLER, David Edwin. b 56. Jes Coll Ox BA 79 BA 86 ACA 83. St Steph Ho Ox MA 87. **d** 87 **p** 88. C Hulme Ascension *Man* 87-90; V Patricroft 90-94; PtO *Liv* 97-03; *Man* from 03; *Blackb* from 03; Hon C Prestwich St Hilda *Man* 00-01. *16 St George's Road, Nelson BB9 0YA*

BUTLER, Derek John. b 53. Aston Univ BSc 74 St Jo Coll York PGCE 75. Cranmer Hall Dur 79. **d** 82 **p** 83. C Bramcote *S'well* 82-86; Lon and SE Co-ord CPAS 86-88; NSM Bromley Ch Ch *Roch* 88-91; NSM Chesham Bois *Ox* 92-10; PtO from 10. *121 Woodside Road, Amersham HP6 6AL* T: (01494) 724577

BUTLER, Donald Arthur. b 31. **d** 79 **p** 80. Hon C Apsley End *St Alb* 79-80; Hon C Chambersbury 80-04; PtO from 04. *143 Belswains Lane, Hemel Hempstead HP3 9UZ*

BUTLER, George James. b 53. AKC 74 Kent Univ MA 95. St Aug Coll Cant 75. **d** 76 **p** 77. C Ellesmere Port *Ches* 76-79; C Eastham 79-81; Chapl RAF 81-83; C W Kirby St Bridget *Ches* 83-84; V Newton 84-86; CF 86-91; V Folkestone St Sav *Cant* 91-99; P-in-c Wool and E Stoke *Sarum* 99-04; P-in-c Mansfield St Mark *S'well* 04-10; AD Mansfield 06-10; V Goring-by-Sea *Chich* from 10. *The Vicarage, 12 Compton Avenue, Goring-by-Sea, Worthing BN12 4UJ* T: (01903) 242525
E: revgjb@btinternet.com

BUTLER, Canon George William. b 52. CITC. **d** 90 **p** 91. C Drung w Castleterra, Larah and Lavey etc *K, E & A* 90-93; I 93-95; I Castlemacadam w Ballinaclash, Aughrim etc *D & G* from 95; Can Ch Ch Cathl Dublin from 03. *Dunamon, Fiddler's Lane, Ballinabarney, Redcross, Wicklow, Republic of Ireland* M: (00353) 87-679 5625 E: gwb2@hotmail.com

BUTLER, Mrs Helen Carole. b 66. Bath Coll of HE BEd 87. Dioc OLM tr scheme 02. **d** 04 **p** 05. NSM Mirfield *Leeds* from 04. *1A Holmdene Drive, Mirfield WF14 9SZ* T: (01924) 496189 M: 07764-187988 E: curate-stmary@cofe-mirfield.org.uk

BUTLER, Huw. b 63. Univ of Wales (Ban) BSc 84. St Mich Coll Llan BTh 95. **d** 95 **p** 96. C Llantwit Fardre *Llan* 95-00; R Llangynhafal w Llanbedr DC and Llanychan *St As* 00-02; R Llanbedr DC w Llangynhafal, Llanychan etc 02-10; P-in-c Llanynys 10; AD Dyffryn Clwyd 10; TR Llantwit Major *Llan* from 10. *The Rectory, High Street, Llantwit Major CF61 1SS* T: (01446) 794670 E: huw.butler@tesco.net

BUTLER, Jane. See BUTLER, Virginia Jane

BUTLER, John. b 38. Gwent Coll Newport CertEd 77. St Mich Coll Llan. **d** 68 **p** 69. C Ebbw Vale *Mon* 68-70; TV 70-75; PtO 76-77 and 79-88; P-in-c Crumlin 77-78; R Gt and Lt Casterton w Pickworth and Tickencote *Pet* 88-91; R Woolstone w Gotherington and Oxenton etc *Glouc* 91-97; Hon C Dawlish *Ex* 98-01; P-in-c Chevington w Hargrave, Chedburgh w Depden etc *St E* 01-02; R 02-03; rtd 03; C Shaldon, Stokeinteignhead, Combeinteignhead etc *Ex* 03-06. *3 Pine Tree Close, Dawlish Warren, Dawlish EX7 0RD*

BUTLER, John Frederick. Yorks Min Course. **d** 14 **p** 15. NSM Heaton St Barn *Leeds* from 14; NSM Heaton St Martin from 14. *48 Toller Grove, Bradford BD9 5NP* M: 07785-624117 T: (01274) 409085 E: revdjohnbutler@icloud.com

BUTLER, John Philip. b 47. Leeds Univ BA 70. Coll of Resurr Mirfield 70. **d** 72 **p** 73. C Elton All SS *Man* 72-75; C Bolton St Pet 75-78; Chapl Bolton Colls of H&FE 75-78; Asst Chapl Bris Univ 78-81; Hon C Clifton St Paul 78-81; V Llansawel w Briton Ferry Llan 81-84; Warden Bp Mascall Cen *Heref* 84-88; Vice-Prin Glouc Sch for Min 85-88; Chapl Univ of Wales (Ban) 88-07; rtd 07; PtO *Ban* from 11. *Cefn Engan, Llangybi, Pwllheli LL53 6LZ* T: (01766) 810046

BUTLER, Mrs Lesley Ann. b 52. Cov Univ BSc 75 Nottm Univ MA 05. EMMTC 08. **d** 10 **p** 12. NSM Loughborough Em and St Mary in Charnwood *Leic* 10-11; NSM Kegworth, Hathern, Long Whatton, Diseworth etc from 11. *1 Cheriborough Road, Castle Donington, Derby DE74 2RY* T: (01332) 391780 M: 07505-384527 E: revlesley.butler@gmail.com

BUTLER, Mrs Linda. b 51. Liv Univ CertEd 72. Cranmer Hall Dur 01. **d** 03 **p** 04. C Middlewich w Byley *Ches* 03-06; R Ditchingham, Hedenham, Broome, Earsham etc *Nor* 06-12; P-in-c Hartlepool St Luke *Dur* from 12. *St Luke's Vicarage, 5 Tunstall Avenue, Hartlepool TS26 8NF* T: (01429) 271280 E: revlbutler@aol.com

BUTLER, Canon Linda Jane. b 56. SRN 77. St Jo Coll Nottm 85. **d** 88 **p** 94. C Burbage w Aston Flamville *Leic* 88-91; Asst Chapl Leic R Infirmary 91-93; Asst Chapl Towers Hosp Humberstone 93-95; Chapl 95-97; Chapl Leics and Rutland Healthcare NHS Trust 97-03; Chapl amongst Deaf People *Pet* 03-10; P-in-c Kingsthorpe 10-14; TR from 14; Can Pet Cathl from 14. *The Rectory, 16 Green End, Kingsthorpe, Northampton NN2 6RD* T: (01604) 717133 M: 07773-018260 E: revjane94@me.com

BUTLER, Mrs Louise Gail Nesta. b 53. **d** 04 **p** 05. OLM Blewbury, Hagbourne and Upton *Ox* 04-06; OLM S w N

Moreton, Aston Tirrold and Aston Upthorpe 05-06; OLM The Churn from 06. *Penridge, Church Road, Blewbury, Didcot OX11 9PY* T: (01235) 851011 E: louisegbutler@aol.com

BUTLER, Malcolm. b 40. Linc Th Coll 76. **d** 78 **p** 79. C Whickham *Dur* 78-82; V Leam Lane 82-87; R Penshaw 87-90; rtd 90; PtO *Dur* from 90. *Lincoln Lodge, Front Street, Castleside, Consett DH8 9AR* T: (01207) 507672

BUTLER, Canon Michael. b 41. St Mich Coll Llan 62 St Deiniol's Hawarden 63. **d** 64 **p** 65. C Welshpool *St As* 64; C Welshpool w Castle Caereinion 65-73; TV Aberystwyth *St D* 73-80; Chapl Univ of Wales (Abth) 73-80; V St Issell's and Amroth 80-09; V St Issell's and Amroth w Crunwere 09-12; V St Issell's and Amroth w Crunwere and Marros 12-13; AD Narberth 94-09; AD Pembroke 10-13; Can St D Cathl 01-13; rtd 13; PtO *St D* from 13. *Roxborough, 45 Whitlow, Saundersfoot SA69 9AE* T: (01834) 810475

BUTLER, Canon Michael Weeden. b 38. Clare Coll Cam BA 60 MA 65. Westcott Ho Cam 63. **d** 65 **p** 66. C Bermondsey St Mary w St Olave, St Jo etc *S'wark* 65-68; Ind Chapl 68-72; Sierra Leone 73-77; Ind Chapl and R Gt Chart *Cant* 77-86; RD E Charing 81-86; V Glouc St Jas and All SS 86-04; RD Glouc City 94-99; Hon Can Glouc Cathl 96-04; rtd 04; Clergy Retirement Officer *Glouc* from 05. *121 London Road, Gloucester GL2 0RR* T: (01452) 421563

E: michael121@blueyonder.co.uk

BUTLER, Ms Pamela. b 53. Nottm Univ BTh 86 CertEd 74. Linc Th Coll 83. **dss** 86 **d** 87 **p** 94. Rotherhithe H Trin *S'wark* 86-87; Par Dn 87-88; Par Dn Old Trafford St Jo *Man* 88-89; Par Dn Claremont H Angels 90-94; C 94-95; C Pendleton 95-97; Chapl Asst Univ Hosp of S Man NHS Foundn Trust from 96. *St Mary's Vicarage, 18 Rushcroft Road, Shaw, Oldham OL2 7PR* T: (01706) 847455 *or* 0161-291 2298 *or* 998 7070

BUTLER, Patrick. b 61. All Nations Chr Coll 89. **d** 07 **p** 07. V Asunción St Andr Paraguay 07-09; C Stoughton *Guildf* 09-13; Min Elvetham Heath LEP from 13. *1 Dunley Drive, Fleet GU51 1BH* T: (01252) 695067 M: 07847-121092

E: patrickbutler61@hotmail.com

BUTLER, Paul David. b 67. Sheff Univ BA 88. Linc Th Coll 92. **d** 92 **p** 93. C Handsworth Woodhouse *Sheff* 92-96; V Bellingham St Dunstan *S'wark* 96-06; AD E Lewisham 99-06; R Deptford St Paul from 06; AD Deptford from 13. *St Paul's Rectory, Mary Ann Gardens, London SE8 3DP* T: (020) 8692 7449 E: paulredbutler@btinternet.com

BUTLER, Paul Harnett. b 58. Perkins Sch of Th (USA) MTS 96 Girton Coll Cam MPhil 99. Ridley Hall Cam 05. **d** 07 **p** 08. C Histon and Impington *Ely* 07-11; C Landbeach from 12; C Waterbeach from 12. *The Vicarage, 8 Chapel Street, Waterbeach, Cambridge CB25 9HR* T: (01223) 860353 M: 07903-904599 E: revpbutler@gmail.com

✠**BUTLER, The Rt Revd Paul Roger.** b 55. Nottm Univ BA 77. Wycliffe Hall Ox 82. **d** 83 **p** 84 **c** 04. C Wandsworth All SS *S'wark* 83-87; Inner Lon Ev Scripture Union 87-92; Dep Hd of Miss 92-94; NSM E Ham St Paul *Chelmsf* 87-94; P-in-c Walthamstow St Mary w St Steph 94-97; P-in-c Walthamstow St Luke 94-97; TR Walthamstow 97-04; AD Waltham Forest 00-04; Suff Bp Southampton *Win* 04-09; Bp S'well and Nottm 09-14; Bp Dur from 14; Hon Can Byumba from 01. *Auckland Castle, Bishop Auckland DL14 7NR* T: (01388) 602576 F: 605264 E: bishop.of.durham@durham.anglican.org

BUTLER, Perry Andrew. b 49. York Univ BA 70 Lon Univ PGCE 75 Jes Coll Ox DPhil 78 FRHistS. Linc Th Coll 78. **d** 80 **p** 81. C Chiswick St Nic w St Mary *Lon* 80-83; C S Kensington St Steph 83-87; V Bedford Park 87-95; Angl Adv Lon Weekend TV 87-99; P-in-c Bloomsbury St Geo w Woburn Square Ch Ch *Lon* 95-02; R 02-09; Dioc Dir of Ords 96-09; rtd 09. *6 Mikyle Court, 39 South Canterbury Road, Canterbury CT1 3LH* T: (01227) 767692 E: holmado@aol.com

BUTLER, Richard Charles Burr. b 34. St Pet Hall Ox BA 59 MA 62. Linc Th Coll 58. **d** 60 **p** 61. C St John's Wood *Lon* 60-63; V Kingstanding St Luke *Birm* 63-75; R Lee St Marg *S'wark* 75-00; rtd 00. *21 Defoe House, Barbican, London EC2Y 8DN* T: (020) 7628 0527

E: eleanorandrichardbutler@btinternet.com

BUTLER, Canon Robert Edwin. b 37. Ely Th Coll 60. **d** 62 **p** 63. C Lewisham St Jo Southend *S'wark* 62-65; C Eastbourne St Elisabeth *Chich* 65-69; V Langney 69-86; TR 86-96; Can and Preb Chich Cathl 94-97; rtd 96; PtO *Chich* from 97. *10 Langdale Close, Langney, Eastbourne BN23 8HS* T: (01323) 461135

BUTLER, Sandra. *See* BARTON, Sandra

BUTLER, Canon Simon. b 64. UEA BSc 86 RN Coll Dartmouth 86. St Jo Coll Nottm MA 92. **d** 92 **p** 93. C Chandler's Ford *Win* 92-94; C Northolt St Jos *Lon* 94-97; V Streatham Immanuel and St Andr *S'wark* 97-04; RD Streatham 01-04; Lambeth Adnry Ecum Officer 99-02; P-in-c

Sanderstead All SS 04-05; TR Sanderstead 05-11; V Battersea St Mary from 11; Hon Can S'wark Cathl from 04. *St Mary's Vicarage, 32 Vicarage Crescent, London SW11 3LD* T: (020) 7228 8141 M: 07941-552407 E: simon.butler7@gmail.com

BUTLER, Simon Richard. b 80. Oak Hill Th Coll BA 03 Ripon Coll Cuddesdon MTh 06. **d** 06 **p** 07. C W Bridgford *S'well* 06-10; C Ashtead *Guildf* from 10. *1 Oakfield Road, Ashtead KT21 2RE* M: 07803-909284

E: sib@christiansinmotorsport.org.uk

BUTLER, Stephen Ian. b 59. Edin Univ BA BSc 80. Trin Coll Bris BA 84. **d** 97 **p** 98. C Edin St Pet 97-99; R Edin St Jas 99-08; LtO *Glas* 09-11; Hon C Dumfries 11-13; R Edin St Jas from 13. *71 Restalrig Road, Edinburgh EH6 8BG* M: 07939-069699 E: steviebutler@gmail.com *or* rector@stjamesleith.org

BUTLER, Mrs Susan Jane. b 60. Anglia Ruskin Univ BA 99. Ridley Hall Cam 08. **d** 11 **p** 12. C Cambridge St Phil *Ely* from 11. *The Vicarage, 8 Chapel Street, Waterbeach, Cambridge CB25 9HR* M: 07985-406371 T: (01223) 977496

E: susybu@gmail.com

✠**BUTLER, The Rt Revd Thomas Frederick.** b 40. Leeds Univ BSc 61 MSc 62 PhD 72. Coll of Resurr Mirfield 62. **d** 64 **p** 65 **c** 85. C Wisbech St Aug *Ely* 64-66; C Folkestone St Sav *Cant* 66-67; Lect Univ of Zambia 68-73; Chapl Kent Univ *Cant* 73-80; Six Preacher Cant Cathl 79-84; Adn Northolt *Lon* 80-85; Area Bp Willesden 85-91; Bp Leic 91-98; Bp S'wark 98-10; rtd 10; Hon Asst Bp Wakef 10-14. *Overtown Grange Cottage, The Balk, Walton, Wakefield WF2 6JX*

E: bishop.tombutler@wakefield.anglican.org

BUTLER, Valerie Joyce. *See* WHITE, Valerie Joyce

BUTLER, Virginia Jane. **d** 15. C Mynyddislwyn *Mon* from 15. *The Vicarage, Central Avenue, Oakdale, Blackwood NP12 0JS* T: (01495) 225445 E: oakdalevicarage@yahoo.co.uk

BUTLIN, David Francis Grenville. b 55. Bris Univ BA 77 Ox Univ CertEd 78. Sarum & Wells Th Coll 85. **d** 87 **p** 88. C Bedford St Andr *St Alb* 87-90; C Milton *Portsm* 90-92; V Hurst Green *S'wark* 92-12; RD Godstone 04-08; Chapl Heart of Kent Hospice from 12; Chapl R Marsden NHS Foundn Trust from 14; PtO *S'wark* from 13. *Heart of Kent Hospice, Preston Hall, Royal British Legion Village, Aylesford ME20 7PU* T: (01622) 792200

BUTLIN, Timothy Greer. b 53. St Jo Coll Dur BA 75 Ox Univ CertEd 76 Spurgeon's Coll MTh 05. Wycliffe Hall Ox 85. **d** 87 **p** 88. C Eynsham and Cassington *Ox* 87-91; V Loudwater from 91. *The Vicarage, Treadaway Hill, Loudwater, High Wycombe HP10 9QL* T: (01628) 526087 F: 529354

E: vicar@loudwater.org

BUTT, Adrian. b 37. **d** 71 **p** 72. C Umtata Cathl S Africa 71-76; C Ilkeston St Mary *Derby* 76-79; R N and S Wheatley w W Burton *S'well* 79-84; P-in-c Bole w Saundby 79-84; P-in-c Sturton w Littleborough 79-84; R N Wheatley, W Burton, Bole, Saundby, Sturton etc 84-85; R Kirkby in Ashfield 85-05; rtd 05. *25 Searby Road, Sutton-in-Ashfield NG17 5JQ* T: (01623) 555650 E: adrian@shopfront.freeserve.co.uk

BUTT, Mrs Catherine. b 76. St Hilda's Coll Ox BA 99 MA 02 St Jo Coll Dur BA 02. Cranmer Hall Dur 00. **d** 03 **p** 04. C Bletchley *Ox* from 03. *1 Ashburnham Close, Bletchley, Milton Keynes MK3 7TR* T: (01908) 631050 M: 07971-714223

E: butties01@yahoo.co.uk

BUTT, The Very Revd Christopher Martin. b 52. St Pet Coll Ox BA 74 Fitzw Coll Cam BA 77. Ridley Hall Cam 75. **d** 79 **p** 80. C Cambridge St Barn *Ely* 79-82; Hong Kong 82-89; P-in-c Windermere *Carl* 89-98; TR S Gillingham *Roch* 98-09; Dean St Chris Cathl Bahrain from 09. *St Christopher's Cathedral, PO Box 36, Manama, Bahrain* T: (00973) 1725 3866 F: 1724 6436

E: revbutt@ymail.com

BUTT, Edward. b 46. CQSW 80. Trin Coll Bris 86. **d** 88 **p** 89. C Erith St Paul *Roch* 88-92; C Shirley *Win* 92-99; V Stourbridge St Mich Norton *Worc* 99-12; rtd 12. *Fleurette, Brixham Road, Paignton TQ4 7BD*

BUTT, Martin James. b 52. Sheff Univ LLB 75. Trin Coll Bris 75. **d** 78 **p** 79. C Aldridge *Lich* 78-84; C Walsall 84-87; TV 87-94; P-in-c Farewell 94-12; P-in-c Gentleshaw 94-12; C Hammerwich 96-03; P-in-c 03-12; rtd 12. *36 Buttermere Avenue, Nuneaton CV11 6ET* T: (024) 7767 6068

BUTT, William Arthur. b 44. Kelham Th Coll 70 Linc Th Coll 71. **d** 71 **p** 72. C Mackworth St Fran *Derby* 71-75; C Aston cum Aughton *Sheff* 76-79; V Dalton 79-88; TR Staveley and Barrow Hill *Derby* 88-11; rtd 12. *17 Ramsey Avenue, Chesterfield S40 3EF* T: (01246) 239131

BUTTANSHAW, Graham Charles. b 59. TCD BA(Econ) 80 BA 85. St Jo Coll Nottm 88. **d** 91 **p** 92. C Toxteth St Cypr w Ch Ch *Liv* 91-94; CMS 94-99; Uganda 95-99; V Otley *Leeds* from 99. *The Vicarage, Vicarage Gardens, Otley LS21 3PD* T: (01943) 462240 E: graham.buttanshaw@bradford.anglican.org

BUTTERFIELD, Amanda Helen. *See* DIGMAN, Amanda Helen

BUTTERFIELD, The Ven David John. b 52. Lon Univ BMus 73. St Jo Coll Nottm. **d** 77 **p** 78. C Southport Ch Ch *Liv* 77-81; Min Aldridge St Thos CD *Lich* 81-91; V Lilleshall, Muxton and Sheriffhales 91-07; RD Edgmond and Shifnal 97-01; RD Shifnal 99-00; RD Edgmond and Shifnal 01-06; Adn E Riding *York* 07-14; Can and Preb York Minster 07-14; Adn for Generous Giving and Can Res York Minster from 14. *2A Minster Court, York YO1 7JJ*
E: archdeacondavid@yorkminster.org

BUTTERFIELD, John Kenneth. b 52. Nottm Univ BCombStuds. Linc Th Coll 79. **d** 82 **p** 83. C Cantley *Sheff* 82-84; C Doncaster St Leon and St Jude 84-86; TV Ilfracombe, Lee, Woolacombe, Bittadon etc *Ex* 86-88; V Thurcroft *Sheff* 88-96; Chapl Chesterfield and N Derbyshire NHS Trust 96-14; rtd 14. *11 Bolsover Road, Glapwell, Chesterfield S44 5NJ*

BUTTERFIELD, Mrs Katharine Mary. Aston Univ BSc 79. LCTP 13. **d** 15. NSM Morland, Thrimby, Gt Strickland and Cliburn *Carl* from 15. *Strickland Well, Great Strickland, Penrith CA10 3DF* T: (01932) 712052 M: 07867-533131
E: kmbutterfield@btinternet.com

BUTTERFIELD, Peter Graham. b 60. Lanc Univ BSc 82 Trent Poly PGCE 83. SWMTC 11. **d** 13 **p** 14. NSM Gulval and Madron *Truro* from 13. *4 Vellanhoggan Mews, Vellanhoggan, Gulval, Penzance TR18 3DN* T: (01736) 350243 M: 07812-959460 E: peter.butterfield@physics.org

BUTTERFIELD, Canon Antony James. b 51. Hull Univ BSc 73. Trin Coll Bris 73. **d** 76 **p** 77. C Halliwell St Pet *Man* 76-81; V Werneth 81-90; V Tonge Fold 90-06; V Pennington from 06; Hon Can Man Cathl from 11. *Pennington Vicarage, Schofield Street, Leigh WN7 4HT* T: (01942) 673619
E: tony@penningtonchurch.com

BUTTERWORTH, David Frederick. b 48. Oak Hill Th Coll BA 88. **d** 88 **p** 89. R Telegraph Creek Canada 88-92; R Barrhead and Westlock 92-94; R Yellowknife 94-98; V Hanmer, Bronington, Bettisfield, Tallarn Green *St As* 98-04; PtO from 09. *Bettisfield Hall, Bettisfield, Whitchurch SY13 2LB* T: (01948) 710525

BUTTERWORTH, Elsie. b 27. Linc Th Coll 81. **dss** 83 **d** 87 **p** 94. OHP 83-85; Derringham Bank *York* 85-87; Par Dn 87-88; Par Dn Filey 88-94; C 94-97; rtd 97; PtO *York* from 97. *32 Dulverton Hall, Esplanade, Scarborough YO11 2AR*

BUTTERWORTH, Frederick. *See* BUTTERWORTH, David Frederick

BUTTERWORTH, George John. b 58. Liv Univ BA 85. Chich Th Coll 92. **d** 92 **p** 93. C Mayfield *Chich* 92-93; C Hastings St Clem and All SS 93-96; TV Brighton Resurr 96-02; P-in-c Saltdean 02-09; V 09-14; rtd 15. *146 Manor Hall Road, Southwick, Brighton BN42 4NP* E: butt21158@aol.com

BUTTERWORTH, Canon George Michael. b 41. Man Univ BSc 63 Lon Univ BD 67 PhD 89 Nottm Univ MPhil 71. Tyndale Hall Bris. **d** 67 **p** 68. C S Normanton *Derby* 67-71; India 72-79; Lect United Th Coll Bangalore 77-80; Lect Oak Hill Th Coll 80-96; Prin SAOMC *Ox* 97-05; Prin Ox Min Course 05-06; Prin ERMC 05-06; Hon Can St Alb *St Alb* 02-06; PtO from 06; *Ox* from 11; Hon C Walton H Trin 06-09; Hon C Broughton 09-11. *3 Horseshoe Close, Cheddington, Leighton Buzzard LU7 0SB* T: (01296) 661903 M: 07870-242250
E: mikebutterworth@waitrose.com

BUTTERWORTH, Canon Gillian. b 49. Man Univ BA 71 Dur Univ PGCE 72. NOC 96. **d** 99. C Barnsley St Mary *Wakef* 99-03; Hon Par Dn Outwood 03-14; Hon Par Dn *Leeds* 03-14; Min Development Officer *Wakef* 13-14; *Leeds* 03-14; Asst Chapl Wakefield Hospice 03-14; Hon Can Wakef Cathl 10-14; rtd 15. *Address temp unknown*

BUTTERWORTH, Ian Eric. b 44. Aber Univ MA 67 MTh 79. Edin Th Coll 67. **d** 69 **p** 70. C Langley All SS and Martyrs *Man* 69-71; Prec St Andr Cathl 71-75; V Bolton St Matt w St Barn *Man* 75-85; C-in-c Lostock CD 85-92; Laity Development Officer (Bolton Adnry) 85-92; Teacher Fairfield High Sch Droylsden 92-99; PtO *Man* 96-99; Hon C Sudden St Aidan 00-05; P-in-c Castleton Moor 00-05; V 05-10; AD Heywood and Middleton 07-10; rtd 10; PtO *Man* from 10. *7 Bruce Street, Rochdale OL11 3NH* T: (01706) 522264
E: i.butterworth@tesco.net

BUTTERWORTH, James Frederick. b 49. St Chad's Coll Dur BA 70 Birm Univ MA 99. Cuddesdon Coll 70. **d** 72 **p** 73. C Kidderminster St Mary *Worc* 72-76; P-in-c Dudley St Barn 76-79; V 79-82; Prec and Min Can Worc Cathl 82-88; TR Bridgnorth, Tasley, Astley Abbotts, etc *Heref* 88-94; Can Res and Treas Heref Cathl 94-99; Preb 94-06; P-in-c Ewyas Harold w Dulas, Kenderchurch etc *Heref* 99-06; RD Abbeydore 02-06; V Cirencester *Glouc* 06-08; rtd 08. *Meadows View, Orcop, Hereford HR2 8SF* T: (01981) 540887

BUTTERWORTH, James Kent. b 49. Southn Univ BTh 79 PGCE 12. Chich Th Coll 75. **d** 79 **p** 80. C Heckmondwike *Wakef* 79-83; V Wrenthorpe 83-95; V Staincross 95-14; rtd 14; V Staincross *Leeds* from 14; CF (TA) 82-86. *Address temp unknown* E: jim@radiouk.com

BUTTERWORTH, Mrs Janet Mary. b 49. Bris Univ CertEd 70. SNWTP 09. **d** 12 **p** 13. OLM Heatons Man from 12. *71 Berwick Avenue, Stockport SK4 3AA* T: 0161-431 3851
E: janet@butterworth.madasafish.com

BUTTERWORTH, John Walton. b 49. St Jo Coll Dur BSc 70. Cranmer Hall Dur. **d** 74 **p** 75. C Todmorden *Wakef* 74-77; Chapl Wakef Cathl 77-78; C Wakef Cathl 77-78; V Outwood *Leeds* from 78. *Outwood Vicarage, 424 Leeds Road, Wakefield WF1 2JB* T: (01924) 823150
E: johnbutterworth@blueyonder.co.uk

BUTTERWORTH, Canon Julia Kay. b 42. Edin Univ MA 64 Bris Univ CertEd 66. Linc Th Coll 73. **dss** 77 **d** 87 **p** 94. Cov E 77-79; Cant Cathl 79-84; Dioc Adv in Women's Min 82-92; Faversham 84-92; Par Dn 87-92; Team Dn Whitstable 92-94; TV 94-97; P-in-c Tenterden St Mich 97-07; Dioc Adv in Spirituality 97-07; Hon Can Cant Cathl 96-07; rtd 07; PtO *Cant* from 07. *14 Cobham Close, Canterbury CT1 1YL* T: (01227) 472806 E: jkbutterworth@btinternet.com

BUTTERWORTH, Michael. *See* BUTTERWORTH, George Michael

BUTTERWORTH, Mildred Jean. b 42. Leeds Univ MB, ChB 65 FRCOG 84. St Jo Coll Nottm. **d** 00 **p** 01. NSM Moldgreen and Rawthorpe *Wakef* 00-03; NSM Almondbury w Farnley Tyas 03-11; rtd 11. *1 Furnbrook Gardens, Kirkheaton, Huddersfield HD5 0DY* T: (01484) 664455
E: mildred@mildredjb.plus.com

BUTTERWORTH, Roy. b 31. Selw Coll Cam BA 55 MA 59. Wells Th Coll 55. **d** 57 **p** 58. C Bathwick w Woolley *B & W* 57-61; Prec St Paul's Cathl Dundee 61-63; V Dearnley *Man* 63-81; V Tyldesley w Shakerley 81-83; V Healey 83-94; rtd 94. *102 Greenbank Road, Rochdale OL12 0EN* T: (01706) 350808

BUTTERY, Bernard. b 36. Culham Coll Ox CertEd 58 LCP 75. OLM course 96. **d** 99 **p** 00. OLM Stafford *Lich* 99-11; PtO from 12. *7 Dearnsdale Close, Tillington, Stafford ST16 1SD* T: (01785) 244771 E: bb.ngb@talktalk.net

BUTTERY, Graeme. b 62. York Univ BA 84. St Steph Ho Ox 85. **d** 88 **p** 89. C Peterlee *Dur* 88-91; C Sunderland 91-92; TV 92-94; V Horsley Hill St Lawr 94-05; AD Jarrow 01-05; V Hartlepool St Oswald from 05. *St Oswald's Clergy House, Brougham Terrace, Hartlepool TS24 8EY* T: (01429) 273201
E: buttery.stl@virgin.net

BUTTERY, Nathan James. b 72. Em Coll Cam BA 94 MA 97. Wycliffe Hall Ox BA 98. **d** 00 **p** 01. C Hull St Jo Newland *York* 00-08; C Cambridge H Sepulchre *Ely* from 09. *1 Pretoria Road, Cambridge CB4 1HD* T: (01223) 518299
E: nathan.buttery@stag.org

BUTTIMER, Mrs Cynthia Margaret. b 45. STETS 07. **d** 08 **p** 09. OLM Clarendon *Sarum* 08-12; NSM 12-15; rtd 15; PtO *Sarum* from 15. *Willow Cottage, Gunville Road, Winterslow, Salisbury SP5 1PP* T: (01980) 862017
E: cynthiabuttimer@hotmail.com

BUTTLE, Leslie Albert. b 32. Open Univ BA 89. Edin Th Coll 61. **d** 64 **p** 65. C Sowerby Bridge w Norland *Wakef* 64-66; C Plymstock *Ex* 66-69; C Ilfracombe H Trin 69-71; V Woolfardisworthy and Buck Mills 71-76; C Sticklepath 76-77; Asst Chapl HM Pris Leeds 77-80; LtO *Ripon* 77-80; Chapl HM Youth Cust Cen Hindley 80-84; PtO *Ex* 86-93; Hon C Braunton from 93; rtd 97. *63 Caen View, Braunton EX33 1FE* T: (01271) 817022

BUTTON, David Frederick. b 27. St Chad's Coll Dur BA 53. **d** 54 **p** 55. C S Shields St Mary *Dur* 54-58; C Seacroft *Ripon* 58-60; V Holland Fen *Linc* 60-64; PC Surfleet 64-68; V 68-71; R Belton SS Pet and Paul 71-78; V Barkston w Syston 72-78; V Honington 73-78; R Gunhouse w Burringham 78-82; P-in-c Gt w Lt Hockham w Wretham w Illington *Nor* 82-84; P-in-c Shropham w Larling and Snetterton 82-84; V Hockham w Shropham Gp of Par 84-91; rtd 91; PtO *Nor* 91-96. *6 Vallibus Close, Oulton, Lowestoft NR32 3DS*

BUXTON, Alyson Christina. b 65. Chelt & Glouc Coll of HE BA 00 Nottm Univ MA 03 RGN 86. St Jo Coll Nottm MTh 01. **d** 02 **p** 03. C New Sleaford *Linc* 02-05; Dioc Lay Min Co-ord and PV Linc Cathl 05-08; P-in-c Horncastle Gp 08-10; R 10-12; R Asterby Gp 10-12; R Hemingby Gp 10-12; RD Horncastle 11-12; Dir Min *Ely* 13-14; Hon Can Ely Cathl 13-14; TR Boston *Linc* from 14. *The Vicarage, Wormgate, Boston PE21 6NP* T: (01205) 355302

BUXTON, Canon Derek Major. b 31. Lon Univ BD 63. Ripon Hall Ox 58. **d** 60 **p** 61. C Leic St Nic 60-64; Chapl Leic Univ 60-64; Chapl Leic Coll of Art and Tech 61-65; Min Can Leic Cathl 64-69; Prec 67; R Ibstock *Leic* 69-76; R Ibstock w Heather 76-87; Chapl ATC from 78; OCF and Cen and E Regional Chapl from 87; RD Akeley S *Leic* 84-87; P-in-c Woodhouse Eaves 87-91; V Woodhouse and Woodhouse Eaves 91-98; Chapl Roecliffe Manor Cheshire Home from 87; Hon Can Leic Cathl from 88; rtd 98; PtO *Leic* from 99. *Shepherd's Hill, 74 Pitsford Drive, Loughborough LE11 4NY* T: (01509) 216663

BUXTON, Francis Edmund. b 42. Trin Coll Cam MA 68 Sheff Univ MA 93. Linc Th Coll 65. **d** 67 **p** 68. C Wanstead St Mary *Chelmsf* 67-70; C Cambridge Gt St Mary w St Mich *Ely* 70-73; C Barking St Marg w St Patr *Chelmsf* 74-75; Chapl Vellore Hosp S India 75-79; Chapl Bath Univ *B & W* 79-89; TR Willenhall H Trin *Lich* 89-96; Chapl Team Leader Univ Hosp Birm NHS Foundn Trust 96-07; rtd 07; Hon C St Briavels w Hewelsfield *Glouc* 08-12. *Bridge Cottage, Mill Lane, Govilon, Abergavenny NP7 9SA* M: 07899-673096 T: (01873) 831424
E: fjbuxton@yahoo.co.uk

BUXTON, James Andrew Denis. b 64. Newc Univ BA 86 CCC Cam MA 11. Westcott Ho Cam 95. **d** 97 **p** 98. C Portsea St Mary *Portsm* 97-01; Succ S'wark Cathl 01-07; Chapl Guy's Campus K Coll Lon 01-07; Fell CCC Cam from 07; Chapl 07-11; Dean of Chpl from 11; Tutor Westcott Ho Cam from 08. *Corpus Christi College, Trumpington Street, Cambridge CB2 1RH* T/F: (01223) 338002 E: jb225@cam.ac.uk

BUXTON, Nicholas Alexander Vavasseur. b 66. Wolfs Coll Cam BA 02 Trin Hall Cam MPhil 03 PhD 07. St Steph Ho Ox MTh 08. **d** 08 **p** 09. C and Hon Min Can Ripon Cathl 08-12; P-in-c Newc St Jo from 12; Dioc Ch and Soc Adv from 12. *3 Crossway, Jesmond, Newcastle upon Tyne NE2 3QH* T: 0191-212 0181 E: buxton.nicholas@gmail.com

BUXTON, Richard Fowler. b 40. Lon Univ BScEng 62 Linacre Coll Ox BA 67 MA 71 Ex Univ PhD 73 Surrey Univ Hon BUniv 11. St Steph Ho Ox 65. **d** 68 **p** 69. C Whitley Ch Ch *Ox* 68-70; C Pinhoe *Ex* 70-71; Asst Chapl Ex Univ 71-73; Tutor Sarum & Wells Th Coll 73-77; Vice-Prin 77; Chapl *Ches* 77-97; Lect Liturgy Man Univ 80-94; PtO *Man* 81-94; Subwarden St Deiniol's Lib Hawarden 94-97; PtO *Ban* from 96; *St As* from 97; *Ely* from 13. *The New Room, 8 Orchard Close, Harston, Cambridge CB22 7PT* T: (01223) 870115
E: cynhaearn@lineone.net

BUXTON, Canon Trevor George. b 57. Ex Univ BEd 78. Chich Th Coll 81. **d** 83 **p** 84. C Hove All SS *Chich* 83-87; C Burgess Hill St Jo 87-91; V Brighton St Aug and St Sav 91-03; P-in-c Sidley 02-04; V 04-11; V Brighton St Martin w St Wilfrid and St Alban from 11; Can and Preb Chich Cathl from 01. *St Martin's Vicarage, Upper Wellington Road, Brighton BN2 3AN* T: (01273) 604687 M: 07885-942901
E: hojoe@waitrose.com

BUYERS, Stanley. b 39. Leeds Univ CertEd 71 Sunderland Poly BEd 78 Newc Univ MEd 90. NEOC 97. **d** 00 **p** 01. NSM E Boldon *Dur* 00-03; P-in-c Boldon 03-09; rtd 09; PtO *Dur* from 09. *37 Tarragon Way, South Shields NE34 8TB* T: 0191-519 0370 M: 07979-693153
E: stanbuyers@btinternet.com

BYARD, Nigel Gordon. b 65. Leic Poly BEng 88 CEng MIMechE. Ox Min Course 06. **d** 09 **p** 10. NSM Sunningdale *Ox* 09-11; TV Penrith w Newton Reigny and Plumpton Wall *Carl* 11-14; P-in-c Droitwich Spa *Worc* from 14; P-in-c Salwarpe and Hindlip w Martin Hussingtree from 14. *1 Ombersley Close, Droitwich WR9 8JY* T: (01905) 778265
E: nigelbyard@btinternet.com

BYATT, John William. b 55. St Jo Coll Nottm 99. **d** 01 **p** 02. C Heanor *Derby* 01-05; C Ilkeston St Jo 05-07; P-in-c Whipton *Ex* from 07. *The Vicarage, 9 Summer Lane, Exeter EX4 8BY* T: (01392) 462206 M: 07773-906919

BYE, Paul Andrew. b 82. Nottm Univ BSc 04. Wycliffe Hall Ox BTh 12. **d** 12 **p** 13. C Blackb Ch Ch w St Matt from 12. *31 Britten Close, Blackburn BB2 3TD* M: 07923-552339
E: p_bye@hotmail.com

BYE, Canon Peter John. b 39. Lon Univ BD 65. Clifton Th Coll 62. **d** 67 **p** 68. C Hyson Green S'well 67-70; C Dur St Nic 70-73; V Lowestoft Ch Ch *Nor* 73-80; V Carl St Jo 80-04; Hon Can Carl Cathl 98-04; RD Carl 00-04; Chapl Carl Hosps NHS Trust 80-98; rtd 04; PtO Carl from 08. *21 McIlmoyle Way, Carlisle CA2 5GY* T: (01228) 596256
E: peterbye@mcilmoyleway.plus.com

BYFIELD, Andrew Thornton James. b 77. St Pet Coll Ox MA 99 Selw Coll Cam BTh 09. Ridley Hall Cam 07. **d** 09 **p** 10. C Wimbledon Em Ridgway Prop Chpl *S'wark* 09-12; V Moulton *Pet* from 12. *The Vicarage, 30 Cross Street, Moulton, Northampton NN3 7RZ* T: (01604) 491060
M: 07925-421085 E: a.byfield@spc.oxon.org *or* atjbyfield@googlemail.com

BYFORD, The Ven Edwin Charles. b 47. Aus Nat Univ BSc 70 Melbourne Coll of Div BD 73 Univ of Chicago MA 76 Man Univ PhD 85. Trin Coll Melbourne 70. **d** 73 **p** 73. C Qeanbeyan Ch Ch Australia 73-75; Chapl Univ of Chicago USA 75-76; Hon C Chorlton-cum-Hardy St Werburgh *Man* 76-79; Australia from 79; Chapl Woden Valley Hosp 80-83; Asst P Wagga Wagga 83-84; Asst P Ainslie All SS 84-87; Chapl Aus Nat Univ 87-91; R Binda 91-95; R Broken Hill St Pet and Adn The Darling from 95. *PO Box 185, Broken Hill NSW*

2880, Australia T/F: (0061) (8) 8087 3221 M: 409-467981
E: e-byford-4@alumni.uchicago.edu

BYLES, Canon Raymond Vincent. b 30. Univ of Wales (Lamp) BA 52. St Mich Coll Llan 52. **d** 54 **p** 55. C Llanfairisgaer *Ban* 54-57; C Llandudno 57-59; V Carno 59-64; V Trefeglwys 63; V Newmarket and Gwaenysgor *St As* 64-72; R Llysfaen 72-80; V Bodelwyddan and St George 80-84; V Bodelwyddan 85-95; Hon Can St As Cathl from 89; rtd 95. *20 Lon Dderwen, Tan-y-Goppa Parc, Abergele LL22 7DW* T: (01745) 833604

BYLLAM-BARNES, Preb Paul William Marshall. b 38. Birm Univ BCom Lon Univ MSc. Sarum & Wells Th Coll. **d** 84 **p** 85. C Gt Bookham *Guildf* 84-87; R Cusop w Blakemere, Bredwardine w Brobury etc *Heref* 87-03; RD Abbeydore 96-00; Preb Heref Cathl 99-03; rtd 03. *90 Granger Avenue, Maldon CM9 6AN* T: (01621) 858978

BYNON, William. b 43. St Aid Birkenhead 63. **d** 66 **p** 67. C Huyton St Mich *Liv* 66-69; C Maghull 69-72; TV 72-75; V Highfield 75-82; V Southport All SS 82-88; P-in-c Southport All So 86-88; V Newton in Makerfield St Pet 88-94; V Caerhun w Llangelynin w Llanbedr-y-Cennin *Ban* 94-06; rtd 06. *Swn-y-Don, Maes Hyfryd, Moelfre LL72 8LR* T: (01248) 410749
E: william@pontwgan.freeserve.co.uk

BYRNE, Bryn. *See* BYRNE, Ronald Brendan Anthony

BYRNE, David Patrick. b 48. PGCE 96. St Jo Coll Nottm 74. **d** 77 **p** 78. C Bordesley Green *Birm* 77-79; C Weoley Castle 79-82; TV Kings Norton 82-92; TV Hodge Hill 92-94; PtO 94-97; Chapl Asst Birm Heartlands and Solihull NHS Trust 96-98; Chapl NW Lon Hosp NHS Trust 98-13; Chapl Harrow and Hillingdon Healthcare NHS Trust 98-13; rtd 13; Hon C Greenhill St Jo *Lon* from 11. *214 Currie Court, Harrow HA1 3GX*

BYRNE, David Rodney. b 47. St Jo Coll Cam BA 70 MA 73. Cranmer Hall Dur 71. **d** 73 **p** 74. C Maidstone St Luke *Cant* 73-77; C Patcham *Chich* 77-83; TV Stantonbury *Ox* 83-87; TV Stantonbury and Willen 87-92; TV Woodley 92-02; V Patchway *Bris* 02-10; rtd 11. *4 Pound Lane, Topsham, Exeter EX3 0NA* T: (01392) 758557

BYRNE, Canon Georgina Ann. b 72. Trin Coll Ox BA 92 MA 96 CCC Cam MPhil 98. Westcott Ho Cam. **d** 97 **p** 98. NSM W Bromwich All SS *Lich* 97-98; C 98-01; Hon Asst Chapl CCC Cam 97-98; Chapl to Bp Kensington *Lon* 01-04; Hon C Twickenham St Mary 01-04; TV Halas *Worc* 04-09; Can Res Worc Cathl from 09; Dir of Ords 09-15; Convenor for Women's Min from 05. *15B College Green, Worcester WR1 2LH* T: (01905) 732938 M: 07740-706448

BYRNE, Ian Barclay. b 53. Ripon Coll Cuddesdon 01. **d** 03 **p** 04. C Blyth St E 03-06; P-in-c Bungay H Trin w St Mary 06-13; C Wainford 06-13; V Bungay from 13; C S Elmham and Ilketshall from 14. *The Vicarage, 3 Trinity Gardens, Bungay NR35 1HH* T: (01986) 892553 E: rev.ib@btinternet.com

BYRNE, Canon John Victor. b 47. FCA. St Jo Coll Nottm LTh 73. **d** 73 **p** 74. C Gillingham St Mark *Roch* 73-76; C Cranham Park *Chelmsf* 76-80; V Balderstone *Man* 80-87; V Southsea St Jude *Portsm* 87-06; P-in-c Southsea St Pet 95-03; Hon Can Portsm Cathl 97-06; RD Portsm 01-06; V Branksome Park All SS *Sarum* 06-12; rtd 12; Chapl to The Queen from 03; PtO *Portsm* from 13. *4 St Georges Terrace, Southwick Road, Denmead, Waterlooville PO7 6FR* T: (023) 9225 3621
E: byrne.jv@gmail.com

BYRNE, Lynda. *See* BUNTING, Lynda

BYRNE, Miriam Alexandra Frances. b 46. Westcott Ho Cam. **d** 87 **p** 94. Par Dn Beoley *Worc* 87-90; C Ayr *Glas* 90-92; Dn-in-c Dumbarton 92-94; P-in-c 94-98; Provost St Paul's Cathl Dundee 98-06; R Dundee St Paul 98-06; rtd 06. *rue de la Bonnacherie, 16700 Salles-de-Villefagnan, France* T: (0033) 6 31 66 58 34

BYRNE, Rodney Edmund. b 18. **d** 84 **p** 84. Hon C Leckhampton SS Phil and Jas w Cheltenham St Jas *Glouc* 84-88; rtd 88; PtO *Glouc* 88-03. *39 Collum End Rise, Cheltenham GL53 0PA* T: (01242) 526428

BYRNE, Ronald Brendan Anthony (Bryn). b 31. Reading Univ BA 72. Westcott Ho Cam 86. **d** 64 **p** 65. Chapl Cov Cathl 87-91; Chapl Lanchester Poly 87-90; LtO 91-94; Chapl Limerick Univ *L & K* 94-98; Chapl Villier's Sch Limerick 95-98; rtd 96; Chapl Lanzarote *Eur* 98-00; PtO *Lon* 02-07. *6 Newton Terrace, Crown Lane, Bromley BR2 9PH* M: 07960-319294 E: brynbyrne@aol.com *or* roybyrne@eircom.net

BYRNE, Canon Roy Harold. b 71. Westmr Coll Ox BTh 97 Irish Sch of Ecum MPhil 00. CITC 97. **d** 99 **p** 00. C Dublin Ch Ch Cathl Gp 99-03; I Killeshin w Cloydagh and Killabban *C & O* 03-08; I Dublin Drumcondra w N Strand *D & G* from 08; Can Ch Ch Cathl Dublin from 12. *The Rectory, 74 Grace Park Road, Drumcondra, Dublin 9, Republic of Ireland* T: (00353) (1) 837 2505 M: 86-346 7920
E: roybyrne@eircom.net

BYROM, Alan. b 51. Magd Coll Ox BA 72 Bris Univ MA 85 Man Univ MPhil 99 Leeds Univ PGCE 73. NOC 97. **d** 99 **p** 00. C Leyland St Andr *Blackb* 99-03; TV Solway Plain *Carl* 03-10; P-in-c Blackpool Ch Ch w All SS *Blackb* 10-13; V from 13. *The Vicarage, 23A North Park Drive, Blackpool FY3 8LR* T: (01253) 390272 E: arm@abyrom.freeserve.co.uk

BYROM, Catherine Mary. b 66. Nottm Univ BA 88 MA 04. St Jo Coll Nottm 11. **d** 13 **p** 14. C Skegby w Teversal *S'well* from 13. *64 Fackley Way, Stanton Hill, Sutton-in-Ashfield NG17 3HT* T: 0115-960 9877 M: 07527-548644 E: katebyrom@hotmail.co.uk *or* kate@skegbyparish.org.uk

BYROM, Canon Malcolm Senior. b 37. Edin Th Coll 65. **d** 67 **p** 68. C Allerton *Bradf* 67-69; C Padstow *Truro* 69-72; V Hessenford 72-77; P-in-c St Martin by Looe 72-77; C Kenwyn 77-91; R Kenwyn w St Allen 91-99; Hon Can Truro Cathl 92-00; RD Powder 88-90; Sub-Warden Community of the Epiphany Truro 85-01; Warden from 01; rtd 99; PtO *Truro* from 00. *West Haven, Dobbin Lane, Trevone, Padstow PL28 8QP* T: (01841) 520242 E: malcolmbyrom@supanet.com

BYRON, Terence Sherwood. b 26. Keble Coll Ox BA 50 MA 54. Linc Th Coll 50. **d** 52 **p** 53. C Melton Mowbray w Burton Lazars, Freeby etc *Leic* 52-55; C Whitwick St Jo the Bapt 55-60; India 60-76; C-in-c Beaumont Leys (Extra-paroch Distr) *Leic* 76-85; V Beaumont Leys 85-86; RD Christianity N 86-92;

P-in-c Leic St Phil 86-88; V 88-92; rtd 93; PtO *Leic* from 93. *84 Flax Road, Leicester LE4 6QD* T: 0116-266 1922

BYSOUTH, Paul Graham. b 55. Oak Hill Th Coll. **d** 84 **p** 85. C Gorleston St Andr *Nor* 84-87; C Ripley *Derby* 87-91; TV N Wingfield, Clay Cross and Pilsley 91-00; V Blagreaves from 00. *St Andrew's Vicarage, 5 Greenburn Close, Littleover, Derby DE23 1FF* T: (01332) 773877 E: paulbysouth4@yahoo.co.uk *or* paemlu@googlemail.com

BYTHEWAY, Phillip James. b 35. MIIExE 89 BA 93. **d** 97. OLM Church Stretton *Heref* 97-00; rtd 00; PtO *Heref* from 00. *Buxton Cottage, All Stretton, Church Stretton SY6 6JU* T: (01694) 723907 M: 07778-391088 E: philip.bytheway@btinternet.com

BYWORTH, Canon Christopher Henry Briault. b 39. Oriel Coll Ox BA 61 MA 65 Bris Univ BA 63. Lon Coll of Div 64. **d** 65 **p** 66. C Low Leyton *Chelmsf* 65-68; C Rusholme H Trin *Man* 68-70; LtO *Lon* 71-75; TR Thetford *Nor* 75-79; Warden Cranmer Hall Dur 79-83; TR Fazakerley Em *Liv* 83-90; P-in-c St Helens St Helen 90-94; TR 94-04; AD St Helens 90-00; Hon Can Liv Cathl 99-04; rtd 04. *11 Oakleigh, Skelmersdale WN8 9QU* T: (01744) 886481

BYWORTH, Mrs Ruth Angela. b 49. Cranmer Hall Dur BA 82. dss 83 **d** 92 **p** 94. Kirkby *Liv* 83-89; Aintree St Pet 89-97; Dn-in-c 92-94; P-in-c 94-97; P-in-c St Helens St Mark 97-98; C Sutton 98-03; TV 03-04; rtd 04. *11 Oakleigh, Skelmersdale WN8 9QU* T: (01744) 886481

C

CABLE, Kevin John. b 74. Ripon Coll Cuddesdon BA 08. **d** 08 **p** 09. C Bromley Common St Aug *Roch* C 08-11; NSM Brenchley 12-14; C Perry Street from 14; TV Northfleet and Rosherville from 14. *The Vicarage, Perry Street, Northfleet, Gravesend DA11 8RD* M: 07739-539448 T: (01474) 534398 E: fr.kevin@btopenworld.com

CABLE, Patrick John. b 50. AKC 72. **d** 74 **p** 75. C Herne *Cant* 74-78; CF 78-05; Rtd Officer Chapl RAChD from 05. *c/o MOD Chaplains (Army)* T: (01799) 550466

CACKETT, Janice Susan. b 39. Goldsmiths' Coll Lon BA 76 Surrey Univ MSc 83. SWMTC 99. **d** 99 **p** 00. NSM Clyst St Mary, Clyst St George etc *Ex* 99-03; P-in-c E Budleigh w Bicton and Otterton 03-10; rtd 10. *27 Elm Grove Road, Topsham, Exeter EX3 0EJ* T: (01392) 877468 E: jcackett@ukgateway.net

CACOURIS, Alexander Xenophon. b 71. St Mellitus Coll. **d** 13 **p** 14. C E Twickenham St Steph *Lon* from 13. *68 Heathfield South, Twickenham TW2 7SS* T: (020) 8892 1561 M: 07919-117780 E: acacouris@hotmail.co.uk

CADDELL, Richard Allen. b 54. Auburn Univ Alabama BIE 77. Trin Coll Bris BA 88. **d** 88 **p** 89. C Uphill *B & W* 88-94; PtO 94-96; TV Beaconsfield *Ox* 96-07; P-in-c Lamp 07-09; R from 09; AD Newport 13-15. *The Rectory, High Street, Haversham, Milton Keynes MK19 7DT* T: (01908) 312136 E: caddells@holtspur.plus.com

CADDEN, Brian Stuart. b 58. BSc BTh TCD. **d** 89 **p** 90. C Lecale Gp *D & D* 89-92; C Killowen *D & R* 92-95; I Muckamore *Conn* 95-06; I Castlewellan w Kilcoo *D & D* from 06. *5 Cedar Heights, Bryansford, Newcastle BT33 0PJ* T: (028) 4372 3198 E: castlewellan@dromore.anglican.org

CADDEN, Canon Terence John. b 60. TCD BTh 89. CITC 86. **d** 89 **p** 90. C Coleraine *Conn* 89-92; C Lurgan Ch the Redeemer *D & D* 92-93; Past Dir 93-01; I Gilford 01-06; I Seagoe from 06; Can Dromore Cathl from 10. *Seagoe Rectory, 8 Upper Church Lane, Portadown, Craigavon BT63 5JE* T: (028) 3833 2538 *or* 3835 0583 F: 3833 0773 M: 07894-987702 E: cadden@talktalk.net *or* seagoechurch@btinternet.com

CADDICK, Jeremy Lloyd. b 60. St Jo Coll Cam BA 82 MA 86 K Coll Lon MA 93. Ripon Coll Cuddesdon BA 86 MA 91. **d** 87 **p** 88. C Kennington St Jo w St Jas *S'wark* 87-90; Chapl Lon Univ 90-94; Chapl R Free Medical Sch 90-94; Chapl R Veterinary Coll Lon 90-94; PV Westmr Abbey 92-94; Dean Em Coll Cam from 94. *Emmanuel College, Cambridge CB2 3AP* T: (01223) 334264 *or* 330195 F: 334426 E: jlc24@cam.ac.uk

CADDICK, Canon Lloyd Reginald. b 31. Bris Univ BA 56 St Cath Coll Ox BA 58 MA 62 Nottm Univ MPhil 73 K Coll Lon PhD 78 Open Univ Hon MA 79. St Steph Ho Ox 56. **d** 59 **p** 59. C N Lynn w St Marg and St Nic *Nor* 59-62; Chapl Oakham Sch 62-66; P-in-c Bulwick, Harringworth w Blatherwycke and Laxton *Pet* 66-67; R Bulwick, Blatherwycke w Harringworth and Laxton 67-77; V Oundle 77-96; Can

Pet Cathl 94-96; rtd 96; PtO *Pet* from 96. *102 West Street, Kings Cliffe, Peterborough PE8 6XA* T: (01780) 470332 E: gill.lloyd.c@btinternet.com

CADDOO (née BLAKELY), Mrs Denise Irene. b 69. QUB BD 91 PGCE 92. CITC 93. **d** 95 **p** 96. C Holywood *D & D* 95-99; C Portadown St Columba *Arm* 99-00; I Carrowdore w Millisle *D & D* 00-04; C Holywood 04-06; I Gilford from 06. *The Vicarage, 18 Scarva Road, Gilford, Craigavon BT63 6BG* T: (028) 3883 1130

CADDY, Canon Michael George Bruce Courtenay. b 45. K Coll Lon. **d** 71 **p** 72. C Walton St Mary *Liv* 71-76; C Solihull *Birm* 76-79; TV 79-81; V Shard End 81-87; TR Shirley 87-00; P-in-c Tanworth St Patr Salter Street 97-00; TR Salter Street and Shirley 00-13; AD Shirley 97-02; Hon Can Birm Cathl 99-13; Dioc Chapl MU 07-11; rtd 13; Bps' Dom Chapl *B & W* 13-15. *12 Dial Hill Road, Clevedon BS21 7HJ* E: ann@acaddy.wanadoo.co.uk

CADDY, Ms Susan. b 50. Westcott Ho Cam 99. **d** 01 **p** 02. C Sutton in Ashfield St Mary *S'well* 01-05; P-in-c Shelton and Oxon *Lich* 05-10; TV Retford Area *S'well* from 10. *The Rectory, Hine Close, Retford DN22 7ZH* T: (01777) 703322 E: suecee123@btinternet.com

CADE, Mrs Margaret Elizabeth. b 34. Dioc OLM tr scheme 99. **d** 00. OLM Portland All SS w St Andr *Sarum* 00-07; PtO 07-14. *27 Avalanche Road, Portland DT5 2DJ* T: (01305) 821317 F: 826453 M: 07974-696892 E: margaretcade@fsmail.net

CADE, Simon Peter Vincent. b 69. Univ of Wales BA 90. Westcott Ho Cam 92. **d** 94 **p** 95. C Calne and Blackland *Sarum* 94-98; Chapl St Mary's Sch Calne 94-97; TV Basingstoke *Win* 98-05; TR Redruth w Lanner and Treleigh *Truro* 05-14; P-in-c 14; Dioc Dir of Educn and Discipleship from 14; Public Preacher from 14. *Church House, Woodlands Court, Truro Business Park, Threemilestone, Truro TR4 9NH* T: (01872) 247214. E: simon.cade@truro.anglican.org

CADMAN, Robert Hugh. b 49. St Jo Coll Nottm 77. **d** 78 **p** 79. C Ecclesall *Sheff* 78-82; C Worting *Win* 82-84; C-in-c Winklebury CD 84-87; R Woldford *Chelmsf* 87-94; Chapl Anglia Poly Univ 94-95; NSM Brentwood St Thos 01-03; TV Southend 03-08; V Prittlewell St Pet w Westcliff St Cedd 08-14; rtd 14; PtO *Chelmsf* from 14. *68 Marlborough Road, Braintree CM7 9LR* T: (01376) 408079 E: robcadman@me.com

CADMORE, Albert Thomas. b 47. Open Univ BA 81 UEA MA 94 Lon Inst of Educn CertEd 68. EAMTC 85. **d** 88 **p** 89. NSM Gorleston St Andr *Nor* 88-96; NSM Winterton w E and W Somerton and Horsey 94-96; NSM Flegg Coastal Benefice 96-12; rtd 12; PtO *Nor* from 12. *10 Upper Cliff Road, Gorleston, Great Yarmouth NR31 6AL* T: (01493) 668762 E: acadmore@ntlworld.com

CADOGAN, Paul Anthony Cleveland. b 47. AKC 74. **d** 75 **p** 76. C Fishponds St Jo *Bris* 75-79; C Swindon New Town 79-81; P-in-c Swindon All SS 81-82; V 82-90; R Lower Windrush *Ox* 90-94. *2 Malthouse Close, Ashbury, Swindon SN6 8PB* T: (01793) 710488

CADOGAN, Percil Lavine. b 41. WMMTC. **d** 01 **p** 02. NSM Bournville *Birm* 01-05; NSM Bordesley St Benedict 05-14; P-in-c 12-14; rtd 14; PtO *Birm* from 14. *76 Highway Road, Birmingham B14 7QW* T: 0121-680 9595
E: percil.cadogan@gmail.com

CADWALLADER, Michael Godfrey. b 56. Bris Univ BEd 79 St Jo Coll Dur BA 06. Cranmer Hall Dur 05. **d** 07 **p** 08. C Kingston upon Hull St Aid Southcoates *York* 07-11; P-in-c Burton Dassett *Cov* from 11; P-in-c Avon Dassett w Farnborough and Fenny Compton from 11; P-in-c Gaydon w Chadshunt from 11. *Burton Dassett Vicarage, Bottom Street, Northend, Southam CV47 2TH* T: (01295) 770400
E: cadwalladermg@waitrose.com

CAESAR, Canon Anthony Douglass. b 24. LVO 87 CVO 91. Magd Coll Cam BA 47 MA 49 MusB 47 FRCO 47. St Steph Ho Ox 59. **d** 61 **p** 62. C Kensington St Mary Abbots w St Geo *Lon* 61-65; Chapl RSCM 65-70; Asst Sec CACTM 65-66; Asst Sec ACCM 65-70; Dep P in O 67-68; P in O 68-70; C Bournemouth St Pet *Win* 70-73; Prec and Sacr Win Cathl 74-79; Hon Can Win Cathl 75-76 and 79-91; Can Res Win Cathl 76-79; Dom Chapl to The Queen 79-91; Extra Chapl to The Queen from 91; Sub Almoner and Dep Clerk of the Closet 79-91; Sub Dean of HM Chpls Royal 79-91; rtd 91; Chapl St Cross Hosp 91-93; PtO *Portsm* 93-06. *26 Capel Court, The Burgage, Prestbury, Cheltenham GL52 3EL* T: (01242) 577541

CAFFYN, Douglas John Morris. b 36. Peterho Cam MA 60 Nairobi Univ MSc 69 Westmr Coll Ox DipEd 61 ACIS 77. S Dios Minl Tr Scheme 87. **d** 90 **p** 91. NSM Hampden Park *Chich* 90-94; Chapl among Deaf People 94-97; Jt Sec Cttee for Min among Deaf People 95-97; PtO *Chich* from 97; rtd 01. *255 King's Drive, Eastbourne BN21 2UR* T: (01323) 500977

CAGE, Doreen. b 43 **p** 14. Asst Chapl Málaga *Eur* from 13. *Buzón 40, La Parrilla, 21930 Villanueva de Algaidas, (Málaga), Spain* T: (0034) 952 745 028 E: jmnct123@gmail.com

CAHILL, Canon Nigel. b 59. St Mich Coll Llan. **d** 82 **p** 83. C Whitchurch *Llan* 82-86; V Tonypandy w Clydach Vale 86-96; RD Rhondda 93-96; V Fairwater 96-03; V Caerau w Ely 03-08; AD Llan 06-08; TR Aberavon from 08; Can Llan Cathl from 09. *The Rectory, Forge Road, Port Talbot SA13 1US* T: (01639) 883630 E: rector@parishofaberavon.org

CAHUSAC, Henry William James. b 73. Wycliffe Hall Ox BTh 06. **d** 06 **p** 07. C Tollington *Lon* 06-10; C Onslow Square and S Kensington St Aug from 10. *17 Nevinson Close, London SW18 2TF*

CAIN, Andrew David. See FORESHEW-CAIN, Andrew David

CAIN, Andrew Paul. b 76. St Jo Coll Nottm. **d** 08 **p** 09. C Hinckley H Trin *Leic* 08-11; C Bosworth and Sheepy Gp 11-12; V Cuddington *Guildf* from 12. *St Mary's Vicarage, St Mary's Road, Worcester Park KT4 7JL*

CAIN, Frank Robert. b 56. Oak Hill Th Coll BA 88. **d** 88 **p** 89. C Aughton Ch Ch *Liv* 88-91; P-in-c Toxteth Park St Clem 91-99; V Toxteth St Bede w St Clem 99-04; AD Toxteth and Wavertree 01-04; Hon Can Liv Cathl 03-04; Chapl N Mersey Community NHS Trust 96-04; V New Brighton St Jas w Em *Ches* from 04; RD Wallasey 07-09. *The Vicarage, 14 Albion Street, Wallasey CH45 9LF* T: 0151-639 5844
E: vicarfrank@btinternet.com

CAIN, Jonathan Michael Field. b 69. Nottm Univ BEng 90 Bradf Univ MBA 03. Yorks Min Course 13. **d** 15. C Bolton Abbey *Leeds* from 15. *6 Longcroft Road, Ilkley LS29 8SE* T: (01943) 871149 M: 07957-713387 E: jonathonmfcain@icloud.com or jonathan.cain@westyorkshiredales.anglican.org

CAIN, Michael Christopher. b 68. St Jo Coll Dur BA 90 K Coll Lon MA 92 Selw Coll Cam BA 94. Ridley Hall Cam 92. **d** 95 **p** 96. C Wimbledon Em Ridgway Prop Chpl *S'wark* 95-99; Asst Chapl Leipzig *Eur* 99-02; C Clifton Ch Ch w Em *Bris* 02-10; Pioneer Min Clifton Em from 11. *60 Clifton Park Road, Bristol BS8 3HN* T: 0117-973 3729
E: mike@emmanuelbristol.org.uk

CAIN, Michael John Patrick. b 62. Chich Th Coll 88. **d** 91 **p** 92. C Cainscross w Selsley *Glouc* 91-94; C Mackworth St Fran *Derby* 94-97; V Derby St Luke 97-02; C Paignton St Jo *Ex* 02-07; rtd 07. *124 Forest Road, Torquay TQ1 4JY* T: (01803) 316046 E: cainfamily@toucansurf.co.uk

CAINE, Diane. b 56. Ex Univ BTh 12. SWMTC 09. **d** 12. NSM Dawlish *Ex* 12-15; NSM Dawlish, Cofton and Starcross from 15. *2 Charlemont Road, Teignmouth TQ14 8RP* T: (01626) 680187 E: nigedi.caine@hotmail.co.uk

CAINES, Julia Clare. See CHARD, Julia Clare

CAINK, Richard David Somerville. b 37. Lich Th Coll 68. **d** 71 **p** 72. C Prittlewell St Mary *Chelmsf* 71-74; C Gt Yarmouth *Nor* 74-76; P-in-c Blickling w Ingworth 76-80; P-in-c Saxthorpe and Corpusty 76-80; P-in-c Oulton SS Pet and Paul 76-80; R Cheddington w Mentmore and Marsworth *Ox* 80-87; P-in-c Wooburn 87-90; V 90-96; P-in-c Lacey Green 96-98;

TV Risborough 98-02; rtd 02; PtO *St E* from 11. *1 Whitlock Drive, Great Yeldham, Halstead CO9 4EE* T: (01787) 236091

✠**CAIRD, The Rt Revd Prof Donald Arthur Richard.** b 25. TCD BA 49 MA 55 BD 55 HDipEd 59 Hon DD 88 Hon LLD 93. TCD Div Sch 49. **d** 50 **p** 51 **c** 70. C Dundela St Mark *D & D* 50-53; Chapl and Asst Master Portora R Sch Enniskillen 53-57; Lect St D Coll Lamp 57-59; I Rathmichael *D & G* 60-69; Asst Master St Columba's Coll Dub 60-62; Lect TCD 62-64; Lect in Philosophy of Relig Div Hostel 64-69; Dean Ossory *C & O* 69-70; Can Leighlin Cathl 69-70; I Kilkenny 69-70; Bp Limerick, Ardfert and Aghadoe *L & K* 70-76; Bp M & K 76-85; Abp Dublin *D & G* 85-96; Preb Cualaun St Patr Cathl Dublin 85-96; rtd 96; Visiting Prof Gen Th Sem New York USA from 97. *3 Crofton Avenue, Dun Laoghaire, Co Dublin, Republic of Ireland* T: (00353) (1) 280 7869 F: 230 1053

CAIRNS, Dorothy Elizabeth. b 66. Wilson Carlile Coll 87 CITC 07. **d** 09 **p** 10. CA from 90; C Portadown St Columba *Arm* 09-11; I 11-13; I Mullavilly from 13. *The Rectory, 89 Mullavilly Road, Tandragee, Craigavon BT62 2LX* M: 07719-857187 T: (028) 3884 0221 E: ecairns@talk21.com

CAISSIE, Mrs Elizabeth Anne. b 40. CBDTI 07. **d** 08 **p** 09. NSM Keighley St Andr *Bradf* 08-13; PtO *Leeds* from 13; *York* from 14. *2A Turmer Avenue, Bridlington YO15 2HJ* T: (01262) 229763 E: elizabethcaissie581@btinternet.com

CAITHNESS, Mrs Joyce Marigold. b 45. **d** 06 **p** 07. OLM Bris St Matt and St Nath from 06. *383 Southmead Road, Westbury-on-Trym, Bristol BS10 5LT* T: 0117-983 3755
E: jm.caithness@blueyonder.co.uk

CAKE, Nichola Carla. See CHATER, Nichola Carla

CAKE, Simon Charles Eagle. b 61. Wilson Carlile Coll 91 Cranmer Hall Dur 08. **d** 10 **p** 11. C Hebburn St Jo *Dur* 10-14; TV Egremont and Haile Carl from 14; Chapl N Cumbria Univ Hosps NHS Trust from 14. *The Vicarage, 1 Bridge End Park, Egremont CA22 2RH* T: (01946) 821567 M: 07710-523856 E: cakekands@btinternet.com

CALAM, Mrs Josephine Mary. b 54. Qu Coll Birm 13. **d** 15. NSM Areley Kings *Worc* from 15. *13 Larches Road, Kidderminster DY11 7AA*

CALCOTT-JAMES, Colin Wilfrid. b 25. Bris Univ BSc 48. S'wark Ord Course 77. **d** 80 **p** 81. NSM Barnes H Trin *S'wark* 80-85; C Hykeham *Linc* 85-88; R Barrowby 88-92; rtd 92; PtO *Lon* 93-94; *S'wark* from 93. *23 Gwendolen Avenue, London SW15 6ET* T: (020) 8788 6591

CALDER, David Ainsley. b 60. NE Lon Poly BSc 86 St Jo Coll Dur BA 95. Cranmer Hall Dur 93. **d** 96 **p** 97. C Ireland Wood *Ripon* 96-00; V Woodhouse and Wrangthorn 00-10; Chapl Leeds Metrop Univ 02-10. *2 Halcyon Hill, Leeds LS7 3PU* M: 07947-535044

CALDER, Canon Ian Fraser. b 47. York Univ BA 68 CertEd 69. Glouc Sch of Min 84. **d** 87 **p** 88. NSM Lydney w Aylburton *Glouc* 87-91; C Cirencester 91-95; V Coney Hill 95-01; RD Glouc City 99-01; R Bishop's Cleeve 01-08; AD Tewkesbury and Winchcombe 02-07; Hon Can Glouc Cathl 03-08; rtd 08. *11 Riversley Road, Elmbridge, Gloucester GL2 0QU* T: (01452) 537845 E: revian@blueyonder.co.uk

CALDERHEAD, Christopher Conrad. b 62. Princeton Univ AB 84. Seabury-Western Th Sem MDiv 98. **d** 98 **p** 99. C Chesterton Gd Shep *Ely* 98-02; USA from 02. *3075 Thirty-third Street Apt 4A, Astoria NY 11102, USA* T: (001) (718) 278 3098 E: cccalderhead@yahoo.com

CALDERIN (née AVISON), Mrs Sara Jane. b 41. Florida Internat Univ BSc 79 MSc 95. **d** 00. Dn Miami Ven Bede USA 00-03; Dn Stamford Ch Ch *Linc* 04-12; rtd 12; PtO *Linc* from 12. *3 Glen Crescent, Stamford PE9 1SW* T: (01780) 754290
E: janecalderin@hotmail.co.uk

CALDERWOOD, Emma Louise. See WILLIAMS, Emma Louise

CALDWELL, Alan. b 29. Oak Hill Th Coll 65. **d** 67 **p** 68. C Aldershot H Trin *Guildf* 67-69; C New Malden and Coombe *S'wark* 69-73; C-in-c Edgware St Andr CD *Lon* 73-78; P-in-c Pettaugh and Winston w Framsden *St E* 78; R Helmingham w Framsden and Pettaugh w Winston 78-87; R Cowden w Hammerwood *Chich* 87-94; rtd 94; PtO *Ban* from 94. *Ael-y-Bryn, Druid Road, Menai Bridge LL59 5BY* T: (01248) 713550 E: alancaldwell3d@btinternet.com

CALDWELL, Alan Alfred. b 48. Loughb Univ BSc 70 PhD 83. Linc Th Coll 70. **d** 73 **p** 74. C Bulwell St Mary *S'well* 73-80; Chapl Nottm Univ 80-87; R Baxterley w Hurley and Wood End and Merevale etc *Birm* 87-91; PtO *S'well* from 06. *33 The Spinney, Bulcote, Nottingham NG14 5GX* T: 0115-931 4556

CALDWELL, Ian Charles Reynolds. b 43. St Mich Coll Llan 68. **d** 70 **p** 71. C Oakham w Hambleton and Egleton *Pet* 70-74; C Swindon New Town *Bris* 74-78; P-in-c Honicknowle *Ex* 78-80; V 80-88; V Norton St Mich *Dur* 88-94; rtd 03. *Address withheld by request*

CALDWELL, Jacob Wilson (Jim). b 84. St Andr Univ MA 07 AVCM 04. TCD Div Sch MTh 09. **d** 11 **p** 12. Intern Dn Magherafelt *Arm* 11-12; C Larne and Inver *Conn* 12-15; CF from 15. *c/o MOD Chaplains (Army)* M: 07564-418252 T: (01264) 383430 F: 381824

CALDWELL, Mrs Jill. b 47. Lon Univ BPharm 69 MRPharmS 70. S Dios Minl Tr Scheme 89. **d** 92 **p** 94. NSM Yiewsley *Lon* 92-97; NSM St Marylebone w H Trin 97-02; Chapl St Marylebone Girls' Sch Lon 97-98; Chapl R Academy of Music 97-98; Chapl Lon Sch of Pharmacy 97-98; Chapl Liv Cathl 03-04; PtO *Derby* 04-05; NSM Darley Abbey 05-10; NSM Allestree St Edm and Darley Abbey 10-13; PtO *Ox* from 14. *1 Pheasants Ridge, Marlow SL7 3QT* E: jill-caldwell@talk21.com

CALDWELL, Roger Fripp. b 31. Cranmer Hall Dur. **d** 64 **p** 65. C Gosforth St Nic *Newc* 64-67; C Sugley 67-74; R Greatworth and Helmdon w Stuchbury and Radstone *Pet* 74-91; rtd 91. *Silver House, Silver Street, Ditcheat, Shepton Mallet BA4 6QY* T: (01749) 860239

CALDWELL, Sarah Louise. *See* HARE, Sarah Louise

CALE, Canon Clifford Roy Fenton. b 38. St Mich Coll Llan 65. **d** 67 **p** 68. C Griffithstown *Mon* 67-72; V Cwm 72-73; V Abersychan 73-79; V Abersychan and Garndiffaith 79-82; R Goetre w Llanover and Llanfair Kilgeddin 82-84; R Goetre w Llanover 85-01; RD Raglan-Usk 90-01; Can St Woolos Cathl 98-01; rtd 01. *3 Trelawny Close, Usk NP15 1SP* T: (01291) 672252

CALE, Mrs Heather. b 68. Ches Coll of HE BEd 90. St Mich Coll Llan 12. **d** 14 **p** 15. NSM Haverfordwest *St D* from 14. *St Martin's Vicarage, Barn Street, Haverfordwest SA61 1TD* T: (01437) 762303 E: heather.cale@btinternet.com

CALE, Nicholas. b 66. St Mich Coll Llan. **d** 92 **p** 93. C Tenby *St D* 92-95; R Begelly w Ludchurch and Crunwere 95-01; V Wiston w Walton E and Clarbeston 01-14; P-in-c Haverfordwest from 14; AD Daugleddau from 12. *St Martin's Vicarage, Barn Street, Haverfordwest SA61 1TD* T: (01437) 762303 E: nickthevic@parishofhaverfordwest.co.uk

CALITIS, Juris. Maryland Univ BA Latvia Univ DD. Harvard Div Sch STB. **d** 98 **p** 98. Chapl Riga, Latvia *Eur* from 98; Dean Faculty of Th Univ of Latvia from 99; Assoc Prof Bibl Studies from 99; Co-ord Bible Translation (Latvian Bible Soc) from 99. *Anglikanu iela 2A, Riga, LV1050, Latvia* T: (00371) 721 1390 *or* 721 1288 E: juris.calitis@lu.lv

CALLADINE, Joanne Elizabeth. b 71. Liv Inst of Educn BA 93. Cranmer Hall Dur 95. **d** 97 **p** 98. NSM Blurton *Lich* 97-98; C Stoke-upon-Trent 98-01; PtO *Man* 07-12; Chapl HM Pris Man from 12. *HM Prison Manchester, 1 Southall Street, Manchester M60 9AH* T: 0161-817 5600 E: jo.calladine@lineone.net

CALLADINE, Matthew Robert Michael. b 65. St Jo Coll Dur BSc 87 BA 95 Reading Univ MSc 89. Cranmer Hall Dur 93. **d** 96 **p** 97. C Blurton *Lich* 96-01; P-in-c Moston St Mary *Man* from 01. *St Mary's Rectory, 47 Nuthurst Road, Moston, Manchester M40 0EW* T: 0161-681 1201 E: matthew.calladine@lineone.net

CALLAGHAN, Canon Harry. b 34. AKC 59 Open Univ BA 83. **d** 60 **p** 61. C Sheff St Cecilia Parson Cross 60-63; Br Guiana 63-66; Guyana 66-70; Barbados 70-74; LtO *Man* 74-84; Miss to Seamen 74-76; Area Sec USPG Blackb, Man and S & M 76-84; P-in-c Wythenshawe St Martin *Man* 84-85; V 85-91; V Bolton St Jo 91-98; Hon Can Massachusetts from 92; rtd 98; PtO *Man* 98-14; *Derby* from 99; *Blackb* from 14. *32 Fosbrook House, 8 Clifton Drive, Lytham St Annes FY8 5RQ* T: (01253) 667021 M: 07778-988523 E: canoncallaghan@gmail.com

CALLAGHAN, Martin Peter. b 57. Edin Th Coll 91. **d** 93 **p** 94. C Ayr *Glas* 93-96; C Girvan 93-96; C Maybole 93-96; P-in-c Gretna from 96; P-in-c Eastriggs from 96; P-in-c Annan from 97; P-in-c Lockerbie from 97; P-in-c Moffat from 97; Clergy Ldr Annandale Gp from 03. *South Annandale Rectory, 28 Northfield Park, Annan DG12 5EZ* T: (01461) 202924 E: martinpcallaghan@btinternet.com

CALLAGHAN, Michael James. b 63. Clare Coll Cam BA 85. SEITE 94. **d** 97 **p** 98. NSM Blackheath Park St Mich *S'wark* 97-08; PtO *Guildf* 12-14; NSM Egham from 14. *3 College Avenue, Egham TW20 8NR* T: (01784) 435678

CALLAGHAN, Robert Paul. b 59. K Coll Lon BD 81 Kent Univ MA 04. Linc Th Coll 81. **d** 83 **p** 85. C Winchmore Hill St Paul *Lon* 83-85; C Paddington St Jo w St Mich 85-91; V Dartford St Edm *Roch* 91-11; Nat Co-ordinator Inclusive Ch from 11; PtO *Glouc* from 14. *4 Ferney, Dursley GL11 5AB* M: 07989-178558 E: bcall@hotmail.co.uk

CALLAGHAN, Yvonne Susan. b 58. St Jo Coll Nottm 06. **d** 08 **p** 09. C Middleham w Coverdale and E Witton etc *Ripon* 08-13; V Easby w Skeeby and Brompton on Swale etc *Leeds* from 13. *The Vicarage, St Paul's Drive, Brompton on Swale, Richmond DL10 7HQ* T: (01748) 811748 E: callaghans1992@ntlworld.com

CALLAN, Canon Terence Frederick. b 26. CITC 55. **d** 57 **p** 58. C Monaghan *Clogh* 57-58; I Clogh 58-64; C Derriaghy *Conn* 64-66; P-in-c Ballymacash 67-70; I Belfast St Aid 70-79; I Agherton 79-94; Can Conn Cathl from 86; Treas Conn Cathl from 90; rtd 94. *18 Central Avenue, Portstewart BT55 7BS* T: (028) 7083 2704

CALLAN, Ms Wendy Mary. b 52. Ox Brookes Univ BA 93. SAOMC 96. **d** 99 **p** 00. C Bicester w Bucknell, Caversfield and Launton *Ox* 99-03; V Shipton-under-Wychwood w Milton, Fifield etc 03-10; I Killala w Dunfeeny, Crossmolina, Kilmoremoy etc *T, K & A* 10-13; Dean Killala 12-13; TV The Claydons and Swan *Ox* from 13. *The Rectory, Queen Catherine Road, Steeple Claydon, Buckingham MK18 2PY* T: (01296) 738055 E: revwendycallan@googlemail.com

CALLAN-TRAVIS, Anthony. b 46. NOC 90. **d** 93 **p** 94. C Tong *Bradf* 93-97; C Harrogate St Wilfrid *Ripon* 97-03; TV Knaresborough 03-08; rtd 09. *3 Providence Terrace, Harrogate HG1 5EX* T: (01423) 529266

CALLARD, Canon David Kingsley. b 37. St Pet Coll Ox BA 61 MA 65. Westcott Ho Cam 61. **d** 63 **p** 64. C Leamington Priors H Trin *Cov* 63-66; C Wyken 66-68; C Bp's Hatfield *St Alb* 68-73; R Bilton *Cov* 73-83; TR Swanage and Studland *Sarum* 83-93; TR Oakdale 93-02; Can and Preb Sarum Cathl 95-02; rtd 02; PtO *B & W* from 05. *Woodlands, 29 Folkestone Road, Salisbury SP2 8JP* T: (01722) 501200 E: katcallard@ntlworld.com

CALLEN, Nicola Geraldine. b 48. Open Univ BA 85. Trin Coll Bris 09. **d** 11 **p** 12. OLM Fishponds St Jo *Bris* from 11; OLM Bristol St Aid w St Geo from 15; OLM Two Mile Hill St Mich from 15. *164 Ridgeway Road, Bristol BS16 3EG* E: ng.callen@gmail.com

CALLENDER, Francis Charles. b 48. TCD BA 70 DipEd 71 MA 73. TCD Div Sch 76. **d** 79 **p** 80. C Bandon *C, C & R* 79-82; New Zealand 82-88 and from 90; USA 88-90. *31 Grampian Street, Casebrook, Christchurch 8051, New Zealand* T: (0064) (3) 359 4568 F: 337 8236

CALLER, Laurence Edward Harrison. b 19. Lon Univ BMus 77 MA 82. Lich Th Coll 39. **d** 42 **p** 43. C Ipswich St Matt *St E* 42-45; C Walsall St Pet *Lich* 45-46; C Hednesford 46-48; R Stafford St Mary 48-55; Subchanter Lich Cathl 55-57; V Shrewsbury St Alkmund *Lich* 57-63; V Harlescott 63-67; rtd 84. *103 Fronks Road, Dovercourt, Harwich CO12 4EG* T: (01255) 504501

CALLIS, Gillian Ruth. *See* TURNER-CALLIS, Gillian Ruth

CALLIS, Stephen Harby. b 49. Keele Univ MA 97. SNWTP 10. **d** 11 **p** 12. NSM Prestbury *Ches* from 11; NSM Upton Priory from 11. *2 Fieldbank Road, Macclesfield SK11 8PZ* T: (01625) 427002 M: 07720-181978 E: paraprexis@sky.com

CALLON, Andrew McMillan. b 56. Chich Th Coll 77. **d** 80 **p** 81. C Wigan All SS *Liv* 80-85; V Abram 85-90; V Bickershaw 89-90; Chapl RN 90-12; rtd 12. *Kings Living, Prigg Lane, South Petherton TA13 5BX* T: (01460) 242537 M: 07777-670319 E: a.mcallon@btinternet.com

CALLWAY, Peter Stanley. b 55. SEITE 06. **d** 09 **p** 10. C Paddock Wood *Roch* 09-13; R Coxheath, E Farleigh, Hunton, Linton etc from 13. *The Rectory, 144 Heath Road, Coxheath, Maidstone ME17 4PL* T: (01622) 747570 E: peter@callways.co.uk

CALOW, Jacqueline. b 60. SNWTP. **d** 11 **p** 12. C Langley *Man* 11-14; NSM Saddleworth from 14. *Address temp unknown* E: jackie.2026309@hotmail.com

CALOW, Timothy. b 58. **d** 10 **p** 11. NSM Sutton w Cowling and Lothersdale *Leeds* from 10. *3 Laurel Close, Embsay, Skipton BD23 6RS* T: (01756) 799517 E: tim@calows.me.uk

CALVELEY, Mrs Susan. b 47. **d** 02 **p** 03. OLM Birkdale St Pet *Liv* 02-06; NSM 06-11; rtd 11. *1 Balfour Road, Southport PR8 6LE* E: revd.sue@gmail.com

CALVER, Canon Gillian Margaret. b 47. Qu Eliz Coll Lon BSc 68. Cant Sch of Min 89. **d** 92 **p** 94. NSM Folkestone H Trin w Ch Ch *Cant* 92-95; P-in-c Alkham w Capel le Ferne and Hougham 95-01; V 01-02; Chapl Dover Coll 95-99; R Staplehurst *Cant* 02-11; AD Weald 06-10; Hon Can Cant Cathl 08-11; rtd 11; PtO *Cant* from 12; Chapl to The Queen from 08. *6 Grand Court, Grand Parade, Littlestone, New Romney TN28 8NT* T: (01797) 366082 E: gill.calver@btinternet.com

CALVER, Nicholas James. b 58. Nottm Univ BTh 83 Dur Univ MA 90. Cranmer Hall Dur 86. **d** 88 **p** 89. C Forest Hill Ch Ch *S'wark* 88-91; C Forest Hill 91-92; P-in-c Mottingham St Edw 92-95; V 95-97; Voc Adv Lewisham Adnry 94-97; V Redhill St Jo *S'wark* 97-14; P-in-c Burstow w Horne 14-15; C S Nutfield w Outwood 14-15; R The Windmill from 15. *The Rectory, 5 The Acorns, Redehall Road, Smallfield, Horley RH6 9QJ* T: (01342) 842224 E: nicholas.calver@btinternet.com

CALVERLEY, Mrs Denise Marie. b 66. Trin Coll Bris 10. **d** 12 **p** 13. C Saltford w Corston and Newton St Loe *B & W* 12-14;

C Keynsham from 14. *2 Fenton Close, Saltford, Bristol BS31 3AT* T: (01225) 920387 M: 07849-821588 E: dmcalverley@icloud.com

CALVERT, Geoffrey Richard. b 58. Edin Univ BSc 79 PhD 84 Leeds Univ BA 86. Coll of Resurr Mirfield 84. **d** 87 **p** 88. C Curdworth w Castle Vale *Birm* 87-90; C Barnsley St Mary *Wakef* 90-92; TV Halifax 92-94; V Halifax H Trin 95-99; V Luton St Aug Limbury *St Alb* 99-09; P-in-c Watford St Mich 09-12; V from 12. *St Michael's Vicarage, 5 Mildred Avenue, Watford WD18 7DY* T: (01923) 232460 E: geoffreycalvert@virginmedia.com

CALVERT, Canon Jean. b 34. Lightfoot Ho Dur IDC 63. **dss** 87 **d** 87 **p** 94. S Bank *York* 78-84; Chapl Asst Rampton Hosp Retford 84-88; Dn-in-c Dunham w Darlton, Ragnall, Fledborough etc *S'well* 88-94; P-in-c 94-04; Hon Can S'well Minster 93-04; rtd 04; PtO *S'well* from 06. *The Rafters, Lincoln Road, Darlton, Newark NG22 0TF* T: (01777) 228758

CALVERT, John Raymond. b 42. Lon Coll of Div 64. **d** 67 **p** 68. C Kennington St Mark *S'wark* 67-70; C Southborough St Pet w Ch Ch and St Matt *Roch* 70-72; C Barton Seagrave *Pet* 72-73; C Barton Seagrave w Warkton 73-75; Asst Master Shaftesbury High Sch 78-79; Dioc Children's Officer *Glouc* 79-87; P-in-c S Cerney w Cerney Wick and Down Ampney 87-89; V 89-07; P-in-c Siddington w Preston 02-07; rtd 07. *46 Penn Lane, Brixham TQ5 9NR*

CALVERT, John Stephen. b 27. Lon Univ BSc 53. Wycliffe Coll Toronto BTh 61. **d** 61 **p** 62. Canada 61-63; C Preston St Jo *Blackb* 63-70; rtd 92; PtO *Blackb* 92-11. *17 Leyster Street, Morecambe LA4 5NF* T: (01524) 424491

CALVERT, Mrs Judith. b 50. NOC 04. **d** 07 **p** 08. NSM Woodchurch *Ches* 07-12; NSM Neston from 12. *33 Centurion Drive, Wirral CH47 7AL* T: 0151-632 4729 E: rev.judithcalvert@btinternet.com

CALVERT, Canon Peter Noel. b 41. Ch Coll Cam BA 63 MA 67. Cuddesdon Coll 64. **d** 66 **p** 67. C Brighouse *Wakef* 66-71; V Heptonstall 71-82; V Todmorden 82-07; P-in-c Cross Stone 83-93; RD Calder Valley 84-06; Hon Can Wakef Cathl 92-07; rtd 07; P-in-c Leven Valley *Carl* 07-11; TV Cartmel Peninsula 12-15; Chapl to The Queen 98-11. *26 Stonemere Avenue, Todmorden OL14 5RW* E: pncalvert@btinternet.com

CALVERT, Philip. b 62. St Steph Ho Ox 00. **d** 02 **p** 03. C Holbrooks *Cov* 02-06; P-in-c Kingstanding St Mark *Birm* 06-10; V from 10; AD Handsworth from 14. *St Mark's Clergy House, Bandywood Crescent, Birmingham B44 9JX* T: 0121-360 7288 M: 07969-362577 E: frphilipcalvert@aol.com

CALVIN, Alison Noeleen. Ulster Univ BA QUB BTh PGCE. CITC. **d** 09 **p** 10. Bp's C Killeshandra w Killegar and Derrylane *K, E & A* 09-12; I from 12. *The Rectory, Killeshandra, Co Cavan, Republic of Ireland* T: (00353) (49) 433 4307 E: alisoncalvin@gmail.com *or* killeshandra@kilmore.anglican.org

CALVIN-THOMAS, David Nigel. b 43. Univ of Wales (Cardiff) BSc 64 Lon Univ BD 77. St Mich Coll Llan 77. **d** 78 **p** 79. C Pontypridd St Cath *Llan* 78-80; Malawi 81-84; V Rastrick St Matt *Wakef* 84-88; V Birchencliffe 88-93; Chapl Huddersfield R Infirmary 88-93; R Aberdeen St Pet *Ab* 93-01; P-in-c Cove Bay 93-01; TV Glenrothes *St And* 01-07; R 07-09; R Leven and Lochgelly 07-09; rtd 09. *2 Ruthin Way, Tonteg, Pontypridd CF38 1TF* T: (01443) 203633 E: davidcalvinthomas@btinternet.com

CAM, Julian Howard. b 48. York Univ BA 69 Man Univ MA 99. Qu Coll Birm 73. **d** 75 **p** 76. C St Ives *Truro* 75-80; C Lelant 78-80; V Flookburgh *Carl* 80-82; V St Stephen by Saltash *Truro* 82-83; V Low Marple *Ches* 83-08; rtd 08; PtO *Ches* from 08; *Derby* from 08; *Man* from 15. *14 High Lea Road, New Mills, High Peak SK22 3DP* T: (01663) 744065 E: julian.angela.cam08@btinternet.com

CAMBER, Mrs Victoria Clare. b 69. Man Univ BA 91 Leeds Univ BA 10. Yorks Min Course 07. **d** 10 **p** 11. C Wales *Sheff* 10-12; C Todwick 12-13; P-in-c from 13. *The Rectory, 15 Rectory Gardens, Todwick, Sheffield S26 1JU* T: (01909) 771101 E: vicky_camber@yahoo.co.uk

CAMBRIDGE, Benedict Howard. b 73. Westmr Coll Ox BTh 95. Cranmer Hall Dur 99. **d** 01 **p** 02. C Chilwell *S'well* 01-05; Sen Chapl Staffs Univ *Lich* 05-12; TV Littleham w Exmouth *Ex* 12-13; C Lympstone and Woodbury w Exton 12-13; TV Littleham-cum-Exmouth w Lympstone from 13. *The Vicarage, 96 Littleham Road, Exmouth EX8 2RD* M: 07535-480077 E: rev.benedict@btinternet.com

CAMBRIDGE, Archdeacon of. *See* HUGHES, The Ven Alexander James

✠**CAMERON, The Rt Revd Andrew Bruce.** b 41. Edin Th Coll 61. **d** 64 **p** 65 **c** 92. C Helensburgh *Glas* 64-67; C Edin H Cross 67-71; Prov and Dioc Youth Chapl 69-75; Chapl St Mary's Cathl 71-75; R Dalmahoy 75-82; Chapl Heriot-Watt Univ 75-82; TV Livingston LEP 82-88; R Perth St Jo *St And*

88-92; Convener Prov Miss Bd 88-92; Bp Ab 92-06; Primus 00-06; rtd 06; LtO *St And* from 07. *2 Newbigging Grange, Coupar Angus, Blairgowrie PH13 9GA* T: (01821) 650482 M: 07715-323119 E: bruce2541@gmail.com

CAMERON, David Alan. b 59. Glas Univ MA 81 DipEd 82 PGCE 82. Ripon Coll Cuddesdon 88. **d** 91 **p** 92. C Farncombe *Guildf* 91-93; C Guildf H Trin w St Mary 93-96; V Fenton *Lich* 96-15; R Forfar *St And* from 15. *Address temp unknown*

CAMERON, David Alexander. b 42. Reading Univ BA 63 MRTPI. St And Dioc Tr Course 80. **d** 90 **p** 93. NSM Blairgowrie *St And* from 90; NSM Coupar Angus from 90; NSM Alyth from 90. *Firgrove, Golf Course Road, Blairgowrie PH10 6LF* T: (01250) 873272 *or* 874583 E: dacameron@talk21.com

✠**CAMERON, The Rt Revd Douglas MacLean.** b 35. Edin Th Coll 59. **d** 62 **p** 63 **c** 93. C Falkirk *Edin* 62-65; Miss P Eiwo Papua New Guinea 66-67; Miss P Movi 67-72; R Goroka and Adn New Guinea Mainland 72-74; P-in-c Edin St Fillan 74-78; R 78-88; R Edin St Hilda 77-88; R Dalkeith 87-92; R Lasswade 88-92; Can St Mary's Cathl 90-91; Syn Clerk 90-91; Dean Edin 91-92; Bp Arg 93-03; rtd 03; LtO *Edin* from 04. *23 Craigs Way, Rumford, Falkirk FK2 0EU* T: (01324) 714137

✠**CAMERON, The Rt Revd Gregory Kenneth.** b 59. Linc Coll Ox BA 80 MA 84 Down Coll Cam BA 82 MA 85 Univ of Wales (Cardiff) MPhil 92 LLM 95. St Mich Coll Llan 82. **d** 83 **p** 84 **c** 09. C Newport St Paul *Mon* 83-86; Tutor St Mich Coll Llan 86-89; C Llanmartin *Mon* 86-87; TV 87-88; Chapl Wycliffe Coll Glos 88-94; Dir Bloxham Project 94-00; Research Fell Cardiff Univ Cen for Law and Relig 98-00; Chapl to Abp Wales 00-03; Dir Ecum Relns ACC 03-04; Dep Sec 04-09; Hon Can St Woolos Cathl 03-09; Bp St As from 09. *Esgobty, St Asaph LL17 0TW* T: (01745) 583503 E: bishop.stasaph@churchinwales.org.uk

CAMERON, Mrs Janice Irene. b 43. Reading Univ BA. TISEC 93. **d** 96 **p** 96. C Blairgowrie *St And* 96-98; C Coupar Angus 96-98; C Alyth 96-98; R Dunblane 99-08; Can St Ninian's Cathl Perth 05-08; rtd 08; LtO *St And* from 08; Hon C Alyth from 10. *Firgrove, Golf Course Road, Blairgowrie PH10 6LF* T: (01250) 873272 E: janicecameron@freeola.net

CAMERON, Mrs Laura Bluebell. b 55. SRN 77. STETS 10. **d** 13 **p** 14. NSM Shedfield and Wickham *Portsm* from 13. *Wentworth, Heath Road, Wickham, Fareham PO17 6LA* T: (01329) 830145 M: 07562-217104 E: revdlauracameron@gmail.com

CAMERON, Preb Margaret Mary. b 48. Qu Mary Coll Lon BA 69 Ex Univ MA 95. SWMTC 87. **d** 90 **p** 94. NSM Budleigh Salterton *Ex* 90-95; C Whipton 95-97; R Hemyock w Culm Davy, Clayhidon and Culmstock 97-03; RD Cullompton 99-03; V Plympton St Mary 03-13; Preb Ex Cathl 05-13; rtd 13. *Belair, 9 Cyprus Road, Exmouth EX8 2DZ* T: (01395) 223395 E: margaretcameron271@btinternet.com

CAMERON, Michael John. b 41. Linc Th Coll 91. **d** 92 **p** 93. C Dinnington *Sheff* 92-96; V Beighton 96-06; AD Attercliffe 99-02; rtd 07. *17 Western Street, Barnsley S70 2BP* T: (01226) 249573

CAMERON, Ms Monica Eunice. b 58. ERMC 12. **d** 15. C Gt Shelford *Ely* from 15. *16 Chelwood Road, Cambridge CB1 9LX* T: (01223) 779728 E: monica-cameron@sky.com

CAMERON, Peter Scott. b 45. Edin Univ LLB 67 BD 76 Cam Univ PhD 79 LRAM 64. **d** 97 **p** 97. C Perth St Jo *St And* 97-98; R Dunkeld 98-04; R Strathtay 98-04; rtd 04. *Hope Cottage, Strathtay, Pithlochry PH9 0PG* T/F: (01887) 840212

CAMERON, Ms Sheila. b 34. TCert 54. Gilmore Ho 65. **d** 98 **p** 99. NSM Catford St Laur *S'wark* 98-02; PtO from 02. *52 Engleheart Road, London SE6 2HW* T: (020) 8698 9282 *or* 8698 9706 E: sheilacameron@rocketmail.com

CAMERON, Sheila Helen MacLeod. b 46. St Andr Univ MA 68 Stirling Univ MLitt 83 St Andr Univ MLitt 15 Cam Univ MA 96 Anglia Ruskin Univ MA 06. ERMC 04. **d** 06 **p** 07. NSM Cherry Hinton St Andr *Ely* 06-07; NSM Chesterton St Geo 07-09; P-in-c Dunbar *Edin* 09-12; NSM Lasswade and Dalkeith 12-13; NSM N Tyne and Redesdale *Newc* from 13. *7 Redesmouth Court, Bellingham, Hexham NE48 2ES* T: (01434) 220900 M: 07432-504308 E: shmcameron@btinternet.com

CAMERON, Thomas Edward. b 46. d 06. NSM St Paul's Cathl 06-11; NSM Clayton w Keymer *Chich* from 11. *11 The Spinney, Hassocks BN6 8EJ* T: (01273) 846274 E: tomecam1@aol.com

CAMERON, William Hugh Macpherson. b 59. Edin Univ LLB 82 BD 86. Edin Th Coll 83. **d** 86 **p** 87. C Cheadle Hulme All SS *Ches* 86-89; Asst Chapl and Hd RS Wellington Coll Berks 89-93; Chapl K Sch Bruton 93-00; PtO *Chich* from 01. *Cranesden, West Street, Mayfield TN20 6DS* T: (01435) 872991

CAMINER, Mrs Miriam. b 54. Lanc Univ BA 77. Ox Min Course 09. **d** 11 **p** 12. NSM Old Windsor *Ox* 11-13; PtO from 13. *9 The Grange, Old Windsor, Windsor SL4 2PS*

CAMMIDGE, Jacqueline. d 15. NSM Hampton Hill *Lon* from 15. *Address temp unknown*

CAMP, Mrs Carole Ann. b 48. Qu Coll Birm. d 08 p 09. NSM Chelmsley Wood *Birm* 08-13; rtd 13; PtO *St Alb* from 14. *19 Fouracres Walk, Hemel Hempstead HP3 9LB* M: 07762-564426 E: revcarolecamp@gmail.com

CAMP, Lin. b 47. Loughb Univ MA 07. SNWTP 07. d 10 p 11. OLM Ormskirk *Liv* from 10. *9 Whiterails Drive, Ormskirk L39 3BE* T: (01695) 574152 E: lin.camp@mypostoffice.co.uk

CAMP, Michael Maurice. b 52. Southn Univ BTh 83 K Coll Lon MA 99 Brentwood Coll of Educn CertEd 73. Sarum & Wells Th Coll 78. d 81 p 82. C Loughton *St Jo Chelmsf* 81-84; C Chingford SS Pet and Paul 84-87; V Northfleet *Roch* 87-94; V Hadlow 94-01; RD Paddock Wood 99-01; V Bromley SS Pet and Paul 01-12; AD Bromley 06-11; Hon Can Roch Cathl 11-13; Abp's Chapl *Cant* 12-13; Hon C Stockwell St Andr and St Mich *S'wark* 12-13; R Parkstone St Pet and St Osmund w Branksea *Sarum* from 13. *The Rectory, 19 Springfield Road, Poole BH14 0LG* T: (01202) 801802 M: 07734-424996 E: rector@stpetersparkstone.org.uk

CAMPBELL, Andrew Philip. b 82. QUB BA MTh. d 12 p 13. C Belfast St Anne *Conn* 12-13; C Bangor Abbey *D & D* from 13. *9 Pinehill Crescent, Bangor BT19 6SF* T: (02891) 477182 E: acampbell31@qub.ac.uk

CAMPBELL, Mrs Brenda. b 47. St Jo Coll Nottm 92. d 94 p 95. C Rothley *Leic* 94-97; C Market Bosworth, Cadeby w Sutton Cheney etc 97-00; TV Bosworth and Sheepy Gp 00-07; rtd 07; PtO *Leic* from 13. *28 Ashfield Drive, Moira, Swadlincote DE12 6HQ* T: (01530) 413534 E: brendajones101@sky.com *or* brendajones101@tiscali.co.uk

CAMPBELL, David. b 70. St Andr Univ MTheol 92 New Coll Edin MTh 94. Edin Th Coll 92. d 94 p 95. C Perth St Jo *St And* 94-96; P-in-c Tayport and Newport-on-Tay 96-99; R Dunfermline 99-07; Dioc Youth Officer 96-07; Chapl Fettes Coll Edin 07-12; Chapl Marlborough Coll from 12. *Marlborough College, Bath Road, Marlborough SN8 1PA* T: (01672) 514557 M: 07786-353619 E: frdavid.campbell@btinternet.com

CAMPBELL, Miss Elizabeth Hume. b 53. Glas Univ MA 74 Hamilton Coll of Educn TCert 75. St Jo Coll Nottm 01. d 02 p 03. NSM Alstonfield, Butterton, Ilam etc *Lich* 02-08; NSM Stonehaven and Catterline *Bre* 08-10; P-in-c Dundee St Luke 10-12; Chapl Grampian Univ Hosp NHS Trust 12-13; NSM Muchalls, Stonehaven and Catterline *Bre* 12-15; P-in-c S Shields St Simon *Dur* from 15; C Jarrow from 15. *St Simon's Vicarage, 134 Wenlock Road, South Shields NE34 9AL* M: 07809-830556 T: 0191-454 8834 E: lizziecampbell@o2.co.uk

CAMPBELL, George St Clair. b 32. Lon Univ BSc 53. Clifton Th Coll 58. d 60 p 61. C Tunbridge Wells St Pet *Roch* 60-64; C Clitheroe St Jas *Blackb* 64-70; V Tibshelf *Derby* 70-86; V W Bromwich H Trin *Lich* 86-97; Chapl Heath Lane Hosp 87-97; rtd 97; PtO *Guildf* from 98. *2 Doreen Close, Farnborough GU14 9HB* T: (01276) 31639

CAMPBELL, Mrs Hilary Anne. b 58. UMIST BSc 80. SAOMC. d 01 p 02. C Goring w S Stoke *Ox* 01-05; TV Kidlington w Hampton Poyle 05-13; V Shires' Edge from 13; AD Deddington from 15. *The Vicarage, High Street, Cropredy, Banbury OX17 1NG* T: (01295) 750385 E: vicar@thecampbells.demon.co.uk

CAMPBELL, Ian George. b 47. FRICS 74 FBEng 93. SEITE 96. d 99 p 00. NSM Chilham w Challock and Molash *Cant* 99-01; P-in-c Crundale w Godmersham 01-12; NSM King's Wood 12-14; C A20 Benefice from 14. *The Rectory, Bower Road, Mersham, Ashford TN25 6NN* T: (01233) 501039 E: ian@godmersham.com

CAMPBELL, James Duncan. b 55. Qu Eliz Coll Lon BSc 77 Oak Hill Th Coll MA 00. Cranmer Hall Dur 85 Oak Hill Th Coll MA 00. d 87 p 88. C Hendon St Paul Mill Hill *Lon* 87-92; V Stevenage St Hugh and St Jo *St Alb* 92-13; RD Stevenage 11-13; V Watford Ch Ch from 13. *Christ Church Vicarage, Leggatts Way, Watford WD24 5NQ* T: (01923) 674142

CAMPBELL, James Larry. b 46. Indiana Univ BSc 69 E Kentucky Univ MA 73 Hull Univ MA 91. Linc Th Coll 86. d 88 p 89. C N Hull St Mich *York* 88-92; C Hessle 92-95; V Burton Pidsea and Humbleton w Elsternwick 95-12; rtd 12. *The Mullburys, Bardney Road, Wragby, Market Rasen LN8 5QZ* T: (01673) 857646 E: campbell822@aol.com

CAMPBELL, James Malcolm. b 55. MRICS 81. Wycliffe Hall Ox 89. d 91 p 92. C Scole, Brockdish, Billingford, Thorpe Abbots etc *Nor* 91-95; R Bentley and Binsted *Win* 95-08; RD Alton 02-08; Hon Can Win Cathl 08; R The Lavingtons, Cheverells, and Easterton *Sarum* from 08. *The Vicarage, 14 Church Street, Market Lavington, Devizes SN10 4DT* E: lavingtonrector@gmail.com

CAMPBELL, Canon James Norman Thompson. b 49. BTh MA. d 86 p 87. C Arm St Mark w Aghavilly 86-89; I Belfast H Trin and Ardoyne *Conn* 89-95; I Dundela St Mark *D & D* 95-01; I Portadown St Mark *Arm* 01-15; Can Arm Cathl 09-15; rtd 15. *Address temp unknown* E: j.campbell147@btinternet.com

CAMPBELL, Jane Judith. *See* BAKKER, Jane Judith

CAMPBELL, Kenneth Scott. b 47. BA 82. Oak Hill Th Coll. d 82 p 83. C Aughton St Mich *Liv* 82-85; V Brough w Stainmore Carl 85-90; R Brough w Stainmore, Musgrave and Warcop 90-92; rtd 92. *4 Quarry Close, Kirkby Stephen CA17 4SS* T: (01768) 372390

CAMPBELL, Kenneth William. b 66. Oak Hill Th Coll. d 10 p 11. C Leyland St Andr *Blackb* 10-13; PtO *Ox* from 13; R Chinnor, Sydenham, Aston Rowant and Crowell from 14. *32 Stile Road, Headington, Oxford OX3 8AQ* E: kencampbell66@gmail.com

CAMPBELL, Lerys William. b 85. Win Univ BA 06. Trin Coll Bris MA 14. d 14 p 15. C Ringwood *Win* from 14. *3 Waterside Close, Ringwood BH24 1SB* M: 07952-303970 T: (01425) 291945 E: revlerys@gmail.com

CAMPBELL, Mrs Margaret Ruth. b 62. Trin Coll Bris BA 02. d 02 p 03. C Yeovil w Kingston Pitney *B & W* 02-06; TV Wellington and Distr 06-11; R Backwell w Chelvey and Brockley from 11. *The Rectory, 72 Church Lane, Backwell, Bristol BS48 3JJ* T: (01275) 462391 E: jmbt2001@hotmail.com

CAMPBELL, Patrick Alistair. b 36. Qu Coll Birm 64. d 67 p 68. C Paston *Pet* 67-71; C Stockton Heath *Ches* 71-73; V Egremont St Jo 73-78; V Bredbury St Mark 78-85; R Astbury and Smallwood 85-91; V Wybunbury w Doddington 91-97; rtd 97; PtO *Ches* from 97; Warden Coll of St Barn Lingfield 01-07. *8 Brookside, Crawley Down, Crawley RH10 4UU* T: (01342) 713667

CAMPBELL, Robin William. b 41. TCD BA 63 MA 67. Ridley Hall Cam 63. d 65 p 66. C Netherton *Liv* 65-68; C Liv Our Lady and St Nic w St Anne 68-70; V Hooton *Ches* 70-99; rtd 99. *77 Seaview Parade, Lakes Entrance Vic 3909, Australia* T: (0061) (3) 5155 2157

CAMPBELL, Roger Stewart. b 40. Birm Univ BSc 61 PhD 65 St Jo Coll Dur BA 71. Cranmer Hall Dur 68. d 71 p 72. C Jesmond Clayton Memorial *Newc* 71-77; V St Jo and St Marg Singapore 78-85; C Nottingham St Nic *S'well* 86-90; V Holloway St Mark w Em *Lon* 90-92; TR Tollington 92-97; Chapl Leeds Teaching Hosps NHS Trust 97-04; rtd 04; PtO *Carl* from 05. *Redesdale Cottage, Lazonby, Penrith CA10 1AJ* T: (01768) 870695

CAMPBELL, Stephen James. b 60. TCD BTh 91. CITC 88. d 91 p 92. C Lisburn Ch Ch *Conn* 91-95; I Kilcronaghan w Draperstown and Sixtowns *D & R* 95-00; I Dunluce *Conn* 00-03; PtO *Eur* from 04. *94A Mountsandel Road, Coleraine BT52 1TA* E: sjmimc@yahoo.com

CAMPBELL, Stephen Lloyd. b 46. St Andr Univ LLB 67 Solicitor 72. SEITE 95. d 98 p 99. NSM Quantoxhead *B & W* 98-07; NSM Quantock Coast from 07; RD Quantock 06-12. *Hodderscombe Lodge, Holford, Bridgwater TA5 1SA* T/F: (01278) 741329 M: 07808-967046 E: stephencampbell0@tiscali.co.uk

CAMPBELL-SMITH, Robert Campbell. b 38. CCC Cam BA 61 MA 66 Ibadan Univ Nigeria 62. Linc Th Coll 61. d 63 p 64. C Norbury St Steph *Cant* 63-66; C W Wickham St Mary 66-71; Ind Chapl 65-76; V Croydon St Aug 71-81; Acting RD Croydon Cen 77-81; Spiritual Development Adv Nat Assn of Boys' Clubs 77-89; V Goudhurst *Cant* 81-87; Chapl Kent Assn of Boys' Clubs 81-97; RD W Charing *Cant* 82-89; P-in-c Kilndown 83-87; V Goudhurst w Kilndown 87-99; Hon Can Cant Cathl 94-99; Chapl Kent Youth Trust 97-99; TR Modbury, Bigbury, Ringmore w Kingston etc *Ex* 99-04; rtd 04. *Even Keel, Pillory Hill, Noss Mayo, Plymouth PL8 1ED* T: (01752) 872559

CAMPBELL-SMYTH, Jonathan. d 11 p 12. C Coleraine *Conn* 11-13; C Jordanstown from 13. *9 Lenamore Avenue, Newtown-abbey BT37 0PF* T: (028) 9086 0471 M: 07808-479649

CAMPBELL-TAYLOR, William Goodacre. b 65. Ox Univ BA 87 Cam Univ BA 93 MA 95 Princeton Th Sem DMin 11. Westcott Ho Cam 90. d 94 p 95. C Chingford SS Pet and Paul *Chelmsf* 94-97; Chapl Lon Guildhall Univ 97-02; Chapl Lon Metrop Univ 02-04; Research Fell St Ethelburga's Cen for Reconciliation and Peace 05-08; Hon C Hoxton St Anne w St Columba *Lon* 05-09; V Stamford Hill St Thos from 09; P-in-c Upper Clapton St Matt from 14. *The Vicarage, 1 Clapton Terrace, London E5 9BW* T: (020) 8806 1463 E: fatherwilliamtaylor@hotmail.com

CAMPBELL-WILSON, Allan. b 43. Dur Univ BEd 74. NEOC 79. d 82 p 83. NSM Boosbeck w Moorsholm *York* 82-85; R Easington w Skeffling, Kilnsea and Holmpton 85-87; P-in-c Middlesbrough St Jo the Ev 89-95; V 95-99; V Cayton w Eastfield 99-12; rtd 12; PtO *York* from 12. *51 Oak Road, Scarborough YO12 4AP* T: (01723) 362426 E: campbellwilson165@btinternet.com

CAMPEN, William Geoffrey. b 50. Liv Univ CertEd 71 Southn Univ BTh 81 Lon Univ MA 08. Sarum & Wells Th Coll 76. d 79 p 80. C Peckham St Jo w St Andr *S'wark* 79-83; P-in-c

Mottingham St Edw 83-92; R Charlwood from 92; R Sidlow Bridge from 92. *The Rectory, The Street, Charlwood, Horley RH6 0EE* T: (01293) 862343 E: w.g.campen@bigfoot.com

CAMPION, Keith Donald. b 52. S Dios Minl Tr Scheme. **d** 84 **p** 87. NSM Is of Scilly *Truro* 84-96. *20 Launceston Close, St Mary's TR21 0LN* T: (01720) 422606

CAMPION (formerly HOUSEMAN), Mrs Patricia Adele. b 39. St Mich Coll Llan. **d** 93 **p** 97. C St Issell's and Amroth *St D* 93-95; C Llanegryn w Aberdyfi w Tywyn *Ban* 95-97; rtd 97. *3 Mariners Reach, The Strand, Saundersfoot SA69 9EX* T: (01834) 811047

CAMPION, Canon Peter Robert. b 64. Bp's Univ Canada BA 87 TCD BTh 90 MA 93 MPhil 97 Homerton Coll Cam PGCE 94. **d** 90 **p** 91. C Belfast H Trin and Ardoyne *Conn* 90-93; C Taney *D & G* 94-00; Dean's V St Patr Cathl Dublin 96-00; Chapl Netherwood Sch Rothesay Canada 00-05; Chapl K Hosp Sch Dub from 05; Treas V St Patr Cathl Dublin 05-11; Prec Ch Ch Cathl Dublin from 08. *The King's Hospital, Palmerstown, Dublin 20, Republic of Ireland* T: (00353) (1) 626 5933 F: 623 0349

CAMPION-SPALL, Ms Kathryn May. b 79. York Univ BA 02 Fitzw Coll Cam BA 09. Westcott Ho Cam 07. **d** 10 **p** 11. C Merton St Mary *S'wark* 10-14; C Bris St Mary Redcliffe w Temple etc from 14. *2 Colston Parade, Bristol BS1 6RA* T: 0117-929 1519 M: 07960-588015 or 929 1605 E: kat.campion-spall@stmaryredcliffe.co.uk

CAMPLING, Camilla Anne. *See* CAMPLING-DENTON, Camilla Anne

CAMPLING, The Very Revd Christopher Russell. b 25. St Edm Hall Ox BA 50 MA 54. Cuddesdon Coll 50. **d** 51 **p** 52. C Basingstoke *Win* 51-55; Chapl Lancing Coll 60-68; P-in-c Birlingham w Nafford *Worc* 68-75; V Pershore w Wick 68-75; V Pershore w Pinvin, Wick and Birlingham 75-76; RD Pershore 70-76; Hon Can Worc Cathl 74-84; Dioc Dir of Educn 76-84; Adn Dudley 76-84; P-in-c Dodderhill 76-84; Dean Ripon 84-95; Chmn CCC 88-94; rtd 95; PtO *Chich* from 95. *Pebble Ridge, Aglaia Road, Worthing BN11 5SW* T: (01903) 246598

CAMPLING, Doreen Elizabeth. b 31. K Coll Lon BSc 55. **d** 01 **p** 02. OLM Bridport *Sarum* 01-08. *Harbour Lights, Coneygar Park, Bridport DT6 3BA* T: (01308) 425670

CAMPLING, Michael. b 27. Trin Coll Cam BA 50 MA 61. Wells Th Coll 51. **d** 53 **p** 54. C Calne *Sarum* 53-57; C Roehampton H Trin *S'wark* 57-61; V Crowthorne *Ox* 61-75; P-in-c Foleshill St Laur *Cov* 75-81; V 81-83; R Old Alresford and Bighton *Win* 83-92; rtd 92; Chapl St Marg Convent E Grinstead 92-99; Hon C Bexhill St Pet *Chich* 99-05. *9 Orchard Grove, Bloxham, Banbury OX15 4NZ* T: (01295) 721599

CAMPLING-DENTON, Camilla Anne. b 76. St Andr Univ MA 98 Jes Coll Cam MPhil 04. Westcott Ho Cam 02. **d** 05 **p** 06. C Fountains Gp *Ripon* 05-07; C Caerleon w Llanhennock *Mon* 07-09; C Caerleon and Llanfrechfa 09-10; Hon C Washburn and Mid-Wharfe *Leeds* 12-14; R Walkingham Hill from 14. *The Rectory, Main Street, Staveley, Knaresborough HG5 9LD* M: 07817-386070 E: camilla.cd@cantab.net or milly@c-d.eclipse.co.uk

CAMPOS DE SANTANA, Levy Henrique. b 85. **d** 13 **p** 14. C High Wycombe *Ox* from 13. *175 Dashwood Avenue, High Wycombe HP12 3DB* T: (01494) 474996 M: 07950-212347 E: levysantana@me.com

CANADA, Primate of. *See* HUTCHISON, The Most Revd Andrew Sandford

CANBERRA AND GOULBURN, Bishop of. *See* ROBINSON, Stuart Peter

CANDELAND, Thomas Blyde. b 37. **d** 99 **p** 00. OLM Lyng, Sparham, Elsing, Bylaugh, Bawdeswell etc *Nor* 99-08; RD Sparham 05-08; PtO from 08. *2 Hammond Place, Lyng, Norwich NR9 5RQ* T: (01603) 871674

CANDOW, Brian Gordon. b 58. Memorial Univ Newfoundland BComm 82 BEd 83. Qu Th Coll Newfoundland MDiv 89. **d** 89 **p** 89. C Fogo Is Canada 89-91; R Botwood 91-95; R Summerside and St Eleanor 00-04; Hon C Skirbeck Quarter *Linc* 04-05; Assoc P Gander Canada from 05. *2 Lindberg Road, Gander NL A1V 2E7, Canada* T: (001) (709) 256 3700 E: candows@bostonengland.freeserve.co.uk

CANDY, Julia Elaine. b 80. K Coll Cam BA 01 QUB PhD 06 Jes Coll Cam BA 09. Westcott Ho Cam 07. **d** 10 **p** 11. C Dur St Giles 10-13; C Shadforth and Sherburn 10-13; P-in-c Aberdeen St Jas *Ab* 13; P-in-c Aberdeen St Clem 13; Asst Chapl Univ Coll Lon Hosps NHS Foundn Trust from 14. *University College London Hospitals, 250 Euston Road, London NW1 2PG* T: (020) 3456 7890 E: jec1492@hotmail.com

CANE, Canon Anthony William Nicholas Strephon. b 61. Cape Town Univ BA 81 Birm Univ MPhil 93 PhD 03. Westcott Ho Cam 87. **d** 90 **p** 91. C Kings Heath *Birm* 90-93; Chapl Brighton Univ *Chich* 93-99; P-in-c Torquay St Luke *Ex* 99-01; Dioc Adv in Adult Tr 99-01; C Ringmer and Dioc Adv for Educn and Tr of Adults *Chich* 01-07; Can Res and Chan Chich Cathl from

07. *The Residentiary, 2 Canon Lane, Chichester PO19 1PX* T: (01243) 813594 E: chancellor@chichestercathedral.org.uk

CANE, Geoffrey Brett Salkeld. **d** 80. Canada 80-12; Lect Trin Coll Bris 12-15; Canada from 14.

CANESSA, Jonathan. b 70. Ox Brookes Univ BA 02. Westcott Ho Cam 11. **d** 13 **p** 14. C Cambridge St Paul *Ely* from 13. *31 Thornton Close, Girton, Cambridge CB3 0NF* T: (01223) 576899 E: curate@centrestpauls.org.uk or joncanessa@gmail.com

CANEY, Canon Robert Swinbank. b 37. St Jo Coll Cam 57. Lich Th Coll 58. **d** 61 **p** 62. C Kingswinford H Trin *Lich* 61-64; C Castle Church 64-67; V Bradwell *Derby* 67-73; V Fairfield 73-84; RD Buxton 78-84; P-in-c Peak Forest and Wormhill 79-83; R Wirksworth w Alderwasley, Carsington etc 84-92; TR Wirksworth 92-02; Hon Can Derby Cathl 93-02; rtd 02; PtO *Derby* from 02. *2 Erica Drive, South Normanton, Alfreton DE55 2ET* T: (01773) 581106 E: randjcaney@gmail.com

CANHAM, Frances Elizabeth. b 55. MCIPD 93. St Mich Coll Llan 05. **d** 07 **p** 08. NSM Thanington *Cant* 07-10; Asst Chapl Salisbury NHS Foundn Trust 10-13; Chapl from 13. *Chaplain's Office, Salisbury District Hospital, Salisbury SP2 8BJ* T: (01258) 489331 E: frances.canham@cox.net

CANHAM, John Graham. b 33. Univ of Wales (Lamp) BA 55. Chich Th Coll 55. **d** 57 **p** 58. C Hawarden *St As* 57-64; Asst Chapl Ellesmere Coll 64-66; Chapl Ches Cathl Choir Sch 66-73; Chapl Choral Ches Cathl 66-73; Asst Chapl Rossall Sch Fleetwood 73-76 and 83-93; Chapl 76-83; V Minera *St As* 93-05; V Bwlchgwyn and Minera 05-08; AD Minera 01-08; rtd 08; PtO *St As* from 10. *2 Parkers Close, Wrexham LL11 2RR* T: (01978) 291166

CANNAM, Martin Stafford John. b 68. Jes Coll Ox BA 90 MA 95. Wycliffe Hall Ox 93. **d** 96 **p** 97. C Childwall All SS *Liv* 96-00; V Biddulph *Lich* from 00; RD Leek from 13. *The Vicarage, 7 Wrexham Close, Biddulph, Stoke-on-Trent ST8 6RZ* T: (01782) 513247 or 513891 E: martin@cannam.fsnet.co.uk

CANNELL, Anthea Marjorie. b 45. UEA MA 85. EAMTC 01. **d** 02 **p** 03. NSM Theydon Bois *Chelmsf* 02-10; P-in-c Roydon 10-15; rtd 15. *118 High Street, Roydon, Harlow CM19 5EF* T: (01279) 792543 E: amcannell@btinternet.com

CANNING, Canon Arthur James. b 45. St Jo Coll Dur BA 66 Linacre Coll Ox BA 70 MA 74 Lambeth STh 90. Ripon Hall Ox 67. **d** 71 **p** 72. C Coleshill *Birm* 71-74; C Frome St Jo *B & W* 75-76; V Frizington and Arlecdon *Carl* 76-80; P-in-c Foleshill St Paul *Cov* 80-81; V 81-12; Hon Can Cov Cathl 00-12; rtd 12; PtO *Cov* from 12. *13 Broadlands Close, Coventry CV5 7AJ* T: (024) 7671 3220 E: jcxwx@aol.com

CANNING, Peter Christopher. b 52. Birm Poly CQSW. St Jo Coll Nottm 87. **d** 89 **p** 90. C Cov St Mary 89-93; V Hartshill 93-96; rtd 96. *11 Thackeray Close, Galley Common, Nuneaton CV10 9RT* T: (024) 7639 8828

CANNINGS, Karen Rachel. *See* SKIDMORE, Karen Rachel

CANNON, Elizabeth Mary. b 50. EAMTC 94. **d** 97 **p** 98. NSM New Catton Ch Ch *Nor* 97-00; P-in-c Cross Roads cum Lees *Bradf* 00-06; TV Blyth Valley *St E* 06-15; rtd 15. *The Vicarage, Beccles Road, Holton, Halesworth IP19 8NG* T: (01986) 874548

CANNON, Mark Harrison. b 60. Keble Coll Ox BA 82. Cranmer Hall Dur 83. **d** 85 **p** 86. C Skipton Ch Ch *Bradf* 85-88; Dioc Youth Officer 88-92; C Baildon 88-92; P-in-c Church Coniston *Carl* 92-00; P-in-c Torver 92-00; P-in-c Brindle *Blackb* 00-10; Dioc Voc Adv 00-05; NSM E Lonsdale 10-11; P-in-c from 11. *The Rectory, Main Street, Wray, Lancaster LA2 8QF* T: (01524) 221030 E: mhcannon@fsmail.net

CANNON, Ms Rebekah Lindsey. b 77. Man Metrop Univ BA 99 Middx Univ MA 00 PGCE 06 SS Coll Cam BTh 09. Westcott Ho Cam 07. **d** 10 **p** 11. C Whyke w Rumboldswhyke and Portfield *Chich* 10-14; Chapl RAF from 14. *Chaplaincy Services (RAF), HQ Air Command, RAF High Wycombe HP14 4UE* T: (01494) 496800 F: 496343 E: canon@whyke.info

CANNON, Tony Arthur. b 57. Oak Hill Th Coll 94. **d** 96 **p** 97. C Church Stretton *Heref* 96-00; P-in-c Kingham w Churchill, Daylesford and Sarsden *Ox* 00-01; TV Chipping Norton 01-10; V Woking St Jo *Guildf* from 11. *The Vicarage, St John's Hill Road, Woking GU21 7RQ* T: (01483) 761253 E: tonyacannon@virginmedia.com

CANSDALE, George Graham. b 38. Mert Coll Ox BA 60 MA 64 DipEd 61. Clifton Th Coll 62. **d** 64 **p** 65. C Heatherlands St Jo *Sarum* 64-67; BCMS Kenya 68-76; P-in-c Clapham *St Alb* 76-80; V 80-89; Asst Chapl Bedford Sch 89-97; LtO *St Alb* 93-01; PtO *Leeds* from 01; rtd 03. *Serendipity, 4 Brier Hey Lane, Mytholmroyd, Hebden Bridge HX7 5PJ* T: (01422) 706761 E: graham.cansdale@virgin.net

CANSDALE, Michael Cranmer. b 70. Bradf Univ BA 93 St Jo Coll Dur BA 06. Cranmer Hall Dur 04. **d** 06 **p** 07. C Silsden *Bradf* 06-09; P-in-c Riddlesden *Leeds* from 09; P-in-c Morton St Luke from 09. *The Vicarage, St Mary's Road, Riddlesden, Keighley BD20 5PA* T: (01535) 603419 M: 07545-566898 E: mike@stlukesmorton.org.uk

CANSDALE, Philip John. b 73. Keble Coll Ox BA 95 MA 99. Trin Coll Bris BA 98 MA 99. **d** 99 **p** 00. C Cant St Mary Bredin 99-03; C Penn Lich 03-09; V Meole Brace from 09. *The Vicarage, Vicarage Road, Shrewsbury SY3 9EZ* T: (01743) 231744

CANSDALE, Simon James Lee. b 68. Keble Coll Ox BA 90. Wycliffe Hall Ox 93. **d** 95 **p** 96. C Bletchley Ox 95-98; C Cambridge H Trin Ely 98-01; R W Bridgford S'well 01-08; TR Gt Chesham Ox from 08. *The Rectory, Church Street, Chesham HP5 1HY* T/F: (01494) 783629
E: rector@cheshamchurch.co.uk

CANT, Anthony David. b 59. Middx Univ BA 04. NTMTC 01. **d** 04 **p** 05. C Walthamstow Chelmsf 04-07; TV 07-10; Chapl Anglia Ruskin Univ from 10. *4 Bishops Court Gardens, Chelmsford CM2 6AZ* T: (01245) 261700 M: 07980-291940
E: revtonyc@googlemail.com

CANT, Christopher Somerset Travers. b 51. Keble Coll Ox BA 72 MA 76 Ex Univ PGCE 77. All Nations Chr Coll 80 Wycliffe Hall Ox 93. **d** 87 **p** 90. Pakistan 87-92; LtO Cov 92-93; Warden St Clem Family Cen Ox 93-95; C Gt Ilford St Andr Chelmsf 95-98; V Hainault 98-10; rtd 10; C Aylesbeare, Clyst St George, Clyst St Mary etc Ex from 11. *15 Stoneborough Lane, Budleigh Salterton EX9 6HL* T: (01395) 488178
E: chriscant@tiscali.co.uk

CANT, David Edward. b 49. Sheff Univ LLB 70. Oak Hill Th Coll 87. **d** 89 **p** 90. C Newburn Newc 89-92; C N Shields 92-93; TV 93-98; Chapl Tynemouth Coll 94-98; P-in-c Wylam Newc 98-11; Dioc Ecum Officer 08-11; rtd 11. *17 Farrier's Rise, Shilbottle, Alnwick NE66 2EN* T: (01665) 575349

CANT, Joseph Clifford. b 72. UEA BA 94 MA 98 DipSW 98 Cam Univ BTh 08. Westcott Ho Cam 06. **d** 08 **p** 09. C Hilton w Marston-on-Dove Derby 08-11; TV Uttoxeter Area Lich from 11. *The Vicarage, Moisty lane, Marchington, Uttoxeter ST14 8JY* M: 07847-125341 E: cant740@btinternet.com

CANT, Miss Sheila Phyllis. b 59. All SS Cen for Miss & Min 13. **d** 15. OLM Denton St Lawr Man from 15. *3 Ashlands Drive, Audenshaw, Manchester M34 5EL* T: 0161-336 1566
E: sheila.cant@btinternet.com

CANTACUZENE, Mrs Mary. b 52. **d** 05 **p** 06. OLM Bures w Assington and Lt Cornard St E 05-13; NSM from 13. *Peartree Barn, Peartree Hill, Mount Bures, Bures CO8 5BA* T: (01787) 227616 F: 227220 M: 07932-033019
E: mary.cantacuzene@gmail.com

CANTERBURY, Archbishop of. See WELBY, The Most Revd and Rt Hon Justin Portal

CANTERBURY, Archdeacon of. See WATSON, The Ven Sheila Anne

CANTERBURY, Dean of. See WILLIS, The Very Revd Robert Andrew

CANTRELL, David Grindon. b 59. Bris Univ BSc 80 Nottm Univ PhD 83 Pemb Coll Cam BA 88. Ridley Hall Cam 86. **d** 89 **p** 90. C Low Harrogate St Mary Ripon 89-90; C Horsforth 90-94; Chapl Nottm Trent Univ S'well 94-97; V Porchester 97-00; Chapl York Univ 00-04; PtO 04-11. *52 Tranby Avenue, York YO10 3NJ* T: (01904) 427146
E: david.cantrell@ukgateway.net

CANTRILL, Mark James. b 67. Lanc Univ BEd 89. St Jo Coll Nottm 00. **d** 02 **p** 03. C Warsop S'well 02-07; TV Retford Area from 07. *Clarborough Vicarage, Church Lane, Clarborough, Retford DN22 9NA* T: (01777) 711530 M: 07985-160694
E: revmark.cantrill@btinternet.com

CANTY, Mrs Katherine Anne. b 52. York Univ BA 74 Coll of Ripon & York St Jo PGCE 75. NOC 05. **d** 07 **p** 08. Asst Chapl HM Pris Altcourse 03-07; Chapl from 07; NSM Gateacre Liv from 07. *HM Prison Altcourse, Higher Lane, Liverpool L9 7LH* T: 0151-522 2000 ext 2395

CAPEL, Luke Thomas. See IRVINE-CAPEL, Luke Thomas

CAPEL-EDWARDS, Maureen. b 38. Southn Univ BSc 60 Reading Univ PhD 69. St Alb Minl Tr Scheme 84. **d** 87 **p** 94. NSM Ware St Mary St Alb 87-90; Chapl Hertf Regional Coll of FE 87-00; NSM Hertford All SS St Alb 90-94; NSM Aspenden and Layston w Buntingford 94-95; NSM Aspenden, Buntingford and Westmill 95-00; P-in-c Ardeley and Cottered w Broadfield and Throcking 00-05; rtd 05; PtO Portsm from 05. *Capeland, High Street, Soberton, Southampton SO32 3PN* T: (01489) 878192 E: capeland@waitrose.com

CAPELIN-JONES, Kevin Stuart. b 73. Huddersfield Univ BMus 96. Oak Hill Th Coll BA 02. **d** 02 **p** 03. C Croglin and Holme Eden and Wetheral w Warwick Carl 02-06; Chapl RAF from 06. *Chaplaincy Services (RAF), HQ Air Command, RAF High Wycombe HP14 4UE* T: (01494) 496800 F: 496343
E: rev.kev@virgin.net

CAPERON, John Philip. b 44. Bris Univ BA 66 Open Univ MPhil 80 Ox Univ MSc 83 Kent Univ MA 99. Ox NSM Course 80. **d** 83 **p** 84. NSM Hook Norton w Gt Rollright, Swerford etc Ox 83-86; NSM Knaresborough Ripon 86-92; Dep Hd St Aid Sch Harrogate 86-92; Hd and Chapl Bennett Memorial Dioc Sch Tunbridge Wells 92-04; rtd 04; PtO Chich 98-03; Hon C Mayfield from 03; Dir Bloxham Project from 06. *Sarum, 5 Twyfords, Beacon Road, Crowborough TN6 1YE* T: (01892) 667207 E: johncaperon@btinternet.com

CAPES, Dennis Robert. b 34. Handsworth Coll Birm 55 Linc Th Coll 65. **d** 64 **p** 65. In Methodist Ch (Sarawak) 59-63; C Lt Coates Linc 64-66; R Miri Malaysia 66-69; V Gosberton Clough Linc 69-71; V Kirton in Holland 71-80; Area Sec USPG Cov, Heref and Worc 80-87; Chapl Copenhagen w Aarhus Eur 87-93; TV Liv Our Lady and St Nic w St Anne 93-99; rtd 99. *35 Hardwick Avenue, Newark NG24 4AW* T: (01636) 672874

CAPIE, Fergus Bernard. b 47. Auckland Univ BA 68 MA 71. Wycliffe Hall Ox BA 77. **d** 77 **p** 78. C Ox St Mich w St Martin and All SS 77-80; Chapl Summer Fields Sch Ox 80-91; Hon C Wolvercote w Summertown Ox 87-91; PtO St E 91; TV E Ham w Upton Park and Forest Gate Chelmsf 91-95; P-in-c Brondesbury St Anne w Kilburn H Trin Lon 95-01; V 01-12; Chapl NW Lon Coll 95-12; rtd 12; P-in-c Bure Valley Nor from 13. *The Beeches, 24 Brook Street, Buxton, Norwich NR10 5HF* M: 07977-740400 T: (01603) 279630
E: ferguscapie@yahoo.co.uk

CAPITANCHIK, Sophie Rebecca. See JELLEY, Sophie Rebecca

CAPLE, Stephen Malcolm. b 55. Chich Th Coll 86. **d** 88 **p** 89. C Newington St Mary S'wark 88-92; V Eltham St Sav 92-97; V Salfords 97-07; P-in-c S Kensington St Aug Lon 07-10; V Whitton St Aug from 10; Dir Evang Kensington Area from 07. *St Augustine's Vicarage, Hospital Bridge Road, Twickenham TW2 6DE* T: (020) 8894 3764
E: stephencaple@blueyonder.co.uk

CAPON, Canon Anthony Charles. b 26. Trin Coll Cam BA 51 MA 55. Wycliffe Coll Toronto BD 65 DD 82 Oak Hill Th Coll 51. **d** 53 **p** 54. C Portman Square St Paul Lon 53-56; Canada from 56; Hon Can Montreal from 78; Prin Montreal Dioc Th Coll 78-91; rtd 91. *5 Loradean Crescent, Kingston ON K7K 6X9, Canada* T: (001) (613) 545 9781
E: acapon@cgocable.net

CAPON, The Very Revd Gerwyn Huw. b 65. Liv Jo Moores Univ BSc 92. St Steph Ho Ox 01. **d** 03 **p** 04. C W Derby St Mary Liv 03-07; Chapl to Abp Wales and Dir of Ords Llan 07-09; P-in-c Bolton-le-Sands Blackb 09-12; Chapl to Abp Wales Llan 12-14; Dean Llan from 14; V Llandaff from 14. *The Deanery, The Cathedral Green, Cardiff CF5 2YF* T: (029) 2056 1545
E: thedean@llandaffcathedral.org.uk

CAPORN, David Richard. b 78. St Jo Coll Cam BA 00 MA 04 ACA 03. Trin Coll Bris MA 13. **d** 13 **p** 14. C Highworth w Sevenhampton and Inglesham etc Bris from 13; C Broad Blunsdon from 13. *14 Brookfield, Highworth, Swindon SN6 7HY* T: (01793) 766243 M: 07900-55390
E: david.caporn@gmail.com

CAPPER, Alan. See CAPPER, William Alan

CAPPER, Mrs Elizabeth Margaret. b 31. St Chris Coll Blackheath 52. dss 79 **d** 87 **p** 94. The Dorothy Kerin Trust Burrswood 79; Whitstable Cant 80-96; Hon Par Dn 87-94; Hon C 94-96; rtd 91. *Brocastle Manor Care Home, Brocastle Estate, Ewenny, Bridgend CF35 5AU* T: (01656) 679120

CAPPER, Mrs Katherine Frances. b 64. Warwick Univ BA 86. SEITE 07. **d** 10 **p** 11. NSM Horley S'wark 10-14; NSM Betchworth and Buckland from 14. *12 Beaufort Close, Reigate RH2 9DG* T: (01737) 217191
E: kate@thecappers.co.uk

CAPPER, Lorraine. **d** 10 **p** 11. C Drumragh w Mountfield D & R from 10. *12 Crevenagh Way, Omagh BT79 0JE* T: (028) 8224 1527 E: lorraine.capper@googlemail.com

CAPPER, Canon Richard. b 49. Leeds Univ BSc 70 Fitzw Coll Cam BA 72 MA 79. Westcott Ho Cam 70. **d** 73 **p** 74. C Wavertree H Trin Liv 73-76; P-in-c Ince St Mary 76-79; V 79-83; V Gt Crosby St Faith 83-97; AD Bootle 89-97; Can Res Wakef Cathl 97-05; Can Res Nor Cathl 05-14; P-in-c Nor St Mary in the Marsh 05-14; rtd 15; PtO Nor from 15. *3 Kingfisher Walk, Loddon, Norwich NR14 6FB* T: (01603) 665210

CAPPER, Canon Robert Melville. b 52. Chu Coll Cam BA 74 MA 80. Wycliffe Hall Ox 74. **d** 77 **p** 78. C Maindee Newport Mon 77-81; TV Aberystwyth St D 81-87; Chapl Univ of Wales (Abth) 81-87; V Malpas Mon 87-00; V Gabalfa Llan from 00; P-in-c Tremorfa St Phil CD from 05; AD Cardiff from 13; Hon Can Llan Cathl from 14. *St Mark's Vicarage, 208 North Road, Gabalfa, Cardiff CF14 3BL* T: (029) 2061 3286

CAPPER, William Alan. QUB BTh. **d** 88 **p** 89. C Dundonald D & D 88-91; C Lisburn Ch Ch Conn 91-94; I Tamlaght O'Crilly Upper w Lower D & R 94-96; I Lack Clogh 03-09; I Lisnaskea from 09. *3 Castlebalfour Road, Lisnaskea, Enniskillen BT92 0LT* T: (028) 6772 2413 or 6772 3977
E: lisnaskea@clogher.anglican.org

CAPPLEMAN, Graham Robert (Sam). b 56. Chelsea Coll Lon BSc 79 Sheff Univ PhD 83. SAOMC 94. **d** 97 **p** 98. NSM Bedf St Mark *St Alb* from 97. *107 Dover Crescent, Bedford MK41 8QR* T: (01234) 266952   F: 402624   M: 07836-784051
E: sam_cappleman@hotmail.com *or* nsm@thisischurch.com

CAPPLEMAN, Mrs Jennifer Margaret. b 53. C F Mott Coll of Educn CertEd 74. SAOMC 97. **d** 00 **p** 01. NSM Bedford St Pet w St Cuth *St Alb* 00-03; C Goldington 03-07; TV Ouzel Valley 07-13; rtd 13; PtO *St Alb* 13-14; NSM Keysoe w Bolnhurst and Lt Staughton from 14. *107 Dover Crescent, Bedford MK41 8QR* T: (01234) 405253   M: 07714-701008
E: jennie.cappleman@btinternet.com

CAPRIELLO (née BUR), Patricia Margaret. b 59. SEITE. **d** 99 **p** 01. C Clapham Team *S'wark* 99-01; C Nunhead St Antony w St Silas 01-03; P-in-c N Woolwich w Silvertown *Chelmsf* 03-12; Ind Chapl 04-12; rtd 12. *2 Deering Close, St Mary's Island, Chatham ME4 3SX* E: stjohnse16@hotmail.co.uk

CAPRON, Canon David Cooper. b 45. Open Univ BA 80. Sarum & Wells Th Coll 71. **d** 75 **p** 76. C Cov St Mary 75-79; V Shottery St Andr 79-86; TV Stratford-on-Avon w Bishopton 79-86; V Shottery St Andr 86; V Newton Aycliffe *Dur* 86-89; TR 89-90; P-in-c Alcester and Arrow w Oversley and Weethley *Cov* 90-95; R 95-12; P-in-c Kinwarton w Gt Alne and Haselor 06-12; P-in-c Coughton 06-12; Hon Can Cov Cathl 07-12; Chapl Warks Fire and Rescue Service 93-09; rtd 13; PtO *Cov* from 13; *Worc* from 13. *19 Holbrook Road, Stratford-upon-Avon CV37 9DZ* T: (01789) 762904   M: 07780-707521
E: canon@caprons.co.uk

CAPRON, Mark Andrew. b 80. Staffs Univ BA 02. Ridley Hall Cam 09. **d** 12 **p** 13. C Pakefield *Nor* from 12; C Carlton Colville and Mutford from 12. *9 Ryedale, Carlton Colville, Lowestoft NR33 8TB* E: revmarkcapron@gmail.com

CAPRON, Ronald Beresford. b 35. Clifton Th Coll. **d** 62 **p** 63. Canada 62-65; C Evington *Leic* 65-67; R Gaddesby w S Croxton 67-71; R Beeby 67-71; Chapl RAF 71-83; rtd 95. *107 Coverside Road, Great Glen, Leicester LE8 9EB* T: 0116-259 2809

CAPSTICK, Mrs Jean Rose. b 43. **d** 09 **p** 10. NSM Sodbury Vale *Glouc* 09-11; NSM Winterbourne *Bris* 12-13; NSM Frenchay and Winterbourne Down 12-13; NSM Frampton Cotterell and Iron Acton 12-13; NSM Coalpit Heath 12-13. *Lerryn, Wotton Road, Rangeworthy, Bristol BS37 7LZ* T: (01454) 228236
E: jean.capstick@homecall.co.uk

CAPSTICK, John Nowell. b 30. AKC 54. **d** 55 **p** 56. C Skipton Ch Ch *Bradf* 55-57; C Buxton *Derby* 57-61; V Codnor and Loscoe 61-63; C-in-c Rawthorpe CD *Wakef* 63-64; V Rawthorpe 64-70; V Netherthong 70-89; V Upper Holme Valley 89-95; rtd 95; PtO *Leeds* from 96. *8 Town End Avenue, Holmfirth HD9 1QW* T: (01484) 688708

CAPSTICK, William Richard Dacre. b 32. Pemb Coll Ox. Chich Th Coll 61. **d** 64 **p** 65. C Hunslet St Mary and Stourton St Andr *Ripon* 64-67; C Knaresborough H Trin 67-71; V Stratfield Mortimer *Ox* 71-76; P-in-c St Marylebone Ch Ch w St Paul *Lon* 76-78; TV St Marylebone Ch Ch 78-79; TR Newbury *Ox* 79-89; TV Brighton St Pet and St Nic w Chpl Royal *Chich* 89-97; rtd 97. *28 Bloomsbury Street, Brighton BN2 1HQ* T: (01273) 681171

CARBERRY, Derek William. b 65. Leeds Univ BA 03 SEN 88. Coll of Resurr Mirfield 01. **d** 03 **p** 04. C Tynemouth Cullercoats St Paul *Newc* 03-08; P-in-c Horton 08-14. *Address temp unknown* E: d.wc@btopenworld.com

CARBERRY, Leon Carter. b 54. Penn State Univ BSc 76. St Steph Ho Ox 81. **d** 84 **p** 85. C Peterlee *Dur* 84-87; C Newton Aycliffe 87-89; V Choral York Minster 89-94; Chapl St Pet Sch York 94-95; V Fylingdales and Hawsker cum Stainsacre *York* 95-01; Chapl Burrswood Chr Cen *Roch* 01-03; V Beckenham St Jas from 03; AD Beckenham 12-15; P-in-c Beckenham St Mich w St Aug from 15. *The Vicarage, 15 St James' Avenue, Beckenham BR3 4HF* T/F: (020) 8650 0420   E: leoncarberry@gmail.com

CARBY, Stuart Graeme. b 51. Man Univ BSc 73 Open Univ MA 96 Leeds Univ PGCE 74 CBiol 77 MIBiol 77 LRSC 78. St Jo Coll Nottm 92. **d** 92 **p** 93. C Magor w Redwick and Undy *Mon* 92-96; TV Cyncoed from 96. *100 Hillrise, Llanederyn, Cardiff CF23 6UL* T: (029) 2073 3915

CARD, Terence Leslie. b 37. K Coll Lon BD 68 AKC 68 Heythrop Coll Lon MTh 84. **d** 69 **p** 70. C Thundersley *Chelmsf* 69-72; LtO *Bradf* 72-75; V Chingford St Anne *Chelmsf* 75-81; RD Waltham Forest 78-81; R Springfield All SS 81-83; C Becontree St Jo 85-87; rtd 87; PtO *Ely* 96-00. *11 Harvey Goodwin Gardens, Cambridge CB4 3EZ* T: (01223) 367715

CARD-REYNOLDS, Charles Leonard. b 67. Lon Univ BD 92 Hughes Hall Cam BA 94 MA 98 FRSA 13. St Steph Ho Ox 96. **d** 98 **p** 99. C Reading H Trin *Ox* 98-06; C Reading St Mark 98-06; V Stamford Hill St Bart *Lon* from 06. *The Vicarage, 31 Craven Park Road, London N15 6AA* T: (020) 8800 1554
E: c.cardreynolds@me.com

CARDALE, Edward Charles. b 50. CCC Ox BA 72 MA 73. Cuddesdon Coll 72 Union Th Sem (NY) STM 74. **d** 74 **p** 75. C E Dulwich St Jo *S'wark* 74-77; Asst P Bainbridge Is USA 77-80; V Ponders End St Matt *Lon* 80-84; V Lytchett Minster *Sarum* 84-98; Dir Past Studies Coll of the Resurr Mirfield 98-02; P-in-c Lemsford *St Alb* 02-05; TV Bp's Hatfield, Lemsford and N Mymms 05-14; Tutor SAOMC 02-05; Dir Past Studies ERMC 05-14; rtd 14. *28 Warren Way, Welwyn AL6 0DH*
E: edward.cardale@btopenworld.com

CARDELL-OLIVER, John Anthony. b 43. Em Coll Cam BA 67 MA 72 Univ of W Aus BEd 75 MEd 85. Westcott Ho Cam 86. **d** 86 **p** 88. C Subiaco w Leederville Australia 86-88; PtO *Ely* 88-89; C Stansted Mountfitchet *Chelmsf* 89-92; R Langham w Boxted 92-02; rtd 02. *40 Halesworth Road, Jolimont, Perth WA 6014, Australia* T/F: (0061) (8) 9383 7381
E: jcardelloliver@optusnet.com.au

CARDEN, Edwin William. b 54. Cranmer Hall Dur 85. **d** 87 **p** 88. C Thundersley *Chelmsf* 87-91; CUF 91-93; NSM Poplar *Lon* 91-93; Chapl Pathfinder Mental Health Services NHS Trust 93-99; Chapl SW Lon and St George's Mental Health NHS Trust 99-00; Selection Sec Min Division 00-05; NSM Maldon St Mary w Mundon *Chelmsf* 00-02; Dioc Dep Chief Exec 03-08; PtO from 08; Chief Exec WHCM from 08. *21 Plume Avenue, Maldon CM9 6LB* T: (01621) 854908
E: mudmonkeys4@btinternet.com

CARDIGAN, Archdeacon of. See STRANGE, The Ven William Anthony

CARDINAL, Ian Ralph. b 57. Qu Coll Birm 81. **d** 84 **p** 85. C Whitkirk *Ripon* 84-87; C Knaresborough 87-89; R Ancaster Wilsford Gp *Linc* 89-94; P-in-c Wigginton *Lich* 94-07; Warden of Readers 96-03; P-in-c Stone St Mich and St Wulfad w Aston St Sav 07-08; R from 08. *11 Farrier Close, Stone ST15 8XP* T: (01785) 812747   M: 07778-055993
E: ian.cardinal@ukonline.co.uk

CARDWELL, Edward Anthony Colin. b 42. Trin Coll Cam BA 63 MA 68. St Jo Coll Nottm 73. **d** 75 **p** 76. C Stapenhill w Cauldwell *Derby* 75-78; C Bramcote *S'well* 78-81; V S'well H Trin 81-92; R Eastwood 92-07; rtd 07. *49 Bramcote Road, Beeston, Nottingham NG9 1DW* T: 0115-925 5866

CARDWELL, Joseph Robin. b 47. Qu Coll Cam BA 68 MA 77. Trin Coll Bris 73. **d** 76 **p** 77. C Bromley Ch Ch *Roch* 76-79; C Shirley *Win* 79-82; V Somborne w Ashley 82-90; V Derry Hill *Sarum* 90-94; V Derry Hill w Bremhill and Foxham 94-00; Community Affairs Chapl 90-94; V Lyddington and Wanborough and Bishopstone etc *Bris* 00-12; rtd 12; PtO *Ox* from 13. *Winter's Tale, 18 Stainswick Lane, Shrivenham, Swindon SN6 8DX* T: (01793) 783822   E: r.cardwell1@btinternet.com

CAREW, Richard Clayton. b 72. York Univ BA 94 PGCE 96 St Jo Coll Dur BA 04. Cranmer Hall Dur 02. **d** 05 **p** 06. C Beverley Minster *York* 05-10; Abp's Dom Chapl from 10. *Bishopthorpe Palace, Bishopthorpe, York YO23 2GE* T: (01904) 707021 *or* 772381   F: 709204   E: richard.carew@archbishopofyork.org

CAREY, Alan Lawrence. b 29. K Coll Lon AKC 53. **d** 54 **p** 55. C Radford *Cov* 54-57; C Burnham *Ox* 57-65; C-in-c Cippenham CD 65-77; rtd 94. *12 Ormsby Street, Reading RG1 7YR* T: 0118-961 2309

CAREY, Charles John. b 29. K Coll Lon BD 53 AKC 53. St Aug Coll Cant 71. **d** 72 **p** 73. C Spring Park *Cant* 72-74; C Ifield *Chich* 74-78; C Burgess Hill St Jo 78-80; Chapl Rush Green Hosp Romford 80-94; Chapl Oldchurch Hosp Romford 80-94; rtd 94. *Address withheld by request*

CAREY, Christopher Lawrence John. b 38. St Andr Univ BSc 61 Lon Univ BD 64. Clifton Th Coll 61. **d** 64 **p** 65. C Battersea Park St Sav *S'wark* 64-67; CMS Kenya 68-79; Overseas Regional Sec for E and Cen Africa CMS 79-98; NSM Chislehurst Ch Ch *Roch* 79-98; R Stickney Gp *Linc* 99-04; RD Bolingbroke 02-03; rtd 04; PtO *Mon* from 04. *83 Wentwood View, Caldicot NP26 4QH* T: (01291) 425010   E: crcandkili@tiscali.co.uk

CAREY, Donald Leslie. b 50. ACII 78. CBDTI 01. **d** 04 **p** 05. OLM Ashton-on-Ribble St Mich w Preston St Mark *Blackb* 04-06; OLM W Preston 06-07; NSM 07-08; P-in-c Fairhaven 08-11; V 11-15; rtd 15; PtO *Carl* from 15. *31 Roman Way, Kirkham, Preston PR4 2YG* E: frdonaldcarey@gmail.com

CAREY, Mark Jonathan. b 65. St Jo Coll Nottm BTh 94. **d** 94 **p** 95. C S Ossett *Wakef* 94-97; C Chapeltown *Sheff* 97-99; V Grenoside 99-07; P-in-c Low Harrogate St Mary *Ripon* 07-13; Pioneer Min *Leeds* from 13. *St Mary's Vicarage, 22 Harlow Oval, Harrogate HG2 0DS* T: (01423) 701848   E: mpjcarey@aol.com

CAREY, Philip John. d 15. NSM Rhosllanerchrugog and Penycae *St As* from 15. *146 Stockwell Grove, Wrexham LL13 7HJ* T: (01978) 312604   E: carey711@btinternet.com

CAREY, Canon Ronald Clive Adrian. b 21. K Coll Cam BA 46 MA 48. Chich Th Coll 47. **d** 48 **p** 49. C Harborne St Pet *Birm* 48-50; Bp's Dom Chapl *Chich* 50-52; C Keighley *Bradf* 52-55; V Illingworth *Wakef* 55-59; Asst in Relig Broadcasting BBC 59-68; PtO *S'wark* 59-68; V Claygate *Guildf* 68-78; RD Emly

72-77; Hon Can Guildf Cathl 78-86; R Guildf H Trin w St Mary 78-86; RD Guildf 84-86; rtd 86; PtO *Roch* 86-04; *Linc* from 04. *23 Moores Court, Jermyn Street, Sleaford NG34 7UL* T: (01529) 303698

CAREY, Mrs Wendy Marion. b 45. Bris Univ BA 66 Lon Inst of Educn CertEd 67. WMMTC 90. **d** 93 **p** 94. NSM Milton Keynes *Ox* 93-96; Sub Chapl HM Pris Woodhill 93-96; Chapl HM Pris Bullingdon 96-00; Ecum Tr Officer HM Pris Service Chapl 00-06; rtd 06; PtO *Ox* from 00. *46 Parklands, Great Linford, Milton Keynes MK14 5DZ* T: (01908) 605997

✠**CAREY OF CLIFTON, The Rt Revd and Rt Hon Lord (George Leonard).** b 35. PC 91. Lon Univ BD 62 MTh 65 PhD 71 Dur Univ Hon DD 93 Open Univ Hon DD 95 FRSA 91 FKC 93. ALCD 61. **d** 62 **p** 63 **c** 87. C Islington St Mary *Lon* 62-66; Lect Oak Hill Th Coll 66-70; Lect St Jo Coll Nottm 70-75; V Dur St Nic 75-82; Chapl HM Rem Cen Low Newton 77-81; Prin Trin Coll Bris 82-87; Hon Can Bris Cathl 84-87; Bp B & W 87-91; Abp Cant 91-02; rtd 02. *Rosemount, Garden Close Lane, Newbury RG14 6PR* E: carey.george01@googlemail.com

CARGILL, Christine Elizabeth. b 68. Chas Sturt Univ NSW BA(Ed) 91 New England Univ NSW MLitt 99 Sydney Univ MA 03. NTMTC 07. **d** 10 **p** 11. C Kilburn St Mary w All So and W Hampstead St Jas *Lon* 10-13; V Brondesbury St Anne w Kilburn H Trin from 13. *125 Salusbury Road, London NW6 6RG* M: 07906-067569 T: (020) 7624 5306 E: motherchristinenw6@gmail.co.uk

CARGILL THOMPSON, Edmund Alwyn James. b 72. St Jo Coll Ox BA 94. Cranmer Hall Dur 98. **d** 00 **p** 01. C St Jo on Bethnal Green *Lon* 00-03; V Barkingside H Trin *Chelmsf* 03-13; V Pimlico St Pet w Westmr Ch Ch *Lon* 13-14; V Northolt Park St Barn from 14. *The Vicarage, Raglan Way, Northolt UB5 4SX* M: 07908-949166 T: (020) 8422 3775 E: father.edmund@ntlworld.com

CARHART, John Richards. b 29. Bris Univ BA 50 Salford Univ MSc 77 Liv Univ MTh 99 FRSA. St Deiniol's Hawarden 63. **d** 65 **p** 66. C Ches St Oswald w Lt St Jo 65-72; Lect Ches Coll of HE 63-72; Prin Lect from 72; Dean Academic Studies 88-94; C Ches 72; LtO 73-85; Hon C Ches St Mary 85-00; rtd 00; PtO *Ches* from 00. *29 Abbot's Grange, Chester CH2 1AJ* T: (01244) 380923 E: jcarhart@nepc.co.uk

CARLESS, Canon Frank. b 22. Lon Univ BD 56. St Aid Birkenhead 53. **d** 56 **p** 57. C Normanton *Wakef* 56-59; V Rashcliffe 59-64; V Warley 64-87; RD Halifax 82-86; Hon Can Wakef Cathl 86-87; rtd 87; PtO *Leeds* from 87. *8 Joseph Crossley Almshouses, Arden Road, Halifax HX1 3AA* T: (01422) 348379

CARLILL, Adam Jonathan. b 66. Keble Coll Ox BA 88. Linc Th Coll 88. **d** 90 **p** 91. C Romford St Edw *Chelmsf* 90-94; C Uckfield *Chich* 94-98; V Tilehurst St Geo *Ox* 98-12; P-in-c Tilehurst St Mary 02-12; V Tilehurst St Geo and St Mary from 12. *St George's Vicarage, 98 Grovelands Road, Reading RG3 2PD* T: 0118-958 8354 E: adamcarlill@me.com

CARLILL, Richard Edward. b 38. Westcott Ho Cam 77. **d** 79 **p** 80. C Prittlewell *Chelmsf* 79-83; TV Saffron Walden w Wendens Ambo and Littlebury 83-89; V Langtoft w Foxholes, Butterwick, Cottam etc *York* 89-94; V Gt and Lt Driffield 94-03; RD Harthill 99-02; rtd 03; PtO *Newc* from 03. *31 Riverdene, Tweedmouth, Berwick-upon-Tweed TD15 2JD* T: (01289) 303701

CARLIN, Philip Charles. b 49. St Cath Coll Cam MA 71 Didsbury Coll of Educn PGCE 72. **d** 09 **p** 10. OLM Hurst *Man* 09-14. *1 Sunderland Avenue, Ashton-under-Lyne OL6 8PF* T: 0161-330 5530 M: 07708-398699 E: carlin@phonecoop.coop

CARLIN, William Patrick Bruce. b 53. St Steph Ho Ox 75. **d** 78 **p** 79. C Penistone *Wakef* 78-81; C Barnsley St Mary 81-83; V Stockton St Chad *Dur* 83-93; V Hedworth 93-01; TR Kippax w Allerton Bywater *Ripon* 01-11; V Bury, Roch Valley *Man* 11-13; rtd 13. *120 Huddersfield Road, Elland HX5 0EE* T: (01422) 252711 E: brucecarlin@cooptel.net

CARLING, Mrs Bronwen Noël. b 43. SRN 65 SCM 73. Linc Th Coll 89. **d** 91 **p** 94. C Blakeney w Cley, Wiveton, Glandford etc *Nor* 91-94; C Trunch 94-96; TV 96-01; rtd 01; PtO *Nor* 01-04. *Meadowbank, Rathdermot, Bansha, Co Tipperary, Republic of Ireland* T: (00353) (62) 54891 E: bncarling@sagainternet.co.uk

CARLISLE, Matthew David. b 74. Man Univ BA 96. Westcott Ho Cam 99. **d** 02 **p** 03. C E Crompton *Man* 02-06; TV Heywood 06-11; V Heywood St Jo and St Luke 11-15; V Gatley *Ches* from 15. *St James's Vicarage, 14 Elm Road, Gatley SK8 4LY* M: 07870-760746 E: matthewcarlisle@aol.com

CARLISLE, Archdeacon of. *See* ROBERTS, The Ven Kevin Thomas

CARLISLE, Bishop of. *See* NEWCOME, The Rt Revd James William Scobie

CARLISLE, Dean of. *See* BOYLING, The Very Revd Mark Christopher

CARLSON, Blair Truett. b 52. Wheaton Coll Illinois BA 74. Cranmer Hall Dur 00. **d** 02 **p** 03. C Hailsham *Chich* 02-05; USA from 05. *4619 Arden Avenue, Edina MN 55424, USA* T: (001) (952) 924 9062 E: btcarlson@gmail.com

CARLSSON, Miss Siw Ebba Christina. b 43. **d** 92 **p** 94. Par Dn Barnes St Mary *S'wark* 92-93; C Mitcham SS Pet and Paul 93-98; Asst Chapl SW Lon and St George's Mental Health NHS Trust 99-00; Chapl Ipswich Hosp NHS Trust 00-08; rtd 08; PtO *St E* from 08. *60 Bury Hill, Melton, Woodbridge IP12 1JD* T: (01394) 384281

CARLTON, Preb Roger John. b 51. **d** 80 **p** 81. NSM Downend *Bris* 80-83; NSM Heavitree w Ex St Paul 83-87; Chapl Ex Sch and St Marg Sch 83-87; TV Bickleigh (Plymouth) *Ex* 87-91; TR 91-93; TR Bickleigh and Shaugh Prior 94-10; RD Ivybridge 93-98; V Paignton St Jo from 10; Preb Ex Cathl from 06. *The Vicarage, Palace Place, Paignton TQ3 3AQ* T: (01803) 551866 E: roger.carlton@btinternet.com

CARLYON, Miss Catherine Rachel. b 67. RN 89. Ripon Coll Cuddesdon BTh 06. **d** 02 **p** 03. C Launceston *Truro* 02-06; C Crediton, Shobrooke and Sandford etc *Ex* 06-14; Chapl w Deaf People 06-14; Chapl among Deaf and Deafblind People *Lon* from 14. *2 Anatola Road, London N19 5HN* E: catherinecarlyon@btinternet.com

CARMAN, Jill Youde. b 37. Cartrefle Coll of Educn CertEd 69 Liv Univ DipEd 86. SAOMC 97. **d** 99 **p** 00. NSM Markyate Street *St Alb* 99-02; NSM Quinton *Glouc* 02-05; NSM Quinton and Welford w Weston 05-06; NSM Bourton-on-the-Water w Clapton etc 06-13; rtd 13; PtO *Pet* from 13; *Portsm* from 14. *The Castle, Duver Road, St Helens, Ryde PO33 1XY* E: jillcarman777@btinternet.com

CARMAN, Philip Gordon. b 80. York St Jo Coll BA 01 St Jo Coll Dur BA 07. Cranmer Hall Dur 04. **d** 07 **p** 08. C Acomb St Steph and St Aid *York* 07-10; C Huntington from 10. *402 Huntington Road, York YO31 9HU* T: (01904) 619852 E: philcarman3@gmail.com

CARMARTHEN, Archdeacon of. *See* HUGHES, The Ven William Roger

CARMICHAEL, Elizabeth Dorothea Harriet. b 46. MBE 95. LMH Ox MA 73 BM 73 BCh 73 Worc Coll Ox BA 83 Ox Univ DPhil 91. **d** 91 **p** 92. S Africa 91-96; Chapl and Tutor St Jo Coll Ox 96-11; rtd 11; Research Fell from 11. *St John's College, Oxford OX1 3JP* T: (01865) 277351 F: 277435 E: liz.carmichael@sjc.ox.ac.uk

CARMODY, Canon Dermot Patrick Roy. b 41. CITC 77. **d** 77 **p** 78. C Dublin Zion Ch *D & G* 77-79; I Dunganstown w Redcross 79-84; TV Dublin Ch Ch Cathl Gp 84-93; Can Ch Ch Cathl Dublin 84-92; Preb Ch Ch Cathl Dublin 92-93; I Mullingar, Portnashangan, Moyliscar, Kilbixy etc *M & K* 93-08; Dir of Ords (Meath) 97-08; Can Meath 98-08; Can Kildare Cathl 98-08; Treas Kildare Cathl 00-08; P-in-c Rathmolyon w Castlerickard, Rathcore and Agher 00-07; rtd 08. *15 Gleann Alain, Collinstown, Mullingar, Co Westmeath, Republic of Ireland* T/F: (00353) (44) 966 6232 M: 86-829 0183 E: patkcarmody@gmail.com

CARMYLLIE, Mrs Kathryn Ruth. b 61. Cov Poly BA 84 CQSW 84 Univ Coll Ches BTh 04. NOC 01. **d** 04 **p** 05. C Leigh St Mary *Man* 04-07; TV Worsley 07-12; TR Atherton and Hindsford w Howe Bridge 12-14; PtO from 15. *St Stephen's Vicarage, 7 Holbeck, Astley, Tyldesley, Manchester M29 7DU* T: (01942) 883313 E: k.carmyllie@btinternet.com

CARMYLLIE, Robert Jonathan. b 63. Cov Poly BSc 85. Cranmer Hall Dur 85. **d** 88 **p** 89. C Horwich *Man* 88-92; P-in-c Edgeside 92-99; P-in-c Astley 99-06; TR Astley, Tyldesley and Mosley Common 06-15; AD Leigh 12-15; V W Pendleside *Blackb* from 15. *The Vicarage, 40 The Sands, Whalley, Clitheroe BB7 9TL* T: (01254) 824679 E: j.carmyllie@btinternet.com

CARNALL, Mrs Nicola Jane. b 66. St Jo Coll Nottm 99. **d** 01 **p** 02. C Edwinstowe *S'well* 01-05; P-in-c Sowerby *York* 05-12; V from 12; P-in-c Sessay 05-12; R from 12; V Thirkleby w Kilburn and Bagby from 12. *The Vicarage, 5 The Close, Sowerby, Thirsk YO7 1JA* T: (01845) 522814 E: vicar@stoswaldsowerby.org.uk *or* njcarnall@tiscali.co.uk

CARNE, Canon Brian George. b 29. FSA Liv Univ BCom 50. Qu Coll Birm 53. **d** 55 **p** 56. C Swindon St Aug *Bris* 55-58; C Bris St Andr w St Bart 58-60; R Lydiard Millicent w Lydiard Tregoz 60-68; V Bris St Andr Hartcliffe 68-74; V Almondsbury 74-91; RD Westbury and Severnside 80-86; Hon Can Bris Cathl 82-91; P-in-c Littleton on Severn w Elberton 83-91; P-in-c Olveston 83-91; rtd 91; PtO *Bris* from 92; *Glouc* 92-98 and from 01. *Whitehouse Farm, English Bicknor, Coleford GL16 7PA* T: (01594) 860200

CARNEGIE, Ms Rachel Clare. b 62. New Hall Cam BA 84 Sussex Univ MA 94. SEITE 01. **d** 04 **p** 05. NSM Richmond St Mary w St Matthias and St Jo *S'wark* 04-09; Abp's Sec for Internat Development *Cant* 09-13; Co-Dir Angl Alliance from 13. *Anglican Communion Office, 16 Tavistock Crescent, London W11 1AP* T: (020) 7313 3922 E: rachel.carnegie@aco.org

CARNELL, Canon Geoffrey Gordon. b 18. St Jo Coll Cam BA 40 MA 44. Cuddesdon Coll 40. **d** 42 **p** 43. C Abington *Pet* 42-49; Chapl and Lect St Gabr Coll Camberwell 49-53; R Isham and V Gt w Lt Harrowden *Pet* 53-71; Dir of Post-Ord Tr and Dir of Ords 62-85; Can Pet Cathl 65-85; R Boughton 71-85; Dioc Lib Ecton Ho 67-93; Chapl to The Queen 81-88; rtd 85; PtO *Pet* 86-07. *52 Walsingham Avenue, Kettering NN15 5ER* T: (01536) 511415

CARNELLEY, The Ven Desmond. b 29. Open Univ BA 77 Leeds Univ CertEd. Ripon Hall Ox 59. **d** 60 **p** 61. C Aston cum Aughton *Sheff* 60-63; C-in-c Ecclesfield St Paul CD 63-67; V Balby w Hexthorpe 67-73; P-in-c Mosbrough 73-74; V 74-85; RD Attercliffe 79-84; Adn Doncaster 85-94; Dioc Dir of Educn 91-94; rtd 94; PtO *Sheff* from 94; *Derby* from 94. *11 Fairways, Wickersley, Rotherham S66 1AE* T: (01709) 544927

CARNELLEY, Ms Elizabeth Amy. b 64. St Aid Coll Dur BA 85 Selw Coll Cam MPhil 87. Ripon Coll Cuddesdon 88. **d** 90 **p** 94. Par Dn Sharrow St Andr *Sheff* 90-93; Par Dn Is of Dogs Ch Ch and St Jo w St Luke *Lon* 93-94; C 94-95; P-in-c Woolfold *Man* 95-99; TV Man Whitworth 99-02; Chapl Man Univ and Man Metrop Univ 99-02; Policy Officer Chs' Regional Commn for Yorks and the Humber 02-06; Chief Exec 06-11; Near Neighbours Progr Dir CUF from 11. *Church Urban Fund, Church House, Great Smith Street, London SW1P 3AZ* M: 07812-984818 E: elizabeth.carnelley@cuf.org.uk

CARNEY, David Anthony. b 42. Salford Univ BSc 77. Linc Th Coll 77. **d** 79 **p** 80. C Wythenshawe St Martin *Man* 79-81; CF 81-84; Chapl Canadian Armed Forces Canada 84-87; R Burford H Trin Ontario 87-91; P-in-c Whaplode *Linc* 91-97; V 97-02; P-in-c Holbeach Fen 91-97; V 97-02; R Colsterworth Gp 02-05; P-in-c Kirton in Holland 05-09; rtd 09. *6 South Road, Bourne PE10 9JD* T: (01778) 426061

CARNEY, Mrs Mary Patricia. b 42. Univ of Wales (Ban) BSc 62. Wycliffe Hall Ox. **d** 90 **p** 94. Par Dn Carterton *Ox* 90-93; Par Dn Harwell w Chilton 93-94; C 94-01; P-in-c Ray Valley 01-07; rtd 07; PtO *Ox* from 07. *104 Pensclose, Witney OX28 2EQ* T: (01993) 358139 E: marypcarney@tiscali.co.uk

CARNEY, The Ven Richard Wayne. b 52. Lon Teachers' Coll Ontario TCert 73 Toronto Univ BA 79. Trin Coll Toronto MDiv 84. **d** 84 **p** 85. C Scarborough St Andr Canada 84-86; I Roche's Pt 86-91; P Asst Newmarket St Paul 91-93; Assoc P 93-95; I Clonfert Gp *L & K* 95-03; I Birr w Lorrha, Dorrha and Lockeen from 03; Adn Killaloe, Kilfenora, Clonfert etc from 02; Preb Taney St Patr Cathl Dublin from 12. *The Rectory, Birr, Co Offaly, Republic of Ireland* T: (00353) (57) 912 0021 M: 87-786 5234 E: mapleire@eircom.net *or* archdeacon@killaloe.anglican.org

⌖**CARNLEY, The Rt Revd Peter Frederick.** b 37. AO 98. Melbourne Univ BA 66 Cam Univ PhD 69 Gen Th Sem NY Hon DD 84 Newc Univ Aus Hon DLitt 00 Univ of W Aus Hon DLitt 00. St Jo Coll Morpeth. **d** 62 **p** 64 **c** 81. LtO Melbourne Australia 63-65; C Parkes 66; LtO *Ely* 66-69; Chapl Mitchell Coll Bathurst Australia 70-71; Research Fell St Jo Coll Cam 71-72; Warden St Jo Coll Brisbane Australia 72-81; Can Res Brisbane 75-81; Abp Perth 81-05; Primate of Australia 00-05; rtd 05. *PO Box 221, Nannup WA 6275, Australia* T: (0061) (8) 9756 0420

CAROLAN (née STUART-BLACK), Mrs Veronica. b 52. St Jo Coll Dur BA 75. Cranmer Hall Dur. **dss** 82 **d** 87 **p** 08. Par Dn Stevenage St Mary Shephall w Aston *St Alb* 87-88; Hon C 08-14; PtO 98-08; V Lower Esk *York* from 14. *The Vicarage, 22 Eskdaleside, Sleights, Whitby YO22 5EP* E: vronca@hotmail.co.uk

CAROLAN-EVANS, Stewart James. b 65. Salford Univ BSc 88 CEng 95 MICE 95. SEITE 04. **d** 06 **p** 07. NSM Dover St Mary *Cant* 06-13; NSM Bewsborough from 13. *Springfield, Eythorne Road, Shepherdswell, Dover CT15 7PW* T: (01304) 832248 F: 830641 M: 07940-544748 E: sjkgcarolan@tesco.net

CARPANI, Karl Augustus. b 65. St Jo Coll Nottm 96. **d** 98 **p** 99. C Biggin Hill *Roch* 98-01; V Green Street Green and Pratts Bottom from 01. *The Vicarage, 46 World's End Lane, Orpington BR6 6AG* T: (01689) 852905 E: karl.carpani@diocese-rochester.org *or* karl@carpani.org

CARPENTER, Canon Bruce Leonard Henry. b 32. Lon Univ BA 54. St Chad's Coll Dur. **d** 59 **p** 60. C Portsea N End St Mark *Portsm* 59-63; C Fareham SS Pet and Paul 63-67; V Locks Heath 67-74; TR Fareham H Trin 74-84; RD Alverstoke 71-76; Hon Can Portsm Cathl 79-84; V Richmond St Mary w St Matthias and St Jo *S'wark* 84-91; Chapl Ch Ch High Sch Ashford 91-93; P-in-c S Ashford Ch Ch *Cant* 94-97; rtd 97; Chapl Huggens Coll Northfleet 97-02; PtO *Portsm* from 02; Hon Chapl MU from 03. *48 Summerson Lodge, 94 Alverstone Road, Southsea PO4 8GS* T: (023) 9307 6722

CARPENTER, David. b 60. **d** 12 **p** 13. NSM Bury St Edmunds Ch Ch *St E* from 12. *40 Tollgate Lane, Bury St Edmunds IP32 6DE* T: (01284) 705990 E: d.carpenter3@homecall.co.uk

CARPENTER, David James. b 52. Trin Coll Carmarthen CertEd 74. St Steph Ho Ox 74. **d** 76 **p** 77. C Newport St Julian *Mon* 76-77; C Pontypool 77-79; C Ebbw Vale 79-81; TV 81-85; V Pontnewynydd 85-88; V Bedwellty 88-00; Chapl Aberdargoed Hosp 88-99; V Staincliffe and Carlinghow *Wakef* 00-05; Chapl Yorks Ambulance Service 05-11; PtO *Wakef* 10-11; P-in-c Birkby and Woodhouse *Leeds* from 11. *The Vicarage, 43 Ashbrow Road, Huddersfield HD2 1DX* T: (01484) 424669 E: carpenterdj@aol.com

CARPENTER, Canon Derek George Edwin. b 40. K Coll Lon BD 62 AKC 62. **d** 63 **p** 64. C Friern Barnet All SS *Lon* 63-66; C Chingford SS Pet and Paul *Chelmsf* 66-70; V Dartford St Alb *Roch* 70-79; R Crayford 79-90; RD Erith 82-90; R Beckenham St Geo 90-02; Hon Can Roch Cathl 97-02; rtd 02; PtO *Roch* from 04. *39 Chatfield Way, East Malling, West Malling ME19 6QD* T: (01732) 874420 E: derek.carpenter@rochester.anglican.org

CARPENTER, Donald Arthur. b 35. Roch Th Coll 65. **d** 67 **p** 68. C Thornton Heath St Jude *Cant* 67-73; V Earby *Bradf* 73-78; V Skipton Ch Ch 78-88; V Baildon 88-91; P-in-c Perivale *Lon* 91-96; rtd 96; PtO *Lon* 96-05. *Le Moulin Verneau, 49390 Parcay-les-Pins, France* T: (0033) 2 41 51 42 22 M: 6 77 98 48 07 E: sue.carpenter@numeo.fr

CARPENTER, Giles Michael Gerard. b 67. Trin Coll Bris BA 10. **d** 10 **p** 11. C Shottermill *Guildf* 10-14; V Eastbourne St Jo *Chich* from 14. *9 Buxton Road, Eastbourne BN20 7LL* T: (01323) 721105 M: 07710-498906 E: giles.rev@gmail.com

CARPENTER, Canon Judith Margaret. b 47. Birm Univ BA 68 CertEd 69. Trin Coll Bris BA 95. **d** 95 **p** 96. C Warmley, Syston and Bitton *Bris* 95-99; V Withywood 99-12; Hon Can Bris Cathl 06-12; rtd 12. *Dawes Orchard, Latchen, Longhope GL17 0QB* E: judith.carpenter1@btinternet.com

CARPENTER, Leonard Richard. b 32. EMMTC 82. **d** 85 **p** 86. NSM Leic H Apostles 85-90; P-in-c Barlestone 90-98; rtd 98; PtO *Leic* from 98; *Derby* from 98. *10 Main Street, Albert Village, Swadlincote DE11 8EW* T: (01283) 229335 E: lenpia7@gmail.com

CARPENTER, Michael John Anselm. *See* PHILLIPS, Michael John Anselm

CARPENTER, William Brodie. b 35. St Alb Minl Tr Scheme 76. **d** 79 **p** 80. NSM Hemel Hempstead *St Alb* 79-85; C Bp's Hatfield 85-88; C Caversham St Pet and Mapledurham etc *Ox* 88-89; V Caversham St Andr 89-99; rtd 99; PtO *St Alb* 00-02; P-in-c Wigginton 02-05; PtO *Ox* from 07. *33 Elm Tree Walk, Tring HP23 5EB* T: (01442) 824585 E: billcarp@supanet.com

CARR, Alan Cobban. b 49. Nottm Univ BTh 88. Linc Th Coll 85. **d** 88 **p** 89. C Rustington *Chich* 88-92; V Highbrook and W Hoathly 92-10; C St Giles-in-the-Fields *Lon* 10-15; R from 15. *15A Gower Street, London WC1E 6HW* T: (020) 7274 0407 E: alancarr17@gmail.com

CARR, Mrs Amanda Helen. b 70. Univ of Wales (Cardiff) BA 91 Kent Univ MA 97. SEITE 01. **d** 04 **p** 05. C Meopham w Nurstead *Roch* 04-07; P-in-c Lamberhurst and Matfield 07-09; V 09-15; RD Paddock Wood 12-15; V Sevenoaks Weald from 15. *St George's Vicarage, Church Road, Weald, Sevenoaks TN14 6LT* M: 07866-675015 E: mandy.carr@diocese-rochester.org *or* reverendmandy@btinternet.com

CARR, Anthony Howard. b 62. Ex Univ BA. **d** 92 **p** 93. C Taverham w Ringland *Nor* 92-97; P-in-c S Darley, Elton and Winster *Derby* 97-03; R E Peckham and Nettlestead *Roch* from 03. *The Rectory, Bush Road, East Peckham, Tonbridge TN12 5LL* T: (01622) 871278

CARR, The Very Revd Arthur Wesley. b 41. KCVO 06. Jes Coll Ox BA 64 MA 67 Jes Coll Cam BA 66 MA 70 Sheff Univ PhD 75 Hon DLitt 03 UWE Hon DLitt 97. Ridley Hall Cam 65. **d** 67 **p** 68. C Luton w E Hyde *St Alb* 67-71; Tutor Ridley Hall Cam 70-71; Chapl 71-72; Hon C Ranmoor *Sheff* 72-74; Chapl Chelmsf Cathl 74-78; Can Res 78-87; Dep Dir Cathl Cen for Research and Tr 74-82; Dioc Dir of Tr 76-84; Dean Bris 87-97; Dean Westmr 97-06; rtd 06. *16 Church Road, Romsey SO51 8EY* T: (01794) 511143

CARR, David Scott. b 72. Derby Univ BA 97 MCIM 05. NEOC 06. **d** 09 **p** 10. NSM Horden *Dur* 09-14. *Glen View, 26 Station Avenue, Brandon, Durham DH7 8QQ* M: 07990-775054 T: 0191-378 0126 E: david@carrd.fsbusiness.co.uk

CARR, Derrick Charles. b 43. MCIPD. SAOMC 99. **d** 02 **p** 03. NSM Amersham *Ox* 02-13; AD 09-12; PtO from 13. *52 Warren Wood Drive, High Wycombe HP11 1EA* T/F: (01494) 452389 M: 07768-507391 E: carrd@btopenworld.com

CARR, Mrs Elaine Susan. b 46. LTCL 82. SAOMC 99. **d** 02 **p** 03. NSM High Wycombe *Ox* 02-09; Bp's NSM Officer (Bucks) from 09. *52 Warren Wood Drive, High Wycombe HP11 1EA* T/F: (01494) 452389 E: revcarr@btinternet.com

CARR, Miss Eveline. b 45. Cranmer Hall Dur 91. **d** 93 **p** 95. NSM Eighton Banks *Dur* 93-98; NSM Gateshead 98-12; rtd 12; PtO *Dur* from 12. *10 Lanchester Avenue, Gateshead NE9 7AJ* T: 0191-482 1157 E: e-carr@supanet.com

CARR, Jeremy Barnardo Quintin. b 75. Wycliffe Hall Ox 13. **d** 15. C St Margaret's-on-Thames *Lon* from 15. *24 Kings Road, Twickenham TW1 2QS*

CARR, John Bernard. b 53. Lindisfarne Regional Tr Partnership 11. **d** 13 **p** 14. NSM Jesmond H Trin *Newc* from 13. *19 Bourne Avenue, Newcastle upon Tyne NE4 9XL* T: 0191-274 0901 E: jbcarr@btinternet.com

CARR, John Henry Percy. b 52. NTMTC 95. **d** 98 **p** 99. C Hackney Wick St Mary of Eton w St Aug *Lon* 98-01; R Walesby *Linc* from 01. *The Rectory, Otby Lane, Walesby, Market Rasen LN8 3UT* T: (01673) 838513 E: carr.ide@btinternet.com

CARR, John Robert. b 40. ACII 62. Oak Hill Th Coll 63. **d** 66 **p** 67. C Tonbridge St Steph *Roch* 66-70; C Cheadle Hulme St Andr *Ches* 70-79; R Widford *Chelmsf* 79-87; TV Becontree W 87-93; V Basildon St Andr w H Cross 93-05; rtd 05; PtO *Chelmsf* from 06. *3 Windsor Way, Rayleigh SS6 8PE* T: (01268) 741065 E: john316+wendycarr@talktalk.net

CARR, Miss Joy Vera. b 32. DipEd 52. Dalton Ho Bris 56. **dss** 80 **d** 87 **p** 94. Par Dn Kingston upon Hull St Matt w St Barn *York* 87-89; Par Dn Elloughton and Brough w Brantingham 89-92; rtd 92; PtO *York* from 92. *15 Sea View Gardens, Scarborough YO11 3JD* T: (01723) 376986

CARR, Leighton Westwood. b 60. Trin Coll Bris. **d** 09 **p** 10. NSM Kingswood *Bris* 09-14; NSM Hanham 13-14; NSM Clifton Ch Ch w Em from 14. *19 Nutgrove Avenue, Bristol BS3 4QE* T: 0117-983 2605

CARR, Mandy. *See* CARR, Amanda Helen

CARR, Paul Anthony. b 62. Univ of Wales MA 13. Aston Tr Scheme 93 Oak Hill Th Coll 95. **d** 97 **p** 98. C Handforth *Ches* 97-01; V Chadwell Heath *Chelmsf* 01-08; TR Billericay and Lt Burstead from 08. *The Rectory, 40 Laindon Road, Billericay CM12 9LD* T: (01277) 658055 E: revpaulcarr@btinternet.com

CARR, Richard George. b 43. AKC 65. St Boniface Warminster 65. **d** 66 **p** 67. C Fenham St Jas and St Basil *Newc* 66-69; C Alnwick St Mich 69-73; Ind Chapl *Llan* 73-77; PtO *Chelmsf* from 80. *Nelmes, Mill Lane, Birch, Colchester CO2 0NG* T: (01206) 330521 E: richardcarr@nelmes.fsnet.co.uk

CARR, Wesley. *See* CARR, Arthur Wesley

CARRINGTON, David John. b 63. Cam Univ MA 85 Reading Univ MSc 88. Trin Coll Bris BA 09. **d** 09 **p** 10. C Bovey Tracey SS Pet, Paul and Thos w Hennock *Ex* 09-12; C Brampford Speke, Cadbury, Newton St Cyres etc 12-15; TV Bideford, Northam, Westward Ho!, Appledore etc from 15. *The Vicarage, Meeting Street, Appledore, Bideford EX39 1RJ* T: (01237) 423026 E: revdavidcarrington@gmail.com

CARRINGTON, Mrs Elizabeth Ashby. b 46. Open Univ BA 02. EMMTC 86. **d** 90 **p** 94. NSM Nottingham St Ann w Em *S'well* 90-91; C Basford w Hyson Green 92-97; Lect Nottingham St Mary and St Cath 97-00; Assoc P W Bingham Deanery 00; PtO 00-01; Chapl Woodford Ho Sch New Zealand 01-10; NSM Napier Cathl 03-06; rtd 11. *98 Repton Road, West Bridgford, Nottingham NG2 7EL* T: 0115-914 2504 M: 07900-417275 E: carringtonpe@yahoo.co.uk

CARRINGTON, Margaret Elizabeth. b 46. **d** 09. NSM York St Luke from 09. *202 Boroughbridge Road, York YO26 6BD* T: (01904) 798916 E: carringtonpe@btinternet.com

CARRINGTON, Philip John. b 48. **d** 85 **p** 86. C W Acklam *York* 85-88; V Middlesbrough St Agnes 88-92; Chapl S Cleveland Hosp 88-92; Trust Chapl S Tees Hosps NHS Trust 92-06; V Guernsey St Steph *Win* 06-13; Hd Chapl Services States of Guernsey Bd of Health 07-13; rtd 13; PtO *Leeds* from 13. *Stonecroft, Hackforth Road, Little Crakehall, Bedale DL8 1HY* T: (01677) 425077 E: pandlcarrington@btinternet.com

CARRIVICK, Derek Roy. b 45. Birm Univ BSc 66. Ripon Hall Ox 71. **d** 74 **p** 75. C Enfield St Jas *Lon* 74-78; C-in-c Woodgate Valley CD *Birm* 78-83; TR Chelmsley Wood 83-92; Dioc Ecum Officer 86-96; R Baxterley w Hurley and Wood End and Merevale etc 92-99; AD Polesworth 96-99; P-in-c Helland and Blisland w St Breward *Truro* 99-04; P-in-c Devoran 04-11; Hon C 11-12; Hon C Chacewater w St Day and Carharrack 11-12; Hon C St Stythians w Perranarworthal and Gwennap 11-12; Hon C Feock 11-12; Bp's Dom Chapl 04-09; rtd 09. *30 Par Green, Par PL24 2AF* T: (01726) 813566 E: pjc87@tutor.open.ac.uk

CARROLL, James Thomas. b 41. Pittsburgh Univ MA 85. St Deiniol's Hawarden 89 Oblate Fathers Sem Dub 59. **d** 63 **p** 64. C Dublin St Patr Cathl Gp 89-92; Min Can St Patr Cathl Dublin 90-96; I Raheny w Coolock *D & G* 92-13; Chan V St Patr Cathl Dublin 96-01; rtd 13. *8 Castle Terrace Court, St Margaret's Road, Malahide, Co Dublin, Republic of Ireland* E: midnight@indigo.ie

CARROLL, John Hugh. b 31. Bris Univ BA 57. Tyndale Hall Bris 54. **d** 58 **p** 59. C Slough *Ox* 58-61; V S Lambeth St Steph *S'wark* 61-72; V Norwood St Luke 72-81; P-in-c Purley Ch Ch 81-85; V 85-93; rtd 93; PtO *S'wark* 93-13. *11 Manormead, Tilford Road, Hindhead GU26 6RA* E: jonthel.carroll@virgin.net

CARROLL, Laurence William. b 44. Birm Univ CertEd 66 Open Univ BA 73 Leic Univ BEd 74 FRHS 66 ACP 67 LCP 68. **d** 95 **p** 96. OLM Mid Marsh Gp *Linc* from 95. *15 Grantavon House, Brayford Wharf East, Lincoln LN5 7WA* T: (01522) 523643

CARROLL, Ruth Ellen. b 68. **d** 14 **p** 15. C Boston *Linc* 14-15; C Willoughby from 15. *The Rectory, Station Road, Willoughby, Alford LN13 9NA* E: americanruth@gmail.com

CARROLL WALLIS, Ms Joy Ann. b 59. SS Mark & Jo Univ Coll Plymouth BEd 82. Cranmer Hall Dur 85. **d** 88 **p** 94. Par Dn Hatcham St Jas *S'wark* 88-93; Par Dn Streatham Immanuel and St Andr 93-94; C 94-97; USA from 97. *1305 Fairmont Street NW, Washington DC 20009, USA* T: (001) (202) 483 0119 E: joycwallis@aol.com

CARRUTHERS, Arthur Christopher (Kester). b 35. Lon Coll of Div ALCD 60 LTh 73. **d** 60 **p** 61. C Addiscombe St Mary *Cant* 60-62; Prec Bradf Cathl 62-64; CF 64-92; R W Tanfield and Well w Snape and N Stainley *Ripon* 92-00; rtd 00; PtO *Guildf* from 00. *3 Park View Court, Woking GU22 7SE* T: (01483) 721995

CARSON, Christopher John. b 69. QUB BA 91 TCD BTh 94. **d** 94 **p** 95. C Bangor St Comgall *D & D* 94-97; Bp's C Kilmegan w Maghera 97-98; I from 98. *The Rectory, 50 Main Street, Dundrum, Newcastle BT33 0LY* T: (028) 4375 1225 M: 07758-722617

CARSON, Claire. b 76. St Martin's Coll Lanc BA 98 Birm Univ MA 99. Qu Coll Birm 00. **d** 03 **p** 04. C Streetly *Lich* 03-04; C Stafford 04-05; C Lich St Mich w St Mary and Wall 05-07; Chapl R Free Hampstead NHS Trust 07-10; Chapl Imp Coll Healthcare NHS Trust 10-11; Chapl SW Lon and St George's Mental Health NHS Trust from 11. *20 Courthope Road, London NW3 2LB* M: 07891-180023 E: claire.carson3@btinternet.com

CARSON, Canon James Irvine. b 59. TCD BA MTh. **d** 84 **p** 85. C Willowfield *D & D* 84-87; C Lecale Gp 87-89; I Devenish w Boho *Clogh* 89-95; Dioc Youth Adv 91-95; Dioc Communications Officer 93-95; I Belfast Upper Malone (Epiphany) *Conn* 95-99; I Lisburn St Paul from 99; Preb Conn Cathl from 11. *St Paul's Rectory, 3 Ballinderry Road, Lisburn BT28 1UD* T: (028) 9266 3520 E: jamescarson203@btinternet.com

CARSON, Tom Patrick. b 83. Regent's Park Coll Ox MA 09 Heythrop Coll Lon MA 10 K Coll Lon PGCE 06. Ripon Coll Cuddesdon MTh 12. **d** 12 **p** 13. C Mortlake w E Sheen *S'wark* from 12. *5 Vernon Road, London SW14 8NH* M: 07974-080946 E: tompcarson@gmail.com

CARSON-FEATHAM, Lawrence William. b 53. AKC. **d** 78 **p** 79. SSM from 77; C Walton St Mary *Liv* 78-82; Chapl Bolton Colls of H&FE 82-87; C Bolton St Pet *Man* 82-87; TV Oldham 87-92; V Ashton St Jas 92-95; PtO *Liv* 95-97; C Leeds Belle Is St Jo and St Barn *Ripon* 97-01; TV Accrington Ch the King *Blackb* 01-13; V Accrington St Andr, St Mary and St Pet from 13. *St Mary Magdalen's Vicarage, 5 Queen's Road, Accrington BB5 6AR* T: (01254) 233763 E: carsonfeatham@btinternet.com

CARTER, Arthur Edward. b 32. CITC. **d** 97 **p** 98. C Clonmel w Innislounagh, Tullaghmelan etc *C & O* from 97. *Suir Villa, Barnora, Cahir, Co Tipperary, Republic of Ireland* T: (00353) (52) 744 1524 E: nacarter@eircom.net

CARTER, Ashley Stuart Bourn. b 79. Lanc Univ BA 00. Oak Hill Th Coll 10. **d** 14 **p** 15. C Mayfair Ch Ch *Lon* from 14. *164 Tranmere Road, London SW18 3QU*

CARTER, Barry Graham. b 54. K Coll Lon BD 76 AKC 76. St Steph Ho Ox 76. **d** 77 **p** 78. C Evesham *Worc* 77-81; C Amblecote 81-84; TV Ovingdean w Rottingdean and Woodingdean *Chich* 84-85; V Woodingdean 85-95; V Lancing St Mich from 95. *The Vicarage, 117 Penhill Road, Lancing BN15 8HD* T: (01903) 753653 E: frbaz@saintmichaels.plus.com

CARTER, Benjamin Huw. b 77. Ex Univ BA 99 St Cath Coll Cam MPhil 00 Middx Univ PhD 04. Cranmer Hall Dur 08. **d** 10 **p** 11. C Monkseaton St Mary *Newc* 10-14; V Haydon Bridge and Beltingham w Henshaw from 14. *The Vicarage, Haydon Bridge, Hexham NE47 6LL* M: 07985-412542 T: (01434) 684307 E: benj_carter@yahoo.co.uk

CARTER, Carl. b 56. LCTP 11. **d** 14 **p** 15. NSM Millom *Carl* from 14. *13 Pepper Hall Walk, Haverigg, Millom LA18 4HT* T: (01229) 774427 M: 07738-618350

CARTER, Celia. b 38. JP 74 MBE 12. Glouc Sch of Min 86. **d** 89 **p** 94. NSM Avening w Cherington *Glouc* 89-13; P-in-c 95-13; Asst Chapl Severn NHS Trust 89-05; Asst Chapl Glos Primary Care Trust 05-13; rtd 13. *Avening Park, West End, Avening, Tetbury GL8 8NE* T: (01453) 836390

CARTER (née SMITH), Mrs Christine Lydia. b 43. SRN 64 SCM 67. Trin Coll Bris 89. **d** 91 **p** 94. Par Dn Penkridge *Lich* 91-94; C 94-96; PtO *Blackb* 96-97; NSM Blackb Sav 97-01; Chapl Asst St Helens and Knowsley Hosps NHS Trust 97-01; NSM Elmdon St Nic *Birm* 01-11; PtO *Lich* from 12. *Elmdon, 4 Goods Station Lane, Penkridge, Stafford ST19 5AU* T: (01785) 710809 E: chris@tworevs.co.uk

CARTER, Christopher Franklin. b 37. Wadh Coll Ox BA 59 MA 63. Wycliffe Hall Ox 60. **d** 64 **p** 65. C Clifton St Jas *Sheff* 64-67; C Handsworth 67-70; C Clun w Chapel Lawn *Heref* 70-74; LtO 74-76; P-in-c Ironbridge 76-78; C Coalbrookdale, Iron-Bridge and Lt Wenlock 78-80; V Llansilin w Llangadwaladr and Llangedwyn *St As* 80-05; RD Llanfyllin 88-05; rtd 05; PtO *St As* from 09. *Ysgubor Goch, Cefn Coch, Llanrhaeadr-ym-Mochnant, Oswestry SY10 0BQ* T: (01691) 860577

CARTER, Christopher Paul. b 43. CCC Cam BA 64. SAOMC 02. **d** 05 **p** 06. NSM W Buckingham *Ox* 05-13; rtd 13; PtO *Ox* from 13. *The Mount, Upper Street, Tingewick, Buckingham MK18 4QN* T/F: (01280) 848291 E: rev.c.carter@btinternet.com

CARTER, Colin John. b 56. Fitzw Coll Cam BA 77 MB, BChir 80 MA 81 FRCS 86 FRCOphth 89. Trin Coll Bris BA 93. **d** 93 **p** 94. C Ripley *Derby* 93-97; TV Horsham *Chich* 97-00. *Duke Elder Eye Unit, Blackshaw Road, London SW17 0QT* T: (020) 8266 6111

CARTER, Duncan Robert Bruton. b 58. Univ of Wales (Cardiff) BA 79 Cam Univ BA 83 MA 89. Ridley Hall Cam 81. **d** 84 **p** 85. C Harold Wood *Chelmsf* 84-88; C S Kensington St Luke *Lon* 88-90; V Henley H Trin *Ox* from 90; AD Henley 02-06. *Holy Trinity Vicarage, Church Street, Henley-on-Thames RG9 1SE* T: (01491) 574822 E: drbcarter@hotmail.com

CARTER, Canon Edward John. b 67. Ex Univ BA 88. Ripon Coll Cuddesdon BA 96 MA 01. **d** 97 **p** 98. C Thorpe St Matt *Nor* 97-00; Min Can and Dean's V Windsor 00-04; P-in-c Didcot St Pet *Ox* 04-12; AD Wallingford 07-12; Can Th Chelmsf Cathl from 12. *2 Harlings Grove, Chelmsford CM1 1YQ* T: (01245) 294489 E: edward.carter@chelmsfordcathedral.org.uk

CARTER, Grayson Leigh. b 53. Univ of S California BSc 76 Ch Ch Ox DPhil 90. Fuller Th Sem California MA 84 Wycliffe Hall Ox 89. **d** 90 **p** 91. C Bungay H Trin w St Mary *St E* 90-92; Chapl BNC Ox 92-96; Hon C Ox St Mary V w St Cross and St Pet 93-96; USA from 96; Assoc Prof Methodist Coll Fayetteville 96-03; Asst R Fayetteville H Trin 96-03; Assoc Prof Fuller Th Sem from 03. *1602 Palmcroft Drive SW, Phoenix AZ 85007-1738, USA* T: (001) (602) 252 5582 *or* 220 0400 F: 220 0444 E: gcarter10@yahoo.com *or* gcarter@fuller.edu

CARTER, Hazel June. b 48. Doncaster Coll of Educn CertEd 72. Carl Dioc Tr Inst 89. **d** 92 **p** 94. C Dalston and Raughton Head w Gatesgill 92-98; TV Carl H Trin and St Barn 98-02; TR 02-07; rtd 07; PtO *Carl* from 08. *4 Wandales Lane, Natland, Kendal LA9 7QY* T: (015395) 60429

CARTER, Heather Ruth. b 62. Trin Coll Bris 85. **d** 02 **p** 04. Dn Montevideo Cathl Uruguay 02-04; Chapl among Deaf People 02-04; NSM Dalston w Cumdivock, Raughton Head and Wreay *Carl* 04-10; Chapl to the Deaf and Hard of Hearing 05-10; Chapl N Cumbria Acute Hosps NHS Trust 05-10; V Blackbird Leys *Ox* from 12. *Church House, 5 Cuddesdon Way, Oxford OX4 6JH* T: (01865) 778728 E: revhev2@gmail.com

CARTER, Ian Sutherland. b 51. Trin Coll Ox BA 73 MA 77 DPhil 77 Leeds Univ BA 80. Coll of Resurr Mirfield 78. **d** 81 **p** 82. C Shildon *Dur* 81-84; C Darlington H Trin 84-87; Chapl Liv Univ 87-93; V Hindley St Pet 93-98; Chapl Oldham NHS Trust 98-02; Chapl Pennine Acute Hosps NHS Trust 02-03; Chapl Salford R NHS Foundn Trust 03-14; P-in-c Hamer *Man* 14-15; P-in-c Healey 14-15; V Hamer and Healey from 15. *All Saints' Vicarage, Foxholes Road, Rochdale OL12 0EF* T: (01706) 355591 E: ianscarter@aol.com

CARTER (née O'NEILL), Mrs Irene. b 44. Worc Coll of Educn CertEd 65. EMMTC 92. **d** 93. NSM N and S Leverton *S'well* 93-11; NSM Retford Area from 11. *38 St Martin's Road, North Leverton, Retford DN22 0AU*

CARTER, Mrs Jacqueline Ann. b 50. St Mich Coll Llan 01. **d** 03 **p** 04. C Ebbw Vale *Mon* 03-06; TV 06-11; V Rhosllannerchrugog *St As* 11; V Rhosllannerchrugog and Penycae from 11. *The Vicarage, Wrexham Road, Johnstown, Wrexham LL14 1PE* T: (01978) 844535 E: jackiecarter16@hotmail.com

CARTER, Canon John Howard Gregory. b 55. York Univ BA 76 Leeds Univ CertEd 77 Nottm Univ MA 96. St Jo Coll Nottm LTh 87. **d** 87 **p** 88. C Nailsea H Trin *B & W* 87-91; TV Camberley St Paul *Guildf* 91-97; Chapl Elmhurst Ballet Sch 91-97; Dioc Communications Officer *Leeds* from 97; Bp's Press Officer *Ripon* 00-14; Hon Can Ripon Cathl from 10.

7 Blenheim Court, Harrogate HG2 9DT T: (01423) 530369 F: 08717-333778 M: 07798-652707 E: jhgcarter@aol.com

CARTER, Mrs Linda Susan. b 61. STETS 11. **d** 14 **p** 15. C Broadstone *Sarum* from 14. *The Curate's House, 1A Mission Road, Broadstone BH18 8JJ* T: (01202) 690947 E: lscarter@btinternet.com

CARTER, Marian. b 40. Whitelands Coll Lon TCert 61 Lon Univ BD 67 Nottm Univ MPhil 79 Man Univ MA 84 Ex Univ PhD 05. N Bapt Coll 81. **d** 92 **p** 94. Par Dn Kempshott *Win* 92-93; Tutor SWMTC 92-96; Tutor Coll of SS Mark and Jo Plymouth 93-00; NSM Plymstock and Hooe *Ex* 94-98; NSM Widecombe-in-the-Moor, Leusdon, Princetown etc 98-00; Chapl St Eliz Hospice Ipswich 00-05; rtd 05; PtO *St E* from 06. *Shalom, 80 Woodlands, Chelmondiston, Ipswich IP9 1DU* T: (01473) 780259

CARTER, Canon Michael John. b 32. St Alb Minl Tr Scheme 81. **d** 84 **p** 85. NSM Radlett *St Alb* 84-88; Chapl SW Herts HA 88-94; Chapl Watford Gen Hosp 88-94; LtO *St Alb* 88-99; Chapl Mt Vernon and Watford Hosps NHS Trust 94-99; Bp's Adv for Hosp Chapl *St Alb* 95-99; Hon Can St Alb 96-99; rtd 99; PtO *St Alb* from 99; Hon Chapl Peace Hospice Watford from 99. *4 Field View Rise, Bricket Wood, St Albans AL2 3RT* T: (01923) 279870 E: mail@mjcarter.com

CARTER, Michael William. b 33. Newland Park Teacher Tr Coll TCert 56. Dioc OLM tr scheme 98. **d** 01 **p** 02. OLM Lingfield and Crowhurst *S'wark* 01-04; rtd 04; PtO *S'wark* from 04. *Redwood House, 76 Godstone Road, Lingfield RH7 6BT* T: (01342) 833843 E: mandjcarter@talktalk.net

CARTER, Nicholas Adrian. b 47. Ripon Hall Ox 71. **d** 74 **p** 75. C Sowerby *Wakef* 74-79; V Hanging Heaton 79-83; CF 83-86; V Elton All SS *Man* 86-90; C Milton *Win* 90-94; P-in-c Boscombe St Andr 94-00; V 00-09; rtd 09; TV Winchcombe *Glouc* from 09. *The Vicarage, Church Road, Alderton, Tewkesbury GL20 8NR* T: (01242) 620238 E: cdevildodger@aol.com

CARTER, Nigel John. b 53. Bolton Inst of Educn CertEd 89. Sarum & Wells Th Coll 91. **d** 93 **p** 94. C Burntwood *Lich* 93-96; V Bentley 96-04; RD Wolverhampton 00-02; V Walsall Wood from 04. *The Vicarage, 2 St John's Close, Walsall Wood, Walsall WS9 9NH* T: (01543) 360558 *or* 372284 E: nigel.carter@02.co.uk

CARTER, Noel William. b 53. Birm Univ BSc 75 Bris Univ CertEd 76 Nottm Univ BSc 83. Linc Th Coll. **d** 83 **p** 84. C Penrith w Newton Reigny and Plumpton Wall *Carl* 83-86; C Barrow St Matt 86-87; V Netherton 87-91; TR Penrith w Newton Reigny and Plumpton Wall 91-97; P-in-c Jersey St Brelade *Win* 97-98; R 98-01; Vice-Dean Jersey 00-01; P-in-c Brymbo and Southsea *St As* 05-07; P-in-c Brymbo, Southsea and Tanyfron 07-14; AD Minera 08-12; TR Rhos-Cystennin from 14; AD Llanrwst and Rhos from 15; PtO *Ban* from 15. *8 Llys Helyg, Deganwy, Conwy LL31 9BN* T: (01492) 339521

CARTER, Canon Norman. b 23. Leeds Univ BSc 48. Coll of Resurr Mirfield 48. **d** 50 **p** 51. C Liv Our Lady and St Nic w St Anne 50-54; C Orford St Marg 54-56; V 56-71; PC Knotty Ash H Spirit 71-74; V Dovecot 74-83; RD W Derby 78-83; Hon Can Liv Cathl 82-88; V Formby St Pet 83-88; rtd 88; PtO *Liv* from 88. *34 Granby Close, Southport PR9 9QG* T: (01704) 232821

CARTER, Paul Joseph. b 67. St Chad's Coll Dur BA 88. St Steph Ho Ox 89. **d** 91 **p** 92. C Ipswich All Hallows *St E* 91; C Newmarket St Mary w Exning St Agnes 91-94; V Thorpe-le-Soken *Chelmsf* 94-04; V Ipswich St Bart *St E* from 04. *St Bartholomew's Vicarage, Newton Road, Ipswich IP3 8HQ* T: (01473) 727441 E: frpaul@stbarts.freeserve.co.uk

CARTER, Paul Mark. b 56. BA 78 MA 90 Cranfield Univ MBA 95. Ridley Hall Cam 79. **d** 81 **p** 82. C Kidsgrove *Lich* 81-84; CF 84-00; Asst P Vancouver St Phil Canada 00-03. *1655 West 41st Avenue, Vancouver BC V6M 1X9, Canada* T: (001) (604) 222 4497 E: paulcarter@acinw.org

CARTER, Paul Rowley. b 45. Lon Univ BD 69 Lon Bible Coll ALBC 69 Southn Univ PGCE 70. Trin Coll Bris. **d** 91 **p** 92. C Penkridge *Lich* 91-96; V Blackb Sav 96-01; R Elmdon St Nic *Birm* 01-11; rtd 11; PtO *Birm* 11; *Lich* from 12. *Elmdon, 4 Goods Station Lane, Penkridge, Stafford ST19 5AU* T: (01785) 710809 E: paul@tworevs.co.uk

CARTER, Richard Anthony. b 59. Univ of Wales (Abth) BA 80 Melbourne Coll of Div BD 94 Leeds Univ MA 02 Lon Inst of Educn PGCE 87. Bp Patteson Th Coll (Solomon Is) 90. **d** 91 **p** 92. Lect Bp Patteson Th Coll 91-00; Miss and Tr Co-ord Melanesian Brotherhood 00-05; Chapl 94-00 and 02-05; PtO *Lon* 00-06; C St Martin-in-the-Fields from 06. *Flat 1, 6 St Martin's Place, London WC2N 4JJ* T: (020) 7766 1100 F: 7839 5163 E: richard.carter@smitf.org

CARTER, Richard William. b 75. Newc Univ BSc 96. Westcott Ho Cam 04. **d** 07 **p** 08. C Llanbedr DC w Llangynhafal, Llanychan etc *St As* 07-10; P-in-c 10; P-in-c Clocaenog and

Gyffylliog from 10; P-in-c Llanfair DC, Derwen, Llanelidan and Efenechtyd from 10. *The Vicarage, Bron y Clwyd, Llanfair Dyffryn Clwyd, Ruthin LL15 2SB*   T: (01824) 703867 M: 07769-727985 E: reverendcarter@gmail.com

CARTER, Robert Desmond. b 35. Cranmer Hall Dur 62. **d** 65 **p** 66. C Otley *Bradf* 65-69; C Keighley 69-73; V Cowling 73-00; rtd 00; PtO *Leeds* from 00. *1 Quincy Close, Eccleshill, Bradford BD2 2EP*   T: (01274) 638385

CARTER, Robert Edward. b 44. Univ of Wales (Ban) BSc 66. St Jo Coll Nottm 79. **d** 81 **p** 82. C Caverswall *Lich* 81-86; V Biddulph 86-94; V Wolverhampton St Jude 94-10; rtd 11; PtO *Lich* from 11; NSM Penn Fields from 12. *17 The Spinney, Wolverhampton WV3 9HE*

CARTER, Robert Thomas. b 49. Moore Th Coll Sydney 72 Ridley Coll Melbourne ThL 75. **d** 75 **p** 76. C Traralgon St Jas Australia 75-76; P-in-c Endeavour Hills St Matt 77-79; V 80-84; Assoc Min Kew St Hilary 85-91; V Blackburn N St Alfred 92-00; C Fisherton Anger *Sarum* 00-02; Australia from 02. *224 Maroondah Highway, Croydon, Melbourne VIC 3136, Australia*

CARTER, Robin. b 46. Cam Univ MSt 02. Chich Th Coll 71. **d** 74 **p** 75. C Wortley-de-Leeds *Ripon* 74-76; C Hutton *Chelmsf* 76-78; C Wickford 78-81; TV Wickford and Runwell 81-83; Chapl HM Pris Leeds 83-85; Chapl HM Pris Reading 85-89; Chapl HM YOI Huntercombe and Finnamore 85-89; Chapl HM YOI Finnamore Wood Camp 86-89; Gov 5, Hd of Operations, HM Pris Channings Wood 89-94; Gov 4, Hd of Operations/Régime and Throughcare, HM Pris Woodhill 94-99; Gov HM Pris E Sutton Park 99-05; Sen Operational Pris Service Manager 05-08; Chapl Costa Blanca *Eur* 08-12; rtd 12; PtO *Ox* from 13. *1 Symington Court, Shenley Lodge, Milton Keynes MK5 7AN* E: robincarter@yahoo.com

CARTER, Ronald George. b 31. Leeds Univ BA 58. Coll of Resurr Mirfield 58. **d** 60 **p** 61. C Wigan St Anne *Liv* 60-63; Prec Wakef Cathl 63-66; V Woodhall *Bradf* 66-77; Chapl Qu Marg Sch Escrick Park 77-83; Min Can, Prec and Sacr Pet Cathl 83-88; R Upper St Leonards St Jo *Chich* 88-94; rtd 94; PtO *York* from 95. *5 Greenwich Close, York YO30 5WN*   T: (01904) 610237

CARTER, Russell James Wigney. b 29. Chich Th Coll 80. **d** 82 **p** 83. C Aldwick *Chich* 82-86; R Buxted and Hadlow Down 86-90; rtd 90; PtO *Chich* from 90. *6 Lucerne Court, Aldwick, Bognor Regis PO21 4XL*   T: (01243) 862858

CARTER, Samuel. b 49. St Jo Coll Dur BA 71. Cranmer Hall Dur 73. **d** 74 **p** 75. C Kingswinford St Mary *Lich* 74-77; C Shrewsbury H Cross 77-84; V Normacot 84-94. *Address withheld by request*

CARTER, Sarah Helen Buchanan. *See* GORTON, Sarah Helen Buchanan

CARTER, Stanley Reginald. b 24. St Jo Coll Dur BA 49. **d** 50 **p** 51. C Stoughton *Guildf* 50-53; C Bucknall and Bagnall *Lich* 53-56; R Salford St Matthias w St Simon *Man* 56-62; V Highbury New Park St Aug *Lon* 62-69; V Sneinton St Chris w St Phil *S'well* 69-89; rtd 89; PtO *S'well* from 89. *31 Pateley Road, Nottingham NG3 5QF*   T: 0115-953 2122 E: stan.carter@dunelm.org.uk

CARTER, Canon Stephen. b 56. Univ of Wales (Lamp) BA 77 Southn Univ BTh 81. Sarum & Wells Th Coll 78. **d** 81 **p** 82. C Halstead St Andr w H Trin and Greenstead Green *Chelmsf* 81-84; C Loughton St Jo 84-89; V N Shoebury 89-95; R Lexden 95-09; RD Colchester 01-06; V Maldon All SS w St Pet from 09; Hon Can Chelmsf Cathl from 07. *All Saints' Vicarage, Church Walk, Maldon CM9 4PY*   T: (01621) 854179 E: revscarter@googlemail.com

CARTER, Stephen Howard. b 47. City Univ BSc 72. St Jo Coll Nottm 83. **d** 85 **p** 86. C Hellesdon *Nor* 85-88; Chapl Birm Children's Hosp 88-91; Chapl Birm Maternity Hosp 88-91; TV Tettenhall Wood *Lich* 91-98; Chapl Compton Hospice 91-98; P-in-c Coalbrookdale, Iron-Bridge and Lt Wenlock *Heref* 98-00; R 00-07; Asst Dioc Co-ord for Evang 00-01; P-in-c Darby End *Worc* 07-08; V 08-12; P-in-c Netherton St Andr 07-08; V 08-12; V Darby End and Netherton 12-14; RD Dudley 10-13; rtd 14; PtO *Cov* from 15. *Address temp unknown* E: stevecarter@fastmail.net

CARTER, Stephen Paul. b 55. Cartrefle Coll of Educn CertEd 76. Trin Coll Bris BA 88. **d** 98 **p** 99. Dn-in-c Montevideo H Spirit Uruguay 98-99; P-in-c 00-04; V Dalston w Cumdivock, Raughton Head and Wreay *Carl* from 04. *The Vicarage, Townhead Road, Dalston, Carlisle CA5 7JF*   T/F: (01228) 710215 E: stevecarter194@gmail.com

CARTER, Stuart Conway. b 58. Lon Bible Coll 81 St Jo Coll Nottm 90. **d** 92 **p** 93. C Birm St Luke 92-96; C The Quinton 96-10; V Castle Bromwich St Clem from 10; AD Coleshill from 13. *The Vicarage, Lanchester Way, Castle Bromwich, Birmingham B36 9JG*   T: 0121-218 6118 E: stuwcarter@btinternet.com

CARTER, Terence John. b 31. K Coll Lon BD 57 AKC 57 Lon Univ BA 68 PGCE 69. **d** 58 **p** 59. C Winchmore Hill H Trin *Lon*

58-60; PV S'wark Cathl 60-63; Sacr S'wark Cathl 60-61; Succ S'wark Cathl 61-63; R Ockham w Hatchford *Guildf* 63-69; LtO *S'wark* 69-78; *Portsm* 78-82; PtO from 82; rtd 91. *15 Balliol Road, Portsmouth PO2 7PP*   T: (023) 9269 9167 M: 07811-474020 E: terence.carter1@ntlworld.com

CARTER, Timothy Stephen. b 76. Somerville Coll Ox MEng 99. St Jo Coll Nottm 06. **d** 08 **p** 09. C Hanley H Ev *Lich* 08-11; C Priors Lee and St Georges' from 11. *16 Highgrove Meadow, Priorslee, Telford TF2 9RJ*   M: 07772-956146 E: tim@carterclan.me.uk

CARTER, Mrs Wendy Elise Grace. b 46. Battersea Coll of Educn TCert 67. Qu Coll Birm 01. **d** 04 **p** 05. C Kingshurst *Birm* 04-07; P-in-c High Wych and Gilston w Eastwick *St Alb* 07-10; rtd 10; PtO *Birm* 13-14; Hon C Salter Street and Shirley from 14. *134 Shakespeare Drive, Shirley, Solihull B90 2AR* T: 0121-744 8589 M: 07753-676973 E: revwendy@sky.com

CARTLEDGE, Margery. *See* TÖLLER, Margery Elizabeth

CARTLEDGE, Mark John. b 62. Lon Bible Coll BA 85 Univ of Wales PhD 00. Oak Hill Th Coll MPhil 89. **d** 88 **p** 89. C Formby H Trin *Liv* 88-91; CMS Nigeria 91-93; Chapl Liv Univ 93-98; Chapl and Tutor St Jo Coll Dur 98-03; Lect Univ of Wales (Lamp) 03-06; Sen Lect Th Birm Univ 08-15; PtO *Birm* from 09. *Address temp unknown* E: m.j.cartledge@bham.ac.uk

CARTMELL, Canon Richard Peter Watkinson. b 43. Cranmer Hall Dur 77. **d** 79 **p** 80. C Whittle-le-Woods *Blackb* 79-85; V Lower Darwen St Jas 85-03; RD Darwen 91-96; P-in-c S Shore H Trin 03-08; Hon Can Blackb Cathl 98-08; rtd 08; PtO *Blackb* from 08. *4 Salwick Avenue, Blackpool FY2 9BT* T: (01253) 590083

CARTMILL, Canon Ralph Arthur. b 40. St Jo Coll Dur BA 62 Em Coll Cam MA 64. Ridley Hall Cam 63. **d** 65 **p** 66. C Dukinfield St Jo *Ches* 65-68; C Wilmslow 68-69; Warden Walton Youth Cen Liv 69-70; Asst Master Aylesbury Gr Sch 70-74; PtO *Ox* 72-74; V Terriers 74-85; P-in-c Chinnor w Emmington and Sydenham 85-86; R Chinnor w Emmington and Sydenham etc 86-98; Hon Can Ch Ch 97-98; rtd 98; PtO *Nor* from 00. *6 Longview Close, Snettisham, King's Lynn PE31 7RD* T: (01485) 543357 E: r.cartmill58@btinternet.com

CARTWRIGHT, Alan John. b 44. Liv Univ BEng 66 Birm Univ MSc 68 Warwick Univ PhD 95 CEng 72 MIMechE 72. WMMTC 04. **d** 07 **p** 08. OLM Rugby W *Cov* 07-12; NSM Warmington w Shotteswell and Radway w Ratley 12-14; NSM Edgehill Churches from 14. *Address temp unknown* M: 07981-667534 E: alan@stmatthews.org.uk

CARTWRIGHT, Mrs Amanda Jane. b 58. St Jo Coll Nottm 00. **d** 02 **p** 03. C Beeston *S'well* 02-07; P-in-c Bilborough St Jo 07-13; V from 13; P-in-c Bilborough w Strelley 07-13; R from 13. *St John's Vicarage, Graylands Road, Nottingham NG8 4FD* T: 0115-854 3628 E: revdmand@hotmail.com

CARTWRIGHT, Julia Ann. b 58. Nottm Univ BA 80. Linc Th Coll 84. **dss** 86 **d** 87 **p** 94. Asst Chapl HM Pris Morton Hall 85-90; Linc St Jo 86-88; Hon C 87-88; Hon C Bardney 88-97; Chapl Linc Co Hosp 90-93; Chapl St Geo Hosp Linc 90-93; Chapl Linc Distr Health Services and Hosps NHS Trust 93-97; Chapl S Bucks NHS Trust 97-04; LtO *Ox* 97-04; Chapl S Warks Combined Care NHS Trust 04-12; Chapl N Devon Healthcare NHS Trust from 12. *North Devon District Hospital, Raleigh Park, Barnstaple EX31 4JB*   T: (01271) 322362

CARTWRIGHT, Michael. *See* CARTWRIGHT, William Michael

CARTWRIGHT, Michael John. b 42. Qu Coll Birm 67. **d** 70 **p** 71. C Astwood Bank w Crabbs Cross *Worc* 70-75; P-in-c Worc St Mich 75-77; V Stockton St Paul *Dur* 77-87; V Market Rasen *Linc* 87-12; R Linwood 87-12; V Legsby 87-12; R Wickenby Gp 95-00; V Lissington 00-12; RD W Wold 89-01; rtd 12. *The Coach House, Main Road, Welbourn, Lincoln LN5 0PA* T: (01400) 279062 E: pontiac57@hotmail.com

CARTWRIGHT, Paul. b 71. Leeds Metrop Univ BA 99 Leeds Univ BA 08 MA 13 Huddersfield Univ PGCE 06. Coll of Resurr Mirfield 06. **d** 08 **p** 09. C Athersley *Wakef* 08-11; C Carlton 10-11; P-in-c Barnsley St Pet and St Jo *Leeds* from 11. *The Vicarage, 1 Osborne Mews, Barnsley S70 1UU*   T: (01226) 282220 M: 07852-174303 E: fr.paul.cartwright@gmail.com

CARTWRIGHT, Ms Ruth. b 59. St Mellitus Coll BA 14. **d** 14 **p** 15. C Grays Thurrock *Chelmsf* from 14. *19 Grove Road, Rayleigh SS6 8PU* M: 07432-599404 T: (01375) 370884 E: ruth@cartmann.eclipse.co.uk

CARTWRIGHT, Samuel. b 27. Cuddesdon Coll 71. **d** 72 **p** 72. C Rochdale *Man* 72-76; V Roundthorn 76-83; V Ashton Ch Ch 83-93; rtd 93; PtO *Derby* 93-13. *8 Wentworth Avenue, Walton, Chesterfield S40 3JB*   T: (01246) 232252 E: elsieandsam@yahoo.co.uk

CARTWRIGHT, Simon John. b 71. R Holloway Coll Lon BA 93 Sheff Univ MA 95. St Jo Coll Nottm MTh 05. **d** 06 **p** 07. C Ward End w Bordesley Green *Birm* 06-11; TV Walbrook Epiphany *Derby* from 11. *The Vicarage, 81 Palmerston Street, Derby DE23 6PF* T: (01332) 762573 M: 07720-769631 E: revscartwright@gmail.com

CARTWRIGHT, William Michael. b 44. Birm Univ CertEd 67. Coll of Resurr Mirfield 83. **d** 83 **p** 84. Hd Master Chacombe Sch 83-85; Hon C Middleton Cheney w Chacombe *Pet* 83-85; Hd Master Chacombe Sch Banbury 83-85; C Kettering SS Pet and Paul 85-86; PtO 86-88; Chapl Northaw Prep Sch Win 89-92; P-in-c Altarnon w Bolventor, Laneast and St Clether *Truro* 92-97; V Treverbyn 97-01; V Bempton w Flamborough, Reighton w Speeton *York* 01-03; V Ampleforth w Oswaldkirk, Gilling E etc 03-09; rtd 09; P-in-c Barningham w Matlaske w Baconsthorpe etc *Nor* 09-14; PtO from 14. *11 Dairy Farm Cottages, Barningham, Norwich NR11 7JY* T: (01263) 577865 E: williamcartwright606@btinternet.com

CARUANA, Mrs Rosemary Anne. b 38. St Alb Minl Tr Scheme 81. **dss** 84 **d** 87 **p** 94. Hertford St Andr *St Alb* 84-87; Par Dn Hertingfordbury 87-94; C 94-98; P-in-c 98-05; rtd 05. *36 Holly Croft, Hertford SG14 2DR* T: (01992) 306427 M: 07769-658756 E: r.caruana@ntlworld.com

CARVER, Miss Elizabeth Ann. b 36. Bp Otter Coll BA 00 Chich Univ MA 09 ACIB 72. **d** 99. NSM Littlehampton and Wick *Chich* 99-15; rtd 15. *13 Hearnfield Road, Littlehampton BN17 7PR* T: (01903) 713169

CARVETH, Mrs Marlene. b 51. Ex Univ BA 07. SWMTC 04. **d** 07 **p** 08. NSM Camborne *Truro* 07-13; NSM Camborne and Tuckingmill 13-14; NSM St Illogan from 15. *Trelowarren, 5 Rosevale Crescent, Camborne TR14 7LU* T: (01209) 713175 E: roseyvale@tiscali.co.uk

CARVOSSO, John Charles. b 45. ACA 71 FCA 79. Oak Hill Th Coll 75. **d** 78 **p** 79. C Chelsea St Jo w St Andr *Lon* 78-81; Chapl RAF 81-84; P-in-c Tawstock *Ex* 84-85; TV Newport, Bishops Tawton and Tawstock 85-96; TV Newton Tracey, Horwood, Alverdiscott etc 96-11; RD Torrington 97-02; rtd 11. *45 Trafalgar Drive, Torrington EX38 7AD* M: 07507-369127 E: revjcc@gmail.com

CASE, Preb Catherine Margaret. b 44. Ripon Coll Cuddesdon 86. **d** 88 **p** 94. C Blurton *Lich* 88-92; TD Hanley H Ev and Min to Hanley Care Agencies 92-94; P-in-c Wrockwardine Wood *Lich* 95-98; R 98-00; V Gnosall 00-06; V Gnosall and Moreton 06-07; Preb Lich Cathl 02-07; rtd 07; PtO *Lich* 07-14; C Barlaston from 14. *2 Fulmar Place, Stoke-on-Trent ST3 7QF* T: (01782) 399291

CASE, Clive Anthony. b 70. St Andr Univ MTheol 93 Surrey Univ BA 05 St Jo Coll Dur PGCE 94. STETS 02. **d** 05 **p** 06. NSM Epsom St Martin *Guildf* 05-11; Asst Chapl Epsom Coll 05-07; Chapl St Jo Sch Leatherhead 08-11; Sen Chapl Charterhouse Sch Godalming from 11. *Charterhouse School, Brook Hall, Charterhouse, Godalming GU7 2DX* T: (01483) 291741 M: 07801-288943 E: cac@charterhouse.org.uk

CASEBOW, Ronald Philip. b 31. Roch Th Coll 59. **d** 61 **p** 62. C Southgate Ch Ch *Lon* 61-64; C Oseney Crescent St Luke w Camden Square St Paul 64-70; Warden St Paul's Ho Student Hostel 64-70; V Colchester St Steph *Chelmsf* 70-74; V Burnham 74-89; rtd 89; PtO *Nor* from 95. *The Priory, Priory Road, Palgrave, Diss IP22 1AJ* T: (01379) 651804

CASEY, Christopher Noel. b 61. Open Univ BA 95. St Jo Coll Nottm BA 01. **d** 01 **p** 02. C Penrith w Newton Reigny and Plumpton Wall *Carl* 01-06; P-in-c Mirehouse from 06. *The Vicarage, Hollins Close, Whitehaven CA28 8EX* T: (01946) 693565 E: kc.family@btopenworld.com

CASH, Simon Andrew. b 62. St Jo Coll Nottm 99. **d** 01 **p** 02. C Aston cum Aughton w Swallownest and Ulley *Sheff* 01-04; P-in-c Worksop St Anne *S'well* from 04; P-in-c Norton Cuckney from 05; AD Bassetlaw and Bawtry from 14. *The Vicarage, 11 Poplar Close, Worksop S80 3BZ* T: (01909) 472069 E: simon_cash@sky.com

CASHEL, Dean of. *See* FIELD, The Very Revd Gerald Gordon

CASHEL, WATERFORD AND LISMORE, Archdeacon of. *See* LONG, The Ven Christopher William

CASHEL, WATERFORD, LISMORE, OSSORY, FERNS AND LEIGHLIN, Bishop of. *See* BURROWS, The Rt Revd Michael Andrew James

CASSAM, Victor Reginald. b 33. Chich Univ BA 05. Chich Th Coll 59. **d** 62 **p** 63. C Portsea St Jo Rudmore *Portsm* 62-64; C W Leigh CD 64-66; C Torquay St Martin Barton *Ex* 66-69; C Stanmer w Falmer and Moulsecoomb *Chich* 69-73; P-in-c Catsfield 73-76; R Catsfield and Crowhurst 76-81; R Selsey 81-01; RD Chich 96-01; rtd 01; PtO *Chich* from 01; *Portsm* from 01. *195 Oving Road, Chichester PO19 7ER* T/F: (01243) 783998 M: 07976-757451 E: frvictor@gmail.com

CASSELTON, John Charles. b 43. Univ of Wales (Swansea) MA 95. Oak Hill Th Coll 64. **d** 68 **p** 69. C Upton *Ex* 68-73; C Braintree *Chelmsf* 73-80; V Ipswich St Jo *St E* 80-92; RD Ipswich 86-92; Chapl St Clem Hosp Ipswich 92-98; Chapl St Eliz Hospice Ipswich 92-00; Dir Inspire Chr Counselling 00-05; rtd 05; PtO *St E* from 00. *Rose Cottage,*

41 North Hill Road, Ipswich IP4 2PN T: (01473) 401638 M: 07951-700479 E: johnandmidge@hotmail.co.uk

CASSERLY-FARRAR, Caroline. **d** 13 **p** 14. NSM Enniscorthy w Clone, Clonmore, Monart etc *C & O* 13-14; NSM Gorey w Kilnahue, Leskinfere and Ballycanew from 14. *Havish Japa, Glen Road, Delgany, Co Wicklow, Republic of Ireland* E: revdccasserlyfarrar@gmail.com

CASSIDY, Brian Ross. b 31. Cape Town Univ. St Bede's Coll Umtata 88. **d** 89 **p** 91. S Africa 89-92; C Lymington *Win* 92-93; P-in-c Hyde Common 93-96; P-in-c Ellingham and Harbridge and Ibsley 95-96; V Ellingham and Harbridge and Hyde w Ibsley 96-03; rtd 03. *The Vicarage, Hyde, Fordingbridge SP6 2QJ* T: (01425) 653216 E: cassidy@btinternet.com

✠**CASSIDY, The Rt Revd George Henry.** b 42. QUB BSc 65 Lon Univ MPhil 67. Oak Hill Th Coll 70. **d** 72 **p** 73 **c** 99. C Clifton Ch Ch w Em *Bris* 72-75; V Sea Mills 75-82; V Portman Square St Paul *Lon* 82-87; Adn Lon and Can Res St Paul's Cathl 87-99; P-in-c St Ethelburga Bishopgate 89-91; Bp S'well and Nottm 99-09; rtd 09; Hon Asst Bp B & W from 10. *Darch House, 17 St Andrew's Road, Stogursey, Bridgwater TA5 1TE* T: (01278) 732625 E: georgecassidy123@btinternet.com

CASSIDY, Ian David. b 59. NOC 94. **d** 97 **p** 98. NSM Everton St Geo *Liv* 97-07; NSM Liv N Deanery 07-11; NSM Liv All SS from 11. *79 Gilroy Road, Liverpool L6 6BG* T: 0151-263 9751 M: 0780-1933654

CASSIDY, Patrick Nigel. b 40. TCD BA 63 MA 66. Sarum Th Coll 64. **d** 66 **p** 67. C Heaton St Barn *Bradf* 66-68; Asst Chapl Brussels *Eur* 68-70; Chapl SW France 70-72; V Oseney Crescent St Luke w Camden Square St Paul *Lon* 72-83; Chapl Strasbourg w Stuttgart and Heidelberg *Eur* 83-84; PtO *Chich* 86-90; Chapl Marseille w Aix-en-Provence *Eur* 90-05; Hon Chapl Miss to Seafarers 90-05; rtd 05; PtO *Eur* from 05. *73 La Canebière (Appt 83), 13001 Marseille, France* T: (0033) 4 91 90 18 81

CASSIDY, Canon Ronald. b 43. Lon Univ BD 66 Man Univ MPhil 85 Liv Univ PhD 00. Tyndale Hall Bris 63. **d** 68 **p** 69. C Kirkdale St Lawr *Liv* 68-70; C Bolton Em *Man* 70-74; V Roughtown 74-89; R Denton St Lawr 89-07; AD Ashton-under-Lyne 97-03; Hon Can Man Cathl 02-07; rtd 07; PtO *Man* from 07; AD Ardwick from 15. *19 Broomfields, Denton, Manchester M34 3TH* T: 0161-320 6955 M: 07841-892028 E: roncassidy60@gmail.com

CASSON, David Christopher. b 41. Qu Coll Cam BA 64 MA 68. Ridley Hall Cam 65. **d** 67 **p** 68. C Birm St Martin 67-72; C Luton St Mary *St Alb* 72-77; P-in-c Luton St Fran 77; V 77-84; V Richmond H Trin and Ch Ch *S'wark* 84-97; R Acle w Fishley, N Burlingham, Beighton w Moulton *Nor* 97-04; rtd 04; PtO *Nor* from 04. *70 The Street, Brundall, Norwich NR13 5LH* T: (01603) 712092

CASSON, Canon James Stuart. b 32. Liv Univ BA 54 Nottm Univ MPhil 70. Ridley Hall Cam. **d** 61 **p** 62. C Eccleston Ch Ch *Liv* 61-64; C Littleover *Derby* 64-67; V Dearham *Carl* 67-76; V Holme Eden 76-98; RD Brampton 91-96; Hon Can Carl Cathl 93-98; P-in-c Croglin 93-98; rtd 98; PtO *Carl* from 01. *5 High Woodbank, Brisco, Carlisle CA4 0QR* T: (01228) 525692

CASSWELL, Canon David Oriel. b 52. Loughb Coll of Educn DipEd 74 CQSW 79. Oak Hill Th Coll 85. **d** 87 **p** 88. C Acomb St Steph and St Aid *York* 87-91; Dep Chapl HM Pris Leeds 91-92; Chapl HM Pris Everthorpe 92; Chapl HM Pris Wolds 92-98; V Clifton *York* from 98; Can and Preb York Minster from 13. *Clifton Vicarage, Clifton, York YO30 6BH* T: (01904) 655071 F: 654796 E: david.casswell@cliftonparish.org.uk

CASTER, John Forristall. b 71. Texas A&M Univ BA 93. St Steph Ho Ox BTh 05. **d** 05 **p** 06. C Hendon St Alphage *Lon* 05-09; TV Old St Pancras 09-12; P-in-c Tunbridge Wells St Barn *Roch* from 12. *The Clergy House, 114 Upper Grosvenor Road, Tunbridge Wells TN1 2EX* T: (01892) 525656 E: john.caster@ssho.oxon.org

✠**CASTLE, The Rt Revd Brian Colin.** b 49. Lon Univ BA 72 Ox Univ BA 77 MA 80 Birm Univ PhD 89. Cuddesdon Coll 74. **d** 77 **p** 78 **c** 02. C Limpsfield and Titsey *S'wark* 77-81; USPG Zambia 81-84; Lect Ecum Inst WCC Geneva 84-85; V N Petherton w Northmoor Green *B & W* 85-92; Dir Past Studies and Vice-Prin Cuddesdon Coll 92-01; Suff Bp Tonbridge *Roch* from 02; Hon Can Roch Cathl from 02. *Bishop's Lodge, 48 St Botolph's Road, Sevenoaks TN13 3AG* T: (01732) 456070 F: 741449 E: bishop.tonbridge@rochester.anglican.org

CASTLE, Brian Stanley. b 47. Oak Hill Th Coll 70. **d** 73 **p** 74. C Barnsbury St Andr w St Thos and St Matthias *Lon* 73-76; C Lower Homerton St Paul 76-79; P-in-c Bethnal Green St Jas Less 79-82; V 82-98; V Tile Cross *Birm* 98-08; P-in-c Garretts Green 03-08; V Garretts Green and Tile Cross from 08; P-in-c Sheldon from 12; AD Coleshill 06-13. *The Vicarage,*

Haywood Road, Birmingham B33 0LH   T/F: 0121-779 2739
M: 07710-251790 E: revbcastle@aol.com
CASTLE, John Arthur. b 61. G&C Coll Cam BA 83 St Jo Coll Dur
BA 95. Aston Tr Scheme 90 Cranmer Hall Dur 92. **d** 95 **p** 96.
C Southborough St Pet w Ch Ch and St Matt *Roch* 95-99; Miss
Partner CMS 99-04; P-in-c Sandhurst *Ox* 04-10; R from 10. *The
Rectory, 155 High Street, Sandhurst GU47 8HR*   T: (01252)
872168 E: rector@stmichaels-sandhurst.org.uk
CASTLE, Martin Roger. b 69. Leic Univ BA 92 Liv Univ MCD 95
St Edm Coll Cam BTh 09. Ridley Hall Cam. **d** 09 **p** 10. C Leic
Martyrs 09-12; P-in-c Earl Shilton w Elmesthorpe from 12. *The
Vicarage, Maughan Street, Earl Shilton, Leicester LE9 7BA*
CASTLE, Michael David. b 38. Wells Th Coll 69. **d** 71 **p** 72.
C Acocks Green *Birm* 71-75; C Weoley Castle 76-78; V 78-08;
rtd 08. *12 West Pathway, Birmingham B17 9DU*
T: 0121-427 2914
CASTLE, Phillip Stanley. b 43. **d** 97 **p** 98. OLM E Farnworth
and Kearsley *Man* 97-09; OLM Farnworth, Kearsley and
Stoneclough 10-13; rtd 13; PtO *Man* from 13. *73 Bradford
Street, Farnworth, Bolton BL4 9JY*   T: (01204) 571439
E: phillip@stjohnsfarnworth.co.uk
CASTLE, Roger James. b 39. St Jo Coll Cam BA 62 MA 66.
Clifton Th Coll 63. **d** 65 **p** 66. C Rushden w Newton
Bromswold *Pet* 65-68; C Stapenhill w Cauldwell *Derby* 68-72;
V Hayfield 72-89; R Coxheath, E Farleigh, Hunton, Linton etc
Roch 89-04; Chapl Invicta Community Care NHS Trust 91-04;
rtd 04; PtO *Bris* from 04. *10 College Park Drive, Bristol BS10 7AN*
T: 0117-950 7028
CASTLETON, Mark Peter. b 82. Bath Spa Univ BA 04 Cam
Univ BTh 09. Ridley Hall Cam 06. **d** 09 **p** 10. C Salisbury
St Mark *Sarum* 09-13; C Aldridge *Lich* from 13. *The Vicarage,
14 St Thomas Close, Aldridge, Walsall WS9 8SL*
E: markcastleton@ymail.com
CASWELL, Roger John. b 47. St Chad's Coll Dur BA 70. St Steph
Ho Ox 75. **d** 77 **p** 78. C Brighton Resurr *Chich* 77-83; TV
Crawley 83-90; TR Littlehampton and Wick from 90; Chapl
Worthing Priority Care NHS Trust from 90. *St Mary's Vicarage,
18 Church Street, Littlehampton BN17 5PX*   T: (01903) 724410
or 726875
CATALLO, Leon Peter. b 84. Down Coll Cam MSci 06. Wycliffe
Hall Ox BA 14. **d** 15. C Plymouth St Andr *Ex* from 15.
117 Lipson Road, Plymouth PL4 7NQ
E: leoncatallo@googlemail.com
CATCHPOLE, Geoffrey Alan. b 47. AKC. Westcott Ho Cam 76.
d 77 **p** 78. C Camberwell St Luke *S'wark* 77-80; C Dulwich
St Barn 80-82; TV Canvey Is *Chelmsf* 82-87; Ind Chapl 83-87;
P-in-c Bradwell on Sea 87-92; P-in-c St Lawrence 87-92;
V Holland-on-Sea 92-00; P-in-c Witchford w Wentworth
Ely 00-02; Adult Educn and Tr Officer 00-02; R Colchester
St Mich Myland *Chelmsf* 02-07; rtd 07; PtO *Chelmsf* from 09.
Shobita's Ship, 21 Empire Road, Harwich CO12 3QA
T: (01255) 508525 E: pole@pole97.fsnet.co.uk
CATCHPOLE, Richard James Swinburne. b 65. St Steph Ho
Ox 92. **d** 95 **p** 96. C Eastbourne St Andr *Chich* 95-98;
C Eastbourne St Mary 98-00; C E Grinstead St Swithun 00-07.
23 Nineveh Shipyard, Arundel BN18 9SU   M: 07951-427384
E: rjscatchpole@hotmail.co.uk
CATCHPOLE, Roy. b 46. Sheff Univ MMinTheol 95. St Jo Coll
Nottm LTh 74 ALCD 74. **d** 74 **p** 75. C Rainham *Chelmsf*
74-76; C Hyson Green *S'well* 76-79; V Broxtowe 79-86;
V Calverton 86-94; Hilfield Friary Dorchester 95-01; rtd 01;
PtO *Sarum* from 06; B & W from 11. *60 Gainsborough, Milborne
Port, Sherborne DT9 5BB*   T: (01963) 250040
E: rev.catch@virgin.net
CATER, Lois May. b 37. S Dios Minl Tr Scheme 81. **dss** 84 **d** 87
p 94. Calne and Blackland *Sarum* 84-89; Hon Par Dn 87-89;
Hon Par Dn Devizes St Jo w St Mary 89-94; Hon C 94-96;
Hon TV Alderbury Team 96-01; Hon TV Clarendon 01-07.
18 St Margaret's Close, Calne SN11 0UQ   T: (01249) 819432
CATERER, James Albert Leslie Blower. b 44. New Coll Ox BA 67
MA 81. Sarum & Wells Th Coll 79. **d** 81 **p** 82. C Cheltenham
St Luke and St Jo *Glouc* 81-85; V Standish w Haresfield and
Moreton Valence etc 85-96; P-in-c Glouc St Steph 96-09;
rtd 09. *Copelands, 180 Stroud Road, Gloucester GL1 5JX*
T/F: (01452) 524694 E: jimscicaterer@googlemail.com
CATHCART, Adrian James. *See* MATTHEWS, Adrian James
CATHERALL, Mark Leslie. b 64. Chich Th Coll BTh 93. **d** 93
p 94. C Lancing w Coombes *Chich* 93-95; C Selsey 95-98;
Chapl RN 98-04; V S Thornaby *York* from 04. *St Peter's
Rectory, White House Road, Thornaby, Stockton-on-Tees TS17 0AJ*
T: (01642) 888403 E: frmark.catherall@ntlworld.com
CATHERINE JOY, Sister. *See* MOON, Catherine Joy
CATHIE, Sean Bewley. b 43. Univ Tor BA 67 Birkbeck Coll
Lon MSc 04. Cuddesdon Coll 67. **d** 69 **p** 70. C Kensal Rise
St Martin *Lon* 69-73; C Paddington H Trin w St Paul 73-75;
P-in-c Bridstow w Peterstow *Heref* 76-79; Hon C Westmr St Jas

Lon 85-97; Hon C St Marylebone w H Trin 99-06; Hon C
St Marylebone St Cypr 99-06; rtd 06. *Little Adawent, Garway
Hill, Hereford HR2 8RX*   T: (01981) 580380
E: scathie@waitrose.com
CATLEY, John Howard. b 37. AKC 60. K Coll Lon 57 St Boniface
Warminster 60. **d** 61 **p** 62. C Sowerby Bridge w Norland *Wakef*
61-64; C Almondbury 64-67; V Earl's Heaton 67-75;
V Brownhill 75-86; V Morley St Pet w Churwell 86-92;
V St Annes St Marg *Blackb* 92-98; RD Kirkham 94-98; rtd 98;
PtO *Blackb* from 98. *Flat 6, Herne Hill Lodge, 598 Lytham Road,
Blackpool FY4 1RB*   T: (01253) 408129
CATLEY, Marc. b 59. Liv Univ BA 82 Lon Bible Coll BA 85 Man
Poly PGCE 90. St Jo Coll Nottm MTh 06. **d** 07 **p** 08. C E Green
Cov 07-11; V Packwood w Hockley Heath *Birm* from 11. *The
Vicarage, Nuthurst Lane, Hockley Heath, Solihull B94 5RP*
T: (01564) 783121   M: 07952-456846
E: marc.catley@yahoo.co.uk
CATLING, Michael David. b 56. Goldsmiths' Coll Lon
CertEd 77 DipEd 84 Newc Univ MLitt 06. Cranmer Hall
Dur 88. **d** 90 **p** 91. C Cullercoats St Geo *Newc* 90-94; TV
Glendale Gp 94-01; V Whittingham and Edlingham w
Bolton Chapel 01-09; R Wigmore Abbey *Heref* from 09.
The Rectory, Dark Lane, Leintwardine, Craven Arms SY7 0LJ
T: (01547) 540235 E: mikecat7@btinternet.com
CATO (*formerly* LEGGETT), Ms Vanessa Gisela. b 51. St Osyth
Coll of Educn TCert 75. Westcott Ho Cam 93. **d** 93 **p** 94.
C Southchurch H Trin *Chelmsf* 93-97; R Orsett and Bulphan
and Horndon on the Hill 97-03; Chapl Basildon and Thurrock
Gen Hosps NHS Trust 99-03; P-in-c Sandridge and Herts Area
Children's Work Adv *St Alb* 03-11; R Ogden Gd Shep USA
from 11. *The Church of the Good Shepherd, 2374 Grant Avenue,
Ogden UT 84401, USA*
CATON, Philip Cooper. b 47. Oak Hill Th Coll 79. **d** 81 **p** 82.
C Much Woolton *Liv* 81-85; TV Parr 85-98; V Birkdale
St Jo 98-11; rtd 11. *Cooper's Cottage, 23 Alma Road, Southport
PR8 4AN*   T: (01704) 565785 E: p.caton@sky.com
CATTELL, Angela Kathleen. b 48. Trin Coll Bris. **d** 12 **p** 13.
OLM Stoke Bishop *Bris* from 12. *9 Eastmead Lane, Bristol
BS9 1HW*   T: 0117-968 3069
E: angela.cattell@blueyonder.co.uk
CATTELL, Mrs Rosemary Ann. b 51. Open Univ BA 87 Univ
Coll Chich BA 04 Chich Univ MA 09. SEITE 10. **d** 12 **p** 13.
NSM Warnham *Chich* from 12. *Whitegates, Salisbury Road,
Horsham RH13 0AL*   T: (01403) 264396
E: r.a.cattell@btinternet.com
CATTERALL, David Arnold. b 53. Lon Univ BSc 74 ARCS 74.
Cranmer Hall Dur. **d** 78 **p** 79. C Swinton St Pet *Man* 78-81;
C Wythenshawe St Martin 81-83; R Heaton Norris Ch w
All SS 83-88; I Fanlobbus Union *C, C & R* 88-95; Can Cork
and Ross Cathls 93-95; Warden Ch's Min of Healing in
Ireland 95-02; I Templemichael w Clongish, Clooncumber
etc *K, E & A* from 02. *Amberley, The Belfry, Co Longford,
Republic of Ireland*   T: (00353) (43) 334 6442
E: djcatt@eircom.net
CATTERALL, Canon Janet Margaret. b 53. Univ of Wales (Ban)
BA 74. Cranmer Hall Dur 77. **dss** 81 **d** 87 **p** 90. Par Dn Heaton
Norris Ch w All SS *Man* 87-88; C Bandon Union *C, C & R*
88-89; Dioc Youth Adviser (Cork) 89-94; Dioc Youth Chapl
94-95; I Drung w Castleterra, Larah and Lavey etc *K,
E & A* 95-02; P-in-c Mostrim w Granard, Clonbroney, Killoe
etc from 02; Preb Mulhuddart St Patr Cathl Dublin from
05. *Amberley, The Belfry, Co Longford, Republic of Ireland*
T: (00353) (43) 334 6442 E: djcatt@eircom.net
CATTERICK, Matthew John. b 68. W Sussex Inst of HE BA 90
Heythrop Coll Lon MA 11. St Steph Ho Ox BTh 95. **d** 95 **p** 96.
C Colchester St Jas and St Paul w All SS etc *Chelmsf* 95-98;
C Leic Resurr 98-99; TV 99-04; TR Wembley Park *Lon* 04-11;
V Pimlico St Sav from 11. *59 Aylesford Street, London
SW1V 3RY*   T: (020) 7592 9733 E: vicar@stsp.org.uk
CATTLE, David James. b 75. ACCA 05 FCCA 05. Trin Coll Bris
BA 06 MA 07. **d** 07 **p** 08. C Firswood and Gorse Hill *Man*
07-10; TV Digswell and Panshanger *St Alb* from 11.
71 Haldens, Welwyn Garden City AL7 1DH   T: (01707) 372316
M: 07891-148884 E: david_cattle@hotmail.com
CATTLE, Canon Richard John. b 40. WMMTC 88. **d** 90 **p** 91.
NSM Brixworth Deanery *Pet* 90-91; NSM Welford w Sibbertoft
and Marston Trussell 91-92; V 92-97; Bp's Dioc Chapl 97-00;
Dioc Sec 98-00; Can Pet Cathl 98-02; rtd 01; PtO *Pet* from 02;
Dean's Asst from 05. *18 Minster Precincts, Peterborough
PE1 1XX*   T: (01733) 209275 *or* 355315   F: 355316
E: richard.cattle@peterborough-cathedral.org.uk
CATTLEY, Richard Melville. b 49. Trin Coll Bris. **d** 73 **p** 74.
C Kendal St Thos *Carl* 73-77; Nat Sec Pathfinders CPAS 77-82;
Exec Sec 82-85; V Dalton-in-Furness *Carl* 85-90; V Dulwich
St Barn *S'wark* 90-99; Chapl Alleyn's Foundn Dulwich 90-99;

V Milton Keynes *Ox* 99-05; AD 01-05; V Dorking w Ranmore *Guildf* 05-10; rtd 11. *9 St Margaret's Road, Maidenhead SL6 5DZ*

CATTON, Canon Cedric Trevor. b 36. JP . Lambeth STh 94. Wells Th Coll 70. **d** 72 **p** 73. C Solihull *Birm* 72-74; R Hawstead and Nowton w Whepstead and Brockley *St E* 74-75; R Hawstead and Nowton w Stanningfield etc 74-79; Dioc Stewardship Adv 77-83; R Cockfield 79-83; V Exning St Martin w Landwade 83-99; Chapl Mid Anglia Community Health NHS Trust 85-99; Hon Can St E Cathl 90-02; Dioc Par Resources and Stewardship Officer 99-02; Asst Can Past St E Cathl 02; Acting Can Past 03-05; rtd 02; Dioc Clergy Retirement Officer *St E* 02-10. *60 Sextons Meadows, Bury St Edmunds IP33 2SB* T/F: (01284) 749429
E: moretee@vicar1.freeserve.co.uk

CATTON, Stanley Charles. b 44. **d** 99 **p** 00. NSM Bermondsey St Jas w Ch Ch and St Crispin *S'wark* 99-13; NSM Bermondsey St Jas and St Anne 13-14; PtO from 14. *4 Reverdy Road, London SE1 5QE* T: (020) 7237 7703 or 7274 0913
E: scatton4@btinternet.com

CAUDWELL, Juliet Lesley. *See* STRAW, Juliet Lesley

CAUNT, Mrs Margaret. b 55. Coll of Ripon & York St Jo MA 97. NOC 93. **d** 97 **p** 98. NSM Brightside w Wincobank *Sheff* 97-00; C Ecclesfield 00-02; TV Gleadless 02-07; V Anston from 07; AD Laughton from 15. *The Vicarage, 17 Rackford Road, North Anston, Sheffield S25 4DE* T: (01909) 563447 *or* 519459
E: caunt@sky.com *or* margaret.caunt@sheffield.anglican.org

CAVAGAN, Raymond. b 35. Hull Univ MA 86 PhD 87. **d** 63 **p** 64. C Upper Holloway St Pet *Lon* 63-66; C Hurworth *Dur* 66-68; V New Shildon 68-76; V Toxteth Park St Mich *Liv* 76-77; P-in-c Toxteth Park St Andr Aigburth Road 76-77; V Toxteth Park St Mich w St Andr 78-88; V Stamfordham w Matfen *Newc* 88-05; Hon CF from 90; rtd 05; PtO *Ches* from 05. *1 Leys Road, Timperley, Altrincham WA14 5AT* T: 0161-969 5603

CAVAGHAN, Dennis Edgar. b 45. Ex Univ MA 99. St Jo Coll Nottm BTh 74. **d** 74 **p** 75. C Hartford *Ches* 74-77; C Plymouth St Andr w St Paul and St Geo *Ex* 77-80; V Cofton w Starcross 80-88; P-in-c W Exe 88-93; PtO *B & W* 94-02; Hon C Taunton St Mary 02-14; Hon C Taunton St Mary and St Jo from 14. *Combe House, Corfe, Taunton TA3 7BU* T: (01823) 421013
M: 07810-796025 E: dennis.cavaghan@btinternet.com

CAVALCANTI, Canon Joabe Gomes. b 69. Federal Univ of Pernambuco BA 97 Trin Coll Bris MA 00. Nordeste Th Sem BA 91. **d** 98 **p** 98. PtO *Bris* 99; *S'wark* 01-05; Chapl St Sav and St Olave's Sch Newington 05-08; C Bermondsey St Hugh CD 05-08; V Mitcham St Barn from 08; Hon Can Rio de Janeiro from 15. *St Barnabas' Vicarage, 46 Thirsk Road, Mitcham CR4 2BD* T: (020) 8648 2571 M: 07940-444241
E: joabec@gmail.com

CAVALIER, Mrs Sandra Jane. b 48. Guildf Dioc Min Course 98. **d** 00 **p** 01. OLM Guildf Ch Ch w St Martha-on-the-Hill 00-04; NSM Westborough 04-08; NSM Wrecclesham from 08. *107 Campbell Fields, Aldershot GU11 3TZ* T: (01252) 325567
M: 07990-658445 E: revcav@hotmail.co.uk

CAVAN, Lawrence Noel. b 38. Trin Coll Bris 72. **d** 75 **p** 76. C Lurgan Ch the Redeemer *D & D* 75-78; C Chorleywood Ch Ch *St Alb* 78-82; I Kilmocomogue w Snave, Durrus and Rooska *C, C & R* 82-85; I Portarlington w Cloneyhurke and Lea *M & K* 85-90; TV Eston w Normanby *York* 90-03; rtd 03; PtO *Derby* 05-13; *Sheff* from 11. *22 Wentworth Road, Dronfield Woodhouse, Dronfield S18 8ZU* T: (01246) 418814
E: thecavans@hotmail.com

CAVANAGH, Anthony James. b 49. Ushaw Coll Dur 72. **d** 79 **p** 80. In RC Ch 79-95; C Goole *Sheff* 99-01; TV Cullercoats St Geo *Newc* 01-06; V Billy Mill 06-09; V Marden w Preston Grange 06-09; P-in-c Shilbottle 09-11; P-in-c Gosforth St Hugh 11-14; rtd 14; PtO *Dur* from 15. *7 Westfield Drive, Crook DL15 9NX* T: (01388) 762064
E: cavanaghtony@aol.com

CAVANAGH, Capt Kenneth Joseph. b 41. CA Tr Coll 60. **d** 77 **p** 77. CA from 64; Paraguay 70-83; P-in-c Gt w Lt Snoring *Nor* 83-85; R Gt w Lt Snoring w Kettlestone and Pensthorpe 85-88; R Glencarse *Bre* 88-94; CA Co-ord (Scotland/Ireland) & Regional Voc Adv 90-95; R Dundee St Luke *Bre* 95-06; rtd 06. *PD Barranquets, Calle 38 Casa 18, 03779 Els Poblets (Alicante), Spain* E: kscavanagh@tiscali.co.uk

CAVANAGH, Lorraine Marie. b 46. Lucy Cavendish Coll Cam BA 97 MA 01 PhD 03. Ridley Hall Cam 00. **d** 01 **p** 02. PtO *Ely* 01-03; Chapl Fitzw Coll Cam 03; Chapl Cardiff Univ *Llan* 04-09; rtd 09. *Cae Hedd, Talycoed Lane, Llantilio Crossenny, Abergavenny NP7 8TL* T: (01600) 780244

CAVANAGH, Michael Richard. b 49. Salford Univ MSc 00. NOC 89. **d** 92 **p** 93. NSM Stalybridge H Trin and Ch Ch *Ches* 92-98; P-in-c Over Tabley and High Legh 98-03; V 03-10; P-in-c Kenmare w Sneem, Waterville etc *L & K* from 10. *St Patrick's*

Rectory, Kenmare, Co Kerry, Republic of Ireland T: (00353) (64) 664 8566 M: 87-160 6312
E: michael@balmoralconsulting.co.uk

CAVANAGH, Canon Peter Bernard. b 49. Sarum & Wells Th Coll 71. **d** 73 **p** 74. C Gt Crosby St Faith *Liv* 73-76; C Stanley 76-79; V Anfield St Columba 79-97; V Lancaster St Mary w St John and St Anne *Blackb* 97-09; P-in-c Scorton and Barnacre and Calder Vale 06-09; Hon Can Blackb Cathl 00-09; rtd 09; PtO *Blackb* from 09. *6 Lunesdale Court, Derwent Road, Lancaster LA1 3ET* T: (01524) 62786 E: manderley552@btinternet.com

CAVE, Anthony Sidney. b 32. EMMTC. **d** 84 **p** 85. C Immingham *Linc* 84-88; V Keelby 88-89; V Riby 88-89; V Keelby w Riby and Aylesby 89-98; rtd 99; PtO *Linc* from 00. *Polruan, The Bungalow, Cherry Lane, Barrow-upon-Humber DN19 7AX* T: (01469) 532350

CAVE, Bill. *See* CAVE-BROWNE-CAVE, Bernard James William

CAVE, Brian Malcolm. b 37. St Cath Soc Ox BA 60 MA 64. Oak Hill Th Coll. **d** 63 **p** 64. C Streatham Park St Alb *S'wark* 63-66; C Ruskin Park St Sav and St Matt 66-68; C Tunbridge Wells St Jas *Roch* 68-71; V Bootle St Leon *Liv* 71-75; Min St Mary w St John Bootle 73-75; Area Sec Leprosy Miss 75-81; V Hurst Green *Bradf* 81-82; P-in-c Mitton 81-82; V Hurst Green and Mitton 82-91; rtd 91; PtO *B & W* from 97. *63 Westway, Nailsea, Bristol BS48 2NB* T: (01275) 854892

CAVE, Mrs Margaret. b 62. Van Mildert Coll Dur BSc 84. SEITE 07. **d** 10 **p** 11. C Kidbrooke St Jas *S'wark* 10-13; TR E Greenwich from 13. *3 Hardy Road, London SE3 7NS* M: 07740-859958 E: margaret.cave@btinternet.com

CAVE BERGQUIST, Julie Anastasia. b 59. St Jo Coll Dur BA 80 Franciscan Univ Rome STL 87. St Steph Ho Ox 85. **d** 87 **p** 98. Par Dn Kennington *Cant* 87-89; Chapl Trin Coll Cam 89-94; Chapl Westcott Ho Cam 94-97; C St Alb St Steph *St Alb* 98-02; P-in-c S Kensington H Trin w All SS *Lon* 02-06; Dir of Ords Two Cities Area 02-06; Nat Voc Adv and Selection Sec Min Division 06-10; PtO *Lon* from 06; Dioc Dir of Ords *Ox* 10-15. *St John's House, St John's Wood High Street, London NW8 7NE*

CAVE-BROWNE-CAVE, Bernard James William (Bill). b 54. Trin Hall Cam BA 76 MA 80 Bradf Univ MA 90. Westcott Ho Cam 77. **d** 79 **p** 80. C Chesterton Gd Shep *Ely* 79-83; Chapl Lanc Univ *Blackb* 83-95; Chapl HM Pris Service 95-14; rtd 14. *Address temp unknown*
E: bill@cave_browne_cave.freeserve.co.uk

CAVEEN, David Francis. b 44. Univ of Wales (Cardiff) BSc 66 DipEd 67. STETS 95. **d** 98 **p** 99. C Swaythling *Win* 98-02; V Lord's Hill 02-09; rtd 09; PtO *Win* from 09; *Cov* from 14. *2A Long Furlong, Rugby CV22 5QS* T: (01788) 815938
E: davidcaveen@tinyworld.co.uk

✠**CAVELL, The Rt Revd John Kingsmill.** b 16. Qu Coll Cam BA 39 MA 44. Wycliffe Hall Ox 39. **d** 40 **p** 41 **c** 72. C Folkestone H Trin *Cant* 40; C Addington 40-44; LtO *Ox* 45-52; Area Sec (Dio Ox) CMS 44-52; Dio Pet 44-49; Tr Officer 49-52; V Cheltenham Ch Ch *Glouc* 52-62; V Plymouth St Andr *Ex* 62-70; V E Stonehouse 68-70; V Plymouth St Andr w St Paul and St Geo 70-72; RD Plymouth 67-72; Preb Ex Cathl 67-72; Suff Bp Southampton *Win* 72-84; Hon Can Win Cathl 72-84; rtd 84; PtO *Win* 84-14; Hon Asst Bp Sarum from 88; Can and Preb Sarum Cathl from 88. *143 The Close, Salisbury SP1 2EY* T: (01722) 334782 F: 413112

CAVELL-NORTHAM, Canon Cavell Herbert James. b 32. St Steph Ho Ox 53. **d** 56 **p** 57. C W Wycombe *Ox* 56-61; CF (TA) 60-63; V Lane End *Ox* 61-68; V Stony Stratford 68-97; P-in-c Calverton 69-72; R 72-97; Hon Can Ch Ch 91-97; rtd 97; LtO *Ox* 97-04; PtO from 04. *The Glebe House, Finings Road, Lane End, High Wycombe HP14 3EU* T: (01494) 881552

CAW (*née* FINLAY), Alison Mary. b 40. Natal Univ BA 62 Ox Univ PGCE 64. Ox Min Course 90. **d** 93 **p** 94. NSM Beaconsfield *Ox* 93-04; NSM Penn and Tylers Green 04-08; PtO from 08. *1 Westway, Beaconsfield HP9 1DQ* T: (01494) 674524

CAW, Hannah Mary. *See* JEFFERY, Hannah Mary

CAWDELL, Mrs Sarah Helen Louise. b 65. St Hugh's Coll Ox BA 88 MA 91 Trin Coll Cam BA 94 MA 99 K Coll Lon MA 99. Ridley Hall Cam 92. **d** 95 **p** 96. C Belmont *S'wark* 95-98; PtO *Heref* 98-00; Hon C Claverley w Tuckhill 00-10; CME Officer 06-09; Public Preacher 10-11; TV Bridgnorth, Tasley, Astley Abbotts, etc 11. *The Rectory, 16 East Castle Street, Bridgnorth WV16 4AL* T: (01746) 761573
E: s.h.cawdell@btinternet.com

CAWDELL, Preb Simon Howard. b 65. Univ Coll Dur BA 86 K Coll Lon MA 99. Ridley Hall Cam 91. **d** 94 **p** 95. C Cheam Common St Phil *S'wark* 94-98; V Claverley w Tuckhill *Heref* 98-10; TR Bridgnorth, Tasley, Astley Abbotts, etc from 10; V Morville w Aston Eyre from 10; RD Bridgnorth 09-13; Preb Heref Cathl from 15. *The Rectory, 16 East Castle Street, Bridgnorth WV16 4AL* T: (01746) 761573
E: s.h.cawdell@btinternet.com

CAWLEY, David Lewis. b 44. AKC 71 FSA 81. St Aug Coll Cant 71. **d** 72 **p** 73. C Sprowston *Nor* 72-75; Chapl HM Pris

Nor 74-75; C Wymondham *Nor* 75-77; C Buckland in Dover w Buckland Valley *Cant* 77-83; V Eastville St Anne w St Mark and St Thos *Bris* 83-95; V Leic St Mary 95-09; TV Leic H Spirit 97-02; Chapl Trin Hosp Leic 96-09; rtd 09; C Margate All SS *Cant* from 09. *All Saints' Vicarage, All Saints' Avenue, Margate CT9 5QL* T: (01843) 290845
E: davidl.cawley@btinternet.com

CAWRSE, Christopher William. b 60. Birkbeck Coll Lon BA 97 Qu Mary and Westf Coll Lon MA 00. Westcott Ho Cam 82. **d** 84 **p** 85. C Stoke Newington St Mary *Lon* 84-86; Chapl St Mark's Hosp Lon 86-90; C Islington St Jas w St Pet *Lon* 86-90; Chapl Asst Charing Cross Hosp Lon 90-93; PtO *Lon* 93-06; P-in-c St Pancras H Cross w St Jude and St Pet from 06. *Holy Cross Vicarage, 47 Argyle Square, London WC1H 8AL* T: (020) 7278 6263 E: chriscawrse@blueyonder.co.uk

CAWTE, Canon David John. b 30. St Mich Coll Llan. **d** 65 **p** 66. C Chorley St Laur *Blackb* 65-67; C Boyne Hill *Ox* 67-74; C-in-c Cox Green CD 75-78; V Cox Green 78-94; Hon Can Ch Ch 88-94; rtd 94; PtO *Win* from 94. *6 Broadfields Close, Milford on Sea, Lymington SO41 0SE* T: (01590) 642793
E: david.cawte@tinyworld.co.uk

CAWTE, Martin Charles. b 51. Jes Coll Ox BA 73 MA 77 IPFA 76. SEITE 97. **d** 00 **p** 01. NSM Sanderstead All SS *S'wark* 00-03; NSM Greenham *Ox* 03-06; NSM Hermitage 06-12; P-in-c Lambourn 12-13; P-in-c Eastbury and E Garston 12-13; V Lambourn Valley from 13. *The Vicarage, 4 Newbury Street, Lambourn, Hungerford RG17 8PD* T: (01488) 73920
E: martin_cawte@hotmail.com

CAWTHORNE, Paul Howarth. b 66. St Hild Coll Dur BA 88. Cuddesdon Coll 98. **d** 98 **p** 99. C Cen Telford *Lich* 98-01; TV Wrockwardine Deanery 01-13; TV Dorchester *Ox* from 13. *The Vicarage, Cherwell Road, Berinsfield, Wallingford OX10 7PB* T: (01865) 340460 E: paulcawthorne@tiscali.co.uk

CAYTON, John. b 32. Bps' Coll Cheshunt 54. **d** 57 **p** 58. C Hindley All SS *Liv* 57-59; C Littleham w Exmouth *Ex* 59-63; V Burnley St Cath *Blackb* 63-72; V Marton 72-87; V Fleetwood St Pet 87-97; Miss to Seamen 87-97; rtd 97; PtO *Blackb* 97-11. *19 Parkstone Avenue, Thornton-Cleveleys FY5 5AE* T: (01253) 854088

CECIL, John Richard. b 75. Univ of Wales (Lamp) BA 97 Univ of Wales (Abth) PGCE 98. St Mich Coll Llan 11. **d** 13 **p** 14. NSM Hubberston *St D* 13-14; NSM Hubberston and Herbrandston from 15. *Sunnybank, Liddeston, Milford Haven SA73 3PY* T: (01646) 692974 E: revjohncecil@btinternet.com

CECIL, Kevin Vincent. b 54. BA PGCE. St Mich Coll Llan. **d** 82 **p** 83. C Llanilid w Pencoed *Llan* 82-85; C Coity w Nolton 85-88; Area Co-ord CMS St D, Llan, Mon and S & B 88-05; P-in-c Dixton *Heref* 05-08; V Wye Reaches Gp from 08. *The Vicarage, 38 Hillcrest Road, Wyesham, Monmouth NP25 3LH* T: (01600) 713459 E: vincent_cecil@yahoo.com

CECILE, Sister. See HARRISON, Cécile

CERMAKOVA, Ms Helena Maria Alija. b 43. **d** 88 **p** 95. NSM Roath *Llan* 88-91; Asst Chapl Univ Hosp of Wales NHS Trust 92-95; Chapl United Bris Healthcare NHS Trust 95-99; Lead Chapl Jersey Gp of Hosps 99-06; Tutor St Mich Coll Llan 06-12. *9 Orchard View, Wear Farm, Newton Road, Bishopsteignton, Teignmouth TQ14 9PU*
E: helenacermakova@talktalk.net

CERRATTI, Christa Elisabeth. See PUMFREY, Christa Elisabeth

CHABALA, Patches. b 78. St Jo Coll Nottm BA 11. **d** 11 **p** 12. C Plas Newton *Ches* 11-15; TV Hampreston *Sarum* from 15. *The Vicarage, Albert Road, Ferndown BH22 9HE* M: 07791-250300 E: pcchabala@yahoo.com

CHADD, Jeremy Denis. b 55. Jes Coll Cam BA 77 MA 81. Coll of Resurr Mirfield 78. **d** 81 **p** 82. C Seaton Hirst *Newc* 81-84; C N Gosforth 84-88; V Sunderland St Chad *Dur* from 88. *St Chad's Vicarage, Charter Drive, Sunderland SR3 3PG* T: 0191-528 2397

CHADD, Canon Leslie Frank. b 19. Leeds Univ BSc 41. Coll of Resurr Mirfield 41. **d** 43 **p** 44. C Portsea All SS w St Jo Rudmore *Portsm* 43-46; Chapl RNVR 46-48; C Greenford H Cross *Lon* 48-54; C Littlehampton St Mary *Chich* 54-58; V Hanworth All SS *Lon* 58-65; V Fareham SS Pet and Paul *Portsm* 65-92; Relig Adv STV 72-81; Hon Can Portsm Cathl 81-92; rtd 92; PtO *Portsm* 92-12. *56 Mountjoy Road, Huddersfield HD1 5QQ* T: (01484) 519254

CHADDER, Philip Thomas James. b 66. Ex Univ BA 88. Oak Hill Th Coll 01. **d** 03 **p** 04. C Gt Chesham *Ox* 03-07; Chapl HM Pris Brixton from 07. *HM Prison Brixton, Jebb Avenue, London SW2 5XF* T: (020) 8588 6052 M: 07796-815285
E: philchadder@yahoo.co.uk

CHADWICK, Alan Michael. b 61. St Cath Coll Cam BA 83 MA 87. Wycliffe Hall Ox 96. **d** 98 **p** 99. C Hubberston *St D* 98-01; R 01-11; P-in-c Llanstadwel from 11; AD Roose from 10. *The Vicarage, 68 Church Road, Llanstadwell, Milford Haven SA73 1EB* T: (01646) 600227
E: alanandmarychadwick@btinternet.com

CHADWICK, Arnold. See CHADWICK, Francis Arnold Edwin

CHADWICK, Carolyn Ann. b 52. Westhill Coll Birm CertEd 73 Birm Univ BMus 93 ABSM 78. WMMTC 04. **d** 07 **p** 08. NSM Pontesbury I and II *Heref* 07-08; NSM Minsterley 08-13; NSM Minsterley, Habberley and Hope w Shelve from 13. *The Hermitage, Asterley, Minsterley, Shrewsbury SY5 0AW* T/F: (01743) 792421 M: 07766-832547
E: carolyn.chadwick@googlemail.com

CHADWICK, Charles John Peter. b 59. Birm Univ BA 81 Southn Univ BTh 90. Sarum & Wells Th Coll 85. **d** 88 **p** 89. C Chalfont St Peter *Ox* 88-91; C Gt Marlow 91-93; TV Gt Marlow w Marlow Bottom, Lt Marlow and Bisham 93-95; P-in-c Stokenchurch and Ibstone 95-01; Asst Dir Chiltern Ch Tr Course 95-01; V Bridgwater St Mary and Chilton Trinity *B & W* 01-14; Preb Wells Cathl 11-14; Par Development Adv *Ox* from 14. *39 Bluebell Way, Carterton OX18 1JY* T: (01993) 359210 E: cjpchad9@aol.com

CHADWICK, David Emmerson. b 73. Lincs & Humberside Univ BA 96. Ridley Hall Cam BTh 00. **d** 00 **p** 01. C Whickham *Dur* 00-06; V Ryhope from 06. *St Paul's Vicarage, Ryhope Street North, Sunderland SR2 0HH* T: 0191-523 7884

CHADWICK, David Guy Evelyn St Just. b 36. Bps' Coll Cheshunt 61. **d** 68 **p** 69. C Edmonton All SS *Lon* 68-71; C Edmonton St Mary w St Jo 71-72; C Greenhill St Jo 72-74; Bp's Dom Chapl *Truro* 74-79; Chapl Community of the Epiphany *Truro* 77-78; P-in-c Crantock *Truro* 79-83; R Clydebank *Glas* 83-87; R Renfrew 87-94; rtd 94. *Alverna, 1 Nithsdale Crescent, Bearsden, Glasgow G61 4DF*

CHADWICK, Francis Arnold Edwin. b 30. AKC 54. **d** 55 **p** 56. C Chapel Allerton *Ripon* 55-58; C Hayes *Roch* 58-61; V Arreton *Portsm* 61-67; V Newchurch 61-67; V Kingshurst *Birm* 67-73; V York Town St Mich *Guildf* 73-83; P-in-c Long Sutton w Long Load *B & W* 83-87; R Stockbridge and Longstock and Leckford *Win* 87-93; rtd 93; Chapl Helsinki w Tallinn *Eur* 95-98; PtO *B & W* 98-03; *Sarum* from 02. *Hillway, Wickfield, Devizes SN10 5DU* T: (01380) 721489

CHADWICK, Helen Jane. See MARSHALL, Helen Jane

CHADWICK, Mark William Armstrong. b 67. Coll of Resurr Mirfield. **d** 05 **p** 06. C Colwyn Bay w Brynymaen *St As* 05-08; V Kerry, Llanmerewig, Dolfor and Mochdre 08-13; V Shrewsbury St Chad, St Mary and St Alkmund *Lich* from 13. *St Chad's Vicarage, Claremont Hill, Shrewsbury SY1 1RD* T: (01743) 343761 E: croeso123@gmail.com

CHADWICK, Philip Edward. b 41. AMICE 63 IEng 65. **d** 07 **p** 08. OLM Elland *Leeds* from 07. *26 Crestfield Avenue, Elland HX5 0LN* T: (01422) 373298 E: pechadwick@hotmail.com

CHAFFEY, Jane Frances. b 59. Somerville Coll Ox BA 80 MA 84 St Jo Coll Dur BA 86. Cranmer Hall Dur 84. **d** 88 **p** 94. Par Dn Roby *Liv* 88-90; NSM Finningley w Auckley *S'well* 95-96; PtO *Pet* 96-99; *Linc* 98-01; Chapl Wycombe Abbey Sch from 08. *Wycombe Abbey School, Abbey Way, High Wycombe HP11 1PE* T: (01494) 520381

CHAFFEY, The Ven Jonathan Paul Michael. b 62. St Chad's Coll Dur BA 83. Cranmer Hall Dur 84. **d** 87 **p** 88. C Gateacre *Liv* 87-90; Chapl RAF 90-14; Chapl-in-Chief RAF from 14; Adn RAF from 14; Can and Preb Linc Cathl from 14. *Chaplaincy Services (RAF), HQ Air Command, RAF High Wycombe HP14 4UE* T: (01494) 496800 F: 496343

CHAFFEY, Michael Prosser. b 30. Lon Univ BA 51. St Steph Ho Ox 53. **d** 55 **p** 56. C Victoria Docks Ascension *Chelmsf* 55-59; C Leytonstone H Trin and St Aug Harrow Green 59-62; V Walthamstow St Mich 62-69; R Cov St Jo 69-85; P-in-c Cov St Thos 69-74; Hon C Bideford *Ex* 85; P-in-c Charlestown *Man* 85-88; V Sutton St Mich *York* 88-96; rtd 96; PtO *York* from 96. *17 Highcliffe Court, St Annes Road, Bridlington YO15 2JZ* T: (01262) 602758

CHALCRAFT, Christopher Warine Terrell (Kit). b 37. Oak Hill Th Coll. **d** 67 **p** 68. C Egham *Guildf* 67-70; P-in-c Slough *Ox* 70-73; TV Bramerton w Surlingham *Nor* 73-87; P-in-c Cockley Cley w Gooderstone 87-95; P-in-c Gt and Lt Cressingham w Threxton 87-95; P-in-c Didlington 87-95; P-in-c Hilborough w Bodney 87-95; P-in-c Oxborough w Foulden and Caldecote 87-95; PtO from 02. *The Malthouse, 39 London Street, Swaffham PE37 7DD* T: (01760) 724805 E: k.chalcraft@btinternet.com

CHALCRAFT, Mrs Sharon Anita. b 62. Ex Univ BTh 09. SWMTC 05. **d** 08 **p** 09. NSM Lelant, Towednack and Zennor *Truro* 08-09; NSM Breage w Godolphin and Germoe 09-14; Public Preacher from 14. *Summerhill Cottage, Nancledra, Penzance TR20 8AY* T: (01736) 350779 M: 07889-406326 E: sharon@m8trix.ltd.uk

CHALK, Francis Harold. b 25. Lich Th Coll 61. **d** 62 **p** 63. C Linc St Nic w St Jo Newport 62-64; R Kirkby Laythorpe w Asgarby 64-69; V Ewerby w Evedon 65-69; R Gt Gonerby 69-89; rtd 89; PtO *Truro* from 90. *Chalkleigh, 3 Church Street, St Just, Penzance TR19 7HA* T: (01736) 787925

CHALKLEY, Andrew William Guy. b 64. Aston Tr Scheme 90 St Jo Coll Nottm BTh 92. **d** 95 **p** 96. C Liskeard, St Keyne, St Pinnock, Morval etc *Truro* 95-99; TV Uphill *B & W* 99-07; P-in-c Beckington w Standerwick, Berkley, Rodden etc 07-10; R from 10. *8 Church Street, Beckington, Frome BA11 6TG* T: (01373) 830314 E: rector@beckington.org.uk

CHALLEN (née O'DONNELL), Paula Ella. b 72. ERMC 11. **d** 14. C Towcester w Caldecote and Easton Neston etc *Pet* from 14. *35 Hazel Crescent, Towcester NN12 6UQ* T: (01327) 323106 E: revpaula@btinternet.com

CHALLEN, Canon Peter Bernard. b 31. Clare Coll Cam BA 56 MA 60 FRSA 94. Westcott Ho Cam 56. **d** 58 **p** 59. C Goole *Sheff* 58-61; V Dalton 61-67; Sen Ind Chapl *S'wark* 67-96; R S'wark Ch Ch 67-96; Hon Can S'wark Cathl 74-96; rtd 96; PtO *S'wark* from 96. *21 Bousfield Road, London SE14 5TP* T/F: (020) 7207 0509 E: peterchallen@gmail.com

CHALLENDER, John Clifford. b 32. CITC 67. **d** 67 **p** 68. C Belfast St Luke *Conn* 67-70; Bp's V and Lib Kilkenny Cathl and C Kilkenny w Aghour and Odagh *C & O* 70-71; I Fenagh w Myshall and Kiltennel 71-76; I Fenagh w Myshall, Aghade and Ardoyne 76-79; I Crosspatrick Gp 79-95; Preb Ferns Cathl 85-88; Dioc Glebes Sec (Ferns) 86-91; Treas Ferns Cathl 88-91; Chan Ferns Cathl 91-95; I Killeshin w Cloydagh and Killabban 95-02; Can Ossory and Leighlin Cathls 00-02; rtd 02. *3 Adare Close, Killincarrig, Greystones, Co Wicklow, Republic of Ireland* T: (00353) (1) 201 7268 *or* 287 6359 M: 86-243 3678 E: challen1@eircom.net

CHALLENGER, Ann. b 54. Leeds Univ BA 09. NOC 06. **d** 09 **p** 10. NSM Bradf St Aug Undercliffe *Leeds* from 09; NSM Bradf St Clem from 09. *304 Undercliffe Street, Bradford BD3 0PH* T: (01274) 640410 M: 07832-293751 E: ann_challenger@hotmail.co.uk

CHALLENGER, Peter Nelson. b 33. St Jo Coll Cam BA 57 MA 61. Ripon Hall Ox 57. **d** 59 **p** 60. C Bushbury *Lich* 59-62; V Horsley Woodhouse *Derby* 62-67; V Derby St Barn 67-75; Brazil 75-80; TV New Windsor *Ox* 80-89; V Wootton (Boars Hill) 89-98; rtd 99. *39 Moorland Road, Witney OX28 6LS* T: (01993) 774630

CHALLICE, John Richard. b 34. ACP 65. Sarum & Wells Th Coll 73. **d** 75 **p** 76. C Warminster St Denys *Sarum* 75-78; R Longfield *Roch* 78-00; rtd 00; PtO *Roch* from 00. *Magnolia, Allhallows Road, Lower Stoke, Rochester ME3 9SL* T: (01634) 272468

CHALLIS, Mrs Clare Elizabeth. b 78. Wycliffe Hall Ox 09. **d** 12 **p** 13. C Bursledon *Win* from 12. *13 Redcroft Lane, Bursledon, Southampton SO31 8GS* T: (023) 8040 5172 M: 07887-702021 E: clareec7@aol.com *or* challisclare@gmail.com

CHALLIS, Douglas James. b 21. Selw Coll Cam BA 48 MA 55. Cuddesdon Coll 49. **d** 51 **p** 58. Kimbolton Sch 53-58; Chapl Summer Fields Sch Ox 58-60; Asst Chapl Stowe Sch 60-64; Chapl St Bees Sch Cumbria 64-67; Chapl Reed's Sch Cobham 67-80; rtd 80; PtO *Cant* 89-07; Chapl Crowhurst Chr Healing Cen 05-06; LtO *Mor* 07-10; PtO from 10. *7 Milinclarin Way, Church Hill Road, Lairg IV27 4BL* T: (01549) 402108

CHALLIS, Ian. b 46. St Jo Coll Nottm 82. **d** 84 **p** 85. C Heatherlands St Jo *Sarum* 84-86; C Lytchett Minster 86-88; PtO 88-95 and 00-08; NSM Canford Magna 95-00. *50 Constitution Hill Road, Poole BH14 0QD* T: (01202) 248400 E: ianchallis@ntlworld.com

CHALLIS, John William Anthony. b 68. St Steph Ho Ox 98. **d** 00 **p** 01. C Ifield *Chich* 00-04; P-in-c Buxted and Hadlow Down 04-09; R Beeding and Bramber w Botolphs from 09. *The Rectory, Sele Priory Church, Church Lane, Upper Beeding BN44 3HP* T: (01903) 810265

CHALLIS, Terence Peter. b 40. St Aid Birkenhead 65. **d** 68 **p** 69. C Billericay St Mary *Chelmsf* 68-71; Admin Sec Dio Maseno S Kenya 72-75; Bp's Chapl 72-74; P-in-c Sparkbrook Ch Ch *Birm* 76-80; V Enfield St Jas *Lon* 80-89; V Astley Bridge *Man* 89-98; P-in-c Leigh St Mary and Leigh St Jo 99-02; rtd 02; PtO *Blackb* from 03. *48 Wilson Square, Thornton-Cleveleys FY5 1RF* T: (01253) 864534

CHALLIS, Canon William George. b 52. Keble Coll Ox BA 73 K Coll Lon MTh 75. Oak Hill Th Coll 73. **d** 75 **p** 76. C Islington St Mary *Lon* 75-79; Lect Trin Coll Bris 79-81; C Stoke Bishop *Bris* 79-81; Lect Oak Hill Th Coll 82; Burundi 82-85; P-in-c Bishopston *Bris* 86-89; TR *Birm* 89-92; Vice-Prin Wycliffe Hall Ox 93-98; V Bitterne *Win* 98-03; Dir of Ords *Guildf* from 03; Hon Can Guildf Cathl from 13. *80 York Road, Woking GU22 7XR* T: (01483) 769759 *or* 790322 E: ddo@cofeguildford.org.uk

CHALMERS, Canon Brian. b 42. Oriel Coll Ox BA 64 MA 68 DPhil 70 BA 71. Wycliffe Hall Ox 71. **d** 72 **p** 73. C Luton St Mary *St Alb* 72-76; Chapl Cranfield Inst of Tech 76-81; Chapl Kent Univ Cant 81-89; Six Preacher Cant Cathl 85-96; V Charing w Charing Heath and Lt Chart 89-05; AD Ashford 98-03; Hon Can Cant Cathl 97-05; rtd 05; PtO *Cant* from 05.

The Chantry, Pilgrims Lane, Chilham, Canterbury CT4 8AB T: (01227) 730669 E: brian.chalmers@tesco.net

CHAMBERLAIN, Allen Charles William. b 29. Lon Univ CertEd 52 Birkbeck Coll Lon BSc 56. **d** 96 **p** 97. OLM Gunton St Pet *Nor* 96-99; rtd 99; PtO *Nor* 99-13. *28 Yarmouth Road, Lowestoft NR32 4AG* T: (01502) 573637

CHAMBERLAIN, David (Bernard). b 28. Fitzw Ho Cam BA 51. Linc Th Coll 52. **d** 54 **p** 55. C Brighouse *Wakef* 54-57; C Sheff St Cecilia Parson Cross 57-61; CR 63-85; S Africa 68-70; Bp's Adv on Community Relns *Wakef* 71-85; Bp's Adv Community Relns & Inter-Faith Dialogue *Bris* 86-93; V Easton All Hallows 86-93; rtd 93; PtO *B & W* from 94. *43 Bath Road, Wells BA5 3HR* T: (01749) 679369

CHAMBERLAIN, Elizabeth Ann. b 58. St Jo Coll Nottm 08. **d** 10 **p** 11. C Walsall St Matt *Lich* 10-14; V Shenstone and Stonnall from 14. *The Vicarage, St John's Hill, Shenstone, Lichfield WS14 0JB* T: (01543) 480286 E: lizchamberlainuk@yahoo.co.uk

CHAMBERLAIN, Helen. b 66. **d** 09 **p** 10. NSM Farnham Royal w Hedgerley *Ox* 09-14; C The Cookhams from 14. *St John's House, Spring Lane, Cookham, Maidenhead SL6 9PN* T: (01753) 251635

CHAMBERLAIN, Jane Louise. b 62. Bedf Coll Lon BSc 84. WEMTC 04. **d** 07 **p** 08. NSM Blagdon w Compton Martin and Ubley *B & W* 07-11; R from 11; RD Chew Magna from 14. *Grove House, The Street, Compton Martin, Bristol BS40 6JF* T: (01761) 220070 M: 07949-037548 E: revjanechamberlain@gmail.com

CHAMBERLAIN, The Ven Malcolm Leslie. b 69. York Univ BA 92 Liv Hope Univ MPhil 11. Wycliffe Hall Ox BTh 96. **d** 96 **p** 97. C Walsall Pleck and Bescot *Lich* 96-99; C Mossley Hill St Matt and St Jas *Liv* 99-02; Asst Chapl Liv Univ 99-02; Chapl Liv Univ and Dioc 18-30s Officer 02-08; P-in-c Wavertree St Mary 08-11; R 11-14; AD Toxteth and Wavertree 12-14; Adn Sheff and Rotherham from 14. *34 Wilson Road, Sheffield S11 8RN* T: 0114-418 3917 *or* (01709) 309110 E: malcolm.chamberlain@sheffield.anglican.org

✠**CHAMBERLAIN, The Rt Revd Neville.** b 39. Nottm Univ BA 61 MA 73 CQSW 73. Ripon Hall Ox 61. **d** 63 **p** 64. C Balsall Heath St Paul *Birm* 63-64; C Hall Green Ascension 64-66; C-in-c Gospel Lane CD 66-69; V Gospel Lane St Mich 69-72; LtO *Linc* 73-74; Soc Resp Sec 74-82; Can and Preb Linc Cathl 79-98; R Edin St Jo 82-97; Bp Bre 97-05; rtd 05; Master Hugh Sexey's Hosp Bruton 05-12. *Wessex House, Quaperlake Street, Bruton BA10 0HG* T: (01749) 813797

CHAMBERLAIN, Nicholas Alan. b 63. St Chad's Coll Dur BA 85 PhD 91 New Coll Edin BD 91. Edin Th Coll 88. **d** 91 **p** 92. C Cockerton *Dur* 91-94; C Newton Aycliffe 94-95; TV 95-96; TV Gt Aycliffe 96-98; P-in-c Burnmoor 98-06; Bp's Adv for CME 98-06; V Newc St Geo and St Hilda from 06. *St George's Vicarage, St George's Close, Newcastle upon Tyne NE2 2TF* T: 0191-281 1628

CHAMBERLAIN, Paul Martin. b 74. Southn Univ MChem 97 Bris Univ PhD 02. Ripon Coll Cuddesdon 08. **d** 10 **p** 11. C Thame *Ox* 10-14; P-in-c Lee-on-the-Solent *Portsm* from 14. *21 Elson Road, Gosport PO12 4BL* T: (023) 9200 6184 E: revdr.paulchamberlain@gmail.com

CHAMBERLAIN, Roger Edward. b 53. Culham Coll of Educn BEd 75. Trin Coll Bris BA 87. **d** 87 **p** 88. C Plymouth Em w Efford *Ex* 87-90; C Selly Park St Steph and St Wulstan *Birm* 90-94; V Yardley St Cypr Hay Mill 94-96; PtO 96-10; P-in-c Baddesley Ensor w Grendon 10-14; V from 14. *The Vicarage, 75 Newlands Road, Baddesley Ensor, Atherstone CV9 2BY* T: (01827) 713245 E: revrog@hotmail.co.uk

CHAMBERLAIN, Roy Herbert. b 44. Oak Hill Th Coll 91 NOC 95. **d** 96 **p** 97. C Gee Cross *Ches* 96-98; PtO *Blackb* from 01. *125 Lancaster Road, Morecambe LA4 5QJ* T: (01524) 409070

CHAMBERLAIN, Russell Charles. b 51. Univ of Wales (Cardiff) LLM 00. Oak Hill Th Coll 76. **d** 78 **p** 79. C Harold Hill St Geo *Chelmsf* 78-80; C Uckfield *Chich* 80-83; R Balcombe 83-90; V Okehampton w Inwardleigh *Ex* 90-94; TR Okehampton w Inwardleigh, Bratton Clovelly etc 94-01; RD Okehampton 93-98; R Worborough and Ogwell 01-15; rtd 15; St Jo Hosp Heytesbury from 15. *96 The Butts, Westbury BA13 3EZ* M: 07770-270019 E: russell.chamberlain70@gmail.com

CHAMBERLAIN, David John. b 56. St Jo Coll Nottm. **d** 94 **p** 95. C Chatham St Phil and St Jas *Roch* 94-97; R Swardeston w E Carleton, Intwood, Keswick etc *Nor* 97-04; RD Humbleyard 03-04; R Milton *Ely* from 04; P-in-c Landbeach from 12; P-in-c Waterbeach from 12. *The Rectory, 24 Church Lane, Milton, Cambridge CB24 6AB* T: (01223) 861511 M: 07805-083300 E: rector@allsaintsmilton.org.uk

CHAMBERLAIN, John Malcolm. b 38. Carl Dioc Tr Course 84. **d** 87 **p** 88. NSM Cockermouth w Embleton and Wythop *Carl* 87-97; Master St Mary Magd and H Jes Trust 97-05; Hon C

Newc St Jo 98-05; rtd 05. *45 Wansbeck Avenue, North Shields NE30 3DU* T: 0191-253 0022
E: johnchamberlin@btinternet.com

CHAMBERLIN, Mrs Julia Joanne. b 61. St Mellitus Coll 12. **d** 15. C Bluntisham cum Earith w Colne and Holywell etc *Ely* from 15. *24 Church Lane, Milton, Cambridge CB24 6AB* T: (01223) 861511

CHAMBERS, Canon Anthony Frederick John. b 40. ACII 69. Sarum Th Coll 69. **d** 71 **p** 72. C Hall Green St Pet *Birm* 71-74; C Holdenhurst *Win* 74-77; P-in-c Ropley w W Tisted 77-79; R Bishop's Sutton and Ropley and W Tisted 79-83; V Pokesdown St Jas 83-99; RD Bournemouth 95-99; P-in-c Heckfield w Mattingley and Rotherwick 99-02; V 02-04; Chapl N Foreland Lodge Sch Basingstoke 99-04; Hon Can Win Cathl 03-04; rtd 05; PtO *Ex* from 05. *4 J H Taylor Drive, Northam, Bideford EX39 1TU* T: (01237) 421306
E: anthony.chambers1@virgin.net

CHAMBERS, Miss Barbara Ada. b 51. **d** 98 **p** 99. OLM Gt Crosby St Luke *Liv* 98-15; rtd 15. *12 Vale Road, Crosby, Liverpool L23 5RZ* T: 0151-924 5851

CHAMBERS, Mrs Barbara Mary Sinnott. b 43. SRN 65 RM 67 HVCert 75 Keele Univ TCert 77. WMMTC 87. **d** 93 **p** 94. Par Dn Blurton *Lich* 93-94; C 94-96; Chapl Asst Qu Medical Cen Nottm Univ Hosp NHS Trust 96-03; Chapl 03-07; Chapl United Lincs Hosps NHS Trust from 07. *51 Mill Lane, Woodhall Spa LN10 6QZ* T: (01526) 354872
E: barbara.chambers@ulh.nhs.uk

CHAMBERS, Carl Michael. b 68. Pemb Coll Cam BA 90 Oak Hill Th Coll BA 00. **d** 01 **p** 02. C Hove Bp Hannington Memorial Ch *Chich* 01-05; C Preston St Jo w Brighton St Aug and St Sav from 05. *24 Stanford Avenue, Brighton BN1 6EA* T: (01273) 553207

CHAMBERS, Mrs Christine. b 55. St Mellitus Coll BA 10. **d** 10 **p** 11. C E Ham St Paul *Chelmsf* 10-14; TV Barking from 14. *Christ Church Vicarage, Bastable Avenue, Barking IG11 0NG* T: (020) 3509 6067 M: 07941-823783
E: christinechambers@hotmail.co.uk

CHAMBERS, George William. b 24. TCD BA 46 MA 57. CITC 47. **d** 47 **p** 48. C Conwall *D & R* 47-50; Chapl Portora R Sch Enniskillen 50-51; I Tullyaughnish w Milford *D & R* 51-61; I Adare *L & K* 61-81; Dioc Registrar (Limerick etc) 62-81; Adn Limerick 69-81; Dean Limerick 81-86; I Limerick City 81-86; I Killeshin w Cloydagh and Kullabban *C & O* 86-95; Can Ossory and Leighlin Cathls 90-92; Treas Ossory and Leighlin Cathls 92-95; rtd 95. *c/o Wingfield, Gorey, Co Wexford, Republic of Ireland*

CHAMBERS, John Richard. b 50. EMMTC 01. **d** 04 **p** 05. C Farnsfield *S'well* 04-07; C Kirklington w Hockerton 04-07; C Bilsthorpe 04-07; C Eakring 04-07; C Maplebeck 04-07; C Winkburn 04-07; P-in-c E Bridgford and Kneeton 07-10; P-in-c Flintham 08-10; P-in-c Car Colston w Screveton 08-10; R Richmond w Hudswell and Downholme and Marske *Leeds* from 10. *The Rectory, Church Wynd, Richmond DL10 7AQ* T: (01748) 821241 M: 07875-348245
E: j_echambers@btinternet.com

CHAMBERS, Mrs Lynn. b 53. Northd Coll of Educn TCert 74 Greenwich Univ MA 96. St Mich Coll Llan 03. **d** 05 **p** 06. Dioc Children's Officer *St D* 01-06; NSM Carmarthen St Pet 05-08; P-in-c Brechfa w Abergorlech etc 08-09; P-in-c Brechfa and Llanfihangel Rhos-y-corn from 09; AD Llandeilo 12-15. *Llwyn Aderyn, Brechfa, Carmarthen SA32 7BL* T: (01267) 202763
E: chambers@bromihangel.freeserve.co.uk

CHAMBERS, Marion Patricia. *See* HINKS, Marion Patricia

CHAMBERS, Canon Peter Lewis. b 43. Imp Coll Lon BScEng 64. St Steph Ho Ox 64. **d** 66 **p** 67. C Llandaff w Capel Llanilltern *Llan* 66-70; Chapl Ch in Wales Youth Coun 70-73; Youth Chapl *Bris* 73-78; V Bedminster St Mich 78-84; RD Bedminster 81-84; Adv Ho of Bps Marriage Educn Panel Gen Syn 84-88; Dir Dioc Coun for Soc Resp *Guildf* 88-94; Hon Can Guildf Cathl 89-94; Dir Tr *Sheff* 95-00; P-in-c Harthill and Thorpe Salvin 00-07; Dioc Min Teams Officer 00-04; Hon Can Sheff Cathl 96-07; rtd 07. *5 Henley Grove, Bristol BS9 4EQ* T: 0117-307 9427

CHAMBERS, Rachel Jill. *See* GANNEY, Rachel Jill

CHAMBERS, Robert Anthony. b 46. **d** 05 **p** 06. OLM Kirkburton *Leeds* from 05. *Address temp unknown*
E: robert.chambers27@ntlworld.com

CHAMBERS, Simon Paul. b 65. Liv Univ BEng 87 PhD 91. Ripon Coll Cuddesdon 00. **d** 02 **p** 03. C Parkstone St Pet and St Osmund w Branksea *Sarum* 02-05; P-in-c Ashwell w Hinxworth and Newnham *St Alb* 05-10; TV Shaftesbury *Sarum* from 10. *St James's Vicarage, 34 Tanyards Lane, Shaftesbury SP7 8HW* T: (01747) 852193 E: simon@simonchambers.com

CHAMBEYRON, Mrs Julia Lynne. b 46. Univ of Wales (Ban) BTh 06. ERMC 03. **d** 06 **p** 07. C La Côte *Eur* 06-11; Asst Chapl from 11. *1199 rue Guy de Maupassant, 01220 Divonne les Bains, France* T: (0033) 4 50 20 19 37 E: julia.chambeyron@orange.fr

CHAMP, Darren David. b 60. Kent Univ BA 93. Linc Th Coll MA 95. **d** 95 **p** 96. C Ashford *Cant* 95-97; PtO 02-03. *154 Beaver Road, Ashford TN23 7SS* T: (01233) 663090
E: daz@dazchamp.co.uk

CHAMPION, Arthur. b 51. Loughb Univ BSc 76 Aston Univ MSc 77 CEng 88 MIMechE 88 FIOSH 88. WEMTC 03. **d** 08 **p** 09. NSM Badgeworth, Shurdington and Witcombe w Bentham *Glouc* 08-13; NSM Bourton-on-the-Water w Clapton etc 13-14; Public Preacher from 14; NSM Churn Valley from 15. *The New Rectory, Cowley, Cheltenham GL53 9NJ* M: 07768-658723 T: (01242) 870402
E: championarthur@gmail.com

CHAMPION, Canon John Oswald Cecil. b 27. St Chad's Coll Dur BA 49. **d** 51 **p** 52. C Worc St Martin 51-53; Chapl RN 53-57; C Cant St Martin w St Paul 57-60; C-in-c Stourbridge St Mich Norton CD *Worc* 60-64; V Astwood Bank w Crabbs Cross 64-68; V Redditch St Steph 68-75; R Fladbury, Wyre Piddle and Moor 75-93; RD Pershore 79-85; Hon Can Worc Cathl 81-93; rtd 93; PtO *Worc* from 93. *Black Horse Cottage, 3 Church Row, Pershore WR10 1BL* T: (01386) 552403

CHAMPNEYS, Michael Harold. b 46. LRAM 66 GRSM 67 ARCO 67. Linc Th Coll 69. **d** 72 **p** 73. C Poplar *Lon* 72-73; C Bow w Bromley St Leon 73-75; P-in-c Bethnal Green St Barn 75-76; C Tewkesbury w Walton Cardiff *Glouc* 76-78; V Bedford Park *Lon* 78-83; V Shepshed *Leic* 84-87; Community Educn Tutor Bolsover 88-93; PtO *Derby* 90-92; NSM Bolsover 92-93; V Potterspury, Furtho, Yardley Gobion and Cosgrove *Pet* 93-98; RD Towcester 94-98; V Shap w Swindale and Bampton w Mardale *Carl* 98-01; R Calow and Sutton cum Duckmanton *Derby* 01-10; rtd 10. *1 New Road, Holymoorside, Chesterfield S42 7EW* T: (01246) 566172
E: michaelchampneys@yahoo.co.uk

CHANCE, David Newton. b 44. Univ of Wales (Lamp) BA 68. St Steph Ho Ox 68. **d** 70 **p** 71. C Selsdon St Jo w St Fran *Cant* 70-73; C Plymstock *Ex* 73-77; P-in-c Northam 77-79; TR Northam w Westward Ho! and Appledore 79-93; V Banstead *Guildf* 93-10; rtd 10; PtO *Cant* from 11. *3 Norman Road, Westgate-on-Sea CT8 8RR* T: (01843) 836882
E: david.chance93@ntlworld.com

CHAND, Richard. b 62. SAOMC 02. **d** 05 **p** 06. NSM Headington St Mary *Ox* 05-09; NSM Cowley St Jas from 09. *Moore House, 15 Beauchamp Lane, Oxford OX4 3LF* T: (01865) 701948 M: 07590-431903 E: richardchandrw@hotmail.co.uk

CHAND, Wazir. b 29. Punjab Univ BA 56 BT 59. Ox NSM Course. **d** 90 **p** 91. NSM Cowley St Jas *Ox* 90-04; PtO from 04. *38 Garsington Road, Oxford OX4 2LG* T: (01865) 714160 or 433015

CHANDA, Daniel Khazan. b 28. Punjab Univ BA 57 MA 62 Saharanputh Coll. **d** 70 **p** 70. Hon C Handsworth St Jas *Birm* 70-83; Hon C Perry Barr 83-89; C Small Heath 89-98; rtd 98; PtO *Birm* from 98. *173 Wood Lane, Handsworth, Birmingham B20 2AG* T: 0121-551 0725

CHANDLER, Anthony. b 43. Lon Inst of Educn CertEd 65. EAMTC 94. **d** 97 **p** 98. Dioc Youth Officer *Ely* 96-00; NSM March St Mary 97-00; R 00-12; P-in-c 12-15; NSM March St Pet 97-00; R 00-12; P-in-c 12-15; rtd 12; PtO *Ely* from 15. *17 St Peter's Road, March PE15 9NA* T/F: (01354) 652894
E: anthony.chandler@ely.anglican.org

CHANDLER, Barbara Janet. b 58. Newc Univ BMedSci 79 MB, BS 82 MD 93 FRCP 00. NEOC 04. **d** 07 **p** 08. NSM Ponteland *Newc* 07-11; PtO *Mor* from 11. *Highfield House, Lentran, Inverness IV3 8RN* T: (01463) 704393 M: 07989-673801 E: chandlernorth@gmail.com

CHANDLER, Derek Edward. b 67. Southn Univ BTh 91 Nottm Univ MDiv 93. Linc Th Coll 91. **d** 93 **p** 94. C Bitterne Park *Win* 93-97; C Sholing 97-00; R Emmer Green w Caversham Park *Ox* from 00. *20 St Barnabas Road, Emmer Green, Reading RG4 8RA* T: 0118-947 8239 E: rev.derek.chandler@virgin.net

CHANDLER, The Ven Ian Nigel. b 65. K Coll Lon BD 89 AKC 89. Chich Th Coll 92. **d** 92 **p** 93. C Hove *Chich* 92-96; Bp's Dom Chapl 96-00; V Haywards Heath St Rich 00-10; RD Cuckfield 04-06; Adn Plymouth *Ex* from 10. *St Mark's House, 46A Cambridge Road, Plymouth PL2 1PU* T: (01752) 202401
E: archdeacon.of.plymouth@exeter.anglican.org

CHANDLER, John. b 49. ACIB 73. NTMTC 05. **d** 07 **p** 08. NSM Colchester St Mich Myland *Chelmsf* from 07; P-in-c Wormingford, Mt Bures and Lt Horkesley from 14. *4 Longdryve, Wavell Avenue, Colchester CO2 7HH* T: (01206) 366930 M: 07951-160558 E: john@mylandchurch.org.uk or vicar@wormingford.com

CHANDLER, John Charles. b 46. Solicitor . Oak Hill Th Coll 91. **d** 94 **p** 95. C Tonbridge St Steph *Roch* 94-98; V Felsted and Lt Dunmow *Chelmsf* 98-05; V Hildenborough *Roch* 05-13; rtd 13; PtO *Nor* from 13. *1 Beach Close, Overstrand, Cromer NR27 0PJ* T: (01263) 576970
E: jm@chandler464.freeserve.co.uk

CHANDLER, The Very Revd Michael John. b 45. Lambeth STh 80 K Coll Lon PhD 87. Linc Th Coll 70. **d** 72 **p** 73. C Cant St Dunstan w H Cross 72-75; C Margate St Jo 75-78; V Newington w Bobbing and Iwade 78-83; P-in-c Hartlip w Stockbury 80-83; V Newington w Hartlip and Stockbury 83-88; RD Sittingbourne 84-88; R Hackington 88-95; RD Cant 94-95; Can Res Cant Cathl 95-03; Dean Ely 03-11; rtd 11; PtO Cant from 12. *218 Tankerton Road, Whitstable CT5 2AT* T: (01227) 262937

CHANDLER, Quentin David. b 62. Anglia Ruskin Univ MA 08. Aston Tr Scheme 87 Trin Coll Bris BA 92. **d** 92 **p** 93. C Goldington *St Alb* 92-96; TV Rushden w Newton Bromswold *Pet* 96-00; V Rushden St Pet 00-03; Dir Tr for Past Assts 03-08; Dir Studies Dioc Lay Min Course 08-11; R Burton Latimer 03-11; CME Officer and Lic Lay Min Officer from 11; C Gt w Lt Harrowden and Orlingbury and Isham etc from 12. *Diocese of Peterborough, 1 Bouverie Court, The Lakes, Northampton NN4 7YD* T: (01604) 887042 *or* (01536) 725111 M: 07909-542060 E: q.chandler@btopenworld.com

CHANDLER, Stephen Michael. b 54. NTMTC. **d** 09 **p** 10. NSM Victoria Docks St Luke *Chelmsf* 09-12; NSM W Ham from 12. *117 Atkinson Road, London E16 3LT* T: (020) 7474 2083 E: smchandler@lineone.net

CHANDLER, Mrs Susan May. b 54. WMMTC 06. **d** 09 **p** 10. NSM Olton *Birm* from 09. *14 Hollyberry Avenue, Solihull B91 3UA* T: 0121-709 1512 M: 07970-791288 E: j14chand@aol.com

CHANDRA, Kevin Douglas Naresh. b 65. Lon Bible Coll BA 91. Qu Coll Birm 94. **d** 96 **p** 97. C Walmley *Birm* 96-00; P-in-c Erdington St Chad 00-02; TV Erdington 02-05; Chapl St Pet Sch Ex from 06. *St Peter's C of E Aided School, Quarry Lane, Exeter EX2 5AP* T: (01392) 204764 E: kc@chandra.plus.com

CHANDY, Sugu John Mathai. b 40. Kerala Univ BSc 61 Serampore Univ BD 66. Wycliffe Coll Toronto 67. **d** 66 **p** 68. India 66-74 and from 80; C Ormesby *York* 74-77; C Sutton St Jas and Wawne 78-80; rtd 99. *Matteetha, Muttambalam, Kottayam, Kerala 686 004, India* T: (0091) (481) 572438 *or* 572590

✠**CHANG-HIM, The Rt Revd French Kitchener.** b 38. Lich Th Coll. **d** 62 **p** 63 **c** 79. C Goole *Sheff* 62-63; R Praslin Seychelles 63-67; C Sheff St Leon Norwood 67-68; C Mahé Cathl Mauritius 68-70; Missr Praslin Seychelles 70-73; R Anse Royale St Sav 73-79; adn Seychelles 73-79; Bp Seychelles 79-04; rtd 04. *PO Box 44, Victoria, Seychelles* T/F: (00248) 248151 E: changhim@seychelles.sc

CHANNER, Christopher Kendall. b 42. K Coll Lon BD 64 AKC 64. St Boniface Warminster 64. **d** 65 **p** 66. C Norbury St Steph *Cant* 65-68; C S Elmsall *Wakef* 68-70; V Dartford St Edm *Roch* 70-75; Chapl Joyce Green Hosp Dartford 73-75; V Bromley St Andr *Roch* 75-81; V Langton Green 81-94; Chapl Holmewood Ho Sch Tunbridge Wells 94-98; P-in-c Lewes All SS, St Anne, St Mich and St Thos *Chich* 98-00; R Lewes St Mich and St Thos at Cliffe w All SS 00-08; rtd 08. *Toath House, Ockley Road, Hawkhurst, Cranbrook TN18 4DZ* T: (01580) 752105

CHANT, Edwin John. b 14. Lon Univ BA 62. K Coll Lon 39 Clifton Th Coll 46. **d** 47 **p** 48. C Erith St Paul *Roch* 47-49; C Darfield *Sheff* 49-51; C Conisbrough 51-53; C Cliftonville *Cant* 53-56; V Gentleshaw *Lich* 56-80; V Farewell 56-80; rtd 80; PtO *Lich* from 80. *The Old Vicarage Nursing Home, 160 High Street, Chasetown, Burntwood WS7 3XG*

CHANT, Harry. b 40. Oak Hill Th Coll. **d** 78 **p** 79. C Heatherlands St Jo *Sarum* 78-81; P-in-c Bramshaw 81-83; P-in-c Landford w Plaitford 81-83; R Bramshaw and Landford w Plaitford 83-87; V Fareham St Jo *Portsm* 87-00; rtd 00; PtO *Truro* from 00. *Paradise Cottage, 34 Nanscober Place, Helston TR13 0SP* T/F: (01326) 561916 E: handrchant@aol.com

CHANT, Kenneth William. b 37. St Deiniol's Hawarden 67. **d** 70 **p** 71. C Ynyshir *Llan* 70-74; C Bargoed and Deri w Brithdir 74; P-in-c Aberpergwm and Blaengwrach 74-77; V 77-81; V Cwmavon 81-02; rtd 02. *22 Chalice Court, Port Talbot SA12 7DA* T: (01639) 813456

CHANT, Maurice Ronald. b 26. Chich Th Coll 51. **d** 54 **p** 55. C Mitcham St Mark S'wark 54-57; C Surbiton St Matt 57-60; P-in-c Cookridge H Trin *Ripon* 60-64; V 64-67; Chapl Miss to Seamen Tilbury 67-71; Chapl Miss to Seamen Gt Yarmouth 71-77; Australia 77-84 and 85-91; Singapore 84-85; rtd 91. *c/o Mrs Anne Klose, 15 Marcel Place, Wellington Point QLD 4160, Australia*

CHANTER, Canon Anthony Roy. b 37. ACP 60 Open Univ BA 72 Lon Univ MA 75. Sarum Th Coll 64. **d** 66 **p** 67. C W Tarring *Chich* 66-69; Chapl St Andr Sch Worthing 69-70; Hd Master Bp King Sch Linc 70-73; Hon PV Linc Cathl 70-73; Hd Master Grey Court Comp Sch Richmond 73-76; Hon C Kingston All SS S'wark 73-76; Hd Master Bp Reindorp Sch Guildf 77-84; Dir of Educn *Guildf* 84-01; Hon Can Guildf Cathl 84-01; rtd 02; PtO *Chich* from 02. *Thalassa, 62 Sea*

Avenue, Rustington, Littlehampton BN16 2DJ T: (01903) 774288 E: tonychanter@hotmail.com

CHANTREY, Preb David Frank. b 48. K Coll Cam BA 70 PhD 73 MA 74. Westcott Ho Cam 83. **d** 86 **p** 87. C Wordsley *Lich* 86-89; C Beckbury 89-90; P-in-c 90-93; C Badger 89-90; P-in-c 90-93; C Kemberton, Sutton Maddock and Stockton 89-90; P-in-c 90-93; C Ryton 89-90; P-in-c 90-93; R Beckbury, Badger, Kemberton, Ryton, Stockton etc 93-08; TR Wrockwardine Deanery from 08; RD Wrockwardine from 08; Preb Lich Cathl from 99. *The Rectory, Wrockwardine, Telford TF6 5DD* T: (01952) 251857 M: 07785-524495 E: david@wdtm.org.uk

CHANTRY, Canon Helen Fiona. b 59. Bradf Univ BSc 82 Leeds Univ CertEd 83. Trin Coll Bris BA 89. **d** 89 **p** 94. NSM Hyde St Geo *Ches* 89-92; Dioc Youth Officer 92-00; NSM Barrow 94-99; C Acton and Worleston, Church Minshull etc 00-04; P-in-c Audlem 04-11; Bp's Adv for Women in Min 05-09; V Wybunbury and Audlem w Doddington from 11; RD Nantwich from 13; Hon Can Ches Cathl from 10. *St James's Vicarage, 66 Heathfield Road, Audlem, Crewe CW3 0HG* T: (01270) 811543 E: helenchantry@btopenworld.com

CHANTRY, Peter Thomas. b 62. Bradf Univ BSc 83. Trin Coll Bris BA 89. **d** 89 **p** 90. C Hyde St Geo *Ches* 89-92; Dioc Youth Officer 91-99; P-in-c Barrow 94-99; R Nantwich 99-12; Hon C Edstaston, Fauls, Prees, Tilstock and Whixall *Lich* 13; V Betley from 13; V Madeley from 13. *St James's Vicarage, 66 Heathfield Road, Audlem, Crewe CW3 0HG* T: (01270) 811543 E: peterchantry@hotmail.com

CHANTRY, Mrs Sandra Mary. b 41. Cam Inst of Educn CertEd 63. EMMTC 83. dss 86 **d** 87 **p** 94. Loughb Gd Shep *Leic* 86-87; Par Dn 87-89; Par Dn Belton and Osgathorpe 89-90; Par Dn Hathern, Long Whatton and Diseworth w Belton etc 90-94; C 94-97; P-in-c 97-01; rtd 01; PtO *Derby* from 07. *4 The Toft, Mill Lane, Belton, Loughborough LE12 9UL* T: (01530) 222678 E: sandrachantry@aol.com *or* s.chantry41@btinternet.com

CHAPLIN, Ann. b 39. Em Coll Boston (USA) MA 93 LRAM 59 TCert 75. WEMTC 95. **d** 98 **p** 99. NSM Heref S Wye 98-02; NSM St Weonards w Orcop, Garway, Tretire etc 02-05; P-in-c Belmont St Andr USA 06-09; Asst R Cambridge St Pet from 09. *St Peter's Church, PO Box 390390, Cambridge MA 02139, USA* T: (001) (617) 547 7788

CHAPLIN, Colin. b 33. Edin Dioc NSM Course 74. **d** 76 **p** 77. NSM Penicuik *Edin* 76-91; P-in-c Peebles 89-90; NSM Bathgate 91-95; rtd 95; Asst P Edin St Mark 97-00; Asst P Innerleithen from 00; Asst P Peebles from 00; P-in-c Galashiels 02-03. *26 Broomhill Road, Penicuik, Edinburgh EH26 9EE* T: (01968) 672050

CHAPLIN, Douglas Archibald. b 59. Em Coll Cam BA 81. St Jo Coll Nottm. **d** 86 **p** 87. C Glouc St Geo w Whaddon 86-89; C Lydney w Aylburton 89-93; R Worc St Clem 93-01; TV Droitwich Spa 01-13; Dioc Miss Development Officer from 13. *The Old Palace, Deansway, Worcester WR1 2JE* T: (01905) 20537 M: 07905-842565 E: fatherdoug@actually.me.uk

CHAPLIN, Paul. b 57. Hull Univ BA 80 CertEd 81 K Coll Lon MA 89. St Steph Ho Ox 85. **d** 87 **p** 88. C Ex St Jas 87-90; C Wokingham St Paul *Ox* 90-98; V Stratfield Mortimer and Mortimer W End etc from 98. *The Vicarage, 10 The Avenue, Mortimer, Reading RG7 3QY* T: 0118-933 1718 *or* 933 3704

CHAPMAN, Andrew John. b 81. Leeds Univ BA 03 St Jo Coll Dur BA 09. Cranmer Hall Dur 06. **d** 09 **p** 10. C Hykeham *Linc* 09-12; Chapl RAF from 12. *Chaplaincy Services (RAF), HQ Air Command, RAF High Wycombe HP14 4UE* T: (01494) 496800 F: 496343 E: a.j.chapman@live.co.uk

CHAPMAN, Canon Ann Beatrice. b 53. Hull Coll of Educn BEd 77 Leeds Univ BA 87. St Jo Coll Nottm MA 95. **d** 95 **p** 96. C Burley *Ripon* 95-98; TV Sheff Manor 98-01; P-in-c Askrigg w Stallingbusk *Leeds* 01-15; Dir Practical Th NEOC 04-08; P-in-c Hawes and Hardraw *Leeds* 09-15; Hon Can Ripon Cathl from 13; V Upper Wensleydale from 15. *The Vicarage, Burtersett Road, Hawes DL8 3NP* T: (01969) 667553 E: ann681@btinternet.com

CHAPMAN, Barry Frank. b 48. Trin Coll Bris 83. **d** 82 **p** 83. NSM Bradford-on-Avon Ch Ch *Sarum* 82-11; Assoc Chapl Bath Univ *B & W* from 83; NSM N Bradford on Avon and Villages *Sarum* from 11. *16 Church Acre, Bradford-on-Avon BA15 1RL* T: (01225) 866861 *or* 461244 E: ann.barry.chapman@btinternet.com

CHAPMAN, Carl Lewis. b 46. Matlock Coll of Educn CertEd 67. **d** 12 **p** 13. NSM Malin Bridge *Sheff* from 12. *38 Wisewood Lane, Sheffield S6 4WA* T: 0114-220 6820 M: 07941-812155 E: chappie@blueyonder.co.uk

CHAPMAN, Mrs Celia. b 32. Whitelands Coll Lon TCert 53 Open Univ BA 82. WMMTC 84. **d** 87 **p** 94. NSM Bilston *Lich* 87-93; Chapl St Pet Colleg Sch Wolv and Ind Chapl Black Country Urban Ind Miss 93-98; rtd 99; PtO *Glouc* from 99; *Worc* from 99. *5 Tyne Drive, Evesham WR11 7FG* T: (01386) 765878 E: peter_celia@yahoo.co.uk

CHAPMAN, Canon Christopher Robin. b 37. Ripon Hall Ox 72. **d** 73 **p** 74. C Kidbrooke St Jas *S'wark* 73-77; V Corton *Nor* 77-80; V Hopton 77-80; V Hopton w Corton 80-92; RD Lothingland 80-86; P-in-c Loddon w Sisland 92-93; P-in-c Loddon, Sisland w Hales and Heckingham 93-98; P-in-c Chedgrave w Hardley and Langley 97-98; V Loddon, Sisland, Chedgrave, Hardley and Langley 98-03; RD Loddon 95-98; Hon Can Nor Cathl 96-03; Chapl Langley Sch Nor 00-03; rtd 04; PtO *Chelmsf* 04-06; *St E* from 06. *Preveli, 16 Riley Close, Ipswich IP1 5QD* T: (01473) 462109

CHAPMAN, Claire Louise. *See* CULLINGWORTH, Claire Louise

CHAPMAN, Colin Gilbert. b 38. St Andr Univ MA 60 Lon Univ BD 62 Birm Univ MPhil 94. Ridley Hall Cam 62. **d** 64 **p** 65. C Edin St Jas 64-67; Asst Chapl Cairo Cathl Egypt 68-73; Tutor Crowther Hall CMS Tr Coll Selly Oak 73-75; Prin 90-97; Lebanon 75-82; Chapl Limassol St Barn 82-83; Lect Trin Coll Bris 83-90; Dir Faith to Faith Consultancy 97-99; Lect Near E Sch of Th Lebanon 99-03; rtd 04; PtO *Ely* from 07. *West Lodge, 17 Knights Way, Milton, Cambridge CB24 6DE* T: (01223) 862169 E: beirutchapman@hotmail.com

CHAPMAN, Mrs Deborah Herath. b 55. Fort Lewis Coll (USA) BA 76 Lon Bible Coll MA 94. NTMTC 04. **d** 05 **p** 06. C Hanwell St Mellitus w St Mark *Lon* 05-08; C Northolt St Jos 08-13; PtO Cyprus and the Gulf 13-14. *St George, Horacio 38, 08022 Barcelona, Spain* E: bee@rechord.com

CHAPMAN, Mrs Dorothy. b 38. EMMTC. **d** 89 **p** 94. Par Dn Bingham *S'well* 89-92; Sub-Chapl HM Pris Whatton 89-92; C Lenton *S'well* 92-98; rtd 98; PtO *S'well* from 04. *86 Kenrick Road, Nottingham NG3 6FB* T: 0115-950 3088

CHAPMAN, Drummond John. b 36. Cant Sch of Min 80. **d** 83 **p** 86. C Kington w Huntington, Old Radnor, Kinnerton etc *Heref* 83-84; C Llanidloes w Llangurig *Ban* 86-90; V Llanwnnog and Caersws w Carno 90-06; rtd 06. *Wgi Fawr, Carno, Caersws SY17 5LX*

CHAPMAN, Mrs Elizabeth Ann. b 57. SEITE 05. **d** 09 **p** 10. NSM Gillingham St Mary *Roch* 09-11; Chapl Pilgrims Hospice Cant 11-13; NSM Cant St Pet w St Alphege and St Marg etc 11-13; PtO 13-15. *93 Hempstead Road, Hempstead, Gillingham ME7 3RH* T: (01634) 233477 M: 07961-337083 E: l.chapman431@btinternet.com

CHAPMAN, Preb Gorran. b 55. Dur Univ BA. Westcott Ho Cam 78. **d** 80 **p** 81. C Par *Truro* 80-82; C Kenwyn 82-84; P-in-c Penwerris 84-89; V 89-92; V Torquay St Martin Barton *Ex* from 92; PtO *Truro* from 92; Preb Ex Cathl from 07. *St Martin's Vicarage, Beechfield Avenue, Barton, Torquay TQ2 8HU* T: (01803) 327223

CHAPMAN, Guy Godfrey. b 33. Southn Univ BSc 57. Clifton Th Coll 60. **d** 62 **p** 63. C Chadderton Ch Ch *Man* 62-67; V Edgeside 67-70; P-in-c Shipton Bellinger *Win* 70-72; V 72-83; RD Andover 75-85; Hon Can Win Cathl 79-91; R Over Wallop w Nether Wallop 83-91; V Ambrosden w Merton and Piddington *Ox* 91-00; RD Bicester and Islip 95-00; rtd 00; PtO *Sarum* from 01; *Win* 01-15. *65 St Ann Place, Salisbury SP1 2SU* T: (01722) 335339 E: gandachapman@tiscali.com

CHAPMAN, Henry Davison. b 31. Bris Univ BA 55. Tyndale Hall Bris 52. **d** 56 **p** 57. C St Helens St Mark *Liv* 56-60; R Clitheroe St Jas *Blackb* 60-67; V Tipton St Martin *Lich* 67-68; SW Area Sec CPAS 68-72; V Eccleston St Luke *Liv* 72-78; P-in-c Ringshall w Battisford, Barking w Darmsden etc *St E* 78-80; R 80-93; RD Bosmere 87-91; rtd 93; PtO *Sarum* from 93. *Daracombe, 4 The Clays, Market Lavington, Devizes SN10 4AY* T: (01380) 813774

CHAPMAN (née CRAVEN), Canon Janet Elizabeth. b 58. St Jo Coll Dur BSc 80 MA 92. Cranmer Hall Dur 84. **d** 87 **p** 95. Par Dn Darlington St Cuth *Dur* 87-92; NSM Edin Gd Shep 93-95; NSM Long Marston and Rufforth w Moor Monkton and Hessay *York* 95-98; Chapl Qu Ethelburga's Coll York 97-99; Chapl Harrogate Ladies' Coll 00; P-in-c Banbury *Ox* 01-08; Can Res Birm Cathl from 08. *4 Nursery Drive, Handsworth, Birmingham B20 2SW* T: 0121-262 1840 E: canonliturgist@birminghamcathedral.com

CHAPMAN, John Brown. b 54. Strathclyde Univ BSc 76 Lon Bible Coll BA 80. NTMTC 00. **d** 02 **p** 03. C W Ealing St Jo w St Jas *Lon* 02-05; C Northolt St Mary 05-08; Chapl for Internat Chs 08-13; Chapl Sharjah and Asst Chapl Dubai UAE 13-14; Chapl Barcelona *Eur* from 14. *St George, Horacio 38, 08022 Barcelona, Spain* T: (0034) 934 178 867 F: 932 128 433 E: stgeorgeschurch@telefonica.net

CHAPMAN (née WHITFIELD), Mrs Joy Verity. b 46. SRN 67 SCM 71. Trin Coll Bris BA 88. **d** 88 **p** 94. C Littleover *Derby* 88-92; Par Dn Bucknall and Bagnall *Lich* 92-94; TV 94-97; Chapl LOROS Hospice 97-03; rtd 03; PtO *Leic* from 03. *15 Templar Way, Rothley, Leicester LE7 7RB* T: 0116-230 1994 E: joychapman@btinternet.com

CHAPMAN, Mrs Lesley. b 61. NEOC 02. **d** 05 **p** 06. C Fenham St Jas and St Basil *Newc* 05-09; P-in-c Kenton Ascension from

09. *Kenton Vicarage, Creighton Avenue, Newcastle upon Tyne NE3 4UN* T: 0191-285 7803 E: lesley.chapman414@btopenworld.com

CHAPMAN, Mrs Linda. b 46. Lon Univ BSc 67 Lon Inst of Educn PGCE 68. Guildf Dioc Min Course 98. **d** 00 **p** 01. NSM Ewell St Fran *Guildf* 00-04; NSM Cheswardine, Childs Ercall, Hales, Hinstock etc *Lich* 04-14; TV 11-14; rtd 14. *Dalrigh, 12 Lords Mount, Berwick upon Tweed TD15 1LY* T: (01289) 307466 M: 07956-429116 E: rev.linda@btinternet.com

CHAPMAN, Linda Rosa. *See* HILLIER, Linda Rosa

CHAPMAN, Miss Lynn Marie. b 71. Coll of Ripon & York St Jo BEd 93 Cant Ch Ch Univ MA 98. ERMC 08. **d** 11 **p** 12. C Sheringham *Nor* 11-14; P-in-c Brooke, Kirstead, Mundham w Seething and Thwaite 14. *The Vicarage, 105 The Street, Brooke, Norwich NR15 1JU* T: (01508) 558479 E: chapman.lynn@btinternet.com

CHAPMAN, Margaret. *See* FLINTOFT-CHAPMAN, Margaret

CHAPMAN, Mark David. b 60. Trin Coll Ox MA 83 DPhil 89. Ox Min Course 93. **d** 94 **p** 95. Lect Ripon Coll Cuddesdon from 92; NSM Dorchester *Ox* 94-99; NSM Wheatley 99-14; NSM Garsington, Cuddesdon and Horspath from 14. *Ripon College, Cuddesdon, Oxford OX44 9EX* T: (01865) 874310 E: mchapman@ripon-cuddesdon.ac.uk

CHAPMAN, The Ven Michael Robin. b 39. Leeds Univ BA 61. Coll of Resurr Mirfield 61. **d** 63 **p** 64. C Southwick St Columba *Dur* 63-68; Chapl RN 68-84; V Hale *Guildf* 84-91; RD Farnham 88-91; Adn Northn and Can Pet Cathl 91-04; rtd 04; PtO *Pet* 04-07. *Dolphin House, High Street, Caenby, Market Rasen LN8 2EE* T: (01673) 876190 E: chapmanhome@btinternet.com

CHAPMAN, Nigel Leonard. b 58. York St Jo Coll MA 02. Cranmer Hall Dur 04. **d** 05 **p** 06. NSM Coxwold and Husthwaite York from 05. *The Vicarage, Coxwold, York YO61 4AD* T: (01347) 868287 M: 07877-793179 E: nigel.chapman@yorkdiocese.org

CHAPMAN, Miss Patricia Ann. b 42. dss 84 **d** 87 **p** 94. Rainworth *S'well* 84-96; Par Dn 87-94; C 94-96; P-in-c Mansfield Oak Tree Lane 96-07; rtd 07. *28 St John's View, Mansfield NG18 1QP* T: (01623) 423344

CHAPMAN, Peter Harold White. b 40. AKC 64. **d** 65 **p** 66. C Havant *Portsm* 65-69; C Stanmer w Falmer and Moulsecoomb *Chich* 69-73; Chapl RN 73-86; Chapl Chigwell Sch Essex 86-90; P-in-c Stapleford Tawney w Theydon Mt *Chelmsf* 87-01. *Unit F, 33/F, Block 6, Tung Chung Crescent, 2 Mei Tung Street, Lantau, Hong Kong, China* E: phwchapman@aol.com

CHAPMAN, Peter John. b 50. ERMC 05. **d** 08 **p** 09. NSM Lt Barningham, Blickling, Edgefield etc *Nor* 08-11; NSM Trunch 11-12; NSM Roughton and Felbrigg, Metton, Sustead etc from 12; Chapl Qu Eliz Hosp King's Lynn NHS Foundn Trust 12-14. *Pump Cottage, The Street, Bessingham, Norwich NR11 7JR* T: (01263) 577782 E: mail@peterminachapman.plus.com

CHAPMAN, Peter John. b 33. Dur Univ BA 56. Cranmer Hall Dur. **d** 59 **p** 60. C Boulton *Derby* 59-62; Uganda 63-70; P-in-c Southampton St Matt *Win* 71-73; TV Southampton (City Cen) 73-78; V Bilston St Leon *Lich* 78-79; P-in-c Bilston St Mary 78-79; TR Bilston 80-98; RD Wolverhampton 89-98; rtd 99; PtO *Glouc* from 99; *Worc* from 99. *5 Tyne Drive, Evesham WR11 6FG* T: (01386) 765878 E: peter_celia@yahoo.co.uk

CHAPMAN, Rachel Grace. *See* WIGRAM, Rachel Grace

CHAPMAN, Raymond. b 41. Linc Th Coll 68. **d** 71 **p** 72. C Dronfield *Derby* 71-74; C Delaval *Newc* 75-76; TV Whorlton 76-79; V Newc St Hilda 79-83; V Blyth St Cuth 83-89; Hon C Fareham SS Pet and Paul *Portsm* 95-98; PtO 98-00 and from 05; C Purbrook 00-05. *170 White Hart Lane, Fareham PO16 9AX* T: (023) 9232 4537 F: 9264 4237 M: 07944-1245467

CHAPMAN, Canon Rex Anthony. b 38. Univ Coll Lon BA 62 St Edm Hall Ox BA 64 MA 68. Wells Th Coll 64. **d** 65 **p** 66. C Stourbridge St Thos *Worc* 65-68; Chapl Aber Univ *Ab* 68-78; Can St Andr Cathl 76-78; Bp's Adv for Educn *Carl* 78-85; Dir of Educn 85-04; Can Res Carl Cathl 78-04; rtd 04; LtO *Ab* from 06; Chapl to The Queen 97-08. *The Cottage, Myreside, Finzean, Banchory AB31 6NB* T: (01330) 850645 E: rex.chapman@btinternet.com

CHAPMAN, Robert Bertram. b 68. St Jo Coll Nottm BA 00. **d** 00 **p** 01. C Daybrook *S'well* 00-03; P-in-c Colwick and Netherfield 03-11; V Hanwell St Thos *Lon* from 11. *St Thomas's Vicarage, 182 Boston Road, London W7 2AD* T: (020) 8566 0443 E: robertsarah@talktalk.net

CHAPMAN, Rodney Andrew. b 53. AKC 75. St Aug Coll Cant 75. **d** 76 **p** 77. C Hartlepool St Aid *Dur* 76-81; LtO 81-83; C Owton Manor 83-87; P-in-c Kelloe 87-92; V Sharlston *Wakef* 92-01; V Stainland w Outlane *Leeds* from 01; C Elland from 06. *The Vicarage, 345 Stainland Road, Stainland, Halifax HX4 9HF* T: (01422) 311848

CHAPMAN, Roger. b 60. Leic Univ BSc 82. Westcott Ho Cam 04. **d** 06 **p** 07. C Norton *St Alb* 06-09; P-in-c Eaton Bray w Edlesborough 09-10; rtd 10. *13 The Pastures, Hatfield AL10 8PB* M: 07905-891890 E: r.chapman27@ntlworld.com

CHAPMAN, Roger John. b 34. AKC 58. **d** 59 **p** 60. C Guildf Ch Ch 59-61; Kenya 61-67; R S Milford *York* 68-77; RD Selby 72-77; V Beverley St Mary 77-88; RD Beverley 85-88; V Desborough *Pet* 88-95; R Brampton Ash w Dingley and Braybrooke 88-95; rtd 95; PtO *York* from 95. *14 Scrubwood Lane, Beverley HU17 7BE* T: (01482) 881267

CHAPMAN, Ruth Elizabeth. *See* WYLD, Ruth Elizabeth

CHAPMAN, Sally Anne. b 55. Lanchester Poly Cov BSc 76 Univ of Wales (Swansea) PGCE 77. WMMTC 87. **d** 90 **p** 94. Par Dn Glascote and Stonydelph *Lich* 90-93; Par Dn Willenhall H Trin 93-94; C 94-96; TV 96-99; V Streetly 99-05; Dioc Adv for Women in Min 99-04; RD Walsall 04-05; Preb Lich Cathl 04-05; Lect Stourbridge Coll from 05. *41 Hunters Gate, Much Wenlock TF13 6BW* T: (01952) 727569 E: robert@furzebank.freeserve.co.uk

CHAPMAN, Mrs Sarah Jean. b 55. Lon Univ DipCOT 77. Sarum & Wells Th Coll 86. **d** 89 **p** 94. NSM Rogate w Terwick and Trotton w Chithurst *Chich* 89-94; NSM Easebourne 94-96; PtO *Portsm* 96-97; V Sheet 97-02; V Bitterne Park *Win* 02-12; Chapl The Living Well and Dioc Adv for Healing and Wholeness *Cant* from 12. *The Vicarage, Vicarage Lane, Nonington, Dover CT15 4JT* T: (01304) 842847 E: revsarah@sargil.co.uk

CHAPMAN, Simon Jon. b 75. Bris Bapt Coll 04 Trin Coll Bris 07. **d** 08 **p** 09. C Broxbourne w Wormley *St Alb* 08-11; CF(V) 09-11; Chapl RAF 11-14; Chapl Aldenham Sch Herts from 14. *4 The Orchard, Aldenham School, Aldenham Road, Elstree, Borehamwood WD6 3RL* E: simon@chapsters.org.uk

CHAPMAN (formerly WOOD), Canon Sylvia Marian. b 40. Univ of Wales (Lamp) BA 09. Gilmore Ho 77. **dss** 80 **d** 87 **p** 94. Tolleshunt Knights w Tiptree *Chelmsf* 80-83; Leigh-on-Sea St Jas 83-86; Canvey Is 86-92; Par Dn 87-92; Miss to Seamen 87-92; Warder of Ords *Chelmsf* 89-92; C Hutton and CME Officer 92-97; Ind Chapl 97-99; V Moulsham St Luke 99-06; rtd 06; Hon Can Chelmsf Cathl 01-06; PtO *Nor* 00-05; *St E* from 05. *Preveli, 16 Riley Close, Ipswich IP1 5QD* T: (01473) 462109 E: canons.chapman@btinternet.com

CHAPMAN, Stephen Gerard. b 61. Man Univ BSc 83 Sheff Univ BA 15. Yorks Min Course 13. **d** 15. C Sheff Manor from 15. *666 Abbey Lane, Sheffield S11 9NB* M: 07980-065236 E: steve.chapman2015@gmail.com

CHAPMAN, Thomas Graham. b 33. Trin Coll Bris 73. **d** 75 **p** 76. C Branksome St Clem *Sarum* 75-81; V Quarry Bank *Lich* 81-93; V *Worc* 93-99; rtd 99; PtO *Worc* from 99. *8 Somerset Drive, Wollaston, Stourbridge DY8 4RH* T: (01384) 373921 E: thomas.chapman1@btinternet.com

CHAPMAN, Tristan David. b 79. K Alfred's Coll Win BA 01. Ripon Coll Cuddesdon BTh 07. **d** 07 **p** 08. C Bocking St Mary *Chelmsf* 07-10; TV Chipping Barnet *St Alb* from 10. *St Mark's Vicarage, 56 Potters Road, Barnet EN5 5HY* T: (020) 8440 7490 E: fr.tristan@googlemail.com

CHAPMAN, Miss Yvonne Hazel. b 35. Serampore Th Coll BRE 63 Brighton Coll of Educn CertEd 55. EAMTC 95. **d** 96 **p** 97. NSM Duston *Pet* 96-02; NSM Officer 99-02; rtd 02; PtO *Pet* from 02. *18 Sundew Court, Northampton NN4 9XH* T: (01604) 762091 E: rev.yhc@btinternet.com

CHAPPELL, Frank Arnold. b 37. Dur Univ BA 58. Bps' Coll Cheshunt. **d** 60 **p** 61. C Headingley *Ripon* 60-65; V Beeston Hill St Luke 65-73; R Garforth 73-91; V Dacre w Hartwith and Darley w Thornthwaite 91-02; rtd 02; PtO *York* from 02; *Leeds* from 02. *14 Nelsons Lane, York YO24 1HD* T: (01904) 709566

CHAPPELL, Michael Paul. b 35. Selw Coll Cam BA 57 MA 61. Cuddesdon Coll 60. **d** 62 **p** 63. C Pershore w Pinvin, Wick and Birlingham *Worc* 62-65; Malaysia 65-67; V Choral and Chapl Heref Cathl 67-71; Min Can Dur Cathl 71-76; Prec 72-76; Chapl H Trin Sch Stockton 76-87; C-in-c Stockton Green Vale H Trin CD *Dur* 82-87; V Scarborough St Luke *York* 87-01; Chapl Scarborough Gen Hosp 87-91; rtd 01; PtO *York* from 01. *26 Dulverton Hall, Esplanade, Scarborough YO11 2AR* T: (01723) 340126

CHARD, Mrs Julia Clare. b 54. Trin Coll Bris 09. **d** 11 **p** 12. OLM Soundwell *Bris* from 11. *8 Glenside Close, Bristol BS16 2QY* T: 0117-902 1774 E: juliachard@hotmail.com

CHARD, Reginald Jeffrey. b 40. Univ of Wales (Lamp) BA 62 CQSW 75. Coll of Resurr Mirfield 62. **d** 64 **p** 65. C Ystrad Mynach *Llan* 64-67; C Aberdare St Fagan 67-71; V Hirwaun 71-74; Hon C Stechford *Birm* 74-78; TV Banbury *Ox* 78-86; Ind Chapl 86-09; P-in-c Claydon w Mollington 86-96; R Ironstone 96-09; rtd 09. *15 The Glen, Yarmouth PO41 0PZ* T: (01983) 760554 E: jeffreychard@btinternet.com

CHARING CROSS, Archdeacon of. *See* JACOB, The Ven William Mungo

CHARKHAM, Rupert Anthony. b 59. Ex Univ BA 81. Wycliffe Hall Ox 83. **d** 89 **p** 89. C Ox St Aldate w St Matt 89-92; P-in-c Fisherton Anger *Sarum* 92-99; R 99-03; V Cambridge H Trin *Ely* from 03. *Holy Trinity Vicarage, 1 Selwyn Gardens, Cambridge CB3 9AX* T: (01223) 354774 or 355397 E: rupert.charkham@htcambridge.org.uk

CHARLES, Ms Beverley Maria. b 65. Trin Coll Bris 13. **d** 15. C Yate *Bris* from 15. *22 Hampden Close, Yate, Bristol BS37 5UW* T: (01454) 319416 E: beverleycharles@blueyonder.co.uk

CHARLES, Cecilia. *See* CHARLES, Mary Cecilia

CHARLES, David Gordon. b 79. Ex Coll Ox BA 01 MA 04 CCC Cam BA 05 MA 09. Westcott Ho Cam 03. **d** 06 **p** 07. C Willingdon *Chich* 06-10; P-in-c Waldron 10-12; V Eastbourne Ch Ch and St Phil from 12; Chapl to Bp Lewes from 10. *Christ Church Vicarage, 18 Addingham Road, Eastbourne BN22 7DY* T: (01323) 728522 E: davidgcharles@hotmail.com

CHARLES, George Edward. b 41. St Jo Coll Morpeth 63. **d** 66 **p** 67. C Bentleigh St Jo Australia 66-67; C Broadmeadows 67-70; I Montgomery 70-74; I Mooroolbark 74-81; I Bacchus Marsh 81-86; I Sorrento 86-93; I Altona 93-98; I Inverleigh, Bannockburn and Meredith 98-01; TV Hanley H Ev *Lich* 02-06; rtd 06; PtO *Lich* 06-10; RD Alstonfield 09-10. *140 Geelong Road, Portarlington Vic 3223, Australia* E: gpsecharles@ntlworld.com

CHARLES, James Richard. b 67. St Edm Hall Ox BA 90 CertEd 91. Oak Hill Th Coll BA 03. **d** 03 **p** 04. C Throop *Win* 03-07; P-in-c Bexleyheath St Pet *Roch* 07-11; V from 11. *St Peter's Vicarage, 50 Bristow Road, Bexleyheath DA7 4QA* T: (020) 8303 8713 E: jimrcharles@mac.com

CHARLES, Canon Jonathan. b 42. St Luke's Coll Ex CertEd 64. Ripon Hall Ox 72 Ripon Coll Cuddesdon 78. **d** 79 **p** 80. C Leagrave *St Alb* 79-82; Chapl Denstone Coll Uttoxeter 82-86; Chapl Malvern Girls' Coll 86-89; Chapl K Sch Worc 89-95; Min Can Worc Cathl 89-95; R Burnham Gp of Par *Nor* 95-09; RD Burnham and Walsingham 00-08; Hon Can Nor Cathl 05-09; rtd 09; PtO *Nor* from 09. *Michaelmas Cottage, 8 Back Street, South Creak, Fakenham NR21 9PG* T: (01328) 823072 E: revj.charles@virgin.net

CHARLES, Kevin. b 58. EMMTC 08. **d** 11 **p** 12. NSM Annesley w Newstead *S'well* 11-15; Chapl E Midl Ambulance Service from 15; NSM Kirkby in Ashfield St Thos *S'well* from 15. *6 Boughton Close, Sutton-in-Ashfield NG17 4NJ* T: (01623) 514294 E: kevin.charles1@btinternet.com

CHARLES, Martin. *See* CHARLES, William Martin Darrell

CHARLES, Mary Cecilia. b 49. Univ of Wales BEd. Trin Coll Carmarthen. **d** 96 **p** 97. NSM Letterston w Llanfair Nant-y-Gof etc *St D* 96-08; NSM Maenclochog and New Moat etc 08-09; V Borth and Eglwys-fach 09-12; V Borth and Eglwys-fach and Llangynfelyn 12-15; P-in-c Gwendraeth Fawr from 15. *The Vicarage, 56 Llannon Road, Pontyberem, Llanelli SA15 5LY* T: (01970) 871889 E: marycharles@btinternet.com

CHARLES, Meedperdas Edward. b 28. Fitzw Ho Cam BA 60 MA 64. Bangalore Th Coll BD 54. **d** 54 **p** 55. C Malacca Malaya 54-55; P-in-c Singapore St Paul and St Pet Singapore 55-58; PtO *Ely* 58-60; V Sheff St Bart Langsett Road 60-64; Chapl Univ of Singapore 64-66; V Gravelly Hill *Birm* 66-78; V Endcliffe *Sheff* 79-90; rtd 91; PtO *Sheff* from 91. *60 Ringinglow Road, Sheffield S11 7PQ* T: 0114-266 4980

CHARLES, Nathan John. b 80. Wycliffe Hall Ox. **d** 13 **p** 14. C Broadwell, Evenlode, Oddington, Adlestrop etc *Glouc* from 13. *The Vicarage, Chapel Lane, Bledington, Chipping Norton OX7 6UZ* T: (01608) 659508 E: njcharles@gmail.com

CHARLES, Robert Sidney James. b 40. Lon Univ CertEd 77 Open Univ BA 79 Univ of Wales LLM 97. St Mich Coll Llan. **d** 65 **p** 66. C Merthyr Tydfil *Llan* 65-68; C Shotton *St As* 68-70; R Stock and Lydlinch *Sarum* 70-74; R Hubberston *St D* 74-76; PtO *Chelmsf* 81-83; V Crossens *Liv* 83-97; V Budleigh Salterton *Ex* 97-10; rtd 10; PtO *Ex* from 11. *8 Old Bystock Drive, Exmouth EX8 5RB* T: (01395) 223419 E: r.charles@btinternet.com

CHARLES, Robin. b 50. Sarum & Wells Th Coll. **d** 86 **p** 87. C Chesterton *Lich* 86-89; C Rugeley 89-90; TV 90-97; TV E Scarsdale *Derby* 97-01; C Chesterfield St Mary and All SS 01-04; V Worc Dines Green St Mich and Crown E, Rushwick from 04. *3 Grove Farm, Farmbrook Close, Worcester WR2 5UG* T/F: (01905) 749995 M: 07788-724581 E: robin@maize45.freeserve.co.uk

CHARLES, Mrs Susan Jane. b 67. Cant Ch Ch Univ BA 12. SEITE 05. **d** 08 **p** 09. NSM Eltham H Trin *S'wark* 08-13; NSM Mottingham St Edw from 13. *109 Tarnwood Park, London SE9 5PE* T: (020) 8850 0189 M: 07909-037690 E: susanjcharles@aol.com

CHARLES, William Martin Darrell. b 40. **d** 90 **p** 91. C Market Harborough *Leic* 90-91; P-in-c Higham-on-the-Hill w Fenny Drayton and Witherley 91-99; P-in-c Breedon cum Isley Walton and Worthington 99-02; rtd 02; PtO *Leic* from 14. *37 Whatton Road, Kegworth, Derby DE74 2EZ* T: (01509) 672040

CHARLES-EDWARDS, David Mervyn. b 38. Trin Coll Cam BA 61. Linc Th Coll 62. **d** 64 **p** 89. C Putney St Mary *S'wark* 64-65; Chief Exec Officer Br Assn for Counselling 82-87; Gen Manager Lon Lighthouse AIDS Project 87-88; Consultant in leadership and team building from 88; NSM Rugby *Cov* 89-99; P-in-c Clifton upon Dunsmore and Newton 99-03; PtO from 03. *3 Pudding Bag Lane, Thurlaston, Rugby CV23 9JZ* T: (01788) 815395 E: adce@btinternet.com

CHARLESWORTH, Eric Charlesworth. b 29. Kelham Th Coll 49. **d** 54 **p** 56. C Woodbridge St Mary *St E* 54-57; Asst Chapl Oslo St Edm *Eur* 57-59; Canada 60-66; R Huntingfield w Cookley *St E* 66-70; R Slimbridge *Glouc* 70-96; rtd 96; PtO *Glouc* from 96; *Ox* 04-12. *Gardener's Cottage, Fairford Park, Fairford GL7 4JQ* T: (01285) 712411

CHARLESWORTH, Ian Peter. b 65. Lanc Univ BA 87. St Mich Coll Llan 91. **d** 93 **p** 94. C Caereithin *S & B* 93-95; C Oystermouth 95-97; R Llandefalle and Llyswen w Boughrood etc from 97. *The Rectory, Church Lane, Llyswen, Brecon LD3 0UU* T: (01874) 754255 E: ian.charlesworth@btinternet.com

CHARLESWORTH, Philip. b 55. Sheff City Poly BSc 85 Anglia Poly MSc 92. **d** 07 **p** 08. OLM Sprowston w Beeston *Nor* 07-13; NSM Taverham from 13. *63 Wroxham Road, Norwich NR7 8TN* T: (01603) 411316 M: 07545-968435 E: revdphilcharlesworth@gmail.com

CHARLEY, Canon Julian Whittard. b 30. New Coll Ox BA 55 MA 58. Ridley Hall Cam 55. **d** 57 **p** 58. C St Marylebone All So w SS Pet and Jo *Lon* 57-64; Lect Lon Coll of Div 64-70; Vice-Prin St Jo Coll Nottm 70-74; TR Everton St Pet *Liv* 74-87; Warden Shrewsbury Ho 74-87; P-in-c Gt Malvern St Mary *Worc* 87-97; Hon Can Worc Cathl 91-97; rtd 97; PtO *Worc* from 97; *Heref* from 97. *2 Sunrise, Malvern WR14 2NJ* T: (01684) 569801 E: claire_charley@hotmail.com

CHARLTON, Mrs Elizabeth Anne. b 55. STETS BA 08. **d** 08 **p** 09. C W Moors *Sarum* 08-11; C Budleigh Salterton *Ex* 11-12; P-in-c 12-13; C E Budleigh w Bicton and Otterton 11-12; P-in-c 12-13; V Budleigh Salterton, E Budleigh w Bicton etc from 13. *The New Vicarage, Vicarage Road, East Budleigh, Budleigh Salterton EX9 7EF* T: (01395) 444276 M: 07541-069078 E: eacharlton@btinternet.com

CHARLTON, Dr Fraser Graham. b 67. Lindisfarne Regional Tr Partnership 12. **d** 15. NSM Wallsend St Jo *Newc* from 15. *17 Northumberland Avenue, Forest Hall, Newcastle upon Tyne NE12 9NR*

CHARLTON, Hazel. b 66. Qu Coll Birm. **d** 12 **p** 13. C Worc SE from 12. *23 Mortlake Avenue, Worcester WR5 1QD*

CHARLTON, Helen. b 47. **d** 09 **p** 10. NSM Wokingham All SS *Ox* from 09. *36 Rances Lane, Wokingham RG40 2LH* T: 0118-978 9153 E: helenjcharlton@btinternet.com

CHARLTON, Thomas David. b 53. York St Jo Univ BA 12 IEng MIET 80. Cranmer Hall Dur 12. **d** 13 **p** 14. NSM Whorlton w Carlton and Faceby *York* 13-15; NSM Eston w Normanby from 15. *28 Brougham Close, Ingleby Barwick, Stockton-on-Tees TS17 5GH* T: (01642) 767176 M: 07805-388165 E: td.charlton@btinternet.com

CHARMAN, Canon Jane Ellen Elizabeth. b 60. St Jo Coll Dur BA 81 Selw Coll Cam BA 84 MA 88. Westcott Ho Cam 82. **d** 87 **p** 94. C Glouc St Geo w Whaddon 87-90; Chapl and Fell Clare Coll Cam 90-95; R Duxford *Ely* 95-04; V Hinxton 95-04; V Ickleton 95-04; RD Shelford 03-04; Dir of Min *Sarum* 04-07; Dir of Learning for Discipleship and Min from 07; Can and Preb Sarum Cathl from 07. *4 The Sidings, Downton, Salisbury SP5 3QZ* T: (01722) 411944 M: 07867-146524 E: jane.charman@salisbury.anglican.org

CHARMLEY, Mark Richard. b 71. Ex Univ BA 93. Qu Coll Birm MA 01. **d** 01 **p** 02. C Blurton *Lich* 01-04; P-in-c Banbury St Leon *Ox* 04-10; P-in-c Guernsey St Sav *Win* 10-13; P-in-c Guernsey St Marguerite de la Foret 10-13; TR Guernsey W Par from 13. *The Rectory, Le Neuf Chemin Road, St Saviour, Guernsey GY7 9FQ* T: (01481) 263045 E: charmley@cwgsy.net

CHARMLEY, Mrs Tracy-Belinda. b 72. Ex Univ BA 93 St Luke's Coll Ex PGCE 95 Birm Univ MEd. Ripon Coll Cuddesdon 07. **d** 10 **p** 11. NSM Guernsey St Martin *Win* 10-14; NSM Guernsey W Par from 14; NSM Guernsey St Pierre du Bois from 14; NSM Guernsey St Sav from 14. *The Rectory, Le Neuf Chemin Road, St Saviour, Guernsey GY7 9FQ* T: (01481) 263045 E: charmley@cwgsy.net

CHARNLEY, Anthony Keith. Dur Univ BSc 71 PhD 76 FHEA 07. STETS. **d** 12 **p** 13. NSM N Bradford on Avon and Villages *Sarum* from 12; Visiting Prof Chongqing Univ China from 08. *41 Leigh Park Road, Bradford-on-Avon BA15 1TF* T: (01225) 866515 E: keith@a-charnley.freeserve.co.uk

CHARNOCK, Deryck Ian. b 47. Oak Hill Th Coll 78. **d** 80 **p** 81. C Rowner *Portsm* 80-84; TV Southgate *Chich* 84-90; V Penge St Paul *Roch* 90-98; V Whitwick St Jo the Bapt *Leic* 98-06;

R Hollington St Leon *Chich* from 06. *The Rectory, Tile Barn Road, St Leonards-on-Sea TN38 9PA* T: (01424) 852257 E: deryck8@aol.com

CHARNOCK, Ms Tracy. b 75. Leeds Univ BA 97 BA 08. Coll of Resurr Mirfield 06. **d** 08 **p** 09. C Man Victoria Park 08-11; P-in-c S Shore H Trin *Blackb* 11-13; V from 13; P-in-c S Shore St Pet 11-13; V from 13. *92 Watson Road, Blackpool FY4 2DE* T: (01253) 344773 M: 07778-163920 E: tracy.charnock@hotmail.co.uk

CHARRETT, Geoffrey Barton. b 36. ALCM Nottm Univ BSc 57. Ridley Hall Cam 65. **d** 67 **p** 68. C Clifton *York* 67-68; LtO *Blackb* 69-80; C Walthamstow St Mary w St Steph *Chelmsf* 81-82; TV 82-87; Chapl Gordon's Sch Woking 87-94; P-in-c Hambledon *Guildf* 94-97; rtd 97; PtO *Linc* from 00. *2 Station Road, Sutton-on-Sea, Mablethorpe LN12 2HN* T: (01507) 443525

CHARTERIS, Hugo Arundale. b 64. Witwatersrand Univ BA 88. Cranmer Hall Dur 90. **d** 93 **p** 94. C Byker St Mark and Walkergate St Oswald *Newc* 93-97; P-in-c New Ferry *Ches* 97-02; V 02-05. *26 Rothbury Terrace, Newcastle upon Tyne NE6 5XH* T: 0191-209 2508 E: hugo@charteris.org.uk

CHARTERS, Alan Charles. b 35. Trin Hall Cam BA 60 MA 63 FCollP 88. Linc Th Coll 60. **d** 62 **p** 63. C Gt Grimsby St Mary and St Jas *Linc* 62-65; Chapl and Hd RE Eliz Coll Guernsey 65-70; P-in-c Guernsey St Jas the Less 65-70; Dep Hd Master Park Sen High Sch Swindon 70-73; Chapl St Jo Sch Leatherhead 73-83; Dep Hd Master 76; Visiting Lect and Tutor Lon Univ Inst of Ed 76-80; Headmaster The K Sch Glouc 83-92; V Aberedw w Llandeilo Graban and Llanbadarn etc *S & B* 92-00; Bp's Visitor to Schs 92-00; rtd 00; PtO *Eur* 00-03; P-in-c Dinard 03-06. *Crescent House, Church Street, Talgarth, Brecon LD3 0BL* T: (01874) 711135 E: alan@ccharterss.net.uk

⊕CHARTRES, The Rt Revd and Rt Hon Richard John Carew. b 47. PC 96 KCVO 09. Trin Coll Cam BA 68 MA 73 BD 83 Hon DLitt 98 Hon DD 99 FSA 99 Hon FGCM 97. Cuddesdon Coll 69 Linc Th Coll 72. **d** 73 **p** 74 **c** 92. C Bedford St Andr *St Alb* 73-75; Bp's Dom Chapl 75-80; Abp's Chapl *Cant* 80-84; P-in-c Westmr St Steph w St Jo *Lon* 86-92; Dir of Ords 85-92; Prof Div Gresham Coll 86-92; Six Preacher Cant Cathl 91-97; Area Bp Stepney *Lon* 92-95; Bp Lon from 95; Dean of HM Chpls Royal and Prelate of OBE from 95. *The Old Deanery, Dean's Court, London EC4V 5AA* T: (020) 7248 6233 F: 7248 9721 E: bishop@londin.clara.co.uk

CHASE, Mrs Elizabeth. b 41. Wycliffe Hall Ox. **d** 09 **p** 10. NSM Headbourne Worthy *Win* from 09; NSM King's Worthy from 09. *The Greetings, Grange Road, Winchester SO23 9RT*

CHATER, John Augustus. b 43. SEITE 99. **d** 04 **p** 05. NSM St Peter-in-Thanet *Cant* 04-07; Ramsgate Town Cen Missr 07-13; rtd 13; PtO *Cant* from 13. *125 High Street, Ramsgate CT11 9UA* T: (01843) 596175 E: johnchater@rya-online.net

CHATER, John Leathely. b 29. Qu Coll Cam BA 54 MA 58. Ridley Hall Cam 54. **d** 56 **p** 57. C Bath Abbey w St Jas *B & W* 56-60; V Bermondsey St Anne *S'wark* 60-64; Ind Chapl 60-64; V Heslington *York* 64-69; Chapl York Univ 64-69; V Lawrence Weston *Bris* 69-73; PtO 74-80; P-in-c Wraxall *B & W* 80-82; R 82-84; V Battle *Chich* 84-90; Dean Battle 84-90; RD Battle and Bexhill 86-90; R St Marylebone w H Trin *Lon* 90-96; rtd 96; PtO *Chich* 96-11. *High Ridge, London Road, Halesworth IP19 8LR* T: (01986) 875876

CHATER (née CAKE), Nichola Carla. b 58. Liv Univ BSc 79 MB, ChB 85 MRCGP FRCP 08. Cranmer Hall Dur 05. **d** 07 **p** 08. NSM Dur St Marg and Neville's Cross St Jo from 07. *37 Hill Meadows, High Shincliffe, Durham DH1 2PE* T: 0191-383 1869 E: nicky_chater@yahoo.co.uk

CHATFIELD, Adrian Francis. b 49. Leeds Univ BA 71 MA 72 MPhil 89 PhD 97. Coll of Resurr Mirfield 71. **d** 72 **p** 73. Trinidad and Tobago 72-83; TV Barnstaple, Goodleigh and Landkey *Ex* 83-84; TV Barnstaple 85; TR 85-88; Lect St Jo Coll Nottm 88-98; S Africa 99-05; Tutor Wycliffe Hall Ox 05-07; Hon C Wallingford *Ox* 05-07; Co-ord Mixed Mode Tr Ridley Hall Cam 07-15; Tutor from 15; Dir Simeon Cen from 07. *12 Barrons Way, Comberton, Cambridge CB23 7EQ* T: (01223) 263009 or 746590 E: adrian.chatfield@btinternet.com *or* ac588@cam.ac.uk

CHATFIELD, Mrs Gillian. b 50. Leeds Univ BA 71 PGCE 72. St Jo Coll Nottm MA 94. **d** 94 **p** 95. C Greasley *S'well* 94-98; Miss Partner Th Coll by Ext S Africa 99-05; TV Wallingford *Ox* 05-07; Past Tutor Ridley Hall Cam 07-13; Hon C Lordsbridge *Ely* from 13. *12 Barrons Way, Comberton, Cambridge CB23 7EQ* T: (01223) 263009 M: 07758-591430 E: jill.chatfield@btinternet.com

CHATFIELD, Michael Francis. b 75. York Univ BSc 96 Fitzw Coll Cam BA 99 MA 03. Ridley Hall Cam. **d** 00 **p** 01. C Attenborough *S'well* 00-03; P-in-c Chaguanas St Thos Trinidad and Tobago 04-09; Chapl RAF from 09. *Chaplaincy*

Services (RAF), HQ Air Command, RAF High Wycombe HP14 4UE
T: (01494) 496800 F: 496343 M: 07540-848758
E: thechatalots@hotmail.com

CHATFIELD, Canon Norman. b 37. Fitzw Ho Cam BA 59 MA 68. Ripon Hall Ox 60. **d** 62 **p** 63. C Burgess Hill St Jo *Chich* 62-65; C Uckfield 65-69; V Lower Sandown St Jo *Portsm* 69-76; V Locks Heath 76-83; R Alverstoke 83-91; Hon Can Portsm Cathl 85-91; Can Res Glouc Cathl 91-02; rtd 02; PtO *Portsm* from 03. *Ellwood, Garfield Road, Bishop's Waltham SO32 1AT* T: (01489) 891995 E: chat.field@btinternet.com

CHATTELL, David Malcolm. b 63. St Luke's Coll Ex BEd 93. Wycliffe Hall Ox 03. **d** 05 **p** 06. C Bucklebury w Marlston *Ox* 05-11; R Farleigh, Candover and Wield *Win* from 11. *The Rectory, Alresford Road, Preston Candover, Basingstoke RG25 2EE* T: (01256) 389474 E: davidchattell172@btinternet.com

CHATTEN, Mrs Sophie. b 79. **d** 15. C Stoughton *Guildf* from 15. *12 Grange Close, Guildford GU2 9QJ* M: 07969-604514
E: sophiebish@gmail.com

CHATTERLEY, Mrs Marion Frances. b 55. Edin Th Coll 95. **d** 98 **p** 99. C Edin Gd Shep 98-00; C Edin Ch Ch 00-05; Hon C Edin St Mich and All SS 07-11; Chapl Edin Napier Univ from 00; Dioc Dir of Ords from 06. *102 Relugas Road, Edinburgh EH9 2LZ* T: 0131-667 6847 M: 07771-982163
E: marion.chatterley@blueyonder.co.uk

CHATTERTON, Mrs Nicola Mary. b 63. Qu Coll Birm BA 15. **d** 14 **p** 15. NSM Stratford-upon-Avon, Luddington etc *Cov* from 14. *Address temp unknown*

CHATTERTON, Thomas William. b 50. SEITE. **d** 99 **p** 00. C Blackheath All SS *S'wark* from 99; C Thamesmead 11-14; Chapl Greenwich Foundn from 14. *44 Harland Road, London SE12 0JA* T: (020) 8851 6813
E: williamchatterton@hotmail.co.uk

CHATWIN, Ronald Ernest. b 34. St Aid Birkenhead 58. **d** 60 **p** 61. C Selsdon *Cant* 60-64; C Crawley *Chich* 64-68; V Coldwaltham 68-74; TV Ovingdean w Rottingdean and Woodingdean 74-83; V Saltdean 83-91; V Hellingly and Upper Dicker 91-02; rtd 02; PtO *Chich* from 03. *Cold Waltham, 29A New Road, Hellingly, Hailsham BN27 4EW* T: (01323) 843346

CHAUDHARY, Jaisher Masih. b 56. Qu Coll Birm. **d** 08 **p** 09. NSM Handsworth St Mich *Birm* from 08; NSM Handsworth Good News Asian Ch from 12. *29 George Street, Handsworth, Birmingham B21 0EG* T: 0121-551 6279
E: jaisher@hotmail.com

CHAVE, Preb Brian Philip. b 51. Open Univ BA. Trin Coll Bris. **d** 84 **p** 85. C Cullompton *Ex* 84-87; TV Bishopsnympton, Rose Ash, Mariansleigh etc 87-93; Chapl for Agric *Heref* 93-96; Communications Adv and Bp's Staff Officer 97-01; Bp's Dom Chapl 97-01; TV W Heref from 01; Preb Heref Cathl from 97; Can Heref Cathl 97-01; RD Heref City 04-07; Bp's Dom Chapl from 15. *The Vicarage, Vowles Close, Hereford HR4 0DF* T: (01432) 273086 E: chave@hfddiocesan.freeserve.co.uk

CHAVE-COX, Guy. b 56. St Andr Univ BSc 79. Wycliffe Hall Ox 83. **d** 86 **p** 87. C Wigmore Abbey *Heref* 86-88; C Bideford *Ex* 88-91; TV Barnstaple from 91. *St Paul's Vicarage, Old Sticklepath Hill, Barnstaple EX31 2BG* T: (01271) 344400
E: vicar@barnstaple-st-paul.org.uk

CHAVNER, Robert. b 59. ALCM 82 AGSM 85 FGMS 00 FRSA 06. Linc Th Coll 90. **d** 92 **p** 93. C Beckenham St Geo *Roch* 92-96; V Sevenoaks St Luke 96-06; P-in-c Brighton St Nic *Chich* 06-11; V from 11. *The Vicarage, 8 Prestonville Road, Brighton BN1 3TL* T: (01273) 709045 E: robert.chavner@ntlworld.com

CHEATLE, Adèle Patricia. b 46. York Univ BA 73. Trin Coll Bris 76. **d** 87 **p** 98. Par Dn Harborne Heath *Birm* 87; NSM 92-93; PtO *Heref* 96-97; NSM Burghill and Stretton Sugwas 97-99; NSM Heref St Pet w St Owen and St Jas 99-04; NSM Ches Square St Mich w St Phil *Lon* 04-07; PtO *Birm* from 11. *26 Oakham Road, Harborne, Birmingham B17 9DG* T: 0121-427 5362 E: thecheatles@googlemail.com

CHEDZEY, Canon Derek Christopher. b 67. Univ of Wales MA 12. Trin Coll Bris BA 93. **d** 93 **p** 94. C Bedgrove *Ox* 93-95; C Haddenham w Cuddington, Kingsey etc 95-98; TV High Wycombe 98-01; Deanery Tr Officer and C Washfield, Stoodleigh, Withleigh etc *Ex* 01-04; P-in-c Frenchay and Winterbourne Down *Bris* 04-06; Dioc Dir Lay Min 04-08; Adv for Initial Minl Educn 08-15; Warden of Readers 04-15; Hon C Yate 09-15; Asst Adn 13-15; Hon Can Bris Cathl 11-15; Hd of Min Development from 15; Can Res Bris Cathl from 15. *The Rectory, Rectory Road, Frampton Cotterell, Bristol BS36 2BP* T: 0117-906 0100 M: 07811-878774
E: derek.chedzey@bristoldiocese.org

CHEEK, Jane Elizabeth. *See* VLACH, Jane Elizabeth

CHEEK, Richard Alexander. b 35. Lon Univ LDS 60 RCS 60. Ox NSM Course 72. **d** 75 **p** 76. NSM Maidenhead St Luke *Ox* 75-94 and 05-12; Asst Chapl Heatherwood and Wexham Park Hosps NHS Trust 94-04; PtO *Ox* from 12. *Windrush,*

26 Sheephouse Road, Maidenhead SL6 8EX T: (01628) 628484
E: r.a.cheek@dialpipex.com

CHEESEMAN (née DUNHAM), Mrs Angela Mary. b 40. New Hall Cam MB, BChir 66 MRCOG 74 FRCSEd 75 FRCOG 96. **d** 05 **p** 06. OLM Eastling w Ospringe and Stalisfield w Otterden *Cant* 05-10. *New House Farm, Otterden Road, Eastling, Faversham ME13 0BN* T: (01795) 892124
E: angiecheeseman45@hotmail.com

CHEESEMAN, Colin Henry. b 47. Reading Univ BA 69 Kent Univ PhD 00. Sarum & Wells Th Coll 82. **d** 84 **p** 85. C Cranleigh *Guildf* 84-87; C Godalming 87-89; V Cuddington 89-96; Chapl HM Pris Wealstun 96-97; P-in-c Tockwith and Bilton w Bickerton *York* 97-01; RD New Ainsty 99-01; P-in-c Roundhay St Jo *Leeds* from 01; Dioc Ecum Adv *Ripon* 09-14. *Scatwell House, Church Fenton Lane, Ulleskelf, Tadcaster LS24 9DW*

CHEESEMAN, Janet. *See* GOODAIR, Jan

CHEESEMAN, John Anthony. b 50. Oriel Coll Ox BA 73 MA 75. Trin Coll Bris. **d** 76 **p** 77. C Sevenoaks St Nic *Roch* 76-79; C Egham *Guildf* 79-82; V Leyton Ch Ch *Chelmsf* 82-90; V Westgate St Jas *Cant* 90-01; V Eastbourne H Trin *Chich* 01-10; rtd 10; PtO *Cant* from 11. *7 Meadow Road, Margate CT9 5JJ* T: (01843) 230733 E: jcpreach@gmail.com

CHEESEMAN, Nicholas James. b 72. Qu Mary and Westf Coll Lon BA 94 Leeds Univ BA 02. Coll of Resurr Mirfield 00. **d** 03 **p** 04. C Wantage *Ox* 03-07; V Reading St Mark and All SS from 07. *All Saints' Vicarage, 14 Downshire Square, Reading RG1 6NH* T: 0118-957 2000 M: 07732-252709
E: njcheeseman@gmail.com

CHEESEMAN, Trevor Percival. b 38. Auckland Univ PhD 64 Lon Univ BD 67. K Coll Lon and St Boniface Warminster AKC 67. **d** 68 **p** 69. C Warmsworth *Sheff* 68-71; New Zealand from 71. *49 Birdwood Avenue, Papatoetoe, Manukau 2025, New Zealand* T: (0064) (9) 277 6145 E: tpandhmc@middleearth.net.nz

CHEESMAN, Canon Andrew Walford. b 36. St Mark's Coll Adelaide BA 58. Cuddesdon Coll 59. **d** 61 **p** 62. C Man St Aid 61-63; P-in-c Keith Australia 64-68; Prec St Pet Cathl Adelaide 68-70; Chapl Flinders Univ 68-70; Asst Chapl St Pet Coll Adelaide 70-73; P-in-c Tea Tree Gully 73-76; R Mitcham Adelaide 76-01; Adn Torrens 85-93; Can Adelaide from 85. *1/4 Torrens Street, Mitcham SA 5062, Australia* T/F: (0061) (8) 8272 1864 E: mousal@bigbutton.com.au

CHEESMAN, Peter. b 43. ACA 65 FCA 76 MCMI. Ridley Hall Cam 66. **d** 69 **p** 70. C Herne Bay Ch Ch *Cant* 69-74; TV Lowestoft St Marg *Nor* 75-78; TV Lowestoft and Kirkley 79-81; Ind Chapl *Glouc* 81-84; P-in-c Saul w Fretherne and Framilode 84-85; V Frampton on Severn, Arlingham, Saul etc 85-08; rtd 08. *Frampton Court, The Green, Frampton on Severn, Gloucester GL2 7EX* T: (01452) 740533
E: peter@the-cheesman.net

CHEETHAM, David Andrew. b 69. **d** 12 **p** 13. NSM Kenilworth St Jo *Cov* 12-13; NSM Olton *Birm* from 13. *75 Solihull Road, Shirley, Solihull B90 3HJ* T: 0121-744 4407
E: d.cheetham@bham.ac.uk

CHEETHAM (née MUMFORD), Mrs Lesley Anne. b 51. Man Univ BA 73. NOC 01. **d** 04 **p** 05. C Halifax *Wakef* 04-08; V Easby w Skeeby and Brompton on Swale etc *Ripon* 08-12; Chapl Overgate Hospice from 12. *Overgate Hospice, 30 Hullen Edge Road, Elland HX5 0QY* T: (01422) 387110 M: 07963-620391 E: lesley_cheetham@btinternet.com

✠**CHEETHAM, The Rt Revd Richard Ian.** b 55. CCC Ox BA 77 CertEd 78 MA 82 Lon Univ PhD 99. Ripon Coll Cuddesdon 85. **d** 87 **p** 88 **c** 02. C Newc H Cross 87-90; V Luton St Aug Limbury *St Alb* 90-99; RD Luton 95-98; Adn St Alb 99-02; Area Bp Kingston *S'wark* from 02. *Kingston Episcopal Area Office, 620 Kingston Road, London SW20 8DN* T: (020) 8545 2440 *or* 8789 3218 F: 8545 2441
E: bishop.richard@southwark.anglican.org

CHEGE, James Gathioro. b 57. St Paul's Coll Limuru BD 94. NTMTC. **d** 09 **p** 10. NSM Grays Thurrock *Chelmsf* 09-15; Dir Maasai Educn Cen Kenya from 15. *PO Box 23026, Nairobi, Kenya* M: (00254) 763-181808 E: captjchege@aol.com

CHEGWIN HALL, Elaine. *See* HALL, Elaine Chegwin

CHELASHAW, Godfrey Kiprotich (Kip). b 76. Oak Hill Th Coll BA 08 MA 10. **d** 10 **p** 11. C Audley *Lich* 10-15; C Talke 14-15; C Alsagers Bank 14-15; C Alsagers Bank, Audley and Talke from 15. *St John's Vicarage, High Street, Alsagers Bank, Stoke-on-Trent ST7 8BQ* E: kchelashaw@yahoo.com

CHELMSFORD, Bishop of. *See* COTTRELL, The Rt Revd Stephen Geoffrey

CHELMSFORD, Dean of. *See* HENSHALL, The Very Revd Nicholas James

CHELTENHAM, Archdeacon of. *See* SPRINGETT, The Ven Robert Wilfred

CHENERY, Mrs Janice Marienne. b 46. **d** 07 **p** 08. OLM Mid Loes St E 07-12; rtd 12. *316 Calder Street, Glasgow G42 7NH*

CHERRY, David. b 30. Roch Th Coll 59. **d** 61 **p** 62. C Seacroft *Ripon* 61-67; R Bamford *Derby* 67-75; Chapl Málaga w Almuñécar *Eur* 83-91; rtd 91; NSM Waltham St Lawrence *Ox* 97-01; PtO *Leic* from 01. *2 Church Lane, Rearsby, Leicester LE7 4YE* T: (01664) 424099

CHERRY, David Warwick. b 61. Cape Town Univ BMus 86 Leeds Univ BA 91. Coll of Resurr Mirfield 92. **d** 92 **p** 93. C Hammersmith SS Mich and Geo White City Estate CD *Lon* 92-01; C Hammersmith St Luke 94-01; Chapl Greenwich Univ *S'wark* 01-03; Chapl Univ of Westmr *Lon* 03-10; Hon C St Marylebone St Cypr 06-08; V Pimlico St Mary Bourne Street 10-15; V Pimlico St Barn 10-15. *Address temp unknown* M: 07939-553547

CHERRY, Revd Stephen Arthur. b 58. St Chad's Coll Dur BSc 79 Fitzw Coll Cam BA 85 MA 90 K Coll Lon PhD 95. Westcott Ho Cam 83. **d** 86 **p** 87. C Baguley and Asst Chapl Wythenshawe Hosp Man 86-89; Chapl K Coll Cam 89-94; R Loughborough All SS w H Trin *Leic* 94-06; RD Akeley E 96-99; Hon Can Leic Cathl 04-06; Dir Min and Tr *Dur* 06-14; Can Res Dur Cathl 06-14; Dean K Coll Cam from 14. *King's College, Cambridge CB2 1ST* T: (01223) 331419 E: sacherry@btinternet.com *or* dean@kings.cam.ac.uk

CHESHER, Michael. b 52. Open Univ BA 84. EAMTC 97. **d** 00 **p** 01. C Littleport *Ely* 00-03; V Chelmsf All SS 03-04; P-in-c W Walton and Walpole St Peter w Walpole St Andrew *Ely* 04-11; PtO 11-12; C Spalding St Mary and St Nic *Linc* from 12; C Spalding St Paul from 12. *18 Maple Grove, Spalding PE11 2LE* T: (01775) 712502 M: 07903-883267 E: m.chesher559@btinternet.com

CHESHIRE, Mrs Charlotte. b 77. St Jo Coll Nottm 11. **d** 14 **p** 15. C Shifnal and Sheriffhales *Lich* from 14; C Tong from 14. *18 Gresham Drive, Telford TF3 5ES* M: 07553-432657 E: revcharlotte@yahoo.co.uk

CHESHIRE, James Wilson. b 73. Univ of Florida BA 05. Gordon-Conwell Th Sem MDiv 00 CITC 13. **d** 14. C Bangor Abbey *D & D* from 14. *5 Lineybrook Cottages, Bangor BT19 7EA* T: (028) 9107 5141 M: 07751-576954 E: revjimcheshire@gmail.com

CHESNEY, David Vince. b 69. UMIST BSc 99. NTMTC BA 08. **d** 08 **p** 09. C Springfield H Trin *Chelmsf* 08-12; V Victoria Docks Ascension from 12. *75 Baxter Road, London E16 3HJ* E: dave.chesney@btinternet.com

✠**CHESSUN, The Rt Revd Christopher Thomas James.** b 56. Univ Coll Ox BA 78 MA 82 Trin Hall Cam BA 82. Westcott Ho Cam. **d** 83 **p** 84 **c** 05. C Sandhurst *Ox* 83-87; C Portsea St Mary *Portsm* 87-89; Min Can and Chapl St Paul's Cathl 89-93; Voc Adv 90-05; R Stepney St Dunstan and All SS 93-01; AD Tower Hamlets 97-01; Adn Northolt 01-05; Area Bp Woolwich *S'wark* 05-11; Bp S'wark from 11. *Bishop's House, 38 Tooting Bec Gardens, London SW16 1QZ* T: (020) 8769 3256 *or* 7939 9420 F: 8769 4126 E: bishop.christopher@southwark.anglican.org

CHESTER, David Kenneth. b 50. Dur Univ BA 73 Aber Univ PhD 78 CGeol 92 FGS 88. NOC 93. **d** 96 **p** 97. NSM Hoylake *Ches* 96-04; NSM W Kirby St Bridget from 04. *Yenda, Grange Old Road, West Kirby, Wirral CH48 4ET* T: 0151-625 8004 E: jg54@liv.ac.uk

CHESTER, Irene Mary. *See* GREENMAN, Irene Mary

CHESTER, Mark. b 55. Lanc Univ BA 79. Wycliffe Hall Ox 86. **d** 88 **p** 89. C Plymouth St Andr w St Paul and St Geo *Ex* 88-94; V Burney Lane *Birm* 94-99; V Camberley St Paul *Guildf* 99-15; Sen Chapl Waterways from 15; PtO *Guildf* from 15; CF (TA) from 89. *Berisay, Guildford Road, Frimley Green GU16 6NS* E: markwith29@gmail.com

CHESTER, Maureen Olga. b 47. Univ of Wales (Swansea) BA 70. NEOC 94. **d** 97 **p** 98. NSM Morpeth *Newc* 97-11; rtd 11. *10 Leland Place, Morpeth NE61 2AN* T: (01670) 514569 E: mochester@classicfm.com

CHESTER, Philip Anthony Edwin. b 55. Birm Univ LLB 76. Cranmer Hall Dur 77. **d** 80 **p** 81. C Shrewsbury St Chad *Lich* 80-85; C St Martin-in-the-Fields *Lon* 85-88; Chapl K Coll Lon 88-95; P-in-c Westmr St Matt *Lon* 95-03; V from 03; P-in-c St Mary le Strand w St Clem Danes from 14; AD Westmr St Marg from 05; PV Westmr Abbey from 90. *St Matthew's House, 20 Great Peter Street, London SW1P 2BU* T: (020) 7222 3704 F: 7233 0255 E: paec@stmw.org

CHESTER, Mrs Violet Grace. b 50. WEMTC 97. **d** 00 **p** 01. OLM Dymock w Donnington and Kempley *Glouc* 00; OLM Redmarley D'Abitot, Bromesberrow, Pauntley etc from 00. *1 Longbridge, Dymock GL18 2DA* T: (01531) 890633 F: 635919 E: vi@vichester.orangehome.co.uk

CHESTER, Archdeacon of. *See* GILBERTSON, The Ven Michael Robert

CHESTER, Bishop of. *See* FORSTER, The Rt Revd Peter Robert

CHESTER, Dean of. *See* MACPHATE, The Very Revd Gordon Ferguson

CHESTERFIELD, Archdeacon of. *See* WILSON, The Ven Christine Louise

CHESTERFIELD-TERRY, John Darcy Francis Malcolm. b 82. Kingston Univ BEng 05. Ripon Coll Cuddesdon 12. **d** 15. C Portsea St Mary *Portsm* from 15. *166 Shearer Road, Portsmouth PO1 5LS* M: 07917-397832 E: fr.darcy@hotmail.com

CHESTERMAN, Canon George Anthony (Tony). b 38. Man Univ BSc 62 DipAdEd Nottm Univ PhD 89. Coll of Resurr Mirfield 62. **d** 64 **p** 65. C Newbold w Dunston *Derby* 64-68; C Derby St Thos 68-70; Adult Educn Officer 70-79; R Mugginton and Kedleston 70-89; Vice-Prin EMMTC 79-86; Can Res Derby Cathl and Dioc Clergy In-Service Tr Adv *Derby* 89-03; rtd 03; Chapl to The Queen 98-08. *7 Hillside, Lesbury, Alnwick NE66 3NR* T: (01665) 833124

✠**CHESTERS, The Rt Revd Alan David.** b 37. CBE 07. St Chad's Coll Dur BA 59 St Cath Soc Ox BA 61 MA 65 Ches Univ Hon DTheol 10. St Steph Ho Ox 59. **d** 62 **p** 63 **c** 89. C Wandsworth St Anne *S'wark* 62-66; Hon C 66-68; Chapl Tiffin Sch Kingston 66-72; Hon C Ham St Rich *S'wark* 68-72; Dioc Dir of Educn *Dur* 72-85; R Brancepeth 72-85; Hon Can Dur Cathl 75-85; Adn Halifax *Wakef* 85-89; Bp Blackb 89-03; rtd 03; Hon Asst Bp Ches 03-10; Eur 05-09; St As 09-10; S'wark 11-14; Chich from 11. *14 Pegasus Court, Deanery Close, Chichester PO19 1EA* T: (01243) 788053 E: achesters1937@gmail.com

CHESTERS, David Nigel. b 45. OBE . BA FRSA FSAScot. **d** 04 **p** 05. NSM Wallasey St Hilary *Ches* 04-06; V Ches St Jo from 06. *48 Elizabeth Crescent, Chester CH4 7AZ* T: (01244) 676567 E: rector@parishofchester.co.cc

CHESTERS, Simon. b 66. Rob Coll Cam BA 87 MA 91. Wycliffe Hall Ox BA 94. **d** 95 **p** 96. C Bidston *Ches* 95-99; P-in-c Runcorn St Jo Weston 99-03; Dioc Min Development Officer 03-09; Hon C Lache cum Saltney 03-09; Dir Reader Tr 99-09; Regional Leadership Development Adv (NW) CPAS 10-11; Dir Studies Dioc Lifelong Learning *Liv* from 11; Lic Preacher *Man* from 10. *25 Marlston Avenue, Chester CH4 8HE* T: (01244) 679311 E: chesters.simon@gmail.com

CHESWORTH (née NAYLOR), Mrs Alison Louise. b 68. St Andr Univ MTheol 97 Edin Univ MTh 99. TISEC 98. **d** 00 **p** 01. C Ayr, Girvan and Maybole *Glas* 00-03; R Glas All SS and P-in-c Glas H Cross 03-10; TV Ipswich St Mary at Stoke w St Pet and St Fran *St E* from 10. *St Francis' House, 190 Hawthorn Drive, Ipswich IP2 0QQ* T: (01473) 688339 E: alichesworth@sky.com

CHESWORTH, John Martin. b 44. Leeds Univ BSc 67 PhD 71 FRSC 80. S Dios Minl Tr Scheme 90. **d** 92 **p** 93. Oman 92-95; PtO *Ab* 96-98; *Ches* 98-03; C Egremont St Jo 03-04; V Tranmere St Paul w St Luke 04-09; rtd 09; PtO *Lich* from 10. *21 Oerley Way, Oswestry SY11 1TD* T: (01691) 653922 E: jchesworth44@tiscali.co.uk

CHEVERTON, Miss Jill. b 48. Cranmer Hall Dur 93. **d** 93 **p** 94. Par Dn Bilton *Ripon* 93-94; C 94-96; V Burmantofts St Steph and St Agnes 96-03; Min Binley Woods LEP *Cov* 03-13; rtd 13; PtO *York* from 14. *51 Fairway, Selby YO8 9AF* T: (01757) 428876 E: jc@revchev.org.uk

CHEVILL, Elizabeth Jane. *See* PITKETHLY, Elizabeth Jane

✠**CHEW, The Most Revd John Hiang Chea.** b 47. Nanyang Tech Univ Singapore BA 69 MA 77 Lon Univ BD 77 Sheff Univ PhD 82. **d** 77 **p** 78 **c** 00. C St Andr Cathl Singapore 77-85; Hon Can Singapore 85-00; Lect Trin Th Coll Singapore 82-99; Dean of Studies 85-88; Prin 91-99; Bp Singapore from 00; Abp SE Asia from 06. *1 Francis Thomas Drive, #01-01 Singapore 359340, Republic of Singapore* T: (0065) 6288 7585 F: 6288 5574 E: bpoffice@anglican.org.sg

CHEW, Philip Vivian Frederick. b 62. St Martin's Coll Lanc BA 96. Qu Coll Birm 96. **d** 98 **p** 99. C Chorley St Laur *Blackb* 98-02; V Burnley St Steph 02-08; P-in-c Blackb St Fran and St Aid 08-10; R Llanbedr DC, Llangynhafal, Llanychan etc. *St As* from 10; AD Dyffryn Clwyd from 10. *The Rectory, Llanbedr Dyffryn Clwyd, Ruthin LL15 1UP* T: (01824) 705755 E: revpchew@gmail.com

CHEW, Susan. b 55. **d** 10 **p** 11. NSM Haughton le Skerne *Dur* from 10; NSM Sadberge from 14. *59 Saltersgate Road, Darlington DL1 3DX* T: (01325) 355520 E: suechew@f2s.com

CHICHESTER, Caroline Margaret. b 60. STETS. **d** 09 **p** 10. NSM Winterborne Valley and Milton Abbas *Sarum* from 09. *Kingston Farmhouse, West Street, Winterborne Kingston, Blandford Forum DT11 9AX* E: cmchichester@tiscali.co.uk

CHICHESTER, Archdeacon of. *See* MACKITTRICK, The Ven Douglas Henry

CHICHESTER, Bishop of. *See* WARNER, The Rt Revd Martin Clive

CHICHESTER, Dean of. *See* WAINE, The Very Revd Stephen John

CHIDLAW, Richard Paul. b 49. St Cath Coll Cam BA 71 MA. Ripon Hall Ox 71. **d** 74 **p** 81. C Ribbesford w Bewdley and Dowles *Worc* 74-76; NSM Coaley *Glouc* 81-83; NSM Frampton on Severn 81-83; NSM Arlingham 81-83; NSM Saul w Fretherne and Framilode 83-84; NSM Cam w Stinchcombe

85-90; PtO 90-91; NSM Berkeley w Wick, Breadstone, Newport, Stone etc from 91. *38 May Lane, Dursley GL11 4HU* T: (01453) 547838
E: richardandpauline@chidlaw.freeserve.co.uk

CHIDWICK, Alan Robert. b 49. MA MIL. Oak Hill NSM Course. **d** 84 **p** 85. NSM Pimlico St Pet w Westmr Ch Ch *Lon* 84-06; rtd 06; PtO *Nor* from 06. *85 Claremont House, 14 Aerodrome Road, London NW9 5NW* T: (020) 8457 1246
E: montclare85@btinternet.com

CHIGUMIRA, Godfrey. St Mich Coll Llan. **d** 99 **p** 00. In RC Ch 99-08; C Hawarden *St As* 08-12; TV Rhos-Cystennin from 12; PtO *Ban* from 15. *5 Traeth Penrhyn, Penrhyn Bay, Llandudno LL30 3RN* T: (01492) 330357 E: gchigumira@hotmail.co.uk

CHIKE, Chigor. b 66. Glos Univ BA 93. St Jo Coll Nottm 05. **d** 06 **p** 07. C Victoria Docks St Luke *Chelmsf* 06-10; V Forest Gate Em w Upton Cross from 10; P-in-c Forest Gate All SS from 13. *Emmanuel Vicarage, 2B Margery Park Road, London E7 9JY* T: (020) 8534 6796 M: 07905-155494
E: chigor.chike@sky.com

CHILCOTT, Mark David. b 62. Ch Coll Cam BA 83 MA 87 PhD 88. Ripon Coll Cuddesdon BA 92. **d** 93 **p** 94. C Warrington St Elphin *Liv* 93-99; P-in-c Westbrook St Jas 99-01; V 01-02. *Estates Branch, Sedgley Park Centre, Sedgley Park Road, Prestwich, Manchester M25 0JT* T: 0161-856 0505 F: 856 0506

CHILD, Corin James. b 73. Man Univ BA 95. Trin Coll Bris BA 02 MA 03. **d** 03 **p** 04. C Sanderstead *S'wark* 03-07; V King's Lynn St Jo the Ev *Nor* 07-14; Chapl Coll of W Anglia 07-14; Chapl Nor Sch from 14; Hon PV Nor Cathl from 14. *The Chaplain's Office, Norwich School, 70 The Close, Norwich NR1 4DD* T: (01603) 728450 E: corin.child@sky.com *or* cchild@norwich-school.org.uk

CHILD, Canon David Francis. b 44. Birm Univ MB, ChB 67 FRCP 88. St As Minl Tr Course 02. **d** 04 **p** 05. NSM Gresford *St As* 04-07; NSM Bangor Isycoed Deanery 08-12; P-in-c Overton and Erbistock *St As* from 12; AD Dee Valley 12-14; Hon Can St As Cathl from 13. *Whitegate Farm, Gyfelia, Wrexham LL13 0YH* T: (01978) 823396
E: d_f_child@yahoo.co.uk

CHILD, James John. b 79. St Jo Coll Ox BA 00. Oak Hill Th Coll BTh 10. **d** 10 **p** 11. C St Helen Bishopsgate w St Andr Undershaft etc *Lon* from 10. *26 Walcot Square, London SE11 4TZ* T: (020) 7283 2231 E: jamiejchild@hotmail.com

CHILD, Margaret Mary. *See* MASLEN, Margaret Mary

CHILD, Paul William David. b 78. Ripon Coll Cuddesdon 11. **d** 13 **p** 14. C Monkwearmouth *Dur* from 13. *1 Ormesby Road, Sunderland SR6 9HS* T: 0191-549 7421
E: revpaulchild@gmail.com

CHILDS, Christopher. b 59. **d** 05 **p** 06. NSM Gt Finborough w Onehouse, Harleston, Buxhall etc *St E* 05-11; P-in-c from 11; P-in-c Combs and Lt Finborough from 13. *The Rectory, 135 Poplar Hill, Stowmarket IP14 2AY* T: (01449) 673280
E: revcchilds@aol.com

CHILDS, David Robert. b 64. Univ Coll Lon BSc 86 Regent's Park Coll Ox MA 95. Ripon Coll Cuddesdon 99. **d** 99 **p** 00. C Bloxham w Milcombe and S Newington *Ox* 99-02; TV Witney 02-06; TR 06-08; P-in-c Hadleigh St Jas *Chelmsf* from 08; P-in-c Hadleigh St Barn from 12. *The Rectory, 50 Rectory Road, Hadleigh, Benfleet SS7 2ND* T: (01702) 389532 E: dekm@sky.com

CHILDS, Emma Jane. *See* WESTERMANN-CHILDS, Emma Jane

CHILDS, Ernest Edmund. b 23. Lich Th Coll 63. **d** 65 **p** 66. C Billesley Common *Birm* 65-68; C Elland *Wakef* 68-69; Clerical Org Sec CECS *Pet, Leic* and *Ely* 69-72; V Staverton w Helidon and Catesby *Pet* 72-76; rtd 77; PtO *Nor* 77-91; Hon C W Lynn *Ely* 92-94; P-in-c 94-95; PtO from 95; *Nor* from 96. *4 Fieldview Court, Fakenham NR21 8PB* T: (01328) 856595

CHILDS, Michael Thomas. b 79. Hull Univ BA 01. St Steph Ho Ox BTh 10. **d** 10 **p** 11. C Swinton *Sheff* 10-13; C Ponders End St Matt *Lon* from 13; C Edmonton St Alphege from 13. *St Matthew's Vicarage, Church Road, Enfield EN3 4NT* E: michaelchilds79@gmail.com

✠**CHILLINGWORTH, The Most Revd David Robert.** b 51. TCD BA 73 Oriel Coll Ox BA 75 MA 81. Ripon Coll Cuddesdon 75. **d** 76 **p** 77 **c** 05. C Belfast H Trin *Conn* 76-79; Ch of Ireland Youth Officer 79-83; C Bangor Abbey *D & D* 83-86; I Seagoe 86-05; Dean Dromore 95-02; Adn Dromore 02-05; Bp St And from 05; Primus from 09. *Perth Diocesan Centre, 28A Balhousie Street, Perth PH1 5HJ* T: (01738) 443173 *or* 564432 F: 443174 M: 07921-168666 E: bishop@standrews.anglican.org

CHILLMAN, David James. b 59. Southn Univ BA 82. Trin Coll Bris 83. **d** 95 **p** 96. C Yateley *Win* 95-99; V Halifax All So and St Aug *Wakef* 99-07; V Bagshot *Guildf* 07-14; R Lantzville Canada from 14. *3039 Glen Eagle Crescent, Nanaimo BC V9T 1S2, Canada*

CHILTON, Janice Marguerite. b 49. **d** 08. NSM Wallingford *Ox* 08-13; rtd 13; PtO *Ox* from 13. *2 Fairthorne Memorial, West End, Brightwell-cum-Sotwell, Wallingford OX10 0RY* T: (01491) 836661 E: jchilton894@btinternet.com

CHIN, Michael Shoon Chion. b 41. Lon Univ BD 71 Melbourne Univ BA 76 DipEd 79. Trin Th Coll Singapore BTh 64 Melbourne Coll of Div. **d** 64 **p** 65. Malaysia 64-68; Australia 69-80 and 87-91 and from 97; Miss to Seamen 72-81 and 83-89; USA 81-82; Gen Sec Internat Chr Maritime Assn 91-96. *7/1 Bouverie Street, Charlton Vic 3053, Australia* T/F: (0061) (3) 9347 0005 M: 40-859 7966 E: mschin22@goldenit.net.au

CHINDABATA, Miss Unesu Audrey. b 74. Birkbeck Coll Lon BSc 06 K Coll Lon BA 13. Westcott Ho Cam 13. **d** 15. C Is of Dogs Ch Ch and St Jo w St Luke *Lon* from 15. *14 Forge Square, London E14 3GY* M: 07534-582578 E: unesu@yahoo.com

CHING, Derek. b 37. St Cath Coll Cam BA 58 MA Cam Inst of Educn CertEd 59. Qu Coll Birm 81. **d** 83 **p** 84. C Finham *Cov* 83-87; V Butlers Marston and the Pillertons w Ettington 87-96; rtd 96; PtO *Leeds* from 96. *25 Kirkby Road, Ripon HG4 2EY* T: (01765) 609419

CHIPLIN, Christopher Gerald. b 53. Lon Univ BSc 75. St Steph Ho Ox BA 77 MA 81. **d** 78 **p** 79. C Chesterfield St Mary and All SS *Derby* 78-80; C Thorpe St Andr *Nor* 80-84; V Highbridge *B & W* 84-94; V Midsomer Norton w Clandown from 94. *The Vicarage, 42 Priory Close, Midsomer Norton, Radstock BA3 2HZ* T: (01761) 412118 E: cchi759070@aol.com

CHIPLIN, Gareth Huw. b 50. Worc Coll Ox BA 71 MA. Edin Th Coll 71. **d** 73 **p** 74. C Friern Barnet St Jas *Lon* 73-75; C Eastcote St Lawr 76-79; C Notting Hill St Mich and Ch Ch 79-84; V Hammersmith St Matt from 84. *St Matthew's Vicarage, 1 Fielding Road, London W14 0LL* T: (020) 7603 9769

CHIPLIN, Howard Alan. b 43. Sarum & Wells Th Coll 84. **d** 86 **p** 87. C Caerleon *Mon* 86-89; V Ferndale w Maerdy *Llan* 89-91; V Ysbyty Cynfyn w Llantrisant and Eglwys Newydd *St D* 91-95; R Narberth w Mounton w Robeston Wathen and Crinow 95-02; V Grwp Bro Ystwyth a Mynach 02-08; rtd 08; PtO *Ban* 08-14; AD Arwystli from 11. *Minffordd, 15 Hafren Terrace, Llanidloes SY18 6AT*

CHIPLIN, Malcolm Leonard. b 42. St Mich Coll Llan 86. **d** 88 **p** 89. C Newton Nottage *Llan* 88-91; V Pwllgwaun w Llanddewi Rhondda 91-03; V Mountain Ash and Miskin 03-08; rtd 08; PtO *Llan* from 08. *3 Maes y Ffynon Grove, Aberaman, Aberdare CF44 6PJ* T: (01685) 874720
E: malcolmchiplin@aol.com

CHIPPENDALE, Peter David. b 34. Dur Univ BA 55. Linc Th Coll 57. **d** 59 **p** 60. C Claines St Jo *Worc* 59-63; V Defford w Besford 63-73; P-in-c Eckington 66-69; V 69-73; V Kidderminster St Geo 73-76; V The Lickey *Birm* 76-96; rtd 96. *1 Fairways, Pershore WR10 1HA* T: (01386) 553478

CHIPPENDALE, Robert William. b 42. Ox Univ BA 79 Dip Teaching 84. St Fran Coll Brisbane 64. **d** 67 **p** 68. C Maryborough Australia 67-69; C Hollinwood 70-72; V Shaw *Man* 72-78; R Beaudesert Australia 79-84; Chapl St Hilda's Sch Southport 85-03; rtd 03. *31 Gladioli Court, PO Box 1124, Caboolture Qld 4510, Australia* T: (0061) (7) 5495 4514

CHISHOLM, Canon Ian Keith. b 36. AKC 62. **d** 63 **p** 64. C Lich St Chad 63-66; C Sedgley All SS 66-69; V Rough Hills 69-77; V Harrow Weald All SS *Lon* 77-88; V W Moors *Sarum* 88-01; Can and Preb Sarum Cathl 00-01; rtd 01; PtO *Sarum* from 02. *33 Meadoway, Shrewton, Salisbury SP3 4HE* T: (01980) 620579 E: ian.chisholm250@btinternet.com

CHISHOLM, Ian Stuart. b 37. ALCD 63. **d** 63 **p** 64. C Worksop St Jo *S'well* 63-66; Succ Sheff Cathl 66-68; Bp's Chapl for Soc Resp 68-72; C Ox St Andr 72-76; Tutor Wycliffe Hall Ox 72-76; V Conisbrough *Sheff* 76-94; Chapl Conisbrough Hosp 76-94; RD W Doncaster *Sheff* 82-87 and 93-94; V Chilwell *S'well* 94-99; rtd 99; PtO *Sheff* from 94; *Linc* from 00; *S'well* from 03. *72 Broadbank, Louth LN11 0EW* T: (01605) 605970 E: ianchisholm700@btinternet.com

CHISLETT, David Norman Hilton. b 61. Kingston Poly BSc 83 UEA PGCE 84. Ridley Hall Cam 00. **d** 02 **p** 03. C Highley w Billingsley, Glazeley etc *Heref* 02-05; TV Eston w Normanby *York* 05-09; C Bridlington Quay Ch Ch 09-14; C Bessingby 09-14. *Address temp unknown* E: dave.chislett@btinternet.com

CHITHAM, Ernest John. b 57. LSE BSc 79 Leeds Univ PGCE 80 Dur Univ MA 84. NEOC 88. **d** 91 **p** 92. C Swanborough *Sarum* 91-94; CMS 94-99; R Beirut All SS Lebanon 95-98; TV Worthing Ch the King *Chich* 99-05; P-in-c 05-08; V Worthing St Matt from 08. *85 Heene Road, Worthing BN11 4PP* T: (01903) 218026 E: john.chitham@ntlworld.com

CHITTENDEN, John Bertram d'Encer. b 24. ASCA. Lon Coll of Div 56. **d** 58 **p** 59. C St Mary-at-Lambeth *S'wark* 58-64; R Acrise *Cant* 64-82; R Hawkinge 64-82; R Hawkinge w Acrise and Swingfield 82-90; rtd 91; PtO *Cant* from 91. *19 Hasborough Road, Folkestone CT19 6BQ* T: (01303) 241773

✠**CHIU, The Rt Revd Joshua Ban It.** b 18. K Coll Lon LLB 41 AKC 41 Barrister-at-Law (Inner Temple) 41. Westcott Ho Cam 43. **d** 45 **p** 46 **c** 66. C Bournville *Birm* 45-47; Malaya 47-50; Singapore 50-59 and 66-82; Hon Can St Andr Cathl 56-59; Australia 59-62; Fell St Aug Coll Cant 65-66; Bp Malaya and Bp Singapore 66-70; 70-82; Member Cen Cttee WCC 68-75; Member ACC 75-79; rtd 82; PtO *Sarum* 82-00; *Chelmsf* from 02. *40 Beverley Crescent, Woodford Green IG8 9DD* T: (020) 8924 6490

CHIUMBU, Esther Tamisa. *See* PRIOR, Esther Tamisa

CHIVERS, Canon Christopher Mark. b 67. Magd Coll Ox BA 88 MA 92 Selw Coll Cam BA 96 MA 00. Westcott Ho Cam 94. **d** 97 **p** 98. C Friern Barnet St Jas *Lon* 97-99; Can Prec St Geo Cathl Cape Town S Africa 99-01; Min Can and Prec Westmr Abbey 01-05; Can Res and Chan Blackb Cathl 05-10; V Mill Hill Jo Keble Ch *Lon* 10-15; C Mill Hill St Mich 11-15; AD W Barnet 14-15; PV Westmr Abbey from 12; Hon Can Saldhana Bay S Africa from 14; Prin Westcott Ho Cam from 15. *John Keble Vicarage, 142 Deans Lane, Edgware HA8 9NT* T: (020) 8959 1312

CHIVERS, Ernest Alfred John. b 34. Bris & Glouc Tr Course. **d** 83 **p** 84. NSM Bedminster *Bris* 83-87; NSM Whitchurch 87-98; NSM Knowle St Martin 98-00; Sen Asst P Chard and Distr *B & W* 00-04; P-in-c 04-05; rtd 05; PtO *B & W* from 05. *40 Calcott Road, Bristol BS4 2HD* T: 0117-977 7867 M: 07867-865754

E: ernieandmargaretchivers@btinternet.com

CHIVERS, Royston George. b 34. Glouc Th Course. **d** 83 **p** 84. NSM Gorsley w Cliffords Mesne *Glouc* 83-85; NSM Newent and Gorsley w Cliffords Mesne from 85. *Mayfield, Gorsley, Ross-on-Wye HR9 7SJ* T: (01989) 720492

CHO, Paul Hang-Sik. b 61. Kent Univ MA 96 PhD 04. Chr Th Sem & Div Sch of Korea BTh 93. **d** 00 **p** 01. C Munster Square Ch Ch and St Mary Magd *Lon* 00-07; Chapl Angl Korean Community 00-07; Consultant for Institutional Advancement Ox Cen for Miss Studies 08-11; Prof St Andr Th Sem from 10. *25 Corunna Crescent, Oxford OX4 2RB* E: frpaulcho@hotmail.com

CHOI, Soon-Han. b 64. Bapt Sem Seoul BA 94 Surrey Univ MA 99. **d** 10. NSM St Marylebone Annunciation Bryanston Street *Lon* from 10. *Flat 8, 33 Lexham Gardens, London W8 5JR* T: (020) 7373 5025 M: 07984-452169

E: soonpray@gmail.com

CHOLDCROFT, Graham Charles. b 49. Ripon Coll Cuddesdon 07. **d** 10 **p** 11. NSM Thame *Ox* from 10; Chapl Thames Valley Police from 10. *100 Aylesbury Road, Thame OX9 3AY* T: (01844) 216979 M: 07851-191842 E: graham-choldcroft@supanet.com

CHORLTON, John Samuel Woodard. b 45. Newc Univ BSc 67. Wycliffe Hall Ox 89. **d** 89 **p** 91. Jerusalem 79-92; C Ox St Aldate 92-04; AD Ox 99-04; TV W Slough 04-08; V Britwell 08-14; Voc Adv 98-14; rtd 14; PtO *Ox* from 14. *6 Martin Close, Botley, Oxford OX2 9GU* M: 07517-454433

E: jsw@chorlton.org

CHOUFAR, Joseph Oriho Abulemoi. b 57. Nile Th Coll Khartoum BA 95 ICI Univ Amman BA 98. **d** 87 **p** 88. Sudan 87-96; All SS Cathl Khartoum 87-88 and 91-96; Torit SS Congregation Lologo Displaced Camp 88-90; NSM Ealing St Pet Mt Park *Lon* from 00. *11 Bromyard House, Bromyard Avenue, London W3 7BE* T: (020) 8762 0714

E: abulemoi@hotmail.com

CHOW, Ting Suie Roy. b 46. Brasted Th Coll 68 Sarum & Wells Th Coll 70. **d** 72 **p** 73. C Weaste *Man* 72-74; C Swinton St Pet 74-78; R Blackley St Paul 78-85; Sec SPCK (Dio Man) from 80; R Burnage St Nic *Man* 85-95; P-in-c Man Gd Shep 95-97; P-in-c Openshaw 95-97; R Manchester Gd Shep and St Barn 97-13; rtd 13; PtO *Man* from 13. *66 Bluestone Road, Manchester M40 9HY* T: 0161-681 6215

CHOW, Wai Meng. b 65. Bris Univ BSc 89 ACA 93. Trin Coll Bris BA 97 MA 02. **d** 02 **p** 03. NSM Westminster St Jas the Less *Lon* 02-12; NSM Ealing St Mary from 12. *29 Carillon Court, Oxford Road, London W5 3SX* T: (020) 8810 1651 M: 07968-776557

E: waimeng.chow@jpmorgan.com

CHOWN, William Richard Bartlett. b 27. AKC 54. **d** 55 **p** 56. C Egremont *Carl* 55-58; C Upminster *Chelmsf* 58-61; R Romford St Andr 61-78; R Newton Longville w Stoke Hammond, Whaddon etc *Ox* 78-83; P-in-c Kidmore End 83-85; V 85-90; rtd 90; NSM Harpsden *Ox* 93-94; PtO 94-03; Hon C Shiplake w Dunsden and Harpsden 03-05; PtO *Guildf* from 07. *3 Coniston Court, Weybridge KT13 9YR* T: (01932) 821936

CHRICH, Andrew James. b 70. Girton Coll Cam BA 92 MA 96. Cranmer Hall Dur BA 96. **d** 96 **p** 97. C Gerrards Cross and Fulmer *Ox* 96-99; Chapl Trin Coll Cam 99-04; R Linton in Craven *Bradf* 04-09; P-in-c Burnsall w Rylstone 04-09; V Trumpington *Ely* from 09. *The Vicarage, 28 Wingate Way, Trumpington, Cambridge CB2 9HD* M: 07540-108240

E: andychrich@virginmedia.com *or* vicar@trumpingtonchurch.org.uk

CHRICH-SMITH, Joanne Elizabeth. b 71. Qu Coll Cam BA 93 MA 97. Cranmer Hall Dur BA 96 Ripon Coll Cuddesdon 96. **d** 97 **p** 98. C Amersham on the Hill *Ox* 97-99; PtO *Ely* 99-04; Chapl Girton Coll Cam 00-02; PtO *Bradf* 04-09. *The Vicarage, 28 Wingate Way, Trumpington, Cambridge CB2 9HD*

CHRISMAN, John Aubrey. b 33. US Naval Academy BS 58. Westcott Ho Cam 86. **d** 88 **p** 89. NSM Orwell *Ely* 88-89; NSM Wimpole 88-89; NSM Arrington 88-89; NSM Croydon w Clopton 88-89; Asst Chapl Oslo St Edm *Eur* 89-91; R Newport St Geo USA 91-01; rtd 01. *7118 Treymore Court, Sarasota FL 34243, USA* T: (001) (941) 351 3177

E: fatherjack@comcast.net

CHRIST THE KING, Bishop of. *See* LEE, Peter John

CHRISTENSEN, Mrs Carole Glenda. b 45. Qu Coll Birm 07. **d** 09 **p** 10. NSM Blackheath *Birm* from 09. *73 John Street, Rowley Regis B65 0EN* T: 0121-561 5761

E: christensen_250@hotmail.com

CHRISTENSEN, Canon Norman Peter. b 37. St D Coll Lamp BA 63. Ridley Hall Cam 63. **d** 65 **p** 66. C Barnston *Ches* 65-70; V Over St Jo 70-77; R Bromborough 77-92; RD Wirral S 86-92; Hon Can Ches Cathl 90-02; Chapl Arrowe Park Hosp Wirral 92-96; V Higher Bebington *Ches* 96-02; rtd 02; PtO *Ches* from 02. *13 Howbeck Close, Prenton CH43 6TH* T: 0151-652 9869 E: canonpc@talktalk.net

CHRISTIAN, Canon Alison Jean. b 51. S Dios Minl Tr Scheme 88. **d** 91 **p** 94. Par Dn Uxbridge *Lon* 91-94; C 94-95; Chapl Uxbridge Coll 91-95; V Sudbury St Andr *Lon* 95-02; R Gt Stanmore 02-12; Warden Laude Abbey *Leic* from 12; P-in-c Loddington from 12; Hon Can Leic Cathl from 15. *The Warden's House, Launde Road, Launde, Leicester LE7 9XB* T: (01572) 717780 *or* 717254

E: alison.christian1@btopenworld.com *or* warden@launde.org.uk

CHRISTIAN, Brother. *See* PEARSON, Christian David John

CHRISTIAN, Daniel Chung. b 85. St Jo Coll Dur BA 07. Wycliffe Hall Ox MSt 10. **d** 12 **p** 13. C Chester le Street *Dur* from 12. *2 Glencoe Avenue, Chester le Street DH2 2JJ* T: 0191-388 0167 M: 07841-835711 E: dan.christian@dunelm.org.uk

CHRISTIAN, Helen. *See* HORNBY, Helen

CHRISTIAN, Mark Robert. b 58. Linc Th Coll 95. **d** 95 **p** 96. C Stockport SW *Ches* 95-98; CF 98-08; Sen CF 08-11; Dep Asst Chapl Gen 11-15; rtd 15; Hon C Whitchurch w Tufton and Litchfield *Win* from 15. *Red House Bungalow, Litchfield, Whitchurch RG28 7PT* M: 07702-516518 T: (01256) 8969888 E: mark@padre.me.uk

CHRISTIAN, Paul. b 49. Cant Sch of Min 84. **d** 87 **p** 88. C Folkestone St Sav *Cant* 87-91; R Temple Ewell w Lydden from 91. *The Rectory, Green Lane, Temple Ewell, Dover CT16 3AS* T: (01304) 822865

CHRISTIAN, Richard. b 37. Nottm Univ DipEd 74 Ox Univ MA 81. AKC 62. **d** 63 **p** 65. C Camberwell St Mich w All So w Em *S'wark* 63-66; C Woolwich St Mary w H Trin 66-70; Chapl and Lect Bp Lonsdale Coll Derby 70-74; P-in-c Hurley *Ox* 76-79; Chapl Lancing Coll 79-81; Chapl Harrow Sch 82-89; Chapl R W Sussex Hosp Chich 89-91; P-in-c Cowley *Lon* 91-95; Chapl Hillingdon Hosp NHS Trust 91-11; PtO *Leic* from 12; Pet from 12. *The Warden's House, Launde Road, Launde, Leicester LE7 9XB* T: (01572) 717780

CHRISTIAN-EDWARDS, Canon Michael Thomas. b 36. Down Coll Cam BA 60 MA 64. Clifton Th Coll 60. **d** 62 **p** 63. C Ex St Leon w H Trin 62-67; V Trowbridge St Thos *Sarum* 67-75; R Wingfield w Rowley 67-75; P-in-c Fisherton Anger 75-81; R 81-92; Ind Chapl 85-92; RD Salisbury 85-90; Can and Preb Sarum Cathl 87-92; V Crofton *Portsm* 92-00; rtd 00; PtO *Win* from 02. *Rivendell, Westbeams Road, Sway, Lymington SO41 6AE* T: (01590) 682353 E: mmce@ukpiglet.com

CHRISTIAN-IWUAGWU, Canon Amatu Onundu. b 73. Port Harcourt Univ Nigeria BEng 93. **d** 00 **p** 01. NSM Stonebridge St Mich *Lon* 00-03; NSM Welwyn *St Alb* 04-05; NSM Stonebridge St Mich *Lon* 05-07; V Harmondsworth from 07; Can Ideato from 03. *St Mary's Vicarage, High Street, Harmondsworth, West Drayton UB7 0AQ* T: (020) 8897 2385 M: 07961-593880 E: iwuagwuoa@yahoo.co.uk

CHRISTIANSON, Canon Rodney John (Bill). b 47. St Paul's Coll Grahamstown. **d** 72 **p** 73. C St Sav Cathl Pietermaritzburg S Africa 72-76; Miss to Seafarers 76-09; Min Sec Miss to Seamen 93-00; Sec Gen Miss to Seafarers 00-09; R Richard's Bay S Africa 82-91; Chapl Hull Miss to Seamen 91-93; LtO *Lon* 94-97; V St Mich Paternoster Royal 00-09; PtO *Lon* from 09; Hon Can Bloemfontein Cathl from 93. *45 Wimbledon Park Court, Wimbledon Park Road, London SW19 6NN* E: bill.christianson@btinternet.com

CHRISTIE, Alexander Robert. b 58. Qu Coll Cam BA 79 LLM 80. Oak Hill Th Coll 92. **d** 94 **p** 95. C W Norwood St Luke *S'wark* 94-98; C Wandsworth All SS 98-03;

V Blackheath Park St Mich from 03. *St Michael's Vicarage, 2 Pond Road, London SE3 9JL* T: (020) 8852 5287
E: ar.christie@virgin.net

CHRISTODOULOU, Kostakis. b 53. Southn Univ CertEd 76 BEd 76. St Mellitus Coll BA 10. **d** 10 **p** 11. NSM Edgware *Lon* from 10. *226 East End Road, London N2 8AX* T: (020) 8883 9971 E: kostakis_christodoulou2002@yahoo.co.uk

CHRISTOPHER, Miss Barbara. b 58. Univ of Wales (Swansea) BA 80. **d** 09 **p** 10. OLM Saddleworth *Man* 09-14. *2 St Mary's Crest, Greenfield, Oldham OL3 7DS* T: (01457) 876802
E: barbara.christopher@tiscali.co.uk

CHRISTOPHER, Richard. b 53. NTMTC 94. **d** 97 **p** 98. C Southall Green St Jo *Lon* 97-04; C Reading St Luke w St Bart *Ox* from 04. *107 Anderson Avenue, Earley, Reading RG6 1HA* T: 0118-987 1495 E: rev.r.christopher@yahoo.com

CHRISTOU, Sotirios. b 51. St Jo Coll Nottm 84. **d** 88 **p** 92. C Berechurch St Marg w St Mich *Chelmsf* 88-89; C Goodmayes All SS 89-90; NSM Harston w Hauxton *Ely* 92-94; LtO 94-95; C Burgess Hill St Andr *Chich* 95-98; PtO *Ely* from 98. *18 Bullen Close, Cambridge CB1 8YU* T: (01223) 977764
E: christousotirios@hotmail.co.uk

CHRYSOSTOMOU, Stefan. b 87. R Holloway Coll Lon BA 08 SS Coll Cam BA 11. Westcott Ho Cam 09. **d** 12 **p** 13. C Finchley St Mary *Lon* from 12. *28 Hendon Lane, London N3 1TR* T: (020) 8248 4194 E: revstef@me.com

CHUBB, Richard Henry. b 45. Univ of Wales (Cardiff) BMus 67 Bris Univ PGCE 76. Linc Th Coll 67. **d** 70 **p** 71. C Chippenham St Andr w Tytherton Lucas *Bris* 71-72; C-in-c Stockwood CD 72-73; C Bris Ch the Servant Stockwood 73-76; PtO 76-79; Min Can and Succ Bris Cathl 79-88; Chapl w Deaf People 83-02; Chapl Qu Eliz Hosp Sch Bris 87-92; rtd 02. *22B Westfield Road, Westbury-on-Trym, Bristol BS9 3HG* T/F: 0117-983 2842 E: richard.chubb@lineonet.net

CHUDLEY, Cyril Raymond. b 29. Lon Univ BA 53 DipEd. Wells Th Coll 70. **d** 72 **p** 73. C Newark St Mary *S'well* 72-75; C Egg Buckland *Ex* 75-77; P-in-c Plymouth St Aug 77-80; V 80-83; V Milton Abbot, Dunterton, Lamerton etc 83-91; TV Wickford and Runwell *Chelmsf* 91-95; rtd 95; PtO *Truro* from 95. *Ten Acres, Coxpark, Gunnislake PL18 9BB* T: (01822) 832345

CHUKUKA, Ifeanyi Emmanuel Chukwunonso. b 76. **d** 09 **p** 10. PtO *Chelmsf* 12-15; NSM Victoria Docks St Luke from 15. *105 Shepherds Close, Romford RM6 5AJ* M: 07930-614660
E: ifeanchuks@yahoo.com

CHUMBLEY, Lore Elinor Jane. b 59. **d** 12 **p** 13. NSM Stockton Heath *Ches* from 12. *7 Higher Lane, Lymm WA13 0AR*

CHUMU MUTUKU, Norbert. b 68. Urbanian Univ Rome BA 89 St Jo Fisher Coll USA MSc 00. St Mathias Mulumba Sem Kenya 89. **d** 93 **p** 94. In RC Ch 93-02; C Milton *Portsm* 03-06; C Pitsea w Nevendon *Chelmsf* 06-11; TV Wickford and Runwell from 11. *The Rectory, 120 Southend Road, Wickford SS11 8EB* T: (01268) 733147 E: nchumu@yahoo.com

CHURCH, Mrs Annette Marie. b 56. **d** 09 **p** 10. C Caldicot *Mon* 09-14; P-in-c Shaldon, Stokeinteignhead, Combeinteignhead etc *Ex* 14-15; R from 15. *The Rectory, Torquay Road, Shaldon, Teignmouth TQ14 0AX* T: (01626) 873173 M: 07789-778312
E: anniechurch@hotmail.com *or* revannie@hotmail.co.uk

CHURCH, Canon Linda Ann. b 51. MCSP 73. EMMTC 88. **d** 91 **p** 94. NSM Kirkby in Ashfield St Thos *S'well* 91-95; NSM Skegby and Teversal 95-98; P-in-c Annesley w Newstead 98-03; TR Hucknall Torkard 03-09; Hon Can *S'well* Minster 07-09; R Fowlmere, Foxton, Shepreth and Thriplow *Ely* 09-13; RD Shingay 13; Dir Min from 14; Hon Can Ely Cathl from 14. *Diocesan Office, Bishop Woodford House, Barton Road, Ely CB7 4DX* T: (01353) 652701
E: canonlinda.church@btinternet.com

CHURCH, William John. b 41. Qu Coll Cam MA 62 Solicitor . SAOMC 96. **d** 99 **p** 00. NSM Bengeo *St Alb* 99-01; NSM Gt Amwell w St Margaret's and Stanstead Abbots 01-05; NSM Hertford from 05. *115 Queen's Road, Hertford SG13 8BJ* T: (01992) 410469 F: 583079 E: bill.church@hertscc.gov.uk *or* churchwj@hotmail.com

CHURCHER, Ms Mandy. b 54. Brunel Univ MEd 92 Surrey Univ PGCE 87 RN 75 RM 77. NTMTC 96. **d** 99 **p** 00. C Wolverhampton St Matt *Lich* 99-02; Assoc Chapl Plymouth Hosps NHS Trust 02-06; Chapl S Devon Healthcare NHS Foundn Trust 06-11; NSM Malmesbury w Westport and Brokenborough *Bris* from 11. *The Old Squash Court, Holloway, Malmesbury SN16 9BA* T: (01666) 826666
E: mandy@malmesburyabbey.com

CHYNCHEN, John Howard. b 38. FRICS 72. Sarum & Wells Th Coll 88. **d** 89 **p** 90. Bp's Dom Chapl *Sarum* from 89; Hon Chapl Hong Kong Cathl 90-07; Chapl from 07. *St John's Cathedral, 4-8 Garden Road, Hong Kong* T: (00852) 2523 4157 F: 3487 6404 E: chynchen@stjohnscathedral.org.hk

CIANCHI, Dalbert Peter. b 28. Lon Univ BSc 57. Westcott Ho Cam 69. **d** 70 **p** 71. C Harpenden St Nic *St Alb* 70-74; TV Woughton *Ox* 74-80; P-in-c Wavendon w Walton 74-80; P-in-c

Lavendon w Cold Brayfield 80-84; R Lavendon w Cold Brayfield, Clifton Reynes etc 84-94; rtd 94. *20 Fisken Crescent, Kambah ACT 2902, Australia* T: (0061) (2) 6231 8556
E: pcianchi@cyberone.com.au

CIECHANOWICZ, Edward Leigh Bundock. *See* BUNDOCK, Edward Leigh

CINNAMOND, Andrew Victor. b 71. St Andr Univ MA 94 Lon Sch of Th PhD 12. Wycliffe Hall Ox BA 00. **d** 01 **p** 02. C Clapham H Trin and St Pet *S'wark* 01-05; C Wandsworth All SS 05-11; TV S Cotswolds *Glouc* from 11. *The Vicarage, Sherborne Street, Lechlade GL7 3AH* T: (01367) 253651
E: andrew_cinnamond@hotmail.com

CLABON, Ronald Oliver Edwin. b 30. **d** 97. NSM Pontnewydd *Mon* 97-03. *72 Anthony Drive, Caerleon, Newport NP18 3DX* T: (01633) 420790

CLACEY, Derek Phillip. b 48. St Jo Coll Nottm 76. **d** 79 **p** 80. C Gt Parndon *Chelmsf* 79-82; C Walton H Trin *Ox* 82-88; R Bramshaw and Landford w Plaitford *Sarum* 88-04; P-in-c Redlynch and Morgan's Vale 03-04; TV E Greenwich *S'wark* 04-13; rtd 13. *39 Coombe Way, Plymouth PL5 2HA*
E: derekclacey@aol.com

CLACK (née JERWOOD), Mrs Eleanor Alice Jerwood. b 80. Bath Univ BSc 03. St Jo Coll Nottm 05. **d** 08 **p** 09. C New Milverton *Cov* 08-11; PtO from 11. *198 Rugby Road, Leamington Spa CV32 6DU* T: (01926) 738662 E: ellieclack@hotmail.co.uk

CLACK, Robert John Edmund. b 63. Lanc Univ BA 85. Coll of Resurr Mirfield 89. **d** 92 **p** 93. C Bury St Pet *Man* 92-95; Chapl Bury Colls of FE 93-95; TV New Bury *Man* 95-97; R Ashton-upon-Mersey St Martin *Ches* 97-11; V Ches St Oswald and St Thos from 11; Chapl Ches Univ from 15. *The Vicarage, 33 Abbots Grange, Chester CH2 1AJ* T: (01244) 399990 E: robertjec@btinternet.com

CLACKER, Martin Alexander. b 56. Trin Coll Bris 93. **d** 95 **p** 96. C Yate New Town *Bris* 95-98; V Southmead 98-00; C Portishead *B & W* 00-02; TV 02-03; PtO *Bris* 06-08; P-in-c Winterbourne from 08; C Frampton Cotterell and Iron Acton 08-13; P-in-c from 13; C Frenchay and Winterbourne Down from 08. *Orchard House, 70 High Street, Winterbourne, Bristol BS36 1JQ* T: (01454) 771856
E: presbyter.mc@googlemail.com

CLAMMER, Canon Thomas Edward. b 80. Sussex Univ BA 01 CCC Cam BA 04 MA 09. Westcott Ho Cam 02. **d** 05 **p** 06. C Wotton St Mary *Glouc* 05-08; P-in-c Deerhurst and Apperley w Forthampton etc 08-12; Dioc Worship Officer 08-12; C Tewkesbury w Walton Cardiff and Twyning 10-12; Can Res Sarum Cathl from 12. *54 The Close, Salisbury SP1 2EF*
E: tomclammer@gmail.com *or* precentor@salcath.co.uk

CLANCY, Michael. b 24. Kensington Univ (USA) BA 82. Glas NSM Course 76. **d** 79 **p** 80. Hon C Glas St Silas 79-96; PtO from 96. *33 Highfield Drive, Clarkston, Glasgow G76 7SW* T: 0141-638 4469

CLAPHAM, Christopher Charles. b 69. Man Univ BA 91 St Jo Coll Dur BA 96. Cranmer Hall Dur 94 Union Th Sem (NY) STM 98. **d** 99 **p** 00. NSM Withington St Chris *Man* 99-01; C Didsbury Ch Ch 01-03; P-in-c Swinton H Rood 03-08; Chapl Keele Univ *Lich* 08-12; TV Wolstanton 12-14; V 14-15; V Hammersmith St Pet *Lon* from 15. *17 Ravenscourt Road, London W6 0UH* E: charlesclapham@lineone.net

CLAPHAM, George Henry James. b 52. Trin Coll Bris. **d** 08 **p** 09. C Wellington and Distr *B & W* 08-12; V Wilton from 12. *Wilton Vicarage, Fons George, Taunton TA1 3JT* T: (01823) 284253 E: jamesclapham@talktalk.net

CLAPHAM, John. b 47. Open Univ BA 76. Sarum & Wells Th Coll 77. **d** 80 **p** 81. Dep PV Ex Cathl from 80; C Lympstone 85-87; P-in-c 87-99; P-in-c Woodbury 97-99; RD Aylesbeare 96-01; R Lympstone and Woodbury w Exton 99-09; rtd 09. *375 Topsham Road, Exeter EX2 6HB* T: (01392) 873345
E: johnclaphamuk@btinternet.com

CLAPHAM, Kenneth. b 47. Trin Coll Bris 76. **d** 78 **p** 79. C Pemberton St Mark Newtown *Liv* 78-81; C Darfield *Sheff* 81-83; P-in-c Over Kellet *Blackb* 83-88; V from 88. *The Vicarage, 3 Kirklands Road, Over Kellet, Carnforth LA6 1DP* T/F: (01524) 734189 E: ukvicar@gmail.com

CLAPHAM, Stephen James. b 61. Portsm Poly BSc 84 Ches Coll of HE BTh 04. NOC 01. **d** 04 **p** 05. C Nantwich *Ches* 04-06; V Crewe All SS and St Paul w St Pet from 07. *All Saints' Vicarage, 79 Stewart Street, Crewe CW2 8LX* T: (01270) 560310 E: steve.clapham@virgin.net

CLAPPERTON, Mrs Carolin Beryl. b 43. Westcott Ho Cam 04. **d** 05 **p** 06. NSM Faversham *Cant* 05-08; NSM The Brents and Davington w Oare and Luddenham 08-11; NSM from 11; PtO *Cant* 12-13; *Ox* from 13. *Address temp unknown* M: 07946-420745 E: carolinclapperton226@btinternet.com

CLAPSON, Clive Henry. b 55. Leeds Univ BA 76. Trin Coll Toronto MDiv 79. **d** 79 **p** 80. C Belleville St Thos Canada 79-80; R Loughborough 80-83; V Alpine Ch the K USA 83-88; C Hawley H Trin *Guildf* 88-90; R Invergordon St Ninian

Mor 90-00; Prin Moray Ord and Lay Tr Course 90-94; Can St Andr Cathl Inverness 97-00; R Aberdeen St Mary *Ab* 00-05; R Dundee St Salvador *Bre* from 05. *St Salvador's Rectory, 9 Minard Crescent, Dundee DD3 6LH* T: (01382) 221785 E: father.clive@blueyonder.co.uk

CLAPTON, Timothy. b 59. Westmr Coll Ox MTh 92. Westcott Ho Cam 96. **d** 98 **p** 99. C Wimborne Minster *Sarum* 98-02; Ecum Chapl Milton Keynes Gen NHS Trust 02-05; Milton Keynes Miss Partnership Development Chapl *Ox* 05-10; PtO *S'wark* from 11; *Lon* 14-15; Hon C St Geo-in-the-East w St Paul from 15. *78 Ruskin Park House, Champion Hill, London SE5 8TH* M: 07958-182077 T: (020) 7501 9167 E: timclapton@talktalk.net

CLARE, Christopher. b 52. Sheff Univ BSc 73 Nottm Univ PGCE 74. Ox Min Course 89. **d** 92 **p** 93. NSM Chesham Bois *Ox* from 92. *5 Lime Tree Walk, Amersham HP7 9HY* T: (01494) 766513 E: cc@challoners.com

CLARE, Ms Johanna Howard. b 64. Bris Univ BSc 86 Heythrop Coll Lon MA 98. Ridley Hall Cam 97. **d** 99 **p** 00. C Coulsdon St Jo *S'wark* 99-02; TV Morden 02-09; Dioc Continuing Professional Development Officer 09-14; PtO 14; *Truro* from 14. *Trelowen, 16 Forth An Cos, Ponsanooth, Truro TR3 7RJ* M: 07919-186307 T: (01872) 864129 E: rev.johanna.clare@gmail.com

CLARE, Sister. *See* LOCKHART, Clare Patricia Anne

CLARIDGE, Antony Arthur John. b 37. Hull Univ MA LRAM. Bris & Glouc Tr Course. **d** 84 **p** 85. NSM Keynsham *B & W* 84-97; Bp's Officer for NSMs 90-10; Min Bath Ch Ch Prop Chpl 97-10; rtd 10; PtO *B & W* from 11. *62 Cranwells Park, Bath BA1 2YE* T: (01225) 427462 M: 07988-745721 E: antony.claridge@btinternet.com

CLARIDGE, Michael John. b 61. MCIEH. Qu Coll Birm 89 Bossey Ecum Inst Geneva 91. **d** 92 **p** 93. C Harlescott *Lich* 92-95; P-in-c Wellington Ch Ch 95-97; V 97-03; V W Bromwich St Andr w Ch Ch from 03; RD W Bromwich from 13. *St Andrew's Vicarage, Oakwood Street, West Bromwich B70 9SN* T: 0121-553 1871 E: mjclaridge@me.com

CLARINGBULL (née DAVID), Canon Faith Caroline. b 55. St Aid Coll Dur BA 77. Ripon Coll Cuddesdon 87. **d** 89 **p** 94. Par Dn Is of Dogs Ch Ch and St Jo w St Luke *Lon* 89-93; Asst Chapl R Lon Hosps NHS Trust 93-98; NSM Wheatley *Ox* 98-00; Asst Dioc Dir of Ords *Worc* 00-04; Dioc CME Officer 02-04; Dioc Dir of Ords *Birm* from 04; Dean of Women's Min from 04; Hon Can Birm Cathl from 05. *The Church of England, 1 Colmore Road, Birmingham B3 2BJ* E: faith@birmingham.anglican.org

CLARINGBULL, Keith. b 49. Ripon Coll Cuddesdon 98. **d** 00 **p** 01. SSF 69-89; C Droitwich Spa *Worc* 00-04; P-in-c Hampton in Arden *Birm* 04-10; P-in-c Bickenhill 04-10; Chapl Univ Hosp Birm NHS Foundn Trust 13-14; PtO from 14. *20 Spring Road, Edgbaston, Birmingham B15 2HG* T: 0121-446 5797 E: keithclaringbull@hotmail.com

CLARK, Andrew. b 76. Anglia Poly Univ BA 97. Oak Hill Th Coll BA 08. **d** 08 **p** 09. C Heref St Pet w St Owen and St Jas 08-11; C Barton Seagrave w Warkton *Pet* from 11. *Rectory Cottage, St Botolph's Road, Barton Seagrave, Kettering NN15 6SR* T: (01536) 660363 E: lurpak@aol.com *or* andy@stbots.org.uk

CLARK, Antony. b 61. York Univ BA 83 St Andr Univ PhD. Wycliffe Hall Ox 84. **d** 88 **p** 89. C Ashton-upon-Mersey St Mary Magd *Ches* 88-92; Chapl Lee Abbey 92-95; LtO *Ex* 92-95; Chapl Univ of Westmr Lon 95-98; C Bletchley *Ox* 98-00; Chapl Fettes Coll Edin from 12. *Fettes College, Carrington Road, Edinburgh EH4 1QX* T: 0131-332 2281

CLARK, Bernard Charles. b 34. Open Univ BA 81. S'wark Ord Course 65. **d** 68 **p** 69. C Pemberton St Jo *Liv* 68-71; C Winwick 71-73; P-in-c Warrington St Barn 74-76; V 76-78; V Hindley All SS 78-83; PtO 86-94; R Glazebury w Hollinfare 94-99; rtd 99; PtO *Man* 00-08 and from 11. *31 Linkfield Drive, Worsley, Manchester M28 1JU* T: 0161-799 7998 E: bckathcain31@aol.com

CLARK, Canon Caroline Robbins (Robbin). b 45. Mt Holyoke Coll USA BA 67 Columbia Univ BS 70 Univ of California MS 74. Ch Div Sch of Pacific MDiv 81 Ripon Coll Cuddesdon 79. **d** 81 **p** 82. C Upland St Mark USA 81-84; R Santa Fé St Bede 85-93; R Berkeley St Mark 93-10; Dean of Women Clergy *Glouc* from 11; Hon Can Glouc Cathl from 12. *36 Lurkhay Road, Hucclecote, Gloucester GL3 3NS* T: (01452) 547469 M: 07986-148701 E: rclark@glosdioc.org.uk

CLARK, Cecil. b 44. Sarum Th Coll. **d** 98 **p** 99. OLM Canford Magna *Sarum* from 98. *Fermain Cottage, 133 Magna Road, Bearwood, Bournemouth BH11 9NE* T: (01202) 577898 *or* 663275 E: firmain@ntlworld.com

CLARK, Mrs Christine Margaret. b 44. SAOMC 01. **d** 01 **p** 02. NSM Croxley Green St Oswald *St Alb* 01-06; P-in-c Odell 06-14; rtd 14. *99 High Street, Clapham, Bedford MK41 6AQ* M: 07812-524992 T: (01234) 918985

CLARK, Christopher Austin. b 52. Liv Univ BSc 73. **d** 10 **p** 11. NSM Worthing St Geo *Chich* 10-11; NSM Rustington 11-14;

P-in-c Westham from 14. *The Vicarage, 6 Rattle Road, Westham, Pevensey BN24 5DE* T: (01323) 762294 E: chris@austinclark.co.uk

CLARK, Daniel Alastair. b 74. St Jo Coll Dur BA 96. Wycliffe Hall Ox BA 99. **d** 00 **p** 01. C Rusholme H Trin *Man* 00-06; NSM 04-06; C Clifton Ch Ch w Em *Bris* 06-12; P-in-c Shirley *Win* from 12. *The Vicarage, 2B Wordsworth Road, Southampton SO15 5LX*

CLARK, David. b 30. Nottm Univ BSc 51. St Aid Birkenhead 55. **d** 57 **p** 58. C Tyldesley w Shakerley *Man* 57-60; V Ashton St Jas 60-64; rtd 93; PtO *Eur* from 07. *30 Dulverton Hall, Esplanade, Scarborough YO11 2AR* T: (01723) 340130 E: d2aclark@wanadoo.fr

CLARK, Canon David George Neville. b 25. Linc Coll Ox BA 49 MA 59. Wells Th Coll 49. **d** 51 **p** 52. C Sanderstead All SS *S'wark* 51-54; C Lewisham St Jo Southend 54-59; V Sutton New Town St Barn 59-72; R Charlwood 72-90; P-in-c Sidlow Bridge 76-77; R 77-90; P-in-c Buckland 85-87; P-in-c Leigh 87-90; Hon Can S'wark Cathl 88-90; rtd 90; PtO *Cov* from 90. *12 Marlborough Road, Coventry CV2 4EP* T: (024) 7644 2400 E: david@revdgnc.plus.com

CLARK, David Gordon. b 29. Clare Coll Cam BA 52 MA 57. Ridley Hall Cam 52. **d** 54 **p** 55. C Walthamstow St Jo *Chelmsf* 54-57; V 60-69; C Gt Ilford St Andr 57-60; R Stansted *Roch* 69-82; R Stansted w Fairseat and Vigo 82-94; rtd 94; PtO *Sarum* 94-06; *Roch* from 07. *4 St Marys Close, Platt, Sevenoaks TN15 8NH* T: (01732) 883191

CLARK, David Humphrey. b 39. G&C Coll Cam BA 60. Wells Th Coll 62. **d** 64 **p** 65. C Leigh St Mary *Man* 64-68; Min Can and Prec Man Cathl 68-70; Ind Chapl *Nor* 70-85; P-in-c Nor St Clem and St Geo 70-76; P-in-c Nor St Sav w St Paul 70-76; V Norwich-over-the-Water Colegate St Geo 76-79; Hon Asst P Nor St Pet Mancroft 79-85; TR Oadby *Leic* 85-98; C Leic St Jas 98-04; rtd 04; PtO *Leic* from 04. *46 St James Road, Leicester LE2 1HQ* T: 0116-255 8988 E: dhclark2@btinternet.com

CLARK, David John. b 61. Bretton Hall Coll BA 82 MA 06 PGCE 83 Sheff Univ BA 13. Yorks Min Course 10. **d** 13 **p** 14. C Gildersome *Leeds* from 13; C Drighlington from 13. *The Vicarage, Back Lane, Drighlington, Bradford BD11 1LS* T: (01132) 853276 M: 07891-329614 E: dave@djccreativeteaching.co.uk

CLARK, David John. b 40. Surrey Univ MPhil 75 CEng MIStructE. Ridley Hall Cam 81. **d** 83 **p** 84. C Combe Down w Monkton Combe and S Stoke *B & W* 83-89; Voc Adv Bath Adnry 89-96; R Freshford, Limpley Stoke and Hinton Charterhouse *B & W* 89-05; rtd 05; PtO *B & W* from 05. *14 Barn Close, Frome BA11 4ER* T: (01373) 461073 M: 07710-507327 E: david@astrorev.co.uk

CLARK, Dennis Henry Graham. b 26. St Steph Ho Ox 52. **d** 55 **p** 56. C Southall St Geo *Lon* 55-58; C Barbourne *Worc* 58-61; Chapl RAF 61-78; Asst Chapl-in-Chief RAF 78-82; Chapl St Clem Danes (RAF Ch) 79-82; V Godmanchester *Ely* 82-91; rtd 91; PtO *Ely* from 91. *8 Arran Way, St Ives PE27 3DT* T: (01480) 301951

CLARK, Diane Catherine. *See* FITZGERALD CLARK, Diane Catherine

CLARK, Edward Robert. b 39. Ex Coll Ox BA 61 MA 65. St Steph Ho Ox 61. **d** 63 **p** 64. C Solihull *Birm* 63-67; PtO *Bris* 67-69; *Leic* 69-71; *Ox* 71-80; *St Alb* 80-84; *Cant* from 84; rtd 04. *3 Hunters Bank, Old Road, Elham, Canterbury CT4 6SS* T: (01303) 840134 E: edward.clark.elham@gmail.com

CLARK, Ellen Jane. *See* CLARK-KING, Ellen Jane

CLARK, Frederick Albert George. b 15. MBE 68. ACP 66. **d** 67 **p** 68. Hon C Stroud *Glouc* 67-84; Hon C Stroud and Uplands w Slad 84-85; PtO 85-97. *Address temp unknown*

CLARK, Harold Clive. b 28. Whitwatersrand Univ LTh 53. St Paul's Coll Grahamstown. **d** 54 **p** 55. C Orange Gove S Africa 54-56; R Mayfair 56-60; P-in-c Morden *S'wark* 60-62; R Verulam S Africa 62-68; Chapl Michaelhouse 68-77; V Green Island New Zealand 77-85; V Kaitaia 85-92; Chapl Kristin Sch Albany from 92. *351 East Coast Road, Mairangi Bay, North Shore City 0630, New Zealand* T: (0064) (9) 479 3434 E: hr.clark@clear.net.nz

CLARK, Ian Duncan Lindsay. b 35. K Coll Cam BA 59 MA 63 PhD 64. Ripon Hall Ox 62. **d** 64 **p** 65. C Willington *Newc* 64-66; India 66-76; Lect Bp's Coll Calcutta 66; Vice-Prin 69-74; Chapl St Cath Coll Cam 76; Fell 77-85; Tutor 78-85; Dean of Chpl and Lect 85-95; Select Preacher Cam Univ 82; Hon Asst P Kelso *Edin* 85-06. *4 Yewtree Lane, Yetholm, Kelso TD5 8RZ* T: (01573) 420323 E: revbirdbath@gmail.com

CLARK, Jacqueline Mary. b 58. **d** 08 **p** 09. OLM Canalside Benefice *Sarum* 08-12; NSM Devizes St Jo w St Mary from 12. *3 Stonelea, Trowbridge Road, Hilperton, Trowbridge BA14 7QQ* T: (01225) 769940 M: 07948-089865 E: revjclark@hotmail.co.uk

CLARK, Miss Janet Elizabeth. b 44. Derby Coll of Educn CertEd 65 Open Univ BA 75. Oak Hill Th Coll BA 92. **d** 92

p 94. Par Dn Edmonton All SS w St Mich *Lon* 92-94; C 94-96; V Ealing St Steph Castle Hill 96-08; rtd 08; PtO *Ox* from 09. *55 Cranwells Lane, Farnham Common, Slough SL2 3GW* T: (01753) 646546 E: jan@fortaguada.freeserve.co.uk

CLARK, Mrs Jean Robinson. b 32. K Coll Lon AKC BD 79. **dss** 85 **d** 87 **p** 94. Cov E 85-88; C 87-88; NSM Upper Mole Valley Gp *S'wark* 89-90; Hon Par Dn Charlwood 89-90; LtO *Cov* 90-92; rtd 92; PtO *Cov* from 92. *12 Marlborough Road, Coventry CV2 4EP* T: (024) 7644 2400
E: david@revdgnc.plus.com

CLARK, Jeremy James. b 66. Cant Univ (NZ) BA 88. St Jo Coll Auckland BTh 97. **d** 94 **p** 95. C Shirley St Steph New Zealand 94-97; C Upton (Overchurch) *Ches* 97-01; P-in-c Ilfracombe SS Phil and Jas w W Down *Ex* 01-08; C Alphington, Shillingford St George and Ide 08-11; TV Pinhoe and Broadclyst 11-13; C Aylesbeare, Rockbeare, Farringdon etc 11-13; TV Broadclyst, Clyst Honiton, Pinhoe, Rockbeare etc 13-15; RD Aylesbeare 14-15; rtd 15. *Address temp unknown*
E: jemkiwi@aol.com

CLARK, John David Stanley. b 36. Dur Univ BA 64. Ridley Hall Cam 64. **d** 66 **p** 67. C Benchill *Man* 66-69; C Beverley Minster *York* 69-74; PtO *S'well* 74-76; LtO 76-77; Miss to Seamen 77-80; PtO *York* 80-83; V Egton w Grosmont 83-89; R Thornton Dale w Ellerburne and Wilton 89-01; R Thornton Dale w Allerston, Ebberston etc 01-05; rtd 05; PtO *York* from 05. *22 Swainsea Lane, Pickering YO18 8AP* T: (01751) 476118
E: jdsclark@btinternet.com

CLARK, John Edward Goodband. b 49. Leeds Univ MA 01. Chich Th Coll 70. **d** 73 **p** 74. C Thorpe St Andr *Nor* 73-76; C Earlham St Anne 76-78; Chapl RN 78-82; P-in-c Tittleshall w Godwick, Wellingham and Weasenham *Nor* 82-85; P-in-c Helhoughton w Raynham 82-85; R S Raynham, E w W Raynham, Helhoughton, etc 85-90; R Taverham w Ringland 90-96; V Eggleston and R Middleton-in-Teesdale w Forest and Frith *Dur* 96-03; AD Barnard Castle 00-03; R Caston, Griston, Merton, Thompson etc *Nor* 03-05; PtO from 07. *Old Orchards, Gateley Road, Brisley, Dereham NR20 5LR* T: (01362) 667879

CLARK, John Michael. b 35. EMMTC 87. **d** 90 **p** 91. Chapl to the Deaf *Linc* 86-00; NSM Bracebridge Heath 90-00; rtd 00; PtO *Linc* from 00. *3 Hawthorn Road, Cherry Willingham, Lincoln LN3 4JU* T: (01522) 751759

CLARK, John Patrick Hedley. b 37. St Cath Coll Cam BA 61 MA 65 Worc Coll Ox BA 63 MA 72 BD 74 Lambeth Hon DD 89. St Steph Ho Ox 61. **d** 64 **p** 65. C Highters Heath *Birm* 64-67; C Eglingham *Newc* 67-72; P-in-c Newc St Anne 72-77; V Longframlington w Brinkburn 77-95; C Chevington 95-02; rtd 02; PtO *Dur* from 02. *6 The Cottage, West Row, Greatham, Hartlepool TS25 2HW* T: (01429) 870203

CLARK, Canon John Ronald Lyons. b 47. TCD BA 69 MA 72. Div Hostel Dub 67. **d** 70 **p** 71. C Dundela St Mark *D & D* 70-72; CF 72-75; C Belfast St Aid and Ballymacarrett Conn 75-76; I Stranorlar w Meenglas and Kilteevogue *D & R* 76-81; Chapl Wythenshawe Hosp Man 81-95; I Kilgariffe Union *C, C & R* 95-96; Chapl Blackb, Hyndburn and Ribble Valley NHS Trust 96-03; Chapl Co-ord E Lancs Hosps NHS Trust 03-09; Chapl E Lancs Hospice 96-05; Hon Can Blackb Cathl 06-09; rtd 09. *10 Castle Meadow Link, Cloughey, Newtownards BT22 1RU*
M: 07823-380179 T: (028) 4277 2426
E: rcronnieclark@googlemail.com

✠**CLARK, The Rt Revd Jonathan Dunnett.** b 61. Ex Univ BA 83 Bris Univ MLitt 90 Southn Univ MA 96. Trin Coll Bris 84. **d** 88 **p** 89 **c** 12. C Stanwix *Carl* 88-92; Chapl Bris Univ 92-93; Dir of Studies STETS 94-97; Chapl Lon Metrop Univ 97-03; AD Islington 99-03; R Stoke Newington St Mary 03-12; P-in-c Brownswood Park 04-11; Area Bp Croydon *S'wark* from 12. *St Matthew's House, 100 George Street, Croydon CR0 1PE* T: (020) 8256 9630 *or* 8686 1822 F: 8256 9631 M: 07968-845698
E: bishop.jonathan@southwark.anglican.org

CLARK, Jonathan Giles. b 72. **d** 14. C Stroud Team *Glouc* from 14. *106 Jack Russell Close, Stroud GL5 4EJ*

CLARK, Canon Jonathan Jackson. b 57. Linc Coll Ox 79 Down Coll Cam 83. Ridley Hall Cam 81. **d** 84 **p** 85. C W Derby St Luke *Liv* 84-87; C Gt Clacton *Chelmsf* 87-93; V Hammersmith St Simon *Lon* 93-03; AD Hammersmith and Fulham 96-01; TR Leeds St Geo from 03; Hon Can Ripon Cathl from 12. *St George's Vicarage, 208 Kirkstall Lane, Leeds LS5 2AB* T: 0113-274 4367 E: jonathan.clark@stgeorgesleeds.org.uk

CLARK, Julia Ann. b 62. Linc Sch of Th and Min 10. **d** 13 **p** 14. NSM Brumby *Linc* from 13. *13 Rivelin Crescent, Scunthorpe DN16 2AL* T: (01724) 862273
E: julia.clark23@virginmedia.com

CLARK, Kathleen Christine. *See* ENGLAND, Kathleen Christine

CLARK, Kenneth William. b 69. R Holloway Coll Lon BA 92 Trin Coll Cam BA 99 MA 04. Westcott Ho Cam 97. **d** 00 **p** 01.

C Bromley St Mark *Roch* 00-04; R Stone from 04. *The Rectory, Church Road, Greenhithe DA9 9BE* T: (01322) 382076
E: kenneth.clark@diocese-rochester.org

CLARK, Lance Edgar Dennis. b 52. MBE 93. Linc Th Coll 74. **d** 77 **p** 78. C Arnold *S'well* 77-82; V Brinsley w Underwood 82-87; Chapl RAF 87-02; Chapl Cardiff and Vale NHS Trust 02-10; rtd 10. *Hafod, Gileston, Vale of Glamorgan CF62 4HX* T: (01446) 751077 E: lanceedclark@aol.co.uk

CLARK, Lee Robert. b 82. St Steph Ho Ox BTh 15. **d** 15. C Pimlico St Gabr *Lon* from 15. *The Basement, 30 Warwick Square, London SW1V 2AD* M: 07908-675619
E: lee.clark82@gmail.com

CLARK, Lynn. *See* PURVIS-LEE, Lynn

CLARK, Canon Martin Hudson. b 46. K Coll Lon BD 68 AKC 68 MTh 91 Birm Univ PGCE 89. **d** 71 **p** 72. C S'wark H Trin 71-74; C Parkstone St Pet w Branksea and St Osmund *Sarum* 74-77; V E Wickham *S'wark* 77-86; V Wandsworth St Anne 86-98; RD Wandsworth 90-95; V Angell Town St Jo 98-07; RD Brixton 01-05; Hon Can S'wark Cathl 05-07; rtd 07; PtO *Cant* 07-08 and from 11; Hon C Deal St Leon w St Rich and Sholden etc 08-10. *27 Century Walk, Deal CT14 6AL* T: (01304) 366586
E: eveandmartin@hotmail.com

CLARK, Michael Arthur. b 46. S Dios Minl Tr Scheme. **d** 83 **p** 84. NSM Monkton Farleigh, S Wraxall and Winsley *Sarum* 83-05; PtO *Chich* from 05. *5 Park West, Southdowns Park, Haywards Heath RH16 4SG* T: (01444) 440831
E: mike_clark55@hotmail.com

CLARK, Michael David. b 45. Ox Univ MA 68. Trin Coll Bris. **d** 72 **p** 73. C Cheadle *Ches* 72-76; Brazil 77-86; Bolivia 86-88; C Wilton *B & W* 89-90; TV 90-99; C Tollington *Lon* 99-01; TR Edgware 01-15; rtd 15; Hon C Bisley, Chalford, France Lynch, and Oakridge and Bussage w Eastcombe *Glouc* from 15. *Address temp unknown* E: mikeclark@wayfarer99.go-plus.net

CLARK, Michael James. b 71. Univ of Wales (Cardiff) BSc 92. Trin Coll Bris BA 02. **d** 02 **p** 03. C Tiverton St Geo and St Paul *Ex* 02-07; TV Newton Tracey, Horwood, Alverdiscott etc from 07. *The Rectory, High Bickington, Umberleigh EX37 9AY* T: (01769) 560870 E: revmikeclark@yahoo.co.uk

CLARK, Pamela Ann. b 45. Garnett Coll Lon CertEd 72 Ch Ch Coll Cant PGCE 93. SEITE 00 St Jo Coll Nottm 03. **d** 04 **p** 05. NSM Orlestone w Snave and Ruckinge w Warehorne etc *Cant* 04-06; NSM Hythe 06-09; Asst Chapl St Mich Hospice 06-07; PtO *Cant* 09-10; Chapl Dover Immigration Removal Cen 10-11; PtO *Cant* from 12. *20 Wakefield Way, Hythe CT21 6HT*

CLARK, Miss Patricia Mary. b 36. Liv Univ BSc. **d** 88 **p** 94. Par Dn Leasowe *Ches* 88-92; Bp's Officer for Women in Min 89-97; Par Dn Davenham 92-94; C 94-97; rtd 97; PtO *Ches* 97-12; *Blackb* from 12. *31 Fosbrooke House, 8 Clifton Drive, Lytham St Annes FY8 5RQ* T: (01253) 667052

CLARK, Peter. b 45. Sarum & Wells Th Coll 87. **d** 89 **p** 90. C Portsea St Cuth *Portsm* 89-92; TV Rye *Chich* 92-96 and 04-08; P-in-c Chiddingly w E Hoathly 96-98; R 98-04; rtd 08. *44 Ingrams Way, Hailsham BN27 3NP* T: (01323) 841809
E: clucksville@tiscali.co.uk

CLARK, Peter. b 47. DipCOT 92. ERMC 04. **d** 07 **p** 08. NSM Vange *Chelmsf* 07-11; Public Preacher 11-13; NSM Thundersley 13-15. *283 Church Road, Basildon SS14 2NE* T: (01268) 527570 M: 07828-641518
E: frpeterclark@hotmail.co.uk

CLARK, Canon Peter. b 39. Ch Coll Cam BA 61 MA 65. Chich Th Coll 61. **d** 63 **p** 64. C Huddersfield SS Pet and Paul *Wakef* 63-67; C Notting Hill St Jo *Lon* 67-74; Grenada 75-79; C Hove All SS *Chich* 79; P-in-c Hove St Patr 79-82; V Hove St Patr w Ch Ch and St Andr 82-83; V Battersea Ch Ch and St Steph *S'wark* 83-08; RD Battersea 90-01; Hon Can S'wark Cathl 96-08; rtd 08; PtO *S'wark* from 08. *46 Havil Street, London SE5 7RS* T: 020-7708 8915 M: 07773-164134
E: peterclark263@btinternet.com

CLARK, Peter Rodney. b 58. Oriel Coll Ox BA 81 MCIH 93. NOC 97. **d** 00 **p** 01. C Stone St Mich and St Wulfad w Aston St Sav *Lich* 00-03; TV Hanley H Ev 03-12; RD Stoke N 08-12; R Lich St Chad from 12. *St Chad's Rectory, The Windings, Lichfield WS13 7EX* E: revrod@tiscali.co.uk

CLARK, Mrs Prudence Anne. b 44. Man Coll of Educn CertEd 78. NOC 89. **d** 92 **p** 94. NSM Royton St Anne *Man* 92-94; Hon C 94-95; NSM Haughton St Anne 95-09; PtO from 09. *1 Hereford Way, Stalybridge SK15 2TD* T: 0161-338 5275

CLARK, Miss Rebekah Amy. b 91. UEA BA 12. Ridley Hall Cam 12. **d** 15. C Weston super Mare Ch Ch and Em *B & W* from 15. *3 The Drive, Weston-super-Mare BS23 2SR*
M: 07749-162996 E: rebekah.clark36@gmail.com

CLARK, Richard Martin. b 60. Ch Coll Cam MA 81 Nottm Univ MA 99. Trin Coll Bris BA 86. **d** 86 **p** 87. C Orpington Ch Ch *Roch* 86-89; C Marple All SS *Ches* 89-92; V Nottingham St Andr *S'well* 92-13; AD Nottingham Cen 08-13; TR Redditch H Trin *Worc* from 13; V Tardebigge from 15. *The Vicarage, 20 Church Road, Webheath, Redditch B97 5PG* M: 07970-823462

CLARK, Rodney. See CLARK, Peter Rodney

CLARK, Ronald. See CLARK, John Ronald Lyons

CLARK, The Ven Sarah Elizabeth. b 65. Loughb Univ BA 86 Keele Univ MBA 94. St Jo Coll Nottm MA 97. d 98 p 99. C Porchester *S'well* 98-02; R Carlton-in-Lindrick and Langold w Oldcotes 02-09; AD Worksop 06-09; TR Clifton 09-14; Dean of Women's Min 10-14; Hon Can S'well Minster 10-14; Adn Nottingham from 14. *4 Victoria Crescent, Nottingham NG5 4DA* T: 0115-960 6334 *or* (01636) 817206 E: archd-nottm@southwell.anglican.org

CLARK, Simon Peter John. b 68. Westcott Ho Cam 95. d 98 p 99. C Bocking St Mary *Chelmsf* 98-02; C Edmonton St Alphege *Lon* 02-07; C Ponders End St Matt 02-07; P-in-c Noel Park St Mark from 07; Chapl NE Lon Coll from 07. *St Mark's Vicarage, Ashley Crescent, London N22 6LJ* T: (020) 8888 3442 E: fr.simon@btinternet.com

CLARK, Canon Stephen Kenneth. b 52. Bris Univ BEd 74. Wycliffe Hall Ox 80. d 83 p 84. C Pitsea *Chelmsf* 83-86; Chapl Scargill Ho 86-89; R Elmley Castle w Bricklehampton and Combertons *Worc* 89-96; Chapl Burrswood Chr Cen *Roch* 96-01; Chapl Team Ldr 01-07; I Annagh w Drumaloor, Cloverhill and Drumlane *K, E & A* 07-12; Can Kilmore Cathl 10-12; Dep Chapl Crowhurst Chr Healing Cen from 13. *Crowhurst Christian Healing Centre, The Old Rectory, Forewood Lane, Crowhurst, Battle TN33 9AD* T: (01424) 830204 E: skclar@googlemail.com

CLARK, Terence Paul. b 62. Leeds Univ BSc 85 PGCE 94 St Jo Coll Ox DPhil 91. Wycliffe Hall Ox 98. d 00 p 01. C Whitfield *Derby* 00-10; TR Deane *Man* from 10; AD from 12. *Deane Rectory, 234 Wigan Road, Bolton BL3 5QE* T: (01204) 61819 E: deanechurchoffice@btinternet.com

CLARK-KING (née CLARK), The Ven Ellen Jane. b 62. Newnham Coll Cam BA 85 MA 89 Lon Univ MA 99 Lanc Univ PhD 03. Ripon Coll Cuddesdon 89. d 92 p 94. C Colwall w Upper Colwall and Coddington *Heref* 92-95; Chapl SS Coll Cam 95-00; NSM N Shields *Newc* 00-05; Asst Dioc Dir of Ords 01-05; Canada from 05; Adn Burrard from 07. *402-1025 Gilford Street, Vancouver BC V6G 2P2, Canada* T: (001) (604) 682 3848 ext 25 E: ejck@lineone.net *or* ellen@cathedral.vancouver.bc.ca

CLARK-KING (formerly KING), Jeremy Norman. b 66. K Coll Lon BD 88 AKC 88 Lon Univ MA 99. Ripon Coll Cuddesdon 88. d 90 p 91. C Ashby-de-la-Zouch St Helen w Coleorton *Leic* 90-93; C Ledbury w Eastnor *Heref* 93-96; C Cambridge Gt St Mary w St Mich *Ely* 96-00; Chapl Girton Coll Cam 96-99; Chapl Cam Univ 96-99; V Byker St Ant *Newc* 00-05; R N Vancouver St Martin Canada 05-11. *402-1025 Gilford Street, Vancouver BC V6G 2P2, Canada* E: anglican@uniserve.com

CLARK-MAXWELL, James Michael Gilchrist. b 75. Edin Univ BSc 98 MSc 99 Imp Coll Lon MB, BS 04. TISEC 06 St Jo Coll Nottm 06. d 11. NSM Dumfries *Glas* from 11. *Speddoch, Dumfries DG2 9UB* T: (01556) 610355 M: 07720-455253 E: james@speddoch.com

CLARKE, Alan John. b 55. St Jo Coll Dur BA 77 MA 85 PGCE. Westcott Ho Cam 78. d 80 p 81. C Heworth St Mary *Dur* 80-83; C Darlington St Jo 83-87; Asst Chapl Bryanston Sch 87-91; Chapl St Pet High Sch Ex 93-99; Chapl and Hd RS Reed's Sch Cobham from 99. *Clover, Reed's School, Sandy Lane, Cobham KT11 2EP* T: (01932) 869006 *or* 869080 E: alanjohn@ajclarke.fsnet.co.uk

CLARKE, Alexandra Naomi Mary. b 75. Trin Coll Cam BA 96 MA 99 MPhil 97 SS Hild & Bede Coll Dur PhD 02 Anglia Poly Univ BA 04. Westcott Ho Cam 02. d 05 p 06. C Papworth *Ely* 05-09; R Upper Itchen *Win* 09-11; TV Papworth *Ely* from 11; Chapl St Bede's Coll Cam 09-11. *The Rectory, 2 Short Street, Bourn, Cambridge CB23 2SG* T: (01954) 710426 E: alexandra.clarke@ely.anglican.org

CLARKE, Miss Alison Clare. b 33. MCST 54 Open Univ BA 85. EAMTC 90. d 93 p 94. NSM Lt Ilford St Mich *Chelmsf* 93-98; Asst Chapl Newham Healthcare NHS Trust Lon 93-98; PtO *Lon* 94-98; NSM Woodford St Mary w St Phil and St Jas *Chelmsf* 98-03; rtd 03; PtO *Chelmsf* 03-04. *20 Manor Court Lodge, 175 High Street, London E18 2PD*

CLARKE, Andrew John. b 58. New Coll Edin BD 82 Graduate Soc Dur PGCE 89. Linc Th Coll 84. d 86 p 87. C High Harrogate Ch Ch *Ripon* 86-88; RE Teacher Royds Hall High Sch Huddersfield 89-91; C Thornbury *Bradf* 91-93; P-in-c Bingley H Trin 93-99; V Leeds from 99; RD Airedale *Bradf* 00-05. *6 Woodvale Crescent, Bingley BD16 4AL* T: (01274) 562278 E: andrew@bradford.anglican.org

CLARKE, Ann. See CLARKE, Geraldine Ann

CLARKE (née HARWOOD), Mrs Ann Jane. b 73. SEITE. d 08. C Winslow w Gt Horwood and Addington *Ox* 08-11; C Lee Gd Shep w St Pet *S'wark* from 11. *56 Weigall Road, London SE12 8HF* M: 07903-652927 E: annharwood73@googlemail.com

CLARKE, Anne. b 51. d 04 p 05. OLM E Dulwich St Jo *S'wark* from 04. *62 Oakhurst Grove, London SE22 9AQ* T: (020) 8693 1276 E: anne@oakhurstgrove.com

CLARKE, Miss Audrey May. b 35. Gilmore Ho 65. dss 75 d 87 p 94. Chapl Asst Middx Hosp Lon 80-84; Par Dn Mottingham St Andr w St Alban *S'wark* 87-89; C Westborough *Guildf* 89-95; rtd 95; Hon C St Mary's Bay w St Mary-in-the-Marsh etc *Cant* 95-98; Hon C New Romney w Old Romney and Midley 95-98; PtO *Pet* 98-10; *Leic* from 13. *3 Stuart Court, High Street, Kibworth, Leicester LE8 0LR* T: 0116-279 2592 E: audrey@revaclarke.freeserve.co.uk

CLARKE, Canon Barbara. b 51. Bradf Univ BA 87 Leeds Univ PGCE 89 MA 07. NOC 04. d 07 p 08. NSM Addingham *Leeds* from 07; Hon Can Bradf Cathl from 14. *3 Radley Court, Mirfield WF14 9FD* T: (01924) 506575 M: 07913-176370 E: blarke3@virginmedia.com *or* nutbrownhare@me.com

CLARKE, Bernard Ronald. b 53. MBE 12. Nottm Univ MA 97 FRGS. Ridley Hall Cam 74. d 77 p 78. C Leigh Park *Portsm* 77-78; C Petersfield w Sheet 78-81; Chapl RN from 81; Dir of Ords RN 93-03; QHC from 08. *Royal Naval Chaplaincy Service, Mail Point 1-2, Leach Building, Whale Island, Portsmouth PO2 8BY* T: (023) 9262 5055 F: 9262 5134

CLARKE, Mrs Caroline Anne. b 49. Girton Coll Cam BA 75 MA 79 K Coll Lon PGCE 76. SEITE 97. d 00 p 01. NSM Clapham H Trin and St Pet *S'wark* from 00; Chapl Trin Hospice Lon 03-11. *42 The Chase, London SW4 0NH* T: (020) 7622 0765 F: 7652 4555 M: 07808-858674 E: clarkecaroline@hotmail.com

CLARKE, Charles David. b 37. Univ of Wales BA 76 MA 93 PhD 98 Cam Univ DipEd 77 MEd Lambeth MA 95 LCP 77. St Mich Coll Llan 88. d 90 p 91. C Whitchurch *Llan* 90-93; V Graig 93-96; P-in-c Cilfynydd 93-96; TV Cyncoed *Mon* 96-98; R Neath w Llantwit *Llan* 98-01; TR Neath 01-02; rtd 02; PtO *Llan* from 10. *Lough Cutra, 11 Davies Andrews Road, Tonna, Neath SA11 3EU* T: (01639) 638049

CLARKE, Canon Christopher George. b 43. Sarum Th Coll 67. d 68 p 69. C Sprowston *Nor* 68-72; V Hemsby 72-77; V Sutton Courtenay w Appleford *Ox* 77-84; TR Bracknell 84-97; RD 90-96; Hon Can Ch Ch 95-08; P-in-c Sonning 97-98; V 98-08; rtd 08. *Oak Lodge, Upton Snodsbury, Worcester WR7 4NH* T: (01905) 381146 E: cgandcgclarke@googlemail.com

CLARKE, Claire Margaret Alice. b 74. d 14 p 15. C Upper Sunbury St Sav *Lon* from 14. *41 Wolsey Road, Sunbury-on-Thames TW16 7TU* M: 07810-543197

CLARKE, Canon David James. b 55. Univ of Wales (Abth) BSc(Econ) 77 Keele Univ MA 78 PhD 83. Trin Coll Bris. d 84 p 85. C Cardigan w Mwnt and Y Ferwig *St D* 84-87; P-in-c Llansantffraed and Llanbadarn Trefeglwys etc 87-88; V 88-91; Chapl Coll of SS Mark and Jo Plymouth 91-96; V Lindfield *Chich* from 96; Can and Preb Chich Cathl from 06. *The Vicarage, High Street, Lindfield, Haywards Heath RH16 2HR* T: (01444) 482386

CLARKE, Dominic James. b 71. Surrey Univ BA 07. STETS 04. d 07 p 08. C Petersfield *Portsm* 07-11; P-in-c Blackmoor and Whitehill from 11. *The Vicarage, Blackmoor, Liss GU33 6BN* T: (01420) 489418

CLARKE, Douglas Charles. b 33. Bps' Coll Cheshunt 65. d 66 p 67. C Chingford SS Pet and Paul *Chelmsf* 66-72; V Romford Ascension Collier Row 72-79; V Bembridge *Portsm* 79-83; V Bournemouth St Mary *Win* 83-87; R High Wych and Gilston w Eastwick *St Alb* 87-00; rtd 00; PtO *Linc* from 00; *St Alb* from 00. *36 Tennyson Drive, Bourne PE10 9WD* T: (01778) 394840

CLARKE, Duncan James Edward. b 54. Wycliffe Hall Ox 75. d 78 p 79. C Newport St Andr *Mon* 78-80; C Griffithstown 80-82; Trinidad and Tobago 82-84 and 95-99; NSM Fleckney and Kilby *Leic* 92-95; USPG 95-99; C Wednesfield *Lich* 99; TV 99-01; Asst Chapl HM Pris Wormwood Scrubs 01-02; Chapl HM Pris Haverigg 02-07; Chapl HM Pris Garth 07-09; P-in-c Leyland St Ambrose *Blackb* 09-11; V from 11. *St Ambrose Vicarage, 85 Moss Lane, Leyland, Preston PR25 4XA* T: (01772) 623426 M: 07946-668786 E: namabiah@msn.com

CLARKE, Mrs Elizabeth Hazel. b 55. Ridley Hall Cam 02. d 04 p 05. C Frankby w Greasby *Ches* 04-09; P-in-c Dodleston 09-11; R from 11. *St Mary's Rectory, Pulford Lane, Dodleston, Chester CH4 9NN* T: (01244) 660257 E: hazelclarke@jcscomputers.co.uk

CLARKE, Eric Samuel. b 26. Nottm Univ BSc 51 St Cath Coll Ox BA 69 MA 69. Wycliffe Hall Ox 51. d 54 p 55. C Gedling *S'well* 54-57; C Nottingham St Pet and St Jas 57-69; PtO *Derby* 63-02; rtd 02. *Hillcrest, Cottington Mead, Sidmouth EX10 8HB*

CLARKE (née GILMARTIN), Mrs Frances. b 53. Reading Univ BSc 75 PGCE 02. d 11 p 12. OLM Skellingthorpe w Doddington *Linc* from 11. *12 Shaftesbury Avenue, Lincoln LN6 0QN* T: (01522) 685487 E: frances_clarke@hotmail.co.uk

CLARKE, Francis Alfred. b 46. MCLIP 67 MCMI 82. **d** 08 **p** 09. OLM Weybourne Gp *Nor* from 08. *7 Alexandra Road, Sheringham NR26 8HU* T: (01263) 825677 E: f.clarke46@btinternet.com

CLARKE, Canon Geraldine Ann. b 46. Hockerill Coll of Educn CertEd 68 ACP 81. NTMTC 93. **d** 96 **p** 97. NSM Aldersbrook *Chelmsf* 96-01; TR Becontree S 01-09; P-in-c N Bersted *Chich* from 09; Can and Preb Chich Cathl from 14. *The Vicarage, 330 Chichester Road, North Bersted, Bognor Regis PO21 5AU* T: (01243) 823800 E: annclarke@talktalk.net

CLARKE, Canon Harold George. b 29. St D Coll Lamp 58. **d** 61 **p** 62. C Ebbw Vale Ch Ch *Mon* 61-64; C Roath St German *Llan* 64-73; Chapl Wales Poly 73-74; V Glyntaff 73-84; V Roath St Martin 84-00; RD Cardiff 89-99; Can Res Llan Cathl 91-99; rtd 00. *12 St Margaret's Crescent, Cardiff CF23 5AU* T: (029) 2046 2280

CLARKE, Hazel. *See* CLARKE, Elizabeth Hazel

CLARKE, Mrs Helen. b 57. **d** 13 **p** 14. C Heref St Pet w St Owen and St Jas from 13. *The Vicarage, 10 St Barnabas Close, Hereford HR1 1EY* T: (01432) 276963 E: revhelenspsj@gmail.com

CLARKE, Hilary James. b 41. JP . Univ of Wales (Lamp) BA 64 Ox Univ DipEd 65. St Steph Ho Ox 64. **d** 66 **p** 67. C Kibworth Beauchamp *Leic* 66-68; Chapl to the Deaf 68-71; Prin Officer Ch Miss for Deaf Walsall 71-73; Prin Officer & Sec Leic and Co Miss for the Deaf 73-89; Hon C Leic St Anne 73-98; TV Leic H Spirit 82-89; Hon Can Leic Cathl 88-96; Bp's Press Relns and Dio Communications Officer 95-96; Sec Gen Syn Coun for the Deaf 88-02; rtd 02; PtO *Carl* from 05. *The Gate House, Brough, Kirkby Stephen CA17 4DS* M: 07730-002570

CLARKE, James. *See* CLARKE, David James

CLARKE, Jason Philip. b 66. Lon Hosp BDS. Oak Hill Th Coll 99. **d** 01 **p** 02. C Fulwood *Sheff* 01-06; Dir Staff Tr UCCF from 06; PtO *Sheff* from 06. *469 Redmires Road, Sheffield S10 4LF* T: 0114-230 9345

CLARKE, Jason Scott. b 65. Leeds Univ BA 87. Coll of Resurr Mirfield 89. **d** 91 **p** 92. C Hendon St Mary *Lon* 91-95; V Enfield St Geo 95-01; V Ditchling *Chich* 01-06; CF from 06. *c/o MOD Chaplains (Army)* F: 381824 T: (01264) 383430

CLARKE, John Charles. b 31. St Jo Coll Nottm 91. **d** 92 **p** 93. NSM Winshill *Derby* 92-95; P-in-c Stanley 95-98; rtd 98; PtO *Win* from 98. *4 Campion Drive, Romsey SO51 7RD* T: (01794) 523945

CLARKE, Canon John David Maurice. b 60. **d** 89 **p** 90. C Dublin Whitechurch *D & G* 89-92; Asst Chapl St Vin Hosp Donnybrook 89-92; I Navan w Kentstown, Tara, Slane, Painestown etc *M & K* from 92; Can Meath from 00; Can Kildare Cathl from 00; Can St Patr Cathl Dublin from 09. *The Rectory, Boyne Road, Navan, Co Meath, Republic of Ireland* T/F: (00353) (46) 902 1172 E: johndmclarke@eircom.net

CLARKE, The Very Revd John Martin. b 52. Edin Univ BD 76 Hertf Coll Ox BA 89 MA 89. Edin Th Coll 73. **d** 76 **p** 77. C Kenton Ascension *Newc* 76-79; Prec St Ninian's Cathl Perth 79-82; Info Officer to Gen Syn of Scottish Episc Ch 82-87; Greece 87-88; V Battersea St Mary *S'wark* 89-96; Prin Ripon Coll Cuddesdon 97-04; Can and Preb Linc Cathl 00-04; Dean Wells *B & W* from 04. *The Dean's Lodging, 25 The Liberty, Wells BA5 2SZ* T/F: (01749) 670278 E: thedeanofwells@googlemail.com

CLARKE, John Patrick Hatherley. b 46. Pemb Coll Ox BA 68 Man Univ MBA 73. St Jo Coll Nottm. **d** 83 **p** 84. C Leic H Trin w St Jo 83-87; C Selly Park St Steph and St Wulstan *Birm* 87-92; Hon C Woking St Mary *Guildf* 92-94; V Greenham *Ox* 94-14; rtd 14; Hon C The Churn *Ox* from 14. *The Rectory, Church Lane, South Moreton, Didcot OX11 9AF* T: (01235) 512987 E: john@clarke1662.freeserve.co.uk

CLARKE, John Percival. b 44. TCD BA 67 MA 98. **d** 69 **p** 70. C Belfast St Simon *Conn* 69-72; C Monkstown *D & G* 72-76; Asst Chapl TCD 76-78; I Kilmocomogue w Snave, Durrus and Rooska *C, C & R* 79-82; I Carrigrohane Union 82-89; Tanzania 89-92; I Wicklow w Killiskey *D & G* 92-13; Abp's Dom Chapl 95-97; Can Ch Ch Cathl Dublin 97-13; rtd 13. *22 Church Gate, Station Road, Wicklow Town, Co Wicklow, Republic of Ireland* T: (00353) (404) 6925 M: 85-705 5916

CLARKE, John Philip. b 31. Trin Hall Cam BA 54 MA 62. Linc Th Coll. **d** 57 **p** 58. C Walworth Lady Marg w St Mary *S'wark* 57-59; C Warlingham w Chelsham and Farleigh 59-62; C Mottingham St Andr w St Alban 62-67; C Eltham Park St Luke 67-72; Chapl Leeds Gen Infirmary 72-91; C Far Headingley St Chad *Ripon* 91-96; Bp's Adv on Chr Healing 91-96; rtd 96; PtO *Leeds* from 96. *13 Bishop Garth, Pateley Bridge, Harrogate HG3 5LL* T: (01423) 711646

CLARKE, Mrs Joy Irene. b 44. **d** 98 **p** 02. OLM Ditton St Mich w St Thos *Liv* 98-10; rtd 10. *55 Spinney Avenue, Widnes WA8 8LB* T: 0151-424 8747

CLARKE, Judith Irene. b 46. SRN 67 SCM 69. EAMTC 97. **d** 00 **p** 01. NSM Shingay Gp *Ely* 00-02; P-in-c Gt Staughton 02-05; P-in-c Hail Weston and Southoe 04-05; R Gt Staughton w

Hail Weston w Southoe from 05. *The Vicarage, Causeway, Great Staughton, St Neots PE19 5BF* T: (01480) 861215 E: judi195@btinternet.com

CLARKE (née PULLIN), Kathleen Jean Rebecca. b 58. Qu Coll Birm BA 07. **d** 07 **p** 08. C Kings Norton *Birm* 07-11; V Highters Heath from 11. *Immanuel Vicarage, 5 Pickenham Road, Birmingham B14 4TG* T: 0121-430 7578 E: rebeccapullin@hotmail.com

✠**CLARKE, The Rt Revd Kenneth Herbert.** b 49. TCD BA 71. **d** 72 **p** 73 **c** 01. C Magheralin *D & D* 72-75; C Dundonald 75-78; Chile 78-81; I Crinken *D & G* 82-86; I Coleraine *Conn* 86-01; Chmn SAMS (Ireland) from 94; Can Conn Cathl 96-98; Adn Dalriada 98-01; Bp K, E & A 01-12; Miss Dir SAMS (Ireland) from 13. *SAMS, 1 Irwin Crescent, Lurgan, Craigavon BT66 7EZ* T: (028) 3831 0144 E: ken@atnaf.freeserve.co.uk

CLARKE, Miss Kirsty Ann. b 81. Qu Coll Birm 12. **d** 15. C Leominster *Heref* from 15. *8 Radnor View, Leominster HR6 8TF* M: 07720-323916 E: kclarke1981@yahoo.co.uk

CLARKE, Mrs Lynnette Jean. b 46. Qu Coll Birm 05. **d** 08 **p** 09. OLM Allesley Park and Whoberley *Cov* 08-13; OLM Cov E from 13. *14 High Park Close, Coventry CV5 7BE* T: (024) 7646 7097 M: 07890-048210 E: lynnette@mountnod.co.uk

CLARKE, Canon Margaret Geraldine. b 33. Dalton Ho Bris 62. **dss** 68 **d** 87 **p** 94. Par Dn Easthampstead *Ox* 87-94; C 94; Hon Can Ch Ch 90-94; rtd 94; Hon C Bracknell *Ox* from 97. *Hermon, London Road, Bracknell RG12 2XH* T: (01344) 427451

CLARKE, Martin Howard. b 47. AKC 70. St Aug Coll Cant 70. **d** 71 **p** 72. C Saffron Walden w Wendens Ambo *Chelmsf* 71-74; C Ely 74-78; V Messing w Inworth *Chelmsf* 78-90; V Layer de la Haye 90-96; R Layer de la Haye and Layer Breton w Birch etc 96-12; rtd 12; PtO *Chelmsf* from 14. *Saddlers, 2 Stable Close, West Mersea, Colchester CO5 8HP* T: (01206) 383952

CLARKE, Ms Mary Margaret. b 65. K Coll Lon BD 86 AKC 86. Linc Th Coll 89. **d** 89 **p** 94. Par Dn Northampton St Jas *Pet* 89-93; Chapl Nene Coll of HE Northn 92-93; Team Dn Coventry Caludon *Cov* 93-94; TV 94-01; PtO *Lon* 01-08; C Notting Dale St Clem w St Mark and St Jas from 12. *1 Porchester Gardens, London W2 3LA* T: (020) 7229 6359 E: mary.clare@stclementjames.org.uk

CLARKE, Maurice Harold. b 30. K Alfred's Coll Win CertEd 56 Sussex Univ MA 79 LCP 69. Cuddesdon Coll 65. **d** 67 **p** 68. Hd Master Co Sec Sch Cowplain (Lower Sch) 67-72; Dep Hd Master Thamesview High Sch 72-80; Hd Master Eltham Green Comp Sch 80-83; Hon C Waterlooville *Portsm* 67-70; Hon C Fareham SS Pet and Paul 70-72; Hon C Higham and Merston *Roch* 72-83; V Hamble le Rice *Win* 83-90; rtd 91; PtO *Win* 91-14; *Chich* from 92. *10 Worcester Road, Chichester PO19 8DJ* T: (01243) 775646

CLARKE, Michael. b 39. Ely Th Coll 60. **d** 62 **p** 63. C S Stoneham *Win* 62-64; C N Greenford All Hallows *Lon* 64-69; Hon C Milton *Portsm* 69-74; Chapl St Jas Hosp Portsm 69-91; Chapl Hurstpierpoint Coll 91-92; R Highnam, Lassington, Rudford, Tibberton etc *Glouc* 92-98; rtd 99; PtO *Glouc* 99-01; *Portsm* from 02. *Little Barns, 77 Fishbourne Lane, Ryde PO33 4EX* T: (01983) 883858

CLARKE, Canon Neil Malcolm. b 53. OBE 05. Solicitor 79. WMMTC 89. **d** 92 **p** 93. NSM Desborough, Brampton Ash, Dingley and Braybrooke *Pet* from 92; Can Pet Cathl from 04. *53 Breakleys Road, Desborough, Kettering NN14 2PT* T: (01536) 760667 E: revnclarke@aol.com

CLARKE, Nicholas John. b 57. Lon Univ BA 78 Lon Inst of Educn PGCE 80. Ridley Hall Cam 95. **d** 97 **p** 98. C Attleborough *Cov* 97-00; V Fillongley and Corley 00-07; Chapl Chantilly *Eur* from 07. *7A avenue du Bouteiller, 60500 Chantilly, France* T: (0033) 3 44 58 53 22 E: chaplain@stpeterschantilly.info

CLARKE, Norman. b 28. Keble Coll Ox BA 52 MA 58. St Steph Ho Ox 52. **d** 54 **p** 55. C Ellesmere Port *Ches* 54-57; C Kettering St Mary *Pet* 57-60; Chapl and Tutor St Monica Mampong Ghana 60-62; C Friern Barnet All SS *Lon* 62-63; LtO *Leic* 63-74; C Knighton St Mary Magd 74-81; Dioc Communications Officer *St E* 81-88; P-in-c Sproughton w Burstall 81-88; P-in-c Dunsford and Doddiscombsleigh *Ex* 88-95; P-in-c Cheriton Bishop 88-95; rtd 95; PtO *Ex* 95-08; RD Ottery 02-03; PtO St Helena from 96. *78 Malden Road, Sidmouth EX10 9NA* T: (01395) 515849

CLARKE, Paul Ian. b 72. W Suffolk Coll BA 09. Trin Coll Bris BA 11. **d** 11 **p** 12. C Haughley w Wetherden and Stowupland *St E* 11-14; P-in-c Coxley w Godney, Henton and Wookey *B & W* from 14. *The Vicarage, Vicarage Lane, Wookey, Wells BA5 1JT* M: 07456-936475 E: revpaulclarke@me.com

CLARKE, Paul Wordsworth. b 74. Trevelyan Coll Dur LLB 97. Oak Hill Th Coll BA 06. **d** 07. C St Helen Bishopsgate w St Andr Undershaft etc *Lon* 07-13. *1 Dempster Terrace, St Andrews KY16 9QQ*

CLARKE, Preb Peter Gerald. b 38. Cuddesdon Coll 74. **d** 76 **p** 77. NSM Marston Magna w Rimpton *B & W* 76-79; NSM Queen Camel, Marston Magna, W Camel, Rimpton etc 79-87; NSM Chilton Cantelo, Ashington, Mudford, Rimpton etc 87-88; V Rtinhull w Chilthorne Domer, Yeovil Marsh etc 88-94; TV Weston-super-Mare Cen Par 94-95; V Weston super Mare All SS and St Sav 96-06; Preb Wells Cathl 02-08; rtd 06; PtO *B & W* from 06. *6 West Camel Farm, West Camel, Yeovil BA22 7HH* T: (01935) 850408 E: peter2117@lycos.com

CLARKE, Peter John. b 36. Qu Coll Ox BA 60 MA 64 Lon Univ BD 79. Clifton Th Coll 62. **d** 62 **p** 63. C Upper Tulse Hill St Matthias *S'wark* 62-64; CMJ 64-96; Dir for S America 88-96; rtd 97. *Pedro Moran 4414, C 1419 HLH Buenos Aires, Argentina* T/F: (0054) (11) 4501 4629

CLARKE, Philip John. b 44. Bris Univ BA 65 Univ of Wales (Abth) DipEd 66. NOC 84. **d** 87 **p** 88. NSM Crewe Ch Ch and St Pet *Ches* 87-88; NSM Coppenhall 88-90; LtO 90-91; C Altrincham St Geo 91-95; C Odd Rode 95-97; P-in-c Peterchurch w Vowchurch, Turnastone and Dorstone *Heref* 97-98; V Llansantffraid Glyn Ceirog and Llanarmon etc *St As* 98-09; rtd 09; P-in-c Caerwys and Bodfari *St As* 09-11; P-in-c Lowther and Askham and Clifton and Brougham *Carl* 11-12; PtO *St As* from 12. *17 Plas y Waun, Chapel Lane, Chirk, Wrexham LL14 5NP* T: (01691) 239481 E: revphilipjclarke@aol.com

CLARKE, Rachel Frances. *See* HARTLAND, Rachel Frances

✠**CLARKE, The Most Revd Richard Lionel.** b 49. TCD BA 71 MA 79 PhD 90 K Coll Lon BD 75 AKC 75. **d** 75 **p** 76 **c** 96. C Holywood *D & D* 75-77; C Dublin St Bart w Leeson Park *D & G* 77-79; Dean of Residence TCD 79-84; I Bandon Union *C, C & R* 84-93; Dir of Ords 85-93; Cen Dir of Ords 82-97; Can Cork and Ross Cathls *C, C & R* 91-93; Dean Cork 93-96; I Cork St Fin Barre's Union 93-96; Chapl Univ Coll Cork 93-96; Bp M & K 96-12; Abp Arm from 12; Hon Can St Ninian's Cathl Perth from 04. *Church House, 46 Abbey Street, Armagh BT61 7DZ* T: (028) 3752 7144 E: archbishop@armagh.anglican.org

CLARKE, Canon Robert George. b 36. St Jo Coll Dur BA 65 Natal Univ PhD 83. Cranmer Hall Dur 65. **d** 67 **p** 68. C Basingstoke *Win* 67-70; R Ixopo S Africa 71-74; C Pietermaritzburg Cathl 75-80; Dir Pietermaritzburg Urban Min Project 77-83; R Grahamstown St Bart 84-87; Lect St Paul's Coll 84-87; Ecum Officer Albany Regional Coun of Chs 88-95; Hon Can Grahamstown from 05. *26 Somerset Street, Grahamstown, 6139 South Africa* T: (0027) (046) 622 7803 E: bobandmaggy@imaginet.co.za

CLARKE, Robert Graham. b 28. S Dios Minl Tr Scheme 78. **d** 81 **p** 82. NSM Woolston *Win* 81-89; NSM Portswood St Denys 89-93; Chapl Torrevieja *Eur* 93-95; PtO *Win* from 95; *Eur* from 95. *10 River Green, Hamble, Southampton SO31 4JA* T: (023) 8045 4230

CLARKE, Robert Michael. b 45. Oak Hill Th Coll BD 71 Sarum & Wells Th Coll 78. **d** 78 **p** 79. Hon C Glastonbury St Jo w Godney *B & W* 78-81; Asst Hd Master Edington Sch 78-81; Chapl Felsted Sch 81-84; Asst Chapl and Ho Master 85-92; Hd Master Brocksford Hall 92-94; Hd Master The Park Sch Bath 94-96; Chapl Seaford Coll Petworth 96-99; Hd Master Bredon Sch 99-00; PtO *Lich* from 01. *17 Top Street, Whittington, Oswestry SY11 4DR* T: (01691) 662548

CLARKE, Robert Sydney. b 35. OBE 00. K Coll Lon AKC 64 MA 65. **d** 65 **p** 66. C Hendon St Mary *Lon* 65-69; C Langley Marish *Ox* 69-70; Chapl New Cross Hosp Wolv 70-74; Chapl Dorchester Hosps 74-79; Sen Chapl Chelsea and Westmr Hosp Lon 80-85; Sen Chapl Win Hosps 88-94; Sen Chapl Win and Eastleigh Healthcare NHS Trust 94-00; Chapl to The Queen 87-05; Sec and Dir Tr Gen Syn Hosp Chapl Coun 94-00; PtO *S'wark* from 95; *Lon* 95-00; rtd 00; PtO *Win* from 05. *3 Brook Court, Middlebridge Street, Romsey SO51 8HR* T: (01794) 524215

CLARKE, Canon Robert William. b 56. CITC. **d** 83 **p** 84. C Cloughfern *Conn* 83-85; C Drumragh w Mountfield *D & R* 85-87; I Edenderry w Clanabogan from 87; Can Derry Cathl from 05. *Edenderry Rectory, 91 Crevenagh Road, Omagh BT79 0EZ* T: (028) 8224 5525 E: rw.clarke@btinternet.com

CLARKE, Canon Roger David. b 58. Man Univ BA Ox Univ MA. Ripon Coll Cuddesdon 80. **d** 83 **p** 84. C Frodsham *Ches* 83-86; C Wilmslow 86-88; V High Lane 88-93; V Heald Green St Cath 93-99; R W Kirby St Bridget 99-10; V Hale Barns w Ringway from 10; Hon Can Ches Cathl from 15. *Ringway Vicarage, 35 Burnside, Hale Barns, Altrincham WA15 0SG* T: 0161-980 8944 E: yficerdy@btopenworld.com

CLARKE, Ronald George. b 31. Oak Hill Th Coll. **d** 64 **p** 65. C Carlton-in-the-Willows *S'well* 64-68; V Bestwood St Matt 68-76; V Barnsbury St Andr w St Thos and St Matthias *Lon* 76-77; V Barnsbury St Andr 77-78; V Barnsbury St Andr w H Trin 79-80; P-in-c Battle Bridge All SS w Pentonville St Jas 79-80; V Barnsbury St Andr and H Trin w All SS 81-86;

TR Bath Twerton-on-Avon *B & W* 86-94; rtd 94; P-in-c Churchstanton, Buckland St Mary and Otterford *B & W* 94-97; PtO from 97. *Myrtle Cottage, 35 High Street, Chard TA20 1QL* T: (01460) 65495 E: rgclarke31@gmail.com

CLARKE, Stephen Robert. b 77. Southn Univ BA 99. Trin Coll Bris BA 10. **d** 10 **p** 11. C Pioneer Min Glouc City 10-14; V Whitehall Park *Lon* from 14. *St Andrew's Vicarage, 43 Dresden Road, London N19 3BG* T: (020) 3712 6501 E: steve@standrewsn19.org *or* steveclarkey@gmail.com

CLARKE, Steven Peter. b 61. Oak Hill Th Coll 93. **d** 97 **p** 98. C Frinton *Chelmsf* 97-01; C Woodford Wells 01-12; V Highams Park All SS from 12. *All Saints' Vicarage, 12A Castle Avenue, London E4 9QD* T: (020) 8531 5107 E: sclarke24@btinternet.com

CLARKE (formerly GARDNER), Mrs Susan Carol. b 54. SRN 75. St Jo Coll Nottm 02. **d** 04 **p** 05. C Abington *Pet* 04-07; P-in-c Woodhouse *Wakef* 07-08; V Birkby and Woodhouse 08-10; P-in-c Thornhill and Whitley Lower *Leeds* from 10. *Thornhill Rectory, 51 Frank Lane, Dewsbury WF12 0JW* T: (01924) 520861 M: 07732-189485 E: sue@suegardner1.wanadoo.co.uk

CLARKE (née DAVIS), Canon Susan Elizabeth Mary. b 50. St Thos Hosp Lon MB, BS 74 Univ Coll Lon MSc 81 FRCP 84 FRCR 03. SEITE 03. **d** 06 **p** 07. NSM W Streatham St Jas *S'wark* 06-12; NSM Streatham St Paul 10-12; Hon TV Furzedown from 12; Hon Can S'wark Cathl from 15. *26 Abbotsleigh Road, London SW16 1SP* T: (020) 8769 5117 M: 07710-744006 E: sue.clarke@kcl.ac.uk

CLARKE, Timothy John. b 69. Jes Coll Cam BA 91 MA 95 Barrister 92. WMMTC 00. **d** 03 **p** 04. NSM Birm Cathl from 03. *15B College Green, Worcester WR1 2LH* T: (01905) 732938 E: timclarke@waitrose.com

CLARKE, Ms Valerie Diane. b 45. St Jo Coll Nottm BA 00. NOC 91. **d** 95 **p** 96. C Sherburn in Elmet w Saxton *York* 95-97; C Brayton 97-99; Chapl Scargill Ho 00-03; P-in-c Barnburgh w Melton on the Hill etc *Sheff* 03-09; rtd 09; PtO *Wakef* 09-12; *Sheff* 11-12; Hon C Beverley Minster *York* from 12. *34 Carter Drive, Beverley HU17 9GL* T: (01482) 860185 M: 07974-698468 E: valclarke@googlemail.com

CLARKE, Mrs Yvonne Veronica. b 58. CA Tr Coll. **dss** 86 **d** 87 **p** 94. Par Dn Nunhead St Silas *S'wark* 87-90; Par Dn Nunhead St Antony w St Silas 90-91; Par Dn Mottingham St Andr w St Alban 91-94; C 94-98; V Spring Park All SS from 98. *All Saints' Vicarage, 1 Farm Drive, Croydon CR0 8HX* T: (020) 8777 2775 F: 8777 5228

CLARKSON, The Ven Alan Geoffrey. b 34. Ch Coll Cam BA 57 MA 61. Wycliffe Hall Ox 57. **d** 59 **p** 60. C Penn *Lich* 59-60; C Oswestry St Oswald 60-63; C Wrington *B & W* 63-65; V Chewton Mendip w Emborough 65-74; Dioc Ecum Officer 65-75; V Glastonbury St Jo w Godney 74-84; P-in-c W Pennard 80-84; P-in-c Meare 81-84; P-in-c Glastonbury St Benedict 82-84; V Glastonbury w Meare, W Pennard and Godney 84; Hon Can Win Cathl 84-99; Adn Win 84-99; V Burley Ville 84-99; rtd 99; PtO *Chelmsf* from 99; Ely from 99; St E from 99. *Cantilena, 4 Harefield Rise, Linton, Cambridge CB21 4LS* T: (01223) 892988 E: agclarkson@hotmail.co.uk

CLARKSON, David James. b 42. St Andr Univ BSc 66. NOC 85. **d** 88 **p** 89. NSM Slaithwaite w E Scammonden *Wakef* 88-89; C Morley St Pet w Churwell 89-91; R Cumberworth w Denby Dale 91-93; P-in-c Denby 91-93; R Cumberworth, Denby and Denby Dale 93-02; rtd 03; LtO *Glas* from 04. *Waulkmill Cottage, Westerkirk, Langholm DG13 0NJ* T: (01387) 370279

CLARKSON, Eric George. b 28. St Jo Coll Dur BA 48. **d** 50 **p** 51. C Birkdale St Jo *Liv* 50-52; C Grassendale 52-54; PC W Derby St Luke 54-66; V Blackb St Mich 66-75; V Blackb St Mich w St Jo 75; V Chapeltown *Sheff* 75-86; C Ranmoor 86-87; V Crosspool 87-92; rtd 92; PtO *York* 92-10. *2 Harewood Drive, Filey YO14 0DE* T/F: (01723) 513957

CLARKSON, Geoffrey. b 35. AKC 61. **d** 62 **p** 63. C Shildon *Dur* 62-65; Asst Chapl HM Pris *Liv* 65-66; Chapl HM Borstal Feltham 66-71; Development Officer Br Assn of Settlements 71-74; Dir Community Projects Foundn 74-87; Chapl HM Rem Cen Ashford 88-90; Chapl HM Pris Coldingley 90-99; Chapl HM Pris Send 92-94; rtd 00; Hon C Hampton St Mary *Lon* 71-05; PtO from 05. *109 Cambridge Road, Teddington TW11 8DF* T: (020) 8977 1434 E: gfclarkson@aol.com

CLARKSON, Canon John Thomas. b 30. AKC 53. St Boniface Warminster 54. **d** 54 **p** 55. C Luton St Sav *St Alb* 54-59; Brotherhood of St Barn Australia 59-64; R Mundingburra 64-72; V Dallington *Pet* 73-77; R W Wyalong St Barn Australia 77-82; R Blayney Ch Ch 82-95; Hon Can Bathurst 95-96; rtd 96. *134 Mitre Street, Bathurst NSW 2795, Australia* T: (0061) (2) 6332 6032 E: clarkson@netwit.net.au

CLARKSON, Michael. *See* CLARKSON, Richard Michael

CLARKSON, Michael Livingston. b 48. California Univ BA 70 Loyola Univ JD 73. Wycliffe Hall Ox 87. **d** 89 **p** 90. C Kensington St Barn *Lon* 89-93; Min Oak Tree Angl Fellowship 93-04; Oman 04-06; C Bluffton Ch of the Cross USA 07-08; R Johns Island Our Sav 08-13; rtd 13. *37 Maldon Road, London W3 6SZ*

CLARKSON, Canon Richard. b 33. Man Univ BSc 54 Ball Coll Ox DPhil 57. Oak Hill Th Coll 58. **d** 91 **p** 92. NSM Sunnyside w Bourne End *St Alb* from 91; RD Berkhamsted 97-02; Hon Can St Alb from 02. *Kingsmead, Gravel Path, Berkhamsted HP4 2PH* T: (01442) 873014
E: r.sclarkson@btopenworld.com

CLARKSON, Richard Anthony. b 85. Nottm Univ BSc 06. Trin Coll Bris BA 14. **d** 14 **p** 15. C Whitchurch *Lich* from 14. *8 Bark Hill Mews, Whitchurch SY13 1DS* M: 07763-909110
E: revrichclarkson@gmail.com

CLARKSON, Richard Michael. b 38. St Jo Coll Dur BA 60 Lanc Univ PGCE 68. Cranmer Hall Dur 60. **d** 62 **p** 63. C Heyhouses on Sea *Blackb* 62-66; C Lancaster St Mary 66-68; Asst Master Kirkham Gr Sch 68-90; Asst Master Hurstpierpoint Coll 90-91; Asst Master St Mary's Hall Brighton 92-98; Chapl 96-98; rtd 93; PtO *Chich* from 93. *121 College Lane, Hurstpierpoint, Hassocks BN6 9AF* T: (01273) 834117

CLARKSON, Robert Christopher. b 32. Dur Univ BA 53 DipEd 54. S Dios Minl Tr Scheme 85. **d** 87 **p** 88. NSM Lower Dever Valley *Win* 87-03; PtO from 03. *27 Wrights Way, South Wonston, Winchester SO21 3HE* T: (01962) 881692

CLARRIDGE, Mrs Ann. b 44. Bournemouth Univ BSc 89 S Bank Univ MSc 94. SEITE 01. **d** 04 **p** 05. NSM Shepherd's Bush St Steph w St Thos *Lon* 04-07; NSM Whitton St Aug 07-11; NSM Northwood H Trin from 11. *3 Lees Avenue, Northwood HA6 1HT* E: annclarridge@hotmail.co.uk

CLARRIDGE, Donald Michael. b 41. DipOT 86. Oak Hill Th Coll 63. **d** 66 **p** 67. C Newc St Barn and St Jude 66-70; C Pennycross *Ex* 70-76; R Clayhanger 76-83; R Petton 76-83; R Huntsham 76-83; V Bampton 76-83. *Winkley, Broad Road, Hambrook, Chichester PO18 8RF* T: (01243) 576535
E: donjanwinkley@btinternet.com

CLASBY, Michael Francis Theodore. b 37. Univ Coll Lon BA 59. Chich Th Coll 59. **d** 61 **p** 62. C Leigh-on-Sea St Marg *Chelmsf* 61-64; C Forest Gate St Edm 64-69; V Walthamstow St Mich 69-70; Chapl Community of Sisters of the Love of God 87-89; PtO *St Alb* 87-89; NSM Hemel Hempstead 90-93; PtO 93-98; rtd 02. *2 Heritage Close, High Street, St Albans AL3 4EB* T: (01727) 869818 M: 07506-785442
E: michael.clasby@gmail.com

CLASPER, John. b 42. AKC 67. **d** 68 **p** 69. C Leeds All Hallows w St Simon *Ripon* 68-71; C Hawksworth Wood 72-74; Ind Chapl *Dur* 74-97; TV Jarrow St Paul 75-77; TV Jarrow 77-91; Dioc Urban Development Officer 90-91; TR E Darlington 91-97; V Fenham St Jas and St Basil *Newc* 97-02; RD Newc W 98-02; rtd 03; PtO *Newc* from 03; *Dur* from 15. *103 Warkworth Woods, Newcastle upon Tyne NE3 5RB* T: 0191-217 1325
M: 07710-078945 E: jclasper1@aol.com

CLASSON, Michael Campbell. b 32. TCD BA 52 HDipEd 54 MA 55. CITC 87. **d** 89 **p** 91. NSM Conwal Union w Gartan *D & R* 89-90; NSM Ardara w Glencolumbkille, Inniskeel etc from 90. *Summy, Portnoo, Co Donegal, Republic of Ireland* T: (00353) (74) 954 5242

CLATWORTHY, Jonathan Richard. b 48. Univ of Wales BA 70. Sarum & Wells Th Coll 71. **d** 76 **p** 77. C Man Resurr 76-78; C Bolton St Pet 78-81; V Ashton St Pet 81-85; Chapl Sheff Univ 85-91; V Denstone w Ellastone and Stanton *Lich* 91-98; Chapl Liv Univ 98-02; rtd 02; PtO *Liv* from 04. *9 Westward View, Aigburth, Liverpool L17 7EE* T: 0151-727 6291
E: jonathan@clatworthy.org

CLAVIER, Mark Forbes Moreton. b 70. Coll of Wm & Mary (USA) AB 93 Duke Univ (USA) MTS 95 St Chad's Coll Dur PhD 11. **d** 95 **p** 96. C Langley Park, Hamsteels, Esh and Waterhouses *Dur* 09-10; P-in-c Steeple Aston w N Aston and Tackley *Ox* 11-13; Dean of Res Tr St Mich Coll Llan from 13; PtO *Llan* from 14. *St Michael's College, 54 Cardiff Road, Llandaff, Cardiff CF5 2YJ* T: (029) 2056 3379
M: 07531-856943 E: mark.clavier@gmail.com

CLAXTON, Mrs Claire Marie. b 58. R Academy of Music BMus 79 LRAM 78 K Alfred's Coll Win PGCE 80. STETS 12. **d** 14 **p** 15. NSM Guernsey St Martin *Win* from 14. *Carillon, Rue des Bailleuls, St Andrew, Guernsey GY6 8XB* T: (01481) 238815 M: 07781-433225 E: carillon@cwgsy.net

CLAY, Canon Colin Peter. b 32. Ch Coll Cam BA 55 MA 59. Em Coll Saskatoon Hon DD 91 Wells Th Coll 55. **d** 57 **p** 58. C Malden St Jas *S'wark* 57-59; C Sudbury Epiphany Canada 59-60; R Sudbury St Jas 60-69; C Sudbury St George 60-64; R French River St Thos 64-69; Asst Prof RS Laurentian Univ 69-72; R Capreol St Alb 70-77; Chapl Saskatchewan Univ 77-00; Hon Can Saskatoon from 97; Interim I St Jo Cathl 00-01; Hon Asst from 01. *812 Colony Street, Saskatoon SK SN7 0S1, Canada* T: (001) (306) 664 4628
E: clay@sask.usask.ca

CLAY, Canon Elizabeth Jane. b 50. MBE 06. Ridley Hall Cam. **dss** 86 **d** 87 **p** 94. Birstall *Wakef* 86-87; Hon Par Dn Lupset 87-90; Par Dn 90-94; C 94-96; Chapl HM Pris and YOI New Hall 96-10; Hon Can Wakef Cathl 00-10; rtd 10. *43 Hollybank Avenue, Upper Cumberworth, Huddersfield HD8 8NY* T: (01484) 603051 E: ejclay@ejclay.demon.co.uk

CLAY, Geoffrey. b 51. CertEd. Ridley Hall Cam. **d** 86 **p** 87. C Birstall *Wakef* 86-90; V Lupset 90-03; P-in-c Marsden 03-10; P-in-c Kirkburton *Leeds* from 10; P-in-c Cumberworth, Denby and Denby Dale from 10; Min Development Officer from 03. *43 Hollybank Avenue, Upper Cumberworth, Huddersfield HD8 8NY* T: (01484) 603051 E: geoff@ejclay.demon.co.uk

CLAY, Peter Herbert. b 31. Lich Th Coll 62. **d** 64 **p** 65. C Ross *Heref* 64-67; C Leamington Priors All SS *Cov* 67-70; P-in-c Temple Grafton w Binton 70-73; V 73-75; P-in-c Exhall w Wixford 70-73; R 73-75; TV Cen Telford *Lich* 75-86; USPG 86-90; V Loughb Gd Shep *Leic* 90-96; rtd 96; PtO *Leic* from 96; *Cov* from 96. *c/o T Clay Esq, 8 Queensferry Close, Rugby CV22 7LH*

CLAY, Timothy Francis. b 61. St Mark & St Jo Coll Lon BA 85 Ealing Coll of Educn 89. Linc Th Coll 95. **d** 95 **p** 96. C Wickford and Runwell *Chelmsf* 95-98; C S Ockendon 98-01; C S Ockendon and Belhus Park 01-02; P-in-c Ashingdon w S Fambridge 02-10; P-in-c Canewdon w Paglesham 03-10; R Ashingdon w S Fambridge, Canewdon and Paglesham from 10. *The Rectory, Church Road, Rochford SS4 3HY* T: (01702) 549318 E: timbo9@hotmail.com

CLAYDEN, David Edward. b 42. Oak Hill Th Coll 74. **d** 76 **p** 77. C Worksop St Jo *S'well* 76-79; V Clarborough w Hayton 79-84; C Bloxwich *Lich* 87-90; TV 90-93; TV Tollington *Lon* 93-99; P-in-c Thorndon w Rishangles, Stoke Ash, Thwaite etc *St E* 99-00; P-in-c Thornhams Magna and Parva, Gislingham and Mellis 99-00; R S Hartismere 00-06; rtd 06. *151 Southview Road, Carlton, Nottingham NG4 3QT* T: 0115-987 2690
E: david.clayden@boltblue.com

CLAYDON, Preb Graham Leonard. b 43. K Coll Lon BA 65. Clifton Th Coll 66. **d** 68 **p** 69. C Walthamstow St Mary w St Steph *Chelmsf* 68-71; C St Marylebone All So w SS Pet and Jo *Lon* 71-73; Hon C 73-81; Warden All So Clubhouse 71-81; V Islington St Mary *Lon* 81-99; Dioc Ev (Stepney) and C Highbury Ch Ch w St Jo and St Sav 99-03; TV Hackney Marsh 03-06; Preb St Paul's Cathl 92-06; rtd 07. *Acre End, Tangmere Road, Tangmere, Chichester PO20 2HW* T: (01243) 536789 E: graham@lclaydon.fsnet.co.uk

CLAYDON, John Richard. b 38. St Jo Coll Cam BA 61 MA 65. Trin Coll Bris 71. **d** 73 **p** 74. C Finchley Ch Ch *Lon* 73-76; Asst Chapl K Edw Sch Witley 76-77; C Macclesfield St Mich *Ches* 77-81; V Marple All SS 81-91; CMJ Israel 91-99; V Blackb Redeemer 99-02; rtd 02; PtO *Chelmsf* from 03. *54 Old Forge Road, Layer-de-la-Haye, Colchester CO2 0LH* T: (01206) 734056
E: john@claydon4295.freeserve.co.uk

CLAYTON, Adam. b 78. Keble Coll Ox BA 99. Westcott Ho Cam 00. **d** 02 **p** 03. C Far Headingley St Chad *Ripon* 02-06; TV Seacroft 06-08; Chapl Leeds Teaching Hosps NHS Trust from 10. *47 St James Approach, Leeds LS14 6JJ* T: 0113-294 0414 M: 07834-827294 E: revdaclayton@aol.com

CLAYTON, Adam Jonathan Barnett. b 56. **d** 06 **p** 07. OLM Icknield *Ox* 06-12; P-in-c Myddle *Lich* from 12; P-in-c Broughton from 12; P-in-c Loppington w Newtown from 12; RD Wem and Whitchurch from 15. *The Rectory, Myddle, Shrewsbury SY4 3RX* T: (01939) 291801
E: adam@ajbc.fsnet.co.uk

CLAYTON, Benjamin Theo. b 90. Nottm Univ BA 11. Wycliffe Hall Ox 13. **d** 15. C Nottingham St Jude *S'well* from 15. *21 Corby Road, Nottingham NG3 5HF*

CLAYTON, Geoffrey Buckroyd. b 26. Newc Univ BA 67. Roch Th Coll 62. **d** 64 **p** 65. C Newc St Geo 64-67; C Byker St Ant 67-68; Chapl Salonika *Eur* 68-69; C Cheddleton *Lich* 69-72; V Arbory *S & M* 72-97; RD Castletown 82-97; V Santan 88-97; rtd 97; PtO *St D* from 97. *The Cottage, Hendre Mynach Caravan Park, Llanaber Road, Barmouth LL42 1YR* T: (01341) 280409 E: revgbclayton@hotmail.co.uk

CLAYTON, Canon John. b 11. Leeds Univ BA 33 MA 43. Wells Th Coll 34. **d** 35 **p** 36. C Dewsbury Moor *Wakef* 35-38; C Halifax St Jo Bapt 38-41; Lect 40-41; V Lupset 41-51; Chapl Snapethorpe Hosp 49-51; V Bolton St Jas *Bradf* 51-65; RD Calverley 56-65; V Otley 65-76; RD 68-73; Hon Can Bradf Cathl 63-76; rtd 76; PtO *Leeds* from 76. *24 Ashcroft House, 18 Leeds Road, Bramhope, Leeds LS16 9BQ* T: 0113-284 1272

CLAYTON, Melanie Yvonne. *See* SANTORINI, Melanie Yvonne

CLAYTON, Paul. b 47. Cranmer Hall Dur 03. **d** 04 **p** 05. NSM Elton and Preston-on-Tees and Longnewton *Dur* 04-06; NSM Bishopton w Gt Stainton 06-13; NSM Redmarshall 06-13; NSM Grindon, Stillington and Wolviston 06-13;

NSM Billingham St Mary 09-13; rtd 13; PtO *Dur* from 13. *144 Darlington Lane, Stockton-on-Tees TS19 0NG* T: (01642) 607233 E: pclayton@tinyonline.co.uk

CLAYTON, William Alan. b 32. Liv Univ BSc 54 Lon Univ BD 60. **d** 63 **p** 64. C Wallasey St Hilary *Ches* 63-67; R Burton Agnes w Harpham *York* 67-69; V Batley St Thos *Wakef* 69-72; LtO *Ripon* 73-85; Hon C Grinton 75-85; R Barningham w Hutton Magna and Wycliffe *Ripon* 85-97; rtd 97; PtO *Newc* from 00. *Halidon View, 1 The Pastures, Tweedmouth, Berwick-upon-Tweed TD15 2NT*

CLEALL, Mary Jane Anne. *See* LINDSAY, Mary Jane Anne

CLEALL-HILL, Malcolm John. b 51. Salford Univ Man Metrop Univ. **d** 01 **p** 02. OLM Chorlton-cum-Hardy St Werburgh *Man* 01-11; rtd 11; PtO *Man* from 11. *62 Buckingham Road, Chorlton cum Hardy, Manchester M21 0RP* T: 0161-881 7024 *or* 247 2288 E: m.cleall-hill@mmu.ac.uk

CLEATON, John. b 39. Open Univ BA 86. S Dios Minl Tr Scheme 89. **d** 92 **p** 93. NSM Wareham *Sarum* 92-02. *1 Avon Drive, Wareham BH20 4EL* T: (01929) 553149

CLEATON, Mrs Nancy Thomas. b 45. Lon Bible Coll BD 67. WEMTC 05. **d** 07 **p** 08. NSM Church Stretton *Heref* 07-12; P-in-c Hope Bowdler w Eaton-under-Heywood 12-13; P-in-c Rushbury 12-13; P-in-c Cardington 12-13; R Apedale Gp from 13. *The Rectory, Hope Bowdler, Church Stretton SY6 7DD* T: (01694) 328132 E: nancy.cleaton@tiscali.co.uk

CLEATON, Sheena Faith. b 74. Colchester Inst BA 97 R Holloway Coll Lon MMus 02 PhD 07. Ripon Coll Cuddesdon 09. **d** 11 **p** 12. C Bourne *Linc* from 11. *20 Tilia Way, Bourne PE10 0QR* T: (01778) 395626 E: sheena_cleaton@hotmail.com

CLEAVER, Gordon Philip. b 29. SWMTC. **d** 78 **p** 79. NSM St Ruan w St Grade *Truro* 78-86; PtO from 86. *Bryn-Mor, Cadgwith, Ruan Minor, Helston TR12 7JZ* T: (01326) 290328

CLEAVER, John Martin. b 42. K Coll Lon BD 64 AKC 64. St Boniface Warminster 61. **d** 65 **p** 66. C Bexley St Mary *Roch* 65-69; C Ealing St Steph Castle Hill *Lon* 69-71; P-in-c Bostall Heath *Roch* 71-76; V Green Street Green 76-85; Primary Adv Lon Dioc Bd for Schs 85-92; V Teddington St Mary w St Alb 92-08; rtd 08. *5 Oaklands, Westham, Pevensey BN24 5AW* T: (01323) 769964 E: jmcleaver@hotmail.co.uk

CLEAVER, Stuart Douglas. b 46. ACIS. Oak Hill Th Coll. **d** 83 **p** 84. C Portsdown *Portsm* 83-86; C Blendworth w Chalton w Idsworth etc 86-88; P-in-c Whippingham w E Cowes 88-98; R 98-01; rtd 01. *The Crest, Soake Road, Waterlooville PO7 6HY* T: (023) 9226 2277

CLEE, Mrs Norma. b 53. Lindisfarne Regional Tr Partnership 13. **d** 15. NSM Eighton Banks *Dur* from 15. *19 Cromarty, Outston, Chester le Street DH2 1LA* T: 0191-492 0293 M: 07964-029986 E: normaclee@icloud.com

CLEEVE, Admire William. b 43. Ox Univ MTh 96 ACIS 78 MBIM 81. Sierra Leone Th Hall 78. **d** 82 **p** 83. Sierra Leone 82-86; NSM Douglas St Geo and St Barn *S & M* 87-91; TV Langley Marish *Ox* 91-97; P-in-c Tilehurst St Mary 97-02; rtd 02. *5346 Bressler Drive, Hilliard OH 43026-9401, USA* T: (001) (614) 219 8407

CLEEVE, Martin. b 43. Bp Otter Coll TCert 65 ACP 67 Open Univ BA 80. Oak Hill Th Coll 69. **d** 72 **p** 73. C Margate H Trin *Cant* 72-76; V Southminster *Chelmsf* 76-86; Teacher Castle View Sch Canvey Is 86-91; Hd RE Bromfords Sch Wickford 91-94; Hd RE Deanes Sch Thundersley 94-98; P-in-c Gt Mongeham w Ripple and Sutton by Dover *Cant* 99-04; rtd 04; PtO *Cant* from 04; Chapl Kent & Medway NHS and Soc Care Partnership Trust from 08. *Euphony, Waldershare Road, Ashley, Dover CT15 5JA* E: martincleeve@mcleeve.freeserve.co.uk

CLEEVES, David John. b 56. Univ of Wales (Lamp) BA Fitzw Coll Cam MA 85. Westcott Ho Cam. **d** 82 **p** 83. C Cuddington *Guildf* 82-85; C Dorking w Ranmore 85-87; V Ewell St Fran 87-94; P-in-c Rotherfield w Mark Cross *Chich* 94-01; V Masham and Healey *Leeds* from 01; Jt AD Ripon 04-05; AD 05-09. *The Vicarage, Rodney Terrace, Masham, Ripon HG4 4JA* T: (01765) 689255 E: cleevesmasham@onetel.com

CLEGG, Anthony. *See* CLEGG, John Anthony Holroyd

CLEGG, Canon John Anthony Holroyd. b 44. Kelham Th Coll 65. **d** 70 **p** 71. C Heyhouses on Sea *Blackb* 70-74; C Lancaster St Mary 74-76; V Lower Darwen St Jas 76-80; TV Shaston *Sarum* 80-86; Chapl HM Youth Cust Cen Guys Marsh 80-86; R Poulton-le-Sands w Morecambe St Laur *Blackb* 86-97; RD Lancaster 89-94; TR Cartmel Peninsula *Carl* 97-04; RD Windermere 01-04; P-in-c Appleby 04-08; P-in-c Ormside 04-08; TR Heart of Eden 08-09; RD Appleby 04-09; Hon Can Carl Cathl 01-09; rtd 09; PtO *Carl* from 09; *Blackb* from 10. *33 Mayfield Road, Holme, Carnforth LA6 1PT* T: (01524) 784752 E: anthonyclegg@talktalk.net

CLEGG, John Lovell. b 48. Qu Coll Ox BA 70 MA 74. Trin Coll Bris. **d** 75 **p** 76. C Barrow St Mark *Carl* 75-79; R S Levenshulme

Man 79-98; P-in-c Blackley St Paul 98-10; rtd 10; PtO *Man* from 11. *5 Mough Lane, Chadderton, Oldham OL9 9NT* T: 0161-684 1226

CLEGG, Patricia Ann. b 45. STETS 96. **d** 99 **p** 00. NSM Harnham *Sarum* 99-03; PtO 03-05; NSM Bemerton 05-07; NSM Arle Valley *Win* 07-11; rtd 11. *24 Arle Close, Alresford SO24 9BG* T: (01962) 736566 E: pat@clegg1.demon.co.uk

CLEGG, Peter Douglas. b 49. Sarum & Wells Th Coll 83. **d** 85 **p** 86. C Hangleton *Chich* 85-88; C-in-c Portslade Gd Shep CD 88-94; V Portslade Gd Shep 94-09; rtd 10. *11 Maplehurst Road, Portslade, Brighton BN41 2LR* T: (01273) 382913 E: fatherpeterclegg_ssc@yahoo.co.uk

CLEGG, Roger Alan. b 46. St Jo Coll Dur BA 68 Nottm Univ CertEd 69. St Jo Coll Nottm 75. **d** 78 **p** 79. C Harwood *Man* 78-81; TV Sutton St Jas and Wawne *York* 81-87; V Kirk Fenton w Kirkby Wharfe and Ulleskelfe 87-09; Chapl HM Pris Askham Grange from 95; PtO *York* from 09. HM Prison Askham Grange, *Askham Richard, York YO23 3FT* T: (01904) 772014 *or* (01757) 268060 M: 07957-474030 E: rogclegg@dunelm.org.uk

CLELAND, Miss Lucy Eleanor. b 74. Aston Univ BSc 97 Cam Univ BTh 05. Ridley Hall Cam 02. **d** 05 **p** 06. C Yaxley and Holme w Conington *Ely* 05-08; P-in-c Landbeach and Waterbeach 08-11; Bp's Dom Chapl *S'well* from 11. *Jubilee House, Westgate, Southwell NG25 0JH* T: (01636) 817996 E: chaplain@southwell.anglican.org *or* lecleland@hotmail.com

CLELAND, Richard. b 26. Belf Coll of Tech MPS 47. St Aid Birkenhead 58. **d** 60 **p** 61. C Lisburn Ch Ch *Conn* 60-63; C Ballynafeigh St Jude *D & D* 63-66; C Portman Square St Paul *Lon* 66-67; V Ilkley All SS *Bradf* 67-83; Master Wyggeston's Hosp Leic 83-97; PtO *S'well* 97-02; rtd 97. *23 Stuart Court, High Street, Kibworth, Leicester LE8 0LR* T: 0116-279 6245

CLELAND, Trevor. b 66. QUB BTh 94 TCD MPhil 97. CITC 94. **d** 96 **p** 97. C Lisburn Ch Ch *Conn* 96-99; C Carrickfergus 99-03; I Belfast Upper Falls 03-12; I Ballinderry from 12. *Ballinderry Rectory, 124 Ballinderry Road, Ballinderry Upper, Lisburn BT28 2NL* T: (028) 9265 0134 M: 07875-361682 E: tcleland@btinternet.com

CLEMAS, Preb Nigel Antony. b 53. Wycliffe Hall Ox. **d** 83 **p** 84. C Bootle St Mary w St Paul *Liv* 83-87; V Kirkdale St Mary and St Athanasius 87-91; TV Netherthorpe *Sheff* 91-93; V Netherthorpe St Steph 93-98; R Chapel Chorlton, Maer and Whitmore *Lich* from 98; RD Eccleshall from 00; Preb Lich Cathl from 13. *The Rectory, Snape Hall Road, Whitmore, Newcastle ST5 5HS* T: (01782) 680258 E: nclemas@hotmail.com

CLEMENCE, Paul Robert Fraser. b 50. St Edm Hall Ox MA 90 MRTPI 82. Wycliffe Hall Ox 88. **d** 90 **p** 91. C Lancaster St Mary *Blackb* 90-94; Chapl HM Pris Lanc Castle 90-94; V Lt Thornton *Blackb* from 94; AD Poulton 00-09. *St John's Vicarage, 35 Station Road, Thornton-Cleveleys FY5 5HY* T/F: (01253) 825107 E: p.clemence@tiscali.co.uk

CLEMENT, Geoffrey Paul. b 69. **d** 94 **p** 96. Jardines del Hipódromo St Aug Uruguay 94-96; Colón St Jas Miss 95-97; Barrio Fátima Salto St Luke w H Spirit 97-01; TV Wilford Peninsula *St E* 01-07; R Holbrook, Stutton, Freston, Woolverstone etc from 07. *The Rectory, 15 Denmark Gardens, Holbrook, Ipswich IP9 2BG* T: (01473) 327141 M: 07955-721332 E: revgclement@btinternet.com

CLEMENT, Paskal. b 63. Punjab Univ BA 92 Univ of Wales MA 08. Nat Catholic Inst of Th Karachi 82. **d** 88 **p** 88. Pakistan 88-01; NSM Hounslow H Trin w St Paul and St Mary *Lon* 04-08; C Oadby *Leic* 08-13; P-in-c Leic Resurr from 13. *St Alban's House, Weymouth Street, Leicester LE4 6FN* M: 07727-286905 E: paskalm@yahoo.com

CLEMENT, Peter James. b 64. UMIST BSc 88 Man Univ MA 98. Qu Coll Birm 89. **d** 92 **p** 93. C Grange St Andr *Ches* 92-95; C Man Apostles w Miles Platting 95-97; TV Uggeshall w Sotherton, Wangford and Henham *St E* 97-99; TV Sole Bay 99-00; Dioc Youth Officer 01-02; V Fairweather Green *Bradf* 02-07; Assoc Dioc Dir of Ords 04-07; Dioc Dir of Ords *Ripon* 07-14; Dir of Ords *Leeds* 14-15; Voc Development Officer and Dir of Ords; Carl from 15. *Church House, West Walls, Carlisle CA3 8UE* T: (01228) 522573

CLEMENT, Richard Percy. b 63. Bris Univ BA 85. ERMC 04. **d** 06 **p** 08. C Framlingham w Saxtead *St E* 06-09; Chapl RAF from 09. *Chaplaincy Services (RAF), HQ Air Command, RAF High Wycombe HP14 4UE* T: (01494) 496800 F: 496343 E: revd.richard@btinternet.com

CLEMENT, Thomas Gwyn. b 51. Lon Univ BMus 73 Goldsmiths' Coll Lon PGCE 74 LRAM 73 LTCL 74. St Steph Ho Ox. **d** 93 **p** 94. C Friern Barnet St Jas *Lon* 93-96; V Edmonton St Alphege 96-04; P-in-c Ponders End St Matt 02-04; AD Enfield 01-04; V Hendon St Mary and Ch Ch from 04; Warden of Readers Edmonton Area from 08; AD W

Barnet 09-14. *The Vicarage, 34 Parson Street, London NW4 1QR* T: (020) 8203 2884 E: fr.gwyn@btinternet.com

CLEMENT, Canon Timothy Gordon. b 54. Trin Coll Bris 92. **d** 94 **p** 95. C Chepstow *Mon* 94-97; R Bettws Newydd w Trostrey etc 97-14; R Raglan Gp from 14; Rural Min Adv from 02; AD Raglan-Usk from 05; Can St Woolos Cathl from 08. *The Rectory, Bettws Newydd, Usk NP15 1JN* T: (01873) 880258 E: timtherec@outlook.com

CLEMENTS, Alan Austin. b 39. Newc Univ MA 93 ACIB 66 FCIE 05. Linc Th Coll 74. **d** 76 **p** 77. C Woodley St Jo the Ev *Ox* 76-79; C Wokingham All SS 79-83; V Felton *Newc* 83-95; P-in-c Wallsend St Pet 95-01; rtd 01; PtO *Newc* 01-06; *Blackb* from 07; *Man* from 09. *15 Carleton Road, Chorley PR6 8TQ* T/F: (01257) 271782 E: fr_alan@btinternet.com

CLEMENTS, Andrew. b 48. K Coll Lon BD 72 AKC 72 Leeds Univ MA 02. St Aug Coll Cant 72. **d** 73 **p** 74. C Langley All SS and Martyrs *Man* 73-76; C Westhoughton 76-81; R Thornton Dale w Ellerburne and Wilton *York* 81-89; Prec Leic Cathl 89-91; V Market Weighton *York* 91-97; R Goodmanham 91-97; V Osbaldwick w Murton from 97; RD Derwent from 11. *The Vicarage, 80 Osbaldwick Lane, York YO10 3AX* T: (01904) 416763 E: andrew@ozmurt.freeserve.co.uk

CLEMENTS, Miss Christine Hilda. b 49. Ex Univ BTh 04. SWMTC 99. **d** 02 **p** 03. C Halsetown *Truro* 02-05; Zambia 05-07; PtO *Nor* 07; TR Thamesmead *S'wark* 07-13; rtd 13. *20 Penbeagle Crescent, St Ives TR26 2JG* T: (01736) 796454 M: 07852-476805 E: chris_clements1@btinternet.com

CLEMENTS, Canon Doris Thomasina Sara. b 46. TCD BA 68 MA 90. CITC 92. **d** 95 **p** 96. NSM Killala w Dunfeeny, Crossmolina, Kilmoremoy etc *T, K & A* 95-14; Dioc C from 14; Can Achonry Cathl 05-11 and from 13; Can Tuam Cathl from 11. *Doobeg House, Bunninadden, Ballymote, Co Sligo, Republic of Ireland* T: (00353) (71) 918 5425 F: 918 5255 M: 86-249 7806 E: doristsclements@gmail.com

CLEMENTS, Miss Mary Holmes. b 43. Bedf Coll Lon BA 64 Lon Inst of Educn PGCE 69. Ox Min Course 92. **d** 94 **p** 95. NSM High Wycombe *Ox* 94-01; C N Petherton w Northmoor Green and N Newton w St Michaelchurch, Thurloxton etc *B & W* 01-03; C Alfred Jewel 03-10; rtd 10; PtO *B & W* from 12. *18 Meadway, Woolavington, Bridgwater TA7 8HA* T: (01278) 683099 E: kharaclements@btinternet.com

CLEMENTS, Philip Christian. b 38. K Coll Lon BD 64 AKC 64. **d** 65 **p** 66. C S Norwood St Mark *Cant* 65-68; Chapl R Russell Sch Croydon 68-75; Asst Chapl Denstone Coll Uttoxeter 75-76; Chapl 76-81; Chapl Lancing Coll 82-90; R Ninfield *Chich* 90-99; V Hooe 90-99; rtd 99; PtO *Cant* from 95; Chapl St Bart Hosp Sandwich from 04; Hon Chapl Northbourne Park Sch from 12. *21 Swaynes Way, Eastry, Sandwich CT13 0JP* T: (01304) 617413 or 613982 E: philip@philipclements.co.uk

CLEMENTS, Philip John Charles. b 42. Nottm Univ CertEd 64 Loughb Univ Hon BA 09. Ridley Hall Cam. **d** 85 **p** 86. C Aylestone St Andr w St Jas *Leic* 85-87; P-in-c Swinford w Catthorpe, Shawell and Stanford 87-91; V 91-99; Dioc Rural Officer 91-96; RD Guthlaxton II 94-99; P-in-c N w S Kilworth and Misterton 96-99; P-in-c Barrowden and Wakerley w S Luffenham *Pet* 99-02; R Barrowden and Wakerley w S Luffenham etc 03-06; RD Barnack 00-06; rtd 06; PtO *Pet* from 06; *Leic* from 07. *Clementine Cottage, 51 Laughton Road, Lubenham, Market Harborough LE16 9TE* T/F: (01858) 432548 E: pipclements2@tiscali.co.uk

CLEMENTS, Robert Williams. **d** 12 **p** 13. C Dublin Rathfarnham *D & G* 12-13; C Enniskillen *Clogh* from 13. *2 Halls Lane, Enniskillen BT74 7DR* M: 07902-896806 T: (028) 6632 2421 E: rob4t@hotmail.com *or* rclements@clogher.anglican.org

CLEMENTS, Canon Roy Adrian. b 44. St Chad's Coll Dur BA 68 MA 74. **d** 69 **p** 70. C Royston *Wakef* 69-73; V Clifton 73-77; V Rastrick St Matt 77-84; Dioc Communications Officer 84-98; V Horbury Junction 84-92; Bp's Chapl 92-00; V Battyeford 00-08; Hon Can Wakef Cathl 94-08; rtd 08; PtO *Leeds* from 08. *12 Castle Crescent, Sandal, Wakefield WF2 7HX* T: (01924) 251834 E: royaclements@tiscali.co.uk

CLEMENTS, Mrs Virginia. b 47. Weymouth Coll of Educn CertEd 68. **d** 13 **p** 14. OLM Apedale Gp *Heref* from 13. *Rock Edge, 3 Windle Hill, Church Stretton SY6 7AP* T: (01694) 724078 E: virginia_clements@me.com

CLEMETT, Peter Thomas. b 33. Univ of Wales (Lamp) BA 60. Sarum Th Coll 59. **d** 61 **p** 62. C Tredegar St Geo *Mon* 61-63; Chapl St Woolos Cathl 63-66; CF 66-99; Chapl R Memorial Chpl Sandhurst 84-88; rtd 88; OCM from 99; PtO *Win* from 01. *Silver Birches, Gardeners Lane, East Wellow, Romsey SO51 6AD* T: (023) 8081 4261

CLEMOW (née WINDER), Cynthia Frances. b 48. SWMTC 02. **d** 05 **p** 06. NSM Bodmin w Lanhydrock and Lanivet *Truro* from 05. *Denton, 2 Boxwell Park, Bodmin PL31 2BB* T: (01208) 73306

CLENCH, Brian Henry Ross. b 31. Ripon Coll Cuddesdon. **d** 82 **p** 83. C Fulham All SS *Lon* 82-85; Ind Chapl *Truro* 85-92; P-in-c St Mewan 85-92; rtd 92; PtO *Sarum* from 96. *Stable Cottage, St Tudy, Bodmin PL30 3NP* T: (01208) 851809

CLEPHANE, Alexander Honeyman. b 48. **d** 97 **p** 98. OLM Flixton St Mich *Man* 97-11; NSM from 11. *306 Church Road, Urmston, Manchester M41 6JJ* T: 0161-747 8816 M: 07798-613291

CLEUGH, David Robert. b 80. New Coll Ox MA 07. Ripon Coll Cuddesdon BTh 09. **d** 09 **p** 10. C Dorchester *Ox* 09-13; P-in-c Leadgate *Dur* from 13; P-in-c Ebchester from 14; P-in-c Medomsley from 14. *The Vicarage, St Ives Road, Consett DH8 7SN* T: (01207) 509654 M: 07805-332979 E: david.cleugh@btinternet.com

CLEUGH, Hannah Felicity. b 81. Worc Coll Ox MA 08 MSt 04 DPhil 07. Ripon Coll Cuddesdon 07. **d** 09 **p** 10. C Dorchester *Ox* 09-12; Chapl Univ Coll Dur from 13. *University College, The Castle, Palace Green, Durham DH1 3RW* T: 0191-334 4116 *or* (01207) 509654 M: 07854-143605 E: hannah.cleugh@dur.ac.uk *or* hannah.cleugh@yahoo.co.uk

CLEVELAND, Michael Robin. b 52. Warwick Univ BA 73. St Jo Coll Nottm 86 Serampore Th Coll BD 88. **d** 88 **p** 89. C Bushbury *Lich* 88-92; V Foleshill St Laur *Cov* from 92. *St Laurence's Vicarage, 142 Old Church Road, Coventry CV6 7ED* T: (024) 7668 8271

CLEVELAND, Archdeacon of. *See* RUSHTON, The Ven Samantha Jayne

CLEVERLEY, Michael Frank. b 36. Man Univ BScTech 57. Wells Th Coll 61. **d** 63 **p** 64. C Halifax St Aug *Wakef* 63; C Huddersfield St Jo 63-66; C Brighouse 66-69; V Gomersal 69-83; P-in-c Clayton W w High Hoyland 83-89; P-in-c Scissett St Aug 83-89; R High Hoyland, Scissett and Clayton W 89-96; rtd 96; Hon C Leathley w Farnley, Fewston and Blubberhouses *Bradf* 96-04; PtO *Leeds* from 04. *86 Riverside Park, Otley LS21 2RW* E: michael.cleverley@bradford.anglican.org

CLEVERLY, Canon Charles St George. b 51. St Jo Coll Ox MA 75 Goldsmiths' Coll Lon PGCE 76. Trin Coll Bris 79. **d** 82 **p** 83. C Cranham Park *Chelmsf* 82-89; V 89-92; Crosslinks Paris 92-02; R Ox St Aldate from 02; Hon Can Ch Ch from 15. *Holy Trinity House, 19 Turn Again Lane, Oxford OX1 1QL* T: (01865) 254800 E: charlie.cleverly@staldates.org.uk

CLEWS, Nicholas. b 57. SS Coll Cam BA 80 MA 84 Leeds Univ BA 87 CIPFA 85. Coll of Resurr Mirfield 85. **d** 88 **p** 89. C S Elmsall *Wakef* 88-91; V Featherstone 91-07; P-in-c Purston cum S Featherstone 04-07; P-in-c Thornbury *Leeds* from 07; P-in-c Woodhall from 07. *St James's Vicarage, Galloway Lane, Pudsey LS28 8JR* T: (01274) 662735 M: 07985-091748 E: n.clews@sky.com

CLIFF, Frank Graham. b 38. St Paul's Coll Chelt TCert 60. Clifton Th Coll 63. **d** 66 **p** 67. C Leic St Chris 66-69; C Whitton and Thurleston w Akenham *St E* 69-71; Asst R Houston St Thos USA 71-72; Asst R Waco St Alb 72-74; Asst R Potomac St Jas 74-78; R Denton Ch Ch 78-85; V Pittsburgh St Phil 86-87; R Pittsburgh Advent Ch 87-94; R Honesdale Grace Ch 94-03. *15 Bede Circle, Honesdale PA 18431-7625, USA* T: (001) (570) 253 4535 E: cliffam@ptd.net

CLIFF, Frank William. b 51. ERMC. **d** 14 **p** 15. OLM Gt Yarmouth *Nor* from 14. *2 Barrack Road, Great Yarmouth NR30 3DR* T: (01493) 851097 E: fwc1234@gmail.com

CLIFF, Julian Arnold. b 41. Univ Coll Ches BEd 86. Cranmer Hall Dur 63. **d** 66 **p** 67. C Bowdon *Ches* 66-69; C Poynton 69-73; P-in-c Crewe St Barn 73-74; V 74-79; Hon C Higher Bebington 98-00; PtO from 06. *15 Sandy Lane, Heswall, Wirral CH60 5SX* T: 0151-342 3230 M: 07980-379699 E: julianann.cliff@talktalk.net

CLIFFE, Canon Christopher George. b 47. CITC 94. **d** 97 **p** 98. C Fiddown w Clonegam, Guilcagh and Kilmeaden *C & O* 97-00; I 00-13; Bp's Dom Chapl 97-13; Can Ossory Cathl 07-13; rtd 13. *Hawthorn, 51 Fan Glas, Kilmeaden, Waterford, Republic of Ireland* M: 87-236 8682 T: (00353) (51) 399699 E: cgc2@eircom.net

CLIFFORD, Bruce Douglas. b 52. Birm Univ BA 73 Southn Univ MSocSc 76. Trin Coll Bris 09. **d** 11 **p** 12. NSM Glouc St Cath 11-15; NSM Glouc St Geo w Whaddon 15; V from 15. *10 Carne Place, Gloucester GL4 3BE* T: (01452) 302238 E: clifftopps@btinternet.com

CLIFFORD, Erin Chrisanne. b 77. James Madison Univ USA BS 98. Gordon-Conwell Th Sem MDiv 06. **d** 08 **p** 09. C Ches Square St Mich w St Phil *Lon* 08-11; C Onslow Square and S Kensington St Aug 11-13; USA from 13. *Address temp unknown* E: clifford_erin@yahoo.com

CLIFFORD, Paula Margaret. b 45. **d** 11 **p** 12. NSM Ox St Giles and SS Phil and Jas w St Marg 11-13; NSM Akeman 13-14; P-in-c Minster Lovell from 14; Deanery Miss Enabler from 14. *3 Pound Close, Kirtlington, Kidlington OX5 3JR* T: (018869) 350806 E: pm.clifford@virgin.net

CLIFFORD, Raymond Augustine. b 45. Coll of Resurr Mirfield 91. **d** 93 **p** 94. C Saltdean *Chich* 93-96. *124 Arnold Estate, Druid Street, London SE1 2DT* T: (020) 7232 2439 E: raylondonbb@hotmail.com

CLIFFORD, Miss Susan Frances. b 58. Qu Univ Kingston Ontario BA 87. Westcott Ho Cam 02. **d** 04 **p** 05. C Winchmore Hill St Paul *Lon* 04-08; Canada from 08. *54 Kinsman Crescent, Arnprior ON K7S 1V6, Canada* E: susanclif@hotmail.com

CLIFTON, Canon Robert Walter. b 39. Solicitor . Westcott Ho Cam 82. **d** 84 **p** 85. C Bury St Edmunds St Geo *St E* 84-87; P-in-c Culford, W Stow and Wordwell 87-88; R Culford, W Stow and Wordwell w Flempton etc 88-95; P-in-c Fornham All SS and Fornham St Martin w Timworth 93-95; RD Thingoe 93-95; P-in-c Orford w Sudbourne, Chillesford, Butley and Iken 95-00; P-in-c Eyke w Bromeswell, Rendlesham, Tunstall etc 98-99; TR Wilford Peninsula 00-05; RD Woodbridge 96-04; Hon Can St E Cathl 00-05; rtd 05; PtO *Nor* from 05; *St E* from 05. *12 Stan Petersen Close, Norwich NR1 4QJ* T: (01603) 631758 M: 07713-237754 E: cliftonrobert@sky.com

CLIFTON, Canon Roger Gerald. b 45. ACA 70 FCA. Sarum & Wells Th Coll 70. **d** 73 **p** 74. C Winterbourne *Bris* 73-76; P-in-c Brislington St Cuth 76-83; P-in-c Colerne w N Wraxall 83-95; RD Chippenham 88-94; Hon Can Bris Cathl 94-09; TR Gtr Corsham 95-01; TR Gtr Corsham and Lacock 01-09; rtd 09; PtO *B & W* from 11. *20 Southcot Place, Bath BA2 4PE* T: (01225) 330211 M: 07762-324596 E: rogerclifton@btinternet.com

CLIFTON, Sharon. b 66. **d** 07 **p** 08. C St Illogan *Truro* 07-11; TV Godrevy 11-13; TR from 13. *The Rectory, 22 Forth An Tewennow, Phillack, Hayle TR27 4QE* T: (01736) 753549

CLIFTON-SMITH, Gregory James. b 52. Goldsmiths' Coll Lon BMus 82 GGSM 73 Lon Univ TCert 74 Leeds Univ MA 02. Sarum & Wells Th Coll 87. **d** 89 **p** 90. C Welling *S'wark* 89-93; V Tattenham Corner and Burgh Heath *Guildf* 93-97; Asst Chapl R Berks and Battle Hosps NHS Trust 97-99; Chapl Isle of Wight NHS Primary Care Trust 99-12; rtd 12; PtO *Portsm* from 12; Close V and Min Can Win Cathl from 12. *Prospect Cottage, 20 West Street, Ventnor PO38 1NQ* T: (01962) 857251 *or* 857231 M: 07790-089981 E: gregory.clifton-smith@winchester-cathedral.org.uk

CLINCH, Christopher James. b 60. Nottm Univ BEd 82 BTh 89. Linc Th Coll 86. **d** 89 **p** 90. C Newc St Geo 89-92; C Seaton Hirst 92-94; TV Ch the King 94-00; V Newc St Fran 00-09; Chapl K Sch Tynemouth from 09. *The King's School, Huntingdon Place, North Shields NE30 4RF* T: 0191-258 5995 E: ccne12747@blueyonder.co.uk

CLINES, Emma Christine. *See* LOUIS, Emma Christine

CLINES, Jeremy Mark Sebastian. b 68. Birm Univ PhD 11. Cranmer Hall Dur. **d** 97 **p** 98. C Birm St Martin w Bordesley St Andr 97-99; Chapl York St Jo Univ 99-10; Chapl Sheff Univ from 10. *119 Ashdell Road, Sheffield S10 3DB* T: 0114-268 3260 *or* 222 4098 E: jeremyclines@gmail.com *or* j.clines@sheffield.ac.uk

CLITHEROW, Canon Andrew. b 50. St Chad's Coll Dur BA 72 Ex Univ MPhil 87. Sarum & Wells Th Coll 78. **d** 79 **p** 80. Hon C Bedford Ch Ch *St Alb* 79-84; Asst Chapl Bedford Sch 79-84; Chapl Caldicott Sch Farnham Royal 84-85; C Penkridge w Stretton *Lich* 85-88; Min Acton Trussell w Bednall 85-88; Chapl Rossall Sch Fleetwood 89-94; V Scotforth *Blackb* 94-00; Dioc Dir of Tr and Can Res Blackb Cathl 00-07; Hon Can Blackb Cathl from 07; P-in-c Lytham St Cuth 07-12; P-in-c Lytham St Jo 08-12; Chapl Cen Lancs Univ from 12; Chapl to The Queen from 08. *The Multi-Faith Centre, 34-35 St Peter's Square, Preston PR1 2HE* T: (01772) 892615 E: candrew@uclan.ac.uk

CLOAKE, David Michael. b 72. Ripon Coll Cuddesdon 07. **d** 08 **p** 09. C Aylesbury *Ox* 08-11; V Whitton SS Phil and Jas *Lon* from 11; CF (ACF) from 10. *The Vicarage, 205 Kneller Road, Twickenham TW2 7DY* T: (020) 8894 1932 M: 07758-289702 E: fatherdavid@ntlworld.com

CLOCKSIN, Prof William Frederick. b 55. BA 76 St Cross Coll Ox MA 81 Trin Hall Cam MA 87 PhD 93. EAMTC 91. **d** 94 **p** 95. Asst Chapl Trin Hall Cam 94-01; Acting Dean 00-01. *5 Stansfield Close, Oxford OX3 8TH* T: (01865) 426022 E: wfc@brookes.ac.uk

CLODE, Arthur Raymond Thomas. b 35. Roch Th Coll 67. **d** 69 **p** 70. C Blackheath *Birm* 69-72; V Londonderry 73-75; R Kirkbride *S & M* 75-79; UAE 80-83; Min Stewartly LEP 86-90; C Wootton *St Alb* 86-90; C St Alb St Paul 90-94; rtd 94; PtO *Glouc* from 01. *60 Albemarle Gate, Cheltenham GL50 4PJ* T: (01242) 577521

CLOETE, Richard James. b 47. AKC 71. St Aug Coll Cant 72. **d** 72 **p** 73. C Redhill St Matt *S'wark* 72-76; V Streatham St Paul 76-84; P-in-c W Coker w Hardington Mandeville, E Chinnock etc *B & W* 84-88; R 88; R Wincanton and Pen Selwood 88-97; Sec and Treas Dioc Hosp Chapl Fellowship 91-97; PtO *Lon*

97-98; *Ex* 99-02; C Sampford Peverell, Uplowman, Holcombe Rogus etc 02-11; rtd 11; PtO *B & W* from 12. *19 Mount Nebo, Taunton TA1 4HG* T: (01823) 338428 M: 07855-493868 E: r.j.cloete@btinternet.com

CLOGHER, Archdeacon of. *See* STEED, The Ven Helene

CLOGHER, Bishop of. *See* MACDOWELL, The Rt Revd Francis John

CLOGHER, Dean of. *See* HALL, The Very Revd Kenneth Robert James

CLONMACNOISE, Dean of. *See* BOGLE, The Very Revd Paul David

CLOSE, Brian Eric. b 49. St Chad's Coll Dur BA 74 MA 76. Ridley Hall Cam 74. **d** 76 **p** 77. C Far Headingley St Chad *Ripon* 76-79; C Harrogate St Wilfrid 79-80; C Harrogate St Wilfrid and St Luke 80-82; P-in-c Alconbury cum Weston *Ely* 82-83; V 83-86; P-in-c Buckworth 82-83; R 83-86; P-in-c Upton and Copmanford 82-83; Chapl Reed's Sch Cobham 86-96; Chapl Malvern Coll 96-01; Chapl Uppingham Sch 01-04; R Easington, Easington Colliery and S Hetton *Dur* 04-09; rtd 09. *9 Ivy Cottages, Hilton, Yarm TS15 9LD*

CLOSE (née HITCHEN), Mrs Carol Ann. b 47. St Mary's Coll Ban CertEd 69 St Martin's Coll Lanc DipEd 91 Ches Coll of HE BTh 02. NOC 99. **d** 02 **p** 03. NSM Hindley St Pet *Liv* 02-07; PtO *Man* 08-11; NSM Hindley Green *Liv* 11-14; NSM Newton from 15. *271 Warrington Road, Abram, Wigan WN2 5RQ* T: (01942) 861670

CLOSE, Mrs Jane. b 48. WMMTC 00. **d** 03 **p** 04. NSM Fillongley and Corley *Cov* 03-06; P-in-c Leam Valley from 06. *The Vicarage, Lower Street, Willoughby, Rugby CV23 8BX* T: (01788) 899226 M: 07958-685423 E: revj.close@btinternet.com

CLOSE, Mark Wesley. b 78. **d** 14 **p** 15. C Trull w Angersleigh *B & W* from 14. *5 Barton Green, Trull, Taunton TA3 7NA* M: 07891-792661 T: (01823) 710174 E: mark_close@hotmail.com

CLOSE, Canon Timothy John. b 68. QUB BA 91 Leic Univ MSc 95 TCD BTh 00. CITC 97. **d** 00 **p** 01. C Glenageary *D & G* 00-03; Dean's V Belf Cathl 03-09; Can Belf Cathl 07-09; I Eglantine *Conn* 11-14. *Address temp unknown* M: 07772-704232

CLOSS-PARRY, The Ven Selwyn. b 25. Univ of Wales (Lamp) BA 50. St Mich Coll Llan 50. **d** 52 **p** 53. C Dwygyfylchi *Ban* 52-58; V Treuddyn *St As* 58-66; R Llangystennin 66-71; V Holywell 71-77; Can St As Cathl 76-82; Prec 82-84; Preb 82-90; V Colwyn *St As* 77-84; Adn St As 84-90; R Trefnant 84-90; rtd 91. *3 Llys Brompton, Brompton Avenue, Rhos-on-Sea LL28 4TB* T: (01492) 545801

CLOTHIER, Gerald Harry. b 34. Oak Hill Th Coll 75. **d** 78 **p** 79. Hon C Highwood *Chelmsf* 78-79; Hon C Writtle w Highwood 79-83; P-in-c Westhall w Brampton and Stoven *St E* 83-86; TV Beccles St Mich 86-93; R Rougham, Beyton w Hessett and Rushbrooke 93-97; rtd 97; PtO *Nor* from 97; P-in-c Tenerife Sur *Eur* 01-02. *57 Eckling Grange, Dereham NR20 3BB* T: (01362) 694949

CLOUSTON, Eric Nicol. b 63. G&C Coll Cam BA 85 MA 88 PhD 89. Ridley Hall Cam 03. **d** 05 **p** 06. C Chatham St Phil and St Jas *Roch* 05-08; CMS India from 09. *c/o V Duraikan Esq, 29 Aylesford Way, Stapleford, Cambridge CB22 5DP* E: eclouston@btinternet.com

CLOVER, Brendan David. b 58. G&C Coll Cam BA 79 MA 83 LTCL 74. Ripon Coll Cuddesdon 79. **d** 82 **p** 83. C Friern Barnet St Jas *Lon* 82-85; C W Hampstead St Jas 85-87; Chapl Em Coll Cam 87-92; Dean 92-94; P-in-c St Pancras w St Jas and Ch Ch *Lon* 94-99; P-in-c St Pancras H Cross w St Jude and St Pet 96-99; Can Res Bris Cathl 99-06; Sen Provost Woodard Corp from 06; PtO *Lich* from 06. *The Woodard Corporation, High Street, Abbots Bromley, Rugeley WS15 3BW* T: (01283) 840670 *or* 840120 E: brendanclover@woodard.co.uk

CLOW, Laurie Stephen. b 65. Man Univ BA 86 MA 88. Wycliffe Hall Ox 96. **d** 98 **p** 99. C Trentham *Lich* 98-01; TV Hampreston *Sarum* 01-15; R Chesham Bois *Ox* from 15. *The Rectory, 1 Glebe Way, Amersham HP6 5ND* T: (01494) 728318 M: 07825-135616 E: w.m.clow@uclan.ac.uk *or* isclow@ccssite.freeserve.co.uk

CLOWES, John. b 45. AKC 67. **d** 68 **p** 69. C Corby St Columba *Pet* 68-71; R Itchenstoke w Ovington and Abbotstone *Win* 71-73; R New Alresford w Ovington and Itchen Stoke 73-74; V Acton w Gt and Lt Waldingfield *St E* 74-80; Asst Dioc Chr Stewardship Ad*v*r 75-80; TV Southend St Jo w St Mark, All SS w St Fran etc *Chelmsf* 80-82; TV Southend 82-85; Ind Chapl 80-85; R Ashwick w Oakhill and Binegar *B & W* 85-91; P-in-c Brompton Regis w Upton and Skilgate 91-97; rtd 98. *The Tythings, Tythings Court, Minehead TA24 5NT* M: 07808-200619

CLOWES, Mrs Lindsay Joan. b 48. **d** 13 **p** 14. OLM Biddulph *Lich* from 13. *10 York Close, Biddulph, Stoke-on-Trent ST8 6SE* T: (01782) 514413 E: lindsay48@hotmail.co.uk

CLOYNE, Dean of. *See* MARLEY, The Very Revd Alan Gordon

CLUCAS, Anthony John. b 56. Portsm Poly BA 77. WMMTC 96. d 99 p 00. NSM Erdington *Birm* 99-04; NSM Nechells 04-05; P-in-c Shard End 05-12; V from 12. *Apartment 1, 11 York Crescent, Birmingham B34 7NS* T: 0121-747 3299
E: clucas@btinternet.com

CLUCAS, Robert David. b 55. Cranmer Hall Dur. d 82 p 83. C Gateacre *Liv* 82-86; P-in-c Bishop's Itchington *Cov* 86-93; CPAS Staff 93-98; Freelance Tr GodStuff from 99; PtO *Cov* 93-09; C Priors Hardwick, Priors Marston and Wormleighton from 09; C Napton-on-the-Hill, Lower Shuckburgh etc from 09. *4 Highfield Cottages, Bishops Itchington, Southam CV47 2SR* T: (01926) 613739 E: bob@godstuff.org.uk

CLUER, Donald Gordon. b 21. S'wark Ord Course 61. d 64 p 65. C Malden St Jas *S'wark* 64-68; C Bexhill St Pet *Chich* 68-73; V Shoreham Beach 73-77; V Heathfield St Rich 77-86; C Eastbourne St Mary 86-90; rtd 90; PtO *Ox* from 90. *St John's Home, St Mary's Road, Oxford OX4 1QE* T: (01865) 241658

CLUES, David Charles. b 66. K Coll Lon BD 87 Lon Univ PGCE 95. St Steph Ho Ox 88. d 90 p 91. C Notting Hill All SS w St Columb *Lon* 90-94; NSM 94-96; NSM Notting Hill St Mich and Ch Ch 96-98; Asst Chapl HM Pris Wormwood Scrubs 97-98; C Paddington St Mary Magd *Lon* 98-03; C Paddington St Mary 98-03; C Paddington St Sav 98-03; V Willesden St Mary 03-11; P-in-c Brighton St Bart *Chich* from 11. *16 Richmond Terrace, Brighton BN2 9SA* T: (01273) 685142 E: transpontem@aol.com

CLUETT, Preb Michael Charles. b 53. Kingston Poly BSc 78. St Steph Ho Ox 84. d 86 p 87. C Pontesbury I and II *Heref* 86-90; TV Wenlock 90-99; P-in-c Canon Pyon w Kings Pyon and Birley 99-04; V Canon Pyon w King's Pyon, Birley and Wellington from 04; RD Leominster 08-14; Preb Heref Cathl from 10. *The Vicarage, Brookside, Canon Pyon, Hereford HR4 8NY* T: (01432) 830802 E: mccluett@aol.com

CLUNE, David Julian. b 60. Open Univ BSc 03. Wilson Carlile Coll 99 St Jo Coll Nottm LTh 07. d 07 p 08. C Spalding St Mary and St Nic *Linc* 07-11; TV Sutton St Jas and Wawne *York* 11-12; V Sutton St Jas from 12. *The Rectory, Church Street, Sutton, Hull HU7 4TL* T: (01482) 782154
E: david@clune.org.uk

CLUNIE, Grace. b 60. Ulster Univ BA 82 MA 91. CITC BTh 95. d 95 p 96. C Newtownards *D & D* 95-99; C Seagoe 99-01; I Belfast St Nic *Conn* 01-07; Dir Celtic Spirituality Arm Cathl from 07; Dom Chapl to Abp Arm from 09; Chapl S Area Hospice Services from 11. *The Garden House, 23 Drumilly Road, Armagh BT61 8RG* T: (028) 3887 0667
E: contact@celtic-spirituality.net

CLUTTERBUCK, Miss Elizabeth Lesieli. b 81. LSE BA 02 K Coll Lon MA 04. St Mellitus Coll BA 14. d 15. C Highbury Ch Ch w St Jo and St Sav *Lon* from 15. *Christ Church Vicarage, 155 Highbury Grove, London N5 1SA* M: 07763-852258 T: (020) 7354 0741 E: liz.clutterbuck@gmail.com

CLUTTERBUCK, Miss Marion Isobel. b 56. Oak Hill Th Coll BA 91. d 92 p 94. C Lindfield *Chich* 92-96; TV Alderbury Team *Sarum* 96-01; TV Clarendon 01-05; PtO *Win* from 13. *3 Hillside Close, West Dean, Salisbury SP5 1EX* T: (01794) 342377 E: miclutterbuck@hotmail.co.uk

CLUTTON, Canon Barbara Carol. b 47. WMMTC 00. d 04 p 05. NSM Draycote Gp *Cov* 04-14; P-in-c 08-14; Rural Life Officer 07-14; Hon Can Cov Cathl 11-14; rtd 14. *Church Cottage, Main Street, Grandborough, Rugby CV23 8DQ* M: 07808-137550 T: (01788) 810372 E: barbaraclutton@igberthouse.co.uk

CLYDE, John. b 39. Univ of Wales (Lamp) MA 99 Greenwich Univ PhD. CITC. d 71 p 72. C Belfast St Aid *Conn* 71-74; I Belfast St Barn 74-80; I Belfast H Trin 80-87; I Belfast H Trin and St Silas 88-89; Bp's C Acton and Drumbanagher *Arm* 89-94; I Desertlyn w Ballyeglish 94-02; rtd 02. *25 Castleoak, Castledawson, Magherafelt BT45 8RX* T: (028) 7946 9153 E: jc@rclyde.freeserve.co.uk

CLYNES, William. b 33. Sarum & Wells Th Coll 78. d 79 p 80. C Winterbourne *Bris* 79-83; TV Swindon St Jo and St Andr 83-91; rtd 91. *34 Sandown Court, 22-62 Bromley Drive, Cardiff CF5 5EZ*

COAD, Dominic John. b 82. Ex Univ BA 02 MA 06 PhD 10. Westcott Ho Cam 10. d 12 p 13. C Oakham, Ashwell, Braunston, Brooke, Egleton etc *Pet* from 12. *45 Trent Road, Oakham LE15 6HE* T: (01572) 770024 M: 07713-165193 E: dominic@oakhamteam.org.uk

COAKLEY (née FURBER), Prof Sarah Anne. b 51. New Hall Cam BA 73 PhD 82. Harvard Div Sch ThM 75. d 00 p 01. Edw Mallinckrodt Jr Prof Div Harvard Div Sch 95-07; Visiting Prof 07-08; Hon C Waban The Gd Shep 00-08; Hon C Littlemore *Ox* 00-07; Norris-Hulse Prof Div Cam Univ from 07; LtO *Ely* from 08; Hon Can Ely Cathl from 11. *Faculty of Divinity, West Road, Cambridge CB3 9BS* T: (01223) 763002 E: sc545@cam.ac.uk

COATES, Alan Thomas. b 55. St Jo Coll Nottm 87. d 89 p 90. C Heeley *Sheff* 89-90; C Bramley and Ravenfield 90-92; V Askern 92-96; Chapl RAF 96-12; V Metheringham w

Blankney and Dunston *Linc* from 15. *The Vicarage, 30 Lincoln Road, Metheringham, Lincoln LN4 2EE* T: (01526) 569979 E: alanthomascoates@hotmail.com

COATES, Archie. See COATES, Richard Michael

COATES, Canon Christopher Ian. b 59. Qu Coll Birm 81. d 84 p 85. C Cottingham *York* 84-87; TV Howden 87-91; V Sherburn in Elmet 91-94; V Sherburn in Elmet w Saxton 94-02; V Bishopthorpe from 02; V Acaster Malbis from 02; P-in-c Appleton Roebuck w Acaster Selby 07-12; V from 12; RD New Ainsty from 11; Hon Can Ho from 10. *The Vicarage, 48 Church Lane, Bishopthorpe, York YO23 2QG* T: (01904) 707840 E: chriscoates@hotmail.co.uk

COATES, David Martin. b 57. Sheff Univ BSc 78 Reading Univ MSc 80 Birm Univ PhD 83. STETS 04. d 07 p 08. NSM Salisbury St Mark *Sarum* 07-10; NSM Bourne Valley from 10. *2 St Matthew's Close, Bishopdown, Salisbury SP1 3FJ* T: (01722) 325944 E: dmc50@waitrose.com

COATES, Jean. b 55. Linc Univ BA 10. d 13 p 14. OLM Bolingbroke Deanery *Linc* from 13. *The Vicarage, Church Street, Spilsby PE23 5EF* T: (01790) 752526 E: coatesjean@yahoo.co.uk

COATES, Canon Jean Margaret. b 47. Sussex Univ BSc 68 Reading Univ PhD 77 MSB CBiol. SAOMC 93. d 96 p 97. C Wallingford *Ox* 96-99; P-in-c Watercombe *Sarum* 99-02; R 02-13; Rural Officer (Dorset) 99-13; Can and Preb Sarum Cathl 05-13; rtd 13. *Three Gables, Colesbrook, Gillingham SP8 4HH* T: (01747) 229168 E: jean@coates.ctlconnect.co.uk

COATES, John David Spencer. b 41. St Jo Coll Dur BA 64. Cranmer Hall Dur 64. d 66 p 67. C Chipping Campden w Ebrington *Glouc* 66-68; CF 69-96; rtd 96; PtO *B & W* from 96. *4 The Poplars, Hawkcombe, Porlock, Minehead TA24 8QN* T: (01643) 862772 M: 07791-027884

COATES, Maxwell Gordon. b 49. Lon Univ CertEd 70 Open Univ BA 83 UEA MA 86. Trin Coll Bris. d 77 p 78. C Blackheath Park St Mich *S'wark* 77-79; Chapl Greenwich Distr Hosp Lon 77-79; Asst Teacher Saintbridge Sch Glouc 79-81; Teacher Gaywood Park High Sch King's Lynn 81-85; Teacher St Jo *Nor* 81-85; Dep Hd Teacher Winton Comp Sch Bournemouth 85-90; Hd Teacher St Mark's Comp Sch Bath 90-97; NSM Canford Magna *Sarum* 85-90 and 99-05; NSM Stoke Gifford *Bris* 93-96; PtO *B & W* 91-96; rtd 97. *3 Oakley Road, Wimborne BH21 1QJ* T: (01202) 883162

COATES, Michael David. b 60. Ches Coll of HE BTh 01. NOC 98. d 01 p 02. C Orrell Hey St Jo and St Jas *Liv* 01-07; P-in-c Edge Hill St Cypr w St Mary 07-10; C Liv All SS 11-14; V from 14. *The Vicarage, 48 John Lennon Drive, Liverpool L6 9HT* T: 0151-260 6351 E: mike@allsaintsliverpool.org

COATES, Canon Nigel John. b 51. Reading Univ BSc MA. Trin Coll Bris. d 83 p 84. C Epsom St Martin *Guildf* 83-86; C Portswood Ch Ch *Win* 86-88; Chapl Southn Univ 89-97; Chapl Southn Inst of HE 89-95; P-in-c Freemantle 97-00; R 00-05; Can Res S'well Minster from 05. *3 Vicars Court, Southwell NG25 0HP* T: (01636) 817296
E: nigelcoates@southwellminster.org

COATES, Canon Peter Frederick. b 50. K Coll Lon BD 79 AKC 79. St Steph Ho Ox 79. d 80 p 81. C Woodford St Barn *Chelmsf* 80-83; C E and W Keal *Linc* 83-86; R The Wainfleets and Croft 86-94; R The Wainfleet Gp 94-03; RD Calcewaithe and Candleshoe 92-03; P-in-c Spilsby Gp 03-13; TR Bolingbroke Deanery from 14; RD Bolingbroke from 03; Can and Preb Linc Cathl from 02. *The Vicarage, Church Street, Spilsby PE23 5DU* T: (01790) 752526
E: peter.coates50@yahoo.com

COATES, Richard Michael (Archie). b 70. Birm Univ BA 92. Wycliffe Hall Ox BA 99. d 00 p 01. C Ashtead *Guildf* 00-03; C Brompton H Trin w Onslow Square St Paul *Lon* 03-09; V Brighton St Pet *Chich* from 09; P-in-c Whitehawk from 13. *10 West Drive, Brighton BN2 0GD* T: (01273) 695064
E: coates@archieandson.co.uk

COATES, Robert. b 63. Aston Tr Scheme 87 St Steph Ho Ox 89. d 92 p 93. C Heavitree w Ex St Paul 92-95; Chapl RN 95-00; V Bexhill St Aug *Chich* from 00. *St Augustine's Vicarage, St Augustine's Close, Bexhill-on-Sea TN39 3AZ* T/F: (01424) 210785 E: ert@rcoates42.freeserve.co.uk

COATES, Robert Charles. b 44. Open Univ BA 76. Cant Sch of Min 83. d 86 p 87. C Deal St Leon and St Rich and Sholden *Cant* 86-89; V Loose 89-00; V Barnwood *Glouc* 00-06; rtd 06; PtO *B & W* from 06. *4 The Poplars, Weston-super-Mare BS22 6RB* T: (01934) 249387 M: 07874-202318 E: robert.coates@hotmail.co.uk

COATES, Stuart Murray. b 49. Lon Univ BA 70 Edin Univ MTh 91. Wycliffe Hall Ox 72. d 75 p 76. C Rainford *Liv* 75-78; C Orrell 78-79; V 79-86; Chapl Strathcarron Hospice Denny from 86; Hon C Stirling *Edin* 86-90; NSM Aberfoyle *St And* 89-94; NSM Doune 89-12; R 12-14. *Westwood Smithy, Chalmerston Road, Stirling FK9 4AG* T: (01786) 860531 or (01324) 826222 E: stuart@stuartcoates.wanadoo.co.uk

COATS, Maureen Quin. b 43. **d** 10 **p** 11. NSM Eastham *Ches* from 10. *24 Stanley Lane, Wirral CH62 0AG*

COATSWORTH, Mrs Deborah Margaret. b 58. **d** 13 **p** 14. NSM Baschurch and Weston Lullingfield w Hordley *Lich* from 13. *Oakmere House, 69 Hill Park, Dudleston Heath, Ellesmere SY12 9LB* T: (01691) 690261
E: deborahcoatsworth@btinternet.com

COATSWORTH, Nigel George. b 39. Trin Hall Cam BA 61 MA. Cuddesdon Coll 61. **d** 63 **p** 64. C Hellesdon *Nor* 63-66; Ewell Monastery 66-80; TV Folkestone H Trin and St Geo w Ch Ch *Cant* 83-85; C Milton next Sittingbourne 85-86; P-in-c Selattyn *Lich* 86-91; P-in-c Weston Rhyn 88-91; R Weston Rhyn and Selattyn 91-05; rtd 05; PtO *Lich* 05-09. *Oakmere House, 69 Hill Park, Dudleston Heath, Ellesmere SY12 9LB* T: (01691) 690261
E: rev.coatsworth@micro-plus-web.net

COBB, George Reginald. b 50. Oak Hill Th Coll BA 81. **d** 81 **p** 82. C Ware Ch Ch *St Alb* 81-84; C Uphill *B & W* 84-89; R Alresford *Chelmsf* 89-99; Chapl Mt Vernon and Watford Hosps NHS Trust 99-00; Chapl E and N Herts NHS Trust 00-15; rtd 15; PtO *St Alb* from 15. *25 Church Meadows, St Neots PE19 1PR* M: 07890-091973 E: george.cobb@cobbweb.co.uk

COBB, Canon John Philip Andrew. b 43. Man Univ BSc 65 New Coll Ox BA 67 MA 71. Wycliffe Hall Ox 66. **d** 68 **p** 69. C Reading St Jo *Ox* 68-71; C Romford Gd Shep *Chelmsf* 71-73; SAMS Chile 74-08; Can from 99; Dioc Ecum Officer 00-06; rtd 08; LtO Chile from 08. *Casilla 330, Correo Paine, Paine, Region Metropolitana, Chile* T: (0056) (2) 259 4099
E: jn.cobb@yahoo.co.uk

COBB, Miss Marjorie Alice. b 24. St Chris Coll Blackheath IDC 52. **dss** 61 **d** 87. CSA 56-85; rtd 85; PtO *Cant* 87-12; Chapl Jes Hosp Cant 90-12. *c/o Mowll and Mowll Solicitors, Trafalgar House, Gordon Road, Whitfield, Dover CT16 3PN*

COBB, Mark Robert. b 64. Lanc Univ BSc 86 Keele Univ MA 99 Liv Univ PhD 13. Ripon Coll Cuddesdon 88. **d** 91 **p** 92. C Hampstead St Jo *Lon* 91-94; Asst Chapl Derbyshire R Infirmary NHS Trust 94-96; Palliative & Health Care Chapl Derbyshire R Infirmary NHS Trust 96-98; Chapl Manager Cen Sheff Univ Hosps NHS Trust 98-02; Sen Chapl 98-04; Sen Chapl Sheff Teaching Hosps NHS Foundn Trust from 04. *Chaplaincy Services, Royal Hallamshire Hospital, Glossop Road, Sheffield S10 2JF* T: 0114-271 3327 E: mark.cobb@sth.nhs.uk

COBB, Peter Graham. b 27. St Jo Coll Cam BA 48 MA 52. Ridley Hall Cam 66. **d** 68 **p** 69. C Porthkerry *Llan* 68-71; P-in-c Penmark 71-72; V Penmark w Porthkerry 72-81; V Magor w Redwick and Undy *Mon* 82-95; rtd 95. *2 Talycoed Court, Talycoed, Monmouth NP25 5HR* T: (01600) 780309

COBBOLD, Richard Nevill. b 55. Bris Univ BScEng 76. Local Minl Tr Course. **d** 11 **p** 12. NSM N Farnborough *Guildf* from 11. *4 Penns Wood, Farnborough GU14 6RB* T: (01252) 515547 M: 07776-352240 E: richard@cobbold.plus.com

COBURN, Mrs Sharron Dawn. b 73. Trin Coll Bris MA 13. **d** 13 **p** 14. C Stanton, Hopton, Market Weston, Barningham etc *St E* from 13. *8 St Andrews Close, Barningham, Bury St Edmunds IP31 1EQ* T: (01359) 221946 M: 07739-250135
E: sha.coburn@me.com

COCHRANE, Alan George. b 28. S'wark Ord Course. **d** 82 **p** 83. NSM Clapham Old Town *S'wark* 82-85; C Spalding St Jo w Deeping St Nicholas *Linc* 85-87; R Southery and Hilgay *Ely* 87-98; V Fordham St Mary 87-91; rtd 98; PtO *Nor* from 99. *34 Pightle Way, Lyng, Norwich NR9 5RL* T: (01603) 872795

COCHRANE, Mrs Anthea Mary. b 38. **d** 02 **p** 03. OLM Clarendon *Sarum* 02-07; PtO 07-08. *Old Timbers, Silver Street, Alderbury, Salisbury SP5 3AN* T: (01722) 710503
E: antheaa.cochrane@tiscali.co.uk

COCHRANE, Philip Andrew. b 70. Reading Univ BA 92. Trin Coll Bris BA 07. **d** 07 **p** 08. C Fareham H Trin *Portsm* 07-09; TV 09-12; V Win St Barn 12-15; V Caerleon and Llanfrechfa *Mon* from 15. *The Vicarage, High Street, Caerleon, Newport NP18 1AZ* T: (01633) 420248

COCKAYNE, Gordon. b 34. RMN 73. **d** 92 **p** 93. NSM Owlerton *Sheff* 92-94; Ind Chapl 92-94; NSM Brightside w Wincobank 94-99; PtO from 99. *6 Austin Close, Loxley, Sheffield S6 6QD* T: 0114-220 6626

COCKAYNE, Mark Gary. b 61. UEA LLB 82. St Jo Coll Nottm BTh 92 MA 93. **d** 93 **p** 94. C Armthorpe *Sheff* 93-96; V Malin Bridge 96-05; AD Hallam 02-05; C Haydock St Mark *Liv* 05-08; V 08-14; AD St Helens 06-14; Hon Can Liv Cathl 06-14; Dir Par Support Team *Sheff* from 14. *2 Heather Close, Rotherham S60 2TQ* E: cockayne120@btinternet.com

COCKBILL, Douglas John. b 53. Chicago Univ BA 75. Gen Th Sem (NY) MDiv 78. **d** 78 **p** 79. Virgin Is 79-80; Bahamas 80-83; USA 84-90; P-in-c Roxbourne St Andr *Lon* 90-92; V 92-04; USA 05-06; Chapl Larnaca St Helena Cyprus 06-09; USA from 09. *428 King Street, Wenatchee WA 98801-2846, USA* E: dcockbill22@yahoo.com

COCKBURN, Kathleen. b 50. NEOC 04. **d** 07 **p** 08. NSM Walker *Newc* 07-10; NSM N Shields from 10. *92 Paignton Avenue, Whitley Bay NE25 8SZ* T: 0191-252 0710
E: kath.co@blueyonder.co.uk

COCKE, James Edmund. b 26. Wadh Coll Ox BA 50 MA 55. Wells Th Coll 50. **d** 52 **p** 53. C Christchurch *Win* 52-57; V Highfield *Ox* from 57; Chapl Wingfield-Morris Hosp Ox 57-90; Chapl Nuffield Orthopaedic Centre NHS Trust 90-12; Chapl Ox Univ Hosps NHS Trust from 12. *All Saints' Vicarage, 85 Old Road, Oxford OX3 7LB* T: (01865) 762536

COCKELL, Ms Helen Frances. b 69. Trin Hall Cam BA 90 MA 94. Qu Coll Birm BD 94. **d** 95. C Bracknell *Ox* 95-98; PtO *Cov* from 00; Chapl S Warks Gen Hosps NHS Trust from 09. *The New Rectory, Pool Close, Rugby CV22 7RN* T: (01788) 812613
E: nell.cockell@btinternet.com

COCKELL, Timothy David. b 66. Qu Coll Birm BTheol 95. **d** 95 **p** 96. C Bracknell *Ox* 95-98; C Rugby *Cov* 98-99; TV 99-04; P-in-c Bilton 04-08; R from 08. *The New Rectory, Pool Close, Rugby CV22 7RN* T: (01788) 812613
E: tim.cockell@btopenworld.com

COCKER (née BENTLEY), Mrs Frances Rymer (Sister Frances Anne). b 22. Man Univ BSc 48 TDip 49 PGCE 49. **d** 95 **p** 95. Mother Superior CSD 87-00; PtO *Sarum* from 95. *7 St Nicholas Hospital, St Nicholas Road, Salisbury SP1 2SW* T: (01722) 339761 M: 07702-659609

COCKERELL, David John. b 47. Univ of Wales (Cardiff) BA 71 Univ of Wales (Swansea) MA 74 Qu Coll Cam BA 75. Westcott Ho Cam 73. **d** 76 **p** 77. C Chapel Allerton *Ripon* 76-79; C Farnley 79-81; TV Hitchin *St Alb* 81-89; TV Dorchester *Ox* 89-92; Adult Educn and Tr Officer *Ely* 92-00; R Raddesley Gp 00-06; rtd 06. *44 Humberley Close, Eynesbury, St Neots PE19 2SE* T: (01480) 218225 E: david@cockerell.co.uk

COCKERTON, Canon John Clifford Penn. b 27. Liv Univ BA 48 St Cath Soc Ox BA 54 MA 58. Wycliffe Hall Ox 51. **d** 54 **p** 55. C St Helens St Helen *Liv* 54-58; Tutor Cranmer Hall Dur 58-60; Chapl 60-63; Warden 68-70; Vice-Prin St Jo Coll Dur 63-70; Prin 70-78; R Wheldrake *York* 78-84; R Wheldrake w Thorganby 84-92; Can and Preb York Minster 87-92; rtd 92; PtO *York* from 98. *42 Lucombe Way, New Earswick, York YO32 4DS* T: (01904) 765505

COCKETT, The Ven Elwin Wesley. b 59. Aston Tr Scheme 86 Oak Hill Th Coll BA 91. **d** 91 **p** 92. C Chadwell Heath *Chelmsf* 91-94; Chapl W Ham United Football Club 92-12; C Harold Hill St Paul *Chelmsf* 94-95; P-in-c 95-97; V 97-00; TR Billericay and Lt Burstead 00-07; RD Basildon 04-07; Adn W Ham from 07. *86 Aldersbrook Road, London E12 5DH* T: (020) 8989 8557 E: a.westham@chelmsford.anglican.org

COCKFIELD, Mrs Marisa. **d** 14. *Meadow View, 15 Andrews Park, Stoke Gabriel, Totnes TQ9 6FF* T: (01803) 782994

COCKFIELD, Mrs Myrtle Jacqueline. b 51. S Bank Univ BSc 96. SEITE 05. **d** 08 **p** 09. NSM Mitcham SS Pet and Paul *S'wark* from 08. *28 Garden Avenue, Mitcham CR4 2EA* T: (020) 8646 2333 M: 07722-568604 E: jackiecockfield@yahoo.co.uk

COCKING, Ann Louisa. b 44. **d** 03 **p** 04. OLM The Lavingtons, Cheverells, and Easterton *Sarum* 03-12; rtd 12. *High Acre, Eastcott, Devizes SN10 4PH* T: (01980) 812763
E: alc.highacre@btinternet.com

COCKING, Mrs Anne Frances Patricia. b 60. SEITE 12. **d** 15. NSM Clapham Common St Barn *S'wark* from 15. *Address temp unknown*

COCKING, Martyn Royston. b 53. Trin Coll Bris 83. **d** 85 **p** 86. C Weston-super-Mare Cen Par *B & W* 85-88; C Kingswood *Bris* 88-89; TV 89-93; V Pill w Easton in Gordano and Portbury *B & W* 93-96; PtO *Man* from 12. *39 Down Green Road, Bolton BL2 3QD*

COCKRAM, Anthony John. b 44. Leeds Univ BSc 65 Birm Univ MEd 83 Ex Univ BA 04. SWMTC 98. **d** 01 **p** 02. NSM Seaton *Ex* 01-03; NSM Seaton and Beer 03-04; Asst Chapl R Devon and Ex NHS Foundn Trust 04-05; TV Aberavon *Llan* 05-10; rtd 10. *1 Hillymead, Seaton EX12 2LF* T: (01297) 21887
E: ajcockram@hotmail.co.uk

COCKS, Canon Howard Alan Stewart. b 46. St Barn Coll Adelaide 78. **d** 80 **p** 81. C Portland Australia 80-82; C Prestbury *Glouc* 82-87; P-in-c Stratton w Baunton 87-94; P-in-c N Cerney w Bagendon 91-94; R Stratton, N Cerney, Baunton and Bagendon 95-98; V Leic St Aid 98-04; RD Christianity 03-04; R Winchelsea and Icklesham *Chich* 04-12; rtd 12; PtO *Lon* from 13; Can The Murray from 06. *The Charterhouse, Charterhouse Square, London EC1M 6AN* T: (020) 7253 2892 E: hcocks@btinternet.com

COCKS, Michael Dearden Somers. b 28. Univ of NZ MA 50 St Cath Coll Ox BA 53 MA 57. Ripon Hall Ox. **d** 53 **p** 54. C Merivale New Zealand 53-56; V Geraldine 56-58; V Ross and S Westland 58-60; V Hinds 60-63; V St Martins 63-70; V Barrington Street w Speydon St Nic 70-79; V Hororata 79-93; Chapl Gothenburg w Halmstad, Jönköping etc *Eur*

93-98; rtd 98. *23 Fairfield Avenue, Addington, Christchurch 8020, New Zealand* T/F: (0064) (3) 377 7053
E: michaelandgertrud@gmail.com

COCKSEDGE, Hugh Francis. b 26. Magd Coll Cam BA 50 MA 52. **d** 88 **p** 89. NSM Alton All SS *Win* 88-89; LtO 89-91; Chapl Ankara *Eur* 91-96; rtd 96; PtO *Win* from 96; *Eur* from 97; *Portsm* from 01; *Guildf* from 06. *4 Riverside Mews, The Spain, Petersfield GU32 3FJ* T: (01730) 859078
E: hughcocksedge@talktalk.net

COCKSEDGE, Simon Hugh. b 56. Univ Coll Lon BSc 78 New Coll Ox BM, BCh 81 Man Univ MD 03 FRCGP 96. NOC 05. **d** 07 **p** 08. NSM Hayfield and Chinley w Buxworth *Derby* 07-11; P-in-c Edale from 11. *Corrour, Hall Hill, Chapel-en-le-Frith, High Peak SK23 9RX*

COCKSEDGE, Stuart John. b 78. Ex Univ BA 99 Univ Coll Lon MSc 07. St Jo Coll Nottm 11. **d** 13 **p** 14. C Hinckley St Jo *Leic* from 13. *2 Brascote Road, Hinckley LE10 0YE* M: 07779-345852 E: stuart.cocksedge@gmail.com

✠**COCKSWORTH, The Rt Revd Christopher John.** b 59. Man Univ BA 80 PhD 89 PGCE 81. St Jo Coll Nottm 84. **d** 88 **p** 89 **c** 08. C Epsom Common Ch Ch *Guildf* 88-92; Chapl K Holloway and Bedf New Coll 92-97; Dir STETS 97-01; Hon Can Guildf Cathl 99-01; Prin Ridley Hall Cam 01-08; Bp Cov from 08. *The Bishop's House, 23 Davenport Road, Coventry CV5 6PW* T: (024) 7667 2244 F: 7671 3271
E: bishop@bishop-coventry.org

CODLING, Timothy Michael. b 62. Trin Coll Ox BA 84 MA 91. St Steph Ho Ox 89. **d** 91 **p** 92. C N Shoebury *Chelmsf* 91-97; V Tilbury Docks from 97; Hon Chapl Miss to Seafarers from 97. *St John's Vicarage, Dock Road, Tilbury RM18 7PP* T: (01375) 842417 E: tim@frcodling.fsnet.co.uk

CODRINGTON-MARSHALL, Louise. b 64. Westcott Ho Cam 06. **d** 08 **p** 09. C Mortlake w E Sheen *S'wark* 08-11; P-in-c Deptford St Nic and St Luke 11-14; V from 14. *11 Evelyn Street, London SE8 5RQ* T: (020) 8876 7162 E: revdlouise@blueyonder.co.uk

CODY (*née* TAYLOR), Julia Mary. b 73. Reading Univ LLB 94. Ridley Hall Cam 06. **d** 08 **p** 09. C Penkridge *Lich* 08-12; TV Tettenhall Wood and Perton from 12. *Church House, 23 Portrush Road, Perton, Wolverhampton WV6 7YZ* T: (01902) 750232 M: 07990-976859 E: jules.m.taylor@googlemail.com

CODY, Paul James Luke. b 73. Westcott Ho Cam. **d** 08 **p** 09. C Cen Wolverhampton *Lich* 08-12; Chapl St Pet Colleg Sch Wolv from 12. *Church House, 23 Portrush Road, Perton, Wolverhampton WV6 7YZ* T: (01902) 750232 M: 07834-345269 E: paulcody@hotmail.co.uk

COE, Andrew Derek John. b 58. Nottm Univ BTh 86. St Jo Coll Nottm 83. **d** 86 **p** 87. C Pype Hayes *Birm* 86-88; C Erdington St Barn 88-91; C Birm St Martin w Bordesley St Andr 91-96; P-in-c Hamstead St Bernard 96; V 96-02; P-in-c Newdigate *Guildf* 02-03; TR Surrey Weald from 03; RD Dorking 04-09. *The Rectory, Church Road, Newdigate, Dorking RH5 5DL* T: (01306) 631469 E: revdandrewdj.coe@btinternet.com

COE, David. b 45. **d** 69 **p** 70. C Belfast St Matt *Conn* 69-72; C Belfast St Donard *D & D* 72-75; I Tullylish 75-81; I Lurgan St Jo 81-89; I Ballymacarrett St Patr 89-02; I Richhill *Arm* 02-11; rtd 11. *49 Toberhewny Lodge, Lurgan, Craigavon BT66 7FL* T: (028) 3834 2579 M: 07794-356030
E: davidcoe144@aol.com

COE, John Norris. b 31. Oak Hill Th Coll 57. **d** 59 **p** 60. C Stoughton *Guildf* 59-61; C Guernsey St Michel du Valle *Win* 61-63; C Norbiton *S'wark* 63-67; V Bath Widcombe *B & W* 67-84; R Publow w Pensford, Compton Dando and Chelwood 84-96; rtd 96; PtO *B & W* from 96. *30 Minerva Court, St John's Road, Bathwick, Bath BA2 6PL* T: (01225) 789752 E: coej@sky.com

COE, Michael Stephen. b 63. Bath Univ BSc 85. Wycliffe Hall Ox. **d** 00 **p** 01. C Moulton *Pet* 00-03; P-in-c Silverhill St Matt *Chich* 03-05; R from 05; RD Hastings from 13. *The Rectory, 9 St Matthew's Road, St Leonards-on-Sea TN38 0TN* T: (01424) 430262 E: mikelisac@aol.com

COE, Noelle Elizabeth. b 60. Anglia Ruskin Univ BA 10. **d** 08 **p** 09. NSM N Holmwood *Guildf* 08-10; NSM Westcott 10-12; NSM Surrey Weald from 12. *The Rectory, Church Road, Newdigate, Dorking RH5 5DL* T: (01306) 631469
E: noellecoe@btinternet.com

COE, Stephen David. b 49. Ch Coll Cam MA 72 Oak Hill Th Coll MA 99. Ox Min Course 90. **d** 93 **p** 94. NSM Abingdon *Ox* 93-97; Assoc Min Ox St Andr 97-05; V Wallington H Trin *S'wark* from 05. *Holy Trinity Vicarage, Maldon Road, Wallington SM6 8BL* T: (020) 8401 8177 E: sdcoe@btinternet.com

COEKIN, Philip James. b 64. Wye Coll Lon BScAgr 87. Oak Hill Th Coll BA 93. **d** 96 **p** 97. C Eastbourne All SS *Chich* 96-00; V Hastings Em and St Mary in the Castle 00-11; V Eastbourne H Trin from 11. *Holy Trinity Vicarage, 2 Hartington Place, Eastbourne BN21 3BE* T: (01323) 325421
E: philipcoekin@talktalk.net

COEKIN, Richard John. b 61. Solicitor 86 Jes Coll Cam BA 83 MA 87. Wycliffe Hall Ox 89. **d** 91 **p** 92. C Cheadle *Ches* 91-95; NSM Wimbledon Em Ridgway Prop Chpl *S'wark* from 95; PtO *Lon* from 02. *264 Worple Road, London SW20 8RG* T: (020) 8545 2734 E: richard.coekin@dundonald.org

COFFEY, Helen Theresa. b 63. Salford Univ BA 08 Sheff Univ BA 12. Coll of Resurr Mirfield 10. **d** 12 **p** 13. C Ashton-in-Makerfield St Thos *Liv* from 12. *79 Greenfields Crescent, Ashton-in-Makerfield, Wigan WN4 8QY* M: 07742-590672
E: helentcoffey@gmail.com

COFFEY, Hubert William (Bill). b 15. MBE 46. TCD BA 37 MA 40. TCD Div Sch Div Test 38. **d** 38 **p** 39. C Errigle Keerogue w Ballygawley and Killeshil *Arm* 38-41; Chapl RN 41-47; I Milltown *Arm* 47-52; Chapl Miss to Seamen 52-64; V Melbourne S Australia 64-80; PtO Melbourne from 80; rtd 80. *23 Hawthorn Avenue, Caulfield North VIC 3161, Australia* T: (0061) (3) 9527 7875

COFFIN, Pamela. *See* PENNELL, Pamela

COFFIN, Stephen. b 52. Pemb Coll Ox BA 74 MA 79. Trin Coll Bris 74. **d** 77 **p** 78. C Illogan *Truro* 77-80; C Liskeard w St Keyne and St Pinnock 80-82; CMS Burundi 82-86; V St Germans *Truro* 86-00; Chapl Grenoble *Eur* 00-12; rtd 13. *7 Impasse du Four, 73130 Notre Dame du Cruet, France*
E: coffin@onetelnet.fr

COGGINS, Glenn. b 60. Warwick Univ BA 81. Cranmer Hall Dur 93. **d** 95 **p** 96. C Cley Hill Warminster *Sarum* 95-99; R Doddington w Benwick and Wimblington *Ely* 99-06; V E Ardsley *Leeds* from 06; Bp's Adv for Ecum Affairs from 07. *The Vicarage, Church Lane, East Ardsley, Wakefield WF3 2LJ* T: (01924) 822184 M: 07951-651952

COGHLAN, Jennifer Mary. *See* WILTSHIRE, Jennifer Mary

COGHLAN, Canon Patrick John. b 47. Down Coll Cam BA 69. St Jo Coll Nottm MA 73. **d** 73 **p** 74. C Crookes St Thos *Sheff* 73-78; Brazil 78-92; V Anston *Sheff* 92-06; V Malin Bridge 06-13; Hon Can Sheff Cathl 07-13; rtd 13; PtO *Sheff* from 13. *1 Bradway Road, Sheffield S17 4QQ* T: 0114-236 9483
E: patrick.coghlan@sheffield.anglican.org

COHEN, The Ven Clive Ronald Franklin. b 46. ACIB 71. Sarum & Wells Th Coll 79. **d** 81 **p** 82. C Esher *Guildf* 81-85; R Winterslow *Sarum* 85-00; RD Alderbury 89-93; Can and Preb Sarum Cathl 92-00; Adn Bodmin *Truro* 00-11; Hon Can Truro Cathl 00-11; rtd 11; Chapter Can Ex Cathl from 11. *86 Moor View Drive, Teignmouth TQ14 9UZ* T: (01626) 775704
E: cliveandjunecohen@btinternet.com

COHEN, Canon David Mervyn Stuart. b 42. Sydney Univ BA 63 MA 78. **d** 67 **p** 68. Exec Sec Bible Soc Mauritius 67-69; Dep Gen Sec Bible Soc New Zealand 70-72; Regional Sec (Africa) Bible Soc 73-75; C-in-c Sylvania Australia 75-77; R Manly St Matt 78-85; Gen Dir Scripture Union (England and Wales) 86-93; Team Leader Tear Fund UK Zaïre 93-96; Nat Dir Chr Nationals Evang Coun Australia from 96; Hon Can Antsiranana from 06. *1 Currawong Place, East Blaxland NSW 2774, Australia* E: davidc@moringa-au.com

COHEN, Grant Geoffrey. b 71. Regents Th Coll BA 08. Ridley Hall Cam 09. **d** 11 **p** 12. C Sale St Anne *Ches* 11-14; TV Sanderstead *S'wark* from 14. *St Mary's Vicarage, 85 Purley Oaks Road, South Croydon CR2 0NY* M: 07717-170386
E: grant_cohen@hotmail.co.uk

COHEN, Canon Ian Geoffrey Holland. b 51. Nottm Univ BA 74. Ripon Coll Cuddesdon 77. **d** 79 **p** 80. C Sprowston *Nor* 79-83; TV Wallingford w Crowmarsh Gifford etc *Ox* 83-88; V Chalgrove w Berrick Salome from 88; Hon Can Ch Ch from 11. *The Vicarage, 58 Brinkinfield Road, Chalgrove, Oxford OX44 7QX* T: (01865) 890392 E: ianghcohen@hotmail.com

COHEN, Janet Elizabeth. *See* GASPER, Janet Elizabeth

COHEN, Malcolm Arthur. b 38. Canberra Coll of Min. **d** 78 **p** 79. C Moruya, Bega and Cootamundra Australia 79-80; R Braidwood 82-83; R Stifford *Chelmsf* 84-92; Chapl Asst Thurrock Community Hosp Grays 84-86; Hon Chapl ATC from 86; P-in-c Mayland and Steeple *Chelmsf* 92-95; C Prittlewell 95-99; C Greenstead 99-00; TV Greenstead w Colchester St Anne 00-03; rtd 03; PtO *Chelmsf* from 08. *177 Straight Road, Colchester CO3 5DG* T: (01206) 573231

COKE, Canon William Robert Francis. b 46. St Edm Hall Ox BA 68 MA 79 Lon Univ BD 78. Trin Coll Bris 75. **d** 79 **p** 80. C Blackb Sav 79-83; V Fence in Pendle 83-84; P-in-c Newchurch-in-Pendle 83-84; V Fence and Newchurch-in-Pendle 84-89; Switzerland 89-95; Chapl Ardingly Coll 95-96; V Ambleside w Brathay *Carl* 96-10; P-in-c Langdale 97-08; TR Loughrigg 10-11; RD Windermere 04-10; Hon Can Carl Cathl 08-11; V Lt LtO *Mor* from 13. *Anancaun Cottage, Kinlochewe, Achnasheen IV22 2PA* T: (01445) 760364
E: robertricia.coke@homecall.co.uk

COKE-WOODS, Sylvia Jessie. b 47. Sheff Univ BA 69. Qu Coll Birm 81 NOC 98. **d** 99 **p** 00. C Widnes St Mary *Liv* 99-03; PtO *B & W* 04-10. *35 Bridge Street, Hatherleigh, Okehampton EX20 3HZ*

COKER, Alexander Bryan. b 48. Fourah Bay Coll (Sierra Leone) LDiv 73 K Coll Lon BD 75 MTh 76 Brunel Univ MA 84 MEd 89 AKC 76 MCollP 84. St Aug Coll Cant 75. **d** 86 **p** 87. NSM Belsize Park *Lon* 86-90; C Croydon Woodside *S'wark* 90-93; C Cheam Common St Phil 93-94; PtO *Lon* 02-04. *The Mission House, 19 Rosehill Park West, Sutton SM1 3LA* T: (020) 8641 8690

COKER, Canon Barry Charles Ellis. b 46. K Coll Lon BD 69 AKC 69. **d** 70 **p** 71. C Newton Aycliffe *Dur* 70-74; R Marabella H Cross Trinidad and Tobago 74-78; R Matson *Glouc* 78-90; V Stroud and Uplands w Slad 90-11; P-in-c The Edge, Pitchcombe, Harescombe and Brookthorpe 00-01; RD Bisley 94-06; Hon Can Glouc Cathl 98-11; rtd 11. *St Petroc, 30 Highfield Road, Lydney GL15 5NA* T: (01594) 840890

COLAM (*née* TAVERNER), Mrs Lorraine Dawn. b 61. SRN 82 RSCN 86. **d** 07 **p** 08. OLM Tilehurst St Cath and Calcot *Ox* from 07; Chapl R Berks NHS Foundn Trust from 14. *120 Chapel Hill, Tilehurst, Reading RG31 5DH* T: 0118-943 2001 M: 07790-076450 E: lorraine.colam@virginmedia.com

COLBOURN, John Martin Claris. b 30. Selw Coll Cam BA 52 MA 56. Ridley Hall Cam 52. **d** 54 **p** 55. C Cheadle *Ches* 54-58; V Trowbridge St Thos *Sarum* 59-65; V Fareham St Jo *Portsm* 65-87; V Crich *Derby* 87-95; RD Alfreton 88-95; rtd 95; PtO *Derby* from 95. *Stanton View Cottage, Dale Road North, Darley Dale, Matlock DE4 2HX* T: (01629) 733284 E: john@colbourn.freeserve.co.uk

COLBY, David Allan. b 33. Ox NSM Course 78. **d** 81 **p** 82. NSM Gt Faringdon w Lt Coxwell *Ox* 81-83; TV Ewyas Harold w Dulas, Kenderchurch etc *Heref* 83-91; V Westbury-on-Severn w Flaxley and Blaisdon *Glouc* 91-99; rtd 99; PtO *Ox* 01-10. *Solway House, Faringdon Road, Kingston Bagpuize, Abingdon OX13 5AQ* T: (01865) 820360

COLCHESTER, Archdeacon of. See COOPER, The Ven Annette Joy

COLCHESTER, Area Bishop of. See MORRIS, The Rt Revd Roger Anthony Brett

✠**COLCLOUGH, The Rt Revd Michael John.** b 44. Leeds Univ BA 69. Cuddesdon Coll 69. **d** 71 **p** 72 **c** 96. C Burslem St Werburgh *Lich* 71-75; C Ruislip St Mary *Lon* 75-79; P-in-c Hayes St Anselm 79-85; V 85-86; AD Hillingdon 85-92; P-in-c Uxbridge St Marg 86-88; P-in-c Uxbridge St Andr w St Jo 86-88; TR Uxbridge 88-92; Adn Northolt 92-94; P-in-c St Vedast w St Mich-le-Querne etc 94-96; Bp's Sen Chapl 94-96; Dean of Univ Chapls from 94; Dep P in O 95-96; Area Bp Kensington *Lon* 96-08; Can Res St Paul's Cathl 08-13; rtd 13; Hon Asst Bp Lon from 13; Hon Asst Bp Eur from 14. *12 Grosvenor Court, 99 Sloane Street, London SW1X 9PF* T: (020) 3612 3135 E: michaeljcolclough@gmail.com

COLDERWOOD, Alfred Victor. b 26. Bps' Coll Cheshunt 58. **d** 60 **p** 61. C Oakwood St Thos *Lon* 60-63; C Enfield St Jas 63-66; V Edmonton St Aldhelm 66-91; rtd 91; PtO *Cant* 91-09. *28 Elliot Close, South Woodham Ferrers, Chelmsford CM3 5YN* T: (01245) 324758

COLDHAM, Miss Geraldine Elizabeth. b 35. FLA 66 Trevelyan Coll Dur BA 80. Cranmer Hall Dur 82. **dss** 83 **d** 87 **p** 94. S Normanton *Derby* 83-87; Par Dn 87; Par Dn Barking St Marg w St Patr *Chelmsf* 87-90; Par Dn Stifford 90-94; C 94-95; rtd 95; PtO *Glouc* from 01. *27 Capel Court, The Burgage, Prestbury, Cheltenham GL52 3EL* T: (01242) 576425

COLDICOTT, Mrs Christine Mary. b 51. EMMTC 04. **d** 07 **p** 08. NSM Ascension TM *Leic* 07-11; NSM Fosse 11-15; rtd 15. *5 Wayfarer Drive, East Goscote, Leicester LE7 3QZ* T: 0116-260 2437 E: chris_grand2004@yahoo.co.uk

COLDICOTT, Richard Spencer. b 69. Leeds Univ BSc 90 PhD 93 PGCE 94. Trin Coll Bris 06. **d** 08 **p** 09. C Aspley *S'well* 08-11; TV Horsham *Chich* from 11. *St Mark's House, North Heath Lane, Horsham RH12 4PJ* T: (01403) 260435 M: 07742-014444 E: richardcoldicott@btinternet.com

COLDWELL, Canon John Philip. b 62. Trin Coll Bris 04. **d** 06 **p** 07. C Inglewood Gp *Carl* 06-09; P-in-c Douglas St Ninian *S & M* 09-13; V from 13; Dioc Communications Officer from 10; Hon Can St German's Cathl from 14. *St Ninian's Vicarage, 58 Ballanard Road, Douglas, Isle of Man IM2 5HE* T: (01624) 621694 M: 07624-203395 E: media@sodorandman.im

COLDWELL, Rosemary Anne. b 52. Bretton Hall Coll CertEd 75 Open Univ BA 82 LTCL 74 LLCM 74. STETS 04. **d** 07 **p** 08. NSM Blandford Forum and Langton Long *Sarum* 07-12; PtO *Bradf* 12-13. *3 Shell Lane, Calverley, Pudsey LS28 5NR* M: 07929-090948 E: rosemarycoldwell@btinternet.com

COLE, Adrian Peter. See ROBBINS-COLE, Adrian Peter

COLE, Canon Alan John. b 35. Bps' Coll Cheshunt 63. **d** 66 **p** 67. C Boreham Wood All SS *St Alb* 66-69; C St Alb St Mich 69-72; V Redbourn 72-80; R Thorley w Bishop's Stortford H Trin 80-87; Chapl St Edw K and Martyr Cam *Ely* 87-94; Chapl Arthur Rank Hospice Cam 87-94; P-in-c Gamlingay w Hatley St George and E Hatley *Ely* 94-99; Hon Can Ely Cathl 96-00; P-in-c Everton w Tetworth 98-99; R Gamlingay and Everton

99-00; rtd 01; PtO *St E* from 01; *Ely* from 01. *73 Finchams Close, Linton, Cambridge CB21 4ND* T: (01223) 892286 E: alan73@waitrose.com

COLE, Alan Michael. b 40. Melbourne Univ DipEd 74 BA 74. ACT. **d** 66 **p** 67. Australia 66-75 and 90-97; Chapl Bp Otter Coll Chich 76-77; Chapl Ardingly Coll 77-82; Chapl Bonn w Cologne *Eur* 82-86; Chapl Helsinki w Moscow 86-90; P-in-c Ilkeston H Trin *Derby* 97-01; V 02-10; rtd 10; PtO *Pet* from 10. *30 St Mary's Paddock, Wellingborough NN8 1HJ*

COLE, Canon Brian Robert Arthur. b 35. Nottm Univ BA 57. Ridley Hall Cam 59. **d** 61 **p** 62. C Tye Green w Netteswell *Chelmsf* 61-64; C Keighley *Bradf* 64-67; V Copley *Wakef* 67-73; Chapl Halifax Gen Hosp 67-73; R Gt w Lt Dunham *Nor* 73-82; R Gt w Lt Fransham 74-82; P-in-c Sporle w Gt and Lt Palgrave 81-82; R Gt and Lt Dunham w Gt and Lt Fransham and Sporle 83-03; P-in-c 03-06; rtd 06; PtO *Nor* from 06; RD Brisley and Elmham 93-08; Hon Can Nor Cathl 98-08. *15 Wroxham Avenue, Swaffham PE37 7SD* T: (01760) 725585 E: bra.cole15@gmail.com

COLE, David Henry. See GIFFORD-COLE, David Henry

COLE, Guy Spenser. b 63. Univ of Wales (Ban) BA 84 Jes Coll Cam BA 88 MA 91. Westcott Ho Cam 85. **d** 88 **p** 89. C Eastville St Anne w St Mark and St Thos *Bris* 88-92; P-in-c Penhill 92-95; V 95-01; R Easthampstead *Ox* from 01. *The Rectory, Crowthorne Road, Easthampstead, Bracknell RG12 7ER* T: (01344) 423253 *or* 425205 E: guycole@guycole.freeserve.co.uk

COLE, Jennifer Ann. b 52. Open Univ MBA 04. STETS 07. **d** 09 **p** 10. NSM Kilmersdon w Babington and Radstock w Writhlington *B & W* 09-13; PtO 13-14; NSM Wells St Cuth w Wookey Hole from 14. *8 The Grange, Easton Hill, Easton, Wells BA5 1DU* M: 07749-079276 E: jennifer.cole@bathwells.anglican.org

COLE, John Gordon. b 43. Magd Coll Cam BA 65 MA 69. Cuddesdon Coll 66. **d** 68 **p** 69. C Leeds St Pet *Ripon* 68-71; C Moor Allerton 71-75; P-in-c Pendleton *Blackb* 75-86; Dioc Communications Officer 75-86; Dioc Missr *Linc* 86-98; Ecum Development Officer 98-02; Nat Adv for Unity in Miss 03-08; rtd 08. *Pelham House, Little Lane, Wrawby, Brigg DN20 8RW* T: (01652) 657484 E: johngcole@btinternet.com

COLE, John Spensley. b 39. Clare Coll Cam BA 62 MA 66 FCA 65. Linc Th Coll 78. **d** 80 **p** 81. C Cowes St Mary *Portsm* 80-83; C Portchester 83-87; V Modbury *Ex* 87-95; R Aveton Gifford 87-95; TR Modbury, Bigbury, Ringmore w Kingston etc 95-98; P-in-c Alne and Brafferton w Pilmoor, Myton-on-Swale etc *York* 98-05; rtd 05. *11 Long Meadow, Farnsfield, Newark NG22 8DR* T: (01623) 883595 E: johnlizcole@firenet.uk.net

COLE, Michael Berkeley. b 44. Cuddesdon Coll. **d** 72 **p** 73. C Shepshed *Leic* 72-76; V Leic St Chad 76-79; Hon C Painswick w Sheepscombe *Glouc* 94-97; Hon C Painswick w Sheepscombe and Cranham 97-98; Hon C Painswick and Kempsford w Whelford 98-04; TR Redhorn *Sarum* 04-09; rtd 09. *Homestead, Church End, Twyning, Tewkesbury GL20 6DA* E: mbcole@uwclub.net

COLE, Michael George. b 35. CD 75. Wesley Th Sem Washington DMin 88. Kelham Th Coll 56 Lich Th Coll 57. **d** 60 **p** 61. C Doncaster Ch Ch *Sheff* 60-63; Chapl RAF 63-68; Canada 68-82; USA from 82; rtd 98. *1202 Stonegate Way, Crozet VA 22932-3150, USA* E: mvgrcr6@comcast.net

COLE, Canon Michael John. b 34. St Pet Hall Ox BA 56 MA 60. Ridley Hall Cam 56. **d** 58 **p** 59. C Finchley Ch Ch *Lon* 58; C Leeds St Geo *Ripon* 58-61; Travelling Sec IVF 61-64; V Crookes St Thos *Sheff* 64-71; R Rusholme H Trin *Man* 71-75; V Woodford Wells *Chelmsf* 75-00; Chapl Leytonstone Ho Hosp 85-00; Hon Can Chelmsf Cathl 89-00; RD Redbridge 95-00; rtd 00; PtO *Chelmsf* 00-06. *1 Paradise Drive, Eastbourne BN20 7SX* T: (01323) 723425

COLE, Canon Norma Joan. b 46. EAMTC 93. **d** 96 **p** 97. C Ipswich St Mary at Stoke w St Pet *St E* 96-97; C Ipswich St Mary at Stoke w St Pet and St Fran 97-99; V Gt Cornard 99-04; V Rushen *S & M* 04-10; Hon Can St German's Cathl 09-10; rtd 10. *6 St Ninian's Court, St Ninian's Road, Douglas, Isle of Man IM2 4BY* T: (01624) 614695

COLE, Canon Peter George Lamont. b 27. Pemb Coll Cam BA 49 MA 52. Cuddesdon Coll 50. **d** 52 **p** 53. C Aldershot St Mich *Guildf* 52-55; C St Jo Cathl Bulawayo S Rhodesia 55-59; P-in-c Riverside All SS 55-59; R 59-62; Chapl St Steph Coll Balla Balla 63-65; V Bromley St Andr *Roch* 65-72; V Folkestone St Mary and St Eanswythe *Cant* 72-87; Hon Can Cant Cathl 80-87; V E and W Worldham, Hartley Mauditt w Kingsley etc *Win* 87-92; RD Alton 89-92; rtd 92; RD Petworth *Chich* 94-95; PtO from 95. *29 Swan View, Pulborough RH20 2BF* T: (01798) 873238

COLE, Timothy Alexander Robertson. b 60. Aber Univ MA 83 Edin Univ BD 86. Edin Th Coll 83. **d** 86 **p** 87. C Dunfermline *St And* 86-89; Vice-Provost St Andr Cathl Inverness 89-90;

R Inverness St Andr 89-90; R Edin St Mich and All SS 90-95; CF from 95; Chapl R Memorial Chpl Sandhurst 07-08. *c/o MOD Chaplains (Army)* F: 381824　T: (01264) 383430

COLE, Mrs Vanessa Anne. b 73. K Alfred's Coll Win BA 94. Trin Coll Bris BA 03. **d** 04 **p** 05. C Congresbury w Puxton and Hewish St Ann *B & W* 04-09; TV Portway and Danebury *Win* from 09. *The Rectory, Over Wallop, Stockbridge SO20 8HT* T: (01264) 782615　E: vanessa@cole.org.uk

COLE, William. b 45. Oak Hill Th Coll BA 96. **d** 96 **p** 97. NSM St Keverne *Truro* 96-99; P-in-c St Ruan w St Grade and Landewednack 99-10; rtd 10; PtO *Carl* from 11. *16 Copperas Close, Lowca, Whitehaven CA28 6QU*　T: (01946) 599614　E: billcole124@btinternet.com

COLE-BAKER, Peter Massey. b 58. New Univ of Ulster BSc 80 TCD BTh 98. CITC 95. **d** 98 **p** 99. C Ballywillan *Conn* 98-01; I Templemore w Thurles and Kilfithmone *C & O* 01-14; Can Ossory Cathl 12-14; rtd 14. *The Bungalow, Springfield, Clonard Road, Wexford, Republic of Ireland* E: pcolebaker@eircom.net

COLEBROOK, Canon Christopher John. b 36. Qu Mary Coll Lon BA 60 BD 69. St D Coll Lamp 60. **d** 62 **p** 63. C Llandeilo Tal-y-bont *S & B* 62-66; C Llansamlet 66-71; V Nantmel w St Harmon's and Llanwrthwl 71-76; V Glantawe 76-85; V Gowerton 85-01; RD Llwchwr 93-00; Hon Can Brecon Cathl 97-01; Prec 00-01; rtd 01. *79 Vivian Road, Sketty, Swansea SA2 0UN*　T: (01792) 521966

COLEBROOK, Peter Acland. b 29. Coates Hall Edin 52. **d** 55 **p** 56. C Northfield *Birm* 58-62; C Bideford *Ex* 62-66; rtd 89; PtO *Sarum* from 01. *Danes Lee, Ham Lane, Marnhull, Sturminster Newton DT10 1JN*　T: (01258) 820246

COLEBROOKE, Andrew. b 50. Imp Coll Lon BSc 71 MSc 72 PhD 75. Ridley Hall Cam 92. **d** 94 **p** 95. C Shrub End *Chelmsf* 94-98; R Mistley w Manningtree and Bradfield 98-09; RD Harwich 04-09; R Icknield Way Villages from 09. *The Rectory, 1 Hall Lane, Great Chishill, Royston SG8 8SG*　T: (01763) 838703　E: andy.colebrooke@icknieldwayparish.com

COLEBY, Andrew Mark. b 59. Linc Coll Ox MA 85 DPhil 85 Dur Univ BA 90 FRHistS 88. Cranmer Hall Dur 88. **d** 91 **p** 92. C Heeley *Sheff* 91-93; TV Gleadless 94-97; Chapl Ox Brookes Univ 97-01; P-in-c Didcot All SS 01-06; Dioc FE Officer and Chapl Abingdon and Witney Coll 06-09; Soc Resp Adv *St Alb* 09-13; R Shipston-on-Stour w Honington and Idlicote *Cov* from 13; PtO *Ox* from 11. *Shipston Rectory, 8 Glen Close, Shipston-on-Stour CV36 4ED*　T: (01608) 661210　E: am.coleby@btopenworld.com

COLEMAN, Aidan William. b 56. St Jo Coll Nottm 97. **d** 99 **p** 00. C Llandudno *Ban* 99-02; TV Bangor and P-in-c Llandygai and Maes y Groes 02-05; P-in-c Rhosymedre w Penycae *St As* 05-12; V Holywell from 12; AD from 14. *The Vicarage, 1 Lys Bychan, Holywell CH8 7SX*　T: (01352) 710010　E: a.coleman560@btinternet.com

COLEMAN, Andrew David. b 78. Monash Univ BA 00. Melbourne Coll of Div MDiv 08. **d** 07 **p** 08. C Kilmore Australia 07-09; C Port Elliot w Goolwa 09-11; V Longford *Cov* from 13; P-in-c Ansty and Shilton from 13. *The Vicarage, 65 Hurst Road, Longford, Coventry CV6 6EL*　T: (024) 7636 6635　M: 07517-373587　E: andrewdavidcoleman@hotmail.com

COLEMAN, Mrs Ann Valerie. b 51. K Coll Lon BD 72 Heythrop Coll Lon MA 03. St Aug Coll Cant. **dss** 80 **d** 87 **p** 94. Hampstead Garden Suburb *Lon* 80-84; Golders Green 85-87; Selection Sec and Voc Adv ACCM 87-91; Teacher Bp Ramsey Sch 92-93; Chapl 93-99; Dir of Ords Willesden Area *Lon* 96-99; Course Leader NTMTC 99-04; Hon C Eastcote St Lawr *Lon* 93-04; Dir Wydale Hall *York* 04-08; Dioc Moderator Reader Tr 05-08; Tutor St Mellitus Coll *Lon* 08-12; Asst Dean St Mellitus Coll and Dir NTMTC 12-15; Hon C Doddinghurst *Chelmsf* from 14; NSM Bentley Common, Kelvedon Hatch and Navestock from 14. *The Rectory, Church Lane, Doddinghurst, Brentwood CM15 0NJ* E: annvc@tiscali.co.uk

COLEMAN, Brian James. b 36. K Coll Cam BA 58 MA 61. Ripon Hall Ox 58. **d** 60 **p** 61. C Allestree *Derby* 60-65; V Allestree St Nic 65-69; Chapl and Lect St Mich Coll Salisbury 69-77; P-in-c Matlock Bank *Derby* 77-86; R Frimley *Guildf* 86-92; V Guildf All SS 92-02; rtd 02; PtO *Sarum* from 03. *6 Kingfisher Close, Salisbury SP2 8JE*　T: (01722) 410034　E: coleman.sarum@virgin.net

COLEMAN, Brian Ray. b 71. California State Univ Fullerton BPhil 94. Seabury-Western Th Sem MDiv 98. **d** 98 **p** 99. Assoc R Los Angeles St Jas USA 98-01; C Sheff St Leon Norwood 01-03; Chapl N Gen Hosp NHS Trust Sheff 01-03; P-in-c Sheff St Pet Abbeydale 03-08; P-in-c Sheff St Oswald 03-08; R Battle Creek St Thos USA from 08. *St Thomas's Rectory, 252 Chestnut Street, Battle Creek MI 49017-3348, USA* E: frbrian@btopenworld.com

COLEMAN, David. b 61. **d** 14 **p** 15. C Horley *S'wark* from 14. *St Francis' Vicarage, 84 Balcombe Road, Horley RH6 9AY* T: (01293) 771088　M: 07958-997455　E: davidmcoleman61@gmail.com

COLEMAN, Preb David. b 49. K Coll Lon BD 72 AKC 72. St Aug Coll Cant 72. **d** 73 **p** 74. C Is of Dogs Ch Ch and St Jo w St Luke *Lon* 73-77; C Greenford H Cross 77-80; V Cricklewood St Pet 80-85; V Golders Green 85-90; V Eastcote St Lawr 90-04; P-in-c Upper Ryedale and CME Officer Cleveland Adnry *York* 04-08; V Heston *Lon* 08-15; Preb St Paul's Cathl 13-15; rtd 15; PtO *Chelmsf* from 15. *The Rectory, Church Lane, Doddinghurst, Brentwood CM15 0NJ* E: frdavid.coleman@tiscali.co.uk

COLEMAN, David Kenneth. b 60. SWMTC 06. **d** 09 **p** 10. NSM Bickleigh and Shaugh Prior *Ex* from 09. *4 Torbridge Road, Horrabridge, Yelverton PL20 7SD*　T: (01822) 853311　E: deekaycee@hotmail.com

COLEMAN, Frank. b 58. Hull Univ BA 79. St Steph Ho Ox BA 83 MA 87. **d** 83 **p** 84. C Brandon *Dur* 83-85; C Newton Aycliffe 85-88; V Denford w Ringstead *Pet* 88-00; P-in-c Islip 95-00; V Caldecote, Northill and Old Warden *St Alb* from 00. *The Vicarage, 2A Biggleswade Road, Upper Caldecote, Biggleswade SG18 9BL*　T: (01767) 315578　F: 317988　M: 07738-357458　E: frankcoleman@ntlworld.com

COLEMAN, John Harold. b 38. Cant Sch of Min 83. **d** 86 **p** 87. NSM Dover St Martin *Cant* 86-92; V St Mary's Bay w St Mary-in-the-Marsh etc 92-03; P-in-c New Romney w Old Romney and Midley 95-03; rtd 03; PtO *Cant* from 03. *13 Alexandra Road, Capel-le-Ferne, Folkestone CT18 7LN* T: (01303) 489705　E: john.coleman8@btinternet.com

COLEMAN, Jonathan Mark. b 59. Kent Univ BA 81. Qu Coll Birm MA 99. **d** 99 **p** 00. C Warrington St Elphin *Liv* 99-02; P-in-c Liv St Chris Norris Green 02-07; Area Dean W Derby and Hon Can Liv Cathl 06-07; P-in-c W Derby St Mary 07-09; P-in-c W Derby St Jas 07-09; V W Derby St Mary and St Jas 09-14; R Rochdale *Man* from 14. *The Vicarage, Sparrow Hill, Rochdale OL16 1QT*　E: markcoleman@bigfoot.com

COLEMAN, Ms Julie Victoria. b 62. Cant Ch Cn Univ PGCE 08. St Jo Coll Nottm 09. **d** 11 **p** 12. C Aylesham w Adisham and Nonington *Cant* 11-14; P-in-c Romney Marsh from 14. *The Vicarage, North Street, New Romney TN28 8DR* M: 07583-774857　E: jvcoleman@btinternet.com

COLEMAN, Michael. b 28. Nat Coll Div LTh 90. **d** 95. NSM E Kilbride *Glas* 95-99; NSM Motherwell 99-01; NSM Wishaw 99-01; rtd 01; LtO *Glas* from 01. *26 Wingate Park, East Kilbride, Glasgow G74 3PR*　T: (01355) 902523

COLEMAN, Neil Geoffrey. b 77. Trin Coll Bris BA 11. **d** 11 **p** 12. C N Mundham w Hunston and Merston *Chich* 11-15; V St Paul's Cray St Barn *Roch* from 15. *The Vicarage, Rushet Road, Orpington BR5 2PU*　M: 07826-850273　E: n-coleman@hotmail.co.uk

COLEMAN, Ms Nicola Jane. b 63. Goldsmiths' Coll Lon BA 86. Ripon Coll Cuddesdon 99. **d** 01 **p** 02. C Croydon St Jo *S'wark* 01-05; P-in-c S Norwood H Innocents 05-12; P-in-c The Lulworths, Winfrith Newburgh and Chaldon *Sarum* from 12. *The Rectory, West Road, West Lulworth, Wareham BH20 5RY* T: (01929) 400550　E: rev.niccoleman@gmail.com

COLEMAN, Patrick Francis. b 58. Pontifical Univ Rome PhB 79 STB 82 STL 84. Ven English Coll Rome 77. **d** 82 **p** 83. In RC Ch 82-92; NSM Abergavenny St Mary w Llanwenarth Citra *Mon* 96-99; Asst Chapl Milan w Genoa and Varese *Eur* 99-01; R Goetre w Llanover *Mon* 01-06; Dir CME 01-06; P-in-c Abertillery w Cwmtillery 06-10; V Abertillery w Cwmtillery w Llanhilleth etc 10-14; V Chesterfield St Mary and All SS *Derby* from 14. *The Vicarage, 28 Cromwell Road, Chesterfield S40 4TH* T: (01246) 462866　E: abervicar@me.com

COLEMAN, Canon Peter Nicholas. b 42. St Mich Coll Llan 83. **d** 85 **p** 86. C Skewen *Llan* 85-88; R Ystradyfodwg 88-07; P-in-c Treorchy and Treherbert 04-07; RD Rhondda 96-04; Can Llan Cathl 04-07; rtd 07; PtO *Llan* from 07. *15 Pant Hendre, Pencoed, Bridgend CF35 6LN*

COLEMAN, Richard Ian. b 70. Open Univ BSc 00. Wycliffe Hall Ox 05. **d** 07 **p** 08. C Peterlee *Dur* 07-11; P-in-c Barton in Fabis *S'well* from 11; P-in-c Gotham from 11; P-in-c Kingston and Ratcliffe-on-Soar from 11; P-in-c Thrumpton from 11. *The New Rectory, 39 Leake Road, Gotham, Nottingham NG11 0HW* T: 0115-983 0608　E: coleman@orpheusmail.co.uk

COLEMAN, Stephen Paul Losack. b 80. St Benet's Hall Ox BA 02 MSt 03. Westcott Ho Cam 12. **d** 14 **p** 15. C Winchmore Hill St Paul *Lon* from 14. *St Paul's Lodge, 58 Church Hill, London N21 1JA*　T: (020) 8882 1921　E: stephen@spwh.org

COLEMAN, Canon Sybil Jean. b 30. St Deiniol's Hawarden 83. **d** 85 **p** 97. NSM Manselton *S & B* 85-90; C Swansea St Mark and St Jo 90-94; P-in-c 94-98; V 98-00; Hon Can Brecon Cathl 98-00; rtd 00. *Beckley, 25 Beverley Gardens, Fforestfach, Swansea SA5 5DR*　T: (01792) 584280

COLEMAN, Timothy. b 57. Southn Univ BSc 79 MBACP. Ridley Hall Cam 87. **d** 89 **p** 90. C Bisley and W End *Guildf* 89-93; C Hollington St Jo *Chich* 93-97; V Aldborough Hatch *Chelmsf* 97-02; Chapl Princess Alexandra Hosp NHS Trust 02-04; Chapl Barking Havering and Redbridge Hosps NHS Trust from 04. *The Chaplain's Office, Queen's Hospital, Rom Valley Way, Romford RM7 0AG* T: (01708) 503201
E: tim.coleman@bhrhospitals.nhs.uk

COLERIDGE, William Paul Hugh. b 76. Newc Univ LLB 98 Solicitor 01. Wycliffe Hall Ox 07. **d** 09 **p** 10. C Ches Square St Mich w St Phil *Lon* 09-12; C Bayswater from 12; C Paddington St Steph w St Luke from 12. *The Vicarage, 27 St Petersburgh Place, London W2 4LA* T: (020) 7229 2192
E: will@stmatthewsbayswater.org.uk

COLES, Canon Alasdair Charles. b 67. St Andr Univ BSc 90 Homerton Coll Cam PGCE 91 Heythrop Coll Lon PhD 03. Ripon Coll Cuddesdon 96. **d** 96 **p** 97. C Wymondham *Nor* 96-99; Min Can and Sacr St Paul's Cathl 99-04; P-in-c Pimlico St Mary Bourne Street 04-07; V 07-09; P-in-c Pimlico St Barn 04-07; V 07-09; Asst Vice Prin and Chapl All SS Academy Dunstable from 09; PV Westmr Abbey from 04; Hon Can Mampong Ghana from 14. *All Saints Academy, Houghton Road, Dunstable LU5 5AB* F: 619701 M: 07729-962723 T: (01582) 619700 ext 7105
E: alasdaircoles@allsaintsacademydunstable.org

COLES, Alasdair John. b 66. Pemb Coll Ox BA 87 Green Coll Ox BM, BCh 90 CCC Cam PhD 98 MRCP 94. ERMC 05. **d** 08 **p** 09. NSM Chesterton St Andr *Ely* from 08. *Department of Neurology, Box 165, Addenbrooke's Hospital, Cambridge CB2 2QQ* T: (01223) 216751 F: 336941 E: ajc1020@medschl.cam.ac.uk

COLES, Preb Alison Elizabeth. b 60. St Mary's Coll Dur BA 81. Ripon Coll Cuddesdon 95. **d** 97 **p** 98. C Leckhampton SS Phil and Jas w Cheltenham St Jas *Glouc* 97-00; Asst Chapl Dudley Gp of Hosps NHS Trust 00-04; Chapl Walsall Hosps NHS Trust from 04; Preb Lich Cathl from 15. *Walsall Hospitals NHS Trust, Manor Hospital, Moat Road, Walsall WS2 9PS* T: (01922) 656216

COLES, Christopher Wayne. b 58. St Mich Coll Llan 97. **d** 99 **p** 00. C Coity w Nolton *Llan* 99-02; C Canton Cardiff 02-07; P-in-c Porth Newydd 07-13; P-in-c Skewen from 13. *New Skewen Vicarage, 39 Hill Road, Neath Abbey, Neath SA10 7NP* T: (01792) 814116

COLES (*formerly* **OLDHAM), David Christian.** b 76. Surrey Univ MSc 07 RN 98. Ripon Coll Cuddesdon 09. **d** 10 **p** 11. C Wymondham *Nor* 10-11; NSM Wellingborough All SS and Wellingborough All Hallows *Pet* 12-15. *The Vicarage, Church Hill, Finedon, Wellingborough NN9 5NR* T: (01933) 681786 M: 07840-700277 E: oldhamd@hotmail.com

✠**COLES, The Rt Revd David John.** b 43. Auckland Univ MA 67 Otago Univ BD 69 MTh 71 Man Univ PhD 74. St Jo Coll Auckland 66. **d** 68 **p** 69 **c** 90. C Remuera New Zealand 68-70; Chapl Selwyn Coll Dunedin 70-71; Hon C Fallowfield *Man* 72-74; Chapl Hulme Gr Sch Oldham 73-74; V Glenfield New Zealand 74-76; V Takapuna 76-80; Dean Napier 80-84; Dean Christchurch 84-90; Bp Christchurch from 90. *PO Box 4438, Christchurch 8140, New Zealand* T: (0064) (3) 351 7711 or 363 0913 F: 372 3357 E: bishop@chch.ang.org.nz

COLES, Preb Francis Herbert. b 35. Selw Coll Cam BA 59 MA 63. Coll of Resurr Mirfield 59. **d** 61 **p** 62. C Wolvercote *Ox* 61-65; C Farnham Royal 65-69; V Lynton and Brendon *Ex* 69-73; V Countisbury 70; V Lynton, Brendon, Countisbury and Lynmouth 70-73; TR Lynton, Brendon, Countisbury, Lynmouth etc 73-76; P-in-c Iffley *Ox* 76-88; V Ivybridge w Harford *Ex* 88-00; Preb Ex Cathl from 98; rtd 00; PtO *Ex* from 00. *8 Glenthorne Road, Exeter EX4 4QU* T: (01392) 420238

COLES, Graham Robert. b 60. Qu Coll Birm 07. **d** 09 **p** 10. C Lillington and Old Milverton *Cov* 09-12; C Leamington Spa H Trin 09-12; P-in-c Cubbington 12-14; V from 14. *St Mary's Vicarage, 15 Pinehurst, Cubbington, Leamington Spa CV32 7XA* T: (01926) 330596

COLES, Preb John Spencer Halstaff. b 50. Hertf Coll Ox BA 72 MA 76. Wycliffe Hall Ox 72. **d** 75 **p** 76. C Reading Greyfriars Ox 75-79; C Clifton Ch Ch w Em *Bris* 79-82; V Woodside Park St Barn *Lon* 82-06; C 06-11; Dir New Wine Internat Min from 11; Preb St Paul's Cathl from 11. *33 Arnos Road, London N11 1AP* T: (020) 3441 5264

COLES, Matthew Simon Robert. b 79. UEA BA 02. Ridley Hall Cam 06. **d** 09 **p** 10. C Gt Chesham *Ox* 09-12; CF from 12. *c/o MOD Chaplains (Army)* T: (01264) 383430 F: 381824 M: 07736-464537 E: mattsr7@yahoo.com

COLES, Mrs Olivia Mary Kana. b 64. ERMC 12. **d** 15. NSM Histon *Ely* from 15; NSM Impington from 15. *Address temp unknown*

COLES, Mrs Pamela. b 39. Nottm Univ CertEd 59. NOC 04. **d** 05 **p** 06. NSM Clayton *Bradf* 05-09; PtO *Leeds* from 09. *4 Ferndale Avenue, Clayton, Bradford BD14 6PG* T: (01274) 427956 E: pamcolesclayton@yahoo.com

COLES, Richard Keith Robert. b 62. K Coll Lon BA 94 AKC 94 Leeds Univ MA 05 Northn Univ Hon PhD 12 FRSA 12. Coll of Resurr Mirfield 03. **d** 05 **p** 06. C Boston *Linc* 05-07; C Wilton Place St Paul *Lon* 07-11; Chapl R Academy of Music 07-08; P-in-c Finedon *Pet* from 11. *St Mary's Vicarage, Church Hill, Finedon, Wellingborough NN9 5NR* T: (01933) 681786
E: revdrichardcoles@yahoo.co.uk

COLES, Canon Robert Reginald. b 47. Surrey Univ BSc 69. Cant Sch of Min 82. **d** 85 **p** 86. NSM Sittingbourne St Mich *Cant* 85-87; C St Laur in Thanet 87-93; P-in-c St Nicholas at Wade w Sarre and Chislet w Hoath 93-13; P-in-c Minster w Monkton 96-13; Hon Can Cant Cathl 09-13; rtd 13; PtO *Cant* from 14. *4 Millfield, St Margaret-at-Cliffe, Dover CT15 6JL* T: (01304) 852091

COLES, Preb Stephen Richard. b 49. Univ Coll Ox BA 70 MA 74 Leeds Univ BA 80. Coll of Resurr Mirfield 78. **d** 81 **p** 82. C Stoke Newington St Mary *Lon* 81-84; Chapl K Coll Cam 84-89; V Finsbury Park St Thos *Lon* from 89; Preb St Paul's Cathl from 13. *25 Romilly Road, London N4 2QY* T: (020) 7359 5741 E: cardinal.jeoffry@btconnect.com

COLES, Mrs Sylvia Margaret. b 48. ERMC 04. **d** 07 **p** 08. NSM Northampton St Benedict *Pet* 07-10; NSM Duston 10-14; NSM Dallington from 14; NSM Northampton St Jas from 14. *37 Delapre Crescent Road, Northampton NN4 8NG* T: (01604) 767305 E: lizziesgranny@talktalk.net

COLEY (*née* **JOHNSON), Mrs Emma Louise.** b 76. Ex Univ BA 97 PGCE 98. Wycliffe Hall Ox BTh 04. **d** 04 **p** 05. C Wendover and Halton *Ox* 04-09; C Kennington and Radley and Sunningwell 09-12; P-in-c Sandridge *St Alb* 12-14; V from 14; Asst Dir of Ords from 12. *The Vicarage, 2 Anson Close, Sandridge, St Albans AL4 9EN* T: (01727) 866089
E: emcoley@me.com

COLEY, Peter Leonard. b 45. Bath Univ BSc 67 City Univ MSc 84 CEng MIMechE. Oak Hill Th Coll 85. **d** 87 **p** 88. C Mile Cross *Nor* 87-92; R Stratton St Mary w Stratton St Michael etc 92-01; R Kirby-le-Soken w Gt Holland *Chelmsf* 01-10; rtd 10; PtO *Portsm* from 11. *6 Forest Rise, Liss GU33 7AU* T: (01730) 300659 M: 07706-037108
E: rev.petercoley@googlemail.com

COLLARD, Canon Harold. b 27. Wycliffe Hall Ox 51. **d** 53 **p** 54. C Rainham *Chelmsf* 53-56; C Kingston upon Hull H Trin *York* 56-59; V Upper Armley *Ripon* 59-68; R Chesterfield H Trin *Derby* 68-77; P-in-c Matlock Bath 77-83; V 83-92; Hon Can Derby Cathl 87-92; RD Wirksworth 88-92; rtd 92; PtO *Leeds* from 92. *10 Kirkby Avenue, Ripon HG4 2DR* T: (01765) 606306

COLLARD, Norton Harvey. b 22. Open Univ BA 80. Roch Th Coll 63. **d** 65 **p** 66. C Swanley St Mary *Roch* 65-67; C Dartford H Trin 67-70; V Grantham St Anne *Linc* 70-87; rtd 87; PtO *Linc* 87-02. *1 Kenwick Drive, Grantham NG31 9DP* T: (01476) 577345

COLLEDGE, Ms Anthea June. b 78. St Jo Coll Ox BA 00 Imp Coll Lon MSc 06 MPhil 09 St Jo Coll Dur BA 10. Cranmer Hall Dur 08. **d** 10 **p** 11. C Wortley-de-Leeds *Ripon* 10-13; C Wortley and Farnley *Leeds* 13-14; Chapl Sheff Univ from 14. *University of Sheffield Chaplaincy, Octagon Centre, Clarkson Street, Sheffield S10 2TQ* M: 07518-319475 T: 0114-222 9750
E: a.j.colledge@googlemail.com or a.colledge@sheffield.ac.uk

COLLEDGE, Christopher Richard. b 58. Chich Th Coll. **d** 82 **p** 83. C Deal St Leon and St Rich and Sholden *Cant* 82-85; Bermuda 85-88; TV Wickford and Runwell *Chelmsf* 88-90; Chapl Runwell Hosp Wickford 88-90; Chapl RAD 90-03; rtd 04; PtO *Win* from 12. *Address withheld by request*
E: chriscolledge1@talktalk.net

COLLESS, Mrs Salma. b 55. SRN 77 RM 80. EAMTC 89. **d** 92 **p** 94. NSM Chesterton St Andr *Ely* 92-93; Hon Dn Chapman Australia 93; C Curtin 94-96; Chapl Brindabella Gardens 96; P Worker Bernie Court 97; Asst P Woden 97-98. *12 Sollya Place, Rivett ACT 2611, Australia* T: (0061) (2) 6288 7835 M: 414-755756

COLLETT, George Ernest. b 48. Cant Sch of Min 01. **d** 04 **p** 05. NSM Bromley H Trin *Roch* from 04; P-in-c Bromley Common St Luke from 15. *Holy Trinity Cottage, 1 Church Lane, Bromley BR2 8LB* T: (020) 8462 7561 E: george.collett@outlook.com

COLLETT-WHITE, Thomas Charles. b 36. Trin Coll Cam BA 61 MA 86. Ridley Hall Cam 60. **d** 62 **p** 63. C Gillingham St Mark *Roch* 62-66; V 79-90; C Normanton *Wakef* 66-69; V Highbury New Park St Aug *Lon* 69-76; R Huntingdon w Ormstown Canada 76-79; Chapl Medway Hosp Gillingham 79-85; P-in-c Clerkenwell St Jas and St Jo w St Pet *Lon* 90-96; rtd 01; PtO *Cant* from 06. *77 The Street, Boughton-under-Blean, Faversham ME13 9BE* T: (01227) 750770

COLLEY, Elizabeth Jane. b 51. Open Univ BA 89 DipSW 96. **d** 13 **p** 14. NSM Crewe All SS and St Paul w St Pet *Ches* from 13. *8 Tatton Drive, Sandbach CW11 1DR* T: (01270) 748669 E: ejmmcc@aol.com

COLLEY, Mrs Karen. b 68. Sheff Hallam Univ BA 96 Leeds Metrop Univ MSc 01. Yorks Min Course 11. **d** 13 **p** 14. NSM Sheff Manor from 13. *4 Bramley Hall Road, Handsworth, Sheffield S13 8TX* E: revdkaren@btinternet.com *or* karen.colley@manorparish.co.uk

COLLEY, Leonard Noel. b 51. Qu Coll Birm 12. **d** 15. C Nanpantan St Mary in Charnwood *Leic* from 15. *Address temp unknown*

COLLICUTT McGRATH, Joanna Ruth. b 54. LMH Ox BA 76 MA 85 Lon Univ MPhil 78 Ox Brookes Univ PhD 98. Wycliffe Hall Ox 00 Ripon Coll Cuddesdon 05. **d** 06 **p** 07. NSM Witney *Ox* from 06; Tutor Ripon Coll Cuddesdon 07; Lect from 10; Dioc Adv for Spiritual Care for Older People *Ox* from 10. *Ripon College, Cuddesdon, Oxford OX44 9EX* T: (01865) 877404 E: jcollicutt@aol.com *or* joanna.collicutt@hmc.ox.ac.uk

COLLIE, Canon Bertie Harold Guy. b 28. Glas Univ MB, ChB 56. Glas NSM Course 75. **d** 76 **p** 77. NSM Ayr *Glas* 76-84; NSM Maybole 76-04; NSM Girvan 84-04; NSM Pinmore 84-04; Dioc Supernumerary 91-99; Can St Mary's Cathl 96-99; Hon Can St Mary's Cathl from 99; LtO from 99. *4 Savoy Park, Ayr KA7 2XA* T: (01292) 285889 E: b.collie@sky.com

COLLIER, Anthony Charles. b 45. Peterho Cam BA 68 MA 72 Whitelands Coll Lon PGCE 76. Cuddesdon Coll 68. **d** 71 **p** 72. C N Holmwood *Guildf* 71-75; PtO *S'wark* 75-79; Chapl Colfe's Sch Lon 80-10; rtd 10; Hon C Shirley St Jo *Cant* 80-84; Hon C *S'wark* 85-13; PtO from 13. *56 Bennetts Way, Croydon CR0 8AB* T: (020) 8777 6456 E: accollier@hotmail.com

COLLIER, Clive. *See* COLLIER, Paul Clive

COLLIER, Capt David Leslie. b 60. Wilson Carlile Coll 02 Qu Coll Birm 12. **d** 14 **p** 15. C Birkdale St Pet *Liv* from 14. *St Peter's Vicarage, 2 St Peter's Road, Southport PR8 4BY* E: davecollier3@blueyonder.co.uk

COLLIER, Canon Janice Margaret. b 57. MCSP 79. Cam Th Federation 99. **d** 01 **p** 02. C Formby H Trin *Liv* 01-05; P-in-c Hale 05-10; TR S Widnes from 10; AD Widnes from 13; Hon Can Liv Cathl from 13. *The Vicarage, 2 Vicarage Close, Hale Village, Liverpool L24 4BH* T: 0151-425 3195

COLLIER, John Alfred. **d** 13 **p** 13. NSM Mamhilad w Monkswood and Glascoed Chapel *Mon* 13-14; R from 14. *The Rectory, Nantyderry, Abergavenny NP7 9DW* T: (01873) 880378 E: collierjohn1@aol.com

COLLIER, Michael Francis. b 29. Wycliffe Hall Ox 71. **d** 73 **p** 74. C Hamstead St Paul *Birm* 73-75; P-in-c Castleton *Derby* 75-80; P-in-c Hope 78-80; V Hope and Castleton 80-97; RD Bakewell and Eyam 90-95; rtd 97; PtO *Derby* from 97. *Buffers Cottage, Station Road, Hope, Hope Valley S33 6RR* T: (01433) 620915

COLLIER, Paul Clive. b 53. Trin Coll Bris 80. **d** 82 **p** 83. C Hazlemere *Ox* 82-90; V from 90. *The New Vicarage, 260 Amersham Road, High Wycombe HP15 7PZ* T: (01494) 439404 E: clive.collier@hazlemere.org

COLLIER, Paul Edward. b 58. Mert Coll Ox BA 85 Lon Univ PGCE 87 Solicitor 93. S'wark Ord Course 91. **d** 94 **p** 95. C E Dulwich St Jo *S'wark* 94-97; C-in-c Bermondsey St Hugh CD 97-02; Chapl Goldsmiths' Coll Lon 03-09; Hon C Dulwich St Barn 09-11; C Peckham St Sav 11; P-in-c 11-13; V from 13. *173 Choumert Road, London SE15 4AW* M: 07545-305798 E: collier.paul@coplestoncentre.org.uk

COLLIER, Richard John Millard. b 45. FRSA 92. EAMTC 78. **d** 81 **p** 82. NSM Nor St Pet Mancroft w St Jo Maddermarket 81-97; NSM Thurton 99-09; NSM Rockland St Mary w Hellington, Bramerton etc 09-12; PtO 12-14; NSM Docking, the Birchams, Stanhoe and Sedgeford from 14. *The Old Buck, Church Lane, Sedgeford, Hunstanton PE36 5NA* T: (01485) 579091 E: rjsjc@yahoo.com

COLLIER, Stefan John. b 74. Man Univ BSc 95 St Andr Univ PhD 99 Cam Univ BTh 09. Ridley Hall Cam 07. **d** 09 **p** 10. C E Win 09-11; C Itchen Valley 11-13; R Esher *Guildf* from 13. *The Rectory, 4 Esher Place Avenue, Esher KT10 8PY*

COLLIER, Stephen John. b 46. St Pet Coll Ox MA 68 Univ of Wales (Cardiff) DipSW 74. Qu Coll Birm 92. **d** 94 **p** 95. C Thorpe St Andr *Nor* 94-98; C Nor St Pet Mancroft w St Jo Maddermarket 98-01; R Kessingland, Gisleham and Rushmere 01-05; rtd 05; Hon C N Greenford All Hallows *Lon* from 06. *9 Drew Gardens, Greenford UB6 7QF* T: (020) 8903 9697

COLLIER, Steven Philip. b 84. Wycliffe Hall Ox. **d** 12. C Upper Sunbury St Sav *Lon* 12-13; C Isleworth All SS 13-15; C Broadwater *Chich* from 15. *53 Lavington Road, Worthing BN14 7SL* M: 07725-743194 E: stevencollier@hotmail.co.uk

COLLIER, Susan Margaret. b 47. Cam Univ MB, BChir 73. NOC 95. **d** 98 **p** 99. NSM Dringhouses *York* 98-12; PtO from 12. *12 St Helen's Road, York YO24 1HP* T: (01904) 706064 F: 708052

COLLIN, Mrs Fiona Maria. b 62. RGN 83. Cranmer Hall Dur 11. **d** 13 **p** 14. C Sunderland Minster *Dur* from 13. *21 Thornhill Terrace, Sunderland SR2 7JL* M: 07743-589429 E: fionamariacollin@gmail.com

COLLIN, Terry. b 39. St Aid Birkenhead 65. **d** 67 **p** 68. C Bolton St Jas w St Chrys *Bradf* 67-71; C Keighley 71-74; V Greengates 74-04; rtd 04; PtO *Bradf* 05-11. *275 Leeds Road, Eccleshill, Bradford BD2 3LD* T: (01274) 200855

COLLING, Terence John. b 47. Linc Th Coll 84. **d** 86 **p** 87. C Wood End *Cov* 86-90; V Willenhall 90-02; V Wolvey w Burton Hastings, Copston Magna etc 02-14; rtd 14; PtO *Cov* from 14; *Leic* from 14. *2 Roman Close, Claybrooke Magna, Lutterworth LE17 5DU* E: tc@vicwolvey.fsnet.co.uk

COLLINGBOURNE, David Edward. b 42. St D Coll Lamp. **d** 01. Treas Dioc Coun of Educn *Mon* from 94; NSM Bishton 01-06; NSM Newport Ch 06-08; NSM Bedwas w Machen w Rudry 08-12; P-in-c Marshfield w St Bride's Wentloog from 12. *The Vicarage, Church Lane, Marshfield, Cardiff CF3 2UF* T: (01633) 680687 E: davidcollingbourne42@tiscali.co.uk

COLLINGBOURNE, Mrs Susan Lynne. b 48. Caerleon Coll of Educn TCert 75 Univ of Wales (Cardiff) BEd 82 MEd 94. **d** 09 **p** 10. NSM Maesglas and Duffryn *Mon* 09-12; P-in-c Marshfield w St Bride's Wentloog from 12; Dioc Child Protection Officer from 98. *The Vicarage, Church Lane, Marshfield, Cardiff CF3 2UF* T: (01633) 680687 E: susan.collingbourne@tinyworld.co.uk

COLLINGE, Mrs Christine Elizabeth. b 47. Doncaster Coll of Educn CertEd 68. SAOMC 95. **d** 98 **p** 99. NSM W Slough *Ox* 98-04; TV Stantonbury and Willen 04-12; rtd 12; PtO *Ox* from 13. *26 Bell Close, Slough SL2 5UQ* T: (01753) 575332 E: chriscollinge@hotmail.com

COLLINGRIDGE, Graham Ian. b 58. Pemb Coll Ox BA 80 MA 84 Bedf Coll Lon MSc 84 Anglia Ruskin Univ MA 10. Ridley Hall Cam 07. **d** 09 **p** 10. C Bitterne Park *Win* 09-13; V Long Buckby w Watford and W Haddon w Winwick *Pet* from 13. *The Vicarage, 10 Hall Drive, Long Buckby, Northampton NN6 7QU* T: (01327) 842204 E: vicar.longbuckby@btinternet.com

COLLINGRIDGE, Susan Rachel. b 61. St Mary's Coll Dur BA 83. Cranmer Hall Dur 85. **d** 88 **p** 94. Par Dn Luton St Mary *St Alb* 88-93; PtO *Ex* 93-94; NSM Parkham, Alwington, Buckland Brewer etc 94-98; TV Cove St Jo *Guildf* 98-03; V Guildf Ch Ch w St Martha-on-the-Hill 03-11; PtO *Ches* 11-14; NSM Antrobus from 14. *Glebe House, Knutsford Road, Antrobus, Northwich CW9 6JW* T: (01606) 892951 M: 07734-879224 E: susie.collingridge@gmail.com

COLLINGS, Ms Helen Mary. b 67. Warwick Univ BA 88 St Jo Coll Dur BA 06 Jes Coll Ox PGCE 90. Cranmer Hall Dur 04. **d** 06 **p** 07. C Ossett and Gawthorpe *Wakef* 06-09; P-in-c Sandal St Cath *Leeds* from 09. *9 Sandal Cliff, Wakefield WF2 6AU* T: (01924) 254480 M: 07708-066063 E: helen@trinityossett.org.uk

COLLINGTON, Cameron James. b 68. Wycliffe Hall Ox BTh 01. **d** 01 **p** 02. C Ealing St Paul *Lon* 01-05; V Hammersmith St Simon from 05. *153 Blythe Road, London W14 0HL* T: (020) 7602 1043 E: cameron@stsimons.com

COLLINGWOOD, Canon Christopher Paul. b 54. Birm Univ BMus 76 PGCE 77 Ox Univ BA 82 MA 87 K Coll Lon MA 01 PhD 07 LRSM 04. Ripon Coll Cuddesdon 80. **d** 83 **p** 84. C Tupsley *Heref* 83-86; Prec St Alb Abbey *St Alb* 86-90; V Bedford St Paul 90-97; Can Res and Prec Guildf Cathl 97-99; Hon C Loughton St Jo *Chelmsf* 99-09; Chapl Chigwell Sch Essex 99-09; Sen Tutor 01-09; R Minchinhampton w Box and Amberley *Glouc* 09-13; AD Stroud 11-13; Can Res and Chan York Minster from 13. *3 Minster Court, York YO1 7JJ* T: (01904) 557267 *or* 557204 E: christopherc@yorkminster.org

COLLINGWOOD, Deryck Laurence. b 50. St Jo Coll Cam BA 72. Edin Th Coll BD 85. **d** 85 **p** 85. Chapl Napier Poly *Edin* 85-88; C Edin Ch Ch 85-88; TV 88-89; Tutor Edin Th Coll 89-94; Asst P Edin St Hilda and Edin St Fillan 94-03; Chapl Edin Napier Univ 95-03; P-in-c Dalmahoy 03-06; R from 06. *St Mary's Rectory, Dalmahoy, Kirknewton EH27 8EB* T: 0131-333 1312 E: dcollingwood131@btinternet.com

COLLINGWOOD, Graham Lewis. b 63. Open Univ BA 92 Ex Univ MA 98. St Steph Ho Ox 92. **d** 95 **p** 96. C Heavitree w Ex St Paul 95-97; CF 97-99; C St Marychurch *Ex* 99-00; C Cottingham *York* 00-02; Chapl RAF 02-11; V New Rossington *Sheff* 11-13; PtO *York* from 14. *11 Kingtree Avenue, Cottingham HU16 4DS* T: (01482) 842476 E: rafglc@hotmail.co.uk

COLLINGWOOD, John Jeremy Raynham. b 37. Barrister 64 CCC Cam BA 60 MA 68 Lon Univ BD 78. Trin Coll Bris 75. **d** 78 **p** 79. C Henleaze *Bris* 78-80; P-in-c Clifton H Trin, St Andr and St Pet 80-81; V 81-91; RD Clifton 84-87; Bp's Officer for Miss and Evang 87-91; V Guildf Ch Ch 91-98; V Guildf Ch Ch w St Martha-on-the-Hill 98-02; RD Guildf 95-00; rtd 02. *The Old Manse, 55 Audley Road, Saffron Walden CB11 3HD* T: (01799) 529055 E: mporokoso@aol.com

COLLINS, Adelbert Andrew. b 15. Lich Th Coll. **d** 61 **p** 62. C Sedgley All SS *Lich* 61-77; P-in-c Enville 77-81 and 86-87;

179

R 81-86; C Kinver and Enville 87-90; rtd 90; PtO *Lich* from 90; *Worc* from 90. *West Cottage, Bridgnorth Road, Enville, Stourbridge DY7 5JA* T: (01384) 873733

COLLINS, Mrs Ann Maureen. b 62. St Pet Coll Ox BA 83 Cam Univ PGCE 84. St Jo Coll Nottm 11. **d** 13 **p** 14. C Wilford *S'well* from 13. *7 Chancery Court, Wilford, Nottingham NG11 7EQ* T: 0115-919 3860 E: maureencolli@gmail.com

COLLINS, Anthony James. b 63. NEOC 04. **d** 07 **p** 08. NSM Fountains Gp *Ripon* 07-08; NSM Dacre w Hartwith and Darley w Thornthwaite *Leeds* from 08. *Harvest Cottage, Sawley, Ripon HG4 3EQ* T: (01765) 620393 M: 07971-245780

COLLINS, Barry Douglas. b 47. Kelham Th Coll 66. **d** 70 **p** 71. C Peel Green *Man* 70-73; C Salford St Phil w St Steph 73-75; R Blackley H Trin 75-79; PtO *Ripon* 80-82; *Pet* 83-93; *Cov* 85-93; *Ox* 93-97; P-in-c Bengeworth *Worc* 98-99; V 99-11; rtd 11. *9 Holbrook Avenue, Rugby CV21 2QG* T: (01788) 878993 E: barry2047@btinternet.com

COLLINS, Ms Cheryl Anne. b 62. Rob Coll Cam BA 85 MA 89 MCA 90. Ripon Coll Cuddesdon 91. **d** 93 **p** 94. C Sharrow St Andr *Sheff* 93-95; Chapl Sheff Univ 95-01; Hon C Endcliffe 96-01; P-in-c Barton *Ely* 01-10; P-in-c Coton 01-10; P-in-c Dry Drayton 01-10; RD Bourn 03-10; Miss P Red Lodge *St E* 10-12; P-in-c Chevington w Hargrave, Chedburgh w Depden etc from 12; RD Clare from 14. *The Rectory, New Road, Chevington, Bury St Edmunds IP29 5QL* T: (01284) 850843 E: cheryl62collins@btinternet.com

COLLINS, Christopher. b 46. K Coll Lon BSc 67 AKC 67 Pemb Coll Ox BA 70. St Steph Ho Ox 68. **d** 71 **p** 72. C Pennywell St Thos and Grindon St Oswald CD *Dur* 71-74; C Pallion, Millfield St Mary and Bishopwearmouth Gd Shep 74-76; C Harton Colliery 76-78; TV Winlaton 78-85; V Grangetown 85-11; rtd 12. *15 Linthorpe Avenue, Seaham SR7 7JW* T: 0191-581 7186 E: christopher_collins@lineone.net

COLLINS, Canon Christopher David. b 43. Sheff Univ BA(Econ) 64. Tyndale Hall Bris 65. **d** 68 **p** 69. C Rusholme H Trin *Man* 68-71; C Bushbury *Lich* 71-74; V Fairfield *Liv* 74-81; V Tunbridge Wells St Jo *Roch* 81-92; R Luton Ch Ch and Chapl Thames Gateway NHS Trust 92-05; Chapl Medway NHS Trust 92-99; RD Roch 94-00; P-in-c Cobham w Luddesdowne and Dode 05-08; Hon Can Roch Cathl 98-08; rtd 08. *2 Courtenay Gardens, Alphington, Exeter EX2 8UH* T: (01392) 203975 E: canonchris@blueyonder.co.uk

COLLINS, Christopher Philip. b 80. Wycliffe Hall Ox 10. **d** 13 **p** 14. C Hartford *Ches* from 13. *The Propagator's House, Greenbank Lane, Hartford, Northwich CW8 1JJ* M: 07766-833032 E: chris_collins42@btinternet.com

COLLINS, Darren Victor. b 69. NTMTC. **d** 05 **p** 06. C Chingford SS Pet and Paul *Chelmsf* 05-07; Min Can St Alb Abbey *St Alb* 07-11; P-in-c Norton 11-13; V from 13. *Norton Vicarage, 17 Norton Way North, Letchworth Garden City SG6 1BY* T: (01462) 685059 *or* 678133 E: frdarren@yahoo.com

COLLINS, Mrs Debra Michelle. b 67. **d** 11 **p** 12. NSM Cofton Hackett w Barnt Green *Birm* 11-14; C Balsall Heath and Edgbaston SS Mary and Ambrose from 15. *72 Brookvale Road, Solihull B92 7HZ* T: 0121-708 0751 E: debracollins21@hotmail.com

COLLINS, Donard Michael. b 55. Oak Hill Th Coll BA 83. **d** 83 **p** 84. C Lurgan Ch the Redeemer *D & D* 83-87; I Ardmore w Craigavon 87-98; I Killowen *D & R* from 98. *St John's Rectory, 4 Laurel Hill, Coleraine BT51 3AT* T: (028) 7034 2629 E: revdonard@yahoo.co.uk

COLLINS, Elaine Judith. b 56. **d** 12 **p** 13. NSM The Bourne and Tilford *Guildf* from 12. *49 Carlton Road, Headley Down, Bordon GU35 8JT* T: (01428) 714385 E: ej.collins@tiscali.co.uk

COLLINS, The Ven Gavin Andrew. b 66. Trin Hall Cam BA 89 MA 93. Trin Coll Bris BA 96 MA 97. **d** 97 **p** 98. C Cambridge St Barn *Ely* 97-02; V Chorleywood Ch Ch *St Alb* 02-11; RD Rickmansworth 06-11; Hon Can St Alb 09-11; Adn The Meon *Portsm* from 11; Warden of Readers from 14. *Victoria Lodge, 36 Osborn Road, Fareham PO16 7DS* T: (01329) 608895 E: gavin-collins@supanet.com *or* admeon@portsmouth.anglican.org

COLLINS, Guy James Douglas. b 74. St Andr Univ MTheol 96 Peterho Cam PhD 00. Westcott Ho Cam 96. **d** 00 **p** 01. C Barnes *S'wark* 00-03; R Huntington Valley USA from 03. *The Rectory, 2122 Washington Lane, Huntingdon Valley PA 19006-5824, USA*

COLLINS, Mrs Helen Marie. b 83. Magd Coll Ox BA 04 K Coll Lon MA 08. Trin Coll Bris 10. **d** 12 **p** 13. C Bris Ch the Servant Stockwood from 12. *7 Petherton Road, Bristol BS14 9BP* T: (01275) 839444 E: helenmariecollins@me.com

COLLINS, Canon Ian Geoffrey. b 37. Hull Univ BA 60 CertEd. Sarum Th Coll 60. **d** 62 **p** 63. C Gainsborough All SS *Linc* 62-65; Min Can Windsor 65-81; Succ Windsor 67-81; R Kirkby in Ashfield *S'well* 81-85; Can Res S'well Minster 85-02; P-in-c Edingley w Halam 91-00; rtd 02. *2 Marston Moor Road, Newark NG24 2GN* T: (01636) 702866

COLLINS, Miss Janet May. b 55. Qu Mary Coll Lon BA 78 St Jo Coll Dur BA 84. Cranmer Hall Dur 82. **dss** 85 **d** 87 **p** 94. Willington *Newc* 85-88; C 87-88; Par Dn Stevenage St Hugh Chells *St Alb* 88-90; Par Dn Goldington 90-93; Team Dn Witney *Ox* 93-94; TV 94-96; Tutor SAOMC 96-01; TV Langtree 99-01; P-in-c Weldon w Deene *Pet* 01-08; P-in-c Gt and Lt Oakley 01-08; RD Corby 02-07; P-in-c Pet H Spirit Bretton 08-10; P-in-c Corby SS Pet and Andr 10-15; P-in-c Gt and Lt Oakley 10-15; rtd 15; PtO *Pet* from 15. *81 Furnace Lane, Nether Heyford, Northampton NN7 3JS* M: 07984-060768 T: (01327) 341276 E: revjan.jc@gmail.com *or* rev.jan@btinternet.com

COLLINS, John Gilbert. b 32. S'wark Ord Course 67. **d** 71 **p** 72. C Coulsdon St Jo *S'wark* 71-75; Chapl St Fran Hosp Haywards Heath 75-84; Chapl Hurstwood Park Hosp Haywards Heath 75-84; R Stedham w Iping, Elsted and Treyford-cum-Didling *Chich* 84-92; rtd 92; PtO *Chich* 94-00. *12 Exeter Road, Broyle, Chichester PO19 5EF* T: (01243) 536861

COLLINS, Preb John Theodore Cameron Bucke. b 25. Clare Coll Cam BA 49 MA 52. Ridley Hall Cam 49. **d** 51 **p** 52. C St Marylebone All So w SS Pet and Jo *Lon* 51-57; V Gillingham St Mark *Roch* 57-71; Chapl Medway Hosp Gillingham 70-71; V Canford Magna *Sarum* 71-80; RD Wimborne 79-80; V Brompton H Trin w Onslow Square St Paul *Lon* 80-85; C 85-89; AD Chelsea 84-88; Preb St Paul's Cathl 85-89; rtd 89; PtO *Lon* 89-90; *Win* 89-97. *27 Woodstock Close, Oxford OX2 8DB* T: (01865) 556228

COLLINS, John William Michael. b 54. Bp Otter Coll 95. **d** 98 **p** 07. NSM S Patcham *Chich* 98-06; NSM Moulsecoomb from 06. *2 Buxted Rise, Brighton BN1 8FG* T: (01273) 509388

COLLINS, Mrs Joy Christina. b 53. K Coll Lon MA. STETS. **d** 14 **p** 15. NSM Westfield and Guestling *Chich* from 14. *23 Croft Road, Hastings TN34 3HP* T: (01424) 447643 E: joycollins3591@gmail.com

COLLINS, Kathryne Broncy. b 51. Portland State Univ BSc 75 Lon Univ MSc 76. Linc Th Coll 92. **d** 94 **p** 95. C Bishop's Castle w Mainstone *Heref* 94-98; P-in-c 98-01; V Bishop's Castle w Mainstone, Lydbury N etc 01-03; TV Wrexham *St As* 03-05; NSM 05-12; Chapl NE Wales NHS Trust 03-14; Hon Can St As Cathl 14; P-in-c Strathnairn St Paul *Mor* from 14. *St Paul's Parsonage, Croachy, Inverness IV2 6UB* T: (01808) 521388 E: kathy.collins@virgin.net

COLLINS, Ms Linda Kathleen. b 56. Girton Coll Cam BA 77 MA 80. Bris Univ PGCE 78. WMMTC 99. **d** 02 **p** 03. C Harborne St Pet *Birm* 02-05; C Cen Wolverhampton *Lich* 05-09; TV 09-10; Chapl K Sch Wolv and St Pet Colleg Sch Wolv 05-10; C Lich St Mich w St Mary and Wall from 10. *17 Leyfields, Lichfield WS13 7NJ* M: 07985-033476 E: lindacollins4@hotmail.co.uk

COLLINS, Mrs Lindsay Rosemary Faith. b 70. K Coll Lon BD 91 AKC 91 PGCE 92. Ripon Coll Cuddesdon MTh 95. **d** 97 **p** 98. C Witney *Ox* 97-99; NSM 00-01; Chapl Cokethorpe Sch Witney 00-01; Chapl and Hd RE St Paul's Girls' Sch Hammersmith 01-04; Chapl K Coll Sch Wimbledon 04-10; Hon C Barnes *S'wark* 04-10; Chapl Sherborne Sch from 10. *Rosslyn House, 11 Acreman Street, Sherborne DT9 3NU* T: (01935) 813846 E: lcollins@sherborne.org

COLLINS, Louise Ridley. b 59. Lanc Univ BA 81 LGSM 83. Cranmer Hall Dur 01. **d** 03 **p** 04. C Sheff St Cuth 03-07; V from 07. *St Cuthbert's Vicarage, 7 Horndean Road, Sheffield S5 6UJ* T: 0114-261 1605

COLLINS, Margaret Ruth. **d** 14 **p** 15. NSM Warminster Ch Ch *Sarum* from 14. *Address temp unknown*

COLLINS, Martin. *See* COLLINS, William Francis Martin

COLLINS, Maureen. *See* COLLINS, Ann Maureen

COLLINS, Canon Norman Hilary. b 33. Mert Coll Ox BA 55 MA 58. Wells Th Coll 58. **d** 60 **p** 61. C Ystrad Mynach *Llan* 60-62; C Gelligaer 62-67; V Maerdy 67-77; R Penarth w Lavernock 77-98; RD Penarth and Barry 87-98; Can Llan Cathl 92-98; rtd 98; PtO *Llan* from 04. *4 Llys Steffan, Llantwit Major CF61 2UF* T: (01446) 794976

COLLINS, Paul David Arthur. b 50. Lanc Univ MSc 91. K Coll Lon BD 72 AKC 72 St Aug Coll Cant 73. **d** 73 **p** 74. C Rotherhithe St Mary w All SS *S'wark* 73-76; C Stocking Farm *Leic* 76-78; V 78-83; R Husbands Bosworth w Mowsley and Knaptoft etc 83-87; Soc Resp Officer *Blackb* 87-94; R Worc City St Paul and Old St Martin etc 94-03; Min Can Worc Cathl 95-03; P-in-c Bishop's Castle w Mainstone, Lydbury N etc *Heref* 03-10; RD Clun Forest 05-08; rtd 10. *79 Lower Chestnut Street, Worcester WR1 1PD* E: nb.wcycrown@hotmail.co.uk

COLLINS, Paul Michael. b 71. St Jo Coll Nottm 06. **d** 08 **p** 09. C Chenies and Lt Chalfont, Latimer and Flaunden *Ox* 08-10; Chapl RAF 11-14; C Warfield *Ox* from 14. *Glen Lossie, Goughs Lane, Bracknell RG12 2PL* M: 07973-838003 E: pmcollins2@yahoo.co.uk *or* paulcollins@warfield.org.uk

COLLINS, Paul Myring. b 53. St Jo Coll Dur BA 75 Ox Univ BA 78 MA 83 K Coll Lon PhD 95. St Steph Ho Ox 76. **d** 79

p 80. C Meir *Lich* 79-82; C Fenton 82-83; TV Leek and Meerbrook 83-87; Tutor in Th and Liturgy Chich Th Coll 87-94; Dir of Studies 90-94; V Brighton Gd Shep Preston *Chich* 94-96; Tutor Qu Coll Birm 96-01; V Bournville *Birm* 01-02; Reader Chr Th Chich Univ 02-11; V Holy Is *Newc* from 11. *The Vicarage, Holy Island, Berwick-upon-Tweed TD15 2RX* T: (01289) 389216 E: pmcollins1@btinternet.com

COLLINS, Peter Graham. b 60. Anglia Ruskin Univ MA 07. EMMTC 99 Westcott Ho Cam 05. **d** 07 **p** 08. C S Lawres Gp *Linc* 07-11; P-in-c Upper Wreake *Leic* 11-14; R Hykeham *Linc* from 14. *The Rectory, Mill Lane, North Hykeham, Lincoln LN6 9PA* M: 07896-066302 E: revdpeter@msn.com

COLLINS, Canon Philip Howard Norton. b 50. AKC 73. St Aug Coll Cant 73. **d** 74 **p** 75. C Stamford Hill St Thos *Lon* 74-78; C Upwood w Gt and Lt Raveley *Ely* 78-81; C Ramsey 78-81; R Leverington 81-92; P-in-c Wisbech St Mary 89-92; RD Wisbech 90-92; TR Whittlesey and Pondersbridge 92-95; TR Whittlesey, Pondersbridge and Coates 95-02; R New Alresford w Ovington and Itchen Stoke *Win* 02-07; R Arle Valley from 07; RD Alresford from 09; Hon Can Win Cathl from 14. *The Rectory, 37 Jacklyns Lane, Alresford SO24 9LF* T: (01962) 732105 E: philhcollinsrector@yahoo.co.uk

COLLINS (née SHIRRAS), Rachel Joan. b 66. Univ of Wales (Abth) BSc 88. St Jo Coll Nottm 88. **d** 91 **p** 94. Par Dn Ockbrook *Derby* 91-94; C Bris St Matt and St Nath 94-97; V Beckton St Mark *Chelmsf* 97-02; NSM Wandsworth St Steph *S'wark* 02-06; NSM Wandsworth St Mich 02-06; NSM Wandsworth St Mich w St Steph 06-11; PtO 12-13; *Ex* from 13. *20 Orchard Grove, Croyde, Braunton EX33 1NF* T: (01271) 890588 E: racheljcollins@aol.com

COLLINS, Richard Andrew. b 65. K Coll Lon BD 92 AKC 92 Dur Univ MA 00. St Steph Ho Ox 92. **d** 94 **p** 95. C Whickham *Dur* 94-97; C Bensham 97-98; TV 98-03; P-in-c Greatham and Chapl Greatham Hosp 03-09; Local Min Officer *Dur* 03-09; P-in-c Lumley from 09; Dir of Ords from 09. *Christ Church Vicarage, Great Lumley, Chester le Street DH3 4ER* T: 0191-388 2228 *or* 374 6015 E: ddo@durham.anglican.org

COLLINS, Roger Richardson. b 48. Birm Univ BPhil 88. WMMTC 78. **d** 81 **p** 82. NSM Cotteridge *Birm* from 81. *6 Chesterfield Court, Middleton Hall Road, Birmingham B30 1AF* T: 0121-459 4009 E: roger@rrcollins.freeserve.co.uk

COLLINS, Ross Nicoll Ferguson. b 64. Edin Univ MA 87 Ven English Coll Rome 91 Pontifical Univ Rome 91. Ripon Coll Cuddesdon BA 91. **d** 92 **p** 93. C Goring w S Stoke *Ox* 92-96; P-in-c N Leigh 96-01; TR Barnes *S'wark* 01-10; NSM Sherborne w Castleton, Lillington and Longburton *Sarum* from 10. *Rosslyn House, 11 Acreman Street, Sherborne DT9 3NU* M: 07738-478548 T: (01935) 816091 E: rossnfcollins@btinternet.com

COLLINS, Canon Stella Vivian. b 32. S Dios Minl Tr Scheme 74. **dss** 77 **d** 87 **p** 94. Harnham *Sarum* 77-88; Hon Par Dn 87-88; Dioc Lay Min Adv 82-97; Adv for Women's Min 82-97; Hon Par Dn Wilton w Netherhampton and Fugglestone *Sarum* 88-94; Hon C 94-97; RD Wylye and Wilton 89-94; Can and Preb Sarum Cathl 93-97; rtd 97; PtO *Sarum* 97-01. *Address temp unknown*

COLLINS, Canon William Francis Martin. b 43. St Cath Coll Cam BA 66 MA 70. Cuddesdon Coll 68. **d** 70 **p** 71. C Man Victoria Park 70-73; P-in-c Ancoats 73-78; Chapl Abraham Moss Cen 78-91; Hon C Cheetham Hill 81-84; Chs' FE Officer for Gtr Man 84-91; V Norbury *Ches* 91-08; Hon Can Ches Cathl 05-08; rtd 08. *9 Milldale Avenue, Buxton SK17 9BE* T: (01298) 74906 M: 07866-505589 E: martin.collins1@o2.co.uk

COLLINS, Winfield St Clair. b 41. Univ of W Indies BA 83 Man Univ BA 88 MEd 91. Codrington Coll Barbados. **d** 76 **p** 76. Asst Chapl HM Pris Wakef 76; C St Jo Barbados 76; P-in-c St Mark and St Cath 77-84; Asst Chapl HM Pris Wandsworth 85; Chapl HM YOI Thorn Cross 85-91; Chapl HM Pris Pentonville 91-01; Can Res Barbados 01-02; rtd 02. *92 Barclay Road, London N18 1EQ* T: (020) 8245 4145

COLLINSON, Mrs Amanda. b 74. Luton Univ BA 96. Ripon Coll Cuddesdon 07. **d** 09 **p** 10. C Catherington and Clanfield *Portsm* 09-13; P-in-c Gurnard 13-14; P-in-c Cowes St Faith 13-14; V Gurnard w Cowes St Faith from 14; P-in-c Northwood 13-14; R from 14. *The Rectory, Chawton Lane, Cowes PO31 8PR* T: (01983) 294913 E: amanda.collinson@ntlworld.com

COLLINSON, Leslie Roland. b 47. St Jo Coll Nottm 90. **d** 92 **p** 93. C Gorleston St Andr *Nor* 92-96; TV Banbury *Ox* 96-98; V Banbury St Paul 98-00; V Darwen St Barn *Blackb* from 00. *St Barnabas' Vicarage, 68 Park Road, Darwen BB3 2LD* T: (01254) 702732 E: revles@talktalk.net

COLLINSON, Canon Mark Peter Charles. b 68. City Univ BSc 90 Fitzw Coll Cam BA 97 MA 01 Vrije Univ Amsterdam MA 10. Ridley Hall Cam 95. **d** 98 **p** 99. C Ashton-upon-

Mersey St Mary Magd *Ches* 98-01; Chapl Amsterdam w Den Helder and Heiloo *Eur* 01-15; Hon Can 12-15; Can Res Win Cathl from 15; Prin Win Sch of Miss from 15. *The Vicarage, Church Lane, Twyford, Winchester SO21 1NT, or School of Mission, Wolvesey, Winchester SO23 9ND* T: (01962) 710970 E: mark.collinson@winchester.anglican.org

COLLINSON, Roger Alfred. b 36. St Jo Coll Dur BA 58. BA 58 Cranmer Hall Dur 60. **d** 63 **p** 97. C Liv St Mich 63-64; NSM Ormside *Carl* 97-06; NSM Appleby 97-06; PtO from 06. *1 Caesar's View, Appleby-in-Westmorland CA16 6SH* T: (017683) 52886

COLLIS, Janet Mary. b 57. Plymouth Poly BA 78 PhD 83 SS Mark & Jo Univ Coll Plymouth MA 03. SWMTC 08. **d** 10 **p** 11. NSM Plympton St Mary *Ex* 10-12; Chapl Plymouth Community Healthcare Trust 12-13; Chapl Plymouth Hosps NHS Trust from 13. *Derriford Hospital, Derriford Road, Derriford, Plymouth PL6 8DH* T: (01752) 792313 E: jan.collis@gmail.com

COLLIS, Jonathan. b 69. Selw Coll Cam BA 91 MA 94. Aston Tr Scheme 96 Westcott Ho Cam 97. **d** 99 **p** 00. C St Neots *Ely* 99-02; Chapl Jes Coll Cam 02-09; V Thorpe Bay *Chelmsf* from 09. *The Vicarage, 86 Tyrone Road, Southend-on-Sea SS1 3HB* T: (01702) 587597 E: jonathan.collis@cantab.net

COLLIS, Michael Alan. b 35. K Coll Lon BD 60 AKC 60. **d** 61 **p** 62. C Worc St Martin 61-63; C Dudley St Thos and St Luke 63-66; C St Peter-in-Thanet *Cant* 66-70; V Croydon H Trin 70-77; P-in-c Norbury St Steph 77-81; V 81-82; V Sutton Valence w E Sutton and Chart Sutton 82-89; R New Fishbourne *Chich* 89-00; P-in-c Appledram 89-00; rtd 00; PtO *Chich* from 00. *66 Orchard Way, Barnham, Bognor Regis PO22 0HY* T: (01243) 552429

COLLIS, Canon Stephen Thomas. b 47. MHCIMA 94. Cranmer Hall Dur 80. **d** 82 **p** 83. C Crewe All SS and St Paul *Ches* 82-84; C Wilmslow 84-86 and 95-98; Chapl RAF 86-95; P-in-c Barthomley *Ches* 98-00; S Cheshire Ind Chapl 98-00; Chapl Abu Dhabi UAE 00-02; Dean St Paul's Cathl and Chapl Nicosia 02-09; Adn Cyprus 06-09; Hon Can Cyprus and the Gulf from 09; R Montrose and Inverbervie *Bre* 09-12; rtd 12; PtO *Bre* from 12; *Eur* from 12. *5 Martins Lane, Brechin DD9 6AS* M: 07791-618320 T: (01356) 625150 E: collis.steve@hotmail.com

COLLISHAW, Ashley Stuart. b 66. Wycliffe Hall Ox 03. **d** 05 **p** 06. C Worc City 05-09; Hon C Cheltenham H Trin and St Paul *Glouc* from 09. *22 Greatfield Drive, Charlton Kings, Cheltenham GL53 9BY* M: 07932-045598 E: crockfords@collishaw.net

COLLISON, Christopher John. b 48. Oak Hill Th Coll 68. **d** 72 **p** 73. C Cromer *Nor* 72-75; C Costessey 76-78; V 87-95; C Heckmondwike *Wakef* 78-79; P-in-c Shepley and Dioc Communications Officer 79-83; Chapl Flushing Miss to Seamen *Eur* 83-85; Asst Min Sec Miss to Seamen 85-87; C St Mich Paternoster Royal *Lon* 85-87; P-in-c Swainsthorpe w Newton Flotman *Nor* 95-97; TV Newton Flotman, Swainsthorpe, Tasburgh, etc 98-02; R Henfield w Shermanbury and Woodmancote *Chich* 02-09; Dioc Evang Officer 04-09; RD Hurst *Chich* 04-09; P-in-c Hartlepool St Hilda *Dur* from 09; AD Hartlepool 10-13; Chapl Miss to Seafarers from 09. *The Rectory, Church Close, Hartlepool TS24 0PW* T: (01429) 267030 E: revchris@hartlepool-sthilda.org.uk

COLLISON, Ms Elizabeth. b 38. Man Univ CertEd 58. NOC 85. **d** 88 **p** 94. C Huyton St Mich *Liv* 88-94; C Rainhill 94-05; rtd 05. *25 Lowther Drive, Rainhill, Prescot L35 0NG* T: 0151-426 3853 E: liz_collison@yahoo.co.uk

COLLYER, David John. b 38. JP . Keble Coll Ox BA 61 MA 86. Westcott Ho Cam 61. **d** 63 **p** 64. C Perry Beeches *Birm* 63-65; P-in-c Deritend 66-70; Bp's Chapl for Special Youth Work 65-70; Bp's Youth Chapl and Dioc Youth Officer 70-73; R Northfield 73-78; Hon Chapl Birm Cathl 78-81; Hon C Birm St Geo 81-86; V Handsworth St Andr 86-97; Dioc Development Officer 97-01; Hon Can Birm Cathl 95-06; PtO from 01. *19 Birch Close, Bournville, Birmingham B30 1NA*

COLLYER, Leon John. b 72. SS Hild & Bede Coll Dur BSc 95 Leeds Univ BA 00. Coll of Resurr Mirfield 98. **d** 01 **p** 02. C Airedale w Fryston *Wakef* 01-04; P-in-c Crofton and Warmfield 04-10; C Reading St Agnes w St Paul and St Barn *Ox* from 10. *St Barnabas' Rectory, 14 Elm Road, Reading RG6 5TS* T: 0118-327 9389 M: 07714-986462 E: leoncollyer@gmail.com

COLMAN, Geoffrey Hugh. b 29. Univ Coll Ox BA 53 MA 68. Wells Th Coll 67. **d** 68 **p** 69. C Wanstead St Mary *Chelmsf* 68-72; V Barking St Erkenwald 72-77; Youth Chapl 78-81; C Maidstone All SS and St Phil w Tovil *Cant* 85-88; P-in-c Norton 88-93; R 93-96; P-in-c Teynham 88-93; P-in-c Lynsted w Kingsdown 88-93; V Teynham w Lynsted and Kingsdown 93-96; rtd 96; PtO *Cant* 98-99. *c/o Mrs G H Fulcher, 98 Barnham Road, Barnham, Bognor Regis PO22 0EW*

COLMAN, Susan. b 59. **d** 12 **p** 13. NSM Onslow Square and S Kensington St Aug *Lon* from 12; PtO *Win* from 14. *117 Queen's Gate, London SW7 5LP* E: sue_colman59@yahoo.co.uk

COLMER, Andrew John. b 68. De Montfort Univ Leic BSc 90. St Jo Coll Nottm MA 96 LTh 97. **d** 97 **p** 98. C Roby *Liv* 97-01; C Litherland St Andr 01-02; P-in-c Liv All So Springwood 02-10; Chapl Enterprise S Liv Academy from 10. *Enterprise South Liverpool Academy, Horrocks Avenue, Liverpool L19 5PF* E: a.colmer@esla.org.uk

COLMER, The Ven Malcolm John. b 45. Sussex Univ MSc 67. St Jo Coll Nottm BA 73. **d** 73 **p** 74. C Egham *Guildf* 73-76; C Chadwell *Chelmsf* 76-79; V S Malling *Chich* 79-85; V Hornsey Rise St Mary w St Steph *Lon* 85-87; TR Hornsey Rise Whitehall Park Team 87-96; AD Islington 90-94; Adn Middx 96-05; Adn Heref 05-10; Can Res Heref Cathl 05-10; rtd 10; PtO *St D* 12-15. *Pantdafydd, Maesllyn, Llandysul SA44 5LL* T: (01239) 851731 E: malcom_colmer@hotmail.com

COLPUS (née EDWARDS), Mrs Anita Carolyn. b 71. Trin Coll Bris 01. **d** 03 **p** 04. C Notting Hill *St Pet Lon* 03-06; NSM Sittingbourne St Mary and St Mich *Cant* 07-10; P-in-c Reigate St Luke *S'wark* from 10; Jt Dir of IME Croydon Area from 13. *St Luke's House, 3 Church Road, Reigate RH2 8HY* T: (01737) 243846 E: anitacolpus@tesco.net

COLSON, Ian Richard. b 65. Wolv Poly BSc 86 Nottm Univ BTh 89 Warwick Univ MA 03. Linc Th Coll 86. **d** 89 **p** 90. C Nunthorpe *York* 89-92; C Thornaby on Tees 92-93; Chapl RAF 93-00; V Sunbury *Lon* 00-02; Chapl Ardingly Coll 02-09; Sen Chapl Ch Hosp Horsham 09-10; CF(V) 08; CF from 10. *c/o MOD Chaplains (Army)* F: 381824 T: (01264) 383430 E: ianrcolson@aol.com

COLSTON, Canon John Edward. b 43. Open Univ BA 91 Leeds Univ MA 94. Lich Th Coll 65. **d** 68 **p** 69. C Bromsgrove All SS *Worc* 68-71; C Tettenhall Wood *Lich* 71-74; V Alrewas and Wychnor 74-88; R Ainderby Steeple w Yafforth and Kirby Wiske etc *Ripon* 88-95; V High Harrogate Ch Ch 95-07; Warden of Readers 90-96; AD Harrogate 01-05; Hon Can Ripon Cathl 06-07; rtd 08. *15 Sycamore Road, Ripon HG4 2LR* T: (01765) 600747 E: john.colston@yahoo.co.uk

COLTON, Mrs Christine Ann. b 56. Univ of Wales (Cardiff) BA 00 MTh 06. St Mich Coll Llan 01. **d** 06 **p** 07. NSM Cen Cardiff *Llan* 06-07; NSM Radyr 07-13; PtO *S'wark* 14; P-in-c Kingswood from 14. *St Mark's Vicarage, 8 Alma Road, Reigate RH2 0DA* T: (01737) 241161 M: 07941-011337 E: chris.colton@ntlworld.com

COLTON, Christopher Francis. b 52. **d** 12 **p** 14. NSM Holme-in-Cliviger w Worsthorne *Blackb* 12-13; NSM Oswaldtwistle from 13. *1 Western Avenue, Burnley BB11 4JW* T: (01282) 451425 E: fr.chriscolton@gmail.com

COLTON, Martin Philip. b 67. Sheff Univ BMus 89 MMus 92 FRCO 92 Open Univ PGCE 97. St Mich Coll Llan BA 03. **d** 03 **p** 04. C Whitchurch *Llan* 03-06; TV Canton Cardiff 06-14; V Reigate St Mark *S'wark* from 14. *St Mark's Vicarage, 8 Alma Road, Reigate RH2 0DA* T: (01737) 241161 E: martin.colton@ntlworld.com

✠**COLTON, The Rt Revd William Paul.** b 60. NUI BCL 81 TCD MPhil 87 Univ of Wales (Cardiff) LLM 06. **d** 84 **p** 85 **c** 99. C Lisburn St Paul *Conn* 84-87; Bp's Dom Chapl 85-90; V Choral Belf Cathl 87-90; Min Can Belf Cathl 89-90; PV, Registrar and Chapter Clerk Ch Ch Cathl Dub 90-95; I Castleknock and Mulhuddart w Clonsilla 90-99; Co-ord Protestant Relig Progr RTE 93-99; Hon Chapl Actors' Ch Union 94-96; Area Chapl (Ireland) Actors' Ch Union 96-97; Can Ch Ch Cathl Dublin 97-99; Bp C, C & R from 99. *St Nicholas' House, 14 Cove Street, Cork, Republic of Ireland* T: (00353) (21) 500 5080 F: 432 0960 E: bishop@corkchurchofireland.com

COLVER, Mrs Sarah Marianne. b 63. RGN 85. Westcott Ho Cam. **d** 13 **p** 14. C Aston cum Aughton w Swallownest and Ulley *Sheff* from 13. *The Vicarage, 27 Skipton Road, Swallownest, Sheffield S26 4NQ* T: 0114-287 7421 M: 07975-689403 E: smcolver@hotmail.com *or* sarah.colver@sheffield.anglican.org

COLVILLE, Gary Stanley. b 59. Sarum & Wells Th Coll 90. **d** 92 **p** 94. C Plaistow St Mary *Roch* 92-94; P-in-c Foots Cray 94-96; R 96-00; P-in-c N Cray 97-00; R Pembroke Bermuda 01-04; V Roch 04-14; Ind Chapl from 14. *15 Oaks Dene, Chatham ME5 9HN* M: 07766-302809 E: gcolville@blueyonder.co.uk

COLWELL, Ms Katherine Elizabeth. b 57. Man Univ BA 78 Nottm Univ MA 08 Man Poly PGCE 79. EMMTC 05. **d** 08 **p** 09. C Barton upon Humber *Linc* 08-11; P-in-c Kirton in Lindsey w Manton from 11; P-in-c Bishop Norton, Waddingham and Snitterby from 11; P-in-c Grayingham from 11. *The Vicarage, 28 South Cliff Road, Kirton Lindsey, Gainsborough DN21 4NR* T: (01652) 640552 E: katherine.colwell@btinternet.com

COLWILL, James Patrick (Jay). b 68. Man Poly BA 91. St Jo Coll Nottm BTh 93 MA 94. **d** 94 **p** 95. C Reading St Agnes w St Paul *Ox* 94-97; C Easthampstead 97-03; V Orpington Ch Ch *Roch* from 03; AD Orpington 10-15. *The Vicarage, 165 Charterhouse Road, Orpington BR6 9EP* T: (01689) 870923 M: 07941-752513 E: jay.colwill@diocese-rochester.org

COMBE, The Very Revd John Charles. b 33. TCD BA 53 MA 56 BD 57 MLitt 65 PhD 70. **d** 56 **p** 57. C Cork St Luke w St Ann *C, C & R* 56-58; C Ballynafeigh St Jude *D & D* 58-61; I Crinken *D & G* 61-66; Hon Clerical V Ch Ch Cathl Dublin 63-66; C Belfast St Bart *Conn* 66-70; I Belfast St Barn 70-74; I Portadown St Mark *Arm* 74-84; I Arm St Mark w Aghavilly 84-90; Can Arm Cathl 85-90; Dean Kilmore *K, E & A* 90-96; I Kilmore w Ballintemple, Kildallan etc 90-96; rtd 96. *24 Kensington Park, Maxwell Road, Bangor BT20 3RF* T: (028) 9146 6123

COMBER, Mrs Alison. b 47. **d** 94 **p** 95. OLM New Bury *Man* 94-04; PtO 04-14. *12 Seymour Grove, Farnworth, Bolton BL4 0HF* T: (01204) 397745

COMBER, The Ven Anthony James. b 27. Leeds Univ BSc 49 MSc 52. St Chad's Coll Dur 53. **d** 56 **p** 57. C Manston *Ripon* 56-60; V Oulton 60-69; V Hunslet St Mary 69-77; RD Armley 72-75 and 79-81; R Farnley 77-82; Hon Can Ripon Cathl 80-92; Adn Leeds 82-92; rtd 92; PtO *Leeds* from 92; *Bradf* 93-99. *28 Blayds Garth, Woodlesford, Leeds LS26 8WN* T: 0113-288 0489 M: 07840-763818 E: tony.comber@btinternet.com

COMBER, Michael. b 35. Carl Dioc Tr Inst. **d** 72 **p** 72. CA 59-72; C Carl H Trin and St Barn 72-73; C Upperby St Jo 73-76; V Dearham 76-81; V Harraby 81-84; R Orton and Tebay w Ravenstonedale etc 84-90; I Clonfert Gp *L & K* 90-94; I Convoy w Monellan and Donaghmore *D & R* 94-97; I Tamlaght O'Crilly Upper w Lower 97-02; rtd 02; PtO *Carl* from 03. *87 Pinecroft, Kingstown, Carlisle CA3 0DB* T: (01228) 401428 M: 07742-392124 E: m.comber@talk21.com

COMBES, The Ven Roger Matthew. b 47. K Coll Lon LLB 69. Ridley Hall Cam 72. **d** 74 **p** 75. C Onslow Square St Paul *Lon* 74-77; C Brompton H Trin 76-77; C Cambridge H Sepulchre w All SS *Ely* 77-86; R Silverhill St Matt *Chich* 86-03; RD Hastings 98-02; Adn Horsham 03-14; rtd 14; PtO *Chich* from 14. *3 Aldingbourne Close, Ifield, Crawley RH11 0QJ* T: (01293) 538161 E: rogercombes@gmail.com

COMER, Michael John. b 30. St Mich Coll Llan 79. **d** 81 **p** 82. C Bistre *St As* 81-84; R Llanfyllin and Bwlchycibau 84-91; V Hattersley *Ches* 91-94; rtd 94; PtO *St As* from 09. *8 Cae Camlas, Newtown SY16 2HT* T: (01686) 624557

COMERFORD, Canon Patrick. b 52. Pontifical Univ Maynooth BD 87 FRSAI 87. CITC 99. **d** 00 **p** 01. NSM Dublin Whitechurch *D & G* from 00; Dir Spiritual Formation CITC 06-11; Lect from 11; Can Ch Ch Cathl Dublin from 07. *75 Glenvara Park, Knocklyon, Dublin 16, Republic of Ireland* T: (00353) (1) 495 0934 M: 87-663 5116 E: revpatrickcomerford@gmail.com

COMERFORD, Mrs Suzanne Lyn. b 46. SAOMC 97. **d** 00 **p** 01. OLM Woodley *Ox* 00-08. *110 Lower Drayton Lane, Portsmouth PO6 2HE* M: 07786-224247

COMFORT, Alan. b 64. Ridley Hall Cam 91. **d** 94 **p** 95. C Chadwell Heath *Chelmsf* 94-97; V Buckhurst Hill 97-98; TV 98-03; V Loughton St Mary 03-09; TR Gt Baddow 09-10; V Walthamstow St Jo 10-14; R Standon and The Mundens w Sacombe *St Alb* from 14. *The Vicarage, Kents Lane, Standon, Ware SG11 1PJ* E: alancomfort11@googlemail.com

COMLEY, Thomas Hedges. b 36. Leeds Univ BA 62. Coll of Resurr Mirfield 62. **d** 64 **p** 65. C Leadgate *Dur* 64-67; C Shirley *Birm* 67-71; V Smethwick St Alb 71-76; PtO 76-82; V N Wembley St Cuth *Lon* 82-92; V Taddington, Chelmorton and Flagg, and Monyash *Derby* 92-01; rtd 01; PtO *Derby* from 01. *19 Wentworth Avenue, Walton, Chesterfield S40 3JB* T: (01246) 270911 E: tom_comley@lineone.net

COMMANDER, David James. b 58. Cranfield Inst of Tech MSc 84. SEITE 07. **d** 10 **p** 11. C Tunbridge Wells St Jas *Roch* 10-13; V Benenden and Sandhurst *Cant* from 13. *The Vicarage, The Green, Benenden, Cranbrook TN17 4DL* T: (01580) 240658 M: 07710-416978 E: david@dc-uk.co.uk

COMMIN, Robert William. b 47. Cape Town Univ BA 79. St Paul's Coll Grahamstown. **d** 70 **p** 71. S Africa 70-80 and from 89; Chapl Loretto Sch Musselburgh 80-84; TV Thetford *Nor* 84-89. *42 Earl Street, Woodstock, 7925 South Africa* M: 82-202 5303 E: bcommin@netactive.co.za

COMPTON, Barry Charles Chittenden. b 33. Linc Th Coll 60. **d** 62 **p** 63. C Beddington *S'wark* 62-65; C Limpsfield and Titsey 66-68; Hon C N 71-94; R Ridley *Roch* 69-70; R Ash 69-70; PtO *S'wark* from 70; rtd 94; PtO *Roch* from 11. *14 Hallsland Way, Oxted RH8 9AL* T: (01883) 714896 F: 722842 E: bccompton@aol.com

CONALTY, Julie Anne. b 63. SEITE. **d** 99 **p** 00. NSM E Wickham *S'wark* 99-04; NSM Charlton 04-10; C Plumstead Common 10-12; V Erith Ch Ch *Roch* from 12; AD Erith from 15. *Christ Church Vicarage, Victoria Road, Erith DA8 3AN* T: (01322) 334729 E: julie@littleheath.demon.co.uk

CONANT, Alan Richard. b 67. Kent Univ BSc 89 PhD 92. St Jo Coll Nottm 09. **d** 11 **p** 12. C Maghull and Melling *Liv* 11-14; V Rainhill from 14. *The Vicarage, 1 View Road, Rainhill, Prescot L35 0LE* T: 0151-426 4666 E: revd_al@btinternet.com

CONANT, Fane Charles. b 44. Oak Hill Th Coll 83. **d** 85 **p** 86. C Hoole *Ches* 85-89; V Kelsall 89-01; P-in-c Seer Green and Jordans *Ox* 01-06; rtd 06; Partner Evang Luis Palau Evang Assn from 06. *1 Spring Bank, Shrewsbury Road, Church Stretton SY6 6HA* T: (01694) 722610 E: fanesue@aol.com

CONANT (née PARR), Mrs Vanessa Caroline. b 78. Lanc Univ BA 00. Trin Coll Bris BA 07. **d** 08 **p** 09. C Hoddesdon *St Alb* 08-11; C Edin St Paul and St Geo 11-15; TR Walthamstow *Chelmsf* from 15. *The Rectory, 117 Church Hill, London E17 3BD* M: 07811-444435 T: (020) 3722 2041 E: vcconant@gmail.com

CONAWAY, Barry Raymond. b 41. CertEd 69 Nottm Univ BEd 70. Sarum & Wells Th Coll 86. **d** 88 **p** 89. C Ross w Brampton Abbotts, Bridstow and Peterstow *Heref* 88-91; R Bishop's Frome w Castle Frome and Fromes Hill 91-96; P-in-c Acton Beauchamp and Evesbatch w Stanford Bishop 91-96; P-in-c Charminster and Stinsford *Sarum* 96-01; rtd 01; PtO *Glouc* 01-02; *Sarum* from 03. *9 Constable Way, West Harnham, Salisbury SP2 8LN* T: (01722) 334870

CONDER, Paul Collingwood Nelson. b 33. St Jo Coll Cam BA 56 MA 60. Ridley Hall Cam 56. **d** 58 **p** 59. C Grassendale *Liv* 58-61; Tutor St Jo Coll Dur 61-67; R Sutton *Liv* 67-74; TR 74-75; V Thames Ditton *Guildf* 75-86; RD Emly 82-86; V Blundellsands St Mich *Liv* 86-99; rtd 99; PtO *York* from 00. *112 Strensall Road, Earswick, York YO32 9SJ* T: (01904) 763071

✠**CONDRY, The Rt Revd Edward Francis.** b 53. UEA BA 74 Ex Coll Ox BLitt 77 DPhil 80 Open Univ MBA 02. Linc Th Coll 80. **d** 82 **p** 83 **c** 12. C Weston Favell *Pet* 82-85; V Bloxham w Milcombe and S Newington *Ox* 85-93; TR Rugby *Cov* 93-02; Can Res Cant Cathl 02-12; Dir Post-Ord Tr 02-06; Treas and Dir of Educn 06-12; Area Bp Ramsbury *Sarum* from 12; Can and Preb Sarum Cathl from 12. *Ramsbury Office, Church House, Crane Street, Salisbury SP1 2QB* T: (01722) 438662 E: bishop.ramsbury@salisbury.anglican.org

CONEY, Joanna Margery. b 39. Culham Coll of Educn CertEd 75 Open Univ BA 83. Ox Min Course 90. **d** 93 **p** 94. C Wolvercote w Summertown *Ox* 93-97; Hon C New Marston 97-06; Hon C Wolvercote w Summertown 06-07; Hon C Wolvercote 07-10; OLM Tr Officer (Ox Adnry) 97-00; Dioc Portfolio Officer 00-04; rtd 04; Dioc Adv to Lic Lay Min *Ox* 02-09; NSM Voc Adv from 09; Min Prov (Eur) Third Order SSF 09-12; Hon C Wolvercote and Wytham *Ox* from 10. *4 Rowland Close, Wolvercote, Oxford OX2 8PW* T/F: (01865) 556456 E: joanna.coney@gmail.com

CONEYS, Canon Stephen John. b 61. Sheff Univ LLB 82. St Jo Coll Nottm 87. **d** 90 **p** 91. C Plymouth Em w Efford *Ex* 90-92; C Plymouth Em, Efford and Laira 93-94; TV Whitstable *Cant* 94-02; TR from 02; Hon Can Cant Cathl from 08; Jt AD Reculver from 12. *The Vicarage, 11 Kimberley Grove, Seasalter, Whitstable CT5 4AY* T: (01227) 276795 E: steveconeys@btinternet.com

CONGDON, John Jameson. b 30. St Edm Hall Ox BA 53 MA 57. Wycliffe Hall Ox 53. **d** 55 **p** 56. C Aspley *S'well* 55-58; C-in-c Woodthorpe CD 58-63; V Woodthorpe 63-70; V Spring Grove St Mary *Lon* 70-84; V Woodley St Jo the Ev *Ox* 84-89; Chapl W Middx Univ Hosp Isleworth 89-95; rtd 95; PtO *Lon* from 95; *Ox* 06-09. *23 Pates Manor Drive, Feltham TW14 8JJ* T: (020) 8893 1823 E: john.congdon@btinternet.com

CONLEY, James Alan. b 29. Dur Univ BSc 51. St Jo Coll Nottm. **d** 87 **p** 88. NSM Cropwell Bishop w Colston Bassett, Granby etc *S'well* 87-97; PtO *Sarum* 97-07. *30 The Waldrons, Thornford, Sherborne DT9 6PX* T: (01935) 872672

CONLIN, Tiffany Jane Kate. b 71. K Coll Lon BA 93 MA 94 PhD 00 AKC 93. Westcott Ho Cam 03. **d** 05 **p** 06. C Wisbech St Aug and Wisbech SS Pet and Paul *Ely* 05-08; Chapl Fitzw Coll Cam 08-11; Dir Past Studies Westcott Ho Cam 11-14. *Address withheld by request* M: 07778-330855 E: tiffanyjanekatie@gmail.com

CONLON, Shaun. b 69. Birm Univ BA 90. Ripon Coll Cuddesdon 91. **d** 93 **p** 94. C Castle Bromwich SS Mary and Marg *Birm* 93-97; C Hockerill *St Alb* 97-00; V St Mary-at-Latton *Chelmsf* 00-07; V Prittlewell 07-14; P-in-c Ashton-upon-Mersey St Martin *Ches* from 14. *St Martin's Rectory, 367 Glebelands Road, Sale M33 5GG* T: 0161-973 4204 E: shaunconlon@tiscali.co.uk

CONN, Alistair Aberdein. b 37. Down Coll Cam BA 60 MA 64. Linc Th Coll 60. **d** 62 **p** 63. C W Hartlepool St Paul *Dur* 62-65; Uganda 65-66; Chapl Shrewsbury Sch 66-73; R Coupar Angus *St And* 73-78; V Ravenshead *S'well* 78-93; RD Newstead 90-93; R Collingham w S Scarle and Besthorpe and Girton 93-02; RD Newark 95-02; rtd 02; PtO *S'well* from 02. *17 Beacon Heights, Newark NG24 2JS* T: (01636) 706291

CONN, Christopher Kenneth. b 83. Dur Univ BSc 05. Oak Hill Th Coll BA 15. **d** 15. C Laleham *Lon* from 15. *346 Worple Road, Staines-upon-Thames TW18 1HB* M: 07917-191303 E: c.conn@hotmail.co.uk

CONNELL, Anthony. **d** 12. NSM Dolton *Ex* from 12; NSM Iddesleigh w Dowland from 12; NSM Monkokehampton from 12. *Long Parks, Coldridge, Crediton EX17 6BA* E: tonyandjeanconnell@gmail.com

CONNELL, Clare. *See* CONNELL, Penelope Clare

CONNELL, Frederick Philip Richard John. b 45. St Jo Coll Nottm MA 98. **d** 99 **p** 00. Deacon Jos St Piran Nigeria 99-00; V 00-01; NSM Nottingham St Pet and All SS *S'well* 01-03; PtO 03-04; NSM Nottingham St Nic 04-07; C Leic Martyrs 07-09; TV Vale of Belvoir 09-15; rtd 15. *Colston Bassett House, Church Gate, Colston Bassett, Nottingham NG12 3FE* T: (01949) 81424 E: frederick.connell@tiscali.co.uk

CONNELL, John Richard. b 63. K Coll Lon BD 84. St Mich Coll Llan 92. **d** 94 **p** 96. C Caldicot *Mon* 94-97; C Risca 97-00; V Llantilio Pertholey w Bettws Chpl etc 00-05; P-in-c Wokingham St Paul *Ox* 05-11; Chapl R Berks NHS Foundn Trust 11-12; R Chingford SS Pet and Paul *Chelmsf* 12-15; V Rumney *Mon* from 15. *St Augustine's Vicarage, 702 Newport Road, Rumney, Cardiff CF3 4FF* T: (029) 2241 5848 E: frjohnconnell@gmail.com

CONNELL, Julie. b 58. **d** 08 **p** 09. NSM Brixton Road Ch Ch *S'wark* 08-12; NSM Furzedown from 12. *8 Helix Road, London SW2 2JS* T: (020) 8671 0481 *or* 7587 0375 F: 7582 7421

CONNELL, Mrs Penelope Clare. b 44. EMMTC. **d** 03 **p** 04. NSM Whatton w Aslockton, Hawksworth, Scarrington etc *S'well* 03-06; NSM Nottingham St Nic 06-07; NSM Ironstone Villages *Leic* 07-12; rtd 12. *Colston Bassett House, Church Gate, Colston Bassett, Nottingham NG12 3FE* T: (01949) 81424 M: 07866-495720 E: clare.connell@tiscali.co.uk

CONNELL, Sister Sharon Margaret. b 65. Cardiff Univ MTh 11. Wilson Carlile Coll 86 St Jo Coll Nottm BA 03. **d** 03 **p** 04. C S Hackney St Jo w Ch Ch *Lon* 03-06; C Stepney St Dunstan and All SS 06-08; Ecum Chapl Chelsea and Westmr Hosp NHS Found Trust 08-13; Dep Hd Multi-Faith Chapl from 13. *Chelsea and Westminster Hospital, 369 Fulham Road, London SW10 9NH* T: (020) 3315 8083 E: sharon.connell@chelwest.nhs.uk

CONNER, Mrs Cathryn. b 42. Birm Univ BSc 64. NEOC 91. **d** 94 **p** 95. NSM Bainton w N Dalton, Middleton-on-the-Wolds etc *York* 94-98; NSM Woldsburn 98-04; rtd 04; PtO *York* from 04. *Centre House, North Dalton, Driffield YO25 9XA* T: (01377) 217265

✠**CONNER, The Rt Revd David John.** b 47. KCVO 10. Ex Coll Ox BA 69 MA 77. St Steph Ho Ox 69. **d** 71 **p** 72 **c** 94. Asst Chapl St Edw Sch Ox 71-73; Chapl 73-80; Hon C Summertown *Ox* 71-76; TV Wolvercote w Summertown 76-80; Chapl Win Coll 80-87; V Cambridge Gt St Mary w St Mich *Ely* 87-94; RD Cambridge 89-94; Suff Bp Lynn *Nor* 94-98; Dean Windsor and Dom Chapl to The Queen from 98; Bp HM Forces 01-09. *The Deanery, Windsor Castle, Windsor SL4 1NJ* T: (01753) 865561 F: 819002 E: david.conner@stgeorges-windsor.org

CONNING, Dowell Paul. b 64. Univ of Wales (Cardiff) MTh 12. Ripon Coll Cuddesdon BTh 00. **d** 00 **p** 01. C Leckhampton St Pet *Glouc* 00-03; CF from 03; Hon Min Can Ripon Cathl from 05; Chapl Guards Chpl Lon from 14. *c/o MOD Chaplains (Army)* F: 381824 T: (01264) 383430 E: dconning@googlemail.com

CONNOLL, Miss Helen Dorothy. b 45. Oak Hill Th Coll BA 86. **dss** 86 **d** 87 **p** 94. Leytonstone St Jo *Chelmsf* 86-90; Par Dn 87-90; Asst Chapl Grimsby Distr Gen Hosp 90-93; Chapl Kent and Cant Hosp 93-94; Chapl Kent and Cant Hosps NHS Trust 94-99; Chapl E Kent Hosps NHS Trust 99-01; Hon C Aylesham w Adisham and Nonington w Wymynswold and Goodnestone etc *Cant* 01-09; rtd 09; PtO *Cant* from 09. *5 White House, Farm Court, Easole Street, Nonington, Dover CT15 4NJ* T: (01304) 840271 E: helen.therev@virgin.net

CONNOLLY, Daniel. b 51. BEng. St Jo Coll Nottm 82. **d** 84 **p** 85. C Bedgrove *Ox* 84-87; C-in-c Crookhorn Ch Cen CD *Portsm* 87-88; V Crookhorn 88-97; R Sutton Coldfield H Trin *Birm* 97-98; V Reigate St Mary *S'wark* 98-05; RD Reigate 03-05; P-in-c Kenilworth St Jo *Cov* 05-08; Adnry Miss Enabler 08-09; P-in-c Blackpool St Jo *Blackb* 09-13; V from 13. *32 Forest Gate, Blackpool FY3 9AW* T: (01253) 623190 E: dan@famcon.co.uk

CONNOLLY, Lewis Alexander. b 88. Lon Sch of Th BA 10. Westcott Ho Cam 10. **d** 13 **p** 14. C W Leigh *Portsm* 13-15. *6 Idsworth Close, Horndean, Waterlooville PO8 0DW* M: 07581-524067 E: lewisconnolly@live.co.uk

CONNOLLY, Miss Lynne. b 53. Aston Tr Scheme 88 Linc Th Coll 92. **d** 92 **p** 94. Par Dn Hurst *Man* 92-94; C 94-96; R Burnage St Nic 96-02; V Spotland 02-10; P-in-c E Crompton 10-14; V from 14. *St James's Vicarage, Vicarage Street, Shaw, Oldham OL2 7TE* T: (01706) 847454 E: tyc@clara.co.uk

CONNOLLY, Canon Sydney Herbert. b 40. Leeds Univ BA 66. Coll of Resurr Mirfield 66. **d** 68 **p** 69. C W Derby St Mary *Liv* 68-71; C Prescot 71-74; V Burtonwood 74-80; V Walker *Newc* 80-89; TR Whorlton 89-96; V Chapel House 96-99; TR N Shields 99-06; Hon Can Newc Cathl 04-06; rtd 06. *222 Brunton Walk, Newcastle upon Tyne NE3 2TL* T: 0191-271 1473 E: sydandpat@blueyonder.co.uk

CONNOP PRICE, Martin Randall. *See* PRICE, Martin Randall Connop

CONNOR, Canon Geoffrey. b 46. K Coll Lon BD 73 AKC 73. St Aug Coll Cant. **d** 74 **p** 75. C Cockerton *Dur* 74-79; Dioc Recruitment Officer 79-87; Chapl St Chad's Coll 84-87; R Edin St Mary and Vice Provost St Mary's Cathl 87-90; Dioc Dir of Ords Edin and Arg 87-90; V Whitechapel w Admarsh-in-Bleasdale *Blackb* 90-00; Dir of Ords 90-00; TR Epping Distr *Chelmsf* from 00; RD Epping Forest 04-10; Hon Can Chelmsf Cathl from 12. *The Rectory, Hartland Road, Epping CM16 4PD* T: (01992) 572906 E: geoffrey_connor@priest.com

CONNOR, Archdeacon of. *See* MACBRIDE, The Ven Stephen Richard

CONNOR, Bishop of. *See* ABERNETHY, The Rt Revd Alan Francis

CONNOR, Dean of. *See* BOND, The Very Revd John Frederick Augustus

CONRAD, Canon Paul Derick. b 54. Worc Coll Ox BA 74 MA 82. St Steph Ho Ox 78. **d** 80 **p** 81. C Wanstead St Mary *Chelmsf* 80-83; C Somers Town *Lon* 83-85; P-in-c Kentish Town St Martin w St Andr 85-91; V 91-95; P-in-c Hampstead Ch Ch 95-97; V from 97; Chapl R Free London NHS Foundn Trust from 95; Can Wiawso Ghana from 09. *Christ Church Vicarage, 10 Cannon Place, London NW3 1EJ* T/F: (020) 7435 6784 E: paulconrad@btinternet.com

CONROY, Kevin. **d** 14. Stillorgan w Blackrock *D & G* from 14. *Address temp unknown*

CONSTABLE, Douglas Brian. b 40. Lon Univ BA 62 Southn Univ MPhil 05. Linc Th Coll 63. **d** 65 **p** 66. C Stockwood CD *Bris* 65-70; Asst Chapl Bris Univ 70-72; Hon C Clifton St Paul 70-72; Chapl Lee Abbey 72-77; V Derby St Thos 77-85; TV Southampton (City Cen) *Win* 85-92; rtd 92; PtO *Win* 92-00; *St D* from 05. *Y Bwthyn, 9 Church Street, Llandeilo SA19 6BH* T: (01558) 823518 E: douglasconstable@btinternet.com

CONSTABLE, Mrs Sharon Joanne. b 57. STETS 95. **d** 98 **p** 99. NSM Hutton *B & W* 98-01; Bp's Officer for NSMs 01-04; C E Clevedon w Clapton in Gordano etc 01-04; Chapl St Jo Cathl Hong Kong 04-10; TV Melton Mowbray *Leic* 10-15; Bp's Adv for Women's Min 10-14; TR Broughton Astley and Croft w Stoney Stanton from 15. *The Rectory, St Marys Close, Broughton Astley, Leicester LE9 6ES* E: sharonconstable@msn.com

CONSTABLE, Mrs Sybil Margaret. b 43. **d** 00 **p** 01. NSM Montgomery and Forden and Llandyssil *St As* 00-04; P-in-c Slindon, Eartham and Madehurst *Chich* 04-09; rtd 09. *Stubbs Oak, Straight Half Mile, Maresfield, Uckfield TN22 3DN* T: (01825) 760715

CONSTANTINE, Leonard. b 30. AKC 57. **d** 58 **p** 59. C W Hartlepool St Aid *Dur* 58-61; C Sheff St Geo and St Steph 61-62; Malawi 62-69; V W Pelton *Dur* 69-73; V Shotton 73-78; V Stillington 78-80; V Grindon and Stillington 80-82; V Corbridge w Halton and Newton Hall *Newc* 82-95; Chapl Charlotte Straker Hosp 82-95; rtd 95; PtO *Wakef* 95-10. *13 Stuart Court, High Street, Kibworth, Leicester LE8 0LR* T: 0116-279 2347

CONVERY, Canon Arthur Malcolm. b 42. Sheff Univ BSc 63 DipEd 64. NOC 79. **d** 82 **p** 83. NSM Parr *Liv* 82-87; V Marown *S & M* 87-04; V Onchan 04-10; Can St German's Cathl 99-10; rtd 10; P-in-c German St Jo *S & M* 10-12; C Michael 10-12. *50 Faaie ny Cabbal, Kirk Michael, Isle of Man IM6 2HU* T: (01624) 878855

CONWAY, Alfred Sydney. b 22. Kelham Th Coll 40. **d** 45 **p** 46. C Fulham St Oswald w St Aug *Lon* 45-49; PC Allenton and Shelton Lock *Derby* 49-55; P-in-c Chaddesden St Phil 55-63; V Croxley Green All SS *St Alb* 63-81; V Walton St Jo *Liv* 81-89; rtd 89; PtO *Ex* from 89. *58 Millhead Road, Honiton EX14 1RA* T: (01404) 46052

CONWAY, Catherine Mary. *See* VICKERS, Catherine Mary

CONWAY, Canon Glyn Haydn. b 38. St Mich Coll Llan. **d** 65 **p** 66. C Wrexham *St As* 65-71; TV 71-77; V Holywell 77-83; V Upton Ascension *Ches* 83-05; rtd 05; Hon Can Accra

from 03; PtO *St As* from 07; *St D* from 10. *15 Penygraig, Aberystwyth SY23 2JA* T: (01970) 612637 E: glyn.conway@btinternet.com

CONWAY, John Arthur. b 67. Leeds Univ BEng 90 Edin Univ BD 97. Linc Th Coll 94 TISEC 95. **d** 97 **p** 98. C Edin St Mary 97-01; R Edin St Martin from 01; Dioc IME Co-ord 04-07 and from 09; Chapl Edin Sick Children's NHS Trust 98-99; Chapl Lothian Univ Hosps NHS Trust 99-01. *15 Ardmillan Terrace, Edinburgh EH11 2JW* T: 0131-337 5471 E: john.conway@stmartinsedinburgh.org.uk

CONWAY, Philip James. b 66. Liv Inst of Educn BA 91. St Steph Ho Ox 92. **d** 95 **p** 96. C High Harrogate Ch Ch *Ripon* 95-99; P-in-c Menheniot *Truro* 99-08; C St Ive and Pensilva w Quethiock 02-08; P-in-c Lostwithiel, St Winnow w St Nectan's Chpl etc from 08; P-in-c Lanlivery from 08; C Lanreath, Pelynt and Bradoc from 08. *The Rectory, 3 Springfield Close, Lostwithiel PL22 0ER* E: church_centre@yahoo.co.uk

CONWAY, Robert. b 51. Bris Poly MBA 90. Trin Coll Bris 09. **d** 12 **p** 13. OLM Filton *Bris* from 12. *71 Juniper Way, Bradley Stoke, Bristol BS32 0BR* T: (01454) 612661 M: 07733-228878 E: bob.conway1@btinternet.com

CONWAY, Mrs Sandra Coralie. b 45. Bris Univ BA 66. S'wark Ord Course 89. **d** 92 **p** 00. NSM Kenley *S'wark* 92-05; PtO 06-07; *Guildf* 07-09; NSM E Horsley and Ockham w Hatchford and Downside from 09. *Rowan Tree Cottage, Norrels Drive, East Horsley, Leatherhead KT24 5DR* T: (01483) 281497 E: sandyconwayrtc@btinternet.com

✠**CONWAY, The Rt Revd Stephen David.** b 57. Keble Coll Ox BA 80 MA 84 CertEd 81 Selw Coll Cam BA 85. Westcott Ho Cam 83. **d** 86 **p** 87 **c** 06. C Heworth St Mary *Dur* 86-89; C Bishopwearmouth St Mich w St Hilda 89-90; Dir of Ords and Hon C Dur St Marg 90-94; P-in-c Cockerton 94-96; V 96-98; Bp's Sen Chapl and Communications Officer 98-02; Adn Dur and Can Res Dur Cathl 02-06; Area Bp Ramsbury *Sarum* 06-10; Bp Ely from 10. *The Bishop's House, The College, Ely CB7 4DW* T: (01353) 662749 F: 669477 E: bishop@ely.anglican.org

CONWAY, Thomas Robertson. b 36. **d** 86 **p** 87. C Bangor Abbey *D & D* 86-95; I Dungiven w Bovevagh *D & R* 89-95; I Carrowdore w Millisle *D & D* 95-00; rtd 00. *6 Rosstulla Drive, Newtownabbey BT37 0QJ* T: (028) 9086 0523

COOGAN, The Ven Robert Arthur William. b 29. Univ of Tasmania BA 51. St Jo Coll Dur 51. **d** 53 **p** 54. C Plaistow St Andr *Chelmsf* 53-56; R Bothwell Australia 56-62; V N Woolwich *Chelmsf* 62-73; P-in-c W Silvertown St Barn 62-73; V Hampstead St Steph *Lon* 73-77; P-in-c N St Pancras All Hallows 74-77; RD S Camden 75-81; P-in-c Old St Pancras w Bedford New Town St Matt 76-80; V Hampstead St Steph w All Hallows 77-85; P-in-c Kentish Town St Martin w St Andr 78-81; AD N Camden 78-83; Preb St Paul's Cathl 82-85; Adn Hampstead 85-94; rtd 94; PtO *Chich* 94-00. *Salters Hall West, Stour Street, Sudbury CO10 2AX* T: (01787) 370026

COOK, Alan. b 27. St Deiniol's Hawarden 79. **d** 80 **p** 81. Hon C Gatley *Ches* 80-83; Chapl Man R Eye Hosp 83-86; Chapl Asst Man R Infirmary 80-83 and 86-88; V Congleton St Jas *Ches* 89-93; rtd 93; PtO *Ches* from 93. *15 Buttermere Road, Gatley, Cheadle SK8 4RQ* T: 0161-428 4350

COOK, Anesia. *See* NASCIMENTO COOK, Anesia

COOK, Sister Anita Isabel. b 44. Whitelands Coll Lon CertEd 66 Toronto Univ BA 93. **d** 06 **p** 07. CSC from 67; PtO *S'wark* from 10; Hon C E Clevedon w Clapton in Gordano etc *B & W* from 10. *St Gabriel's, 27A Dial Hill Road, Clevedon BS21 7HL* T: (01275) 544471 E: anita@sistersofthechurch.org.uk

COOK, Canon Brian Edwin. b 36. Sarum & Wells Th Coll 78. **d** 80 **p** 81. C E Wickham *S'wark* 80-83; C Petersfield w Sheet *Portsm* 83-86; R Liss 86-01; RD Petersfield 91-96; Acting RD 99; Hon Can Portsm Cathl 96-01; rtd 01; PtO *Chich* from 01. *Daubeney Cottage, Bersted Street, South Bersted, Bognor Regis PO22 9QE* T: (01243) 828379 E: daubeney@tesco.net

COOK, Brian Robert. b 43. Chich Th Coll 83. **d** 85 **p** 86. C Whyke w Rumboldswhyke and Portfield *Chich* 85-87; C Worth 87-90; TV 90-94; P-in-c Chidham 94-99; V 99-04; RD Westbourne 99-04; P-in-c E Blatchington 04-08; R E Blatchington and Bishopstone 08-11; rtd 11; Hon C Wymering *Portsm* from 11; Hon C Cosham from 11. *269 Hawthorn Crescent, Cosham, Portsmouth PO6 2TL* T: (023) 9237 5882

COOK, Celia Jane. b 66. DipCOT 94. ERMC 07. **d** 10 **p** 11. C Aldeburgh w Hazlewood *St E* 10-14; TV Thurstable and Winstree *Chelmsf* 14-15; P-in-c Gt and Lt Bealings w Playford and Culpho *St E* from 15. *5 Brook Lane, Playford, Ipswich IP6 9DY* M: 07857-823617 E: thecooksonline@hotmail.co.uk

COOK, Canon Charles Peter. b 32. St Jo Coll Dur BA 54. Cranmer Hall Dur. **d** 58 **p** 59. C Kingston upon Hull H Trin *York* 58-64; V High Elswick St Paul *Newc* 64-74; V Cheadle

Hulme St Andr *Ches* 74-98; Hon Can Ches Cathl 91-98; rtd 98; PtO *Newc* 00-05; *Carl* 01-05; *Ches* from 05. *4 Moseley Grange, Cheadle Hulme, Cheadle SK8 5EZ* T: 0161-485 1702

COOK, Christopher. *See* COOK, James Christopher Donald

COOK, Christopher. b 44. Qu Coll Birm 68. **d** 69 **p** 70. C Gt Ilford St Mary *Chelmsf* 69-72; C Corringham 72-77; R E Donyland 77-84; R Pentlow, Foxearth, Liston and Borley 84-88; Chapl RAD Essex Area 88-89; rtd 89; PtO *Chelmsf* 89-04. *c/o Mrs A Philpott, Plains Farm Barn, Little Totham, Maldon CM9 8JF*

COOK, Canon Christopher Arthur. Edin Th Coll 53. **d** 56 **p** 58. C Motherwell *Glas* 56-59; S Africa 59-64; Area Sec Wakef and Sheff USPG 65-70; R Grahamstown St Matt Miss S Africa 70-95; Adn Grahamstown 80-95; Hon Can Grahamstown from 96; rtd 96. *PO Box 7641, East London, 5200 South Africa* T: (0027) (431) 385357

COOK, Christopher Charles Holland. b 56. K Coll Lon BSc 77 MB, BS 81 MD 95 MRCPsych 87. SEITE 97. **d** 00 **p** 01. Prof Psychiatry Alcohol Misuse Kent Inst of Medicine and Health Science 97-03; NSM Otham w Langley *Cant* 00-03; Chapl and Prof Fell St Chad's Coll Dur 03-05; Prof Research Fell Dur Univ from 05; Tutor and Lect Cranmer Hall Dur 08-13. *Department of Theology and Religion, Abbey House, Palace Green, Durham DH1 3RS* T: 0191-334 3885 E: c.c.h.cook@durham.ac.uk

COOK, David. b 46. Hertf Coll Ox BA MA 72. Wycliffe Hall Ox 69. **d** 73 **p** 74. C Stranton *Dur* 74-75; Lect Qu Coll Birm 75-81; Chapl Cranbrook Sch Kent 81-11; rtd 11; PtO *Cant* from 11. *33 Oatfield Drive, Cranbrook TN17 3LA* T: (01580) 713310 E: senor_aardvark@hotmail.com

COOK, David Arthur. b 50. St Jo Coll Dur BA 74. St Steph Ho Ox 86. **d** 88 **p** 89. C S Bank *York* 88-91; C Up Hatherley *Glouc* 91-93; P-in-c Cumbernauld *Glas* 93-04; P-in-c Helensburgh from 04. *The Rectory, 16 William Street, Helensburgh G84 8BD* T: (01436) 672500 E: rector@stmichaelhelensburgh.org.uk

COOK, Canon David Charles Murray. b 41. MA. Wycliffe Hall Ox 65. **d** 67 **p** 68. C Chatham St Phil and St Jas *Roch* 67-71; S Africa 71-89; TR Newbury *Ox* 89-02; RD 98-02; Hon Can Ch Ch 02; P-in-c Chipping Campden w Ebrington *Glouc* 02-13; rtd 13. *Laverton Cottage, Lansdowne, Bourton-on-the-Water, Cheltenham GL54 2AR*

COOK, David Smith. b 47. Hull Univ BTh 88 MA 93. Lich Th Coll 68. **d** 71 **p** 72. C Tudhoe Grange *Dur* 71-75; C Bishopwearmouth St Mary V w St Pet CD 75-77; V Copley *Wakef* 77-80; V Birstall 80-83; V Holme upon Spalding Moor *York* 83-98; R Holme and Seaton Ross Gp 98-01; RD S Wold 96-01; V Copmanthorpe 01-07; P-in-c Askham Bryan 01-07; Chapl Askham Bryan Coll 01-04; P-in-c Eskdaleside w Ugglebarnby and Sneaton *York* 07-09; V Lower Esk 09-13; RD Whitby 08-13; rtd 13; PtO *York* from 13. *15 Farndale Drive, Guisborough TS14 8JD* E: revcook@btinternet.com

COOK, Elspeth Jean. b 34. Edin Univ BSc 56 PhD 66. S Dios Minl Tr Scheme 85. **d** 88 **p** 94. C Yateley *Win* 88-91; Assoc Chapl Ld Mayor Treloar Hosp Alton 91-93; NSM Dunfermline *St And* 93-99; P-in-c Aberdour 96-01; rtd 01. *12 River View, Dalgety Bay, Dunfermline KY11 9YE* T: (01383) 825222 E: andrewandjean.cook@btinternet.com

COOK, Geoffrey John Anderson. b 64. St Steph Ho Ox. **d** 97 **p** 98. C St Leonards Ch Ch and St Mary *Chich* 97-99; Hon Asst P Brighton St Mich 00-02; Hon C Southwick St Mich 02-03; Asst Chapl Univ Coll Lon Hosps NHS Foundn Trust 03-05; Chapl W Herts Hosps NHS Trust 05-06; Chapl E Sussex Hosps NHS Trust from 06. *The Chaplain's Office, Eastbourne District General Hospital, King's Drive, Eastbourne BN21 2UD* T: (01323) 417400

COOK, Ian. b 63. Trin Coll Bris. **d** 09 **p** 10. C Plymouth St Jude *Ex* 09-13; R Wellington St Mark New Zealand from 13. *10 Karepa Street, Brooklyn, Wellington, New Zealand* E: ianruthcook@aol.com

COOK, Ian Bell. b 38. NW Ord Course 70. **d** 73 **p** 74. C Oldham St Paul *Man* 73-75; Ind Chapl 76-79; P-in-c Newton Heath St Wilfrid and St Anne 76-79; V Middleton Junction 79-08; rtd 08; PtO *Man* from 09. *109 Hollin Lane, Middleton, Manchester M24 5LA* T: 0161-654 7724 E: ian.cook13@btopenworld.com

COOK, Preb Ian Brian. b 38. Aston Univ MSc 72 Birm Univ MA 76 MBIM 73. Kelham Th Coll 58. **d** 63 **p** 64. C Langley Marish *Ox* 63-66; C Stokenchurch and Cadmore End 66-68; V Lane End 68-72; P-in-c Ibstone w Fingest 68-72; Tutor W Bromwich Coll of Comm and Tech 72-74; Sen Tutor 74-80; NSM W Bromwich St Pet *Lich* 77-80; R Wednesbury St Jas and St Jo 80-03; Dir St Jas Tr Inst 81-03; RD Wednesbury *Lich* 88-03; Preb Lich Cathl 94-03; rtd 03; PtO *Lich* from 03; RD Penkridge 06-11. *4 Orams Lane, Brewood, Stafford ST19 9EA* T: (01902) 850960

COOK, Canon James Christopher Donald. b 49. Ch Ch Ox BA 70 MA 74. St Steph Ho Ox 79. **d** 80 **p** 81. C Witney *Ox* 80-83; CF 83-04; P-in-c Toxteth Park St Agnes and St Pancras

Liv 04-06; V from 06; Can Wiawso Ghana from 09. *St Agnes's Vicarage, 1 Buckingham Avenue, Liverpool L17 3BA* T/F: 0151-733 1742 E: leoclericus@aol.com

COOK, James Robert. b 45. ACCA 68 FCCA 73. Ox Min Course 05. **d** 08 **p** 09. NSM Newbury *Ox* 08-10; NSM W Woodhay w Enborne, Hampstead Marshall etc 10-11; NSM Kintbury w Avington 10-11; NSM Walbury Beacon 11-13; NSM Totland Bay *Portsm* from 13. *The Vicarage, Alum Bay New Road, Totland Bay PO39 0ES* T: (01983) 759091 E: jamesrobertcook@aol.com

COOK, Jean. *See* COOK, Elspeth Jean

COOK, Mrs Joan Lindsay. b 46. SRN 70. Cranmer Hall Dur 86. **d** 88 **p** 94. Par Dn Hartlepool St Hilda *Dur* 88-93; Dn-in-c 93-94; P-in-c 94-96; rtd 96. *10 Peakston Close, Hartlepool TS26 0PN* T: (01429) 231778

COOK, John. b 32. Linc Th Coll 87. **d** 89 **p** 90. C Bourne *Linc* 89-92; R Colsterworth Gp 92-02; rtd 02. *24 Portrush Drive, Grantham NG31 9GD* T: (01476) 569063

COOK, John Edward. b 35. AKC 61. **d** 62 **p** 63. C York Town St Mich *Guildf* 62-67; Singapore 67-77; P-in-c Beoley *Worc* 78-83; V 83-89; V Bromsgrove All SS 89-01; rtd 01; PtO *Cov* from 02. *61 Newport Drive, Alcester B49 5BJ* T: (01789) 762553 F: 400040 E: jcook120@btinternet.com

COOK, John Michael. b 48. Coll of Resurr Mirfield 72. **d** 74 **p** 75. C Weymouth H Trin *Sarum* 74-76; C Felixstowe St Jo *St E* 76-79; P-in-c Gt and Lt Whelnetham 79-84; P-in-c Cockfield 84-85; P-in-c Bradfield St George w Bradfield St Clare etc 84-85; R Cockfield w Bradfield St Clare, Felsham etc 85-87; V Workington St Jo *Carl* 87-14; rtd 14. *28 Braeside, Seaton, Workington CA14 1EH* T: (01900) 267031

COOK, John Richard Millward. b 61. St Jo Coll Dur BA. Wycliffe Hall Ox 83. **d** 85 **p** 86. C Brampton St Thos *Derby* 85-89; C Farnborough *Guildf* 89-92; C Langham Place All So *Lon* 92-98; V Chelsea St Jo w St Andr 98-08; V Wargrave w Knowl Hill *Ox* from 08. *The Vicarage, Station Road, Wargrave, Reading RG10 8EU* T: 0118-940 2202 E: johnrmcook@btinternet.com

COOK (née OBLESBY), Mrs Judith Mary. b 43. Cranmer Hall Dur 07. **d** 08 **p** 09. NSM Middlesbrough St Martin w St Cuth *York* 08-12; NSM Nunthorpe from 12. *8 Windsor Crescent, Nunthorpe, Middlesbrough TS7 0AN* T: (01642) 315482 E: judycook.nunthorpe@googlemail.com

COOK, Kenneth Hugh. b 30. ALAM. AKC 55. **d** 56 **p** 57. C Netherfield *S'well* 56-59; C Newark w Coddington 59-61; V Basford St Aid 61-67; V Gargrave *Bradf* 67-77; Dir of Ords 77-89; Can Res Bradf Cathl 77-95; rtd 95; PtO *Leeds* from 95. *25 Hollins Close, Hampsthwaite, Harrogate HG3 2EH* T: (01423) 772521

COOK (née McCLEAN), Mrs Lydia Margaret Sheelagh. b 72. Ball Coll Ox BA 94 MA 98. Cuddesdon Coll 94. **d** 96 **p** 97. C Brackley St Pet w St Jas 96-99; Chapl Cranford Ho Sch Ox 99-02; NSM Wallingford Deanery *Ox* 01-04; NSM Sandford-on-Thames 04-06. *Tower View Farm, Kingston, Sturminster Newton DT10 2AR* T: (01258) 817914 E: simonandlydia@towerviewfarm.co.uk

COOK, Marcus John Wyeth. b 41. Chich Th Coll 67. **d** 70 **p** 71. C Friern Barnet St Jas *Lon* 70-73; Hon C St Geo-in-the-East w St Paul 73-00. *2 Vic Johnson House, 74 Armagh Raod, London E3 2HT* M: 07890-207726

COOK, Matthew. b 78. Oak Hill Th Coll. **d** 06 **p** 07. C Bispham *Blackb* 06-10; P-in-c Preston St Steph 10-11; V from 11. *6 Woodfield Close, Penwortham, Preston PR1 0SJ* T: (01772) 741308 E: matthewcook741@btinternet.com

COOK, Mrs Myrtle Bridget Weigela. b 47. BA LLM. EMMTC. **d** 04 **p** 05. NSM Kibworth and Smeeton Westerby and Saddington *Leic* 04-08; NSM Church Langton cum Tur Langton etc 08-13; P-in-c 11-13; P-in-c Thundridge *St Alb* from 13; P-in-c High Cross from 13. *St Mary's House, Church Lane, Stapleford, Hertford SG14 3NB* E: mchighcroft@aol.com

COOK, Neil John. b 70. Wolv Univ BA 93. Wycliffe Hall Ox 05. **d** 06 **p** 07. C Roby *Liv* 06-07; C Huyton Quarry 07-10; P-in-c Goose Green from 10; P-in-c Wigan St Jas w St Thos from 14. *21 Colby Road, Wigan WN3 5NP* T: (01942) 242984 M: 07733-296850 E: cookrnj@googlemail.com

COOK, Nicholas Leonard. b 59. Nottm Univ BCombStuds 84 Greenwich Univ PGCE 01 MCGI 12. Linc Th Coll 81. **d** 84 **p** 85. C Leic St Pet 84-85; C Knighton St Mich 85-86; Chapl Asst Towers Hosp Humberstone 86-89; Chapl Leics Mental Health Service Unit 89-91; Chapl Quainton Hall Sch Harrow 91-94; CF(V) 88-94; CF 94-14; Chapl Duke of York's R Mil Sch Dover from 14; Chapl RAuxAF from 14. *Duke of York's Royal Military School, Dover CT15 5EQ* T: (01304) 245014 E: nick.cook@doyrms.com

COOK, Paul Raymond. *See* McLAREN-COOK, Paul Raymond

COOK, Peter. *See* COOK, Charles Peter

COOK, Peter John. b 57. Ridley Hall Cam 93. **d** 95 **p** 96. C Romford Gd Shep *Chelmsf* 95-98; C Colchester St Jo

98-06; V Bangkok Ch Ch Thailand from 06. *11 Convent Road, Bangkok 10500, Thailand* T: (0066) (2) 266 2887
E: vicar@christchurchbangkok.org

COOK, Peter Ralph. b 69. Portsm Univ BA 92 Kent Univ BA 06. SEITE 03. **d** 06 **p** 07. C Hadlow *Roch* 06-09; V Docking, the Birchams, Stanhoe and Sedgeford *Nor* from 09; P-in-c Fring from 14. *The Vicarage, Sedgeford Road, Docking, King's Lynn PE31 8PN* T: (01485) 517157 E: t2andnor@supanet.com

COOK, Mrs Rachel Elizabeth. b 48. **d** 11 **p** 12. NSM Haydon Wick *Bris* 11-13; NSM N Swindon St Andr from 13. *7 Capesthorne Drive, Swindon SN25 1UP* T: (01793) 706142 M: 07584-094104 E: rachelecook@btinternet.com

COOK, Canon Richard John Noel. b 49. Univ Coll Ox BA 70 MA 74 PGCE 72. Wycliffe Hall Ox MA 77. **d** 78 **p** 79. C Fulwood *Sheff* 78-80; C Bolton St Paul w Em *Man* 81-86; TV 86-93; V Goldsworth Park *Guildf* 93-14; RD Woking 99-03; Hon Can Guildf Cathl 10-14; rtd 14; PtO *Ox* from 15. *7 Rye Close, Banbury OX16 1XG* T: (01295) 367944
E: cookingwok@gmail.com

COOK, Canon Robert Bond. b 28. Dur Univ BSc 54. Ripon Hall Ox 54. **d** 56 **p** 57. C Benwell St Jas *Newc* 56-60; C Sugley 60-64; V Denton 64-75; V Haltwhistle 75-88; P-in-c Greenhead 84-88; V Haltwhistle and Greenhead 88-93; RD Hexham 88-93; Hon Can Newc Cathl 92-93; rtd 93; PtO *St E* from 94; RD Lavenham 03-05. *Ashcroft, Heath Road, Woolpit, Bury St Edmunds IP30 9RN* T: (01359) 240670

COOK, Mrs Ruth Anna Margaret. b 52. Bedf Coll of Educn CertEd 74. **d** 09. OLM Smestow Vale *Lich* from 08. *10 Dowells Gardens, Stourbridge DY8 5QA* T: (01384) 835311 M: 07796-615982 E: ruthfromstourbridge@googlemail.com

COOK, Simon David James. b 74. St Cath Coll Ox BA 97 St Jo Coll Dur BA 08. Cranmer Hall Dur 06. **d** 08 **p** 09. C Broughton *Man* 08-11; V Kirklees Valley from 11; Borough Dean Bury from 12. *All Saints' Vicarage, 10 Kirkburn View, Bury BL8 1DL* T: 0161-797 1595 M: 07745-232662
E: simondjcook@aol.com

COOK, Stephen. b 62. JP 05. Brunel Univ BSc(Econ) 84. S'wark Ord Course 89. **d** 92 **p** 93. Hon C Forest Hill St Aug *S'wark* 92-98; P-in-c Eltham St Barn 98-10; V from 11; CF (TA) from 00; Chapl Greenwich Univ *S'wark* from 14. *St Barnabas' Vicarage, 449 Rochester Way, London SE9 6PH* T: (020) 8856 8294 E: cooksca@aol.com

COOK, Stephen William. b 57. Bris Univ BA 80 Lambeth STh 86. Trin Coll Bris 82. **d** 85 **p** 86. C Heref St Pet w St Owen and St Jas 85-89; TV Keynsham *B & W* 89-95; V Hanham *Bris* 95-02; RD Bitton 98-99; AD Kingswood and S Glos 99-02; TR Okehampton w Inwardleigh, Bratton Clovelly etc *Ex* 02-11; TR Okehampton, Inwardleigh, Belstone, Sourton etc from 12; RD Okehampton 05-12. *The Rectory, 1 Church Path, Okehampton EX20 1LW* T: (01837) 659297

COOK, Timothy John. b 62. Cranmer Hall Dur 95. **d** 95 **p** 96. C Dorchester *Sarum* 95-99; TV Ilminster and Distr *B & W* 99-03; R Yeovil H Trin w Barwick 03-12; rtd 12. *38 Southway Drive, Yeovil BA21 3ED* T: (01935) 706042
E: timcook@tesco.net

COOK, Trevor Vivian. b 43. Sarum Th Coll 67. **d** 69 **p** 70. C Lambeth St Phil *S'wark* 69-73; C St Buryan, St Levan and Sennen *Truro* 73-75; V The Ilketshalls *St E* 75-79; P-in-c Rumburgh w S Elmham 75-79; R Rumburgh w S Elmham w the Ilketshalls 79-84; TR Langport Area *B & W* 84-96; P-in-c Rode Major 96-02; C Hardington Vale 02-04; rtd 04; PtO *B & W* from 04. *Hedge End, 5 Queen Street, Keinton Mandeville, Somerton TA11 6EH* T: (01458) 224448
E: sandracook838@btinternet.com

COOKE, Alan. b 50. Nottm Univ BTh 74 Lanc Univ PGCE 75. Kelham Th Coll 69. **d** 75 **p** 76. C Tyldesley w Shakerley *Man* 75-78; C Langley All SS and Martyrs 80-82; TV Langley and Parkfield 82-83; P-in-c Chadderton St Mark 83-85; V 85-14; rtd 14; PtO *Man* from 14. *The Vicarage, Yates Street, Oldham OL1 4AR*

COOKE, Angela Elizabeth. b 42. SRN 65 SCM 67. St Jo Coll Nottm 86. **d** 87 **p** 94. Par Dn Walton H Trin *Ox* 87-92; Par Dn Bexleyheath Ch Ch *Roch* 92-94; C 94-97; V St Mary Cray and St Paul's Cray 97-05; rtd 05. *7 Maytree Gardens, Bexhill-on-Sea TN40 2PE* T: (01424) 213268
E: angelacooke@hotmail.com

COOKE (née LEA), Mrs Carolyn Jane. b 65. Nottm Univ BA 88 PGCE 90. St Jo Coll Nottm MTh 02. **d** 02 **p** 03. C Hyson Green and Forest Fields *S'well* 02-06; TV Clifton 06-10; P-in-c La Côte *Eur* from 10. *7 chemin du Couchant, 1260 Nyon, Switzerland* T: (0041) (22) 364 0160
E: carolyn.cooke@lacotechurch.ch

COOKE, Christopher Stephen. b 54. Lon Univ BA 76 MA 77 Ox Univ BA 81 MA 88. Ripon Coll Cuddesdon 79. **d** 82 **p** 83. C Cen Telford *Lich* 82-86; R Uffington, Upton Magna and Withington 86-95; RD Wrockwardine 92-01; TR Wrockwardine Deanery 95-01; P-in-c Wem and Lee Brockhurst

01-13; P-in-c Loppington w Newtown 01-02; rtd 13. *Broomfield, Station Road, Pontesbury, Shrewsbury SY5 0QY* E: christopher@csc2000.f9.co.uk

COOKE, Daniel Benedict. b 84. Hull Univ BA 06. St Jo Coll Nottm 06. **d** 08 **p** 09. C W Acklam *York* 08-11; R Brimington *Derby* from 11. *The Rectory, Church Street, Brimington, Chesterfield S43 1JG* T: (01246) 273103
E: danielbcooke@hotmail.com

COOKE, David John. b 31. Linc Th Coll 60. **d** 62 **p** 63. C Brighton Gd Shep Preston *Chich* 62-65; C Clayton w Keymer 65-70; R Stone w Hartwell w Bishopstone *Ox* 70-77; R Stone w Dinton and Hartwell 77-07; rtd 07; PtO *Ox* from 08. *5 Astronomy Way, Aylesbury HP19 7WD* T: (01296) 748215

COOKE, David Michael Randle. b 68. Newc Univ BA 90. Wycliffe Hall Ox 05. **d** 07 **p** 08. C Richmond H Trin and Ch Ch *S'wark* 07-12; TV Barnes from 12. *162 Castelnau, London SW13 9ET* M: 07766-900267
E: davidcooke2003@hotmail.com

COOKE, Francis Theodore. b 34. Tyndale Hall Bris 53 Clifton Th Coll 58. **d** 02 **p** 03. NSM Poynton *Ches* 02-03; NSM Woodford 02-09; Ind Missr Bentley Motors 02-13; rtd 13; PtO *Ches* from 09. *13 Maple Avenue, Poynton, Stockport SK12 1PR* T: (01625) 859246

COOKE, Frederic Ronald. b 35. Selw Coll Cam BA 58 MA 61. Ridley Hall Cam 59. **d** 61 **p** 62. C Flixton St Mich *Man* 61-64; C-in-c Flixton St Jo CD 64-67; V Flixton St Jo 68-74; R Ashton St Mich 74-77; Jerusalem 77-80; V Walmsley *Man* 80-85; AD 81-85; Malaysia 85-90; Prin Ho of Epiphany Th Coll Borneo 85-90; P-in-c Accrington *Blackb* 90-91; TR 91-96; P-in-c Ringley w Prestolee *Man* 96-01; rtd 01; PtO *S & M* from 09. *314 Queens Court, St Pauls Square, Ramsey, Isle of Man IM8 1LF* T: (01624) 816747

COOKE, Geoffrey. b 38. Sarum Th Coll 61. **d** 64 **p** 65. C Eastover *B & W* 64-67; Chapl RAF 67-71; C Bridgwater St Jo *B & W* 71-76; R N Newton w St Michaelchurch and Thurloxton 76-78; V Yeovil H Trin 88-96; rtd 96; PtO *B & W* from 96. *Elmar, Stoke St Mary, Taunton TA3 5DG* E: endymion.99@virgin.net

COOKE, Ms Gillian Freda. b 39. Lon Univ BD 73 Leeds Univ MA 87. Linc Th Coll 74. **dss** 78 **d** 87 **p** 94. Chapl Middx Poly *Lon* 78-80; Chapl Leeds Poly *Ripon* 80-87; N Humberside Ind Chapl *York* 87-90; Asst Chapl HM Pris Hull 90-94; Chapl Keele Univ *Lich* 94-97; Assoc Min Betley and Keele 94-97; Chapl Rampton Hosp Retford 97-99; rtd 99; PtO *York* from 00; Chapl HM Pris Wolds 05-12. *7 Northfield, Swanland, North Ferriby HU14 3RG* T: (01482) 633971
E: gilalsrd@gilalsrd.karoo.co.uk

COOKE (née MORRALL), Mrs Heather Lynne. b 55. LMH Ox BA 76 MA 80 MIPR 88. Dioc OLM tr scheme 96. **d** 99 **p** 00. OLM Martlesham w Brightwell *St E* 99-12; PtO from 12. *9 Swan Close, Martlesham Heath, Ipswich IP5 3SD* T: (01473) 623770 M: 07703-568051 E: hcookema@aol.com

COOKE, James Martin. b 46. Trin Coll Ox BA 67 Ox Univ DipEd 68. **d** 07 **p** 08. OLM Wonersh w Blackheath *Guildf* from 07. *7 Durnsford Way, Cranleigh GU6 7LN* T: (01483) 276049 E: james.cooke20@virgin.net

COOKE, John Stephen. b 35. K Coll Lon BD 58 AKC 58. **d** 59 **p** 60. C W Bromwich St Fran *Lich* 59-62; C Chalfont St Peter *Ox* 62-66; V Cross Heath *Lich* 66-72; R Haughton 72-86; P-in-c Ellenhall w Ranton 72-80; V Eccleshall 86-00; Sub Chapl HM Pris Drake Hall 89-95; rtd 00; PtO *Lich* from 00. *1 James Court, High Street, Eccleshall, Stafford ST21 6BF* T: (01785) 850188

COOKE, Mrs Katherine Mary. b 69. Univ of Wales (Lamp) BA 92. Ox Min Course 08. **d** 12 **p** 13. C Eynsham and Cassington *Ox* from 12. *4 The Tennis, Cassington, Witney OX29 4EL* T: (01865) 881366 M: 07540-568055
E: revkathcooke@gmail.com

COOKE, Canon Kenneth John. b 29. Linc Coll Ox BA 53 MA 57. Ely Th Coll 53. **d** 55 **p** 56. C Nuneaton St Mary *Cov* 55-58; C Cov St Thos 58-61; V Willenhall 61-66; V Meriden 66-76; V Cov St Geo 76-84; V Leamington Spa H Trin and Old Milverton 84-94; Hon Can Cov Cathl 92-94; rtd 94; PtO *Cov* from 94. *2 Chantry Crescent, Alcester B49 5BT* T: (01789) 763460

COOKE, Lesley Elizabeth. d 12 **p** 13. NSM Hawarden *St As* from 12. *University of Chester, Parkgate Road, Chester CH1 4BJ* T: (01244) 511136 E: l.cooke@chester.ac.uk

COOKE, Lorraine Mary. b 48. **d** 12 **p** 13. OLM Droylsden St Martin *Man* from 12; OLM Droylsden St Andr from 13. *72 Waverley Crescent, Droylsden, Manchester M43 7WL* E: lorrainecooke@stmartins-droylsden.co.uk

COOKE, Michael David. b 46. New Coll Ox BA 68 MA 71 DPhil 71. Ox NSM Course 75. **d** 78 **p** 79. NSM Newport

Pagnell *Ox* 78-79; NSM Newport Pagnell w Lathbury 79-85; NSM Newport Pagnell w Lathbury and Moulsoe 85-88; NSM Beckenham Ch Ch *Roch* 90-96; P-in-c Seal St Lawr 96-10; P-in-c Underriver 96-10; rtd 10; PtO *Cant* from 11. *92 Dumpton Park Drive, Broadstairs CT10 1RL* T: (01843) 863293 E: mcooke.92@btinternet.com

COOKE, Michael John. b 39. Ab Dioc Tr Course 78. **d** 80 **p** 81. NSM St Andr Cathl 80-81; Chapl Miss to Seamen 81-88; Miss to Seamen Tilbury 88-91; Hon C Immingham *Linc* 81-88; Ind Chapl Teesside *Dur* 91-97; V Kelloe and Coxhoe 97-06; rtd 06. *36 Nuneaton Drive, Hemlington, Middlesbrough TS8 9PR* E: mikecooke8@yahoo.co.uk

COOKE, Patrick Arthur. b 45. **d** 12. NSM Winterton Gp *Linc* from 12. *10 West Street, Winterton, Scunthorpe DN15 9QQ* T: (01724) 734885

COOKE, Philip George. b 66. Plymouth Univ BSc 88 Univ of Wales (Lamp) PhD 96. Lon Bible Coll 99 Ox Min Course 10. **d** 12 **p** 13. NSM Hanborough and Freeland *Ox* from 12. *4 The Tennis, Cassington, Witney OX29 4EL* T: (01865) 881366 M: 07857-822053 E: revphilcooke@gmail.com

COOKE, Raymond. b 34. Liv Univ BSc 56. Wells Th Coll 58. **d** 60 **p** 61. C Newton Heath All SS *Man* 60-64; C-in-c Failsworth H Family CD 64-75; R Failsworth H Family 75-83; P-in-c Man Gd Shep 83-88; V Westleigh St Pet 88-99; rtd 99; PtO *Man* from 99. *136 Victoria Avenue East, Manchester M9 6HF* T: 0161-740 0664

COOKE, Richard James. b 60. Pemb Coll Ox BA 82 MA 88 Bris Univ PhD 96. Trin Coll Bris 85. **d** 88 **p** 89. C Rugby St Matt *Cov* 88-92; V Fletchamstead 92-04; Dir Initial Tr for Readers 97-02; CME Lay Development and Local Min Adv *Cov* 04-07 and 07-08; Dir of Discipleship Development from 09; C Warmington w Shotteswell and Radway w Ratley 07-14; C Kineton 07-14; C Combroke w Compton Verney 07-14; C Edgehill Churches from 14. *Diocesan Office, 1 Hill Top, Coventry CV1 5AB* T: (024) 7652 1200 E: richard.cooke@covcofe.org

COOKE, Roger. b 68. Heriot-Watt Univ BA 90 BArch 91 Edin Univ MTh 02. TISEC 98. **d** 99 **p** 00. C Prestonpans *Edin* 99-02; R 02-09; C Musselburgh 99-02; R 02-09; I Coleraine *Conn* from 09. *St Patrick's Rectory, 28 Mountsandel Road, Coleraine BT52 1JE* T: (028) 7034 3429 E: carrington20@aol.com

COOKE, Stephen. See COOKE, John Stephen

COOKE, Miss Susan Marilyn. b 76. K Coll Lon BA 97 MA 02 AKC 97 PGCE 98. Ridley Hall Cam 10. **d** 12 **p** 13. C Sunningdale *Ox* from 12. *62 Park Crescent, Ascot SL5 0AY* T: (01344) 621886 M: 07780-606124 E: revsuecooke@gmail.com

COOKE, Mrs Susan Patricia. b 63. Ox Brookes Univ MA 99. WEMTC 10. **d** 13 **p** 14. C Barnwood *Glouc* from 13. *12 Windmill Field, Abbeymead, Gloucester GL4 4RQ* M: 07736-770797 E: susan_phil_cooke@hotmail.com

COOKE, Mrs Suzanne. b 65. Westmr Coll Ox BTh 96. Westcott Ho Cam 08. **d** 10 **p** 11. C Watton *Nor* 10-13; P-in-c Upper Tas Valley from 13. *The Rectory, 16 The Fields, Tacolneston, Norwich NR16 1DG* T: (01953) 788227 E: sucooke@hotmail.co.uk

COOKSEY, Miss Diane Marie. b 75. Univ of Cen England in Birm BA 97. St Jo Coll Nottm 09. **d** 11 **p** 12. C Churchill-in-Halfshire w Blakedown and Broome *Worc* 11-14; C Warndon St Nic from 14. *4 Daty Croft, Home Meadow, Worcester WR4 0JB* M: 07974-556514 E: diane_cooksey@hotmail.com

COOKSON, Canon Diane Veronica. b 51. NOC 81. **dss** 84 **d** 87 **p** 94. Gt Sutton *Ches* 84-86; Neston 86-87; Par Dn 87-94; C 94-96; V Stockport St Sav from 96; Ecum Adv (Gtr Man) 00-02; RD Stockport from 12; Hon Can Ches Cathl from 04. *St Saviour's Vicarage, 22 St Saviour's Road, Great Moor, Stockport SK2 7QE* T: 0161-483 2633 E: st.saviours@virgin.net

COOKSON, Canon Graham Leslie. b 37. Sarum Th Coll 64. **d** 67 **p** 68. C Upton Ascension *Ches* 67-69; C Timperley 69-75; V Godley cum Newton Green 75-83; R Tarporley 83-07; Hon Can Ches Cathl 04-07; rtd 07; PtO *Ches* from 08. *15 Dolphin Court, Chester CH4 8JX* T: (01244) 671044 E: g.cookson532@btinternet.com

COOKSON, Matthew James Gathorne. b 51. **d** 09 **p** 10. NSM Kintbury w Avington *Ox* 09-11; NSM W Woodhay w Enborne, Hampstead Marshall etc 09-11; NSM Walbury Beacon from 11. *St Laurence's House, West Woodhay, Newbury RG20 0BL* T: (01488) 669043 E: mjgcookson@gmail.com

COOKSON, Canon William. b 61. **d** 98 **p** 99. C Haydock St Mark *Liv* 98-02; Min Wallington Springfield CH *S'wark* from 02; Dioc Dean of Fresh Expressions from 15; Hon Can S'wark Cathl from 15. *49 Stanley Park Road, Carshalton SM5 3HT* T: (020) 8404 6064 E: willcookson@blueyonder.co.uk

COOLING, Derrick William. b 35. AKC 58 Heref Coll of Educn TCert 68 Lon Univ BD 69 DipEd 71 Univ of Wales (Cardiff) MEd 81. St Boniface Warminster 58. **d** 59 **p** 60. C Haydock St Jas *Liv* 59-61; C Hove St Barn *Chich* 61-63; V Llangattock w St Maughan's etc *Mon* 63-68; R Blaina 68-70; PtO *Sarum* 70-74;

Chapl Windsor Sch Hamm 74-75; Asst Master Croesyceiliog Sch Cwmbran 75-81; PtO *Mon* 79-81; Chapl Epsom Coll 81-84; V Bettws *Mon* 84-95; P-in-c Purleigh, Cold Norton and Stow Maries *Chelmsf* 95-98; rtd 98; PtO *Mon* from 98; *Glouc* from 05. *St Thomas Cottage, The Fence, St Briavels, Lydney GL15 6QG* T: (01594) 530926 E: clericderrick@aol.com

COOLING (*née* YOUNG), Mrs Margaret Dorothy. b 37. K Coll Lon BA 59 AKC Lon Univ BD 69 PGCE 70 MSc 10 Univ of Wales (Cardiff) MEd 81. Mon Dioc Tr Scheme 89. **d** 90 **p** 95. NSM Bettws *Mon* 90-95; NSM Purleigh, Cold Norton and Stow Maries *Chelmsf* 95-98; rtd 98; PtO *Mon* from 98; *Glouc* from 01. *St Thomas Cottage, The Fence, St Briavels, Lydney GL15 6QG* T: (01594) 530926 E: maggieandderrick@outlook.com

COOMBE, James Anthony. b 31. Em Coll Cam BA 53 MA 57 Lon Univ BD 60. Tyndale Hall Bris 57. **d** 60 **p** 61. C Chadderton Ch Ch *Man* 60-63; C Worthing St Geo *Chich* 63-65; V Wandsworth St Mich *S'wark* 65-74; P-in-c Warboys *Ely* 74-76; R 76-87; RD St Ives 83-87; P-in-c Broughton and Wistow 84-87; R Buckworth and V Alconbury cum Weston 87-96; rtd 96; PtO *Cant* 06-13. *12 Nursery Fields, Hythe CT21 4DL* T: (01303) 262151

COOMBE, Canon Michael Thomas. b 31. Lon Univ BA 64. Ox NSM Course 73. **d** 75 **p** 76. Chapl St Piran's Sch Maidenhead 75-81; NSM Furze Platt *Ox* 75-81; C 86-88; Asst Chapl Oslo St Edm *Eur* 81-84; Chapl Belgrade w Zagreb 84-86; Chapl Marseille w St Raphaël, Aix-en-Provence etc 88-89; Chapl Reading Hosps 89-91; P-in-c Clewer St Andr *Ox* 91-92; C New Windsor 92-93; C Reading St Mark 93-95; C Reading H Trin 93-95; Prec Gib Cathl and Port Chapl 95-03; Can Gib Cathl 00-03; rtd 03. *28 Gipsy Lane, Exmouth EX8 3HN* T: (01395) 272923

COOMBER, Ian Gladstone. b 47. Ch Ch Coll Cant CertEd 68 Southn Univ BTh 79. Sarum & Wells Th Coll 73. **d** 76 **p** 77. C Weeke *Win* 76-79; TV Saffron Walden w Wendens Ambo and Littlebury *Chelmsf* 79-82; V Weston *Win* 82-90; R Bedhampton *Portsm* 90-96; R Botley and Durley 96-05; V Curdridge 96-05; RD Bishop's Waltham 98-03; TR Cartmel Peninsula *Carl* 05-09; rtd 09; PtO *B & W* from 09. *Elder Cottage, Throop Road, Templecombe BA8 0HR* T: (01963) 371205 E: iancoomber747@btinternet.com

COOMBES, Frederick Brian John. b 34. Nottm Univ BA 56 Plymouth Poly MPhil 73 FRGS. SWMTC 85. **d** 88 **p** 89. NSM Bodmin w Lanhydrock and Lanivet *Truro* 88-07; PtO from 07. *191 Boslowick Road, Falmouth TR11 4QF* T: (01326) 210788

COOMBES, Gareth John. d 10 **p** 11. NSM Bedwas w Machen w Rudry *Mon* 10-12; C Caerphilly *Llan* 12-15; C Eglwysilan and Caerphilly from 15. *2 Clos Cae'r Wern, Castle View, Caerphilly CF83 1SQ* T: (029) 2088 0357 E: revgareth@aol.com

COOMBS, Christopher. b 48. UWIC MSc 05. Trin Coll Bris 10. **d** 12 **p** 13. OLM Rodbourne Cheney *Bris* from 12. *230 Cheney Manor Road, Swindon SN2 2NZ* T: (01793) 643465 M: 07789-514310 E: chris@theatreskills.fsnet.co.uk

COOMBS, Edward Neve. b 66. Bris Univ BSc 88. Cranmer Hall Dur BA 93. **d** 94 **p** 95. C Edin St Thos 94-96; C Dagenham *Chelmsf* 97-01; P-in-c Banbury St Paul *Ox* 01-13; V from 13. *St Paul's House, Bretch Hill, Banbury OX16 0LR* T: (01295) 264003 E: edward.coombs@virgin.net

COOMBS, John Allen. b 46. Portsm Poly BSc 70. Oak Hill Th Coll 86 Sarum & Wells Th Coll 89. **d** 89 **p** 90. C Leverington and Wisbech St Mary *Ely* 89-93; P-in-c Emneth 93-96; V Emneth and Marshland St James 96-99; P-in-c Papworth Everard 99-00; TV Papworth 00-02; Chapl Papworth Hosp NHS Foundn Trust 99-06; P-in-c Roche *Truro* 06-12; rtd 12; PtO *Ex* 13-14; *Portsm* from 14. *The Little Haven, Castle Road, Ventnor PO38 1LG* T: (01983) 854290 E: john.coombs.7@gmail.com

COOMBS, John Kendall. b 47. Culham Coll Ox BEd 73. Sarum & Wells Th Coll 75. **d** 77 **p** 78. C Fareham H Trin *Portsm* 77-80; C Petersfield w Sheet 80-83; TV Beaminster Area *Sarum* 83-87; TR Preston w Sutton Poyntz, Littlemoor etc 87-97; TR Hermitage *Ox* 97-05; P-in-c Hurst 05-11; rtd 11; PtO *Ox* from 11. *20 Katchside, Sutton Courtenay, Abingdon OX14 4BH* E: jkcoombs@yahoo.co.uk

COOMBS, Martin. See COOMBS, Walter James Martin

COOMBS, The Ven Peter Bertram. b 28. Bris Univ BA 58 MA 61. Clifton Th Coll 55. **d** 60 **p** 61. C Beckenham Ch Ch *Roch* 60-63; R Nottingham St Nic *S'well* 63-68; V New Malden and Coombe *S'wark* 68-75; RD Kingston 71-75; Adn Wandsworth 75-88; Adn Reigate 88-95; rtd 95; PtO *Portsm* from 97. *92 Locks Heath Park Road, Locks Heath, Southampton SO31 6LZ* T: (01489) 577288

COOMBS, Richard Murray. b 63. St Chad's Coll Dur BSc 85 Rob Coll Cam BA 89 MA 90. Ridley Hall Cam 87. **d** 90 **p** 91. C Enfield Ch Ch Trent Park *Lon* 90-94; C St Helen Bishopsgate w St Andr Undershaft etc 94-98; P-in-c Pet Cornhill 95-98; V Burford w Fulbrook, Taynton, Asthall etc *Ox* from 98. *The Vicarage, Church Lane, Burford OX18 4SD* T: (01993) 822275 F: 824699 E: richardcoombs@burfordchurch.org

COOMBS, Stephen John. b 54. Open Univ BA 86. Trin Coll Bris 85. d 87 p 88. C Norton Canes Lich 87-90; Chapl Trowbridge Coll Sarum 90-94; C Studley 90-94. 48 Whitstone Rise, Shepton Mallet BA4 5QB T: (01749) 343750

COOMBS, Canon Walter James Martin. b 33. Keble Coll Ox BA 57 MA 61. Cuddesdon Coll 59. d 61 p 62. C Kennington St Jo S'wark 61-64; Chapl Em Coll Cam 64-68; Bp's Dom Chapl S'wark 68-70; V E Dulwich St Jo 70-77; V Pershore w Pinvin, Wick and Birlingham Worc 77-92; Hon Can Worc Cathl 84-92; RD Pershore 85-91; TV Dorchester Ox 92-98; rtd 98; PtO Ox from 01. 54 Divinity Road, Oxford OX4 1LJ T: (01865) 243865

COONEY, Craig Stephen. Ulster Univ BSc 98 TCD BTh 06. d 06 p 07. C Lurgan Ch the Redeemer D & D 06-11; C Dublin St Cath and St Jas w St Audoen D & G from 11. 17 Emmet Road, Inchicore, Dublin 8, Republic of Ireland M: (00353) 86-722 4660 E: cooneycraig@hotmail.com

COONEY, Canon Michael Patrick. b 55. City of Lon Poly BA 77. Ripon Coll Cuddesdon 77. d 80 p 81. C Cov E 80-83; C Old Brumby Linc 83-85; V Linc St Jo 85-90; V Frodingham 90-05; RD Manlake 99-10; RD Is of Axholme 05-10; Ind Chapl from 05; P-in-c Gainsborough and Morton from 12; Can and Preb Linc Cathl from 04. The Rectory, 32 Morton Terrace, Gainsborough DN21 2RQ T: (01427) 679407 E: mike.cooney@btinternet.com

COONEY, William Barry. b 47. K Coll Lon 69. d 70 p 71. C W Bromwich All SS Lich 70-73; C Wolverhampton St Pet 73-75; C Rugeley 75-78; V Sneyd Green 78-87; R Sandiacre Derby 87-11; rtd 11. 15 Newthorpe Common, Newthorpe, Nottingham NG16 2BX T: (01773) 711549 E: rosemary.c@talk21.com

COOPER, Alexander James Goodenough. b 47. Bath Univ BSc 69. WEMTC 04. d 06 p 07. NSM Soundwell Bris from 06. 1 Deerhurst, Bristol BS15 1XH T: 0117-973 9441 E: linsand@blueyonder.co.uk

COOPER, Alfred Philip. b 50. Bris Univ BA 71. All Nations Chr Coll 72. d 77 p 78. Chile from 75; SAMS from 77. Iglesia Anglicana del Chile, Casilla 50675, Correo Central, Santiago, Chile T: (0056) (2) 226 8794

COOPER, Mrs Alison Beryl. b 51. Ripon Coll Cuddesdon 03. d 04 p 05. NSM Ascot Heath Ox 04-07; NSM Sunninghill and S Ascot 07-10; NSM Limpsfield and Tatsfield S'wark 10-13; PtO from 13. Rosemary Cottage, Oakdale Lane, Crockham Hill, Edenbridge TN8 6RL M: 07747-682139 T: (01732) 669447 E: alison8@talktalk.net

COOPER, Andrew John. b 62. W Sussex Inst of HE BA 87 Greenwich Univ PGCE 03. St Steph Ho Ox 88. d 91 p 92. C Rawmarsh w Parkgate Sheff 91-93; C Mosbrough 93-95; P-in-c Donnington Wood Lich 95-96; CF from 96. c/o MOD Chaplains (Army) F: 381824 T: (01264) 383430

COOPER, Andrew John Gearing. b 48. Sir John Cass Coll Lon BSc 70. Ripon Coll Cuddesdon 73. d 76 p 77. C Potternewton Ripon 76-79; Antigua 79-81; Anguilla 81-87; V W Bromwich St Andr w Ch Ch Lich 88-92. 45 Dimbles Lane, Lichfield WS13 7HW T: (01543) 416020

COOPER, Andrew Richard James. b 81. Lon Metrop Univ BSc 04. Ridley Hall Cam 07. d 10 p 11. C S Harrow St Paul Lon 10-13; Chapl HM YOI Feltham from 13. HM Young Offender Institution, Bedfont Road, Feltham TW13 4ND T: (020) 8844 5000 E: arjcooper@aim.com

COOPER, Miss Angela Jean. b 56. SWMTC 09. d 12 p 13. C St Just-in-Roseland and St Mawes Truro from 12. Penros, Rose Da Mar Cottages, St Just in Roseland, Truro TR2 5JB M: 07753-517304 E: angelajeancooper@hotmail.com

COOPER, Anne. See COOPER, Margaret Anne

COOPER, The Ven Annette Joy. b 53. Open Univ BA 80 Dur Univ MA 13 CQSW 84. S'wark Ord Course 85. d 88 p 94. NSM Pembury Roch 88; Chapl Asst Kent and Sussex Hosp Tunbridge Wells 88-91; Chapl Asst Leybourne Grange Hosp W Malling 88-91; Chapl Bassetlaw Hosp and Community Services NHS Trust 91-96; P-in-c Edwinstowe S'well 96-04; Chapl Center Parcs Holiday Village 96-01; AD Worksop 99-04; Hon Can S'well Minster 02-04; Adn Colchester Chelmsf from 04. 63 Powers Hall End, Witham CM8 1NH T: (01376) 513130 F: 500789 E: a.colchester@chelmsford.anglican.org

COOPER, Arthur. b 47. d 15 p 15. C Stoneycroft All SS Liv from 15. All Saints' Vicarage, 7 Saints Close, Liverpool L13 4AT T: 0151-220 2860 E: akc@f2s.com

COOPER, Canon Bede Robert. b 42. Ex Univ BA 69. Coll of Resurr Mirfield 69. d 71 p 72. C Weymouth H Trin Sarum 71-74; P-in-c Broad Town 74-79; V Wootton Bassett 74-86; R Wilton w Netherhampton and Fugglestone 86-07; Can and Preb Sarum Cathl 88-07; rtd 07; PtO B & W from 09; Win 11-14; Sarum from 13. 205 High Street, Milborne Port, Sherborne DT9 5AG T: (01963) 250503 E: b.cooper789@btinternet.com

COOPER, Benedict Christopher. b 68. K Coll Cam BA 90 Wolfs Coll Ox MPhil 94 DPhil 97 W Sydney Univ PhD 10. Oak Hill Th Coll BA 03. d 03 p 04. C St Helen Bishopsgate w St Andr

Undershaft etc Lon 03-07; Australia 07-10; C Fulwood Sheff from 10. 1 Silver Birch Avenue, Sheffield S10 3TA T: 0114-230 4444 or 229 5567 M: 07402-065857 E: bencooper@fulwoodchurch.co.uk

COOPER, Bert. See COOPER, Herbert William

COOPER, Brian Hamilton. b 35. Keble Coll Ox BA 58 MA 67. Ripon Hall Ox 58. d 60 p 61. C Woolwich St Mary w H Trin S'wark 60-64; Canada 64-66; Vice-Prin Westcott Ho Cam 66-71; R Downham Market w Bexwell Ely 71-82; RD Fincham 80-82; V Chesterfield St Mary and All SS Derby 82-91; V Herringthorpe Sheff 91-00; RD Rotherham 93-98; rtd 00; PtO Sheff from 00. 51 Anston Avenue, Worksop S81 7HU T: (01909) 479306 E: m.y.cooper1723@aol.com

✠**COOPER, The Rt Revd Carl Norman.** b 60. Univ of Wales (Lamp) BA 82 Trin Coll Carmarthen MPhil 99. Wycliffe Hall Ox 82. d 85 p 86 c 02. C Llanelli St D 85-87; P-in-c Llanerch Aeron w Ciliau Aeron and Dihewyd etc 87-88; I 88-93; R Dolgellau w Llanfachreth and Brithdir etc Ban 93-02; Warden of Readers 88-02; Adn Meirionnydd 00-02; Bp St D 02-08. Hafod Lon, 35 Llandeilo Road, Llandybie, Ammanford SA18 3JA

COOPER, Cecil Clive. b 26. TD 75. AKC 52. d 53 p 54. C Chipping Campden Glouc 53-55; C Cheltenham St Mary 55-60; V Stroud 60-65; CF (TA) 63-75; R Woodmansterne S'wark 65-91; RD Sutton 80-90; rtd 91; PtO Pet 91-12; Cov from 91. 10 Mill Close, Braunston, Daventry NN11 7HY T: (01788) 890596

COOPER, Cecil William Marcus. b 32. TCD BA 58 MA 66. CITC 57. d 59 p 60. C Cork St Fin Barre and St Nic C, C & R 59-62; Bp's V, Lib and Registrar Kilkenny Cathl 62-64; C Knockbreda D & D 65-67; Asst Ed Church of Ireland Gazette 66-82; Ed 82-00; I Magheradroll D & D 67-82; Dioc Registrar 81-90; I Drumbeg 82-00; Can Down Cathl 86-00; Prec 90-91; Chan 91-00; rtd 00. c/o D Griffin Esq, 23 Ailesbury Park, Ballsbridge, Dublin 4, Republic of Ireland

COOPER, Clive Anthony Charles. b 38. Lon Univ BEd 74. ALCD 62. d 62 p 63. C Morden S'wark 62-65; SAMS Argentina 65-71; Asst Master St Nic Sch Cranleigh 74-92; Hon C Cranleigh Guildf 78-79; Hon C Ewhurst 80-82; Hon Chapl Duke of Kent Sch Ewhurst 83-92; Chapl Felixstowe Coll 92-93; PtO Ex 94-95; Chapl Puerto Pollensa Eur 95-02; P-in-c Instow and Westleigh Ex 03-07; rtd 08; PtO Eur 08-12; Ex 09-12. 64 Benfer Road, Victoria Point QLD 4165, Australia E: clivecooper141@yahoo.com.au

COOPER, Colin. b 55. Open Univ BA. St Jo Coll Nottm 83. d 86 p 87. C Cheadle Hulme St Andr Ches 86-89; C Tunbridge Wells St Jo Roch 89-93; V Whitfield Derby 93-11; TR N Wingfield, Clay Cross and Pilsley from 11. The Rectory, St Lawrence Road, North Wingfield, Chesterfield S42 5HX T: (01246) 851181 E: revccooper@gmail.com

COOPER, Colin Charles. b 40. Middx Univ BA 94. Oak Hill Th Coll 62. d 66 p 67. C Islington St Andr w St Thos and St Matthias Lon 66-69; Bermuda 69-76; V Gordeston St Andr Nor 77-94; R Emporia Ch Ch w Purdy Grace USA 94-12; rtd 12. 2608 South Anchor Lane, Nags Head NC 27959, USA T: (001) (434) 430 0107 E: colincooper9540@gmail.com

COOPER, Mrs Corynne Elizabeth. b 54. Kent Univ BA 76 PGCE 77 Nottm Univ MA 98. EMMTC 95. d 98 p 99. NSM Kneesall w Laxton and Wellow S'well 98-01; C Widecombe-in-the-Moor, Leusdon, Princetown etc Ex 01-05; TV Ashburton, Bickington, Buckland in the Moor etc from 05. The Vicarage, Holne, Newton Abbot TQ13 7RT T: (01364) 631522 E: corynne.cooper@virgin.net

COOPER, David Philip. b 65. York Univ BA 86. Qu Coll Birm BTheol 94. d 94 p 95. C Burslem Lich 94-98; TV Cen Wolverhampton and Dioc Inter-Faith Officer 98-05; P-in-c Arnside Carl from 05; Dioc Ecum Officer from 14. The Vicarage, 45 Church Hill, Arnside, Carnforth LA5 0DW T: (01524) 761319 E: revdavidcooper@btinternet.com

COOPER, Derek Edward. b 30. Bps' Coll Cheshunt 61. d 62 p 63. C Bishop's Stortford St Mich St Alb 62-66; V Westcliff St Cedd Chelmsf 66-89; R Camerton w Dunkerton, Foxcote and Shoscombe B & W 89-95; rtd 95; PtO Win 95-14. 6 Caerleon Drive, Andover SP10 4DE T: (01264) 362807

COOPER, Donna. d 14. C Edin St Jo from 14. Address temp unknown

COOPER, Eric John. b 22. Cam Univ MA 47. Chich Th Coll 52. d 53 p 54. C Tottenham St Paul Lon 53-55; C Hillingdon St Jo 55-62; C Knowle St Martin Bris 62-66; V Bedminster Down 66-72; rtd 87. 6 Deveron Grove, Keynsham, Bristol BS31 1UJ T: 0117-986 7339

COOPER, Frederick. b 30. Cranmer Hall Dur 68. d 70 p 71. C Preston All SS Blackb 70-72; C Preston St Jude 72-76; TV 76-78; V Higher Walton 78-91; P-in-c Preston All SS 91-95; rtd 95; PtO Blackb from 95. 10 Guardian Close, Fulwood, Preston PR2 8EX T: (01772) 713808

COOPER, Gavin Ashley. b 85. Chich Univ BA 06. St Steph Ho Ox BA 10 MA 15. **d** 11 **p** 12. C Old St Pancras *Lon* 11-14; P-in-c Stamford St Mary and St Martin *Linc* from 14. *St Martin's Rectory, 6 Pinfold Lane, Stamford PE9 2LS* T: (01780) 753356 E: frgavincooper@gmail.com

COOPER, Gordon William. b 54. Aston Tr Scheme 93 Ripon Coll Cuddesdon 95. **d** 97 **p** 98. C Kippax w Allerton Bywater *Ripon* 97-01; V Wyther 01-08; P-in-c Garforth 08-12; R *Leeds* from 12. *The Rectory, Croft Foulds Court, Garforth, Leeds LS25 1NQ* T: 0113-286 3737
E: gordon@williamcooper.freeserve.co.uk

COOPER, Graham Denbigh. b 48. Nottm Univ BTh 75. St Jo Coll Nottm LTh 75. **d** 75 **p** 76. C Collyhurst *Man* 75-78; C Stambermill *Worc* 78-80; V The Lye and Stambermill 80-90; P-in-c Frome H Trin *B & W* 90; V 91-95; Appeals Organiser Children's Soc 95-97; Area Manager Save the Children Fund from 97. *2 Coombe View, Shepton Mallet BA4 5YF* T: (01749) 343157

COOPER, Mrs Gwenda. d 11 **p** 12. NSM Colwyn and Llanelian *St As* from 11. *Bron Digain, Llangernyw, Abergele LL22 8PP* T: (01745) 860349 E: brondigain@googlemail.com

COOPER, Hannah Reveana. b 84. St Mellitus Coll BA 12. **d** 12. C Colchester, New Town and The Hythe *Chelmsf* from 12. *8 Circular Road South, Colchester CO2 7UF* T: (01206) 679105
E: rev.hannahcooper@gmail.com

COOPER, Herbert William. b 29. Chich Th Coll 77. **d** 79 **p** 80. C Leigh Park *Portsm* 79-82; C-in-c Hayling St Pet CD 82-85; V Whitwell and St Lawrence 85-94; P-in-c Niton 89-94; rtd 94; PtO *Heref* 94-04; *Chich* from 05. *10 Andrew Avenue, Felpham, Bognor Regis PO22 7QS* T: (01243) 584212

COOPER, Ian. b 57. St Jo Coll Nottm 00. **d** 02 **p** 03. C Mildenhall *St E* 02-05; TV 05-06; V Blacklands Hastings Ch Ch and St Andr *Chich* 06-10; P-in-c Peacehaven and Telscombe Cliffs 10-13; P-in-c Piddinghoe 10-13; P-in-c Telscombe Village 10-13; V Peacehaven and Telscombe Cliffs w Piddinghoe etc 13-14; Chapl HM Pris Wayland from 15. *HM Prison Wayland, Griston, Thetford IP25 6RL* T: (01953) 804080
E: ian@rpmo.co.uk

COOPER, Ian Clive. b 48. Ex Univ BA 76 K Coll Lon MTh 94 FCA. Linc Th Coll 76. **d** 78 **p** 79. C Sunbury *Lon* 78-81; P-in-c Astwood Bank *Worc* 81-85; P-in-c Feckenham w Bradley 82-85; TV Hemel Hempstead *St Alb* 85-95; R Bushey 95-04; TR Witney *Ox* 04-06; TV Marlborough *Sarum* 06-13; rtd 13; Learning for Discipleship Support Officer *Sarum* 13-15. *73 Bowbridge Lane, Stroud GL5 2JL*
E: iancoopermlboro@aol.com

COOPER, James Peter. b 61. Westf Coll Lon BSc 82 Portsm Univ BA 04 Heythrop Coll Lon MA 12. Sarum & Wells Th Coll 82. **d** 85 **p** 86. C Durrington *Chich* 85-88; C Clayton w Keymer 88-95; TV Chich and Chapl Chich Coll of Tech 95-01; Chapl R W Sussex NHS Trust 01-11; R Cessnock Australia 11-15; P-in-c Donnington *Chich* from 15; Chapl St Wilfrid's Hospice Chich from 15. *The Vicarage, 34 Graydon Avenue, Chichester PO19 8RF*
E: lizandjimcooper@gmail.com

COOPER, Mrs Jennifer Ann Lisbeth. b 45. MCSP 67. **d** 04 **p** 05. OLM Ashwellthorpe, Forncett, Fundenhall, Hapton etc *Nor* 04-13; rtd 13; PtO *Nor* from 13. *12 Valley Road, Tasburgh, Norwich NR15 1NQ* T: (01508) 470141

COOPER, Jennifer Elaine. b 62. Toronto Univ BA 83 Ottawa Univ MA 90 Keble Coll Ox DPhil 05. Ripon Coll Cuddesdon 05. **d** 06 **p** 07. C Cotham St Sav w St Mary and Clifton St Paul *Bris* 06-09; Lect and Tutor Coll of Resurr Mirfield from 09; Visiting Lect Leeds Univ from 09. *College of the Resurrection, Stocks Bank Road, Mirfield WF14 0BW* T: (01924) 481904 E: jcooper@mirfield.org.uk

COOPER, Jeremy John. b 45. Kelham Th Coll 65 Linc Th Coll 71. **d** 71 **p** 72. C Derby St Luke 71-76; TV Malvern Link w Cowleigh *Worc* 76-79; P-in-c Claypole *Linc* 79-80; P-in-c Westborough w Dry Doddington and Stubton 79-80; C Eye w Braiseworth and Yaxley *St E* 80-82; P-in-c Hundon w Barnardiston 82-83; R 83-97; V Hundon 97-99; Chapl St Marg Convent E Grinstead 99-03; Warden, Lect and Preacher Newland Almshouses 03-04. *The College of St Barnabas, Blackberry Lane, Lingfield RH7 6NJ* T: (01342) 870260

COOPER, Jeremy Llewellyn John. b 51. Lanc Univ BA 73 Sussex Univ PGCE 74 York Univ MSc 87. **d** 07 **p** 08. OLM Morpeth *Newc* 07-11; Chapl Northumbria Healthcare NHS Foundn Trust from 11. *Southdown, 13 Curlew Hill, Morpeth NE61 3SH*
E: jeremylcooper@aol.com

COOPER, John. b 47. Sarum & Wells Th Coll 71. **d** 74 **p** 75. C Spring Grove St Mary *Lon* 74-77; C Shepherd's Bush St Steph w St Thos 77-82; V Paddington St Pet 82-89; V Darwen St Cuth w Tockholes St Steph *Blackb* 89-96; V Northampton St Mich w St Edm *Pet* 96-99; PtO *St Alb* from 99; *Lon* from 02. *The Charterhouse, Charterhouse Square, London EC1M 6AN* T: (020) 3560 1336 M: 07749-502929
E: buster6913@yahoo.co.uk

COOPER, John. b 34. BEd. NOC. **d** 83 **p** 84. C Tong *Bradf* 83-87; V Bingley H Trin 87-92; V Silsden 92-99; rtd 99; PtO *Bradf* 01-08; *Blackb* from 10. *15 Fosbrooke House, 8 Clifton Drive, Lytham St Annes FY8 5RQ* T: (01253) 667029

COOPER, John Edward. b 40. K Coll Lon BD 63 AKC 63. **d** 64 **p** 65. C Prittlewell St Mary *Chelmsf* 64-67; C Up Hatherley *Glouc* 67-69; C-in-c Dorridge *Birm* 69-71; V Longford and P-in-c Alkmonton w Yeaveley *Derby* 71-76; TV Canvey Is *Chelmsf* 76-82; R Spixworth w Crostwick *Nor* 82-91; R Frettenham w Stanninghall 82-91; V Gt w Lt Harrowden and Orlingbury *Pet* 91-01; rtd 01; PtO *Leic* from 01; *Pet* 01-12. *Staveley House, 30 Brooke Road, Braunston, Oakham LE15 8QR* T: (01572) 770984

COOPER, Canon John Leslie. b 33. Lon Univ BD 65 MPhil 78. Chich Th Coll 59. **d** 62 **p** 63. C Kings Heath *Birm* 62-65; Asst Chapl HM Pris Wandsworth 65-66; Chapl HM Borstal Portland 66-68; Chapl HM Pris Bris 68-72; P-in-c Balsall Heath St Paul *Birm* 73-81; V 81-82; Adn Aston and Can Res Birm Cathl 82-90; Adn Coleshill 90-93; C Sutton Coldfield H Trin 93-97; Hon Can Birm Cathl 93-97; rtd 97; PtO *Derby* from 98. *4 Ireton Court, Kirk Ireton, Ashbourne, Derby DE6 3JP* T: (01335) 370459 E: johncooper612@btinternet.com

COOPER, John Northcott. b 44. Ox Min Course 89. **d** 92 **p** 93. NSM Burghfield *Ox* 92-99; P-in-c Wootton (Boars Hill) 99-00; V Wootton and Dry Sandford 00-10; AD Abingdon 02-07; rtd 10. *Dinosaur Footprints, 21 Townend Road, Swanage BH19 2PU* T: (01929) 421342 E: dinofoot@hotmail.co.uk

COOPER, Jonathan Mark Eric. b 62. Man Univ BSc 83 Edin Univ BD 88. Edin Th Coll 85. **d** 88 **p** 89. C Stainton-in-Cleveland *York* 88-91; C W Bromwich All SS *Lich* 91-93; P-in-c Ingleby Barwick CD *York* 93-98; P-in-c Hinderwell w Roxby 98-03; R Kirby Misperton w Normanby, Edston and Salton 03-10; V Brompton w Deighton from 10; R Rounton w Welbury from 10. *The Vicarage, Northallerton Road, Brompton, Northallerton DL6 2QA* T: (01609) 772436
E: j.m.e.c@btinternet.com

COOPER, Judith Mary. b 52. Leeds Univ BA 09. NOC 06. **d** 09 **p** 10. C Prestwich St Mary *Man* 09-12; P-in-c Westleigh St Pet 12-15; V from 15; P-in-c Westleigh St Paul from 12. *St Peter's Vicarage, 6 Malham Close, Leigh WN7 4SD* T: (01942) 673626 M: 07752-676007 E: judith.cooper5@virginmedia.com

COOPER, Ms Louise Helena. b 68. Leeds Univ BA 90. Qu Coll Birm. **d** 93 **p** 94. Par Dn Dovecot *Liv* 93-94; C 94-96; Dep Chapl HM YOI Glen Parva 96-01; Chapl HM Pris Styal 01-02; Chapl HM Pris Man 02-09; Chapl HM Pris Nottm 09-11; Chapl HM Pris Dartmoor from 11. *The Chaplaincy, HM Prison Dartmoor, Princetown, Yelverton PL20 6RR* T: (01822) 322000

COOPER, Malcolm Tydeman. b 37. Pemb Coll Ox BA 61 MA 64. Linc Th Coll 63. **d** 63 **p** 64. C Spennithorne *Ripon* 63-66; C Caversham *Ox* 66-71; Hon C Blackbird Leys CD 71-75; LtO *Sarum* 75-78; *B & W* 78-82; NSM Sutton and Witcham w Mepal *Ely* 82-97; P-in-c Coveney 97-06. *8 The Coppice, Merrington, Bomere Heath, Shrewsbury SY4 3QE*
E: mtcm4@waitrose.com

COOPER, Marc Ashley Rex. b 62. Leeds Univ BA 85 MA 95. Linc Th Coll 92. **d** 92 **p** 93. C Bolton St Jas w St Chrys *Bradf* 92-96; P-in-c Fishtoft *Linc* 96-97; R from 97; RD Holland E 03-09. *The Rectory, Rectory Close, Fishtoft, Boston PE21 0RZ* T/F: (01205) 363216 E: revmarccooper@dsl.pipex.com

COOPER, Mrs Margaret Anne. b 54. SRN 76. STETS 11. **d** 14 **p** 15. NSM Guildf St Nic from 14. *68 Horseshoe Lane East, Guildford GU1 2TW* T: (01483) 825191
E: anne.cooper9@btinternet.com

COOPER, Sister Margery. b 26. CA Tr Coll 49. dss 79 **d** 87 **p** 94. CA from 52; Evang Family Miss *Dur*, *Newc* and *York* 79-86; PtO *York* 86-91 and 00-11; NSM Fulford 91-00; rtd 00. *3 Grimston Court, Hull Road, York YO19 5LE* T: (01904) 489343

COOPER, Canon Mark Richard. b 69. Kent Univ BA 98. St Jo Coll Morpeth. **d** 95 **p** 95. C Hamilton Australia 95-96; C Rainham *Roch* 96-98; Assoc P Kincumber Australia 98-02; P-in-c Blue Gum Hills 02-06; Chapl Bp Tyrell Angl Coll 06; Can Res Goulbourn Cathl from 07; Chapl Goulbourn Mental Health Service from 07. *55 Reign Street, Goulbourn NSW 2580, Australia* T: (0061) (2) 4821 1506 or 4821 2206 F: 4822 2634 M: 40-982 8006 E: markcooper1969@hotmail.com

COOPER, Canon Michael Leonard. b 30. St Jo Coll Cam BA 53 MA 58. Cuddesdon Coll 53. **d** 55 **p** 56. C Croydon St Jo *Cant* 55-61; V Spring Park 61-71; V Boxley 71-82; RD Sutton 74-80; V Cranbrook 82-92; Hon Chapl to Bp Dover 93-97; Asst Chapl Kent and Cant Hosps NHS Trust 94-97; Hon Can Cant Cathl 76-97; PtO *Newc* from 97; *Roch* 97-06; rtd 00. *The Rectory, Bellingham, Hexham NE48 2JS* T: (01434) 220019

COOPER, Canon Michael Sydney. b 41. Univ of Wales (Lamp) BA 63. Westcott Ho Cam 63. **d** 65 **p** 66. C Farlington *Portsm* 65-69; Pakistan 70-71; Mauritius 71-73; C-in-c Hayling St Pet CD *Portsm* 74-81; V Carisbrooke St Mary 81-92; V Carisbrooke St Nic 81-92; V Hartplain 92-98; V Portchester 98-06;

RD Fareham 99-04; Hon Can Portsm Cathl 02-06; rtd 06; PtO Portsm from 06. *122 Paxton Road, Fareham PO14 1AE* T: (01329) 822152

COOPER, Nicholas. b 62. Wycliffe Hall Ox. **d** 06 **p** 07. C Tenterden St Mildred w Smallhythe *Cant* 06-09; C Tenterden St Mich 07-09; P-in-c Saltwood 09-13; C Aldington w Bonnington and Bilsington etc 10-13; R Lympne and Saltwood from 13. *The Rectory, Rectory Lane, Saltwood, Hythe CT21 4QA* T: (01303) 266932

COOPER, Nigel Scott. b 53. Qu Coll Cam BA 75 MA 79 PGCE 76 CEnv MIEEM CBiol FIBiol FLS. Ripon Coll Cuddesdon BA 83 MA 88. **d** 83 **p** 84. C Moulsham St Jo *Chelmsf* 83-88; R Rivenhall 88-05; Chapl Anglia Ruskin Univ *Ely* from 05; Bp's Adv on Further Educn from 08. *The Chaplaincy Office, Anglia Ruskin University, East Road, Cambridge CB1 1PT* T: 08451-962398 E: nigel.cooper@anglia.ac.uk

COOPER, Noel. b 49. Oak Hill Th Coll. **d** 88 **p** 89. C Plymouth St Jude *Ex* 88-92; V Clapham Park All SS *S'wark* 92-99; R Bedford St Jo and St Leon St Alb from 99. *St John's Rectory, 36 St John's Street, Bedford MK42 0DH* T: (01234) 354818 E: stjohns@nascr.net

COOPER, Canon Peter David. b 48. Sarum & Wells Th Coll 70. **d** 73 **p** 74. C Yateley *Win* 73-78; C Christchurch 78-81; P-in-c Southampton St Mark 81-83; V 83-98; P-in-c Tadley St Pet 98-02; R Tadley S and Silchester 02-13; rtd 13; PtO *Win* from 13; Hon Can Ife Nigeria from 00. *42 Tuckton Road, Bournemouth BH6 3HS* T: (01202) 986894 E: peter.clairecooper@gmail.com

COOPER, Peter Timothy. b 65. Brunel Univ BSc 95. Ridley Hall Cam 01. **d** 03 **p** 04. C Edgware *Lon* 03-07; China 07-15; V Seacombe w Poulton *Ches* from 15. *Seacombe Vicarage, 5 Brougham Road, Wallasey CH44 6PN* E: pandmcooper@tiscali.co.uk

COOPER, Canon Richard Thomas. b 46. Leeds Univ BA 69. Coll of Resurr Mirfield 69. **d** 71 **p** 72. C Rothwell *Ripon* 71-75; C Adel 75-78; C Knaresborough 78-81; P-in-c Croft 81-90; P-in-c Eryholme 81-90; P-in-c Middleton Tyas and Melsonby 81-90; RD Richmond 86-90; V Aldborough w Boroughbridge and Roecliffe 90-98; RD Ripon 93-96; R Richmond w Hudswell 98-05; R Richmond w Hudswell and Downholme and Marske 05-09; Hon Can Ripon Cathl 97-09; rtd 09; Chapl to The Queen from 03. *26 The Springs, Middelham, Leyburn DL8 4RB* T: (01969) 623844 E: richard@hargill.plus.com

COOPER, Canon Robert Gerard. b 68. Univ of Wales (Abth) BD 91. Linc Th Coll 93. **d** 93 **p** 94. C Whitkirk *Ripon* 93-96; C Leeds Richmond Hill 96-97; Chapl Agnes Stewart C of E High Sch Leeds 96-97; Chapl Chigwell Sch Essex 97-98; V Lightcliffe *Wakef* 98-05; V Pontefract St Giles from 05; AD Pontefract *Leeds* from 06; Hon Can Wakef Cathl from 08. *The Vicarage, 9 The Mount, Pontefract WF8 1NE* T: (01977) 706803 M: 07931-565516 E: robert_cooper@msn.com

COOPER, Robert James. b 52. Bris Univ BA 75. Ridley Hall Cam 76. **d** 78 **p** 79. C Street w Walton *B & W* 78-82; C Batheaston w St Cath 82-86; P-in-c Sadberge *Dur* 86-03; Asst Chapl Arts and Recreation 86-05; Chapl 05-08; Lic to AD Stockton from 08; Chapl N Tees and Hartlepool NHS Trust from 14. *24 North Close, Thorpe Thewles, Stockton-on-Tees TS21 3JY* T: (01740) 630015 E: robert@cooperphoto.co.uk *or* robert.cooper@nth.nhs.uk

COOPER, Canon Roger Charles. b 48. GRSM ARMCM 69 PGCE 70. Coll of Resurr Mirfield 79. **d** 81 **p** 82. C Monkseaton St Mary *Newc* 81-83; C Morpeth 83-87; Min Can and Prec Man Cathl 87-90; V Blackrod 90-15; AD Deane 05-12; C Horwich and Rivington 11-15; Hon Can Man Cathl 11-15; rtd 15; PtO *Man* from 15. *Address temp unknown*

COOPER, Rosanne Elizabeth. d 13 **p** 14. NSM Bradgate Team *Leic* 13-15. *Address temp unknown* E: rosinthegarden@hotmail.com

COOPER, Seth William. b 62. Westcott Ho Cam 94. **d** 96 **p** 97. C Golders Green *Lon* 96-00; TV Uxbridge 00-05; V Walmer *Cant* from 05; AD Sandwich from 10. *Elizabeth House, 32 St Mary's Road, Walmer, Deal CT14 7QA* T: (01304) 366605 E: sethandjen@tinyworld.co.uk

COOPER, Shirley Ann. *See* RUSSELL, Alexandra Blaise

COOPER, Stephen. b 54. Bernard Gilpin Soc Dur 73 Chich Th Coll 74. **d** 77 **p** 78. C Horbury *Wakef* 77-78; C Horbury w Horbury Bridge 78-81; C Barnsley St Mary 81-84; TV Elland 84-91; Hon C Huddersfield St Thos 93-94; P-in-c Middlesbrough St Columba w St Paul *York* 94-08; V from 09; P-in-c Middlesbrough St Jo the Ev 05-08; V from 09; Chapl S Tees Hosps NHS Trust 94-05. *St Columba's Vicarage, 115 Cambridge Road, Middlesbrough TS5 5HF* T: (01642) 824779 E: fr_s_cooper@hotmail.com

COOPER, Stephen Paul Crossley. b 58. Trin Coll Bris 91. **d** 93 **p** 94. C Blackb Redeemer 93-95; C Altham w Clayton le Moors 95-98; V Langho Billington 98-03; Chapl Rossall Sch

Fleetwood 03-09; TV Fellside Team *Blackb* 09-15; TR from 15. *The Vicarage, Goosnargh Lane, Goosnargh, Preston PR3 2BN* T: (01722) 865274 E: revscooper@gmail.com

COOPER, Mrs Susan Elizabeth Courtenay. b 50. Open Univ BA 94 LLAM 70. **d** 10 **p** 12. New Zealand 01-13; NSM Rotherfield Peppard and Kidmore End etc *Ox* from 14. *2 Priory Copse, Peppard Common, Henley-on-Thames RG9 5LH* T: 0118-437 5734 E: coosuron50@gmail.com

COOPER, Mrs Susan Mary. b 45. Westcott Ho Cam 01. **d** 03 **p** 04. C Syston *Leic* 03-06; R Chipping Ongar w Shelley *Chelmsf* 06-14; rtd 14; PtO *Leic* from 14. *89 Scotland Road, Market Harborough LE16 8AY* E: scoople@btinternet.com

COOPER, Susan Mira. *See* RAMSARAN, Susan Mira

COOPER, Mrs Suzanne Tracey. b 62. Ripon Coll Cuddesdon 13. **d** 15. C Blisworth, Alderton, Grafton Regis etc *Pet* from 15. *The Rectory, Barn Corner, Collingtree, Northampton NN4 0NF* E: s.cooper@fsmail.net

COOPER, Thomas Joseph Gerard Strickland. b 46. Lanc Univ PhD 85. Ven English Coll & Pontifical Gregorian Univ Rome PhB 66 PhL 67 STB 69 STL 71. **d** 70 **p** 70. In RC Ch 70-92; Chapl St Woolos Cathl 93-95; V Llandaff N *Llan* 95-08; rtd 08. *Arwel, Cwmdegwel, St Dogmaels, Cardigan SA43 3JH* T: (01239) 614156 E: teilo@woolos.supanet.com

COOPER, Trevor John. b 51. Ex Univ MA 95. Wycliffe Hall Ox 75. **d** 79 **p** 95. C Southsea St Pet *Portsm* 79-80; NSM Heavitree w Ex St Paul 93-96; C Standish *Blackb* 96-99; V Burnley St Cuth 99-03; P-in-c Lytham St Jo 03-06; rtd 06. *119 Emsworth Road, Portsmouth PO2 0BT* E: trevor.j.cooper@btinternet.com

COOPER, Ms Wendy. b 58. **d** 12 **p** 14. NSM Salisbury St Thos and St Edm *Sarum* from 12. *Parish Office, St Thomas's House, St Thomas's Square, Salisbury SP1 1BA* E: mukinge.minstead@yahoo.co.uk

COOPER, William Douglas. b 42. Open Univ BA 83 BSc 11 St Andr Univ MA 08 Aber Univ MA 09. St Jo Coll Nottm 88 Qu Coll Birm 93. **d** 94 **p** 95. NSM Melbourne *Derby* 94-97; C Pennwortham St Mary *Blackb* 97-00; P-in-c Smeeth w Monks Horton and Stowting and Brabourne *Cant* 00-04; rtd 04. *18A Market Street, St Andrews KY16 9NS* T: (01334) 460678

COOPEY, Thomas Peter. b 80. St Martin's Coll Lanc BA 02. St Jo Coll Nottm 11. **d** 13 **p** 14. C Salisbury St Fran and Stratford sub Castle *Sarum* from 13. *20 Thistlebarrow Road, Salisbury SP1 3RT* M: 07771-360147 E: tcoopey@hotmail.com

COORE, Jonathan. b 71. Lon Inst of Educn PGCE 97 GTCL 94. Trin Coll Bris 05. **d** 07 **p** 08. C Heref St Pet w St Owen and St Jas 07-12; Bp's Dom Chapl 08-12; Min Can and Succ St Paul's Cathl 12-14; R S'wark Ch Ch from 14. *35 Oswin Street, London SE11 4TF* E: jonathancoore@gmail.com *or* rectorccs@gmail.com

COOTE, Anthony John. b 54. Qu Coll Birm 95. **d** 97 **p** 98. C Malvern H Trin and St Jas *Worc* 97-01; TV Heref S Wye 01-02; P-in-c Cradley *Worc* 02-04; rtd 04. *43 The Poplars, Stourbridge DY8 5SN* T: (01384) 482446

COOTE, Bernard Albert Ernest. b 28. Lon Univ BD 53. Chich Th Coll 54. **d** 55 **p** 56. C Addiscombe St Mary *Cant* 55-57; C Hawkhurst 57-59; C Sanderstead All SS *S'wark* 59-63; Chapl HM Borstal E Sutton Park 63-74; V Sutton Valence w E Sutton *Cant* 63-76; P-in-c Chart next Sutton Valence 71-76; P-in-c Sutton Valence w E Sutton and Chart Sutton 76; Chapl and Dir R Sch for the Blind Leatherhead 76-91; rtd 91; PtO *Chich* from 91; *Guildf* from 91. *25 Raphael Road, Hove BN3 5QP* T: (01273) 640732

COPE, James Brian Andrew. b 58. Chich Th Coll 80. **d** 83 **p** 84. C Poulton-le-Fylde *Blackb* 83-86; C Fleetwood St Pet 86-87; V Fleetwood St Dav 87-94; P-in-c Somercotes *Derby* 94-99; V Watford St Jo St Alb 99-07; V Castle Vale w Minworth *Birm* from 07. *St Cuthbert's Vicarage, St Cuthbert's Place, Birmingham B35 7PL* T: 0121-747 4041 E: fr.jamescopessc@sky.com

COPE, Judith Diane. b 50. St Hilda's Coll Ox BA 72 Lon Univ MB, BS 75 MRCGP 80. SAOMC 00. **d** 03 **p** 04. NSM Lt Berkhamsted and Bayford, Essendon etc *St Alb* 03-13; rtd 13; PtO *St Alb* from 13. *18 Hatherleigh Gardens, Potters Bar EN6 5HZ* T: (01707) 644391 E: m_cope@btinternet.com

COPE, Mrs Melia Lambrianos. b 53. Cape Town Univ BSocSc 73. St Jo Coll Nottm 80 WMMTC 83. **dss** 86 **d** 93 **p** 94. W Bromwich All SS *Lich* 86-93; NSM 93-94; NSM W Bromwich St Mary Magd CD 93-94; TV Cen Telford 94-02; Chapl HM Pris Shrewsbury 95-98; P-in-c Stokesay *Heref* 02-12; P-in-c Halford w Sibdon Carwood 02-12; P-in-c Acton Scott 02-12; P-in-c Wistanstow 06-12; V E Radnor *S & B* from 12. *The Vicarage, Church Street, Knighton LD7 1AG* T: (01547) 528566 E: revdmeliacope@gmail.com

COPE, Miss Olive Rosemary. b 29. Gilmore Ho 63. **dss** 69 **d** 87 **p** 94. Kentish Town St Martin w St Andr *Lon* 69-72; Enfield St Andr 73-99; Par Dn 87-89; Hon Par Dn 89-94; Hon C 94-99; PtO from 99. *7 Calder Close, Enfield EN1 3TS* T: (020) 8363 8221 E: oliveclose2003@yahoo.co.uk

COPE, Mrs Patricia Millicent. b 51. Man Univ BEd 73 MEd 88. SNWTP 10. **d** 12 **p** 13. NSM Knutsford St Cross *Ches* from 12. *23 North Drive, High Legh, Knutsford WA16 6LX* T: (01925) 754787 M: 07703-470101 E: trishcope2012@btinternet.com

COPE, Peter John. b 42. Mert Coll Ox BA 64 MA 67 Lon Univ MSc 74 Man Univ PhD 91. Cuddesdon Coll 64. **d** 66 **p** 67. C Chapel Allerton *Ripon* 66-69; Ind Chapl *Lon* 69-76; *Worc* 76-85; Min Can Worc Cathl 76-85; P-in-c Worc St Mark 76-81; Ind Chapl W Bromwich and Min W Bromwich St Mary Magd CD *Lich* 85-94; Telford Town Cen Chapl 94-07; W Midl FE Field Officer 94-97; Churches Ind Officer 97-07; rtd 07; PtO *Heref* 96-14; *Lich* 07-10; *S & B* from 12. *The Vicarage, Church Street, Knighton LD7 1AG* T: (01547) 528566

COPE, Ralph Bruce. Sir Geo Williams Univ Montreal BA 60 McGill Univ Montreal BD 62. **d** 60 **p** 61. Canada 60-99 and from 00; P-in-c Sophia Antipolis *Eur* 99-00. *407-4701 Uplands Drive, Nanaimo BC V9T 5Y2, Canada* T: (001) (250) 758 3296 E: ralglo@compuserve.com

COPE, Canon Stephen Victor. b 60. St Jo Coll Ox BA 81 MA 87. Chich Th Coll 86. **d** 89 **p** 90. C Newmarket St Mary w Exning St Agnes *St E* 89-92; C Northampton St Matt *Pet* 92-94; V Rudston w Boynton and Kilham *York* 94-98; V Rudston w Boynton, Carnaby and Kilham 98-06; P-in-c Burton Fleming w Fordon, Grindale etc 00-06; RD Bridlington 98-03; P-in-c Owthorne and Rimswell w Withernsea 06-07; P-in-c Easington w Skeffling, Kilnsea and Holmpton 06-07; R Withernsea w Owthorne and Easington etc 07-14; P-in-c Roos and Garton w Tunstall, Grimston and Hilston 12-14; V Withernsea w Owthorne, Garton-in-Holderness etc 14; RD S Holderness 09-14; R Holme and Seaton Ross Gp from 14; Can and Preb York Minster from 10. *The Vicarage, Market Weighton Road, Holme-on-Spalding-Moor, York YO43 4AG* T: (01964) 611462 E: stephenvcope@tiscali.co.uk

COPELAND, Annabel Susan Mary. b 64. Roehampton Inst BEd 87. Wycliffe Hall Ox 03. **d** 05 **p** 06. C Billericay and Lt Burstead *Chelmsf* 05-14; TV Gt Baddow 08-14; P-in-c Tidworth *Sarum* from 14; Chapl Wellington Academy from 14. *North Tidworth Rectory, St George's Road, Tidworth SP9 7EW* T: (01980) 849007 E: copeland321@btinternet.com

COPELAND, Christopher Paul. b 38. AKC 64. **d** 65 **p** 66. C Luton St Andr *St Alb* 65-67; C Droitwich St Nic w St Pet *Worc* 67-71; C Kings Norton *Birm* 71-72; TV 73-78; V Tyseley 78-88; P-in-c Grimley w Holt *Worc* 88-96; Dioc Stewardship Missr 88-96; P-in-c Forest of Dean Ch Ch w English Bicknor *Glouc* 96-03; rtd 03; PtO *Worc* from 03. *24 Players Avenue, Malvern WR14 1DU* T: (01684) 563323 E: chriscopeland@mypostoffice.co.uk

COPELAND, Derek Norman. b 38. Worc Coll Ox BA 62 MA 68. Westcott Ho Cam 63. **d** 64 **p** 65. C Portsea St Mary *Portsm* 64-71; P-in-c Avonmouth St Andr *Bris* 71-77; P-in-c Chippenham St Paul w Langley Burrell 78-79; Ind Chapl from 78; TR Chippenham St Paul w Hardenhuish etc 79-89; V Kington St Michael 79-89; PtO from 89; *B & W* from 89; *Sarum* from 89; rtd 03. *51B Lowden, Chippenham SN15 2BG* T: (01249) 443879

COPELAND, Ian Trevor. b 51. FCA 83. **d** 99 **p** 00. OLM Werrington *Lich* 99-09; OLM Werrington and Wetley Rocks from 09. *4 Heather Close, Werrington, Stoke-on-Trent ST9 0LB* T: (01782) 303525 E: it.copeland@ntlworld.com

COPELAND, Trevor. b 57. St Jo Coll Nottm 04. **d** 07 **p** 08. S Barrow *Carl* 05-07; C Westfield St Mary 07-11; P-in-c Llangrannog w Llandysiliogogo w Penbryn *St D* from 12. *The Vicarage, Pontgarreg, Llandysul SA44 6AJ* T: (01239) 652882 E: deeandtrev@btinternet.com

COPESTAKE, Mrs Sharon Louise. b 70. Cov Univ BA 94 Cant Ch Ch Univ BA 12. SEITE 09. **d** 12 **p** 13. C Chatham St Phil and St Jas *Roch* 12-15; V Strood St Fran from 15. *The Vicarage, Galahad Avenue, Rochester ME2 2YS* T: (01634) 717162 E: vicar.stfrancisstrood@gmail.com

COPLAND, Miss Carole Jean. b 37. Man Univ BA 60. Wm Temple Coll Rugby 65. **d** 87 **p** 94. NSM Northallerton w Kirby Sigston *York* 87-90; Dioc Adv in Children's Work 81-90; Par Dn Dunnington 90-94; Faith in the City Link Officer 90-96; C Dunnington 94-96; V Ledsham w Fairburn 96-99; rtd 99; PtO *York* from 99. *4 Jedwell Close, New Earswick, York YO32 4DQ* T: (01904) 767110 E: carolecopland@hotmail.com

COPLETON, Roger Boyd. b 62. Edin Univ BD 87. TISEC 02. **d** 97 **p** 98. NSM Haddington and Dunbar *Edin* 97-06. *30 Couston Drive, Dalgety Bay, Dunfermline KY11 9NX* M: 07759-952618

COPLEY, Paul. b 58. NEOC 97. **d** 99 **p** 00. C Hessle *York* 99-02; TV Sutton St Jas and Wawne 02-07; P-in-c Kingston upon Hull St Nic 07-14; V from 14; P-in-c Newington w Dairycoates 07-10. *St Nicholas' Vicarage, 898 Hessle High Road, Hull HU4 6SA* T: (01482) 504088 E: copleypaul@hotmail.com

COPPEN, Colin William. b 53. BCombStuds 85. Linc Th Coll. **d** 85 **p** 86. C Tokyngton St Mich *Lon* 85-88; C Somers Town 88-90; P-in-c Edmonton St Alphege 90-92; V 92-95; P-in-c W Hampstead St Jas 95-97; P-in-c Kilburn St Mary w All So 95-97; TR Wood Green St Mich w Bounds Green St Gabr etc from 97. *St Michael's Rectory, 1A Selborne Road, London N22 7TL* T: (020) 8888 1968 E: rector@woodgreenparish.com

COPPEN, George. See COPPEN, Robert George

COPPEN, Canon Martin Alan. b 48. Ex Univ BA 69. St Jo Coll Nottm 83. **d** 85 **p** 86. C Bitterne *Win* 85-88; V St Mary Bourne and Woodcott 88-99; V Hurstbourne Priors, Longparish etc 00-13; RD Whitchurch 98-03; Hon Can Win Cathl 04-13; rtd 13. *5 Acre Path, Andover SP10 1HJ* E: church@1and3.org.uk

COPPEN, Robert George. b 39. Cape Town Univ BA 66. Cranmer Hall Dur 79. **d** 81 **p** 82. C Douglas St Geo and St Barn *S & M* 81-84; TV Kidlington w Hampton Poyle *Ox* 84-05; Chapl HM Detention Cen Campsfield Ho 84-91; rtd 05; LtO *Mor* from 05. *Taobh Mol, Kildary, Invergordon IV18 0NJ* T: (01862) 842381 E: coppen@dunelm.org.uk

COPPIN, Canon Ronald Leonard. b 30. Birm Univ BA 52. Ridley Hall Cam 54. **d** 56 **p** 57. C Harrow Weald All SS *Lon* 56-59; Bp's Dom Chapl *Man* 59-63; Chapl St Aid Birkenhead 63-65; Vice-Prin 65-68; Selection Sec ACCM 68-74; Sec Cttee for Th Educn 71-74; Can Res and Lib Dur Cathl 74-97; Dir of Clergy Tr 74-96; Warden NEOC 76-84; Dir Post-Ord Tr 86-97; rtd 97; PtO *Lon* from 02. *157 Defoe House, London EC2Y 8ND* T: (020) 7588 9228 E: ronald.coppin@virgin.net

COPPING, Canon Adrian Walter Alexander. b 52. Ridley Hall Cam. **d** 00 **p** 01. C Royston *St Alb* 00-04; R Bangor Monachorum, Worthenbury and Marchwiel *St As* 04-09; AD Bangor Isycoed 05-09; R Cilcain, Gwernaffield, Llanferres etc from 09; AD Mold from 11; Can St As Cathl from 14. *The New Rectory, Rectory Lane, Llanferres, Mold CH7 5SR* T: (01352) 810936 E: adriancopping@hotmail.com

COPPING, John Frank Walter Victor. b 34. K Coll Lon BD 58 AKC 58. **d** 59 **p** 60. C Hampstead St Jo *Lon* 59-62; C Bray and Braywood *Ox* 62-65; V Langley Mill *Derby* 65-71; V Cookham Dean *Ox* 71-03; RD Maidenhead 87-94; rtd 03; PtO *Ox* from 03. *41 Golden Ball Lane, Pinkneys Green, Maidenhead SL6 6NW* T: (01628) 674433 E: johnfcopping@talktalk.net

COPPING, Mary Catriona. b 69. STETS. **d** 12 **p** 13. NSM Win St Matt from 12. *2 Churchill Close, King's Worthy, Winchester SO23 7PD* T: (01962) 881342 E: marycopping@btinternet.com

COPPING, Raymond. b 36. St Mark & St Jo Coll Lon TCert 59. Wycliffe Hall Ox 72. **d** 74 **p** 75. C High Wycombe *Ox* 74-77; TV 77-87; TV Digswell and Panshanger *St Alb* 87-95; P-in-c Charlton Kings H Apostles *Glouc* 95-00; rtd 00; Hon C Thame *Ox* from 04. *20 Friars Furlong, Long Crendon, Aylesbury HP18 9DQ* T: (01844) 208509

COPSEY, Mrs Christine. b 51. Nottm Univ CertEd 73. ERMC 04. **d** 07 **p** 08. NSM Fakenham w Alethorpe *Nor* 07-08; NSM King's Lynn St Marg w St Nic 08-11; Chapl Ind Miss from 11. *5 Back Lane, Castle Acre, King's Lynn PE32 2AR* T: (01760) 755558 E: chriscopsey@btinternet.com

COPSEY, Mrs Janette. b 51. **d** 11 **p** 12. NSM Ben Rhydding *Leeds* from 11. *23 Wheatley Avenue, Ilkley LS29 8PT* T: (01943) 604113 E: jan.copsey@bradford.anglican.org

COPSEY, Nigel John. b 52. K Coll Lon BD 75 AKC 75 Surrey Univ MSc 88 Middx Univ DProf 01. St Aug Coll Cant 72. **d** 76 **p** 77. C Barkingside St Fran *Chelmsf* 76-78; C Canning Town St Cedd 78-80; P-in-c Victoria Docks Ascension 80-87; Chapl E Surrey Mental Health Unit 87-90; Hd Past and Spiritual Care E Surrey Priority Care NHS Trust from 90; Co-ord Past Care Surrey Oaklands NHS Trust 99-05; Hd Past and Spiritual Care Surrey and Borders Partnership NHS Trust from 08; Co-ord Relig Care Newham Community Health Services NHS Trust 99-01; Co-ord Relig Care Newham Primary Care Trust from 01; Team Ldr Spiritual, Relig & Cultural Care E Lon NHS Foundation Trust from 08. *Newham Centre for Mental Health, Glen Road, London E13 8SP* T: (020) 7540 4380 F: 7540 2970 E: nigel.copsey@eastlondon.nhs.uk

COPUS, Brian George. b 36. AKC 59. **d** 60 **p** 61. C Croydon St Mich *Cant* 60-63; C Swindon New Town *Bris* 63-69; V Colebrooke *Ex* 69-73; P-in-c Hittisleigh 69-73; R Perivale *Lon* 73-82; V Ruislip St Mary 82-01; rtd 01; PtO *Win* 02-13. *Le Bec, 84 Carbery Avenue, Bournemouth BH6 3LQ* T: (01202) 428943

COPUS, John Cecil. b 38. TCert 64 Maria Grey Coll Lon DipEd 71 Open Univ BA 78. Cant Sch of Min. **d** 83 **p** 84. Hon C Folkestone H Trin and St Geo w Ch Ch *Cant* 83-85; Hon C Midsomer Norton w Clandown *B & W* 85-91; Dioc Adv for Children's Work *Ex* 91-98; Hon C Aylesbeare, Rockbeare, Farringdon etc 95-98; P-in-c 98-01; rtd 01; PtO *Ex* from 01; Clergy Widow(er)s Officer from 02; C N Creedy

08-10. *The Sidings, Park Road, Lapford, Crediton EX17 6QJ* T: (01363) 83408

COPUS, Jonathan Hugh Lambert. b 44. BNC Ox BA 66 MA 71 LGSM 66 MInstPI 94. S'wark Ord Course 68. **d** 71 **p** 72. C Horsell *Guildf* 71-73; Producer Relig Progr BBC Radio Solent 73-87; V Maenclochog and New Moat etc *St D* 06-07; V Martletwy w Lawrenny and Minwear etc 07; PtO 07-11; rtd 10; P-in-c Crymych Gp *St D* from 11. *Llys Myrddin, Efailwen, Clynderwen SA66 7XG* T: (01994) 419834 M: 07828-510283 E: revjc@dentron.co.uk

CORBAN-BANKS, Edrick Hale. b 53. Victoria Univ Wellington BMus 74 LTCL 79 FTCL 81. St Jo Coll Auckland BTh 91. **d** 91 **p** 92. P Asst Johnsonville St Jo New Zealand 92-94; Ch Planter Churton Park 93-94; V Katikati 94-99; P Missr Alicante Spain 99; R Alicante St Paul 99-00; Chapl Ibiza *Eur* 00-03; V Stoke New Zealand from 04. *523 Main Road, Stoke, Nelson 7001, New Zealand* T: (0064) (3) 547 3478 E: vicar.stbarnabas@paradise.net.nz

CORBETT, Canon Henry. b 53. CCC Cam BA 75. Wycliffe Hall Ox. **d** 78 **p** 79. C Everton St Pet *Liv* 78-84; TV 84-87; TR 87-02; R Everton St Pet w St Chrys from 02; AD Liv N from 03; Hon Can Liv Cathl from 03. *St Peter's Vicarage, Langrove Street, Liverpool L5 3PE* T: 0151-207 1948 E: hjcorbett@shewsy.freeserve.co.uk

CORBETT, The Very Revd Ian Deighton. b 42. St Cath Coll Cam BA 64 MA 67 Cam Univ PGCE 65. Westcott Ho Cam 67. **d** 69 **p** 70. C New Bury *Man* 69-72; C Bolton St Pet 72-75; Chapl Bolton Colls of H&FE 72-75; R Man Victoria Park 75-80; Chapl Salford Univ 80-83; Dioc FE Officer 74-83; R Salford Sacred Trin 83-87; Dir CME and Hon Can Man Cathl 83-87; Warden Lelapa la Jesu Sem Lesotho 88-91; Can Missr Harare Zimbabwe 92-93; Can Missr Botswana 93-95; R Kuruman St Mary S Africa 95-97; Dean Tuam and I Tuam w Cong and Aasleagh *T, K & A* 97-99; R Whitesands Canada 99-01; V Utah Region USA 01-08; Hon C E Clevedon w Clapton in Gordano etc *B & W* 09-13. *6 The Quadrangle, Newland, Malvern WR13 5AX* T: (01684) 574091 E: iancorbett123@btinternet.com

CORBETT, Jocelyn Rory. **d** 05 **p** 06. Aux Min Aghalee *D & D* 05-06; NSM Donaghcloney w Waringstown 06-13; NSM Seapatrick from 13. *Badger Hill, 23 Magherabeg Road, Dromore BT25 1RS* T: (028) 9269 2067 *or* 4062 2744 E: rory.corbett23@gmail.com *or* office@seapatrickparish.com

CORBETT, John David. b 32. Oriel Coll Ox BA 55 MA 59. St Steph Ho Ox 55. **d** 57 **p** 58. C Plymouth St Pet *Ex* 57-64; V Marldon 64-74; TV Bournemouth St Pet w St Swithun, H Trin etc *Win* 74-83; V Beckenham St Barn *Roch* 83-88; V King's Sutton and Newbottle and Charlton *Pet* 88-97; rtd 97; PtO *Portsm* from 98; *Win* 98-14. *38 Meredith Road, Portsmouth PO2 9NN* T: (023) 9236 5609 E: jdc.jdc1@virginmedia.com

CORBETT, Philip Peter. b 81. St Andr Univ MTheol 03 Yale Univ STM 04 Keble Coll Ox MPhil 06. Coll of Resurr Mirfield 06. **d** 08 **p** 09. C Worksop Priory *S'well* 08-11; P Lib and Chapl Pusey Ho 11-13; P-in-c Lewisham St Steph and St Mark *S'wark* from 13. *St Stephen's Vicarage, Cressingham Road, London SE13 5AG* M: 07929-750054 E: philippetercorbett@googlemail.com

CORBETT, Miss Phyllis. b 34. Cranmer Hall Dur 76. **dss** 80 **d** 87 **p** 94. Par Dn Baswich *Lich* 87-94; C 94-95; rtd 95; PtO *Lich* from 95. *9 Redhill Gorse, Crab Lane, Trinity Fields, Stafford ST16 1SW*

CORBETT, Rory. *See* CORBETT, Jocelyn Rory

CORBETT, Stephen Paul. b 57. BA 80. St Jo Coll Nottm 83. **d** 85 **p** 86. C Tollington Park St Mark w St Anne *Lon* 85-86; C Holloway St Mark w Em 86-91; V Chitts Hill St Cuth 91-93; V Springfield *Birm* 93-04; AD Moseley 02-04; V Walmley 04-09; P-in-c Blackb St Gabr 09-11; V from 11. *St Gabriel's Vicarage, 6 Charnwood Close, Blackburn BB2 7BT* T: (01254) 581412

CORBYN, John. b 58. Man Univ BA 79 New English Coll & Pontifical Gregorian Univ Rome 83. Wycliffe Hall Ox BA 83 MA 87. **d** 84 **p** 85. C Deane *Man* 84-87; C Lancaster St Mary *Blackb* 87-90; Sub-Chapl HM Pris Lanc 89-90; V Blackb St Gabr 90-01; V Bearsted w Thurnham *Cant* from 01. *The Vicarage, Church Lane, Bearsted, Maidstone ME14 4EF* T: (01622) 737135 E: vicar@holycrosschurch.co.uk

CORCORAN, Daniel Chad. b 71. Man Metrop Univ BA 93. St Jo Coll Nottm 04. **d** 06 **p** 07. C Stapleford *S'well* 06-10; C Bilborough w Strelley from 10; C Broxtowe from 14. *29 College Way, Nottingham NG8 4JH* M: 07963-332221 E: danchadcorcoran@hotmail.com

CORCORAN, Hilary. **d** 15. C Blackley St Paul *Man* from 15; C Blackley St Pet from 15. *Address temp unknown*

CORCORAN, Jennifer Miriam. b 78. Lanc Univ BA 01. St Jo Coll Nottm BA(MM) 07. **d** 07 **p** 08. C Chilwell *S'well* 07-10; NSM Chilwell and Lenton Abbey 10-13; Tutor St Jo Coll Nottm from 13. *29 College Way, Nottingham NG8 4JH* T: 0115-925 1114

CORCORAN, Michael. b 65. Man Univ BSocSc 86. St Jo Coll Nottm 12. **d** 14 **p** 15. C Brunswick *Man* from 14. *29 Ashbourne House, Oxford Place, Manchester M14 5SF* M: 07825-153455 E: corkie@sky.com

CORCORAN, Mrs Valerie A'Court. b 46. UEA BA 68 Lon Inst of Educn PGCE 69. STETS 99. **d** 02 **p** 03. NSM Boyatt Wood *Win* 02-10; rtd 10; PtO *Win* from 13. *Ashley, Finches Lane, Twyford, Winchester SO21 1QB* T: (01962) 712951 F: 715770 M: 07736-459500 E: v.corcoran@btinternet.com

CORDELL, Derek Harold. b 34. Chich Th Coll 57. **d** 60 **p** 61. C Whitstable All SS *Cant* 60-63; C Moulsecoomb *Chich* 63-69; Chapl Bucharest *Eur* 69-71; V Brighton St Wilfrid *Chich* 71-74; Chapl HM Borstal Roch 74-80; Asst Chapl HM Pris Man 80-81; Chapl HM Pris The Verne 81-89; Chapl HM Pris Channings Wood 89-90; Chapl Milan w Genoa and Varese *Eur* 90-91; Chapl Mojácar 91-94; PtO from 95; rtd 97. *27 Scalwell Mead, Seaton EX12 2DW* T: (01297) 624182

CORDINER, Alan Dobson. b 61. Westmr Coll Ox BA 87. **d** 92 **p** 93. C Upperby St Jo *Carl* 92-98; P-in-c Bootle, Corney, Whicham and Whitbeck 98-05; Asst Chapl HM Pris Haverigg 98-03. *Address temp unknown*

CORDINGLEY, Canon Brian Lambert. b 30. St Aid Birkenhead 55. **d** 57 **p** 58. Ind Chapl *Sheff* 57-63; C Clifton St Jas 57-61; C Rotherham 61-63; Ind Chapl *Man* 63-92; R Old Trafford St Cuth 63-81; V Hamer 81-92; Hon Can Man Cathl 87-92; rtd 92; PtO *Man* from 99. *Wellsprings, 27 Fernthorpe Avenue, Uppermill, Oldham OL3 6EA* T: (01457) 820130

CORFE, David Robert. b 35. Pemb Coll Cam BA 58 MA 60 Lambeth STh 70. Cuddesdon Coll 58. **d** 60 **p** 61. C Wigan All SS *Liv* 60-63; SPG Miss India 63-68; V Lucknow Ch Ch w All SS and St Pet 70-75; C Northwood Em *Lon* 75; V Westwell and Eastwell w Boughton Aluph *Cant* 75-80; V Hildenborough *Roch* 80-91; Lic Preacher Stretford St Bride *Man* 91-98; Interserve 98-00; rtd 00; PtO *Win* from 03. *1 Hartley Court, 12 Winn Road, Southampton SO17 1EN* T: (023) 8058 5557 E: drcorfe@freedomland.co.uk

CORK, Ronald Edward. b 43. Plymouth Poly CQSW 72. NOC 89. **d** 92 **p** 93. Hon C Altrincham St Geo *Ches* 92-96; P-in-c Altrincham St Jo 96-01; rtd 01. *68 Elmfield Crescent, Exmouth EX8 3BW* T: (01395) 223489 E: chrisandroncork@gmail.com

CORK, CLOYNE AND ROSS, Archdeacon of. *See* WILKINSON, The Ven Adrian Mark

CORK, CLOYNE AND ROSS, Bishop of. *See* COLTON, The Rt Revd William Paul

CORK, Dean of. *See* DUNNE, The Very Revd Nigel Kenneth

CORKE, Andrew John. b 55. Bris Univ LLB 77. **d** 98 **p** 99. NSM Canford Magna *Sarum* 98-10; TV Swanage and Studland from 10. *The Vicarage, 5 Redcliffe Road, Swanage BH19 1LZ* T: (01929) 421836 M: 07711-898723 E: vicar@allsaints-swanage.org

CORKE, Bryan Raymond. b 49. Westmr Coll Lon 81. **d** 95 **p** 96. OLM Flixton St Jo *Man* 95-11; NSM Urmston from 11; NSM Davyhulme Ch Ch from 13. *40 Daresbury Avenue, Manchester M41 8GL* T: 0161-748 1827

CORKE, Colin John. b 59. St Pet Coll Ox BA 81. Cranmer Hall Dur 83. **d** 85 **p** 86. C Chapel Allerton *Ripon* 85-88; C Burmantofts St Steph and St Agnes 88-91; P-in-c Tatsfield *S'wark* 91-01; Reigate Adnry Ecum Officer 92-01; V Longbridge *Birm* from 01; Dioc Ecum Officer 02-12; AD Kings Norton 06-12. *St John's Vicarage, 220 Longbridge Lane, Birmingham B31 4JT* T: 0121-475 3484 E: ado67@btinternet.com

CORKE, Francis Bonny. *See* RODRIGUEZ-VEGLIO, Francis Bonny

CORKE, Louise Dorothy. b 59. Southn Univ BSc 80 PGCE 81. Trin Coll Bris BA 94. **d** 97 **p** 98. C Ipsley *Worc* 97-01; TV Bradgate Team *Leic* 01-15; Bp's NSM Officer from 13. *The Rectory, 58 Pymm Ley Lane, Groby, Leicester LE6 0GZ* T: 0116-231 3090 E: standstill@btopenworld.com

CORKE, Roderick Geoffrey. b 58. UEA BEd 79 Open Univ MA 96. St Jo Coll Nottm 90. **d** 92 **p** 93. C Trimley *St E* 92-95; C Walton 95-00; TR Walton and Trimley 00-05; P-in-c Taunton St Mary *B & W* 05-08; V 08-14; V Taunton St Mary and St Jo from 14. *St Mary's Vicarage, Church Square, Taunton TA1 1SA* T: (01823) 272441 E: rodcorke@tiscali.co.uk

CORKER, Mrs Elizabeth Jane. b 42. **d** 99 **p** 00. OLM Martlesham w Brightwell *St E* 99-10; OLM Felixstowe St Jo 10-12; rtd 12. *12 Fairfield Avenue, Felixstowe IP11 9JN* T: (01394) 210793 E: e.corker@ntlworld.com

CORKER, John Anthony. b 37. TD 93. ACIB 75 AKC 63. **d** 64 **p** 65. C Lindley *Wakef* 64-68; V Brotherton 68-72; PtO 72-82; CF (TA) 80-93; Hon C Askham Bryan *York* 82-91; TV York All SS Pavement w St Crux and St Martin etc 91-96; Chapl York Health Services NHS Trust 91-96; Chapl Dudley Gp of Hosps NHS Trust 96-99; Asst P Amblecote *Worc* 96-01; Asst P Dudley St Barn 01-02; rtd 02; PtO *Worc* from 02. *69 Lakeside Court, Brierley Hill DY5 3RQ* T: (01384) 897378 E: the.corkers@talktalk.net

CORLEY, Denise. b 47. **d** 13 **p** 14. OLM N Blackwater *Chelmsf* from 13. *Arden Cottage, Beckingham Street, Tolleshunt Major, Maldon CM9 8LH*

CORLEY, Canon Samuel Jon Clint. b 76. St Aid Coll Dur BA 97 MA 98 Hughes Hall Cam PGCE 99. St Jo Coll Nottm MA 04. **d** 04 **p** 05. C Lancaster St Thos *Blackb* 04-08; Asst Dioc Missr 08-11; P-in-c Ellel w Shireshead 08-11; Can Res Bradf Cathl 11-15; Chapl Bradf Univ 11-15; P-in-c Leeds City from 15; Hon Can Ripon Cathl from 15. *2A Ryder Gardens, Leeds LS8 1JS* M: 07966-524683 E: sam.corley76@gmail.com

CORMACK, Donald Stuart. b 45. Brock Univ Ontario TCert 67 McMaster Univ Ontario BA 71. Regent Coll Vancouver MTh 85. **d** 92 **p** 93. C St Geo Singapore 92-93; P-in-c Phnom Penh Cambodia 93-96; PtO *Glouc* from 06. *305 Gloucester Road, Cheltenham GL51 7AR* T: (01242) 699506 E: don.cormack@hotmail.co.uk

CORNE, Ronald Andrew. b 51. Sarum & Wells Th Coll 87. **d** 89 **p** 90. C Bitterne Park *Win* 89-93; R Headbourne Worthy and King's Worthy 93-01; P-in-c Broughton, Bossington, Houghton and Mottisfont 01-03; R from 03; RD Romsey 06-13. *The Rectory, Rectory Lane, Broughton, Stockbridge SO20 8AB* T: (01794) 301287 E: cronandrew@aol.com

CORNELIUS, Donald Eric. b 31. K Coll Lon BD 52 AKC. Linc Th Coll 84. **d** 84 **p** 85. NSM Crowle *Linc* 84-97; NSM Crowle Gp 97-02; NSM Flixborough w Burton upon Stather 91-02; P-in-c Gunhouse w Burringham 91-02; PtO 02-04. *4 Mulberry Drive, Crowle, Scunthorpe DN17 4JF* T: (01724) 710279

CORNELL, Miss Jean Cranston. b 36. Man Univ CertEd 59 BA 64 York Univ BPhil 71. Ripon Coll Cuddesdon 87 MTh 00. **d** 89 **p** 94. C Matson *Glouc* 89-92; C Bishop's Cleeve 92-96; rtd 96; NSM Winchcombe, Gretton, Sudeley Manor etc *Glouc* 96-01; PtO 01-02. *11 Willow Close, Woodmancote, Cheltenham GL52 9TU* T: (01242) 662869 E: naej@chris47.freeserve.co.uk

CORNELL, Nicholas Simon. b 78. Trin Hall Cam BA 00 MA 03. Oak Hill Th Coll MTh 08. **d** 08 **p** 09. C Eastbourne All SS *Chich* 08-12; R Maresfield from 12; V Nutley from 12. *16 The Paddock, Maresfield, Uckfield TN22 2HQ* T: (01825) 769004 M: 07946-220638 E: nscornell@gmail.com

CORNES, Alan Stuart. b 70. Open Univ BA 98. St Jo Coll Nottm MA 00. **d** 01 **p** 02. C Meole Brace *Lich* 01-04; P-in-c Halliwell St Luke Man 04-11; P-in-c Halliwell 06-11; TR W Bolton from 11. *St Matthew's Vicarage, Stowell Street, Bolton BL1 3RQ* T: (01204) 522810 E: ascornes@yahoo.co.uk

CORNES, Canon Andrew Charles Julian. b 49. CCC Ox BA 70 MA 74. Wycliffe Hall Ox 70 Cranmer Hall Dur 72. **d** 73 **p** 74. C York St Mich-le-Belfrey 73-76; C St Marylebone All So w SS Pet and Jo *Lon* 76-85; R Pittsburgh Ascension USA 85-88; V Crowborough *Chich* 89-15; RD Rotherfield 97-03; Can and Preb Chich Cathl 00-15; Chapl Eastbourne and Co Healthcare NHS Trust 89-02; Chapl Sussex Downs and Weald Primary Care Trust 02-15; rtd 15. *Address temp unknown*

CORNESS, Andrew Stuart. b 69. Bp Otter Coll Chich BA 91 Westmr Coll Ox PGCE 93. Wycliffe Hall Ox MA 05. **d** 01 **p** 02. C Ewood *Blackb* 01-04; Chapl RN from 04. *Royal Naval Chaplaincy Service, Mail Point 1-2, Leach Building, Whale Island, Portsmouth PO2 8BY* T: (023) 9262 5055 F: 9262 5134 E: andrewcorness@hotmail.com

CORNFIELD, Richard James. b 67. St Jo Coll Nottm BA 96. **d** 96 **p** 97. C Cheltenham Ch Ch *Glouc* 96-00; C Aldridge *Lich* 00-03; R 03-11; C Edin St Paul and St Geo from 11; Dioc Dir of Ords from 12. *24 Easter Steil, Edinburgh EH10 5XE* T: 0131-447 1974 *or* 556 1335 M: 07966-165043 E: rich.cornfield@gmail.com *or* richard@pandgchurch.org.uk

CORNISH, Anthony. b 30. Roch Th Coll 64. **d** 67 **p** 68. C Goodmayes All SS *Chelmsf* 67-71; C Buckhurst Hill 71-73; V Westcliff St Andr 73-83; R Rawreth w Rettendon 83-96; rtd 96; PtO *Chelmsf* from 99. *12 Fleetwood Avenue, Clacton-on-Sea CO15 5SE* T: (01255) 813826

CORNISH, Dennis Henry Ronald. b 31. FCIB 72 FCIS 81. S'wark Ord Course 83. **d** 86 **p** 87. NSM Uxbridge *Lon* 86-89; R Lurgashall, Lodsworth and Selham *Chich* 89-96; rtd 96; PtO *Chich* from 96. *Peerley Lodge, 1 Peerley Road, East Wittering, Chichester PO20 8DW* T: (01243) 672481

CORNISH, Gillian Lesley. b 45. ACIB 77. **d** 96 **p** 97. OLM Moston St Mary *Man* 96-08; OLM Blackley St Pet 08-10; rtd 10; PtO *Man* from 10. *11 Rishworth Drive, New Moston, Manchester M40 3PS* T: 0161-681 2839 E: gl.cornish@ntlworld.com

CORNISH, Graham Peter. b 42. Dur Univ BA 67 FLA. NEOC 82. **d** 84 **p** 85. NSM Harrogate St Wilfrid and St Luke *Ripon* 84-96; PtO *York* from 84; NSM Bilton *Ripon* 96-09. *33 Mayfield Grove, Harrogate HG1 5HD* T: (01423) 562747 F: 529928 E: gp-jm.cornish@virgin.net

CORNISH, Ivor. b 40. Reading Univ BSc 61 DipEd 62. Ox Min Course 86. **d** 89 **p** 90. NSM Aston Clinton w Buckland and Drayton Beauchamp *Ox* 89-97; NSM The Lee and Hawridge w Cholesbury and St Leonard 97-10; PtO from 10. *79 Weston Road, Aston Clinton, Aylesbury HP22 5EP* T: (01296) 630345

CORNISH, John Douglas. b 42. Lich Th Coll 67. **d** 70 **p** 71. C Lt Stanmore St Lawr *Lon* 70-73; C Harefield 73-96; PtO from 96. *46 Arnos Grove, London N14 7AR* T: (020) 8372 4510

CORNISH, Peter Andrew. b 55. Ch Ch Ox BA 77 MA 80 Ex Univ CertEd 78. St Jo Coll Nottm 84. **d** 87 **p** 88. C Sanderstead All SS *S'wark* 87-92; TV Cen Telford *Lich* 92-98; R Sturry w Fordwich and Westbere w Hersden *Cant* from 98; Jt AD Cant 11-14. *The Rectory, 2 The Hamels, Sturry, Canterbury CT2 0BL* T: (01227) 710320 E: rector@sturrychurch.org.uk

CORNISH, Mrs Rachel. b 54. **d** 14 **p** 15. NSM Felixstowe St Jo *St E* 14-15; NSM Combs and Lt Finborough from 15; NSM Gt Finborough w Onehouse, Harleston, Buxhall etc from 15. *The Rectory, Woodlands Close, Onehouse, Stowmarket IP14 3HL* T: (01449) 257622 E: rev.rachelcornish@gmail.com

CORNWALL, Valerie Cecilia. *See* SAUNDERS, Valerie Cecilia

CORNWALL, Archdeacon of. *See* STUART WHITE, The Ven William Robert

CORNWELL, Christopher Richard. b 43. Dur Univ BA 67. Cuddesdon Coll 67. **d** 69 **p** 70. C Cannock *Lich* 69-75; P-in-c Hadley 75-80; V 80-81; Bp's Dom Chapl 81-86; Subchanter Lich Cathl 81-86; V Ellesmere 86-89; V Welsh Frankton 86-89; V Ellesmere and Welsh Frankton 89-92; TV Leeds City *Ripon* 92-00; AD Allerton 94-97; V Ireland Wood 00-08; AD Headingley 01-07; Hon C Bishop Monkton and Burton Leonard 08-13; Hon Min Can Ripon Cathl from 08; PtO from 14. *41 Skelldale Close, Ripon HG4 1UH* T: (01765) 602837 E: christophercornwell08@btinternet.com

CORNWELL, Lisa Michele. b 70. Lon Bible Coll BA 94 Westmr Coll Ox PGCE 95 K Coll Lon MA 99. Ridley Hall Cam 00. **d** 02 **p** 03. C Newport Pagnell w Lathbury and Moulsoe *Ox* 02-06; V Crowthorne from 06. *The Vicarage, 56 Duke's Ride, Crowthorne RG45 6NY* T: (01344) 772413 E: revlisacornwell@aol.com

CORP, Ronald Geoffrey. b 51. OBE 12. Ch Ch Ox MA 77. STETS. **d** 98 **p** 99. NSM Kilburn St Mary w All So and W Hampstead St Jas *Lon* 98-02; NSM Hendon St Mary and Ch Ch 02-07; NSM Holborn St Alb w Saffron Hill St Pet from 07. *The Clergy House, 18 Brooke Street, London EC1N 7RD* M: 07956-847792 E: ronald.corp@btconnect.com

CORRIE, Jennifer Sylvia. b 46. RMN 68 SRN 76. **d** 99 **p** 00. OLM Broughton *Man* from 99. *6 Briardene, Back Hilton Street, Salford M7 2GQ*

CORRIE, John. b 48. Imp Coll Lon BScEng 69 MSc 70 PhD 73 Nottm Univ MTh 86. Trin Coll Bris 74. **d** 77 **p** 78. C Kendal St Thos *Carl* 77-80; C Attenborough *S'well* 80-86; ICS Peru 86-91; Tutor and Lect All Nations Chr Coll Ware 91-02; Lect/Development Officer Cen for Angl Communion Studies Selly Oak 02-05; Abp's Internat Project Officer *Cant* 05-06; Tutor Trin Coll Bris from 07; PtO *Birm* from 03. *15 Woodfield Road, Kings Heath, Birmingham B13 9UL* T: 0121-444 2767

CORRIE, Paul Allen. b 43. St Jo Coll Nottm 77. **d** 79 **p** 80. C Beverley Minster *York* 79-82; V Derby St Werburgh 82-84; V Derby St Alkmund and St Werburgh 84-95; Singapore 95-99; R Hawkwell *Chelmsf* 00-05; rtd 06; PtO *Leeds* from 06. *5 Airedale Ings, Cononley, Keighley BD20 8LF* E: plcorrie@btopenworld.com

CORRY, Mrs Sarah. b 57. Sussex Univ BEd 78. SEITE 06. **d** 09 **p** 10. C Crayford *Roch* 09-13. *The Rectory, School Lane, West Kingsdown, Sevenoaks TN15 6JL* T: (01474) 852265 E: sarahcorry@aol.com

CORSIE, Andrew Russell. b 57. Middx Univ BA 97 Birkbeck Coll Lon MSc 11. Trin Coll Bris 91. **d** 93 **p** 94. C Northolt Park St Barn *Lon* 93-97; C Perivale 97-01; P-in-c 01-06; R 06-14; AD Ealing 03-10; Dir Tr and Development Willesden Area from 14. *12A Medway Drive, Perivale, Greenford UB6 8LN* T: (020) 8991 9571 M: 07940-722184 E: andrew.corsie@london.anglican.org

CORWIN, Nigel Trevor. b 47. EAMTC 95. **d** 97 **p** 98. NSM Bury St Edmunds Ch Ch *St E* 97-12; rtd 12; PtO *St E* from 12. *121 Raedwald Drive, Bury St Edmunds IP32 7DG* T: (01284) 725284 F: 725391 M: 07713-769816 E: nigel@corwin.co.uk

CORY, Valerie Ann. *See* DAWSON, Valerie Ann

COSGRAVE-HANLEY, Máirt Joseph. *See* HANLEY, Máirt Joseph

COSH, Roderick John. b 56. Lon Univ BSc 78 Heythrop Coll Lon MA 03. St Steph Ho Ox 78. **d** 81 **p** 82. C Swindon New Town *Bris* 81-86; Chapl Asst R Marsden Hosp 86-91; V Whitton St Aug *Lon* 91-00; P-in-c Staines St Mary and St Pet 00-05; P-in-c Staines Ch Ch 04-05; V Staines 06-13; AD Spelthorne 04-10; AD Burnham and Slough *Ox* from 13; C Colnbrook and Datchet from 13. *The New Vicarage, Mill Street, Colnbrook, Slough SL3 0JJ* T: (01753) 681432 M: 07771-527141 E: rod@tommiez.com

COSLETT, Anthony Allan. b 49. Cuddesdon Coll. **d** 84 **p** 85. C Notting Hill St Clem and St Mark *Lon* 84-85; C Brentford 85-87; C-in-c Hounslow Gd Shep Beavers Lane CD 87-90;

V Hounslow W Gd Shep 90-92; CF 92-08; TR Leic Resurr 08-12; C Broughton Astley and Croft w Stoney Stanton from 12. *The Rectory, Nock Verges, Stoney Stanton, Leicester LE9 4LR*

COSLETT (née SLATER), Mrs Carol Ann. b 63. Univ of Wales (Ban) BD 85 Jes Coll Cam PGCE 86 Lon Inst of Educn MA 92. Ripon Coll Cuddesdon 01. **d** 03 **p** 04. C Horsell *Guildf* 03-07; R Betchworth and Buckland *S'wark* from 07; P-in-c Merstham, S Merstham and Gatton from 13. *The Rectory, Old Reigate Road, Betchworth RH3 7DE* T: (01737) 842102 M: 07803-671256 E: ccoslett@btinternet.com

COSS, Oliver James. b 82. Hull Univ BSc 04 Leeds Univ BA 06 MA 09. Coll of Resurr Mirfield 04. **d** 07 **p** 08. C Cottingham *York* 07-11; V Small Heath *Birm* from 11. *The Clergy House, 85 Jenkins Street, Small Heath, Birmingham B10 0PQ* E: oliver.coss@gmail.com

COSSAR, David Vyvyan. b 34. Lon Univ BA 63. Chich Th Coll 63. **d** 65 **p** 66. C Upper Clapton St Matt *Lon* 65-68; C Withycombe Raleigh *Ex* 68-72; V Honicknowle 72-78; V Brixham w Churston Ferrers 78-86; P-in-c Kingswear 85-86; TR Brixham w Churston Ferrers and Kingswear 86-90; V Lamorbey H Trin *Roch* 90-03; rtd 03; PtO *Roch* from 03. *10 Broadbridge Close, London SE3 7AD* T: (020) 3632 3651 E: dianeanddavidcossar@talktalk.net

COSSINS, John Charles. b 43. Hull Univ BSc 65. Oak Hill Th Coll 65. **d** 67 **p** 68. C Kenilworth St Jo *Cov* 67-70; C Huyton St Geo *Liv* 70-73; TV Maghull 73-79; Chapl Oakwood Hosp Maidstone 79-85; Maidstone Hosp 85-88; Chapl Park Lane Hosp Maghull 88-03; Chapl Moss Side Hosp Liv 88-03; Chapl Ashworth Hosp Maghull 88-03; rtd 03; PtO *Liv* from 03. *9 Longton Drive, Liverpool L37 7ET* T: (01704) 833136 E: jcossins@jcossins.demon.co.uk

COSSINS, Roger Stanton. b 40. K Coll Lon BD 67 AKC 67. **d** 68 **p** 69. C Bramley *Ripon* 68-71; C W End *Win* 71-76; V Bramley 76-91; P-in-c Bournemouth H Epiphany 91-94; V 94-00; rtd 00. *5 Allen Court, Trumpington, Cambridge CB2 9LU* T: (01223) 841726

COSSTICK, Mrs Helen Mary Vaux. b 47. K Alfred's Coll Win TCert 69. NTMTC 06. **d** 09 **p** 10. NSM Hanwell St Mary w St Chris *Lon* from 09. *22 Shakespeare Road, London W7 1LR* T: (020) 8579 6367 M: 07727-902309 E: helen.cosstick@btinternet.com

COSTER, Canon Catherine Anne. b 47. Bris Poly BEd 85. WEMTC 97. **d** 00 **p** 01. NSM Yate New Town *Bris* 00-04; NSM Warmley, Syston and Bitton from 04; Hon Min Can Bris Cathl 04-13; Hon Can from 13. *31 Vayre Close, Chipping Sodbury, Bristol BS37 6NT* T: (01454) 314858 F: 0117-927 7454 E: catherine.coster@bristoldiocese.org

COSTER, David John. b 65. Derby Univ BSc 98. NTMTC BA 09. **d** 09 **p** 10. C Leigh St Clem *Chelmsf* 09-12; P-in-c Rochford and Sutton w Shopland and Stambridge 12-13; PtO from 13. *27 Branksome Avenue, Hockley SS5 5PF* T: (01702) 203756 M: 07747-391083

COSTERTON, Alan Stewart. b 40. Bris Univ BA 67. Clifton Th Coll 67. **d** 69 **p** 70. C Peckham St Mary Magd *S'wark* 69-73; C Forest Gate St Sav w W Ham St Matt *Chelmsf* 73-76; TV 76-79; V Thornton cum Bagworth *Leic* 79-85; V Thornton, Bagworth and Stanton 85-95; TR Sileby, Cossington and Seagrave 95-04; R 04-05; rtd 05; PtO *Leic* from 14. *71 Fowke Street, Leicester LE7 7PJ* T: 0116-234 1026 E: alan.costerton@gmail.com

COSTIGAN, Esther Rose. See FOSS, Esther Rose

COSTIN, Pamela Lindsay. b 49. Ridley Hall Cam 06. **d** 07 **p** 08. C Immingham, Habrough Gp and Keelby Gp *Linc* 07-09; C Scawby, Redbourne and Hibaldstow 09-10; C Bishop Norton, Waddingham and Snitterby 09-10; C Kirton in Lindsey w Manton 09-10; C Grayingham 09-10; S Wolds Community Chapl from 10. *The Rectory, 6 Simons Close, Donington-on-Bain, Louth LN11 9TX* T: (01507) 343345 M: 07756-852907 E: pamcostin@yahoo.co.uk

COSTIN, Richard George Charles. b 38. Liv Univ CertEd 59 Anglia Poly BEd 85 ACP 67 FCollP 82. Coll of Resurr Mirfield 04. **d** 05 **p** 06. NSM Scarborough St Martin *York* from 05. *12 Lightfoots Close, Scarborough YO12 5NR* T: (01723) 376141 M: 07768-856175 E: rcos38@hotmail.com

COTMAN, John Sell Granville (Jan). b 44. St Jo Coll Dur BA 69. Wells Th Coll 70. **d** 73 **p** 74. C Leigh St Mary *Man* 73-76; P-in-c Coldhurst 76-78; TV Oldham 78-82; TV E Ham w Upton Park and Forest Gate *Chelmsf* 82-85; C Hove All SS *Chich* 88-93; TV Hove 93-00; TV W Slough *Ox* 01-08; V Manor Park and Whitby Road 08-13; rtd 13. *6 Riley Close, Aylesbury HP20 2TH* E: jcotman@tiscali.co.uk

COTSON, Tony Arthur. b 53. NEOC 00. **d** 03 **p** 04. C Kingston upon Hull St Nic *York* 03-10; P-in-c Kingston upon Hull St Matt w St Barn 10-11; C Newington w Dairycoates 08-10;

P-in-c 10-11; V Newington w Hull St Andr from 12. *11 Kipling Walk, Summergroves Way, Hull HU4 6SX* T: (01482) 504189 M: 07718-567675 E: tony@cotson.karoo.co.uk

COTTAM, Kenneth Michael David. b 46. St Mich Coll Llan 93. **d** 93 **p** 94. LtO Llangadog and Llandeilo Deanery *St D* 93-96; V Llangadog and Gwynfe w Llanddeusant from 96. *The Vicarage, Walters Road, Llangadog SA19 9AE* T: (01550) 777604

COTTEE, Christopher Paul. b 54. Newc Univ BSc 75. Wycliffe Hall Ox 77. **d** 80 **p** 81. C Much Woolton *Liv* 80-84; C Prescot 84-88; NSM Parr 89-91; V Watford St Pet *St Alb* from 91. *St Peter's Vicarage, 61 Westfield Avenue, Watford WD24 7HF* T: (01923) 226717 E: chris.cottee1@ntlworld.com

COTTEE, Mary Jane. b 43. Open Univ BA 81 CertEd 64. Oak Hill Th Coll 87. **d** 90 **p** 94. NSM Gt Baddow *Chelmsf* 90-95; P-in-c Woodham Ferrers and Bicknacre 95-11; rtd 11; PtO *Chelmsf* from 11. *20 Elm Road, South Woodham Ferrers, Chelmsford CM3 5QE* M: 07735-975423 E: marycottee@btinternet.com

COTTELL, Avril Jane. See GAUNT, Avril Jane

COTTER, Graham Michael. b 50. Univ of Wales (Ban) BA 72. Ridley Hall Cam 75. **d** 78 **p** 79. C Headley All SS *Guildf* 78-81; C Plymouth St Andr w St Paul and St Geo *Ex* 81-84; V Buckland Monachorum from 84; RD Tavistock 93-98. *The Vicarage, Buckland Monachorum, Yelverton PL20 7LQ* T: (01822) 852227 E: cotters@onetel.com

COTTER, Robert Edmund. d 05 p 06. NSM Mossley *Conn* 05-09; NSM Skerry w Rathcavan and Newtowncrommelin 09-13; Aux Min Belfast St Mary Magd from 13. *33 Deerfin Road, Ballymena BT42 4HP* T: (028) 2563 1303 E: robertcotter76@btinternet.com

COTTERELL, Michael Clifford. b 54. Oak Hill Th Coll 81. **d** 84 **p** 85. C Lutterworth w Cotesbach *Leic* 84-87; C Belper *Derby* 87-91; V Locking *B & W* 91-98; V Slough *Ox* from 98. *St Paul's Vicarage, 196 Stoke Road, Slough SL2 5AY* T: (01753) 521497 E: michael.cotterell@btinternet.com

COTTERILL, John Glyn. b 58. **d** 10 **p** 11. NSM Baswich *Lich* 10-13; NSM Stafford St Mary and Marston 13-14; NSM Stafford St Chad 13-14. *11 Bracken View, Brocton, Stafford ST17 0TF* T: (01785) 664072 E: john-cotterill@hotmail.com

COTTERILL, Joseph Charles. b 17. AMCT 38 Lon Univ BD California Coll Peking MA 46. Ox Min Course 92. **d** 93 **p** 94. NSM Marcham w Garford *Ox* 93-98; PtO from 98. *8 Draycott Road, Southmoor, Abingdon OX13 5BY* T: (01865) 820758

COTTON, Charles Anthony. b 50. Linc Coll Ox BA 72 MA 77 PGCE 73. Ridley Hall Cam 89. **d** 91 **p** 92. C Hendon St Paul Mill Hill *Lon* 91-96; C Wandsworth All SS *S'wark* 96-97; V Clapham St Jas 97-08; PtO from 08. *9 Woodcote Avenue, Wallington SM6 0QR* T: (020) 8669 1143 E: revdcharlie@btinternet.com

COTTON, David John. b 65. Linc Sch of Th and Min 12. **d** 14. OLM Lea Gp *Linc* from 14. *42 Meadow Rise, Saxilby, Lincoln LN1 2HW* T: (01522) 702634 M: 07944-669166 E: david.cotton500@ntlworld.com

COTTON, John Horace Brazel. b 28. MIMechE St Jo Coll Cam BA 50 MA 76. St Alb Minl Tr Scheme 78. **d** 81 **p** 82. NSM Lt Berkhamsted and Bayford, Essendon etc *St Alb* 81-87; P-in-c 87-96; rtd 96; PtO *St Alb* from 96. *49 Sherrardspark Road, Welwyn Garden City AL8 7LD* T: (01707) 321815

COTTON, John William. b 53. Oak Hill Th Coll 86. **d** 86 **p** 87. C New Clee *Linc* 86-89; Chapl St Andr Hospice Grimsby 88-89; R Middle Rasen Gp *Linc* 89-95; P-in-c Broughton 95-97; R 97-10; Chapl Humberside Airport 99-00; rtd 11; PtO *Linc* from 11; Chapl United Lincs Hosps NHS Trust 11-12. *47 Ridgeway, Nettleham, Lincoln LN2 2TL* E: revcottonj@yahoo.co.uk

COTTON, Mrs Margaret Elizabeth. b 30. JP 79. Newnham Coll Cam BA 53 MA 66. St Alb Minl Tr Scheme 78. **dss** 82 **d** 87 **p** 94. Lt Berkhamsted and Bayford, Essendon etc *St Alb* 82-87; Hon Par Dn 87-94; Hon C 94-96; rtd 96; PtO *St Alb* from 96. *49 Sherrardspark Road, Welwyn Garden City AL8 7LD* T: (01707) 321815

COTTON, Miss Michelle Susan. b 77. Ox Brookes Univ BA 13. Ripon Coll Cuddesdon 09. **d** 11 **p** 12. C Weston Favell *Pet* 11-15; P-in-c Wellingborough St Andr from 15. *St Andrew's Vicarage, Berrymoor Road, Wellingborough NN8 2HU* M: 07817-905423 E: michelle.cotton123@btinternet.com

COTTON, Miss Patricia Constance. b 32. Gilmore Ho 54. **dss** 60 **d** 87 **p** 94. Forest Gate St Edm *Chelmsf* 60-64; Reading St Giles *Ox* 64-65; Basildon St Martin w H Cross and Laindon *Chelmsf* 65-79; Gt Burstead 79-87; Par Dn Maldon All SS w St Pet 87-91; rtd 92; NSM Holland-on-Sea *Chelmsf* from 96; PtO from 96. *67 Copperfield Gardens, Brentwood CM14 4UD* T: (01277) 224274

COTTON, Patrick Arthur William. b 46. Essex Univ BA 67 Down Coll Cam MA 73 Homerton Coll Cam PGCE 96. Linc Th Coll 68. **d** 71 **p** 72. C Earlham St Anne *Nor* 71-73; Chapl Down Coll Cam 73-78; V Eaton Socon *St Alb* 78-84; TR

Newc Epiphany 84-90; V Tunstall w Melling and Leck *Blackb* 90-95; Chapl Pet High Sch 01-05; P-in-c Debenham and Helmingham *St E* from 06. *The Vicarage, 6 Raedwald Way, Debenham, Stowmarket IP14 6SN* T: (01728) 861073

COTTON, Peter John. b 45. BNC Ox BA 66 CQSW 76. Cuddesdon Coll 67. **d** 69 **p** 70. C Salford St Phil w St Steph *Man* 69-73; Asst Educn Officer *St Alb* 73-75; C Bris St Geo 75; C-in-c Portsea St Geo CD *Portsm* 76-80; Soc Resp Adv 78-88; Can Res Portsm Cathl 84-88; V St Laur in Thanet *Cant* 88-93; TR 93-97; Hon Min Can Cant Cathl 93-97; TR Hemel Hempstead *St Alb* 97-09; RD 03-08; Hon Can St Alb 08-09; rtd 09. *45 Bepton Down, Petersfield GU31 4PR* T: (01730) 233785 E: petercotton2@tiscali.co.uk

COTTON, Canon Richard William. b 35. Hertf Coll Ox BA 58 MA 62. Clifton Th Coll 58. **d** 60 **p** 61. C Harold Wood *Chelmsf* 60-64; C Higher Openshaw *Man* 64-67; LtO 67-71; Ch Youth Fellowships Assn and Pathfinders 67-71; Nat Sec Pathfinders CPAS 71-76; LtO *St Alb* 73-76; V Chislehurst Ch Ch *Roch* 76-92; V Herne Bay Ch Ch *Cant* 92-01; RD Reculver 93-01; Hon Can Cant Cathl 99-01; rtd 01; PtO *Cant* 01-15. *16 Crundale Way, Cliftonville, Margate CT9 3YH* T: (01843) 221970 E: rwcotton67@hotmail.com

COTTON, Canon Robert Lloyd. b 58. Mert Coll Ox MA 79. Westcott Ho Cam 81. **d** 83 **p** 84. C Plaistow St Mary *Roch* 83-86; C Bisley and W End *Guildf* 87-89; P-in-c E Molesey St Paul 89-96; Dir of Reader Tr from 90; R Guildf H Trin w St Mary from 96; Hon Can Highveld S Africa from 06; Hon Can Guildf Cathl from 10. *Holy Trinity Rectory, 9 Eastgate Gardens, Guildford GU1 4AZ* T: (01483) 575489 E: rector@holytrinityguildford.org.uk

COTTON-BETTERIDGE, Mrs Fiona Jane Marson. b 56. Nottm Univ MA 05. EMMTC 02. **d** 05 **p** 06. NSM Burton Joyce w Bulcote and Stoke Bardolph *S'well* 05-08; P-in-c Old Leake w Wrangle *Linc* from 08; P-in-c Friskney from 08. *The Vicarage, Yawling Gate Road, Friskney, Boston PE22 8QF* T: (01754) 820104 E: fionacb@aol.com

COTTRELL, Matthew Brian. b 80. Ban Univ BTh 09. Ripon Coll Cuddesdon 11. **d** 14. C Thornbury and Oldbury-on-Severn w Shepperdine *Glouc* from 14. *Elm Cottage, Church Road, Rudgeway, Bristol BS35 3SQ* M: 07826-522019 E: revmattcottrell@gmail.com

✠**COTTRELL, The Rt Revd Stephen Geoffrey.** b 58. Poly Cen Lon BA 79. St Steph Ho Ox 81. **d** 84 **p** 85 **c** 04. C Forest Hill Ch Ch *S'wark* 84-88; P-in-c Parklands St Wilfrid CD *Chich* 88-93; Asst Dir Past Studies Chich Th Coll 88-93; Dioc Missr *Wakef* 93-98; Bp's Chapl for Evang 93-98; Springboard Missr and Consultant in Evang 98-01; Can Res Pet Cathl 01-04; Area Bp Reading *Ox* 04-10; Bp Chelmsf from 10. *Bishop's Court, Main Road, Margaretting, Ingatestone CM4 0HD* T: (01277) 352001 F: 355374 E: bishopscourt@chelmsford.anglican.org

COTTRILL, Derek John. b 43. MA. Qu Coll Birm. **d** 82 **p** 83. C Southampton Maybush St Pet *Win* 82-85; V Barton Stacey and Bullington etc 85-92; R Bishopstoke 92-06; Asst Chapl Win and Eastleigh Healthcare NHS Trust 92-06; rtd 06. *7 The Old Green, Sherborne DT9 3JY* T: (01935) 816746 E: revdc@live.co.uk

COTTRILL, Mrs Sarah. b 64. **d** 14 **p** 15. C St Jo in Bedwardine *Worc* from 14. *4 Willis Place, Worcester WR2 4BJ*

COUCH, Ms Felicity Anne. b 59. CQSW 85. SEITE 00. **d** 03 **p** 04. NSM Stockwell St Andr and St Mich *S'wark* 03-08; P-in-c Ulceby Gp, Croxton and Brocklesby Park *Linc* 08-11; R Orwell Gp *Ely* from 11. *The Rectory, Fishers Lane, Orwell, Royston SG8 5QX* T: (01223) 207212 M: 07745-905417 E: fcouch@btinternet.com

COUCH, John. b 46. Trin Coll Carmarthen BEd 85. **d** 14 **p** 15. NSM Llansadwrn w Llanwrda and Manordeilo *St D* from 14. *Capel Seion, Llansadwrn, Llanwrda SA19 8HL* T: (01550) 779062 E: john@wales123.plus.com

COUCHMAN, Anthony Denis. b 37. Sarum Th Coll 66. **d** 69 **p** 70. C Barkingside St Fran *Chelmsf* 69-71; C Chingford SS Pet and Paul 71-76; P-in-c Walthamstow St Barn and St Jas Gt 76-80; V 80-07; rtd 07; PtO *Nor* from 08. *Friarscot, Church Street, King's Lynn PE30 5EB* T: (01553) 766643 E: anthony.couchman@yahoo.co.uk

COUCHMAN, Kathryn. b 60. Open Univ BA 92 Coll of Ripon & York St Jo MA 00 MBPsS. NOC 02. **d** 06 **p** 07. C Wetherby *Ripon* 06-08; C Collingham w Harewood 08-10; C Spofforth w Kirk Deighton 08-10; Chapl HM YOI Wetherby 08-11; NSM Bishop Thornton, Burnt Yates, Markington etc *Ripon* 11-12; R Middleham w Coverdale and E Witton etc *Leeds* from 12. *The Rectory, Wensley, Leyburn DL8 4HS* T: (01969) 623736 E: kathycouchman@yahoo.com

COUGHTREY, Mrs Sheila Frances. b 48. RSCN 73 SRN 73 S Bank Poly BSc 79. Qu Coll Birm 79. **dss** 81 **d** 87 **p** 94. Sydenham St Bart *S'wark* 81-85; Roehampton H Trin 85-91; Par Dn 87-91; Par Dn Brixton Hill St Sav 91-94; P-in-c 94-01;

Min King's Acre LEP 91-01; RD Brixton *S'wark* 99-01; P-in-c Pleshey *Chelmsf* 01-15; Warden Dioc Retreat Ho 01-15; rtd 15. *The Vicarage, The Street, Pleshey, Chelmsford CM3 1HA* T: (01245) 237576 E: sheila@scoughtrey.fsnet.co.uk

COULDRIDGE, Janice Evelyn. *See* FOX, Janice Evelyn

COULING, Canon David Charles. b 36. Open Univ BA 89. Qu Coll Birm 61. **d** 63 **p** 64. C Harborne St Faith and St Laur *Birm* 63-66; C E Grinstead St Mary *Chich* 66-70; V Copthorne 70-75; V Eastbourne St Mich 75-82; V Brighton St Matthias 82-83; C-in-c Harton St Lawr CD *Dur* 84-90; V Horsley Hill St Lawr 91-94; P-in-c Greatham 94-97; V 97-01; AD Hartlepool 95-01; Master Greatham Hosp 94-00; Hon Can Dur Cathl 99-01; rtd 01; P-in-c Brancepeth *Dur* 01-04; Chapl Dur Cathl from 04; PtO from 13. *6 Ferens House, Sherburn Hospital, Durham DH1 2SE*

COULSON, Kenneth. b 51. **d** 15. NSM Windy Nook St Alb *Dur* from 15. *13 Beaconsfield Avenue, Low Fell, Gateshead NE9 5XT* T: 0191-487 1544 E: kenc51@sky.com

COULSON, Renée. b 45. **d** 03 **p** 04. OLM Potterne w Worton and Marston *Sarum* 03-09; P-in-c Seend, Bulkington and Poulshot 09-15; rtd 15; PtO *Sarum* from 15. *40 Highlands, Potterne, Devizes SN10 5N* E: renee.coulson.2@googlemail.com *or* revren.d@btinternet.com

COULSON, Canon Stephen Hugh. b 60. St Edm Hall Ox BA 82 MA 88 Lon Univ CertEd 83. Wycliffe Hall Ox 85. **d** 88 **p** 89. C Summerfield *Birm* 88-91; PtO 91-92; CMS Uganda 92-01; Asst V Namirembe 92-96; Can from 96; Prin Uganda Martyrs Sem Namugongo 96-01; V Mitcham St Mark *S'wark* 01-12; AD Merton 09-12; V Kennington St Mark from 12. *St Mark's Vicarage, 56 Kennington Oval, London SE11 5SW* T: (020) 7735 1801 E: steve@scoulson.freeserve.co.uk

COULSON, Thomas Stanley. b 32. TCD BA 54 MA 68. TCD Div Sch 55. **d** 55 **p** 56. C Maghera w Killelagh *D & R* 55-62; I Aghalurcher and Tattykeeran *Clogh* 62-63; I Woodschapel w Gracefield *Arm* 63-97; Preb Arm Cathl 88-97; Treas Arm Cathl 94-96; Chan Arm Cathl 96-97; rtd 97. *Lisadian, 84 Coleraine Road, Portrush BT56 8HN* T: (028) 7082 4202 E: canoncoulson@btinternet.com

COULSON, Tony Erik Frank. b 32. St Edm Hall Ox BA 55 MA 59. Wycliffe Hall Ox 55. **d** 57 **p** 58. C Walthamstow St Mary *Chelmsf* 57-60; C Reading St Jo *Ox* 63-66; V Iver 63-86; R White Waltham w Shottesbrooke 86-97; rtd 97; PtO *Ox* from 98. *30 Ravensbourne Drive, Reading RG5 4LH* T: 0118-969 3556

COULTER, Edmond James. b 60. QUB BSc 82 BD 96. **d** 87 **p** 88. C Ballymena w Ballyclug *Conn* 87-90; C Knockbreda *D & D* 90-92; I Belfast Upper Falls *Conn* 92-97; I Milltown *Arm* 97-03; Supt Dublin Irish Ch Miss *D & G* from 03. *28 Bachelors Walk, Dublin 1, Republic of Ireland* T: (00353) (1) 873 0829 F: 878 4049 E: ejcoulter@iolfree.ie *or* eddie@icm-online.ie

COULTER, Ian Herbert Young. b 54. TCD BA 77 HDipEd 78. **d** 99 **p** 00. LtO Cashel, Waterford and Lismore *C & O* 99-10; NSM Castlecomer w Colliery Ch, Mothel and Bilboa 10-13; NSM Templemore w Thurles and Kilfithmone from 13. *22 Rose Hill Court, Kilkenny, Co Kilkenny, Republic of Ireland* T/F: (00353) (56) 776 2675 M: 86-813 0290 E: ianhycoulter@gmail.com

COULTER (née REEVES), Mrs Maria Elizabeth Ann. b 72. Leeds Univ BA 95 Heythrop Coll Lon MTh 03. St Steph Ho Ox 96. **d** 98 **p** 99. C Newington St Mary *S'wark* 98-02; V Dulwich St Clem w St Pet from 02. *St Clement's Vicarage, 140 Friern Road, London SE22 0AY* T: (020) 8693 1890 E: meareeves@hotmail.com

COULTER, Miss Marilyn Judith. b 48. City of Birm Coll BEd 70 Qu Coll Birm BA 05. WMMTC 02. **d** 05 **p** 06. NSM Brewood *Lich* from 05; NSM Bishopswood from 05; Chapl Mid Staffs NHS Foundn Trust from 08. *14 St Chad's Close, Brewood, Stafford ST19 9DA* T: (01902) 851168 E: coulter14@aol.com

COULTER, Stephen Paul. b 53. Nottm Univ BSc 76 CEng MIMechE. **d** 92 **p** 93. C Oakwood St Thos *Lon* 92-95; V Grange Park St Pet 95-99; I Kells Union *M & K* 99-01; R Pimperne, Stourpaine, Durweston and Bryanston *Sarum* from 01. *The Vicarage, Shaston Road, Stourpaine, Blandford Forum DT11 8TA* T: (01258) 480580 E: stephen.coulter@tiscali.co.uk

COULTHARD, Miss Nina Marion. b 50. CertEd 71 Bp Lonsdale Coll BEd 72. Trin Coll Bris 89. **d** 91 **p** 94. Par Dn Cant St Mary Bredin 91-94; C 94-95; C Bath Abbey w St Jas *B & W* 95-99; Chapl R Nat Hosp for Rheumatic Diseases NHS Trust 95-99; C Northwood Em *Lon* 99-06; V Loughton St Mich *Chelmsf* from 06. *St Michael's House, Roding Road, Loughton IG10 3EJ* T: (020) 8508 1489 E: nina@revnc.wanadoo.co.uk

COULTHURST, Jeffrey Evans. b 38. Man Univ BA 61 Leeds Univ PGCE 62. **d** 84 **p** 85. OLM Ancaster *Linc* 84-89; OLM Ancaster Wilsford Gp 89-05. *152 Cirencester Road, Charlton Kings, Cheltenham GL53 8DY* E: jeff@jcoulthurst.fsnet.co.uk

COULTON, David John. b 45. St Jo Coll Cam BA 67 MA 71 Glos Univ MA 04 CertEd 69. WEMTC 07. **d** 09 **p** 10. NSM Tewkesbury w Walton Cardiff and Twyning *Glouc* from 09; NSM Deerhurst and Apperley w Forthampton etc from 12. *4 Conigree Lane, Abbots Road, Tewkesbury GL20 5TF* T: (01684) 293523 E: davidcoulton@btinternet.com

COULTON, David Stephen. b 41. Bernard Gilpin Soc Dur 63 Sarum Th Coll 64. **d** 67 **p** 68. C Guildf H Trin w St Mary 67-70; Asst Chapl St Luke's Hosp Guildf 67-70; Asst Chapl Radley Coll 70-83; Sen Chapl 83-01; Chapl Eton Coll 01-04; rtd 04. *Address temp unknown*

COULTON, The Very Revd Nicholas Guy. b 40. Lon Univ BD 72 Ox Univ MA 07. Cuddesdon Coll 65. **d** 67 **p** 68. C Pershore w Wick *Worc* 67-70; Bp's Dom Chapl *St Alb* 71-75; P-in-c Bedford St Paul 75-79; V 79-90; Hon Can St Alb 89-90; Dean Newc 90-03; Can Res and Sub-Dean Ch Ch *Ox* 03-08; rtd 08. *123 Merewood Avenue, Headington, Oxford OX3 8EQ* T: (01865) 763790 E: ngc@proscenia.co.uk

COULTON, Philip Ernest. b 31. St Cath Coll Cam BA 54 MA 58 TCD BD 68 Open Univ BA 84. Ely Th Coll 55. **d** 57 **p** 58. Asst Master Perse Sch Cam 54-55; Asst Master Bradf Gr Sch 57; C Newark w Coddington *S'well* 57-61; Min Can and Sacr Cant Cathl 61-63; Min Can Ripon Cathl 63-68; Hd of RE Ashton-under-Lyne Gr Sch 69-84; V Ulceby Gp *Linc* 85-89; P-in-c Ingatestone w Buttsbury *Chelmsf* 89-99; P-in-c Fryerning w Margaretting 89-92; rtd 99; PtO *Sarum* from 01; *B & W* 02-06. *90 Boreham Road, Warminster BA12 9JW* T: (01985) 219353 E: pecoulton@talktalk.net

COUNSELL, Canon Edwin Charles Robert. b 63. Univ of Wales (Cardiff) BA 84 MTh 97. St Steph Ho Ox 85. **d** 88 **p** 89. C Cardiff St Mary and St Steph w St Dyfrig etc *Llan* 88-94; V Pendoylan w Welsh St Donats 94-06; Dioc Dir Statutory Educn from 00; Prov Adv on Educn Ch in Wales from 06; Hon Can Llan Cathl from 14. *The Vicarage, 9 Heol St Cattwg, Pendoylan, Cowbridge CF71 7UG* T: (01446) 760195 *or* T/F: 760210 E: post@llandaffschools.fs.net.co.uk

COUPAR, Thomas. b 50. BA 71 ACE 80. Edin Dioc NSM Course 77. **d** 80 **p** 81. NSM Dunbar *Edin* 80-86; NSM Haddington 80-86; Hd Master Pencaitland Primary Sch E Lothian 80-81; Hd Master K Meadow Sch E Lothian 81-87; Asst Dioc Supernumerary *Edin* 87-89; Primary Educn Adv Fife 88-06; Dioc Supernumerary *Edin* 90-96; Chapl Robin Chpl Edin from 06. *The Robin Chapel, 21/9 Rennie's Isle, Edinburgh EH6 6QB* T: 0131-555 6066 M: 07814-588904 E: tcoupar@hotmail.com

COUPE, Christopher John. b 57. LCTP 10. **d** 12 **p** 13. NSM Lower Darwen St Jas *Blackb* from 12. *Mow Cop, 9 Hesse Street, Darwen BB3 2RU*

COUPER (née WOOD), Mrs Audrey Elizabeth. b 54. Edin Univ BSc 75 Westmr Coll of Educn PGCE 76. ERMC 05. **d** 08 **p** 09. NSM Digswell and Panshanger *St Alb* from 08. *18 Netherfield Road, Harpenden AL5 2AG* T: (01582) 346901 E: audrey@tizmoi.net

COUPER, Jeanette Emily (Jean). b 40. S'wark Ord Course 85. **d** 88. Par Dn Mitcham SS Pet and Paul *S'wark* 88-93; Chapl Asst Guy's Hosp Lon 93-94; PtO *S'wark* 93-04; rtd 00. *Rose Cottage, Wentnor, Bishops Castle SY9 5EE* T: (01588) 650590

COUPER, Jonathan George. b 51. St Jo Coll Dur BA 73. Wycliffe Hall Ox 73. **d** 75 **p** 76. C Clifton *York* 75-78; C Darfield *Sheff* 78-81; V Bridlington Quay Ch Ch *York* from 81; P-in-c Bessingby 99-12; V from 12. *21 Kingston Road, Bridlington YO15 3NF* T: (01262) 400259 *or* 404100 E: joncouper@yahoo.co.uk

COUPER, Simon Piers Mortimer. b 88. Moorlands Coll BA 09 Anglia Ruskin Univ MA 13. Ridley Hall Cam 11. **d** 13. C Tonbridge SS Pet and Paul *Roch* from 13. *14 Salisbury Road, Tonbridge TN10 4PB* T: (01732) 355200 E: simon@tonbridgeparishchurch.org.uk

COUPLAND, Simon Charles. b 59. St Jo Coll Cam BA 82 PGCE 83 MA 85 PhD 87. Ridley Hall Cam 88. **d** 91 **p** 92. C Bath St Luke *B & W* 91-95; TV Broadwater *Chich* 95-04; V Kingston Hill St Paul *S'wark* from 04; AD Kingston from 12. *The Vicarage, 33 Queen's Road, Kingston upon Thames KT2 7SF* T: (020) 8549 8597 *or* 8549 5444 E: simon.coupland@stpaulskingston.org.uk

✠**COURT, The Rt Revd David Eric.** b 58. Southn Univ BSc 80 PhD 83 PGCE 84. Oak Hill Th Coll BA 91. **d** 91 **p** 92 **c** 14. C Barton Seagrave w Warkton *Pet* 91-94; C Kinson *Sarum* 94-97; P-in-c Mile Cross *Nor* 97-99; V 99-03; V Cromer 03-14; RD Repps 10-14; Hon Can Nor Cathl 10-14; Suff Bp Grimsby *Linc* from 14. *Sanderlings, Willingham Road, Market Rasen LN8 3RE* E: revdavidcourt@btinternet.com

COURT, Canon Kenneth Reginald. b 36. AKC 60. **d** 61 **p** 62. C Garforth *Ripon* 61-63; C Harrogate St Wilfrid 63-65; V Thornbury *Bradf* 65-73; Prec Leic Cathl 73-76; V Douglas

St Matt *S & M* 76-84; V Syston *Leic* 84-93; TR 93-98; RD Goscote 90-95; Hon Can Leic Cathl 92-98; rtd 98; PtO *Leic* from 99; *Linc* 01-03; *Pet* 03-08. *12 Lord Burghley's Hospital, Station Road, Stamford PE9 2LD* T: (01780) 754372 E: kenneth@kcourt.wanadoo.co.uk

COURT, Martin Jeremy. b 61. GRNCM 84 Nottm Univ BTh 89. Linc Th Coll 86. **d** 89 **p** 90. C Thurmaston *Leic* 89-92; C Leic St Jas 92-93; TV Leic Resurr 93-98; V Scraptoft from 98; P-in-c Leic St Chad from 08; Dioc Info Tech Co-ord from 96. *All Saints' Vicarage, 331 Scraptoft Lane, Scraptoft, Leicester LE5 2HU* T: 0116-241 3205 M: 07798-876837 E: mcourt@leicester.anglican.org

COURT, Martin John. b 64. Ridley Hall Cam 03. **d** 05 **p** 06. C Blandford Forum and Langton Long *Sarum* 05-09; V Chadwell Heath *Chelmsf* from 09. *The Vicarage, 7 Chadwell Heath Lane, Romford RM6 4LS* T: (020) 8590 2391 M: 07905-612542 E: martin_stchads@live.co.uk

COURT, Nicholas James Keble. b 56. Chich Th Coll 86. **d** 88 **p** 89. C Golders Green *Lon* 88-91; C Westbury-on-Trym H Trin *Bris* 91-94; PV Llan Cathl 94-96; V Graig 96-02; P-in-c Cilfynydd 96-01; Miss P *Mor* from 09. *Cair Paravel, Ardmuir, Ullapool IV26 2TN* T: (01854) 612506 E: nicholas.court@btinternet.com

COURT, Richard Leonard. b 54. Univ of Wales (Ban) BTh 04. EAMTC 94. **d** 97 **p** 98. NSM Framlingham w Saxtead *St E* 97-05; V Badsey w Aldington and Offenham and Bretforton *Worc* 05-15; RD Evesham 10-15; rtd 15. *Address temp unknown* M: 07751-955917 E: richard.court@btinternet.com

COURTIE, John Malcolm. b 42. BNC Ox BA 65 DPhil 72 St Jo Coll Dur BA 76. Cranmer Hall Dur 74. **d** 77 **p** 78. C Mossley Hill St Matt and St Jas *Liv* 77-80; V Litherland St Paul Hatton Hill 80-84; Wellingborough Sch 84-89; Hon C Wollaston and Strixton *Pet* 84-89; V Woodford Halse w Eydon 89-99; R Blisworth and Stoke Bruerne w Grafton Regis etc 99-02; rtd 02; Hon C NW Hants *Win* 09-10; PtO *Ex* from 15. *Brooksong, Longmeadow Road, Lympstone, Exmouth EX8 5LF* T: (01395) 260242 E: thecourties@hotmail.com

COURTNEY (née JORDAN), Mrs Avril Marilyn. b 35. Lon Univ DipEd 56. SWMTC 79. **dss** 82 **d** 87 **p** 94. Highweek and Teigngrace *Ex* 82-88; Par Dn 87-88; Par Dn Ottery St Mary, Alfington, W Hill, Tipton etc 88-94; C 94-99; rtd 99; PtO *Ex* 00-09. *39 Newman Court, Barber Road, Basingstoke RG22 4BW* T: (01256) 479477

COURTNEY, Canon Brian Joseph. b 44. BD 92 MA 97. CITC 70. **d** 73 **p** 74. C Willowfield *D & D* 73-75; P-in-c Knocknagoney 75-78; I Aghavea *Clogh* 78-83; I Carrickfergus *Conn* 83-95; I Enniskillen *Clogh* 95-09; Prec Clogh Cathl 95-09; rtd 09. *10 Berkeley Road, Carrickfergus BT38 9DS* T: (028) 9335 5139 E: briancourtney09@googlemail.com

COURTNEY, Miss Louise Anita Hood. b 48. Ex Univ BTh 04. SWMTC 99. **d** 02 **p** 03. C St Keverne *Truro* 02-05; P-in-c Lanteglos by Fowey 05-15; P-in-c Lansallos 05-15; P-in-c Talland 10-15; C Lanreath, Pelynt and Bradoc 13-15; rtd 15. *Le Pinet, 24500 Razac-d'Eymet, France* E: louiseanitacourtney@gmail.com

COURTNEY, Martin Horace. b 34. SAOMC 95. **d** 98 **p** 99. OLM Flackwell Heath *Ox* from 98. *1 Green Crescent, Flackwell Heath, High Wycombe HP10 9JQ* T: (01628) 526354

COUSANS (née BRADLEY), Mrs Joy Elizabeth. b 63. Sheff Univ BA 85 Fitzw Coll Cam BA 91 MA 95. Ridley Hall Cam 89. **d** 92 **p** 94. Par Dn Wadsley *Sheff* 92-94; C 94-96; C Mosbrough 96-97; V Hillsborough and Wadsley Bridge 97-06; P-in-c High Hoyland, Scissett and Clayton W *Leeds* from 06; Asst Dioc Dir of Ords from 08. *The Rectory, Church Lane, Clayton West, Huddersfield HD8 9LY* T: (01484) 862321 E: joy@daveandjoy.plus.com

COUSINS, Christopher William. b 44. Ox Univ MTh 95. **d** 87 **p** 88. C Wallasey St Hilary *Ches* 87-90; R Rollesby w Burgh w Billockby w Ashby w Oby etc *Nor* 90-94; P-in-c Ormesby w Scratby 92-94; V Ormesby St Marg w Scratby, Ormesby St Mich etc 94-98; RD Gt Yarmouth 94-98; V Altham w Clayton le Moors *Blackb* 98-03; P-in-c Rochford *Chelmsf* 03-10; P-in-c Stambridge 03-10; P-in-c Sutton w Shopland 03-10; RD Rochford 04-08; rtd 10; PtO *Chelmsf* from 10. *180 Manners Way, Southend-on-Sea SS2 6QB* T: (01702) 351584 E: c4cousins@yahoo.com

COUSINS, Mrs Deborah Ann. b 52. LCST 74. ERMC 06. **d** 09 **p** 10. C Earlham *Nor* 09-13; C Bure Valley from 13. *16 Hautbois Road, Badersfield, Norwich NR10 5JL* T: (01603) 738329 E: deb@madmotorbike.fsnet.co.uk

COUSINS, Canon Graham John. b 55. Oak Hill Th Coll BA 91. **d** 91 **p** 92. C Birkenhead St Jas w St Bede *Ches* 91-95; C Bebington 95-01; R Moreton from 01; RD Wallasey from 11; Hon Can Ches Cathl from 12. *The Rectory, Dawpool Drive, Moreton, Wirral CH46 0PH* T: 0151-641 0303 *or* 604 0049 E: rector@christchurchmoreton.org.uk

COUSINS, Peter Gareth. b 37. d 95 p 96. NSM Cwmparc *Llan* 95-02; PtO from 07. *15 Conway Road, Cwmparc, Treorchy CF42 6UW* T: (01443) 773669

COUSINS, Canon Philip John. b 35. K Coll Cam BA 58 MA 62. Cuddesdon Coll 59. d 61 p 62. C Marton *Blackb* 61-63; PV Truro Cathl 63-67; USPG Ethiopia 67-75; V Henleaze *Bris* 75-84; RD Clifton 79-84; Provost All SS Cathl Cairo 84-89; Chan Malta Cathl 89-95; Chapl Valletta w Gozo 89-95; R Llandudno *Ban* 95-04; rtd 04; PtO *York* from 04; *Eur* from 05. *17 Chalfonts, York YO24 1EX* T: (01904) 700316
E: janet.philip@virgin.net

COUSINS, Stephen Michael. b 53. SAOMC 98. d 01 p 02. OLM Caversham St Jo *Ox* 01-03; PtO 03-04; NSM Shiplake w Dunsden and Harpsden 04-11; Chapl Shiplake Coll Henley from 09. *15 Champion Road, Caversham, Reading RG4 8EL* T: 0118-948 1679 M: 07753-166687
E: stephen.cousins@btinternet.com

COUSSENS, Mervyn Haigh Wingfield. b 47. St Jo Coll Nottm BTh 74. d 74 p 75. C Clifton Ch Ch w Em *Bris* 74-77; C Morden *S'wark* 77-83; V Patchway *Bris* 83-91; R Lutterworth w Cotesbach *Leic* 91-98; P-in-c Bitteswell 95-98; R Lutterworth w Cotesbach and Bitteswell 99-12; RD Guthlaxton II 01-05; rtd 12. *8 Chestnut Avenue, Lutterworth LE17 4TJ* T: (01455) 556279

COUSSMAKER, Canon Colin Richard Chad. b 34. OBE 99. Worc Coll Ox BA 57 BSc 58 MA 63 MSc 85. Chich Th Coll 59. d 60 p 61. C Newtown St Luke *Win* 60-64; C Whitley Ch Ch *Ox* 64-67; Chapl Istanbul *Eur* 67-72; Chapl Sliema 72-77; Chapl Antwerp St Boniface 77-93; Can Brussels Cathl 81-00; Chapl Moscow 93-99; rtd 99; Hon Asst Chapl Nice w Vence *Eur* 99-00; PtO from 00. *533 route des Vallettes Sud, 06140 Tourrettes-sur-Loup, France* T: (0033) 4 93 59 28 74

COUTTS, Diana. d 07 p 08. Chapl S Lon Healthcare NHS Trust from 08; PtO *Roch* from 14. *Queen Mary's Hospital, Frognal Avenue, Sidcup DA14 6LT* T: (020) 8302 2678 ext 4399
E: diana.coutts@nhs.net

COUTTS, Ian Alexander. b 56. Warwick Univ BA 77 Jes Coll Ox MSc 80 CQSW 80. St Jo Coll Nottm 87. d 89 p 90. C Hamstead St Bernard *Birm* 89-92; C Warlingham w Chelsham and Farleigh *S'wark* 92-97; TV 97-00; PtO 00-03; *Ox* from 03. *Address temp unknown*

COUTTS, James Allan. b 58. Fitzw Coll Cam MA. St Jo Coll Nottm MTh 84. d 84 p 85. C Thorpe Acre w Dishley *Leic* 84-88; TV Kirby Muxloe 88-99; P-in-c Trowbridge St Thos and W Ashton *Sarum* 99-07; V from 07; Chapl Wilts and Swindon Healthcare NHS Trust from 99. *St Thomas's Vicarage, York Buildings, Trowbridge BA14 8PT* T: (01225) 754826
E: allan@stthomastrowbridge.com

COUTTS, Canon James Walter Cargill. b 35. Univ of Wales (Lamp) BA 57 CCC Cam BA 59. St Mich Coll Llan 59. d 60 p 61. C Cardiff St Mary *Llan* 60-63; C Greenford H Cross *Lon* 63-67; C Swansea St Gabr *S & B* 67-71; V Llanwrtyd w Llanddulas in Tir Abad etc 71-78; V Brecon St Dav 78-80; V Brecon St David w Llanspyddid and Llanilltyd 80-84; V Monmouth *Mon* 84-02; Can St Woolos Cathl 94-02; RD Monmouth 99-01; rtd 02. *The Reynolds, Penallt, Monmouth NP25 4RX* T: (01600) 860277

COUTTS, Canon Mandy Rosalind. b 65. Ox Poly BSc 87 St Jo Coll Dur BA 06 Leeds Univ MA 11 Bath Univ PGCE 88. Cranmer Hall Dur 04. d 06 p 07. C Chapel Allerton *Ripon* 06-10; TV Bramley *Leeds* 10-15; Can Res Bradf Cathl from 15. *2 Cathedral Close, Bradford BD1 4EG* T: (01274) 777728
E: mandy.coutts@virgin.net

COUTTS, Richard Ian Marcus. b 65. Bath Univ BSc 87 PGCE 88 St Jo Coll Dur BA 06. Cranmer Hall Dur 04. d 06 p 07. C Leeds City *Ripon* 06-10; R Stanningley St Thos *Leeds* from 10. *The Rectory, Stanningley Road, Stanningley, Pudsey LS28 6NB* T: 0113-257 5111 M: 07736-180461
E: richard.coutts@virgin.net

COUTTS, Canon Robin Iain Philip. b 52. Portsm Univ MA 00. Sarum & Wells Th Coll 80. d 83 p 84. C Alverstoke *Portsm* 83-86; Min Leigh Park St Clare CD 86-88; V Warren Park 89-91; V Purbrook 91-04; RD Havant 00-04; P-in-c Blendworth w Chalton w Idsworth 04-06; P-in-c Hambledon from 06; Dioc Dir NSM from 04; Dioc Dir of Ords from 06; Hon Can Portsm Cathl from 06. *The Vicarage, Church Lane, Hambledon, Waterlooville PO7 4RT* T: (023) 9263 2717
E: robin.rocket@btinternet.com

COUTURE (née MAWBEY), Mrs Diane. b 55. Birm Univ MMedSc 97. Cranmer Hall Dur. d 89 p 94. Par Dn Menston w Woodhead *Bradf* 89-92; C Barnoldswick w Bracewell 92-93; Chapl Asst Birm Children's Hosp 93-96; Chapl Asst Birm Maternity Hosp 93-96; Chapl Birm Women's Healthcare NHS Trust 96-98; R The Whitacres, Lea Marston, and Shustoke *Birm* from 98. *The Rectory, Dog Lane, Coleshill, Birmingham B46 2DU* T: (01675) 481252 M: 07710-281648

COUVELA, Ms Stephanie Joy. b 68. Sheff City Poly BA 89. Ridley Hall Cam 95. d 98 p 99. C Upper Holloway *Lon* 98-01; TV 01-04; C Busbridge and Hambledon *Guildf* 04-10; Chapl Scargill Ho 10-15; Chapl Keele Univ *Lich* from 15. *Address temp unknown*

COUZENS, Mrs Carolyn Mary. b 67. St Mellitus Coll 13. d 15. C Lilliput *Sarum* from 15. *Address temp unknown*

COVENTRY, Archdeacon of. See GREEN, The Ven John

COVENTRY, Bishop of. See COCKSWORTH, The Rt Revd Christopher John

COVENTRY, Dean of. See WITCOMBE, The Very Revd John Julian

COVERLEY, Mrs Cheryl Joy. b 62. SS Hild & Bede Coll Dur BA 83 PGCE 84. St Jo Coll Nottm MA 07. d 05 p 06. C Birkenhead St Jas w St Bede *Ches* 05-07; V Newton from 07; Asst Warden of Readers from 08. *St Michael's Vicarage, 56 Queensbury, Wirral CH48 6EP* T: 0151-625 8517 E: cheryl.coverley@tiscali.co.uk

COVINGTON, Canon Michael William Rock. b 38. Open Univ BA 78. Sarum Th Coll 60. d 63 p 64. AD Framland *Leic* from 15; C Woolwich St Mary w H Trin *S'wark* 66-68; C Northampton All SS w St Kath *Pet* 68-71; V Longthorpe 71-86; Hon Min Can Pet Cathl 75-86; V Warmington, Tansor, Cotterstock and Fotheringhay 86-95; Warden of Readers 87-95; RD Oundle 89-95; V Oakham, Hambleton, Egleton, Braunston and Brooke 95-03; P-in-c Langham 97-03; RD Rutland 02-03; Can Pet Cathl 86-03; rtd 03; PtO *Leic* 05-06 and 10-13; C Burrough Hill Pars 07-10; P-in-c S Framland from 13. *Hall Farm House, Burrough Road, Little Dalby, Melton Mowbray LE14 2UG* T: (01664) 454015

COWAN, David John. b 47. Selw Coll Cam BA 69 MA 73. SEITE 06. d 09 p 10. NSM Dorking w Ranmore *Guildf* from 09. *Dolphin House, Harrow Road West, Dorking RH4 3BE* T: (01306) 885341 F: 740183 E: david@cowansdorking.co.uk

COWAN, Helen Jane. b 42. d 00 p 01. OLM Redhill H Trin *S'wark* 00-12; PtO from 12. *15 Westway Gardens, Redhill RH1 2JA* T: (01737) 762543 E: cowan@clara.co.uk

COWAN, John Conway. b 71. Trin Coll Bris. d 03 p 04. C Redcar *York* 03-07; V Hull St Cuth from 07; Chapl Hull Univ from 10. *The Vicarage, 112 Marlborough Avenue, Hull HU5 3JX* T: (01482) 342848 E: cowanjohnc@yahoo.com

COWAN, Mrs Lynda Barbette. b 55. ALAM 77. Ban Ord Course 02. d 05 p 06. C Arwystli Deanery *Ban* 05-08; P-in-c Llandinam w Trefeglwys w Penstrowed *Ban* 08-10; V 10-14; V Bro Arwystli from 14. *The Coach House, Old Hall Road, Llanidloes SY18 6PQ* T: (01686) 413099

COWAN, Malcolm. b 60. Ches Coll of HE BTh 04. NOC 01. d 04 p 05. C W Kirby St Bridget *Ches* 04-07; V Witton 07-11; R Christleton from 11. *The Rectory, Birch Heath Lane, Christleton, Chester CH3 7AP* T: (01244) 335663
E: jandmcowan@gmail.com

COWAN, Malcolm. b 45. CBDTI. d 00 p 01. NSM Keswick St Jo *Carl* 00-05; TV Whitehaven 05-07; P-in-c Kirkby Ireleth from 07; C Dalton-in-Furness and Ireleth-with-Askam from 07. *The Vicarage, School Road, Kirkby-in-Furness LA17 7UQ* T: (01229) 889256 E: malcolm-cowan@o2.co.uk

COWAN, Paul Hudson. b 69. Ripon Coll Cuddesdon BTh 05. d 02 p 03. C Wokingham All SS *Ox* 02-05; C Kimberley Cathl S Africa 05-06; TV Newbury *Ox* 06-15; V Newbury St Geo and St Jo from 15. *St George's Vicarage, 206 Andover Road, Newbury RG14 6NU* T: (01635) 41249 E: vicar@st-george-newbury.org

COWAN, Shirley. b 64. d 12 p 13. C Gateacre *Liv* from 12. *24 Lee Vale Road, Gateacre, Liverpool L25 3RW*

COWARD, Colin Charles Malcolm. b 45. MBE 14. Kingston Poly DArch 72. Westcott Ho Cam 75. d 78 p 79. C Camberwell St Geo *S'wark* 78-82; P-in-c Wandsworth St Faith 82-90; V 90-96; Chapl Richmond, Twickenham and Roehampton NHS Trust 96-97; Co-ord Changing Attitude 97-03; Dir 03-15; rtd 15. *6 Norney Bridge, Mill Road, Worton, Devizes SN10 5SF* T: (01380) 724908 E: ccmcoward@aol.com

COWARD, Raymond. b 41. NW Ord Course 79. d 82 p 83. C Turton *Man* 82-84; C Heaton Ch Ch 84-86; V Rochdale St Geo w St Alb 86-92; V Daisy Hill 92-06; rtd 06; PtO *Man* from 06. *433 Hough Fold Way, Bolton BL2 3PY*
E: coward@tinyworld.co.uk

COWBURN, John Charles. b 48. Sarum & Wells Th Coll 88. d 90 p 91. C Andover w Foxcott *Win* 90-94; C Christchurch 94-96; Chapl to the Deaf *Lich* 96-09; P-in-c Church Aston 01-09; Chapl to the Deaf *Sarum* from 09. *The Vicarage, 25 White Street, West Lavington, Devizes SN10 4LW* T: (01380) 816878 E: johnchap@sky.com

COWELL, Anthony. See COWELL, Neil Anthony

COWELL, Christopher Douglas. b 47. Ex Univ BA 90 K Coll Lon PGCE 92 Brunel Univ PGDE 99. d 08 p 09. OLM Frimley Green and Mytchett *Guildf* 08-12; rtd 12. *29 The Glade, Mytchett, Camberley GU16 6BG* T: (01252) 513434

COWELL, Irene Christine. b 58. RGN 80. Ridley Hall Cam 92. d 94 p 95. C Litherland St Phil *Liv* 94-98; R Sefton and

Thornton 98-11; P-in-c Southport Em from 11; Dioc Adv on HIV/AIDS and Sexual Health 97-06; Dioc Dir CME from 02; Dir Leadership and Management Tr from 05. *Emmanuel Vicarage, 12 Allerton Road, Southport PR9 9NJ* T: (01704) 532743 E: irene.cowell@btinternet.com

COWELL, Neil Anthony. b 61. d 98 p 99. OLM New Bury *Man* 98-06; OLM New Bury w Gt Lever from 06. *166 Harrowby Street, Farnworth, Bolton BL4 7DE* T: (01204) 706957

COWEN, Canon Brian. b 45. Nottm Univ BTh 77. Linc Th Coll 73. d 77 p 78. C Hexham *Newc* 77-80; C Ledbury w Eastnor *Heref* 80-81; TV Glendale Gp *Newc* 81-90; V Lesbury w Alnmouth 90-08; V Longhoughton w Howick 98-08; AD Alnwick 93-05; Hon Can Newc Cathl 01-08; rtd 08. *13 Fenton Grange, Wooler NE71 6AW* T: (01668) 281991 E: rev.cowen@btopenworld.com

COWGILL, Canon Michael. b 48. Linc Th Coll 84. d 86 p 87. C Bolton St Jas w St Chrys *Bradf* 86-89; V Buttershaw St Paul 89-93; P-in-c Cullingworth 93-97; Dir Dioc Foundn Course 93-97; V Sutton 97-07; V Sutton w Cowling and Lothersdale *Leeds* 07-14; Hon Can Bradf Cathl 07-14; rtd 14. *2 Garforth Avenue, Steeton, Keighley BD20 6SP* E: michael@cowgill.force9.co.uk

COWIE, Andrew Cameron. b 66. Wycliffe Hall Ox. d 11 p 12. C Woking St Paul *Guildf* from 11. *The Rectory, 28 High Street, Old Woking GU22 9ER* E: thecowies@btinternet.com

COWIE, David James. b 87. Ches Univ BEd 09. Ripon Coll Cuddesdon BTh 14. d 14 p 15. C Ches H Trin from 14. *44 Southway, Blacon, Chester CH1 5NN* E: revd.david.cowie@gmail.com

COWIE, Derek Edward. b 33. S'wark Ord Course 70. d 73 p 74. C Maldon All SS w St Pet *Chelmsf* 73-76; R Bowers Gifford w N Benfleet 76-79; V Chelmsf Ascension 79-84; V Shrub End 84-95; P-in-c Gosfield 95-03; RD Hinckford 01-03; rtd 03; PtO *Nor* from 03. *Bruar Cottage, 68 Wash Lane, Kessingland, Lowestoft NR33 7QY* T: (01502) 740989 M: 07788-662211 E: revcowie73@gmail.com

COWIE, John William Stephen. b 64. Wycliffe Hall Ox BTh 97. d 97 p 98. C Shoreditch St Leon and Hoxton St Jo *Lon* 97-00. *Address withheld by request* E: williamcowie@onetel.com

COWIE, Margaret Harriet. See KING, Margaret Harriet

COWLES, Richard Martin. b 53. Birm Univ BSc 74. Ripon Coll Cuddesdon 91. d 93 p 94. C Iffley *Ox* 93-96; TV Wheatley 96-08; V Bray and Braywood from 08. *The Vicarage, The Churchyard, High Street, Bray, Maidenhead SL6 2AB* T: (01628) 621527 E: vicar@cowles.globalnet.co.uk

COWLEY, Anne. See COWLEY, Judith Anne

COWLEY, Charles Frederick. See HOWARD-COWLEY, Joseph Charles

COWLEY, Mrs Elizabeth Mary. b 47. Bris Univ PQCSW 84. WMMTC 89. d 92 p 94. NSM Wolston and Church Lawford *Cov* 92-97; Soc Resp Officer 97-02; P-in-c Churchover w Willey 97-02; TV Daventry, Ashby St Ledgers, Braunston etc *Pet* 02-13; Adv for Healing Min (Northn Adnry) 06-13; rtd 13; PtO *Pet* from 14. *57 Daventry Road, Barby, Rugby CV23 8TP* T: (01788) 891411 E: liz.cowley@btinternet.com

COWLEY, Herbert Kenneth. b 20. Glouc Sch of Min 75. d 79 p 80. Hon C Lydney w Aylburton *Glouc* 79-89; rtd 89; PtO *B & W* 89-98. *108 Waverley Court, Forth Avenue, Portishead BS20 7NY* T: (01275) 856198

COWLEY, Ian Michael. b 51. Natal Univ BCom 72 BA 75 Sheff Univ MA 83. Wycliffe Hall Ox 75. d 78 p 79. C Scottsville S Africa 78-81; C Norton Woodseats St Chad *Sheff* 81-83; R Hilton S Africa 83-94; R Mutin Ely 94-03; RD Quy 00-02; V Yaxley and Holme w Conington 03-08; Co-ord of Voc and Spirituality *Sarum* from 08; Hon C Clarendon from 15. *The Vicarage, Common Road, Whiteparish, Salisbury SP5 2SU* T: (01794) 884315 E: iancowley@ukonline.co.uk

COWLEY, Jean Louie Cameron. See HERRICK, Jean Louie Cameron

COWLEY, Mrs Judith Anne. b 59. Nottm Univ BSc 80. Ox Min Course. d 08 p 09. NSM Shepherd's Bush St Steph w St Thos *Lon* from 08. *10 Barlby Road, London W10 6AR* T: (020) 8960 9587 M: 07824-511029 E: anne.cowley@ntlworld.com *or* anne.cowley@btinternet.com

COWLEY, Kenneth. See COWLEY, Herbert Kenneth

COWLEY, Paul William. b 55. MBE 14. Middx Univ BA 02. NTMTC 99. d 02 p 03. C Brompton H Trin w Onslow Square St Paul *Lon* 02-11; C Onslow Square and S Kensington St Aug from 11. *72 Archel Road, London W14 9QP* T: (020) 7386 5140 M: 07860-146552 *or* 08456-447544 E: amanda.wilkie@htb.org.uk

COWLEY, Peter. b 53. NOC 06. d 08 p 09. NSM Prescot *Liv* 08-12; NSM Knowsley 12-14; NSM Stockbridge Village 12-14; NSM Huyton St Geo 12-14; NSM W Derby St Luke 12-14; NSM 4Saints Team from 14. *17 Kingsway, Prescot L35 5BG* T: 0151-426 5441 E: petercowley@blueyonder.co.uk

COWLEY, Samuel Henry. b 44. St Jo Coll Nottm 85. d 87 p 88. C Hadleigh w Layham and Shelley *St E* 87-91; P-in-c Ipswich St Mich 91-99; P-in-c Westerfield and Tuddenham w Witnesham 99-10; rtd 10; PtO *St E* from 10. *44 Hunters End, Trimley St Mary, Felixstowe IP11 0XH* T: (01394) 200462 E: sam@familycowley.co.uk

COWLIN, Clare Margaret. b 54. d 13 p 14. NSM Wells St Thos w Horrington *B & W* from 13; NSM Chewton Mendip w Ston Easton, Litton etc from 13. *Garden Cottage, The Liberty, Wells BA5 2SU* E: clarecowlin@aol.com

COWLING, John Francis. b 32. K Coll Cam BA 56. Linc Th Coll 56. d 58 p 59. C Leigh St Mary *Man* 58-61; Sec SCM in Schs Liv and Ches 61-65; V Bolton St Matt *Man* 65-71; V Bolton St Matt w St Barn 71-75; V Southport H Trin *Liv* 75-91; R St Olave Hart Street w All Hallows Staining etc *Lon* 91-05; P-in-c St Kath Cree 02-05; Dir of Ords 92-02; rtd 05; PtO *Cant* 05-12. *13 Colleton Hill, Exeter EX2 4AS*

COWLING, Mark Alasdair. b 71. Loughb Univ BA 92 Man Metrop Univ MA 94. Trin Coll Bris BA 10. d 10 p 11. C Halliwell St Pet *Man* 10-13. *9 Lowside Avenue, Bolton BL1 5XQ*

COWLING, Simon Charles. b 59. G&C Coll Cam BA 80 MA 88 K Coll Lon PGCE 82. Linc Th Coll BTh 91. d 91 p 92. C Potternewton *Ripon* 91-94; C Far Headingley St Chad 94-96; V Roundhay St Edm 96-07; AD Allerton 04-07; Can Res and Prec Sheff Cathl 07-13; R Bolton Abbey *Leeds* from 13; Adn Richmond and Craven from 15. *The Rectory, Bolton Abbey, Skipton BD23 6AL* T: (01756) 710238 E: office@boltonpriory.org.uk

COWPER, Christopher Herbert. b 44. Open Univ BA 76. AKC 67. d 68 p 69. C Pitsmoor *Sheff* 68-71; C Ulverston St Mary w H Trin *Carl* 71-74; R Kirklinton w Hethersgill and Scaleby 74-83; V Bridekirk and Chapl Dovenby Hall Hosp Cockermouth 83-94; P-in-c Wetheral w Warwick *Carl* 94-98; R Barningham w Hutton Magna and Wycliffe *Ripon* 98-09; rtd 09. *6 Darnborough Gate, Ripon HG4 2TF* T: (01765) 692221 E: chrisjchrish@gmail.com

COWPER, Peter James. See SELLICK, Peter James

COX, Alan John. b 34. Lon Coll of Div ALCD 65 LTh. d 65 p 66. C Kirkheaton *Wakef* 65-67; C Keynsham w Queen Charlton *B & W* 67-71; R Chipstable w Huish Champflower and Clatworthy 71-76; TV Strood *Roch* 76-80; V Strood St Fran 80-83; R Keston 83-95; rtd 95; PtO *Roch* from 00. *12 Beech Court, 46 Copers Cope Road, Beckenham BR3 1LD* T: (020) 8639 0082

COX, The Very Revd Albert Horace Montague. b 26. d 86 p 87. C Masvingo Zimbabwe 86-94; P-in-c Mucheke 91-94; Dean Gweru 95-02; V Gen Cen 96-03; Hon C Winchelsea and Icklesham *Chich* 03-10; PtO *Cant* 10-13. *29 Church Road, Murston, Sittingbourne ME10 3RT*

COX, Ms Alison Clare. b 63. MHort(RHS) 89. Ripon Coll Cuddesdon 01. d 03 p 04. C Spalding St Mary and St Nic *Linc* 03-07; P-in-c Dukinfield St Mark *Ches* from 07; RD Mottram from 12. *The Vicarage, 2 Church Square, Dukinfield SK16 4PX* T: 0161-330 2783 E: alisoncox19@hotmail.com

COX, Alison Hilda. b 57. Coll of Ripon & York St Jo BEd 79 Nottm Univ MA 02. EMMTC 99. d 02 p 03. NSM Bakewell *Derby* 02-04; NSM Walton St Jo 04-05; TV Buxton w Burbage and King Sterndale 05-07; Lay Tr Officer *S'well* from 07. *The Cruck Barn, 191 Old Road, Chesterfield S40 3QH* T: (01246) 211179 E: alison.cox@southwell.anglican.org

COX, Canon Anthony James Stuart. b 46. BNC Ox BA 68 MA 74. Qu Coll Birm 69. d 71 p 72. C Smethwick St Matt w St Chad *Birm* 71-74; Chapl Liv Univ 74; Chapl Malosa Secondary Sch Malawi 75-79; Hd Master 80-87; Hon Can S Malawi from 80; Chapl Loughborough Gr Sch 87-09; rtd 09; PtO *Leic* from 87; S'well from 97. *Orchard House, 169 Main Street, Willoughby on the Wolds, Loughborough LE12 6SY* T: (01509) 880861 E: tonycox169@gmail.com

COX, Brian Leslie. b 49. S Dios Minl Tr Scheme 91. d 94 p 95. C Southampton Maybush St Pet *Win* 94-98; P-in-c Knights Enham 98-05; R Knight's Enham and Smannell w Enham Alamein 05-06; P-in-c Freemantle 06-09; R 09-14; rtd 14; PtO *Win* from 14; *Portsm* from 14. *2 Arden Close, Gosport PO12 3RS* M: 07796-070850 E: brianandlys@icloud.com

COX, David John. b 51. Lon Univ BD 97 Man Univ MA 04. Qu Coll Birm 76. d 79 p 80. C Brampton Bierlow *Sheff* 79-82; Miss Partner CMS 82-88; V N Perak W Malaysia 83-88; V Friarmere *Man* 88-96; P-in-c Denton Ch Ch 96-06; rtd 06; PtO *Carl* from 07. *5 Main Street, St Bees CA27 0DE* T: (01946) 821601 E: david.j.cox@hotmail.co.uk

COX (née FRANKLIN), Mrs Dianne Mary. b 48. UEA BA 69 Univ Coll of Swansea PGCE 70. NEOC 03. d 06 p 07. NSM Osbaldwick w Murton *York* 06-09; Chapl Aiglon Coll Switzerland 09-10; NSM Berne w Neuchâtel *Eur* 11-13; rtd 13; PtO *York* from 14. *35 Broughton Way, York YO10 3BG* T: (01904) 421556 E: diannecoxuk@yahoo.co.uk

COX, Elizabeth Anne. b 55. SEITE 01. **d** 04 **p** 05. NSM Newington w Hartlip and Stockbury *Cant* 04-11; Chapl HM Pris Standford Hill 11-13; Chapl HM Pris Swaleside from 13. *HM Prison Swaleside, Church Road, Eastchurch, Sheerness ME12 4AX* T: (01795) 804100 M: 07789-510499
E: lizapple@btopenworld.com

COX, Canon Eric William. b 30. Dur Univ BA 54. Wells Th Coll 54. **d** 56 **p** 57. C Sutton in Ashfield St Mary *S'well* 56-59; Asst Chapl Brussels *Eur* 59-62; V Winnington *Ches* 62-71; V Middlewich 71-76; Chapl Mid Cheshire Hosps Trust 73-95; P-in-c Biley *Ches* 73-76; V Middlewich w Byley 76-95; RD Middlewich 80-94; Hon Can Ches Cathl 84-95; rtd 95; PtO *Ches* from 95; *Lich* from 96. *Lovel Hollow, Church Road, Baschurch, Shrewsbury SY4 2EE* T: (01939) 261258
E: canoneric@lovelhollow.fsnet.co.uk

COX, Geoffrey Sidney Randel. b 33. Mert Coll Ox BA 56 MA 60. Tyndale Hall Bris. **d** 58 **p** 59. C St Paul's Cray St Barn CD *Roch* 58-61; C Bromley Ch H 61-64; V Gorsley w Cliffords Mesne *Glouc* 64-79; V Hucclecote 79-89; V Wollaston and Strixton *Pet* 89-96; rtd 96; PtO *Glouc* from 96. *32 Murvagh Close, Cheltenham GL53 7QY* T: (01242) 251604

COX, Hugh Teversham. b 42. Keble Coll Ox BA 76 MA 82 Trin Evang Div Sch (USA) DMin 99. Moore Th Coll Sydney. **d** 69 **p** 70. C Manuka St Paul Australia 70-71; P-in-c Kameruka 71-74; PtO *Ox* 75-76; P-in-c Canberra Ch Ch Australia 76-82; Tutor and Lect St Mark's Nat Th Cen 77-87; R Lane Cove 82-87; R Castle Hill St Paul 87-01; Tervuren *Eur* 01-06; R E Sydney Australia from 06. *PO Box 465, Kings Cross NSW 1340, Australia* T: (0061) (2) 9360 6844 F: 9360 1759
E: rector@stjohnsanglican.org.au

COX, James David Robert. b 65. Lanc Univ BA 88. Qu Coll Birm BD 92. **d** 93 **p** 94. C Harborne St Pet *Birm* 93-96; C Chelmsley Wood 96-97; TV 97-00; V Smethwick Resurr 00-07; V Taunton St Andr *B & W* 07-09; V Selly Oak St Mary *Birm* from 09. *St Mary's Vicarage, 923 Bristol Road, Selly Oak, Birmingham B29 6ND* T: 0121-472 0250 E: jimcox11@googlemail.com

COX, Janet. b 48. CBDTI 04. **d** 05 **p** 06. NSM Long Marton w Dufton and w Milburn *Carl* 05-08; NSM Heart of Eden 08-13; rtd 13. *Broom Cottage, Long Marton, Appleby-in-Westmorland CA16 6JP* T: (017683) 62896
E: peter_janet_cox@hotmail.com

COX, John Anthony. b 45. Hull Univ BA 67. Qu Coll Birm 71. **d** 73 **p** 74. C Buckingham *Ox* 73-76; C Whitley Ch Ch 76-81; V Reading St Agnes w St Paul 81-83; V Chaddesley Corbett and Stone *Worc* 83-10; rtd 10. *7 Burlington Close, Kidderminster DY10 3DQ* T: (01562) 637966 E: jacm.cox@ukgateway.net

COX, John Edgar. b 26. Lon Univ BSc 50 MSc 69 CEng MIET 56. Bps' Coll Cheshunt 67. **d** 68 **p** 69. NSM Harlow St Mary Magd *Chelmsf* 68-76; C S Petherwin w Trewen *Truro* 77-79; P-in-c 79-82; P-in-c Lawhitton 81-82; P-in-c Lezant 81-82; R Lezant w Lawhitton and S Petherwin w Trewen 82-83; V Breage w Germoe 83-91; rtd 91; PtO *Truro* from 91. *7 Evans Way, Germoe, Penzance TR20 9QZ* T: (01736) 762582

COX, The Ven John Stuart. b 40. Fitzw Ho Cam BA 62 MA 66 Linacre Coll Ox BA 67. Wycliffe Hall Ox 64. **d** 68 **p** 69. C Prescot *Liv* 68-71; C Birm St Geo 71-73; R 73-78; Selection Sec ACCM 78-83; Hon C Orpington All SS *Roch* 78-83; Dioc Dir of Ords *S'wark* 83-91; Can Res and Treas S'wark Cathl 83-91; V Roehampton H Trin 91-95; Adn Sudbury *St E* 95-06; rtd 06; PtO *St E* from 06; Dioc Dir of Educn from 07. *2 Bullen Close, Bury St Edmunds IP33 3JP* T/F: (01284) 766796
E: archdeacon.john@stedmundsbury.anglican.org

COX, Jonathan James. b 63. Wollongong Univ BA 85 DipEd 86. Ridley Hall Cam. **d** 00 **p** 01. C Tonbridge SS Pet and Paul *Roch* 00-03; R Oxley Vale Australia 03-10; P-in-c Menteng Indonesia 10-13; Chapl RAAF Specialist Reserve 03-13; Chapl RAN from 13. *101 Arthur Street, Surry Hills 2010 NSW, Australia*

COX, Julie Margaret. b 55. SAOMC. **d** 00 **p** 01. NSM Luton St Chris Round Green *St Alb* 00-06; NSM Luton St Anne w St Chris 06-08; PtO from 08. *29 Maple Close, Pulloxhill, Bedford MK45 5EF* T: (01525) 717002 E: revjuliecox@hotmail.com

COX, Kenneth Ian Royston. b 54. SEITE 09. **d** 12 **p** 13. NSM St Laur in Thanet *Cant* from 12. *297 Margate Road, Ramsgate CT12 6TE* T: (01843) 594895
E: kennethcox954@btinternet.com

COX, Mrs Linda Jayne. b 66. RGN 88. Qu Coll Birm 10. **d** 12 **p** 13. C Woodfield *Leic* from 12. *The Vicarage, Mill Street, Packington, Ashby-de-la-Zouch LE65 1WL* T: (01530) 411642 M: 07708-015631 E: lindac40@btinternet.com

COX, Martin Brian. b 64. Keele Univ BA 91 CQSW 91. St Jo Coll Nottm 01. **d** 03 **p** 04. C Sale St Anne *Ches* 03-05; V Sandiway 05-10; P-in-c Chorley St Laur *Blackb* 10-11; R from 11. *The Rectory, Rectory Close, Chorley PR7 1QW* T: (01257) 263114
E: martin_b_cox@btopenworld.com

COX, Martin Lloyd. b 57. Wilson Carlile Coll and Sarum & Wells Th Coll. **d** 88 **p** 89. C Risca *Mon* 88-91;

TV Pontypool 91-96; V Monkton *St D* 96-04; TR 04-10; V Gorseinon *S & B* from 10; AD Llwchwr from 13. *40 Princess Street, Gorseinon, Swansea SA4 4US* T: (01792) 892849
E: martinlloydcox@btinternet.com

COX, Nicholas. **d** 10. C Ayr *Glas* from 10; C Girvan from 10; C Maybole from 10. *30 Queens Terrace, Ayr KA7 1DX*

COX, Noel Stanley Bertie. b 65. Auckland Univ LLB 88 LLM 95 PhD 01 MTheol Lambeth MA 05 Univ of Wales (Lamp) LTh 07 FRHistS 04. St Mich Coll Llan 10. **d** 12 **p** 13. Prof Law Aberystwyth Univ *St D* 10-14; NSM Llanbadarn Fawr and Elerch and Penrhyncoch etc 12-15. *19 William Blofield Avenue, Mount Roskill, Auckland 1041, New Zealand*
E: noel.cox34@gmail.com

COX, Ms Patricia Jean. b 44. WEMTC. **d** 00 **p** 01. NSM Coleford, Staunton, Newland, Redbrook etc *Glouc* 00-07; NSM Lydney 07-13; rtd 14. *67 Primrose Hill, Lydney GL15 5SW* T: (01594) 843852 E: revp_cox@tiscali.co.uk

COX, Canon Paul Graham. b 40. Keele Univ BA 62 DipEd 62. Westcott Ho Cam 77. **d** 78 **p** 79. NSM Kemsing w Woodlands *Roch* 78-80; Hd Master and Chapl St Mich Sch Otford 81-90; C Petham and Waltham w Lower Hardres etc *Cant* 90-95; P-in-c 95-97; C Elmsted w Hastingleigh 90-95; P-in-c 95-97; R Biddenden and Smarden 97-06; Bp's Officer for NSM 91-98; Dioc Dir of Reader Selection and Tr 98-00; Bp's Officer for OLM 00-06; Hon Can Cant Cathl 01-06; rtd 06. *31 Waldron Thorns, Heathfield TN21 0AB* T: (01435) 868814
M: 07766-545341 E: pgcox@tiscali.co.uk

COX, Peter Allard. b 55. Univ of Wales (Lamp) BA 76. Wycliffe Hall Ox 77. **d** 79 **p** 80. C Penarth All SS *Llan* 79-82; V Aberpergwm and Blaengwrach 82-86; V Bargoed and Deri w Brithdir 86-97; V Penarth All SS from 97; AD Penarth and Barry from 11; Can Llan Cathl from 15. *All Saints' Vicarage, 2 Lower Cwrt-y-Vil Road, Penarth CF64 3HQ* T: (029) 2070 8952 E: petercox6@virgin.net

COX, Philip Gordon. b 36. St Jo Coll Cam MA 62 Lon Univ PGCE 71. Dioc OLM tr scheme 99. **d** 02 **p** 03. OLM Charing w Charing Heath and Lt Chart *Cant* 02-10; PtO from 11. *Home Meadow, Little Chart Forstal, Little Chart, Ashford TN27 0PU* T: (01233) 840274 E: philip@homemeadow.plus.com

COX, Miss Rosemary Jennifer. b 54. St Aid Coll Dur BA 75 Lon Bible Coll BTh 97 Trin Coll Bris MA 99. Cranmer Hall Dur 01. **d** 03 **p** 04. C Leeds All SS w Osmondthorpe *Ripon* 03-05; C Ireland Wood 05-07; PtO *Dur* from 05. *7 The Paddock, Waterhouses, Durham DH7 9AW* T: 0191-373 1539
E: rosemaryjcox@aol.com

COX, Canon Sheila Margaret. b 54. Nottm Univ BA 76 Reading Univ PGCE 77. SEITE 00. **d** 03 **p** 04. NSM Cranbrook *Cant* 03-08; NSM Mersham w Hinxhill and Sellindge 08-12; NSM Smeeth w Monks Horton and Stowting and Brabourne 08-12; R G7 Benefice from 12; Asst Dir of Ords from 08; Bp's Adv for Women's Min from 13; Hon Can Cant Cathl from 14. *The Vicarage, Pett Lane, Charing, Ashford TN27 0DL* T: (01233) 712598 M: 07985-003095
E: sheila.m.cox@btopenworld.com

COX, Mrs Sheila Stuart. b 41. Aber Coll of Educn CertEd 63. Edin Dioc NSM Course 85. **d** 88 **p** 94. NSM Livingston LEP *Edin* 88-93; Asst Chapl St Jo and Bangour Hosps W Lothian 89-93; Chapl 96-98; Hon C Edin St Mark 93-96; Missr Edin St Andr and St Aid 95-96; NSM Eyemouth 98-05; rtd 05; LtO *Edin* from 06. *5 Northfield Farm Cottages, St Abbs, Eyemouth TD14 5QF* T: (01890) 771764

COX, Canon Simon John. b 53. Qu Mary Coll Lon BSc 74 Liv Univ PhD 81 Selw Coll Cam BA 81 MA 85 Lanc Univ MA 87 MSB 79 CBiol 79. Ridley Hall Cam 79. **d** 82 **p** 83. C Livesey *Blackb* 82-85; C Cheadle Hulme St Andr *Ches* 85-89; V Disley 89-94; R Bispham *Blackb* from 94; P-in-c S Shore St Pet 05-07; AD Blackpool from 04; Hon Can Blackb Cathl from 07. *All Hallows Rectory, 86 All Hallows Road, Blackpool FY2 0AY* T: (01253) 351886 E: drsjcox@yahoo.co.uk

COX, Stephen. b 38. Open Univ BA 80. Bps' Coll Cheshunt 65. **d** 68 **p** 69. C Gaywood, Bawsey and Mintlyn *Nor* 68-72; Youth Chapl 72-82; C N Lynn w St Marg and St Nic 73-82; Chapl Guildf Coll of Tech 82-87; Chapl Surrey Univ *Guildf* 82-91; Tr and Development Manager Jas Paget Hosp Gorleston 91-93; Manager Medical Records 93-96; Consumer Relns and Litigation Manager 96-99; rtd 99. *56 Bately Avenue, Gorleston, Great Yarmouth NR31 6HN* T: (01493) 662061

COX, Stephen John Wormleighton. b 54. New Coll Ox MA 79 Fitzw Coll Cam BA 79. Ridley Hall Cam 77. **d** 80 **p** 81. C Clapton Park All So *Lon* 80-85; TV Hackney Marsh 85-87; V Holloway St Mary w St Jas 87-88; P-in-c Barnsbury St Dav w St Clem 87-88; V Holloway St Mary Magd 88-97; AD Islington 95-99; TR Upper Holloway 97-10; Preb St Paul's Cathl 07-10; Local Miss Adv *Guildf* from 10. *17 Glenmount Road, Mytchett, Camberley GU16 6AY* T: (01483) 790330
E: stephenj.cox@virgin.net *or* stephen.cox@cofeguildford.org.uk

COX, Mrs Susan Margaret. b 55. WEMTC 05. **d** 08 **p** 09. NSM Bourton-on-the-Water w Clapton etc *Glouc* 08-12; NSM The Guitings, Cutsdean, Farmcote etc from 12. *30 Lamberts Field, Bourton-on-the-Water, Cheltenham GL51 8LB* T: (01451) 821641 M: 07903-451932
E: suemcoxuk@yahoo.co.uk

COX, Terence John. **d** 15. NSM Rhondda *Llan* from 15. *8 Nantgwyddon Close, Gelli, Pentre CF41 7RD* T: (01443) 436505 E: cox945@btinternet.com

COX, William John Francis. b 24. SWMTC. **d** 77 **p** 78. NSM Liskeard w St Keyne and St Pinnock *Truro* 77-82; NSM Liskeard w St Keyne, St Pinnock and Morval 82-86; NSM N Hill w Altarnon, Bolventor and Lewannick 86-87; TV Bolventor 87-92; P-in-c North Hill and Lewannick 92-94; rtd 94; PtO *Truro* from 94. *9 Trelawney Rise, Callington PL17 7PT* T: (01579) 384347

COXHEAD, Mrs Margaret. b 40. S Dios Minl Tr Scheme 91. **d** 94 **p** 95. NSM High Hurstwood *Chich* 94-00; P-in-c 00-05; P-in-c Fairwarp 00-05; rtd 05. *Rock Hall, Chillies Lane, High Hurstwood, Uckfield TN22 4AD* T: (01825) 733833

COYNE, Deborah Margaret. b 88. Cranmer Hall Dur 12. **d** 15. C Rural E York from 15. *69A The Village, Stockton on the Forest, York YO32 9UP* T: (01904) 400644 M: 07704-855759
E: rev.deborah.coyne@gmail.com

COYNE, John Edward. b 55. Sheff Univ MA 98. Oak Hill Th Coll BA 79. **d** 79 **p** 80. C Cheadle Hulme St Andr *Ches* 79-81; C Macclesfield St Mich 81-83; V Stalybridge H Trin and Ch Ch 83-88; Chapl RAF 88-03; Command Chapl RAF 03-05; RAF Adv in Evangelism 93-98; Hon C Hemingford Grey *Ely* 96-98; Dean of Coll St Jo Coll Nottm 05-09; Dir Local and Regional Delivery CPAS 09-12; R Aldridge *Lich* from 12. *The Rectory, 14 The Green, Aldridge, Walsall WS9 8NH* T: (01922) 456830 or 458801 E: j2scoyne@hotmail.com

COYNE, Terence Roland Harry. b 37. Chich Th Coll 64. **d** 66 **p** 67. C Meir *Lich* 66-69; C Horninglow 69-72; V Walsall St Gabr Fulbrook 72-10; C Walsall St Mary and All SS Palfrey 97-02; C Caldmore w Palfrey 02-10; rtd 10. *20 Frame Lane, Doseley, Telford TF4 3BQ* T: (01952) 503394

COZENS (née FULLER), Alison Jane. b 61. St Andr Univ MTheol 84. Edin Th Coll 85. **d** 87 **p** 94. C Selkirk *Edin* 87-89; C Melrose 87-89; C Galashiels 87-89; C Edin H Cross 89-92; Dn-in-c Edin St Columba 92-94; R 94-10; Chapl Edin Univ 96-00; P-in-c Leic Presentation 10-15; R Dunfermline *St And* from 15. *17 Ardeer Place, Dunfermline KY11 4YX*
E: mrandmrscozens2012@gmail.com

COZENS, Mrs Audrey Lilian. b 35. St Hugh's Coll Ox BA 56 MA 84. Gilmore Course 79. dss 82 **d** 87 **p** 94. Shenfield *Chelmsf* 82-87; Par Dn 87-89; Par Dn Westcliff St Andr 89-94; C 94-95; P-in-c Chelmsf St Andr 95-02; P-in-c The Chignals w Mashbury 95-02; rtd 02; PtO *Chelmsf* from 02. *56 Victoria Road, Writtle, Chelmsford CM1 3PA* T: (01245) 420165
E: alcozens@btinternet.com

COZENS, Daniel Harry. b 44. Oak Hill Th Coll. **d** 71 **p** 72. C St Paul's Cray St Barn *Roch* 71-74; C Deptford St Nic w Ch Ch *S'wark* 74-76; C Deptford St Nic and St Luke 76-78; Rees Missr *Ely* 78-09; rtd 09; PtO *Ely* from 09; Six Preacher Cant Cathl 94-04. *Walnut Top, High Street, Bury, Ramsey, Huntingdon PE26 2NR*

COZENS, Canon Michael Graeme. b 59. Chich Th Coll 91. **d** 93 **p** 94. C Emscote *Cov* 93-96; C Prestbury *Glouc* 96-03; TV Prestbury and All SS 03-06; P-in-c 06-08; TR N Cheltenham 08-14; P-in-c Dursley from 14; Hon Can Glouc Cathl from 10. *The Rectory, Broadwell, Dursley GL11 4JE* T: (01453) 542035

CRABB, Helen Maria. *See* BARTON, Helen Maria

CRABB, Paul Anthony. b 58. St Chad's Coll Dur BSc 79 Leeds Univ PGCE 80. Qu Coll Birm 90. **d** 91 **p** 92. C Gomersal *Wakef* 91-95; V Drighlington 95-01; TV Dewsbury 01-09; P-in-c Hanging Heaton 09-12; P-in-c Batley St Thos 09-12; P-in-c Bramley *Leeds* from 14. *The Vicarage, 8 Hough Lane, Leeds LS13 3NE* T: 0113-257 8590 or 225 8562 M: 07946-530415
E: paulthepriest.pc@gmail.com

CRABTREE, Derek. b 32. Leic Univ BSc(Econ) 53. Cant Sch of Min 91. **d** 94 **p** 95. NSM Hackington *Cant* 94-02; Asst Chapl Kent Univ 94-02; rtd 02; PtO *Cant* from 02. *19 Monastery Street, Canterbury CT1 1NJ* T: (01227) 471503

CRABTREE, Eric. b 30. Chelt & Glouc Coll of HE BA 99 ACA 55 FCA 68. Premontre Community (RC) 58. **d** 64 **p** 64. In RC Ch 64-90; PtO *Glouc* 00-04; *Ox* from 04. *St Katharine's House, Ormond Road, Wantage OX12 8EA* T: (01235) 769279

CRABTREE, Hazel. b 40. SRN 82 Yorks & Humberside Assn for F&HE TCert 89. **d** 07 **p** 08. OLM Went Valley *Wakef* 07-10; PtO *Leeds* from 10. *11 Hillcroft Close, Darrington, Pontefract WF8 3BD* T: (01977) 793268
E: hazel@darringtonchurch.com

CRABTREE, Martine Charmaine. b 74. Glas Bible Coll BA 96 St Jo Coll Nottm MTh 02. **d** 02 **p** 03. C Kippax w Allerton Bywater *Ripon* 02-06; P-in-c Sowerby *Wakef* 06-12; P-in-c

Norland 09-12; P-in-c Lupset *Leeds* from 12; P-in-c Thornes from 12; Adv on Urban Issues from 12. *Lupset Vicarage, 23C Broadway, Wakefield WF2 8AA* T: (01422) 832830
E: martinecrabtree@aol.com

CRABTREE, Stephen. b 56. Nottm Univ BTh 80. Linc Th Coll 76. **d** 80 **p** 81. C Chorley St Pet *Blackb* 80-83; C Blackpool St Steph 83-84; C Penwortham St Mary 84-88; R Mareham-le-Fen and Revesby *Linc* 88-02; R Hameringham w Scrafield and Winceby 98-02; V Mareham on the Hill 98-02; R Washingborough w Heighington and Canwick 02-14. *2 Ollerdale Avenue, Allerton, Bradford BD15 9BQ* T: (01274) 498273 E: stephencrabtree425@yahoo.com

CRABTREE, Stephen John. b 62. Roehampton Inst BEd 85 Surrey Univ MA 93. SEITE 93. **d** 96 **p** 97. NSM N Farnborough *Guildf* 96-08; NSM Rowledge and Frensham from 08. *40 West Street, Farnham GU9 7DX* T: (01252) 541873
E: stephecrab@aol.com

CRACKNELL, Heather Louise. b 76. UEA BSc 97. ERMC 08. **d** 11 **p** 12. C Cringleford and Colney *Nor* from 11. *5 Poppy Close, Cringleford, Norwich NR4 7JZ* T: (01603) 501364
E: heather.cracknell@gmail.com

CRACKNELL, Paul Allen. b 63. NTMTC. **d** 10 **p** 11. NSM Harlow St Mary Magd *Chelmsf* 10-12. *135 Woodcroft, Harlow CM18 6YB* T: (01279) 423720 E: lastbirder@yahoo.co.uk

CRADDOCK, Jeremy Graham. b 37. Lon Univ BSc 64 Nottm Univ MPhil 72. EAMTC 93. **d** 94 **p** 95. NSM Godmanchester *Ely* 94-99; PtO from 99. *8 Hall Close, Hartford, Huntingdon PE29 1XJ* T: (01480) 458011 E: zen172463@zen.co.uk

CRADDOCK, Mrs Lesley-Ann. b 58. Ridley Hall Cam 10. **d** 12 **p** 13. C Hatfield Hyde *St Alb* from 12. *All Saints House, 7C Hall Grove, Welwyn Garden City AL7 4PJ* M: 07903-020509
E: lesley.craddock@btinternet.com

CRADDUCK, Martin Charles. b 50. Hull Univ BSc 71. St Jo Coll Nottm. **d** 79 **p** 80. C W Kilburn St Luke w St Simon and St Jude *Lon* 79-83; C Oxhey All SS *St Alb* 83-86; Asst Chapl HM Pris Man 86-87; Dep Chapl HM Young Offender Inst Glen Parva 87-89; Chapl HM Pris Stocken 89-95. *35 Worcester Road, Grantham NG31 8SF* T: (01476) 571351

CRADDUCK, Stuart William. b 74. Bp Otter Coll Chich BA 97. Ripon Coll Cuddesdon BTh 00. **d** 00 **p** 01. C W Leigh *Portsm* 00-03; Min Can St Alb Abbey *St Alb* 03-07; R Whyke w Rumboldswhyke and Portfield *Chich* 07-14; R Grantham *Linc* from 14; P-in-c Grantham, Manthorpe from 14. *The Rectory, Church Street, Grantham NG31 6RR*
E: stuart@cradduckmail.freeserve.co.uk

CRAFER, Mrs Jeanette Angela. b 48. Keswick Hall Coll CertEd 78. EAMTC 99. **d** 01 **p** 02. C Ashmanhaugh, Barton Turf etc *Nor* 01-05; P-in-c Martham and Repps w Bastwick, Thurne etc 05-07; V 07-13; rtd 13; PtO *Nor* from 14. *Whispers, Chapel Road, Sea Palling, Norwich NR12 0UQ*
T: (01692) 598590 E: jeanette.crafer@tiscali.co.uk

CRAFT, William Newham. b 46. Lon Univ BSc 68 MCIPD 70. Oak Hill Th Coll 87. **d** 89 **p** 90. C Werrington *Pet* 90-93; C-in-c Norfolk Park St Leonard CD *Sheff* 93-02; P-in-c Sheff St Jo 99-02; V 02-03; V Stapleford *S'well* 03-09; AD Beeston 07-09; rtd 09; PtO *Sheff* from 09. *435 Redmires Road, Sheffield S10 4LF* T: 0114-230 2718 E: billncraft@gmail.com

CRAGG, Edward William Adrian. b 55. St Cath Coll Cam BA 77 MA 81. Cranmer Hall Dur 97. **d** 99 **p** 00. C Clifton *York* 99-02; R Skelton w Shipton and Newton on Ouse 02-09; Chapl York Hosps NHS Foundn Trust 02-09; R Bridlington Priory *York* 09-12; V Wyke *Leeds* from 12. *The Vicarage, 6 Vicarage Close, Wyke, Bradford BD12 8QW* T: (01274) 676059
E: adrian@cragg.myzen.co.uk

CRAGG, Mrs Sandra Anne. b 45. St Hugh's Coll Ox BA 67. SEITE 94. **d** 97 **p** 98. NSM Kingston All SS w St Jo *S'wark* 97-12; NSM Kingston from 12. *10 Lingfield Avenue, Kingston upon Thames KT1 2TN* T: (020) 8546 1997 F: 8541 5281
E: sandy@toadstool.co.uk

CRAGGS, Colin Frederick. b 41. Open Univ BA 80. Sarum & Wells Th Coll 85. **d** 88 **p** 89. NSM Wilton *B & W* 88-90 and 93-06; NSM Taunton St Andr 90-93; Chapl Taunton and Somerset NHS Trust 90-06; rtd 06. *31 Highfield, Taunton TA1 5JG* T/F: (01823) 271989

CRAGGS, Michael Alfred. b 43. Open Univ BA 79. St Mich Coll Llan 66. **d** 69 **p** 70. C Clee *Linc* 69-72; C Old Brumby 72-76; TV Kingsthorpe w Northampton St Dav *Pet* 76-83; P-in-c Gt w Lt Addington 83-89; RD Higham 88-89; TR Corby SS Pet and Andr w Gt and Lt Oakley 89-02; V Corby SS Pet and Andr 02-08; RD Corby 90-95; rtd 08. *1 Johnson Drive, Scotter, Gainsborough DN21 3HA* T: (01724) 764200
E: mikeccorb@aol.com

CRAGO, Geoffrey Norman. b 44. Linc Th Coll 67. **d** 70 **p** 71. C Matson *Glouc* 70-75; V Dean Forest H Trin 75-80; Relig Progr Producer Radio Severn Sound 80-85; P-in-c Huntley *Glouc* 80-82; PtO 82-90; Dioc Communications Officer 84; Gen Syn Broadcasting Dept 85-88; Hon C Highnam, Lassington,

Rudford, Tibberton etc *Glouc* 90-08; Relig Progr Producer BBC Radio Gloucestershire 94-03; Bp's Press Officer and Dioc Communications Officer *Glouc* 97-01; rtd 09. *Milestones, 2 Two Mile Lane, Highnam, Gloucester GL2 8DW*   T: (01452) 750575 F: 08700-940404   E: g.crago@btinternet.com

CRAIG, Canon Alan Stuart. b 38. Leeds Univ BA 59. Cranmer Hall Dur. **d** 61 **p** 62. C Newcastle w Butterton *Lich* 61-65; C Scarborough St Mary w Ch Ch, St Paul and St Thos *York* 65-67; V Werrington *Lich* 67-72; Asst Chapl HM Pris Man 72-73; Chapl HM Borstal Hindley 73-78; Chapl HM Pris Acklington 78-84; V Longhirst *Newc* 84-90; R Morpeth 90-99; RD 84-95; Dir of Ords and Bp's Chapl 99-02; Hon Can Newc Cathl 90-02; Chapl Northd Mental Health NHS Trust 90-99; Chapl to The Queen 95-08; rtd 02; PtO *Newc* from 02. *5 Springfield Meadows, Alnwick NE66 2NY*   T: (01665) 602806 M: 07779-519040

CRAIG, Andrew John. b 54. Selw Coll Cam BA 76 MA 80 PhD 80 Dur Univ MBA 92. NEOC 00. **d** 03 **p** 04. NSM Stranton *Dur* from 03. *25 Egerton Road, Hartlepool TS26 0BW* T: (01429) 422461   E: andrewj.craig@ntlworld.com

CRAIG, David Paul. b 46. Univ of K Coll Halifax NS Hon DD 94. ACT. **d** 84 **p** 85. P Innisfail Australia 84-85; C St Jas Cathl Townsville 85-88; Miss to Seamen Halifax Canada 88-94; Chapl Immingham Seafarers' Cen 94-05; Gen Preacher *Linc* 97-05; P-in-c Denman Australia from 05. *33 Palace Street, Denman NSW 2328, Australia*   T: (0061) (2) 6547 2243 *or* T/F: 6547 1149   F: 6547 2249   M: 41-083 8089 E: denmanap@bigpond.net.au

CRAIG, Eric. b 39. Birm Univ BA 62. Qu Coll Birm 62. **d** 64 **p** 65. C Todmorden *Wakef* 64-68; C Hurstpierpoint *Chich* 68-70; C Cobham *Guildf* 70-73; V Dawley St Jerome *Lon* 73-76; V Stainland *Wakef* 76-87; R Yarnton w Begbroke and Shipton on Cherwell *Ox* 87-04; rtd 04; PtO *Ox* 04-09. *17 Farmers Close, Witney OX28 1NN*   T: (01993) 704892

CRAIG, Gillean Weston. b 49. York Univ BA 72 Qu Coll Cam BA 76 MA 80. Westcott Ho Cam 76. **d** 77 **p** 78. C St Marylebone Ch Ch *Lon* 77-82; C Kings St Barn 82-88; P-in-c St Geo-in-the-East w St Paul 88-89; R 89-02; V Kensington St Mary Abbots w St Geo 02-06; V Kensington St Mary Abbots w Ch Ch and St Phil from 06. *St Mary Abbots Vicarage, Vicarage Gate, London W8 4HN*   T: (020) 7937 6032 E: gillean.craig@stmaryabbotschurch.org

CRAIG, James Owen Maxwell. b 72. Open Univ BA 98. Cranmer Hall Dur 99. **d** 02 **p** 03. C Ch the K *Dur* 02-05; Gateshead and Bensham Community Chapl to Arts from 05; TV Gateshead from 11. *St Columba House, Peterborough Close, Gateshead NE8 1NL*   M: 07918-659088 E: rev.jim@btopenworld.com

CRAIG, Canon John Newcome. b 39. Selw Coll Cam BA 63 MA 67. Linc Th Coll 63. **d** 65 **p** 66. C Cannock *Lich* 65-71; V Gt Wyrley 71-79; TR Wednesfield 79-91; Prec Leic Cathl 91-03; Hon Can Leic Cathl 93-02; Can Res Leic Cathl 03-04; rtd 04; PtO *Birm* from 04. *109 Kingsbury Road, Erdington, Birmingham B24 8QH*   T: 0121-373 2809 E: john.olivia.craig@lineone.net

CRAIG, Judy Howard. *See* CRAIG PECK, Judy Howard

CRAIG, Julie Elizabeth. *See* LEAVES, Julie Elizabeth

CRAIG, Julie Elizabeth. *See* EATON, Julie Elizabeth

CRAIG, Patrick Thomas. b 36. BA. St D Coll Lamp 59 Bps' Coll Cheshunt 59. **d** 61 **p** 62. C Belfast St Mary *Conn* 61-65; C Belfast St Pet 65-69; CF 69-88; R Hartfield w Coleman's Hatch *Chich* 88-01; rtd 01; P-in-c Six Pilgrims *B & W* 03-11; PtO from 11. *Briars, Broadclose Way, Barton St David, Somerton TA11 6BS*   T: (01458) 850825   E: pat.craig092@btinternet.com

CRAIG, Richard Harvey. b 31. Em Coll Cam BA 58. Linc Th Coll. **d** 60 **p** 61. C Bottesford *Linc* 60-65; Bp's Ind Chapl 65-69; Dioc Adv on Laity *Tr Bris* 69-74; V Whitchurch 74-86; TV N Lambeth *S'wark* 86-96; Bp's Ecum Adv 88-96; Ecum Officer 90-96; rtd 96; PtO *St Alb* 96-99; *S'wark* from 01. *18 Holst Court, Westminster Bridge Road, London SE1 7JQ* T: (020) 7928 0495

CRAIG, Robin Joseph. b 43. TCD BA 65 Div Test 66 Birm Univ CertEd 70. **d** 66 **p** 67. C Carrickfergus *Conn* 66-69; Chapl Lord Wandsworth Coll Hook 75-85; Chapl K Sch Macclesfield 85-01; LtO *Ches* 85-01; rtd 01. *5 Winston Court, Lavant Road, Chichester PO19 5RG*   T: (01243) 778636

CRAIG PECK, Judy Howard. b 57. Lon Univ MB, BS 81 MRCGP 86. WMMTC 97. **d** 00 **p** 01. NSM Billing *Pet* 00-07; NSM Yardley Hastings, Denton and Grendon etc 07-15; NSM Officer 03-10; C Guilsborough and Hollowell and Cold Ashby etc from 15. *The Vicarage, 15 Church Mount, Guilsborough, Northampton NN6 8QA* E: judy@peckc.fsnet.co.uk

CRAIG-WILD, Ms Dorothy Elsie (Dhoe). b 54. Birm Univ BA 77. Qu Coll Birm 79. **dss** 81 **d** 87 **p** 94. Middleton St Mary *Ripon* 81-87; Par Dn Chapeltown *Sheff* 88-94; C 94-96; P-in-c Bruntcliffe *Wakef* 96-02; RD Birstall 98-08; Jt P-in-c Morley

St Paul 00-02; P-in-c Roberttown w Hartshead 02-08; C Heckmondwike 05-08; C Liversedge w Hightown 05-08; TV Maltby *Sheff* 08-15; C Thurcroft 09-15; R Whiston from 14. *The Rectory, Rectory Drive, Whiston, Rotherham S60 4JA* E: dhoe.craig-wild@sheffield.anglican.org

CRAIG-WILD, Peter John. b 55. Leeds Univ BA 77. Qu Coll Birm 77. **d** 80 **p** 81. C Rothwell w Lofthouse *Ripon* 80-83; C Beeston 83-87; V Chapeltown *Sheff* 87-96; RD Tankersley 93-96; V Mirfield *Wakef* 96-08; P-in-c Eastthorpe and Upper Hopton 03-07; Hon Can Wakef Cathl 03-08; RD Dewsbury 06-08; TR Maltby *Sheff* 08-14; P-in-c Thurcroft 09-14; rtd 14; PtO *Sheff* from 15. *The Rectory, Rectory Drive, Whiston, Rotherham S60 4JA*   E: peter@craig-wild.me.uk

CRAIGHEAD, Mrs Patricia Anne. b 60. Northumbria Univ BSc 02. NEOC 05. **d** 08 **p** 09. C Monkseaton St Pet *Newc* 08-12; V Long Benton St Mary from 12. *St Mary's Vicarage, Blackfriars Way, Newcastle upon Tyne NE12 8ST*   M: 07967-316615 E: patcraighead@hotmail.co.uk

CRAM, Mrs Ruth Frances Isobel. b 52. Kingston Poly BA 87 Poly Cen Lon MA 92. NOC 94. **d** 97 **p** 98. C E Crompton *Man* 97-99; C Cirencester *Glouc* 99-02; C Broad Blunsdon *Bris* 02; V N Swindon St Andr 02-05; rtd 05. *52 Hague Street, Glossop SK13 8NS*   T: (01457) 868107   E: rc.cram@btinternet.com

CRAMERI, Mrs Mary Barbara. b 44. K Coll Lon BD 65 AKC 91 Lon Inst of Educn PGCE 66. S Dios Minl Tr Scheme 86. **d** 88 **p** 94. C Whitton SS Phil and Jas *Lon* 88-91; Staff Member STETS 91-97; Minl Development Officer 97-98; Vice-Prin Sarum Coll 93-98; Par Dn Bemerton *Sarum* 91-92; TV Pewsey and Swanborough 98-00; TR Whitton 00-01; rtd 01; PtO *Sarum* 02-05; *Ox* from 10; *Cov* from 10; Hon C Chase *Ox* 05-10. *6 Browning Close, Stratford-upon-Avon CV37 7PF* T: (01789) 296650   E: mary.crameri@btinternet.com

CRAMP, Barry Leonard. b 46. St Luke's Coll Ex CertEd 67 CChem 76   MRSC 76. **d** 04 **p** 05. OLM Ditchingham, Hedenham, Broome, Earsham etc *Nor* from 04. *Wyvern, The Street, Earsham, Bungay NR35 2TY*   T: (01986) 895535 E: sue@sbcramp.waitrose.com

CRAMP, Susan Louise. b 53. Univ of Wales (Abth) BSc 74 Leic Univ PGCE 75. **d** 04 **p** 05. OLM Ditchingham, Hedenham, Broome, Earsham etc *Nor* from 04. *Wyvern, The Street, Earsham, Bungay NR35 2TY*   T: (01986) 895535 E: sbcramp@waitrose.com

CRAMPTON, John Leslie. b 41. CITC 64. **d** 67 **p** 68. C Lurgan Ch the Redeemer *D & D* 67-71; C Dundela St Mark 71-73; C Umtali Rhodesia 73-76; R Fort Victoria 73-76; I Killanne w Killegney, Rossdroit and Templeshanbo *C & O* 82-88; Preb Ferns Cathl 85-88; Chapl Wilson's Hosp Sch Multyfarnham *M & K* 88-91; C Mullingar, Portnashangan, Moyliscar, Kilbixy etc 89-91; I Athy w Kilberry, Fontstown and Kilkea *D & G* 91-01; Can Ch Ch Cathl Dublin 95-01; I Geashill w Killeigh and Ballycommon *M & K* 01-06; rtd 06. *41 Beech Avenue, The Paddock, Enniscorthy, Co Wexford, Republic of Ireland* T: (00353) (53) 923 2589   M: 87-907 7981 E: janetcrampton14@gmail.com

CRANE, Miss Alison Mary. b 63. **d** 14 **p** 15. C Hedge End St Luke *Win* from 14. *44 Westbury Court, Hedge End, Southampton SO30 0HN*   T: (01489) 808311 E: alisoncrane2013@gmail.com

CRANE, Mrs Janet. **d** 14 **p** 15. OLM Chell *Lich* from 14. *18 Vickers Road, Stoke-on-Trent ST6 6NR*   T: (01782) 257814 E: jcrane8@googlemail.com

CRANE, John Walter. b 32. Chich Th Coll. **d** 58 **p** 59. C Forest Town *S'well* 58-60; C Primrose Hill St Mary w Avenue Road St Paul *Lon* 60-64; R Greenford H Cross 64-67; Min Can and Chapl Windsor 67-79; Chapl St Geo Sch Ascot 67-79; Warden Dioc Retreat Ho (Holland Ho) Cropthorne *Worc* 79-83; P-in-c Harvington and Norton and Lenchwick 84-87; rtd 87. *16 Allesborough Drive, Pershore WR10 1JH* T: (01386) 556444

CRANE, Mrs Judith. b 53. Matlock Coll of Educn BCombStuds 81. Cranmer Hall Dur 94. **d** 96 **p** 97. C Tadcaster w Newton Kyme *York* 96-99; TV Brayton 99-02; V Blackwell w Tibshelf *Derby* 02-08; Asst Dir of Ords 06-09; PtO from 09. *27 Highfield Road, Little Eaton, Derby DE21 5AG*   T: (01332) 833872   E: judithcrane@yahoo.co.uk

CRANFIELD, Nicholas William Stewart. b 56. Mert Coll Ox BA 77 MA 81 DPhil 88 Leeds Univ BA 81 Selw Coll Cam PhD 95 FSA 07. Coll of Resurr Mirfield 79 Union Th Sem (NY) STM 84. **d** 86 **p** 87. C Ascot Heath *Ox* 86-89; Prin Berks Chr Tr Scheme 89-92; Hon C Reading St Mary the Virgin 89-92; Chapl and Fell Selw Coll Cam 92-99; Dean of Chpl 94-99; Chapl Newnham Coll Cam 92-99; V Blackheath All SS *S'wark* from 99; Chapl St Dunstan's Coll Catford 00-05. *All Saints' Vicarage, 10 Duke Humphrey Road, London SE3 0TY* T: (020) 8852 4280   E: vicar@allsaintsblackheath.org

CRANIDGE, Mrs Wendy Ann. b 31. Sheff Univ CertEd 52. Cant Sch of Min 81. **dss** 84 **d** 87 **p** 94. Roch 84-88; Hon Par

Dn 87-88; Soc Resp Adv *Cant* and *Roch* 86-88; Hon C Washingborough w Heighington and Canwick *Linc* 88-92; PtO 92-93; *Roch* 93-94; C Farnborough 94-96; rtd 96; PtO *Roch* 96-02; *Leeds* from 04. *1 Fern Valley Chase, Todmorden OL14 7HB* T: (01706) 815062

CRANKSHAW, Ronald. b 41. Coll of Resurr Mirfield 74. **d** 76 **p** 77. C Orford St Andr *Liv* 76; C N Meols 76-79; V Abram 79-85; V Wigan St Anne 85-99; AD Wigan W 94-99; V Heston *Lon* 99-07; rtd 07; PtO *Carl* from 09. *Orchard House, Westlinton, Carlisle CA6 6AA* T: (01228) 791434
E: roncrankshaw@sky.com

CRANMER, Ms Elaine. b 56. Hockerill Coll Cam CertEd 77. SEITE 97. **d** 00 **p** 01. C Charlton *S'wark* 00-03; P-in-c Eltham Park St Luke 03-10; V 11-14; AD Eltham and Mottingham 06-13; TR S Chatham H Trin *Roch* from 14. *The Rectory, 18 Marion Close, Chatham ME5 9QA* T: (01634) 685556
E: rev.elaine@virgin.net

CRANMER, John Abery. b 33. K Alfred's Coll Win CertEd 56 Southn Univ MPhil 69. **d** 94 **p** 00. NSM Crawley and Littleton and Sparsholt w Lainston *Win* 94-02; rtd 02; PtO *Win* 02-13. *The Coach House, Crawley, Winchester SO21 2PU* T: (01962) 776214

CRANSHAW, Trevor Raymond. b 58. Trin Coll Bris 00. **d** 03 **p** 04. C Westbury-on-Trym H Trin *Bris* 03-07; P-in-c Wheathill Priory Gp *B & W* 07-14; P-in-c Clevedon St Andr and Ch Ch from 14. *The Vicarage, 10B Coleridge Road, Clevedon BS21 7TB* M: 07753-397404 E: trevcranshaw@hotmail.com

CRANSTON, Andrew David. b 79. Ex Univ MEng 02 PGCE 04 Cam Univ BTh 11. Ridley Hall Cam 08. **d** 11 **p** 12. C Stone Ch Ch and Oulton *Lich* 11-14; Chapl Oswestry Sch from 14. *Oswestry School, Upper Brook Street, Oswestry SY11 2TL* T: (01691) 655711 E: ac@oswestryschool.org.uk

CRANSTON, Miss Margaret Elizabeth. b 56. Newnham Coll Cam BEd 78 Ex Univ BTh 10. SWMTC 04. **d** 07 **p** 08. NSM Heanton Punchardon w Marwood *Ex* 07-13; NSM Isle Valley *B & W* from 13. *55 Adams Meadow, Ilminster TA19 9DB* E: mecranston@btinternet.com

CRANSWICK, James Harvard. b 22. Melbourne Univ BA 47 St Cath Coll Ox BA 50 MA 54 Birm Univ MA 76. Wycliffe Hall Ox 49. **d** 50 **p** 51. C Werneth *Man* 50-51; C St Pancras H Cross w St Jude and St Pet *Lon* 52-54; P-in-c Dartford St Alb *Roch* 54-56; Australia 56-66 and from 70; C Raynes Park St Sav *S'wark* 68-70; rtd 88. *Rhodoglade Retirement Village, 3/1502 Mount Dandenong Tourist Road, Olinda VIC 3788 Australia* T: (0061) (3) 9751 0021 F: 9754 3518
E: jimcranswick@hotmail.com

CRANWELL, Brian Robert. b 32. Sheff Poly MSc Sheff Hallam Univ MPhil 06. Cranmer Hall Dur. **d** 84 **p** 85. C Ecclesfield *Sheff* 84-86; V Handsworth Woodhouse 86-99; rtd 99; PtO *Sheff* from 99; *Derby* from 00. *9 Westview Close, Totley, Sheffield S17 3LT* T: 0114-262 1499 E: brian_cranwell@lineone.net

CRASKE, Leslie Gordon Hamilton. b 29. AKC 54 Lambeth STh 80. **d** 55 **p** 56. C Malden St Jo *S'wark* 55-58; C Streatham St Leon 58-60; S Rhodesia 60-65; Rhodesia 65-66; V Upper Norwood St Jo *Cant* 67-83; R Guernsey St Sav *Win* 83-97; rtd 97; PtO *Win* from 97. *La Gruterie, 3 Mount Row, St Peter Port, Guernsey GY1 1NS* T: (01481) 716027

CRASTON (née FULLALOVE), Mrs Brenda Hurst. b 33. Open Univ BA 75 Man Univ MPhil 86. St Mich Ho Ox 58. **dss** 80 **d** 87 **p** 94. Par Dn Bolton St Paul w Em *Man* 87-93; rtd 93; PtO *Man* from 93. *12 Lever Park Avenue, Horwich, Bolton BL6 7LE* T: (01204) 699972

CRASTON, Canon Richard Colin. b 22. Bris Univ BA 49 Lon Univ BD 51 Lambeth DD 92. Tyndale Hall Bris 46. **d** 51 **p** 52. C Dur St Nic 51-54; V Bolton St Paul *Man* 54-76; P-in-c Bolton Em 64-66; V 66-76; Hon Can Man Cathl 68-95; RD Bolton 72-92; V Bolton St Paul w Em 77-86; TR 86-93; Chapl to The Queen 85-92; rtd 93; PtO *Man* from 93. *12 Lever Park Avenue, Horwich, Bolton BL6 7LE* T: (01204) 699972

CRAVEN, Miss Alison Ruth Miranda. b 63. Cen Sch Speech & Drama BSc 86. Westcott Ho Cam 05. **d** 07 **p** 08. C Chelsea St Luke and Ch Ch *Lon* 07-11; V Wyke *Guildf* from 12. *Wyke Vicarage, Guildford Road, Normandy, Guildford GU3 2DA* T: (01483) 811777
E: alisoncraven584@btinternet.com

CRAVEN, Colin Peter. b 48. Dartmouth RN Coll. St Steph Ho Ox 83. **d** 85 **p** 86. C Holbeach *Linc* 85-88; Chapl Fleet Hosp 86-97; TV Grantham *Linc* 88-97; P-in-c Fairfield *Derby* 97-03; OCM 48-03; CF 03-06; Rtd Officer Chapl RAChD 06-14; rtd 14. *154 Mudeford Lane, Christchurch BH23 3HS* E: revcp@hotmail.com

CRAVEN, David Alex. b 80. Univ of Wales (Ban) BA 01. Wycliffe Hall Ox BTh 06. **d** 06 **p** 07. C Holme Eden and Wetheral w Warwick *Carl* 06-09; R from 09; C Croglin 06-09; P-in-c 09-12. *The Rectory, Warwick Bridge, Carlisle CA4 8RF* T: (01228) 560332 E: dacraven@hotmail.com

CRAVEN, Janet Elizabeth. *See* CHAPMAN, Janet Elizabeth

CRAVEN, Mrs Janet Mary. b 43. Bp Otter Coll TCert 64. **d** 06 **p** 07. OLM Shelley and Shepley *Leeds* from 06. *70 Jenkyn Lane, Shepley, Huddersfield HD8 8AW* T: (01484) 604107
E: jmcraven@btinternet.com

CRAVEN, Rebecca Clare. b 58. Bris Univ BDS 80 Glas Univ MPH 90 Man Univ PhD 97 RCPS FDS 97. **d** 01 **p** 02. OLM Reddish *Man* 01-06; NSM 06-07; NSM Salford Sacred Trin and St Phil from 07. *201 Thornton Road, Fallowfield, Manchester M14 7NS* T: 0161-225 7336
E: rebecca.c.craven@manchester.ac.uk

CRAW, Jane Mary. b 47. **d** 10 **p** 11. NSM Sherborne w Castleton, Lillington and Longburton *Sarum* from 10. *Jubilee Cottage, Lower Kingsbury, Milborne Port, Sherborne DT9 5ED* T: (01963) 251527 E: jane@jubileecottage.plus.com

CRAWFORD, Mrs Anne Elizabeth. b 59. SAOMC 01. **d** 04 **p** 05. C Billington, Egginton, Hockliffe etc *St Alb* 04-08; R Toddington and Chalgrave from 08. *The Rectory, 41 Leighton Road, Toddington, Dunstable LU5 6AL* T: (01525) 872298
E: annie.anselm@btinternet.com

CRAWFORD, Duncan Alexander. b 59. Newc Univ BA 81 MA 83 K Coll Lon CertEd 83. St Jo Coll Nottm 86. **d** 89 **p** 90. C Hatcham St Jas *S'wark* 89-92; PtO 93-02. *Gortestraat 44, 2311 NM Leiden, The Netherlands*

CRAWFORD, Canon Ivy Elizabeth. b 50. Trin Coll Bris 83. **dss** 85 **d** 87 **p** 94. Collier Row St Jas *Chelmsf* 85; Collier Row St Jas and Havering-atte-Bower 86-89; Par Dn 87-89; Par Dn Harlow New Town w Lt Parndon 89-94; C Harlow Town Cen w Lt Parndon 94-95; V Blackmore and Stondon Massey 95-09; RD Ongar 06-09; P-in-c Broxted w Chickney and Tilty etc from 09; CME Adv from 09; Hon Can Chelmsf Cathl from 98. *The Rectory, Park Road, Little Easton, Dunmow CM6 2JJ* T: (01371) 872509
E: ivycrawford@btinternet.com

CRAWFORD, James Robert Harry. b 55. Cumbria Univ BA 09. CBDTI 00. **d** 03 **p** 04. NSM Lower Darwen St Jas *Blackb* 03-10; C Colne and Villages 10-14; C Pendle Deanery from 14. *St Mary's Vicarage, Burnley Road, Trawden, Colne BB8 8PN* T: (01282) 864046 M: 07923-484785
E: jayjay644@btinternet.com

CRAWFORD, Kenneth Ian. b 48. Melbourne Univ BMus 77 Columbia Univ MA 79 MEd 80 MACE 84. Trin Coll Melbourne BD 86. **d** 87 **p** 87. C Ringwood St Paul Australia 87-89; C Cheltenham St Matt 89-90; P-in-c Vermont S H Name 90-93; Can Prec Melbourne Cathl 93-97; P-in-c Warndon St Nic *Worc* 97-03; V Pershore w Pinvin, Wick and Birlingham 03-14; P-in-c Darlington St Jas *Dur* from 14. *The Vicarage, 30 Smithfield Road, Darlington DL1 4DD*

CRAWFORD, Michael Davis. b 45. Oak Hill Th Coll BA 97 K Coll Lon PGCE 98. **d** 00 **p** 01. NSM New Barnet St Jas *St Alb* 00-04; C Limassol St Barn Cyprus 04-08; Chapl SE Cyprus 08-11; PtO *Eur* from 11; Cyprus and the Gulf from 11. *3 Brewers Green Lane, Diss IP22 4QP* T: (01379) 650365 M: 07527-480921 E: rev.michaelcrawford@gmail.com

CRAWFORD JONES, Neil. *See* JONES, Neil Crawford

CRAWFORD-McCAFFERTY, Louise Dorothy Anita. b 60. Oak Hill Th Coll BA 91 Princeton Th Sem MDiv 00. Irish Sch of Ecum MPhil 02. **d** 02 **p** 03. C Drumragh w Mountfield *D & R* 02-05; I Aghadowey w Kilrea from 05. *40 Brone Road, Garvagh, Coleraine BT51 4EQ* T: (028) 7086 9277 M: 07890-745359
E: lcrawfordmccafferty@yahoo.com

CRAWLEY, Alan John. b 58. Trin Coll Cam MA 83. SAOMC 04. **d** 07 **p** 08. NSM Gt Marlow w Marlow Bottom, Lt Marlow and Bisham *Ox* 07-08; C Amersham on the Hill 08-11; P-in-c Badshot Lea and Hale *Guildf* 11-15; NSM from 15. *The Rectory, 25 Upper Hale Road, Farnham GU9 0NX* T: (01252) 820537
E: reverend.alan@gmail.com

CRAWLEY, Canon David. b 47. TD . St Steph Ho Ox 75. **d** 78 **p** 79. C Solihull *Birm* 78-81; TV Newbury *Ox* 81-84; LtO 84-95; Chapl Stoke Mandeville Hosp Aylesbury 84-95; Distr Chapl 88-95; Hd Chapl Services W Suffolk Hosps NHS Trust 95-11; Bp's Adv on Hosp Chapl *St E* from 00; Hon Can St E Cathl from 05; Chapl from 11. *22 Westbury Avenue, Bury St Edmunds IP33 3QE* T: (01284) 750526

CRAWLEY (née FELLOWS), Lesley June. b 70. Salford Univ BEng 91 New Coll Ox DPhil 01. Ox Min Course 04. **d** 07 **p** 08. C Bernwode *Ox* 07-11; NSM Badshot Lea and Hale *Guildf* 12-15; R from 15. *The Rectory, 25 Upper Hale Road, Farnham GU9 0NX* T: (01252) 820537 E: revdlesley@gmail.com

CRAWLEY, Nicholas Simon. b 58. Southn Univ BSc 79 ACIB 82 AIIM 85. Wycliffe Hall Ox 85. **d** 88 **p** 89. C E Twickenham St Steph *Lon* 88-93; R Avondale Zimbabwe 93-99; P-in-c Netherthorpe St Steph *Sheff* 99-04; Network Miss P (Bris Adnry) from 04; P-in-c Clifton H Trin, St Andr and St Pet 10-12. *27 Carnarvon Road, Bristol BS6 7DU* T: 0117-944 1980 E: nick.crawley@blueyonder.co.uk

CRAWLEY, Simon Ewen. b 31. Em Coll Cam BA 57 MA 60. Ridley Hall Cam 56. **d** 58 **p** 59. C Denton Holme *Carl* 58-61;

P-in-c Cinderford St Steph w Littledean *Glouc* 61-67; V Margate H Trin *Cant* 67-74; V Folkestone H Trin w Ch Ch 74-81; R Patterdale *Carl* 81-87; RD Penrith 83-86; R Culworth w Sulgrave and Thorpe Mandeville etc *Pet* 87-95; RD Brackley 89-95; rtd 95; PtO *Ex* 96-03; *York* from 03. *Blacksmith Cottage, Main Street, Healaugh, Tadcaster LS24 8DB* T: (01937) 830160

CRAWSHAW, Clinton. b 70. St Steph Ho Ox. **d** 02 **p** 03. C Hendon St Alphage *Lon* 02-04; rtd 04. *21 Beckmeadow Way, Mundesley, Norwich NR11 8LP* E: revcrawshaw@yahoo.com

CRAWTE, William Richard. b 30. TCD BA 54. **d** 55 **p** 56. C Belfast St Aid *Conn* 55-57; C Newcastle *D & D* 57-59; CF 59-79. *38 Heath Estate, Great Waldingfield, Sudbury CO10 0TZ* T: (01787) 377356

✠**CRAY, The Rt Revd Graham Alan.** b 47. Leeds Univ BA 68. St Jo Coll Nottm 69. **d** 71 **p** 72 **c** 01. C Gillingham St Mark *Roch* 71-75; N Area Co-ord CPAS Youth Dept 75-78; C York St Mich-le-Belfrey 78-82; V 82-92; Prin Ridley Hall Cam 92-01; Six Preacher Cant Cathl 97-01; Suff Bp Maidstone 01-09; Abps' Missr and Team Ldr Fresh Expressions 09-14; Hon Asst Bp Cant 09-14; rtd 14. *The Dovecote, Main Street, Kirby Misperton, Malton YO17 6XL* T: (01653) 669365 E: grahamcray@me.com

CRAY, Mrs Jacqueline. b 49. Glos Coll of Educn CertEd 70. SEITE 01. **d** 04 **p** 05. NSM Gt Chart *Cant* 04-08; P-in-c Maidstone St Faith 08-14; Asst Dir of Ords 09-14; rtd 14; PtO *York* from 14. *The Dovecote, Main Street, Kirby Misperton, Malton YO17 6XL* M: 07889-742973 T: (01653) 669365 E: jackiecray@hotmail.co.uk

CREAN, Patrick John Eugene. b 38. TCD BA 81 MA 84. Edin Th Coll 82. **d** 84 **p** 85. C Perth St Jo *St And* 84-86; P-in-c Liv St Phil w St Dav 86-87; V 87-90; R Cupar and Ladybank *St And* 90-92; P-in-c Sefton *Liv* 92-97; Dioc Children's Officer 92-03; V Aintree St Giles 97-98; V Aintree St Giles w St Pet 98-03; rtd 03; PtO *Liv* from 03. *36 Lingfield Close, Netherton, Bootle L30 1BB* T: 0151-525 8838

CREASER, Canon David Edward. b 35. St Cath Coll Cam BA 58 MA 62. Clifton Th Coll 59. **d** 61 **p** 62. C Cheadle *Ches* 61-67; V Weston *Bradf* 67-69; P-in-c Denton 67-69; V Weston w Denton 69-74 and 82-02; Dir Educn 73-96; V Frizinghall 74-82; V Weston w Denton 82-02; Hon Can Bradf Cathl 80-02; P-in-c Leathley w Farnley, Fewston and Blubberhouses 96-02; rtd 02; PtO *Leeds* from 03. *Rose Cottage, Pant Lane, Austwick, Lancaster LA2 8BH* T: (01542) 51536 E: david.creaser@bradford.anglican.org

CREASEY, Mrs Alison Frances. b 72. Yorks Min Course 12. **d** 15. NSM Dore *Sheff* from 15. *142 Meadowhead, Sheffield S8 7UF* M: 07968-100137

CREASEY, David John. b 46. Univ of Wales (Abth) BSc 69. **d** 06 **p** 07. OLM Ringstone in Aveland Gp *Linc* 06-13; C Corby Glen 14; PtO from 14. *37 Stainfield Road, Hanthorpe, Bourne PE10 0RE* T: (01778) 570553 E: hanthorpefarm@btconnect.com

CREASEY, Graham. *See* GOLDSTONE-CREASEY, Graham

CREBER, Preb Arthur Frederick. b 45. NOC 84. **d** 87 **p** 88. C Rickerscote *Lich* 87-91; V Gt Wyrley 91-99; RD Rugeley 94-98; P-in-c Newcastle w Butterton 99-07; R 07-08; Preb Lich Cathl 04-08; rtd 08; PtO *St As* from 09. *22 Malvern Rise, Rhos-on-Sea, Colwyn Bay LL28 4RX* T: (01492) 547761 E: arthur.creber@btinternet.com

CREDITON, Suffragan Bishop of. *See* MULLALLY, The Rt Revd Dame Sarah Elisabeth

CREE, John Richard. b 44. Open Univ BA 74 Lanc Univ MA 92. Coll of Resurr Mirfield. **d** 83 **p** 84. C Blackb St Jas 83-86; V Feniscowles 86-01; Chapl Blackb Coll 86-01; R Chorley St Laur *Blackb* 01-09; rtd 09; PtO *Bre* from 86; *Blackb* from 09. *5 Bromley Green, Chorley PR6 8TX* T: (01257) 263398 E: john.cree@tiscali.co.uk

CREER, Irene. *See* SHAW, Irene

CREES, David Paul. b 68. Southn Univ BSc 89. Trin Coll Bris BA 99 MA 00. **d** 00 **p** 01. C Patcham *Chich* 00-04; CF from 04. *c/o MOD Chaplains (Army)* F: 381824 T: (01264) 383430

CREES, Geoffrey William. b 35. Open Univ BA 85. Cranmer Hall Dur 65. **d** 67 **p** 68. C Hoddesdon *St Alb* 67-70; C Harwell and Chilton All SS *Ox* 70-73; V Greenham 73-82; TR Marfleet and AD E Hull *York* 82-88; TR Rodbourne Cheney *Bris* 88-99; rtd 99; PtO *Glouc* from 99. *The Thatch, New Road, Popes Hill, Newnham GL14 1JT* T: (01452) 760843

CREGAN, Mark. b 59. Lon Bible Coll BA 91. Wycliffe Hall Ox 95. **d** 97 **p** 98. C Chippenham St Pet *Bris* 97-01; P-in-c Stapleton 01-05; Asst Chapl Colston's Sch Bris 01-03; Chapl 03-05; Chapl Stanley Bay All SS Egypt 05-07; P-in-c Casablanca *Eur* 07-12; PtO *B & W* 13; R Clutton w Cameley, Bishop Sutton and Stowey from 13. *Cameley Rectory, Main Road, Temple Cloud, Bristol BS39 5DA* T: (01761) 451315 M: 07770-295461 E: r.cregan59@gmail.com

CREGEEN, Canon Gary Marshall. b 62. Oak Hill Th Coll BA 00. **d** 00 **p** 01. C Carl St Jo 00-03; P-in-c Scotby and Cotehill w Cumwhinton 03-05; V 06-12; N Area Chapl Cumbria Constabulary 04-12; RD Brampton 09-12; TR S Barrow from 12; RD Barrow from 12; Hon Can Carl Cathl from 14. *The Rectory, 98 Roose Road, Barrow-in-Furness LA13 9RL* T: (01229) 877367 E: gmcregeen@btinternet.com

CREIGHTON, Canon Frederick David. b 50. TCD BTh 88 ACII 74. **d** 88 **p** 89. C Lisburn Ch Ch *Conn* 88-91; I Drumclamph w Lower and Upper Langfield *D & R* 91-00; I Glendermott from 00; Can Derry Cathl from 08. *Glendermott Rectory, 11 Church Brae, Altnagelvin BT47 2LS* T: (028) 7134 3001

CREIGHTON, Mrs Judith. b 36. Reading Univ BSc 57. Trin Coll Bris 80 Edin Th Coll 81. **dss** 83 **d** 87 **p** 94. Greenock *Glas* 83-85; Lawrence Weston *Bris* 85-87; Par Dn Kingswood 87-90; Chapl Stoke Park and Purdown Hosps Stapleton 90-91; Chapl Phoenix NHS Trust 92-93; Hon C Marshfield w Cold Ashton and Tormarton etc *Bris* 93-97; rtd 96; PtO *Bris* from 97. *Rose Cottage, West Littleton, Marshfield, Chippenham SN14 8JE* T: (01225) 891021

CREIGHTON, Ms Rachel Margaret Maxwell. b 64. Br Is Nazarene Coll BTh 86 BD 87 Lon Bible Coll MA 89 Man Univ MA. Cranmer Hall Dur 92. **d** 94 **p** 95. C Basford w Hyson Green *S'well* 94-96; C Nottingham All SS 96-98; P-in-c Broxtowe 98-02; Chapl HM Pris Bedf 02-04; Chapl HM Pris Wellingborough 04-09; I Belfast H Trin and St Silas *Conn* from 09. *The Rectory, 313 Ballysillan Road, Belfast BT14 6RD* T: (028) 9071 3046 M: 07748-063770 E: rachel.creighton64@btinternet.com

CRELLIN, Gary Paul. b 67. Kingston Poly BSc 88 Aston Business Sch MBA 06. WEMTC 11. **d** 14 **p** 15. NSM Stoke Prior, Wychbold and Upton Warren *Worc* from 14. *The Lodge, 11 Turton Gardens, Feckenham, Redditch B96 6JB* T: (01527) 893081 E: revgarycrellin@gmail.com

CRELLIN, Howard Joseph. b 30. Magd Coll Cam BA 52 MA 56 Magd Coll Ox BA 54 MA 56. Wycliffe Hall Ox 53. **d** 55 **p** 56. C Dovercourt *Chelmsf* 55-58; R Theydon Garnon 58-70; Select Preacher Ox Univ 68; PtO *Ox* 70-82; Hon C High Wycombe 72-77; Asst Master K Chas I Sch Kidderminster 74-80; Caldicott Sch Farnham 80-82; PtO *Chelmsf* 82-91; Asst Master Fryerns Sch Basildon 82-88; St Anselm's Sch Basildon 88-91; P-in-c Whatfield w Semer, Nedging and Naughton *St E* 91-98; rtd 98; PtO *St E* from 98; *Eur* from 02. *10 Green Willows, Lavenham, Sudbury CO10 9SP* T: (01787) 247588

CREMIN (née LAKE), Mrs Eileen Veronica. b 58. Aston Tr Scheme 83 Sarum & Wells Th Coll 85. **d** 88 **p** 94. Par Dn Islington St Mary *Lon* 88-92; Asst Chapl Homerton Hosp Lon 92-94; Asst Chapl Hackney Hosp Gp Lon 92-94; P-in-c Brondesbury Ch Ch and St Laur *Lon* 94-01; C Douglas Union w Frankfield *C, C & R* 01-06; I Fermoy Union from 06. *The Rectory, Forglen Terrace, Fermoy, Co Cork, Republic of Ireland* T: (00353) (25) 31016 M: 86-333 0206 E: evcremin@eircom.net *or* ecremin@hotmail.com

CRESSEY, Canon Roger Wilson. b 35. Chich Th Coll 72. **d** 74 **p** 75. C Pontefract St Giles *Wakef* 74-77; Hon C Dewsbury All SS 77-80; Chapl Pinderfields Gen Hosp Wakef 80-94; Chapl Carr Gate Hosp Wakef 80-94; Chapl Fieldhead Hosp Wakef 80-94; Chapl Pinderfields and Pontefract Hosps NHS Trust 94-00; Hon Can Wakef Cathl 98-00; rtd 00. *1 Wellhead Mews, Chapelthorpe, Wakefield WF4 3JG* T: (01924) 258972 E: roger-cressey@supanet.com

CRESSWELL, Howard Rex. b 31. Ely Th Coll 56. **d** 59 **p** 60. C Dovercourt *Chelmsf* 59-61; C Victoria Docks Ascension 61-64; V 64-71; R E w W Harling *Nor* 71-72; TV Quidenham w Eccles and Snetterton 72-75; V Arminghall 75-82; R Caistor w Markshall 75-82; V Trowse 75-82; V Heigham St Barn w St Bart 82-91; rtd 91; PtO *Nor* from 91. *4 Haverscroft Close, Taverham, Norwich NR8 6LU* E: howardcresswell@hotmail.com

CRESSWELL, Jane Stella. b 62. Bris Univ BA 84. SEITE 04. **d** 07 **p** 08. C Sutton *S'wark* 07-11; P-in-c Nork *Guildf* from 11. *St Paul's Vicarage, Warren Road, Banstead SM7 1LG* T: (01737) 353849 E: janecresswell523@btinternet.com

CRESSWELL, Canon Jeremy Peter. b 49. St Jo Coll Ox BA 72 MA 78 K Coll Lon MA 83. Ridley Hall Cam 73. **d** 75 **p** 76. C Wisley w Pyrford *Guildf* 75-78; C Weybridge 78-82; P-in-c E Clandon 82-83; P-in-c W Clandon 82-83; R E and W Clandon 83-90; V Oxshott from 90; RD Leatherhead 03-08; Hon Can Owerri from 01; Hon Can Guildf Cathl from 10. *The Vicarage, Steel's Lane, Oxshott, Leatherhead KT22 0QH* T: (01372) 842071 E: vicar@standrewsoxshott.org.uk

CRESSWELL, Richard James. b 78. Liv Univ BDS 01. St Jo Coll Nottm 13. **d** 15. C Lilleshall and Muxton *Lich* from 15. *3 Wild Thyme Drive, Muxton, Telford TF2 8RU* M: 07974-157862 E: revrichcresswell@gmail.com

CRETNEY, Mrs Antonia Lois. b 48. York Univ BA 69 Bris Univ BA 87 PGCE 89. S Dios Minl Tr Scheme 92. **d** 94 **p** 95. NSM Bedminster *Bris* 94-96; C 96-97; P-in-c Beedon and Peasemore w W Ilsley and Farnborough *Ox* 97-99; R 99-04; Deanery P Wantage from 04; Bp's Adv for Women in Ord Min *Ox* from 05. *8 Elm Farm Close, Grove, Wantage OX12 9FD* T: (01235) 763192 E: antcret@aol.com

CREW, Ruan John. b 70. Bris Univ BSc 92 PGCE 93 All Nations Chr Coll BA 99 Anglia Ruskin Univ MA 10. ERMC 07. **d** 10 **p** 11. C Almondsbury and Olveston *Bris* 10-13; C Pilning w Compton Greenfield 10-13; Chapl Voorschoten *Eur* from 13. *Chopinlaan 17, 2253 BS Voorschoten, Netherlands* T: (0031) (71) 561 3020 E: ruancrew@gmail.com

CRIBB, Mrs Karen Elisabeth. b 63. Liv Univ BA 85 Leeds Univ BA 10. Yorks Min Course 97. **d** 10 **p** 11. NSM Sheff St Mary Bramall Lane from 10; Bp's Adv for SSM from 14. *St Mary's Church, Bramall Lane, Sheffield S2 4QZ* T: 0114-223 0237 E: revkaren@stmarys-church.co.uk

CRICHTON, James Kenneth. b 35. Glouc Sch of Min 78. **d** 80 **p** 80. NSM Minchinhampton *Glouc* 80-83; NSM Nailsworth 83-86; Dep Chapl HM Pris Pentonville 86-87; Chapl HM Pris The Mount 87-97; rtd 97. *Pennant, Horeb, Llandysul SA44 4JG* T: (01559) 362448

CRICK, Peter. b 39. Lon Univ BD 68 NY Univ DMin 84. Wells Th Coll 66. **d** 67 **p** 68. C Horsham *Chich* 67-71; Asst Dioc Youth Officer *Ox* 71-75; R Denham 75-88; Bp's Adv for CME *Dur* 88-97; P-in-c Coniscliffe 88-97; Hon Can Dur Cathl 93-97; R City of Bris 97-04; rtd 04; PtO *Win* from 06. *7 Westfield Common, Hamble, Southampton SO31 4LB* T: (023) 8045 7025 E: pandvcrick@btinternet.com

CRICK, Philip Benjamin Denton (Ben). b 33. Bris Univ BA 63. Clifton Th Coll 60. **d** 64 **p** 65. C Clerkenwell St Jas and St Jo w St Pet *Lon* 64-67; CF 67-72; C Southall Green St Jo *Lon* 72-75; P-in-c Southall H Trin 75-83; P-in-c Kidbrooke St Jas *S'wark* 83-85; TV 85-92; C E Acton St Dunstan w St Thos *Lon* 92-95; Sub-Chapl HM Pris Wormwood Scrubs 92-95; rtd 95; PtO *Cant* from 95; Sub-Chapl HM Pris *Cant* 97-06. *232 Canterbury Road, Birchington CT7 9TD* T: (01843) 846049 M: 07818-040651 E: ben.crick@ormail.co.uk

CRIDLAND, Clarissa Rosemary Dorothea. b 55. STETS 03. **d** 06 **p** 07. NSM Coleford w Holcombe *B & W* from 06. *4 Rock Terrace, Church Street, Coleford, Radstock BA3 5NF* T: (01373) 812705 M: 07800-578967 E: clarissacridland@hotmail.co.uk

CRINKS, Kevin David. b 63. Aston Tr Scheme 86 Sarum & Wells Th Coll BTh 91. **d** 93 **p** 94. C Aylesford *Roch* 93-96; C Hessle *York* 96-97; TV Upholland *Liv* 97-00; V Platt Bridge 00-09; P-in-c Leigh St Mary *Man* 09-12; V from 12; Borough Dean Wigan 10-13. *The Vicarage, Westleigh Lane, Leigh WN7 5NW* T: (01942) 882883 M: 07933-750913 E: kcrinks@btinternet.com

CRIPPS, Martyn Cyril Rowland. b 46. Birm Univ LLB 68 Solicitor 71. Wycliffe Hall Ox 80. **d** 82 **p** 83. C Canford Magna *Sarum* 82-86; V Preston St Cuth *Blackb* 87-94; Warden Les Cotils *Win* 94-96; V Gipsy Hill Ch Ch *S'wark* 96-00; R Ashmanhaugh, Barton Turf etc *Nor* 00-04; P-in-c Davenham *Ches* 04-06; R 06-14; rtd 14; PtO *Blackb* from 14. *11 Lancaster Road, Pilling, Preston PR3 6AU* E: mandmc2@btopenworld.com

CRIPPS, Michael Frank Douglas. b 28. Ch Ch Ox BA 50 MA 53. Ridley Hall Cam 58. **d** 59 **p** 60. C Cambridge Gt St Mary w St Mich *Ely* 59-62; Ceylon 62-66; C-in-c Swindon Covingham CD *Bris* 66-72; V Swindon St Paul 72-73; P-in-c Aldbourne and Baydon *Sarum* 73; TV Whitton 73-81; C Marlborough 81-94; rtd 94; Chapl Pau *Eur* 94-96; PtO *Sarum* from 96. *1 Irving Way, Marlborough SN8 1UE* T: (01672) 512748 E: mkcripps@btinternet.com

CRISPIN, Mrs Mavis Avril. b 46. Stranmillis Coll TCert 69 Open Univ BA 75 Lon Sch of Th BA 03. **d** 06 **p** 09. Peru 06-09; NSM Finchley St Paul and St Luke *Lon* from 09. *47 Etchingham Park Road, London N3 2EB* T: (020) 8346 8698 E: mavecrispin@yahoo.co.uk

CRITCHELL, Denise Eileen. b 49. SAOMC 96. **d** 99 **p** 00. C Flackwell Heath *Ox* 99-03; TV Risborough 03-13; rtd 13; PtO *Cant* from 14. *3 Somerset Close, Whitstable CT5 4RA* T: (01227) 771885 E: denisecritchell@btconnect.com

CRITCHLEY, Colin. b 41. Dur Univ BA 63 Liv Univ MA 69 AFBPsS 94. NW Ord Course 75. **d** 78 **p** 79. NSM Halewood *Liv* 78-06; Dioc Child Protection Adv 96-06; rtd 06. *53 Elwyn Drive, Halewood, Liverpool L26 0UX* T: 0151-487 5710 F: 280 4937

CRITCHLEY, Mrs Patsy Eva. b 49. Reading Univ CertEd 70. ERMC 04. **d** 07 **p** 08. NSM Meppershall and Shefford *St Alb* 07-10; NSM Henlow and Langford 10-15; rtd 15; PtO *St Alb* from 15. *39 Rooktree Way, Haynes, Bedford MK45 3PT* T: (01234) 381510 E: patsy@critchley04.plus.com

CRITCHLOW, Mrs Anne-Louise. b 51. Westf Coll Lon BA 73 Qu Mary Coll Lon MA 75 Leeds Univ MA 05 Grenoble Univ

MèsL 74 Cam Univ PGCE 76. NOC 03. **d** 05 **p** 06. C Eccles *Man* 05-08; TV from 08. *St Andrew's Vicarage, 11 Abbey Grove, Eccles, Manchester M30 9QN* T: 0161-707 9996 E: mmcritchlow@btinternet.com

CRITCHLOW, Daniel Douglas. b 87. QUB BTh 09 MTh 10 SS Coll Cam MPhil 12. Ridley Hall Cam 10. **d** 12 **p** 13. C Firswood and Gorse Hill *Man* from 12. *14 Rosslyn Road, Manchester M16 0FY* T: 0161-657 0793 E: critchlow.daniel@gmail.com

CRITCHLOW (née KHARITONOVA), Mrs Natalia (Tasha). b 74. St Petersburg State Univ MA 98 Dallas Th Sem MTh 04. Westcott Ho Cam 07. **d** 09 **p** 10. C Brondesbury Ch Ch and St Laur *Lon* 09-12; PtO from 12. *St Dunstan's Rectory, Rectory Square, London E1 3NQ* T: (020) 7791 3545 M: 07540-588860 E: tasha.critchlow@googlemail.com

CRITCHLOW, Trevor Francis. b 61. Lanc Univ BA 83 K Coll Lon MA 96. Westcott Ho Cam 88. **d** 90 **p** 91. C Croydon St Jo *S'wark* 90-92; C Lewisham St Mary 92-94; PtO *Ely* 94-05; Development Dir Westmr St Matt *Lon* 95-99; TV Wembley Park *Lon* 05-11; CME Officer Willesden Area 06-10; R Stepney St Dunstan and All SS from 11. *St Dunstan's Rectory, Rectory Square, London E1 3NQ* T: (020) 7790 1920 M: 07850-578193 F: 07092-868327 E: trevor.critchlow@googlemail.com

CRITTALL, Richard Simon. b 47. Sussex Univ BA 69 Linacre Coll Ox BA 71. St Steph Ho Ox 69. **d** 72 **p** 73. C Oswestry H Trin *Lich* 72-75; C E Grinstead St Mary *Chich* 75-78; TV Brighton Resurr 78-83; R E Blatchington 83-95; V Heathfield St Rich 95-07; Dioc Ecum Officer *Ex* 07-12; P-in-c Broadhembury, Payhembury and Plymtree 07-12; rtd 12; PtO *Sarum* from 12. *9 Gate Close, Hawkchurch, Axminster EX13 5TY* T: (01297) 678191 E: simoncrittall@breathmail.net

CROAD, Arthur Robert. b 35. Down Coll Cam BA 58 MA 61. Clifton Th Coll 58. **d** 61 **p** 62. C Sneinton St Chris w St Phil *S'well* 61-64; C Kinson *Sarum* 64-72; R Sherfield English *Win* 72-74; R Awbridge w Sherfield English 74-92; P-in-c Hinton Ampner w Bramdean and Kilmeston 92-01; rtd 01; PtO *Win* from 10. *48 Woodfield Drive, Winchester SO22 5PU* T: (01962) 851978

CROAD, David Richard. b 31. Reading Univ BSc 55. Clifton Th Coll. **d** 57 **p** 58. C Iver *Ox* 57-60; C Rushden *Pet* 60-63; V Loudwater *Ox* 63-72; SW Area Sec CPAS 72-78; V Bovingdon *St Alb* 78-91; Min Hampstead St Jo Downshire Hill Prop Chpl *Lon* 91-94; rtd 94; PtO *Guildf* from 97; *Win* from 97. *8 Compass Court, 42 Winn Road, Southampton SO17 1EZ* T: (023) 8058 2022

CROCKER, Mrs Fiona Jane. b 64. Southn Univ BN 87 Univ of Wales (Lamp) BA 14 RGN 87. St Jo Coll Nottm. **d** 14 **p** 15. C Brailsford w Shirley, Osmaston w Edlaston etc *Derby* from 14. *7 Sundial Close, Brailsford, Ashbourne DE6 3DP* M: 07956-582917 E: fionacrocker@aol.com

CROCKER, The Very Revd Jeremy Robert. b 67. S Bank Univ MA 94 Heythrop Coll Lon MA 98 MCIM 92. Westcott Ho Cam 94 CITC 96. **d** 97 **p** 98. C Stevenage H Trin *St Alb* 97-00; TV Bp's Hatfield 00-04; TR Elstow 04-15; PtO 15; Dean St Paul's Cathl and Chapl Nicosia from 15. *St Paul's Cathedral, PO Box 22014, 1516 Nicosia, Cyprus* T: (00357) (22) 677897 E: jeremy.crocker@live.co.uk

CROCKER, Keith Gwillam. b 49. Lanchester Poly Cov BSc 70. Oak Hill Th Coll 74. **d** 77 **p** 78. C Whitnash *Cov* 77-80; C Gt Horton *Bradf* 80-83; C Grays SS Pet and Paul, S Stifford and W Thurrock *Chelmsf* 83-84; TV Grays Thurrock 84-88; TR Wreningham *Nor* 88-95; P-in-c New Catton Ch 95-99; V from 99. *Christ Church Vicarage, 65 Elm Grove Lane, Norwich NR3 3LF* T: (01603) 408332 E: keith.crocker@which.net

CROCKER, Peter David. b 56. Lon Univ MB, BS 80 MRCGP. Mon Dioc Tr Scheme 93. **d** 96 **p** 97. NSM Bassaleg *Mon* 96-02; TV 02-06; P-in-c Bedwas and Rudry 06-07; R Bedwas w Machen w Rudry 07-14; R Bedwas w Machen w Michaelston-y-Fedw w Rudry from 14. *1A Navigation Street, Trethomas, Caerphilly CF83 8DJ* T: (029) 2088 5220

CROCKER, Richard Campbell. b 54. Nottm Univ BSc 76. Wycliffe Hall Ox BA 81 MA 85. **d** 82 **p** 83. C Summerfield *Birm* 82-84; Chapl K Edw Sch Birm 84-91; R Council Bluffs USA 91-99; Assoc R Truro Episc Ch from 99. *10520 Main Street, Fairfax VA 22030, USA* T: (001) (703) 273 1300 E: rcrocker@trurochurch.org

CROCKETT, Peter James Sinclair. b 44. Sarum & Wells Th Coll 74. **d** 77 **p** 78. C Heavitree *Ex* 77; C Heavitree w Ex St Paul 78-80; TV Ex St Thos and Em 80-87; V Wear 87-09; Chapl St Loyes Tr Coll for the Disabled 87-09; Chapl W of England Sch for those w little or no sight 87-09; PtO 09; CF (TA) from 88. *The Old House, 7 Strete Ralegh House, London Road, Strete Ralegh, Whimple, Exeter EX5 2PT* T: (01404) 823651

CROCKFORD, James Robert William. b 86. Nottm Univ BA 07 Trin Hall Cam BA 13 MPhil 14. Ridley Hall Cam 11. **d** 14. C Crayford *Roch* from 14. *1A Iron Mill Place, Crayford, Dartford DA1 4RT* E: curate@stpaulinus.co.uk

CROFT, Andrew John. b 86. St Mellitus Coll. **d** 13 **p** 14. NSM Soul Survivor Watford *St Alb* from 13. *61 Brighton Road, Watford WD24 5HN*

CROFT, James Stuart. b 57. K Coll Lon BD 80 Leeds Univ MA 95. Ripon Coll Cuddesdon 83. **d** 85 **p** 86. C Friern Barnet St Jas *Lon* 85-88; R Lea *Linc* 88-93; V Knaith 88-93; V Upton 88-93; R Gate Burton 88-93; R Lea Gp 93-97; Chapl N Lincs Coll 90-93; V Froyle and Holybourne *Win* 97-10; P-in-c Chesterfield SS Aug *Derby* 10-15; P-in-c Brampton St Mark 10-15; V Longstone, Curbar and Stony Middleton from 15. *Address temp unknown* E: jamescroft57@fsmail.net

CROFT, Jennifer Sara. b 69. Leeds Univ BSc 94. Ripon Coll Cuddesdon 99. **d** 01 **p** 02. C Lillington *Cov* 01-05; Chapl Cov Univ 05-11; Chapl amongst Deaf People 03-08; V Over Tabley *Ches* 11-14; V High Legh 11-14; Sen Research Fell Warw Univ *Cov* 11-14; Chapl Countess of Chester Hosp NHS Foundn Trust 13-14; V Ormesby *York* from 14. *The Vicarage, 54 Church Lane, Ormesby, Middlesbrough TS7 9AU* T: (01642) 901482 E: jennifer.croft69@btinternet.com

CROFT, Michael Peter. b 60. GradIPM MCIPD 95 FCIPD 08. Trin Coll Bris BA 88. **d** 88 **p** 89. C Drypool *York* 88-91; P-in-c Sandal St Cath *Wakef* 91-95; V 95-07; PtO *Leeds* from 07. *5 College Terrace, Ackworth, Pontefract WF7 7LB* T: (01977) 611251 M: 078139-59066 E: michael@michaelcroftlimited.co.uk

CROFT, Richard. d 15. NSM Bris St Steph w St Jas and St Jo w St Mich etc from 15; NSM Clifton H Trin, St Andr and St Pet from 15. *Address temp unknown*

CROFT, Ronald. b 30. St Aid Birkenhead 61. **d** 63 **p** 64. C Lawton Moor *Man* 63-65; C Withington St Crispin 65-66; R 74-86; C Prestwich St Marg 66-67; V Oldham St Ambrose 67-71; P-in-c Oldham St Jas 67-68; V 68-71; V Prestwich St Hilda 71-74; P-in-c 96-00; R Heaton Norris St Thos 86-96; rtd 00; PtO *Man* from 00. *St Hilda's Cottage, 55 Whittaker Lane, Prestwich, Manchester M25 5ET* T: 0161-773 1642

CROFT, Simon Edward Owen. b 51. Ch Ch Coll Cant CertEd 73. St Steph Ho Ox 75. **d** 78 **p** 79. C Heavitree w Ex St Paul 78-83; V Seaton 83-93; P-in-c Ex St Mark 93-96; P-in-c Ex St Sidwell and St Matt 96; R Ex St Mark, St Sidwell and St Matt 96-09; C Dawlish 09-10; P-in-c 10-15; R Dawlish, Cofton and Starcross from 15. *The Vicarage, 13 West Cliff Road, Dawlish EX7 9EB* T: (01626) 864569 E: simoncdevon@gmail.com

✠**CROFT, The Rt Revd Steven John Lindsey.** b 57. Worc Coll Ox BA 80 MA 83 St Jo Coll Dur PhD 84. Cranmer Hall Dur 80. **d** 83 **p** 84 **c** 09. C Enfield St Andr *Lon* 83-87; V Ovenden *Wakef* 87-96; Dioc Miss Consultant 94-96; Warden Cranmer Hall Dur 96-04; Abps' Missr and Team Ldr Fresh Expressions 04-09; Bp Sheff from 09. *Bishopscroft, Snaithing Lane, Sheffield S10 3LG* T: 0114-230 2170 F: 263 0110 E: bishop@bishopofsheffield.org.uk

CROFT, Canon Warren David. b 36. ACT ThL 62. **d** 61 **p** 62. Australia 61-69 and from 79; Papua New Guinea 69-77; C Mottingham St Andr w St Alban *S'wark* 77-78; rtd 01. *43 Sierra Avenue, PO Box 3078, Bateau Bay NSW 2261, Australia* T: (0061) (2) 4333 3967 M: 425-206621 F: 9553 8594 E: isandwas@bigpond.com

CROFT, Canon William Stuart. b 53. Trin Hall Cam BA 76 MA 79 K Coll Lon MTh 88. Ripon Coll Cuddesdon BA 80. **d** 80 **p** 81. C Friern Barnet St Jas *Lon* 80-83; Tutor Chich Th Coll 83-92; Vice-Prin 88-92; V Fernhurst *Chich* 92-98; Dir of Ords *Pet* 98-03; Prec and Min Can Pet Cathl 98-01; Can Res and Prec 01-04; Liturg Officer 03-04; Non-res Can from 04; P-in-c Longthorpe *Pet* from 04; P-in-c Pet H Spirit Bretton from 11. *The Vicarage, 315 Thorpe Road, Longthorpe, Peterborough PE3 6LU* T: (01733) 263016 E: williamsbill_croft@hotmail.com

CROFTON, Edwin Alan. b 46. Univ Coll Ox BA 68 MA 72. Cranmer Hall Dur. **d** 73 **p** 74. C Hull St Jo Newland *York* 73-77; C Worksop St Jo *S'well* 77-81; Chapl Kilton Hosp Worksop 80-81; V Scarborough St Mary w Ch Ch and H Apostles *York* 81-91; Miss to Seamen 81-91; Chapl St Mary's Hosp Scarborough 82-91; V Cheltenham Ch Ch *Glouc* 91-02; RD Cheltenham 95-00; Hon Can Glouc Cathl 01-02; TR Eccles *Man* 02-11; P-in-c Hope St Jas 07-09; AD Eccles 05-11; rtd 11. *177 Leigh Sinton Road, Malvern WR14 1LB* T: (01886) 833376 E: ea_crofton@msn.com

CROFTON, Robert Edwin. b 75. UEA BSc 98. Ridley Hall Cam 03. **d** 06 **p** 07. C Churchdown *Glouc* 06-09; TV Cheltenham St Mark from 09. *St Barnabas' Vicarage, 152 Alstone Lane, Cheltenham GL51 8HL* T: (01242) 575679 E: rob.crofton@tiscali.co.uk

CROFTS, David Thomas. b 47. Cheshire Coll of Educn CertEd 68 Open Univ BA 76. **d** 99 **p** 00. OLM Thurston St Edmunds St Mary *St E* 99-13; NSM from 13. *8 Linton Gardens, Bury St Edmunds IP33 2DZ* T: (01284) 761801 F: 765501 E: david@pandda.co.uk

CROFTS, Ian Hamilton. b 55. BSc. St Jo Coll Nottm 79. **d** 82 **p** 83. C Leamington Priors St Paul *Cov* 82-86; C Oadby *Leic* 86; TV 86-91; V Maidstone St Faith *Cant* 91-07; V Forty Hill Jes Ch *Lon* from 07. *The Vicarage, Forty Hill, Enfield EN2 9EU* T: (020) 8363 1935 E: ian.crofts@gmail.com

CROFTS, Stephen Andrew. b 76. Ch Ch Coll Cant BA 98 Ox Brookes Univ MA 09. Ripon Coll Cuddesdon 07. **d** 09 **p** 10. C Birstall and Wanlip *Leic* 09-14; V Gravenhurst, Shillington and Stondon *St Alb* from 13; PtO *Leic* from 14. *154-0023 Tokyo, Setagaya-ku, Wakabayashi 4-18-8, Japan* E: crofts.stephen@icloud.com

CROISDALE-APPLEBY, Mrs Carolynn Elizabeth. b 46. Ch Ch Coll Cant CertEd 68. SAOMC 01. **d** 04 **p** 05. NSM Amersham and Gt Coxwell w Buscot, Coleshill etc *Ox* 04-07; NSM Beaconsfield from 07. *Abbotsholme, Hervines Road, Amersham HP6 5HS* T: (01494) 725194 F: 725474 E: revcarolynn@aol.com

CROMARTY, Andrew Robert McKean. b 63. Newc Univ MB, BS 86 Homerton Coll Cam PGCE 89 St Jo Coll Dur BA 04. Cranmer Hall Dur 02. **d** 06 **p** 07. NSM Crook *Dur* 06-10; C Upper Weardale 10-14; V Hipswell *Leeds* from 14. *The Vicarage, 7 Forest Drive, Colburn, Catterick Garrison DL9 4PN* E: andrew.cromarty63@btinternet.com

CROMBIE, Calum Dugald Ferguson. b 81. Nazarene Th Coll Man BA 05 Keele Univ MA 13. LCTP 12. **d** 13 **p** 14. NSM Leyland St Ambrose *Blackb* from 13; Chapl HM Pris Preston 13-15; Chapl HM Pris Wymott from 15. *Chaplaincy Office, HM Prison Wymott, Ulnes Walton Lane, Leyland PR26 8LW* T: (01772) 442000 E: calum.crombie@hmps.gsi.gov.uk

CROMPTON (née KILGOUR), Mrs Christine Mary. b 39. Newnham Coll Cam BA 61 MA York Univ MA 86 Lon Inst of Educn PGCE 62. **d** 06 **p** 07. OLM Newc St Geo and St Hilda from 06. *11 South Bend, Newcastle upon Tyne NE3 5TR* T: 0191-236 3679

CROMPTON, Gillian Kay. *See* STANNING, Gillian Kay

CROMPTON, Canon Roger Martyn Francis. b 47. Sheff Univ BA 69 PGCE 73 St Jo Coll Dur BA 84. Cranmer Hall Dur 82. **d** 85 **p** 86. C Woodford Wells *Chelmsf* 85-89; V Golcar *Wakef* 89-12; P-in-c Longwood 10-12; RD Huddersfield 99-09; Hon Can Wakef Cathl 06-12; rtd 12. *4 Top Row, Armitage Bridge, Huddersfield HD4 7NP* E: rmf4vmc@btinternet.com

CROMPTON-BATTERSBY, Holly Jo. b 74. Bath Coll of HE BA 95. Wycliffe Hall Ox BTh 01. **d** 01 **p** 02. C Luton Lewsey St Hugh *St Alb* 01-04; Chapl Bennett Memorial Dioc Sch Tunbridge Wells 04-07; Chapl Bedgebury Sch Kent 05-06; Chapl St Bede's Sch Cam from 09. *St Bede's Inter-Church School, Birdwood Road, Cambridge CB1 3TD* M: 07761-628335 T: (01223) 568816 ext 210 E: hollycrompton@hotmail.com *or* hcrompton@stbedes.cambs.sch.uk

CROMPTON-THOMAS, Lionel Edrich. b 47. **d** 12. C Walthamstow St Barn and St Jas Gt *Chelmsf* from 13. *49 Steele Road, London E11 3JB* T: (020) 8522 1945 E: lcromptonthomas@yahoo.co.uk

CRONIN, Mrs Linda Nancy. b 61. NTMTC BA 08. **d** 08 **p** 09. C Barrow St Mark *Carl* 08-10; C S Barrow 10-11; TV 11-13; Chapl All SS Academy Cheltenham 13-14; NSM Cheltenham St Mark *Glouc* 13-14; P-in-c Madeley *Heref* from 14. *The Vicarage, Park Lane, Madeley, Telford TF7 5HN* M: 07817-678775 E: croninlinda@sky.com

CRONK, Simon Nicholas. b 59. CQSW 85 Poly of Wales BA 82. Wycliffe Hall Ox 89. **d** 92 **p** 93. C Cheltenham Ch Ch *Glouc* 92-96; V Cinderford St Steph w Littledean 96-02; V Hughenden *Ox* from 02; AD Wycombe from 12. *The Vicarage, Valley Road, Hughenden Valley, High Wycombe HP14 4PF* T: (01494) 563439

CROOK, Colin. b 44. JP 78. Lon Univ BSc(Econ) 74 ALA 67 FLA 93. S'wark Ord Course 87. **d** 90 **p** 91. NSM Dartford Ch Ch *Roch* 90-97; P-in-c Crockenhill All So 97-05; Dioc Ecum Officer 96-04; rtd 05; PtO *Chich* from 06. *57 Martello Court, 3-15 Jevington Gardens, Eastbourne BN21 4SD* E: revcolincrook@yahoo.co.uk

CROOK, David Creighton. b 37. Trin Coll Cam BA 61 MA 68. Cuddesdon Coll 61. **d** 63 **p** 64. C Workington St Mich *Carl* 63-66; C Penrith St Andr 66-68; V Barrow St Jas 70-78; V Maryport 78-81; TV Greystoke, Matterdale and Mungrisdale 81-87; TV Watermillock 84-87; V Hesket-in-the-Forest and Armathwaite 87-98; rtd 98; PtO *Carl* from 01. *11 Lowther Street, Penrith CA11 7UW* T: (01768) 866773

CROOK, David Robert. b 64. Liv Univ BA 85 PGCE 86 Univ of Wales (Swansea) PhD 07. Westcott Ho Cam 13. **d** 15. C Easebourne, Lodsworth and Selham *Chich* from 15. *14 Heathfield Park, Midhurst GU29 9HN* M: 07902-485877 E: david.crook15@btinternet.com

CROOK, Mrs Diana Elizabeth. b 47. Hull Univ BA 73 Open Univ BSc 93 City Univ MSc 97 Middx Univ BA 03 RGN 70 CPsychol. NTMTC 00. **d** 03 **p** 04. NSM Waltham H Cross

Chelmsf 03-07; P-in-c Uley w Owlpen and Nympsfield *Glouc* from 07. *The Rectory, 2 The Green, Uley, Dursley GL11 5SN* T: (01453) 861363 *or* 860249 E: revdiana@dianacrook.org

CROOK, Graham Leslie. b 49. Chich Th Coll 74. **d** 76 **p** 77. C Withington St Crispin *Man* 76-79; C Prestwich St Marg 79-82; V Nelson St Bede *Blackb* 82-92; Chapl Southend Health Care NHS Trust from 92; Bp's Adv for Hosp Chapl (Bradwell Area) *Chelmsf* 98-04; PtO from 09. *Ebenezer, 249 Woodgrange Drive, Southend-on-Sea SS1 2SQ* T: (01702) 613429

✠**CROOK, The Rt Revd John Michael.** b 40. Univ of Wales (Lamp) BA 62. Coll of Resurr Mirfield 62. **d** 64 **p** 65 **c** 99. C Horninglow *Lich* 64-66; C Bloxwich 66-70; R Inverness St Mich *Mor* 70-78; R Inverness St Jo 74-78; Dioc Youth Chapl *St And* 78-86; R Aberfoyle 78-87; R Doune 78-87; R Callander 78-87; Can St Ninian's Cathl Perth 85-99; R Bridge of Allan 87-99; Syn Clerk 97-99; Bp Mor 99-06; rtd 06; LtO *St And* from 07. *8 Buccleuch Court, Dunblane FK15 0AR* T: (01786) 826872 E: johnmichaelcrook@tiscali.co.uk

CROOK, Malcolm Geoffrey. b 53. St Steph Ho Ox 88. **d** 90 **p** 91. C Pet St Jude 90-93; C Barrow St Matt *Carl* 93-96; TV Langley and Parkfield *Man* 96-97; R Man Apostles w Miles Platting 97-03; P-in-c Sneinton St Steph w St Alb *S'well* 03-04; P-in-c Sneinton St Matthias 03-04; V Sneinton St Steph w St Matthias 04-11; P-in-c Sculcoates *York* from 11; P-in-c Hull St Mary Sculcoates from 15. *St Paul's Vicarage, Bridlington Avenue, Hull HU2 0DU* T: (01482) 620341 E: malccrook@hotmail.com

CROOK, Marie Elizabeth. b 46. CBDTI 02. **d** 05 **p** 06. OLM Over Darwen St Jas *Blackb* 05-07; NSM 07-13; NSM Over Darwen St Jas and Hoddlesden from 13. *4 Churchill Avenue, Rishton, Blackburn BB1 4EY* T: (01254) 447900 E: mariecrook500@hotmail.com

CROOK, Rowland William. b 39. Tyndale Hall Bris 61. **d** 64 **p** 65. C Penn Fields *Lich* 64-68; C Lower Broughton St Clem w St Matthias *Man* 68-70; C Bucknall and Bagnall *Lich* 70-76; V New Shildon *Dur* 76-86; V Northwich St Luke and H Trin *Ches* 86-99; P-in-c Helsby and Dunham-on-the-Hill 99-04; rtd 04; PtO *Ches* from 04. *14 Bollington Avenue, Northwich CW9 8SB* T: (01606) 45177 E: rowland.crook@talktalk.net

CROOK, Simon Charles. b 72. Imp Coll Lon BSc 95 Ox Brookes Univ PGCE 97 Sheff Univ BA 14. Coll of Resurr Mirfield 12. **d** 14 **p** 15. C Huddersfield St Pet *Leeds* from 14. *10 The Dell, Huddersfield HD2 2FD* M: 07742-177610 E: sichcrook@gmail.com

CROOK, Timothy Mark. b 68. Oak Hill Th Coll BA 00. **d** 00 **p** 01. C Charles w Plymouth St Matthias *Ex* 00-03; C Harold Wood *Chelmsf* 03-09; V S w N Bersted *Chich* from 09. *121 Victoria Drive, Bognor Regis PO21 2EH* T: (01243) 862018 E: timothycrook@hotmail.com

CROOKES, Keith John. b 54. Sheff Univ BA 94 Leeds Univ PhD 02. NOC 02. **d** 05 **p** 06. NSM Deepcar *Sheff* 05-09; NSM Sheff St Paul from 09; P-in-c from 09. *219 High Greave, Sheffield S5 9GS* T: 0114-240 3790 E: keith.crookes@sheffield.anglican.org

CROOKES, Canon Christopher John (Kip). b 53. St Bede's Coll Dur CertEd 75. Trin Coll Bris BA 90. **d** 90 **p** 91. C The Quinton *Birm* 90-93; V Ince Ch Ch 93-03; R Much Woolton from 03; AD Liv S 06-14; Hon Can Liv Cathl from 06. *The Rectory, 67 Church Road, Woolton, Liverpool L25 6DA* T: 0151-428 1853

CROOKS, Canon David William Talbot. b 52. TCD BA 75 MA 78 BD 83. **d** 77 **p** 78. C Glendermott *D & R* 77-81; C Edin Old St Paul 81-84; I Taughboyne, Craigadooish, Newtowncunningham etc *D & R* from 84; Bp's Dom Chapl 88-07; Can Raphoe Cathl from 91. *Taughboyne Rectory, Churchtown, Carrigans, Lifford, Co Donegal, Republic of Ireland* T: (00353) (74) 914 0135 M: 86-212 5670 E: dcrooks@eircom.net

CROOKS, Mrs Jayne Barbara. b 52. Birm Univ BSc 73 Avery Hill Coll PGCE 74. WMMTC 01. **d** 04 **p** 05. NSM Kings Norton *Birm* 04-08; C 08-11; TV 11-15; rtd 15; PtO *Birm* from 15. *15 Chalgrove Avenue, Birmingham B38 8YP* T: 0121-459 3733 E: jayne.crooks@blueyonder.co.uk

CROOKS, Kenneth Robert. b 36. CEng FIEE FCMI FCIM. S'wark Ord Course 80. **d** 83 **p** 84. NSM Wisley w Pyrford *Guildf* 83-92; PtO *Ex* from 98. *1 Glenside, Manor Road, Sidmouth EX10 8FG* T: (01395) 489254 E: revken.sidmouth@talktalk.net

CROOKS, Kip. *See* CROOKES, Christopher John

CROOKS, Peter James. b 50. MBE 09. St Jo Coll Cam BA 72. Cranmer Hall Dur. **d** 76 **p** 77. C Onslow Square St Paul *Lon* 76-77; C Brompton H Trin w Onslow Square St Paul 77-79; C Wembley St Jo 79-82; CMS 82-92; Lebanon 83-89; Syria 85-89; Dean Jerusalem 89-92; P-in-c Hunningham and Wappenbury w Weston under Wetherley *Cov* 92-01; P-in-c Offchurch 96-01; V Long Itchington and Marton 96-01; CMS Iran 01-02; TV Dolgellau w Llanfachreth and Brithdir etc *Ban* 02-04; Chapl Aden Ch Ch Yemen 04-09; Dir Ras Morbat

Clinics 04-09; rtd 09; P-in-c Arthog w Fairbourne w Llangelynnin w Rhoslefain *Ban* 09-10; PtO 10-14; *Ox* from 14. *25 Radstock Road, Reading RG1 3PS* T: 0118-375 3103 M: 07866-276562 E: petercrooks781@btinternet.com

CROOS, Sebastian John Princely. b 59. Madurai Univ BA 82. Oak Hill Th Coll BA 04. **d** 04 **p** 05. C Becontree St Mary *Chelmsf* 04-07; C E Ham St Paul 07-08; Chapl Lon City Miss 08-11; NSM Forest Gate St Mark *Chelmsf* 11-13; P-in-c N Woolwich w Silvertown from 13. *St John's Vicarage, Manwood Street, London E16 2JY* T: (020) 7474 7008 M: 07449-043579 E: sprincecroos@hotmail.com

CROSBIE, Andrew. b 62. St Steph Ho Ox 96. **d** 98 **p** 99. C St Paul's Cathl St Helena 98-00; CF 00-03; PtO *Blackb* 03-11; Chantry P Shrine of Our Lady of Haddington from 08. *Irish Gait, 29 Irish Street, Dumfries DG1 2PJ* T: (01387) 274033 M: 07791-540535 E: fathercrosbie@btinternet.com

CROSBIE, Timothy John. b 44. ACMA 72. **d** 00 **p** 01. OLM Shotley *St E* 00-08; OLM Shoreline 08-13; NSM 13-14; rtd 14; PtO *St E* from 15. *5 Mill Rise, Holbrook, Ipswich IP9 2QH* T: (01473) 328297 E: txb44@btinternet.com

CROSBY, Anne Denise. b 58. BA. Linc Sch of Th and Min. **d** 14 **p** 15. NSM Birstall and Wanlip *Leic* from 14. *9 Beaumont Leys Lane, Leicester LE4 2BB* T: 0116-261 1576 E: annedcrosby@hotmail.com

CROSBY, Bernard Edward. b 47. Oak Hill Th Coll 86. **d** 88 **p** 89. C Springfield H Trin *Chelmsf* 88-91; C Penn Fields *Lich* 91-94; V St Leonards St Ethelburga *Chich* 94-02; R Fairlight, Guestling and Pett 02-10; rtd 10. *4 Willowbed Walk, Hastings TN34 2QL* T: (01424) 435800 E: bernardcrosby@supanet.com

CROSBY, David Edward. b 48. SAOMC 96. **d** 99 **p** 00. NSM Newbury *Ox* 99-01; C The Bourne and Tilford *Guildf* 01-04; P-in-c Hurst Green and Mitton *Bradf* 04. *7 Murfitt Way, Gamlingay, Sandy SG19 3EW* E: davidec@live.co.uk

CROSLAND, Sarah Rosita. *See* WILLIAMS, Sarah Rosita

CROSS, Alan. *See* CROSS, Thomas Alan

CROSS, Canon Alan. b 43. Chich Th Coll 68. **d** 70 **p** 71. C Bordesley St Oswald *Birm* 70; C S Yardley St Mich 70-73; C Colchester St Jas, All SS, St Nic and St Runwald *Chelmsf* 73-77; V Leigh-on-Sea St Jas 77-89; V Woodford St Barn 89-09; Hon Can Chelmsf Cathl 97-09; rtd 09; PtO *Chelmsf* from 09. *11 Grayling Drive, Colchester CO4 3EN* T: (01206) 790984

CROSS, Preb Elizabeth Mary. b 46. Leeds Univ BA 69 CertEd 70. Sarum Th Coll 80. **dss** 83 **d** 87 **p** 94. Wootton Bassett *Sarum* 83-86; Westbury 86-87; Par Dn 87-89; C Glastonbury w Meare, W Pennard and Godney *B & W* 89-95; Asst Dir of Ords 89-95; Preb Wells Cathl 93-07; V Wedmore w Theale and Blackford 95-07; rtd 07. *7 Carpenters Close, Stratton, Dorchester DT2 9SR* T: (01305) 260499 E: lizmcross@btinternet.com

CROSS, Canon Greville Shelly. b 49. Sarum & Wells Th Coll 73. **d** 76 **p** 77. C Kidderminster St Mary *Worc* 76-80; P-in-c Worc St Mark 80-81; TV Worc St Martin w St Pet, St Mark etc 81-85; R Inkberrow w Cookhill and Kington w Dormston 85-98; RD Evesham 93-97; R Old Swinford Stourbridge 98-11; RD Stourbridge 01-04; rtd 11; NSM Upton-on-Severn, Ripple, Earls Croome etc *Worc* 11-14; NSM Hanley Castle, Hanley Swan and Welland 11-14; Hon Can Worc Cathl from 05. *The Chaplain's House, St Oswald's Hospital, Upper Tything, Worcester WR1 1HR* E: canon.cross@btinternet.com

CROSS, James Stuart. b 36. Magd Coll Ox BA 65 MA 71. Ripon Hall Ox 62. **d** 65 **p** 66. C Leckhampton SS Phil and Jas *Glouc* 65-66; CF 66-92; QHC 89-92; R Stretford St Pet *Man* 92-00; rtd 00. *St Davids, Redbrook Road, Monmouth NP25 3LY* T/F: (01600) 715977 E: jimcross1@aol.com

CROSS, Jeremy Burkitt. b 45. St Pet Coll Ox BA 68 MA 71. Wycliffe Hall Ox 67. **d** 69 **p** 70. C Mildenhall *St E* 69-72; C Lindfield *Chich* 72-77; V Framfield 77-89; R St Leonards St Leon 89-01; R Birling, Addington, Ryarsh and Trottiscliffe *Roch* 01-10; rtd 10; PtO *Roch* 10-14. *Les Sapins Verts, Branla, 56140 Reminiac, France* T: (0033) 2 97 93 25 63 E: jandscross@aol.com

CROSS, John Henry Laidlaw. b 30. Peterho Cam BA 53 MA 57. Ridley Hall Cam 53. **d** 55 **p** 56. C Ealing Dean St Jo *Lon* 55-58; C Gt Baddow *Chelmsf* 58-60; V Maidenhead St Andr and St Mary *Ox* 60-68; News Ed C of E Newspaper 68-71; Assoc Ed 71-72; Ed 72-75; Hon C St Pet Cornhill *Lon* 68-87; P-in-c 87-95; Hon C Chelsea All SS 76-93; rtd 95. *2 Wren Park, Whittlesford, Cambridge CB22 4LY* E: revjhlcross@aol.com

CROSS, Katie Louise. b 70. Ox Brookes Univ BA 08. St Jo Coll Nottm 11. **d** 13 **p** 14. C Newton Tracey, Horwood, Alverdiscott etc *Ex* from 13. *The Rectory, Beaford, Winkleigh EX19 8NN* T: (01805) 603113 M: 07976-263514 E: katie.cross@gmx.com

CROSS, Kenneth James. b 69. Trin Coll Bris BA 09. **d** 09 **p** 10. C Alcombe *B & W* 09-12; R Old Cleeve, Leighland

and Treborough from 12. *The Rectory, Roadwater, Watchet TA23 0QZ* T: (01984) 641808 M: 07951-568703
E: kennethjcross@gmail.com

CROSS, Kingsley James. b 50. SWMTC 09. **d** 11 **p** 12. NSM N Creedy *Ex* from 11. *9 Church Close, Puddington, Tiverton EX16 8PJ* T: (01884) 860382
E: kingsleycross@btinternet.com

CROSS, Mrs Linda Ann. b 57. St Jo Coll Dur BA 79 Wye Coll Lon MSc 80. **d** 10 **p** 11. OLM Wye w Brook and Hastingleigh etc *Cant* 10-14; OLM Wye from 14. *Yew Tree House, The Street, Brook, Ashford TN25 5PF* T: (01233) 813360
E: jandlcross@btinternet.com

CROSS, Max David. b 68. **d** 14 **p** 15. C Sheet *Portsm* from 14. *20 Bramble Road, Petersfield GU31 4HL* M: 07590-608766
E: max@maxcross.com

CROSS, Canon Michael Anthony. b 45. Leeds Univ BA 67 BA 69. Coll of Resurr Mirfield 68. **d** 70 **p** 71. C Bloemfontein Cathl S Africa 70-73; C Adel *Ripon* 74-76; Chapl Birm Univ 76-81; V Chapel Allerton *Ripon* 81-92; V Headingley 92-04; AD 96-01; P-in-c Wetherby 04-10; Hon Can Ripon Cathl 06-10; rtd 11; PtO *York* from 11. *1 Angram Close, York YO30 5ZN* T: (01904) 347051 E: mandacross@yahoo.co.uk

CROSS, Mrs Rachel Beth. b 73. Ox Brookes Univ BA 95. STETS 06. **d** 09 **p** 11. C Ponteland *Newc* 09-10; C Benwell 10-13; NSM Kenton Ascension 14; TV Thame *Ox* from 14. *22 Stuart Way, Thames OX9 3WP* T: (01844) 212344 M: 07795-292280 E: rachel@thecrosses.f9.co.uk

CROSS, Ronald. b 72. Trin Coll Bris 10. **d** 12. C Cullompton, Willand, Uffculme, Kentisbeare etc *Ex* 12-15; V Upper Sunbury St Sav *Lon* from 15. *The Vicarage, 205 Vicarage Road, Sunbury-on-Thames TW16 7TP* M: 07539-021385
E: r.cross001@yahoo.co.uk *or* revroncross@gmail.com

CROSS, Samuel John. See McNALLY-CROSS, Samuel John

CROSS, Stephanie (Stevie). b 53. Essex Univ BSc 74 Loughb Univ MSc 76 Bris Univ BA 01 Reading Univ PGCE 93. Trin Coll Bris 99. **d** 01 **p** 02. C Lytchett Minster *Sarum* 01-05; TV Wheatley *Ox* 05-11; R Aston-le-Walls, Byfield, Boddington, Eydon etc *Pet* from 11. *The Rectory, 55 Church Street, Byfield, Daventry NN11 6XN* T: (01327) 260783
E: crossstevie@hotmail.com

CROSS, Thomas Alan. b 58. CITC BTh 05. **d** 05 **p** 06. C Drumglass w Moygashel *Arm* 05-08; I Lissan from 08; Hon V Choral Arm Cathl from 06; Dom Chapl to Abp Arm from 09. *Lissan Rectory, 150 Moneymore Road, Cookstown BT80 8PY* T: (028) 8676 6112 M: 07795-436918
E: tacross@btinternet.com

CROSSE, Mrs Anne-Marie. b 48. **d** 99 **p** 09. NSM W Worthing St Jo *Chich* 99-02; NSM Arundel w Tortington and S Stoke 02-05; PtO 05-14; P-in-c Brightling, Mountfield and Netherfield from 14. *The Rectory, Brightling, Robertsbridge TN32 5HE* T: (01424) 838504 E: annemariecrosse@btinternet.com

CROSSEY, The Very Revd Nigel Nicholas. b 59. Cam Univ BA. **d** 84 **p** 85. C Drumglass w Moygashel *Arm* 84-87; I Magheraculmoney *Clogh* 87-93; CF 93-09; Chapl St Columba's Coll Dub 09-15; Dean Kilmore *K, E & A* from 15; I Kilmore w Ballintemple, Kildallan etc from 15. *The Deanery, Danesfort, Cavan, Republic of Ireland* M: (00353) 86-067 2528

CROSSLAND, June Marcia. b 44. **d** 01. OLM Monk Bretton *Leeds* from 01; OLM Staincross from 05. *16 Deacons Way, Barnsley S71 2HU* T: (01226) 203895

CROSSLAND, Richard Henry. b 49. Ex Univ BA 72. S'wark Ord Course 91. **d** 94 **p** 96. NSM Surbiton St Andr and St Mark *S'wark* 94-95; NSM Linc Cathl 95-98; NSM Spring Line Gp 10-14; NSM Owmby Gp 10-14; V Nettleham from 14; RD Lawres from 12. *The Vicarage, 2 Vicarage Lane, Nettleham, Lincoln LN2 2RH* T: (01522) 754752
E: rcrossland@voxhumana.co.uk

CROSSLEY, Mrs Charmain Janice. b 47. Sarum Th Coll 07. **d** 09 **p** 10. OLM Shaftesbury *Sarum* 09-12; NSM from 12. *Tanders, Elm Hill, Motcombe, Shaftesbury SP7 9HR* T: (01747) 852545
E: jancrossley.may1594@gmail.com

CROSSLEY, Dennis Thomas. b 23. AKC 52 St Boniface Warminster. **d** 53 **p** 54. C Crofton Park St Hilda *S'wark* 53-56; C Beddington 56-59; C Talbot Village *Sarum* 59-62; R Finchampstead *Ox* 62-97; rtd 97; PtO *Ox* from 97. *1 Larkswood Close, Sandhurst, Camberley GU47 8QJ* T: (01344) 751456 E: dtcrossley@web-hq.com

CROSSLEY, George Alan. b 34. St Jo Coll Dur BA 56. Cranmer Hall Dur. **d** 60 **p** 61. C Blackb St Steph 60-63; C Ashton-on-Ribble St Andr 63-65; V Oswaldtwistle St Paul 65-72; R Dufton *Carl* 72-73; P-in-c Milburn w Newbiggin 72-73; R Long Marton w Dufton and w Milburn 73-76; P-in-c Beckermet St Jo 76-78; V Beckermet St Jo and St Bridget w Ponsonby 78-84; Chapl Furness Gen Hosp 84-89; TV Newbarns w Hawcoat *Carl* 84-89; Chapl Princess R Hosp Telford 89-97; rtd 95; P-in-c Bilsborrow *Blackb* 97-99; PtO from 00. *44 Dewhurst Road, Bolton BL2 3NE* T: (01204) 396592

CROSSLEY, George John. b 57. Bradf Univ BA 81 PhD 84. NOC 91. **d** 94 **p** 95. C Balderstone *Man* 94-98; V Branston w Tatenhill *Lich* 98-02; RD Tutbury 00-02; Chapl Burton Hosps NHS Foundn Trust from 04; P-in-c Burton St Chad *Lich* from 09. *St Chad's Vicarage, 113 Hunter Street, Burton-on-Trent DE14 2SS* T: (01283) 564044 M: 07976-979755
E: george@gcrossley.wanadoo.co.uk

CROSSLEY, James Salter Baron. b 39. Linc Th Coll 70. **d** 72 **p** 74. C Chesterfield St Mary and All SS *Derby* 72-75; Chapl Doncaster R Infirmary and Montagu Hosp NHS Trust 75-95; Chapl Asst Tickhill Road Hosp Doncaster 75-92; Chapl Asst St Cath Hosp Doncaster 75-92; Hon C Doncaster Intake *Sheff* 78-95; rtd 95; PtO *Sheff* 95-99; *Leeds* from 00. *South View, Reeth, Richmond DL11 6SN* T: (01748) 886429

CROSSLEY, Janice. *See* CROSSLEY, Charmain Janice

CROSSLEY, Jeremy. *See* CROSSLEY, William Jeremy Hugh

CROSSLEY, Joan Winifred. b 57. Sussex Univ BA 78 Leic Univ MA 80 Univ Coll Lon PhD 85. SAOMC 97. **d** 00 **p** 01. C Goldington *St Alb* 00-02; C Bedf St Mark 02-08; Asst Chapl Gt Ormond Street Hosp for Children NHS Trust 03-05; Asst Chapl Westmr Sch 08-10; PV Westmr Abbey 08-10; Chapl K Coll Sch Wimbledon from 10. *King's College School, Southside Common, London SW19 4TT* T: (020) 8255 5300
E: jwcrossley@aol.com

CROSSLEY, John Eric. b 51. St Martin's Coll Lanc BA 92. Carl Dioc Tr Inst 92. **d** 94 **p** 95. C Westfield St Mary *Carl* 94-97; P-in-c Penrith w Newton Reigny and Plumpton Wall 97-02; Chapl Newton Rigg Coll of H&FE 97-02; TV Cartmel Peninsula *Carl* 02-09; rtd 09; PtO *Carl* from 10. *The Vicarage, Vicarage Road, Levens, Kendal LA8 8PY* T: (015395) 60223
E: rjoncros@aol.com

CROSSLEY, Kenneth Ernest. b 38. NEOC 01. **d** 03 **p** 04. NSM Ripon Cathl from 03. *11 Station Drive, Ripon HG4 1JA* T: (01765) 692499 E: kennethecrossley@aol.com

CROSSLEY, Canon Robert Scott. b 36. Lon Univ BSc 61 BD 68 PhD 75. ALCD 64. **d** 64 **p** 65. C Beckenham St Jo *Roch* 64-68; C Morden *S'wark* 68-72; Chapl Ridley Hall Cam 72-75; V Camberley St Paul *Guildf* 75-83; TR 83-98; RD Surrey Heath 81-84; Hon Can Guildf Cathl 89-98; rtd 98; PtO *Guildf* 98-01 and from 07; Hon C Camberley St Mich Yorktown 01-07. *20 Highbury Crescent, Camberley GU15 1JZ* T: (01276) 500036
E: robertcrossley@ntlworld.com

CROSSLEY, Mrs Ruth Joy. b 54. Cranmer Hall Dur 00. **d** 02 **p** 03. C Cartmel Peninsula *Carl* 02-06; P-in-c Levens from 06; Bp's Adv for CME 06-11. *The Vicarage, Vicarage Road, Levens, Kendal LA8 8PY* T: (015395) 60223 E: rcross3357@aol.com

CROSSLEY, Preb William Jeremy Hugh. b 55. St Jo Coll Dur BA 76. Cranmer Hall Dur 81. **d** 84 **p** 85. C Gillingham St Mark *Roch* 84-87; C Ches Square St Mich w St Phil *Lon* 87-94; V Westminster St Jas the Less 94-00; R St Marg Lothbury and St Steph Coleman Street etc from 00; P-in-c St Edm the King and St Mary Woolnoth etc from 11; AD The City 06-09; Dir Post-Ord Tr from 06; Dir of Ords Two Cities Area from 08; Preb St Paul's Cathl from 11. *The Rectory, 1 St Olave's Court, London EC2V 8EX* T: (020) 7600 2379 *or* 7726 4878 M: 07963-441212 E: the.rector@stml.org.uk

CROSSMAN, Maria Antoinette (Manette). b 64. ERMC 09. **d** 12 **p** 13. C Haverhill w Withersfield *St E* 12-15; C Haughley w Wetherden and Stowupland 15; V Gt Barton and Thurston from 15. *The Vicarage, Church Road, Great Barton, Bury St Edmunds IP31 2QR* M: 07947-737789
E: revmcrossman@gmail.com

CROSSMAN, Ms Sharon Margaret Joan. b 65. DipCOT 87. Linc Th Coll BTh 93. **d** 93 **p** 94. Par Dn Chippenham St Andr w Tytherton Lucas *Bris* 93-94; C 94-96; Chapl UWE 96-02; Hon C Almondsbury 97-98; Hon C Almondsbury and Olveston 98-02; Chapl Würzburg Univ Germany 02-03; TV Portishead *B & W* 03-10; V Highbridge from 10; C Huntspill from 13; RD Axbridge from 15; Chapl MU from 05. *The Vicarage, 81A Church Street, Highbridge TA9 3HS* T: (01278) 789290
E: sharon.crossman@btopenworld.com

CROSTHWAITE, George Roger. b 38. Dur Univ BSc 62 Fuller Th Sem California DMin 83. Ridley Hall Cam 62. **d** 65 **p** 66. C Bradf Cathl Par 65-67; C Ox St Aldate w H Trin 67-70; Youth Adv CMS 70-73; P-in-c Derby St Werburgh 73-78; V 78-82; C La Crescenta St Luke USA 77-78; V Anston *Sheff* 82-83; Registrar St Giles-in-the-Fields *Lon* 83-86; V Barnes St Mich *S'wark* 86-88; PtO *Guildf* 88-93; Dir Cen Essential Psychology from 92; PtO *Derby* 01-04; *Chich* 04-07; P-in-c Findon w Clapham and Patching 07-09; P-in-c Bexhill St Barn and Hon C Bexhill St Pet from 09-12. *49 Clausentum Road, Southampton SO14 6RX* M: 07528-761048
E: rogercrosthwaite@yahoo.com

CROSTHWAITE, Howard Wellesley. b 37. St Cuth Soc Dur BA 59. St Steph Ho Ox 59. **d** 61 **p** 62. C Workington St Mich *Carl* 61-63; Grenada 63-64; C Barnsley St Mary *Wakef* 64-68; V Milnsbridge 68-70; V Thurgoland 70-79; rtd 99; PtO *Sheff*

from 08. *50 Low Road West, Warmsworth, Doncaster DN4 9LE* T: (01302) 811164 E: howard@yogadon.co.uk

CROTON, John Barry. b 43. **d** 09 **p** 10. NSM Reading Ch Ch *Ox* 09-13; PtO from 13. *35 Vine Crescent, Reading RG30 3LT* T: 0118-954 3134 M: 07704-858928 E: revjohnc@virginmedia.com

CROUCH, Prof David Bruce. b 53. Univ of Wales (Cardiff) BA 75 PhD 84 FRHistS 86. NEOC 95. **d** 98 **p** 99. NSM Scarborough St Martin *York* 98-01; NSM Scarborough St Columba 01-07. *Department of History, Hull University, Hull HU6 7RX* T: (01482) 465613 E: d.crouch@hull.ac.uk

CROUCH, Keith Matheson. b 45. Whitelands Coll Lon CertEd 71 Westhill Coll Birm BPhil 00. K Coll Lon AKC 70. **d** 72 **p** 73. C Hill *Birm* 72-75; C-in-c Woodgate Valley CD 75-77; V Bishop's Castle w Mainstone *Heref* 91-98; Vice-Prin WEMTC 98-04; TV Tenbury Wells 98-02; Public Preacher 02-04; Chapl Dorothy House Hospice Winsley 05-10; rtd 10; PtO *B & W* 05-11; *Heref* 12-15. *3 Julian Road, Ludlow SY8 1HA* T: (01584) 875567 E: keithandjoyc@gmail.com

CROUCHER, James Christopher William. b 84. Univ Coll Ox MChem 06. Oak Hill Th Coll BA 12. **d** 12 **p** 13. C Harold Wood *Chelmsf* from 12. *48 Harold Court Road, Romford RM3 0YX* T: (01708) 371804 *or* 342080 M: 07902-096783 E: james_croucher@yahoo.com

CROUCHER, Jonathan Edward. b 68. Trin Coll Cam BA 90 MA 93. SEITE 01. **d** 04 **p** 05. NSM Lee Gd Shep w St Pet *S'wark* 04-08; C Blackheath Park St Mich 08-12; P-in-c Gipsy Hill Ch Ch 12-13; V from 13. *Christ Church Vicarage, 1 Highland Road, London SE19 1DP* T: (020) 8670 0799 M: 07766-072750 E: revjec@hotmail.co.uk

CROUCHMAN, Eric Richard. b 30. Bps' Coll Cheshunt 64. **d** 66 **p** 67. C Ipswich H Trin *St E* 66-69; C Ipswich All Hallows 69-72; R Crowfield w Stonham Aspal and Mickfield 72-81; R Combs 81-90; RD Stowmarket 84-90; P-in-c Lydgate w Ousden and Cowlinge 90-95; R Wickhambrook w Lydgate, Ousden and Cowlinge 95-96; rtd 96; PtO *St E* from 97. *6 Mitre Close, Woolpit, Bury St Edmunds IP30 9SJ* T/F: (01359) 240070 E: ericthecleric@lineone.net

CROW, Michael John. b 35. AKC 63. **d** 64 **p** 65. C Welwyn Garden City *St Alb* 64-67; C Sawbridgeworth 67-69; C Biscot 69-71; V Luton St Aug Limbury 71-79; TR Borehamwood 79-87; V Markyate Street 87-00; P-in-c Flamstead 98-00; rtd 00; PtO *Ex* from 00. *216 Pinhoe Road, Exeter EX4 7HH* T: (01392) 424804

CROWDER, George Timothy. b 74. Liv Univ MEng 96. Oak Hill Th Coll MTh 07. **d** 07 **p** 08. C Hartford *Ches* 07-11; V Over St Jo from 11. *St John's Vicarage, Delamere Street, Winsford CW7 2LY* T: (01606) 594651 E: george@stjohnover.org.uk

CROWE, Anthony Murray. b 34. St Edm Hall Ox BA 58 MA 61. Westcott Ho Cam 57. **d** 59 **p** 60. C Stockingford *Cov* 59-62; C New Eltham All SS *S'wark* 62-66; V Clapham St Jo 66-73; R Charlton St Luke w H Trin 73-94; rtd 94; Sub-Chapl HM Pris Elmley 94-97; Sub-Chapl HM Pris Swaleside 94-99; PtO *Cant* from 94. *4 South Lodge Close, Whitstable CT5 2AD* T: (01227) 273046 E: tonycrowe34@btinternet.com

CROWE, Brian David. b 39. QUB BA 92 PhD 95 TCD BA 98. **d** 98 **p** 99. C Ballynure and Ballyeaston *Conn* 98-01; I Galloon w Drummully *Clogh* 01-02. Ulster Unionist Party, First Floor, 174 Albertbridge Road, Belfast BT5 4GS E: brian.crowe@uup.org

CROWE, Eric Anthony. b 29. St Jo Coll Dur BA 53 MA 98. Cuddesdon Coll 53. **d** 55 **p** 56. C Huddersfield St Jo *Wakef* 55-58; C Barnsley St Pet 58-60; R High Hoyland w Clayton W 60-68; V Battyeford 68-74; P-in-c Pitminster w Corfe *B & W* 75-76; V 76-90; rtd 90; PtO *Ex* 95-01; *B & W* 02-08. *8 Gracey Court, Woodland Road, Broadclyst, Exeter EX5 3GA* T: (01392) 460759

CROWE, Grant Norman. b 74. Keele Univ LLB 96. Cranmer Hall Dur 00. **d** 03 **p** 04. C Burton All SS w Ch Ch *Lich* 03-07; TV Cen Telford from 07. *The Vicarage, 40 Church Road, Dawley, Telford TF4 2AS* T: (01952) 501655

CROWE, Canon John Yeomans. b 39. Keble Coll Ox BA 62 MA 66. Linc Th Coll 62. **d** 64 **p** 65. C Tettenhall Regis *Lich* 64-67; C Caversham *Ox* 67-71; V Hampton *Worc* 72-76; P-in-c Leek St Edw *Lich* 76-79; TR Leek 79-83; TR Leek and Meerbrook 83-87; RD Leek 82-87; TR Dorchester and V Warborough *Ox* 87-04; RD Aston and Cuddesdon 93-02; Hon Can Ch Ch 94-04; rtd 04. *9 Pierrepont Road, Leominster HR6 8RB* T: (01568) 611081 E: john.crowe90@ntlworld.com

CROWE, Leonard Charles. b 25. S Dios Minl Tr Scheme 80. **d** 82 **p** 83. Hon NSM Buxted and Hadlow Down *Chich* 82-84; NSM Fairlight 84-86; P-in-c 86-89; V 89-92; RD Rye 93-95; PtO 95-98; Hon C Ashburnham w Penhurst 98-99; rtd 99; PtO *Chich* from 99. *c/o Mrs L G Charles, Oak House, Stoneyfield Bank, Belper DE56 1GA*

CROWE, Canon Philip Anthony. b 36. Selw Coll Cam BA 60 MA 64. Ridley Hall Cam 60. **d** 62 **p** 63. Tutor Oak Hill Th Coll

62-67; C Enfield Ch Ch Trent Park *Lon* 62-65; Ed *C of E Newspaper* 67-71; Lect Birm St Martin 71-76; R Breadsall *Derby* 77-88; Prin and Tutor Sarum & Wells Th Coll 88-95; Can and Preb Sarum Cathl 91-95; R Overton and Erbistock and Penley *St As* 95-97; Dir St As and Ban Minl Tr from 96; rtd 97; PtO *Lich* from 01; *St As* from 09. *Alder Lea, Babbinswood, Whittington, Oswestry SY11 4PQ* T: (01691) 671698

CROWE, Miss Rebecca Helena. b 80. Salford Univ BA 01. Trin Coll Bris BA 12. **d** 12 **p** 13. C Penwortham St Mary *Blackb* from 12. *4 Hill Road, Penwortham, Preston PR1 9XH* M: 07793-018893 E: rebeccahcrowe@hotmail.com

CROWE, Canon Sydney Ralph. b 32. Edin Th Coll 61. **d** 63 **p** 64. C Bingley H Trin *Bradf* 63-66; C Bierley 66-69; V Toller Lane St Chad *Leeds* from 69; Hon Can Bradf Cathl from 85; RD Airedale *Bradf* 95-99. *The Vicarage, St Chad's Road, Toller Lane, Bradford BD8 9DE* T: (01274) 543957 E: ralph.crowe@bradford.anglican.org

CROWE, Toby Nicholas. b 70. Oriel Coll Ox BA 94 Univ of Wales (Swansea) PGCE 97 Cam Univ BTh 09. Ridley Hall Cam 07. **d** 09 **p** 10. C Alperton *Lon* 09-12; R Elmdon St Nic *Birm* from 12. *Elmdon Rectory, 86 Tanhouse Farm Road, Solihull B92 9EY* T: 0121-743 6336 E: toby.crowe@rocketmail.com

CROWHURST, Preb David Brian. b 40. Qu Coll Birm 77. **d** 80 **p** 81. NSM Ribbesford w Bewdley and Dowles *Worc* 80-82; Hon Chapl Birm Cathl 81-82; C Kidderminster St Jo *Worc* 82-83; C-in-c Wribbenhall 83-84; P-in-c 84-87; V Oswestry St Oswald *Lich* 87-94; P-in-c Oswestry H Trin 93-94; V Oswestry 94-08; P-in-c Rhydycroesau 90-91; R 91-08; RD Oswestry 95-01; Preb Lich Cathl 00-08; rtd 08; PtO *Heref* from 08; *Lich* from 08. *The Old Hall Coach House, Main Road, Dorrington, Shrewsbury SY5 7JD* T: (01743) 718049 M: 07885-021878 E: d.crowhurst@btinternet.com

CROWIE, Hermon John. b 41. Kelham Th Coll 61. **d** 69 **p** 73. C Sneinton St Cypr *S'well* 69; C Balderton 72-75; V Basford St Aid 75-78; R Everton and Mattersey w Clayworth 78-84; St Helena 84-89; Chapl HM Pris Nor 89-91; Chapl HM Pris Cant 91-02; Bulgaria from 02. *Nova Mahala 6191, Municipality Nikolaevo, Stara Zagora, Bulgaria*

CROWLE, Sarah Ann. *See* BROUGH, Sarah Ann

CROWLEY, Mrs Jennifer Eileen. b 55. CITC 00. **d** 03 **p** 04. NSM Waterford w Killea, Drumcannon and Dunhill *C & O* 03-07; NSM New w Old Ross, Whitechurch, Fethard etc 07-10; Chapl Waterford Regional Hosp from 10. *Glen, Stradbally, Kilmacthomas, Co Waterford, Republic of Ireland* T: (00353) (51) 293143 M: 87-780 0257 E: jcrowleyglen@gmail.com

CROWLEY, Melanie. b 55. **d** 10 **p** 11. NSM St Alb St Mich *St Alb* 10-13; TV Hitchin from 13. *St Faith's Vicarage, 31 Meadowbank, Hitchin SG4 0HY* E: melaniecrowley@ntlworld.com

CROWN, Ola. b 42. **d** 06 **p** 07. NSM Walworth St Jo *S'wark* from 06. *23 Dawes House, Orb Street, London SE17 1RE*

✠**CROWTHER, The Rt Revd Clarence Edward.** b 29. Leeds Univ BA 50 LLB 52 LLM 53 California Univ PhD 75. Cuddesdon Coll 55. **d** 56 **p** 57 **c** 65. C Ox SS Phil and Jas 56-59; Episc Chapl California Univ USA 59-64; Dean Kimberley S Africa 64-65; Bp Kimberley and Kuruman 65-67; Asst Bp California 70-84; Asst Bp Los Angeles from 84. *289 Moreton Bay Lane Nr 2, Goleta CA 93117, USA* T: (001) (805) 683 1016 E: cctravel@west.net

CROWTHER, Donald James. b 23. Oak Hill NSM Course 80. **d** 82 **p** 83. NSM Seal St Lawr *Roch* 82-85; NSM Sevenoaks St Nic 85-87; P-in-c Sevenoaks Weald 87-90; PtO 90-08. *2 Summerhill Court, 9-11 South Park, Sevenoaks TN13 1DR* T: (01732) 461179 E: djcrowther@btinternet.com

CROWTHER, Frank. b 28. Qu Coll Birm 68. **d** 69 **p** 70. C Bulwell St Mary *S'well* 69-72; TV Clifton 72-77; V Kirkby in Ashfield St Thos 77-85; rtd 86; PtO *S'well* from 86; *Derby* 86-00. *30 Bramley Court, Sutton-in-Ashfield NG17 4AT* T: (01623) 443251

CROWTHER, Gordon Allan. b 63. Rhodes Univ BA 85 LLB 87 Spurgeon's Coll BD 94 St Jo Coll Dur MA. Spurgeon's Coll BD 94 Cranmer Hall Dur 98 St Jo Coll Dur MA 98. **d** 00 **p** 01. C Lancaster St Thos *Blackb* 00-03; Miss P Newcastle and Stoke *Lich* 03-08; C Kirstenhof H Spirit S Africa from 09. *38 Raapkraal Road, Kirstenhof, Cape Town, 7945 South Africa* T: (0027) (21) 701 201

CROWTHER, Mrs Hildred Anne. b 49. ERMC 05. **d** 08 **p** 09. NSM Oakham, Ashwell, Braunston, Brooke, Egleton etc *Pet* from 08. *6 The Limes, Market Overton, Oakham LE15 7PX* T: (01572) 767779 E: hildred.c@btinternet.com

CROWTHER, Ms Sheila Ann. b 52. Ox Min Course 12. **d** 15. C Osney *Ox* from 15. *Address temp unknown*

CROWTHER-ALWYN, Benedict Mark. b 53. Kent Univ BA 74. Qu Coll Birm 74. **d** 77 **p** 78. C Fenny Stratford and Water Eaton *Ox* 77-80; C Moulsecoomb *Chich* 80-81; TV 81-83; R Glas St Serf and Baillieston *Glas* 83-87; R Bassingham *Linc* 87-90; V Aubourn w Haddington 87-90; V Carlton-le-

Moorland w Stapleford 87-90; R Thurlby w Norton Disney 87-90; V Elmton *Derby* 90-03; P-in-c Matlock 03-05; R 05-14; R Matlock, Dethick, Lea and Holloway from 14. *The Rectory, 116 Church Street, Matlock DE4 3BZ* T: (01629) 582199
E: mcrowther-alwyn@tiscali.co.uk

CROWTHER-GREEN, Michael Leonard. b 36. K Coll Lon 56. d 60 p 61. C Caterham *S'wark* 60-64; C Lewisham St Jo Southend 64-69; Chr Aid Area Sec (Berks, Oxon and Bucks) 69-78; LtO *Ox* 78-83; Dioc Stewardship Adv 83-92; rtd 92; PtO *Ox* from 92. *8 Egerton Road, Reading RG2 8HQ* T: 0118-987 2502

CROYDON, Archdeacon of. *See* SKILTON, The Ven Christopher John

CROYDON, Area Bishop of. *See* CLARK, The Rt Revd Jonathan Dunnett

CRUDDAS, Mrs Valerie Mary. b 52. Univ of Wales (Swansea) BSc 73 St Mark & St Jo Coll Lon PGCE 75. St Jo Coll Nottm 05 MA 10. d 07 p 08. NSM Leatherhead and Mickleham *Guildf* 07-11; TV Schorne *Ox* from 11. *The Rectory, Rectory Drive, Waddesdon, Aylesbury HP18 0JQ* T: (01296) 655069
E: marycruddas@yahoo.co.uk

CRUICKSHANK, Ian Morison. QUB BTh. d 04 p 05. C Bray *D & G* 04-07; I Kilcooley w Littleon, Crohane and Fertagh *C & O* 07-13; I Errigle Keerogue w Ballygawley and Killeshil *Arm* 13-15; P-in-c Belfast St Brendan *D & D* from 15. *St Brendan's Rectory, 36 Circular Road, Belfast BT4 2GA*
E: ian.mcruickshank@btopenworld.com

CRUICKSHANK, Jonathan Graham. b 52. K Coll Lon BD 74 AKC 74 Keble Coll Ox PGCE 75. St Aug Coll Cant 75. d 76 p 77. C Stantonbury *Ox* 76-79; C Burnham 79-82; Chapl RNR 80-83; TV Burnham w Dropmore, Hitcham and Taplow *Ox* 82-83; Chapl RN 83-89; TV New Windsor *Ox* 89-01; R Itchen Valley *Win* 01-09; RD Alresford 01-09; R Newton Ferrers w Revelstoke *Ex* 09-11; P-in-c Holbeton 09; V from 09; V St Peter-in-Thanet *Cant* 11-15; Min Harvest New Angl Ch 12-15; Corps Chapl Sea Cadet Corps 95-10; V Mamble w Bayton, Rock w Heightington etc *Worc* from 15. *The Vicarage, Church Lane, Far Forest, Kidderminster DY14 9TT*
E: jcruickshank60@btinternet.com

CRUICKSHANKS, Mrs Arlene Elizabeth Henderson. b 42. d 06 p 07. OLM Gt Finborough w Onehouse, Harleston, Buxhall etc *St E* 06-12; rtd 12; PtO *St E* from 12. *23 Ash Road, Onehouse, Stowmarket IP14 3HA* T: (01449) 676123 E: arleron@aol.com

CRUISE, Brian John Alexander. Bris Univ BA 86 TCD BTh 88. d 88 p 89. C Lurgan Ch the Redeemer *D & D* 88-92; I Kildress w Altedesert *Arm* from 92. *Kildress Rectory, 6 Rectory Road, Cookstown BT80 9RX* T: (028) 7965 1215
E: brian@aonet.org.uk

CRUMP (formerly WARREN), Mrs Barbara. b 46. d 08 p 09. NSM Rocester and Croxden w Hollington *Lich* 08-11; NSM Uttoxeter Area 08-15; rtd 15; PtO *Lich* from 15. *1 Lake Drive, Doveridge, Ashbourne DE6 5NW* T: (01889) 564195
E: barbarawarren149@btinternet.com

CRUMPLER, Peter George. b 56. ERMC. d 13 p 14. NSM Sandridge *St Alb* from 13. *57 Kingshill Avenue, St Albans AL4 9QH* T: (01727) 847760 E: sandridgecurate@gmail.com

CRUMPTON, Colin. b 38. AKC 61 Sheff Univ Dip Leadership, Renewal & Miss Studies 97. d 64 p 65. C Billingham St Cuth *Dur* 64-66; C Shirley *Birm* 66-69; V Mossley *Ches* 69-75; Miss to Seamen 75-77; V Burslem St Paul *Lich* 77-82; V Edensor 82-97; V Llanrhaeadr-ym-Mochnant etc *St As* 97-00; Dir Accra Retreat Cen Ghana 00-01; rtd 02; Hon C Redmarley D'Abitot, Bromesberrow, Pauntley etc *Glouc* 02-03; PtO *Lich* from 03; Ches from 04. *1 Dennis Round Court, Hall Drive, Alsager, Stoke-on-Trent ST7 2YD* T: (01270) 882666 M: 07799-183971 E: colin.crumpton@virgin.net

CRUSE, Jack. b 35. ARIBA 67. Sarum & Wells Th Coll 76. d 79 p 80. NSM W Teignmouth *Ex* 79-85; C Ideford, Luton and Ashcombe 85-89; C Bishopsteignton 85-89; R Broadhempston, Woodland, Staverton etc 90-98; RD Totnes 94-98; rtd 98; PtO *Ex* from 98. *41 Butts Close, Honiton EX14 2FS* T: (01404) 46567 E: jack@jcruse.freeserve.co.uk

CRUSE, John Jeremy. b 58. Univ of Wales (Lamp) BA 79 Hughes Hall Cam CertEd 87. Sarum & Wells Th Coll 81. d 82 p 83. C Newton St Pet *S & B* 82-84; P-in-c Newbridge-on-Wye and Llanfihangel Brynpabuan 84-86; PtO *Heref* 88-89; C Waltham H Cross *Chelmsf* 89-91; TV Yatton Moor *B & W* 91-00; V Shalford *Guildf* from 00. *The Vicarage, East Shalford Lane, Shalford, Guildford GU4 8AE* T/F: (01483) 562396 M: 07889-919928 E: vicar@stmary-shalford.org.uk

CRUSE, Mrs Susan Elizabeth. b 51. Middx Univ BA 04. NTMTC 01. d 04 p 05. NSM Eastington w Fryerning *Chelmsf* 04-11; TV Halstead Area from 11. *The Vicarage, Church Road, Gosfield, Halstead CO9 1UD* T: (01787) 273434 M: 07885-909837 E: sue.cruse@sky.com

CRUST, Mrs Erica Doreen. b 51. d 10 p 11. NSM Moulton *Linc* 10-14; NSM Mid Elloe Gp from 14. *3 St Guthlac's Close, Crowland, Peterborough PE6 0ES* T: (01733) 321077 M: 07751-323584 E: erica@thecrusts.freeserve.co.uk

CRUTCHLEY, John Hamilton. b 62. Kingston Poly LLB 85. Trin Coll Bris 99. d 01 p 02. C Barnstaple *Ex* 01-06; R Ardingly *Chich* from 06. *The Rectory, Church Lane, Ardingly, Haywards Heath RH17 6UR* T: (01444) 892332
E: crutchleyfam@tesco.net

CRYER, Gordon David. b 34. St D Coll Lamp BA 63. d 64 p 65. C Mortlake w E Sheen *S'wark* 64-67; C Godstone 67-70; Chapl St Dunstan's Abbey Sch Plymouth 71-02; R Stoke Damerel *Ex* 71-02; P-in-c Devonport St Aubyn 88-02; rtd 02; PtO *Truro* from 02. *9 St Stephens Road, Saltash PL12 4BG* T: (01752) 510436

CUBA, Bishop of. *See* HURTADO, The Rt Revd Jorge A Perera

CUBITT, Paul. b 64. Sheff Univ BA 86. Cranmer Hall Dur 95. d 97 p 98. C Bromyard *Heref* 97-01; V Elloughton and Brough w Brantingham *York* 01-07; R Blofield w Hemblington *Nor* 07-14; RD Blofield 08-14; V N Walsham and Edingthorpe from 14. *The Vicarage, 28A Yarmouth Road, North Walsham NR28 9AT* T: (01692) 406380 E: revpcubitt@btinternet.com

CUDBY, Paul Edward Frank. b 66. Hatf Poly BSc 88. Ridley Hall Cam 99. d 02 p 03. C Bedford St Andr *St Alb* 02-06; V Tanworth *Birm* from 06; Bp's Adv for New Relig Movements from 12. *The Vicarage, Vicarage Hill, Tanworth-in-Arden, Solihull B94 5EB* T: (01564) 742565 E: paulcudby@ntlworld.com

CUFF, Gregor John. b 61. Keele Univ BSc 82 Liv Hope Univ MA 12 LTCL 07. Ridley Hall Cam 93. d 95 p 96. C Stanley *Liv* 95-99; V Waterloo Ch Ch and St Jo from 99; Hon Chapl Mersey Miss to Seafarers from 06. *The Vicarage, 22 Crosby Road South, Liverpool L22 1RQ* T/F: 0151-920 7791
E: gregor.cuff@btinternet.com

CUFF, Preb Pamela. b 47. MCSP 68. S Dios Minl Tr Scheme 89. d 92 p 94. NSM Nether Stowey w Over Stowey *B & W* 92-93; NSM Quantoxhead 93-07; NSM Quantock Coast 07-12; Asst Chapl Taunton Hosps 93-94; Asst Chapl Taunton and Somerset NHS Trust 94-05; Bp's Officer for Ord NSM (Taunton Adnry) *B & W* 06-09; PtO from 12; Preb Wells Cathl from 08. *Millands, Kilve, Bridgwater TA5 1EA* T: (01278) 741229
E: pam.cuff@hotmail.co.uk

CUFF, Simon Lloyd. b 88. Keble Coll Ox BA 09 MSt 10 DPhil 14. Ox Min Course 10. d 13 p 14. C Ealing Ch the Sav *Lon* from 13. *28 Castlebar Road, London W5 2DD* T: (020) 8621 5061
E: frsimon@ymail.com

CULL, John. b 31. Oak Hill Th Coll 56. d 59 p 60. C Radipole *Sarum* 59-66; Chapl Mariners' Ch Glouc 66-70; R Woodchester *Glouc* 70-90; RD Stonehouse 85-89; V Walton *St E* 90-94; rtd 94; PtO *Glouc* from 94. *Hillgrove Stables, Bear Hill, Woodchester, Stroud GL5 5DH* T: (01453) 872145

CULLEN, Canon John Austin. b 43. Auckland Univ BA 67 Otago Univ BD 76 Keble Coll Ox DPhil 86 FRSA 89. St Jo Coll Auckland 66. d 69 p 70. C Papatoetoe New Zealand 69-73; Assoc P Mt Albert St Luke 73-75; P-in-c 74; Hon C Remuera St Aiden 75-78; Asst Chapl Keble Coll Ox 79-82; PtO *Lon* 82-84; Chapl and Lect Worc Coll Ox 84-86; C St Botolph Aldgate w H Trin Minories *Lon* 86-87; Dir Inst of Chr Studies 87-91; Hon C St Marylebone All SS 87-91; Dir of Min Development *Win* 91-01; Hon Can Win Cathl 96-02; Sen Asst to Bp Lon 02-04; P-in-c St Geo-in-the-East w St Paul 03-04; V Palmers Green St Jo 05-12; rtd 12. *73 Stanhope Road, London N11 2LB* T: (020) 8350 5616 E: john.cullen1@virgin.net

CULLENS, Lynne Susan. b 64. Man Univ BA 86 GradICSA 90. SNWTP 09. d 12 p 13. C Congleton *Ches* 12-15; C Sandbach Heath w Wheelock from 15. *16A New Street, Elworth, Sandbach CW11 3JF* T: (01270) 529089 M: 07561-167567
E: lynne.cullens@sky.com

CULLIFORD, Jane Margaret. b 48. Lon Univ MB, BS 73. STETS 03. d 06 p 07. NSM Dorchester *Sarum* 06-14; NSM Dorchester and the Winterbournes from 14; Bp's Adv for Wholeness and Healing from 10. *8 Grosvenor Road, Dorchester DT1 2BB* T: (01305) 264360 E: janeculliford@aol.com

CULLIMORE, Jeremy Stuart. b 53. TD . Westcott Ho Cam. d 06 p 07. C New Sleaford *Linc* 06-10; P-in-c Linc St Pet-at-Gowts and St Andr from 10; P-in-c Linc St Botolph from 10; P-in-c Linc St Mary-le-Wigford w St Benedict etc from 10. *St Peter-at-Gowts Vicarage, 1 Sibthorpe Street, Lincoln LN5 7SP* T: (01522) 530256 M: 07733-114280
E: jscullimore@btinternet.com

CULLING, Elizabeth Ann. *See* HOARE, Elizabeth Ann

CULLINGWORTH, Anthony Robert. b 42. BSc. Ox NSM Course. d 83 p 84. NSM Slough *Ox* 83-99; NSM Denham 99-02; NSM Morton St Luke *Bradf* 02-04; PtO *Leeds* from 04. *2 Thurleston Court, East Morton, Keighley BD20 5RG* T: (01535) 601187
E: thecullies@aol.com

CULLINGWORTH (née CHAPMAN), Mrs Claire Louise. b 74. St Anne's Coll Ox BA 96 St Jo Coll Dur BA 08. Cranmer Hall

Dur 06. **d** 08 **p** 09. C Tadcaster w Newton Kyme *York* 08-12; V Windy Nook St Alb *Dur* from 12. *The Vicarage, Coldwell Park Drive, Gateshead NE10 9BY* T: 0191-442 2499
E: claire@secondmouse.co.uk

CULLIS, Andrew Stanley Weldon. b 48. Hertf Coll Ox BA 69 LTh. St Jo Coll Nottm 70. **d** 73 **p** 74. C Reigate St Mary *S'wark* 73-78; C Yateley *Win* 78-82; V Dorking St Paul *Guildf* 82-00; RD Dorking 94-99; P-in-c Chilwell *S'well* 00-04; R Fisherton Anger *Sarum* 04-13; rtd 13. *76 Fernside Road, Poole BH15 2JL*

CULLWICK, Christopher John. b 53. Hull Univ BA 75. Wycliffe Hall Ox BA 80 MA 85. **d** 81 **p** 82. C Nottingham St Jude *S'well* 81-84; C York St Mich-le-Belfrey 84-87; TV Huntington 87-03; Ind Chapl 02-10; Ldr York Community Chapl 10-13; rtd 13; PtO *York* from 13. *64 Strensall Road, Huntington, York YO32 9SH* T: (01904) 764608 M: 07792-565805
E: cullwick@lineone.net

CULLY, Miss Elizabeth Faith. b 46. SRN 67 SCM 69 RGN 72. Trin Coll Bris BA 88. **d** 88 **p** 94. Par Dn Filton *Bris* 88-92; Par Dn Fishponds St Jo 92-94; C 94-95; P-in-c Brinsley w Underwood *S'well* 95-98; V 98-02; P-in-c Farnsfield 02-08; P-in-c Kirklington w Hockerton 02-08; P-in-c Bilsthorpe 02-08; P-in-c Eakring 02-08; P-in-c Maplebeck 02-08; P-in-c Winkburn 02-08; rtd 08; Hon C Salcombe and Malborough w S Huish *Ex* from 08. *26 Weymouth Park, Hope Cove, Kingsbridge TQ7 3HD* T: (01548) 561081 E: faith.cully@btinternet.com

CULVERWELL, Martin Phillip. b 48. Sarum & Wells Th Coll 72. **d** 75 **p** 76. C Ashford St Hilda *Lon* 75-78; C Chelsea St Luke 78-80; Chapl RN 80-83; TV Yeovil *B & W* 83-87; P-in-c Sarratt *St Alb* 87-90; NSM Bradford w Oake, Hillfarrance and Heathfield *B & W* 90-92; R Rode Major 92-96; PtO 07-09; *Portsm* from 09. *8 Sandisplatt, Fareham PO14 3AG* T: (01329) 841358 E: stbeon@gmail.com

CUMBERLAND, The Very Revd Barry John. b 44. Birm Univ BA 67 Worc Coll Ox DipEd 68. Trin Coll Singapore MDiv 88. **d** 88 **p** 89. NSM Westmr St Matt *Lon* 88-90; PtO 90-96; Philippines 90-96, 98-01, and from 03; Dean Manila 92-96; Chapl Stockholm w Gävle and Västerås *Eur* 96-98; P-in-c Las Palmas 01-03; rtd 09. *85A Aurora Pijuan Street, BFRV, Las Pinas City 1740, Metro Manila, Philippines* T: (0063) (2) 875 3528
E: barrycumberland@yahoo.co.uk

CUMBERLAND, John Allan. b 51. Chu Coll Cam BA 73 MA 78. WEMTC 07. **d** 10 **p** 11. NSM Wenlock *Heref* from 10. *Priory Cottage, 5 The Bull Ring, Much Wenlock TF13 6HS* T: (01952) 727386 E: jacumberland@btinternet.com

CUMBERLEGE, Francis Richard. b 41. AKC 65. **d** 66 **p** 67. C Leigh Park St Fran CD *Portsm* 66-71; P-in-c Gona Papua New Guinea 71-75; R Popondetta 79-81; Adn N Papua 74-81; R Hastings St Clem and All SS *Chich* 81-86; V Broadwater Down 86-91; V Tunbridge Wells St Mark *Roch* 91-99; RD Tunbridge Wells 96-99; P-in-c Brockenhurst *Win* 99-03; V 03-06; rtd 06; P-in-c Ashburnham w Penhurst *Chich* 09-12; PtO *Win* from 14. *Kairos, 10 Forward Drive, Pennington, Lymington SO41 8GA* T: (01590) 719421
E: cumberlege@littleoaks.net

CUMBERLIDGE, Anthony Wynne. b 49. ACIB 75. Sarum & Wells Th Coll 79. **d** 82 **p** 83. C Llanrhos *St As* 82-85; R Llanfair Talhaearn and Llansannan etc 85-87; CF 87-04; P-in-c Lambourn and Eastbury and E Garston *Ox* 04-11; rtd 12. *17 Juniper Close, Bilsthorpe, Newark NG22 8UN* T: (01623) 871883

CUMINGS, Llewellyn Frank Beadnell. b 29. Natal Univ BA 50 St Cath Coll Cam CertEd 53. Ridley Hall Cam 65. **d** 67 **p** 68. C Leamington Priors St Mary *Cov* 67-70; V Lobley Hill *Dur* 70-74; R Denver *Ely* 74-82; V Ryston w Roxham 74-82; R St Leonards St Leon *Chich* 82-88; V Billinghay *Linc* 88-93; rtd 93; PtO *St As* from 09. *Y Bwthyn, Coedllan, Llanfyllin SY22 5BP* T: (01691) 648013

CUMMING, Miss Catriona Mary. b 82. York Univ BA 04 MA 05. Westcott Ho Cam 11. **d** 14 **p** 15. C Melton Mowbray *Leic* from 14. *1 Palmerston Road, Melton Mowbray LE13 0SS* E: catriona.cumming@yahoo.com

CUMMING, Canon Nigel Patrick. b 42. St Jo Coll Nottm 73. **d** 75 **p** 76. C Castle Hall *Ches* 75-77; C Stalybridge H Trin and Ch Ch 77-78; C Tadley St Pet *Win* 78-82; R Overton w Laverstoke and Freefolk 82-07; RD Whitchurch 89-98; Hon Can Win Cathl 99-07; rtd 07; PtO *Win* from 08. *Pasture House, Whitsbury, Fordingbridge SP6 3QB* T: (01725) 518248
E: nigel.cumming@btinternet.com

CUMMING, Paul James. b 79. Cliff Coll BA 00. St Jo Coll Nottm 09. **d** 11 **p** 12. C Poynton *Ches* 11-14; V Cheadle All Hallows from 14. *All Hallows' Vicarage, 222 Councillor Lane, Cheadle SK8 2JG* T: 0161-478 8789 E: cumming-no-s@hotmail.co.uk *or* revpaul@live.co.uk

CUMMING, Susan Margaret. *See* FORSHAW, Susan Margaret

CUMMING-LATTEY, Mrs Susan Mary Ruth. b 47. Open Univ BA 77 SRN 69. STETS 00. **d** 03 **p** 04. NSM Ash Vale *Guildf* 03-07; NSM Crondall and Ewshot from 07; Chapl Phyllis

Tuckwell Hospice Farnham from 12. *38A Elms Road, Fleet GU51 3EQ* T: (01252) 621295 M: 07761-126354 F: 815882
E: suelattey@btinternet.com

CUMMINGS, Mrs Elizabeth. b 45. St Jo Coll Dur BA 84. NEOC 85. **d** 87 **p** 94. NSM Dur St Giles 87-89; Chapl HM Pris Dur 89-90; Chapl HM Rem Cen Low Newton 90-95; Chapl HM Pris Stocken 95-96; Chapl HM Pris Frankland 96-05; rtd 05; PtO *Dur* from 05. *8 Bridgemere Drive, Framwellgate Moor, Durham DH1 5FG* T: 0191-383 0832

CUMMINGS, John Michael. b 53. Ex Univ BTh 07 Solicitor 87. SWMTC 02. **d** 05 **p** 06. NSM Langport Area *B & W* from 05; Chapl Yeovil Distr Hosp NHS Foundn Trust from 09. *32 Bishops Drive, Langport TA10 9HW* T: (01458) 250449 M: 07966-416675 E: headways1@waitrose.com

CUMMINGS, Canon William Alexander Vickery. b 38. Ch Ch Ox BA 62 MA 64. Wycliffe Hall Ox 61. **d** 64 **p** 65. C Leytonstone St Jo *Chelmsf* 64-67; C Writtle 67-71; R Stratton St Mary w Stratton St Michael *Nor* 71-73; R Wacton Magna w Parva 71-73; R Stratton St Mary w Stratton St Michael etc 73-91; RD Depwade 81-91; Hon Can Nor Cathl 90-91; V Battle Chich 91-04; Dean Battle 91-04; rtd 04; PtO *Win* from 13. *80 Samber Close, Lymington SO41 9LF* T: (01590) 610426

CUMMINS, Ashley Wighton. b 56. St Andr Univ BD 83. Coates Hall Edin 82. **d** 84 **p** 85. C Broughty Ferry *Bre* 84-87; P-in-c Dundee St Ninian 87-92; P-in-c Invergowrie from 92; Chapl Angl Students Dundee Univ 92-07. *27 Errol Road, Invergowrie, Dundee DD2 5AG* T: (01382) 562525
E: ashleycummins@tiscali.co.uk

CUMMINS, Daphne Mary. *See* GREEN, Daphne Mary

CUMMINS, James Ernest. b 32. Brasted Th Coll 56 Westcott Ho Cam 57. **d** 60 **p** 61. C Baswich *Lich* 60-64; V Hales w Heckingham *Nor* 64-70; V Raveningham 70-76; PtO *Heref* 76-08; *S & B* 76-08; rtd 97. *Skyborry, Knighton LD7 1TW* T: (01547) 528369 F: 640677

CUMMINS, Lesley Patricia. b 47. **d** 12 **p** 13. NSM Poynton *Ches* from 12. *20 Distaff Road, Poynton, Stockport SK12 1HN*

CUMMINS, Nicholas Marshall. b 36. CITC 65. **d** 67 **p** 68. C Ballymena w Ballyclug *Conn* 67-70; C Belfast St Nic 70-73; I Buttevant Union *C, C & R* 73-78; I Mallow Union 78-83; I Kilmoe Union 83-96; Can Cork Cathl 90-96; Treas Cork Cathl 95-96; Preb Tymothan St Patr Cathl Dublin 95-01; Dean Killaloe and Clonfert *L & K* 96-01; Dean Kilfenora and Provost Kilmacduagh 96-01; I Killaloe w Stradbally 96-01; rtd 01. *13 Borough Hill, Petersfield GU32 3LQ* T: (01730) 269742

CUNDILL, David James. b 65. Leic Poly BEng 88. St Jo Coll Nottm MTh 05. **d** 05 **p** 06. C Leic Martyrs 05-09; Pioneer Min Leic City Cen 09-15; Chapl De Montfort Univ 10-14; P-in-c Springfield *Birm* 11-15; V from 15. *St Mary's House, The Close, Lichfield WS13 7LD* T: (01532) 306030
E: david.cundill@btinternet.com

CUNLIFFE, Anne. b 48. CBDTI 01. **d** 04 **p** 05. OLM Poulton-le-Sands w Morecambe St Laur *Blackb* 04-07; NSM 04-14; rtd 14; PtO *Blackb* from 14. *14 Coniston Road, Morecambe LA4 5PS* T: (01524) 422509 E: revanne@gmail.com

CUNLIFFE, The Ven Christopher John. b 55. Ch Ch Ox BA 77 MA 81 DPhil 81 Trin Coll Cam BA 82 MA 86 ARHistS 94. Westcott Ho Cam 80. **d** 83 **p** 84. C Chesterfield St Mary and All SS *Derby* 83-85; Chapl Linc Coll Ox 85-89; Chapl City Univ and Guildhall Sch of Music and Drama *Lon* 89-91; Voc Officer and Selection Sec ABM 91-97; Dir Professional Min *Lon* 97-03; Chapl to Bp Bradwell *Chelmsf* 04-06; Adn Derby from 06; Can Res Derby Cathl 06-08. *1 Thatch Close, Derby DE22 1EA* T: (01332) 553455 *or* 382233 F: 552322 *or* 292969
E: archderby@derby.anglican.org

CUNLIFFE, Harold. b 28. St Aid Birkenhead 57. **d** 60 **p** 61. C Hindley All SS *Liv* 60-64; V Everton St Chad w Ch Ch 64-69; R Golborne 70-93; rtd 93; PtO *Liv* from 93. *51 Greenfields Crescent, Ashton-in-Makerfield, Wigan WN4 8QY* T: (01942) 202956 E: cunliffe@cableinet.co.uk

CUNLIFFE, The Ven Helen Margaret. b 54. St Hilda's Coll Ox BA 77 MA 78. Westcott Ho Cam 81. **dss** 83 **d** 87 **p** 94. Chesterfield St Mary and All SS *Derby* 83-85; Ox St Mary V w St Cross and St Pet 86-89; Par Dn 87-89; Chapl Nuff Coll Ox 86-89; Team Dn Clapham Team *S'wark* 89-94; TV 94-96; Can Res S'wark Cathl 96-03; Chapl Welcare 96-03; Adn St Alb *St Alb* 03-07; rtd 08. *1 Thatch Close, Derby DE22 1EA* T: (01332) 553455

CUNLIFFE (née LEESE), Mrs Katherine Helen. b 79. Coll of Resurr Mirfield 13. **d** 15. C Man Gd Shep from 15. *Address temp unknown* T: 0161-223 5481
E: katycunliffe@hotmail.com

CUNLIFFE, Peter Henry. b 54. Univ of Wales MA 93 SRN 77 RSCN 79 RCNT 83. Trin Coll Bris 92. **d** 94 **p** 95. C Carshalton Beeches *S'wark* 94-95; C Reigate St Mary 95-02; P-in-c Hemingford Grey *Ely* 02-04; V from 04; P-in-c Hemingford

Abbots from 04. *The Vicarage, 6 Braggs Lane, Hemingford Grey, Huntingdon PE28 9BW* T: (01480) 394378 E: vicar@churchbytheriver.org.uk

CUNNINGHAM, Brian James. b 65. York Univ BA 88. Ripon Coll Cuddesdon BA 91. **d** 92 **p** 93. C Merrow *Guildf* 92-96; C Kennington St Jo w St Jas *S'wark* 96-99; Chapl Pangbourne Coll 99-11; Chapl Oundle Sch from 11. *Oundle School, New Street, Oundle, Peterborough PE8 4GH* T: (01832) 277122 E: bjc@oundleschool.org.uk

CUNNINGHAM, John James. b 50. TCD Div Sch BTh 98. **d** 98 **p** 99. C Drumachose *D & R* 98-01; I Camus-juxta-Bann 01-06; I Ballymoney w Finvoy and Rasharkin *Conn* 06-11; I Ballymacarrett *D & D* from 11. *155 Upper Newtownards Road, Belfast BT4 3HX*

CUNNINGHAM, Canon Philip John. b 52. St Jo Coll Dur BA 74 PGCE 75 MA 85. NOC 93. **d** 95 **p** 96. NSM York St Luke 95-97; NSM York St Olave w St Giles 97-99; TV Haxby w Wigginton 99-02; V Gosforth St Nic *Newc* from 02; AD Newc Cen 05-13; Hon Can Newc Cathl from 11. *The Vicarage, 17 Rectory Road, Gosforth, Newcastle upon Tyne NE3 1XR* T: 0191-285 1326 E: philipcunningham@hotmail.com

CUNNINGHAM, Richard Martin. b 61. Goldsmiths' Coll Lon BEd 84. SAOMC 95. **d** 98 **p** 99. NSM Kingham w Churchill, Daylesford and Sarsden *Ox* 98-01; NSM Chipping Norton 01-02; NSM Ox St Andr from 01. *Churchill Mill, Sarsden Halt, Churchill, Chipping Norton OX7 6NT* T: (01608) 659426 F: 659134 E: richard.cunningham@standrewsoxford.org.uk

CUNNINGHAM, Wendy. b 42. SAOMC 01. **d** 04 **p** 05. NSM Hook Norton w Gt Rollright, Swerford etc *Ox* from 04. *Dewlands, Church End, Great Rollright, Chipping Norton OX7 5RX* T: (01608) 737135 E: wendy@dewlands.me.uk

CUNNINGTON, Canon Andrew Thomas. b 56. Southn Univ BTh 86. Sarum & Wells Th Coll 82. **d** 85 **p** 86. C Ifield *Chich* 85-89; TV Haywards Heath St Wilfrid 89-94; V Midhurst 94-06; R Woolbeding 94-06; RD Midhurst 03-06; V Redhill St Matt *S'wark* from 06; Jt Dir of IME Croydon Area 09-13; AD Reigate from 13; Hon Can S'wark Cathl from 15. *St Matthew's Vicarage, 27 Ridgeway Road, Redhill RH1 6PQ* T: (01737) 761568 E: andrew@stmatthews-redhill.org.uk

CUNNINGTON, Miss Averil. b 41. St Mary's Coll Chelt CertEd 61 Man Univ BA 68 MEd 73. NOC 93. **d** 95 **p** 96. Hd Mistress Counthill Sch Oldham 84-96; NSM Milnrow *Man* 95-98; NSM Hey 98-02; Lic Preacher 02-05; Tutor NOC 98-05; PtO *Heref* 05-10; *Man* from 10. *6 Summerhill View, Denshaw, Oldham OL3 5TB*

CUNNINGTON, Howard James. b 56. Southn Univ BA 77 St Jo Coll Dur PGCE 78. Trin Coll Bris 90. **d** 92 **p** 93. C Ex St Leon w H Trin 92-96; V Sandown Ch Ch and Lower Sandown St Jo *Portsm* 96-04; PtO from 04. *5 The Mall, Lake Hill, Sandown PO36 9ED* E: howard@cunnington.org.uk

CUPITT, Don. b 34. Trin Hall Cam BA 55 MA 58 Bris Univ Hon DLitt 84. Westcott Ho Cam 57. **d** 59 **p** 60. C Salford St Phil w St Steph *Man* 59-62; Vice-Prin Westcott Ho Cam 62-66; Dean Em Coll Cam 66-91; Asst Lect Div Cam Univ 68-73; Lect 73-96; rtd 96; Life Fell Em Coll Cam from 96. *Emmanuel College, Cambridge CB2 3AP* T: (01223) 334200

CURD, Preb Christine Veronica. b 51. Bris Univ BA Leic Univ MSc 05. Oak Hill Th Coll 84 WMMTC 88. **d** 89 **p** 94. NSM Widecombe-in-the-Moor, Leusdon, Princetown etc *Ex* 89-93; NSM Bovey Tracey SS Pet, Paul and Thos w Hennock 94-97; Asst Chapl HM Pris Channings Wood 92-01; Chapl HM Pris Ex 01-10; Bp's Officer for Pris *Ex* 10-13; Hon C Dawlish 13-15; Hon C Dawlish, Cofton and Starcross from 15; Preb Ex Cathl from 05. *St George's, Holcombe Village, Dawlish EX7 0JT* M: 07710-159751 E: stgeorgesholcombe@live.co.uk

CURD, Clifford John Letsom. b 45. SRN RNT. Oak Hill Th Coll 84. **d** 86 **p** 87. C Stone Ch Ch *Lich* 86-89; TV Widecombe-in-the-Moor, Leusdon, Princetown etc *Ex* 89-93; P-in-c Ilsington 93-04; rtd 05. *Address withheld by request* M: 07881-442031 E: cliff-chris@garden2.eclipse.co.uk

CURL, Roger William. b 50. BA BD DPhil. Oak Hill Th Coll. **d** 82 **p** 83. C Cromer *Nor* 82-86; C Sevenoaks St Nic *Roch* 86-88; V Fulham St Mary N End *Lon* from 88. *St Mary's Vicarage, 2 Edith Road, London W14 9BA* T: (020) 7602 1996 E: stmarys.westken@london.anglican.org

CURNEW, Brian Leslie. b 48. Qu Coll Ox BA 69 DPhil 77 MA 77. Ripon Coll Cuddesdon 77. **d** 79 **p** 80. C Sandhurst *Ox* 79-82; Tutor St Steph Ho Ox 82-87; V Fishponds St Mary *Bris* 87-94; TR Ludlow *Heref* 94-09; P-in-c Bitterley w Middleton, Stoke St Milborough etc 09; Preb Heref Cathl 02-09; P-in-c Headcorn *Cant* 09-11; P-in-c Sutton Valence w E Sutton and Chart Sutton 09-11; V Headcorn and The Suttons 11-14; rtd 14. *16 Richmond Road, London N11 2QR* T: (020) 8292 9207 E: briancurnew@gmail.com

CURNOCK, Canon Karen Susan. b 50. Nottm Univ BTh 78. Linc Th Coll 74. **d** 95 **p** 97. NSM Graffoe Gp *Linc* 95-96; Dioc Sec *Sarum* 96-03; NSM Chalke Valley 96-03; V Buckland

Newton, Cerne Abbas, Godmanstone etc 03-10; Can and Preb Sarum Cathl 02-10; RD Dorchester 06-09; rtd 10. *Stoneacre, Castle Hill, Seaton EX12 2QP* E: karen.curnock@gmail.com

CURNOW, Terence Peter. b 37. Univ of Wales (Lamp) BA 62. **d** 63 **p** 64. C Llanishen and Lisvane *Llan* 63-71; Youth Chapl 67-71; Asst Chapl K Coll Taunton 71-74; Chapl Taunton Sch 74-84; Ho Master 84-98; PtO *B & W* from 84; rtd 02. *19 Stonegallows, Taunton TA1 5JW* T: (01823) 330003

CURRAH, Michael Ewart. b 31. Down Coll Cam BA 54 MA 58. Sarum Th Coll 54. **d** 56 **p** 57. C Calne *Sarum* 56-60; V Southbroom 60-69; PtO 70-88; Asst Master Woodroffe Sch Lyme Regis 71-85; Hon C Taunton H Trin *B & W* 88-96; rtd 96; PtO *B & W* 96-06; *Leic* from 06. *14 Latimer Crescent, Market Harborough LE16 8AP* T: (01858) 433706

CURRALL, James Edward Patrick. b 55. Man Univ BSc 76 Aber Univ PhD 81. TISEC 09. **d** 12 **p** 13. C Largs *Glas* from 12. *9 Aitken Street, Dalry KA24 4BX* T: (01294) 833294 E: jcurrall@talktalk.net

CURRAN, John Henry. b 77. Nottm Univ BA 00. Wycliffe Hall Ox 00. **d** 02 **p** 03. C W Bridgford *S'well* 02-05; Youth Chapl P-in-c Wollaton Park 07-11; V from 11; Chapl Nottm Univ 07-11. *St Mary's Vicarage, Wollaton Hall Drive, Nottingham NG8 1AF* T: 0115-978 4914 E: henry@curransonline.co.uk

CURRAN, The Ven Patrick Martin Stanley. b 56. K Coll (NS) BA 80 Southn Univ BTh 84. Chich Th Coll 80. **d** 84 **p** 85. C Heavitree w Ex St Paul 84-87; Bp's Chapl to Students *Bradf* 87-93; Chapl Bonn w Cologne *Eur* 93-00; Chapl Vienna from 00; Can Malta Cathl from 00; Adn E Adnry from 02. *The British Embassy, Jaurèsgasse 12, A-1030 Vienna, Austria* T: (0043) (1) 714 8900 *or* 718 5902 E: office@christchurchvienna.org

CURRAN, Thomas Heinrich. b 49. Toronto Univ BA 72 Dalhousie Univ Canada MA 75 Hatf Coll Dur PhD 91. Atlantic Sch of Th MTS 80. **d** 78 **p** 79. Canada 77-81 and from 92; Chapl Hatf Coll Dur 88-92. *PO Box 28010 RPO Tacoma, Dartmouth NS B2W 6E2, Canada*

CURRELL, Linda Anne. *See* SCOTT, Linda Anne

CURRER, Caroline Mary. b 49. Keele Univ BA 71 Warwick Univ PhD 86 Anglia Ruskin Univ MA 09 CQSW 71. EAMTC 02. **d** 04 **p** 05. NSM Stansted Mountfitchet w Birchanger and Farnham *Chelmsf* 04-09; P-in-c Poynings w Edburton, Newtimber and Pyecombe *Chich* from 09. *The Rectory, The Street, Poynings, Brighton BN45 7AQ* T: (01273) 857456 E: c.currer@btinternet.com

CURREY, Pauline Carol. *See* REES, Pauline Carol

CURRIE, Alan Richard. b 58. St Andr Univ MA 82 Aber Univ DipEd 83. NEOC 97. **d** 00 **p** 01. NSM Haydon Bridge and Beltingham w Henshaw *Newc* 00-05; NSM St John Lee and Warden w Newbrough 05-08; NSM Hexham from 08. *35 Dotland Close, Eastwood Grange, Hexham NE46 1UF* T: (01434) 607614

CURRIE, Daniel Robert. b 71. Trin Coll Bris 07. **d** 09 **p** 10. C Gorleston St Andr *Nor* 09-12; C Marple All SS *Ches* from 12. *125 Church Lane, Marple, Stockport SK6 7LD* E: revdcurrie@gmail.com

CURRIE, John Stuart. b 47. SEITE 94. **d** 97 **p** 98. C S Chatham H Trin *Roch* 97-01; TV 01-13; Dioc Ecum Officer 09-13; rtd 13; PtO *Roch* from 13; *Cant* from 14. *Pilgrim's House, Oxenden Street, Herne Bay CT6 8TD* T: (01227) 364842 M: 07814-670051 E: revjsc@gmail.com

CURRIE, Mrs Katherine Barbara. b 55. Huddersfield Univ BSc 01 York St Jo Univ BA 13 SRN 78. Yorks Min Course 12. **d** 14 **p** 15. NSM High Hoyland, Scissett and Clayton W *Leeds* from 14. *158 Blacker Lane, Netherton, Wakefield WF4 4EZ* T: (01924) 279295 M: 07949-850460 E: kate.currie158@yahoo.co.uk

CURRIE, Lesley Sarah. b 70. Nene Coll Northn BA 95 Herts Univ PGCE 97. All SS Cen for Miss & Min 11. **d** 14 **p** 15. NSM Marple All SS *Ches* from 14. *125 Church Lane, Marple, Stockport SK6 7LD* T: 0161-292 9305 E: dalcurrie5@gmail.com

CURRIE, Canon Stuart William. b 53. Hertf Coll Ox MA 79 Fitzw Coll Cam BA 85 CertEd. Westcott Ho Cam 82. **d** 85 **p** 86. C Whitley Ch Ch *Ox* 85-89; TV Banbury 89-94; V Barbourne *Worc* from 94; Hon Can Worc Cathl from 09. *St Stephen's Vicarage, 1 Beech Avenue, Worcester WR3 8PZ* T: (01905) 452169 E: sw.currie@virgin.net

CURRIN, John. b 56. Keele Univ CertEd 78. St Jo Coll Nottm MA 93. **d** 93 **p** 94. C Eastwood *S'well* 93-97; P-in-c Matlock Bath and Cromford *Derby* 97-02; V 02-06; R Dibden *Win* from 06. *The Rectory, Beaulieu Road, Dibden Purlieu, Southampton SO45 4PT* T: (023) 8084 3204

CURRY, Canon Bruce. b 39. Dur Univ BA 61. Wells Th Coll 61. **d** 63 **p** 64. C Shepton Mallet *B & W* 63-67; C Cheam *S'wark* 67-71; R W Walton *Ely* 71-78; V St Neots 78-94; P-in-c Everton w Tetworth 94-98; P-in-c Abbotsley 94-99; P-in-c Waresley 94-99; P-in-c Gt w Lt Gransden 98-99; R Gt Gransden and Abbotsley and Lt Gransden etc 99-04; RD St Neots 90-02;

Hon Can Ely Cathl 98-04; rtd 04; PtO *Ely* from 05. *10 Ravens Court, Ely CB6 3ED* T: (01353) 661494 E: brucecurry10@gmail.com *or* janeandbruce@waitrose.com

CURRY, George Robert. b 51. JP 90. Bede Coll Dur BA 72 Newc Univ MA 97. Cranmer Hall Dur Oak Hill Th Coll. **d** 76 **p** 77. C Denton Holme *Carl* 76-81; V Low Elswick *Newc* 81-06; P-in-c High Elswick St Paul 97-06; V Elswick from 06. *St Stephen's Vicarage, Clumber Street, Newcastle upon Tyne NE4 7ST* T: 0191-273 4680 E: g.r.curry@btinternet.com

CURRY, James Sebastian. b 63. Hatf Coll Dur BA 84. Ripon Coll Cuddesdon BTh 93. **d** 93 **p** 94. C Four Oaks *Birm* 93-96; C Erdington St Barn 96-99; TV Jarrow *Dur* 99-06; R Aboyne, Ballater and Braemar *Ab* 06-13; P-in-c Golcar *Leeds* from 13; P-in-c Longwood from 13. *The Vicarage, Church Street, Golcar, Huddersfield HD7 4PX* T: (01484) 654647 E: revjamescurry@btinternet.com

CURTIS, Anthony Gordon. b 74. Selw Coll Cam BTh 10. Westcott Ho Cam 07. **d** 10 **p** 11. C Morpeth *Newc* 10-13; V Shiremoor from 13. *St Mark's Vicarage, Brenkley Avenue, Shiremoor, Newcastle upon Tyne NE27 0PP* T: 0191-253 7020 M: 07969-737763 E: tony_curtis@europe.com

CURTIS, Colin. b 47. Open Univ BA 80 ALA 69. St Jo Coll Nottm 83. **d** 93 **p** 94. NSM Clarkston *Glas* 93-10. *78 Auldhouse Road, Glasgow G43 1UR* T: 0141-569 4206 E: colin.curtis540@ntlworld.com

CURTIS, Canon Geoffrey John. b 35. Dur Univ BA 57. Ripon Hall Ox 59. **d** 61 **p** 62. C Gosport Ch Ch *Portsm* 61-65; C Bedhampton 65-68; Producer Schs Broadcasting Dept BBC Lon 68-75; Dioc Communications Adv *Guildf* 75-00; P-in-c Grayswood 75-91; Dir Grayswood Studio 84-00; Hon Can Guildf Cathl 87-00; rtd 00; PtO *Guildf* from 00. *1 Clairville, Woodside Road, Chiddingfold, Godalming GU8 4QY* T: (01428) 685943

CURTIS, Gerald Arthur. b 46. Lon Univ BA 69. Sarum & Wells Th Coll 85. **d** 87 **p** 88. C Allington and Maidstone St Pet *Cant* 87-90; TV Gt Grimsby St Mary and St Jas *Linc* 90-95; P-in-c Morton w Hacconby 95-96; R Ringstone in Aveland Gp 96-02; rtd 03. *Le Val, 61560 Saint-Germain-de-Martigny, France* E: gacurt@btinternet.com

CURTIS, Mrs Jacqueline Elaine. b 60. Sarum & Wells Th Coll 87. **d** 90 **p** 94. Par Dn Bridport *Sarum* 90-94; C 94-95; TV Melbury 95-00; TV Maltby *Sheff* 00-02; TR 02-08; TR Crosslacon *Carl* from 08. *The Vicarage, Trumpet Road, Cleator CA23 3EF* T: (01946) 810510 E: jecurtisx3@gmail.com

CURTIS, Canon Jane Darwent. b 64. Leic Univ BA 86. Linc Th Coll BTh 93. **d** 93 **p** 94. Par Dn Oadby *Leic* 93-94; C 94-96; Chapl De Montfort Univ 96-03; C Leic H Spirit 96-97; TV 97-03; TV Gilmorton, Peatling Parva, Kimcote etc 03-09; Bp's Adv for Women's Min from 04; V Whatborough Gp from 09; Officer for IME 4-7 from 09; Hon Can Leic Cathl from 06. *The Vicarage, Oakham Road, Tilton on the Hill, Leicester LE7 9LB* T: 0116-259 7244 E: jcurtis@leicester.anglican.org

CURTIS, John Durston. b 43. Lich Th Coll 65. **d** 68 **p** 69. C Coseley Ch Ch *Lich* 68-71; C Sedgley All SS 71-74; CF 74-79; P-in-c Newton Valence *Win* 79-82; P-in-c Selborne 79-82; R Newton Valence, Selborne and E Tisted w Colemore 82-87; R Marchwood 87-09; AD Lyndhurst 05-08; rtd 09; PtO *Nor* from 09. *7 Pearce Road, Diss IP22 4YF* T: (01379) 640036 E: linda.john7@btinternet.com

CURTIS, Mrs Julia. b 67. Warwick Univ BSc 89 Anglia Ruskin Univ BA 13 ACA 92. Westcott Ho Cam 13. **d** 15. C Creech St Michael and Ruishton w Thornfalcon *B & W* from 15. *2 Newlands Grove, Ruishton, Taunton TA3 5JJ* M: 07908-925693 E: revjuliacurtis@gmail.com

CURTIS, Layton Richard. b 61. Leic Univ BSc 84 PGCE 85. Linc Th Coll BTh 93. **d** 93 **p** 94. C Knighton St Mary Magd *Leic* 93-96; C Leic St Phil 96-01; P-in-c Wigston Magna 01-12; P-in-c Hallaton and Allexton, w Horninghold, Tugby etc from 12. *The Vicarage, Oakham Road, Tilton-on-the-Hill, Leicester LE7 9LB* T: 0116-259 7244 M: 07855-746041 E: rcurtis@leicester.anglican.org

CURTIS, Mrs Marian Ruth. b 54. Nottm Univ BA 75 CQSW 80. Trin Coll Bris 03. **d** 05 **p** 06. C Blackheath Park St Mich *S'wark* 05-08; Asst Chapl Salisbury NHS Foundn Trust 08-09; P-in-c Slindon, Eartham and Madehurst *Chich* 09-15; rtd 15. *Short Street Farm, Short Street, Chapmanslade, Westbury BA13 4AA* E: mariancurtis@btinternet.com

CURTIS, Peter Bernard. b 35. St Pet Hall Ox BA 60 MA 64. Westcott Ho Cam 60. **d** 62 **p** 63. C Warsop *S'well* 62-65; Chapl Dur Univ 65-69; V Worle *B & W* 69-78; R Crewkerne w Wayford 78-00; rtd 00; PtO *B & W* from 01. *The Old Farmhouse, 28 Millstream Gardens, Wellington TA21 0AA* T: (01823) 662638

CURTIS, Ronald Victor. b 47. SAOMC 98. **d** 01 **p** 02. NSM Shipton-under-Wychwood w Milton, Fifield etc *Ox* 01-05; P-in-c Stourbridge St Thos *Worc* 05-12; rtd 12; PtO *Ox* from 13. *12 Waites Close, Aston, Bampton OX18 2ES*

CURTIS, Mrs Susan Anne. b 51. Birm Univ CertEd 72 Open Univ BA 79. **d** 07 **p** 08. OLM Epsom Common Ch Ch *Guildf* 07-12; NSM from 12. *The Rye, 38C Woodlands Road, Epsom KT18 7HW* E: sacsac@ntlworld.com *or* curtis-s@epsomcollege.org.uk

CURTIS, Thomas John. b 32. Pemb Coll Ox BA 55 MA 59 Lon Univ BD 58. Clifton Th Coll 55. **d** 58 **p** 59. C Wandsworth All SS *S'wark* 58-61; Chile 61-71; R Saxmundham *St E* 71-77; V Cheltenham St Mark *Glouc* 77-84; TR 84-86; V Chipping Norton *Ox* 86-95; rtd 95; Hon Dioc Rep SAMS *St E* 95-01; PtO *St E* 95-01; *Glouc* from 01; *Worc* from 01. *60 Courtney Close, Tewkesbury GL20 5FB* T: (01684) 295298 E: curtistomjon@aol.com

CURWEN, Canon David. b 38. St Cath Coll Cam BA 62. Cuddesdon Coll 62. **d** 64 **p** 65. C Orford St Andr *Liv* 64-67; Ind Chapl *Cant* 67-77 and 83-84; C S'wark Ch Ch 78-83; Ind Chapl *S'wark* 78-83 and 85-88; Dioc Soc Resp Adv *St E* 88-93; Dioc Adv for CME 93-97; R Capel St Mary w Lt and Gt Wenham 97-03; Hon Can St E Cathl 97-03; rtd 03; PtO *St E* from 03. *41 Cuckfield Avenue, Ipswich IP3 8SA* T: (01473) 272706

CURZEN, Prof Peter. b 31. Lon Univ BSc 52 MB, BS 55 MD 66 MRCOG 62 FRCOG 70. Sarum & Wells Th Coll 93. **d** 94 **p** 95. NSM Bemerton *Sarum* 94-98; NSM Wylye and Till Valley 98-00; rtd 01; PtO *Sarum* 01-04. *The Meadows, Hindon Lane, Tisbury, Salisbury SP3 6PZ*

CUSHING, Mrs Barbara Anne. b 51. Doncaster Coll of Educn CertEd 72 Sheff Univ BEd 73. Yorks Min Course 12. **d** 13 **p** 14. NSM Anston *Sheff* from 13. *17 Lindale Close, North Anston, Sheffield S25 4FD* T: (01909) 564905 M: 07854-728444 E: barbara_cush@hotmail.com

CUSHING, Gregory Douglas. b 84. Plymouth Univ BA 05 Cam Univ BTh 12. Ridley Hall Cam 09. **d** 12 **p** 13. C Wandsworth All SS *S'wark* from 12. *74 Haldon Road, London SW18 1QG* M: 07746-721504 E: gregory_cushing@hotmail.com

CUTCLIFFE, Canon Neil Robert. b 50. NUU BA 72 TCD BA 72. **d** 75 **p** 76. C Belfast St Mary *Conn* 75-78; C Lurgan Ch the Redeemer *D & D* 78-80; I Garrison w Slavin and Belleek *Clogh* 80-86; I Mossley *Conn* from 86; Can Belf Cathl from 07. *558 Doagh Road, Mossley, Newtownabbey BT36 6TA* T: (028) 9083 2726 E: rathdune@hotmail.com

CUTHBERT, Canon John. b 52. Edin Univ BSc 76 PhD 80. Coates Hall Edin BD 92. **d** 92 **p** 93. Chapl St Mary's Cathl 92-98; C Edin St Mary 92-98; P-in-c Forres *Mor* 98-03; R Arbroath *Bre* 04-14; R Auchmithie 04-14; Can St Paul's Cathl Dundee 09-14; P-in-c Inverness St Jo *Mor* from 14; P-in-c Inverness St Mich from 14. *Address temp unknown* E: john@cuth100.freeserve.co.uk

CUTHBERT, John Hamilton. b 34. Univ of Wales (Lamp) BA 59. Coll of Resurr Mirfield 59. **d** 61 **p** 62. C Cov St Pet 61-64; Australia 64-69; C Willesden St Andr *Lon* 69-72; CMP from 72; C Sheff St Cecilia Parson Cross 72-74; V Lavender Hill Ascension *S'wark* 74-97; rtd 97; PtO *St Alb* from 97; *Lon* from 99. *29 The Cloisters, Welwyn Garden City AL8 6DU* T: (01707) 376748

CUTHBERT, Mrs Penelope Jane. b 65. Collingwood Coll Dur BA 87 Ox Brookes Univ BA 12. Ox Min Course 09. **d** 12 **p** 13. C Reading St Agnes w St Paul and St Barn *Ox* from 12. *12 Harlech Avenue, Caversham, Reading RG4 6RN* T: 0118-946 4287 M: 07825-331810 E: penny.cuthbert@btinternet.com

CUTHBERT, Vernon John. b 66. Trin Coll Bris 02. **d** 04 **p** 05. C Alvaston *Derby* 04-08; P-in-c Cleadon *Dur* from 08. *The Vicarage, 5 Sunderland Road, Cleadon, Sunderland SR6 7UR* T: 0191-536 7147

CUTHBERT, Victor. b 46. St Alb & Ox Min Course 97. **d** 01 **p** 02. OLM Surbiton St Matt *S'wark* 01-11; PtO from 11. *4 St Thomas Close, Surbiton KT6 7TU* T: (020) 8399 8722 E: victorcuthbert@btinternet.com

CUTHBERTSON, Mrs Amanda. b 54. K Coll Lon BD 92 AKC 92 Open Univ PGCE 98 Loughb Univ MA 00 ALCM 85 LLCM 87. EAMTC 98. **d** 00 **p** 01. C Northampton St Benedict *Pet* 00-03; V Wellingborough St Mark from 03. *St Mark's Vicarage, 142 Queensway, Wellingborough NN8 3SD* T: (01933) 673893 E: revacuthbertson@o2.co.uk *or* amandacuthbertson123@gmail.com

CUTHBERTSON, Raymond. b 52. AKC 75. Coll of Resurr Mirfield 74. **d** 77 **p** 78. C Darlington St Mark w St Paul *Dur* 77-81; C Usworth 81-83; C Darlington St Cuth 83-86; V Shildon w Eldon 86-00; V Shildon 00-04; RD Auckland 94-96; Chapl N Tees and Hartlepool NHS Trust 04-07; Chapl Tees, Esk and Wear Valley NHS Trust from 07; PtO *Dur* from 14. *Tees, Esk and Wear Valley NHS Trust, County Hospital, North Road, Durham DH1 4ST* T: 0191-333 3423 E: raymond.cuthbertson@cddps.nhs.uk

CUTLER, Robert Francis. b 37. Lon Univ BSc 57. Clifton Th Coll 62. **d** 64 **p** 65. C Peckham St Mary Magd *S'wark* 64-68;

C Redhill H Trin 68-70; Travel Sec Inter-Coll Chr Fellowship of IVF 70-74; Hon C Selly Hill St Steph *Birm* 70-74; Interserve Internat Bangladesh 74-93; Internat Fellowship Evang Students 74-85; Bible Students Fellowship of Bangladesh 85-93; V Rochdale Deeplish St Luke *Man* 94-99; TV S Rochdale 00-02; rtd 02; PtO *St Alb* 03-10; *Pet* from 11. *10 Troon Crescent, Wellingborough NN8 5WG* T: (01933) 676322
E: robertcutler@btinternet.com

CUTLER, Roger Charles. b 49. Liv Univ BSc 70 Glas Univ MPhil 98. Coll of Resurr Mirfield 86. **d** 88 **p** 89. C Walney Is *Carl* 88-91; Chapl RN 91-98; PtO *Glas* 91-95; Hon C Challoch w Newton Stewart 95-98; V Gosforth St Nic *Newc* 98-01; P-in-c St John Lee 01-04; R 05-08; P-in-c Warden w Newbrough 01-04; V 05-08; R Kirkcudbright *Glas* 08-14; R Gatehouse of Fleet 08-14; rtd 14. *Address temp unknown*
E: rogercutler49@gmail.com

CUTMORE, Simon Giles. b 72. Trin Coll Bris BA 95 St Jo Coll Dur MA 00. Cranmer Hall Dur 97. **d** 99 **p** 00. C Biggleswade *St Alb* 99-03; TV Chambersbury 03-09; TV Langelei 09-11; P-in-c Mill End and Heronsgate w W Hyde 11-13; V from 13. *St Peter's Vicarage, Berry Lane, Rickmansworth WD3 7HQ* T: (01923) 772785 E: simoncutmore@02.co.uk

CUTTELL, Jeffrey Charles. b 59. Birm Univ BSc 80 PhD 83 Sheff Univ MA 91. Trin Coll Bris 84. **d** 87 **p** 88. C Normanton *Wakef* 87-91; V 91-95; Producer Relig Progr BBC Radio Stoke 95-97; Presenter Relig Progr BBC 97-99; CF (TA) 97-06; R Astbury and Smallwood *Ches* 99-08; RD Congleton 04-08; Assoc Lect Th Univ of Wales (Cardiff) 01-06; Tutor St Mich Coll Llan 01-06; Dean Derby 08-10; Chapl HM YOI Werrington Ho 10-15; R Astbury and Smallwood *Ches* from 15. *Corner Cottage, Pools Lane, Smallwood, Sandbach CW11 2XD* T: (01477) 500536
E: jeffrey.cuttell@btinternet.com

CUTTER, John Douglas. b 31. Lon Univ BD 61. Chich Th Coll 56. **d** 59 **p** 60. C Blyth St Mary *Newc* 59-62; C Rugeley *Lich* 62-65; V Rocester 65-73; V Shrewsbury St Giles 73-83; R Yoxall and Dean's V Lich Cathl 83-91; rtd 91; PtO *Win* from 91; Hon Chapl Win Cathl from 98. *3 Morley College, Market Street, Winchester SO23 9LF* T: (01962) 852203

CUTTING, The Ven Alastair Murray. b 60. Westhill Coll Birm BEd 83 Heythrop Coll Lon MA 03. St Jo Coll Nottm 84. **d** 87 **p** 88. C Woodlands *Sheff* 87-88; C Wadsley 89-91; C Uxbridge *Lon* 91-96; Chapl to the Nave and Uxbridge Town Cen 91-96; V Copthorne *Chich* 96-10; R Henfield w Shermanbury and Woodmancote 10-13; Adn Lewisham and Greenwich *S'wark* from 13. *1 Sydenham Park Road, London SE26 4DY* M: 07736-676106 E: acutting@mac.com

CUTTS, Canon David. b 52. Van Mildert Coll Dur BSc 73. St Jo Coll Nottm BA 79. **d** 80 **p** 81. C Ipswich St Matt *St E* 80-82; Bp's Dom Chapl 82-85; R Coddenham w Gosbeck and Hemingstone w Henley 85-94; RD Bosmere 92-94; V Ipswich St Marg from 94; RD Ipswich 96-01; Hon Can St E Cathl from 00. *St Margaret's Vicarage, 32 Constable Road, Ipswich IP4 2UW* T: (01473) 253906 M: 07733-406552
E: david.cutts3@ntlworld.com

CUTTS, Elizabeth Joan Gabrielle. *See* STRICKLAND, Elizabeth Joan Gabrielle

CUTTS, Nigel Leonard. b 57. Sheff Univ BA 86 BTh. Linc Th Coll 83. **d** 87 **p** 88. C Old Brampton and Loundsley Green *Derby* 87-89; C Chesterfield St Mary and All SS 89-91; V Morecambe St Barn *Blackb* 91-99; V Colwyn *St As* 99-03; rtd 03. *2 Cwm Road, Dyserth, Rhyl LL18 6BB* T: (01745) 571496

CYPRUS, Archdeacon of. *See* HOLDSWORTH, John Ivor

CYRUS, Keyvan Dominic. b 74. Univ of Sistan & Baluchestan BSc 98 Lon Sch of Th MA 11. K Coll Lon 11 Westcott Ho Cam 12. **d** 15. C Tividale *Lich* from 15. *Holy Cross House, Ashleigh Road, Tividale, Oldbury B69 1LL*
E: fr.dominiccyrus@gmail.com

CZERNIAWSKA EDGCUMBE, Mrs Irena Christine. b 59. Trin Coll Ox BA 82. Oak Hill Th Coll 93. **d** 95 **p** 96. NSM De Beauvoir Town St Pet *Lon* 95-99; Chapl Raines Foundn Sch Tower Hamlets 99-04; NSM Bow Common 00-04; P-in-c Hoxton St Anne w St Columba 04-12; Min Development Adv Stepney Area 04-07; Dean of Women's Min Stepney Area 07-12; Dir Tr and Development Stepney Area from 12. *24 Calabria Road, London N5 1JA*
E: irenaczerniawskaedgcumbe@hotmail.com

D

DA SILVA, Carlos Alberto Tome. *See* TOME DA SILVA, Carlos Alberto

DABIN, Susan. *See* ADAMS, Susan

DABORN, Mark Henry. b 55. Magd Coll Cam BA 76 MA 80 MRICS 82. WEMTC 99. **d** 05 **p** 06. NSM Cleobury Mortimer w Hopton Wafers etc *Heref* 05-15; P-in-c Stottesdon w Farlow, Cleeton St Mary from 15. *The Rectory, Stottesdon, Kidderminster DY14 8UE* M: 07808-840992 T: (01746) 718127
E: mark.daborn@hotmail.co.uk

DABORN, Robert Francis. b 53. Keble Coll Ox BA 74 MA 78 Fitzw Coll Cam BA 77. Ridley Hall Cam 75. **d** 78 **p** 79. C Mortlake w E Sheen *S'wark* 78-81; Chapl Collingwood and Grey Coll *Dur* 82-83; V Lapley w Wheaton Aston *Lich* 86-91; P-in-c Blymhill w Weston-under-Lizard 89-91; P-in-c Tibberton w Bolas Magna and Waters Upton 91-99; Shropshire Local Min Adv 91-99; P-in-c Childs Ercall and Stoke upon Tern 92-95; Dir Local Min Development 99-05; Dir Past Studies WEMTC 05-14; Vice-Prin 09-14; Preb Heref Cathl 14; R Newcastle w Butterton *Lich* from 14. *The Rectory, St Giles Church, Seabridge Road, Newcastle ST5 2HS*
E: robert.daborn@btinternet.com

DACK, Miss Margaret Patricia. b 39. Offley Teacher Tr Coll TCert 61. Oak Hill NSM Course 91. **d** 93 **p** 94. NSM Letchworth St Paul w William 93-98. *91 Penn Way, Letchworth Garden City SG6 2SH* T: (01462) 634956

DADD, Alan Edward. b 50. St Jo Coll Nottm 77. **d** 78 **p** 79. C Bishopsworth *Bris* 78-81; V Springfield *Birm* 81-85; Chapl Poly Cen Lon 85-86; V Hanger Lane St Ann 86-93; rtd 93; PtO *Bris* 96-98; *Win* from 10. *C14 Elizabeth Court, Grove Road, Bournemouth BH1 3DU*
E: al.e.dd@btinternet.com

DADD, Canon Peter Wallace. b 38. Sheff Univ BA 59. Qu Coll Birm 59. **d** 61 **p** 62. C Grays Thurrock *Chelmsf* 61-65; C Grantham St Wulfram *Linc* 65-70; C Grantham w Manthorpe 70-72; TV 72-73; V Haxey 73-90; RD Is of Axholme 82-90; V Gainsborough All SS 90-98; Can and Preb Linc Cathl 91-08; P-in-c Flixborough w Burton upon Stather 98-00; V 00-08; rtd 08. *15 Southfields Rise, North Leverton, Retford DN22 0AY* T: (01427) 884191 E: peterdadd@tiscali.co.uk

DADE, Jonathan James. b 88. De Montfort Univ BA 10 Leic Univ MA 13 St Jo Coll Dur BA 15. Cranmer Hall Dur 12. **d** 15. C Northampton St Giles *Pet* from 15. *18 The Avenue, Cliftonville, Northampton NN1 5BT* M: 07824-999038
E: jonnydade@hotmail.co.uk *or* curate@stgilesnorthampton.org.uk

DADSON, Lawrence Michael (Mike). b 29. G&C Coll Cam MA 56 Lon Univ BSc(Econ) 64. St Deiniol's Hawarden 80. **d** 92 **p** 92. NSM Bramhall *Ches* 92-95; PtO from 97. *14 Yew Tree Park Road, Cheadle Hulme, Cheadle SK8 7EP* T: 0161-485 2482

DADSWELL, David Ian. b 58. New Coll Ox BA 80 MA 83 Brunel Univ MPhil 97. Westcott Ho Cam 80. **d** 83 **p** 84. C W Derby St Mary *Liv* 83-87; Chapl Brunel Univ *Lon* 87-96; PtO 96-04; 99-04; Hon C New Windsor from 04. *243 St Leonards Road, Windsor SL4 3DR* T: (01753) 864827
E: d.dadswell@me.com

DADSWELL, The Ven Richard Edward. b 46. CITC BTh 98. **d** 98 **p** 99. C Cork St Fin Barre's Union *C, C & R* 98-01; Min Can Cork Cathl 00-01; I Ballisodare w Collooney and Emlaghfad *T, K & A* 01-09; Dioc Dir of Ords 03-09; Adn Killala and Achonry 05-09; rtd 09. *8 Fox Ridge, Rathfriland, Newry BT34 5FR* T: (028) 4063 1154

DADY (formerly MARTIN), Elizabeth Anne. b 60. Sheff Univ BMedSci 82. ERMC 05. **d** 09 **p** 10. C Gaywood *Nor* 09-14; R Blakeney w Cley, Wiveton, Glandford etc from 14. *The Rectory, Wiveton Road, Blakeney, Holt NR25 7NJ* M: 07503-747484 E: reverend.libby@yahoo.co.uk

D'AETH, Mrs Emma Louise Alice. b 63. Portsm Univ BA 03. STETS 04. **d** 07. NSM Portsea St Mary *Portsm* 07-11; PtO from 11. *52 Belmont Street, Southsea PO5 1ND* T: (023) 9286 2108 E: emmadaeth@yahoo.co.uk

DAFFERN, Canon Adrian Mark. b 68. St Jo Coll Dur BA 89 MA 06 FRCO 98 FRSA 99. St Steph Ho Ox 90. **d** 92 **p** 93. C Lich St Chad 92-95; TV Stafford 95-00; V Walsall Wood 00-03; Treas V Lich Cathl 97-03; Can Res and Prec Cov Cathl 03-10; TR Blenheim *Ox* from 10. *The Rectory, Rectory Lane, Woodstock OX20 1UQ* T: (01993) 811415
E: rectorblenheim@btinternet.com

DAFFERN, Mrs Megan Isobel Jane. b 80. Ex Coll Ox BA 02 MA 06 DPhil 14 SS Coll Cam BA 05 MA 09. Westcott Ho Cam 03. **d** 06 **p** 07. C Rugby *Cov* 06-09; Chapl Jes Coll Ox from 09; PtO *Cov* from 09. *Jesus College, Oxford OX1 3DW* T: (01865) 279757 E: chaplain@jesus.ox.ac.uk

DAFIS, Lyn Lewis. d 15. C Llanbadarn Fawr and Elerch and Penrhyncoch etc *St D* from 15. *Y Ficerdy, Garth, Penrhyncoch, Aberystwyth SY23 3EP* T: (01970) 820462 E: lyndafis@gmail.com

DAGGER, Ms Rose-Mary Anne. d 14 p 15. OLM Llandogo w Whitebrook Chpl and Tintern Parva *Mon* from 14. *Fox Cottage, Llandogo, Monmouth NP25 4TA* T: (01594) 530700 E: maryrosedagger@btinternet.com

DAGGETT, Michael Wayne. b 47. Portland State Univ BSc 72. Ridley Hall Cam 84. **d** 86 **p** 87. C Tyldesley w Shakerley *Man* 86-90; V Swinton H Rood 90-02; Chapl Eccles Sixth Form Coll 90-02; rtd 02. *138 Elliott Street, Tyldesley, Manchester M29 8FJ* T: (01942) 883437

DAGLEISH, John. b 38. Goldsmiths' Coll Lon MA 01 ACIB 74. S'wark Ord Course 75. **d** 78 **p** 79. NSM Riddlesdown *S'wark* 78-99; NSM All Hallows by the Tower etc *Lon* 79-89; Chapl Asst Guy's Hosp Lon 87-89. *42 Brancaster Lane, Purley CR8 1HF* T/F: (020) 8660 6060

DAGLISH, John David. b 44. RMCS BSc 70. Cranmer Hall Dur 74. **d** 77 **p** 78. C Ormesby *York* 77-79; C Kirk Ella 79-82; V Hull St Cuth 82-97; NSM Beverley St Mary 00-01; P-in-c Thorpe Edge *Bradf* 01-05; V St Marsden w Nelson St Phil *Blackb* 05-09; rtd 09. *13 St Barnabas Close, Gloucester GL1 5LH* E: john.daglish2@ntlworld.com

DAGNALL, Canon Bernard. b 44. K Coll Lon BSc 65 AKC 65 Ox Univ BA 75 MA 78 CChem MRSC MSOSc 88 CSci 04. St Steph Ho Ox 72. **d** 75 **p** 76. C Stanningley St Thos *Ripon* 75-76; C Lightbowne *Man* 76-78; C-in-c Grahame Park St Aug CD *Lon* 78-84; V Earley St Nic *Ox* 84-91; Ind Chapl 85-91; TR N Huddersfield *Wakef* 91-93; TV Newbury *Ox* 93-09; Chapl W Berks Priority Care Services NHS Trust 93-01; Chapl Newbury and Community Primary Care Trust 01-06; Chapl Berks W Primary Care Trust 06-09; Superior Soc of Retreat Conductors 00-05; rtd 09; PtO *Ox* from 10; *Lon* from 15; Hon Can Ho Ghana from 04. *10 Windsor Street, Headington, Oxford OX3 7AP* T: (01865) 751854 E: bernarddagnall@btinternet.com

DAILEY, Douglas Grant. b 56. Nottm Univ BTh 88. Linc Th Coll 85. **d** 88 **p** 89. C Leominster *Heref* 88-91; Assoc R Hickory Ascension USA 91-93; R Statesville 93-02; R Gainesville Grace Ch from 02. *3603 Tradition Drive, Gainesville GA 30506-3600, USA* T: (001) (770) 536 0126 E: ddailey@gracechurchgainesville.org

DAIMOND, John Ellerbeck. b 39. St Cuth Soc Dur BA 61. Ripon Hall Ox 61. **d** 63 **p** 64. C Caverswall *Lich* 63-66; Chapl RAF 66-85; Asst Chapl-in-Chief RAF 85-91; QHC 89-91; V Shawbury *Lich* 91-95; R Moreton Corbet 91-95; V Stanton on Hine Heath 91-95; rtd 99; P-in-c Pattingham w Patshull *Lich* 02-08; PtO from 08. *The Hollies, Church Street, Uffington, Shrewsbury SY4 4SN* T: (01743) 709034

DAINTREE, Canon Geoffrey Thomas. b 54. Bris Univ BSc 77. Trin Coll Bris 78. **d** 81 **p** 82. C Old Hill H Trin *Worc* 81-85; C Tunbridge Wells St Jo *Roch* 85-89; V Framfield *Chich* 89-00; RD Uckfield 96-00; V Eastbourne St Jo 00-09; Chs Relns Manager Chr Aid from 09; PtO *Chich* from 09; Hon Can Cyangugu (Rwanda) from 97. *5 Upper Wish Hill, Eastbourne BN20 9HB* T: (01323) 501102 E: geoff.daintree@googlemail.com *or* gdaintree@christian-aid.org

DAINTY, James Ernest. b 46. Open Univ BA 86 ALBC 68. Cranmer Hall Dur 71. **d** 73 **p** 74. C Normanton *Wakef* 73-76; C Gillingham St Mark *Roch* 76-78; V Barnsley St Geo *Wakef* 78-88; Chapl Barnsley Distr Gen Hosp 78-88; Chapl Seacroft Hosp Leeds 88-94; Chapl Killingbeck Hosp 88-94; Chapl Meanwood Park Hosp Leeds 88-94; P-in-c Turnham Green Ch Ch *Lon* 94-97; V 97-06; rtd 06; Chapl PtO *Ches* from 06; Maranatha Community Flixton from 08. *10 Albion Street, Wallasey CH45 9LF* T: 0151-638 4425 E: jimdainty@dunelm.org.uk

DAKIN (née HOLLETT), Mrs Catherine Elaine. b 53. Qu Eliz Coll Lon BSc 74. St Jo Coll Nottm 88. **d** 90 **p** 05. Par Dn Horley S'wark 90-93; NSM Heydon, Gt and Lt Chishill, Chrishall etc *Chelmsf* 93-97; NSM Gt and Lt Maplestead w Gestingthorpe 97-99; NSM Knights and Hospitallers Par 99-01; NSM Fulford w Hilderstone *Lich* from 01. *20 Tudor Hollow, Fulford, Stoke-on-Trent ST11 9NP* T: (01782) 397073

DAKIN, Peter David. b 57. Wye Coll Lon BSc 79. St Jo Coll Nottm 91. **d** 91 **p** 92. NSM Southgate *Chich* 91-93; C Heydon, Gt and Lt Chishill, Chrishall etc *Chelmsf* 93-97; P-in-c Gt and Lt Maplestead w Gestingthorpe 97-99; P-in-c Alphamstone w Lamarsh and Pebmarsh 99; V Knights and Hospitallers Par 99-01; P-in-c Fulford w Hilderstone *Lich* 01-15; V from 15;

Rural Officer for Staffs from 01; RD Stone from 07. *20 Tudor Hollow, Fulford, Stoke-on-Trent ST11 9NP* T: (01782) 397073 F: (01780) 761764 E: pdakin@waitrose.com

DAKIN, Reginald James Blanchard. b 25. S'wark Ord Course 66. **d** 70 **p** 71. C Preston Ascension *Lon* 70-74; C Greenhill St Jo 74-76; P-in-c Littleton 76-80; R 80-95; CF (ACF) 78-95; Warden for Readers (Kensington Area) *Lon* 88-95; rtd 95; PtO *Nor* from 95; Chapl Malta 97-99. *22 Heywood Avenue, Diss IP22 4DN* T: (01379) 641167

DAKIN, Mrs Sally. b 58. SRN 79 SCM 82 RHV 85 K Coll Lon MSc 89 TCert 92. SAOMC 02. **d** 04 **p** 05. NSM Ruscombe and Twyford *Ox* 04-12; PtO *Win* from 12. *Wolvesey, Winchester SO23 9ND* T: (01962) 854050 F: 897088 E: sally.dakin@btinternet.com

DAKIN, Canon Stanley Frederick. b 30. CA 52. Roch Th Coll 63. **d** 65 **p** 66. C Meole Brace *Lich* 65-68; V 68-72; R Sutton 68-72; Hosp Chapl Nairobi Kenya 72-75; P-in-c Nettlebed *Ox* 75-81; P-in-c Bix w Pishill 77-81; P-in-c Highmore 78-81; R Nettlebed w Bix and Highmore 81; V Ealing Dean St Jo *Lon* 81-84; V W Ealing St Jo w St Jas 84-92; Hon Can Mombasa from 89; Gen Sec CA Africa from 92; rtd 99; PtO *Lich* 99-02; *Ox* from 02. *71 Rectory Crescent, Middle Barton, Chipping Norton OX7 7BP* T: (01869) 349983

✠**DAKIN, The Rt Revd Timothy John.** b 58. SS Mark & Jo Univ Coll Plymouth BA 86 K Coll Lon MTh 87. **d** 93 **p** 94 **c** 12. Prin Carlile Coll Kenya 93-00; C Nairobi Cathl 94-00; Gen Sec CMS 00-12; Gen Sec SAMS 09-12; Hon C Ruscombe and Twyford *Ox* 00-12; Can Th Cov Cathl 01-12; Bp Win from 11. *Wolvesey, Winchester SO23 9ND* T: (01962) 854050 F: 897088 E: bishop.tim@winchester.anglican.org

DALAIS, Duncan John. b 56. St Paul's Coll Grahamstown. **d** 83 **p** 84. C Pinetown S Africa 83-87; C Chingford SS Pet and Paul *Chelmsf* 87-92; V Aldersbrook 92-02; P-in-c Leytonstone St Andr 02-14; V 14; P-in-c Leytonstone H Trin and St Aug Harrow Green 11-14; Asst Chapl Forest Healthcare NHS Trust Lon 02-09; rtd 14. *Corn Bin House, Chippenham Park, Chippenham, Ely CB7 5PT* T: (01638) 724195 M: 07983-560245 E: duncan.dalais@virgin.net

DALE, Miss Barbara. b 48. Cranmer Hall Dur 78. **dss** 81 **d** 87 **p** 94. N Wingfield, Pilsley and Tupton *Derby* 81-90; Par Dn 87-90; Par Dn N Wingfield, Clay Cross and Pilsley 90-94; TV 94-00; C Eckington and Ridgeway 00-04; TV E Scarsdale 04-13. *89 Pavilion Gardens, New Houghton, Mansfield NG19 8TT*

DALE, Charles William. b 49. **d** 02 **p** 03. OLM Uttoxeter Area *Lich* from 02. *Manor Court, Kingstone, Uttoxeter ST14 8QH* T: (01889) 500428 E: charles.dale@tesco.net

DALE, Ms Christine. b 62. Trin Coll Bris BA 94. **d** 94 **p** 95. C Thatcham *Ox* 94-98; TV Bracknell 98-02; R E Woodhay and Woolton Hill *Win* 02-09; R NW Hants from 09; RD Whitchurch 08-14. *The Rectory, The Mount, Highclere, Newbury RG20 9QZ* T: (01635) 253323 E: revdc@cdsm.wanadoo.co.uk

DALE, John Anthony. b 42. Open Univ BSc 00. Qu Coll Birm 72. **d** 75 **p** 76. C Elmley Castle w Bricklehampton and Combertons *Worc* 75-81; P-in-c 81-83; R 83-88; Hon Can Worc Cathl 87-92; V Hallow 88-92; Dioc Registrar 92; P-in-c Michaelston-y-Fedw *Mon* 03-08; rtd 08; PtO *Ban* from 08. *5 Tan y Bryn, Machynlleth SY20 8TL* T: (01654) 703758 E: jadale@onetel.com

DALE, Mrs Joy. b 57. **d** 13 **p** 14. NSM Penn Fields *Lich* from 13. *17 Haden Hill, Wolverhampton WV3 9PT* T: (01902) 772239 E: steveandjoydale@blueyonder.co.uk

DALE, Martin Nicholas. b 55. Chelsea Coll Lon BSc 76 CPA 83. Wycliffe Hall Ox 99. **d** 01 **p** 02. C Stiffkey and Cockthorpe w Morston, Langham etc *Nor* 01-03; C Stiffkey and Bale 03-04; P-in-c New Romney w Old Romney and Midley *Cant* 04-07; P-in-c St Mary's Bay w St Mary-in-the-marsh etc 04-07; P-in-c Dymchurch w Burmarsh and Newchurch 05-07; P-in-c Upper Wreake *Leic* 07-10; P-in-c S Croxton Gp and Burrough Hill Pars 07-10; V E Marshland *Ely* from 10. *The Vicarage, 37 Church Road, Tilney St Lawrence, King's Lynn PE34 4QQ* T: (01945) 880259 M: 07887-554761 E: mndale@aol.com

DALE (née LIVESEY), Mrs Rachel Elizabeth. b 67. Univ of Wales (Cardiff) BSc 89 MBA 96 Homerton Coll Cam BTh 09 Huddersfield Univ PGCE 99. Ridley Hall Cam 07. **d** 09 **p** 10. C Streetly *Lich* 09-12; R Watershed from 12. *The Vicarage, Pinfold Lane, Wheaton Aston, Stafford ST19 9PD* T: (01785) 840395 M: 07977-310049 E: rachel.livesey@googlemail.com *or* revracheldale@gmail.com

DALEY, David Michael. b 50. Oak Hill Th Coll BA 90. **d** 92 **p** 92. C Enfield Ch Ch Trent Park *Lon* 92-94; V Chitts Hill St Cuth 94-14; rtd 14. *Address temp unknown* E: ddaley24@btinternet.com

DALEY, Judith. b 54. Sheff Univ BA 94 Leeds Univ PhD 03. NOC 03. **d** 04 **p** 05. NSM Sheff St Leon Norwood from 04; Chapl Sheff Teaching Hosps NHS Foundn Trust from 02.

112 Broad Inge Crescent, Chapeltown, Sheffield S35 1RU
T: 0114-246 8824 E: judith.daley@sth.nhs.uk

DALEY, Preb Victor Leonard. b 38. Chich Th Coll 76. **d** 78 **p** 79.
C Durrington *Chich* 78-81; C Somerton w Compton Dundon,
the Charltons etc *B & W* 81-87; P-in-c Cheddar 87-88; V
88-08; P-in-c Rodney Stoke w Draycott 02-03; RD Axbridge
91-03; Preb Wells Cathl 97-08; rtd 08; PtO *B & W* from 09.
Barns, Cheddar Road, Wedmore BS28 4EJ T: (01934) 710404
E: prebvictordaley@tiscali.co.uk

DALGLISH, David John. b 45. Heriot-Watt Univ BSc 70 Open
Univ BA 94 Edin Univ MBA 97. TISEC 07. **d** 08. NSM Melrose
Edin 08-10; R Jedburgh from 10. *Kirkbrae House, The Woll,
Askirk, Selkirk TD7 4NY* T: (01750) 32293 M: 07858-140200
E: david_dalglish@btinternet.com

DALLAS, Lucy Joanne Clair. b 73. Kent Univ BA 95 Herts Univ
PGCE 98. Ripon Coll Cuddesdon BA 11. **d** 12 **p** 13. C Welwyn
St Alb from 12. *St Michael's House, London Road, Woolmer
Green, Knebworth SG3 6JP* E: ljcdallas@gmail.com

DALLAWAY, Philip Alan. b 48. Chich Th Coll 80. **d** 81 **p** 82.
C Newbury *Ox* 81-83; C Newport Pagnell w Lathbury 83-85;
V Stewkley w Soulbury and Drayton Parslow 85-92; P-in-c
Didcot All SS 92-97; R 97-00; V Caversham St Jo 00-07; rtd 07;
PtO *Leeds* from 12. *20 Applehaigh Close, Bradford BD10 9DW*
T: (01274) 614803 E: p.dallaway@btinternet.com

DALLEN, Julia Anne. b 58. Matlock Coll of Educn TCert 79 Ex
Univ BTh 10. SWMTC 07. **d** 10 **p** 11. NSM Brampford Speke,
Cadbury, Newton St Cyres etc *Ex* 10-14; NSM Sark *Win* from
14. *The Vicarage, Sark, Guernsey GY10 1SF* M: 07733-673842
E: juliadallen@btinternet.com

DALLEY, Mrs Gail Margaret. b 53. Cranmer Hall Dur 05. **d** 07
p 08. NSM Pocklington Wold *York* 07-10; V Barmby Moor Gp
10-13; rtd 13; PtO *York* from 14. *63 Algarth Rise, Pocklington,
York YO42 2HX* T: (01759) 301920
E: gaildalley@btinternet.com

DALLING, Roger Charles. b 26. Lon Univ BSc 53. S Dios Minl
Tr Scheme 79. **d** 83 **p** 84. NSM Lewes St Jo sub Castro *Chich*
83-84; NSM Uckfield 84-98; NSM Isfield 84-98; NSM Lt
Horsted 84-98; rtd 98; PtO *Chich* from 98. *1 Avis Close, Denton,
Newhaven BN9 0DN* T: (01273) 515970

DALLISON, Frances Mary. *See* EDWARDS, Frances Mary

DALLISTON, The Very Revd Christopher Charles. b 56. Ox
Univ BA Cam Univ MA. St Steph Ho Ox 81. **d** 84 **p** 85.
C Halstead St Andr w H Trin and Greenstead Green *Chelmsf*
84-87; Bp's Dom Chapl 87-91; V Forest Gate St Edm 91-95;
P-in-c Boston *Linc* 95-97; V 97-03; RD Holland E 97-03; Dean
Newc from 03. *The Cathedral Vicarage, 26 Mitchell Avenue,
Jesmond, Newcastle upon Tyne NE2 3LA* T: 0191-281 6554
or 232 1939 F: 230 0735 E: dean@stnicnewcastle.co.uk

DALLISTON, Mrs Michelle Aleysha Caron. b 67. Qu Mary Coll
Lon BSc 89 St Jo Coll Dur 10. Cranmer Hall Dur 08. **d** 10 **p** 11.
C Gosforth St Nic *Newc* 10-13; C Newc St Gabr 13-14;
C Hexham from 14. *The Cathedral Vicarage, 26 Mitchell Avenue,
Jesmond, Newcastle upon Tyne NE2 3LA* T: 0191-281 6554
E: michelleacd@hotmail.co.uk

DALLOW, Gillian Margaret. b 45. Univ of Wales (Ban) BA 66
DipEd 67 Bris Univ MEd 87. Oak Hill Th Coll 93. **d** 96 **p** 97.
NSM W Ealing St Jo w St Jas *Lon* 96-99; P-in-c Barlestone
and Dioc Children's Min Adv *Leic* 99-08; rtd 08; PtO Lon
08-09; NSM Gabalfa *Llan* 09-15; PtO from 15. *26 Baron's Court
Road, Penylan, Cardiff CF23 9DF* T: (029) 2046 3754
M: 07801-650187 E: g.dallow@btinternet.com

DALLY, Keith Richard. b 47. FCCA 77. St Jo Coll Nottm 80. **d** 82
p 83. C Southend St Sav Westcliff *Chelmsf* 82-85; Ind Chapl
85-93; C Southend 85-86; TV 86-92; C Harold Hill St Geo
92-93; Cen Co-ord Langham Place All So Clubhouse *Lon*
97-02; PtO *Ox* 02-05; *Pet* 05-11; Hon C Northampton Em
11-13; P-in-c King's Beck *Nor* from 13. *The Rectory, Aylsham
Road, Felmingham, North Walsham NR28 0LD*
E: keithdally@aol.com

DALRIADA, Archdeacon of. *See* FORDE, The Ven Stephen
Bernard

DALRYMPLE, Wendy Margaret. b 75. Coll of Resurr Mirfield.
d 07 **p** 08. C Mirfield *Wakef* 07-10; Chapl Sir Robert Woodard
Academy Lancing 10-12; P-in-c Alfold and Loxwood
Guildf 12-15; R Loughborough All SS w H Trin *Leic* from 15.
The Rectory, 69 Westfield Drive, Loughborough LE11 3QL
E: priestwendy@btinternet.com

DALTON, Anthony Isaac. b 57. Em Coll Cam BA 78 MA 82
Leeds Univ BA 82. Coll of Resurr Mirfield. **d** 82 **p** 83.
C Carl St Aid and Ch Ch 82-86; C Caversham St Pet and
Mapledurham etc *Ox* 86-88; P-in-c Accrington St Mary *Blackb*
88-91; V 91-92; Chapl Victoria Hosp Accrington 88-92;
V Sheff St Cecilia Parson Cross 92-96; P-in-c Burnley St Cath w
St Alb and St Paul *Blackb* 96-98; V 98-01; R Orton and Tebay w
Ravenstonedale etc *Carl* 01-07; CF from 07. *c/o MOD Chaplains
(Army)* F: 381824 T: (01264) 383430
E: tonydaltonuk@yahoo.co.uk

DALTON, Bertram Jeremy (Tod). b 32. ACIB 64. Sarum & Wells
Th Coll 81. **d** 83 **p** 84. C Ringwood *Win* 83-86; R Norton sub
Hamdon, W Chinnock, Chiselborough etc *B & W* 86-97;
rtd 97; PtO *B & W* from 97. *Meadow Cottage, 8 Woodbarton,
Milverton, Taunton TA4 1LU* T: (01823) 400302
E: todandjane@hotmail.com

D'ALTON, Craig William. b 68. Melbourne Univ BA 90 MA 94
PhD 99. Melbourne Coll of Div BTheol 98. **d** 00 **p** 00. C S
Yarra Ch Ch Australia 00-03; C Melbourne St Pet 03-07; C Ox
St Mary V w St Cross and St Pet 07-10; P-in-c N Melbourne
St Mary Australia from 10. *St Mary's North Melbourne,
430 Queensberry St, North Melbourne, 3051 Australia*
E: craig.stmarys@gmail.com

DALTON, Derek. b 40. NOC. **d** 84 **p** 85. NSM Pool w Arthington
Ripon 84-87; P-in-c Thornton Watlass w Thornton Steward
87-90; C Bedale 87-90; R Wensley 90-95; V W Witton 90-95;
R Romaldkirk w Laithkirk 95-97; rtd 97; PtO *Leeds* from 98.
North Wing, Thornton Watlass Hall, Ripon HG4 4AS
T: (01677) 425302

DALTON, Kevin. b 32. TCD BA 65. Ch Div Sch of the Pacific
(USA) BD 67 CITC 66. **d** 66 **p** 67. C Stillorgan *D & G* 66-72;
I Dublin Drumcondra w N Strand 72-79; I Monkstown 79-07;
rtd 07. *Norwood Lodge, Shanganagh Road, Ballybrack, Co Dublin,
Republic of Ireland* T: (00353) (1) 282 2778 M: 87-122 4807
E: kevinthehumble@gmail.com

DALTON, Tod. *See* DALTON, Bertram Jeremy

DALTRY, Canon Paul Richard. b 56. St Jo Coll Nottm 90. **d** 92
p 93. C Ipswich St Matt *St E* 92-96; P-in-c Needham Market w
Badley 96-05; RD Bosmere 01-05; R Ipswich St Helen, H Trin,
and St Luke 05-09; Min for Ch and Community Engagement
from 09; Hon Can St E Cathl from 10. *264 Norwich Road,
Ipswich IP1 4BT* E: paul@daltry.co.uk

DALY, Ms Bernadette Theresa. b 45. TCD BTh 94. **d** 97 **p** 98.
C Taney *D & G* 97-00 and 05-06; Dir Past Studies CITC 00-04;
rtd 06. *8 Greenlands, Sandyford, Dublin 16, Republic of Ireland*
T: (00353) (1) 294 8815 M: 86-241 9009 E: berdaly@live.com

DALY, Gary James. b 63. Wycliffe Hall *Ox* 07. **d** 09 **p** 10.
C Muswell Hill St Jas w St Matt *Lon* from 09. *8 St James Lane,
London N10 3DB* T: (020) 8442 2902 M: 07957-154787
E: gazdaly@tinyonline.co.uk

DALY, Jeffrey. b 50. Bris Univ BA 73 Jes Coll Cam PGCE 74 Fitzw
Coll Cam BA 82 MA 86 Westmr Coll Ox MTh 03. Ridley Hall
Cam 80. **d** 83 **p** 84. C Tilehurst St Mich *Ox* 83-89; P-in-c
Steventon w Milton 89-92; Asst Chapl Sherborne Sch 92-96;
Chapl St Pet Sch York 96-11; rtd 11; PtO *Eur* from 07;
York from 11. *3 Shotel Close, York YO30 5FY* T: (01904) 630142
E: fatherj.daly@cantab.net

DALY, Martin Jonathan. b 48. Woolwich Poly BSc 69. **d** 05 **p** 06.
C Upton (Overchurch) *Ches* 05-13; rtd 13. *Fairfield Lodge,
1 Columbia Road, Prenton CH43 6TU* T: 0151-670 1461 *or* 677
1186 M: 07710-242241 E: martin@stm-upton.org.uk

DALZELL, Donald Paul. b 52. Qld Agric Coll BAppSc 74. Trin
Coll Melbourne BD 77 DMin 03. **d** 80 **p** 81. C Geelong All SS
Australia 80-82; Chapl Turana w Winlaton 82-89; P-in-c
Bulleen 90-00; Lect St Fran Th Coll 00-03; P-in-c Alexandra
05-11; P-in-c Montreux w Anzere, Gstaad and Monthey
Eur from 11. *avenue de Chillon 92, CH-1820 Territet, Montreux,
Switzerland* T: (0041) (21) 963 4354 F: 963 4391
E: chaplain@stjohns-montreux.ch

DAMIAN, Brother. *See* KIRKPATRICK, Roger James

DANBY, Shirley Elizabeth. b 49. St Hugh's Coll Ox BA 72
Portsm Univ PhD 76. STETS 07. **d** 09 **p** 10. NSM Cricklade w
Latton *Bris* from 09; NSM Ashton Keynes, Leigh and Minety
from 09. *The Old Manse, 21 High Street, Cricklade, Swindon
SN6 6AP* T: (01793) 751463 M: 07980-548844
E: shirleydanby@tiscali.co.uk

DANCE, Peter Patrick. b 31. Em Coll Saskatoon 66. **d** 69 **p** 69.
R Mannville Canada 69-71; C Hednesford *Lich* 71-75;
P-in-c Westcote Barton and Steeple Barton *Ox* 76-77; P-in-c
Sandford St Martin 76-77; R Westcote Barton w Steeple
Barton, Duns Tew etc 77-89; R Castle Douglas *Glas* 89-97;
rtd 97. *Mannville, High Street, Adderbury, Banbury OX17 3NA*
T: (01295) 811989

DAND, Andrew John. b 80. St Mellitus Coll. **d** 13 **p** 14. C Ealing
St Steph Castle Hill *Lon* from 13. *26 Drayton Gardens, London
W13 0LQ* M: 07775-957814 E: andrewdand1@hotmail.com

DAND, Mrs Angela Jane. b 49. St Andr Univ BSc 70 Newc Univ
PGCE 71. **d** 98 **p** 99. OLM Astley *Man* 98-06; OLM Astley,
Tyldesley and Mosley Common from 06. *20 Acresfield, Astley,
Tyldesley, Manchester M29 7NL* T: (01942) 879608

DANDO, Ms Elaine Vera. b 53. Coll of Resurr Mirfield 94
NOC 98. **d** 00 **p** 01. C Luddenden w Luddenden Foot *Wakef*
00-03; C Halifax 03-04; LtO 04-05; Chapl Univ Coll *Lon*
05-08; C St Pancras w St Jas and Ch Ch 05-08; C Northwood
H Trin 08-10; rtd 10; PtO *Lon* 11-13. *37 Wilderness Road,
Hurstpierpoint, Hassocks BN6 9XD* T: (01273) 835277
E: evd.macrina@btinternet.com

DANDO, Stephen. b 49. Goldsmiths' Coll Lon TCert 70. Coll of Resurr Mirfield 81. **d** 83 **p** 84. C Wandsworth St Anne *S'wark* 83-87; V Stainland *Wakef* 87-99; V Illingworth 99-05; V Eastcote St Lawr *Lon* 05-13; rtd 13. *37 Wilderness Road, Hurstpierpoint, Hassocks BN6 9XD* T: (01273) 835277
E: revstephendando@hotmail.co.uk

DANE, John William. b 52. St Jo Coll Nottm 04. **d** 06 **p** 07. C Deddington w Barford, Clifton and Hempton *Ox* 06-09; Chapl Chich Univ from 09; C Chich St Paul and Westhampnett 12-15. *Chaplaincy, University of Chichester, Bishop Otter Campus, College Lane, Chichester PO19 6PE* T: (01243) 816041 E: chaplain@chi.ac.uk *or* john@ausome.co.uk

DANES, Charles William. b 28. Chich Th Coll 54. **d** 56 **p** 57. C N Greenford All Hallows *Lon* 56-59; C Caversham *Ox* 59-63; V Walsgrave on Sowe *Cov* 63-65; P-in-c Hanworth All SS *Lon* 65-67; V 68-76; P-in-c Wick *Chich* 76-78; V Littlehampton St Jas 76-78; P-in-c Littlehampton St Mary 76-78; V W Worthing St Jo 78-87; Chapl Monte Carlo *Eur* 87-93; rtd 93; PtO *Chelmsf* from 93; *Eur* from 93. *31 Oakley Road, Braintree CM7 5QS* T: (01376) 324586

DANGERFIELD, Canon Andrew Keith. b 63. Univ of Wales (Ban) BD 87. St Steph Ho Ox 87. **d** 89 **p** 90. C St Marychurch *Ex* 89-93; C-in-c Grahame Park St Aug CD *Lon* 93-96; V Tottenham St Paul 96-06; P-in-c Edmonton St Mary w St Jo 98-04; AD E Haringey 00-05; V Kensal Green St Jo 06-12; Miss to Seafarers Yokohama Japan from 12; Hon Can Cape Coast from 04. *Address temp unknown*

DANGERFIELD, Miss Sarah Ann. b 66. Ripon Coll Cuddesdon 09. **d** 11 **p** 12. C Badgeworth, Shurdington and Witcombe w Bentham *Glouc* from 11. *25 Blenheim Orchard, Shurdington, Cheltenham GL51 4TG* T: (01242) 863979
E: s.dangerfield150@btinternet.com

DANIEL, Gaynor Elizabeth. *See* DANIEL-LOWANS, Gaynor Elizabeth

DANIEL, Canon Herrick Haynes. b 38. Open Univ BA 81. Trin Coll Bris 73. **d** 75 **p** 76. C Harlesden St Mark *Lon* 75-78; C Livesey *Blackb* 78-81; V Blackb St Barn 81-08; Hon Can Blackb Cathl 98-08; rtd 08; PtO *Blackb* from 08. *40 Appletree Drive, Lancaster LA1 4QY* T: (01524) 389764
E: herrickdaniel@hotmail.co.uk

DANIEL, Mrs Joy. b 44. Gilmore Course 81 Oak Hill Th Coll 82. **dss** 84 **d** 87 **p** 94. Luton St Fran *St Alb* 84-02; Par Dn 87-94; C 94-02; P-in-c Woodside 02-10; rtd 10; PtO *St Alb* from 10. *22 Rowelfield, Luton LU2 9HN* E: joydaniel1@btinternet.com

DANIEL, Pamela Olive. b 52. Middx Poly BEd 86 K Coll Lon MA 94 Westmr Coll Ox BTh 98. Wycliffe Hall Ox 04. **d** 06 **p** 07. C Kennington St Mark *S'wark* 06-10; P-in-c W Bromwich St Phil *Lich* from 10. *The Vicarage, 33 Reform Street, West Bromwich B70 7PF* M: 07771-633035
E: pamdaniel8@hotmail.com

DANIEL, Philip Sharman. b 62. Man Univ BA 83 Rob Coll Cam CertEd 84. Wycliffe Hall Ox 84. **d** 86 **p** 87. C Macclesfield Team *Ches* 86-89; C Cheadle 89-94; V Disley 94-07; TR Mid Trent *Lich* from 07; RD Stafford from 15. *The Rectory, Stafford Road, Weston, Stafford ST18 0HX* T: (01889) 271870
E: revpsdan@btinternet.com

DANIEL, Rajinder Kumar. b 34. St Steph Coll Delhi 55 Westcott Ho Cam 61. **d** 63 **p** 64. C Purley St Barn *S'wark* 63-66; C Battersea St Pet 66-67; C N Harrow St Alb *Lon* 67-72; TV Beaconsfield *Ox* 72-75; V Smethwick St Matt w St Chad *Birm* 75-87; Dioc Adv on Black Min 87-92; Chapl Birm Gen Hosp 91-92; TR Braunstone *Leic* 92-01; rtd 01; USPG and R Arima St Jude Trinidad and Tobago 03-04; PtO *Birm* from 04. *508 Chester Road, Kingshurst, Birmingham B36 0LG* T: 0121-770 1066

DANIEL-LOWANS, Mrs Gaynor Elizabeth. b 46. Llan Ord Course 98. **d** 98 **p** 99. NSM St Brides Minor w Bettws *Llan* 98-01; C 01-02; C St Brides Minor w Bettws w Aberkenfig 02-04; C Llansantffraid, Bettws and Aberkenfig 04-11; rtd 11; PtO *Llan* from 11. *36 Heol Crwys, Cwmavon, Port Talbot SA12 9NT* T: (01639) 891871

DANIEL-McKEIGUE, Christine Joy. b 63. **d** 13 **p** 14. NSM Carr Mill *Liv* from 13. *7 Galston Avenue, Rainhill, Prescot L35 0NY* T: 0151-493 1944

DANIELL, Robert. b 37. **d** 87 **p** 88. C Camberwell St Giles w St Matt *S'wark* from 10; *Roch* from 12. *4 Glenhouse Road, London SE9 1JQ* T: (020) 8850 4594 E: r.daniell@btinternet.com

DANIELS, Geoffrey Gregory. b 23. St Pet Coll Ox BA 48 MA 53 Lambeth STh 60. Linc Th Coll 73. **d** 73 **p** 75. NSM Diss *Nor* 73-74; NSM Bexhill St Pet *Chich* 74-83; C Eastbourne St Andr 83-84; V Hoam 84-88; rtd 88; Chapl Convent of Dudwell St Mary from 88; NSM Bexhill St Andr CD *Chich* 90-95; PtO from 95. *20 Richmond Grove, Bexhill-on-Sea TN39 3EQ* T: (01424) 211719

DANIELS, Ian Geoffrey. b 72. Univ of Wales (Ban) BEng 93. ERMC 09. **d** 12 **p** 13. NSM Ipswich St Aug *St E* from 12. *44 Lindbergh Road, Ipswich IP3 9QX* T: (01473) 719089
M: 07777-698353 E: iandaniels@btinternet.com

DANIELS, John Wyn. b 60. Southn Univ BSc 82 PhD 87. Trin Coll Bris MA 92. **d** 92 **p** 93. C Roundhay St Edm *Ripon* 92-95; India 96; C Ambleside w Brathay *Carl* 97-01; Chapl St Martin's Coll Lanc 97-01; Res Can Ban Cathl 01-05; Min Development Officer *Bradf* 05-10; C Embsay w Eastby and Skipton H Trin 05-10; Local Min Officer *Heref* from 10; Warden of Readers from 13. *Diocese of Hereford, Unit 8-9, The Business Quarter, Eco Park Road, Ludlow SY8 1FD* T: (01584) 871084
E: j.daniels@hereford.anglican.org *or* jd001@supanet.com

DANIELS, Lee Martin. b 61. Coll of Resurr Mirfield 99. **d** 01 **p** 02. C Toxteth Park St Agnes and St Pancras *Liv* 01-05; TV Staveley and Barrow Hill *Derby* 05-10; P-in-c Blackb St Thos w St Jude 10-13; P-in-c Blackb St Mich w St Jo and H Trin 10-13; V N and E Blackb from 13. *The Vicarage, Didsbury Street, Blackburn BB1 3JL* E: mazdaz@fsmail.net

DANIELS, Philip John. b 70. Southn Univ BA 92 Reading Univ MA 93 PGCE 96. Ox Min Course 09. **d** 12 **p** 13. C Hullavington, Norton and Stanton St Quintin *Bris* 12-15; C Sherston Magna, Easton Grey, Luckington etc 12-15; P-in-c Ashley, Crudwell, Hankerton and Oaksey from 15. *The Rectory, 1 Days Court, Crudwell, Malmesbury SN16 9HG* M: 07515-660190 E: philjdaniels@talktalk.net

DANKS, Alan Adam. b 41. Essex Univ MA 01. Edin Th Coll 61. **d** 64 **p** 65. C Dumfries *Glas* 64-67; C Earl's Court St Cuth w St Matthias *Lon* 68-71; C St Steph Walbrook and St Swithun etc 71-74; C Brookfield St Mary 75-76; C Hendon St Mary 76-85. *327 Hanworth Road, Hampton TW12 3EJ* T: (020) 8941 6055 E: luccas@btinternet.com

DANKS, Mark James. b 71. Qu Coll Birm. **d** 12 **p** 13. C Blakenall Heath *Lich* from 12. *78A Chestnut Road, Walsall WS3 1AP*

DANKS-FLOWER, Marilyn Clare. b 42. **d** 08 **p** 11. Chapl Barts and The Lon NHS Trust 08-10; NSM Egremont and Haile *Carl* from 11; Chapl N Cumbria Univ Hosps NHS Trust from 11. *18 Lamb Lane, Egremont CA22 2AH* T: (01946) 822913
M: 07967-369103 E: kajori1@gmail.com

DANSIE, Bruce John. b 40. Woolwich Poly BSc 67 Univ Coll Lon MSc 71 CEng 72. Linc Th Coll 92. **d** 92 **p** 93. C Ivybridge w Harford *Ex* 92-96; P-in-c Charleton w Buckland Tout Saints etc 96-01; rtd 01. *3 Second Avenue, Murrumbeena, Melbourne VIC 3163, Australia* T: (0061) (3) 9563 2196

DAOUD, Hamdy. b 61. Chich Th Coll 92. **d** 94 **p** 95. Dn All SS Cathl Cairo 94-97; Asst P St Mark's Cathl Alexandria Egypt 94-97; P-in-c Old Cairo 97-08; Chapl and P-in-c Tripoli Libya 08-12; PtO *Sarum* 12-13; P-in-c Algiers H Trin Algeria from 13. *6 Avenue Souiddani Boudjemaa, BP 122K El-Mouradia, Algiers, Algeria* M: 781-306726 T: (00213) (21) 230591 *or* 681719
E: pastorhamdy@yahoo.com *or* info@holytrinityalgiers.org

DAPLYN, Timothy James. b 52. Ripon Coll Cuddesdon 92. **d** 94 **p** 95. C Southmead *Bris* 94-97; P-in-c Abbots Leigh w Leigh Woods 97-99; Dioc Communications Officer 97-99; R Clutton w Cameley *B & W* 99-04; RD Chew Magna 03-04; P-in-c E w W Harptree and Hinton Blewett 04-08; LtO *Mor* 09-10; R Poolewe 10-13; R Kishorn 10-13; P-in-c Lochalsh 10-13; rtd 13. *Coillegillie, Applecross, Strathcarron IV54 8LZ* M: 07747-464833 E: coillegillie@hotmail.com

DARBY, George. b 48. SWMTC 06. **d** 09 **p** 10. NSM Egloskerry, N Petherwin, Tremaine and Tresmere *Truro* 09-10; NSM Egloskerry, N Petherwin, Tremaine, Tresmere etc 10-12; NSM Lezant w Lawhitton and S Petherwin w Trewen 09-10; NSM Altarnon w Bolventor, Laneast and St Clether 10-11; P-in-c Slaidburn *Leeds* 12-15; P-in-c Long Preston w Tosside 12-15; R Slaidburn w Tosside from 15. *The Rectory, Church Street, Slaidburn, Clitheroe BB7 3ER* T: (01200) 446478
E: gdandpd@btinternet.com

DARBY, Michael Barwick. b 34. St D Coll Lamp BA 61 Tyndale Hall Bris 61. **d** 63 **p** 64. C Islington St Andr w St Thos and St Matthias *Lon* 63-66; C Ealing Dean St Jo 66-68; V Broomfleet *York* 68-73; Area Sec CCCS *York* and *Sheff* 68-73; V Paddington Em Harrow Road *Lon* 73-78; Iran 78-79; Brazil 80-83; PtO *Cant* 80-84 and from 01; V Maidstone St Faith 84-90; UAE 90-92; V Platt Bridge *Liv* 93-99; rtd 99. *Paqueta, 79 Sandwich Road, Cliffsend, Ramsgate CT12 5JA* T: (01843) 597228 M: 07947-582469

DARBY, Canon Nicholas Peter. b 50. Kent Univ BA 82 Surrey Univ MSc 02. Sarum & Wells Th Coll 71. **d** 74 **p** 75. C Walton-on-Thames *Guildf* 74-78; C Horsell 78-80; USA 82-84; Chapl Lon Univ 84-89; Chapl R Lon Hosp (Whitechapel) 90-91; V Kew St Phil and All SS w St Luke *S'wark* 91-04; Dean Gaborone Botswana 04-07; V Fenham St Jas and St Basil *Newc* from 99; AD Newc W from 11; Hon Can Newc Cathl from 12. *St James and St Basil Vicarage, Wingrove Road North, Newcastle upon Tyne NE4 9EJ* T: 0191-274 5078

DARBY, Preb Philip William. b 44. Bede Coll Dur TCert 66. Qu Coll Birm. **d** 70 **p** 71. C Kidderminster St Geo *Worc* 70-74; P-in-c Dudley St Jo 74-79; V 79-80; P-in-c Catshill 80-81; P-in-c Catshill and Dodford 81-82; V 82-88; V Ipplepen w Torbryan *Ex* 88-00; V Ipplepen, Torbryan and Denbury 01-02; RD Newton Abbot and Ipplepen 93-01; V Ashburton w Buckland in the Moor and Bickington 02-05; P-in-c Widecombe-in-the-Moor, Leusdon, Princetown etc 04-05; TR Ashburton, Bickington, Buckland in the Moor etc 05-10; Preb Ex Cathl 02-10; rtd 10. *3 Kellett Close, Ashburton, Newton Abbot TQ13 7FB* T: (01364) 652844 M: 07814-272198 E: pwdarby@supanet.com

DARBYSHIRE, Brian. b 48. TD 04. Oak Hill Th Coll BA 83. **d** 83 **p** 84. C Enfield St Jas *Lon* 83-86; R Slaidburn *Bradf* 86-92; V Gt Harwood St Jo *Blackb* 92-02; V Douglas St Ninian *S & M* 02-08; CF (TA) 90-04; V Bingara Australia from 08. *St John's Vicarage, 8 Frazer Street, Bingara NSW 2404, Australia* T: (0061) (2) 7624 1668 E: briandarbyshire@bigpond.com

DARBYSHIRE, Paul. b 50. City Univ BSc 77 Sheff Univ MA 80 N Lon Univ DipSW 97. Linc Sch of Th and Min 11. **d** 14. NSM Quarrington w Old Sleaford *Linc* 14. *Address temp unknown* M: 07938-861643 E: pd@darbyshirehouse.co.uk

DARCH, John Henry. b 52. Univ of Wales (Lamp) BA 73 PhD 97 Lon Univ PGCE 74 MA 77 FRHistS 09 FHEA 04. Trin Coll Bris 80. **d** 82 **p** 83. C Meole Brace *Lich* 82-85; C Hoole *Ches* 85-88; V Hyde St Geo 88-99; P-in-c Godley cum Newton Green 89-93; RD Mottram 91-99; Lect St Jo Coll Nottm 99-06; Chapl 03-06; Public Preacher *S'well* 99-06; PtO *Derby* 03-06; Dir of Ords and Dir IME 4-7 *Blackb* from 06; Hon C Walton-le-Dale St Leon w Samlesbury St Leon 11-13; Hon C Balderstone 11-13; Hon C Mellor 11-13; Hon C Langho Billington 11-13; Hon C Salesbury 11-13. *24 Bosburn Drive, Mellor Brook, Blackburn BB2 7PA* T: (01254) 813544 E: j.darch248@btinternet.com

DARK, Nicholas John. b 62. Leic Univ BA 83 ACIB 92. CITC BTh 98. **d** 98 **p** 99. C Ballyholme *D & D* 98-05; I Magheragall *Conn* from 05. *Magheragall Rectory, 70 Ballinderry Road, Lisburn BT28 2QS* T: (028) 9262 1273 E: magheragall@aol.com

DARKINS, Mrs Judith Rosemary. b 45. **d** 10 **p** 11. OLM Biddenden and Smarden *Cant* 10-12; NSM Wittersham w Stone and Ebony 12-13; C Rother and Oxney from 13; C Tenterden and Smallhythe from 13. *The Rectory, The Street, Wittersham, Tenterden TN30 7EA* T: (01797) 270418 E: judy.darkins@btinternet.com

DARLEY, Canon Shaun Arthur Neilson. b 36. Dur Univ BA 61 Reading Univ MSc 75. Cranmer Hall Dur 61. **d** 63 **p** 64. C Luton w E Hyde St Alb 63-67; Chapl Bris Tech Coll 67-69; Chapl Bris Poly 69-92; Sen Chapl UWE 92-01; Lect 69-75; Sen Lect 75-01; Dir Cen for Performing Arts 85-02; Bp's Cathl Chapl 69-76; Hon Can Bris Cathl 89-01; PtO *B & W* from 98; rtd 01; PtO *Bris* from 02. *Church Paddock, Winscombe Hill, Bristol BS25 1DE* T: (01934) 843633 E: san.darley@btinternet.com

DARLING, Colin. **d** 12 **p** 13. C Saintfield *D & D* 12-13; C Cregagh from 13. *72 Dromara Road, Hillsborough BT26 6PE* T: (028) 9079 6193 M: 07925-672340 E: colin.darling@talktalk.net

DARLING, David Francis. b 55. K Coll Lon BSc 09 Heythrop Coll Lon MA 13. TISEC 93. **d** 96 **p** 97. SSF 88-05; Novice Guardian 99-05; NSM Edin St Ninian 96-98; Chapl W Gen Hosps NHS 96-98; Chapl Edin Sick Children's NHS Trust 96-98; Lic Preacher *Lon* 03-05; PtO from 15. *St Andrew's Vicarage, 28 Old Church Lane, London NW9 8RZ* M: 07811-405835 E: davidfrancis.darling@gmail.com

✠**DARLING, The Rt Revd Edward Flewett.** b 33. TCD BA 55 MA 58. CITC. **d** 56 **p** 57 **c** 85. C Belfast St Luke *Conn* 56-59; C Orangefield *D & D* 59-62; C-in-c Carnalea 62-72; Chapl Ban Hosp 63-72; I Belfast Malone St Jo *Conn* 72-85; Min Can Belf Cathl 78-85; Chapl Ulster Independent Clinic 81-85; Bp L & K 85-00. *15 Beechwood Park, Moira, Craigavon BT67 0LL* T: (028) 9261 2982 E: darling-moira@utvinternet.com

DARLING, John. b 47. Sarum & Wells Th Coll 76. **d** 79 **p** 80. NSM Trowbridge St Thos *Sarum* 79-82; NSM Trowbridge St Thos and W Ashton 82-92; NSM Atworth w Shaw and Whitley 07-13; NSM Melksham 01-13; NSM Broughton Gifford, Gt Chalfield and Holt 07-13; PtO from 13. *43 Horse Road, Hilperton Marsh, Trowbridge BA14 7PF* T: (01225) 777803 E: revjohndarling@yahoo.co.uk

DARLINGTON, Paul Trevor. b 71. Imp Coll Lon BSc 92 K Coll Lon PGCE 93. Oak Hill Th Coll BA 99. **d** 00 **p** 01. C Bispham *Blackb* 00-05; P-in-c Oswestry H Trin *Lich* 05-10; V from 10. *Holy Trinity Vicarage, 29 Balmoral Crescent, Oswestry SY11 2XQ* T: (01691) 652184 E: fwspauldarlington@uwclub.net

DARLISON, Geoffrey Stuart. b 49. MRTPI 80. St Jo Coll Nottm 89. **d** 91 **p** 92. C Horncastle w Low Toynton *Linc* 91-95;

P-in-c Welton and Dunholme w Scothern 95-97; V 97-08; RD Lawres 07-08; P-in-c Thorpe Edge *Leeds* 08-14; P-in-c Greengates 08-14; rtd 14. *Address temp unknown* E: s.darlison@googlemail.com

DARMODY, Canon Richard Arthur. b 52. Lon Univ BD 90. Linc Th Coll MDiv 94. **d** 94 **p** 95. C Cherry Hinton St Jo *Ely* 94-97; I Belfast St Aid *Conn* 97-99; TR The Ramseys and Upwood *Ely* 99-10; R from 10; RD St Ives 02-06; Hon Can Ely Cathl from 08. *The Rectory, 16 Hollow Lane, Ramsey, Huntingdon PE26 1DE* T: (01487) 813271 E: darmodyrichard@hotmail.com

DARRALL, Charles Geoffrey. b 32. Nottm Univ BA 55 MA 57. Qu Coll Birm 56. **d** 57 **p** 58. C Cockermouth All SS w Ch Ch *Carl* 57-63; Chapl Dioc Youth Cen 63-95; V St John's in the Vale w Wythburn 63-95; P-in-c Threlkeld 85-95; rtd 96; PtO *Carl* from 98. *Piper House, Naddle, Keswick CA12 4TF* T: (01768) 774500

DARRALL, John Norman. b 34. Nottm Univ BA 57. Ripon Hall Ox 57. **d** 60 **p** 61. C Nottingham St Mary *S'well* 60-65; Chapl Nottm Children's Hosp 64-65; V Bole w Saundby and Sturton w Littleborough *S'well* 65-66; Chapl Oakham Sch 84-99; rtd 99; PtO *Leic* from 01; *Pet* from 05. *Grange Cottage, 69 Main Street, Cottesmore, Oakham LE15 7DH* T: (01572) 812443 E: johndarrall@googlemail.com

DARRANT, Louis Peter. b 77. Aber Univ BD 00 Leeds Univ MA 03. Coll of Resurr Mirfield 01. **d** 03 **p** 04. C Kennington St Jo w St Jas *S'wark* 03-07; R Maldon St Mary w Mundon *Chelmsf* 07-15. *35 Buckhurst Street, London E1 5QT* M: 07779-103826 E: louis.darrant@btinternet.com

DART, Miss Andrea Elizabeth. b 47. Northd Coll of Educn TCert 68. Lindisfarne Regional Tr Partnership 12. **d** 14 **p** 15. NSM Stanley and S Moor *Dur* from 14. *13 Tweed Terrace, Stanley DH9 6JQ* T: (01207) 237214 E: andrea.dart@btinternet.com

DART, John Peter. b 40. St Jo Coll Ox BA 62. Cuddesdon Coll 62. **d** 64 **p** 65. C W Hartlepool St Aid *Dur* 64-67; C Alverthorpe *Wakef* 67-70; LtO 70-79; rtd 05. *3 Springhill Avenue, Crofton, Wakefield WF4 1HA* T: (01924) 860374 E: mail@dart.eclipse.co.uk

DARVILL, Christopher Mark. b 61. Ox Univ BA 83. St Steph Ho Ox 84. **d** 86 **p** 87. C Tottenham St Paul *Lon* 86-88; C Oystermouth *S & B* 88-90; Chapl Univ of Wales (Swansea) 90-94; Asst Dioc Warden of Ords from 92; V Llansamlet from 94. *The Vicarage, 61 Church Road, Llansamlet, Swansea SA7 9RL* T: (01792) 798845

DARVILL, Canon George Collins. b 36. Kelham Th Coll 56. **d** 61 **p** 62. C Middlesbrough St Chad *York* 61-64; C Manston *Ripon* 64-66; V Kippax 66-79; V Catterick 79-88; RD Richmond 80-86; P-in-c Adel 88-89; R 89-01; RD Headingley 91-96; Hon Can Ripon Cathl 91-01; rtd 01; PtO *Leeds* from 01. *39 Woodlea Lane, Meanwood, Leeds LS6 4SX* T: 0113-275 7973

✠**DARWENT, The Rt Revd Frederick Charles.** b 27. JP 87. ACIB. Wells Th Coll 61. **d** 63 **p** 64 **c** 78. C Pemberton St Jo *Liv* 63-65; R Strichen *Ab* 65-71; R New Pitsligo 65-71; R Fraserburgh w New Pitsligo 71-78; Can St Andr Cathl 71-78; Dean Ab 73-78; Bp Ab 78-92; rtd 92; LtO *Ab* from 92. *107 Osborne Place, Aberdeen AB25 2DD* T: (01224) 646497

DARWENT, Thomas James. b 74. Wycliffe Hall Ox. **d** 07 **p** 08. C Claygate *Guildf* 07-11; C Guildf St Sav from 11. *16 Cunningham Avenue, Guildford GU1 2PE* T: (01483) 566711 E: tom@st-saviours.org.uk

DASH, Mrs Janet Eleanor Gillian. b 47. SRN 69. Cant Sch of Min 89. **d** 93 **p** 94. C Morden *S'wark* 93-96; C S Croydon Em 96-98; P-in-c Borstal and Chapl HM Pris Cookham Wood 98-05; P-in-c Darenth *Roch* 05-10; rtd 10; PtO *Cant* from 11. *5 Edenfield, Birchington CT7 9DE* T: (01843) 448846 M: 07853-844509 E: janet.dash@btinternet.com

DATCHLER, Colin Neil. b 72. Univ Coll Chich BA 01. Ripon Coll Cuddesdon 07. **d** 09 **p** 10. C Hythe *Cant* 09-12; V Waiwhetu New Zealand from 12. *28 Guthrie Street, Waterloo, Lower Hutt 5011, New Zealand* E: colindatchler@hotmail.co.uk

DATE, Stephen James. b 69. LSE BA 90 Dur Univ MA 92. SEITE 99. **d** 02 **p** 03. NSM Brighton Gd Shep Preston *Chich* 02-08; C Uckfield 08-12; P-in-c Woodingdean 13-14; P-in-c Lancing w Coombes from 14. *30 Greenoaks, Lancing BN15 0HE* T: (01903) 750286 M: 07747-895213 E: stephendate@gmail.com

DATSON, Mrs Sheila Mary. b 24. CertEd 67. S'wark Ord Course 76. **dss** 78 **d** 87 **p** 94. Bexleyheath Ch Ch *Roch* 78-91; Hon Par Dn 87-91; rtd 91; PtO *Worc* 91-94 and from 95; NSM Stourport and Wilden 94-95. *17 Moorhall Lane, Stourport-on-Severn DY13 8RB* T: (01299) 823044

DATTA, Adrian. b 66. STETS. **d** 13 **p** 14. NSM Guernsey W Par *Win* from 13. *Les Menages, Les Fries, St Pierre du Bois, Guernsey GY7 9EY*

DAUBNEY, Howard. b 49. Woolwich Poly BA 70. S'wark Ord Course 86. **d** 89 **p** 90. C Roch 89-04; V Strood St Fran 04-14;

rtd 14; PtO *Nor* from 15. *47 The Green, Martham, Great Yarmouth NR29 4PF* M: 07932-384823 T: (01493) 749126 E: howarddaubney@gmail.com

DAUGHTERY, Stephen John. b 61. Kent Univ BSc 82. Trin Coll Bris BA 94. **d** 96 **p** 97. C Guildf Ch Ch 96-98; C Guildf Ch Ch w St Martha-on-the-Hill 98-03; R Southover *Chich* from 03; P-in-c Lewes St Jo sub Castro and S Malling from 14. *The Rectory, Southover High Street, Lewes BN7 1HT* T: (01273) 472018 E: steve@daughtery.plus.com

DAULMAN, John Henry. b 33. Lich Th Coll 60. **d** 62 **p** 63. C Monkseaton St Mary *Newc* 62-65; Min Can Newc Cathl 65-67; Chapl Crumpsall and Springfield Hosp 67-73; V Tyldesley w Shakerley *Man* 73-81; V Turton 81-00; rtd 00; PtO *Blackb* from 01; *Man* 13-14. *17 Higher Bank Street, Withnell, Chorley PR6 8SF* T: (01254) 832597

DAUNTON-FEAR, Andrew. b 45. Univ of Tasmania BSc 64 Qu Coll Cam BA 67 MA 72 St Andr Univ BPhil 76 K Coll Lon PhD 00. Ridley Hall Cam 66. **d** 68 **p** 70. Lect Ridley Coll Melbourne Australia 68-70; C Epping w Thomastown 68-71; P-in-c Islington H Trin Cloudesley Square *Lon* 71-75; Hon C Islington St Mary 71-75; C Stoke Bishop *Bris* 76-79; R Thrapston *Pet* 79-89; R Barming *Roch* 89-03; Lect St Andr Th Sem Philippines 03-15; rtd 15. *20 St Oswald's Court, St Oswald's Road, Bristol BS6 7HX* E: fear.no.evil70@gmail.com

DAVAGE, William Ernest Peter. b 50. MA 94. St Steph Ho Ox 89. **d** 91 **p** 92. C Eyres Monsell *Leic* 91-94; P Lib Pusey Ho 94-11; rtd 11. *7 Hampstead Square, London NW3 1AB* T: (020) 7209 5375 E: william.davage@stx.ox.ac.uk

DAVENPORT (née HILL), Elizabeth Jayne Louise. b 55. St Hugh's Coll Ox BA 77 MA 81 Univ of S California PhD 03. Fuller Th Sem California ThM 89 NOC 79. **dss** 82 **d** 87 **p** 91. Halliwell St Pet *Man* 82-83; Paris St Mich *Eur* 83-85; LtO *St Alb* 85-87; Hon Par Dn Chorleywood St Andr 87-89; USA from 89. *University of Southern California, University Religious Center, Los Angeles, CA 90089-0751, USA* T: (001) (213) 740 1366 E: ejld@usc.edu

DAVENPORT, Canon Ian Arthan. b 54. Linc Th Coll 85. **d** 87 **p** 88. C Ches H Trin 87-91; V Newton 91-97; V Oxton 97-10; RD Birkenhead 05-10; R Malpas and Threapwood 10-11; R Malpas and Threapwood and Bickerton from 11; RD Malpas from 14; Hon Can Ches Cathl from 06. *The Rectory, Church Street, Malpas SY14 8PP* T: (01948) 860922 E: malpas.ian.d@gmail.com

DAVENPORT, Mrs Joy Gwyneth. b 46. Glam Coll of Educn TCert 68. SEITE 01. **d** 04 **p** 07. NSM Rye *Chich* 04-15; Asst Chapl E Sussex Hosps NHS Trust 04-15; rtd 15. *2 The Oakfields, Rye Road, Rye TN31 7UA* T: (01797) 224209

DAVENPORT, Ms Sally Elizabeth. b 59. Lon Bible Coll BA 99. Ripon Coll Cuddesdon 99. **d** 01 **p** 02. C Bishop's Stortford St Mich *St Alb* 01-05; TV Bp's Hatfield, Lemsford and N Mymms 05-10; P-in-c Fareham H Trin *Portsm* from 11. *Bishopsgrove, 26 Osborn Road, Fareham PO16 7DQ* T: (01329) 232688 M: 07500-775926 E: sally.davenport@portsmouth.anglican.org

DAVENPORT, Susan Jane. *See* MILLINCHIP, Susan Jane

DAVENPORT, Miss Sybil Ann. b 36. Nottm Univ CertEd 57. EMMTC 85. **d** 89 **p** 94. NSM Thurgarton w Hoveringham and Bleasby etc *S'well* 89-94; NSM Collingham w S Scarle and Besthorpe and Girton 94-02; rtd 02; PtO *S'well* from 02. *Holmedale, North Muskham, Newark NG23 6HQ* T: (01636) 701552

DAVEY, Andrew John. b 57. Magd Coll Ox BA 78 MA 83. Wycliffe Hall Ox 80. **d** 83 **p** 84. C Bermondsey St Jas w Ch Ch *S'wark* 83-87; Chapl Trin Coll Cam 87-92; Pilsdon Community 94-04. *Kingswood, North Street, Axminster EX13 5QF* T: (01297) 33534

DAVEY, Andrew John. b 53. St Mich Coll Llan. **d** 77 **p** 78. C Gt Stanmore *Lon* 77-79; NSM Watford St Jo *St Alb* 87-92; C Potters Bar 92-95; P-in-c Clenchwarton *Ely* 95-96; P-in-c W Lynn 95-96; R Clenchwarton and W Lynn from 96. *The Rectory, Clenchwarton, King's Lynn PE34 4DT* T/F: (01553) 772089 E: postmaster@andrewdavey.plus.com

DAVEY, Andrew Paul. b 61. Southn Univ BA 82 Sheff Univ DMinTh 98. Tamilnadu Th Sem 84 Westcott Ho Cam 85. **d** 87 **p** 88. C S'wark H Trin w St Matt 87-91; V Camberwell St Luke 91-96; Min Development Officer Woolwich Area Miss Team 96-98; Ho of Bps' Officer for UPAs 96-98; Asst Sec Abps' Coun Bd for Soc Resp 98-03; Nat Adv on Community and Urban Affairs 03-12; V Upper Tooting H Trin w St Aug *S'wark* from 12; Hon Chapl S'wark Cathl from 01. *Holy Trinity Vicarage, 14 Upper Tooting Park, London SW17 7SW* T: (020) 8672 4790 E: ap.davey@btinternet.com

DAVEY, Christopher Mark. b 64. EN(G) 84 RGN 89. St Steph Ho Ox 92. **d** 95 **p** 96. C Leeds Belle Is St Jo and St Barn *Ripon*

95-97; C-in-c Grahame Park St Aug CD *Lon* 97-01; V St Alb St Mary Marshalswick *St Alb* 01-08; P-in-c Leavesden 08-12; V 12-13; P-in-c Coggeshall w Markshall *Chelmsf* from 13; P-in-c Cressing w Stisted and Bradwell etc from 15. *The Vicarage, 4 Church Green, Coggeshall, Colchester CO6 1UD* T: (01376) 561234 E: cdavey2776@aol.com *or* vicarcoggeshall@btinternet.com

DAVEY, Mrs Hilary Margaret. b 49. Bris Univ BSc 70. EAMTC 98. **d** 01 **p** 02. NSM Saffron Walden w Wendens Ambo, Littlebury etc *Chelmsf* 01-07; P-in-c Debden and Wimbish w Thunderley 07-11; TV Saffron Walden and Villages from 12. *Barltrops, High Street, Debden, Saffron Walden CB11 3LE* T: (01799) 522616 E: hilarydavey@btopenworld.com

DAVEY, John. b 35. Birkbeck Coll Lon BSc 84 MPhil 87 PhD 91 FRSH 89 CPsychol 92 AFBPsS 92. Chich Th Coll 67. **d** 69 **p** 70. C Eastbourne St Elisabeth *Chich* 69-72; C Eastbourne St Mary 72-74; V W Wittering 74-77; Min Can and Chapl Windsor 77-81; R The Rissingtons *Glouc* 81-85; R Alfriston w Lullington, Litlington and W Dean *Chich* 85-92; Chapl Bramshill Police Coll *Win* 92-96; rtd 97; P-in-c Amberley w N Stoke and Parham, Wiggonholt etc *Chich* 97-98; PtO 98-08. *20 Holly Avenue, Wilford, Nottingham NG11 7AF*

DAVEY, Julian Metherall. b 40. Jes Coll Ox BA 62 MA 65. Wells Th Coll 62. **d** 64 **p** 65. C Weston-super-Mare St Jo *B & W* 64-66; PtO *St Alb* 66-68; Chapl St Alb Sch 68-73; Chapl Merchant Taylors' Sch Crosby 73-82; PtO *Truro* 82-83; P-in-c Meavy w Sheepstor *Ex* 83-85; P-in-c Walkhampton 83-85; R Meavy, Sheepstor and Walkhampton 85; Chapl Warw Sch 86-89; P-in-c The Winterbournes and Compton Valence *Sarum* 89-94; TV Marshwood Vale 96-98; P-in-c St Gennys, Jacobstow w Warbstow and Treneglos *Truro* 98-02; rtd 02; PtO *Truro* from 02. *18 Pondfield Road, Latchbrook, Saltash PL12 4UA* T: (01752) 840086

DAVEY, Julian Warwick. b 45. LRCPI 70 LRCSI 70. Qu Coll Birm 78. **d** 81 **p** 82. NSM Ipsley *Worc* 81-05; PtO *Cov* from 05; *Worc* from 05. *The Field House, Allimore Lane, Alcester B49 5PR* T: (01789) 764640 E: julianw.davey@yahoo.com

DAVEY, Kenneth William. b 41. Qu Coll Birm 84. **d** 86 **p** 87. C Baswich *Lich* 86-90; V Lostock Gralam *Ches* 90-96; P-in-c Thornton-le-Moors w Ince and Elton 96-07; rtd 07; PtO *Ches* from 08. *4 Firbank, Elton, Chester CH2 4LY* T: (01928) 726166 M: 07977-361059 E: kenzor@daveyk1.fsnet.co.uk

DAVEY, Mark Sydney Henry. b 80. Wycliffe Hall Ox 10. **d** 13 **p** 14. C Herne Bay Ch Ch *Cant* from 13. *66 Linden Avenue, Herne Bay CT6 8TZ* T: (01227) 506403 E: mark.davey@live.co.uk

DAVEY, Peter James. b 59. Bris Univ BSc 81 Loughb Univ MBA 91. Trin Coll Bris BA 00. **d** 00 **p** 01. C Long Eaton St Jo *Derby* 00-04; V Cotmanhay from 04; RD Erewash from 13. *The Vicarage, 197 Heanor Road, Ilkeston DE7 8TA* T: 0115-932 5670 E: petedavey@outlook.com

DAVEY, Peter William. b 44. Culham Coll of Educn TCert 65. Linc Th Coll 93. **d** 93 **p** 94. C Cheadle w Freehay *Lich* 93-96; P-in-c Calton, Cauldon, Grindon and Waterfall 96-99; R Calton, Cauldon, Grindon, Waterfall etc 99-00; R Norton in the Moors 04-09; rtd 09. *24 rue des Vergers, Verdroux, 79120 St Coutant, France*

DAVEY, Piers Damer. b 57. Dur Univ BSc. Coll of Resurr Mirfield 80. **d** 83 **p** 84. C Heworth St Mary *Dur* 83-86; C Barnard Castle w Whorlton 86-89; V Aycliffe 89-95; V Chilton Moor 95-06; R Gawler St Geo Australia from 06. *26 Cowan Street, Gawler SA 5118, Australia* T: (0061) (8) 8523 5677 E: stgeorgegawler@optusnet.com.au

DAVEY, Richard Henry. b 66. Man Univ BA 88 Nottm Univ PhD 06. Linc Th Coll BTh 93. **d** 93 **p** 94. C Parkstone St Pet w Branksea and St Osmund *Sarum* 93-96; Chapl and Min Can St E Cathl 96-99; Can Res S'well Minster 99-04; Chapl Nottm Trent Univ from 04; C Clifton from 04; C Nottingham All SS, St Mary and St Pet from 10. *All Saints Vicarage, 16 All Saints Street, Nottingham NG7 4DP* T: 0115-808 4149 E: rdavey1175@aol.com

DAVID, Brother. *See* JARDINE, David John

DAVID, Faith Caroline. *See* CLARINGBULL, Faith Caroline

DAVID, Gilbert. b 56. Karachi Univ BA 76. Ripon Coll Cuddesdon 08. **d** 11 **p** 12. C New Bury w Gt Lever *Man* 11-15; TV Darlaston and Moxley *Lich* from 15. *Moxley Vicarage, 5 Sutton Road, Wednesbury WS10 8SG* M: 07880-710122 E: gildavid2u@hotmail.com

DAVID, Kaushal. b 65. **d** 15. C Nantwich *Ches* from 15. *22 Beatty Road, Nantwich CW5 5JP 22 Beatty Road, Nantwich CW5 5JP* T: 07824-603592 E: kaushaldavid@hotmail.com

DAVID, Canon Kenith Andrew. b 39. Natal Univ BA(Theol) 64. Coll of Resurr Mirfield 64. **d** 66 **p** 67. C Harpenden St Nic

St Alb 66-69; R Chatsworth Epiphany S Africa 69-71; P-in-c Southwick St Mich *Chich* 71-72; Th Educn Sec Chr Aid 72-75; Project Officer India and Bangladesh 76-81; Hon C Kingston All SS *S'wark* 72-76; Hon C Kingston All SS w St Jo 76-81; LtO Botswana 81-83; Hon C Geneva *Eur* 83-95; Co-ord Urban Rural Miss WCC 83-94; Can Lundi Zimbabwe from 93; V Hessle *York* 95-05; rtd 05; PtO *Cant* 05-11. *5 Randolph Close, Canterbury CT1 3AZ* T/F: (01227) 452009

DAVID, Philip Evan Nicholl. b 31. Jes Coll Ox BA 53 MA 57 Univ of Wales BA 61 Nottm Univ MPhil 86 Leic Univ MEd 88. St Mich Coll Llan 56. **d** 57 **p** 58. C Llanblethian w Cowbridge *Llan* 57-60; C Cardiff St Jo 60-64; Chapl Ch Coll Brecon 64-75; P-in-c Aberyscir and Llanfihangel Nantbran *S & B* 70-75; Chapl Loretto Sch Musselburgh 75-82; Chapl Trent Coll Nottm 83-91; R Llanfyllin and Bwlchycibau *St As* 91-96; P-in-c Llangynog 95-96; rtd 96; P-in-c Newbridge-on-Wye and Llanfihangel Brynpabuan etc *S & B* 98-00; P-in-c Llanwrtyd w Llanddulas in Tir Abad etc 05. *Woodside Cottage, The Bron, Cross Gates, Llandrindod Wells LD1 6RS* T: (01597) 851401

DAVID, Wayne Aldwyn. b 74. Univ of Cen England in Birm BA 97. St Mich Coll Llan 04. **d** 07 **p** 08. NSM Merthyr Tydfil St Dav *Llan* 07-10; NSM Rhydyfelin w Graig 10-11; NSM Glyntaff, Rhydfelin and the Graig from 11. *16 St Illtyd's Road, Church Village, Pontypridd CF38 1DA* T: (01443) 203422
E: wayneadavid@hotmail.com

DAVID, William John. b 57. Ban Univ BTh 07. **d** 04 **p** 05. OLM Eltham St Barn *S'wark* 04-07; NSM 07-09 and 11-15; C Toowoomba St Luke Australia 09-11; Chapl Lewisham and Greenwich NHS Trust from 14. *12 Tarnwood Park, London SE9 5NY* M: 07929-644503 T: (020) 8333 6338
E: williamdavid10@aol.com

DAVID FRANCIS, Brother. *See* DARLING, David Francis

DAVIDGE-SMITH, Mrs Margaret Kathleen. b 53. CQSW 77. STETS 99. **d** 02 **p** 03. NSM E Acton St Dunstan w St Thos *Lon* 02-06; Asst Chapl Ealing Hosp NHS Trust 04-06; Asst Chapl Meadow House Hospice 04-06; Asst Chapl W Middx Univ Hosp NHS Trust 05-06; Asst Chapl W Lon Mental Health NHS Trust 05-06; Chapl Ealing Hosp NHS Trust from 06. *36 Newburgh Road, London W3 6DQ* T/F: (020) 8993 0868
E: mdavidge_s@hotmail.com

DAVIDSON, Canon Charles Hilary. b 29. St Edm Hall Ox BA 52 MA 56 Leic Univ MPhil 89. Lich Th Coll 52. **d** 54 **p** 55. C Abington *Pet* 54-59; C Pet St Jo 59-60; R Sywell w Overstone 60-66; P-in-c Lamport w Faxton 66-76; R Maidwell w Draughton and Scaldwell 67-76; R Maidwell w Draughton, Scaldwell, Lamport etc 77-80; RD Brixworth 77-79; V Roade 80-87; V Roade and Ashton w Hartwell 87-94; RD Towcester 91-94; Can Pet Cathl 79-94; rtd 94; PtO *Pet* from 94. *Croftside, Butlins Lane, Roade, Northampton NN7 2PU* T: (01604) 863016

DAVIDSON, Christopher John. b 45. St Luke's Coll Ex CertEd 67 St Martin's Coll Lanc BEd 74. EAMTC. **d** 91 **p** 92. NSM Taverham w Ringland *Nor* 91-93; Dir of Educn 87-93; P-in-c Whixley w Green Hammerton *Ripon* 93-96; RE Adv 93-96; Dioc Dir of Educn *Ex* 97-01; Assoc P Exminster and Kenn 97-01; R Quidenham Gp *Nor* 01-08; P-in-c Guiltcross 04-08; rtd 08; P-in-c Pyworthy, Pancrasweek and Bridgerule *Ex* 08-11; PtO *Nor* from 11. *2 The Old School, Hinderclay Road, Rickinghall, Diss IP22 1HD* T: (01379) 890465
E: chris.davidson@btinternet.com

DAVIDSON, Mrs Dawn Margaret. b 59. **d** 09 **p** 10. OLM Mulbarton w Bracon Ash, Hethel and Flordon *Nor* 09-14; TV Newton Flotman, Swainsthorpe, Tasburgh, etc from 14. *The Rectory, The Street, Saxlingham Nethergate, Norwich NR15 1AJ* T: (01508) 498924 M: 07784-003432
E: davidsonhome1@btinternet.com

DAVIDSON, Donald. b 52. TISEC 00. **d** 05 **p** 06. C W Highland Region *Arg* from 05. *4 Kearan Road, Kinlochleven, Argyll PH50 4QU* T: (01855) 831444 E: donaldd@btinternet.com

DAVIDSON, Graeme John. b 42. Victoria Univ Wellington BA 64 BA 66 Ox Univ MA 70. St Steph Ho Ox 67. **d** 70 **p** 71. C Maidenhead St Luke *Ox* 70-73; New Zealand 73-77 and from 93; USA 77-88. *3 Tauroa Road, Havelock North, Hawke's Bay 4130, New Zealand* E: graeme.davidson@paradise.net.nz

DAVIDSON, Hilary. *See* DAVIDSON, Charles Hilary

DAVIDSON, Ian George. b 32. LSE BSc(Econ) 54. Linc Th Coll 55. **d** 58 **p** 59. C Waltham Cross *St Alb* 58-60; C St Alb Abbey 61-63; Hon PV S'wark Cathl 63-67; V Gt Cornard *St E* 67-72; R Lt Cornard 67-70; LtO 72-79; Student Counsellor Suffolk Coll 72-79; P-in-c Witnesham w Swilland and Ashbocking *St E* 79-83; Warden Scargill Ho 83-88; Chapl Chr Fellowship of Healing *Edin* 88-97; rtd 97. *28 Fox Spring Crescent, Edinburgh EH10 6NQ* T: 0131-445 3381
E: iangill@foxspring.freeserve.co.uk

DAVIDSON, John Lindsay. b 27. LRCP 51. St Steph Ho Ox. **d** 58 **p** 59. C Croydon St Mich *Cant* 58-61; P-in-c H Cross Miss 62-66; V Kennington Cross St Anselm *S'wark* 67-70;

V Croydon St Mich *Cant* 70-80; V Croydon St Mich w St Jas 80-81; TR N Creedy *Ex* 81-92; RD Cadbury 86-90; rtd 92; PtO *Ex* 92-09. *9 Redvers House, Union Road, Crediton EX173AW* T: (01363) 775998

DAVIDSON, Lynn. b 61. Cov Univ BA 02 DipSW 02. Ridley Hall Cam 13. **d** 14 **p** 15. C Shrewsbury St Geo w Greenfields *Lich* from 14. *5 Bayford Drive, Shrewsbury SY1 3XQ*
M: 07447-932803 E: lynn.davidson3@btinternet.com

DAVIDSON, Ralph. b 38. **d** 01 **p** 02. OLM Birkenshaw w Hunsworth *Leeds* from 01. *Bedale, Moorhouse Lane, Birkenshaw, Bradford BD11 2BA* T: (01274) 681955
E: ralphdavidson@bedale1938.wanadoo.co.uk

DAVIDSON, Trevor John. b 49. CertEd. Oak Hill Th Coll 80. **d** 85 **p** 86. C Drypool *York* 85-88; V Bessingby 88-97; V Carnaby 88-97; Chapl Bridlington and Distr Gen Hosp 88-94; Chapl E Yorks Community Healthcare NHS Trust 94-97; V Felling *Dur* 97-14; CUF Projects Officer 97-14; rtd 14; PtO *Dur* from 15. *10 Alder Grove, Seaham SR7 7RT* T: 0191-435 5685

DAVIE (née JONES), Mrs Alyson Elizabeth. b 58. Ex Univ BA 86. Wycliffe Hall Ox 86. **d** 88 **p** 94. Par Dn Ipswich St Fran *St E* 88-92; PtO *Ox* 92-93; *St Alb* 93-94; NSM E Barnet 94-97; Asst Chapl Oak Hill Th Coll 94-96; P-in-c The Mundens w Sacombe *St Alb* 97-06; V St Paul's Cray St Barn *Roch* 06-14; P-in-c Meopham w Nurstead from 14. *The Rectory, Shipley Hills Road, Meopham, Gravesend DA13 0AD* T: (01474) 812068
E: alyson.davie@btinternet.com

DAVIE, Peter Edward Sidney. b 36. LSE BSc 57 Birm Univ MA 73 K Coll Lon MPhil 78 Kent Univ PhD 90. Coll of Resurr Mirfield 57. **d** 60 **p** 61. C De Beauvoir Town St Pet *Lon* 60-63; C-in-c Godshill CD *Portsm* 63-67; R Upton St Leonards *Glouc* 67-73; Sen Lect Ch Ch Coll of HE *Cant* 73-98; Prin Lect *Cant* Ch Ch Univ Coll 98-01; rtd 01; Hon C Cant St Pet w St Alphege and St Marg etc 79-10; PtO from 10. *8 Brockenhurst Close, Canterbury CT2 7RX* T: (01227) 451572
E: pedavie@dircon.co.uk

DAVIE, Stephen Peter. b 52. S Bank Poly BA 75 MRTPI 77. Oak Hill Th Coll BA 93. **d** 93 **p** 94. C Luton Ch Ch *Roch* 93-97; R Cobham w Luddesdowne and Dode 97-04; P-in-c Horley *S'wark* 04-08; TR 08-12; P-in-c Tong *Leeds* 12-14; AD N Bradford 14; Dir Bradf Sch of Min from 14. *Bradford School of Ministry, Kadugli House, Elmsley Street, Steeton, Keighley BD20 6SE* M: 07918-654956 T: (01943) 510653
E: steve.davie@btinternet.com

DAVIES, Adrian. *See* DAVIES, Glanmor Adrian

DAVIES, Adrian Paul. b 43. K Coll Lon. **d** 69 **p** 70. C Nottingham St Mary *S'well* 69-74; C Gt w Lt Billing *Pet* 74-75; P-in-c Marholm 75-82; R Castor 75; R Castor w Sutton and Upton 76-82; V Byker St Mich w St Lawr *Newc* 82-94; rtd 95. *27 Clougha Avenue, Halton, Lancaster LA2 6NR* T: (01524) 811141

DAVIES, Alan. *See* DAVIES, James Alan

DAVIES, Alan Arthur. b 35. Sarum & Wells Th Coll 83. **d** 85 **p** 86. C Eastleigh *Win* 85-88; C Portsea N End St Mark *Portsm* 88-90; V Lydiate *Liv* 90-00; rtd 00; PtO *Sarum* from 01. *25 St Catherine's, Wimborne BH21 1BE* T: (01202) 848233

DAVIES, Alan Douglas. b 49. ERMC 08. **d** 10 **p** 11. NSM Downham Market and Crimplesham w Stradsett *Ely* from 10. *The Lodge, Wallington Hall, Runcton Holme, King's Lynn PE33 0EP* T: (01553) 810675 E: fralandavies@hotmail.co.uk

DAVIES, Alastair John. b 56. Nottm Univ BA MTh. Westcott Ho Cam. **d** 84 **p** 85. C Eltham St Jo *S'wark* 84-87; C Dulwich St Barn 87-89; Chapl RAF 89-07; P-in-c Lyneham w Bradenstoke *Sarum* 01-03; Sen Chapl R United Hosp Bath NHS Trust from 07. *Royal United Hospital, Combe Park, Bath BA1 3NG* T: (01225) 428331
E: alastair.davies@ruh-bath.swest.nhs.uk

DAVIES, Albert Brian. b 37. Worc Coll of Educn CertEd 60. Wycliffe Hall Ox 03. **d** 04 **p** 05. C Poitou-Charentes *Eur* 04-07; P-in-c The Vendée 07-10; Asst Chapl Aquitaine 11-12; rtd 13. *La Basse Coussaie, 85140 Les Essarts, France*
T: (0033) 2 51 62 96 32 E: briandpam@free.fr

DAVIES, Mrs Alison Margaret. b 57. Nottm Univ BA 78. STETS 96. **d** 99 **p** 00. NSM Win St Barn 99-04; PtO 04-07; *Nor* 07-10 and 13; Chapl King's Lynn and Wisbech Hosps NHS Trust 10-13. *63 Wheatway, Abbeydale, Gloucester GL4 5ET* T: (01452) 551020

DAVIES, Allan Randall. **d** 12 **p** 13. NSM Magor *Mon* from 12. *10 Windsor Gardens, Magor, Caldicot NP26 3NH* T: (01633) 882314 E: allanrdavies@hotmail.com

DAVIES, Mrs Allison Claire. b 65. Qu Coll Birm 12. **d** 15. NSM Redditch H Trin *Worc* from 15. *19 Chelmarsh Close, Church Hill North, Redditch B98 85Q*

DAVIES, Andrew James. b 53. Univ of Wales (Cardiff) BD 00. St Mich Coll Llan 01. **d** 03 **p** 04. C Caerphilly *Llan* 03-06;

P-in-c Rhondda Fach Uchaf 06-12; V Vale of Neath from 12. *The Vicarage, 99A Neath Road, Resolven, Neath SA11 4AN* T: (01639) 711657 M: 07931-370054
E: daviesaj8@yahoo.co.uk

DAVIES, Andrew John. *See* GRACE, Andrew John

DAVIES, Anthony. *See* DAVIES, Vincent Anthony

DAVIES, Anthony. *See* DAVIES, David Anthony

DAVIES, Anthony Paul. b 56. JP 02. Univ of Wales (Swansea) BSc 76 CEng 85. St Mich Coll Llan 03. **d** 06 **p** 07. NSM Penllergaer *S & B* 06-07; NSM Gorseinon 07-12; PtO from 12. *The Gate House, 1 Westend Court, Frome BA11 1ET* M: 07855-237866 T: (01373) 473668
E: anthonypdavies@yahoo.com

DAVIES, Barry Lewis. b 46. Boro Road Teacher Tr Coll CertEd 69 Lon Inst of Educn DipEd 84 MA 86. STETS 02. **d** 05 **p** 06. NSM Hardington Vale *B & W* 05-08; rtd 08; PtO *B & W* 09-13; *Bris* from 10; Chapl Avon and Somerset Constabulary *B & W* from 10; Chapl Partis Coll Bath 10-13; NSM Mells w Buckland Dinham, Elm, Whatley etc *B & W* from 13. *3 The Lays, Goose Street, Beckington, Frome BA11 6RS* T: (01373) 831344
E: bandkdavies@msn.com

DAVIES, Miss Belinda Jane. b 68. Ox Poly BSc 91 Dur Univ MA 11. STETS BA 08. **d** 08 **p** 10. C Yateley *Win* 08-09; C Salisbury St Thos and St Edm *Sarum* 10-13; P-in-c Portsea St Geo *Portsm* from 13; CMD Officer from 13. *The Vicarage, 8 Queen Street, Portsmouth PO1 3HL*
E: belinda.davies@portsmouth.anglican.org

DAVIES, Benjamin John. b 27. Glouc Sch of Min 80 Trin Coll Bris 87. **d** 88 **p** 89. NSM Cinderford St Steph w Littledean *Glouc* 88-98; PtO 98-00. *22 Withy Park, Bishopston, Swansea SA3 3EY* T: (01792) 232352

DAVIES, Canon Bernard. b 34. Lon Univ BD 63. Oak Hill Th Coll 59. **d** 63 **p** 64. C Rawtenstall St Mary *Man* 63-69; Sec Rwanda Miss 69-71; R Widford *Chelmsf* 71-78; V Braintree 78-00; RD 87-95; Hon Can Chelmsf Cathl 92-00; rtd 00; PtO *Nor* from 00; *St E* from 01. *3 Brookwood Close, Worlingham, Beccles NR34 7RJ* T: (01502) 719739

DAVIES, Sister Beverley. b 55. **d** 11 **p** 12. NSM Leic Presentation 11-14; PtO from 14; Chapl LOROS Hospice from 15; Chapl Qu Th Foundn Birm from 15. *St Matthew's House, 25 Kamloops Crescent, Leicester LE1 2HX* T: 0116-253 9158
E: bevcsf@gmail.com

DAVIES, Brian. *See* DAVIES, Albert Brian

DAVIES, Carol Ann. b 50. St Mich Coll Llan BTh 14. **d** 12 **p** 13. NSM Llwynderw *S & B* from 12. *20 Dolycoed, Dunvant, Swansea SA2 7UG* T: (01792) 523293
E: davies773@ntlworld.com

DAVIES, Catharine Mary. *See* FURLONG, Catharine Mary

DAVIES, Mrs Catherine Olive Sarah Skeel. b 61. Univ of Wales (Cardiff) BA 84. WMMTC 03. **d** 06 **p** 07. NSM Wootton Wawen and Claverdon w Preston Bagot *Cov* 06-09; NSM Barford w Wasperton and Sherbourne and Hampton Lucy w Charlecote and Loxley 09-13; PtO from 13. *2 Station Cottages, Danzey Green, Tamworth-in-Arden, Solihull B94 5BE* T: (01564) 742337 E: revcathydavies@aol.com

DAVIES, Ceri John. b 61. Univ of Wales (Lamp) BA 91 Univ of Wales (Abth) PGCE 92 Univ of Wales (Cardiff) BTh 00. St Mich Coll Llan 97. **d** 00 **p** 01. C Carmarthen St Dav *St D* 00-03; TV Llanelli 03-11; C Cynwyl Elfed w Newchurch and Trelech a'r Betws 11-14; P-in-c from 14. *50 Meysydd y Coleg, Carmarthen SA31 3GU* E: cdavies465@btinternet.com

DAVIES, Chris. *See* DAVIES, David Christopher

DAVIES, Christopher Edward. b 72. **d** 03 **p** 04. OLM Bilston *Lich* from 03. *10 Wroxham Glen, Willenhall WV13 3HU* T: (01902) 655305 M: 07952-196204

DAVIES, Christopher John. b 55. St Alb Minl Tr Scheme 83. **d** 86 **p** 87. C Tooting All SS *S'wark* 86-90; V Malden St Jas 90-96; RD Kingston 92-96; TR Wimbledon 96-06; Hon Can S'wark Cathl 06; V Wymondham *Nor* from 06; RD Humbleyard from 08. *The Vicarage, 5 Vicar Street, Wymondham NR18 0PL* T: (01953) 602269
E: vicar@wymondhamabbey.org.uk

DAVIES, Christopher Mark. b 76. Essex Univ BA 97 Sheff Univ BA 13 Southn Inst DipSW 02. Coll of Resurr Mirfield 11. **d** 13 **p** 14. C Grimsby St Mary and St Jas *Linc* from 13. *62A Brighowgate, Grimsby DN32 0QW*
E: cmdavies76@yahoo.co.uk

DAVIES, Canon Clifford Thomas. b 41. Glouc Th Course. **d** 83 **p** 84. NSM Dean Forest H Trin *Glouc* 83-87; C Huntley and Longhope 87; R Ruardean 87-06; Hon Can Glouc Cathl 02-06; rtd 06. *Purbeck, 13 Park View, Ruardean GL17 9YW*

DAVIES, David Anthony (Tony). b 57. Thames Poly BSc 81 MRICS 84. Coll of Resurr Mirfield 85. **d** 88 **p** 89. C Stalybridge *Man* 88-91; C Swinton and Pendlebury 91-92 and 01-02; TV 92-01; V Tonge Moor from 02. *St Augustine's Vicarage, Redthorpe Close, Bolton BL2 2PQ* T/F: (01204) 523899
M: 07866-359864 E: tony@daviese.co.uk

DAVIES, David Berwyn. b 42. St Mich Coll Llan 95. **d** 96 **p** 97. C Llanelli *St D* 96-98; I Llanerch Aeron w Ciliau Aeron and Dihewyd etc 98-07; rtd 07; PtO *St D* from 07. *56 Tyisha Road, Llanelli SA15 1RW* T: (01554) 774391
E: taddavid@aol.com

DAVIES, Canon David Christopher. b 52. Lon Univ BSc 73 UWE MSc 11. Coll of Resurr Mirfield 73. **d** 76 **p** 77. C Bethnal Green St Jo w St Simon *Lon* 76-78; C Bethnal Green St Jo w St Bart 78-80; C-in-c Portsea St Geo CD *Portsm* 80-81; V Portsea St Geo 81-87; Relig Affairs Producer Radio Victory 81-86; Chapl Ham Green Hosp Bris 87-94; Chapl Southmead Hosp Bris 87-94; Chapl Southmead Health Services NHS Trust 94-99; Chapl N Bris NHS Trust 99-05; Hd Spiritual and Past Care 05-13; Hd Spiritual and Past Care Univ Hosps Bris NHS Foundn Trust 05-13; PtO *B & W* 94-13; Hon Can Bris Cathl 99-13; rtd 13; PtO *Bris* from 13. *28 Hortham Lane, Almondsbury, Bristol BS32 4JL* T: (01454) 616608
E: chris.davies1958@talktalk.net

DAVIES, David Geoffrey George. b 24. Univ of Wales (Ban) BA 49 Lon Univ BD 55 Chorley Coll of Educn PGCE 75. St Mich Coll Llan 49. **d** 51 **p** 52. C Brecon St Mary w Battle and Llanhamlach *S & B* 51-54; Min Can Brecon Cathl 53-55; C Oystermouth 55-59; V Cwm *St As* 59-63; Warden of Ords 62-70; V Ruabon 63-70; Hon Can St As Cathl 66-69; Can Cursal St As Cathl 69-70; Hon C W Derby St Jo *Liv* 70-81; Chapl to Welsh Speaking Angl in Liv 74-81 and from 96; TV Bourne Valley *Sarum* 81-87; TR 87-89; Bp's Chapl to Schs 83-89; RD Alderbury 86-89; rtd 89; Hon Chapl Liv Cathl 89-04; Sub-Chapl HM Pris Risley 90-96. *1 Sinclair Drive, Liverpool L18 0HN* T: 0151-722 1415

DAVIES, Canon David Jeremy Christopher. b 46. CCC Cam BA 68 MA 72. Westcott Ho Cam 68. **d** 71 **p** 72. C Stepney St Dunstan and All SS *Lon* 71-74; Chapl Qu Mary Coll 74-78; Chapl Univ of Wales (Cardiff) *Llan* 78-85; Can Res Sarum Cathl 85-12; rtd 12; PtO *Sarum* from 13. *The Old Chapel, The Street, Farley, Salisbury SP5 1AB* T: (01722) 712879
E: jeremy@theoldchapelfarley.co.uk

DAVIES, Canon David Michael Cole. b 44. St D Coll Lamp. **d** 68 **p** 69. C Carmarthen St Pet *St D* 68-72; R Dinas 72-77; V Ty-Croes w Saron 77-79; V Llanedi w Tycroes and Saron 80-90; RD Dyffryn Aman 85-90; V Dafen and Llwynhendy 90-94; V Dafen 94-08; Hon Can St D Cathl 00-08; rtd 08. *30 Bro'r Dderwen, Clynderwen SA66 7NR* E: dcmcd@aol.com

DAVIES, David Peter. b 47. **d** 13 **p** 14. NSM Worc City 13-14; NSM Worc St Nic and All SS w St Helen from 14. *44 Battenhall Rise, Worcester WR5 2DE* T: (01905) 356714

DAVIES, Prof David Protheroe. b 39. CCC Cam BA 62 MA 66 CCC Ox MA 69 BD 69. Ripon Hall Ox 62. **d** 64 **p** 65. C Swansea St Mary w H Trin *S & B* 64-67; Lect Th Univ of Wales (Lamp) 67-75; Sen Lect 75-86; Dean Faculty of Th 75-77 and from 81; Hd Th and RS from 84; Prof Th Univ of Wales (Trin St Dav) from 86; Pro Vice-Chan from 88; Bp's Chapl for Th Educn *S & B* from 79. *University of Wales, Lampeter SA48 7ED* T: (01570) 422351

DAVIES, David Vernon. b 14. AFBpSS 68 Univ of Wales (Swansea) BA 35 BD 38 St Cath Coll Ox MA 40 K Coll Lon PhD 56. St D Coll Lamp 41. **d** 41 **p** 42. C Llanelli Ch Ch *St D* 41-46; Chapl St John's Coll Nassau Bahamas 46-50; Chapl Cane Hill Hosp Coulsdon 50-61; Lect St Luke's Coll Ex 61-65; LtO *Ex* 61-68; Sen Lect St Luke's Coll Ex 65-68; LtO *Llan* from 68; Prin Lect Llan Coll of Educn 68-77; Sen Lect Univ of Wales (Cardiff) 77-79; rtd 79. *41 Cefn Coed Avenue, Cyncoed, Cardiff CF23 6HF* T: (029) 2075 7635

DAVIES, David William. b 55. St Mich Coll Llan. **d** 90 **p** 91. C Newton St Pet *S & B* 90-93; V Llywel and Traean-glas w Llanulid 93-97; CF 97-13; P-in-c Torre All SS *Ex* 13-15. *Address temp unknown*
E: davidwdavies2008@hotmail.com

DAVIES, Derek George. b 47. UWIST BEng 74 Univ of Wales (Lamp) BD 03. St Mich Coll Llan 03. **d** 05 **p** 06. NSM Steynton *St D* from 05; Interfaith Officer from 14. *Ty Llosg, Clarbeston Road, Pembroke SA63 4SG* T: (01437) 563560
E: derekgeorgedavies@hotmail.com

DAVIES, Dewi Gwynfor. b 56. Univ of Wales (Abth) BD 92 MTh 98 RIBA 81. **d** 98 **p** 99. C Llangunnor w Cwmffrwd *St D* 98-99; P-in-c Elerch w Penrhyncoch w Capel Bangor and Goginan 99-00; P-in-c Cil-y-Cwm and Ystrad-ffin w Rhandir-mwyn etc 00-01; V 01-03; V Llanedi w Tycroes and Saron 03-09; V Pen-bre from 09; AD Cydweli from 15. *The Vicarage, Ar-y-bryn, Pembrey, Burry Port SA16 0AJ* T: (01554) 833766
E: frdewivicarage@btinternet.com

DAVIES, Dillwyn. b 30. St Mich Coll Llan 52. **d** 54 **p** 55. C Laugharne w Llansadwrnen and Llandawke *St D* 54-57; LtO *Dur* 57-58; Miss to Seamen 57-58; Ceylon 58-62; R Winthorpe *S'well* 62-71; V Langford w Holme 62-71; V Mansfield Woodhouse 71-85; R Gedling 85-92; RD 85-90; Hon Can

DAVIES, Canon Dorrien Paul. b 64. Univ of Wales (Lamp) BA 95. Llan Dioc Tr Scheme 86. **d** 88 **p** 89. C Llanelli *St D* 88-91; V Llanfihangel Ystrad and Cilcennin w Trefilan etc 91-99; V St Dogmael's w Moylgrove and Monington w Meline 99-10; TV Dewisland from 10; Can St D Cathl from 07. *The Archdeaconry, The Close, St Davids, Haverfordwest SA62 6PE* T: (01437) 720456 E: davies.vicarage1@virgin.net

DAVIES, Prof Douglas James. b 47. St Jo Coll Dur BA 69 St Pet Coll Ox MLitt 72 Nottm Univ PhD 80 DLitt 04 Uppsala Univ Hon DTh 98. Cranmer Hall Dur 71. **d** 75 **p** 76. Lect Nottm Univ 75-97; Sen Lect 90-97; Hon C Wollaton *S'well* 75-83; Hon C Attenborough 83-85; Hon C E Leake 85-91; Hon C Daybrook 91-97; Prof RS Nottm Univ 93-97; Prin SS Hild and Bede Coll Dur 97-00; Prof Th Dur Univ from 97; Prof Study of Relig Dur Univ from 00; PtO *Dur* from 13. *Department of Theology and Religion, Abbey House, Palace Green, Durham DH1 3RS* T: 0191-375 7697 E: douglas.davies@durham.ac.uk

DAVIES, Canon Douglas Tudor. b 20. Univ of Wales (Ban) BA 44. Coll of Resurr Mirfield 44. **d** 46 **p** 47. C Swansea Ch Ch *S & B* 46-52; C Oystermouth 52-57; R Llangynllo and Bleddfa 57-63; C-in-c Treboeth CD 63-65; V Treboeth 65-90; RD Penderi 78-90; Hon Can Brecon Cathl 82-83; Can Brecon Cathl 83-90; rtd 90. *245A Swansea Road, Waunarlwydd, Swansea SA5 4SN* T: (01792) 879587

DAVIES, Edward Earl. b 40. Llan Dioc Tr Scheme 88. **d** 90 **p** 91. C Pontypridd St Cath w St Matt *Llan* 90-93; V Ferndale w Maerdy 93-00; V Cardiff Ch Ch Roath Park 00-09; rtd 09; PtO *Llan* from 10. *4 St Augustine Road, Heath, Cardiff CF14 4BD*

DAVIES, Edward Trevor. b 37. MRSC 62 MInstE 74 CEng 78. NOC 92. **d** 95 **p** 96. Hon Asst Chapl Countess of Chester Hosp NHS Foundn Trust 95-02; Chapl 02-05; NSM Waverton *Ches* 95-99; NSM Hargrave 99-00; C Bunbury and Tilstone Fearnall 00-02; NSM 02-03; PtO 05-10 and from 11; C Waverton w Aldford and Bruera 10-11; rtd 11. *Athergreen, 5 Allansford Avenue, Waverton, Chester CH3 7QH* T: (01244) 332106 E: etdavies1@btinternet.com

DAVIES, Canon Edward William Llewellyn. b 51. St Jo Coll Nottm BTh 77. **d** 78 **p** 79. C Southsea St Jude *Portsm* 78-81; C Alverstoke 81-84; R Abbas and Templecombe w Horsington *B & W* 84-89; PtO *Ches* 89-99; V Sutton St Jas 99-13; RD Macclesfield 05-12; Warden Foxhill Retreat and Conf Cen 13-15; Asst Warden of Readers 02-15; Hon Can Ches Cathl 10-15; rtd 15. *Address temp unknown* E: taffy@parishpump.co.uk

DAVIES, Eileen. *See* DAVIES, Rachel Hannah Eileen

DAVIES, Ms Elizabeth Jane. b 58. Man Univ BA 97 RGN 82 RSCN 88. Qu Coll Birm MA 01. **d** 01 **p** 02. C Spotland *Man* 01-04; Chapl Pennine Acute Hosps NHS Trust 04-05; Chapl Bolton Hospice 05-08; P-in-c Ladybarn *Man* from 08. *St Chad's Rectory, 1 St Chad's Road, Manchester M20 4WH* T: 0161-445 1185

DAVIES, Mrs Elizabeth Jean. b 39. Lon Univ MB, BS 63 MRCS 63 LRCP 63. Chich Th Coll 86. **d** 89 **p** 95. Par Dn Southwick St Mich *Chich* 89-91; Par Dn Littlehampton and Wick 91-95; C Seaford w Sutton 95-97; NSM E Preston w Kingston 97-04; rtd 99; P-in-c Everton and Mattersey w Clayworth *S'well* 04-05; PtO from 06. *Mayfield, Bone Mill Lane, Welham, Retford DN22 9NL* T: (01777) 703727

DAVIES, Mrs Emma Louise. b 67. St Andr Univ MA 89. Ripon Coll Cuddesdon 05. **d** 07 **p** 08. C Market Harborough and The Transfiguration etc *Leic* 07-10; TV Gilmorton, Peatling Parva, Kimcote etc from 10. *The Rectory, Church Lane, Gilmorton, Lutterworth LE17 5LU* T: (01455) 553475 E: emmydavies@aol.com

DAVIES, Éric Brian. b 36. St Jo Coll Nottm. **d** 87 **p** 89. NSM Castle Donington and Lockington cum Hemington *Leic* 87-88; Hon C Hathern, Long Whatton and Diseworth 89-90; Hon C Hathern, Long Whatton and Diseworth w Belton etc 90-93; C Minster-in-Sheppey *Cant* 93-00; rtd 00; NSM Walsall St Gabr Fulbrook *Lich* 00-03; NSM Caldmore 00-02; Hon C Caldmore w Palfrey 02-03; NSM Kinver and Enville 03-08. *1 White Cottages, Gospel Ash Road, Bobbington, Stourbridge DY7 5EF* T: (01384) 221168 E: reverend.ericdavies@kirion.net

DAVIES, Evelyn Dorothy. MBE 99. BEd 72 Liv Univ CertEd 56. **d** 96 **p** 97. NSM Llangynog *St As* 96-00; P-in-c Aberdaron and Llanfaelrhys *Ban* 00-04; R 04-07; rtd 07; PtO *Ban* 07-13; P-in-c Llandysilio and Penrhos and Llandrinio etc *St As* from 13. *The Rectory, Four Crosses, Llanymynech SY22 6RW* T: (01691) 839646 E: melangell@pennant1.demon.co.uk

DAVIES, Mrs Felicity Ann. b 58. Wycliffe Hall Ox. **d** 11 **p** 12. C Wadhurst *Chich* 11-14; C Stonegate 11-14; C Tidebrook 11-14; R Ickenham *Lon* from 14. *St Giles's Rectory, 38 Swakeleys Road, Ickenham, Uxbridge UB10 8BE* T: (01895) 622970 E: fadavies58@gmail.com

DAVIES, Frances Elizabeth. b 38. BA CertEd. Moray Ord Course. **d** 95. Hon C Thurso *Mor* from 95; Hon C Wick from 95. *22 Granville Crescent, Thurso, Caithness KW14 7NP* T: (01847) 892386 E: reallyfed@yahoo.co.uk

✠**DAVIES, The Rt Revd Francis James Saunders.** b 37. Univ of Wales (Ban) BA 60 Selw Coll Cam BA 62 MA 66 Bonn Univ 63. St Mich Coll Llan 62. **d** 63 **p** 64 **c** 00. C Holyhead w Rhoscolyn *Ban* 63-67; Chapl Ban Cathl 67-69; R Llanllyfni 69-75; Can Missr Ban Cathl 75-78; V Gorseinon *S & B* 78-86; RD Llwchwr 83-86; V Cardiff Dewi Sant *Llan* 86-93; R Criccieth w Treflys *Ban* 93-99; adn Meirionnydd 93-99; Bp Ban 99-04; rtd 04. *Ger-y-Nant, 5 Maes-y-Coed, Cardigan SA43 1AP* T: (01239) 615664

DAVIES, Gareth Rhys. b 51. Oak Hill Th Coll. **d** 83 **p** 84. C Gt Warley Ch Ch *Chelmsf* 83-86; C Oxhey All SS *St Alb* 86-90; C Aldridge *Lich* 90-99; V Colney Heath St Mark *St Alb* 99-00; V Sneyd Green *Lich* from 00; Bp's Adv on Healing 09-15. *St Andrew's Vicarage, 42 Granville Avenue, Sneyd Green, Stoke-on-Trent ST1 6BH* T: (01782) 215139

DAVIES, Geoffrey. *See* DAVIES, David Geoffrey George

✠**DAVIES, The Rt Revd Geoffrey Francis.** b 41. Cape Town Univ BA 62 Em Coll Cam BA 67 MA 71. Cuddesdon Coll 67. **d** 69 **p** 70 **c** 87. C W Brompton St Mary *Lon* 69-72; C Serowe St Aug Botswana 72-76; R Kalk Bay H Trin S Africa 77-80; Dir Dept of Miss 81-87; Suff Bp St John 88-91; Bp Umzimvubu 91-03; rtd 03. *Waterfall Cottage, 7 Upper Quarterdeck Road, Kalk Bay, 7990 South Africa* T/F: (0027) (21) 788 6591 E: geoffd@intermail.co.za

DAVIES, Geoffrey Michael. b 43. St D Coll Lamp. **d** 70 **p** 71. C Brynmawr *S & B* 70-73; Coll of Ascension Selly Oak 73-74; C Claremont St Sav S Africa 74-76; R Strand 76-82; R E London St Sav 82-84; Assoc R Constantia Ch Ch 90-91; C Roath *Llan* 91-95; V Llanishen w Trellech Grange and Llanfihangel etc *Mon* 95-99; S Africa from 99; R Graaf-Reinet St Jas 03-09. *2 Candlewood Street, Heather Park, George, 6529 South Africa*

DAVIES, George William. b 51. Open Univ BA 74 MPhil 89 MCIPD. Sarum & Wells Th Coll 83. **d** 85 **p** 86. C Mansfield SS Pet and Paul *S'well* 85-89; Chapl Cen Notts HA 86-89; P-in-c Fobbing and Ind Chapl *Chelmsf* 89-96; Chapl Thurrock Lakeside Shopping Cen 93-96; R Mottingham St Andr w St Alban *S'wark* 96-04; V Lamorbey H Trin *Roch* 04-12; Chapl Rose Bruford Coll 04-12; rtd 12. *106 Kirklington Road, Rufford Grange, Rainworth NG21 0JX* T: (01623) 490653 E: georgeandkatedavies@btinternet.com

DAVIES, Glanmor Adrian. b 51. St D Coll Lamp. **d** 73 **p** 75. C Llanstadwel *St D* 73-78; R Dinas w Llanllawer and Pontfaen w Morfil etc 78-84; V Lamphey w Hodgeston 84-85; V Lamphey w Hodgeston and Carew 85-03; V Borth and Eglwys-fach w Llangynfelyn 03-06. *4 Somerset Place, Park Road, Tenby SA70 7NF*

✠**DAVIES, The Most Revd Glenn Naunton.** b 50. Sydney Univ BSc 72 Sheff Univ PhD 88. Westmr Th Sem (USA) BD 78 ThM 79. **d** 81 **p** 81 **c** 01. Australia 81-85; Hon C Fulwood *Sheff* 85-87; Hon C Lodge Moor St Luke 86-87; Lect Moore Th Coll Australia 87-95; R Miranda 95-01; Bp N Sydney 01-13; Abp from 13. *PO Box Q190, Queen Victoria Building, Sydney NSW 1230, Australia* T: (0061) (2) 9265 1555 F: 9261 1170 E: registry@sydney.anglican.asn.au

DAVIES, Glyndwr George. b 36. Glouc Sch of Min 88. **d** 91 **p** 92. NSM Clodock and Longtown w Craswall, Llanveynoe etc *Heref* 91-02; rtd 02; PtO *Heref* 02-12. *White House Farm, Llanfihangel Crucorney, Abergavenny NP7 8HW* T: (01873) 890251

DAVIES, The Ven Graham James. b 35. Univ of Wales BD 72 St D Coll Lamp BA 56. St Mich Coll Llan 56 Episc Th Sch Cam Mass 58. **d** 59 **p** 60. C Johnston w Steynton *St D* 59-62; C Llangathen w Llanfihangel Cilfargen 62-64; Min Can St D Cathl 64-66; R Burton 66-71; R Hubberston 71-74; Hon C Lenham w Boughton Malherbe *Cant* 74-80; V Cwmdauddwr w St Harmon and Llanwrthwl *S & B* 80-86; V Cydweli and Llandyfaelog *St D* 86-97; Can St D Cathl 92-02; Adn St D 96-02; V Steynton 97-02; rtd 02. *16 Freshwater East Road, Lamphey, Pembroke SA71 5JX*

DAVIES, Canon Henry Joseph. b 38. Univ of Wales (Cardiff) BSc 61. St Mich Coll Llan 75. **d** 76 **p** 77. C Griffithstown *Mon* 76-79; TV Cwmbran 79-85; V Newport St Andr 85-03; Can St Woolos Cathl 98-03; rtd 03; PtO *Mon* 03-11; P-in-c Bettws from 11. *14 Morden Road, Newport NP19 7EU*

DAVIES, Herbert John. b 30. Cheltenham & Glouc Coll of HE BA 97. Glouc Sch of Min 84. **d** 87 **p** 88. NSM Cheltenham St Mark *Glouc* 87-01; PtO from 01. *45 Farmington Road, Benhall, Cheltenham GL51 6AG* T: (01242) 515996

DAVIES, Huw. *See* DAVIES, Philip Huw
DAVIES, Huw. *See* DAVIES, Peter Huw

DAVIES, Hywel John. b 45. Univ of Wales (Abth) BA 67 Univ of Wales (Ban) DipEd 68 Univ of Wales (Cardiff) MA 90 Univ of Wales (Ban) BTh 99. St Mich Coll Llan 94 Qu Coll Birm 96. **d** 97 **p** 98. Min Can Ban Cathl 97-98; C Llandudno 98-99; LtO *Llan* 99-03; NSM Canton Cardiff 03-04; P-in-c Llanarthne and Llanddarog *St D* 04-07; Chapl Coleg Sir Gâr 04-07; rtd 07; P-in-c Cardiff Dewi Sant *Llan* 08-10; PtO from 10. *68 Glas y Gors, Cwmbach, Aberdare CF44 0BQ* T: (01685) 378457 E: hywel33@btinternet.com

DAVIES, Ian. b 45. Man Coll of Educn TCert 74 Open Univ BA 79. Carl Dioc Tr Inst 88. **d** 91 **p** 92. NSM Harraby *Carl* 91-95; C Barrow St Jo 95-96; P-in-c 96-00; P-in-c Beetham and Youth and Sch Support Officer 00-05; V Marown *S & M* 05-11; rtd 11; PtO *Dur* from 12. *10 Capulet Terrace, Sunderland SR2 8JL* ; E: reviand@manx.net

DAVIES, Canon Ian. b 54. Sheff Hallam Univ BA 80 Univ of Wales (Cardiff) MSc(Econ) 86 MBA 92 Bris Univ PhD 01 CQSW 80. Wycliffe Hall Ox 02. **d** 04 **p** 05. C Swansea St Pet *S & B* 04-06; C Waunarllwydd 06-07; P-in-c 07-10; V from 10; Hon Can Brecon Cathl from 12. *The New Vicarage, 59A Victoria Road, Waunarlwydd, Swansea SA5 4SY* T: (01792) 874286 M: 07779-145267 E: iandavies12@hotmail.com

DAVIES, Ian Charles. b 51. Sarum & Wells Th Coll 78. **d** 81 **p** 82. C E Bedfont *Lon* 81-84; C Cheam *S'wark* 84-87; V Merton St Jas 87-96; RD Merton 91-96; Chapl Tiffin Sch Kingston 96-97; P-in-c Kingston St Luke *S'wark* 96-98; V S Beddington St Mich 98-99. *111 Milton Road, London W7 1LG* T: (020) 8621 4450

DAVIES, Canon Ian Elliott. b 64. Univ of Wales (Ban) BD 85. Ridley Hall Cam 86. **d** 88 **p** 89. C Baglan *Llan* 88-90; C Skewen 90-96; C St Marylebone All SS *Lon* 96-01; R Hollywood St Thos USA from 02; Can Los Angeles from 14. *St Thomas's Church, 7501 Hollywood Boulevard, Hollywood CA 90046, USA* T: (001) (323) 876 2102 F: 876 7738 E: frdavies@saintthomashollywood.org

DAVIES, Ion. *See* DAVIES, Johnston ap Llynfi

DAVIES, Canon Ivor Llewellyn. b 35. Univ of Wales BA 56 St Cath Soc Ox BA 58 MA 63. Wycliffe Hall Ox 56. **d** 62 **p** 63. C Wrexham *St As* 62-64; India 65-71; V Connah's Quay *St As* 71-79; P-in-c Gorsley w Cliffords Mesne *Glouc* 79-84; P-in-c Hempsted 89-90; Dir of Ords 84-90; Hon Can Glouc Cathl 89-01; V Parkend 90-01; P-in-c Viney Hill 97-01; rtd 01; PtO *Glouc* from 01; *Heref* from 04. *Rose Cottage, Church Walk, Viney Hill, Lydney GL15 4NY* T: (01594) 564512

DAVIES, James Alan. b 38. Lambeth STh 95. St Jo Coll Nottm. **d** 83 **p** 84. C Fletchamstead *Cov* 83-87; P-in-c Hartshill 87-89; V 89-93; V E Green 93-03; rtd 03; Hon C Mickleton, Willersey, Saintbury etc *Glouc* 04-05; PtO *Cov* from 05. *5 Margetts Close, Kenilworth CV8 1EN* T: (01926) 854337 E: a.davies861@btinternet.com

DAVIES, James William. b 51. Trin Hall Cam BA 72 MA 76 St Jo Coll Dur BA 79. Cranmer Hall Dur 77. **d** 80 **p** 81. C Croydon Ch Ch Broad Green *Cant* 80-83; CMS 83-86; Chapl Bethany Sch Goudhurst 86-90; P-in-c Parkstone St Luke *Sarum* 90-00; Hon C Bournemouth St Andr *Win* from 05. *8 Newton Road, Swanage BH19 2DZ* T: (01929) 475770 E: jameswdavies@btopenworld.com

DAVIES, Preb Jane Ann. b 58. Coll of Ripon & York St Jo MA 97. Aston Tr Scheme 91 WMMTC 93 NOC 94. **d** 96 **p** 97. NSM Heref S Wye 96-97; C 97-00; P-in-c Bishop's Frome w Castle Frome and Fromes Hill 00-08; P-in-c Acton Beauchamp and Evesbatch w Stanford Bishop 00-08; P-in-c Stoke Lacy, Moreton Jeffries w Much Cowarne etc 00-08; V Frome Valley 09-12; P-in-c Lugwardine w Bartestree, Weston Beggard etc 12; P-in-c Withington w Westhide 12; R Bartestree Cross from 12; Preb Heref Cathl from 10. *The Vicarage, Lugwardine, Hereford HR1 4AE* T: (01432) 850244 E: trendy.rev2@btinternet.com

DAVIES, Mrs Jaqueline Ann. b 42. Bris Univ BA 64 CertEd 65 Univ of Wales (Lamp) MA 99. EMMTC 84 St As Minl Tr Course 97. **d** 98 **p** 99. NSM Llanfair DC, Derwen, Llanelidan and Efenechtyd *St As* 98-00; PtO 00-14. *1A Swanbourne Road, Wick, Littlehampton BN17 6HS*

DAVIES, Jeffrey William. b 45. St Cath Coll Cam BA 66 MA 69 LLM 67 Liv Univ MTh 07 Solicitor 69. NOC 01. **d** 04 **p** 05. NSM Ramsbottom and Edenfield *Man* 04-11; NSM Heaton Ch Ch w Halliwell St Marg 11-14; rtd 14; PtO *Man* from 14. *44 Higher Dunscar, Egerton, Bolton BL7 9TF* T/F: (01204) 412503 E: jeffdavies1@ntlworld.com

DAVIES, Jeremy. *See* DAVIES, David Jeremy Christopher

DAVIES, Joanna. b 65. NTMTC. **d** 10 **p** 11. C Onslow Square and S Kensington St Aug *Lon* from 10. *54 Mayford Road, London SW12 8SN* E: jo.davies@htb.org

DAVIES, John. *See* DAVIES, Herbert John

DAVIES, John. *See* DAVIES, Benjamin John

DAVIES, John. *See* PAGE DAVIES, David John

DAVIES, John. *See* DAVIES, Kenneth John

DAVIES, John. b 62. Univ of Wales (Cardiff) BA 88. Ridley Hall Cam 98. **d** 00 **p** 01. C Wavertree H Trin *Liv* 00-04; P-in-c W Derby Gd Shep 04-09; V 09-10; TV Okehampton w Inwardleigh, Bratton Clovelly etc *Ex* 10-11; TV Okehampton, Inwardleigh, Belstone, Sourton etc 12-13; V Whitegate w Lt Budworth *Ches* 13-14; R Cam Vale *B & W* from 14. *The Rectory, Englands Lane, Queen Camel, Yeovil BA22 7NN* T: (01935) 851324 E: john@johndavies.org

DAVIES, John Atcherley. b 27. St Jo Coll Dur BA 55. Wycliffe Hall Ox 55. **d** 57 **p** 58. C Eastbourne St Jo *Chich* 57-61; Chapl RN 61-82; V Hyde Common *Win* 82-92; rtd 92; PtO *Win* 98-13. *14 Cherritt Court, 557 Ringwood Road, Ferndown BH22 9FE* T: (01202) 895997

DAVIES, John Barden. b 47. St D Coll Lamp 70. **d** 71 **p** 72. C Rhosllannerchrugog *St As* 71-75; R Llanbedr-y-Cennin *Ban* 75-86; Adult Educn Officer 86-93; V Betws-y-Coed and Capel Curig w Penmachno etc 86-93; R Llanfrwog and Clocaenog and Gyffylliog *St As* 93-09; AD Dyffryn Clwyd 95-09. *183 Station Road, Deganwy, Conwy LL31 9EX* T: (01492) 593045 M: 07590-465052 E: jbdrtn@hotmail.co.uk

DAVIES, John Daniel Lee. b 55. Trin Coll Carmarthen BEd 79. **d** 00 **p** 00. C Leverburgh *Arg* 00-01; P-in-c Harris Ch Ch from 01. *3A Cluer, Isle of Harris HS3 3EP* T: (01859) 530344

✠**DAVIES, The Rt Revd John David Edward.** b 53. Southn Univ LLB 74 Univ of Wales (Cardiff) LLM 95. St Mich Coll Llan 82. **d** 84 **p** 85 **c** 08. C Chepstow *Mon* 84-86; C-in-c Michaelston-y-Fedw and Rudry 86-89; R Bedwas and Rudry 89-95; V Maindee Newport 95-00; Dean Brecon and V Brecon St Mary w Llanddew *S & B* 00-08; P-in-c Cynog Honddu 05-08; Bp S & B from 08. *Ely Tower, Castle Square, Brecon LD3 9DJ* T: (01874) 622008 E: bishop.swanbrec@churchinwales.org.uk

✠**DAVIES, The Rt Revd John Dudley.** b 27. Trin Coll Cam BA 51 MA 63. Linc Th Coll 52. **d** 53 **p** 54 **c** 87. C Leeds Halton St Wilfrid *Ripon* 53-56; C Yeoville S Africa 57; R Evander 57-61; R Empangeni 61-63; Chapl Witwatersrand Univ 63-71; Sec Chapls in HE Gen Syn Bd of Educn 71-74; P-in-c Keele *Lich* 74-76; Chapl Keele Univ 74-76; Prin USPG Coll of the Ascension Selly Oak 76-81; Preb Lich Cathl 76-87; Can Res, Preb and Sacr St As Cathl 82-85; Dioc Missr 82-87; V Llanrhaeadr-ym-Mochnant, Llanarmon, Pennant etc 85-87; Suff Bp Shrewsbury *Lich* 87-92; rtd 94; PtO *Lich* from 05; *St As* from 09. *Nyddfa, By-Pass Road, Gobowen, Oswestry SY11 3NG* T/F: (01691) 653434 E: davies.johnd@btinternet.com

DAVIES, John Gwylim. b 27. Ripon Hall Ox 67. **d** 70 **p** 71. C Ox St Mich 70-71; C Ox St Mich w St Martin and All SS 71-72; TV New Windsor 73-77; R Hagley *Worc* 77-83; TV Littleham w Exmouth *Ex* 83-92; Asst Dioc Stewardship Adv 83-92; rtd 92; PtO *Ex* from 92. *5 The Retreat, The Retreat Drive, Topsham, Exeter EX3 0LS* T: (01392) 876995

DAVIES, The Very Revd John Harverd. b 57. Keble Coll Ox BA 80 MA 84 CCC Cam MPhil 82 Lanc Univ PhD. Westcott Ho Cam 82. **d** 84 **p** 85. C Liv Our Lady and St Nic w St Anne 84-87; C Pet St Jo 87-90; Min Can Pet Cathl 88-90; V Anfield St Marg *Liv* 90-94; Chapl, Fell and Lect Keble Coll Ox 94-99; V Melbourne *Derby* 99-10; P-in-c Ticknall, Smisby and Stanton by Bridge etc 07-10; V Melbourne, Ticknall, Smisby and Stanton 10; Dioc Dir of Ords 00-09; Hon Can Derby Cathl 10; Dean Derby from 10. *Derby Cathedral Centre, 18-19 Iron Gate, Derby DE1 3GP* T: (01332) 341201 E: dean@derbycathedral.org

DAVIES, John Howard. b 51. EAMTC 98. **d** 01 **p** 02. NSM Walsingham, Houghton and Barsham *Nor* 01-04; NSM Holt w High Kelling 04-06; P-in-c Lake *Portsm* 06-15; P-in-c Shanklin St Sav 06-15; rtd 15. *Address temp unknown* M: 07870-509439 E: john@apostle.co.uk

DAVIES, Canon John Howard. b 29. St Jo Coll Cam BA 50 MA 54 Nottm Univ BD 62. Westcott Ho Cam 54. **d** 55 **p** 56. Succ Derby Cathl 55-58; Chapl Westcott Ho Cam 58-63; Lect Th Southn Univ 63-81; LtO *Win* 63-81; Sen Lect 74-81; Dir Th and RS Southn Univ 81-94; Can Th Win Cathl 81-91; Hon C Southampton St Alb 88-91; Hon C Swaythling 91-94; rtd 94. *13 Glen Eyre Road, Southampton SO16 3GA* T: (023) 8067 9359

DAVIES, John Hugh Conwy. b 42. Bris Univ BSc 64 PhD 67 CEng 72 MICE 72. Linc Th Coll 84. **d** 86 **p** 87. C Limber Magna w Brocklesby *Linc* 86-89; R Wickenby Gp 89-94; R Denbigh and Nantglyn *St As* 94-99; R Denbigh 99-00; V Llanrhaeadr-ym-Mochnant etc 01-07; rtd 07; PtO *St As* 09-14. *1A Swanbourne Road, Wick, Littlehampton BN17 6HS*

DAVIES, Canon John Hywel Morgan. b 45. St D Coll Lamp BA 71 LTh 73. **d** 73 **p** 74. C Milford Haven *St D* 73-77; V 89-11; R Castlemartin w Warren and Angle etc 77-82; R Walton W w Talbenny and Haroldston W 82-89; Can St D Cathl 03-11; rtd 11; PtO *St D* from 11. *6 Waterloo Road, Hakin, Milford Haven SA73 3PB* T: (01646) 692766 E: johnmorgandavies@talk21.com

DAVIES, John Ifor. b 20. ACP DipEd. **d** 80 **p** 81. Hon C Allerton *Liv* 80-84; Hon C Ffynnongroew *St As* 84-87; Hon C Whitford 87-88. *Hafan Deg, Ffordd-y-Graig, Lixwm, Holywell CH8 8LY* T: (01352) 781151

DAVIES, John Keith. b 33. St Mich Coll Llan 80. **d** 82 **p** 83. C Llanbadarn Fawr w Capel Bangor and Goginan *St D* 82-84; V Llandygwydd and Cenarth w Cilrhedyn etc 84-89; V Abergwili w Llanfihangel-uwch-Gwili etc 89-98; RD Carmarthen 93-98; rtd 98. *Tanyfron, 81 Hafod Cwnin, Carmarthen SA31 2AS* T: (01267) 223931

DAVIES, John Melvyn George. b 37. Wycliffe Hall Ox 68. **d** 71 **p** 72. C Norbury *Ches* 71-75; C Heswall 76-78; V Claughton cum Grange 78-83; R Waverton 83-02; RD Malpas 90-97; rtd 02; PtO *Ches* from 03. *15 Tattenhall Road, Tattenhall, Chester CH3 9QQ* T: (01829) 770184

DAVIES, Canon John Oswell. b 27. St D Coll Lamp 74. **d** 75 **p** 76. C Henfynyw w Aberaeron and Llanddewi Aberarth *St D* 75-76; P-in-c Eglwyswenydd w Ysbyty Ystwyth 76-77; V 77-83; R Maenordeifi and Capel Colman w Llanfihangel etc 83-93; RD Cemais and Sub-Aeron 87-93; Hon Can St D Cathl 92-93; rtd 93. *Hafod, Carregwen, Llechryd, Cardigan SA43 2PJ* T: (01239) 682568

✠**DAVIES, The Rt Revd John Stewart.** b 43. Univ of Wales BA 72 Qu Coll Cam MLitt 74. Westcott Ho Cam 72. **d** 74 **p** 75 **c** 99. C Hawarden *St As* 74-78; Tutor St Deiniol's Lib Hawarden 76-83; V Rhosymedre *St As* 78-87; Dir Dioc Minl Tr Course 83-93; Warden of Ords *St As* 83-91; Hon Can St As Cathl 86-91; V Mold 87-92; Adn St As 91-99; R Llandyrnog and Llangwyfan 92-99; Bp St As 99-08; rtd 09; PtO *St As* from 09. *17 Pont y Bedol, Llanrhaeadr, Denbigh LL16 4NF*

DAVIES, Johnston ap Llynfi (Ion). b 28. St D Coll Lamp BA 51 St Mich Coll Llan 51. **d** 53 **p** 54. C Swansea Ch Ch *S & B* 53-55; C Sketty 55-57; Nigeria 57-61; R Whittington *Derby* 61-64; Chapl Broadmoor Hosp Crowthorne 64-66; PtO *Ox* 67-72; *York* 72-86; R Creeksea w Althorne, Latchingdon and N Fambridge *Chelmsf* 86-88; rtd 88; Asst Chapl Costa Blanca *Eur* 89-92; Chapl 92-93; LtO 93-95. *Calle Ponent 1, Apartamentos Esmeralda 41A, 03710 Calpe (Alicante), Spain* T: (0034) 965 838 063

DAVIES, Jonathan Byron. b 69. Univ of Wales (Cardiff) BTh 95. St Mich Coll Llan 94. **d** 96 **p** 97. C Betws w Ammanford *St D* 96-99; Dioc Youth Chapl 96-99; C Newton St Pet *S & B* 99-00; P-in-c Swansea St Luke 03-05; V Manselton and Cwmbwrla from 05; AD Penderi from 12; Chapl Mid and W Wales Fire and Rescue Service from 05. *The Vicarage, Manor Road, Manselton, Swansea SA5 9PA* T: (01792) 464595 M: 07760-210975 E: rev.jbd@sky.com

DAVIES, Judith. b 54. Man Univ BA 75. WEMTC 97. **d** 00 **p** 01. C Harlescott *Lich* 00-04; Chapl Shrewsbury and Telford NHS Trust 04-05; Asst Chapl Severn Hospice Shrewsbury 05-06; PtO *Heref* 05-06; TV Wenlock 06-14; rtd 14; PtO *Lich* from 15. *The Vicarage, Harley Road, Cressage, Shrewsbury SY5 6DF* T: (01952) 510417 E: judydaviesrev@gmail.com

DAVIES, Prof Julia Mary. b 44. Ex Univ BA 65 FCIPD 00. **d** 04 **p** 05. OLM Deane *Man* 04-14; Hon Assoc Dioc Dir of Ords from 10; PtO from 15. *15 Newland Drive, Bolton BL5 1DS* T: (01204) 660260 M: 07966-528877

DAVIES, Julian Edward. b 60. Jes Coll Ox BA 82 MA 86 DPhil 87 Selw Coll Cam BA 92 MA 96. Ridley Hall Cam 90. **d** 94 **p** 95. C Hucknall Torkard *S'well* 94-96; C Eglwysilan *Llan* 96-99; Assoc R St Marylebone w H Trin *Lon* 99-03; Assoc R St Giles-in-the-Fields 03-08; TR Southampton (City Cen) *Win* from 08. *The Deanery House, 100 Chapel Road, Southampton SO14 5GL* T: (023) 8023 5716 E: jed-ihs@o2.co.uk

DAVIES, Mrs Karen Elizabeth. b 44. Univ of Wales (Abth) BA 66 Univ of Wales (Ban) MEd 85. **d** 11 **p** 12. OLM Criftins w Dudleston and Welsh Frankton *Lich* from 11. *Horseshoe Cottage, Horseshoe Lane, Eastwick, Ellesmere SY12 9JT* T: (01691) 690346 M: 07787-324953 E: karendavies2000@btinternet.com

DAVIES, Keith. *See* DAVIES, John Keith

DAVIES, Keith. *See* BERRY-DAVIES, Charles William Keith

DAVIES, Kenneth John. b 42. Ripon Coll Cuddesdon 79. **d** 80 **p** 81. C Buckingham *Ox* 80-83; V Birstall *Wakef* 83-91; TV Crookes St Thos *Sheff* 91-94; TR Huntington *York* 94-07; rtd 07; PtO *York* from 14. *18 Hall Rise, Haxby, York YO32 3LP* T: (01904) 768211 E: johnsuedavies@aol.com

DAVIES, Kevin Godfrey. b 62. Univ Coll Ox BA 84 MA 87. Trin Coll Bris BA 93. **d** 93 **p** 94. C Otley *Bradf* 93-97; P-in-c Scotby *Carl* 97-00; P-in-c Scotby and Cotehill w Cumwhinton 00-02; TR Langtree *Ox* from 02; P-in-c Whitchurch St Mary 02-03; AD Henley from 11. *The Rectory, Checkendon, Reading RG8 0SR* T: (01491) 680252 E: langtreerector@hotmail.com

DAVIES, Lee. b 76. St Jo Coll Nottm 12. **d** 14 **p** 15. C Andover *Win* from 14. *6 Osborne Road, Andover SP10 3HU* T: (01264) 333474 M: 07809-682085 E: revlee@daviestribe.co.uk

DAVIES, Leonard Hamblyn Kenneth. b 57. Birm Univ MA 03 Dur Univ MA 06. Sierra Leone Bible Coll 84. **d** 93 **p** 94. C St Geo Cathl Freetown Sierra Leone 93-96; C Freetown St Jo 96-98; P-in-c Freetown H Spirit 98-01; PtO *Worc* 01-02; *Birm* 02-03; *Chelmsf* 03-08; LtO 08-15; Asst Chapl E Lon Univ 08-09; Asst Chapl YMCA 09-10; C Forest Gate All SS *Chelmsf* 10-15. *28B High Street, London SW19 2AB* M: 07834-971467 E: kendavies90@hotmail.com

DAVIES, The Ven Lorys Martin. b 36. JP 78. Univ of Wales (Lamp) BA 57 ALCM 52. Wells Th Coll 57. **d** 59 **p** 60. C Tenby w Gumfreston *St D* 59-62; Asst Chapl Brentwood Sch 62-66; Chapl Solihull Sch 66-68; V Moseley St Mary *Birm* 68-81; Can Res Birm Cathl 81-92; Dioc Dir of Ords 82-90; Adn Bolton *Man* 92-01; Bp's Adv Hosp Chapl 92-01; Warden of Readers 94-01; rtd 02; PtO *Birm* from 04; *Worc* from 04. *Heol Cerrig, 28 Penshurst Road, Bromsgrove B60 2SN* T: (01527) 577337

DAVIES, Lynda. b 64. Cov Univ BA 87 CQSW 87 Leic Univ MA 09. ERMC 10. **d** 13 **p** 14. C Oundle w Ashton and Benefield w Glapthorn *Pet* from 13. *30 Bellamy Road, Oundle, Peterborough PE8 4NB* T: (01832) 272121 M: 07598-927416 E: lyndadavies559@btinternet.com

DAVIES, Malcolm. b 35. St Mich Coll Llan 82. **d** 84 **p** 85. C Roath *Llan* 84-88; C Pentre 88-94; V Llancarfan w Llantrithyd 94-02; rtd 02; PtO *Llan* from 04. *141 Fontygary Road, Rhoose, Barry CF62 3DU* T: (01446) 710509

DAVIES, Malcolm Thomas. b 36. Open Univ BA 81. St Mich Coll Llan 71. **d** 73 **p** 74. C Betws w Ammanford *St D* 73-76; V Cil-y-Cwm and Ystrad-ffin w Rhandir-mwyn etc 76-80; V Llangyfelach *S & B* 80-85; V Loughor 85-94; V Llanelli St Pet *St D* 94-01; rtd 01. *25 Walters Road, Llanelli SA15 1LR* T: (01554) 770295

DAVIES, Mrs Margaret Adelaide. b 45. Weymouth Coll of Educn CertEd 67. S Dios Minl Tr Scheme 92. **d** 95 **p** 96. NSM Westbury *Sarum* 95-02; NSM White Horse 02-11; TV 07-11; rtd 11; PtO *Sarum* from 12. *20 The Knoll, Westbury BA13 3UB* T: (01373) 228671

DAVIES, Mrs Margot Alison Jane. b 55. SWMTC 02. **d** 05 **p** 06. C St Ives *Truro* 05-09; C Halsetown 05-09; TV Saltash 09-12; P-in-c Menheniot from 12; P-in-c St Ive and Pensilva w Quethiock from 12; C Liskeard and St Keyne from 12. *The Vicarage, Menheniot, Liskeard PL14 3SU* T: (01579) 324705 E: margotaj@tiscali.co.uk

✠**DAVIES, The Rt Revd Mark.** b 62. Leeds Univ BA 85. Coll of Resurr Mirfield 86. **d** 89 **p** 90 **c** 08. C Barnsley St Mary *Wakef* 89-95; R Hemsworth 95-06; Dioc Vocations Adv and Asst Dir of Ords 98-06; RD Pontefract 00-06; Hon Can Wakef Cathl 02-06; Adn Rochdale *Man* 06-08; Suff Bp Middleton from 08. *The Hollies, Manchester Road, Rochdale OL11 3QY* T: (01706) 358550 F: 354851 E: bishopmark@manchester.anglican.org

DAVIES, Martin. *See* DAVIES, William Martin

DAVIES, Martyn John. b 60. Chich Th Coll 82. **d** 85 **p** 86. C Llantrisant *Llan* 85-87; C Whitchurch 87-90; V Porth w Trealaw 90-01; R Merthyr Tydfil St Dav 01-10; R Merthyr Tydfil St Dav and Abercanaid 10-12; AD Merthyr Tydfil 04-12; R Peterston-super-Ely w St Brides-super-Ely from 12; P-in-c St Nicholas w Bonvilston and St George-super-Ely from 12; P-in-c Pendoylan w Welsh St Donats from 12; AD Vale of Glam from 12. *The Rectory, Peterston-super-Ely, Cardiff CF5 6LH* T: (01446) 760498

DAVIES, Melvyn. *See* DAVIES, John Melvyn George

DAVIES, Canon Mervyn Morgan. b 25. Univ of Wales BA 49. Coll of Resurr Mirfield 49. **d** 51 **p** 52. C Penarth w Lavernock *Llan* 51-58; LtO *Wakef* 58-60; C Port Talbot St Theodore *Llan* 60-63; V Pontycymer and Blaengarw 63-69; V Fairwater 69-95; RD Llan 81-95; Jt Ed *Welsh Churchman* 82-95; Can Llan Cathl 84-89; Prec 89-95; rtd 95; PtO *Llan* from 95. *The Vicarage, Dale, Haverfordwest SA62 3RN*

DAVIES, Michael. *See* DAVIES, David Michael Cole

DAVIES, Miss Moira Kathleen. b 41. Cant Sch of Min. **d** 88 **p** 94. Par Dn Walmer *Cant* 88-94; C 94-96; P-in-c Somercotes and Grainthorpe w Conisholme *Linc* 96-99; R 99-06; rtd 06. *9 Amanda Drive, Louth LN11 0AZ* T: (01507) 609960

DAVIES, Canon Mostyn David. b 37. AKC 64. **d** 65 **p** 66. C Corby St Columba *Pet* 65-69; Ind Chapl 69-03; P-in-c Pet St Barn 80-03; Can Pet Cathl 95-03; rtd 03; PtO *Pet* from 03. *92 West End, Langtoft, Peterborough PE6 9LU* T: (01778) 342838 E: mostyn@mostyn.myzen.co.uk

DAVIES, Canon Myles Cooper. b 50. Sarum & Wells Th Coll 71. **d** 74 **p** 75. C W Derby St Mary *Liv* 74-77; C Seaforth 77-80; V 80-84; V Stanley 84-07; P-in-c Liv St Paul Stoneycroft 05-07; V Stanley w Stoneycroft St Paul 07-11; Chapl N Mersey Community NHS Trust 84-05; Dioc Voc Adv Liv 87-02; Hon Can Liv Cathl 01-05; Can Res Liv Cathl from 06; Prec from 08. *2 Cathedral Close, Liverpool L1 7BZ* T: 0151-702 7203 E: myles.davies@liverpoolcathedral.org

DAVIES, Nicholas Duff. b 67. Sheff Univ BA 88 Edin Univ MTh 89 Anglia Ruskin Univ MA 09 FRSA 01. Westcott Ho Cam 06. **d** 08 **p** 09. C S Dulwich St Steph *S'wark* 08-12; TV S Cheltenham *Glouc* from 12. *80 Painswick Road, Cheltenham GL50 2EU* T: (01242) 321268 M: 07801-336144 E: nickduffdavies@gmail.com

DAVIES, Nicola Louise. b 69. STETS. **d** 14 **p** 15. NSM Fordingbridge and Breamore and Hale etc *Win* from 14. *Godshill Wood Cottage, Woodgreen, Fordingbridge SP6 2QU* T: (01725) 512306 E: daviesnicky@live.co.uk

DAVIES, Nicola Louise. b 55. Birm Univ BA 77 Lon Inst of Educn PGCE 78. STETS 02. **d** 05. NSM Rowledge and Frensham *Guildf* 05-06. *16 Netley Court, Surrey Street, Littlehampton BN17 5DZ* E: nickydavies@sky.com

DAVIES, Canon Nigel Lawrence. b 55. Lanc Univ BEd 77. Sarum & Wells Th Coll 84. **d** 87 **p** 88. C Heywood St Luke w All So *Man* 87-91; V Burneside *Carl* 91-07; P-in-c Crosscrake 04-06; P-in-c Skelsmergh w Selside and Longsleddale 06-07; TR Beacon from 07; RD Kendal 03-08; Hon Can Carl Cathl from 06. *St Oswald's Vicarage, The Main Road, Burneside, Kendal LA9 6QX* T: (01539) 722015 F: 07974-448370 T: 795419 E: canon.nigel@beaconteam.org.uk

DAVIES, Noel Paul. b 47. Chich Th Coll 83. **d** 85 **p** 86. C Milford Haven *St D* 85-89; R Jeffreyston w Reynoldston and E Williamston etc 89-09; R Jeffreyston w Reynoldston and Loveston etc 09-12; rtd 12; PtO *St D* from 12. *Hungerford Farm, Loveston, Kilgetty SA68 0NY*

DAVIES, Mrs Pamela Elizabeth. b 55. Oak Hill Th Coll 09. **d** 11 **p** 12. C Berechurch St Marg w St Mich *Chelmsf* 11-15. *3 Helen Ewing Place, Colchester CO2 8WS* T: (01206) 657697 M: 07866-600304

DAVIES, Canon Patricia Elizabeth. b 36. Westf Coll Lon BA 58 Hughes Hall Cam CertEd 59 Leeds Univ MA 74. NEOC 83. **dss** 86 **d** 87 **p** 94. Killingworth *Newc* 86-90; Hon C 87-90; Hon C Newc H Cross 91-96; NSM Newc Epiphany 96-99; NSM Gosforth St Hugh 99-00; P-in-c 00-01; Hon Can Newc Cathl 00-01; rtd 01; PtO *York* from 01. *Applegarth, Middlewood Lane, Fylingthorpe, Whitby YO22 4TT* T: (01947) 881175

DAVIES, Patrick Charles Steven. b 59. Leeds Univ BA 99 Man Univ MA 13 RGN 86 RMN 92 RHV 94. Coll of Resurr Mirfield 97. **d** 99 **p** 00. C Reddish *Man* 99-04; P-in-c Withington St Crispin from 04. *296 Wilbraham Road, Manchester M21 0UU* T: 0161-282 8514 M: 07967-385357 E: fr.patrick@ntlworld.com

DAVIES, Paul. *See* DAVIES, Richard Paul

DAVIES, Paul Lloyd. b 46. Bris Univ LLB 68 Solicitor 71. Trin Coll Carmarthen 84. **d** 87 **p** 88. NSM Newport w Cilgwyn and Dinas w Llanllawer *St D* 87-97; P-in-c Mathry w St Edren's and Grandston etc 97-01; V 01-08; rtd 08. *Treetops, Osborn Park, Neyland, Milford Haven SA73 1SX* T: (01646) 602919

DAVIES, Paul Martin. b 35. Lon Univ BD 75. Sarum & Wells Th Coll 75. **d** 75 **p** 76. C Walthamstow St Mary w St Steph *Chelmsf* 75-79; Kenya 79-86; R Leven w Catwick *York* 86-95; RD N Holderness 90-95; rtd 95; PtO *York* from 95. *54 The Meadows, Cherry Burton, Beverley HU17 7SD* T: (01964) 551739

DAVIES, Paul Scott. b 59. Cranmer Hall Dur 85. **d** 88 **p** 89. C New Addington *S'wark* 88-91; C Croydon H Sav 91-94; P-in-c Norton in the Moors *Lich* 94-99; R 99-03; V Sunbury *Lon* 03-15; Sen P Doha Epiphany Qatar from 15. *The Church of the Epiphany, PO Box 3210, Doha, Qatar* T: (00974) 4416 5726 F: 4416 5729 E: paul@zippor.com

DAVIES, Peter. b 67. Lon Bible Coll BA 97 Cardiff Univ MTh 08. St Mich Coll Llan 06. **d** 07 **p** 08. C Llanelli *St D* 07-10; TV E Carmarthen 10-11; Chapl Cardiff and Vale Univ Local Health Bd from 11. *153 Gabalfa Avenue, Cardiff CF14 2PB* E: peter.davies4@wales.nhs.uk

DAVIES, Peter Huw. b 57. Crewe & Alsager Coll BEd 79. Wycliffe Hall Ox 87. **d** 89 **p** 90. C Moreton *Ches* 89-93; V Weston-super-Mare St Paul *B & W* 93-05; P-in-c Chesham Bois *Ox* 08-13; R Sandy St Alb from 13. *The Rectory, 34 High Street, Sandy SG19 1AQ* T: (01767) 680512 E: daviesp5@aol.com

DAVIES, Peter Richard. b 32. St Jo Coll Ox BA 55 MA 58. Westcott Ho Cam 56. **d** 58 **p** 59. C Cannock *Lich* 58-62; Kenya 63-76; Chapl Bedford Sch 76-85; V Dale and St Brides w Marloes *St D* 85-92; rtd 92. *Canthill Cottage, Dale, Haverfordwest SA62 3QZ* T: (01646) 636535

DAVIES, Preb Peter Timothy William. b 50. Leeds Univ BSc 74. Oak Hill Th Coll 75. **d** 78 **p** 79. C Kingston Hill St Paul *S'wark* 78-81; C Hove Bp Hannington Memorial Ch *Chich* 81-88; V Audley *Lich* 88-15; P-in-c Alsagers Bank 06-15; P-in-c Talke 13-15; Preb Lich Cathl 13-15; rtd 15. *Address temp unknown*

DAVIES, Philip Huw. b 64. Aston Univ BSc 86 MRPharmS 87. St Mich Coll Llan 00. **d** 02 **p** 03. C Llangynwyd w Maesteg *Llan* 02-03; C Betws w Ammanford *St D* 03-07; P-in-c Slebech

and Uzmaston w Boulston 07-08; V Uzmaston 08-11; P-in-c Llawhaden w Bletherston and Llanycefn 07-10; V 10-11; V Llawhaden w Bletherston and Uzmaston from 11. *The Vicarage, Maenclochog, Clynderwen SA66 7LD* T: (01437) 532925

DAVIES, Philip James. b 58. UEA BA 79 Keswick Hall Coll PGCE 80 K Coll Lon MA 92. Ridley Hall Cam 86. **d** 89 **p** 90. C Rainham *Roch* 89-90; C Gravesend St Geo and Rosherville 90-95; V 95-98; Dioc Schs Development Officer *Pet* 98-13; P-in-c King's Cliffe 98-10; C Bulwick, Blatherwycke w Harringworth and Laxton 07-10; R King's Cliffe, Bulwick and Blatherwycke etc from 10; C Ketton, Collyweston, Easton-on-the-Hill etc from 13. *The Rectory, 3 Hall Yard, King's Cliffe, Peterborough PE8 6XQ* T: (01780) 470314 E: p.j.davies@tesco.net

DAVIES, Philip Simon. b 65. Trin Coll Ox BA 87 MA 91. Aston Tr Scheme 93 Ridley Hall Cam 95. **d** 97 **p** 98. C Burntwood *Lich* 97-00; TV Cheswardine, Childs Ercall, Hales, Hinstock etc 00-03; TR 03-04; P-in-c Olney *Ox* 04-08; P-in-c Banbury St Hugh 08-12; PtO from 12. *5 Kedlestone Rise, Banbury OX16 9TX* T: (01295) 255744 E: revdavies@btinternet.com

DAVIES, Canon Philip Wyn. b 50. Univ of Wales BA 72 MA 82. St D Dioc Tr Course 93 St Mich Coll Llan BD 96. **d** 96 **p** 97. C Llandysul *St D* 96-98; V Tregaron w Ystrad Meurig and Strata Florida 98-14; P-in-c Blaenpennal 01-07; V 07-14; V Tregaron Gp from 14; Dioc Archivist from 04; AD Lampeter and Ultra-Aeron from 11. *The Vicarage, Tregaron SY25 6HL* T: (01974) 299010 E: philipwyn@btinternet.com

DAVIES, Canon Rachel Hannah Eileen. b 64. Ban Univ BTh 08. St Mich Coll Llan 01. **d** 04 **p** 05. NSM Lampeter and Llanddewibrefi Gp *St D* 04-06; NSM Bro Teifi Sarn Helen 06-08; P-in-c Llanerch Aeron w Ciliau Aeron and Dihewyd etc from 08; Dioc Adv on Rural Matters from 05; Hon Can St D Cathl 12-14; Can St D Cathl from 14. *Gwndwn, New Inn, Pencader SA39 9BE* T/F: (01559) 384248 M: 07814-272998 E: eileengwndwn@yahoo.co.uk

DAVIES, Raymond Emlyn Peter. b 25. St Mich Coll Llan 51. **d** 53 **p** 54. C Llangeinor *Llan* 53-58; C Llanishen and Lisvane 58-62 and 65-68; R Glyncorrwg w Afan Vale and Cymmer Afan 62-65; V Penrhiwceiber w Matthewstown and Ynysboeth 68-72; C Whitchurch 72-73; V Childs Ercall *Lich* 73-81; R Stoke upon Tern 73-81; P-in-c Hamstall Ridware w Pipe Ridware 81-82; P-in-c Kings Bromley 81-82; P-in-c Mavesyn Ridware 81-82; R The Ridwares and Kings Bromley 83-90; rtd 90; PtO *B & W* from 95. *51 Vereland Road, Hutton, Weston-super-Mare BS24 9TH* T: (01934) 814680

DAVIES, Rebecca Jane. b 75. Clare Coll Cam MA 96. St Mich Coll Llan 01. **d** 03 **p** 04. C Llandeilo Fawr and Taliaris *St D* 03-05; C Llandybie 05-07; P-in-c Maenclochog and New Moat etc 07-10; V from 10. *The Vicarage, Maenclochog, Clynderwen SA66 7LD* T: (01437) 532925

DAVIES, Reginald Charles. b 33. Hull Univ MA 93 Birm Univ MPH 09. Tyndale Hall Bris 58. **d** 64 **p** 65. C Heywood St Jas *Man* 64-66; C Drypool St Columba w St Andr and St Pet *York* 66-69; V Denaby Main *Sheff* from 69. *The Vicarage, Church Road, Denaby Main, Doncaster DN12 4AD* T: (01709) 862297 E: ailsa.reg@hotmail.co.uk

DAVIES, Rendle Leslie. b 29. St Chad's Coll Dur BA 52. **d** 54 **p** 55. C Monmouth *Mon* 54-58; V Llangwm Uchaf w Llangwm Isaf w Gwernesney etc 58-63; V Usk and Monkswood w Glascoed Chpl and Gwehelog 63-99; Chapl HM Pris Usk and Prescoed 63-94; rtd 99; PtO *Heref* from 08. *12 Ridgeway, Wyesham, Monmouth NP25 3JX* T: (01600) 714189

DAVIES, Rhiannon Mary Morgan. *See* JOHNSON, Rhiannon Mary Morgan

DAVIES, Richard. **d** 15. NSM Letterston w Llanfair Nant-y-Gof etc *St D* from 15. *Northgate, Little Newcastle, Haverfordwest SA62 5TD* T: (01348) 881230

DAVIES, The Ven Richard Paul. b 73. Univ of Wales (Lamp) BA 94 Ox Univ MTh 98. Ripon Coll Cuddesdon 94. **d** 97 **p** 98. Min Can St D Cathl 97-00; Succ 00-06; TV Dewisland *St D* 01-06; V Burry Port and Pwll 06-12; Dioc Ecum Officer 02-07; OCM 05-07; Dioc Warden Ords *St D* 11-12; Adn Ban from 12; R Llanfair Mathafarn Eithaf w Llanbedrgoch etc 12-14. *The Archdeaconry, 1 Belmont Road, Bangor LL57 2LL* T: (01248) 354360 E: archdeacon.bangor@churchinwales.org.uk

DAVIES, Richard Paul. b 48. Wycliffe Hall Ox 72. **d** 75 **p** 76. C Everton St Sav w St Cuth *Liv* 75-78; Chapl Asst Basingstoke Distr Hosp 78-80; TV Basingstoke *Win* 80-85; V Southampton Thornhill St Chris 85-94; V Eastleigh 94-13; rtd 13; PtO *Win* from 14. *1 Woodcock Gardens, Warminster BA12 9JH* T: (01985) 300606 E: rp.davies@yahoo.co.uk

DAVIES, Robert Emlyn. b 56. N Staffs Poly BA 79. Coll of Resurr Mirfield 83. **d** 86 **p** 87. C Cardiff St Jo *Llan* 86-90; V Cwmparc 90-97; V Aberdare from 97; AD Cynon Valley 02-08. *13 Tan y Bryn Gardens, Llwydcoed, Aberdare CF44 0TQ*

DAVIES, Robert Gwynant. b 55. **d** 08 **p** 09. NSM Canwell *Lich* from 08; NSM Drayton Bassett from 08; NSM Fazeley from 08. *Middleton House Farm, Tamworth Road, Middleton, Tamworth B78 2BD* T: (01827) 873474 E: rob.jane@tinyonline.co.uk

DAVIES, Roger Charles. b 46. Univ of Wales BD 72. St Mich Coll Llan 67. **d** 73 **p** 74. C Llanfabon *Llan* 73-75; C Llanblethian w Cowbridge and Llandough etc 75-78; CF 78-84; TV Halesworth w Linstead, Chediston, Holton etc *St E* 84-87; R Claydon and Barham 87-91; R Lavant and Chapl Lavant Ho Sch 91-94; TV Gt Aycliffe and Chilton *Dur* 04-08; P-in-c Wheatley Hill and Wingate w Hutton Henry 08-13; rtd 13; PtO *Dur* from 13. *West Lea, Thorpe Road, Easington, Peterlee SR8 3UB* M: 07866-649300 E: r876davies@btinternet.com

DAVIES, Miss Rowan. b 55. Univ of Wales (Swansea) BA 78 PGCE 79. WMMTC 00. **d** 03 **p** 04. NSM Wigginton *Lich* from 03. *16 Queen's Way, Tamworth B79 8QD* T: (01827) 69651 E: rowan.davies1@ukonline.co.uk

DAVIES, Preb Roy Basil. b 34. Bris Univ BA 55. Westcott Ho Cam 57. **d** 59 **p** 60. C Ipswich St Mary le Tower *St E* 59-63; C Clun w Chapel Lawn *Heref* 63-70; V Bishop's Castle w Mainstone 70-83; RD Clun Forest 72-83; Preb Heref Cathl 82-99; P-in-c Billingsley w Sidbury 83-86; P-in-c Chelmarsh 83-86; P-in-c Chetton w Deuxhill and Glazeley 83-86; P-in-c Middleton Scriven 83-86; R Billingsley w Sidbury, Middleton Scriven etc 86-89; RD Bridgnorth 87-89; TR Wenlock 89-99; rtd 99; PtO *Heref* from 00. *13 Courtnay Rise, Hereford HR1 1BP* T: (01432) 341154

DAVIES, Mrs Sally Jane. b 63. Linc Coll Ox BA 86. Trin Coll Bris BA 92. **d** 92 **p** 94. C E Molesey St Paul *Guildf* 92-96; C Chalfont St Peter *Ox* 96-99; Chapl RN Coll Greenwich and Trin Coll of Music 99-06; Hon C Greenwich St Alfege *S'wark* 99-06; P-in-c Shamley Green *Guildf* 06-11; V from 11. *The Vicarage, Church Hill, Shamley Green, Guildford GU5 0UD* T: (01483) 892030 E: vicar@shamleygreen.net

DAVIES, Canon Sarah Isabella. b 39. Llan Dioc Tr Scheme 87. **d** 91 **p** 97. NSM Pontypridd St Cath w St Matt *Llan* 91-93; C Ferndale w Maerdy 93-00; Chapl Univ Hosp of Wales and Llandough NHS Trust 98-00; Chapl Pontypridd and Rhondda NHS Trust 98-00; C Cardiff Ch Ch Roath Park *Llan* 00-09; Dioc Child Protection Officer 02-09; Hon Can Llan Cathl 06-09; rtd 09; PtO *Llan* from 10. *4 St Augustine Road, Heath, Cardiff CF14 4BD*

DAVIES, Saunders. See DAVIES, Francis James Saunders

DAVIES, Scott Lee. b 73. St Jo Coll Nottm. **d** 06 **p** 07. C Childwall All SS *Liv* 06-10; V Carr Mill from 10. *St David's Vicarage, 27 Eskdale Avenue, St Helens WA11 7EN* T: (01744) 732330

DAVIES, Simon Stanley Miles. b 65. Cranfield Univ BEng 88 MSc 95 Greenwich Univ PGCE 09. Seabury-Western Th Sem 97 Westcott Ho Cam 98. **d** 00 **p** 01. C Llanrhos *St As* 00-03; R Alberton Canada 03-05; Hon C Win St Cross w St Faith 07-12; Chapl Felixstowe Miss to Seafarers *St E* from 12. *Felixstowe Seafarers' Centre, Dock Road, Felixstowe IP11 3TG* T: (01394) 673599 M: 07855-188013

DAVIES, Stephen. b 56. Nottm Univ BSc 77. Wycliffe Hall Ox 01. **d** 03 **p** 04. C Crawley and Littleton and Sparsholt w Lainston *Win* 03-07; V Heacham *Nor* 07-13; RD Heacham and Rising 11-13; Min Abbeydale Ch Ch LEP *Glouc* from 13. *63 Wheatway, Abbeydale, Gloucester GL4 5ET* T: (01452) 551020 E: revdstevedavies@gmail.com

DAVIES, Stephen John. b 55. Bp Otter Coll Chich BA 01 IEng 77. St Steph Ho Ox 96. **d** 98 **p** 99. C Leigh Park and Warren Park *Portsm* 98-02; C Durrington *Chich* 02-05; P-in-c Earnley and E Wittering 05-08; R from 08; Chapl Chich Cathl from 02. *The Rectory, Church Road, East Wittering, Chichester PO20 8PS* T: (01243) 672260

DAVIES, Mrs Susan Anne. b 48. N Co Coll Newc CertEd 69. St Mich Coll Llan 98. **d** 01 **p** 02. NSM Monmouth w Overmonnow etc *Mon* 01-05; NSM Goetre w Llanover 05; TV Rossendale Middle Valley *Man* 05-13; Dioc Rural Officer 07-13; AD Rossendale 08-13; rtd 13; PtO *Sheff* from 13. *10 Grange Mews, Wickersley, Rotherham S66 1YA* T: (01709) 207098 E: susanannedavies@aol.com

DAVIES, Taffy. See DAVIES, Edward William Llewellyn

DAVIES, Canon Timothy Robert. b 64. Bradf Univ BSc 87. Wycliffe Hall Ox BTh 93. **d** 93 **p** 94. C Eynsham and Cassington *Ox* 93-97; C Fulwood *Sheff* 97-03; Crosslinks Assoc Ch Ch Cen from 03; Hon Can Nairobi Cathl from 08. *2. Egerton Hall, Fitzwilliam Street, Sheffield S1 4JR* T: 0114-273 9750 E: tim.davies@christchurchcentral.co.uk

DAVIES, Trevor. See DAVIES, Edward Trevor

DAVIES, Canon Trevor Gwesyn. b 28. Univ of Wales (Ban) BEd 73. St Mich Coll Llan 55. **d** 56 **p** 57. C Holywell *St As* 56-63; V Cwm 63-74; V Colwyn Bay 74-95; Can St As Cathl from 79; rtd 95; PtO *St As* 12-14. *Dalkeith, 37 Brompton Avenue, Rhos on Sea, Colwyn Bay LL28 4TF* T: (01492) 548044

DAVIES, The Ven Vincent Anthony (Tony). b 46. Brasted Th Coll 69 St Mich Coll Llan 71. **d** 73 **p** 74. C Owton Manor CD *Dur* 73-76; C Wandsworth St Faith *S'wark* 76-78; P-in-c 78-81; V Walworth St Jo 81-94; RD S'wark and Newington 88-93; Adn Croydon 94-11; Bp's Adv for Hosp Chapl 00-11; P-in-c Sutton New Town St Barn 04-06; rtd 11; PtO *S'wark* from 11; *Chich* from 12. *1 High Beeches, Worthing BN11 4TJ* M: 07946-640288 E: v.a.davies@hotmail.co.uk

DAVIES, William Martin. b 56. Univ of Wales (Cardiff) BSc 78. Wycliffe Hall Ox 78. **d** 81 **p** 82. C Gabalfa *Llan* 81-84; P-in-c Beguildy and Heyope *S & B* 84-85; V 85-87; V Swansea St Thos and Kilvey 87-93; V Belmont *Lon* 93-03; Asst Chapl Miss to Seafarers 87-03; Area Co-ord Leprosy Miss for Wales 04-07; Area Co-ord Lon and Essex 07-11; V Harefield *Lon* from 11. *The Vicarage, 28 Countess Close, Harefield, Uxbridge UB9 6DL* T: (01895) 825960 M: 07050-042586

DAVIES-COLE, Charles Sylester. b 38. New Coll Dur BA BD. Edin Th Coll 66. **d** 66. Hon C Edin Old St Paul from 66; Prin Teacher Jas Gillespie's High Sch 82-03. *121 Mayburn Avenue, Loanhead EH20 9ER* T: 0131-440 4190

DAVIES-HANNEN, Robert John. b 65. W Glam Inst of HE BEd 89. St Mich Coll Llan BTh 92. **d** 92 **p** 93. C Gorseinon *S & B* 92-95; P-in-c Swansea St Luke 95-02; V Llangyfelach from 02. *The Vicarage, 8 Maes y Dderwen, Llangyfelach, Swansea SA6 6ET* T: (01792) 774120

DAVIES-JAMES, Mrs Roxana Ruth de la Tour. b 56. **d** 05 **p** 06. OLM Cusop w Blakemere, Bredwardine w Brobury etc *Heref* 05-11; P-in-c Credenhill w Brinsop and Wormsley etc from 11. *8 Hillside View, Credenhill, Hereford HR4 7FD* T: (01432) 760443 M: 07870-929040 E: rana.james@virgin.net

DAVILL, Robin William. b 51. SS Paul & Mary Coll Cheltenham CertEd 73 BEd 74 Leic Univ MA 79. Westcott Ho Cam 86. **d** 88 **p** 89. C Broughton *Blackb* 88-91; C Howden *York* 91-93; NSM Crayke w Brandsby and Yearsley 93-97; P-in-c 97-03; P-in-c Thirkleby w Kilburn and Bagby 03-09; P-in-c Topcliffe, Baldersby w Dishforth, Dalton etc 09-12; rtd 12; PtO *York* from 12. *Leyland House, 44 Uppleby, Easingwold, York YO61 3BB* T: (01347) 823472 E: robin@davill.eclipse.co.uk

DAVINA, Sister. See WILBY, Jean

DAVIS, Alan. b 34. Birm Univ BSc 56. Ox NSM Course. **d** 75 **p** 76. NSM Chesham St Mary *Ox* 75-80; NSM Gt Chesham 80-00; rtd 00; PtO *Ox* from 00. *18 Cheyne Walk, Chesham HP5 1AY* T: (01494) 782124

DAVIS, Alan John. b 33. St Alb Minl Tr Scheme 77. **d** 80 **p** 81. NSM Goldington *St Alb* 80-84; C Benchill *Man* 84-86; R Gt Chart *Cant* 86-02; rtd 02; PtO *Cant* from 02. *8 Roberts Road, Greatstone, New Romney TN28 8RL* T: (01797) 361917

DAVIS, The Ven Alan Norman. b 38. Open Univ BA 75. Lich Th Coll 63. **d** 65 **p** 66. C Kingstanding St Luke *Birm* 65-68; C-in-c Ecclesfield St Paul CD *Sheff* 68-73; V Sheff St Paul 73-75; V Shiregreen St Jas and St Chris 75-80; R Maltby 80-81; TR 81-89; Abp's Officer for UPA 90-92; P-in-c Carl St Cuth w St Mary 92-96; Dioc Communications Officer 92-96; Adn W Cumberland and Hon Can Carl Cathl 96-04; RD Solway 98-99; rtd 04; PtO *Cov* from 05; *Leic* from 05; RD Sparkenhoe W 07-08. *71 North Street, Atherstone CV9 1JW* T: (01827) 718210 E: alannorman@aol.com

DAVIS, Preb Andrew Fisher. b 46. St Chad's Coll Dur BA 67 K Coll Lon MA 99 MPhil 06. St Steph Ho Ox 68. **d** 70 **p** 71. C Beckenham St Jas *Roch* 70-74; C Kensington St Mary Abbots w St Geo *Lon* 74-80; V Sudbury St Andr 80-90; AD Brent 85-90; V Ealing Ch the Sav from 90; Preb St Paul's Cathl from 07. *The Clergy House, The Grove, London W5 5DX* T/F: (020) 8567 1288 E: fr.a@btopenworld.com

DAVIS, Andrew George. b 63. Bath Univ BSc Edin Univ BD. Edin Th Coll. **d** 89 **p** 90. C Alverstoke *Portsm* 89-92; C Portsea N End St Mark 92-96; Bp's Dom Chapl 96-98; R Bishop's Waltham and Upham 98-07; V Gosport H Trin from 07; V Gosport Ch Ch from 07; AD Gosport 14-15. *Holy Trinity House, 9 Britannia Way, Gosport PO12 4FZ* T: (023) 9258 0173 E: andy-chris@adavis.fsbusiness.co.uk

DAVIS, Anne. See DAVIS, Maureen Anne

DAVIS, Canon Bernard Rex. b 33. OAM 05. Sydney Univ BA 55 Gen Th Sem (NY) MDiv 60 Newc Univ MA 67 FRSA 87. Coll of Resurr Mirfield 55. **d** 57 **p** 58. C Guildf St Nic 57-59; USA 59-61; R Wickham Australia 62-66; Studies Sec ACC 66-68; Exec Sec Unit 3 WCC Geneva 68-77; Warden Edw K Ho 77-03; Can Res and Subdean Linc Cathl 77-03; PtO *S'well* 01-03; rtd 03; PtO *Lon* from 06; *Eur* from 06. *425 Bromyard House, Bromyard Avenue, London W3 7BY* T: (020) 8743 0181 E: subdean@aol.com

DAVIS, Canon Brian. b 40. AKC 69 BD 69. St Aug Coll Cant 69. **d** 70 **p** 71. C Humberstone *Leic* 70-73; C Kirby Muxloe 73-74; V Countesthorpe w Foston 74-91; RD Guthlaxton I 90-91; V Hinckley St Mary 91-10; RD Sparkenhoe W 92-02; Hon Can Leic Cathl 94-10; Bp's Adv for Wholeness and Healing

04-10; rtd 10; PtO *Leic* 10-13; P-in-c Gaulby from 13. *62 Lubenham Hill, Market Harborough LE16 9DQ* T: (01858) 431843 E: revbdavis@aol.com

DAVIS, Mrs Bryony Elizabeth. b 64. Ban Univ BTh 09 DipCOT 86. EAMTC 99. **d** 02 **p** 03. C Beccles St Mich *St E* 02-05; P-in-c Ottershaw *Guildf* 05-08; rtd 08; Chapl HM Pris Bronzefield from 10; Methodist Min from 10; PtO *Guildf* from 11. *HM Prison Bronzefield, Woodthorpe Road, Ashford TW15 3JZ* T: (01784) 425690 E: bryony@tiscali.co.uk

DAVIS, Christopher James. b 63. Worc Coll Ox BA 85. Cranmer Hall Dur 88. **d** 91 **p** 92. C Margate H Trin *Cant* 91-94; C Cambridge H Sepulchre *Ely* 94-00; C Wimbledon Em Ridgway Prop Chpl *S'wark* 00-04; R Tooting Graveney St Nic from 04. *The Rectory, 20A Rectory Lane, London SW17 9QJ* T: (020) 8672 7691

DAVIS, Clinton Ernest Newman. b 46. Solicitor 71. Wycliffe Hall Ox 78. **d** 80 **p** 81. C Margate H Trin *Cant* 80-84; C St Laur in Thanet 84-87; V Sandgate St Paul 87-92; P-in-c Folkestone St Geo 92; V Sandgate St Paul w Folkestone St Geo 92-97; Chapl HM Pris Standford Hill 97-08; rtd 08; PtO *Cant* from 08. *Springfield, 39 Ashford Road, Maidstone ME14 5DP* T: (01622) 682330 E: clintonendavis@btinternet.com

DAVIS, Colin Anthony John. b 65. St Jo Coll Nottm. **d** 99 **p** 00. C Bletchley *Ox* 99-02; C S Molton w Nymet St George, High Bray etc *Ex* 02-03; TV 03-10; I Carrowdore w Millisle *D & D* from 10. *15 Kilbright Road, Carrowdore, Newtownards BT22 2HQ* E: revcol23@btinternet.com

DAVIS, David John. b 35. St Steph Ho Ox 79. **d** 81 **p** 82. C Reading St Mark *Ox* 81-84; C Gt Grimsby St Mary and St Jas *Linc* 84-85; TV 85-89; V Caistor w Clixby 89-94; TV Louth 98-01; rtd 01; PtO *Linc* from 03; *Nor* from 04. *34 Park Road, Hunstanton PE36 5BY* T: (01485) 534700

DAVIS, Donald Cyril. b 26. Open Univ BA 79. NTMTC 94. **d** 96 **p** 97. NSM N Greenford All Hallows *Lon* 96-13; PtO 13-15. *33 Sherwood Avenue, Greenford UB6 0PG* T: (020) 8864 1060 E: donald.davis07@ntlworld.com

DAVIS, Donald Richard. b 59. Oak Hill Th Coll 92. **d** 94 **p** 95. C Plymouth St Jude *Ex* 94-99; C Devonport St Boniface and St Phil 99-08; V W Norwood St Luke *S'wark* from 08. *The Vicarage, 6 Chatsworth Way, London SE27 9HR* T: (020) 8265 5139 E: dondavis@blueyonder.co.uk

DAVIS, Edward Gabriel Anastasius. b 75. R Holloway Coll Lon BA 97. Trin Coll Bris BA 02. **d** 03 **p** 04. C Boldmere *Birm* 03-06; Chapl Aston Univ 06; Chapl Bris Univ from 07; NSM Inner Ring Partnership from 07. *67 Waverley Road, Bristol BS6 6ET* T: 0117-942 5390 E: ed.davis@bris.ac.uk

DAVIS, Mrs Elizabeth Jane. b 42. S'wark Ord Course 91. **d** 94 **p** 95. NSM Plaistow St Mary *Roch* 94-99; NSM Bromley St Andr from 99. *11 Park Avenue, Bromley BR1 4EF* T: (020) 8460 4672 E: elizabeth.davis@diocese-rochester.org

DAVIS (née GENT), Emily Louise. b 88. Cant Ch Ch Univ BA 10. St Steph Ho Ox BA 13. **d** 14 **p** 15. C Bishop's Stortford St Mich *St Alb* from 14. *Cowell House, 24 Apton Road, Bishop's Stortford CM23 3SN* E: curate.emily@gmail.com

DAVIS, Felicity Ann. See SMITH, Felicity Ann

DAVIS, Geoffrey. See DAVIS, Ronald Geoffrey

DAVIS, George Shaun. b 75. Middx Univ BA 01 Lon Inst of Educn PGCE 02 Leeds Univ BA 10. Coll of Resurr Mirfield 08. **d** 10 **p** 11. C W Bromwich All SS *Lich* 10-14; TV Worc SE from 14. *33 Aconbury Close, Worcester WR5 1JD* E: fr.georgedavis@hotmail.com

DAVIS, Canon Herbert Roger. b 36. Kelham Th Coll 60. **d** 65 **p** 66. C Barkingside St Fran *Chelmsf* 65-69; C Harpenden St Nic *St Alb* 69-73; P-in-c Eaton Bray 73-75; P-in-c Eaton Bray w Edlesborough 75; V 75-81; RD Dunstable 77-81; R Gt Berkhamsted 81-95; Hon Can St Alb 93-95; rtd 99. *6 St Thomas Terrace, St Thomas Street, Wells BA5 2XG* T: (01749) 677195

DAVIS, Ian Andrew. b 58. Sheff Univ BSc 79 PGCE 80 MSB 85 CBiol 85. St Jo Coll Nottm 87. **d** 90 **p** 91. C Hatfield *Sheff* 90-92; C Beighton 92-95; R Thurnscoe St Helen 95-99; P-in-c Chesterfield SS Aug *Derby* 99-01; V 01-05; P-in-c Hope, Castleton and Bradwell 05-11; V from 11. *The Vicarage, Church Street, Bradwell, Hope Valley S33 9HJ* T: (01433) 620485 E: reviandavis@aol.com

DAVIS, Jack. b 35. LRSC 63 CChem 80 MRSC 80 Sheff Univ MSc 88. Oak Hill Th Coll 86. **d** 88 **p** 89. C Owlerton *Sheff* 88-91; V Manea *Ely* 91-93; R Wimblington 91-93; P-in-c Walsoken 93-94; R 94-00; rtd 00; PtO *Sheff* from 00. *5 Pinfold Court, Barnby Dun, Doncaster DN3 1RQ* T/F: (01302) 888065 E: revjackdavis@aol.com

DAVIS, Mrs Jacqueline. b 47. Cant Ch Ch Univ Coll BA 01. **d** 05 **p** 06. OLM Upchurch w Lower Halstow *Cant* 05-13; NSM The Six 13-14. *Mill House, The Street, Lower Halstow, Sittingbourne ME9 7DY* T: (01795) 842557 E: jackytd@eclipse.co.uk

DAVIS, Jennifer Anne Stanway. b 38. SWMTC 04. **d** 05 **p** 06. NSM Cullompton, Willand, Uffculme, Kentisbeare etc *Ex* 06-08; rtd 08; PtO *B & W* from 09. *36 Church Acre, Bradford-on-Avon BA15 1RL* T: (01225) 866479

DAVIS, Mrs Joanna Helen. b 82. Ex Univ BA 04 K Coll Lon PGCE 05. St Jo Coll Nottm MTh 10. **d** 10 **p** 11. C Inglewood Gp *Carl* 10-14; Chapl Milton Abbey Sch Dorset from 14. *Nether Fen, Milton Abbas, Blandford Forum DT11 0DA* E: joannahelendavis@hotmail.com

DAVIS, John Brian. b 33. Linc Th Coll 72. **d** 75 **p** 76. Hon C Bungay H Trin w St Mary *St E* 75-84; P-in-c Barrow 84-85; P-in-c Denham St Mary 84-85; R Barrow w Denham St Mary and Higham Green 85-98; rtd 98; PtO *Nor* from 98; *St E* from 98. *Cherry Tree House, 4 Outney Road, Bungay NR35 1DY* T: (01986) 895574

DAVIS, John George. b 65. Roehampton Inst BSc 87 S Glam Inst HE PGCE 88. St Steph Ho Ox BTh 96. **d** 96 **p** 97. C Newton Nottage *Llan* 96-00; V Tredegar *Mon* from 00. *St George's Vicarage, Church Street, Tredegar NP22 3DU* T: (01495) 722672

DAVIS, John Harold. b 54. St Jo Coll Dur BSc 76 MA 86. Cranmer Hall Dur 76. **d** 79 **p** 80. C Marske in Cleveland *York* 79-82; C Pocklington w Yapham-cum-Meltonby, Owsthorpe etc 82-83; TV Pocklington Team 84-86; V Carlton and Drax 86-95; P-in-c Sessay 95-98; R 98-03; V Sowerby 95-03; Ind Chapl 88-97; Sen Chapl Selby Coalfield Ind Chapl 03-11; Chapl Askham Bryan Coll 04-11; rtd 11; PtO *York* from 11. *46 Sandsacre Avenue, Bridlington YO16 6UG* T: (01262) 228427 E: revjhdavis@gmail.com

DAVIS, John James. b 48. MBE 08. Keele Univ MA 93 Staffs Univ PGCE 98. Qu Coll Birm BA 05. **d** 05 **p** 06. NSM Baswich *Lich* 05-08; NSM Bradeley, Church Eaton, Derrington and Haughton 08-09; NSM Stafford 09-13; NSM Stafford St Mary and Marston from 13; NSM Stafford St Chad from 13; RD Stafford 11-15; CF (ACF) 06-09; Chapl Abbots Bromley Sch 13. *Stockton Croft, 87 Weeping Cross, Stafford ST17 0DQ* T: (01785) 661382 E: revjohndavis@talktalk.net

DAVIS, John Stephen. b 51. N Staffs Poly BSc 75. Wycliffe Hall Ox 75. **d** 78 **p** 79. C Meole Brace *Lich* 78-81; C Bloxwich 81-85; V Walsall St Paul 85-96; Development Officer Prince's Trust 96-01; Hospice Development Manager Walsall Primary Care Trust 01-06; Hon C Halas *Worc* 98-07. *57 Moss Lane, Burscough, Ormskirk L40 4AL*

DAVIS, Miss Judith Alison. b 88. Cam Univ BTh 11. Ridley Hall Cam 08. **d** 11 **p** 12. C Doncaster St Geo *Sheff* 11-14; P-in-c Hathersage w Bamford and Derwent and Grindleford *Derby* from 14. *The Vicarage, Church Bank, Hathersage, Hope Valley S32 1AJ* E: jude.a.davis@cantab.net

DAVIS, Mrs Kathleen Mary. b 37. Derby Coll of Educn TCert 58. **d** 07 **p** 08. OLM Morley *Leeds* from 07. *13 New Park Street, Morley, Leeds LS27 0PT* T: 0113-253 4521

DAVIS, Mrs Lucy Frances. b 72. Keble Coll Ox BA 93 Lon Inst of Educn PGCE 94. ERMC 09. **d** 12 **p** 13. NSM Redbourn *St Alb* from 12. *13 Topstreet Way, Harpenden AL5 5TU* T: (01582) 762644 M: 07803-357891 E: lucy_davis@ntlworld.com

DAVIS, Margaret Ann. b 59. Kingston Poly BA 81 Liv Univ MSc 93 RGN 85. Westcott Ho Cam 06. **d** 08 **p** 09. C Abbots Langley *St Alb* 08-11; P-in-c Clavering and Langley w Arkesden etc *Chelmsf* 11-13; V Clavering w Langley, Arkesden etc from 13. *The Vicarage, 54 Pelham Road, Clavering, Saffron Walden CB11 4PQ* T: (01799) 550703 E: m.davis.sasha@gmail.com

DAVIS, Martin John. b 59. Van Mildert Coll Dur BSc 80. Ox Min Course 07. **d** 09 **p** 10. C Colnbrook and Datchet *Ox* 09-13. *Address unknown* M: 07909-976637 E: martindavis26@tiscali.co.uk

DAVIS, Matthias. See DAVIS, Peter Langdon

DAVIS, Canon Maureen Anne. b 59. St Hilda's Coll Ox BA 80 MA 84. NOC 96. **d** 99 **p** 00. NSM Plemstall w Guilden Sutton *Ches* 99-01; C Ches St Mary 01-03; R Woodchurch from 03; Hon Can Ches Cathl from 11. *The Rectory, Church Lane, Upton, Wirral CH49 7LS* T: 0151-677 5352 M: 07974-816390 E: revannedavis@uwclub.net

DAVIS, Michael James Burrows. b 36. ED JP 87. St Deiniol's Hawarden Ridley Hall Cam. **d** 72 **p** 72. Bermuda from 72. *PO Box SN 74, Southampton SN BX, Bermuda* T: (001441) 238 0236 F: 238 3767

DAVIS, Nicholas Anthony Wylie. b 56. Univ of Wales (Lamp) BA 80. Chich Th Coll 82. **d** 84 **p** 85. C N Lambeth *S'wark* 84-88; TV Catford (Southend) and Downham 88-94; V Camberwell St Phil and St Mark 94-04; V Shrub End *Chelmsf* from 04. *All Saints' Vicarage, 270 Shrub End Road, Colchester CO3 4RL* T: (01206) 570922 E: nicholasdavis676@btinternet.com

DAVIS, Nicholas Edward. b 75. Univ of Wales (Ban) BD 96. Coll of Resurr Mirfield 98. **d** 00 **p** 01. C Darwen St Cuth w Tockholes St Steph *Blackb* 00-05; P-in-c Tarleton 05-11; P-in-c Rufford 07-11; P-in-c Rufford and Tarleton 11-12; R from 12;

P-in-c Hesketh w Becconsall from 07. *The Rectory, 92 Blackgate Lane, Tarleton, Preston PR4 6UT* T/F: (01772) 812614 E: httarleton@hotmail.com

DAVIS, Canon Norman. b 38. FCII 66. Oak Hill Th Coll 77. **d** 79 **p** 80. C Walton *St E* 79-82; P-in-c Grundisburgh w Burgh 82-91; P-in-c Bredfield w Boulge 86-91; R Boulge w Burgh and Grundisburgh 91-03; P-in-c Ufford w Bredfield and Hasketon 01-03; R Boulge w Burgh, Grundisburgh and Hasketon 03-04; RD Woodbridge 90-96; Hon Can St E Cathl 01-04; rtd 04; PtO *St E* from 04. *The Randalls, Front Street, Orford, Woodbridge IP12 2LN* T: (01394) 459449 E: n.l.davis@btinternet.com

DAVIS, Norman John. b 41. Oak Hill Th Coll 63. **d** 66 **p** 67. C Wellington w Eyton *Lich* 66-70; C Higher Openshaw *Man* 70-72; R S Levenshulme 72-79; P-in-c Berrow w Pendock and Eldersfield *Worc* 79-81; V 81-87; R Churchill-in-Halfshire w Blakedown and Broome 87-07; rtd 07; PtO *Worc* from 08. *48 Waterside Grange, Kidderminster DY10 2LA* T: (01562) 750079 M: 07792-119278 E: norsue16@yahoo.co.uk

DAVIS, Paul Montague. b 29. St Jo Coll Dur BA 52. Ely Th Coll 52. **d** 54 **p** 55. C Malden St Jas *S'wark* 54-56; C Boreham Wood All SS *St Alb* 56-57; C Colchester St Jas, All SS, St Nic and St Runwald *Chelmsf* 57-61; Hon C 72-81; CF 61-63; C Leigh St Clem *Chelmsf* 63-67; C Hockley 67-70; V Lt Horkesley 81-85; R The Bromleys 85-94; rtd 94; PtO *Chelmsf* 94-01 and from 12. *5 Coltsfoot Court, Colchester CO4 5UD* T: (01206) 852474

DAVIS, Peter Langdon (Matthias). b 51. Univ of Wales (Cardiff) BD 99 PGCE 00. Westcott Ho Cam 03. **d** 05 **p** 06. C Daventry, Ashby St Ledgers, Braunston etc *Pet* 05-08; R Aylmerton, Runton, Beeston Regis and Gresham *Nor* 08-10; TV Wolstanton *Lich* 10-11; V Somercotes *Derby* 11-14; C Bakewell, Ashford w Sheldon and Rowsley from 14. *Slade Cottage, Monyash Road, Over Haddon, Bakewell DE45 1HZ* T: (01629) 312031 E: plmd.davis@gmail.com

DAVIS, Peter Thomas. b 61. Flinders Univ Aus BTh 87 MThSt 02. St Barn Coll Adelaide 83. **d** 87 **p** 87. C Modbury and Dioc Youth Chapl Adelaide Australia 87-89; C Port Lincoln 89-91; TV Gt and Lt Coates w Bradley *Linc* 91-92; Dioc Youth Officer Adelaide Australia 92-94; P-in-c Parafield Gardens St Barbara 94-98; R Elizabeth H Cross 98-01; Chapl Anglicare S 98-01; V Satley, Stanley and Tow Law *Dur* 01-04. *Address temp unknown* M: 07795-417337 E: montedog2000@yahoo.co.uk

DAVIS, Rex. *See* DAVIS, Bernard Rex

DAVIS, Roger. *See* DAVIS, Herbert Roger

DAVIS, Ronald Geoffrey. b 47. St Jo Coll Nottm 79. **d** 81 **p** 81. C Maidstone St Luke *Cant* 81-84; P-in-c Lostwithiel *Truro* 84-86; P-in-c Lanhydrock 84-86; Asst Dioc Youth Officer 84-86; P-in-c Boughton Monchelsea *Cant* 86-88; V 88-15; Six Preacher Cant Cathl 94-99; C-in-c Parkwood CD 95-98; AD N Downs 99-02; rtd 15. *3 The Links, Falmouth TR11 5UJ*

DAVIS, Ruth Elizabeth. *See* TAIT, Ruth Elizabeth

DAVIS, Simon Charles. b 63. Plymouth Poly BSc 86 Univ of Wales (Lamp) MTh 08 MIET. Trin Coll Bris BA 92. **d** 92 **p** 93. C Bollington St Jo *Ches* 92-96; P-in-c Abbots Bromley w Blithfield *Lich* 96-10; P-in-c Colton, Colwich and Gt Haywood 05-10; R Abbots Bromley, Blithfield, Colton, Colwich etc from 11; RD Rugeley from 15. *The Vicarage, Market Place, Abbots Bromley, Rugeley WS15 3BP* T: (01283) 840242 E: revdsimon@davisfamily.waitrose.com

DAVIS, Susan Elizabeth Mary. *See* CLARKE, Susan Elizabeth Mary

DAVIS, Thomas Henry. b 60. OLM course 97 Coll of Resurr Mirfield 05. **d** 99 **p** 00. OLM Sudbury and Chilton *St E* 99-03; NSM Preston St Jo and St Geo *Blackb* 03-05; C Torrisholme 05-08; C Blackpool St Steph 08-09; PtO 09-10; C Morecambe St Barn 10-12; V from 12. *St Barnabas' Vicarage, 101 Regent Road, Morecambe LA3 1AG* T: (01524) 415216 M: 07854-770360 E: father.tom@live.co.uk

DAVIS, Timothy Alwyn. b 74. Trin Coll Bris BTh. **d** 01 **p** 02. C Crich and S Wingfield *Derby* 01-05; V Leyton St Mary w St Edw and St Luke *Chelmsf* 05-10; V Clifton w Newton and Brownsover *Cov* from 10. *The Vicarage, 43 Bow Fell, Rugby CV21 1JF* T: (01788) 573696 E: timandjo.davis@ntlworld.com

DAVIS, Timothy Charles. b 59. Reading Univ BA 81 Homerton Coll Cam PGCE 82. Trin Coll Bris 89. **d** 91 **p** 92. C Normanton *Wakef* 91-95; C Fisherton Anger *Sarum* 95-99; TV Abingdon *Ox* 99-13; V N Abingdon from 13. *69 Northcourt Road, Abingdon OX14 1NR* T: (01235) 520115 *or* 539172 F: 539179 E: tim@cca.uk.net

DAVIS, Mrs Yvonne Annie. b 30. CQSW 75. **d** 96 **p** 97. OLM Purley St Barn *S'wark* 96-00; PtO from 00. *8 Meadow Hill, Purley CR8 3HL* T: (020) 3441 9348 E: yvonnea.davis@talktalk.net

DAVISON, Andrew Paul. b 74. Mert Coll Ox BA 96 MA 99 DPhil 00 CCC Cam BA 02 MA 08. Westcott Ho Cam 00 Ven English Coll Rome 02. **d** 03 **p** 04. C Bellingham St Dunstan *S'wark* 03-06; Tutor and Fell St Steph Ho Ox 06-10; Jun Chapl Mert Coll Ox 06-10; Tutor Westcott Ho Cam 10-14; Lect Div Cam Univ from 14; Fell CCC Cam from 14. *Faculty of Divinity, West Road, Cambridge CB3 9BS* T: (01223) 763027

DAVISON, Deborah Karin Mary. b 56. Ex Univ BA 79 SRN 83 RHV 85. Ripon Coll Cuddesdon 09. **d** 11 **p** 12. C Boyne Hill *Ox* 11-13; C Wokingham St Paul from 13. *13 Brook Close, Wokingham RG41 1ND* T: 0118-979 0042 M: 07833-935901 E: debbie_moomoo@hotmail.com

DAVISON, The Ven George Thomas William. b 65. St Andr Univ BD 88. Oak Hill Th Coll 88 CITC BTh 92. **d** 92 **p** 93. C Portadown St Mark *Arm* 92-95; I Kinawley w H Trin *K, E & A* 95-09; Dir of Ords 97-09; Preb Kilmore Cathl 02-09; Adn Kilmore 04-09; I Carrickfergus *Conn* from 09; Adn Belfast from 13. *The Rectory, 12 Harwood Gardens, Carrickfergus BT38 7US* M: 07771-812844 T/F: (028) 9336 3244 T: 9336 0061 E: geordie1965@icloud.com

DAVISON, Philip Anthony. b 66. Magd Coll Cam BA 88 MA 93. Cuddesdon Coll BA 98. **d** 98 **p** 99. C Lancaster St Mary w St John and St Anne *Blackb* 98-02; P-in-c Feniscowles 02-08; R Finchley St Mary *Lon* from 08. *St Mary's Rectory, Rectory Close, London N3 1TS* T: (020) 8346 4600 *or* T/F: 8248 3818 E: rector@stmaryatfinchley.org.uk

DAVISON, Canon Richard Ireland. b 42. St Chad's Coll Dur BSc 63. Linc Th Coll 64. **d** 66 **p** 67. C Cockerton *Dur* 66-70; C Houghton le Spring 70-73; V Hawthorn Hill 73-80; Ascension Is 80-82; V Dunston *Dur* 82-85; V Bishopwearmouth Ch Ch 85-98; AD Wearmouth 94-99; P-in-c Dur St Giles 99-00; V 00-08; P-in-c Shadforth and Sherburn 03-08; Hon Can Dur Cathl 97-08; AD Dur 06-08; rtd 08; PtO *Dur* from 08. *16 Loraine Crescent, Darlington DL1 5TF*

DAVISON, Canon Roger William. b 20. Kelham Th Coll 46. **d** 51 **p** 52. C Tonge Moor *Man* 51-55; V 55-65; Hon Can Man Cathl 63-65; V Higham Ferrers w Chelveston *Pet* 65-88; rtd 88; PtO *Roch* 88-05. *The College of St Barnabas, Blackberry Lane, Lingfield RH7 6NJ* T: (01342) 872819

DAVY, Mrs Helen Mary. b 44. **d** 05 **p** 06. OLM Kirton w Falkenham *St E* 05-06; OLM Nacton and Levington w Bucklesham etc 06-13; NSM 13-15; PtO from 15. *9 Roman Way, Felixstowe IP11 9NJ* T: (01394) 270703 E: alan@alandavy.plus.com

DAVY, Mrs Judith Ann. b 60. SRN 82. STETS 01. **d** 04 **p** 05. NSM Jersey St Brelade *Win* 04-12; NSM Jersey All SS from 12; NSM Jersey St Simon from 12. *Brookvale House, Les Grupieaux, St Peter, Jersey JE3 7YW* T: (01534) 507800 M: 07797-730983 E: judithdavy@jerseymail.co.uk

DAVY, Peter Geoffrey. b 31. St Pet Coll Saltley TCert 54. SWMTC 93. **d** 94 **p** 94. NSM St Columb Minor and St Colan Truro 94-99; rtd 99; PtO *Truro* from 00. *9 Tredour Road, Newquay TR7 2EY* T: (01637) 872241

DAVYS, Mark Andrew. b 66. St Cath Coll Ox BA 87 MA 97 Keele Univ MA 01 Qu Coll Birm BA 04 Solicitor 90. WMMTC 01. **d** 04 **p** 05. NSM Colton, Colwich and Gt Haywood *Lich* 04-10; NSM Abbots Bromley, Blithfield, Colton, Colwich etc from 11. *Deer's Leap, Meadow Lane, Little Haywood, Stafford ST18 0TT* T: (01889) 882855 E: revmdavys@deersleap.org.uk

DAW, Geoffrey Martin. b 57. Oak Hill Th Coll 81. **d** 84 **p** 85. C Hollington St Leon *Chich* 84-87; C Seaford w Sutton 87-90; V Iford w Kingston and Rodmell 90-13; V Iford w Kingston and Rodmell and Southease from 13; RD Lewes and Seaford from 08. *The Rectory, 14 Lockitt Way, Kingston, Lewes BN7 3LG* T: (01273) 473665 E: geoffrey.daw@btinternet.com

DAW, Nicholas William. b 69. **d** 13 **p** 14. NSM Worc SE from 13. *21 Oak Avenue, Worcester WR4 9UG* T: (01905) 745645 E: revnickdaw@orangehome.co.uk

DAWE, David Fife Purchas. b 20. Keble Coll Ox BA 41 MA 45. Wells Th Coll 41. **d** 43 **p** 44. C Wolstanton *Lich* 43-46; C Meole Brace 46-47; C Leek All SS 47-50; C Tardebigge *Worc* 50-52; R Stoke Bliss w Kyre Wyard 52-54; R Jackfield *Heref* 54-61; V Criftins *Lich* 61-77; V Dudleston 63-77; P-in-c Alkmonton w Yeaveley *Derby* 77-81; P-in-c Cubley w Marston Montgomery 77-81; R Alkmonton, Cubley, Marston Montgomery etc 81-85; rtd 85; PtO *Derby* 85-94; *Lich* 85-94; *Pet* 94-07. *11 Coaching Walk, Northampton NN3 3EU* T: (01604) 414083

DAWES, Dori Katherine. b 37. ARCM. Oak Hill Th Coll 85. **d** 88 **p** 94. Par Dn Watford St Luke *St Alb* 88-90; Par Dn Watford 90-94; C 94-96; P-in-c Dunton w Wrestlingworth and Eyeworth 96-01; rtd 01; PtO *B & W* from 05. *Orchard House, Upway, Porlock, Minehead TA24 8QE* T: (01643) 862474

DAWES, Mrs Helen Elizabeth. b 74. Trin Coll Cam BA 96 MA 00. Westcott Ho Cam 99. **d** 02 **p** 03. C Chesterton St Andr *Ely* 02-05; P-in-c Sandon, Wallington and Rushden w Clothall *St Alb* 05-09; Dep Public Affairs Sec to Abp Cant 09-13; Abp's Soc and Public Affairs Adv 13-15. *Address temp unknown* E: helen@stmin.org.uk

DAWES, Hugh William. b 48. Univ Coll Ox BA 71 MA 76. Cuddesdon Coll 71. **d** 74 **p** 75. C Purley St Mark *S'wark* 74-77; Chapl G&C Coll Cam 77-82; Chapl Em Coll Cam 82-87; V Cambridge St Jas *Ely* 87-00; Dir Focus Chr Inst Cambridge 87-00; V N Dulwich St Faith *S'wark* 00-10; rtd 10; PtO *S'wark* from 10; *Guildf* from 11. *8 The Wells, Lower Street, Haslemere GU27 2PA* T: (01428) 652466 E: hugh@hughdawes.com

DAWES, Julian Edward. b 27. RAF Coll Cranwell 49. Bps' Coll Cheshunt 58. **d** 59 **p** 60. C Whitton St Aug *Lon* 59-62; Chapl RAF 62-65; V Overbury w Alstone, Teddington and Lt Washbourne *Worc* 65-70; V Cropthorne w Charlton 70-76; Chapl Dioc Conf Cen 70-76; Chapl Exe Vale Hosp Gp 76-84; Chapl Bromsgrove and Redditch Distr Gen Hosp 84-86; rtd 91; PtO *Ex* 91-09. *Maranatha, Exeter Road, Rewe, Exeter EX5 4EU* T: (01392) 841877 F: 841577

✠**DAWES, The Rt Revd Peter Spencer.** b 28. Hatf Coll Dur BA 52. Tyndale Hall Bris 53. **d** 54 **p** 55 **c** 88. C Whitehall Park St Andr Hornsey Lane *Lon* 54-57; C Ox St Ebbe 57-60; Tutor Clifton Th Coll 60-65; V Romford Gd Shep *Chelmsf* 65-80; Hon Can Chelmsf Cathl 78-80; Adn W Ham 80-88; Dioc Dir of Ords 80-86; Bp Derby 88-95; rtd 95; Hon Asst Bp *Ely* from 95. *45 Arundel, Ely CB6 1BQ.* T: (01353) 661241

DAWKES, Peter. b 31. Roch Th Coll 64. **d** 66 **p** 67. C Newbold w Dunston *Derby* 66-69; C Buxton 69-72; V Somercotes 72-93; rtd 93; Hon C Kenton, Mamhead, Powderham, Cofton and Starcross *Ex* 93-15; Hon C Exminster, Kenn, Kenton w Mamhead, and Powderham from 15. *115 Exeter Road, Dawlish EX7 0AN* T: (01626) 862593

DAWKIN, Peter William. b 60. Nottm Univ BTh 88 Open Univ BA 91. St Jo Coll Nottm 85. **d** 88 **p** 89. C Birkdale St Jo *Liv* 88-91; C Netherton 91-93; V Liv Ch Ch Norris Green 93-03; Assoc Min Wigan Deaneries 03-06; V Hough Green St Basil and All SS from 06. *339 Ditchfield Road, Widnes WA8 8XR* T: 0151-420 4963 M: 07852-484802 E: peter.dawkin@blueyonder.co.uk

DAWKINS, Canon Alan Arthur Windsor. b 26. St Aid Birkenhead 53. **d** 55 **p** 56. C Preston Em *Blackb* 55-57; C S Shore H Trin 57-59; V Slade Green *Roch* 59-61; V St Mary Cray and St Paul's Cray 61-63; V White Colne *Chelmsf* 63-66; R Pebmarsh 63-66; P-in-c Mt Bures 65-66; V Westgate St Jas *Cant* 66-74; V Herne Bay Ch Ch 74-83; Hon Can Cant Cathl 79-91; P-in-c Chilham 83-85; Adv for Miss and Unity 85-91; rtd 91; Chapl St Jo Hosp Cant 96-07; PtO *Cant* 96-10. *44 Columbia Avenue, Whitstable CT5 4EH*

DAWKINS (née LEWIS-MORRIS), Mrs Catherine Mary. b 76. St Hilda's Coll Ox MA 98 Qu Mary Coll Lon MSc 01 Peterho Cam BA 08. Ridley Hall Cam 06. **d** 10 **p** 11. C Aden Yemen 10-11; C Dubai UAE 11-12; PtO *S'wark* 12-15; LtO from 15. *41 Harestone Hill, Caterham CR3 6SG*

DAWKINS, Ms Jennifer Claire. b 76. Nottm Univ BA 97 SOAS Lon MSc 05 Wolfs Coll Cam BTh 13. Ridley Hall Cam 11. **d** 13 **p** 14. C Peckham All St *S'wark* from 13. *18 Martock Court, Consort Road, London SE15 2PL* M: 07773-963198 E: jennydawkins@hotmail.com

DAWKINS, John Haswell. b 47. NEOC 98. **d** 01 **p** 02. NSM Barmby Moor Gp *York* 01-11. *9 Fossbeck Close, Wilberfoss, York YO41 5PR* T: (01759) 388144

DAWKINS, Michael Howard. b 44. Bris Univ BTh 68 Man Univ MA 96. Tyndale Hall Bris 67. **d** 69 **p** 69. C Drypool St Columba w St Andr and St Pet *York* 69-73; CF 74-80; P-in-c Bulford *Sarum* 80-81; P-in-c Figheldean w Milston 80-81; R Meriden *Cov* 85-09; rtd 09. *60 Wassell Road, Wollescote, Stourbridge DY9 9DB* T: (01384) 893299 M: 07854-833460 E: mhdawkins@aol.com

DAWKINS, Nigel Jonathan. b 72. St Jo Coll Ox BA 94 MA 97 Univ Coll Lon MSc 97 Peterho Cam BA 05 MA 07. Westcott Ho Cam 03. **d** 06 **p** 07. C Caterham *S'wark* 06-09; Chapl Aden Ch Ch and Yemen 09-11; Chapl Miss to Seafarers Dubai and UAE 11-12; PtO *S'wark* 12-13; Min Can and Sacr St Paul's Cathl 13-14; PtO *S'wark* from 15. *41 Harestone Hill, Caterham CR3 6SG* E: nigeldawkins@gmail.com

DAWKINS, Staffan Anthony. b 59. SEITE 12. **d** 15. C Stanground and Farcet *Ely* from 15. *The Vicarage, Main Street, Farcet, Peterborough PE7 3AN* M: 07481-861817 T: (01733) 245171 E: staffan.dawkins@gmail.com

DAWN, Maggi Eleanor. b 59. Fitzw Coll Cam MA 96 Selw Coll Cam PhD 02. Ridley Hall Cam 96. **d** 99 **p** 00. C Ely 99-01; Chapl K Coll Cam 01-03; Chapl Rob Coll Cam from 03. *Robinson College, Cambridge CB3 9AN* T: (01223) 339140 M: 07743-351467 E: med1000@cam.ac.uk

DAWSON, Alan. b 28. St Jo Coll Dur BA 54 Liv Univ MA 67. Clifton Th Coll 54. **d** 56 **p** 57. C Bowling St Steph *Bradf* 56-59; C Attenborough w Bramcote *S'well* 59-62; V Everton St Jo *Liv* 62-69; V Birkdale St Pet 69-91; NSM Kirkcudbright and Gatehouse of Fleet *Glas* 98-06; PtO *Ches* from 07. *The Bungalow, Church Lane, Guilden Sutton, Chester CH3 7EW* T: (01244) 301685

DAWSON, Alan David Hough. b 67. St Jo Coll Dur BA 09 ACIB 92. Cranmer Hall Dur 07. **d** 09 **p** 10. C Hale and Ashley *Ches* 09-13; V Neston from 13. *The Vicarage, High Street, Neston CH64 9TZ* M: 07919-278104 E: alan.dawson21@btinternet.com

DAWSON, Andrew. See DAWSON, William James Andrew

DAWSON, Andrew. See DAWSON, Francis Andrew Oliver Duff

DAWSON, Miss Anne. b 54. Nottm Univ BA 76 Hull Coll of Educn PGCE 77. NEOC 03. **d** 06 **p** 07. NSM Market Weighton *York* 06-09; P-in-c Sigglesthorne w Nunkeeling and Bewholme 10-11; rtd 11; PtO *York* from 11. *23 Sloe Lane, Beverley HU17 8ND* T: (01482) 862940 E: andaw@andaw.karoo.co.uk

DAWSON, Barry. b 38. Oak Hill Th Coll 63. **d** 66 **p** 67. C Fulham St Mary N End *Lon* 66-69; C St Marylebone All So w SS Pet and Jo 69-73; Bp's Chapl *Nor* 73-76; Gen Sec CEMS 76-81; V Rye Park St Cuth *St Alb* 81-89; V Attenborough *S'well* 89-98; rtd 98; PtO *S'well* from 98. *27 Orlando Drive, Carlton, Nottingham NG4 3FN*

DAWSON, Canon Brian. b 33. Leeds Univ BA 54 Man Univ MA 84 Newc Univ MPhil 01. Coll of Resurr Mirfield 56. **d** 58 **p** 59. C Hollinwood *Man* 58-62; C Rawmarsh w Parkgate *Sheff* 62-63; V Royton St Anne *Man* 63-75; V Urswick *Carl* 75-86; V Bardsea 75-86; R Skelton and Hutton-in-the-Forest w Ivegill 86-98; RD Penrith 91-96; Hon Can Carl Cathl 94-98; rtd 98; PtO *Carl* from 98. *Apple Croft, High Hesket, Carlisle CA4 0HS* T: (016974) 73069

DAWSON, Miss Claire Louise. b 68. Nottm Poly BA 92 CQSW 92 Nottm Univ MA 04. EMMTC 01. **d** 04 **p** 05. C Mansfield Woodhouse *S'well* 04-05; C Sutton in Ashfield St Mary 05-08; C Orrell Hey St Jo and St Jas *Liv* 08-11; P-in-c from 11; P-in-c Litherland St Phil from 15. *20 Mount Avenue, Bootle L20 6DT* T: 0151-284 1359 E: cdawson@blueyonder.co.uk

DAWSON, Canon Cyril. b 34. St Chad's Coll Dur BA 58. **d** 59 **p** 60. C Honicknowle *Ex* 59-63; C Paignton St Jo 63-66; V Heptonstall *Wakef* 66-71; V Todmorden 71-82; RD Calder Valley 75-82; Can Res Wakef Cathl 82-92; Vice-Provost Wakef Cathl 86-92; Hon Can Wakef Cathl 92-99; V Darrington 92-99; rtd 99; PtO *York* from 00; *Leeds* from 00. *24 Beacon Road, Bridlington YO16 6UX* T: (01262) 672911

DAWSON, David. b 57. TISEC 99. **d** 99 **p** 00. NSM Kirkwall *Ab* from 99; P-in-c from 05. *St Olaf's Rectory, Dundas Crescent, Kirkwall, Orkney KW15 1JQ* T: (01856) 872024 M: 07881-932657 E: frdave_473@hotmail.com

DAWSON, Edward. b 50. **d** 81 **p** 83. NSM Newington St Paul *S'wark* 81-85; NSM Walworth St Jo 85-00; Chapl Asst Maudsley Hosp Lon from 87. *3 Ethel Street, London SE17 1NH* T: (020) 7701 8923

DAWSON, Francis Andrew Oliver Duff. b 48. Keble Coll Ox BA 70 MA 74. St Jo Coll Nottm 74. **d** 76 **p** 77. C Billericay St Mary *Chelmsf* 76-77; C Billericay and Lt Burstead 77-80; C Childwall All SS *Liv* 80-84; Chapl St Kath Coll 80-84; V Shevington *Blackb* 84-97; Internat Officer and Team Ldr for Evang Affairs *Man* 97-03; P-in-c Werneth 03-14; rtd 14. *3 Woodside Drive, Hyde SK14 5QB* E: andrewdawson51@hotmail.com

DAWSON, Frederick William. b 44. St Chad's Coll Dur BA 66 Nottm Univ MTh 74. Linc Th Coll 67. **d** 69 **p** 70. C Caversham *Ox* 69-72; C Ranmoor *Sheff* 72-79; R Kibworth Beauchamp *Leic* 79-82; R Kibworth and Smeeton Westerby and Saddington 82-94; R Tilehurst St Mich *Ox* 94-07; P-in-c Mickleton, Willersey w Saintbury etc *Glouc* 07-14; rtd 14. *Address temp unknown* E: fwd@revfwd.plus.com

DAWSON, Hilary. b 64. Univ of Wales (Lamp) BA 85 UWE PGCE 89 Ex Univ MA 08. SWMTC 05. **d** 08 **p** 09. C Thorverton, Cadbury, Upton Pyne etc *Ex* 08-10; C Brampford Speke, Cadbury, Newton St Cyres etc 10-11; P-in-c Colyton, Musbury, Southleigh and Branscombe from 11. *The Vicarage, Vicarage Street, Colyton EX24 6LJ* T: (01297) 553180 E: hilary.dawson2@btinternet.com

DAWSON, Ian Douglas. b 52. Liv Univ BSc 73. NOC 83. **d** 86 **p** 87. NSM Southport SS Simon and Jude *Liv* 86-93; NSM Birkdale St Jas 93-95; NSM Southport St Phil and St Paul 96-01; PtO *Linc* from 01. *18 Park View, Barton-upon-Humber DN18 6AX* T: (01652) 637554

DAWSON, John William Arthur. b 43. EMMTC. **d** 95 **p** 96. NSM Breedon cum Isley Walton and Worthington *Leic* 95-05; NSM Ashby-de-la-Zouch and Breedon on the Hill from 05. *Orchard House, 2 Manor Drive, Worthington, Ashby-de-la-Zouch LE65 1RN* T: (01530) 222673 E: johndawson@benefice.org.uk

DAWSON, Miss Mary. b 51. Loughb Coll ALA 73. EMMTC 85. **d** 90 **p** 94. Par Dn Braunstone *Leic* 90-92; Par Dn Shrewsbury H Cross *Lich* 92-94; C 94-95; P-in-c Glentworth Gp *Linc* 95-97; V 97-10; rtd 10. *20 Newbolt Close, Caistor, Market Rasen LN7 6NY* T: (01472) 859802 E: fenellacoughdrop@btinternet.com

DAWSON, Neil. b 49. Ripon Hall Ox 71. **d** 74 **p** 75. C Putney St Mary *S'wark* 74-78; C Camberwell St Giles 78-80; TV N Lambeth 84-86; V E Dulwich St Clem 86; V Dulwich St Clem w St Pet 86-89; Hon C Wilton Place St Paul *Lon* 92-06; P-in-c Madeira *Eur* 06-14; rtd 14. *Address temp unknown* E: neil.dawson6@btinternet.com

DAWSON, Nicholas Anthony. b 52. St Jo Coll Nottm 88. **d** 90 **p** 91. C Mortomley St Sav High Green *Sheff* 90-95; V Owlerton from 95; P-in-c Hillsborough and Wadsley Bridge 06-09. *Owlerton Vicarage, Forbes Road, Sheffield S6 2NW* T: 0114-234 3560 E: nick.dawson@sheffield.anglican.org

DAWSON, Canon Norman William. b 41. MBE 99. K Coll Lon BD 63 AKC 63. **d** 65 **p** 66. C Salford St Phil w St Steph *Man* 65-68; C Heaton Ch Ch 68-70; R Longsight St Jo 70-75; R Longsight St Jo w St Cypr 75-82; R Withington St Paul 82-99; Chapl Christie Hosp Man 81-91; AD Withington *Man* 91-99; P-in-c Davyhulme St Mary 99-04; Hon Can Man Cathl 98-04; rtd 04; PtO *Blackb* from 04; *Man* 04-12. *Well House, Lowgill, Lancaster LA2 8RA* T: (01524) 262936

DAWSON, Paul Christopher Owen. b 61. Leeds Univ BA 82. Ripon Coll Cuddesdon 83. **d** 85 **p** 86. C Dovecot *Liv* 85-89; V Westbrook St Phil 89-94; Bp's Dom Chapl 94-98; V Witton *Ches* 98-06; R Ches St Mary from 06; RD Ches from 14. *10 Lower Park Road, Chester CH4 7BB* T: (01244) 675199 E: comet411@tiscali.co.uk

DAWSON, Paul Richard. b 67. Bris Univ BSc 89. Oak Hill Th Coll 99. **d** 01 **p** 02. C Wimbledon Em Ridgway Prop Chpl *S'wark* 01-09; V Chelsea St Jo w St Andr *Lon* from 09. *The Vicarage, 43 Park Walk, London SW10 0AU* T: (020) 7352 1675 E: paul@standrewschelsea.org

DAWSON, Peter John. b 44. Local Minl Tr Course. **d** 06 **p** 07. NSM Heckmondwike *Wakef* 06-12; NSM Liversedge w Hightown 06-12; NSM Roberttown w Hartshead 06-12; NSM Heckmondwike (w Norristhorpe) and Liversedge 12-14; NSM Hartshead, Hightown, Roberttown and Scholes 12-14; rtd 14; PtO *Leeds* from 14. *10 Meadow Drive, Liversedge WF15 7QF* T: (01924) 404311 E: manxpeter@yahoo.co.uk

DAWSON, Peter Rodney. b 44. **d** 98 **p** 99. OLM Ashtead *Guildf* 98-05; Asst Chapl Pau *Eur* 05-06; PtO 06-08; P-in-c Biarritz 08-11. *Le Bosquet, 64400 Poey d'Oloron, France* T: (0033) 5 59 27 63 14 E: peter.dawson@free.fr

DAWSON, Ronald Eric John. b 27. St Mark & St Jo Coll Lon TCert 54 Lon Univ BD 64. Bps' Coll Cheshunt 62. **d** 62 **p** 63. C Dartford H Trin *Roch* 62-66; C Fulham St Etheldreda *Lon* 66-74; V Brentford St Faith 74-80; rtd 92. *13 Birkbeck Road, London W5 4ES* T: (020) 8560 3564

DAWSON, Ruth Adelaide. b 44. **d** 15. NSM Heighington and Darlington St Matt and St Luke *Dur* from 15. *27 Wilton Court, Greenfields, Newton Aycliffe DL5 7PU* T: (01325) 321729 M: 07786-154638

DAWSON, Ms Sarah. b 70. **d** 15. C Mitcham St Barn *S'wark* from 15. *All Saints' Vicarage, 10 Deburgh Road, London SW19 1DX* M: 07952-729499 E: sarahdawson39@gmail.com

DAWSON, Stephen Charles. b 70. LCTP 08. **d** 10 **p** 11. C Bentham *Bradf* 10-13; P-in-c Langcliffe w Stainforth and Horton *Leeds* from 13; C Settle from 13; C Giggleswick and Rathmell w Wigglesworth from 13; PtO *Blackb* from 12. *16 Mount Pleasant, Bentham, Lancaster LA2 7LB* T: (01524) 262242 F: 242027 E: scudawson@hotmail.com

DAWSON, Thomas Douglas. b 52. Newc Univ BA. St Steph Ho Ox. **d** 80 **p** 82. C N Gosforth *Newc* 80-81; C Leic St Chad 82-85; TV Catford (Southend) and Downham *S'wark* 85-88; V Chevington *Newc* 88-94; V Cowgate 94-96; P-in-c Cresswell and Lynemouth 96-98; C Blyth St Mary 98-01; rtd 01; PtO *Newc* from 02. *Iona, 2 Hillside, Lesbury, Alnwick NE66 3NR* T: (01665) 830412 M: 07763-122259 E: fr_tom_dawson@hotmail.com

DAWSON, Timothy Charles. b 63. **d** 12 **p** 13. C Newport Deanery *Ox* from 12. *17 Kitelee Close, Hanslope, Milton Keynes MK19 7JT* E: revdawson@gmail.com

DAWSON (formerly CORY), Mrs Valerie Ann. b 44. CertEd 65 Nottm Univ BEd 85. EMMTC 85. **d** 88 **p** 94. Area Sec CMS Linc and Pet 87-91; NSM Grantham *Linc* 88-91; Par Dn Ealing St Mary *Lon* 91-94; Chapl NW Lon Poly 91-92; Chapl Thames Valley Univ 92-96; C Ealing St Mary 94-96; Chapl Birm Cathl 96-99; C Surbiton St Andr and St Mark *S'wark* 99-08; rtd 08. *15A Greengate Close, Chesterfield S40 3SJ* T: (01246) 550445

DAWSON, Canon William James Andrew. b 48. TCD MA 72. CITC 88. **d** 88 **p** 89. NSM Killyman *Arm* 88-91; NSM Pomeroy 91-13; NSM Derryloran from 14; Can Arm Cathl from 98; Preb 98-01. *Tamlaght House, 29 Bridgend Road, Cookstown BT80 0AB* T: (028) 8673 7151 *or* T/F: 8676 2227 E: wjadawson@gmail.com

DAWSON-CAMPBELL, Olive Sheila. b 37. ACIB 70. WEMTC 99. **d** 00 **p** 01. OLM Longden and Annscroft w Pulverbatch *Heref*

00-13; OLM Gt Hanwood and Longden and Annscroft etc from 13. *Sheaves, Lyth Bank, Lyth Hill, Shrewsbury SY3 0BE* T: (01743) 872071

DAWSON-JONES, Garry Alan. b 66. Cliff Coll MA 02. Yorks Min Course 11. **d** 12 **p** 13. C Hackenthorpe *Sheff* 12-15; R Warboys w Broughton and Bury w Wistow *Ely* from 15. *The Rectory, 1 Oaklands, Warboys, Huntingdon PE28 2XH* M: 07976-382681 T: (01487) 824612 E: garrydawsonjones@yahoo.com

DAWSWELL, Jonathan Andrew. b 65. Jes Coll Cam BA 86. Wycliffe Hall Ox BA 91. **d** 92 **p** 93. C Childwall All SS *Liv* 92-96; C Leyland St Andr *Blackb* 96-99; V Knypersley *Lich* 99-09; P-in-c Biddulph Moor 05-09; R Biddulph Moor and Knypersley 09-11; V Westlands St Andr from 11. *St Andrew's Vicarage, 50 Kingsway West, Newcastle ST5 3PU* T: (01782) 619594 E: jadawswell@ntlworld.com

DAWTRY, The Ven Anne Frances. b 57. Westf Coll Lon BA 79 PhD 85. Ripon Coll Cuddesdon 91. **d** 93 **p** 94. C Corfe Mullen *Sarum* 93-96; C Parkstone St Pet w Branksea and St Osmund 96-97; Chapl Bournemouth Univ and Bournemouth and Poole Coll of FE 97-99; Prin OLM and Integrated Tr 99-03; Dir Tr and Prin Dioc OLM Scheme *Man* 03-06; Course Dir SNWTP 06-08; C Chorlton-cum-Hardy St Werburgh 06-08; P-in-c 08-09; R 09-11; Hon Can Man Cathl 06-11; Adn Halifax *Leeds* from 11; Warden of Readers from 12. *2 Vicarage Gardens, Brighouse HD6 3HD* T: (01484) 714553 M: 07772-826577 E: archdeacon.halifax@westyorkshiredales.anglican.org

DAXTER, Preb Gregory. b 42. Chelmer Inst of HE PGCE 76. Oak Hill Th Coll 64. **d** 68 **p** 69. C Paignton St Paul Preston *Ex* 68-72; C Woodford Wells *Chelmsf* 72-75; Hon C Harold Hill St Paul 75-77; Hon C Wilmington *Roch* 77-87; PV Ex Cathl and Chapl Ex Cathl Sch 87-03; Preb Ex Cathl from 02; rtd 03. *36 Lyncombe Crescent, Higher Lincombe Road, Torquay TQ1 2HP*

DAY, Audrey. b 30. CA Tr Coll IDC 57. **d** 88 **p** 94. Par Dn Mildenhall *St E* 88-91; NSM Blackbourne 94-95; rtd 95; PtO *St E* 95-04; *Glouc* from 04. *25 Capel Court, The Burgage, Prestbury, Cheltenham GL52 3EL* T: (01242) 576494

DAY, Canon Charles Ian. b 48. Univ of Wales (Ban) BA 72. St Mich Coll Llan 73. **d** 75 **p** 76. C Llanrhos *St As* 75-79; V Mochdre 79-83; CF 80-91; V Minera *St As* 83-92; Dioc Soc Resp Officer 89-94; V Mold 92-11; AD 03-11; V Rhuddlan and Bodelwyddan from 11; AD St As from 15; Can St As Cathl from 14. *The Vicarage, 19 Tirionfa, Rhuddlan, Rhyl LL18 6LT* T: (01745) 590883 M: 07977-001692 E: revian@spamex.com

DAY, Christine Audrey. b 63. K Alfred's Coll Win BTh 01 Univ of Wales (Lamp) MA(Theol) 06. STETS 02. **d** 04 **p** 05. NSM N Stoneham *Win* 04-08; NSM Swaythling 08-14; Chapl Southn Univ 11-14; Chapl Win Univ from 14. *The University of Winchester, Sparkford Road, Winchester SO22 4NR* M: 07580-968215 T: (01962) 827246 E: revchrisday@gmail.com *or* chaplaincy@winchester.ac.uk

DAY, Canon Colin Michael. b 40. Lon Univ BSc 62 AKC 62 Em Coll Cam BA 66 MA 71. Ridley Hall Cam 65. **d** 67 **p** 68. C Heworth w Peasholme St Cuth *York* 67-70; C Ox St Clem 70-76; V Kidsgrove *Lich* 76-86; Exec Officer Angl Evang Assembly and C of E Coun 86-90; Adv on Miss and Evang *Sarum* 90-95; P-in-c Branksome Park All SS 95-01; V 01-05; Can and Preb Sarum Cathl 94-05; Dioc Tr in Evang 95-05; rtd 05; PtO *Win* from 13. *113 Archery Grove, Southampton SO19 9ET* T: (023) 8043 9854 E: colin.day1@tiscali.co.uk

DAY, David John. b 44. CEng 72 MICE 72. Trin Coll Bris. **d** 90 **p** 91. C Stratton St Margaret w S Marston etc *Bris* 90-94; PtO from 94; Manager SA Addictions Rehab Cen Highworth 98-09; rtd 09. *56 Beechcroft Road, Swindon SN2 7PX* T: (01793) 725721 E: davidjday1@hotmail.co.uk

DAY, David Vivian. b 36. Lon Univ BA 57 Nottm Univ MEd 73 MTh 77. **d** 99 **p** 00. NSM Dur St Nic 99-07; rtd 07; PtO *Dur* from 07. *35 Orchard Drive, Durham DH1 1LA* T: 0191-386 6909 E: dv.day@virgin.net

DAY, Canon David William. b 37. St Andr Univ MA 58 BD 61 CertEd 73. St And Dioc Tr Course 74. **d** 76 **p** 77. C St Andrews All SS *St And* 76-77; P-in-c Dundee St Ninian *Bre* 77-84; Itinerant Priest *Arg* 84-02; R Duror 84-02; P-in-c Gruline 84-02; P-in-c Kinlochart 84-02; P-in-c Kinlochleven 84-02; P-in-c Kinlochmoidart 84-96; P-in-c Lochbuie 84-96; P-in-c Portnacrois 84-02; P-in-c Strontian 84-96; Can St Jo Cathl Oban 99-02; rtd 02; Hon Can Cumbrae *Arg* from 02; Hon C St Andrews All SS *St And* from 03. *10 Doocot Road, St Andrews KY16 8QP* T: (01334) 476991 E: arkvillewest@googlemail.com

DAY, George Chester. b 45. Ex Univ BA 66 Lon Univ BD 70. Clifton Th Coll 67. **d** 71 **p** 72. C Reading St Jo *Ox* 71-75; C Morden *S'wark* 75-81; Sec for Voc and Min CPAS 81-86;

Hon C Bromley Ch Ch *Roch* 83-86; V St Paul's Cray St Barn 86-05; RD Orpington 01-05; V Joydens Wood St Barn 05-10; rtd 10. *5 Abbey Grange Close, Buckfast, Buckfastleigh TQ11 0EU* T: (01364) 643912
E: revgeorgeday@ntlworld.com

DAY, Canon James Alfred. b 23. DFC 44. AKC 49. **d** 50 **p** 51. C Wembley Park St Aug *Lon* 50-52; Mauritius 52-57; V E and W Ravendale w Hatcliffe *Linc* 57-60; R Beelsby 57-60; PC Gt Grimsby St Paul 60-66; V Tattershall 66-80; R Coningsby 66-80; RD Horncastle 73-80; V Heckington 80-89; Can and Preb Linc Cathl 77-05; rtd 89. *Flat 12, Manormead, Tilford Road, Hindhead GU26 6RA* T: (01428) 601512

DAY, Jennifer Ann. *See* BRADSHAW, Jennifer Ann

DAY, John Kenneth. b 58. Hull Univ BA 85. Cranmer Hall Dur 85. **d** 87 **p** 88. C Thornbury *Bradf* 87-90; V 90-96; V Whitkirk *Ripon* 96-01; V Fendalton New Zealand from 01. *7 Makora Street, Fendalton, Christchurch 8041, New Zealand* T: (0064) (3) 351 7392 or 351 7064 E: thedays@clear.net.nz

DAY, Judith Mollie. d 15. NSM Brecon St Mary *S & B* from 15. *Maes yr Haf, Pentrefelin, Sennybridge, Brecon LD3 8TT* T: (01874) 638307 E: judyday.jd@gmail.com

DAY, Martyn John. b 69. Univ Coll Lon BSc 90. St Jo Coll Nottm 07. **d** 09 **p** 10. C Horwich and Rivington *Man* 09-12; C Blackrod 11-12; V Epsom St Geo New Zealand from 12. *St George's Church, 19 Ranfurly Road, Epsom, Auckland 1023, New Zealand* T: (0064) (9) 520 5652

DAY, Canon Mary Elizabeth. b 57. Leic Poly BEd 79. St Jo Coll Nottm 93. **d** 93 **p** 94. C Newbarns w Hawcoat *Carl* 93-98; P-in-c Allonby 98-03; P-in-c Cross Canonby 98-03; P-in-c Dearham 02-03; V Allonby, Cross Canonby and Dearham from 03; Adv for Women in Min from 07; RD Solway 08-11; Hon Can Carl Cathl from 08. *The Vicarage, Crosscanonby, Maryport CA15 6SJ* T: (01900) 814192
E: vicarmary@talktalk.net

DAY, Michael. b 37. AKC 61 RCA(Lon) MA 75. **d** 62 **p** 63. C Hulme St Phil *Man* 62-65; Asst Chapl Newc Univ 65-70; Chapl Chelsea Coll *Lon* 70-85; Chapl R Coll of Art 70-90; Chapl Cen, Chelsea and St Martin's Schs of Art *Lon* 85-90; P-in-c Bloomsbury St Geo w Woburn Square Ch Ch 91-95; C St Pancras w St Jas and Ch Ch 95-02; Chapl Lon Art Colls 95-02; rtd 02. *40 Thistlewaite Road, London E5 0QQ* T: (020) 8985 8568

DAY, Paul Geoffrey. b 51. Dur Univ BEd 75. Trin Coll Bris 76. **d** 78 **p** 79. C Roxeth Ch Ch *Lon* 78-82; TV Barking St Marg w St Patr *Chelmsf* 82-87; V Barrow St Mark *Carl* 87-00; V Eccleston St Luke *Liv* 00-07; TV Eccleston 07-13; rtd 13. *2 St Paul's Villas, King Street, Acrefair, Wrexham LL14 3RW* E: paulgday@btinternet.com

DAY, Peter. b 50. BPharm 71. Coll of Resurr Mirfield 85. **d** 87 **p** 88. C Eastcote St Lawr *Lon* 87-91; C Wembley Park St Aug 91-94; V Glen Parva and S Wigston *Leic* 94-14; C Wigston from 14; rtd 15. *2A Eastfields Close, Gaywood, King's Lynn PE30 4HQ*

DAY, Peter Andrew. b 67. Westmr Coll Ox BTh 98 Bris Univ PhD 03. Ripon Coll Cuddesdon 07. **d** 10 **p** 11. C Wokingham St Paul *Ox* 10-13; P-in-c Reading Ch Ch 13-15; V from 15. *Christ Church Vicarage, Vicarage Road, Reading RG2 7AJ* M: 07702-043857 E: fr.peterday@virginmedia.com

DAY, Roy Frederick. b 24. S'wark Ord Course 63. **d** 67 **p** 68. C Newington St Paul *S'wark* 67-70; C Radlett *St Alb* 70-72; P-in-c Ponsbourne 72-76; R Campton 76-82; V Shefford 76-82; R Shenley 82-89; rtd 89; PtO *St Alb* 89-14. *11 Hill End Lane, St Albans AL4 0TX* T: (01727) 845782

DAY, Miss Sally Ann. b 43. **d** 07 **p** 08. OLM Shifnal and Sheriffhales *Lich* from 07. *11 Cherry Tree Hill, Coalbrookdale, Telford TF8 7EF* T/F: (01952) 433213 M: 07831-101361
E: sallyannday@hotmail.com

DAY, Stephen Michael. b 60. Down Coll Cam BA 82 MA 85 Open Univ BA 00. Ridley Hall Cam 02. **d** 05 **p** 06. C Waltham H Cross *Chelmsf* 05-09; TV Papworth *Ely* from 09. *The Rectory, 1 Barons Way, Papworth Everard, Cambridge CB23 3QJ* T: (01480) 831915 E: revdsmday@tesco.net *or* stephen.day@ely.anglican.org

DAY, Timothy Robert. b 63. WMMTC 07. **d** 10 **p** 11. NSM Leic H Apostles 10-14; TV Fosse from 14. *St Michael's Vicarage, 828 Melton Road, Thurmaston, Leicester LE4 8BE* T: 0116-348 6896 M: 07976-186546 E: revtimday.fosseteam@gmail.com

DAY, Trevor Martin. b 51. STETS 09. **d** 12 **p** 13. NSM Highworth w Sevenhampton and Inglesham etc *Bris* from 12; NSM Broad Blunsdon from 12; Min Can Bris Cathl from 15. *23 Melfort Close, Sparcells, Swindon SN5 5FG* T: (01793) 875373 M: 07918-125826 E: trevor.day@btinternet.com

DAY, William Charles. b 47. Portsm Poly BEd 86. Ripon Coll Cuddesdon 88. **d** 90 **p** 91. C Bishop's Waltham *Portsm* 90-93; P-in-c Greatham w Empshott and Hawkley w Prior's Dean

93-95; R 95-98; V Titchfield 98-09; RD Fareham 04-08; C-in-c Whiteley CD 08-09; rtd 09; PtO *Portsm* from 09. *19 Peter's Road, Locks Heath, Southampton SO31 6EB* T: (01489) 564035
E: carolday@frmail.net

DAY, William George. b 45. SNWTP 14. **d** 14 **p** 15. OLM Derby St Barn from 14. *2 Whenby Close, Mickleover, Derby DE3 0RQ* T: (01332) 518449 E: wwgday@btinternet.com

DAYKIN, Mrs Jean Elizabeth. b 43. **d** 04 **p** 05. NSM Cawthorne and Darton *Leeds* 04-14; rtd 14; PtO *Leeds* from 14. *13 Maltkiln Road, Cawthorne, Barnsley S75 4HH* T: (01226) 793804 M: 07967-767839 E: rev.jean@btinternet.com

DAYKIN, Timothy Elwin. b 54. R Holloway Coll Lon BSc 75 St Jo Coll Dur MA 81 K Coll Lon MPhil 93 MEHS 89. Cranmer Hall Dur 75. **d** 78 **p** 79. C Bourne *Guildf* 78-81; Chapl K Alfred Coll *Win* 82-87; C-in-c Valley Park CD 87-91; V Valley Park 91-92; P-in-c Fordingbridge 92-98; V 98-01; P-in-c Hale w S Charford 94-01; P-in-c Breamore 99-01; TR Fordingbridge and Breamore and Hale etc 01-05; TV Southampton (City Cen) 05-14; Producer/Presenter Relig Progr BBC Radio Solent from 05. *11 Cottage Mews, Fordingbridge SP6 1RJ*
E: tim@fordingbridge.com

DAYNES, Andrew John. b 47. Jes Coll Cam BA 69 MA 73. Westcott Ho Cam 69. **d** 72 **p** 73. C Radlett *St Alb* 72-76; Chapl St Alb Abbey 76-80; Chapl Bryanston Sch 80-08; rtd 08; PtO *B & W* from 09. *Romneya, Claycastle, Haselbury Plucknett, Crewkerne TA18 7PE* T: (01460) 78971 M: 07748-734263
E: hilandandy@googlemail.com

DAZELEY, Mrs Lorna. b 31. CertEd 53 New Hall Cam BA 82 MA 86. EAMTC 82. **dss** 84 **d** 87 **p** 94. Chesterton St Andr *Ely* 84-97; C 87-97; rtd 97; PtO *Ely* from 01. *Chesterton House, Church Street, Chesterton, Cambridge CB4 1DT* T: (01223) 356243 E: lornadazeley@mac.com

DE ALMEIDA FEITAL, Peterson. b 75. Cliff Coll BA 05 MA 09. Ridley Hall Cam 09. **d** 11 **p** 12. C Muswell Hill St Jas w St Matt *Lon* 11-14; Missr to the Arts from 15. *4 Dollings Yard, 3 Bellingdon Road, Chesham HP5 2HA* M: 07791-581745
E: petersonfeital@hotmail.com

DE ALWIS, Anthony Clarence. b 39. Nottm Univ MA 99. EAMTC 96. **d** 99 **p** 00. NSM Carrington *S'well* 99-04; NSM Basford St Leodegarius 04-06; rtd 06. *85 Marlborough Road, Beeston, Nottingham NG9 2HL* T: 0115-967 8097 M: 07974-084514 E: tonydealwis270@hotmail.com

DE ANDRADE LIMA, Luiz Henrique. b 80. Trin Coll Bris BA 14. **d** 14 **p** 15. C Worksop St Anne *S'well* from 14; C Norton Cuckney from 14. *129 Stubbing Lane, Worksop S80 1NF* T: (01909) 472880 M: 07989-674364
E: luizhlima@yahoo.com

de BERRY, Andrew Piers. b 44. St Jo Coll Dur BA 66. Ripon Hall Ox 70. **d** 74 **p** 75. C Aylesbury *Ox* 74-77; USA 78; TV Clyst St George, Aylesbeare, Clyst Honiton etc *Ex* 78-80; Asst Chapl HM Pris Wormwood Scrubs 80-82; Chapl HM Pris Sudbury 82-84; V Blackwell *Derby* 84-91; V Thurgarton w Hoveringham and Bleasby etc *S'well* 91-10; rtd 10; PtO *S'well* from 10. *The Vicarage, Church Road, Clipstone Village, Mansfield NG21 9DG* T: (01623) 623916 E: adeberry@tiscali.co.uk

de BERRY, Barnabas John de la Tour. b 75. Heythrop Coll Lon BA 99. Wycliffe Hall Ox 99. **d** 01 **p** 02. C Derby St Alkmund and St Werburgh 01-04; C Cambridge H Trin *Ely* 04-10; V Cant St Mary Bredin from 10; AD Cant from 14. *St Mary Bredin Vicarage, 57 Nunnery Fields, Canterbury CT1 3JN* T: (01227) 453777 M: 07968-728840
E: barney.deberry@btinternet.com

DE BERRY, Robert Delatour. b 42. Qu Coll Cam BA 64 MA 68. Ridley Hall Cam 65. **d** 67 **p** 68. C Bradf Cathl 67-70; Youth Worker CMS Uganda 71-75; V Attercliffe *Sheff* 75-83; V W Kilburn St Luke w St Simon and St Jude *Lon* 83-97; Gen Sec Mid-Africa Min (CMS) 97-99; P-in-c Kennington St Mark *S'wark* from 99; V 01-08; rtd 08. *27 Cossor Road, Pewsey SN9 5HX* E: robertdeberry@btinternet.com

de BOURCIER, Miss Katherine Elizabeth. b 71. Clare Coll Cam BA 92. St Mellitus Coll BA 12. **d** 12 **p** 13. C Gt Baddow *Chelmsf* from 12. *3 Westbourne Grove, Chelmsford CM2 9RT* T: (01245) 269443

de BOWEN, Alfred William. b 24. St Paul's Coll Grahamstown 76. **d** 78 **p** 86. NSM Port Alfred S Africa 78-86; NSM Cil-y-Cwm and Ystrad-ffin w Rhandir-mwyn etc *St D* 86-88; LtO *Linc* 88-92; rtd 90. *Elmham House, Bay Hill, Ilminster TA19 0AT* T: (01460) 52694

DE CHAIR LADD, Anne. *See* LADD, Anne de Chair

de COSTOBADIE, James Palliser. b 72. G&C Coll Cam BA 94 MA 98. Oak Hill Th Coll BA 01. **d** 02 **p** 03. C Mayfair Ch Ch and St Helen Bishopsgate w St Andr Undershaft etc *Lon* 02-05; P-in-c Sydenham w Beckenham New Zealand from 05. *8A Roxburgh Street, Sydenham, Christchurch 8023, New Zealand* T: (0064) (3) 332 3432
E: jdecostobadie@hotmail.com

de GARIS, Canon Jean Helier Thomson. b 60. K Alfred's Coll Win BA 82 PGCE 83. Sarum & Wells Th Coll BTh 93. **d** 93 **p** 94. C Chandler's Ford *Win* 93-98; P-in-c Lytchett Minster *Sarum* 98-10; TR The Lytchetts and Upton from 10; RD Poole from 09; Can and Preb Sarum Cathl from 14. *The Vicarage, New Road, Lytchett Minster, Poole BH16 6JQ* T: (01202) 622253 E: jean@degaris.freeserve.co.uk

DE GARIS, Juliette Elizabeth Charmaine. *See* ROBILLIARD, Juliette Elizabeth Charmaine

de GAY, Sandra Jane. b 49. NOC. **d** 08 **p** 09. NSM Potternewton *Leeds* from 08. *48 Vesper Way, Leeds LS5 3LN* T: 0113-258 2673 E: j.degay@leedstrinity.ac.uk

de GREY-WARTER, Philip. b 67. Leeds Univ BEng 89. Ridley Hall Cam BA 94. **d** 94 **p** 95. C Bromley Ch Ch *Roch* 94-97; C Sevenoaks St Nic 97-02; P-in-c Fowey *Truro* 02-12; V from 12; P-in-c St Sampson from 02; Chapl Cen Cornwall Primary Care Trust 02-06; Chapl Cornwall and Is of Scilly Primary Care Trust 06-07; Hon Chapl Miss to Seafarers 04-07. *The Vicarage, Church Avenue, Fowey PL23 1BU* T: (01726) 833535 E: philipdegreywarter@me.com

de GRUCHY, Ms Heidi-Maria. b 63. Cardiff Univ BTh 12. St Mich Coll Llan 08. **d** 10 **p** 11. C Bedwellty w New Tredegar *Mon* 10-12; C Bassaleg 12-14; C Tredegar from 14. *St James's Vicarage, Poplar Road, Tredegar MP22 4LH* M: 07877-957503 T: (01495) 722510 E: heididegruchy@hotmail.co.uk

de la BAT SMIT, Reynaud. b 50. St Edm Hall St Aug BA 80 MA 86 Dur Univ PhD 94 FRSA 94. Ripon Coll Cuddesdon. **d** 82 **p** 83. C Headington *Ox* 82-85; Chapl St Hild and St Bede Coll *Dur* 85-96; Chapl Cheltenham Coll 96-11; rtd 11; Sec Chs' Peace Forum CTBI 97-02; PtO *Ox* from 12. *133 Oxford Road, Kidlington OX5 2NP* T: (01865) 420547 M: 07747-734870 E: reynaud1@virginmedia.com

de la HOYDE, Canon Denys Ralph Hart. b 33. G&C Coll Cam BA 57 MA 61. Westcott Ho Cam 57. **d** 59 **p** 60. C Moss Side Ch Ch *Man* 59-60; Chapl G&C Coll Cam 60-64; P-in-c Naini Tal etc India 64-68; C Eltham H Trin *S'wark* 68-69; Chapl Bromsgrove Sch 69-71; Asst Master Harrogate High Sch 71-78; LtO *Ripon* 71-78; V Pool w Arthington 86-98; Dioc Dir of Ords 86-98; Hon Can Ripon Cathl 92-98; rtd 98; PtO *Leeds* from 00. *36 Hookstone Chase, Harrogate HG2 7HS* T: (01423) 548146 E: denys.delahoyde@ntlworld.com

de la MOUETTE, Norman Harry. b 39. Southn Univ BEd 73 MA 98. Sarum & Wells Th Coll 76. **d** 79 **p** 80. NSM Win St Lawr and St Maurice w St Swithun 79-99; Deputation Appeals Org CECS Win and Portsm 83-96; Chapl St Jo Win Charity 96-99; NSM Win St Lawr and St Maurice w St Swithun 99-04; rtd 04; PtO *Win* from 04. *146 Greenhill Road, Winchester SO22 5DR* T: (01962) 853191

DE LYON, Hilary Barbara. b 56. **d** 13 **p** 14. NSM Swaffham and Sporle *Nor* from 13. *Woodford Lodge, Tittleshall, King's Lynn PE32 2PF* T: (01328) 700066 E: hilary@delyon.plus.com

de MELLO, Bridget Dorothea. *See* DEUCHAR de MELLO, Bridget Dorothea

de MELLO, Gualter Rose. b 34. MBE 96. Ridley Hall Cam 63. **d** 64 **p** 65. C S Hackney St Jo w Ch Ch *Lon* 64-66; Toc H Chapl (Hackney) 66-72; Hon C All Hallows by the Tower etc *Lon* from 73; Dir Friends Anonymous Service from 73; Dir Community of Reconciliation and Fellowship from 88; rtd 99. *c/o E White Esq, 2 College Street, Bury St Edmunds IP33 1NH*

de POMERAI, David Ian Morcamp. b 50. Edin Univ BSc 72 Univ Coll Lon PhD 75. EMMTC 90. **d** 93 **p** 94. NSM Sutton in Ashfield St Mary *S'well* 93-96; NSM Clifton 96-02; NSM Walton-on-Trent w Croxall, Rosliston etc *Derby* 02-13; LtO from 13. *74 Woodville Road, Hartshorne, Swadlincote DE11 7ET* T: (01283) 225846 E: david.depomerai@nottingham.ac.uk

DE PURY, Andrew Robert. b 28. K Coll Lon BD 57 AKC 57. **d** 58 **p** 59. C Epping St Jo *Chelmsf* 58-60; C Loughton St Jo 60-65; V Harold Hill St Geo 65-72; Missr Swan Par Gp *Ox* 72-76; TR Swan 76-85; R Worminghall w Ickford, Oakley and Shabbington 85-95; rtd 95; PtO *B & W* 95-06. *8 Russell Pope Avenue, Chard TA20 2JN* T: (01460) 66714

de QUIDT, Mrs Fiona Margaret Munro. b 53. St Andr Univ MTheol 76. NTMTC 97. **d** 00 **p** 01. NSM Kingston Hill St Paul *S'wark* from 00. *10 Norbiton Avenue, Kingston-upon-Thames KT1 3QS* T: (020) 8549 4175

de QUIDT, Marion Elizabeth. b 59. Girton Coll Cam MPhil 83 MA 85 PhD 86. STETS 09. **d** 11 **p** 12. C Fetcham *Guildf* 11-15; P-in-c Whitewater *Win* from 15. *The Vicarage, London Road, Hook RG27 9EG* M: 07866-304516 E: mariondequidt@whitewaterchurches.co.uk

DE ROBECK, Fiona Caroline. *See* GIBBS, Fiona Caroline

DE SALIS, Mary. *See* FANE DE SALIS, Mary

DE SAUSMAREZ, Canon John Havilland Russell. b 26. Lambeth MA 81 Wells Th Coll 54. **d** 56 **p** 57. C N Lynn w St Marg and St Nic *Nor* 56-58; C Hythe *Cant* 58-61; V Maidstone St Martin 61-68; V St Peter-in-Thanet 68-81; RD Thanet 74-81;

Hon Can Cant Cathl 78-81; Can Res Cant Cathl 81-94; rtd 94; PtO *Cant* 94-12. *6 Chantry Court, St Radigunds Street, Canterbury CT1 2AD* T: (01227) 458868

DE SILVA, David Ebenezer Sunil. b 48. **d** 72 **p** 73. Sri Lanka 72-84; C Elm Park St Nic Hornchurch *Chelmsf* 84-87; R Mistley w Manningtree and Bradfield 87-90; TR Stanground and Farcet *Ely* 90-01; V Stanground 01-05; rtd 05. *10 Anson House, Cottesmore Close, Peterborough PE3 9ET*

DE SMET, Andrew Charles. b 58. Ex Univ BSc 79 Southn Univ BTh 88. Sarum & Wells Th Coll 85. **d** 88 **p** 89. C Portsea St Mary *Portsm* 88-93; R Shipston-on-Stour w Honington and Idlicote *Cov* 93-00; Warden Offa Retreat Ho and Dioc Spirituality Adv 00-07; P-in-c Kirkdale w Harome, Nunnington and Pockley *York* 07-14; V from 14; Dioc Adv in Past Care from 07. *Kirkdale Vicarage, Main Road, Nawton, York YO62 7ST* T: (01439) 770760 E: andrewdesmet@btinternet.com

DE VERNY, David Dietrich Schuld. b 55. Trier Univ MTh 81. **d** 83 **p** 83. Asst Chapl Bonn *Eur* 83; C Henfield w Shermanbury and Woodmancote *Chich* 84-86; C Westmr St Sav and St Jas Less *Lon* 86-88; P-in-c Cheddington w Mentmore and Marsworth *Ox* 88-90; Gen Sec Fellowship of St Alb and St Sergius 90-92; Chapl for Migrant Workers *Linc* 06-08; Dioc Link Person for Ethnic Minority Anglicans 06-08; Hon C Boston 05-08; Chapl Hull Univ *York* 08-10; P-in-c Swineshead *Linc* 10-12; P-in-c Bicker, Donington, and Sutterton and Wigtoft 10-12; R Cheriton w Newington *Cant* 12-15; Chapl Haarlem *Eur* from 15. *Address temp unknown* M: 07761-469456 E: david.deverny129@btinternet.com

de VIAL, Raymond Michael. b 39. Oak Hill Th Coll 77. **d** 80 **p** 81. NSM Beckenham St Jo *Roch* 80-84; C Morden *S'wark* 84-88; TV 88-94; V Kingston Hill St Paul 94-04; rtd 04; PtO *S'wark* 04-05; Carl from 05. *39 Helme Drive, Kendal LA9 7JB* T: (01539) 729396 E: revray@btinternet.com

de WAAL, Victor Alexander. b 29. Pemb Coll Cam BA 49 MA 53 Nottm Univ Hon DD 83. Ely Th Coll 50. **d** 52 **p** 53. C Isleworth St Mary *Lon* 52-56; Chapl Ely Th Coll 56-59; Chapl K Coll Cam 59-63; Hon C Nottingham St Mary *S'well* 63-69; Chapl Nottm Univ 63-69; Can Res and Chan Linc Cathl 69-76; Dean Cant 76-86; PtO *Heref* 88-99; rtd 90; Chapl Soc of Sacred Cross Tymawr 90-00; LtO *Mon* 90-02; PtO from 02. *6 St James Close, Bishop Street, London N1 8PH* T: (020) 7354 2741 E: victordewaal@aol.com

DE WIT, Canon John. b 47. Oriel Coll Ox BA 69 MA 73 Clare Coll Cam BA 78 MA 84. Westcott Ho Cam 75. **d** 78 **p** 79. C The Quinton *Birm* 78-81; TV Solihull 81-85; V Kings Heath 85-94; RD Moseley 91-94; P-in-c Hampton in Arden 94-04; Chapl Utrecht w Zwolle *Eur* 04-12; Adn NW Eur 08-12; rtd 12; PtO *Ox* from 12. *21 Harding Close, Faringdon SN7 7SJ* T: (01367) 243331

DE WOLF, Mark Anthony. b 32. BA 55. Ely Th Coll 56. **d** 59 **p** 60. C Hackney Wick St Mary of Eton w St Aug *Lon* 59-64; P-in-c Brooklyn St Jo & Sheepshead Bay Em USA 64-66; R Amityville St Mary 67-75; R Stamford St Andr 75-06; rtd 06. *9 Weetamoe Farm Drive, Bristol RI 02809-5199, USA*

DEACON, Charles Edward. b 57. Westf Coll Lon BSc 78. Ridley Hall Cam 92. **d** 94 **p** 95. C Ex St Jas 94-98; V Shiphay Collaton from 98. *St John's Vicarage, 83 Cadewell Lane, Torquay TQ2 7HP* T: (01803) 401316

DEACON, Donald (Brother Angelo). Chich Th Coll 66. **d** 68 **p** 69. SSF from 63; LtO *Man* 69-70; USA 70-72; C Kennington St Jo *S'wark* 72-74; C Wilton Place St Paul *Lon* 74-75; Angl-Franciscan Rep Ecum Cen Assisi *Eur* 75; PtO *Sarum* 78-82; LtO *Chelmsf* 82-90; *Birm* 90-93; PtO *Linc* 94-97; rtd 98; LtO *Lon* 98-07; *Chich* from 07. *3 Bramwell Lodge, Brighton Road, Woodmancote, Henfield BN5 9SX*

DEACON, John. b 37. Arm Aux Min Course 87. **d** 90 **p** 91. NSM Enniscorthy w Clone, Clonmore, Monart etc *C & O* 90-05; rtd 05. *The Rectory, Creagh, Gorey, Co Wexford, Republic of Ireland* T: (00353) (53) 942 0354

DEACON, Mrs Selina Frances. b 52. SRN 74. Ripon Coll Cuddesdon 01. **d** 03 **p** 04. C White Horse *Sarum* 03-07; P-in-c Studley 07-12; V from 12; RD Bradford from 13. *The Vicarage, 340 Frome Road, Studley, Trowbridge BA14 0ED* T: (01225) 753162 M: 07867-521909 E: selinadeacon@hotmail.com

DEACON, Susan. b 47. **d** 14 **p** 15. OLM Spring Line Gp *Linc* from 14; OLM Owmby Gp from 14. *Parsonage Lodge, High Street, Scampton, Lincoln LN1 2SE* T: (01522) 730167 E: susan.deacon3@btinternet.com

DEACON, Preb Timothy Randall. b 55. Chich Th Coll 79. **d** 80 **p** 81. C Whitleigh *Ex* 80-83; P-in-c Devonport St Aubyn 83-88; P-in-c Newton Ferrers w Revelstoke 88-94; R 94-07; P-in-c Holbeton 93-07; TR Brixham w Churston Ferrers and Kingswear 07-13; RD Ivybridge 98-03; P-in-c Lifton, Broadwoodwidger, Stowford etc from 13; Preb Ex Cathl from 08. *The Rectory, Lifton PL16 0BJ* T: (01566) 784228 E: revtimdeacon@hotmail.co.uk

DEADMAN, Richard George Spencer. b 63. Ex Univ BA 85. Coll of Resurr Mirfield 86. **d** 88 **p** 89. C Grangetown *York* 88-91; P-in-c 91-93; V 93-96; V Wallsend St Luke *Newc* 96-01; V Newc St Phil and St Aug and St Matt w St Mary from 01. *St Matthew's Vicarage, 10 Winchester Terrace, Newcastle upon Tyne NE4 6EY* T: 0191-232 9039 E: richardgsd@aol.com

DEAKIN, Christopher Harold. b 49. ARMCM 72. Qu Coll Birm 02. **d** 04 **p** 05. C Wrockwardine Deanery *Lich* 04-07; P-in-c Bicton, Montford w Shrawardine and Fitz 07-14; P-in-c Leaton and Albrighton w Battlefield 07-14; rtd 14; P-in-c Hargrave *Ches* from 14. *The Vicarage, Church Lane, Hargrave, Chester CH3 7RN* T: (01829) 781378 E: revdeakin@gmail.com

DEAKIN, John David. b 58. Qu Coll Birm BA 03. **d** 03 **p** 04. C Blakenall Heath *Lich* 03-07; TV Willenhall H Trin 07-11; TV Bentley Em and Willenhall H Trin 11-15; TR from 15. *129 Essington Road, Willenhall WV12 5DT* T: (01922) 409460

DEAKIN, Preb John Hartley. b 27. K Coll Cam BA 50 MA 63. Cranmer Hall Dur. **d** 65 **p** 66. C Newcastle St Geo *Lich* 65-70; V Cotes Heath 70-84; RD Eccleshall 82-92; R Standon and Cotes Heath 84-95; Preb Lich Cathl 88-02; Sub Chapl HM Pris Drake Hall 89-95; rtd 95; Hon C Kinver and Enville *Lich* 95-02; PtO *Heref* 04-11. *8C Cliff Road, Bridgnorth WV16 4EY* T: (01746) 762574

DEAKIN, Paul David. b 62. Sheff Univ BA 13. Coll of Resurr Mirfield 11. **d** 13 **p** 14. C Bramhall *Ches* 13-14; C Hale and Ashley from 14. *75 Dairyground Road, Bramhall, Stockport SK7 2QW* M: 07813-368845 E: revdpauldeakin@gmail.com

DEAMER, Mrs Carylle. b 40. SAOMC 96. **d** 99 **p** 00. OLM Riverside *Ox* 99-05; rtd 05; PtO *Ox* 05-08; *B & W* from 09. *7 Coombe Close, Castle Cary BA7 7HJ* T: (01963) 359243 E: rev.carylle@deamer.me.uk

DEAN, The Ven Alan. b 38. Hull Univ BA 61. Qu Coll Birm. **d** 63 **p** 64. C Clitheroe St Mary *Blackb* 63-67; C Burnley St Pet 67-68; CF 68-93; Dep Chapl Gen and Adn for the Army 93-95; QHC 93-95; rtd 96; PtO *York* from 95. *1 Midway Avenue, Nether Poppleton, York YO26 6NT* T: (01904) 785305

DEAN, Andrew James. b 40. FCII ACIArb. WEMTC 92. **d** 95 **p** 96. NSM Rodbourne Cheney *Bris* 95-05; rtd 05; PtO *Bris* from 05. *Koinonia, 2 Wicks Close, Haydon Wick, Swindon SN25 1QH* T: (01793) 725526

DEAN, Canon Arthur. b 32. Southn Univ CQSW 80. Wesley Coll Leeds 55 S Dios Minl Tr Scheme 89. **d** 90 **p** 90. NSM Eastney *Portsm* 90-96; P-in-c Portsea St Alb 96-02; Hon Can Portsm Cathl 02; rtd 02; PtO *Portsm* from 02. *9 Kingsley Road, Southsea PO4 8HJ* T: (023) 9273 5773 M: 07855-146929 E: annenarthur.dean@btopenworld.com

DEAN, Benjamin Timothy Frederic. b 70. Lon Bible Coll BA 93 K Coll Lon MA 94 Selw Coll Cam MPhil 02 PhD 06. Ridley Hall Cam 04. **d** 07. C Georgeham *Ex* 07-08; Lect Geo Whitefield Coll S Africa from 08. *George Whitefield College, PO Box 64, Muizenberg, 7950 South Africa* T: (0027) (21) 788 1652 E: btfd@mac.com

DEAN, Hazel Michaela. b 48. **d** 14 **p** 15. OLM Long Sutton w Lutton etc *Linc* from 14. *Milldean Cottage, Broadgate, Sutton St James, Spalding PE12 0EL* T: (01945) 440347 E: hazel-makaila.dean@sky.com

DEAN, John Milner. b 27. S'wark Ord Course 69. **d** 72 **p** 73. C Lewisham St Mary *S'wark* 72-75; C Merton St Mary 75-77; V S Beddington St Mich 77-97; rtd 97. *69 Groveside Close, Carshalton SM5 2ER* T: (020) 8669 9369

DEAN, Jonathan Charles. b 57. St Cath Coll Cam MA 83. NEOC 04. **d** 07 **p** 08. NSM Gt Ayton w Easby and Newton under Roseberry *York* from 07. *The White House, 2 Dikes Lane, Great Ayton, Middlesbrough TS9 6HJ* T: (01642) 722649 E: jondean@cantab.net

DEAN, Mrs Linda Louise. b 39. **d** 04 **p** 05. NSM Primrose Hill St Mary w Avenue Road St Paul *Lon* 04-13. *52 Lanchester Road, London N6 4TA* T: (020) 8883 5417 E: linda@lindadean52.wanadoo.co.uk

DEAN, Lucas John William. b 57. St Jo Coll Nottm 05. **d** 07 **p** 08. C St Laur in Thanet *Cant* 07-11; V Hollington St Jo *Chich* from 11. *The Vicarage, 94 Lower Glen Road, St Leonards-on-Sea TN37 7AR* T: (01424) 751103 M: 07712-834472 E: ljwdean@hotmail.com

DEAN, Malcolm. b 34. Tyndale Hall Bris 67. **d** 69 **p** 70. C Daubhill *Man* 69-73; P-in-c Constable Lee 73-74; V 74-79; P-in-c Everton St Sav w St Cuth *Liv* 79-86; P-in-c Anfield SS Simon and Jude 81-86; V Walton Breck Ch Ch 86-89; rtd 89; PtO *Man* from 89. *40 Grasmere Road, Haslingden, Rossendale BB4 4EB* T: (01706) 215953

DEAN, Margaret Heath. b 50. Newton Park Coll Bris BEd 72. STETS 05. **d** 07 **p** 08. C Farncombe *Guildf* 07-11; R Reepham, Hackford w Whitwell, Kerdiston etc *Nor* from 11. *The Rectory, 26 Station Road, Reepham, Norwich NR10 4LJ* T: (01603) 879275 E: margaretdean@cnet.org

DEAN, Mark William John. b 58. **d** 10 **p** 11. NSM N Greenford All Hallows *Lon* 10-13; Chapl Univ of the Arts from 13; PtO *S'wark* from 13. *76 Essendine Road, London W9 2LY* T: (020) 7289 7900 M: 07960-793683 E: md@tailbiter.com

DEAN, Simon Timothy Michael Rex. b 62. Liv Univ BEng 83. Ridley Hall Cam 86. **d** 89 **p** 90. C St German's Cathl 89-92; V Castletown 92-05; PtO *Cant* 08-11. *11 Viking Court, St Stephen's Close, Canterbury CT2 7HZ*

DEAN, Timothy Charles Painter. b 50. STETS MA 08. **d** 07 **p** 08. NSM Godalming *Guildf* 07-11; CMD Officer *Nor* from 11; NSM Reepham, Hackford w Whitwell, Kerdiston etc from 11; RD Sparham from 14. *The Rectory, 26 Station Road, Reepham, Norwich NR10 4LJ* T: (01603) 871062 *or* 882339 E: timdean@cnet.org *or* tim.dean@norwich.anglican.org

DEAN, Trevor Stephen. b 58. Lon Hosp MB, BS 81. Trin Coll Bris BA 03. **d** 10 **p** 11. NSM Nailsea H Trin *B & W* from 10. *3 Ilminster Close, Nailsea, Bristol BS48 4YU* T: (01275) 851218 M: 07905-757649 E: trevor.dean@blueyonder.co.uk

DEAN-REVILL, David Frank. b 68. Univ Coll Ches BA 06. NOC 03. **d** 06 **p** 07. C Dinnington w Laughton and Throapham *Sheff* 06-09; P-in-c Shiregreen from 09. *The Vicarage, 510 Bellhouse Road, Sheffield S5 0RG* T: 0114-245 6526 E: daviddeanrevill@hotmail.com

DEANE, Mrs Angela Christine. b 52. WEMTC 00. **d** 04 **p** 05. NSM Credenhill w Brinsop and Wormsley etc *Heref* from 04. *The Oak, Mansel Lacy, Hereford HR4 7HQ* T: (01981) 590615 E: angiestutheoak@lineone.net

DEANE, Canon John. **d** 02 **p** 03. NSM Stranorlar w Meenglas and Kilteevogue *D & R* 02-06; NSM Derg w Termonamongan 06-07; NSM Urney w Sion Mills 07-08; Bp's C Ardara w Glencolumbkille, Inniskeel etc 08-12; I from 12; Can Raphoe Cathl from 14. *The Rectory, Ardara, Co Donegal, Republic of Ireland* T: (00353) (74) 954 1124 E: revjohndeane@yahoo.ie

DEANE, Nicholas Talbot Bryan. b 46. Bris Univ BA 69. Clifton Th Coll 70. **d** 72 **p** 73. C Accrington Ch Ch *Blackb* 72-75; OMF Korea 75-89; P-in-c Newburgh *Liv* 90-93; P-in-c Westhead 90-93; V Newburgh w Westhead 93-97; R Chadwell *Chelmsf* 97-11; rtd 11; C Waverton w Aldford and Bruera *Ches* 11-15. *The Rectory, Green Lake Lane, Aldford, Chester CH3 6HW* T: (01244) 620281 E: nic.deane@btinternet.com

DEANE, Canon Robert William. b 52. CITC. **d** 85 **p** 86. C Raheny w Coolock *D & G* 85-88; I Clonsast w Rathangan, Thomastown etc *M & K* 88-00; Can Kildare Cathl 97-00; Can Meath Cathl 98-00; I Swords w Donabate and Kilsallaghan *D & G* from 00; Can Ch Ch Cathl Dublin from 08. *The Rectory, Church Road, Swords, Co Dublin, Republic of Ireland* T: (00353) (1) 840 2308 E: rwdeane@eircom.net

DEANE, Stuart William. b 45. Sarum & Wells Th Coll 86. **d** 88 **p** 89. C Bromyard *Heref* 88-92; V Astley, Clive, Grinshill and Hadnall *Lich* 92-98; TV Cen Telford 98-00; TR 00-05; rtd 05; PtO *Heref* from 07. *38 Crest Court, Hereford HR1 9QD* T: (01432) 351937

DEANS, Bruce Gibson. b 64. MCIBS 86. Wycliffe Hall Ox 02. **d** 04 **p** 05. C Hartley Wintney, Elvetham, Winchfield etc *Win* 04-08; R Shedfield and Wickham *Portsm* 08-15; P-in-c Fareham St Jo from 15. *3A Upper St Michael's Grove, Fareham PO14 1DN* E: brucedeans@thebearsden.fsnet.co.uk

DEANS, Robert. b 58. Stirling Univ BA 82 Edin Univ MSc 83 Anglia Ruskin Univ MA 12. ERMC 09. **d** 12 **p** 13. NSM Pet St Jo from 12. *8 Minster Precincts, Peterborough PE1 1XS* T: (01733) 735301 M: 07533-425691 E: robert.deans@sky.com

DEAR, Graham Frederick. b 44. St Luke's Coll Ex CertEd 66. Wycliffe Hall Ox 67. **d** 70 **p** 71. C Chigwell *Chelmsf* 70-73; C Chingford SS Pet and Paul 73-75; V Southchurch Ch Ch 75-82; CF 82-89; P-in-c The Cowtons *Ripon* 89-94; RE Adv 89-94; V Startforth and Bowes and Rokeby w Brignall 94-97; Chapl HM Pris Garth 97-01; rtd 09; PtO *Leeds* from 01. *1 The Old Wynd, Bellerby, Leyburn DL8 5QJ* T: (01969) 623960

DEAR, Neil Douglas Gauntlett. b 35. Linc Th Coll 87. **d** 89 **p** 90. C Framlingham w Saxtead *St E* 89-92; P-in-c Eyke w Bromeswell, Rendlesham, Tunstall etc 92-98; Chapl Local Health Partnerships NHS Trust 98-02; Chapl Cen Suffolk Primary Care Trust 02-05; P-in-c Worlingworth, Southolt, Tannington, Bedfield etc *St E* 02-05; rtd 05; PtO *St E* from 05. *Peacehaven, Duke Street, Stanton, Bury St Edmunds IP31 2AB* T: (01359) 252001

DEAR, Virginia Anne. b 65. Westcott Ho Cam. **d** 13 **p** 14. C Hertford *St Alb* from 13. *8 Calton Avenue, Hertford SG14 2EP* E: ginni@blackberry.orange.co.uk

DEARDEN, Geoffrey. b 36. Salford Univ MSc 74. CBDTI 05. **d** 06 **p** 07. NSM Hurst Green and Mitton *Bradf* 06-10; PtO *Leeds* from 10. *14 Church Close, Waddington, Clitheroe BB7 3HX* T: (01200) 427380 E: geoffandann@btinternet.com

DEARDEN, Canon Philip Harold. b 43. AKC 65. **d** 66 **p** 67. C Haslingden w Haslingden Grane *Blackb* 66-69; C Burnley St Pet 69-71; V Langho Billington 71-78; TR Darwen St Pet w

Hoddlesden 78-91; RD Darwen 86-91; V Altham w Clayton le Moors 91-97; RD Accrington 95-97; V Clitheroe St Mary 97-08; Hon Can Blackb Cathl 96-08; rtd 08; PtO *Blackb* from 08; *Carl* from 11. *16 Sun Street, Ulverston LA12 7BX* T: (01229) 480155 E: philip.dearden@btinternet.com

DEARING, Henry Ernest. b 26. Lon Univ BD 53. St Deiniol's Hawarden 55. **d** 55 **p** 56. C Skerton St Chad *Blackb* 55-57; V Huncoat 57-60; rtd 95. *7 Llewelyn Avenue, Llandudno LL30 2ER*

DEARING, Trevor. b 33. Lon Univ BD 58. Qu Coll Birm MA 63. **d** 61 **p** 62. C Todmorden *Wakef* 61-63; V Silkstone 63-66; V Northowram 66-68; C Harlow New Town w Lt Parndon *Chelmsf* 68-70; V Hainault 70-75; Dir Healing Miss 75-79; Hon C Gt Ilford St Andr 75-79; PtO *Linc* 80-81 and 99-02; USA 81-83; rtd 83. *75 Banks Crescent, Stamford PE9 1FF* T: (01780) 751680

DEARMER, Juliet. *See* WOOLLCOMBE, Juliet

DEARNLEY, Miss Helen Elizabeth Booker. b 77. De Montfort Univ LLB 98 Cam Univ BTh 02. Westcott Ho Cam 99. **d** 02 **p** 03. C Knighton St Mary Magd *Leic* 02-06; Co-ord Chapl HM Pris Leic 06-13; HQ Chapl Adv Nat Offender Management Service from 13. T: 03000-476790
E: helen.dearnley@noms.gsi.gov.uk

DEARNLEY, John Wright. b 37. Open Univ BA 81. **d** 99 **p** 05. NSM Llandogo w Whitebrook Chpl and Tintern Parva *Mon* 99-15; P-in-c 07-15; rtd 15. *2 Greenbanks, Llandogo, Monmouth NP25 4TG* T: (01594) 530080

DEARNLEY, Canon Mark Christopher. b 59. Cranmer Hall Dur 84. **d** 87 **p** 88. C Purley Ch Ch *S'wark* 87-91; C Addiscombe St Mary 91-93; C Addiscombe St Mary Magd w St Martin 93-94; V Hook 94-02; R Wendover and Halton Ox from 02; AD Wendover from 04; Hon Can Ch Ch from 14. *The Vicarage, 34A Dobbins Lane, Wendover, Aylesbury HP22 6DH* T: (01296) 622230
E: mark.dearnley@btinternet.com

DEARNLEY, Preb Patrick Walter. b 34. Nottm Univ BA 55 LTh 75. ALCD 64. **d** 64 **p** 65. C New Malden and Coombe *S'wark* 64-68; C Portswood Ch Ch *Win* 68-71; C Leeds St Geo *Ripon* 71-74; Hon C Nottingham St Nic *S'well* 74-77; P-in-c Holloway Em w Hornsey Road St Barn *Lon* 77-85; AD Islington 80-85; Abp's Officer for UPA 85-90; Preb St Paul's Cathl 86-91; P-in-c Waterloo St Jo *Liv* 91-99; rtd 99; PtO *Leeds* from 00. *14 Beanlands Parade, Ilkley LS29 8EW* T: (01943) 603927
E: gilrea@blueyonder.co.uk

DEAS, Leonard Stephen. b 52. New Coll Ox BA 75 CertEd 76 MA 78. St Mich Coll Llan 81. **d** 82 **p** 83. C Dowlais *Llan* 82-84; Chapl St Mich Coll Llan 84-85; Chapl Univ of Wales (Cardiff) *Llan* 85-86; V Newbridge *Mon* 86-93; Can Res St Woolos Cathl 92-96; Master Charterhouse Hull from 96. *The Charterhouse, Charterhouse Lane, Hull HU2 8AF* T: (01482) 329307

DEAVE, Mrs Gillian Mary. b 31. EMMTC 79. **dss** 82 **d** 87 **p** 94. Nottingham St Pet and St Jas *S'well* 82-87; Par Dn 87-91; rtd 91; PtO *S'well* from 91; *Leic* from 91. *Greensmith Cottage, 8 City Road, Stathern, Melton Mowbray LE14 4HE* T: (01949) 860340
E: gilliandeave@btinternet.com

DEAVES, Mrs Hannah Claire. b 73. York Univ BSc 94 Bp Grosseteste Coll PGCE 95 Univ of Wales (Ban) BTh 06. **d** 11 **p** 12. OLM Triangle, St Matt and All SS *St E* 11-15; PtO from 15. *2 Exeter Road, Ipswich IP3 8JL* T: (01473) 399635
M: 07906-372733 E: hannahdeaves@yahoo.co.uk

DEBENHAM, Peter Mark. b 68. Nottm Univ BSc 89 PhD 94. EAMTC 98. **d** 01 **p** 03. NSM Burwell *Ely* 01-02; NSM Swaffham Bulbeck and Swaffham Prior w Reach 01-02; PtO 02-03; NSM Fordham St Pet 03-08; NSM Kennett 03-08; NSM Three Rivers Gp from 08. *23 Burleigh Rise, Burwell, Cambridge CB25 0RS* T: (01638) 603142 E: peter.debenham@ely.anglican.org

DEBNEY, Nicholas Johnathan. b 72. SWMTC 10. **d** 13 **p** 14. C Dartmouth and Dittisham *Ex* from 13. *22 Church Road, Dartmouth TQ6 9HQ* T: (01803) 839162
E: fr.debney@hotmail.co.uk

DEBOO, Canon Alan John. b 45. Qu Coll Cam BA 73 MA 77. Westcott Ho Cam 72. **d** 74 **p** 75. C Brackley St Pet w St Jas 74-77; PtO *Sarum* 85-94; NSM Wexcombe 94-02; NSM Savernake 02-09 and from 13; Bp's Officer for NSMs 03-09; Bp's Adv for Assoc Min from 09; Can and Preb Sarum Cathl from 05. *Mayzells Cottage, Collingbourne Kingston, Marlborough SN8 3SD* T: (01264) 850683 E: alandeboo@aol.com

DEBOYS, David Gordon. b 54. QUB BD 76 Wolfs Coll Ox MLitt. Ridley Hall Cam 90. **d** 92 **p** 93. C Ipswich St Aug *St E* 92-93; C Whitton and Thurleston w Akenham 93-95; R Hardwick *Ely* 95-00; R Toft w Caldecote and Childerley 95-00; V Cambridge St Jas 00-07; Dir Focus Chr Inst Cambridge 00-07; V Ealing St Barn *Lon* 07-12; C Tewkesbury w Walton Cardiff and Twyning *Glouc* 12-15; Dioc Worship Officer 12-15; TV Southampton (City Cen) *Win* from 15. *St Michael's Vicarage, 55 Bugle Street, Southampton SO14 2AG* M: 07773-613172
E: daviddeboys@btconnect.com

DEDMAN, Canon Roger James. b 45. Oak Hill Th Coll 68. **d** 71 **p** 72. C Gresley *Derby* 71-74; C Ipswich St Fran *St E* 74-79; P-in-c Bildeston w Wattisham 79-92; P-in-c Bramford 92-10; P-in-c Somersham w Flowton and Offton w Willisham 94-02; P-in-c Gt and Lt Blakenham w Baylham and Nettlestead 02-10; RD Bosmere 96-01 and 05-07; Hon Can St E Cathl 01-10; rtd 10; PtO *Leeds* from 10; *St E* from 10. *10 St Martin's Field, Otley LS21 2FN* E: roger.dedman@talktalk.net

DEE, Clive Hayden. b 61. Ripon Coll Cuddesdon 86. **d** 89 **p** 90. C Bridgnorth, Tasley, Astley Abbotts, etc *Heref* 89-93; P-in-c Wellington w Pipe-cum-Lyde and Moreton-on-Lugg 93-96. *Ross Cottage, Crumpton Hill Road, Storridge, Malvern WR13 5HE* T: (01886) 832639

DEED, Michael James. b 77. **d** 04 **p** 05. C Notting Dale St Clem w St Mark and St Jas *Lon* 04-07; C Burlington St Chris Canada from 07. *662 Guelph Line, Burlington ON L7R 3M8, Canada* T: (001) (905) 320 6034 E: michael.deed@googlemail.com

DEEDES, Ms Rosemary Anne. b 66. Birm Univ BA 87 City Univ 90. Westcott Ho Cam 94. **d** 96 **p** 97. C St Botolph Aldgate w H Trin Minories *Lon* 96-99; Asst Chapl HM Pris Holloway 99-02; Chapl HM Pris Downview 02-10; Chapl HM Pris Is of Wight 10-15; Chapl Cov Univ from 15. *129A London Road, Coventry CV1 2JQ* T: (024) 7625 2106
E: rosie.deedes@coventry.ac.uk

DEEGAN, Arthur Charles. b 49. CertEd 71 Birm Univ BEd 86. Qu Coll Birm 86. **d** 88 **p** 89. C Leic St Jas 88-91; C Melton Gt Framland 91-92; TV 92-93; TV Melton Mowbray 93-96; R Barwell w Potters Marston and Stapleton 96-08; P-in-c Braunstone Town w Thorpe Astley from 08; CF (TA) from 95; Chapl ACF Leics, Northants, and Rutland from 95. *The Vicarage, 36 Woodcote Road, Leicester LE3 2WD* T: 0116-224 8346 E: ac.deegan@ntlworld.com

DEEGAN, Michael Joseph. b 54. Ripon Coll Cuddesdon. **d** 09 **p** 10. Dir Soc Justice and C Sarum Cathl 09-12; Warden Pilsdon Community from 12. *Pilsdon Manor, Pilsdon, Bridport DT6 5NZ* T: (01308) 868308 F: 868161 M: 07502-216607
E: mdeegan01@aol.com

DEELEY, Mrs Elke Christiane. b 58. Birm Univ BA 81. SWMTC 99. **d** 02 **p** 03. NSM Roche and Withiel *Truro* 02-11; NSM St Columb Major w St Wenn 09-11; NSM St Wenn and Withiel from 11; Chapl Cornwall Partnership NHS Trust from 09. *44 Duporth Bay, St Austell PL26 6AQ* T: (01726) 63083
E: elke1@tinyonline.co.uk

DEEMING, Paul Leyland. b 44. CA Tr Coll 65 CMS Tr Coll Selly Oak 70. **d** 80 **p** 80. CMS Pakistan 71-82; R E and W Horndon w Lt Warley *Chelmsf* 83-89; V Gt Ilford St Andr 89-01; Co-ord Chapl Heatherwood & Wexham Park Hosps NHS Foundn Trust 01-09; rtd 09. *10 Glenthorn Road, Bexhill-on-Sea TN39 3QH* T: (01424) 222287
E: deeming346@btinternet.com

DEENY, David Anthony. b 61. Witwatersrand Univ BA 81. ERMC 03. **d** 06 **p** 07. NSM Alresford *Chelmsf* 06-10; Hon C Alresford and Frating w Thorrington 10-11; Chapl John Wollaston Angl Community Sch Australia from 11. *John Wollaston Anglican Community School, Lake Road, Kelmscott WA 6111, Australia* T: (0061) (8) 9495 8100
E: davedeeny@aol.com

DEER, Diane Antonia. *See* JOHNSON, Diane Antonia

DEES, Miss Marilyn Monica (Mandy). b 34. Nottm Univ BSc 55 PGCE 56. WEMTC 94. **d** 96 **p** 97. NSM Fownhope w Mordiford, Brockhampton etc *Heref* from 96. *9 Fairfield Green, Fownhope, Hereford HR1 4NL* T: (01432) 860369

DEETH, William Stanley. b 38. St Pet Coll Ox BA 59 MA 67. St Steph Ho Ox 66. **d** 68 **p** 69. C Eastbourne St Mary *Chich* 68-71; C Benwell St Jas *Newc* 71-75; C-in-c Byker St Martin CD 75-76; P-in-c Byker St Martin 76; V 76-89; P-in-c Bothal 89-91; R Bothal and Pegswood w Longhirst 91-94; rtd 94; PtO *Newc* 94-08. *2 All Saints Square, Ripon HG4 1FN* T: (01765) 690366

DEGG, Miss Jennifer Margaret. b 39. Open Univ BA 85 Rolle Coll CertEd 64. NOC. **d** 06 **p** 07. NSM Saddleworth *Man* 06-09; PtO from 09. *2 Lowerfields, Dobcross, Oldham OL3 5NW* E: jennydegg@onetel.com

DEHOOP, Brother Thomas Anthony. b 38. Bp's Univ Lennox BA 63 LTh 63. **d** 68 **p** 69. C Fort George w Painthills Canada 68-70; I Mistassini 70-72; R La Tuque 72-75; Assoc P Pierrefonds 75-79; SSF from 79; PtO *Sarum* 79-80; Hon C Toxteth St Marg *Liv* 80-85; Chapl Newsham Gen Hosp Liv 82-85; P-in-c Cambridge St Benedict *Ely* 85-88; V 88-92; PtO *Liv* 92-96; *Ely* 92-96; *Eur* from 94. *Glasshampton Monastery, Shrawley, Worcester WR6 6TQ* T: (01299) 896345
E: glasshamptonssf@franciscans.org.uk

DEIGHTON, Gary. b 61. Dundee Univ MA 83 Nottm Univ MA 89 Heythrop Coll Lon MA 11 PGCE 84. SWMTC 10. **d** 12 **p** 13. C Paignton St Jo *Ex* from 12. *Christchurch Vicarage, 133 Torquay Road, Paignton TQ3 2AG* T: (01803) 540086
E: gary.deighton@hotmail.co.uk

DEIGHTON, William John. b 44. Plymouth Poly CQSW 74. K Coll Lon AKC 68 St Boniface Warminster 68. **d** 69 **p** 70. C Kenwyn *Truro* 69-72; Hon C Winterbourne *Bris* 90-04. *22 Salem Road, Winterbourne, Bristol BS36 1QF* T: (01454) 778847

DEIMEL, Margaret Mary. b 49. CertEd 71. WMMTC 91. **d** 94 **p** 95. NSM Bidford-on-Avon *Cov* 94-97; NSM Studley 97-10; NSM Spernall, Morton Bagot and Oldberrow 07-10; Dioc Adv on New Relig Movements 02-10; NSM Escomb *Dur* 10-14; NSM Etherley 10-14; NSM Witton Park 10-14; NSM Hamsterley and Witton-le-Wear 10-14; rtd 14; Adv on New Spiritual Movements *Newc* from 13. *Sherfield Cottage, Field Row, Crawleyside, Stanhope, Bishop Auckland DL13 2EE*

DEIMEL, Richard Witold. b 49. Lon Univ BA 84. Cranmer Hall Dur 86. **d** 88 **p** 89. C Bilton *Cov* 88-93; P-in-c Studley 93-97; V 97-10; P-in-c Spernall, Morton Bagot and Oldberrow 07-10; RD Alcester 08-10; Dioc Adv on New Relig Movements 02-10; P-in-c Escomb *Dur* 10-14; P-in-c Etherley 10-14; P-in-c Witton Park 10-14; P-in-c Hamsterley and Witton-le-Wear 10-14; rtd 14; Dioc Adv on New Spiritual Movements *Dur* from 10; Adv on New Spiritual Movements *Newc* from 13. *Sherfield Cottage, 3 Field Row, Crawleyside, Stanhope, Bishop Auckland DL13 2EE*

DEKKER, Denise Rosemary Irene. b 43. Th Ext Educn Coll 90. **d** 95 **p** 96. C Stutterheim S Africa 95-99; P-in-c 99-04; P-in-c Kokstad 04-09; PtO *Win* 09-11; P-in-c Guernsey St Andr 11-15; NSM Coventry Caludon *Cov* from 15. *Address temp unknown* M: 07781-469241 E: dekkerd1@hotmail.com

del RIO, Michael Paul Juan. b 73. Univ of Wales (Cardiff) BScEcon 94 PGCE 00. Oak Hill Th Coll MTh 05. **d** 05 **p** 06. NSM Ealing St Mary *Lon* 05-10. *Apartment 19, 21 Whitestone Way, Croydon CR0 4WJ* T: (020) 8840 2208 E: michael@didasko.org.uk

DELAFORCE, Stephen Robert. b 52. Middx Poly BSc 80 Cranfield Inst of Tech MSc 88 Nottm Univ MA 03 CEng MIMechE 83. EMMTC 04. **d** 07 **p** 08. NSM Woodhouse, Woodhouse Eaves and Swithland *Leic* 07-10; C Beaumont Leys 10-15; P-in-c from 15. *97 Halifax Drive, Leicester LE4 2DR* E: steve.delaforce@googlemail.com

DELAMERE, Isaac George. b 71. CITC BTh 02. **d** 02 **p** 03. C Newtownards *D & D* 02-05; I Narraghmore and Timolin w Castledermot etc *D & G* 05-14; I Tullamore w Durrow, Newtownfertullagh, Rahan etc *M & K* from 14. *St Catherine's Rectory, Church Avenue, Tullamore, Co Offaly, Republic of Ireland* T: (00353) (57) 932 1731 M: 86-060 9241 E: revisaacdelamere@eircom.net *or* tullamore@meath.anglican.org

DELANEY, Anthony. b 65. St Jo Coll Nottm BTh 95. **d** 95 **p** 96. C Cullompton *Ex* 95-98; C Maidstone St Luke *Cant* 98-01; P-in-c W Horsley *Guildf* 01-03; R 03-08; PtO *Man* from 09. *97 Barlow Moor Road, Didsbury, Manchester M20 2GP* M: 07881-902966 E: antdel@tiscali.co.uk

DELANEY, Janet. b 50. STETS. **d** 07 **p** 08. C Wootton Bassett *Sarum* 07-11; R Askerswell, Loders, Powerstock and Symondsbury from 11; RD Lyme Bay from 14. *The Vicarage, Loders, Bridport DT6 3SA* T: (01308) 538118 E: reverendjan@thedelaneys.me.uk

DELANEY, The Ven Peter Anthony. b 39. MBE 01. AKC 65. **d** 66 **p** 67. C St Marylebone w H Trin *Lon* 66-70; Chapl Nat Heart Hosp *Lon* 66-70; Res Chapl Univ Ch Ch the K *Lon* 70-73; Can Res and Prec S'wark Cathl 73-77; V All Hallows by the Tower etc *Lon* 77-04; P-in-c St Kath Cree 98-02; Can Cyprus and the Gulf from 88; Preb St Paul's Cathl 95-99; Adn Lon 99-09; P-in-c St Steph Walbrook and St Swithun etc 04-14. *29 Portland Square, London E1W 2QR* T: (020) 7481 1786

DELAP, Ms Dana Lurkse. b 65. St Jo Coll Dur BA 87 MA 93 MATM 11. Cranmer Hall Dur 09. **d** 11 **p** 12. C Fenham St Jas and St Basil *Newc* 11-14; TV Vale and Cotswold Edge *Glouc* from 14. *The Vicarage, High Street, Blockley, Moreton-in-Marsh GL56 9ES* M: 07952-096789 T: (01386) 700676 E: dana@delap.org.uk

DELFGOU, John. b 35. Oak Hill Th Coll 81. **d** 84 **p** 85. NSM Loughton St Mary and St Mich *Chelmsf* 84-90; NSM Loughton St Jo 90-93; C 93-94; TV 94-00; rtd 01; PtO *Chelmsf* from 01. *20 Carroll Hill, Loughton IG10 1NN* T: (020) 8508 6333 E: jd0739@btinternet.com

DELFGOU, Jonathan Hawke. b 63. Aston Tr Scheme 89 Linc Th Coll BTh 94. **d** 94 **p** 95. C Greenstead *Chelmsf* 94-98; TV Wickford and Runwell from 98; Chapl Southend Community Care Services NHS Trust 98-99; Chapl S Essex Mental Health & Community Care NHS Trust from 00. *St Mary's Vicarage, Church End Lane, Runwell, Wickford SS11 7JQ* T: (01268) 732068

DELINGER, Ian Michael. b 70. Truman State Univ (USA) BSc 92 SS Coll Cam BTh 04. Westcott Ho Cam 01. **d** 04 **p** 05. C Chorlton-cum-Hardy St Clem *Man* 04-07; Chapl Ches Univ

from 08. *University of Chester, Warrington Campus, Crab Lane, Warrington WA2 0DB* T: (01925) 534361 E: i.delinger@chester.ac.uk

DELMEGE, Andrew Mark. b 68. Essex Univ BA 91 Southn Univ MTh 98. SWMTC 94. **d** 97 **p** 98. C Kings Heath *Birm* 97-01; V Brandwood from 01; Chapl to Deaf People 01-10; P-in-c Weoley Castle 10-14. *The Vicarage, 77 Doversley Road, Birmingham B14 6NN* T: 0121-456 1535 F: 246 6125 T: 0121-693 0217 *or* 246 6100 E: andydelmege@hotmail.com

DELVE, Eric David. b 42. Trin Coll Bris. **d** 89 **p** 90. NSM Bris St Matt and St Nath 89-92; P-in-c Kirkdale St Lawr *Liv* 93-96; V Maidstone St Luke *Cant* 96-12; AD Maidstone 99-03; Six Preacher Cant Cathl 99-09; rtd 13; PtO *Roch* from 13. *33 Parker Close, Gillingham ME8 9NQ*

DELVES, Canon Anthony James. b 47. Birm Univ BSocSc 70 Hull Univ PhD 94. St Steph Ho Ox 83. **d** 85 **p** 86. C Cantley *Sheff* 85-90; V Goldthorpe w Hickleton 90-07; Hon Can Sheff Cathl 98-07; AD Wath 00-06; rtd 07; PtO *Sheff* from 07; *Leeds* from 07. *4 Balmoral Street, Hebden Bridge HX7 8BJ* T: (01422) 843948 E: ajd@delwood.plus.com

DELVES (formerly MANHOOD), Canon Phyllis. b 32. Aston Tr Scheme 78 Qu Coll Birm 79. **dss** 82 **d** 87 **p** 94. Harwich *Chelmsf* 82-83; Dovercourt and Parkeston 83-85; Fawley *Win* 85-87; Par Dn 87-92; P-in-c Bournemouth St Aug 92-99; Hon Can Win Cathl 96-99; rtd 99; PtO *Win* from 01. *11 Rhyme Hall Mews, Fawley, Southampton SO45 1FX* T: (023) 8089 4450

DELVES BROUGHTON, Simon Brian Hugo. b 33. Ex Coll Ox BA 56 MA 64. Kelham Th Coll 56. **d** 59 **p** 60. Ox Miss to Calcutta India 60-64; C Skirbeck St Nic *Linc* 64-67; Chapl Chittagong E Pakistan/Bangladesh 67-69; V St Thos Cathl Dhaka 69-74; V Northampton Ch Ch *Pet* 74-95; Chapl Northn Gen Hosp 77-87; rtd 95; PtO *Ox* 95-00. *71A Observatory Street, Oxford OX2 6EP* T: (01865) 515463

DEMAIN, Peter James. b 64. Salford Univ BA 85. SNWTP 07. **d** 10 **p** 11. OLM Middleton and Thornham *Man* from 10. *3 St Gabriel's Close, Rochdale OL11 2TG* T: (01706) 522985 M: 07747-398012 E: peterdemain@tiscali.co.uk

DEMERY, Rupert Edward Rodier. b 72. Trin Hall Cam BA 94 MA 01 BTh 01. Ridley Hall Cam 98. **d** 01 **p** 02. C New Borough and Leigh *Sarum* 01-05; Lower Chapl Eton Coll from 05. *136A High Street, Eton, Windsor SL4 6AR* T: (01753) 441629 M: 07801-825671 E: r.demery@etoncollege.org.uk

DEMPSTER, Adrian. b 49. Newc Univ BSc 70. EMMTC 05. **d** 08 **p** 09. NSM Kirkby in Ashfield *S'well* 08-12; NSM Skegby w Teversal from 12. *105 Nottingham Road, Selston, Nottingham NG16 6BU* T: (01773) 811846 F: 0115-950 4646 M: 07971-142829 E: adrian@dempstera.freeserve.co.uk

den HAAN, Canon Peter Albert Percy. b 67. Wycliffe Hall Ox BA 07. **d** 08 **p** 09. C Bedworth *Cov* 08-13; PtO 13-15. *10 Monks Close, Cawston, Rugby CV22 7FP* T: (01788) 817194 E: peter@denhaan.co.uk

DENBY, Canon Paul. b 47. NW Ord Course 73. **d** 76 **p** 77. C Stretford All SS *Man* 76-80; V Stalybridge 80-87; Chapl Tameside Gen Hosp 82-87; Dir of Ords *Man* 87-95; LNSM Officer 91-95; Hon Can Man Cathl 92-95; Bp's Dom Chapl 94-95; Can Admin and Prec Man Cathl 95-07; rtd 07; PtO *Man* 07-08 and from 12. *14 Cranberry Drive, Bolton BL3 3TB* T: (01204) 655157 E: paul@denby94.wanadoo.co.uk

DENCH, Canon Christopher David. b 62. RGN 83. Aston Tr Scheme 86 Sarum & Wells Th Coll 88. **d** 91 **p** 92. C Crayford *Roch* 91-94; P-in-c Leybourne 94-98; R 98-05; Dioc Lay Tr Adv 01-05; Tr Officer for CME 03-10; Min Development Officer 05-10; Bp's Officer for Min and Tr from 10; Hon Can Roch Cathl from 11. *340 New Hythe Lane, Larkfield, Aylesford ME20 6RZ* T: (01732) 220245 E: chris.dench@rochester.anglican.org

DENERLEY, John Keith Christopher. b 34. Qu Coll Ox BA 58 MA 61. St Steph Ho Ox 58. **d** 61 **p** 62. C Airedale w Fryston *Wakef* 61-64; Chapl Sarum Th Coll 64-68; Min Can Cov Cathl 68-76; Chapl Lanchester Poly 70-76; Chapl The Dorothy Kerin Trust Burrswood 76-85; V Trellech and Cwmcarvan *Mon* 85-86; V Penallt 85-86; V Penallt and Trellech 87-99; Chapl Ty Mawr Convent (Wales) 85-90; RD Monmouth *Mon* 93-99; rtd 99; PtO *Glouc* from 00. *1 The Pales, English Bicknor, Coleford GL16 7PQ* T: (01594) 860028

DENGATE, Richard Henry. b 39. Cant Sch of Min 82. **d** 85 **p** 86. NSM Wittersham w Stone and Ebony *Cant* 85; R Sandhurst w Newenden 90-01; rtd 01; PtO *Cant* from 01. *Apuldram, Main Street, Peasemarsh, Rye TN31 6UL* T: (01797) 230980

DENHAM, Anthony Christopher. b 43. Keble Coll Ox BA 65 MA 70. Oak Hill Th Coll 91. **d** 93 **p** 94. C Hythe *Cant* 93-97; V Haddenham w Cuddington, Kingsey etc *Ox* 97-08; rtd 08; PtO *Guildf* from 08. *3 The Larches, Woking GU21 4RE* T: (01483) 823310 E: a.chris.denham@googlemail.com

DENHAM, Nicholas Philip. b 50. Salford Univ BSc 72 Dur Univ MA 10 Birm Univ CertEd 74. Wycliffe Hall Ox 87. **d** 89 **p** 90. C Bishopwearmouth St Gabr *Dur* 89-90; C Chester le Street 90-92; TV Rushden w Newton Bromswold *Pet* 92-95; R Teigh w Whissendine and Market Overton 95-02; P-in-c Greetham and Thistleton w Stretton and Clipsham 01-02; RD Rutland 01-02; TR Bedworth *Cov* 02-05; V Escomb *Dur* 05-08; R Etherley 05-08; V Witton Park 05-08; V Hamsterley and Witton-le-Wear 05-08; rtd 08; PtO *Ox* 09-14; *Ely* from 14. *23 Meadow Way, Mepal, Ely CB6 2GH* E: nickden@btinternet.com

DENHOLM, Robert Jack. b 31. Edin Th Coll 53. **d** 56 **p** 57. C Dundee St Mary Magd *Bre* 56-59; C Edin St Pet 59-61; R Bridge of Allan *St And* 61-69; Chapl Stirling Univ 67-69; R N Berwick *Edin* 69-80; R Gullane 76-80; R Edin St Mark 80-90; Can St Mary's Cathl 88-90; rtd 90. *15 Silverknowes, Midway, Edinburgh EH4 5PP* T: 0131-312 6462 E: jackdenholm@googlemail.com

DENIS LE SEVE, Hilary. *See* LE SEVE, Hilary Jane

DENISON, Canon Keith Malcolm. b 45. Down Coll Cam BA 67 MA 71 PhD 70. Westcott Ho Cam 70. **d** 71 **p** 72. C Chepstow *Mon* 71-72; C Bassaleg 72-75; Post-Ord Tr Officer 75-85; V Mathern and Mounton 75-80; V Mathern and Mounton w St Pierre 80-85; RD Chepstow 82-85; V Risca 85-91; V Goldcliffe and Whitson and Nash 91-96; Dioc Dir of Educn Monmouth 91-11; Hon Can St Woolos Cathl 91-94; Can St Woolos Cathl 94-11; Can Res St Woolos Cathl 96-11; rtd 11. *8 West Mill, Easton on the Hill, Stamford PE9 3NX* E: keith_denison@hotmail.com

DENISON, Philip. b 55. York Univ BA 77 CertEd. St Jo Coll Nottm 83. **d** 86 **p** 87. C Barnoldswick w Bracewell *Bradf* 86-88; P-in-c Basford St Leodegarius *S'well* 88-91; C Basford w Hyson Green 91-94; V Nether Stowey w Over Stowey *B & W* 94-04; R Aisholt, Enmore, Goathurst, Nether Stowey etc 05; RD Quantock 01-05; PtO 06-10; C Alfred Jewel from 10. *15 Sylvan Way, Monkton Heathfield, Taunton TA2 8PH* T: (01823) 410021 E: denisonphil15@hotmail.com

DENLEY, Trevor Maurice. b 47. **d** 06 **p** 07. Partnership P E Bris from 06; OLM Bristol St Aid w St Geo from 06. *31 Dundridge Gardens, Bristol BS5 8SZ* T: 0117-961 4468 M: 07960-329127

DENMAN, Frederick George. b 46. Chich Th Coll 67. **d** 70 **p** 71. C Stafford St Mary *Lich* 70-72; C Ascot Heath *Ox* 72-75; P-in-c Culham 75-77; P-in-c Sutton Courtenay w Appleford 75-77; TV Dorchester 78-81; Chapl Henley Memorial Hosp 81-82; P-in-c W Hill *Ex* 82; TV Ottery St Mary, Alfington and W Hill 82-87; V Sparkwell from 87; V Shaugh Prior 87-93; P-in-c Cornwood from 98. *The Vicarage, Sparkwell, Plymouth PL7 5DB* T: (01752) 837218 E: freddie@sparkwell.fsnet.com

DENNEN, Lyle. b 42. Harvard Univ LLB 67 Trin Coll Cam BA 70 MA 75. Cuddesdon Coll 70. **d** 72 **p** 73. C S Lambeth St Ann *S'wark* 72-75; C Richmond St Mary 75-78; P-in-c Kennington St Jo 78-79; V Kennington St Jo w St Jas 79-99; P-in-c Brixton Road Ch Ch 81-89; RD Brixton 90-99; Hon Can S'wark Cathl 99; Adn Hackney *Lon* 99-10; V St Andr Holborn 99-14; rtd 14; PtO *Lon* from 14. *St Andrew's Vicarage, 5 St Andrew's Street, London EC4A 3AB* T: (020) 7353 3544 F: 7583 2750 E: lyle.dennen@hotmail.com

DENNER-BROWN, Sarah. *See* BROWN, Sarah Romilly Denner

DENNESS, Mrs Linda Christine. b 51. Portsm Dioc Tr Course 88. **d** 89 **p** 01. NSM Milton *Portsm* 89-93; Chapl Asst Portsm Hosps NHS Trust 89-91; NSM Portsea St Mary *Portsm* 93-96; NSM Wymering 96-06; P-in-c Cosham 06-09; P-in-c Wymering 07-09; PtO 09-10; NSM Portsea N End St Mark from 10. *19 Fourth Avenue, Cosham, Portsmouth PO6 3HX* T: (023) 9232 6885 E: linda@ldenness.wanadoo.co.uk

DENNIS, Barbara Christine. *See* HUME, Barbara Christine

DENNIS, David Alan. b 46. St Luke's Coll Ex BSc 90. **d** 05 **p** 06. OLM Alderholt *Sarum* from 05. *18 Oak Road, Alderholt, Fordingbridge SP6 3BL* T: (01425) 655230 E: davidalan.dennis@btinternet.com

DENNIS, Miss Drucilla Lyn. b 49. Ox Univ BEd 71 Southn Univ MA(Ed) 82 Win Univ MA 10. S Dios Minl Tr Scheme 92. **d** 95 **p** 96. NSM Cowes H Trin and St Mary *Portsm* 95-01; TV Dorchester *Sarum* 01-08; Hon C Chale, Shorwell w Kingston and Brighstone and Brooke w Mottistone *Portsm* 08-11; Chapl Earl Mountbatten Hospice and Isle of Wight NHS Primary Care Trust 09-11; P-in-c Brading w Yaverland *Portsm* from 11. *The Vicarage, The Mall, Brading, Sandown PO36 0DE* T: (01983) 401191 E: drucilladennis@hotmail.com

✠**DENNIS, The Rt Revd John.** b 31. St Cath Coll Cam BA 54 MA 59. Cuddesdon Coll 54. **d** 56 **p** 57 **c** 79. C Armley St Bart *Ripon* 56-60; C Kettering SS Pet and Paul 60-62; V Is of Dogs Ch Ch and St Jo w St Luke *Lon* 62-71; V Mill Hill Jo Keble Ch 71-79; RD W Barnet 73-79; Preb St Paul's Cathl 77-79; Suff Bp Knaresborough *Ripon* 79-86; Dioc Dir of Ords 80-86; Bp St E 86-96; rtd 96; PtO *St E* from 96; Hon Asst Bp Win from 99. *7 Conifer Close, Winchester SO22 6SH* T: (01962) 868881 E: 7johndennis@gmail.com

DENNIS, Keith Aubrey Lawrence. b 55. City of Lon Poly BA 79. Cranmer Hall Dur 88. **d** 90 **p** 91. C Bushbury *Lich* 90-94; P-in-c Newcastle St Geo 94-99; TV Kirby Muxloe *Leic* 99-03; C Ashby-de-la-Zouch St Helen w Coleorton 03; C Breedon cum Isley Walton and Worthington 03; Chapl HM Pris Glouc 04-09; PtO Pet 11-15. *6 Rowandean Court, Cinderford GL14 2XQ* M: 07447-918022 E: keith.dennis24@gmail.com

DENNIS, Canon Robert Franklin. b 51. St Paul's Coll Grahamstown 91. **d** 94 **p** 94. C Kuils River S Africa 94-96; C Matroosfontein 96-99; R Maitland 99-03; TR Bredasdorp 03-05; P-in-c Crumpsall *Man* 06-09; Min Can St Woolos Cathl 09-11; P-in-c Llantilio Pertholey w Bettws Chpl etc 11-14; V Connah's Quay *St As* from 14; Hon Can Saldanha Bay S Africa from 14. *8 Eurgain Avenue, Connah's Quay, Deeside CH5 4PW* T: (01244) 830224 E: rfd.stmark2@gmail.com

DENNIS, Samuel James. b 85. Peterho Cam BA 07. Westcott Ho Cam 08. **d** 11 **p** 12. C Catford (Southend) and Downham *S'wark* from 11. *59 Southend Lane, London SE6 3AB* T: (020) 8697 6538 M: 07940-576397 E: fr.sam.dennis@gmail.com

DENNIS, Canon Trevor John. b 45. St Jo Coll Cam BA 68 MA 71 PhD 74. Westcott Ho Cam 71. **d** 72 **p** 73. C Newport Pagnell *Ox* 72-74; Chapl Eton Coll 75-82; Tutor Sarum & Wells Th Coll 82-94; Vice-Prin 89-94; Can Res Ches Cathl 94-10; rtd 10; PtO *Ches* from 11. *11 Anne's Way, Chester CH4 7BA* T: (01244) 638441 E: trevordennis11@gmail.com

DENNISON, Philip Ian. b 52. Nottm Univ BTh 81. St Jo Coll Nottm 77. **d** 81 **p** 82. C Stalybridge H Trin and Ch Ch *Ches* 81-84; C Heswall 84-91; TV Bushbury *Lich* 91-04; V Shevington *Blackb* from 04. *St Anne's Vicarage, Gathurst Lane, Shevington, Wigan WN6 8HW* T: (01257) 252136 E: stannepc.office@googlemail.com

DENNISS, Mrs Amanda Jane. b 57. Univ Coll Lon LLB 78. Oak Hill Th Coll 98 NTMTC 00. **d** 03 **p** 04. C Turnham Green Ch Ch *Lon* 03-06; PtO 06-08 and 13-15; C Westwood *Cov* 08-11; R Itchen Valley *Win* from 15. *Itchen Valley Rectory, Chillandham Lane, Itchen Abbas, Winchester SO21 1AS* T: (01962) 779832 E: amandadenniss@gmail.com

DENNISTON, James Keith Stuart. b 49. Down Coll Cam MA 70 Barrister-at-Law 70. Oak Hill Th Coll DipEd 92. **d** 93 **p** 94. C Harborne Heath *Birm* 93-97; Chapl Lee Abbey 97-02; PtO *Ex* 02-03; TV Chippenham St Paul w Hardenhuish etc *Bris* 03-07. *Rectory Cottage, King's Nympton, Umberleigh EX37 9SS* T: (01769) 581326 E: j-denniston@tiscali.co.uk

DENNO, Basil. b 52. Dundee Univ BSc 74. Oak Hill Th Coll BA 81. **d** 81 **p** 83. C Chaddesden St Mary *Derby* 81-83; Hon C 83-84. *21 Parkside Road, Chaddesden, Derby DE21 6QR* T: (01332) 672687 E: lizziedenno@talk21.com

DENNO, Elizabeth Kate (Skye). b 79. Derby Univ BA 00. St Jo Coll Nottm BA 08. **d** 08 **p** 09. C Dursley *Glouc* 08-12; TV Cowley St Jas *Ox* from 12. *27 Don Bosco Close, Oxford OX4 2LD* M: 07720-768684 T: (01865) 434160 E: joskso@yahoo.co.uk

DENNY, Annita. b 46. **d** 13. NSM Budleigh Salterton, E Budleigh w Bicton etc *Ex* from 13. *119 Cotmaton Road, Sidmouth EX10 8XN* T: (01395) 512735

DENNY, John Peter Sekeford. b 43. RIBA 69. Chich Th Coll 90. **d** 91 **p** 92. C Aylmerton w Runton *Nor* 91-95; P-in-c Barney, Fulmodeston w Croxton, Hindringham etc 95-96; R 96-98; rtd 98; PtO *Truro* 98-04; *Nor* 04-06. *Little Folly, Mutton Dingle, New Radnor, Presteigne LD8 2TL* T: (01544) 350568

DENNY, Lorne Robert. b 58. Pemb Coll Ox MA 84 Lon Inst of Educn PGCE 84. SAOMC 98. **d** 01 **p** 02. NSM Ox St Barn and St Paul 01-04; NSM Cowley St Jo 04-07; P-in-c Milton next Sittingbourne *Cant* 07-12; TV Cheam *S'wark* from 12. *11 Revell Road, Cheam SM1 2ED*

DENNY, Michael Thomas. b 47. Kelham Th Coll 68 St Jo Coll Nottm 71. **d** 73 **p** 74. C Gospel Lane St Mich *Birm* 73-77; P-in-c Frankley 77-82; R 82-07; rtd 07; PtO *Birm* from 07. *Orchard Cottage, Green Lane, Yarpole, Leominster HR6 0BE* T: (01568) 780874 E: michael@revdenny1.freeserve.co.uk

DENT, Canon Christopher Mattinson. b 46. K Coll Lon BA 68 AKC 68 MTh 69 Jes Coll Cam BA 72 MA 76 New Coll Ox MA 76 DPhil 80. Westcott Ho Cam 70. **d** 72 **p** 73. C Chelsea St Luke *Lon* 72-76; Asst Chapl New Coll Ox 76-79; Fell Chapl and Dean Div 79-84; V Hollingbourne and Hucking w Leeds and Broomfield *Cant* 84-93; V Bedford St Andr *St Alb* 93-12; Hon Can St Alb 01-12; RD Bedford 05-10; rtd 12; PtO *Cant* from 13. *20 Ardent Avenue, Walmer, Deal CT14 7UE* T: (01304) 361624 E: dent@tinyworld.net

DENT, Joseph Michael. b 73. Jes Coll Cam BA 94 MA 98. Wycliffe Hall Ox BTh 99. **d** 99 **p** 00. C Plymouth St Andr and Stonehouse *Ex* 99-03; C Sevenoaks St Nic *Roch* 03-13; TR Plymouth St Andr and Stonehouse *Ex* from 13. *St Andrew's Rectory, 13 Bainbridge Avenue, Plymouth PL3 5QZ* T: (01752) 211241 E: josephdent@gmail.com

DENT, Marie Penelope. b 46. K Coll Lon BA 88. Westcott Ho Cam 02. **d** 04 **p** 05. C N Walsham and Edingthorpe *Nor* 04-08;

TV Redditch H Trin *Worc* 08-10; rtd 10; PtO *Nor* from 10. *1 Stirling Road, Norwich NR6 6GE* T: (01603) 487938 M: 07799-220357 E: penelopedent@live.co.uk

DENT, Michael Leslie. b 54. Leeds Univ BEd 76. St Steph Ho Ox 93. **d** 95 **p** 96. C Cockerton *Dur* 95-98; V Escomb 98-03; R Etherley 98-03; V Witton Park 98-03; Chapl Dur Constabulary 02-03; TR E Darlington 03-12; V Darlington St Jo 12-13; V Warkworth and Acklington *Newc* from 13. *The Vicarage, 11 Dial Place, Warkworth, Morpeth NE65 0UR* T: (01665) 711217 E: mikedent54@gmail.com

DENT, Raymond William. b 47. TD 03. Open Univ BA 84 Birm Coll of Educn CertEd 68. Ridley Hall Cam 70. **d** 73 **p** 74. C Hyde St Geo *Ches* 73-76; C Eastham 76-79; TV E Runcorn w Halton 79-80; V Hallwood 80-83; V New Brighton Em 83-94; V Willaston 94-13; rtd 13. *32 Proctor Road, Wirral CH47 4BB* E: raymond@raydent.freeserve.co.uk

DENT, Richard William. b 32. Down Coll Cam BA 56 MA LLB 59. Bris Sch of Min 73. **d** 77 **p** 78. NSM Southmead *Bris* 77-81; NSM Henleaze 81-85; V Highworth w Sevenhampton and Inglesham etc 85-88; TV Oldland 88-91; V Longwell Green 91-93; C Bedminster St Mich 93-97; Chapl Asst Frenchay Healthcare NHS Trust Bris 94-97; rtd 97; PtO *Bris* from 99; *B & W* 03-06 and from 09. *1 Bakers Buildings, Wrington, Bristol BS40 5LQ* T: (01934) 861070 M: 07930-840822 E: richdent@talktalk.net

DENT, Stephen Edward. b 55. STETS 12. **d** 15. NSM Lee-on-the-Solent *Portsm* from 15. *18 North Hill, Fareham PO16 7HP* T: (01329) 237098 E: steve.e.dent@btinternet.com

DENTON, Peter Brian. b 37. Kelham Th Coll 57. **d** 62 **p** 63. C Ellesmere Port *Ches* 62-66; Chapl HM Borstal Hollesley Bay 66-69; CF 69-89; Warden Bridge Cen and C Hounslow H Trin w St Paul *Lon* 89-92; V Northolt Park St Barn 92-04; P-in-c Perivale 97-01; P-in-c N Greenford All Hallows 00-04; rtd 04; PtO *Ely* from 05; *Pet* 05-10; P-in-c Pet All SS 10-13. *52 Lornas Field, Hampton Hargate, Peterborough PE7 8AY* T: (01733) 552353 E: revddenton@aol.com

DENYER, Alan Frederick. b 31. Wycliffe Hall Ox 80. **d** 82 **p** 83. C Rodbourne Cheney *Bris* 82-84; P-in-c Garsdon w Lea and Cleverton 84-87; R Garsdon, Lea and Cleverton and Charlton 87-91; R Lydbury N w Hopesay and Edgton *Heref* 91-97; Asst Dioc Soc Resp Officer 91-97; rtd 97; Hon C Long Preston w Tosside *Bradf* 97-02; PtO *Leeds* from 03. *1 Old Deanery Close, St Marygate, Ripon HG4 1LZ* T: (01765) 602397

DENYER, Christopher Richard Terence. b 79. SEITE 13. **d** 15. C Bethersden w High Halden and Woodchurch *Cant* from 15. *75 Romney Road, Willesborough, Ashford TN24 0RR* E: chrisdenyer1@sky.com

DENYER, Canon Paul Hugh. b 46. Lon Univ BA 68. Ripon Coll Cuddesdon 74. **d** 77 **p** 78. C Horfield H Trin *Bris* 77-82; TV Yate New Town 82-88; V Bris Lockleaze St Mary Magd w St Fran 88-95; Dioc Dir of Ords 02-07; R Warmley, Syston and Bitton 02-13; Hon Can Bris Cathl 99-13; rtd 13. *21 Westfield Close, Hanham, Bristol BS15 3SB* E: paul.joanne4647@btinternet.com

DENYER, Samuel. b 74. Ripon Coll Cuddesdon 07. **d** 09 **p** 10. C Lostwithiel, St Winnow w St Nectan's Chpl etc *Truro* 09-12; C Lanreath, Pelynt and Bradoc 09-12; C Lanlivery 09-12; R Winnersh *Ox* from 12. *The Rectory, 6 St Catherine's Close, Sindlesham, Wokingham RG41 5BZ* T: 0118-977 6221 M: 07827-013808 E: denyer.samuel@gmail.com

DEO, Paul. b 60. Coll of Ripon & York St Jo CertEd 81. St Jo Coll Nottm 95. **d** 97 **p** 98. C Tong *Bradf* 97-00; P-in-c Laisterdyke 00-02; V 02-07; C Baildon 07-12; V Heworth Ch Ch *York* from 12. *Christ Church Vicarage, 23 Lawnsway, York YO31 1JD* T: (01904) 269054 E: pauldeo@sky.com

DERBY, Archdeacon of. *See* CUNLIFFE, The Ven Christopher John

DERBY, Bishop of. *See* REDFERN, The Rt Revd Alastair Llewellyn John

DERBY, Dean of. *See* DAVIES, The Very Revd John Harverd

DERBYSHIRE, Mrs Anne Margaret. b 31. Open Univ BA 87 Lon Univ CertEd 75. SWMTC. **dss** 84 **d** 87 **p** 01. NSM Tiverton St Pet *Ex* 87-90; PtO 90-01 and from 02; NSM Washfield, Stoodleigh, Withleigh etc 01-02. *6 Devenish Close, Weymouth DT4 8RU* T: (01305) 750909

DERBYSHIRE, Douglas James. b 26. **d** 81 **p** 82. NSM Heald Green St Cath *Ches* 81-86; NSM Stockport St Geo 86-89; C 89-91; rtd 91; PtO *Man* 92-95 and 00-06; *Ches* 86-99 from 92. *91 East Avenue, Heald Green, Cheadle SK8 3BR* T: 0161-437 3748

DERBYSHIRE, Philip Damien. b 50. Leic Poly LLB 71. Sarum & Wells Th Coll 80. **d** 82 **p** 83. C Chatham St Wm *Roch* 82-86; R Melfort Zimbabwe 86-88; TV Burnham w Dropmore, Hitcham and Taplow *Ox* 88-92; Chapl HM Pris Reading 92-97; Chapl HM Pris Holloway 97-00; Chapl HM Pris Bullingdon 00-04; C Buckingham *Ox* 04-11; AD 10-11; P-in-c Stewkley w

Soulbury 11-12; TR Cottesloe from 12. *The Vicarage, High Street North, Stewkley, Leighton Buzzard LU7 0HH* T: (01525) 240287 E: revphil5@btinternet.com

DERHAM, Miss Hilary Kathlyn. b 50. Nottm Univ BPharm 71 MRPharmS 71. Chich Th Coll 89. **d** 91 **p** 95. Par Dn Stevenage H Trin *St Alb* 91-94; C 94-98; P-in-c London Colney St Pet 98-03; rtd 03; PtO *St Alb* from 03. *Stuart House, 149 London Road, St Albans AL1 1TA* T: (01727) 842089 E: h.derham@btopenworld.com

DERLÉN, Mrs Eva Teresia Birgitta Andersdotter. b 75. Lund Univ Sweden MTheol 02. Westcott Ho Cam 02. **p** 03. Sweden 03-11; Hon C Prestwood and Gt Hampden *Ox* from 12. *28 Peters Close, Prestwood, Great Missenden HP16 9ET* T: (01494) 868448 E: teresia@htprestwood.org.uk

DEROSAIRE, Leslie John. b 50. Univ of Wales BA 85 Univ of Wales Coll Newport MA 03. St Mich Coll Llan 01. **d** 04 **p** 05. NSM Govilon w Llanfoist w Llanelen *Mon* 04-07; NSM Llanddewi Rhydderch w Llangattock-juxta-Usk etc 07-09; P-in-c 09-11. *Elmgrove, Hereford Road, Mardy, Abergavenny NP7 6HU* T: (01873) 857256 E: derosaire@tiscali.co.uk

DeROY-JONES, Philip Antony. b 49. St Mich Coll Llan 92. **d** 92 **p** 93. C Neath w Llantwit *Llan* 92-95; V Caerau St Cynfelin 95-98; V Pontlottyn w Fochriw 98-14; rtd 14; PtO *Llan* from 14. *Nyth Llyd, 36 Hoo Street, Neath SA11 2PA* T: (01639) 415304 E: fathertony@outlook.com

DERRICK, David John. b 46. S'wark Ord Course. **d** 84 **p** 85. NSM Angell Town St Jo *S'wark* 84-98; NSM St Mary le Strand w St Clem Danes *Lon* 86-93; PtO *Chelmsf* from 12. *Station View, Black Boy Lane, Wrabness, Manningtree CO11 2TL* T: (01255) 880125 E: davidderrick3@btinternet.com

DERRICK, Mrs Dorothy Margaret. b 41. St Mary's Coll Chelt CertEd 63. Ox Min Course 89. **d** 92 **p** 94. NSM Gt Missenden w Ballinger and Lt Hampden *Ox* 92-98; P-in-c Drayton St Pet (Abingdon) 98-04; rtd 04; PtO *Carl* from 05. *33 Parkland Avenue, Carlisle CA1 3GN* T: (01228) 593159 E: dorothyderrick@aol.com

DERRIMAN, Canon Graham Scott. b 39. Bps' Coll Cheshunt 63. **d** 66 **p** 67. C Wandsworth St Mich *S'wark* 66-70; C Merton St Mary 70-74; P-in-c Earlsfield St Andr 74-79; V 79-81; V Camberwell St Luke 81-90; V Croydon St Aug 90-04; Voc Adv Croydon Adnry 93-04; RD Croydon Cen *S'wark* 95-04; Hon Can S'wark Cathl 01-04; rtd 04; PtO *S'wark* from 05. *15 Goodwood Close, Morden SM4 5AW* T: (020) 8648 1550 M: 07952-471515 E: gsd.24@virginmedia.com

DERRY AND RAPHOE, Bishop of. *See* GOOD, The Rt Revd Kenneth Raymond

DERRY, Archdeacon of. *See* MILLER, The Ven Robert Stephen

DERRY, Dean of. *See* MORTON, The Very Revd William Wright

DESBOROUGH, Mrs Margaret Maureen. b 63. Yorks Min Course 13. **d** 15. NSM Skirlaugh, Catwick, Long Riston, Rise, Swine w Ellerby *York* from 15. *8 Old Forge Way, Skirlaugh HU11 5DX* T: (01964) 563048 E: mo.desborough@gmail.com

DESCOMBES, Raymond Patrick Claude. b 51. Birkbeck Coll Lon BA 01. St Mellitus Coll 14. **d** 15. OLM Becontree S *Chelmsf* from 15. *129 Ballards Road, Dagenham RM10 9AR* T: (020) 8592 4691 M: 07918-050491 E: ray.descombes@gmail.com

DESERT, Thomas Denis. b 31. Bps' Coll Cheshunt 54. **d** 56 **p** 57. C Goldington *St Alb* 56-60; C-in-c Luton St Hugh Lewsey CD 60-63; C St Alb St Sav 63-65; C Cheshunt 65-68; V Bedford All SS 68-89; R Northill w Moggerhanger 89-96; rtd 96; PtO *St Alb* from 96. *2 Phillpotts Avenue, Bedford MK40 3UJ* T: (01234) 211413 E: denisdesert@ntlworld.com

DESHPANDE, Lakshmi Anant. *See* JEFFREYS, Lakshmi Anant

DESICS, Robert Anthony. b 77. Bp Grosseteste Coll BA 99 Open Univ MA 00. St Jo Coll Nottm 99. **d** 01 **p** 02. C Potters Bar *St Alb* 01-04; C Rainham w Wennington *Chelmsf* 04-05; V Hemlington *York* from 05. *St Timothy's House, 31 Coatham Close, Hemlington, Middlesbrough TS8 9JW* T: (01642) 590496 E: rob_desics@hotmail.com

DESMOND, Canon Margaret Elspeth. b 49. S Dios Minl Tr Scheme 90. **d** 93 **p** 95. NSM Filton *Bris* from 93; Asst Chapl HM Pris Bris 98-09; Hon Can Bris Cathl from 13. *14 Kenmore Crescent, Bristol BS7 0TN* T: 0117-976 3390 E: ian.desmond@lineone.net

DESON, Rolston Claudius. b 39. Qu Coll Birm 85. **d** 84 **p** 85. NSM Saltley *Birm* 84-86; C Edgbaston St Mary and Ambrose 86-90; V W Bromwich St Phil *Lich* 90-08; rtd 08. *97 Cardington Avenue, Birmingham B42 2PB*

DESROSIERS, Jacques Thomas Maurice. b 55. Qu Univ Kingston Ontario BCom 77. S'wark Ord Course 91. **d** 94 **p** 95. NSM Benenden *Cant* 94-97; C Maidstone All SS and St Phil w Tovil 97-01; TV Pewsey and Swanborough *Sarum* 01-04; P-in-c Rolvenden *Cant* 04-10; P-in-c Newenden and Rolvenden 10-13; R Rother and Oxney 13-14; AD Tenterden 07-11; AD Romney and Tenterden 11-13; P-in-c Warminster St Denys and Upton Scudamore *Sarum* from 14. *The Rectory, 5 Church Street, Warminster BA12 8PG* T: (01985) 213456 E: jtmdesrosiers@gmail.com

d'ESTERRE, Mrs Jennifer Ann. b 48. Coll of St Matthias Bris BEd 77. WEMTC 01. **d** 04 **p** 05. NSM Sharpness, Purton, Brookend and Slimbridge *Glouc* 04-11; C Cromhall, Tortworth, Tytherington, Falfield etc 11-15; rtd 15. *Gossington Cottage, Gossington, Slimbridge, Gloucester GL2 7DN* T: (01453) 890384 M: 07855-243264 E: revdjenny@gmail.com

DETTMER, The Ven Douglas James. b 64. Univ of Kansas BA 86 Yale Univ MDiv 90. Berkeley Div Sch 90. **d** 90 **p** 91. C Ilfracombe, Lee, Woolacombe, Bittadon etc *Ex* 90-94; Bp's Dom Chapl 94-98; P-in-c Thorverton, Cadbury, Upton Pyne etc 98-10; P-in-c Stoke Canon, Poltimore w Huxham and Rewe etc 06-10; R Brampford Speke, Cadbury, Newton St Cyres etc 10-15; Adn Totnes from 15; Preb Ex Cathl from 12. *Blue Hills, Bradley Road, Bovey Tracey, Newton Abbot TQ13 9EU* T: (01626) 832064 E: archdeacon.of.totnes@exeter.anglican.org

DEUCHAR, Canon Andrew Gilchrist. b 55. Southn Univ BTh 86. Sarum & Wells Th Coll 81. **d** 84 **p** 85. C Alnwick *Newc* 84-88; TV Heref St Martin w St Fran 88-90; Adv to Coun for Soc Resp Roch and Cant 90-94; Sec for Angl Communion Affairs 94-00; Hon Prov Can Cant Cathl from 95; R Nottingham St Pet and St Jas *S'well* 00-02; R Nottingham St Pet and All SS 02-07; P-in-c Nottingham St Mary and St Cath 04-07; P-in-c Nottingham All SS, St Mary and St Pet 07-08; Chapl to The Queen 03-08; Dioc Audit Officer *Mor* from 08. *BUILD, The Upper Office, The Dutch Barn, Elm Tree Park, Manton, Marlborough* T: (01672) 861001 E: andrew@build-online.org.uk

DEUCHAR de MELLO, Bridget Dorothea. b 55. Sussex Univ BA 77 Leic Univ PGCE 78. SEITE BA 08. **d** 08 **p** 09. NSM Gt Ilford St Luke *Chelmsf* 08-13; C Leytonstone H Trin and St Aug Harrow Green from 13. *Holy Trinity Vicarage, 4 Holloway Road, London E11 4LD* T: (020) 8539 6067 E: bridget@demello.co.uk

DEVADASON, Jacob. b 61. Madras Bible Sem BTh Serampore Univ BTh Annamalai Univ MA United Th Coll Bangalore MTh. Tamilnadu Th Sem BD NOC. **d** 06 **p** 07. C Man Clayton St Cross w St Paul 06-09; TV Wythenshawe 09-13; P-in-c Croydon Ch Ch *S'wark* from 13; Interfaith Adv Croydon Area from 13. *34 Longley Road, Croydon CR0 3LH* T: (020) 3092 1602 M: 07814-845053 E: 2revjacob@gmail.com

DEVADASON, Mrs Jasmine. b 67. Kakatiya Univ India BA 91 Tamilnadu Th Sem BD 96 United Th Coll Bangalore MTh 99. SNWTP. **d** 08 **p** 09. C W Didsbury and Withington St Chris *Man* 08-11; PtO 12-14. *34 Longley Road, Croydon CR0 3LH* M: 07515-726923 T: (020) 3092 1602 E: jasdevadason@yahoo.co.uk

DEVAL, Mrs Joan Margaret. b 38. Southlands Coll Lon TDip 58. SAOMC 95. **d** 98 **p** 99. OLM Chinnor, Sydenham, Aston Rowant and Crowell *Ox* 98-10; PtO from 10. *3 Orchard Way, Chinnor OX39 4UD* T: (01844) 353404

DEVALL, Elizabeth Jane. b 70. SNWTP. **d** 10 **p** 11. C Royton St Anne *Man* 10-13; C Heyside 12-13; P-in-c Hurst from 13. *St John's Vicarage, 155 Kings Road, Ashton-under-Lyne OL6 8EZ* T: 0161-330 1935 M: 07725-739506 E: lizdevall@btinternet.com

DEVAS, Thomas Christopher. b 86. Nottm Univ BSc 09. Wycliffe Hall Ox BTh 15. **d** 15. C Wollaton Park *S'well* from 15. *11 Robins Wood Road, Nottingham NG8 3LA* M: 07817-458483 E: tom@stmaryswollatonpark.co.uk

DEVENISH, Nicholas Edward. b 64. Ridley Hall Cam 02. **d** 04 **p** 05. C Huntingdon *Ely* 04-07; C Farcet Hampton 07-12; TV Cartmel Peninsula *Carl* from 12. *The Vicarage, Priest Lane, Cartmel, Grange-over-Sands LA11 6PU* T: (015395) 36261 E: nickdevenish@mac.com *or* vicar.cartmel@virgin.net

DEVENNEY, Raymond Robert Wilmont. b 47. TCD BA 69 MA 73. CITC 70. **d** 70 **p** 71. C Ballymena w Ballyclug *Conn* 70-75; C Ballyholme *D & D* 75-81; I Killinchy w Kilmood and Tullynakill 81-00; I Drumbeg 00-12; rtd 12. *6 Windslow Court, Carrickfergus BT38 9DP* T: (028) 9335 5012 E: raydev@hotmail.com

DEVER, Paul. b 71. BSc. Wycliffe Hall Ox. **d** 06 **p** 07. C Fair Oak *Win* 06-10; TV Horwich and Rivington and Dioc Young Adults Missr *Man* 10-12; C Blackrod 11-12; C Howell Hill w Burgh Heath *Guildf* from 12. *18 Nonsuch Walk, Cheam SM2 7NG* E: pauldever@btinternet.com *or* revpaul@gmail.com

DEVERAJ, Jacob Devadason. *See* DEVADASON, Jacob

DEVERELL, Clive David. b 61. Anglia Ruskin Univ BA 09. CA Tr Coll 83 ERMC 04. **d** 07 **p** 08. C Paston *Pet* 07-10; TV W Swindon and the Lydiards *Bris* from 10. *26 The Bramptons, Shaw, Swindon SN5 5SL* T: (01793) 877111 E: clive.deverell@btinternet.com

DEVERELL, Canon William Robert Henry. b 61. CITC 88 St Jo Coll Nottm 90. **d** 92 **p** 93. C Agherton *Conn* 92-95; I Sixmilecross w Termonmaguirke *Arm* 95-99; I Tallaght *D & G* from 99; Can Ch Ch Cathl Dublin from 14. *St Maelruain's Rectory, 6 Sally Park, Firhouse Road, Tallaght, Dublin 24, Republic of Ireland* T: (00353) (1) 462 1044 *or* 462 6006 F: 462 1044 M: 86-803 0239 E: tallaghtparish@gmail.com

DEVEREUX, Canon John Swinnerton. b 32. Lon Univ BSc 53. Wells Th Coll. **d** 58 **p** 59. C Wigan St Mich *Liv* 58-60; C Goring-by-Sea *Chich* 60-69; Ind Chapl 69-97; Can and Preb Chich Cathl 90-97; rtd 97; PtO *Chich* from 97. *4 Pony Farm, Findon, Worthing BN14 0RS* T: (01903) 873638

DEVERILL, Jennifer. b 40. Auckland Medical Sch MSR 62. **d** 96 **p** 97. OLM Battersea St Luke *S'wark* 96-05; Chapl St Geo Healthcare NHS Trust Lon 96-05; PtO *S'wark* from 05; P-in-c Le Gard *Eur* 08-13; rtd 13; PtO *Ox* from 15. *8 rue de l'Eglise, 30140 Bagard, France* T: (0033) 4 6 25 17 63 E: jennifer.deverill@wanadoo.fr

DEVINE, Margaret Rose. b 50. Sunderland Poly BEd 76. NEOC 00. **d** 03 **p** 04. NSM E Boldon *Dur* 03-12; rtd 12; PtO *Dur* from 12. *13 Coniston Close, Belmont, Durham DH1 2UQ* M: 07708-222634 E: devinemargaret@googlemail.com

DEVINE, Maureen Mary. b 37. Cheltenham & Glouc Coll of HE TCert 74. SAOMC 95. **d** 98 **p** 99. NSM Reading St Jo *Ox* 98-01; NSM Beech Hill, Grazeley and Spencers Wood 01-05; NSM Loddon Reach 05-08; PtO from 08. *33 Radstock Lane, Earley, Reading RG6 5RX* T: 0118-921 2767 E: julmar99@aol.com

DEVONISH, Clive Wayne. b 51. Ridley Hall Cam. **d** 96 **p** 97. C Meole Brace *Lich* 96-05; V Greenside *Dur* 05-15; rtd 15. *Maranatha, 3 Dorricotts Place, Yockleton, Shrewsbury SY5 9PH* E: revclivedevo@talktalk.net

DEVONSHIRE, Canon Roger George. b 40. AKC 62. **d** 63 **p** 64. C Rotherhithe St Mary w All SS *S'wark* 63-67; C Kingston Hill St Paul 67-71; Chapl RN 71-95; QHC 92-95; R Pitlochry and Kilmaveonaig *St And* 95-05; Syn Clerk and Can St Ninian's Cathl Perth 00-05; rtd 05; PtO *Portsm* 05-07 and from 10; Chapl QinetiQ 07-10. *4 Chiltern Court, 27 Florence Road, Southsea PO5 2NX* T: (023) 9287 3397 M: 07769-680922 E: rdevonshire@btinternet.com

DEW, Glyn. b 55. Worc Coll of Educn BEd 90. St Jo Coll Nottm MA 97. **d** 97 **p** 98. C Beoley *Worc* 97-01; TV Redditch, The Ridge 01-05; P-in-c Tardebigge 04-05; PtO from 09. *18 Merevale Close, Redditch B98 0HZ* T: (01527) 450068 E: revmodew@btinternet.com

DEW, Lindsay Charles. b 52. Wilson Carlile Coll 76 Cranmer Hall Dur 85. **d** 86 **p** 86. C Knottingley *Wakef* 86-89; V Batley St Thos 89-97; R Thornhill and Whitley Lower 97-09; RD Dewsbury 96-06; Hon Can Wakef Cathl 05-09; P-in-c Dunton w Wrestlingworth and Eyeworth *St Alb* 09-14; R from 14; RD Biggleswade from 11. *22 Angell's Meadow, Ashwell, Baldock SG7 5QS* T: (01462) 743617 M: 07545-878082 E: lindsay.dew@btinternet.com

DEW, Martin John. b 49. CBDTI 00. **d** 04 **p** 05. NSM Natland *Carl* 04-09; NSM Shap w Swindale and Bampton w Mardale 09-13; rtd 13. *Address temp unknown* E: martindew23@live.co.uk

DEW, Maureen. b 51. Univ of Wales (Newport) MA 00. Qu Coll Birm BA 99. **d** 99 **p** 00. C Inkberrow w Cookhill and Kington w Dormston *Worc* 99-02; C Redditch, The Ridge 02-05; TV Redditch Ch the K 05-12; rtd 12. *18 Merevale Close, Redditch B98 0HZ* T: (01527) 450068 E: revmodew@btinternet.com

DEW, Robert David John. b 42. St Pet Coll Ox BA 63. St Steph Ho Ox 63. **d** 65 **p** 66. C Abington *Pet* 65-69; Chapl Tiffield Sch Northants 69-71; Ind Chapl *Pet* 71-79; Liv 79-87; Sen Ind Missr 88-91; V Skelsmergh w Selside and Longsleddale *Carl* 91-06; Bp's Research Officer 91-95; Bp's Adv for CME 95-06; rtd 06; PtO *Carl* from 07. *Tither Crag Barn, Crook, Kendal LA8 8LE* T: (015395) 68680 E: bob.dew@virgin.net

DEWAR, Francis John Lindsay. b 33. Keble Coll Ox BA 56 MA 59. Cuddesdon Coll 58. **d** 60 **p** 61. C Hessle *York* 60-63; C Stockton St Chad *Dur* 63-66; V Sunderland St Chad 66-81; Org Journey Inward, Journey Outward Project 82-07; rtd 07; PtO *B & W* from 01. *Wellspring, Church Road, Wookey, Wells BA5 1JX* T: (01749) 675365 E: dewar@waitrose.com

DEWAR, Ian John James. b 61. Kingston Poly BA 83. Cranmer Hall Dur 89. **d** 92 **p** 93. C Blackb St Gabr 92-95; C Darwen St Cuth w Tockholes St Steph 95-97; V Appley Bridge 97-05; Chapl St Cath Hospice Preston 05-14; Chapl Univ Hosps of Morecambe Bay NHS Trust from 14. *Chaplain's Office, Royal Lancaster Infirmary, Ashton Road, Lancaster LA1 4RP* T: (01524) 65944 E: ijjdewar@hotmail.com *or* ian.dewar@mbht.nhs.uk

DEWAR, John. b 32. Chich Th Coll 58. **d** 61 **p** 62. C Leeds St Hilda *Ripon* 61-63; C Cross Green St Sav and St Hilda 63-65; C Cullercoats St Geo *Newc* 65-69; V Newsham 69-76; V Kenton Ascension 76-86; R Wallsend St Pet 86-92;

V Longhorsley and Hebron 92-96; rtd 96; PtO S'well from 04. *51 Bonner Lane, Calverton, Nottingham NG14 6FU* T: 0115-965 2599 E: jandmedewar@ntlworld.com

DEWES, Ms Deborah Mary. b 59. Homerton Coll Cam BEd 81 St Jo Coll Dur BA 90 MA 93. Cranmer Hall Dur 88. **d** 92 **p** 94. C Stockton St Pet *Dur* 92-96; C Knowle *Birm* 96-03; C Bath Abbey w St Jas *B & W* 03-08; Chapl R United Hosp Bath NHS Trust 03-08; P-in-c Brislington St Luke *Bris* 08-14; V from 14. *The Vicarage, 9 St Luke's Gardens, Bristol BS4 4NW* T: 0117-977 7633 E: vicar@stlukesbrislington.org.uk

DEWEY, David Malcolm. b 43. Lon Univ BA 72 LSE MSc(Econ) 87 Fitzw Coll Cam MPhil 94. Westcott Ho Cam 76. **d** 78 **p** 79. Sen Lect Middx Poly 72-92; Sen Lect Middx Univ 92-01; Hon C Enfield St Mich *Lon* 78-79; Hon C Bush Hill Park St Steph 79-84; Hon C Palmers Green St Jo 84-90; PtO 90-95; *St Alb* 95-98; Hon C Hertford All SS 98-01; P-in-c St Paul's Walden 01-08; rtd 08; PtO *St Alb* from 09. *9 Bowling Road, Ware SG12 7EH* T: (01920) 467287 M: 07813-439463 E: daviddewey8566@fsmail.net

DEWEY, Peter Lewis. b 38. Wycliffe Hall Ox 69. **d** 71 **p** 72. C Hammersmith St Sav *Lon* 71-73; Chapl to Bp Kensington 73-75; C Isleworth All SS 75-81; TV Dorchester *Ox* 81-91; CF (TA) 86-91; Chapl Gordonstoun Sch 92-97; TR St Laur in Thanet *Cant* 97-03; rtd 03; P-in-c Sulhamstead Abbots and Bannister w Ufton Nervet *Ox* 03-10; Hon C 10-12; AD Bradfield 10-11; Chapl Allnutt's Hosp Goring Heath from 12. *Old School Cottage, Goring Heath, Reading RG8 7RR*

DEWEY, Sanford Dayton. b 44. Syracuse Univ AB 67 MA 72. Gen Th Sem (NY) MDiv 79. **d** 79 **p** 80. Assoc Chapl Roosevelt Hosp New York USA 80-81; Assoc Dir Relig Services 81-86; C St Mary le Bow w St Pancras Soper Lane etc *Lon* 87-92; C Hampstead St Steph w All Hallows 92-94; Co-Dir Hampstead Counselling Service 94-00; Dir from 00; NSM Hampstead All Ch *Lon* 94-96; Hon C Grosvenor Chpl from 96; Prov Past Consultant URC from 96; PtO *Lon* from 97. *B908 New Providence Wharf, 1 Fairmont Avenue, London E14 9PJ* E: daytondewey@gmail.com

DEWHIRST, Janice. b 50. EMMTC 99. **d** 02 **p** 03. NSM Forest Town *S'well* 02-04; NSM Mansfield SS Pet and Paul 04-06; P-in-c Ladybrook 06-09; rtd 09. *26 King Street, Mansfield Woodhouse, Mansfield NG19 9AU* T: (01623) 454471 E: revd.jan.d@ntlworld.com

DEWHURST, Gabriel George. b 30. **d** 59 **p** 60. In RC Ch 60-69; C Darlington St Jo *Dur* 70; C Bishopwearmouth St Nic 71-73; C-in-c Stockton St Mark CD 73-81; V Harton 81-86; R Castle Eden w Monkhesleden 86-97; rtd 97; PtO *York* from 98. *9 Knott Lane, Easingwold, York YO61 3LX* T: (01347) 823526

DEWHURST, Russell James Edward. b 77. Magd Coll Ox MPhys 99 Selw Coll Cam BTh 03. Westcott Ho Cam 00. **d** 03 **p** 04. C Blewbury, Hagbourne and Upton *Ox* 03-05; P-in-c Ox St Frideswide w Binsey 05-09; Web Pastor i-church 05-07; Asst Chapl Ex Coll Ox 06-09; V Ewell *Guildf* from 09. *St Mary's Vicarage, 14 Church Street, Ewell, Epsom KT17 2AQ* T: (020) 8393 2643 E: rdewhurst@mac.com *or* vicar@stmarysewell.com

DEWICK, David Richard. b 36. SAOMC 96. **d** 99 **p** 00. NSM Risborough *Ox* 99-10; rtd 10. *Russets, Peters Lane, Monks Risborough, Princes Risborough HP27 0LQ* T: (01844) 343016

DEWING, Robert Mark Eastwood. b 68. Bris Univ BA 90 PGCE 91. Ridley Hall Cam BA 98. **d** 99 **p** 00. C Alverstoke *Portsm* 99-03; V Sheet 03-11; AD Petersfield 09-11; Past Dir Lee Abbey from 11. *Lee Abbey Fellowship, Lee Abbey, Lynton EX35 6JJ* T: (01598) 752621 E: robdewing@hotmail.com

DEWING, William Arthur. b 52. NEOC 99. **d** 02 **p** 03. NSM Middlesbrough St Oswald *York* 02-06; NSM Stainton w Hilton from 06; NSM Brookfield from 14. *19 Monarch Grove, Marton, Middlesbrough TS7 8QQ* T: (01642) 321074 F: 500661 M: 07966-191640 E: bill@revd.me.uk

DEWSBURY, Michael Owen. b 31. St Aid Birkenhead 54. **d** 57 **p** 58. C Hellesdon *Nor* 57-60; C Speke All SS *Liv* 60-62; R Gt and Lt Glemham *St E* 62-67; R W Lynn *Nor* 67-68; R Dongara Australia 69-71; R Nollamara 71-76; Chapl R Perth Hosp 76-79; Chapl Fremantle Hosp 79-99; rtd 99. *8 Thomas Street, South Fremantle WA 6162, Australia* T: (0061) (8) 9335 6852 E: dewsbury@iinet.net.au

DEXTER, Canon Frank Robert. b 40. Cuddesdon Coll 66. **d** 68 **p** 69. C Newc H Cross 68-71; C Whorlton 71-73; V Pet Ch Carpenter 73-80; V High Elswick St Phil *Newc* 80-85; RD Newc W 81-85; V Newc St Geo 85-05; Hon Can Newc Cathl 94-05; P-in-c Newc St Hilda 95-98; rtd 05. *8 Tynedale Terrace, Hexham NE46 3JE* T: (01434) 601759 E: frank.dexter@talk21.com

DEY, Canon Charles Gordon Norman. b 46. Lon Coll of Div. **d** 71 **p** 72. C Almondbury *Wakef* 71-76; V Mixenden 76-85; TR Tong *Bradf* 85-11; C Laisterdyke 08-11; Hon Can Bradf Cathl 00-11; rtd 11. *29 Parsons Road, Bradford BD9 4AY* T: (01274) 499781 E: thedeyteam@blueyonder.co.uk

DEY, John Alfred. b 33. ALCD 57 ALCM 57. **d** 57 **p** 58. C Man Albert Memorial Ch 57-60; C Pennington 60-62; V Mosley Common 62-69; V Chadderton Em 69-79; V Flixton St Jo 79-96; rtd 96; PtO *Man* from 96. *8 Woodlands Avenue, Urmston, Manchester M41 6NE*

DI CASTIGLIONE, James Alexander. b 81. St Jo Coll Nottm. **d** 08 **p** 09. C Mid-Sussex Network Ch *Chich* 08-12; Chapl Sir Robert Woodard Academy Lancing 12-13; R Ashington, Washington and Wiston w Buncton *Chich* from 13. *The Rectory, Mill Lane, Ashington, Pulborough RH20 3BX* T: (01903) 893878 M: 07796-945662 E: jamesdicastiglione@me.com

DI CASTIGLIONE, Nigel Austin. b 57. St Jo Coll Dur BA 78. St Jo Coll Nottm MA 94. **d** 94 **p** 95. C Tamworth *Lich* 94-97; P-in-c Trentham 97-01; V 02-10; V Hanford 02-10; V Harborne Heath *Birm* 10-15; TR Papworth *Ely* from 15. *Elsworth Rectory, The Drift, Elsworth, Cambridge CB23 4JN* M: 07770-697240 E: nigel.dicastiglione@gmail.com

DI CHIARA, Miss Alessandra Maddalena. b 59. Univ of Wales (Swansea) BA 80. Wycliffe Hall Ox 00. **d** 02 **p** 03. C Hooton *Ches* 02-05; P-in-c Millbrook 05-15; P-in-c Micklehurst 14-15; C Douglas St Geo and All SS *S & M* from 15. *62 Ballabrooie Way, Douglas, Isle of Man IM1 4HB*

DIALI, The Ven Daniel Chukwuma. b 47. Portsm Univ BA 80 Surrey Univ MA 04. Basic Ord Course by Ext 85. **d** 84 **p** 86. Nigeria 84-01; V Lagos St Bart 86-92; V Bp Tugwell Ch 92-96; Can Lagos W 96-99; Adn St Paul's 00-01; PtO *S'wark* from 02. *36 Arnold Estate, Druid Street, London SE1 2DU* T: (020) 7231 5357 E: dcdvnd@yahoo.com

DIAMOND, Canon Michael Lawrence. b 37. St Jo Coll Dur BA 60 MA 74 Sussex Univ DPhil 84. ALCD 62. **d** 62 **p** 63. C Wandsworth St Mich *S'wark* 62-64; C Patcham *Chich* 64-69; R Hamsey 70-75; P-in-c Cambridge St Andr Less *Ely* 75-86; V 86-04; Hon Can Ely Cathl 94-04; RD Cambridge 96-04; rtd 04; PtO *S'well* from 04. *16 St Michael's Square, Bramcote, Nottingham NG9 3HG* T: 0115-925 4452

DIAMOND, Capt Richard Geoffrey Colin. b 49. MBE 00. CA Tr Coll. **d** 93 **p** 93. Miss to Seafarers Kenya 90-01; rtd 01; PtO *Win* from 02. *209A Priory Road, Southampton SO17 2LR* T: (023) 8067 8558 E: rgcdiamond@ic24.net

DIANA, Sister. *See* MORRISON, Diana Mary

DIAZ BUTRON, Marcos Máximo. b 72. St Steph Ho Ox 06. **d** 08. C Wantage *Ox* 08-10; PtO from 14. *Address temp unknown* E: maxdiazbutron@yahoo.es

DIBB SMITH, John. b 29. Ex & Truro NSM Scheme 78. **d** 81 **p** 82. NSM Carbis Bay *Truro* 81-82; NSM Carbis Bay w Lelant 82-84; Warden Trelowarren Fellowship Helston 84-89; Chapl 89-91; NSM Halsetown *Truro* 91-97; rtd 98; PtO *Truro* from 00. *Cargease Cottage, Cockwells, Penzance TR20 8DG* T: (01736) 740707

DIBBENS, Canon Hugh Richard. b 39. Lon Univ BA 63 MTh 67 St Pet Coll Ox BA 65 MA 74. Oak Hill Th Coll 60. **d** 67 **p** 68. C Holborn St Geo w H Trin and St Bart *Lon* 67-72; CMS 73-74; Japan 74-77; TR Chigwell *Chelmsf* 78-92; V Hornchurch St Andr 92-06; RD Havering 98-04; Hon Can Chelmsf Cathl 01-06; rtd 06; PtO *Chelmsf* from 07. *9 Stonehill Road, Roxwell, Chelmsford CM1 4PF* T: (01245) 248173 E: hugh@dibbens1.orangehome.co.uk

DIBDEN, Alan Cyril. b 49. Hull Univ LLB 70 Fitzw Coll Cam BA 72 MA 76. Westcott Ho Cam 70 Virginia Th Sem 73. **d** 73 **p** 74. C Camberwell St Luke *S'wark* 73-77; TV Walworth 77-79; TV Langley Marish *Ox* 79-84; C Chalfont St Peter 84-90; TV Burnham w Dropmore, Hitcham and Taplow 90-08; V Taplow and Dropmore from 08. *The Rectory, Rectory Road, Taplow, Maidenhead SL6 0ET* T: (01628) 661182 E: alan.dibden@btinternet.com

DICK, Canon Angela. b 62. Sheff Univ BA 92. St Jo Coll Nottm MA 94. **d** 96 **p** 97. C Mixenden *Wakef* 96-97; C Mount Pellon 97-99; P-in-c Bradshaw 99-00; P-in-c Holmfield 99-00; V Bradshaw and Holmfield 00-10; P-in-c Sowerby Bridge 10-11; V Leeds from 11; Asst Dioc Dir of Ords *Wakef* 13-14; Assoc Dioc Dir of Ords Leeds from 14; Hon Can Wakef Cathl from 10. *The Vicarage, 62 Park Road, Sowerby Bridge HX6 2BJ* T: (01422) 831253 E: angedix110@talktalk.net

DICK, Canon Caroline Ann. b 61. Nottm Univ BTh 88. Linc Th Coll 85. **d** 88 **p** 94. Par Dn Houghton le Spring *Dur* 88-93; Par Dn Hetton le Hole 93-94; C 94-96; Asst Chapl Sunderland Univ 94-98; C Harton 96-09; Development Officer Dioc Bd of Soc Resp 98-09; Adv for Women's Min 02-09; TV Dur N from 09; Hon Can Dur Cathl from 03. *Boldon Rectory, 13 Rectory Green, West Boldon, East Boldon NE36 0QD* T: 0191-454 3804

DICK, Cecil Bates. b 42. TD 97. Selw Coll Cam BA 68 MA 72. EMMTC 73. **d** 76 **p** 78. NSM Cinderhill *S'well* 76-79; Chapl Dame Allan's Schs Newc 79-85; CF (TA) 84-99; C Gosforth All

SS *Newc* 85-87; Chapl HM Pris Dur 88-89; Chapl HM Pris Hull 89-04; rtd 04; PtO *Newc* from 01; *York* from 04. *11 Juniper Chase, Beverley HU17 8GD* T: (01482) 862985

DICK, Malcolm Gordon (Mac). b 40. SWMTC 10. **d** 11 **p** 12. NSM Ottery St Mary, Alfington, W Hill, Tipton etc *Ex* from 11. *Green Hollow, Lower Broad Oak Road, West Hill, Ottery St Mary EX11 1XH* T: (01404) 812494 E: macdick1@aol.com

DICK, Norman MacDonald. b 32. ACIB. Ox NSM Course 87. **d** 90 **p** 91. NSM Bedgrove *Ox* 90-95; NSM Ellesborough, The Kimbles and Stoke Mandeville 95-01; PtO from 01. *21 Camborne Avenue, Aylesbury HP21 7UH* T: (01296) 485530 E: norman.dick@care4free.net

DICK, Canon Raymond Owen. b 53. Edin Univ BD 77. Edin Th Coll 73. **d** 77 **p** 78. C Glas St Mary 77-84; PtO *St Alb* 84-85; P-in-c Edin St Paul and St Geo 85; Edin St Phil 85-86; P-in-c Edin St Marg 85-87; TV Edin Old St Paul 87-88; R Hetton le Hole *Dur* 88-96; V Harton 96-13; P-in-c Cleadon Park 09-13; R The Boldons from 13; AD Jarrow from 14; Hon Can Dur Cathl from 11. *The Rectory, 13 Rectory Green, West Boldon, East Boldon NE36 0QD* T: 0191-908 9102 E: raymonddick@btinternet.com

DICKENS, Adam Paul. b 65. Man Univ BA 89 Nottm Univ MDiv 93. Linc Th Coll 91. **d** 93 **p** 94. C Pershore w Pinvin, Wick and Birlingham *Worc* 93-98; C Portsea St Mary *Portsm* 98-04; Pilsdon Community 04-12; Chapl Derby Univ from 14; Chapl Derby Cathl from 14. *1 Flamsteed Court, Kedleston Old Road, Derby DE22 1GA* E: adampdickens@hotmail.co.uk

DICKENS, John Franklin. b 50. Birm Univ BEd 72 Leeds Univ MEd 82. St Mellitus Coll 12. **d** 13 **p** 14. OLM Maldon St Mary w Mundon *Chelmsf* from 13. *7 Viking Road, Maldon CM9 6JN* T: (01621) 858136　M: 07582-423219 E: john.dickens@talktalk.net

DICKENS, Timothy Richard John. b 45. Leeds Univ BSc 68. Westcott Ho Cam 68. **d** 71 **p** 72. C Meole Brace *Lich* 71-74; C-in-c Stamford Ch Ch CD *Linc* 74-80; V Anlaby St Pet *York* 80-91; V Egg Buckland *Ex* 91-10; P-in-c Estover 04-10; RD Plymouth Moorside 03-09; rtd 10. *52 Budshead Road, Plymouth PL5 2RA* T: (01752) 298570 E: timothy.vicar@tiscali.co.uk

DICKENSON, Charles Gordon. b 29. Bps' Coll Cheshunt 53. **d** 56 **p** 57. C Ellesmere Port *Ches* 56-61; R Egremont St Columba 61-68; V Latchford Ch Ch 68-74; P-in-c Hargrave 74-79; Bp's Chapl 75-79; V Birkenhead St Jas w St Bede 79-83; R Tilston and Shocklach 83-94; rtd 94; PtO *Ches* from 94. *58 Kingsway, Crewe CW2 7ND* T: (01270) 560722 E: cg.dickenson@talktalk.net

DICKENSON, Canon Robin Christopher Wildish. b 44. Lon Univ CertEd 67 Ex Univ BPhil 81 MA 98. SWMTC 94. **d** 97 **p** 98. NSM Week St Mary w Poundstock and Whitstone *Truro* 97-98; P-in-c 98-06; P-in-c St Gennys, Jacobstow w Warbstow and Treneglos 02-06; R Week St Mary Circle of Par 06-13; RD Stratton 05-11; Hon Can Truro Cathl 07-13; rtd 13. *Ranelagh, Week St Mary, Holsworthy EX22 6XA* E: parsonrob@aol.com

DICKER, Ms Jane Elizabeth. b 64. Whitelands Coll Lon BA 87 Anglia Ruskin Univ MA 08 Greenwich Univ PGCE 11. Linc Th Coll 87. **d** 89 **p** 94. Par Dn Merton St Jas *S'wark* 89-93; C Littleham w Exmouth *Ex* 93-97; Chapl Plymouth Univ 93-97; Ecum Chapl for F&HE Grimsby *Linc* 97-02; Chapl Univ of Greenwich *Roch* 02-05; Chapl Kent Inst of Art and Design 02-04; Chapl Univ Coll for the Creative Arts *Roch* 05; Hon PV Roch Cathl 03-05; P-in-c Waltham Cross *St Alb* 05-08; TV Cheshunt from 08. *The Vicarage, 3 Longlands Close, Cheshunt, Waltham Cross EN8 8LW* T: (01992) 633243 M: 07843-667971　E: mthr_jane@btinternet.com

DICKER, Miss Mary Elizabeth. b 45. Girton Coll Cam BA 66 MA 70 Sheff Univ MSc 78. Cranmer Hall Dur 83. **dss** 85 **d** 87 **p** 94. Mortlake w E Sheen *S'wark* 85-88; Par Dn 87-88; Par Dn Irlam *Man* 88-92; Par Dn Ashton Ch Ch 92-94; C 94-97; P-in-c Hopwood 97-98; TV Heywood 98-05; rtd 05; PtO *Man* from 05. *32 Souchay Court, 1 Clothorn Road, Manchester M20 6BR* T: 0161-434 7634

DICKERSON, Richard Keith. b 31. Sir Geo Williams Univ Montreal BA 60 McGill Univ Montreal BD 60. Montreal Dioc Th Coll. **d** 60 **p** 60. C Hampstead St Matt Canada 60-63; R Waterloo St Luke 63-69; PtO *Cant* 72; C Canvey Is *Chelmsf* 73-75; PtO Montreal Canada 75-78; C Georgeville St Geo 78-82; P-in-c 82-91; R Lennoxville St Geo 91-01; rtd 01. *172 McGowan Road, Georgeville QC J0B 1T0, Canada*

DICKIN (née LENTON), Mrs Patricia Margarita. b 72. STETS MA 08. **d** 08 **p** 09. C Epsom Common Ch Ch *Guildf* 08-10; C Oxshott 10-12; P-in-c Mereworth w W Peckham *Roch* from 12. *The Rectory, The Street, Mereworth, Maidstone ME18 5NA*

DICKINSON, Albert Hugh. b 34. Trin Coll Connecticut AB 55. Episc Th Sch Harvard STB 58. **d** 58 **p** 59. USA 58-97; C Portarlington w Cloneyhurke and Lea *M & K* 97-99; USA from 99. *807 Seashore Road, Cold Spring NJ 08204, USA* E: husan@avaloninternet.net

DICKINSON, Canon Anthony William. b 48. New Coll Ox BA 71 MA 74. Linc Th Coll 80. **d** 82 **p** 83. C Leavesden *St Alb* 82-86; TV Upton cum Chalvey *Ox* 86-94; P-in-c Terriers 94-99; V from 99; Chapl Bucks New Univ from 03; Hon Can Ch Ch *Ox* from 05. *St Francis's Vicarage, Amersham Road, High Wycombe HP13 5AB* T: (01494) 520676 E: tony.dickinson@ukonline.co.uk *or* sainsw01@bcuc.ac.uk

DICKINSON, David Charles. b 58. BA 79 Lanc Univ MA 97. CBDTI. **d** 99 **p** 00. NSM Ewood *Blackb* 99-04; NSM Blackb Redeemer 04-05; P-in-c Hoghton 05-12; V 12-13; PtO from 13. *5 Ralph's Wife's Lane, Southport PR9 8ER* M: 07805-598256 T: (01704) 226724　E: dickinsonrev@btinternet.com

DICKINSON, Dyllis Annie. b 52. **d** 01 **p** 02. OLM Stalmine w Pilling *Blackb* 01-07; NSM from 07. *Springfield, Moss Side Lane, Stalmine, Poulton-le-Fylde FY6 0JP* T: (01253) 700011 E: dyllisdickinson@talktalk.net

DICKINSON, Gareth Lee. b 69. Ridley Hall Cam 06. **d** 08 **p** 09. C Bryanston Square St Mary w St Marylebone St Mark *Lon* 08-10; NSM Cheltenham H Trin and St Paul *Glouc* from 10. *Trinity Cheltenham, 100-102 Winchcombe Street, Cheltenham GL52 2NW* M: 07788-742700　T: (01242) 808780 E: garethdickinson@me.com

DICKINSON, Henry. b 29. St Deiniol's Hawarden 84. **d** 86 **p** 87. NSM Blackb St Mich w St Jo and H Trin 86-89; NSM Burnley St Cath w St Alb and St Paul 89-95; PtO from 98. *22 Notre Dame Gardens, Blackburn BB1 5EF* T: (01254) 693414

DICKINSON, The Very Revd the Hon Hugh Geoffrey. b 29. Trin Coll Ox BA 53 MA 56. Cuddesdon Coll 54. **d** 56 **p** 57. C Melksham *Sarum* 56-58; Chapl Trin Coll Cam 58-63; Chapl Win Coll 63-69; P-in-c Milverton *Cov* 69-77; V St Alb St Mich *St Alb* 77-86; Dean Sarum 86-96; rtd 96; PtO *Glouc* from 96. *5 St Peter's Road, Cirencester GL7 1RE* T: (01285) 657710 E: hughanjean@aol.com

DICKINSON, Canon Robert Edward. b 47. Nottm Univ BTh 74. St Jo Coll Nottm 70. **d** 74 **p** 75. C Birm St Martin 74-78; P-in-c Liv St Bride w St Sav 78-81; TV St Luke in the City 81-86; Chapl Liv Poly 86-92; Chapl Liv Jo Moores Univ 92-08; Hon Can Liv Cathl 03-08; rtd 08. *3 Wightman Avenue, Newton-le-Willows WA12 0LS* T: (01925) 271124 E: bobdicko@blueyonder.co.uk

DICKINSON, Simon Braithwaite Vincent. b 34. SAOMC 94. **d** 97 **p** 98. OLM Waddesdon w Over Winchendon and Fleet Marston *Ox* 97-02; OLM Schorne 02-04; PtO from 04. *12A Croft Road, Thame OX9 3JF* T: (01844) 212408 E: dickinson@whitehousewaddesdon.freeserve.co.uk

DICKINSON, Stephen Paul. b 54. SRN 75. NOC 85. **d** 88 **p** 89. NSM Purston cum S Featherstone *Wakef* 88-91; C Goldthorpe w Hickleton *Sheff* 91-94; V New Bentley 94-05; P-in-c Arksey 04-05; V New Bentley w Arksey from 05. *The Vicarage, Victoria Road, Bentley, Doncaster DN5 0EZ* T: (01302) 875266

DICKINSON, Victor Tester. b 48. Univ of Wales (Cardiff) BSc 70. St Steph Ho Ox 70. **d** 73 **p** 74. C Neath w Llantwit *Llan* 73-76; Asst Chapl Univ of Wales (Cardiff) 76-79; TV Willington *Newc* 79-86; V Kenton Ascension 86-97; V Lowick and Kyloe w Ancroft from 97; R Ford and Etal from 97. *The Vicarage, 1 Main Street, Lowick, Berwick-upon-Tweed TD15 2UD* T: (01289) 388229

DICKS, Gareth Roger Milroy. b 80. Ox Brookes Univ BSc 06. Trin Coll Bris BA 13. **d** 13 **p** 14. C Cove St Jo *Guildf* from 13. *14 The Cloisters, Frimley, Camberley GU16 7JR* M: 07939-134261　E: gareth.dicks@btopenworld.com

DICKSON, Adam Anwar. b 83. Hull Univ BSc 05 MSc 06. Qu Coll Birm MA 14. **d** 14 **p** 15. C Wythenshawe *Man* from 14. *St Francis House, 40 Chalford Road, Manchester M23 2RD* E: adam.dickson@gmail.com

DICKSON, Anthony Edward. b 59. Nottm Univ BTh 88. Linc Th Coll 85. **d** 88 **p** 89. C Portsea St Alb *Portsm* 88-91; C Cleobury Mortimer w Hopton Wafers *Heref* 91-94; R Fownhope w Mordiford, Brockhampton etc 94-99; PtO *B & W* 09-11; P-in-c Leigh upon Mendip w Stoke St Michael from 11; P-in-c Nunney and Witham Friary, Marston Bigot etc from 11. *The Rectory, High Street, Nunney, Frome BA11 4LZ* T: (01373) 837337 E: nunney.rectory@gmail.com

DICKSON, Colin James. b 74. St Andr Univ MA 96 MPhil 00 Leeds Univ BA 01. Coll of Resurr Mirfield 99. **d** 02 **p** 03. C Tottenham St Paul *Lon* 02-05; C Croydon St Mich w St Jas *S'wark* 05-10; SSF from 10. *The Friary of St Francis, Alnmouth, Alnwick NE66 3NJ* E: josephemmanuelssf@franciscans.org.uk

DICKSON, Colin Patrick Gavin. b 56. **d** 96 **p** 97. C Grays Thurrock *Chelmsf* 96-00; V Glantawe *S & B* from 00. *The Vicarage, 122 Mansel Road, Bonymaen, Swansea SA1 7JR* T: (01792) 652839 E: cdickson1@sky.com

DICKSON, Samuel Mervyn James. b 41. CITC. **d** 66 **p** 67. C Ballyholme *D & D* 66-70; C Knockbreda 70-75; I Clonallon w Warrenpoint 75-84; I Down H Trin w Hollymount 84-06; Bp's C Rathmullan 00-05; Bp's C Tyrella 00-06; Bp's C Loughinisland 01-06; Can Down Cathl 91-06; Treas Down Cathl 98-00; Prec Down Cathl 00-01; Chan Down Cathl 01-06; rtd 06. *Apartment 1, 40A Main Street, Dundrum, Newcastle BT33 0LY* T: (028) 4375 1112

DIDUK, Sergiy. b 74. Ukranian Nat Academy BA 08. St Jo Coll Nottm MA 11. **d** 11 **p** 12. C Hucknall Torkard *S'well* from 11. *149 Beardall Street, Hucknall, Nottingham NG15 7HA* M: 07817-488425 E: sergius_nd99@hotmail.co.uk

DIETZ, Matthew Paul Richard. b 70. Magd Coll Cam MA 95. Wycliffe Hall Ox 05. **d** 07 **p** 08. C Win Ch Ch 07-08; C Throop 08-11; Chapl Monkton Combe Sch Bath 11-14; Chapl Taunton Sch from 14. *Taunton School, Staplegrove Road, Taunton TA2 6AD* M: 07751-454993 T: (01823) 703703 E: matthew.dietz@btinternet.com

DIFFEY, Margaret Elsie. b 39. MCSP. **d** 02 **p** 03. OLM Nor St Geo Tombland 02-10; rtd 10; PtO *Nor* from 10. *45 Welsford Road, Norwich NR4 6QB* T/F: (01603) 457248 E: maggiediffey@tiscali.co.uk

DIFFIN, Rosie. **d** 12 **p** 13. C Drumglass w Moygashel *Arm* 12-13; C Seapatrick *D & D* 13-15; Dioc C *Arm* from 15. *Address temp unknown* M: 07540-119163 E: rosie.diffin@tesco.net

DIGGINS, Glyn Wingfield. b 62. Cranmer Hall Dur 13. **d** 15. C Malton and Old Malton *York* from 15. *6 Pinfold Garth, Malton YO17 7YQ* E: glynn.diggins@btinternet.com

DIGGLE, Judith Margaret. See BROWN, Judith Margaret

DIGGLE, Richard James. b 47. Lon Inst BA 69 Man Poly CertEd 73. **d** 01 **p** 02. OLM Chorlton-cum-Hardy St Werburgh *Man* 01-05; NSM Bickerton, Bickley, Harthill and Burwardsley *Ches* 05-08; V Antrobus, Aston by Sutton, Lt Leigh etc 08-12; P-in-c Bickley from 12. *Ebnal House, Ebnal Lane, Malpas SY14 8DL* M: 07749-849783 E: diggle163@btinternet.com

DIGGORY, Mrs Susan Jane. b 51. SEITE BA 09. **d** 09 **p** 10. NSM Tunbridge Wells St Mark *Roch* 09-14; V Crockham Hill H Trin from 14. *The Vicarage, Oakdale Lane, Crockham Hill, Edenbridge TN8 6RL* T: (01732) 446466 M: 07799-892583 E: sue.diggory@diocese-rochester.org

DIGMAN (née BUTTERFIELD), Mrs Amanda Helen. b 73. Derby Univ BA 96. St Jo Coll Nottm 07. **d** 09 **p** 10. C Sutton in Ashfield St Mary *S'well* 09-12; C Huthwaite 09-10; P-in-c Carlton from 12; P-in-c Colwick from 12. *The Vicarage, 261 Oakdale Road, Carlton, Nottingham NG4 1BP* M: 07803-625049 E: revamandadigman@gmail.com

DILKES, Nigel Bruce. b 58. Univ of Wales (Ban) BSc 97 Lanc Univ PhD 01. Ridley Hall Cam 03. **d** 05 **p** 06. C Llandudno *Ban* 05-07; C Holyhead 07-09; TV Barnstaple *Ex* from 09. *The Rectory, 4 Northfield Lane, Barnstaple EX31 1QB* T: (01271) 343225 E: nigeldilkes@aol.com

DILL, Nicholas Bayard Botolf. b 63. Toronto Univ BA 86 Lon Univ LLB 89 Barrister 91. Wycliffe Hall Ox 96. **d** 98 **p** 99. C Lindfield *Chich* 98-05; R Pembroke St Jo Bermuda from 05. *St John's Rectory, 15 Langton Hill, Pembroke HM 13, Bermuda* T: (001) (441) 292 5308 F: 296 9173 E: nickdill@logic.bm

DILL, Peter Winston. b 41. ACP 66 K Coll Lon BD 72 AKC 72. St Aug Coll Cant 72. **d** 73 **p** 74. C Warsop *S'well* 73-75; C Rhyl w St Ann *St As* 75-77; C Oxton *Ches* 77-78; V Newton in Mottram 78-82; P-in-c Shelton and Oxon *Lich* 82-84; V 84-87; Chapl Clifton Coll Bris 87-00; C Thorverton, Cadbury, Upton Pyne etc *Ex* 00-01; PtO *Bris* 02-03; Past Co-ord St Monica Trust Westbury Fields 03-06; rtd 06. *85B Pembroke Road, Clifton, Bristol BS8 3EB* T: 0117-973 9769

DILLINGHAM, Robert Paul. b 64. St Mellitus Coll. **d** 12 **p** 13. NSM Crowborough *Chich* from 12. *Thornton, Crowborough Hill, Crowborough TN6 2SE* T: (01892) 660038

DILLON, Gerard Francis. **d** 14 **p** 15. C Glenrothes *St And* from 14; C Leven from 14; C Lochgelly from 14. *Address temp unknown*

DILNOT, Canon John William. b 36. Selw Coll Cam BA 60 MA 64. Cuddesdon Coll 60. **d** 62 **p** 63. C Stafford St Mary *Lich* 62-66; C Stoke upon Trent 66-67; V Leek All SS 67-74; V Leeds w Broomfield *Cant* 74-79; P-in-c Aldington 79-81; P-in-c Bonnington w Bilsington 79-81; P-in-c Fawkenhurst 79-81; R Aldington w Bonnington and Bilsington 81-87; RD N Lympne 82-87; Hon Can Cant Cathl 85-99; V Folkestone St Mary and St Eanswythe 87-99; rtd 99; PtO *Cant* from 99. *Underhill Cottage, The Undercliff, Sandgate, Folkestone CT20 3AT* T: (01303) 248000

DILWORTH, Anthony. b 41. St Deiniol's Hawarden 87. **d** 90 **p** 91. NSM Gt Saughall *Ches* 90-93; P-in-c Cwmcarn *Mon*

93-95; V 95-98; V Abercarn and Cwmcarn 99-01; TV Upholland *Liv* 01-06; PtO *St As* 09-10 and from 12; P-in-c Llansilin w Llangadwaladr and Llangedwyn 10-12. *4 Maes Owain, Glyndyfrdwy, Corwen LL21 9HF* T: (01490) 430586 M: 07773-389179 E: anthonydilworth536@btinternet.com

DIMERY, Richard James. b 76. CCC Cam MA 98 Leeds Univ MA 99. Wycliffe Hall Ox MA 03. **d** 04 **p** 05. C Upper Armley *Ripon* 04-08; P-in-c Woodside *Leeds* from 08; Asst Dir of Ords *Ripon* 13-14; AD Headingley *Leeds* from 13; Assoc Dioc Dir of Ords from 14. *St James's Vicarage, 1 Scotland Close, Horsforth, Leeds LS18 5SG* T: 0113-228 2902 E: richard@dimery.com

DIMES, Stuart Christopher Laurence. b 60. Warwick Univ BSc 81. St Jo Coll Nottm 99. **d** 01 **p** 02. C Branksome St Clem *Sarum* 01-05; P-in-c W Heath *Birm* 05-10; V from 10. *The Vicarage, 54A Lilley Lane, Birmingham B31 3JT* T: 0121-476 7776 E: revsdimes@live.com

DIMMICK, Kenneth Ray. b 55. Texas A&M Univ BA 77. Nashotah Ho MDiv 84. **d** 84 **p** 84. C Shreveport St Matthias USA 84-86; P-in-c 86-87; R St Francisville Grace Ch 87-00; Assoc R Houston Palmer Memorial Ch 00-05; V Anahuac Trin 05-06; P-in-c Stuttgart *Eur* from 06. *Lorenzstaffel 8, 70182 Stuttgart, Germany* T: (0049) (711) 787 8783 M: 151-5798 9140 E: vicar@stcatherines-stuttgart.de

DIMMICK, Mrs Margaret Louisa. b 44. Keswick Hall Coll TCert 66 Open Univ BA 75. SAOMC 97. **d** 00 **p** 02. OLM Caversham St Pet and Mapledurham etc *Ox* 00-03; OLM Emmer Green w Caversham Park 03-14; PtO from 14. *12 Lowfield Road, Caversham, Reading RG4 6PA* T: 0118-947 0258 E: margaret@dimmick33.freeserve.co.uk

DIMOND, Mark James. b 68. Kent Univ BA 90 St Ant Coll Ox MPhil 93 Univ of Wales (Swansea) PhD 04 Cardiff Univ DipEd 06. **d** 11 **p** 12. C Penarth All SS *Llan* 11-14; Chapl to Abp Wales from 14. *Llys Esgob, The Cathedral Green, Cardiff CF5 2YE* T: (029) 2056 2400 E: markdimond@churchinwales.org.uk

DINELEY, Margaret Anne. **d** 15. C Glenrothes *St And* from 15; C Leven from 15; C Lochgelly from 15. *Address temp unknown*

DINES, Edwin Paul Anthony. b 73. Chelt & Glouc Coll of HE BEd 96. Trin Coll Bris BA 11. **d** 11 **p** 12. C Knight's Enham and Smannell w Enham Alamein *Win* 11-14; C Knight's Enham 14-15; P-in-c Win St Barn from 15. *St Barnabas Vicarage, Trussell Crescent, Winchester SO22 6DY* E: eddines@inbox.com

DINNEN, John Frederick. b 42. TCD BA 65 BD 72 QUB MTh 91. CITC. **d** 66 **p** 67. C Belfast All SS *Conn* 66-68; ICM Dub 69-71; C Carnmoney *Conn* 71-73; Asst Dean of Residences QUB 73-74; Dean 74-84; I Hillsborough *D & D* 84-07; Preb Down Cathl 93-96; Dir of Ords 96-06; Dean Down 96-06; rtd 06. *74 Demesne Road, Ballynahinch BT24 8NS* T: (028) 4481 1148 E: jdinnen@btinternet.com

DINNEN, Mrs Judith Margaret. b 48. Open Univ BA 87 Univ of Wales (Cardiff) MA 00 Goldsmiths' Coll Lon TCert 71. WEMTC 01. **d** 05 **p** 06. NSM Madley w Tyberton, Peterchurch, Vowchurch etc *Heref* from 05. *The Hawthorns, Madley, Hereford HR2 9LU* T: (01981) 251866 E: judy@dinnen.plus.com

DINSMORE, Ivan Ernest. b 71. TCD BTh 01. CITC 98. **d** 01 **p** 02. C Glendermott *D & R* 01-04; I Balteagh w Carrick and Tamlaghtard w Aghanloo 04-11; I Ardstraw w Baronscourt, Badoney Lower etc from 11. *The Rectory, 2 Bunderg Road, Newtownstewart BT78 4NQ* T/F: (028) 8166 1342 M: 07918-765428 E: ivandinsmore@hotmail.com

DINSMORE, Stephen Ralph. b 56. Wye Coll Lon BSc 78 Man Univ MA 06. Cranmer Hall Dur 82. **d** 85 **p** 86. C Haughton le Skerne *Dur* 85-88; C Edgware *Lon* 88-93; V Plymouth St Jude *Ex* 93-05; RD Plymouth Sutton 96-01; Dioc Adv for Miss and Par Development *Chelmsf* 05-07; Hon C Cranham Park 05-07; Nat Dir SOMA UK from 07. *SOMA UK, PO Box 69, Merriott TA18 9AP* T: (01460) 279737 E: stephen.dinsmore@somauk.org

DINWIDDY SMITH, Emma Ruth. b 67. **d** 10 **p** 11. C Hampstead St Jo Lon 10-13; C Chelsea St Luke and Ch Ch from 13. *29 Burnsall Street, London SW3 3SR*

DISLEY, Mrs Edith Jennifer. b 51. Sheff Univ BSc 72 Man Univ BD 79. NOC 99. **d** 01 **p** 02. NSM Man Victoria Park 01-10; NSM Withington St Paul 02-10; NSM Wythenshawe 10-12; P-in-c Leesfield 12-15; V from 15. *St Thomas's Vicarage, 2 Wild Street, Lees, Oldham OL4 5AD* T: 0161-624 3731 E: edithdisley@hotmail.com

DITCH, David John. b 45. St Cath Coll Cam BA 67 MA 70 Leeds Univ PGCE 68. WMMTC 88. **d** 91 **p** 92. C Biddulph *Lich* 91-94; V Hednesford 94-02; V Chasetown 02-08; rtd 09; PtO *Derby* from 09. *6 Redwing Croft, Derby DE23 1WF* T: (01332) 271767

DITCHBURN, Hazel. b 44. NEOC 82. **dss** 84 **d** 87 **p** 94. Scotswood *Newc* 84-86; Ind Chapl *Dur* 86-95; TV Gateshead 95-98; AD 92-98; P-in-c Stella 98-04; P-in-c Swalwell 01-04;

R Blaydon and Swalwell 04-06; AD Gateshead W 98-00; Hon Can Dur Cathl 94-06; P-in-c Freshwater Australia 06-09. *2 Woburn Way, Westerhope, Newcastle upon Tyne NE5 5JD* T: 0191-286 0553

DITCHFIELD, Timothy Frederick. b 61. CCC Cam BA 83. Cranmer Hall Dur 85. **d** 88 **p** 89. C Accrington St Jo *Blackb* 88-89; C Accrington St Jo w Huncoat 89-91; C Whittle-le-Woods 91-95; Chapl K Coll Lon from 95. *19 Maunsel Street, London SW1P 2QN, or King's College, Strand, London WC2R 2LS* T: (020) 7828 1772 *or* 7848 2373 F: 7848 2344 E: tim.ditchfield@kcl.ac.uk

DIVALL, David Robert. b 40. New Coll Ox BA 64 Sussex Univ DPhil 74. Sarum & Wells Th Coll 75. **d** 77 **p** 78. Hon C Catherington and Clanfield *Portsm* 77-92; Hon C Rowlands Castle 92-93; PtO from 01. *17 Pipers Mead, Clanfield, Waterlooville PO8 0ST* T: (023) 9259 4845

DIVALL, Stephen Robert. b 70. Pemb Coll Ox MA 92. Ridley Hall Cam 95. **d** 98 **p** 99. C Cheadle *Ches* 98-01; Team Ldr UCCF 01-06; V Kensington St Helen w H Trin *Lon* from 06. *St Helen's Vicarage, St Helen's Gardens, London W10 6LP* T: (020) 8968 7807

DIX, Edward Joseph. b 77. Goldsmiths' Coll Lon BMus 00. Wycliffe Hall Ox BTh 09. **d** 09 **p** 10. C Shadwell St Paul w Ratcliffe St Jas *Lon* 09-13; C Is of Dogs Ch Ch and St Jo w St Luke from 13. *170 Wheat Sheaf Close, London E14 9UZ* T: (020) 7515 5772 M: 07899-075935 E: edjdix@gmail.com

DIXON, Ms Anne Elizabeth. b 56. Leeds Univ LLB 77 Solicitor 80. Westcott Ho Cam. **d** 01 **p** 02. C Guildf H Trin w St Mary 01-05; Chapl HM Pris Bullwood Hall 06-09; PtO *Guildf* from 05; *Blackb* from 10; *S'wark* from 14; *Ox* from 15. *2 Highcroft Court, Bookham, Leatherhead KT23 3QU* T: (01372) 450643 M: 07973-542467

DIXON, Bruce Richard. b 42. Lon Univ BScEng 63. Sarum Th Coll 66. **d** 68 **p** 69. C Walton St Mary *Liv* 68-70; C Harnham *Sarum* 70-73; C Streatham St Leon *S'wark* 73-77; R Thurcaston *Leic* 77-83; R Cranborne w Boveridge, Edmondsham etc *Sarum* 83-02; rtd 02. *East Heddon, Filleigh, Barnstaple EX32 0RY* T: (01598) 760513 E: bandk2d@hotmail.com

DIXON, Bryan Stanley. b 61. St Jo Coll Nottm BTh 93. **d** 93 **p** 94. C Beverley Minster *York* 93-96; C Kingston upon Hull St Aid Southcoates 96-97; Asst Chapl HM Pris Dur 97-98; R Mid Marsh Gp *Linc* 98-03; R Brandesburton and Leven w Catwick *York* 03-10; P-in-c Patrick Brompton and Hunton *Leeds* from 10; P-in-c Crakehall from 10; P-in-c Hornby from 10; P-in-c Spennithorne w Finghall and Hauxwell from 12; AD Wensley *Ripon* 11-13. *The Vicarage, Patrick Brompton, Bedale DL8 1JN* T: (01677) 450985 E: tdogcollar3@tdogcollar3.yahoo.co.uk

DIXON, Campbell Boyd. b 42. Lon Univ BSc 63. **d** 07 **p** 08. NSM Jordanstown *Conn* from 07. *10 Meadowbank, Newtownabbey BT37 0UP* E: campbelldixon@hotmail.co.uk

DIXON, Charles William. b 41. NW Ord Course 78. **d** 81 **p** 82. C Almondbury *Wakef* 81-82; C Almondbury w Farnley Tyas 82-84; P-in-c Shelley 84-88; P-in-c Shepley 84-88; V Shelley and Shepley 88-89; V Ripponden 89-94; V Barkisland w W Scammonden 89-94; P-in-c Thornes 94-98; Chapl among Deaf People *Chelmsf* 98-06; rtd 06; Chapl among Deaf People *Ely* 06-10; PtO from 10. *9 The Paddock, Huntingdon PE29 1BY* T: (01480) 451109 M: 07749-702924 E: c.dixon41@btinternet.com

DIXON, Canon David. b 19. Lich Th Coll 57. **d** 58 **p** 59. C Barrow St Luke *Carl* 58-61; V Westfield St Mary 61-68; Warden Rydal Hall 68-84; P-in-c Rydal 78-84; rtd 84; PtO *Carl* from 84; Hon Can Carl Cathl 84-85. *Rheda, The Green, Millom LA18 5JA* T: (01229) 774300

DIXON, David Hugh. b 40. Chich Th Coll 90. **d** 92 **p** 93. C Launceston *Truro* 92-95; TV Probus, Ladock and Grampound w Creed and St Erme 95-06; rtd 06. *1 Rectory Close, Old Village, Willand, Cullompton EX15 2RH* T: (01884) 839984

DIXON, David Michael. b 58. Preston Poly BA 82 Barrister 83. Coll of Resurr Mirfield BA 98. **d** 98 **p** 99. C Goldthorpe w Hickleton *Sheff* 98-01; P-in-c W Kirby St Andr *Ches* 01-07; V 07-10; P-in-c Scarborough St Martin *York* 10-12; V from 12; P-in-c Scarborough St Sav w All SS 10-12; V from 12. *St Martin's Vicarage, Craven Street, Scarborough YO11 2BY* T: (01723) 363828 E: frdavidstmart@gmail.com

DIXON, Edward Michael. b 42. St Chad's Coll Dur BA 64 Newc Univ MA 93. **d** 66 **p** 67. C Hartlepool H Trin *Dur* 66-70; C Howden *York* 70-73; Chapl HM Pris Liv 73; Chapl HM Pris Onley 74-82; Chapl HM Pris Frankland 82-87; Chapl HM Pris Dur 87-97; Chapl HM Pris Acklington 97-98; Asst Chapl 98-02; P-in-c Shilbottle *Newc* 98-07; P-in-c Chevington 03-07; rtd 07; PtO *Dur* from 07. *2 Crowley Place, Newton Aycliffe DL5 4JH* T: (01325) 312872

DIXON, John Kenneth. b 40. Linc Th Coll 79. **d** 81 **p** 82. C Goldington *St Alb* 81-85; V Cardington 85-94; RD Elstow

89-94; R Clifton 94-95; P-in-c Southill 94-95; R Clifton and Southill 95-05; RD Shefford 95-01; rtd 05. *7 Milton Fields, Brixham TQ5 0BH* T: (01803) 854396 E: eidyn@cainnech.fsworld.co.uk

DIXON, John Scarth. b 69. Aber Univ MA 92. Westcott Ho Cam 95. **d** 98 **p** 99. C Walney Is *Carl* 98-01; R Harrington 01-06; V Hawkshead and Low Wray w Sawrey and Rusland etc from 06. *The Vicarage, Vicarage Lane, Hawkshead, Ambleside LA22 0PD* T: (015394) 36301 E: jjcdixon@btinternet.com

DIXON, Kenneth. See DIXON, John Kenneth

DIXON, Capt Kerry John. b 59. Wilson Carlile Coll 84. **d** 13 **p** 14. LtO *Bre* 13-14; P Missr from 14; P-in-c Dundee St Luke from 14. *6 Dudhope Street, Dundee DD1 1JU* T: (01382) 523911 M: 07711-410017 E: kerry@signpost-international.org

DIXON, Lorraine. b 65. Leeds Univ BA 96. Qu Coll Birm BD 98. **d** 98 **p** 99. C Potternewton *Ripon* 98-01; Chapl Ches Univ 01-05; Min Can Ches Cathl 04-05; Deanery Missr to Young Adults Yardley & Bordsley *Birm* 05-12; PtO from 13. *26-28 Lincoln Street, Birmingham B12 9EX* T: 0121-440 1221 E: l.dixon65@btopenworld.com

DIXON, Margaret Innes Goodwin. b 58. Reading Univ BA 01. Ox Min Course 08. **d** 11 **p** 12. NSM Ellesborough, The Kimbles and Stoke Mandeville *Ox* 11-14; NSM C N Leigh from 14; C Cogges and S Leigh from 14. *The Vicarage, New Yatt Road, North Leigh, Witney OX29 6TT* M: 07773-017636 T: (01993) 880095 E: margaretigdixon@tinyworld.co.uk

DIXON, Michael. See DIXON, Edward Michael

DIXON, Nicholas Scarth. b 30. G&C Coll Cam BA 54 MA 63. Westcott Ho Cam 54. **d** 56 **p** 57. C Walney Is *Carl* 56-59; CF 59-62; V Whitehaven Ch Ch w H Trin *Carl* 62-70; R Blofield w Hemblington *Nor* 70-77; P-in-c Bowness *Carl* 77-79; R 79-81; V Frizington and Arlecdon 81-87; V Barton, Pooley Bridge and Martindale 87-95; rtd 95; PtO *Carl* from 95. *7 Mayburgh Avenue, Penrith CA11 8PA* T: (01768) 892864

DIXON, Peter. b 70. Ex Univ BTh 08. SWMTC 04. **d** 07 **p** 08. C Redruth w Lanner and Treleigh *Truro* 07-10; V Wisborough Green *Chich* 10-13; P-in-c Lanteglos by Camelford w Advent *Truro* from 13; P-in-c St Teath from 13. *The Rectory, Glebe Parc, St Tudy, Bodmin PL30 3AS* E: peter_dixon@btinternet.com

DIXON, Canon Peter. b 36. Qu Coll Ox BA 58 MA 62 Birm Univ BD 65 PhD 75. Qu Coll Birm. **d** 60 **p** 61. C Mountain Ash *Llan* 60-63; C Penrhiwceiber w Matthewstown and Ynysboeth 63-68; P-in-c 68-70; V Bronllys w Llanfilo *S & B* 70-02; Bp's Chapl for Readers 80-02; Bp's Chapl for Th Educn 83-02; Warden of Readers 92-02; RD Hay 90-02; Can Res Brecon Cathl 98-02; rtd 02. *22 The Caerpound, Hay-on-Wye, Hereford HR3 5DU* T: (01497) 820775

DIXON, Peter David. b 48. Edin Univ BSc 71 MIMechE. Edin Dioc NSM Course 75. **d** 79 **p** 80. NSM Prestonpans *Edin* 79-89; NSM Musselburgh 79-89; NSM Wester Hailes St Luke 90; P-in-c Edin St Barn from 91. *8 Oswald Terrace, Prestonpans EH32 9EG* T: (01875) 812985

DIXON, Philip. b 48. Leeds Univ BSc 69 Open Univ BA 91. St Jo Coll Nottm 77. **d** 80 **p** 81. C Soundwell *Bris* 80-82; C Stoke Bishop 82-84; TV Hemel Hempstead *St Alb* 84-85; Chapl Westonbirt Sch 85-11; rtd 11; PtO *Bris* from 86. *27 Downfield Lodge, Downfield Road, Bristol BS8 2TQ* T: 0117-373 8528 E: pdnovenove@yahoo.com

DIXON, Philip Roger. b 54. CCC Ox BA 77 MA 80. Oak Hill Th Coll BA 80. **d** 80 **p** 81. C Droylsden St Mary *Man* 80-84; TV Rochdale 84-91; V Audenshaw St Steph from 91; AD Ashton-under-Lyne 03-08; C Denton Ch Ch from 13; C Denton St Lawr from 13; C Haughton St Anne from 13. *St Stephen's Vicarage, 176 Stamford Road, Audenshaw, Manchester M34 5WW* T: 0161-370 1863 E: ssaudenshaw@aol.com

DIXON, Robert. b 50. Univ of Wales (Lamp) BA 80 Sussex Univ MA 04. Chich Th Coll 80. **d** 81 **p** 82. C Maidstone St Martin *Cant* 81-84; Chapl HM Youth Cust Cen Dover 84-88; C All Hallows by the Tower etc *Lon* 88-90; P-in-c Southwick H Trin *Dur* 90-97; R 97; R Etchingham *Chich* 97-10; V Hurst Green 97-10; V Bedford Leigh *Man* from 10. *St Thomas's Vicarage, 121 Green Lane, Leigh WN7 2TW* T: (01942) 673519 M: 07779-121169 E: sussexrob@aol.com

DIXON, Roger John. b 33. Magd Coll Cam BA 58 MA 61. EAMTC 78. **d** 79 **p** 80. NSM Fakenham w Alethorpe *Nor* 79-82; C Brandeston w Kettleburgh *St E* 82-84; P-in-c 84-99; Asst Chapl Framlingham Coll 82-99; RD Loes *St E* 97-98; rtd 99; PtO *Nor* 99-05; *Llan* from 05. *9 The Crescent, Fairwater, Cardiff CF5 3DF* T: (029) 2056 6031

DIXON, Stephen. b 65. Lindisfarne Regional Tr Partnership 13. **d** 15. Pioneer Min Willington Quay and Tynemouth *Newc* 08-15; C Gosforth All SS from 15. *27 Otterburn Avenue, Newcastle upon Tyne NE3 4RR* T: 0191-262 1539 M: 07729-393580 E: s.d.dixon@bigfoot.com *or* s.c.dixon@hotmail.co.uk

DIXON, Stephen William. b 53. Nottm Univ BA 75 Liv Univ MTh 00 Ches Univ DProf 12 Man Metrop Univ PGCE 88. NOC 96. **d** 99 **p** 00. NSM Meltham *Wakef* 99-02; NSM Upper Holme Valley *Leeds* from 02; Lic Preacher *Man* from 01. *83 Totties, Holmfirth HD9 1UJ* T: (01484) 687376
E: familymasondixon@uwclub.net

DIXON, Mrs Teresa Mary. b 61. Southn Univ BSc 82 Ball Coll Ox PGCE 83. EAMTC 99. **d** 02 **p** 03. NSM Sutton and Witcham w Mepal *Ely* 02-04; C Littleport 04-06; NSM Witchford w Wentworth from 06. *Ash Tree Farm, Furlong Drove, Little Downham, Ely CB6 2EW* T: (01353) 699552
E: revteresa@googlemail.com

DNISTRIANSKYJ, Stefan Mykola. b 61. Leic Univ BSc 82 Ches Coll of HE BTh 02. NOC 99. **d** 02 **p** 03. C Halliwell St Luke *Man* 02-06; TV New Bury w Gt Lever 06-09; P-in-c Anchorsholme *Blackb* 09-12; V from 12. *The Vicarage, 36 Valeway Avenue, Thornton-Cleveleys FY5 3RN* T: (01253) 823904 M: 07931-785598 E: dnists@gmail.com

DOARKS, Andrew John. b 68. Leic Univ BA 91 De Montfort Univ MSc 92. St Mellitus Coll BA 08. **d** 11 **p** 12. C Brislington St Luke *Bris* 11-14; P-in-c Bedminster from 14. *Bedminster Rectory, 287 North Street, Bedminster, Bristol BS3 1JP* M: 07970-495654 E: adoarks@gmail.com

DOBBIE, Charles William Granville. b 49. OBE 92. Wycliffe Hall Ox 94. **d** 96 **p** 97. C Morriston *S & B* 96-00; Asst Chapl Morriston Hosp/Ysbyty Treforys NHS Trust 97-98; Asst Chapl Swansea NHS Trust 99-00; V Lyonsdown H Trin *St Alb* from 00. *Holy Trinity Vicarage, 18 Lyonsdown Road, Barnet EN5 1JE* T: (020) 8216 3786 E: charles@holytrinitylyonsdown.org.uk

DOBBIE, Gary William. b 51. St Andr Univ MA 75 BD 77 Magd Coll Cam CertEd 80 FRSA 98 FSAScot. Coll of Resurr Mirfield 83. **d** 83 **p** 83. Kimbolton Sch 83-84; Hon C Kimbolton *Ely* 83-84; Sen Chapl Ch Hosp Horsham 86-96; Asst Chapl 96-03; Housemaster 93-03; Chapl Shrewsbury Sch from 03. *Shrewsbury School, Kingsland, Shrewsbury SY3 7BA* T: (01743) 280550 M: 07879-426056
E: chaplain@shrewsbury.org.uk

DOBBIN, Canon Charles Philip. b 51. MBE 14. Jes Coll Cam BA 73 MA 77 Oriel Coll Ox BA 75 MA 88. St Steph Ho Ox 74. **d** 76 **p** 77. C New Addington *Cant* 76-79; C Melton Mowbray w Thorpe Arnold *Leic* 79-83; V Loughb Gd Shep 83-89; V Ashby-de-la-Zouch St Helen w Coleorton 89-00; RD Akeley W 93-00; Hon Can Leic Cathl 94-00; TR Moor Allerton *Ripon* 00-09; TR Moor Allerton and Shadwell *Leeds* from 09; Dioc Interfaith Relns Officer from 09. *St John's Rectory, 1 Fir Tree Lane, Leeds LS17 7BZ* T: 0113-268 4598 E: cdobbin@aol.com

DOBBIN, Harold John. b 47. Liv Univ BSc 69. St Steph Ho Ox 70. **d** 73 **p** 74. C Newbold w Dunston *Derby* 73-77; C Leckhampton SS Phil and Jas w Cheltenham St Jas *Glouc* 77-80; V Hebburn St Cuth *Dur* 80-86; R Barlborough *Derby* 86-95; P-in-c Alfreton 95-00; V 00-04; RD 02-04; P-in-c Clifton 04-08; P-in-c Norbury w Snelston 04-08; rtd 08. *21 Dale Close, Fritchley, Belper DE56 2HZ* T: (01773) 857002
E: harolddobbin@yahoo.co.uk

DOBBIN, Miss Penelope Jane. b 59. GRSC 88. SAOMC 96. **d** 99 **p** 00. C Bideford, Northam, Westward Ho!, Appledore etc *Ex* 99-05; TV 05-11; V Minehead *B & W* 11-14; rtd 14. *1 Riverside Close, Bideford EX39 2RX* T: (01237) 477264
E: penelopedobbin@outlook.com

DOBBINS, Lorraine Sharon. b 72. Ripon Coll Cuddesdon BTh 01. **d** 01 **p** 02. C Talbot Village *Sarum* 01-05; TV Preston w Sutton Poyntz, Littlemoor etc from 05; Asst Dioc Dir of Ords from 13. *2 Primula Close, Weymouth DT3 6SL* T: (01305) 835921 E: vicarlorraine@gmail.com

DOBBS, George Christopher. b 48. Linc Th Coll 66. **d** 68 **p** 69. C Hykeham *Linc* 68-71; Asst Master Heneage Sch Grimsby 71-78; PtO *S'well* 78-80; TV Chelmsley Wood *Birm* 80-84; TV Rochdale *Man* 84-99; V Sudden St Aidan and C Castleton Moor 00-08; rtd 08; PtO *Man* from 08. *9 Highlands, Littleborough OL15 0DS* T: (01706) 377688
E: g3rjv@gqpr.demon.co.uk

DOBBS, Matthew Joseph. b 62. St Mich Coll Llan BTh 04. **d** 04 **p** 05. C Llantwit Major *Llan* 04-08; TV Monkton *St D* 08-09. *4 rue de la Bergère, St Just-Luzac, 17320 Charente-Maritime, France* E: matthew@mdobbs.freeserve.co.uk

DOBBS, Michael John. b 48. Linc Th Coll 74. **d** 77 **p** 78. C Warsop *S'well* 77-82; V Worksop St Paul 82-89; P-in-c Mansfield St Mark 89-03; V Kirk Hallam *Derby* 03-05; rtd 05; PtO *S'well* from 06. *30 Waverley Road, Mansfield NG18 5AG* E: mjdmjd@ntlworld.com

DOBELL (née PRICE), Mrs Alison Jane. b 63. Open Univ BA 98. Aston Tr Scheme 91 Westcott Ho Cam 93. **d** 95 **p** 96. C Upper Norwood All SS *S'wark* 95-99; V Mitcham St Barn 99-07; Chapl St Jo Win Charity from 11. *74 Radway Road, Southampton SO15 7PJ* T: (023) 8077 3631
E: alisonjane.price@btinternet.com

DOBLE, Dominic Julian Anderson. b 71. Wye Coll Lon BSc 92 Univ of Wales (Ban) MSc 99 Leeds Univ BA 10. Coll of Resurr Mirfield 08. **d** 10 **p** 11. C Crediton, Shobrooke and Sandford etc *Ex* 10-14; R Watercombe *Sarum* from 14. *The Rectory, Main Street, Broadmayne, Dorchester DT2 8EB* T: (01305) 852435 M: 07743-554955 E: dominic.doble@thephone.coop

DOBLE, Mrs Maureen Mary Thompson. b 44. RGN 65. S Dios Minl Tr Scheme 90. **d** 93 **p** 94. NSM Kingston St Mary w Broomfield etc *B & W* 93-07; Chapl Taunton and Somerset NHS Trust 03-07; rtd 07; PtO *B & W* from 07. *Rosebank, Lyngford Lane, Taunton TA2 7LL* T: (01823) 286772
E: rosebank@maureendoble.co.uk

DOBLE, Peter. b 29. Univ of Wales (Cardiff) BA 51 Fitzw Coll Cam BA 54 MA 58 St Edm Hall Ox MA 68 Leeds Univ PhD 92. Wesley Ho Cam 52. **d** 55 **p** 58. In Ch of S India 55-60; In Meth Ch 60-64; Hd of RE Qu Mary Sch Lytham St Annes *Blackb* 64-67; Lect RS Culham Coll Abingdon Ox 67-69; Sen Lect 69-74; Prin Lect and Hd Relig Studies 74-80; PtO *York* from 80; Dir York RE Cen 80-94; Sen Fell Th and RS Leeds Univ *Ripon* 95-98; Hon Lect *Leeds* from 98. *6 Witham Drive, Huntington, York YO32 9YD* T: (01904) 761288
E: peter.doble@btinternet.com

DOBSON, Catherine Heather. b 71. ERMC. **d** 09 **p** 10. NSM Broughton w Loddington and Cransley etc *Pet* 09-11; C 11-14; C Rothwell w Orton, Rushton w Glendon and Pipewell 11-14; R Bacton, Happisburgh, Hempstead w Eccles etc *Nor* from 14. *The Rectory, The Hill, Happisburgh, Norwich NR12 0PW* E: revcdobson@live.com

DOBSON, Christopher John. b 62. Univ of Wales (Abth) BA 83. Wycliffe Hall Ox BA 88. **d** 89 **p** 90. C Biggin Hill *Roch* 89-92; C Tunbridge Wells St Jas w St Phil 92-95; USPG Zimbabwe 95-99; V Paddock Wood *Roch* 00-08; Dioc Ecum and Global Partnership Officer *Bris* from 08; Hon C Downend from 09. *23 Ducie Road, Staple Hill, Bristol BS16 5JZ* M: 07904-831829 E: chris.j.dobson@gmail.com *or* chris.dobson@bristoldiocese.org

DOBSON, Geoffrey Norman. b 46. Leeds Univ CertEd 68 Open Univ BA 77 MA 05 ACP 70. Wells Th Coll 71. **d** 74 **p** 75. C Wanstead H Trin Hermon Hill *Chelmsf* 74-76; Colchester Adnry Youth Chapl 76-78; C Halstead St Andr w H Trin and Greenstead Green *Chelmsf* 76-78; Asst Dir Educn (Youth) *Carl* 78-82; P-in-c Kirkandrews-on-Eden w Beaumont and Grinsdale 78-82; V Illingworth *Wakef* 82-86; V Roxton w Gt Barford *St Alb* 86-93; Chapl N Man Health Care NHS Trust 93-98; P-in-c Newton Heath St Wilfrid and St Anne *Man* 93-97; C Newton Heath 97-98; P-in-c Alconbury cum Weston *Ely* 98-00; P-in-c Buckworth 98-00; P-in-c Gt w Lt Stukeley 98-00; PtO from 02. *30 Lees Lane, Southoe, St Neots PE19 5YG* T: (01480) 475474 E: geoffreyndobson@aol.com

DOBSON, Mrs Joanna Jane Louise. b 61. Coll of Ripon & York St Jo BEd 83. NEOC 98. **d** 01 **p** 02. NSM Scalby *York* 01-04; V Bridlington Em 04-08; P-in-c Skipsea w Ulrome and Barmston w Fraisthorpe 04-08; Pioneer Min Retford Deanery *S'well* 08-10; P-in-c Mitford and Hebron *Newc* from 10. *The Vicarage, Stable Green, Mitford, Morpeth NE61 3PZ* T: (01670) 511468 M: 07828-181506 E: revjoannadobson@yahoo.co.uk

DOBSON, The Very Revd John Richard. b 64. Van Mildert Coll Dur BA 87. Ripon Coll Cuddesdon 87. **d** 89 **p** 90. C Benfieldside *Dur* 89-92; C Darlington St Cuth 92-96; C-in-c Blackwell All SS and Salutation CD 96-98; V Blackwell All SS and Salutation 98-14; P-in-c Coniscliffe 04-14; AD Darlington 01-14; Hon Can Dur Cathl 08-14; Dean Ripon *Leeds* from 14. *Minster House, Bedern Bank, Ripon HG4 1PE* T: (01765) 602609 E: j.dobson991@btinternet.com

DOBSON, Owen James. b 83. Ex Univ BA 04. Westcott Ho Cam 08. **d** 10 **p** 11. C St John's Wood *Lon* 10-14; C Paddington St Jas from 14. *61 Pembroke House, Hallfield Estate, London W2 6HQ* M: 07891-890837
E: owenjamesdobson@hotmail.com

DOBSON, Peter David. b 88. St Andr Univ MTheol 10 Jes Coll Cam MPhil 11. Westcott Ho Cam 10. **d** 12 **p** 13. C Ch the King *Newc* from 12. *24 Chipchase Mews, Newcastle upon Tyne NE3 5RH* T: 0191-236 8876 M: 07940-706123
E: peterdobsonuk@yahoo.co.uk

DOBSON, Philip Albert. b 52. Lanc Univ BA 73 CertEd 74. Trin Coll Bris 89. **d** 89 **p** 90. C Grenoside *Sheff* 89-92; C Cove St Jo *Guildf* 92-93; TV 93-96; V Camberley St Martin Old Dean 96-07; TR Bushbury *Lich* 07-13; rtd 13; PtO *Man* from 14. *134 Old Moat Lane, Manchester M20 1DE* T: 0161-283 9697
E: philipdobson1@tiscali.co.uk

DOBSON, Stuart Joseph. b 51. Westmr Coll Ox BA 85. Chich Th Coll 86. **d** 88 **p** 89. C Costessey *Nor* 88-90; C Chaddesden St Phil *Derby* 90-92; C Friern Barnet St Jas *Lon* 92-93; TV Plymouth Em, Efford and Laira *Ex* 93-96; P-in-c Laira 96; R Withington St Crispin *Man* 96-98; P-in-c Beguildy and

Heyope *S & B* 98-00; P-in-c Whitton and Pilleth and Cascob etc 99-00; TV Bruton and Distr *B & W* 00-01; Community Chapl *Linc* 09-11; rtd 11; PtO *Blackb* from 13. *St Wilfrid's Vicarage, 8 Langdale Road, Blackpool FY4 4RT* T: (01253) 764369 E: stuartdobson141@btinternet.com

DOCHERTY, William Sales Hill. b 54. Open Univ BA 96 Callendar Park Coll of Educn Falkirk DipEd 75. TISEC 98. **d** 05 **p** 06. C Broughty Ferry *Bre* 05-09; C Heswall *Ches* 09-11; V Grange St Andr from 11. *The Vicarage, 37 Lime Grove, Runcorn WA7 5JZ* T: (01928) 574411
E: therevdoch@gmail.com

DOCKREE, Peter Martin. b 74. Keele Univ BA 96 Ox Univ MSc 00. Ox Min Course 07. **d** 10 **p** 11. C Wolverton *Ox* 10-14; V Swaythling *Win* from 14. *The Vicarage, 357 Burgess Road, Southampton SO16 3BD* M: 07972-439865 T: (023) 8055 4231
E: peter.dockree@outlook.com

DODD, Canon Andrew Patrick. b 68. Hatf Poly BEng 91 Selw Coll Cam BTh 00. Westcott Ho Cam 97. **d** 00 **p** 01. C New Addington *S'wark* 00-04; R Newington St Mary 04-11; AD S'wark and Newington 07-11; P-in-c Gt Grimsby St Mary and St Jas *Linc* 11-13; TR from 13; AD Grimsby and Cleethorpes from 11; Can and Preb Linc Cathl from 12. *The Rectory, 49 Park Drive, Grimsby DN32 0EG* T: (01472) 358610
E: andrew@vincerdodd.co.uk

DODD, Miss Denise Kate. b 72. Cranmer Hall Dur 07. **d** 09 **p** 10. C Porchester *S'well* 09-14; Bp's Dom Chapl *Dur* from 14. *Auckland Castle, Bishop Auckland DL14 7NR* T: (01388) 602576 F: 605264 E: denisekdodd@yahoo.co.uk

DODD, Jane. b 33. Loughb Univ ALA 51 FLA 51. **d** 98 **p** 99. OLM Wroxham w Hoveton and Belaugh *Nor* 98-08; PtO from 08. *Locheil, Tunstead Road, Hoveton, Norwich NR12 8QN*
T: (01603) 782509

DODD, Mrs Jean. b 47. **d** 98 **p** 99. OLM Irlam *Man* from 98; OLM Cadishead from 09. *75 Harewood Road, Manchester M44 6DL* T: 0161-775 9125

DODD, John Stanley. b 24. Huron Coll Ontario 46. **d** 50 **p** 51. C Kitchener Canada 50-52; Leeds St Jo Ev *Ripon* 52-54; C High Harrogate Ch Ch 54-58; V Stainburn 58-65; V Weeton 58-64; V Meanwood 65-89; rtd 89; PtO *Leeds* from 89. *3 Shawdene, Burton Crescent, Leeds LS6 4DN* T: 0113-278 9069

DODD, Malcolm Ogilvie. b 46. Dur Univ BSc 67 Loughb Univ MSc 90. Edin Th Coll 67. **d** 70 **p** 71. C Hove All SS *Chich* 70-73; C Crawley 73-78; P-in-c Rusper 79-83; Chapl Brighton Coll Jun Sch 83; Chapl Stancliffe Hall Sch 84-97; rtd 01. *210 chemin des Villecrozes, 26170 Buis-les-Baronnies, France* T: (0033) 4 75 28 05 99 E: m.et.j.dodd@wanadoo.fr

DODD, Michael Christopher. b 33. Ch Coll Cam BA 55 MA 59. Ridley Hall Cam 57. **d** 59 **p** 60. C Stechford *Birm* 59-62; V Quinton Road W St Boniface 62-72; TV Paston *Pet* 72-77; TR Hodge Hill *Birm* 77-89; rtd 90; PtO *Birm* from 90. *39 Regency Gardens, Birmingham B14 4JS* T: 0121-474 6945

DODD, Canon Peter Curwen. b 33. St Jo Coll Cam BA 57 FRSA 93. Linc Th Coll 58 Wm Temple Coll Rugby 59. **d** 60 **p** 61. C Eastwood *Sheff* 60-63; Ind Chapl 63-67; *Newc* 67-98; RD Newc E 78-83 and 92-95; Hon Can Newc Cathl 82-98; rtd 98; PtO *Newc* from 98. *Glenesk, 26 The Oval, Benton, Newcastle upon Tyne NE12 9PP* T: 0191-266 1293

DODDS, Alan Richard. b 46. Greenwich Univ BA 92 K Coll Lon MA 94. **d** 95 **p** 96. C Deal St Geo *Cant* 95-99; C-in-c Deal, The Carpenter's Arms 98-99; Prin OLM Course 99-01; TV Cullompton, Willand, Uffculme, Kentisbeare etc *Ex* 02-07; rtd 07. *Green Pastures, Smithincott Farm, Uffculme, Cullompton EX15 3EF* T: (01884) 841801
E: alan.and.chris@tesco.net

DODDS, Barry. *See* DODDS, Norman Barry

DODDS, Brian Martin. b 37. AKC 62. **d** 63 **p** 64. C Morpeth *Newc* 63-67; C Georgetown Cathl Guyana 67-69; V Morawhanna 69-71; V Willington *Newc* 71-74; TV Brayton *York* 75-79; V Gravelly Hill *Birm* 79-83; V Winterton *Linc* 83-85; V Winterton Gp 85-90; V Gainsborough St Jo 90-96; V Morton 95-96; R Walesby 96-00; rtd 00; PtO *Linc* from 01. *69 Pennell Street, Lincoln LN5 7TD* T: (01522) 512593
E: bmdodds@talk21.com

DODDS, Canon Graham Michael. b 58. Liv Univ MA 01 Bris Univ PhD 08 LTCL 80 GTCL 80 York Univ PGCE 81. Trin Coll Bris 84. **d** 84 **p** 85. C Reigate St Mary *S'wark* 84-91; P-in-c Bath Walcot *B & W* 91-93; R Wing *Nor* 96; Dir Reader Studies from 96; Lay Tr Adv 96-01; Asst Dir Min Development 01-04; Dir of Learning Communities *B & W* from 04; Preb Wells Cathl 03-10; Can Res and Treas Wells Cathl from 10. *2 The Liberty, Wells BA5 2SU* T: (01749) 670607 or 670777 F: 674240
M: 07702-658687 E: graham.dodds@bathwells.anglican.org

DODDS, Linda. b 54. **d** 08 **p** 09. OLM Bishop Auckland Woodhouse Close CD *Dur* 08-15; rtd 15. *30 Low Etherley, Bishop Auckland DL14 0EU* T: (01388) 832756
E: linda_dodds@yahoo.co.uk

DODDS, Canon Norman Barry. b 43. Open Univ BA. CITC 73. **d** 76 **p** 77. C Ballynafeigh St Jude *D & D* 76-80; I Belfast St Mich *Conn* 80-14; Chapl HM Pris Belfast 84-14; Can Belf Cathl 98-14; Adn Belfast *Conn* 07-13; rtd 14. *85 Bangor Road, Newtownards BT23 7BZ* M: 07763-935160
T: (028) 9107 1347 E: doddscavehill@yahoo.com

DODDS, Peter. b 35. WMMTC 88 Qu Coll Birm 88. **d** 91 **p** 92. NSM Hartshill *Cov* 91-93; NSM Nuneaton St Mary 94-95; Hon Chapl Geo Eliot Hosp NHS Trust Nuneaton from 95; Hon Chapl Mary Ann Evans Hospice from 95; NSM Camp Hill w Galley Common *Cov* 99-01; PtO from 02. *Wem House, 51 Magyar Crescent, Nuneaton CV11 4SQ* T: (024) 7638 4061
E: pvdodds@googlemail.com

DODGE, Robin Dennis. b 58. Cornell Univ NY BA 80 Boston Univ JD 83. Virginia Th Sem MDiv 99. **d** 98 **p** 99. C Arlington St Mary USA 98-02; C Bris St Mary Redcliffe w Temple etc 02-05; R Washington St Dav USA from 05. *5150 Macomb Street NW, Washington DC 20016, USA* T: (001) (202) 966 2093
F: 966 3437 E: robindodge@starpower.net

DODGSON, David. b 46. **d** 13 **p** 14. NSM Sandal St Cath *Leeds* from 13. *c/o St Catherines Church, Doncaster Road, Belle Vue, Wakefield WF1 5HL* M: 07508-053587

DODHIA, Hitesh Kishorilal. b 57. Cranmer Hall Dur 85. **d** 88 **p** 89. C Leamington Priors All SS *Cov* 88-91; Chapl HM YOI Glen Parva 91-92; Asst Chapl 94-98; Chapl HM Pris Roch 92-94; The Mount 98-01; PtO *St Alb* from 02. *HM Prison Wormwood Scrubs, Du Cane Road, London W12 0AE* T: (020) 8588 3200 M: 07546-033740 E: hiteshdodhia@yahoo.co.uk

DODSON, Canon Gordon. b 31. Em Coll Cam BA 54 MA 58 LLB 55 LLM 01 Barrister 56. Ridley Hall Cam 57. **d** 59 **p** 60. C Belhus Park *Chelmsf* 59-60; C Barking St Marg 60-63; CMS 63-67; C New Malden and Coombe *S'wark* 67-69; V Snettisham *Nor* 69-81; RD Heacham and Rising 76-81; P-in-c Reepham and Hackford w Whitwell and Kerdiston 81-83; P-in-c Salle 81-83; P-in-c Thurning w Wood Dalling 81-83; R Reepham, Hackford w Whitwell, Kerdiston etc 83-94; Hon Can Nor Cathl 85-94; rtd 94; PtO *Nor* from 94. *Poppygate, 2 The Loke, Cromer NR27 9DH* T: (01263) 511811

DODSON, James Peter. b 32. Lich Th Coll 58. **d** 61 **p** 62. C Chasetown *Lich* 61-63; C Hednesford 63-68; V Halifax St Hilda *Wakef* 68-76; V Upperthong 76-85; TV York All SS Pavement w St Crux and St Martin etc 85-90; rtd 92; PtO *Leeds* from 92. *Roseville, Studley Road, Ripon HG4 2QH*
T: (01765) 602053

DODSWORTH, George Brian Knowles. b 34. Open Univ BSc 94. St Mich Coll Llan 59. **d** 62 **p** 63. C Kidderminster St Mary *Worc* 62-67; Asst Chapl HM Pris Man 67-68; Chapl HM Pris Eastchurch 68-70; Chapl HM Pris Wakef 70-74; Chapl HM Pris Wormwood Scrubs 74-83; Asst Chapl Gen of Pris (SE) 83-90; Asst Chapl Gen of Pris (HQ) 90-94; Chapl HM Pris Brixton 94-95; rtd 95; PtO *S'wark* 95-14; *Lon* from 14. *19 Farnsworth Court, West Parkside, London SE10 0QF*
T/F: (020) 8305 0283 E: briandodsworth611@btinternet.com

DODWELL, Andrew. b 75. Man Univ BSc 96 MSc 98. SWMTC 06. **d** 08 **p** 09. C Barnstaple *Ex* from 08. *28 Old School Road, Barnstaple EX32 9DP* T: (01271) 371068
E: andyandcarolyn.dodwell@virgin.net

DOE, Martin Charles. b 54. Lon Univ BSc(Econ) 75 PGCE 87 MA 95. St Steph Ho Ox 89. **d** 91 **p** 92. C Portsea St Mary *Portsm* 91-94; Chapl Abbey Grange High Sch 94-00; Sen Angl Chapl Scarborough and NE Yorks Healthcare NHS Trust 00-14; Sen Chapl York Teaching Hosp NHS Foundn Trust from 14. *The Chaplaincy Centre, York Hospital, Wigginton Road, York YO31 8HE* T: (01904) 725579 E: martin.doe@york.nhs.uk

✤**DOE, The Rt Revd Michael David.** b 47. St Jo Coll Dur BA 69 Bath Univ Hon LLD 02. Ripon Hall Ox 69. **d** 72 **p** 73 **c** 94. C St Helier *S'wark* 72-76; Hon C 76-81; Youth Sec BCC 76-81; C-in-c Blackbird Leys CD *Ox* 81-88; V Blackbird Leys 88-89; RD Cowley 86-89; Soc Resp Adv *Portsm* 89-94; Can Res Portsm Cathl 89-94; Suff Bp Swindon *Bris* 94-04; Gen Sec USPG 04-11; rtd 11; Preacher Gray's Inn from 11; Asst Bp S'wark from 04. *405 West Carriage House, Royal Carriage Mews, London SE18 6GA* T: (020) 3259 3841 E: michaeldd@btinternet.com

DOE, Mrs Priscilla Sophia. b 41. LRAM 61. SEITE 97. **d** 00 **p** 01. NSM Maidstone All SS and St Phil w Tovil *Cant* 00-11; PtO from 11. *Mount St Laurence, High Street, Cranbrook TN17 3EW*
T: (01580) 712330

DOEL, Patrick Stephen. b 71. Peterho Cam BA 92 MA 97. Wycliffe Hall Ox BA 01 MA 06 MSt 03. **d** 03 **p** 04. C Blackheath St Jo *S'wark* 03-06; P-in-c Deptford St Nic and St Luke 06-08; V 08-10; V Walmley *Birm* from 10. *The Vicarage, 2 Walmley Road, Sutton Coldfield B76 1QN* E: steve@doel.org

DOERR, Mrs Anne. b 55. Man Univ BA 76. SEITE 06. **d** 09 **p** 10. NSM Belmont *S'wark* 09-13; NSM St Helier from 13; Chapl R Marsden NHS Foundn Trust from 14. *14 Central Way, Carshalton SM5 3NF* T: (020) 8669 2494 M: 07811-908731
E: aedoerr@btinternet.com

DOGGETT, Margaret Ann. b 36. Open Univ BA 78 Homerton Coll Cam PGCE 79. **d** 96 **p** 97. OLM Pulham Market, Pulham St Mary and Starston *Nor* 96-99; OLM Dickleburgh and The Pulhams 99-01; rtd 02; PtO *Nor* from 02. *Antares, Station Road, Pulham St Mary, Diss IP21 4QT* T/F: (01379) 676662 M: 07710-621547 E: john.doggett@btinternet.com

DOHERTY, Mrs Christine. b 46. SEN 72. STETS 97. **d** 00 **p** 01. NSM Framfield *Chich* 00-03; C Seaford w Sutton 03-11; rtd 11. *27 Hawth Park Road, Seaford BN25 2RF* T: (01323) 351243 E: chris.doh@tiscali.co.uk

DOHERTY, Deana Rosina Mercy. b 21. St Aid Coll Dur BA 55. **dss** 82 **d** 87 **p** 94. Sutton St Jas and Wawne *York* 82-95; Par Dn 87-94; C 94-95; PtO 95-99; rtd 98. *Alana, Chapel Street, Lismore, Co Waterford, Republic of Ireland* T: (00353) 58 54418

DOHERTY, Sean William. b 07 **p** 08. C Cricklewood St Gabr and St Mich *Lon* 07-10; Lect St Paul's Th Cen 08-10; Tutor from 10. *50 Waynflete Square, London W10 6UD* M: 07710-515800 E: sean.doherty@stmellitus.org

DOHERTY, Thomas Alexander. b 48. Chich Th Coll 73. **d** 76 **p** 77. V Choral Derry Cathl 76-79; C Llandaff w Capel Llanilltern *Llan* 79-80; PV Llan Cathl 80-84; V Penmark w Porthkerry 84-90; R Merthyr Dyfan 90-02; V Margam 02-15; rtd 15; PtO *Llan* from 15. *Riverside Bungalow, 2 Library Lane, Port Talbot SA13 1LQ*

DOICK, Paul Stephen James. b 70. Chich Univ BA 10. Ripon Coll Cuddesdon 03. **d** 05 **p** 06. C Hove *Chich* 05-09; TV 09-10; V Hove St Jo 10-14; R Henfield w Shermanbury and Woodmancote from 14. *Henfield Vicarage, Church Lane, Henfield BN5 9NY* T: (01273) 492017 M: 07742-868602 E: p.doick@btinternet.com

DOIDGE, Charles William. b 44. Univ Coll Lon BSc 65 MSc 67 PhD 72. EMMTC 93. **d** 93 **p** 94. NSM Blaby *Leic* 93-96; P-in-c Willoughby Waterleys, Peatling Magna etc 96-04; rtd 04. *21 Brunel Mews, Solsbro Road, Torquay TQ2 6QA* T: (01803) 690548 E: doidge@dmu.ac.uk

DOIDGE, Valerie Gladys. b 49. STETS 98. **d** 01 **p** 02. C St Leonards St Ethelburga *Chich* 01-07; C Hollington St Leon 07-12; rtd 12. *6 Collinswood Drive, St Leonards-on-Sea TN38 0NU* T: (01424) 425651 E: valrod@rdoidge.freeserve.co.uk

DOIG, Allan George. b 51. Univ of BC BA 69 K Coll Cam BA 73 MA 80 PhD 82 FSA 98. Ripon Coll Cuddesdon 86. **d** 88 **p** 89. C Abingdon *Ox* 88-91; Chapl LMH Ox from 91; Fell from 96; Select Preacher *Ox* 95-96. *Lady Margaret Hall, Oxford OX2 6QA* T: (01865) 274386 M: 07585-003240 E: allan.doig@lmh.ox.ac.uk

DOLAN, Miss Louise. b 68. St Paul's Coll Chelt BA 89 Reading Univ PGCE 90. Aston Tr Scheme 92 Linc Th Coll 94 Westcott Ho Cam MA 95. **d** 96 **p** 97. C N Stoneham *Win* 96-99. *19 Ipswich Grove, Norwich NR2 2LU* T: (01603) 469865

DOLAN, Mary Ellen. b 44. Gen Th Sem NY STM 90. **d** 95 **p** 95. USA 97-06; American Chs in Eur 07-14; Chapl Málaga *Eur* from 14. *Address temp unknown* T: (0034) 952 401 945 E: chaplain@stgeorgemalaga.org

DOLBY, Mrs Christine Teresa. b 54. Nottm Univ MA 01 SRN 80. EMMTC 98. **d** 01 **p** 02. C Cropwell Bishop w Colston Bassett, Granby etc *S'well* 01-05; P-in-c Ancaster Wilsford Gp *Linc* 05-08; Chapl Qu Medical Cen Nottm Univ Hosp NHS Trust from 08. *16 Morley's Close, Lowdham, Nottingham NG14 7HN* T: 0115-966 5890 M: 07738-851181 E: ca.dolby263@btinternet.com

DOLL, Canon Peter Michael. b 62. Yale Univ BA 84 Ch Ch Ox DPhil 89. Cuddesdon Coll BA 94. **d** 95 **p** 96. C Cowley St Jo *Ox* 95-99; Chapl Worc Coll Ox 98-02; TV Abingdon *Ox* 02-09; Can Res Nor Cathl from 09. *56 The Close, Norwich NR1 4EG* T: (01603) 218336 E: canonlibrarian@cathedral.org.uk

DOLLERY, Anne Mary Elizabeth. b 55. Hull Univ BA 78. Ridley Hall Cam 02. **d** 04. C Thundersley *Chelmsf* 04-09; V Walthamstow St Andr 09-15; V Feltham *Lon* from 15. *The Vicarage, St Elmo, Cardinal Road, Feltham TW13 5AL* T: (020) 8890 8347 E: annedollery@yahoo.co.uk

DOLMAN, Derek Alfred George Gerrit. b 40. ALCD 64. **d** 65 **p** 66. C St Alb St Paul *St Alb* 65-68; C Bishopwearmouth St Gabr *Dur* 68-72; R Jarrow Grange 72-80; V New Catton St Luke *Nor* 80-98; V New Catton St Luke w St Aug 98-00; R S Croxton Gp *Leic* 00-06; rtd 06; PtO *Leic* 06-12; *Derby* from 07; *Lich* from 07. *17 Kestrel Way, Burton-on-Trent DE15 0DJ* T: (01283) 845330 E: derekdolman@uwclub.net

DOLMAN, William Frederick Gerrit. b 42. JP . K Coll Lon MB, BS 65 Lon Univ LLB 87 MRCS 65 LRCP 65. SEITE 04. **d** 06 **p** 07. NSM Beckley and Peasmarsh *Chich* 06-14; rtd 15. *Little Bellhurst Cottage, Hobbs Lane, Beckley, Rye TN31 6TT* T: (01797) 260203 E: hmcwd@aol.com

DOLPHIN, Mark Patrick (Pads). b 58. Man Univ BSc 81. St Jo Coll Nottm 06. **d** 08 **p** 09. C Reading Greyfriars *Ox* 08-11;

P-in-c Reading St Matt 11-14; V from 14. *St Matthew's Vicarage, 205 Southcote Lane, Reading RG30 3AX* T: 0118-957 3755 M: 07866-754770

DOMINIAK, Paul Anthony. b 78. Univ of the S (USA) BA 05 SS Coll Cam BA 07 MPhil 08. Westcott Ho Cam 05. **d** 08 **p** 09. C Ingleby Barwick *York* 08-11; Chapl Trin Coll Cam from 11. *Trinity College, Cambridge CB2 1TQ* T: (01223) 338472 E: pad39@cam.ac.uk

DOMINIC MARK, Brother. *See* IND, Dominic Mark

DOMINY, Canon Peter John. b 36. Qu Coll Ox BA 60 MA 64 Aber Univ MLitt 83 Ex Univ PhD 11. Oak Hill Th Coll 60. **d** 62 **p** 63. C Bedworth *Cov* 62-66; Nigeria 67-84; Sudan United Miss 67-72; V Jos St Piran 72-84; R Broadwater St Mary *Chich* 84-92; TR Broadwater 92-98; P-in-c Danehill 98-99; V 99-03; Can and Preb Chich Cathl 93-03; RD Uckfield 00-03; rtd 03; PtO *Sarum* from 03. *32 Bedwin Street, Salisbury SP1 3UT* T: (01722) 238635 E: peterd@uwclub.net

DOMMETT, Simon Paul. b 58. Warwick Univ BSc 79. St Jo Coll Nottm MA 99. **d** 99 **p** 00. C Weston Favell *Pet* 99-02; P-in-c Gt w Lt Harrowden and Orlingbury 02-06; P-in-c Isham w Pytchley 05-06; R Gt w Lt Harrowden and Orlingbury and Isham etc 06-12; R Aynho and Croughton w Evenley etc from 12; RD Brackley from 13. *The Rectory, Croughton Road, Aynho, Banbury OX17 3BD* T: (01869) 810903 E: the.revd.simon@gmail.com

DOMONEY, Canon Lynette May (Lyndy). b 44. Th Ext Educn Coll 90. **d** 92 **p** 93. S Africa 92-06; P-in-c Kessingland, Gisleham and Rushmere *Nor* 06-08; R 08-14; rtd 14; PtO *Nor* from 15. *25 Victory Court, Diss IP22 4GN* T: (01379) 650445 E: l.domoney@btinternet.com

DONAGHEY, Thomas Alfred. b 67. Trin Coll Bris 06. **d** 08 **p** 09. C Whittle-le-Woods *Blackb* 08-13; V Baxenden from 13. *The Vicarage, Langford Street, Accrington BB5 2RF* T: (01254) 384179 M: 07974-457544 E: tdonaghey@hotmail.com

DONAGHY, Paul Robert Blount. b 56. **d** 00 **p** 01. OLM Goldsworth Park *Guildf* 00-14. *Address temp unknown* E: p.donaghy@hotmail.co.uk

DONALD, Andrew William. b 19. St Jo Coll Morpeth 47 ACT ThL 50. **d** 49 **p** 50. C Claremont Australia 49-50; C Perth Cathl 50-52; R Wyalkatchem 52-56; PtO *Lon* 57-58; Chapl Gothenburg *Eur* 58-65; Chapl Lausanne 65-68; Asst P Mt Lawley Australia 68-70; R Bellevue and Darlington 70-79; R Toodyay and Goomalling 79-84; rtd 84. *Eriswell, 18A Cobham Way, Camillo WA 6111, Australia* T: (0061) (8) 9390 8425

DONALD, Brother. *See* GREEN, Donald Pentney

DONALD, Dennis Curzon. b 38. Oak Hill Th Coll 68. **d** 70 **p** 71. C Carl St Jo 70-73; LtO 73-77; Warden Blaithwaite Ho Chr Conf Cen Wigton 73-90; Chapl Cumberland Infirmary 85-92; Chapl Eden Valley Hospice Carl 92-98; rtd 98; PtO *Carl* from 77. *5 The Old Bakery, Gretna DG16 5FZ* T: (01461) 338053

DONALD, Mrs Philippa Jane. b 58. Bath Univ BA 79 Moray Ho Edin DipEd 80. WEMTC 08. **d** 11 **p** 12. NSM Churchdown St Jo and Innsworth *Glouc* from 11. *8 Seabrooke Road, Gloucester GL1 3JH* T: (01452) 528569 E: talk2philippa@hotmail.com

DONALD, Robert Francis. b 49. St Jo Coll Nottm BTh 75 LTh. **d** 75 **p** 76. C New Barnet St Jas *St Alb* 75-79; C St Alb St Paul 79-86; C St Alb St Mary Marshalswick 86-87; LtO from 87; Dir Chr Alliance Housing Assn Ltd 87-98. *24 Meadowcroft, St Albans AL1 1UD* T: (01727) 841647 M: 07973-208289

DONALD, Rosemary Anne. b 52. STETS 99. **d** 02 **p** 03. NSM Blendworth w Chalton w Idsworth *Portsm* 02-07; P-in-c from 07. *1A Havant Road, Horndean, Waterlooville PO8 0DB* T: (023) 9259 1719 E: rosemary.donald3@gmail.com

DONALD, Steven. b 55. CertEd 76 Hull Univ MA 99. Oak Hill Th Coll BA 88. **d** 88 **p** 89. C Cheadle All Hallows *Ches* 88-91; C Ardsley *Sheff* 91; V Kendray 92-99; P-in-c Chadderton Ch Ch *Man* 99-03; V 03-05; V Carl St Jo from 05. *St John's Vicarage, London Road, Carlisle CA1 2QQ* T: (01228) 521601 E: stevedon1@aol.com

DONALDSON, Alastair Philip. d 14. Fivemiletown *Clogh* 14-15; C Roscommon w Donamon, Rathcline, Kilkeevin etc *K, E & A* from 15. *Address temp unknown*

DONALDSON, Miss Elizabeth Anne. b 55. Univ of Wales (Ban) BSc 76 Surrey Univ MSc 80 Nottm Univ BA 82. St Jo Coll Nottm 80. **dss** 83 **d** 87 **p** 94. Guildf Ch Ch 83-86; Coulsdon 86-90; C 87-90; C Keresley and Coundon *Cov* 90-99; V Gt Amwell w St Margaret's and Stanstead Abbots *St Alb* from 00. *The Vicarage, 25 Hoddesdon Road, Stanstead Abbotts, Ware SG12 8EG* T: (01920) 870115 E: vicar@3churches.net *or* anne.donaldson@ntlworld.com

DONALDSON, Mrs Janet Elizabeth. b 53. GTCL 74 Whitelands Coll Lon CertEd 75. EAMTC 95. **d** 98 **p** 99. NSM Tolleshunt Knights w Tiptree and Gt Braxted *Chelmsf* 98-02; V Knights and Hospitallers Par 02-11; P-in-c Deeping St James *Linc* 11-13;

P-in-c Welford w Sibbertoft and Marston Trussell *Pet* from 13. *The Vicarage, 35 The Leys, Welford, Northampton NN6 6HS* T: (01858) 571101 E: rev.janet@donaldsonfamily.org.uk

DONALDSON, Malcolm Alexander. b 48. Cranmer Hall Dur 84. **d** 86 **p** 87. C Heworth H Trin *York* 86-89; Chapl York Distr Hosp 86-89; C Marfleet *York* 89-90; TV 90-96; R Collyhurst *Man* 96-05; rtd 05. *12 Clove Court, Tweedmouth, Berwick-upon-Tweed TD15 2FJ*

DONALDSON, Canon Roger Francis. b 50. Jes Coll Ox BA 71 MA 75. Westcott Ho Cam 72. **d** 74 **p** 75. C Mold *St As* 74-78; V Denio w Abererch *Ban* 78-95; TR Llanbeblig w Caernarfon and Betws Garmon etc from 95; AD Arfon 04-09; Hon Can Ban Cathl from 04. *The Rectory, 4 Ffordd Menai, Caernarfon LL55 1LF* T: (01286) 673750

DONALDSON, William Richard. b 56. St Cath Coll Cam BA 78 MA 81. Ridley Hall Cam 79. **d** 82 **p** 83. C Everton St Sav w St Cuth *Liv* 82-85; C Reigate St Mary *S'wark* 85-89; V Easton H Trin w St Gabr and St Lawr and St Jude *Bris* 89-99; V W Ealing St Jo w St Jas *Lon* 99-07; Dir of Ords Willesden Area 06-07; Dir Chr Leadership Wycliffe Hall Ox 07-12; Course Dir Part-Time Tr 12-13; Chapl St Edm Hall Ox from 13; C Ox St Aldate from 12; AD Ox from 15. *St Edmund Hall, Queens Lane, Oxford OX1 4AR* T: (01865) 279021 M: 07745-363540 E: w.r.donaldson@btinternet.com

DONCASTER, Archdeacon of. See WILCOCKSON, The Ven Stephen Anthony

DONCASTER, Suffragan Bishop of. See BURROWS, The Rt Revd Peter

DONE, Mrs Margaret. b 43. LNSM course 84 Linc Th Coll 91. **d** 92 **p** 94. OLM Coningsby w Tattershall *Linc* 92-06; OLM Bain Valley Gp from 06. *43 Park Lane, Coningsby, Lincoln LN4 4SW* T: (01526) 343013

DONE, Nigel Anthony. b 68. Wye Coll Lon BSc 89 St Jo Coll Dur BA 98. Cranmer Hall Dur. **d** 98 **p** 99. C Pilton w Croscombe, N Wootton and Dinder *B & W* 98-02; R Hardington Vale 02-12; V Ilminster and Whitelackington from 12. *21 Higher Beacon, Ilminster TA19 9AJ* T: (01460) 250802 E: nigel.done@btinternet.com

DONE, Roy Edward. b 46. **d** 11. NSM Bain Valley Gp *Linc* from 11. *43 Park Lane, Coningsby, Lincoln LN4 4SW* T: (01526) 343013 E: roy.done@btinternet.com

DONEGAN-CROSS, Guy William. b 68. St Aid Coll Dur BA 90. Trin Coll Bris BA 98. **d** 99 **p** 00. C Swindon Ch Ch *Bris* 99-03; V Saltburn-by-the-Sea *York* 03-10; V Harrogate St Mark *Leeds* from 10. *St Mark's Vicarage, 15 Wheatlands Road, Harrogate HG2 8BB* T: (01423) 504959 E: guydonegancross@yahoo.co.uk

DONELLA, Sister. See MATHIE, Patricia Jean

DONEY, Malcolm Charles. b 50. Lon Univ BA 71 Middx Univ BA 05. NTMTC 02. **d** 05 **p** 06. NSM Tufnell Park St Geo and All SS *Lon* 05-07; NSM W Holloway St Luke 07; NSM All Hallows Lon Wall from 07; PtO *St E* from 10. *21 Jacobs Court, 19 Plumbers Row, London E1 1AE* T: (020) 7377 9284 M: 07812-566520 E: malcolmdoney@me.com

DONKERSLEY, Mrs Christine Mary. b 44. K Alfred's Coll Win CertEd 65. STETS 98. **d** 01 **p** 02. NSM Baltonsborough w Butleigh, W Bradley etc *B & W* 01-06; P-in-c Fosse Trinity 06-13; rtd 13. *17 Church Close, Martock TA12 6DS* T: (01935) 825260 M: 07866-531917 E: cm.donkersley@btinternet.com

DONKIN, Canon Robert. b 50. St Mich Coll Llan 71. **d** 74 **p** 75. C Mountain Ash *Llan* 74-77; C Coity w Nolton 77-79; V Oakwood 79-84; V Aberaman and Abercwmboi 84-91; V Aberaman and Abercwmboi w Cwmaman 91-99; R Penarth w Lavernock 99-04; R Penarth and Llandough 04-08; AD Penarth and Barry 04-08; R Caerphilly 08-14; AD 10-14; AD Merthyr Tydfil and Caerphilly 12-14; Hon Can Llan Cathl 06-14; rtd 14; PtO *Llan* from 14. *4 Heol-y-Gelli, Aberdare CF44 6LN* T: (01685) 884645 E: robert.donkin@hotmail.com

DONMALL, Michael Charles. b 53. Univ Coll Lon BSc 75 PhD 84 K Coll Lon PGCE 06. Yorks Min Course 12. **d** 14 **p** 15. NSM Saddleworth *Man* from 14. *7 Higher Arthurs, Greenfield, Oldham OL3 7BE* T: (01457) 870427 E: m.donmall@manchester.ac.uk

DONN, Mrs Julie. b 61. Lincs & Humberside Univ BA 98 Hull Univ BA 07. EMMTC 08. **d** 10 **p** 11. C Skegness Gp *Linc* 10-15; C Immingham Gp from 15. *18 Danial Close, Skegness PE25 1RQ* T: (01754) 766877 M: 07885-843207 E: revjulie.donn@btinternet.com

DONNE, Miranda. b 49. **d** 04 **p** 05. NSM Whitchurch *Ex* from 04. *Whitchurch House, Whitchurch, Tavistock PL19 9EL* T: (01822) 614552

DONNELLY, Ms Juliet Ann. b 70. K Coll Lon BD 92 AKC 92 PGCE 93. Ripon Coll Cuddesdon 01. **d** 05 **p** 06. C Bexley St Jo *Roch* 05-07; C Sidcup St Jo 07-08; Chapl Bp Justus C of E Sch Bromley 09-15; Chapl Trin Sch Lewisham

from 15. *The Vicarage, 40 Dartmouth Row, London SE10 8AP* M: 07910-166491 E: juliet.blessed@virgin.net

DONNELLY, Trevor Alfred. b 71. K Coll Lon BA 93 AKC 93. Cuddesdon Coll 94. **d** 97 **p** 98. C Southgate Ch Ch *Lon* 97-01; V Hinchley Wood *Guildf* 01-05; Sen Chapl Medway Secure Tr Cen 06-09; TV Deptford St Jo w H Trin and Ascension *S'wark* from 09. *The Vicarage, 40 Dartmouth Row, London SE10 8AP* T: (020) 8694 1074 E: trevordonnelly@mac.com

DONOGHUE, William Noel. b 80. Trin Coll Bris 13. **d** 15. C Willowfield *D & D* from 15. *8 Jocelyn Gardens, Belfast BT6 9BA*

DONOHOE, Olive Mary Rose. b 58. TCD BA 79 BTh 94 MA 95 CPA 83. CITC 91. **d** 95 **p** 96. C Bandon Union C, C & R 95-98; I Mountmellick w Coolbanagher, Rosenallis etc *M & K* 98-10; P-in-c Stradbally w Ballintubbert, Coraclone etc *C & O* 10-14; I Athy w Kilberry, Fontstown and Kilkea *D & G* from 14. *The Rectory, Church Road, Athy, Co Kildare, Republic of Ireland* M: 87-220 9945 T: (00353) (59) 863 1446 E: revol@elive.ie

DONOHOE, Simon James. b 83. **d** 15. C Cheadle *Ches* from 15. *39 Oakfield Avenue, Cheadle SK8 1EF* M: 07875-836054 E: simondonohoe@hotmail.com

DONOVAN, Mrs Rosalind Margaret. b 48. Birm Univ LLB 69 Bedf Coll Lon DASS 73. SAOMC 95. **d** 98 **p** 99. NSM Seer Green and Jordans *Ox* 98-03; P-in-c Wexham 03-13; rtd 13; PtO *Ox* from 14. *2 The Dell, Chalfont St Peter, Gerrards Cross SL9 0JA* T: (01494) 871573 E: rev.ros.donovan@gmail.com

DONOVAN, Mrs Rosemary Ann. b 71. La Sainte Union Coll BTh 92 Birm Univ PGCE 93. Qu Coll Birm MA 01. **d** 01 **p** 02. C Kings Heath *Birm* 01-04; C Moseley St Mary and St Anne 04-11; V Epsom Common Ch Ch *Guildf* from 11. *Christ Church Vicarage, 20 Christ Church Road, Epsom KT19 8NE* T: (01372) 720302 E: rosemary.donovan@o2.co.uk *or* vicar@christchurchepsom.org.uk

DONSON, Miss Helen Cripps. b 32. Somerville Coll Ox DipEd 55 MA 58. Dalton Ho Bris 58 Gilmore Ho 69. **dss** 79 **d** 87. Staines St Pet *Lon* 80-83; Staines St Mary and St Pet 83-90; Par Dn 87-90; Par Dn Herne Bay Ch Ch *Cant* 90-92; rtd 93; Hon Par Dn Bexhill St Aug *Chich* 93-97; PtO 97-07. *Flat 27, Manormead, Tilford Road, Hindhead GU26 6RA* T: (01428) 601527

DONSON, Margaret Christine. See BARROW, Margaret Christine

DOODES, Peter John. b 45. STETS 98. **d** 01. NSM Ninfield and Hooe *Chich* 01-02; NSM Hastings H Trin 02-07; PtO *Roch* 09-14. *Catslide, The Common, Hooe, Battle TN33 9EF* T: (01424) 892329 M: 07718-302115 E: pjdoodes@hotmail.com

DOOGAN, Canon Simon Edward. b 70. Univ of Wales (Abth) LLB 92 Univ of Wales (Cardiff) LLM 01 TCD BTh 97. CITC 94. **d** 97 **p** 98. C Cregagh *D & D* 97-01; Dom Chapl to Bp Horsham *Chich* 01-04; I Aghalee *D & D* 04-08; I Ballyholme from 08; Dioc Registrar from 07; Can St Patr Cathl Dublin from 11. *Ballyholme Rectory, 3 Ward Avenue, Bangor BT20 5JW* T: (028) 9127 4901 *or* 9127 4912 F: 9146 6357 E: simon_doogan@hotmail.com

DOOLAN, Mrs Alison Ruth. b 59. Yorks Min Course 13. **d** 15. NSM Beverley St Mary *York* from 15. *8 Norfolk Street, Beverley HU17 7DN* T: (01482) 864707 E: alidoolan@googlemail.com

DOOLAN, Benjamin. b 87. Sheff Univ BA 08 Anglia Ruskin Univ MA 13. Ridley Hall Cam 11. **d** 13 **p** 14. C York St Mich-le-Belfrey from 13. *Bede House, Heslington Lane, York YO10 5ED* M: 07849-024523 E: ben.doolan@belfrey.org

DOOLAN, Canon Leonard Wallace. b 57. St Andr Univ MA 79 Ox Univ BA 82 MA 88. Ripon Coll Cuddesdon 80. **d** 83 **p** 84. C High Wycombe *Ox* 83-85; C Bladon w Woodstock 85-88; C Wootton by Woodstock 85-88; P-in-c 88-90; C Kiddington w Asterleigh 85-88; P-in-c 88-90; P-in-c Glympton 88-90; R Wootton w Glympton and Kiddington 90-91; TR Halesworth w Linstead, Chediston, Holton etc *St E* 91-98; RD Halesworth 95-98; TR Ifield *Chich* 98-08; V Cirencester *Glouc* from 08; AD 11-15; Hon Can Douala Cameroon from 09; Hon Can Glouc Cathl from 12. *The Vicarage, 1 Dollar Street, Cirencester GL7 2AJ* T: (01285) 653142 E: vicarcirencester@hotmail.com

DOOR, Hazel Lesley. b 48. Open Univ BSc 99. EAMTC 01. **d** 04 **p** 05. C Poitou-Charentes *Eur* 05-07; P-in-c Brittany 07-10; Asst Chapl Poitou-Charentes 10-11; Chapl from 12. *3 rue des Ebaupins, Fortran, 86400 Linazay, France* T: (0033) 5 49 87 71 45 *or* 5 49 97 04 21 E: rev.hazel@wanadoo.fr

DOORES, Jennifer Mary. See McKENZIE, Jennifer Mary

DOORES, Canon Peter George Herbert. b 46. Hull Univ BSc 67 Birm Univ PGCE 68. Linc Th Coll 92. **d** 92 **p** 93. C N Stoneham *Win* 92-96; V St Leonards and St Ives 96-03; P-in-c Alton St Lawr 03-09; V Alton 10-13; Hon Can Win Cathl 09-13; rtd 13; PtO *Win* from 13. *5 Cranford Gardens, Chandler's Ford, Eastleigh SO53 1PU* T: (023) 8025 3778 E: peterdoores@lineone.net *or* peter@doores.myzen.co.uk

DORAGH (née ELLIOTT), Mrs Sonya Jacqueline. b 72. Ox Brookes Univ BA 95. Trin Coll Bris MA 12. **d** 12 **p** 13. C Much Woolton *Liv* from 12. *25 Linkside Road, Liverpool L25 9NX* M: 07852-244537 E: sonya@doragh.co.uk

DORAN, Clive. b 58. St Jo Coll Nottm 99. **d** 01 **p** 02. C Maghull *Liv* 01-05; V Huyton St Geo 05-13; TV Parr from 13; Bp's Adv on Children and Communion from 06. *St Paul's Vicarage, 75 Chain Lane, St Helens WA11 9QF* T: (01744) 734335 E: revclivedoran@yahoo.co.uk

DORAN, Edward Roy. b 47. St Jo Coll Nottm. **d** 85 **p** 86. C Roby *Liv* 85-88; V Ravenhead 88-07; TV Eccleston 07-09; V Knotty Ash St Jo from 09. *St John's Vicarage, Thomas Lane, Liverpool L14 5NR* T: 0151-228 2396

DORBER, The Very Revd Adrian John. b 52. St Jo Coll Dur BA 74 K Coll Lon MTh 91. Westcott Ho Cam 76. **d** 79 **p** 80. C Easthampstead *Ox* 79-85; P-in-c Emmer Green 85-88; Chapl Portsm Poly 88-92; Chapl Portsm Univ 92-97; Lect 91-97; Public Orator 92-97; Hon Chapl Portsm Cathl 92-97; P-in-c Brancepeth *Dur* 97-01; Dir Min and Tr 97-05; Hon Can Dur Cathl 97-05; Dean Lich from 05. *The Deanery, 16 The Close, Lichfield WS13 7LD* T: (01543) 306250 F: 306109 E: adrian.dorber@lichfield-cathedral.org

DORCHESTER, Archdeacon of. *See* FRENCH, The Ven Judith Karen

DORCHESTER, Area Bishop of. *See* FLETCHER, The Rt Revd Colin William

DORÉ, Eric George. b 47. S Dios Minl Tr Scheme 87. **d** 90 **p** 91. NSM Hove Bp Hannington Memorial Ch *Chich* 90-92; C Burgess Hill St Andr 92-95; R Frant w Eridge 95-00; V Framfield 00-07; rtd 07; PtO *St E* from 08. *Oak House, 86A Southwold Road, Wrentham, Beccles NR34 7JF* T: (01502) 675777 E: ericdore@onetel.com

DOREY, Miss Alison. b 77. Sheff Univ BA 98 Sheff Hallam Univ PGCE 01 St Jo Coll Dur MA 08. Cranmer Hall Dur 05. **d** 07 **p** 08. C Askern *Sheff* 07-11; Miss Development Co-ord N Sheff Estates from 11; Dir Tr Fresh Expressions from 15. *85 Malton Street, Sheffield S4 7EA* T: 0114-272 6855 E: ali.dorey@sheffield.anglican.org *or* alidorey1@gmail.com

DOREY, Trevor Eric. b 30. ACIS 53. S Dios Minl Tr Scheme 87. **d** 90 **p** 91. NSM E Woodhay and Woolton Hill *Win* 90-96; P-in-c Manaccan w St Anthony-in-Meneage and St Martin *Truro* 96-99; rtd 99; PtO *Sarum* 01-05; *Ox* from 07. *6 Marshall Court, Speen Lane, Newbury RG14 1RY* T: (01635) 551956 E: tandvdorey@btinternet.com

DORGU, Woyin Karowei. b 58. MB, BS 85. Lon Bible Coll BA 93 Oak Hill Th Coll 93. **d** 95 **p** 96. C Tollington *Lon* 95-98; C Upper Holloway 98-00; TV 00-12; V *St John's Vicarage, 51 Tytherton Road, London N19 4PZ* T/F: (020) 7272 5309 E: wdorgu@yahoo.com

DORKING, Archdeacon of. *See* BRYER, The Ven Paul Donald

DORKING, Suffragan Bishop of. *See* BRACKLEY, The Rt Revd Ian James

DORLING, Philip Julian. b 69. Edin Univ BSc 90. Ripon Coll Cuddesdon BTh 09. **d** 05 **p** 06. C Ulverston St Mary w H Trin *Carl* 05-09; R Vryheid St Pet S Africa 10-12; R Inglewood Gp *Carl* from 13. *St Mary's Vicarage, High Hesket, Carlisle CA4 0HU* T: (01697) 473320 E: philipdorling123@btinternet.com

DORMANDY, Richard Paul. b 59. Univ Coll Lon BA 81 St Edm Ho Cam BA 88. Ridley Hall Cam 86. **d** 89 **p** 90. C Sydenham H Trin *S'wark* 89-93; V 93-01; V Westminster St Jas the Less *Lon* 01-09; V Tulse Hill H Trin and St Matthias *S'wark* from 09. *Holy Trinity Vicarage, 49 Trinity Rise, London SW2 2QP* T: (020) 8674 6721 E: richard@dormandy.co.uk

DORMOR, Duncan James. b 67. Magd Coll Ox BA 88 Lon Univ MSc 89. Ripon Coll Cuddesdon BA 94. **d** 95 **p** 96. C Wolverhampton *Lich* 95-98; Chapl St Jo Coll Cam 98-02; Fell and Dean from 02. *St John's College, Cambridge CB2 1TP* T: (01223) 338633 E: djd28@cam.ac.uk

DORMOR, Preb Duncan Stephen. b 36. St Edm Hall Ox BA 60. Cuddesdon Coll 60. **d** 62 **p** 63. C Headington *Ox* 62-66; USA 66-72; R Hertford St Andr St Alb 72-88; RD Hertford 77-83; TR Tenbury Wells *Heref* 88-01; R Burford I, Nash and Boraston 88-01; R Whitton w Greete and Hope Bagot 88-01; R Burford III w Lt Heref 88-01; V Tenbury St Mich 94-01; RD Ludlow 96-01; Preb Heref Cathl 99-02; C Tenbury Wells 01-02; C Burford I, Nash and Boraston 01-02; C Whitton w Greete and Hope Bagot 01-02; C Burford III w Lt Heref 01-02; C Tenbury St Mich 01-02; rtd 02; PtO *Heref* 02-14. *30 Queen Anne Road, West Mersea, Colchester CO5 8BB*

DORNAN, Michael. CITC. **d** 09 **p** 10. C Hillsborough *D & D* 09-14; I Desertmartin w Termoneeny *D & R* from 14. *The Rectory, 25 Dromore Road, Desertmartin, Magherafelt BT45 5JZ* M: 07858-597416 T: (028) 7963 2455 E: mikedornan@gmail.com

DORRELL, Martin Christopher. b 57. STETS. **d** 09 **p** 10. NSM Portsea St Sav *Portsm* 09-14; PtO from 14. *284B Allaway Avenue, Portsmouth PO6 4QR* T: (023) 9238 8689 E: martin.dorrell1@ntlworld.com

DORRIAN, Adrian Terence Warren. b 82. QUB BA 03 TCD BTh 06. CITC 04. **d** 06 **p** 07. C Newtownards *D & D* 06-09; I Belfast St Pet and St Jas *Conn* 09-12; I Dundela St Mark *D & D* from 12. *St Mark's Rectory, 4 Sydenham Avenue, Belfast BT4 2DR* M: 07760-664337 E: adriandorrian@gmail.com

DORRINGTON, Brian Goodwin. b 32. Leeds Univ CertEd 55. St Deiniol's Hawarden 65. **d** 66 **p** 67. C Poynton *Ches* 66-71; PtO Truro 71-78; Hd Master Veryan Sch Truro 71-84; Hon C Veryan *Truro* 78-83; Hon C Veryan w Ruan Lanihorne 83-84; C N Petherwin 84-87; C Boyton w N Tamerton 84-87; TV Bolventor 87-90; R Kilkhampton w Morwenstow 90-97; RD Stratton 92-97; rtd 97; PtO *Truro* from 00. *Southcroft, 18 Elm Drive, Bude EX23 8EZ* T: (01288) 352467

DORRINGTON, Richard Bryan. b 48. Linc Th Coll 79. **d** 81 **p** 82. C Streetly *Lich* 81-84; C Badger, Ryton and Beckbury 84-85; R 85-88; V Geddington w Weekley *Pet* 88-98; P-in-c Bradworthy *Ex* 98-99; P-in-c Abbots Bickington and Bulkworthy 98-99; P-in-c Bradworthy, Sutcombe, Putford etc 99-00; R 00-13; RD Holsworthy 99-11; rtd 13. *3 Wassail Close, Bodmin PL14 6LJ* T: (01208) 79156 E: r2b2d2@btinternet.com

DORSET, Archdeacon of. *See* WAINE, The Very Revd Stephen John

DORSET, Archdeacon of. *See* MACROW WOOD, The Ven Antony Charles

DORSETT, Mark Richard. b 63. Univ of Wales (Lamp) BA 84 MTh 86 Birm Univ PhD 90. Ripon Coll Cuddesdon 91. **d** 93 **p** 94. C Yardley St Edburgha *Birm* 93-96; Chapl K Sch Worc from 96; Min Can Worc Cathl from 96. *12A College Green, Worcester WR1 2LH* T: (01905) 25837

DOSE, Lara Ellen. b 70. De Pauw Univ USA BA 92 Trin Hall Cam BTh 08 Heythrop Coll Lon MA 09. Westcott Ho Cam 06. **d** 09 **p** 10. C Birch-in-Rusholme St Agnes w Longsight St Jo etc *Man* 09-12; P-in-c Romford St Andr *Chelmsf* from 12. *St Andrew's Rectory, 119 London Road, Romford RM7 9QD* T: (01708) 728583 E: lara-dose@hotmail.com

DOSSOR, Timothy Charles. b 70. Birm Univ BEng 94. Ridley Hall Cam BTh 99. **d** 99 **p** 00. C Ipswich St Jo *St E* 99-03; Asst Ldr Iwerne Holidays Titus Trust from 03; PtO *Ox* from 08. *31 Southdale Road, Oxford OX2 7SE* T: (01865) 553226 *or* 310513 M: 07748-184503 E: tim@dossor.org

DOTCHIN, Andrew Steward. b 56. Federal Th Coll S Africa. **d** 84 **p** 85. C Standerton w Evender S Africa 84-87; Asst P St Martin's-in-the-Veld 87-89; R Belgravia St Jo the Divine 89-94; Chapl St Martin's Sch Rosettenville 94-01; TV Blyth Valley *St E* 01-04; P-in-c Whitton and Thurleston w Akenham 04-09; R 09-15; P-in-c Felixstowe St Jo from 15; RD Colneys from 15. *The Rectory, 176 Flrcroft Road, Ipswich IP1 6PS* T: (01473) 741389 M: 07814-949828 E: revdotchin@gmail.com

DOTCHIN, Canon Joan Marie. b 47. NEOC 84. **d** 87 **p** 94. C Newc St Gabr 87-92; Team Dn Willington 92-94; TV 94-95; TR 95-03; V Fenham St Jas and St Basil 03-08; Hon Can Newc Cathl 01-08; rtd 08. *22 Astley Gardens, Seaton Sluice, Whitley Bay NE26 4JJ* T: 0191-237 3030 E: revj.dotchin@goldserve.net

DOUBLE, Richard Sydney (Brother Samuel). b 47. K Coll Lon BD 69 AKC 69. St Aug Coll Cant 69. **d** 70 **p** 71. C Walton St Mary *Liv* 70-74; SSF from 75; Guardian Hilfield Friary Dorchester 92-01; Can and Preb Sarum Cathl 95-01 and from 09; V Cambridge St Benedict *Ely* 01-05. *The Friary, Hilfield, Dorchester DT2 7BE* T: (01300) 341345

DOUBTFIRE, Canon Barbara. b 39. LMH Ox BA 61 MA 65. **d** 91 **p** 94. Par Development Adv *Ox* 88-04; NSM Kidlington w Hampton Poyle 91-04; Hon Can Ch Ch 98-04; rtd 04. *6 Meadow Walk, Woodstock OX20 1NR* T: (01993) 812095 E: spidir@oxford.anglican.org

DOUBTFIRE, Samuel. b 33. Edin Th Coll 63. **d** 66 **p** 66. C Knottingley *Wakef* 66-68; V Ripponden 68-76; V Crosthwaite Keswick *Carl* 76-81; V Barrow St Matt 81-87; R N Reddish *Man* 87-92; rtd 92; PtO *Bradf* 92-06. *21 Lichfield Lane, Mansfield NG18 4RA* T: (01623) 633266

DOUGAL, Stephen George. b 62. FICS. **d** 06 **p** 07. OLM Lyminge w Paddlesworth, Stanford w Postling etc *Cant* from 06. *Berefortal Farm Bungalow, Canterbury Road, Elham, Canterbury CT4 6UE* T: (01303) 840750

DOUGHTY, The Ven Andrew William. b 56. K Coll Lon BD AKC. Westcott Ho Cam 80. **d** 82 **p** 83. C Alton St Lawr *Win* 82-85; TV Basingstoke 85-91; V Chilworth w N Baddesley 91-95; R Warwick St Mary V Bermuda from 95; Adn Bermuda from 04. *PO Box WK 530, Warwick WK BX, Bermuda* T: (001) (441) 236 5744 F: 236 3667 E: adoughty@ibl.bm

DOUGLAS, Ann Patricia. b 49. Lon Univ CertEd 71. Oak Hill NSM Course 85. **d** 88 **p** 94. Par Dn Chorleywood Ch Ch *St Alb*

88-94; V Oxhey All SS 94-02; TR Woodley *Ox* 02-06; rtd 06; Development Officer Li Tim-Oi Foundn from 06; PtO *Sarum* from 07. *20 Passage Close, Weymouth DT4 9GE*
M: 07809-467717 T: (01305) 788310
E: anniedouglas@btopenworld.com

DOUGLAS, Anthony Victor. b 51. St Jo Coll Nottm 74. **d** 76 **p** 77. C Gt Crosby St Luke *Liv* 76-79; TV Fazakerley Em 79-84; TR Speke St Aid 84-90; TR Gt and Lt Coates w Bradley *Linc* 90-97; TR E Ham w Upton Park and Forest Gate *Chelmsf* 97-02; R Holkham w Egmere w Warham, Wells and Wighton *Nor* 02-12; Co-ord Chapl HM Pris Holme Ho from 12. *HM Prison Holme House, Holme House Road, Stockton-on-Tees TS18 2QU*
T: (01642) 744000 E: anthony.douglas123@btinternet.com

DOUGLAS, Gavin Allan. b 52. OBE 00. Cardiff Univ BTh 08. St Mich Coll Llan 03. **d** 05 **p** 06. C Week St Mary Circle of Par *Truro* 05-08; R Castle Bromwich SS Mary and Marg *Birm* from 08. *67 Chester Road, Castle Bromwich, Birmingham B36 9DP*
T: 0121-747 8546 E: gavinadouglas@yahoo.co.uk

DOUGLAS, Miss Janet Elizabeth. b 60. SS Paul & Mary Coll Cheltenham BEd 83. Cranmer Hall Dur 88. **d** 90 **p** 94. Par Dn Yardley St Edburgha *Birm* 90-93; Par Dn Hamstead St Paul 93-94; C 94-00; PtO 00-04; C Birm St Martin w Bordesley St Andr 04-11; rtd 11; PtO *Birm* 11-14. *6 Baxter Court, 96 School Road, Moseley, Birmingham B13 9TP* T: 0121-449 3763

DOUGLAS, Jonathan William Dixon. b 75. QUB BSc 96 K Coll Lon MA 01 Keele Univ MBA 03 DUniv 09 Spurgeon's Coll MTh 09. **d** 11 **p** 12. C Spitalfields Ch Ch w All SS *Lon* 11-14; C Northwood Em from 15. *4 Church Close, Northwood HA6 1SG* M: 07799-072845
E: revjohnnydouglas@gmail.com

DOUGLAS, Maureen Eleanor. b 43. Open Univ BA 87 Worc Coll of Educn CertEd 65. SWMTC 10. **d** 12. NSM Littleham w Exmouth *Ex* 12-13; NSM Littleham-cum-Exmouth w Lympstone from 13. *8A Elwyn Road, Exmouth EX8 2EL*
T: (01395) 225963 M: 07530-259773
E: medouglas@uwclub.net

DOUGLAS, Michael Williamson. b 51. Birm Univ BSc 72 Liv Univ PGCE 74. Trin Coll Bris 00. **d** 02 **p** 03. C Macclesfield Team *Ches* 02-06; TV Hawarden *St As* 06-10. *46 Far Meadow Lane, Wirral CH61 4XW* E: mikedougie@yahoo.co.uk

DOUGLAS, Pamela Jean. *See* WELCH, Pamela Jean

DOUGLAS, Patrick John. b 62. Ox Brookes Univ BA 05. St Mellitus Coll BA 13. **d** 13 **p** 14. C Walbrook Epiphany *Derby* from 13. *27 Clarence Road, Derby DE23 6LN* T: (01332) 602319 M: 07968-503447 E: patrickdouglas62@gmail.com *or* revive67@virginmedia.com

DOUGLAS, Peter Melvyn. b 47. **d** 96 **p** 97. NSM Prestwick *Glas* 96-01; Chapl HM Pris Dovegate 01-03; P-in-c Kilmarnock *Glas* 07-14; rtd 14. *Address temp unknown*

DOUGLAS, Richard Norman Henry. b 37. SAOMC 94. **d** 97 **p** 98. NSM Watercombe *Sarum* 97-02; PtO 02-04; Ox 04-06; NSM Grove 06-07; rtd 07; PtO *Ox* from 07. *6 Vale Avenue, Grove, Wantage OX12 7LU* T: (01235) 767753
E: dickannan@talktalk.net

DOUGLAS, Simon Alexander. b 70. Nottm Univ BEng 92. Qu Coll Birm 09. **d** 11 **p** 12. C Tettenhall Regis *Lich* 11-15; TV from 15. *76 Tyningham Avenue, Wolverhampton WV6 9PW*
E: simon@sdouglas.org

DOUGLAS LANE, Charles Simon Pellew. b 47. BNC Ox MA 71 MCIPD 79. Oak Hill Th Coll 91. **d** 94 **p** 95. C Whitton St Aug *Lon* 94-97; P-in-c Hounslow W Gd Shep 97-02; V 02-05; TV Riverside *Ox* 05-08; V Horton and Wraysbury 08-13; rtd 13; PtO *Lon* from 13. *1 Magnolia Villas, 30A Belgrade Road, Hampton TW12 2AZ* T: (020) 8941 5027
E: simondouglaslane@tiscali.co.uk

DOUGLAS-PENNANT, Oliver Andrew. b 79. Edin Univ MA 06. Trin Coll Bris 08. **d** 10 **p** 11. C Kidderminster E *Worc* 10-13; Canada 13-14; C Brentford *Lon* 14-15; TV from 15. *122 Windmill Road, Brentford TW8 9NA* M: 07950-878051
E: olidpennant@gmail.com

DOUGLASS, Michael Crone. b 49. Open Univ BA 96. NEOC 02. **d** 05 **p** 06. NSM Gosforth St Nic *Newc* from 05. *44 Regent Road, Newcastle upon Tyne NE3 1ED* T: 0191-285 0977
E: m.douglass@blueyonder.co.uk

DOUGLASS, Preb Philip. b 48. Open Univ BA 88. St Steph Ho Ox 87. **d** 89 **p** 90. C Peterlee *Dur* 89-92; V Crowan w Godolphin *Truro* 92-97; V Crowan and Treslothan 98-13; P-in-c Penponds 01-13; Preb St Endellion 02-13; rtd 13. *31 Bay View Terrace, Hayle TR27 4JY*
E: philip@thedouglasses.freeserve.co.uk

DOULL, Canon Iain Sinclair. b 43. St Mich Coll Llan 86. **d** 88 **p** 89. C Malpas *Mon* 88-91; P-in-c Newport All SS 91-98; V 98-02; V Newport Ch Ch 02-12; Hon Can St Woolos Cathl 11-12; rtd 12. *Ty'r Ydlan, Fachelich, St Davids, Haverfordwest SA62 6QL*

DOULTON, Dick. b 32. St Cath Coll Cam BA 60 MA 64. Ridley Hall Cam 61. **d** 63 **p** 64. C Gedling *S'well* 63-65; C Danbury *Chelmsf* 65; LtO *Ox* 88-90; L & K from 90. *Ballygriffin, Kenmare, Killarney, Co Kerry, Republic of Ireland* T: (00353) (64) 41743

DOULTON, Roderick John. b 55. Oak Hill Th Coll 91. **d** 93 **p** 94. C Hoddesdon *St Alb* 93-96; P-in-c Caldecote All SS 96-98; P-in-c Old Warden 97-98; V Caldecote, Northill and Old Warden 98-99; TV Macclesfield Team *Ches* 99-07; Chapl W Park Hosp Macclesfield 99-07; P-in-c Heydon, Gt and Lt Chishill, Chrishall etc *Chelmsf* 07-08; PtO *Ely* from 14. *7A Doddington Road, Chatteris PE16 6UA*

DOVE, Giles Wilfred. b 62. St Andr Univ MA 85 MPhil 88 FSAScot FRSA. TISEC 03. **d** 05 **p** 06. NSM Dunblane *St And* 05-07; Chapl Glenalmond Coll from 07. *The Chaplain's House, Glenalmond College, Glenalmond, Perth PH1 3RY* T: (01738) 880479 E: gilesdove@glenalmondcollege.co.uk

DOVE, Lionel John. b 38. **d** 06 **p** 07. OLM N Bradley, Southwick, Heywood and Steeple Ashton *Sarum* from 06. *Chobham Cottage, Acreshot Lane, Steeple Ashton, Trowbridge BA14 6HD*
T: (01380) 870013 E: lionel@dove8569.freeserve.co.uk

DOVE, Richard. b 54. EMMTC. **d** 99 **p** 00. NSM Dronfield w Holmesfield *Derby* 99-15; LtO from 15. *29 Hollins Spring Avenue, Dronfield S18 1RN* T: (01246) 412502
E: rdove1553@aol.com *or* dick.dove@dwhparish.org.uk

DOVER, Suffragan Bishop of. *See* WILLMOTT, The Rt Revd Trevor

DOVEY, Andrew Michael Stanley. b 59. SEITE 00. **d** 06 **p** 07. NSM Selsdon St Jo w St Fran *S'wark* 06-10; PtO 10-14; NSM Shirley St Geo from 14; NSM Shirley St Jo from 14. *6 Stokes Road, Croydon CR0 7SD* T: (020) 8656 9911
E: andrewdovey136@btinternet.com

DOW, Canon Andrew John Morrison. b 46. Univ Coll Ox BA 67 MA 71. Oak Hill Th Coll 69. **d** 71 **p** 72. C Watford St Luke *St Alb* 71-74; C Chadderton Ch Ch *Man* 75-78; V Leamington Priors St Paul *Cov* 78-88; V Knowle *Birm* 88-97; RD Solihull 95-97; V Clifton Ch Ch w Em *Bris* 97-04; P-in-c Cheltenham St Mary, St Matt, St Paul and H Trin *Glouc* 04-07; R Cheltenham St Mary w St Matt 07-10; AD Cheltenham 06-10; Hon Can Glouc Cathl 08-10; rtd 10; PtO *Cov* from 10. *17 Brownlow Drive, Stratford-upon-Avon CV37 9QS*
T: (01789) 417852 E: andrewdow451@btinternet.com

✠**DOW, The Rt Revd Geoffrey Graham.** b 42. Qu Coll Ox BA 63 MA 68 BSc 65 MSc 81 Nottm Univ MPhil 82. Clifton Th Coll 66. **d** 67 **p** 68 **c** 92. C Tonbridge SS Pet and Paul *Roch* 67-72; Chapl St Jo Coll Ox 72-75; Lect St Jo Coll Nottm 75-81; V Cov H Trin 81-92; Can Th Cov Cathl 88-92; Area Bp Willesden *Lon* 92-00; Bp Carl 00-09; rtd 09; Hon Asst Bp Ches from 09; Hon Asst Bp Man from 11. *34 Kimberley Avenue, Romiley, Stockport SK6 4AB* T: 0161-494 9148
E: graham@gdow.co.uk

DOWD, Garfield George. b 60. QUB BSc. **d** 86 **p** 87. C Monkstown *D & G* 86-90; I Carlow w Urglin and Staplestown *C & O* 90-05; Can Ossory Cathl 96-05; I Glenageary *D & G* from 05. *St Paul's Vicarage, Silchester Road, Glenageary, Co Dublin, Republic of Ireland* T/F: (00353) (1) 280 1616 M: 87-926 6558 E: glenageary@dublin.anglican.org

DOWDESWELL, Anne Marjory. b 68. **d** 06 **p** 07. C Leckhampton St Pet *Glouc* 06-10; TV Ex St Thos and Em 10-14; P-in-c Heref S Wye from 14. *1 Prinknash Close, Hereford HR2 7XA* T: (01432) 371292
E: anne.dowdeswell@hotmail.co.uk

DOWDING, Ms Clare Alice Elizabeth. b 74. Ch Ch Coll Cant BA 98 Greenwich Univ PGCE 99. Westcott Ho Cam BA 02. **d** 03 **p** 05. USA 03-04; C Longsight St Luke *Man* 04-07; Chapl Man HE Institutions 07-11; R Earlham *Nor* 11-14; R St Marylebone St Paul *Lon* from 14. *St Paul's House, 9 Rossmore Road, London NW1 6NJ* M: 07970-661534 T: (020) 7262 9443 *or* 7724 8517 E: caedowding@gmail.com

DOWDING, Canon Edward Brinley. b 47. St Mich Coll Llan 70 St D Coll Lamp BA 71. **d** 72 **p** 73. C Canton St Cath *Llan* 72-75; C Aberdare 75-78; V Aberavon H Trin 78-85; R Sully 85-13; R Wenvoe and St Lythans 10-13; RD Penarth and Barry 98-04; Hon Can Llan Cathl 11-13; rtd 13; PtO *Llan* from 13. *10 Clos Tawe, Barry CF62 7BN* T: (01446) 737180
E: edward.dowding@btinternet.com

DOWDING, Mrs Elizabeth Jean. b 43. Bath Coll of HE TCert 67. SAOMC 00. **d** 04 **p** 05. NSM Goring w S Stoke *Ox* 04-07; NSM Goring and Streatley w S Stoke from 07. *30 Milldown Avenue, Goring, Reading RG8 0AS* T: (01491) 873140
E: elizdowding@aol.com

DOWDING, Jeremy Charles. b 51. St Steph Ho Ox 89. **d** 91 **p** 92. C Newport St Steph and H Trin *Mon* 91-94; C Risca 94-96; P-in-c Whitleigh *Ex* 96-05; P-in-c Thorpe-le-Soken *Chelmsf* from 05. *The Vicarage, Mill Lane, Thorpe-le-Soken, Clacton-on-Sea CO16 0ED* T: (01255) 861234

DOWDLE, Canon Cynthia. b 48. Cranmer Hall Dur 88. **d** 90 **p** 94. C Allerton *Liv* 90-94; TR Halewood 94-00; V Knowsley

00-11; Hd Spiritual Care Adelaide Ho Probation Hostel from 11; Dean of Women's Min from 01; Hon Can Liv Cathl 01-10; Can Res Liv Cathl from 10. *19 Belvedere House, 2-4 Ullet Road, Liverpool L8 3SR* T: 0151-727 5766
E: cynthiadowdle@hotmail.com

DOWDY, Simon Mark Christopher. b 67. Trin Hall Cam BA 89 MA 93. Wycliffe Hall Ox 93. **d** 96 **p** 97. C Beckenham Ch Ch *Roch* 96-00; C St Helen Bishopsgate w St Andr Undershaft etc *Lon* 00-05; P-in-c St Botolph without Aldersgate from 02. *45 Woodwarde Road, London SE22 8UN* T: (020) 8299 1631
E: mail@stbotolphsaldersgate.org.uk

DOWER, Frances Helen. b 45. Lon Univ MB, BS 69. **d** 09 **p** 10. OLM Kirkwhelpington, Kirkharle, Kirkheaton and Cambo *Newc* 09-14; NSM from 14. *Cambo House, Front Row, Cambo, Morpeth NE61 4AY* T: (01670) 774297
E: frances.dower@dower.org.uk

DOWIE, Winifred Brenda McIntosh. b 57. Callendar Park Coll of Educn Falkirk DipEd 78. Trin Coll Bris BA 91. **d** 92 **p** 94. Par Dn Downend *Bris* 92-94; C 94-95; Chapl Asst Southmead Health Services NHS Trust 95-98; Chapl St Pet Hospice Bris 98-13; Hon Can Bris Cathl 02-13; Chapl Glos Hosps NHS Foundn Trust from 13. *Trust Headquarters, 1 College Lawn, Cheltenham GL53 7AG* T: 0300-422 2222 *or* (01242) 222222

DOWLAND, Martin John. b 48. Lon Univ BD 70 Southn Univ PGCE 71. Wycliffe Hall Ox 75. **d** 77 **p** 78. C Jesmond Clayton Memorial *Newc* 77-80; C Chadderton Ch Ch *Man* 80-85; R Haughton St Mary 85-14; rtd 14. *11 Overdale Drive, Glossop SK13 6GA* E: m.dowland@ntlworld.com

DOWLAND-OWEN, Edward Farrington. b 73. St D Coll Lamp BA 95 Trin Coll Carmarthen PGCE 96 FVCM 99. S Wales Ord Course 00 St Mich Coll Llan 03. **d** 04 **p** 05. C Llandaff *Llan* 04-08; P-in-c Llandyfodwg and Cwm Ogwr 08-10; C Penarth and Llandough 10-13; TV Cowbridge from 13; Dioc Spirituality Adv from 12; P Assoc Shrine of Our Lady of Walsingham from 05. *The Vicarage, 2 Court Close, Aberthin, Cowbridge CF71 7EH* T: (01446) 775381 M: 07403-935555
E: revedward@dowlandowen.co.uk

DOWLAND-PILLINGER, Catherine Louise. b 60. New Hall Cam BA 82 MA 86 PhD 89. SEITE 05. **d** 08 **p** 09. C Addington *S'wark* 08-12; PtO 12-13; Chapl S'wark Cathl 13; TV Caterham from 13. *Address temp unknown* M: 07768-065301
E: rev.catherine1@googlemail.com

DOWLEN, Isabella McBeath. b 45. Man Univ CertEd 86 Edin Univ MTh 06 RGN 67 SCM 68 HVCert 69. STETS 96. **d** 99 **p** 01. NSM Branksome St Clem *Sarum* 99-04; NSM Clarkston *Glas* 04-06; P-in-c Glas St Oswald 06-08; R Pittenweem *St And* 10-14; R Elie and Earlsferry 10-14; rtd 14. *24 Baird Place, Elie, Level KY9 1EH* T: (01333) 330003 M: 07974-084657
E: isabel.dowlen@gmail.com

DOWLER, Robert Edward Mackenzie. b 67. Ch Ch Ox BA 89 Selw Coll Cam BA 93 Dur Univ PhD 07. Westcott Ho Cam 91. **d** 94 **p** 95. C Southgate Ch Ch *Lon* 94-97; C Somers Town 97-01; Tutor and Dir Past Th St Steph Ho Ox 01-09; Vice Prin 03-09; Asst Chapl Malvern Coll 09-10; V Clay Hill St Jo and St Luke *Lon* from 10; CME Officer Edmonton Area from 13. *St Luke's Vicarage, 92 Browning Road, Enfield EN2 0HG* T: (020) 8363 6055

DOWLEY, Mrs Ruth Ada. b 49. St Mellitus Coll 13. **d** 14 **p** 15. OLM Becontree St Cedd *Chelmsf* from 14. *68 Malvern Drive, Ilford IG3 9DW* T: (020) 8597 1988 M: 07817-163203
E: ruthdowley@hotmail.com

DOWLING, Donald Edward. b 43. St Andr Univ MA 66. Cranmer Hall Dur. **d** 74 **p** 75. C Thame w Towersey *Ox* 74-77; C Norton *St Alb* 77-80; V Wilbury 81-99; V Stevenage St Nic and Graveley 99-10; rtd 10. *56 Caslon Way, Letchworth Garden City SG6 4QL* E: rev_don@virgin.net

DOWLING, Graham Paul. b 62. NTMTC BA 09. **d** 09 **p** 10. C Rainham w Wennington *Chelmsf* 09-13; TV Barking from 13. *St Patrick's Vicarage, 79 Sparsholt Road, Barking IG11 7YG* T: (020) 8594 1960 M: 07889-286308
E: revgpd@btinternet.com

DOWLING, Canon Kingsley Avery Paul. b 60. Open Univ BA. Aston Tr Scheme 93 Ripon Coll Cuddesdon 95. **d** 97 **p** 98. C Headingley *Ripon* 97-99; C Far Headingley St Chad 99-01; V Wortley-de-Leeds 01-13; P-in-c Farnley 10-13; AD Armley 08-13; Hon Can Ripon Cathl 13-14; R Wortley and Farnley *Leeds* 13-15; V Meanwood from 15; Hon Can Ripon Cathl from 13. *Meanwood Vicarage, 9 Parkside Green, Leeds LS6 4NY* T: 0113-263 8867 M: 07810-212127
E: kingsley.dowling@hotmail.com

DOWLING, Tracy Anne. b 59. SEITE 08. **d** 11 **p** 12. NSM Merton Priory *S'wark* 11-14; C Dundee St Paul *Bre* from 14. *St Paul's Cathedral, High Street, Dundee DD1 1TD* M: 07788-239798 T: (01382) 224486 *or* (01241) 410935
E: chaplain@saintpaulscathedral.net

DOWMAN, Jonathan Robert. b 76. Westmr Coll Ox BEd 00. Trin Coll Bris 04. **d** 07 **p** 08. C Anglesey Gp *Ely* 07-10; Deanery Missr *Birm* 10-14; Bp's Adv on Fresh Expressions *Leic* from 14; PtO from 15. *8 Main Street, Marston Trussell, Market Harborough LE16 9TY* T: 0116-261 5307
E: jonathandowman@icloud.com *or* jonathan.dowman@leccofe.org

DOWMAN, Peter Robert. b 52. City Univ BSc 76. Wycliffe Hall Ox 82. **d** 84 **p** 85. C Cheltenham Ch Ch *Glouc* 84-87; C Danbury *Chelmsf* 87-90; R Woodham Ferrers and Bicknacre 90-95; Consultant E England CPAS 95-03; R Warboys w Broughton and Bury w Wistow *Ely* 03-14; rtd 14. *1 Oaklands, Warboys, Huntingdon PE28 2XH* T: (01487) 824612
E: rector@4parishes.org

DOWN, Andrew Stuart. b 77. Ex Univ BSc 99. Ripon Coll Cuddesdon BTh 14. **d** 14. C Ex St Jas from 14. *17 Culverland Close, Exeter EX4 6HR* M: 07443-458487
E: rev.andrewdown@gmail.com

DOWN, Martin John. b 40. Jes Coll Cam BA 62 MA 68. Westcott Ho Cam 63. **d** 65 **p** 66. C Bury St Mary *Man* 65-68; C Leigh St Mary 68-70; R Fiskerton *Linc* 70-75; V Irnham w Corby 75-79; RD Beltisloe 76-84; P-in-c Swayfield and Creeton w Swinstead 78-79; V Corby Glen 79-84; Good News Trust 84-88; PtO *Linc* 84-88; *Pet* 86-88; P-in-c Ashill w Saham Toney *Nor* 88-94; R 94-00; C Watton w Carbrooke and Ovington 00-05; rtd 05; PtO *Nor* 05-12; *Ox* from 12. *36 Beechgate, Witney OX28 4JL* T: (01993) 709743

DOWN, Peter Michael. b 54. K Coll Lon BD 78 AKC. Coll of Resurr Mirfield 78. **d** 79 **p** 80. C Swindon Ch Ch *Bris* 79-82; C Southmead 82-84; TV Cannock *Lich* 84-92; V Coleford w Holcombe *B & W* 92-01; Hon C Westfield 01-02; PtO 07-11; P-in-c Tintinhull w Chilthorne Domer, Yeovil Marsh etc from 11. *The Rectory, Vicarage Street, Tintinhull, Yeovil BA22 8PY* M: 07971-308671 T: (01935) 829058
E: peterdown836@btinternet.com

DOWN, The Venn Philip Roy. b 53. Hull Univ MA 93. Melbourne Coll of Div BTh 82 MTh 88. **d** 89 **p** 89. C Gt Grimsby St Mary and St Jas *Linc* 89-91; TV 91-95; R Hackington *Cant* 95-02; AD Cant 99-02; Adn Maidstone 02-11; Adn Ashford from 11. *The Archdeaconry, Pett Lane, Charing, Ashford TN27 0DL* T: (01233) 712649 E: pdown@archdeacashford.org

✠**DOWN, The Rt Revd William John Denbigh.** b 34. St Jo Coll Cam BA 57 MA 61 FNI 91. Ridley Hall Cam 57. **d** 59 **p** 60 **c** 90. C Fisherton Anger *Sarum* 59-63; Miss to Seamen 63-90; Australia 71-74; Dep Gen Sec Miss to Seamen 75; Gen Sec 76-90; Hon C Gt Stanmore *Lon* 75-90; Chapl St Mich Paternoster Royal 76-90; PtO *St Alb* 78-90; Hon Can Gib Cathl 85-90; Hon Can Koba Japan from 87; Bp Bermuda 90-95; Asst Bp Leic 95-01; P-in-c Humberstone 95-01; P-in-c Thurnby Lodge 01; rtd 01; Hon Asst Bp Ox from 01. *54 Dark Lane, Witney OX28 6LX* T: (01993) 706615
E: bishbill@aol.com

DOWN AND DROMORE, Bishop of. See MILLER, The Rt Revd Harold Creeth

DOWN, Archdeacon of. See MACCLAY, The Ven David Alexander

DOWN, Dean of. See HULL, The Very Revd Thomas Henry

DOWNER, Barry Michael. b 58. STETS 99. **d** 02 **p** 07. NSM Lake and Shanklin St Sav *Portsm* 02-05; NSM Bonchurch, Ventnor H Trin and Ventnor St Cath 05-08; NSM Oakfield St Jo 09-14; NSM Brading w Yaverland 14. *44 Landguard Road, Shanklin PO37 7JX* E: barry.downer@southwight.com

DOWNER, Cuthbert John. b 18. S'wark Ord Course 60. **d** 74 **p** 75. Hon C Kirdford *Chich* 74-76; C Halesworth w Linstead and Chediston *St E* 76-79; P-in-c Knodishall w Buxlow 79-80; P-in-c Friston 79-80; R Bacton w Wyverstone 80-83; P-in-c Cotton and Wickham Skeith 80-83; R Bacton w Wyverstone and Cotton 83-84; rtd 84; PtO *St E* 84-87; *B & W* 88-95 and from 97. *Abbeyfield Society, 43-49 Westbury Road, Westbury-on-Trym, Bristol BS9 3AU*

DOWNES, Andrew Victor John. b 65. STETS 10. **d** 13 **p** 14. C Chiswick St Nic w St Mary *Lon* from 13. *32 Lysia Street, London SW6 6NG* T: (020) 7386 5079 M: 07939-290265
E: andrewvjd@gmail.com

DOWNES, Gregory Charles. b 69. Roehampton Inst BSc 91 Hughes Hall Cam PGCE 92. Wycliffe Hall Ox BA 95 MA 01. **d** 96 **p** 97. C Hazlemere *Ox* 96-99; Chapl HM Pris Ashfield 99-01; Lect Lon Sch of Th 01-04; Chapl Pemb Coll Ox 04-05; Chapl Ox Pastorate 05-06; PtO *Truro* 06-09; Dir Cen for Missional Leadership Watford 10-14; PtO *St Alb* 10-14; Y Stre St Mich-le-Belfrey from 14. *12 Muncastergate, York YO31 9LA* M: 07920-128029
E: greg.downes@belfrey.org

DOWNES, Richard John. b 63. Cranmer Hall Dur 91. **d** 94 **p** 95. C Bishopwearmouth St Gabr *Dur* 94-97; CF from 97. *c/o MOD Chaplains (Army)* F: 381824 T: (01264) 383430

DOWNEY, Jocelyn Stewart. b 69. Surrey Univ BSc 92 Lon Univ PhD 98 St Edm Coll Cam MPhil 14 Ch Coll Cam BTh 13. Ridley Hall Cam 11. **d** 14 **p** 15. C Bermondsey St Jas and St Anne *S'wark* from 14. *Salmon Youth Centre, 43 Old Jamaica Road, London SE16 4TE* T: (020) 7394 2448

DOWNEY, Canon John Stewart. b 38. QUB CertEd 60 Open Univ BA 76. Oak Hill Th Coll 63. **d** 66 **p** 67. C Londonderry St Aug *D & R* 66-71; I Dungiven w Bovevagh 71-82; Bp's Dom Chapl 75-82; V Bishopwearmouth St Gabr *Dur* 82-91; V New Malden and Coombe *S'wark* 91-06; Hon Can S'wark Cathl 97-06; rtd 06; PtO *S'wark* from 08. *171 Kenton Road, Newcastle upon Tyne NE3 4NR* T: 0191-597 2892

DOWNEY, Olivia Margaret Grace. **d** 14. Aughaval w Achill, Knappagh, Dugort etc *T, K & A* 14-15; C Enniskillen *Clogh* from 15. *Address temp unknown*

DOWNHAM, Canon Peter Norwell. b 31. Man Univ BA 52. Ridley Hall Cam 54. **d** 56 **p** 57. C Cheadle *Ches* 56-62; V Rawtenstall St Mary *Man* 62-68; Chapl Rossendale Gen Hosp 62-68; V Denton Holme *Carl* 68-79; V Reading Greyfriars *Ox* 79-95; Hon Can Ch Ch 90-95; rtd 95; Hon C Cotehill and Cumwhinton *Carl* 95-00; PtO 98-07; *Ox* from 07. *17 Grange Close, Goring, Reading RG8 9DY* T: (01491) 875983

DOWNHAM, Simon Garrod. b 61. K Coll Lon LLB 84 Solicitor 87. Wycliffe Hall Ox BA 93. **d** 94 **p** 95. C Brompton H Trin w Onslow Square St Paul *Lon* 94-99; P-in-c Hammersmith St Paul 00-06; V from 06. *14 Lena Gardens, London W6 7PZ* T: (020) 7603 9662 *or* 8748 3855
E: simon.downham@sph.org.uk

DOWNING, Francis Gerald. b 35. Qu Coll Ox BA 56 MA 60. Linc Th Coll. **d** 58 **p** 59. C Filwood Park CD *Bris* 58-60; Tutor Linc Th Coll 60-64; V Unsworth *Man* 64-80; Tutor NOC 80-82; Vice-Prin 82-90; V Bolton SS Simon and Jude *Man* 90-97; rtd 97; PtO *Blackb* from 97. *33 Westhoughton Road, Chorley PR7 4EU* T: (01257) 474240

DOWNS, Caroline Rebecca. b 58. UWIST BA 80 Univ of Wales (Cardiff) PGCE 81. St Mich Coll Llan 98. **d** 02 **p** 03. C Roath *Llan* 02-07; P-in-c Cathays from 07; Warden of Readers from 14. *6 Newminster Road, Roath, Cardiff CF23 5AP* T: (029) 2049 5699 E: carolinerebecca.downs@btinternet.com

DOWNS, Miss Geinor. b 47. UEA BA 72 Southn Univ BTh 89 Birm Univ MA 05. Chich Th Coll 85. **d** 87 **p** 94. Par Dn Wellingborough All SS *Pet* 87-89; Development Officer Chich Th Coll 89-92; C Durrington *Chich* 92-95; Chapl City Hosp NHS Trust Birm 95-02; Chapl Sandwell and W Birm Hosps NHS Trust 02-06. *Address temp unknown*

DOWNS, John Alfred. b 58. Leic Univ BSc 79 PGCE 80 CBiol 80 MSB 80. EMMTC 90. **d** 93 **p** 94. NSM Barlestone *Leic* 93-96; NSM Markfield, Thornton, Bagworth and Stanton etc 96-11; NSM Newbold de Verdun, Barlestone and Kirkby Mallory from 11; PtO *Cov* from 13. *29 Meadow Road, Barlestone, Nuneaton CV13 0JG* T: (01455) 290195
E: revjohndowns@hotmail.co.uk

DOWNS, Mrs Lynsay Marie. b 75. Hull Univ BA 98. Ripon Coll Cuddesdon BTh 05. **d** 05 **p** 06. C Tettenhall Wood and Perton *Lich* 05-09; TV Brereton and Rugeley 09-13; R Penicuik *Edin* from 13. *The Rectory, 23 Broomhill Road, Penicuik EH26 9EE* T: (01968) 672862 E: stjandstmrector@icloud.com

DOWSE, Ivor Roy. b 35. ARHistS MRSL. St Deiniol's Hawarden 66. **d** 68 **p** 70. C Harrow St Pet *Lon* 68-69; C Sudbury St Andr 69-71; C Weeke *Win* 71-73; Min Can Ban Cathl 73-78; V Hollym w Welwick and Holmpton *York* 78-81; R Bearwood *Ox* 81-82; P-in-c Rothesay *Arg* 83-86; C Boxmoor St Jo *St Alb* 86-92; Hon C Cowes H Trin and St Mary *Portsm* 92-94; PtO 94-98; P-in-c St Hilary w Perranuthnoe *Truro* 98-00; rtd 01; PtO *Win* from 06; Hon Chapl Win Cathl from 06; Hon Asst Chapl St Jo Win Charity from 09. *10 St Mary Magdalen Almshouses, Colebrook Street, Winchester SO23 9LR* T: (01962) 890877

DOWSETT, Alan Charles. b 27. Selw Coll Cam BA 51 MA 55 Bris Poly CQSW 76. Cuddesdon Coll 51. **d** 53 **p** 54. C Portsea St Mary *Portsm* 53-57; C Wokingham All SS *Ox* 57-60; V Water Orton *Birm* 60-64; Chapl Colston's Sch Bris 64-65; C Stoke Bishop *Bris* 65-68; LtO 69-89; rtd 89. *23 Upper Cranbrook Road, Bristol BS6 7UW* T: 0117-924 3227

DOWSETT, Andrew Christopher. b 72. Sheff Univ BA 95 PhD 99. St Jo Coll Nottm 07. **d** 09. C Clubmoor *Liv* 09-11; C Birkdale St Jas and Birkdale St Pet 11-13; Min Sunderland Minster *Dur* from 13. *20 Beechwood Terrace, Thornhill, Sunderland SR2 7LY* M: 07783-760012
E: andrew@dowsetts.net *or*
minsterpriest@sunderlandminster.org

DOWSETT, Ian Peter. b 71. Liv Univ BA 95 Lon Inst of Educn PGCE 96. Wycliffe Hall Ox BA 01. **d** 02. C Kensington St Helen w H Trin *Lon* 02-09; V S Harrow St Paul from 09. *St Paul's Vicarage, Findon Close, Harrow HA2 8NJ* T: (020) 8864 0362 M: 07985-726465 E: irdowsett@talk21.com

DOWSETT, Canon Marian Ivy Rose. b 40. **d** 88 **p** 97. NSM Rumney *Mon* 88-94; C St Mellons and Michaelston-y-Fedw 94-96; C St Mellons 96-03; V Llanrumney 03-10; rtd 10; P-in-c Llanrumney *Mon* from 10; Hon Can St Woolos Cathl 09-11. *114 Ridgeway Road, Rumney, Cardiff CF3 4AB* T: (029) 2079 2635

DOWSON, Ruth Helen. b 59. Sheff Univ BA 81 Bradf Univ MBA 85 Leeds Univ MA 12 Leeds Metrop Univ PGCE 09. Yorks Min Course 09. **d** 12 **p** 13. *22 Windermere Road, Bradford BD7 4RQ* T: (01274) 579143 M: 07971-189599
E: r.dowson@leedsmet.ac.uk

DOWSON, Simon Paul. b 63. Bris Univ BSc 85 Cam Univ PGCE 89. Cranmer Hall Dur 95. **d** 97 **p** 98. C Bradf St Aug Undercliffe 97-99; C Werrington *Pet* 99-04; V Skirbeck H Trin *Linc* 04-14; RD Holland 13-14; TR Bilton *Ripon* from 14. *Bilton Vicarage, Bilton Lane, Harrogate HG1 3DT* T: (01205) 363657
E: simondowson64@gmail.com *or* rector.bilton@gmail.com

DOXSEY, Canon Roy Desmond. b 41. St D Coll Lamp 64. **d** 67 **p** 68. C Pembroke St Mary w St Mich *St D* 67-70; C Milford Haven 70-73; C Loughton *Ox* 73-75; Chapl Llandovery Coll 75-81 and 92-96; Zambia 81-86; Chapl Epsom Coll 86-92; V Roath St German *Llan* 96-11; Hon Can Llan Cathl 09-11; PtO from 12. *St Anne's Clergy House, 3 Snipe Street, Cardiff CF24 3RB* T: (029) 2048 9313

DOYLE, Andrew Michael. b 63. K Coll Lon BD 85 AKC 85. Ripon Coll Cuddesdon 86. **d** 88 **p** 89. C Lytchett Minster *Sarum* 88-92; TV Kirkby *Liv* 92-97; V Rotherhithe H Trin *S'wark* from 97; AD Bermondsey 00-08. *Holy Trinity Vicarage, Bryan Road, London SE16 5HF* T: (020) 7237 4098

DOYLE, Edward Michael. b 70. St Mich Coll Llan BTh 93. **d** 94 **p** 95. C Sketty *S & B* 94-96; C Llwynderw 96-00; R Rogate w Terwick and Trotton w Chithurst *Chich* from 00. *The Vicarage, Fyning Lane, Rogate, Petersfield GU31 5EE* T: (01730) 821576
E: edwarddoyle@uwclub.net

DOYLE, Eileen Ann. b 53. SEITE 08. **d** 11 **p** 12. NSM Coxheath, E Farleigh, Hunton, Linton etc *Roch* from 11. *63 Felderland Close, Maidstone ME15 9YD* T: (01622) 236170
E: eileen@leedoyle.co.uk

DOYLE, Graham Thomas. b 48. St Barn Coll Adelaide ThL 73 ThSchol 77 Worc Coll Ox BA 85 MA 90. **d** 73 **p** 74. Australia 73-83; PtO *Ox* 83-85; C Cobbold Road St Sav w St Mary *Lon* 86; P-in-c Bradf St Oswald Chapel Green 86-91; Chapl Belgrade w Zagreb *Eur* 91-93; Chapl Belgrade 93-97; Taiwan 97-00; I Killeshandra w Killegar and Derrylane *K, E & A* 00-03; I Athlone w Benown, Kiltoom and Forgney *M & K* from 03. *St Mary's Rectory, Killion Hill Street, Bonavalley, Athlone, Co Westmeath, Republic of Ireland* T/F: (00353) (90) 647 8350 E: gtdoyleathlone@eircom.net

DOYLE, Janet Mary. b 51. **d** 13 **p** 14. OLM Westbury-on-Trym St Alb *Bris* from 13. *26 Rodbourne Road, Bristol BS10 5AS*

DOYLE, Michael Christopher. b 64. St Jo Coll Nottm 06. **d** 08 **p** 09. C Ashbourne St Oswald w Mapleton *Derby* 08-12; R N Beltisloe Gp *Linc* from 12. *The Rectory, 12 School Lane, Ropsley, Grantham NG33 4BT* T: (01476) 586963
E: mike_c_doyle@hotmail.com

DOYLE, Nigel Paul. b 55. MHort(RHS) 82. St Mich Coll Llan 00. **d** 03 **p** 04. NSM Landore w Treboeth *S & B* 03-09; NSM Gower Deanery from 09. *3 Ael-y-Bryn, Penclawdd, Swansea SA4 3LF* T: (01792) 850659 E: tadnigel@yahoo.co.uk

DOYLE, Robin Alfred. b 43. Dur Univ BA 65. Westcott Ho Cam 66. **d** 68 **p** 69. C Edgbaston St Geo *Birm* 68-70; C Erdington St Barn 70-73; P-in-c Oldbury 73-81; R Maker w Rame *Truro* 81-11; rtd 11. *9 Camperknowle Close, Millbrook, Torpoint PL10 1QB* T: (01752) 822302
E: robin@robindoyle.wanadoo.co.uk

DOYLE, Mrs Sara. b 66. **d** 12 **p** 13. NSM St Luke in the City *Liv* from 12. *4 Elstree Road, Liverpool L6 8NU*

DOYLE, Mrs Tracey Elizabeth. b 58. Open Univ BA 00. SAOMC 94. **d** 97 **p** 98. OLM Winslow w Gt Horwood and Addington *Ox* 97-99; C 00-04; P-in-c Ivinghoe w Pitstone and Slapton 04-08; V Ivinghoe w Pitstone and Slapton and Marsworth 08-14. *Stables Cottage, Nethergrove, High Bickington, Umberleigh EX37 9BQ* M: 07814-538208
E: mick.doyle@virgin.net

DOYLE-BRETT, Mrs Jacqueline Margaret. b 62. Hull Univ BA 99 PGCE 00 Sheff Univ MA 13. Yorks Min Course 11. **d** 13 **p** 14. C Tadcaster *York* from 13. *The Vicarage, Church Street, Church Fenton, Tadcaster LS24 9RD* T: (01937) 558221 M: 07793-545755 E: jackiemdb@gmail.com

DRACUP, John Stuart. b 75. Cranmer Hall Dur 13. **d** 15. C Coley *Wakef* from 15. *The Vicarage, 1 Church Walk, Northowram, Halifax HX3 7HF* M: 07753-987668
E: fionadracup@hotmail.co.uk

DRACKLEY, John Oldham. b 36. Em Coll Cam BA 57 MA 61. Wells Th Coll 57. **d** 59 **p** 60. C Eckington *Derby* 59-62;

C Lee Gd Shep w St Pet *S'wark* 62-63; C Derby St Thos 63-67; C Matlock and Tansley 67-77; P-in-c Radbourne 77-82; P-in-c Dalbury, Long Lane and Trusley 77-82; P-in-c Longford 77-82; Sec Dioc Cttee for Care of Chs 82-98; rtd 95; PtO *Derby* from 98. *26 Highfield Drive, Matlock DE4 3FZ* T: (01629) 55902

DRAFFAN, Canon Ian William. b 42. Aston Univ BSc 65 MSc 66 FBCS 77 CEng 88. NOC 83. **d** 86 **p** 87. NSM Millhouses H Trin *Sheff* 86-04; NSM Endcliffe 04-10; P-in-c 08-10; Hon Can Sheff Cathl from 05; PtO from 10. *13 Bocking Lane, Sheffield S8 7BG* T: 0114-236 4523 E: ian.draffan@sheffield.anglican.org

DRAIN, Walter. b 39. JP 75. Open Univ BA 76 ACP 66. NW Ord Course 76. **d** 79 **p** 80. NSM Cheadle *Ches* 79-81; C 81-84; V Chatburn *Blackb* 84-02; Sub Chapl HM Pris Preston 94-02; rtd 02; PtO *Blackb* from 02. *Angels, 28 The Croft, Euxton, Chorley PR7 6LH* T: (01257) 249646

DRAISEY, Damon Allan. b 67. STETS 10. **d** 13 **p** 14. C Warblington w Emsworth *Portsm* from 13. *1 Godwin Close, Emsworth PO10 7XT* M: 07906-346498 E: damon.rev@googlemail.com

DRAKE, Graham. b 46. Linc Th Coll 81. **d** 83 **p** 85. C Alford w Rigsby *Linc* 83-84; PtO *Wakef* 84-85; Hon C Purston cum S Featherstone 85-89; NSM Castleford All SS 89-92; C Cudworth 92-95; rtd 11. *8A Broomhill, Castleford WF10 4QP* T: (01977) 518407 E: alison-drake@btinternet.com

DRAKE, Canon Graham Rae. b 45. Fitzw Coll Cam BA 68 MA 72. Qu Coll Birm 70. **d** 73 **p** 74. C New Windsor *Ox* 73-77; TV 77-78; P-in-c Bath Ascension *B & W* 78-81; TV Bath Twerton-on-Avon 81-86; P-in-c Buxton w Oxnead *Nor* 86-90; P-in-c Lammas w Lt Hautbois 86-90; R Buxton w Oxnead, Lammas and Brampton 90-95; RD Ingworth 88-94; P-in-c Cockley Cley w Gooderstone 95-01; P-in-c Gt and Lt Cressingham w Threxton 95-01; P-in-c Didlington 95-01; P-in-c Hilborough w Bodney 95-01; P-in-c Oxborough w Foulden and Caldecote 95-01; P-in-c Mundford w Lynford 99-01; P-in-c Ickburgh w Langford 99-01; P-in-c Cranwich 99-01; V Thorpe St Matt 01-10; Hon Can Nor Cathl 99-10; rtd 10; PtO *Nor* from 10. *13 Needham Place, St Stephen's Square, Norwich NR1 3SD* T: (01603) 886084 E: grahamrdrake@btinternet.com

DRAKE, Jonathan Charles. b 81. Down Coll Cam MEng 03 MA 05. Wycliffe Hall Ox BA 11. **d** 12 **p** 13. C Wargrave w Knowl Hill *Ox* from 12. *Houndsford Cottage, 103 High Street, Wargrave, Reading RG10 8DD* T: 0118-940 6857 M: 07715-123856 E: jon.drake1981@gmail.com

DRAKE, Leslie Sargent. b 47. Boston Univ BA 69 MTh 72 Hull Univ BPhil 74 Anglia Poly Univ MSc 93. Coll of Resurr Mirfield 78. **d** 78 **p** 79. C Oldham *Man* 78-81; TV Rochdale 81-83; V Palmers Green St Jo *Lon* 83-89; St Mary's Sch Cheshunt 89-91; Hd RE St Mary's Sch Hendon 91-99; TV Wimbledon *S'wark* 99-03; V Clay Hill St Jo and St Luke *Lon* 03-09; V Aiken St Aug USA 09-12; V S Benfleet *Chelmsf* from 12. *St Mary's Vicarage, 105 Vicarage Hill, Benfleet SS7 1PD* T: (01268) 754268 E: frldrake@btinternet.com

DRAKE-SMITH, Jacqueline Ann. b 59. Ripon Coll Cuddesdon 12. **d** 14 **p** 15. C Merrow *Guildf* from 14. *42 Finches Rise, Guildford GU1 2UW* M: 07806-775974 E: jackieds8@hotmail.com

DRAKELEY, Stephen Richard Francis. b 51. Aston Univ BSc 73. Chich Th Coll 76. **d** 76 **p** 77. C Yardley Wood *Birm* 76-79; V Rednal 79-89; TV Bodmin w Lanhydrock and Lanivet *Truro* 89-99; P-in-c Falmouth All SS from 99. *All Saints' Vicarage, 72 Dracaena Avenue, Falmouth TR11 2EN* T/F: (01326) 317474 E: srfd@compuserve.com

DRAPER, Charles James. b 59. Dur Univ BSc 80 Cam Univ BA 86. Ridley Hall Cam 84. **d** 87 **p** 88. C Wareham *Sarum* 87-90; C Maltby *Sheff* 90-93; R The Claydons *Ox* 93-99; R Chinnor w Emmington and Sydenham etc 99-02; P-in-c Gt Faringdon w Lt Coxwell 02-07; V from 07; AD Vale of White Horse from 13. *The Vicarage, Coach Lane, Faringdon SN7 8AB* T: (01367) 240106 E: 6drapers@cdraper.fslife.co.uk

DRAPER, Christine. b 46. **d** 06 **p** 07. OLM Newburgh w Westhead *Liv* from 06. *Arenal, 38 Hoscar Moss Road, Lathom, Ormskirk L40 4BQ* T: (01704) 893081

DRAPER, Derek Vincent. b 38. Linc Th Coll 65. **d** 68 **p** 69. C Orpington All SS *Roch* 68-72; C Bramley *Guildf* 72-74; P-in-c Kempston All SS *St Alb* 74-76; Min Kempston Transfiguration CD 77-78; V Kempston Transfiguration 79-84; RD Bedford 79-84; V Bromham w Oakley 84-88; P-in-c Stagsden 84-88; V Bromham w Oakley and Stagsden 88-03; RD Elstow 00-02; Chapl Bromham Hosp 84-03; rtd 03; PtO *Ely* from 03; *St Alb* from 03. *24 Wilkinson Close, Eaton Socon, St Neots PE19 8HJ* T: (01480) 384031 E: drapers24@ntlworld.com

DRAPER, Elizabeth Ann. See BRADLEY, Elizabeth Ann

DRAPER, Ivan Thomas. b 32. Aber Univ MB, ChB 56 FRCP FRCPGlas. St Jo Coll Nottm 87. **d** 90 **p** 91. NSM Glas St Bride

from 90; P-in-c 96-99. *13/1 Whistlefield Court, 2 Canniesburn Road, Bearsden, Glasgow G61 1PX* T: 0141-943 0954

DRAPER, Jean Margaret. b 31. **d** 80 **p** 97. NSM Pontnewydd *Mon* 80-83; BRF 82-83; NSM Llantilio Pertholey w Bettws Chpl etc *Mon* 83-94; NSM Newport St Andr 94-03. *Govilon House, Merthyr Road, Govilon, Abergavenny NP7 9PT* T: (01873) 830380

DRAPER, Canon John William. b 54. Win Univ MA 13. Qu Coll Birm 88. **d** 90 **p** 91. C Stepney St Dunstan and All SS *Lon* 90-94; C Leigh Park and Warren Park *Portsm* 94-96; R Rowner from 96; V Bridgemary 04-08; AD Gosport 09-14; Hon Can Portsm Cathl from 13. *The Rectory, 174 Rowner Lane, Gosport PO13 9SU* T: (023) 9258 1834 E: rownerrector@btinternet.com

DRAPER, The Very Revd Jonathan Lee. b 52. Gordon Coll Mass BA 76 St Jo Coll Dur BA 78 PhD 84. Ripon Coll Cuddesdon 83. **d** 83 **p** 84. C Baguley *Man* 83-85; Dir Academic Studies Ripon Coll Cuddesdon 85-92; V Putney St Mary *S'wark* 92-00; Can Res York Minster 00-12; Dean Ex from 12. *The Deanery, 10 Cathedral Close, Exeter EX1 1EZ* T: (01392) 431266 *or* 273509 E: dean@exeter-cathedral.org.uk

DRAPER, Canon Martin Paul. b 50. OBE 98. Birm Univ BA 72 Southn Univ BTh 79. Chich Th Coll 72. **d** 75 **p** 76. C Primrose Hill St Mary w Avenue Road St Paul *Lon* 75-78; C Westmr St Matt 79-84; Chapl Paris St Geo *Eur* 84-02; Adn France 94-02; Can Gib Cathl 94-02. *112 Bolanachi Building, Enid Street, London SE16 3EX* E: martin.draper@sfr.fr

DRAPER, Patrick Hugh. b 43. S Dios Minl Tr Scheme 91. **d** 94 **p** 95. NSM Boscombe St Jo *Win* 94-99; P-in-c Southbourne St Chris 99-02; rtd 02; PtO *Win* 02-14. *82 Tuckton Road, Bournemouth BH6 3HT* T: (01202) 420190

DRAPER, The Very Revd Paul Richard. b 64. Glas Univ MA 87 TCD BTh 90. **d** 90 **p** 91. C Drumragh w Mountfield *D & R* 90-94; I Ballydehob w Aghadown *C, C & R* 94-09; Can Cork and Ross Cathls 98-09; Bp's Dom Chapl 99-09; Dean Lismore *C & O* from 09; I Lismore w Cappoquin, Kilwatermoy, Dungarvan etc from 09; Dioc Dir of Ords from 10. *The Deanery, The Mall, Lismore, Co Waterford, Republic of Ireland* T: (00353) (58) 54105 E: dean@lismore.anglican.org

DRAPER (née TRIMMER), Mrs Penelope Marynice. b 65. STETS 01. **d** 04 **p** 05. C Talbot Village *Sarum* 04-08; TV Dunstable *St Alb* from 08. *St Augustine's Vicarage, 83 Halfmoon Lane, Dunstable LU5 4AE* T: (01582) 668019 M: 07733-172460 E: p.trimmer1@ntlworld.com

DRAPER, Peter Raymond. b 57. Leeds Poly BSc 86 Leeds Univ CertEd 88 Hull Univ PhD 94 SRN 80. NEOC 01. **d** 04 **p** 05. NSM S Cave and Ellerker w Broomfleet *York* from 04. *122 The Stray, Smith Cave, Brough HU15 2AL* T: (01430) 425486 M: 07956-531002 E: p.r.draper@hull.ac.uk

DRAPER, Raymond James. b 48. Ex Coll Ox BA 70 MA 75 Em Coll Cam BA 73 MA 78. Ridley Hall Cam 71. **d** 74 **p** 75. C Sheff Manor 74-78; Ind Chapl 78-82; R Wickersley 82-00; V Leytonstone St Jo *Chelmsf* 00-13; rtd 13. *Address withheld by request*

DRAPER, Mrs Sylvia Edith. b 39. ARCM 60. NOC 86. **d** 89 **p** 94. C Aughton St Mich *Liv* 89-92; Par Dn Wigan St Jas w St Thos 92-94; Asst Chapl Wigan and Leigh Health Services NHS Trust 92-97; C Wigan St Jas w St Thos *Liv* 94-97; TV Walton-on-the-Hill 97-02; rtd 02; PtO *Liv* from 03. *6 Brookfield Lane, Aughton, Ormskirk L39 6SP* T: (01695) 422138

DRAX, Elizabeth Margaret. See ANSON, Elizabeth Margaret

DRAY, John. b 66. St Chad's Coll Dur BSc 87. St Steph Ho Ox BTh 95. **d** 95 **p** 96. C Byker St Ant *Newc* 95-98; C Cullercoats St Geo 98-01; P-in-c Platt *Roch* 01-05; Chapl to the Deaf 01-05. *51 Widmere Lodge Road, Bromley BR1 2QE* E: john.dray@bigfoot.com

DRAYCOTT, John. b 53. Sheff Univ BA 84. Linc Th Coll 85. **d** 85 **p** 86. In Wesleyan Reform Union 77-82; C Wombwell *Sheff* 85-87; V W Bessacarr 87-92; V Erith Ch Ch *Roch* 92-11; P-in-c Erith St Jo 92-95; rtd 11. *Oakdale, Hertford Drive, Fobbing, Stanford-le-Hope SS17 9HL* T: (01268) 423021 E: johnd1662@gmail.com

DRAYCOTT, John Edward. b 54. EMMTC 99. **d** 01 **p** 02. C Calverton, Epperstone, Gonalston and Oxton *S'well* 01-05; TV Parr *Liv* 05-13; P-in-c E Scarsdale *Derby* 13-15; TR from 15. *The Rectory, Rectory Road, Upper Langwith, Mansfield NG20 9RE* T: (01623) 618972 E: john.draycott@sky.com

DRAYCOTT, Philip John. b 27. Sarum & Wells Th Coll. **d** 83 **p** 84. C Bishop's Cleeve *Glouc* 83-86; V Chedworth, Yanworth and Stowell, Coln Rogers etc 86-93; rtd 94; PtO *B & W* from 94. *April Cottage, Newton Road, North Petherton, Bridgwater TA6 6NA* T: (01278) 662487

DRAYCOTT, Tina. b 57. Win Univ BA 11. STETS 08. **d** 11 **p** 12. OLM Avon River *Sarum* from 11. *1 Crusader Cottages, High Street, Netheravon, Salisbury SP4 9QP* T: (01980) 670609 M: 07747-033585 E: tina_draycott@hotmail.com

✠**DRAYSON, The Rt Revd Nicholas James Quested.** b 53. Keble Coll Ox BA 75 MA 83. Wycliffe Hall Ox 82. **d** 79 **p** 79 **c** 09. SAMS Argentina 79-82; 92-00; Pastor Tartagal and Chapl to Chorote Indians 79-82; P-in-c Seville Ascension Spain 83-91; Adn Andalucia 89-91; Translations Co-ord 92-98; Pastor Salta St Andr 98-00; C Beverley Minster *York* 00-09; Suff Bp N Argentina from 09. *Casilla 187, 4400 Salta, Argentina* T: (0054) (387) 431 1718 E: diaan.epi@gmail.com *or* nicobispo@gmail.com

DRAYTON, James Edward. b 30. St Deiniol's Hawarden 81. **d** 84 **p** 86. Hon C Heald Green St Cath *Ches* 84-88; C Bollington St Jo 88-92; P-in-c Lt Leigh and Lower Whitley 92-96; P-in-c Aston by Sutton 92-96; P-in-c Antrobus 92-96; rtd 96; PtO *York* from 96. *87 Wharfedale, Filey YO14 0DP* T: (01723) 512662

DREDGE, David John. b 32. Cranmer Hall Dur 69. **d** 71 **p** 72. C Goole *Sheff* 71-74; P-in-c Eastoft 74-77; V Whitgift w Adlingfleet 74-77; V Whitgift w Adlingfleet and Eastoft 77-78; V Walkley 78-81; TV Bicester w Bucknell, Caversfield and Launton *Ox* 81-86; V N Brickhill and Putnoe *St Alb* 86-90; P-in-c Sarratt 90-95; rtd 95; PtO *Lich* 95-14. *19 Waterdale, Wombourne, Wolverhampton WV5 0DH* T: (01902) 897467

DREDGE, David Julian. b 36. ALA 74 Sheff Univ BA 59. Cranmer Hall Dur 61 Ban Ord Course 85. **d** 87 **p** 88. NSM Dwygyfylchi *Ban* 87-92; R Llanllechid 92-97; rtd 97; PtO *Ban* from 97. *Westfield, Treforris Road, Penmaenmawr LL34 6RH* T: (01492) 623439 M: 07721-941861 F: 0870-056 7258 E: david@djdredge.plus.com

DREW, Gerald Arthur. b 36. Bps' Coll Cheshunt 59. **d** 61 **p** 62. C Lyonsdown H Trin *St Alb* 61-67; C Tring 67-71; R Bramfield w Stapleford and Waterford 71-78; V Langleybury St Paul 78-90; P-in-c Hormead, Wyddial, Anstey, Brent Pelham etc 90-95; V 95-01; rtd 01; PtO *St E* from 01; *St Alb* from 01. *33 The Glebe, Lavenham, Sudbury CO10 9SN* T: (01787) 248133

DREW (née ROY), Mrs Jennifer Pearl. b 53. SRN 75 CSS 91. Cranmer Hall Dur. **d** 01 **p** 02. C Hebburn St Jo and Jarrow Grange *Dur* 01-05; NSM Broom Leys *Leic* 05-08; PtO 08-11; NSM Loughborough Em and St Mary in Charnwood 11-14; PtO from 14. *5 Balmoral Road, Coalville LE67 4RF* T: (01530) 836329 E: revjen03@hotmail.co.uk

DREW, Jo Ann. b 57. Ripon Coll Cuddesdon 09. **d** 11 **p** 12. C Milton next Gravesend Ch Ch *Roch* 11-14; PtO *Blackb* from 15. *80 Main Street, Warton, Carnforth LA5 9PG* E: revjodrew@btinternet.com

DREW, Michael Edgar Cecil. b 31. Oriel Coll Ox BA 55 MA 59. St Steph Ho Ox 55. **d** 57 **p** 58. C Plymouth St Pet *Ex* 57-63; Missr Pemb Coll Cam Miss Walworth 63-67; Asst Chapl All Hallows Sch Rousdon 67-75; Chapl 80-81; Chapl Ex Sch 81-83; V Scraptoft *Leic* 83-97; V Hungarton 83-97; P-in-c Leic St Eliz Nether Hall 87-97; rtd 97. *28 St Mary's Paddock, Wellingborough NN8 1HJ* T: (01933) 277407

DREW, Canon Rosemary. b 43. SRN 64. EAMTC 90. **d** 93 **p** 94. NSM Gt Dunmow *Chelmsf* 93-96; NSM Gt Dunmow and Barnston 96-11; Hon Can Chelmsf Cathl 01-11; rtd 11; Area Adv for Healing and Deliverance Min *Chelmsf* from 04; PtO from 13. *The Bowling Green, 8 The Downs, Dunmow CM6 1DT* T/F: (01371) 872662 E: rose.drew@btinternet.com

DREW, Simon Mark. b 68. Liv Univ BEng 89 CEng 94 MICE 94. St Jo Coll Nottm MA 98. **d** 99 **p** 00. C Torquay St Matthias, St Mark and H Trin *Ex* 99-03; V Marshfield w Cold Ashton and Tormarton etc *Bris* 03-11; V Middlewich w Byley *Ches* from 11; RD Middlewich from 12. *The Rectory, Poplar Fell, Nantwich Road, Middlewich CW10 9HG* T: (01606) 833440 E: revsdrew@btinternet.com

DREWETT, Mrs Susan. b 56. **d** 06 **p** 07. NSM Bemerton *Sarum* from 06. *Melford House, 36 Bulford Road, Durrington, Salisbury SP4 8DJ* T: (01980) 652751 E: rev.susandrewett@btinternet.com

DREYER, Rodney Granville. b 55. Lon Univ MPhil 91 AKC 91. St Paul's Coll Grahamstown 79. **d** 81 **p** 82. S Africa 81-84; NSM Headstone St Geo *Lon* 84-86; NSM Northolt St Mary 86-87; C Portsea St Mary *Portsm* 87-90; V Sudbury St Andr *Lon* 90-94; Adn W and S Free State S Africa 94-95; V Hawkhurst *Cant* from 98. *The Vicarage, Moor Hill Road, Hawkhurst, Cranbrook TN18 4QB* T: (01580) 753397 E: rodneydreyer@sky.com

DRING (née PETTY), Alicia Christina Margaret. b 64. Wycliffe Hall Ox 01. **d** 03 **p** 04. C Ockbrook *Derby* 03-07; P-in-c Sawley 07-10; R 10-13; V Littleover from 13; Dean of Women's Min from 11. *The Vicarage, 35 Church Street, Littleover, Derby DE23 6GF* T: (01332) 767802 E: alicia@stpeterlittleover.org.uk

DRISCOLL, Canon David. b 42. Lon Univ BSc 64. Linc Th Coll 68. **d** 71 **p** 72. C Walthamstow St Jo *Chelmsf* 71-76; Chapl NE Lon Poly 71-79; C-in-c Plaistow St Mary 76-79; P-in-c

Stratford St Jo and Ch Ch w Forest Gate St Jas 79-89; V Theydon Bois 89-01; RD Epping Forest 92-00; Hon Can Chelmsf Cathl 01; C All Hallows by the Tower etc *Lon* 01-07; rtd 07; Educn Tutor R Foundn of St Kath in Ratcliffe 05-10; Exec Officer Miss in London's Economy 07-10; PtO *Chelmsf* 07-10; *Lon* 07-10; *Sarum* from 11; *B & W* from 11. *24 Baileys Barn, Bradford-on-Avon BA15 1BX* T: (01225) 865314 E: david_driscoll@btopenworld.com

DRIVER, Arthur John Roberts. b 44. SS Coll Cam MA 70 FCIPA 73. Linc Th Coll 73. **d** 76 **p** 77. C S'wark H Trin w St Matt 76-80; TV N Lambeth 80-85; CMS Sri Lanka 86-92; V Putney St Marg *S'wark* 92-97; V Streatham St Paul 97-09; rtd 09; PtO *Chelmsf* from 09. *91 Ernest Road, Wivenhoe, Colchester CO7 9LJ* T: (01206) 822135 E: ajrdriver@gmail.com

DRIVER, Bruce Leslie. b 42. Lon Univ LLB 73. Linc Th Coll 76. **d** 78 **p** 79. C Dunstable *St Alb* 78-81; TV 81-86; V Rickmansworth 86-98; RD 91-98; V Northwood Hills St Edm *Lon* 98-08; rtd 08; PtO *Roch* from 09; *S'wark* from 12. *7 Bromley College, London Road, Bromley BR1 1PE* T: (020) 8290 0366 E: bruced river@gmx.com

DRIVER, Mrs Deborah Jane. b 59. **d** 10 **p** 11. OLM Poringland *Nor* from 10. *50 Rectory Lane, Poringland, Norwich NR14 7SL* T: (01508) 494641 F: 494948 M: 07719-281531 E: debbie.driver@virgin.net

DRIVER, Geoffrey. b 41. Chich Th Coll 86. **d** 88 **p** 89. C Pontefract St Giles *Wakef* 88-91; V Glass Houghton 91-97; Chapl Pinderfields and Pontefract Hosps NHS Trust 97-99; R Southwick H Trin *Dur* 99-03; TR N Wearside 03-11; rtd 11; PtO *Dur* from 12. *115 Killingworth Drive, High Barnes, Sunderland SR4 8QX* T: 0191-528 5142 E: geoffreydriver@msn.com

DRIVER, Geoffrey Lester. b 59. Liv Poly BA 83. Chich Th Coll 86. **d** 89 **p** 90. C Walton St Mary *Liv* 89-92; C Selsey *Chich* 92-95; V Cowfold 95-07; LtO from 07; Chapl St Mich Hospice from 08. *St Michael's Hospice, 25 Upper Maze Hill, St Leonards-on-Sea TN38 0LB* T: (01424) 438587 M: 07871-488224

DRIVER, Gordon Geoffrey. b 32. Garnett Coll Lon Dip Teaching 59. Trin Coll Bris. **d** 95 **p** 96. NSM Radipole and Melcombe Regis *Sarum* 95-03; rtd 03; PtO *Sarum* from 03. *11 Greenway Close, Weymouth DT3 5BQ* T: (01305) 812784

DRIVER (née FRENCH), Janet Mary. b 43. Leeds Univ BA 65 PGCE 66 Surrey Univ BA 98. Linc Th Coll 74. **dss** 80 **d** 92 **p** 94. St Paul's Cathl 80-82; N Lambeth *S'wark* 80-85; CMS Sri Lanka 86-92; NSM Putney St Marg *S'wark* 97-09; Hon C Streatham St Paul 97-09; rtd 09; PtO *Chelmsf* from 11. *91 Ernest Road, Wivenhoe, Colchester CO7 9LJ* T: (01206) 822135 E: janet@janetdriver.co.uk

DRIVER, Jennifer. b 63. Kent Univ BA. SEITE 05. **d** 08 **p** 09. NSM Farnborough *Roch* 08-13; NSM Orpington All SS from 13. *3 Starts Hill Road, Orpington BR6 7AR* T: (01689) 858766 M: 07599-957969 E: jen.driver63@gmail.com

DRIVER, John. *See* DRIVER, Arthur John Roberts

DRIVER, The Ven Penelope May. b 52. NOC. **d** 87 **p** 94. Dioc Youth Adv *Newc* 86-88; C Cullercoats St Geo 87-88; Youth Chapl *Ripon* 88-96; Dioc Adv on Women's Min 91-06; Assoc Dir of Ords 96-98; Dioc Dir of Ords 98-06; Min Can Ripon Cathl 96-06; Hon Can Ripon Cathl 98-06; Adn Ex 06-12; P-in-c Dawlish 09-10; Adn Westmorland and Furness *Carl* from 12. *The Vicarage, Windermere Road, Lindale, Grange-over-Sands LA11 6LB* T: (015395) 34717 E: archdeacon.south@carlislediocese.org.uk

DRIVER, Canon Roger John. b 64. Liv Univ MA 08. Trin Coll Bris BA 88. **d** 90 **p** 91. C Much Woolton *Liv* 90-93; C Fazakerley Em 93-94; TV 94-00; P-in-c Bootle St Matt 00-03; P-in-c Bootle St Leon 00-03; P-in-c Litherland St Andr 00-03; TR Bootle from 04; AD from 07; Hon Can Liv Cathl from 07. *The Vicarage, 70 Merton Road, Bootle L20 7AT* T: 0151-922 3316 E: rogerdriver@btinternet.com

DROBIG, Marion. *See* WOOD, Marion

DROMORE, Archdeacon of. *See* WEST, The Ven Thomas Roderic

DROMORE, Dean of. *See* KERR, The Very Revd Bryan Thomas

DROWLEY, Arthur. b 28. Oak Hill Th Coll 54. **d** 56 **p** 57. C Longfleet *Sarum* 56-59; C Wallington *S'wark* 59-62; V Taunton St Jas *B & W* 62-73; RD Taunton N 72-73; V Rodbourne Cheney *Bris* 73-87; R Bigbury, Ringmore and Kingston *Ex* 87-94; rtd 94; PtO *Ex* 95-02; *Man* 03-08; *Lich* from 05. *4 Inglis Road, Park Hall, Oswestry SY11 4AN* T: (01691) 671994

DROWN, Richard. b 19. BNC Ox BA 41 MA 43. Wycliffe Hall Ox 41. **d** 42 **p** 43. C St Helens St Helen *Liv* 42-45; Chapl K Coll Budo Uganda 46-65; Hd Master St Andr Sch Turi Kenya 65-73; Hd Master Edin Ho Sch New Milton 73-84; rtd 84; Hon C Brockenhurst *Win* from 85. *3 Waters Green Court, Brockenhurst SO42 7QR* T: (01590) 624038

DRUCE, Brian Lemuel. b 31. MRICS 55. Bps' Coll Cheshunt 58. **d** 60 **p** 61. C Whitton St Aug *Lon* 60-63; C Minehead *B & W* 63-66; R Birch St Agnes *Man* 66-70; V Overbury w Alstone, Teddington and Lt Washbourne *Worc* 70-81; Ind Chapl 81-91; rtd 91; PtO *Worc* from 91. *Park Cottage, Elmley Castle, Pershore WR10 3HU* T: (01386) 710577 E: bravo.delta@uwclub.net

DRUCE, John Perry. b 34. Em Coll Cam BA 57 MA 61 Lambeth STh 97 ALCM 86. Wycliffe Hall Ox 57. **d** 59 **p** 60. C Wednesbury St Bart *Lich* 59-62; C Bushbury 62-64; V Walsall Wood 64-74; R Farnborough *Roch* 74-87; R E Bergholt *St E* 87-99; P-in-c Bentley w Tattingstone 95-99; rtd 99. *9 Fullers Close, Hadleigh, Ipswich IP7 5AS* T: (01473) 827242 E: jgdruce@realemail.co.uk

DRUMMOND, Canon Christopher John Vaughan. b 26. Magd Coll Ox MA 51 Magd Coll Cam MA 56. Ridley Hall Cam 51. **d** 53 **p** 54. C Barking St Marg *Chelmsf* 53-56; Tutor Ridley Hall Cam 56-59; LtO *Ely* 57-62; Chapl Clare Coll Cam 59-62; Nigeria 63-69; V Walthamstow St Jo *Chelmsf* 69-74; P-in-c Stantonbury *Ox* 74-75; R 75-84; P-in-c Ducklington 84-88; Dioc Ecum Officer 84-88; Can Ibadan from 87; Home Sec Gen Syn Bd for Miss and Unity 88-91; rtd 91; P-in-c Colton *Lich* 91-94; PtO 94-99; *Guildf* from 97. *77 Markham Road, Capel, Dorking RH5 5JT* T: (01306) 712637 M: 07966-518681

DRUMMOND, John Malcolm. b 44. Nottm Univ CertEd 65. Edin Th Coll 68. **d** 71 **p** 72. C Kirkholt *Man* 71-74; C Westleigh St Pet 74-76; Hd of RE Leigh High Sch from 76; Lic Preacher *Man* 76-84; Hon C Leigh St Jo 84-90; Hon C Tonge Moor 90-10; PtO from 10. *14 Bull's Head Cottages, Tottington Road, Turton, Bolton BL7 0HS* T: (01204) 852232 E: rev.m.drummond@btinternet.com

DRUMMOND, Joscelline Maurice Vaughan. b 29. Lon Univ BD 70. Wycliffe Hall Ox 55. **d** 58 **p** 59. C Tunbridge Wells St Jo *Roch* 58-60; C Walthamstow St Mary *Chelmsf* 60-62; V Oulton *Lich* 62-68; V Leyton St Cath *Chelmsf* 71-85; Gen Dir CMJ 85-94; Public Preacher *St Alb* 88-94; rtd 94; PtO *St Alb* from 94. *3 Fryth Mead, St Albans AL3 4TN* T: (01727) 857620

DRUMMOND, Ms Judi. b 74. Cranmer Hall Dur. **d** 06 **p** 07. C Kirkby *Liv* 06-09; C Rainhill 09-11; Chapl E Lon Univ *Chelmsf* 11-14. *281 Central Park Road, London E6 3AF* T: (020) 8471 7193 M: 07748-965856 E: drummondjudi@gmail.com

DRUMMOND, Matthew James. b 77. Roehampton Inst BSc 98 Birkbeck Coll Lon MSc. Westcott Ho Cam 12. **d** 14 **p** 15. C Limpsfield and Tatsfield *S'wark* from 14. *24 Padbrook, Oxted RH8 0DW* T: (01883) 716809 E: revd.matt.drummond@gmail.com

DRURY, Anthony Desmond. b 42. NOC. **d** 99 **p** 00. NSM New Ferry *Ches* from 99. *61 Church Road, Bebington, Wirral CH63 3DZ* T: 0151-334 4797 E: des@stmarksnewferry.org.uk

DRURY, Benjamin Guy. b 84. Worc Coll Ox BA 05 MA 11 MPhil 07. St Steph Ho Ox BA 13. **d** 14. C Stony Stratford w Calverton *Ox* from 14. *9 Bunsty Court, Stony Stratford, Milton Keynes MK11 1NJ* E: benjamin.drury@gmail.com

DRURY, Mrs Carol. b 61. SRN 83. Trin Coll Bris BA 02. **d** 01 **p** 02. NSM Soundwell *Bris* 01-03; CMS Uganda 04-05; C Motueka New Zealand from 06. *St Thomas's Church, 101 High Street, Motueka, New Zealand* T: (0064) (3) 528 8825

DRURY, Caroline Nora. See BURNETT, Caroline Nora

DRURY, Desmond. See DRURY, Anthony Desmond

DRURY, The Very Revd John Henry. b 36. Trin Hall Cam MA 66. Westcott Ho Cam 61. **d** 63 **p** 64. C St John's Wood *Lon* 63-66; Chapl Down Coll Cam 66-69; Chapl Ex Coll Ox 69-73; Can Res Nor Cathl 73-79; Vice-Dean 78-79; Lect Sussex Univ 79-81; Dean K Coll Cam 81-91; Dean Ch Ch *Ox* 91-03; rtd 03; Chapl and Fell All So Coll Ox from 03. *All Souls College, Oxford OX1 4AL* T: (01865) 279379 F: 279299

DRURY, Michael Dru. b 31. Trin Coll Ox BA 55 MA 59. Wycliffe Hall Ox. **d** 58 **p** 59. C Fulham St Mary N End *Lon* 58-62; C Blackheath St Jo *S'wark* 62-64; Asst Master Canford Sch 64-80; Chapl and Teacher Fernhill Manor Sch New Milton 80-81; P-in-c Stowe *Ox* 82-92; Asst Master Stowe Sch 82-92; R Rampton w Laneham, Treswell, Cottam and Stokeham *S'well* 92-96; rtd 96; PtO *Sarum* from 96. *Tanfield, Giddylake, Wimborne BH21 2QT* T: (01202) 881246 E: michaeldrury@talktalk.net

DRURY, Richard Alexander. b 63. Lon Univ BD 85 Avery Hill Coll PGCE 86 ACII 91. Trin Coll Bris MA 00. **d** 00 **p** 01. C Kingswood *Bris* 00-03; CMS Uganda 04-05; V Motueka New Zealand from 06. *St Thomas's Church, 101 High Street, Motueka, New Zealand* T: (0064) (3) 528 8825

DRURY, Stephen Roger. b 45. Univ Coll Lon LLB 66 York St Jo Univ MA 11 Solicitor 70. Coll of Resurr Mirfield 06. **d** 07 **p** 08. NSM Seamer w East Ayton *York* 07-15; P-in-c Scarborough St Columba from 15. *74 Garth End Road, West Ayton, Scarborough YO13 9JH* T: (01723) 862044 E: stephen_drury@hotmail.com

DRURY, Valerie Doreen. b 40. Univ of Wales (Cardiff) BA 62 K Coll Lon PGCE 63 MBATOD 80. Oak Hill Th Coll 85. **d** 87 **p** 94. NSM Becontree St Alb *Chelmsf* 87-89; NSM Becontree S 89-02; rtd 02; PtO *Chelmsf* from 02. *37 Blunts Hall Road, Witham CM8 1ES* T: (01376) 517330 E: vdrury@tiscali.co.uk

DRYDEN, Barry Frederick. b 44. Ches Coll of HE BTh 00. NOC 97. **d** 00 **p** 01. C Formby St Pet *Liv* 00-03; V Woolston 03-10; rtd 10; PtO *Leic* from 13. *5 Briton Lodge Close, Moira, Swadlincote DE12 6DD* T: (01283) 550920 E: revbarrydryden@ntlworld.com

DRYDEN, Martin John. b 57. Loughb Univ BA 80 Univ of Wales (Lamp) MA 09. STETS 07. **d** 09 **p** 10. NSM Jersey St Clem *Win* from 09. *Mont Ubé House, La rue de la Blinerie, St Clement, Jersey JE2 6QT* T: (01534) 874668 M: 07797-729525 E: martin@mont-ube.net

DRYDEN, Sally Jane. b 65. St Mellitus Coll BA 15. **d** 15. C Golders Green *Lon* from 15. *24 Brook Meadow, London N12 7DB* M: 07941-192699 E: sallydryden@talk21.com

DRYE, Douglas John. b 37. Man Univ BSc 61. Clifton Th Coll. **d** 63 **p** 64. C Whalley Range St Edm *Man* 63-66; C Drypool St Columba w St Andr and St Pet *York* 66-68; V Worsbrough Common *Sheff* 68-86; R Armthorpe 86-92; rtd 92; PtO *Pet* from 92. *25 Willow Crescent, Oakham LE15 6EQ* T: (01572) 770429 E: djwillowoak@uwclub.net

DRYER, Richard. **d** 14 **p** 15. NSM Wimbledon Em Ridgway Prop Chpl *S'wark* from 14. *Address temp unknown*

D'SOUZA, Derek Emile. b 54. Trin Coll Bris. **d** 07 **p** 08. C Edgbaston St Germain *Birm* 07-11; P-in-c Prince's Park *Roch* from 11. *6 Thrush Close, Chatham ME5 7TG* T: (01634) 685828 E: helennderek@yahoo.co.uk

du SAIRE, Ms Michele Marie. b 55. Leeds Poly BSc 78. ERMC 06. **d** 09 **p** 10. C Leavesden *St Alb* 09-13; R Sarratt and Chipperfield from 13. *The New Vicarage, The Street, Chipperfield, Kings Langley WD4 9BJ* T: (01923) 265848 E: micheledusairehcstp@gmail.com

DUBLIN (Christ Church), Dean of. See DUNNE, The Very Revd Dermot Patrick Martin

DUBLIN, Archbishop of, and Bishop of Glendalough. See JACKSON, The Most Revd Michael Geoffrey St Aubyn

DUBLIN, Archdeacon of. See PIERPOINT, The Ven David Alfred

DUBREUIL, Yann. b 70. Birm Univ BA 04. Wycliffe Hall Ox 05. **d** 07 **p** 08. C Four Marks *Win* 07-11; R Bentley, Binsted and Froyle from 11. *Holy Cross Vicarage, Church Street, Binsted, Alton GU34 4NX* M: 07777-684533 E: yann@benbinfro.org

DUCE, Miss Catherine Veronica. b 81. Westcott Ho Cam 12. **d** 15. C Westmr St Steph w St Jo *Lon* from 15. *Flat C, 16 Hide Place, London SW1P 4NJ* M: 07948-980024 E: cath.duce@hotmail.com

DUCKERS, Miss Linda Jean. b 62. Univ of Wales (Abth) BSc 84 PGCE 85 Rob Coll Cam BTh 06. Ridley Hall Cam 04. **d** 06 **p** 07. C Leek and Meerbrook *Lich* 06-10; TV Warwick *Cov* from 10. *St Nicholas' Vicarage, 184 Myton Road, Warwick CV34 6PS* T: (01926) 496209 E: linda.duckers@googlemail.com

DUCKERS, Paul Gerrard. b 42. Qu Coll Birm 07. **d** 09 **p** 10. NSM Sutton Coldfield H Trin *Birm* 09-12; PtO from 12. *5 Moor Meadow Road, Sutton Coldfield B75 6BU* T: 0121-378 1835 E: paulduckers@talktalk.net

DUCKETT, Canon Brian John. b 45. ALCD 70. **d** 70 **p** 71. C S Lambeth St Steph *S'wark* 70-73; C Norwood St Luke 73-75; C Bushbury *Lich* 75-77; TV 77-79; V Dover St Martin *Cant* 79-92; TR Swindon Dorcan *Bris* 92-00; RD Highworth 95-99; V Clifton H Trin, St Andr and St Pet 00-09; Vulnerable Adults Policy Officer 07-09; Hon Can Bris Cathl 98-09; rtd 09. *52 The Fieldings, Southwater, Horsham RH13 9LZ* T: (01403) 733417

DUCKETT, Ms Helen Lorraine. b 71. Keble Coll Ox BA 92 Sheff Univ MA 94 Birm Univ MPhil 98. Qu Coll Birm 95. **d** 98 **p** 99. C Cannock *Lich* 98-01; TV Wednesfield 01-10; TV Cen Wolverhampton 10-14. *167 Colman Avenue, Wolverhampton WV11 3RU* E: helen.duckett@sky.com

DUCKETT, John Dollings. b 41. Nottm Univ BA 62 BTh 81. Linc Th Coll 79. **d** 81 **p** 82. C Boston *Linc* 81-84; V Baston 84-86; V Langtoft Gp 86-88; V Sutterton and Wigtoft 88-89; R Sutterton w Fosdyke and Algarkirk 89-92; P-in-c Chapel St Leonards w Hogsthorpe 92-97; V 97-00; V Bracebridge 00-06; rtd 06. *Old Post Office, Faldingworth Road, Spridlington, Market Rasen LN8 2DF* T: (01673) 860116

DUCKETT, Keith Alexander. b 69. Worc Coll of Educn BA 93. Qu Coll Birm BD 97 MA 98. **d** 98 **p** 99. C Willenhall H Trin *Lich* 98-01; TV Blakenall Heath 01-03; Asst Chapl Sandwell and W Birm Hosps NHS Trust 03-06; Chapl K Sch Wolv from 12; Spiritual Care Lead John Taylor Hospice Birm 13. *167 Colman Avenue, Wolverhampton WV11 3RU* E: keith.duckett@sky.com

DUCKETT, Lee Christopher James. b 67. Wycliffe Hall Ox BTh 04. **d** 04 **p** 05. C Cranham Park *Chelmsf* 04-08; C Purley Ch Ch *S'wark* 08-12; V Ore Ch Ch *Chich* from 12. *103 Fairlight Road, Hastings TN35 5EJ* T: (01424) 715193 M: 07979-191747 E: lee@christchurchore.org

DUCKETT, Matthew Robert. b 64. UEA BSc 85 PGCE 88. NTMTC BA 09. **d** 09 **p** 10. NSM Old St Pancras *Lon* 09-13; P-in-c Friern Barnet St Pet le Poer from 13. *Little Ilford Rectory, 124 Church Road, London E12 6HA* T: (020) 8478 2182 E: m.duckett@ucl.ac.uk

DUCKETT, Raphael Thomas Marie James. b 65. N Staffs Poly BA 87. Cranmer Hall Dur 01. **d** 03 **p** 04. C Madeley *Heref* 03-06; V Bradley St Martin *Lich* from 06. *St Martin's Vicarage, 7 King Street, Bradley, Bilston WV14 8PQ* T: (01902) 650101 E: revraphael@blueyonder.co.uk

DUCKWORTH, Angela Denise. *See* WATTS, Angela Denise

DUCKWORTH, Annette Jacqueline. b 54. Univ of Wales (Ban) BSc 75 PGCE 76. **d** 00 **p** 01. OLM Moxley *Lich* 00-14; OLM Darlaston and Moxley from 14; Chapl Blue Coat Comp Sch Walsall 07-10. *1 Sutton Road, Wednesbury WS10 8SG* E: annette.duckworth@hotmail.co.uk

DUCKWORTH, Brian George. b 47. Edin Th Coll 85. **d** 87 **p** 88. C Sutton in Ashfield St Mary *S'well* 87-95; C Sutton in Ashfield St Mich 89-95; P-in-c 95-98; TV Hucknall Torkard 98-03; R S Ockendon and Belhus Park *Chelmsf* 03-12; rtd 12; PtO *Cant* from 13. *24 Aspen Drive, Whitfield, Dover CT16 2EX* T: (01304) 827239 E: brian288@btinternet.com

DUCKWORTH, Patrick Richard Stephen. b 52. **d** 77 **p** 77. C Bendigo Australia 77-79; C Swan Hill 80; R Ouyen 80-83; Chapl Launceston Ch Gr Sch 88-98; Chapl St Pet Coll Adelaide 97-10; P-in-c Barnsley St Mary *Wakef* 10-14; Chapl All SS Coll Perth Australia from 14. *All Saints' College, Ewing Avenue, Bull Creek WA 6149, Australia* T: (0061) (8) 9313 9333 E: duckworth52@btinternet.com

DUDDLES (formerly MOORES), Mrs Samantha Jane. b 73. Man Metrop Univ BEd 96 Southn Univ MSc 01. Ripon Coll Cuddesdon. **d** 12 **p** 14. C Upper Dever *Win* from 12. *20 Cundell Way, Kings Worthy, Winchester SO23 7NP* T: (01962) 809931 M: 07740-505271 E: samjmoores@gmail.com

DUDLEY, Mrs Janet Carr. b 36. EMMTC 86. **d** 89 **p** 94. NSM Countesthorpe w Foston *Leic* 89-94; NSM Arnesby w Shearsby and Bruntingthorpe 94-01; rtd 01; PtO *Leic* 01-02 and from 10; NSM Market Harborough and The Transfiguration etc 02-10. *13 The Broadway, Market Harborough LE16 7LZ* T: (01858) 467619

DUDLEY, John Donald Swanborough. b 34. Ox Univ BTh 95. SAOMC 96. **d** 97 **p** 98. NSM Emmer Green *Ox* 97-02; PtO from 02. *26 Russet Glade, Emmer Green, Reading RG4 8UJ* T/F: 0118-954 6664

DUDLEY, Ms Josephine. b 52. ERMC 04. **d** 06 **p** 07. NSM Tolleshunt Knights w Tiptree and Gt Braxted *Chelmsf* 06-11; P-in-c Lonan *S & M* 11-14; P-in-c Laxey 11-14; TV Onchan, Lonan and Laxey from 14. *The Vicarage, 56 Ard Reayrt, Ramsey Road, Laxey, Isle of Man IM4 7QQ* M: 07704-431790 E: jo@dudley.plus.com

DUDLEY, Martin Raymond. b 53. K Coll Lon BD 77 AKC 77 MTh 78 PhD 94 City Univ MSc 07 Hon DArts 14 FRHistS 95 FRSA 06 FSA 97. St Mich Coll Llan 78. **d** 79 **p** 80. C Whitchurch *Llan* 79-83; V Weston *St Alb* 83-88; P-in-c Ardeley 87-88; V Owlsmoor *Ox* 88-95; Lect Simon of Cyrene Th Inst 92-95; R Smithfield St Bart Gt *Lon* 95-15; P-in-c St Bart Less 12-15; R Smithfield Gt St Bart from 15. *The Parish Office, Church House, Cloth Fair, London EC1A 7JQ* T: (020) 7600 0400 E: rector@greatstbarts.com

DUDLEY, Miss Wendy Elizabeth. b 46. City of Sheff Coll CertEd 68. Cranmer Hall Dur 79. **dss** 81 **d** 87 **p** 94. Cumnor *Ox* 81-89; Par Dn 87-89; Par Dn Hodge Hill *Birm* 89-94; C 94-95; TV 95-98; TV Bucknall *Lich* 98-06; rtd 06; PtO *Lich* from 08. *26 Swallow Croft, Lichfield WS13 7HF* T: (01543) 306509 E: wed.btm@tinyworld.co.uk

DUDLEY-SMITH, James. b 66. Fitzw Coll Cam BA 89 MA 92. Wycliffe Hall Ox BTh 94. **d** 97 **p** 98. C New Borough and Leigh *Sarum* 97-01; C Hove Bp Hannington Memorial Ch *Chich* 01-06; R Yeovil w Kingston Pitney *B & W* from 06; RD Yeovil from 15. *The Rectory, 41 The Park, Yeovil BA20 1DG* T: (01935) 475352

✠**DUDLEY-SMITH, The Rt Revd Timothy.** b 26. OBE 03. Pemb Coll Cam BA 47 MA 51 Lambeth MLitt 91 Dur Univ Hon DD 09. Ridley Hall Cam 48. **d** 50 **p** 51 **c** 81. C Erith St Paul *Roch* 50-53; LtO *S'wark* 53-62; Hd of Cam Univ Miss Bermondsey 53-55; Chapl 55-60; Ed Sec Evang Alliance and Ed Crusade 55-59; Asst Sec CPAS 59-65; Gen Sec 65-73; Adn Nor 73-81; Suff Bp Thetford 81-91; rtd 92; PtO *Sarum* from 12. *9 Ashlands, Ford, Salisbury SP4 6DY* T: (01722) 326417

DUDLEY, Archdeacon of. *See* GROARKE, The Ven Nicola Jane

DUDLEY, Suffragan Bishop of. *See* USHER, The Rt Revd Graham Barham

DUERDEN, Martin James. b 55. Liv Poly BA 77. Oak Hill Th Coll 86. **d** 88 **p** 89. C Tunbridge Wells St Jas *Roch* 88-92; V Southport SS Simon and Jude *Liv* 92-98; P-in-c Maghull 98-02; TR 02-07; P-in-c Marsh Green w Newtown 07; V 08-13; V Salesbury *Blackb* from 13; Hon C Langho Billington from 13. *St Peter's Vicarage, 49A Ribchester Road, Blackburn BB1 9HU* T: (01254) 248072 E: martinduerden@hotmail.com

DUERR, Robert Kenneth. b 54. Univ of S California BMus 77 MMus 80. Ridley Hall Cam 99. **d** 04 **p** 06. NSM Cambridge Gt St Mary w St Mich *Ely* 04-05; C Marton-in-Cleveland *York* 06-07; C Scarborough St Martin and Scarborough St Sav w All SS 07-10. *258 Christiana Street, North Tonawanda NY 14120, USA* M: (904) 671 2916 E: robert@robertduerr.com

DUFF, Alison. *See* FINCH, Alison

DUFF, Andrew John. b 57. Open Univ BSc 07. Sarum & Wells Th Coll 92. **d** 92 **p** 93. C Banbury *Ox* 92-95; C Bracknell 95-96; TV 96-98; CF 98-04; Chapl RN 04-12; rtd 12. *Address temp unknown*

DUFF, Miss Emma Cameron. b 73. St Andr Univ MA 95 Solicitor 99. Qu Coll Birm 12. **d** 14 **p** 15. C Willington *Newc* from 14. *2 Burlington Court, Wallsend NE28 9YH* T: 0191-257 2405 E: eduff.willington@gmail.com

DUFF, Garden Ian. b 34. Imp Coll Lon BScEng 56. Sarum & Wells Th Coll 92. **d** 93 **p** 94. NSM Ashton Gifford *Sarum* 93-97; TV Upper Wylye Valley 97-03; rtd 03. *Trinity Trees Cottage, 58 Upton Lovell, Warminster BA12 0JP* T/F: (01985) 850291 E: giandsduff@waitrose.com

DUFF, Jeremy. b 71. MA DPhil. **d** 06 **p** 07. NSM Toxteth St Philemon w St Gabr and St Cleopas *Liv* 06-10; Dir Lifelong Learning and Can Liv Cathl 04-10; TV S Widnes *Liv* from 10. *St Paul's Vicarage, Victoria Square, Widnes WA8 7QU* E: jeremy.duff@liverpool.anglican.org

DUFF, Jillian Louise Calland. b 72. Ch Coll Cam BA 93 MA 97 Worc Coll Ox DPhil 96. Wycliffe Hall Ox BA 02. **d** 03. C Litherland St Phil *Liv* 03-05; Lic to Adn Liv 05-11; Dir Tr for Ords from 11; Dir St Mellitus NW from 13. *St Paul's Vicarage, Victoria Square, Widnes WA8 7QU* E: jillduff@btinternet.com

DUFF, John Alexander. b 57. York Univ BA 78. EMMTC 91. **d** 94 **p** 95. NSM Linc St Geo Swallowbeck 94-00; PtO *Leeds* from 02. *37 Mornington Crescent, Harrogate HG1 5DL* T: (01423) 549987 M: 07788-432009 E: ffudnhoj@hotmail.com

DUFF, Michael Ian. b 63. Ox Univ BA 85. Trin Coll Bris BA 98 MA 99. **d** 99 **p** 00. C Southsea St Jude *Portsm* 99-03; CMS Bandung Indonesia 03-07; V Southsea St Jude *Portsm* from 07. *St Jude's Vicarage, 7 Hereford Road, Southsea PO5 2DH* T: (023) 9234 9622 E: all@theduffs.me.uk

DUFF, Timothy Cameron. b 40. G&C Coll Cam BA 62 LLM 63 MA 66 Solicitor 65. NEOC 90. **d** 93 **p** 94. NSM Tynemouth Priory *Newc* 93-96; NSM N Shields 96-00; Hon TV 00-05; rtd 05; PtO *Newc* from 05. *24A Percy Gardens, Tynemouth, North Shields NE30 4HQ* T: 0191-257 1463 E: timothy@timothyduff.co.uk

DUFFELL, Lucy Margaret. *See* GARDNER, Lucy Margaret

DUFFETT, Canon Paul Stanton. b 33. Keble Coll Ox BA 55 MA 59. Ripon Hall Ox. **d** 59 **p** 60. C Portsea St Cuth *Portsm* 59-63; C Inhlwathi S Africa 63-65; R Isandhlwana 65-68; Chapl Nqutu Hosp 68-70; R Vryheid 71-79; Hon Can Zululand from 87; Accredited Rep Zululand and Swaziland Assn from 89; P-in-c Greatham w Empshott *Portsm* 80-85; R 85-88; R Papworth Everard *Ely* 88-98; Chapl Papworth Hosps 88-98; rtd 98; Hon Chapl MU from 97; PtO *Ely* from 99. *11 Roman Hill, Barton, Cambridge CB23 7AX* T: (01223) 262831 E: duffett@ifightpoverty.com

DUFFETT-SMITH (née RUSHTON), Ms Patricia Mary. b 54. Lon Univ BPharm 76 Anglia Poly Univ MA 99 MRPharmS 77. EAMTC 94. **d** 97 **p** 98. NSM Haddenham and Wilburton *Ely* 97-00; Asst Chapl Hinchingbrooke Health Care NHS Trust from 99. *Holme House, 4B The Avenue, Godmanchester, Huntingdon PE29 2AF* M: 07788-668900 E: trishads@googlemail.com

DUFFIELD, Ian Keith. b 47. K Coll Lon BD 71 AKC 71 MTh 73. NY Th Sem DMin 84. **d** 73 **p** 74. C Broxbourne *St Alb* 73-77; C Harpenden St Nic 77-81; TV Sheff Manor 81-87; V Walkley 87-02; V Sheff St Leon Norwood 02-13; rtd 13. *17 Springwell Drive, Beighton, Sheffield S20 1XA*

DUFFIELD, John Ernest. b 55. BA 86. Oak Hill Th Coll 83. **d** 86 **p** 87. C Walton Breck Ch Ch *Liv* 86-89; TV Fazakerley Em 89-00; Chapl N Cheshire Hosps NHS Trust 00-08; Chapl Warrington and Halton Hosps NHS Foundn Trust from 08. *Warrington Hospital, Lovely Lane, Warrington WA5 1QG* T: (01925) 662146 F: 662048 E: john.duffield@nch.nhs.uk

DUFFIELD, Ronald Bertram Charles. b 26. Hull Univ Coll BA 49 TCert 50. Sarum & Wells Th Coll 91. **d** 92 **p** 93. NSM E

Knoyle, Semley and Sedgehill *Sarum* 92-94; P-in-c 94-95; rtd 95; PtO *York* 95-99 and from 01; P-in-c Isfield *Chich* 99-01. *16 Wylies Road, Beverley HU17 7AP* T: (01482) 880983

DUFFUS, Barbara Rose. *See* HOBBS, Barbara Rose

DUGDALE, Angela Marion. b 33. DL 92 MBE 06. ARCM 52 GRSM 54 UEA Hon MA 89. **d** 97 **p** 98. OLM Weybourne Gp *Nor* 97-03; rtd 03; PtO *Nor* from 03. *The Old Carpenter's Shop, Kelling, Holt NR25 7EL* T: (01263) 588389 F: 588594 E: dugdale@freeuk.com

DUGMORE, Barry John. b 61. STETS. **d** 01 **p** 02. C Cowplain *Portsm* 01-04; C-in-c Whiteley CD and Dioc Ecum Officer 04-07; P-in-c Tiverton St Geo and St Paul *Ex* 07-15; RD Tiverton and Cullompton 12-15; RD Cullompton from 12; Dioc Miss Enabler from 15. *St Paul's Vicarage, Bakers Hill, Tiverton EX16 5NE* T: (01884) 255705 E: b.dugmore@ukgateway.net

DUGUID, Alison Audrey. b 52. STETS 99. **d** 02 **p** 03. C Appledore w Brookland, Fairfield, Brenzett etc *Cant* 02-06; P-in-c The Brents and Davington w Oare and Luddenham 06-12; P-in-c Eastling w Ospringe and Stalisfield w Otterden 06-12; V Marden from 12; Dir Dioc Poverty and Hope Appeal from 07; AD Weald from 14. *The Vicarage, Haffenden Close, Marden, Tonbridge TN12 9DR* E: ali@dogooders.co.uk

DUGUID, Reginald Erskine. b 29. S'wark Ord Course. **d** 88 **p** 89. NSM Notting Hill All SS w St Columb *Lon* 88-99; PtO from 99. *53 Sandbourne, Dartmouth Close, London W11 1DS* T: (020) 7221 4436

DUKE, Canon Alan Arthur. b 38. Tyndale Hall Bris 59. **d** 64 **p** 65. C Whalley Range St Marg *Man* 64-67; C Folkestone H Trin w Ch Ch *Cant* 67-71; V Queenborough 71-76; V Bearsted w Thurnham 76-86; P-in-c Torquay St Luke *Ex* 86-91; R Barham w Bishopsbourne and Kingston *Cant* 91-00; Dioc Communications Officer 91-95; Hon Can Cant Cathl 99-03; Chapl to Bp Dover 00-03; Bp's Media Link Officer 00-03; rtd 03; PtO *Cant* from 03. *Roundways, Derringstone Hill, Barham, Canterbury CT4 6QD* T: (01227) 831817 F: 784985 M: 07751-833670

DUKE, David Malcolm. b 40. Ch Ch Ox BA 61 MA 65 Newc Poly MPhil 80 CQSW 81. Cuddesdon Coll 63. **d** 65 **p** 66. C Sunderland Pennywell St Thos *Dur* 65-68; C Dur St Oswald 68-70; C Harton 70-74; PtO 85-96; Hon C Heworth 96-13; Hon C The Boldons from 13; PtO from 13. *43 Coquet Street, Jarrow NE32 5SW* T: 0191-430 1200 F: 537 4409 M: 07979-036977

DUKE, Miss Judith Mary. b 47. Leeds Univ LLB 68. Cranmer Hall Dur 03. **d** 04 **p** 05. NSM Buckrose Carrs *York* 04-07; R 07-12; rtd 12. *13 Sledgate Garth, Rillington, Malton YO17 8JS* T: (01944) 758189 E: m.j.duke@btinternet.com

DULFER, John Guidi. b 37. Lich Th Coll 62. **d** 64 **p** 65. C Fenny Stratford and Water Eaton *Ox* 64-67; C Cheshunt *St Alb* 67-68; C Kennington Cross St Anselm *S'wark* 68-73; C N Lambeth 74-76; P-in-c Kensington St Phil Earl's Court *Lon* 76-79; V 79-84; V Jersey City St Jo & Jersey City St Matt USA 84-85; R New York Resurr 00-01; P-in-c Castleton 02-06. *110 West 15 Street, Apartment 1, New York NY 10011-6724, USA* E: johndulfer@hotmail.com

DUMAT, Mrs Jennifer. b 42. ARCM 62. Qu Coll Birm 80 EMMTC 82. **dss** 83 **d** 87 **p** 94. Chapl Asst Pilgrim Hosp Boston 83-94; P-in-c Friskney *Linc* 94-04; rtd 04. *11 Sea Lane, Butterwick, Boston PE22 0EY* T: (01205) 760883

DUMBRECK, Geoffrey James William. b 84. Peterho Cam BA 05 MA 09 MPhil 06 PhD 10. Ripon Coll Cuddesdon 11. **d** 13 **p** 14. C Cambridge Ascension *Ely* from 13; Chapl Peterho Cam from 15. *258 Milton Road, Cambridge CB4 1LQ* M: 07727-968985 E: geoff.dumbreck@gmail.com

DUNBAR, Peter Lamb. b 46. Bede Coll Dur DipEd 68. Lambeth STh 77 NOC 78. **d** 81 **p** 82. NSM Knaresborough *Ripon* 81-82; C 82-84; R Farnham w Scotton, Staveley, Copgrove etc 84-92; V Upper Nidderdale 92-12; Chapl St Aid Sch Harrogate 86-94; rtd 12. *4 Chapel Mews, Bridgehouse Gate, Pateley Bridge, Harrogate HG3 5HG* T: (01423) 711762 E: lion.lamb@virgin.net

DUNCAN, Mrs Amanda Jayne. b 58. Balls Park Coll Hertford BEd 79. ERMC 08. **d** 11 **p** 12. C Harpenden St Jo *St Alb* 11-15; TV Bp's Hatfield, Lemsford and N Mymms from 15. *47 Heron Way, Hatfield AL10 8QT* M: 07506-715026 E: amanda.duncan@virginmedia.com *or* vicar@stjohns-hatfield.co.uk

DUNCAN, Canon Bruce. b 38. MBE 93. Leeds Univ BA 60 FRSA. Cuddesdon Coll 65. **d** 67 **p** 68. C Armley St Bart *Ripon* 67-69; Dir Children's Relief Internat 69-71; Hon C Cambridge St Mary Less *Ely* 69-70; Chapl OHP and St Hilda's Sch Whitby 70-71; Chapl Vienna w Budapest and Prague *Eur* 71-75; V Crediton *Ex* 75-82; R Crediton and Shobrooke 82-86; RD Cadbury 76-81 and 84-86; Can Res Man Cathl 86-95; Prin Sarum Coll and Can and Preb Sarum Cathl 95-02; rtd 02;

Chapl Ex Univ 03-04; PtO 02-08; *Sarum* from 08; Hon C Salisbury St Martin and Laverstock 10-13; Hon C Salisbury St Martin from 13. *92 Harnham Road, Salisbury SP2 8JW* T: (01722) 502227 M: 07851-737230 E: churchpath1@ntlworld.com

DUNCAN, Christopher Robin. b 41. AKC 71. **d** 72 **p** 73. C Allington *Cant* 72-73; C Allington and Maidstone St Pet 73-77; P-in-c Wittersham 77-82; R Wittersham w Stone and Ebony 82-85; V Chilham 85-92; P-in-c Challock w Molash 87-92; V Chilham w Challock and Molash 92-11; RD W Bridge 92-95 and 02-03; rtd 12; PtO *Cant* from 12. *173 Shalmsford Street, Chartham, Canterbury CT4 7QP* T: (01227) 733813 E: rev.chris.duncan@gmail.com

DUNCAN, Colin Richard. b 34. SS Coll Cam BA 58 MA 60. Ripon Coll Cuddesdon 83. **d** 85 **p** 86. C Stafford *Lich* 85-89; C Wednesfield 89-90; TV 90-99; rtd 99; PtO *Glouc* from 99. *92 Kingfisher Road, Portishead, Bristol BS20 7QD* T: (01275) 818607 M: 07891-528295 E: duncan.firtree@tiscali.co.uk

DUNCAN, Graham Charles Dewar. b 65. Sheff Univ BSc 87. NTMTC 95. **d** 98 **p** 99. NSM Dawley St Jerome *Lon* 98-00; NSM Sheff St Mary Bramall Lane from 00; Manager St Mary's Ch Community Cen from 00. *11 Coverdale Road, Sheffield S7 2DD* T: 0114-258 7275 *or* 272 5596 F: 275 3892

DUNCAN, Richard. b 87. Wycliffe Hall Ox 12. **d** 15. *Address temp unknown*

✠**DUNCAN, The Rt Revd Gregor Duthie.** b 50. Glas Univ MA 72 Clare Coll Cam PhD 77 Oriel Coll Ox BA 83. Ripon Coll Cuddesdon 81. **d** 83 **p** 84 **c** 10. C Oakham, Hambleton, Egleton, Braunston and Brooke *Pet* 83-86; Chapl Edin Th Coll 87-89; R Largs *Glas* 89-99; Dean Glas 96-10; R Glas St Ninian 99-10; Bp Glas from 10. *Bishop's Office, Diocesan Centre, 5 St Vincent Place, Glasgow G1 2DH* T: 0141-221 6911 F: 221 7014 E: bishop@glasgow.anglican.org

DUNCAN, The Ven John Finch. b 33. Univ Coll Ox BA 57 MA 63. Cuddesdon Coll 57. **d** 59 **p** 60. C S Bank *York* 59-61; SSF 61-62; C Birm St Pet 62-65; Chapl Birm Univ 65-76; V Kings Heath 76-85; Hon Can Birm Cathl 83-85; Adn Birm 85-01; rtd 01; PtO *Birm* from 01; *Pet* from 01. *66 Glebe Rise, King's Sutton, Banbury OX17 3PH* T: (01295) 812641 E: jfduncan66@googlemail.com

DUNCAN, Thomas James. b 37. **d** 97 **p** 98. NSM Poplar *Lon* from 97. *1 Chardwell Close, London E6 5RR* T: (020) 7474 9965 *or* 7538 9198 M: 07732-666434 E: duncant1@sky.com

DUNCAN, The Ven William Albert. b 30. TCD BA 53 MA 61 BD 66. CITC 54. **d** 54 **p** 55. C Bangor Abbey *D & D* 54-57; C Larne and Inver *Conn* 57-61; Hd of Trin Coll Miss Belf 61-66; I Rasharkin w Finvoy *Conn* 66-78; I Ramoan w Ballycastle and Culfeightrin 78-96; Adn Dalriada 93-96; rtd 96. *8 Beech Hill, Rallymoney BT53 6DB* T: (028) 7066 4285

DUNCANSON, Derek James. b 47. TD 93. AKC 69 Open Univ BA 80 Lon Univ MA(Ed) 93 FCollP 94. St Aug Coll Cant 69. **d** 70 **p** 71. C Norbury St Oswald *Cant* 70-72; CF (TAVR) 71-76 and 79-95; C Woodham *Guildf* 72-76; CF 76-79; V Burneside *Carl* 79-84; R Coppull St Jo *Blackb* 84-86; Chapl Bloxham Sch 86-99; V Pet St Mary Boongate 99-04; RD Pet 01-04; Chapl Pet Regional Coll 00-04; Chapl Heathfield Sch Ascot 04-08; rtd 08; PtO *Cant* from 08; rtd 08. *Old Forge Cottage, 235 Canterbury Road, Birchington CT7 9TB* T: (01843) 843289 E: dmduncanson@btinternet.com

DUNCOMBE, Maureen Barbara. *See* WHITE, Maureen Barbara

DUNDAS, Edward Paul. b 67. NUU BSc 88. TCD Div Sch BTh 91. **d** 91 **p** 92. C Portadown St Mark *Arm* 91-95; I Ardtrea w Desertcreat 95-00; Dioc Youth Adv to Abp Armagh 99-00; I Belfast St Aid *Conn* 00-05; I Lisburn Ch Ch from 05. *Christ Church Rectory, 27 Hillsborough Road, Lisburn BT28 1JL* T: (028) 9266 2163 *or* 9267 3271 M: 07740-589465 E: paul_dundas@yahoo.com

DUNDAS, Gary Walter. b 56. EMMTC 04. **d** 07 **p** 08. NSM Stanton-by-Dale w Dale Abbey and Risley *Derby* 07-14; NSM Wilne and Draycott w Breaston from 14. *17-19 Victoria Road, Draycott, Derby DE72 3PS* T: (01332) 872893 F: 875371 M: 07971-783083 E: gwdundas@aol.com

DUNDEE, Provost of. *See* AULD, The Very Revd Jeremy Rodger

DUNFORD, Malcolm. b 34. FCA 74. EMMTC 73. **d** 76 **p** 77. NSM Frodingham and New Brumby *Linc* from 76. *57 Rowland Road, Scunthorpe DN16 1SP* T: (01724) 840859

DUNGAN, Hilary Anne. b 46. TCD BA 98 ARCM 68. CITC 98. **d** 00 **p** 01. C Arm St Mark 00-03; I Maryborough w Dysart Enos and Ballyfin *C & O* 03-11; Chapl Midlands and Portlaoise Pris 03-11; Chapl Midland Regional Hosp Portlaoise 03-11; rtd 11. *46 The Drive, Woodbrook Glen, Bray, Co Dublin, Republic of Ireland* T: (00353) (1) 200 5959 M: 087-6418125 E: hildungan@gmail.com

DUNGAN, Ivan Francis. b 49. CITC 06. **d** 09 **p** 10. NSM Bunclody w Kildavin, Clonegal and Kilrush *C & O* 09-14;

NSM Ferns w Kilbride, Toombe, Kilcormack etc from 14. *Brookhaven, Lower Southknock, New Ross, Co Wexford, Republic of Ireland* T: (00353) (51) 422281 E: ivandungan@gmail.com

DUNHAM, Angela Mary. *See* CHEESEMAN, Angela Mary

DUNK, Mrs Carol Ann. b 65. EMMTC 08. **d** 11 **p** 13. NSM Retford Area *S'well* 11-12; NSM Tuxford w Weston, Markham Clinton etc 12-15; NSM Ollerton w Boughton from 15. *42 Whitehall Road, Retford DN22 6HX* T: (01777) 709092 M: 07527-081388 E: dunkavicar@hotmail.co.uk

DUNK, Carolyn Margaret. b 55. Wycliffe Hall Ox 04. **d** 06 **p** 07. C Uxbridge *Lon* 06-09; C W Ealing St Jo w St Jas from 09. *23A Culmington Road, London W13 9NJ* T: (020) 8566 3459 E: caz.dunk@stjamesealing.org.uk *or* revcaz@tiscali.co.uk

DUNK, Michael Robin. b 43. Oak Hill Th Coll BA 82. **d** 82 **p** 83. C Northampton All SS w St Kath *Pet* 82-86; Ind Chapl *Birm* 86-96; P-in-c Warley Woods 96; V 96-08; AD Warley 01-06; rtd 08; Hon C Shepshed and Oaks in Charnwood *Leic* 08-10; PtO *Birm* 11-14; *Guildf* from 15. *Glenesk, Church Street, Ewell, Epsom KT17 2AQ* T: (020) 3609 8013 E: michael.dunk@talk21.com

DUNK, Peter Norman. b 43. Sarum Th Coll 67. **d** 69 **p** 70. C Sheff St Mary w St Simon w St Matthias 69-71; C Margate St Jo *Cant* 71-74; Dioc Youth Officer *Birm* 74-78; R Hulme Ascension *Man* 78-83; V E Farleigh and Coxheath *Roch* 83; P-in-c Linton w Hunton 83; R Coxheath w E Farleigh, Hunton and Linton 83-88; R Swanbourne Australia 88-99; rtd 00. *7 Raffan View, Gwelup WA 6018, Australia* T: (0061) (8) 9447 8877

DUNKERLEY, James Hobson. b 39. Seabury-Western Th Sem BD 69 STh 70. **d** 64 **p** 65. C Stirchley *Birm* 64-66; C Perry Barr 66-70; R Chicago St Pet USA from 70. *6033 N Sheridan Road, Unit 44B, Chicago IL 60660-3059, USA* T: (001) (772) 275 2773

DUNKLEY, Canon Christopher. b 52. Edin Univ MA 74 Ox Univ BA 77 MA 81. St Steph Ho Ox 75. **d** 78 **p** 79. C Newbold w Dunston *Derby* 78-82; C Chesterfield St Mary and All SS 82; Chapl Leic Univ 82-85; TV Leic Ascension 85-92; Chapl Leics Hospice 85-87; V Leic St Aid 92-97; V Holbrooks *Cov* from 97; Hon Can Cov Cathl from 07. *St Luke's Vicarage, Rotherham Road, Coventry CV6 4FE* T: (024) 7668 8604 E: kitdunkley@virginmedia.com

DUNKLING, Miss Judith Mary. b 77. Westcott Ho Cam 01 Bossey Ecum Inst Geneva 03. **d** 04 **p** 05. C Holbeach *Linc* 04-07; TV Maryport, Netherton and Flimby *Carl* 07-08; TV Tenbury *Heref* 08-11; P-in-c Sutton Bridge and The Suttons w Tydd *Linc* 11-12; PtO *Ely* 13-14; V Dovecot *Liv* from 14. *Holy Spirit Vicarage, Dovecot Avenue, Liverpool L14 7QJ* T: 0151-220 6611 E: j.dunkling@btinternet.com

DUNLOP, Andrew James. b 76. Collingwood Coll Dur BSc 97 PGCE 98. Wycliffe Hall Ox BTh 07. **d** 07 **p** 08. C Plymouth St Andr and Stonehouse *Ex* 07-10; Pioneer Min Gtr Northampton Deanery *Pet* 10-15; TV Duston from 15. *22 Berrywood Drive, Duston, Northampton NN5 6GB* T: (01604) 948255 E: revajdunlop@gmail.com

DUNLOP, Mrs Anne. b 44. NSM Ex St Thos and Em from 14. *14 Otterbourne Court, 6 Coastguard Road, Budleigh Salterton EX9 6HB* T: (01395) 446458

DUNLOP, Brian Kenneth Charles. b 49. Ex Univ BSc 73. WEMTC 07. **d** 10 **p** 11. NSM S Cheltenham *Glouc* from 10. *31 Pickering Road, Cheltenham GL53 0LF* T: (01242) 580731 E: dogcollar@quinweb.net

DUNLOP, Mrs Frances Jane. b 57. New Hall Cam MA 82 ACA 84. STETS 06. **d** 09 **p** 10. NSM Clarendon *Sarum* from 09. *Little Paddock, Romsey Road, Whiteparish, Salisbury SP5 2SD* T: (01794) 884793 M: 07795-836653 E: fjdunlop@hotmail.com

DUNLOP, Mrs Jennifer Mary. b 51. Yorks Min Course 13. **d** 15. NSM Dukinfield St Mark *Ches* from 15. *180A Dowson Road, Hyde SK14 5BW* T: 0161-368 2149 M: 07946-586188 E: jennydunlop2004@yahoo.co.uk

DUNLOP, Neil Stuart. b 78. Qu Coll Birm. **d** 11. C Lighthorne *Cov* 10-12; C Newbold Pacey w Moreton Morrell 10-12; C Chesterton 10-12; Chapl N Warks and Hinckley Coll of FE from 13; C Arden Marches *Cov* from 13. *12 Queensway, Bidford-on-Avon, Alcester B50 4BA* E: nsdunlop@googlemail.com

DUNLOP, Peter John. b 44. TCD BA 68 MA 72 Dur Univ CertEd 71. Cranmer Hall Dur. **d** 71 **p** 72. C Barking St Marg w St Patr *Chelmsf* 71-75; C Gt Malvern Ch Ch *Worc* 75-78; Chapl K Sch Tynemouth 78-89; V Monkseaton St Pet *Newc* 90-96; rtd 96; PtO *Newc* from 96. *19 Cliftonville Gardens, Whitley Bay NE26 1QJ* T: 0191-251 0983

DUNN, Canon Alastair Matthew Crusoe. b 40. Lon Univ LLB 64 AKC 64. Wycliffe Hall Ox 78. **d** 80 **p** 81. C Yardley St Edburgha *Birm* 80-83; R Bishop's Sutton and Ropley and W Tisted *Win* 83-90; V Milford 90-04; Hon Can Win Cathl 03-04; C Harrogate St Mark *Ripon* 04-05; Hon C 05-07; rtd 05; PtO *York* from 08. *13 Littlefield Close, Nether Poppleton, York YO26 6HX* T: (01904) 798487 E: asdunn@talk21.com

DUNN, Mrs Anne. b 36. **d** 03 **p** 04. OLM Weymouth H Trin *Sarum* from 03. *6 Ilchester Road, Weymouth DT4 0AW* T: (01305) 770066 E: annedunn73@talktalk.net

DUNN, Mrs Barbara Anne. b 42. Man Univ BA 72 Sheff Univ CQSW 76. NOC 92. **d** 95 **p** 96. NSM Stretford St Matt *Man* 95-02; PtO 02-12. *36 Alcester Road, Sale M33 3QP* E: bnsdunn@btinternet.com

DUNN, Christopher George Hunter. b 28. Pemb Coll Cam BA 49 MA 53. Oak Hill Th Coll 51. **d** 53 **p** 54. C Tunbridge Wells H Trin *Roch* 53-54; C Broadwater St Mary *Chich* 54-58; R Garsdon w Lea and Cleverton *Bris* 59-74; Chapl Marie Curie Foundn (Tidcombe Hall) 74-95; V Tiverton St Geo *Ex* 74-01; RD Tiverton 84-91; rtd 01; PtO *Sarum* from 02. *8 Counter Close, Blandford Forum DT11 7XJ* T: (01258) 456843 E: cghdunn@uwclub.net

DUNN, David James. b 47. Leeds Univ CertEd 79 BA 82. Trin Coll Bris 88. **d** 90 **p** 91. C Magor w Redwick and Undy *Mon* 90-92; Chapl Toc H from 90; C St Mellons and Michaelston-y-Fedw *Mon* 92-93; V Pontnewydd 93-11; P-in-c Llanfair Caereinion, Llanllugan and Manafon *St As* from 11. *5 Lon Cafnant, Llanfair Caereinion, Welshpool SY21 0RA* T: (01938) 811929 E: vicarddunn@btinternet.com

DUNN, Canon David Michael. b 47. AKC 70. St Aug Coll Cant 70. **d** 71 **p** 72. C Padgate *Liv* 71-74; C Halliwell St Marg *Man* 74-76; V Lever Bridge 76-84; V Bradshaw 84-01; TR Turton Moorland 01-12; Hon Can Man Cathl 12; rtd 12; PtO *Man* from 13. *1 Tottington Fold, Bolton BL2 4DX*

DUNN, Derek William Robert. b 48. Open Univ BA 81 MA 01 Stranmillis Coll CertEd 70 AMusTCL 74 LTCL 75. **d** 85 **p** 87. Aux Min Carnalea *D & D* 85-97; Aux Min Bangor Abbey 97-05; C Ballymena w Ballyclug *Conn* 05-09; Bp's C Acton and Drumbanagher *Arm* from 09; V Choral Arm Cathl from 14. *Drumbanagher Vicarage, 1 Church Hill, Newry BT35 6FT* T: (028) 3082 1556 E: derek@mambolo.freeserve.co.uk

DUNN, Florence Patricia. b 37. Ches Coll of HE BTh 02. NOC 99. **d** 02 **p** 03. NSM Basford *Lich* from 02. *213 Newcastle Road, Trent Vale, Stoke-on-Trent ST4 6PU* T: (01782) 846417 E: rev.patdunn@tesco.net

DUNN, John Frederick. b 44. Trin Coll Bris 71. **d** 74 **p** 75. C Carl St Jo 74-77; C Tooting Graveney St Nic *S'wark* 77-82; V Attleborough *Cov* 85; PtO *Cant* 86-02; V Tipton St Martin and St Paul *Lich* 02-14; rtd 14. *16 School Crescent, Godshill, Ventnor PO38 3JL*

DUNN, Julian. b 46. Open Univ BA 83. K Coll Lon 67 St Aug Coll Cant 70. **d** 71 **p** 72. C Hanworth All SS *Lon* 71-74; C Kidlington *Ox* 74-76; C-in-c Cleethorpes St Fran CD *Linc* 76-77; TV Cleethorpes 77-85; Chapl Friarage and Distr Hosp Northallerton 85-88; Chapl Broadmoor Hosp Crowthorne 88; Ind Chapl *York* 88-89; P-in-c Micklefield 88-89; PtO *Ox* from 95; rtd 11. *timbles brewery (sic), 1 Lewington Close, Great Haseley, Oxford OX44 7LS* T: (01844) 279687 E: eisendora@aol.com

DUNN, Kevin Lancelot. b 62. Newc Univ BSc 83. St Steph Ho Ox 89. **d** 92 **p** 93. C Tynemouth Cullercoats St Paul *Newc* 92-95; C Newc St Matt w St Mary 95-97; P-in-c Kirkholt *Man* 97-00; Chapl Rochdale Healthcare NHS Trust 00-02; Chapl Pennine Acute Hosps NHS Trust 02-07; Chapl Christie Hosp NHS Trust Man from 07. *Christie Hospital, Wilmslow Road, Manchester M20 4BX* T: 0161-446 3000

DUNN (née LEE), Mrs Mary Elizabeth. b 49. Open Univ BA 81 Bp Grosseteste Coll CertEd 78. St Mich Coll Llan 08. **d** 09 **p** 10. NSM Malpas *Mon* 09-11; NSM Llanfair Caereinion, Llanllugan and Manafon *St As* from 11. *5 Lon Cafnant, Llanfair Caereinion, Welshpool SY21 0RA* T: (01938) 811929 E: ourmarylou@googlemail.com

DUNN, Michael Henry James. b 34. Em Coll Cam BA 56 MA 62. Cuddesdon Coll 57 and 62. **d** 62 **p** 63. C Chatham St Steph *Roch* 62-66; C Bromley SS Pet and Paul 66-70; V Roch St Justus 70-83; P-in-c Malvern Wells and Wyche *Worc* 83-85; P-in-c Lt Malvern, Malvern Wells and Wyche 85-97; rtd 97; PtO *Worc* from 97. *253 Oldbury Road, Worcester WR2 6JT* T: (01905) 429938 E: michaelandbery1@talk21.com

DUNN, Nicholas Roger (Jack). b 78. New Coll Ox DPhil 07. Ripon Coll Cuddesdon 09. **d** 11 **p** 12. C Chelsea St Luke and Ch Ch *Lon* 11-13; Chapl Linc Coll Ox 13-15; P-in-c Leytonstone St Andr *Chelmsf* from 15. *St Andrew's Vicarage, 7 Forest Glade, London E11 1LU* M: 07960-512433 T: (020) 8989 0942 E: jackdunn@hotmail.com

DUNN, Pat. *See* DUNN, Florence Patricia

DUNN, Paul James Hugh. b 55. Dur Univ PhD 93. Ripon Coll Cuddesdon. **d** 83 **p** 84. C Wandsworth St Paul *S'wark* 83-87; C Richmond St Mary w St Matthias and St Jo 88-92; TV

Wimbledon 92-98; V Ham St Rich from 98. *The Vicarage, Ashburnham Road, Ham, Richmond TW10 7NL* T: (020) 8948 3758 E: revpdunn@aol.com

DUNN, Reginald Hallan. b 31. Oak Hill NSM Course 79. **d** 82 **p** 83. NSM Enfield St Andr *Lon* 82-88; NSM Forty Hill Jes Ch 88-92; NSM Enfield Chase St Mary 92-97; rtd 97; PtO *Lon* from 97. *3 Conway Gardens, Enfield EN2 9AD* T: (020) 8366 3982

DUNN, Sharon Louise. *See* GOBLE, Sharon Louise

DUNN, Simon David. b 69. Trin Coll Bris BA 08. **d** 08 **p** 09. C Stoke Gifford *Bris* 08-11; TV Chippenham St Paul w Hardenhuish etc 11-14; P-in-c from 14; TV Kington St Michael 11-14. *1 Hardenhuish Avenue, Chippenham SN15 1NL* T: (01249) 445816 M: 07904-733141 E: simon_dunn@hotmail.co.uk

DUNN, Canon Struan Huthwaite. b 43. Ch Coll Hobart 66 Moore Th Coll Sydney ThL 68 Clifton Th Coll 68. **d** 70 **p** 71. C Orpington Ch Ch *Roch* 70-74; C Cheltenham St Mary *Glouc* 74-76; C Welling *Roch* 76-79; Chapl Barcelona w Casteldefels *Eur* 79-83; R Addington w Trottiscliffe *Roch* 83-89; P-in-c Ryarsh w Birling 83-89; P-in-c S Gillingham 89-90; TR 90-96; RD Gillingham 91-96; R Meopham w Nurstead 96-08; Hon Can Roch Cathl 97-08; rtd 08; PtO *Cant* from 08; *Roch* from 08; Chapl HM Pris Standford Hill from 09. *18 Blenheim Avenue, Faversham ME13 8NR* T: (01795) 531700

DUNNAN, Donald Stuart. b 59. Harvard Univ AB 80 AM 81 Ch Ch Ox BA 85 MA 90 DPhil 91. Gen Th Sem (NY) 86. **d** 86 **p** 87. USA 86-87; Lib Pusey Ho 87-89; LtO *Ox* 87-92; PtO *Cant* 87-92; Chapl Linc Coll Ox 90-92; USA from 92. *St James School, 17641 College Road, St James MD 21781-9900, USA* E: dsdunnan@stjames.edu

DUNNE, The Very Revd Dermot Patrick Martin. b 59. Dub City Univ BA 04. St Patr Coll Maynooth 78 CITC 98. **d** 83 **p** 84. In RC Ch 83-95; Dean's V Ch Ch Cathl Dublin 99-01; I Crosspatrick Gp *C & O* 01-08; Prec Ferns Cathl 04-08; Adn Ferns 07-08; Dean Ch Ch Cathl Dublin from 08. *19 Mountainview Road, Ranelagh, Dublin 6, Republic of Ireland* T: (00353) (1) 498 3608 *or* 677 8099 F: 679 8991 M: 87-986 5073 E: dean@cccclub.ie

DUNNE, Kevin Headley. b 43. Cranmer Hall Dur 85. **d** 87 **p** 88. C Chester le Street *Dur* 87-90; V S Hetton w Haswell 90-94; P-in-c Oxclose 94-02; R Chester le Street 02-08; AD Chester-le-Street 97-02 and 04-08; rtd 08; Chapl Sherburn Hosp Dur 09-13; PtO *Dur* from 13. *78 Chesterton Road, South Shields NE34 9HJ* T: 0191-537 4804 E: revdunne@btopenworld.com

DUNNE, The Very Revd Nigel Kenneth. b 66. TCD BA 88 BTh 90 MA 00 MPhil 00. **d** 90 **p** 91. C Dublin St Bart w Leeson Park *D & G* 90-93; C Taney 93-95; I Blessington w Kilbride, Ballymore Eustace etc 95-03; Can Ch Ch Cathl Dublin 01-03; I Bandon Union *C, C & O* 03-07; Dean Cork from 07; I Cork St Fin Barre's Union from 07. *The Deanery, Gilabbey Street, Cork, Republic of Ireland* T: (00353) (21) 431 8073 E: dean@cork.anglican.org

DUNNETT, John Frederick. b 58. SS Coll Cam MA 84 Worc Coll Ox MSc 83 CQSW 82. Trin Coll Bris BA 87. **d** 88 **p** 89. C Kirkheaton *Wakef* 88-93; V Cranham Park *Chelmsf* 93-06; Gen Dir CPAS from 06. *39 Crescent Road, Warley, Brentwood CM14 5JR* T: (01277) 221419 *or* (01926) 458427 E: jd@johndunnett.co.uk *or* jdunnett@cpas.org.uk

DUNNETT, Keith Owen. b 66. Cranfield Inst of Tech BSc 87. Trin Coll Bris BA 00. **d** 00 **p** 01. C Walton and Trimley *St E* 00-03; V Clayton *Bradf* 03-11; C Abingdon *Ox* 11-13; C N Abingdon from 13. *102 Gibsons Close, Abingdon OX14 1XT* T: (01235) 209145 M: 07974-081354 E: keith@cca.uk.net

DUNNETT, Nigella. *See* YOUNGS-DUNNETT, Elizabeth Nigella

DUNNETT, Robert Curtis. b 31. SS Coll Cam BA 54 MA 58. Oak Hill Th Coll 56. **d** 58 **p** 59. C Markfield *Leic* 58-60; C Bucknall and Bagnall *Lich* 60-73; PtO *Birm* from 72; Chapl and Tutor Birm Bible Inst 72-79; Vice-Prin 84-92; Hon Vice-Prin 92-05; rtd 96. *72 Chadbrook Crest, Richmond Hill Road, Birmingham B15 3RN*

DUNNILL, Canon John David Stewart. b 50. UEA BA 72 Ox Univ CertEd 76 Birm Univ PhD 88. Ripon Coll Cuddesdon 86. **d** 88 **p** 89. C Tupsley *Heref* 88-92; Lect Glouc Sch for Min 89-91; Sen Lect Murdoch Univ Australia from 92; Dir Bibl and Th Studies Angl Inst of Th from 92; Can Perth from 99. *School of Social Inquiry, Murdoch University, Murdoch WA 6150, Australia* T: (0061) (8) 9360 6369 *or* 9383 4403 F: 9360 6480 E: j.dunnill@murdoch.edu.au

DUNNING, Adam Jonathan. b 73. Regent's Park Coll Ox BA 95 MA 99 Birm Univ PhD 00 Wolv Univ CertEd 05. Westcott Ho Cam 97. **d** 99 **p** 00. C Evesham w Norton and Lenchwick *Worc* 99-02; C Hamstead St Paul *Birm* 02-03; Hon C Moseley St Mary and Moseley St Anne 03-05; P-in-c The Ortons, Alwalton and Chesterton *Ely* 06-10; V Orton Longueville w

Bottlebridge 10-11; Sen Chapl Cheltenham Coll from 11. *4 Waterfield Close, Cheltenham GL53 7NL* T: (01242) 228774 M: 07970-503909 E: a.dunning@cheltenhamcollege.org

DUNNING, Martyn Philip. b 51. Reading Univ MSc 79 Dur Univ MA 95 MRTPI 77. Cranmer Hall Dur 89. **d** 92 **p** 93. C Beverley Minster *York* 92-96; P-in-c Brandesburton 96-97; P-in-c Leven w Catwick 96-97; R Brandesburton and Leven w Catwick 97-02; RD N Holderness 97-02; P-in-c Scarborough St Mary w Ch Ch and H Apostles 02-04; V from 04; RD Scarborough 04-11. *St Mary's Vicarage, 1 North Cliff Gardens, Scarborough YO12 6PR* T: (01723) 371354 E: parish.office@scarborough-stmarys.org.uk

DUNNINGS, Reuben Edward. b 36. Clifton Th Coll 62. **d** 66 **p** 67. C Longfleet *Sarum* 66-70; C Melksham 70-73; TV 73-78; R Broughton Gifford w Gt Chalfield 78-84; V Holt St Kath 78-84; R Broughton Gifford, Gt Chalfield and Holt 85-86; V Salisbury St Fran 86-99; P-in-c Stratford sub Castle 98-99; V Salisbury St Fran and Stratford sub Castle 99-01; rtd 01; PtO *Sarum* from 01. *11 Cornbrash Rise, Hilperton, Trowbridge BA14 7TS* T: (01225) 768834

DUNSETH, George William. b 52. Multnomah Sch of the Bible Oregon BRE 79. Oak Hill Th Coll BA 85. **d** 85 **p** 86. C Cheadle All Hallows *Ches* 85-88; C New Borough and Leigh *Sarum* 88-91; V Thurnby w Stoughton *Leic* 91-06; PtO 07-08; P-in-c Leic St Leon CD 08-14; rtd 14. *33 Nutfield Road, Leicester LE3 1AN* E: george.dunseth@sky.com

DUNSTAN, The Very Revd Gregory John Orchard. b 50. Cam Univ MA 75 TCD BTh 90. CITC 87. **d** 90 **p** 91. C Ballymena w Ballyclug *Conn* 90-93; I Belfast St Matt 93-11; Preb Swords St Patr Cathl Dublin 07-11; Dean Arm and Keeper of Public Lib from 11. *The Deanery, Library House, 43 Abbey Street, Armagh BT61 7DY* M: 07986-327333 T: (028) 3751 8447 *or* 3752 3142 E: dean@armagh.anglican.org

DUNSTAN, Kenneth Ian. b 40. Goldsmiths' Coll Lon BEd 71 ACP. Oak Hill NSM Course 86. **d** 88 **p** 89. NSM Creeksea w Althorne, Latchingdon and N Fambridge *Chelmsf* 88-94; P-in-c Woodham Mortimer w Hazeleigh 94-98; P-in-c Woodham Walter 94-98; NSM Bradwell on Sea 99-05; rtd 05; PtO *Chelmsf* 05-13; P-in-c Mayland 13-15. *35 Ely Close, Southminster CM0 7AQ* T: (01621) 772199 E: kandk@uwclub.net

DUNSTAN, Mark Philip. b 70. Middx Univ BSc 93. Oak Hill Th Coll BA 03. **d** 03 **p** 04. C Stranton *Dur* 03-06; P-in-c Hunsdon w Widford and Wareside *St Alb* 06-15; R from 15. *The Rectory, Acorn Street, Hunsdon, Ware SG12 8PB* T: (01920) 877276 E: dunstan_mark@hotmail.com

DUNSTAN-MEADOWS, Victor Richard. b 63. Chich Th Coll BTh 90. **d** 90 **p** 91. C Clacton St Jas *Chelmsf* 90-93; C Stansted Mountfitchet 93-95; CF 95-00; Chapl RAF 00-10; P-in-c Up Hatherley *Glouc* 10-13; V from 13. *The Vicarage, Hatherley Road, Cheltenham GL51 6IIX* T: (01242) 210673 M: 07712-050629 E: rev.rdm@gmail.com

DUNTHORNE, Paul. b 63. K Coll Lon LLB 85 St Jo Coll Dur BA 90 Dur Univ MA 98. Cranmer Hall Dur 88. **d** 91 **p** 92. C Heacham and Sedgeford *Nor* 91-95; C Eastbourne H Trin *Chich* 95-98; P-in-c Preston and Ridlington w Wing and Pilton *Pet* 98-00; Local Min Officer 98-00; CME Officer *Heref* 00-06; TR Ledbury 06-14; Preb Heref Cathl 12-14; Miss and Tr Adv *Win* from 14. *School of Mission, Wolvesey, Winchester SO23 9ND* T: (01962) 710980 E: paul.dunthorne@winchester.anglican.org

DUNWOODY, Stephen John Herbert. b 71. Glam Univ BA 92. St Steph Ho Ox BTh 96. **d** 96 **p** 97. C Skewen *Llan* 96-98; C Roath 98-99; C Stanley *Liv* 99-02; TV Colyton, Southleigh, Offwell, Widworthy etc *Ex* 02-03; V Offwell, Northleigh, Farway, Cotleigh etc 03-05; CF from 05. *c/o MOD Chaplains (Army)* F: 381824 T: (01264) 383430 E: stephendunwoody@hotmail.com

DUNWOODY, Thomas Herbert Williamson. b 35. TCD BA 58 MA 64. TCD Div Sch Div Test 59. **d** 59 **p** 60. C Newcastle *D & D* 59-61; Asst Missr Ballymacarrett St Martin 61-63; C Lurgan Ch the Redeemer 63-66; I Ardglass w Dunsford 66-74; OCM 66-74; V Urmston *Man* 74-85; I Wexford w Ardcolm and Killurin *C & O* 85-93; Can Ferns Cathl 88-93; I Newry *D & D* 93-02; rtd 02. *36 Godfrey Avenue, Bangor BT20 5LS* T: (028) 9145 3918 E: thw_d@tiscali.co.uk

DUPRÉ, Robin Charles. b 50. Nottm Univ BA 72 Worc Coll of Educn PGCE 76. SWMTC 08. **d** 11 **p** 12. NSM Jersey Grouville *Win* from 11. *Le Picachon, 4 Le Clos Royale, La Rue de la Ville es Renauds, Grouville, Jersey JE3 9DF* T: (01534) 856378 M: 07829-936250 E: dupre@freeuk.com

DUPREE, Hugh Douglas. b 50. Univ of the South (USA) BA 72 Virginia Th Sem MDiv 75 Ch Ch Ox MA 86 Ball Coll Ox DPhil 88. **d** 75 **p** 76. USA 75-80; Hon C Ox St Mich w St Martin and All SS 80-87; Asst Chapl Ball Coll Ox 84-87; Chapl 87-14; Dean 07-14; Chapl HM Pris Ox 88-97; rtd 14; R

Bp's Inst for Min Florida USA from 15. *Diocesan House, 325 N Market Street, Jacksonville, Florida 32202 USA* T: (001) (904) 356 1328   M: 904-504-7042 E: ddupree@diocesefl.org

DUPUY, Alan Douglas William. b 48. SEITE 98. **d** 00 **p** 01. NSM Forest Hill St Aug *S'wark* 00-01; NSM S Dulwich St Steph 01-04; NSM Perry Hill St Geo w Ch Ch and St Paul 04-12; NSM Forest Hill w Lower Sydenham from 12. *323A Stansted Road, London SE6 4UE* T: (020) 3560 9100 M: 07837-011573 E: alandupuy1@aol.com

DURAND, Noel Douglas. b 33. Jes Coll Cam BA 57 MA 61 BD 76. Westcott Ho Cam 72. **d** 74 **p** 75. C Eaton *Nor* 74-78; V Cumnor *Ox* 78-01; rtd 01; PtO *Nor* from 01. *74 Amderley Drive, Norwich NR4 6JH* T: (01603) 501764 E: douglas@ismene.fsnet.co.uk

DURAND, Canon Stella Evelyn Brigid, Lady. b 42. TCD BA 64 Sorbonne Univ Paris DèS 65. CITC BTh 99. **d** 00. C Kiltegan w Hacketstown, Clonmore and Moyne *C & O* 00-03; I from 03; Can Ossory Cathl from 14. *The Rectory, Kiltegan, Co Wicklow, Republic of Ireland* T/F: (00353) (59) 647 3368 E: stelladurand@eircom.net

DURANT, Lucas Crain. b 85. Wheaton Coll Illinois BA 07 Leuven Univ Belgium MA 08. Wycliffe Hall Ox 15. **d** 15. C Wootton *St Alb* from 15. *9 Studley Road, Wootton, Bedford MK43 9DL* M: 07727-409641 E: lucas.durant@gmail.com

DURANT, Samuel John. b 85. Univ Coll Lon LLB 06. Wycliffe Hall Ox 12. **d** 15. C Linc St Pet in Eastgate from 15. *23 Montaigne Crescent, Lincoln LN2 4QN* E: mrsamuel@gmail.com

DURANT, William John Nicholls. b 55. K Coll Lon BA 76 Southn Univ PGCE 11. St Jo Coll Nottm 77. **d** 80 **p** 81. C Norwood St Luke *S'wark* 80-83; C Morden 83-88; TV 88-92; V Frindsbury w Upnor *Roch* 92-00; CF 00-13; V Vale *Ox* from 13. *The Vicarage, Main Street, Grove, Wantage OX12 7LQ* T: (01235) 766484 E: vicar@valebenefice.org.uk

DURANT-STEVENSON, Mrs Helen Mary. b 53. Saffron Walden Coll TCert 74. Trin Coll Bris BA 04. **d** 04 **p** 05. C S Croydon Em *S'wark* 04-08; C New Malden and Coombe from 08. *2 California Road, New Malden KT3 3RU* T: (020) 8942 0544

DURBIN, James. b 70. Victoria Univ Wellington 83 MA 96. Oak Hill Th Coll BA 13. **d** 13 **p** 14. C Barnston *Ches* from 13. *109 Somerset Road, Heswall, Wirral CH61 8SS* T: 0151-648 8785 M: 07411-226948 E: durbin1970@gmail.com

DURBIN, Roger. b 41. Bris Sch of Min 83. **d** 85 **p** 86. NSM Bedminster *Bris* 85-91; NSM Henbury 91-94; NSM Clifton All SS w St Jo from 94. *13 Charbury Walk, Bristol BS11 9UU* T: 0117-985 8404

DURELL, Miss Jane Vavasor. b 32. Bedf Coll Lon BSc 55 Lambeth STh 64. Gilmore Ho 61. **dss** 86 **d** 87 **p** 94. Par Dn Banbury *Ox* 87-92; rtd 92; PtO *Nor* 92-94 and from 02; NSM Nor St Mary Magd w St Jas 94-02. *44 Corton House, City Road, Norwich NR1 3AP* T: (01603) 627949

DURHAM, Miss Bethany Helen. b 58. Cranmer Hall Dur 86. **d** 89 **p** 94. C Newark *S'well* 89-93; rtd 93; PtO *S'well* from 93. *c/o Crockford, Church House, Great Smith Street, London SW1P 3AZ*

DURHAM, Mrs Eleanore Jane. b 62. St Andr Univ MTheol 84. Trin Coll Bris MA 01. **d** 01 **p** 02. C Childwall All SS *Liv* 01-05; P-in-c Hunts Cross 05-12; TV Halewood and Hunts Cross from 12. *The Vicarage, 7 Kingsmead Drive, Liverpool L25 0NG* T: 0151-486 1220 E: jane.durham@dsl.pipex.com

DURHAM, Archdeacon of. *See* JAGGER, The Ven Ian

DURHAM, Bishop of. *See* BUTLER, The Rt Revd Paul Roger

DURHAM, Dean of. *See* SADGROVE, The Very Revd Michael

DURIE, David James. b 63. Cen Lancs Univ BA 93 St Martin's Coll Lanc MA 99. CBDTI 97. **d** 99 **p** 00. C Briercliffe *Blackb* 99-01; P-in-c Edin St Dav 02-13. *20 Brucehaven Crescent, Limekilns, Dunfermline KY11 3JJ* T: (01890) 781542 E: patricia.durie@btinternet.com

DURING, Arthur Christopher. b 59. Sierra Leone Th Hall 80. **d** 83 **p** 85. C Freetown H Trin Sierra Leone 83-85; C St Geo Cathl 85-86; PtO *S'wark* 00-05. *22 Challice Way, London SW2 3RD* T: (020) 8671 7678

DURKAN, Barbara Isobel Mary. b 43. Kent Univ BSc 71 MPhil 00 Ch Ch Coll Cant MA 95 Sarum Dioc Tr Coll CertEd 65. SEITE 99. **d** 01 **p** 02. Aux Chapl HM Pris Standford Hill 01-08; PtO *Cant* 08-09; Hon C Minster-in-Sheppey 09-12; Hon C Queenborough 09-12; Hon C Sheerness H Trin w St Paul 09-12; Hon C W Sheppey 12-13; PtO from 13. *69 Darlington Drive, Minster-on-Sea, Sheerness ME12 3LG*

DURKIN, Anthony Michael. b 45. Sarum & Wells Th Coll 87. **d** 89 **p** 90. C Faversham *Cant* 89-92; V St Margarets-at-Cliffe w Westcliffe etc 92-09; rtd 09. *Church Cottage, Leigh, Sherborne DT9 6HL* T: (01935) 872117 E: tony@durkin6595.freeserve.co.uk

DURKIN, Mrs Derath May. b 52. N Staffs Poly LLB 87. SAOMC 01. **d** 02 **p** 03. C Harlington Ch Ch CD *Lon* 02-06; TV Brentford 06-14; rtd 14. *35 Fore Street, Newlyn, Penzance TR18 5JP* T: (01736) 369176 M: 07962-168440

DURLEY, Jonathan Richard Hall. b 66. Wolv Univ BA 97 Ch Ch Coll Cant MA 01. S Wales Ord Course 04. **d** 05 **p** 06. C Canton Cardiff *Llan* 05-07; C Newton Nottage 07-10; P-in-c Kenfig Hill from 10. *The Vicarage, 5 Redman Close, Kenfig Hill, Bridgend CF33 6BF* T: (01656) 670148 E: fatherjon@btinternet.com

DURNDELL, Miss Irene Frances. b 43. Trin Coll Bris 84. **dss** 86 **d** 87 **p** 94. Erith Ch Ch *Roch* 86-93; Par Dn 87-93; Par Dn Erith St Paul 93-94; C 94-98; Asst Dir of Tr 93-98; V Falconwood 98-07; rtd 07. *17A Buxton Drive, Bexhill-on-Sea TN39 4BA* T: (01424) 810477 E: renee.durndell@btinternet.com

DURNFORD, Canon Catherine Margaret. b 36. St Mary's Coll Dur BA 57. Gilmore Course 78 NW Ord Course 77. **d** 87 **p** 94. Area Sec USPG York and Ripon 82-89; Par Dn Whitby *York* 89-92; Par Dn Redcar 92-94; C Selby Abbey 94-97; V New Marske and Wilton 97-03; Can and Preb York Minster 01-03; rtd 03; PtO *York* from 03. *18 Canongate, Cottingham HU16 4DG* T: (01482) 844868 E: cmdurnford@gmail.com

DURNFORD, John Edward. b 30. CCC Cam BA 53 MA 61. Linc Th Coll 53. **d** 55 **p** 56. C Selby Abbey *York* 55-58; C Newland St Jo 58-62; C Umtali S Rhodesia 62-64; R Mazoe Valley Rhodesia 74-76; V Hebden Bridge *Wakef* 76-84; RD Calder Valley 82-84; P-in-c Blanchland w Hunstanworth *Newc* 84-90; P-in-c Edmundbyers w Muggleswick *Dur* 84-90; R Blanchland w Hunstanworth and Edmundbyers etc *Newc* 90-94; RD Corbridge 88-93; rtd 94; PtO *Newc* 94-05; *Cant* 06-09. *19 Sunburst Close, Marden, Tonbridge TN12 9TS*

DUROSE, Harry William. **d** 14 **p** 15. OLM Stoke-upon-Trent *Lich* from 14. *48 Lime Street, Stoke-on-Trent ST4 4EF* T: (01782) 863956 E: badger_bill1954@yahoo.co.uk

DURRAN, Ms Margaret. b 47. Surrey Univ MSc 96 Lady Spencer Chu Coll of Educn CertEd 70. S'wark Ord Course 88. **d** 91 **p** 94. Par Dn Brixton St Matt *S'wark* 91-94; C Streatham St Leon 94-95; V Walworth St Chris 95-99; Hon C S'wark St Geo w St Alphege and St Jude 99-09; Hist Churches Project Officer *Lon* 99-07; rtd 08; PtO *Ox* from 09. *8 Bath Terrace, Victoria Road, Bicester OX26 6PR* M: 07739-988742 E: maggie.durran@virginmedia.com

DURRANS, Mrs Janet. b 58. Westcott Ho Cam 09. **d** 11 **p** 12. C Chislehurst St Nic *Roch* from 11. *Southbeech, Old Perry Street, Chislehurst BR7 6PP* T: (020) 8295 4111 M: 07585-660621 E: jandurrans@googlemail.com

DURRANT, Christopher Wayne. b 82. Ex Univ BSc 03 MSc 04. SWMTC 12. **d** 15. *3 Cowley View, Glenthorne Road, Exeter EX4 4XA* M: 07811-671729 E: curate@stdavidschurchexeter.org.uk

DURRANT, Melvyn Richard Bloomfield. b 59. Leeds Univ BA 82 St Luke's Coll Ex PGCE 86. Trin Coll Bris 01. **d** 03 **p** 04. C Watercombe *Sarum* 03-06; C Moreton and Woodsford w Tincleton 03-06; P-in-c Sixpenny Handley w Gussage St Andrew etc from 06; C Chase from 06. *The Vicarage, 60 High Street, Sixpenny Handley, Salisbury SP5 5ND* T: (01725) 552608 E: durrant@talktalk.net

DURRANT, Simon James. b 82. R Academy of Music BMus 04 LRAM 03. Trin Coll Bris BA 11. **d** 12. C Tiverton St Geo and St Paul *Ex* from 12. *St George's Vicarage, St Andrew Street, Tiverton EX16 6PH* T: (01884) 252699 M: 07898-350791 E: si_dur@yahoo.com

DURSTON, Canon David Michael Karl. b 36. Em Coll Cam BA 60 MA 64. Clifton Th Coll 61. **d** 63 **p** 64. C Wednesfield Heath *Lich* 63-66; Project Officer Grubb Inst 67-78; Ind Chapl *Lich* 78-84; P-in-c W Bromwich St Paul 78-82; V 82-84; Adult Educn Officer 84-92; Preb Lich Cathl 89-92; Can Res and Chan Sarum Cathl 92-03; Can and Preb Sarum Cathl 03-06; TR Wylye and Till Valley 03-06; rtd 06. *26 Mill Road, Salisbury SP2 7RZ* T: (01722) 334017 E: david.durston36@btinternet.com

DURUEKE, Collins. b 71. St Mellitus Coll 12. **d** 12. PtO *S'wark* from 15. *83 Dawes House, Orb Street, London SE17 1RD* T: (020) 3561 6910 M: 07862-285672 E: collinsdurueke@yahoo.com

DURWARD, Rosemary. b 60. **d** 10 **p** 11. NSM Notting Hill St Jo *Lon* 10-12; PtO *Win* from 14. *Loral, Miles Lane, Cobham KT11 2EA* E: rdurward@msn.com

DUSSEK, Canon Jeremy Neil James Christopher. b 70. St Jo Coll Dur BA 92. Westcott Ho Cam 96. **d** 97 **p** 98. C Whickham *Dur* 97-00; C Fareham H Trin *Portsm* 00-01; TV 01-07; V Moseley St Mary and St Anne *Birm* 07-14; Can Res Ches Cathl from 14. *9 Abbey Street, Chester CH1 2JF* T: (01244) 500967 E: canon.precentor@chestercathedral.com

DUST, Simon Philip. b 63. Oak Hill Th Coll BA 95. **d** 95 **p** 96. C Chesham Bois *Ox* 95-00; C-in-c Bushmead CD *St Alb* 00-04; V Bushmead 04-08; TV High Wycombe *Ox* from 08.

15 The Brackens, High Wycombe HP11 1EB T: (01494) 529668
E: simon@sac-hw.org.uk

DUTFIELD, Canon Alan. b 20. Linc Th Coll 54. **d** 55 **p** 56.
C Kimberworth *Sheff* 55-60; V New Rossington 60-71; R Old
Brumby *Linc* 71-77; TR 77-86; Can and Preb Linc Cathl 81-86;
RD Manlake 82-86; rtd 86; PtO *Linc* 89-94 and from 01; *S'well*
from 03. *30 Barnes Green, Scotter, Gainsborough DN21 3RW*
T: (01724) 764220

DUTHIE, Elliot Malcolm. b 31. Clifton Th Coll 63. **d** 66 **p** 67.
C Eccleston St Luke *Liv* 66-69; Malaysia 70-75; P-in-c Bootle
St Leon *Liv* 76-78; V 78-81; V Charlton Kings H Apostles *Glouc*
81-94; rtd 94; PtO *Glouc* 94-00; Ex 02-05; *Derby* from 06.
11 Fairisle Close, Oakwood, Derby DE21 2SJ T: (01332) 668238
E: emduthie@btinternet.com

DUTHIE, John. b 39. **d** 04 **p** 05. NSM Aberdeen St Pet *Ab* 04-07;
Chapl NHS Grampian from 06; P-in-c Insch *Ab* 08-09; R from
09. *Moraine, Inchmarlo, Banchory AB31 4BR* T: (01330) 824108
M: 07826-158180 E: johnduthie@nhs.net

DUTTON, Andrew Rivers George. b 49. Bris Univ BSc 71
PGCE 72 Reading Univ MSc 79. EAMTC 98. **d** 98 **p** 99. NSM
Kettering SS Pet and Paul 98-03; NSM Broughton w
Loddington and Cransley etc 04-09; P-in-c Kettering All SS
from 09; Chapl Bp Stopford Sch 99-10. *10 Beardsley Gardens,
Kettering NN15 5UB* T: (01536) 392401 M: (07708) 188818
E: andrew.allsaints@gmail.com

DUTTON, Antony John. b 82. Newc Univ BA 04 Liv Univ
MTh 08 Ches Univ PGCE 08. Ripon Coll Cuddesdon BA 11
MSt 12. **d** 12 **p** 13. C Malpas and Threapwood and Bickerton
Ches 12-14; V Gt Sutton from 14. *15 The Paddock, Great Sutton,
Ellesmere Port CH66 2NN* M: 07976-819114
E: ant_sjd@hotmail.com

DUTTON, Leonard Arthur. b 35. Bps' Coll Cheshunt 63. **d** 66
p 67. C Knighton St Jo *Leic* 66-70; C Chilvers Coton w Astley
Cov 70-73; R Harthern *Leic* 73-79; V Ashby-de-la-Zouch H Trin
79-04; rtd 04; PtO *Leic* from 04. *8 Merganser Way, Coalville
LE67 4QA* T: (01530) 815420 E: lenmeg@uwclub.net

DUTTON, Sandra Rosemary. b 50. Ripon Coll Cuddesdon 03.
d 04 **p** 05. NSM Chatham St Steph *Roch* 04-08; TV Hartshill,
Penkhull and Trent Vale *Lich* 08-12; TR 12-13; R 13-14; P-in-c
Rackheath and Salhouse *Nor* from 14. *The Rectory, 56 Green
Lane West, Rackheath, Norwich NR13 6PG* T: (01782) 744224
E: sandydutton@hotmail.com

DUVALL, Michael James. b 31. **d** 79 **p** 80. Hon C Kings Langley
St Alb 79-89; Hon C Selworthy and Timberscombe and
Wootton Courtenay *B & W* 89-95; Hon C Luccombe 89-95;
Hon C Selworthy, Timberscombe, Wootton Courtenay etc
95-97; rtd 97; PtO *B & W* from 97. *Dovery Edge, 19 Hawkcombe
View, Porlock, Minehead TA24 8NB* T: (01634) 862834

DUXBURY, Brian. b 59. **d** 13 **p** 14. NSM Drighlington *Leeds* from
13; NSM Gildersome from 13. *27 Highfield Drive, Morley, Leeds
LS27 7DW* T: 0113-252 6949 E: briandux@t2s.com

DUXBURY, Clive Robert. b 49. Open Univ BA(ThM) 06.
St Jo Coll Nottm 90. **d** 92 **p** 93. C Horwich and Rivington
Man 92-96; P-in-c Bury St Paul and Bury Ch King 98-00;
P-in-c Freethorpe, Wickhampton, Halvergate w Tunstall
Nor 00-02; P-in-c Reedham w Cantley w Limpenhoe and
Southwood 00-02; R Freethorpe, Wickhampton, Halvergate
etc 02-05; RD Blofield 04-05; R High Ongar w Norton
Mandeville *Chelmsf* 05-08; Chapl HM Pris Everthorpe
08-14; Hon C Elloughton and Brough w Brantingham *York*
11-14; rtd 14; P-in-c S Rodings *Chelmsf* from 14. *The Rectory,
Stortford Road, Leaden Roding, Dunmow CM6 1GY*
M: 07777-602980 E: duxbury@duxbury.karoo.co.uk

DUXBURY, Canon James Campbell. b 33. Tyndale Hall Bris 58.
d 61 **p** 62. C Southover SS Simon and Jude *Liv* 61-65;
V Tittensor *Lich* 65-70; V Bromwich Gd Shep w St Jo
70-75; P-in-c Wellington w Eyton 75-80; V 80-85; V Padiham
Blackb 85-01; Hon Can Blackb Cathl 97-01; rtd 01; PtO *Blackb*
from 01. *1 Gills Croft, Clitheroe BB7 1LJ* T: (01200) 429261
E: theduxburys@talktalk.net

DUXBURY, Miss Margaret Joan. b 30. JP 81. DipEd 52.
St Jo Coll Nottm 83. **dss** 84 **d** 87 **p** 94. Thornthwaite w
Thruscross and Darley *Ripon* 84-86; Middleton St Cross 86-90;
C 87-90; Par Dn Dacre w Hartwith and Darley w Thornthwaite
90-94; C 94-96; rtd 97; NSM Bishop Monkton and Burton
Leonard *Ripon* 97-02; PtO *Leeds* from 01. *Scot Beck House, Low
Lane, Darley, Harrogate HG3 2QN* T: (01423) 780451

DYAS, Stuart Edwin. b 46. Lon Univ BSc 67. Ridley Hall
Cam 78. **d** 80 **p** 81. C Bath Weston St Jo w Kelston *B & W*
80-83; C Tunbridge Wells St Jas *Roch* 83-90; V Nottingham
St Jude *S'well* 90-99; AD Nottingham Cen 93-98; V Long Eaton
St Jo *Derby* 99-05; rtd 05; PtO *Derby* from 05; *S'well* from 14.
Flat 1, 22A Huntington Road, York YO31 8RD
T: (01904) 655355

DYAS, Sylvia Denise (Dee). b 51. Bedf Coll Lon BA 72
Nottm Univ PhD 99. St Jo Coll Nottm MA 00. **d** 00 **p** 01.
Dir Cen for Study of Christianity and Culture *York* from 99;

Tutor St Jo Coll Nottm 00-12; PtO *Derby* 00-04; *S'well*
from 12. *Flat 1, 22A Huntington Road, York YO31 8RD*
T: (01904) 655355 E: dee.dyas@york.ac.uk

DYBLE, Ian Hugh. b 64. Anglia Poly LLB 85 Leic Univ MSc 98.
Ridley Hall Cam 08. **d** 10 **p** 11. C Onslow Square and S
Kensington St Aug *Lon* 10-13; P-in-c Heigham St Thos *Nor*
from 13. *St Thomas's Vicarage, 77 Edinburgh Road, Norwich
NR2 3RL* T: (01603) 624390 M: 07770-592733
E: iandyble@live.co.uk *or* ian@stthomasnorwich.org

DYE, Mrs Margaret Mary. b 48. NOC 95. **d** 98 **p** 99. C Morley
St Pet w Churwell *Wakef* 98-02; TV Morley 02-08; TR 08-13;
rtd 13; PtO *York* from 13. *5 Church Lane, Hutton, Driffield
YO25 9PS* E: thedyes5@btinternet.com

DYE, Stephen. b 49. NOC 01. **d** 04 **p** 05. C Gildersome *Wakef*
04-08; Chapl St Geo Crypt Leeds *Ripon* 08-13; Chapl to the
Homeless 10-13; rtd 13; PtO *York* from 13. *5 Church Lane,
Hutton, Driffield YO25 9PX* M: 07720-975688
E: thedyes5@btinternet.com

DYER, Adrian Louis. b 67. Cant Univ (NZ) BA 02 Auckland Univ
BTheol 03. **d** 04 **p** 05. C Methven New Zealand 05-06;
V Ellesmere 06-09; Chapl RAF from 09. *Chaplaincy Services
(RAF), HQ Air Command, RAF High Wycombe HP14 4UE*
T: (01494) 496800 F: 496343

DYER, Canon Anne Catherine. b 57. St Anne's Coll Ox MA 80
Lon Univ MTh 89. Wycliffe Hall Ox 84. **d** 87 **p** 94. NSM
Beckenham St Jo *Roch* 87-88; NSM Beckenham St Geo 88-89;
Hon Par Dn Luton Ch Ch 89-94; Chapl for Evang 93-98; NSM
Istead Rise 94-98; Min Development Officer 98-04; Hon Can
Roch Cathl 00-04; Warden Cranmer Hall Dur 05-11; Hon
Can Dur Cathl 08-11; R Haddington *Edin* from 11. *The Rectory,
6 Church Street, Haddington EH41 3EX* T: (01620) 824158
E: rect.holytrinityhadd@btinternet.com

DYER, Ms Catherine Jane. b 46. Westf Coll Lon BA 68. Ox NSM
Course 85. **d** 88 **p** 94. NSM Wokingham All SS *Ox* 88-90;
C 90-95; TV W Slough 95-01; P-in-c Linslade 01-07;
AD Mursley 03-06; rtd 07. *45 Shady Bower, Salisbury SP1 2RG*
E: catherine.dyer46@hotmail.co.uk

DYER, Canon Christine Anne. b 53. Nottm Univ BEd 75 MA 97.
EMMTC 81. **dss** 84 **d** 87 **p** 94. Mickleover St Jo *Derby*
85-90; Par Dn 87-90; Dioc Voc Adv 86-90; Par Educn Adv
90-98; Dioc Youth Officer 91-98; P-in-c Morton and
Stonebroom 98-99; P-in-c Shirland 98-99; R Morton and
Stonebroom w Shirland 99-06; P-in-c Allestree 06-10;
P-in-c Darley Abbey 06-10; V Allestree St Edm and Darley
Abbey 10-15; Hon Can Derby Cathl 02-15; PtO *Roch* from 13;
Derby from 15. *7 Devonshire Drive, Mickleover, Derby DE3 9HA*
T: (01332) 513397 E: c.a.dyer.t21@btinternet.com *or*
c.a.dyer@talk21.com

DYER, Fraser Colin. b 65. SEITE. **d** 09 **p** 10. C De Beauvoir Town
St Pet *Lon* 09-12; P-in-c S Lambeth St Anne and All SS *S'wark*
from 12. *The Vicarage, 179 Fentiman Road, London SW8 1JY*
T: (020) 7735 3191 E: revdfraserdyer@gmail.com

DYER, Mrs Gillian Marie. b 50. Sheff Univ BA 71 Leic Univ
PGCE 72. S Dios Minl Tr Scheme 81. **dss** 84 **d** 87 **p** 94. Witney
Ox 84-85; Carl St Cuth w St Mary 86-89; Par Dn 87-89;
Dioc Communications Officer 86-89; Par Dn Kirkbride w
Newton Arlosh 89-91; Par Dn Carl H Trin and St Barn 91-94;
TV 94-97; P-in-c Arbroath *Bre* 01-03; P-in-c Lower Deerann
St Jas *Blackb* 03-10; P-in-c Whalley 10-12; P-in-c Sabden
and Pendleton 10-12; V W Pendleside 12-15; PtO from 15.
Fairwinds, 61 Glendale Drive, Mellor, Blackburn BB2 7HB
T: (01254) 813530 E: revvygilly141@btinternet.com

DYER, Canon James Henry. b 14. ALCD 39. **d** 39 **p** 40. C S
Hackney St Jo w Ch Ch *Lon* 39-43; C New Malden and
Coombe *S'wark* 43-50; V Murchison New Zealand 50-56;
V Collingwood 56-59; V Spring Creek 59-67; V Amuri 67-70;
V Motupiko 70-77; Hon Can Nelson Cathl 85. *7 Talbot Street,
Richmond, Nelson, New Zealand* T: (0064) (3) 554 8638
E: james.dyer@xtra.co.nz

DYER, Janet. b 35. LNSM course 77. **dss** 85 **d** 86 **p** 94. Balerno
Edin 85-86; NSM 86-93; Chapl Edin R Infirmary 88-93; Dn-in-c
Roslin (Rosslyn Chpl) *Edin* 93-94; P-in-c 94-97; NSM
Livingston LEP 97-00; Chapl Livingstone St Jo Hosp 97-00;
NSM Dalmahoy *Edin* 02-11. *499 Lanark Road West, Balerno
EH14 7AL* T: 0131-449 3767 E: jdyer499@googlemail.com

DYER, Mrs Kay. Lon Sch of Th. **d** 15. C Shottery St Andr *Cov*
from 15. *Address temp unknown*

DYER, Ronald Whitfield. b 29. Solicitor 51. Guildf Dioc Min
Course 91. **d** 95 **p** 96. NSM Fleet *Guildf* 95-99; rtd 99; PtO
Guildf from 99. *7 Dukes Mead, Fleet GU51 4HA*
T: (01252) 621457

DYER, Stephen Roger. b 57. Brunel Univ BSc. Wycliffe Hall
Ox 83. **d** 86 **p** 87. C Beckenham St Jo *Roch* 86-89; C Luton
Ch Ch 89-94; V Istead Rise 94-01; V Frindsbury w Upnor
01-04; Hon C Easington, Easington Colliery and S Hetton
Dur 05-09. *The Rectory, 6 Church Street, Haddington EH41 3EX*
T: (01620) 824158 E: revrogdyer@aol.com

DYER, Miss Sylvia Mary. b 30. Westf Coll Lon BA 66. Ab Dioc Tr Course 90. **d** 95 **p** 98. NSM Turriff *Ab* 95-06; NSM Cuminestown 95-06; rtd 06; PtO *Bre* from 07. *Lily Cottage, 19 Long Row, Westhaven, Carnoustie DD7 6BE* T: (01241) 851341 E: sylviadyer@talktalk.net

DYER, Terence Neville. b 50. Sheff Univ BEng 71 Leic Univ PGCE 72. Carl Dioc Tr Course 86. **d** 89 **p** 90. NSM Kirkbride w Newton Arlosh *Carl* 89-91; NSM Carl H Trin and St Barn 91-97; NSM Arbroath *Bre* 01; P-in-c Monifieth 01-03; P-in-c Over Darwen St Jas *Blackb* 03-13; C Darwen St Pet w Hoddlesden 08-10; P-in-c Hoddlesden 10-13; V Over Darwen St Jas and Hoddlesden from 13. *Fairwinds, 61 Glendale Drive, Mellor, Blackburn BB2 7HB* M: 07919-543475 T: (01254) 813530 E: terry255dyer@btinternet.com

DYKE, The Ven Elizabeth Muriel. b 55. St Mary's Coll Dur BSc 77 St Martin's Coll Lanc PGCE 78. Oak Hill Th Coll 92. **d** 94 **p** 95. C High Wycombe *Ox* 94-95; C W Wycombe w Bledlow Ridge, Bradenham and Radnage 95-97; TV Bedworth *Cov* 97-02; V Dunchurch 02-09; R Kidman Park and Mile End Australia 09-14; Adn Sturt 13-14; R Queanbeyan and Distr from 14; Adn Queanbeyan, Monaro and Alpine Region from 14. *39 Rutledge Street, Queanbeyan NSW 2620, Australia* E: elizabethdyke@bigpond.com

DYKE, Kevin Robert. b 59. Sheff Univ BA 13. Coll of Resurr Mirfield 11. **d** 13 **p** 14. C Gainsborough and Morton *Linc* from 13. *The Vicarage, Morton Front, Gainsborough DN21 3AD* T: (01427) 616701 M: 07814-260467 E: kevinfirestorm@virginmedia.com

DYKES, John Edward. b 33. Trin Coll Bris 82. **d** 84 **p** 85. C Rushden w Newton Bromswold *Pet* 84-87; R Heanton Punchardon w Marwood *Ex* 87-97; rtd 97; PtO *Guildf* 98-01; *B & W* from 02. *42 Ashley Road, Taunton TA1 5BP* T: (01823) 282507 E: john@dykes42.plus.com

DYKES, Mrs Katrina Mary. b 66. Trin Coll Bris BA 90. Guildf Dioc Min Course 03. **d** 04 **p** 05. NSM Windlesham *Guildf* 04-07; Chapl St Swithun's Sch Win from 08. *St Swithun's School, Alresford Road, Winchester SO21 1HA* T: (01962) 835700 E: dykesk@stswithuns.com

DYKES, Philip John. b 61. Loughb Univ BSc 83. Trin Coll Bris 88. **d** 91 **p** 92. C Morden *S'wark* 91-95; C St Helier 95-98; TV Camberley St Paul *Guildf* 98-99; V Camberley Heatherside 99-08; Chapl Win Univ 08-11; Dioc Adult Discipleship

Adv *Win* from 11. *The Diocesan Office, Old Alresford Place, Old Alresford, Alresford SO24 9DH* T: (01962) 737354 E: phil.dykes@winchester.anglican.org

DYMOND, Canon Rosemary Carmen. b 70. Ox Univ MEng 94 Aber Univ MSc 95 Bremen Univ Dr rer nat 99. Wycliffe Hall Ox BA 02. **d** 03 **p** 04. C The Hague *Eur* 03-06; Asst Chapl 06-07; V Bedwellty and New Tredegar *Mon* from 07; Can St Woolos Cathl from 14. *The Rectory, Church Street, Aberbargoed, Bargoed CF81 9FF* T: (01443) 829555 E: rosiedymond@yahoo.com

DYSON, Mrs Clare Louise. b 63. WMMTC 02. **d** 05 **p** 06. C Tupsley w Hampton Bishop *Heref* 05-08; P-in-c Kingstone w Clehonger, Eaton Bishop etc 08-10; R Cagebrook 10-14; NSM Cheltenham St Mary w St Matt and St Luke *Glouc* from 14. *Address temp unknown* E: clared@stmstm.org.uk

DYSON, Mrs Debra Anne. b 62. **d** 08 **p** 09. C Lich St Mich w St Mary and Wall 08-11; V Wigginton from 11; RD Tamworth from 14. *The Vicarage, Comberford Lane, Wigginton, Tamworth B79 9DT* T: (01827) 690380 E: debdyson@btinternet.com

DYSON, Michael John. b 57. **d** 12 **p** 13. OLM Kersal Moor *Man* from 12. *15 Moorside Road, Salford M7 3PJ* T: 0161-792 1098 M: 07730-811200 E: beardandsandals@gmail.com

DYSON, Peter Whiteley. b 51. Man Univ BA 73 LLB 75. Qu Coll Birm 77. **d** 81 **p** 82. C Swindon Ch Ch *Bris* 81-84; P-in-c Brislington St Luke 84-91; V Bourne *Guildf* 91-92; PtO 02-04; P-in-c Herriard w Winslade and Long Sutton etc *Win* 04-08; P-in-c Newnham w Nately Scures w Mapledurwell etc 04-08; R N Hants Downs from 08; RD Odiham from 11. *The Vicarage, Church Street, Upton Grey, Basingstoke RG25 2RB* T: (01256) 861750 E: pwdyson@btinternet.com

DYSON, Steven John. b 79. Univ of Wales (Ban) BSc 00. Trin Coll Bris BA 11. **d** 11 **p** 12. C Pinhoe and Broadclyst *Ex* 11-13; C Aylesbeare, Rockbeare, Farringdon etc 11-13; C Broadclyst, Clyst Honiton, Pinhoe, Rockbeare etc from 13. *The Vicarage, Broadclyst, Exeter EX5 3EW* M: 07779-594037 E: revstevedyson@gmail.com

DYTHAM, Linda Alison. b 52. STETS 02. **d** 05 **p** 06. NSM Savernake *Sarum* 05-14; PtO from 14; Chapl Fitzwarren Ho and Standon Lodge from 07. *14 Nutley Court, Eastcourt Road, Marlborough SN8 3AJ* M: 07921-123422 T: (01672) 811025 E: ladytham@btinternet.com

E

EADE, John Christopher. b 45. Ch Coll Cam BA 68 MA 72. Linc Th Coll 68. **d** 70 **p** 71. C Portsea N End St Mark *Portsm* 70-73; C Henleaze *Bris* 73-77; V Slad *Glouc* 77-82; V N Bradley, Southwick and Heywood *Sarum* 82-91; R Fovant, Sutton Mandeville and Teffont Evias etc 91-08; C Nadder Valley 06-08; TR 08-11; rtd 11; PtO *Sarum* from 15. *Odd Acre, Ryall Road, Ryall, Bridport DT6 6EG* T: (01297) 489633 E: johneade.me.uk

EADES, Preb Jonathan Peter. b 51. Dundee Univ MA 74 Edin Univ BD 77. Coates Hall Edin 74. **d** 77 **p** 78. Chapl St Paul's Cathl Dundee 77-88; Chapl Dundee Univ 79-88; TV Leek and Meerbrook *Lich* 88-96; RD Leek 93-96; V Wolstanton 96-08; P-in-c Ashley and Mucklestone 08-09; C Broughton w Croxton and Cotes Heath w Standon 08-09; R Ashley and Mucklestone and Broughton and Croxton from 09; Preb Lich Cathl from 08. *The Rectory, Charnes Road, Ashley, Market Drayton TF9 4LQ* T: (01630) 672210

EADON, Benjamin Myles. b 85. Univ Coll Dur BA 07 Clare Coll Cam BA 10. Westcott Ho Cam 08. **d** 11 **p** 12. C Sunderland St Chad *Dur* 11-15; C Durrington *Chich* from 15. *The Vicarage, Bramble Lane, Worthing BN13 3JE* T: (01903) 694827 E: ben.eadon@btinternet.com

EADY, David Robert. b 43. Salford Univ BSc. Glouc Th Course 82. **d** 85 **p** 86. NSM Highnam, Lassington, Rudford, Tibberton etc *Glouc* 85-95; NSM Stratton, N Cerney, Baunton and Bagendon 95-99; P-in-c Swindon and Elmstone Hardwicke w Uckington 99-08; P-in-c N Cheltenham 08-10; rtd 10; PtO *Glouc* from 10. *117 Sussex Gardens, Hucclecote, Gloucester GL3 3SP* E: davideady@hotmail.com

EADY, Timothy William. b 57. Open Univ BA. Cranmer Hall Dur 82. **d** 85 **p** 86. C Boulton *Derby* 85-88; C Portchester *Portsm* 88-92; R Brighstone and Brooke w Mottistone 92-07; Relig Progr Adv Ocean Sound Radio 88-07; V Iver *Ox* 07-12; Miss Partner Bangkok Ch Th Thailand from 12. *Christ Church, 11 Convent Road, Bangkok 10500, Thailand* E: timothy_eady@yahoo.co.uk

EAGER, Ms Rosemary Anne McDowall. b 65. St Andr Univ MA 87 Strathclyde Univ 88. Ridley Hall Cam 92. **d** 95 **p** 96. C Walthamstow St Mary w St Steph *Chelmsf* 95-97; C Walthamstow 97-01; TV Bushbury *Lich* 01-05; PtO 05-07. *37 Park Dale East, Wolverhampton WV1 4TD* T: (01902) 710340 *or* 553945 E: revdrosie@yahoo.co.uk

EAGGER, Mrs Christine Mary. b 32. **d** 94 **p** 95. NSM Upper w Lower Gravenhurst *St Alb* 94-03; PtO *S'well* from 05. *27 Lancaster Road, Coddington, Newark NG24 2TA* T: (01636) 643885

EAGLE, Canon Julian Charles. b 32. Qu Coll Cam BA 56 MA 60. Westcott Ho Cam. **d** 58 **p** 59. C Billingham St Aid *Dur* 58-61; C Eastleigh *Win* 61-65; Ind Chapl 65-97; Hon Can Win Cathl 83-97; rtd 97; PtO *Win* 97-13. *123 Cranleigh Road, Bournemouth BH6 5JY* T: (01202) 429639

EAGLES, The Ven Peter Andrew. b 59. K Coll Lon BA 82 AKC 82 Ox Univ BA 88. St Steph Ho Ox 86. **d** 89 **p** 90. C Ruislip St Martin *Lon* 89-92; CF from 92; Chapl Guards Chpl Lon 07-08; Asst Chapl Gen from 08; Adn for the Army from 11. *c/o MOD Chaplains (Army)* F: 381824 T: (01264) 383430 E: peter.eagles330@mod.uk

EALES, Geoffrey Pellew. b 50. Trin Coll Bris 95. **d** 97 **p** 98. C Uphill *B & W* 97-00; C Weston super Mare Em 00-05; Chapl Weston Area Health NHS Trust 00-05; V Milton *B & W* 05-09; P-in-c Kewstoke w Wick St Lawrence 08-09; V Milton and Kewstoke from 09. *St Peter's Vicarage, Baytree Road, Weston-super-Mare BS22 8HG* T: (01934) 624247 E: geoffeales@aol.com

EALES, Canon Howard Bernard. b 46. Sarum & Wells Th Coll 73. **d** 76 **p** 77. C Timperley *Ches* 76-78; C Stockport St Thos 78-82; V Wythenshawe Wm Temple Ch *Man* 82-95; V Cheadle Hulme All SS *Ches* 95-11; RD Cheadle 02-09; Hon Can Ches Cathl 06-11; rtd 11; PtO *Ches* from 11. *8 Taxmere Close, Sandbach CW11 1WT* T: (01270) 763965

EAMAN, Michael Leslie. b 47. Ridley Hall Cam 87. d 89 p 90. C Wharton *Ches* 89-93; V Buglawton 93-98; TV Congleton 98-10; rtd 10; Hon C Alcester and Arrow w Oversley and Weethley *Cov* 10-13; Hon C Kinwarton w Gt Alne and Haselor 10-13; P-in-c Potters Green from 13. *St Philip's Vicarage, Ringwood Highway, Coventry CV2 2GF* E: mike.eaman123@btinternet.com

EAMES, Charles George. b 69. CITC 05. d 08 p 09. NSM Magheracross *Clogh* from 08. *79 The Limes, Drumlyon, Enniskillen BT74 5NB* M: 07792-191565 E: charles@charleseames.orangehome.co.uk

EAMES, David John. b 80. Liv Hope Univ Coll BA 01 MA 04 St Jo Coll Dur MA 08. Cranmer Hall Dur 06. d 08 p 09. C Brigg, Wrawby and Cadney cum Howsham *Linc* 08-11; P-in-c Broughton from 11; P-in-c Scawby, Redbourne and Hibaldstow from 11. *St Hybald's Vicarage, Vicarage Lane, Scawby, Brigg DN20 9LX* T: (01652) 600860

✠EAMES, The Most Revd and Rt Hon Lord. b 37. OM 07. QUB LLB 60 PhD 63 Hon LLD 89 TCD Hon LLD 92 Cam Univ Hon DD 94 Lanc Univ Hon LLD 94 Aber Univ Hon DD 97 Ex Univ Hon DD 99 Hon FGCM 88. TCD Div Sch Div Test 60. d 63 p 64 c 75. C Bangor St Comgall *D & D* 63-66; I Gilnahirk 66-74; Bp's Dom Chapl 70-72; I Dundela St Mark 74-75; Bp D & R 75-80; Bp D & D 80-86; Abp Arm 86-06; rtd 06. *3 Downshire Crescent, Hillsborough BT26 6DD* T: (028) 9268 9913

EARDLEY, John. b 38. Ch Coll Cam BA 61. Ridley Hall Cam 60. d 62 p 63. C Barnston *Ches* 62-65; C Wilmslow 65-67; V Hollingworth 67-75; V Leasowe 75-81; Chapl Leasowe Hosp 75-82; RD Wallasey *Ches* 86-91; V Church Hulme and Chapl Cranage Hall Hosp 91-03; rtd 03; PtO *Ches* from 03. *7 Banks Road, Heswall, Wirral CH60 9JS* T: 0151-342 9537 E: johneardley@talktalk.net

EARDLEY, Canon John Barry. b 35. MBE 97. MEd 87. AKC 62. d 63 p 64. C Merton St Jas *S'wark* 63-66; C St Helier 66-69; C Bilton *Cov* 69-70; C Canley CD 70-74; P-in-c Church Lawford w Newnham Regis 74-80; P-in-c Leamington Hastings and Birdingbury 82-88; Dioc Educn Officer 82-00; Hon Can Cov Cathl 87-00; rtd 01; PtO *Cov* from 01. *8 Margetts Close, Kenilworth CV8 1EN* T: (01926) 748313 E: johnbarry.eardley@ntlworld.com

EARDLEY, Robert Bradford. b 44. St Alb Minl Tr Scheme 90. d 93 p 94. NSM Digswell and Panshanger *St Alb* 93-96; NSM Wheathampstead 97-98; NSM Tewin 98-05; P-in-c 98-04; rtd 05; PtO *St Alb* 05-07. *Bridge Cottage, Martin, Fordingbridge SP6 3LD* T: (01725) 519423 M: 07941-345895 E: rob.eardley@virgin.net

EARDLEY, William Robert. b 56. Oak Hill Th Coll 94. d 96 p 97. C Whitfield *Derby* 96-99; TV Dronfield w Holmesfield from 99. *The Vicarage, Vicarage Close, Holmesfield, Dronfield S18 7WZ* T: 0114-289 1425 E: william.eardley@dwhparish.org.uk

EAREY, Mark Robert. b 65. Loughb Univ BSc 87 St Jo Coll Dur BA 91. Cranmer Hall Dur 88. d 91 p 92. C Glen Parva and S Wigston *Leic* 91-94; C Luton Ch Ch *Roch* 94-97; Praxis Nat Educn Officer Sarum Coll 97-02; TR Morley *Wakef* 02-07; Tutor Qu Foundn Birm from 07. *The Queen's Foundation, Somerset Road, Edgbaston, Birmingham B15 2QH* T: 0121-452 2667 E: m.earey@queens.ac.uk

EARIS, Canon Stanley Derek. b 50. Univ Coll Dur BA 71 BCL 80. Ripon Hall Ox BA 73 MA 80. d 74 p 75. C Sutton St Jas and Wawne *York* 74-77; C Acomb St Steph and St Aid 77-81; V Skelmanthorpe *Wakef* 81-87; R Market Deeping *Linc* 87-02; V N Walsham and Edingthorpe *Nor* 02-13; C Bacton w Edingthorpe w Witton and Ridlington 04-07; Hon Can Nor Cathl 10-13; rtd 13; C York St Olave w St Giles from 13; C York St Denys from 13; C York St Helen w St Martin from 13; C York All SS Pavement w St Crux and St Mich from 13. *49 St John Street, York YO31 7QR* T: (01904) 654767 E: dereke569@gmail.com

EARL (formerly LAMB), Mrs Alison. b 60. Ches Coll of HE BTh 04. NOC 01. d 04 p 05. C Rossington *Sheff* 04-08; V Worsbrough w Elscar from 08. *The Vicarage, Wath Road, Elsecar, Barnsley S74 8HJ* T: (01226) 351806 E: alison.lamb@sheffield.anglican.org

EARL, Andrew John. b 61. Huddersfield Univ CertEd 01 Ches Coll of HE BTh 04. NOC. d 04 p 05. NSM Barnsley St Mary *Wakef* 04-08; NSM S Kirkby 08-09; Chapl W Yorks Police 04-09; CF from 09. *c/o MOD Chaplains (Army)* T: (01264) 383430 F: 381824 M: 07557-362130 E: padreearl@hotmail.co.uk

EARL, David Arthur. b 34. Hartley Victoria Coll 63 Coll of Resurr Mirfield. d 83 p 83. In Meth Ch 67-83; P-in-c Paddock *Wakef* 83-84; C Huddersfield St Pet and All SS 84-99; rtd 99; PtO *Leeds* from 99. *2 Clifton Court, Cleveland Road, Huddersfield HD1 4PU* T: (01484) 535608

EARL, The Very Revd David Kaye Lee. b 28. TCD BA 54. d 55 p 56. C Chapelizod *D & G* 55-58; I Rathkeale *L & K* 58-65; I Killarney 65-79; Prec Limerick Cathl 77-79; Dean Ferns *C & O* 79-94; I Ferns w Kilbride, Toombe, Kilcormack etc 79-94; rtd 94. *Random, Seafield, Tramore, Co Waterford, Republic of Ireland* T: (00353) (51) 390503

EARL, Simon Robert. b 50. Culham Coll of Educn CertEd 71 Open Univ BA 82. Linc Th Coll 94. d 96 p 97. C Bexhill St Aug *Chich* 96-99; R Ninfield 99-15; V Hooe 99-15; rtd 15. *6 Frant Avenue, Bexhill-on-Sea TN39 4NG* T: (01424) 842179 E: srearl@btopenworld.com

EARL, Stephen Geoffrey Franklyn. b 53. Lon Univ BA 76 Goldsmiths' Coll Lon PGCE 77. Ridley Hall Cam 91. d 93 p 94. C Sawston *Ely* 93-96; V Burwell w Reach 96-10; RD Fordham and Quy 02-10; Hon Can Ely Cathl 07-10; P-in-c Lavenham w Preston *St E* 10-12; R from 12; RD Lavenham from 12. *The Rectory, Church Street, Lavenham, Sudbury CO10 9SA* T/F: (01787) 247244 E: earls2222@btinternet.com

EARLE, Mrs Sylvia. b 51. St Aid Coll Dur BA 72. Cranmer Hall Dur 05. d 07 p 08. C Whitkirk *Ripon* 07-11; P-in-c Collingham w Harewood *Leeds* from 12; P-in-c Spofforth w Kirk Deighton from 12. *The Vicarage, Church Lane, Collingham, Wetherby LS22 5AU* T: (01937) 573975 E: sylvia.earle@tesco.net

EARLEY, Stephen John. b 48. Trin Coll Bris 91. d 93 p 94. C Stroud H Trin *Glouc* 93-98; C Leckhampton SS Phil and Jas w Cheltenham St Jas 98-02; V Nailsworth w Shortwood, Horsley etc 02-13; rtd 13. *17 Whitecroft, Nailsworth, Stroud GL6 0NS* E: stevearl@earleys.f9.co.uk

EARNEY, Preb Graham Howard. b 45. AKC 67. d 68 p 69. C Auckland St Helen *Dur* 68-72; C Corsenside *Newc* 72-76; P-in-c 76-79; TV Willington 79-83; TR 83-87; Dioc Soc Resp Officer *B & W* 87-95; Dir Bp Mascall Cen *Heref* 95-02; Hon TV Ludlow, Ludford, Ashford Carbonell etc 95-02; Dioc Development Rep 96-02; Local Min Officer 02-10; RD Condover 03-06; Preb Heref Cathl 02-10; rtd 10. *The Coppice, Castle Pulverbatch, Pulverbatch, Shrewsbury SY5 8DS* T: (01743) 718930 E: gandsearney@btinternet.com

EARNGEY, Mark. Univ of NSW BSc 03. Moore Th Coll Sydney BD 11. d 12. C Toongabbie Australia 12-14; PtO *Ox* from 15. *2 Court Place Gardens, Iffley, Oxford OX4 4EW* M: 07943-910520 E: mark.earngey@theology.ox.ac.uk

EARNSHAW, Alan Mark. b 36. CQSW 81. Lon Coll of Div LTh 60. d 60 p 61. C Fazakerley Em *Liv* 60-65; V Ovenden *Wakef* 65-79; NSM Halifax St Jude 79-90; V Coley 90-99; rtd 99; PtO *Leeds* from 00. *67 Smithy Clough Lane, Ripponden, Sowerby Bridge HX6 4LG* T: (01422) 822833

EARNSHAW, Robert Richard. b 42. NOC 78. d 81 p 82. NW Area Sec Bible Soc 78-85; NSM Liv All So Springwood 81-85; R Hinton Ampner w Bramdean and Kilmeston *Win* 85-87; Chapl HM YOI Huntercombe and Finnamore 87-92; Chapl HM YOI Finnamore Wood Camp 87-92; R Spaxton w Charlynch, Goathurst, Enmore etc *B & W* 92-98; R Old Cleeve, Leighland and Treborough 98-03; rtd 03; PtO *Cov* 03-10; *Portsm* from 10; *Win* from 13. *11 Chesterton Place, Whiteley, Fareham PO15 7EZ* T: (01489) 886687 E: bobjen@sagainternet.co.uk or bobjen1@virginmedia.com

EARP, John William. b 19. Jes Coll Cam BA 42 MA 45. Ridley Hall Cam 42. d 43 p 44. C Portman Square St Paul *Lon* 43-46; Tutor Ridley Hall Cam 46-48; Chapl 48-51; Vice-Prin 51-56; Chapl Eton Coll 56-62; V Hartley Wintney and Elvetham *Win* 62-77; RD Odiham 76-83; V Hartley Wintney, Elvetham, Winchfield etc 77-88; rtd 88; PtO *Nor* from 89. *Woodland View, The Fairstead, Cley, Holt NR25 7RJ* T: (01263) 740902

EARWAKER, John Clifford. b 36. Keble Coll Ox BA 59 MA 63 Man Univ MEd 71. Linc Th Coll 59. d 61 p 62. C Ecclesall *Sheff* 61-64; Succ St Mary's Cathl 64-65; LtO *Man* 65-69; *Sheff* 69-93; Chapl and Lect Sheff Poly 81-92; Chapl and Lect Sheff Hallam Univ 92-93; rtd 93; PtO *Sheff* from 93. *89 Dransfield Road, Crosspool, Sheffield S10 5RP* T: 0114-230 3487

EARWICKER, Matthew Charles. b 77. St Jo Coll Ox BA 00 MA 03. Ridley Hall Cam 12. d 14 p 15. C Salisbury St Mark and Laverstock *Sarum* from 14. *4 St Joseph's Close, Bishopdown, Salisbury SP1 3FX* M: 07539-384084 E: matthew@earwicker.me.uk

EASEMAN, Robert Leslie. b 44. d 00 p 01. OLM Hunstanton St Mary w Ringstead Parva etc *Nor* 00-09; rtd 09; PtO *Nor* from 09. *5 Lighthouse Close, Hunstanton PE36 6EL* T/F: (01485) 535258 M: 07941-323218 E: robert.easeman@virgin.net

EAST, Bryan Victor. b 46. Oak Hill Th Coll 91. d 93 p 94. C Waltham Cross *St Alb* 93-96; C Wotton St Mary *Glouc* 96-99; V Humberston *Linc* 99-12; rtd 12. *8 Ashway Court, Stroud GL5 4LL* E: bryan.east@ntlworld.com

EAST, Mark Richard. b 57. Trin Coll Bris BA 89. d 89 p 90. C Dalton-in-Furness *Carl* 89-93; TV Bucknall and Bagnall *Lich*

93-00; P-in-c Church Coniston *Carl* 00-12; P-in-c Torver 00-12; P-in-c Haughton le Skerne *Dur* 12-15; R from 15; P-in-c Sadberge 14-15; R from 15. *7 St Andrew's Close, Darlington DL1 2EB* E: east793@btinternet.com

EAST, Martin James. b 47. STETS. **d** 10 **p** 11. NSM N Hants Downs *Win* 10-13; PtO from 13; NSM Hartley Wintney, Elvetham, Winchfield etc from 13. *South Lodge, 112 London Road, Holybourne, Alton GU34 4EW* M: 07828-423762 T: (01420) 549595 E: martineast@btinternet.com

EAST, Peter Alan. *See* OSTLI-EAST, Peter Alan

EAST, Canon Richard Kenneth. b 47. Oak Hill Th Coll 86. **d** 88 **p** 89. C Necton w Holme Hale *Nor* 88-92; R Garsdon, Lea and Cleverton and Charlton *Bris* 92-12; P-in-c Gt Somerford, Lt Somerford, Seagry, Corston etc 10-12; C Brinkworth w Dauntsey 10-12; RD Malmesbury 93-99; Hon Can Bris Cathl 10-12; rtd 12. *6 Ryeland Way, Trowbridge BA14 7SH* T: (01225) 282902 E: richardeast@homecall.co.uk

EAST, Stuart Michael. b 50. Chich Th Coll 86. **d** 88 **p** 89. C Middlesbrough St Martin *York* 88-92; R Upper Ryedale 92-97; V Macclesfield St Paul *Ches* 97-01; C Maidstone St Luke *Cant* 01-03; R Peopleton and White Ladies Aston w Churchill etc *Worc* 03-10; V Nunthorpe *York* 10-12; rtd 12. *12 Avon Drive, Guisborough TS14 8AX* M: 07754-244929 E: stuart@the-rectory.fsnet.co.uk

EAST KERALA, Bishop of. *See* SAMUEL, Kunnumpurathu Joseph

EAST RIDING, Archdeacon of. *See* BROOM, The Ven Andrew Clifford

EASTELL, Jane Rosamund. b 47. Sheff Univ BA 68 Univ of Wales (Lamp) MA 68 RIBA 73. Trin Coll Bris BA 99. **d** 99 **p** 00. C Backwell w Chelvey and Brockley *B & W* 99-03; C Chew Stoke w Nempnett Thrubwell 03-08; C Chew Magna w Dundry and Norton Malreward 03-08; Hon C Taunton St Jo 09-13; P-in-c 13-14; Hon C Taunton St Mary and St Jo from 14; Dioc Adv in Prayer and Spirituality from 04. *Meadowside, Wild Oak Lane, Trull, Taunton TA3 7JT* T: (01823) 321069 E: jane.eastell@bathwells.anglican.org

EASTER, Canon Ann Rosemarie. SRN 68 Univ of E Lon MBA 94. Gilmore Ho 78. **dss** 80 **d** 87 **p** 94. Stratford St Jo and Ch Ch w Forest Gate St Jas *Chelmsf* 80-89; Par Dn 87-89; Chapl Asst Newham Gen Hosp 80-89; PtO *Chelmsf* 89-08; Chief Exec Officer The Renewal Programme from 95; AD Newham 97-07; NSM W Ham 08-10; NSM E Ham w Upton Park and Forest Gate from 11; Hon Can Chelmsf Cathl from 00; Chapl to The Queen from 07. *The Renewal Programme, 2nd Floor, Durning Hall, Earlham Grove, London E7 9AB* T: (020) 8221 3880 M: 07889-799290 E: ann@renewalprogramme.org.uk

EASTERN ARCHDEACONRY, Archdeacon of the. *See* CURRAN, The Ven Patrick Martin Stanley

EASTOE, Canon Robin Howard Spenser. b 53. Lon Univ BD 75 AKC 75. Coll of Resurr Mirfield 77. **d** 78 **p** 79. C Gt Ilford St Mary *Chelmsf* 78-81; C Walthamstow St Sav 81-84; V Barkingside St Fran 84-92; V Leigh-on-Sea St Marg 92-08; RD Hadleigh 00-08; Chapl Southend Health Care NHS Trust 96-08; Hon Can Chelmsf Cathl 06-08; P-in-c Heavitree and St Mary Steps *Ex* 08-14; TR from 14. *The Rectory, 10 Victoria Park Road, Exeter EX2 4NT* T: (01392) 677150 E: theeastoes@btinternet.com

EASTON, Christopher Richard Alexander. b 60. TCD BA 81. **d** 84 **p** 85. C Belfast St Donard *D & D* 84-89; I Inishmacsaint *Clogh* 89-95; I Magheralin w Dollingstown *D & D* 95-01; I Coleraine *Conn* 01-09; P-in-c Belfast Whiterock 09-14; I Armoy w Loughguile and Drumtullagh from 14. *The Rectory, 181 Glenshesk Road, Armoy, Ballymoney BT53 8RJ* T: (028) 2075 1565 E: stpat@btinternet.com

EASTON, Donald Fyfe. b 48. St Edm Hall Ox BA 69 MA 85 Nottm Univ CertEd 70 Univ Coll Lon MA 76 PhD 90 Clare Hall Cam MA 85. Westcott Ho Cam 89. **d** 90 **p** 91. NSM Fulham St Andr *Lon* 90-97; Lic Preacher from 97. *12 Weltje Road, London W6 9TG* T: (020) 8741 0233

EASTON, John. b 41. Nor City Coll 71. **d** 97. OLM New Catton Ch Ch *Nor* 97-11; PtO from 11. *14 Carterford Drive, Norwich NR3 4DW* T: (01603) 412589 E: jejo@waitrose.com

EASTON, John. b 34. St Cath Soc Ox BA 59 MA 63. Chich Th Coll 59. **d** 61 **p** 62. C Rugeley *Lich* 61-64; TR 72-87; C Shrewsbury All SS 64-66; Ind Chapl *Sheff* 66-72; V Bolsover *Derby* 87-99; RD Bolsover and Staveley 93-98; rtd 99; PtO *Derby* 99-11; *York* from 11. *27 Dulverton Hall, Esplanade, Scarborough YO11 2AR*

EASTON, Robert Paul Stephen. b 62. Bris Univ BA 84. St Steph Ho Ox BTh 00. **d** 00 **p** 01. C Stoke Newington St Mary *Lon* 00-03; Chapl Brighton Coll from 03. *The Chaplaincy, Brighton College, Eastern Road, Brighton BN2 2AL* T: (01273) 606524 E: roberteaston1@onetel.com

EASTON-CROUCH, Jonathan Brian. b 65. SEITE 96. **d** 99 **p** 00. C Mitcham SS Pet and Paul *S'wark* 99-02; Hon C S Wimbledon H Trin and St Pet 03-06; C New Addington 06-09;

P-in-c Merton St Jas 09-15; P-in-c New Addington from 15. *St Edward's Vicarage, Cleves Crescent, Croydon CR0 0DL* M: 07939-121252 E: jonathan.ec@virgin.net

EASTWOOD, Colin Foster. b 34. Leeds Univ BA 56 MA 66. Linc Th Coll 65. **d** 67 **p** 68. C Cottingham *York* 67-70; C Darlington St Cuth *Dur* 70-75; V Eighton Banks 75-81; V Sutton St Jas *Ches* 81-99; rtd 99; PtO *Glouc* from 00. *14 Ross Close, Chipping Sodbury, Bristol BS37 6RS* T: (01454) 317594

EASTWOOD, Canon David Dean. b 54. Newc Univ LLB 77. Ridley Hall Cam 06. **d** 08 **p** 09. C Westbrook St Phil *Liv* 08-10; P-in-c St Helens St Helen 10; TR St Helens Town Cen from 10; AD St Helens from 14; Hon Can Liv Cathl from 14. *The Vicarage, 51A Rainford Road, Dentons Green, St Helens WA10 6BZ* T: (01744) 27446 M: 07785-542594 E: davideastwood86@googlemail.com

EASTWOOD, Harry. b 26. Man Univ BSc 48. Ridley Hall Cam 81. **d** 82 **p** 83. NSM Barton Seagrave w Warkton *Pet* 82-00; PtO 00-13. *22 Poplars Farm Road, Kettering NN15 5AF* T: (01536) 513271 E: harry.eastwood@virginmedia.com

EASTWOOD, Canon Janet. b 54. Wycliffe Hall Ox 83. **dss** 86 **d** 87 **p** 94. Ainsdale *Liv* 86-90; Par Dn 87-90; Team Dn Kirkby Lonsdale *Carl* 90-94; TV 94-95; Dioc Youth Officer 90-94; R Wavertree H Trin *Liv* from 95; P-in-c Wavertree St Thos 95-97; Hon Can Liv Cathl from 06; Chapl Blue Coat Sch Liv from 96. *Wavertree Rectory, Hunters Lane, Liverpool L15 8HL* T: 0151-733 2172 E: janet@holytrinitywavertree.co.uk

EASTWOOD, Mrs Nicola. b 63. **d** 11 **p** 12. C Upton (Overchurch) *Ches* from 11. *34 Birch Road, Prenton CH43 5UA* T: 0151-653 3910 E: nikkieastwood@gmail.com

EATOCK, John. b 45. Lanc Univ MA 82. Lich Th Coll 67. **d** 70 **p** 71. C Crumpsall St Mary *Man* 70-73; C Atherton 73-74; C Ribbleton *Blackb* 74-77; V Ingol 77-83; V Laneside 83-92; RD Accrington 90-92; PtO 92-08; *Truro* from 08. *29 Wellington Road, Camborne TR14 7LH* T: (01209) 714899 E: john.eatock@tiscali.co.uk

EATON, Barry Anthony. b 50. St Martin's Coll Lanc MA 98. CBDTI 94. **d** 97 **p** 98. C W Burnley All SS *Blackb* 97-99; Dep Chapl HM Pris Leeds 99-00; Chapl HM Pris Buckley Hall 00-07; Chapl HM Pris Styal 07-10; Chapl HM Pris Preston from 10. *HM Prison Preston, 2 Ribbleton Lane, Preston PR1 5AB* T: (01772) 444550

EATON, Benjamin. *See* EATON, Oscar Benjamin

EATON, David Andrew. b 58. MBE 06. Man Univ BSc 79 ACA 83 FCA. Trin Coll Bris BA 89. **d** 89 **p** 90. C Barking St Marg w St Patr *Chelmsf* 89-92; C Billericay and Lt Burstead 92-95; P-in-c Vange 95-05; TV Sole Bay *St E* 05-10; CF (TA) from 94; rtd 10; PtO *St E* from 10. *The Cedars, School Lane, Great Barton, Bury St Edmunds IP31 2RQ* T: (01284) 787718 M: 07841-215182 E: davidaeaton@lineone.net

EATON, Canon David John. b 45. Nottm Univ LTh BTh 74. St Jo Coll Nottm 70. **d** 74 **p** 75. C Headley All SS *Guildf* 74-77; Ind Chapl *Worc* 77-82; TV Halesowen 80-82; V Rowledge *Guildf* 82-89; V Leatherhead 89-01; R Leatherhead and Mickleham 01-09; RD Leatherhead 93-98; Hon Can Guildf Cathl 02-09; rtd 09; PtO *Guildf* from 10; *S'wark* from 09. *Two Way House, Wheelers Lane, Brockham, Betchworth RH3 7LA* T: (01737) 843915 E: rev_davideaton@hotmail.com

✠**EATON, The Rt Revd Derek Lionel.** b 41. MA 78. Trin Coll Bris. **d** 71 **p** 71 **c** 90. C Barton Hill St Luke w Ch Ch *Bris* 71-72; Chapl Br Emb Tunisia 72-78; Provost All SS Cathl Cairo 78-83; Chapl Br Emb Egypt 78-83; Hon Can All SS Cathl Cairo 85; Assoc P Papanui St Paul New Zealand 84; V Sumner-Redcliffs 85-90; Bp Nelson 90-06; rtd 06. *67 Grove Street, The Wood, Nelson 7010, New Zealand* T: (0064) (3) 545 6998

EATON (née CRAIG), Mrs Julie Elizabeth. b 57. Open Univ BA 08 SEN 81. Trin Coll Bris 87. **d** 89 **p** 94. Par Dn Gt Ilford St Andr *Chelmsf* 89-92; NSM Billericay and Lt Burstead 92-95; C 95-96; TV 96-01; Chapl Thameside Community Healthcare NHS Trust 92-95; PtO *Chelmsf* 01-05; TV Sole Bay *St E* 05-10. *The Cedars, School Lane, Great Barton, Bury St Edmunds IP31 2RQ* T: (01284) 787718 E: juliecraigeaton@tiscali.co.uk

EATON, Margaret Anne. b 44. Ab Dioc Tr Course 82. **dss** 84 **d** 86 **p** 94. NSM Ellon and Cruden Bay *Ab* 84-95; C Bridge of Don 95-00; Co-ord Scottish Episc Renewal Fellowship 00-04; C Ellon *Ab* 01-03; C Elgin w Lossiemouth *Mor* 03-04 and 06-10; C Aberlour and Dufftown 06-10; LtO from 11. *Grianach, Tom-na-Muidh Road, Dufftown, Keith AB55 4AT* T: (01340) 821478 E: maggie-e@hotmail.co.uk

EATON, Canon Oscar Benjamin. b 37. Puerto Rico Th Coll STB 66. **d** 66 **p** 67. Ecuador 66-69; C Wandsworth St Anne *S'wark* 69-71; C Aldrington *Chich* 71-73; TV Littleham w Exmouth *Ex* 74-79; R Alphington 79-84; Chapl Barcelona w Casteldefels *Eur* 84-87; Barcelona 88; Chapl Maisons-Laffitte 88-02; rtd 02; P-in-c St Raphaël *Eur* 02-10; Can Malta Cathl

96-10. *6 Belle Vue House, 19 Belle Vue Road, Exmouth EX8 3AS*
E: revbeaton@aol.com

EATON, The Very Revd Peter David. b 58. K Coll Lon BA 82 AKC 82 Qu Coll Cam BA 85 MA 89 Magd Coll Ox MA 90. Westcott Ho Cam 83. **d** 86 **p** 87. C Maidstone All SS and St Phil w Tovil *Cant* 86-89; Fells' Chapl Magd Coll Ox 89-91; LtO *Ox* 89-06; PtO from 14; Assoc R Salt Lake City St Paul USA 91-95; R Lancaster St Jas Penn 95-01; Hon Can Th Utah 91-01; Dean St Jo Cathl Denver from 02; Adjunct Angl Studies Iliff Sem Denver from 05. *The Diocese of Southeast Florida, 525 NE 15th Street, Miami FL 33132, USA* F: 375 8054 T: (001) (305) 373 0881 E: coadjutor@diosef.org

EATON, Miss Phyllis Mary. b 42. Qu Eliz Coll Lon BSc 63 UNISA BA 79 SRD. WMMTC 87. **d** 90 **p** 94. NSM Washwood Heath *Birm* 90-91; NSM Edgbaston SS Mary and Ambrose 91-95; PtO 95-05; NSM Oldbury, Langley and Londonderry 05-13; PtO from 13. *7 Milton Court, Sandon Road, Smethwick B66 4AD* T: 0121-420 3488 E: phyllis.eaton@btinternet.com

EAVES, Alan Charles. b 37. Tyndale Hall Bris 62. **d** 65 **p** 66. C Southport SS Simon and Jude *Liv* 65-66; C Eccleston Ch Ch 66-70; V Earlestown 70-79; V Orpington Ch Ch *Roch* 79-02; rtd 02; PtO *Ely* from 03. *4 Chervil Close, Folksworth, Peterborough PE7 3SZ* T: (01733) 241644 M: 07904-357476 E: vaeaves@talktalk.com

EAVES, Brian Maxwell. b 40. Tyndale Hall Bris 66. **d** 69 **p** 70. C Wolverhampton St Jude *Lich* 69-72; C Fazeley 72-75; TV Ipsley *Worc* 75-79; Chapl Amsterdam *Eur* 79-86; Chapl Bordeaux w Riberac, Cahors, Duras etc 86-91; Monaco 91-93; TV Buckhurst Hill *Chelmsf* 93-96; R Culworth w Sulgrave and Thorpe Mandeville etc *Pet* 96-03; rtd 03. *13 Blenheim Drive, Newent GL18 1TU* T: (01531) 822760

EBBSFLEET, Suffragan Bishop of (Provincial Episcopal Visitor). *See* GOODALL, The Rt Revd Jonathan Michael

EBELING, Mrs Barbara. b 44. Hull Univ BA 67. St Alb Minl Tr Scheme 87. **d** 94 **p** 95. C Stevenage St Hugh and St Jo *St Alb* 94-99; R Riversmeet 99-08; rtd 08; PtO *St Alb* 08-09; *Chelmsf* from 09; V High Cross *St Alb* 10-13; V Thundridge 10-13. *7 Wicklands Road, Hunsdon, Ware SG12 8PD* T: (01279) 842086 E: barbara.ebeling@sky.com

ECCLES, James Henry. b 30. DipEd. Wycliffe Hall Ox 86. **d** 87 **p** 88. NSM Llandudno *Ban* 87-91; rtd 91; NSM Llanrhos *St As* 94-00; PtO from 97. *Lowlands, 7 St Seiriol's Road, Llandudno LL30 2YY* T: (01492) 878524

ECCLES, Mrs Vivien Madeline. b 44. **d** 92 **p** 94. OLM Old Trafford St Bride *Man* from 92. *479 Barton Road, Stretford, Manchester M32 9TA* T: 0161-748 9795

ECCLESTON, Mrs Frances Mary. b 61. Jes Coll Cam BA 83 York St Jo Coll MA 05 CQSW 88. NOC 00. **d** 03 **p** 04. C Ranmoor *Sheff* 03-06; C Sheff St Leon Norwood 06-09; P-in-c Crosspool 09-14; V from 14; Dioc Ecum Officer 10-14; Bp's Adv in Past Care and Reconciliation from 14. *The Vicarage, 1 Barnfield Road, Sheffield S10 5TD* T: 0114-230 2531
E: frances.eccleston@sheffield.anglican.org

ECCLESTONE, Canon Gary Edward. b 73. Ex Univ BA 95 PGCE 96. Cuddesdon Coll BTh 99. **d** 99 **p** 00. C Salisbury St Martin and Laverstock *Sarum* 99-03; P-in-c Hanslope w Castlethorpe *Ox* 03-09; V from 09; Hon Can Ho Ghana from 14. *The Vicarage, Park Road, Hanslope, Milton Keynes MK19 7LT* T: (01908) 337936

ECKERSLEY, Mrs Nancy Elizabeth. b 50. York Univ BA 72 Leeds Univ CertEd 73. NEOC 86. **d** 89 **p** 94. C Clifton *York* 89-00; Chapl York Distr Hosp 90-93; Lay Tr Officer *York* 93-00; V Heslington 00-11; rtd 11; PtO *York* from 12. *14 Church Close, Flamborough, Bridlington YO15 1AF* T: (01626) 850515
E: nancyeckersley@yahoo.co.uk

EDDY, Paul Anthony. b 67. St Jo Coll Nottm 07. **d** 09 **p** 10. C Grove *Ox* 09-12; V Stanford in the Vale w Goosey and Hatford from 13; Dioc Missr from 11. *The Vicarage, 24 Church Green, Stanford in the Vale, Faringdon SN7 8HU* T: (01367) 710267 M: 07958-905716 E: paul@pauleddy.org

EDE, The Ven Dennis. b 31. Nottm Univ BA 55 Birm Univ MSocSc 73. Ripon Hall Ox 55. **d** 57 **p** 58. C Sheldon *Birm* 57-60; C Castle Bromwich SS Mary and Marg 60-64; Chapl E Birm Hosp 60-76; C-in-c Hodge Hill CD *Birm* 64-70; V Hodge Hill 70-72; TR 72-76; Chapl Sandwell Distr Gen Hosp 76-90; V W Bromwich All SS *Lich* 76-90; P-in-c W Bromwich Ch Ch 76-79; RD W Bromwich 76-90; Preb Lich Cathl 83-90; Adn Stoke 90-97; rtd 97; Hon C Tilford *Guildf* 97-99; Hon C The Bourne and Tilford 99-02; PtO from 03; *Guildf* from 03. *Tilford, 13 Park Close, Carshalton SM5 3EU* T: (020) 8647 5891 M: 07946-324299 E: dennisangelaede@aol.co.uk

EDELL, Philip Stephen. b 69. American Univ of Paris BA 92 Brighton Univ PGCE 07. St Steph Ho Ox 11. **d** 14. C W Worthing St Jo *Chich* from 14. *4 Lansdowne Road, Worthing BN11 4LY* T: (01903) 869775 M: 07766-496132 E: philip.edell@mac.com

EDEN, Grenville Mervyn. b 37. Bris Univ BA 58 Lon Univ MPhil 78. Ox Min Course 88. **d** 95 **p** 96. NSM Burnham w Dropmore, Hitcham and Taplow *Ox* 95-06; PtO from 06. *Langdale, Grays Park Road, Stoke Poges, Slough SL2 4JG* T: (01753) 525962

EDEN, Henry. b 36. G&C Coll Cam BA 59 MA 64. Ox NSM Course. **d** 87 **p** 88. NSM Abingdon w Shippon *Ox* 87-88; Chapl Brentwood Sch 88-95; TV Beaconsfield *Ox* 95-00; PtO *St E* from 01; *Ely* from 03. *Address temp unknown* E: heden@btinternet.com

EDEN, Mrs Lesley Patricia. b 54. Liv Univ MTh 99. NOC 93. **d** 96 **p** 97. C Wallasey St Hilary *Ches* 96-98; C Oxton 98-01; Min Review Officer 01-07; V Whitegate w Lt Budworth 01-12; rtd 12; RD Middlewich *Ches* 10-12. *New Holding, Watling Street, Craven Arms SY7 8DX* E: lesley_eden88@hotmail.com

EDEN, Mervyn. *See* EDEN, Grenville Mervyn

EDEN, Michael William. b 57. Nottm Univ BTh 86. Linc Th Coll 83. **d** 86 **p** 87. C Daventry *Pet* 86-89; TV Northampton Em 89-92; V Corby St Columba 92-03; P-in-c Stowmarket *St E* 03-10; V from 10. *The Vicarage, 7 Lockington Road, Stowmarket IP14 1BQ* T: (01449) 678623 or T/F: 774652 E: theedens@talk21.com

EDGAR, David. b 59. Newc Univ BA 81. Linc Th Coll BTh 86. **d** 86 **p** 87. C Wednesbury St Paul Wood Green *Lich* 86-91; V Winterton Gp *Linc* 91-00; C Linc St Swithin 00-01; P-in-c 01-14; P-in-c Linc All SS from 06; Chapl N Lincs Coll from 00. *1 St Giles Avenue, Lincoln LN2 4PE* T: (01522) 528199 E: david.edgar1@tesco.net

EDGCUMBE, Irena Christine. *See* CZERNIAWSKA EDGCUMBE, Irena Christine

EDGE, Darren. b 69. Man Metrop Univ BEd 99. SNWTP 10. **d** 13 **p** 14. C Werrington and Wetley Rocks *Lich* 13-14; NSM from 14. *2 East Drive, Cheddleton, Leek ST13 7DN* T: (01538) 361999 M: 07940-555540 E: d.s.edge@hotmail.co.uk

EDGE, John Nicholson. b 53. **d** 99 **p** 00. OLM Flixton St Jo *Man* 99-14; PtO from 14. *5 Devon Road, Flixton, Manchester M41 6PN* T: 0161-748 4736

EDGE, Michael MacLeod. b 45. St Andr Univ BSc 68 Qu Coll Cam BA 70 MA 74. Westcott Ho Cam 68. **d** 72 **p** 73. C Allerton *Liv* 72-76; R Bretherton *Blackb* 76-82; P-in-c Kilpeck *Heref* 82-84; P-in-c St Devereux w Wormbridge 82-84; TR Ewyas Harold w Dulas, Kenderchurch etc 82-93; RD Abbeydore 84-90; V Enfield St Andr *Lon* 93-13; rtd 13. *19 Abbeyfields, Bury St Edmunds IP33 1AQ* T: (01284) 724178 E: michaeledge@cantab.net

EDGE, Philip John. b 54. Ripon Coll Cuddesdon 77. **d** 80 **p** 81. C N Harrow St Alb *Lon* 80-83; C St Giles Cripplegate w St Bart Moor Lane etc 83-86; P-in-c Belmont 86-88; V 88-92; V Ellesmere and Welsh Frankton *Lich* 92-97; V Ellesmere from 97; RD 10-13. *The Vicarage, Church Hill, Ellesmere SY12 0HB* T: (01691) 622571

EDGE, Ms Renate Erika. b 50. Cranmer Hall Dur 86. **d** 88. Par Dn Leic H Spirit 88-89; Asst Chapl Leic and Co Miss for the Deaf 88-89; Par Dn Leic H Apostles 89-94. *Flat 3, 1 Stuart Court, Stuart Square, Edinburgh EH12 8UU* E: mail@renata.org.uk or renata.edge@hotmail.co.uk

EDGE, Timothy Peter. b 55. Brighton Poly BSc 80 K Coll Lon MA 10 CEng 85 MIET 85 FRAS 80. Westcott Ho Cam 85. **d** 88 **p** 89. C Norton *Ches* 88-91; C Bedworth *Cov* 91-96; TV Witney *Ox* 96-02; Asst Chapl HM Pris Bullingdon 02-04; Chapl 04-09; NSM Cogges and S Leigh *Ox* 03-11; PtO from 11. *27 Burford Road, Witney OX28 6DP* T: (01993) 773438 E: tim.edge@talk21.com

EDGELL, Hugh Anthony Richard. b 31. ARHistS 84. AKC 57. **d** 58 **p** 59. C N Lynn w St Marg and St Nic *Nor* 58-64; R S Walsham 64-74; V Upton w Fishley 64-74; R Hingham 74-81; R Hingham w Woodrising w Scoulton 81-85; V Horning 85-89; P-in-c Beeston St Laurence w Ashmanhaugh 85-89; R Horning w Beeston St Laurence and Ashmanhaugh 89-95; Prior St Benet's Abbey Horning 87-95; rtd 95; PtO *Nor* from 95. *Brambles, Brimbelow Road, Hoveton, Norwich NR12 8UJ* T: (01604) 782206

EDGERTON, Ms Hilary Ann. b 66. R Holloway & Bedf New Coll Lon BSc 88. Wycliffe Hall Ox BTh 93. **d** 93 **p** 94. Par Dn S Cave and Ellerker w Broomfleet *York* 93-94; C 94-97; TV Howden 97-00; V Hayfield and Chinley w Buxworth *Derby* from 00. *8 Bluebell Close, Hayfield, High Peak SK22 2PG* T: (01663) 743350 E: hedgerton356@btinternet.com

EDIE, Jennifer Mary. b 40. Edin Univ MA 62 Hong Kong Univ PGCE 77. **d** 03 **p** 04. NSM Eyemouth *Edin* 03-09; P-in-c 06-09; rtd 09; LtO *Edin* from 09. *12 Barefoots Avenue, Eyemouth TD14 5JH* T: (01289) 386338 E: rev.jennifer@gmail.com

EDINBOROUGH, David. b 36. Nottm Univ BA 58 MEd 74. EMMTC 79. **d** 82 **p** 83. NSM Bramcote *S'well* 82-01; P-in-c 94-01; Dioc Officer for NSMs 89-94; rtd 01; PtO *S'well* 01-02; P-in-c Radford St Pet 02-04; PtO from 04; Bp's Chapl for

Rtd Clergy from 09. *105A Derby Road, Beeston, Nottingham NG9 3GZ* T: 0115-925 1066
E: david.edinborough@btopenworld.com

EDINBURGH, Bishop of. *See* ARMES, The Rt Revd John Andrew

EDINBURGH, Dean of. *See* MACDONALD, The Very Revd Susan Elizabeth

EDINBURGH, Provost of. *See* FORBES, The Very Revd Graham John Thompson

EDIS, John Oram. b 26. Open Univ BA 81 ACIS 50 ACP 52 FCollP 89. Ox NSM Course 85. **d** 88 **p** 89. Hon Warden and Chapl E Ivor Hughes Educn Foundn from 88; NSM Gt Chesham *Ox* 88-96; PtO *Lon* 96-03; *Ox* from 96. *2 Meades Lane, Chesham HP5 1ND* T: (01494) 774242

EDLIN-WHITE, Glenys Rowena Dexter. b 48. **d** 11 **p** 12. NSM Lowdham w Caythorpe, and Gunthorpe *S'well* 11-14; PtO from 15. *Willow House, 11 Frederick Avenue, Carlton, Nottingham NG4 1HP* T: 0115-987 3135
E: ro@edlin-white.net

EDMANS, Mrs Jennifer. b 56. **d** 07 **p** 08. OLM Bernwode *Ox* 07-10; C from 10. *2 The Bungalow, Coldharbour Farm, Brill, Aylesbury HP18 9UA* T: (01844) 237855 M: 07808-347276
E: jennyedmans@aol.com

EDMEADS, Andrew. b 53. Linc Th Coll 84. **d** 86 **p** 87. C Sholing *Win* 86-89; R Knights Enham 89-97; rtd 97; PtO *Win* 97-13; Chapl St Mich Hospice Basingstoke 00-13; Chapl Naomi Ho Hospice from 13. *10 Altona Gardens, Andover SP10 4LG* T: (01264) 391464

EDMONDS (née HARRIS), Mrs Catherine Elizabeth. b 52. Leic Coll of Educn CertEd 73 ACP 79. S Dios Minl Tr Scheme 91. **d** 95 **p** 96. NSM Basing *Win* 95-99; C Yeovil H Trin w Barwick *B & W* 99-01; Chapl Coll of SS Mark and Jo Plymouth *Ex* 01-06; TV Ottery St Mary, Alfington, W Hill, Tipton etc from 06; C Broadhembury, Payhembury and Plymtree from 09; Dioc Youth Adv from 06; RD Ottery from 14. *The Rectory, Station Road, Feniton, Honiton EX14 3DF* T: (01404) 851401
E: cateedmonds@me.com

EDMONDS, Clive Alway. b 42. ACII. S'wark Ord Course 78. **d** 81 **p** 82. C Horsell *Guildf* 81-85; R Bisley and W End 85-92; RD Surrey Heath 90-92; R Haslemere 92-00; Chapl Wispers Sch Haslemere 92-00; P-in-c Westbury-on-Severn w Flaxley and Blaisdon *Glouc* 00-02; V Westbury-on-Severn w Flaxley, Blaisdon etc 03-06; rtd 06; PtO *Heref* from 07. *3 Church Road, Longhope GL17 0LH* T: (01452) 831545
E: alwayedmonds@hotmail.com

EDMONDS, Michelle Kay. b 70. S Bank Univ BSc 98. Ripon Coll Cuddesdon BTh 08. **d** 06 **p** 07. C Croydon St Matt *S'wark* 06-09; TV Warlingham w Chelsham and Farleigh from 09; Asst Dir of Ords Croydon Area from 13. *The Vicarage, 2 Chelsham Road, Warlingham CR6 9EQ* T: (01883) 623011
M: 07799-713957 E: revmichelle@btinternet.com

EDMONDS (née MAGUIRE), Mrs Sarah Alison. b 65. Univ Coll Lon BSc 87 Southn Univ MSc 93. STETS 95. **d** 98 **p** 99. C Warwick St Paul *Cov* 98-02; P-in-c Hampton Lucy w Charlecote and Loxley 02-06; Hon C Ilmington w Stretton-on-Fosse etc from 14; Hon C Tredington and Darlingscott from 14. *Tredington Rectory, Tredington, Shipston-on-Stour CV36 4NG*

EDMONDS, Stephen Harry James. b 77. SS Hild & Bede Coll Dur BA 99 Leeds Univ MA 08. Coll of Resurr Mirfield 06. **d** 08 **p** 09. C Hendon *Dur* 08-12; V Edlington and Hexthorpe *Sheff* from 12. *The Vicarage, 17 Heaton Gardens, Edlington, Doncaster DN12 1SY* T: (01709) 858358 M: 07882-443025
E: fr.s.edmonds@gmail.com

EDMONDS, Stephen Philip Augustine. b 83. Kent Univ BA 05 Heythrop Coll Lon MA 10. Westcott Ho Cam 10. **d** 15. C Sydenham St Bart *S'wark* from 15. *Address withheld by request* T: (020) 8676 8925 E: curate@sedmonds.co.uk

EDMONDS, Tony Ernest. b 50. R Holloway Coll Lon BSc 71 Imp Coll Lon MSc 73 PhD 75 Nottm Univ MA 05. EMMTC 02. **d** 05 **p** 06. NSM Barrow upon Soar w Walton le Wolds *Leic* 05-10; TV Kegworth, Hathern, Long Whatton, Diseworth etc from 10; Warden of Readers 10-13; AD Akeley E from 11. *The Vicarage, Present Lane, Belton, Loughborough LE12 9UN* T: (01530) 223447 M: 07837-009147
E: t.e.edmonds@btconnect.com

EDMONDS-SEAL, John. b 34. FFARCS 63 Lon Univ MB, BS 58. Ox NSM Course. **d** 90 **p** 91. NSM Ox St Aldate w St Matt 90-94; NSM Wheatley 95-14; NSM Albury w Tiddington, Holton, Waterperry, Waterstock and Wheatley from 14. *Otway, Woodperry Road, Oxford OX3 9UY* T: (01865) 351582
E: edmondsseal@doctors.org.uk

✠**EDMONDS, The Rt Revd Christopher Paul.** b 50. St Jo Coll Dur BA 71 MA 81. Cranmer Hall Dur 71. **d** 73 **p** 74 **c** 08. C Kirkheaton *Wakef* 73-79; V Ovenden 79-86; Bp's Adv on Evang 81-86; Dioc Officer for Evang *Carl* 86-92; P-in-c Bampton w Mardale 86-92; V Shipley St Pet *Bradf* 92-02; Warden Lee Abbey 02-08; Suff Bp Bolton *Man* from 08.

Bishop's Lodge, Walkden Road, Worsley, Manchester M28 2WH T: 0161-790 8289 F: 703 9157
E: bishopchrisedmondson@manchester.anglican.org

EDMONDSON, The Very Revd John James William. b 55. St Jo Coll Dur BA 83 MA 91 PhD 04. Cranmer Hall Dur 80. **d** 83 **p** 84. C Gee Cross *Ches* 83-86; C Camberley St Paul *Guildf* 86-88; TV 88-90; Chapl Elmhurst Ballet Sch 86-90; V Foxton w Gumley and Laughton and Lubenham *Leic* 90-94; R Bexhill St Mark *Chich* 94-05; V Battle from 05; Dean Battle from 05; P-in-c Sedlescombe w Whatlington 05-08; Dioc Voc Adv 98-02; Asst Dir of Ords 02-05; RD Battle and Bexhill 13-15; Can and Preb Chich Cathl from 14. *The Deanery, Caldbec Hill, Battle TN33 0JY* T/F: (01424) 772693
E: dean@johnedmondson.org

EDMONDSON, Paul. b 58. Qu Coll Birm. **d** 10 **p** 11. NSM Shottery St Andr *Cov* from 10. *Shakespeare Centre, Henley Street, Stratford-upon-Avon CV37 6QW*

EDMONTON, Area Bishop of. *See* WHEATLEY, The Rt Revd Peter William

EDMUND, Brother. *See* BLACKIE, Richard Footner

EDMUNDS, Andrew Charles. b 57. Whitelands Coll Lon BEd 80 CQSW 83. Oak Hill NSM Course 87. **d** 89 **p** 90. NSM Hawkwell *Chelmsf* 89-95; C Torquay St Matthias, St Mark and H Trin *Ex* 95-97; V Ripley *Derby* 97-09; RD Heanor 06-09; PtO 09-11; R Yateley *Win* from 11. *The Vicarage, 99 Reading Road, Yateley GU46 7LR* T: (01252) 873133 M: 07715-377225
E: a.edmunds@me.com

EDSON, John Benedict. b 73. Wolv Univ BSc 95 York St Jo Coll MA 02. NOC 06. **d** 08 **p** 09. C Brunswick *Man* 08-11; TV Didsbury St Jas and Em from 11. *453 Parrswood Road, East Didsley, Manchester M20 5NE* E: ben@benedson.co.uk

EDSON, The Ven Michael. b 42. Birm Univ BSc 64 Leeds Univ BA 71. Coll of Resurr Mirfield 69. **d** 72 **p** 73. C Barnstaple St Pet w H Trin *Ex* 72-77; TV Barnstaple and Goodleigh 77-79; TV Barnstaple, Goodleigh and Landkey 79-82; V Roxbourne St Andr *Lon* 82-89; AD Harrow 85-89; P-in-c S Harrow St Paul 86-89; Warden Lee Abbey 89-94; LtO *Ex* 89-94; Adn Leic 94-02; Bp's Insp of Par Registers and Records 94-02; TR Bideford, Northam, Westward Ho!, Appledore etc *Ex* 02-09; rtd 09. *43 Old Torrington Road, Barnstaple EX31 3AS* T: (01271) 327917 E: ven.mike.edson@googlemail.com

EDWARDS, Canon Aled. b 55. OBE 06. Univ of Wales (Lamp) BA 77. Trin Coll Bris 77. **d** 79 **p** 80. C Glanogwen *Ban* 79-82; V Llandinorwig w Penisa'r-waen 82-85; R Botwnnog 85-93; V Cardiff Dewi Sant *Llan* 93-99; Nat Assembly Liaison Officer from 99; Hon Chapl Llan Cathl from 99; Metrop Can Llan Cathl from 14. *20 Hilltop Avenue, Cilfynydd, Pontypridd CF37 4HZ* T: (01443) 407310 E: aled@globalnet.co.uk

EDWARDS, Allen John. b 50. Univ of Wales (Cardiff) BSc 72 Imp Coll Lon PhD 81 CEng 81 EurIng 88 FIMechE 93 FNucI 95 MCMI 95 MAPM 95. SAOMC 00. **d** 02 **p** 03. NSM Didcot All SS *Ox* 02-11; PtO *Eur* from 10; *Sarum* 12; NSM Warminster Ch Ch from 12. *10 Southdown Way, Warminster BA12 8FP*
E: allen.edwards@btinternet.com

EDWARDS, Andrew Colin. b 55. ACA 81 Pemb Coll Cam BA 77 MA 80. St Mich Coll Llan BD 89. **d** 89 **p** 90. C Newport St Paul *Mon* 89-91; C Newport St Woolos 91-93; Min Can St Woolos Cathl 91-93; P-in-c Ynysddu 93-95; TV Mynyddislwyn 95-97; rtd 97. *197 Heritage Park, St Mellons, Cardiff CF3 0DU* T: (029) 2079 2715

EDWARDS, Canon Andrew David. b 42. Tyndale Hall Bris 67. **d** 70 **p** 71. C Blackpool Ch Ch *Blackb* 70-73; C W Teignmouth *Ex* 73-76; P-in-c Ilfracombe SS Phil and Jas 76-85; C-in-c Lundy Is 79-89; V Ilfracombe SS Phil and Jas w W Down 85-89; TV Canford Magna *Sarum* 89-98; R Moresby *Carl* 98-07; RD Calder 02-07; Hon Can Carl Cathl 05-07; rtd 07; PtO *Carl* 07-14. *21 Grovelands Road, Headington, Oxford OX3 8HZ* T: (01865) 751591 E: a.edwards432@btinternet.com

EDWARDS, Andrew James. b 54. York Univ BA 76. Wycliffe Hall Ox 77. **d** 80 **p** 81. C Beckenham St Jo *Roch* 80-83; C Luton Ch Ch 83-87; V Skelmersdale Ch at Cen *Liv* 87-95; V Netherton 95-02; V Southport St Phil and St Paul 02-11; C Southport All SS 03-11; V W Derby Gd Shep from 11. *4 Christchurch Close, Liverpool L11 3EN* T: 0151-474 1444
E: andrew@ajedwards.freeserve.co.uk

EDWARDS, Andrew Jonathan Hugo (Joe). b 56. Ex Univ BA 78. Sarum & Wells Th Coll BTh 93. **d** 93 **p** 94. C Honiton, Gittisham, Combe Raleigh, Monkton etc *Ex* 93-97; P-in-c Queen Thorne *Sarum* 97-01; Chapl Clayesmore Sch Blandford 01-10; P-in-c Bridge Par *Sarum* from 11; Chapl Qu Eliz Sch Wimborne 11-12; P-in-c Spetisbury w Charlton Marshall etc *Sarum* from 13. *The Vicarage, Newton Road, Sturminster Marshall, Wimborne BH21 4BT* T: (01258) 857620
E: joe@bridgeparishes.co.uk

EDWARDS, Anita Carolyn. *See* COLPUS, Anita Carolyn

EDWARDS, Mrs Anne Joan. b 67. Lanc Univ BA·89. NOC 97. **d** 00 **p** 01. C Elton All SS *Man* 00-04; Chapl Bolton Hosps NHS Trust 02-04; Chapl Team Ldr Wrightington Wigan and Leigh NHS Trust from 04; Bp's Adv for Healthcare Chapl *Man* from 15. *9 Stocks Courts, 2 Harriet Street, Worsley, Manchester M28 3JW* E: anna.edwards@dsl.pipex.com *or* anne.j.edwards@wwl.nhs.uk

EDWARDS, Canon Arthur John. b 42. Qu Mary Coll Lon BA 64 MPhil 66. St Mich Coll Llan 66. **d** 68 **p** 69. C Newport St Woolos *Mon* 68-71; V Llantarnam 71-74; Chapl Bp of Llan High Sch 74-78; V Griffithstown *Mon* 78-86; Dioc Dir RE 86-91; TR Cwmbran 86-95; Hon Can St Woolos Cathl 88-91; Can St Woolos Cathl 91-12; V Caerleon 95-02; V Caerleon w Llanhennock 02-09; V Caerleon and Llanfrechfa 09-12; AD Newport 98-09; rtd 12; P-in-c Mynyddislwyn *Mon* 12-14. *31 Candwr Park, Ponthir, Newport NP18 1HL* T: (01633) 430768

EDWARDS, Carl Flynn. b 63. Cranmer Hall Dur 03. **d** 05 **p** 06. C Scartho *Linc* 05-09; P-in-c Fairfield *Derby* from 09; C Buxton w Burbage and King Sterndale 09-12; P-in-c Peak Forest and Dove Holes from 12. *Fairfield Vicarage, Cherry Tree Drive, Fairfield, Buxton SK17 7JN* T: (01298) 23629 E: carl.mara@tiscali.co.uk *or* revcarl@live.co.uk

EDWARDS, Miss Carol Rosemary. b 46. Trin Coll Bris 74. **dss** 81 **d** 87 **p** 94. Dn-in-c Brislington St Chris *Bris* 87-94; P-in-c 94-99; P-in-c Brislington St Chris and St Cuth 99-00; Hon Can Bris Cathl 93-00; P-in-c California *Ox* 00-10; rtd 10; PtO *B & W* from 11. *44 Godwin Drive, Nailsea, Bristol BS48 2XF* T: (01275) 858168 M: 07879-536218 E: carol.edwards789@btinternet.com

EDWARDS, Charles Grayson. b 37. Macalester Coll (USA) BSc 59. Ripon Hall Ox 64. **d** 66 **p** 67. C Bletchley *Ox* 66-68; C Ware St Mary *St Alb* 68-73; TV Basingstoke *Win* 73-80; P-in-c Sandford w Upton Hellions *Ex* 80-82; R 82-94; PtO from 95; rtd 97. *The Peak, Higher Road, Crediton EX17 2EU* T: (01363) 772530

EDWARDS, Christopher Alban. b 27. Hertf Coll Ox. Th Ext Educn Coll. **d** 89 **p** 92. C Pietersburg Ch Ch S Africa 89; C Montagu 90-96; C Harare Cathl Zimbabwe 96-01; PtO *Ripon* 01; *York* from 01. *1 Hastings House, Holyrood Lane, Ledsham, South Milford, Leeds LS25 5LL* T: (01977) 682117 M: 07780-543114 E: chrisalban@btopenworld.com

EDWARDS, David Arthur. b 26. Wadh Coll Ox BA 50 MA 51. Wycliffe Hall Ox 50. **d** 52 **p** 53. C Didsbury St Jas and Em *Man* 52-55; Liv Sec CECS 55-58; Chapl Liv Univ 55-58; R Burnage St Nic *Man* 58-65; V Yardley St Edburgha *Birm* 65-73; Org Sec CECS Blackb, Carl and Man 73-78; R Man Resurr 78-81; V Lorton and Loweswater w Buttermere *Carl* 81-87; USPG 87-92; Malaysia 87-92; rtd 92; PtO *Carl* from 00. *Wood Close, 11 Springs Road, Keswick CA12 4AQ* T: (01768) 780274

EDWARDS, David John. b 60. Loughb Univ BA 81 Homerton Coll Cam PGCE 82 Kent Univ MA 95. CA Tr Coll 86 EAMTC 94. **d** 95 **p** 96. C High Ongar w Norton Mandeville *Chelmsf* 95-98; Prin Taylor Coll Saint John Canada 98-05; P-in-c Saint John St Jas 98-00; R Saint John St Mark (Stone D) from 00. *31 Carlile Crescent, Saint John NB E2J 5C3, Canada* T: (001) (506) 634 1474 E: david.edwards@anglican.nb.ca

EDWARDS, The Very Revd David Lawrence. b 29. OBE 95. Magd Coll Ox BA 52 MA 56 Lambeth DD 90. Westcott Ho Cam 53. **d** 54 **p** 55. Fell All So Coll Ox 52-59; Tutor Westcott Ho Cam 54-55; SCM Sec 55-58; C Hampstead St Jo *Lon* 55-58; C St Martin-in-the-Fields 58-66; Ed SCM Press 59-66; Gen Sec SCM 65-66; Dean K Coll Cam 66-70; Six Preacher Cant Cathl 69-76; Can Westmr Abbey 70-78; I Westmr St Marg 70-78; Chapl to Speaker of Ho of Commons 72-78; Sub Dean Westmr 74-78; Chmn Chr Aid 71-78; Dean Nor 78-83; Provost S'wark 83-94; rtd 94; PtO *Win* 95-14; Hon Chapl Win Cathl from 95. *4 Morley College, Market Street, Winchester SO23 9LF*

EDWARDS, Canon Diana Clare. b 56. Nottm Univ BTh 86 SRN 77 RSCN 81. Linc Th Coll 83. **dss** 86 **d** 87 **p** 94. S Wimbledon H Trin and St Pet *S'wark* 86-90; Par Dn 87-90; Par Dn Lingfield and Crowhurst 90-94; C 94-95; Chapl St Piers Hosp Sch Lingfield 90-95; R Bletchingley *S'wark* 95-04; RD Godstone 98-04; Hon Can S'wark Cathl 01-04; Dean of Women's Min 03-04; Can Res Cant Cathl from 04. *22 The Precincts, Canterbury CT1 2EP* T: (01227) 865227 E: canonclare@canterbury-cathedral.org

EDWARDS (née DALLISON), Canon Frances Mary. b 39. RSCN 61 SRN 64. Cranmer Hall Dur IDC 71. **d** 92 **p** 94. NSM Skerton St Chad *Blackb* 92-97; Asst Chapl R Albert Hosp Lanc 92-94; Chapl 94-96; Regional Co-ord (NW) Ch Action on Disability 96-04; Hon Can Blackb Cathl 00-04; rtd 04; PtO *Blackb* from 04. *9 Rochester Avenue, Morecambe LA4 4RH* T: (01524) 421224 F: 413661 E: frances@floray.fsnet.co.uk

EDWARDS, Preb Geraint Wyn. b 47. Univ of Wales (Ban) BTh 93. St D Coll Lamp. **d** 71 **p** 72. C Llandudno *Ban* 71-73; C Ban St Mary 73-74; V Penisarwaen and Llanddeiniolen 74-77; V Llandinorwig w Penisarwaen and Llanddeiniolen 77-78; R Llanfechell w Bodewryd w Rhosbeirio etc 78-13; RD Twrcelyn 94-01; AD 01-11; Hon Can Ban Cathl 97-99; Prec 99-11; Preb 11-13; rtd 13; PtO *Ban* from 13. *14 Y Fron Estate, Cemaes Bay LL67 0LW* E: geraintedwards@fsmail.net

EDWARDS, Canon Gerald Lalande. b 30. Bris Univ MEd 72. Glouc Th Course 75. **d** 76 **p** 76. NSM Pittville All SS *Glouc* 76-79; NSM Cheltenham St Mich 79-96; Hon Can Glouc Cathl 91-96; rtd 96; PtO *Glouc* 96-97. *26 Monica Drive, Cheltenham GL50 4NQ* T: (01242) 516863

EDWARDS, Graham Charles. b 40. Qu Coll Birm 80. **d** 82 **p** 83. C Baswich *Lich* 82-86; C Tamworth 86-88; R Hertford St Andr *St Alb* 88-05; RD Hertford and Ware 96-99; rtd 05; PtO *Lich* from 06. *2 The Old Forge, Main Road, Great Haywood, Stafford ST18 0RZ* T: (01889) 882868

EDWARDS, Guy. *See* EDWARDS, Jonathan Guy

EDWARDS, Harold James. b 50. Lon Univ CertEd 72. Ridley Hall Cam 84 Qu Coll Birm 78. **d** 81 **p** 82. NSM The Quinton *Birm* 81-84; C Highters Heath 84-85; V Llanwddyn and Llanfihangel-yng-Nghwynfa etc *St As* 85-88; V Ford *Heref* 88-97; V Alberbury w Cardeston 88-97; Chapl Team Ldr Severn Hospice from 96; PtO *St As* from 13. *Severn Hospice, Bicton Heath, Shrewsbury SY3 8HS* T: (01743) 236565 M: 07713-639447 E: harrye@severnhospice.org.uk

EDWARDS, Harry Steadman. b 37. St Aid Birkenhead 64. **d** 66 **p** 67. Hon C Handsworth St Jas *Birm* 66-83; Hon C Curdworth w Castle Vale 83-85; P-in-c Small Heath St Greg 85-88; V High Crompton *Man* 88-98; rtd 98; PtO *Man* from 99. *42 Manor Road, Shaw, Oldham OL2 7JJ* T: (01706) 672820

EDWARDS, Helen. *See* HINGLEY, Helen

EDWARDS (née BENNETT), Canon Helen Anne. b 69. Coll of Ripon & York St Jo BEd 91 Bris Univ BA 01. Trin Coll Bris 99. **d** 01 **p** 02. C Beverley Minster *York* 01-05; P-in-c Liv Ch Ch Norris Green 05-09; V from 09; Hon Can Liv Cathl from 13. *4 Christchurch Close, Liverpool L11 3EN* T: 0151-474 1444 E: helenedwards@ymail.com

EDWARDS, Helen Glynne. *See* WEBB, Helen Glynne

EDWARDS, Canon Henry Victor. b 48. AKC 71 Open Univ BA 85 Middx Univ MSc 00. St Aug Coll Cant 72. **d** 73 **p** 74. C W Leigh CD *Portsm* 73-77; V Cosham 77-84; V Reydon *St E* 84-86; V Blythburgh w Reydon 86-96; Chapl St Felix Sch Southwold 86-96; Chapl Blythburgh Hosp 86-96; P-in-c Campsea Ashe w Marlesford, Parham and Hacheston *St E* 96-00; R 00-14; P-in-c Brandeston w Kettleburgh and Easton 07-14; Hon Can St E Cathl 00-14; rtd 14; PtO *St E* from 14; Dioc Adv for Counselling and Past Care from 96. *Dunwich View, The Green, Walberswick, Southwold IP18 6TP* T: (01502) 722928 M: 07748-986022 E: harry@psalm23.demon.co.uk

EDWARDS, Herbert Joseph. b 29. Nottm Univ BA 51. Wells Th Coll 54. **d** 56 **p** 57. C Leic St Pet 56-61; C-in-c Broom Leys CD 61-64; V Broom Leys 65-68; Lect Lich Th Coll 68-71; Rhodesia 71-79; Botswana 74-75; V Bloxwich *Lich* 80-84; R Asfordby *Leic* 84-92; R N w S Kilworth and Misterton 92-96; rtd 96; PtO *Leic* from 97; *Lich* from 00. *Beechfields Nursing Home, 1 Wissage Road, Lichfield WS13 6EJ* T: (01543) 418351 *or* 418354

EDWARDS, Canon James Frederick. b 36. ALCD 62. **d** 62 **p** 63. C Kenwyn *Truro* 62-68; V Tuckingmill 68-76; V St Columb Minor and St Colan 76-01; RD Pydar 84-93; Hon Can Truro Cathl 92-01; rtd 01; PtO *Truro* from 01. *45 Tretherras Road, Newquay TR7 2TF* T: (01637) 870967

EDWARDS, Jane. *See* EDWARDS, Wendy Jane

EDWARDS, Janet Margaret. b 41. TCert 62 Lon Bible Coll BD 73. WEMTC 98. **d** 01 **p** 02. NSM Coalbrookdale, Iron-Bridge and Lt Wenlock *Heref* from 01. *2 Madeley Wood View, Madeley, Telford TF7 5TF* T: (01952) 583254

EDWARDS, Mrs Jill Kathleen. b 48. Man Univ BA 69 CQSW 72. S'wark Ord Course 90. **d** 93 **p** 95. NSM Grays Thurrock and Ind Chapl *Chelmsf* 93-07; Asst Dioc Soc Resp Officer *Truro* from 07; Public Preacher 07-08; P-in-c Gerrans w St Anthony-in-Roseland and Philleigh from 08. *Trelowen, Rosevine, Portscatho, Truro TR2 5EW* T: (01872) 580117 E: jill@jilledwards.com

EDWARDS, Joe. *See* EDWARDS, Andrew Jonathan Hugo

EDWARDS, Joel Kim. b 69. Oak Hill Th Coll BA 02. **d** 09 **p** 10. NSM Leyton Ch Ch *Chelmsf* 09-14; PtO 14-15; P-in-c Dagenham from 15. *The Vicarage, Church Lane, Dagenham RM10 9UL* M: 07903-516456 T: (020) 8215 2962 E: joel.dagenham@gmail.com

EDWARDS, Canon John Ralph. b 50. Bris Univ BSc 71 FCA 74. SAOMC 98. **d** 01 **p** 02. NSM California *Ox* 01-06; NSM Finchampstead 06-11; NSM Finchampstead and California from 11; Hon Can Ch Ch from 13. *Green Hedges, 25 St John's Street, Crowthorne RG45 7NJ* T: (01344) 774586 F: 774056 M: 07850-602488

EDWARDS, Jonathan Guy. b 63. Bris Univ BA 85. Ridley Hall Cam BA 93 MA 96. d 94 p 95. C Preston Plucknett *B & W* 94-98; C Clevedon St Andr and Ch Ch 98-02; V Farrington Gurney 02-06; V Paulton 02-06; P-in-c High Littleton 05-06; V Paulton w Farrington Gurney and High Littleton from 07. *The Vicarage, Church Street, Paulton, Bristol BS39 7LG* T: (01761) 416581 E: guyedwards455@btinternet.com

EDWARDS, Joseph. *See* EDWARDS, Herbert Joseph

EDWARDS, Judith Sarah. *See* McARTHUR-EDWARDS, Judith Sarah

EDWARDS (née EVANS), Mrs Linda Mary. b 49. Univ of Wales (Cardiff) BA 71 K Coll Lon BD 74 AKC 74. Yale Div Sch STM 76. dss 76 d 80 p 99. Llanishen and Lisvane *Llan* 76-78; Wrexham *St As* 78-80; C 80-82; Chapl Maudsley Hosp Lon 82-84; Chapl Bethlem R Hosp Beckenham 82-84; Chapl Lon Univ 84-87; NSM Llanfair-pwll and Llanddaniel-fab etc *Ban* 99-03; P-in-c Llangynog *St As* 03-06; C Llanrhaeadr ym Mochnant etc 07-10; rtd 10; PtO *St As* from 14. *15 The Meadows, Llandudno Junction LL31 9LP* T: (01492) 585063 E: eleme@tiscali.co.uk

EDWARDS, Lynda. b 67. Qu Coll Birm. d 11 p 12. NSM Allesley *Cov* 11-15; NSM Meriden from 15. *3 Torbay Road, Coventry CV5 9JY* T: (024) 7671 3235

EDWARDS, Malcolm Ralph. b 27. Man Univ 49. Cranmer Hall Dur 57. d 59 p 60. C Withington St Paul *Man* 59-62; C Chadderton Em 62-64; R Longsight St Jo 64-70; V Halliwell St Thos 70-81; V Milnrow 81-92; rtd 92; PtO *Man* from 92. *20 Upper Lees Drive, Westhoughton, Bolton BL5 3UE* T: (01942) 813279

EDWARDS, Mrs Marie. b 73. NEOC 06. d 09 p 10. NSM Middlesbrough St Agnes *York* from 09; Chapl S Tees Hosps NHS Trust from 13. *76 Hesleden Avenue, Middlesbrough TS5 8RN* T: (01642) 509381 M: 07908-608605 E: medwards15@ntlworld.com

EDWARDS, Mark Anthony. b 61. MBE 10. Cranmer Hall Dur 91. d 95 p 97. C Ulverston St Mary w H Trin *Carl* 95-97; C Barrow St Jo 97-00; TV Barrow St Matt 00-08; TV Ch the King *Newc* from 08; Chapl Northumbria Police 08-12. *The Vicarage, 2 East Acres, Dinnington, Newcastle upon Tyne NE13 7NA* T: (01661) 872320 E: hayden@fox9411.freeserve.co.uk

EDWARDS, Mrs Mary. b 47. St Jo Coll York CertEd 69 Birkbeck Coll Lon BSc 74 New Coll Edin BD 93. S Dios Minl Tr Scheme 96. d 96 p 97. NSM Avon Valley *Sarum* 96-00; TV Wexcombe 00-02; TV Savernake 02-12; RD Pewsey 10-12; rtd 12. *The Coach House, Glenmayne, Galashiels TD1 3NR* T: (01896) 668383 E: mary_avonvalley@hotmail.com

EDWARDS, Michael Norman William. b 34. Bp Gray Coll Cape Town 61 St Paul's Coll Grahamstown 62. d 63 p 65. C Woodstock S Africa 63-66; C Plumstead 66-69; P-in-c Lansdowne All SS 69-72; R Hoetjes Bay 73-78; R Parrow St Marg 78-80; Chapl Tristan da Cunha 81-83; R Aston-on-Trent and Weston-on-Trent *Derby* 84-87; V Derby St Thos 87-95; P-in-c Blackwell 95-01; rtd 01; PtO *Win* from 02. *16 Ridley Close, Holbury, Southampton SO45 2NR* T: (023) 8089 2924 E: mnwedwards.novaforest@googlemail.com

EDWARDS, Preb Nicholas John. b 53. UEA BA 75 Fitzw Coll Cam BA 77 MA 80. Westcott Ho Cam 75. d 78 p 79. C Kirkby *Liv* 78-81; V Cantril Farm 81-87; V Hale 87-94; R Chingford SS Pet and Paul *Chelmsf* 94-04; R Colyton, Musbury, Southleigh and Branscombe *Ex* 04-10; P-in-c Ex St Thos and Em from 10; Preb Ex Cathl from 13. *Emmanuel Vicarage, 49 Okehampton Road, Exeter EX4 1EL* T: (01392) 202583 E: nicholas_edwards@ntlworld.com

EDWARDS, Mrs Nita Mary. b 50. Univ of Wales (Ban) BD 72 Nottm Univ PGCE 73. Cranmer Hall Dur 93. d 93 p 94. C Ormesby *York* 93-95; C Billingham St Aid *Dur* 95-97; V 97-02; V Clayton *Lich* from 02. *The Vicarage, Clayton Lane, Newcastle ST5 3DW* T/F: (01782) 614500 E: nita.edwards@ntlworld.com

EDWARDS, Mrs Patricia Anne. b 52. EMMTC 76. dss 79 d 87 p 94. Hon Par Dn Clifton *S'well* 87-91; NSM Edwalton 91-12; NSM E and W Leake, Stanford-on-Soar, Rempstone etc from 12. *Le Petit Champ, Widmerpool Road, Wysall, Nottingham NG12 5QW* T: (01509) 880385

EDWARDS, Canon Peter Clive. b 50. Lon Univ BA 72. St Steph Ho Ox 83. d 85 p 86. C Lee St Aug *S'wark* 85-90; V Salfords 90-97; R Newington St Mary 97-03; Chapl Costa Blanca *Eur* 04-09; Sen Chapl 09-15; Hon Can 12-15; rtd 15. *Apdo Correos 158, 03420 Castalla (Alicante), Spain* T: (0034) 966 560 716 E: pce11@yahoo.com

EDWARDS, Peter Daniel. b 81. St Aid Coll Dur BA 02 Peterho Cam BA 09. Ridley Hall Cam 07. d 10 p 11. C Gt Malvern St Mary *Worc* 10-14. *107 Court Road, Malvern WR14 3EF* T: (01684) 563077 E: peter.edwards@cantab.net

EDWARDS, Peter Richard Henderson. b 65. Nottm Univ BA 86. St Steph Ho Ox 03. d 05 p 06. C Uppingham w Ayston and Wardley w Belton *Pet* 05-08; TV Bridport *Sarum* 08-13; P-in-c Bath Bathwick *B & W* from 13. *The Rectory, Sham Castle Lane, Bath BA2 6JL* E: frpeteredwards@sky.com

EDWARDS, Canon Philip John. b 28. Lon Univ MRCS 51 LRCP 51. Chich Th Coll 58. d 60 p 61. C Orpington St Andr *Roch* 60-67; C Mayfield *Chich* 67-71; V Haywards Heath St Rich 71-91; Can and Preb Chich Cathl 84-91; rtd 91; PtO *Chich* from 91. *22 Hamsey Road, Sharpthorne, East Grinstead RH19 4PA* T: (01342) 810210

EDWARDS, Phillip Gregory. b 52. Lon Univ BSc 73 ARCS 73 MSOSc 90. Qu Coll Birm 78. d 81 p 82. C Lillington *Cov* 81-85; P-in-c Cov St Alb 85-86; TV Cov E 86-01; C Bury St Paul and Bury Ch King *Man* 01-03; Chapl Bolton Univ 03-15; C Westhoughton and Wingates 04-05; C Leverhulme 05-07; Lic Preacher from 11. *St Stephen and All Martyrs Vicarage, Radcliffe Road, Bolton BL2 1NZ* T: (01204) 528300 E: phil@edwards.clara.co.uk

EDWARDS, Richard John. b 47. Univ of Qld BA 85. St Fran Coll Brisbane 83. d 85 p 85. C St Lucia Australia 85-87; C Olveston *Bris* 87-88; R N Pine Australia 88-96; R Kingston St Mary w Broomfield etc *B & W* 96-10; rtd 10. *PO Box 181, Franklin Tas 7113, Australia*

EDWARDS, Robert James. b 52. Chich Univ BA 07. Cranmer Hall Dur 01. d 03 p 04. C Broadwater *Chich* 03-08; TV Southgate from 08. *Holy Trinity House, Titmus Drive, Crawley RH10 5EU* T: (01293) 618214 E: rev.rob@ctlconnect.co.uk

EDWARDS, Roger Brian. b 41. Sarum & Wells Th Coll 87. d 89 p 90. C Wellington and Distr *B & W* 89-92; V Hursley and Ampfield *Win* 92-06; rtd 06; PtO *Win* from 06. *34 Heatherstone Avenue, Dibden Purlieu, Southampton SO45 4LH* T: (023) 8087 9689 E: rogerbedwards@yahoo.co.uk

EDWARDS, Canon Rowland Thomas. b 62. Univ of Wales BTh 91. St Mich Coll Llan 85. d 88 p 89. C Llangiwg *S & B* 88-90; C Morriston 90-91; V Llangorse, Cathedine, Llanfihangel Talyllyn etc 91-01; V Llyn Safaddan 01-06; V Talgarth w Bronllys w Llanfilo from 06; AD Hay from 02; Can Res Brecon Cathl from 08. *The Vicarage, Bronllys, Brecon LD3 0HS* T: (01874) 711200

EDWARDS, Rupert Quintin. b 67. Bris Univ LLB 89. Wycliffe Hall Ox BTh 94. d 97 p 98. C Bromley Ch Ch *Roch* 97-00; C Hammersmith St Paul *Lon* 00-02; Hon C 06-11; Hon C Shadwell St Paul w Ratcliffe St Jas from 11. *27 Ropemakers Fields, London E14 8BX* T: (020) 7680 2772 E: ropefield@gmail.com

EDWARDS, Canon Ruth Blanche. b 39. Girton Coll Cam BA 61 MA 65 PhD 68 Aber Coll of Educn PGCE 75. Ab Dioc Tr Course 77. d 87 p 94. Lect Aber Univ *Ab* 77-90; Sen Lect 90-96; NSM Aberdeen St Jas 87-88; NSM Aberdeen St Jo 88-96; Lect Ripon Coll Cuddesdon 96-99; Hon Can St Andr Cathl from 97; rtd 00; NSM Aberdeen St Jas *Ab* from 00. *99 Queen's Den, Aberdeen AB15 8BN* T: (01224) 312688

EDWARDS, Mrs Sandra May. b 48. STETS 96. d 99 p 01. NSM Denmead *Portsm* 99-05; P-in-c 05-06; V from 06. *The Vicarage, Ludcombe, Waterlooville PO7 6TL* T: (023) 9225 5490 E: sandra@pinoy.fsnet.co.uk

EDWARDS, Scott. b 71. Wolv Univ LLB 93 St Jo Coll Dur BA 00. Cranmer Hall Dur 97. d 00 p 01. C Halas *Worc* 00-03; V Frimley Green and Mytchett *Guildf* 03-12; V Chessington from 12. *The Vicarage, 1 Garrison Lane, Chessington KT9 2LB* T: (020) 8397 3016 E: scott_edwards@btinternet.com

EDWARDS, Stephen. b 44. S'wark Ord Course. d 82 p 83. C Benhilton *S'wark* 82-86; P-in-c Clapham Ch Ch and St Jo 86-87; TV Clapham Team 87-94; Chapl HM Pris Wormwood Scrubs 94-96; Chapl HM Pris Maidstone 96-01; Chapl HM Pris Wandsworth 01-04; rtd 04; PtO *S'wark* from 04. *12 Bucharest Road, London SW18 3AR* T: (020) 8870 1991

EDWARDS, Stephen Michael. b 72. Lanc Univ BSc 93 Anglia Poly Univ MA 99. Westcott Ho Cam 93. d 96 p 97. C Colwyn Bay *St As* 96-99; C Colwyn 99-02; P-in-c Brynymaen 99-02; P-in-c Birch-in-Rusholme St Agnes w Longsight St Jo etc *Man* 02-12; R 12; TR Wythenshawe from 12; AD Withington from 13. *William Temple Vicarage, Robinswood Road, Manchester M22 0BU* T: 0161-437 3194 E: revstephenedwards@hotmail.com

EDWARDS, Steven Charles. b 58. Lanc Univ BSc 82 PhD 86. Linc Th Coll 94. d 94 p 95. C Bradshaw *Man* 94-98; P-in-c Bolton Breightmet St Jas 98-04; TR Walkden and Lt Hulton 04-10; rtd 10; PtO *Man* from 10; *Blackb* from 12. *9 Stocks Courts, 2 Harriet Street, Worsley, Manchester M28 3JW* E: steve@sajm.net

EDWARDS, Stuart. b 46. Lanc Univ BA 73. Kelham Th Coll 66. d 71 p 72. C Skerton St Luke *Blackb* 71-76; C Ribbleton 76-80; TV 80-82; V Blackb St Mich w St Jo and H Trin 82-91;

V Blackpool H Cross 91-12; RD Blackpool 93-94; P-in-c S Shore St Pet 00-05; rtd 12. *221 Heysham Road, Heysham, Morecambe LA3 1NN*

EDWARDS, Mrs Susan. b 54. R Holloway Coll Lon BSc 75 SS Hild & Bede Coll Dur PGCE 76. Qu Coll Birm 78. **dss** 81 **d** 87 **p** 94. Lillington *Cov* 81-85; Cov E 85-01; Par Dn 87-94; C 94-01; P-in-c Woolfold *Man* 01-07; TV Leverhulme 07-12; TR from 12. *St Stephen and All Martyrs Vicarage, Radcliffe Road, Bolton BL2 1NZ* T: (01204) 528300
E: sue@edwards.clara.co.uk

EDWARDS, Mrs Susan Diane. b 48. St Alb Minl Tr Scheme 86 Cranmer Hall Dur 91. **d** 92 **p** 94. Par Dn Borehamwood *St Alb* 92-94; C 94-96; V Arlesey w Astwick 96-13; rtd 13. *31 School Road, Meadowbank, Winsford CW7 2PG*
E: susan.d.edwards@ntlworld.com

EDWARDS, Timothy Mark. b 79. St Aid Coll Dur BA 00. Oak Hill Th Coll MA 12. **d** 12 **p** 13. C Eden, Gelt and Irthing *Carl* from 12. *The New Vicarage, Irthington, Carlisle CA6 4NJ*
M: 07980-826365 T: (016977) 41864
E: timothy.mark.edwards@gmail.com

EDWARDS, Wendy Jane. b 49. Bingley Coll of Educn CertEd 71 Kent Univ BA 07. SEITE 03. **d** 06 **p** 07. C Riverhead w Dunton Green *Roch* 06-11; P-in-c Belvedere All SS 11-12; V from 12. *c/o Crockford, Church House, Great Smith Street, London SW1P 3AZ* M: 07858-483652
E: revjaneedwards@btinternet.com

EDWARDSON, Joseph Philip. b 28. Dur Univ BA 52 Leeds Univ PGCE 53. Wells Th Coll 61. **d** 63 **p** 64. C Macclesfield St Mich *Ches* 63-66; V Egremont St Jo 66-72; V Eastham 72-81; V Poulton 81-94; rtd 94; PtO *Ches* from 94. *Keppler, 38 Hazel Grove, Irby, Wirral CH61 4UZ* T: 0151-648 2661

EDY, Robert James. b 48. Southn Univ BA 70 CertEd 71. Ox Min Course 90. **d** 93 **p** 94. Dep Hd Master Henry Box Sch Witney 90-08; NSM Ducklington *Ox* 93-99; P-in-c 99-13; R 13-15; PtO from 15; Chapl Rendcomb Coll Cirencester from 15. *The Rectory Cottage, Rendcomb, Cirencester GL7 7EZ* T: (01285) 831391 E: bobedy21@gmail.com

EDYE, Ian Murray. b 21. K Coll Lon BD AKC. S'wark Ord Course 66. **d** 69 **p** 70. NSM E Grinstead St Swithun *Chich* 69-00; PtO 00-02. *Bramcote House, Town Street, Bramcote, Nottingham NG9 3DP* T: 0115-925 7316

EFIRD, David Hampton. b 74. Duke Univ (USA) BA 94 Princeton Th Sem MDiv 98 Edin Univ MSc 99 Ox Univ DPhil 02. Yorks Min Course 08. **d** 10 **p** 11. NSM York Minster 10-13; NSM York St Clem w St Mary Bishophill from 13. *1 Bleachfield, Heslington, York YO10 5DB* T: (01904) 323226 *or* 433266 M: 07930-754045 E: david.efird@york.ac.uk

EGAR, Miss Judith Anne. b 57. Somerville Coll Ox BA 79 MA 84 Solicitor 83. STETS 01. **d** 04 **p** 05. NSM Brighton St Nic *Chich* 04-07; LtO 09-12; NSM Lewes St Anne and St Mich and St Thos etc from 15; PtO *Lon* 08-10; NSM Lewes All SS, St Anne, St Mich and St Thos *Chich* from 15. *15 St Peter's Place, Lewes BN7 1YP*

EGERTON, George. b 28. S'wark Ord Course 70. **d** 73 **p** 74. NSM Shere *Guildf* 73-94; PtO from 94. *Weyside, Lower Street, Shere, Guildford GU5 9HX* T: (01483) 202549

EGERTON, Mrs Susan Doreen. b 52. MCSP 75. **d** 09 **p** 10. OLM Surrey Weald *Guildf* 09-15; rtd 15. *Hollington, Horsham Road, Capel, Dorking RH5 5LF* T: (01306) 711299

EGGLESTON, Hugh Patrick. b 60. LSE BSc(Econ) 82 Leeds Univ BA 10. Coll of Resurr Mirfield 08. **d** 10 **p** 11. C E Dulwich St Jo *S'wark* 10-14; TR Thamesmead from 14. *Thamesmead Rectory, 22 Manor Close, London SE28 8EY* T: (020) 8310 6814 M: 07788-563253 E: peggleston@ymail.com

EGGLETON, Michael John. b 50. SAOMC 96 ERMC 06. **d** 07 **p** 08. NSM Northchurch and Wigginton *St Alb* from 07. *St Bartholomew's Vicarage, Vicarage Road, Wigginton, Tring HP23 6DZ* T: (01442) 823273 M: 07962-145398
E: mikeeggleton7@btopenworld.com

EGHTEDARIAN, Mohammad Reza. b 76. Wycliffe Hall Ox 12. **d** 15. C Liv Cathl from 15. *Liverpool Cathedral, St James Road, Liverpool L1 7AZ* M: 07709-903764
E: mohammad.e@liverpoolcathedral.org.uk

EGLIN, Ian Charles. b 55. St Jo Coll Dur BA 76. Coll of Resurr Mirfield 77. **d** 79 **p** 80. C Cov St Mary 79-83; TV Kingsthorpe w Northampton St Dav *Pet* 83-87; P-in-c Pitsford w Boughton 85-87; Chapl RN 87-03; V Ipplepen, Torbryan and Denbury *Ex* 03-12; RD Newton Abbot and Ipplepen 07-12; rtd 12. *27 Riverside Walk, Yealmpton, Plymouth PL8 2LU* T: (01752) 881996 E: ianeglin@talktalk.net

EJIAKU, Sebastian Chidozie. b 58. Herts Univ MSc 95. NTMTC 02. **d** 05 **p** 06. NSM Hoxton St Jo w Ch Ch *Lon* 05-09; NSM St John-at-Hackney from 09. *13 Dellwood Gardens, Clayhall, Ilford IG5 0EH* M: 07952-950681 T: (020) 8550 9715 E: sejiaku123@btinternet.com

EJINKONYE, Prorenata Emeka. b 52. **d** 08 **p** 09. OLM Victoria Docks St Luke *Chelmsf* 08-10; Hon C from 10. *26 Boreham Avenue, London E16 3AG* T: (020) 3538 5076
E: emeka12@hotmail.com

EKIN, Tom Croker. b 29. Linc Th Coll 59. **d** 60 **p** 61. C Leamington Priors All SS *Cov* 60-63; R Ilmington w Stretton-on-Fosse 63-72; S Africa 72-77; R Moreton-in-Marsh w Batsford *Glouc* 77-83; R Moreton-in-Marsh w Batsford, Todenham etc 83-94; rtd 95; Hon C Theale and Englefield *Ox* 96-04; PtO *B & W* from 04. *6 Old Bell Court, Wrington, Bristol BS40 5QH* T: (01934) 862398

EL KISS MIHANNY, Canon Medhat Sabry. b 60. Cairo Univ BSc 83 San Francisco Th Sem DMin 02. Trin Coll Bris 83. **d** 86 **p** 87. C Alexandria St Mark Egypt 86-89; V Heliopolis St Mark 89-10; V Old Cairo Jes Light of the World 10-13; P-in-c Casablanca *Eur* from 13. *7 Impasse Chasseur Jules Gros, Quartier Oasis, 20100 Casablanca, Morocco* E: canonms@hotmail.com

EL SALVADOR, Bishop of. *See* BARAHONA, Martin de Jesus

ELBOURNE, Keith Marshall. b 46. Nottm Univ BTh 74 Lon Univ BD 76. St Jo Coll Nottm 70. **d** 74 **p** 75. C Romford Gd Shep *Chelmsf* 74-78; C Victoria Docks St Luke 78-81; P-in-c 81-92; V Walthamstow St Pet 92-02; TR Tettenhall Wood and Perton *Lich* 02-10; rtd 10; PtO *Lich* from 10. *11 Windsor Gardens, Codsall, Wolverhampton WV8 2EX*
E: keith.elbourne@dsl.pipex.com

ELBOURNE, Timothy. b 60. Selw Coll Cam BA 81 MA 85 PGCE 82. Westcott Ho Cam 84. **d** 86 **p** 87. C Tottenham H Trin *Lon* 86-88; Chapl York Univ 88-94; P-in-c Thorp Arch w Walton 94-98; Dir of Educn *Ely* 98-12; Hon Can Ely Cathl 99-12; Dir of Educn *Chelmsf* from 13; Public Preacher from 13. *10 Sherwood Way, Feering, Colchester CO5 9LJ*
T: (01245) 294400 F: 294477 P: (04325) 320796
E: telbourne@chelmsford.anglican.org

ELCOCK, Jonathan. b 64. Westcott Ho Cam 07. **d** 09 **p** 11. C Aberavon *Llan* 09; C Salford All SS *Man* 10-13; R Failsworth St Jo from 13. *St John's Rectory, Pole Lane, Failsworth, Manchester M35 9PB*

ELDER, Andrew John. b 49. Sunderland Poly BSc 72 MSc 76. NEOC 91. **d** 94 **p** 95. NSM Wallsend St Luke *Newc* 94-02; NSM Wallsend St Pet and St Luke 02-03; C Monkseaton St Pet 03-06; V Blyth St Mary from 06. *St Mary's Vicarage, 51 Marine Terrace, Blyth NE24 2JP* T: (01670) 353417
E: andy.elder@btinternet.com

ELDER, David. b 28. Brechin NSM Ord Course 75. **d** 79 **p** 80. NSM Dundee St Salvador *Bre* 79-93; rtd 93; P-in-c Dundee St Martin *Bre* 93-08; PtO from 09. *235 Arbroath Road, Dundee DD4 7PT* T: (01382) 827844

ELDER, Nicholas John. b 51. Hatf Poly BA 73. Cuddesdon Coll 73. **d** 76 **p** 77. C Mill End and Heronsgate w W Hyde *St Alb* 76-79; TV Borehamwood 79-85; V Bedford St Mich 85-90; V Bedford All SS 90-00; V Camberwell St Geo *S'wark* from 00; Warden Trin Coll Cen Camberwell from 00. *St George's Vicarage, 115 Wells Way, London SE5 7SZ* T: (020) 7703 2895 *or* 7703 9855 E: nicholas.elder@virgin.net

ELDERGILL, Sharon Alice. b 62. **d** 13 **p** 14. NSM Burnham *B & W* from 13. *Flat 4, 15 Esplanade, Burnham-on-Sea TA8 1BG*
E: sharon.eldergill@yahoo.co.uk

ELDRIDGE, John Frederick. b 48. Loughb Univ BSc 70 Golden Gate Sem (USA) MDiv 83 Fuller Th Sem California DMin 96. Oak Hill Th Coll 90. **d** 92 **p** 93. C Maidstone St Luke *Cant* 92-97; Min Prince's Park CD *Roch* 97-02; P-in-c Wickham Market w Pettistree *St E* 02-07; V from 07. *The Vicarage, Crown Lane, Wickham Market, Woodbridge IP13 0SA* T: (01728) 746026 E: jeldridge@supanet.com

ELDRIDGE, John Kenneth Tristan. b 59. St Steph Ho Ox 90. **d** 92 **p** 93. C Brighton Resurr *Chich* 92-96; C Hangleton 96-98; TR Moulsecoomb 98-05; V W Worthing St Jo from 05; Chapl Sussex Beacon Hospice from 00. *St John's Vicarage, 15 Reigate Road, Worthing BN11 5NF* T: (01903) 247340

ELDRIDGE, Stephen William. b 50. Open Univ BA 98. Chich Th Coll 87. **d** 89 **p** 90. C Stroud and Uplands w Slad *Glouc* 89-92; C Glouc St Mary de Crypt w St Jo and Ch Ch 92-95; C Glouc St Mary de Lode and St Nic 92-95; Bp's Chapl 92-93; P-in-c Kingswood w Alderley and Hillesley 95-00; P-in-c Cheltenham St Pet 00-08; TV N Cheltenham from 08. *St Peter's Vicarage, 375 Swindon Road, Cheltenham GL51 9LB* T/F: (01242) 524369 E: stephen.eldridge@northchelt.org.uk

ELEY, John Edward. b 49. Sarum & Wells Th Coll 74. **d** 77 **p** 78. C Sherborne w Castleton and Lillington *Sarum* 77-80; Min Can Carl Cathl 80-84; V Bromsgrove All SS *Worc* 84-88; PtO *St E* 90-98; V Stourhead 98-10; rtd 10. *5 Church Walks, Bury St Edmunds IP33 1NJ* T: (01284) 763564 M: 07783-584651 E: john.eley5@btopenworld.com

ELEYAE, Mrs Adeola Winifred. b 63. Lagos Univ LLB 85 LLM 90 Bris Univ LLM 13. St Mellitus Coll 11. **d** 14 **p** 15. NSM E Ham St Paul *Chelmsf* from 14. *6 Heather Drive, Romford RM1 4SP* T: (01708) 722562 M: 07821-710521
E: aweleyae333@gmail.com

266

ELFICK, Brian Richard. b 76. Ex Coll Ox BA 98 Selw Coll Cam BA 04 MPhil 05. Ridley Hall Cam 02. **d** 06 **p** 07. C Cambridge H Sepulchre *Ely* 06-12; TR Toxteth St Philemon w St Gabr and St Cleopas *Liv* from 12. *The Vicarage, 40 Devonshire Road, Toxteth L8 3TZ* E: brian.elfick@stag.org

ELFORD, Keith Anthony. b 59. Em Coll Cam BA 80 MA 84. Wycliffe Hall Ox 87. **d** 90 **p** 91. C Chertsey *Guildf* 90-94; P-in-c Ockham w Hatchford 94-98; Bp's Chapl 94-98; PtO 98-00; LtO from 01. *15 Canford Drive, Addlestone KT15 2HH* T: (01932) 885137 E: keith.elford@lineone.net

ELFORD, Canon Robert John. b 39. Man Univ MA 71 Ex Univ PhD 74. Brasted Th Coll 64 Ridley Hall Cam 66. **d** 68 **p** 69. C Denton St Lawr *Man* 68-71; P-in-c Gwinear *Truro* 71-74; R Phillack w Gwithian and Gwinear 74-78; Lect Man Univ 78-87; Hon C Withington St Paul *Man* 79-83; Warden St Anselm Hall 82-87; LtO *Man* 84-87; Pro-R Liv Inst of HE 88-99; Can Th Liv Cathl 92-04; rtd 04. *The Penthouse, 120 The Cliff, Wallasey CH45 2HW*

ELFRED, Michael William. b 48. BA 76 MPhil. Linc Th Coll 77. **d** 79 **p** 80. C Boultham *Linc* 79-82; C Croydon H Sav *Cant* 82-84; C Upper Norwood All SS *S'wark* 84-88; V Sanderstead St Mary 88-01; P-in-c Tadworth 01-11; V from 11. *The Vicarage, 1 The Avenue, Tadworth KT20 5AS* T: (01737) 813152 M: 07931-463661 E: michael.elfred@talk21.com

ELGAR, Richard John. b 50. Charing Cross Hosp Medical Sch MB, BS 73 LRCP 73 MRCS 73 MRCGP 80. St Jo Coll Nottm 92. **d** 92 **p** 93. NSM Derby St Alkmund and St Werburgh 92-96; P-in-c Derby St Barn 96-01; V 01-08; RD Derby N 05-06; rtd 08. *38 Holborn Drive, Derby DE22 4DX* T: (01332) 342553 or 344895 E: relgar1015@aol.com

ELIZABETH, The Ven Danny Rollan Henry. b 67. Seychelles Poly DipEd 87 Edith Cowan Univ (Aus) BEd 93 Rhodes Univ BTh 00. Coll of Transfiguration Grahamstown 97. **d** 99 **p** 00. R St Paul's Cathl Seychelles 00-05; PtO *Lon* 05-06; NSM Hanwell St Mellitus w St Mark 06-08; V Hayes St Anselm 08-10; Adn Seychelles from 10. *PO Box 44, Victoria, Mahe, Seychelles* E: dannyelizabeth@btinternet.com

ELIZABETH, Sister. *See* WEBB, Marjorie Valentine

ELIZABETH MARY, Sister. *See* NOLLER, Hilda Elizabeth Mary

ELKINGTON, The Ven Audrey Anne. b 57. St Cath Coll Ox BA 80 UEA PhD 83. St Jo Coll Nottm 85 EAMTC 86. **dss** 88 **d** 92 **p** 94. Monkseaton St Mary *Newc* 88-91; Ponteland 91-93; Par Dn 92-93; C Prudhoe 93-02; RD Corbridge 99-02; Bp's Adv for Women in Min 01-11; Bp's Chapl 02-11; Dir of Ords 02-11; Hon Can Newc Cathl 06-11; Adn Bodmin *Truro* from 11. *4 Park Drive, Bodmin PL31 2QF* T: (01208) 892811 M: 07766-822872 E: audrey@truro.anglican.org

ELKINGTON, Canon David John. b 51. Nottm Univ BTh 76 Leic Univ MEd 81 Dur Univ MATM 05. St Jo Coll Nottm 73. **d** 76 **p** 77. C Leic Martyrs 76-78; C Kirby Muxloe 78-80; Asst Chapl Leic Univ 80-82; Hon C Leic H Spirit 82; Chapl UEA *Nor* 82-88; TV Newc Epiphany 88-91; TR 91-93; P-in-c Prudhoe 93-98; V 98-02; Can Res Newc Cathl 02-11; C St Tudy w St Mabyn and Michaelstow *Truro* from 11; C Bodmin w Lanhydrock and Lanivet from 11; RD Trigg Minor and Bodmin from 13. *4 Park Drive, Bodmin PL31 2QF* T: (01208) 892811 E: djelk@btinternet.com

ELKINS, Alan Bernard. b 47. Sarum & Wells Th Coll 70. **d** 73 **p** 74. C Wareham *Sarum* 73-77; P-in-c Codford, Upton Lovell and Stockton 77-79; P-in-c Boyton w Sherrington 77-79; R Bishopstrow and Boreham 79-92; R Corfe Mullen 92-03; V W Byfleet *Guildf* 03-08; P-in-c 08-14; Bp's Adv for Spirituality 08-14; rtd 14; PtO *Nor* from 14. *4 The Lawn, Fakenham NR21 8DT* T: (01328) 855075 E: alanelkins@btinternet.com

ELKINS, Mrs Joy Kathleen. b 45. S Tr Scheme 93. **d** 96 **p** 97. NSM Corfe Mullen *Sarum* 96-03; NSM W Byfleet *Guildf* 03-08; C 08-14; rtd 14; PtO *Nor* from 14. *4 The Lawn, Fakenham NR21 8DT* T: (01328) 855075 E: joyelkins@btinternet.com

ELKINS, Canon Patrick Charles. b 34. St Chad's Coll Dur BA 57 DipEd 58. **d** 60 **p** 61. C Moordown *Win* 60-63; C Basingstoke 64-67; V Bransgore 67-04; Hon Can Win Cathl 89-04; rtd 04; PtO *Win* from 04. *1 Tyrrells Court, Bransgore, Christchurch BH23 8BU* T: (01425) 673103

ELKS, Roger Mark. b 60. Imp Coll Lon BSc 83. Wycliffe Hall Ox 89. **d** 92 **p** 93. C St Austell *Truro* 92-95; V Carbis Bay w Lelant 95-01; I Holywood *D & D* 01-15. *Address temp unknown* M: 07954-406680 E: vicarroger@ntlworld.com

ELLAM, Stuart William. b 53. Westcott Ho Cam. **d** 85 **p** 86. C Ditton St Mich *Liv* 85-88; C Greenford H Cross *Lon* 88-91; PtO 91-94. *243 St Leonards Road, Windsor SL4 3DR* T: (01753) 864827

ELLEM, Peter Keith. b 58. Nottm Univ BTh 90 Leeds Univ MA 99 CQSW. St Jo Coll Nottm 87. **d** 90 **p** 91. C Islington St Mary *Lon* 90-94; C Leeds St Geo *Ripon* 94-99; R Yagoona Australia from 00. *211 Auburn Road, Yagoona NSW 2199, Australia* T: (0061) (2) 9790 6281 F: 9796 6201 E: prellem@bigfoot.com

ELLENS, Gordon Frederick Stewart. b 26. Columbia Univ (NY) MPhil 62 PhD 68 FRAS. K Coll Lon BD 52 AKC 52 St Boniface Warminster 52. **d** 53 **p** 54. C Old Street St Luke w St Mary Charterhouse etc *Lon* 53-55; C Chiswick St Mich 55-57; Canada 57-60; USA 62-66; Asst Prof Relig St Sophia Univ Tokyo Japan 70-75; Rikkyo Women's Univ 75-84; Prof Humanities Ueno Gakueu 84-88; rtd 92. *45 Ullswater Drive, Tilehurst, Reading RG31 6RS*

ELLERTON, Mrs Mary Diane. b 45. RGN 67 Southn Univ RHV 68. NOC 90. **d** 93 **p** 94. NSM Upper Holme Valley *Leeds* from 93; TV from 10; Chapl Calderdale and Huddersfield NHS Foundn Trust from 01. *13 Liphill Bank Road, Holmfirth, Huddersfield HD9 2LQ* T: (01484) 684207 or 482266 or 343437 E: diane.ellerton@btopenworld.com

ELLERY, Arthur James Gabriel. b 28. St Jo Coll Dur BSc 49. Linc Th Coll 51. **d** 53 **p** 54. C Milton next Sittingbourne *Cant* 53-56; C St Laur in Thanet 56-58; C Darlington St Cuth *Dur* 58-62; V Tanfield 62-70; Chapl St Olave's Sch York 70-78; V Gt Ayton w Easby and Newton-in-Cleveland *York* 78-81; Chapl Bancroft's Sch Woodford Green 81-86; V Chipperfield St Paul *St Alb* 86-93; rtd 93; PtO *Pet* 93-05. *7 Church Drive, Orton Waterville, Peterborough PE2 5EX* T: (01733) 231800

ELLERY, Ian Martyn William. b 56. K Coll Lon BD AKC. Chich Th Coll. **d** 82 **p** 83. C Hornsey St Mary w St Geo *Lon* 82-85; V Choral York Minster 85-89; Subchanter 86-89; R Patrington w Hollym, Welwick and Winestead 89-97; TR Howden 97-05; RD 97-02; P-in-c Cawood w Ryther and Wistow 05-11; R from 11. *Cawood Vicarage, Rythergate, Cawood, Selby YO8 3TP* T: (01757) 268273 E: ianmwellery@hotmail.co.uk

ELLIN, Lindsey Jane. b 66. UEA BA 87 St Jo Coll Dur BA 92. Cranmer Hall Dur 90. **d** 93 **p** 94. C Bishopsworth *Bris* 93-96; PtO *Ely* 96-97; Hon C Cambridge St Mark 97-01; PtO *York* 01-07; Hon C Fulford 07-08; PtO *Dur* 08-09; Hon C Dur St Nic from 09. *1 Hastings Avenue, Durham DH1 3QG* T: 0191-374 0607 E: ljegoodhew@gmail.com

ELLINGTON, David John. b 39. Oriel Coll Ox BA 63 MA. Cuddesdon Coll 63. **d** 65 **p** 66. C Sheff St Mark Broomhall 65-68; C Timperley *Ches* 68-72; P-in-c Altrincham St Ju 72-74; V 74-80; P-in-c Ashley 82-86; rtd 86; PtO *Ches* 87-00. *Flat 1, 46 High Street, Woodstock OX20 1TG* T: (01993) 815808 E: davidellington@btinternet.com

ELLINGTON, Mrs Joanna Elisabeth. b 68. Leeds Univ BSc 89. Ripon Coll Cuddesdon. **d** 14 **p** 15. OLM The Cookhams *Ox* from 14. *Frith Coppice, Church Road, Cookham, Maidenhead SL6 9UH* M: 07787-178231 E: revjo.ellington@gmail.com

ELLIOT, Neil Robert Minto. b 63. Hatf Poly BEng 87 Herts Univ CertEd 93 Kingston Univ PhD 11. St Jo Coll Nottm 94. **d** 96 **p** 97. C Walbrook Epiphany *Derby* 96-00; Chapl Univ of Cen England in Birm 00-05; V Trail SS Andr and Geo Canada from 05. *St Andrew's Church, 1347 Pine Avenue, Trail BC V1R 4E7, Canada* T: (001) (250) 368 5581 E: rev.nelli@virgin.net

ELLIOT, William Brunton. b 41. Edin Dioc NSM Course 81. **d** 84 **p** 85. NSM Lasswade *Edin* 84-92; NSM Dalkeith 84-92; Assoc P Edin St Pet 92-94; R Selkirk 94-06; rtd 06; LtO *Edin* from 06. *157 Newbattle Abbey Crescent, Dalkeith EH22 3LR* T: 0131-663 1369 E: bille157@aol.com

ELLIOT-NEWMAN, Christopher Guy. b 43. Bede Coll Dur TCert 67 Hull Univ BTh 83 MEd 87. Westcott Ho Cam 67. **d** 70 **p** 71. C Ditton St Mich *Liv* 70-73; C Hazlemere *Ox* 73-77; R Stockton-on-the-Forest w Holtby and Warthill *York* 77-87; Dir of Educn *Cant* 87-94; P-in-c Warden w Newbrough *Newc* 99-01; PtO 95-99 and from 02. *15 Hextol Terrace, Hexham NE46 2DF* T: (01434) 600547 M: 07951-471189 E: christopher@firststandardltd.co.uk

ELLIOT, Anne. *See* ELLIOTT, Elizabeth Anne

ELLIOTT, Mrs Antonia. b 66. St Mellitus Coll BA 14. **d** 14 **p** 15. C N Farnborough *Guildf* from 14. *14 Wilton Court, Farnborough GU14 7EL* M: 07871-047490 E: antonia_elliott@btinternet.com

ELLIOTT, Ben. *See* ELLIOTT, William Henry Venn

ELLIOTT, Brian. b 49. Dur Univ BA 73. Coll of Resurr Mirfield 73. **d** 75 **p** 76. C Nunthorpe *York* 75-77; CF 77-09; Dep Asst Chapl Gen 96-09; rtd 09; PtO Cyprus and the Gulf from 09; PtO *Win* from 09; OCM from 09. *St Paul's Cathedral, PO Box 22014, 1516 Nicosia, Cyprus* T: (01904) 898941 E: brian@newpost.org

ELLIOTT, Christopher John. b 67. Southn Univ 93. Chich Th Coll 94. **d** 94 **p** 95. C Alton St Lawr *Win* 94-97; PtO *Guildf* 99-02. *77 Wickham Place, Church Crookham, Fleet GU52 6NQ* M: 07788-195548

ELLIOTT, Christopher John. b 44. Sarum Th Coll 66. **d** 69 **p** 70. C Walthamstow St Pet *Chelmsf* 69-71; C Witham 71-74; P-in-c Gt and Lt Bentley 74-80; R Colchester Ch Ch w St Mary V

80-85; R Sible Hedingham 85-93; V Leigh-on-Sea St Aid 93-98; P-in-c Thornton Gp *Linc* 98-01; RD Horncastle 98-01; P-in-c Gt Leighs *Chelmsf* 01-05; P-in-c Lt Leighs 01-05; P-in-c Lt Waltham 01-05; R Gt and Lt Leighs and Lt Waltham 05-06; RD Chelmsf N 04-06; rtd 06; PtO *Chelmsf* 06-10; P-in-c Middleton-in-Teesdale w Forest and Frith *Dur* 10-13; P-in-c Eggleston 10-13; PtO *St E* from 14. *20 Orchard Drive, Wickham Market, Woodbridge IP13 0RU* T: (01728) 747575
E: christopher@malus.co.uk

ELLIOTT, Colin David. b 32. AKC 55. **d** 56 **p** 57. C W Wickham St Jo *Cant* 56-59; C Dover St Mary 59-64; V Linton 64-66; V Gillingham H Trin *Roch* 66-81; V Belvedere All SS 81-88; V Bromley St Jo 88-97; rtd 97; PtO *S'wark* 98-14; *Roch* 99-03. *Flat 3, 160 George Lane, London SE13 6JF* T: (020) 8698 4901

ELLIOTT, David Reed. b 62. Lon Bible Coll BA 91. Oak Hill Th Coll 91. **d** 93 **p** 94. C Luton Lewsey St Hugh *St Alb* 93-98; Dioc Communications Officer 98-00; Chapl W Herts Hosps NHS Trust 07-10; Chapl Bucks Hosps NHS Trust from 10. *Wycombe Hospital, Queen Alexandra Road, High Wycombe HP11 2TT* T: (01494) 526161

ELLIOTT, Elizabeth Anne. b 52. Lon Bible Coll BA 03. STETS 09. **d** 11 **p** 12. NSM Pennington *Win* from 11. *19 Heron Close, Sway, Lymington SO41 6ET* M: 07553-552540
E: anne19elliott@gmail.com

ELLIOTT, Miss Eveline Mary. b 39. Bedf Coll Lon BA 60 Cam Univ 92 ALA 63. EAMTC 92. **d** 95 **p** 96. NSM Bury St Edmunds St Mary *St E* 95-97; NSM Lark Valley 97-07; rtd 07; PtO *St E* from 07. *4 St Michael's Close, Northgate Street, Bury St Edmunds IP33 1HT* T: (01284) 753592
E: me@larkvalley57.fsnet.co.uk

ELLIOTT, Gordon. b 25. St Aid Birkenhead 63. **d** 65 **p** 66. C Latchford St Jas *Ches* 65-68; C Bollington St Jo 68-70; V Dukinfield St Mark 70-73; TV Tenbury Wells *Heref* 74-78; V Bromfield 78-82; R Culmington w Onibury 78-82; V Stanton Lacy 78-82; P-in-c Withybrook w Copston Magna *Cov* 82-83; P-in-c Wolvey, Burton Hastings and Stretton Baskerville 82-83; V Wolvey w Burton Hastings, Copston Magna etc 83-90; rtd 90; PtO *Worc* from 90; *Heref* 90-95. *12 Handbury Road, Malvern WR14 1NN* T: (01684) 569388

ELLIOTT, Ian David. b 40. Qu Coll Cam BA 61 MA 65. Tyndale Hall Bris 64. **d** 66 **p** 67. C Halewood *Liv* 66-71; C Gt Crosby St Luke 71-74; C-in-c Dallam CD 74-80; V Dallam 80-83; TV Fazakerley Em 83-92; V Warrington H Trin 92-05; rtd 05; PtO *Carl* from 07. *High Bank, 1 West End Road, Orton, Penrith CA10 3RT* T: (015396) 24441 E: iandelliott@tiscali.co.uk

ELLIOTT, Jane. b 49. **d** 08 **p** 09. NSM Hatcham St Cath *S'wark* from 08. *13 Seymour Gardens, London SE4 2DN* T: (020) 7277 7968 E: jane.elliott@kcl.ac.uk

ELLIOTT, Mrs Joanna Margaret. b 64. Bris Univ BA 85. STETS 03. **d** 06 **p** 07. NSM Haywards Heath St Wilfrid *Chich* from 06. *20 Courtlands, Haywards Heath RH16 4JD* T: (01444) 413799 M: 07710-273299 E: joanna@ctsn.co.uk

ELLIOTT, John Andrew. b 44. ACIB 68. SAOMC 95. **d** 98 **p** 99. NSM Bedgrove *Ox* 98-01; C Modbury, Bigbury, Ringmore w Kingston etc *Ex* 01-09; rtd 09; PtO *Ex* from 10. *Little Cumery, Aveton Gifford, Kingsbridge TQ7 4NN* T: (01548) 830688

ELLIOTT, John Philip. b 37. MIChemE 61 MBIM Salford Univ CEng. Glouc Th Course 79. **d** 80 **p** 80. NSM Brimscombe *Glouc* 80-86; C Caverswall *Lich* 86-91; R Tredington and Darlingscott w Newbold on Stour *Cov* 91-97; rtd 97; PtO *Glouc* from 97. *Pipers Barn, 69 Bownham Park, Stroud GL5 5BZ*

ELLIOTT, Kathryn Georgina. b 50. **d** 08. NSM Manston *Ripon* 08-12; NSM Holbeck *Leeds* from 12. *19 Roper Avenue, Leeds LS8 1LQ* T: 0113-217 7805 M: 07979-954472
E: kelliott@ntlworld.com

ELLIOTT, Capt Keith Alcock. b 51. CA Tr Coll 83 Cranmer Hall Dur 94. **d** 95 **p** 96. C Chulmleigh, Chawleigh w Cheldon, Wembworthy etc *Ex* 95-99; TV Barnstaple and C-in-c Roundswell CD 99-08; V Thorpe Acre w Dishley *Leic* from 08; Warden of Ev from 14. *The Vicarage, Thorpe Acre Road, Loughborough LE11 4LF* T: (01509) 211656
E: elliottkeith@btinternet.com

ELLIOTT (née JUTSUM), Mrs Linda Mary. b 56. St Pet Coll Birm CertEd 77. WMMTC 92. **d** 95 **p** 96. NSM Longthorpe *Pet* 95-99; P-in-c Etton w Helpston and Maxey 99-04; Chapl Thorpe Hall Hospice 04-09; PtO *Pet* from 09. *68 Bradwell Road, Peterborough PE3 9PZ* T: (01733) 261793
E: revlinda.elliott@googlemail.com

ELLIOTT, Marilyn Elizabeth. b 53. Ex Univ BTh 10. SWMTC 05. **d** 08 **p** 09. C Stoke Climsland *Truro* 08-13; C Linkinhorne 08-13; P-in-c Lanreath, Pelynt and Bradoc from 13; C Lanteglos by Fowey 13-15; P-in-c from 15; C Talland 13-15; P-in-c from 15; C Lansallos 13-15; P-in-c from 15. *The Rectory, Lanreath, Looe PL13 2NU* T: (01503) 221159
E: marilynelliottm@btinternet.com

ELLIOTT, Mary. *See* ELLIOTT, Eveline Mary

ELLIOTT, Canon Maurice John. b 65. St Andr Univ MA 87 TCD BTh 92 MPhil 93 QUB PhD 01. CITC 89. **d** 93 **p** 94. C Coleraine *Conn* 93-98; I Greenisland 98-02; I Lurgan Ch the Redeemer *D & D* 02-08; Dir Ch of Ireland Th Inst from 08; Can Ch Ch Cathl Dublin from 15. *7 Coolgraney, Nutgrove Park, Clonskeagh, Dublin 14, Republic of Ireland* T: (00353) (1) 260 5737 or 492 3506 F: 492 3082 M: 87-968 5218
E: mauriceelliott@theologicalinstitute.ie

ELLIOTT, Michael James. b 58. St Jo Coll Nottm 80. **d** 83 **p** 84. C Pontypridd St Cath *Llan* 83-86; C Leamington Priors St Paul *Cov* 86-89; Chapl RAF 89-06 and from 07; Chapl Kimbolton Sch 06-07. *Chaplaincy Services (RAF), HQ Air Command, RAF High Wycombe HP14 4UE* T: (01494) 496800 F: 496343

ELLIOTT, Neil Raymond. b 78. Trin Coll Bris 13. **d** 15. C Whalley Range St Edm and Moss Side etc *Man* from 15. *Address temp unknown*

ELLIOTT, Nigel Harvey. b 55. St Jo Coll Nottm 90. **d** 92 **p** 93. C Radcliffe *Man* 92-95; V Kilnhurst *Sheff* 95-08; R Wombwell 08-14; AD Wath 06-11; P-in-c Sinfin *Derby* from 14. *St Stephen's Vicarage, 313 Sinfin Lane, Derby DE24 9GP* T: (01332) 760135
E: nigel520@btinternet.com

ELLIOTT, The Ven Peter. b 41. Hertf Coll Ox BA 63 MA 68. Linc Th Coll 63. **d** 65 **p** 66. C Gosforth All SS *Newc* 65-68; C Balkwell 68-72; V High Elswick St Phil 72-80; V N Gosforth 80-87; V Embleton w Rennington and Rock 87-93; RD Alnwick 89-93; Hon Can Newc Cathl 90-93; Adn Northd and Can Res Newc Cathl 93-05; rtd 05. *56 King Street, Seahouses NE68 7XS* T: (01665) 721133

ELLIOTT, Peter Wolstenholme. b 31. CChem MRSC. NEOC 78. **d** 81 **p** 82. NSM Yarm *York* 81-02; PtO from 02. *48 Butterfield Drive, Eaglescliffe, Stockton-on-Tees TS16 0EZ* T: (01642) 652698 E: revdpeter@hotmail.com

ELLIOTT, Philip. *See* ELLIOTT, John Philip

ELLIOTT, Philip. b 78. Westcott Ho Cam. **d** 11 **p** 13. C Bradford-on-Avon H Trin *Sarum* 11-12; C Weymouth H Trin from 12. *Weldon Lodge, 65 Rodwell Road, Weymouth DT4 8QX* T: (01305) 459971 M: 07990-604890
E: philipelliott78@gmail.com

ELLIOTT, Richard David Clive. b 53. Portsm Poly BSc 74 MICE 79 MIStructE. STETS 03. **d** 06 **p** 07. NSM Sway *Win* from 06. *19 Heron Close, Sway, Lymington SO41 6ET* T: (01590) 683778 M: 07836-760150 E: richard.elliott@uwclub.net

ELLIOTT, Mrs Rosemary Miriam. b 37. Toronto Univ BPaed 62 Birm Univ BPhil 86. **d** 04 **p** 05. Asst Chapl Birm Specialist Community Health NHS Trust 04-05; rtd 06; PtO *Carl* from 07. *10 Homethwaite House, Erskin Street, Keswick CA12 4DG* T: (017687) 72513 M: 07721-855007
E: rosemary.elliott@btinternet.com

ELLIOTT, Simon Mark. b 76. Liv Hope Univ Coll BA 97. Ridley Hall Cam 05. **d** 08 **p** 09. C Gt Crosby St Luke *Liv* 08-12; C Netherton 12-14; TV from 14. *22 Moorbridge Close, Bootle L30 7RL* E: sielliott76@btinternet.com

ELLIOTT, Simon Richard James. b 66. Lon Univ BSc 88. Cranmer Hall Dur BA 95. **d** 95 **p** 96. C Hendon St Paul Mill Hill *Lon* 95-99; V Hull St Martin w Transfiguration *York* from 99. *St Martin's Vicarage, 942 Anlaby Road, Hull HU4 6AH* T: (01482) 352995 M: 07776-143084
E: st.martins-hull@live.co.uk

ELLIOTT, Sonya Jacqueline. *See* DORAGH, Sonya Jacqueline

ELLIOTT, Stuart. b 75. Univ of Wales (Ban) BTh 98 MTh 00. St Mich Coll Llan 05. **d** 07 **p** 08. C Holywell *St As* 07-10; V Llanasa and Ffynnongroew 10-15; P-in-c Betws-y-Coed and Capel Curig w Penmachno etc *Ban* from 15. *The Vicarage, Vicarage Road, Betws-y-Coed LL24 0AD* T: (01690) 710313
E: stu@stubiedoo.co.uk

ELLIOTT, William. b 20. Lon Univ BA 56. Ripon Hall Ox 60. **d** 61 **p** 62. C Kidderminster St Mary *Worc* 61-70; V Bewdley Far Forest 70-78; V Rock w Heightington w Far Forest 78-82; V Mamble w Bayton, Rock w Heightington etc 82-85; rtd 85; PtO *Heref* from 85; *Worc* from 85. *8 Lea View, Cleobury Mortimer, Kidderminster DY14 8EE* T: (01299) 270993

ELLIOTT, William Henry Venn (Ben). b 34. K Coll Cam BA 55 MA 59. Wells Th Coll 59. **d** 61 **p** 62. C Almondbury *Wakef* 61-66; V Bramshaw *Sarum* 66-81; P-in-c Landford w Plaitford 77-81; V Mere w W Knoyle and Maiden Bradley 81-99; rtd 99. *3 St George's Close, Salisbury SP2 8HA* T: (01722) 338409

ELLIOTT, William James. b 38. Jes Coll Cam BA 62 MA 66 Birm Univ MA 69 PhD 74. Qu Coll Birm 62. **d** 64 **p** 65. C Hendon St Paul Mill Hill *Lon* 64-67; C St Pancras w St Jas and Ch Ch 67-69; P-in-c Preston St Paul *Blackb* 69-74; Chapl Preston R Infirmary 69-74; R Elstree *St Alb* 74-00; Research Fell Birm Univ 00-03; rtd 03; PtO *Nor* from 00. *23 Neil Avenue, Holt NR25 6TG* T/F: (01263) 713853
E: bill.elliott@akainternet.co.uk

ELLIS

ELLIOTT DE RIVEROL, Mrs Jennifer Kathleen. b 52. St Pet Coll Birm CertEd 75 UEA MA 88. ERMC 09. d 11 p 12. C Puerto de la Cruz Tenerife *Eur* from 11. *El Búho, Calle Tamarahoya 1, El Paso, 38750 La Palma, Canary Islands* T: (0034) 922 497 446 M: 670 813 599 E: jkelliottderiverol@hotmail.com

ELLIS, Anthony. *See* ELLIS, John Anthony

ELLIS, Anthony Colin. b 56. Keble Coll Ox BA 77 Man Univ PhD 80. Linc Th Coll 80. d 81 p 82. C Mill Hill Jo Keble Ch *Lon* 81-83; Staff Tutor in RS Man Univ from 83; Dir Cen for Continuing Educn from 99; C Stretford St Pet *Man* 83-87; NSM Shore 87-89; Lic Preacher from 89. *2 Crowther Terrace, Blackshaw, Hebden Bridge HX7 6DE* T: (01422) 844242 *or* 0161-275 3302

ELLIS, Brian Eric James. b 50. STETS 05. d 08 p 09. NSM Preston w Sutton Poyntz, Littlemoor etc *Sarum* from 08; NSM Bincombe w Broadwey, Upwey and Buckland Ripers from 12. *27 Fisherbridge Road, Preston, Weymouth DT3 6BT* T: (01305) 832427 M: 07533-941686 E: brian-ellis@talktalk.net

ELLIS, Canon Bryan Stuart. b 31. Qu Coll Cam BA 54 MA 58. Ridley Hall Cam 55. d 57 p 58. C Ramsgate St Luke *Cant* 57-59; C Herne Bay Ch Ch 59-62; V Burmantofts St Steph and St Agnes *Ripon* 62-81; RD Wakef 81-96; V Wakef St Andr and St Mary 81-00; Hon Can Wakef Cathl 89-00; rtd 00; PtO *Leeds* from 01. *302 Oakwood Lane, Leeds LS8 3LE* T: 0113-240 3122

ELLIS, Charles Harold. b 50. NOC 78. d 81 p 82. C Davyhulme St Mary *Man* 81-85; V Tonge w Alkrington 85-91; P-in-c Radcliffe St Thos and St Jo 91; P-in-c Radcliffe St Mary 91; TR Radcliffe 91-99; AD Radcliffe and Prestwich 96-99; P-in-c Newchurch 99-00; TR Rossendale Middle Valley 00-04; AD Rossendale 00-04; V Ingleton w Chapel le Dale *Bradf* 04-14; TV Bentham, Burton-in-Lonsdale, Chapel-le-Dale etc *Leeds* from 14. *St Mary's Vicarage, Main Street, Ingleton, Carnforth LA6 3HF* T: (015242) 41440 E: chasellis@btinternet.com

ELLIS, Christopher Charles. b 55. Edin Univ BD 78 Hull Univ MA 80. Edin Th Coll 76 Irish Sch of Ecum 78. d 79 p 80. C Selby Abbey *York* 79-82; C Fulford 82-85; Dioc Ecum Officer 81-98; Dioc Ecum Adv 90-98; Lect Ecum Th Hull Univ from 84; P-in-c Kexby w Wilberfoss *York* 85-90; Ecum Officer S Cleveland and N Yorks Ecum Coun 88-98; P-in-c Bulmer w Dalby, Terrington and Welburn *York* 98-01; R Howardian Gp 01-05; P-in-c Sheriff Hutton, Farlington, Stillington etc 05-06; V Forest of Galtres from 06. *The Vicarage, Main Street, Sutton-on-the-Forest, York YO61 1DW* T: (01347) 810251 E: benefice.admin@googlemail.com

ELLIS, Christopher Duncan. b 67. Anglia Ruskin Univ BA 09. ERMC 05. d 08 p 09. C Thorpe St Andr *Nor* 08-11; V Thorpe St Matt 11-15; R Rockland St Mary w Hellington, Bramerton etc from 15; Hon PV Nor Cathl from 14. *The Rectory, 29 Ashby Road, Thurton, Norwich NR14 6AX* E: chris.ellis23@btinternet.com

ELLIS, Canon David Craven. b 34. Man Univ BA 56 MA 57. St Aid Birkenhead 59. d 61 p 62. C St Crosby St Luke *Liv* 61-65; Hong Kong 65-69; P-in-c Sawrey *Carl* 69-74; Dioc Youth Officer 69-74; V Halifax St Aug *Wakef* 74-84; R Greystoke, Matterdale and Mungrisdale *Carl* 84-87; R Watermillock 84-87; TR Greystoke, Matterdale, Mungrisdale etc 88-91; RD Penrith 87-91; TR Carl H Trin and St Barn 91-96; Hon Can Carl Cathl 91-96; rtd 96; PtO *Carl* 97-02 and from 04; *Cov* from 13; NSM Cartmel Peninsula *Carl* 02-04. *55 Cherry Orchard, Stratford-upon-Avon CV37 9AP* T: (01789) 269409 E: dandbellis4@btinternet.com

ELLIS, Dorothy Pearson. b 43. Sheff Univ BA 66 MA 67. Dioc OLM tr scheme 05. d 07 p 08. NSM Oakenshaw, Wyke and Low Moor *Bradf* 07-12; Hon C Low Moor and Oakenshaw *Leeds* from 12. *2 Woodrow Drive, Low Moor, Bradford BD12 0JU* T: (01274) 679048

ELLIS, Mrs Emma Louise. b 79. Coll of Ripon & York St Jo BA 00 Heythrop Coll Lon MTh 03. Ridley Hall Cam 05. d 07 p 08. C Addiscombe St Mary Magd w St Martin *S'wark* 07-10; TV Limpsfield and Tatsfield from 10. *The Rectory, Ricketts Hill Road, Tatsfield, Westerham TN16 2NA* M: 07949-697075 E: rev.louiseellis@googlemail.com

ELLIS, Gay Winifred. b 48. Oak Hill Th Coll 94. d 96 p 97. NSM Nazeing *Chelmsf* 96-99; C 99-00; P-in-c Chingford St Anne 00-02; V 02-04; P-in-c Lambourne w Abridge and Stapleford Abbotts 04-10; Ind Chapl 04-10; rtd 10; PtO *Chelmsf* 11-12; TV Halstead Area from 12. *16 Church Ponds, Castle Hedingham, Halstead CO9 3BZ* M: 07749-838769 E: gayellis@aol.com

ELLIS, Gillian Patricia. b 34. d 99 p 00. OLM Blymhill w Weston-under-Lizard *Lich* 99-00; OLM Lapley w Wheaton Aston 00-09; OLM Watershed 09-12; rtd 12; PtO *Lich* 12-14. *18 Ashleigh Crescent, Wheaton Aston, Stafford ST19 9PN* T: (01785) 840925 E: gellis3011@toucansurf.com

ELLIS, Hugh William. b 54. Sussex Univ BSc 76. Ridley Hall Cam 88. d 90 p 91. C Reading St Jo *Ox* 90-93; P-in-c Bradfield

and Stanford Dingley 93-97; R 97-03; TR Langport Area *B & W* 03-12; TR High Wycombe *Ox* from 12. *The Vicarage, 6 Priory Avenue, High Wycombe HP13 6SH* E: hughelli@aol.com

ELLIS, Canon Ian Morton. b 52. QUB BD 75 MTh 82 TCD PhD 89. CITC. d 77 p 78. C Portadown St Columba *Arm* 77-79; C Arm St Mark w Aghavilly 79-85; Chapl Arm R Sch 79-85; Hon V Choral Arm Cathl 82-93; I Mullavilly 85-93; Dom Chapl to Abp Arm 86-93; Tutor for Aux Min (Arm) 90-93; I Newcastle *D & D* from 93; Can Belf Cathl from 00; Ed *The Church of Ireland Gazette* from 01; Preb Newcastle St Patr Cathl Dublin from 01. *The Rectory, 1 King Street, Newcastle BT33 0HD* T: (028) 4372 2439 F: 4372 5977 E: ian.m.ellis@btinternet.com

ELLIS, Ian William. b 57. QUB BSc 78 CertEd 79 TCD BTh 89. CITC 86. d 89 p 90. C Arm St Mark 89-91; I Loughgall w Grange 91-02; Sec Gen Syn Bd of Educn 02-15; I Rossorry *Clogh* from 15. *Rossorry Rectory, Derrygonnelly Road, Kinarla, Enniskillen BT74 5PX* T: (028) 6632 0239

ELLIS, Jean Miriam. b 35. St Mich Coll Llan 92. d 95 p 97. NSM Llanelli *S & B* 95-98; NSM Rockfield and St Maughen's w Llangattock etc *Mon* 99-04; NSM Rockfield and Dingestow Gp 05-09; PtO from 12. *2 New Bungalows, Watery Lane, Monmouth NP25 5AT* T: (01600) 719562

ELLIS, Jenny Susan. b 56. Bp Grosseteste Coll BEd 80. STETS 08. d 11 p 12. NSM Martock w Ash *B & W* 11-12; PtO *Ox* from 13. *The Vicarage, 6 Priory Avenue, High Wycombe HP13 6SH* E: ellisjene@aol.com

ELLIS, John Anthony. b 47. Open Univ BA 80. Coll of Resurr Mirfield 70. d 72 p 73. C Sketty *S & B* 72-75; C Duston *Pet* 75-80; R Lichborough w Maidford and Farthingstone 80-85; V Stratfield Mortimer *Ox* 85-98; P-in-c Mortimer W End w Padworth 85-98; TR Kidlington w Hampton Poyle 98-12; AD Ox 04-12; Hon Can Ch Ch 07-12; rtd 13; PtO *Heref* from 13. *The Skirrid, Ullingswick, Hereford HR1 3JG* T: (01432) 820759 E: janthonychurchkid@gmail.com

ELLIS, John Beaumont. b 45. Univ of Wales (Lamp) BA 67 LTh 69. Bp Burgess Hall Lamp. d 69 p 70. C Abergavenny St Mary w Llanwenarth Citra *Mon* 69-72; C Swansea St Gabr *S & B* 72-75; V Llanbister and Llanbadarn Fynydd w Llananno 75-77; V Newport St Andr *Mon* 77-80; V Risca 80-84; V Cheadle Heath *Ches* 84-94. *12 Upper Hibbert Lane, Marple, Stockport SK6 7HX* T: 0161-427 1963

ELLIS, John Franklyn. b 34. Leeds Univ BA 58. Linc Th Coll 58. d 60 p 61. C Ladybarn *Man* 60-63; C Stockport St Geo *Ches* 63-66; V High Lane 66-81; V Chelford w Lower Withington 81-99; rtd 99; PtO *Ches* from 00. *3 Millers Croft, Adlington Street, Macclesfield SK10 1BD*

ELLIS, Canon John Keith Randolph. b 44. Univ of Wales MEd Man Univ CertEd. Westcott Ho Cam 98. d 01 p 02. C Glanogwen w St Ann's w Llanllechid *Ban* 01-04; Min Can Ban Cathl 04-09; rtd 09; Hon Can Ban Cathl from 12. *Glan Arthur, Penisarwaun, Caernarfon LL55 3PW* T: (01286) 873623 E: randolph@afoncegin.freeserve.co.uk

ELLIS, John Raymond. b 63. St Steph Ho Ox 95. d 97 p 98. C Clare w Poslingford, Cavendish etc *St E* 97-00; P-in-c Bury St Edmunds St Jo 00-02; P-in-c Bury St Edmunds St Geo 00-02; TV Bury St Edmunds All SS w St Jo and St Geo 02-04; Chapl RAF from 04. *Chaplaincy Services (RAF), HQ Air Command, RAF High Wycombe HP14 4UE* T: (01494) 496800 F: 496343

ELLIS, John Roland. b 32. Wells Th Coll 67. d 69 p 70. C Kettering SS Pet and Paul 69-71; C Kingsthorpe 71-73; TV 73; TV Kingsthorpe w Northampton St Dav 73-74; TV Ebbw Vale *Mon* 74-76; V Llanddewi Rhydderch w Llanvapley etc 76-83; Miss to Seamen 79-86; V New Tredegar *Mon* 83-86; V Llanelli *S & B* 86-98; RD Crickhowell 91-98; rtd 99; P-in-c Rockfield and St Maughen's w Llangattock etc *Mon* 99-05; Hon C Rockfield and Dingestow Gp 05-07; PtO from 12. *2 New Bungalows, Watery Lane, Monmouth NP25 5AT* T: (01600) 719562

ELLIS, Canon John Wadsworth. b 42. MBE 98. TCD BA 64. d 66 p 67. C Lisburn Ch Ch Cathl 66-69; C Norbiton *S'wark* 69-72; C New Clee *Linc* 72-85; V 85-11; RD Grimsby and Cleethorpes 94-99; Can and Preb Linc Cathl 98-11; rtd 11. *9 Abbots Way, Grimsby DN32 0HB* E: johnellis55@gmail.com

ELLIS, Kevin Stuart. b 67. Newc Univ BA 91 Lon Bible Coll PhD 97. Qu Coll Birm 99. d 01 p 02. C Matson *Glouc* 01-04; TV Maryport, Netherton and Flimby *Carl* 04-07; TR 07-09; V Bartley Green *Birm* 09-14; V Bro Cybi *Ban* from 14. *Holy Island Vicarage, Trearddur House Mews, Lon St Ffraid, Trearddur Bay, Holyhead LL65 2UD* T: (01407) 861845 M: 07535-557632 E: holyislandvicar@gmail.com

ELLIS, Sister Lilian. b 44. Keswick Hall Coll TCert 66. Oak Hill Th Coll 95. d 96 p 97. C Vange *Chelmsf* 96-00; C Pitsea w Nevendon 00-02; rtd 02; PtO *Chelmsf* from 02. *9 The Poplars, Basildon SS13 2ER* T: (01268) 551018 E: lilian.ellis@tesco.net

ELLIS, Malcolm Railton. b 35. LTCL 71 Univ of Wales (Lamp) BA 56. Sarum Th Coll 56. **d** 58 **p** 59. C Llangynwyd w Maesteg *Llan* 58-61; C Llantrisant 61-67; V Troedrhiwgarth 67-70; PV Truro Cathl 70-73; V Egloshayle 73-81; V Margam *Llan* 81-87; V Cardiff St Jo 87-00; TR Cen Cardiff 00-02; Prec and Can Llan Cathl 96-02; rtd 02. *5 Llanedeyrn Road, Penylan, Cardiff CF23 4DT*

ELLIS, Preb Mark Durant. b 39. Ex Univ BA 62. Cuddesdon Coll 62. **d** 64 **p** 65. C Lyngford *B & W* 64-67; V Weston-super-Mare St Andr Bournville 67-76; TV Yeovil 76-88; V Yeovil St Mich 88-09; Preb Wells Cathl 90-09; RD Yeovil 94-04; rtd 09; Hon C Bruton and Distr *B & W* from 09. *The Parsonage, Gold Hill, Batcombe, Shepton Mallet BA4 6HF* T: (01749) 850074

ELLIS, Paul. b 49. **d** 07 **p** 08. NSM Wakef St Jo *Leeds* from 07. *98 Bradford Road, Wakefield WF1 2AH* T: (01924) 367976

ELLIS, Paul. b 56. Aston Tr Scheme 88 Trin Coll Bris 92. **d** 92 **p** 93. C Pennington *Man* 92-96; TV Deane 96-06; P-in-c Grassendale *Liv* 06-14; V from 14; P-in-c Liv All So Springwood 11-14; V from 14. *The Vicarage, 22 Eaton Road, Cressington, Liverpool L19 0PN* T: 0151-427 1474
E: rev_paul_e@btinternet.com *or* rev.paul.ellis@gmail.com

ELLIS, Peter Andrew. b 46. St D Coll Lamp 65. **d** 69 **p** 70. C Milford Haven *St D* 69-71; R Walwyn's Castle w Robeston W 71-74; Miss to Seafarers 74-11; Hong Kong 74-75 and 92-11; Singapore 75-82; The Tees and Hartlepool 82-92; rtd 11; PtO *York* from 13. *The Forge, Home Farm, Hutton Village Road, Guisborough TS14 8EL* T: (01287) 348371
E: ellishongkong@gmail.com

ELLIS, Randolph. *See* ELLIS, John Keith Randolph

ELLIS, Richard. b 47. **d** 02 **p** 03. OLM Leiston *St E* 02-13; NSM from 13. *9 Kings Road, Leiston IP16 4DA* T: (01728) 832168 M: 07759-349057 E: us@rellis41.freeserve.co.uk

ELLIS, Robert Albert. b 48. K Coll Lon BD 70 AKC 70. St Aug Coll Cant 70. **d** 72 **p** 73. C Liv Our Lady and St Nic w St Anne 72-76; P-in-c Meerbrook *Lich* 76-80; Producer Relig Progr BBC Radio Stoke 76-80; V Highgate All SS *Lon* 80-81; P-in-c Longdon *Lich* 81-87; Dioc Communications Officer 81-01; Chapl Palma de Mallorca *Eur* 01-11; rtd 11; PtO *Lich* from 11. *The Pump House, Jacks Lane, Marchington, Uttoxeter ST14 8LW* T: (01283) 820732 E: robertellis1948@gmail.com

ELLIS, Roger Henry. b 40. Natal Univ BA 61 Selw Coll Cam BA 64 MA 68 Linacre Coll Ox BLitt 69. **d** 66 **p** 67. C Ox St Mich 66-68; Sen Lect Univ of Natal S Africa 68-76; Hon C Pietermaritzburg Cathl 68-76; P-in-c Wortham *St E* 77; V Wheatley Hills *Sheff* 77-84; Chapl St Edm Sch Cant 84-00; P-in-c Dymchurch w Burmarsh and Newchurch *Cant* 00-04; AD Romney 01-03; rtd 05. *5 Bishops Reach, Wyndham Lane, Allington, Salisbury SP4 0BB* T: (01980) 610797
E: ellisrhdm@yahoo.co.uk

ELLIS, Susannah Margaret. b 44. Open Univ BA 82 New Coll Dur CertEd 88. EAMTC 93. **d** 96 **p** 97. NSM S Elmham and Ilketshall *St E* 96-98; Warden Quiet Waters Chr Retreat Ho 96-98; C Worlingham w Barnby and N Cove *St E* 98-01; C Beccles St Mich 98-01; P-in-c Worlingham w Barnby and N Cove 01-03; R 03-14; rtd 14. *27 Lowestoft Road, Worlingham, Beccles NR34 7DZ* T: (01502) 715403

✠**ELLIS, The Rt Revd Timothy William.** b 53. AKC 75 York Univ DPhil 98. St Aug Coll Cant 75. **d** 76 **p** 77 **c** 06. C Old Trafford St Jo *Man* 76-80; V Pendleton St Thos 80-87; Chapl Salford Coll of Tech 80-87; V Sheff St Leon Norwood 87-01; P-in-c Shiregreen St Hilda 94-01; RD Ecclesfield 94-99; Hon Can Sheff Cathl 00-01; Adn Stow *Linc* 01-06; Suff Bp Grantham 06-13; Dean Stamford 05-11; Can and Preb Linc Cathl 01-13; rtd 13; Hon Asst Bp Linc from 13; Hon Asst Bp Sheff from 14. *8 Mason Grove, Sheffield S13 8LL*
E: fatherowl@googlemail.com

ELLISDON, Canon Patrick Leon Shane. b 61. St Jo Coll Nottm 99. **d** 01 **p** 02. C Margate St Phil *Cant* 01-04; P-in-c Cliftonville 04-14; V from 14; Hon Can Cant Cathl from 14. *St Paul's Vicarage, 18 Devonshire Gardens, Margate CT9 3AF* T: (01843) 226832 M: 07932-734932

ELLISON, John. b 37. FCA 64. Qu Coll Birm. **d** 04 **p** 05. NSM Northanger *Win* 04-07; PtO from 07. *High Candovers, Hartley Mauditt, Alton GU34 3BP* T: (01420) 511346
E: revjohnellison@hotmail.com

✠**ELLISON, The Rt Revd John Alexander.** b 40. ALCD 67. **d** 67 **p** 68 **c** 88. C Woking St Paul *Guildf* 67-70; SAMS from 71; C Belgrano St Sav Argentina 80-83; R Aldridge *Lich* 83-88; Bp Paraguay 88-07; rtd 07; Hon Asst Bp Win from 08. *The Furrow, Evingar Road, Whitchurch RG28 7EU* T: (01256) 892126

ELLISON, Mrs Margaret Helen. b 50. Edin Univ BSc 77 Leeds Univ BA 09 RN 72. Yorks Min Course 07. **d** 09 **p** 10. NSM York St Hilda and York St Lawr w St Nic 09-13; PtO 13-15; NSM Stamford Bridge Gp from 15. *17 Foresters Walk, Stamford Bridge, York YO41 1BB* T: (01759) 372696
E: maggs.ellison@googlemail.com

ELLISON, Ms Sandra Anne. b 53. Anglia Poly Univ BA 96 RMN 74. EAMTC 99. **d** 02 **p** 03. C Hunstanton St Mary w Ringstead Parva etc *Nor* 02-05; R Ashmanhaugh, Barton Turf etc from 05. *11 Pinewood Drive, Horning, Norwich NR12 8LZ* T: (01692) 630216

ELLISON, Simon John. b 51. SEITE 99. **d** 02 **p** 03. NSM Caterham *S'wark* 02-08; Asst Chapl Newcastle upon Tyne Hosps NHS Foundn Trust 08-09; Chapl Epsom and St Helier Univ Hosps NHS Trust from 09; PtO *S'wark* 09-14; NSM Caterham from 14. *Trust Headquarters, St Helier Hospital, Wrythe Lane, Carshalton SM5 1AA* T: (020) 8296 2000
E: simon.ellison@epsom-sthelier.nhs.uk

ELLISTON, John Ernest Nicholas. b 37. ALCD 61. **d** 61 **p** 62. C Gipsy Hill Ch Ch *S'wark* 61-64; C Whitton and Thurleston w Akenham *St E* 64-68; P-in-c New Clee *Linc* 68-71; V 75-76; V Grimsby St Steph 71-75; P-in-c Mildenhall *St E* 77-79; RD 81-84; R Barton Mills, Beck Row w Kenny Hill etc 80-84; V Ipswich St Aug 84-96; R Guernsey St Peter Port *Win* 96-02; Chapl Princess Eliz Hosp Guernsey 96-02; rtd 02; PtO *St E* from 03. *27 Wyvern Road, Ipswich IP3 9TJ* T: (01473) 726617 *or* 720036

ELLMORE, Peter Robert. b 44. Portsm Univ MA. Sarum & Wells Th Coll 84. **d** 86 **p** 87. C Bridgemary *Portsm* 86-89; C Portsea N End St Mark 89-91; Asst Chapl St Mary's Hosp Portsm 91-92; Chapl Qu Alexandra Hosp Portsm 91-93; Chapl Team Ldr Portsm Hosps NHS Trust 93-97; P-in-c Cosham *Portsm* 97-99; Angl Chapl Univ Coll Lon Hosps NHS Trust 99-01; Chapl Team Ldr United Bris Healthcare NHS Trust 01-04; Lead Chapl (S) Caring for the Spirit NHS Project 04-07; Chapl St Pet Hospice Bris 07-09; rtd 09. *2 Westover Drive, Bristol BS9 3LX* T: 0117-950 2927
E: peter.ellmore@lineone.net

ELLOR, Preb Michael Keith. b 52. St Jo Coll Nottm 92. **d** 94 **p** 95. C Stafford St Jo and Tixall w Ingestre *Lich* 94-97; TV Bucknall and Bagnall 97-03; TR Bucknall 03-09; RD Stoke 02-06; V Branston from 09; Local Min Adv (Stafford) 09-14; Local Par Development Adv Stafford Area 10-14; P-in-c Burton All SS w Ch Ch from 14; Preb Lich Cathl from 09. *The Vicarage, Church Road, Branston, Burton-on-Trent DE14 3ER* T: (01283) 567017 E: ellors@bucknall12.fsnet.co.uk

ELLSON, Montague Edward. b 33. Birm Univ BA 56 Cam Univ CertEd 67 Univ of Wales (Lamp) MA 08. EAMTC 84. **d** 87 **p** 88. Hon C Freethorpe w Wickhampton, Halvergate etc *Nor* 87-90; C Gaywood, Bawsey and Mintlyn 90-92; Miss to Seafarers from 90; R Pulham *Nor* 92-94; P-in-c Starston 93-94; R Pulham Market, Pulham St Mary and Starston 94-97; Dioc NSM Officer 94-97; RD Redenhall 95-97; rtd 97; PtO *Nor* from 97. *Barn Cottage, Neatishead Road, Horning, Norwich NR12 8LB* T: (01692) 630251 E: revmonty@btinternet.com

ELLSWORTH, Lida Elizabeth. b 48. Columbia Univ (NY) BA 70 Girton Coll Cam PhD 76. EMMTC 85. **d** 88 **p** 94. NSM Bakewell *Derby* 88-07; PtO 07-11; NSM Longstone, Curbar and Stony Middleton from 11. *Apple Croft, Granby Gardens, Bakewell DE45 1ET* T/F: (01629) 814255 E: lide.el@virgin.net

ELLWOOD, Mrs Ethney. **d** 06 **p** 07. OLM Uttoxeter Area *Lich* 06-11; rtd 11; PtO *Win* from 11. *1A Elmsway, Bournemouth BH6 3HU* T: (01202) 427463
E: revethneyellwood@hotmail.co.uk

ELLWOOD, Keith Brian. b 36. Curwen Coll Lon BA 58 MMus 65 Bede Coll Dur CertEd 59 Hon DD 99 AIGCM 58 FRSA 64 ACP 66 FCollP 83. Bps' Coll Cheshunt 64. **d** 64 **p** 65. Asst Master R Wanstead Sch 66-66; Chapl 64-66; C Wanstead St Mary *Chelmsf* 64-66; CF 66-70; OCM 70-71 and 76-79; Chapl St Paul's Coll Hong Kong 70-71; P-in-c Bicknoller *B & W* 71-73; Chapl Roedean Sch Brighton 73-76; PtO *B & W* 74-79; Chapl Windsor Boys' Sch Hamm W Germany 76-79; Chapl Trin Coll Glenalmond 79-81; Hd Master St Chris Sch Burnham-on-Sea 82-86; Hon C Burnham *B & W* 82-86; R Staple Fitzpaine, Orchard Portman, Thurlbear etc 86-89; P-in-c Hugill and Dioc Educn Adv *Carl* 89-93; P-in-c Coldwaltham and Hardham *Chich* 93-95; rtd 96; PtO *Chich* 96-04; *Sheff* from 04. *21 Fiddlers Drive, Armthorpe, Doncaster DN3 3TS* T: (01302) 834031 E: k.b.e@btinternet.com

ELMAN, Simon Laurie. b 57. NTMTC. **d** 99 **p** 00. C Loughton St Jo *Chelmsf* 99-01; C Tye Green w Netteswell 01-07; PtO from 08. *26 Pakes Way, Theydon Bois, Epping CM16 7NA* T: (01992) 813057 E: simon.elman@btinternet.com

ELMES, Amanda Jane. b 53. Lon Univ BDS 76 RCS LDS 77 Herts Univ PhD 04. ERMC 06. **d** 08 **p** 09. NSM W w E Mersea *Chelmsf* 08-10; NSM W w E Mersea, Peldon, Gt and Lt Wigborough 10-14; P-in-c Langham w Boxted from 14; P-in-c W Bergholt and Gt Horkesley from 14. *The Rectory, 1 Church Close, West Bergholt, Colchester CO6 3JZ* T: (01206) 240906
E: revmandyelmes@btinternet.com

ELMES, Sister Evelyn Sandra. b 61. **d** 97 **p** 98. C Southchurch H Trin *Chelmsf* 97-00; PtO *Win* 01-13; Chapl Hants Hosps

NHS Foundn Trust 13-15; PtO *Win* from 15. *Address temp unknown* T: (01256) 473202 E: eveelmes@tesco.net

ELMES, Ruth Katherine. b 65. TCD BTh 09 RGN 83. CITC 06. **d** 09 **p** 10. C Stillorgan w Blackrock *D & G* 09-12; I Crosspatrick Gp *C & O* from 12. *The Rectory, Churchlands, Tinahely, Co Wicklow, Republic of Ireland* T: (00353) (402) 28922 M: 86-062 1009 E: relmes@eircom.net

ELMQVIST, Gunilla. *See* AQUILON-ELMQVIST, Gunilla

ELMS, Christian Grant. b 71. Salford Univ BSc 04. Trin Coll Bris 07. **d** 09 **p** 10. C Pennington *Man* 09-12; TV Worle *B & W* from 12. *Church Cottage, 2A St Marks Road, Weston-super-Mare BS22 7PW* T: (01934) 515438 M: 07796-988907 E: chriselms1@gmail.com

ELPHICK, Robin Howard. b 37. ALCD 63. **d** 64 **p** 65. C Clapham Common St Barn *S'wark* 64-67; C Woking St Pet *Guildf* 67-71; R Rollesby w Burgh w Billockby *Nor* 71-80; P-in-c Ashby w Oby, Thurne and Clippesby 79-80; R Rollesby w Burgh w Billockby w Ashby w Oby etc 80-84; R Frinton *Chelmsf* 84-94; P-in-c W w E Mersea and Peldon w Gt and Lt Wigborough 94-02; rtd 02; PtO *Nor* from 02. *1 Barn Cottages, Dodma Road, Weasenham, King's Lynn PE32 2TJ* T: (01328) 838340 E: robinelphick@btinternet.com

ELPHICK, Canon Vivien Margaret. b 53. Kent Univ BA 74 Solicitor 77. Trin Coll Bris BA 90. **d** 90 **p** 94. C Oulton Broad *Nor* 90-94; P-in-c Burlingham St Edmund w Lingwood, Strumpshaw etc 94-06; RD Blofield 98-04; Hon Can Nor Cathl 03-06; P-in-c Measham *Leic* 06-08; P-in-c Packington w Normanton-le-Heath 06-08; P-in-c Donisthorpe and Moira w Stretton-en-le-Field 06-08; TR Woodfield from 08; AD NW Leics from 11. *The Vicarage, High Street, Measham, Swadlincote DE12 7HZ* T: (01530) 270354 E: vivien@rectorybarn.wanadoo.co.uk

ELPHIN AND ARDAGH, Archdeacon of. *See* LINTON, The Ven Barry Ian

ELPHIN AND ARDAGH, Dean of. *See* WILLIAMS, The Very Revd Arfon

ELSDON, Bernard Robert. b 29. Roch Th Coll 65. **d** 67 **p** 68. C Wallasey St Hilary *Ches* 67-71; C Liv Our Lady and St Nic w St Anne 71-72; V Anfield St Marg 73-89; Dioc Exec Dir for Chr Resp 80-83; rtd 89; PtO *Man* 89-08; *Ches* from 89. *31 Douglas Road, Hazel Grove, Stockport SK7 4JE* T: 0161-292 1858 E: bernard.hillcrest@ntlworld.com

ELSDON, Mrs Janice Margaret. b 49. CITC 92. **d** 95 **p** 96. NSM Cloughfern *Conn* 95-99; NSM Ahoghill w Portglenone 99-02; NSM Belfast St Thos 02-05; LtO 05-08; NSM Belfast St Bart 08-13; NSM Belfast St Anne from 13. *128 Station Road, Greenisland, Carrickfergus BT38 8UW* T: (028) 9085 1963 E: janice@belfastcathedral.org

ELSDON, Ronald. b 44. St Jo Coll Cam BA 66 Trin Hall Cam PhD 69 K Coll Lon BD 86 Milltown Inst Dub PhD. CITC 97. **d** 99 **p** 00. C Ballymena w Ballyclug *Conn* 99-02; I Belfast St Bart 02-13; rtd 13. *128 Station Road, Greenisland, Carrickfergus BT38 8UW* T: (028) 9085 1963 E: elsdon.rj@nireland.com

ELSMORE, Canon Guy Charles. b 66. Edin Univ BSc 88. Ridley Hall Cam 93. **d** 93 **p** 94. C Huyton St Mich *Liv* 93-98; V Hough Green St Basil and All SS 98-05; AD Widnes and Hon Can Liv Cathl 03-05; P-in-c St Luke in the City 05-10; TR from 10; AD Toxteth and Wavertree from 14; Hon Can Liv Cathl from 14. *7 Crossley Drive, Liverpool L15 8AJ* T: 0151-709 2788 M: 07787-848229

ELSMORE, (née HANOVA), Ms Petra. b 70. Chas Univ Prague BA 97. Ridley Hall Cam 00. **d** 03 **p** 04. C Toxteth St Philemon w St Gabr and St Cleopas *Liv* 03-06; P-in-c Everton St Geo 06-09. *7 Crossley Drive, Liverpool L15 8AJ* T: 0151-709 2788 E: petra.elsmore@yahoo.co.uk

ELSON, Christopher John. b 52. K Coll Lon BD 75 AKC 75. St Aug Coll Cant. **d** 76 **p** 77. C New Haw *Guildf* 76-79; C Guildf H Trin w St Mary 79-82; C Hale 85-87; V Ripley from 87; Sub Chapl HM Pris Send 88-92. *The Vicarage, 8 Grove Heath North, Ripley, Woking GU23 6EN* T: (01483) 211460 M: 07956-103289 E: chris@elsons.org.uk *or* vicar@ripleychurch.org.uk

ELSON, John Frederick. Roch Th Coll 62. **d** 64 **p** 65. C Tenterden St Mildred w Smallhythe *Cant* 64-68; P-in-c Chart next Sutton Valence 68-71; V Fletching *Chich* 71-93; Chapl Wivelsfield Green Hospice 91-93; rtd 93; PtO *Chich* from 93. *1 Manor House Court, Regency Close, Uckfield TN22 1DS* T: (01825) 763217

ELSON, Sharon Anne. b 50. WEMTC 99. **d** 00 **p** 01. OLM Heref St Pet w St Owen and St Jas from 00. *100 Green Street, Hereford HR1 2QW* T: (01432) 370417 M: 07718-481318 E: upinalms@btinternet.com

ELSTOB, Stephen William. b 57. Sarum & Wells Th Coll. **d** 86 **p** 87. C Sunderland Springwell w Thorney Close *Dur* 86-88;

C Upholland *Liv* 88-89; TV 89-96; V Cinnamon Brow 96-07; TV N Wearside *Dur* 07-11; TR from 11. *The Vicarage, Bootle Street, Sunderland SR5 4EY5* T: 0191-537 3744

ELSTON, Mrs Anthea Elizabeth Lynne. b 64. **d** 10 **p** 11. NSM Berrow w Pendock, Eldersfield, Hollybush etc *Worc* from 10. *The Plough, Eight Oaks, Castlemorton, Malvern WR13 6BU* T: (01684) 833557 E: revanth@eightoaks.com

ELSTON, James Ian. b 70. City Univ BSc 95. SEITE 01. **d** 04 **p** 05. NSM Old St Pancras *Lon* 04-12; TV 12-15; TR from 15. *23 Albert Street, London NW1 7LU* T: (020) 7387 4193 E: fr.jameselston@googlemail.com

ELSTON, Philip Herbert. b 35. RD 80 and Bar 90. Leeds Univ MA 76 K Coll Lon AKC 63 Leic Coll of Educn CertEd 67. St Boniface Warminster 63. **d** 64 **p** 65. C Thurnby Lodge *Leic* 64-66; Hon C 66-67; Chapl RNR 67-90; Chapl Malosa Sch Malawi 68-75; Hon C Far Headingley St Chad *Ripon* 75-79; V Knowl Hill w Littlewick *Ox* 79-84; Chapl RN Sch Haslemere 85-89; C Felpham w Middleton *Chich* 89-90; Asst S Regional Dir Miss to Seamen 91-93; Dep S Regional Dir 93-97; S Regional Dir 97-00; PtO *Win* 93-14; *Cant* 94-00; *Chich* from 97; Corps Chapl Sea Cadet Corps 83-95; rtd 00; Hon C Witchampton, Stanbridge and Long Crichel etc *Sarum* 00-04; Hon Chapl Miss to Seafarers from 00. *East Farm Cottage, Dinton Road, Wylye, Warminster BA12 0RE* T: (01985) 248598 E: dee.elston1@btinternet.com

ELSWORTH, Mrs Teresa Karen. b 60. Cape Town Univ BSc 82. SEITE 03. **d** 06 **p** 07. NSM Yalding w Collier Street *Roch* 06-10; PtO *Cant* 07-10; NSM Goudhurst w Kilndown 10-14. *10 Lurkins Rise, Goudhurst, Cranbrook TN17 1ED* T: (01580) 211550 E: karenelsworth@hotmail.com

ELTON, Canon Derek Hurley. b 31. Lon Univ BSc 52. Wycliffe Hall *Ox* 53. **d** 55 **p** 56. C Ashton-on-Ribble St Andr *Blackb* 55-57; Miss C of S India 58-70; R Wickmere w Lt Barningham and Itteringham *Nor* 71-79; R Lt w Gt Ellingham 79-83; P-in-c Rockland All SS and St Andr w St Pet 81-83; R Lt w Gt Ellingham w Rockland 83-88; Chapl Wayland Hosp Norfolk 84-88; Miss to Seamen 89-98; Chapl Algiers H Trin 89-94; Chapl Asmara St Geo Eritrea 94-98; rtd 96; PtO *Nor* from 00. *22 Alfred Road, Cromer NR27 9AN* T: (01263) 511730 E: jedclef@paston.co.uk

ELTRINGHAM, Anna. b 74. St Jo Coll Dur BA 96. SEITE 05. **d** 08 **p** 09. C S Norwood H Innocents *S'wark* 08-14; TV Oxted from 14. *The Vicarage, 14 Oast Road, Oxted RH8 9DU* M: 07826-524038 T: (01883) 712674 E: revd.anna@gmail.com

ELTRINGHAM, Mrs Fiona Ann. b 48. Bp Grosseteste Coll CertEd 69. NEOC 86. **d** 89 **p** 94. Chapl HM Willington *Newc* 89-92; Chapl HM YOI Castington 92-95; Chapl HM Pris Dur 95-07; rtd 07; PtO *Dur* from 07. *Granary Cottage, Stockley House Farm, Oakenshaw, Crook DL15 0TJ* T: (01388) 746058 E: davefi@tiscali.co.uk

ELVERSON, Ronald Peter Charles. b 50. St Edm Hall Ox BA 73 MA 86. St Jo Coll Nottm 84. **d** 86 **p** 87. C Whitnash *Cov* 86-90; V Dunchurch 90-01; R Dersingham w Anmer and Shernborne *Nor* 01-05; P-in-c Ore Ch Ch *Chich* 05-08; V 08-11; rtd 11; PtO *Pet* from 12. *7 Cheltenham Close, Rushden NN10 0NY* T: (01933) 355716 E: ronelverson@hotmail.co.uk

ELVEY, Ms Charlotte Evanthia. b 44. St Anne's Coll Ox BA 66 Bris Univ CertEd 67. S'wark Ord Course 91. **d** 94 **p** 95. C Sydenham St Bart *S'wark* 94-98; P-in-c Worcester Park Ch Ch w St Phil 98-03; V 03-14; rtd 14. *29 Percy Street, Shrewsbury SY1 2QQ* E: c.elvey@btinternet.com

ELVIDGE, Mrs Joanna. b 55. FCIPD 84. STETS BA 06. **d** 06 **p** 07. NSM Horsham *Chich* 06-14; P-in-c Hythe *Win* from 14. *The Vicarage, 14 Atheling Road, Hythe, Southampton SO45 6BR* T: (023) 8084 4336 E: joanna.elvidge@btinternet.com

ELVIN, Jonathan Paul Alistair. b 65. Bris Univ BSc 90 Fitzw Coll Cam BA 94. Ridley Hall Cam 92. **d** 95 **p** 96. C Gravesend St Geo *Roch* 95-98; C Ex St Leon w H Trin 98-07; Min Ex Trin CD 07-13; V Ex H Trin from 13. *23 Couper Meadows, Exeter EX2 7TF* T: (01392) 363627 E: jonny@trinityexeter.com

ELVY, Canon Peter David. b 38. Lon Univ BA 62 Fitzw Ho Cam BA 64 MA 68 Edin Univ PhD 95. Ridley Hall Cam. **d** 65 **p** 66. C Herne Cant 65-66; C New Addington 66-68; C Addiscombe St Mildred 69-71; Youth Chapl *Chelmsf* 71-80; V Gt Burstead 75-92; Can Chelmsf Cathl 80-92; V Chelsea All SS *Lon* 92-05; Can Ughelli from 98; Preb St Paul's Cathl from 05; rtd 05; PtO *Lon* from 05; *Roch* from 12; S'wark 12-14. *2 Honiton Mansions, Flood Street, London SW3 5TU* T: (020) 7795 0084 E: peterelvy@gmail.com

ELWIS, Malcolm John. b 42. Melbourne Univ DipEd 74 ACT ThL 74. St Jo Coll Morpeth 69. **d** 70 **p** 72. C Bentleigh St Jo Australia 70-72; C St Paul's Cathl Sale 72-73; PtO Melbourne 73-80; PtO *Chich* from 80; Chapl Eastbourne and Co Healthcare NHS Trust 88-02; Chapl E Sussex Co Healthcare NHS Trust 02-06; Chapl Sussex Partnership NHS

Foundn Trust 06-13; Sub Chapl HM Pris Lewes 92-04; Chapl 04-06; rtd 13. *Old Place, 83 Church Street, Willingdon, Eastbourne BN22 0HS* T: (01323) 657349
E: malcolmelwis21@hotmail.co.uk

ELWOOD, Alan Roy. b 54. Sarum & Wells Th Coll 90. **d** 92 **p** 93. C Street w Walton *B & W* 92-96; V Kingsbury Episcopi w E Lambrook, Hambridge etc 96-12. *Woodend Farm, Bishopswood, Chard TA20 3RZ*

ELY, Nigel Patrick. b 62. Thames Poly BA 83 Southn Univ BTh 92. Chich Th Coll 89. **d** 92 **p** 93. C Rustington *Chich* 92-93; C Bexhill St Pet 93-96; Chapl St Geo Post 16 Cen *Birm* 96-99; PtO 02-06; *Lich* 11-13; Asst Chapl R Wolv Hosps NHS Trust from 13; PtO *Birm* 14-15; C Lich St Mary from 15. *136 Trinity Road South, West Bromwich B70 6NF* T: 0121-293 4058 E: nigel_stgeorge@excite.com

ELY, Bishop of. *See* CONWAY, The Rt Revd Stephen David

ELY, Dean of. *See* BONNEY, The Very Revd Mark Philip John

EMBLIN, Canon Richard John. b 48. BEd 71 MA 81. S Dios Minl Tr Scheme 83. **d** 86 **p** 87. C S w N Hayling *Portsm* 86-89; P-in-c Wootton 89-95; V Cowes H Trin and St Mary 95-13; RD W Wight 01-07; Hon Can Portsm Cathl 05-13; rtd 13. *Address temp unknown* E: cowesvic@yahoo.com

EMERSON, Arthur Edward Richard. b 24. Lich Th Coll 69. **d** 72 **p** 73. C Barton upon Humber *Linc* 72-74; V Chapel St Leonards 75-88; P-in-c Hogsthorpe 77-88; V Chapel St Leonards w Hogsthorpe 88-91; rtd 91; PtO *Linc* 91-09. *119 Folkestone Road, Southport PR8 5PH* T: (01704) 514778

EMERSON, Mrs Jan Vivien. b 44. S Dios Minl Tr Scheme 89. **d** 92 **p** 95. NSM Chich St Paul and St Pet 92-94; NSM Bosham 94-02; Asst Chapl R W Sussex NHS Trust 02-09; Asst Chapl W Sussex Hosps NHS Foundn Trust from 09. *Lea-Rig, 3 Elm Park, Bosham, Chichester PO18 8PD* T: (01243) 574948
E: janvemerson@aol.com

EMERTON, Andrew Neil. b 72. York Univ BSc 93 Qu Coll Ox DPhil 96 Down Coll Cam BTh 05. Ridley Hall Cam 02. **d** 05 **p** 06. C Brompton H Trin w Onslow Square St Paul *Lon* 05-07; Asst Dean St Mellitus Coll and Dir St Paul's Th Cen from 08. *18 Collingham Road, London SW5 0LX* M: 07815-498162 E: andy.emerton@stmellitus.org

EMERTON, David Mark. b 78. Edin Univ MA 01 K Coll Lon MA 11. St Mellitus Coll BA 11. **d** 11 **p** 12. C E Twickenham St Steph *Lon* 11-14. *5 Tullylumb Terrace, Perth PH1 1BA* M: 07951-602102 E: dmemerton@gmail.com

EMERTON, Prof John Adney. b 28. CCC Ox BA 50 MA 54 CCC Cam MA 55 BD 60 St Jo Coll Cam DD 73 Edin Univ Hon DD 77 FBA 79. Wycliffe Hall Ox 50. **d** 52 **p** 53. C Birm Cathl 52-53; Asst Lect Th Birm Univ 52-53; Lect Hebrew and Aramaic Dur Univ 53-55; Lect Div Cam Univ 55-62; Fell St Pet Coll Ox 62-68; Reader in Semitic Philology Ox Univ 62-68; Regius Prof Hebrew Cam Univ 68-95; Fell St Jo Coll Cam from 70; Hon Can Jerusalem from 84; PtO *Ely* from 98. *34 Gough Way, Cambridge CB3 9LN* T: (01223) 363219

EMERY, Karen Maureen. *See* BECK, Karen Maureen

EMERY, Sandra Faith. b 45. **d** 10 **p** 11. NSM Minchinhampton w Box and Amberley *Glouc* from 10. *The Old Carriage House, Edge, Stroud GL6 6PQ* T: (01452) 814148
E: emery31@btinternet.com

EMINSON, Mark Franklin. b 79. Mert Coll Ox BA 01 MSt 03 MA 06 Trin Coll Cam BA 07. Westcott Ho Cam 05. **d** 08 **p** 09. C E Grinstead St Swithun *Chich* 08-12; V Pagham from 12. *38 Kings Drive, Bognor Regis PO21 4PZ* T: (01243) 261823 E: eminsons@btinternet.com

EMM, Robert Kenneth. b 46. K Coll Lon BD 68 AKC 68. **d** 69 **p** 70. C Hammersmith SS Mich and Geo White City Estate CD *Lon* 69-72; C Keynsham *B & W* 72-75; C Yeovil 75-80; TV Gt Grimsby St Mary and St Jas *Linc* 80-85; R N Thoresby 85-94; R Grainsby 85-94; V Waithe 85-94; R The North-Chapel Parishes from 94. *The Rectory, Church Lane, North Thoresby, Grimsby DN36 5QG* T/F: (01472) 840029
E: bob@bobemm.demon.co.uk

EMMANUEL, Rufin. b 63. Punjab Univ BA 87. Nat Catholic Inst of Th Pakistan 89. **d** 96 **p** 96. In RC Ch 96-09; Chapl Mid-Essex Hosp Services NHS Trust 09-11; Chapl Lewisham Healthcare NHS Trust 12-14; Chapl Lewisham and Greenwich NHS Trust from 14. *8 Mendip Place, Chelmsford CM1 2WT* T: (01245) 357579 M: 07583-087984 E: rufi49@hotmail.com *or* rufin.emmanuel@nhs.net

EMMEL, Canon Malcolm David. b 32. Qu Coll Birm. **d** 58 **p** 59. C Hessle *York* 58-62; Canada 62-66; V Catterick *Ripon* 66-73; V Pateley Bridge and Greenhow Hill 73-77; P-in-c Middlesmoor w Ramsgill 76-77; V Upper Nidderdale 77-88; RD Ripon 79-86; Hon Can Ripon Cathl 84-97; R Bedale 88-97; P-in-c Leeming 88-97; rtd 97; PtO *Leeds* from 97. *29 Greystone Close, Burley in Wharfedale, Ilkley LS29 7RS* T: (01943) 865047

EMMETT, Kerry Charles. b 46. St Jo Coll Dur BA 68. St Jo Coll Nottm 71. **d** 73 **p** 74. C Attenborough w Chilwell *S'well* 73-75; C Chilwell 75-76; C Wembley St Jo *Lon* 76-79; V Hanworth

St Rich 79-89; R Ravenstone and Swannington *Leic* 89-04; RD Akeley S 97-03; P-in-c Mountsorrel Ch Ch and St Pet 04-13; rtd 13; PtO *Leic* from 13. *1 Chamberlain's Field, Birstall, Leicester LE4 3LD* T: 0116-319 4736

EMMOTT, David Eugene. b 41. St Chad's Coll Dur BA 63. **d** 66 **p** 67. C Bingley H Trin *Bradf* 66-69; C Anfield St Marg *Liv* 69-70; C Kirkby 70-75; Chapl Newc Poly 75-78; Hon C Toxteth Park St Marg *Liv* 78-80; TV Upholland 80-88; V Southfields St Barn *S'wark* 88-99; TV Liv Our Lady and St Nic w St Anne 99-06; rtd 06. *6A Eastern Drive, Liverpool L19 0NB* T: 0151-281 5493 E: davidemmott@mac.com

EMMOTT, Douglas Brenton. b 45. K Coll Lon BD 78 AKC 78 York Univ MA 97. Linc Th Coll 79. **d** 80 **p** 81. C Kingston upon Hull St Alb *York* 80-83; V Scarborough St Sav w All SS 83-91; V York St Chad 91-99; V Leeds All So *Ripon* 99-07; rtd 07. *Le Moulin de Vernay, 72500 Dissay-sous-Courcillon, France* T: (0033) 2 43 46 53 82 M: 6 37 79 26 45
E: douglas.emmott@mac.com

EMMOTT, John Charles Lionel. b 32. SEITE 96. **d** 96 **p** 97. NSM Tenterden St Mich *Cant* 96-02; rtd 02; PtO *Cant* from 02. *58 Grange Crescent, St Michaels, Tenterden TN30 6DZ* T: (01580) 762092 E: emmott@connectfree.co.uk

EMPEY, Clement Adrian. b 42. TCD BA 64 MA 68 PhD 71. CITC. **d** 74 **p** 75. C Dublin St Ann *D & G* 75-76; I Kells-Inistioge Gp *C & O* 76-84; I Clane w Donadea and Coolcarrigan *M & K* 84-88; Hon Chapl Miss to Seafarers from 88; Sen Chapl Miss to Seamen (Irish Republic) 97-08; I Dublin St Ann and St Steph *D & G* 88-01; Preb Tassagard St Patr Cathl Dublin 82-89; Treas St Patr Cathl Dublin 89-91; Chan St Patr Cathl Dublin 91-96; Prec St Patr Cathl Dublin 96-01; Chapl Rotunda Hosp 98-08; Prin CITC 01-08; Prec Ch Ch Cathl Dublin 01-08; rtd 08. *5 Callenders Mill, Simmonstown Manor, Celbridge, Co Kildare, Republic of Ireland* T: (00353) (1) 503 7797 M: 87-902 2169 E: adrianempey@gmail.com

✠**EMPEY, The Rt Revd Walton Newcome Francis.** b 34. TCD BA 57 Hon FGCM 02. K Coll (NS) BD 68. **d** 58 **p** 59 **c** 81. C Glenageary *D & G* 58-60; Bp's C Grand Falls New Brunswick Canada 60-63; I Madawaska 63-66; I Stradbally *C & O* 66-71; Dean Limerick *L & K* 71-81; I Limerick St Mich 71-81; Preb Taney St Patr Cathl Dublin 73-81; Bp L & K 81-85; Bp M & K 85-96; Abp Dublin *D & G* 96-02; Preb Cualaun St Patr Cathl Dublin 96-02; rtd 02. *Rathmore Lodge, Rathmore, Tullow, Co Carlow, Republic of Ireland* T: (00353) (59) 916 1891
E: louempey@hotmail.com

EMTAGE, Miss Susan Raymond. b 34. St Mich Ho Ox 63. **dss** 79 **d** 87 **p** 94. SW Area Sec CPAS Women's Action 75-82; Leic St Chris 82-86; Bramerton w Surlingham *Nor* 86-88; C 87-88; C Rockland St Mary w Hellington, Bramerton etc 88-89; Par Dn W Bromwich St Jas and St Paul 89-94; C 94; rtd 94; Hon C Stapleton *Bris* 96-04. *23 Capel Court, The Burgage, Prestbury, Cheltenham GL52 3EL* T: (01242) 577535
E: sue.emtage@ukonline.co.uk

ENDALL, Peter John. b 38. Linc Th Coll 83. **d** 85 **p** 86. C Burley in Wharfedale *Bradf* 85-88; V Thwaites Brow 88-03; RD S Craven 96-02; rtd 03; Hon C Tamworth *Lich* 04-08; PtO from 08; *Leic* from 09. *19 Cordwell Close, Castle Donington, Derby DE74 2JL* T: (01332) 390863

ENDEAN, Michael George Devereux. b 33. Ox NSM Course. **d** 84 **p** 85. NSM Wantage Downs *Ox* 84-93. *87 Brookmead Drive, Wallingford OX10 9BH* T: (01491) 824231

ENDICOTT, Michael John. b 45. **d** 97. NSM Pontnewydd *Mon* 97; NSM Well Chr Healing Cen from 97. *Address temp unknown* T: (01633) 483660

ENEVER, John William. b 44. MBE 92. Open Univ BA 80. NTMTC 94. **d** 97 **p** 98. NSM Waltham H Cross *Chelmsf* 97-02; NSM Gt Ilford St Andr 02-08; Asst Chapl St Ormond Street Hosp for Children NHS Trust 08-10. *197 Pinhoe Road, Exeter EX4 8AB* T: (01392) 200510 E: johnenever@gmail.com

ENEVER, Canon Rosemary Alice Delande. b 45. Oak Hill Th Coll 86. **d** 88 **p** 94. NSM Gt Ilford St Jo *Chelmsf* 88-94; TV Waltham H Cross 94-02; Asst Area Dean Epping Forest 00-01; V Gt Ilford St Andr 02-10; RD Redbridge 06-08; Hon Can Chelmsf Cathl 06-10; rtd 10. *197 Pinhoe Road, Exeter EX4 8AB* T: (01392) 200510 E: rosemaryenever@googlemail.com

ENEVER, Mrs Susan Elizabeth. b 33. WMMTC 87. **d** 92 **p** 94. NSM Rugby *Cov* 92-97; PtO 97-05; Pet 98-05; *Worc* from 00. *7 Rocheberie Way, Rugby CV22 6EG* T: (01788) 813135

ENEVER, Vivian John. b 61. Collingwood Coll Dur BA 82 Cam Univ PGCE 85 Man Univ BPhil 99. Westcott Ho Cam 88. **d** 91 **p** 92. C Gt Crosby St Faith *Liv* 91-95; C Cantril Farm 95-97; TV Halas *Worc* 97-03; TR Newark w Coddington *S'well* 03-13; R Queen Thorne *Sarum* from 13; RD Sherborne from 14. *The Rectory, Trent, Sherborne DT9 4SL* T: (01935) 851118

ENGA, Mrs Charis Amelia. b 84. Dur Univ BA 05. St Mellitus Coll 10. **d** 12 **p** 13. C Highbury Ch Ch w St Jo and St Sav *Lon* from 12. *7 Lyndon Court, 67A Kelvin Road, London N5 2PP* T: (020) 7354 0741 E: curate@christchurchhighbury.com

ENGEL, Jeffrey Davis. b 38. Man Univ BA 59 Liv Univ PGCE 60 Aston Univ MSc 82 FCP 83. St Deiniol's Hawarden 86. **d** 89 **p** 90. NSM Formby St Pet *Liv* 89-92; C Prescot 92-94; P-in-c Hale 94-03; Dioc Adv for Past Care and Counselling 94-03; rtd 04; Chapl MU from 05. *Church View, West Street, Prescot L34 1LQ*

ENGELSEN, Christopher James. b 57. Nottm Univ BTh 86. Linc Th Coll 83. **d** 86 **p** 87. C Sprowston *Nor* 86-89; C High Harrogate Ch Ch *Ripon* 89-92; TV Seacroft 92-95; P-in-c Foulsham w Hindolveston and Guestwick *Nor* 95-01; P-in-c Hevingham w Hainford and Stratton Strawless 01-05; R Coltishall w Gt Hautbois, Frettenham etc from 05. *The Rectory, Rectory Road, Coltishall, Norwich NR12 7HL* T: (01603) 737255 E: christopher.engelsen@btinternet.com

ENGH, Dwayne Darcy. b 72. Westcott Ho Cam 13. **d** 15. C Cov St Mary from 15. *5 The Oaklands, Fletchamstead, Coventry CV4 9SY* M: 07425-606421 E: dwayneengh@shaw.ca

ENGLAND, Mrs Elizabeth Anne. b 73. Qu Coll Birm BA 15. **d** 15. C Codsall *Lich* from 15. *9 Windsor Gardens, Codsall, Wolverhampton WV8 2EX* M: 07930-264857 E: reverendelizabethengland@gmail.com

ENGLAND (née CLARK), Mrs Kathleen Christine. b 33. Newton Park Coll Bris TCert 53. St Mich Ho Ox 56 Trin Coll Bris 90. **d** 90 **p** 02. Personnel Sec SAMS 83-91; Asst Gen Sec 87-92; rtd 92; NSM Eastbourne H Trin *Chich* 90-02; NSM Eastbourne St Jo 02-08; PtO from 08. *11 Holywell Close, Eastbourne BN20 7RX* T: (01323) 640294 E: katieengland8@gmail.com

ENGLAND, Richard Alan. b 74. Sheff Univ BA 97 Dur Univ MA 07. Wycliffe Hall Ox 06. **d** 08 **p** 09. C Whitfield *Derby* 08-13; C Gillingham St Mark *Roch* from 13. *The Garden House, Vicarage Road, Gillingham ME7 5JA* E: richardalanengland@gmail.com

ENGLAND-SIMON, Haydn Henry. b 57. Llan Dioc Tr Scheme 92. **d** 96 **p** 97. NSM Penydarren *Llan* 96-97; C Caerphilly 97-01; V Pentre 01-07; V Ystradyfodwg from 07; AD Rhondda from 11. *The Vicarage, St David's Close, Pentre CF41 7AX* T: (01443) 433651

ENGLER, Mrs Margaret Dorothy. b 44. Lon Univ TCert 77. S'wark Ord Course 90. **d** 93 **p** 94. NSM Harlesden All So *Lon* 93-97; Dep Chapl HM Pris Wandsworth 97; Acting Chapl HM Pris Wormwood Scrubs 97-98; Chapl HM Pris High Down 98-04; rtd 04; PtO *Lon* 04-07; NSM Harlesden All So 07-13; PtO from 13. *33 Sheppard's Colleges, London Road, Bromley BR1 1PE* M: 07929-300048 E: margaretengler@waitrose.com

ENGLISH, Dana Leigh. **d** 12 **p** 13. C Rome *Eur* from 12. *via del Babuino 153, 00187 Rome, Italy* T: (0039) (06) 3600 1881 E: dlenglish@aya.yale.edu

ENGLISH, Helen Margaret (Sister Helen Julian). b 55. Newc Poly BA 76. Ripon Coll Cuddesdon 12. **d** 13. NSM Hanborough and Freeland *Ox* 13-14; NSM Edwinstowe *S'well* from 14; NSM Clipstone from 14; NSM Perlethorpe from 14. *St Mary's Convent, Wroslyn Road, Freeland, Witney OX29 8AJ, or Meden View, Budby, Newark NG22 9EX* E: helenjuliancsf@franciscans.org.uk

ENGLISH, Peter Gordon. b 31. Edin Univ MA 55. Ripon Hall Ox 59. **d** 61 **p** 62. C Bingley All SS *Bradf* 61-64; V Cottingley 64-66; Sugden Head 72; rtd 86; PtO *Sarum* from 96. *9 Carlton Row, Trowbridge BA14 0RJ* T: (01225) 752243

ENGLISH, Philip Trevor. b 37. Dur Univ BSc 60 FLIA 81 MITPA 84. Cranmer Hall Dur 60. **d** 62 **p** 63. C Hall Green Ascension *Birm* 62-66; Chapl St Jo Cathl Hong Kong 66-67; V Dorridge *Birm* 67-72; PtO *Ox* from 04. *Churchlands, Appletree Road, Chipping Warden, Banbury OX17 1LN* T: (01295) 660222 F: 660725 M: 07831-446421 E: pteifs@aol.com

ENNION, Peter. b 56. Aston Tr Scheme 85 Coll of Resurr Mirfield 87. **d** 89 **p** 90. C Middlewich w Byley *Ches* 89-91; C Aylestone St Andr w St Jas *Leic* 91-92; C Coppenhall *Ches* 92-94; P-in-c Newton in Mottram 94-99; P-in-c Tranmere St Paul w St Luke 99-04; V Torrisholme *Blackb* 04-11; P-in-c Blackpool St Mary 11-13; V from 13; V Blackpool H Cross from 13. *Holy Cross Vicarage, 388 Central Drive, Blackpool FY1 6LA* T: (01253) 343824 E: ennionpeter@gmail.com

ENNIS, Mrs Lesley. b 47. Bp Lonsdale Coll CertEd 68 Open Univ BA 84. OLM course 97. **d** 99 **p** 00. NSM Sowerby *Wakef* 99-13; NSM Norland 09-13; NSM Ryburn *Leeds* from 13. *26 Springfield, Sowerby Bridge HX6 1AD* T: (01422) 832747 M: 07703-628897 F: 842747 E: lesleyennis@hotmail.co.uk

ENNIS, Martin Michael. b 58. Man Univ BSc 80 MCollP 84. Sarum & Wells Th Coll 87. **d** 89 **p** 90. C Newquay *Truro* 89-92; C Tewkesbury w Walton Cardiff *Glouc* 92-95; P-in-c Brockworth 95-96; V 96-03; Hon C Wotton St Mary 09-10; V Tividale *Lich* from 10; P-in-c Wednesbury St Jas and St Jo from 14. *26 View Point, Tividale, Oldbury B69 1UU* T: (01384) 257888 E: frmennis@gmail.com

ENOCH, William Frederick Palmer. b 30. EMMTC 76. **d** 79 **p** 80. NSM Ilkeston St Mary *Derby* 79-85; P-in-c Ilkeston H Trin 85-95; rtd 95; PtO *Derby* 95-13. *82 Derby Road, Ilkeston DE7 5EZ* T: 0115-944 3003

ENSOR, Paul George. b 56. Ripon Coll Cuddesdon. **d** 82 **p** 83. C Newington St Mary *S'wark* 82-87; TV Croydon St Jo 87-91; P-in-c Brandon and Santon Downham *St E* 91-92; R Brandon and Santon Downham w Elveden 92-95; V Mitcham St Olave *S'wark* 95-13; V Kennington Park St Agnes from 13. *St Agnes Vicarage, 37 St Agnes Place, London SE11 4BB* T: (020) 7091 7342 E: pedrazzini@ukgateway.net

ENSOR, Canon Terence Bryan. b 45. K Coll Lon BD 78 AKC 78. Westcott Ho Cam 78. **d** 79 **p** 80. C Bermondsey St Hugh CD *S'wark* 79-82; Seychelles 82-85; V Northampton St Benedict *Pet* 85-90; Uruguay 90-93; Fieldworker USPG Blackb, Bradf, Carl and Wakef 93-96; V Blackb St Jas 96-02; Assoc P Caracas Venezuela 02-03; Hon Can Venezuela and Curazao from 02; TV Ribbleton *Blackb* 03-06; C Standish 06-11; rtd 11; PtO *Blackb* from 11. *18 Kingfisher Close, Blackburn BB1 8NS* T: (01254) 580227 E: ensor@hotmail.co.uk

ENTICOTT, Ian Peter. b 59. Sheff Univ BA 82 St Jo Coll Dur MA 00. Cranmer Hall Dur 97. **d** 99 **p** 00. C Higher Bebington *Ches* 99-02; P-in-c Kelsall 02-10; Dir African Pastors' Fellowship 10-14; PtO *Cov* 10-14; V Accrington St Jas and St Paul *Blackb* from 14. *St Paul's Vicarage, Barnfield Street, Accrington BB5 2AQ* T: (01254) 433590 M: 07941-389621 E: ian.enticott@dunelm.org.uk

ENTWISLE, George Barry. b 43. St Jo Coll Ox BA 66 MA 72 Massey Univ (NZ) MEd 99. Linc Th Coll 73. **d** 75 **p** 76. C Rawmarsh w Parkgate *Sheff* 75-78; C Ashburton New Zealand 78-80; V Upper Clutha 80-84; V Gore 84-94; Can St Paul's Cathl Dunedin 87-94; Hon C Upper Clutha 01-06; rtd 08. *5 Bruce Street, Cromwell 9310, New Zealand* T/F: (0064) (3) 445 1797 M: 27-426 5539 E: b.entwisle@xtra.co.nz

ENTWISTLE, Christopher John. b 47. NOC 79. **d** 82 **p** 83. NSM Colne H Trin *Blackb* 82-84; C Poulton-le-Fylde 84-87; V Blackpool St Paul 87-96; RD Blackpool 94-96; P-in-c Overton 96-01; V Ashton-on-Ribble St Andr 01-06; TV W Preston 06-10; AD Preston 04-09; rtd 10; PtO *Blackb* from 10. *9 Chatsworth Avenue, Warton, Preston PR4 1BQ* T: (01772) 460435 E: revcjentwistle@yahoo.co.uk

ENTWISTLE, Frank Roland. b 37. Dur Univ BA 59. Cranmer Hall Dur 59. **d** 61 **p** 62. C Harborne Heath *Birm* 61-65; S Area Sec BCMS 65-66; Educn Sec 66-73; Hon C Wallington *S'wark* 68-73; UCCF 73-02; Hon C Ware Ch Ch *St Alb* 73-76; Hon C Leic H Trin w St Jo 76-02; rtd 02. *50 Redlands Road, Fremington, Barnstaple EX31 2NY* T: (01271) 342449 E: entwistles@cwcom.net

ENWUCHOLA, Canon Benjamin Ameh. b 56. Lon Bible Coll BA 94. **d** 95 **p** 98. NSM S Tottenham St Ann *Lon* 96-99; NSM W Kilburn St Luke w St Simon and St Jude 99-13; NSM W Kilburn St Luke and Harrow Road Em from 13; Chapl Nigerian Congregation from 99; Hon Can Ondo from 02. *The Nigerian Chaplaincy Office, 79 Alderney Gardens, Northolt UB5 5BT* T: (020) 3719 5856 E: benwuchola@yahoo.co.uk *or* nigerianchaplaincy@yahoo.co.uk

EPPS, Christopher Derek. b 54. ACII 79. Linc Th Coll 95. **d** 95 **p** 96. C Clevedon St Jo *B & W* 95-98; R St John w Millbrook *Truro* 98-03; P-in-c Truro St Geo and St Jo 03-15; P-in-c Truro St Paul and St Clem 03-12; C 12-15; V Truro St Paul, St Geo and St Jo from 15. *St George's Vicarage, St George's Road, Truro TR1 3NR* T: (01872) 272630 F: 823559 E: frcdepps@btinternet.com

EPPS, Gerald Ralph. b 31. Open Univ BA 79. Oak Hill Th Coll 52 K Coll Lon 54. **d** 57 **p** 58. C Slade Green *Roch* 57-60; V Freethorpe w Wickhampton *Nor* 60-70; P-in-c Halvergate w Tunstall 62-67; V 67-70; R Pulham St Mary Magd 70-80; P-in-c Alburgh 76-77; P-in-c Denton 76-77; P-in-c Pulham St Mary V 76-80; R Pulham 80-91; rtd 91; PtO *Nor* from 91. *10 Lime Close, Harleston IP20 9DG* T: (01379) 854532

EPPS (formerly REEVE), Mrs Sally Ann. b 55. SEITE 07. **d** 10 **p** 11. C Ringmer *Chich* 10-14; P-in-c Burwash from 14. *The Rectory, Rectory Close, Etchingham Road, Burwash, Etchingham TN19 7BH* T: (01435) 882301 E: sally.epps@btinternet.com

EPTON, John Alan. b 47. EMMTC 08. **d** 10 **p** 11. NSM Morton and Stonebroom w Shirland *Derby* from 10. *Phare, 22 Fernwood Close, Shirland, Alfreton DE55 6BW* T: (01773) 834153

EQUEALL, Canon David Edward Royston. b 41. Open Univ BA. St Mich Coll Llan 68. **d** 71 **p** 72. C Mountain Ash *Llan* 71-74; C Gabalfa and Chapl Asst Univ Hosp of Wales Cardiff 74-77; Chapl 77-79; Chapl N Gen Hosp Sheff 79-94; Chapl N Gen Hosp NHS Trust Sheff 94-02; Chapl Manager Sheff Teaching Hosps NHS Trust 02-06; Hon Can Sheff Cathl 98-06; rtd 06. *4 Riverside Court, Dinnington, Sheffield S25 3PH* T: (01909) 655355

ERIKSSON, Olaf Lennart. b 62. Ridley Hall Cam 03. **d** 05 **p** 06. C Cockerton *Dur* 05-09; P-in-c Millfield St Mark and Pallion St Luke 09-14; Chapl Maisons-Laffitte *Eur* from 14. *Holy Trinity, 15 avenue Carnot, 78600 Maisons-Laffitte, France* T/F: (0033) 1 39 62 34 97 E: revdolaf@googlemail.com *or* htcml@aol.com

ERLANDSON, Samuel Benjamin. b 88. Ban Univ BA 10 Cardiff Univ BTh 13. St Mich Coll Llan 10. **d** 13 **p** 14. C LLay, Rossett and Isycoed *St As* from 13. *19 Acacia Court, Llay, Wrexham LL12 0TX* T: (01978) 639781 M: 07775-778469 E: s.erlandson@hotmail.co.uk

ERLEBACH, Jonathan Bartholomew (Bart). b 77. York Univ BSc 99. Oak Hill Th Coll BA 05. **d** 05 **p** 06. C Hove Bp Hannington Memorial *Chich* 05-09; C Surbiton Hill Ch Ch *S'wark* from 09. *181 Elgar Avenue, Surbiton KT5 9JX* T: (020) 8399 1503 M: 07714-379836 E: bartbev@erlebach.org.uk

✠**ERNEST, The Most Revd Gerald James Ian.** b 54. **p** 85 **c** 01. Bp Mauritius from 01; Abp Indian Ocean from 08. *Bishop's House, Nalletamby Avenue, Phoenix, Mauritius* T: (00230) 686 5158 F: 697 1096 E: dioang@intnet.mu

ERREY, Rosalind Elisabeth. *See* RUTHERFORD, Rosalind Elisabeth

ERRIDGE, David John. b 45. Tyndale Hall Bris 66. **d** 69 **p** 70. C Bootle St Matt *Liv* 69-72; C Horwich H Trin *Man* 72-77; R Blackley St Andr 77-00; AD N Man 85-94; V Acomb St Steph and St Aid *York* 00-10; rtd 10; PtO *York* from 11. *51 Barlow Street, Acomb, York YO26 5HS* T: (01904) 797614 E: davidandsusan51@hotmail.co.uk

ERRIDGE, Timothy John. b 65. Wye Coll Lon BSc 86 Croydon Coll CertEd 90. St Jo Coll Nottm 08. **d** 10 **p** 11. C Congresbury w Puxton and Hewish St Ann *B & W* 10-14; P-in-c Bleadon from 14. *The Rectory, 17 Coronation Road, Bleadon, Weston-super-Mare BS24 0PG* T: (01934) 815404 E: revtimerridge@gmail.com

ERRINGTON, Mrs Sarah. b 67. UEA BA 90. Wycliffe Hall Ox BTh 94. **d** 97 **p** 98. C Gateacre *Liv* 97-02; TV Halewood 02-10; TV Wrexham *St As* from 10. *The Vicarage, 160 Borras Road, Wrexham LL13 9ER* T: (01978) 266018 E: vicarstjohnswxm@gmail.com

ERVING, Ms Christel Estelle Ann. b 79. Liv Univ BSc 01 St Jo Coll Dur BA 15. Cranmer Hall Dur 13. C Walton St Luke *Liv* from 15. *166 Wadham Road, Bootle L20 2DF* M: 07477-594790 E: christel.erving@outlook.com

ESAU, John Owen. b 39. St Mich Coll Llan 93. **d** 95 **p** 96. Min Can St D Cathl 95-97; V Llanpumsaint w Llanllawddog 97-01; V Cydweli and Llandyfaelog 01-03; R Aberporth w Tremain w Blaenporth and Betws Ifan 03-04; rtd 04. *Nursery Cottage, 14 Grove Place, Cardiff CF14 4QS* T: (029) 2061 2190

ESCOLME, Miss Doreen. b 29. St Jo Coll Nottm 82. **dss** 83 **d** 87 **p** 94. Hunslet Moor St Pet and St Cuth *Ripon* 83-87; C 87-88; Par Dn Wyther 88-94; C 94; rtd 94; PtO *Leeds* from 94. *6 Heather Gardens, Leeds LS13 4LF* T: 0113-257 9055

ESCRITT, Canon Margaret Ruth. b 37. Selly Oak Coll IDC 62. **d** 87 **p** 94. Hon C Selby Abbey *York* 87-90; C Kexby w Wilberfoss 93-94; Asst Chapl HM Pris Full Sutton 92-94; Chapl HM Pris Everthorpe 95-98; Can and Preb York Minster 95-01; rtd 97; PtO *York* from 01. *73 Heslington Lane, York YO10 4HN* T: (01904) 639444

ESDAILE, Canon Adrian George Kennedy. b 35. Mert Coll Ox BA 57 MA 61. Wells Th Coll 59. **d** 61 **p** 62. C St Helier *S'wark* 61-64; C Wimbledon 64-68; V Hackbridge and N Beddington 68-80; RD Sutton 76-80; TR Chipping Barnet w Arkley *St Alb* 80-01; RD Barnet 89-94; Hon Can St Alb 94-01; rtd 01; PtO *S'wark* from 01; *Guildf* from 02. *29 Hereford Close, Epsom KT18 5DZ* T/F: (01372) 723770 E: esdaileadrian@yahoo.co.uk

ESHUN, Daniel Justice. b 69. Cape Coast Univ Ghana BA 93 K Coll Lon MA 97 PhD 00 St Jo Coll Dur MA 03. Cranmer Hall Dur 00. **d** 03 **p** 04. C Staines *Lon* 03-06; C Kensal Town St Thos w St Andr and St Phil 06-07; Chapl Roehampton Univ *S'wark* from 07. *Whitelands College, Holybourne Avenue, London SW15 4JD* T: (020) 8392 3500 E: daniel.eshun@yahoo.co.uk

ESPIN-BRADLEY, Richard John. b 61. Lanc Univ BSc 84. Oak Hill Th Coll 93. **d** 95 **p** 96. C Brundall w Braydeston and Postwick *Nor* 95-98; C St Helier *S'wark* 98-02; V Wolverhampton St Luke *Lich* from 02. *St Luke's Vicarage, 122 Goldthorn Hill, Wolverhampton WV2 3HU* T: (01902) 340261 E: vicar@stlukeswolverhampton.org *or* richardeb@idnet.com

ESSEX, Mary Rose. b 50. **d** 02 **p** 03. NSM E and W Leake, Stanford-on-Soar, Rempstone etc *S'well* 02-08; P-in-c Kirkby Woodhouse 08-15; rtd 15. *1A Bley Avenue, East Leake, Loughborough LE12 6NX* T: (01509) 856521 E: rev.maryessex@btopenworld.com

ETCHES, Haigh David. b 45. St Jo Coll Dur BA 71. Cranmer Hall Dur. **d** 73 **p** 74. C Whitnash *Cov* 73-77; C Wallingford w Crowmarsh Gifford etc *Ox* 77-83; P-in-c Bearwood 83-86; R 86-11; rtd 11. *Silver Birches, 6 Chelmick Drive, Church Stretton SY6 7BP* T: (01694) 723266 E: haigh.etches@btinternet.com

ETHERIDGE, Alastair. b 60. **d** 10 **p** 11. NSM Woking Ch Ch *Guildf* 10-15; NSM Fisherton Anger *Sarum* from 15. *Address temp unknown*

ETHERIDGE, Canon Richard Thomas. b 32. Lon Univ BD 62. ALCD 61. **d** 62 **p** 63. C Wilmington *Roch* 62-65; C Rainham 65-69; V Langley St Jo *Birm* 69-01; P-in-c Oldbury 83-01; P-in-c Langley St Mich 95-01; Hon Can Birm Cathl 97-01; rtd 01; PtO *Birm* 01-12; *Worc* from 02. *23 Scobell Close, Pershore, Worcester WR10 1QJ* T: (01386) 554745

ETHERINGTON (née SMITH), Mrs Elizabeth Anne. b 68. Keele Univ BA 95. Ridley Hall Cam 04. **d** 06 **p** 07. C E Twickenham St Steph *Lon* 06-11; C Hounslow H Trin w St Paul and St Mary 12-15; V Hounslow St Paul and Gd Shep from 15. *183 Bath Road, Hounslow TW3 3BU* M: 07903-112082 E: libbyetherington@hotmail.com

ETHERINGTON, Mrs Ferial Mary Gould. b 44. Open Univ BA. St Alb Minl Tr Scheme 86. **d** 93 **p** 94. NSM Luton St Chris Round Green *St Alb* 93-04; Selection Sec and Co-ord for OLM Min Division 97-04; rtd 04; PtO *Carl* 04-10; Dioc Min Review Officer 05-11; TV Cartmel Peninsula 10-14. *North View, Durdar, Carlisle CA2 4TX* E: ferial.etherington@btinternet.com

ETHERINGTON, Robert Barry. b 37. Man Univ BA 62. Linc Th Coll 62. **d** 64 **p** 65. C Linc St Jo 64-67; C Frodingham 67-69; V Reepham 69-78; Ind Chapl 70-78; *St Alb* 78-88; V Luton St Chris Round Green 88-04; RD Luton 98-02; rtd 04; PtO *Carl* from 05. *North View, Durdar, Carlisle CA2 4TX*

ETHERTON, Christopher Charles. b 47. UMIST BSc 68. STETS 04. **d** 07 **p** 08. NSM Lower Sandown St Jo and Sandown Ch Ch *Portsm* 07-10; P-in-c Binstead 10-14; P-in-c Havenstreet St Pet 10-14; NSM Bourton-on-the-Water w Clapton etc *Glouc* from 14. *The Vicarage, 6 De Havilland Road, Upper Rissington, Cheltenham GL54 2NZ* M: 07906-238368 T: (01451) 798651 E: revd.etherton@uwclub.net

ETHERTON, Geoffrey Robert. b 74. Univ of Cen England in Birm BMus 96. Trin Coll Bris BA 01. **d** 02 **p** 03. C Trentham and Hanford *Lich* 02-03; C Hanley H Ev 03-06; Pioneer Min 04-06. *c/o Crockford, Church House, Great Smith Street, London SW1P 3AZ*

EUNSON, Ms Lisa Kei. b 54. San Francisco State Univ BA 78. Ch Div Sch of the Pacific (USA) MDiv 01. **d** 01 **p** 02. C Burlingame USA 01-06; R Banchory *Ab* from 06; R Kincardine O'Neil from 06. *The Rectory, High Street, Banchory AB31 5TB* T: (01330) 826045 *or* 822783 M: 07917-886672 E: lisa.eunson@googlemail.com

EUROPE, Bishop of Gibraltar in. *See* INNES, The Rt Revd Robert Neil

EUROPE, Suffragan Bishop in. *See* HAMID, The Rt Revd David

EUSTICE, Peter Lafevre. b 32. AKC 56. **d** 57 **p** 58. C Finsbury Park St Thos *Lon* 57-60; C Redruth *Truro* 60-63; V Treslothan 63-71; V Falmouth All SS 71-76; R St Stephen in Brannel 76-97; rtd 97; PtO *Truro* from 97. *21 Gloucester Avenue, Carlyon Bay, St Austell PL25 3PT* T: (01726) 817343

EVANS, Adrian John. b 81. St Jo Coll Nottm BA 13. **d** 13 **p** 14. C Walmley *Birm* from 13. *90 Walmley Ash Road, Sutton Coldfield, Birmingham B76 1JB* M: 07961-375769 E: adrianevans007@gmail.com

EVANS, Miss Alison Jane. b 66. Sheff Univ BSc 87 Bris Univ PGCE 93. Trin Coll Bris BA 04. **d** 04 **p** 05. C Finham *Cov* 04-08; V Cov St Geo from 08. *St George's Vicarage, 101 Moseley Avenue, Coventry CV6 1HR* T: (024) 7659 1994 E: aevans@talktalk.net

EVANS, The Ven Alun Wyn. b 47. Down Coll Cam BA 70 MA 73. Cuddesdon Coll 70. **d** 72 **p** 73. C Bargoed w Brithdir *Llan* 72-74; C Bargoed and Deri w Brithdir 74-75; C Coity w Nolton 75-77; V Cwmavon 77-81; Warden of Ords 80-81; V Llangynwyd w Maesteg 81-86; Prov Officer for Soc Resp 86-93; V Cardiff Ch Ch *Llan* 93-99; V Swansea St Mary w H Trin *S & B* 99-00; TR Cen Swansea 00-04; Can Res Brecon Cathl 00-04; V Cynwil Elfed and Newchurch *St D* 04-06; V Cynwyl Elfed w Newchurch and Trelech a'r Betws 06-09; P-in-c Llanarthne and Llanddarog 09-14; Adn Carmarthen 04-12; rtd 14; PtO *St D* from 14. *Gwili Cottage, 7 Glangwili, Carmarthen SA31 2PP* T: (01267) 220330

EVANS, Andrew. *See* EVANS, John Andrew

EVANS, Andrew. b 57. Southn Univ BEd 80. S Dios Minl Tr Scheme 88. **d** 91 **p** 92. NSM Cricklade w Latton *Bris* 91-97; C Yatton Keynell 97-99; TV By Brook 99-00; R Hullavington, Norton and Stanton St Quintin 00-09; P-in-c Sherston Magna, Easton Grey, Luckington etc 06-09; Bp's Adv for Rural Min 00-09; Hon Can Bris Cathl 05-09; AD N Wilts 06-09;

TR Bridport *Sarum* from 09; OCM from 00. *The Rectory, 84 South Street, Bridport DT6 3NW* T: (01308) 422138 M: 07931-616329 E: canonandrewevans@gmail.com

EVANS, Andrew Eric. b 58. Sheff Univ LLB 80 Solicitor 83. Trin Coll Bris 01. **d** 03 **p** 04. C Gt Bookham *Guildf* 03-06; P-in-c Broughton Gifford, Gt Chalfield and Holt *Sarum* 06-14; R from 14; C Atworth w Shaw and Whitley from 07; C Melksham 07-10; TR 10-14; RD Bradford 08-13. *The Rectory, Ham Green, Holt, Trowbridge BA14 7PZ* T: (01225) 782289 E: goodevansitsandrew@tiscali.co.uk

EVANS (née HADFIELD), Mrs Ann Elizabeth Mary. b 78. Mt Allison Univ Canada BMus 99 Ex Univ MA 07. St Mich Coll Llan 09. **d** 12 **p** 13. C Three Cliffs *S & B* 12-15; C Hawarden *St As* from 15. *St Mary's Vicarage, Church Road, Broughton, Chester CH4 0QB* M: 07952-680167 T: (01244) 796668 E: revmaryevans@sky.com

EVANS, Anne. b 47. Ches Coll of HE MTh 99. **d** 05 **p** 06. OLM Broughton *Lich* from 05; OLM Myddle from 05; OLM Loppington w Newtown from 05. *The Fields, Welshampton, Ellesmere SY12 0NP* T: (01948) 710206

EVANS, Canon Anthony Nigel. b 53. Nottm Univ BA 74 Fitzw Coll Cam BA 76. Westcott Ho Cam 74. **d** 77 **p** 78. C Sneinton St Cypr *S'well* 77-80; C Worksop Priory 80-83; V Nottingham St Geo w St Jo 83-88; R Ordsall 88-95; P-in-c Sutton in Ashfield St Mary 95-07; AD Newstead 01-05; Bp's Dom Chapl 07-11; Hon Can S'well Minster 04-11; P-in-c Edwinstowe from 11; P-in-c Perlethorpe from 11; P-in-c Clipstone from 11. *5 West Lane, Edwinstowe, Mansfield NG21 9QT* T: (01623) 822430 E: frtony@care4free.net

EVANS, Ashley Francis. b 58. Birm Univ BA 79. WEMTC 00. **d** 03 **p** 04. C Kington w Huntington, Old Radnor, Kinnerton etc *Heref* 03-07; P-in-c Ewyas Harold w Dulas, Kenderchurch etc 07-10; R from 11; RD Abbeydore 09-14. *The Rectory, Ewyas Harold, Hereford HR2 0EZ* T: (01981) 240079 M: 07763-070177 E: revd@penandashley.co.uk

EVANS, Brian. b 34. Open Univ BA 86. St Deiniol's Hawarden 70. **d** 71 **p** 72. C Porthkerry *Llan* 71-72; C Barry All SS 72-75; V Abercynon 75-82; V Pendoylan w Welsh St Donats 82-87; R Maentwrog w Trawsfynydd *Ban* 87-99; rtd 99; PtO *Ban* 99-14. *Madryn, 46 Glan Ysgethin, Talybont LL43 2BB* T: (01341) 247965

EVANS, Canon Caroline Mary. b 46. Ban Coll CertEd 69. St Jo Coll Nottm. **d** 86 **p** 97. C Llanbeblig w Caernarfon and Betws Garmon etc *Ban* 86-88; Dn-in-c Bodedern w Llechgynfarwy and Llechylched etc 88-97; V 97; RD Llifon and Talybolion 96-97; R Llanfairfechan w Aber 97-11; Can Cursal Ban Cathl 03-11; rtd 11; PtO *Ban* 11-14; Hon C Llanrwst, Llanddoged w Capel Garmon etc *St As* 12-14; PtO from 14; *Ban* from 15. *15 Parc Sychnant, Conwy LL32 8SB*

EVANS, Mrs Christine Elizabeth. b 54. RGN 75 RMHN 77. STETS. **d** 12 **p** 13. NSM Kingswood *Bris* from 12; NSM Hanham from 12. *3 Teewell Hill, Bristol BS16 5PA* T: 0117-957 0731 E: se007a4909_2@blueyonder.co.uk

EVANS, Christopher Idris. b 51. Chich Th Coll 74. **d** 77 **p** 78. C Gelligaer *Llan* 77-80; C St Andrews Major w Michaelston-le-Pit 80-81; V Llangeinor 81-87; V Watlington w Pyrton and Shirburn *Ox* 87-97; R Icknield from 97. *The Vicarage, Hill Road, Watlington OX49 5AD* T: (01491) 612494 E: c.idris.evans@gmail.com

EVANS, Christopher James Catherall. b 75. Oak Hill Th Coll. **d** 11 **p** 12. C Chadderton Ch Ch *Man* from 11. *23 Lindale Avenue, Chadderton, Oldham OL9 9DW* T: 0161-628 1616

EVANS, Christopher Jonathan. b 43. AKC 67 and 88. **d** 68 **p** 69. C Wednesfield St Thos *Lich* 68-71; C Dorridge *Birm* 71-74; V Marston Green 74-81; V Acocks Green 81-86; RD Yardley 84-86; V Hill 86-88; Area Officer COPEC Housing Trust 88-91; V Harborne St Pet *Birm* 91-08; rtd 08; PtO *Heref* from 08. *5 The Square, Clun, Craven Arms SY7 9EY* T: (01588) 640439 E: jo@evansj84.fsnet.co.uk

EVANS, Clive Richard. b 49. WEMTC 99. **d** 00 **p** 01. OLM Heref S Wye 00-13; rtd 13; PtO *Heref* from 14. *14 St Vincents Cross, Lower Bullingham, Hereford HR2 6EL* T: (01432) 270838 E: clivelinda@cliveevans11.wanadoo.co.uk

EVANS, Clive Roger. b 59. Worc Coll Ox BA 80 MA 84. St Jo Coll Nottm 94. **d** 94 **p** 95. C Barton Seagrave w Warkton *Pet* 94-97; V Long Buckby w Watford 97-11; P-in-c W Haddon w Winwick and Ravensthorpe 03-11; V Long Buckby w Watford and W Haddon w Winwick 11-13; RD Brixworth 01-09; Can Pet Cathl 09-13; V Bromyard and Stoke Lacy *Heref* from 13. *The Vicarage, 28 Church Lane, Bromyard HR7 4DZ* T: (01885) 788275 E: cliveevans@tiscali.co.uk

EVANS, Canon Colin Rex. b 24. Reading Univ BA 49. Linc Th Coll. **d** 57 **p** 58. C Boultham *Linc* 57-59; C Linc St Nic w St Jo

Newport 59-62; V Linc St Mary-le-Wigford w St Martin 62-66; P-in-c Linc St Faith 63-66; R Bassingham 66-74; V Aubourn w Haddington 66-74; V Carlton-le-Moorland w Stapleford 66-74; R Skinnand 66-74; R Thurlby w Norton Disney 66-74; RD Graffoe 69-74; RD Elloe E 74-89; Can and Preb Linc Cathl 74-89; V Holbeach 74-89; rtd 90; Hon C Dawlish *Ex* 90-97; RD Kenn 95-97; PtO from 97. *87 West Cliff Park Drive, Dawlish EX7 9EL* T: (01626) 865191

EVANS, Daniel Barri. b 70. St Steph Ho Ox 01. **d** 03 **p** 04. C Weymouth H Trin *Sarum* 03-07; V Llwynderw *S & B* 07-15; TV Hawarden *St As* from 15. *St Mary's Vicarage, Church Road, Broughton, Chester CH4 0QB* M: 07948-692927 T: (01244) 796668 E: revdannyevans@sky.com

EVANS, Miss Daphne Gillian. b 41. Bible Tr Inst Glas 67 Trin Coll Bris IDC 75. **dss** 83 **d** 87. Team Dn Wenlock *Heref* 87-88; rtd 88. *Address temp unknown*

EVANS, Canon David. b 37. Keble Coll Ox BA 60 MA 65 Lon Univ BD 64. Wells Th Coll 62. **d** 64 **p** 65. Min Can Brecon Cathl 64-68; C Brecon w Battle 64-68; C Swansea St Mary and H Trin 68-71; Chapl Univ of Wales (Swansea) 68-71; Bp's Chapl for Samaritan and Soc Work *Birm* 71-75; Jt Gen Sec Samaritans 75-84; Gen Sec 84-89; R Heyford w Stowe Nine Churches *Pet* 89-96; R Heyford w Stowe Nine Churches and Flore etc 96-01; Chapl Northants Police 89-01; RD Daventry *Pet* 96-00; Can Pet Cathl 97-01; rtd 01; PtO *Ex* from 01. *Curlew River, The Strand, Starcross, Exeter EX6 8PA* T: (01626) 891712

EVANS, David. b 37. Open Univ BA 73 FRSA 95. St Mich Coll Llan 65. **d** 67 **p** 68. C Swansea St Pet *S & B* 67-70; C St Austell *Truro* 70-75; R Purley *Ox* 75-90; RD Bradfield 85-90; R Bryanston Square St Mary w St Marylebone St Mark *Lon* 90-99; P-in-c St Marylebone Ch Ch 90-91; R Nuthurst and Mannings Heath *Chich* 99-07; P-in-c 07-11; rtd 11. *10 Eastgate Mews, Brighton, Horsham RH13 5AW* T: (01403) 581394

EVANS, David Burton. b 35. Open Univ BA 87 Goldsmiths' Coll Lon BMus 93. K Coll Lon 58 Edin Th Coll 60. **d** 62 **p** 63. C Leeds St Hilda *Ripon* 62-63; C Cross Green St Sav and St Hilda 63-67; Min Can Dur Cathl 67-71; PV Chich Cathl 71-74; Chapl Prebendal Sch Chich 71-74; R Lynch w Iping Marsh *Chich* 74-79; V Easebourne 79-86; Chapl K Edw VII Hosp Midhurst 77-86; R St Mich Cornhill w St Pet le Poer etc *Lon* 86-96; rtd 96; Pau *Eur* 96-01; PtO from 05. *128 Little Breach, Chichester PO19 5UA* T: (01243) 773266 M: 07795-662991 E: evtherev7@btinternet.com

EVANS, David Elwyn. b 43. St Mich Coll Llan 71. **d** 73 **p** 74. C Llandybie *St D* 73-75; C Llanelli 75-78; V Tre-lech a'r Betws w Abernant and Llanwinio 78-02; rtd 02. *8 Ger y Llan, The Parade, Carmarthen SA31 1LY*

EVANS, David Frederick Francis. b 35. Univ of Wales BSc 59. Wells Th Coll 59. **d** 61 **p** 62. C Eltham St Jo *S'wark* 61-64; C Banbury *Ox* 64-69; V Brize Norton and Carterton 69-73; V Tilehurst St Geo 73-84; V Lydney w Aylburton *Glouc* 84-95; V Lydney 95-02; RD Forest S 90-95; Chapl Severn NHS Trust 94-02; rtd 02. *2 Bodforis, Braichmelyn, Bethesda, Bangor LL57 3PU* T: (01248) 601994

EVANS, David Julian James. b 65. Rob Coll Cam BA 87. Westcott Ho Cam 03. **d** 05 **p** 06. SSF 93-99; C W Hackney St Barn *Lon* 05-08; C St John-at-Hackney 08-10; V Walworth St Chris *S'wark* from 10; Warden Pemb Coll Miss Walworth from 10. *76 Tatum Street, London SE17 1QR* T: (020) 7740 6382 E: davidjjevans@me.com

EVANS, David Leslie Bowen. b 28. Univ of Wales (Lamp) BA 52 LTh 54. **d** 54 **p** 55. C Cardigan *St D* 54-57; C Llangathen w Llanfihangel Cilfargen 57-58; C Betws w Ammanford 58-60; V Betws Ifan 60-64; V Burry Port and Pwll 64-76; V Cardiff Dewi Sant *Llan* 76-86; Asst Chapl HM Pris Cardiff 76-86; V Llan-llwch w Llangain and Llangynog *St D* 86-95; Can St D Cathl 89-90; rtd 95. *35 Ger y Capel, Llangain, Carmarthen SA33 5AQ* T: (01267) 241916

EVANS, David Meurig Ashton. b 56. Univ of Wales (Cardiff) BSc 78 PhD 82 Lon Bible Coll BA 90. SEITE 12. **d** 13 **p** 14. C Lewisham St Mary *S'wark* from 13. *14 Keats Close, London SE1 5TZ* T: (020) 7231 6104 M: 07919-416900 E: davidmaevans1@gmail.com

EVANS, Capt David Raymond. b 48. **d** 11 **p** 12. C Dale and St Brides w Marloes etc *St D* 11-14. *11 Lapwing Gardens, Weston-super-Mare BS22 8UP* M: 07814-699336 E: landevans79@aol.com

EVANS, David Richard. b 47. St Steph Ho Ox 68. **d** 72 **p** 73. C Cardiff St Jo *Llan* 72-76; PV Llan Cathl 76-80; V Cleeve Prior and The Littletons *Worc* 80-12; rtd 12. *Stone Barn, Main Street, Evesham WR11 8LG* E: father.richard@tesco.net

✠**EVANS, The Rt Revd David Richard John.** b 38. G&C Coll Cam BA 63 MA 66. Clifton Th Coll 63. **d** 65 **p** 66 **c** 78. C Enfield Ch Ch Trent Park *Lon* 65-68; SAMS Argentina 69-77;

Peru 77-88; Bp Peru 78-88; Bp Bolivia 82-88; Asst Bp Bradf 88-93; Gen Sec SAMS 93-03; Hon Asst Bp Chich 94-97; Hon Asst Bp Roch 95-97; Hon Asst Bp Birm 97-03; rtd 03; Hon Asst Bp Cov from 03; Hon C Alderminster and Halford 03-07; Hon C Butlers Marston and the Pillertons w Ettington 03-07; Hon C Stourdene Gp 07-10. *30 Charles Street, Warwick CV34 5LQ* T: (01926) 258791
E: bishopdrjevans@talktalk.com

EVANS, David Russell. b 36. Liv Univ BA 57. Ripon Hall Ox 59. d 61 p 62. C Netherton CD *Liv* 61-65; Chapl Canon Slade Sch Bolton 65-93; Lic Preacher *Man* 65-09; PtO from 09. *2 Rushford Grove, Bolton BL1 8TD* T: (01204) 592981

EVANS, Derek. b 38. St As Minl Tr Course 93. d 97 p 98. NSM Llangollen w Trevor and Llantysilio *St As* 97-00; NSM Corwen and Llangar w Gwyddelwern and Llawrybetws 00-02; NSM Betws Gwerful Goch w Llangwm, Gwyddelwern etc 02-05; P-in-c Gwyddelwern 05-08; rtd 09; PtO *St As* from 09. *Fern Mount, 68 Berwyn Street, Llangollen LL20 8NA* T: (01978) 861893

EVANS, Canon Derek. b 45. St D Coll Lamp. d 68 p 69. C Pembroke Dock *St D* 68-74; V Ambleston, St Dogwells, Walton E and Llysyfran 74-77; V Wiston w Ambleston, St Dogwells and Walton E 78-81; V Wiston w Ambleston, St Dogwells, Walton E etc 81-85; R Haverfordwest St Mary and St Thos w Haroldston 85-09; Dep Dioc Dir of Educn 92-97; Dir 97-09; Can St D Cathl 99-09; RD Roose 00-04; rtd 09. *Thimble Cottage, Milford Road, Haverfordwest SA61 1PJ* E: derek.evans0@talk21.com

EVANS, Desmond. b 26. Univ of Wales (Lamp) BA 48 St Cath Soc Ox BA 50 MA 54. St Steph Ho Ox 48. d 51 p 52. C Clydach *S & B* 51-54; V 82-87; Chapl Cranleigh Sch Surrey 54-59; LtO *Ban* 59-78; St Mary's Coll Ban 59-78; V Llanwrtyd w Llanddulas in Tir Abad etc *S & B* 78-82; RD Builth 79-82; V Abercraf and Callwen 87-94; rtd 95. *26 Palleg Road, Lower Cwmtwrch, Swansea SA9 2QE* T: (01639) 845389

EVANS, Canon Edward John. b 47. St Mich Coll Llan 67. d 71 p 72. C Llantwit Fardre *Llan* 71-77; R Eglwysilan 77-88; V Laleston w Tythegston and Merthyr Mawr 88-09; V Laleston and Merthyr Mawr 09-13; V Laleston and Merthyr Mawr w Penyfai 13-15; RD Bridgend 94-04; AD 12-15; Hon Can Llan Cathl 07-15. *The Vicarage, Rogers Lane, Laleston, Bridgend CF32 0LB* T/F: (01656) 654254 M: 07968-044583
E: edward@laleston.org.uk

EVANS, Elaine. *See* JENKYNS, Elaine

EVANS, Elaine. *See* EVANS, Jennifer Elaine

EVANS, Elwyn David. b 36. Keble Coll Ox BA 58 MA 62. St Steph Ho Ox 58 St Mich Coll Llan 60. d 61 p 62. C Aberystwyth H Trin *St D* 61-63; C Llanelli St Paul 63-66; C Roath St German *Llan* 66-69; V Crynant 69-78; R Llanilid w Pencoed 79-95; rtd 95; PtO *Llan* from 95; *S & B* 95-14. *23 Christopher Rise, Pontlliw, Swansea SA4 9EN* T: (01792) 891961

EVANS, Frances Margaret Bethan. *See* GUTTRIDGE, Frances Margaret Bethan

EVANS, Canon Freda Christine. b 48. MBE 89. NTMTC 96. d 99 p 00. C Hampton Hill *Lon* 99-02; V Kingshurst *Birm* 02-08; TR Erdington from 08; Hon Can Birm Cathl from 14. *The Vicarage, 26 Church Road, Birmingham B24 9AX* T: 0121-373 0884

EVANS, Mrs Freda Mary Ann (Frieda). b 54. St D Coll Lamp 95. d 00 p 05. OLM Malpas *Mon* 00-09; NSM Caerleon and Llanfrechfa 09-13; NSM Cwmbran from 13. *3 The Firs, Malpas, Newport NP20 6YD* T: (01633) 850600 M: 0411-650088
E: frieda@evafirs.freeserve.co.uk

EVANS, Canon Frederick John Margam. b 31. Magd Coll Ox BA 53 MA 57. St Mich Coll Llan 53. d 54 p 55. C New Tredegar *Mon* 54-58; C Chepstow 58-60; Asst Chapl United Sheff Hosps 60-62; Chapl Brookwood Hosp Woking 62-70; V Crookham *Guildf* 70-98; RD Aldershot 78-83; Hon Can Guildf Cathl 89-98; rtd 98; PtO *Guildf* from 98. *4 Radford Close, Farnham GU9 9AB* T/F: (01252) 710594
E: johnjunee@btinternet.com

EVANS, Gareth Rae. b 48. Ripon Coll Cuddesdon 96. d 98 p 99. C Chepstow *Mon* 98-00; TV Cwmbran 00-07; Hon C Torquay St Martin Barton *Ex* 07-12; C Stoke Gabriel and Collaton 12-14; TV Totnes w Bridgetown, Berry Pomeroy etc 14; rtd 15. *9 Mill Hill Court, Stoke Gabriel, Totnes TQ9 6SU*
E: evansgareth50@yahoo.com

EVANS, Genevieve Sarah. b 62. Univ of Wales (Cardiff) BA 04. St Mich Coll Llan 02. d 04 p 05. C Whalley Range St Edm and Moss Side etc *Man* 04-08; V Walsall Pleck and Bescot *Lich* from 08; C Walsall St Matt from 08; C Walsall St Paul from 08. *St John's Vicarage, Vicarage Terrace, Walsall WS2 9HB* T: (01922) 639805 E: rev.gen@btinternet.com

EVANS, Geoffrey David. b 44. Ex Univ PGCE 74. K Coll Lon BD 69 AKC 69 St Aug Coll Cant 69. d 70 p 71. C Lawrence

Weston *Bris* 70-73; Chapl Grenville Coll Bideford 74-79; Chapl Eastbourne Coll 79-82; Chapl Taunton and Somerset Hosp 83-91; Chapl Musgrove Park Hosp 83-91; Chapl Taunton Sch 92-04; rtd 09. *10 Chaucer Road, Bath BA2 4QU*
E: bidabid@yahoo.co.uk

EVANS, Mrs Gillian. b 39. Imp Coll Lon BSc 61. Mon Dioc Tr Scheme 84. d 88 p 94. NSM Penallt and Trellech *Mon* 88-89; NSM Overmonnow w Wonastow and Michel Troy 89-92; Dioc Ecum Officer and C Ludlow, Ludford, Ashford Carbonell etc *Heref* 92-95; Pakistan 95-96; PtO *Heref* 96-06; Hon C Dawlish *Ex* 97-98; TV Golden Cap Team *Sarum* 98-01; rtd 01; PtO *Cov* 01-06; *Mon* 01-06; Hon C Wolford w Burmington *Cov* 06-08; Hon C Cherington w Stourton 06-08; Hon C Barcheston 06-08; Hon C Long Compton, Whichford and Barton-on-the-Heath 06-08; Hon C S Warks Seven Gp from 08. *16 The Long Close, Stourton, Shipston-on-Stour CV36 5HT* T: (01608) 685773

EVANS, Canon Glyn. b 59. Nene Coll Northn BA 80 Leic Univ BA 80 Ch Ch Coll Cant CertEd 82 Kent Univ PGCE 82. Qu Coll Birm 85. d 88 p 89. C Denton *Newc* 88-92; V Choppington 92-97; P-in-c Longhorsley and Hebron 97-01; Chapl HM Pris Acklington 97-01; P-in-c Newc St Andr and St Luke from 01; City Cen Chapl from 01; Chapl Northumbria Police from 11; Hon Can Newc Cathl from 11. *12 The Glebe, Stannington, Morpeth NE61 6HW* T: 0191-232 7935 *or* 222 0259

EVANS, Canon Glyn Peter. b 54. Leeds Univ BA 75. Ripon Coll Cuddesdon 76. d 77 p 78. C Binley *Cov* 77-80; C Clifton upon Dunsmore w Brownsover 80-84; P-in-c Lacock w Bowden Hill *Bris* 84-89; P-in-c Lt Compton w Chastleton, Cornwell etc *Ox* 89-00; Agric Chapl 89-00; Dioc Rural Officer from 00; Hon Can Ch Ch from 05. *Chelmscote Cottage, Brailes, Banbury OX15 5JJ* T: (01608) 686749 M: 07581-491713
E: glynevansrro@tiscali.co.uk *or* glynevans@goldserve.net

EVANS, Godfrey. *See* EVANS, Joseph Henry Godfrey

EVANS, Canon Gwyneth Mary. b 43. Stamford Ho 69 Linc Th Coll 70. dss 74 d 87 p 94. Stamford Hill St Thos *Lon* 74-79; Chapl Asst R Free Hosp Lon 79-89; Chapl Salisbury Health Care NHS Trust 89-01; Can and Preb Sarum Cathl 96-01; rtd 01; PtO *Sarum* from 01. *39 The Close, Salisbury SP1 2EL* T: (01722) 412546 E: gwyneth175@btinternet.com

EVANS, Ms Heather Rhiannon. d 14 p 15. NSM Llanbadarn Fawr and Elerch and Penrhyncoch etc *St D* from 14. *Melindwr, Capel Bangor, Aberystwyth SY23 3LU* T: (01970) 880469
E: heather.melindwr@live.co.uk

EVANS, Canon Henry Thomas Platt. b 28. Selw Coll Cam BA 51 MA 55. Linc Th Coll 51. d 53 p 54. C Lt Ilford St Barn *Chelmsf* 53-56; C-in-c Stocking Farm CD *Leic* 56-58; V Stocking Farm 58-67; R Stretford St Matt *Man* 67-73; V Knighton St Mary Magd *Leic* 73-83; Hon Can Leic Cathl 76-93; RD Christianity S 81-83; Warden Launde Abbey 83-93; P-in-c Loddington 83-92; rtd 93; PtO *Leic* from 93. *157 Avenue Road, Leicester LE2 3ED* E: htpe@talktalk.net

EVANS (née TAYLOR), Mrs Hilary Elizabeth. b 57. d 03 p 04. OLM Reddish *Man* 03-11; NSM Hulme Ascension 11-13. *13 Lindfield Road, Stockport SK5 6SD* T: 0161-442 3023
E: hilary@mojomusica.freeserve.co.uk

EVANS, Hilary Margaret. b 49. Redland Coll of Educn TDip 71 Ches Coll of HE BTh 97. NOC 94. d 97 p 98. C Heald Green St Cath Ches 97-00; P-in-c Davyhulme Ch Ch *Man* 00-03; P-in-c Blackley St Pet 03-09; AD N Man 06-08; rtd 09; Hon C SW Gower *S & B* 09-14; PtO from 14. *10 Meadow Croft, Southgate, Swansea SA3 2DF* T: (01792) 234230
E: hilary@evanses.plus.com

EVANS, Huw David. b 68. Sheff Univ BEng 90 PGCE 91. Trin Coll Bris BA 98. d 98 p 02. C Sherborne w Castleton and Lillington *Sarum* 98-99; NSM Martock w Ash *B & W* 01-04; CF from 04. *c/o MOD Chaplains (Army)* F: 381824 T: (01264) 383430

EVANS, Ian David. b 61. Qu Coll Birm 13. d 15. NSM Ipsley *Worc* from 15. *27 Belmont Close, Redditch B97 5AW*

EVANS, Mrs Jane. b 59. W Midl Coll of Educn BEd 81. d 03 p 04. OLM Lilleshall and Muxton *Lich* from 03. *5 Collett Way, Priorslee, Telford TF2 9SL* T: (01952) 291340
E: revjane@talktalk.net

EVANS, Mrs Jennifer. b 41. Ilkley Coll DipEd 62. Sarum Th Coll 88. d 88 p 08. Par Dn Bramshott *Portsm* 88-91; Par Dn Bramshott and Liphook 91-92; Par Dn Whippingham w E Cowes 92-95; Par Dn Sarisbury 95-05; Hon C Llawhaden w Bletherston and Llanycefn *St D* 08-10; Hon C Slebech and Uzmaston w Boulston 08; Hon C Uzmaston 08-10; Hon C Chaffcombe, Cricket Malherbie etc *B & W* from 10. *34 Tansee Hill, Thorncombe, Chard TA20 4LQ* T: (01460) 30844
E: jennie.honeycombs@virgin.net

EVANS, Mrs Jennifer. b 43. d 01. NSM New Tredegar *Mon* 01-05; NSM Bedwellty and New Tredegar 05-15. *4 Glynsifi, Elliots Town, New Tredegar NP24 6DE* T: (01443) 836798

EVANS, Jennifer Elaine. b 59. Wolv Univ BA 92. Qu Coll Birm 00. d 02 p 03. C Stafford St Jo and Tixall w Ingestre *Lich* 02-06; TV Stafford 06-13; V Stafford St Bertelin and Whitgreave St Jo from 13. *St Bertelin's Vicarage, 36 Holmcroft Road, Stafford ST16 1JF* T: (01785) 252874

EVANS, Jill. See EVANS, Gillian

EVANS, Mrs Joan. b 36. Nor Tr Coll TCert 57 UEA BEd 94. d 02 p 03. OLM Loddon, Sisland, Chedgrave, Hardley and Langley *Nor* 02-06; rtd 06; PtO *Nor* from 06. *13 Drury Lane, Loddon, Norwich NR14 6LB* T: (01508) 528656
E: joanevans936@btinternet.com

EVANS, John. See EVANS, Frederick John Margam

EVANS, John Andrew. b 53. Hull Univ BSc 74 Univ of Wales MSc 75 Bris Univ BA 96. Trin Coll Bris 94. d 96 p 97. C Walton H Trin *Ox* 96-98; C Caversham St Pet and Mapledurham etc 98-01; R Bradford Abbas and Thornford w Beer Hackett *Sarum* 01-09; V N Hayes St Nic *Lon* from 09. *St Nicholas' Vicarage, Raynton Drive, Hayes UB4 8BG* T: (020) 8573 4122 M: 07725-805437 E: j_andrew_evans@btconnect.com

EVANS, John David Vincent. b 41. CQSW 78. Lich Th Coll 66. d 68 p 70. C Kingsthorpe *Pet* 68-69; C Corby Epiphany w St Jo 69-72; Bp's Adv in Children's Work 72-74; Probation Officer 74-90; PtO *Pet* 88-90; R Greens Norton w Bradden and Lichborough 90-96; V Northampton Ch Ch 96-06; rtd 06; PtO *Pet* 06-09. *Ivy Cottage, Creaton Road, Hollowell, Northampton NN6 8RP* T: (01604) 743878
E: revjohnwenevans@yahoo.co.uk

EVANS, Canon John Griffiths. b 37. Glouc Th Course 76. d 77 p 77. Hd Master Corse Sch Glos 86-90; C Hartpury w Corse and Staunton *Glouc* 77-79; P-in-c Corse 79-09; P-in-c Maisemore 01-09; Hon Can Glouc Cathl 96-09; rtd 09. *Elm House, Gadfield Elms, Staunton, Gloucester GL19 3PA* T: (01452) 840302

EVANS, John Laurie. b 34. Pretoria Univ BSc 54 Imp Coll Lon BSc 55 Rhodes Univ BA 59. Ripon Coll Cuddesdon 84. d 86 p 87. C Bruton and Distr *B & W* 86-89; P-in-c Ambrosden w Merton and Piddington *Ox* 89-91; C Pet St Mary Boongate 91-93; V Michael *S & M* 93-96; R Ballaugh 93-96; rtd 96; Chapl Allnutt's Hosp Goring Heath 96-99; P-in-c Fochabers *Mor* 99-00; P-in-c Strathnairn St Paul 00-03; TV Langtree *Ox* 03-07; Hon C Kelso *Edin* from 07; Hon C Coldstream from 07. *2 Pressen Farm Cottage, Cornhill-on-Tweed TD12 4RS* T: (01890) 850309 M: 07909-986369
E: jonevansscotland@btinternet.com

EVANS, John Miles. b 39. Yale Univ BA 61 JD 67 St Cath Coll Cam BA 64 MA 68. NY Th Sem MDiv 93. d 95 p 95. Chapl St Jo Cathl Oban 95-97; Interim R Lynbrook Ch Ch USA 98-99; R Davidsonville All Hallows 99-05. *PO Box 1272, Portsmouth NH 03802-1272, USA*

EVANS, John Rhys. b 45. Hull Univ BSc 66. Sarum & Wells Th Coll 77. d 79 p 80. C Alton St Lawr *Win* 79-82; C Tadley St Pet 82-85; V Colden 85-91; V Bitterne Park 91-01; C Ringwood 01-11; Chapl R Bournemouth and Christchurch Hosps NHS Trust 01-11; rtd 11. *The Cottage, Alderley, Wotton-under-Edge GL12 7QT* E: johnrhysevans@yahoo.co.uk

EVANS, John Ronald. b 16. Univ of Wales BA 40. St Mich Coll Llan 41. d 42 p 44. C Rhosllannerchrugog *St As* 42-45; C Holywell 45-54; V Glyndyfrdwy 54-81; RD Edeyrnion 64-81; Dioc Sec SPCK 66-81; rtd 81. *22 Glebe Avenue, Hardingstone, Northampton NN4 6DG*

EVANS, John Stuart. b 57. Univ of Wales (Abth) BA 78 Bretton Hall Coll PGCE 81. Trin Coll Bris BA 98. d 98 p 99. C Connah's Quay *St As* 98-02; V Rhosllannerchrugog 02-10; AD Llangollen 05-10; R Ruthin w Llanrhydd and Llanfwrog from 10. *The Cloisters, School Road, Ruthin LL15 1BL* T: (01824) 702068 E: jsevans@surfaid.org

EVANS, Canon John Thomas. b 43. St Mich Coll Llan 66. d 67 p 68. C Connah's Quay *St As* 67-71; C Llanrhos 71-74; Chapl Rainhill Hosp Liv 74-78; TV Wrexham *St As* 78-83; V Holywell 83-96; RD 95-96; V Colwyn Bay 96-99; V Colwyn Bay w Brynymaen 99-02; RD Rhos 00-02; R Caerwys and Bodfari 02-08; Can Cursal St As Cathl 96-08; rtd 08; PtO *St As* from 09. *25 Everard Road, Rhos-on-Sea, Colwyn Bay LL28 4EY* T: (01492) 540506 M: 07905-861174 E: johnbethevans@btinternet.com

✠**EVANS, The Rt Revd John Wyn.** b 46. FSA 88 FRHistS 94 Univ of Wales (Cardiff) BA 68 BD 71. St Mich Coll Llan 68. d 71 p 72 c 08. C St D Cathl 71-72; Min Can St D Cathl 72-75; PtO *Ox* 75-77; Dioc Archivist *St D* 76-92; R Llanfallteg w Clunderwen and Castell Dwyran etc 77-82; Warden of Ords 78-83; Dioc Dir of Educn 82-92; Chapl Trin Coll Carmarthen 82-90; Dean of Chpl 90-94; TR Hd and RS 91-94; Hon Can St D Cathl 88-90; Can St D Cathl 90-94; Dean St D 94-08; V St D Cathl 94-01; TR Dewisland 01-08; Bp St D from 08. *Llys Esgob, Abergwili, Carmarthen SA31 2JG* T: (01267) 236597 E: bishop.stdavids@churchinwales.org.uk

EVANS, Jonathan Alan. b 53. Fitzw Coll Cam BA 75 PGCE 77 MA 79. St Jo Coll Nottm MA 95. d 95 p 96. C Drypool *York* 95-98; V Beverley St Nic 98-12; V Rye Park St Cuth *St Alb* from 12. *The Vicarage, 8 Ogard Road, Hoddesdon EN11 0NU* E: jonathan@familyevans.org.uk

EVANS, Joseph Henry Godfrey. b 31. Univ of Wales (Lamp) BA 50 St Mary's Coll Chelt CertEd 75 Kingston Poly 89. Qu Coll Birm 53. d 55 p 56. C Hackney St Jo *Lon* 55-58; C Stonehouse *Glouc* 58-60; V Selsley 60-65; V Cheltenham St Pet 65-74; R Willersey w Saintbury 74-77; Chapl Tiffin Sch Kingston 77-94; rtd 95; PtO *S'wark* 01-11. *300 Raeburn Avenue, Surbiton KT5 9EF* T: (020) 8390 0936

EVANS, Mrs Judith Ann. b 55. SEITE 99. d 02 p 03. C Crayford *Roch* 02-06; P-in-c Kells *Carl* 06-13; Chapl N Cumbria Univ Hosps NHS Trust 06-13; V Northampton St Alb *Pet* from 13. *St Alban's Vicarage, Broadmead Avenue, Northampton NN3 2RA* M: 07929-978523
E: revdjudyevans@btinternet.com

EVANS, Mrs Kathryn Louise. b 63. Birm Univ MHSc 96 RGN 86 RM 88. St Jo Coll Nottm 12. d 14 p 15. C Blackheath *Birm* from 14. *25 Garland Crescent, Halesowen B62 9NJ* T: 0121-421 5432 M: 07813-076628 E: kathrynevans3@sky.com

EVANS, Canon Keith. b 57. Trin Coll Carmarthen CertEd 81 BEd 82. St D Coll Lamp BA 84 Sarum & Wells Th Coll 84. d 85 p 86. C Swansea St Thos and Kilvey *S & B* 85-87; C Gorseinon 87-89; V Oxwich w Penmaen and Nicholaston 89-94; Dir Post-Ord Tr from 93; R Ystradgynlais 94-98; V Oystermouth from 98; Hon Can Brecon Cathl from 04. *The Vicarage, 9 Western Close, Mumbles, Swansea SA3 4HF* T: (01792) 369971 E: revkeithevans@talktalk.net

EVANS, Kenneth. b 50. Bp Burgess Hall Lamp. d 74 p 75. C Llanaber w Caerdeon *Ban* 74-79; C Upper Clapton St Matt *Lon* 79-82; P-in-c Tottenham St Phil 82-95; V 95-12; rtd 13. *10 Exeter Road, Croydon CR0 6EG* E: fr_kenmjd@tiscali.co.uk

EVANS, Kevin Stuart. b 56. Bris Poly CQSW 80. Qu Coll Birm 93. d 95 p 96. C Madeley *Heref* 95-98; P-in-c Wombridge *Lich* from 98; TV Cen Telford 05-14; C Priors Lee and St Georges' from 14. *Wombridge Vicarage, Wombridge Road, Telford TF2 6HT* T: (01952) 613334

EVANS, Mrs Linda Joyce. b 54. Trin Coll Bris BA 06. d 06 p 07. NSM Weston super Mare Ch Ch and Em *B & W* 06-10; P-in-c Dale and St Brides w Marloes *St D* 10-11; P-in-c Herbrandston and Hasguard w St Ishmael's etc 10-11; P-in-c Dale and St Brides w Marloes etc 11-14; rtd 14. *11 Lapwing Gardens, Weston-super-Mare BS22 8UP* E: landevans79@aol.com

EVANS, Linda Mary. See EDWARDS, Linda Mary

EVANS, Lloyd Russell. d 15. NSM Talgarth w Bronllys w Llanfilo *S & B* from 15. *Lower Dingle, Penbont Road, Talgarth, Brecon LD3 0BU* T: (01874) 711690 E: l.evans758@btinternet.com

EVANS, Miss Madeleine Thelma Bodenham. b 30. K Coll Lon BD 76 AKC 76. Gilmore Course 80. dss 85 d 87 p 94. Chapl Pipers Corner Sch 85-91; Par Dn Calne and Blackland *Sarum* 91-94; C 94-00; Chapl St Mary's Sch Calne 91-99; rtd 00; PtO *Sarum* from 00. *11 Fairway, Rookery Park, Calne SN11 0LB* T/F: (01249) 814755

EVANS, Ms Margaret Elizabeth. b 48. Leeds Univ BA 69 Lon Inst of Educn CertEd 70. Oak Hill Th Coll 91. d 94 p 95. NSM Canonbury St Steph *Lon* from 94. *St Stephen's Canonbury, 17 Canonbury Road, London N1 2DF* T: (020) 7226 7526 or 7359 4343 E: margareteevans@hotmail.com

EVANS, Margaret Rose. b 48. d 12. NSM Ensbury Park *Sarum* from 12. *179 Redhill Drive, Bournemouth BH10 6AH* T: (01202) 513154 E: mrevans@alnwick48.plus.com

EVANS, Ms Marina Anne. d 14 p 15. NSM Pembroke Dock *St D* from 14. *43 Arthur Street, Pembroke Dock SA72 6EN* T: (01646) 683891 E: rev.marina.evans@hotmail.com

EVANS, Mark Roland John. b 55. St Cath Coll Cam MA 81 Bris Univ PGCE 78. WEMTC 01. d 04 p 05. NSM Frenchay and Winterbourne Down *Bris* 04-08; NSM Frampton Cotterell and Iron Acton 08; NSM Winterbourne 08. *60 High Street, Thornbury, Bristol BS35 2AN* T: (01454) 414101 M: 07702-289385 E: mark.evans@bathwells.anglican.org

EVANS, Martin Lonsdale. b 69. Man Univ BA 91. Ripon Coll Cuddesdon 93. d 95 p 96. C Morpeth *Newc* 95-98; Chapl RN from 98. *Royal Naval Chaplaincy Service, Mail Point 1-2, Leach Building, Whale Island, Portsmouth PO2 8BY* T: (023) 9262 5055 F: 9262 5134

EVANS, Martyn Hywel. b 63. Univ of Wales (Cardiff) BScEcon 86 Glam Univ MBA 99. St Mich Coll Llan 10. d 12 p 13. C Tredegar *Mon* 12-14; C Lower Islwyn from 14. *The Vicarage, 1 Gelli Crescent, Risca, Newport NP11 6QG* T: (01633) 619425 E: martynevans01@btinternet.com

EVANS, Mary. See EVANS, Ann Elizabeth Mary

EVANS, Matthew Scott. b 72. Grey Coll Dur BA 93. Cranmer Hall Dur 96. d 98 p 99. C Fountains Gp *Ripon* 98-03; P-in-c Dacre w Hartwith and Darley w Thornthwaite *Leeds* 03-15; Jt AD Ripon 09-11; AD *Leeds* 11-15. *Christ Church Vicarage, 11 St Hilda's Road, Harrogate HG2 8JX*

EVANS, Miss Merewyn Abigail. b 80. Univ of Wales (Ban) BA 02 MTh 04 Warwick Univ PGCE 04. Cranmer Hall Dur 12. **d** 14 **p** 15. C Blurton and Dresden *Lich* from 14. *51 Ripon Road, Stoke-on-Trent ST3 3BS* M: 07982-239783

EVANS, Michael. b 49. St Jo Coll Nottm 88. **d** 90 **p** 91. C Beeston *S'well* 90-93; P-in-c Kirkby in Ashfield St Thos 93-97; V 97-08; Chapl Notts Healthcare NHS Trust 93-08; rtd 08. *2 Westminster Avenue, Kirkby-in-Ashfield, Nottingham NG17 7HY* T: (01623) 759537 M: 07825-223189 E: munnamonk@aol.com

EVANS, Michael John. b 53. **d** 00 **p** 01. OLM Longnor, Quarnford and Sheen *Lich* 00-04; OLM Ipstones w Berkhamsytch and Onecote w Bradnop 04-11; P-in-c 11-15; V from 15. *The Vicarage, Church Lane, Ipstones, Stoke-on-Trent ST10 2LF* T: (01538) 266313 E: revdmjevans@btinternet.com

EVANS, Neil Robert. b 54. Lon Univ MA 93 K Coll Lon DMin 10. Coll of Resurr Mirfield. **d** 84 **p** 85. C Bethnal Green St Jo w St Bart *Lon* 84-86; C St Jo on Bethnal Green 87-88; P-in-c Stoke Newington Common St Mich 88-95; V 95-98; V Twickenham All Hallows 98-05; Kensington Area CME Officer 98-05; Par Min Development Adv Willesden Area 05-07; Area Dir Tr and Development 07-13; Dir Tr and Development Two Cities Area from 13; Dioc Dir of Min from 07. *23 St Albans Avenue, London W4 5LL* T: (020) 8987 7332 E: neil.evans@london.anglican.org

EVANS, Nicholas Anthony Paul. b 60. Sheff Univ BA 81 Liv Univ PGCE 86. Qu Coll Birm 81. **d** 84 **p** 87. C Ludlow *Heref* 84-85; C Sunbury *Lon* 86-92; Hd RE Guildf Co Sch 93-99; NSM Crookham *Guildf* 94-99; CF 99-02; V Shenley Green *Birm* 02-15; R Newport Pagnell w Lathbury and Moulsoe *Ox* from 15. *The Rectory, 81 High Street, Newport Pagnell MK16 8AB* M: 07769-550204 T: (01908) 611145 E: nickevans49@btinternet.com

EVANS, Nigel William Reid. b 70. Sheff Hallam Univ BEd 96. Ridley Hall Cam BTh 01. **d** 01 **p** 02. C Ossett and Gawthorpe *Wakef* 01-05; V Loddon, Sisland, Chedgrave, Hardley and Langley *Nor* 05-10; RD Loddon 06-10; TR Bucknall *Lich* from 10; RD Stoke from 14. *The Rectory, 151 Werrington Road, Bucknall, Stoke-on-Trent ST2 9AQ* T: (01782) 280667

EVANS, Norman Cassienet. b 30. Keble Coll Ox MA 54. Guildf Dioc Min Course 91. **d** 95 **p** 96. OLM Seale, Puttenham and Wanborough *Guildf* 95-00; PtO from 00. *Hoplands, Riversmeet, Tilford, Farnham GU10 2BW* T: (01252) 782933 E: norman@thereverend.fsnet.co.uk

EVANS, The Ven Patrick Alexander Sidney. b 43. Linc Th Coll 70. **d** 73 **p** 74. C Lyonsdown H Trin *St Alb* 73-76; C Royston 76-78; V Gt Gaddesden 78-82; V Tenterden St Mildred w Smallhythe *Cant* 82-89; Adn Maidstone 89-02; Hon Can Cant Cathl 89-02; Dir of Ords 89-93; Adn Cant and Can Res Cant Cathl 02-07; rtd 07. *Wills Tenement, Trehan, Saltash PL12 4QN* T: (01752) 847011 E: patrickevans120@hotmail.co.uk

EVANS, Paul David. b 54. Pemb Coll Cam BA 75 MA 79 Lon Inst of Educn PGCE 76. SWMTC 11. **d** 14. NSM Cockington *Ex* from 14; NSM Torre All SS from 14. *3 Hermosa, Higher Woodfield Road, Torquay TQ1 2LB* T: (01803) 215462 M: 07715-535007 E: revpaulevans@gmail.com

EVANS, Peter. b 35. St Aid Birkenhead 57. **d** 60 **p** 61. C Higher Bebington *Ches* 60-63; C W Kirby St Bridget 63-66; P-in-c Lower Tranmere 66-68; V Flimby *Carl* 68-74; V Kirkby Ireleth 74-79; P-in-c Kirkbride w Newton Arlosh 79-80; R 80-85; V Beckermet St Jo and St Bridget w Ponsonby 85-97; rtd 97; PtO *Carl* from 98. *26 Gelt Close, Carlisle CA3 0HJ*

EVANS, Peter. b 40. S'wark Ord Course 75. **d** 75 **p** 76. C Welling *S'wark* 75-78; C Sutton New Town St Barn 78-81; C Kingston All SS w St Jo 81-87; V Croydon Woodside 87-99; TV Sanderstead All SS 99-03; rtd 03; PtO *Leic* from 13. *174 Main Street, Stanton-under-Bardon, Markfield LE67 9TP* T: (01530) 245470

EVANS, Peter Anthony. b 36. Imp Coll Lon BScEng 57. St Steph Ho Ox 58. **d** 60 **p** 61. C Surbiton St Mark *S'wark* 60-63; Asst Chapl Lon Univ 63-64; C S Kensington St Luke 64-68; C Surbiton St Andr and St Mark *S'wark* 68-69; C Loughton St Jo *Chelmsf* 69-74; P-in-c Becontree St Geo 74-82; PtO 82-89; NSM Romford St Alb 89-93; NSM Coopersale 93-95; NSM Epping Distr 95-96; rtd 97; PtO *Chelmsf* from 97. *6 Woodhall Crescent, Hornchurch RM11 3NN* T: (01708) 509399

EVANS, Peter Gerald. b 41. Man Univ BA 71. AKC 65. **d** 65 **p** 66. C Kidbrooke St Jas *S'wark* 65-68; C Fallowfield *Man* 68-71; C Brockley Hill St Sav *S'wark* 71-73; P-in-c Colchester St Botolph w H Trin and St Giles *Chelmsf* 74-79; V 79-92; PtO from 93. *97 Northgate Street, Colchester CO1 1EY* T: (01206) 543297

EVANS, Peter Kenneth Dunlop. b 38. Ch Coll Cam BA 60. St D Coll Lamp 72. **d** 74 **p** 75. C Roath *Llan* 74-77; V Buttington and Pool Quay *St As* 77-87; V Llanfair Caereinion w

Llanllugan 87-03; rtd 03; PtO *St As* from 09. *Stepaside, Llanfair Caereinion, Welshpool SY21 0HU* T: (01686) 627076

EVANS, Richard. *See* EVANS, David Richard

EVANS, Richard Gregory. b 50. St Mich Coll Llan 69. **d** 73 **p** 74. C Oystermouth *S & B* 73-76; C Clydach 76-79; CF 78-81; V Llanddew and Talachddu *S & B* 79-83; Youth Chapl 79-83; Hon Min Can Brecon Cathl 79-83; Chapl Huntley Sch New Zealand 83-87; Chapl Nga Tawa Sch 83-90; Chapl Wanganui Sch from 90. *Wanganui Collegiate School, Private Bag 3002, Wanganui 4540, New Zealand* F: 348 8302 T: (0064) (6) 349 0281 ext 8750 E: rgevans@collegiate.school.nz

EVANS, Richard Trevor. b 33. Jes Coll Ox MA 58 DipEd 58. St And Dioc Tr Course 73. **d** 76 **p** 76. NSM Leven *St And* 76-95; NSM St Andrews St Andr from 95. *33 Huntingtower Park, Whinnyknowe, Glenrothes KY6 3QF* T/F: (01592) 741670 E: revans9973@blueyonder.co.uk

EVANS, Robert. *See* EVANS, Simon Robert

EVANS, Robert Arnold Hughes. b 90. Ridley Hall Cam 12. **d** 15. C Cambridge St Andr Less *Ely* from 15. *Address temp unknown*

EVANS, Canon Robert Arthur. b 24. Univ of Wales (Cardiff) BA 48. St Mich Coll Llan 48. **d** 50 **p** 51. C Aberdare St Fagan *Llan* 50-52; C Roath 52-57; C Llandaff w Capel Llanilltern 57-61; Asst Chapl Mersey Miss to Seamen 61-62; Chapl Supt Mersey Miss to Seamen 62-74 and 79-89; Chapl RNR 67-89; V Rainhill *Liv* 74-79; PtO *Ches* 79-91; Hon Can Liv Cathl 88-89; rtd 89; PtO *Liv* 89-05. *10 Fulwood Court, 529 Aigburth Road, Liverpool L19 7DN*

EVANS, Robert Charles. b 55. K Coll Lon BA 77 AKC 77 MA 78 MTh 89 Qu Coll Cam BA 80 MA 83 CertEd 85. Westcott Ho Cam 79. **d** 81 **p** 87. C St Breoke *Truro* 81-83; C St Columb Minor and St Colan 83-84; Chapl Rob Coll Cam 87-92; Lect Ches Univ from 92. *University of Chester, Parkgate Road, Chester CH1 4BJ* T: (01244) 510000

EVANS, Robert George Roger. b 49. Cam Univ MA. Trin Coll Bris 74 St Jo Coll Nottm 94. **d** 77 **p** 78. C Bispham *Blackb* 77-80; C Chadwell *Chelmsf* 80-84; V Ardsley *Sheff* 84-09; P-in-c Kendray 04-09; Chapl Barnsley Community & Priority Services NHS Trust 98-00; rtd 09. *73 High Street, Wombwell, Barnsley S73 8HS* T: (01226) 345635 E: rgrevans@gmail.com

EVANS, Robert Stanley. b 51. Univ of Wales (Lamp) BA 72 Univ of Wales (Cardiff) PGCE 73. St Mich Coll Llan 90. **d** 92 **p** 93. C Penarth All SS *Llan* 92-95; R Gelligaer 95-99; V Roath 99-04; R Coychurch, Llangan and St Mary Hill 04-06; rtd 06. *Ty Tudful, 5 Cook Road, Barry CF62 9HD* T: (01446) 420011

EVANS, Ronald. b 47. St Mich Coll Llan 85. **d** 87 **p** 88. C Flint *St As* 87-91; TV Wrexham 91-97; V Rhosymedre 97-99; V Rhosymedre w Penycae 99-05; PV Connah's Quay 05-11; rtd 11; PtO *St As* from 11. *29 Blackbrook Avenue, Hawarden, Deeside CH5 3HJ* T: (01244) 534340 E: godshelp2002@yahoo.com

EVANS, Ronald Wilson. b 47. Windsor Univ Ontario BA 69 Dalhousie Univ MA 83. Trin Coll Toronto MDiv 73. **d** 72 **p** 73. R Springhill Canada 73-76; Chapl Univ of Prince Edw Is 76-79; Lect 82-85; Chapl King's-Edgehill Sch 85-87; R Clements 87-98; Lect Bilgi Univ Istanbul Turkey 98-00; Asst Chapl Izmir (Smyrna) w Bornova 00-03; P-in-c 03-04; Chapl from 04. *PK 1005, Pasaport, Izmir 35120, Turkey* T: (0090) (232) 463 7263 *or* T/F: 464 5753 E: seljuk85@hotmail.com

EVANS, Roy Clifford. b 39. Qu Coll Birm 04. **d** 05 **p** 05. Chapl Univ Hosp Birm NHS Foundn Trust 05-07; NSM Billesley Common *Birm* 05-07; Chapl Countess of Chester Hosp NHS Foundn Trust 07-11; PtO *Ches* from 08; *Lich* from 08; Clergy Widows Visitor from 11. *Hawthorn Cottage, Llandrinio, Llanymynech SY22 6SB* T: (01691) 831389 M: 07791-398923 E: brother.evans@tesco.net

EVANS, Rupert Alexander. b 81. St Cath Coll Cam BA 02. Wycliffe Hall Ox MTh 10. **d** 10 **p** 11. C Crowborough *Chich* 10-14; Team Ldr Titus Trust from 14. *17 Clive Road, London SE21 8DA* T: (020) 8670 2736 E: rupertaevans@gmail.com

EVANS, Mrs Sarah Rosemary. b 64. Trevelyan Coll Dur BA 85. STETS 05. **d** 08 **p** 09. NSM Hullavington, Norton and Stanton St Quintin *Bris* 08-12; NSM Sherston Magna, Easton Grey, Luckington etc 08-12; NSM By Brook from 12. *Ashdown, Littleton Drew, Chippenham SN14 7NA* T: (01249) 782885 E: rev.sarahevans@gmail.com

EVANS, Sheila Jean. *See* ROBERTSON, Sheila Jean

EVANS, Canon Simon. b 55. Newc Univ BA 77 Heythrop Coll Lon MA 06. St Steph Ho Ox 78. **d** 80 **p** 81. C Pet St Jude 80-84; Chapl Asst Pet Distr Hosp 80-84; C Wantage *Ox* 84-87; V W Leigh *Portsm* 87-96; Chapl E Hants Primary Care Trust 88-96; V Ruislip St Martin *Lon* from 96; AD Hillingdon 08-13; Can Wiawso Ghana from 08. *The Vicarage, 13 Eastcote Road, Ruislip HA4 8BE* T: (01895) 633040 *or* 625456 E: frsimon@waitrose.com

EVANS, Simon Andrew. b 59. Sarum & Wells Th Coll 81. **d** 84 **p** 85. C Norbury St Steph and Thornton Heath *S'wark* 84-88;

C Putney St Mary 88-92; P-in-c Telford Park St Thos 92-94; V 94-04; V Ensbury Park *Sarum* from 04. *St Thomas's Vicarage, 42 Coombe Avenue, Bournemouth BH10 5AE* T: (01202) 519735 E: simon@evansonline.info *or* vicar@ensburypark.org.uk

EVANS, Simon Robert. b 58. Reading Univ BSc 79. NOC 99. **d** 02 **p** 03. C Pudsey St Lawr and St Paul *Bradf* 02-04; P-in-c Low Moor 04-05; TV Oakenshaw, Wyke and Low Moor 06-07; TR 07-10; P-in-c Harden and Wilsden 10-13; P-in-c Denholme 10-13; P-in-c Cullingworth 10-13; TR Harden and Wilsden, Cullingworth and Denholme *Leeds* from 13. *The Vicarage, Wilsden Old Road, Harden, Bingley BD16 1JD* T: (01535) 273758 E: vicarbob@talktalk.net *or* bob.evans@bradford.anglican.org

EVANS, Stanley George. b 43. CITC 00. **d** 03 **p** 04. Aux Min Killaloe w Stradbally *L & K* 03-04; P-in-c Killarney w Aghadoe and Muckross 04-05; Aux Min Leighlin w Grange Sylvae, Shankill etc *C & O* 05-09; PtO *L & K* 09-13; P-in-c Omey w Ballynakill, Errislannan and Roundstone *T, K & A* from 13. *The Rectory, Clifden, Co Galway, Republic of Ireland* T: (00353) (95) 21147 M: 87-636 9473 E: revdstanevans@gmail.com

EVANS, Stanley Munro. b 30. AKC 53. **d** 54 **p** 55. C Norbury St Oswald *Cant* 54-57; C St Laur in Thanet 57-63; V Bredgar 63-71; V Bredgar w Bicknor and Huckinge 71-72; V Westgate St Sav 72-01; rtd 01; PtO *Cant* from 01. *40 Queen Bertha Road, Ramsgate CT11 0ED* T: (01843) 594459

EVANS, Stephen John. b 60. Dartmouth RN Coll 81 St Steph Ho Ox BA 85 MA 89 Aber Univ MPhil 94. **d** 86 **p** 87. Prec St Andr Cathl Inverness 86-89; R Montrose and P-in-c Inverbervie *Bre* 89-91; Miss to Seamen 89-91; V Northampton St Paul *Pet* 91-98; CME Officer 94-00; Liturg Officer 96-03; P-in-c Ecton and Warden Ecton Ho 98-00; R Uppingham w Ayston and Wardley w Belton *Pet* 00-10; Can Pet Cathl 03-10; RD Rutland 03-10; R St Marylebone w H Trin *Lon* from 10. *21 Beaumont Street, London W1G 6DQ* T: (020) 7935 8965 E: rector@stmarylebone.org

EVANS, Steven Edward. b 52. CBDTI 97. **d** 00 **p** 01. NSM Caton w Littledale *Blackb* 00-05; NSM Hornby w Claughton and Whittington etc 05-06; NSM Slyne w Hest and Halton w Aughton 06-08; PtO from 08. *Evans Marquee Hire, Butler Works, Wyresdale Road, Lancaster LA1 3JJ*

EVANS, Stuart. *See* EVANS, John Stuart

EVANS, Ms Susan Mary. b 55. St Jo Coll Dur BA 76 CertEd 77 Nottm Univ BCombStuds 84. Linc Th Coll 81. **dss** 84 **d** 87 **p** 94. Weaste *Man* 84-88; Par Dn 87-88; Par Dn Longsight St Luke 88-92; Par Dn Claydon and Barham *St E* 92-94; C 94-99; P-in-c Coddenham w Gosbeck and Hemingstone w Henley 95-99; Chapl HM YOI Hollesley Bay Colony 99-02; NSM Henley, Claydon and Barham *St E* 02-06; Chapl HM Pris Whatton 06-09. *8 Abbey Road, Bardney, Lincoln LN3 5XA* T: (01526) 397101

EVANS, Terence. b 35. St Mich Coll Llan 67. **d** 69 **p** 70. C Loughor *S & B* 69-73; C Gowerton w Waunarlwydd 73-77; V Llanbister and Llanbadarn Fynydd w Llananno 77-82; V Llanyrnewydd 82-01; rtd 01. *28 Orchard Court, New Orchard Street, Swansea SA1 SEN*

EVANS, Terence Robert. b 45. NOC 82. **d** 85 **p** 86. C Warrington St Elphin *Liv* 85-88; V Cantril Farm 88-94; V Rainhill 94-03; R Odd Rode *Ches* 03-10; rtd 10; PtO *Ches* from 10. *11 Harpur Crescent, Alsager, Stoke-on-Trent ST7 2SX* T: (01270) 878209 E: evans338@btinternet.com

EVANS, Timothy Simon. b 57. York Univ BA 79 Sussex Univ MA 81 Fitzw Coll Cam BA 85 MA 88. Ridley Hall Cam 83. **d** 87 **p** 88. C Whitton St Aug *Lon* 87-90; C Ealing St Steph Castle Hill 90-93; P-in-c Shireshead *Blackb* 93-97; Asst Chapl Lanc Univ 93-97; Vice Prin LCTP 97-09; P-in-c Natland *Carl* 97-09; C Old Hutton and New Hutton 06-09; RD Kendal 00-03; Hon Can Carl Cathl 00-09; Dir Past Studies and Tutor Yorks Min Course from 09. *The Yorkshire Ministry Course, The Mirfield Centre, Stocks Bank Road, Mirfield WF14 0BW* T: (01924) 481926 E: tim@ymc.org.uk

EVANS, Trevor Owen. b 37. Univ of Wales BSc 59. Coll of Resurr Mirfield 59. **d** 61 **p** 62. C Llanaber w Caerdeon *Ban* 61-64; C Llandudno 64-70; TV 70-75; V Llanidloes w Llangurig 75-89; RD Arwystli 75-89; Can and Preb Ban Cathl 82-98; Spirituality Officer 84-03; R Trefdraeth 89-90; Dir of Min 89-98; R Llanfairpwll w Penmynydd *Ban* 90-97; R Llanfairpwll w Penmynydd and Llanddaniel-fab etc 98; Dean Ban 98-03; RD Ogwen 99-00; rtd 03. *Hafan, 3 Coed y Castell, Bangor LL57 1PH* T: (01248) 352855

EVANS, Mrs Wendy Nicola. b 59. St Jo Coll Dur BA 11. Cranmer Hall Dur 09. **d** 11 **p** 12. C Oulton Broad *Nor* 11-14; TV Diss from 14. *61 Roydon Road, Diss IP22 4LW* M: 07971-082603 E: wendy.evans2009@gmail.com

EVANS, William James Lynn. b 30. St D Coll Lamp 73. **d** 75 **p** 76. P-in-c Penbryn and Blaenporth *St D* 75-76; V Penbryn

and Betws Ifan w Bryngwyn 77-79; V Penrhyncoch and Elerch 79-83; V Cynwil Elfed and Newchurch 83-87; V Llandybie 87-95; rtd 95. *5 Dolau Tywi, Manordeilo, Llandeilo SA19 7BL* T: (01550) 777944

EVANS, Wyn. *See* EVANS, John Wyn

EVANS-HILLS, Ms Bonnie Jean. b 57. Westcott Ho Cam. **d** 09 **p** 10. C Leic Resurr 09-10; C Oadby 10-14; Bp's Interfaith Adv 12-14; Dioc Interfaith Adv *St Alb* from 14; P-in-c Kimpton w Ayot St Lawrence from 15. *The Vicarage, 11 High Street, Kimpton, Hitchin SG4 8RA* T: (01483) 833419

EVANS-SMITH, Brian George. b 49. **d** 02 **p** 03. OLM S Ramsey St Paul *S & M* 02-06; P-in-c Lezayre 06-12; P-in-c Bride, Lezayre and N Ramsey 12-14; R from 14. *41 Barrule Park, Ramsey, Isle of Man IM8 2BR* T: (01624) 817322

EVASON, Stuart Anthony. b 44. Salford Univ BSc. Chich Th Coll 79. **d** 81 **p** 82. C Heref St Martin 81-85; TV Cleethorpes *Linc* 85-87; TV Howden *York* 87-92; V Heywood St Jas *Man* 92-03; P-in-c Barrow St Jas *Carl* 03-10; TR Barrow St Matt 06-09; rtd 10; PtO *Man* from 10. *17 Drake Hall, Westhoughton, Bolton BL5 2RA* T: (01942) 810128 E: s.evason@gmail.com

EVE, David Charles Leonard. b 45. AKC 74. St Aug Coll Cant 74. **d** 75 **p** 76. C Hall Green Ascension *Birm* 75-79; TV Kings Norton 79-84; V Rowley Regis 84-93; PtO *Heref* 94-98 and from 01; NSM Hallow and Grimley w Holt *Worc* 98-05; PtO from 05. *14 Orchard End, Cleobury Mortimer, Kidderminster DY14 8BA* T: (01299) 270510 E: gabrielle.davideve@btinternet.com

EVE, Gary Henry. b 68. SWMTC 12. **d** 15. NSM St Germans *Truro* from 15. *11 Rowse Gardens, Calstock PL18 9RB* T: (01822) 834306 E: gary.eve@btinternet.com

EVE, Hilary Anne. *See* FIFE, Hilary Anne

EVE, Canon Ian Halliday. b 33. St Paul's Coll Grahamstown LTh 59. **d** 59 **p** 60. S Africa 59-80 and from 81; P-in-c Salcombe *Ex* 80-81; Can Cape Town from 86. *Christ Church Rectory, Main Road, Constantia, 7800 South Africa* T: (0027) (21) 794 6352 *or* 794 5051 F: 794 1065

EVELEIGH, Raymond. b 36. Univ of Wales (Cardiff) BSc 58. NW Ord Course 73. **d** 76 **p** 77. NSM S Cave and Ellerker w Broomfleet *York* 76-79; P-in-c Kingston upon Hull St Mary 79-82; Chapl Hull Coll of FE 79-01; V Anlaby Common St Mark *York* 82-94; V Langtoft w Foxholes, Butterwick, Cottam etc 94-01; rtd 01; PtO *York* from 01. *Pasture Lodge, West End, Kilham, Driffield YO25 4RR* T: (01262) 420060 E: rev@revray.co.uk

EVENS, Jonathan Adrian Harvey. b 63. Middx Poly BA 84 Middx Univ BA 03 ACIPD 90. NTMTC 00. **d** 03 **p** 04. C Barking St Marg w St Patr *Chelmsf* 03-06; V Gt Ilford St Jo 06-15; P-in-c St Steph Walbrook and St Swithun etc *Lon* from 15; C St Martin-in-the-Fields from 15. *43 Auriel Avenue, Dagenham RM10 8BT* T: (020) 7766 1100 *or* 7626 9000 E: jonathan.evens@smitf.org *or* priest@ststephenwalbrook.net

EVENS, Robert Alan. b 51. **d** 00 **p** 01. NSM Sharnbrook and Knotting w Souldrop *St Alb* 00-03; P-in-c Wymington w Podington 03-05; R Sharnbrook, Felmersham and Knotting w Souldrop 05-15; RD Sharnbrook 12-15; R Ashwell w Hinxworth and Newnham from 15. *109 High Street, Ashwell, Baldock SG7 5PQ* T: (01462) 742277 E: robert.evens@lineone.net

✠**EVENS, The Rt Revd Robert John Scott.** b 47. ACIB 74. Trin Coll Bris 74. **d** 77 **p** 78 **c** 04. C Southsea St Simon *Portsm* 77-79; C Portchester 79-83; V Locks Heath 83-96; RD Fareham 93-96; Adn Bath and Preb Wells Cathl 96-04; Suff Bp Crediton *Ex* 04-12; rtd 12; Hon Asst Bp Glouc from 13. *30 Highland Road, Charlton Kings, Cheltenham GL53 9LT* T: (01242) 251411 E: robertevens@hotmail.co.uk

EVEREST, Canon John Cleland. b 45. Sarum Th Coll 66. **d** 68 **p** 69. C Moulsecoomb *Chich* 68-71; C Easthampstead *Ox* 71-74; C Southwick St Mich *Chich* 74-77; Dioc Soc Services Adv *Worc* 77-84; Ind Chapl 84-93; R Worc City St Paul and Old St Martin etc 84-93; RD Worc E 89-93; TR Halas 93-10; RD Dudley 95-98; Hon Can Worc Cathl 90-10; rtd 10. *18 Tunnel Hill, Worcester WR4 9RP* T: (01905) 723305 E: cleland@tunnelhill.plus.com

EVERETT, Alan Neil. b 57. St Cath Coll Ox BA 79 DPhil 96 SS Coll Cam BA 84. Westcott Ho Cam 82. **d** 85 **p** 86. C Hindley All SS *Liv* 85-88; Chapl Qu Mary Coll *Lon* 88-91; V S Hackney St Mich w Haggerston St Paul 94-10; V Notting Dale St Clem w St Mark and St Jas from 10. *12 St Anns Villas, London W11 4RS* T: (020) 7221 3548 E: alan@n16.org.uk

EVERETT, Anthony William. b 60. S Bank Poly BA 82. Oak Hill Th Coll BA 89. **d** 89 **p** 90. C Hailsham *Chich* 89-92; C New Malden and Coombe *S'wark* 92-97; V Streatham Park St Alb 97-02; V Herne Bay Ch Ch *Cant* from 02; Asst Dir of Ords 05-09; Jt AD Reculver 12-13. *Christ Church Vicarage, 38 Beltinge Road, Herne Bay CT6 6BU* T: (01227) 374906 *or* 366640 E: anthony@fayland.freeserve.co.uk

EVERETT, Mrs Christine Mary. b 46. St Osyth Coll of Educn CertEd 67. Westcott Ho Cam 90. **d** 92 **p** 94. Par Dn Ipswich St Fran *St E* 92-94; C 94-95; C Gt and Lt Bealings w Playford and Culpho 96; P-in-c 96-02; P-in-c The Creetings and Earl Stonham w Stonham Parva 02-11; rtd 11; PtO *St E* from 11. *35 Chainhouse Road, Needham Market, Ipswich IP6 8TB* T: (01449) 720319 M: 07980-023236
E: chrisev1@btinternet.com

EVERETT, Colin Gerald Grant. b 44. Open Univ BA 77 Keswick Hall Coll CertEd. Ripon Coll Cuddesdon 79. **d** 81 **p** 82. C Aston cum Aughton *Sheff* 81-84; R Fornham All SS and Fornham St Martin w Timworth *St E* 84-92; P-in-c Old Newton w Stowupland 92-94; C Ipswich All Hallows 94-95; TV Ipswich St Fran 95-97; TV Ipswich St Mary at Stoke w St Pet and St Fran 97-09; rtd 09; PtO *St E* from 09. *35 Chainhouse Road, Needham Market, Ipswich IP6 8TB* T: (01449) 720319
E: revcolin@btinternet.com

EVERETT, David John. b 51. Leeds Univ BA 07. NOC 04. **d** 07 **p** 08. NSM Moor Allerton and Shadwell *Ripon* 07-11; V Market Weighton *York* from 11; R Goodmanham from 11; V Sancton from 11. *The Vicarage, 38 Cliffe Road, Market Weighton, York YO43 3BN* T: (01430) 872808
E: david.j.everett51@gmail.com

EVERETT, Nevsky James. b 89. G&C Coll Cam BA 10. Westcott Ho Cam 10. **d** 13 **p** 14. C Norton *St Alb* from 13. *2 Common View, Letchworth Garden City SG6 1DA* M: 07791-910050
E: nevsky.everett@hotmail.co.uk

EVERETT, Robert Henry. b 60. Em Coll Cam BA 82 MA 86 Ox Univ BA 85 MA 90 Ex Univ MPhil 95. St Steph Ho Ox 83. **d** 86 **p** 87. C Ex St Thos and Em 86-88; C Plymstock 88-91; R St Dominic, Landulph and St Mellion w Pillaton *Truro* 91-96; P-in-c Reading All SS *Ox* 96-98; V 98-07; P-in-c Paddington St Mary Magd *Lon* 07-09; P-in-c Paddington St Pet 07-09; V Paddington St Mary Magd and St Pet from 09. *The Vicarage, 2 Rowington Close, London W2 5TF* T: (020) 7289 1818 *or* 7289 2011 E: frhenry@yahoo.uk

EVERETT, Canon Simon Francis. b 58. Oak Hill Th Coll BA 89. **d** 89 **p** 90. C Wroughton *Bris* 89-93; TV Wexcombe *Sarum* 93-98; P-in-c The Iwernes, Sutton Waldron and Fontmell Magna 98-01; V Iwerne Valley 01-14; RD Milton and Blandford 01-13; TR Wareham from 14; Can and Preb Sarum Cathl from 09. *The Rectory, 22 Worgret Road, Wareham BH20 4PN* E: reveverett@btinternet.com

EVERETT-ALLEN, Canon Clive. b 47. AKC 70. St Aug Coll Cant 69. **d** 70 **p** 71. C Minera *St As* 70-72; C Hatcham St Cath *S'wark* 72-75; TV Beaconsfield *Ox* 75-83; R Southwick St Mich *Chich* 83-98; V E Grinstead St Swithun 98-15; RD E Grinstead 05-10; Chapl Qu Victoria Hosp NHS Trust East Grinstead 98-15; Can and Preb Chich Cathl 98-15; rtd 15. *2 Keble Park Crescent, Bishopthorpe, York YO23 2SY* E: clive47@gmail.com

EVERINGHAM, Georgina Wendy. b 32. Tyndale Hall Bris BA 57. **d** 58 **p** 59. C Broadwater St Mary *Chich* 58-61; V Shipton Bellinger w S Tidworth *Win* 61-70; V Bournemouth St Paul 70-84; V Throop 84-95; rtd 95; PtO *Worc* from 96. *3 Harlech Close, Berkeley Alford, Worcester WR4 0JU* T: (01905) 754394 M: 07940-851495
E: gina@wordoflife.uk.com

EVERITT, Anthony David. b 64. Ex Univ BA 85 ACA 88. STETS 09. **d** 12 **p** 13. NSM Knowle St Martin *Bris* from 12. *23 Dunford Road, Bristol BS3 4PN* T: 0117-966 0563 M: 07792-330836 E: fr.anthony.everitt@btinternet.com

EVERITT, Mrs Jane. b 57. St Jo Coll Nottm 08. **d** 10 **p** 11. C Poulton Carleton and Singleton *Blackb* 10-14; TR Launceston *Truro* from 14. *The Rectory, Dunheved Road, Launceston PL15 9JE* T: (01566) 451089 M: 07762-811170
E: revdjane@theeveritts.co.uk

EVERITT, Mark. b 34. Linc Coll Ox BA 58 MA 62. Wells Th Coll. **d** 60 **p** 61. C Hangleton *Chich* 60-63; Chapl Mert Coll Ox 63-02; rtd 02. *48 Annandale Avenue, Bognor Regis PO21 2EX* T: (01243) 823852

EVERITT, The Ven Michael John. b 68. K Coll Lon BD 90 AKC 90. Qu Coll Birm 90 English Coll Rome 91. **d** 92 **p** 93. C Cleveleys *Blackb* 92-95; Succ Bloemfontein Cathl S Africa 95-98; Prec 96-98; Chapl and Asst Lect Univ of Orange Free State 96-98; Sen Chapl St Martin's Coll *Blackb* 98-02; Asst Dir of Ords 00-02; R Standish 02-11; P-in-c Appley Bridge 06-09; AD Chorley 04-11; Hon Can Blackb Cathl 10-11; Adn Lancaster from 11. *6 Eton Park, Fulwood, Preston PR2 9NL* T: (01772) 700337 E: michael.everitt@blackburn.anglican.org

EVERITT, William Frank James. b 38. Dur Univ BA 68 FCA 63. Cranmer Hall Dur 65. **d** 69 **p** 70. C Leic St Phil 69-73; P-in-c Prestwold w Hoton 73-77; R Settrington w N Grimston and Wharram *York* 77-84; RD Buckrose 80-84; V Cheltenham St Pet *Glouc* 84-99; rtd 99; PtO *Leeds* from 03. *27 Lark Hill Crescent, Ripon HG4 2HN* T: (01765) 603683
E: reveveritt@yahoo.com

EVERY, Harriet Mary. **d** 12. NSM Chagford, Gidleigh, Throwleigh etc *Ex* from 12. *Furlong Mill, Sandy Park, Chagford, Newton Abbot TQ13 8JW* T: (01647) 432402
E: hmevery@aol.com

EVES, Barry. b 51. Cranmer Hall Dur 86. **d** 88 **p** 89. C Tadcaster w Newton Kyme *York* 88-91; C York St Paul 91-93; V Bubwith w Skipwith 93-04. *8 Marina Avenue, Sunderland SR6 9AL* T: 0191-549 1742

EVETTS-SECKER, Ms Josephine. b 42. Univ Coll Lon BA 63 MPhil 65. Coll of Resurr Mirfield 06. **d** 07 **p** 08. NSM Hinderwell, Roxby and Staithes etc *York* 07-12; PtO from 12. *Lidgate, Victoria Square, Lythe, Whitby YO21 3RW* T/F: (01947) 893338 M: 07717-061343 E: revj@evetts-secker.co.uk

EWART, John. b 66. QUB BA 89. CITC BTh 02. **d** 02 **p** 03. C Derryloran *Arm* 02-05; China 05-07; I Bright w Ballee and Killough *D & D* 07-13; Min Can Down Cathl 10-13; OMF Internat from 13. *Flat 8, 221 Belmont Road, Belfast BT4 2AH* E: john.ewart@yahoo.co.uk

EWBANK, Mark Robert. b 59. Qu Coll Ox MA 86 Heythrop Coll Lon MTh 05. Westcott Ho Cam 84. **d** 86 **p** 87. Zimbabwe 86-00; Asst P N End St Marg Bulawayo 87-88; P-in-c Pumula St Luke 88-96; R Famona St Mary 96-00; C Chalfont St Peter *Ox* 00-06; V Englefield Green *Guildf* from 06; CF (ACF) from 01; CF (TA) from 05. *The Vicarage, 21 Willow Walk, Englefield Green, Egham TW20 0DQ* T: (01784) 432553
E: v.ewbank@btinternet.com *or* vicar@stjudeschurch.info

EWBANK, Canon Robin Alan. b 42. Ex Coll Ox BA 64 MA 88 Lon Univ BD 68. Clifton Th Coll 66. **d** 69 **p** 70. C Woodford Wells *Chelmsf* 69-72; Warden Cam Univ Miss Bermondsey 72-76; TV Sutton St Jas and Wawne *York* 76-82; R Bramshott Portsm 82-91; R Bramshott and Liphook 91-99; Hon Can Koforidua from 96; P-in-c Hartley Wintney, Elvetham, Winchfield etc *Win* 99-02; V 02-12; RD Odiham 04-11; rtd 12; Hon C Northanger *Win* from 12. *The Vicarage, The Plestor, Selborne, Alton GU34 3JQ* T: (01420) 511098
E: robin.ewbank@googlemail.com

EWEN, Keith John McGregor. b 43. Sarum & Wells Th Coll 77. **d** 79 **p** 80. C Kington w Huntington *Heref* 79-82; C Kington w Huntington, Old Radnor, Kinnerton etc 82-83; P-in-c Culmington w Onibury 83-89; P-in-c Bromfield 83-89; P-in-c Stanton Lacy 83-89; R Culmington w Onibury, Bromfield etc 90-01; R Llangenni and Llanbedr Ystrad Yw w Patricio *S & B* 01-08; rtd 08. *Ty Goleuddydd, 5 Goylands Close, Llandrindod Wells LD1 5RB* T: (01597) 825183

EWER, Edward Sydney John (Jonathan). b 36. Univ of New England BA 69 Lanc Univ MPhil 91 Ch Div Sch of the Pacific (USA) DMin 02. St Mich Th Coll Crafers ThL 63. **d** 62 **p** 63. Australia 62-83; SSM from 68; PtO *Blackb* 83-84; LtO Dur 84-98; Prior SSM Priory Dur 85-98; Dioc Dir of Ords Dur 94-98; PtO *S'wark* 00-05; Hon C Pimlico St Mary Bourne Street *Lon* 05-06; PtO from 06; Ox from 09. *The Well, Newport Road, Willen, Milton Keynes MK15 9AA* T: (01908) 242741 M: 07915-377554 E: j_ewer@yahoo.com

EWINGTON, John. b 43. MRICS 65. Chich Th Coll 74. **d** 78 **p** 79. C Walthamstow St Jo *Chelmsf* 78-81; Papua New Guinea 81-87; V Southend St Sav Westcliff *Chelmsf* 87-96; TV Bideford, Northam, Westward Ho!, Appledore etc *Ex* 96-11; rtd 11. *The Ingle, Newland, Landkey, Barnstaple EX32 0LZ* T: (01271) 830949 E: ewingtons@hotmail.co.uk

EWINS, Tiffany-Alice Letitia. b 74. Mansf Coll Ox BA 97. St Mellitus Coll MA 13. **d** 13 **p** 14. C Brixton St Paul w St Sav *S'wark* from 13. *66 Gayville Road, London SW11 6JP* T: (020) 7738 7259 M: 07970-259580
E: tiffewins@gmail.com

EXCELL, Robin Stanley. b 41. AKC 64. St Boniface Warminster 64. **d** 65 **p** 66. C Ipswich St Mary Stoke *St E* 65-68; C Melton Mowbray w Thorpe Arnold *Leic* 68-70; TV 70-71; R Gt and Lt Blakenham w Baylham *St E* 71-76; R Gt and Lt Blakenham w Baylham and Nettlestead 76-86; RD Bosmere 84-86; NSM Sproughton w Burstall 91-94; R Rattlesden w Thorpe Morieux, Brettenham etc 94-05; rtd 05; PtO *St E* from 05. *Hollywater, Upper Street, Baylham, Ipswich IP6 8JR* T: (01473) 830228 E: robin.excell@tesco.net

EXELL, Ernest William Carter. b 28. Qu Coll Cam BA 52 MA 53. Tyndale Hall Bris 49. **d** 52 **p** 53. C Sydenham H Trin *S'wark* 52-54; C E Ham St Paul *Chelmsf* 54-57; Uganda 57-65; Tanzania 66-70; R Abbess and Beauchamp Roding *Chelmsf* 70-71; P-in-c White Roding w Morrell Roding 70-71; R Abbess Roding, Beauchamp Roding and Berners Roding 71-94; RD Roding 75-79; rtd 94; PtO *St E* from 94. *8 Ickworth Drive, Bury St Edmunds IP33 3PX* T: (01284) 724726

EXELL, Michael Andrew John. b 45. FHCIMA MRIPHH 67 MICA 70. Sarum & Wells Th Coll 87. **d** 89 **p** 90. C Ryde H Trin Portsm 89-93; C Swanmore St Mich w Havenstreet 89-92; C Swanmore St Mich 92-93; P-in-c Carisbrooke St Mary 93-99;

V 99-10; P-in-c Carisbrooke St Nic 93-99; V 99-10; rtd 10; PtO *Portsm* from 10. *3 Glossop Close, East Cowes PO32 6PD* T: (01983) 293686 E: mikeexell@aol.com

EXETER, Archdeacon of. *See* FUTCHER, The Ven Christopher David

EXETER, Bishop of. *See* ATWELL, The Rt Revd Robert Ronald

EXETER, Dean of. *See* DRAPER, The Very Revd Jonathan Lee

EXLEY, Malcolm. b 33. Cranmer Hall Dur. **d** 67 **p** 68. C Sutton St Jas *York* 67-71; C Sutton St Jas and Wawne 71-73; V Mappleton w Goxhill 73-77; V Market Weighton 77-90; P-in-c Goodmanham 77-78; R 78-90; V Bridlington Em 90-98; rtd 98; PtO *York* from 00. *11 The Chase, Driffield YO25 7FJ* T: (01377) 272312

EXLEY-STIEGLER, Canon George Ebdon. b 16. Syracuse Univ BS 51. Berkeley Div Sch STM 53. **d** 53 **p** 54. R Camden Trin USA 53-57; R Brockport St Luke 57-64; R Rochester Calvary-St Andr 64-79; rtd 79; Hon C Knowsley *Liv* 80-81; Hon C Upholland 81-89; Lect Upholland N Inst 80-84; USA from 89. *168 Dalaker Drive, Rochester NY 14624, USA* E: geoes@frontiernet.net

EXON, Helier John Philip. b 44. MBE 87. BSc 70 CEng 87 MIET 87. STETS 96. **d** 99 **p** 00. NSM Milton Abbas, Hilton w Cheselbourne etc *Sarum* 99-05; NSM Piddletrenthide w Plush, Alton Pancras etc 02-05; NSM Piddle Valley, Hilton, Cheselbourne etc 05-14; rtd 14; PtO *Sarum* from 14. *The Monk's House, Hilton, Blandford Forum DT11 0DG* T: (01258) 880396 E: helier@exon.me.uk

EYDEN, Christopher David. b 59. RSAMD BA 81. St Steph Ho Ox 88. **d** 91 **p** 92. C Tottenham St Paul *Lon* 91-93; C Ealing St Pet Mt Park 93-96; TV Wimbledon *S'wark* 96-04; PtO 04-05; C Putney St Mary 05-10; TV from 10; Dir of Ords Kingston Area from 13. *All Saints' Vicarage, 70 Fulham High Street, London SW6 3LG* T: (020) 7384 0115 M: 07951-600924 E: chriseyden@talk21.com

EYEONS, Keith James. b 70. Clare Coll Cam BA 92 MA 96 Down Coll Cam PhD 10 Lon Inst of Educn PGCE 95. St Jo Coll Nottm MA(MM) 03. **d** 01 **p** 02. C Iffley *Ox* 01-03; Chapl Down Coll Cam from 03. *Downing College, Cambridge CB2 1DQ* T: (01223) 334810 E: kje11@cam.ac.uk

EYLES, Anthony John. b 34. Bris Univ BSc 57. Sarum Th Coll 61. **d** 63 **p** 64. C Wellington w W Buckland *B & W* 63-67; C Wilton 67-74; Ind Chapl *Dur* 74-85; *Worc* 85-90; P-in-c Bickenhill w Elmdon *Birm* 90; P-in-c Bickenhill 90-00; Chapl Birm Airport 90-00; rtd 00; PtO *Ex* from 00. *5 Kersbrook Lane, Kersbrook, Budleigh Salterton EX9 7AD* T: (01395) 446084

EYNON, John Kenneth. b 56. Nottm Univ BA 77 BArch 80. **d** 96 **p** 97. OLM Croydon Ch Ch *S'wark* 96-05. *21 Rye Close, Saltdean, Brighton BN2 8PP* T: (01273) 308397 M: 07789-877541 E: johneynon@btinternet.com

EYNSTONE, Ms Sarah Francesca Louise. b 75. Univ Coll Lon BA 96 Fitzw Coll Cam BA 04. Westcott Ho Cam 02. **d** 05 **p** 06. C Hampstead St Jo *Lon* 05-09; Min Can and Chapl St Paul's Cathl 10-15. *Address temp unknown* E: sarah.eynstone@cantab.net

EYRE, Canon Richard Stuart. b 48. Bris Univ BEd 81 Nottm Univ MTh 86. Linc Th Coll 74. **d** 77 **p** 78. C Henbury *Bris* 77-81; C Bedminster 81-82; TV 82-84; Chapl Bp Grosseteste Coll Linc 84-95; Sen Tutor 89-95; P-in-c Long Bennington w Foston *Linc* 95; P-in-c Saxonwell 95-97; R 97-01; RD Grantham 96-01; TR Hykeham 01-13; R 13; RD Graffoe 02-09; Can and Preb Linc Cathl 03-13; rtd 13. *20 Quintin Close, Bracebridge Heath, Lincoln LN4 2LW* E: richard.eyre3@ntlworld.com

EZAT, Timothy. b 83. Wycliffe Hall Ox BTh 12. **d** 12 **p** 13. C Eastbourne All SS *Chich* 12-14; C Eastbourne St Mary from 14. *1F Grassington Road, Eastbourne BN20 7BP* M: 07809-679421 E: timothy.ezat@gmail.com

EZE, Geoffrey Ejike. b 73. Trin Coll Bris 06. **d** 08 **p** 09. C Gt Ilford St Jo *Chelmsf* 08-12; TV Stoke-upon-Trent *Lich* from 12. *23 Mere Side Close, Stoke-on-Trent ST1 5GH* T: (01782) 265129 E: geoffrey_eze@o2.co.uk

F

FACCINI (née LEGG), Sandra Christine. b 55. Surrey Univ BSc 78 PhD 82 Univ of Wales (Ban) BTh 07. **d** 04 **p** 05. OLM Howell Hill w Burgh Heath *Guildf* 04-09; P-in-c Ottershaw 09-14; V from 14. *50 Slade Road, Ottershaw, Chertsey KT16 0HZ* T: (01932) 873160 M: 07743-675633 E: sandra@faccinis.freeserve.co.uk *or* sandrafster@gmail.com

FACER, Miss Rosemary Jane. b 44. Hull Univ BA 65 Reading Univ CertEd 66 LTCL 72. Trin Coll Bris 78. **dss** 80 **d** 87 **p** 98. St Paul's Cray St Barn *Roch* 80-88; Par Dn 87-88; C Cheltenham St Mark *Glouc* 88-01; C Clifton *York* 01-09; rtd 09; PtO *Carl* from 10. *16 Garborough Close, Crosby, Maryport CA15 6RZ* T: (01900) 810776 E: rjfacer@talk21.com

FACEY, Miss Jane (BJ). b 54. EMMTC 05. **d** 07 **p** 08. NSM W Hallam and Mapperley w Stanley *Derby* 07-11; V Chellaston from 11. *The Vicarage, Swarkestone Road, Chellaston, Derby DE73 6UT* T: (01332) 704835 E: bjfacey@btinternet.com

FAGAN, Jeremy David. b 75. Qu Coll Ox BA 98. Wycliffe Hall Ox 99. **d** 01 **p** 02. C Chell *Lich* 01-04; TV Kirkby *Liv* 04-12; TR from 12. *27 Shakespeare Avenue, Liverpool L32 9SH* T: 0151-547 2133 E: faganj@mac.com

FAGAN, John Raymond. b 32. Lon Univ BD 69. Ripon Hall Ox 71. **d** 72 **p** 73. C Stalybridge *Man* 72-74; C Madeley *Heref* 74-79; V Amington *Birm* 79-91; P-in-c Stonnall *Lich* 91-97; Chapl HM YOI Swinfen Hall 91-97; rtd 97; C Stonnall *Lich* 97; Res Min Elford 98-07. *19 Homewelland House, Leicester Road, Market Harborough LE16 7BT* T: (01858) 419988

FAGAN, Thomas. b 27. MCIOB 67 Man Univ CertEd 70. NW Ord Course 78. **d** 81 **p** 82. NSM Rainhill *Liv* 81-90; NSM Prescot 90-97; rtd 97; PtO *Liv* 97-03. *4 Wensleydale Avenue, Prescot L35 4NR* T: 0151-426 4788

FAGBEMI, Olubunmi Ayobami (Bunmi). b 57. Lagos Univ LLB 78 LSE LLM 81 Qu Mary Coll Lon PhD 91 Solicitor 79. Ripon Coll Cuddesdon 95. **d** 97 **p** 98. C Enfield St Andr *Lon* 97-01; V Tottenham H Trin from 01; AD E Haringey from 11. *Holy Trinity Vicarage, Philip Lane, London N15 4GZ* T: (020) 8801 3021 E: bunmif@btinternet.com

FAGBEMI, The Ven Stephen Ayodeji Akinwale. b 67. St Jo Coll Nottm BTh 96 Kent Univ PhD 04. Immanuel Coll Ibadan 87. **d** 90 **p** 91. C Iyere St Jo Nigeria 90-91; C Owo St Patr 91-92; P-in-c Wakajaye-Etile Ch Ch 92-93; V Emure-Ile St Sav 96-00; Can Owo from 99; PtO *Cant* 00-03; Hon C Murston w Bapchild and Tonge 03-05; Co-ord Chapl Sunderland Univ *Dur* 05-11; Hon C Sunderland Minster 05-11; Nigeria from 11. *Archbishop Vining College of Theology, Oke-Emeso, PMB 727, Akure, Ondo State, Nigeria* E: saaf95@hotmail.com *or* saaf90@yahoo.co.uk

FAGERSON, Joseph Leonard Ladd. b 35. Harvard Univ BA 57. Ridley Hall Cam 61. **d** 63 **p** 64. C Tonbridge SS Pet and Paul *Roch* 63-67; Afghanistan 67-74; P-in-c Marbury *Ches* 74-75; P-in-c Kinloch Rannoch *St And* 75-00; Chapl Rannoch Sch Perthshire 75-00; rtd 00; Hon C Killin *St And* 00-12. *Westgarth, Tomnacroich, Fortingall, Aberfeldy PH15 2LJ* T: (01887) 830569

FAHIE, Mrs Stephanie Bridget. b 48. St Jo Coll Nottm 85. **d** 87 **p** 94. Par Dn Leic St Chris 87-90; Chapl Scargill Ho 90-95; P-in-c Hickling w Kinoulton and Broughton Sulney *S'well* 95-00; R 00-10; rtd 11; PtO *Lich* from 12. *61 Monkmoor Avenue, Shrewsbury SY2 5ED* T: (01743) 588307

FAINT, Paul Edward. b 38. Qu Coll Birm 85. **d** 87 **p** 88. C Cradley *Worc* 87-90; V Hanley Castle, Hanley Swan and Welland 90-94; V Northwood H Trin *Lon* 94-97; Miss to Seafarers from 97; Chapl Larnaca Cyprus 97-01; rtd 01; PtO *Ox* from 01; Hon Chapl Miss to Seafarers from 02. *17 Priory Orchard, Wantage OX12 9EL* T: (01235) 772297 E: thefaints@lineone.net

FAIR, Dorothy Enid. b 48. **d** 11 **p** 12. OLM Swinton H Rood *Man* 11-15; P-in-c from 15; NSM Worsley from 13. *375 Worsley Road, Swinton, Manchester M27 0EJ* T: 0161-794 0010 E: de.fair@uwclub.net

FAIRALL, Hannah Marie. *See* MEARS, Hannah Marie

FAIRALL, Michael John. b 45. SWMTC 88. **d** 90 **p** 91. NSM Southway *Ex* 90-00; NSM Bickleigh and Shaugh Prior from 00. *25 Buzzard Road, Whitchurch, Tavistock PL19 9FZ* T: (01822) 610926 E: m.j.fairall@talk21.com

FAIRBAIRN, Andrew Graham. b 48. SEITE 06. **d** 09 **p** 10. NSM Surbiton Hill Ch Ch *S'wark* 09-12; NSM High Ongar w Norton Mandeville *Chelmsf* from 13. *1 Apple Gate, Pilgrims Hatch, Brentwood CM14 5PL* T: (01277) 375574 M: 07789-992843 E: gandlfairbairn@btinternet.com

FAIRBAIRN, Francis Stephen. b 41. **d** 98 **p** 99. OLM Orrell *Liv* 98-13; rtd 13. *27 Greenslate Road, Billinge, Wigan WN5 7BQ* T: (01695) 623127 *or* (01722) 812176 F: 815398

FAIRBAIRN, John Alan. b 46. Trin Coll Cam BA 67 MA 72. Wycliffe Hall Ox 84. **d** 86 **p** 87. C Boscombe St Jo *Win* 86-89; C Edgware *Lon* 89-95; R Gunton St Pet *Nor* 95-11; Chapl Jas

Paget Healthcare NHS Trust 96-08; rtd 11; PtO *Win* from 11. *28 Clifton Road, Bournemouth BH6 3PA* T: (01202) 424466 E: jfairbairn@fsmail.net

FAIRBAIRN, Stella Rosamund. b 41. **d** 87 **p** 94. NSM Banbury *Ox* 87-99; PtO *Pet* 88-94. *Hillside, Overthorpe, Banbury OX17 2AF* T: (01295) 710648

FAIRBAIRN, Stephen. *See* FAIRBAIRN, Francis Stephen

FAIRBANK, Brian Douglas Seeley. b 53. AKC 75. St Steph Ho Ox 77. **d** 78 **p** 79. C Newton Aycliffe *Dur* 78-81; C Stocking Farm *Leic* 81-84; TV Ratby cum Groby 84-91; Chapl RN 91-04; R Bramfield, Stapleford, Waterford etc *St Alb* 04-12; R Culworth w Sulgrave and Thorpe Mandeville etc *Pet* from 12. *The Rectory, Queen's Street, Culworth, Banbury OX17 2AT* T: (01295) 768994 E: brianfairbank487@btinternet.com

FAIRBROTHER, Robin Harry. b 44. Ho of Resurr Mirfield 64 Wells Th Coll 68. **d** 69 **p** 70. C Wrexham *St As* 69-74; C Welshpool w Castle Caereinion 74-77; V Bettws Cedewain and Tregynon 77-80; V Betws Cedewain and Tregynon and Llanwyddelan 80-92; TR Marshwood Vale *Sarum* 92-98; TR Golden Cap Team 98-05; rtd 06. *28 bis avenue Ernest Leotard, 11150 Bram, France* E: robin.fairbrother2356@freeserve.co.uk

FAIRCLOUGH, Miss Amanda Ann Catherine. b 68. Man Univ BSc 89. St Jo Coll Nottm 06 SNWTP 08. **d** 10 **p** 11. NSM Orford St Marg *Liv* 10-14; NSM Warrington E from 14. *7 Time Park, Whiston, Prescot L35 7NU* T: 0151-426 6114 M: 07788-101178 E: a.fairclough@amandafairclough.co.uk

FAIRCLOUGH, Clive Anthony. b 54. TISEC 01. **d** 04 **p** 05. C Nadder Valley *Sarum* 04-08; R Abberton, The Flyfords, Naunton Beauchamp etc *Worc* 08-14; P-in-c Fladbury, Hill and Moor, Wyre Piddle etc 11-14; C Peopleton and White Ladies Aston w Churchill etc 11-14; Chapl Moscow *Eur* from 14. *British Embassy - Moscow, FCO, King Charles Street, London SW1A 2AH* T/F: (007) (495) 629 0990 E: chaplain@standrewsmoscow.org

FAIRCLOUGH, John Frederick. b 40. St Jo Coll Dur BA 63 MA 68 MBIM. Coll of Resurr Mirfield 81. **d** 83 **p** 84. C Horninglow *Lich* 83-87; V Skerton St Luke *Blackb* 87-94; V Thornton-le-Fylde 94-00; rtd 00; PtO *Blackb* from 01. *18 Crossfield Avenue, Bury BL9 5NX* T: (01706) 825664

FAIREY, Michael. b 51. NEOC. **d** 08 **p** 10. NSM York St Hilda 08-12; PtO from 12. *10 Mallard Close, York YO10 3BS* T: (01904) 399655 E: mike@fairey-consulting.com

FAIRHURST, John Graham. b 39. Linc Th Coll 86. **d** 88 **p** 89. C Whiston *Sheff* 88-91; V Elsecar 91-04; AD Tankersley 01-04; Chapl Barnsley Community & Priority Services NHS Trust 98-04; rtd 04; PtO *Sheff* from 04. *30 Barberry Way, Ravenfield, Rotherham S65 4RE* T: (01709) 548206

FAIRHURST, Canon Rosemary Anne. b 63. Newnham Coll Cam BA 85 MA 85 Heythrop Coll Lon MTh 97 Lon Inst of Educn PGCE 86. Wycliffe Hall Ox MA 92. **d** 93 **p** 94. C Hackney Marsh *Lon* 93-97; C Islington St Mary 97-02; Dir Miss and Min Ripon Coll Cuddesdon 02-06; Organizational Analyst Grubb Inst 07-12; C St Martin-in-the-Fields *Lon* 98-12; PtO 12-14; Can Res and Chan Leic Cathl from 14. *The Chancellor's House, 23 St Martins, Leicester LE1 5DE* T: 0116-251 9197 M: 07766-451316 E: rosy.fairhurst@leccofe.org

FAIRHURST, Susan. **d** 14 **p** 15. NSM Lillington and Old Milverton *Cov* from 14. *Address temp unknown*

FAIRLAMB, Neil. b 49. Univ of Wales (Ban) BA 71 Jes Coll Ox BPhil 73 Pemb Coll Cam CertEd 74 Univ of Wales (Abth) MTh 00. S'wark Ord Course 90. **d** 93 **p** 94. Hon C Dulwich St Barn *S'wark* 93-95; P-in-c Elerch w Penrhyncoch w Capel Bangor and Goginan *St D* 95-96; V 96-98; R Arthog w Fairbourne w Llangelynnin w Rhoslefain *Ban* 98-03; R Beaumaris 03-11; R Beaumaris w Llanddona and Llaniestyn 11-13; R Beaumaris w Llanddona from 13. *The Rectory, 5 Tros yr Afon, Beaumaris LL58 8BN* T/F: (01248) 811402 E: rheithor@aol.com

FAIRLESS, Elizabeth Jane. *See* JONES, Elizabeth Jane

FAIRWEATHER, David James. b 35. Keele Univ BEd 79. Wycliffe Hall Ox 70. **d** 72 **p** 73. C Trentham *Lich* 72-76; C Cheddleton 76; C Hanley H Ev 77-79; C Rugeley 79-86; V Brown Edge 86-03; rtd 03; PtO *Lich* from 09. *2 Lockwood Close, Kingsley Holt, Stoke-on-Trent ST10 2BN* T: (01538) 267054 E: father.david222@googlemail.com

FAIRWEATHER, John. b 39. K Coll Lon AKC 66 BD 72. **d** 67 **p** 68. C Plymouth St Jas Ham *Ex* 67-69; C Townstal w St Sav and St Petrox w St Barn 69-73; R Corringham w Springthorpe *Linc* 73-78; P-in-c Blyborough 76-78; P-in-c Heapham 76-78; P-in-c Willoughton 76-78; V Pinchbeck 78-82; V Exwick *Ex* 82-04; rtd 04. *52 Woodman's Crescent, Honiton EX14 2DY* T: (01404) 549711 E: john.fairweather6@btinternet.com

FAIRWEATHER, Sally Helen. *See* ROSS, Sally Helen

FALASCHI-RAY, Sonia Ofelia. Surrey Univ BSc 79 Wolfs Coll Cam BA 02 MA 06 CEng 86. Ridley Hall Cam 03. **d** 05 **p** 06.

NSM Fowlmere, Foxton, Shepreth and Thriplow *Ely* 05-09; PtO *St Alb* 09-10; *Ely* from 09; NSM Barkway, Reed and Buckland w Barley *St Alb* from 10. *27 Church Lane, Barkway, Royston SG8 8EJ* T: (01763) 849057 M: 07747-844265 E: sonia.falaschi-ray@virgin.net

FALCONER, Ian Geoffrey. b 40. BNC Ox BA 62 Newc Univ MA 93. Cuddesdon Coll 62. **d** 64 **p** 65. C Chiswick St Nic w St Mary *Lon* 64-68; C-in-c Hounslow Gd Shep Beavers Lane CD 68-76; P-in-c Hammersmith St Matt 76-84; P-in-c Byker St Silas *Newc* 84-93; V 93-95; P-in-c Newc St Phil and St Aug 95-98; P-in-c Newc St Matt w St Mary 95-98; P-in-c Newc St Phil and St Aug and St Matt w St Mary 98-00; V Seghill 00-06; rtd 06. *70 Lowgates, Staveley, Chesterfield S43 3TU* T: (01246) 471913 E: frianfalc@yahoo.co.uk

FALKINGHAM (née MOORE), Mrs Caroline Judith. b 57. Coll of Ripon & York St Jo BA 78 Leeds Univ MA 07. NOC 05. **d** 07 **p** 08. C Bilton *Ripon* 07-11; NSM Fountains Gp 11-12; R *Leeds* from 12. *The Rectory, Ringbeck Road, Kirkby Malzeard, Ripon HG4 3SL* E: carolinefalkingham@talktalk.net

FALKNER, Jonathan Michael Shepherd. b 47. Open Univ BA 74. Cranmer Hall Dur. **d** 79 **p** 80. C Penrith w Newton Reigny *Carl* 79-81; C Penrith w Newton Reigny and Plumpton Wall 81-82; C Dalton-in-Furness 82-84; V Clifton 84-90; P-in-c Dean 85-89; R Rumburgh w S Elmham w the Ilketshalls *St E* 90-92; R S Elmham and Ilketshall 92-99; RD Beccles and S Elmham 94-99; Hon Can St E Cathl 98-99; P-in-c W Newton and Bromfield w Waverton *Carl* 99-02; P-in-c Holme Cultram St Mary 00-02; P-in-c Holme Cultram St Cuth 00-02; TR Solway Plain 02-05; P-in-c Gosforth w Nether Wasdale and Wasdale Head 05-12; P-in-c Beckermet St Jo and St Bridget w Ponsonby 12; rtd 12. *22 Whole House Road, Seascale CA20 1QY* T: (019467) 21852 E: southcalder@falconfleet.org.uk

FALLA, Miles. b 43. MCIM. EAMTC 93. **d** 96 **p** 97. NSM Buckden *Ely* 96-98; P-in-c Gretton w Rockingham *Pet* 98-99; V Gretton w Rockingham and Cottingham w E Carlton 99-04; RD Corby 01-02; rtd 04; PtO *Ely* from 05. *Bowlings, Silver Street, Buckden, St Neots PE19 5TS* T: (01480) 811335 E: miles@falla.ndo.co.uk

FALLON, James Anthony. b 62. Qu Coll Birm. **d** 11 **p** 12. C Chard St Mary w Combe St Nicholas, Wambrook etc *B & W* 11-15; R Blackdown from 15. *The Vicarage, Pitminster, Taunton TA3 7AZ* E: revfallon@btinternet.com

FALLONE, Christopher. b 55. Aston Tr Scheme 85 Oak Hill Th Coll 87. **d** 90 **p** 91. C Rochdale *Man* 90-93; P-in-c Thornham w Gravel Hole 93-94; TV Middleton w Thornham 94-08; P-in-c Collyhurst from 08. *The Rectory, Eggington Street, Collyhurst, Manchester M10 7RN* T: 0161-205 2808 M: 07976-624124 E: chrisfallone@bigfoot.com

FALLOWS, Stuart Adrian. b 50. Moray Ho Edin 75. **d** 78 **p** 79. Hon C Forres w Nairn *Mor* 78-81; Hon C Elgin w Lossiemouth 81-86; Hon Dioc Chapl 86; C Brighton St Geo w St Anne and St Mark *Chich* 86-89; V Wivelsfield 89-98; P-in-c Kieth, Huntly and Aberchirder *Mor* 98-02; P-in-c Ringwould w Kingsdown *Cant* 02-04; R Ringwould w Kingsdown and Ripple etc 05-09; R W Highland Region *Arg* 09-15; rtd 15. *Duncroft, 25 Murray Crescent, Lamlash, Isle of Arran KA27 8NS* T: (01855) 811987 E: afallows222@aol.co.uk

FALSHAW, Simon Meriadoc. b 60. Leeds Univ BSc 82. Oak Hill Th Coll BA 93. **d** 93 **p** 94. C Stapleford *S'well* 93-99; Miss Partner Crosslinks 99-00; P-in-c The Lye and Stambermill *Worc* from 01; RD Stourbridge 04-07. *Christ Church Vicarage, High Street, Lye, Stourbridge DY9 8LF* T: (01384) 423142 *or* 894948 E: christchurchlye@classicfm.net

FALUDY, Alexander Raban Spencer. b 83. Peterho Cam BA 01 MA 05 Linc Coll Ox MSt 04. Coll of Resurr Mirfield 05. **d** 08 **p** 09. C Tynemouth Cullercoats St Paul *Newc* 08-11; C Willington 11-13; P-in-c Wallsend St Jo from 14. *St John's Vicarage, Station Road, Wallsend NE28 8DT* T: 0191-289 5135 E: wallsend.vicar@gmail.com

FALVEY, Mrs Imogen Rosalind. b 62. Somerville Coll Ox BA 84 Solicitor 88. ERMC 11. **d** 14 **p** 15. NSM Sawtry and Glatton *Ely* from 14. *171 Eagle Way, Hampton Vale, Peterborough PE7 8EL* M: 07903-098982 E: falvey12@btinternet.com

FANCOURT, Graeme. b 77. St Jo Coll Dur BA 00 DThM 11. Ripon Coll Cuddesdon 09. **d** 10 **p** 11. C Caversham Thameside and Mapledurham *Ox* 10-13; P-in-c Reading St Luke w St Bart 13-14; V from 14. *The Vicarage, 50 London Road, Reading RG1 5AS* E: fancourt@gmail.com

FANE DE SALIS, Mrs Mary. b 88. **d** 14 **p** 15. C Clothall, Rushden, Sandon, Wallington and Weston *St Alb* from 14. *14 Munts Meadow, Weston, Hitchin SG4 7AE* M: 07866-890402 E: marydesalis@hotmail.com

FANTHORPE, Robert Lionel. b 35. Open Univ BA 80 CertEd 63 FCMI 81 FCP 90. Llan Dioc Tr Scheme. **d** 87 **p** 88. NSM Roath

St German *Llan* 87-00; LtO from 00. *Rivendell, 48 Claude Road, Roath, Cardiff CF24 3QA* T: (029) 2049 8368 F: 2049 6832 M: 07767-207289 E: fanthorpe@aol.com

FARADAY, John. b 49. Leeds Univ BSc 71 MICE 78. Oak Hill Th Coll 81. **d** 83 **p** 84. C Sutton *Liv* 83-86; C Rainhill and Chapl Whiston Hosp 86-89; V Over Darwen St Jas *Blackb* 89-02; TR S Rochdale *Man* 02-08; TR Gorton and Abbey Hey 08-15; rtd 15; PtO *Man* from 15. *1 Magpie Lane, Oldham OL4 5PB* E: john.faraday@sky.com

FARAGHER, James Philip. b 77. St Jo Coll Nottm 12. **d** 14 **p** 15. C St Alb St Paul *St Alb* from 14. *46 Brampton Road, St Albans AL1 4PT* M: 07800-908396 E: jamesfaragher@yahoo.co.uk

FARAH, Mones Anton. b 64. Trin Coll Bris BA 88. **d** 88 **p** 89. C Aberystwyth *St D* 88-91; Chapl St D Coll Lamp 91-98; TV Gt Baddow *Chelmsf* 98-14; P-in-c Aberystwyth *St D* from 14. *The Rectory, 7 Laura Place, Aberystwyth SY23 2AU* T: (01970) 617184 E: monesf@yahoo.com

FARBRIDGE, Nicholas Brisco. b 33. FCA. Sarum & Wells Th Coll 75. **d** 77 **p** 78. C Gt Bookham *Guildf* 77-80; C Ewell 80-83; V Addlestone 83-89; R Shere 89-95; rtd 96; PtO *Guildf* from 96. *55 Curling Vale, Guildford GU2 7PH* T: (01483) 531140 E: nickfarbridge@msn.com

FARDELL, Rebecca Susan. b 70. Reading Univ BA 92 Leic Univ MA 94 Qu Coll Cam PGCE 93. Ridley Hall Cam 11. **d** 13 **p** 14. C Itchen Valley *Win* from 13. *28 Longfield Road, Winchester SO23 0NT* E: rebecca.itchenvalley@gmail.com

FARDON, Raymond George Warren. b 30. St Pet Hall Ox BA 52 MA 56. Ridley Hall Cam 54. **d** 59 **p** 60. C High Wycombe All SS *Ox* 59-63; Chapl Bedford Secondary Modern Sch 63-68; Dep Hd Dunstable Secondary Modern Sch 68-72; Hd Master K Sch Grantham 72-82; Travelling Ev from 82; Hon C Longfleet *Sarum* 82-83; PtO 83-05; *S'well* from 05; rtd 95. *9 Somerby Court, Bramcote, Nottingham NG9 3NB* T: 0115-928 0810

FAREY, David Mark. b 56. St Jo Coll Dur BA 85. Cranmer Hall Dur 82. **d** 86 **p** 87. C Brackley St Pet w St Jas 86-89; TV Kingsthorpe w Northampton St Dav 89-96; R Laughton w Ripe and Chalvington *Chich* 96-10; Chapl to Bp Lewes 96-10; Dioc Communications Officer 10-14; V Hellingly and Upper Dicker from 14. *14 Orchard Grange, Lower Dicker, Hailsham BN27 3PA* T: (01323) 440450 M: 07512-370221 E: vicar.hellingly@btinternet.com

FARGUS, Gavin James Frederick. b 30. AKC 54. K Coll Lon. **d** 55 **p** 57. C Salisbury St Mark *Sarum* 55-57; C Wareham w Arne 57-60; C Marlborough 60-63; P-in-c Davidstow w Otterham *Truro* 63-65; R Nether Lochaber *Arg* 65-81; R Kinlochleven 65-81; rtd 81; LtO *Arg* 82-94. *61 Loan Fearn, Ballachulish, Argyll PH49 4JB* T: (01855) 811851

FARISH, Alan John. b 58. Lanc Univ BA. St Jo Coll Nottm 83. **d** 86 **p** 87. C Bishopwearmouth St Gabr *Dur* 86-89; C Fatfield 89-98; P-in-c Preston on Tees 98-03; V Preston-on-Tees and Longnewton 03-10; P-in-c Stockton from 08. *23 Deepdale Avenue, Stockton-on-Tees TS18 2QE*

FARLEY, David Stuart. b 53. Univ Coll Dur BA 75 Westmr Coll Ox MTh 00. St Jo Coll Nottm. **d** 84 **p** 85. C Bath Weston All SS w N Stoke *B & W* 84-87; Chapl Scargill Ho 87-90; Min Hedge End N Coll *Win* 90-94; V Hedge End St Luke 94-00; Dep Chapl HM Pris Belmarsh 00; Chapl HM Pris Shrewsbury 00-13; Chapl HM Pris Featherstone from 13. *HM Prison, Featherstone, Wolverhampton WV10 7PU* T: (01902) 703000

FARLEY, Ian David. b 56. Linc Coll Ox BA 78 MA 87 Dur Univ PhD 88. Cranmer Hall Dur 84. **d** 87 **p** 88. C Thorpe Acre w Dishley *Leic* 87-92; V S Lambeth St Steph *S'wark* 92-99; V Bacton w Edingthorpe w Witton and Ridlington *Nor* 99-03; Ind Chapl 99-03; TR Buckhurst Hill *Chelmsf* from 03. *St John's Rectory, High Road, Buckhurst Hill IG9 5RX* T: (020) 8504 1931 E: parish-office@buckhursthill.free-online.co.uk

FARLEY, James Trevor. b 37. IEng MIET FRSA. EMMTC 80. **d** 82 **p** 83. NSM Grantham *Linc* from 82; PtO *Leic* from 14. *Highfield Cottage, Station Road, Bottesford, Nottingham NG13 0EN* T/F: (01949) 843860 M: 07768-360592 E: jimfarley@talktalk.net

FARLEY, Ronald Alexander. b 30. Oak Hill NSM Course. **d** 79 **p** 80. NSM Stoke Newington St Faith, St Matthias and All SS *Lon* 79-97; NSM Upper Clapton St Matt 99-04; rtd 04; PtO *Lon* from 04. *2 St James Close, Bishop Street, London N1 8PH* T: (020) 7354 2231

FARLEY-MOORE, Peter James. b 72. Sheff Univ BA 94 UEA MA 00. Ridley Hall Cam. **d** 00 **p** 01. C Chapeltown *Sheff* 00-03; Miss Cell Adv CMS 04-05; Asst Min Kowloon St Andr Hong Kong 05-07; V Blackheath St Jo *S'wark* 07-14; TR Deptford St Jo w H Trin and Ascension from 14. *St John's Vicarage, St John's Vale, London SE8 4EA* E: peter.stjohnsdeptford@gmail.com

FARMAN, Joanne Margaret. b 46. Birkbeck Coll Lon BA 81 Leeds Univ MA 08 Southlands Coll Lon PGCE 82. SEITE 97. **d** 00 **p** 01. NSM Limpsfield and Titsey *S'wark* 00-04;

Chapl St Geo Healthcare NHS Trust Lon 00-10; Lead Chapl R Hosp for Neuro-Disability 04-05; PtO *S'wark* from 10; *Roch* from 12. *10 Detillens Lane, Limpsfield, Oxted RH8 0DJ* T: (01883) 713086 *or* (020) 8725 3070 E: joannefarman086@btinternet.com

FARMAN, Robert Joseph. b 54. Ridley Hall Cam 86. **d** 88 **p** 89. C Sutton St Nic *S'wark* 88-90; C Cheam Common St Phil 90-92; R Wootton w Glympton and Kiddington *Ox* 92-00; TV Kings Norton *Birm* 00-04; Chapl St Mary's Hospice 04-12; Chapl R Orthopaedic Hosp NHS Trust 05-06; Chapl Birm and Solihull Mental Health Trust 06-07; rtd 12. *58 Station Road, Kings Norton, Birmingham B30 1DA* T: 0121-451 1234 M: 07766-054137 E: robfarman@evemail.net

FARMAN, Mrs Roberta. b 48. Aber Univ MA 70 Cam Univ CertEd 72. Qu Coll Birm 78. **dss** 82 **d** 87 **p** 01. Ovenden *Wakef* 80-82; Scargill Ho 83-84; Coulsdon St Jo *S'wark* 85-86; Hon Par Dn Cambridge St Mark *Ely* 86-88; Hon Par Dn Sutton St Nic *S'wark* 88-92; Hon Par Dn Wootton w Glympton and Kiddington *Ox* 92-00; NSM Kings Norton *Birm* 01-04; Chapl Univ Hosp Birm NHS Foundn Trust 01-05. *58 Station Road, Kings Norton, Birmingham B30 1DA* T: 0121-451 1234 *or* 627 1627 E: bj@robfarman.evesham.net

FARMBOROUGH, James Laird McLelland (Mac). b 22. MBE 90. Magd Coll Cam BA 49 MA 54. Tyndale Hall Bris. **d** 52 **p** 53. C Wolverhampton St Luke *Lich* 52-55; C Holloway St Mary w St Jas *Lon* 55-56; C Broadwater St Mary *Chich* 56-58; Chapl All SS Niteroi Brazil 58-64; Org Sec SAMS 65-70; V Marple All SS *Ches* 70-80; Chapl Vina del Mar St Pet Chile 80-92; Miss to Seamen 80-92; rtd 92. *Flat 8, Manormead, Tilford Road, Hindhead GU26 6RA*

FARMER, Mrs Anne Louise. b 61. Warwick Univ BEd 84. Trin Coll Bris 04. **d** 06 **p** 07. NSM Stoke Bishop *Bris* 06-09; TV Worle *B & W* from 09. *21 Westmarch Way, Weston-super-Mare BS22 7JY* T: (01934) 515610 E: annefarmer21@o2.co.uk

FARMER, Diane Marcia (Diana). b 61. Warwick Univ BSc 82 PGCE 83. WMMTC 97 Cranmer Hall Dur 00. **d** 01 **p** 02. C Allesley Park and Whoberley *Cov* 01-05; Hd Tr and Development Rethink from 05; Hon C Pensnett *Worc* 05-07; PtO 07-09; Hon C Wollaston from 09. *13 Rectory Street, Stourbridge DY8 5QT* T: (01384) 295205 E: diana@farmerfamilyuk.fsnet.co.uk *or* diana.farmer@rethink.org

FARMER, Lorelie Joy. Southn Univ BA 65 MA 68 Univ of Mass EdD 88. Cranmer Hall Dur 97. **d** 99 **p** 00. C Newbury *Ox* 99-03; C Stratford-upon-Avon, Luddington etc *Cov* 03-05; C Warmington w Shotteswell and Radway w Ratley 05-06; rtd 08; Hon C Witchampton, Stanbridge and Long Crichel etc *Sarum* 08-10; Hon C Wimborne Minster from 12. *1 Oakdene Close, Wimborne BH21 1TJ* E: loreliefarmer@dunelm.org.uk

FARMER, Robert James. b 65. WMMTC 03. **d** 06 **p** 07. C Lich St Chad 06-10; C Longdon 08-10; P-in-c Longdon and C Heath Hayes 10-11; V Shelfield and High Heath from 11. *Church House, 25 Green Lane, Shelfield, Walsall WS4 1RN* T: (01922) 692550 E: robert@farmer2181.freeserve.co.uk

FARMER, Robert John Thayer. b 62. Kent Univ BA 84. St Steph Ho Ox 91. **d** 93 **p** 94. C Leigh St Clem *Chelmsf* 93-96; P-in-c Wellingborough St Mary *Pet* 96-00; V from 00; Chapl Northants Healthcare NHS Trust from 99. *St Mary's Vicarage, 193 Midland Road, Wellingborough NN8 1NG* T: (01933) 225626 E: vicar@stmarywellingborough.org.uk

FARMER, Simon John. b 60. Birm Univ BSc 82. St Jo Coll Nottm 86. **d** 89 **p** 90. C Ulverston St Mary w H Trin *Carl* 89-92; CF 92-97; Chapl HM Pris Lowdham Grange 97-00; CF (TA) from 99; PtO *S'well* 00-14; Operations Dir (Africa) ACCTS Mil Min Internat from 00. *26 Halloughton Road, Southwell NG25 0LR* T: (01636) 814441 M: 07824-838411 E: farmer@f2s.com

FARMILOE, Preb Trevor James. b 42. Sarum & Wells Th Coll. **d** 82 **p** 82. C S Petherton w The Seavingtons *B & W* 82-85; R Norton St Philip w Hemington, Hardington etc 85-93; Chapl Rural Affairs Wells Adnry 87-92; RD Frome 89-93; V Martock w Ash 93-07; RD Ivelchester 95-01 and 04-07; Preb Wells Cathl 96-07; rtd 07; PtO *B & W* 07-11; C Yeovil St Mich 11-12. *38 Ashmead, Yeovil BA20 2SQ* T: (01935) 428952 E: revtrev.martock@btinternet.com

FARNHAM, Douglas John. b 30. SS Mark & Jo Univ Coll Plymouth TCert 52 Ex Univ MEd 75. S Dios Minl Tr Scheme 80. **d** 83 **p** 84. Lect Bp Otter Coll Chich 70-78; Sen Lect W Sussex Inst of HE 78-92; NSM Barnham and Eastergate *Chich* 83-85; NSM Aldingbourne, Barnham and Eastergate 85-92; R 92-96; rtd 96; PtO *Chich* from 96. *12 Summersdale Court, The Drive, Chichester PO19 5RF* T: (01243) 532251

FARNWORTH, Ms Joanna Helen. b 66. Jes Coll Cam BA 88 MA 92. St Jo Coll Nottm BTh 98 MA 99. **d** 99 **p** 00. C Middleton w Thornham *Man* 99-03; TV Ashton 03-11;

P-in-c Droylsden St Martin from 11. *St James's Vicarage, Union Street, Aston-under-Lyne OL6 9NQ* T: 0161-330 4925
E: joannafarnworth@aol.com

FARNWORTH, Roger. b 60. Man Univ BSc 81. St Jo Coll Nottm MA 99. **d** 99 **p** 00. C Tonge w Alkrington *Man* 99-03; TV Ashton 03-05; TR from 05; AD Ashton-under-Lyne from 08. *St James's Vicarage, Union Street, Ashton-under-Lyne OL6 9NQ* T: 0161-330 2771 E: rogerfarnworth@aol.com

FARQUHAR, Iain. b 45. **d** 05 **p** 06. OLM Catford St Laur *S'wark* from 05. *18 Birkhall Road, London SE6 1TE* T: (020) 8698 7438 E: iain@thefarquhars.freeserve.co.uk

FARQUHAR, Preb Patricia Ann. b 42. **dss** 78 **d** 87 **p** 94. Par Dn S Hackney St Jo w Ch Ch *Lon* 87-94; C 94-01; Preb St Paul's Cathl 97-01; rtd 01; PtO *Nor* from 15. *8 Holme Terrace, Bishopgate, Norwich NR1 4EJ* T: (01603) 610112

FARQUHARSON, The Very Revd Hunter Buchanan. b 58. ALAM LLAM. Edin Th Coll 85. **d** 88 **p** 89. C Dunfermline *St And* 88-91; R Glenrothes 91-97; R Leven 95-97; R Dunfermline 97-99; Provost St Ninian's Cathl Perth from 99. *St Ninian's Cathedral, North Methven Street, Perth PH1 5PP* T/F: (01738) 850497 T: 632053 E: huntfar@gmail.com *or* provost@perthcathedral.co.uk

FARR, John. *See* FARR, William John

FARR (née ROSE), Margaret. b 37. Man Univ BDS, LDS 60 Birm Univ MB, ChB 69 MD 85. WMMTC 99. **d** 02 **p** 03. NSM Handsworth St Jas *Birm* 02-09; Hon Chapl Sandwell and W Birm Hosps NHS Trust 07-11; PtO *Birm* from 11. *35 West Drive, Handsworth, Birmingham B20 3ST* T: 0121-554 0909

FARR, Richard William. b 55. Ridley Hall Cam. **d** 83 **p** 84. C Enfield Ch Ch Trent Park *Lon* 83-87; C Eastbourne H Trin *Chich* 87-90; P-in-c Henham and Elsenham w Ugley *Chelmsf* 90-91; V 91-09; C Tunbridge Wells St Jo *Roch* from 09. *112 Sandhurst Road, Tunbridge Wells TN4 9QA* T: (01892) 540897 E: dickthevic@btopenworld.com

FARR, William John. b 66. QUB BTh 05 MTh 07. **d** 08 **p** 09. NSM Muckamore and Killead w Gartree *Conn* 08-11; P-in-c Stoneyford from 11. *1 Ballyvannon Road, Ballinderry Upper, Lisburn BT28 2LB* T: (028) 9442 2158 M: 07808-399579 E: j20far@hotmail.com

FARRAN, Canon George Orman. b 35. Worc Coll Ox BA 58 MA 62. Wycliffe Hall Ox 58. **d** 60 **p** 61. C Tyldesley w Shakerley *Man* 60-62; Tutor Wycliffe Hall Ox 62-64; V Netherton *Liv* 64-73; R Sefton 69-73; R Credenhill w Brinsop, Mansel Lacey, Yazor etc *Heref* 73-83; RD Heref Rural 81-83; R Ditcheat w E Pennard and Pylle *B & W* 83-94; Dir of Ords 86-89; Can and Chan Wells Cathl 85-97; rtd 97; PtO *B & W* from 97. *6 The Empire, Grand Parade, Bath BA2 4DF* T: (01225) 339365

FARRANT, David Stuart. b 38. Ripon Coll Cuddesdon 82. **d** 84 **p** 85. C Woodford St Mary w St Phil and St Jas *Chelmsf* 84-87; R Clymping and Yapton w Ford *Chich* 87-92; Dioc Schs Admin Officer 92-95; Chapl Qu Alexandra Hosp Home Worthing 95-04; P-in-c Amberley w N Stoke and Parham, Wiggonholt etc *Chich* 04-10; rtd 10. *3 Fairlands, East Preston, Littlehampton BN16 1HS*

FARRANT, Canon Martyn John. b 38. AKC 61. **d** 62 **p** 63. C Hampton St Mary *Lon* 62-65; C Shere *Guildf* 65-67; V Stoneleigh 67-75; V Addlestone 75-83; V Dorking w Ranmore 83-98; RD Dorking 89-94; Hon Can Guildf Cathl 96-98; rtd 98; PtO *Guildf* from 98; Chapl Phyllis Tuckwell Hospice Farnham 98-01. *42 Hampstead Road, Dorking RH4 3AE* T: (01306) 740916

FARRAR, Caroline. *See* CASSERLY-FARRAR, Caroline

FARRAR, James Albert. b 27. TCD BA 55 MA 57. CITC 56. **d** 56 **p** 57. C Dublin Drumcondra w N Strand *D & G* 56-59; C Dublin Rathmines 59-61; I Ballinaclash 61-72; I Dunganstown w Redcross 72-79; Warden Ch Min of Healing 79-95; Hon Clerical V Ch Ch Cathl Dublin 79-92; Can Ch Ch Cathl Dublin 92-95; rtd 95. *Tree Tops, Brides Glen Road, Shankill, Dublin 18, Republic of Ireland* T: (00353) (1) 282 0150

FARRAR, Prof Roy Alfred. b 39. Imp Coll Lon BSc 60 PhD 67 FWeldI 85. Wycliffe Hall Ox 99. **d** 00 **p** 01. NSM Portswood St Denys *Win* 00-04; P-in-c Lille *Eur* 04-06; PtO *Bris* from 07. *20 Orchard Court, Arches Lane, Malmesbury SN16 0ED* T: (01666) 826700

FARRAR, Ruth. b 43. Matlock Coll of Educn CertEd 64. **d** 04 **p** 05. OLM Leesfield *Man* 04-13; rtd 13; PtO *Man* from 13. *Belvoir, 43 Coverhill Road, Grotton, Oldham OL4 5RE* T: 0161-633 0374

FARRELL, Mrs Joanna Susan Elizabeth. b 53. Southn Univ LLB 95. STETS 03. **d** 06 **p** 07. NSM Steep and Froxfield w Privett *Portsm* from 06; Asst Chapl Portsm Hosps NHS Trust from 12. *Hurst Farm Cottage, Hurst Lane, Privett, Alton GU34 3PL* T: (01730) 828450
E: joanna@hurstfarmcottage.co.uk

FARRELL, Ms Katherine Lucy Anne. b 61. Westcott Ho Cam 00. **d** 02 **p** 03. C Forest Gate E w Upton Cross *Chelmsf* 02-03; C Lt Ilford St Mich 03-07; V Bellingham St Dunstan *S'wark* 07-11; C Croydon St Jo 11-13; PtO 13-15; TV Gt Grimsby St Mary and St Jas *Linc* from 15. *St Hugh's Vicarage, 4 Freshney Drive, Grimsby DN31 1TP* M: 07904-653180
E: k.farrell916@btinternet.com

FARRELL, Ms Margaret Ruth. b 57. Linc Inst Melbourne BAppSc(OT) 78. **d** 02 **p** 03. C Bury St Edmunds All SS w St Jo and St Geo *St E* 02-06; P-in-c Woolpit w Drinkstone 06-08; R from 08. *The Rectory, Rectory Lane, Woolpit, Bury St Edmunds IP30 9QP* T: (01359) 242244

FARRELL, Peter Godfrey Paul. b 39. Sarum & Wells Th Coll 72. **d** 74 **p** 75. C St Just in Roseland *Truro* 74-77; C Kenwyn 77-80; V Knighton St Jo *Leic* 80-86; TR Clarendon Park St Jo w Knighton St Mich 86-89; V Woodham *Guildf* 89-99; V Wells St Cuth w Wookey Hole *B & W* 99-09; rtd 09; P-in-c E w W Harptree and Hinton Blewett *B & W* 09-12. *Close Cottage, 1 Great Gardens, Gaol Lane, Shepton Mallet BA4 5LF* T: (01749) 345443 E: pgpfvic@gmail.com

FARRELL, Robert Edward. b 54. Univ of Wales (Abth) BA 74 Jes Coll Ox BA 77 MA 81. Qu Coll Birm 85. **d** 86 **p** 87. C Llanrhos *St As* 86-88; C Prestwich St Marg *Man* 89-91; V Moulsham St Luke *Chelmsf* 91-98; V Thorpe Bay 98-08; R Ardleigh and The Bromleys 08-13; rtd 13; PtO *Cant* from 14. *Villa Derwen, 135 London Road, Temple Ewell, Dover CT16 3BY* E: robert_farrell21@hotmail.com

FARRELL, Ronald Anthony. b 57. Edin Univ BD 84 Birm Univ MA 86. Qu Coll Birm 84. **d** 86 **p** 87. C Shard End *Birm* 86-87; C Shirley 87-89; Bp's Officer for Schs and Young People 89-93; V Kingstanding St Mark 93-01; TR Swinton and Pendlebury *Man* 01-05; P-in-c Lower Broughton Ascension 02-05; V W Bromwich St Fran *Lich* from 05. *Friar Park Vicarage, Freeman Road, Wednesbury WS10 0HJ* T: 0121-556 5823
E: father.ron@btinternet.com

FARRELL, Stephen Andrew. b 84. Jes Coll Ox BA 05. CITC BTh 08. **d** 08 **p** 09. C Taney *D & G* 08-11; I Dublin Zion Ch from 11; Prov and Dioc Registrar from 12. *Zion Rectory, 18 Bushy Park Road, Rathgar, Dublin 6, Republic of Ireland* T: (00353) (1) 492 2365 *or* 406 4730
E: zion@dublin.anglican.org

FARRELL, Thomas Stanley. b 32. Lon Univ BD 71. Ridley Hall Cam 69. **d** 71 **p** 72. C Much Woolton *Liv* 71-73; C Gt Sankey 73-74; Asst Chapl Dulwich Coll 74-76; Chapl 76-81; P-in-c Wonersh *Guildf* 81-86; V 86-90; RD Cranleigh 87-90; R St Marg Lothbury and St Steph Coleman Street etc *Lon* 90-00; P-in-c St Botolph without Aldersgate 90-97; rtd 00; Hon C Burford w Fulbrook, Taynton, Asthall etc *Ox* 00-04; PtO from 04. *Candle Cottage, 23 Frogmore Lane, Long Crendon, Aylesbury HP18 9DZ* T: (01844) 208683

FARRER, Canon Carol Elizabeth. b 47. Open Univ BA 88. Cranmer Hall Dur 81. **dss** 83 **d** 87 **p** 94. Newbarns w Hawcoat *Carl* 83-86; Egremont and Haile 86-91; Par Dn 87-91; Team Dn Penrith w Newton Reigny and Plumpton Wall 91-94; TV 94-01; Dioc Lay Min Adv 87-88; Assoc Dir of Ords 88-97; 97-00; Dioc OLM Officer 00-05; TV S Barrow 01-07; Hon Can Carl Cathl 01-07; rtd 08; PtO *St As* from 09. *3 Marlow Terrace, Mold CH7 1HH* T: (01352) 756011

FARRER, Canon Michael Robert Wedlake. b 22. St Pet Hall Ox BA 52 MA 57. Tyndale Hall Bris 47. **d** 52 **p** 53. C Ox St Ebbe 52-56; Tutor Clifton Th Coll 56-65; R Barton Seagrave *Pet* 65-73; R Barton Seagrave w Warkton 73-78; V Cambridge St Paul *Ely* 78-92; RD Cambridge 84-89; Hon Can Ely Cathl 88-92; rtd 92; Bp's Sen Chapl *Ely* 92-95; PtO 92-03. *2 Houghton Gardens, Ely CB7 4JN* T: (01353) 665654

✣**FARRER, The Rt Revd Ralph David.** b 44. St Barn Coll Adelaide ThL 68. **d** 68 **p** 69 **c** 98. C Plympton w Richmond Australia 68-71; P-in-c Hillcrest 71-73; C Melbourne St Pet 73-75; V Brunswick 75-90; V Melbourne St Pet 90-98; Can La Trobe 85-98; Adn La Trobe 94-96; Adn Melbourne 96-98; Bp Wangaratta 98-08; V Arundel w Tortington and S Stoke *Chich* 08-15; Hon Asst Bp Chich 09-15; rtd 15. *Unit 3, 7 Sinclair Street, Elsternwick VIC 3185, Australia* T: (0061) 43-259 3929
E: stnicholasarundel@btconnect.com

FARRIMOND, Sarah Lucy. b 67. Hertf Coll Ox BA 89 Leeds Univ BA 99 Dur Univ PhD 09. Qu Coll Birm 12. **d** 14 **p** 15. C Birkby and Birchencliffe *Leeds* from 14. *38 Holly Grove, Lindley, Huddersfield HD3 3NS* T: (01484) 768583 M: 07943-738638
E: revsarahfarrimond@yahoo.co.uk

FARRINGTON, Canon Christine Marion. b 42. Birkbeck Coll Lon BA 65 Nottm Univ DASS 66 Middx Poly MA 75. St Alb Minl Tr Scheme 79. **dss** 82 **d** 87 **p** 94. Redbourn *St Alb* 82-87; Dir Past Studies Linc Th Coll 86-87; HM Pris Linc 86-87; Dir Sarum Chr Cen 87-93; Dn Sarum Cathl 87-93; Co-Dir of Ords and Dir of Women's Min *Ely* 93-02; Hon Can Ely Cathl 93-02; C Cambridge Gt St Mary w St Mich 93-96; V Cambridge

St Mark 96-02; Chapl Wolfs Coll Cam 97-02; rtd 02; PtO *St Alb* 97-04; RD Wheathampstead 04-07; Chapl to The Queen 98-12. *42 East Common, Redbourn, St Albans AL3 7NQ* T: (01582) 793409

FARRINGTON, Mrs Lynda June. b 59. WMMTC. **d** 01 **p** 02. NSM Cannock *Lich* 01-07; NSM Abbots Bromley w Blithfield 07-10; NSM Abbots Bromley, Blithfield, Colton, Colwich etc from 11; Officer for NSMs 06-08. *Blithford Farm, Blithbury, Rugeley WS15 3JB* T: (01283) 840253 or 502131
E: revmumlynda@aol.com

FARROW, Edward. b 38. Sarum Th Coll 69. **d** 71 **p** 72. C Parkstone St Pet w Branksea *Sarum* 71-74; R Tidworth 74-79; P-in-c W and E Lulworth 79-80; P-in-c Winfrith Newburgh w Chaldon Herring 79-80; R The Lulworths, Winfrith Newburgh and Chaldon 80-83; V Ensbury Park 83-03; Chapl Talbot Heath Sch Bournemouth 83-97; rtd 03; P-in-c Marseille w Aix-en-Provence *Eur* 05-08. *21 Avenue de Bourgogne, 13600 La Ciotat, France* T: (0033) 4 42 83 03 20

FARROW, Elizabeth Maura. b 43. Edin Th Coll. **d** 91 **p** 96. NSM Glas H Cross 91-96; TV Bearsden w Milngavie 96-00 and 03-05. *5 Campsie Road, Strathblane G63 9AB* T: (01360) 770936

FARROW, Ian Edmund Dennett. b 38. S'wark Ord Course 70. **d** 72 **p** 73. C Tunbridge Wells St Jo *Roch* 72-78; Chapl N Cambs Gen Hosp Gp 78-92; P-in-c Walsoken *Ely* 78-80; R 80-92; V Bisley, Oakridge, Miserden and Edgeworth *Glouc* 92-04; rtd 04. *Wellspring, Brook Lane, Stonesfield, Witney OX29 8PR* T: (01993) 891293

FARROW, Canon Keith. b 59. Leeds Univ BA 05. NOC 02. **d** 05 **p** 06. C Sprotbrough *Sheff* 05-07; C Hillsborough and Wadsley Bridge 07-09; P-in-c 09-11; V 11-14; Can Missr Sheff Cathl from 14; Dir IME 4-7 from 12. *62 Kingfield Road, Sheffield S11 9AU* T: 0114-255 9093
E: keith.farrow@sheffield.anglican.org

FARROW, Peter Maurice. b 44. St Chad's Coll Dur BSc 65. **d** 68 **p** 69. C Gt Yarmouth 68-71; C N Lynn w St Marg and St Nic 71-75; P-in-c Sculthorpe w Dunton and Doughton 75-77; PtO 78-89; TV Lowestoft and Kirkley 89-94; Ind Miss 89-94; Sen Ind Chapl 94-99; TV Gaywood 95-02; P-in-c Mundford w Lynford, Cranwich and Ickburgh w Langford 02-09; rtd 09; PtO *Nor* from 09. *129 Carlton Road, Lowestoft NR33 0LZ* T: (01502) 521817 E: farrpm@btinternet.com

FARTHING, Michael Thomas. b 28. St Cuth Soc Dur 48 Lambeth STh 81 Ox Univ CertHE 08. St Steph Ho Ox. **d** 58 **p** 59. C St Marylebone St Mark w St Luke *Lon* 58-63; C Newport Pagnell *Ox* 63-69; R Standlake 69-74; R Yelford 69-74; R Lower Windrush 74-82; V Wheatley w Forest Hill and Stanton St John 82-95; rtd 95; PtO *Ox* from 95. *32 Falstaff Close, Eynsham, Oxford OX29 4QA* T: (01865) 883805

FARTHING, Paul Andrew. b 58. McGill Univ Montreal BA 80 STM 82. Montreal Dioc Th Coll. **d** 83 **p** 84. C Montreal W St Phil Canada 83-85; R Montreal St Jo Divine 85-96; R Montreal St Jo Ev 96-99; P-in-c Burton *Lich* 99-05; V Burton St Aid and St Paul 05-13; PV Lich Cathl 12-13; V Chislehurst Annunciation *Roch* from 13. *The Vicarage, 2 Foxhome Close, Chislehurst BR7 5XT* T: (020) 8467 3606
E: pafarthing@fmail.co.uk

FARTHING, Ronald Edward. b 27. Oak Hill Th Coll. **d** 58 **p** 59. C Tollington Park St Anne *Lon* 58-61; C Tollington Park St Mark 58-61; V Clodock and Longtown w Craswell and Llanveyno *Heref* 61-67; R Langley *Cant* 67-72; V Bapchild w Tonge and Rodmersham 72-80; TV Widecombe, Leusden and Princetown etc *Ex* 80-84; P-in-c Riddlesworth w Gasthorpe and Knettishall *Nor* 84-87; P-in-c Garboldisham w Blo' Norton 84-87; R Garboldisham w Blo' Norton, Riddlesworth etc 88-92; rtd 92; PtO *Nor* from 92; *St E* from 92. *23 Home Close, Great Ellingham, Attleborough NR17 1HW* T: (01953) 456750

FASS, Michael John. b 44. Trin Coll Cam MA 75. Edin Dioc NSM Course 89. **d** 95 **p** 95. NSM Penicuik *Edin* 95-97; NSM W Linton 95-97; NSM Roslin (Rosslyn Chpl) 97-06; Bp's Officer for Min 03-09; LtO from 06. *Old Gore Coach House, Old Gore, Ross-On-Wye HR9 7QT* E: michael.fass@btinternet.com

FATHERS, Jeremy Mark. b 54. Crewe & Alsager Coll BEd 78. WMMTC 93. **d** 96 **p** 97. NSM Baxterley w Hurley and Wood End and Merevale etc *Birm* 96-00; C Sheldon 00-03; Chapl N Warks NHS Trust 00-02; R Chelmsley Wood *Birm* 03-14; rtd 14; PtO *Birm* from 14. *1 Colebridge Crescent, Coleshill, Birmingham B46 1HF* T: (01675) 464047 M: 07769-780306
E: jeremyfathers@btinternet.com

FAUCHON-JONES, Susan Gurmito. b 61. **d** 06 **p** 07. NSM Eynsford w Farningham and Lullingstone *Roch* 06-08; NSM Southborough St Pet w Ch Ch and St Matt etc 08-13; C Horsmonden 13-14; R from 14. *The Rectory, Goudhurst Road, Horsmonden, Tonbridge TN12 8JU* T: (01892) 722274
E: suefj@live.com

FAULDS, Ian Craig. b 48. **d** 03 **p** 04. NSM Maughold *S & M* 03-12; NSM Maughold and S Ramsey 12-13; PtO 13-14; Min Can and Prec St German's Cathl from 14. *The Lynague, Ramsey Road, Lynague, Peel, Isle of Man IM5 2AQ* T: (01624) 842045

FAULKNER, Mrs Anne Elizabeth. b 38. Bp Otter Coll BA 58. **d** 00 **p** 01. NSM Aylesbury *Ox* 00-04; Chapl to Bp Buckingham 02-04; rtd 04; Hon C Wroxall *Portsm* 04-05; P-in-c 05-11; P-in-c St Lawrence 08-10; Hon C N Swindon St Andr *Bris* from 11. *8 Figsbury Close, Swindon SN25 1UA* T: (01793) 702715
E: aefaulkner77@gmail.com

FAULKNER, Brian Thomas. b 48. S Dios Minl Tr Scheme. **d** 84 **p** 85. C W Leigh *Portsm* 84-88; R Foulsham w Hindolveston and Guestwick *Nor* 88-93; P-in-c Erpingham w Calthorpe, Ingworth, Aldborough etc 93-94; R 94-13; RD Ingworth 10-13; rtd 13; PtO *Nor* 14-15; Hon C Barningham w Matlaske w Baconsthorpe etc from 15; Hon C Lt Barningham, Blickling, Edgefield etc from 15. *Oak Tree Cottage, Cherrytree Road, Plumstead, Norwich NR11 7LQ* T: (01263) 577868
E: brian.faulkner@btinternet.com

FAULKNER, Bruce Stephen. b 63. Trin Coll Bris BA 97 St Jo Coll Dur MA 08. Cranmer Hall Dur 06. **d** 08 **p** 09. C Somerton w Compton Dundon, the Charltons etc *B & W* 08-12; P-in-c Ilchester w Northover, Limington, Yeovilton etc from 12; RD Ivelchester from 13. *3 The Paddocks, West Street, Ilchester, Yeovil BA22 8PS* T: (01935) 849441 M: 07796-283766
E: bsfaulkner1@aol.com

FAULKNER, Mrs Catherine Evelyn. b 43. Man Poly RHV 82. **d** 01 **p** 02. OLM Urmston *Man* 01-11; P-in-c 11-14; NSM Davyhulme Ch Ch 13-14; rtd 14; PtO *Man* from 14. *5 Barnfield, Urmston, Manchester M41 9EW* T: 0161-748 3226
E: catherine.faulkner@ntlworld.com

FAULKNER, David Ernest. b 43. St Mich Coll Llan 65. **d** 66 **p** 67. C Aberystwyth St Mich *St D* 66-67; C Aberystwyth 67-68; C Tenby and Gumfreston 68-69; C Burry Port and Pwll 69-73; R Jeffreyston w Reynalton and E Williamston 73-79; R Jeffreyston w Reynoldston and E Williamston etc 79-89; V Whitland w Cyffig and Henllan Amgoed etc 89-96; V Llawhaden w Bletherston and Llanycefn 96-06; rtd 06. *Littledean, Maes Abaty, Whitland SA34 0HQ* T: (01994) 241464

FAULKNER, Henry Odin. b 35. G&C Coll Cam BA 56 MA 59. St Jo Coll Nottm 70. **d** 74 **p** 75. C Heigham H Trin *Nor* 74-76; C Heeley *Sheff* 76-80; TV Netherthorpe 80-84; PtO *St Alb* from 84; rtd 00. *69 Holywell Hill, St Albans AL1 1HF* T: (01727) 854177 M: 07719-642479

FAULKNER, Iain Stuart. b 58. **d** 12 **p** 14. NSM Balham St Mary and St Jo S'wark from 12. *Christ Church Vicarage, 3 Christchurch Road, London SW2 3ET* E: iainsfaulkner@hotmail.com

FAULKNER (*née* RITCHIE), Ms June. b 41. UCD BA 64. **d** 05 **p** 06. OLM New Windsor *Ox* 05-11; PtO from 11. *69 Springfield Road, Windsor SL4 3PR* T: (01753) 622808

FAULKNER, Margaret Evelyn. *See* WHITFORD, Margaret Evelyn

FAULKNER, Martin Trevor. b 62. Salford Univ BSc 83 Bretton Hall Coll PGCE 88 Leeds Univ BA 10. Coll of Resurr Mirfield 09. **d** 11 **p** 12. C Spilsby Gp *Linc* 11-14; C Bolingbroke Deanery from 14. *3 Woodlands View, Spilsby PE23 5GD* T: (01790) 755615 E: rev.martin@hotmail.co.uk

FAULKNER, Peter Graham. b 47. Lon Univ CertEd 69. Oak Hill Th Coll BA 87. **d** 82 **p** 83. C Crofton *Portsm* 87-89; R Mid Marsh Gp *Linc* 89-98; V S Cave and Ellerker w Broomfleet *York* 98-13; P-in-c N Cave w Cliffe 09-12; P-in-c Hotham 09-12; RD Howden 05-10; rtd 13. *9 Hurn Close, Ruskington, Sleaford NG34 9FE* T: (01526) 832184 E: faulkner47peter@gmail.com

FAULKNER, Canon Roger Kearton. b 36. AKC 62. **d** 63 **p** 64. C Oxton *Ches* 63-67; C Ellesmere Port 67-69; V Runcorn H Trin 69-73; TV E Runcorn w Halton 73-76; V Altrincham St Geo 76-90; Chapl Altrincham Gen Hosp 80-93; Chapl Trafford Healthcare NHS Trust 94-96; Hon Can Ches Cathl 88-96; V Higher Bebington 90-96; rtd 96; PtO *Ches* 96-98. *33 Arncliffe Road, Liverpool L25 9PA* T: 0151-428 6752

FAULKNER, Mrs Susan Ann. b 70. Lanc Univ BA 96. Ripon Coll Cuddesdon 97. **d** 99 **p** 00. C Scotswood *Newc* 99-03; P-in-c Byker St Silas 03-10; P-in-c Badby w Newham and Charwelton w Fawsley etc *Pet* 10-12; R from 12. *The Vicarage, 24A High Street, Silverstone, Towcester NN12 8US* T: (01327) 857996 M: 07786-265422 E: revsuefaulkner@aol.com

FAULKS, David William. b 45. EMMTC 82. **d** 86 **p** 87. C Market Harborough *Leic* 86-88; C Wootton Bassett *Sarum* 88-90; R Clipston w Naseby and Haselbech w Kelmarsh *Pet* 90-13; rtd 13; PtO *Leic* from 14. *7 Pochin Drive, Market Harborough LE16 7LP* E: david.faulks@btinternet.com

FAULKS, Simon George. b 73. Moorlands Th Coll BA 99. St Jo Coll Nottm 09. **d** 11 **p** 12. C Warminster Ch Ch *Sarum* 11-15; V Newton Longville, Mursley, Swanbourne etc *Ox* from 15. *The Rectory, 7 Main Street, Mursley, Milton Keynes MK17 0RT* M: 07795-154222 E: revsimon@notashamed.co.uk

FAULL, Mrs Janet Dorothy. b 60. SS Paul & Mary Coll Cheltenham PGCE 86 LGSM 82. WEMTC 05. **d** 08 **p** 09. C Cheltenham Ch Ch *Glouc* 08-12; V Tuffley from 12; AD Glouc City from 15. *St Barnabas' Vicarage, 200 Reservoir Road, Gloucester GL4 6SB* M: 07986-650459 T: (01452) 545366 E: janetfaull@btinternet.com

FAULL, The Very Revd Vivienne Frances. b 55. St Hilda's Coll Ox BA 77 MA 82 Clare Coll Cam MA 90. St Jo Coll Nottm BA 81. **dss** 82 **d** 87 **p** 94. Mossley Hill St Matt and St Jas *Liv* 82-85; Chapl Clare Coll Cam 85-90; Chapl Glouc Cathl 90-94; Can Res Cov Cathl 94-00; Vice-Provost 95-00; Provost Leic 00-02; Dean Leic 02-12; Dean York from 12. *Church House, 10-14 Ogleforth, York YO1 7JN* T: (01904) 557202 F: 557204 E: viviennef@yorkminster.org

FAULTLESS, Mrs Patricia Doreen. b 53. **d** 05 **p** 06. OLM Glascote and Stonydelph *Lich* from 05. *40 Stephenson Close, Glascote, Tamworth B77 2DQ* T: (01827) 287171 M: 07980-434897 E: patfaultless@hotmail.com

FAURE WALKER, Edward William. b 46. DL 01. SAOMC 01. **d** 04 **p** 05. NSM Stevenage All SS Pin Green *St Alb* from 04. *Sandon Bury, Sandon, Buntingford SG9 0QY* T/F: (01763) 287753 M: 07801-175009 E: e.faure.walker@farming.me.uk

FAUX, Steven Paul. b 58. UEA BA 79. Trin Coll Bris BA 07. **d** 07 **p** 08. C Bath St Mich w St Paul *B & W* 07-14; PtO from 14. *Fleetlands, Weston Park, Bath BA1 4AL* T: (01225) 313145 E: steven@stevenfaux.com

FAWCETT, Mrs Diane Elizabeth. b 49. Cant Univ (NZ) BA 72 Kent Univ MA 03. Westcott Ho Cam 03. **d** 04 **p** 05. C Egerton w Pluckley *Cant* 04-08; PtO 08-10; P-in-c St Margarets-at-Cliffe w Westcliffe etc from 10. *The Vicarage, Sea Street, St Margarets-at-Cliffe, Dover CT15 6AR* T: (01304) 852179 E: fawcett38@hotmail.com

FAWCETT, Mrs Joanna Mary. b 45. SRN 67 SCM 69. EAMTC 01. **d** 04 **p** 05. NSM Blakeney w Cley, Wiveton, Glandford etc *Nor* 04-12; PtO from 12. *14 The Cornfield, Langham, Holt NR25 7DQ* T: (01328) 830415 E: jofawcett@btinternet.com

FAWCETT, Mrs Laura Joy. b 82. Westcott Ho Cam 13. **d** 15. C Putney St Mary *S'wark* from 15. *88 Hayward Gardens, London SW15 3BZ* M: 07815-115826 E: laurajoyfawcett@gmail.com

FAWCETT, Canon Pamela Margaret. b 29. Univ Coll Lon BA 51 DipEd 75. EAMTC 83. **dss** 86 **d** 87 **p** 94. Stiffkey and Cockthorpe w Morston, Langham etc *Nor* 86-90; Hon C 87-90; Hon Asst Min Repps Deanery 91-92; Hon C Trunch *Nor* 92-01; Asst Dir of Ords 93-99; Bp's Consultant for Women's Min 93-01; Hon Can Nor Cathl 94-01; PtO from 01. *Seekings, 47A High Street, Mundesley, Norwich NR11 8JL* T: (01263) 721752 E: pam.seekings@tinyworld.co.uk

FAWCETT, Timothy John. b 44. K Coll Lon BD 66 AKC 67 PhD 71. St Boniface Warminster 66. **d** 67 **p** 68. C Blackpool St Steph *Blackb* 67-70; Hon C St Marylebone All SS *Lon* 68-70; C Southgate St Mich 70-72; Sacr Dur Cathl 72-75; V Wheatley Hill 75-79; V Torrisholme *Blackb* 79-84; V Thaxted *Chelmsf* 84-89; NSM Holt Deanery *Nor* 89-06; C Stiffkey and Bale 06-09; rtd 09; PtO *Nor* from 09. *Dowitchers, 14 The Cornfield, Langham, Holt NR25 7DQ* T: (01328) 830415 E: tjfawcett@btinternet.com

FAWNS, Lynne. b 56. Thames Valley Univ BA 95. NTMTC 97. **d** 00 **p** 01. C Hillingdon All SS *Lon* 00-03; V London Colney St Pet *St Alb* from 03. *The Vicarage, Riverside, London Colney, St Albans AL2 1QT* T: (01727) 769797 E: lynne@ffamily.freeserve.co.uk

FAYERS, Canon Robert Stanley. b 48. St Steph Ho Ox 82. **d** 84 **p** 85. C Deptford St Paul *S'wark* 84-88; V Beckenham St Mich w St Aug *Roch* 88-00; V Brighton St Mich *Chich* 00-11; P-in-c Brighton St Paul 06-11; V Brighton St Mich and St Paul 11-14; Can and Preb Chich Cathl 12-14; rtd 14; PtO *Nor* from 15. *Grampus House, 32 Pilot Street, King's Lynn PE30 1QL* E: rsfayers@gmail.com

FAYLE, David Charles Wilfred. b 51. Sarum & Wells Th Coll. **d** 83 **p** 84. C Parkstone St Pet w Branksea and St Osmund *Sarum* 83-87; TV Dorchester 87-96; P-in-c Taunton All SS *B & W* 96-97; V from 97. *All Saints' Vicarage, Roman Road, Taunton TA1 2DE* T: (01823) 324730 E: dfayle@freeserve.co.uk

FAZZANI, Keith. b 47. Portsm Poly BSc 70. Cant Sch of Min 93. **d** 96 **p** 97. NSM Appledore w Brookland, Fairfield, Brenzett etc *Cant* 96-01 and 05-13; Chapl Team Ldr E Kent Hosps NHS Trust 01-12; rtd 13; PtO *Cant* from 13. *Oakhouse Farm, Appledore, Ashford TN26 2BB* T: (01233) 758322 E: kfazzani@btinternet.com

FEAK, Christopher Martin. b 52. Keele Univ BA 75. Trin Coll Bris 92. **d** 94 **p** 95. C Handsworth St Mary *Birm* 94-97; P-in-c Perry Common 97-00; V 00-05; AD Aston 01-05; P-in-c Sandown Ch Ch *Portsm* 05-15; P-in-c Lower Sandown St Jo 05-15; AD E Wight 12-14; P-in-c Towyn *St As* from 15. *The Rectory, 7 Parc Gwellyn, Kinmel Bay, Rhyl LL18 5HN* T: (01745) 353955 E: c.feak123@btinternet.com

FEAR, Mrs Susan. b 59. **d** 11 **p** 12. C Werrington *Pet* from 11. *21 Riverside, Deeping Gate, Peterborough PE6 9AJ* T: (01778) 348857 E: sue.fear@googlemail.com

FEARNLEY, Andrew Anthony. b 84. Nottm Univ BA 06. Oak Hill Th Coll MTh 13. **d** 13. C Sevenoaks St Nic *Roch* from 13. *40 South Park, Sevenoaks TN13 1EJ* M: 07709-448080 E: andyfearnley1@gmail.com

FEARNLEY, Jeffrey Malcolm. b 46. Newc Univ BSc 69. St Jo Coll Nottm 90. **d** 92 **p** 93. C Bispham *Blackb* 92-95; C Bolton w Ireby and Uldale *Carl* 95-00; TV Binsey 00-02; C 02-07; rtd 07; PtO *Blackb* from 07. *32 Chestnut Court, Leyland PR25 3GN* T: (01772) 458696

FEARNSIDE, Mary Ingrid. b 44. OLM course 98. **d** 98 **p** 99. OLM Shelton and Oxon *Lich* 98-08; Chapl Uplands Care Home 08-14; Chapl R Shrewsbury Hosps NHS Trust 98-04; Chapl Shrewsbury and Telford NHS Trust from 04; PtO *Lich* from 11. *23 Eastwood Road, Shrewsbury SY3 8YJ* T: (01743) 353290 E: mary.fearnside@btinternet.com

FEARON, Mrs Doris Ethel Elizabeth. b 26. Gilmore Ho 66. **dss** 72 **d** 87. Lingfield *S'wark* 68-75; Farnborough *Roch* 75-77; Bitterne *Win* 78-86; rtd 86; Bexhill St Pet *Chich* 86-87; Hon Par Dn 87-89; PtO 89-95; New Zealand from 96; Hon Asst Dn One Tree Hill St Oswald 99-02. *Waiatarua Mercy Parklands, 12 Umere Crescent, Ellerslie, Auckland 1051, New Zealand*

FEARON, Mrs Irene. b 51. CBDTI 00. **d** 03 **p** 04. NSM Maryport, Netherton and Flimby *Carl* 03-08; NSM Camerton, Seaton and W Seaton from 08. *Kirkborough Lodge, Ellenborough, Maryport CA15 7RD* T: (01900) 813108 E: irene@kirklodge.com

FEASTER, Mrs Sarah Catherine. b 67. St Hugh's Coll Ox BA 89 Sheff Univ BA 13. Yorks Min Course 10. **d** 13 **p** 14. C Manston Leeds from 13. *The Old Manse, 13 Austhorpe Road, Leeds LS15 8BA* T: 0113-390 9201 E: sarahfeaster@btinternet.com

FEATHERSTON, Margery. See GRANGE, Alice Margery

FEATHERSTONE, Canon Andrew. b 53. St Chad's Coll Dur BA 74 MA 93. Sarum & Wells Th Coll 78. **d** 80 **p** 81. C Newc H Cross 80-83; C Seaton Hirst 83-86; TV 86-87; R Crook *Dur* 87-99; V Stanley 87-99; AD Stanhope 94-99; V Stockton 99-05; Can and Chan Wells Cathl from 05. *8 The Liberty, Wells BA5 2SU* T: (01749) 679587 E: andrew.featherstone@btinternet.com

FEATHERSTONE, Gray. b 42. Stellenbosch Univ BA 62 LLB 64. Cuddesdon Coll 65. **d** 67 **p** 68. C Woodstock S Africa 67-70; Asst Master Waterford Sch Swaziland 70-72; P-in-c Maputo St Steph and St Lawr Mozambique 73-76; Miss to Seamen 73-80; V Upper Clapton St Matt *Lon* 80-83; V Stamford Hill St Thos 80-89; Chr Aid Area Sec (N & W Lon) 89-06; Chr Aid Area Sec (Lon) 06-07; rtd 07; PtO *Lon* from 97. *20 Richmond Road, London N2 7JT* T: (020) 3602 2788 E: gray.featherstone@htef.org.uk

FEATHERSTONE, John. b 32. Man Univ BA 53 St Cath Soc Ox MTh 59 Dur Univ DipEd 66. Wycliffe Hall Ox 57. **d** 60 **p** 61. C Newland St Aug *York* 60-62; C Kidderminster St Jo and H Innocents *Worc* 62-65; Hd RE Co Gr Sch Pet 66-70; Hd RE Qu Anne Gr Sch York 70-85; Chapl Tangier *Eur* 86-87; 90-93; Chapl Pau w Biarritz 87-88; C Mexborough *Sheff* 88-90; rtd 93; PtO *York* from 93. *39 Cambridge Avenue, Marton-in-Cleveland, Middlesbrough TS7 8EH* T: (01642) 318181

FEATHERSTONE, Robert Leslie. b 54. Leeds Univ MA 04 LLCM 74 Lon Univ CertEd 75. Chich Th Coll 84. **d** 86 **p** 87. C Crayford *Roch* 86-89; V Belvedere St Aug 89-94; V Crowborough St Jo *Chich* 94-01; P-in-c New Brompton St Luke *Roch* 01-06; Hon Succ Roch Cathl 03-06; PtO 07-08; P-in-c Hastings St Clem and All SS *Chich* from 09. *The Rectory, 7 High Street, Hastings TN34 3EY* T: (01424) 422023 M: 07878-237312 E: frrobertf@live.co.uk

FEAVER, Nigel Conway McDonald. b 51. Leeds Univ BA 73 Brunel Univ MA 76 CQSW 76. Ripon Coll Cuddesdon 03. **d** 05 **p** 06. C Oxton *Ches* 05-08; R Wincanton *B & W* from 08; R Pen Selwood from 08. *The Rectory, 3 Bayford Court, Bayford Hill, Wincanton BA9 9GY* T: (01963) 31507 E: revnigelfeaver@googlemail.com

FEENEY, Damian Prescott Anthony. b 62. Grey Coll Dur BA 83 PGCE 84 ALCM 81. Chich Th Coll BTh 94. **d** 94 **p** 95. C Harrogate St Wilfrid *Ripon* 94-96; C Preston St Jo and St Geo *Blackb* 96-99; Bp's Miss P to Longsands 99-01; TR Ribbleton 01-04; V Woodplumpton 04-09; Vice-Prin St Steph Ho Ox 09-15; PtO *Ox* from 12; V Ettingshall *Lich* from 15. *Holy Trinity Vicarage, Farrington Road, Wolverhampton WV4 6QH* T: (01902) 478679 E: damian.feeney@ssho.ox.ac.uk

FEIST, Canon Nicholas James. b 45. Solicitor 70. St Jo Coll Nottm. **d** 76 **p** 77. C Didsbury St Jas *Man* 76-80; TV Didsbury St Jas and fam 80; V Friarmere 80-88; R Middleton 88-94; TR Middleton w Thornham 94-10; R Middleton and Thornham 10-14; AD Heywood and Middleton 99-07; Hon Can Man Cathl 98-14; rtd 14; PtO *Man* from 14; *Ches* from 15. *86 Rossendale Road, Heald Green, Cheadle SK8 3HF* M: 07808-159339 T: 0161-286 9440 E: njfeist@gmail.com

FEITAL, Peterson. See DE ALMEIDA FEITAL, Peterson

FELCE, Brian George. b 30. Jes Coll Ox BA 54 MA 57. Oak Hill Th Coll. **d** 58 **p** 59. C E Twickenham St Steph *Lon* 58-60; C Ramsgate St Luke *Cant* 60-64; R Bedingfield w Southolt *St E* 64-73; V Preston All SS *Blackb* 73-86; rtd 86. *11 St Barnabas Road, Sutton SM1 4NL* T: (020) 8642 7885

FELIX, Canon David Rhys. b 55. Univ of Wales (Cardiff) LLB 76 Solicitor 81. Ripon Coll Cuddesdon 83. **d** 86 **p** 87. C Bromborough *Ches* 86-89; V Grange St Andr 89-99; Chapl Halton Gen Hosp NHS Trust 95-99; P-in-c Runcorn H Trin *Ches* 96-99; RD Frodsham 98-99; V Daresbury from 99; Sen Ind Chapl from 00; Hon Can Ches Cathl from 06. *All Saints' Vicarage, Daresbury Lane, Daresbury, Warrington WA4 4AE* T: (01925) 740348 F: 740799 E: david.felix@btinternet.com

FELL, Canon Alan William. b 46. Ball Coll Ox BA 69. Coll of Resurr Mirfield 68. **d** 71 **p** 72. C Woodchurch *Ches* 71-74; C Man Clayton St Cross w St Paul 74-75; C Prestwich St Marg 75-77; V Hyde St Thos *Ches* 77-80; R Tattenhall and Handley 80-86; V Sedbergh, Cautley and Garsdale *Bradf* 86-12; Hon C Firbank, Howgill and Killington 86-06; P-in-c 06-12; Hon Can Bradf Cathl 96-12; RD Ewecross 00-05; rtd 12; PtO *Lich* from 13. *The Wharfinger's House, Maesbury Marsh, Oswestry SY10 8JB* E: vixed@btopenworld.com

FELL, David Edward. b 61. Bradf Univ BSc 84 Brunel Univ BA 05. ERMC 05. **d** 07 **p** 08. C Wootton *St Alb* 07-11; TV Barnsbury *Lon* from 11. *2 Brooksby Street, London N1 1HA* T: (020) 7697 4400 M: 07989-203429 E: ted_fell@hotmail.com

FELLINGHAM, Wendy Margaret. b 48. St Mich Coll Sarum BEd 70. STETS 03. **d** 06 **p** 07. NSM Swanage and Studland *Sarum* 06-13; rtd 13. *47 Bay Crescent, Swanage BH19 1RB* T: (01929) 426454 E: wendy.fellingham@btinternet.com

FELLOWS, Grant. b 56. K Coll Lon BD 77 AKC 77. Coll of Resurr Mirfield 79. **d** 80 **p** 81. C Addington *Cant* 80-84; C S Gillingham *Roch* 84-86; V Heath and Reach *St Alb* 86-94; V Radlett 94-03; RD Aldenham 98-03; V Leighton Buzzard w Eggington, Hockliffe etc 03-05; TR Billington, Egginton, Hockliffe etc 06-08; TR Ouzel Valley from 08. *The Vicarage, Pulford Road, Leighton Buzzard LU7 1AB* T: (01525) 373217 E: rev.grant.fellows@gmail.com

FELLOWS, Ian Christopher. b 73. Univ Coll Ox BA 94 MA 98 St Jo Coll Dur BA 99. Cranmer Hall Dur 96. **d** 99 **p** 00. C Bucknall and Bagnall *Lich* 99-03; TV Broughton *Man* 03-07; P-in-c Blackley St Andr from 07. *St Andrew's Vicarage, Churchdale Road, Higher Blackley, Manchester M9 8NE* T: 0161-740 2961 E: pointlessvicar@gmail.com

FELLOWS, John Lambert. b 35. LTCL 67 SS Mark & Jo Coll Chelsea CertEd 58. Portsm Dioc Tr Course 86. **d** 88. NSM Portsea St Cuth *Portsm* 88-94; NSM Farlington 94-05; PtO from 05. *7 Court Lane, Portsmouth PO6 2LG* T: (023) 9237 7270

FELLOWS, Canon John Michael. b 46. Oriel Coll Ox MA 77. Coll of Resurr Mirfield 74. **d** 77 **p** 78. C Kings Heath *Birm* 77-80; TV E Ham w Upton Park and Forest Gate *Chelmsf* 80-85; P-in-c Wormingford 85-90; P-in-c Mt Bures 85-90; P-in-c Lt Horkesley 85-90; V Wormingford, Mt Bures and Lt Horkesley 90; R Compton w Shackleford and Peper Harow *Guildf* 90-12; RD Godalming 07-12; Chapl Prior's Field Sch 90-12; Hon Can Guildf Cathl 12; rtd 12. C Balsham, Weston Colville, W Wickham etc *Ely* from 12; Hon C Gt w Lt Abington from 12; Hon C Hildersham from 12. *The Vicarage, The Causeway, West Wratting, Cambridge CB21 5NA* T: (01223) 291265 E: j.fellows321@btinternet.com

FELLOWS, Lesley June. See CRAWLEY, Lesley June

FELLOWS, Peter William. b 48. CertEd 70 DipEd 79. Chich Th Coll 86. **d** 88 **p** 89. C Westmr St Steph w St Jo *Lon* 88-93; R Deptford St Paul *S'wark* 93-05; TV Redruth w Lanner and Treleigh *Truro* 05-11; rtd 11. *12 Penmare Court, Hayle TR27 4RD*

FELLOWS, Mrs Susan Elizabeth. b 46. ATCL 65 LTCL 66 GTCL 67. SAOMC 99. **d** 02 **p** 03. NSM Weston Turville *Ox* from 02. *65 Craigwell Avenue, Aylesbury HP21 7AG* T: (01296) 424982 M: 07712-226999 E: susan.sefellows@btinternet.com

FELTHAM, Keith. b 40. **d** 75 **p** 76. In Bapt Ch 66-75; C Plympton St Mary *Ex* 75-79; TV Northam w Westward Ho! and Appledore 79-82; TR Lynton, Brendon, Countisbury, Lynmouth etc 82-85; P-in-c Bickleigh (Plymouth) 85-86; TR 86-91; Chapl R Bournemouth Gen Hosp 91-95; P-in-c Whimple, Talaton and Clyst St Lawr *Ex* 95-00; rtd 00; PtO *Ex* from 00. *16 Jefferson Walk, Plymouth PL3 4HN* T: (01792) 254383

FELTHAM-WHITE, Antony James. b 67. Ox Brookes Univ BSc 92 Reading Univ MA 94. Wycliffe Hall Ox 99. **d** 01 **p** 02. C Bernwode *Ox* 01-05; CF from 05. *c/o MOD Chaplains (Army)* F: 381824 T: (01264) 383430

FENBY, Andrew Robert. b 66. Loughb Univ BSc 88. St Steph Ho Ox 03. **d** 05 **p** 06. C Leigh-on-Sea St Marg *Chelmsf* 05-09; V Barkingside St Fran 09-14; R Beddington *S'wark* from 14. *The Rectory, 18 Bloxworth Close, Wallington SM6 7NL* T: (020) 8647 1973 E: frandrew@me.com

FENBY, Mrs Sarah Louise. b 66. Kent Univ BA 88 Lon Bible Coll BA 96. Trin Coll Bris MA 00. **d** 00 **p** 01. C Stoke Gifford *Bris* 00-04; C S Croydon Em *S'wark* 04-10; Min Selsdon St Fran CD 07-10; P-in-c Lydney *Glouc* from 10; P-in-c Woolaston w Alvington and Aylburton from 10. *5 Raglan Gardens, Lydney GL15 5GZ* T: (01594) 842321 E: revfenby@live.co.uk

FENN, Norman Alexander. b 20. Kelham Th Coll 37. **d** 43 **p** 44. C Tunstall Ch Ch *Lich* 43-47; C Leek St Edw 47-51; V Tilstock 51-55; V Milton 55-61; V Ellesmere 61-85; V Welsh Frankton 62-85; RD Ellesmere 70-85; rtd 85; PtO *Lich* from 85. *1 Larkhill Road, Oswestry SY11 4AW* T: (01691) 659411

FENNELL (née PAVYER), Mrs Jennifer Elizabeth. b 75. Ex Univ BSc 96 Cam Univ BTh 02 Lon Univ MA 05. Westcott Ho Cam 99. **d** 02 **p** 03. C Stevenage St Andr and St Geo *St Alb* 02-05; C Harpenden St Nic 05-10; P-in-c Welwyn Garden City 10-14; V from 14. *The Vicarage, 48 Parkway, Welwyn Garden City AL8 6HH* T: (01707) 320960 E: jennyfennell@virginmedia.com

FENNELL, Julian. b 56. Dioc OLM tr scheme. **d** 08 **p** 09. OLM Ipswich St Mary at Stoke w St Pet and St Fran *St E* 08-13; NSM 13-14; C Bramford from 14; C Gt and Lt Blakenham w Baylham and Nettlestead from 14. *The Beeches, Sycamore Way, Little Blakenham, Ipswich IP8 4LX* T: (01473) 833250 M: 07449-972663 E: julianfennell@hotmail.co.uk

FENNEMORE, Canon Nicholas Paul. b 53. Wycliffe Hall Ox 76. **d** 79 **p** 80. C N Mymms *St Alb* 79-82; C Chipping Barnet w Arkley 82-83; TV 83-84; TV Preston w Sutton Poyntz, Littlemoor etc *Sarum* 84-86; Chapl St Helier Hosp Carshalton 86-90; Chapl Jo Radcliffe Hosp Ox 90-94; Chapl Ox Radcliffe Hosp NHS Trust 94-96; Sen Chapl Ox Radcliffe Hosps NHS Trust 96-06; Hon Can Ch Ch *Ox* 03-06; Hd Chapl Services Portsm Hosps NHS Trust 06-11; Dioc Adv for Healing *Portsm* 08-11; Chapl Martlets Hospice Hove 11-12; Lead Chapl St Wilfrid's Hospice Chich 12-14; Chapl Southern Health NHS Foundn Trust from 14. *Southern Health NHS Foundation Trust, Tatchbury Mount Hospital, Calmore, Southampton SO40 2RZ* M: 07919-547508 E: canonfennemore@btinternet.com

FENSOME, Canon Anthony David. b 49. Open Univ BA 89. Sarum & Wells Th Coll 82. **d** 84 **p** 85. C Gtr Corsham *Bris* 84-88; P-in-c Lyddington w Wanborough 88-91; P-in-c Bishopstone w Hinton Parva 88-91; P-in-c Lyddington and Wanborough and Bishopstone etc 91; V 91-93; V Chippenham St Pet 93-08; RD Chippenham 94-99; AD 06-08; Hon Can Bris Cathl 98-08; rtd 08. *42 Francis Crescent, Tiverton EX16 4EP* E: tonyfens@aol.com

FENTIMAN, David Frank. b 43. RIBA 74 Roehampton Inst PGCE 94. S Dios Minl Tr Scheme 90. **d** 93 **p** 94. NSM Hastings St Clem and All SS *Chich* 93-98; P-in-c Blacklands Hastings Ch Ch and St Andr 98-01; V 01-05; rtd 05. *4 Barnfield Close, Hastings TN34 1TS* T: (01424) 421821 E: xxblacklands@tiscali.co.uk

FENTON, Ms Allison Jane. b 66. Grey Coll Dur BA 87 Dur Univ PGCE 90 St Jo Coll Dur MATM 08. Cranmer Hall Dur 06. **d** 08 **p** 09. C Newc St Geo and St Hilda 08-10; C Newc Ch Ch w St Ann 10-12; P-in-c Scotswood 12-14; NSM Dur St Giles from 14; NSM Shadforth and Sherburn from 14. *St Mary's Vicarage, 89 Front Street, Sherburn Village, Durham DH6 1HD* T: 0191-372 1501 E: allisonjfenton@gmail.com

FENTON, Barry Dominic. b 59. Leeds Univ BA 85. Coll of Resurr Mirfield 85. **d** 87 **p** 88. C Leigh Park *Portsm* 87-90; Chapl and Prec Portsm Cathl 90-95; Min Can and Prec Westmr Abbey 95-02; Chapl N Middx Hosp NHS Trust from 02; PV Westmr Abbey from 04. *North Middlesex Hospital, Sterling Way, London N18 1QX* T: (020) 8887 2000 or 8887 2724 E: dominic.fenton@nmh.nhs.uk

FENTON, Christopher Miles Tempest. b 28. Qu Coll Cam BA 50 LLB 51 MA 55 LLM. Ridley Hall Cam 52. **d** 54 **p** 55. C Welling *Roch* 54-57; Chapl Malsis Prep Sch Keighley 57-63; C Hove Bp Hannington Memorial Ch *Chich* 63-65; V Ramsgate Ch Ch *Cant* 65-71; Hd Dept of Gp Studies Westmr Past Foundn 71-83; P-in-c Mottingham St Andr w St Alban *S'wark* 71-73; Sen Tutor Cambs Consultancy in Counselling 73-85; Co-ord of Tr St Alb Past Foundn 80-88; Dir St Anne's Trust for Psychotherapy Ledbury from 85; PtO *Heref* from 85; rtd 93. *The Leys, Aston, Kingsland, Leominster HR6 9PU* T: (01568) 708632

FENTON, David Frank. b 43. Open Univ BA 79 Matlock Coll of Educn CertEd 67. Wycliffe Hall Ox 07. **d** 08 **p** 09. NSM Win Ch Ch 08-12; PtO from 12. *5 Glenwood Avenue, Southampton SO16 3PY* T: (023) 8076 9574 M: 07967-419169 E: dave.fenton1@btinternet.com

FENTON, Geoffrey Eric Crosland. b 54. St Jo Coll Ox BA 75 MSc 76. WEMTC 98. **d** 01 **p** 02. NSM Wedmore w Theale and Blackford *B & W* 01-05; NSM Greinton and W Poldens 05-08; C Mark w Allerton 08-10; P-in-c 10-11; TV Ashburton, Bickington, Buckland in the Moor etc *Ex* from 11. *The Vicarage, Widecombe-in-the-Moor, Newton Abbot TQ13 7TF* T: (01364) 621334 E: geoffrey.fenton@wildyeast.co.uk

FENTON, Heather. b 48. Trin Coll Bris. **d** 87 **p** 97. C Corwen and Llangar *St As* 87-89; C Corwen and Llangar w Gwyddelwern and Llawrybetws 89-98; Dioc Rural Min Co-ord 87-98; LtO 98-01; C Deanery of Penllyn 01-03; P-in-c Bryneglwys 03-11; P-in-c Gwyddelwern 09-11; P-in-c Corwen w Llangar w Glyndyfrdwy etc 11; AD Penllyn and Edeirnion 10-12; PtO from 13. *Coleg y Groes, The College, London Road, Corwen LL21 0DR* T: (01490) 412169 E: revheather@btconnect.com

FENTON, Keith John. b 54. Coll of Resurr Mirfield 01. **d** 03 **p** 04. C St Annes St Anne *Blackb* 03-07; TV Ribbleton 07-12; C 12-14; R from 14. *140 Teil Green, Fulwood, Preston PR2 9PE* T: (01772) 791144 M: 07773-630784 E: keithjfenton@yahoo.co.uk

FENTON, Michael John. b 42. Linc Th Coll 67. **d** 69 **p** 70. C Guiseley *Bradf* 69-72; C Heswall *Ches* 72-75; TV Birkenhead Priory 75-81; V Alvanley 81-91; Chapl Crossley Hosp Cheshire 82-91; V Holbrook and Lt Eaton *Derby* 91-03; V Allenton and Shelton Lock 03-07; rtd 07; PtO *Derby* from 07. *11 Nethercroft Lane, Danesmoor, Chesterfield S45 9DE* T: (01246) 250071 E: michaeljfenton@yahoo.co.uk

FENTON, Mrs Nicola Jane. b 70. York Univ BSc 91 Leeds Univ PGCE 94 St Jo Coll Dur BATM 12. Cranmer Hall Dur 10. **d** 12 **p** 13. C Nottingham St Ann w Em *S'well* from 12. *18 Boyce Gardens, Nottingham NG3 3FB* T: 0115-941 4878 M: 07811-957913 E: njfenton@aol.com

FENTON, Miss Penelope Ann. b 41. Leic Univ BSc 64. Cant Sch of Min 92. **d** 95 **p** 96. NSM Eastling w Ospringe and Stalisfield w Otterden *Cant* 95-00; P-in-c 00-05; Asst to Bp's Officer for NSM 99-05; rtd 05; PtO *Cant* from 05. *9 Brogdale Road, Faversham ME13 8SX* T: (01795) 536366 E: penny.fenton@lineone.net

FENTON, Vincent Thompson. b 52. Cranmer Hall Dur 94. **d** 96 **p** 97. C Heworth St Mary *Dur* 96-99; C-in-c Bishop Auckland Woodhouse Close CD 99-06; Chapl S Durham Healthcare NHS Trust 01-02; Chapl Co Durham and Darlington Acute Hosps NHS Trust 02-05; P-in-c Crook *Dur* from 06; AD Stanhope from 07. *The Rectory, 14 Hartside Close, Crook DL15 9NH* T: (01388) 760939 E: vincent.fenton@durham.anglican.org

FENTON, Canon Wallace. b 32. TCD. **d** 64 **p** 65. C Glenavy *Conn* 64-67; I Tullaniskin w Clonoe *Arm* 67-87; Bp's C Sallaghy *Clogh* 87-96; Warden of Readers 91-96; Preb Clogh Cathl 95-96; I Kilwarlin Upper w Kilwarlin Lower *D & D* 96-99; rtd 99. *2 Beech Green, Doagh, Ballyclare BT39 0QB* T: (028) 9334 0576

FENWICK, Canon Malcolm Frank. b 38. Cranmer Hall Dur 62. **d** 65 **p** 66. C Tynemouth Cullercoats St Paul *Newc* 65-68; C Bywell 68-73; V Alnmouth 73-75; CF (TAVR) 75-83; V Lesbury w Alnmouth *Newc* 75-80; V Delaval 80-91; RD Bedlington 83-88; V Riding Mill 91-01; P-in-c Whittonstall 91-01; Chapl Shepherd's Dene Retreat Ho from 91; RD Corbridge *Newc* 93-99; P-in-c Slaley 97-99; P-in-c Healey 99-01; Hon Can Newc Cathl 97-01; rtd 01; PtO *Newc* from 01. *21 Welburn Close, Ovingham, Prudhoe NE42 6BD* T: (01661) 835565

✠**FENWICK, The Rt Revd Richard David.** b 43. Univ of Wales (Lamp) BA 66 MA 86 TCD MusB 79 MA 92 Univ of Wales (Lamp) PhD 95 FLCM 68 FTCL 76 Hon FGCM 04. Ridley Hall Cam 66. **d** 68 **p** 69 **c** 11. C Skewen *Llan* 68-72; C Penarth w Lavernock 72-74; PV, Succ and Sacr Roch Cathl 74-78; Min Can St Paul's Cathl 78-79; Min Can and Succ 79-83; Warden Coll Min Cans *Lon* 81-83; PV Westmr Abbey 83-90; V Ruislip St Martin *Lon* 83-90; Can Res and Prec Guildf Cathl 90-97; Sub-Dean 96-97; Dean Mon 97-11; V Newport St Woolos 97-11; Warden Guild of Ch Musicians 98-11; Bp St Helena from 11. *Bishopsholme, PO Box 62, St Helena, South Atlantic Ocean* T: (00290) 4471 F: 4728 E: richard.d.fenwick@googlemail.com

FEREDAY, Harold James Rodney. b 46. St Jo Coll Nottm 87. **d** 89 **p** 90. C Rastrick St Matt *Wakef* 89-92; V Siddal 92-99; Dir Chr Care 99-11; rtd 11; PtO *Leeds* from 01; *York* from 11. *7 Burlyn Road, Hunmanby, Filey YO14 0QA*

FERGUS, David. b 52. Imp Coll Lon BSc 74. St Jo Coll Nottm 00. **d** 02 **p** 03. C Ilkeston St Mary *Derby* 02-06; P-in-c Kirk Hallam 06-14; rtd 14; PtO *Derby* from 14. *19 Alexandra Road, Burton-upon-Trent DE15 0JD* T: (01283) 749217 E: revdave.fergus@ntlworld.com

FERGUSON, Aean Michael O'Shaun. b 39. CITC 87. **d** 90 **p** 91. NSM Kilmallock w Kilflynn, Kilfinane, Knockaney etc *L & K* 90; NSM Killaloe w Stradbally 90-94; NSM Adare and Kilmallock w Kilpeacon, Croom etc 94-97; C Killala w Dunfeeny, Crossmolina, Kilmoremoy etc *T, K & A* 97-00; I Skreen w Kilmacshalgan and Dromard 00-08; Can Killala Cathl 05-08; rtd 08; Dioc Information Officer *T, K & A* 04-09. *Rathlee, Easkey, Co Sligo, Republic of Ireland* T: (00353) (96) 49865 M: 87-812 1020 E: amferguson@iol.ie

FERGUSON, Caroline Maria. b 64. Sunderland Univ BA 08. Lindisfarne Regional Tr Partnership 10. **d** 13 **p** 14. NSM Darlington St Mark w St Paul *Dur* from 13. *Moss Glen, 248 North Road, Darlington DL1 2EN* T: (01325) 244907 M: 07816-154355 E: caroline.ferguson@ntlworld.com

FERGUSON, David Edward. **d** 04 **p** 05. NSM Antrim All SS *Conn* 04-11; I Ramoan w Ballycastle and Culfeightrin from 11. *12 Novally Road, Ballycastle BT54 6HB* T: (028) 2076 2010 M: 07773-051603 E: davidedwardferguson@gmail.com

FERGUSON, Edith Constance May (Joy). b 37. Ch of Ireland Tr Coll DipEd 60. CITC 99. **d** 02 **p** 03. NSM Bandon Union *C, C & R* from 02. *Telkador, Kinure, Oysterhaven, Co Cork, Republic of Ireland* T: (00353) (21) 477 0663 M: 86-350 3138

FERGUSON, Canon Ian John. b 51. Aber Univ BD 77. Trin Coll Bris 77. **d** 78 **p** 79. C Folkestone St Jo *Cant* 78-82; C Bieldside *Ab* 82-86; Dioc Youth Chapl 82-86; P-in-c Westhill 86-96; R from 96; Can St Andr Cathl from 01. *1 Westwood Drive, Westhill, Skeene AB32 6WW* T: (01224) 740007 E: ianferguson@westhill-episcopal.org

FERGUSON, John Aitken. b 40. Glas Univ BSc 64 Strathclyde Univ PhD 74 CEng MICE ARCST 64. Linc Th Coll 79. **d** 81 **p** 82. C Morpeth *Newc* 81-85; V Whittingham and Edlingham w Bolton Chapel 85-96; rtd 00. *Cold Harbour Cottage, Cold Harbour, Berwick-upon-Tweed TD15 2TQ*

FERGUSON, Joy. *See* FERGUSON, Edith Constance May

FERGUSON, Mrs Kathleen. b 46. LMH Ox BA 68 MA 72 ALA 76. St As Minl Tr Course 86. **d** 88 **p** 97. NSM Llanidloes w Llangurig *Ban* 88-01; P-in-c Llandinam w Trefeglwys w Penstrowed 01-02; V 02-04; AD Arwystli 02-04; NSM Shelswell Ox 04-07; rtd 07; PtO *Ban* from 07. *Trawsnant, 18 Maes Trannon, Trefeglwys, Caersws SY17 5QX* T: (01686) 430666 E: kathy@oerle.co.uk

FERGUSON, Marie Dorothy Michelle. b 58. Ottawa Univ BA 78. Cranmer Hall Dur 93. **d** 95 **p** 96. NSM Gt Aycliffe *Dur* 95-97; Chapl Asst HM Pris Holme Ho 97-98; NSM Heighington *Dur* 99-04; R Hurworth 04-09; R Dinsdale w Sockburn 04-09; Chapl Ian Ramsey Sch Stockton 10-11; PtO *Car* 11-12; I Sturgeon Falls Canada from 12. *St Mary Magdalene Anglican Church, 253 King Street, Sturgeon Falls, ON P2B 3A1, Canada* T: (001) (705) 753 4249

✠**FERGUSON, The Rt Revd Paul John.** b 55. New Coll Ox BA 76 MA 80 K Coll Cam BA 84 MA 88 FRCO 75. Westcott Ho Cam 82. **d** 85 **p** 86 **c** 14. C Ches St Mary 85-88; Sacr and Chapl Westmr Abbey 88-92; Prec 92-95; Can Res and Prec York Minster 95-01; Adn Cleveland 01-14; Warden of Readers 04-14; Suff Bp Whitby from 14; Can and Preb York Minster from 01. *21 Thornton Road, Stainton, Middlesbrough TS8 9DS* T: (01642) 593273 E: bishopofwhitby@yorkdiocese.org

FERGUSON, Peter Armstrong. **d** 10 **p** 11. C Carrickfergus *Conn* 10-15; I Derg w Termonamongan *D & R* from 15. *The Rectory, 13 Strabane Road, Castlederg BT81 7HZ* T: (028) 8167 9433 E: peteferg50@hotmail.com *or* derg@derry.anglican.org

FERGUSON, Raymond. *See* FERGUSON, Wallace Raymond

FERGUSON, Richard Archie. b 39. Dur Univ BA 62. Linc Th Coll 62. **d** 64 **p** 65. C Stretford St Matt *Man* 64-68; Bp's Dom Chapl 68-69; C Newc St Geo 69-71; V Glodwick *Man* 71-77; V Tynemouth Ch Ch *Newc* 77-82; V Tynemouth Ch Ch w H Trin 82-87; P-in-c Tynemouth St Aug 82-87; TR N Shields 87-90; TR Upton cum Chalvey *Ox* 90-95; V Kirkwhelpington, Kirkharle, Kirkheaton and Cambo *Newc* 95-04; AD Morpeth 95-04; rtd 04. *6 Green Close, Stannington, Morpeth NE61 6PE* T: (01670) 789795 E: frgsno@aol.com

FERGUSON, Robert Garnett Allen. b 48. Leeds Univ LLB 70 Clare Coll Cam. Cuddesdon Coll 71. **d** 73 **p** 74. C Wakef Cathl 73-76; V Lupset 76-83; Chapl Cheltenham Coll 83-87; Sen Chapl Win Coll 87-05; PtO *S & M* from 09. *Follaton, Highfield Drive, Baldrine, Isle of Man IM4 6EE*

FERGUSON, Robin Sinclair. b 31. Worc Coll Ox BA 53 MA 57 Lon Univ CertEd 63. ALCD 55 Wycliffe Coll Toronto 55. **d** 57 **p** 58. C Brompton H Trin *Lon* 57-60; C Brixton St Matt *S'wark* 60-63; Hon C Framlingham w Saxtead *St E* 63-65; Hon C Haverhill 65-67; Chapl St Mary's Sch Richmond 67-75; C Richmond St Mary *S'wark* 68-76; P-in-c Shilling Okeford *Sarum* 76-87; Chapl Croft Ho Sch Shillingstone 76-87; R Milton Abbas, Hilton w Cheselbourne etc *Sarum* 87-96; rtd 96; PtO *Sarum* from 98. *Durnovria, East Walls, Wareham BH20 4NJ* T: (01929) 551340 E: revrob@btinternet.com

FERGUSON, Ronald Leslie. b 36. Open Univ BA 86 BA 89. Chich Th Coll 65. **d** 68 **p** 69. C Toxteth Park St Marg *Liv* 68-72; C Oakham w Hambleton and Egleton *Pet* 72-74; Asst Chapl The Dorothy Kerin Trust Burrswood 74-76; V Castleside *Dur* 76-96; C Washington 96-99; P-in-c Eighton Banks 99-06; Chapl Gateshead Health NHS Trust 96-06; rtd 06; PtO *Dur* from 07. *2 Lapwing Court, Burnopfield, Newcastle upon Tyne NE16 6LP* T: (01207) 271559

FERGUSON (née PAMPLIN), Mrs Samantha Jane. b 71. St Andr Univ MTheol 06. TISEC 06. **d** 08 **p** 09. C Aberdeen St Pet and Aberdeen St Jo *Ab* 08-10; P-in-c Aberdeen St Ninian 10-14; Chapl Aber Univ 11-14; Chapl NHS Grampian 12-13; R Montrose *Bre* from 14; R Inverbervie from 14. *The Rectory, 12 Mallard Drive, Montrose, Angus DD10 9ND* M: 07971-231709 E: samferguson@fsmail.net

FERGUSON, Wallace Raymond. b 47. Qu Coll Birm BTheol CITC 76. **d** 78 **p** 79. C Lurgan Ch the Redeemer *D & D* 78-80; I Newtownards w Movilla Abbey 80-84; I Mullabrack w Markethill and Kilcluney *Arm* 84-00; I Carnteel and Crilly 00-05; Hon V Choral Arm Cathl 86-05; Dioc Chapl to Retired Clergy 92-05; Dean Kilmore *K, E & A* 05-14; I Kilmore w Ballintemple 05-14; All-Ireland Chapl MU 12-14; rtd 14. *81 Drumady Road, Stralustin, Newtownbutler, Enniskillen BT92 6NP* T: (028) 6775 1386
E: deanraymondferguson@gmail.com

FERGUSON, Mrs Zoë Marie. b 75. ERMC 09. **d** 12 **p** 13. C Trunch *Nor* 12-14; C Gaywood from 14. *28 Jermyn Road, King's Lynn PE30 4AE* T: (01553) 763479 M: 07767-878721
E: revzoe@hotmail.co.uk

FERGUSON-STUART, Hamish. b 51. Open Univ BA 92 Cardiff Univ MTh 10 RGN. **d** 99 **p** 00. OLM Burton St Chad *Lich* 99-05; Asst Chapl Rotherham NHS Foundn Trust from 05. *Rotherham District General Hospital, Moorgate Road, Rotherham S60 2UD* T: (01709) 820000
E: hamish.ferguson-stuart@rothgen.nhs.uk

FERGUSSON, Mrs Norma. b 52. St Hugh's Coll Ox BA 73 MA 83. **d** 11 **p** 12. NSM Rowde and Bromham *Sarum* 11-14; NSM Shrivenham and Ashbury *Ox* from 14; PtO *Sarum* from 14. *St Mary's House, 8 Chapel Lane, Ashbury, Swindon SN6 8LS* T: (01793) 710055 M: 07799-545035
E: rev.n.fergusson@btinternet.com

FERMER, Michael Thorpe. b 30. Lon Univ BSc 52 ARCS 52 St Cath Soc Ox BA 54. Wycliffe Hall Ox 52. **d** 54 **p** 55. C Upper Holloway All SS *Lon* 54-57; C Plymouth St Andr *Ex* 57-59; V Tamerton Foliot 59-63; Asst Chapl United Sheff Hosps 63-64; Chapl 64-66; LtO *Sheff* 66-73; V Holmesfield *Derby* 73-79; TR Old Brampton and Loundsley Green 79-83; V Brightside w Wincobank *Sheff* 83-89; V Loscoe *Derby* 89-94; rtd 94; PtO *Derby* from 94; *Sheff* from 13. *39 Elm Lane, Sheffield S5 7TR* T: 0114-281 1267
E: marieandmichael7@virginmedia.com

FERMER, Richard Malcolm. b 71. St Pet Coll Ox BA 94 K Coll Lon MA 95 PhD 02 Surrey Univ PGCE 96. Coll of Resurr Mirfield 00. **d** 02 **p** 03. C Palmers Green St Jo *Lon* 02-05; USPG Brazil 05-09; Asst Chapl Paris St Geo *Eur* 09-12; P-in-c Grosvenor Chpl *Lon* from 12. *24 South Audley Street, London W1K 2PA* T: (020) 7499 1684 E: richard.fermer@tiscali.co.uk

FERN, John. b 36. Nottm Univ BA 57 MA 88. Coll of Resurr Mirfield 57. **d** 59 **p** 60. C Carlton *S'well* 59-61; C Hucknall Torkard 61-68; V Rainworth 68-97; rtd 97; PtO *S'well* from 03. *4 Fosbrooke House, 8 Clifton Drive, Lytham St Annes FY8 5RQ*

FERNANDES, José Augusto dos Santos (Joseph). b 70. Lisbon Univ BA 95. Ripon Coll Cuddesdon BTh 15. **d** 15. C Horton and Wraysbury *Ox* from 15. *3 Montagu Road, Datchet, Slough SL3 9DT* M: 07879-687301 E: joaufer@hotmail.com

FERNANDES, Sheila Maud. b 45. Punjab Univ MB, BS 69. NTMTC 05. **d** 08 **p** 09. NSM Leyton Em *Chelmsf* 08-12; NSM Tye Green w Netteswell from 12. *19 Wedgewood Drive, Harlow CM17 9PX* T: (01279) 629791 E: fernandesgideon@aol.com

FERNANDEZ, Hugo. See ADAN-FERNANDEZ, Hugo Federico

FERNANDEZ, Mrs Valerie Anne. b 48. WMMTC 03. **d** 05 **p** 06. C Mile Cross *Nor* 05-08; P-in-c Doddington w Benwick and Wimblington *Ely* 08-11; rtd 11; PtO *Llan* from 11. *51 Glyn Bedw, Llanbradach, Caerphilly CF83 3PF* T: (029) 2088 2725
E: revval@btinternet.com

FERNANDEZ-VICENTE, Lorenzo Michel Manuel. b 68. Louvain Univ BA 92 MA 97 STL 97. **d** 97 **p** 97. C Battersea St Mary *S'wark* 04-08; V Malden St Jas from 08. *St James's Vicarage, 7 Bodley Road, New Malden KT3 5QD* T: (020) 8942 5070 M: 07780-914434 E: lorenzo.fernandez@mac.com

FERNANDO, Percy Sriyananda. b 49. St And Dioc Tr Course 85. **d** 88 **p** 89. NSM Blairgowrie *St And* 88-93; NSM Alyth and Coupar Angus 89-93. *Gowrie Cottage, Perth Road, Blairgowrie PH10 6QB*

FERNELEY, Alastair John. b 69. Roehampton Inst BA 93 K Coll Lon MA 94 Birm Univ MPhil 98 St Jo Coll Dur MA 02. Cranmer Hall Dur 00. **d** 02 **p** 03. C Skipton Ch Ch *Bradf* 02-05; P-in-c Scalby *York* 05-14; V from 14; P-in-c Scarborough St Luke 05-14; V from 14; V Ravenscar and Staintondale from 14; V Hackness w Harwood Dale from 14; V Scalby from 14. *The Vicarage, 48 High Street, Scalby, Scarborough YO13 0PS* T: (01723) 362740 E: irreverend@btinternet.com

FERNS, Stephen Antony Dunbar. b 61. St Chad's Coll Dur BA 84 MA 94. Ripon Coll Cuddesdon BA 87 MA 91. **d** 88 **p** 89. C Billingham St Cuth *Dur* 88-90; Chapl Dur Univ 91; Chapl Van Mildert and Trevelyan Colls Dur 91-95; V Norton St Mary 95-97; Bp's Dom Chapl *Blackb* 97-01; Voc Officer and Selection Sec Min Division 01-06; Sen Selection Sec 06-15; PtO *Lon* from 04; Senior Chapl to Bp Chich from 15. *The Palace, Chichester PO19 1PY* T: (01243) 782161
E: stephen.ferns@chichester.anglican.org

FERNS, Archdeacon of. See LONG, The Ven Christopher William

FERNS, Dean of. See MOONEY, The Very Revd Paul Gerard

FERNYHOUGH, Timothy John Edward. b 60. Leeds Univ BA 81. Linc Th Coll 81. **d** 83 **p** 84. C Daventry *Pet* 83-86; Chapl Tonbridge Sch 86-92; Chapl Dur Sch 92-02; Hd RS and Asst Chapl Radley Coll from 02. *Radley College, Radley, Abingdon OX14 2HR* T: (01235) 543000 F: 543106

FERRAR, Andrew Nicholas. b 46. Em Coll Cam MA 70 Liv Univ PhD 70. **d** 06 **p** 07. NSM St Alb St Sav *St Alb* from 06. *2 Tiberius Square, St Albans AL3 4GE* T: (01727) 685903
E: andrew.ferrar@gmail.com

FERRIS, Amanda Jane. b 61. RGN 83. SAOMC 00. **d** 03 **p** 04. NSM Letchworth St Paul w Willian *St Alb* from 03; Chapl E and N Herts NHS Trust 07-12; Chapl Milton Keynes Hosp NHS Foundn Trust from 12. *Rivendell, 33B Stotfold Road, Arlesey SG15 6XL* T: (01462) 834627 *or* (01908) 660033 M: 07780-670651 E: amanda.ferris@btinternet.com

FERRIS, Robert Joseph. b 82. Ulster Univ BSc 05 QUB PGCE 06. CITC BTh 09. **d** 09 **p** 10. C Knock *D & D* 09-12; C Carrigrohane Union *C, C & R* from 12. *24 Ard Darra View, Station Road, Blarney, Co Cork, Republic of Ireland* T: (0353) (21) 451 6620 E: rferris281@gmail.com

FERRIS, Samuel Albert. b 41. Open Univ BA 80. S & M Dioc Tr Inst 98. **d** 99 **p** 00. OLM Douglas All SS *S & M* 99-14; OLM Douglas St Geo and All SS from 15. *27 Hillberry Meadows, Governors Hill, Douglas, Isle of Man IM2 7BJ* T/F: (01624) 619631

FERRIS, Samuel Christopher. b 77. Univ of Wales (Lamp) BA 98. Trin Coll Bris 02. **d** 04 **p** 05. C Tunbridge Wells St Mark *Roch* 04-07; TV S Gillingham 07-11; C St John-at-Hackney *Lon* 11-14; Chapl Hackney Free and Paroch Sch 11-14; TR Chipping Barnet *St Alb* from 14. *The Rectory, 38 Manor Road, Barnet EN5 2JJ* M: 07910-077885 T: (020) 8275 0648
E: frchris@ymail.com

FERRITER, Felicity Eunicé Myfanwy. b 54. Sheff Univ BA 76 Nottm Univ MA 98. EMMTC 95. **d** 98 **p** 99. NSM Retford S'well 98-03; Asst Chapl Rampton Hosp Retford 99-01; Asst Chapl Notts Healthcare NHS Trust 01-02; Chapl 02-03; Asst to AD Retford 03-04; C Rampton w Laneham, Treswell, Cottam and Stokeham *S'well* 04-11; C N and S Leverton 04-11; TV Retford Area 11-14; rtd 14. *The Gables, Treswell Road, Rampton, Retford DN22 0HU* T: (01777) 248580
E: felicityferriter@yahoo.com

FERRY, Canon David Henry John. b 53. TCD BTh 88. **d** 88 **p** 89. C Enniskillen *Clogh* 88-90; I Leckpatrick w Dunnalong *D & R* 90-01; I Donagheady 01-12; I Balteagh w Carrick from 12; I Tamlaghtard w Aghanloo from 12; Bp's Dom Chapl from 96; Can Derry Cathl from 05. *Balteagh Rectory, 115 Drumsurn Road, Limavady BT49 0PD* T: (028) 7776 5806 M: 07813-983772 E: hdjferry@hotmail.com

FERRY, Malcolm Ronald Keith. b 66. QUB BEd 88. CITC BTh 96. **d** 96 **p** 97. C Agherton *Conn* 96-99; I Kilwaughter w Cairncastle and Craigy Hill 99-03; I Castlerock w Dunboe and Fermoyle *D & R* 03-08; I Clooney w Strathfoyle 08-14; I Londonderry St Aug from 14. *St Augustine's Rectory, 4 Bridgewater, Londonderry BT47 6YA* T: (028) 7136 6041 *or* 7132 9551 E: weechurch@btinternet.com

FESSEY, Mrs Annis Irene. b 40. St Mary's Coll Chelt CertEd 60. Ripon Coll Cuddesdon 88. **d** 90 **p** 94. Par Dn Bris St Andr Hartcliffe 90-94; C The Lydiards 94-95; C Penhill 95-00; rtd 00; PtO *Bris* 00-03; *Portsm* from 03. *Tintern, 17 Mayfield Road, Ryde PO33 3PR* T: (01983) 616466

FESSEY, Canon Brian Alan. b 39. Bris Univ CertEd 61 Leeds Univ DipEd 71. Ripon Coll Cuddesdon 88. **d** 90 **p** 91. Hon C Bishopsworth *Bris* 90; C Withywood CD 91-94; V Purton 94-03; Hon Can Bris Cathl 01-03; rtd 03; PtO *Portsm* from 03. *Tintern, 17 Mayfield Road, Ryde PO33 3PR* T: (01983) 616466

FEWINGS, Peter Trenchard. b 53. WEMTC 12. **d** 14 **p** 15. NSM Sodbury Vale *Glouc* from 15. *8 Highlands Drive, North Nibley, Dursley GL11 6DX* T: (01453) 436703

FEWKES, Jeffrey Preston. b 47. Derby Univ MA 99 DMin 04. Wycliffe Hall Ox 72. **d** 75 **p** 76. C Chester le Street *Dur* 75-78; C Kennington St Mark *S'wark* 78-81; V Bulwell St Jo *S'well* 81-98; V Stapleford 98-02; Victim Support Nottinghamshire 02-12; rtd 12; PtO *Derby* from 06. *3 Monks Close, Ilkeston DE7 5EY* T: 0115-930 2482 E: j.fewkes@btopenworld.com

FFRENCH (née WILLIAMS), Mrs Janet Patricia (Trish). b 59. Bradf Univ BTech 81. Trin Coll Bris BA 02. **d** 02 **p** 03. C Quinton Road W St Boniface *Birm* 02-05; C Mamble w Bayton, Rock w Heightington etc *Worc* 05-07; C Elmsett w Aldham, Hintlesham, Chattisham etc from 07. *The Rectory, Hadleigh Road, Elmsett, Ipswich IP7 6ND* T: (01473) 658803 M: 07801-257959 E: revsff@btinternet.com

FFRENCH, Timothy Edward. b 58. Ball Coll Ox MA 86. Trin Coll Bris BA 01 MA 03. **d** 03 **p** 04. C Pedmore *Worc* 03-07; R Elmsett w Aldham, Hintlesham, Chattisham etc *St E* from 07. *The Rectory, Hadleigh Road, Elmsett, Ipswich IP7 6ND* T: (01473) 658803 M: 07801-492126 E: revsff@gmail.com

FFRENCH-HODGES, Christina Caroline. b 64. RGN 86. Aston Tr Scheme 94. **d** 99 **p** 00. C Castle Church *Lich* 99-02; C Rugby *Cov* 02-03; TV 03-05; PtO *Sheff* 06-07; NSM Arbourthorne and Norfolk Park 07-14; P-in-c Sheff St Jo from 14. *St John's Vicarage, 91 Manor Oaks Road, Sheffield S2 5EA* T: 0114-272 8349 M: 07850-660513 E: transformationisforall@gmail.com

FFRENCH-HODGES, Jasper Tor. *See* HODGES, Jasper Tor

FICKE, Michael John. b 46. **d** 97 **p** 98. OLM Marnhull *Sarum* 97-07; rtd 07; PtO *Sarum* from 07. *13 Plowman Close, Marnhull, Sturminster Newton DT10 1LB* T: (01258) 820509

FIDDIAN-GREEN, Anthony Brian. b 39. Sussex Univ MA 88 Birm Univ CertEd 60 ACP 66. Bps' Coll Cheshunt 62. **d** 64 **p** 65. C Batheaston w St Cath *B & W* 64-67; Chapl Aiglon Coll and Chapl Villars *Eur* 67-71; Hd Master Battisborough Sch Holbeton 71-81; Chapl R Gr Sch Worc 81-83; Hd Master Frewen Coll Rye 83-96; P-in-c New Groombridge *Chich* 97-11; rtd 11. *21 Chatham Green, Eastbourne BN23 5PQ* T: (01323) 478533 E: revtfg@googlemail.com

FIDDYMENT, Alan John. b 40. Cant Sch of Min 91. **d** 94 **p** 95. NSM Chatham St Wm *Roch* 94-96; NSM Spalding St Mary and St Nic *Linc* 96-99; R Barkston and Hough Gp 99-07; rtd 07; PtO *Pet* from 14. *5 Ascot Close, Spalding PE11 3BZ* T: (01775) 712837 M: 07930-434126 E: alan.fiddyment@tiscali.co.uk

FIDLER, John Harvey. b 49. Hatf Poly BSc 72. St Alb Minl Tr Scheme 84. **d** 87 **p** 88. NSM Royston *St Alb* from 87; PtO *Ely* from 00. *8 Stamford Avenue, Royston SG8 7DD* T: (01763) 241886

FIELD, David Hibberd. b 36. K Coll Cam BA 58. Oak Hill Th Coll 58. **d** 60 **p** 61. C Aldershot H Trin *Guildf* 60-63; C Margate H Trin *Cant* 63-66; Sec Th Students Fellowship 66-68; Tutor Oak Hill Th Coll 68-93; Vice Prin 79-93; Dean Minl Tr Course 88-93; Dir Professional Min Div CPAS 94-00; Patr Sec CPAS 94-00; PtO *Cov* from 94; rtd 00. *25 Field Barn Road, Hampton Magna, Warwick CV35 8RX* T: (01926) 410291

FIELD, The Very Revd Gerald Gordon. b 54. K Coll Lon BD 75 AKC 75. Coll of Resurr Mirfield 76. **d** 77 **p** 78. C Broughton *Blackb* 77-79; C Blackpool St Steph 79-82; V Skerton St Luke 82-86; NSM Westleigh St Pet *Man* 92-93; V Shap w Swindale and Bampton w Mardale *Carl* 93-97; P-in-c Netherton 97; V 98-01; I Tullamore w Durrow, Newtownfertullagh, Rahan etc *M & K* 01-14; Can Meath 10-14; Can Kildare Cathl 10-14; Dean Cashel *C & O* from 14; I Cashel w Magorban, Tipperary, Clonbeg etc from 14. *The Deanery, Boherclogh Street, Cashel, Co Tipperary, Republic of Ireland* T: (00353) (62) 61232 M: 87-908 3821 E: dean@cashel.anglican.org

FIELD, James Lewis. b 46. Open Univ BSc 96. SEITE 94. **d** 97 **p** 98. NSM Chatham St Mary w St Jo *Roch* 97-00; R Gravesend H Family w Ifield 00-08; P-in-c New Romney w Old Romney and Midley *Cant* 08-12; R Romney Marsh 12-14; rtd 14. *14 York Road, Littlehampton BN17 6EN* T: (01903) 726425 M: 07942-931006 E: revjimfield@googlemail.com

FIELD, Jeremy Mark. b 75. St Jo Coll Dur BA 96. Ridley Hall Cam 10. **d** 10 **p** 11. C Onslow Square and S Kensington St Aug *Lon* 10-13; LtO from 13. *198 Broom Road, Teddington TW11 9PQ* M: 07767-784011 E: jerryfield@hotmail.com

FIELD, Martin Richard. b 55. Keswick Hall Coll CertEd 76 Leic Univ MA 87. St Jo Coll Nottm BTh 82. **d** 82 **p** 83. C Gaywood, Bawsey and Mintlyn *Nor* 82-85; PtO *Leic* 85-87; Hon C S'well Minster 87-88; Hon C Stand *Man* 88-89; Dioc Press and Communications Officer 88-91; CUF 91-95; PtO *Cant* 96-99; Fundraising and Campaigns Dir Children's Soc 04-09; UK Dir of Fundraising Barnardo's from 09. *40 Elm Grove Road, Salisbury SP1 1JW* T: (01722) 502910 or (020) 8498 7647 E: martin.field@barnardos.org.uk

FIELD, Peold Olwen Joyce. b 53. St Jo Coll Nottm 86. **d** 88 **p** 94. Par Dn Kensal Rise St Mark and St Martin *Lon* 88-91; Par Dn Northwood H Trin 91-94; C 94-95; Chapl Mt Vernon Hosp 91-99; P-in-c W Drayton 99-03; V 03-12; V Preston from 12;

Dean of Women's Min Willesden Area 01-03; AD Hillingdon 03-08; Dir of Ords Willesden Area from 09; Preb St Paul's Cathl from 10. *The Rectory, 319 Preston Road, Harrow HA3 0QQ* T: (020) 8904 4062 M: 07901-563426 E: olwenfield123@btinternet.com

FIELD, Richard Colin. b 33. St Cath Soc Ox BA 54 MA 63. Clifton Th Coll 63. **d** 65 **p** 66. C Highbury Ch Ch *Lon* 65-70; V Hanger Lane St Ann 70-85; V Leytonstone St Jo *Chelmsf* 85-98; rtd 98; PtO *Chich* from 99. *21 Rufus Close, Lewes BN7 1BG* T: (01273) 472884

FIELD, Canon Susan Elizabeth. b 59. York Univ BA 80 Birm Univ CertEd 81 Ox Univ MTh 98. Qu Coll Birm 84. **d** 87 **p** 94. C Coleshill *Birm* 87-90; Chapl Loughb Univ *Leic* 91-98; TV Loughborough Em and St Mary in Charnwood 98-14; V Nanpantan St Mary in Charnwood from 15; Dir Post-Ord Tr 95-04; Bp's Adv for Women's Min 97-04; Dir of Ords from 04; Hon Can Leic Cathl from 04. *134 Valley Road, Loughborough LE11 3QA* T: (01509) 234472 E: sue.field134@gmail.com

FIELDEN, Elizabeth Ann. b 42. TCert 63. **d** 99 **p** 00. OLM Broughton Gifford, Gt Chalfield and Holt *Sarum* 99-12; OLM Atworth w Shaw and Whitley 07-12; OLM Melksham 07-12; rtd 12. *19 The Street, Broughton Gifford, Melksham SN12 8PW* T: (01255) 782509 E: annfielden@btconnect.com

FIELDEN, Hugh. b 66. BNC Ox BA 88 Birm Univ PGCE 90. Qu Coll Birm 91. **d** 93 **p** 94. C Sholing *Win* 93-97; TV Bramley *Ripon* 97-02; TV Bingley All SS *Bradf* 02-07; P-in-c Earby 07; P-in-c Kelbrook 07; V Earby w Kelbrook *Leeds* from 08. *The Vicarage, 40 Brookfield Way, Earby, Barnoldswick BB18 6YQ* T: (01282) 844877 E: hugh.fielden@bradford.anglican.org

FIELDEN, Mrs Janice Winifred. b 46. Warwick Univ BEd 82 MEd 89. SAOMC 99. **d** 02 **p** 03. NSM Chipping Norton *Ox* 02-05; NSM Churchdown w Shorthampton from 05; AD Chipping Norton 12-15. *The Vicarage, Church Lane, Charlbury, Chipping Norton OX7 3PX* T/F: (01608) 810286 E: jan@charlburyvicarage.co.uk

FIELDEN, Robert. b 32. Linc Th Coll 65. **d** 67 **p** 68. C Bassingham *Linc* 67-72; R Anderby w Cumberworth 72-88; P-in-c Huttoft 72-88; P-in-c Mumby 77-88; R Fiskerton 88-90; rtd 90; PtO *Carl* 91-99; *Linc* from 91. *Woodlands, 8 Fiskerton Road, Reepham, Lincoln LN3 4EB* T: (01522) 750480 E: robert@rfielden.freeserve.co.uk

FIELDER, Joseph Neil. b 67. Univ of Wales BSc 89. Wycliffe Hall Ox 93. **d** 96 **p** 97. C Cheadle All Hallows *Ches* 96-00; V Preston St Steph *Blackb* 00-09; P-in-c Baxenden 09-12; Supernumerary P Blackb and Darwen Deanery 12-13; Chapl Bradf Hosps NHS Trust from 13. *St Luke's Hospital, Little Horton Lane, Bradford BD5 0NA* T: (01274) 365819 M: 07944-182058 E: joe.fielder@bthft.nhs.uk

FIELDGATE, John William Sheridan. b 44. St Jo Coll Dur BA 68. Ox NSM Course 75. **d** 79 **p** 80. NSM Haddenham w Cuddington, Kingsey etc *Ox* 79-90; C Northleach w Hampnett and Farmington *Glouc* 90-92; C Cold Aston w Notgrove and Turkdean 90-92; P-in-c Upper and Lower Slaughter w Eyford and Naunton 92-01; P-in-c The Guitings, Cutsdean and Farmcote 92-01; V Acton w Gt Waldingfield *St E* 01-09; rtd 09; PtO *St E* from 09; *Chelmsf* from 09. *Patmos, 23 Woodfield Drive, West Mersea, Colchester CO5 8PX* T: (01206) 386851 E: jandjfieldgate@tiscali.co.uk

FIELDING, John Joseph. b 29. TCD BA 53 MA 65 QUB DipEd 57. TCD Div Sch Div Test 54. **d** 54 **p** 55. C Belfast St Luke *Conn* 54-57; C Belfast St Mary Magd 57-60; Chapl Windsor Boys' Sch Hamm W Germany 61-69; Chapl St Edw Sch Ox 69-73; V Highgate St Mich *Lon* 73-95; rtd 95; PtO *Guildf* from 95; *S'wark* from 99. *30 Sackville Mews, Sackville Road, Sutton SM2 6HS* E: j.j.fielding@btinternet.com

FIELDING, Mrs Pamela Florence. b 46. **d** 10 **p** 11. OLM Sherington w Chicheley, N Crawley, Astwood etc *Ox* from 10. *4 Griggs Orchard, Sherington, Newport Pagnell MK16 9PL* T: (01908) 616763 E: john_fielding@hotmail.com

FIELDING, Robert David. b 67. Liv Univ BA 89 St Jo Coll Dur BA 08. Cranmer Hall Dur 07. **d** 08 **p** 09. C Formby St Pet *Liv* 08-10; Chapl Mersey Care NHS Trust 10-14; PtO *Blackb* 14-15; P-in-c Read and Simonstone from 15. *The Vicarage, George Lane, Read, Burnley BB12 7RQ* M: 07951-173434 E: robertdfielding@gmail.com

FIELDING, Stephen Aubrey. b 67. Ulster Univ BSc 89 TCD BTh 93. CITC 90. **d** 93 **p** 94. C Bangor Abbey *D & D* 93-97; I Templepatrick w Donegore *Conn* 97-07; I Agherton from 07. *The Rectory, 59 Strand Road, Portstewart BT55 7LU* T: (028) 7083 2538 or 7083 3277 E: agherton@connor.anglican.org

FIELDING, Canon Stephen Lister. b 52. Ch Ch Ox BA 73 MA 77 Barrister 74. SAOMC 04. **d** 07 **p** 08. NSM Welwyn *St Alb* 07-11; TV Albury, Braughing, Furneux Pelham, Lt Hadham etc 11-14; Can Res Cov Cathl from 14. *The Cottage, 10 Smith Street, Warwick CV34 4HH* M: 07760-287614 E: slfielding@hotmail.com

FIELDSEND, John Henry. b 31. Nottm Univ BSc 54 Lon Univ BD 61. Lon Coll of Div ALCD 59. **d** 61 **p** 62. C Pennington *Man* 61-64; C Didsbury Ch Ch 64-66; P-in-c Bayston Hill *Lich* 66-67; V 67-88; UK Dir CMJ 89-91; Dir and Min at Large CMJ 91-96; rtd 96; PtO *St Alb* 96-00; Hon C Thame *Ox* from 01. *58 Cedar Crescent, Thame OX9 2AU* T: (01844) 212559 E: john@tehillah.freeserve.co.uk

FIELDSON, Canon Robert Steven. b 56. Qu Coll Cam BA 78 MA 81 Wye Coll Lon MSc 79. St Jo Coll Nottm BA 86. **d** 87 **p** 88. C Walmley *Birm* 87-90; Chapl Protestant Ch in Oman 90-95; P-in-c Cofton Hackett w Barnt Green *Birm* 95-98; V from 98; AD Kings Norton 00-06; Hon Can Birm Cathl from 14. *The Vicarage, 8 Cofton Church Lane, Barnt Green, Birmingham B45 8PT* T: 0121-445 1269 E: rob@fieldson.co.uk

FIFE (née EVE), Hilary Anne. b 57. Lon Univ BEd 80. Ripon Coll Cuddesdon 89. **d** 91 **p** 94. Par Dn Coulsdon St Andr *S'wark* 91-94; C 94-95; Chapl Croydon Coll 92-94; Asst Chapl Mayday Healthcare NHS Trust Thornton Heath 94-02; Sen Chapl from 02; Chapl Harestone Marie Curie Cen Caterham 94-98; Hon C Shirley St Geo *S'wark* from 08. *19 Greenview Avenue, Croydon CR0 7QW* T: (020) 8654 8685 *or* 8401 3105 E: hilary.fife@croydonhealth.nhs.uk

FIFE, Janet Heather. b 53. Sussex Univ BA 77 Man Univ MPhil 98. Wycliffe Hall Ox 84. **d** 87 **p** 94. Chapl Bradf Cathl 87-89; Par Dn York St Mich-le-Belfrey 89-92; Chapl Salford Univ *Man* 92-00; Hon TV Pendleton St Thos w Charlestown 92-95; Hon TV Pendleton 95-96; V Upton Priory *Ches* 00-10; P-in-c Marske in Cleveland *York* 10-14; rtd 14. *Address temp unknown* E: j.fife@virgin.net

FIGG, Robin Arthur Rex. b 62. RN Eng Coll Plymouth BScEng 84. Westcott Ho Cam 91. **d** 94 **p** 95. C Old Cleeve, Leighland and Treborough *B & W* 94-97; C Gt Berkhamsted *St Alb* 97-01; V Kildwick *Leeds* from 01. *The Vicarage, Kildwick, Keighley BD20 9BB* T: (01535) 633307 E: robin.figg@bradford.anglican.org

FILBERT-ULLMANN, Mrs Clair. b 44. Leuven Univ Belgium BTh 94 MA 94. Virginia Th Sem 95. **d** 94 **p** 96. USA 94-95; Asst Chapl Charleroi *Eur* 95-00; P-in-c Leuven 99-02; Asst Chapl Tervuren w Liège 99-01; PtO from 02. *Mühlbach am Hochkönig 437, A-5505, Austria* T: (0043) (6467) 20107 E: crullmann2001@yahoo.com

FILLERY, Paul. b 61. SWMTC 08. **d** 11 **p** 12. NSM Crediton, Shobrooke and Sandford etc *Ex* from 11. *Green Pastures, Sandford, Crediton EX17 4LP* T: (01363) 777372 M: 07596-080462 E: paul@fillery.plus.com

FILLERY, William Robert. b 42. Univ of Wales (Swansea) BA 65 St D Coll Lamp BD 69 PGCE 72 Surrey Univ MA 96. Bp Burgess Hall Lamp 65. **d** 68 **p** 69. C Llangyfelach *S & B* 68-71; C Morriston 71-72; LtO *Ox* 73-76; Chapl Windsor Girls's Sch Hamm W Germany 76-81; OCM 79-81; Chapl Reed's Sch Cobham 81-86; V Oxshott *Guildf* 86-89; P-in-c Seale 89-91; P-in-c Puttenham and Wanborough 89-91; Hd RE Streatham Hill & Clapham Sch for Girls 91-03; V Llanybydder and Llanwenog w Llanllwni *St D* 03-10; rtd 10; PtO *St D* from 10. *Afon Del, Falcondale Drive, Lampeter SA48 7SB* T: (01570) 421425 M: 07792-958431 E: fillerybill@gmail.com

FILLINGHAM, Richard James. b 58. Man Univ BA 80 Cliff Coll MA 03 ACA 83. All Nations Chr Coll 90 Wycliffe Hall Ox 97. **d** 98 **p** 99. C Brinsworth w Catcliffe and Treeton *Sheff* 98-01; C Ecclesall 01-05; PtO 05-13; V Newburn *Newc* from 13. *The Vicarage, High Street, Newburn, Newcastle upon Tyne NE15 8LQ* T: 0191-229 0522 E: rick@rfillingham22.plus.com

FILMER, Paul James. b 58. Open Univ BA 88. Aston Tr Scheme 93 Oak Hill Th Coll 95. **d** 97 **p** 98. C Petham and Waltham w Lower Hardres etc *Cant* 97-00; P-in-c Patrixbourne w Bridge and Bekesbourne 00-06; P-in-c Stone Street Gp 00-06; Chapl Univ of Greenwich *Roch* 06-09; Chapl Univ for the Creative Arts 06-09; V Yalding w Collier Street from 09; Chapl Kenward Trust from 11. *The Vicarage, Vicarage Road, Yalding, Maidstone ME18 6DR* T: (01622) 814182 M: 07595-176797 E: revpfilmer@mac.com

FILTNESS, Trevor Moshe. b 50. MNI MInstD. STETS 05. **d** 08 **p** 09. NSM Farlington *Portsm* 08-11; NSM Rowlands Castle 11-13; P-in-c from 13. *9 College Close, Rowland's Castle PO9 6AJ* M: 07785-568056 E: trevor@filtness.org

FINCH, Alan James. b 51. **d** 06 **p** 07. OLM Orrell Hey St Jo and St Jas *Liv* 06-15; NSM Litherland St Phil from 15. *1 Kirkstone Road North, Liverpool L21 7NP* T: 0151-928 3919 E: alan@chesed.freeserve.co.uk

FINCH, Mrs Alison. b 59. SEN 79. Sarum & Wells Th Coll 90. **d** 92 **p** 94. Par Dn Banbury *Ox* 92-94; C 94-95; C Wokingham All SS 95-98; C Binfield 98-99; C St Peter-in-Thanet *Cant* 99-02; R Kirkwall and P-in-c Stromness *Ab* 02-05; Ind Chapl and C Colchester St Pet and St Botolph *Chelmsf* 05-13; TV High Wycombe *Ox* from 13. *St James's Vicarage, Plomer Hill, Downley, High Wycombe HP13 5NB* T: (01494) 526896 M: 07762-744977 E: chaplain@alisonfinch.com

FINCH, Christopher. b 41. Lon Univ BA 63 AKC 63 BD 69. Sarum Th Coll 63. **d** 65 **p** 66. C High Wycombe *Ox* 65-69; Prec Leic Cathl 69-73; R Lt Bowden St Nic 73-81; V Evington 81-99; P-in-c Leic St Phil 95-99; P-in-c Lower Dever Valley *Win* 99-00; R 00-07; rtd 07; PtO *Portsm* from 07; *Win* from 10. *7 Arundel Drive, Fareham PO16 7NP* T: (01329) 829015

FINCH, Canon David Walter. b 40. Cam Univ MA 74 FIBMS 69. Ridley Hall Cam. **d** 91 **p** 92. C Ixworth and Bardwell *St E* 91-92; C Blackbourne 92-94; P-in-c Stoke by Nayland w Leavenheath 94-00; P-in-c Polstead 95-00; P-in-c Fressingfield, Mendham, Metfield, Weybread etc 00-08; C Hoxne w Denham, Syleham and Wingfield 06-08; RD Hoxne 00-07; Hon Can St E Cathl 05-08; rtd 08; PtO *St E* from 08; LtO *Ab* 08-12; Hon C Cen Buchan 10-12. *3 Fleetwood Avenue, Felixstowe IP11 9HR* T: (01394) 277061 E: canondavidfinch@btinternet.com

FINCH, Frank. b 33. Qu Coll Birm 72. **d** 74 **p** 75. C Bilston St Leon *Lich* 74-78; R Sudbury and Somersal Herbert *Derby* 78-87; Chapl HM Pris Sudbury 78-87; HM Det Cen Foston Hall 80-87; V Lilleshall and Sheriffhales *Lich* 87-90; R The Ridwares and Kings Bromley 90-98; rtd 98; PtO *Lich* from 00. *11 Ferrers Road, Yoxall, Burton-on-Trent DE13 8PS* T: (01543) 472065

FINCH, Jeffrey Walter. b 45. Man Univ BA(Econ) 66 Liv Univ DASE 80. Linc Th Coll 82. **d** 84 **p** 85. C Briercliffe *Blackb* 84-87; P-in-c Brindle and Asst Dir of Educn 87-93; V Laneside 93-00; TV Fellside Team 00-08; TR 08-14; rtd 14; PtO *Blackb* from 14. *21 Cock Robin Lane, Catterall, Preston PR3 1YL* T: (01995) 601171

FINCH, John. b 20. Bps' Coll Cheshunt 59. **d** 61 **p** 62. C Middlesbrough St Paul *York* 61-64; V Easington w Skeffling and Kilnsea 64-68; V Habergham Eaves St Matt *Blackb* 68-75; V Garstang St Helen Churchtown 75-86; rtd 86; PtO *Blackb* 86-11. *Bushells House, Mill Lane, Goosnargh, Preston PR3 2BJ* T: (01772) 865225

FINCH, Jonathan Mark. b 86. **d** 14 **p** 15. C Oseney Crescent St Luke *Lon* from 14. *Flat 2, 22D Lady Margaret Road, London NW5 2XL* M: 07816-122687 E: jon.finch@slkt.org.uk

FINCH, Morag Anne Hamilton. b 64. EAMTC 97. **d** 00 **p** 01. C Cranham *Chelmsf* 00-05; V Gidea Park 05-13; V Shortlands *Roch* from 13. *The Vicarage, 37 Kingswood Road, Bromley BR2 0HG* T: (020) 8464 8065 E: revfinch@btinternet.com

FINCH, Paul William. b 50. Oak Hill Th Coll Lon Bible Coll. **d** 75 **p** 76. C Hoole *Ches* 75-78; C Charlesworth *Derby* 78-87; C Charlesworth and Dinting Vale 87-88; TV Radipole and Melcombe Regis *Sarum* 88-01; V Malvern St Andr and Malvern Wells and Wyche *Worc* 01-14; TR Malvern Chase 14-15; rtd 15. E: paulwfinch@gmail.com

FINCH, Richard William. b 62. Westcott Ho Cam 95. **d** 97 **p** 98. C Saffron Walden w Wendens Ambo and Littlebury *Chelmsf* 97-00; C Elm Park St Nic Hornchurch 00-01; V 01-10; Chapl and Faith Support Officer Forest YMCA from 10; Hon C Gidea Park *Chelmsf* 11-13; Public Preacher from 13; NSM Shortlands *Roch* from 13. *The Vicarage, 37 Kingswood Road, Bromley BR2 0HG* T: (020) 8464 8065 E: rfinch@forestymca.org.uk

FINCH, Miss Rosemary Ann. b 39. Leeds Univ CertEd 60. **d** 93 **p** 94. OLM S Elmham and Ilketshall *St E* 93-00; Asst Chapl Ipswich Hosp NHS Trust 00-11; rtd 11; PtO *St E* from 11. *Grace House, 15 Weston Park, Weston under Penyard, Ross-on-Wye HR9 7FR* T: (01989) 565019 E: revrosie.finch@btinternet.com

FINCH, Canon Stanley James. b 31. Mert Coll Ox BA 55 MA 58. Wells Th Coll 55. **d** 57 **p** 58. C Lancaster St Mary *Blackb* 57-61; C Leeds St Pet *Ripon* 61-65; V Habergham All SS *Blackb* 65-73; V S Shore H Trin 73-84; V Broughton 84-98; RD Preston 86-92; Hon Can Blackb Cathl 91-98; rtd 98; P-in-c Alderton, Gt Washbourne, Dumbleton etc *Glouc* 98-02; PtO from 02. *14 Bellflower Road, Walton Cardiff, Tewkesbury GL20 7SB* T: (01684) 850544

FINCH, Mrs Susan. b 59. St Mellitus Coll 12. **d** 15. OLM Gt Baddow *Chelmsf* from 15. *68 Vicarage Lane, Great Baddow, Chelmsford CM2 8HY*

FINCH, Thomas. b 20. Lon Univ BD 57. Edin Th Coll 48. **d** 51 **p** 51. C Dur St Andr Cathl 51-55; C St Marylebone St Cypr *Lon* 55-58; V Warmington *Pet* 58-67; RD Oundle 62-67; V Wellingborough St Mary 67-88; rtd 88; PtO *Blackb* from 88. *18 Royal Avenue, Leyland, Preston PR25 1BQ* T: (01772) 433780

FINCHAM, Nicholas Charles. b 56. St Jo Coll Dur BA 78 MA 80. Westcott Ho Cam 80 Bossey Ecum Inst Geneva 81. **d** 82 **p** 83. C Seaham w Seaham Harbour *Dur* 82-85; C Lydney w Aylburton *Glouc* 85-87; C Isleworth All SS *Lon* 87-95; P-in-c Chiswick St Mich 95-10; rtd 10. *7 Harding Avenue, Eastbourne BN22 8PH* T: (01323) 638273 E: nicholas.fincham@talk21.com

FINDLAY, Canon Brian James. b 42. Wellington Univ (NZ) BA 62 MA 63 BMus 66 Magd Coll Ox MA 75. Qu Coll Birm.

d 72 **p** 73. C Deptford St Paul *S'wark* 72-75; Chapl and Dean of Div Magd Coll Ox 75-84; V Tonge Moor *Man* 84-02; Hon Can Man Cathl 00-03; R Monks Eleigh w Chelsworth and Brent Eleigh etc *St E* 03-11; rtd 11. *The Bull Pen, Hallthwaites, Millom LA18 5HP* T: (01229) 770049
E: briankirsty@onetel.com

FINDLAY, James. b 68. Bp Otter Coll BA 90 Westmr Coll Ox PGCE 92. Wycliffe Hall Ox 02. **d** 04 **p** 05. C Gillingham St Mark *Roch* 04-07; P-in-c Salisbury St Mark *Sarum* 07-13; V Salisbury St Mark and Laverstock from 13; Asst Dioc Dir of Ords from 13. *St Mark's Vicarage, 62 Barrington Road, Salisbury SP1 3JD* T: (01722) 323767 or 340368 M: 07854-510569
E: jim.magsfindlay@btinternet.com

FINDLAYSON, Roy. b 44. Man Univ MA 89 CQSW 69. Sarum & Wells Th Coll 80. **d** 82 **p** 83. C Benwell St Jas *Newc* 82-83; Hon C 83-85; C Morpeth 85-88; C N Gosforth 88; TV Ch the King 88-94; V Newc St Fran 94-98; Asst Chapl Newcastle upon Tyne Hosps NHS Trust 98-06; Chapl Marie Curie Cen Newc 98-06; rtd 06. *3 Balmoral Terrace, Stockton-on-Tees TS18 4DD* T: (01642) 601702

FINDLEY, Peter. b 55. Trin Coll Ox BA 77 MA 80 Barrister-at-Law (Gray's Inn) 78. Trin Coll Bris 90. **d** 92 **p** 93. C Yateley *Win* 92-97; V Westwood *Cov* 97-14; P-in-c Canley 09-14; Sen Miss P Philadelphia St Thos *Sheff* from 14. *30 Victoria Road, Sheffield S10 2DL* M: 07941-998830 E: peterfindley@gmail.com

FINDLOW, Robert Charles. b 69. All SS Cen for Miss & Min 12. **d** 15. NSM Bury St Mary *Man* from 15. *Address withheld by request*

FINDON, John Charles. b 50. Keble Coll Ox BA 71 MA 75 DPhil 79. Ripon Coll Cuddesdon. **d** 77 **p** 78. C Middleton *Man* 77-80; Lect Bolton St Pet 80-83; V Astley 83-91; V Baguley 91-98; P-in-c Bury St Mary 98-05; R from 05. *St Mary's Rectory, Tithebarn Street, Bury BL9 0JR* T: 0161-764 2452 E: bpc.office@tiscali.co.uk

FINKENSTAEDT, Harry Seymour. b 23. Yale Univ BA 49 Univ of Mass MA 68. Episc Th Sch Cam Mass BD 50. **d** 53 **p** 54. USA 53-71; C Hazlemere *Ox* 71-73; C Huntingdon St Mary w St Benedict *Ely* 73-75; R Castle Camps 75-84; R Shudy Camps 75-84; P-in-c W Wickham 79-84; P-in-c Horseheath 79-81; P-in-c Gt w Lt Stukeley 84-88; rtd 88; PtO *Ely* 84-01. *13761 Charismatic Way, Gainesville VA 20155-3119, USA* T: (001) (703) 743 5787

FINLAY, Alison Mary. *See* CAW, Alison Mary

FINLAY, Canon Hueston Edward. b 64. TCD BA 85 BAI 85 BTh 89 MA 92 Cam Univ MA 98 Lon Univ PhD 99. CITC 86. **d** 89 **p** 90. C Kilkenny w Aghour and Kilmanagh *C & O* 89-92; Bp's Dom Chapl 89-92; Bp's V and Lib Kilkenny Cathl 90-92; Chapl Girton Coll Cam 92-95; C Cambridge Gt St Mary w St Mich *Ely* 92-95; Chapl and Fell Magd Coll Cam 95-99; Dean of Chpl 99-04; Can Windsor from 04; Treas St Patr Cathl Dublin from 11. *8 The Cloisters, Windsor Castle, Windsor SL4 1NJ* T: (01753) 867094 F: 833806
E: hueston.finlay@stgeorges-windsor.org

FINLAY, Malcolm Armstrong. b 85. Univ Coll Lon BSc 10. Wycliffe Hall Ox BTh 13. **d** 13 **p** 14. C Southall Green St Jo *Lon* from 13. *21 Ellison Gardens, Southall UB2 4EW*
E: rev.malcolm.finlay@gmail.com

FINLAY, Canon Michael Stanley. b 45. NOC 78. **d** 81 **p** 82. C Padgate *Liv* 81-85; V Newton-le-Willows 85-90; V Orford St Marg 90-98; P-in-c Warrington St Elphin 98-00; R 00-11; Hon Can Liv Cathl 07-11; rtd 11. *40 Chatteris Park, Runcorn WA7 1XE* T: (01928) 579354 E: finlay289@btinternet.com

FINLAY, Nicholas. b 47. Regent Coll Vancouver MCS 00. St Jo Coll Nottm 01. **d** 02 **p** 03. C Haydock St Mark *Liv* 02-03; C Bootle 03-04; Lic to Adn Warrington 04-05; V Sittingbourne St Mary and St Mich *Cant* 05-09; rtd 09; C Upper Ithon Valley and Lower Ithon Valley *S & B* from 13; PtO *Lich* from 13. *7 Lawford Gardens, Gobowen, Oswestry SY11 3GX* M: 07771-688812 E: nick.finlay047@gmail.com

FINLAYSON, Duncan. b 24. **d** 76 **p** 76. NSM Bridge of Allan *St And* 76-94; NSM Alloa 77-94; NSM Dollar 77-94; Hon AP Hillfoots Team 80-87; rtd 94. *Address temp unknown* T: (01786) 833074

FINLAYSON, Mrs Gladys Victoria. b 49. TCert 67. ERMC 05. **d** 09 **p** 10. NSM Luton St Anne w St Chris *St Alb* 09-11. *St Andrew's Vicarage, 11 Blenheim Crescent, Luton LU3 1HA* T: (01582) 732380 E: gladysfinlayson@sky.com

FINLAYSON, Grantley Adrian. b 55. Wilson Carlile Coll 74 Chich Th Coll 87. **d** 89 **p** 90. Bedford All SS *St Alb* 84-87; C Watford St Mich 89-92; TV W Slough *Ox* 92-97; Dioc Officer for Race Relations *Glouc* 97-02; V Luton St Andr *St Alb* from 02. *St Andrew's Vicarage, 11 Blenheim Crescent, Luton LU3 1HA* T/F: (01582) 481711 E: grantleyfinlayson11@sky.com

FINLINSON, Paul. b 58. St Chad's Coll Dur BA 79 St Martin's Coll Lanc PGCE 81. Carl Dioc Tr Course 86. **d** 89 **p** 90. NSM

Kirkby Lonsdale *Carl* 89-99; Chapl Worksop Coll Notts from 99; Chapl Ranby Ho Sch Retford from 11. *Worksop College, Sparken Hill, Worksop S80 3AP* T: (01909) 537166 or (01524) 69652 E: pf@worksopcollege.notts.sch.uk

FINN, Andrew David. b 79. Cant Ch Ch Univ Coll BA 00 PGCE 01 Glos Univ MA 14. Ridley Hall Cam 13. **d** 15. C Ingatestone w Fryerning *Chelmsf* from 15; C Margaretting w Mountnessing and Buttsbury from 15. *39 The Furlongs, Ingatestone CM4 0AJ* M: 07818-675100
E: revandyfinn@outlook.com

FINN, Gordon Frederick. b 33. Dur Univ BA 60. Ely Th Coll 60. **d** 62 **p** 63. C Kingswinford St Mary *Lich* 62-65; C Northampton St Mary *Pet* 65-67; Chapl Barnsley Hall Hosp Bromsgrove 67-71; Chapl Lea Hosp Bromsgrove 67-71; C Swanage *Sarum* 71-73; P-in-c Ford End *Chelmsf* 73-79; V S Shields St Oswin *Dur* 79-98; rtd 98. *58 Hutton Lane, Guisborough TS14 8AW* T: (01287) 619132

FINN, Canon Ian Michael. b 58. AKC. Chich Th Coll 81. **d** 82 **p** 83. C Habergham All SS *Blackb* 82-83; C W Burnley All SS 83-85; C Torrisholme 85-87; V Lancaster Ch Ch w St Jo and St Anne 87-91; P-in-c Tillingham and Dengie w Asheldham *Chelmsf* 91-97; Chapl R Gr Sch Worc 97-99; P-in-c Denston w Stradishall and Stansfield *St E* 99-01; P-in-c Wickhambrook w Lydgate, Ousden and Cowlinge 00-01; R Bansfield 02-07; V Haverhill w Withersfield from 07; RD Clare 06-14; Hon Can St E Cathl from 11. *The Rectory, 10 Hopton Rise, Haverhill CB9 7FS* T: (01440) 708768 E: ian.finn1@btinternet.com

FINN, Miss Sheila. b 30. LMH Ox BA 68 MA 69. Gilmore Ho 68. **dss** 78 **d** 87 **p** 94. Par Dn The Ridwares and Kings Bromley *Lich* 87-94; C 94-95; rtd 95; PtO *Lich* from 97. *15 Leacroft Road, Penkridge, Stafford ST19 5BU* T: (01785) 716018

FINNEMORE, James Christopher. b 59. Pemb Coll Cam BA 81 MA 85. Coll of Resurr Mirfield. **d** 85 **p** 86. C Manston *Ripon* 85-88; C Hessle *York* 88-92; R Bishop Wilton w Full Sutton, Kirby Underdale etc 92-99; R Garrowby Hill from 99; RD S Wold 07-12. *The Rectory, Bishop Wilton, York YO42 1SA* T: (01759) 368230 E: j.c.finnemore@btinternet.com

FINNEMORE, Thomas John. b 79. Hull Univ BA 01. Wycliffe Hall Ox 05. **d** 07 **p** 08. C Crookes St Thos *Sheff* 07-11; C Cambridge St Barn *Ely* from 11. *80 St Barnabas Road, Cambridge CB1 2DE* E: tom.finnemore@stbs.org.uk

FINNERTY, Cynthia Ann. b 46. **d** 05 **p** 06. OLM E Greenwich *S'wark* from 05. *33 Ruthin Road, London SE3 7SJ* T: (020) 8858 2883 E: cynthiafin@hotmail.com

FINNEY, Canon David. b 41. St Mich Coll Llan 68. **d** 70 **p** 71. C Wythenshawe Wm Temple Ch *Man* 70-73; C Bedford Leigh 73-75; V Royton St Anne 75-81; V Dearnley 81-94; TV Rochdale 94-07; Hon Can Man Cathl 04-07; rtd 07; PtO *Man* from 09. *59 Knowl Road, Rochdale OL1 4BB* T: (01706) 346384

✠**FINNEY, The Rt Revd John Thornley.** b 32. Hertf Coll Ox BA 55. Wycliffe Hall Ox 56. **d** 58 **p** 59 **c** 93. C Highfield *Ox* 58-61; C Weston Turville 61-65; R Tollerton *S'well* 65-71; V Aspley 71-80; Bp's Adv on Evang 80-89; Bp's Research Officer 88-89; Hon Can *S'well* Minster 84-89; Officer for Decade of Evang in C of E 90-93; Suff Bp Pontefract *Wakef* 93-98; rtd 98; Hon Asst Bp *S'well* and Nottm from 98. *Greenacre, Crow Lane, South Muskham, Newark NG23 6DZ* T/F: (01636) 679791 E: john.finney2@ntlworld.com

FINNEY, Ms Melva Kathleen. b 24. LTh 76. St Jo Coll Auckland 47 Gilmore Ho 56. **dss** 57 **d** 78. E Dulwich St Jo *S'wark* 56-59; Community of Sisters of the Love of God Ox 59-61; Asst Chapl Christchurch New Zealand 61-62; Fendalton St Barn 62-63; Asst Chapl Womens and Templeton Hosp 63-72; Asst Chapl Princess Marg Hosp 63-72; Chapl Princess Marg Hosp 72-86; rtd 86. *22 Gunns Crescent, Cashmere, Christchurch 8022, New Zealand* T: (0064) (3) 332 7100

FINNIMORE, Keith Anthony. b 36. AKC 59. **d** 60 **p** 61. C Wanstead H Trin Hermon Hill *Chelmsf* 60-63; C Kingswood *S'wark* 63-65; V Bolney *Chich* 65-67; V Elmstead *Chelmsf* 67-73; R Pentlow, Foxearth, Liston and Borley 73-77; NSM Cockfield w Bradfield St Clare, Felsham etc *St E* 89-91; R Hawstead and Nowton w Stanningfield etc 91-96; P-in-c 96-01; rtd 96; PtO *St E* 01-09; *Chelmsf* from 09. *52B Summerhill Road, Saffron Walden CB11 4AJ* T: (01799) 521763

FIRBANK, Michael John. b 73. R Holloway Coll Lon BA 94 St Mary's Coll Twickenham PGCE 94. St Jo Coll Nottm MTh 05. **d** 05 **p** 06. C St Illogan *Truro* 05-07; P-in-c Camborne 07-13; P-in-c Tuckingmill 12-13; R Camborne and Tuckingmill 13-14; V Gresley *Derby* from 14. *The Vicarage, 120 Church Street, Church Gresley, Swadlincote DE11 9NR* M: 07814-033183 E: mjfirbank@hotmail.com

FIRMIN, Paul Gregory. b 57. Win Univ MA 11 ACIB 80. Trin Coll Bris BA 87. **d** 87 **p** 88. C Swindon Ch Ch *Bris* 87-91; V Shrewsbury H Trin w St Julian *Lich* 91-99; V Astley, Clive, Grinshill and Hadnall 99-01; V Southampton St Mary Extra

Win 01-10; V Shrewsbury H Cross *Lich* from 10. *1 Underdale Court, Underdale Road, Shrewsbury SY2 5DD* T: (01743) 245300 E: nimrifs@sky.com *or* vicar@shrewsburyabbey.com

FIRMSTONE, Ian Harry. b 44. Qu Coll Birm. **d** 82 **p** 83. C Warminster St Denys *Sarum* 82-84; C N Stoneham *Win* 84-88; R Freemantle 88-90; V Littleport *Ely* 90-91; TV Stanground and Farcet 91-97; P-in-c Holme w Conington 95-96; rtd 97; PtO *Birm* from 15. *Cotswold Cottage, School Lane, Alvechurch, Birmingham B48 7SA* T: 0121-445 1318 E: ianfirmstone@gmail.com

FIRTH, Mrs Ann Neswyn. b 40. St As Minl Tr Course 95. **d** 98 **p** 99. NSM Llanidloes w Llangurig *Ban* 98-05; LtO 05-11; PtO from 11. *Springfield, Westgate Street, Llanidloes SY18 6HJ* T: (01686) 413098 E: davidandneswyn@firth19.freeserve.co.uk

FIRTH, Christopher John Kingsley. b 37. St Mich Coll Llan. **d** 66 **p** 67. C Sutton in Ashfield St Mary *S'well* 66-70; V Langold 70-74; C Falmouth K Chas *Truro* 74-77; P-in-c Mabe 77-81; V 81-95; RD Carnmarth S 90-94; rtd 99. *1 Boscawen, Cliff Road, Falmouth TR11 4AW* T: (01326) 316734

FIRTH, Geoffrey David. b 74. Lincs & Humberside Univ BA 96. Oak Hill Th Coll BA 08. **d** 06 **p** 07. C Poynton *Ches* 06-10; Chapl RAF from 10. *Chaplaincy Services (RAF), HQ Air Command, RAF High Wycombe HP14 4UE* T: (01494) 496800 F: 496343 E: geoffreyfirth@gmail.com

FIRTH, Mrs Jennifer Anne. b 52. Goldsmiths' Coll Lon BMus 75 Kingston Poly PGCE 83. **d** 07 **p** 08. OLM Dorking St Paul *Guildf* from 07. *33 Downsview Gardens, Dorking RH4 2DX* T: (01306) 887189 M: 07970-102987 E: jennyafirth@aol.com *or* jenny@stpaulsdorking.org.uk

FIRTH, Matthew Paul. b 83. Magd Coll Cam BA 04 MA 08. Wycliffe Hall Ox BTh 09. **d** 09 **p** 10. C Triangle, St Matt and All SS *St E* 09-12; Chapl Cumbria Univ *Carl* from 12; 18-30 Pioneer Min from 12. *University of Cumbria Chaplaincy, Fusehill Street, Carlisle CA1 2HH* T: (01228) 513201 M: 07932-482929 E: mpf1983@hotmail.com

FIRTH, Neswyn. *See* FIRTH, Ann Neswyn

✠**FIRTH, The Rt Revd Peter James.** b 29. Em Coll Cam BA 52 MA 63. St Steph Ho Ox 53. **d** 55 **p** 56 **c** 83. C Barbourne *Worc* 55-58; C Malvern Link St Matthias 58-62; R Abbey Hey *Man* 62-66; Asst Network Relig Broadcasting BBC Man 66-67; Sen Producer/Org Relig Progr TV & Radio BBC Bris 67-83; Hon Can Bris Cathl 74-83; Suff Bp Malmesbury 83-94; Angl Adv HTV West 84-94; rtd 94; Hon Asst Bp Glouc from 03; Hon Asst Bp Bris from 09. *Mill House, Silk Mill Lane, Winchcombe, Cheltenham GL54 5HZ* T: (01242) 603669 E: peter@firth7.fsbusiness.co.uk

FIRTH, Peter William Simpson. b 39. **d** 11. NSM New Romney w Old Romney and Midley *Cant* 11-12; NSM Romney Marsh 12-13; PtO from 13. *114 Leonard Road, Greatstone, New Romney TN28 8RZ* T: (01797) 367296 E: firth166@btinternet.com

FIRTH, Mrs Rachel Naomi. b 73. Huddersfield Univ BA 97 Leeds Univ BA 08. NOC 05. **d** 08 **p** 09. C Halifax *Wakef* 08-11; V Lindley *Leeds* from 11; Adv for Women's Min Huddersfield Area from 15. *The Vicarage, 2 The Clock Tower, Lidget Street, Huddersfield HD3 3JB* T: (01484) 650996 M: 07793-709988 E: vicaroflindley@hotmail.co.uk

FIRTH, Richard Geoffrey. b 48. **d** 06 **p** 07. OLM Dur St Marg and Neville's Cross St Jo 06-08; PtO *York* from 08. *6 Vicarage Close, Seamer, Scarborough YO12 4QS* T: (01723) 867957 E: afirth9819@aol.com

FISH, Mrs Jacqueline Wendy. b 42. NTMTC 02. **d** 04 **p** 05. NSM Enfield Chase St Mary *Lon* from 04. *41 Churchbury Lane, Enfield EN1 3TX* T: (020) 8366 2235 E: jacquiefishie@aol.com *or* curate@saintmarymagdalene.org.uk

FISH, Michael. b 61. Lanc Univ BA 05. CBDTI 01. **d** 04 **p** 05. NSM Blackb St Mich w St Jo and H Trin 04-07; NSM Blackb St Thos w St Jude 04-07; P-in-c Cen Buchan *Ab* 07-08; P-in-c Shrewsbury All SS w St Mich *Lich* from 08. *All Saints' Vicarage, 5 Lingen Close, Shrewsbury SY1 2UN* T: (01743) 244879 M: 07867-760110 E: fr.michaelfish@btinternet.com

FISH, Thomas Ronald Huxley. b 59. Chu Coll Cam BA 81. Oak Hill Th Coll 11. **d** 13 **p** 14. C The Lye and Stambermill *Worc* from 13. *43 Bredon Avenue, Stourbridge DY9 7NR* E: tomhelen@2fishes.org.uk

FISH, Winthrop. b 40. Dalhousie Univ Canada BA 63 BEd Birm Univ BPhil 76 MEd 78. K Coll (NS) 62. **d** 64 **p** 65. I Arichat Canada 64-66; I Neil's Harbour and Baddeck 66-67; I Cut Knife 68-70; PtO Nova Scotia 70-74; PtO *Birm* 74-77; Asst Chapl Solihull Sch 77-79; Chapl Wroxall Abbey Sch 79-82; C Newquay *Truro* 82-84; V Highertown and Baldhu 84-89; P-in-c Newlyn St Newlyn 89-97; Dioc Children's Adv 89-97; Dioc Adv in RE 95-97; rtd 98; PtO *Ex* 98-11. *Birkdale, Fraser Place, Kemnay, Inverurie AB51 5NH* T: (01467) 642660

FISHER, Mrs Alison. b 48. Cranmer Hall Dur 04. **d** 05 **p** 06. NSM The Thorntons and The Otteringtons *York* 05-11; rtd 11; PtO *York* from 11. *31 Church Close, Marske-by-the-Sea, Redcar TS11 7AW* T: (01642) 488682 E: ali.fisher913@btinternet.com

FISHER, Andrew John. b 72. St Jo Coll Nottm BA 02 St Mich Coll Llan MTh 13. **d** 02 **p** 03. C Ilkeston St Jo *Derby* 02-05; P-in-c Hodge Hill *Birm* 05-08; Chapl Worcs Acute Hosps NHS Trust 08-13; V Wood End *Cov* from 13. *St Chad's Vicarage, Hillmorton Road, Coventry CV2 1FY* T: (024) 7661 2909 E: the_fisherfamily@btinternet.com

FISHER, Brian Robert. b 36. **d** 02 **p** 03. OLM Sole Bay *St E* 02-07; rtd 07; PtO *St E* from 07. *Green Gates, The Street, Walberswick, Southwold IP18 6UH* T: (01502) 723023 M: 07766-216111 E: fishell@btopenworld.com

FISHER, David Benjamin. b 52. Bp Lonsdale Coll CertEd 74. Chich Th Coll 75. **d** 78 **p** 79. C Dovecot *Liv* 78-81; C Weymouth St Paul *Sarum* 81-82; R Lower Broughton Ascension *Man* 82-86; PtO *S'well* 10-14; *Derby* 14-15; P-in-c Salisbury St Martin *Sarum* from 15. *The Rectory, 42 Tollgate Road, Salisbury SP1 2JJ* M: 07734-200314 T: (01722) 500896 E: benevans002@mac.com

FISHER, Canon David Stephen. b 66. Ripon Coll Cuddesdon BTh 98. **d** 98 **p** 99. C Stockport SW *Ches* 98-01; V Gatley 01-06; V Gt Sutton 06-13; RD Wirral S 11-13; Can and Prec Ban Cathl from 13. *The Canonry, Glanrafon, Bangor LL57 1LH* T: (01248) 352954 E: daifisher@aol.com *or* pencantor@gmail.com

FISHER, Eric Henry George. b 48. NTMTC 94. **d** 97 **p** 98. NSM Heydon, Gt and Lt Chishill, Chrishall etc *Chelmsf* 97-03; P-in-c Gt Oakley w Wix and Wrabness 03-08; rtd 08; PtO *Chelmsf* from 09; *St E* from 09. *Sheldon, 12 Joseph Close, Hadleigh, Ipswich IP7 5FH* T: (01473) 832626 E: eric.fisher@ukgateway.net

FISHER, Eric William. b 30. Birm Univ BA 53. Coll of Resurr Mirfield 70. **d** 72 **p** 73. C Styvechale *Cov* 72-75; C Chesterfield St Mary and All SS *Derby* 75-78; Chapl Buxton Hosps 78-84; TV Buxton w Burbage and King Sterndale *Derby* 78-84; R Shirland 84-89; V Sheff St Matt 89-95; rtd 95; PtO *Lich* from 95. *6 Wickstead Row, Main Road, Betley, Crewe CW3 9AB* T: (01270) 820653

FISHER, Frank. *See* FISHER, Kenneth Francis McConnell

FISHER, George Arnold. b 54. Lon Univ BD 75. NOC 81. **d** 84 **p** 85. C Conisbrough *Sheff* 84-92; V Blackpool St Thos *Blackb* 92-07; Dir Par Miss *Lich* from 07; Hon C Walsall St Matt from 07. *14 Gorway Gardens, Walsall WS1 3BJ* T: (01922) 650063 M: 07814-166951 E: george.fisher@lichfield.anglican.org

FISHER, Gordon. b 44. NW Ord Course 74. **d** 77 **p** 78. NSM Airedale w Fryston *Wakef* 77-81; C Barkisland w W Scammonden 81-84; C Ripponden 81-84; V Sutton St Mich *York* 84-87; V Marton-in-Cleveland 87-96; R Kettering SS Pet and Paul 96-02; rtd 02. *8 Mount Pleasant Avenue, Marske-by-the-Sea, Redcar TS11 7BW* T: (01642) 489489 E: gandgmf@tiscali.co.uk

FISHER, Humphrey John. b 33. Harvard Univ AB 55 Ox Univ DPhil 59. Heythrop Coll Lon MA. **d** 91 **p** 92. NSM Bryngwyn and Newchurch and Llanbedr etc *S & B* 91-06; PtO from 06. *Rose Cottage, Newchurch, Kington, Hereford HR5 3QF* T: (01544) 370632

FISHER, Ian St John. b 59. Down Coll Cam BA 80 MA 84 Leic Univ PhD 84. St Steph Ho Ox BA 88. **d** 88 **p** 89. C Colwall w Upper Colwall and Coddington *Heref* 88-91; Chapl Surrey Univ *Guildf* 92-97; V Hurst *Man* 97-04; V N Shoebury *Chelmsf* from 04. *The Vicarage, 2 Weare Gifford, Shoeburyness, Southend-on-Sea SS3 8AB* T: (01702) 584053 E: ian.fisher@btclick.com

FISHER, Mrs Joan. b 52. **d** 00 **p** 01. NSM Blackpool St Mark *Blackb* 00-04; NSM Blackpool St Thos 04-07; C Aldridge *Lich* 08-14; rtd 14. *14 Gorway Gardens, Walsall WS1 3BJ* T: (01922) 650063

FISHER, John Andrew. b 63. Bath Univ BSc 85 MA 97. Wycliffe Hall Ox BA 93. **d** 94 **p** 95. C Rayleigh *Chelmsf* 94-98; V Burton Joyce w Bulcote and Stoke Bardolph *S'well* 98-09; AD Gedling 00-05; Regional Leadership Adv (Midl) CPAS 09-11; Patr Sec from 11; PtO *Sheff* 10-13. *CPAS, Unit 3, Sir William Lyons Road, University of Warwick Science Park, Coventry CV4 7EZ* T: 03001-230780 ext 4387 E: jfisher@cpas.org.uk

FISHER, Canon Kenneth Francis McConnell (Frank). b 36. K Coll Lon 57. **d** 61 **p** 62. C Sheff St Geo and St Steph 61-63; Chapl Sheff Univ 64-69; Chapl Lon Univ 69-75; Th-in-c Dean *Carl* 75-80; Soc Resp Officer 75-80; TR Melksham *Sarum* 80-90; P-in-c Stapleford *Ely* 90-01; Dioc Ecum Officer 90-01; RD Shelford 94-03; Hon Can Ely Cathl 96-06; rtd 01; P-in-c Grantchester *Ely* 01-06; PtO *B & W* from 06. *Hollybrook, Station Road, Castle Cary BA7 7BU* T: (01963) 351304 E: frankfisher@waitrose.com

FISHER, Mark Simon. b 52. K Coll Lon BD 76 AKC 76 Trin Coll Ox MA 82 DPhil 83. Kelham Th Coll 70 Perkins Sch of Th (USA) 76. **d** 78 **p** 78. SSF 78-80; Hon C Victoria Docks Ascension *Chelmsf* 78-79; LtO *Eur* 78-80; *Lon* 78-80; *Ox* 78-87; Chapl LMH Ox 80-86; R Glas St Matt 87-89; Hon Asst P W Derby St Jo *Liv* 97-05. *29A Rodney Street, Liverpool L1 9EH* T: 0151-707 9748

FISHER, Mary Christine. b 43. Bris Univ BA 64. LCTP 07. **d** 08 **p** 09. NSM Heaton St Barn *Leeds* from 08; PtO from 13. *423 Toller Lane, Bradford BD9 5NN* T: (01274) 541238

FISHER, Canon Michael Harry. b 39. Ex Univ BA 61. St Steph Ho Ox 61. **d** 63 **p** 64. C Wolverhampton St Pet *Lich* 63-67; C Newquay *Truro* 67-70; V Newlyn St Pet 70-75; P-in-c Launceston St Steph w St Thos 75-82; V Carbis Bay w Lelant 82-95; V Newquay 95-99; Hon Can Truro Cathl 85-99; RD Penwith 88-93; Chapl Costa del Sol W *Eur* 99-00; rtd 00; PtO *Truro* from 00; *Eur* from 04. *Chymedda, Southway, Windmill, Padstow PL28 8RN* T: (01841) 521544 M: 07970-865049 E: mfisher39@aol.com

FISHER, Michael John. b 43. Leic Univ BA 64 Keele Univ MA 67. Qu Coll Birm 75. **d** 78 **p** 79. NSM Stafford St Mary and St Chad *Lich* 78-79; NSM Stafford 79-13; rtd 13; PtO *Lich* from 14. *35 Newland Avenue, Stafford ST16 1NL* T: (01785) 245069

FISHER, Nicholas. b 48. Newc Univ BA 71 MLitt 87 Man Univ MA 98 Leeds Univ PhD 04 Birm Univ BA 09. Qu Coll Birm 06. **d** 08 **p** 09. NSM Northleach w Hampnett and Farmington etc *Glouc* 08-13; P-in-c Sherborne, Windrush, the Barringtons etc from 13; Dioc NSM Officer from 13. *Providence House, High Street, Northleach, Cheltenham GL54 3EU* T: (01451) 861195 E: nick@5fishers.co.uk

FISHER, Paul Vincent. b 43. Worc Coll Ox BA 66 MA 70 ARCM 73. Qu Coll Birm. **d** 70 **p** 71. C Redditch St Steph *Worc* 70-73; C Chorlton upon Medlock *Man* 73-79; Chapl Man Univ 73-79; Exec Sec Community Affairs Division BCC 79-81; Asst Dir of Tr and Dir of Lay Tr *Carl* 81-86; P-in-c Raughton Head w Gatesgill 81-85; Lay Tr Team Ldr *S'wark* 86-90; Dir of Tr 90-94; V Kingswood 94-00; rtd 00; PtO *Leeds* from 01. *3 Buxton Park, Langcliffe, Settle BD24 9NQ* T: (01729) 824058 E: paul.fisher@ukonline.co.uk

FISHER, Peter Francis Templer. b 36. CCC Cam BA 60 MA. Wells Th Coll 62. **d** 63 **p** 64. C Gt Ilford St Mary *Chelmsf* 63-67; C Colchester St Mary V 67-70; C-in-c Basildon St Andr CD 70-72; P-in-c Edstaston *Lich* 83-87; P-in-c Whixall 83-87; P-in-c Tilstock 84-87; V Shelton and Oxon 87-97; rtd 97; PtO *Derby* from 07; *Sheff* from 10. *1 Cherry Tree Close, Sheffield S11 9AF* T: 0114-327 4718

FISHER, Canon Peter Timothy. b 44. Dur Univ BA 68 MA 75. Cuddesdon Coll 68. **d** 70 **p** 71. C Bedford St Andr *St Alb* 70-74; Chapl Surrey Univ *Guildf* 74-78; Sub-Warden Linc Th Coll 78-83; R Houghton le Spring *Dur* 83-94; RD Houghton 87-92; Prin Qu Coll Birm 94-02; V Maney *Birm* 02-10; Hon Can Birm Cathl 00-10; rtd 10. *Eden, Unicorn View, Bowes, Barnard Castle DL12 9HW* T: (01833) 628001 E: peter.fisher@onetel.net

FISHER, Richard John. b 60. K Coll Lon BA 82 AKC 82 Selw Coll Cam BA 87 MA 95. Ridley Hall Cam 85. **d** 88 **p** 89. C Woodley St Jo the Ev *Ox* 88-91; C Acomb St Steph and St Aid *York* 91-95; Chapl Preston Acute Hosps NHS Trust 98-02; Chapl Lancs Teaching Hosps NHS Trust 02-06; PtO *Blackb* 08-09; NSM Rufford and Tarleton 09; C Loughton St Jo *Chelmsf* from 09. *24 The Summit, Loughton IG10 1SW* T: (020) 8281 1389 E: reverendrichard@virginmedia.com

FISHER, Mrs Sheila Janet. b 50. WEMTC 01. **d** 04 **p** 05. NSM Cam w Stinchcombe *Glouc* 04-11; NSM Thornbury and Oldbury-on-Severn w Shepperdine from 11. *Court Hayes, Rockhampton, Berkeley GL13 9DU* T: (01454) 269700 E: ashmead.fishers@btinternet.com

FISHER, Simon John Plumley. b 80. St Jo Coll Dur BA 01. Ripon Coll Cuddesdon BA 04. **d** 05 **p** 06. C Bath Bathwick *B & W* 05-09; P-in-c Brigstock w Stanion and Lowick and Sudborough *Pet* 09-11; P-in-c Weldon w Deene 09-11; V W Derby St Jo *Liv* from 11. *The Vicarage, 685 West Derby Road, Liverpool L13 0BH* T: 0151-228 2023 M: 07525-617067

FISHER, Stephen Newson. b 46. Univ of Wales (Swansea) BSc 67 CEng 82 MIET 82. Linc Th Coll 84. **d** 86 **p** 87. C Nunthorpe *York* 86-89; P-in-c Middlesbrough St Oswald 89-90; V 90-94; V Redcar 94-02; P-in-c The Thorntons and The Otteringtons 02-11; Chapl N Yorks Police 01-11; PtO *Bradf* 02-11; rtd 11; PtO *York* from 11. *31 Church Close, Marske-by-the-Sea, Redcar TS11 7AW* T: (01642) 488682 E: stephen.fisher913@btinternet.com

FISHER, Stuart Frederick. b 48. **d** 11 **p** 12. OLM Swindon Dorcan *Bris* from 11; PtO *Ox* from 15. *30 Blakeney Avenue, Swindon SN3 3NL* T: (01793) 497169 M: 07774-205640 E: sfisher111@btinternet.com

FISHER, Susan. b 49. Yorks Min Course 09. **d** 11. NSM Gomersal *Wakef* 11-12; NSM Griffin, Mango Hill and North Lakes Australia from 12. *Address temp unknown* E: suefisher21@yahoo.co.uk

FISHER, Susan Alexandra. *See* NORTON, Susan Alexandra

FISHER, Thomas Ruggles. b 20. Cranmer Hall Dur 58. **d** 60 **p** 61. C Melton Mowbray w Thorpe Arnold *Leic* 60-63; R Husbands Bosworth 63-74; R Husbands Bosworth w Mowsley and Knaptoft etc 74-82; PtO 82-96; *Pet* 83-04; rtd 85. *12 The Dell, Oakham LE15 6JG* T: (01572) 757630

FISHER-BAILEY, Mrs Carol. b 56. **d** 96 **p** 97. C Eccleshill *Bradf* 96-99; TV Sutton St Jas and Wawne *York* 99-12; V Wawne 12; V Keyingham w Ottringham and Sunk Island 12-14; V Easington w Skeffling, Keyingham, Ottringham etc from 14. *The Rectory, Northside, Patrington, Hull HU12 0PB* E: ladyvicar@googlemail.com

FISHLOCK, Christopher Douglas. b 70. Anglia Poly BA 91. Oak Hill Th Coll BA 06. **d** 07. C St Helen Bishopsgate w St Andr Undershaft etc *Lon* from 07. *St Helen's Church Office, Great St Helens, London EC3A 6AT* E: c.fishlock@st-helens.org.uk

FISHLOCK, Mrs Margaret Winifred (Peggy). b 28. Cant Sch of Min 87. **d** 97 **p** 98. NSM Deal St Leon and St Rich and Sholden *Cant* 97-04; PtO from 04. *58 Gilford Road, Deal CT14 7DQ* T: (01304) 365841

FISHWICK, Alan. b 46. Chich Th Coll 87. **d** 89 **p** 90. C Laneside *Blackb* 89-92; C Accrington 92-93; TV 93-96; V Blackb St Aid 96-02; V Scorton and Barnacre and Calder Vale 02-05; P-in-c Coppull St Jo 05-09; rtd 09. *3 Burnside Cottages, Rye Hill Road, Flimby, Maryport CA15 8PJ*

FISHWICK, Mrs Ann. b 40. St Barn Coll Adelaide 91 Trin Coll Melbourne 93. **d** 91 **p** 94. Chapl Charters Towers Hosp and Home Australia 91-94; Dn Charters Towers St Paul 91-94; Asst P 94-97; PtO *Heref* 98-99; NSM Worthen 99-02; NSM Hope w Shelve 99-02; NSM Middleton 99-02; Asst P Weipa Australia 02-04; Asst P Innisfail 04-08. *217 Edward Road, Meru WA 6530, Australia* T: (0061) (8) 9921 5537 E: rayannf@bigpond.com

FISHWICK, Ian Norman. b 54. Lanc Univ BEd E Lon Univ MA 99. **d** 82 **p** 83. C High Wycombe *Ox* 82-87; V Walshaw Ch Ch *Man* 87-93; Area Voc Adv 88-93; V W Ealing St Jo w St Jas *Lon* 93-98; Dir of Ords Willesden Area 94-98; E Region Area Co-ord for CA 98-99; Operations Dir 99-04; Par Development Adv *Ox* 05-07; Lead Org Consultant S Lon and Maudsley NHS Foundn Trust from 07. *89 Carver Hill Road, High Wycombe HP11 2UB* T: (01494) 538775

FISHWICK, Raymond Allen. b 42. St Fran Coll Brisbane 93 N Queensland Coll of Min ACP 96. **d** 91 **p** 92. P-in-c Charters Towers Australia 92-94; R 94-97; P-in-c Worthen *Heref* 98-02; P-in-c Hope w Shelve 98-02; P-in-c Middleton 98-02; P-in-c Weipa Australia 02-04; P-in-c Innisfail 04-08; CF 02-08; rtd 08. *217 Edward Road, Geraldton WA 6530, Australia* T: (0061) (8) 9921 5537 E: rfi64412@bigpond.net.au

FISKE, Paul Francis Brading. b 45. St Jo Coll Dur BA 68 PhD 72. Wycliffe Hall Ox 72. **d** 73 **p** 74. C Sutton *Liv* 73-76; TV Cheltenham St Mary, St Matt, St Paul and H Trin *Glouc* 76-80; C-in-c Hartplain CD *Portsm* 80-84; Hd of Miss UK CMJ 84-86; Hon C Edgware *Lon* 84-86; R Broughton Gifford, Gt Chalfield and Holt *Sarum* 86-95; TV Bourne Valley 95-97; Adv Chr Action 95-97; P-in-c Princes Risborough w Ilmer *Ox* 97-98; TR Risborough 98-08; rtd 08; PtO *Cov* from 09. *30 Elmdene Road, Kenilworth CV8 2BX* T: (01926) 857118 E: paulfiske@live.co.uk

FISON, Geoffrey Robert Martius. b 34. Dur Univ BA 59. Ely Th Coll 59. **d** 61 **p** 62. C Heavitree *Ex* 61-64; Australia 64-69; BSB 64-69; C Southampton Maybush St Pet *Win* 70-73; TV Swindon *Roch* 73-79; TV Swindon Dorcan *Bris* 79-83; P-in-c Brislington St Cuth 83-99; rtd 99; PtO *Glouc* from 99; *Bris* from 99. *88 Oakleaze Road, Thornbury, Bristol BS35 2LP* T: (01454) 850678

FITCH, Capt Alan John. b 45. Open Univ BA 82 Warwick Univ MA 84. Wilson Carlile Coll 64 Qu Coll Birm 92. **d** 92 **p** 93. C Glouc St Jas and All SS 92-97; NSM Wotton St Mary 93-97; V Douglas All SS and St Thos *S & M* 97-02; Chapl HM Pris Is of Man 97-02; TR Walbrook Epiphany *Derby* 02-09; Dioc Adv on Racial Justice from 02; rtd 09. *16 Nether Slade Road, Ilkeston DE7 8ET* T: 0115-930 5768 E: a.fitch@virgin.net *or* iom123@btinternet.com

FITTER, Matthew Douglas. b 59. City of Lon Poly BSc 81. Trin Coll Bris MA 03. **d** 03 **p** 04. C Purley Ch Ch *S'wark* 03-07; C Beckenham Ch Ch *Roch* 07-10; TR Anerley from 10; P-in-c Penge St Jo from 13. *The Vicarage, 234 Anerley Road, London SE20 8TJ* T: (020) 8778 4800 E: matthewfitter@hotmail.com

FITTER, Mrs Ruth Patricia. b 69. Chelt & Glouc Coll of HE BEd 90. WEMTC 08. **d** 11 **p** 12. C S Cheltenham *Glouc* 11-14; V Glouc St Paul and St Steph from 14. *84 Frampton Road, Gloucester GL1 5QB* M: 07876-170964 E: ruthfitter1@googlemail.com

FITZGERALD, John Edward. b 44. Leic Univ MSc 98. Oak Hill Th Coll. d 76 p 77. C Rainham *Chelmsf* 76-79; C Cambridge St Andr Less *Ely* 79-86; Min Cambridge St Steph CD 79-83; Min Cambridge St Phil 84-86; V Holmesfield *Derby* 86-88; Chapl HM Pris Wakef 88-90; Whatton 90-93; Nottm 90-98; Chapl HM YOI Glen Parva 98-05; Chapl Leic Constabulary 05-10; rtd 11. *288A Derby Road, Bramcote, Nottingham NG9 3JN* T: 0115-939 9664 M: 07768-507883

FITZGERALD, Miss Melanie Anne. b 52. Sheff Univ BMus 75. Westcott Ho Cam 96. d 98 p 99. C Rotherham *Sheff* 98-01; C Stannington 01-02; P-in-c Walkley 02-05; V from 05. *St Mary's Vicarage, 150 Walkley Road, Sheffield S6 2XQ* T: 0114-234 5029 E: melanie.fitzgerald@zen.co.uk

FITZGERALD, Sarah. b 65. DipCOT 87. St Jo Coll Nottm 06. d 08 p 09. C Folkestone Trin *Cant* 08-12; TV Gt Marlow w Marlow Bottom, Lt Marlow and Bisham *Ox* from 12. *The Vicarage, 18 Oak Tree Road, Marlow SL7 3EE* T: (01628) 481167 E: sarah.vicar@googlemail.com

FITZGERALD CLARK, Mrs Diane Catherine. b 54. Rhode Is Univ BA 76. Gen Th Sem NY MDiv 86. d 86 p 87. USA 86-95; NSM Hampstead Em W End *Lon* 96-99; Chapl St Alb High Sch for Girls from 98; Assoc Min St Alb Abbey from 98. *13 Eleanor Avenue, St Albans AL3 5TA* T: (01727) 860099 E: dfc@stahs.org.uk

FITZGIBBON, Kevin Peter. b 49. St Jo Coll Nottm BTh 81. d 81 p 82. C Corby St Columba *Pet* 81-85; V Newborough 85-99; V Eaton Socon *St Alb* 99-07; Min Consultant CPAS from 07; P-in-c Christchurch and Manea and Welney *Ely* 07-15; P-in-c Doddington w Benwick and Wimblington 11-15; rtd 15. *127 High Street, Eye, Peterborough PE6 7UX* E: k.fitzgibbon@care4free.net

FITZHARRIS, Barry. b 47. Lon Univ BA 69 W Ontario Univ MA 70 K Coll Lon BD 72 AKC 72. St Aug Coll Cant 72. d 73 p 74. C Whitstable All SS *Cant* 73-75; C Whitstable All SS w St Pet 75-76; Hon C Clapham Old Town *S'wark* 77-79; Asst Chapl Abp Tenison's Sch Kennington 78-84; Chapl and Hd RS 87-89; Hon C Streatham Ch Ch *S'wark* 80-84; R Radwinter w Hempstead *Chelmsf* 84-87; Hon C Streatham St Pet *S'wark* 87-89 and 97-98. *8 Holmlea Court, Chatsworth Road, Croydon CR0 1HA*

FITZHARRIS, The Ven Robert Aidan. b 46. Sheff Univ BDS 71. Linc Th Coll 87. d 89 p 90. C Dinnington *Sheff* 89-92; V Bentley 92-01; RD Adwick 95-01; Hon Can Sheff Cathl 98-01; Adn Doncaster 01-11; rtd 12; PtO *Sheff* from 12. *Amberley, Old Bawtry Road, Finningley, Doncaster DN9 3BY* T: (01302) 773220 M: 07767-355357 E: lesleyfitzharris@waitrose.com

FITZMAURICE, Arthur William John. b 65. Leeds Univ BA 99 Heythrop Coll Lon MA 04 K Coll Lon PhD 14 Lon Inst of Educn PGCE 92 AGSM 89. Coll of Resurr Mirfield 97. d 99 p 00. C Spondon *Derby* 99-02; P-in-c Emscote *Cov* 02-03; TV Warwick 03-15; Dir of Ords *Worc* from 15. *15 Ingram Avenue, Worcester WR2 5GQ* T: (01905) 428055 E: john@fmaurice.freeserve.co.uk

FITZPATRICK, Paul Kevin. b 60. Open Univ BA 99 Univ of Wales (Lamp) MTh 05 Univ of Wales (Cardiff) PhD 11 Plymouth Univ PGCE 07. Cuddesdon Coll 96. d 98 p 99. C Okehampton w Inwardleigh, Bratton Clovelly etc *Ex* 98-02; P-in-c Whipton 02-04; V 04-07; RD Christianity 05-06; Chapl Cardiff Metrop Univ *Llan* from 07. *Cardiff Metropolitan University, Chaplaincy, Cyncoed Campus, Cyncoed Road, Cardiff CF23 6XD* T: (029) 2041 7252 M: 07917-818524 E: pfitzpatrick@uwic.ac.uk

FITZPATRICK, Victor Robert Andrew. b 75. Milltown Inst Dub BA 00 Pontifical Univ Maynooth BD 03 Cant Ch Ch Univ MA 04. CITC 08. d 03 p 04. Chapl Cork Univ Hosp 03; C Bray *D & G* 04-07; C Dublin St Ann and St Steph 09-10; C Castleknock and Mulhuddart w Clonsilla 10-13; I Kilcooley w Littleon, Crohane and Fertagh *C & O* from 13. *The Rectory, Grange, Barna, Thurles, Co Tipperary, Republic of Ireland* T: (00353) (56) 883 4147 M: 86-397 4035 E: prayspot@live.ie

FITZSIMONS, Canon Kathryn Anne. b 54. Bedf Coll of Educn CertEd 78. NEOC 87. d 90 p 13. NSM Bilton *Ripon* 90-01; Soc Resp Development Officer Richmond Adnry 92-99; Urban Min Officer *Ripon* 99-14; P-in-c Leeds Gipton Epiphany from 14; Hon Can Ripon Cathl from 04. *Epiphany Vicarage, 227 Beech Lane, Leeds LS9 6SW* E: kathrynfitzsimons@hotmail.com

FLACH, (née ROLLINS), Canon Deborah Mary Rollins. b 54. Sarum & Wells Th Coll 88. d 94 p 97. C Chantilly *Eur* 94-96; C Maisons-Laffitte 96-04; Asst Chapl 04-07; P-in-c Lille from 07; Can Gib Cathl from 07. *Christ Church, 14 rue Lyderic, 59000 Lille, France* T/F: (0033) 3 28 52 66 36 E: debbieflach@gmail.com

FLACK, Miss Heather Margaret. b 47. d 95 p 96. C Shenley Green *Birm* 95-00; TV Kings Norton 00-07; rtd 07; PtO *Birm* from 07. *23 Stourport Road, Bewdley DY12 1BB* T: (01299) 400691 E: hm.flack@btinternet.com

✠**FLACK, The Rt Revd John Robert.** b 42. Leeds Univ BA 64. Coll of Resurr Mirfield 64. d 66 p 67 c 97. C Armley St Bart *Ripon* 66-69; C Northampton St Mary *Pet* 69-72; V Chapelthorpe *Wakef* 72-81; V Ripponden and Barkisland w W Scammonden 81-85; Chapl Rishworth Sch Ripponden 81-85; V Brighouse *Wakef* 85-88; TR Brighouse St Martin 88-92; RD Brighouse and Elland 86-92; Hon Can Wakef Cathl 89-92; Adn Pontefract 92-97; Suff Bp Huntingdon and Hon Can Ely Cathl 97-03; Abp's Rep H See and Dir Angl Cen Rome 03-08; P-in-c Nassington w Yarwell and Woodnewton w Apethorpe *Pet* 08-12; Can Pet Cathl 04-12; Hon Asst Bp Pet and Eur from 03; Ely from 13; Bp's Adv for Healing Min *Pet* from 14. *The Rectory, 38 West Street, Easton on the Hill, Stamford PE9 3LS* T: (01780) 753901 M: (07810) 330263 E: johnflack67@yahoo.com

FLAGG, David Michael. b 50. CCC Cam BA 71 MA 75. St Jo Coll Nottm BA 76. d 77 p 78. C Hollington St Leon *Chich* 77-80; C Woodley St Jo the Ev *Ox* 80-86; Chapl The Dorothy Kerin Trust Burrswood 86-94; R Knockholt w Halstead *Roch* 94-99; Dir Chapl Services Mildmay UK 99-02; Hd Chapl Services Qu Eliz Hosp NHS Trust 02-11; Hd Chapl Services S Lon Healthcare NHS Trust 11-13; rtd 13; PtO *S'wark* from 13. *61 Church Street, Edenbridge TN8 5BQ* T: (01732) 866058 E: david.pastoral@mail.com

FLAHERTY, Jane Venitia. *See* ANDERSON, Jane Venitia

FLAHERTY, Ms Mandy Carol. b 63. Ches Coll of HE BA 86 Leic *Leic* 04-08; PtO *Ely* 09-10; NSM Alconbury cum Weston 10-14; Chapl K Sch Pet from 14; Chapl All SS C of E Primary Sch from 15. *The King's Cathedral School, Park Road, Peterborough PE1 2UE* T: (01733) 751541 E: flaherty.m@kings.peterborough.sch.uk

FLANAGAN, Kevin Joseph. b 60. Middx Poly BA 87 Newman Coll Birm PGCE 80. St Jo Coll Nottm 04. d 06 p 07. C Allesley Park and Whoberley *Cov* 06-09; V Wolston and Church Lawford from 09. *The Vicarage, Brook Street, Wolston, Coventry CV8 3HD* T: (024) 7654 0778 *or* 7654 2722 E: vicar.kevin@wolston.me.uk

FLANAGAN, Miss Vivienne Lesley. b 66. Liv Poly BA 89 Nottm Univ PGCE 90. St Jo Coll Nottm MA 98. d 98 p 99. C Huthwaite *S'well* 98-02; P-in-c Lenton Abbey 02-08; Chapl Bp Bell Sch 08-13; Chapl St Pet Academy Stoke-upon-Trent from 13; C Stoke-upon-Trent *Lich* from 13. *St Peter's Academy, Fenton Manor, Stoke-on-Trent ST4 2RR* T: (01782) 882500

FLASHMAN, Sarah. b 63. d 13 p 14. NSM Southbourne w W Thorney *Chich* from 13. *70 Winterbourne Road, Chichester PO19 6PB* T: (01243) 539129

FLASHMAN, Stephen. b 49. Spurgeon's Coll Lon 69. d 08 p 10. NSM Chich St Paul and Westhampnett from 08. *70 Winterbourne Road, Chichester PO19 6PB* T: (01243) 539129 M: 07950-000910 E: steve@ontheboxmission.com

FLATT, Lynn Patricia. b 47. Univ of Wales (Ban) BA 73 Birm Univ MSocSc 75 Ex Univ DipSW 79 RGN 68. SWMTC 12. d 14. NSM S Molton w Nymet St George, High Bray etc *Ex* from 14. *1 Widgery Drive, South Molton EX36 4DP* T: (01769) 572076 E: lynnflatt@btinternet.com

FLATT, Stephen Joseph. b 57. SRN 79 RSCN 81. Sarum & Wells Th Coll 92. d 92 p 93. C Limpsfield and Titsey *S'wark* 92-96; TV Pewsey *Sarum* 96-97; Staff Nurse R Free Hampstead NHS Trust 97-99; Charge Nurse 99-00; Asst Chapl Univ Coll Lon Hosps NHS Trust 00-01; Chapl 01-03; PtO *S'wark* 98-99; NSM Clapham H Trin and St Pet 99-02; Lead Chapl St Mary's NHS Trust Paddington 03-10; Hd Spiritual and Past Care Imp Coll Healthcare NHS Trust 10-13; Clinical Service Manager W Middx Univ Hosp NHS Trust from 13. *West Middlesex University Hospital, Twickenham Road, Isleworth TW7 6AF* T: (020) 8560 2121

FLATTERS, Clive Andrew. b 56. Sarum & Wells Th Coll 83. d 86 p 88. C Weston Favell *Pet* 86-87; C Old Brumby *Linc* 88-91; C Syston *Leic* 91-93; TV 93-99; V Knottingley *Wakef* 99-02; TR Knottingley and Kellington w Whitley *Leeds* from 02. *The Vicarage, Chapel Street, Knottingley WF11 9AN* T: (01977) 672267

FLAVELL, Paul William Deran. b 44. St Mich Coll Llan 67. d 68 p 69. C W Cairns Australia 68-71; C Blaenavon w Capel Newydd *Mon* 71-74; V Ynysddu 74-84; R Llanaber w Caerdeon *Ban* 84-00; V Llanstadwel *St D* 00-10; rtd 10; PtO *St As* from 10; *Ban* from 10. *7 Park Grove, Abergele LL22 7NE* T: (01745) 823648 E: fish.foulkes1811@btinternet.com

FLEET, Daniel James Russell. b 60. Wye Coll Lon BSc 84 Keele Univ PGCE 02. St Jo Coll Nottm 86. d 89 p 90. C Boldmere *Birm* 89-92; C Caverswall and Weston Coyney w Dilhorne

Lich 92-95; V Alton w Bradley-le-Moors and Oakamoor w Cotton 95-01; rtd 01; PtO *Lich* 01-10. *124 Byrds Lane, Uttoxeter ST14 7NB* T: (01889) 560214 E: byrdfleet@tiscali.co.uk

FLEETNEY, Colin John. b 33. Cant Sch of Min. **d** 83 **p** 84. NSM Upper Hardres w Stelling *Cant* 83-85; Chapl Asst St Aug Hosp Cant 85-86; NSM Petham and Waltham w Lower Hardres etc *Cant* 85-86; V Lezayre *S & M* 86-90; rtd 98; PtO *S & M* from 10. *43 Magherchirrym, Port Erin, Isle of Man IM9 6DB* T: (01624) 835249

FLEETWOOD, Zachary William Maddrey. b 50. Guilford Coll USA BA 73. Virginia Th Sem MDiv 87. **d** 87 **p** 88. C Arlington St Mary USA 87-89; C Washington Ch Ch Georgetown 89-90; R The Plains 90-97; R Morristown St Pet 97-03; Dean H Trin Cathl Paris 03-11; R Edin St Columba 11-15; rtd 15. *Address temp unknown* M: 07870-638969

FLEMING (formerly LOOKER), Miss Clare Margaret. b 55. Liv Univ CertEd 78. Westcott Ho Cam 85. **d** 87 **p** 02. Par Dn Prestwood and Gt Hampden *Ox* 87-90; Hon C Olney w Emberton 90-92; Hon C Blunham, Gt Barford, Roxton and Tempsford etc *St Alb* 01-03; P-in-c Welford w Sibbertoft and Marston Trussell *Pet* 03-04; PtO *St Alb* 04-05; Hon C Wilden w Colmworth and Ravensden 05-08; PtO *Ely* from 11; *St E* from 12. *3 Bracken Row, Thurston, Bury St Edmunds IP31 3PT* T: (01359) 230987   M: 07519-590767 E: fleming.clare@yahoo.co.uk

FLEMING, The Ven David. b 37. Kelham Th Coll 58. **d** 63 **p** 64. C Walton St Marg Belmont Road *Liv* 63-67; Chapl HM Borstal Gaynes Hall 68-76; V Gt Staughton *Ely* 68-76; RD St Neots 72-76; V Whittlesey 76-85; RD March 77-82; Hon Can Ely Cathl 82-01; P-in-c Ponds Bridge 83-85; Adn Wisbech 84-93; V Wisbech St Mary 85-89; Chapl Gen of Pris 93-01; Chapl to The Queen 95-07; PtO *Ely* from 01. *Fair Haven, 123 Wisbech Road, Littleport, Ely CB6 1JJ* T: (01353) 862498 E: davidfleming@hotmail.com

FLEMING, Elizabeth Julie. b 57. Westhill Coll Birm CertEd 79 Ches Coll of HE BTh 00. NOC 97. **d** 00 **p** 01. C Widnes St Jo *Liv* 00-03; P-in-c Walton Breck Ch Ch 03-04; V Walton Breck 04-08; V Becontree St Mary *Chelmsf* from 08; AD Barking and Dagenham from 13. *The Vicarage, 191 Valence Wood Road, Dagenham RM8 3AH* T: (020) 8592 2822 E: juliestmary@gmail.com

FLEMING, George. b 39. CITC. **d** 78 **p** 79. C Donaghcloney w Waringstown *D & D* 78-80; C Newtownards 80; I Movilla 80; C Heref St Pet w St Owen and St Jas 80-85; V Holmer w Huntington 85-96; P-in-c Worfield 96-98; V 98-04; rtd 04; PtO *Truro* 05-08. *The Rectory, Kenwin Close, Swindon SN3 4NY* T: (01793) 831239

FLEMING, Canon Kathryn Claire. b 60. Trin Coll Cam BA 82 MA 91 Montessori TDip 92. WEMTC 01. **d** 04 **p** 05. C Charlton Kings St Mary *Glouc* 04-08; P-in-c Cainscross w Selsley 08-13; TV Stroud Team 13-14; Can Res Cov Cathl from 14. *Coventry Cathedral, 1 Hill Top, Coventry CV1 5AB* T: (024) 7652 1200   F: 7652 1220   E: revkathryn@googlemail.com

FLEMING (formerly JOHNSTON), Mrs Patricia Anne. b 42. Qu Coll Birm 05. **d** 06 **p** 07. NSM Rubery *Birm* 06-09; P-in-c Allens Cross from 09. *9 Dowles Close, Birmingham B29 4LE* T: 0121-475 6190

FLEMING, Penelope Rawling. *See* SMITH, Penelope Rawling

FLEMING, Ronald Thorpe. b 29. Codrington Coll Barbados 52. **d** 56 **p** 57. Barbados 56-61; C Delaval *Newc* 61-64; V Cambois 64-69; V Ancroft w Scremerston 69-81; V Longhirst 81-84; Chapl Preston Hosp N Shields 84-94; Chapl N Tyneside Hosps 84-94; rtd 94; PtO *Newc* 94-04; LtO *Mor* from 04. *49 Woodside Drive, Forres IV36 2UF* T: (01309) 671101

FLEMING, Victoria Rosalie. b 58. WEMTC 01. **d** 04 **p** 05. NSM St Breoke and Egloshayle *Truro* 04-08; TV Stratton St Margaret w S Marston etc *Bris* 08-11; P-in-c from 11. *The Rectory, Kenwin Close, Swindon SN3 4NY* T: (01793) 831239 E: revs.fleming@tiscali.co.uk

FLEMING, William Edward Charlton. b 29. TCD BA 51 MA 65. CITC 52. **d** 52 **p** 53. C Dublin Santry *D & G* 52-56; C Arm St Mark w Aghavilly 56-61; I Tartaraghan 61-80; Prov Registrar 79-96; I Tartaraghan w Diamond 80-96; Can Arm Cathl 86-96; Treas Arm Cathl 88-92; Chan Arm Cathl 92-96; rtd 96. *65 Annareagh Road, Drumorgan, Richhill, Armagh BT61 9JT* T: (028) 3887 9612

FLENLEY, Benjamin Robert Glanville. b 50. Sarum & Wells Th Coll 86. **d** 88 **p** 89. C Eastleigh *Win* 88-92; V Micheldever and E Stratton, Woodmancote etc 92-03; R Bentworth, Lasham, Medstead and Shalden 03-15; rtd 15; Hon C Quantock Towers *B & W* from 15. *Shardloes, Staple Lane, West Quantoxhead, Taunton TA4 4DE* E: flenbenley@aol.com

FLENLEY, Kathryn Alison. b 69. STETS. **d** 12 **p** 13. NSM Bentworth, Lasham, Medstead and Shalden *Win* 12-15. *Address temp unknown*

FLETCHER, Mrs Angela. b 59. EMMTC 04. **d** 07 **p** 08. C Edwinstowe and Perlethorpe *S'well* 07-10; P-in-c Warsop 10-11; R from 11. *The Rectory, Church Road, Warsop, Mansfield NG20 0SL* T: (01623) 843290 E: angela_fletcher43@hotmail.com

FLETCHER, Anthony. *See* FLETCHER, James Anthony

FLETCHER, Anthony Peter Reeves. b 46. Bede Coll Dur CertEd Nottm Univ BTh 78. Ridley Hall Cam 71. **d** 74 **p** 75. C Luton St Mary *St Alb* 74-78; Chapl RAF 78-00; P-in-c Lyneham w Bradenstoke *Sarum* 98-99; P-in-c Kyrenia St Andr and Chapl N Cyprus 00-04; P-in-c Lyneham w Bradenstoke *Sarum* 04-07; rtd 07. *Glentworth House, Giles Avenue, Cricklade, Swindon SN6 6HS* T: (01793) 751333

FLETCHER, Barbara. b 41. ALAM 79. WMMTC 93. **d** 96 **p** 97. NSM Smethwick *Birm* 96-97; C 97-02; rtd 02; PtO *Birm* from 02. *231 Abbey Road, Smethwick B67 5NN* T: 0121-429 9354 E: bfletcher@talktalk.net

FLETCHER, Bryce Clifford. b 52. ACIB. Cranmer Hall Dur. **d** 08 **p** 09. NSM Arle Valley *Win* 08-14; rtd 14; PtO *Win* from 14. *Robinia House, 23 Rosebery Road, Alresford SO24 9HQ* T: (01962) 734670

✠**FLETCHER, The Rt Revd Colin William.** b 50. OBE 00. Trin Coll Ox BA 72 MA 76. Wycliffe Hall Ox 72. **d** 75 **p** 76 **c** 00. C Shipley St Pet *Bradf* 75-79; Tutor Wycliffe Hall Ox 79-84; Hon C Ox St Andr 79-84; V Margate H Trin *Cant* 84-93; RD Thanet 88-93; Abp's Chapl 93-00; Area Bp Dorchester Ox from 00; Hon Can Dallas from 93. *Arran House, Sandy Lane, Yarnton, Kidlington OX5 1PB* T: (01865) 208218   F: 849003 E: bishopdorchester@oxford.anglican.org

FLETCHER, David Clare Molyneux. b 32. Worc Coll Ox BA 55 MA 59. Wycliffe Hall Ox 56. **d** 58 **p** 59. C Islington St Mary *Lon* 58-62; Hon C 62-83; Field Worker Scripture Union 62-86; R Ox St Ebbe w H Trin and St Pet 86-98; rtd 98; PtO *Ox* from 06. *32 Linkside Avenue, Oxford OX2 8JB* T: (01865) 552420

FLETCHER, David Ernest. b 53. Worc Coll of Educn BEd 76 Open Univ MTh 01. St Jo Coll Nottm 99. **d** 01 **p** 02. C Mixenden *Wakef* 01-04; P-in-c 04-10; V Mixenden and Illingworth 10-11; Dioc Urban Officer 08-11; P-in-c Waggoners *York* from 11; P-in-c Woldsburn from 11; RD Harthill from 12. *The Vicarage, 4 Pulham Lane, Wetwang, Driffield YO25 9XT* T: (01377) 236189   M: 07702-385885 E: de.fletcher@hotmail.co.uk

FLETCHER, David Mark. b 56. Chich Th Coll 84. **d** 87 **p** 88. C Taunton St Andr *B & W* 87-91; P-in-c Chard, Furnham w Chaffcombe, Knowle St Giles etc 91-95; P-in-c Tiverton St Andr *Ex* 95-11; RD Tiverton 02-08; Chapl Mid Devon Primary Care Trust 95-11; C Barnstaple *Ex* from 11. *The Vicarage, Sowden Lane, Barnstaple EX32 8BU* T: (01271) 373837 E: davidfletcher56@btinternet.com

FLETCHER, Douglas. b 40. Coll of Resurr Mirfield 67. **d** 68 **p** 69. C Notting Hill St Jo *Lon* 68-73; C Cambridge St Mary Less *Ely* 73-74; C Fulham St Jo Walham Green *Lon* 74-76; C Walham Green St Jo w St Jas 76-84; P-in-c Kensal Town St Thos w St Andr and St Phil 84-92; V 92-06; rtd 06; PtO *Lon* 07-13. *68 Clarendon Road, London W11 2HW* T: (020) 7229 8146

FLETCHER, Capt Frank. b 40. Wilson Carlile Coll 71 EAMTC 94. **d** 96 **p** 96. Asst Chapl HM Pris Highpoint *Ches* 90-97; Chapl HM Pris Wealstun 97-05; rtd 05; PtO *York* from 05. *6 Kingsclere, Huntington, York YO32 9SF* T: (01904) 758453

FLETCHER, Gordon Wolfe (Robin). b 31. Edin Th Coll. **d** 62 **p** 63. C Eston *York* 62-65; C Harton Colliery *Dur* 65-68; V Pelton 68-81; V Ryhope 81-96; rtd 96; PtO *Dur* from 04. *23 Swinburne Road, Darlington DL3 7TD* T: (01325) 265994 E: gordon.fletcher@btinternet.com

FLETCHER, Ian Paul. b 76. **d** 09 **p** 10. C Holdenhurst and Iford *Win* 09-13; P-in-c Eastleigh from 14. *Eastleigh Vicarage, 1 Cedar Road, Eastleigh SO50 9NR* E: ianpaulfletcher@gmail.com

FLETCHER, James Anthony. b 36. St Edm Hall Ox BA 60 MA 66. St Steph Ho 60. **d** 62 **p** 63. C Streatham St Pet *S'wark* 62-65; C Hobs Moat CD *Birm* 65-66; C Hobs Moat 67-68; C Cowley St Jo *Ox* 68-77; V Hanworth All SS *Lon* 77-02; P-in-c Hanworth St Geo 89-91; rtd 02; PtO *Cant* from 02. *19 Strand Street, Sandwich, Kent CT13 9OX* T: (01304) 620506

FLETCHER, James Arthur. b 71. Reading Univ BA 99. Trin Coll Bris 03. **d** 05 **p** 06. Bexleyheath Ch Ch *Roch* 05; C 05-08; R Fawkham and Hartley from 08. *The Rectory, 3 St John's Lane, Hartley, Longfield DA3 8ET* T: (01474) 703819 E: rector@fawkhamandhartley.org.uk

FLETCHER, James John Gareth. b 79. Aber Univ MA 02 Cam Univ BA 08. Ridley Hall Cam 06. **d** 09 **p** 10. C Tooting Graveney St Nic *S'wark* 09-13; C Ox St Ebbe w H Trin and St Pet from 13. *81 Marlborough Road, Oxford OX1 4LX* T: (01865) 240438   M: 07809-291992 E: jfletcher@stables.org.uk

FLETCHER, Miss Janet. b 59. Lanc Univ MA 07. Cranmer Hall Dur. **d** 00 **p** 01. C Ainsdale *Liv* 00-04; TV Walton-on-the-Hill and Hon Chapl Liv Cathl 04-09; C Prescot 09-11; TV Bangor *Ban* 11-14; TV Bro Deiniol 14-15; Spirituality Officer from 15; C Bro Ystumanner from 15. *65 Faenol Isaf, Tywyn LL36 0DW* T: (01654) 711792 E: revjfletcher@btinternet.com

FLETCHER, Jeremy James. b 60. Dur Univ BA 81. St Jo Coll Nottm 85. **d** 88 **p** 89. C Stranton *Dur* 88-91; C Nottingham St Nic *S'well* 91-94; P-in-c Skegby 94-00; P-in-c Teversal 96-00; Bp's Dom Chapl 00-02; Can Res and Prec York Minster 02-09; V Beverley Minster from 09; P-in-c Routh from 09; RD Beverley from 12. *The Minster Vicarage, Highgate, Beverley HU17 0DN* T: (01482) 881434 *or* 868540
E: vicar@beverleyminster.org.uk *or* jeremy@jjfletcher.co.uk

FLETCHER, Canon John Alan Alfred. b 33. Oak Hill Th Coll 58. **d** 61 **p** 62. C Erith St Paul *Roch* 61-64; C Rushden *Pet* 64-67; R Hollington St Leon *Chich* 67-86; V Chadwell Heath *Chelmsf* 86-00; RD Barking and Dagenham 91-00; Chapl Chadwell Heath Hosp Romford 86-93; Chapl Redbridge Health Care NHS Trust 93-00; Hon Can Chelmsf Cathl 99-00; rtd 00; PtO *Chich* from 01. *41 Parkstone Road, Hastings TN34 2NR* T: (01424) 712343 M: 07860-128912 E: jaaf@btinternet.com

FLETCHER, Jonathan James Molyneux. b 42. Hertf Coll Ox BA 66 MA 68. Wycliffe Hall Ox 66. **d** 68 **p** 69. C Enfield Ch Ch Trent Park *Lon* 68-72; C Cambridge St Sepulchre *Ely* 72-73; C Cambridge H Sepulchre w All SS 73-76; C St Helen Bishopsgate w St Martin Outwich *Lon* 76-81; Min Wimbledon Em Ridgway Prop Chpl *S'wark* 82-12; rtd 12; PtO *S'wark* from 12. *11 Preston Road, London SW20 0SS* T: (020) 8946 4728

FLETCHER, Keith. b 47. Chich Th Coll 79. **d** 80 **p** 81. C Hartlepool St Paul *Dur* 80-82; V Eighton Banks 82-85; V Haydon Bridge *Newc* 85-96; RD Hexham 93-96; P-in-c Beltingham w Henshaw 93-96; R Ashmanhaugh, Barton Turf etc *Nor* 96-99; rtd 99. *2 Churchill Terrace, Sherburn Hill, Durham DH6 1PF* T: 0191-372 0362

FLETCHER, Ms Linda Edith. b 72. Man Univ BA 93. Trin Coll Bris BA 09. **d** 09 **p** 10. C Coulsdon St Jo *S'wark* 09-12; P-in-c Swindon St Jo and St Andr *Bris* from 12. *The Vicarage, Verwood Close, Swindon SN3 2LE* T: (01793) 611473 M: 07852-911598 E: revlindafletcher@live.co.uk

FLETCHER, Linden Elisabeth. b 50. Lon Univ BEd 73 MA 80. St Jo Coll Nottm 87. **d** 89 **p** 94. C Fakenham w Alethorpe *Nor* 89-93; C Cumnor *Ox* 93-02; P-in-c Ringshall w Battisford, Barking w Darmsden etc *St E* 02-08; P-in-c Somersham w Flowton and Offton w Willisham 02-08; V Llanfair Caereinion, Llanllugan and Manafon *St As* 08-11; rtd 11. *Tanrallt, Cwrtnewydd, Llanybydder SA40 9YJ*

FLETCHER, Mrs Margaret. b 44. MBE . **d** 04 **p** 05. NSM Thurstaston *Ches* 04-07; V Thornton-le-Moors w Ince and Elton 07-14; rtd 14. *1 Coombe Road, Wirral CH61 4UN* T: 0151-648 1025 E: revmfletcher@o2.co.uk

FLETCHER, Mark. b 72. Staffs Poly BSc 93. Oak Hill Th Coll BA 00. **d** 00 **p** 01. C Paddington Em Harrow Road *Lon* 00-03; C W Kilburn St Luke w St Simon and St Jude 00-03; C Barnsbury from 04. *43 Matilda Street, London N1 0LA* T: (020) 7278 5208 E: mark@midwinter.org.uk

FLETCHER, Martin. b 60. Bradf Univ BEng 83 CEng MIMechE. Ripon Coll Cuddesdon. **d** 00 **p** 01. C Oatlands *Guildf* 00-04; R Tolleshunt Knights w Tiptree and Gt Braxted *Chelmsf* 04-10; V Hersham *Guildf* from 10. *The Vicarage, 5 Burwood Road, Walton-on-Thames KT12 4AA* T: (01932) 227445
E: fletcher_martin@yahoo.co.uk

FLETCHER, Martin James. b 48. Ex Univ BA 03 MIFA 89. SWMTC 99. **d** 02 **p** 03. NSM Wolborough and Ogwell *Ex* 02-05; NSM Chudleigh w Chudleigh Knighton and Trusham from 05. *11 Troarn Way, Chudleigh, Newton Abbot TQ13 0PP* T: (01626) 853998 E: m.fletcher@uwclub.net

FLETCHER, Maurice. *See* FLETCHER, Ralph Henry Maurice

FLETCHER, Mrs Patricia. b 34. K Alfred's Coll Win CertEd 74. Chich Th Coll 94. **d** 94. NSM Droxford *Portsm* 94-97; NSM Meonstoke w Corhampton cum Exton 94-97; PtO 97-00; NSM Blendworth w Chalton w Idsworth 00-04; rtd 04; PtO *Portsm* from 04. *17 Maylings Farm Road, Fareham PO16 7QU* T: (01329) 311489 E: patfletch2004@yahoo.co.uk

FLETCHER, Paul Gordon MacGregor. b 61. St Andr Univ MTheol 84. Edin Th Coll 84. **d** 86 **p** 87. C Cumbernauld *Glas* 86-89; C-in-c Glas H Cross 89-93; P-in-c Bearsden w Milngavie 93-99; R Clarkston 99-07; LtO *Arg* 08-10; R E Kilbride *Glas* from 10. *6 Kelvin Crescent, East Kilbride, Glasgow G75 0TY* T: (01355) 224895 E: paulmcgregorfletcher@hotmail.com

FLETCHER, Ralph Henry Maurice. b 43. St Luke's Coll Ex CertEd 65. St Steph Ho *Ox* 71. **d** 74 **p** 75. C Chislehurst Annunciation *Roch* 74-77; Chapl Quainton Hall Sch Harrow 77-87 and 94-00; Hon C Hillingdon All SS *Lon* 87-94; PtO 94-00; *Roch* 00-02; *Leeds* from 05. *6 Joseph Court, Joseph Street, Barnsley S70 1LJ* T: (012260) 779928

FLETCHER, Robert Alexander. b 52. Ridley Hall Cam. **d** 84 **p** 85. C Chalfont St Peter *Ox* 84-88; C Bushey *St Alb* 88-93; TV Digswell and Panshanger 93-00; P-in-c Aldenham 00-05; TV Aldenham, Radlett and Shenley from 05. *The Vicarage, Church Lane, Aldenham, Watford WD25 8BE* T/F: (01923) 854209
E: r.a.fletcher@btinternet.com

FLETCHER, Robin. *See* FLETCHER, Gordon Wolfe

FLETCHER, Canon Robin Geoffrey. b 32. Nottm Univ BA 57. Ridley Hall Cam 57. **d** 59 **p** 60. C S Mimms Ch Ch *Lon* 59-64; V Wollaton Park *S'well* 64-71; V Clifton *York* 71-97; Chapl Clifton Hosp York 71-88; RD City of York 86-97; Can and Preb York Minster 89-00; rtd 98; PtO *York* 00-04; *Leeds* from 04. *14 South Avenue, Fartown, Huddersfield HD2 1BY* T: (01484) 510266 E: rgfletcher@tiscali.co.uk

FLETCHER, Mrs Sarah Louise. b 72. Cranmer Hall Dur. **d** 14 **p** 15. C New Bury w Gt Lever *Man* from 14. *9 Wanless Terrace, Durham DH1 1RU* M: 07717-002472
E: s.l.fletcher@durham.ac.uk

FLETCHER, Mrs Sheila Elizabeth. b 35. Nottm Univ BA 57 CertEd 58. NEOC 84. **d** 87 **p** 94. NSM Dringhouses *York* 87-90; Par Dn 90-94; C 94-97; P-in-c Sutton on the Forest 97-02; rtd 02; PtO *York* from 02. *68 Huntsman's Walk, York YO24 3LA* T: (01904) 796876 E: sheeliz@tiscali.co.uk

FLETCHER, Stephen. b 57. Man Univ BA 79 MA 84. St Jo Coll Nottm 82. **d** 84 **p** 85. C Didsbury St Jas and Em *Man* 84-88; R Kersal Moor 88-91; TR Horwich and Rivington from 01; C Blackrod from 11. *The Rectory, Chorley Old Road, Horwich, Bolton BL6 6AX* T/F: (01204) 468263
E: stephen@fletchers.freeserve.co.uk

FLETCHER, Stephen William. b 62. Wolv Poly BA 84. Qu Coll Birm 85. **d** 88 **p** 89. C Rainham *Roch* 88-91; C Shottery St Andr *Cov* 91-97; Min Bishopton St Pet 91-97; V Llanrumney *Mon* 97-02; V Adderbury w Milton from 02. *11 Walton Avenue, Adderbury, Banbury OX17 3JY* T: (01295) 810309
E: revfletcher@btconnect.com

FLETCHER, Steven John Carylon. b 60. NCTJ 83. Aston Tr Scheme 89 Ripon Coll Cuddesdon 89. **d** 92 **p** 15. C Newquay *Truro* 92-93; NSM St Stythians w Perranarworthal and Gwennap from 15; NSM Chacewater w St Day and Carharrack from 15; NSM Feock from 15; NSM Devoran from 15. *5 Scorrier Street, St Day, Redruth TR16 5LH* T: (01209) 822584
E: steven.fletcher@btinternet.com

FLETCHER, Timothy John. b 63. Sheff Univ BA 88 St Jo Coll Dur MA 04. Cranmer Hall Dur 01. **d** 03 **p** 04. C Four Marks *Win* 03-06; V Walton le Soken *Chelmsf* 06-14; P-in-c Stannington *Sheff* from 14; Dir IME 4-7 from 14. *The Vicarage, 214 Oldfield Road, Stannington, Sheffield S6 6DY* T: 0114-234 9247
E: tim906fletcher@btinternet.com

FLETCHER, Victor James Daniel. b 56. **d** 12 **p** 13. OLM Holcombe and Hawkshaw *Man* from 12. *32 Moor Way, Hawkshaw, Bury BL8 4LF* T: (01204) 882750
M: 07977-668836 E: v.fletcher@talktalk.net

FLEWKER, David William. b 53. Birm Univ BA 75. Wycliffe Hall Ox 76. **d** 78 **p** 79. C Netherton *Liv* 78-82; C Prescot 82-84; V Seaforth 84-88; TV Whitstable *Cant* 88-96; Miss to Seamen 88-96; V Bethersden w High Halden *Cant* 96-08; Asst Dir of Ords 02-06; P-in-c Deal St Leon w St Rich and Sholden etc 08-13; R from 13. *St Leonard's Rectory, Addelam Road, Deal CT14 9BZ* T: (01304) 374076 E: d.flewker@btinternet.com

FLEWKER-BARKER, Miss Linda. b 68. Redcliffe Coll BA 02 St Jo Coll Dur MA 04. Cranmer Hall Dur 02. **d** 04 **p** 05. C Cheltenham Ch Ch *Glouc* 04-07; Chapl RAF 07-15; R Kwinana Australia from 15. *All Saints Church, Chisham Avenue, Parmelia WA 6167, Australia* T: (0061) (8) 9439 6854
E: lindafbarker@yahoo.com *or*
revlinda@kwinana.perth.anglican.org

FLIGHT, Michael John. b 41. Sarum Th Coll 68. **d** 71 **p** 72. C Wimborne Minster *Sarum* 71-75; R Tarrant Gunville, Tarrant Hinton etc 75-78; P-in-c Tarrant Rushton, Tarrant Rawston etc 77-78; R Tarrant Valley 78-80; V Westbury 80-00; RD Heytesbury 83-87 and 96-00; R Broad Town, Clyffe Pypard, Hilmarton etc 00-07; RD Calne 03-06; rtd 07. *11 Nursteed Close, Devizes SN10 3EU* T: (01380) 738493
E: michael@flightfamily.co.uk

FLINN, Canon John Robert Patrick. b 30. CITC. **d** 65 **p** 66. C Dublin Rathfarnham *D & G* 65-67; I Baltinglass w Ballynure etc *C & O* 67-76; I Castlepollard and Oldcastle w Loughcrew etc *M & K* 76-84; rtd 84; Treas Ossory and Leighlin Cathls *C & O* 90-92; Chan Ossory and Leighlin Cathls 96-01. *The Old School House, Kells, Co Kilkenny, Republic of Ireland* T: (00353) (56) 772 8297

FLINT, Edward Benedict William. b 80. **d** 08 **p** 09. C Bryanston Square St Mary w St Marylebone St Mark *Lon* from 09. *Hawthorn House, Garford, Abingdon OX13 5PF* E: edflint@gmail.com

FLINT, Howard Michael. b 59. Edge Hill Coll of HE BEd 81. Cranmer Hall Dur 95. **d** 97 **p** 98. C Chipping Campden w Ebrington *Glouc* 97-00; V Upper Wreake *Leic* 00-06; RD Framland 02-06; V Tunbridge Wells H Trin w Ch Ch *Roch* from 06. *The Vicarage, 63 Claremont Road, Tunbridge Wells TN1 1TE* T: (01892) 526644 *or* 522323 F: 529300
E: rev4howard@hotmail.com

FLINT, Nicholas Angus. b 60. Chich Th Coll 84. **d** 87 **p** 88. C Aldwick *Chich* 87-91; Bp's Asst Chapl for the Homeless *Lon* 91-92; TV Ifield *Chich* 92-96; R Rusper w Colgate from 96. *The Rectory, High Street, Rusper, Horsham RH12 4PX* T: (01293) 871251 E: nick.flint@totalise.co.uk

FLINT, Simon Paul. b 67. Trin Coll Bris 11. **d** 13 **p** 14. C Bath Weston All SS w N Stoke and Langridge *B & W* from 13. *23 Lucklands Road, Bath BA1 4AX* T: (01225) 444790
M: 07864-910953 E: simonfredflint@gmail.com

FLINT, Toby. b 76. Wycliffe Hall Ox BA 08. **d** 08 **p** 09. C Brompton H Trin w Onslow Square St Paul *Lon* 08-11; C Onslow Square and S Kensington St Aug from 11. *Holy Trinity Brompton, Brompton Road, London SW7 1JA*
T: 08456-447533 E: tobyflint@hotmail.co.uk

FLINTHAM, Alan Jenkinson. b 45. Leeds Univ BSc 66 PGCE 67 MEd 74. EMMTC 98. **d** 00 **p** 01. NSM Melbourne *Derby* 00-10; NSM Melbourne, Ticknall, Smisby and Stanton 10-15; PtO *Linc* from 15. *50 Burlington Way, Mickleover, Derby DE3 9BD* T: (01332) 512293 E: flintham@flinthams.org.uk

FLINTOFT, Canon Ian Hugh. b 74. Pemb Coll Cam BA 97 MA 99 MPhil 98. Westcott Ho Cam 01. **d** 04 **p** 05. C Newc St Geo 04-06; C Newc St Geo and St Hilda 06-07; C Ch the King 07-08; TV 08-11; Bp's Chapl and Dioc Dir of Ords from 11; Hon Can Newc Cathl from 14. *The Bishop's House, 29 Moor Road South, Newcastle upon Tyne NE3 1PA* T: 0191-285 2220 *or* 232 1750 E: i.flintoft@newcastle.anglican.org *or* ianflintoft@hotmail.com

FLINTOFT-CHAPMAN, Mrs Margaret. b 47. Leeds Univ BA 68. NTMTC 03. **d** 05 **p** 06. NSM Barkingside St Cedd *Chelmsf* 05-12; NSM Barkingside H Trin from 12. *84 Roding Lane North, Woodford Green IG8 8NG* T: (020) 8504 6750

FLIPPANCE, Kim Sheelagh May. *See* STEPHENS, Kim Sheelagh May

FLIPSE, Miss Adriana Maria (Marja). b 82. Leiden Univ MA 05. St Mich Coll Llan 07. **d** 08 **p** 09. C Roath *Llan* 08-11; C Newton Nottage 11-14; TV Whitchurch from 14. *All Saints' Vicarage, 59 Station Road, Llandaff North, Cardiff CF14 2FB* T: (029) 2031 2510 E: marjaflipse@btinternet.com

FLITCROFT, Jonathan Fredrick. b 62. Leeds Univ BA 85. Qu Coll Birm 13. **d** 15. C Four Oaks *Birm* from 15. *2 Knightsbridge Close, Sutton Coldfield B74 4UQ* T: 0121-565 2368
M: 07905-975601 E: johnflit@hotmail.co.uk *or* allsaintsfouroaks@yahoo.co.uk

FLOATE, Herbert Frederick Giraud. b 25. Keble Coll Ox BA 50 MA 54. Qu Coll Birm 50. **d** 61 **p** 62. Seychelles 61; Hon C Quarrington w Old Sleaford *Linc* 63-65; P-in-c Mareham le Fen 65-66; Australia 66-72; R Stroxton *Linc* 72-74; R Harlaxton w Wyville and Hungerton 72-74; Lect Shenston New Coll Worcs 74-78; P-in-c Redditch St Geo *Worc* 78-79; LtO 80-84; R Upton Snodsbury and Broughton Hackett etc 84-89; Chapl Mojácar *Eur* 89-91; rtd 91; PtO *Heref* 97-13. *15 Progress Close, Ledbury HR8 2QZ* T: (01531) 635509

FLOATE, Mrs Rhona Cameron. b 59. Univ of Wales (Cardiff) BA 80. Trin Coll Bris 01. **d** 03 **p** 04. C Lighthorne *Cov* 03-07; C Chesterton 03-07; C Newbold Pacey w Moreton Morrell 03-07; P-in-c Wool and E Stoke *Sarum* 07-15; R from 15; RD Purbeck from 15. *The Vicarage, Vicarage Close, Wool, Wareham BH20 6EB* T: (01929) 462215 E: vicar@holyroodwool.org.uk *or* rhonafloate@aol.com

FLOCKHART, Mrs Ruth. b 56. TISEC 96. **d** 99 **p** 00. NSM Strathpeffer *Mor* from 99; NSM Dingwall from 99. *Kilmuir Farm Cottage, North Kessock, Inverness IV1 3ZG* T: (01463) 731580 E: kilmuirseabreeze@btinternet.com

FLOOD, Emma Louise. *See* ANTOINE, Emma Louise

FLOOD, Mrs Jean Anne. b 51. Liv Hope Univ MEd 00 Liv Univ CertEd 95. NOC 06. **d** 08 **p** 09. NSM Fazakerley Em *Liv* 08-11; Co-ord Miss in the Economy from 11; NSM Walton-on-the-Hill from 11. *19 Palm Close, Liverpool L9 1JD* T: 0151-525 0304 E: floods@merseymail.com

FLOOD, John Leslie. b 45. Yorks Min Course 10. **d** 11 **p** 12. NSM Todmorden *Wakef* 11-13; NSM Todmorden w Cornholme and Walsden *Leeds* from 13. *52 Stansfield Street, Todmorden OL14 5EB* T: (01706) 813539 M: 07976-209480
E: aestus@talk21.com

FLOOD, Kenneth. b 75. St Chad's Coll Dur BSc 96. St Steph Ho Ox BTh 01. **d** 01 **p** 02. C Hulme Ascension *Man* 01-05; C Wokingham St Paul *Ox* 05-08; P-in-c Chorlton-cum-Hardy St Clem *Man* 08-09; R from 09; AD Hulme from 13. *The Rectory, 6 Edge Lane, Manchester M21 9JF* T: 0161-881 3063 E: ken@mightyflood.org.uk

FLOOD, Nicholas Roger. b 42. FCA. Ripon Hall Ox 71. **d** 92 **p** 93. NSM Romsey *Win* 92-94; Chapl Win and Eastleigh Healthcare NHS Trust 94-08; rtd 08; PtO *Win* from 09. *The Sanctuary, Salisbury Road, Plaitford, Romsey SO51 6EE* T: (01794) 323731

FLORANCE, James Andrew Vernon. b 44. MCIOB. Linc Th Coll 84. **d** 86 **p** 87. C Lt Ilford St Mich *Chelmsf* 86-90; TV Becontree S 90-93; R Orsett and Bulphan and Horndon on the Hill 93-97; P-in-c Liscard St Mary w St Columba *Ches* 97-02; RD Wallasey 99-02; Chapl St D Foundn Hospice Care Newport 02-03; P-in-c Abersychan and Garndiffaith *Mon* 03-08; rtd 08; PtO *Heref* 08-10; *Mon* 08-10; *St E* from 10. *1 Woodlands, Leiston IP16 4BT* T: (01728) 768124
E: jandp2florance@gmail.com

FLORANCE (née WAINWRIGHT), Mrs Pauline Barbara. b 40. St Deiniol's Hawarden 83. **dss** 84 **d** 87 **p** 94. New Ferry *Ches* 84-90; Par Dn 87-90; Par Dn Hallwood 90-94; C 94-00; rtd 00; PtO *Ches* 00-03; *Mon* 04-08; *Heref* 08-10; Bp's Adv in Past Care and Counselling *Mon* 07-10; PtO *St E* from 10. *1 Woodlands, Leiston IP16 4BT* T: (01728) 768124
E: jandp2florance@gmail.com

FLORENTINUS, Erik. ERMC. **d** 09 **p** 10. C Amsterdam w Den Helder and Heiloo *Eur* from 09; C Haarlem from 12. *0Z Achterburgwal 100, NL-1012 DS Amsterdam, The Netherlands*

FLORY, John Richard. b 35. Clare Coll Cam BA 59 MA 63. Westcott Ho Cam 69. **d** 71 **p** 72. C Shirehampton *Bris* 71-74; V Patchway 74-82; R Lydiard Millicent w Lydiard Tregoz 82-86; TR The Lydiards 86-93; R Box w Hazlebury and Ditteridge 93-01; rtd 01; PtO *Derby* from 02. *Beechbank, 3 Ivonbrook Close, Darley Bridge, Matlock DE4 2JX* T: (01629) 734707 E: johnjean@johnflory.wanadoo.co.uk

FLOWERDAY, Andrew Leslie. b 53. Imp Coll Lon BSc 75. St Jo Coll Nottm. **d** 90 **p** 91. C Farnborough *Guildf* 90-95; TV Morden *S'wark* 95-12; V Patcham *Chich* from 12. *All Saints' Vicarage, 12 Church Hill, Brighton BN1 8YE* T: (01273) 552157

FLOWERDEW, Martin James. b 56. Herts Coll CertEd 78 Pemb Coll Cam BEd 79. Sarum & Wells Th Coll 89. **d** 91 **p** 92. C Leagrave *St Alb* 91-95; C Radlett 95-99; TV Wilford Peninsula *St E* 99-01; V St Osyth *Chelmsf* 01-09; V Hoylake *Ches* 09-12; V Foremark and Repton w Newton Solney *Derby* from 12. *St Wystan's Vicarage, Willington Road, Repton, Derby DE65 6FH* T: (01283) 619686
E: theblacksheep@tinyworld.co.uk

FLOWERS, John Henry. b 33. Qu Coll Birm 63. **d** 65 **p** 66. C Aberdare St Fagan *Llan* 65-68; C Llantrisant 68-72; V Nantymoel w Wyndham 72-76; Asst Chapl HM Pris Wormwood Scrubs 76-78; Chapl HM Pris Birm 78-80; Chapl HM Pris Albany 80-93; rtd 93; PtO *Portsm* from 93. *1 Ulster Crescent, Newport PO30 5RU* T: (01983) 525493

FLUX, Brian George. b 39. Oak Hill Th Coll 68. **d** 71 **p** 72. C Chadderton Ch Ch *Man* 71-74; C Preston All SS *Blackb* 74-76; Min Preston St Luke 76-81; CF (TA) from 78; R Higher Openshaw *Man* 81-88; Chapl HM Pris Haverigg 88-92; rtd 92. *65 Crosby Street, Maryport CA15 6DR* T: (01900) 810635

FLYNN, Anna Therese. *See* LINDLEY, Anna Therese

FLYNN, Mrs Diane Mary. b 62. Yorks Min Course. **d** 09 **p** 10. C Roundhay St Edm *Ripon* 09-13; TV Kippax w Allerton Bywater *Leeds* from 13. *St Mary's Rectory, Wakefield Road, Swillington, Leeds LS26 8DS* E: dianeflynn888@btinternet.com

FLYNN, Peter Murray. b 35. Oak Hill Th Coll 76. **d** 79 **p** 80. NSM Finchley St Mary *Lon* 79-83; NSM Mill Hill Jo Keble Ch 84-86; C Mill End and Heronsgate w W Hyde *St Alb* 86-92; V Chessington *Guildf* 92-05; rtd 05; PtO *Roch* from 05. *16 The Street, Plaxtol, Sevenoaks TN15 0QQ* T: (01732) 811304
E: revpeterflynn@yahoo.co.uk

FOALE, Rosemary. *See* MASON, Sheila Rosemary

FOALE, Sheila Rosemary. *See* MASON, Sheila Rosemary

FOBISTER, Mrs Wendy Irene. b 44. Lon Inst of Educn TCert 65. **d** 07 **p** 08. OLM Charminster and Stinsford *Sarum* 07-11; NSM 11-15; PtO from 15. *44 Meadow View, Charminster, Dorchester DT2 9RE* T: (01305) 251681 E: wenfob@gmail.com

FODEN, Mrs Janice Margaret. b 54. Sheff Univ BA 76 Sheff City Poly PGCE 77. NOC 98. **d** 01 **p** 02. NSM Kimberworth *Sheff* 01-05; P-in-c Barnby Dun 05-13; R Armthorpe from 13; AD Doncaster from 10. *The Rectory, Church Street, Armthorpe, Doncaster DN3 3AD* T: (01302) 831231
E: janfoden@hotmail.com *or* jan.foden@sheffield.anglican.org

FODEN-CURRIE, Mary Agnes. b 43. Bp Grosseteste Coll BEd 64. St Jo Coll Nottm MA 97. **d** 98 **p** 99. NSM Skegby *S'well* 98-02; NSM Skegby w Teversal 02-03; rtd 03; PtO *S'well* from 03. *40 Harvey Road, Mansfield NG18 4ES* T: (01623) 479838

FOGDEN, Canon Elizabeth Sally. b 40. MBE 04. MCSP 61. Qu Coll Birm 76. **dss** 78 **d** 87 **p** 94. Chevington w Hargrave and Whepstead w Brockley *St E* 78-84; Honington w Sapiston and Troston 84-92; Par Dn 87-92; Par Dn Euston w Barnham,

Elvedon and Fakenham Magna 90-92; Team Dn Blackbourne 92-94; TV 94-06; Chapl Center Parc Elvedon from 90; Dioc Adv for Women's Min *St E* 90-06; Hon Can St E Cathl 92-06; rtd 06; PtO *St E* from 06. *Meadow Farm, Coney Weston Road, Sapiston, Bury St Edmunds IP31 1RX* T: (01359) 268923 M: 07860-101980

FOGDEN, Mrs Patricia Lily Margaret. b 51. SRN 73. **d** 03 **p** 04. OLM Orlestone w Snave and Ruckinge w Warehorne etc *Cant* 03-10; NSM 10-11; NSM Appledore w Brookland, Fairfield, Brenzett etc 11-13; NSM Wittersham w Stone and Ebony 11-13; C Rother and Oxney from 13; C Tenterden and Smallhythe from 13. *The Vicarage, Appledore, Ashford TN26 2DB* T: (01233) 758250 M: 07885-285636 E: patricia.fogden@btinternet.com

FOGG, Cynthia Mary (Sister Mary Clare). b 34. Bp Grosseteste Coll TCert 54. LNSM course 94. **d** 95 **p** 96. NSM Westgate Common *Wakef* 95-09; rtd 09. *Gadged Well House, 14 Spring End Road, Horbury, Wakefield WF4 6DB*

FOGG, Mrs Margaret. b 37. CBDTI 04. **d** 05 **p** 06. NSM Allonby, Cross Canonby and Dearham *Carl* 05-08; PtO from 08. *Green Pastures, 59 Sycamore Road, Maryport CA15 7AE* T: (01900) 816203 E: margaret.fogg@btinternet.com

FOLEY, Geoffrey Evan. b 30. Univ of New England BA 71 DipEd 73 MEd 79. St Jo Coll Morpeth 51. **d** 53 **p** 54. C Murwillumbah Australia 53-59; R Mallanganee 59-65; R Woodburn 65-72; P-in-c Lismore 84-85; P-in-c Bangalow 87-88; P-in-c Alstonville 88-89; PtO *S'wark* 90-91; Chapl Hamburg w Kiel *Eur* 91; C Stoke-upon-Trent *Lich* 91; rtd 93; PtO Grafton Australia from 93; Dioc Archivist from 97. *198 Dawson Street, Lismore NSW 2480, Australia* T: (0061) (2) 6621 4684 E: gefoley@bigpond.net.au

FOLEY, James Frank. b 50. MBE 91. Reading Univ BSc 72. STETS 03. **d** 99 **p** 00. C St Illogan *Truro* 99-03; P-in-c Droxford and Meonstoke w Corhampton cum Exton *Portsm* 03-08; C Balham Hill Ascension *S'wark* 09-11; rtd 11; P-in-c Lower Sydenham St Mich *S'wark* 11-12; TV Forest Hill w Lower Sydenham from 12. *The Vicarage, Champion Crescent, London SE26 4HH* M: 07545-831961 E: james.stmikes@google.com

✠**FOLEY, The Rt Revd Ronald Graham Gregory.** b 23. St Jo Coll Dur BA 49. **d** 50 **p** 51 **c** 82. C S Shore H Trin *Blackb* 50-54; V Blackb St Luke 54-60; Dir RE *Dur* 60-71; R Brancepeth 60-71; Hon Can Dur Cathl 65-71; Hon Can Ripon Cathl 71-82; V Leeds St Pet 71-82; Chapl to The Queen 77-82; Area Bp Reading *Ox* 82-89; rtd 89; Hon Asst Bp York from 95. *3 Poplar Avenue, Kirkbymoorside, York YO62 6ES* T: (01751) 432439

FOLKARD, Oliver Goring. b 41. Nottm Univ BA 63. Lich Th Coll 64. **d** 66 **p** 67. C Carlton *S'well* 66-67; C Worksop Priory 67-68; C Brewood *Lich* 68-71; C Folkingham w Laughton *Linc* 72-75; P-in-c Gedney Hill 76-77; V 77-84; V Whaplode Drove 76-84; V Sutton St Mary 84-94; RD Elloe E 89-94; P-in-c Scotter w E Ferry 94-99; R 99-06; R Scotton w Northorpe 99-06; rtd 06; PtO *Nor* from 06. *1 Barons Close, Fakenham NR21 8BE* T: (01328) 851468

FOLKS, Andrew John. b 42. St Jo Coll Dur BA 65. Cranmer Hall Dur. **d** 69 **p** 70. C Stranton *Dur* 69-72; Chapl Sandbach Sch 73-80; Chapl Casterton Sch Lancs 80-85; Hd Master Fernhill Manor Sch New Milton 85-97; NSM Langdale *Carl* 97-07; rtd 07; PtO *Leeds* from 09. *10 Winfield Road, Sedbergh LA10 5AZ* T: (01539) 621314 E: folksandrew@yahoo.co.uk

FOLKS, Peter William John. b 30. FRCO 56 ARCM. Launde Abbey 72. **d** 72 **p** 73. C Leic St Aid 72-76; V Newfoundpool 76-84; V Whetstone 84-94; rtd 94; PtO *Leic* from 94. *4 Beaufort Close, Desford, Leicester LE9 9HS* T: (01455) 828090 E: peterfolks@hotmail.com

FOLLETT, Jeremy Mark. b 60. Jes Coll Cam BA 82. St Jo Coll Nottm 90. **d** 91 **p** 92. C Newark *S'well* 91-95; C Hellesdon *Nor* 95-01; V St Alb Ch Ch from 01. *Christ Church Vicarage, 5 High Oaks, St Albans AL3 6DJ* T: (01727) 857592

FOLLETT, Neil Robert Thomas. b 50. RMCS BSc 75 Open Univ BA 85. EAMTC 86. **d** 89 **p** 90. C Godmanchester *Ely* 89-92; V 92-00; V Wilton Place St Paul *Lon* 00; rtd 00. *Address withheld by request*

FOLLIN, Michael Stuart. b 62. UMIST BSc 84. St Jo Coll Nottm MTh 02. **d** 02 **p** 03. C Aughton Ch Ch *Liv* 02-06; TV Maghull 06-09; TV Maghull and Melling from 09. *St Peter's Vicarage, 1 St Peter's Row, Liverpool L31 5LU* T: 0151-526 3434 M: 07813-794252 E: michael.follin@gmail.com

FOLLIS, Bryan Andrew. b 61. Ulster Poly BA 83 QUB PhD 90 TCD BA 98. CITC 95. **d** 98 **p** 99. C Portadown St Mark *Arm* 98-01; I Belfast All SS *Conn* 01-14; I Hillsborough *D & D* from 14. *The Rectory, 17A Dromore Road, Hillsborough BT26 6HS* T: (028) 9268 2949 *or* 9268 8839 M: 07743-549890 E: b.a.follis@hotmail.co.uk

FONTAINE, Mrs Marion Elizabeth. b 39. RN 61 RM 62. SAOMC 96. **d** 99 **p** 00. OLM Thatcham *Ox* from 99. *24 Ferndale Court, Thatcham RG19 4PW* T: (01635) 827746

FOOKS, George Edwin. b 25. Trin Hall Cam BA 49 MA 52 Reading Univ AdDipEd 70. Linc Th Coll 49. **d** 51 **p** 52. C Portsea St Cuth *Portsm* 51-53; C Fareham SS Pet and Paul 53-55; Chapl Earnseat Sch 55-59; V Sheff St Cuth 59-64; Hd Careers Fairfax Gr Sch Bradf 64-66; Hd RE/Careers Buttershaw Comp Sch Bradf 66-70; Counsellor Ifield Sch Crawley 70-73; Hd Guidance Hengrove Sch Bris 73-78; Counsellor w Hearing Impaired Children (Avon) 78-89; PtO *Bris* from 83; Chapl Southmead Hosp Bris 89-90; Chapl Qu Eliz Hosp Bris 90-96; Chapl Thornbury Hosp from 90; rtd 90; PtO *Glouc* 90-97. *26 Rudgeway Park, Rudgeway, Bristol BS35 3RU* T: (01454) 614072

FOOT, Adam Julian David. b 58. Thames Poly BSc 80 Garnett Coll Lon CertEd 87. Trin Coll Bris 93. **d** 97 **p** 98. C Luton Ch Ch *Roch* 97-00; V Welling from 00. *St John's Vicarage, Danson Lane, Welling DA16 2BQ* T: (020) 8303 1107 E: adam.foot@diocese-rochester.org

FOOT, Daniel Henry Paris. b 46. Peterho Cam BA 67 MA 74. Ridley Hall Cam 77. **d** 79 **p** 80. C Werrington *Pet* 79-82; P-in-c Cranford w Grafton Underwood 82; R Cranford w Grafton Underwood and Twywell from 83; P-in-c Slipton from 94. *The Rectory, Rectory Hill, Cranford, Kettering NN14 4AH* T: (01536) 330263 E: katinafoot@gmail.com

FOOT, Daniel James. b 87. Trin Coll Bris 12. **d** 15. C Sandy *St Alb* from 15. *17 Station Road, Sandy SG19 1AW* T: (01767) 449032 E: danieljamesfoot@yahoo.co.uk

FOOT, Elizabeth Victoria Anne. b 55. St Mich Coll Sarum BEd 77. Trin Coll Bris BA 04. **d** 04 **p** 05. C Linkinhorne and Stoke Climsland *Truro* 04-07; C Godrevy 07-08; TV 08-11; P-in-c Zennor from 11; P-in-c Towednack from 11; C Halsetown from 11. *St John's in the Fields, Hellesvean, St Ives TR26 2HG* T: (01736) 794899 E: godrevyvic@hotmail.co.uk

FOOT, Jeremy Michael. b 67. Qu Mary Coll Lon BSc 88. St Mellitus Coll 07. **d** 10 **p** 11. NSM Enfield St Jas *Lon* from 10. *24 St Andrews Road, Enfield EN1 3UB* T: (020) 8366 1456 M: 07725-474769 E: jeremy@thefeet.net *or* jeremy.foot@stjameschurch.cc

FOOT, Joachim Paul Winwaloe. b 85. Collingwood Coll Dur BA 08 K Coll Lon MA 12. Westcott Ho Cam 13. **d** 15. C Duloe, Herodsfoot, Morval and St Pinnock *Truro* from 15. *5 Salter Close, St Martin, Looe PL13 1FE* E: jpwfoot@outlook.com

FOOT, Keith George. b 45. Surrey Univ BSc 70 Lon Univ PhD 73 MRSC CChem. NTMTC 96. **d** 99 **p** 00. C New Thundersley *Chelmsf* 99-03; Min Prince's Park CD *Roch* 03-07; V Prince's Park 07-10; rtd 10; PtO *Roch* from 10. *51 Elmshurst Gardens, Tonbridge TN10 3QT* T: (01732) 365185 E: rev.keith.foot@btinternet.com

FOOT, Lynda. b 43. Reading Univ BEd 75 Loughb Univ MSc 82 Nottm Univ MA 00. EMMTC 97. **d** 00 **p** 01. NSM Coalville and Bardon Hill *Leic* 00-03; NSM Hickling w Kinoulton and Broughton Sulney *S'well* 04-05; NSM Bingham 05-08; rtd 08. *34 White Furrows, Cotgrave, Nottingham NG12 3LD* T: 0115-989 9724 M: 07799-662852 E: lyndafoot@btinternet.com

FOOT, Paul. b 41. Lon Univ BA 64. Chich Th Coll 65. **d** 67 **p** 68. C Portsea N End St Mark *Portsm* 67-72; C Grimsbury *Ox* 72-74; V Cury w Gunwalloe *Truro* 74-80; P-in-c Port Isaac 80-83; P-in-c St Kew 80-83; V St Day 83-91; rtd 95. *Aeaea, 39 New Road, Llandovery SA20 0EA* T: (01550) 720140

FOOTE, Desmond. b 46. S Dios Minl Tr Scheme. **d** 82 **p** 83. NSM Furze Platt *Ox* 82-88; NSM Ruscombe and Twyford 88-05; NSM Woolhampton w Midgham and Beenham Valance 05-08; NSM Aldermaston w Wasing and Brimpton 05-08; NSM Aldermaston and Woolhampton 08-13; rtd 13; PtO *Ox* from 14. *33 Mill Lane, Chinnor OX39 4QU* T: (01844) 355945 E: desfoote@dsl.pipex.com

✠**FOOTTIT, The Rt Revd Anthony Charles.** b 35. K Coll Cam BA 57 MA 70. Cuddesdon Coll 59. **d** 61 **p** 62 **c** 99. C Wymondham *Nor* 61-64; C Blakeney w Lt Langham 64-67; P-in-c Hindringham w Binham and Cockthorpe 67-71; P-in-c Yarlington *B & W* 71-75; R N Cadbury 71-75; P-in-c Sutton Montis 75; TR Camelot Par 76-81; RD Cary 79-81; Dioc Missr *Linc* 81-87; Can and Preb Linc Cathl 86-87; Dioc Rural Officer *Nor* 87; Adn Lynn 87-99; Suff Bp Lynn 99-03; rtd 03; Hon Asst Bp Nor from 04; Dioc Environmental Officer 04-09. *Ivy House, Whitwell Street, Reepham, Norwich NR10 4RA* T: (01603) 870340 E: acfoottit@hotmail.com

FORAN, Andrew John. b 55. Aston Tr Scheme 84 Linc Th Coll 86. **d** 88 **p** 89. C Epping St Jo *Chelmsf* 88-92; TV Canvey Is 92-97; C Dorking w Ranmore *Guildf* 97-99; Chapl HM Pris Send 97-09; Chapl HM Pris Bullingdon from 09. *HM Prison Bullingdon, PO Box 50, Bicester OX25 1PZ* T: (01869) 353100 E: andrew.foran@hmps.gsi.gov.uk

FORBES, Mrs Angela Laura. b 47. Ox Min Course 91. **d** 94 **p** 96. NSM Cowley St Jo *Ox* 94-04; PtO from 04. *6 Elm Crescent, Charlbury, Chipping Norton OX7 3PZ* T: (01608) 819121

FORBES, The Very Revd Graham John Thompson. b 51. CBE 04. Aber Univ MA 73 Edin Univ BD 76. Edin Th Coll 73. **d** 76 **p** 77. C Edin Old St Paul 76-82; Can St Ninian's Cathl Perth 82-90; R Stanley 82-88; Provost St Ninian's Cathl Perth 82-90; R Perth St Ninian 82-90; Provost St Mary's Cathl from 90; R Edin St Mary from 90. *8 Lansdowne Crescent, Edinburgh EH12 5EQ* T: 0131-225 2978 *or* 225 6293 M: 07711-199297 F: 226 1482 *or* 225 3181 E: provost@cathedral.net

FORBES, Iain William. b 56. Ex Univ BA 81. Chich Th Coll 83. **d** 85 **p** 86. C Upper Norwood St Jo *S'wark* 85-88; C Lewisham St Mary 88-90; Chapl St Martin's Coll of Educn *Blackb* 90-94; P-in-c Woodplumpton 94-99; Dioc Voc Adv 94-99; V Woodham *Guildf* from 99. *The Vicarage, 25 Woodham Waye, Woking GU21 5SW* T: (01483) 762857 E: fatheriainforbes@aol.com

FORBES, Canon John Francis. b 29. CITC 85. **d** 88 **p** 90. Aux Min Ferns w Kilbride, Toombe, Kilcormack etc *C & O* 88-04; Treas Ferns Cathl 98-03; rtd 04. *Ballinabarna House, Enniscorthy, Co Wexford, Republic of Ireland* T: (00353) (53) 923 3353 M: 87-237 9319

FORBES, Canon John Franey. b 33. AKC 57. **d** 58 **p** 59. C Darlington H Trin *Dur* 58-62; C St Geo Cathl Cape Town S Africa 62-65; R Hoedjies Bay 65-69; Warden Zonnebloem Coll Cape Town 69-75; Dean Pietermaritzburg 76-03; rtd 03. *PO Box 481, Noordhoek, 7979 South Africa* T/F: (0027) (21) 789 2227

FORBES, Canon Joyce Brinella. b 52. **d** 03 **p** 04. OLM Norbury St Steph and Thornton Heath *S'wark* from 03; Hon Can S'wark Cathl from 14. *36 Dalmeny Avenue, London SW16 4RT* T: (020) 8240 0283 *or* 7525 7982 E: petnard36@aol.com

FORBES, Patrick. b 38. Open Univ BA 82. Linc Th Coll 64. **d** 66 **p** 67. C Yeovil *B & W* 66-69; C Plumstead Wm Temple Ch Abbey Wood CD *S'wark* 69-70; Thameshead Ecum Gp 70-73; TV Thameshead *S'wark* 73-78; Dioc Communications Officer *St Alb* 78-90; P-in-c Offley w Lilley 78-82; Info Officer Communications Dept CA Ho Lon 91-95; Press Officer Miss to Seamen 95-99; rtd 99; PtO *St Alb* from 04. *18 Francis Road, Hinxworth, Baldock SG7 5HL* T: (01462) 742015 E: fool1@patrickforbes.plus.com

FORBES, Raymond John. b 34. ALCD 58. **d** 58 **p** 59. C Wandsworth St Steph *S'wark* 58-61; C Kewstoke *B & W* 61-63; V Fordcombe *Roch* 63-73; R Ashurst 64-73; P-in-c Morden w Almer and Charborough *Sarum* 73-76; P-in-c Bloxworth 73-76; V Red Post 76-84; P-in-c Hamworthy 84-92; P-in-c Symondsbury and Chideock 92-96; rtd 96; PtO *Sarum* from 96. *3 Shelley Court, Library Road, Ferndown BH22 9JZ* T: (01202) 897567

FORBES, Stuart. b 33. Lon Univ BD 59. Oak Hill Th Coll 56. **d** 61 **p** 62. C Halliwell St Pet *Man* 61-64; P-in-c Wicker w Neepsend *Sheff* 64-69; V Stainforth 69-77; V Salterhebble All SS *Wakef* 77-89; V Toxteth Park St Mich w St Andr *Liv* 89-98; rtd 98; PtO *Lich* from 00. *29 Firbeck Gardens, Wildwood, Stafford ST17 4QR* T: (01785) 663658

FORBES, Susan Margaret. *See* VAN BEVEREN, Susan Margaret

FORBES ADAM, Sir Stephen Timothy Beilby Bt. b 23. Ball Coll Ox. Chich Th Coll 59. **d** 61 **p** 62. C Guisborough *York* 61-64; R Barton in Fabis *S'well* 64-70; V Thrumpton 65-70; P-in-c S Stoke *B & W* 74-81; C Combe Down w Monkton Combe w Stoke 81-83; PtO 83-86; *Ox* 86-87; NSM Epwell w Sibford, Swalcliffe and Tadmarton 87-92; rtd 88; PtO *York* 88-11. *Woodhouse Farm, Escrick, York YO19 6HT* T: (01904) 878827

FORBES STONE, Elizabeth Karen (Buff). b 61. Birm Univ MB, ChB 85 MRCGP 89. Ridley Hall Cam BA 99. **d** 00 **p** 01. C Brentford Lon 00-02; C Shaw cum Donnington *Ox* 02-08; Chapl R Berks NHS Foundn Trust 09-10; PtO *Cov* 10-12; C Cov St Fran N Radford from 12. *55 Cotswold Drive, Coventry CV3 6EZ* T: (024) 7641 9831 M: 07954-652824 E: buff@dandb.org.uk

FORCE-JONES, Graham Roland John. b 41. Sarum Th Coll 65. **d** 68 **p** 69. C Calne and Blackland *Sarum* 68-73; TV Oldbury 73-78; R 78-80; TR Upper Kennet 80-94; RD Marlborough 90-94; P-in-c Atworth w Shaw and Whitley 94-06; Chapl Stonar Sch Melksham 01-06; rtd 06. *Le Petit Cormy, 86700 Vaux-en-Couche, France*

FORD, Adam. b 40. Lanc Univ MA 72 K Coll Lon BD 63 AKC 63. **d** 65 **p** 65. C Cirencester *Glouc* 65-70; V Hebden Bridge *Wakef* 70-76; Chapl St Paul's Girls' Sch Hammersmith 77-01; LtO *Lon* 77-98; P in o 84-91; rtd 05. *Bramble, Weaver's Lane, Alfriston BN26 5TH* E: adamfordspgs@hotmail.com

FORD, Alun James. b 73. Ex Univ BA 94 MA 96 Man Univ PhD 09 St Jo Coll Cam BA 11. Westcott Ho Cam 08. **d** 11 **p** 12. C Newc St Geo and St Hilda 11-14; V Sugley from 14. *Sugley Vicarage, Sugley Village, Lemington, Newcastle upon Tyne NE15 8RD* T: 0191-267 4633 E: alun.ford@gmail.com

FORD, Canon Amanda Kirstine. b 61. Middx Univ BA 83 Open Univ MA 97. St Steph Ho Ox 98. **d** 00 **p** 01. C Leic Resurr 00-05; P-in-c Beaumont Leys 05-09; V 09-14; P-in-c Stocking Farm 11-14; AD City of Leic 11-14; Dioc CUF Officer 04-14; Hon Can Leic Cathl 13-14; Can Res and Chan S'wark Cathl from 14; Dir Minl Educn from 14. *483C Southwark Park Road, London SE16 2JP* E: mandyford@btinternet.com

FORD, Anthony. b 60. Oak Hill Th Coll 06. **d** 08 **p** 09. C Chadderton Ch Ch *Man* 08-11; P-in-c Balderstone 11-13; V from 13. *St Mary's Vicarage, The Sett, Badger Lane, Rochdale OL16 4RQ* T: (01706) 649886 M: 07816-596878 E: tonyford227@btinternet.com

FORD, Mrs Avril Celia. b 43. St Mary's Coll Dur BSc 64 Chelsea Coll Lon PGCE 65. **d** 92 **p** 94. OLM Horncastle w Low Toynton *Linc* 92-98; NSM 98-06; OLM High Toynton 92-98; NSM 98-06; OLM Greetham w Ashby Puerorum 92-98; NSM 98-06; NSM Horncastle Gp from 06. *Frolic, Reindeer Close, Horncastle LN9 5AA* T: (01507) 526234 *or* 525600

FORD, Brian. b 40. OBE 89. Imp Coll Lon BSc 62 Nottm Univ MSc 66 PhD 74 Ox Univ MA 74 CMath FIMA ARCS. SAOMC 96. **d** 99 **p** 00. NSM Witney Ox 99-02; NSM Forest Edge 02-15; rtd 15; PtO *Ox* from 15. *Ramsden Farmhouse, Ramsden, Oxford OX7 3AU* T: (01993) 868343 F: 868322 E: brian@nag.co.uk

FORD, Mrs Carol Mary. b 67. NUI BA 88 HDipEd 89 Lon Inst of Educn MA 07 St Jo Coll Dur BA 13. Cranmer Hall Dur 11. **d** 13 **p** 14. C Cowgate *Newc* from 13. *Sugley Vicarage, Sugley Drive, Lemington, Newcastle upon Tyne NE15 8RD* T: 0191-267 4633 E: cmuford@yahoo.co.uk

FORD (née HARRISON-WATSON), Mrs Carole. b 44. Reading Univ BSc 66 St Martin's Coll Lanc PGCE 79. Carl Dioc Tr Inst 92. **d** 95 **p** 96. NSM Windermere *Carl* 95-98; NSM Borrowdale 98-01; NSM Thornthwaite cum Braithwaite, Newlands etc 01-05; rtd 05; PtO *Carl* from 05. *Croft View, Low Lorton, Cockermouth CA13 9UW* T: (01900) 85519

FORD, Canon Christopher Simon. b 51. Leeds Univ MPhil 86 PhD 91. AKC 74. **d** 75 **p** 76. C Wythenshawe Wm Temple Ch *Man* 75-77; C New Bury 77-80; R Old Trafford St Jo 80-94; R Moston St Jo 94-05; P-in-c Davyhulme St Mary 05-09; V from 09; Bp's Adv on Archives from 93; AD N Man 94-00; Hon Can Man Cathl from 04; Borough Dean Trafford from 11. *St Mary's Vicarage, 13 Vicarage Road, Urmston, Manchester M41 5TP* T: 0161-748 2210 E: christopher.ford5@btinternet.com

FORD, David John. b 38. Lon Coll of Div BD 68. **d** 69 **p** 70. C Blackheath St Jo *S'wark* 69-71; C Westlands St Andr *Lich* 71-75; V Sheff St Steph w St Phil and St Ann 75-77; R Netherthorpe 77-80; TR 80-84; R Thrybergh 82-84; R Thrybergh w Hooton Roberts 84-94; Ind Chapl 86-87; TV Parkham, Alwington, Buckland Brewer etc *Ex* 94-01; r-d 03; Hon C Knaresborough *Ripon* 01-05; PtO *York* from 07. *10 Grove Hill Road, Filey YO14 9NL* T: (01723) 518292 E: shielandavid@4afairworld.co.uk

FORD, David Stuart. b 61. City of Lon Poly BA 82 Qu Coll Birm MA 09. WMMTC 06. **d** 09 **p** 10. C Bramhope and Ireland Wood *Ripon* 09-10; C Leeds City 10-11; Chapl Chapl Abbey Grange High Sch 09-11; TV Hucknall Torkard *S'well* 11-14; Chapl Nat C of E Academy Hucknall 11-14; P-in-c Northleach w Hampnett and Farmington etc *Glouc* from 14. *The Vicarage, Northleach, Cheltenham GL54 3HL* M: 07973-412625 E: revdavidford09@googlemail.com

FORD, Mrs Deborah Perrin. b 59. Leeds Univ BA 81 Birm Univ MSocSc 85 Univ of Wales (Ban) BTh CQSW 85. EAMTC 00. **d** 03 **p** 04. NSM Cambridge St Benedict *Ely* 03-12; NSM Cambridge St Jas from 12; Chapl Cam Univ Hosps NHS Foundn Trust from 03. *102 Millington Lane, Cambridge CB3 9HA* T: (01223) 329321 *or* 363113 E: debbie.ford@addenbrookes.nhs.uk

FORD, Derek Ernest. b 32. St Mich Coll Llan 56. **d** 58 **p** 59. C Roath St Martin *Llan* 58-61; C Newton Nottage 61-67; V Abercanaid 67-70; PtO *Win* 70-80; SSF from 72; LtO *Sarum* 73-80; *Newc* 75-80; USA from 80; Min Prov American Province SSF 02-05; P-in-c Siparia Trinidad and Tobago 06-09. *St Francis' Friary, 2449 Sichel Street, Los Angeles CA 90031, USA* E: broderekssf@aol.com

FORD, Canon Henry Malcolm. b 33. Em Coll Cam BA 54 MA 58. Ely Th Coll 58. **d** 59 **p** 69. C Ipswich St Matt *St E* 59-61; Hon C Bury St Edmunds St Jo 66-76; Hon C Hawstead and Nowton w Stanningfield etc 76-89; Hon Can St E Cathl 86-97; NSM Cockfield w Bradfield St Clare, Felsham etc 89-98; PtO from 09. *Thatch on the Green, Cross Green, Cockfield, Bury St Edmunds IP30 0LG* T: (01284) 828479

FORD, John. *See* FORD, William John

✠**FORD, The Rt Revd John Frank.** b 52. Chich Univ MA 04. Chich Th Coll 76. **d** 79 **p** 80 **c** 05. C Forest Hill Ch Ch *S'wark* 79-82; V Lee St Aug 82-91; V Lower Beeding and Dom Chapl to Bp Horsham *Chich* 91-94; Dioc Missr 94-00; Can and Preb Chich Cathl 97-00; Can Res and Prec Chich Cathl 00-05; Suff Bp Plymouth *Ex* 05-13; Asst Bp Truro 11-13; Bp The Murray Australia from 13. *Diocese of The Murray, PO Box 394, Murray Bridge SA 5253, Australia* T: (0061) (8) 8532 2270 F: 8532 5760 E: registry@murray.anglican.org

FORD, Jonathan Laurence. *See* ALDERTON-FORD, Jonathan Laurence

FORD, Joyce. b 42. Qu Coll Birm 97. **d** 00 **p** 01. NSM Bentley *Lich* 00-04; NSM Wednesfield 04-06; PtO from 07. *33 Bowness Grove, Willenhall WV12 5DB* T: (01922) 408420

FORD, Mrs Kimberley Kaye. b 65. St Jo Coll Nottm 09. **d** 11 **p** 12. C Market Harborough and The Transfiguration etc *Leic* 11-14; P-in-c Glen Magna cum Stretton Magna etc from 14. *St Cuthbert's Vicarage, Church Road, Great Glen, Leicester LE8 9FE* E: kimberleykford@aim.com

FORD, Michael Andrew. Bris Univ BA 87 Liv Univ PhD 02. Ripon Coll Cuddesdon 11. **d** 12. C E Clevedon w Clapton in Gordano etc *B & W* 12-13; C Taunton H Trin 13. *Address withheld by request* M: 07967-181810 E: frmichaelford@gmail.com

FORD, Nancy Celia. b 48. Open Univ BA 02 FCIPD 00. STETS 98. **d** 01 **p** 02. NSM Crookham *Guildf* 01-04; NSM Aldershot St Mich 04-07; Asst Dioc Dir of Ords 04-05; Bp's Chapl 05-10; rtd 10; Min Can Guildf Cathl 07-14. *40 Orchard Avenue, Worthing BN14 7QB* T: (01903) 411523 E: nancyc.ford@sky.com

FORD, Peter. b 46. York Univ MA 96 Bede Coll Dur TCert 72 ACP 75. Linc Th Coll 76. **d** 78 **p** 79. OGS from 72; C Hartlepool H Trin *Dur* 78-81; Dioc Youth Officer *Wakef* 81-84; C Mirfield Eastthorpe St Paul 82-84; C Upper Hopton 82-84; V Dodworth 84-88; Chapl and Hd RS Rishworth Sch Ripponden 88-97; Ho Master 94-97; P-in-c Accrington St Mary *Blackb* 97-99; C Torrisholme 99-01; V Warton St Paul 01-08; Dioc Ecum Officer 01-08; Germany 08-09; P-in-c Las Palmas *Eur* 09-13; P-in-c Oporto 13; rtd 13. *Edificio Carlita 5F, Paseo de Maritimo 84, Los Boliches, 29640 Fuengirola, Spain* E: pford@ogs.net

FORD, Canon Peter Hugh. b 43. St Cath Coll Cam BA 65 MA 69. Cuddesdon Coll 65. **d** 67 **p** 68. C Is of Dogs Ch Ch and St Jo w St Luke *Lon* 67-70; C Tillsonburg St Jo Canada 70-71; St Catherine's St Thos 71-73; P-in-c Thorold South Resurr 71-73; R Port Colborne St Brendan 73-78; R Milton Grace Ch 78-80; Can Pastor Ch Ch Cathl Hamilton 80-86; Adn Lincoln 86-91; R Niagara-on-the-Lake St Mark 86-91; Hon Chapl Niagara from 91; Hon C Montserrat St Geo Canada 91; R Saba 92-98; PtO *Chich* 98-99; V Newchurch and Arreton *Portsm* 99-07; rtd 07. *11 Vokins Rise, Esplanade, Ryde PO33 2AX* T: (01983) 568286 E: islandpeter@btinternet.com

FORD, Richard. b 47. Grey Coll Dur BA 69 PGCE 70 FRSA 94. SEITE 06. **d** 09 **p** 10. NSM Sanderstead *S'wark* 09-15; NSM W Wickham St Fran and St Mary from 15; NSM W Wickham St Jo from 15. *7 Sylvan Way, West Wickham BR4 9HA* T: (020) 8289 2432 M: 07706-998272 E: richard.ford73@ntlworld.com

FORD, Richard Graham. b 39. AKC 65 Open Univ BA 96. **d** 66 **p** 67. C Morpeth *Newc* 66-71; C Fordingbridge w Ibsley *Win* 71-73; TV Whorlton *Newc* 73-80; Chapl RNR 75-92; V Choppington *Newc* 80-92; V Tynemouth Priory 92-04; rtd 04. *43 Farriers Rise, Shilbottle, Alnwick NE66 2EN* T: (01665) 581115

FORD, Roger James. b 33. Sarum & Wells Th Coll 81. **d** 83 **p** 84. C Sidcup St Jo *Roch* 83-86; V Dartford 86-98; rtd 98; PtO *Cov* 02-04. *21 Hawthorn Way, Shipston-on-Stour CV36 4FD* T: (01608) 664875 E: roger585413@gmail.com

FORD, Roger Lindsay. b 47. Ex Univ LLB 68. Llan Dioc Tr Scheme 87. **d** 91 **p** 92. NSM Fairwater *Llan* 91-96; NSM Llandaff 96-01; NSM Arthog w Fairbourne w Llangelynnin w Rhoslefain *Ban* 12-14; NSM Bro Cymer from 14. *The Rectory, Llwyngwril LL37 2JB* T: (01341) 250888 E: lindsayrectory@hotmail.org.uk

FORD, Mrs Shirley Elsworth. b 40. AIMLS 67. Sarum & Wells Th Coll 89. **d** 91 **p** 94. C Farnham *Guildf* 91-96; V Wrecclesham 96-04; rtd 04; PtO *Chich* from 05. *North House, Queen's Park Mews, Queen's Park Rise, Brighton BN2 9YY* T: (01273) 674061

FORD, Simone Louise. *See* BENNETT, Simone Louise

FORD, Canon William John. b 50. Linc Th Coll 89. **d** 91 **p** 92. C Marton-in-Cleveland *York* 91-94; V Whorlton w Carlton and Faceby 94-02; P-in-c Stainton w Hilton 02-12; P-in-c Brookfield 11-12; R Yarm from 12; RD Stokesley from 03; Can and Preb York Minster from 13. *The Rectory, 6 Westgate, Yarm TS15 9QT* T: (01642) 964664 E: revjohnford@sky.com

FORDE, Barry George. **d** 07 **p** 08. C Coleraine *Conn* 07-10; Chapl and Dean of Residence QUB from 10. *20 Elmwood Avenue, Belfast BT9 6AY* T: (028) 9066 7754 or 9573 5980 E: barry@thehubbelfast.org

FORDE, The Ven Stephen Bernard. b 61. Edin Univ BSc. TCD Div Sch. **d** 86 **p** 87. C Belfast St Mary w H Redeemer *Conn* 86-89; Chapl QUB 89-95; Min Can Belf Cathl 89-91; Bp's Dom Chapl *Conn* 90-95; I Dublin Booterstown *D & G* 95-99; Dean of Res UCD 95-99; I Larne and Inver *Conn* from 99; I Glynn w Raloo from 99; Adn Dalriada from 06. *The Rectory, 8 Lower Cairncastle Road, Larne BT40 1PQ* T: (028) 2827 2788 or 2827 4633 E: stephenforde@btinternet.com

FORDHAM, Richard George. b 34. AIMarE 60 TEng(CEI) 71 FBIM 74. **d** 91 **p** 92. NSM Cookham *Ox* 91-94; NSM Hedsor and Bourne End 94-01; PtO 01-03; *Ely* from 03. *6 Sorrel Way, Downham Market PE38 9UD* T: (01366) 384271 E: richardfordham939@btinternet.com

FORD-WHITCOMBE, William. *See* WHITCOMBE, William Ashley

FORDYCE, Andrew Ian. b 70. K Alfred's Coll Win BA 94 Southn Univ PGCE 96. Trin Coll Bris BA 03. **d** 03 **p** 04. C Bramshott and Liphook *Portsm* 03-07; V Berechurch St Marg w St Mich *Chelmsf* from 07. *The Vicarage, 348 Mersea Road, Colchester CO2 8RA* T: (01206) 576859 M: 07790-543304 E: revdyce@googlemail.com

FOREMAN, Canon Patrick Brian. b 41. CertEd. St Jo Coll Nottm 77. **d** 79 **p** 80. C Gainsborough All SS *Linc* 79-83; V Thornton St Jas *Bradf* 83-91; R Hevingham w Hainford and Stratton Strawless *Nor* 91-99; RD Ingworth 94-99; V Heacham 99-06; Hon Can Nor Cathl 03-06; rtd 06; PtO *Nor* 06-14; RD Burnham and Walsingham from 14; Bp's Officer for Rtd Clergy and Widows 08-15. *Seorah, 7 Mallard Close, Fakenham NR21 8PU* T: (01328) 853691 E: patrick@pandmforeman.eclipse.co.uk

FOREMAN, Mrs Penelope. b 47. Lon Inst of Educn TCert 68 Ch Ch Coll Cant BEd 90 MA 93. SEITE 04. **d** 06 **p** 07. NSM Roch St Justus 06-15; P-in-c Chatham St Mary w St Jo from 15; AD Roch from 14. *28 Kingsway, Chatham ME5 7HT* T: (01634) 571220 E: penny.foreman@btinternet.com

FOREMAN, Timothy. b 56. K Coll Lon BD 77. SEITE 97. **d** 99 **p** 00. C Camberwell St Giles w St Matt *S'wark* 99-02; R Buckland-in-Dover *Cant* 02-13; Hon Min Can Cant Cathl 04-13; V Walker *Newc* from 13. *Walker Vicarage, Middle Street, Newcastle upon Tyne NE6 4DB* T: 0191-262 3666 E: fr.timforeman@gmail.com

FORESHEW-CAIN, Andrew David. b 63. Aber Univ BSc 86. Ripon Coll Cuddesdon BA 89. **d** 90 **p** 91. C Walworth St Jo *S'wark* 90-94; Bp's Dom Chapl *Ox* 94-98; P-in-c Kilburn St Mary w All So *Lon* 98-01; P-in-c W Hampstead St Jas 98-01; V Kilburn St Mary w All So and W Hampstead St Jas from 01; AD N Camden 07-14. *St Mary's Vicarage, 134A Abbey Road, London NW6 4SN* T/F: (020) 7624 5434 E: vicaragekilburn@btopenworld.com

FORGAN, Eleanor. b 44. St Andr Univ MA 66 Aber Univ DipEd 67. St And Dioc Tr Course. **d** 89 **p** 95. NSM Alloa *St And* from 89. *18 Alexandra Drive, Alloa FK10 2DQ* T: (01259) 212836 E: eleanor.forgan@btinternet.com

FORMAN, Alastair Gordon. b 48. St Jo Coll Nottm 78. **d** 80 **p** 81. C Pennycross *Ex* 80-83; C Woking St Jo *Guildf* 83-88; V Luton Lewsey St Hugh *St Alb* 88-95; P-in-c Jersey Millbrook St Matt *Win* 95-01; P-in-c Jersey St Lawr 95-01; PtO from 14. *5 Riverdale, Wrecclesham, Farnham GU10 4PH* T: (01252) 712546 E: alastair.forman@gmail.com

FORMAN, Carolyn Dawn. b 45. SEITE. **d** 07 **p** 08. NSM Meopham w Nurstead *Roch* from 07. *Aysgarth, White Hill Road, Meopham, Gravesend DA13 0NZ* T: (01474) 812373 E: acform@btinternet.com

FORMAN, Deborah Jayne. b 56. LMH Ox BA 78 MA 83 PGCE 79 Lambeth STh 07. STETS 05. **d** 08 **p** 09. C Churchdown St Jo and Innsworth *Glouc* 08-11; P-in-c Pebworth, Dorsington, Honeybourne etc 11-14; C Quinton and Welford w Weston 11-14; TV Vale and Cotswold Edge from 14. *The Vicarage, Stratford Road, Honeybourne, Evesham WR11 5PP* T: (01386) 830302 M: 07985-943371 E: deborah.forman2@btinternet.com

FORRER, Michael Dennett Cuthbert. b 34. St Pet Hall Ox BA 59 MA 63. Wycliffe Hall Ox 59. **d** 60 **p** 61. C Westwood *Cov* 60-63; C Cov Cathl 63-71; Ind Chapl 63-69; Sen Ind Chapl 69-71; Hon C All Hallows by the Tower etc *Lon* 76-99; Asst P Bangkok Ch Ch Thailand 81-89; PtO *Sarum* from 99; *Ox* 01-02 and from 11; Hon C Sonning 02-11; rtd 04. *36 Ravensbourne Drive, Woodley, Reading RG5 4LJ* M: 07899-926020

FORREST, Antony William. b 60. Imp Coll Lon BSc 82 Sussex Univ PGCE 83 Leic Univ MBA 06 Win Univ MA 12 ARCS 82 FCollP 08. STETS 08. **d** 11 **p** 12. C Portsea N End St Mark *Portsm* 11-15; Chapl Portsm Coll 12-15; R Meon Bridge *Portsm* from 15. *The Rectory, Rectory Lane, Meonstoke, Southampton SO32 3NF*

FORREST, The Very Revd Leslie David Arthur. b 46. TCD BA 68 MA 86. CITC 70. **d** 70 **p** 71. C Conwall *D & R* 70-73;

I Tullyaughnish 73-80; I Galway w Kilcummin *T, K & A* 80-95; Dir of Ords 84-95; Can Tuam Cathl 86-95; Provost Tuam 91-95; Dean Ferns *C & O* 95-11; I Ferns w Kilbride, Toombe, Kilcormack etc 95-11; Preb Tassagard St Patr Cathl Dublin 91-11; rtd 11. *Tassagard, Coolamurry, Davidstown, Enniscorthy, Co Wexford, Republic of Ireland* T: (00353) (53) 923 0651
E: ldaforrest@eircom.net

FORREST, Michael Barry Eric. b 38. Lon Univ BA 87 MA 89. NZ Bd of Th Studies LTh 62 Chich Th Coll 64. **d** 66 **p** 67. C Beckenham St Jas *Roch* 66-70; P-in-c Cape Vogel Papua New Guinea 70-73; P-in-c Alotau 74; R Lae 74-76; C Altarnon and Bolventor *Truro* 76-78; TV N Hill w Altarnon, Bolventor and Lewannick 78-79; R St Martin w E and W Looe 79-84; V Kensington St Phil Earl's Court *Lon* 84-04; rtd 04; PtO *Chich* from 04. *12 Riley Road, Brighton BN2 4AH* T: (01273) 690231

FORREST, Canon Robin Whyte. b 33. Edin Th Coll 58. **d** 61 **p** 62. C Glas St Mary 61-66; R Renfrew 66-70; R Motherwell 70-79; R Wishaw 75-79; R Forres *Mor* 79-98; R Nairn 79-92; Can St Andr Cathl Inverness 88-98; Hon Can St Andr Cathl Inverness from 98; Syn Clerk 91-92; Dean Mor 92-98; rtd 98. *Landeck, Cummingston, Elgin IV30 5XY*
T/F: (01343) 835539 E: robin.forrest33@btinternet.com

FORREST-REDFERN, Mrs Susan Michéle. b 57. S Bank Poly BEd 86. St Jo Coll Nottm 01. **d** 03 **p** 04. C Lostock St Thos and St Jo *Man* 03-06; C Bolton St Bede 05-06; Ch/Sch Missr E Bolton from 06; C Tonge Fold 07-10; Chapl St Cath Academy Bolton from 11. *7 Alford Close, Bolton BL2 6NR*
E: revsuefr@yahoo.co.uk

FORRESTER, Ian Michael. b 56. Chich Th Coll. **d** 82 **p** 83. C Leigh-on-Sea St Marg *Chelmsf* 82-84; Min Can, Succ and Dean's V Windsor 84-86; Prec and Chapl Chelmsf Cathl 86-91; Chapl Lancing Coll 91-99; P-in-c Boxgrove *Chich* from 99; Dioc Liturgy and Music Consultant from 95. *The Vicarage, Boxgrove, Chichester PO18 0ED* T: (01243) 774045
E: iforrester@hotmail.com

FORRESTER, James Oliphant. b 50. SS Coll Cam BA 72 MA 76. Wycliffe Hall Ox 73. **d** 76 **p** 77. C Hull St Jo Newland *York* 76-80; C Fulwood *Sheff* 80-87; V Lodge Moor St Luke 87-90; V Ecclesfield 90-01; AD 99-01; P-in-c Kingston upon Hull H Trin *York* 01-02; V and Lect 02-09; V Longnor, Quarnford and Sheen *Lich* from 09; RD Alstonfield from 12. *The Vicarage, Gauledge Lane, Longnor, Buxton SK17 0PA* T: (01298) 83742

FORRESTER, Matthew Agnew. b 31. Univ of Wales (Cardiff) BA 64. Trin Coll Bris 70. **d** 72 **p** 73. C Tonbridge SS Pet and Paul *Roch* 72-77; Chapl Elstree Sch Woolhampton 77-78; Chapl Duke of York's R Mil Sch Dover 78-96; rtd 96; PtO *Cant* 96-12. *4 Abbots Place, Canterbury CT1 2AH* T: (01227) 458882

FORRESTER, Robin William. b 43. Kent Univ MA 84 Aston Univ MSc 90. All Nations Chr Coll 64. **d** 04 **p** 05. NSM Wharton *Ches* 04-06; P-in-c Moulton 06-11; rtd 11; PtO *Ches* from 11. *27 Levens Avenue, Winsford CW7 3TA* T: (01606) 215248
E: robin.forrester@tiscali.co.uk

FORRYAN, Thomas Quested. b 64. Pemb Coll Cam BA 85. Wycliffe Hall Ox 87. **d** 90 **p** 91. C Cheadle Hulme St Andr *Ches* 90-93; C Aberavon *Llan* 93-94; UCCF 94-98. *1 Grosvenor Road, Watford WD1 2QS*

FORSDIKE, Alan William. b 55. **d** 05 **p** 06. NSM Westerfield and Tuddenham w Witnesham *St E* from 05. *Hill House, 2 Henley Road, Ipswich IP1 3SF* T: (01473) 252904
E: alan.forsdike@btinternet.com

FORSDIKE, Mrs Catherine Agnes. b 57. **d** 10 **p** 11. OLM Westerfield and Tuddenham w Witnesham *St E* 10-13; NSM from 13. *2 Henley Road, Ipswich IP1 3SF* T: (01473) 252904

FORSE, Reginald Austin. b 43. Oak Hill Th Coll 77. **d** 79 **p** 80. C Crofton *Portsm* 79-84; NSM Purbrook *Portsm* Ch Ch 91-96; NSM Alverstoke 96-13; PtO from 13. *40 Osprey Gardens, Lee-on-the-Solent PO13 8LJ* T: (023) 9255 3395 E: regforse@yahoo.co.uk

FORSHAW, David Oliver. b 27. Trin Coll Cam BA 50 MA 52. Qu Coll Birm. **d** 53 **p** 54. C Glen Parva and S Wigston *Leic* 53-55; Singapore 55-59; V Heptonstall *Wakef* 59-66; V Whitehaven St Nic *Carl* 66-76; P-in-c Whitehaven Ch Ch w H Trin 73-76; V Benchill *Man* 76-89; C Elton All SS 89-92; rtd 92; PtO *Carl* from 92. *Tynashee, Church Street, Broughton-in-Furness LA20 6HJ* T: (01229) 716068

FORSHAW, Mrs Frances Ann. b 52. Edin Univ BSc 74 Glas Univ MN 91 RGN 76 SCM 78. Moray Ord Course 91. **d** 98 **p** 02. NSM Elgin w Lossiemouth *Mor* 98-01; NSM Perth St Jo *St And* 01-05; P-in-c Pitlochry and Kilmaveonaig 05-09; NSM St Ninian's Cathl Perth 09-10; Miss P Fochabers *Mor* from 11. *40 Castle Street, Fochabers IV32 7DW* T: (01343) 829094
E: jandfforshaw@tiscali.co.uk *or* gordonchapel@btinternet.com

FORSHAW, Janet Elisabeth. *See* BUFTON, Janet Elisabeth

FORSHAW, Mrs Susan Margaret. b 47. Man Univ BSc 68 Makerere Univ Kampala DipEd 69. EMMTC 82. **dss** 82 **d** 87 **p** 95. Cinderhill *S'well* 82-85; Dioc Adv in Adult Educn 85-92;

Par Dn Nottingham St Mary and St Cath 93-95; Lect 95-97; Asst Chapl Qu Medical Cen Nottm Univ Hosp NHS Trust 97-03; Sen Chapl 03-07; rtd 07; PtO *Leic* from 08. *33 Upton Close, Millers Reach, Castle Donington, Derby DE74 2GN*
T: (01332) 858267 E: susanforshaw@talktalk.net

FORSTER, The Ven Andrew James. QUB BA 89. CITC BTh 92. **d** 92 **p** 93. C Willowfield *D & D* 92-95; Dean of Res QUB 95-02; C of I Adv Downtown Radio Newtownards 96-02; I Drumcliffe w Lissadell and Munninane *K, E & A* 02-07; Adn Elphin and Ardagh 02-07; I Drumglass w Moygashel *Arm* from 07; Adn Ardboe from 15. *The Rectory, 26 Circular Road, Dungannon BT71 6BE* T: (028) 8772 2614
E: drumglass@armagh.anglican.org

FORSTER, Gregory Stuart. b 47. Worc Coll Ox BA 69 MA 73. Wycliffe Hall Ox 69. **d** 72 **p** 73. C Bath Walcot *B & W* 72-74; C Bolton Em *Man* 74-76; C Bolton St Paul w Em 77-79; R Northenden from 79. *The Rectory, Ford Lane, Northenden, Manchester M22 4NQ* T: 0161-998 2615
E: gsfm22@tiscali.co.uk

FORSTER, Ian Duncan. b 51. St Mich Coll Llan 95. **d** 97 **p** 98. C Lampeter Pont Steffan w Silian *St D* 97-00; C Llandysul w Bangor Teifi and Llanfairollwyn etc 00-03; V Llangrannog w Llandysiliogogo w Penbryn 03-10; TV Hawarden *St As* 10-14; rtd 14. *11 Maesafallon, Penegoes, Machynlleth SY20 8PB*
T: (01654) 702910

FORSTER, Kenneth. b 27. St Jo Coll Cam BA 50 MA 52 Salford Univ MSc 77 PhD 80. NEOC 83. **d** 86 **p** 87. NSM Hessle *York* 86-92; Chapl Humberside Univ 87-92; rtd 92; NSM Hull St Mary Sculcoates *York* 92-95; PtO 95-09; *Ox* 04-09; *Portsm* 09-14. *3 Ventnor Way, Fareham PO16 8RU* M: 07542-527466

✠**FORSTER, The Rt Revd Peter Robert.** b 50. Mert Coll Ox MA 73 Edin Univ BD 77 PhD 85. Edin Th Coll 78. **d** 80 **p** 81 **c** 96. C Mossley Hill St Matt and St Jas *Liv* 80-82; Sen Tutor St Jo Coll Dur 83-91; V Beverley Minster *York* 91-96; C Routh 91-96; Bp Ches from 96. *Bishop's House, 1 Abbey Street, Chester CH1 2JD* T: (01244) 350864 F: 314187
E: bpchester@chester.anglican.org

FORSTER, Canon Thomas Shane. b 72. QUB BA 93. CITC BTh 93. **d** 96 **p** 97. C Drumglass w Moygashel *Arm* 96-99; Hon V Choral Arm Cathl 97-99; I Donaghmore w Upper Donaghmore 99-06; I Ballymore from 06; Sen Dom Chapl to Abp Arm from 06; Dioc Communications Officer 02-09; Asst Dioc and Prov Registrar from 09; Can St Patr Cathl Dublin from 14. *Ballymore Rectory, 10 Glebe Hill Road, Tandragee, Craigavon BT62 2DP* T: (028) 3884 0234
E: ballymore@armagh.anglican.org

FORSTER, William. b 50. NOC 92. **d** 95 **p** 96. C Ashton-in-Makerfield St Thos *Liv* 95-00; TR Fazakerley Em 00-08; TV Eccleston from 08. *The Vicarage, Chapel Lane, Eccleston, St Helens WA10 5DA* T: (01744) 22698
E: william.forster1@btopenworld.com

FORSYTH, Jeanette Mary Shaw. b 48. Aber Coll of Educn ACE 78. St Jo Coll Nottm 85. **d** 89. NSM Old Deer *Ab* 89-92; NSM Longside 89-92; NSM Strichen 89-92; NSM Fraserburgh w New Pitsligo 92-94; Tanzania 95-96, 97-98 and 99-00. *Moss-side of Durno, Bogensourie, Strichen AB43 7TU* T: (01771) 637230 E: jeanetteforsyth@hotmail.com

FORSYTH, John Warren. b 38. Univ of W Aus BA 62 Princeton Th Sem DMin 98. St Mich Th Coll Crafers 65. **d** 65 **p** 66. C Busselton Australia 65-68; R Kondinin 68-72; C Warwick St Mary *Cov* 72-74; C Edin St Pet 74-76; R E Fremantle and Palmyra Australia 76-79; Chapl Abp Perth 79-82; Warden Wollaston 79-82; R Midland 82-89; Sen Angl Chapl R Perth Hosp 89-06; rtd 06; PtO Dio Perth Australia from 06. *40B Cookham Road, Lathlain WA 6100, Australia* T: (0061) (8) 9472 1893 M: 89-472 1893 E: forsyth@iinet.net.au

FORSYTHE, John Leslie. b 27. CITC. **d** 65 **p** 66. C Cloughfern *Conn* 65-67; C Carnmoney 67-71; I Mossley 71-80; I Antrim All SS 80-95; Preb Conn Cathl 94-95; rtd 95. *c/o Mrs A Rooke, Dunadooan Cottage, 18 Dunadooan Road, Coleraine BT52 1SF*

FORTNUM, Brian Charles Henry. b 48. Hertf Coll Ox MA Imp Coll Lon MSc. Wycliffe Hall Ox 82. **d** 84 **p** 85. C Tonbridge St Steph *Roch* 84-87; V Shorne 87-94; P-in-c Speldhurst w Groombridge and Ashurst 94-98; R 98-01; V Tunbridge Wells St Mark 01-12; rtd 12; PtO *Roch* from 13. *27 Ames Way, Kings Hill, West Malling ME19 4HT*
E: brian.fortnum@btinternet.com

FORWARD, Canon Eric Toby. b 50. Nottm Univ BEd 72 Hull Univ MA 93. Cuddesdon Coll 74. **d** 77 **p** 78. C Forest Hill Ch Ch *S'wark* 77-80; Chapl Goldsmiths' Coll Lon 80-84; Chapl Westwood Ho Sch Pet 84-86; V Brighton St Aug and St Sav *Chich* 86-90; PtO *York* 90-95; V Kingston upon Hull St Alb 95-05; Can Res and Prec Liv Cathl 05-07; rtd 07. *2 Kingsway, Liverpool L22 4RQ* T: 0151-928 0681

FORWARD, Miss Frances Mary. b 43. Bp Otter Coll Chich TCert 64. SEITE 96. **d** 99 **p** 00. NSM Ham St Andr *S'wark*

99-09; NSM Ham St Rich 09-13; NSM Petersham 09-13; PtO from 13. *66 Tudor Drive, Kingston upon Thames KT2 5QF* T: (020) 8546 1833

FORWARD, Canon Ronald George. b 25. Selw Coll Cam BA 50 MA 54. Ridley Hall Cam 50. **d** 52 **p** 53. C Denton Holme *Carl* 52-55; C-in-c Mirehouse St Andr CD 55-60; C-in-c Mirehouse 61; V 61-66; V Kendal St Thos 66-90; V Crook 78-90; Hon Can Carl Cathl 79-90; rtd 90; PtO *Carl* from 90. *51 Mayo Park, Cockermouth CA13 0BJ* T: (01900) 824359

FORWARD, Toby. *See* FORWARD, Eric Toby

FOSBUARY, David Frank. b 32. Leeds Univ BA 63. Coll of Resurr Mirfield 63. **d** 65 **p** 66. C Fleetwood St Pet *Blackb* 65-68; Lesotho 69-76; C Dovercourt *Chelmsf* 76-78; TV 78-79; TV Basildon St Martin w H Cross and Laindon etc 79-82; R Colsterworth *Linc* 82-84; R Colsterworth Gp 84-90; RD Beltisloe 89-90; R Lawshall w Shimplingthorne and Alpheton *St E* 90-96; rtd 96; PtO *St E* from 96. *c/o Mrs O Fosbuary, 56 Lindisfarne Road, Bury St Edmunds IP33 2EH* T: (01284) 767687

FOSKETT, Canon John Herbert. b 39. St Cath Coll Cam BA 62 Lambeth MA 04. Chich Th Coll 62. **d** 64 **p** 65. C Malden St Jo *S'wark* 64-70; P-in-c Kingston St Jo 70-76; Chapl Maudsley Hosp Lon 76-94; Chapl Bethlem R Hosp Beckenham 76-94; Hon Can *S'wark* Cathl 88-94; rtd 94; PtO *B & W* 95-01 and from 06. *Victoria Cottage, 8 Cornwall Road, Dorchester DT1 1RT* T: (01305) 264955 E: jfoskett@btinternet.com

FOSS, David Blair. b 44. Bris Univ BA 65 Dur Univ MA 66 Fitzw Coll Cam BA 68 MA 72 K Coll Lon PhD 86. St Chad's Coll Dur 68. **d** 69 **p** 70. C Barnard Castle *Dur* 69-72; Sierra Leone 72-74; Chapl St Jo Coll York 74-75; Chapl Ch Ch Coll of HE Cant 75-80; Chapl Elmslie Girls' Sch Blackpool 80-83; Tutor Coll of Resurr Mirfield 83-88; V Battyeford *Wakef* 88-99; V Ryde All SS *Portsm* 99-01; TR Rochdale *Man* 01-09; R 09-10; rtd 10; PtO *Man* from 10. *11 Sims Close, Ramsbottom, Bury BL0 9NT* T: (01706) 828248

FOSS, Esther Rose. b 79. Regent's Park Coll Ox BA 00 MA 04 Clare Hall Cam MPhil 04 Univ of Wales (Trin St Dav) MA 12. Westcott Ho Cam 03. **d** 05 **p** 06. C Altrincham St Geo *Ches* 05-07; C Bramhall 07-09; TV Knaresborough *Leeds* 09-15; P-in-c Coulsdon St Andr *S'wark* from 15. *4 Mitchley Avenue, Purley CR8 1EA* E: esther.foss@live.co.uk

FOSSETT, Michael Charles Sinclair. b 30. Dur Univ BSc 54 CEng 59 MIMechE 59. NEOC 82. **d** 90 **p** 91. NSM Nether w Upper Poppleton *York* from 90. *20 Fairway Drive, Upper Poppleton, York YO26 6HE* T: (01904) 794712

FOSSEY (née HIRST), Margaret. b 52. Huddersfield Univ BA 96. NOC 06. **d** 09 **p** 10. NSM Birkby and Birchencliffe *Leeds* from 09. *103 Kirkstone Avenue, Dalton, Huddersfield HD5 9ES* T: (01484) 301242 E: m.fossey@ntlworld.com

FOSTEKEW, Canon Dean James Benedict. b 63. Bulmershe Coll of HE BEd. Chich Th Coll 89. **d** 92 **p** 93. C Boyne Hill *Ox* 92-95; P-in-c Lockerbie and Annan *Glas* 95-97; P-in-c Dalmahoy *Edin* 97-02; TV Edin St Mary 02-09; R Edin Gd Shep from 09; Dioc Miss 21 Co-ord 97-11; Prov Miss 21 Co-ord 01-11; Can St Mary's Cathl from 15. *The Rectory, 9 Upper Coltbridge Terrace, Edinburgh EH12 6AD* T: 0131-346 4127 M: 07968-099470 E: therector@uwclub.net *or* mission21@edinburgh.anglican.org

FOSTER, Anthony Stuart. b 47. K Coll Lon BD 69 Peterho Cam BA 72 MA 74 Lon Inst of Educn PGCE 70. Pontifical Beda Coll Rome 82. **d** 85 **p** 86. In RC Ch 85-98; NSM Leighton-cum-Minshull Vernon *Ches* 05-07; rtd 07; PtO *Ches* from 07; *Ban* from 10. *10 Uppergate Street, Conwy LL32 8RF* T: (01492) 562658 E: revtonyfoster@btinternet.com

FOSTER, Antony John. b 39. Down Coll Cam BA 61 MA 65. Ridley Hall Cam 65. **d** 66 **p** 67. C Sandal St Helen *Wakef* 66-69; Uganda 69-74; V Mount Pellon *Wakef* 74-92; rtd 92; PtO *Leeds* from 92. *32 Savile Drive, Halifax HX1 2EU* T: (01422) 344152

✠**FOSTER, The Rt Revd Christopher Richard James.** b 53. Univ Coll Dur BA 75 Man Univ MA 77 Trin Hall Cam BA 79 MA 83 Wadh Coll Ox MA 83. Westcott Ho Cam 78. **d** 80 **p** 81 **c** 01. C Tettenhall Regis *Lich* 80-82; Chapl Wadh Coll Ox 82-86; C Ox St Mary V w St Cross and St Pet 82-86; V Southgate Ch Ch Lon 86-94; CME Officer 88-94; Can Res and Sub-Dean St Alb *St Alb* 94-01; Suff Bp Hertford 01-10; Bp Portsm from 10. *Bishopsgrove, 26 Osborn Road, Fareham PO16 7DQ* T: (01329) 280247 E: bishop@portsmouth.anglican.org

FOSTER, David Brereton. b 55. Selw Coll Cam BA 77 MA 81 Ox Univ BA 80. Wycliffe Hall Ox 78. **d** 81 **p** 82. C Luton St Mary *St Alb* 81-84; C Douglas St Geo and St Barn *S & M* 84-87; V S Ramsey St Paul 87-91; Dir Dioc Tr Inst 88-91; Asst Dir Buckingham Adnry Chr Tr Progr *Ox* 91-95; Dir 95-97; C W Wycombe w Bledlow Ridge, Bradenham and Radnage 91-97; TV High Wycombe 97-07; Tr Officer CME and Laity Development *Man* 07-12; Bp's Officer for Ord and Initial Tr

Nor from 12. *St Mary's Vicarage, Norwich Road, Watton, Thetford IP25 6DB* E: rev.dbf@ntlworld.com *or* david.foster@norwich.anglican.org

FOSTER, Edward Philip John. b 49. Trin Hall Cam BA 70 MA 74. Ridley Hall Cam 76. **d** 79 **p** 80. C Finchley Ch Ch *Lon* 79-82; C Marple All SS *Ches* 82-86; P-in-c Cambridge St Matt *Ely* 86-90; V 90-07; rtd 07. *1 Barnfield, Common Lane, Hemingford Abbots, Huntingdon PE28 9AX* T: (01480) 399098

FOSTER, Frances Elizabeth. *See* TYLER, Frances Elizabeth

FOSTER, Canon Gareth Glynne. b 44. Open Univ BA. Chich Th Coll 66. **d** 69 **p** 70. C Fairwater *Llan* 69-71; C Merthyr Tydfil and Cyfarthfa 71-76; TV 76-87; P-in-c Abercanaid and Dioc Soc Resp Officer 87-10; Exec Officer Dioc Bd Soc Resp 95-10; Can Llan Cathl 00-10; rtd 10; PtO *Llan* from 12. *19 The Walk, Merthyr Tydfil CF47 8RW* T: (01685) 722375 M: 07850-823038

FOSTER, Gavin Richard. b 76. Regent's Park Coll Ox BA 97 MA 01 Cardiff Univ LLM 13 Barrister-at-Law (Gray's Inn) 98. Wycliffe Hall Ox BTh 09. **d** 09 **p** 10. C Radipole and Melcombe Regis *Sarum* 09-12; Bp's Dom Chapl *Win* from 12. *Wolvesey, Winchester SO23 9ND* T: (01962) 854050 F: 897088 E: gavin.foster@winchester.anglican.org

FOSTER, Mrs Gemma Michelle. b 81. St Mellitus Coll 13. **d** 15. C Letchworth St Paul w William 15. St Alb from 15. *89 Howard Drive, Letchworth Garden City SG6 2BX* M: 07775-761518 E: mrsgemmafoster@icloud.com

FOSTER, Mrs Geraldine. b 55. RGN 77. SAOMC 00. **d** 03 **p** 04. C Flackwell Heath *Ox* 03-07; C Ashton-upon-Mersey St Mary Magd *Ches* 07-12; PtO *Nor* 12-13; C Wroxham w Hoveton and Belaugh 13-14; V Watton from 14; C Gt and Lt Cressingham w Threxton from 14. *St Mary's Vicarage, Norwich Road, Watton, Thetford IP25 6DB* M: 07730-586839 E: rev.gf@ntlworld.com

FOSTER, Mrs Gillian Susan. b 62. Leeds Univ BA 09. NOC 06. **d** 09 **p** 10. C Frankby w Greasby *Ches* 09-13; C Ellesmere Port from 13. *4 Deeside Close, Whitby, Ellesmere Port CH65 6TH* M: 07970-522365 E: gillian.foster9495@o2.co.uk

FOSTER, Graham Paul. b 66. Univ of W Aus BSc 86 DipEd 87 BEd 88 Murdoch Univ Aus BD 99 Qu Coll Ox MSt 00 DPhil 02. **d** 04 **p** 05. Lect NT Edin Univ from 03; NSM Edin St Mary from 04. *University of Edinburgh, Faculty of Divinity, New College, Mound Place, Edinburgh EH1 2LX*

FOSTER, James. b 29. Man Univ BA 52 MA 55 Lon Univ CertEd 53 Leeds Univ MEd 74. NEOC 82. **d** 85 **p** 86. NSM Aldborough w Boroughbridge and Roecliffe *Ripon* 85-91; P-in-c Kirby-on-the-Moor, Cundall w Norton-le-Clay etc 91-97; rtd 97; PtO *Leeds* from 97. *Shippen Bower, Marton, Marton cum Grafton, York YO51 9QY* T: (01423) 323133

FOSTER, Mrs Jessica Beatrice. b 70. Qu Coll Birm 12. **d** 15. C Hall Green St Pet *Birm* from 15. *59 Addison Road, Kings Heath, Birmingham B14 7EN* T: 0121-443 2752 E: jessbfoster3@gmail.com *or* jess@nearneighbours.com

FOSTER, Mrs Joan Alison. b 46. ARMCM 67. NOC 95. **d** 98 **p** 99. NSM Blundellsands St Nic *Liv* 98-02; Asst Chapl Southport and Ormskirk NHS Trust 98-02; V N Harrow St Alb *Lon* from 02. *St Alban's Vicarage, Church Drive, Harrow HA2 7NS* T: (020) 8868 6567 M: 07713-819012 E: revjoanfoster@yahoo.co.uk

FOSTER, Jonathan Guy Vere. b 56. Goldsmiths' Coll Lon BA 78. Wycliffe Hall Ox 83. **d** 86 **p** 87. C Hampreston *Sarum* 86-90; Chapl Chantilly *Eur* 90-97; V Branksome St Clem *Sarum* from 97. *The Vicarage, 7 Parkstone Heights, Branksome, Poole BH14 0QE* T: (01202) 748058 E: vicar@stclementschurch.co.uk

FOSTER, Mrs Julia. b 58. RGN RSCN. STETS 03. **d** 06 **p** 07. NSM Chilworth w N Baddesley *Win* 06-10; NSM Ampfield 07-10; NSM Ampfield, Chilworth and N Baddesley 10-11; NSM N Waltham and Steventon, Ashe and Deane from 11. *11 West Lane, North Baddesley, Southampton SO52 9GB* T: (023) 8041 0682 E: juliafoster58@hotmail.com

FOSTER, Leslie. b 49. Linc Th Coll 89. **d** 91 **p** 92. C Coseley Ch Ch *Lich* 91-93; C *Worc* 93-95; V Firbank, Howgill and Killington *Bradf* 95-00; Hon C Sedbergh, Cautley and Garsdale 95-00; Dioc Rural Adv 96-00; P-in-c Ruyton XI Towns w Gt and Lt Ness *Lich* 00-10; V 10-14; RD Ellesmere 08-10; rtd 14. *1 Cambridge Court, Ellesmere SY12 0FN* E: lesfoster@lunevic.freeserve.co.uk

FOSTER, Luke Richard. b 78. St Anne's Coll Ox MA 00. Oak Hill Th Coll MTh 11. **d** 11 **p** 12. C Banbury St Paul *Ox* 11-15; Chile from 15. *2 Blenheim Court, High Street, Eynsham, Witney OX29 4NU* E: lukerichardfoster@gmail.com

FOSTER, Michael John. b 52. St Steph Ho Ox 76. **d** 79 **p** 80. C Wood Green St Mich *Lon* 79-82; TV Clifton *S'well* 82-85; P-in-c Aylesbury *Ox* 85-87; Dep Warden Durning Hall Chr Community Cen 87-89; V Lydbrook *Glouc* 89-97; R Hemsby, Winterton, E and W Somerton and Horsey *Nor* 97-99; P-in-c Tarrant Valley *Sarum* 99-01; P-in-c Tollard Royal w Farnham,

Gussage St Michael etc 99-01; R Chase from 01; C Sixpenny Handley w Gussage St Andrew etc from 06. *The Rectory, Church Hill, Tarrant Hinton, Blandford Forum DT11 8JB* T: (01258) 830764 E: drmjf@church.prestel.co.uk

FOSTER, Paul. *See* FOSTER, Graham Paul

FOSTER, Paul. b 60. MAAT 80. Oak Hill Th Coll 91. **d** 93 **p** 94. C New Clee *Linc* 93-96; P-in-c Aldington w Bonnington and Bilsington *Cant* 96-02; P-in-c Sellindge w Monks Horton and Stowting etc 00-02; Chapl HM Pris Aldington 96-02; Chapl HM YOI Feltham from 02. *HM Young Offender Institution, Bedfont Road, Feltham TW13 4ND* T: (020) 8890 0061 *or* 8844 5325 E: pfozzy@hotmail.com *or* paul.foster01@hmps.gsi.gov.uk

FOSTER, Philip. *See* FOSTER, Edward Philip John

FOSTER, Miss Samantha. b 80. Sunderland Univ BA 01 St Jo Coll Dur BA 04. Cranmer Hall Dur 01. **d** 04 **p** 05. C Fulford *York* 04-08; Pioneer Min Scarborough Deanery 08-15; C Cayton w Eastfield from 15. *9 Green Lane, Scarborough YO12 6HL* T: (01723) 503809 E: samantha.foster7@btinternet.com

FOSTER, Simon John Darby. b 57. Qu Mary Coll Lon BSc 78. Wycliffe Hall Ox 85. **d** 88 **p** 89. C Bedgrove *Ox* 88-92; C Glyncorrwg w Afan Vale and Cymmer Afan *Llan* 92-94; R Breedon cum Isley Walton and Worthington *Leic* 94-98; R Anstey 98-06; R Anstey and Thurcaston w Cropston 06-10; V Croydon St Matt *S'wark* from 10. *The Vicarage, 7 Brownlow Road, Croydon CR0 5JT* T: (020) 8688 5055 E: revsimonfoster@ntlworld.com

FOSTER, Stephen. b 80. St Anne's Coll Ox BA 02 MA 11. Ridley Hall Cam 10. **d** 14 **p** 15. C Onslow Square and S Kensington St Aug *Lon* from 14. *165 Trentham Street, London SW18 5DH*

FOSTER, Stephen. b 47. Leeds Univ CertEd 69. NEOC 83. **d** 86 **p** 87. NSM Kingston upon Hull St Nic *York* 86-87; NSM Aldbrough, Mappleton w Goxhill and Withernwick 87-98; TV Howden 98-05; RD 02-05; Chapl HM Pris Wolds 03-05; rtd 05; PtO *York* from 05; Chapl Costa Blanca *Eur* from 13. *Buzon 3, La Cometa 18, 03729 Senija (Alicante), Spain* M: 07791-547727 E: sf@rhbay.com

FOSTER, Stephen. b 52. **d** 06 **p** 07. OLM Halliwell *Man* 06-08; OLM Turton Moorland from 08; Chapl Bolton Hosps NHS Trust from 07. *68 Adrian Road, Bolton BL1 3LQ* T: (01204) 841382

FOSTER, Canon Stephen Arthur. b 54. Lon Univ BMus 75 BA 78 Potchefstroom Univ PhD 98. Coll of Resurr Mirfield 75. **d** 78 **p** 79. C Ches H Trin 78-82; C Tranmere St Paul w St Luke 82-83; V Grange St Andr 83-88; V Cheadle Hulme All SS 88-94; P-in-c Stockport St Matt 94-00; Asst Dir of Ords 96-04; V Sale St Anne 00-04; Can Res Leic Cathl 04-10; Prec Leic Cathl 04-10; Chapl Leic Univ from 10; Hon Can Leic Cathl from 11. *290 Victoria Park Road, Leicester LE2 1XE* E: stephen.foster@leccofe.org

FOSTER, Steven Francis. b 55. Lon Univ BD 76 AKC 76 Open Univ BA 91 FRSA 90. Coll of Resurr Mirfield 77. **d** 78 **p** 79. C Romford St Edw *Chelmsf* 78-80; C Leigh St Clem 80-83; Ed Mayhew McCrimmon Publishers 84-86; Hon C Southend *Chelmsf* 85-86; P-in-c Sandon 86-90; R 90-91; R Wanstead St Mary 91-93; R Wanstead St Mary w Ch Ch 93-00; PtO 00-05; Asst to Master R Foundn of St Kath in Ratcliffe 00-04; P-in-c Brighton Annunciation *Chich* 05-09; rtd 10; PtO *Chich* from 11. *45 Holland Mews, Hove BN3 1JG* T: (01273) 206478 M: 07901-554866 E: stevenffoster@aol.com

FOSTER, Stuart Jack. b 47. Oak Hill Th Coll BA 80 Lambeth STh 86. **d** 80 **p** 81. C Worting *Win* 80-84; C-in-c Kempshott CD 84-88; R Hook 88-95; Chapl and Warden Bp Grosseteste Coll *Linc* 95-99; R Grayingham and Kirton in Lindsey w Manton *Linc* 99-05; P-in-c Vale of Belvoir *Leic* 05-09; OCM 99-04; Chapl ATC 04-09; rtd 09; PtO *Leic* 10-14. *Sans Souci, 3 Marigold Close, Lincoln LN2 4SZ* T: (01522) 524918 M: 07887-701876 E: rafikimusoma@gmail.com

FOSTER, Susan. b 58. Nottm Univ BMedSci 80 BM, BS 82. WEMTC 00. **d** 03 **p** 05. NSM Tenbury *Heref* from 03; Chapl Kemp Hospice Kidderminster from 07. *Little Oaks Cottage, Hope Bagot, Ludlow SY8 3AE* T: (01584) 891092 E: thefosters@littleoakshb.fsnet.uk

FOSTER, Susan Anne. b 53. Trin Coll Bris BA 97. **d** 98 **p** 99. C Watton w Carbrooke and Ovington *Nor* 98-02; Min S Wonston CD *Win* 02-07; P-in-c Micheldever and E Stratton, Woodmancote etc 05-07; V Upper Dever from 07. *The Rectory, Micheldever, Winchester SO21 3DA* T: (01962) 774379

FOSTER, Thomas Andrew Hayden. b 43. CITC 70. **d** 73 **p** 74. C Dublin Clontarf *D & G* 73-78; I Drumcliffe w Clare Abbey and Kildysart *L & K* 78-80; P-in-c Polstead *St E* 78; I Kilscoran w Killinick and Mulrankin *C & O* 80-85; I Fanlobbus Union *C, C & R* 85-86; R Lasswade and Dalkeith *Edin* 86-87; C Woodford St Mary w St Phil and St Jas *Chelmsf* 87-88; I New w Old Ross, Whitechurch, Fethard etc *C & O* 89-91; Dioc Info

Officer (Ferns) 90-91; I Whitehouse *Conn* 03-10; rtd 10. *18 Marguerite Park, Belfast BT10 0HF* T: (028) 9061 6472 M: 07595-348856 E: tahf@me.com

FOTHERBY, Miss Doreen. b 41. **d** 05 **p** 06. OLM Shipdham w Bradenham *Nor* 05-13; rtd 13; PtO *Nor* from 13. *6 Pound Green Lane, Shipdham, Thetford IP25 7LF* T: (01362) 821481 E: d.fotherby@btinternet.com

FOTHERGILL, Richard Patrick. b 61. Newc Univ BA 83. Trin Coll Bris 91. **d** 95 **p** 96. C E Twickenham St Steph *Lon* 95-97; Assoc R Kirstenhof S Africa 97-04; Network Miss P *Bris* 04-06; Hon C Peasedown St John w Wellow and Foxcote etc *B & W* from 08; PtO *Ox* from 12. *Flossie's Cottage, Hodshill, South Stoke, Bath BA2 7ED* T: (01225) 832806 M: 07835-263706 E: fothers@talktalk.net

FOUHY, Giles. b 71. Oak Hill Th Coll. **d** 07 **p** 08. C Shoreditch St Leon w St Mich *Lon* 07-13; C W Hackney from 13. *16 Albion Drive, London E8 4ET* E: gilesfouhy@hotmail.com

FOULGER, Wendy. b 43. St D Coll Lamp BA 90. St Jo Coll Nottm 04. **d** 11 **p** 12. NSM Cil-y-Cwm and Ystrad-ffin w Rhandir-mwyn etc *St D* 11-12; rtd 12. *20 Gilders Paddock, Bishops Cleeve, Cheltenham GL52 8UJ* E: defld6@aol.com

FOULIS BROWN, Canon Graham Douglas. b 50. JP 87. St Steph Ho Ox 80. **d** 82 **p** 83. C Hungerford and Denford *Ox* 82-84; Chapl Hungerford Hosp 83-84; C Bicester w Bucknell, Caversfield and Launton *Ox* 84-85; TV 85-90; V Kidmore End and Sonning Common 90-03; P-in-c Rotherfield Peppard 02-03; R Rotherfield Peppard and Kidmore End etc 03-15; AD Henley 06-11; Hon Can Ch Ch 11-15; rtd 15; PtO *Ox* from 15. *3 Hillview Place, West Street, Newbury RG14 1BF* M: 07703-267133 E: foulisbrown@gmail.com

FOULKES, Simon. b 58. Ox Poly BA 81. Oak Hill Th Coll BA 89. **d** 89 **p** 90. C St Austell *Truro* 89-92; C Boscombe St Jo *Win* 92-94; P-in-c Portswood St Denys 94-99; Par Evang Adv *Wakef* 99-04; TR Almondbury w Farnley Tyas 02-05; PtO *Cant* 07-09; P-in-c Bethersden w High Halden 09-11; Asst Dir of Educn from 11. *53 Littlestone Road, Littlestone, New Romney TN28 8LN* T: (01797) 364517 E: vicar@idnet.co.uk

FOUNTAIN, David Roy (Brother Malcolm). b 48. Qu Coll Birm 85. **d** 87 **p** 88. SSF from 72; NSM Handsworth St Mich *Birm* 87-92; LtO *Sarum* 92-95; PtO *Worc* 95-00; Newc 00-02; *Lon* 02-03; V Bentley *Sheff* 03-13; rtd 13. *St Anthony's Vicarage, Enslin Gardens, Newcastle upon Tyne NE6 3ST* T: 0191-276 0117 E: malcolmssf@talktalk.net

FOUNTAIN, John Stephen. b 43. RAF Coll Cranwell 65 Solicitor 80. LNSM course 91. **d** 93 **p** 94. NSM Nacton and Levington w Bucklesham and Foxhall *St E* 93-03; NSM Taddington, Chelmorton and Flagg, and Monyash *Derby* 03-11; NSM Taddington, Chelmorton and Monyash etc from 11. *The Old School, Chelmorton, Buxton SK17 9SL* T: (01298) 85009 E: johnfountain@fastmail.fm

FOUNTAIN, Miss Stephanie Ann Cecilia. b 58. Lon Univ BMus 81 Roehampton Inst PGCE 88. Westcott Ho Cam 00. **d** 02 **p** 03. C Tadworth *S'wark* 02-06; TV Boston *Linc* 07-10; P-in-c Bishop's Castle w Mainstone, Lydbury N etc *Heref* from 10; P-in-c Churchstoke w Hyssington and Sarn from 10 and from 10. *The Vicarage, Church Lane, Bishops Castle SY9 5AF* T: (01588) 638095 E: stephaniefountain@yahoo.co.uk

FOUTS, Arthur Guy. b 44. Washington Univ BA 72 Seabury-Western Th Sem DMin 98. Ridley Hall Cam 78. **d** 81 **p** 82. C Alperton *Lon* 81-84; R Pinxton *Derby* 84-87; R Dublin St Patr USA 88-89; Pastor Warren St Mark 90-91; R Silver Spring St Mary Magd 91-99; Chapl St Andr Sch 99-00; P-in-c Point of Rocks St Paul 01-08. *3901 Park Avenue, Union City NJ 07087-6127, USA* E: rubberduck301@yahoo.com

FOWELL, Preb Graham Charles. b 48. Southn Univ BTh 85. Chich Th Coll. **d** 82 **p** 83. C Clayton *Lich* 82-86; C Uttoxeter w Bramshall 86-90; V Oxley 90-95; P-in-c Shifnal 95-07; V Shifnal and Sheriffhales 07-08; RD Edgmond and Shifnal 06-08; TR Stafford 08-13; V Stafford St Mary and Marston 13-14; V Stafford St Chad 13-14; Preb Lich Cathl 08-14; rtd 14; PtO *Lich* 14-15; Hon C Fenton from 15. *2 The Millway, Swynnerton, Stone ST15 0PN*

FOWLER, Anthony Lewis. b 57. Oak Hill Th Coll BA 93. **d** 93 **p** 94. C Walton *St E* 93-96; P-in-c Combs 96-00; P-in-c Hitcham w Lt Finborough 98-00; R Combs and Lt Finborough 00-04; Chapl Suffolk Coll 00-04; Chapl HM Pris Coldingley 04-05; Chapl HM Pris Blundeston 05-07; Chapl HM Pris Swinfen Hall 07-09; Chapl HM Pris Highpoint from 09. *HM Prison Highpoint, Stradishall, Newmarket CB8 9YG* T: (01440) 743232 E: tony.fowler@hmps.gsi.gov.uk *or* alfowler@supanet.com

FOWLER, Canon Colin. b 40. Linc Th Coll 80. **d** 82 **p** 83. C Barbourne *Worc* 82-85; TV Worc St Martin w St Pet, St Mark etc 85-86; TV Worc SE 86-92; P-in-c Moulton *Linc* 92-95; Chapl Puerto de la Cruz Tenerife *Eur* 95-01; Hon Can Madrid

Cathl from 99; R Tangmere and Oving *Chich* 01-05; rtd 05; PtO *Nor* from 07. *10 Drakes Heath, Lowestoft NR32 2QQ* T: (01502) 564707 E: cancol07@btinternet.com

FOWLER, Canon David Mallory. b 51. Ian Ramsey Coll Brasted 74 Trin Coll Bris 75. **d** 78 **p** 79. C Rainhill *Liv* 78-81; C Houghton *Carl* 81-84; P-in-c Grayrigg 84-89; P-in-c Old Hutton w New Hutton 84-89; V Kirkoswald, Renwick and Ainstable 89-99; P-in-c Gt Salkeld w Lazonby 98-99; R Kirkoswald, Renwick w Croglin, Gt Salkeld etc from 00; RD Penrith 99-06; Hon Can Carl Cathl from 99. *The Vicarage, Kirkoswald, Penrith CA10 1DQ* T: (01768) 898176 E: revdmf@aol.com

FOWLER, Mrs Janice Karen Brenda. b 56. Middx Univ BA 97. Oak Hill Th Coll 91. **d** 93 **p** 94. NSM Walton *St E* 93-96; Chapl Ipswich Hosp NHS Trust 94-00; NSM Combs *St E* 96-00; NSM Combs and Lt Finborough 98-00; C 00-04; P-in-c 04; C S Hartismere 04-07; PtO *Lich* 08-09; C Lich St Chad 09-10; P-in-c Worlingworth, Southolt, Tannington, Bedfield etc *St E* 10-11; NSM S Hartismere 11-13; PtO from 13; Chapl Havebury Housing Partnership from 13; Chapl HM Pris Highpoint from 14. *HM Prison Highpoint, Stradishall, Newmarket CB8 9YN* T: (01440) 743500 *or* (01449) 782107 E: jan.fowler@tesco.net

FOWLER, John Ronald. b 30. Ely Th Coll 55. **d** 58 **p** 59. C Surbiton St Andr *S'wark* 58-61; C St Sidwell Lodge Br Guiana 61-62; V Morawhanna 62-65; R Plaisance Guyana 65-70; and 83-89; V Sydenham All SS *S'wark* 70-81; V Wood End *Cov* 81-83; Adn Demarara and Can St Geo Cathl 86-89; V Bedford St Mich *St Alb* 90-95; rtd 95. *12 St Marys Paddock, Wellingborough NN8 1HL* T: (01933) 228691

FOWLER, John Thomas. b 42. EAMTC. **d** 01 **p** 02. NSM Stoke by Nayland w Leavenheath and Polstead *St E* 01-11; rtd 11; PtO *St E* from 11. *Warners, Thorington Street, Stoke by Nayland, Colchester CO6 4SP* T/F: (01206) 337229 E: twam.johnf@googlemail.com

FOWLER, Josephine Margaret. b 47. Worc Coll of Educn TCert 69 BEd 70. **d** 12 **p** 12. OLM Oulton Broad *Nor* from 12. *1 Swonnells Court, Lowestoft NR32 3PY* T: (01502) 572302 E: josephinefowler@talktalk.net

FOWLER, Margaret Joan. b 47. St Mellitus Coll 06. **d** 14 **p** 15. OLM Billericay and Lt Burstead *Chelmsf* from 14. *4 Chestwood Close, Billericay CM12 0PB* T: (01277) 630144 M: 07974-720510 E: margaret.fowler@billericaychurches.org

FOWLES, Canon Christopher John. b 31. Lich Th Coll 54. **d** 58 **p** 59. C Englefield Green *Guildf* 58-63; C Worplesdon 63-69; V Chessington 69-77; V Horsell 77-95; RD Woking 92-94; Hon Can Guildf Cathl 94-95; rtd 95; PtO *Guildf* 95-15. *78 St Jude's Road, Egham TW20 0DF* T: (01784) 439457

FOX, Mrs Carole Ann. b 36. TISEC 98. **d** 99 **p** 00. NSM Ellon *Ab* from 99. *4 Mavis Bank, Newburgh, Ellon AB41 6FB* T: (01358) 789693 E: charlesandcarole@btinternet.com

FOX, Charles Edward. b 36. Lich Th Coll 62. **d** 66 **p** 67. C S Bank *York* 66-69; C Stokesley 69-72; V Egton w Grosmont 72-82; P-in-c Ugthorpe 72-82; P-in-c Newbold Verdon *Leic* 82-83; R Newbold de Verdun and Kirkby Mallory 84-04; rtd 04; PtO *Leic* from 04. *White Rose Cottage, 6 Brascote Lane, Newbold Verdon, Leicester LE9 9LF* T: (01455) 822103

FOX, Christopher. b 79. UWE BSc 01. Trin Coll Bris BA 10. **d** 11 **p** 12. C Ealing St Paul *Lon* from 11. *2 Nightingale Road, London W7 1DG* M: 07974-320324 E: chrispfox@gmail.com

FOX, Colin George. b 46. TD . Sarum & Wells Th Coll 73. **d** 75 **p** 76. C N Hammersmith St Kath *Lon* 75-79; CF (TA) 76-90; C Heston *Lon* 79-81; TV Marlborough *Sarum* 81-90; P-in-c Pewsey 90-91; TR 91-98; TR Pewsey and Swanborough 98-03; Chapl Pewsey Hosp 90-95; P-in-c Avon Valley *Sarum* 03-11; C Durrington 08-11; rtd 11; PtO *Sarum* from 12. *The Pightle, The Street, Teffont, Salisbury SP3 5QP* T: (01722) 716010 E: foxy.col@talk21.com

FOX, Harvey Harold. b 27. Lich Th Coll 58. **d** 60 **p** 61. C Birchfield *Birm* 60-62; C Boldmere 62-65; V Sparkbrook Em 65-71; V Dordon 71-77; V Four Oaks 77-82; V Packwood w Hockley Heath 82-90; rtd 90; PtO *Cov* from 90. *37 Meadow Road, Henley-in-Arden B95 5LB* T: (01564) 795302

FOX, Canon Ian James. b 44. Selw Coll Cam BA 66 MA 70. Linc Th Coll 66. **d** 68 **p** 69. C Salford St Phil w St Steph *Man* 68-71; C Kirkleatham *York* 71-73; TV Redcar w Kirkleatham 73-77; V Bury St Pet *Man* 77-85; V Northallerton w Kirby Sigston *York* 85-03; RD Northallerton 85-91; Chapl Northallerton Health Services NHS Trust 88-03; P-in-c Barlby and Riccall *York* 03-09; P-in-c Hemingbrough 06-09; rtd 09; Can and Preb York Minster from 95; PtO from 10. *21 Springfield Close, Thirsk YO7 1FH* T: (01845) 526889 E: ianfox321@btinternet.com

FOX, Preb Jacqueline Frederica. b 43. Ripon Coll of Educn CertEd 66 Leeds Univ BEd 74 MEd 84 HonRCM 85. S Dios Minl Tr Scheme 83. **dss** 85 **d** 87 **p** 94. RCM *Lon* 85-86; Dioc FE Officer 87-96; Hon C Acton St Mary 87-96; R 96-08; Dean of Women's Min 96-08; Dir of Ords Willesden Area 01-08; Preb

St Paul's Cathl 01-08; rtd 08. *52 North Street, Ripon HG4 1EN* T: (01765) 603698 E: jackie@actonfox.co.uk

FOX, Mrs Jane. b 47. Open Univ BA 91 Bp Otter Coll Chich CertEd 75 ALA 70. S Dios Minl Tr Scheme 92. **d** 95 **p** 96. NSM W Blatchington *Chich* 95-98; C Peacehaven and Telscombe Cliffs 98-01; C Telscombe w Piddinghoe and Southease 98-01; TV Hitchin *St Alb* 01-08; P-in-c Harrold and Carlton w Chellington from 08. *Church House, 3 The Moor, Carlton, Bedford MK43 7JR* T: (01234) 720262 E: janefox_1@btinternet.com

FOX (née COULDRIDGE), Mrs Janice Evelyn. b 49. Bognor Regis Coll of Educn CertEd 71. Glouc Sch of Min 89. **d** 92 **p** 94. C Tupsley w Hampton Bishop *Heref* 92-96; P-in-c Orleton w Brimfield 96-01; Dioc Ecum Officer 96-01; TV Worc SE 01-05; rtd 05; PtO *Worc* from 05. *6 Malvern View, Wichenford, Worcester WR6 6YY* T: (01886) 888637 E: janfox2@googlemail.com

FOX, Jeremy Robin. b 68. St Chad's Coll Dur BA 89 MA 92 Leeds Univ BA 94. Coll of Resurr Mirfield 92. **d** 95 **p** 96. C S Shields All SS *Dur* 95-99; C Tottenham St Paul *Lon* 99-04; C Edmonton St Mary w St Jo 99-04; Chapl Belgrade *Eur* from 04. *c/o FCO (Belgrade), King Charles Street, London SW1A 2AH* T: (00381) (11) 402315 E: robin.fox@sbb.co.yu

FOX, John Brian. b 38. **d** 94 **p** 95. NSM Phillack w Gwithian and Gwinear *Truro* 94-96; NSM Godrevy 96-03; Chapl St Mich Mt from 04. *Abbeydale, 26 Tresdale Parc, Connor Downs, Hayle TR27 5DX* T: (01736) 753935

FOX, Jonathan Alexander. b 56. St Jo Coll Nottm LTh 77 BTh 78. **d** 81 **p** 82. C Chasetown *Lich* 81-85; TV Fazakerley Em *Liv* 85-89; NSM Swanwick and Pentrich *Derby* 89-92; Miss Aviation Fellowship Kenya 92-96; TV Madeley *Heref* 97-02; Co-ord Chapl HM Pris Onley 04-13; P-in-c Revel Gp *Cov* 13-14; PtO 14-15; R Revel Gp from 15. *Kirby Moynes House, 1 Gate Farm Drive, Monks Kirby, Rugby CV23 0RY*

FOX, Leonard. b 41. AKC 66. **d** 67 **p** 68. C Salford Stowell Memorial *Man* 67-68; C Hulme St Phil 68-72; C Portsea All SS w St Jo Rudmore *Portsm* 72-75; V Oakfield St Jo 75-92; P-in-c Portsea All SS 92-06; V 06; Dir All SS Urban Miss Cen 92-06; rtd 06; PtO *Portsm* from 07. *Middle Reach, Ashlake Farm Lane, Wootton Bridge, Ryde PO33 4LF* T: (01983) 880138

FOX, Linda Margaret. b 58. **d** 08 **p** 09. NSM S Croydon St Pet and St Aug *S'wark* from 08. *67 Kingsdown Avenue, South Croydon CR2 6QJ* E: linda.southcroydonbenefice@gmail.com

FOX, Mark. b 70. Surrey Univ BA Birkbeck Coll Lon MSc St Steph Ho Ox BTh. St Mellitus Coll and Ripon Coll Cuddesdon. **d** 13 **p** 14. NSM St Marg Lothbury and St Steph Coleman Street etc *Lon* from 13. *66 Walnut Tree Walk, London SE11 6DN* E: mark.fox@fsmail.net *or* mark.fox@bsa-org.com

FOX, Maurice Henry George. b 24. Lon Univ BD 58. St Aid Birkenhead 47. **d** 49 **p** 50. C Eccleshill *Bradf* 49-52; C Bingley All SS 52-56; V Cross Roads cum Lees 56-62; V Sutton 62-79; V Grange-over-Sands *Carl* 79-88; rtd 89. *7 Manor Close, Topcliffe, Thirsk YO7 3RH* T: (01845) 578322

FOX, Michael Adrian Orme. b 47. Bris Univ BSc 68 PhD 72. WMMTC 01. **d** 04 **p** 05. NSM Codsall *Lich* from 04; Ind Chapl Black Country Urban Ind Miss 04-12. *1 Windsor Gardens, Codsall, Wolverhampton WV8 2EX* T: (01902) 843442 E: mike@maofox.me.uk

FOX, Michael Frederick. b 58. St Pet Coll Ox BA 80. SNWTP 12. **d** 14 **p** 15. NSM Bollington *Ches* from 14. *Hordern Farm, Buxton New Road, Macclesfield SK11 0AN* M: 07714-216665 E: therevdfox@gmail.com

FOX, The Ven Michael John. b 42. Hull Univ BSc 63. Coll of Resurr Mirfield 64. **d** 66 **p** 67. C Becontree St Elisabeth *Chelmsf* 66-70; C Wanstead H Trin Hermon Hill 70-72; V Victoria Docks Ascension 72-76; V Chelmsf All SS 76-88; P-in-c Chelmsf Ascension 85-88; RD Chelmsf 86-88; R Colchester St Jas, All SS, St Nic and St Runwald 88-93; Hon Can Chelmsf Cathl 91-93; Adn Harlow 93-95; Adn W Ham 95-07; rtd 07; PtO *Chelmsf* from 08. *17A Northgate Street, Colchester CO1 1EZ* T: (01206) 710701 E: michael.fox510@ntlworld.com

FOX, Michael John Holland. b 41. Lon Univ BD 68. Oak Hill Th Coll 64. **d** 69 **p** 70. C Reigate St Mary *S'wark* 69-73; NSM 76-01; C Guildf St Sav 73-76; Asst Chapl Reigate Gr Sch 76-81; Chapl 81-01; NSM Reigate St Pet CD *S'wark* 96-01; P-in-c Reigate St Luke w Doversgreen 01-09; rtd 09; Hon C Reigate St Mary *S'wark* from 09; PtO from 09. *71 Blackborough Road, Reigate RH2 7BU* T: (01737) 226616 E: mikejh.fox@virgin.net

FOX, Norman Stanley. b 39. Wolv Univ LLB 97 Birm Univ LLM 09. St Mich Coll Llan 61. **d** 64 **p** 65. C Brierley Hill *Lich* 64-67; C Tettenhall Regis 67-70; V Cradley *Worc* 70-73; Asst Chapl HM Pris Wakef 73-74; Chapl HM Pris The Verne 74-76; R Clayton W w High Hoyland *Wakef* 76-81; R Cumberworth 81-84; C Tettenhall Wood *Lich* 85-89; TV 89-91; V Pensnett 91-93; rtd 99. *54 Lyndon Road, Solihull B92 7RQ* T: 0121-707 8216 E: nsfox390@hotmail.co.uk

FOX, Paul Alexander. b 60. d 12 p 13. NSM Ackworth *Leeds* from 12. *5 Andrews Grove, Ackworth, Pontefract WF7 7NU* T: (01977) 613834 E: pafox7@aol.com

✠**FOX, The Rt Revd Peter John.** b 52. AKC 74. St Aug Coll Cant 74. d 75 p 76 c 02. C Wymondham *Nor* 75-79; Miss P Papua New Guinea 79-85; R Gerehu 80-85; Dioc Sec Port Moresby 84-85; P-in-c E w W Rudham *Nor* 85-88; P-in-c Syderstone w Barmer and Bagthorpe 85-88; P-in-c Tatterford 85-88; P-in-c Tattersett 85-88; P-in-c Houghton 85-88; R Coxford Gp 88-89; TR Lynton, Brendon, Countisbury, Lynmouth etc *Ex* 89-95; RD Shirwell 92-95; P-in-c Harpsden *Ox* 95-02; Gen Sec Melanesian Miss 95-02; Bp Port Moresby Papua New Guinea 02-06; Hon Asst Bp Nor from 06; P-in-c Nor Lakenham St Jo and All SS and Tuckswood 06-07; V from 07. *The Vicarage, Harwood Road, Norwich NR1 2NG* T: (01603) 625679 E: peterandangiefox@yahoo.co.uk

FOX, Raymond. b 46. QUB BSc 69. CITC 71. d 71 p 72. C Holywood *D & D* 71-75; C Min Can Down Cathl 75-78; I Killinchy w Kilmood and Tullynakill 78-81; I Belfast St Mary *Conn* 81-87; I Killaney w Carryduff *D & D* 88-02; Can Down Cathl 98-02; Chapter Clerk and V Choral Belf Cathl 00-02; I Donegal w Killymard, Lough Eske and Laghey *D & R* 02-10; Can Raphoe Cathl 09-10; rtd 10. *14 St Helens Court, High Street, Holywood BT18 9SS* M: 07511-752160 T: (028) 9042 4560 E: canonfox@btinternet.com

FOX, Robert. b 54. Man Univ BEd 76. NOC 89. d 91 p 92. NSM Stalybridge *Man* 91; NSM Ashton from 91. *36 Norman Road, Stalybridge SK15 1LY* T: 0161-338 8481 E: rob.foxesbridge@tiscali.co.uk

FOX, Robin. See FOX, Jeremy Robin

FOX, Sidney. b 47. Nottm Univ BTh 79 PhD 93. Linc Th Coll 75. d 79 p 80. C Middlesbrough St Oswald *York* 79-81; P-in-c 81-86; V 86-87; V Newby 87-92; R Brechin and Tarfside *Bre* 92-05; P-in-c Auchmithie 92-00; Can St Paul's Cathl Dundee 98-05; V Broughton *Blackb* 05-13; rtd 13; PtO *York* from 13. *15 Rawson Way, Hornsea HU18 1DH* E: revsfox@yahoo.co.uk

FOX, Timothy William Bertram. b 37. CCC Cam BA 61. Qu Coll Birm 66. d 68 p 69. C Cannock *Lich* 68-72; C Bilston St Leon 72-75; V Essington 75-81; R Buildwas and Leighton w Eaton Constantine etc 81-92; RD Wrockwardine 88-92; R Bradeley, Church Eaton and Moreton 92-04; rtd 04; Hon C Hanbury, Newborough, Rangemore and Tutbury *Lich* 04-08; PtO *Leeds* from 09. *40 Lakeber Avenue, High Bentham, Lancaster LA2 7JN* T: (01524) 262575 E: editimfox@btinternet.com

FOX-WILSON, Francis James. b 46. Nottm Univ BTh 73. Linc Th Coll 69. d 73 p 74. C Eastbourne St Elisabeth *Chich* 73-76; C Seaford w Sutton 76-78; P-in-c Hellingly 78-79; P-in-c Upper Dicker 78-79; V Hellingly and Upper Dicker 79-85; V Goring-by-Sea 85-93; R Alfriston w Lullington, Litlington and W Dean 93-08; rtd 08; Hon C Isfield *Chich* 08-13; PtO 13-15; Hon C Arlington, Berwick, Selmeston w Alciston etc from 15. *The Vicarage, The Street, Wilmington, Polegate BN26 5SL* E: frank.fox-wilson@fastnet.co.uk

FOXWELL, Rupert Edward Theodore. b 54. Magd Coll Cam BA 76 MA 80 Solicitor 79. Wycliffe Hall Ox 91. d 93 p 94. C Tonbridge SS Pet and Paul *Roch* 93-98. *24 Cheviot Close, Tonbridge TN9 1NH* T/F: (01732) 358535 E: foxwell@harvester.org.uk

FOY, Malcolm Stuart. b 48. Univ of Wales (Lamp) BA 71 Magd Coll Cam CertEd 72 K Coll Lon MA 89 ACP 80 FCollP FRSA. Ox NSM Course 84. d 87 p 88. NSM Tilehurst St Mich *Ox* 87-90; C Ireland Wood *Ripon* 90-96; Adv RE Leeds Adnry 90-96; Dir Educn *Bradf* 96-99; C Otley 99; PtO 00-05; Hon C Keighley All SS *Leeds* from 05; rtd 13. *45 The Chase, Keighley BD20 6HU* T: (01535) 665112

FOY, Peter James. b 59. d 08 p 09. NSM Warminster Ch Ch *Sarum* 08-15. *122 High Street, Chapmanslade, Westbury BA13 4AW* T: (01373) 832088 E: pjfoy@blueyonder.co.uk

FRAIS, Jonathan Jeremy. b 65. Kingston Poly LLB 87. Oak Hill Th Coll BA 92. d 92 p 93. C Orpington Ch Ch *Roch* 92-96; Asst Chapl Moscow *Eur* 96-99; Chapl Kiev 99-05; R Bexhill St Mark *Chich* from 05; RD Battle and Bexhill from 15. *St Mark's Rectory, 11 Coverdale Avenue, Bexhill-on-Sea TN39 4TY* T/F: (01424) 843733 E: frais@tiscali.co.uk

FRAMPTON, Miss Marcia Ellen. b 36. SRN 65 SCM 66. Ripon Coll Cuddesdon 86. d 88 p 95. Par Dn Paston *Pet* 88-89; Par Dn Burford w Fulbrook and Taynton *Ox* 90-92; Par Dn Witney 92-93; NSM Heref S Wye 94-01; rtd 01; PtO *Heref* from 02. *18 Brook Farm Court, Belmont, Hereford HR2 7TZ* T: (01432) 509007 E: revmframpton@talktalk.net

FRAMPTON-MORGAN, Anthony Paul George. See MORGAN, Anthony Paul George

FRANCE, Alistair. See FRANCE, Robert Alistair

FRANCE, Andrew. See FRANCE, John Andrew

FRANCE, Canon Charles Malcolm. b 48. ACA 71 FCA 76. EAMTC 94. d 97 p 98. C Gt Grimsby St Mary and St Jas *Linc* 97-02; P-in-c Skegness and Winthorpe 02-04; P-in-c Ingoldmells w Addlethorpe 02-04; R Skegness Gp 04-14; rtd 14; Can and Preb Linc Cathl from 14. *Address temp unknown* E: malcolmfrance@aol.com

FRANCE (née PIERCY), Mrs Elizabeth Claire. b 66. Qu Mary Coll Lon BSc 87. Wycliffe Hall Ox 97. d 99 p 00. C Dronfield w Holmesfield *Derby* 99-03; V Allestree 03-05; P-in-c Etchingham *Chich* 11-12; PtO *Lon* from 13. *The Rectory, 46 The Avenue, London NW6 7NP* E: lizfrance@btinternet.com

FRANCE, Evan Norman Lougher. b 52. Jes Coll Cam BA 74 MA 78. Wycliffe Hall Ox 76. d 79 p 80. C Hall Green Ascension *Birm* 79-82; CMS 82-84; C Bexhill St Pet *Chich* 84-87; V Westfield 87-11; R Buxted and Hadlow Down from 11. *The Rectory, Church Road, Buxted, Uckfield TN22 4LP* T: (01825) 733103 E: enlfrance@gmail.com

FRANCE, Geoffrey. b 37. S Dios Minl Tr Scheme 87. d 90 p 91. NSM Uckfield *Chich* 90-92; C 92-94; R Warbleton and Bodle Street Green 94-02; rtd 02. *Little Croft, 19 James Avenue, Herstmonceux, Hailsham BN27 4PB* T: (01323) 831840

FRANCE, John Andrew. b 68. Edin Univ MA 90 Leeds Univ BA 00 Dur Univ MA 09. Coll of Resurr Mirfield 98. d 00 p 01. C Hartlepool H Trin *Dur* 00-04; Co-ord Chapl HM Pris Low Newton 04-05; V Earsdon and Backworth *Newc* from 05. *The Vicarage, 5 Front Street, Earsdon, Whitley Bay NE25 9JU* T: 0191-252 9393 E: andrewfrance1968@hotmail.com

FRANCE, Malcolm. See FRANCE, Charles Malcolm

FRANCE, Robert Alistair. b 71. Ox Poly BA 92. Oak Hill Th Coll BA 97. d 97 p 98. C Hartford *Ches* 97-02; P-in-c Stokenchurch and Ibstone *Ox* from 02. *The Vicarage, Wycombe Road, Stokenchurch, High Wycombe HP14 3RG* T: (01494) 483384 E: revalistair@aol.com

FRANCE, Stephen Mark. b 66. Wycliffe Hall Ox BTh 00. d 00 p 01. C Newbold w Dunston *Derby* 00-03; P-in-c Darley Abbey 03-05; Dioc Duty Press Officer 03-04; P-in-c Burwash *Chich* 05-06; R 06-12; R Brondesbury Ch Ch and St Laur *Lon* from 12. *The Rectory, 46 The Avenue, London NW6 7NP* E: revfrance@tiscali.co.uk

FRANCE, William Michael. b 43. Sydney Univ BA 68 Lon Univ BD 72 Chas Sturt Univ NSW MEd 96. Moore Th Coll Sydney LTh 70. d 73 p 73. C Turramurra Australia 73-75; C Barton Seagrave w Warkton *Pet* 76-78; R Dundas Australia 79-82; Chapl The K Sch 83-94; Chapl Sydney C of E Girls' Gr Sch 94-99; Assoc Chapl St Andr Cathl Sch 99-04; R Murchison 04-08; rtd 08. *6 Wesson Road, West Pennant Hills NSW 2125, Australia* T: (0061) (2) 9945 0939 E: billandjackie@optusnet.com.au *or* wfrance@sacs.nsw.edu.au

FRANCE-WILLIAMS, Andrew David Azariah. b 75. Man Univ BA 97 Sheff Univ MA 04. Trin Coll Bris 08. d 10 p 11. C Onslow Square and S Kensington St Aug *Lon* 10-14; C Kensington St Helen w H Trin from 14. *St Clement's Church, 95 Sirdar Road, London W11 4EQ* M: 07818-422586 E: azariah10@gmail.com

FRANCE, Archdeacon of. See NAYLOR, The Ven Ian Frederick

FRANCES, Nicolas Francis. b 61. MBE 98. NOC 92. d 95 p 96. NSM Anfield St Columba *Liv* 95-98; Australia from 98; Acting Dir Health and Welfare Chapls Melbourne 98-99; Exec Dir Brotherhood of St Laur from 99. *15 Traill Street, Northcote Vic 3070, Australia* T: (0061) (3) 9481 7373 *or* 9483 1347 F: 9486 9724 E: nic@bsl.org.au

FRANCES ANNE, Sister. See COCKER, Frances Rymer

FRANCIS (formerly WARD), Alisoun Mary. b 52. Univ of Wales BA 74 Liv Univ MA 05. Ridley Hall Cam 94. d 96 p 97. C S Woodham Ferrers *Chelmsf* 96-00; TV Southend 00-02; Chapl HM Pris Maidstone from 13. *HM Prison, 36 County Road, Maidstone ME14 1UZ* T: (01622) 775300 E: alisoun.francis@hmps.gsi.gov.uk

FRANCIS, Miss Annette. b 44. Trin Coll Bris 91. d 93 p 94. NSM Belmont *Lon* 93; C 94-97; C Swansea St Pet *S & B* 97-99; V Llanelli 99-11; rtd 11; PtO *Mon* from 11; *Llan* 12-15. *58 Garden City, Rhymney, Tredegar NP22 5JZ* T: (01685) 840465 E: rev.a.francis@btinternet.com

FRANCIS, David Carpenter. b 45. Southn Univ BSc 66 Loughb Univ MSc 71 Sussex Univ MA 83. Westcott Ho Cam 85. d 87 p 88. C Ealing St Mary *Lon* 87-90; Chapl Ealing Coll of HE 87-90; Chapl Clayponds Hosp Ealing 88-90; P-in-c Wembley St Jo *Lon* 90-93; Chapl Wembley Hosp 90-93; V Platt *Roch* 93-01; Post Ord Tr Officer 93-98; RD Shoreham 99-01; R Stow on the Wold, Condicote and The Swells *Glouc* 01-11; AD Stow 04-09; rtd 11. *East Forches, Alexandra Road, Crediton EX17 2DH* T: (01363) 777606 M: 07799-410370

FRANCIS, David Everton Baxter. b 45. St Deiniol's Hawarden 76. d 77 p 78. C Llangyfelach *S & B* 77-78; C Llansamlet 78-80; V Llanrhaeadr-ym-Mochnant,

Llanarmon, Pennant etc *St As* 80-85; V Penrhyncoch and Elerch *St D* 85-93; V Borth and Eglwys-fach w Llangynfelyn 93-02; V Garthbeibio w Llanerfyl w Llangadfan etc *St As* 02-11; AD Caereinion 02-11; rtd 12. *53 Rhoslan, Guilsfield, Welshpool SY21 9NR*

FRANCIS, Miss Gillian Cartwright. b 40. CertEd 61. Dalton Ho Bris 69. **dss** 85 **d** 87 **p** 94. Par Dn Blackheath *Birm* 87-94; P-in-c Stechford 94-03; rtd 03; PtO *Glouc* from 03. *22 Ince Castle Way, Gloucester GL1 4DT* T: (01452) 503059

FRANCIS, Canon Graham John. b 45. St Mich Coll Llan 66. **d** 70 **p** 71. C Llanblethian w Cowbridge and Llandough etc *Llan* 70-76; V Penrhiwceiber w Matthewstown and Ynysboeth 76-02; V Cardiff St Mary w St Dyfrig and St Samson from 02; V Grangetown from 05; Can Llan Cathl from 02. *St Mary's Vicarage, 2 North Church Street, Cardiff CF10 5HB* T/F: (029) 2048 7777 E: fathergraham@aol.com

FRANCIS, Canon James More MacLeod. b 44. Edin Univ MA 65 BD 68 PhD 74 Yale Univ STM 69. New Coll Edin 65. **d** 87 **p** 87. Sen Lect RS Sunderland Univ *Dur* from 82; NSM Sunderland St Chad 87-98; TV Sunderland 98-07; NSM Sunderland Minster 07-09; Tutor NEOC 89-98; Bp's Adv for NSM *Dur* 99-10; Prin Dioc OLM Course 02-09; Hon Can Dur Cathl 00-10; rtd 10; PtO *Dur* from 14. *Woodside, David Terrace, Bowburn, Durham DH6 5EF* T: 0191-377 9215 E: jamesfrancis@mac.com

FRANCIS, James Stephen. b 66. FInstD 97 FRSA 99. SEITE 95. **d** 99 **p** 07. NSM St Botolph Aldgate w H Trin Minories *Lon* 99-02; NSM Soho St Anne w St Thos and St Pet 02-05; Chapl RNR 05-07; NSM St Mary le Strand w St Clem Danes *Lon* 07; Chapl RN from 07. *Royal Naval Chaplaincy Service, Mail Point 1-2, Leach Building, Whale Island, Portsmouth PO2 8BY* T: (023) 9262 5055 F: 9262 5134 M: 07961-123811 E: james.francis118@hotmail.co.uk

FRANCIS, Canon James Woodcock. b 28. OBE 97. Wilberforce Univ Ohio AB 57 Payne Th Sem Ohio BD 58. Bexley Hall Div Sch Ohio 59. **d** 59 **p** 60. USA 59-84; Bermuda from 85; Can Res Bermuda 85-99; R Devonshire Ch Ch Bermuda from 99. *PO Box HM 627, Hamilton HM CX, Bermuda* T: (001809) 295 1125 F: 292 5421

FRANCIS, Jennifer Anne Harrison. b 45. JP . Southn Univ BSc 67 Brunel Univ MA 74 CQSW 73. WEMTC 07. **d** 07 **p** 08. NSM Stow on the Wold, Condicote and The Swells *Glouc* 07-11; rtd 11. *East Forches, Alexandra Road, Crediton EX17 2DH* T: (01363) 776606 M: 07881-953769 E: jennyfrancis@btinternet.com

FRANCIS, Jeremy Montgomery. b 31. BNC Ox BA 53 MA 56. Glouc Sch of Min 84. **d** 87 **p** 88. NSM Chedworth, Yanworth and Stowell, Coln Rogers etc *Glouc* 87-90; NSM Coates, Rodmarton and Sapperton etc 90-01; NSM Daglingworth w the Duntisbournes and Winstone 95-97; NSM Brimpsfield w Birdlip, Syde, Daglingworth etc 97-00; PtO from 01. *Old Barnfield, Duntisbourne Leer, Cirencester GL7 7AS* T: (01285) 821370

FRANCIS, John. b 56. Bris Poly BA 78 MCIH 81. **d** 98 **p** 99. OLM Hatcham Park All SS *S'wark* from 98. *Flat 2, 133 Deptford High Street, London SE8 4NS* T: (020) 8691 3145 *or* 8875 5942 E: franci@threshold.org.uk

FRANCIS, John Sims. b 25. Fitzw Ho Cam BA 54 MA 58. St D Coll Lamp BA 47 LTh 49. **d** 49 **p** 50. C Swansea St Barn *S & B* 49-52; C Chesterton St Andr *Ely* 52-54; C Swansea St Mary and H Trin *S & B* 54-58; V Newbridge-on-Wye and Llanfihangel Brynpabuan 58-65; R Willingham *Ely* 65-82; RD N Stowe 78-82; R Rampton 82; P-in-c Buckden 82-85; V 85-91; rtd 91; PtO *Linc* 92-01. *3 The Brambles, Bourne PE10 9TF* T: (01778) 426396

FRANCIS, Julian Montgomery. b 60. Selw Coll Cam BA 83 MA 83. S'wark Ord Course 88. **d** 91 **p** 92. C S Wimbledon H Trin and St Pet *S'wark* 91-95; V Cottingley *Bradf* 95-99; Minority Ethnic Angl Concerns Officer *Lich* 99-02; C W Bromwich St Andr w Ch Ch 99-02; TR Coventry Caludon *Cov* 02-08; Nat Tr Co-ord for Minority Ethnic Anglicans 08-11; V Edgbaston St Geo *Birm* from 11. *The Vicarage, 3 Westbourne Road, Birmingham B15 3TH* T: 0121-454 4204 E: j.francis@queens.ac.uk

FRANCIS, Miss Katherine Jane. b 67. St Jo Coll Dur BA 08 RGN 88 RM 92. Cranmer Hall Dur 06. **d** 08 **p** 09. C Sprotbrough *Sheff* 08-10; Chapl Newcastle upon Tyne Hosps NHS Foundn Trust from 10. *The Freeman Hospital, High Heaton, Newcastle upon Tyne NE7 7DN* T: 0191-244 8680 E: katherine.francis@nuth.nhs.uk

FRANCIS, Kenneth. b 30. Em Coll Cam BA 56 MA 60. Coll of Resurr Mirfield. **d** 58 **p** 59. C De Beauvoir Town St Pet *Lon* 58-61; P-in-c Lusaka St Phil Zambia 62-70; Sub-Warden St Jo Th Sem 62-65; Chapl 65-70; V Harlow St Mary Magd *Chelmsf* 70-76; V Felixstowe St Jo *St E* 76-97; rtd 98. *43 Harvest House, Cobbold Road, Felixstowe IP11 7SP*

FRANCIS, Kenneth Charles. b 22. Oak Hill Th Coll 46. **d** 50 **p** 51. C Wandsworth All SS *S'wark* 50-53; V Deptford St Nic w Ch Ch 53-61; V Summerstown 61-77; R Cratfield w Heveningham and Ubbeston etc *St E* 77-87; rtd 87; PtO *Truro* from 87. *Wheal Alfred, Chapel Hill, Bolingey, Perranporth TR6 0DQ* T: (01872) 571317

FRANCIS, Kevin. b 52. Glas Univ MA 83 PhD 88. TISEC 08. **d** 11 **p** 12. Hon C Glas St Bride from 11; Hon Chapl Glas Univ from 11. *33 Maxwell Avenue, Bearsden, Glasgow G61 1PA* T: 0141-570 0990 E: rev.kevinfrancis@gmail.com

FRANCIS, Prof Leslie John. b 47. Pemb Coll Ox BA 70 MA 74 BD 90 DD 01 Nottm Univ MTh 76 Qu Coll Cam PhD 76 ScD 97 Lon Univ MSc 77 Univ of Wales (Ban) DLitt 07 FBPsS 88 FCP 94. Westcott Ho Cam 70. **d** 73 **p** 74. C Haverhill *St E* 73-77; P-in-c Gt Bradley 78-82; P-in-c Gt w Lt Wratting 79-82; Research Officer Culham Coll Inst 82-88; P-in-c N Cerney w Bagendon *Glouc* 82-85; PtO 85-95; Fell Trin Coll Carmarthen 89-99; Dean of Chpl 95-99; Prof Th Univ of Wales (Lamp) 92-99; Prof Practical Th Univ of Wales (Ban) 99-07; Prof Religions and Educn Warw Univ *Cov* from 07; PtO *Ox* 95-01; *Ban* 99-06; Hon C Llanfair-pwll and Llanddaniel-fab etc 06-12; Hon C Seintiau Braint a Chefni 12-14; Hon C Bro Dwynwen from 15; Hon Can St D Cathl 98-99; Hon Can and Can Th Ban Cathl from 06. *Llys Onnen, Abergwyngregyn, Llanfairfechan LL33 0LD* T: (01248) 681877

FRANCIS, Mark Simon. b 77. Dur Univ BSc 98. Oak Hill Th Coll BA 10. **d** 10 **p** 11. C Egham *Guildf* 10-13; P-in-c Felbridge *S'wark* from 13. *The Vicarage, 8 The Glebe, Felbridge, East Grinstead RH19 2QT* E: thefranos@gmail.com

FRANCIS, Martin Rufus. b 37. Pemb Coll Ox BA 60 MA 64. Linc Th Coll 60. **d** 63 **p** 64. C W Hartlepool St Paul *Dur* 63-67; C Yeovil St Jo w Preston Plucknett *B & W* 67-69; Chapl Tonbridge Sch 69-83; Chapl and Dep Hd St Jo Sch Leatherhead 83-94; R Herstmonceux and Wartling *Chich* 94-01; rtd 01; PtO *Sarum* from 02. *4 Abbots Way, Sherborne DT9 6DT* E: venetiakfrancis@hotmail.co.uk

FRANCIS, Canon Paul Edward. b 52. Southn Univ BTh 84. Sarum & Wells Th Coll 78. **d** 81 **p** 82. C Biggin Hill *Roch* 81-85; R Fawkham and Hartley 85-90; V Aylesford 90-99; V Riverhead w Dunton Green 99-11; Chapl Dioc Assn of Readers 01-11; RD Sevenoaks 05-11; R Beckenham St Geo from 11; Hon Can Roch Cathl from 10. *The Rectory, 14 The Knoll, Beckenham BR3 5JW* T: (020) 8650 0983 E: paul.francis@diocese-rochester.org

FRANCIS, Peter Alan. b 73. Wycliffe Hall Ox. **d** 09 **p** 10. C Horsham *Chich* 09-13; P-in-c Woodchester and Brimscombe *Glouc* from 13. *The Vicarage, Burleigh Lane, Walls Quarry, Brimscombe, Stroud GL5 2PA* E: peterfrancis777@gmail.com

FRANCIS, Peter Brereton. b 53. St Andr Univ MTheol 77. Qu Coll Birm 77. **d** 78 **p** 79. C Hagley *Worc* 78-81; Chapl Qu Mary Coll *Lon* 81-87; R Ayr *Glas* 87-92; Miss to Seamen 87-92; Provost St Mary's Cathl 92-96; R Glas St Mary 92-96; Warden and Lib Gladstone's Lib Hawarden from 97; Visiting Prof Glyndwr Univ from 09. *Gladstone's Library, Church Lane, Hawarden, Deeside CH5 3DF* T: (01244) 532350 E: peter.francis@gladlib.org

FRANCIS, Peter Philip. b 48. St Jo Coll Dur BA 73. Wycliffe Hall Ox 73. **d** 75 **p** 76. C Folkestone St Jo *Cant* 75-78; C Morden *S'wark* 78-83; P-in-c Barford St Martin, Dinton, Baverstock etc *Sarum* 83-88; P-in-c Fovant, Sutton Mandeville and Teffont Evias etc 83-86; R Newick *Chich* 88-14; rtd 14. *12 Downland Copse, Uckfield TN22 1SX* T: (01825) 763557 E: pandnfrancis@btinternet.com

FRANCIS, Philip Thomas. b 58. TD 03. St D Coll Lamp BA 81 Regent's Park Coll Ox MTh 99. Chich Th Coll 81. **d** 82 **p** 83. C Llanelli St Paul *St D* 82-84; C Barnsley St Mary *Wakef* 84-87; V Burton Dassett *Cov* 87-10; V Gaydon w Chadshunt 87-10; P-in-c Avon Dassett w Farnborough and Fenny Compton 07-10; CF (TA) 88-10; CF from 10. *c/o MOD Chaplains (Army)* F: 381824 T: (01264) 383430 E: philip.francis@regents.ox.ac.uk

FRANCIS, Mrs Sharon Edwina. b 57. Westmr Coll Ox BTh 99 Heythrop Coll Lon MA 11. SEITE 98. **d** 08 **p** 09. NSM Langton Green *Roch* 08-12; P-in-c New Groombridge *Chich* from 12. *The Vicarage, Corseley Road, Groombridge, Tunbridge Wells TN3 9SE* T: (01892) 864265 E: revsharon.francis@gmail.com

FRANCIS, Younis. b 66. **d** 95 **p** 95. C Addington *S'wark* 05-07; TV Cheam 07-11; P-in-c Norbury St Phil from 11. *39 Pollards Hill South, London SW16 4LW* M: 07504-721294 E: younis_francis@hotmail.com

FRANCIS-DEHQANI, Gulnar Eleanor (Guli). b 66. Nottm Univ BA 89 Bris Univ MA 94 PhD 99. SEITE 95. **d** 98 **p** 99. C Mortlake w E Sheen *S'wark* 98-02; Chapl R Academy of Music *Lon* 02-04; Chapl St Marylebone C of E Sch 02-04; PtO *Pet* 04-11; C Tr Officer from 11; Adv in Women's Min from 12. *Bouverie Court, 6 The Lakes, Bedford Road, Northampton NN4 7YD* M: 07771-948190 E: guli.fd@btinternet.com

FRANCIS-DEHQANI, Canon Lee Thomas. b 67. Nottm Univ BA 89. Sarum & Wells Th Coll 92 Trin Coll Bris BA 95. **d** 95 **p** 96. C Putney St Mary *S'wark* 95-98; TV Richmond St Mary w St Matthias and St Jo 98-04; P-in-c Oakham, Hambleton, Egleton, Braunston and Brooke *Pet* 04-10; P-in-c Langham 04-10; C Teigh w Whissendine and Market Overton 04-10; C Cottesmore and Barrow w Ashwell and Burley 04-10; TR Oakham, Ashwell, Braunston, Brooke, Egleton etc from 11; RD Rutland from 10; Can Pet Cathl from 10. *The Vicarage, Vicarage Road, Oakham LE15 6EG* T/F: (01572) 722108 M: 07827-668169 E: lee.fd@btinternet.com

FRANCIS-MULLINS, Ms Vienna Jane Eileen. b 89. LMH Ox BA 12. Westcott Ho Cam 12. **d** 15. C Eltham H Trin *S'wark* from 15. *59A Southend Crescent, London SE9 2SD* T: (020) 8859 5936 E: mtr.vienna@ht-e.org.uk

FRANCK, Mrs Janet. b 53. MCSP 75. **d** 14 **p** 15. OLM Egham Hythe *Guildf* from 14. *56 Hazel Grove, Staines TW18 1JL* T: (01784) 465879 E: janetf56@aol.com

FRANK, Derek John. b 49. Imp Coll Lon BScEng 70 Warwick Univ MSc 71. Cranmer Hall Dur 83. **d** 85 **p** 86. C Clay Cross *Derby* 85-87; C Crookes St Thos *Sheff* 87-90; TV 90-93; Chapl Vevey w Château d'Oex and Villars *Eur* 93-02; rtd 07. *1741 chemin des Anciens Combattants, 06140 Vence, France* E: derek@ebeg.ch

FRANK, Penelope Edith. b 45. WMMTC 96. **d** 99 **p** 00. NSM Edgbaston St Geo *Birm* 99-02; PtO *Cov* 03-04; NSM Stoneleigh w Ashow 04-10; CPAS 87-06; rtd 06; Asst Chapl Vevey w Château d'Oex *Eur* 10-12. *Address temp unknown* E: pennyfrank@mail.com

FRANK, Canon Richard Patrick Harry. b 40. St Chad's Coll Dur BA 66. **d** 68 **p** 69. C Darlington H Trin *Dur* 68-72; C Monkwearmouth St Andr 72-74; C-in-c Harlow Green CD 74-79; R Skelton and Hutton-in-the-Forest w Ivegill *Carl* 79-86; V Carl St Luke Morton 86-92; RD Carl 88-89; P-in-c Thursby 89-90; P-in-c Kirkbride w Newton Arlosh 89-92; TR Greystoke, Matterdale, Mungrisdale etc 92-98; P-in-c Patterdale 95-98; TR Gd Shep TM 98-99; RD Penrith 96-99; Hon Can Carl Cathl 97-99; rtd 99; PtO *Carl* 00-02; *York* from 02. *8 Taylors Rise, Walkington, Beverley HU17 8SF* T: (01482) 872262 E: richardandann.frank@virgin.net

FRANK, Richard Stephen. b 70. Keble Coll Ox MEng 93 Fitzw Coll Cam MA 98. Ridley Hall Cam 96. **d** 99 **p** 00. C Cranham Park *Chelmsf* 99-04; P-in-c St Margaret's-on-Thames *Lon* 05-11; V from 11; AD Hounslow from 15. *295 St Margarets Road, Twickenham TW1 1PN* T: (020) 8891 3504 M: 07973-719730 E: richardfrank@allsoulschurch.org.uk

FRANKLAND, Angela Tara. b 69. Lon Bible Coll BA 96 MB. EAMTC 97. **d** 99 **p** 00. C Hornchurch St Andr *Chelmsf* 99-03; TV Wickford and Runwell 03-11; P-in-c Aveley and Purfleet 11-13; TR Mardyke from 13. *The Vicarage, Mill Road, Aveley, South Ockendon RM15 4SR* T: (01708) 891471 E: tfrankland@btinternet.com

FRANKLIN, David John. b 67. Selw Coll Cam BA 88 MA 92. St Jo Coll Nottm MTh 06. **d** 06 **p** 07. C Windermere *Carl* 06-10; Hon C Bramley *Sheff* 10-12; V Askern from 12. *The Vicarage, Church Street, Askern, Doncaster DN6 0PH* T: (01302) 708081 E: david@franklind.freeserve.co.uk

FRANKLIN, Dianne Mary. *See* COX, Dianne Mary

FRANKLIN (*formerly* WILKES), **Mrs Elizabeth Ann.** b 76. St Jo Coll Dur BA 97 UEA MA 01. **d** 13 **p** 14. C Blackheath Park St Mich *S'wark* from 13. *1A Pond Road, London SE3 9JL* T: (020) 8852 6498 *or* 8852 1205 E: wilkes_liz@hotmail.com

FRANKLIN, Hector Aloysius. b 32. NOC 94. **d** 97 **p** 98. NSM Chapeltown *Sheff* 97-99; P-in-c Sheff St Paul 99-02; rtd 02; PtO *Sheff* from 04. *108 Mackenzie Crescent, Burncross, Sheffield S35 1US* T: 0114-245 7160

FRANKLIN, Mrs Janet. b 67. Selw Coll Cam VetMB 91 MA 92 Cumbria Univ BA 10. LCTP 06. **d** 10 **p** 11. C Maltby and Thurcroft *Sheff* 10-13; P-in-c Stainforth from 13. *The Vicarage, Church Street, Askern, Doncaster DN6 0PH* T: (01302) 708081 E: janet.franklin@sheffield.anglican.org

FRANKLIN, Canon Lewis Owen. b 46. Natal Univ BSc 67. S'wark Ord Course 68. **d** 73 **p** 74. C Durban St Paul S Africa 74-75; R Newcastle H Trin 76-79; Dir St Geo Cathl Cen Cape Town 80-83; Chapl St Geo Gr Sch 84-86; R Sea Pt H Redeemer 87-89; R Cape Town St Paul 89-90; Subdean and Prec Kimberley Cathl 91-94; Hon Can from 93; Dioc Sec Kimberley and Kuruman 94-96; Subdean and Prec Kimberley Cathl 96-99; C Altrincham St Geo *Ches* 99-00; P-in-c Newcastle St Paul *Lich* 00-05; R Bryanston St Mich S Africa 05-09; rtd 08. *414 Carlingford, Randjes Estate, PO Box 565, Highlands North, 2037 South Africa* T/F: (0027) (11) 440 1857 E: fr.owen@gmail.com

FRANKLIN, Miss Ola. b 55. Balls Park Coll Hertford CertEd 76 Open Univ BA 92 Birkbeck Coll Lon MA 95. NTMTC BA 09. **d** 09 **p** 10. C Harlow St Mary and St Hugh w St Jo the Bapt *Chelmsf* 09-13; PtO 13-14; V Woodford Bridge from 14. *St Paul's Vicarage, 4 Cross Road, Woodford Green IG8 8BS* T: (020) 8506 0662 E: ofrank@btinternet.com

FRANKLIN, Paul. b 79. **d** 13 **p** 14. NSM Kidbrooke St Nic *S'wark* from 13. *Address temp unknown*

FRANKLIN, Canon Richard Charles Henry. b 48. Ch Ch Coll Cant CertEd 70 Heythrop Coll Lon MA 08. Sarum & Wells Th Coll 75. **d** 78 **p** 79. C Pershore w Pinvin, Wick and Birlingham *Worc* 78-80; Educn Chapl 80-85; V Wollescote 85-92; V Fareham SS Pet and Paul *Portsm* 92-98; V Luton All SS w St Pet *St Alb* 98-12; RD Luton 02-07; Hon Can St Alb 09-12; rtd 13. *Baldwin's Oak, Castle Tump, Newent GL18 1LS* T: (01531) 890289 E: richardfranklin@mail2world.com

FRANKLIN, Canon Richard Heighway. b 54. Southn Univ BA 75 MPhil 83. Sarum & Wells Th Coll 75. **d** 78 **p** 79. C Thame w Towersey *Ox* 78-81; Asst Chapl Southn Univ *Win* 81-83; Dir of Studies Chich Th Coll 83-89; P-in-c Stalbridge *Sarum* 89-94; V Weymouth H Trin from 94; Can and Preb Sarum Cathl from 02; RD Weymouth 04-08. *Holy Trinity Vicarage, 7 Glebe Close, Weymouth DT4 9RL* T: (01305) 760354 *or* 774597 E: richardfranklin@iname.com

FRANKLIN (*née* WESTMACOTT), **Mrs Rosemary Margaret.** b 41. WEMTC 03. **d** 05 **p** 06. NSM Cirencester *Glouc* 05-13; rtd 13. *Waterton Farm House, Ampney Crucis, Cirencester GL7 5RR* T: (01285) 654282 E: revrmf@btinternet.com

FRANKLIN, Roxanne Fay. *See* HUNTE, Roxanne Fay

FRANKLIN, Preb Simon George. b 54. Bris Univ BA 75. Ridley Hall Cam 77. **d** 79 **p** 80. C Woodmansterne *S'wark* 79-83; C St Peter-in-Thanet *Cant* 83-86; R Woodchurch 86-96; P-in-c Ottery St Mary, Alfington, W Hill, Tipton etc *Ex* 96-99; TR 99-12; P-in-c Feniton and Escot 07-12; P-in-c Moretonhampstead, Manaton, N Bovey and Lustleigh 12-15; R from 15; Preb Ex Cathl from 07. *The Rectory, 3 Grays Meadow, Moretonhampstead, Newton Abbot TQ13 8NB* T: (01647) 441413 E: safranklin@btinternet.com

FRANKLIN, Stephen Alaric. b 58. Lon Univ BD 87. Sarum & Wells Th Coll 87. **d** 89 **p** 90. C Chenies and Lt Chalfont, Latimer and Flaunden *Ox* 89-93; CF from 93. *c/o MOD Chaplains (Army)* F: 381824 T: (01264) 383430

FRANKS, John Edward. b 29. **d** 61 **p** 62. C Plymouth St Matthias *Ex* 61-66; V Upton Grey w Weston Patrick and Tunworth *Win* 66-77; V Upton Grey, Weston Patrick, Tunworth etc 77-79; P-in-c Wolverton cum Ewhurst and Hannington 79-80; R Baughurst, Ramsdell, Wolverton w Ewhurst etc 81-94; rtd 94. *Victoria, 57 Triq Santa Lucija, Naxxar, NXR 1507, Malta GC* T: (00356) 2143 7006

FRANKS, John William. b 45. K Alfred's Coll Win BEd 87 DAES 94 MISM 89. STETS 97. **d** 00 **p** 01. NSM Fareham H Trin *Portsm* 00-03; Hon Chapl Pitmore Sch Chandler's Ford 00; Hon Chapl Fareham Coll of F&HE 01-03; C Rowner *Portsm* 03-07; C Bridgemary 05-07; P-in-c Banwell *B & W* 08-13; Hon C Dunster, Carhampton, Withycombe w Rodhuish etc 13-15; rtd 15. *Church House, Carhampton, Minehead TA24 6LX* T: (01643) 822302

FRANKUM, Matthew David Hyatt. b 65. Leic Poly BSc 87 Univ of Wales MA 13. Trin Coll Bris 97. **d** 99 **p** 00. C Bath St Luke *B & W* 99-03; TV Worle 03-08; P-in-c Bath St Luke from 08. *St Luke's Vicarage, Hatfield Road, Bath BA2 2BD* T: (01225) 311904 E: matthew@stlukesbath.com

FRANSELLA, Cortland Lucas. b 48. Trin Hall Cam BA 70 MA 74 Heythrop Coll Lon MA 00 Open Univ BSc 05 MSc 11. NTMTC 95. **d** 98 **p** 99. NSM Palmers Green St Jo *Lon* 98-03 and 09-12; NSM Hornsey St Mary w St Geo 03-08; PtO from 08; Asst Chapl to Abp Cant 11-13; Lambeth Awards Officer from 14; Asst P Chpl R St Pet-ad-Vincula at HM Tower of Lon from 12. *17 Warner Road, London N8 7HB* T: (020) 8340 7706 E: fransella@btinternet.com

FRASER, Alan Richard. b 69. Leeds Univ BA 91 MA 94. WMMTC 04. **d** 07 **p** 08. NSM Gravelly Hill *Birm* from 07. *41 Hobhouse Close, Birmingham B42 1HB* E: alan-fraser@blueyonder.co.uk

FRASER, Andrew Thomas. b 52. Newc Univ Aus BA 81. St Jo Coll (NSW) ThL 79. **d** 81 **p** 82. Australia 81-87; C Prestbury *Glouc* 87-91; C Wotton St Mary 91-92. *79 Victoria Street, Gloucester GL1 4EP* T: (01452) 381082

FRASER, Ann. *See* FRASER, Elizabeth Ann

FRASER, Beverly. b 49. **d** 10 **p** 11. NSM Sutton *S'wark* from 10. *53 Sherwood Park Road, Sutton SM1 2SG* T: (020) 8661 7448 *or* 7735 8338 M: 07799-580570 E: beverly.fraser1@googlemail.com

FRASER, Charles Ian Alexander. b 45. Ex Univ BA Cam Univ PGCE Open Univ MA MCMI. ERMC. **d** 10 **p** 11. NSM Cherry Hinton St Jo *Ely* 10-13; NSM Lordsbridge from 13; Asst Master The Leys Sch from 10. *The Leys School, Fen Causeway, Cambridge CB2 7AD* T: (01223) 264974 *or* 508916 M: 07889-019157 E: ciaf@theleys.net *or* revd.charlesfraser@gmail.com

FRASER, Christine Nancy. b 61. TISEC 98. **d** 02 **p** 03. NSM St Ninian's Cathl Perth 02-13; Chapl Perth High Sch 09-13; R Kirkcaldy *St And* from 13; R Kinghorn from 13. *1 Longbraes Garden, Kirkcaldy KY2 5YJ* T: (01592) 204208 E: cnfraser@btinternet.com

FRASER, Darren Anthony. b 71. Wilson Carlile Coll 02. **d** 08 **p** 09. C Bucknall *Lich* 08-12; R Biddulph Moor and Knypersley from 12. *St John's Vicarage, 62 Park Lane, Knypersley, Stoke-on-Trent ST8 7AU* M: 07766-198455

FRASER, David Ian. b 32. Em Coll Cam BA 54 MA 58. Oak Hill Th Coll 56. **d** 58 **p** 59. C Bedford St Jo *St Alb* 58-61; C Cheadle Hulme St Andr *Ches* 61-64; R Fringford w Hethe and Newton Purcell *Ox* 64-67; V Preston St Luke *Blackb* 67-71; V Surbiton Hill Ch Ch *S'wark* 71-91; rtd 91; PtO *Ox* from 97. *7 Godwyn Close, Abingdon OX14 1BU* T: (01235) 532049 E: david@ab-frasers.freeserve.co.uk

FRASER, Duncan Piers. b 71. Bris Univ BA 93 Ch Ch Coll Cant PGCE 98. Wycliffe Hall Ox 11. **d** 13 **p** 14. C Eastbourne H Trin *Chich* from 13. *22 Chamberlain Road, Eastbourne BN21 1RU* M: 07810-324088 E: duncanpfraser@gmail.com

FRASER, Mrs Elizabeth Ann. b 44. **d** 07 **p** 08. OLM Witley *Guildf* 07-14; PtO from 14. *Oakwood, Petworth Road, Milford, Godalming GU8 5BS* T: (01483) 417190 M: 07966-513450 E: ann.fraser@btinternet.com

FRASER, Mrs Gemma Elaine. b 81. St Mellitus Coll BA 14. **d** 14 **p** 15. C Galleywood Common *Chelmsf* from 14. *The Vicarage, Vicarage Road, Chelmsford CM2 9PH* M: 07540-152561 E: frasergem@gmail.com

FRASER, Geoffrey Michael. b 29. Sarum Th Coll. **d** 59 **p** 60. C Thames Ditton *Guildf* 59-63; C Shere 63-65; C Dunsford and Doddiscombsleigh *Ex* 65-70; V Uffculme 70-92; rtd 92; PtO *Worc* from 92. *Dalvey House, 46 Priory Road, Malvern WR14 3DB* T: (01684) 576302

FRASER, Canon Giles Anthony. b 64. Newc Univ BA 84 Ox Univ BA 92 MA 97 Lanc Univ PhD 99. Ripon Coll Cuddesdon. **d** 93 **p** 94. C Streetly *Lich* 93-97; C Ox St Mary V w St Cross and St Pet 97-00; Chapl Wadh Coll Ox 97-00; V Putney St Mary *S'wark* 00-04; TR 04-09; Can Res and Chan St Paul's Cathl 09-12; P-in-c Newington St Mary *S'wark* from 12; Hon Can Sefwi-Wiawso Ghana from 09. *The Rectory, 57 Kennington Park Road, London SE11 4JQ* T: (020) 7735 3779 *or* 7582 6771 E: giles.fraser@guardian.co.uk

FRASER, Mrs Helen Jane. b 77. Man Univ LLB 98. Trin Coll Bris BA 11. **d** 11 **p** 12. C Chipstead *S'wark* 11-14; C Reigate St Mary from 14. *63 Chart Lane, Reigate RH2 7EA* E: fraserhj@gmail.com

FRASER, Canon Jane Alicia. b 44. Man Univ BA. Glouc Sch of Min 86. **d** 89 **p** 94. NSM Upton on Severn *Worc* 89-00; NSM Ripple, Earls Croome w Hill Croome and Strensham 97-00; Faith Adv Dept of Health's Adv Gp on Teenage Pregnancy from 00; NSM Upton-on-Severn, Ripple, Earls Croome etc *Worc* 00-14; Hon Can Worc Cathl 05-14; PtO from 14. *The Campanile, Church Lane, Stoulton, Worcester WR7 4RE* T: (01905) 840266 E: training@revjane.demon.co.uk

FRASER, Jeremy Stuart. b 58. **d** 08 **p** 09. C E Greenwich *S'wark* 08-13; P-in-c Stratford St Paul and St Jas *Chelmsf* from 13; AD Newham from 15. *St Paul's Vicarage, 65 Maryland Road, London E15 1JL* T: (020) 8534 1164 M: 07970-139881 E: jeremy@fraserwireless.co.uk

FRASER, Leslie John. b 60. **d** 99 **p** 00. NSM Thamesmead *S'wark* 99-04; PtO 05-07. *4 Goldcrest Close, London SE28 8JA* T: (020) 8473 4736 E: les.fraser@virgin.net

FRASER, Mark Adrian. b 69. Warwick Univ BSc 90 Birm Univ MSc 91. St Jo Coll Nottm MTh 04. **d** 05 **p** 06. C Astley Bridge *Man* 05-08; P-in-c Gamston and Bridgford *S'well* 08-11; V from 11; P-in-c Edwalton from 14. *10 Scafell Close, West Bridgford, Nottingham NG2 6RJ* M: 07963-397688 E: mark.fraser@tiscali.co.uk *or* mark@st-lukes-gamston.org

FRASER, Mrs Pamela Jean. b 49. **d** 98 **p** 98. C Forster w Tuncurry Australia 99-00; Singleton 01-02; R The Entrance 02-09; P-in-c Clarencetown and Stroud from 09; R Hemingby Gp *Linc* from 15; R Asterby Gp from 15. *The Rectory, 6 Simons Close, Donington-on-Bain, Louth LN11 9TX*

FRASER-SMITH, Keith Montague. b 48. St Jo Coll Dur BA 70. Trin Coll Bris. **d** 73 **p** 74. C Bishopsworth *Bris* 73-75; CMS 76-84; Egypt 76-80; Jerusalem 80-84; Asst Chapl Marseille w St Raphaël, Aix-en-Provence etc *Eur* 84-90; Media Dir Arab World Min 84-92; E Area Dir 92-97; Dep Internat Dir 97-98; NSM Worthing Ch the King *Chich* 90-93; Cyprus 93-97; NSM Tranmere St Cath *Ches* 97-98; P-in-c Barnton 98-03; Dir Global Mobilisation Arab World Min 03-10; Min Ldr UK 10-13; rtd 13; PtO *Ches* 03-15. *8 Cockshott Close, Leeds LS12 2RJ* E: keith.fraser-smith@tiscali.co.uk

FRAY, Bernard Herbert. b 44. Open Univ BA 73 Worc Coll of Educn CertEd 65 LTCL 67. Cranmer Hall Dur 02. **d** 03 **p** 04. NSM Long Marston *York* 03-06; NSM Rufforth w Moor Monkton and Hessay 03-06; NSM Healaugh w Wighill, Bilbrough and Askham Richard 03-06; NSM Tockwith and Bilton w Bickerton 03-06; P-in-c Aberford w Micklefield 06-11; rtd 11; PtO *York* from 11; *Eur* from 11. *11 Trafalgar House, Piccadilly, York YO1 9QP* T: (01904) 626911 M: 07967-232535 E: fraybernard985@gmail.com

FRAY, Vernon Francis. b 41. FCIOB 79. S'wark Ord Course 91. **d** 94 **p** 95. NSM Heston *Lon* 94-96; NSM Twickenham All Hallows 96-02; NSM Teddington St Mark and Hampton Wick 02-08; NSM Whitton SS Phil and Jas 08-11; PtO from 11; *S'wark* from 15. *10 Hall Farm Drive, Twickenham TW2 7PQ* T: (020) 8894 6399 E: v.fray@btinternet.com

FRAYLING, The Very Revd Nicholas Arthur. b 44. Ex Univ BA 69 Liv Univ Hon LLD 01. Cuddesdon Coll 69. **d** 71 **p** 72. C Peckham St Jo *S'wark* 71-74; V Tooting All SS 74-83; Can Res and Prec Liv Cathl 83-87; R Liv Our Lady and St Nic w St Anne 87-90; TR 90-02; Hon Can Liv Cathl 89-02; Dean Chich 02-14; rtd 14; PtO *Portsm* from 14. *Flat 5, 27 South Parade, Southsea PO5 2JF* T: (023) 9281 7041 E: nicholasfrayling@gmail.com

FRAYNE, The Very Revd David. b 34. St Edm Hall Ox BA 58 MA 62. Qu Coll Birm 58. **d** 60 **p** 61. C E Wickham *S'wark* 60-63; C Lewisham St Jo Southend 63-67; V N Sheen St Phil and All SS 67-73; R Caterham 73-83; RD 80-83; Hon Can *S'wark* Cathl 82-83; V Bris St Mary Redcliffe w Temple etc 83-92; RD Bedminster 86-92; Hon Can Bris Cathl 91-92; Provost Blackb 92-00; Dean Blackb 00-01; rtd 01; PtO *Sarum* from 02; *B & W* from 12. *30 Coleridge Vale Road South, Clevedon BS21 6PB* T: (01275) 873799 M: 07788-795698 E: davidfrayne666@btinternet.com

FRAZER, David. b 60. QUB BSSc. TCD Div Sch. **d** 84 **p** 85. C Taney *D & G* 84-87; C Dublin Ch Ch Cathl Gp 87-88; I Clane w Donadea and Coolcarrigan *M & K* 88-05; Dioc P and Soc Officer from 05. *3 The Glen, Inse Bay, Laytown, Co Meath, Republic of Ireland* T: (00353) (41) 988 8229 M: 89-216 3339 E: dublinblackdog@yahoo.ie

FRAZER, Deborah. b 58. Open Univ BA 90 PGCE 96. Th Ext Educn Coll 89. **d** 92 **p** 95. C Pretoria St Fran S Africa 92-93; PtO *S'wark* 93-94; NSM Merton St Mary 94-96; Asst Chapl HM Pris Brixton 96-97; P-in-c Barton Hill St Luke w Ch Ch and Moorfields *Bris* 02-12; AD City 06-10; R Bow w Bromley St Leon *Lon* from 12. *28 Coborn Street, London E3 2AB* T: (020) 8981 7916 M: 07891-692656 E: revdebbiefrazer@gmail.com

FRAZER, Ian Martin. b 44. QUB BTh. **d** 91 **p** 93. LtO *D & D* 91-98; Aux Min Orangefield w Moneyreagh 98-04; Aux Min Ballymacarrett from 04. *The Stacks, Deramore Park South, Belfast BT9 5JY* T: (028) 9066 7100 E: genie.frazer@gmail.com

FRAZER, Canon James Stewart. b 27. TCD Div Sch. **d** 57 **p** 58. C Belfast Whiterock *Conn* 57-59; C Belfast St Matt 59-61; I Lack *Clogh* 61-64; I Camlough w Mullaglass *Arm* 64-65; I Milltown 65-70; I Heathcote w Axedale Australia 70-72; I Kangaroo Par w Marong, Lockwood etc 72-74; I Dromore *Clogh* 74-82; Bp's Dom Chapl 82; I Derryvullen S w Garvary 82-90; Can Clogh Cathl 83-85; Preb Clogh Cathl 85-94; I Clogh w Errigal Portclare 90-94; Glebes Sec 91-94; Chan Clogh Cathl 93-94; rtd 94. *8 Carsons Avenue, Ballygowan, Newtownards BT23 5GD* T: (028) 9752 1562

FREAR, Canon Philip Scott. b 45. Univ of Wales (Lamp) BA 66. Bris & Glouc Tr Course 77. **d** 80 **p** 81. Hon C Purton *Bris* 80-81; C Rodbourne Cheney 81-85; V Hengrove 85-95; V Braddan *S & M* 95-12; Chapl Isle of Man Dept of Health and Social Security 98-12; Can St German's Cathl 04-12; rtd 12. *37 Hutchinson Square, Douglas, Isle of Man IM2 4HW*

FREARSON, Andrew Richard. b 57. Wolv Univ BA 80. Wycliffe Hall Ox. **d** 83 **p** 84. C Acocks Green *Birm* 83-86; C Moseley St Mary 86-89; P-in-c Holme *Blackb* 89-96; P-in-c Norcross Ch Ch USA 97-06; TV Bracknell *Ox* 06-10; R Dollar *St And* from 10. *St James's Rectory, 12 Harviestown Road, Dollar FK14 7HF* E: andrewfrearsontron@hotmail.co.uk

FREATHY, Nigel Howard. b 46. Lon Univ BA 68 CertEd. Sarum & Wells Th Coll 79. **d** 81 **p** 82. C Crediton *Ex* 81-82; C Crediton and Shobrooke 82-84; TV Ex St Thos and Em 84-86; V Beer and Branscombe 86-01; P-in-c Stockland, Dalwood, Kilmington and Shute 01-03; V Kilmington, Stockland, Dalwood, Yarcombe etc 03-08; RD Honiton 96-99; rtd 08. *5 Mill Lane, Branscombe, Seaton EX12 3DS* T: (01297) 680424 E: nigelfreathy@hotmail.co.uk

FREDERICK, David George. b 68. Birm Univ BSc 92. Ridley Hall Cam 08. **d** 10 **p** 11. C Cromer *Nor* 10-13; Pioneer Min *Ex* from 13. *26 Thompson Road, Exeter EX1 2UB* M: 07766-051948 E: dgfrederick@hotmail.com

FREDERICK, John Bassett Moore. b 30. Princeton Univ BA 51 Birm Univ PhD 73. Gen Th Sem (NY) MDiv 54. **d** 54 **p** 55. C Cheshire St Pet USA 54-56; C All Hallows Barking *Lon* 56-58; C Ox SS Phil and Jas 58-60; R New Haven St Jo USA 61-71;

R Bletchingley *S'wark* 74-95; Reigate Adnry Ecum Officer 90-95; RD Godstone 92-95; rtd 95. *32 Chestnut Street, Princeton NJ 08542-3806, USA* T: (001) (609) 924 7590 F: 924 1694 E: jf9642@netscape.net

FREDERICK, Warren Charles. b 47. Univ of Illinois BSc. Qu Coll Birm 86. **d** 88 **p** 89. C W Leigh *Portsm* 88-91; V N Holmwood *Guildf* 91-00; R Cumberland H Cross USA 00-04; R Worceser St Mich 04-12; rtd 12. *3502 Lower Cove Run Road, Mathias WV 26812, USA*

FREDRIKSEN, Martin. b 47. St Chad's Coll Dur BA 69 Univ of Wales (Lamp) MA 03. **d** 70 **p** 71. C Bideford *Ex* 70-73; C Guildf St Nic 73-76; R Cossington *B & W* 76-82; V Woolavington 76-82; Asst Chapl K Coll Taunton 82-84; C Bp's Hatfield *St Alb* 84-94; P-in-c Broadstone *Sarum* 94; V 94-12; rtd 12; PtO *Sarum* from 12. *129 Stour View Gardens, Corfe Mullen, Wimborne BH21 3TN* T: (01202) 900198 E: fr.fred@fsmail.net

FREE, Canon James Michael. b 25. K Coll Lon BD 50 AKC 50. **d** 51 **p** 52. C Corsham *Bris* 51-54; Trinidad and Tobago 54-62; PC Knowle St Barn *Bris* 62-67; V Pilning 67-75; P-in-c Lydiard Millicent w Lydiard Tregoz 75-82; Hon Can Bris Cathl 76-82; Can Res, Prec and Sacr Bris Cathl 82-83; Can Treas Bris Cathl 83-90; Bp's Adv for Miss 82-87; Bp's Officer for Miss and Evang 87-89; rtd 90; PtO *Bris* from 90; *B & W* 90-03 and from 06; P-in-c Haselbury Plucknett, Misterton and N Perrott 03-05. *Well House, Silver Street, Misterton, Crewkerne TA18 8NG* T: (01460) 271133 E: jim.free@tiscali.co.uk

FREEBAIRN-SMITH, Canon Jane. b 36. St Chris Coll Blackheath IDC 60. **d** 88 **p** 94. NSM Uddingston *Glas* 88-91; NSM Cambuslang 88-91; Dioc Missr 88-92; Dioc Past Cllr 92-95; NSM Baillieston 91-92; C St Mary's Cathl 92-95; TV Hykeham *Linc* 95-03; Can and Preb Linc Cathl 02-03; rtd 04. *12 Bell Grove, Lincoln LN6 7PL* T: (01522) 705421

FREELAND, Nicolas John Michell. b 65. FNMSM 99 FCMI 10. STETS 07. **d** 10 **p** 11. NSM Jersey St Pet *Win* 10-13; C from 13. *Le Vieux Ménage, Rue de la Ville au Neveu, St Ouen, Jersey JE3 2DU* T: (01534) 618284 M: 07797-736023 E: nicolas.freeland@jerseymail.co.uk

FREEMAN, Anthony John Curtis. b 46. Ex Coll Ox BA 68 MA 72. Cuddesdon Coll 70. **d** 72 **p** 73. C Worc St Martin 72-74; C Worc St Martin w St Pet 74-75; Bp's Dom Chapl *Chich* 75-78; C-in-c Parklands St Wilfrid CD 78-82; V Durrington 82-89; P-in-c Staplefield Common 89-94; Bp's Adv on CME 89-93; Asst Dir of Ords 89-93. *6 Winchester Drive, Chichester PO19 5DE* T: (01243) 783136 E: anthony.jcs@gmail.com

FREEMAN, Mrs Dorothy Lloyd (Dee). b 54. Lon Inst of Educn BEd 76. EMMTC 06. **d** 09 **p** 10. NSM Linc St Geo Swallowbeck from 09. *Bethany, 69 Lincoln Road, Bassingham, Lincoln LN5 9JR* T: (01522) 788942 E: freemen@btinternet.com

FREEMAN, Gordon Bertie. b 37. CITC BTh 95. **d** 95 **p** 96. C Lecale Gp *D & D* 95-98; I Ardara w Glencolumbkille, Inniskeel etc *D & R* 98-07; Bp's Dom Chapl 06-07; rtd 07. *3 Leyland Meadow, Ballycastle BT54 6JX* T: (028) 2076 8458

FREEMAN, Canon Jane. b 54. Dur Univ BA 75 PhD 80. Qu Coll Birm BD 00. **d** 00 **p** 01. C Waterloo St Jo w St Andr *S'wark* 00-03; TV E Ham w Upton Park and Forest Gate *Chelmsf* 03-11; TR Wickford and Runwell from 11; Hon Can Chelmsf Cathl from 09. *8 Friern Walk, Wickford SS12 0HZ* T: (01268) 734077 M: 07702-922818 E: email@janefreeman.fsnet.co.uk

FREEMAN, Mrs Karen Lynn. b 62. San Diego State Univ USA BS 86 Leeds Univ BA 09. NOC 06. **d** 09 **p** 10. C New Brighton St Jas w Em *Ches* 09-12; P-in-c Birkenhead Ch Ch from 13. *The Vicarage, 7 Palm Grove, Prenton CH43 1TE* E: k.freeman62@gmail.com

FREEMAN, Preb Karl Fredrick. b 57. St Luke's Coll Ex BEd 80. **d** 90 **p** 91. C Plymouth St Andr w St Paul and St Geo *Ex* 90-95; TV Plymouth St Andr and Stonehouse 95-96; Chapl Coll of SS Mark and Jo Plymouth 96-01; TR Plymouth Em, St Paul Efford and St Aug from 01; Preb Ex Cathl from 14; RD Plymouth City from 15. *The Rectory, 9 Seymour Drive, Plymouth PL3 5BG* T: (01752) 248601 *or* 260317 E: karldesk@blueyonder.co.uk

FREEMAN, Keith Ian. b 66. St Jo Coll Nottm 10. **d** 12 **p** 13. C Shelley and Shepley *Leeds* from 12. *6 Stonecroft Gardens, Shepley, Huddersfield HD8 8EX* T: (01484) 522483 M: 07958-328289 E: keithfreeman66@hotmail.com

FREEMAN (formerly MARSHALL), Kirstin Heather. b 64. St Jo Coll Nottm 90 TISEC 95. **d** 93 **p** 95. NSM Glas St Marg 93-96; Hon Asst P Glas St Mary 96-99; P-in-c E Kilbride 99-09; TR Bearsden w Milngavie from 09. *67 Stockiemuir Avenue, Bearsden, Glasgow G61 3JJ* T: 0141-931 5649 E: revkirstin@freemanhome.co.uk

FREEMAN, Malcolm Robin. b 48. Master Mariner 78. St And NSM Tr Scheme 85. **d** 88 **p** 89. NSM Kirkcaldy *St And* 88-94; NSM Westbury *Sarum* 99-02; R Tidworth, Ludgershall and Faberstown 02-13; rtd 13; PtO *Win* from 14. *26 Home*

Farm Gardens, Charlton, Andover SP10 4AX M: 07810-862740 E: fgmastermariner@ntlworld.com

FREEMAN, Martin. *See* FREEMAN, Philip Martin

FREEMAN, Michael Charles. b 36. Magd Coll Cam BA 61 MA 68 Lon Univ BD 69 PhD 93. Clifton Th Coll 67. **d** 69 **p** 70. C Bedworth *Cov* 69-72; C Morden *S'wark* 72-77; P-in-c Westcombe Park St Geo 77-85; V Kingston Vale St Jo 85-94; rtd 99; PtO *B & W* from 11. *6 Wristland Road, Watchet TA23 0DH* T: (01984) 634378 E: freemmic@talktalk.net

FREEMAN, Michael Curtis. b 51. Lanc Univ BA 72 Liv Hope Univ Coll MA 96 PhD 05. Cuddesdon Coll 72. **d** 75 **p** 76. C Walton St Mary *Liv* 75-78; C Hednesford *Lich* 78-81; TV Solihull *Birm* 81-86; V Yardley Wood 86-90; V Farnworth *Liv* 90-03; AD Widnes 02-03; P-in-c Blundellsands St Mich 03-12; V 12; P-in-c Thornton and Crosby 05-12; rtd 12. *5 Lincoln Crescent, Bootle L20 7EB* E: mcfreeman@btinternet.com

FREEMAN, Michael Raymond. b 58. Chu Coll Cam BA 80 MA 84 Ox Univ BA 87. St Steph Ho Ox 85. **d** 88 **p** 89. C Clifton All SS w St Jo *Bris* 88-92; TV Elland *Wakef* 92-01; V Horninglow *Lich* from 01; RD Tutbury from 10. *Horninglow Vicarage, 14 Rolleston Road, Burton-on-Trent DE13 0JZ* T: (01283) 568613 E: cft-rfreeman@supanet.com

FREEMAN, Preb Pamela Mary. b 45. Univ of Wales (Lamp) MA 08. WMMTC 83. **dss** 86 **d** 87 **p** 94. Cannock *Lich* 86-88; Par Dn 87-88; Min for Deaf (Salop Adnry) 88-95; Par Dn Shelton and Oxon *Lich* 88-94; C 94-95; TV Stafford 95-00; P-in-c High Offley and Norbury 00-02; R Adbaston, High Offley, Knightley, Norbury etc 02-10; Preb Lich Cathl 07-10; rtd 10; PtO *Lich* from 11; Chapl Severn Hospice from 11. *14 Meadow Close, Trentham Road, Wem, Shrewsbury SY4 5HP* T: (01939) 234672 E: p.m.freeman@btinternet.com

FREEMAN, Peter Cameron Jessett. b 41. **d** 05 **p** 06. OLM Sturry w Fordwich and Westbere w Hersden *Cant* 05-11; rtd 11; PtO *Cant* from 11. *29 Cedar Road, Sturry, Canterbury CT2 0HZ*

FREEMAN, Philip Martin. b 54. Westcott Ho Cam 76. **d** 79 **p** 80. C Stanley *Liv* 79-82; C Bromborough *Ches* 82-84; V Runcorn H Trin 84-91; Chapl Halton Gen Hosp 84-91; R Ashton-upon-Mersey St Martin *Ches* 91-96; SSF 96-06; PtO *Sarum* 96-99; Asst Chapl HM Pris Birm 98-99; PtO *Lon* 99-02; *Ely* 02-05; Chapl Barts and The Lon NHS Trust 00-02 and 05-08; Chapl Guy's and St Thos' NHS Foundn Trust 05-08; PtO *S'wark* 05-08; Chapl Univ Coll Lon Hosps NHS Foundn Trust from 08; Hon C Smithfield St Bart *Lon* 06-15; Hon C Smithfield Gt St Bart from 15. *Flat 1, 48 Huntley Street, London WC1E 6DD* T: (020) 7419 9095 M: 07985-512436 E: martin.freeman@uclh.nhs.uk

FREEMAN, Richard Alan. b 52. Ripon Coll Cuddesdon. **d** 83 **p** 84. C Crayford *Roch* 83-86; V Slade Green 86-94; R Eynsford w Farningham and Lullingstone 94-01; P-in-c Shoreham 01-12; V 12-15; Chapl St Mich Sch Otford 01-15; R Bradworthy, Sutcombe, Putford etc *Ex* from 15. *The New Rectory, St Peters Well Lane, Bradworthy, Holsworthy EX22 7TG* T: (01409) 241315 E: ricktherec@aol.com

✠**FREEMAN, The Rt Revd Robert John.** b 52. St Jo Coll Dur BSc 74 Fitzw Coll Cam BA 76 MA. Ridley Hall Cam 74. **d** 77 **p** 78 **c** 11. C Blackpool St Jo *Blackb* 77-81; TV Chigwell *Chelmsf* 81-85; V Leic Martyrs 85-99; Hon Can Leic Cathl 94-03; RD Christianity S 95-98; Nat Adv in Evang 99-03; LtO *Leic* 99-03; Adn Halifax *Wakef* 03-11; Suff Bp Penrith *Carl* from 11. *Holm Croft, 13 Castle Road, Kendal LA9 7AU* T: (01539) 727836 E: bishop.penrith@carlislediocese.org.uk

FREEMAN, Rodney. *See* FREEMAN, William Rodney

FREEMAN, Rosemary. b 47. **d** 03 **p** 04. NSM Madeley *Heref* from 03. *5 Rowley Close, Madeley, Telford TF7 5RR* T: (01952) 583460

FREEMAN, Terence. b 40. Wells Th Coll 67. **d** 70 **p** 71. C Hanham *Bris* 70-75; C Cockington *Ex* 75-77; R Sampford Spiney w Horrabridge 77-89; V Wembury 89-08; rtd 08. *85 Blackstone Close, Plymouth PL9 8UW* E: revkarl.freeman@lineone.net

FREEMAN, William Rodney. b 35. Ch Coll Cam MA 63 FCA 73. **d** 95 **p** 96. OLM Chelmondiston and Erwarton w Harkstead *St E* 95-05; PtO *St E* from 05. *Lavender Cottage, Harkstead, Ipswich IP9 1BN* T: (01473) 328381 E: revrod@lavcot.freeserve.co.uk

FREESTONE, Anne Elizabeth. b 52. Bp Otter Coll Chich CertEd 73 Coll of Ripon & York St Jo MA 00. NEOC 04. **d** 07 **p** 08. NSM Middleton-in-Teesdale w Forest and Frith *Dur* 07-11; PtO from 11; *Ripon* from 14; Chapl Castle Howard from 15. *22 Birch Road, Barnard Castle DL12 8JR* T: (01833) 631018 M: 07939-964011 E: annefreestone22@btinternet.com

FREETH, Barry James. b 35. Birm Univ BA 60. Tyndale Hall Bris 60. **d** 62 **p** 64. C Selly Hill St Steph *Birm* 62-63; C Birm St Jo Ladywood 63-71; Chapl RAF 71-75; P-in-c Crudwell w Ashley *Bris* 75-81; P-in-c Lanreath *Truro* 81-84; R 84-87; P-in-c

Pelynt 81-84; V 84-87; R Harvington and Norton and Lenchwick *Worc* 87-93; V Ramsden, Finstock and Fawler, Leafield etc *Ox* 93-99; rtd 99; PtO *Derby* 99-03; *Ox* from 08. *16 Broad Meadow, Leonard Stanley, Stonehouse GL10 3PG* T: (01453) 823890

FREETH, John Stanton. b 40. Selw Coll Cam BA 62 MA 66. Ridley Hall Cam 64. **d** 66 **p** 67. C Gillingham St Mark *Roch* 66-72; TV Heslington *York* 72-80; Chapl York Univ 72-80; TR Wynberg St Jo S Africa 80-93; Adn Athlone 88-93. *15 Wellington Road, Wynberg, 7800 South Africa* T: (0027) (21) 761 0908 E: jill@pdg.co.za

FREETH, Mrs Patricia. b 48. Wycliffe Hall Ox BTh 95. **d** 95 **p** 96. NSM Ramsden, Finstock and Fawler, Leafield etc *Ox* 95-99; TV Buxton w Burbage and King Sterndale *Derby* 99-03; V Shires' Edge *Ox* 03-12; AD Deddington 10-12; rtd 12; PtO *Glouc* from 13. *16 Broad Meadow, Leonard Stanley, Stonehouse GL10 3PG* T: (01453) 823890 E: pfreeth@toucansurf.com

FREMMER, Ludger. b 56. Ridley Hall Cam 02. **d** 04 **p** 05. C Mattishall w Mattishall Burgh, Welborne etc *Nor* 04-07; P-in-c Kibworth and Smeeton Westerby and Saddington *Leic* from 07. *The Rectory, 25 Church Road, Kibworth, Leicester LE8 0NB* T: 0116-279 2294 M: 07753-213145 E: ludger.fremmer@tesco.net

FRENCH, Mrs Christine. b 68. Nottm Trent Univ PGCE 05. EMMTC MA 08 Qu Coll Birm MPhil 09. **d** 09 **p** 10. C Keyworth and Stanton-on-the-Wolds and Bunny etc *S'well* 09-13; P-in-c Norwell w Ossington, Cromwell and Caunton 13-14; P-in-c Kirk Hallam *Derby* from 14. *The Vicarage, 71 Ladywood Road, Ilkeston DE7 4NF* T: 0115-783 1793 E: chrisclayton18@btinternet.com

FRENCH, Canon Clive Anthony. b 43. AKC 70. St Aug Coll Cant 70. **d** 71 **p** 72. C Monkseaton St Mary *Newc* 71-73; Dioc Youth Adv 73-76; Chapl RN 76-97; Dir of Ords RN 85-90; Chapl RN Coll Greenwich 95-97; R Cheam *S'wark* 97-06; TR Catford (Southend) and Downham 06-09; Hon Can *S'wark* Cathl 08-09; rtd 09; PtO *S'wark* 10 and from 14. *17 Kingslea, Leatherhead KT22 7SN* T: (01372) 375418

FRENCH, Daniel Alain. b 68. Kent Univ BSc 91. St Jo Sem Wonersh BTh 97. **d** 97 **p** 98. In RC Ch 97-01; P-in-c Aberdeen St Clem *Ab* 03-08; Chapl Robert Gordon Univ 04-08; V Salcombe and Malborough w S Huish *Ex* from 08; RD Woodleigh from 12. *The Vicarage, Devon Road, Salcombe TQ8 8HJ* T: (01548) 842853 E: cybervicar@gmail.com

FRENCH, Canon Dendle Charles. b 29. Lon Univ BD 56. ALCD 55. **d** 56 **p** 57. C Gt Yarmouth *Nor* 56-63; Jamaica 63-66; V Sedgeford w Southmere *Nor* 66-71; P-in-c Gt Ringstead 66-67; R 67-71; TV Thetford 71-74; Chapl Hockerill Coll Bishop's Stortford 74-78; P-in-c St Paul's Walden *St Alb* 78-85; V 85-94; RD Hitchin 84-89; Hon Can St Alb 91-94; rtd 94; Chapl Glamis Castle 94-10. *4 Curtis Close, Collingham, Newark NG23 7QW* T: (01636) 892217 E: dendle.french@talk21.com

FRENCH, Derek John. b 47. Man Univ BA 03. Ripon Coll Cuddesdon 93. **d** 95 **p** 96. C Stand *Man* 95-98; TV E Farnworth and Kearsley 98-00; P-in-c Halliwell St Marg 00-09; P-in-c Ringley w Prestolee 06-09; P-in-c Elton St Steph 09-11; V 11-15; rtd 15. *Address temp unknown* E: revdelboy@gmail.com

FRENCH, George Leslie. b 47. AIFST NE Lon Poly BSc 70. S'wark Ord Course 86. **d** 89 **p** 90. NSM Reading St Barn *Ox* 89-99. *Hawthorne House, 2 Cutbush Close, Lower Earley, Reading RG6 4XA* T: 0118-986 1886

FRENCH, Janet. b 54. Anglia Poly Univ MA 05. EAMTC 99. **d** 02 **p** 03. C Thetford *Nor* 02-06; R Thyrbergh *Sheff* 06-11; V Heaton Ch Ch w Halliwell St Marg *Man* from 11. *The Vicarage, 2 Towncroft Lane, Bolton BL1 5EW* T: (01204) 840430 E: frenchrevj@hotmail.com

FRENCH, Janet Mary. *See* DRIVER, Janet Mary

FRENCH, Jonathan David Seabrook. b 60. Westcott Ho Cam 84. **d** 87 **p** 88. C Loughton St Jo *Chelmsf* 87-90; Chapl St Bede's Ch for the Deaf Clapham 90-92; C Richmond St Mary w St Matthias and St Jo *S'wark* 92-95; TV 96-03; V Downham St Barn 03-10; Chapl RAD 92-03; Dioc Adv for Min of Deaf and Disabled People *S'wark* 03-10; R Southwick *Chich* from 10. *The Rectory, 22 Church Lane, Southwick, Brighton BN42 4GB* T: (01273) 592389 E: jo.nathan@btinternet.com

FRENCH, The Ven Judith Karen. b 60. St D Coll Lamp BA 89. St Steph Ho Ox 89. **d** 91 **p** 94. Par Dn Botley *Portsm* 91-94; C Bilton *Cov* 94-97; V Charlbury w Shorthampton *Ox* 97-14; AD Chipping Norton 07-12; Hon Can Ch Ch 12-14; Adn Dorchester from 14. *11 Broad Field Road, Yarnton, Kidlington OX5 1UL* M: 07460-888482 E: archdeacon.dorchester@oxford.anglican.org

FRENCH, Julia. b 57. **d** 06 **p** 07. NSM Plympton St Maurice *Ex* 06-15. *1 Mitre Court, Taunton TA1 3ER* T: (01823) 710798

FRENCH, Michael Anders. b 61. Ch Coll Cam BA 83 MA 87 Ridley Hall Cam BA 91 Man Univ MA(Econ) 96. **d** 92 **p** 93. C Norbury *Ches* 92-96; Chapl Univ Coll Ches 96-01; Chapl Geneva *Eur* 01-08; Dir Advocacy World Vision UK from 08; PtO *Ox* from 09; *St Alb* 09-14. *175 route de la Douane, F-01220 Sauverny, France* T: (0041) (79) 668 7592 *or* 207 6814 E: m.french@bluewin.ch

FRENCH, Michael John. b 37. WEMTC 92. **d** 95 **p** 96. OLM Cheltenham St Pet *Glouc* 95-01; NSM 01-08; NSM N Cheltenham from 08. *8 Alexandria Walk, Cheltenham GL52 5LG* T: (01242) 236661

FRENCH, Peter Robert. b 65. Man Univ BTh 87. Qu Coll Birm 88. **d** 90 **p** 91. C Unsworth *Man* 90-93; C Bury Ch King w H Trin 93-95; V Bury Ch King 95-98; V Handsworth St Andr *Birm* 98-06; Sch Support Officer from 06. *Diocesan Office, 1 Colmore Row, Birmingham B3 2BJ* T: 0121-426 0400 E: pfrench@birmingham.anglican.org *or* peterfrench55@aol.com

FRENCH, Richard John. b 34. Open Univ BA 82. Tyndale Hall Bris 62. **d** 64 **p** 65. C Rustington *Chich* 64-68; C Walton H Trin *Ox* 68-72; V Grove 72-99; rtd 99; PtO *Chich* from 01. *5 Green Meadows, The Welkin, Haywards Heath RH16 2PE* T: (01444) 487842

FRENCH, Stephen Robert James. b 52. St Jo Coll Nottm. **d** 87 **p** 88. C Chell *Lich* 87-91; TV 91-94; V Wednesfield Heath 94-01; TV Hemel Hempstead *St Alb* 01-06; P-in-c Bugbrooke w Rothersthorpe Pef 06-10; P-in-c Kislingbury and Harpole 06-10; R Bugbrooke, Harpole, Kislingbury etc from 10. *The Rectory, Church Lane, Bugbrooke, Northampton NN7 3PB* T: (01604) 831621 E: srjfrench@hotmail.co.uk

FRENCH, William Stephen. b 49. STETS 07. **d** 10 **p** 11. NSM Verwood *Sarum* from 10. *Hollow Tree House, Chalbury, Wimborne BH21 7ER* T: (01258) 841061 M: 07771-560128 E: william.french4@btinternet.com

FRERE, Christopher Michael Hanbury. b 21. Roch Th Coll 65. **d** 67 **p** 68. C Spilsby w Hundleby *Linc* 67-71; V N Kelsey 71-76; V Cadney 71-76; P-in-c Aisthorpe w W Thorpe and Scampton 75-79; P-in-c Brattleby 75-79; R Fillingham 76-78; V Ingham w Cammeringham 76-78; RD Lawres 78-84; V Ingham w Cammeringham w Fillingham 79-86; R Aisthorpe w Scampton w Thorpe le Fallows etc 79-86; rtd 86; PtO *Linc* from 86. *164 Newark Road, North Hykeham, Lincoln LN6 8LZ* T: (01522) 806326 E: cmh.frere@ntlworld.com

FRESHNEY, June. b 46. EMMTC 95. **d** 98 **p** 99. NSM Washingborough w Heighington and Canwick *Linc* 98-05; Asst Chapl St Barn Hospice Linc 03-05; P-in-c Caythorpe *Linc* 05-15. *Address temp unknown* M: 07798-840015 E: revjune@supanet.com

FRESTON, John Samuel Kern. b 28. Lich Th Coll 70. **d** 72 **p** 73. C Walsall *Lich* 72-75; TV Trunch w Swafield *Nor* 75-77; TV Trunch 77-82; R W Winch 82-91; Chapl St Jas Hosp King's Lynn 82-85; Chapl Qu Eliz Hosp King's Lynn 85-90; rtd 91; PtO *Nor* from 91; *Ely* from 91. *71 Howdale Road, Downham Market PE38 9AH* T: (01366) 385936

FRETT, Daniel Calvin. b 60. Univ of S Carolina 85. NTMTC 95 Oak Hill Th Coll BA 99. **d** 98 **p** 99. NSM Clerkenwell St Jas and St Jo w St Pet *Lon* 98-00; NSM Chelsea St Jo w St Andr 00-05; NSM Tulse Hill H Trin and St Matthias *S'wark* 05-08; NSM Cranleigh *Guildf* from 09. *3 Edgefield Close, Cranleigh GU6 8PX* T: (01483) 275861 E: dfrett@me.com

FRETWELL, Brian George. b 34. TD . CEng MIMechE. Chich Th Coll 79. **d** 81 **p** 82. C Bude Haven *Truro* 81-82; C Saltash 82-85; C Walthamstow St Sav *Chelmsf* 85-87; V Doncaster Intake *Sheff* 87-97; rtd 99. *55 Bankside, Woking GU21 3DZ* T: (01483) 721182

FRETWELL, Cynthia Mary. b 37. EMMTC 90. **d** 91 **p** 94. Chapl Asst Doncaster R Infirmary and Montagu Hosp NHS Trust 91-92; Chapl Tickhill Road Hosp Doncaster 91-92; Chapl St Cath Hosp Doncaster 91-92; Chapl Asst Doncaster R Infirmary and Montagu Hosp NHS Trust 92-95; Chapl 95-96; rtd 96. *55 Bankside, Woking GU21 3DZ* T: (01483) 721182

FREY, Christopher Ronald. b 44. AKC 69 Uppsala Univ BD 73 MTh 77. St Aug Coll Cant 69. **d** 70 **p** 71. C Addington *Ox* 70-72; LtO *Eur* 73-78; Chapl Stockholm w Uppsala 78-85; Can Brussels Cathl 81-85; Chapl Casterton Sch Lancs 85-89; Chapl Epsom Coll 89-91; Chapl Worksop Coll Notts 91-94; rtd 96. *Koriandergatan 42, 261 61 Landskrona, Sweden* T: (0046) (418) 20953

FREYHAN, Daniel Jonathan. b 83. Oriel Coll Ox MMath 06. Oak Hill Th Coll BA 14. **d** 14 **p** 15. C Stevenage St Nic and Graveley *St Alb* from 14. *89 Ripon Road, Stevenage SG1 4LW* E: daniel.freyhan@oriel.oxon.org

FRIARS, Ian Malcolm George. b 50. Sarum & Wells Th Coll 83. **d** 85 **p** 86. C Norton *St Alb* 85-88; C Ramsey *Ely* 88-90; TV The Ramseys and Upwood 90-93; P-in-c Cottenham 93-94;

R 94-01; P-in-c Long Melford *St E* 01-02; R Chadbrook 02-13; rtd 13; PtO *Ely* from 12; *St Alb* from 13; *St E* from 13. *Clanjenian, Swan Street, Ashwell, Baldock SG7 5NY* T: (01462) 742441 E: ianfriars@btinternet.com

FRIDD, Nicholas Timothy. b 53. Ch Ch Ox BA 74 MA 78. STETS 05. **d** 08 **p** 09. NSM Wells St Thos w Horrington *B & W* from 08. *The Old Bakery, 30 St Thomas Street, Wells BA5 2UX* M: 07831-209240

FRIEDRICH, Robert Edmund. b 48. Houghton Coll (USA) BA 70 Gordon-Conwell Th Sem MDiv 74 DMin 96. MDiv 74 Gen Th Sem NY 86 86. **d** 86 **p** 86. C Westfield Atonement USA 86-88; Springfield Dio W MA 86-99; R Penfield 88-92; R Newport Epiphany 92-97; Meriden All SS 99-02; W Haven St Jo 04; Las Vegas Grace in the Desert 04-06; Olean 06-07; PtO *St As* from 15. *Polyanna Cottage, Castle Street, Conwy LL32 8AY* E: bobfriedrich@gmail.com

FRIEND, Adam Lyndon David. b 76. St Martin's Coll Lanc BA 98. Cranmer Hall Dur 99. **d** 02 **p** 03. C Witton *Ches* 02-05; V Over St Chad 05-10; V Tarvin *Ches* from 10. *St Andrew's Vicarage, Church Street, Tarvin, Chester CH3 8EB* T: (01829) 740354 E: friendie@talk21.com *or* tarvinparish@gmail.com

FRIENDSHIP, Roger Geoffrey (John-Francis). b 46. ACII 72. WMMTC 90. **d** 93 **p** 94. SSF 76-02; NSM Harborne St Faith and St Laur *Birm* 93-94; Asst Novice Guardian Hilfield Friary 94-97; Novice Guardian 97-99; Gen Sec SSF 99-01; C Clerkenwell H Redeemer and St Mark *Lon* 00-01; R Romford St Andr *Chelmsf* 01-11; rtd 11; PtO *S'wark* from 12. *22 The Old Fire Station, Eaglesfield Road, London SE18 3BT* T: (020) 3583 9312 M: 07808-500717 E: jff2209@yahoo.com

FRIGGENS, Canon Maurice Anthony. b 40. Sheff Univ BA 65. Westcott Ho Cam 65. **d** 67 **p** 68. C Stocksbridge *Sheff* 67-70; C St Buryan, St Levan and Sennen *Truro* 70-72; R 72-84; RD Penwith 82-84; R St Columb Major w St Wenn 84-91; Dioc Dir of Ords 87-93; Hon Can Truro Cathl 87-00; V St Cleer 91-00; rtd 00; PtO *Ban* from 00; *Eur* from 01. *Tŷ Cernyw, Rhiw, Pwllheli LL53 8AF* T: (01758) 780365

FRISWELL, Caroline Anne. b 52. St Mary's Coll Chelt BEd 78 Sunderland Poly MA 90 Dur Univ PhD 99. Cranmer Hall Dur 06. **d** 09 **p** 10. NSM Greenside *Dur* 09-12; P-in-c Byers Green from 12. *12. Westholme, Durham Moor, Durham DH1 5AH* T: 0191-384 0191 E: caroline.friswell@btinternet.com

FRITH, Canon Christopher John Cokayne. b 44. Ex Coll Ox BA 65 MA 69. Ridley Hall Cam 66. **d** 68 **p** 69. C Crookes St Thos *Sheff* 68-71; C Rusholme H Trin *Man* 71-74; R Haughton St Mary 74-85; R Brampton St Thos *Derby* 85-02; V Alvaston 02-09; Hon Can Derby Cathl 99-09; rtd 09. *Cover Point, Back Lane, Bredon, Tewkesbury GL20 7LH* T: (01684) 773164 E: cjcfrith@gmail.com

FRITH, Mrs Gillian. b 43. EAMTC 99. **d** 02 **p** 03. NSM Chipping Ongar w Shelley *Chelmsf* 02-06; P-in-c Doddinghurst 06-13; rtd 13; PtO *Chelmsf* from 14. *29 Windmill Fields, Coggeshall, Colchester CO6 1PJ* M: 07890-376779 E: g.frith@waitrose.com

FRITH, Jonathan Paul (Jonty). b 72. Jes Coll Cam BA 94 MA 97. Wycliffe Hall Ox 95. **d** 97 **p** 98. C Houghton *Carl* 97-00; Chapl Cranleigh Sch Surrey 00-04; C Crowborough *Chich* 04-15; R Bathampton w Claverton *B & W* from 15. *The Vicarage, Bathampton Lane, Bathampton, Bath BA2 6SW* E: jp@jpfrith.freeserve.co.uk

FRITH, Richard John. b 77. Warwick Univ BA 98 Sheff Univ MA 99 Trin Hall Cam PhD 04. Ripon Coll Cuddesdon BA 10. **d** 11 **p** 12. C Ox St Mary Magd 11-14; V Halifax H Trin and St Jude *Leeds* from 14. *Holy Trinity Vicarage, 9 Love Lane, Halifax HX1 2BQ* M: 07754-524206 T: (01422) 352446 E: richard.frith@ymail.com

✠**FRITH, The Rt Revd Richard Michael Cokayne.** b 49. Fitzw Coll Cam BA 72 MA 76. St Jo Coll Nottm 72. **d** 74 **p** 75 **c** 98. C Mortlake w E Sheen *S'wark* 74-78; TV Thameshead 78-83; TR Keynsham *B & W* 83-92; Preb Wells Cathl 91-98; Adn Taunton 92-98; Suff Bp Hull *York* 98-14; Bp Heref from 14. *The Bishop's House, The Palace, Hereford HR4 9BN* T: (01432) 271355 F: 373346 E: bishop@hereford.anglican.org

FRITZE-SHANKS, Miss Annette. Sydney Univ BA 86 DipEd 87 LLB 89 Solicitor . SEITE 01. **d** 04 **p** 05. NSM Kilburn St Mary w All So and W Hampstead St Jas *Lon* 04-08; PtO 08-10; NSM Hampstead Em W End from 10. *13 Elm Grove, London NW2 3AE* M: 07771-544201 E: afritze-shanks@btinternet.com

FROGGATT, Mrs Alison. b 35. Dur Univ BA 56 Bradf Univ MA 79. NOC 96. **d** 98 **p** 98. NSM Bingley H Trin *Bradf* 98-01; rtd 01; PtO *Leeds* from 01. *87 Warren Lane, Bingley BD16 3BY* T: (01274) 565716 E: alison.froggatt@bradford.anglican.org

FROGGATT, Mrs Elaine Muriel. b 43. **d** 00 **p** 01. OLM Skirwith, Ousby and Melmerby w Kirkland *Carl* 00-04; NSM Cross Fell Gp 04-10; rtd 10. *Address temp unknown*

FROGGATT, Peter Michael. b 65. St Hild Coll Dur BA 86 PGCE 88. Wycliffe Hall Ox BTh 95. **d** 95 **p** 96. C Bebington *Ches* 95-00; V Rock Ferry 00-11; RD Birkenhead 10-11; V Barnston from 11; RD Wirral N from 15. *The Vicarage, 87 Barnston Road, Heswall, Wirral CH61 1BW* T: 0151-648 1776 *or* 648 2404 E: peter@froggatt.org.uk

FRONDIGOUN, Mrs Marjorie Elizabeth. b 46. Open Univ BA 87 MSc 94. **d** 08 **p** 09. OLM Cannock and Huntington *Lich* 08-11; NSM 11-13; rtd 13; PtO *Lich* from 13. *12 Adamson Close, Cannock WS11 1TJ* T: (01543) 571199 M: 07889-359358 E: elizabeth.frondigoun@btinternet.com

FROOM, Ian Leonard John. b 42. Sarum Th Coll 69. **d** 71 **p** 72. C Gillingham and Fifehead Magdalen *Sarum* 71-75; C Parkstone St Pet w Branksea and St Osmund 75-78; V Sedgley St Mary *Lich* 78-85; TV Weston-super-Mare Cen Par *B & W* 85-94; PtO 94-97; V Truro St Geo and St Jo 97-03; rtd 03; PtO *Truro* from 03. *11 Marlborough Crescent, Falmouth TR11 2RJ* T: (01326) 311760

FROST, Alan Sydney. b 26. K Coll Lon BD 50 AKC 50. **d** 51 **p** 52. C Folkestone St Sav *Cant* 51-56; C Sneinton St Steph *S'well* 56-59; C Croydon Woodside *Cant* 60-63; Asst Chapl Mersey Miss to Seamen 63-66; rtd 91. *Address withheld by request*

FROST, Alex David John. b 69. LCTP 12. **d** 15. C Burnley St Matt w H Trin *Blackb* from 15. *St Mark's Vicarage, 9 Rossendale Road, Burnley BB11 5DQ*

FROST, David John. b 48. **d** 86 **p** 87. Hon C Upper Norwood All SS *S'wark* 86-89; C Battersea St Luke 90-94; V Shirley St Geo 94-12; rtd 12; PtO *S'wark* from 12. *19 Reculver Avenue, Birchington CT7 9NT* T: (01843) 844511 E: revdfrost1@gmail.com

FROST, Canon David Richard. b 54. Ridley Hall Cam 84. **d** 86 **p** 87. C Burgess Hill St Andr *Chich* 86-90; TV Rye 90-94; V Bexhill St Steph 94-10; RD Battle and Bexhill 06-10; TR Rye from 10; RD from 11; Can and Preb Chich Cathl from 10. *The Rectory, Gungarden, Rye TN31 7HH* T: (01797) 222430 M: 07970-746545 E: david@drfrost.org.uk

FROST, Derek Charles. b 47. Lich Th Coll 69. **d** 71 **p** 72. C Woodley St Jo the Ev *Ox* 71-76; V Bampton w Clanfield 76-81; V Minster Lovell and Brize Norton 81-88; TV Upper Kennet *Sarum* 88-92; P-in-c Seend and Bulkington 92-97; P-in-c Seend, Bulkington and Poulshot 95-97; V 97-01; V Derry Hill w Bremhill and Foxham 01-10; rtd 10; PtO *Sarum* from 10. *Longhope Cottage, 93 North Street, Calne SN11 0HJ* T: (01249) 811565

FROST, The Ven George. b 35. Dur Univ BA 56 MA 61. Linc Th Coll 57. **d** 60 **p** 61. C Barking St Marg *Chelmsf* 60-64; C-in-c Marks Gate CD 64-70; V Tipton St Matt *Lich* 70-77; V Penn 77-87; RD Trysull 84-87; Preb Lich Cathl 85-87; Adn Salop 87-98; V Tong 87-98; P-in-c Donington 97-98; Adn Lich and Can Res and Treas Lich Cathl 98-00; rtd 00; PtO *Lich* from 00. *23 Darnford Lane, Lichfield WS14 9RW* T: (01543) 415109 E: frost151@btinternet.com

FROST, Mrs Jane Helena. b 59. St Aid Coll Dur BA 81 Newc Univ PGCE 82. SWMTC 12. **d** 15. NSM Totnes w Bridgetown, Berry Pomeroy etc *Ex* from 15. *The Vicarage, Week, Dartington, Totnes TQ9 6JL* T: (01803) 865196 M: 07564-979258 E: janehfrost@aol.com

FROST, Jeremy James. b 74. New Coll Ox BA 96 MA 99. Wycliffe Hall Ox BA 99. **d** 00 **p** 01. C Wellington All SS w Eyton *Lich* 00-04; Min Can and Prec Cant Cathl 04-09; Chapl Greenwich Univ *S'wark* 09-14; Chapl RN Coll Greenwich 09-14; Chapl Trin Coll of Mus 09-14. *40 Vanburgh Park, London SE3 7AA* T: (020) 8853 1969 E: jeremy@jamesfrost.fsnet.co.uk

✠**FROST, The Rt Revd Jonathan Hugh.** b 64. Aber Univ BD 88 Nottm Univ MTh 99 Surrey Univ DUniv 12 MSSTh 91 FRSA 06. Ridley Hall Cam 91. **d** 93 **p** 94 **c** 10. C W Bridgford *S'well* 93-97; Police Chapl Trent Division 94-97; R Ash *Guildf* 97-02; Tutor Local Min Progr 99-10; Can Res Guildf Cathl 02-10; Chapl Surrey Univ 02-10; Co-ord Chapl 08-10; Bp's Adv Inter-Faith Relns *Guildf* 07-10; Suff Bp Southampton *Win* from 10. *Bishop's House, St Mary's Church Close, Southampton SO18 2ST* T: (023) 8067 2684 E: bishop.jonathan@winchester.anglican.org

FROST, Canon Julian. b 36. Bris Univ BA 61 MA 65 Lon Univ CertEd 70 Solicitor 57. Clifton Th Coll 64. **d** 65 **p** 66. C Welling Roch 65-69; Hon C 70-73; Dep Dir Schs Coun RE Project Lanc Univ 73-78; V New Beckenham St Paul *Roch* 78-01; Hon Can Roch Cathl 00-01; rtd 01; PtO *Blackb* from 01. *93 Scotforth Road, Lancaster LA1 4JN* T: (01524) 841967 E: julian@canonfrost.plus.com

FROST, Linda May. b 59. CITC MTh 14. **d** 13 **p** 14. Howth *D & G* 13-14; C Mohill w Farnaught, Aughavas, Oughteragh etc *K, E & A* from 14. *Corbo, Kilrooskey, Co Roscommon, Republic of Ireland* M: (00353) 86-601 0895 E: welcomefrost@iol.ie

FROST, Michael John. b 42. Westmr Coll Ox TCert 64. **d** 95 **p** 96. OLM Harwood *Man* 95-12; rtd 12; PtO *Man* from 12. *86 Harden Drive, Harwood, Bolton BL2 5BX* T: (01204) 418596

FROST, Paul William. b 75. Sheff Univ BA 97 Ox Univ PGCE 98. Wycliffe Hall Ox MTh 08. **d** 08 **p** 09. C Kettering Ch the King *Pet* 08-12; P-in-c Corby Epiphany w St Jo from 12. *16 Streather Drive, Corby NN17 1TN* M: 07979-547279
E: frost.pw@gmail.com

FROST, Richard John. b 49. Ch Ch Coll Cant CertEd 71 BA 00. SWMTC 95. **d** 97 **p** 98. NSM Bideford, Northam, Westward Ho!, Appledore etc *Ex* 97-00; C 00-03; TV 03-09; rtd 09; Chapl Kyrenia St Andr Cyprus 11-13; PtO *St E* from 15. *Cana, 2 Tarka Falls, Old Barnstaple Road, Bideford EX39 4FL*
E: richardjohnfrost@hotmail.co.uk

FROST, Ronald Andrew. b 48. Univ of S Carolina BTh 81. Ridley Hall Cam 86. **d** 87 **p** 88. C Gt Wilbraham *Ely* 87-89; P-in-c Kimbolton 89-91; V 91-10; P-in-c Stow Longa 89-91; V 91-10; P-in-c Covington and Tilbrook 07-10; rtd 10; PtO *Cant* from 12. *41 Botany Road, Broadstairs CT10 3SA* T: (01843) 869788 M: 07866-648493
E: ronfrostis@gmail.com

FROST, Stanley. b 37. Univ of Wales BSc 61 Liv Univ MSc 65 PhD 68 MSB 66 CBiol 66 FAEB 82. NOC 79. **d** 82 **p** 83. NSM Lower Kersal *Man* 82-87; NSM Patricroft 87-89; NSM Convenor 87-95; Lic Preacher 89-03; P-in-c Pittenweem and Elie and Earlsferry *St And* 03-04; rtd 04; PtO *Derby* from 04. *25 Somersall Park Road, Chesterfield S40 3LD* T: (01246) 567184 E: stan.frost@homecall.co.uk

FROST, Preb William Selwyn. b 29. Wells Th Coll 61. **d** 62 **p** 63. C Cheddleton *Lich* 62-67; V Longdon-upon-Tern 67-81; R Rodington 67-81; RD Wrockwardine 77-84; Preb Lich Cathl 81-96; R Longdon-upon-Tern, Rodington, Uppington etc 81-84; R Whittington St Jo 84-86; C Trysull 86-89; TV Wombourne w Trysull and Bobbington 89-96; rtd 96; PtO *Heref* from 96. *Ty Ffos, Dilwyn, Hereford HR4 8HZ* T: (01544) 318703

FROSTICK, Canon John George. b 23. Wells Th Coll 52. **d** 54 **p** 55. C Loughborough St Pet *Leic* 54-57; C Knighton St Mary Magd 57-58; V Frisby-on-the-Wreake w Kirby Bellars 58-71; V Shepshed 71-83; R Kirton w Falkenham *St E* 83-90; Hon Can Leic Cathl 80-83; rtd 90; PtO *Leic* from 91. *68 Melton Road, Barrow-upon-Soar, Loughborough LE12 8NX* T: (01509) 620110

FROSTICK, Paul Andrew. b 52. Stockwell Coll of Educn CertEd 73. Ripon Hall Ox 74. **d** 77 **p** 78. C Shepton Mallet *B & W* 77-80; TV Barton Mills, Beck Row w Kenny Hill etc *St E* 80-85; TV Mildenhall 85-86; TV Raveningham *Nor* 86-89; V Bottisham and P-in-c Lode and Longmeadow *Ely* 89-90; V Bottisham and Lode w Long Meadow 90-94; Hd RE Brittons Sch Romford 94-97; Hd RE The Grove Sch St Leonards 97-00; rtd 00; Assoc P Bexhill St Aug *Chich* from 99. *18 The Ridings, Bexhill-on-Sea TN39 5HU* T: (01424) 218126
E: paul@frostickrev.freeserve.co.uk

FROUD, Andrew William. b 65. Mansf Coll Ox BA 87 St Cath Coll Cam MPhil 92. Westcott Ho Cam 90. **d** 93 **p** 94. C Almondbury w Farnley Tyas *Wakef* 93-96; P-in-c Wootton *Portsm* 96-00; R 00-01; V Thornton-le-Fylde *Blackb* 01-05; Chapl St Geo C of E Sch Blackpool 05-09; P-in-c Clitheroe St Mary 09-13; V from 13; P-in-c Chatburn and Downham from 14. *The Vicarage, Church Street, Clitheroe BB7 2DD* T: (01253) 764467 E: andyfroud@googlemail.com

FROUDE (née WOOLCOCK), The Ven Christine Ann. b 47. ACIB 73. S Dios Minl Tr Scheme 92. **d** 95 **p** 96. NSM Stoke Bishop *Bris* 95-99; Chapl United Bris Healthcare NHS Trust 99-01; P-in-c Shirehampton *Bris* 01-11; Dean Women's Min 00-11; Hon Can Bris Cathl 01-11; Adn Malmesbury from 11; Adn Bris from 12. *1 Orchard Close, Winterbourne, Bristol BS36 1BF* T: (01454) 778366 *or* 0117-906 0100
E: christine.froude@bristoldiocese.org

FRUEHWIRTH, Robert Alan. b 69. **d** 97 **p** 97. PtO *Nor* 11-13; Dir Julian Cen 13-15; C Nor St Pet Mancroft w St Jo Maddermarket 13-15; USA from 15. *302 Chesapeake Way, Chapel Hill NC 27516, USA* M: (001) (540) 406 3304
E: r.fruehwirth@icloud.com

FRY, Alison Jacquelyn (Sister Alison). b 65. Newnham Coll Cam BA 86 MA 90 Hertf Coll Ox DPhil 90 St Jo Coll Dur BA 95. Cranmer Hall Dur 93. **d** 96 **p** 97. C Milton *B & W* 96-00; V Batheaston w St Cath 00-12; OSB from 12; PtO *Worc* from 12. *Mucknell Abbey, Mucknell Farm Lane, Soulton, Worcester WR7 4RB* T: (01905) 345900 E: revajfry@gmail.com

FRY, Canon Barry James. b 49. K Alfred's Coll Win MA 03 ACIB. Ripon Coll Cuddesdon 81. **d** 83 **p** 84. C Highcliffe w Hinton Admiral *Win* 83-87; V Southampton St Barn from 87; Hon Can Ruvuma Cathl Tanzania from 02. *St Barnabas' Vicarage, 12 Rose Road, Southampton SO14 6TE* T: (023) 8022 3107

FRY, David William. b 51. St Jo Coll Nottm. **d** 08 **p** 09. C Heeley and Gleadless Valley 08-10 and 12; V Ardsley 10-12; V Heeley from 12; AD Attercliffe from 13. *Heeley Vicarage, 151 Gleadless Road, Sheffield S2 3AE* T: 0114-255 7718
E: davidfry242@btinternet.com

FRY, Mrs Florence Marion. b 24. WMMTC 87. **d** 88 **p** 94. Chapl and Welfare Officer to the Deaf 70-94; Chapl Cov Cathl 88-94; Chmn Cov Coun of Chs 88-91; rtd 94; PtO *St Alb* from 96. *37 Grace Gardens, Bishop's Stortford CM23 3EU* T: (01279) 652315

FRY, John Edward. b 80. Univ of Wales (Swansea) BSc 01 PGCE 03. Wycliffe Hall Ox BTh 13. **d** 13 **p** 14. C Theydon Bois and Theydon Garnon *Chelmsf* from 13. *2 Slade End, Theydon Bois CM16 7EP* M: 07719-469029
E: johnedwardfry@btinternet.com

FRY, Lynn Jane. b 60. **d** 03 **p** 04. OLM E. w W Harling, Bridgham w Roudham, Larling etc *Nor* from 03. *40 White Hart Street, East Harling, Norwich NR16 2NE* T: (01953) 717423
E: fryfam@talktalk.net

FRY, Marion. *See* FRY, Florence Marion

FRY, Michael John. b 59. Nottm Univ BA 80 Sheff Univ CQSW 83 Cam Univ BA 85. Westcott Ho Cam 83. **d** 86 **p** 87. C Upholland *Liv* 86-89; C Dovecot 89-91; TV St Luke in the City 91-14. *Address temp unknown*

FRY, Nigel. b 49. Kent Univ BA 95 Cant Ch Ch Univ MA 06. SEITE 97. **d** 00 **p** 01. NSM Len Valley *Cant* 00-03; C Hollingbourne and Hucking w Leeds and Broomfield 03-11; P-in-c 11-15; Chapl HM Pris E Sutton Park 02-10; rtd 15. *15 Atwater Court, Lenham, Maidstone ME17 2PW* M: 07821-189909 T: (01622) 859086
E: nigel.fry1@btinternet.com

FRY, Nigel Edward. b 57. St Jo Coll Nottm 91. **d** 93 **p** 94. C Wellingborough All Hallows *Pet* 93-96; R Peakirk w Glinton and Northborough 96-05; V Pet Ch Carpenter from 05. *The Vicarage, Chestnut Avenue, Peterborough PE1 4PE* T: (01733) 567140 E: enfrys@gmail.com

FRY, Roger Joseph Hamilton. b 29. Em Coll Cam BA 52 MA 56. Clifton Th Coll 52. **d** 54 **p** 55. C Walcot *B & W* 54-57; C Gresley *Derby* 57-61; P-in-c Bowling St Bart and St Luke *Bradf* 61-65; V Bowling St Jo 61-87; V Ingleton w Chapel le Dale 87-95; rtd 95; PtO *Leeds* from 95. *5 Margerison Crescent, Ilkley LS29 8QZ* T: (01943) 608738

FRYDAY, Canon Barbara Yvonne. b 47. Ch of Ireland Tr Coll TCert 67. CITC 90. **d** 92 **p** 93. NSM Cashel w Magorban, Tipperary, Clonbeg etc *C & O* 93-96; C Kilcooley w Littleon, Crohane and Fertagh 96-99; I 99-07; I Clonmel w Innislounagh, Tullaghmelan etc from 07; Can Ossory Cathl from 03; Warden of Readers from 08. *The Rectory, 7 Linden Lea, Silversprings, Clonmel, Co Tipperary, Republic of Ireland* T/F: (00353) (52) 618 7464 M: 86-275 0735
E: frydayb@gmail.com

FRYER, Alison Jane. *See* BOWNASS, Alison Jane

FRYER, Cora Lynette. *See* YARRIEN, Cora Lynette

FRYER, Mrs Jenifer Anne. b 43. NOC 89. **d** 92 **p** 94. Par Dn Ecclesfield *Sheff* 92-94; C 94-95; Asst Chapl Cen Sheff Univ Hosps NHS Trust 93-96; Chapl Weston Park Hosp Sheff 94-96; Chapl Asst N Gen Hosp NHS Trust Sheff 96-04; Chapl Asst Sheff Teaching Hosps NHS Foundn Trust 04-07; rtd 07; PtO *Sheff* from 07. *5 Nursery Drive, Ecclesfield, Sheffield S35 9XU* T: 0114-246 1027 E: jeni_fryer@talktalk.net

FRYER, Jonathan. b 56. **d** 12 **p** 13. NSM Chilvers Coton w Astley *Cov* from 12. *7 Croft Close, Wolvey, Hinckley LE10 3LE*

FRYER, Michael Andrew. b 56. St Jo Coll Nottm 88. **d** 90 **p** 91. C Hull St Martin w Transfiguration *York* 90-95; V Kingston upon Hull St Aid Southcoates 95-14; AD E Hull 06-13; P-in-c Elloughton and Brough w Brantingham from 14. *55 Stockbridge Park, Elloughton, Brough HU15 1JQ* T: (01482) 667431 E: mickfryer55@gmail.com

FRYER-SPEDDING, Mrs Clare Caroline. b 47. St Aid Coll Dur BA 69. LCTP 06. **d** 09 **p** 10. NSM Binsey *Carl* from 09. *West Mirehouse, Underskiddaw, Keswick CA12 4QE*
E: cfs@mirehouse.com

FUDGE, Prof Erik Charles. b 33. Ch Coll Cam BA 55 MA 59 Southn Univ CertEd 58 Cam Univ PhD 68. Ox Min Course 91. **d** 93 **p** 94. NSM Wokingham St Sebastian *Ox* from 93. *4 South Close, Wokingham RG40 2DJ* T: 0118-978 6081

FUDGER, David John. b 53. Sheff Univ MMin 96. K Coll Lon 73 Coll of Resurr Mirfield 76. **d** 77 **p** 78. C Sutton in Ashfield St Mary *S'well* 77-80; P-in-c Duston *Pet* 80-82; V Radford All So w Ch Ch and St Mich *S'well* 82-91; Min Bermondsey St Hugh CD *S'wark* 91-97; P-in-c Blackheath Ascension 97-04; Hon Chapl S'wark Cathl 91-01; P-in-c Mansfield SS Pet and Paul *S'well* 04-11; V from 11; P-in-c Mansfield St Mark 12-14; V from 14. *The Vicarage, Lindhurst Lane, Mansfield NG18 4JE* T: (01623) 642546 *or* T/F: 640250 E: revfudger@mistral.co.uk

FUDGER, Michael Lloyd. b 55. K Coll Lon BD 77 AKC 77. Coll of Resurr Mirfield 77. **d** 78 **p** 79. C Weston Favell *Pet* 78-82; C Pet H Spirit Bretton 82-84; V Irchester 84-90; TV Darnall-cum-Attercliffe *Sheff* 90-96; TV Attercliffe, Darnall and Tinsley

96-97; TR 97-03; TR Attercliffe and Darnall 03-05; V 05-06; Chapl Nine o'Clock Community 04-06; RD Attercliffe 91-96; Hon Can Sheff Cathl 00-06; R Bedford St Pet w St Cuth *St Alb* from 06. *St Peter's Rectory, 36 De Parys Avenue, Bedford MK40 2TP* T: (01234) 354543 E: fudgerml@yahoo.co.uk

FUERTE, Antonio. *See* GARCIA FUERTE, Antonio

FUHRI, Tessa Jane. b 66. **d** 14 **p** 15. C Heatherlands St Jo *Sarum* from 14. *24 Jubilee Road, Poole BH12 2NY* M: 07789-602682 E: tessafuhri@gmail.com

FULFORD, Alison Jane. b 79. CCC Cam BA 00 MA 04. Ridley Hall Cam 01. **d** 04 **p** 05. C Old Catton *Nor* 04-07; Hon Chapl St Jo Coll Nottm 08-11; P-in-c Hickling w Kinoulton and Broughton Sulney *S'well* 11-13; R 13-14; P-in-c Baddiley and Wrenbury w Burleydm *Ches* from 14; Dean of Women in Min from 15. *The Vicarage, The Green, Wrenbury, Nantwich CW5 8EY* E: revalisonfulford@hotmail.co.uk

FULFORD, Susan Yvonne. b 61. **d** 03. OLM Pemberton St Mark Newtown *Liv* 03-07; OLM Marsh Green w Newtown 08-14; OLM Newtown from 14. *13 Mitchell Street, Wigan WN5 9BY* T: (01942) 242369 E: sueandmike2003@yahoo.co.uk

FULHAM, Suffragan Bishop of. *See* BAKER, The Rt Revd Jonathan Mark Richard

FULKER, Lois Valerie. b 42. Keele Univ BA 64. Cranmer Hall Dur 03. **d** 04 **p** 05. NSM Egremont and Haile *Carl* 04-08; PtO from 08. *3 Mill Farm, Calderbridge, Seascale CA20 1DN* T: (01946) 841475 E: m.l.fulker@btinternet.com

FULLAGAR, Michael Nelson. b 35. SS Coll Cam BA 57 MA 61. Chich Th Coll 57. **d** 59 **p** 60. C Camberwell St Giles *S'wark* 59-61; C Northolt Park St Barn *Lon* 61-64; C Hythe *Cant* 64-66; R Chipata Zambia 66-70; P-in-c Livingstone 70-75; P-in-c Chingola 75-78; R Freemantle *Win* 78-87; P-in-c Westbury w Turweston, Shalstone and Biddlesden *Ox* 87-94; Chapl S Bucks NHS Trust 94-96; rtd 96; P-in-c Burwash Weald *Chich* 97-04; PtO from 04. *1 Roffrey Avenue, Eastbourne BN22 0AE* T: (01323) 503212 E: michaelfullagar@aol.com

FULLALOVE, Brenda Hurst. *See* CRASTON, Brenda Hurst

FULLARTON, Mrs Heather Mary. b 42. Whitelands Coll Lon TCert 63. Qu Coll Birm 90. **d** 92 **p** 94. Par Dn Colwich w Gt Haywood *Lich* 92-94; C 94-97; P-in-c Swindon and Himley 97-01; V Prees and Fauls 01-02; rtd 02; PtO *Sarum* from 03. *3 Rivers Arms Close, Sturminster Newton DT10 1DL* T: (01258) 471895 M: 07703-379684 E: hfullarton@aol.com

FULLER, Alison Jane. *See* COZENS, Alison Jane

FULLER, Christopher John. b 53. Chich Th Coll 85. **d** 87 **p** 88. C Swinton and Pendlebury *Man* 87-90; C Chiswick St Nic w St Mary *Lon* 90-92; V Hounslow W Gd Shep 92-96; V Stoke Newington St Faith, St Matthias and All SS 96-05; V Enfield St Geo 05-13; P-in-c S Shields St Hilda w St Thos *Dur* from 13; Chapl Miss to Seafarers from 13. *St Hilda's Vicarage, 40 Lawe Road, South Shields NE33 2EU* T: 0191-454 1414 E: frcfuller1@btinternet.com

FULLER, Canon Graham Drowley. b 33. AKC 58. **d** 59 **p** 60. C E Grinstead St Swithun *Chich* 59-62; C Coulsdon St Andr *S'wark* 62-64; Chapl RN 64-68; V Battersea St Luke *S'wark* 68-75; V S Stoneham *Win* 75-90; R Eversley 90-96; Bp's Ecum Officer 84-95; Hon Can Win Cathl 93-96; rtd 96; PtO *Portsm* from 03. *Brookside Dairy, Nunnery Lane, Newport PO30 1YR* T: (01983) 525976 E: teazle@metronet.co.uk

FULLER, Canon John James. b 38. SS Coll Cam BA 63 MA 66. Chich Th Coll 63 Union Th Sem (NY) STM 64. **d** 65 **p** 66. C Westmr St Steph w St Jo *Lon* 65-71; Tutor Cuddesdon Coll 71-75; Tutor Ripon Coll Cuddesdon 75-77; Prin S Dios Minl Tr Scheme 77-96; Can and Preb Sarum Cathl 83-96; V Wheatley w Forest Hill and Stanton St John *Ox* 96-97; TR Wheatley 97-03; rtd 03. *11 Ratcliffs Garden, Shaftesbury SP7 8HJ* T: (01747) 850079

FULLER, Mark Joseph Tobias. b 82. Ridley Hall Cam 12. **d** 15. C Yaxley and Holme w Conington *Ely* from 15. *26 Daimler Avenue, Yaxley, Peterborough PE7 3AU* T: (01223) 522113 M: 07766-310509 E: markfuller82@btinternet.com

FULLER, Matthew John. b 74. Birm Univ MA 95 PGCE 96. Oak Hill Th Coll BA 05. **d** 05 **p** 06. C St Helen Bishopsgate w St Andr Undershaft etc *Lon* from 05. *54 Monkton Street, London SE11 4TX* T: (020) 7735 2494 M: 07903-045667 E: matt@thebibletalks.org

FULLER, Michael George. b 46. Chich Th Coll 90. **d** 92 **p** 93. C Fulham All SS *Lon* 92-94; C Kensington St Mary Abbots w St Geo 94-06; V Holland Park 06-12; Dir Post-Ord Tr Kensington Area 94-99; Bp Kensington's Liaison Officer to Metrop Police *Lon* 99-12; rtd 12; R Vancouver St Jo Shaughnessy Canada from 15. *#2305, 1501 Haro Street, Vancouver V6G 1G4, Canada* T: (001) (604) 731 4966 E: rector@sjs.net

FULLER, Canon Michael Jeremy. b 63. Worc Coll Ox BA 85 MA 89 DPhil 89 Qu Coll Cam BA 91. Westcott Ho Cam 89.

d 92 **p** 93. C High Wycombe *Ox* 92-95; C Edin St Jo 95-00; Prin TISEC 00-02; IME Officer from 02; Pantonian Prof from 00; Can St Mary's Cathl from 00; Hon Research Fell Glas Univ from 08. *TISEC, Forbes House, 21 Grosvenor Crescent, Edinburgh EH12 5EE* T: 0131-225 6357 *or* 667 7273 F: 346 7247 E: michaelf@scotland.anglican.org

FULLER, Canon Terence James. b 30. Bris Univ BA 55. Clifton Th Coll 55. **d** 56 **p** 57. C Uphill *B & W* 56-60; V Islington St Jude Mildmay Park *Lon* 60-67; V Southgate *Chich* 67-80; R Stoke Climsland *Truro* 80-95; RD Trigg Major 85-91; P-in-c Lezant w Lawhitton and S Petherwin w Trewen 93-95; Hon Can Truro Cathl 94-96; rtd 96; PtO *Truro* from 96. *9 Westover Road, Callington PL17 7EW* T: (01579) 384958

FULLERTON, Hamish John Neville. b 45. Ball Coll Ox BA 68 MA 73. S'wark Ord Course 76. **d** 79 **p** 80. Hd English Abp Tenison's Sch Kennington 79-88; Hon C Clapham Old Town *S'wark* 79-82; PtO 82-89; Hon C Brixton Road Ch Ch 89-91; C Streatham Ch Ch 91-96; C Purley St Mark 96-98; Asst P Tooting St Aug 98-01; PtO from 03. *Flat 4, 21 Offerton Road, London SW4 0DJ* T: (020) 7622 7890

FULLJAMES, Mrs Janet Kathleen Doris. b 43. Open Univ BA 79 Birm Univ MA 93. Qu Coll Birm 85. **d** 87 **p** 94. Par Dn Harborne St Pet *Birm* 87-93; Par Dn Smethwick SS Steph and Mich 93-94; C 94-95; C Smethwick Resurr 95-98; P-in-c Dudley St Thos and St Luke *Worc* 98-04; P-in-c Dudley St Jo 98-04; rtd 04; PtO *B & W* from 04. *12 Obridge Road, Taunton TA2 7PX* T: (01823) 333585 E: fulljames23@btinternet.com

FULLJAMES, Michael William. b 36. OBE 94. K Coll Lon AKC 60. St Boniface Warminster 60. **d** 61 **p** 62. C Armley St Bart *Ripon* 61-64; C E Wells *B & W* 64-67; Chapl Mendip Hosp Wells 64-67; R Stanningley St Thos *Ripon* 67-73; Chapl St Aug Hosp Cant 73-88; Chapl St Martin's Hosp Cant 82-88; RD W Bridge *Cant* 87-88; Chapl Rotterdam *Eur* 88-94; Sen Chapl Rotterdam Miss to Seamen 88-94; Sen Chapl Burrswood Chr Cen *Roch* 94-01; rtd 01; PtO *Cant* from 01. *40 Somner Close, Canterbury CT2 8LJ* T: (01227) 766950 E: m.fulljames@gmail.com

FULLJAMES, Peter Godfrey. b 38. BNC Ox BA 60 MA 64 Birm Univ PhD 91. Qu Coll Birm. **d** 62 **p** 63. C Mexborough *Sheff* 62-65; Chapl Union Chr Coll India 65-69; Asst Master Wednesfield High Sch Wolverhampton 69-71; Asst Master Moorside High Sch Werrington 71-79; NSM Nairobi St Mark Kenya 80-85; Asst Master Nairobi High Sch 80-85; Research Fell Qu Coll Birm 85-87; Tutor WMMTC 87-90; Vice-Prin 90-93; Tutor Qu Coll Birm 93-94; Tutor Crowther Hall CMS Tr Coll Selly Oak 94-00; Hon Lect Th Birm Univ 97-03; rtd 00; PtO *B & W* from 04. *12 Obridge Road, Taunton TA2 7PX* T: (01823) 333585 E: fulljames23@btinternet.com

FULTON, Miss Ann Elizabeth. b 47. SWMTC 01. **d** 04 **p** 05. NSM Kingston St Mary w Broomfield etc *B & W* 04-11; NSM W Monkton 10-11; NSM W Monkton w Kingston St Mary, Broomfield etc 11-14; Chapl St Marg Hospice Taunton from 14. *St Margaret's Somerset Hospice, Heron Drive, Bishops Hull, Taunton TA1 5HA* T: (01823) 259394 M: 07765-925236 E: annfulton29@yahoo.co.uk

FULTON, John William. b 49. Ex Coll Ox BA 71 BPhil 72 MA 75 MPhil 79. Wycliffe Hall Ox 72. **d** 76 **p** 77. C Bexleyheath Ch Ch *Roch* 76-79; C Ealing Dean St Jo *Lon* 79-83; V Aldborough Hatch *Chelmsf* 83-87; Chapl Chantilly *Eur* 87-90; R Hepworth, Hinderclay, Wattisfield and Thelnetham *St E* 90-14; RD Ixworth 09-14; rtd 15; PtO *St E* from 15. *11 Chancellery Mews, Bury St Edmunds IP33 3AB* T: (01284) 765744 E: jwfulton@btinternet.com

FUNNELL, Preb Norman Richard James. b 40. Univ of Wales (Lamp) BA 64. Ripon Hall Ox 64. **d** 66 **p** 67. C Hackney *Lon* 66-70; Hon C 71-85; TV 85-93; R S Hackney St Jo w Ch Ch 93-08; Chapl St Joseph's Hospice Hackney 93-08; Preb St Paul's Cathl 05-08; rtd 08. *37 Brunel Quays, Great Western Village, Lostwithiel PL22 0JB* T: (01208) 873867 M: 07966-238934 E: jamesfunnell@btinternet.com

FURBER, Mrs Jennifer Margaret. b 50. WEMTC 98. **d** 01 **p** 02. NSM Malvern Link w Cowleigh *Worc* 01-08; rtd 09; PtO *Win* from 09. *3 Ravenswood, 23 Wimborne Road, Bournemouth BH2 6LZ* T: (01202) 296886 E: jenny@furber.me.uk

FURBER, Peter. b 43. Ex Univ BA. Sarum & Wells Th Coll 83. **d** 85 **p** 86. C Stanmore *Win* 85-88; TV Basingstoke 88-95; C Ringwood 95-98; P-in-c Gt Malvern Ch Ch *Worc* 98-99; V 99-08; rtd 09; PtO *Win* from 09. *3 Ravenswood, 23 Wimborne Road, Bournemouth BH2 6LZ* T: (01202) 296886 E: peter@furber.me.uk

FURBER, Sarah Anne. *See* COAKLEY, Sarah Anne

FURBEY, Mrs Linda Alice. b 49. Hockerill Coll of Educn CertEd 70 Wolfs Coll Cam BEd 71 Coll of Ripon & York St Jo MA 03. NOC 00. **d** 03 **p** 04. NSM Crosspool *Sheff* 03-07 and from 08; PtO 07-08; Chapl Sheff Children's NHS Foundn Trust 08-10. *20 Crimicar Avenue, Sheffield S10 4EQ* T: 0114-230 6356 E: linda.furbey1@btinternet.com

FURBY, Penelope. b 51. Middx Univ 06. NTMTC BA 03. **d** 06 **p** 07. NSM Leigh-on-Sea St Aid *Chelmsf* 06-11; PtO from 11. *72A Cliffsea Grove, Leigh-on-Sea SS9 1NQ* T: (01702) 711067 M: 07817-766513 E: penny.furby@btinternet.com

FURLONG, Andrew William Ussher. b 47. TCD BA 69 Jes Coll Cam BA 71. Westcott Ho Cam 70 CITC 72. **d** 72 **p** 73. C Dundela St Mark *D & D* 72-76; C Dublin St Ann w St Mark and St Steph *D & G* 76-83; Zimbabwe 83-94; Adn W Harare 88-89; Can Harare 89-94; Asst Chapl Leeds Teaching Hosps NHS Trust 94-97; Dean Clonmacnoise *M & K* 97-02; I Trim and Athboy Gp 97-02; Prec Kildare Cathl 98-02. *12 Tubbermore Road, Dalkey, Co Dublin, Republic of Ireland* T: (00353) (1) 285 9817 E: tiripo@gofree.indigo.ie

FURLONG (*née* DAVIES), Mrs Catharine Mary. b 48. Philippa Fawcett Coll CertEd 73. EMMTC 85. **d** 88 **p** 95. C Spalding St Mary and St Nic *Linc* 88-92; Zimbabwe 92-94; C Gt w Lt Gidding and Steeple Gidding *Ely* 94-96; P-in-c 96-06; P-in-c Brington w Molesworth and Old Weston 96-06; P-in-c Leighton Bromswold 96-06; P-in-c Winwick 96-06; P-in-c Gt Gransden and Abbotsley and Lt Gransden etc from 06; Asst Chapl Hinchingbrooke Health Care NHS Trust from 06. *The Vicarage, 4 Webb's Meadow, Great Gransden, Sandy SG19 3BL* T: (01767) 677227 E: catherinemfurlong@tiscali.co.uk

FURNESS, Barry Keith. b 47. Open Univ BSc 93. **d** 04 **p** 05. OLM High Oak, Hingham and Scoulton w Wood Rising *Nor* 04-09; P-in-c Smallburgh w Dilham w Honing and Crostwight 09-11; R 11-15; rtd 15; PtO *Nor* from 15. *Church View, 6 Alderfen Way, Hoveton NR12 8GA* T: (01692) 536812 E: barry.furness@norwich.anglican.org *or* barry.furness6@btinternet.com

FURNESS, Christine Anne. b 51. Leic Coll of Educn CertEd 73 Open Univ BA 76 Man Univ MEd 84 PhD 91 Ches Coll of HE MTh 02. NOC 99. **d** 02 **p** 03. C Offerton *Ches* 02-06; V Brinnington w Portwood 06-12; rtd 13; PtO *Lich* from 13. *Address withheld by request* M: 07771-601615 E: anne@afurness.co.uk

FURNESS, Dominic John. b 53. Bris Univ BA 76. Ridley Hall Cam 82. **d** 84 **p** 85. C Downend *Bris* 84-88; V Stoke Hill *Guildf* 88-05; V Milford *Win* from 05; AD Lyndhurst 08-13. *The Vicarage, Lymington Road, Milford on Sea, Lymington SO41 0QN* T: (01590) 643289 E: dominic.furness@talktalk.net

FURNESS, Edward Joseph. b 41. S'wark Ord Course 74. **d** 77 **p** 78. NSM S Lambeth St Steph *S'wark* 77-81; Warden Mayflower Family Cen Canning Town *Chelmsf* 82-96; P-in-c Aston St Jas *Birm* 96-00; V 00-05; rtd 05; PtO *Birm* from 05. *304 New Oscott Village, 25 Fosseway Drive, Birmingham B23 5GP* T: 0121-377 5304

FURSE, Adrian Thomas. b 76. Bris Univ BA 99 Univ of Wales (Swansea) MA 01 Leeds Univ PhD 06. St Steph Ho Ox 08. **d** 10 **p** 11. C Wistow *Leic* 10-14; TV Dewisland *St D* from 14; Min Can St D Cathl from 14. *The Vicarage, Whitchurch, Solva, Haverfordwest SA62 6UD* T: (01437) 721281 M: 07890-020849 E: adrian.t.furse@gmail.com

FURST, John William. b 41. Bris Sch of Min 81 Ripon Coll Cuddesdon. **d** 84 **p** 85. C Bris Ch the Servant Stockwood 84-88; V Hanham 88-94; PtO *Llan* 98-99; V Gosberton, Gosberton Clough and Quadring *Linc* 99-05; P-in-c Hasfield w Tirley and Ashleworth *Glouc* 05-06; Hon C Redmarley D'Abitot, Bromesberrow, Pauntley etc *Glouc* 11-13. *The Rectory, Albright Lane, Bromesberrow, Ledbury HR8 1RU* T: (01531) 650202 E: sandj.furst@btinternet.com

FUTCHER, Mrs Anne Elizabeth. b 57. Portsm Poly BA 78 Univ of Wales (Swansea) MEd 83 PGCE 80. Ripon Coll Cuddesdon 13. **d** 15. C Colyton, Musbury, Southleigh and Branscombe *Ex* from 15. *Emmanuel House, Station Road, Ide, Exeter EX2 9RS* T: (01392) 420972 M: 07551-007123 E: aefutcher@gmail.com

FUTCHER, The Ven Christopher David. b 58. Edin Univ BD 80 Lon Univ MTh 04 K Coll Lon MA 11. Westcott Ho Cam 80. **d** 82 **p** 83. C Borehamwood *St Alb* 82-85; C Stevenage All SS Pin Green 85-88; V 88-96; V St Alb St Steph 96-00; R Harpenden St Nic 00-12; Adn Ex from 12. *Emmanuel House, Station Road, Ide, Exeter EX2 9RS* T: (01392) 425577 E: archdeacon.of.exeter@exeter.anglican.org

FUTERS, Michael Roger. b 58. Trin & All SS Coll Leeds BEd 80. St Jo Coll Nottm 82. **d** 85 **p** 86. C Narborough and Huncote *Leic* 85-87; C Spondon *Derby* 87-90; P-in-c Derby St Jas 90-95; TV Walbrook Epiphany 95-99; Hon C Derby St Mark 99-09; Community Development Officer Home Housing from 99; Hon C Chaddesden St Phil w Derby St Mark from 09. *3 St Pancras Way, Derby DE1 3TH* T: (01332) 203075 E: michaelf@derwentliving.com

FYFE, Mrs Deirdre Bettina. b 44. STETS 05. **d** 07 **p** 08. NSM S Petherton w The Seavingtons *B & W* 07-12; NSM Winsmoor from 12. *1 Waldock Barton, South Petherton TA13 5NZ* T: (01460) 241977 E: dbfyfe@btinternet.com

FYFE, Gordon Boyd. b 63. Aber Univ BD 93 Edin Univ MTh 95. TISEC 94. **d** 96 **p** 97. C Ayr *Glas* 96-99; C Maybole 96-99; C Girvan 96-99; R Airdrie and Coatbridge 99-09; Chapl to Primus 06-09; R Largs *Glas* from 09. *St Columba's Rectory, Aubrey Crescent, Largs KA30 8PR* T: (01475) 673143 M: 07523-128493 E: gordon.fyfe@virginmedia.com

FYFE, Stewart John. b 69. City Univ BSc 91. Ridley Hall Cam 03. **d** 05 **p** 06. C Barony of Burgh *Carl* 05-10; P-in-c Bolton from 10; P-in-c Crosby Ravensworth from 10; P-in-c Morland, Thrimby, Gt Strickland and Cliburn from 10; RD Appleby from 13. *The Vicarage, Morland, Penrith CA10 3AX* T: (01931) 714620 M: 07985-900477 E: stewart.fyfe@btinternet.com

FYFFE, Robert Clark. b 56. Edin Univ BD 78 Napier Univ Edin MBA 98. Edin Th Coll 74. **d** 79 **p** 80. C Edin St Jo 79-83; Youth Chapl *B & W* 83-87; Prov Youth Officer Scottish Episc Ch 87-92; R Perth St Jo *St And* 93-06; Co-ord Internat Angl Youth Network 88-92; Can St Ninian's Cathl Perth 96-06; Gen Sec CTBI from 06. *26 Bothwell Gardens, Dunbar EH42 1PZ* T: (01368) 860885 E: bobfyffe@btopenworld.com *or* bob.fyffe@ctbi.org.uk

FYFFE, Timothy Bruce. b 25. New Coll Ox MA 54. Westcott Ho Cam 54. **d** 56 **p** 57. C Lewisham St Mary *S'wark* 56-60; V Enugu All SS Nigeria 60-68; TV Lowestoft St Marg *Nor* 69-80; Chapl HM Pris Blundeston 70-78; TV Tettenhall Regis *Lich* 80-85; Chapl Compton Hospice 85-87; rtd 90; NSM Wolverhampton St Andr *Lich* 88-10; PtO from 10. *40 Glentworth Gardens, Wolverhampton WV6 0SG* T: (01902) 716510 E: tim@timfyffe.plus.com

FYLES, Gordon. b 39. Trin Coll Bris 76. **d** 77 **p** 78. C Islington St Mary *Lon* 77-81; Ext Sec BCMS 81-88; C Wimbledon Em Ridgway Prop Chpl *S'wark* 88-97; I Crinken *D & G* 97-04; rtd 04. *1 Marlowe House, 147 Durham Road, London SW20 0DQ* T: (020) 8715 1894 E: gordonandyvonne@yahoo.co.uk

FYSH, Leslie David. b 35. Glouc Sch of Min 88. **d** 91 **p** 92. NSM Stonehouse *Glouc* 91-95; Asst Chapl Wycliffe Coll Glos 91-95; NSM W Walton *Ely* 95-00; PtO 00-11; Nor 08-12; PV Ely Cathl 03-06; Sub-Warden Coll of St Barn Lingfield from 14. *The College of St Barnabas, Blackberry Lane, Lingfield RH7 6NJ* T: (01342) 872866 E: revfysh@gmail.com

G

GABB-JONES, Adrian William Douglas. b 43. MRICS. Ripon Coll Cuddesdon 79. **d** 81 **p** 82. C Northolt Park St Barn *Lon* 81-84; C Ruislip St Martin 84-89; V Minster Lovell and Brize Norton *Ox* 89-03; V Minster Lovell 03-13; rtd 13; PtO *Chelmsf* from 14. *25 Newcastle Avenue, Colchester CO3 9XE* T: (01206) 563898

GABBADON, Kenneth Fitz Arthur. b 53. NOC 97. **d** 99 **p** 00. C Burnage St Marg *Man* 99-01; C Bury St Jo w St Mark 01-03; P-in-c Newton Heath 03-08; R 08-09; Chapl HM Pris Leeds 09-14; Chapl HM Pris Wealstun from 14; P-in-c Clifford *York* from 09. *HM Prison Wealstun, Walton Road, Wetherby LS23 7AZ* T: (01937) 444400 *or* 541165 E: ken.gabbadon@hmps.gsi.gov.uk *or* kgabba7036@aol.com

GABEL, Lee. b 75. Ripon Coll Cuddesdon 11. **d** 14 **p** 15. C Frodingham and New Brumby *Linc* from 14. *25 Fenners Avenue, Scunthorpe DN17 2GH* T: (01724) 487178 M: 07999-538824 E: leebbgabel@gmail.com

GABLE, Michael David. b 70. Poly of Wales BEng 92. St Mich Coll Llan BTh 95. **d** 95 **p** 96. C Newton Nottage *Llan* 95-99; V Aberavon H Trin 99-01; TV Aberavon 01-05; P-in-c Rhydyfelin w Graig 05-11; V Glyntaff, Rhydfelin and the Graig from 11; AD Pontypridd from 11. *St John's Vicarage, 28 Llantrisant Road, Graig, Pontypridd CF37 1LW* T: (01443) 650336 E: michaeldgable@gmail.com

GABORONE, Dean of. *See* McKERAN, The Very Revd James Orville

GADD, Alan John. b 44. Imp Coll Lon BSc 65 PhD 69 FRMetS 67. S'wark Ord Course 68. **d** 71 **p** 72. Asst Chapl Lon Univ 71-72; PtO S'wark 73-91; C Battersea Park All SS 91-95; P-in-c 95-96; C Battersea Fields 96-05; rtd 05; PtO S'wark from 05. *24 Holmewood Gardens, London SW2 3RS* T: (020) 8678 8977 E: alangadd@yahoo.co.uk

GADD, Brian Hayward. b 33. Hatf Coll Dur BA 54 DipEd 55. Glouc Sch of Min 82. **d** 85 **p** 87. NSM Cleobury Mortimer w Hopton Wafers etc *Heref* 85-98; rtd 98; PtO *Heref* 99-12. *34 Lower Street, Cleobury Mortimer, Kidderminster DY14 8AB* T: (01299) 270758

GADD, Bryan Stephen Andrew. b 56. Dur Univ BA Ox Univ CertEd Univ of Qld MPhil Cen Qld Univ MLitt. Chich Th Coll. **d** 81 **p** 82. C Newlyn St Pet *Truro* 81-86; R St Mawgan w St Ervan and St Eval 86-90; Chapl Summer Fields Sch Ox 90-02; PtO *Truro* 90-00; Chapl Southport Sen Sch Australia 02-09; Sen Chapl Angl Ch Gr Sch from 09. *Anglican Church Grammar School, Oaklands Parade, East Brisbane QLD 4169, Australia* T: (0061) (7) 3896 2281 F: 3891 5976 E: bryan.gadd@churchie.com.au

GADEN, Timothy John. b 64. Melbourne Univ BA 86 Monash Univ Aus PhD 96. Melbourne Coll of Div BD 90. **d** 91 **p** 91. Australia 91-96; C Battersea St Mary *S'wark* 97-01; Dir Post-Ord Tr Kingston Area 99-01; R Camberwell St Jo Australia from 01. *15 The Grove, Camberwell Vic 3124, Australia* T: (0061) (3) 9889 6456 or 9882 4851 F: 9882 0086 M: 41-911 4697 E: gaden@stjohnscamberwell.org.au

GADSBY, Alison. See HOGGER-GADSBY, Alison

GADSBY, Julian Timothy David Moritz. b 74. K Coll Lon BA 96 AKC 96. Oak Hill Th Coll 02. **d** 04 **p** 05. C Chadwell *Chelmsf* 04-09; P-in-c Bucklebury w Marlston Ox from 09. *The Vicarage, Burdens Heath, Upper Bucklebury, Reading RG7 6SX* T: (01635) 866731 or 860220 E: j_gadsby@tiscali.co.uk

GAFFIN, Jennifer Clare. b 78. Mansf Coll Ox BA 99 Man Univ MA 00 Win Univ PhD 06. Ripon Coll Cuddesdon 07. **d** 09 **p** 10. C Parkstone St Pet and St Osmund w Branksea *Sarum* 09-12; Bp's Dom Chapl *Portsm* from 12. *Bishopsgrove, 26 Osborn Road, Fareham PO16 7DQ* T: (01329) 280247 M: 07855-024789 E: jennygaffin@hotmail.com

GAGE, Aëlla Rupert Fitzehardinge Berkeley. b 66. Reading Univ BEd 92. Oak Hill Th Coll 98. **d** 00. C Muswell Hill St Jas w St Matt *Lon* 00-05; C Hadley Wood St Paul Prop Chpl 05-08; C Highgate Australia 08-10; C Fordham *Chelmsf* 10-14; C Colchester St Pet and St Botolph from 14. *31 St Peter's Street, Colchester CO1 1ES* M: 07796-475130 E: aella.gage@gmail.com

GAGE, Alan William. b 52. Univ of Wales (Cardiff) BMus 72 PGCE 73 Bris Univ MEd 90. WEMTC 98. **d** 00 **p** 01. NSM Tuffley *Glouc* 00-08; NSM Hardwicke and Elmore w Longney 08-09. *Chadburn, 83 Dinglewell, Hucclecote, Gloucester GL3 3HT* T: (01452) 614892 E: curatealan@blueyonder.co.uk

GAGE, Jennifer Anne. b 50. Girton Coll Cam MA 75 Open Univ BA 85 PhD 05 Keele Univ PGCE 86. ERMC 07. **d** 09 **p** 10. NSM Three Rivers Gp *Ely* 09-15; NSM Haddenham from 15; NSM Wilburton from 15; NSM Witchford w Wentworth from 15; Bp's Adv for Self-Supporting Min from 14. *51 Henley Way, Ely CB7 4YH* T: (01353) 666426 E: jennygage3@talktalk.net or 3rivers.jenny@gmail.com

GAGE, Canon Robert Edward. b 47. Whitman Coll Washington BA 69. Cuddesdon Coll BA 75 MA 81. **d** 76 **p** 77. C Cheshunt *St Alb* 76-79; C Harpenden St Nic 79-81; V S Mymms 81-82; P-in-c Ridge 81-82; V S Mymms and Ridge 82-97; Prec and Can Res Wakef Cathl 97-05; Can Res Newc Cathl 05-09; rtd 09. *44 Warkworth Avenue, Whitley Bay NE26 3PS* E: robertgage1@yahoo.co.uk

GAGEN, Mrs Valerie Elizabeth. b 52. Ripon Coll of Educn BEd 75. NTMTC BA 10. **d** 10 **p** 11. NSM N Hinckford *Chelmsf* 10-14; NSM Pastrow *Win* from 14. *Enham Trust, Enham Industries, Enham Alamein, Andover SP11 6JS* T: (01264) 345800 M: 07874-067371 E: valgagen@hotmail.com

GAINER, Canon Jeffrey. b 51. Jes Coll Ox BA 73 MA 77 Univ of Wales LLM 94. Wycliffe Hall Ox 74. **d** 77 **p** 78. C Baglan *Llan* 77-81; V Cwmbach 81-85; V Tonyrefail w Gilfach Goch and Llandyfodwg 85-87; Dir NT Studies and Dir Past Studies St Mich Coll Llan 87-92; V Meidrim and Llanboidy and Merthyr *St D* from 92; P-in-c Abernant from 07; AD St Clears 03-13; Cursal Can St D Cathl from 11. *The Vicarage, Meidrim, Carmarthen SA33 5QF* T: (01994) 231378

GAINES, Miss Atalie Clodia. b 78. Brighton Univ BA 00 Cam Univ BTh 14. Westcott Ho Cam 12. **d** 14 **p** 15. C Bedford St Andr *St Alb* from 14. *5 St Minver Road, Bedford MK40 3DQ* T: (01234) 216587 E: curate@standrewsbedford.org

GAINSBOROUGH, Prof Jonathan Martin. b 66. SOAS Lon MA 91 MSc 95 PhD 01. STETS MA 10. **d** 10 **p** 11. NSM Barton Hill St Luke w Ch Ch and Moorfields *Bris* 10-13; P-in-c from

13; Prof Development Politics Bris Univ from 12. *21 Cotham Lawn Road, Bristol BS6 6DS* E: martin.gainsborough@virgin.net

GAIR, Andrew Kennon. b 62. Westcott Ho Cam 88. **d** 91 **p** 92. C Clare w Poslingford, Cavendish etc *St E* 91-95; R Debden and Wimbish w Thunderley *Chelmsf* 95-06. *18-20 High Street, Wrentham, Beccles NR34 7HB* E: andrew.gair@btinternet.com

✠**GAISFORD, The Rt Revd John Scott.** b 34. St Chad's Coll Dur BA 59 MA 76. **d** 60 **p** 61 **c** 94. C Audenshaw St Hilda *Man* 60-62; C Bramhall *Ches* 62-65; V Crewe St Andr 65-86; RD Nantwich 74-85; Hon Can Ches Cathl 80-86; Adn Macclesfield 86-94; Suff Bp Beverley (PEV) *York* 94-00; Asst Bp Ripon and Leeds 96-00; rtd 00; PtO *Ches* from 00; *Man* from 04. *5 Trevone Close, Knutsford WA16 9EJ* T: (01565) 633531 M: 07429-340155 E: jandg.gaisford@tiscali.co.uk

GAIT, Canon David James. b 48. BNC Ox BA 71 BSc 72 MA 77 MSc 83. Ridley Hall Cam 71. **d** 74 **p** 75. C Litherland St Paul Hatton Hill *Liv* 74-77; C Farnworth 77-80; V Widnes St Jo 80-13; TV E Widnes 13; Chapl Widnes Maternity Hosp 86-90; AD Widnes *Liv* 07-13; Hon Can Liv Cathl 05-13; rtd 13. *Bryn Celyn, Betws Gwerfil Goch, Corwen LL21 9PP* T: (01490) 420759 E: dave.gait@btinternet.com

GALANZINO, Diego. b 80. St Steph Ho Ox BTh 11. **d** 11 **p** 12. C St Ives *Truro* 11-15; C Halsetown 11-15; P-in-c Houghton Regis *St Alb* from 15. *Clergy House, Lowry Drive, Houghton Regis, Dunstable LU5 5SJ* E: frdiego@mail.com

GALBRAITH, Alexander Peter James. b 65. Qu Coll Ox BA 86 MA 90. Wycliffe Hall Ox 87. **d** 90 **p** 91. C Southport Em *Liv* 90-94; C Mossley Hill St Matt and St Jas 94-97; V Kew from 97; Chapl Southport and Ormskirk NHS Trust 97-11. *20 Markham Drive, Kew, Southport PR8 6XR* T: (01704) 547758 E: alexgalbraith20@hotmail.com

GALBRAITH, Jane Alexandra. **d** 95 **p** 96. NSM Kildare w Kilmeague and Curragh *M & K* 95-97; NSM Newbridge w Carnalway and Kilcullen 97-99; C Limerick *L & K* 03-14; C Tralee w Kilmoyley, Ballymacelligott etc 14-15; I Roscrea w Kyle, Bourney and Corbally from 15. *St Cronan's Rectory, Rosemount, Roscrea, Co Tipperary, Republic of Ireland* M: 87-382 5336 T: (00353) (505) 21725 E: galbraithjane@gmail.com

GALBRAITH, John Angus Frame. b 44. Sarum Th Coll 68. **d** 71 **p** 72. C Richmond St Mary *S'wark* 71-74; Chapl W Lon Colls 74-79; R S'wark H Trin w St Matt 79-95; V New Addington 95-02; Asst Chapl HM Pris Wandsworth 02-04; Chapl 04-09; rtd 09; PtO *S'wark* from 09. *35 Joseph Hardcastle Close, London SE14 5RN* T: (020) 7635 3607 E: angus.galbraith@talktalk.net

GALBRAITH, Peter John. b 59. QUB BA MTh. CITC. **d** 85 **p** 86. C Knockbreda *D & D* 85-88; C Ballynafeigh St Jude 88-91; I Broomhedge *Conn* from 91. *Broomhedge Rectory, 30 Lurganure Road, Broughmore, Lisburn BT28 2TR* T: (028) 9262 1229

GALE, Ms Charlotte. b 70. Leeds Univ BEng 92 Nottm Univ MA 00. St Jo Coll Nottm 98. **d** 01 **p** 02. C Whitnash *Cov* 01-05; P-in-c Potters Green 05-08; P-in-c Lillington and Old Milverton 08-14; V from 14; C Leamington Spa H Trin from 08; AD Warwick and Leamington from 14. *The Vicarage, Vicarage Road, Lillington, Leamington Spa CV32 7RH* T: (01926) 424674 or 470449 E: charlotte.gale@tiscali.co.uk

GALE, Canon Christopher. b 44. ALCD 67. **d** 68 **p** 69. C Balderton *S'well* 68-72; C Bilborough St Jo 72-75; P-in-c Colwick 75-78; V Radford St Pet 78-84; V Sherwood 84-98; AD Nottm N 90-98; P-in-c Bulwell St Mary 98-02; R 02-07; Hon Can S'well Minster 03-07; rtd 08. *11 Cliff Road, Carlton, Nottingham NG4 1BS* T: 0115-844 0209 E: rev.chrisgale@gmail.com

GALE, Colin Edward. b 49. Lon Univ PGCE 74. St Jo Coll Nottm BTh 73. **d** 79 **p** 80. C Hoole *Ches* 79-82; C Woodley St Jo the Ev Ox 82-87; V Clapham St Jas *S'wark* 87-96; V Sutton Ch Ch 96-05; R Burstow w Horne 05-14; rtd 14. *Mariner's Cottage, 9 Park Lane, Selsey, Chichester PO20 0HD* E: revceg@aol.com

GALE, The Ven John. b 34. Univ of Wales (Lamp) 67. **d** 69 **p** 70. C Aberdare *Llan* 69-71; C Merthyr Dyfan 71-74; R Walmer St Sav S Africa 74-82; R Knysna St Geo 82-00; Adn Knysna 93-00; LtO *St D* from 00. *3 Connacht Way, Pembroke Dock SA72 6FB* T/F: (01646) 622219

GALE, Keith George. b 44. St Jo Coll Lusaka 68 Sarum Th Coll 69. **d** 70 **p** 71. C Sheff St Cuth 70-77; P-in-c Brightside All SS 72-77; C Birm St Martin 77-81; C Dwangwa Malawi 81-83; R Lilongwe St Pet 83-93; Adn Lilongwe 89-92; TV Sampford Peverell, Uplowman, Holcombe Rogus etc *Ex* 94-09; rtd 09. *101 Chapel Street, Tiverton EX16 6BU* T: (01884) 821879 E: keith@gale5.eclipse.co.uk

GALE, Ms Lucille Catherine. b 67. Sarum & Wells Th Coll 92. **d** 94 **p** 95. C Welling *S'wark* 94-97; Chapl Greenwich Univ 97-00; V Welling 00-09; Officer Lay Min and Miss 09-14; Officer for Reader Tr 12-14; Dir of Ords *Chich* from 14. *6 Patcham Grange, Brighton BN1 8UR* E: lugale2@gmail.com

GALE, Peter Simon. b 56. Welsh Coll of Music & Drama 73 K Alfred's Coll Win PGCE 78. St Mich Coll Llan BD 83. **d** 83 **p** 84. C Caerphilly *Llan* 83-89; Chapl RN 89-93; V Ystrad Rhondda w Ynyscynon *Llan* 93-07; V Pont Rhondda from 07. *St Stephen's Vicarage, Ystrad, Pentre CF41 7RR* T: (01443) 434426

GALE, Stephen. d 15. C S Hackney St Jo w Ch Ch *Lon* from 15. *Address temp unknown*

GALES, Alan. b 29. Sarum Th Coll 56. **d** 59 **p** 60. C Greenside *Dur* 59-60; C Peterlee 60-63; Ind Chapl 60-70; V Marley Hill 63-94; Asst Chapl HM Pris Dur 74-81; rtd 94. *46 Corsair, Whickham, Newcastle upon Tyne NE16 5YA* T: 0191-488 7352

GALES, Bernard Henry. b 27. Lon Univ BSc(Econ) 51 Open Univ BA 02. Wells Th Coll 62. **d** 64 **p** 65. C Sholing *Win* 64-67; C Fordingbridge w Ibsley 67-71; C S Molton w Nymet St George *Ex* 71-73; C Thelbridge 73-77; P-in-c 77-78; P-in-c Creacombe 77-78; P-in-c W w E Worlington 77-78; P-in-c Meshaw 77-78; P-in-c Witheridge 77-78; C Witheridge, Thelbridge, Creacombe, Meshaw etc 79-80; R Bow w Broad Nymet 80-93; V Colebrooke 80-93; R Zeal Monachorum 80-93; RD Cadbury 90-93; rtd 93; PtO *Ex* from 93. *8 Old Rectory Gardens, Morchard Bishop, Crediton EX17 6PF* T: (01363) 877601

GALES, Simon Richard. b 59. CEng 87 MICE 87 Jes Coll Cam BA 81 MA 84. Wycliffe Hall Ox 91. **d** 93 **p** 94. C Houghton *Carl* 93-97; V Lindow *Ches* from 97. *St John's Vicarage, 137 Knutsford Road, Wilmslow SK9 6EL* T: (01625) 583251 *or* 586329 E: simon@srgales.freeserve.co.uk

GALLACHER, Owen Thomas. b 85. Nottm Univ BA 07. Wycliffe Hall Ox BA 13. **d** 14 **p** 15. C Worc St Nic and All SS w St Helen from 14. *160 Bath Road, Worcester WR5 3EP*

GALLAGHER, Mrs Barbara Jean. b 53. Ex Univ BA 73 Coll of Ripon & York St Jo PGCE 76 Open Univ MA 99. **d** 08 **p** 09. OLM The Creetings and Earl Stonham w Stonham Parva *St E* 08-13; NSM from 13. *Primrose Cottage, Forward Green, Stowmarket IP14 5HJ* T: (01449) 711337 E: barbarajg@btopenworld.com

GALLAGHER, Canon Ian. BTh. **d** 90 **p** 91. C Annagh w Drumgoon, Ashfield etc *K, E & A* 90-93; I Drumcliffe w Lissadell and Munninane 93-01; Can Elphin Cathl 97-01; Dioc Sec (Elphin and Ardagh) 97-01; Preb Mulhuddart St Patr Cathl Dublin 98-01; I Stillorgan w Blackrock *D & G* from 01. *The Rectory, St Brigid's Church Road, Stillorgan, Blackrock, Co Dublin, Republic of Ireland* T: (00353) (1) 288 1091 F: 278 1833 M: 86-811 9544 E: istillorgan@dublin.anglican.org

GALLAGHER, Ian Míceál. b 71. Oberlin Coll (USA) BMus 93 Duke Univ (USA) MA 95. Westcott Ho Cam 06. **d** 08 **p** 09. C Walton-on-the-Hill *Liv* 08-12; R Frankfurt am Main Ch the K Germany 12-14; V Enfield St Jas *Lon* from 14. *St James's Vicarage, 144 Hertford Road, Enfield EN3 5AY* E: imgall@gmx.net

GALLAGHER, Mrs Margaret. b 60. SRN 82 RM 84. Westcott Ho Cam 09. **d** 11 **p** 12. C Carrington *S'well* 11-14; V S Elmsall *Leeds* from 14. *St Mary's Vicarage, Doncaster Road, South Elmsall, Pontefract WF9 2HS* T: (01977) 642861 E: revmgallagher@btinternet.com

GALLAGHER, Matthew Edward. b 51. Glas Univ BSc 75. EAMTC. **d** 00 **p** 01. NSM Northampton St Jas *Pet* 00-02. *11 Penfold Gardens, Great Billing, Northampton NN3 9PG* T: (01604) 416972 E: me.gallagher@virgin.net

GALLAGHER, Michael Collins Francis. b 48. St Jo Coll Dur BA 70. Sarum Th Coll 79. **d** 82 **p** 83. C Bridport *Sarum* 82-86; V Downton 86-01; RD Alderbury 93-99; R Crewkerne w Wayford *B & W* 01-07; R Wulfric Benefice 07-14; rtd 14; PtO *Heref* from 15. *Ridgeway, Woodleigh Road, Ledbury HR8 2BG* T: (01531) 635844 E: mcfgallagher@gmail.com

GALLAGHER, Neville Roy. b 45. Birm Univ CertEd 66 K Coll Lon AKC 70 BD 76 Open Univ BA 97. **d** 71 **p** 72. C Folkestone St Mary and St Eanswythe *Cant* 71-74; Hon C Sutton Valence w E Sutton and Chart Sutton 74-76; TV Cen Telford *Lich* 76-78; P-in-c Gt Mongeham *Cant* 78-80; P-in-c Ripple 78-80; R Gt Mongeham w Ripple and Sutton by Dover 80-83; V Kennington 83-88; Chapl and Dep Hd Bedgebury Sch Kent 88-05; P-in-c Appledore w Brookland, Fairfield, Brenzett etc *Cant* 05-11; P-in-c Woodchurch 06-11; P-in-c Wittersham w Stone and Ebony 08-11; AD Romney 08-10; rtd 11; PtO *Cant* from 11. *1 Church Cottages, Church Road, Kilndown, Cranbrook TN17 2SF* T: (01892) 890424 E: nrwg45@aol.com

GALLAGHER, Canon Padraig Francis Majella. b 52. **d** 81 **p** 82. P-in-c Caereithin *S & B* 05-09; V from 09; Can Res Brecon Cathl from 11. *Caereithin Vicarage, 64 Cheriton Close, Portmead, Swansea SA5 5LA* T: (01792) 583646 E: mail@teilo.org.uk

GALLAGHER, Robert. b 43. St Chad's Coll Dur BSc 65. **d** 67 **p** 68. C Crosland Moor *Wakef* 67-69; C Huddersfield SS Pet and Paul 69-71; Chapl Huddersfield Poly 72-79; Min Coulby Newham LEP *York* 79-90; V Toxteth St Marg *Liv* 90-13; rtd 13. *Address temp unknown*

GALLAGHER, Canon Stephen. b 58. Southn Univ BTh 89. Chich Th Coll 86. **d** 89 **p** 90. C S Shields All SS *Dur* 89-92; C Hartlepool St Paul and Chapl Hartlepool Gen Hosp 92-94; R Loftus and Carlin How w Skinningrove *York* 94-97; P-in-c Lower Beeding and Dioc Youth Officer *Chich* 97-09; Shrine P and Youth Missr Shrine of Our Lady of Walsingham from 09. *The Shrine of Our Lady of Walsingham, The College, Knight Street, Walsingham NR22 6EF* T: (01328) 824203 E: shrine.pr@olw-shrine.org.uk

GALLANT, Mrs Joanna-Sue Sheena. b 62. SAOMC 99. **d** 02 **p** 03. C Amersham on the Hill *Ox* 02-05; NSM Gt Missenden w Ballinger and Lt Hampden 06-10; NSM Chenies and Lt Chalfont, Latimer and Flaunden 10-12. *50 Frances Street, Chesham HP5 3ER* M: 07813-886805

GALLEY, Giles Christopher. b 32. Qu Coll Cam BA 56 MA 60. Linc Th Coll 56. **d** 58 **p** 59. C Gt Yarmouth *Nor* 58-62; C N Lynn w St Marg and St Nic 62-66; C Leeds St Pet *Ripon* 66-69; V N Hull St Mich *York* 70-79; V Strensall 79-00; RD Easingwold 82-97; rtd 00; PtO *York* from 00. *19 St John's Road, Stamford Bridge, York YO41 1PH* T: (01759) 371592

✠GALLIFORD, The Rt Revd David George. b 25. Clare Coll Cam BA 49 MA 51. Westcott Ho Cam. **d** 51 **p** 52 **c** 75. C Newland St Jo *York* 51-54; C Eton w Boveney *Ox* 54-56; Min Can Windsor 54-56; V Middlesbrough St Oswald *York* 56-61; R Bolton Percy 61-71; Dioc Adult Tr Officer 61-71; Can and Preb York Minster 69-70; Can Res and Treas York Minster 70-75; Suff Bp Hulme *Man* 75-84; Suff Bp Bolton 84-91; rtd 91; Hon Asst Bp York from 95. *10 St Mary's Mews, Greenshaw Drive, Wigginton, York YO32 2SE* T: (01904) 761489

GALLIGAN, Ms Adrienne. TCD BA 81 HDipEd 82. CITC BTh 03. **d** 03 **p** 04. C Seapatrick *D & D* 03-08; I Dublin Crumlin w Chapelizod *D & G* 08-15; I Dublin Rathfarnham from 15. *The Rectory, 41 Rathfarnham Road, Terenure, Dublin 6W, Republic of Ireland* T: (00353) (1) 490 5543 M: 086-039 0866 E: adriennegalligan@gmail.com

GALLON, Mrs Audrey Kay. b 41. SEITE 94. **d** 97 **p** 98. NSM Gt Mongeham w Ripple and Sutton by Dover *Cant* 97-98; NSM Eastry and Northbourne w Tilmanstone etc 97-98; NSM Walmer 98-04; PtO 04-05; *Roch* from 07. *12 Arne Close, Tonbridge TN10 4DH* T: (01732) 355633 E: audreygallon@talktalk.net

GALLOWAY, Prof Peter John. b 54. JP 89 OBE 96. Goldsmiths' Coll Lon BA 76 K Coll Lon PhD 87 Brunel Univ Hon DLitt 09 FRSA 88 FSA 00. St Steph Ho Ox 80. **d** 83 **p** 84. C St John's Wood *Lon* 83-86; C St Giles-in-the-Fields 86-90; Warden of Readers (Lon Episc Area) 87-92; P-in-c Hampstead Em W End *Lon* 90-95; V 95-08; AD N Camden 02-07; Chapl to RVO and Qu Chpl of the Savoy from 08; Hon Fell Goldsmiths' Coll Lon from 99; Visiting Prof Brunel Univ *Lon* from 08. *The Queen's Chapel of the Savoy, Savoy Hill, London WC2R 0DA* T: (020) 7379 8088 E: peter.galloway@sja.org.uk

GALT, Ian Ross. b 34. Leeds Univ BSc 56. **d** 76 **p** 77. NSM Newport St Julian *Mon* 76-87; NSM Newport St Teilo 87-98. *47 Brynglas Avenue, Newport NP20 5LR* T: (01633) 821499

GALVIN, Mrs Linda Susan. b 59. Ox Min Course 13. **d** 15. NSM W End *Win* from 15. *11A Westbury Court, Hedge End, Southampton SO30 0HN* T: (01489) 788880 E: linda.s.galvin@ntlworld.com

GALWAY, Gary Ford. d 04 **p** 07. C Donaghadee *D & D* 04-06; C Portadown St Mark *Arm* 06-08; I Drumcree from 08. *78 Drumcree Road, Portadown, Craigavon BT62 1PE* T: (028) 3833 2503 E: ggalway@drumcree.org

GAMBLE, Bronwen. *See* GAMBLE, Edana Bronwen

GAMBLE, David Lawrence. b 34. AKC 61. **d** 62 **p** 63. C-in-c Shrub End All SS CD *Chelmsf* 62-65; C Colchester St Jas, All SS, St Nic and St Runwald 65-69; V Chelmsf St Andr 69-73; P-in-c Hatfield Heath 69-73; C 74-77; TV Hemel Hempstead *St Alb* 77-82; P-in-c Renhold 82-90; Chapl HM Pris Bedf 82-90; P-in-c Petersham *S'wark* 90-96; Chapl HM Pris Latchmere Ho 90-96; P-in-c Portsea St Geo *Portsm* 96-99; rtd 99; Hon C Yarmouth and Freshwater *Portsm* 99-04. *35 Kings Chase, Andover SP10 3TH* T: (01264) 338017

GAMBLE, Diane Mary. b 36. BSc. **d** 00 **p** 01. NSM Sanderstead *S'wark* 00-07; PtO 07-10. *14 Barnfield Road, Sanderstead CR2 0EY* T: (020) 8651 0700

GAMBLE, Miss Dianne Elizabeth. b 71. Hull Univ BSc 92 PGCE 94. Cranmer Hall Dur 13. **d** 15. C Sowerby *York* from 15. *3 Herriot Way, Thirsk YO7 1FL* M: 07761-125748 E: 229club.dg@gmail.com

GAMBLE, Donald William. b 67. NUU BSc 88. TCD Div Sch BTh 91. **d** 91 **p** 92. C Belfast St Mich *Conn* 91-95; I Dromore *Clogh* 95-00; P-in-c Renewal and Outreach in the City *Conn* from 00; Chapl Belfast Health and Soc Care Trust from 09. *5 Fernridge Road, Newtownabbey BT36 5SP* T: (028) 9084 2171 *or* 9074 1099 M: 07738-297884 E: dongamble1@btinternet.com

GAMBLE, Mrs Edana Bronwen. b 56. Hull Univ BSc(Econ) 78 Nottm Univ MA 02 FCA 82. EMMTC 99. **d** 02 **p** 03. NSM Nuthall *S'well* 02-06; R Cropwell Bishop w Colston Bassett, Granby etc from 06. *The Rectory, 2 Dobbin Close, Cropwell Bishop, Nottingham NG12 3GR* T: 0115-989 3172

GAMBLE, Miss Gillian Florence. b 78. Glos Univ BA 08. Ripon Coll Cuddesdon 13. **d** 15. C Oadby *Leic* from 15. *62 Fairstone Hill, Oadby, Leicester LE2 5RJ* M: 07725-520667 E: gamble.gillian@gmail.com

GAMBLE, Ian Robert. b 66. Ulster Univ BA 90 MA 98 TCD BTh 93. CITC 90. **d** 93 **p** 94. C Bangor St Comgall *D & D* 93-96; C Bangor Primacy 93-96; Bp's C Belfast Whiterock *Conn* 96-99; R Donaghadee *D & D* from 99. *The Rectory, 3 The Trees, New Road, Donaghadee BT21 0EJ* T: (028) 9188 2594

GAMBLE, Kenneth Wesley. b 52. Ulster Univ BA 81. CITC 04. **d** 07 **p** 08. NSM Ballymacash *Conn* from 07. *21 Dalboyne Park, Lisburn BT28 3BU* T: (028) 9267 7498 E: ken_gamble@talktalk.net

GAMBLE, Norman Edward Charles. b 50. TCD BA 72 HDipEd 73 PhD 78. CITC 76. **d** 79 **p** 80. C Bangor St Comgall *D & D* 79-83; I Dunleckney w Nurney, Lorum and Kiltennel *C & O* 83-90; Warden of Readers 84-90; P-in-c Leighlin w Grange Sylvae, Shankill etc 89-90; Can Leighlin Cathl 89-90; Preb Ossory Cathl 89-90; I Malahide w Balgriffin *D & G* from 90; Abp's Dom Chapl 95-03. *The Rectory, Church Road, Malahide, Co Dublin, Republic of Ireland* T/F: (00353) (1) 845 4770 M: 86-815 3277 E: normanegamble@iol.ie

GAMBLE, Canon Robin Philip. b 53. Oak Hill Th Coll 74. **d** 77 **p** 78. C Kildwick *Bradf* 77-78; C Laisterdyke 78-80; C York St Paul 80-82; V Bradf St Aug Undercliffe 82-95; Dioc Adv in Evang 93-01; Can Ev Man Cathl 01-08; P-in-c Idle *Leeds* from 08; Dioc Ev from 08; Hon Can Bradf Cathl from 13. *The Vicarage, 470 Leeds Road, Idle, Bradford BD10 9AA* T: (01274) 419754 or 615411 M: 07748-943541 E: robinp.gamble@blueyonder.co.uk

GAMBLE, Ronald George. b 41. Cant Sch of Min 92. **d** 95 **p** 96. NSM Loose *Cant* 95-00; P-in-c Boxley w Detling 00-07; Chapl NHS Ambulance Trust 99-07; rtd 07; PtO *Cant* from 07; *Roch* from 13. *18 Copper Tree Court, Maidstone ME15 9RW* T: (01622) 744455 E: r-gamble@sky.com

GAMBLE, Stanley Thomas Robert. b 82. QUB BA 03 MTh 05. CITC 05. **d** 07 **p** 08. C Knockbreda *D & D* 07-12; I Killinchy w Kilmood and Tullynakill from 12. *Killinchy Rectory, 11 Whiterock Road, Killinchy, Newtownards BT23 6PR* T: (028) 9754 1249 E: stanleygamble@gmail.com

GAMBLE, Stephen Robert. b 69. York Univ BA 91. Cranmer Hall Dur 07. **d** 08 **p** 09. C Loughborough All SS w H Trin *Leic* 08-12; P-in-c Middleton, Newton and Sinnington *York* 12; R from 12; P-in-c Kirby Misperton w Normanby, Edston and Salton 12; V Kirby Misperton w Normanby and Salton from 12. *St Andrew's House, 15 Carr Lane, Middleton, Pickering YO18 8PU* T: (01751) 747691 E: revsrgamble@hotmail.com

GAMBLE, Thomas Richard. b 42. K Coll Lon BD 64 AKC. **d** 65 **p** 66. C Gt Ilford St Jo *Chelmsf* 65-68; Hon C 68-73; Asst Master Pettits Sec Sch Romford 68-73; Hall Mead Sch Upminster 73-75; Tabor High Sch Braintree 75-77; Chapl Warminster Sch 77-80; Norway from 80. *Holmen 35, 4842 Arendal, Norway* T: (0047) 3701 6811 or 9974 7494 E: gamble@c2i.net

GAMBLING, Paul Anthony. b 62. Middx Univ BA 06. NTMTC 03. **d** 06 **p** 07. C Warley Ch Ch and Gt Warley St Mary *Chelmsf* 06-10; TV Billericay and Lt Burstead from 10. *The Vicarage, 7A Horace Road, Billericay CM11 1AA* T: (01277) 656266 E: paul.gambling@btinternet.com

GAMLEN, Laurence William. b 59. STETS BA 07. **d** 07 **p** 08. NSM Chertsey, Lyne and Longcross *Guildf* 07-12; C from 12. *The Vicarage, Lyne Lane, Lyne, Chertsey KT16 0AJ* T: (01932) 874405 M: 07939-094851 E: laurence@intermissio.org or laurence@lyneparish.org.uk

GAMMON, Elizabeth Angela Myfanwy. b 47. SWMTC 06. **d** 09 **p** 10. NSM Sidmouth, Woolbrook, Salcombe Regis, Sidbury etc *Ex* 09-12; P-in-c Burley Ville *Win* from 12. *The Vicarage, Church Corner, Burley, Ringwood BH24 4AP* E: revd.angie@gmail.com

GAMMON, William Paul Lachlan. b 60. SS Hild & Bede Coll Dur BA 82. St Steph Ho Ox 89. **d** 91 **p** 92. C Chalfont St Peter *Ox* 91-94; Lect Bolton St Pet *Man* 94-98; R Woodston *Ely* from 98; P-in-c Fletton from 98. *The Rectory, 2 Rectory Gardens, Peterborough PE2 8HN* T: (01733) 562786

✠GANDIYA, The Rt Revd Chad Nicholas. b 53. Nottm Univ BTh 80 Univ of Zimbabwe MA 84 DPhil 06 Michigan State Univ MA 95. St Jo Coll Nottm 77. **d** 80 **p** 81 **c** 09. C Avondale Zimbabwe 80-83; R Mabelreign St Peter 83-85; Chapl Michigan Univ USA 86-87; Asst P Harare Cathl 88; Warden Bp Gaul Coll 88-91; USA 92-95; R Marlborough St Paul 95-96; Prin Bp Gaul Coll 96-01; Tutor United Coll of Ascension Selly Oak 01-05; Regional Desk Officer USPG 05-09; Tanzania and Cen Africa 05-06; Africa and Indian Ocean 06-09; Bp Harare from 09. *Bishopsmount Close, PO Box UA7, Harare, Zimbabwe* T: (00263) (4) 702253 or 702254 F: 700419

GANDIYA, Leonard Farirayi (Lee). b 64. Boston Coll (USA) MA 92. Gordon-Conwell Th Sem 90 Ridley Hall Cam 92. **d** 94 **p** 95. NSM Camberwell St Luke *S'wark* 94-95; C Lowestoft St Marg *Nor* 95-98; Dioc Rep for Black Anglican Concerns 96-98; CF from 98. *c/o MOD Chaplains (Army)* F: 381824 T: (01264) 383430

GANDON, Andrew James Robson. b 54. St Jo Coll Dur BA 76. Ridley Hall Cam 76. **d** 78 **p** 79. C Aston SS Pet and Paul *Birm* 78-82; CMS 82-95; Zaïre 82-88; Kenya 89-94; V Harefield *Lon* 95-10; Chapl R Brompton and Harefield NHS Trust 95-05; V Exhall *Cov* from 10. *36 St Giles Road, Coventry CV7 9HA* T: (024) 7767 7461

GANDON, James Noel. b 84. Leic Univ BSc 05. Trin Coll Bris BA 14. **d** 14 **p** 15. C Linc St Geo Swallowbeck from 14. *28 Sycamore Crescent, Lincoln LN6 0RR* T: (01522) 255177 E: gandonjames@gmail.com

GANDON, James Philip. b 31. ALCD 56. **d** 56 **p** 57. C Westcliff St Mich *Chelmsf* 56-58; Canada from 58; rtd 92. *62 Cambria Road North, Goderich ON N7A 2P3, Canada* E: phil.gandon@odyssey.on.ca

GANDY, Nicholas John. b 53. Westf Coll Lon BSc 75 Reading Univ MSc 76 Ex Coll Ox CertEd 78 CBiol 79 MSB. St Steph Ho Ox 86. **d** 88 **p** 89. C Crowthorne *Ox* 88-89; C Tilehurst St Mary 89-93; P-in-c Didcot St Pet 93-97; V 97-03; V Brackley St Pet w St Jas from 03; OGS from 96. *The Vicarage, Old Town, Brackley NN13 7BZ* T: (01280) 702767 E: nicholas.gandy@btinternet.com

GANE, Canon Christopher Paul. b 33. Qu Coll Cam BA 57 MA 61. Ridley Hall Cam 57. **d** 59 **p** 60. C Rainham *Chelmsf* 59-62; C Farnborough *Guildf* 62-64; V Erith St Paul *Roch* 64-71; V Ipswich St Marg *St E* 71-88; Hon Can St E Cathl 82-98; R Hopton, Market Weston, Barningham etc 88-98; rtd 98; PtO *St E* from 98. *1 Post Office Lane, Thurston, Bury St Edmunds IP31 3RW* T: (01359) 271152

GANE, Nicholas. b 57. St Jo Coll Nottm 93. **d** 95 **p** 96. C Keynsham *B & W* 95-99; TV 99-02. *10 Ludlow Court, Willsbridge, Bristol BS30 6HB* E: nick.gane@virgin.net

GANGA, Jeremy Franklin. b 62. Cape Town Univ BSocSc 86 Lon Bible Coll BA 92 St Jo Coll Nottm MA 93. Ridley Hall Cam 93. **d** 95 **p** 96. C St Peter-in-Thanet *Cant* 95-98; Chapl Felsted Sch 98-00; Past Chapl St Paul's Sch Barnes 00-02; NSM Fulham St Pet *Lon* 00-02; P-in-c 02-06; Tutor Reader Min Tr 03-10; Tutor and Registrar NTMTC 06-10; Progr Dir Angl Inst for Sch Leadership from 10. *Address temp unknown* E: jeremy.ganga@btinternet.com

GANJAVI, John Farhad. b 57. Imp Coll Lon BSc 79. Ridley Hall Cam 79. **d** 82 **p** 83. C Yardley St Edburgha *Birm* 82-85; C Knowle 85-89; P-in-c Beaudesert and Henley-in-Arden w Ullenhall *Cov* 89-92; R from 92; RD Alcester 92-99. *The Rectory, Beaudesert Lane, Henley-in-Arden B95 5JY* T: (01564) 792570 E: bdesert@btinternet.com

GANN, Canon Anthony Michael. b 37. TCD BA 60 MA 64 BD 64. **d** 62 **p** 63. V Choral Derry Cathl 62-66; Lesotho 66-74; Dioc Officer for Miss and Unity *Carl* 75-80; P-in-c Bampton and Mardale 75-80; TV Cen Telford *Lich* 80-89; TR Wolvercote w Summertown *Ox* 89-02; RD Ox 95-99; rtd 02; PtO *Worc* from 02. *Avalon, 84 Pickersleigh Road, Malvern WR14 2RS* T: (01684) 568114 E: connielightowler@agann.plus.com

GANN, John West. b 29. Ex Coll Ox BA 55 MA 59. Wells Th Coll 55. **d** 57 **p** 58. C Wendover *Ox* 57-59; C Walton St Mary *Liv* 59-62; R Didcot *Ox* 62-70; R Newbury St Nic 70-73; TR Newbury 73-78; V Twickenham St Mary *Lon* 78-87; Dir of Ords 81-87; TR Bridport *Sarum* 87-94; RD Lyme Bay 89-92; rtd 94; PtO *Glouc* from 94; *Bris* from 96. *3 Buttercross Lane, Prestbury, Cheltenham GL52 5SF* T: (01242) 220787 E: jandhgann@btinternet.com

GANNEY (née CHAMBERS), Mrs Rachel Jill. b 73. Hull Univ BSc 94 MSc 96 Selw Coll Cam BTh 04. Ridley Hall Cam 01. **d** 04 **p** 05. C Sutton St Jas and Wawne *York* 04-10; TV Plaistow and N Canning Town *Chelmsf* 10-14. *26 Pentreath Close, Fowey PL23 1ER* E: rachel@ganney.net

GANNON, James (Dub). b 75. W Sydney Univ BComm 98 BAppSc(Agric) 98. Moore Th Coll Sydney BTheol 08. **d** 10 **p** 11. NSM Henham and Elsenham w Ugley *Chelmsf* 10-13; P-in-c High and Gd Easter w Margaret Roding from 13; P-in-c Gt Canfield w High Roding and Aythorpe Roding from 13; Rural Evang Adv Colchester Area from 13. *The Rectory, 3 Old Vicarage Close, High Easter, Chelmsford CM1 4RW* T: (01245) 231795 E: dub1994@hotmail.com

GANT, Canon Brian Leonard. b 45. Ox Univ MTh 01. K Coll Lon 72. **d** 73 **p** 74. C Hillmorton *Cov* 73-75; C Cov St Geo 76; P-in-c Maldon St Mary *Chelmsf* 76-79; R Muthill, Crieff and Comrie *St And* 79-81; V Walsall St Paul *Lich* 81-84; Chapl K

Sch Worc and Min Can Worc Cathl 84-89; V Tunbridge Wells K Chas *Roch* 89-95; Hon Can Kumasi from 94; V Wymondham *Nor* 95-01; P-in-c York All SS N Street 01-03; TV Haxby and Wigginton 03-09; CME Officer York Adnry 01-07; rtd 09; PtO *York* 09-14; *Worc* from 14. *122 Henwick Road, Worcester WR2 5PB*   M: 07800-922985 T: (01905) 923247 E: brianlgant@aol.com

GANT, Joanna Elizabeth. *See* NORTHEY, Joanna Elizabeth

GANT, Peter Robert. b 38. BNC Ox BA 60 MA 64 G&C Coll Cam BA 62 MA 67. Ridley Hall Cam 61. **d** 63 **p** 64. C Portsea St Mary *Portsm* 63-67; V Blackheath *Birm* 67-73; Asst Master Harold Malley Gr Sch Solihull 73-75; PtO *Birm* 73-75; *Guildf* from 75; rtd 93. *8 Sandon Close, Esher KT10 8JE* T: (020) 8398 5107

GANT, Russell William. b 77. Suffolk Coll BA 02 St Jo Coll Dur BA 13. Cranmer Hall Dur 09. **d** 12 **p** 13. C Camberley St Paul *Guildf* from 12. *Cornerways, 3 Upper Gordon Road, Camberley GU15 2HJ* T: (01276) 700303   M: 07414-631359 E: russell.gant@stpaulscamb.co.uk

GANT, Trevor Malcolm. b 56. Leeds Univ BSc 97. NEOC 05. **d** 08 **p** 09. NSM York St Luke from 08. *6 Lumley Road, York YO30 6DB* T: (01904) 654784 E: t.gant@st-peters.york.sch.uk

GANZ, Timothy Jon. b 36. Univ Coll Ox BA 58 MA 62 ARCM 63. St Mich Ho Ox 58. **d** 61 **p** 62. C Shrewsbury H Cross *Lich* 61-65; Asst Chapl Hurstpierpoint Coll 65-69; Chapl 69-73; Chapl Univ of Wales (Swansea) *S & B* 74-75; P-in-c Hanley All SS *Lich* 75-80; TV Stoke-upon-Trent 80-81; V Tutbury 81-04; rtd 04. *3 Warren Close, Stretton, Burton-on-Trent DE13 0DD* T: (01283) 749171

GARBETT, Capt Phillip Ronald. b 52. EAMTC 95. **d** 97 **p** 98. C Ipswich St Mary at Stoke w St Pet and St Fran *St E* 97-00; TV Walton and Trimley 00-09; TR Blackbourne from 09. *The Vicarage, Commister Lane, Ixworth, Bury St Edmunds IP31 2HE* T: (01359) 234415   M: 07884-212218 E: philip.garbett@ntlworld.com

GARBUTT, Gerald. b 41. St Aid Birkenhead 65. **d** 67 **p** 68. C Stretford All SS *Man* 67-70; LtO 70-72; R Salford St Bart 72-74; V Lower Kersal 74-79; TR Bethnal Green St Jo w St Bart *Lon* 79-90; P-in-c Stepney St Pet w St Benet 85-87; Chapl Furness Gen Hosp 90-94; Chapl S Cumbria HA 90-94; Hosp Services Chapl Furness Hosps NHS Trust 94-98; Chapl Westmorland Hosps NHS Trust 94-98; Chapl Morecambe Bay Hosps NHS Trust 98-06; rtd 06; P-in-c Beetham *Carl* 06-07. *20 Highbury Road, Stockport SK4 5AZ* T: 0161-975 9110

GARBUTT, Canon Mary Yvonne. b 45. Ridley Hall Cam 00. **d** 02 **p** 03. C Desborough, Brampton Ash, Dingley and Braybrooke *Pet* 02-05; P-in-c Arthingworth, Harrington w Oxendon and E Farndon 05-07; R 07-15; P-in-c from 15; P-in-c Maidwell w Draughton, Lamport w Faxton 05-07; R 07-15; P-in-c from 15; RD Brixworth 09-15; Can Pet Cathl 12-15. *The Rectory, Harlestone Road, Church Brampton, Northampton NN6 8AU* T: (01858) 461992 E: mary@familygarbutt.plus.com

GARCIA FUERTE, Antonio. b 77. St Damasus Univ Madrid BST 02. Westcott Ho Cam 13. **d** 15. C Paddington St Jo w St Mich *Lon* from 15. *23 Archery Close, London W2 2BE* M: 07939-997819 E: a.g.fuerte@gmail.com

GARCIA-MONTIEL, The Rt Revd Martiniano. Bp Cuernavaca 01-04; Acting Primate of Mexico 03-04; rtd 04. *Apartado Postal 538, Admon 4, CP 62431 Cuernavaca, Morelos, Mexico* T/F: (0052) (73) 152870 E: diovca@giga.com.mx

GARDEN, Robert Andrew (Robin). b 26. Edin Univ BSc 49 Kent Univ MA 95 MInstP 58 FIMA 72. Cant Sch of Min 87. **d** 90 **p** 91. NSM Wingham *Cant* 90-97; Chapl St Bart Hosp Sandwich 91-00; PtO *Cant* from 97. *Naini, 164 St George's Road, Sandwich CT13 9LD* T: (01304) 612116

GARDHAM, Mrs Linda Elizabeth. b 49. Leeds Univ BA 70 Warwick Univ PGCE 71. Cranmer Hall Dur 04. **d** 05 **p** 06. NSM Monkseaton St Pet *Newc* 05-08; NSM Cornhill w Carham 08-13; NSM Branxton 08-13; rtd 13. *Address temp unknown* E: leg@lgardham.freeserve.co.uk

GARDINER, Anthony Reade. b 35. Univ of NZ BA 59. Cuddesdon Coll 60. **d** 62 **p** 63. C Gosforth All SS *Newc* 62-65; V Waikohu New Zealand 65-69; V Edgecumbe 69-74; V Eltham 74-78; V Trentham 78-81; V Waipukurau 81-88; Chapl Nelson Cathl 88-92; C Highcliffe w Hinton Admiral *Win* 93-94; TV N Creedy *Ex* 94-00; rtd 00; PtO Wellington New Zealand from 00. *1 Puriri Street, Eastbourne, Lower Hutt 5013, New Zealand* T: (0064) (4) 562 6177 E: nantony2@paradise.net.nz

GARDINER, Mrs Cathrine Leigh. b 64. STETS 05. **d** 08 **p** 09. C Bedminster *Bris* 08-11; TV Anerley *Roch* 11-15; P-in-c Filwood Park *Bris* from 15. *St Barnabas' Vicarage, 64 Daventry Road, Bristol BS4 1DQ* E: cathrinegardiner@gmail.com

GARDINER, Charles Graham. b 18. AKC 49. St Boniface Warminster. **d** 50 **p** 51. C Clapham H Trin *S'wark* 50-54; S Africa from 54. *55 Weltevreden Avenue, Rondebosch, 7700 South Africa* T: (0027) (21) 689 1111

GARDINER, David Andrew. b 81. Surrey Univ BA 03 Fitzw Coll Cam BTh 08. Westcott Ho Cam 05. **d** 08 **p** 09. C N Cheltenham *Glouc* 08-12; TV Richmond St Mary w St Matthias and St Jo *S'wark* from 12. *St Matthias' House, 22 Cambrian Road, Richmond TW10 6JQ* T: (020) 8948 7217

GARDINER, Gerald. *See* GARDINER, William Gerald Henry

GARDINER (née SAYERS), Mrs Karen Jane. b 69. Sheff Univ BMus 90 Lon Univ MA 11. Ripon Coll Cuddesdon 00. **d** 02 **p** 03. C Dunstable *St Alb* 02-05; TV Elstree and Borehamwood 05-15; Hon C Escrick and Stillingfleet w Naburn *York* from 15; Hon C Bubwith w Skipwith from 15. *The Vicarage, 2 Highfield Road, Bubwith, Selby YO8 6LY* T: (01757) 289266 E: revkarenjg@gmail.com

GARDINER, Canon Kenneth Ashton. b 27. S'wark Ord Course 60. **d** 63 **p** 64. C Sydenham H Trin *S'wark* 63-67; C Macclesfield St Mich *Ches* 67-70; V Chatham St Phil and St Jas *Roch* 70-93; RD Roch 88-93; Hon Can Roch Cathl 88-93; rtd 93; PtO *Roch* from 93. *30 The Queen Mother Court, Borstal Road, Rochester ME1 3JF* T: (01634) 846445 E: kn.gardiner@btinternet.com

GARDINER, Richard Allen. b 51. St Steph Ho Ox 12. **d** 13 **p** 14. Asst Chapl Bonn w Cologne *Eur* from 13. *Auf dem Kälberhof 12, D-53797 Lohmar-Krahwinkel, Germany* T: (0049) (2247) 1472 M: 172-532 8025 E: richard.gardiner@web.de

GARDINER, Wendy Doreen. b 49. SRN 71. Trin Coll Bris 10. **d** 12 **p** 13. OLM Barton Hill St Luke w Ch Ch and Moorfields *Bris* from 12. *55 Whitehall Road, Bristol BS5 9BG* T: 0117-954 1645 M: 07902-318663 E: wdgardiner@btopenworld.com

GARDINER, Preb William Gerald Henry. b 46. Lon Univ BD 72. Oak Hill Th Coll 68. **d** 72 **p** 73. C Beckenham St Jo *Roch* 72-75; C Cheadle *Ches* 75-81; P-in-c Swynnerton *Lich* 81-83; P-in-c Tittensor 81-83; R Swynnerton and Tittensor 83-86; V Westlands St Andr 86-11; RD Newcastle 97-11; Preb Lich Cathl 05-11; rtd 11; PtO *Lich* from 12. *4 The Lindens, Stone ST15 0BD*

GARDNER, Canon Anthony Brian. b 32. Lon Coll of Div 62. **d** 64 **p** 65. C Stoke *Cov* 64-68; R Whitnash 68-98; RD Leamington 78; RD Warwick and Leamington 79-87; Hon Can Cov Cathl 83-98; rtd 98; PtO *Cov* from 99. *4 Mark Antony Drive, Heathcote, Warwick CV34 6XA* T: (01926) 832690

GARDNER, Brian Charles. b 46. FIBMS 71. **d** 04 **p** 05. OLM Bodicote *Ox* from 04. *11 Farm Way, Banbury OX16 9TB* T: (01295) 253309   M: 07967-859457 E: bri.jen@btopenworld.com

GARDNER, Christine. *See* GARDNER, Mary Christine

GARDNER, Clive Bruce. b 67. Selw Coll Cam BA 89 MA 93. Wycliffe Hall Ox BA 95 MA 01. **d** 96 **p** 97. C Beverley Minster *York* 96-98; Bp's Dom Chapl *Liv* 98-01; V Cumnor *Ox* 01-06; TV Wimbledon *S'wark* from 11. *55 Alwyne Road, London SW19 7AE* T: (020) 8944 0184 E: clivegardner@tesco.net

GARDNER, David. b 57. Oak Hill Th Coll BA 87. **d** 87 **p** 88. C Ogley Hay *Lich* 87-91; TV Mildenhall *St E* 91-98; P-in-c Woodbridge St Jo 98-00; V 00-03; V Woodbridge St Jo and Bredfield 03-12; P-in-c Ufford w Bredfield and Hasketon 01-03; Dir Miss from 12. *St Nicholas Centre, 4 Cutler Street, Ipswich IP1 1UQ* T: (01473) 298500   F: 298501

GARDNER, Elizabeth Mary. b 47. Nottm Univ BA 01. Trin Coll Bris 72 St Jo Coll Nottm 00. **d** 01 **p** 02. C Swindon Dorcan *Bris* 01-04; P-in-c Runcorn St Jo Weston *Ches* 04-09; V 09-13; rtd 13; Dioc Clergy Widows and Retirement Officer *Ches* 07-10; Chapl Countess of Chester Hosp NHS Foundn Trust from 13. *69 Ford Road, Wirral CH49 0TD*

GARDNER, Geoffrey Maurice. b 28. K Coll Lon BA 51 Lon Inst of Educn PGCE 52 Bris Univ DipEd 74. Cranmer Hall Dur. **d** 59 **p** 60. C Bowling St Jo *Bradf* 59-62; Nigeria 62-72; Hon C Bath St Luke *B & W* 72-73; PtO 73-90 and 94-99; NSM Bath Widcombe 90-94; rtd 94; PtO *Ex* from 99. *15 Bramley Gardens, Whimple, Exeter EX5 2SJ* T: (01404) 823235

GARDNER, Mrs Helen Elizabeth. b 56. ERMC 05. **d** 08 **p** 09. C Sunnyside w Bourne End *St Alb* 08-12; V Totternhoe, Stanbridge and Tilsworth from 12. *The Vicarage, Mill Road, Stanbridge, Leighton Buzzard LU7 9HX* T: (01525) 211917 E: helerevg@aol.com

GARDNER, Helen Jane. b 39. Man Univ BSc 61 PGCE 62. WEMTC 93. **d** 96 **p** 97. NSM Stow on the Wold *Glouc* 96-00; NSM Stow on the Wold, Condicote and The Swells 00-02; PtO 04-07; NSM Stow on the Wold, Condicote and The Swells 07-12; rtd 12. *6 St Mary's Close, Lower Swell, Cheltenham GL54 1LJ* T: (01451) 832553 E: gardner269@btinternet.com

GARDNER, Ian Douglas. b 34. St Pet Hall Ox BA 58 MA 62. Oak Hill Th Coll 58. **d** 60 **p** 61. C Biddulph *Lich* 60-63; C Weston St Jo *B & W* 64; Nigeria 65-76; P-in-c Hurstbourne Tarrant and

Faccombe *Win* 77-79; V Hurstbourne Tarrant, Faccombe, Vernham Dean etc 79-85; R Nursling and Rownhams 85-99; rtd 99; LtO *St D* from 99. *Wilderness Cottage, Haroldston Hill, Broad Haven, Haverfordwest SA62 3JP* T: (01437) 781592

GARDNER, Ian Norman. b 52. Open Univ BSc 96. WEMTC 03. **d** 05 **p** 06. NSM Dursley *Glouc* from 05. *9 Chestal Lodge, Chestal, Dursley GL11 5AA* T: (01453) 546895
M: 07960-287403 E: ian@chestal.freeserve.co.uk

GARDNER, Mrs Jacqueline Anne. b 49. WEMTC 95. **d** 98 **p** 99. NSM Fairford and Kempsford w Whelford *Glouc* 98-02; NSM Cirencester 02-05; PtO *Ox* 05-07; NSM Hanborough and Freeland 07-13; PtO from 13. *15 Oakdale Road, Witney OX28 1AX* T: (01993) 866110 E: jackiegardner@hotmail.com

GARDNER, Jane. *See* GARDNER, Helen Jane

GARDNER, Canon John Phillip Backhouse. b 21. St Aid Birkenhead 49. **d** 52 **p** 53. C Ashtead *Guildf* 52-55; C Bromley SS Pet and Paul *Roch* 55-57; V New Hythe 57-63; V Roch St Justus 63-69; R Wisley w Pyrford *Guildf* 70-87; RD Woking 82-87; Hon Can Guildf Cathl 86-87; rtd 87; PtO *Pet* 87-98; *Guildf* from 98. *42 Godley Road, Byfleet, West Byfleet KT14 7ER* T: (01932) 347431

GARDNER, Mrs Lorna. b 54. **d** 14 **p** 15. NSM Blaydon and Swalwell *Dur* from 14. *1 Kirkstone Close, Blaydon-on-Tyne NE21 6SY* T: 0191-414 5300 E: lornagardner6@gmail.com

GARDNER (née DUFFELL), Mrs Lucy Margaret. b 67. St Jo Coll Ox BA 90 MA 96. Ox Min Course 11. **d** 12 **p** 13. Tutor St Steph Ho Ox from 05; NSM Wheatley *Ox* 12-14; NSM Albury w Tiddington, Holton, Waterperry, Waterstock and Wheatley from 14. *St Stephen's House, 16 Marston Street, Oxford OX4 1JX* T: (01865) 613500 E: lucy.gardner@ssho.ox.ac.uk

GARDNER, Mrs Marian Elizabeth. b 50. Ripon Coll of Educn DipEd 71. WMMTC 00. **d** 03 **p** 04. NSM Kirkleatham *York* 03-07; P-in-c Easington w Liverton from 07. *The Rectory, Grinkle Lane, Easington, Saltburn-by-the-Sea TS13 4NT* T: (01287) 641348 M: 07736-350643
E: marian@thegardners.org.uk

GARDNER, Canon Mark Douglas. b 58. TCD BA 80 MA 83. **d** 83 **p** 84. C Ballymacarrett St Patr *D & D* 83-87; C Belfast St Steph w St Luke *Conn* 87-89; C Hendon and Sunderland *Dur* 89-90; TV Sunderland 90-95; I Dublin Santry w Glasnevin and Finglas *D & G* 95-01; PV and Chapter Clerk Ch Ch Cathl Dublin 96-10; Min Can St Patr Cathl Dublin 96; Treas V 96-01; Can Ch Ch Cathl Dublin from 08; V Dublin St Patr Cathl Gp 10-12; I Dublin St Cath and St Jas w St Audoen from 12; Preb Tipperkevin St Patr Cathl Dublin 10-12; Preb Maynooth from 12. *248 South Circular Road, Dolphin's Barn, Dublin 8, Republic of Ireland* T: (00353) (1) 454 2274 M: 87-266 0228
E: markgardner@eircom.net

GARDNER, Mary Christine. b 42. SRN 64 SCM 66. St Jo Coll Nottm 80. **dss** 82 **d** 85 **p** 94. Ches St Paul 82-87; Macclesfield St Mich 84-85; Macclesfield Team 85-87; Par Dn 87; Chapl Asst Nottm City Hosp 87-93; Chapl St Chris Hospice Lon 93-01; V Over St Jo *Ches* 01-03; rtd 03. *2 Leeks Close, Southwell NG25 0BA* T: (01623) 812823

GARDNER, Michael Ronald. b 53. Trin Coll Bris 95. **d** 97 **p** 98. C Stanmore *Win* 97-01; V from 01. *St Luke's Vicarage, Mildmay Street, Winchester SO22 4BX* T: (01962) 865240

GARDNER, Neil Kenneth. b 65. Univ of Wales (Swansea) BA 92 Peterho Cam BA 00 Univ of Wales (Cardiff) PhD 01. Westcott Ho Cam 98. **d** 01 **p** 02. C Wisbech SS Pet and Paul *Ely* from 01; C Wisbech St Aug 03-04; P-in-c from 04. *The Rectory, 35 Gorefield Road, Leverington, Wisbech PE13 5AS* T/F: (01945) 585850 M: 07855-111794 E: n.gardner952@btinternet.com

GARDNER (née JAMES), Mrs Sandra Kay. b 66. Westcott Ho Cam 97. **d** 99 **p** 00. C Whittlesey, Pondersbridge and Coates *Ely* 99-02; R Leverington 02-04; V Southea w Murrow and Parson Drove 02-04; R Leverington, Newton and Tydd St Giles from 05. *The Rectory, 35 Gorefield Road, Leverington, Wisbech PE13 5AS* T: (01945) 585850
E: sandra.gardner@ely.anglican.org

GARDNER, Mrs Stephanie Yvonne. b 63. SEITE. **d** 14. NSM Beeding and Bramber w Botolphs *Chich* from 14. *18 Heyshott Close, Lancing BN15 0QJ*

GARDNER, Stephen John. b 70. Southn Univ MEng 92. St Jo Coll Nottm 00. **d** 02 **p** 03. C Brinsworth w Catcliffe and Treeton *Sheff* 02-03; C Rivers Team 03-05; V Woodlands from 05. *All Saints' Vicarage, 9 Great North Road, Woodlands, Doncaster DN6 7RB* T: (01302) 339618
M: 07740-200942 E: stephen.gardner@sheffield.anglican.org

GARDNER, Susan Carol. *See* CLARKE, Susan Carol

GARDNER, Vincent Lyndon. b 62. K Coll Lon MA 98 Robert Gordon Univ Aber BFA 90. St Steph Ho Ox 02. **d** 04 **p** 05. C Carew *St D* 04-07; V Reading St Jo *Ox* from 08. *The Vicarage, 5A Alexandra Road, Reading RG1 5PE* T: 0118-926 9906 M: 07901-737649 E: vincent_gardner@hotmail.com

GARDOM, Francis Douglas. b 34. Trin Coll Ox BA 55 MA 59. Wells Th Coll 58. **d** 60 **p** 61. C Greenwich St Alfege w St Pet *S'wark* 60-68; C Lewisham St Steph and St Mark 68-76; Hon C from 76. *79 Maze Hill, London SE10 8XQ* T: (020) 8858 7052 *or* 8852 1474 E: francisgardom@aol.com

GARDOM, James Theodore Douglas. b 61. St Anne's Coll Ox BA 83 K Coll Lon PhD 92. Ripon Coll Cuddesdon 88. **d** 90 **p** 91. C Witney *Ox* 90-92; Dean of Studies Bp Gaul Coll Harare Zimbabwe 93-97; V Chesterton St Andr *Ely* 97-06; Dean and Chapl Pemb Coll Cam from 06. *Pembroke College, Cambridge CB2 1RF* T: (01223) 338147 F: 338163 E: jtdg2@cam.ac.uk

GARLAND, Christopher John. b 47. Ex Univ BA 69 PhD 72. Qu Coll Birm 78. **d** 80 **p** 81. C Beckenham St Jas *Roch* 80-82; C Roch 82-84; Papua New Guinea 85-93; Australia 94-95; R Copford w Easthorpe and Messing w Inworth *Chelmsf* 95-12; R Stroud Australia from 12. *The Rectory, 83 Cowper Street, Stroud NSW 2425, Australia* T: (0061) (2) 4994 5193 E: garlandc79@aol.com

GARLAND, Canon Michael. b 50. Sarum & Wells Th Coll 72. **d** 73 **p** 74. C Swansea St Thos and Kilvey *S & B* 73-76; C Boldmere *Birm* 76-79; V Kingshurst 79-88; P-in-c Curdworth w Castle Vale 88-90; R Curdworth 90-03; P-in-c Wishaw 99-00; V Charlton Kings St Mary *Glouc* from 03; Hon Can Glouc Cathl from 13. *The Vicarage, 63 Church Street, Charlton Kings, Cheltenham GL53 8AT* T: (01242) 253402 M: 07974-066929 E: michaelgarland368@btinternet.com

GARLICK, Canon David. b 37. Nottm Univ BA 62. St Steph Ho Ox 62. **d** 64 **p** 65. C Kennington St Jo *S'wark* 64-66; Hon C Newington St Paul 66-68; P-in-c Vauxhall St Pet 68-79; V Lewisham St Mary 79-07; RD E Lewisham 92-99; Hon Can S'wark Cathl 93-07; rtd 07; PtO *S'wark* from 10. *Limekilns Farmhouse, Braidley, Horsehouse, Leyburn DL8 4TX* T: (01969) 640280 M: 07952-243668 E: lewi346@yahoo.co.uk

GARLICK, Preb Kathleen Beatrice. b 49. Leeds Univ BA 71 Birm Univ PGCE 72. Glouc Sch of Min 87. **d** 90 **p** 94. NSM Much Birch w Lt Birch, Much Dewchurch etc *Heref* 90-03; P-in-c 03-07; R Wormelow Hundred 07-09; Chapl Heref Sixth Form Coll 96-03; Chapl Heref Cathl 09-14; Preb Heref Cathl 99-14; rtd 14; PtO *Heref* from 14; Chapl to The Queen from 11. *Birch Lodge, Much Birch, Hereford HR2 8HT* T: (01981) 540666 M: 07812-995442 E: kaygarlick@hotmail.com

GARLICK, Canon Peter. b 34. AKC 57. **d** 58 **p** 59. C Swindon New Town *Bris* 58-63; St Kitts-Nevis 63-66; V Heyside *Man* 66-73; R Stretford All SS 73-79; RD Wootton *Pet* 79-88; V Duston 79-91; TR 91-94; Can Pet Cathl 85-94; rtd 94; PtO *Pet* from 04. *120 Worcester Close, Northampton NN3 9GD* T: (01604) 416511 E: mail@pandcgarlick.plus.com

GARLICK, William Frederick. b 51. **d** 98 **p** 99. OLM Bermondsey St Jas w Ch Ch and St Crispin *S'wark* 98-06. *33 Penfolds Place, Arundel BN18 9SA*

GARMAN, Mrs Elaine. **d** 15. C Dunoon *Arg* from 15; C Rothesay from 15. *Grianan, Ascog, Isle of Bute PA20 9ET* T: (01700) 505617 E: elainegarman@aol.com

GARNER, Alexander David. b 86. Dur Univ BA 07. St Steph Ho Ox BA 14. **d** 15. C Hendon St Alphage *Lon* from 15. *18 Montrose Avenue, Edgware HA8 0DW* T: (020) 3573 4138 M: 07528-513433 E: a.d.garner86@gmail.com

GARNER, Alistair Ross. b 58. Pemb Coll Ox BA 81 MA 86. St Jo Coll Nottm 90. **d** 92 **p** 93. C Ashton-upon-Mersey St Mary Magd *Ches* 92-96; P-in-c Bredbury St Mark 96-01; V 01-09; Miss Growth Team Ldr *Roch* 09-12; TR Walkden and Lt Hulton *Man* from 12. *St John's Vicarage, Algernon Road, Worsley, Manchester M28 3RD* T: 0161-790 2338
E: revrossgarner@gmail.com

GARNER, Canon Carl. b 42. Rhodes Univ BA 62 Keble Coll Ox BA 64 MA 70. St Paul's Coll Grahamstown 66. **d** 67 **p** 68. C Pietersburg S Africa 67-71; R Louis Trichardt 71-75; Chapl St Paul's Coll Grahamstown 75-84; Dioc Missr *St Alb* 84-98; Can Res St Alb 84-98; P-in-c Digswell and Panshanger 98-06; TR 06-12; Hon Can St Alb 99-12; Jt RD Welwyn Hatfield 01-12; rtd 12; PtO *St Alb* from 12. *2 Hill House, 38 Park Street, Hatfield AL9 5AZ*

GARNER, Mrs Carole. b 61. LCTP 05. **d** 08 **p** 09. NSM Oswaldtwistle St Paul *Blackb* 08-12; NSM Oswaldtwistle from 12. *17 Spinning Mill Close, Oswaldtwistle, Accrington BB5 4AB* E: carole.garner@blackburn.anglican.org

GARNER, David Henry. b 40. Trin Coll Bris 70. **d** 73 **p** 74. C Tunstead *Man* 73-75; C Fazeley *Lich* 76-78; V Sparkhill St Jo *Birm* 78-85; V Blackheath 85-01; Deanery P Warley Deanery 01-05; rtd 05; PtO *Birm* from 05; Chapl Sandwell and W Birm Hosps NHS Trust from 06; PtO *Worc* from 06. *94 Honeybourne Road, Halesowen B63 3HD* T: 0121-550 2498
M: 07779-948333 E: davidhenrygarner@yahoo.co.uk

GARNER, Geoffrey Walter. b 40. Ripon Hall Ox 69. **d** 71 **p** 72. C Stoke *Cov* 71-75; V Tile Hill 76-80; TV Hackney *Lon* 80-89; R Bow w Bromley St Leon 89-06; rtd 06. *98 Wordsworth Road, Plymouth PL2 2JQ*

GARNER, John David. b 47. d 03. OLM Kirkdale St Lawr *Liv* 03-15; rtd 15. *10 Doon Close, Liverpool L4 1XW* T: 0151-284 0388 E: johngarner65@aol.com

GARNER, John Howard. b 45. Univ of Wales (Swansea) BSc 67 Univ of Wales (Ban) PhD 75. SWMTC 95. d 98 p 99. NSM Upton *Ex* from 98; Sen Chapl S Devon Healthcare NHS Foundn Trust from 06. *Highgrove Lodge, Sunbury Hill, Upton, Torquay TQ1 3ED* T: (01803) 293640 *or* 654186 E: johngarner@onetel.net.uk

GARNER, Mark William John. b 50. Melbourne Univ BA 71 DipEd 73 Essex Univ MA 75 Aber Univ MTheol 08. TISEC 09. d 11. C Turriff *Ab* 11-12; Hd of Whitelands Coll Roehampton Univ *S'wark* from 12. *Whitelands College, Holybourne Avenue, London SW15 4JD* T: (020) 8392 3501 E: mark.garner@roehampton.ac.uk

GARNER, Canon Peter. b 35. Lon Univ BSc 56 Leeds Univ MEd 91 PhD 11. Wycliffe Hall Ox 56. d 58 p 59. C Walthamstow St Jo *Chelmsf* 58-61; V Hainault 61-70; R Theydon Garnon 70-73; P-in-c Kirby-le-Soken 73-74; V 74-82; P-in-c Fountains *Ripon* 82-88; P-in-c Kirkby Malzeard w Grewelthorpe and Mickley etc 82-88; Par Development Adv 88-93; P-in-c Birstwith 91-93; R Walkingham Hill 93-01; Hon Can Ripon Cathl 99-01; rtd 01; PtO *Leeds* from 02. *Firtops, 2 Shirley Avenue, Ripon HG4 1SP* T: (01765) 601543 M: 07864-528425 E: petergarner2@sky.com

GARNER, Canon Rodney George. b 48. Lon Univ BA 87 Hull Univ MPhil 96 Man Univ PhD 01 MCIPD 75. Qu Coll Birm 75. d 78 p 79. C Tranmere St Paul w St Luke *Ches* 78-81; V Eccleston St Thos *Liv* 81-90; P-in-c Sculcoates St Paul w Ch Ch and St Silas *York* 90-95; Lay Tr Officer (E Riding Adnry) 90-95; P-in-c Southport H Trin *Liv* 95-96; V from 96; Dioc Th Consultant from 95; Hon Can Liv Cathl from 07. *Holy Trinity Vicarage, 24 Roe Lane, Southport PR9 9DX* T/F: (01704) 538560 E: anglican@garnerr.freeserve.co.uk

GARNER, Ross. *See* GARNER, Alistair Ross

GARNER, Mrs Selina Clare. b 69. Newnham Coll Cam BA 90 K Coll Lon PGCE 93. EAMTC 00. d 06 p 07. C Fulbourn *Ely* 06-09; C Gt Wilbraham 06-09; C Lt Wilbraham 06-09; C Cullompton, Willand, Uffculme, Kentisbeare etc *Ex* from 09; Pioneer Youth Min Cullompton Deanery from 09. *The Vicarage, Bridge Street, Uffculme, Cullompton EX15 3AX* T: (01884) 841001 E: selina@thegarners.me.uk

GARNER, Thomas Richard. b 43. K Coll Lon. d 69 p 70. C Tynemouth Ch Ch *Newc* 69-73; C Fenham St Jas and St Basil 73-76; V Hamstead St Bernard *Birm* 76-80; V Greytown New Zealand 80-87; V Levin 87-96; Can Wellington 96-99; V Upper Riccarton w Yaldhurst New Zealand 99-05; rtd 05. *267 Chester Road, RD 1, Carterton 5791, New Zealand*

GARNETT, Alyson Susan. *See* PEBERDY, Alyson Susan

GARNETT, The Ven David Christopher. b 45. Nottm Univ BA 67 Fitzw Coll Cam BA 69 MA 73. Westcott Ho Cam 67. d 69 p 70. C Cottingham *York* 69-72; Chapl Selw Coll Cam 72-77; P-in-c Patterdale *Carl* 77-80; Dir of Ords 78-80; V Heald Green St Cath *Ches* 80-87; R Christleton 87-92; TR Ellesmere Port 92-96; Adn Chesterfield *Derby* 96-09; P-in-c Beeley and Edensor 07-10; Hon Can Derby Cathl 96-10; rtd 10. *5 South Crescent Avenue, Filey YO14 9JN* T: (01723) 514680 E: davidcgarnett@yahoo.co.uk

GARNETT, Preb Ralph Henry. b 28. Cuddesdon Coll 58. d 60 p 61. C Broseley w Benthall *Heref* 60-64; V Leintwardine 64-69; P-in-c Downton w Burrington and Aston and Elton 66-69; RD Ludlow 72-75; R Whitton w Greete and Hope Bagot 69-87; R Burford III w Lt Heref 69-87; P-in-c Burford I, Nash and Boraston 72-74; R 74-87; V Tenbury Wells 69-74; TR 74-87; Preb Heref Cathl 82-93; P-in-c Fownhope 87-93; P-in-c Brockhampton w Fawley 87-93; RD Heref Rural 92-93; rtd 93; PtO *Heref* 93-12. *8 Butlers Place, Portsmouth Road, Milford, Godalming GU8 5EX*

GARNSEY, George Christopher. b 36. Qu Coll Ox BA 63. d 60 p 60. LtO *Wakef* 78-79; C Lupset 80; Prin St Jo Coll Morpeth Australia 80-91; R Gresford w Paterson 93-01; Lect St Jo Coll Morpeth from 01; rtd 01. *17 James Street, Morpeth NSW 2321, Australia* T: (0061) (2) 4934 2658 F: 4921 6898 E: jan@maths.newcastle.edu.au

GARRARD, Mrs Christine Ann. b 51. Open Univ BA 86 LCST 75. EAMTC 87. d 90 p 94. Par Dn Kesgrave *St E* 90-94; C 94-96; V Ipswich All Hallows 96-02; R Higham, Holton St Mary, Raydon and Stratford 02-08; Asst Dioc Dir of Ords 03-08; Sen Chapl Burrswood Chr Hosp 08-14; rtd 14. *40 Oakbury Drive, Weymouth DT3 6JE* T: (01305) 833475 E: revdchris@aol.com

GARRARD, Mrs Elizabeth Helen. b 65. Dundee Univ BN 11 RGN 89. ERMC 09. d 11 p 12. OLM Broadside *Nor* from 11; Chapl Norfolk Community Health and Care NHS Trust from

14. *Colman Hospital, Priscilla Bacon Lodge, Unthank Road, Norwich NR13 6DQ* M: 07920-528282 T: (01603) 255728 E: elisabeth.garrard@nchc.nhs.uk

GARRARD, Canon James Richard. b 65. Dur Univ BA 88 Keble Coll Ox DPhil 92 Leeds Univ MA 01. Westcott Ho Cam. d 94 p 95. C Elland *Wakef* 94-97; TV Brighouse and Clifton 98-01; P-in-c Balderstone *Blackb* 01-08; Warden of Readers 01-08; Can Res Ely Cathl from 08. *The Precentor's House, 32 High Street, Ely CB7 4JU* T: (01353) 660335 *or* 660300 F: 665658 E: j.garrard@elycathedral.org

GARRARD, Canon Nicholas James Havelock. b 62. Leeds Univ BA 83. Westcott Ho Cam 86. d 88 p 89. C Scotforth *Blackb* 88-91; C Eaton *Nor* 91-95; V Heigham St Thos 95-06; RD Nor S 03-06; R Broadside from 06; RD Blofield from 14; Hon Can Nor Cathl from 14. *The Rectory, 23 The Street, South Walsham, Norwich NR13 6DQ* T: (01603) 270769 E: nickgarr39@aol.com

✠**GARRARD, The Rt Revd Richard.** b 37. K Coll Lon BD 60 AKC 60. d 61 p 62 c 94. C Woolwich St Mary w H Trin *S'wark* 61-66; C Cambridge Gt St Mary w St Mich *Ely* 66-68; Chapl Keswick Hall Coll of Educn 68-74; Prin Wilson Carlile Coll of Evang 74-79; Can Res and Chan S'wark Cathl 79-87; Dir of Tr 79-87; Can Res St E Cathl 87-94; Dioc Adv for CME 87-91; Adn Sudbury 91-94; Suff Bp Penrith *Carl* 94-01; Hon Can Carl Cathl 94-01; Abp's Rep H See and Dir Angl Cen Rome 01-03; Hon Asst Bp Eur from 01; rtd 03; PtO *Nor* from 03; Hon Asst Bp Nor from 03. *26 Carol Close, Stoke Holy Cross, Norwich NR14 8NN* T: (01508) 494165 E: garrard.r.a@btinternet.com

GARRARD, Miss Valerie Mary. b 48. K Alfred's Coll Win TCert 69 St Paul's Coll Chelt BEd 84. d 03 p 04. OLM Wylye and Till Valley *Sarum* 03-11; TV Lower Wylye and Till Valley from 11. *Cowslip Cottage, Wylye Road, Hanging Langford, Salisbury SP3 4NW* T: (01722) 790739 E: vmgarrard@btinternet.com

GARRATT, Alan. b 54. d 04 p 05. NSM Hazlemere *Ox* 04-08; TR Thame from 08; AD Aston and Cuddesdon from 13. *The Rectory, 3 Fish Ponds Lane, Thame OX9 2BA* T: (01844) 212225 E: alan.garratt@hotmail.co.uk

GARRATT, David John. b 66. Leic Poly BA 98. Wycliffe Hall Ox 05. d 07 p 08. C Southover *Chich* 07-14; Chapl Bp Bell Sch from 14. *4 Priory Row, Lewes BN7 1TJ* T: (01273) 474387 M: 07963-988618 E: david.garratt@macmail.com

GARRATT, Mrs Helen Louise Fontana. b 66. Univ Coll Lon BSc 88 MSc 96. SEITE BA 11. d 11 p 12. NSM Southover *Chich* from 11. *4 Priory Row, Lewes BN7 1TJ* T: (01273) 474387

GARRATT, Malcolm John. b 52. Nottm Univ BSc 73. Trin Coll Bris 97. d 99 p 00. C Bawtry w Austerfield and Misson *S'well* 99-00; C Hucknall Torkard 00-03; P-in-c Clipstone 03-10; P-in-c Dunchurch *Cov* 10-15; rtd 15; PtO *Cov* from 15. *4 Gabor Close, Rugby CV21 1XQ* T: (01788) 333993 E: malcolm.garratt@ntlworld.com

GARRATT, Peter James. b 37. ALCD 64. d 64 p 65. C Bingham *S'well* 64-67; C Mansfield SS Pet and Paul 67-69; V Purlwell *Wakef* 69-73; R Kirk Sandall and Edenthorpe *Sheff* 73-82; R Whippingham w E Cowes *Portsm* 82-87; V Soberton w Newtown 87-01; rtd 02; PtO *Portsm* from 02. *35 Fair Isle Close, Fareham PO14 3RT* T: (01329) 661162

GARRATT, Roger Charles. b 50. St Jo Coll Dur BA 72. Cranmer Hall Dur 72. d 74 p 75. C Leamington Priors St Paul *Cov* 74-77; Chapl Emscote Lawn Sch Warw 77-99; Chapl and Dep Hd Arden Lawn Sch 77-00; TV Warwick *Cov* 02-08; rtd 08; PtO *Cov* from 08. *8 Wasdale Close, Leamington Spa CV32 6NF* T: (01926) 335474 E: roger.garratt@btinternet.com

GARRETT, Ms Celia Joy. b 60. RGN 81 RM 85. Cant Sch of Min 92. d 95. C S Ashford St Fran *Cant* 95-98; NSM 98-05. *Address withheld by request*

GARRETT, Christopher Hugh Ahlan. b 35. Sarum & Wells Th Coll 72. d 75 p 76. C Addiscombe St Mildred *Cant* 75-81; V Thornton Heath St Jude w St Aid *S'wark* 81-00; rtd 00; PtO *Glouc* from 01. *Edge View, 18 Gloucester Road, Painswick GL6 6RA* T: (01452) 813688

GARRETT, Clive Robert. b 54. Sheff Univ BA 75 PhD 80 Ex Univ PGCE 88. St Jo Coll Nottm MA 98. d 98 p 99. C Bath Weston St Jo w Kelston *B & W* 98-02; R from 02. *The Rectory, 8 Ashley Avenue, Bath BA1 3DR* T: (01225) 317323 E: crg@cix.co.uk

GARRETT, Miss Elizabeth Clare. b 46. Trin Coll Bris. d 94 p 95. C Ewyas Harold w Dulas, Kenderchurch etc *Heref* 94-96; C Tupsley w Hampton Bishop 96-00; TV Uttoxeter Area *Lich* 00-05; P-in-c Gt Canfield w High Roding and Aythorpe Roding *Chelmsf* 05-11; rtd 11. *10 Culverwell Gardens, Winchester SO23 9JG* M: 07790-878307 E: ecgarrett@btinternet.com

GARRETT, Geoffrey David. b 57. Oak Hill Th Coll 83. d 86 p 87. C Trentham *Lich* 86-90; V Rhodes *Man* 90-00; P-in-c Bardsley 00-05; V 05-08; V Watton *Nor* 08-13; C Cockley Cley w Gooderstone 10-13; R Condover w Frodesley, Acton Burnell etc *Heref* from 13. *The Rectory, Condover, Shrewsbury SY5 7AA* T: (01743) 872251 E: revgeoff@live.co.uk

GARRETT, Ian Lee. b 60. MCSP 81. Sarum & Wells Th Coll 86. **d** 89 **p** 90. C Maidstone St Martin *Cant* 89-95; P-in-c S Ashford St Fran 95-07; TV Bishopsworth and Bedminster Down *Bris* 07-13; P-in-c Brislington St Anne from 13; C Brislington St Chris and St Cuth 07-08; P-in-c Brislington St Cuth from 08. *35 Wick Crescent, Bristol BS4 4HG* T: 0117-971 0523 E: ianlgarrett@gmail.com

GARRETT, Kevin George. b 48. Oak Hill Th Coll BA 86. **d** 86 **p** 87. C Hoddesdon *St Alb* 86-89; C Loughton St Mary and St Mich *Chelmsf* 89-90; TV 90-95; P-in-c Loughton St Mich 95-96; Public Preacher 97; V Dover St Martin *Cant* from 97; TV Dover Town from 14. *St Martin's Vicarage, 339 Folkestone Road, Dover CT17 9JG* T: (01304) 339273 E: kevin.garrett@nltworld.com

GARRETT (née KIRK), Natalie Roberta. b 71. Leeds Univ BA 93. Wycliffe Hall Ox 03. **d** 05 **p** 06. C Gipsy Hill Ch Ch *S'wark* 05-06; Hon C Burford w Fulbrook, Taynton, Asthall etc *Ox* 06-10; Hon C Twickenham Common H Trin *Lon* from 10. *Holy Trinity Vicarage, 1 Vicarage Road, Twickenham TW2 5TS* T: (020) 8898 1168

GARRETT, Timothy Michael. b 70. Univ of Wales (Abth) BA 91. Wycliffe Hall Ox BA 01. **d** 02 **p** 03. C Ox St Andr 02-06; C Burford w Fulbrook, Taynton, Asthall etc 06-10; V Twickenham Common H Trin *Lon* from 10. *Holy Trinity Vicarage, 1 Vicarage Road, Twickenham TW2 5TS* T: (020) 8898 1168 E: revgaz@hotmail.com

GARRISH (née SMITH), Elaine Joan. b 46. NTMTC BA 07. **d** 07 **p** 08. NSM Roxbourne St Andr *Lon* 07-10; PtO from 10. *37 Farthings Close, Pinner HA5 2QR* T: (020) 8429 0659 M: 07780-904402 E: elainegarrish370@btinternet.com

GARROD, Mrs Christine Anne. b 49. EAMTC. **d** 00 **p** 01. C N w S Wootton *Nor* 00-04; P-in-c Brinklow *Cov* 04-09; P-in-c Harborough Magna 04-09; P-in-c Monks Kirby w Pailton and Stretton-under-Fosse 04-09; P-in-c Churchover w Willey 04-09; R Gt and Lt Plumstead w Thorpe End and Witton *Nor* 09-14; rtd 14; PtO *Nor* from 14. *17 Philip Nurse Road, Dersingham, King's Lynn PE31 6WJ* T: (01485) 543708 E: cagarrod@hotmail.com

GARROW, Alan John Philip. b 67. Lon Bible Coll BA 90 Wycliffe Hall Ox MPhil 94 Jes Coll Ox DPhil 00. **d** 93 **p** 94. C Waltham H Cross *Chelmsf* 93-97; C Akeman *Ox* 00-04; Tutor SAOMC 00-04; Dir Studies Ox Min Course 05-06; V Th Bath Abbey w St Jas *B & W* 06-14. *112 Cowlishaw Road, Sheffield S11 8XH* E: alan.garrow@gmail.com

GARRUD, Christopher Charles. b 54. Cranmer Hall Dur. **d** 85 **p** 86. C Watford *St Alb* 85-89; C Ireland Wood *Ripon* 89-95; Chapl Cookridge Hosp Leeds 93-95; R Farnley *Ripon* 95-02. *75 Hill Court Drive, Leeds LS13 2AN*

GARSIDE, Geoffrey Malcolm. b 43. Huddersfield Poly CertEd Huddersfield Univ BEd. **d** 05 **p** 06. OLM Almondbury w Farnley Tyas *Wakef* 05-10; P-in-c Marsden *Leeds* 10-15; rtd 15. *16 Mountfield Avenue, Huddersfield HD5 8RD* E: ggarside@aol.com

GARSIDE, Melvin. b 42. NOC 85. **d** 88 **p** 89. C Lindley *Wakef* 88-91; C Shelf *Bradf* 91-93; V Lundwood *Wakef* 93-97; V Hanging Heaton 97-01; V Woodhouse and Bp's Adv in Racial Justice 01-05; rtd 05. *5 Hawthorne Close, Nether Poppleton, York YO26 6HP* M: 07803-250258 E: melgarside@melgarside.demon.co.uk

GARTLAND, Christopher Michael. b 49. Man Univ BA 78 Leeds Univ MEd 99 Univ Coll Lon MSc 04. Coll of Resurr Mirfield 82. **d** 84 **p** 85. C Almondbury w Farnley Tyas *Wakef* 84-87; P-in-c Upperthong 87-89; TV Upper Holme Valley 89-91; Chapl Stanley Royd Hosp Wakef 91-94; Chapl Wakef HA (Mental Health Services) 91-95; Chapl Wakef and Pontefract Community NHS Trust 95-01; Hd Past/Spiritual Care SW Yorks Partnership NHS Foundn Trust from 02. *2 Weirside, Marsden, Huddersfield HD7 6BU* T: (01924) 327498 E: mike.gartland@swyt.nhs.uk *or* michaelgartland4@aol.com

GARTON, Mrs Anne-Marie. b 48. BA MSW CQSW. **d** 02 **p** 03. NSM Caterham *S'wark* 02-10 and from 14; PtO 10-14. *The Vicarage, 2 Churchview Close, Caterham CR3 6EZ* T: (01883) 343188

GARTON, Capt Jeremy. b 56. Wilson Carlile Coll 78 SEITE 94. **d** 96 **p** 97. C Clapham Team *S'wark* 96-00; P-in-c Caterham Valley 00-03; TV Caterham from 03. *The Vicarage, 2 Churchview Close, Caterham CR3 6EZ* T: (01883) 343188 F: (020) 7863 4120 E: jerry@garton.com

✠**GARTON, The Rt Revd John Henry.** b 41. Worc Coll Ox BA 67 MA. Cuddesdon Coll 67. **d** 69 **p** 70 **c** 96. CF 69-73; Lect Linc Th Coll 73-78; TR Cov E 78-86; V Cuddesdon and Prin Ripon Coll Cuddesdon 86-96; Hon Can Worc Cathl 87-96; Suff Bp Plymouth *Ex* 96-05; rtd 05; Hon Asst Bp Ox from 05. *c/o P M Garton Esq, 68 Stapleton Road, Headington, Oxford OX3 7LU*

GARTSIDE, Philip Oswin. b 60. Pemb Coll Ox BA 82 MA 86 Leeds Univ BA 92. Coll of Resurr Mirfield 93. **d** 93 **p** 94. C Walton-on-the-Hill *Liv* 93-97; CR from 97. *House of the Resurrection, Stocks Bank Road, Mirfield WF14 0BN* T: (01924) 483327

GARVIE, Mrs Anna-Lisa Karen. b 48. Luton Univ BA 99 Leeds Univ MA 05. St Alb Minl Tr Scheme 89. **d** 96 **p** 97. NSM Caddington *St Alb* 96-99; NSM St Paul's Walden 99-01; Chapl Chelsea and Westmr Hosp NHS Foundn Trust 98-01; Co-ord Chapl Hinchingbrooke Health Care NHS Trust 01-09; Chapl Thorpe Hall Hospice 09-12; Chapl NHS Borders 12-13. *Address temp unknown*

GARVIE, Peter Francis. b 84. Univ Coll Dur BA 08. St Steph Ho Ox 09. **d** 11 **p** 12. C Sunderland St Mary and St Pet *Dur* 11-15; Chapl RN from 15. *Royal Naval Chaplaincy Service, 113 Holborn Road, Mail Point 1.2, Leach Building, Whale Island, Portsmouth PO2 8BY* M: 07568-593748 T: (023) 9262 5055 F: 9262 5134 E: ptrgarvie@gmail.com

GARWOOD, Simon Frederick. b 62. Reading Univ BA 85 Lon Univ PGCE 93 Birm Univ BD 99. Qu Coll Birm MA 00. **d** 00 **p** 01. C Chelmsf All SS 00-03; TV Witham 03-14; P-in-c Kelvedon and Feering from 14. *The Vicarage, Church Street, Kelvedon, Colchester CO5 9AH* T: (01376) 573701 E: simon.garwood18@btinternet.com

GASCOIGNE, Philip. b 27. Oak Hill Th Coll. **d** 62 **p** 63. C Blackpool Ch Ch *Blackb* 62-65; V Bootle St Leon *Liv* 65-71; Staff Evang CPAS 71-74; V St Helens St Mark *Liv* 74-77; V Blackpool Ch Ch *Blackb* 77-81; V Blackpool Ch Ch w All SS 81-97; rtd 98; PtO *Blackb* from 98. *18 Grange Road, Blackpool FY3 8EJ* T: (01253) 315607

GASH, Christopher Alan Ronald. b 39. EMMTC 83. **d** 86 **p** 87. C Thurmaston *Leic* 86-89; P-in-c Stoke Golding w Dadlington 89-01; rtd 01; PtO *Cov* 01-03; *Sarum* 03-04; *Cov* 04-06; St E 06-09; *Leic* from 09. *13 Warwick Lane, Market Bosworth, Nuneaton CV13 0JU* T: (01455) 292998

GASH, Canon Wilfred John. b 31. St Aid Birkenhead 60. **d** 62 **p** 63. C St Mary Cray and St Paul's Cray *Roch* 62-65; C Bexley St Jo 65-67; R Levenshulme St Pet *Man* 67-72; V Clifton 72-94; AD Eccles 81-87; Hon Can Man Cathl 86-97; Can Emer Man Cathl from 97; P-in-c Pendlebury Ch Ch 86-87; P-in-c Pendlebury St Aug 86-87; TR Bolton St Paul w Em 94-96; C Urmston 96-97; Dioc Adv on Evang 89-97; rtd 98; PtO *Ches* 98-06; *Blackb* from 08. *7 East Bank, Barrowford, Nelson BB9 6HD* T: (01282) 611419

GASKELL, Barrie Stuart. b 56. SNWTP 07. **d** 10 **p** 11. NSM Bolton St Pet *Man* 10-11; NSM Bolton St Pet w St Phil from 11; Chapl R Bolton Hosp NHS Foundn Trust from 10; Chapl Gtr Man W Mental Health NHS Foundn Trust from 13. *1 Old Vicarage Mews, Westhoughton, Bolton BL5 2EQ* T: (01942) 818797 E: barrie.gaskell@rbh.nhs.uk

GASKELL, David. b 48. Lon Univ BD 76. Trin Coll Bris 72. **d** 76 **p** 77. C Eccleston Ch Ch *Liv* 76-80; C Rainhill 80-83; V Over Darwen St Jas *Blackb* 83-88; V Livesey 88-95; V Preston St Cuth 95-01; V Copp w Inskip 01-13; rtd 13; PtO *Blackb* from 13. *4 St James Gardens, Leyland PR26 7XA* T: (01772) 452045 E: dabberoarer@btinternet.com

GASKELL, Canon Ian Michael. b 51. Nottm Univ BTh 81. Linc Th Coll 77. **d** 81 **p** 82. C Wakef St Jo 81-83; Ind Chapl *Sheff* 83-86; V Cleckheaton St Luke and Whitechapel *Wakef* 86-93; V Birkenshaw w Hunsworth 93-98; RD Birstall 96-98; Can Res Wakef Cathl 98-05; Dioc Soc Resp Adv 98-06; V Chapelthorpe *Leeds* from 06; Hon Can Wakef Cathl 05-14; rtd 15. *21 Stoney Lane, Chapelthorpe, Wakefield WF4 3JN* T: (01924) 255360

GASKELL, Preb John Bernard. b 28. Jes Coll Ox BA 52 MA 58. Chich Th Coll 59. **d** 60 **p** 61. C Beckenham St Jas *Roch* 60-64; C St Marylebone All SS *Lon* 64-68; C-in-c Grosvenor Chpl 68-79; Warden Liddon Ho Lon 68-79; V Holborn St Alb w Saffron Hill St Pet *Lon* 79-93; AD S Camden 81-86; Preb St Paul's Cathl 85-93; rtd 93; PtO *Lon* 93-02 and from 07; Hon C St Marylebone All SS 02-07. *12 Up The Quadrangle, Morden College, 19 St Germans Place, London SE3 0PW* T: (020) 8858 9589

GASKELL, Marion Ingrid. b 52. Wilson Carlile Coll 74 NOC 96. **d** 99 **p** 00. C Thorpe Edge *Bradf* 99-02; TV Shelf w Buttershaw St Aid 02-04; TR *Leeds* from 04. *8 Redwing Drive, Bradford BD6 3YD* T: (01274) 881701 E: marion.gaskell@bradford.anglican.org

GASKELL, Mary. b 50. Nottm Univ BTh 81 Bradf and Ilkley Coll CertEd 89. Linc Th Coll 77. **dss** 81 **d** 89 **p** 94. Wakef St Jo 81-83; NSM Cleckheaton St Luke and Whitechapel 89-93; NSM Birkenshaw w Hunsworth 93-95; Asst Chapl St Jas Univ Hosp NHS Trust Leeds 95-97; Chapl Rishworth Sch Ripponden 97-99; P-in-c Purlwell *Wakef* 00-01; Chapl Dewsbury Health Care NHS Trust 01-02; Chapl Mid Yorks Hosps NHS Trust 02-10; rtd 11. *21 Stoney Lane, Chapelthorpe, Wakefield WF4 3JN* T: (01924) 255360

GASKELL, Peter John. b 70. Bris Univ MS 93 ChB 93. Oak Hill Th Coll BA 03. **d** 03 **p** 04. NSM Poulton Lancelyn H Trin *Ches* 03-07; NSM Rusholme H Trin *Man* from 09. *47 Linden Park, Manchester M19 2PQ* M: 07769-682142 E: peter@glod.co.uk

GASPER (née COHEN), Mrs Janet Elizabeth. b 47. Birm Univ CertEd 70. WMMTC 93. **d** 96 **p** 97. NSM Leominster *Heref* 96-99; C Letton w Staunton, Byford, Mansel Gamage etc 99-01; Hon Chapl RAF 97-01; R Baxterley w Hurley and Wood End and Merevale etc *Birm* 01-13; P-in-c Kingsbury 04-13; rtd 13; P-in-c The Langtons and Shangton *Leic* from 14; P-in-c Welham, Glooston and Cranoe and Stonton Wyville from 14. *26 Jordan Close, Market Harborough LE16 8EW* T: (01858) 434817 E: janet.gasper@hotmail.co.uk

GASSON, Mrs Siân. b 68. **d** 12 **p** 13. C Collyhurst *Man* 12-15; V Bryn *Liv* from 15. *St Peter's Vicarage, 12 Bryn Road, Ashton-in-Makerfield, Wigan WN4 0AA* T: (01942) 589255 E: siangasson@gmail.com

GASTON, Mrs Lydia Madeleine. b 79. St Andr Univ MA 03 Rob Coll Cam BTh 09. Ridley Hall Cam 06. **d** 09 **p** 10. C Erdington Ch the K *Birm* 09-14; V Yardley Wood from 14. *The Vicarage, School Road, Yardley Wood, Birmingham B14 4EP* M: 07779-006178 E: lydgaston@hotmail.co.uk

GASTON, Raymond Gordon. b 62. Leeds Univ BA 94. Linc Th Coll MTh 94. **d** 96 **p** 97. C Leeds Gipton Epiphany *Ripon* 96-99; V Leeds St Marg and All Hallows 99-07; Tutor Qu Coll Birm from 08; PtO *Birm* from 14. *30 Passey Road, Birmingham B13 9NU* T: 0121-778 1730 E: r.gaston@queens.ac.uk

GATENBY, Canon Simon John Taylor. b 62. Nottm Univ BA 83. St Jo Coll Nottm 84. **d** 87 **p** 88. C Haughton St Mary *Man* 87-90; C Newburn *Newc* 90-93; P-in-c Brunswick *Man* 93-96; R from 96; AD Hulme 99-05; Hon Can Man Cathl from 13. *The Rectory, Hartfield Close, Brunswick, Manchester M13 9YX* T: 0161-273 2470 E: simon@brunswickchurch.org.uk

GATER, Jamie. b 84. Chich Univ BA 07 MA 13 PGCE 08. St Steph Ho Ox BA 14. **d** 15. C Ifield *Chich* from 15. *1 Francis Edward Way, Crawley RH11 8GG* M: 07800-937056 E: jamiegater@hotmail.com

GATES, Alan Raymond. b 46. EAMTC 98. **d** 01 **p** 02. C W w E Mersea and Peldon w Gt and Lt Wigborough *Chelmsf* 01-05; P-in-c Gt Barton *St E* 05-12; P-in-c Thurston 12-14; V Gt Barton and Thurston 12-14; RD Thingoe 08-14; rtd 14. *121 High Road, Layer-de-la-Haye, Colchester CO2 0EA* M: 07528-087733 E: alan.gates@virgin.net

GATES, Mrs Frances Margaret. b 44. STETS 01. **d** 04 **p** 05. NSM Portsea St Mary, Portsea St Geo and Portsea All SS *Portsm* 04-11; rtd 11; PtO *Portsm* from 11. *114 Kings Road, Southsea PO5 4DW* T: (023) 9282 0326 M: 07951-062226

GATES, John Michael. b 35. Dur Univ BA 56. Cranmer Hall Dur 58. **d** 60 **p** 61. C Felixstowe St Jo *St E* 60-67; R Boyton w Capel St Andrew and Hollesley 67-98; P-in-c Shottisham w Sutton 87-92; rtd 98. *9 Foxgrove Lane, Felixstowe IP11 7JS* T: (01394) 276886

GATES, Richard James. b 46. Oak Hill Th Coll BA 85. **d** 85 **p** 86. C Heald Green St Cath *Ches* 85-89; V Norton 89-98; V Bunbury and Tilstone Fearnall 98-11; rtd 12; Chapl St Luke's Cheshire Hospice from 13. *Vicarage Cottage, Church Street, Tarvin, Chester CH3 8EB* T: (01829) 749134 M: 07715-178750 E: rick@prayer.fsnet.co.uk

GATES, The Ven Simon Philip. b 60. St Andr Univ MA 82 St Jo Coll Dur BA 86. Cranmer Hall Dur 84. **d** 87 **p** 88. C Southall Green St Jo *Lon* 87-91; Assoc Min St Andr Ch Hong Kong 91-95; V Clapham Park St Steph *S'wark* 96-06; P-in-c Telford Park St Thos 05-06; V Telford Park 06-13; AD Lambeth S 06-13; Adn Lambeth from 13. *The Vicarage, 7 Hoadly Road, London SW16 1AE* T: (020) 8545 2440 E: simon.gates@southwark.anglican.org

GATFORD, The Ven Ian. b 40. AKC 65. **d** 67 **p** 68. C Clifton w Glapton *S'well* 67-71; TV Clifton 71-75; V Sherwood 75-84; Can Res Derby Cathl 84-99; Adn Derby and Hon Can Derby Cathl 93-05; rtd 05; PtO *Derby* from 05. *9 Poplar Nook, Allestree, Derby DE22 2DW* T: (01332) 557567

GATISS, Lee. b 72. New Coll Ox BA 96 MA 01 Westmr Th Sem Philadelphia ThM 09 Cam Univ PhD 14. Oak Hill Th Coll BA 00. **d** 01 **p** 02. C Barton Seagrave w Warkton *Pet* 01-04; C St Helen Bishopsgate w St Andr Undershaft etc *Lon* 04-09; PtO *Ely* from 06; Dir Ch Soc from 13. *Church Society, Ground Floor, Centre Block, Hille Business Estate, 132 St Albans Road, Watford WD24 4AE* T: (01923) 235111 F: 800362 E: director@churchsociety.org

GATLIFFE, David Spenser. b 45. Keble Coll Ox BA 67 Fitzw Coll Cam BA 69. Westcott Ho Cam 67. **d** 69 **p** 70. C Oxted *S'wark* 69-72; C Roehampton H Trin 72-75; C S Beddington St Mich 76-77; TV Clapham Old Town 78-87; P-in-c Clapham Ch Ch and St Jo 81-87; TV Clapham Team 87-89; V S Wimbledon H Trin and St Pet 89-01; R Lee St Marg 01-10; Ldr Ppost Ord Tr

Woolwich Area 04-09; rtd 10. *47 Catherine Street, Frome BA11 1DA* T: (01373) 228757 M: 07527-424526 E: dgatliffe@yahoo.com

GATRILL, Adrian Colin. b 60. Southn Univ BTh 82 FRSA 99. Linc Th Coll 83. **d** 85 **p** 86. C W Bromwich St Andr *Lich* 85-88; C W Bromwich St Andr w Ch Ch 88-89; Chapl RAF 89-11; Dir of Ords 06-11; Sen Chapl Dur Constabulary from 11; PtO *St D* 90-95; *Leeds* from 00. *Durham Constabulary Headquarters, Aykley Heads, Durham DH1 5TT* T: 0191-375 2361 E: adrian.gatrill@durham.pnn.police.uk

GAU, Justin Charles. b 65. Univ Coll Lon LLB 87 Down Coll Cam BTh 11. Westcott Ho Cam 09. **d** 11 **p** 12. Dep Chan *Linc* from 01; Dep *B & W* from 11; *Bris* from 11; NSM S Hackney St Jo w Ch Ch *Lon* 11-15; NSM Brownswood Park from 15. *27 Arlington Square, London N1 7DP* T: (020) 7353 0711 M: 07771-711114 E: j.gau@pumpcourtchambers.com

GAUGE, Canon Barrie Victor. b 41. St D Coll Lamp BA 62 Selw Coll Cam BA 64 MA 74. Bp Burgess Hall Lamp. **d** 65 **p** 66. C Newtown w Llanllwchaiarn w Aberhafesp *St As* 65-68; C Prestatyn 68-73; R Bodfari and Dioc RE Adv 73-76; PtO *Ches* 76-84; V Birkenhead St Jas w St Bede 84-90; Dir of Resources 90-98; Hon Can Ches Cathl 94-98; C Lache cum Saltney 95-98; Par Development Adv *Derby* 98-06; Can Res Derby Cathl 99-06; Dioc Miss Adv 01-04; rtd 06; PtO *St As* from 09; *Ches* from 10; *S & B* 11-14. *40 Saxon Street, Wrexham LL13 7BD* T: (01978) 353715 E: barrie.gauge@talk21.com

GAUNT, Adam. b 79. St Jo Coll Dur BA 00 MA 02. St Steph Ho Ox 03. **d** 05 **p** 06. C Middlesbrough Ascension *York* 05-09; R Loftus and Carlin How w Skinningrove from 09. *The Rectory, 11 Micklow Lane, Loftus, Saltburn-by-the-Sea TS13 4JE* T: (01287) 644047 E: adamgaunt@btinternet.com

GAUNT (née COTTELL), Mrs Avril Jane. b 50. SRN 72 SCM 74. S Dios Minl Tr Scheme 92. **d** 95 **p** 97. NSM Yatton Moor *B & W* 95-96 and 97-02; NSM Bourne *Guildf* 96-97; Chapl N Bris NHS Trust 02-14; rtd 14; PtO *B & W* from 05. *Myrtle Cottage, Ham Lane, Kingston Seymour, Clevedon BS21 6XE* T: (01934) 832995

GAUNTLETT, Gilbert Bernard. b 36. Oriel Coll Ox BA 59 MA 62. Wycliffe Hall Ox 59. **d** 61 **p** 62. C Maidenhead St Andr and St Mary *Ox* 61-64; C Ox St Ebbe w St Pet 64-68; R Nottingham St Nic *S'well* 68-72; Asst Master Leys High Sch Redditch 73-79; Asst Master Stourport High Sch 79-85; rtd 97. *The Tower, Brynygwin Isaf, Dolgellau LL40 1YA* T: (01341) 423481

GAUSDEN, Canon Peter James. b 32. Qu Coll Birm 57. **d** 60 **p** 61. C Battersea St Pet and Chapl S Lon Ind Miss *S'wark* 60-63; C St Peter-in-Thanet *Cant* 63-68; V Sturry 68-74; R Sturry w Fordwich and Westbere w Hersden 74-97; Dioc Ecum Officer 91-96; Hon Can Cant Cathl 96-97; rtd 97; PtO *Cant* 97-99 and from 04; Hon C St Nicholas at Wade w Sarre and Chislet w Hoath 99-04. *2 The Paddocks, Collards Close, Monkton, Ramsgate CT12 4JZ* T: (01843) 825374 E: peter.gausden374@btinternet.com

GAVIGAN, Canon Josephine Katherine. b 49. Univ Coll Chich BA 00. Sarum Th Coll 93. **d** 96. NSM Boxgrove *Chich* 96-00; C 00-03; Dn-in-c Maybridge 03-14; RD Worthing 05-10; Can and Preb Chich Cathl 07-14; rtd 14. *56 The Boulevard, Worthing BN13 1LA* T: (01903) 249463 M: 07760-277262

GAVIN, David Guy. b 63. Birm Univ BA 85 St Jo Coll Dur BA 90. Cranmer Hall Dur 88. **d** 91 **p** 92. C Parr *Liv* 91-95; TV Toxteth St Philemon w St Gabr and St Cleopas 95-02; P-in-c 02-06; TR 06-11; TV from 11. *St Cleopas' Vicarage, Beresford Road, Liverpool L8 4SG* T: 0151-727 0633 E: gavins@uwclub.net

GAVIN (née GREGORY), Mrs Judith Rosalind. b 61. Open Univ BA 97. St Jo Coll Nottm 99. **d** 01 **p** 02. C Moss Side St Jas w St Clem *Man* 01-04; C Whalley Range St Edm 01-04; C Rhyl w St Ann *St As* 04-05. *82 Grosvenor Avenue, Rhyl LL18 4HB* T: (01745) 332224 E: judithanddarrell.gavin@btinternet.com

GAWITH, Canon Alan Ruthven. b 24. Lich Th Coll 54. **d** 56 **p** 57. C Appleby and Murton cum Hilton *Carl* 56-59; C Newton Aycliffe *Dur* 59-61; C-in-c Owton Manor CD 61-67; V Kendal St Geo *Carl* 67-74; Soc Resp Officer *Man* 74-89; Hon Can Man Cathl 82-89; Bp's Adv on AIDS 88-92; rtd 90; PtO *Man* 90-12. *7 Redwaters, Leigh WN7 1JD* T: (01942) 676641

GAWNE-CAIN, John. b 38. G&C Coll Cam BA 61 MA 66 CEng MICE. Cuddesdon Coll 74. **d** 76 **p** 77. C Cowley St Jas *Ox* 76-80; P-in-c Ox St Giles 80-85; V Ox St Giles and SS Phil and Jas w St Marg 85-92; P-in-c Uffington w Woolstone and Baulking 92-93; P-in-c Shellingford 92-93; R Uffington, Shellingford, Woolstone and Baulking 93-03; rtd 03; PtO *Ox* 04-08; *Win* from 10. *14 St Johns Street, Winchester SO23 0HF* T: (01962) 851366 E: j.gawne-cain@ruralnet.org.uk

GAWTHROP-DORAN, Mrs Sheila Mary. b 37. Birm Univ CertEd. Dalton Ho Bris 68. **dss** 79 **d** 87. Par Dn New Bury

Man 87-89; Par Dn Tonge w Alkrington 89-94; rtd 94; PtO York from 95. *35 Swarthdale, Haxby, York YO32 3NZ* T: (01904) 761247

GAWTHROPE, Julie Anne. b 57. **d** 10 **p** 11. C Cherry Hinton St Jo *Ely* 10-15; TV Albury, Braughing, Furneux Pelham, Lt Hadham etc *St Alb* from 15. *The Vicarage, 1 Pentlows, Braughing, Ware SG11 2QD* M: 07789-838084 E: julie.gawthrope@ntlworld.com

GAY, Adam Garcia Hugh. b 57. STETS 02. **d** 05 **p** 06. C Bitterne *Win* 05-09; V Hedge End St Luke *Win* 09-13; PtO from 13; *Portsm* from 13. *14 Sissinghurst Road, Fareham PO16 9YA* T: (01329) 237126 E: adamgay@totalise.co.uk

GAY, Colin James. b 37. Univ of Wales (Lamp) BA 63. Chich Th Coll 63. **d** 65 **p** 66. C W Hackney St Barn *Lon* 65-69; C Hitchin H Sav *St Alb* 69-74; P-in-c Apsley End 74-80; TV Chambersbury 80-85; V Barnet Vale St Mark 85-03; rtd 03; PtO *St Alb* from 03. *Colters, 14 Barleyfield Way, Houghton Regis, Dunstable LU5 5ER* T: (01582) 862309

GAY, John Charles Nankervis. b 58. ERMC 03. **d** 06 **p** 07. C Wilton *B & W* 06-10; R Itchingfield w Slinfold *Chich* 10-14; TV Brixham w Churston Ferrers and Kingswear *Ex* from 14. *13 Warborough Road, Churston Ferrers, Brixham TQ5 0JY* T: (01803) 845692 E: revjohngay@googlemail.com

GAY, John Dennis. b 43. St Pet Coll Ox BA 64 MA 68 DPhil 69 MSc 78. Ripon Hall Ox 64. **d** 67 **p** 68. C Paddington St Jas *Lon* 67-71; P-in-c 71-72; Chapl Culham Coll Abingdon 72-79; Lect Ox Univ 78-80; Dir Culham Inst 80-11; Research Fell Dept of Educn Ox Univ from 11; PtO *Ox* from 15. *Department of Education, 15 Norham Gardens, Oxford OX2 6PY* T: (01865) 611072 E: john.gay@education.ox.ac.uk

GAY, Canon Perran Russell. b 59. St Cath Coll Cam BA 81 MA 85 Ex Univ PGCE 82 FRGS 97. Ripon Coll Cuddesdon BA 86. **d** 87 **p** 88. C Bodmin w Lanhydrock and Lanivet *Truro* 87-90; Bp's Dom Chapl 90-94; Dioc Officer for Unity 90-94; Can Res and Chan Truro Cathl from 94; Prec from 01; Dir of Tr Truro 94-99; Chapl Epiphany Ho from 06. *52 Daniell Road, Truro TR1 2DA* T: (01872) 276782 or 276491 F: 277788 E: perran@perrangay.com or perran@trurocathedral.org.uk

GAY, Stuart. b 66. Oak Hill Th Coll BA 94. **d** 00 **p** 01. C Sunningdale *Ox* 00-04; V Margate St Phil *Cant* from 04. *St Philip's Vicarage, 82 Crundale Way, Margate CT9 3YH* T: (01843) 221589 E: stuartgay@btinternet.com

GAYFORD, John. b 37. Lon Univ BDS 61 MB, BS 65 MD 78 Nottm Univ MA 13 FDSRCS 64 FRCPsych 86 Heythrop Coll Lon MA 05 Univ of Wales (Lamp) MTh 09. St Jo Sem Wonersh 02. **d** 03 **p** 04. NSM E Grinstead St Mary *Chich* from 03; PtO *S'wark* from 15. *Third Acre, 217 Smallfield Road, Horley RH6 9LR* T: (01342) 842752

GAYLE, Steve Anthony. b 74. Univ of W Indies BA 03 Heythrop Coll Lon MA 09. Ripon Coll Cuddesdon 13. **d** 15. C S Hackney St Jo w Ch Ch *Lon* from 15. *9 Stanford Mews, London E8 1JA* M: 07903-175038

GAYLER, Canon Roger Kenneth. b 44. Lich Th Coll 68. **d** 70 **p** 71. C Chingford St Anne *Chelmsf* 70-75; P-in-c Marks Gate 75-81; V 81-14; RD Barking and Dagenham 04-13; Hon Can Chelmsf Cathl 09-14; rtd 14; P-in-c Lambourne w Abridge and Stapleford Abbotts *Chelmsf* from 14. *1 The Poplars, Abridge, Romford RM4 1BB* E: r-gayler@o2.co.uk

GAYNOR, Christopher Thomas. b 68. **d** 08 **p** 09. C Banbury St Fran *Ox* 08-13; V from 13. *26 Meadowsweet Way, Banbury OX16 1WE* T: (01295) 277141 E: allrevedup@hotmail.co.uk

GAYNOR, Mrs Mieke Aaltjen Cornelia. b 43. UEA BA 79. St Jo Coll Nottm 02. **d** 03 **p** 04. NSM Hambleden Valley *Ox* 03-09; C Wollaton *S'well* 09-13; rtd 13. *5 Lodge Close, Marlow SL7 1RB* M: 07856-844554 E: mieke.gaynor@btopenworld.com

GAZE, Canon Sally Ann. b 69. SS Coll Cam BA 91 MA 95 Birm Univ MPhil 98 PGCE 92. Qu Coll Birm 94. **d** 96 **p** 97. C Martley and Wichenford, Knightwick etc *Worc* 96-00; C Crickhowell w Cwmdu and Tretower *S & B* 00-02; TR Newton Flotman, Swainsthorpe, Tasburgh, etc *Nor* from 02; Dioc Fresh Expressions Facilitator from 09; Hon Can Nor Cathl from 15. *The Rectory, Church Road, Newton Flotman, Norwich NR15 1QB* T: (01508) 470762 E: sally@tasvalley.org

GBEBIKAN, Angela Maria Abike. b 56. Lon Univ MA 07. Westcott Ho Cam 02. **d** 04 **p** 05. C Norbury St Steph and Thornton Heath *S'wark* 04-07; P-in-c S Beddington and Roundshaw 07-08; V from 08; Asst Dir of Ords and Adv in Women's Min Croydon Area from 13. *St Michael's Vicarage, Milton Road, Wallington SM6 9RP* T: (020) 8647 1201 E: gbebikan@cantab.net

GBONDA, Egerton Joe Fode. b 67. Univ of Sierra Leone BSc 94 MSc 03. **d** 06 **p** 08. Sierra Leone 06-09; PtO *S'wark* 10-12; NSM Deptford St Jo w H Trin and Ascension 12-14; NSM Bermondsey St Kath w St Bart from 14. *36 Queensberry Place, London E12 6UN* T: (020) 8470 8786 M: 07882-872830 E: father.egerton.gbonda@gmail.com

GEACH, Canon Michael Bernard. b 26. Qu Coll Cam BA 51 MA 56. Westcott Ho Cam 51. **d** 53 **p** 54. C Kenwyn *Truro* 53-56; C Bodmin 56-59; C Helland 56-59; R St Dominic 59-65; Chapl Cotehele Ho Chapl Cornwall 60-65; V Linkinhorne *Truro* 65-84; R Veryan w Ruan Lanihorne 84-96; Hon Can Truro Cathl 92-96; rtd 96; PtO *Truro* from 96. *10 Adelaide Terrace, Truro TR1 3EJ* T: (01872) 262927

GEACH, Canon Sarah Jane. b 50. Trin Coll Carmarthen CertEd 73. WEMTC 96. **d** 99 **p** 00. C Pill w Easton in Gordano and Portbury *B & W* 99-02; TV Ross *Heref* 02-07; P-in-c Begelly w Ludchurch and Crunwere *St D* 07-09; P-in-c Begelly w Ludchurch and E Williamston 09-10; R 10-15; Dioc Tourism Officer 12-15; Can St D Cathl 13-15; rtd 15; PtO *St D* from 15. *Maenwen, Glanymor Road, Goodwick SA64 0ER* E: sgeach@btinternet.com

GEAR, John Arthur. b 37. St Aid Birkenhead 62. **d** 64 **p** 66. C Attleborough *Cov* 64-66; C Attercliffe *Sheff* 66-68; C Sheerness H Trin w St Paul *Cant* 68-73; Asst Youth Adv *S'wark* 73-78; Youth Chapl *Lich* 78-88; V Stafford St Jo and Tixall w Ingestre 88-92; Gen Sec NCEC 92-97; rtd 97; PtO *Lich* 01-02 and 04-13; P-in-c Shrewsbury H Cross 02-03. *50 Cadgwith Drive, Derby DE22 2AE*

✠**GEAR, The Rt Revd Michael Frederick.** b 34. Dur Univ BA 59. Cranmer Hall Dur 59. **d** 61 **p** 62 **c** 93. C Bexleyheath Ch Ch *Roch* 61-64; C Ox St Aldate w H Trin 64-67; V Clubmoor *Liv* 67-71; Rhodesia 71-76; Tutor Wycliffe Hall Ox 76-80; V Macclesfield St Mich *Ches* 80-85; RD Macclesfield 84-88; TR Macclesfield Team 85-88; Adn Ches 88-93; Hon Can Ches Cathl 86-88; Suff Bp Doncaster *Sheff* 93-99; rtd 99; Hon Asst Bp Roch from 99; Hon Asst Bp Cant from 00. *10 Acott Fields, Yalding, Maidstone ME18 6DQ* T: (01622) 817388 E: mike.gear@rochester.anglican.org

GEARY, John Martin. b 52. LRSC 77. **d** 08 **p** 09. OLM Heywood *Man* 08-10; OLM Heywood St Marg and Heap Bridge 10-13; NSM Bagillt *St As* from 13; NSM Flint from 13. *The Vicarage, 1 Vicarage Road, Bagillt CH6 6DB* T: (01352) 730487 M: 07753-462460 E: john@johngeary.co.uk

GEARY, Mrs Paula June. b 48. NUI BSc 69 HDipEd 70. CITC 06. **d** 06 **p** 07. NSM Moviddy Union C, *C & R* from 06. *Lehenaghbeg Farm, Lehenaghbeg, Togher, Cork, Republic of Ireland* E: pjgeary650@hotmail.com

GEBAUER, George Gerhart. b 25. Sarum & Wells Th Coll 71. **d** 73 **p** 74. C Portsdown *Portsm* 73-78; V Purbrook 78-91; rtd 91; PtO *Portsm* from 91. *52 St John's Road, Locks Heath, Southampton SO31 6NF* T: (01489) 575172

GEDDES, Peter Henry. b 51. Trin Coll Bris 84. **d** 86 **p** 87. C Blackpool St Mark *Blackb* 86-88; C Barnston *Ches* 88-92; V Haslington w Crewe Green 92-04; V Partington and Carrington from 04. *St Mary's Vicarage, Manchester Road, Partington, Manchester M31 4FB* T: 0161-775 3542

GEDDES, Roderick Charles. b 47. Man Univ MPhil 85 DipEd 78. NOC 88. **d** 91 **p** 93. C Alverthorpe *Wakef* 91-92; C S Ossett 92-94; R Andreas, V Jurby and V Andreas St Jude *S & M* 94-03; P-in-c Gargrave *Bradf* 03-09; P-in-c Gargrave w Coniston Cold 09-12; rtd 12. *13 School Lane, Earby, Barnoldswick BB18 6QF* T: (01282) 844047 E: roderick.geddes@btinternet.com

GEDGE, Lloyd Victor. b 23. Cuddesdon Coll 54. **d** 57 **p** 58. C Headington *Ox* 57-60; P-in-c Virden Canada 60-63; V Riverton New Zealand 63-66; C All SS Cathl Edmonton Canada 66-68; P-in-c Edmonton St Steph 68-72; I Edgerton 72-76; I Hanna 76-80; P-in-c N Creake *Nor* 82-83; P-in-c S Creake 82-83; R N and S Creake w Waterden 84-86; rtd 86. *6 Vialta Seniors Lodge, Box 780, 5128-51 Avenue, Viking AB T0B 4N0, Canada* T: (001) (780) 366 3210

GEDGE, Richard John Anthony. b 70. Bath Univ BEng 92 CEng 96 MIMechE 96. St Jo Coll Nottm MTh 09. **d** 09 **p** 11. C Much Woolton *Liv* from 09. *48 Babbacombe Road, Liverpool L16 9JW* E: rjagedge@googlemail.com

GEE, Anne Alison. b 43. OBE 99. Man Univ MB, ChB 66. STETS BA 01. **d** 01 **p** 02. NSM Canford Magna *Sarum* 01-06; NSM Horton, Chalbury, Hinton Martel and Holt St Jas 06-13; P-in-c 11-13; NSM Witchampton, Stanbridge and Long Crichel etc 06-13; P-in-c 11-13; rtd 13. *37 Floral Farm, Wimborne BH21 3AT* E: a.gee@doctors.org.uk

GEE, Mrs Dorothy Mary. b 33. St Jo Coll Nottm 88. **d** 89 **p** 94. Chapl Asst Univ Hosp Nottm 89-95; NSM Plumtree *S'well* 95-97; P-in-c 97-01; rtd 01; PtO *S'well* from 01. *Address temp unknown* E: mary.gee@microhelpuk.net

GEE, Canon Edward. b 28. St Deiniol's Hawarden 59. **d** 61 **p** 62. C Hanging Heaton *Wakef* 61-65; V Brownhill 65-75; V Alverthorpe 75-84; R Castleford All SS 84-92; Hon Can Wakef Cathl 87-92; rtd 92; PtO *Leeds* from 92. *1 Holme Ghyll, Colne Road, Glusburn, Keighley BD20 8RG* T: (01535) 630060 E: mandegee@btinternet.com

GEEN, James William. b 50. Chich Th Coll 76. **d** 79 **p** 80. C Brandon *Dur* 79-84; C Sunderland Red Ho 84-86; P-in-c N Hylton St Marg Castletown 86-89; V 89-91; Dep Chapl HM Pris Dur 91-92; Chapl HM YOI Lanc Farms 92-95; Chapl HM Pris Long Lartin 95-01; Chapl HM Pris Blakenhurst 01-06; Chapl HM Pris Kilmarnock 07-09; Chapl Colnbrook Immigration Removal Cen from 09; PtO *Glas* from 09; CMP from 96. *9 Clockston Road, Galston KA4 8LW* M: 07834-144175 E: geen_j@yahoo.co.uk

GEERING, Preb Anthony Ernest. b 43. Columbia Pacific Univ BSc. Kelham Th Coll 62. **d** 68 **p** 69. C Cov St Mary 68-71; New Zealand 71-75; P-in-c Brinklow *Cov* 75-77; R 77-81; V Monks Kirby w Pailton and Stretton-under-Fosse 77-81; R Harborough Magna 77-81; V Pilton w Ashford *Ex* 81-86; P-in-c Shirwell w Loxhore 83-86; R Crediton and Shobrooke 86-01; P-in-c Sandford w Upton Hellions 00-01; R Crediton, Shobrooke and Sandford etc 01; RD Cadbury 93-97; R Chagford, Drewsteignton, Hittisleigh etc 01-09; P-in-c 09-10; RD Okehampton 02-05; Preb Ex Cathl 02-09; rtd 09. *20 Iter Park, Bow, Crediton EX17 6BY*

GEILINGER, John Edward. b 27. Lon Univ BSc 53 BD 58 BA 76 MPhil 79. Tyndale Hall Bris. **d** 59 **p** 60. C Plymouth St Jude *Ex* 59-61; Lect Trin Th Coll Umuahia Nigeria 63-72; Lect Th Coll of N Nigeria 72-77; PtO *Portsm* from 79; rtd 92. *Emmaus House, Colwell Road, Freshwater PO40 9LY* T: (01983) 753030

GEISOW, Hilary Patricia. b 46. Salford Univ BSc 67 Warwick Univ PhD 71 Nottm Univ PGCE 94. St Jo Coll Nottm 01. **d** 03 **p** 04. C Linc St Faith and St Martin w St Pet 03-06; P-in-c Colsterworth Gp 06-08; P-in-c Peakirk w Glinton and Northborough *Pet* from 08; P-in-c Etton w Helpston and Maxey 08-12. *The Rectory, 11 Lincoln Road, Glinton, Peterborough PE6 7JR* T: (01733) 253638 E: hilary.geisow@btinternet.com

GELDARD, Preb Mark Dundas. b 50. Liv Univ BA 71 Bris Univ MA 75. Trin Coll Bris 73. **d** 75 **p** 76. C Aughton Ch Ch *Liv* 75-78; Tutor Trin Coll Bris 78-84; V Fairfield *Liv* 84-88; Dioc Dir of Ords *Lich* 88-07; C Lich St Mich w St Mary and Wall 95-07; P-in-c Wigginton 07-08; V 08-11; Preb Lich Cathl 00-11; rtd 11. *6 Strand Court, Harsfold Road, Rustington, Littlehampton BN16 2NT* T: (01903) 786665 E: mark.geldard2@btinternet.com

GELL, Canon Anne Elizabeth. b 63. St Hugh's Coll Ox BA 85 MA 01 R Free Hosp Sch of Medicine MB, BS 90 Surrey Univ BA 01. STETS 98. **d** 01 **p** 02. C Headley All SS *Guildf* 01-05; V Wrecclesham from 05; RD Farnham from 10; Hon Can Guildf Cathl from 13. *The Vicarage, 2 King's Lane, Wrecclesham, Farnham GU10 4QB* T: (01252) 716431 E: annegell@lineone.net

GELL, Miss Margaret Florence. b 30. **d** 00 **p** 01. NSM Madeley *Lich* 00-04; rtd 04; PtO *Lich* 04-14. *19 Pear Tree Drive, Madeley, Crewe CW3 9EN* T: (01782) 750669

GELLI, Frank Julian. b 43. Birkbeck Coll Lon BA 78 K Coll Lon MTh 82. Ripon Coll Cuddesdon 84. **d** 86 **p** 87. C Chiswick St Nic w St Mary *Lon* 86-89; Chapl Ankara *Eur* 89-91; C Kensington St Mary Abbots w St Geo Lon 91-99; rtd 03. *58 Boston Gardens, Brentford TW8 9LP* T: (020) 8847 4533 E: numapomp@talk21.com

GELSTON, Anthony. b 35. Keble Coll Ox BA 57 MA 60 DD 85. Ridley Hall Cam 59. **d** 60 **p** 61. C Chipping Norton *Ox* 60-62; Lect Th Dur Univ 62-76; Sen Lect 76-88; Dean Div Faculty 77-79; Reader 89-95; LtO 62-95; rtd 95; PtO *Dur* from 95. *Lesbury, Hetton Road, Houghton le Spring DH5 8JW* T: 0191-584 2256 E: agelston35@btinternet.com

GEMMELL, Canon Ian William Young. b 52. ALAM. St Jo Coll Nottm. **d** 77 **p** 78. C Old Hill H Trin *Worc* 77-81; C Selly Park St Steph and St Wulstan *Birm* 81-83; V Leic St Chris 83-93; RD Christianity S 92-93; P-in-c Gt Bowden w Welham, Glooston and Cranoe 93-02; P-in-c Church Langton w Tur Langton, Thorpe Langton etc 93-99; P-in-c Church Langton cum Tur Langton etc 99-02; R Gt Bowden w Welham, Glooston and Cranoe etc 02-06; RD Gartree I 97-06; Hon Can Leic Cathl 03-06; P-in-c Welford w Sibbertoft and Marston Trussell *Pet* 06-12; P-in-c Foxton w Gumley and Laughton *Leic* from 12. *The Vicarage, Vicarage Drive, Foxton, Market Harborough LE16 7RJ* E: bud.gemmell@btopenworld.com

GENDALL, Stephen Mark. b 63. **d** 89 **p** 90. Lundi St Apollos Zimbabwe 89-01; Youth Chapl 93-01; Can Cen Zimbabwe 00-01; V Lingfield and Crowhurst *S'wark* 02-12; Chapl Crowhurst Chr Healing Cen from 12. *Crowhurst Christian Healing Centre, The Old Rectory, Crowhurst, Battle TN33 9AD* T: (01424) 830204 M: 07752-063150 E: steve@thegendalls.freeserve.co.uk

GENDERS, Nigel Mark. b 65. Oak Hill Th Coll BA 92. **d** 92 **p** 93. C New Malden and Coombe *S'wark* 92-96; C Enfield Ch Ch Trent Park *Lon* 96-98; P-in-c Eastry and Northbourne w

Tilmanstone etc *Cant* 98-03; P-in-c Woodnesborough w Worth and Staple 03-08; AD Sandwich 06-08; Min to Sandwich Secondary Schs 03-08; Dir of Educn *Cant* 08-12; C Margate H Trin 11-12; Hd of Sch Policy Bd of Educn and Dep Sec Nat Soc 12-14; Chief Educn Officer Abps' Coun from 14; PtO *Cant* from 12. *Church House, Great Smith Street, London SW1P 3AZ* T: (020) 7898 1789 E: nigel.genders@churchofengland.org

GENEREUX, Patrick Edward. b 47. William Carey Coll BSc 73 Univ of the South (USA) MDiv 78. **d** 78 **p** 79. USA 78-81 and from 82; C Spalding St Mary and St Nic *Linc* 81-82. *621 North 5th Street, Burlington IA 52601-0608, USA* T: (001) (319) 754 6420 E: pgenereux@aol.com

GENOE, Simon Alfred. b 82. Stranmillis Coll BEd 06 TCD BTh 09. CITC 06. **d** 09 **p** 10. C Lisburn Ch Ch Cathl 09-13; V from 13. *82 Thornleigh Drive, Lisburn BT28 2DS* T: (028) 9267 6499 M: 07501-288941 E: simon.genoe@gmail.com

GENT, David Robert. b 71. Surrey Univ BSc 94. Qu Coll Birm BD 97. **d** 98 **p** 99. C Wotton-under-Edge w Ozleworth and N Nibley *Glouc* 98-02; Chapl Yeovil Coll and C Yeovil H Trin w Barwick *B & W* 02-08; P-in-c Martock w Ash 08-14; P-in-c Kingsbury Episcopi w E Lambrook, Hambridge etc 13-14; V Martock w Kingsbury Episcopi and Ash from 14. *The Vicarage, 10 Water Street, Martock TA12 6JN* T: (01935) 826113 E: vicar.martock@gmail.com

GENT, Emily Louise. *See* DAVIS, Emily Louise

GENT, Mrs Miriam. b 29. Leeds Univ BA 51. SWMTC 84. **d** 87 **p** 94. NSM Pinhoe and Broadclyst *Ex* 87-02; Dioc Adv in Adult Tr 96-99; PtO from 02. *Moss Hayne Cottage, West Clyst, Exeter EX1 3TR* T: (01392) 467288 F: 462980

GENT, Miss Susan Elizabeth. K Coll Lon LLB 78 Brunel Univ BA 95. Wycliffe Hall Ox MPhil 96. **d** 97 **p** 98. C Notting Hill St Jo and St Pet *Lon* 97-00; Chapl to City law firms 00-12; Hon Assoc P St Paul's Cathl 00-12; Dioc Visitor 01-02; P-in-c St Martin Ludgate 05-12; Tutor Trin Coll Bris from 12. *24 Stoke Hill, Bristol BS9 1JW* T: 0117-968 2803 E: sue.gent@trinity-bris.ac.uk

GENTILELLA, Barbara Catherine. b 55. SEITE 05. **d** 08 **p** 09. NSM Shirley St Jo *S'wark* 08-12; NSM Addington from 12. *42 Devonshire Way, Croydon CR0 8BR* T: (020) 8777 4462 E: bb2ke@sky.com

GENTRY, Michael John. b 66. St Steph Ho Ox BTh 95. **d** 98 **p** 99. C Bromley SS Pet and Paul *Roch* 98-02; V Langton Green from 02. *The Vicarage, The Green, Langton Green, Tunbridge Wells TN3 0JB* T/F: (01892) 862072 T: 861889 E: michael.gentry@diocese-rochester.org

GEOGHEGAN, Luke. b 62. SS Hild & Bede Coll Dur BA 83 Bedf Coll Lon MSc 87 CQSW 87 Bedfordshire Univ MA 13 FRSA 93. SAOMC 87. **d** 00 **p** 01. NSM Spitalfields Ch Ch w All SS *Lon* 00-03; NSM Gt Berkhamsted *St Alb* 03-05; NSM Gt Berkhamsted, Gt and Lt Gaddesden etc from 05; NSM Hemel Hempstead from 14; Warden Toynbee Hall 98-08; Visiting Prof Lon Metrop Univ 00-08; Chapl Ashridge Business Sch from 08. *1 Clapton Terrace, London E5 9BW*

GEORGE, Alexander Robert. b 46. K Coll Lon BD 69 AKC 69. St Aug Coll Cant. **d** 70 **p** 71. C Newmarket St Mary w Exning St Agnes *St E* 70-74; C Swindon Ch Ch *Bris* 74-76; C Henbury 76-79; LtO 79-80; TV Oldland 80-88; C Ipswich St Aug *St E* 89; C Hadleigh w Layham and Shelley 89-90; P-in-c Assington 90-91; R Assington w Newton Green and Lt Cornard 91-00; P-in-c Hundon 00-03; Hon C 03-04; C Stour Valley 04-11; Dioc Moderator for Reader Tr 95-03; Asst Liturg Officer (Formation and Educn) 00-03; Nat Moderator for Reader Tr 04-08; rtd 11; PtO *St E* from 11. *103 Bixley Road, Ipswich IP3 8NP* E: alecrg@btinternet.com

GEORGE, David. b 64. Wycliffe Hall Ox 01. **d** 03 **p** 04. C Inkberrow w Cookhill and Kington w Dormston *Worc* 03-07; P-in-c Dudley St Jo 07-10; TV Kidderminster St Jo and H Innocents from 10. *9 Sutton Park Road, Kidderminster DY11 6LB* T: (01562) 740114 E: revdave.george@virgin.net

GEORGE, David Michael. b 45. Selw Coll Cam BA 66 MA 70. Chich Th Coll 70. **d** 73 **p** 74. C Chiswick St Nic w St Mary *Lon* 73-76; C Kensington St Mary Abbots w St Geo 76-78; C Northolt Park St Barn 78-81; R Martinez St Mich Argentina 82-00; R St Jo Cathl Buenos Aires 00-08; Adn River Plate 84-02; rtd 08. *Pje Dr Rodolfo Rivarola 112-4-10, C1015AAB Buenos Aires, Argentina* T: (0054) (11) 4372 4596 E: davidmg@ciudad.com.ar

GEORGE, Mrs Elizabeth Ann. b 33. Westf Coll Lon BA 56. S Dios Minl Tr Scheme 84. **d** 87 **p** 94. NSM Basingstoke *Win* 87-05; PtO from 05. *71 Camrose Way, Basingstoke RG21 3AW* T: (01256) 464763 E: elizabethgeorge@compuserve.com

GEORGE, The Ven Frederick. b 39. St Luke's Coll Ex TCert 61. Chich Th Coll 82. **d** 72 **p** 83. Australia 72-75; Brunei 75-80; The Gambia 80-82 and 83-88; Prin Angl Tr Cen Farefeni 85-88; P-in-c Ringsfield w Redisham, Barsham, Shipmeadow etc *St E* 89-92; R Wainford 92-97; V Jamestown St Helena 97-03;

Adn St Helena 99-03; rtd 03; PtO *Chich* from 03; PtO St Helena from 04. *PO Box 87, Woody Ridge, St Helena, STHL 1ZZ, South Atlantic* T/F: (00290) 3140

GEORGE, Henderson Rudolph. b 44. Open Univ BA 80 Chelsea Coll Lon MEd 85. NTMTC BA 07. **d** 07 **p** 08. NSM Clapton St Jas *Lon* 07-11; NSM Enfield St Jas from 11. *12 Cowland Avenue, Enfield EN3 7DX* T: (020) 8804 9224
E: hendersonrgeorge@googlemail.com *or*
henderson.george@stjameschurch.cc

GEORGE, Nicholas Paul. b 58. St Steph Ho Ox 86. **d** 89 **p** 90. C Leeds St Aid *Ripon* 89-92; C Leeds Richmond Hill 92-96; Chapl Agnes Stewart C of E High Sch Leeds 93-96; V Leeds Halton St Wilfrid *Ripon* 96-02; V Camberwell St Giles w St Matt *S'wark* from 02. *St Giles's Vicarage, 200 Benhill Road, London SE5 7LL* T/F: (020) 7703 4504 M: 07771-603217
E: mail@nickgeorge.org.uk

✠**GEORGE, The Rt Revd Randolph Oswald.** b 24. Codrington Coll Barbados 46. **d** 50 **p** 51 **c** 76. Barbados 50-53; C Leigh *Lich* 53-55; C Ardwick St Benedict *Man* 55-57; C Bedford Park *Lon* 57-58; C Lavender Hill Ascension *S'wark* 58-60; Dom Chapl to Bp Trinidad and Tobago 60-62; Chapl Colonial Hosp 60-62; R Couva 62-67; R Port of Spain All SS 67-71; Hon Can Trinidad 68-71; Dean Georgetown Guyana 71-76; Suff Bp Stabroek 76-80; Bp Guyana 80-08; rtd 08. *590 Republic Park, Peter's Hall, East Bank Demerara, Guyana* T: (00592) (233) 6522

GEORGE, Robert Henry. b 45. FCCA 73. WEMTC 99. **d** 01 **p** 02. OLM S Cerney w Cerney Wick and Down Ampney *Glouc* 01-05; NSM Brimpsfield w Birdlip, Syde, Daglingworth etc from 05. *Jedems, Berkeley Close, South Cerney, Cirencester GL7 5UN* T: (01285) 860973
E: member@jedems.wanadoo.co.uk

GEORGE, Mrs Shuna. b 64. SS Coll Cam BA 86 MA 89 Nottm Univ MA 11. EMMTC 08. **d** 11. NSM Bridport *Sarum* 11-12. *Address withheld by request* M: 07971-759997
E: shuna@bridport-team-ministry.org

GEORGE, Sunny. b 58. **d** 15. C Leic Resurr from 15. *20 Kerrysdale Avenue, Leicester LE4 7GH* T: 0116-212 7562
E: jesus4sungeo@yahoo.co.uk

GEORGE-JONES, Canon Gwilym Ifor. b 26. K Coll (NS) 56. **d** 57 **p** 57. R Seaforth St Jas Canada 57-61; V Kirton in Lindsey *Linc* 61-71; R Grayingham 61-71; R Manton 61-71; V Alford w Rigsby 71-92; R Maltby 71-92; R Well 71-92; V Bilsby w Farlesthorpe 71-92; R Hannah cum Hagnaby w Markby 71-92; R Saleby w Beesby 71-92; RD Calcewaithe and Candleshoe 77-85 and 87-89; Can and Preb Linc Cathl 81-01; rtd 92. *42 Kelstern Road, Lincoln LN6 3NJ* T: (01522) 691896

GEORGE-ROGERS, Gillian Jean Richeldis. See WILLIAMS, Gillian Jean Richeldis

GEORGESTONE, Arthur Raymond William. b 51. K Coll Lon MA 95. Sierra Leone Th Hall 78. **d** 82 **p** 83. C Freetown Bp Crowther Memorial Ch Sierra Leone 82-83; C St Geo Cathl Freetown 83-85; P-in-c Goderich St Luke 85-87; PtO *Chelmsf* 87-04; Ox from 10. *117 Langcliffe Drive, Heelands, Milton Keynes MK13 7LD* T: (01908) 315261 M: 07535-163379
E: georgestone93@gmail.com

GERAERTS, Virginia Gwynneth. b 50. **d** 15. NSM Davenham *Ches* from 15. *18 Comboy Drive, Rudheath, Northwich CW9 7JU* T: (01606) 333543 M: 07709-049079
E: virginia_gray@hotmail.com

GERARD, Patrick Hoare. b 64. Man Univ BSc 86 MSc 88. Qu Coll Birm 04. **d** 06 **p** 07. C Solihull *Birm* 06-10; R Baddesley Clinton from 10; R Lapworth from 10; Bp's Adv for the Environment from 12. *The Rectory, Church Lane, Lapworth, Solihull B94 5NX* T: (01564) 782098 M: 07905-967930
E: patrick@gerard.net

GERARDO, Brother. See ROMO-GARCIA, Gerardo

GERD, Sister. See SWENSSON, Gerd Inger

GERRANS, Daniel. b 58. Em Coll Cam LLB 80 MA 83 Barrister-at-Law (Middle Temple) 81. SEITE 02. **d** 05 **p** 06. NSM De Beauvoir Town St Pet *Lon* 05-11; Chapl to Bp Stepney 07-11; V S Hackney St Mich w Haggerston St Paul from 11. *97 Lavender Grove, London E8 3LR* T: (020) 7249 2627
E: daniel.gerrans@xxiv.co.uk

GERRARD, David Ian. b 82. Lanc Univ BA 04. Trin Coll Bris BA 11 MPhil 12. **d** 12 **p** 13. C Shevington *Blackb* from 12. *53 Churchfield, Shevington, Wigan WN6 8BE* M: 07753-417339
E: digerrard@hotmail.com

GERRARD, The Ven David Keith Robin. b 39. St Edm Hall Ox BA 61. Linc Th Coll 61. **d** 63 **p** 64. C Stoke Newington St Olave *Lon* 63-66; C Primrose Hill St Mary w Avenue Road St Paul 66-69; V Newington St Paul *S'wark* 69-79; V Surbiton St Andr and St Mark 79-89; RD Kingston 84-88; Hon Can S'wark Cathl 85-89; Adn Wandsworth 89-04; rtd 05; PtO *Guildf* from 05; S'wark from 05. *15 Woodbourne Drive, Claygate, Esher KT10 0DR* T: (01372) 467295
E: david.gerrard@btinternet.com

GERRARD, Paul Christian Francis. b 58. St Steph Ho Ox 92. **d** 94 **p** 01. C Longton *Lich* 94-95; NSM New Radnor and Llanfihangel Nantmelan etc *S & B* 01-04; NSM E Radnor 04-07; PtO 07-09. *The Old Vicarage, Norton, Presteigne LD8 2EN* T: (01544) 260038

GERRISH, David Victor. b 38. St Jo Coll Dur BSc 61 MA 65. Oak Hill Th Coll 61. **d** 64 **p** 65. C Fareham St Jo *Portsm* 64-66; Asst Chapl K Sch Roch 67-71; Asst Chapl Bryanston Sch 71-73; Chapl 73-77; Chapl Mon Sch 77-86; Chapl Warminster Sch 86-89; R Portland All SS w St Pet *Sarum* 89-96; Chapl Aquitaine *Eur* 96-00; rtd 00; PtO *Sarum* from 01. *Flat 8, 6 Ricketts Close, Weymouth DT4 7UP* T: (01305) 789319

GERRY, Brian John Rowland. b 38. Oak Hill Th Coll 69. **d** 71 **p** 72. C Hawkwell *Chelmsf* 71-74; C Battersea Park St Sav *S'wark* 74-77; C Battersea St Geo w St Andr 74-77; V Axmouth w Musbury *Ex* 77-86; R Upton 86-04; rtd 04. *49 Peasland Road, Torquay TQ2 8PA* T: (01803) 322788

GERRY, Ulric James. b 67. Bris Univ BEng 89. Wycliffe Hall Ox BA 96. **d** 97 **p** 98. C Hemel Hempstead *St Alb* 97-00; PtO 01-02; Crosslinks Tanzania 02-11; P-in-c Glas St Oswald 11-14. *Address temp unknown* M: 07758-004487
E: ulricgerry@gmail.com

GHEORGHIU GOULD, Helen Elizabeth-Anne. b 65. Lanc Univ BA 87. St Mellitus Coll BA 10. **d** 10 **p** 11. C Epping Distr *Chelmsf* 10-14; C Nazeing 14-15; P-in-c from 15. *76 The Plain, Epping CM16 6TW* T: (01992) 560999
E: hsgheorghiu@btinternet.com

GHEST, Richard William Iliffe. b 31. Em Coll Cam BA 53 MA 57 Lon Univ BA 66. Wells Th Coll 53. **d** 55 **p** 56. C Weston-super-Mare St Jo *B & W* 55-57; India 58-63; C Holborn St Geo w H Trin and St Bart *Lon* 63-67; Ceylon 67-68; C Combe Down *B & W* 68-73; C Combe Down w Monkton Combe 73-74; R Tickenham 74-96; rtd 96. *120 Cottrell Road, Roath, Cardiff CF24 3EX* T: (029) 2048 1597

GHINN, Edward. b 45. Oak Hill Th Coll 71. **d** 74 **p** 75. C Purley Ch Ch *S'wark* 74-77; Chile 77-82; V Sevenoaks Weald *Roch* 82-86; Chapl HM Pris Hull 86-89; Chapl HM Pris Pentonville 89-91; Chapl HM Pris Maidstone 91-96; Brazil 96-98; Min Parkwood CD *Cant* 98-01; Chapl HM Pris Grendon and Spring Hill 01-03; Chapl HM Pris Stocken 03-11; rtd 11; PtO *Cant* from 11. *Raigersfeld Lodge, Ashford Road, Weavering, Maidstone ME14 4AE* E: e.ghinn@virgin.net

GHOSH, Dipen. b 43. St Jo Coll Nottm 71. **d** 74 **p** 75. C Bushbury *Lich* 74-77; Hon C 86-89; C Wednesfield Heath 89-91; TV Wolverhampton 91-98; TV Bushbury 98-02; Chapl Compton Hospice 98-02; V Wolverhampton St Matt *Lich* 02-12; rtd 13; PtO *Lich* from 13. *59 Primrose Avenue, Wolverhampton WV10 8AP*

GIBB, Canon David Richard Albert. b 68. Lon Bible Coll BA 90 Cov Univ MPhil 95. **d** 95 **p** 96. C Ox St Ebbe w H Trin and St Pet 95-01; V Leyland St Andr *Blackb* from 01; Hon Can Blackb Cathl from 11. *St Andrew's Vicarage, 1 Crocus Field, Leyland PR25 3DY* T: (01772) 621645 E: d.gibb@talktalk.net

GIBBARD, Roger. b 48. Southn Univ BA 73. Cuddesdon Coll 73. **d** 75 **p** 76. C Portsea St Mary *Portsm* 75-79; P-in-c New Addington *Cant* 79-81; C Ditton St Mich *Liv* 81-82; TV 82-88; Asst Chapl HM Pris Liv 88-89; Chapl HM YOI Hindley 89-92; Chapl HM Pris Risley 92-00; V Wigan St Mich *Liv* 01-04. *97 Barnsley Street, Wigan WN6 7HB* T: (01942) 233465
E: thegibbards@blueyonder.co.uk

GIBBENS, Gwyneth Andrea. b 52. Nottm Univ BA 73 PhD 78. WEMTC 07. **d** 10 **p** 11. NSM Kemble, Poole Keynes, Somerford Keynes etc *Glouc* 10-13; V Wotton St Mary from 13. *Holy Trinity Vicarage, Church Road, Longlevens, Gloucester GL2 0AJ* T: (01452) 524129
E: revgwynethgibbens@gmail.com

GIBBINS, John Grenville. b 53. Aston Tr Scheme 89 Linc Th Coll 89. **d** 91 **p** 92. C Market Harborough *Leic* 91-95; P-in-c Blaby from 95. *The Rectory, Wigston Road, Blaby, Leicester LE8 4FU* T: 0116-277 2588 E: ggibbins@leicester.anglican.org

GIBBINS, Mrs Megan Ceinwen. b 59. Birm Univ MSc 03. St Jo Coll Nottm 12. **d** 14 **p** 15. C Selly Park Ch Ch *Birm* from 14. *38 Bond Street, Stirchley, Birmingham B30 2LA* M: 07896-499640 T: 0121-345 2277
E: megan.gibbins@talk21.com

GIBBON, Matthew. b 79. Trin Coll Carmarthen BA 00. St Steph Ho Ox BTh 03. **d** 03 **p** 04. C Caerau w Ely *Llan* 03-05; C Aberavon 05-08; P-in-c Treharris, Trelewis and Bedlinog 08-11; P-in-c Treharris, Trelewis, Bedlinog and Llanfabon from 11. *The Vicarage, 13 The Oaks, Quakers Yard, Treharris CF46 5HQ* T: (01443) 410280
E: frmatthewgibbon@talktalk.net

GIBBONS, David Austen. b 63. York Univ BSc 84. Ch Div Sch of Pacific 93 Ripon Coll Cuddesdon BA 94. **d** 94 **p** 95. C Ryde H Trin *Portsm* 94-97; C Swanmore St Mich 94-97; C Gosport Ch Ch 97-01; R Havant 01-08; R Barrington Hills USA from 08. *337 Ridge Road, Barrington IL 60010-2331, USA* T: (001) (847) 381 0596 E: dgibbons.stmarks@gmail.com

GIBBONS, David Robin Christian. b 36. Chich Th Coll 82. **d** 84 **p** 85. C Seaford w Sutton *Chich* 84-87; R Harting 87-93; R Harting w Elsted and Treyford cum Didling 93-04; rtd 04. *Richmond Villas, 102 East Street, Selsey, Chichester PO20 0BX* T: (01243) 602978

GIBBONS, Erik. b 47. Sarum & Wells Th Coll 69. **d** 72 **p** 73. C New Haw *Guildf* 72-76; C Hawley H Trin 76-79; P-in-c Blackheath and Chilworth 79-90; V 90-98; C Shere, Albury and Chilworth 98-99; P-in-c Tongham 99-04; rtd 04; PtO *Guildf* from 06. *38 Ambleside Close, Farnborough GU14 0LA* T: (01252) 540586 E: erikthecleric@ntlworld.com

GIBBONS, Harvey Lloyd. b 62. Open Univ BA 12. Ripon Coll Cuddesdon 97. **d** 99 **p** 00. C Verwood *Sarum* 99-00; C Gillingham 00-02; Dioc Voc Adv and P-in-c Upavon w Rushall and Charlton 02-07; R Warminster St Denys and Upton Scudamore 07-13; Asst Dioc Dir of Ords 11-13; P-in-c Swindon All SS w St Barn *Bris* from 13; P-in-c Swindon St Aug from 13. *St Barnabas' Vicarage, 2 Ferndale Road, Swindon SN2 1EX* E: harveygibbons@me.com

GIBBONS, Jayne Lisa. See LEWIS, Jayne Lisa

GIBBONS, The Ven Kenneth Harry. b 31. Man Univ BSc 52. Cuddesdon Coll 54. **d** 56 **p** 57. C Fleetwood St Pet *Blackb* 56-60; NE Sch Sec SCM 60-62; Hon C Leeds St Pet *Ripon* 60-62; C St Martin-in-the-Fields *Lon* 62-65; V New Addington *Cant* 65-70; V Portsea St Mary *Portsm* 70-81; RD Portsm 73-79; Hon Can Portsm Cathl 76-81; Dir Post-Ord Tr *Blackb* 81-83; Dir of Ords and Dir IME 4-7 82-90; Adn Lancaster 81-97; P-in-c Weeton 81-85; V St Michaels-on-Wyre 85-97; rtd 97; P-in-c St Magnus the Martyr w St Marg New Fish Street *Lon* 97-03; P-in-c St Clem Eastcheap w St Martin Orgar 99-08. *84 Whitgift House, 76 Brighton Road, South Croydon CR2 6AB* T: (020) 8686 7505 E: margyandken@btinternet.com

GIBBONS, Lissa Melanie. See SCOTT, Lissa Melanie

GIBBONS, Paul James. b 37. JP . Chich Th Coll 63. **d** 65 **p** 66. C Croydon St Mich *Cant* 65-72; V Maidstone St Mich 72-12; rtd 12. *19 Sterling Avenue, Maidstone ME16 0AY* T: (01622) 754812

GIBBONS, Mrs Susan Janet. b 51. St Mary's Coll Dur BA 73 Birm Univ PGCE 74. WMMTC 89. **d** 92 **p** 94. NSM Fladbury w Wyre Piddle and Moor etc *Worc* 92-00; PtO from 00. *The Old School, Bricklehampton, Pershore WR10 3HJ* T: (01386) 710475

GIBBONS, Thomas Patrick. b 59. St Jo Coll Dur BA 82. St Steph Ho Ox 88. **d** 90 **p** 91. C Whorlton *Newc* 90-94; C Gosforth St Nic 94-96; R Radley and Sunningwell *Ox* 96-04; P-in-c Lenborough 04-07; TV Monkwearmouth *Dur* 07-13; Chapl Co Durham and Darlington NHS Foundn Trust from 07. *Chaplaincy, University Hospital of North Durham, North Road, Durham DH1 5TW* T: (01388) 455451 E: tp.gibbons@btinternet.com

GIBBONS, Mrs Valerie Mary Lydele. b 49. St Aid Coll Dur BA 72 Solicitor 75. Wycliffe Hall Ox 98. **d** 03 **p** 04. OLM Cholsey and Moulsford *Ox* from 03. *Kilifi, Caps Lane, Cholsey, Wallingford OX10 9HF* T/F: (01491) 651377 E: val.gibbons@btinternet.com

GIBBONS, William Jacob. b 84. **d** 11 **p** 12. C E Carmarthen *St D* 11-12; C Carmarthen St Pet 12-13; P-in-c Newtown *Liv* from 13. *The Vicarage, 65 Plane Avenue, Wigan WN5 9PT* T: (01942) 211194 E: willgibbons@hotmail.co.uk

GIBBONS, William Simpson. b 32. TCD BA 60 MA 64. **d** 61 **p** 62. C Londonderry Ch Ch *D & R* 61-65; I Kilbarron w Rossnowlagh and Drumholm 65-70; C Dublin St Ann w St Steph *D & G* 70-72; I Kill 72-95; Can Ch Ch Cathl Dublin 91-95; rtd 95. *Muthaiga, 3 Glenageary Terrace, Dun Laoghaire, Co Dublin, Republic of Ireland* T/F: (00353) (1) 214 8699 M: 87-218 7771 E: wsgibbons@eircom.net

GIBBS, Mrs Claire Anne. b 76. York Univ BA 99 MA 01. Cranmer Hall Dur 12. **d** 13 **p** 14. C Evenwood *Dur* from 13; C Cockfield from 13; C Lynesack from 13. *The Vicarage, Brookside, Evenwood, Bishop Auckland DL14 9RA* T: (01388) 834594 M: 07968-235688 E: protorevclaire@gmail.com

GIBBS, Colin Hugh. b 35. St Mich Coll Llan 82. **d** 84 **p** 85. C Bistre St As 84-87; V Penycae 87-92; rtd 92. *Asaph, 26 Cil y Coed, Ruabon, Wrexham LL14 6TA* T: (01978) 823550

GIBBS, Colin Wilfred. b 39. Man Univ BA 62 Birm Univ CertEd 63. St Jo Coll Nottm 71. **d** 73 **p** 74. C Crowborough *Chich* 73-76; C Rodbourne Cheney *Bris* 76-77; C Bickenhill w Elmdon *Birm* 77-80; CF 80-96; Dir Ichthus Ho Homestay 96-06; Chapl Grenville Coll Bideford 99-02; P-in-c Cowden w Hammerwood *Chich* 06-10. *11 The Gorses, Bexhill-on-Sea TN39 3BE* T: (01424) 845299 E: ichthushouse@tiscali.co.uk

GIBBS, Edmund. b 38. Fuller Th Sem California DMin 81. Oak Hill Th Coll BD 62. **d** 63 **p** 64. C Wandsworth All SS *S'wark* 63-66; SAMS Chile 66-70; Educn Sec SAMS 70-77; Ch Progr

Manager Bible Soc 77-84; USA from 84; Assoc Prof Evang and Ch Renewal Fuller Th Sem 84-93; Prof Ch Growth from 96; Assoc R Beverly Hills All SS 93-96. *625 W Commonwealth Avenue, Apt 314, Alhambra CA 91801-3652, USA* E: eddgibbs@fuller.edu

GIBBS (née DE ROBECK), Mrs Fiona Caroline. b 74. St Martin's Coll Lanc BA 96. St Jo Coll Nottm MA(TS) 99. **d** 00 **p** 01. C Bitterne *Win* 00-05; C Chandler's Ford 05-13; P-in-c Hedge End St Luke from 13. *16 Elliot Rise, Hedge End, Southampton SO30 2RU* T: (01489) 795443

GIBBS, Mrs Fiorenza Silvia Elisabetta. b 49. SRN 71. St Alb Minl Tr Scheme 90. **d** 93 **p** 99. NSM Hitchin *St Alb* 93-96; NSM Pirton 97-99; Asst Chapl N Herts NHS Trust 99-00; Asst Chapl E and N Herts NHS Trust 00-02; Chapl 02-10; NSM Hitchin *St Alb* from 10. *12 Bunyon Close, Pirton, Hitchin SG5 3RE* T: (01462) 711846

GIBBS, Ian Edmund. b 47. Lon Univ BEd 69. St Steph Ho Ox 72. **d** 75 **p** 76. C Stony Stratford *Ox* 75-79; V Forest Town *S'well* 79-83; R Diddlebury w Munslow, Holdgate and Tugford *Heref* 83-12; R Abdon 83-12; rtd 12; PtO *Heref* from 12. *Dhustone Cottage, 10 High Street, Clee Hill, Ludlow SY8 3LZ*

GIBBS, James Millard. b 28. Univ of Michigan BSE 51 Nottm Univ PhD 68. Seabury-Western Th Sem BD 57. **d** 57 **p** 57. USA 57-60; LtO *S'well* 61-62 and 65-66; C Brandon *Dur* 62-64; Vice-Prin Lich Th Coll 66-71; LtO *Lich* 66-71; India 72-77; Tutor Qu Coll Birm 78-84; V Stechford *Birm* 84-93; rtd 93; PtO *Birm* from 93. *13 Lingfield Court, 60 High Street, Harbourne, Birmingham B17 9NE* T: 0121-426 2108 E: jmanddagibbs@aol.com

GIBBS, Jane Anne. b 46. W Midl Coll of Educn CertEd 67. EMMTC 03. **d** 06 **p** 07. NSM Hinckley St Mary *Leic* from 06. *4 Kirfield Drive, Hinckley LE10 1SX* T: (01455) 635934

✠**GIBBS, The Rt Revd Jonathan Robert.** b 61. Jes Coll Ox MA 89 Jes Coll Cam PhD 90. Ridley Hall Cam 84. **d** 89 **p** 90 **c** 14. C Stalybridge H Trin and Ch Ch *Ches* 89-92; Chapl Basle w Freiburg-im-Breisgau *Eur* 92-98; R Heswall *Ches* 98-14; Suff Bp Huddersfield *Leeds* from 14. *Stone Royd, 9 Valley Head, Huddersfield HD2 2DH* E: bishop.jonathan@westyorkshiredales.anglican.org

GIBBS, Marcus Timothy. b 73. UMIST BSc 95. Trin Coll Bris BA 10. **d** 10 **p** 11. C Northampton St Giles *Pet* 10-13; V Balham Hill Ascension *S'wark* from 13. *5 Rossiter Road, London SW12 9RY* T: (020) 8675 8626 F: 8673 3796 E: marcus.gibbs@ascensionbalhamhill.org

GIBBS, Michael Robin. b 42. Th Ext Educn Coll 74. **d** 83 **p** 84. NSM Malawi 83-04; Can Upper Shire from 03; Chapl Essex Chs Coun for Ind and Commerce *Chelmsf* from 05. *120 St John's Road, London E17 4JQ* T/F: (020) 8523 1375 E: micgibbs@talktalk.net

GIBBS, Mrs Patricia Louise. b 39. S'wark Ord Course 91. **d** 94 **p** 95. NSM Croydon H Sav *S'wark* 94-07; Chapl Asst Mayday Healthcare NHS Trust Thornton Heath 94-05; rtd 05. *41 Sandringham Road, Thornton Heath CR7 7AX* T: (020) 8684 9720

GIBBS, Peter Winston. b 50. Ex Univ BA 72 CQSW 75. St Jo Coll Nottm. **d** 90 **p** 91. C Hampreston *Sarum* 90-94; P-in-c Ipswich St Matt *St E* 94-99; Assoc P Attenborough *S'well* 99-01; V Toton 01-08; TV N Poole Ecum Team *Sarum* from 08. *St Paul's Vicarage, 16 Rowbarrow Close, Poole BH17 9EA* T: (01202) 565187 E: ladybird1@ntlworld.com

GIBBS, Canon Philip Roscoe. b 33. Codrington Coll Barbados 57. **d** 60 **p** 61. C St Jo Cathl Belize Br Honduras 61-63; P-in-c S Distr Miss 63-70; V Pomona St Matt 70-71; R Corozal Belize 71-74; Hon Can Belize from 71; V Stoke Newington Common St Mich *Lon* 74-87; R Johnsonville New Zealand 87-96; rtd 96. *13 Sim Street, Johnsonville 6037, New Zealand* E: philip.g@actrix.co.nz

GIBBS, Raymond George. b 55. NTMTC 94. **d** 97 **p** 98. NSM Becontree S *Chelmsf* 97-99; C Dedham 99-04; C Colchester St Mich Myland 04-08; P-in-c from 08; Area Youth Officer 04-08. *352 Mill Road, Mile End, Colchester CO4 5JF* T: (01206) 843926 E: raymond359gibbs@btinternet.com

GIBBS, Mrs Rebecca Ann. b 75. **d** 14 **p** 15. C Cheadle Hulme All SS *Ches* from 14. *3 Hulme Hall Crescent, Cheadle Hulme, Cheadle SK8 6LG* E: beckyd_77@hotmail.com

GIBBS, Richard James. b 68. St Paul's Coll Chelt BSc 90. St Jo Coll Nottm MTh 01. **d** 01 **p** 02. C Southport Ch Ch *Liv* 01-05; Min Banks St Steph CD 05-12; C Southport St Phil and St Paul from 12. *37 Lethbridge Road, Southport PR8 6JA* E: ppwvicar@hotmail.co.uk

GIBBS, Stewart Henry. b 77. CCC Cam BA 98 MA PGCE 99 Anglia Poly Univ BTh 05. Ridley Hall Cam 02. **d** 05 **p** 06. C Grays North *Chelmsf* 05-10; R Hatfield Heath and Sheering 10-15. *The Vicarage, Broomfields, Hatfield Heath, Bishop's Stortford CM22 7EH* T: (01279) 730288 M: 07899-753559 E: stewarthgibbs@hotmail.co.uk

GIBBS, Miss Valerie Edwina. b 47. Sussex Univ BEd 78 Open Univ BA 98. STETS 07. **d** 10. *Address withheld by request* T: (01424) 814278 E: valeriegibbs@aol.com

GIBBS, Canon William Gilbert. b 31. Bps' Coll Cheshunt 55. **d** 58 **p** 59. C Wellington w W Buckland *B & W* 58-61; C Kensington St Mary Abbots w St Geo *Lon* 61-68; V Guilsborough *Pet* 68; V Guilsborough w Hollowell 68-74; V Guilsborough w Hollowell and Cold Ashby 74-98; Jt P-in-c Cottesbrooke w Gt Creaton and Thornby 83-98; Jt P-in-c Maidwell w Draughton, Lamport w Faxton 88-98; Can Pet Cathl 88-98; rtd 98; PtO *Pet* 98-01 and from 03; P-in-c W Haddon w Winwick and Ravensthorpe 01-03. *Paines Close, Maidwell, Northampton NN6 9JB* T: (01604) 686424

GIBBS, William John Morris. b 71. Birm Univ BSc 94. Ripon Coll Cuddesdon BTh 00. **d** 00 **p** 01. C Staines St Mary and St Pet *Lon* 00-03; C Kensington St Mary Abbots w St Geo 03-06; V Redbourn *St Alb* from 06; RD Wheathampstead from 10. *The Vicarage, 49 Church End, Redbourn, St Albans AL3 7DU* T: (01582) 791669

GIBLIN, Brendan Anthony. b 64. K Coll Lon BD 86 AKC 93 Leeds Univ MA 95. Wycliffe Hall Ox 90. **d** 92 **p** 93. C Tadcaster w Newton Kyme *York* 92-96; R Stockton-on-the-Forest w Holtby and Warthill 96-02; P-in-c Middleham w Coverdale and E Witton etc *Ripon* 02-03; R 03-11; AD Wensley 10-11; P-in-c Wetherby *Leeds* from 11; AD Harrogate from 13. *3 Lazenby Drive, Wetherby LS22 6WL* T: (01937) 520951 E: bgiblin@me.com

GIBLING, Derek Vivian. b 31. Wadh Coll Ox BA 56 MA 63. Wycliffe Hall Ox 70. **d** 72 **p** 73. C Fisherton Anger *Sarum* 72-74; C Yatton Keynell *Bris* 74-77; C Castle Combe 74-77; C Biddestone w Slaughterford 74-77; P-in-c Youlgreave *Derby* 77-82; P-in-c Stanton-in-Peak 77-82; V Youlgreave, Middleton, Stanton-in-Peak etc 82-88; P-in-c Hartington and Biggin 88-90; V Hartington, Biggin and Earl Sterndale 90-96; rtd 96; PtO *Linc* 96-02; RD Bolingbroke 00-02. *15 Howards Meadow, Glossop SK13 6PZ* T: (01457) 851423

GIBRALTAR, Archdeacon of. *See* JOHNSTON, The Ven Geoffrey Stanley

GIBRALTAR, Dean of. *See* PADDOCK, The Very Revd John Allan Barnes

GIBSON, Anthony Richard. b 43. Ridley Hall Cam 83. **d** 85 **p** 86. C Rushmere *St E* 85-88; R N Tawton, Bondleigh, Sampford Courtenay etc *Ex* 88-93; R Okehampton 92-93; P-in-c Tiverton St Pet and Chevithorne w Cove 93-03; rtd 03. *Le Bourg, 82210 Fajolles, France* T: (0033) 5 63 94 14 83

GIBSON, Brenda. b 55. St Mary's Coll Dur BSc 77 PhD 80 Hughes Hall Cam PGCE 81 Surrey Univ BA 04. STETS 01. **d** 04 **p** 05. NSM Wimborne Minster *Sarum* from 04; NSM Witchampton, Stanbridge and Long Crichel etc from 15; NSM Horton, Chalbury, Hinton Martel and Holt St Jas from 15. *12 Meadow Court, Leigh Road, Wimborne BH21 2BG* T: (01202) 881472 E: rev.brenda.gibson@btinternet.com

GIBSON, Catherine Snyder. b 39. Parson's Sch of Design (NY) 57. Ab Dioc Tr Course 81 Edin Th Coll 92. **d** 86 **p** 94. Colombia 86-87; NSM Aberdeen St Marg *Ab* 87-88; Dioc Hosp Chapl 88-92; C Aberdeen St Mary 93-94; Bp's Chapl for Tr and Educn 93-94; P-in-c Ballater 95-96; R 96-98; P-in-c Aboyne 95-96; R 96-98; P-in-c Braemar 95-97; Assoc P Fort Lauderdale USA 98-03; I Fermoy Union *C, C & R* 04-06; P-in-c Lugano *Eur* 06-07; P-in-c Dayton St Matt USA 09-10; Assoc P W Palm Beach 11-12; rtd 10; Dioc Supernumerary *Ab* from 13. *Carlene Cottage, Tarland, Aboyne AB34 4YX* T: (01339) 881140 M: 07775-244640 E: ecscanair@gmail.com

GIBSON, Charles Daniel. b 48. **d** 03 **p** 04. OLM Wisley w Pyrford *Guildf* from 03. *The Corner Cottage, Send Marsh Road, Ripley, Woking GU23 6JN* T: (01483) 225317 F: 223681 E: charles@chasdi.freeserve.co.uk

GIBSON, Colin Taylor. b 54. Trin Coll Cam BA 77. Oak Hill Th Coll 86. **d** 88 **p** 89. C Thrybergh w Hooton Roberts *Sheff* 88-91; P-in-c Tinsley 91-96; TV Attercliffe, Darnall and Tinsley 96-02; TR Walsall *Lich* 02-11; R Walsall St Matt 11-13; Hon C Walsall St Paul 05-13; Hon C Walsall Pleck and Bescot 05-13; V Horton and Wraysbury *Ox* from 13. *The Vicarage, 55 Welley Road, Wraysbury, Staines-upon-Thames TW19 5ER* T: (01784) 481258 E: vicar.hortonandwraysbury@gmail.com

GIBSON, David Innes. b 31. Oak Hill Th Coll 56. **d** 59 **p** 60. C S Croydon Em *Cant* 59-62; C Washfield *Ex* 62-63; Chapl and Asst Master Blundell's Sch Tiverton 63-64; Chapl Sutton Valence Sch Kent 64-68; Chapl Dean Close Sch Cheltenham 68-75; Asst Chapl and Ho Master 75-85; Asst Master Brightlands Sch Newnham-on-Severn 85-90; C Cheltenham St Mary, St Matt, St Paul and H Trin *Glouc* 91-96; rtd 96; PtO *Glouc* 96-97 and from 01. *2 Withyholt Park, Charlton Kings, Cheltenham GL53 9BP* T: (01242) 511612

GIBSON, Douglas Harold. b 20. Portsm Dioc Tr Course. **d** 87. NSM Portsea St Luke *Portsm* 87-92; PtO from 92. *83 Middle Street, Southsea PO5 4BW* T: (023) 9282 9769

GIBSON, Mrs Fiona Ruth. b 70. Homerton Coll Cam BEd 93. Oak Hill Th Coll MTh 11. **d** 11 **p** 12. C Bedford Ch Ch *St Alb* 11-14; V Cople, Moggerhanger and Willington from 14. *The Vicarage, 3 Grange Lane, Cople, Bedford MK44 3TT* T: (01234) 838145 E: fiona.gibson@mac.com

GIBSON, The Ven George Granville. b 36. Cuddesdon Coll 69. **d** 71 **p** 72. C Tynemouth Cullercoats St Paul *Newc* 71-73; TV Cramlington 73-77; V Newton Aycliffe *Dur* 77-85; R Bishopwearmouth St Mich w St Hilda 85-90; TR Sunderland 90-93; RD Wearmouth 85-93; Hon Can Dur Cathl 88-01; Adn Auckland 93-01; rtd 01; PtO *Dur* from 04. *12 West Crescent, Darlington DL3 7PR* T: (01325) 462526 E: granville.gibson@durham.anglican.org

GIBSON, Canon Ian. b 48. Open Univ BA 85 Wolv Univ MSc 95 Liv Jo Moores Univ MA 09 FCIPD. S Dios Minl Tr Scheme 82. **d** 85 **p** 86. NSM Uckfield *Chich* 85-88; NSM Lt Horsted 85-88; NSM Isfield 85-88; V Fairwarp 88-93; P-in-c 94-00; NSM 00-04; V High Hurstwood 88-93; P-in-c 94-00; RD Uckfield 03-04; Bp's Dom Chapl and Research Asst 04-09; Episc V for Min and Bp's Sen Chapl 09-13; Can Res and Treas Chich Cathl 09-14. *Windwhistle Down, Upton Lane, Seavington, Ilminster TA19 0PZ* T: (01460) 249566

GIBSON, James Campbell Ramsay. b 70. Southn Univ BEng 92 Cranfield Univ MSc 97 CEng 96 MIMechE 96. Trin Coll Bris 10. **d** 12 **p** 13. C Busbridge and Hambledon *Guildf* from 12. *2 South Hill, Godalming GU7 1JT* T: (01483) 421267 E: jcrgibson@gmail.com

GIBSON, John Murray Hope. b 35. Dur Univ BA 58. Cranmer Hall Dur 58. **d** 60 **p** 61. C Chester le Street *Dur* 60-63; C Stockton 63-68; V Denton and Ingleton 68-75; V Swalwell 75-00; Chapl Dunston Hill Hosp Gateshead 80-93; Chapl Gateshead Health NHS Trust 94-99; rtd 00; PtO *Dur* from 01; *Newc* from 01. *2 Cathedral Court, London Road, Gloucester GL1 3QE* T: (01452) 416397

GIBSON, Canon John Noel Keith. b 22. MBE 89. Ch Coll Cam MA 48 Lon Univ BD 59. Coll of Resurr Mirfield 45. **d** 47 **p** 48. C S Elmsall *Wakef* 47-51; Antigua 51-56; Virgin Is 56-13; Can All SS Cathl 89-92; rtd 92. *College of St Barnabas, Blackberry Lane, Lingfield RH7 6NJ*

GIBSON, Kenneth George Goudie. b 54. Glas Univ MA 83 Edin Univ BD 87 Strathclyde Univ PGCE 95. Edin Th Coll 83. **d** 88 **p** 89. C Glas St Marg 88-90; R E Kilbride 90-98; R Carnoustie *Bre* 98-07; PtO 08-14; P-in-c Monifieth from 14. *39 Durham Street, Monifieth, Dundee DD5 4PF* T: (01382) 533493 E: kenneth.gibson1@btinternet.com

GIBSON, Laura Mary. *See* WILFORD, Laura Mary

GIBSON, Lynne Margaret. b 65. St Andr Univ MA 88 TCD BTh 10. CITC 08. **d** 10 **p** 11. C Dundela St Mark *D & D* from 10. *29 Marmont Park, Belfast BT4 2GR* T: (028) 9076 1967 M: 07828-516799 E: lynnetigger@gmail.com

GIBSON, Nigel Stephen David. b 53. St Barn Coll Adelaide 84. **d** 87 **p** 87. C N Adelaide Ch Ch Australia 87-89; Lect Boston *Linc* 90-91; P-in-c Stamford St Mary and St Mich 91-92; P-in-c Stamford Baron 91-92; R Stamford St Mary and St Martin 92-98; PtO 98-00; V Kempston Transfiguration *St Alb* 00-04; Chapl Milan w Cadenabbia and Varese *Eur* 04-10; Chapl St Jo Cathl and P-in-c Pokfulam Em Hong Kong from 10. *St John's Cathedral, 4-8 Garden Road, Central, Hong Kong, China* T: (00852) 2523 4157 E: frnigelgibson@gmail.com

GIBSON, Mrs Patricia Elizabeth. b 57. Nottm Univ MA 02. EMMTC 99. **d** 02 **p** 03. C Wigston Magna *Leic* 02-06; TV Gt Berkhamsted, Gt and Lt Gaddesden etc *St Alb* 06-10; Bp's Adv for Women in Min 07-10. *Venskab Barn, Morebath, Tiverton EX16 9AQ* E: revteg1@btinternet.com

GIBSON, Paul Saison. b 32. BA LTh Huron Coll Ontario Hon DD 90. Coll of Em and St Chad Hon DD 88 Vancouver Sch of Th Hon DD 95 Montreal Dioc Th Coll Hon DD 98 Trin Coll Toronto Hon DD 99. **d** 56 **p** 57. C Bloomsbury St Geo w St Jo *Lon* 56-59; R Homer St Geo Canada 59-60; Chapl McGill Univ Montreal 60-66; Prin Union Th Coll Hong Kong 66-72; Consultant Angl Ch of Canada 72-82; Liturg Officer 82-98. *588 Millwood Road, Toronto ON M4S 1K8, Canada* T: (001) (416) 487 2008

GIBSON, Philip Nigel Scott. b 53. St Jo Coll Dur BA 78. Cranmer Hall Dur 79. **d** 79 **p** 80. C Yardley St Edburgha *Birm* 79-82; C Stratford-on-Avon w Bishopton *Cov* 82-84; Chapl SW Hosp Lon 84-91; Chapl St Thos Hosp Lon 84-91; Assoc P Newington St Paul *S'wark* 91-92; Chapl Charing Cross Hosp Lon 92-93; Chapl R Lon Hosp (Whitechapel) 93-94; Chapl Bedford Hosp NHS Trust 95-08. *Sillwood, 1 Wood Lane, Aspley Guise, Milton Keynes MK17 8EJ* E: philip.gibson912@btinternet.com

GIBSON (*née* JENKINSON), **Rachel Elisabeth.** b 66. Somerville Coll Ox BA 87 Cranfield Univ MBA 99. Ridley Hall Cam 05. **d** 07 **p** 08. C Chorleywood Ch Ch *St Alb* 07-11; C Chorleywood St Andr 11-15; R Ox St Clem from 15. *St Clement's Rectory, 58 Rectory Road, Oxford OX4 1BW*

GIBSON, Raymond. b 23. Ely Th Coll 60. **d** 62 **p** 63. C Leic St Jas 62-67; Succ Leic Cathl 67-68; Chapl Leic R Infirmary 67-68; Chapl Nottm City Hosp 68-84; V Barlings *Linc* 84-88; rtd 88. *11 Cornell Drive, Nottingham NG5 8RF*

GIBSON, The Ven Terence Allen. b 37. Jes Coll Cam BA 61 MA 65. Cuddesdon Coll 61. **d** 63 **p** 64. C Kirkby *Liv* 63-66; TV 72-75; TR 75-84; Warden Cen 63 66-75; Youth Chapl *Liv* 66-72; RD Walton 79-84; Adn Suffolk *St E* 84-87; Adn Ipswich 87-05; rtd 05; PtO *St E* from 05. *5 Berry Close, Purdis Farm, Ipswich IP3 8SP* T: (01473) 714756
E: archdeaconterry@dsl.pipex.com

GIBSON, Thomas Thomson. b 23. Sarum Th Coll 62. **d** 63 **p** 64. C E w W Harnham *Sarum* 63-66; V Rowde 66-74; R Poulshot 67-74; V Badminton w Acton Turville *Glouc* 74-84; P-in-c Hawkesbury 81-84; V Badminton w Lt Badminton, Acton Turville etc 84-93; rtd 93; PtO *Glouc* 93-96 and from 01; *B & W* from 95; *Sarum* from 95; *Eur* from 99. *3 Lansdown Place West, Bath BA1 5EZ* T: (01225) 337903 F: 483676

GIBSON, Timothy John. b 80. Ex Univ BA 01 MA 02 PhD 06. SWMTC 12. **d** 14 **p** 15. NSM Isle Valley *B & W* from 14; Dir Reader Tr and Lay Educn SWMTC from 11. *Wayside, Hare Lane, Broadway, Ilminster TA19 9LN* T: (01460) 54182
E: tim@swmtc.org.uk

GIDDINGS, Mrs Jaqueline Mary. b 44. St Aid Coll Dur BA 67. SWMTC 91. **d** 94 **p** 95. C Plympton St Mary *Ex* 94-02; rtd 02. *Grange End, Harrowbeer Lane, Yelverton PL20 6EA* T: (01822) 854825

GIFFORD, David Christopher. b 53. Lon Univ BEd 75 Sussex Univ MA 85 Ox Brookes Univ BA 11. Ripon Coll Cuddesdon 08. **d** 11 **p** 12. Chief Exec Coun of Chrs and Jews 06-14; NSM Benson *Ox* 11-14; R Port Glas from 14; R Bridge of Weir from 14; R Kilmacolm from 14. *St Mary's Rectory, Bardrainney Avenue, Port Glasgow PA14 6HB* M: 07720-555858
E: dgdavid706@gmail.com

GIFFORD, Ms Elizabeth Ann. b 47. St Kath Coll Liv CertEd 72 Open Univ BSc 96. STETS 99. **d** 02 **p** 09. NSM Trowbridge H Trin *Sarum* 02-09; NSM Studley from 09. *14 Innox Mill Close, Trowbridge BA14 9BA* T: (01225) 752756 M: 07903-269587
E: revgif@aol.com

GIFFORD, Patricia Rose. b 45. **d** 10 **p** 11. NSM Glouc St Jas and All SS and Ch Ch from 10. *49 Ducie Street, Gloucester GL1 4NZ* T: (01452) 306746 E: patgifford@btopenworld.com

GIFFORD-COLE, David Henry. b 30. San Francisco Th Sem DMin 87 ALCD 56. **d** 56 **p** 57. C Ashtead *Guildf* 56-59; C Farnham 59-60; Canada from 60. *225 Hoylake Road West, Qualicum Beach BC V9K 1K5, Canada*

✠**GILBERT, The Rt Revd Bruce Carlyle.** b 38. CNZM 02. Auckland Univ BSc 59. St Jo Coll Auckland STh 74. **d** 62 **p** 64 **c** 85. C Devonport New Zealand 62-64; C Ponsony and Grey Lynn 65; P Asst Panmure 66-68; V Avondale 68-71; Ind Chapl and C Eaglescliffe *Dur* 71-73; Dir Ind Miss Wellington New Zealand 73-79; Dir Th Educn by Ext 80-85; Bp Auckland 85-94; P-in-c Albany Greenhithe New Zealand 95-00; P-in-c Tamaki St Thos 96-00; Chapl K Sch 97-00; rtd 00. *81 Manaia Road, Tairua 3508, New Zealand* T: (0064) (7) 864 8727 F: 864 8240

GILBERT, Anthony John David. b 54. Open Univ BA 91 LRSC 83 MRSC 01. Ripon Coll Cuddesdon 83. **d** 86 **p** 87. C Exning St Martin w Landwade *St E* 86-89; Chapl RAF 89-14; QHC 10-14; TR Three Valleys *Sarum* from 14. *The Rectory, Church Road, Thornford, Sherborne DT9 6QE* T: (01935) 873044 M: 07810-760680 E: rector3valleys@gmail.com

GILBERT, Canon Barry. b 46. Leeds Univ BA 67. Coll of Resurr Mirfield 67. **d** 69 **p** 70. C Malvern Link w Cowleigh *Worc* 69-73; P-in-c Bromsgrove All SS 73-81; V 81-83; P-in-c Lower Mitton 83-88; V 88-92; V Stourport and Wilden 92-06; RD Stourport 93-00 and 02-06; P-in-c Brierley Hill 06-07; TR 07-11; Hon Can Worc Cathl 09-11; rtd 11; PtO Glas from 11. *Allandale, High Street, New Galloway, Castle Douglas DG7 3RL* T: (01644) 420665 E: barry_gilbert@talk21.com

GILBERT, Clive Franklyn. b 55. City of Liv Coll of HE CertEd 76 BEd 77. SEITE 01. **d** 02 **p** 03. C Paddock Wood *Roch* 02-06; V Dartford St Alb 06-11; V Watchet and Williton *B & W* from 11. *The Vicarage, 16 Bridge Street, Williton, Taunton TA4 4NR* M: 07952-235762 E: clive.gilbert@btinternet.com

GILBERT, Frederick Joseph. b 29. Lich Th Coll 58. **d** 59 **p** 60. C Westhoughton *Man* 59-62; V Goodshaw 62-68; R Crumpsall St Matt 68-75; RD Cheetham 70-74; RD N Man 74-75; V Rochdale St Aid 75-78; TV Rochdale 78-80; V Westhoughton 80-84; TR 84-87; AD Deane 85-87; R W Bowbrook *Worc* 87-89; R Bowbrook N 89-93; rtd 93; PtO *Worc* from 93. *Freshways, Main Road, Peopleton, Pershore WR10 2EG* T: (01905) 841629 E: fsgilbert@btinternet.com

GILBERT, Hilda. b 57. Lon S Bank Univ BSc 01 Spurgeon's Coll BD 11 RGN 82. St Mellitus Coll 13. **d** 14 **p** 15. NSM Leyton St Mary w St Edw and St Luke *Chelmsf* from 14. *13 Priory Avenue, London E17 7QP* T: (020) 8521 8048 M: 07946-407294 E: gilberhil@aol.com

GILBERT, Howard Neil. b 73. Southn Univ BA 96. Ripon Coll Cuddesdon BTh 05. **d** 05 **p** 06. C Dulwich St Barn *S'wark* 05-08; C Cirencester *Glouc* from 09; AD from 15. *The Parsonage, 32 Watermoor Road, Cirencester GL7 1JR* T: (01285) 885109 M: 07887-800478 E: father.howard@gmail.com

GILBERT, Mark. *See* GILBERT, Philip Mark

GILBERT, Ms Mary Rose. b 63. Ridley Hall Cam 94. **d** 97 **p** 97. C Walsall Wood *Lich* 97-00; TV Bilston 00-07; AD Wolverhampton 03-07; V Birm St Paul from 07. *71 Wellington Road, Edgbaston, Birmingham B15 2ET* T: 0121-440 2337 E: mgdartford@aol.com

GILBERT, Michael Victor. b 61. Dur Univ BA 84. Trin Coll Bris 92. **d** 94 **p** 95. C Chapeltown *Sheff* 94-97; V Brightside w Wincobank 97-07; Adult Educator Wilson Carlile Coll of Evang 07-12; R Baslow and Eyam *Derby* from 12. *The Rectory, Church Street, Eyam, Hope Valley S32 5QH* T: (01433) 639637 E: thegilberts@thegilberts.f9.co.uk or rector@eyamchurch.org

GILBERT, Philip Mark. b 62. Liv Univ BA 84. Coll of Resurr Mirfield 84. **d** 87 **p** 88. C Frodsham *Ches* 87-89; C Stockton Heath 89-92; R Tangmere and Oving *Chich* 92-01; Chapl Seaford Coll and P-in-c Graffham w Woolavington 01-09; P-in-c Chich St Wilfrid 09-10; V 10-15; Chapl Bp Luffa Sch Chich from 09; RD Chich 11-15; P-in-c Petworth from 15; P-in-c Egdean from 15. *The Rectory, Rectory Lane, Petworth GU28 0DB* M: 07810-004062 T: (01798) 345278 E: frmarkssc@msn.com

GILBERT, Raymond. b 34. AKC 61. **d** 62 **p** 63. C Newbold w Dunston *Derby* 62-66; PV and Succ S'wark Cathl 66-68; P-in-c Stuntney *Ely* 68-74; Prec and Sacr Ely Cathl 68-74; Min Can Cant Cathl 74-79; Hon Min Can from 79; P-in-c Patrixbourne w Bridge and Bekesbourne *Cant* 79-81; V 81-00; RD E Bridge 92-98; rtd 00; PtO *Cant* from 09. *16 Green Acres, Eythorne, Dover CT15 4LX* T: (01304) 831485

GILBERT, Raymond Frederick. b 44. **d** 93 **p** 94. OLM Stowmarket *St E* 93-10; rtd 10; PtO *St E* from 10. *3 Violet Hill Road, Stowmarket IP14 1NE* T: (01449) 677700

GILBERT, Mrs Rebecca. b 76. Univ of Wales (Lamp) BA. Ridley Hall Cam. **d** 10 **p** 11. C Ely 10-13; C Three Rivers Gp 13-14; TV Lordsbridge from 14. *The Vicarage, Broad Lane, Haslingfield, Cambridge CB23 1JF* E: becgilb@gmail.com

GILBERT, Robert John Crispin. b 74. Hatf Coll Dur BSc 95 Leic Univ PhD 99 Magd Coll Ox MA 05. Ripon Coll Cuddesdon 09. **d** 11 **p** 12. NSM Wolvercote and Wytham *Ox* from 11. *Magdalen College, High Street, Oxford OX1 4AU* T: (01865) 276070 E: gilbert@strubi.ox.ac.uk

GILBERT, Roger Charles. b 46. Ex Coll Ox BA 69 MA 74 Nottm Univ MEd 81. St Steph Ho Ox 69. **d** 71 **p** 72. NSM Bridgwater St Mary w Chilton Trinity *B & W* 71-74; NSM Rugeley *Lich* 74-81; NSM Cannock 81-83; NSM Wednesbury St Jas and St Jo 83-12; NSM Tividale 08-11; NSM W Bromwich St Pet 11-12; NSM Ettingshall from 12. *41 Stafford Road, Cannock WS11 4AF* T: (01543) 570531 E: roger.gilbert@talk21.com

GILBERT, Canon Roger Geoffrey. b 37. K Coll Lon BD 69 AKC 69. **d** 70 **p** 71. C Walton-on-Thames *Guildf* 70-74; R St Mabyn and P-in-c Helland *Truro* 74-81; P-in-c Madron 81-86; R Falmouth K Chas 86-02; Hon Can Truro Cathl 94-02; RD Carnmarth S 94-00; Chapl to The Queen 95-02; rtd 02; PtO *Eur* from 98. *2 rue de Plouzon, 22690 Pleudihen-sur-Rance, France* T: (0033) 2 96 88 28 69

GILBERT, Sean William. b 89. St Steph Ho Ox 12. **d** 15. C St Leonards Ch Ch and St Mary etc *Chich* from 15. *17 Alfred Street, St Leonards-on-Sea TN38 0HD* M: 07535-445512 E: seanwgilbert@msn.com

GILBERTSON, The Ven Michael Robert. b 61. New Coll Ox BA 82 MA 92 St Jo Coll Dur BA 93 Dur Univ PhD 97. Cranmer Hall Dur. **d** 97 **p** 98. C Surbiton St Matt *S'wark* 97-00; V Stranton Dur 00-10; AD Hartlepool 02-10; Hon Can Dur Cathl 08-10; Adn Ches from 10. *Church House, 5500 Daresbury Park, Daresbury, Warrington WA4 4GE* M: 07921-040154 T: (01928) 718834 ext 253 E: michael.gilbertson@chester.anglican.org

GILCHRIST, Mrs Alison Roxanne. b 62. Dur Univ BA 05. Cranmer Hall Dur 02. **d** 04 **p** 05. C Preston St Cuth *Blackb* 04-06; C Fulwood Ch Ch 06-08; TV Marfleet *York* 08-12; V Bassendean and Dioc Evang Enabler Perth Australia from 12. *Address temp unknown* E: twiggy256@twiggy256.karoo.co.uk

GILCHRIST, David John. b 51. Mert Coll Ox BA 75 MA 79 Maryvale Inst PGCE 08. St Jo Coll Nottm. **d** 79 **p** 80. C Gt Ilford St Andr *Chelmsf* 79-81; C Buckhurst Hill 81-84; Chapl Dover Coll 84-95; Chapl Brentwood Sch 95-12;

rtd 12. *18B The Granville, Hotel Road, St Margarets Bay, Dover CT15 6DX* T: (01304) 851805 E: djgilx@btinternet.com

GILCHRIST, Gavin Frank. b 53. AKC 74. Coll of Resurr Mirfield 76. **d** 77 **p** 78. C Newbold w Dunston *Derby* 77-80; C Addlestone *Guildf* 80-84; V Blackpool St Mary *Blackb* 84-92; P-in-c Carl St Herbert w St Steph 92-97; V 97-01; V Tynemouth Cullercoats St Paul *Newc* from 01. *The Vicarage, 53 Grosvenor Drive, Whitley Bay NE26 2JR* T/F: 0191-252 4916 E: gg002l7513@blueyonder.co.uk

GILCHRIST, Lawrence Edward. b 29. Liv Univ BSc 52. NW Ord Course 74. **d** 76 **p** 77. NSM Buxton w Burbage and King Sterndale *Derby* 76-83; V Chinley w Buxworth 83-94; rtd 94; PtO *St E* 94-03. *9 Santingley Lane, New Crofton, Wakefield WF4 1LG* T: (01924) 860262

GILDAY, Patrick Edward. b 84. Jes Coll Ox BA 05 MSt 07 DPhil 12 LRSM 02. Wycliffe Hall Ox BA 13. **d** 14 **p** 15. C Ascot Heath *Ox* from 14. *The Parsonage, King Edward's Road, Ascot SL5 8PD* T: (01344) 890198 E: patrick.gilday@all-saints-ascot.org

GILDERSLEVE, Paul. b 43. Lon Univ BD. Ridley Hall Cam. **d** 06 **p** 07. NSM Papworth *Ely* from 06. *Manor Farm, 14 Alms Hill, Bourn, Cambridge CB23 2SH* T: (01954) 713989 *or* 719318 E: paulg@miscom.co.uk

GILES, Anthony John. b 50. Aston Univ BSc 71 Surrey Univ MSc 78 Homerton Coll Cam PGCE 86 CEng 80 MIET 80. SAOMC 01. **d** 04 **p** 05. NSM Stevenage H Trin *St Alb* 04-09; NSM Norton 09-11; P-in-c High Wych and Gilston w Eastwick 11-15; R from 15; RD Bishop's Stortford from 14. *The Rectory, 1 Dovedale, High Wych, Sawbridgeworth CM21 0DT* T: (01279) 727676 E: anthony.giles@ntlworld.com

GILES, Anthony Richard. b 68. St Jo Coll Nottm MA 00. **d** 01 **p** 02. C Chellaston *Derby* 01-06; P-in-c Epperstone, Gonalston, Oxton and Woodborough *S'well* 06-13; R from 13. *The Vicarage, 12 Lingwood Lane, Woodborough, Nottingham NG14 6DX* T: 0115-965 3727 E: ant.dianne@btopenworld.com

GILES, Brother. *See* SPRENT, Michael Francis

GILES, Edward Alban. b 34. Bps' Coll Cheshunt. **d** 58 **p** 59. C Colne St Bart *Blackb* 58-61; C Warrington St Paul *Liv* 61-63; C Knysna S Africa 63-66; R Eersterus w Silverton 66-70; Chapl HM Pris Camp Hill 70-75; Chapl HM Pris Stafford 75-83; Chapl HM YOI Hollesley Bay Colony 83-94; rtd 94; Sub-Chapl HM Pris Blundeston from 94; PtO *Nor* 94-00; *St E* from 94. *The Hollies, Ferry Farm Drive, Sutton Hoo, Woodbridge IP12 3DR* T: (01394) 387486 E: eag1@onetel.net.uk

GILES, Canon Eric Francis. b 34. Sarum Th Coll 61. **d** 63 **p** 64. C Plympton St Mary *Ex* 63-71; R Dumbleton w Wormington *Glouc* 71-77; P-in-c Toddington w Stanley Pontlarge 71-77; R Dumbleton w Wormington and Toddington 77-79; V Churchdown St Jo 79-99; Hon Can Glouc Cathl 95-99; rtd 99; PtO *Glouc* from 99; *Worc* from 99. *34 Centre Quay, Port Marina, Portishead BS20 7AX* T: (01275) 217851

GILES, Gordon John. b 66. Lanc Univ BA 88 Magd Coll Cam BA 95 MLitt 95 Middx Univ PhD 13. Ridley Hall Cam 92. **d** 95 **p** 96. C Chesterton Gd Shep *Ely* 95-98; Min Can and Succ St Paul's Cathl 98-03; V Enfield Chase St Mary from 03; Dir Post-Ord Tr Edmonton Area from 08. *St Mary Magdalene Vicarage, 30 The Ridgeway, Enfield EN2 8QH* T: (020) 8363 1875 E: gordongiles@me.com

GILES, Graeme John. b 56. Linc Th Coll 82. **d** 85 **p** 86. C Prestbury *Glouc* 85-88; C Paulsgrove *Portsm* 88-96; V Friern Barnet St Pet le Poer *Lon* 96-04. *30A Vine Road, East Molesey KT8 9LF* M: 07981-708606 E: graeme@priest.com

GILES (née WILLIAMS), Mrs Gwenllian. b 34. RSCN 55 SRN 58 SCM 60. WMMTC 88. **d** 92 **p** 94. NSM Bromsgrove St Jo *Worc* 92-00; PtO 00-03; *Ex* from 06; P-in-c Clifton-on-Teme, Lower Sapey and the Shelsleys *Worc* 03-04. *4 Tidal View Close, Fore Street, Aveton Gifford, Kingsbridge TQ7 4LT* T: (01548) 559164

GILES, Canon John Robert. b 36. Em Coll Cam BA 60 MA 65. Ripon Hall Ox 60. **d** 61 **p** 62. C Lowestoft St Marg *Nor* 61-65; Chapl UEA 65-72; R Kidbrooke St Jas *S'wark* 72-79; Sub-Dean Greenwich 74-79; V Sheff St Mark Broomhall 79-87; Ind Chapl 79-92; Can Res Sheff Cathl 87-92; V Lee Gd Shep w St Pet *S'wark* 92-98; rtd 98; PtO *St E* from 99. *25 The Terrace, Aldeburgh IP15 5HJ* T: (01728) 452319

GILES, Kevin Norman. b 40. Lon Univ BD 69 Dur Univ MA 74. ACT ThL 67 MTh 78 ThD 90. **d** 68 **p** 69. C Mosman St Clem Australia 68-69; C Wollongong 69; Chapl Wollongong Univ Coll 70-72; TV Chester le Street *Dur* 73-74; Chapl Tubingen Univ W Germany 75; Chapl Armidale Univ Australia 75-80; R Kensington 81-95; I Carlton N from 96. *44 Arnold Street, North Carlton Vic 3054, Australia* T: (0061) (3) 9387 7214 *or* 9380 6387 F: 9388 9050 E: giles@melbpc.org.au

GILES, Mrs Penelope Sylvia. b 66. SEITE 08. **d** 11 **p** 12. NSM Angmering *Chich* from 11. *4 The Chantrelles, Angmering, Littlehampton BN16 4GR* T: (01903) 770567 M: 07717-152205 E: p.giles2@sky.com

GILES, Peter Michael Osmaston. b 40. Solicitor 65. S Dios Minl Tr Scheme 85. **d** 88 **p** 89. Hon C Wootton Bassett *Sarum* 88-90; Lic to RD Calne from 91; RD Calne 98-03; Chapl St Mary's Sch Calne from 00. *The Old Vicarage, Honeyhill, Royal Wootton Bassett, Swindon SN4 7DY* T: (01793) 852643 F: 853191 E: gilesoldvic@talk21.com

GILES, The Very Revd Richard Stephen. b 40. Newc Univ BA 63 MLitt 88 MRTPI 71. Cuddesdon Coll 64. **d** 65 **p** 66. C Higham Ferrers w Chelveston *Pet* 65-68; PtO *Ox* 69; C Oakengates *Lich* 70; C Stevenage St Geo *St Alb* 71-75; P-in-c Howdon Panns *Newc* 75-76; TV Willington 76-79; Bp's Adv for Planning *Pet* 79-87; V Pet St Jude 79-87; Par Development Officer *Wakef* 87-99; P-in-c Huddersfield St Thos 87-93; V 93-99; Hon Can Wakef Cathl 94-99; Can Th Wakef Cathl 98-99; Dean Philadelphia USA 99-08; rtd 08; PtO *Newc* from 09. *5 Lovaine Row, North Shields NE30 4HF* T: 0191-258 7621 E: tynegiles@talktalk.net

GILES, Sarah Jayne. *See* MORRIS, Sarah Jayne

GILES, Susan Jane. b 58. BSc. dss 83 **d** 92 **p** 94. Balsall Heath St Paul *Birm* 83-85; Asst Chapl Southmead Hosp Bris 86-90; Asst Chapl HM Rem Cen Pucklechurch 90-96; Asst Chapl HM Pris Bris 92-98; Chapl HM Pris Shepton Mallet 98-01; P-in-c Stockton H Trin *Dur* 01-09; P-in-c Stockton H Trin w St Mark 09-12; Chapl Ian Ramsey Sch Stockton 01-09; V Anglesey Gp *Ely* from 12. *The Vicarage, 86 High Street, Bottisham, Cambridge CB5 9BA* T: (01223) 812726 E: suethevic@btinternet.com

GILES, Canon Timothy David. b 46. FCA 69. Oak Hill Th Coll 88. **d** 90 **p** 91. C Ipswich St Marg *St E* 90-94; C Reigate St Mary *S'wark* 94-99; P-in-c W Wickham St Jo 99-03; V 03-10; rtd 10; Hon Can Offa Nigeria from 06. *Lea Cottage, Hillhead Road, Kergilliack, Falmouth TR11 5PA* T: (01326) 377094 E: timgiles04@googlemail.com

GILKES, Donald Martin. b 47. St Jo Coll Nottm 78. **d** 80 **p** 81. C Conisbrough *Sheff* 80-84; P-in-c Balne 84-86; P-in-c Hensall 84-86; TV Gt Snaith 86-88; V Whittle-le-Woods *Blackb* 88-02; V Normanton *Wakef* 02-12; rtd 12. *35 Tradescant Drive, Meopham, Gravesend DA13 0EL* E: don.gilkes1@gmail.com

GILKS, Peter Martin. b 51. Nottm Univ BMus 72 SRN 77. Ripon Coll Cuddesdon 82. **d** 84 **p** 85. C Bitterne Park *Win* 84-87; TV Basingstoke 87-93; R Abbotts Ann and Upper and Goodworth Clatford 93-98; V Boyatt Wood 98-06; V Chilworth w N Baddesley 06-10; P-in-c Ampfield 08-10; V Ampfield, Chilworth and N Baddesley 10-15; TR Portway and Danebury from 15. *The Vicarage, 17 Millway Road, Andover SP10 3EU* T: (01264) 335245 E: peter.gilks@ntlworld.com

GILL, Canon Alan Gordon. b 42. Sarum & Wells Th Coll 73. **d** 75 **p** 76. C Wimborne Minster *Sarum* 75-78; R Winterbourne Stickland and Turnworth etc 78-86; V Verwood 86-00; TR Gillingham 00-04; V Gillingham and Milton-on-Stour 04-08; Can and Preb Sarum Cathl 99-08; rtd 09; PtO *Sarum* from 09. *1 Cheshire Close, Salisbury SP2 9JT* T: (01722) 325239 E: erznmine@houseofgill.org

GILL, Alec John. b 79. Trin Coll Bris 11. **d** 13 **p** 14. C Thatcham *Ox* from 13. *47A Station Road, Thatcham RG19 4PU* E: revalec@hotmail.co.uk

GILL, Mrs Carol Ann. b 42. Lady Mabel Coll TCert 71. NOC 96. **d** 99 **p** 00. NSM Hanging Heaton *Wakef* 99-07; P-in-c 02-07; rtd 07; PtO *Leeds* from 08. *6 Queen's Crescent, Ossett WF5 8AU* T: (01924) 276820 M: 07946-038562 E: rev@cgill2.fsnet.co.uk

GILL, Christopher John Sutherland. b 28. Selw Coll Cam BA 52 MA 70. Ely Th Coll 52. **d** 54 **p** 55. C Portslade St Nic *Chich* 54-58; C Goring-by-Sea 58-60; Chapl St Edm Sch Cant 60-76; Chapl Bennett Memorial Dioc Sch Tunbridge Wells 76-92; Hon C Tunbridge Wells K Chas *Roch* 77-93; rtd 93; PtO *Roch* from 93. *Flat 1, Hurstleigh, Hurstwood Lane, Tunbridge Wells TN4 8YA* T: (01892) 528409

GILL, Daud. b 66. Punjab Univ BA 90. St Jo Coll Nottm 13. **d** 15. C Levenshulme *Man* from 15. *The Rectory, 27 Errwood Road, Manchester M19 2PN* M: 07513-913756 T: 0161-224 5877 E: daudgill@hotmail.co.uk

GILL, David Alan. b 64. Coll of Resurr Mirfield 98. **d** 00 **p** 01. C Devizes St Jo w St Mary *Sarum* 00-04; P-in-c Brockworth *Glouc* 04-10; V 10-11; P-in-c Abenhall w Mitcheldean from 11; C Westbury-on-Severn w Flaxley, Blaisdon etc from 11; C Huntley and Longhope, Churcham and Bulley from 12. *The Rectory, Hawkers Hill, Mitcheldean GL17 0BS* T: (01594) 542952 E: dgill@houseofgill.org

GILL, David Brian Michael. b 55. Southn Univ BTh 88. Sarum & Wells Th Coll 83. **d** 86 **p** 87. C Honiton, Gittisham, Combe Raleigh, Monkton etc *Ex* 86-89; C Teignmouth, Ideford w Luton, Ashcombe etc 89-91; TV Ex St Thos and Em 91-05; RD Christianity 03-05; P-in-c Tamerton Foliot from 05; C Southway from 06; RD Plymouth Moorside from 09. *The Vicarage, 53 Whitson Cross Lane, Tamerton Foliot, Plymouth PL5 4NT* T: (01752) 771033 E: david@dbmg.freeserve.co.uk

GILL, Mrs Gabrielle Mary (Gay). d 90 p 94. NSM Timperley *Ches* 90-96; rtd 96; PtO *Ches* from 97. *The Croft, 3 Harrop Road, Hale, Altrincham WA15 9BU* T: 0161-928 1800

GILL, Gary George. b 44. Culham Coll Ox CertEd 70. Cant Sch of Min 85. d 87 p 88. C Addlestone *Guildf* 87-90; C Buckland in Dover w Buckland Valley *Cant* 90-98; Chapl Buckland Hosp Dover 90-94; Chapl S Kent Hosps NHS Trust 94-98; C Birchington w Acol and Minnis Bay *Cant* 98-99; rtd 04. *9 Tooting Bec Road, London SW17 8BS* T: (020) 8672 2179

GILL, Miss Helen Barbara. b 61. K Alfred's Coll Win BEd 87. Cranmer Hall Dur. d 99 p 00. C Newc St Gabr 99-04; P-in-c Tynemouth St Jo from 04. *St John's Vicarage, St John's Terrace, Percy Main, North Shields NE29 6HS* T: 0191-257 1819 E: helen@gill1999.freeserve.co.uk

GILL, Michael John. b 59. K Coll Lon BA 81 AKC 81 Univ of Wales (Cardiff) BD 85. St Mich Coll Llan 82. d 85 p 86. Min Can St Woolos Cathl 85-90; Chapl St Woolos Hosp Newport 87-90; Succ Heref Cathl and C Heref St Jo 90-93; TV Ebbw Vale *Mon* 93-96; V Tonypandy w Clydach Vale *Llan* 96-09; R Cranford *Lon* from 09. *The Rectory, 34 High Street, Cranford, Hounslow TW5 9RG* T: (020) 8897 8836

GILL, Paul Joseph. b 45. Melbourne Coll of Div MMin 07. Ridley Coll Melbourne 73. d 74 p 74. C Applecross Australia 74-76; C Birm St Martin 77-79; V Pype Hayes 79-89; PtO Perth Australia 89-93; R Perth St Paul 93-00; Sen Chapl HM Min of Justice 00-10; rtd 10; Hon C Heref S Wye 11-13; PtO from 13. *7 Camelot Close, Hereford HR4 9XH* M: 07765-660418 E: pandagill@talktalk.net

GILL, Peter Stephen. b 48. FCA 79. d 09 p 10. OLM Exning St Martin w Landwade *St E* 09-13; NSM from 13. *11 Isinglass Close, Newmarket CB8 8HX* T: (01638) 660335 M: 07762-608031 E: petergill861@btinternet.com

GILL, Canon Robin Morton. b 44. K Coll Lon BD 66 AKC 66 Lon Univ PhD 69 Birm Univ MSocSc 72. d 68 p 69. C Rugby St Andr *Cov* 68-71; Papua New Guinea 71-72; Lect Th Edin Univ 72-86; Sen Lect 86-88; Assoc Dean Faculty of Div 85-88; P-in-c Edin SS Phil and Jas 73-75; P-in-c Ford *Newc* 75-87; P-in-c Coldstream *Edin* 87-92; Wm Leech Prof Applied Th Newc Univ 88-92; Mich Ramsey Prof Modern Th Kent Univ 92-11; Prof Th from 11; Hon Prov Can Cant Cathl from 92; AD N Downs 02-09; P-in-c Hollingbourne and Hucking w Leeds and Broomfield 03-11; Hon C 11-14; PtO from 14; Can Th *Eur* from 12. *2 Copse End, Hadley Gardens, Hollingbourne, Maidstone ME17 1UF* T: (01622) 884120 E: r.gill@kent.ac.uk

GILL, Mrs Ruth Montcrieff. b 48. CITC 01. d 04 p 05. NSM Cloughjordan w Borrisokane etc *L & K* 04-06; NSM Birr w Lorrha, Dorrha and Lockeen from 06. *Kilgolan House, Kilcormac, Birr, Co Offaly, Republic of Ireland* T: (00353) (57) 913 5341 M: 87-948 4402 E: ruth_gill40@hotmail.com

GILL, Miss Sandra Julie. b 67. N Riding Coll of Educn BEd 90 Rolle Coll MEd 01 Ex Univ BTh 08. SWMTC 03. d 06 p 07. NSM Kingsteignton and Teigngrace *Ex* from 06. *58 Furze Cap, Kingsteignton, Newton Abbot TQ12 3TF* T: (01626) 355287

GILL, Miss Sarah Siddique. b 77. Punjab Univ BA 96 MA 01. Qu Coll Birm 08. d 11 p 12. C Shipley St Paul *Leeds* 11-15; C-in-c Bishop Auckland Woodhouse Close CD *Dur* from 15. *18 Watling Road, Bishop Auckland DL14 6RP* M: 07584-498390 E: sarah_siddique_gill@yahoo.co.uk

GILL, Simon David. b 66. Southn Univ BSc 87 PhD 91. St Jo Coll Nottm BTh 00. d 01 p 02. C Frinton *Chelmsf* 01-05; P-in-c Sudbury w Ballingdon and Brundon *St E* from 05. *5 Clermont Avenue, Sudbury CO10 1ZJ* T: (01787) 375334 E: sallie.simon@tinyworld.co.uk

GILL, Stanley. b 34. Sarum Th Coll 66. d 68 p 69. C Ipswich St Mary at Stoke w St Pet etc *St E* 68-73 and 78-80; TV 80-82; V Bury St Edmunds St Geo 73-78; P-in-c Childe Okeford, Manston, Hammoon and Hanford *Sarum* 82-89; R The Lulworths, Winfrith Newburgh and Chaldon 89-94; R Hazelbury Bryan and the Hillside Par 94-99; rtd 99; PtO *Ex* 99-02; *Sarum* 00-02; *York* from 11. *Abbeyfield Society, White Lodge, 36 Holbeck Hill, Scarborough YO11 3BJ* T: (01723) 500702

GILL, Timothy Charles. b 66. Newc Univ BA 88 Jes Coll Cam MPhil 93 Leeds Univ PhD 08. Westcott Ho Cam 89. d 92 p 93. C N Hull St Mich *York* 92-96; P-in-c Sculcoates St Paul w Ch Ch and St Silas 96-98; P-in-c Hull St Mary Sculcoates 96-98; V York St Luke 98-02; R Adel *Ripon* 02-08; V Roby *Liv* from 08. *The Vicarage, 11 Church Road, Roby, Liverpool L36 9TL* T: 0151-489 1438 E: ttimgill@aol.com

GILL, Wilson Ernest. b 55. SAOMC. d 05 p 06. C Walton H Trin *Ox* 05-09; V Southall Em *Lon* from 09. *37 Dormers Wells Lane, Southall UB1 3HX* T: (020) 8843 9556 E: wilsongill37@gmail.com *or* vicar.ecs@googlemail.com

GILLARD, David John. b 66. Ridley Hall Cam 96. d 98 p 99. C Seaford w Sutton *Chich* 98-02; P-in-c Eastbourne St Elisabeth 02-06; V from 06. *The Vicarage, 11 Baldwin Avenue, Eastbourne BN21 1UJ* T: (01323) 649728 E: djgillard@tiscali.co.uk

GILLARD-FAULKNER, Mrs Sarah Kate. b 80. Coll of Ripon & York St Jo BA 01 Glos Univ PGCE 02. St Mich Coll Llan BTh 06. d 09. C Abertillery w Cwmtillery *Mon* 09-10; C Abertillery w Cwmtillery w Llanhilleth etc 10-12; PtO *Llan* 13-14; Dn and Sub-Prior Abergavenny St Mary w Llanwenarth Citra *Mon* from 14; Bp's Chapl from 14. *Holy Trinity Vicarage, Baker Street, Abergavenny NP7 5BH* M: 07900-393358 T: (01873) 855889 E: sarah_gillard@hotmail.com

GILLESPIE, Canon David Ivan. b 68. TCD BTh 01. CITC 98. d 01 p 02. C Agherton *Conn* 01-04; I Moy w Charlemont *Arm* 04-09; I Dublin St Ann and St Steph *D & G* from 09; Can Ch Ch Cathl Dublin from 14. *88 Mount Anville Wood, Lower Kilmacud Road, Dublin 14, Republic of Ireland* T: (00353) (1) 288 0663 M: 86-026 7528 *or* 676 7727 E: digillespie@eircom.net

GILLESPIE, Michael David. b 41. EMMTC 86. d 89 p 90. NSM Countesthorpe w Foston *Leic* from 89. *3 Penfold Drive, Countesthorpe, Leicester LE8 3TP* T: 0116-278 1130 E: mick.gillespie@btinternet.com

GILLESPIE, Canon Nancy Gillian. b 41. TCD MA 68. d 97 p 98. Bp's V and Lib Kilkenny Cathl and C Kilkenny w Aghour and Kilmanagh *C & O* 97-00; I Stradbally w Ballintubbert, Coraclone etc 00-09; P-in-c Maryborough w Dysart Enos and Ballyfin 02-03; Can Ossory Cathl 06-09; rtd 09; C Carlow w Urglin and Staplestown *C & O* 10-11. *1 Fisherman's Lock, Leighlinbridge, Co Carlow, Republic of Ireland* T: (00353) (59) 972 2643 M: 87-232 2574 E: ngilles@iol.ie

GILLETT, Brian Alan Michael. b 42. MRICS 73. Chich Th Coll. d 82 p 83. C Tupsley *Heref* 82-86; R Kingstone w Clehonger, Eaton Bishop etc 86-97; V Baltonsborough w Butleigh, W Bradley etc *B & W* 97-09; Warden of Readers Wells Adnry 00-02; rtd 09; PtO *Bris* from 09. *1 Barn Close, Somerton TA11 6PH* T: (01458) 272738 E: gillett546@btinternet.com

✠**GILLETT, The Rt Revd David Keith.** b 45. Leeds Univ BA 65 MPhil 68. Oak Hill Th Coll 66. d 68 p 69 c 99. C Watford St Luke *St Alb* 68-71; Sec Pathfinders and CYFA N Area 71-74; Lect St Jo Coll Nottm 74-79; Ch of Ireland Renewal Cen 80-82; V Luton Lewsey St Hugh *St Alb* 82-88; Prin Trin Coll Bris 88-99; Hon Can Bris Cathl 91-99; Suff Bp Bolton *Man* 99-08; rtd 08; Hon Asst Bp Nor from 08; Dioc Interfaith Adv from 10. *10 Burton Close, Diss IP22 4YJ* T: (01379) 640309 E: dkgillett@btinternet.com

GILLEY, Margaret Mary. b 54. St Andr Univ MTheol 76 Dur Univ PhD 97. NEOC 97. d 00 p 01. C Birtley *Dur* 00-03; P-in-c Stockton St Mark 03; V 03-09; V Elton 03-09; Assoc P Lanchester Deanery 09-11; V Bensham and Teams from 11. *St Chad's Vicarage, Dunsmuir Grove, Gateshead NE8 4QL* T: 0191-478 6338 E: meg.gilley@durham.anglican.org

GILLHAM, Catherine Anne. b 73. Southn Univ BN 95. Trin Coll Bris BA 09. d 09 p 10. C Kempshott *Win* 09-13; CF from 13. *c/o MOD Chaplains (Army)* T: (01264) 383430 F: 381824 M: 07873-525602 E: catgillham@hotmail.com

GILLHAM, Martin John. b 45. Wilson Carlile Coll IDC 66 Qu Coll Birm 72. d 75 p 76. C Whitley Ch Ch *Ox* 75-78; TV Crowmarsh Gifford w Newnham Murren 78-79; TV Wallingford w Crowmarsh Gifford etc 79-83; V Kintbury w Avington 83-94; Dioc Lay Min Adv and Warden of Readers 89-97; P-in-c W Wycombe w Bledlow Ridge, Bradenham and Radnage 94-00; R 00; Prov Chapl Third Order SSF 95-99; P-in-c Norham and Duddo *Newc* 04-09; P-in-c Cornhill w Carham 00-09; P-in-c Branxton 00-09; AD Norham 05-09; rtd 09; PtO *Newc* 10-13; P-in-c Shilbottle from 13. *The Vicarage, Middle Road, Shilbottle, Alnwick NE66 2XS* T: (01665) 575855 E: martingillham@btinternet.com

GILLHAM, Mrs Patricia Anne. b 40. Wilson Carlile Coll IDC 66 Ox Min Course 90. d 93 p 94. Par Dn Kintbury w Avington *Ox* 93-94; C 94-95; C W Wycombe w Bledlow Ridge, Bradenham and Radnage 95-00; rtd 00; PtO *Newc* from 00. *The Vicarage, Middle Road, Shilbottle, Alnwick NE66 2XS* T: (01665) 575855

GILLIAN, Ronald Trevor. b 57. Ulster Univ MTD 78 QUB BEd 89 TCD BTh 93. CITC 90. d 93 p 94. C Belfast St Donard *D & D* 93-96; I Aghalurcher w Tattykeeran, Cooneen etc *Clogh* 96-11; Dir of Ords 04-11; Preb Donaghmore St Patr Cathl Dublin 05-11. *18 Garlaw Road, Clogher BT76 0TN* T: (028) 8554 8547 M: 07977-157637 E: colebrooke_clogher@hotmail.com

GILLIBRAND, John Nigel. b 60. Ox Univ BA 82 MA 86 Lon Univ PGCE 83. St Steph Ho Ox BTh 87. d 88 p 89. C Dolgellau w Llanfachreth and Brithdir etc *Ban* 88-90; C Llanbeblig w Caernarfon and Betws Garmon etc 90-91; R Ffestiniog w Blaenau Ffestiniog 91-97; V Llandegfan w Llandysilio 97-02; Nat Co-ord (Wales) Nat Autistic Soc 02-04; P-in-c Llangeler w Pen-Boyr *St D* 04-10; V from 10. *The Vicarage, Llangeler, Llandysul SA44 5EX* T: (01559) 371170

GILLIBRAND, Margaret Ann Jane. b 43. d 01 p 02. OLM Deal St Leon and St Rich and Sholden *Cant* 01-04; PtO *Eur* 04-07; Asst Chapl Poitou-Charentes 07-09; NSM Whitstable *Cant* 11-13; rtd 13. *128 Devonshire Road, Chorley PR7 2DJ* E: cornerstone161@yahoo.co.uk

GILLIES, Mrs Jennifer Susan. b 63. Westmr Coll Ox BEd 85. SNWTP 07. d 10 p 11. C Bidston *Ches* 10-13; R Bromborough from 13. *The Rectory, Mark Rake, Wirral CH62 2DH* E: revjennygillies@gmail.com

✠**GILLIES, The Rt Revd Robert Arthur.** b 51. Edin Univ BD 77 St Andr Univ PhD 91. Edin Th Coll 73. d 77 p 78 c 07. C Falkirk *Edin* 77-80; C Edin Ch St 80-84; Chapl Napier Tech Coll 80-84; Chapl Dundee Univ *Bre* 84-90; R St Andrews St Andr *St And* 91-07; Dioc Dir of Ords 96-07; Can St Ninian's Cathl Perth 97-07; Dean St Andr 07; Bp Ab from 07. *Diocesan Office, St Clement's Church House, Mastrick Drive, Aberdeen AB16 6UF* T: (01224) 662247 F: 662168 E: bishop@aberdeen.anglican.org

GILLIES, Miss Sheila Jennifer. b 52. St Martin's Coll Lanc TCert 71. d 06 p 07. OLM Childwall All SS *Liv* from 06. *190 Thomas Drive, Liverpool L14 3LE* T: 0151-228 4304

GILLINGHAM, Canon John Bruce. b 48. Ch Ch Ox BA 69 MA 74. St Jo Coll Nottm BA 73. d 73 p 74. C Plymouth St Andr w St Paul and St Geo *Ex* 73-77; C Ox St Aldate w H Trin 78; Chapl Jes Coll Ox 78-88; Chapl Ox Pastorate 79-88; Dioc Missr *Birm* 88-92; R Ox St Clem 92-14; AD Cowley 07-14; Hon Can Ch Ch 12-14; rtd 14; PtO *Ox* from 15. *58 Church Street, Kidlington OX5 2BB*

GILLINGHAM, Michael John. b 46. Hull Univ MA 90. Chich Th Coll 68. d 71 p 72. C Llanharan w Peterston-super-Montem *Llan* 71-73; C Skewen 73-76; PtO 79-80; TV Kirkby *Liv* 76-77; Youth Chapl Woodchurch *Ches* 77-79; Sen Youth Worker (Bedfordshire) *St Alb* 80-83; PtO 80-83; TV Sheff Manor 83-88; R Frecheville from 88; Chapl RNR 90-92; Chapl S Yorks Police *Sheff* from 93. *Frecheville Rectory, Brackenfield Grove, Sheffield S12 4XS* T: 0114-239 9555 M: 07764-606456 E: mgillingham@talktalk.net

GILLINGHAM, Mrs Stephanie Ruth. b 60. W Lon Inst of HE CertEd 82 Open Univ BA 86 Man Univ MEd 06. NTMTC BA 09. d 09 p 10. C Galleywood Common *Chelmsf* from 09; P-in-c Widford from 13; C Moulsham St Jo from 13; C Moulsham St Luke from 13. *Widford Rectory, 3 Canuden Road, Chelmsford CM1 2SU* T: (01245) 477818 E: stephaniegillingham@hotmail.co.uk

GILLINGS, The Ven Richard John. b 45. St Chad's Coll Dur BA 67. Linc Th Coll 68. d 70 p 71. C Altrincham St Geo *Ches* 70-75; P-in-c Stockport St Thos 75-77; R 77-83; P-in-c Stockport St Pet 78-83; TR Birkenhead Priory 83-93; V Bramhall 93-05; RD Birkenhead 85-93; Hon Can Ches Cathl 92-94; Adn Macclesfield 94-10; rtd 11; PtO *Ches* from 11; Hon C Rothiemurchus *Mor* from 11; Hon C Grantown-on-Spey from 11. *Culvardie, Deshar Road, Boat of Garten PH24 3BN* T: (01479) 831365 E: richard.gillngs698@btinternet.com

GILLINGS, Mrs Ruth Elizabeth. b 63. d 12 p 15. NSM Atworth w Shaw and Whitley *Sarum* from 12. *31 Westlands Lane, Beanacre, Melksham SN12 7QE* T: (01225) 700278 E: ruthgillings@sky.com

✠**GILLION, The Rt Revd Alan Robert.** b 51. LRAM. Sarum & Wells Th Coll 81. d 83 p 84 c 14. C E Dereham *Nor* 83-86; C Richmond St Mary w St Matthias and St Jo *S'wark* 86-90; P-in-c Discovery Bay Ch Hong Kong 90-98; Chapl Shek Pik Pris 90-98; Bp Kensington's Officer for Evang *Lon* 98-01; P-in-c Upper Chelsea St Sav and St Simon 01-02; V 02-08; R Upper Chelsea H Trin 08-11; R Upper Chelsea H Trin and St Sav 11-14; AD Chelsea 04-11; Bp Riverina Australia from 14. *Linton Lodge, 58 Arthur Street, Narrandera 2700 NSW, Australia* T: (0061) (2) 6959 1648 F: 6959 2903 E: rivdio@bigpond.com

GILLIONS, Michael George. b 37. Ch Ch Ox MA 65 Keele Univ PGCE 74. WEMTC 93. d 96 p 97. NSM Dorrington w Leebotwood, Longnor, Stapleton etc *Heref* 96-00; NSM Condover w Frodesley, Acton Burnell etc from 00; PtO *Lich* from 14. *The Maltsters, Dorrington, Shrewsbury SY5 7JD* T: (01743) 718550

GILLON, Patrick. b 51. WMMTC 05. d 08 p 09. NSM Kingstanding St Mark *Birm* 08-11; PtO *Lich* 11-14; NSM Small Heath *Birm* 12-13; Chapl HM Pris Birm from 13. *HM Prison Birmingham, Winson Green Road, Birmingham B18 4AS* T: 0121-598 8000 M: 07792-635831 E: frpatrickgillon@yahoo.co.uk

GILLUM, Thomas Alan. b 55. Ex Univ BSc 76. Cranmer Hall Dur 87. d 89 p 90. C Brompton H Trin w Onslow Square St Paul *Lon* 89-94; P-in-c Paddington St Steph w St Luke 94-04; P-in-c S Kensington St Jude 04-06; Warden Community of St Jude 06-11; P-in-c Isleworth St Jo 11-12; V 12-14; V Isleworth St Jo w St Mary from 15. *The New Vicarage, St John's Road, Isleworth TW7 6NY* T: (020) 8560 2881

GILMARTIN, Frances. *See* CLARKE, Frances

GILMORE, Canon Henry. b 51. Man Univ BA 72 TCD BD 82. CITC 75. d 75 p 76. C Arm St Mark w Aghavilly 75-78; C Dublin St Patr Cathl Gp 78-81; I Stranorlar w Meenglas and Kilteevogue *D & R* 81-84; I Achill w Dugort, Castlebar and Turlough *T, K & A* 84-90; I Moville w Greencastle, Donagh, Cloncha etc *D & R* 91-11; I Tullyaughnish w Kilmacrennan and Killygarvan from 11; Can Raphoe Cathl from 01. *The Rectory, Ramelton, Letterkenny, Co Donegal, Republic of Ireland* T: (00353) (74) 915 1013 E: tkkgparishes@hotmail.com

GILMOUR, Ian Hedley. b 57. Ex Univ LLB Lon Univ BD. Wycliffe Hall Ox 80. d 83 p 84. C Harold Wood *Chelmsf* 83-86; C Thame w Towersey Ox 86-91; V Streatham Vale H Redeemer *S'wark* from 91. *The Vicarage, Churchmore Road, London SW16 5UZ*

GILPIN, Canon Richard John. b 45. Lon Univ BSc 66. Wells Th Coll 67. d 70 p 71. C Davyhulme Ch Ch *Man* 70-74; Pastor Gustav Adolf Berlin EKD 74-77; R Heaton Norris Ch w All SS *Man* 77-83; R Chorlton-cum-Hardy St Clem 83-99; AD Hulme 95-99; V Norley, Crowton and Kingsley *Ches* 99-07; RD Frodsham 03-06; Hon Can Ches Cathl 04-06; rtd 07; PtO *Ches* from 08. *4 Smithy Close, Shocklach, Malpas SY14 7BX* T: (01829) 250413 E: richard.gilpin21@btinternet.com

GILPIN, The Ven Richard Thomas. b 39. Lich Th Coll 60. d 63 p 64. C Whipton *Ex* 63-66; C Tavistock and Gulworthy 66-69; V 73-91; V Swimbridge 69-73; Preb Ex Cathl from 82; RD Tavistock 87-90; Dioc Dir of Ords 90-91; Adv for Voc and Dioc Dir of Ords 91-96; Sub Dean Ex Cathl 92-96; Adn Totnes 96-05; rtd 05. *7 The Strand, Shaldon, Teignmouth TQ14 0DL* T: (01626) 873443 E: richard.gilpin2@btinternet.com

GILROY, Peter William. b 62. Univ of Wales (Ban) MTh 09. Ridley Hall Cam 09. d 11 p 12. C Stapleford *S'well* 11-14; TV Eccleston *Liv* from 14. *St Luke's Vicarage, 31 Mulberry Avenue, St Helens WA10 4DE* E: peterwgilroy@gmail.com

GIMPEL, Gerardo. Catholic Univ of Chile BSc BEng Cen of Public Studies BTh. d 12. C Knockbreda *D & D* from 12. *28 Church Road, Newtownbreda, Belfast BT8 7AQ* T: (028) 9069 4217 E: gerardo.gimpel@gmail.com

GIMSON, Francis Herbert. b 54. Reading Univ BSc 79. St Jo Coll Nottm 83. d 86 p 87. C Menston w Woodhead *Bradf* 86-89; C Barnoldswick w Bracewell 89-91; V Langleybury St Paul *St Alb* 91-02; P-in-c Downton *Sarum* 02-06; P-in-c Redlynch and Morgan's Vale 04-06; TR Forest and Avon from 06. *The Vicarage, Barford Lane, Downton, Salisbury SP5 3QA* T: (01725) 510326 E: fhg@jf1990.co.uk

GINEVER, Paul Michael John. b 49. AKC 71. d 72 p 73. C Davyhulme Ch Ch *Man* 72-75; Australia 76-77; C Tettenhall Wood *Lich* 77-80; C Halesowen *Worc* 80; TV 80-86; P-in-c Gt Malvern Ch Ch 86-98; V S Hayling *Portsm* 98-14; rtd 14. *Address temp unknown*

GINGELL, Mrs Diane. b 56. d 12 p 13. NSM Sturminster Newton, Hinton St Mary and Lydlinch *Sarum* 12-15; NSM Hazelbury Bryan and the Hillside Par from 15. *Meadow View, Wonston, Hazelbury Bryan, Sturminster Newton DT10 2EE* E: diane.gingell@googlemail.com

GINGELL, John Lawrence. b 27. Lon Univ BD 55. ALCD 55. d 55 p 56. C Normanton *Derby* 55-58; C Ilkeston St Bart CD 58-61; Toc H Staff Padre 61-70; Asst Chapl S Lon Ind Miss 61-64; LtO *S'wark* 61-66; *Liv* 67-70; V Somercotes *Derby* 70-72; Bp's Ind Adv 72-80; rtd 92. *18 Bournville Road, London SE6 4RN* T: (020) 8690 0148

GINGRICH, Dale Robert. b 64. Midland Lutheran Coll (USA) BSc 86 Lutheran Th Sem Gettysburg MDiv 93. EAMTC 03. d 04 p 05. NSM Shingay Gp *Ely* 04-08; TV Gaywood *Nor* from 08; Dioc Ecum Officer from 09. *Church Bungalow, Gayton Road, Gaywood, King's Lynn PE30 4DZ* T: (01553) 765167 M: 07766-706773 E: dale.gingrich@norwich.anglican.org

GINN, Daniel Vivian. b 33. Univ of Wales (Cardiff) BSc 55 DipEd 56. Llan Dioc Tr Scheme 79. d 82 p 83. NSM Llantwit Major *Llan* 82-02; TV 88-02; RD Llantwit Major and Cowbridge *Llan* 94-02; PtO from 02. *Chenet, 24 Voss Park Drive, Llantwit Major CF61 1YE* T: (01446) 792774

GINN, Canon Richard John. b 51. Lon Univ BD 77 Dur Univ MLitt 05 ACIB 73 Lambeth STh 85. Oak Hill Th Coll 75 Cranmer Hall Dur 77. d 79 p 80. C Hornsey Ch Ch *Lon* 79-82; C Highgate St Mich 82-85; V Westleton w Dunwich *St E* 85-08; V Darsham 85-08; P-in-c Yoxford, Peasenhall and Sibton 01-08; P-in-c Middleton cum Fordley and Theberton w Eastbridge 01-08; V Yoxmere 08-13; Hon Can St E Cathl 01-13; rtd 13. *Wisteria Cottage, The Street, Hacheston, Woodbridge IP13 0DS* E: r.ginn@btinternet.com

GINNELLY, Yvonne Anne. d 11 p 12. NSM Monkstown *D & G* from 11. *Alexandra College, Milltown Road, Milltown, Dublin 6, Republic of Ireland* M: (00353) 87-699 8238 E: ivangin@eircom.net

GINNO, Albert Charles. b 31. CA Tr Coll 51 Lon Coll of Div 66. **d** 68 **p** 69. C Kemp Town St Mark and St Matt *Chich* 68-72; P-in-c E Hoathly 72-83; V Westham 83-96; rtd 96; PtO *Chich* from 96. *106 Sorrel Drive, Eastbourne BN23 8BJ* T: (01323) 761479   F: 768920

GIRARD, Canon William Nicholas Charles. b 35. Coll of Resurr Mirfield 65. **d** 67 **p** 68. C Yate *Glouc* 67-70; C Westbury-on-Trym St Alb *Bris* 70-73; Chapl K Sch Ely 73-76; V Fenstanton and Hilton *Ely* 76-85; R Balsham and Fen w Wickham 85-99; P-in-c Horseheath 85-96; RD Linton 93-94 and 96-99; Hon Can Ely Cathl 97-03; C Alconbury cum Weston 99-00; Hon C 00-03; C Buckworth 99-00; Hon C 00-03; C Gt w Lt Stukeley 99-00; Hon C 00-03; rtd 00; P-in-c Hamerton *Ely* 00-04; RD Leightonstone 00-02; PtO *Pet* from 05; *Ely* from 05. *Ferrar House, Little Gidding, Huntingdon PE28 5RJ* T: (01832) 293083 *or* 293383 E: girar774@btinternet.com

GIRLING, Andrew Martin. b 40. Em Coll Cam BA 63 MA 67. Wycliffe Hall Ox 63. **d** 65 **p** 66. C Luton w E Hyde *St Alb* 65-69; Chapl Hull Univ *York* 69-75; V Dringhouses 75-00; Can and Preb York Minster 97-00; P-in-c Thurlestone w S Milton *Ex* 00-02; R Thurlestone, S Milton, W Alvington etc 02-08; rtd 08. *2 Mead Drive, Thurlestone, Kingsbridge TQ7 3TA* E: sueand@talktalk.net

GIRLING, David Frederick Charles. b 33. Kelham Th Coll 49 Edin Th Coll 58. **d** 61 **p** 62. C Caister *Nor* 61-65; C Leigh St Clem *Chelmsf* 65-66; CF 66-83; V Prittlewell St Luke *Chelmsf* 83-98; rtd 98; PtO *Nor* 98-13. *37 Dell Road East, Lowestoft NR33 9LA* T: (01502) 567426

GIRLING, Ian John. b 53. Oak Hill Th Coll 03. **d** 05 **p** 06. C Hubberston *St D* 05-08; TV Aberystwyth from 08. *Holy Trinity Vicarage, Buarth Road, Aberystwyth SY23 1NB* T: (01970) 617015 E: iangirling@yahoo.co.uk

GIRLING, Stephen Paul. b 61. Southn Univ BSc 83. Trin Coll Bris BA 91. **d** 91 **p** 92. C Ogley Hay *Lich* 91-95; TV S Molton w Nymet St George, High Bray etc *Ex* 95-01; RD S Molton 97-01; V Crofton *Portsm* 01-15; RD Fareham 08-13; Hon Can Portsm Cathl 11-15; C Bath Abbey w St Jas *B & W* from 15. *48 Devonshire Buildings, Bath BA2 4SU* E: spgirling@gmail.com

GIRLING, Canon Timothy Havelock. b 43. St Aid Birkenhead 63. **d** 67 **p** 68. C Wickford *Chelmsf* 67-70; C Luton w E Hyde *St Alb* 70-74; C Luton All SS w St Pet 74-80; Chapl Luton and Dunstable Hosp 74-80; R Northill w Moggerhanger *St Alb* 80-89; Chapl Glenfield Hosp NHS Trust Leic 89-00; Chapl Glenfrith Hosp 89-93; Chapl Univ Hosps Leic NHS Trust 00-04; Hon Can Leic Cathl 97-04; rtd 04; Chapl Leics Partnership NHS Trust from 04; PtO *Pet* 04-08; *Leic* from 04. *36 Winton Avenue, Leicester LE3 1DH* T: 0116-291 3795 M: 07879-418721 E: tgirling@ntlworld.com

GIRTCHEN, John Christopher. b 54. Linc Th Coll 94. **d** 96 **p** 97. C Bourne *Linc* 96-00; V Barrow and Goxhill from 00. *The Vicarage, Thornton Street, Barrow-upon-Humber DN19 7DG* T: (01469) 530357 E: jcgirtchen@lineone.net

GISBOURNE, Michael Andrew. b 65. Leeds Univ BA 87 St Martin's Coll Lanc MA 09. St Jo Coll Nottm BTh 91. **d** 92 **p** 93. C Gateacre *Liv* 92-95; C Marton *Blackb* 95-98; V Freckleton 98-03; V Garstang St Thos 03-10; Chapl Cumbria Univ 10-11; V Scotforth from 11. *St Paul's Vicarage, 24 Scotforth Road, Lancaster LA1 4ST* T: (01524) 32106 E: michael.gisbourne@phonecoop.coop

GISBY, Mrs Vivien Barbara. b 56. Wolv Poly BSc 78 Leeds Univ BA 08. NOC 05. **d** 08 **p** 09. C Sutton St Jas *Ches* 08-14; V Runcorn St Jo Weston from 14; Warden of Past Workers from 11. *St John's Vicarage, 225 Heath Road South, Weston, Runcorn WA7 4LY* T: (01928) 573798 E: vivien.gisby@btinternet.com

GITTINGS, Graham. b 46. Qu Coll Birm 75. **d** 78 **p** 79. C Caverswall *Lich* 78-81; C Wolverhampton St Matt 81-82; C Walthamstow St Mary w St Steph *Chelmsf* 82-83; C Dagenham 83-89; V Earl Shilton w Elmesthorpe *Leic* 89-11; rtd 11; PtO *Leic* from 11; *Lich* from 12. *21 Princetown Close, Stoke-on-Trent ST3 7WN* T: (01782) 388866 M: 07711-46063 E: graham.gittings77@btinternet.com

GITTOES, Canon Julie Anne. b 76. Trevelyan Coll Dur BA 98 Graduate Soc Dur MA 99 Selw Coll Cam PhD 04. Westcott Ho Cam 99. **d** 03 **p** 04. C Hampton Hill *Lon* 03-06; V Hampton All SS 06-12; Can Res Guildf Cathl from 12. *4 Cathedral Close, Guildford GU2 7TL* T: (01483) 566499 M: 07702-151173 E: juliegittoes@googlemail.com

GIVEN, Canon Harold Richard. b 54. Oak Hill Th Coll 75. **d** 78 **p** 79. C Belfast St Clem *D & D* 78-80; C Belfast St Donard 80-83; I Tamlaght O'Crilly Upper w Lower *D & R* 83-92; I Tamlaghtfinlagan w Myroe from 92; Can Derry Cathl from 14. *Finlagan Rectory, 77 Ballykelly Road, Limavady BT49 9DS* T: (028) 7176 2743

GLADSTONE, Canon Robert Michael. b 60. Ch Ch Ox BA 82 MA 86. Wycliffe Hall Ox 92. **d** 94 **p** 95. C Trentham *Lich* 94-97; C Heigham H Trin *Nor* 97-01; V Rothley *Leic* from 01; AD Goscote from 06; Hon Can Leic Cathl from 10. *The Vicarage, 128 Hallfields Lane, Rothley, Leicester LE7 7NG* T: 0116-230 2241 E: rob.gladstone@btconnect.com

✤**GLADWIN, The Rt Revd John Warren.** b 42. Chu Coll Cam BA 65 MA 68. Cranmer Hall Dur. **d** 67 **p** 68 **c** 94. C Kirkheaton *Wakef* 67-71; Tutor St Jo Coll Dur 71-77; Dir Shaftesbury Project 77-82; Sec Gen Syn Bd for Soc Resp 82-88; Preb St Paul's Cathl 84-88; Provost Sheff 88-94; Angl Adv Yorkshire TV 88-94; Bp Guildf 94-03; Bp Chelmsf 03-09; rtd 09. *131A Marford Road, Wheathampstead, St Albans AL4 8NH* T: (01582) 834223 E: johnwgladwin@hotmail.com

GLADWIN, Thomas William. b 35. St Alb Minl Tr Scheme 78. **d** 81 **p** 82. NSM Hertford St Andr *St Alb* 81-82; NSM Digswell and Panshanger 82-86; C 86-96; rtd 96; PtO *St Alb* from 96. *99 Warren Way, Welwyn AL6 0DL* T: (01438) 714700

GLAISTER, James Richard. b 30. Oak Hill Th Coll 81. **d** 83 **p** 84. NSM Shrub End *Chelmsf* 83-85; NSM Lawshall w Shimplingthorne and Alpheton *St E* 85-87; NSM Lavenham 87-88; C Felixstowe St Jo 88-95; rtd 95; PtO *St E* 95-01; *Carl* 00-02; *Blackb* 02-05. *Les Planchettes, 61350 Saint-Roche-sur-Egrenne, France*

GLAISYER, Canon Hugh. b 30. Oriel Coll Ox BA 51 MA 55. St Steph Ho Ox 51. **d** 56 **p** 56. C Tonge Moor *Man* 56-62; C Sidcup St Jo *Roch* 62-64; V Milton next Gravesend Ch Ch 64-81; RD Gravesend 74-81; V Hove All SS *Chich* 81-91; Can and Preb Chich Cathl 82-91; RD Hove 82-91; P-in-c Hove St Jo 87-91; Adn Lewes and Hastings 91-97; rtd 97; PtO *Chich* 97-03; LtO from 03. *Florence Villa, Hangleton Lane, Ferring, Worthing BN12 6PP* T/F: (01903) 244688 M: 07712-317118 E: h.glaisyer@virgin.net

GLANVILLE-SMITH, Canon Michael Raymond. b 38. Leeds Univ MA 95 AKC 61. **d** 62 **p** 63. C St Marylebone St Mark w St Luke *Lon* 62-64; C Penzance St Mary *Truro* 64-68; R Worc St Andr and All SS w St Helen 68-74; Dioc Youth Chapl 68-74; V Catshill 74-80; P-in-c Worc St Martin w St Pet 80-81; TR Worc St Martin w St Pet, St Mark etc 81-86; TR Worc SE 86-90; Hon Can Worc Cathl 83-90; Can Res Ripon Cathl 90-07; RD Ripon 96-97; rtd 07; PtO *Leeds* from 13. *13 Ure Bank Terrace, Ripon HG4 1JG* T: (01765) 609428 M: 07792-014055 E: mglansmith@hotmail.com

GLARE, Michael Francis. b 28. Southn Univ BA 54. St Steph Ho Ox 56. **d** 57 **p** 58. C Withycombe Raleigh *Ex* 57-62; C-in-c Goodrington CD 62-65; C Tamerton Foliot 65-70; R Weare Giffard w Landcross 70-76; RD Hartland 74-76; P-in-c Babbacombe 76-80; V 80-87; V Ilsington 87-93; rtd 93; PtO *Ex* from 94. *Poplar Lodge, 23 Albion Street, Shaldon, Teignmouth TQ14 0DF* T: (01626) 872679

GLASBY, Alan Langland. b 46. St Jo Coll Nottm 74. **d** 77 **p** 78. C Erith St Paul *Roch* 77-80; C Moor Allerton *Ripon* 80-81; TV 81-87; V Middleton St Mary 87-92; V Bilton 92-00; V Barton and Manfield and Cleasby w Stapleton 00-04; TR E Richmond 04-11; rtd 11; PtO *Leeds* from 13. *23 Westwinn View, Leeds LS14 2HY* T: 0113-265 5992 M: 07970-712484 E: alanglasby@btinternet.com

GLASGOW AND GALLOWAY, Bishop of. *See* DUNCAN, The Rt Revd Gregor Duthie

GLASGOW AND GALLOWAY, Dean of. *See* BARCROFT, The Very Revd Ian David

GLASGOW, Provost of. *See* HOLDSWORTH, The Very Revd Kelvin

GLASS, Mrs Yvonne Elizabeth. b 58. EMMTC 94. **d** 97 **p** 98. NSM Bingham *S'well* 97-00; Chapl Nottm City Hosp NHS Trust 00-11; rtd 11. *25 Valley Road, West Bridgford, Nottingham NG2 6HG* T: 0115-846 2125

GLASS GOWER, Caroline Mary. b 57. Southn Univ BSc 79 Open Univ MA(Ed) 01. Trin Coll Bris BA 06. **d** 06 **p** 07. C Redhill H Trin *S'wark* 06-10; V Tunbridge Wells St Luke *Roch* from 10. *St Luke's Vicarage, 158 Upper Grosvenor Road, Tunbridge Wells TN1 2EQ* T: (01892) 521374 M: 07910-066837 E: caroline.glass957@btinternet.com

GLASSPOOL, John Martin. b 59. Kent Univ BA 83 Heythrop Coll Lon MTh 95 Leeds Univ MA 05 RGN 87. Westcott Ho Cam 88. **d** 90 **p** 91. C Forest Gate Em w Upton Cross *Chelmsf* 90-93; P-in-c Theydon Garnon 93-95; Chapl St Marg Hosp Epping 93-99; TV Epping Distr *Chelmsf* 95-99; Asst Chapl R Free Hampstead NHS Trust 99-02; Chapl Surrey and Sussex Healthcare NHS Trust from 02. *Chaplaincy Department, East Surrey Hospital, Canada Avenue, Redhill RH1 5RH* T: (01737) 768511 ext 6120 E: john.glasspool@sash.nhs.uk

GLEADALL, John Frederick. b 39. Ripon Hall 66 Sarum Th Coll 69. **d** 70 **p** 71. C S Ashford Ch Ch *Cant* 70-76; P-in-c Hothfield 76-83; P-in-c Westwell 81-83; P-in-c Eastwell w Boughton Aluph 81-83; V Westwell, Hothfield, Eastwell and

Boughton Aluph 84-03; rtd 03; Hon C Old Leake w Wrangle *Linc* 03-07; Chapl HM Pris N Sea Camp 03-07. *2 Pinewood Gardens, North Cove, Beccles NR34 7PG* T: (01502) 476483

GLEAVES, John. b 39. Alsager Coll of Educn CertEd 60 Westmr Coll Ox BTh 03. NOC 99. **d** 00 **p** 01. NSM Alsager St Mary *Ches* 00-03; P-in-c Alvanley 03-08; rtd 08; PtO *Ches* from 10. *46 Linley Grove, Alsager, Stoke-on-Trent ST7 2PS* T: (01270) 878169 E: j.gleaves@btinternet.com

GLEDHILL, Alan. b 43. Lon Univ BSc(Econ) 73. NOC 81. **d** 84 **p** 85. C Knaresborough *Ripon* 84-87; P-in-c Easby 87-88; P-in-c Bolton on Swale 87-88; V Easby w Brompton on Swale and Bolton on Swale 88-96; Teacher St Fran Xavier Sch Richmond 96-08; PtO *Ripon* 96-08; rtd 08; Hon C Gilling and Kirkby Ravensworth *Leeds* from 08. *75 High Street, Gilling West, Richmond DL10 5JW* T: (01748) 824466 M: 07906-195390 E: gledhill356@btinternet.com

✠**GLEDHILL, The Rt Revd Jonathan Michael.** b 49. Keele Univ BA 72 Hon DUniv 07 Bris Univ MA 75. Trin Coll Bris 72. **d** 75 **p** 76 **c** 96. C Marple All SS *Ches* 75-78; C Folkestone H Trin w Ch Ch *Cant* 78-83; V Cant St Mary Bredin 83-96; Tutor Cant Sch of Min 83-96; RD Cant 88-94; Hon Can Cant Cathl 92-96; Suff Bp Southampton *Win* 96-03; Bp Lich from 03. *Bishop's House, 22 The Close, Lichfield WS13 7LG* T: (01543) 306000 F: 306009 E: bishop.lichfield@lichfield.anglican.org

GLEESON, Robert Godfrey. b 49. Man Univ CQSW 74. Qu Coll Birm 83. **d** 85 **p** 86. C Hall Green St Pet *Birm* 85-88; Asst Chapl Mental Health & Elderly Care Services Birm HA 88-90; Chapl 90-94; Chapl Moseley Hall Hosp Birm 90-94; Chapl S Birm Mental Health NHS Trust 94-03; PtO *Birm* 03-12; rtd 14. *180 Pineapple Road, Birmingham B30 2TY* T: 0121-444 2793 *or* 678 2002 M: 07966-188006

GLEGHORN, Timothy. b 69. York Univ BA 92. St Jo Coll Nottm 10. **d** 12 **p** 13. C Win Ch Ch from 12. *8 Juniper Close, Winchester SO22 4LU* T: (01962) 843739 M: 07754-801151 E: thegleghorns@btinternet.com

GLEN, Mrs Dawn Andrea. b 64. Liv Univ BA 86. Westcott Ho Cam 07. **d** 09 **p** 10. C Derby Cathl 09-11; C Kirk Langley 11-15; C Mackworth All SS 11-15; C Mugginton and Kedleston 11-15; C Brailsford w Shirley, Osmaston w Edlaston etc from 15. *41 Letchworth Crescent, Beeston, Nottingham NG9 5LL* T: 0115-783 8103 E: revdawnglen@gmail.com

GLENDALOUGH, Archdeacon of. *See* ROUNTREE, The Ven Richard Benjamin

✠**GLENFIELD, The Rt Revd Samuel Ferran.** b 54. QUB BA 76 TCD MLitt 90 MA 94 Ox Univ MTh 99. Wycliffe Hall Ox 88. **d** 91 **p** 92 **c** 13. C Douglas Union w Frankfield *C, C & R* 91-94; I Rathcooney Union 94-96; I Kill *D & G* 96-12; I Hillsborough *D & D* 12-13; Bp K, E & A from 13. *The See House, Kilmore, Cavan, Republic of Ireland* T: (00353) (49) 437 1551 E: bishop@kilmore.anglican.org

GLENNON, James Joseph. b 37. St Mary's Coll Strawberry Hill TCert 69 BA 70. Franciscan Ho of Studies. **d** 62 **p** 63. C S Woodford *Chelmsf* 64-65; NSM Hadleigh w Layham and Shelley *St E* 88-95; C Hadleigh 95-02; rtd 02; PtO *St E* from 02. *5 Carlford Court, 112 Parliament Road, Ipswich IP4 5EL* T: (01473) 721072

GLENNY, Robert Michael. b 90. **d** 14 **p** 15. C Marston w Elsfield *Ox* from 14. *21 Croft Road, New Marston, Oxford OX3 0JZ* M: 07871-644811 E: robertglenny@gmail.com

GLEW, Mark Roy. b 78. Bris Univ BSc 99 ACA 03. Oak Hill Th Coll BA 12. **d** 13 **p** 14. C Rusholme H Trin *Man* from 13. *2 The Grange, Manchester M14 5NY* E: markglew@hotmail.com

GLITHERO, Mrs Helen Elizabeth. b 60. Nottm Univ BA 81 CQSW 83. Qu Coll Birm 11. **d** 14 **p** 15. NSM Highters Heath *Birm* from 14. *61 Stonerwood Avenue, Birmingham B28 0AX* T: 0121-778 3925 E: hglithero@btinternet.com

GLOSSOP, Jonathan Mark. b 55. Open Univ BA 91 Bradf Univ MA 93 Eaton Hall Coll of Educn CertEd 76. Linc Sch of Th and Min 10. **d** 14 **p** 15. C Wolds Gateway Group *Linc* from 14. *23 Pilgrims Way, Immingham DN40 2HD* T: (01469) 574522 E: jmseglossop@tiscali.co.uk

GLOUCESTER, Archdeacon of. *See* SEARLE, The Ven Jacqueline Ann

GLOUCESTER, Bishop of. *See* TREWEEK, The Rt Revd Rachel

GLOUCESTER, Dean of. *See* LAKE, The Very Revd Stephen David

GLOVER, Alan. b 47. SWMTC 96. **d** 99 **p** 00. NSM Bideford, Northam, Westward Ho!, Appledore etc *Ex* from 99. *West Fordlands, Heywood Road, Northam, Bideford EX39 3QA* T: (01237) 479542

GLOVER, Canon David Charles. b 66. St Jo Coll Dur BA 87 St Jo Coll Cam MPhil 91. Ridley Hall Cam 87. **d** 90 **p** 91. C Wath-upon-Dearne w Adwick-upon-Dearne *Sheff* 90-92; Chapl Hatf Coll Dur 92-00; P-in-c Dur St Marg 95-00; R Dur St Marg and Neville's Cross St Jo 00-05; P-in-c Washington 05-07;

R from 07; AD Chester-le-Street from 08; Hon Can Dur Cathl from 11. *27 Wroxton, Washington NE38 7NU* T: 0191-418 7911 M: 07886-289311 E: htcwashington@tiscali.co.uk

GLOVER, Mrs Diana Mary. b 50. Kent Univ BA 73 MA 75. SAOMC. **d** 01 **p** 02. C Aylesbury *Ox* 01-05; P-in-c Amersham on the Hill 05-08; V 08-15; rtd 15; PtO *Ox* from 15. *11 Hamilton Close, Bicester OX26 2HX* E: diana.glover@btinternet.com

GLOVER, Elisabeth Ann. b 53. Univ Coll Ches BTh 99. **d** 98 **p** 99. NSM Thurstaston *Ches* 98-99; C Stockton Heath 00-04; V Eastham from 04; RD Wirral S from 13. *The Vicarage, 29 Ferry Road, Eastham, Wirral CH62 0AJ* T: 0151-327 2182 E: beth.glover@tesco.net

GLOVER, Janet Mary. b 58. Natal Univ BSc 79 UED 80. EAMTC 98. **d** 01 **p** 02. NSM Cambridge St Phil *Ely* 01-04; NSM Histon from 04; NSM Impington from 04; Hon Asst Dir of Ords from 07. *139 Waterbeach Road, Landbeach, Cambridge CB25 9FA* T: (01223) 864931 E: janet@theglovers.name

GLOVER, Canon John. b 48. Kelham Th Coll 67. **d** 71 **p** 72. C Foley Park *Worc* 71-75; TV Sutton *Liv* 75-79; P-in-c Churchill w Blakedown *Worc* 79-84; R 84-87; R Belbroughton w Fairfield and Clent 87-91; Chapl Children's Family Trust 91-13; NSM Flint *St As* 92-93; R Halkyn w Caerfallwch w Rhesycae 93-97; V Rhyl w St Ann 97-13; Can Cursal St As Cathl 02-08; Sacr 08-13; rtd 13. *Bryn Oswald, James Park, Dyserth, Rhyl LL18 6AG* T: (01745) 571473 E: gloverjohn@btinternet.com

GLOVER, Canon Judith Rosalind. b 53. NEOC 93. **d** 95 **p** 96. C Glendale Gp *Newc* 95-99; P-in-c Alwinton w Holystone and Alnham 99-04; R Upper Coquetdale 04-09; R Alston Moor 09-13; V Beadnell from 13; V N Sunderland from 13; Hon Can Newc Cathl from 10. *The Vicarage, South Lane, North Sunderland, Seahouses NE68 7TU* T: (01665) 720202 E: judy@alwinton.net

GLOVER, Michael John Myers. b 28. Lon Univ BSc 48 CEng MICE MSAICE. Cuddesdon Coll 54. **d** 56 **p** 57. C Leic St Pet 56-60; S Africa 60-73 and from 86; TR Northampton Em *Pet* 74-86; Bp's Chapl E Area Northn 73-74; rtd 93. *PO Box 447, Nongoma, 3950 South Africa* T: (0027) (358) 310044 F: 310457

GLOVER, Richard John. b 47. Nottm Univ BTh 77. Linc Th Coll 73. **d** 77 **p** 78. C Barrow St Geo w St Luke *Carl* 77-79; C Netherton 79-80; P-in-c Addingham 80-83; P-in-c Edenhall w Langwathby and Culgaith 80-83; V Addingham, Edenhall, Langwathby and Culgaith 83-84; V Bishops Hull *B & W* 84-89; V Shilbottle *Newc* 89-96; V Whittingham and Edlingham w Bolton Chapel 96-00; P-in-c Barton, Pooley Bridge and Martindale *Carl* 00-04; Dioc Adv for Spiritual Direction and Healing 00-04; R Lower Swale *Ripon* 04-12; rtd 13. *45 Grovehill Road, Filey YO14 9NL* E: richard@richardglover.wanadoo.co.uk

GLOVER, Thomas Edward. b 85. Grey Coll Dur BA 06 Clare Coll Cam BA 09. Westcott Ho Cam 07. **d** 10 **p** 11. C Dur N 10-14; R Winlaton from 14. *St Paul's Rectory, Scotland Head, Blaydon-on-Tyne NE21 6PL* T: 0191-414 3165 M: 07711-576522 E: rectorofwinlaton@gmail.com

GLYN, Aneirin. b 75. St Hugh's Coll Ox MMath 98 DPhil 02. Oak Hill Th Coll MTh 09. **d** 09 **p** 10. C St Helen Bishopsgate w St Andr Undershaft etc *Lon* from 09. *15 Morgan Street, London E3 5AA* M: 07905-288078 E: aneirin@gmail.com

GLYN-JONES, Alun. b 38. JP . CCC Cam BA 59 MA 63. Bps' Coll Cheshunt 60. **d** 61 **p** 62. C Portsea St Mary *Portsm* 61-65; Chapl Hampton Sch Middx 65-76; Hd Master Abp Tenison's Gr Sch Croydon 76-88; V Twickenham St Mary *Lon* 88-01; rtd 01; PtO *B & W* from 01; *Bris* from 01; *Sarum* from 01; *Eur* from 01. *23 Bainton Close, Bradford-on-Avon BA15 1SE* T: (01225) 866874 E: alunandchrisgj@googlemail.com

GLYNN, Simon Adrian. b 59. Van Mildert Coll Dur BSc 80 Univ Coll Ches BTh 99. NOC 96. **d** 99 **p** 00. NSM Carr Mill *Liv* 99-04; C Burscough Bridge 04-09; P-in-c Douglas *Blackb* 09-12; C Appley Bridge 09-12; V Appley Bridge and Parbold from 12. *The Vicarage, 5 Tan House Lane, Parbold, Wigan WN8 7HG* T: (01257) 462350 E: simon@simonglynn.plus.com

GOALBY, George Christian. b 55. Leeds Univ BA 77. St Jo Coll Nottm 79. **d** 81 **p** 82. C Wakef St Andr and St Mary 81-84; Asst Chapl HM Pris Wakef 84-85; Chapl HM Youth Cust Cen Deerbolt 85-87; Chapl HM Pris Frankland 87-89; V Swinderby *Linc* from 89; CF (ACF) from 04. *All Saints' Vicarage, 27 Station Road, Swinderby, Lincoln LN6 9LY* T/F: (01522) 868430

GOATCHER, Mrs Sara Jacoba Helena. b 46. Oak Hill NSM Course 86. **d** 89 **p** 94. NSM S Croydon Em *S'wark* 89-95; C 95-96; R Sutton St Nic 96-06; Asst Chapl Old Palace Sch Croydon 06-11; C Croydon St Jo *S'wark* 07-12; rtd 13; PtO *S'wark* from 13. *8 Hornchurch Hill, Whyteleafe CR3 0DA* T: (020) 8660 6198 M: 07785-230983 E: sara.goatcher@btinternet.com

GOATER, Canon Michael Robert. b 46. York Univ BA MA. NOC 89. **d** 92 **p** 93. C Norton *Sheff* 92-94; V Endcliffe 94-99;

Chapl Sheff Ind Miss 94-95; Assoc Chapl Sheff Hallam Univ 95-99; Asst Post-Ord Tr Officer 95-99; Dioc Voc Officer 96-99; C Stratford-upon-Avon, Luddington etc *Cov* 99-02; P-in-c Gt Shelford *Ely* 02-11; RD Shelford 04-09; RD Granta 09-11; Hon Can Ely Cathl 10-11; rtd 11; Master St Nic Hosp Salisbury from 11. *St Nicholas Hospital, 5 St Nicholas Road, Salisbury SP1 2SW* T: (01722) 336874 E: michael@mickthevic.org.uk

GOATLY, Ms Ruth Christine. b 50. Leic Univ LLB 72 Herts Univ MA 98 CQSW 74. Westcott Ho Cam 08. **d** 09 **p** 10. NSM Boxmoor St Jo *St Alb* 09-13; NSM St Alb St Mary Marshalswick 13-15; NSM St Alb St Luke from 15. *30 Newgate Close, St Albans AL4 9JE* M: 07961-980158 T: (01727) 751542 E: ruthgoatly@hotmail.com

GOBBETT, Michael George Timothy. b 64. St Chad's Coll Dur BSc 86. St Steph Ho Ox BA 89 MA 98. **d** 90 **p** 91. CMP from 91; C Hartlepool St Aid *Dur* 90-94; P-in-c Norton St Mich 94-95; V 95-05; TR Upper Skerne from 05. *The Rectory, 2 Durham Road, Sedgefield, Stockton-on-Tees TS21 3DW* T: (01740) 620274 E: michael.gobbett@btinternet.com

GOBEY, Ian Clifford. b 48. WEMTC 94. **d** 96 **p** 97. NSM Whiteshill and Randwick *Glouc* 96-00; NSM Painswick, Sheepscombe, Cranham, The Edge etc 00-07; P-in-c Westbury-on-Severn w Flaxley, Blaisdon etc 07-13; C Abenhall w Mitcheldean 11-13; C Huntley and Longhope, Churcham and Bulley 12-13; rtd 13. *18 Blenheim Orchard, Shurdington, Cheltenham GL51 4TG* E: gobey910@btinternet.com

GOBLE, Christopher. b 75. Univ of Wales (Lamp) BA 96. Trin Coll Bris 96. **d** 98 **p** 99. C St Jo in Bedwardine *Worc* 98-01; P-in-c Worc St Clem 01-02; R Brington w Whilton and Norton etc *Pet* 02-08; P-in-c Ilmington w Stretton-on-Fosse etc *Cov* from 08; P-in-c Tredington and Darlingscott from 08. *The Rectory, Valenders Lane, Ilmington, Shipston-on-Stour CV36 4LB* T: (01608) 682282 E: ilmingtonrectory@btinternet.com

GOBLE, Clifford David. b 41. Oak Hill Th Coll 69. **d** 72 **p** 73. C Erith St Paul *Roch* 72-76; C Tunbridge Wells St Jas 76-79; R Southfleet 79-05; RD Gravesend 94-05; Hon Can Roch Cathl 99-05; rtd 05; PtO *Cant* from 06. *15 Martindown Road, Whitstable CT5 4PX* T: (01227) 263333

GOBLE (née DUNN), Sharon Louise. b 71. Univ of Wales (Swansea) BA 93 Fitzw Coll Cam BA 97 MA 01. Ridley Hall Cam 95. **d** 98 **p** 99. C Malpas *Mon* 98-01; C Cyncoed 01-02; R Heyford w Stowe Nine Churches and Flore etc *Pet* 02-04; PtO 04-08; Chapl Shakespeare Hospice 08-11; PtO *Cov* 08-13; P-in-c Stoneleigh w Ashow from 13. *The Rectory, Valenders Lane, Ilmington, Shipston-on-Stour CV36 4LB* T: (01608) 682282 M: 07799-220407 E: sharon.goble@btinternet.com

GODBER, Francis Giles. b 48. Open Univ BA 88. Ridley Hall Cam 72. **d** 75 **p** 76. C Blackheath Birm 75-78; C Wolverhampton St Matt *Lich* 78-80; TV Washfield, Stoodleigh, Withleigh etc *Ex* 80-85; R Shenley and Loughton *Ox* 85-88; TR Watling Valley 88-96; Chapl Heatherwood and Wexham Park Hosps NHS Trust 96-00; P-in-c Geddington w Weekley *Pet* 00-13; Dioc Ecum Officer 00-12; Can Pet Cathl 03-12; rtd 13. *8 Barrington Way, Wellington TA21 9BA* E: ecuman.gilbar@talktalk.net

GODBOLD, Michelle Joanne. b 80. Bradf Univ BSc 01 BA 13. Linc Sch of Th and Min 09. **d** 13 **p** 14. C Boultham *Linc* from 13. *10 Abbottsford Way, Lincoln LN6 8DG* T: (01522) 394569 E: michelle.godbold@hotmail.co.uk

GODDARD, Canon Andrew John. b 67. St Jo Coll Ox BA 88 MA 93 DPhil 96. Cranmer Hall Dur 94. **d** 96 **p** 97. C Cogges and S Leigh *Ox* 96-99; Tutor Wycliffe Hall Ox 99-08; Tutor Trin Coll Bris from 08; PtO *Lon* from 11; Hon Can Win Cathl from 12; Hon C Westminster St Jas the Less *Lon* from 13. *56 Tachbrook Street, London SW1V 2NA* T: (020) 7834 1343 M: 07786-907946 E: goddardaj@gmail.com

GODDARD, Canon Charles Douglas James. b 47. CITC 67. **d** 70 **p** 71. C Orangefield *D & D* 70-73; C Stormont 73-75; Miss to Seafarers from 75; Sen Chapl and Sec N Ireland 77-09; rtd 10; Can Belf Cathl from 05. *9 Governors Gate Manor, Hillsborough BT26 6FZ* T: (028) 9268 3592 E: cdjgoddard@googlemail.com

GODDARD, Christopher. b 45. Sarum & Wells Th Coll 79. **d** 81 **p** 82. C Whitehaven *Carl* 81-83; C Barrow St Geo w St Luke 83-85; P-in-c Hayton St Mary 85-90; V Brigham 90-98; V Mosser 90-98; PtO 00-03; Hon C Cockermouth w Embleton and Wythop 03-05; TV Cockermouth Area 05-10; rtd 10; PtO *Carl* from 11. *5 Craig Drive, Whitehaven CA28 6JX* E: chrisgoddardmail@gmail.com

GODDARD, Derek George. b 38. St Martin's Coll Lanc BA 97 CEng FIMechE FIMarEST FCMI. Cranmer Hall Dur 94 CBDTI 95. **d** 97 **p** 98. NSM Windermere St Mary and Troutbeck *Carl* 97-01; P-in-c Leven Valley 01-06; P-in-c Palermo w Taormina *Eur* 06-09; PtO *Blackb* 09-10; P-in-c Overton 10-12; rtd 13; PtO *Blackb* from 13. *3 Chapel Barn, Chapel View, Overton, Morecambe LA3 3EP* T: (01524) 858739 E: d.d.goddard@hotmail.co.uk

GODDARD, Mrs Doris. b 48. St Mary's Coll Twickenham CertEd 70 Open Univ BA 80. S'wark Ord Course 93. **d** 96 **p** 97. Chapl John Nightingale Sch W Molesley 96-00; NSM Addlestone *Guildf* 96-98; NSM Botleys and Lyne 98-04; NSM Long Cross 98-04; NSM Chertsey, Lyne and Longcross 04-05; NSM Blackdown *B & W* 05-09; P-in-c Puriton and Pawlett from 09; Chapl Bridgwater Hosp from 15. *The Vicarage, 1 The Rye, Puriton, Bridgwater TA7 8BZ* T: (01278) 683500 E: rev.doris.goddard@btinternet.com

GODDARD, Douglas. *See* GODDARD, Charles Douglas James

GODDARD, Mrs Elaine Clare. b 53. K Alfred's Coll Win CertEd 78. WEMTC 96. **d** 99 **p** 00. C Leominster *Heref* 99-04; P-in-c St Weonards 04-07; R 07-15; RD Ross and Archenfield 07-13; rtd 15. *Address temp unknown* E: email@ecgoddard.co.uk

GODDARD, Elisabeth Ann. b 64. St Hugh's Coll Ox BA 89 MA 99. Cranmer Hall Dur 94. **d** 96 **p** 97. C Cogges and S Leigh *Ox* 96-99; Chapl Jes Coll Ox 99-04; Tutor Wycliffe Hall Ox 04-08; Hon C Ox St Andr 04-08; Hon C Stoke Bishop *Bris* 09-10; V Westminster St Jas the Less *Lon* from 10. *56 Tachbrook Street, London SW1V 2NA* T: (020) 7834 1343 E: goddardea@gmail.com

GODDARD, Canon Giles William. b 62. Clare Coll Cam MA 84. S'wark Ord Course 92. **d** 95 **p** 96. C N Dulwich St Faith *S'wark* 95-98; R Walworth St Pet 98-09; AD S'wark and Newington 02-07; P-in-c Waterloo St Jo w St Andr 09-14; V from 14; Hon Can S'wark Cathl from 07. *St John's Vicarage, 1 Secker Street, London SE1 8UF* T: (020) 7633 9819 E: gileswgoddard@googlemail.com

GODDARD, Canon Harold Frederick. b 42. Keble Coll Ox BA 63 MA 69. Cuddesdon Coll 64. **d** 66 **p** 67. C Birm St Pet 66-70; Chapl Dudley Road Hosp Birm 66-70; Chapl HM Pris Birm 68-70; C Alverstoke *Portsm* 70-72; Chapl Gosport Cottage Hosp Portsm 70-72; Chapl HM Det Cen Haslar 70-72; P-in-c Portsea St Geo CD *Portsm* 72-76; Chapl Portsm Cathl 73-76; Asst Chapl Portsm Gr Sch 73-75; P-in-c Stoke Prior *Worc* 76-78; P-in-c Wychbold and Upton Warren 77-78; R Stoke Prior, Wychbold and Upton Warren 78-80; Chapl Forelands Orthopaedic Hosp Worc 77-80; Chapl R Marsden Hosp 80-83; R Martley and Wichenford *Worc* 83-88; P-in-c Knightwick w Doddenham, Broadwas and Cotheridge 85-88; R Martley and Wichenford, Knightwick etc 89-90; Bp's Adv on Min of Healing 84-99; Chapl St Richard's Hospice Worc 87-94; RD Martley and Worc W 88-90; Chapl Kidderminster Gen Hosp 90-92; P-in-c Hallow *Worc* 91-92; P-in-c Sedgeberrow w Hinton-on-the-Green 92-00; Chapl Evesham Hosp 93-00; Chapl Worcs Community Healthcare NHS Trust 97-00; Co-ord W Midl Healing Advisers 94-99; RD Evesham *Worc* 97-00; TR Kidderminster St Jo and H Innocents 00-08; Hon Can Worc Cathl 03-08; rtd 08; PtO *Worc* 08-15; Hon C Gt Malvern Ch Ch from 15. *1 Springfield House, Como Road, Malvern WR14 2HS* T: (01684) 563350 M: 07768-106287 E: hgoddard@hotmail.com

GODDARD, John David. b 42. Guy's Hosp Medical Sch MB, BS 64 MRCP 73. **d** 03 **p** 04. OLM Morden *S'wark* 03-12; rtd 12; PtO *S'wark* from 12. *58 Queen Mary Avenue, Morden SM4 4JR* T: (020) 8540 5082 E: jdg13@blueyonder.co.uk

✠**GODDARD, The Rt Revd John William.** b 47. St Chad's Coll Dur BA 69. **d** 70 **p** 71 **c** 00. C S Bank *York* 70-74; C Cayton w Eastfield 74-75; V Middlesbrough Ascension 75-82; RD Middlesbrough 81-87; V Middlesbrough All SS 82-88; Can and Preb York Minster 87-88; Vice-Prin Edin Th Coll 88-92; TR Ribbleton *Blackb* 92-00; Suff Bp Burnley 00-14; Bp's Adv on Hosp Chapls 01-14; Co-ord for Interfaith Work 07-14; rtd 14; PtO *Blackb* from 14. *39 Kearsley Avenue, Tarleton, Preston PR4 6BP* T: (01772) 812532 M: 07779-786114 E: john.goddard39@gmail.com

GODDARD, Mrs Margaret. b 51. **d** 01 **p** 02. NSM Cockermouth Area *Carl* 01-10; rtd 10; PtO *Carl* from 11. *5 Craig Drive, Whitehaven CA28 6JX* E: margaret@cateam.org.uk

GODDARD, Ms Marion. b 54. Sarum & Wells Th Coll 87. **d** 89 **p** 94. Par Dn Lewisham St Swithun *S'wark* 89-94; C 94-95; TV Thamesmead 96-04; rtd 04. *1 Hollows Close, Salisbury SP2 8JU* T: (01722) 338562

GODDARD, Matthew Francis. b 45. Kelham Th Coll 65. **d** 69 **p** 70. C Mansfield St Mark *S'well* 69-72; C Northolt Park St Barn *Lon* 72-78; P-in-c Acton Green St Pet 78-87; R Norwood St Mary 87-96. *27 Hounslow Avenue, Hounslow TW3 2DZ* T: (020) 8230 6591 E: mattandtrace@hotmail.com

GODDARD, Mrs Pamela Gay. b 53. LSE BSc(Econ) 74 CQSW 77. SAOMC 95 EAMTC 97. **d** 98 **p** 99. C New Catton St Luke w St Aug *Nor* 98-03; PtO 03-05; NSM Hamworthy *Sarum* 05-07; C Throop *Win* 07-08; C Hamworthy *Sarum* from 08. *The Rectory, 1 St Michael's Close, Poole BH15 4QT* T: (01202) 674878 E: pam.goddard@googlemail.com

GODDARD, Mrs Rosemary Joy. b 48. Philippa Fawcett Coll CertEd 69. EAMTC 00. **d** 03 **p** 04. C Linc St Nic w St Jo Newport 03-05; P-in-c Bicker 05-08; P-in-c Donington 08; P-in-c Fleet w Gedney 08-13; P-in-c Holbeach Marsh 08-13; rtd 13. *9B Church Lane, Donington, Spalding PE11 4UD* M: 07740-203149 E: rosemaryjg@aol.com

GODDARD, Stuart David. b 53. Cen Sch of Art Lon BA 76 Middx Poly PGCE 82. Trin Coll Bris 91. **d** 93 **p** 94. C Watling Valley *Ox* 93-97; P-in-c Bowthorpe *Nor* 97-00; TV 00-05; P-in-c Hamworthy *Sarum* 05-09; R from 09. *The Rectory, 1 St Michael's Close, Poole BH15 4QT* T: (01202) 674878 E: goddard.stuart@gmail.com

GODDARD, Trevor Paul. b 63. NTMTC 03. **d** 06 **p** 07. NSM Kensal Rise St Mark and St Martin *Lon* 06-11; NSM Kensal Rise St Mark 11-13; NSM S Kenton from 13. *194 Windermere Avenue, Wembley HA9 8QT* T: (020) 8908 2252 E: trevorgoddard@mac.com

GODDEN, Canon Peter David. b 47. Leeds Univ BA 69 MA 04 ARCO 70. Linc Th Coll 85. **d** 87 **p** 88. C Bearsted w Thurnham *Cant* 87-90; C Hykeham *Linc* 90-91; TV 91-95; P-in-c Linc St Pet-at-Gowts and St Andr 95-99; Hon PV Linc Cathl 90-99; R Armthorpe *Sheff* 99-00; R Owmby Gp *Linc* 00-12; RD Lawres 05-06 and 09-12; P-in-c Spring Line Gp 08-12; Can and Preb Linc Cathl 10-12; rtd 12; PtO *York* from 13. *Flat 1, 28 Esplanade, Scarborough YO11 2AQ* E: pd.godden@btinternet.com

GODDEN, Peter James Howard. b 86. St Jo Coll Dur BA 08 Clare Coll Cam BA 13. Westcott Ho Cam 11. **d** 14 **p** 15. C Northwood H Trin *Lon* from 14. *5 Tanworth Close, Northwood HA6 2GF* M: 07835-770610 E: pjhgodden@btinternet.com

GODDEN, Timothy Richard James. b 62. Univ Coll Lon BA 84. St Jo Coll Nottm 89. **d** 89 **p** 90. C Tulse Hill H Trin and St Matthias *S'wark* 89-93; TV Horsham *Chich* 93-01; TR Bishopsworth and Bedminster Down *Bris* from 01. *St Peter's Vicarage, 61 Fernsteed Road, Bristol BS13 8HE* T/F: 0117-964 2734 E: goddenfamily@blueyonder.co.uk

GODFREY, Ann Veronica. *See* MacKEITH, Ann Veronica

GODFREY, Canon Brian Ernest Searles. b 37. Lon Univ BSc 60 MSc 63 PhD 72. S'wark Ord Course 78. **d** 81 **p** 82. NSM Hayes *Roch* 81-86; C 86-88; R Kingsdown 88-93; R Sundridge w Ide Hill 93-02; RD Sevenoaks 95-00; Hon Can Roch Cathl 99-03; rtd 02; PtO *Sarum* from 03. *Rowans, Kingcombe Road, Toller Porcorum, Dorchester DT2 0DG* T: (01300) 320833 E: brian@rowanstp41.fsnet.co.uk

GODFREY, David Samuel George. b 35. CITC 64. **d** 66 **p** 67. C Londonderry Ch Ch *D & R* 66-68; I Tomregan w Drumlane *K, E & A* 68-72; I Cloonclare 72-79; I Templebreedy *C, C & R* 79-85; I Bray *D & G* 85-97; Can Ch Ch Cathl Dublin 95-97; Dean Kilmore *K, E & A* 97-04; I Kilmore w Ballintemple 97-04; Preb Mulhuddart St Patr Cathl Dublin 01-04; rtd 04. *37 Earlsfort Meadows, Earlsfort, Lucan, Co Dublin, Republic of Ireland* T: (00353) (1) 624 1906 M: 86-238 9686 E: godfreyd@o12.ie *or* dsggodfrey@gmail.com

✠**GODFREY, The Rt Revd Harold William.** b 48. AKC 71. St Aug Coll Cant 71. **d** 72 **p** 73 **c** 87. C Warsop *S'well* 72-75; TV Hucknall Torkard 75-86; Bp's Ecum Officer 81-82; United Soc 86-14; R and Adn Montevideo and Can Buenos Aires 86-88; Asst Bp Argentina and Uruguay 87-88; Bp Uruguay 88-98; Bp Peru from 98. *Calle Alcalá 336, Urb la Castellana, Santiago de Surco, Lima 33, Peru* T: (0051) (1) 440 0060 *or* 448 0024 E: hwgodfrey@gmail.com

GODFREY, Ian. b 56. **d** 01 **p** 02. NSM Mill Hill Jo Keble Ch *Lon* 01-11; V Goostrey w Swettenham *Ches* from 11. *The Vicarage, Blackden Lane, Goostrey, Crewe CW4 8PG* T: (01477) 532109 E: goostreyvicarage@btinternet.com

GODFREY, Jennifer Olwen. b 48. Hamilton Coll of Educn DipEd 70. TISEC 99. **d** 02 **p** 03. NSM Dalkeith *Edin* from 02; NSM Lasswade from 02. *131 Newbattle Abbey Crescent, Dalkeith EH22 3LP* T: 0131-660 6145 M: 07812-923159 E: jennie.o@googlemail.com

GODFREY, John Michael. **d** 11 **p** 12. C Galway w Kilcummin *T, K & A* from 11. *77 Knocknacarra Park, Knocknacarra, Galway, Republic of Ireland* T: (00353) (91) 722567 M: 87-900 8085 E: reverendjohngodfrey@gmail.com

GODFREY, Kesari Freeda. b 73. Nesamony Memorial Chr Coll Marthandam BSc 93 United Th Coll Bangalore BD 99. Princeton Th Sem ThM 01. **p** 05. PtO *Birm* 05-07; C Bridlington Priory *York* 07-10; V Southwater *Chich* from 10. *The Vicarage, Church Lane, Southwater, Horsham RH13 9BT* T: (01403) 730229 M: 07709-947056 E: revdgodfrey@yahoo.co.uk

GODFREY, Matthew Fenton. b 69. Univ Coll Dur BA 91 K Coll Lon MA 94. Ripon Coll Cuddesdon MTh 04. **d** 04 **p** 05. C Bodmin w Lanhydrock and Lanivet *Truro* 04-09; Chapl RN

from 09. *Royal Naval Chaplaincy Service, Mail Point 1-2, Leach Building, Whale Island, Portsmouth PO2 8BY* T: (023) 9262 5055 F: 9262 5134 E: nitrogen_narcosis@hotmail.com

GODFREY, Michael. b 49. K Coll Lon BD 70 Wolv Univ PGCE 97. St Aug Coll Cant AKC 72. **d** 72 **p** 73. C Birtley *Dur* 72-75; Ind Chapl 76-79; TV Bilston *Lich* 79-86; TV Wolverhampton 86-93; Chapl Black Country Urban Ind Miss 79-86; Team Ldr 86-93; Preb Lich Cathl 87-93; PtO *Worc* 04-08; *Cov* 05-08; R Newport Pagnell w Lathbury and Moulsoe *Ox* 08-14; rtd 14. *2 Dugdale Avenue, Bidford-on-Avon, Alcester B50 4QE* T: (01908) 611145 E: rev.michael.godfrey@gmail.com

GODFREY, Michael James. b 50. Sheff Univ BEd 77. St Jo Coll Nottm 79. **d** 82 **p** 83. C Walton H Trin *Ox* 82-86; C Chadderton Ch Ch *Man* 86-91; V Woodlands *Sheff* 91-03; V Wythall *Birm* 03-11; TV Morley *Leeds* from 11. *The Vicarage, Rooms Lane, Morley, Leeds LS27 9PA* T: 0113-252 6836 E: mikegodfrey@btinternet.com

GODFREY, Myles. *See* GODFREY, Rumley Myles

GODFREY, The Very Revd Nigel Philip. b 51. Ripon Coll Cuddesdon BA 78 MA 84 Lon Guildhall Univ MBA 00 K Coll Lon MSc 09 MRTPI 76. Ripon Coll Cuddesdon 77. **d** 79 **p** 80. C Kennington St Jo w St Jas *S'wark* 79-89; Community of Ch the Servant 84-93; V Brixton Road Ch Ch *S'wark* 89-01; Prin OLM Scheme 01-07; Chapl S'wark Cathl 02-07; V German *S & M* 07-12; P-in-c Patrick 11-12; V W Coast from 12; Vice-Dean St German's Cathl 07-11; Dean St German's Cathl from 11; Dir Voc and Tr from 10. *4 The Net Loft, Mariners Wharf, Peel, Isle of Man IM5 1AR* T: (01624) 844830 *or* 842608 E: dean@sodoramdman.im

GODFREY, Mrs Patricia Ann. b 54. SEITE 01. **d** 04 **p** 05. NSM Dover St Mary *Cant* 04-14; NSM Dover Town from 14; NSM Dover St Martin from 14. *8 Longfield Road, Dover CT17 9QU* T: (01304) 206019 E: trish@godfrey88.screaming.net

GODFREY (née ROGERS), Mrs Pauline Ann. b 58. LMH Ox BA 79 MA 83 Ox Univ Inst of Educn PGCE 80. S Dios Minl Tr Scheme 89. **d** 92 **p** 94. NSM Headley All SS *Guildf* 92-96; C 96-99; P-in-c Wyke 99-01; V 01-11; Past Tutor Local Min Progr 96-11; Dioc Voc Officer *Glouc* from 11. *23 Oak View, Hardwicke, Gloucester GL2 4AT* T: (01452) 835548 E: p.a.g@talktalk.net

GODFREY, Rumley Myles. b 48. S'wark Ord Course. **d** 83 **p** 84. NSM Dorchester *Ox* 83-11; PtO from 11. *The Old Malt House, Warborough, Wallingford OX10 7DY* T: (01865) 858627 E: myles@warborough.fsnet.co.uk

GODFREY, Mrs Sarah Joy. b 64. Southn Univ BSc 85 Bath Univ PGCE 86. STETS 02. **d** 05 **p** 06. NSM Puddletown, Tolpuddle and Milborne w Dewlish *Sarum* 05-14; Asst Dioc Dir of Ords 11-14; V Milborne Port w Goathill etc *B & W* from 14. *The Vicarage, Bathwell Lane, Milborne Port, Sherborne DT9 5AN* T: (01963) 250248 E: sarah.godfrey@tiscali.co.uk

GODFREY, Canon Simon Henry Martin. b 55. TD 00. K Coll Lon BD 80 AKC 80. St Steph Ho Ox 80. **d** 81 **p** 82. C Kettering SS Pet and Paul 81-84; R Crick and Yelvertoft w Clay Coton and Lilbourne 84-89; V Northampton All SS w St Kath 89-98; R Northampton All SS w St Kath and St Pet 98-09; Sen Chapl Malta and Gozo *Eur* from 09; Can and Chan St Paul's Pro-Cathl Valetta from 09; CF (TA) from 88. *St Paul's Anglican Pro-Cathedral, Independence Square, Valletta VLT12, Malta GC* T: (00356) 2122 5714 F: 2122 5867 E: simonhmgodfrey@googlemail.com

GODFREY, William. *See* GODFREY, Harold William

GODIN, Mrs Mary Louise. b 42. SRN 64 QN 66. Oak Hill NSM Course 89. **d** 92 **p** 94. NSM Surbiton Hill Ch Ch *S'wark* 92-03; Chapl Kingston and Distr Community NHS Trust 97-01; Team Chapl SW Lon and St George's Mental Health NHS Trust 01-03; Chapl Taunton and Somerset NHS Trust 03-11; C Beercrocombe w Curry Mallet, Hatch Beauchamp etc *B & W* from 11. *The Stables, Capland Court, Capland Lane, Hatch Beauchamp, Taunton TA3 6TP* T: (01823) 480606 E: mary.godin@o2.co.uk

GODLINGTON, Ian Denis. b 58. All SS Cen for Miss & Min 13. **d** 14 **p** 15. OLM Mickleover All SS *Derby* 14; OLM Mickleover St Jo 14; OLM Mickleover from 14; Chapl Rolls-Royce Derby from 14. *46 Bren Way, Hilton, Derby DE65 5HP* T: (01283) 730832 M: 07788-417819 E: godlingtons46@gmail.com

GODSALL, Canon Andrew Paul. b 59. Birm Univ BA 81. Ripon Coll Cuddesdon 86. **d** 88 **p** 89. C Gt Stanmore *Lon* 88-91; C Ealing All SS 91-94; V Hillingdon All SS 94-01; Dir of Ords Willesden Area 99-01; Bp's Chapl and Asst *Ex* 01-06; Dioc Dir of Min 06-14; PV Ex Cathl 04-06; Can Res and Chan Ex Cathl 06-14; Miss Community Development Officer from 14. *20 Newcourt Way, Exeter EX2 7SA* E: andrew.godsall@exeter.anglican.org

GODSALL, Canon Ralph Charles. b 48. Qu Coll Cam BA 71 MA 75. Cuddesdon Coll 73. **d** 75 **p** 76. C Sprowston *Nor*

75-78; Chapl Trin Coll Cam 78-84; V Hebden Bridge *Wakef* 84-93; V Westmr St Steph w St Jo *Lon* 93-01; Can Res Roch Cathl 01-08; rtd 08; PV Westmr Abbey from 08. *39 Vincent Square, London SW1P 2NP* T: (020) 7976 5899
M: 07786-959540 E: canonralph@hotmail.co.uk

GODSELL, Kenneth James Rowland. b 22. Birm Coll of Educn Dip Teaching 50. Qu Coll Birm 75. **d** 76 **p** 77. Sen Lect Westhill Coll of HE Birm 74-85; Hon C Selly Hill St Steph *Birm* 76-81; Hon C Selly Park St Steph and St Wulstan 81-90; rtd 90; LtO *Birm* 90-96; PtO *Worc* from 96. *The Quest, Dock Lane, Tewkesbury GL20 7LN* T: (01684) 772469

GODSMARK, Susan Mary. d 14. OLM Gt Totham and Lt Totham w Goldhanger *Chelmsf* from 14. *57 Mill Road, Great Totham, Maldon CM9 8DH* E: suegodsmark@aol.com

GODSON, Alan. b 31. Ch Coll Cam BA 61 MA 65. Clifton Th Coll 61. **d** 63 **p** 64. C Preston All SS *Blackb* 63-66; LtO *Man* 66-69; Asst Chapl Emb Ch Paris 69; Dioc Ev *Liv* 69-01; P-in-c Edge Hill St Mary 72-78; V 78-01; rtd 01; PtO *Liv* from 01. *28 Handley Court, Aigburth, Liverpool L19 3QS* T: 0151-427 0255

GODSON, Mark Rowland. b 61. K Coll Lon BD 83 AKC 83 CertEd 84. Linc Th Coll 84. **d** 86 **p** 87. C Hurst Green *S'wark* 86-88; C Fawley *Win* 88-90; TV Wimborne Minster and Holt *Sarum* 90-95; P-in-c Horton and Chalbury 90-93; P-in-c Vale of Allen 93-95; P-in-c Stalbridge 95-96; Chapl Forest Healthcare NHS Trust Lon 96-00; P-in-c Bicton, Montford w Shrawardine and Fitz *Lich* 00-06; Chapl Shropshire Co Primary Care Trust 01-06; TR Fordingbridge and Breamore and Hale etc *Win* 06-10; Dir 10-12; AD Christchurch 10-12; Lon Cen for Spirituality from 12. *The London Centre for Spirituality, The Church of St Edmund the King, Lombard Street, London EC3V 9EA* T: (020) 7621 1391

GODWIN, Canon David Harold. b 45. Glos Univ BA 09. Kelham Th Coll 67. **d** 71 **p** 72. C Camberwell St Phil and St Mark *S'wark* 71-75; Asst Chapl The Lon Hosp (Whitechapel) 75-79; Chapl R E Sussex Hosp Hastings 79-86; Chapl Over Hosp Glouc 86-92; Chapl Glos R Hosp 86-94; Chapl Glos R Hosp NHS Trust 94-02; Chapl Glos Hosps NHS Foundn Trust 02-05; Hon Can Glouc Cathl 03-05; rtd 05; PtO *Glouc* from 05. *61 The Barge Arm, The Docks, Gloucester GL1 2DN* T: (01452) 730435 M: 07989-046118
E: davidhgodwin@live.co.uk

GODWIN, Canon Michael Francis Harold. b 35. Nottm Univ BSc 57. Ely Th Coll 59. **d** 61 **p** 62. C Farnborough *Guildf* 61-65; V Epsom St Barn 66-85; V Bramley and Grafham 85-98; Hon Can Guildf Cathl 89-98; rtd 00. *14 Lemmington Way, Horsham RH12 5JG* T: (01403) 273411

GOFF, Philip Francis Michael. b 52. K Coll Lon BD 73 AKC 73 FBS 00 FSA 08. St Aug Coll Cant 74. **d** 75 **p** 76. C Ruislip St Martin *Lon* 75-79; Chapl Aldenham Sch Herts 79-82; V Tokyngton St Mich *Lon* 82-89; In RC Ch 89-91; Primary Care Cllr NHS 91-98; PtO *Lon* 99-00; Chapl to Bp Edmonton 00-04; Asst Dir Post-Ord Tr Edmonton Area 03-06; P-in-c Highgate St Aug 04-14; V 14-15; AD W Haringey 11-14; rtd 15. *St Augustine's Vicarage, Langdon Park Road, London N6 5QG* T: (020) 8374 6985 M: 07768-920506
E: phildress@blueyonder.co.uk

GOFTON, Canon William Alder. b 31. Dur Univ BA 54. Coll of Resurr Mirfield 59. **d** 61 **p** 62. C Benwell St Aid *Newc* 61-64; C N Gosforth 64-69; V Seaton Hirst 69-77; V Newc H Cross 77-89; RD Newc W 85-89; Hon Can Newc Cathl 88-96; R Bolam w Whalton and Hartburn w Meldon 89-96; P-in-c Nether Witton 89-95; V 95-96; Chapl Kirkley Hall Coll 90-96; rtd 96; PtO *Newc* from 96. *4 Crossfell, Ponteland, Newcastle upon Tyne NE20 9EA* T: (01661) 820344
E: aggofton@yahoo.co.uk

GOGGIN, Philip Frederick de Jean. b 46. Rhodes Univ BA 66 Lon Univ MA 73 Keele Univ PhD 89 Leeds Univ MA 05. NOC 03. **d** 05 **p** 06. NSM Sandbach Heath w Wheelock *Ches* 05-07; P-in-c Leighton-cum-Minshull Vernon 07-11; V Leighton-cum-Minshull Vernon and Warmingham from 11. *The Vicarage, Middlewich Road, Minshull Vernon, Crewe CW1 4RD* T: (01270) 522213 E: gail.philip@virgin.net

GOLD, Stephen Eric. b 67. St Mellitus Coll 12. **d** 15. C Hillmorton *Cov* from 15. *80 South Road, Clifton upon Dunsmore, Rugby CV23 0BZ* T: (01788) 550479 E: steve.gold2@me.com

GOLDBY, Miss Emma Lucy. b 73. Glos Univ BEd 97. Ripon Coll Cuddesdon 12. **d** 14 **p** 15. C Malvern H Trin and St Jas *Worc* from 14. *103 West Malvern Road, Malvern WR14 4NG*
E: revdemmagoldby@gmail.com

GOLDEN, Stephen Gerard. b 61. Lon Univ BA 84. St Steph Ho Ox 84. **d** 86 **p** 87. C Reading St Luke w St Bart *Ox* 86-90; CF 90-94; PtO *Lon* 07-13. *Flat 1, 35 Lonsdale Road, London SW13 9JP* T: (020) 8748 5306 E: sggolden@btinternet.com

GOLDENBERG, Ralph Maurice. b 45. City Univ FBCO 67 FBOA 67. Trin Coll Bris 88. **d** 90 **p** 91. C Kinson *Sarum* 90-93;

C Edgware *Lon* 93-97; TV Roxeth 97-01; V Bayston Hill *Lich* 01-10; rtd 10. *2 Golf Links, Ferndown BH22 8BY*
E: r.goldenberg@btopenworld.com

GOLDER, Rebecca Marie. *See* ROGERS, Rebecca Marie

GOLDIE, Prof James Stuart. b 46. Edin Univ BEd 73 Hon MEd 00 Cairo Univ Hon PhD 06. Lon Coll of Div BDQ 67 BTh 70 ALCD 69. **d** 69 **p** 70. C Blackpool St Paul *Blackb* 69-70; C Gt Sankey *Liv* 70-73; C-in-c Penketh CD 70-73; Asst Chapl Greystone Heath Sch 70-73; Chapl Kilmarnock Academy 73-75; V Flixton St Jo *Man* 75-78; Chapl Friars Sch Man 75-78; V Skelmersdale St Paul *Liv* 78-80; Chapl Trin Sch Liv 78-80; Lect Man Bible Coll and Dir Man City Miss 80-83; Hon Prof Cam Univ from 81; Chapl Westbrook Hay Sch Hemel Hempstead 83-89; V Pennington w Lindal and Marton *Carl* 89-90; Chapl Bp Wand Sch *Lon* 90-95; Chapl Queenswood Sch Herts 96-97; Hd Master Westcliff Prep Sch 97-03; V Red Sea Area (w ecum oversight) Egypt 04-12; Prin El Gouna Internat Sch 04-12; rtd 12. *23 Ffordd Naddyn, Glan Conway, Colwyn Bay LL28 4NH* T: (01492) 593996

GOLDIE, Katrina Ruth. *See* SCOTT, Katrina Ruth

GOLDING, Neil Christopher. b 47. Warwick Univ BA 69. S'wark Ord Course 92. **d** 95 **p** 96. C Mitcham Ascension *S'wark* 95-00; P-in-c Croydon Woodside 00-05; V 05-15; rtd 15. *Address temp unknown* E: rev_neil@btopenworld.com

GOLDING, The Ven Simon Jefferies. b 46. CBE 02. Brasted Place Coll 70. Linc Th Coll 72. **d** 74 **p** 75. C Wilton *York* 74-77; Chapl RN 77-97; Chapl of the Fleet 97-98 and 00-02; Adn for the RN 97-02; Dir Gen Naval Chapl Service 00-02; QHC 97-02; Hon Can Gib Cathl 98-02; rtd 02; PtO *Ripon* 02-11; Dioc Adv for NSM 08-11; Hon C E Richmond *Leeds* from 11. *Arlanza, Hornby Road, Appleton Wiske, Northallerton DL6 2AF* T: (01609) 881185 E: perce.2000@virgin.net

GOLDING, Stephen. b 57. Keele Univ BA 79 CertEd 79 Lon Bible Coll BA 86 Heythrop Coll Lon MA 09. Cant Sch of Min 93. **d** 95 **p** 96. NSM Ramsgate St Luke *Cant* 95-98; Chapl St Lawr Coll Ramsgate 95-98; Chapl Berkhamsted Sch Herts 98-10; Chapl Ch Hosp Horsham from 10. *Cornerways, Christ's Hospital, Horsham RH13 0LD*

GOLDING, Trevor. b 58. Ridley Hall Cam 07. **d** 09 **p** 10. C Highbury Ch Ch w St Jo and St Sav *Lon* 09-12; V Ipswich St Aug *St E* from 13. *St Augustine's Vicarage, 2 Bucklesham Road, Ipswich IP3 8TJ* M: 07511-870694
E: trevor.golding@googlemail.com

GOLDINGAY, Prof John Edgar. b 42. Keble Coll Ox BA 64 Nottm Univ PhD 83 Lambeth DD 97. Clifton Th Coll 64. **d** 66 **p** 67. C Finchley Ch Ch *Lon* 66-69; Lect St Jo Coll Nottm 70-75; Dir Studies 76-79; Registrar 79-85; Vice-Prin 85-88; Prin 88-97; Prof OT Fuller Th Sem Pasadena from 97. *111 South Orange Grove Apt 108, Pasadena CA 91105-1756, USA* T: (001) (626) 405 0626 E: johngold@fuller.edu

GOLDING, Mrs Philippa Elizabeth Vincent. b 58. Southn Univ LLB 79 Spurgeon's Coll BD 05. SEITE BA 10. **d** 10 **p** 11. C Wednesfield Heath *Lich* 10-14; PtO 14-15; Hon C Heath Town from 15. *2A Victoria Road, Wednesfield, Wolverhampton WV11 1RZ* T: (01902) 732698

GOLDSMITH, Brian Derek. b 36. Leeds Univ BA 64. Coll of Resurr Mirfield 64. **d** 66 **p** 67. C Littlehampton St Mary *Chich* 66-69; C Guildf St Nic 69-73; V Aldershot St Aug 73-81; C-in-c Leigh Park St Clare CD *Portsm* 82-85; C Rowner 85-96; r-d 97; C Catherington and Clanfield *Portsm* 97-01; PtO *Win* 98-14. *27 White Dirt Lane, Catherington, Waterlooville PO8 0NB* T: (023) 9259 9462

✠**GOLDSMITH, The Rt Revd Christopher David.** b 54. York Univ BA 76 DPhil 79. NTMTC 97. **d** 00 **p** 01 **c** 13. NSM Pitsea w Nevendon *Chelmsf* 00-04; V Warley Ch Ch and Gt Warley St Mary 04-13; Suff Bp St Germans *Truro* from 13; Dioc Warden of Readers from 13. *Vounder, Tresillian, Truro TR2 4BW* T: (01872) 520192 M: 07981-912576
E: bishopofstgermans@truro.anglican.org

GOLDSMITH, Mrs Ellen Elizabeth. b 48. York Univ BA 77 Middx Univ BA 06. NTMTC 03. **d** 06 **p** 07. NSM Bentley Common, Kelvedon Hatch and Navestock *Chelmsf* 06-10; NSM Warley Ch Ch and Gt Warley St Mary 10-13; TV Probus, Ladock and Grampound w Creed and St Erme *Truro* from 14. *Vounder, Tresillian, Truro TR2 4BW* T: (01872) 520192 M: 07906-979321 E: ellen.goldsmith@btinternet.com

GOLDSMITH, John Oliver. b 46. K Coll Lon BD 69 AKC 69. St Aug Coll Cant 69. **d** 70 **p** 71. C Dronfield *Derby* 70-73; C Ellesmere Port *Ches* 73-74; TV 74-81; P-in-c Pleasley *Derby* 81-87; P-in-c Pleasley Hill *S'well* 83-87; V Matlock Bank *Derby* 87-97; RD Wirksworth 92-97; P-in-c Kirk Hallam 97-01; V 01-02; P-in-c Taddington, Chelmorton and Flagg, and Monyash 02-11; P-in-c Hartington, Biggin and Earl Sterndale 02-11; V Taddington, Chelmorton and Monyash etc 11; RD Buxton 02-11; rtd 11. *9 Highfield Gardens, Highfield Road, Derby DE22 1HT* T: (01332) 209392
E: goldsmith681@btinternet.com

GOLDSMITH, Lesley Anne. NTMTC 02. **d** 05 **p** 06. C E Ham w Upton Park and Forest Gate *Chelmsf* 05-08; V Chingford St Edm from 08. *St Edmund's Vicarage, Larkswood Road, London E4 9DS* T: (020) 8529 5226
E: lesley.goldsmith@btinternet.com

GOLDSMITH, Canon Mary Louie. b 48. K Coll Lon BA 70 AKC 70. Qu Coll Birm 91. **d** 93 **p** 94. NSM Matlock Bank *Derby* 93-97; NSM Kirk Hallam 97-02; NSM Taddington, Chelmorton and Monyash etc 00-11; Hon Can Derby Cathl from 05. *9 Highfield Gardens, Highfield Road, Derby DE22 1HT* T: (01332) 209392 E: goldsmith681@btinternet.com

GOLDSMITH, Mrs Pauline Anne. b 40. Linc Th Coll 82. **dss** 84 **d** 87 **p** 94. Waddington *Linc* 86-88; Par Dn 87-88; Par Dn Gt and Lt Coates w Bradley 88-94; TV 94-96; TV Kidderminster St Mary and All SS w Trimpley etc *Worc* 96-01; rtd 01; PtO *Derby* from 01; *Sheff* from 01. *143 Ravencar Road, Eckington, Sheffield S21 4JR* T: (01246) 430083

GOLDSMITH, Stephen. b 32. Edin Th Coll. **d** 76 **p** 77. SPCK Staff 53-97; Bookshops Regional Manager SPCK 87-97; NSM Penicuik *Edin* 76-81; NSM Linc St Nic w St Jo Newport 81-90; NSM Gt and Lt Coates w Bradley 94-96; NSM Kidderminster St Mary and All SS w Trimpley etc *Worc* 96-01; PtO *Derby* from 01; *Sheff* from 01. *143 Ravencar Road, Eckington, Sheffield S21 4JR* T: (01246) 430083

GOLDSPINK, David. b 35. Open Univ BA 81. Lon Coll of Div 62. **d** 65 **p** 66. C Mile Cross *Nor* 65-68; C St Austell *Truro* 68-70; TV Bramerton w Surlingham *Nor* 70-73; Min Gunton St Pet 73-75; R Mutford w Rushmere w Gisleham w N Cove w Barnby 75-81; Asst Chapl HM Pris Man 81-82; Chapl HM Youth Cust Cen Hollesley Bay Colony 82-84; Chapl HM Pris Blundeston 84-88; PtO *St E* 87-01; rtd 88; PtO *Nor* from 88. *14 Deepdale, Carlton Colville, Lowestoft NR33 8TU* T: (01502) 537769

GOLDSTONE-CREASEY, Graham. b 51. Trent Poly BA 73. Cranmer Hall Dur 80. **d** 83 **p** 84. C Birstall and Wanlip *Leic* 83-87; C-in-c Wheatley Park St Paul CD *Sheff* 87-92; V Wheatley Park 92-95; P-in-c Gleadless Valley 95-98. *281 Fleetwood Road North, Thornton-Cleveleys FY5 4LE* T: (01253) 862668 E: grahamgc10@gmail.com

GOLDTHORP, Ms Ann Lesley. b 59. Qu Coll Birm 08. **d** 11 **p** 12. C Harbury and Ladbroke *Cov* 11-15; V Deddington w Barford, Clifton and Hempton *Ox* from 15. *The Vicarage, 1 Earls Close, Deddington OX15 0TJ* T: (01869) 336880
E: reverendannie@hotmail.com

GOLDTHORPE, Ms Shirley. b 42. Linc Th Coll 70. **dss** 76 **d** 87 **p** 94. Thornhill Lees *Wakef* 76-78; Birkenshaw w Hunsworth 78-80; Batley St Thos 80-85; Batley All SS 80-85; Purlwell 80-92; Par Dn 87-88; Dn-in-c 88-92; Dn-in-c Horbury Junction 92-94; P-in-c 94-01; rtd 02; PtO *Leeds* from 02. *10 Orchid View, Alverthorpe, Wakefield WF2 0FG* T: (01924) 383181
M: 07885-462837

GOLLEDGE, Miss Patricia Anne. b 55. Trin Coll Bris BA 00. **d** 00 **p** 01. C Pontypool *Mon* 00-03; TV 03-09; V Griffithstown 09-13; R Panteg and Griffithstown from 13. *St Hilda's Vicarage, 2 Sunnybank Road, Griffithstown, Pontypool NP4 5LT* T: (01495) 763641 E: p.golledge@virgin.net

GOLLOP, Michael John. b 58. Keble Coll Ox BA 81 MA 85. St Mich Coll Llan BD 85. **d** 85 **p** 86. C Newport St Mark *Mon* 85-87; C Bassaleg 87-91; V St Hilary Greenway 91-93; V Itton and St Arvans w Penterry and Kilgwrrwg w Devauden from 93. *The Vicarage, Wyndcliffe View, St Arvans, Chepstow NP16 6ET* T: (01291) 622064 E: frmichael1@aol.com

GOLTON, Alan Victor. b 29. St Jo Coll Ox BA 51 MA 54 DPhil 54. **d** 85 **p** 86. P-in-c Barston *Birm* 87-95; PtO 95-96; Hon C Grenoble *Eur* 97-00. *Chant du Matin, Les Michallons, 38250 St Nizier du Moucherotte, France* T: (0033) 4 76 53 43 77 E: avgolton@hotmail.com

GOMERSALL, Canon Ian Douglass. b 56. Birm Univ BSc 77 Fitzw Coll Cam BA 80 MA 85 Dur Univ MA 94. Westcott Ho Cam 78. **d** 81 **p** 82. C Darlington St Mark w St Paul *Dur* 81-84; C Barnard Castle w Whorlton 84-86; Chapl HM YOI Deerbolt 85-90; P-in-c Cockfield *Dur* 86-88; R 88-90; Dep Chapl HM Pris Wakef 90-91; Chapl HM Pris Full Sutton 91-97; P-in-c Kexby w Wilberfoss *York* 93-97; TV Man Whitworth 97-03; P-in-c Man Victoria Park 98-09; R from 09; Chapl Man Univ 97-03; Hon Chapl from 03; AD Ardwick 08-15; Hon Can Man Cathl from 11. *St Chrysostom's Rectory, 38 Park Range, Manchester M14 5HQ* T: 0161-224 6971 M: 07711-670225 E: fatherian@priest.com

GOMERSALL, Richard. b 45. FCA 68. NOC 90. **d** 93 **p** 94. NSM Thurcroft *Sheff* 93-96; NSM Sheff St Matt 96-03; Ind Chapl 98-03; C-in-c Southey Green St Bernard CD 03-11. *Dale View House, 14 Wignall Avenue, Wickersley, Rotherham S66 2AX* T: (01709) 546441 F: 701900 E: fr.gomersall@btinternet.com

GOMES, Canon Jules Francis Paulinus. b 66. Bombay Univ BA 86 United Th Coll Serampore MTh 97 Selw Coll Cam PhD 04. Union Bibl Sem Serampore BD 94. **d** 98 **p** 98. India

98-04; Co-ord Chapl Greenwich Univ *S'wark* 04-08; Lect Lon Sch of Th 08-10; NSM Harefield *Lon* 08-09; Can Res Liv Cathl 11-12; P-in-c Arbory and Castletown *S & M* 12-14; V from 14; Can St German's Cathl from 12. *The Vicarage, Arbory Road, Castletown, Isle of Man IM9 1ND* T: (01624) 823509 M: 07981-570384

✠**GOMEZ, The Rt Revd Drexel Wellington.** b 37. Dur Univ BA 59. Codrington Coll Barbados 55. **d** 59 **c** 72. Tutor Codrington Coll Barbados 64-68; Sec and Treas Dio Bahamas 70-72; Bp Barbados 72-93; Asst Bp Nassau and Bahamas 93-95; Bp Coadjutor 95-96; Dioc Bp Bahamas and Turks and Caicos Is 96-01; Bp 01-08; Abp W Indies 98-08; rtd 09. *PO Box N-7107, Nassau, Bahamas*

GOMM, Timothy Frank. b 64. St Jo Coll Nottm 00. **d** 02 **p** 03. C Kinson *Sarum* 02-04; C Heatherlands St Jo and Community Chapl Rossmore Community Coll 04-10; C Longfleet *Sarum* 10-11; TR Portland from 11. *St John's Vicarage, Ventnor Road, Portland DT5 1JE* T: (01305) 820103
E: rev.gomm@btinternet.com

GOMPERTZ, Adam Charles John. b 73. Trin Coll Bris 11. **d** 13 **p** 14. C Lt Aston *Lich* from 13. *19 Mawgan Drive, Lichfield WS14 9SD* T: (01543) 325640 M: 07917-248973
E: revagomp@gmail.com

GOMPERTZ, Helen Morey. b 40. **d** 06 **p** 07. NSM Kettering St Andr *Pet* from 06. *19 Grendon Drive, Barton Seagrave, Kettering NN15 6RW* T: (01536) 481017
E: morey.gompertz@btinternet.com

GOMPERTZ, Canon Peter Alan Martin. b 40. ALCD 63. **d** 64 **p** 65. C Eccleston St Luke *Liv* 64-69; Scripture Union 69-73; C Yeovil *B & W* 73-75; V Northampton St Giles *Pet* 75-96; R Aynho and Croughton w Evenley etc 96-06; P-in-c Gt w Lt Addington and Woodford 06-10; Can Pet Cathl 88-10; rtd 10; PtO *Pet* 11-14; Hon C Kettering St Andr from 14. *19 Grendon Drive, Barton Seagrave, Kettering NN15 6RW* T: (01536) 481017 M: 07771-615364
E: p.gompertz@btinternet.com

GONIN, Christopher Willett. b 33. Man Univ DACE 87 MBA 92. AKC 59. **d** 60 **p** 61. C Camberwell St Geo *S'wark* 60-64; C Stevenage H Trin *St Alb* 64-69; C Bletchley *Ox* 70-73; R Newington St Mary *S'wark* 73-76; PtO *Bris* 76-77; Hon C Horfield H Trin 77-89; Hon C City of Bris 89-91; V Milton Ernest *St Alb* 92-97; V Thurleigh 92-97; rtd 97; PtO *St E* from 97. *15 The Gables, Leiston IP16 4UZ* T: (01728) 635549 E: christopher@gonin.wanadoo.co.uk

GONZALEZ PENA, Heller. b 72. **d** 11 **p** 12. C La Coruña H Cross Spain 11-12; R 12-15; C Port Glas from 15; C Kilmacolm from 15; C Bridge of Weir from 15. *5 Balmore Court, Kilmacolm PA13 4LX* T: (01505) 872961 M: 07496-841775
E: hellerg@hotmail.com

GOOCH, John Ellerton. b 46. Natal Univ BEcon 70. Trin Coll Bris 73. **d** 75 **p** 76. C Pinetown Ch Ch S S Africa 75-77; P-in-c Escombe 77-79; P-in-c E London St Sav 80-81; R E London St Mich 81-82; TV Beacon Bay 82-83; P-in-c Casablanca *Eur* 98-07; PtO from 07. *109 rue Mozart/Kouttoubia, Amerchich 40000, Marrakech, Morocco* T: (00212) (24) 311600 M: 63-203174 E: johnpen@swissmail.net

GOOCH, Michael Anthony. b 44. Nottm Coll of Educn TCert 66. Cant Sch of Min 90. **d** 93 **p** 94. NSM New Romney w Old Romney and Midley *Cant* 93-97; P-in-c Teynham w Lynsted and Kingsdown 97-08; Bp's Officer for NSM 98-03; rtd 08; PtO *Cant* from 08. *Little Owls, Tookey Road, New Romney TN28 8ET* T: (01797) 367858 E: mgooch@connectfree.co.uk

GOOD, Alan Raymond. b 39. Bris Sch of Min 83. **d** 85 **p** 86. NSM Horfield St Greg *Bris* 85-97; Chapl Asst Southmead Health Services NHS Trust 97-99; Chapl Asst N Bris NHS Trust from 99. *Southmead Hospital, Westbury-on-Trym, Bristol BS10 5NB* T: 0117-959 5447, 950 5050 or (01454) 415778

GOOD, Andrew Ronald. b 60. Bris Univ BA 82. Linc Th Coll 83. **d** 85 **p** 86. C Epping St Jo *Chelmsf* 85-88; C Cheshunt *St Alb* 88-91; R Spixworth w Crostwick and Frettenham *Nor* 91-04; PtO 04-10; P-in-c Ashwellthorpe, Forncett, Fundenhall, Hapton etc 11-12; R Holkham w Egmere w Warham, Wells and Wighton 12-14. *Ferrar House, Little Gidding, Huntingdon PE28 5RJ* E: andrewrgood@hotmail.com

GOOD, Anthony Ernest. b 28. ARIBA 51 Heriot-Watt Univ MSc 73. Wells Th Coll 54. **d** 56 **p** 57. C Maidstone All SS *Cant* 56-60; C Reading St Mary V *Ox* 60-62; R Sandhurst 62-70; PtO *Ex* 71-82; TR Wallingford w Crowmarsh Gifford etc *Ox* 82-92; RD Wallingford 85-91; rtd 92; PtO *Ex* from 92. *Corts Weir Quay, Bere Alston, Yelverton PL20 7BX* T: (01822) 840524

GOOD, David Howard. b 42. Glouc Sch of Min 84. **d** 87 **p** 88. NSM Bromyard *Heref* 87-92; C Pontesbury I and II 92-95; P-in-c Ditton Priors w Neenton, Burwarton etc 95-98; R 98-02; rtd 02; PtO *Heref* from 02. *26 Farjeon Close, Ledbury HR8 2FU* T: (01531) 636474

GOOD, Preb John Hobart. b 43. Bps' Coll Cheshunt 66 Coll of Resurr Mirfield 68. **d** 69 **p** 70. C Ex St Jas 69-73; C Cockington 73-75; C Wolborough w Newton Abbot 75-78; P-in-c Exminster and Kenn 78-80; R 80-95; RD Kenn 89-95; TR Axminster, Chardstock, All Saints etc 95-09; Preb Ex Cathl 02-09; Chapl All Hallows Sch Rousdon 98-09; rtd 09; Hon C The Winterbournes and Compton Valence *Sarum* 09-13; Hon C Dorchester 09-13. *3 Home Farm Court, Deane Road, Stokeinteignhead, Newton Abbot TQ12 4QF*
E: johngood.martinstown@hotmail.co.uk

✠**GOOD, The Rt Revd Kenneth Raymond.** b 52. TCD BA 74 Nottm Univ BA 76 NUI HDipEd 81 MEd 84. St Jo Coll Nottm 75. **d** 77 **p** 78 **c** 02. C Willowfield *D & D* 77-79; Chapl Ashton Sch Cork 79-84; I Dunganstown w Redcross and Conary *D & G* 84-90; I Lurgan Ch the Redeemer *D & D* 90-02; Adn Dromore 97-02; Bp *D & R* from 02. *The See House, 112 Culmore Road, Londonderry BT48 8JF* T: (028) 7135 1206 *or* 7137 7013 F: 7135 2554 E: bishop@derry.anglican.org

GOOD, The Ven Kenneth Roy. b 41. K Coll Lon BD 66 AKC 66. **d** 67 **p** 68. C Stockton St Pet *Dur* 67-70; Chapl Antwerp Miss to Seamen *Eur* 70-74; Chapl Kobe Japan 74-79; Asst Gen Sec Miss to Seamen and Asst Chapl St Mich Paternoster Royal *Lon* 79-85; Hon Can Kobe from 85; V Nunthorpe *York* 85-93; RD Stokesley 90-93; Adn Richmond *Ripon* 93-06; rtd 06; PtO *York* from 07; *Dur* from 10. *18 Fox Howe, Coulby Newham, Middlesbrough TS8 0RU* T: (01642) 594158
E: joken.good@ntlworld.com

GOOD, Stuart Eric Clifford. b 37. Wycliffe Hall Ox 63. **d** 64 **p** 65. C Walton H Trin *Ox* 64-67; Australia from 66; Dir Chapl Services Angl Homes Inc 85-05; rtd 05. *135/27 Pearson Drive, Success WA 6164, Australia* M: 41-894 3337
E: sbargood@bigpond.net.au

GOODACRE, Canon David Leighton. b 36. AKC 59. **d** 60 **p** 61. C Stockton St Chad *Dur* 60-63; C Birtley 63-68; Chapl Sunderland Gen Hosp 69-74; P-in-c Ryhope *Dur* 75-81; V Ovingham *Newc* 81-01; Hon Can Newc Cathl 92-01; rtd 01; PtO *Newc* from 01. *9 Wilmington Close, Newcastle upon Tyne NE3 2SF* T: 0191-271 4382

GOODACRE, Philip James. b 81. Ox Brookes Univ BA 04 Birm Univ MA 06 Anglia Ruskin Univ MA 13. Ridley Hall Cam 09. **d** 11 **p** 12. C Brightside w Wincobank *Sheff* 11-14; P-in-c Hillsborough and Wadsley Bridge from 14. *Christ Church Vicarage, 218 Fox Hill Road, Sheffield S6 1HJ* T: 0114-234 9376
E: philipgoodacre@gmail.com

GOODAIR, Jan. b 59. K Coll Lon BA 81 Leeds Univ PhD 02 Roehampton Inst PGCE 82. NEOC 97. **d** 00 **p** 01. NSM Tockwith and Bilton w Bickerton *York* 00-01; NSM York St Olave w St Giles 00-01; Chapl Harrogate Ladies' Coll 01-10; Chapl Haberdashers' Aske's Sch Elstree 10-15; Chapl Pocklington Sch from 15. *47 North Moor Estate, Huntington, York YO32 9RX* M: 07840-731137
E: jan.cheeseman@ntlworld.com

GOODALL, Alice Elizabeth. b 58. Keele Univ BA 80. STETS 09. **d** 12 **p** 13. C St Bartholomew *Sarum* from 12. *The Rectory, Donhead St Andrew, Shaftesbury SP7 9DZ* T: (01747) 828827 M: 07447-933140 E: alicegoodall313@gmail.com

GOODALL, George. b 24. LCP. **d** 86 **p** 87. NSM Bretby w Newton Solney *Derby* 86-94; PtO from 94; *Lich* 06-10. *Brizlincote Farm, Middle Lane, Wythall, Birmingham B47 6LD*

GOODALL, Canon John William. b 45. Hull Univ BA 69. Ripon Hall Ox 69. **d** 71 **p** 72. C Loughborough Em *Leic* 71-74; C Dorchester *Ox* 74-75; TV 75-80; Tutor Sarum & Wells Th Coll 80-88; Vice Prin S Dios Minl Tr Scheme 80-88; P-in-c Gt Wishford *Sarum* 80-83; P-in-c Colehill 88-96; V 96-13; Dioc Dir of Readers 88-95; Can and Preb Sarum Cathl 07-13; rtd 13; PtO *Sarum* from 13. *27 Fishers Close, Blandford Forum DT11 7EL* E: jwgoodall123@btinternet.com

✠**GOODALL, The Rt Revd Jonathan Michael.** b 61. R Holloway Coll Lon BMus 83. Wycliffe Hall Ox 86. **d** 89 **p** 90 **c** 13. C Bicester w Bucknell, Caversfield and Launton *Ox* 89-92; Asst Chapl HM Pris Bullingdon 90-92; Min Can, Chapl, and Sacr Westmr Abbey 92-98; Bp's Chapl and Research Asst *Eur* 98-05; Can Gib Cathl from 05; Abp's Personal Chapl and Ecum Sec *Cant* 05-13; Hon C Westmr St Matt *Lon* 99-03; PV Westmr Abbey from 04; Suff Bp Ebbsfleet (PEV) *Cant* from 13; Asst Bp Lich from 13; Asst Bp Ox from 13; Asst Bp Worc from 13; Asst Bp Cov from 14; Asst Bp Ex from 14; Asst Bp Bris from 15. *Hill House, Treetops, The Mount, Caversham, Reading RG4 7RE* T: 0118-948 1038 E: office@ebbsfleet.org.uk

GOODBODY, Ruth Vivien. b 68. Surrey Univ BA 02. Wycliffe Hall Ox 96 STETS 00. **d** 02 **p** 03. C Bourne Valley *Sarum* 02-06; C Stebbing and Lindsell w Gt and Lt Saling *Chelmsf* 06-10; rtd 10; PtO *Chelmsf* from 12. *The Vicarage, 7 Ruffels Place, Stebbing, Dunmow CM6 3TJ* T: (01371) 856080
E: thegoodbodies@btinternet.com

GOODBODY, Steven John. b 70. Univ of Wales (Cardiff) BD 92. Wycliffe Hall Ox 00. **d** 02 **p** 03. C Tunbridge Wells St Jo *Roch* 02-05; C Ex St Leon w H Trin 05-10; TR Washfield, Stoodleigh, Withleigh etc 10-15; V Fremington from 15. *19 Lane End Close, Instow, Bideford EX39 4LG*
M: 07768-645172 T: (01271) 861082
E: stevegoodbody@btinternet.com

GOODBODY, Timothy Edward. b 66. York Univ BA 89. Wycliffe Hall Ox BTh 98. **d** 98 **p** 99. C Blandford Forum and Langton Long *Sarum* 98-02; NSM Bourne Valley 02-06; P-in-c Stebbing and Lindsell w Gt and Lt Saling *Chelmsf* from 06. *The Vicarage, 7 Ruffels Place, Stebbing, Dunmow CM6 3TJ* T: (01371) 856080 E: thegoodbodies@btinternet.com

GOODBURN, David Henry. b 41. S'wark Ord Course 73. **d** 76 **p** 77. NSM Enfield SS Pet and Paul *Lon* 76-82; PtO 83-85; NSM Potters Bar *St Alb* 85-88; Chapl RN 88-96; V Luton St Sav *St Alb* 96-09; rtd 09; PtO *Cant* from 12. *Major's, Barrack Hill, Hythe CT21 4BZ* T: (01303) 262736

GOODCHILD, Andrew Philip. b 55. CertEd 80. Oak Hill Th Coll BA 85. **d** 85 **p** 86. C Barnston *Ches* 85-88; C Hollington St Leon *Chich* 88-89; P-in-c Millbrook *Ches* 89-94; Chapl and Hd RE Kimbolton Sch 94-03. *Sand Pit Lodge, 72 Lynn Road, Dersingham, King's Lynn PE31 6LB* T: (01485) 543743
M: 07748-815479 E: mel-andy@tiscali.co.uk

GOODCHILD, Canon John McKillip. b 42. Clare Coll Cam BA 64 MA 68 Oriel Coll Ox CertEd 69. Wycliffe Hall Ox 67. **d** 69 **p** 70. C Clubmoor *Liv* 69-72; CMS Nigeria 72-83; Hon Can Aba from 74; V Ainsdale *Liv* 83-89; TR Maghull 89-98; Prin Dioc Minl Course and Dir OLM Tr *Nor* 98-06; rtd 06. *39 St Michael's Road, Aigburth, Liverpool L17 7AN*

GOODCHILD, Mrs Penelope Faith. b 53. **d** 11 **p** 12. OLM Pinxton *Derby* from 11. *89 Market Street, South Normanton, Alfreton DE55 2AA* T: (01773) 811460
E: pennygoodchild@btinternet.com

GOODDEN, John Maurice Phelips. b 34. Sarum & Wells Th Coll 70. **d** 72 **p** 75. C Weymouth H Trin *Sarum* 72-74; C Harlow New Town w Lt Parndon *Chelmsf* 74-78; Ind Chapl and Chapl Princess Alexandra Hosp Harlow 78-82; V Moulsham St Jo *Chelmsf* 86-90; R Chipstead and Adv Rural Min *S'wark* 90-04; rtd 04; PtO *B & W* from 05. *9 Royston House, 5 Duke Street, Bath BA2 4AH* T: (01225) 282246
E: goodden@msn.com

GOODDEN, Stephanie Anne. *See* NADARAJAH, Stephanie Anne

GOODE, Claire Elizabeth. b 60. Nottm Univ BSc 82. EMMTC 04. **d** 08 **p** 09. C S Notts Cluster of Par *S'well* 08-11; P-in-c Thurgarton w Hoveringham and Bleasby etc 11-14; P-in-c Rolleston w Fiskerton, Morton and Upton 11-14; V Nottingham St Andr from 14. *St Andrew's Vicarage, 1 Chestnut Grove, Nottingham NG3 5AD* T: 0115-912 0098
E: cegoodec@btinternet.com

GOODE, John Laurence. b 48. W Cheshire Coll of Tech TEng 70 Federal Univ Minas Gerais Brazil Dip Teaching 78. Chich Th Coll 81. **d** 83 **p** 84. C Crewe St Andr *Ches* 83-86; USPG 87-94; Brazil 91-94; TV Ches 94-00; V Latchford Ch Ch from 00; P-in-c Latchford St Jas from 15. *Christ Church Vicarage, Wash Lane, Warrington WA4 1HT* T: (01925) 630846
E: dida1@btopenworld.com

GOODE, Jonathan. b 67. St Martin's Coll Lanc BA 89. Qu Coll Birm. **d** 00 **p** 01. C Middleton St Mary *Ripon* 00-04; P-in-c Hartlepool St Hilda *Dur* 04-08; Chapl St Hilda's Sch 04-08; V Denton *Newc* 08-12. *St Hilda's Vicarage, Preston Gate, North Shields NE29 9QB* T: 0191-280 3555
E: revjgoode@yahoo.com

GOODE, Michael Arthur John. b 40. K Coll Lon BD AKC 63. **d** 64 **p** 65. C Sunderland Springwell w Thorney Close *Dur* 64-68; C Solihull *Birm* 68-70; R Fladbury, Wyre Piddle and Moor *Worc* 70-75; P-in-c Foley Park 75-81; V 81-83; RD Kidderminster 81-83; TR Crawley *Chich* 83-93; TR Abingdon and V Shippon *Ox* 93-05; rtd 05; PtO *Worc* from 07. *13 Britannia Square, Worcester WR1 3DG* T: (01905) 616982
E: maj.goode@btinternet.com

GOODE, Canon Peter William Herbert. b 23. Oak Hill Th Coll 60. **d** 62 **p** 63. C Woodford Wells *Chelmsf* 62-65; V Harold Hill St Paul 65-76; V Gt Warley Ch Ch 76-93; RD Brentwood 89-93; Hon Can Chelmsf Cathl 90-93; rtd 93; PtO *St Alb* from 93. *52 Slimmons Drive, St Albans AL4 9AP* T: (01727) 852166

GOODE, Timothy. b 69. Huddersfield Poly BA 90 Roehampton Inst PGCE 91. Ripon Coll Cuddesdon 07. **d** 09 **p** 10. C Croydon St Jo *S'wark* 09-12; TV Caterham from 12; Dioc Disability Adv from 13. *The Vicarage, 8 Whyteleafe Hill, Whyteleafe CR3 0AA* T: (020) 8660 4015
E: musicgoode@hotmail.com

GOODER, Canon Martin Lee. b 37. Sheff Univ BSc 58. Oak Hill Th Coll 58. **d** 60 **p** 61. C Barrow St Mark *Carl* 60-63; C Halliwell St Pet *Man* 63-66; R Chorlton on Medlock

St Sav 66-71; R Brunswick 71-92; P-in-c Bacup Ch Ch 92-02; Hon Can Man Cathl 98-02; rtd 02; PtO *Man* from 02. *12 Walton Close, Bacup OL13 9RE* T: (01706) 872418
E: gooder@btopenworld.com

GOODERHAM, Daniel Charles. b 24. St Fran Coll Brisbane 49. **d** 52 **p** 53. Australia 52-60; C Staveley *Derby* 60-61; C Ipswich St Thos *St E* 61-64; V Ipswich St Bart 64-71; R Drinkstone 71-78; R Rattlesden 71-78; RD Lavenham 75-78; V Beckenham St Mich w St Aug *Roch* 78-87; P-in-c Whiteparish *Sarum* 87-89; rtd 89; PtO *St E* from 89. *58 Millfield, Eye IP23 7DE*
T: (01379) 871589

GOODEY, Philip Julian Frank. b 61. Aston Tr Scheme 87 Trin Coll Bris 89. **d** 92 **p** 93. C Iver *Ox* 92-94; C Hornchurch St Andr *Chelmsf* 94-99; V Wickham Market w Pettistree *St E* 99-01; TR Parkham, Alwington, Buckland Brewer etc *Ex* 01-06; P-in-c Lundy Is 01-06; R Botley *Portsm* 06-11; V Curdridge 06-11; R Durley 06-11; TR Drypool *York* 11-15; V Boughton Monchelsea *Cant* from 15. *The Vicarage, Church Hill, Boughton Monchelsea, Maidstone ME17 4BU* E: phil.goodey@gmail.com

GOODFELLOW, Ian. b 37. St Cath Coll Cam BA 61 MA 65 Lon Univ PGCE 76 Dur Univ PhD 83. Wells Th Coll 61. **d** 63 **p** 64. C Dunstable *St Alb* 63-67; Chapl Haileybury Coll 67-71; Asst Chapl St Bede Coll Dur 71-74; Lect and Tutor 71-75; Sen Lect and Tutor SS Hild and Bede Coll Dur 75-78; Sen Cllr Open Univ (SW Region) 78-97; PtO *Ex* from 89; rtd 02. *Crosslea, 206 Whitchurch Road, Tavistock PL19 9DQ* T: (01822) 612069 E: goodfellow1@lineone.net

GOODGER, The Very Revd Kenneth Andrew. b 67. Univ of Qld BA 96. St Fran Coll Brisbane BTh 97. **d** 93 **p** 96. C Milton Australia 93-96; C Caloundra 96-99; C Pimlico St Pet w Westmr Ch Ch *Lon* 99-02; R Moorooka and Salisbury Australia 02-06; R Caloundra 06-14; R Wangaratta and Dean H Trin Cathl from 14. *2 The Close, Wangaratta VIC 3677, Australia* T: (0061) (3) 5721 8292 E: kagoodger67@gmail.com

GOODHEW, David John. b 65. Collingwood Coll Dur BA 86 CCC Ox DPhil 92 St Jo Coll Dur BA 92. Cranmer Hall Dur 90. **d** 93 **p** 94. C Bedminster *Bris* 93-96; Chapl and Fell St Cath Coll Cam 96-01; V Fulford *York* 01-08; P-in-c York St Denys 01-04; Dir Minl Practice Cranmer Hall Dur from 08. *St John's College, 3 South Bailey, Durham DH1 3RJ* T: 0191-334 3863
F: 334 3501 E: d.j.goodhew@durham.ac.uk

GOODHEW, Lindsey Jane. *See* ELLIN, Lindsey Jane

GOODHEW, Roy William. b 41. Reading Univ BA Univ of Wales (Cardiff) PGCE. S Dios Minl Tr Scheme. **d** 89 **p** 90. C Southampton Maybush St Pet *Win* 89-94; V Hound 94-05; rtd 05; PtO *Lon* from 06. *121 Edgecot Grove, London N15 5HH* T: (020) 8802 5101 E: roygoodhew@btinternet.com

GOODING, Canon Ian Eric. b 42. Leeds Univ BSc 63 BCom 65 CEng 69 MIProdE 68. St Jo Coll Nottm 70. **d** 73 **p** 74. C Wandsworth All SS *S'wark* 73-77; P-in-c Stanton-by-Dale w Dale Abbey *Derby* 77-87; R 87-00; P-in-c Risley 94-00; R Stanton-by-Dale w Dale Abbey and Risley 00-12; RD Erewash 98-12; Bp's Ind Adv 77-12; Hon Can Derby Cathl 02-12; rtd 12; PtO *Derby* from 12; Older People's Adv from 13. *Holly Tree Cottage, 17 Bostocks Lane, Sandiacre, Nottingham NG10 5NL* T: 0115-849 8726 M: 07974-370330
E: ian.e.gooding@gmail.com

GOODING, Ian Peter Slade. b 56. Imp Coll Lon BScEng 77 MBCS 88. Qu Coll Birm 90. **d** 92 **p** 93. C Swindon Dorcan *Bris* 92-96; TV Langley Marish *Ox* 96-02; Internet Manager Scripture Union from 02; Hon C Woughton *Ox* 09-12. *5 Pipston Green, Kents Hill, Milton Keynes MK7 6HT* T: (01908) 673651 E: goodingip@clara.co.uk

GOODING, John Henry. b 47. St Jo Coll Nottm. **d** 84 **p** 85. C Charles w Plymouth St Matthias *Ex* 84-88; C Leeds St Geo *Ripon* 88-93; TV Liskeard, St Keyne, St Pinnock, Morval etc *Truro* 93-94; Lon and SE Consultant CPAS 94-00; Hon C Egham *Guildf* 96-00; Dioc Par Resource Officer 00-03; Dioc Dir Miss, Evang and Par Development 03-12; rtd 12. *26 St Georges Road, Worthing BN11 2DR*
E: johngooding@btinternet.com

GOODING, Ms Karen Ann. b 55. LRAM 76 ARCM 77. **d** 11. OLM Alford w Rigsby *Linc* 11-12; NSM Enfield St Mich *Lon* from 12. *110 Lowther Drive, Enfield EN2 7JR* T: (020) 8245 6450 E: karenanngooding@gmail.com

GOODING, Paul David Buchanan. b 76. Pemb Coll Ox MA 98 Green Coll Ox PGCE 01. Ox Min Course 06. **d** 08. NSM Grove *Ox* 08-12; NSM Vale from 12; Asst Chapl Abingdon Sch from 10. *c/o Crockford, Church House, Great Smith Street, London SW1P 3AZ* E: pdbgooding@hotmail.com

GOODING, Robert Henry. b 60. ACII 87. Trin Coll Bris 08. **d** 10 **p** 11. C Walton le Soken *Chelmsf* 10-13; V Iver *Ox* from 13. *The Vicarage, Delaford Close, Iver SL0 9JX* T: (01255) 677978
E: rev.robert@goodingonline.co.uk

GOODISON, Miss Eleanor Mary. b 57. Leeds Univ BA 78. ERMC 11. **d** 14 **p** 15. NSM S Hartismere *St E* from 14.

Catelyn's House, Wingfield, Diss IP21 5QZ T: (01379) 384181 M: 07437-406997 E: eleanor.goodison@gmail.com

GOODLAD, Canon Martin Randall. b 39. Sheff City Coll of Educn TDip 60. Linc Th Coll 63. **d** 66 **p** 67. C Bramley *Ripon* 66-69; TV Daventry *Pet* 69-71; Asst Dioc Youth Officer 69-71; Asst Dir of Educn *Wakef* 71-74; Youth Work Officer Gen Syn Bd of Educn 74-83; P-in-c Cheam Common St Phil *S'wark* 83-85; V 85-97; RD Sutton 90-97; Hon Chapl St Raphael's Hospice 87-97; V Coulsdon St Andr *S'wark* 97-05; Hon Can S'wark Cathl 96-05; rtd 05; PtO *S'wark* from 06. *3 Cromer Mansions, Cheam Road, Sutton SM1 2SR* T: (020) 8915 0555
E: m.goodlad@sky.com

GOODLAND, Michael Eric. b 53. WEMTC 97. **d** 97 **p** 98. NSM Ilminster and Distr *B & W* 97-02; NSM Crewkerne w Wayford 02-07; PtO *Truro* 07-10; P-in-c Lanreath, Pelynt and Bradoc 10-12; P-in-c St Germans 12-14; V from 14; C Saltash from 12; RD E Wivelshire from 12. *The Vicarage, Quay Road, St Germans, Saltash PL12 5LY* T: (01503) 230275
E: michaelgoodland07@googlemail.com

GOODLEY, Christopher Ronald. b 47. K Coll Lon BD 72 AKC 72. **d** 73 **p** 74. C Shenfield *Chelmsf* 73-77; C Hanley H Ev *Lich* 77-78; TV 78-83; Chapl Whittington Hosp Lon 83-86; Chapl St Crispin's Hosp Northampton 88-94; Chapl Northampton Community Healthcare NHS Trust 94-01; Chapl Northants Healthcare NHS Trust 01-12; rtd 12; PtO *Pet* from 12. *19 Weggs Farm Road, Duston, Northampton NN5 6HD* T: (01604) 758347 E: pandcgoodley@o2.co.uk

GOODMAN, Ms Alice Abigail. b 58. Harvard Univ BA 80 Girton Coll Cam BA 82 MA 86 Boston Univ MDiv 97. Ripon Coll Cuddesdon 00. **d** 01 **p** 03. C Redditch, The Ridge *Worc* 01-02; C Kidderminster St Mary and All SS w Trimpley etc 02-06; Chapl Trin Coll Cam 06-11; R Fulbourn *Ely* from 11; V Gt Wilbraham from 11; R Lt Wilbraham from 11. *The Rectory, 2 Apthorpe Street, Fulbourn, Cambridge CB21 5EY* T: (01223) 880337 E: goodhill@appleinter.net

GOODMAN, Andrew Francis Malby. b 56. Lon Univ BA 79 Birm Univ MSocSc 88 CQSW 88. Qu Coll Birm 01. **d** 03 **p** 04. C Hamstead St Paul *Birm* 03-07; Co-ord Chapl Bedfordshire Univ *St Alb* from 07. *The Rectory, Church Road, Meppershall, Shefford SG17 5NA* T: (01582) 743360
E: goodmanco@yahoo.co.uk

GOODMAN, Canon Derek George. b 34. Keble Coll Ox BA 57 MA 60. Ridley Hall Cam 59. **d** 61 **p** 62. C Attenborough *S'well* 61-65; R Eastwood 65-84; Dioc Chief Insp of Schs 65-89; V Woodthorpe 84-89; Dioc Dir of Educn *Leic* 89-96; Hon Can Leic Cathl 90-96; rtd 96; PtO *Leic* from 96. *1 Brown Avenue, Quorn, Loughborough LE12 8RH* T: (01509) 415692

GOODMAN, Garry Gordon. b 52. **d** 09 **p** 10. OLM Bure Valley *Nor* 09-12; NSM Horsford, Felthorpe and Hevingham from 12. *Heath Farm House, Coltishall Road, Buxton, Norwich NR10 5JD* T: (01603) 279393 E: garry.goodman@btinternet.com

GOODMAN, John Dennis Julian. b 35. Sarum & Wells Th Coll 74. **d** 76 **p** 77. C Cotmanhay *Derby* 76-79; TV Old Brampton and Loundsley Green 79-86; R Finningley w Auckley *S'well* 86-96; rtd 96; PtO from 96. *Address temp unknown* T: (01832) 731194
E: johndi.goodman@btinternet.com

GOODMAN, John Paul. b 84. Trin Coll Bris BA 13 MA 14. **d** 14 **p** 15. C Banbury St Fran *Ox* from 14. *St Francis House, Highlands, Banbury OX16 1FA* T: (01865) 522123 M: 07726-971772 E: goodmanjpf@gmail.com

GOODMAN, Brother Kevin Charles. b 54. Surrey Univ BA 06. STETS 03. **d** 06 **p** 07. NSM Buckland Newton, Cerne Abbas, Godmanstone etc *Sarum* 06-09; PtO *Cant* 09-10; C Cant St Dunstan w H Cross from 10. *The Master's Lodge, 58 St Peter's Street, Canterbury CT1 2BE* T: (01227) 479364
E: kevinssf@franciscans.org.uk

GOODMAN, Mrs Mairion Kim (Mars). b 73. Leeds Univ BA 95. Trin Coll Bris BA 03. **d** 05 **p** 06. NSM Redland *Bris* 05-10 and 13-15. *6 Willoughby Road, Horfield, Bristol BS7 8QX* T: 0117-989 2597 E: mars@redland.org.uk

GOODMAN, Mark Alexander Scott. b 61. Lanc Univ BA 82 Nottm Univ BTh 90 New Coll Edin MTh 97. Linc Th Coll 87. **d** 90 **p** 91. C Denton St Lawr *Man* 90-93; R Dalkeith and Lasswade *Edin* 93-06; Dioc Communications Officer 96-06; Can St Mary's Cathl and Syn Clerk 02-06; Chapl Stamford Sch from 06. *Address temp unknown* M: 07947-032739

GOODMAN, Mrs Penelope Jane. b 52. ERMC 06. **d** 09 **p** 10. OLM Bure Valley *Nor* 09-12; NSM Horsford, Felthorpe and Hevingham from 12. *Heath Farm House, Coltishall Road, Buxton, Norwich NR10 5JD* T: (01603) 279393
E: garry.goodman@btinternet.com

GOODMAN, Peter William (Bill). b 60. St Cath Coll Cam BA 82 Sheff Univ MPhil 98 PhD 11 Linc Univ PGCE 13. St Jo Coll Nottm 85. **d** 89 **p** 90. C Stapenhill w Cauldwell *Derby* 89-92; C Ovenden *Wakef* 92-94; P-in-c Halifax St Aug 94-98;

Crosslinks Ethiopia 98-05; C Leic H Trin w St Jo 05-08; CMD Officer *Linc* from 14; PtO *Leic* from 13. *Edward King House, The Old Palace, Lincoln LN2 1PU* M: 07528-504392 T: (01522) 504923 E: goodmans@cooptel.net *or* bill.goodman@lincoln.anglican.org

GOODMAN, Veronica Mary. b 57. Newman Coll Birm BEd 80. Qu Coll Birm 06. **d** 08 **p** 09. C Dunstable *St Alb* 08-12; V Meppershall and Shefford from 12. *The Rectory, Church Road, Meppershall, Shefford SG17 5NA* E: ronigoodman@yahoo.co.uk

GOODMAN, Victor Terence. b 46. Liv Univ BSc 67 CEng 92 MBCS 74. EMMTC 82. **d** 85 **p** 86. NSM Barwell w Potters Marston and Stapleton *Leic* 85-89; NSM Croft and Stoney Stanton 89-94; P-in-c Whetstone 94-03; TV Hugglescote w Donington, Ellistown and Snibston 03-07; C Coalville w Bardon Hill and Ravenstone 07-10; rtd 10; PtO *Leic* from 13. *21 New Inn Close, Broughton Astley, Leicester LE9 6SU* T: (01455) 285410 E: victor.goodman@btinternet.com

GOODMAN, Mrs Victoria Elizabeth Stuart. b 51. RGN 74. Trin Coll Bris. **d** 98 **p** 99. C Ilminster and Distr *B & W* 98-02; R Blagdon w Compton Martin and Ubley 02-10; Dioc Chapl MU 01-10; rtd 10; PtO *Sarum* from 12. *Underhill, Castle Hill Lane, Mere, Warminster BA12 6JB* T: (01747) 860070 E: vickieplum51@btinternet.com

GOODMAN, William. *See* GOODMAN, Peter William

GOODRICH, The Very Revd Derek Hugh. b 27. Selw Coll Cam BA 48 MA 54. St Steph Ho Ox 50. **d** 52 **p** 53. C Willesden St Andr *Lon* 52-57; W Lodge St Sidwell Guyana 57-67; V Port Mourant 67-71; R New Amsterdam All SS 71-84; Adn Berlice 81-84; V Gen Dio Guyana 82-94; Dean Georgetown 84-93; P-in-c St Aloysius 93-00; rtd 00; PtO *S'wark* 03-14. *The College of St Barnabas, Blackberry Lane, Lingfield RH7 6NJ* T: (01342) 872873

GOODRICH, Mrs Nancy Elisabeth. b 66. St Hilda's Coll Ox BA 88 MA 09 ACA 93. WMMTC 06. **d** 09 **p** 10. C St Annes St Thos *Blackb* 09-12; V Bolton-le-Sands from 12. *The Vicarage, 117 Main Road, Bolton le Sands, Carnforth LA5 8DX* T: (01524) 823106 M: 07974-250466 E: nancy@goodrich.myzen.co.uk

GOODRICH, Canon Peter. b 36. Dur Univ BA 58. Cuddesdon Coll 60. **d** 62 **p** 63. C Walton St Jo *Liv* 62-66; C Prescot 66-68; V Anfield St Marg 68-72; V Gt Crosby St Faith 72-83; P-in-c Seaforth 76-80; RD Bootle 78-83; TR Upholland 83-94; R Halsall 94-02; Dir Dioc OLM Scheme 94-02; Hon Can Liv Cathl 89-02; rtd 03; PtO *Liv* from 03. *Dunelm, 16 Hillside Avenue, Ormskirk L39 4TD* T: (01695) 573285

GOODRIDGE, Elizabeth Jane. b 57. SEITE 06. **d** 09 **p** 10. NSM S Beddington and Roundshaw *S'wark* 09-13; NSM Kenley from 13; NSM Purley St Barn from 13. *47 Chatsworth Road, Cheam SM3 8PL* M: 07788-755752 E: elizabeth.goodridge1@btinternet.com

GOODRIDGE, John Francis James. b 49. Open Univ BA 86. WEMTC 04. **d** 07 **p** 08. Partnership P E Bris 07-13; NSM Two Mile Hill St Mich 07-13; NSM Hanham from 13; NSM Kingswood from 13. *153 Whittucks Road, Bristol BS15 3PY* T: 0117-940 1508

GOODRIDGE, Paul Charles. b 54. Leic Univ MSc 98 MCIPD 88. **d** 04 **p** 05. OLM Cheam *S'wark* 04-08; C Beddington 08-10; R Godstone and Blindley Heath 10-14. *Address temp unknown* E: paul_goodridge1@btinternet.com

GOODRIDGE, Peter Warren. b 66. Liv Univ BA 87. Wycliffe Hall Ox 07. **d** 09 **p** 10. C Tonbridge SS Pet and Paul *Roch* 09-13; R Elmswell *St E* from 13. *The Rectory, Church Road, Elmswell, Bury St Edmunds IP30 9DY* T: (01359) 240512 E: elmswellrector@gmail.com

GOODSELL, Patrick. b 32. BA 88. Linc Th Coll 62. **d** 64 **p** 65. C Thornton Heath St Jude *Cant* 64-65; C Croydon St Jo *S'wark* 65-70; V Tenterden St Mich *Cant* 70-78; P-in-c Sellindge w Monks Horton and Stowting 78-84; P-in-c Lympne w W Hythe 82-84; V Sellindge w Monks Horton and Stowting etc 84-92; V Nonington w Wymynswold and Goodnestone etc 92-98; rtd 98; PtO *Cant* from 98. *3 James Close, Lyminge, Folkestone CT18 8NL* T: (01303) 863976 E: pat_goodsell@sky.com

GOODSON, Sally Louise. b 64. BSc. STETS. **d** 13 **p** 14. C Win St Bart and St Lawr w St Swithun from 13. *Bartholomew House, 1 Abbey Hill Close, Winchester SO23 7AZ* M: 07840-926507 E: sallylgoodson@googlemail.com

GOODWIN, Canon Barry Frederick John. b 48. Birm Univ BSc 69 PhD 77. St Jo Coll Nottm 86. **d** 88 **p** 89. C Ware Ch Ch *St Alb* 88-91; P-in-c Stanstead Abbots 91-96; P-in-c Gt Amwell w St Marg 95-96; V Gt Amwell w St Margaret's and Stanstead Abbots 96-99; RD Hertford and Ware 96-99; V Clapham Park All SS *S'wark* 99-05; RD Clapham 02-05; Soc Resp (Par Development) Adv Croydon Ad'ry 05-11; Hon C Addiscombe St Mildred 09-11; Hon Can S'wark Cathl 11-13; rtd 13; PtO *S'wark* from 13. *57 Southway, Croydon CR0 8RH* M: 07967-917151 E: barry@bcgoodwin.me.uk

GOODWIN, Bruce William. b 64. Univ of W Aus BA 84 DipEd 85. Trin Coll Bris 07. **d** 09 **p** 10. C Thornbury and Oldbury-on-Severn w Shepperdine *Glouc* 09-12; Sen Chapl Glos Univ from 12. *University of Gloucestershire, The Park, Cheltenham GL50 2RH* T: (01242) 714592 M: 07720-772190 E: bgoodwin@glos.ac.uk *or* goodwins07@gmail.com

GOODWIN, Daphne Mary. b 35. Lon Univ MB, BS 60. STETS 94. **d** 97 **p** 98. NSM Ifield *Chich* from 97. *150 Buckswood Drive, Gossops Green, Crawley RH11 8JF* T: (01293) 612906 E: dapheter.goodwin@ukgateway.net

GOODWIN, David Wayne. b 71. Univ of Wales BD 95. Cranmer Hall Dur 95. **d** 97 **p** 98. C Ches H Trin 97-00; Dep Chapl HM Pris Dur 00-01; Chapl HM YOI Thorn Cross 01-04; Chapl HM Pris Liv 04-07; Chapl HM Pris Kennet 07-11; Chapl HM Pris Garth from 11. *HM Prison Garth, Ulnes Walton Lane, Leyland PR26 8NE* T: (01772) 443300

GOODWIN, Mrs Gillian Sheila. b 54. NOC MTh 99. **d** 99 **p** 00. C Penkridge *Lich* 99-02; TV Wrockwardine Deanery 02-15; rtd 15. *4 Gloucester Road, Hyde SK14 5JG* E: gill.goodwin@btinternet.com

GOODWIN, Canon John Fletcher Beckles. b 20. Jes Coll Cam BA 43 MA 46. Ridley Hall Cam 42. **d** 45 **p** 46. C Southall H Trin *Lon* 45-48; C Drypool *York* 48-49; Niger 50-57; Vice-Prin Ripon Hall Ox 57-62; V Merton *Ox* 62-70; V Heanor *Derby* 70-74; V Hazlewood 74-85; V Turnditch 74-85; Adv for In-Service Tr and Chapl to Bp 74-88; Hon Can Derby Cathl 81-85; rtd 85; PtO *Derby* 85-99. *1 Kirby Place, Oxford OX4 2RX* T: (01865) 712356

GOODWIN, Mrs Josephine Anne. b 64. Ripon Coll Cuddesdon 09. **d** 12 **p** 13. C Stow on the Wold, Condicote and The Swells *Glouc* from 12. *Rose Cottage, St Margaret's Road, Alderton, Tewkesbury GL20 8NN* T: (01242) 620391 M: 07718-089099 E: revdjosie.goodwin@btinternet.com

GOODWIN, Ronald Victor. b 33. S'wark Ord Course. **d** 86 **p** 87. NSM Wickford and Runwell *Chelmsf* 86-98; PtO 98-01; NSM W Hanningfield 01-03; P-in-c 03-06; rtd 06; PtO *Chelmsf* from 06. *164 Southend Road, Wickford SS11 8EH* T: (01268) 734447

GOODWIN, Stephen. b 58. Sheff Univ BA 80 Wolv Univ BSc 14. Cranmer Hall Dur 82. **d** 85 **p** 86. C Lytham St Cuth *Blackb* 85-87; C W Burnley All SS 88-90; TV Headley All SS *Guildf* 90-98; NSM Leek and Meerbrook *Lich* 98-03; Chapl Univ Hosp of N Staffs NHS Trust 03-08; Chapl Douglas Macmillan Hospice Blurton from 08. *2 Lordshire Mews, Armshead Road, Werrington, Stoke-on-Trent ST9 0HJ* T: (01782) 302418 *or* 344300 E: stephen.goodwin@talktalk.net

GOODWIN, Mrs Susan Elizabeth. b 51. Leeds Poly BSc 74 Leeds Univ MSc 76. Cranmer Hall Dur 82. **dss** 84 **d** 87 **p** 94. Norton Woodseats St Chad *Sheff* 84-87; Par Dn 87; Chapl Scargill Ho 87-89; NSM W Burnley All SS *Blackb* 89-90; NSM Headley All SS *Guildf* 90-98; Past Asst Acorn Chr Healing Trust 91-93; P-in-c Wetley Rocks *Lich* 98-09; P-in-c Werrington 08-09; V Werrington and Wetley Rocks from 09; RD Cheadle from 14. *2 Lordshire Mews, Armshead Road, Werrington, Stoke-on-Trent ST9 0HJ* T: (01782) 302418 E: revsuegoodwin@orange.net

GOODWIN-HUDSON, Anthony James Philip. b 76. **d** 14 **p** 15. C Appley Bridge and Parbold *Blackb* from 14. *All Saints' Vicarage, Finch Lane, Appley Bridge, Wigan WN6 9DT*

GOODWIN HUDSON, Brainerd Peter de Wirtz. b 34. K Coll Lon BD 57 AKC 57. Westcott Ho Cam 57. **d** 59 **p** 60. C Morden *S'wark* 59-60; Australia 61-65; Asst Sec CCCS 65-68; Chapl St Lawr Coll Ramsgate 68-74; Chapl Repton Sch Derby 74-94; Chapl Santiago Chile 94-01; rtd 99; Hon C Broadwell, Evenlode, Oddington, Adlestrop etc *Glouc* 02-06. *Brea Heights, Trebetherick, Wadebridge PL27 6SE* E: brainerd@freeuk.com

GOODWINS, Christopher William Hedley. b 36. St Jo Coll Cam BA 58 MA 62. Linc Th Coll 62. **d** 64 **p** 65. C Lowestoft St Marg *Nor* 64-69; V Tamerton Foliot *Ex* 69-98; P-in-c Southway 78-82; rtd 98; P-in-c Isleham *Ely* 99-04; PtO from 05; *St E* from 10. *102 The Causeway, Isleham, Ely CB7 5ST* T: (01638) 780284 E: cwhgoodwins@gmail.com

GOODYEAR, Benjamin. b 76. LSE BSc 98. Ridley Hall Cam 03. **d** 06 **p** 07. C Balham Hill Ascension *S'wark* 06-09; P-in-c Brixton St Paul w St Sav 09-13; V from 13. *73 Baytree Road, London SW2 5RR* M: 07866-774354 E: thegoodyears@gmail.com

GOODYER, Canon Edward Arthur. b 42. Witwatersrand Univ BA 63 SS Coll Cam BA 67 MA 70 Rhodes Univ MTh 91. St Paul's Coll Grahamstown 68. **d** 68 **p** 69. C Rosebank S Africa 69; R Vanderbijlpark 71-72; Chapl St Jo Coll Houghton Estate 73-75; R Stellenbosch 76-84; Can Cape Town 80-84; R Bramley S Africa 84-87; Chapl St Andr Coll Grahamstown 88-92; P-in-c Sidbury 90-92; R Alverstoke *Portsm* 92-12; P-in-c Gosport Ch Ch 97-01; rtd 12; Chapl Huggens Coll Northfleet from 12; Hon Can Wusasa Nigeria from 99. *Chaplain's House,*

Huggens College, College Road, Northfleet, Gravesend DA11 9DL
T: (01474) 533091 M: 07952-194187 E: ego.lizg@virgin.net

GOOLD, Peter John. b 44. Lon Univ BD 74. St Steph Ho Ox 67. **d** 70 **p** 71. C Chiswick St Nic w St Mary *Lon* 70-73; Chapl Asst R Masonic Hosp Lon 73-74; Chapl Asst Basingstoke Distr Hosp 74-77; Chapl R Marsden Hosp 77-80; Chapl N Hants Hosp 80-94; Chapl N Hants Hosps NHS Trust 94-00; Chapl N Hants Loddon Community NHS Trust 94-00; PtO *Guildf* 94-00; rtd 09. *Aepelford Acre, The Sands, Woodborough, Pewsey SN9 5PR* T: (01672) 851942

GOOLJARY, Yousouf Azad. b 59. Ex Univ BSc 80 Man Poly PGCE 82. SEITE 07. **d** 10 **p** 11. C Greenwich St Alfege *S'wark* 10-13; Chapl Dagenham Park C of E Sch from 13; C Becontree S *Chelmsf* from 13. *144 Maybank Avenue, Hornchurch RM12 5SH* M: 07563-366811 E: revgooljary@aol.com

GORDON, Alan Williamson. b 53. Strathclyde Univ BA 75 MCIBS 79. Wycliffe Hall Ox 98. **d** 98 **p** 99. C Win Ch *Ch* 98-02; R Headbourne Worthy 02-15; RD Win 07-13; V Tamworth *Lich* from 15. *The Vicarage, Hospital Street, Tamworth B79 7EE* T: (01827) 66776
E: alan.gordon98@ntlworld.com

GORDON, The Very Revd Alexander Ronald. b 49. Nottm Univ BPharm 71. Coll of Resurr Mirfield 74. **d** 77 **p** 78. C Headingley *Ripon* 77-80; C Fareham SS Pet and Paul *Portsm* 80-83; V Cudworth *Wakef* 83-85; P-in-c Tain *Mor* 85-87; P-in-c Lairg Miss 87-01; P-in-c Brora *Mor* 88-01; P-in-c Dornoch 88-01; Dioc Dir of Ords 89-01; Can St Andr Cathl Inverness 95-01; Hon Can St Andr Cathl Inverness from 02; Chapl Strasbourg *Eur* 02-05; Provost St Andr Cathl Inverness 05-14; Geneva *Eur* from 14. *Holy Trinity, 14 bis Rue du Mont Blanc, CH-1201 Geneva, Switzerland* T: (0041) (22) 731 5155
E: canonalexgordon@btconnect.com

GORDON, Alexander Strathearn. b 77. Edin Univ MA 00. St Mellitus Coll BA 12. **d** 12 **p** 13. C Onslow Square and S Kensington St Aug *Lon* from 12. *Holy Trinity Brompton, Ennismore Gardens Mews, London SW7 1JA*
E: al.gordon@htb.org.uk

GORDON, Anne. *See* LE BAS, Anne Jennifer

✠**GORDON, The Rt Revd Archibald Ronald McDonald.** b 27. Ball Coll Ox BA 50 MA 52. Cuddesdon Coll 50. **d** 52 **p** 53 **c** 75. C Stepney St Dunstan and All SS *Lon* 52-55; Chapl Cuddesdon Coll 55-59; LtO *Ox* 57-59; V Birm St Pet 59-68; Lect Qu Coll Birm 60-62; Can Res Birm Cathl 67-71; V Ox St Mary V w St Cross and St Pet 71-75; Bp Portsm 75-84; Bp at Lambeth (Hd of Staff) *Cant* 84-91; Asst Bp S'wark 84-91; Bp HM Forces 85-90; Can Res and Sub-Dean Ch Ch *Ox* 91-96; rtd 96; Hon Asst Bp Ox from 91. *c/o The Ven J A Morrison, 39 Crown Road, Wheatley, Oxford OX33 1UJ*
E: ronaldgordon.ab@btinternet.com

GORDON, Mrs Avis Patricia. b 52. Man Univ BA 73. **d** 08 **p** 09. OLM Clifton *Man* 08-12; NSM from 15. *47 Agecroft Road West, Prestwich, Manchester M25 9RF* T: 0161-798 8018

GORDON, Bruce Harold Clark. b 40. Edin Univ MTh 96. Cranmer Hall Dur 65. **d** 68 **p** 69. C Edin St Jas 68-71; C Blackheath St Jo *S'wark* 71-74; R Duns *Edin* 74-90; R Lanark and Douglas *Glas* 90-05; rtd 05; LtO *Edin* from 05. *52 Foxknowe Place, Livingston EH54 6TX* T: (01506) 418466 M: 07769-927195 E: brucehc.gordon@virgin.net

GORDON, Donald Ian. b 30. Nottm Univ BA 52 PhD 64. Westcott Ho Cam 71. **d** 71 **p** 72. NSM Newport *Chelmsf* 71-75; NSM Creeksea w Althorne, Latchingdon and N Fambridge 76-00; rtd 00; PtO *Chelmsf* from 01. *Holden House, Steeple Road, Latchingdon, Chelmsford CM3 6JX* T: (01621) 740296
E: barbaragordon@tiscali.co.uk

GORDON, Edward John. b 32. Univ of Wales BA 52. St Mich Coll Llan 52. **d** 55 **p** 56. C Baglan *Llan* 55-61; C Newcastle w Laleston and Tythegston 61-64; V Ynyshir 65-69; C Bramhall *Ches* 69-72; V Cheadle Hulme All SS 72-79; V Tranmere St Paul w St Luke 79-88; V Sandbach Heath 88-97; Chapl Arclid Hosp 90-93; RD Congleton *Ches* 92-97; P-in-c Wheelock 95-97; rtd 97; PtO *B & W* from 97. *55 Greenslade Gardens, Nailsea, Bristol BS48 2BJ* T: (01275) 853404

GORDON, Jonathan Andrew. b 61. Keele Univ BA 83 MPhil 98 Southn Univ BTh 88 Southn Inst MPhil 04. Sarum & Wells Th Coll 84. **d** 87 **p** 88. C Wallingford w Crowmarsh Gifford etc *Ox* 87-91; C Tilehurst St Mich 91-93; TV Stoke-upon-Trent *Lich* 93-97; Chapl Southn Solent Univ 98-05; R Northchurch and Wigginton *St Alb* from 05; RD Berkhamsted from 14. *St Mary's Rectory, 80 High Street, Northchurch, Berkhamsted HP4 3QW* T: (01442) 871547
E: ebenezer@jonathangordon.wanadoo.co.uk

GORDON, Canon Kenneth Davidson. b 35. Edin Univ MA 57 Univ of Wales MTh 08. Tyndale Hall Bris 58. **d** 60 **p** 61. C St Helens St Helen *Liv* 60-66; V Daubhill *Man* 66-71; R Bieldside *Ab* 71-01; Can St Andr Cathl 81-01; Syn Clerk 96-01; rtd 01; Hon Can St Andr Cathl from 01; PtO *Blackb*

01-07; *Liv* 01-07; Bp's Warrant *Ab* 06-12; Bp's Commn from 12; P-in-c Aberdeen St Clem *Ab* from 12. *16 Reidford Gardens, Drumoak, Banchory AB31 5AW* T: (01330) 810260 M: 07715-169548 E: canonken@btinternet.com

GORDON, Kristy. *See* PATTIMORE, Kristy

GORDON, Martin Lewis. b 73. Edin Univ MA 97. Wycliffe Hall Ox BA 09. **d** 10 **p** 11. C Stoke Gifford *Bris* 10-14; P-in-c Telford Park *S'wark* from 14. *2 Thornton Road, London SW12 0JU*
E: martingordon2@gmail.com

GORDON, Noel. **d** 10. NSM Willowfield *D & D* 10-12; NSM Ballybeen from 12. *4 Falcon Drive, Newtownards BT23 4GH*
T: (028) 9182 0223

GORDON, Mrs Pamela Anne. b 48. Brighton Coll of Educn CertEd 69 BEd 70. SAOMC 99. **d** 02 **p** 03. NSM Wargrave w Knowl Hill *Ox* 02-12; PtO from 12. *Rebeny, 2A Hawthorn Road, Caversham, Reading RG4 6LY* T: 0118-946 3727 M: 07714-256272 E: revdpamgordon@virginmedia.com

GORDON, Sister Patricia Ann. b 44. SAOMC. **d** 00 **p** 01. CSMV from 80; NSM Didcot St Pet *Ox* 00-07; NSM Wantage Downs 07-11. *Address temp unknown* M: 07884-196004
E: sisterpatriciaann@hotmail.co.uk

GORDON, Robert Andrew. b 42. Llan Dioc Tr Scheme 82. **d** 84 **p** 85. C Bargoed and Deri w Brithdir *Llan* 84-87; V Aberpergwm and Blaengwrach 87-94; R Johnston w Steynton *St D* 94-97; R Cosheston w Nash and Upton 97-04; TV Carew 04-07; rtd 07. *6 Oakridge Acres, Tenby SA70 8DB* T: (01834) 844735

GORDON, Robert John. b 56. Edin Univ MA 81. Wycliffe Hall Ox 87. **d** 89 **p** 90. C Wilnecote *Lich* 89-91; C Bideford *Ex* 91-95; P-in-c Feniton, Buckerell and Escot 95-05; P-in-c Tiverton St Pet and Chevithorne w Cove 05-15; R from 15; P-in-c Tiverton St Andr from 11; RD Tiverton and Cullompton from 05. *St Peter's Vicarage, 29 Moorlands, Tiverton EX16 6UF* T: (01884) 254079 E: robert.j.gordon@btopenworld.com

GORDON, Ronald. *See* GORDON, Archibald Ronald McDonald

GORDON, The Very Revd Thomas William. b 57. QUB BEd 80 Univ of Ulster MA 86 TCD BTh 89. CITC 85. **d** 89 **p** 90. C Ballymacash *Conn* 89-91; Min Can Belf Cathl 91-95; Chapl and Tutor CITC 91-96; Dir Extra-Mural Studies 96-10; Lect Past Th and Liturgy 01-10; Consultant Dir Past Formation and NSM 06-09; PV Ch Ch Cathl Dublin 96-10; Co-ord Relig Progr RTE 99-10; Dean Leighlin *C & O* from 10; I Leighlin w Grange Sylvae, Shankill etc from 10. *The Deanery, Old Leighlin, Co Carlow, Republic of Ireland* T: (00353) (59) 972 1570 M: 87-276 7562 E: dean.leighlin@gmail.com

GORDON CLARK, John Vincent Michael. b 29. FCA. S'wark Ord Course 73. **d** 76 **p** 77. NSM Guildf H Trin w St Mary 76-81; NSM Albury w St Martha 81-91; Dioc Chapl to MU 92-95; LtO 95-99; Hon C Guildf Cathl 91-99; PtO 99-12. *Bethany, 250 Western Way, Ponteland, Newcastle upon Tyne NE20 9ND*

GORDON-CUMMING, Henry Ian. b 28. Barrister-at-Law (Gray's Inn) 56. Oak Hill Th Coll 54. **d** 57 **p** 58. C Southsea St Jude *Portsm* 57-60; Chapl to Bp Ankole-Kigezi Uganda 61-65; Chapl Ntari Sch 65-67; V Virginia Water *Guildf* 68-78; R Busbridge 78-87; R Lynch w Iping Marsh and Milland *Chich* 87-94; rtd 94; PtO *Chich* from 94. *Bay Cottage, Brookside, Runcton, Chichester PO20 1PX* T: (01243) 783395

GORDON-TAYLOR, Benjamin Nicholas. b 69. St Jo Coll Dur BA 90 MA 92 Leeds Univ BA 94 Dur Univ PhD 08 FRSA 99. Coll of Resurr Mirfield 92. **d** 95 **p** 96. C Launceston *Truro* 95-97; C Northampton St Matt *Pet* 97-99; Fell and Chapl Univ Coll Dur 99-04; Lect and Tutor Coll of Resurr Mirfield from 05; Visiting Lect Leeds Univ from 05; Dir Mirfield Liturg Inst from 08; Dioc Liturg Adv *Eur* from 13. *College of the Resurrection, Stocks Bank Road, Mirfield WF14 0BW* T: (01924) 490441
E: bgordon-taylor@mirfield.org.uk

GORDON-WALKER, Caroline. b 37. LMH Ox BA 59. Cranmer Hall Dur 01. **d** 02 **p** 03. NSM Poitou-Charentes *Eur* 02-05; C Aquitaine 05-07; Asst Chapl 07-12; rtd 12; PtO *Eur* from 12. *La Vieille Ferme, 24170 St Germain-de-Belvès, France*
T: (0033) 5 53 29 36 03 E: carolinegw@wanadoo.fr

GORE, Canon John Charles. b 29. Leeds Univ BA 52. Coll of Resurr Mirfield 52. **d** 54 **p** 55. C Middlesbrough St Jo the Ev *York* 54-59; N Rhodesia 59-64; Zambia 64-75; Can Lusaka 70-75; R Elland *Wakef* 75-84; TR 84-86; RD Brighouse and Elland 77-86; V Wembley Park St Aug *Lon* 86-95; P-in-c Tokyngton St Mich 89-90; AD Brent 90-95; rtd 95; P-in-c Heptonstall *Wakef* 95-99; PtO *Leeds* from 99. *3 Navigation Square, Skipton BD23 1XB* T: (01756) 792297

GORE, Canon John Harrington. b 24. Em Coll Cam BA 49 MA 52. Westcott Ho Cam 49. **d** 51 **p** 52. C Deane *Man* 51-54; C Whitstable All SS w St Pet *Cant* 54-59; CF 59-62; V Womenswold *Cant* 62-67; C-in-c Aylesham CD 62-67; R Deal St Leon 67-75; RD Sandwich 70-78; P-in-c Sholden 74-75; R Deal St Leon w Sholden 75-80; R Southchurch

H Trin *Chelmsf* 80-90; RD Southend 84-89; Hon Can Chelmsf Cathl 86-90; rtd 90; PtO *St E* from 90; *Chelmsf* from 90. *8 De Burgh Place, Clare, Sudbury CO10 8QL* T: (01787) 278558

GORE, Mrs Margaret Lesley. b 44. Westf Coll Lon BA 66. ERMC 05. **d** 07 **p** 08. NSM Cherry Hinton St Jo *Ely* 07-09; NSM Linton 09-13; rtd 13; PtO *Ely* from 13. *38 Symonds Lane, Linton, Cambridge CB21 4HY* T: (01223) 891970
E: lesley@lawngore.plus.com

GORHAM, Canon Andrew Arthur. b 51. Bris Univ BA 73 Birm Univ MA 87. Qu Coll Birm 77. **d** 79 **p** 80. C Plaistow St Mary *Roch* 79-82; Chapl Lanchester Poly *Cov* 82-87; TV Warwick 87-95; Chapl Birm Univ 95-00; Bp's Dom Chapl 00-11; Hon Can Birm Cathl 06-11; Master St Jo Hosp Lich from 11. *St John's Hospital, St John Street, Lichfield WS13 6PB* T: (01543) 251884

GORHAM, The Ven Karen Marisa. b 64. Trin Coll Bris BA 95. **d** 95 **p** 96. C Northallerton w Kirby Sigston *York* 95-99; P-in-c Maidstone St Paul *Cant* 99-07; Asst Dir of Ords 02-07; AD Maidstone 03-07; Hon Can Cant Cathl 06-07; Adn Buckingham *Ox* from 07. *The Rectory, Stone, Aylesbury HP17 8RZ* T: (01865) 208264 F: (01296) 747424
E: archdbuc@oxford.anglican.org

GORICK, David Charles. b 32. Reading Univ BA 55 Nottm Univ DipEd 72. EMMTC 81. **d** 84 **p** 85. NSM W Bridgford *S'well* 84-89; C Gotham 89-97; C Kingston and Ratcliffe-on-Soar 89-97; C Barton in Fabis 89-97; C Thrumpton 89-97; P-in-c Gotham 97-99; rtd 99; PtO *S'well* from 03. *11 Brookfields Way, East Leake, Loughborough LE12 6HD* T: (01509) 856960

GORICK, Janet Margaret. b 30. Reading Univ BA 54. EMMTC 84. **dss** 86 **d** 87 **p** 94. Hon Par Dn W Bridgford *S'well* 87-95; NSM Gotham 95-99; NSM Barton in Fabis 95-99; NSM Kingston and Ratcliffe-on-Soar 95-99; NSM Thrumpton 95-99; rtd 99; PtO *S'well* from 03. *11 Brookfields Way, East Leake, Loughborough LE12 6HD* T: (01509) 856960

GORICK, The Ven Martin Charles William. b 62. Selw Coll Cam BA 84 MA 88. Ripon Coll Cuddesdon 85. **d** 87 **p** 88. C Birtley *Dur* 87-91; Bp's Dom Chapl *Ox* 91-94; V Smethwick *Birm* 94-01; AD Warley 97-01; R Stratford-upon-Avon, Luddington etc *Cov* 01-13; Adn Ox and Can Res Ch Ch from 13. *Archdeacon's Lodgings, Christ Church, Oxford OX1 1DP* T: (01865) 208245 E: archdoxf@oxford.anglican.org

GORING, Charles Robert. b 60. Nottm Univ BA 91. Linc Th Coll 91. **d** 93 **p** 94. C Thornbury *Glouc* 93-96; PtO *Chich* 97-98; C Mayfield 98-00; V The Hydneye 00-07; C Eastbourne Ch Ch and St Phil 07-12; Asst Chapl E Sussex Hosps NHS Trust 01-12; C Peacehaven and Telscombe Cliffs w Piddinghoe etc *Chich* from 12. *73 Ambleside Avenue, Telscombe Cliffs, Peacehaven BN10 7LN* T: (01273) 973298
E: jc.goring@gmail.com

GORRIE, Richard Bingham. b 27. Univ Coll Ox BA 49 MA 51. Ridley Hall Cam 49. **d** 51 **p** 52. C Ox St Clem 51-54; C Morden *S'wark* 54-56; Scripture Union Rep (Scotland) 56-92; Chapl Fettes Coll Edin 60-74; Dir Inter-Sch Chr Fellowship (Scotland) 74-80; rtd 92; PtO *Glas* from 92. *20 Auchlochan Courtyard, New Trows Road, Lesmahagow, Lanark ML11 0GS* T: (01555) 895076 E: gorries@silas57.freeserve.co.uk

GORRINGE, Christine. b 44. **d** 13 **p** 14. OLM N Blackwater *Chelmsf* from 13. *2 Wilkin Drive, Tiptree, Colchester CO5 0QP* T: (01621) 819166 M: 07961-129422
E: christine.gorringe@btinternet.com

GORRINGE, Edward George Alexander. b 63. TD . QUB BA 85 Strathclyde Univ MBA 00 FCMA 06. CITC 04. **d** 07 **p** 08. NSM Aghalee *D & D* 07-09; CF from 09. *c/o MOD Chaplains (Army)* T: (01264) 381140 F: 381824
E: edward.gorringe@virginmedia.com

GORRINGE, Prof Timothy Jervis. b 46. St Edm Hall Ox BA 69 MPhil 75. Sarum Th Coll 69. **d** 72 **p** 73. C Chapel Allerton *Ripon* 72-75; C Ox St Mary V w St Cross and St Pet 76-78; India 79-86; Chapl St Jo Coll Ox 86-96; Reader St Andr Univ from 96; Prof Th Ex Univ from 99. *Department of Theology, Exeter University, Queen's Building, The Queen's Drive, Exeter EX4 4QH* T: (01392) 264242 E: t.j.gorringe@exeter.ac.uk

GORTON, Angela Deborah. See WYNNE, Angela Deborah

GORTON, Anthony David Trevor. b 39. Lon Univ BSc 65. Oak Hill Th Coll 78. **d** 81 **p** 82. NSM Colney Heath St Mark *St Alb* 81-00; NSM Watford St Pet from 00. *Waterdell, Lane End, Hatfield AL10 9AG* T: (01707) 263605
E: tonygorton@hotmail.com

GORTON, Ian Charles Johnson. b 62. Bp Otter Coll BA 84. Sarum & Wells Th Coll 86. **d** 89 **p** 90. C Wythenshawe Wm Temple Ch *Man* 89-92; C Man Apostles w Miles Platting 92-95; P-in-c Abbey Hey 95-03; P-in-c Moston St Chad 03-11; P-in-c Moston St Jo 05-11; TV Salford All SS from 11. *The Vicarage, 43 Derby Road, Salford M6 5YD* T: 0161-736 5819
E: charles.gorton@talk21.com

GORTON (née CARTER), Sarah Helen Buchanan. b 44. St Andr Univ BSc 65 DipEd 66. TISEC 93. **d** 96 **p** 98. NSM Lenzie *Glas* 96-01; P-in-c Alexandria 01-12; Chapl Argyll and Clyde NHS 01-12; rtd 12. *Northbank Gardens, 6B Northbank Road, Kirkintilloch, Glasgow G66 1EZ* T: 0141-775 1204
E: shbgorton@btinternet.com

GOSDEN, Angela. b 50. Ox Min Course 07. **d** 11 **p** 12. NSM Stanford in the Vale w Goosey and Hatford *Ox* 11-14; PtO 14-15; Chapl Gt Western Hosps NHS Foundn Trust from 15. *Upper Bockhampton Farmhouse, Bockhampton Road, Lambourn, Hungerford RG17 7LS* T: (01488) 73996 F: 72517
E: angela_gosden@btconnect.com

GOSDEN, Timothy John. b 50. Open Univ BA 86. Chich Th Coll 74. **d** 77 **p** 78. C Cant All SS 77-81; Asst Chapl Loughb Univ *Leic* 81-85; LtO *Cant* 85-87; Chapl Ch Ch Coll of HE Cant 85-87; Sen Chapl Hull Univ 87-94; V Taunton Lyngford *B & W* 94-98; V Harrow St Mary *Lon* 98-15; rtd 15. *St Mary's Vicarage, Church Hill, Harrow HA1 3HL* T: (020) 8422 2652
E: timgosden@tiscali.co.uk

GOSHAI, Miss Veja Helena. b 32. SRN 57 SCM 59 City Univ BSc 99. Trin Coll Bris 75. **d** 87 **p** 94. Asst Chapl St Barts Hosp Lon 87-97; rtd 92; PtO *S'wark* 99-03. *Grace, 26 Bilston Road, Crawford, Cape Town, 7780 South Africa*

GOSLING, David. b 27. SAOMC 95. **d** 98 **p** 99. OLM High Wycombe *Ox* 98-03; PtO 02-09; *Nor* from 10. *18 Parsons Mead, Norwich NR4 6PG* T: (01603) 506025
E: greygoose@talktalk.net

GOSLING, David Lagourie. b 39. Man Univ MSc 63 Fitzw Coll Cam MA 69 Lanc Univ PhD 74 MInstP 69 CPhys 84. Ridley Hall Cam 63. **d** 73 **p** 74. Hon C Lancaster St Mary *Blackb* 73-74; Hon C Kingston upon Hull St Matt w St Barn *York* 74-77; Hon C Cottingham 78-83; Asst Chapl Geneva *Eur* 84-89; C Cambridge Gt St Mary w St Mich *Ely* 89-90; C Dry Drayton 90-94; USPG India 95-99; PtO *York* from 95; *Ely* from 01; Fell Clare Hall Cam from 01; Prin Edwardes Coll Peshawar Pakistan from 06. *Clare Hall, Herschel Road, Cambridge CB3 9AL* T: (01223) 352450 F: 332333 E: dlg26@cam.ac.uk

GOSLING, Ms Dorothy Grace. b 57. St Martin's Coll Lanc BA 94 K Coll Lon MA 06. SNWTP 07. **d** 10 **p** 11. NSM Ches Cathl 10-14; Chapl Ches Univ 11-14; C Llanbedr DC, Llangynhafal, Llanychan etc. *St As* from 14. *7 Maes Celyn, Llanbedr Dyffryn Clwyd, Ruthin LL15 1YR* M: 07976-274459 T: (01824) 520236
E: dotchka@icloud.com

GOSLING, James Albert. b 41. Oak Hill Th Coll 81. **d** 84 **p** 85. NSM Victoria Docks St Luke *Chelmsf* 84-96; Hon C Gt Mongeham w Ripple and Sutton by Dover *Cant* 96-01; Hon C Eastry and Northbourne w Tilmanstone etc 96-01; C Kenton, Mamhead, Powderham, Cofton and Starcross *Ex* 01-02. *2 Wordsworth Close, Exmouth EX8 5SQ* T: (01395) 225278
E: jimandjan@jimandjan.fsnet.co.uk

GOSLING, John William Fraser. b 34. St Jo Coll Dur BA 58 MA 71 Ex Univ PhD 78 Win Univ MA 12. Cranmer Hall Dur 58. **d** 60 **p** 61. C Plympton St Mary *Ex* 60-68; V Newport 68-78; Org Sec CECS St Alb and Ox 78-82; C Stratford sub Castle *Sarum* 83-86; Adv on CME 83-86; PtO 86-91 and from 95; C Swindon Ch Ch *Bris* 91-95; rtd 95. *1 Wiley Terrace, Wilton, Salisbury SP2 0HN* T: (01722) 742788
E: jwfgosling@gmail.com

GOSNEY, Jeanette Margaret. b 58. Bath Univ BA 81 Univ Coll Ches MA 05 Nottm Univ PGCE 82. St Jo Coll Nottm BTh 93 MPhil 95. **d** 95 **p** 96. C Ipswich St Marg *St E* 95-98; Chapl Loughb Univ *Leic* 98; Sen Chapl 98-01; Tutor Trin Coll Bris 01-04; Chapl Repton Sch Derby 04-05; TV Albury, Braughing, Furneux Pelham, Lt Hadham etc *St Alb* 06-10; Par Development Officer from 10. *1 Linden Glade, Hemel Hempstead HP1 1XB* T: (01442) 239428
E: jgosney@stalbans.anglican.org

GOSS, David James. b 52. Nottm Univ BCombStuds 83 York St Jo Univ MA 10. Linc Th Coll 80. **d** 83 **p** 84. C Wood Green St Mich w Bounds Green St Gabr etc *Lon* 83-86; TV Gleadless Valley *Sheff* 86-89; TR 89-95; V Wheatley Hills 95-15; V Wheatley Hills w Intake from 15. *The Vicarage, 18 Central Boulevard, Doncaster DN2 5PE* T: (01302) 342047
E: davidjamesgoss@gmail.com *or* david.goss@sheffield.anglican.org

GOSS, Kevin Ian. b 56. LRAM 75 LTCL 76 GRSM 77 LGSM 80 Hughes Hall Cam PGCE 78 Heythrop Coll Lon MA 08. S Dios Minl Tr Scheme 89. **d** 92 **p** 93. NSM Ardingly *Chich* 92-98; Asst Chapl Ardingly Coll 92-98; Min Can, Prec and Sacr Cant Cathl 98-03; P-in-c Hockerill *St Alb* 04-13; V 13-14; Chapl Herts and Essex Community NHS Trust 04-14; RD Bishop's Stortford *St Alb* 12-14; V Bedford St Paul from 14. *St Paul's Vicarage, 12 The Embankment, Bedford MK40 3PD* T: (01234) 364638

GOSS, Michael John. b 37. Chich Th Coll 62. **d** 65 **p** 66. C Angell Town St Jo *S'wark* 65-68; C Catford St Laur 68-71; P-in-c Lewisham St Swithun 71-81; V Redhill St Jo 81-88;

V Dudley St Thos and St Luke *Worc* 88-98; C Small Heath *Birm* 98-02; rtd 02; PtO *Birm* from 02. *8 Mayland Road, Birmingham B16 0NG* T: 0121-429 6022 E: michael.goss@tinyworld.co.uk

GOSTELOW (née THOMPSON), Mrs Ruth Jean. b 47. St Alb Minl Tr Scheme 85. **d** 90 **p** 94. Par Dn Stonebridge St Mich *Lon* 90-94; C Ealing St Paul 94-96; TV W Slough *Ox* 96-03; V New Haw *Guildf* 03-13; rtd 13. *34 North Salts, Rye TN31 7NU* T: (01797) 227972 E: rev.ruth@btinternet.com

GOSWELL, Geoffrey. b 34. SS Paul & Mary Coll Cheltenham CertEd 68. Glouc Th Course 70. **d** 71 **p** 72. C Cheltenham Em *Glouc* 71-73; C Lydney w Aylburton 73-76; P-in-c Falfield w Rockhampton 76-79; Chapl HM Det Cen Eastwood Park 76-79; Area Sec CMS *Ely* 79-81; PtO *Linc* 79-86; *Pet* 79-86; Dep Regional Sec (UK) CMS 86-97; P-in-c Orton Waterville *Ely* 90-96; TV The Ortons, Alwalton and Chesterton 96-97; rtd 97; PtO *Pet* 01-07. *8 Lapwing Close, Northampton NN4 0RT* T: (01604) 701572 E: g.goswell@hotmail.co.uk

GOTHARD, Mrs Anne Marie. b 51. STETS. **d** 00 **p** 11. NSM E Meon and Langrish *Portsm* 00-04; NSM Catherington and Clanfield from 04. *27 Green Lane, Clanfield, Waterlooville PO8 0JU* T: (023) 9259 6315 M: 07939-472796 E: rev_gothard@hotmail.com

GOTT, Stephen. b 61. St Jo Coll Nottm 92. **d** 94 **p** 95. C Mount Pellon *Wakef* 94-97; V Greetland and W Vale 97-06; TR Em TM *Leeds* from 06. *The Rectory, 42 Beaumont Park Road, Huddersfield HD4 5JS* E: stephen.gott1@hotmail.co.uk

GOUGH, Canon Andrew Stephen. b 60. Sarum & Wells Th Coll 83. **d** 86 **p** 87. C St Leonards Ch Ch and St Mary *Chich* 86-88; C Broseley w Benthall *Heref* 88-90; V Ketley and Oakengates *Lich* 90-93; TV Bickleigh (Plymouth) *Ex* 93; TV Bickleigh and Shaugh Prior 94; P-in-c St Day *Truro* 94-96; V Chacewater w St Day and Carharrack 96-09; P-in-c St Ives from 09; P-in-c Halsetown from 09; Hon Can Truro Cathl from 14. *St Johns in the Fields Vicarage, Hellesvean, St Ives TR26 6HG* M: 07590-695515 E: goughfr@hotmail.com

GOUGH, Andrew Walter. b 55. Bris Univ BA 78. Trin Coll Bris 90. **d** 92 **p** 93. C Mossley Hill St Matt and St Jas *Liv* 92-94; C Wavertree H Trin 94-96; Chapl Warw Sch from 96. *9 Griffin Road, Warwick CV34 6QX* T: (01926) 400533 *or* 776416 E: awg@warwickschool.co.uk

GOUGH, Canon Colin Richard. b 47. St Chad's Coll Dur BA 69. Cuddesdon Coll 73. **d** 75 **p** 76. C Lich St Chad 75-78; C Codsall 78-84; V Wednesbury St Paul Wood Green 84-92; TR Tettenhall Wood 92-99; TR Tettenhall Wood and Perton 99-01; P-in-c Stannington *Newc* 01-10; Dioc Adv for CME 01-10; AD Morpeth 08-10; Hon Can Newc Cathl 06-10; rtd 10. *44 Tyelaw Meadows, Shilbottle NE66 2JJ* T: (01665) 581100 E: colingough@onetel.com

GOUGH, David Kenneth. b 44. St Mark & St Jo Coll *Lon* TCert 66 Open Univ BA 93. **d** 07 **p** 08. OLM Kinnerley w Melverley and Knockin w Maesbrook *Lich* 07-12; PtO from 12. *Ainsdale House, Maesbrook, Oswestry SY10 8QP*

GOUGH, David Norman. b 42. Oak Hill Th Coll 70. **d** 70 **p** 71. C Penn Fields *Lich* 70-73; C Stapenhill w Cauldwell *Derby* 73-77; V Heath 77-86; P-in-c Derby St Chad 86-95; TV Walbrook Epiphany 95-03; P-in-c Codnor and Loscoe 03-07; rtd 07. *7 Mulberry Close, Belper DE56 1RQ* T: (01773) 599013 E: thevic@dsl.pipex.com *or* heyhogough@yahoo.co.uk

GOUGH, David Richard. b 71. St Jo Coll Nottm 06. **d** 08 **p** 09. C Sheff St Jo 08-11; P-in-c Woodhouse St Jas 11-15; V from 15. *St James's Vicarage, 65 Cardwell Avenue, Sheffield S13 7XB* T: 0114-348 4621 M: 07913-083656 E: david.gough@sheffield.anglican.org

GOUGH, Derek William. b 31. Pemb Coll Cam BA 55 MA 59. St Steph Ho Ox 55. **d** 57 **p** 58. C E Finchley All SS *Lon* 57-60; C Roxbourne St Andr 60-66; V Edmonton St Mary w St Jo 66-98; rtd 98; PtO *Chelmsf* 98-07; *St Alb* 00-07. *43A Church Street, Market Deeping, Peterborough PE6 8AN* T: (01778) 341421

GOUGH, Elizabeth. b 54. CBDTI 97. **d** 00 **p** 01. OLM Eden, Gelt and Irthing *Carl* 00-06; TV 06-14; rtd 14. *Brackenside Barn, Brampton CA8 2QX* T: (016977) 746252 E: elizabeth.gough3@btinternet.com

GOUGH, Canon Ernest Hubert. b 31. TCD BA 53 MA 57. TCD Div Sch Div Test 54. **d** 54 **p** 55. C Glenavy *Conn* 54-57; C Lisburn Ch Ch 57-61; P-in-c Belfast St Ninian 61-62; I 62-71; I Belfast St Bart 71-85; I Templepatrick w Donegore 85-97; Can Conn Cathl from 91; rtd 97. *The Cairn, 15 Swilly Road, Portstewart BT55 7DJ* T: (028) 7083 3253 E: ehg@thecaim.eu

GOUGH, Frank Peter. b 32. Lon Coll of Div 66. **d** 68 **p** 69. C Weymouth St Mary *Sarum* 68-70; C Attenborough w Chilwell *S'well* 70-73; R Barrow *Ches* 73-77; P-in-c Summerstown *S'wark* 77-88; RD Tooting 80-88; Dioc Past Sec 88-93; Tutor and Chapl Whittington Coll Felbridge 93-98; rtd 98; PtO *Roch* 03-07; *S'wark* from 13. *24 Whittington College, London Road, Felbridge, East Grinstead RH19 2QU* M: 07970-199135 E: frank_gough@msn.com

GOUGH, Canon Jonathan Robin Blanning. b 62. Univ of Wales (Lamp) BA 83 Westmr Coll Ox MTh 96 FRSA 03. St Steph Ho Ox 83. **d** 85 **p** 86. C Braunton *Ex* 85-86; C Matson *Glouc* 86-89; CF 89-01; Abp's Officer for Ecum *Cant* 01-05; Can Gib Cathl 02-05; Hon Can Nicosia from 06; CF 05-08; Sen CF from 08; Chapl R Memorial Chpl Sandhurst 08-11. *c/o MOD Chaplains (Army)* F: 381824 T: (01264) 383430 E: jonathan.gough443@mod.uk

GOUGH, Miss Lynda Elizabeth. b 54. SS Hild & Bede Coll Dur BA 94 RGN 83. Wycliffe Hall Ox 97. **d** 99 **p** 00. C Stranton *Dur* 99-03; V Spennymoor and Whitworth 03-11; C Darlington H Trin from 11; AD Darlington from 14. *32 Skeldale Grove, Darlington DL3 0GW* T: (01325) 282456

GOUGH, Martyn John. b 66. Univ of Wales (Cardiff) BTh 87 Univ of Wales (Lamp) MA 05 FRSA 04. St Steph Ho Ox 88. **d** 90 **p** 91. C Port Talbot St Theodore *Llan* 90-92; C Roath 92-94; Asst Chapl Milan w Genoa and Varese *Eur* 95-98; Chapl RN 98-14; Asst Dir of Ords RN and Voc Advr 07-09; Voc Advr 07-14; Dir 09-14; Dep Chapl of the Fleet from 14. *Royal Naval Chaplaincy Service, Mail Point 1-2, Leach Building, Whale Island, Portsmouth PO2 8BY* F: 9262 5134 T: (023) 9262 5193 M: 07733-001365 E: martyn.gough656@mod.uk

GOUGH, Stephen William Cyprian. b 50. Alberta Univ BSc 71. Cuddesdon Coll BA 80 MA. **d** 79 **p** 80. C Walton St Mary *Liv* 79-83; V New Springs 83-87; V Childwall St Dav 87-06; V Stoneycroft All SS 04-06; Co-ord Chapl HM Pris Risley 06-08; P-in-c Rainford *Liv* 08-11; V 11-13; TV Walton-on-the-Hill from 13. *49 Grange Lane, Gateacre, Liverpool L25 4SA* T: 0151-421 1213 M: 07881-648037 E: gough_stephen@btopenworld.com

GOULD, Christine. b 52. **d** 10. NSM Darwen St Pet *Blackb* 10-14; rtd 14; PtO *Blackb* from 14. *10 King's Drive, Hoddlesden, Darwen BB3 3RB* T: (01254) 773172 E: b.gould@yahoo.com

GOULD, David Robert. b 59. Cov Poly BA 81. Cranmer Hall Dur 87. **d** 90 **p** 91. C Rugby *Cov* 90-93; CF 93-94; PtO *Cov* 01-05; TV Kings Norton *Birm* 05-08; V Smethwick Resurr from 08. *The Vicarage, 69 South Road, Smethwick, Warley B67 7BP* T: 0121-558 0373 M: 07787-199998 E: davidgould1@btinternet.com

GOULD, Helen Elizabeth-Anne. *See* GHEORGHIU GOULD, Helen Elizabeth-Anne

GOULD, Ms Janet. b 63. LTCL 85. Westcott Ho Cam 92. **d** 95 **p** 96. C Pet St Mary Boongate 95-98; C Fleet *Guildf* 98-04; C St Mellons *Mon* 04-05; P-in-c Glan Ely *Llan* from 06. *Church House, Grand Avenue, Cardiff CF5 2YJ* T: (029) 2067 9833 E: jan.gould2@btinternet.com

GOULD, Jonathan George Lillico. b 58. Bris Univ LLB 79. Wycliffe Hall Ox 86. **d** 89 **p** 91. Australia 89-93; Schs Worker Scripture Union Independent Schs 93-95; PtO *S'wark* 93-95; Min Hampstead St Jo Downshire Hill Prop Chpl *Lon* from 95. *The Parsonage, 64 Pilgrim's Lane, London NW3 1SN* T: (020) 7794 8946 *or* T/F: 7435 8404 E: jonathan@sjdh.org

GOULD, Mrs Pamela Rosemarie. b 41. **d** 01 **p** 02. NSM New Bilton *Cov* 01-03; Asst Chapl HM YOI Onley 01-03; NSM Clifton upon Dunsmore and Newton *Cov* 03-05; P-in-c 05-06; PtO from 07. *19 Church Road, Church Lawford, Rugby CV23 9EG* T: (024) 7654 5745 E: revpamgould@aol.com

GOULD, Peter Richard. b 34. Univ of Wales BA 57. Qu Coll Birm. **d** 62 **p** 63. C Rothwell *Ripon* 62-68; Chapl Agnes Stewart C of E High Sch Leeds 65-68; V Allerton Bywater *Ripon* 68-73; Asst Master S'well Minster Gr Sch 73-76; Chapl Lic Victuallers' Sch Ascot 76-93; V Aberavon H Trin *Llan* 93-99; rtd 99. *Amber Cottage, 1 Load Lane, Weston Zoyland, Bridgwater TA7 0EQ* T: (01278) 691029

GOULD, Robert Ozburn. b 38. Williams Coll Mass BA 59 St Andr Univ PhD 63. **d** 78 **p** 83. NSM Edin St Columba 78-80; TV from 83; Hon Dioc Supernumerary 80-83; Hon Chapl Edin Univ 00-04. *33 Charterhall Road, Edinburgh EH9 3HS* T: 0131-667 7230 E: bob@gould.ca

GOULD, Susan Judith. *See* MURRAY, Susan Judith

GOULDER, Canon Catherine Helen. b 44. Hull Univ BA 65 MA 67 Ox Univ DipEd 68. NEOC 96. **d** 98 **p** 99. NSM Sutton St Mich *York* 98-02; P-in-c Hotham and N Cave w Cliffe 02-08; PtO from 08; Can and Preb York Minster from 05. *5 Bishops Croft, Beverley HU17 8JY* T: (01482) 880553 E: kategoulder@kategoulder.karoo.co.uk

GOULDING, Amanda. b 53. STETS. **d** 07 **p** 08. NSM Upper Dever *Win* 07-08; NSM Win St Bart 08-10; NSM Win St Bart and St Lawr w St Swithun from 10. *Long Valley, Deane Down Drove, Littleton, Winchester SO22 6PP* T: (01962) 884585 E: agoulding@btinternet.com

GOULDING, John Gilbert. b 29. Univ Coll Dur BA 54 MA 59. **d** 88 **p** 89. NSM Kemsing w Woodlands *Roch* 88-91; Hon Nat Moderator for Reader Tr ACCM 90-91; ABM 91-94; NSM Sevenoaks St Luke CD *Roch* 91-96; PtO from 97. *Springwood, 50 Copperfields, Kemsing, Sevenoaks TN15 6QG* T: (01732) 762558

GOULDING, Nicolas John. b 56. Southn Univ BSc 78 PhD 82. NTMTC 94. **d** 97 **p** 98. NSM St Bart Less *Lon* 97-05; Chapl St Bart's and RLSMD Qu Mary and Westf Coll from 97; PtO *St Alb* from 99. *5 Greatfield Close, Harpenden AL5 3HP* T: (01582) 461293 *or* (020) 7882 6128 F: 7982 6076
E: n.j.goulding@qmul.ac.uk

GOULDTHORPE, Rachel Carolyn. b 72. Bp Otter Coll 00. **d** 03 **p** 10. NSM Hove *Chich* 03-05; C Moulsecoomb 05-11; TV 11-12; V Bolsover *Derby* from 12. *The Vicarage, Church Street, Bolsover, Chesterfield S44 6HB* T: (01273) 824888
M: 07859-066557 E: rachelgouldthorpe@gmail.com

GOULSTON, Jeremy Hugh. b 68. St Aid Coll Dur BA 90. Ripon Coll Cuddesdon 01. **d** 03 **p** 04. C Henfield w Shermanbury and Woodmancote *Chich* 03-07; TV Wallingford *Ox* 07-15; R Uffington, Shellingford, Woolstone and Baulking from 15. *The Vicarage, Broad Street, Uffington, Farington SN7 7RA* T: (01491) 837626 E: jgoulston@btinternet.com

GOUNDREY-SMITH, Stephen John. b 67. Brighton Poly BSc 88 MRPharmS 89 City Univ MSc 94. Aston Tr Scheme 96 Wycliffe Hall Ox BTh 01. **d** 99 **p** 00. C Happisburgh, Walcott, Hempstead w Eccles etc *Nor* 99-01; PtO *Pet* 02-03; NSM Chenderit 03-08; PtO 09-11; P-in-c Chedworth, Yanworth and Stowell, Coln Rogers etc *Glouc* from 10; Hon C Northleach w Hampnett and Farmington etc from 10; Hon C Sherborne, Windrush, the Barringtons etc from 10. *The Vicarage, Cheap Street, Chedworth, Cheltenham GL54 4AA* T: (01285) 720392
M: 07771-741009
E: stephen@goundrey-smith.freeserve.co.uk

GOUNDRY, Canon Ralph Walter. b 31. St Chad's Coll Dur BA 56. **d** 58 **p** 59. C Harton Colliery *Dur* 58-62; Prec Newc Cathl 62-65; V Sighill 65-72; V Long Benton 72-96; Hon Can Newc Cathl 94-96; rtd 96; PtO *York* 96-98. *16 Old Manor Way, Chislehurst BR7 5XS* T: (020) 8249 9992

GOURDIE, Janice Elizabeth. *See* BROWN, Janice Elizabeth

GOURLAY, Wendy Elizabeth. b 50. DipOT 71. ERMC 08. **d** 11 **p** 12. NSM Boulge w Burgh, Grundisburgh and Hasketon *St E* 11-13; NSM Carlford from 13. *Tubric Cottage, The Street, Cretingham, Woodbridge IP13 7BL* T: (01728) 685335
E: rev.gourlay@gmail.com

GOURLEY, Malcolm Samuel. b 37. MRPharmS 58. NEOC 94. **d** 98 **p** 98. NSM Gt Smeaton w Appleton Wiske and Birkby etc *Ripon* 98-00; NSM Ainderby Steeple w Yafforth and Kirby Wiske etc 00-02; NSM Herrington, Penshaw and Shiney Row *Dur* 02-07; rtd 07; PtO *Dur* from 07. *10 Weymouth Drive, Houghton le Spring DH4 7TQ* T: 0191-385 4076

GOVAN, Kesh Rico. b 66. St Jo Coll Dur BA 96. Cranmer Hall Dur 93. **d** 96 **p** 97. C Astley Bridge *Man* 96-00; TV Walkden and Lt Hulton 00-04; I Blessington w Kilbride, Ballymore Eustace etc *D & G* 04-07; C Uttoxeter Area *Lich* 07-10; C Rocester and Croxden w Hollington 07-10; V 10-14; Chapl JCB Academy 10-14; R Nelson Bay Australia from 14. *29 Tomaree Street, Nelson Bay NSW 2315, Australia* T: (0061) (2) 4981 1839 E: revkesh@sky.com *or* allsaint@nelsonbay.com

GOVENDER, The Very Revd Rogers Morgan. b 60. Natal Univ BTh 97. St Paul's Coll Grahamstown 83. **d** 85 **p** 86. C Overport Ch Ch S Africa 85-87; R Greyville St Mary 88-92; R Hayfields St Matt 93-98; Adn Pietermaritzburg 97-98; R Berea St Thos S Africa 99-00; P-in-c Didsbury Ch Ch *Man* 01-06; P-in-c Withington St Chris 03-06; AD Withington 04-06; Dean Man from 06. *1 Booth Clibborn Court, Salford M7 4PJ* T: 0161-792 2801 *or* 833 2220 F: 839 6218
E: dean@manchestercathedral.org

GOW, Iain Douglas. b 60. Denver Univ USA BA 83 MIM 85. Trin Coll Bris MA 94. **d** 94 **p** 95. C Kenilworth St Jo *Cov* 94-97; C Birm St Martin w Bordesley St Andr 97-05; AD Birm City Cen 02-04; New Zealand from 05. *2/82 Knights Road, Rothesay Bay, North Shore, Auckland 1311, New Zealand* T: (0064) (9) 478 4894

GOWDEY, Michael Cragg. b 32. Oriel Coll Ox BA 56 MA 58 Keele Univ CertEd 73. Qu Coll Birm. **d** 58 **p** 59. C Ashbourne w Mapleton and Clifton *Derby* 58-63; V Chellaston 63-69; Asst Chapl Ellesmere Coll 69-74; Chapl Trent Coll Nottm 74-81; Educn Chapl *Worc* 81-97; Chapl K Edw Sixth Form Coll Worc 81-97; rtd 97; P-in-c Beeley and Edensor *Derby* 97-02; PtO from 02. *18 Moorhall Estate, Bakewell DE45 1FP* T: (01629) 814121
E: jandmgowdey@uwclub.net

GOWEN, John Frank. b 30. **d** 87 **p** 89. Aux Min Lecale Gp and Cregagh *D & D* 87-91; LtO 89-99; Aux Min Stormont 99-01; Aux Min Knock 01-05; rtd 05. *36 Downshire Road, Belfast BT6 9JL* T: (028) 9070 1640 M: 07815-301818
E: jgowen212@btinternet.com

GOWER, Canon Christopher Raymond. b 45. Nottm Univ BA 73 Heythrop Coll Lon MA 96 Univ of Wales MTh 02 FRSA 84. St Jo Coll Nottm 70. **d** 73 **p** 74. C Hounslow H Trin *Lon* 73-76; Hon C N Greenford All Hallows 76-77; P-in-c Willesden Green St Gabr 77-83; P-in-c Brondesbury St Anne w

Kilburn H Trin 81-82; PtO 82-84; P-in-c Yiewsley 84-96; R St Marylebone w H Trin 97-09; P-in-c St Marylebone St Cypr 99-02; Preb St Paul's Cathl 07-09; rtd 09; PtO *Win* 10-13; S'wark from 14; Ox from 15; Hon Can Ilesa from 04. *14 Kensington Mews, Windsor SL4 3FA* T: (01753) 864644

GOWER, Denys Victor. b 33. Cant Sch of Min 85. **d** 87 **p** 88. NSM Gillingham H Trin *Roch* 87-91; NSM Gillingham St Aug 89-91; C Perry Street 91-93; P-in-c Wateringbury w Teston and W Farleigh 93-96; R 96-00; rtd 00; PtO *Roch* from 00; Ind Chapl from 02; PtO *Cant* 03-09; Hon Chapl Medway NHS Foundn Trust from 05; PV Roch Cathl from 07. *4 Locarno Avenue, Gillingham ME8 6ET* T: (01634) 375765
M: 07985-781161

GOWER, Nigel Plested. b 37. SS Coll Cam BA 62 MA 65 Lon Univ PGCE 68. Ridley Hall Cam 61. **d** 63 **p** 64. C Walthamstow St Jo *Chelmsf* 63-66; CMS Nigeria 67-78; P-in-c Loscoe *Derby* 78-79; V 79-88; RD Heanor 84-88; R Bamford 88-98; Dioc World Development Officer 90-96; P-in-c Bradwell 96-98; Assoc P Alfreton Deanery 98-02; rtd 02; PtO *Heref* 02-08. *New Cottage, Llanbister Road, Llandrindod Wells LD1 5UW* T: (01547) 550318

GOWER, Miss Patricia Ann. b 44. Wilson Carlile Coll IDC 79 Sarum & Wells Th Coll 88. **d** 88 **p** 94. Chapl Bris Univ 88-91; Hon Par Dn Clifton St Paul 88-91; Par Dn Spondon *Derby* 91-94; C 94-95; P-in-c Hatton 95-98; Asst Chapl HM Pris Sudbury 95-98; Chapl 98-04; rtd 04; PtO *Derby* from 04. *19 Heronswood Drive, Spondon, Derby DE21 7AX* T: (01332) 671031 E: pgower217@btinternet.com

GOWER, Miss Paulette Rose-Mary de Garis. b 70. Plymouth Univ BEd 93 St Jo Coll Dur MA 08. Cranmer Hall Dur 01. **d** 03 **p** 04. C Shrewsbury St Geo w Greenfields *Lich* 03-07; TV Hawarden *St As* 07-14; V Gwersyllt from 14. *The Vicarage, Old Mold Road, Gwersyllt, Wrexham LL11 4SB* T: (01978) 756391
E: paulettegower@gwersyllt.plus.com

GOWER, Mrs Sarah Catherine. b 63. Ex Univ BA 84 Cam Univ BTh 09. Westcott Ho Cam 07. **d** 09 **p** 10. C St Neots *Ely* 09-13; C Eynesbury 12-13; Min Orton Goldhay CD from 13. *Christ Church House, 1 Benstead, Orton Goldhay, Peterborough PE2 5JJ* E: sarahcgower@btinternet.com

GOWER, Archdeacon of. *See* WILLIAMS, The Ven Robert John

GOWERS, Nicholas Stephen. b 78. Jes Coll Cam MEng 02 MA 05. Oak Hill Th Coll MTh 08. **d** 08 **p** 09. C Ex St Leon w H Trin 08-13; V Old Hill H Trin *Worc* from 13. *The Vicarage, 58 Wrights Lane, Cradley Heath B64 6RD*

GOWING, Wilfred Herbert. b 50. QUB BSc 72. NEOC 03. **d** 06 **p** 07. NSM Ripon H Trin *Leeds* from 06. *Littlemead, 20 Springfield Rise, Great Ouseburn, York YO26 9SE* T: (01423) 331177 F: 331178 E: wilfgowing@btinternet.com

GOWING-CUMBER, Alexander John. b 72. Fitzw Coll Cam MA 00 Moorlands Th Coll BA 94. Ridley Hall Cam 98. **d** 00 **p** 03. C Vange *Chelmsf* 00-02; C Rayleigh 02-05; TV Grays Thurrock 05-15; rtd 15; PtO *Chelmsf* from 15. *Trinity House, 5 Nevada Road, Canvey Island SS8 8EX* T: (01268) 698414
E: fralexgc@aol.com

GOY, Andrew Robert. b 85. St Jo Coll Dur BA 07. Ridley Hall Cam 12. **d** 15. C Crookhorn *Portsm* from 15. *5 Chilsdown Way, Waterlooville PO7 5DT* M: 07540-810616

GOYMOUR, Mrs Joanna Leigh. b 58. Reading Univ BA 79. **d** 02 **p** 03. OLM Bures w Assington and Lt Cornard *St E* 02-13; NSM from 13. *Dorking Tye House, Dorking Tye, Bures CO8 5JY* T: (01787) 227494 E: jo@acgoymour.freeserve.co.uk

GRACE, Alexandra. d 12 **p** 13. C Tenby *St D* 12-14; C Manorbier and St Florence 14-15; P-in-c from 15; Voc Adv from 15. *The Rectory, Church Park, Tenby SA70 7EE* T: (01834) 842068

GRACE, Canon Andrew John. b 54. Univ of Wales (Abth) BMus 76 St Martin's Coll Lanc PGCE 78 FRCO 75 FTCL 76 LRAM 75. Sarum & Wells Th Coll 79. **d** 81 **p** 82. C Tenby w Gumfreston *St D* 81-84; C Llanelli 84-86; V Monkton 86-91; V Fairfield *Derby* 91-96; P-in-c Barlborough 96-01; R Barlborough and Renishaw 01-03; V Pembroke Dock *St D* 03-04; TR Carew 04-08; TR Tenby from 08; AD Pembroke from 13. *The Rectory, Church Park, Tenby SA70 7EE* T: (01834) 842068 E: andrewgrace1919@gmail.com

GRACE, David Leonard. b 55. Wilson Carlile Coll 89 Ripon Coll Cuddesdon 97. **d** 99 **p** 00. C St Leonards and St Ives *Win* 99-04; V 04-09; Chapl Basingstoke and N Hants NHS Foundn Trust 09-11; Chapl Hants Hosps NHS Foundn Trust 12-13; Chapl Weston Area Health NHS Trust from 13. *The Chaplaincy, Weston General Hospital, Grange Road, Uphill, Weston-super-Mare BS23 4TQ* M: 07825-896388 T: (01934) 636363 ext 3611 E: david.grace1@nhs.net

GRACE, Mrs Irene. b 36. Nottm Univ BSc 58. Guildf Dioc Min Course 96. **d** 98 **p** 99. OLM Stoneleigh *Guildf* 98-06; PtO from 06. *33 Woodstone Avenue, Stoneleigh, Epsom KT17 2JS* T: (020) 8393 7280

GRACE, Louise Sarah. b 68. Girton Coll Cam BA 89. Ripon Coll Cuddesdon BA 97 Ch Div Sch of Pacific 97. **d** 98 **p** 99. C Wordsley *Worc* 98-02; R Teme Valley N 03-15; RD Stourport 07-13; V Topsham and Wear *Ex* from 15. *The Vicarage, Globefield, Topsham, Exeter EX3 0EZ* M: 07779-585908 E: revgrace@hotmail.co.uk

GRACE, Miss Michelle Elizabeth. b 69. St Jo Coll Nottm BA 12. **d** 12. C Chell *Lich* 12-13; C Oswestry from 13. *10 Cae Melin Avenue, Oswestry SY11 2US* T: (01691) 570684

GRACIE, Canon Bryan John. b 45. MBE 06. Open Univ BA 81. AKC 67. **d** 68 **p** 69. C Whipton *Ex* 68-72; Chapl St Jo Sch Tiffield 72-73; Chapl HM Borstal Stoke Heath 74-78; Asst Chapl HM Pris Liv 74; Chapl HM Youth Cust Cen Feltham 78-85; Chapl HM Pris Birm 85-10; Hon Can Birm Cathl 05-10; rtd 10; PtO *Birm* from 10. *346 Eachelhurst Road, Sutton Coldfield B76 1ER* T: 0121-351 6532

GRADY, Gary Brian. b 69. Bris Poly BA 92. WEMTC 10. **d** 13 **p** 14. C Cirencester *Glouc* from 13. *54 Alexander Drive, Cirencester GL7 1UH* T: (01285) 655092 M: 07713-654074 E: garygrady@btinternet.com

GRAEBE, Canon Denys Redford. b 26. Qu Coll Cam BA 48 MA 51. Westcott Ho Cam 50. **d** 51 **p** 52. C Hitchin St Mary *St Alb* 51-57; R Gt Parndon *Chelmsf* 57-72; V Norton *St Alb* 72-83; R Kimpton w Ayot St Lawrence 83-92; RD Wheathampstead 87-92; Hon Can St Alb Abbey 90-92; rtd 92; PtO *St E* from 92. *5 Sancroft Way, Fressingfield, Eye IP21 5QN* T: (01379) 588178

GRAESSER, Adrian Stewart. b 42. Tyndale Hall Bris 63. **d** 67 **p** 68. C Nottingham St Jude *S'well* 67-69; C Slaithwaite w E Scammonden *Wakef* 69-72; CF 72-75; V Earl's Heaton *Wakef* 75-81; R Norton Fitzwarren *B & W* 81-86; R Bickenhill w Elmdon *Birm* 86-90; R Elmdon St Nic 90-00; P-in-c Dolton *Ex* 00-05; P-in-c Iddesleigh w Dowland 00-05; P-in-c Monkokehampton 00-05; RD Torrington 02-05; rtd 05; PtO *Worc* from 09. *7 Mortlake Drive, Martley, Worcester WR6 6QU* T: (01886) 888628 E: adrian.graesser@sky.com

GRAHAM, Alan Robert. b 44. St Edm Hall Ox BA 67 MA 71. St Steph Ho Ox BA 70. **d** 70 **p** 71. C Clifton All SS *Bris* 70-74; C Tadley St Pet *Win* 74-77; P-in-c Upper Clatford w Goodworth Clatford 77-79; R Abbotts Ann and Upper and Goodworth Clatford 79-84; V Lyndhurst and Emery Down 84-92; P-in-c Over Wallop w Nether Wallop 92-02; rtd 02; PtO *Win* from 08. *44 New Forest Drive, Brockenhurst SO42 7QW* T: (01590) 622324 E: agwvgraham@waitrose.com

GRAHAM, Alexander. *See* GRAHAM, Andrew Alexander Kenny

GRAHAM, Alfred. b 34. Bris Univ BA 57. Tyndale Hall Bris. **d** 58 **p** 59. C Chaddesden St Mary *Derby* 58-61; C Bickenhill w Elmdon *Birm* 61-64; V Kirkdale St Lawr *Liv* 64-70; V Stapleford *S'well* 70-83; V Burton Joyce w Bulcote 83-95; V Burton Joyce w Bulcote and Stoke Bardolph 95-97; rtd 97; PtO *S'well* 03-11; *Blackb* from 11. *16 Meadow View, Clitheroe BB7 2NT* T: (01200) 426805

GRAHAM, Alistair. *See* GRAHAM, Michael Alistair

✠**GRAHAM, The Rt Revd Andrew Alexander Kenny (Alec).** b 29. St Jo Coll Ox BA 54 MA 57 Lambeth DD 95. Ely Th Coll 53. **d** 55 **p** 56 **c** 77. C Hove All SS *Chich* 55-58; Chapl, Lect Th, and Tutor Worc Coll Ox 58-70; Warden Linc Th Coll 70-77; Can and Preb Linc Cathl 70-77; Suff Bp Bedford *St Alb* 77-81; Bp Newc 81-97; Chmn ACCM 84-87; Chmn Doctrine Commn 87-95; rtd 97; Hon Asst Bp Carl from 97. *Fell End, Butterwick, Penrith CA10 2QQ* T: (01931) 713147

GRAHAM, Canon Anthony Nigel. b 40. Univ of Wales (Abth) BA 62 CertEd 70. Ripon Hall Ox 62. **d** 64 **p** 65. C Heref H Trin 64-67; C Birm St Martin 67-69; C Selly Oak St Mary 71-75; V Edgbaston SS Mary and Ambrose 75-83; CMS Miss Partner Nigeria 84-88; Hon Can Jos from 88; V Highworth w Sevenhampton and Inglesham etc *Bris* 88-95; RD Highworth 93-95; P-in-c Coalpit Heath 95-99; V 99-00; rtd 00. *19 Dormer Road, Cheltenham GL51 0AX*

GRAHAM, Anthony Stanley David. b 34. SS Coll Cam BA 56 MA 60. Cuddesdon Coll 58. **d** 60 **p** 61. C Welwyn Garden City *St Alb* 60-64; Asst Chapl Ipswich Sch 64-65; C Margate St Jo *Cant* 65-68; Chr Aid Area Sec Chich 68-99; rtd 99; PtO *Chich* from 05. *48 Springfield Road, Crawley RH11 8AH* T: (01293) 526279 E: tonygraham@dsl.pipex.com

GRAHAM, Bruce. *See* GRAHAM, William Bruce

GRAHAM, Christopher John. b 55. EMMTC. **d** 03 **p** 04. NSM Ripley *Derby* 03-08; NSM Ilkeston St Jo from 08. *41 Lathkill Drive, Ripley DE5 8HW* T: (01773) 747223 E: chris@graham-family.freeserve.co.uk

GRAHAM, Clifton Gordon. b 53. ARCM 72 GRSM 74 FRCO 75 Coll of Ripon & York St Jo PGCE 76. St Steph Ho Ox 90. **d** 92 **p** 93. C Northfield *Birm* 92-93; C Perry Beeches 93-97; P-in-c S Yardley St Mich 97-00; V 00-06; Chapl Birm City Univ 06-10; Chapl Ex Univ 10-13; rtd 13. *Springwell, 31 Olympian Way, Cullompton EX15 1GB* T: (01884) 32545 E: jgccgg@gmail.com

GRAHAM, David. *See* GRAHAM, George David

GRAHAM, Fiona Karen. *See* WHEATLEY, Fiona Karen

GRAHAM, Frederick Lawrence. b 35. TCD BA 65. CITC 66. **d** 66 **p** 67. C Belfast St Matt *Conn* 66-69; TV Chelmsley Wood *Birm* 69-73; Ch of Ireland Youth Officer 73-78; Bp's C Stoneyford *Conn* 78-88; Bp's C Fahan Lower and Upper *D & R* 88-91; Can Raphoe Cathl 90-01; I Donagheady 91-01; Can Derry Cathl 95-01; rtd 01. *14 Greenmount Gardens, Lisburn BT27 5HD* T: (028) 9258 2639 M: 07719-529989 E: freka1@virginmedia.com

GRAHAM, George David. b 42. Jes Coll Cam BA 64 MA 68. St Jo Coll Nottm LTh Lon Coll of Div 66. **d** 71 **p** 72. C Corby St Columba *Pet* 71-74; C Deptford St Jo *S'wark* 74-77; P-in-c Deptford St Pet 77-82; C-in-c Wheatley Park St Paul CD *Sheff* 82-87; TV Dunstable *St Alb* 87-92; V Bromley Common St Luke *Roch* 92-02; R Hayes 02-12; rtd 12; PtO *Roch* from 13. *129 Warren Road, Orpington BR6 6JE* T: (01689) 850656 E: gd.graham77@gmail.com

GRAHAM, Canon George Edgar. b 55. QUB BA 91. Sarum & Wells Th Coll 74 CITC 77. **d** 78 **p** 79. C Lisburn Ch Ch *Conn* 78-81; C Mossley 81-83; I Broomhedge 83-91; I Derriaghy w Colin 91-96; I Ballywillan 96-05; I Dunluce from 05; Can Conn Cathl from 05; Preb from 06. *Dunluce Rectory, 17 Priestland Road, Bushmills BT57 8QP* T: (028) 2073 1221 or 2073 0537 E: g.k.graham@btinternet.com *or* admindunluce@btconnect.com

GRAHAM, George Gordon. b 17. OBE 96. St Chad's Coll Dur BA 48 MSc 71. **d** 50 **p** 51. C Luton Ch Ch *St Alb* 50-53; C Bakewell *Derby* 53-56; P-in-c Wheatley Hill *Dur* 56-69; V Hunwick 69-88; Chapl Homelands Hosp Dur 80-94; Chapl Bishop Auckland Hospitals NHS Trust 94-98; Chapl S Durham Healthcare NHS Trust 98-02; rtd 88. *3 The Willows, Bishop Auckland DL14 7HH* T: (01388) 602758

GRAHAM, George Gordon. b 34. Harvard Univ BA 55 MDiv JD 71. **d** 96 **p** 97. C Walkden and Lt Hulton *Man* 96-99; Chapl Salford Coll of Tech 96-99; P-in-c Edgeside *Man* 99-00; TV Rossendale Middle Valley 00-02; Gen Sec Miss without Borders (UK) Ltd from 02. *69 Eyre Court, Finchley Road, London NW8 9TX* T: (020) 7586 8336 or 7940 1370 F: 7403 7348 E: info_uk@mwbi.org

GRAHAM, Gordon. *See* GRAHAM, Lawrence Gordon

GRAHAM, Gordon Cecil. b 31. JP . Ch Coll Cam BA 53 MA 57. Ripon Hall Ox 53. **d** 55 **p** 56. C Didsbury St Jas and Em *Man* 55-58; C Rochdale 58-60; R Heaton Mersey 60-67; Chapl Hulme Gr Sch Oldham 67-74; LtO *Ches* 72-92; rtd 92. *21 The Crescent, Davenport, Stockport SK3 8SL* T: 0161-483 6011

GRAHAM, Harry John. b 52. Magd Coll Cam BA 75 MA 86. Trin Coll Bris BA 94. **d** 96 **p** 97. C Walkden and Lt Hulton *Man* 96-99; Chapl Salford Coll of Tech 96-99; P-in-c Edgeside *Man* 99-00; TV Rossendale Middle Valley 00-02; Gen Sec Miss without Borders (UK) Ltd from 02. *69 Eyre Court, Finchley Road, London NW8 9TX* T: (020) 7586 8336 or 7940 1370 F: 7403 7348 E: info_uk@mwbi.org

GRAHAM, Ian Maxwell. b 50. CertEd 76. Chich Th Coll 86. **d** 88 **p** 89. C Middlesbrough St Thos *York* 88-90; C Stainton-in-Cleveland 90-93; V Hemlington 93-00; V Grangetown 00-14; rtd 14. *19 Whitehouse Road, Thornaby, Stockton-on-Tees TS17 0AJ* T: (01642) 882323 E: ianmgraham50@gmail.com

GRAHAM, James Hamilton. b 54. Trin Hall Cam BA 76 MA 80 Solicitor 78. Ripon Coll Cuddesdon BA 83 MA 87. **d** 84 **p** 85. C Harlescott *Lich* 84-88; C Adderley 88-93; C Drayton in Hales 88-93; C Moreton Say 88-93; R Hodnet 93-00; RD 97-00; V Eccleshall from 00. *The Vicarage, Church Street, Eccleshall, Stafford ST21 6BY* T: (01785) 850351

GRAHAM, Kevin. *See* GRAHAM, Terence Kevin Declan

GRAHAM, Prof Lawrence Gordon. b 49. OBE 96. St Andr Univ MA Dur Univ MA PhD 75 FRSE 99. St Steph Ho Ox 90. **d** 05. Regius Prof Moral Philosophy Aber Univ 96-05; C Aberdeen St Mary *Ab* 05-06; Prof Philosophy and Arts Princeton Th Sem USA from 06. *Princeton Theological Seminary, PO Box 821, Princeton NJ 08542, USA* T: (001) (609) 497 7849

GRAHAM, Matthew John. b 78. Lon Guildhall Univ BSc 00. Oak Hill Th Coll BA 13. **d** 13 **p** 14. C Lt Heath *St Alb* from 13. *Church Office, Great North Road, Potters Bar EN6 1JN* T: (01707) 662460 E: curate@cclh.org.uk

GRAHAM, Michael. b 51. CITC BTh 95. **d** 95 **p** 96. C Cork St Fin Barre's Union *C, C & R* 95-98; Min Can Cork Cathl 97-98; I Drogheda w Ardee, Collon and Termonfeckin *Arm* from 98; Ch of Ireland Internet Co-ord 99-05; I Kilsaran w Drumcar, Dunleer and Dunany *Arm* from 07. *St Peter's Rectory, Drogheda, Co Louth, Republic of Ireland* T: (00353) (41) 983 8791 E: office.drogheda@armagh.anglican.org

GRAHAM, Michael Alistair. b 47. CITC 67. **d** 70 **p** 71. C Dublin Clontarf *D & G* 71-75; C Ox St Mich w St Martin and All SS 76-78; P-in-c Dublin Sandymount *D & G* 80-86; I Stillorgan w Blackrock 86-00; Soc Worker E Health Bd Dub 00-09; I Mullingar, Portnashangan, Moyliscar, Kilbixy etc *M & K*

from 09. *The Rectory, Gaol Hill, Mullingar, Co Westmeath, Republic of Ireland* T: (00353) (44) 934 8376　M: 87-787 0985
E: agkilliney@hotmail.com

GRAHAM, Nigel. *See* GRAHAM, Anthony Nigel

GRAHAM, The Ven Olivia Josephine. b 56. UEA BA 84. SAOMC 94. **d** 97 **p** 98. NSM Wheatley *Ox* 97-98; C Risborough 98-01; TV Burnham w Dropmore, Hitcham and Taplow 01-07; Par Development Adv 07-13; Hon Can Ch Ch 12-13; Adn Berks from 13. *Foxglove House, Love Lane, Donnington, Newbury RG14 2JG* T: (01865) 208274
E: archdber@oxford.anglican.org

GRAHAM, Peter. b 32. CEng MIMechE. **d** 86 **p** 87. NSM Minchinhampton *Glouc* 86-96; PtO 96-97; NSM Alderminster and Halford *Cov* 98-02; NSM Butlers Marston and the Pillertons w Ettington 98-02; rtd 02; PtO *Cov* 02-12. *21 Brick Meadow, Bishops Castle SY9 5DH* T: (01588) 638176

GRAHAM, Richard William. b 63. Poly of Wales BA 86 ACA 91. Trin Coll Bris 03. **d** 05 **p** 06. C Savernake *Sarum* 05-09; TV Hemel Hempstead *St Alb* from 09. *St Barnabas Vicarage, Everest Way, Hemel Hempstead HP2 4HY* T: (01442) 253681
E: randmgraham@hotmail.com

GRAHAM, Ronald Gaven. b 27. **d** 90 **p** 91. NSM Adare w Kilpeacon and Croom *L & K* 90-92; Dioc Info Officer (Limerick) 91-95; NSM Rathkeale w Askeaton and Kilcornan 92-96; NSM Wexford w Ardcolm and Killurin *C & O* 97-03; rtd 03. *8 Chestnut Grove, Fernyhill, Killinick, Co Wexford, Republic of Ireland* T: (00353) (53) 915 8369
E: rvgraham@eircom.net

GRAHAM, Rory Malise. b 75. Southn Univ BSc 97. Oak Hill Th Coll BA 12. **d** 12 **p** 13. C Hove Bp Hannington Memorial Ch *Chich* from 12. *47 Nevill Avenue, Hove BN3 7NB*
E: rorybigfoot@gmail.com

GRAHAM, Roy Richard Arthur. b 39. Lon Univ BD 63 Open Univ BA 78. ALCD 62. **d** 63 **p** 64. C Southsea St Jude *Portsm* 63-66; C Morden *S'wark* 66-70; V Tittensor *Lich* 70-79; R Hurworth and Dinsdale w Sockburn *Dur* 79-02; rtd 02. *The School House, Eaglesfield, Lockerbie DG11 3PA* T: (01461) 500499 E: rragraham@onenet.co.uk

GRAHAM, Stig. *See* GRAHAM, William Stig

GRAHAM, Mrs Susan Lochrie. b 46. Sheff Univ PhD 01. Yale Div Sch MDiv 90. **d** 90 **p** 91. Cow Head Par Canada 90-92; P-in-c Kinsway All SS, St Hilary, Bolton 92-96; NSM Ilminster and Distr *B & W* 96-97; PtO 97-03; NSM Glastonbury w Meare 03-08; NSM Combe Martin, Berrynarbor, Lynton, Brendon etc *Ex* 08-11. *Address temp unknown*

GRAHAM, Terence Kevin Declan. b 67. NUI BSc 89 TCD BTh 02. CITC 99. **d** 02 **p** 03. C Knock *D & D* 02-05; I Carrowdore w Millisle 05-09; I Movilla 09-13; I Belfast St Bart *Conn* from 13. *St Bartholomew's Rectory, 16 Mount Pleasant, Belfast BT9 5DS* T: (028) 9066 9995　M: 07964-663745
E: stbartholomew@connor.anglican.org

GRAHAM, Mrs Wendy. b 41. **d** 01 **p** 02. OLM Chalfont St Peter *Ox* from 01. *The Box, Hillfield Road, Chalfont St Peter, Gerrards Cross SL9 0DU* T: (01753) 885066

GRAHAM, William Bruce. b 37. Univ of New Mexico BA 60 Yale Univ MDiv 90. **d** 90 **p** 91. Canada 90-97 and from 09; P-in-c W Poldens *B & W* 97-08; P-in-c Greinton 05-08; RD Glastonbury 03-08. *17635 Pierrefonds Boulevard Apt 5, Pierrefonds QC H9J 3L1, Canada* T: (001) (514) 696 4797
E: wbg@bell.net

GRAHAM, William Stig. b 53. Newc Univ BSc 75. NEOC. **d** 99 **p** 00. C W Acklam *York* 99-02; Chapl Myton Hamlet Hospice from 02. *2 Winyates Road, Lighthorne Heath, Leamington Spa CV33 9TU* T: (01926) 640811 *or* 492518
E: stiggraham@netscape.net *or*
stig.graham@mytonhospice.org

GRAHAM-BROWN, John George Francis. b 34. CA 60. Wycliffe Hall *Ox* 60. **d** 63 **p** 64. C Darlington St Cuth *Dur* 63-67; C Rufforth w Moor Monkton and Hessay *York* 67-73; Sec York Dioc Redundant Chs Uses Cttee 69-89; Asst Sec DBF 73-84; Dioc Past Cttee *York* 73-89; Hon C York St Barn 73-85; P-in-c 85-92; TV Marfleet 92-99; rtd 99; PtO *St Alb* from 00. *40 Hunters Oak, Hemel Hempstead HP2 7SW* T: (01482) 402226
E: f.graham-brown@tinyonline.co.uk

GRAHAM-ORLEBAR, Ian Henry Gaunt. b 26. New Coll Ox BA 49 MA 56. Cuddesdon Coll 60. **d** 62 **p** 63. C Hemel Hempstead *St Alb* 62-70; R Barton-le-Cley w Higham Gobion 70-80; R Barton-le-Cley w Higham Gobion and Hexton 80-92; rtd 92; PtO *Ex* 94-11. *Hole Farm, Bickington, Newton Abbot TQ12 6PE* T: (01626) 821298

GRAINGER, Canon Bruce. b 37. Nottm Univ BA 62 Hull Univ MA 83. Cuddesdon Coll 62. **d** 64 **p** 65. C Bingley All SS *Bradf* 64-67; Chapl K Sch Cant 67-72; Hon Min Can Cant Cathl 69-72; V Baildon *Bradf* 72-88; V Oxenhope 88-04; Hon Can Bradf Cathl 84-04; Dir of Ords 88-96; Dioc Ecum Officer 96-04; Tutor Bradf Univ 99-03; RD S Craven 02-03; rtd 04; PtO *Leeds*

04-15; Hon Chapl Bradf Cathl from 15. *Aspen Lodge, Low Shann Farm, High Spring Gardens Lane, Keighley BD20 6LN* T: (01535) 611989 E: bruce@graspen.gotadsl.co.uk

GRAINGER, Horace. b 34. Carl Dioc Tr Course 82. **d** 85 **p** 86. NSM Barrow St Matt *Carl* 85-89; C Carl St Herbert w St Steph 89-91; TV Penrith w Newton Reigny and Plumpton Wall 91-96; P-in-c Holme Cultram St Mary 96-00; P-in-c Holme Cultram St Cuth 96-00; rtd 00; Hon C S Barrow *Carl* 01-08; PtO from 08. *15 Maylands Avenue, Barrow-in-Furness LA13 0AL* T: (01229) 828603

GRAINGER, Ian. b 66. Cranmer Hall Dur 89. **d** 92 **p** 93. C Whitehaven *Carl* 92-94; C Walney Is 94-97; P-in-c Barrow St Aid 97-02; V Camerton, Seaton and W Seaton from 02; Dioc World Development Officer from 11. *The Vicarage, Ling Beck Park, Seaton, Workington CA14 1JQ* T: (01900) 602162
E: ian.grainger66@btinternet.com

GRAINGER, Michael Noel Howard. b 40. Trin Coll Carmarthen. **d** 91 **p** 92. NSM Haverfordwest St Martin w Lambston *St D* 91-95; V Maenclochog and New Moat etc 95-05; rtd 05. *1 impasse Edith Piaf, Kerbregent, Plumeliau 56930, France* T: (0033) 2 97 51 91 28　M: 8 79 39 24 61

GRAINGER, Prof Roger Beckett. b 34. Birm Univ MA 70 Leeds Univ PhD 79 Lon Univ BA 80 DD 90 Huddersfield Poly MPhil 88 Bris Univ PhD 92 Leeds Metrop Univ BSc 98 PhD(Educ) 01 Lambeth STh 83 FRSA 85 FRAI 85 CPsychol 96 AFBPsS 99. Lich Th Coll 64. **d** 66 **p** 69. C W Bromwich All SS *Lich* 66-68; C Walsall 69-73; Chapl Stanley Royd Hosp Wakef 73-90; rtd 91; Hon C Wakef St Jo *Leeds* from 93; Dioc Drama Adv from 98; Prof Extraordinary Potchefstroom Univ S Africa from 01; Hon Chapl Wakef Cathl from 02. *7 Park Grove, Horbury, Wakefield WF4 6EE* T: (01924) 272742

GRAINGER-SMITH, James Edward. b 71. Nottm Univ BA 92. St Jo Coll Nottm MA 02. **d** 02 **p** 03. C Hordle *Win* 02-07; R Beeford w Frodingham and Foston *York* from 07; P-in-c Brandesburton and Leven w Catwick 11-13; V Brandesburton and Leven from 13; RD N Holderness from 12. *The Rectory, 11 Glebe Gardens, Beeford, Driffield YO25 8BF* T: (01262) 488042
E: j.grainger-smith@sky.com

GRANDEY, Frederick Michael. b 56. St Jo Coll Ox MA 83 BM, BCh 84 Newc Univ MSc 98 MRCGP 90 FFPH 04. St Jo Coll Nottm 06. **d** 09 **p** 10. C Haxby and Wigginton *York* 09-13; P-in-c S Molton w Nymet St George, High Bray etc *Ex* from 13. *The Rectory, Parsonage Lane, South Molton EX36 3AX* E: m.grandey@talk21.com

GRANGE (née FEATHERSTON), Mrs Alice Margery. b 55. Teesside Univ BA 97. NEOC. **d** 99 **p** 00. C Pickering w Lockton and Levisham *York* 99-02; TV Crosslacon *Carl* 02-07; P-in-c Middlesbrough St Agnes *York* from 07; Chapl S Tees Hosps NHS Trust from 07. *St Agnes' Vicarage, 1 Broughton Avenue, Middlesbrough TS4 3PX* T: (01642) 321770
E: margery-grange@sky.com

GRANNER, Mrs Linda. b 52. Westmr Coll Ox BTh 00. WMMTC 01. **d** 03 **p** 04. NSM Bearwood *Birm* 03-06; C Edgbaston St Bart 06-08; C Edgbaston St Geo 06-08; P-in-c Hobs Moat from 08. *St Mary's House, 30 Hobs Meadow, Solihull B92 8PN* T: 0121-743 4955　E: l.granner@sky.com

GRANT, Amanda Rose Anna. b 63. Ripon Coll Cuddesdon 09. **d** 11 **p** 12. C N Hants Downs *Win* 11-12; C Win St Matt from 12. *18 Lynford Way, Winchester SO22 6BW* M: 07745-130033
E: amandagrant1@hotmail.com

GRANT, Andrew James. b 68. Cranmer Hall Dur 09. **d** 11 **p** 12. C Bramham *York* 11-15; V Marton-in-Cleveland from 15. *The Vicarage, Stokesley Road, Marton-in-Cleveland, Middlesbrough TS7 8JU* M: 07519-423552
E: andygrant1968@btinternet.com *or*
vicar@stcuthbertmarton.org.uk

GRANT, Canon Andrew Richard. b 40. Univ of Wales BA 62. Chich Th Coll 63. **d** 65 **p** 66. C Kennington St Jo *S'wark* 65-68; Hon C 70-72; Hon C Stockwell Green St Andr 68-70; V Nunhead St Antony 72-79; TR N Lambeth 79-92; USPG Ghana 92-99; Hon Can Kumasi from 02; C Paddington St Jo w St Mich *Lon* 99-01; P-in-c Stockwell St Mich *S'wark* 01-03; P-in-c Stockwell St Andr and St Mich 03-04; V 04-09; rtd 09; PtO *S'wark* 09-13 and from 15. *48 Stannard Court, Culverley Road, London SE6 2LE* M: 07448-583179
E: arg.stockwell@hotmail.co.uk

GRANT, Antony Richard Charles. b 34. Ch Ch Ox BA 59 MA 64. Coll of Resurr Mirfield 72. **d** 74 **p** 75. C St John's Wood *Lon* 74-77; Novice CR 77-79; CR from 79; LtO *Leeds* from 80; rtd 99. *House of the Resurrection, Stocks Bank Road, Mirfield WF14 0BN* T: (01924) 483332　F: 490489
E: agrant@mirfield.org.uk

GRANT, Miss Frances Mary. b 52. Qu Coll Birm. **d** 12 **p** 13. NSM Etwall w Egginton *Derby* from 12. *177 Drewry Lane, Derby DE22 3QT* T: (01332) 364617　M: 07714-780668
E: franmgrant@gmail.com

GRANT, Canon Geoffrey Leslie. b 33. Trin Coll Cam BA 57 MA 61. Ridley Hall Cam 57. **d** 59 **p** 60. C Chelsea St Luke *Lon* 59-64; R Nacton w Levington *St E* 64-78; P-in-c Bucklesham w Brightwell and Foxhall 75-76; R Nacton and Levington w Bucklesham and Foxhall 78-06; P-in-c Kirton w Falkenham 96-06; R Nacton and Levington w Bucklesham etc 06-14; RD Colneys 86-11; Hon Can St E Cathl 94-14; Chapl Orwell Park Sch Nacton 64-14; rtd 14; PtO *St E* from 14. *Daisy Chain, The Common, Lavenham, Sudbury CO10 9RL* T: (01787) 247343 E: geoffrey@john-lewis.com

GRANT, James Neil. b 57. Toorak Coll of Educn BEd 80. Trin Coll Melbourne BTh 84. **d** 85 **p** 86. C E Frankston Australia 85-87; C Feltham *Lon* 87-89; Chapl Peninsula Sch Mt Eliza Melbourne Australia 89-03; Assoc P Mt Eliza 99-03; Assoc P Richmond St Steph 04; P-in-c Preston All SS 05-08; P-in-c Jika Jika from 08. *PO Box 81, Preston VIC 3072, Australia* T: (0061) (3) 99471 9191 M: 425-721962 E: frjames.ststephens@keypoint.com.au *or* james@jikajika.com

GRANT, James Nikolas. b 78. Glas Univ MA 07 Anglia Ruskin Univ MA 11. Westcott Ho Cam 09. **d** 11 **p** 12. C Chorlton-cum-Hardy St Clem *Man* 11-14; C Worth, Pound Hill and Maidenbower *Chich* from 15. *St Barnabas' Vicarage, 2 Crawley Lane, Crawley RH10 7EB* M: 07753-456210 E: frjames.grant@gmail.com

GRANT, John Brian Frederick. b 47. Bris Univ BSc 68 MB, ChB 71 MD 76 FRCS 76. Coll of Resurr Mirfield 91. **d** 93 **p** 94. C Doncaster Ch Ch *Sheff* 93-95; C Doncaster H Trin 95-96; Chapl Asst Salford R Hosps NHS Trust 96-07; Hon C Man Victoria Park 08-10; PtO 10-15. *179 Manley Road, Manchester M21 0GY* T: 0161-860 7488

GRANT, Ms Kes. b 65. SEITE 00. **d** 03 **p** 04. NSM Eltham St Sav *S'wark* 03-09; C Bermondsey St Hugh CD 09-11; Chapl Lewisham Hosp NHS Trust 05-09; Chapl St Sav and St Olave's Sch Newington *S'wark* 09-11; Chapl St Aug Academy Maidstone from 11. *St Augustine Academy, Oakwood Road, Maidstone ME16 8AE* T: (01622) 693789 M: 07805-482244 E: revkes@ntlworld.com

GRANT, Canon Malcolm Etheridge. b 44. Edin Univ BSc 66 BD 69. Edin Th Coll 66. **d** 69 **p** 70. C St Mary's Cathl 69-72; C Grantham w Manthorpe *Linc* 72; TV Grantham 72-78; P-in-c Invergordon St Ninian *Mor* 78-81; Provost St Mary's Cathl 81-91; R Glas St Mary 81-91; Provost St Andr Cathl Inverness 91-02; R Inverness St Andr 91-02; P-in-c Culloden St Mary-in-the-Fields 91-97; R Strathnairn St Paul 91-97; Hon Can St Andr Cathl Inverness from 02; V Eaton Bray w Edlesborough *St Alb* 02-09; RD Dunstable 04-09; rtd 09; PtO *St Alb* from 09; *Ox* from 09. *13 Rock Lane, Leighton Buzzard LU7 2QQ* T: (01525) 372771

GRANT, Murray William. b 36. Chich Th Coll 64. **d** 66 **p** 67. C Stanley *Liv* 66-70; C Munster Square St Mary Magd *Lon* 70-74; C Westmr St Sav and St Jas Less 74-82; P-in-c Albany Street Ch Ch 82; P-in-c Hammersmith H Innocents 83-94; V 94-99; Chapl Naples w Sorrento, Capri and Bari *Eur* 99-03; rtd 04; PtO *Lon* from 12. *12 Ashdown Crescent, London NW5 4QB* T: (020) 7319 2519 E: mwgrant@gmail.com

GRANT, Patrick Iain Douglas. b 67. K Alfred's Coll Win BA 88. Cuddesdon Coll BTh 93. **d** 96 **p** 97. C Croydon Woodside *S'wark* 96-99; V S Beddington and Roundshaw 99-07; R Perth St Jo *St And* 07-14; rtd 14. *Aberdeen House, 13 Pitcullen Crescent, Perth PH2 7HT* T: (01738) 625394 M: 07948-270941

GRANT, Richard. b 83. Leeds Univ BA 08. St Mellitus Coll MA 13. **d** 13 **p** 14. C Crookes St Thos *Sheff* from 13. *29 Fitzgerald Road, Sheffield S10 1GX* T: 0114-267 1090 M: 07930-516839 E: richgrantuk@gmail.com *or* rich.grant@stthomascrookes.org

GRANT, Canon Rodney Arthur. b 26. AKC 52. K Coll Lon St Boniface Warminster. **d** 53 **p** 54. C Edin St Jas 53-56; C Musselburgh 56-59; P-in-c Prestonpans 59-60; P-in-c Edin St Aid Miss Niddrie Mains 60-72; R Edin St Jas 72-80; R Edin Ch Ch 72-80; R Edin Ch Ch-St Jas 80-86; R Edin SS Phil and Jas 86-92; Chapl St Columba's Hospice Edin 86-92; rtd 92; P-in-c Edin St Vin 98-14; Hon Can St Mary's Cathl from 91. *1F1, 29 Bruntsfield Gardens, Edinburgh EH10 4DY* T: 0131-229 1857

GRANT, Stuart Peter. b 64. Leeds Poly BSc 87 Leeds Univ BA 11. Yorks Min Course 10. **d** 12 **p** 13. NSM Gt and Lt Driffield *York* from 12; NSM Langtoft w Foxholes, Butterwick, Cottam etc from 12. *Rectory Farm, Station Road, Lockington, Driffield YO25 9SQ* T: (01430) 810202 M: 07795-560065 E: stuart@hastpace.co.uk

GRANTHAM, David George. b 70. **d** 07 **p** 08. C Bury St Edmunds Ch Ch *St E* 07-11; V Jersey All SS *Win* from 11; V Jersey St Simon from 11. *All Saints' Vicarage, Savile Street, St Helier, Jersey JE2 3XF* T: (01534) 768323 E: godistheguy@hotmail.com

GRANTHAM, Michael Paul. b 47. Linc Th Coll. **d** 84 **p** 85. C Gainsborough All SS *Linc* 84-87; R S Kelsey Gp 87-94; R Dunster, Carhampton and Withycombe w Rodhuish *B & W* 94-06; RD Exmoor 03-05; P-in-c Peakirk w Glinton and Northborough *Pet* 06-07; P-in-c Etton w Helpston and Maxey 06-07; rtd 07; Hon C Wheatley *Ox* 13-14; Hon C Albury w Tiddington, Holton, Waterperry, Waterstock and Wheatley from 14. *The Vicarage, Holton, Oxford OX33 1PN* E: michael.grantham@o2.co.uk *or* michaelgrantham@tiscali.co.uk

GRASBY, Derek. b 56. Bris Univ BA 80 MA 82. Wesley Coll Bris 77 EAMTC 95. **d** 95 **p** 96. C Harlescott *Lich* 95-96; C W Bromwich St Andr w Ch Ch 96-98; R Newton Heath *Man* 98-02; Chapl UWE *Bris* 02-03; R Farnley *Ripon* 03-09; rtd 09; PtO *Ripon* 10-13; *Nor* from 14. *9 Boundary Avenue, Norwich NR6 5HY* T: (01603) 291211 M: 07834-276382 E: derek.grasby@gmail.com

GRASHAM, Mrs Frances Mary. b 68. Roehampton Inst BA 89 Kingston Poly PGCE 90. Yorks Min Course 11. **d** 13 **p** 14. NSM Steeton *Leeds* from 13. *12 Railway Street, Keighley BD20 6AQ* T: (01535) 609293 M: 07777-699676 E: fran.grasham@live.co.uk

GRASSKE, Christopher Karl. b 65. Ripon Coll Cuddesdon 12. **d** 14. C Chagford, Gidleigh, Throwleigh etc *Ex* from 14. *The Rectory, South Tawton, Okehampton EX20 2LQ* T: (01837) 849100 E: cgrasske@gmail.com

GRATION, Phillip John. b 83. **d** 12 **p** 13. Chapl HM Pris Linc 12-15; C Linc St Pet-at-Gowts and St Andr 12-15; C Linc St Botolph 12-15; C Linc St Mary-le-Wigford w St Benedict etc 12-15; Chapl Ellesmere Coll from 15. *Ellesmere College, Ellesmere SY12 9AB* T: (01691) 622321

GRATTON, Patricia Margaret. *See* MAGUIRE, Patricia Margaret

GRATY, Canon John Thomas. b 33. Univ Coll Ox BA 58 MA 60. Coll of Resurr Mirfield 58. **d** 60 **p** 61. C Cov St Mark 60-63; C Hitchin St Mary *St Alb* 63-67; R Cov St Alb 67-75; P-in-c Radway w Ratley 75-77; P-in-c Warmington w Shotteswell 75-77; RD Dassett Magna 76-78; R Warmington w Shotteswell and Radway w Ratley 77-84; Hon Can Cov Cathl 80-96; P-in-c Nuneaton St Mary 84-89; V 89-96; rtd 96; PtO *Cov* from 96. *10 Kendall Avenue, Stratford-upon-Avon CV37 6SG* T: (01789) 298856 E: gratysenior@aol.com

GRAVELING, Hannah. *See* PATTON, Hannah

GRAVELL, Canon John Hilary. b 45. Univ of Wales (Abth) BA 65 DipEd 66. Bp Burgess Hall Lamp 66. **d** 68 **p** 69. C Aberystwyth *St D* 68-72; R Llangeitho w Blaenpennal 72-73; V Llangeitho, Blaenpennal and Betws Leucu 73-81; V Betws Leuci 73-81; V Llan-non 81-95; Can St D Cathl 92-09; V Llandybie 95-09; AD Dyffryn Aman 01-07; rtd 09. *16 Stewart Drive, Ammanford SA18 3BH* T: (01269) 5943

GRAVES, John Ivan. b 44. **d** 10 **p** 11. OLM Romney Deanery Romney Marsh *Cant* 10-14; PtO 15. *Gaynes House, St Andrews Road, Littlestone, New Romney TN28 8PZ* T: (01797) 364011 E: jigbag@btinternet.com

GRAVES, Peter. b 33. EMMTC 78. **d** 81 **p** 82. NSM Roughey *Chich* 81-89; NSM Itchingfield w Slinfold 89-98; PtO *S'well* from 98. *5 Fletcher Court, The Woodlands, Farnsfield, Newark NG22 8LY* T: (01623) 882987 E: gravesp1@btinternet.com

GRAY, Alison Jane. b 63. New Hall Cam MB, BChir 87 MA 89 Birm Univ MMedSc 01 MRCPsych 95. Qu Coll Birm 07. **d** 10 **p** 11. NSM Malvern St Andr and Malvern Wells and Wyche *Worc* 10-14; NSM Gt Malvern St Mary from 14. *42 Wyche Road, Malvern WR14 4EG* T: (01684) 893637 E: a.j.gray@doctors.net.uk

GRAY, Andrew Stuart. b 70. LCTP. **d** 11 **p** 12. C Clitheroe St Jas *Blackb* from 11. *125 Henthorn Road, Clitheroe BB7 2QF* T: (01200) 427561 E: andyg@mrgiraffee.freeserve.co.uk

GRAY, Canon Angela Margery. b 46. St D Coll Lamp. **dss** 73 **d** 80 **p** 97. Aberystwyth *St D* 73-80; C Dafen and Llwynhendy 80-90; C-in-c 90-94; C-in-c Dafen 94-97; V Llwynhendy 97-11; Hon Can St D Cathl 01-11; rtd 11; PtO *St D* from 11. *10 Bryn Isaf, Llanelli SA14 9EX* T: (01554) 774213

GRAY, Ms Ann. b 54. Newc Univ BEd 79. LCTP 09. **d** 12 **p** 13. NSM Lanercost, Walton, Gilsland and Nether Denton *Carl* from 12. *Nook Cottage, Irthington, Carlisle CA6 4NJ* T: (016977) 3385 E: anniegray19@aol.com

GRAY, Brett Christopher. b 71. Lon Bible Coll BA 95 Selw Coll Cam MPhil 04. Ridley Hall Cam 02. **d** 04 **p** 05. C Sunnyside w Bourne End *St Alb* 04-07; V St Alb St Mich 07-11; Asst Chapl Selw Coll Cam from 11. *Selwyn College, Cambridge CB3 9DQ* T: (01223) 311825 E: bcg24@cam.ac.uk

GRAY, Charles Malcolm. b 38. Lich Th Coll 67. **d** 69 **p** 70. C St Geo-in-the-East St Mary *Lon* 69-72; C Bush Hill Park St Mark 72-75; V Winchmore Hill H Trin 75-07; rtd 07; PtO *Lon* 07-13; *York* from 13. *7 Dulverton Hall, Esplanade, Scarborough YO11 2AR* T: (01723) 347107 *or* 351432 M: 07721-664178 E: frcmg.upnorth@btinternet.com

GRAY, Ms Christine Angela (Kit). b 46. Nottm Univ BA 67 CertEd 68. Cranmer Hall Dur 71. **dss** 80 **d** 87 **p** 94. Rawthorpe *Wakef* 74-81; Chapl Nottm Univ *S'well* 81-88; C Rushmere *St E* 88-94; P-in-c Ringshall w Battisford, Barking w Darmsden etc 94-00; P-in-c Nayland w Wiston 00-10; rtd 10; PtO *St E* from 10; *Chelmsf* from 12. *Threeways, Bounstead Hill, Layer-de-la-Haye, Colchester CO2 0LG* T: (01206) 734353
E: kit.gray@keme.co.uk

GRAY, Dale Armitage. b 42. Edin Th Coll 62. **d** 92 **p** 93. Dioc Missr *Arg* 92-98; Chapl St Jo Cathl Oban 92-95; P-in-c Cumbrae (or Millport) 95-98; rtd 98; PtO *Edin* from 05. *The Dovecote, Duke Street, Coldstream TD12 4BN* T: (01890) 883247

GRAY, David. b 55. Oak Hill Th Coll. **d** 00 **p** 01. C Bestwood Em w St Mark *S'well* 00-04; P-in-c Bulwell St Jo 04-06; V from 06. *St John's Vicarage, Snape Wood Road, Bulwell, Nottingham NG6 7GH* T: 0115-927 8025 E: davidgray72@hotmail.com

GRAY, David Bryan. b 28. RD 77. Roch Th Coll 59. **d** 61 **p** 62. C Linc St Giles 61-65; V Thurlby 65-67; P-in-c Ropsley 67-75; P-in-c Sapperton w Braceby 67-75; P-in-c Somerby w Humby 67-75; R Trimley *St E* 75-82; R Orford w Sudbourne, Chillesford, Butley and Iken 82-94; rtd 94; PtO *St E* 94-10. *The College of St Barnabas, Blackberry Lane, Lingfield RH7 6NJ* T: (01342) 870260

GRAY, David Cedric. b 53. RMN 77. **d** 97 **p** 98. OLM Gorton Em w St Jas *Man* 97-06; OLM Gorton and Abbey Hey 06-11. *39 Jessop Street, Gorton, Manchester M18 8TZ* T: 0161-355 6605 M: 07854-465393 E: rev.elation4.1@ntlworld.com

GRAY, David Michael. b 57. St Jo Coll Dur BA 99 ACIBS 80. CA Tr Coll 90 Cranmer Hall Dur 97. **d** 99 **p** 00. C Newc H Cross 99-02; V Long Benton St Mary 02-11; V Killingworth from 11. *The New Vicarage, West Lane, Killingworth Village, Newcastle upon Tyne NE12 6BL* T: 0191-268 3242
E: revdavegray@aol.com

GRAY, Canon Donald Clifford. b 30. TD 70 CBE 98. Liv Univ MPhil 81 Man Univ PhD 85 FRHistS 88 FSA 07. AKC 55. **d** 56 **p** 57. C Leigh St Mary *Man* 56-60; CF (TA) 58-67; V Westleigh St Pet *Man* 60-67; V Elton All SS 67-74; CF (TAVR) 67-77; QHC 74-77; R Liv Our Lady and St Nic w St Anne 74-87; RD Liv 75-81; Hon Can Liv Cathl 82-87; Chapl to The Queen 82-00; Can Westmr Abbey 87-98; I Westmr St Marg 87-98; Chapl to Speaker of Ho of Commons 87-98; rtd 98; PtO *Linc* from 98. *3 Barn Hill Mews, Stamford PE9 2GN* T: (01780) 765024

GRAY, Evan William. b 43. Oak Hill Th Coll 86. **d** 88 **p** 89. C Street w Walton *B & W* 88-92; V Blackpool St Mark *Blackb* 92-03; V Ellel w Shireshead 03-08; rtd 08; PtO *Blackb* from 08. *39 Boyes Avenue, Catterall, Preston PR3 0HB* T: (01995) 604092
E: evan.gray@virgin.net

GRAY, James William. b 59. SAOMC. **d** 05 **p** 06. NSM Crich and S Wingfield *Derby* 05-15; PtO from 15. *Holmleigh, Market Place, Crich, Matlock DE4 5DD* T: (01773) 857921
E: jimlynda.gray@btopenworld.com

GRAY (née ROBERTS), Mrs Jennifer. b 55. R Holloway Coll Lon BA 76 Somerville Coll Ox PGCE 77. SAOMC 00. **d** 03 **p** 04. C Welwyn Garden City *St Alb* 03-13; P-in-c Bramfield, Stapleford, Waterford etc from 13. *The Rectory, Church Lane, Watton-at-Stone, Hertford SG14 3RD*
E: jennygraywgc@aol.com

GRAY, Joan. *See* BURKITT-GRAY, Joan Katherine

GRAY, John David Norman. b 38. Oak Hill Th Coll 84. **d** 86 **p** 87. C Portsdown *Portsm* 86-88; C Worthing St Geo *Chich* 88-91; TV Swanborough *Sarum* 91-98; rtd 98; PtO *Ex* 00-03; *Portsm* from 03. *15 Charminster Court, 46 Craneswater Park, Southsea PO4 0NU* T: (023) 9285 1299

GRAY, John Howard. b 39. St Aid Birkenhead 61. **d** 65 **p** 66. C Old Trafford St Cuth *Man* 65-68; C Urmston 68-74; V Oldham Moorside 74-08; rtd 08; Hon C Dulverton w Brushford, Brompton Regis etc *B & W* 08-13. *The Vicarage, Brompton Regis, Dulverton TA22 9NL* T: (01398) 371438
E: johnhoward980@btinternet.com

GRAY, Mrs Joy Dora. b 24. SRN 46 SCM 48. Gilmore Ho 79. **dss** 81 **d** 87 **p** 95. Newick *Chich* 81-94; Hon Par Dn 87-94; NSM Fletching 94-98; PtO from 98. *10 High Hurst Close, Newick, Lewes BN8 4NJ* T: (01825) 722965

GRAY, Julian Francis. b 64. Univ of Wales (Lamp) BA 86 MA 09. Coll of Resurr Mirfield 86. **d** 88 **p** 89. Min Can St Woolos Cathl 88-91; C Bassaleg 91-93; V Overmonnow w Wonastow and Michel Troy 93-98; V King's Sutton and Newbottle and Charlton *Pet* 98-00; V Usk and Monkswood w Glascoed Chpl and Gwehelog *Mon* 00-03; V Usk and Gwehelog w Llantrisant w Llanllowell 03-14; P-in-c Llantilio Pertholey w Bettws Chpl etc from 14. *The Vicarage, 10 The Pines, Mardy, Abergavenny NP7 6HQ* T: (01873) 859881 E: mardyvicarage@yahoo.co.uk

GRAY, Lindsay Doreen. b 50. Open Univ BA 83 Leic Univ PhD 87. Coll of Resurr Mirfield 05. **d** 06 **p** 07. NSM Firbank, Howgill and Killington *Bradf* 06-09; NSM Sedbergh, Cautley and Garsdale 06-09; TV Egremont and Haile *Carl* 09-13; P-in-c

Seascale and Drigg from 13; Ind Chapl from 09. *The Vicarage, The Banks, Seascale CA20 1QT* T: (019467) 21110
E: lgray782@btinternet.com

GRAY, Malcolm. *See* GRAY, Charles Malcolm

GRAY, The Ven Martin Clifford. b 44. Westcott Ho Cam 78. **d** 80 **p** 81. C Gaywood, Bawsey and Mintlyn *Nor* 80-84; V Sheringham 84-94; TR Lowestoft St Marg 94-99; Chapl Lothingland Hosp 95-99; RD Lothingland *Nor* 97-99; Adn Lynn 99-09; rtd 09; PtO *Nor* from 09. *11 Canns Lane, Hethersett, Norwich NR9 3JE* T: (01603) 812610
E: mandpgray@btinternet.com

GRAY, Melvyn Dixon. b 38. Lon Univ BD 86 Dur Univ MA 89 PhD 07. NEOC 84. **d** 87 **p** 88. C Richmond w Hudswell *Ripon* 87-90; P-in-c Downholme and Marske 88-90; P-in-c Forcett and Aldbrough and Melsonby 90-91; R 91-00; R Mobberley *Ches* 00-04; rtd 04; PtO *Dur* from 04; *Leeds* from 13. *19 Windgroves, Chilton, Ferryhill DL17 0RS* T: (01388) 721870
E: melandanne@gray19.plus.com

GRAY, Natty. *See* GRAY, Renate Kathrina

GRAY, Neil Kenneth. b 48. Kelham Th Coll 67. **d** 71 **p** 72. C Chorley St Laur *Blackb* 71-74; C S Shore H Trin 74-78; P-in-c Preston St Oswald 78-83; C Blackpool St Steph 83-87; Chapl Bolton HA from 87; Chapl Bolton Hosps NHS Trust from 90; Co-ord Spiritual and Cultural Care 90-03; Hd of Chapl from 04; Bp's Adv for Healthcare Chapl *Man* from 08. *The Chaplains' Office, Royal Bolton Hospital, Minerva Road, Farnworth, Bolton BL4 0JR* T: (01204) 390770 *or* 390390
E: neil.gray@rbh.nhs.uk

GRAY, Neil Ralph. b 53. MA. St Steph Ho Ox. **d** 82 **p** 83. C Kennington St Jo w St Jas *S'wark* 82-85; C Somers Town *Lon* 85-88. *3 Parsonage Close, High Wycombe HP13 6DT* T: (01494) 531875

GRAY, Mrs Patricia Linda. b 51. Univ of Wales (Swansea) BA 73 Ches Coll of HE BTh 02. NOC 99. **d** 02 **p** 03. C Glazebury w Hollinfare *Liv* 02-12; rtd 12. *14 Bollin Close, Culcheth, Warrington WA3 5DU* T: (01925) 763150 M: 07747-772345
E: pat.gray@virgin.net

GRAY, Patrick. *See* GRAY, Sidney Patrick

GRAY, Penelope Jane. *See* GRAYSMITH, Penelope Jane

GRAY, Canon Philip Charles. b 67. Nottm Univ BA 91. St Steph Ho Ox 91. **d** 93 **p** 94. C Scarborough St Martin *York* 93-97; TV Leek and Meerbrook *Lich* 97-01; Bp's Dom Chapl *Blackb* 02-07; P-in-c Ilkley St Marg *Bradf* 07-12; V *Leeds* from 12; Hon Can Ho Ghana from 04; AD Ilkley *Leeds* from 14. *St Margaret's Vicarage, Wells Road, Ilkley LS29 9JH* T: (01943) 607015 *or* 607210

GRAY, Philip Thomas. b 41. Lon Univ BA 65. Chich Th Coll 66. **d** 68 **p** 69. C Leigh St Clem *Chelmsf* 68-74; P-in-c Wickham Skeith *St E* 86-97; V Mendlesham from 74. *The Vicarage, Old Station Road, Mendlesham, Stowmarket IP14 5RS* T: (01449) 766359

GRAY, Renate Kathrina (Natty). b 52. SNWTP. **d** 13 **p** 14. OLM Deeplish and Newbold *Man* from 13. *669 Oldham Road, Rochdale OL16 4PE* T: (01706) 358550 M: 07577-825371
E: renate.gray@ntlworld.com

GRAY, Canon Robert James. b 70. TCD BA 92 HDipEd 93 MA 95 Irish Sch of Ecum MPhil 97. CITC 94. **d** 96 **p** 97. C Clooney w Strathfoyle *D & R* 96-99; I Ardamine w Kiltennel, Glascarrig etc *C & O* from 99; Treas Ferns Cathl from 04. *Ardamine Rectory, Courtown Harbour, Gorey, Co Wexford, Republic of Ireland* T/F: (00353) (53) 942 5423 M: 86-684 7621
E: ardamine@ferns.anglican.org

GRAY, Sidney Patrick. b 19. Worc Ord Coll. **d** 63 **p** 63. C Skegness *Linc* 63-65; V Dunholme 65-71; R Cliffe at Hoo w Cooling *Roch* 72-78; V Gillingham St Aug 78-84; rtd 84; PtO *Cant* 84-08; *Roch* 84-08. *The White House, Rampton Road, Laneham, Retford DN22 0NE*

GRAY, Stephen James Norman. b 66. Lon Univ BA 89 Hughes Hall Cam PGCE 91. Ridley Hall Cam MA 00. **d** 00 **p** 01. C Cheltenham Ch Ch *Glouc* 00-03; Chapl RN 03-04; Chapl Sherborne Sch 04-10; Chapl Seaford Coll Petworth 10-13; P-in-c Graffham w Woolavington *Chich* 10-13; Chapl Bradfield Coll Berks from 14. *Bradfield College, Bradfield, Reading RG7 6AU* T: 0118-964 4746
E: chaplain@bradfieldcollege.org.uk

GRAY, Mrs Susan Hazel. b 49. Kingston Univ BA 06. **d** 09 **p** 10. OLM Hersham *Guildf* from 09. *39 Misty's Field, Walton-on-Thames KT12 2BG* T: (01932) 242838
E: suehgray@btinternet.com

GRAY, Mrs Trudy Ann Jennifer. b 48. Univ of Wales (Abth) BSc 69 Aston Univ MSc 72. **d** 05 **p** 06. NSM Gt Finborough w Onehouse, Harleston, Buxhall etc *St E* 05-10; NSM Upper Coquetdale *Newc* 10-13; rtd 13. *1 Greenside Avenue, Berwick-upon-Tweed TD15 1BZ* T: (01289) 331722
E: tajgrayfin@aol.com

GRAY, Mrs Ursula Mary. b 33. K Coll Lon BD 56 AKC 91 Univ of Wales (Lamp) MA 02. **d** 04 **p** 05. NSM Shaston *Sarum* 04-08; PtO 09. *Rowans, Chavenage Lane, Tetbury GL8 8JW* T: (01666) 504548 E: umg@shaston.plus.com

GRAY-HAMMOND, Betsy. b 58. Ripon Coll Cuddesdon BA 10. **d** 10 **p** 11. C Brighton St Nic *Chich* 10-14; TV Moulsecoomb from 14. *The Vicarage, Selham Drive, Brighton BN1 9EL* T: (01273) 601854 E: revbetsy@btinternet.com

GRAY-STACK, Martha Mary Stewart. b 35. QUB BA 57. **d** 90 **p** 91. NSM Limerick City *L & K* 90-93; Warden of Readers 90-93; NSM Clara w Liss, Moate and Clonmacnoise *M & K* 93-00; Chapl Kingston Coll Mitchelstown 00-10. *16 Kingston College, Mitchelstown, Co Cork, Republic of Ireland* T/F: (00353) (25) 258 5975

GRAYSHON, Matthew Richard. b 47. St Jo Coll Nottm BTh 81. **d** 81 **p** 82. C Beverley Minster *York* 81-85; V Hallwood *Ches* 85-93; R Hanwell St Mary w St Chris *Lon* from 93. *The Rectory, 91 Church Road, London W7 3BJ* T: (020) 8567 6185 F: 8579 8755 E: matthewg@tesco.net

GRAYSHON, Paul Nicholas Walton. b 50. Cranmer Hall Dur 81. **d** 83 **p** 84. C Walkden Moor *Man* 83-87; V Radcliffe St Andr 87-07; P-in-c Matlock Bath and Cromford *Derby* from 07. *Holy Trinity Vicarage, 8 Derby Road, Matlock DE4 3PU* T: (01629) 583924 E: nickgrayshon@btopenworld.com

GRAYSMITH (née GRAY), Mrs Penelope Jane. b 63. SS Hild & Bede Coll Dur BA 85 Em Coll Cam MPhil 88. Westcott Ho Cam 86. **d** 89 **p** 94. Par Dn Evington *Leic* 89-92; Par Dn Cannock *Lich* 92-94; C 94-96; Chapl Asst Mid Staffs Gen Hosps NHS Trust 96-07; Hd Chapl Services Mid Staffs NHS Foundn Trust from 07; Chapl Kath Ho Hospice Stafford from 96. *The Vicarage, 97 Baswich Lane, Stafford ST17 0BN* T: (01785) 251057 *or* 230930 E: penny.graysmith@midstaffs.nhs.uk

GRAYSMITH, Peter Alexander. b 62. UEA BSc 83. Westcott Ho Cam 85. **d** 88 **p** 89. C Tettenhall Regis *Lich* 88-89; C Cannock 89-92; TV 92-99; V Rocester and Croxden w Hollington 99-01; V Baswich from 01. *The Vicarage, 97 Baswich Lane, Stafford ST17 0BN* T: (01785) 251057 E: petergraysmith@talktalk.net

GRAYSON, Jane Elizabeth. b 71. **d** 07 **p** 08. OLM Moston St Mary *Man* from 07. *296 St Mary's Road, Manchester M40 0BD* T: 0161-688 7073 E: janegrayson@aol.com

GRAYSON, Robin John. b 53. Mert Coll Ox BA 74 DPhil 78. Wycliffe Hall Ox 00. **d** 02 **p** 03. C Beaconsfield *Ox* 02-06; P-in-c Langley Marish 06-08; TR from 08. *The Vicarage, 3 St Mary's Road, Slough SL3 7EN* T: (01753) 542068 M: 07801-280475 E: r.j.grayson@btinternet.com

GREADY, Andrew John. b 63. Univ Coll Lon BSc 84 Newc Univ MA 93 Surrey Univ BSc 05. St Jo Coll Nottm 86. **d** 89 **p** 90. C Monkwearmouth St Andr *Dur* 89-92; C Bramley St Cath S Africa 92-96; R Sunninghill St Steph 96-99; Chapl St Pet Prep Sch 99; V Shottermill *Guildf* 00-06; Chapl Amesbury Sch 01-06; P-in-c Wynberg St Jo S Africa 06-08; Chapl W Prov Prep Sch 07-12; R 08-12; Chapl The Hague *Eur* from 13. *Riouwstraat 2, 2585 HA The Hague, The Netherlands* T: (0031) (70) 306 0758 *or* 355 5339 M: 6-2054 0258 E: chaplain@stjohn-stphilip.org

GREANY, Canon Richard Andrew Hugh. b 44. Qu Coll Ox BA 67 MA 83. Coll of Resurr Mirfield 67. **d** 69 **p** 70. C Hartlepool St Oswald *Dur* 69-72; C Clifton All SS *Bris* 72-75; Tutor Coll of Resurr Mirfield 75-78; V Whitworth w Spennymoor *Dur* 78-83; P-in-c Byers Green 78-79; Asst Prin St Alb Minl Tr Scheme 83-88; V Flamstead *St Alb* 83-88; V Hessle *York* 88-94; V Cambridge St Mary Less *Ely* 94-11; Dioc Spirituality Officer 99-06; Hon Can Ely Cathl 05-11; RD Cambridge S 06-11; rtd 11; Chapl Laslett's *Worc* 11-14; Hon C Worc City 11-14; PtO *York* from 14. *1 Hall Mews, 2A Main Street, Bishop Wilton, York YO42 1RX* T: (01759) 368880 E: andrewgreany@btinternet.com

GREANY, Mrs Virginia Clare. b 52. Bris Univ BA 74 PGCE 75 Hull Univ MSc 94. Westcott Ho Cam 96 EAMTC 97. **d** 98. Bp's Dn to Local Government *Ely* 98-99; Asst to Dean Trin Hall Cam 98-00. *Trinity Hall, Cambridge CB2 1TJ* T: (01223) 332500

GREAR, Hugh Massey. b 60. Bris Univ LLB 82. SEITE. **d** 00 **p** 01. C Warlingham w Chelsham and Farleigh *S'wark* 00-04; V Upper Tooting H Trin w St Aug 04-10; R Worplesdon *Guildf* from 10. *The Rectory, Perry Hill, Worplesdon, Guildford GU3 3RE* T/F: (01483) 234616 E: hugh.grear@sky.com *or* rector@worplesdonparish.com

GREASLEY, James Kenneth. b 39. K Coll Lon BD 66 AKC 66. **d** 67 **p** 68. C Stoke upon Trent *Lich* 67-70; P-in-c Lusaka St Pet Zambia 70-76; V Gt Staughton *Ely* 76-81; Chapl HM Borstal Gaynes Hall 76-81; V Melbourn and Meldreth *Ely* 81-96; RD Shingay 82-96; R Chalfont St Peter *Ox* 96-04; rtd 04; PtO *Heref* from 05. *Bank Cottage, Norton, Presteigne LD8 2EN* T: (01544) 267567 E: jk.greasley@btinternet.com

GREATOREX, Mrs Susan Kathleen. b 58. St Hilda's Coll Ox BA 79 MA 04 Univ of Wales (Cardiff) PGCE 80. WEMTC 01. **d** 04 **p** 05. C Keynsham *B & W* 04-08; R Radstock w Writhlington from 08; R Kilmersdon w Babington from 08. *28 Wells Road, Radstock BA3 3RL* T: (01761) 433917 E: susangreatorex@blueyonder.co.uk

GREATREX, Richard Quintin. b 65. K Coll Lon BD 86 Surrey Univ BA 02. STETS 99. **d** 02 **p** 03. NSM Westbury-on-Trym St Alb *Bris* 02-06; NSM Flax Bourton and Barrow Gurney *B & W* 06-09; NSM Long Ashton w Barrow Gurney and Flax Bourton from 09. *The Rectory, Main Road, Flax Bourton, Bristol BS48 3QJ* T: (01275) 461179 E: rqg1@fsmail.net

GREAVES, Canon John Neville. b 29. Newc Univ MA 96 Dur Univ MLitt 03. St Aid Birkenhead 58. **d** 61 **p** 62. C Pendleton St Ambrose *Man* 61-62; P-in-c 62-63; C Benchill 63-65; C-in-c Wythenshawe St Rich CD 65-71; V Wythenshawe St Rich 71-73; R Sadberge *Dur* 73-78; V Dur St Cuth 78-94; Chapl New Coll Dur 78-92; Lect NEOC 79-84; Chapl Dur Co Fire Brigade 85-94; RD Dur 80-93; Dep Dir of Clergy Tr 91-94; Hon Can Dur Cathl 91-94; rtd 94; PtO *Ches* 94-97; P-in-c Salt and Sandon w Burston *Lich* 97-00; Past Aux Eccleshall Deanery 00-01; PtO 01-02; *Heref* from 03; *S & B* from 10. *3 Sitwell Close, Bucknell SY7 0DD* T: (01547) 530152

GREAVES, Kevin Adam Nathanael. b 65. Sheff Univ BA 13. Yorks Min Course 10. **d** 13 **p** 14. C Castleford *Leeds* from 13. *St Paul's Vicarage, Churchfield Lane, Castleford WF10 4BP* T: (01977) 512404 E: fr.kevin@minister.com

GREBE, Matthias. b 82. Tübingen Univ BA 07 Hughes Hall Cam MPhil 08 Ch Coll Cam PhD 12. Ridley Hall Cam 09. **d** 13 **p** 14. Asst Chapl Bonn w Cologne *Eur* 13-15; C Regent's Park St Mark *Lon* from 15. *9 Crown Terrace, Bishops Stortford CM23 2DP* M: 07919-445378 E: mgrebe471@gmail.com *or* grebe@uni-bonn.de

GREED, Frederick John. b 44. Trin Coll Bris 79. **d** 81 **p** 82. C Yateley *Win* 81-85; R Ore St Helen and St Barn *Chich* 85-95; R Street w Walton *B & W* 95-09; RD Glastonbury 08-09; rtd 09; PtO *B & W* from 09. *40 St Cleers Orchard, Somerton TA11 6QU* T: (01458) 272754 M: 07887-366698 E: john_greed@btinternet.com

GREEDY, Tegryd Joseph. b 31. St D Coll Lamp 59. **d** 61 **p** 62. C Newbridge *Mon* 61-64; C Bassaleg 64-66; V Newport St Teilo 66-74; Hon C Newport St Mark 80-83; V Goldcliffe and Whitson and Nash 83-90; Ind Chapl 83-90; V Marshfield and Peterstone Wentloog etc 90-96; rtd 96. *42 Churchward Drive, Newport NP19 4SB* T: (01633) 282159

GREEN, Adrian Paul. b 66. Trin Coll Bris 06. **d** 08 **p** 09. NSM Willowfield *D & D* 08-11; I Mt Merrion from 11; Dir of Ords from 15. *122 Mount Merrion Avenue, Belfast BT6 0FS* T: (028) 9029 4676 *or* 9045 7654 M: 07914-290193 E: adrian-green@hotmail.co.uk

GREEN, Preb Alan John Enrique. b 56. Worc Coll Ox BA 78 MA 83. Linc Th Coll 83. **d** 85 **p** 86. C Kirkby *Liv* 85-88; TV 88-94; Chapl Knowsley Community Coll 87-90; Chapl Worc Coll and C Ox St Giles and SS Phil and Jas w St Marg 94-98; TR 12-... on Bethnal Green *Lon* from 98; AD Tower Hamlets 06-12; Preb St Paul's Cathl from 10. *St John's Rectory, 30 Victoria Park Square, London E2 9PB* T/F: (020) 8980 1742 E: alan.green@virgin.net

GREEN, Alison Iola. b 58. Glas Caledonian Univ MB, ChB 81 Lon Univ MSc 97 MRCPCH 96. Westcott Ho Cam 11. **d** 13 **p** 14. C Chich Cathl from 13. *2nd Floor Flat, 1 St Richard's Walk, Chichester PO19 1QA* M: 07581-070669 T: (01243) 531315 E: iolag1@yahoo.com

GREEN, Alison Mary. b 51. Boro Road Teacher Tr Coll BEd 74 Wesley Coll Bris MA 03 Roehampton Univ PhD 07. STETS 02. **d** 04 **p** 05. NSM Bath St Barn w Englishcombe *B & W* 04-06; NSM Monmouth w Overmonnow etc *Mon* 06-13; NSM Bradford on Avon H Trin, Westwood and Wingfield *Sarum* from 14. *36 Budbury Close, Bradford-on-Avon BA15 1QG* E: alig9@btinternet.com

GREEN, Arthur Edward. b 27. Chich Th Coll 58. **d** 59 **p** 60. C Malden St Jas *S'wark* 59-62; C Caterham 62-67; R Burgh Parva w Briston *Nor* 67-75; V Middleton 75-76; V Middleton w E Winch 76-84; R Neatishead w Irstead 84-90; V Barton Turf 84-90; R Neatishead, Barton Turf and Irstead 90-92; r-d 92; PtO *Portsm* from 92. *10 James Butcher Court, 16 Eastern Villas Road, Southsea PO4 0TD* T: (023) 9275 0701

GREEN, Barrie. b 51. SS Coll Cam BA 72 MA 76. Wycliffe Hall Ox 75. **d** 78 **p** 79. C Castle Vale *Birm* 78-81; V W Heath 81-96; RD Kings Norton 87-95; TR Dronfield w Holmesfield *Derby* 96-09; P-in-c Bris St Paul's 09-15; rtd 15. *5 Boucherie, 33220 Riocaud, France*

GREEN, Benjamin Charles. b 83. Magd Coll Cam BA 04 MA 08. Wycliffe Hall Ox MTh 08. **d** 08 **p** 14. C Stockton *Dur* 08-09; C Arden Marches *Cov* from 13. *8 Abbeyfields Drive, Studley B80 7BF* T: (01527) 850429 M: 07985-490173 E: revbcg@gmail.com

GREEN, Brian Robert. b 31. Bris Univ BA 55. Tyndale Hall Bris 52. **d** 56 **p** 57. C Toxteth Park St Philemon *Liv* 56-58; V Toxteth Park St Philemon w St Silas 58-69; P-in-c Toxteth Park St Gabr 64-69; P-in-c Toxteth Park St Jo and St Thos 64-69; P-in-c Toxteth Park St Jas and St Matt 68-69; V Elsenham *Chelmsf* 69-85; V Henham 69-85; P-in-c Ugley 84-85; V Henham and Elsenham w Ugley 85-89; RD Newport and Stansted 87-89; PtO *Ex* 90-91; V Tidenham w Beachley and Lancaut *Glouc* 91-97; RD Forest S 95-97; rtd 97; PtO *Ex* 97-11. *3 Crosbys, Burbage, Marlborough SN8 3TL* T: (01672) 811655 E: pasturesgreenoffwell@tiscali.co.uk

GREEN, Brutus Zachary. b 78. Ex Univ BA 99 PhD 07 St Edm Coll Cam MPhil 04. Westcott Ho Cam 07. **d** 09 **p** 10. C Paddington St Jo w St Mich *Lon* 09-14; CF from 14. *c/o MOD Chaplains (Army)* F: 381824 T: (01264) 383430 E: brutuszgreen@gmail.com

GREEN, Catherine Isabel. *See* HITCHENS, Catherine Isabel

GREEN, Christopher Frederick. b 46. Nottm Univ BTh 75 Birm Univ DipEd 85 Univ of Wales (Abth) MEd 94. Bp Otter Coll CertEd 69 Linc Th Coll 71. **d** 75 **p** 76. C Hodge Hill *Birm* 75-77; C S Lafford *Linc* 77-79; P-in-c Worc St Mich 79-82; Hd RS and Lib RNIB New Coll Worc 82-96; V Clipstone *S'well* 96-02; rtd 02; PtO *Linc* from 03. *Cobwebs, Middlefield Lane, Glentham, Market Rasen LN8 2ET* T: (01673) 878633

GREEN, Christopher Martyn. b 58. New Coll Edin BD 80. Cranmer Hall Dur 82. **d** 83 **p** 84. C Virginia Water *Guildf* 83-87; C Bromley Ch Ch *Roch* 87-91; Study Asst the Proclamation Trust 91-92; C Surbiton Hill Ch Ch *S'wark* 92-00; Vice Prin Oak Hill Th Coll 00-13; PtO *Lon* 02-13; V Muswell Hill St Jas w St Matt from 14. *St James's Vicarage, 2 St James's Lane, London N10 3DB* T: (020) 8442 2900

GREEN, Mrs Clare Noreen. b 30. SWMTC 84. **d** 88. NSM Bideford *Ex* 88-90; PtO 90-09. *30 Rosebarn Lane, Exeter EX4 5DX* T: (01392) 272505

GREEN, Daphne Mary. b 55. K Coll Cam BA 77 Bradf Univ MBA 91 Leeds Univ PhD 01 Lon Inst of Educn PGCE 79. NOC 95. **d** 98 **p** 99. C Headingley *Ripon* 98-02; Chapl Leeds Metrop Univ 00-02; R Stanningley St Thos 02-08; Abp's Chapl and Researcher *York* from 08. *Bishopthorpe, York YO23 2GE* T: (01904) 707021 F: 709204 M: 07796-084264 E: daphne.green@archbishopofyork.org

GREEN, David Allen. b 61. Sheff City Poly BA 90. Cranmer Hall Dur 00. **d** 02 **p** 03. C Huyton St Geo *Liv* 02-06; TV Walkden and Lt Hulton *Man* 06-10; P-in-c Thorne *Sheff* 10-14; V from 14. *The Vicarage, 2 Brooke Street, Thorne, Doncaster DN8 4AZ* T: (01405) 814055 E: green426@btinternet.com

GREEN, David Michael. b 69. **d** 02 **p** 13. NSM Ruislip St Martin *Lon* from 12. *8 Blaydon Close, Ruislip HA4 8AD* T: (01895) 633189 M: 07962-057767 E: fr.david@live.co.uk

GREEN, David Norman. b 37. Magd Coll Cam BA 60. Clifton Th Coll 60. **d** 62 **p** 63. C Islington St Mary *Lon* 62-65; C Burley *Ripon* 65-68; Kenya 69-80; P-in-c Brimscombe *Glouc* 81-90; R Woodchester and Brimscombe 90-96; P-in-c Coberley w Cowley 96-97; P-in-c Colesborne 96-97; P-in-c Coberley, Cowley, Colesbourne and Elkstone 97-04; Dioc Rural Adv 96-04; rtd 04; Tanzania 04-13. *8 Cherrywood Gardens, Nottingham NG3 6LQ* T: 0115-950 2958

GREEN, David Robert John. b 73. Sheff Univ BA 96. Ridley Hall Cam 06. **d** 08 **p** 09. C Chatham St Phil and St Jas *Roch* 08-11; P-in-c W Malling w Offham from 11. *The Vicarage, 138 High Street, West Malling ME19 6NE* T: (01732) 842245 E: mail@revdgreen.org.uk

GREEN, David William. b 53. CertEd 75 Nottm Univ BCombStuds 84. Linc Th Coll 81. **d** 84 **p** 85. C S Merstham *S'wark* 84-88; C Walton-on-Thames *Guildf* 88-91; V Gillingham H Trin and Chapl Lennox Wood Elderly People's Home *Roch* 91-99; V Strood St Nic w St Mary from 99; RD Strood from 12. *The Vicarage, 3 Central Road, Strood, Rochester ME2 3HF* T: (01634) 719052 E: david.green@diocese-rochester.org

GREEN, Denise Penelope. b 57. Bedf Coll of Educn BEd 80 MPhil 96. EMMTC 03. **d** 06 **p** 07. C Skirbeck H Trin *Linc* 06-10; P-in-c S Lawres Gp 10-14; R from 14; V Barlings from 14. *The Vicarage, 14 Church Lane, Cherry Willingham, Lincoln LN3 4AB* T: (01522) 595596 M: 07812-006295 E: revdpg@virginmedia.com

GREEN, Donald Henry. b 31. Selw Coll Cam BA 54 Lon Inst of Educn PGCE 55. Qu Coll Birm 81. **d** 83 **p** 84. C Dudley St Aug Holly Hall *Worc* 83-85; V Dudley St Barn 85-90; rtd 96. *The Cuckoo's Nest, 12 Mill Green, Knighton LD7 1EE* T: (01547) 528289

GREEN, Donald Pentney (Brother Donald). b 25. Leeds Univ BA 50. Coll of Resurr Mirfield 50. **d** 52 **p** 53. C Ardwick St Benedict *Man* 52-55; SSF from 55; Sec for Miss SSF 78-96; Chapl HM Pris Kingston (Portsm) 72-76; LtO *Edin* 76-77;

Org Sec Catholic Renewal 77; LtO *Lich* from 78; rtd 95. *85 Crofton Road, London E13 8QT* T: (020) 7474 5863 E: donaldssf@freeuk.com

GREEN, Mrs Dorothy Mary. b 36. Westf Coll Lon BA 58. Selly Oak Coll 60. **dss** 83 **d** 87 **p** 94. Ryde All SS *Portsm* 83-91; C 87-91; Hon C Hempnall *Nor* 91-96; rtd 96; PtO *B & W* 97-07. *12 Monica Wills House, Cromwell Street, Bristol BS3 3NH* T: 0117-239 4257 E: revdern17@yahoo.co.uk

GREEN, The Ven Duncan Jamie. b 52. Sarum & Wells Th Coll 82. **d** 84 **p** 85. C Uckfield *Chich* 84-87; Dioc Youth Officer *Chelmsf* 87-96; Warden and Chapl St Mark's Coll Res Cen 93-96; TR Saffron Walden w Wendens Ambo, Littlebury etc *Chelmsf* 96-07; RD Saffron Walden 05-07; C of E Olympic and Paralympic Co-ord 07-13; Hon Can Chelmsf Cathl 03-13; Adn Northolt *Lon* from 13. *9 Sheridan Gardens, Harrow HA3 0JT* T: (020) 7932 1274 E: archdeacon.northolt@london.anglican.org

GREEN, Edward Bryan. b 75. Westcott Ho Cam 02. **d** 05 **p** 06. C Soham and Wicken *Ely* 05-09; TV Cherwell Valley *Ox* 09-13; V Leavesden *St Alb* from 13. *All Saints' Vicarage, Horseshoe Lane, Watford WD25 7HJ* M: 07595-435752 T: (01869) 340 562 E: eddiebgreen@gmail.com

GREEN, Edward John. b 35. Lich Th Coll. **d** 59 **p** 60. C Longford *Cov* 59-61; C Wigston Magna *Leic* 61-65; V 73-00; V Ellistown 65-73; rtd 00; PtO *Leic* from 00. *Holly Mount, 27 Greendale Road, Glen Parva, Leicester LE2 9HD* T: 0116-277 2479

GREEN, Edward Marcus. b 66. Mert Coll Ox BA 88 MA 92. Wycliffe Hall Ox 90. **d** 94 **p** 95. C Glyncorrwg w Afan Vale and Cymmer Afan *Llan* 94-96; C Aberystwyth *St D* 96-99; P-in-c Pontypridd St Cath *Llan* 00-01; V 01-11; PtO *Bradf* 11-13; R Steeple Aston w N Aston and Tackley *Ox* from 13. *The Rectory, Fir Lane, Steeple Aston, Bicester OX25 4SF* T: (01869) 340903 E: steeplerector@hotmail.co.uk

GREEN, Canon Edward Michael Bankes. b 30. Ex Coll Ox BA 53 MA 56 Qu Coll Cam BA 57 MA 61 BD 66 Toronto Univ DD 92 Lambeth DD 96. Ridley Hall Cam 55. **d** 57 **p** 58. C Eastbourne H Trin *Chich* 57-60; Lect Lon Coll of Div 60-69; Prin St Jo Coll Nottm 69-75; Can Th Cov Cathl 70-76; R Ox St Aldate w H Trin 75-82; R Ox St Aldate w St Matt 82-86; Prof Evang Regent Coll Canada 87-92; Abps' Adv Springboard for Decade of Evang 92-96; rtd 96; Six Preacher Cant Cathl 93-99; Sen Research Fell Wycliffe Hall Ox from 97; PtO *Ox* from 99. *7 Little Acreage, Marston, Oxford OX3 0PS* T: (01865) 248387 F: 792083 E: michael.green@wycliffe.ox.ac.uk

GREEN, Mrs Elizabeth Pauline Anne. b 29. Gilmore Ho 69. **dss** 76 **d** 87 **p** 94. Chorleywood Ch Ch *St Alb* 76-87; Par Dn 87-90; C Chipping Sodbury and Old Sodbury *Glouc* 90-95; Asst Dioc Missr 90-95; rtd 95; NSM Chipping Sodbury and Old Sodbury *Glouc* 95-99; PtO from 99; *Bris* from 99. *The Old House, The Common, Chipping Sodbury, Bristol BS37 6PX* T: (01454) 311936 E: p.green@care4free.net

GREEN, Ernest James. b 31. Pemb Coll Cam BA 55 MA 62. Linc Th Coll 58. **d** 57 **p** 58. C Rawmarsh w Parkgate *Sheff* 57-60; Sec Th Colls Dept SCM 60-62; Prec and Sacr Bris Cathl 62-65; Min Can 62-65; V Churchill *B & W* 65-78; RD Locking 72-78; V Burrington and Churchill 78-82; Preb Wells Cathl 81-82; V Ryde All SS *Portsm* 82-91; P-in-c Ryde H Trin 82-86; RD E Wight 83-88; TR Hempnall *Nor* 91-96; rtd 96; PtO *B & W* 97-07. *12 Monica Wills House, Cromwell Street, Bristol BS3 3NH* T: 0117-239 4257 E: revdern17@yahoo.co.uk

GREEN, Ms Fiona Jenifer. b 67. Ridley Hall Cam 02. **d** 05 **p** 06. C Highbury Ch Ch w St Jo and St Sav *Lon* 05-08; C St Jo on Bethnal Green 08-12; Co-ord Reader Tr Stepney Area 08-12; Intern Programme Dir from 12. *The Rectory Flat, Hereford Street, London E2 6EX* M: 07786-541559 E: fionajgreen@yahoo.co.uk

GREEN, Canon Fleur Estelle. b 72. Univ of Wales (Ban) BD 94. Ripon Coll Cuddesdon 95. **d** 97 **p** 98. C Blackpool St Jo *Blackb* 97-00; C Lancaster St Mary w St John and St Anne 00-03; P-in-c Blackb St Luke w St Phil 03-04; P-in-c Witton 03-04; V Blackb Christ the King 04-12; V Darwen St Pet from 12; Asst Dir of Ords 06-12; Women's Min Adv from 11; Hon Can Blackb Cathl from 11. *The Rectory, St Peter's Close, Darwen BB3 2EA* T: (01254) 702411 E: chauntry1@live.co.uk

GREEN, Frank Gilbert. b 23. Kelham Th Coll 46. **d** 50 **p** 51. C Sheff St Cecilia Parson Cross 50-56; SSM from 52; C Nottingham St Geo w St Jo *S'well* 56-58; Basutoland 59-62; S Africa 62-69 and 84-88; Lesotho 69-84; LtO *Ox* from 88; rtd 93. *Society of the Sacred Mission, 1 Linford Lane, Willen, Milton Keynes MK15 9DL* T: (01908) 663749

GREEN, Gary Henry. b 64. Univ of Wales (Cardiff) BD 87. St Mich Coll Llan 93. **d** 95 **p** 96. C Baglan *Llan* 95-97; C Neath w Llantwit 97-01; TV Neath 01-02; V Llangiwg *S & B* from 02. *1 Clos yr Hen Ysgol, Pontardawe, Swansea SA8 4AZ* T: (01792) 862003 E: gary.green890@btinternet.com

GREEN, George James. b 26. Cuddesdon Coll 69. **d** 69 **p** 70. C Handsworth St Mary *Birm* 69-76; R Croughton w Evenley *Pet* 76-87; R Aynho and Croughton w Evenley 87-95; rtd 95; PtO *Cov* from 95. *Dibbinsdale, Langley Road, Claverdon, Warwick CV35 8PU*

GREEN, Gillian. b 41. Balls Park Coll Hertford TCert 61 Open Univ BA 83. EAMTC 03. **d** 05 **p** 06. NSM Stour Valley *St E* 05-11; PtO from 11. *7 Haling Way, Thetford IP24 1EY* E: revgillgreen@yahoo.co.uk

GREEN, Gloria. *See* SHERBOURNE, Gloria

GREEN, Gordon Sydney. b 33. Ridley Hall Cam 77. **d** 79 **p** 80. C Ipswich St Marg *St E* 79-83; TV Barton Mills, Beck Row w Kenny Hill etc 83-85; TV Mildenhall 85-86; rtd 86; PtO *St E* from 97. *28 Upton Close, Ipswich IP4 2QQ* T: (01473) 252188

GREEN, Graham Herbert. b 53. City Univ BSc 74. Westcott Ho Cam 75. **d** 78 **p** 79. C Hatcham St Cath *S'wark* 78-82; C S Ashford Ch Ch *Cant* 82-88; V Cheriton All So w Newington 88-97; P-in-c Milton next Sittingbourne 97-02; V 02-06; PtO *Roch* 12-13; V Helsby and Dunham-on-the-Hill *Ches* from 13; Dioc Adv in Spirituality from 13. *St Paul's Vicarage, Vicarage Lane, Helsby, Frodsham WA6 9AB* T: (01928) 722151 M: 07988-850261 E: millett1006@btinternet.com

GREEN, Graham Reginald. b 48. Sarum & Wells Th Coll 71. **d** 74 **p** 75. C Chorley St Laur *Blackb* 74-76; C Padiham 76-79; V Osmondthorpe St Phil *Ripon* 79-94. *3 Northwood Gardens, Colton, Leeds LS15 9HH* T: 0113-264 3558

GREEN, Imogen Elizabeth. *See* VIBERT, Imogen Elizabeth

GREEN, James Edwin McKibben. **d** 14 **p** 15. C Edin St Paul and St Geo from 14. *Church Office, 10 Broughton Street, Edinburgh EH1 3RH* T: 0131-556 1335 E: james@pandgchurch.org.uk

GREEN, Mrs Janice Anne. b 48. NTMTC BA 07. **d** 07 **p** 08. NSM Gt Hallingbury and Lt Hallingbury *Chelmsf* from 07; P-in-c from 09. *The Rectory, Wrights Green Lane, Little Hallingbury, Bishop's Stortford CM22 7RE* E: rev.janicegreen@btinternet.com

GREEN, Jeffrey. b 43. Chich Th Coll 76. **d** 78 **p** 79. C Crewkerne w Wayford *B & W* 78-81; C Cockington *Ex* 81-83; R Ripple, Earls Croome w Hill Croome and Strensham *Worc* 83-87; PtO *Glouc* 02-03; Hon C Boxwell, Leighterton, Didmarton, Oldbury etc 03-06; Hon C Nailsworth w Shortwood, Horsley etc 03-06; rtd 06. *7 Cherry Tree Close, Nailsworth, Stroud GL6 0DX* T: (01453) 836910

GREEN, Miss Jennifer Mary. b 55. SEN 78 SRN 81 RM 84. Trin Coll Bris 87. **d** 90 **p** 95. C Tong *Bradf* 90-93; Chapl Bradf Cathl 93; CMS from 94; Uganda from 94. *Muhabura Diocese, PO Box 22, Kisoro, Uganda*

GREEN, Jeremy Nigel. b 52. St Andr Univ MA. St Jo Coll Nottm 80. **d** 83 **p** 84. C Dorridge *Birm* 83-86; V Scrooby *S'well* 86-94; V Bawtry w Austerfield and Misson 94-06; AD Bawtry 01-06; P-in-c Haxey *Linc* 06-12; V from 12; P-in-c Owston 06-12; V from 12. *The Vicarage, Church Street, Haxey, Doncaster DN9 2HY* T: (01427) 754137 E: jngreen@live.co.uk

GREEN, John. *See* GREEN, Edward John

GREEN, The Ven John. b 53. CB 10. Nottm Univ BCombStuds 83. Linc Th Coll 80. **d** 83 **p** 84. C Watford St Mich *St Alb* 83-86; C St Alb St Steph 86-91; Chapl RN 91-06; Chapl of the Fleet and Adn for the RN 06-10; QHC 06-10; Hon Can Portsm Cathl 06-10; PtO *Cov* 11-12; Adn Cov from 12; C Cov St Mary from 14; PtO *Birm* from 12. *Cathedral and Diocesan Office, 1 Hill Top, Coventry CV1 5AB* T: (024) 7652 1337 M: 07947-953191 E: john.green@covcofe.org

GREEN, John David. b 29. Lon Univ BD 66. Roch Th Coll 63. **d** 66 **p** 66. C Roch 66-72; V Oxshott *Guildf* 72-85; R Weybridge 85-94; rtd 94; PtO *Guildf* from 94. *103 Bitterne Drive, Woking GU21 3JX* T: (01483) 727936

GREEN, Canon John Francis Humphrey. b 44. Ex Univ BA 65 Heythrop Coll Lon MA 96. Westcott Ho Cam 91. **d** 93 **p** 94. C Tadworth *S'wark* 93-96; Chapl St Geo Sch Harpenden 96-01; P-in-c Flamstead *St Alb* 01-12; P-in-c Markyate Street 01-12; V Flamstead and Markyate Street 12-14; RD Wheathampstead 09-10; Hon Can St Alb 13-14; rtd 14; P-in-c Barlavington, Burton w Coates, Sutton and Bignor *Chich* from 14. *The Rectory, The Street, Sutton, Pulborough RH20 1PS* T: (01798) 869023 E: johnfhgreen@gmail.com

GREEN, Canon John Henry. b 44. K Coll Lon BD 72 AKC. **d** 73 **p** 74. C Tupsley *Heref* 73-77; Asst Chapl Newc Univ 77-79; V Stevenage St Hugh Chells *St Alb* 79-85; V St Jo in Bedwardine *Worc* 85-92; Dir of Ords 92-08; P-in-c Guarlford and Madresfield w Newland 92-99; C Fladbury w Wyre Piddle and Moor etc 99-08; P-in-c Bowbrook N 08-12; P-in-c Bowbrook S 08-12; Hon Can Worc Cathl 94-12; rtd 12. *25 Station Road, Alcester B49 5ET* T: (01789) 400213 M: 07778-585746 E: ddocropthorne@waitrose.com

GREEN, Jonathon Samuel McKibbin. b 58. LCTP 10. **d** 13 **p** 14. NSM Windermere St Mary and Troutbeck *Carl* 13-14; NSM Grasmere from 14; NSM Rydal from 14. *The Coach House, Rydal Hall, Rydal, Ambleside LA22 9LX* T: (015394) 31980 E: jakjsgreen@hotmail.com

GREEN, Mrs Joy Elizabeth. b 53. Open Univ BA 00. SEITE 04. **d** 07 **p** 08. NSM Maidstone St Martin *Cant* 07-14; rtd 14. *50 Anglesey Avenue, Maidstone ME15 9SU* T: (01622) 741616 E: joy.green50@tiscali.co.uk

GREEN, Julia Ann. *See* CARTWRIGHT, Julia Ann

GREEN, Canon Karina Beverley. b 61. Ripon Coll Cuddesdon 87. **d** 90 **p** 94. C Lee-on-the-Solent *Portsm* 90-93; Dioc Youth Officer *Guildf* 94-99; Youth and Children's Work Adv *Portsm* 99-03; P-in-c Portsea St Geo 03-05; V 05-12; P-in-c W Leigh from 12; CME Officer 03-13; AD Havant from 14; Hon Can Portsm Cathl from 06. *St Alban's Vicarage, Martin Road, Havant PO9 5TE* E: canonkarina@talktalk.net

✠**GREEN, The Rt Revd Laurence Alexander.** b 45. K Coll Lon BD 68 AKC 68 NY Th Sem STM 69 DMin 82. St Aug Coll Cant 70. **d** 70 **p** 71 **c** 93. C Kingstanding St Mark *Birm* 70-73; V Erdington St Chad 73-83; Prin Aston Tr Scheme 83-89; Hon C Birchfield *Birm* 84-89; TR Poplar *Lon* 89-93; Area Bp Bradwell *Chelmsf* 93-11; rtd 11; Hon Asst Bp Chich from 11. *Belclare, 86 Belle Hill, Bexhill-on-Sea TN40 2AP* T: (01424) 217872 M: 07891-938647 E: mail@lauriegreen.org

GREEN, Mrs Linda Anne. b 60. Westcott Ho Cam 84. **dss** 86 **d** 87 **p** 94. Borehamwood *St Alb* 86-89; Par Dn 87-89; Par Dn Sheff St Cuth 89-90; Chapl Asst N Gen Hosp Sheff 89-91; Chapl 91-95; Chapl Qu Mary's Sidcup NHS Trust 96-05; P-in-c Crockenhill All So *Roch* 06-10; P-in-c Brasted 10-12; R from 12. *The Rectory, Coles Lane, Brasted, Westerham TN16 1NR* T: (01959) 565829 E: revlindagreen@aol.com

GREEN, Canon Linda Jeanne. b 50. R Holloway Coll Lon BSc 72 RGN 74 RCNT 79. SAOMC 01. **d** 04 **p** 05. C Headington Quarry *Ox* 04-09; P-in-c Banbury 09-13; R from 13; Hon Can Ch Ch from 14. *The Vicarage, 89 Oxford Road, Banbury OX16 9AJ* T: (01295) 262370 M: 07973-802863 E: linda@revgreen.wanadoo.co.uk

GREEN, Marcus. *See* GREEN, Edward Marcus

GREEN, Mrs Margaret Elizabeth. b 34. St Mich Ho Ox 60. **dss** 84 **d** 87 **p** 94. Ecclesall *Sheff* 84-87; Par Dn 87-90; C Doncaster St Jas 90-94; rtd 95; PtO *Sheff* from 95. *91 Littemoor Lane, Doncaster DN4 0LQ* T: (01302) 361481

GREEN, Martin Charles. b 59. Bris Univ BA 81 MPhil 86. Wycliffe Hall Ox 82. **d** 84 **p** 85. C Margate H Trin *Cant* 84-88; V Kingston upon Hull St Aid Southcoates *York* 88-94; P-in-c Bishop's Itchington *Cov* from 94; Dioc Children's Officer 94-05; P-in-c Radford Semele from 05. *The Vicarage, 1 Manor Road, Bishop's Itchington, Southam CV47 2QJ* T: (01926) 613466 E: revmcg@kerrins.net

GREEN, Martyn. b 41. FCA. Ridley Hall Cam 78. **d** 80 **p** 81. C Wetherby *Ripon* 80-83; V Leeds St Cypr Harehills 83-90; V Ossett cum Gawthorpe *Wakef* 90-99; TR Haxby w Wigginton *York* 99-07; rtd 07. *29 Park Row, Knaresborough HG5 0BJ* T: (01423) 797560

GREEN, Mrs Maureen. b 49. Avery Hill Coll CertEd 70 Lon Univ BEd 71. EAMTC 95. **d** 98 **p** 02. NSM Ipswich St Jo *St E* 98-10; Asst Chapl Ipswich Hosp NHS Trust 98-05; Asst Chapl Local Health Partnerships NHS Trust 98-02; Asst Chapl Cen Suffolk Primary Care Trust 02-05; PtO *Ox* 11-15; *St E* from 15. *Church House, Lower Farm Road, Ringshall, Stowmarket IP14 2JE* T: (01473) 657472 E: maureengreen@talk21.com

GREEN, Michael. *See* GREEN, Edward Michael Bankes

GREEN, Neil Howard. b 57. New Coll Ox BA 80 PGCE 81. Wycliffe Hall Ox 87. **d** 90 **p** 91. C Finchley St Paul and St Luke *Lon* 90-94; C Muswell Hill St Jas w St Matt 94-98; V Eastbourne All So *Chich* 98-10; Asst Master Eastbourne Coll 10-14; Chapl Cranleigh Prep Sch Surrey from 14. *Cranleigh Preparatory School, Horseshoe Lane, Cranleigh GU6 8QH* T: (01483) 542058 E: nhgreen@hotmail.co.uk

GREEN, Nicholas. b 67. Cranmer Hall Dur 07. **d** 08 **p** 09. C Marton-in-Cleveland *York* 08-11; C Brookfield 11-13; R Dunblane *St And* from 13. *St Mary's Rectory, Smithy Loan, Dunblane FK15 0HQ* M: 07970-164175 E: greennick@live.co.uk

GREEN, Paul. b 25. RD . Sarum & Wells Th Coll 72. **d** 74 **p** 75. C Pinhoe *Ex* 74-77; P-in-c 77-79; V 79-85; P-in-c Bishopsteignton 85-88; P-in-c Ideford, Luton and Ashcombe 85-88; rtd 88; PtO *Ex* 88-08. *58 Maudlin Drive, Teignmouth TQ14 8SB* T: (01626) 777312

GREEN, Paul John. b 48. Sarum & Wells Th Coll 72. **d** 73 **p** 74. C Tuffley *Glouc* 73-76; C Prestbury 76-82; P-in-c Highnam w Lassington and Rudford 82-83; P-in-c Tibberton w Taynton 82-83; R Highnam, Lassington, Rudford, Tibberton etc 84-92; Hon Min Can Glouc Cathl 85-96; V Fairford 92-96; RD 93-96; rtd 96; PtO *Glouc* from 98. *19 Prices Road, Abbeymead, Gloucester GL4 4PD* T: (01452) 614259

GREEN, Pauline. *See* GREEN, Elizabeth Pauline Anne

GREEN, Penny. *See* GREEN, Denise Penelope

GREEN, Peter. b 38. Ex Univ BSc 59. Sarum Th Coll 59. **d** 61 **p** 62. C Romford St Edw *Chelmsf* 61-66; Chapl Trin Coll Kandy Ceylon 66-70; V Darnall *Sheff* 71-80; TV Stantonbury *Ox* 80-87; TV Stantonbury and Willen 87-91; Dep Chapl HM Pris Belmarsh 91-92; Chapl HM Pris Woodhill 92-03; rtd 03; PtO *Ox* from 04. *34 North Twelfth Street, Milton Keynes MK9 3BT* T: (01908) 240634 F: 240635 M: 07808-556213 E: peter@pg34.eclipse.co.uk

GREEN, Peter Geoffrey. b 59. St Andr Univ MA 83 Open Univ MA 01 PhD 10 BA 12. Coll of Resurr Mirfield 85. **d** 88 **p** 89. C Pershore w Pinvin, Wick and Birlingham *Worc* 88-91; V Dudley St Barn 91-99; V W Bromwich St Fran *Lich* 99-04; RD W Bromwich 02-04; Chapl Abbots Bromley Sch 04-12; P-in-c Hoar Cross w Newchurch *Lich* 07-12; Dean of Chpl and Chapl Bp Grosseteste Univ from 13. *Bishop Grosseteste University, Longdales Road, Lincoln LN1 3DY* T: (01522) 583607 E: peter.green@bishopg.ac.uk

GREEN, Peter Jamie. b 63. Aston Tr Scheme 87 Oak Hill Th Coll BA 93. **d** 93 **p** 94. C Brigg *Linc* 93-97; C Brigg, Wrawby and Cadney cum Howsham 97; P-in-c Billinghay 97-01; V Carr Dyke Gp 01-02; R Kelsey Gp 02-09; P-in-c St Mark's Bermuda 09-12; R Old Brampton and Great Barlow *Derby* from 12; P-in-c Loundsley Green from 12. *The Rectory, 25 Oldridge Close, Chesterfield S40 4UF* T: (01246) 558112 E: peter.green_99@tiscali.co.uk

GREEN, Canon Philip Charles. b 53. NOC 91. **d** 94 **p** 95. C Southport Em *Liv* 94-98; P-in-c Crossens 98-03; TV N Meols 03-05; TR from 05; AD from 09; Hon Can Liv Cathl from 09. *St John's Vicarage, Rufford Road, Southport PR9 8JH* T: (01704) 227662 E: revphilgreen@talktalk.net

GREEN, Canon Philip Harry. b 19. ALCD 50. **d** 50 **p** 51. C Keighley *Bradf* 50-53; V Everton St Sav *Liv* 53-57; V Barnoldswick w Bracewell *Bradf* 57-64; V Shipley St Paul 64-77; V Gargrave 77-82; Hon Can Bradf Cathl 77-82; rtd 82; PtO *Bradf* 82-94; *Carl* 82-09. *The Villa, Hornby, Northallerton DL6 2JQ* T: (01609) 881288

GREEN, Philip Stuart. b 69. Man Poly BA 90 Man Univ PGCE 91. ERMC 11. **d** 14 **p** 15. NSM Winton Colney St Pet *St Alb* from 14. *38 Oakfield Close, Potters Bar EN6 2BE* T: (01707) 660025 M: 07934-335793 E: revphilipgreen@btinternet.com

GREEN, Richard Alistair. b 76. Ex Univ BA 97. St Steph Ho Ox BA 01. **d** 01 **p** 02. C Cockerton *Dur* 01-05; TV Ludlow *Heref* 05-13; Chapl Shropshire Co Primary Care Trust 05-13; V Aberdare St Fagan *Llan* from 13. *The Vicarage, 5 Redwood Court, Aberdare CF44 8RX* T: (01685) 881435 E: vicar.stfagans@btconnect.com

GREEN, Richard Charles. b 49. K Coll Lon 68 St Aug Coll Cant 73. **d** 74 **p** 75. C Broseley w Benthall *Heref* 74-79; TV Heref St Martin w St Fran 80-95; C Heref S Wye 95-99; rtd 99; Hon Chapl Heref S Wye 99-02. *5 Bardolph Close, Hereford HR2 7QA* T: (01432) 354588 *or* 353717 M: 07976-910881 E: rghswtm@aol.com

GREEN, Robert Henry. b 57. K Coll Lon BD 79. Wycliffe Hall Ox 81. **d** 83 **p** 84. C Norbury *Ches* 83-86 and from 91; C Knutsford St Jo and Toft 86-88; rtd 88. *122 Cavendish Road, Hazel Grove, Stockport SK7 6JH* T: (01625) 858680 E: rob.green122@ntlworld.com

GREEN, Robert Leonard. b 44. Sarum & Wells Th Coll. **d** 84 **p** 85. C Battersea St Luke *S'wark* 84-89; CF 89-04; P-in-c Southwick w Boarhunt *Portsm* from 05. *The White House, High Street, Southwick, Fareham PO17 6EB* T: (023) 9237 7568 E: revdbobgreen@talktalk.net

GREEN, Robert Stanley. b 42. Dur Univ BA 65. Wells Th Coll 65. **d** 67 **p** 68. C Ashford *Cant* 67-73; R Otham 73-80; V Bethersden w High Halden 80-87; R Winterbourne Stickland and Turnworth etc *Sarum* 87-99; R Monkton Farleigh, S Wraxall and Winsley 99-05; rtd 05. *The Bungalow, Wootton Grove, Sherborne DT9 4DL* T: (01935) 817066 E: green@homecall.co.uk

GREEN, Robin. b 47. St As Minl Tr Course. **d** 06 **p** 07. NSM Llangystennin *St As* 06-09; NSM Rhos-Cystennin 09-11; rtd 11; PtO *St As* from 12; *Ban* from 15. *140 Queens Road, Llandudno LL30 1UE* T: (01492) 876451 E: rev.robin@tiscali.co.uk

GREEN, Robin Christopher William. b 43. Leeds Univ BA 64 Fitzw Ho Cam BA 67. Ridley Hall Cam 65. **d** 68 **p** 69. C S'wark H Trin 68-71; C Englefield Green *Guildf* 71-73; Chapl Whitelands Coll of HE *S'wark* 73-78; Team Ldr Dioc Lay Tr Team 78-84; V W Brompton St Mary w St Pet *Lon* 84-87; USPG 87-90; PtO *S'wark* 88-90; rtd 03. *The Catch, 53 Sandown Road, Deal CT14 6PE* T: (01304) 389050

GREEN, Roderick Ernest Alexander. b 74. Reading Univ BA 95 Brunel Univ MA 99. Wycliffe Hall Ox MTh 07. **d** 07 **p** 08. C Spitalfields Ch Ch w All SS *Lon* 07-11; C Shadwell St Paul w

Ratcliffe St Jas 11-14; V W Harrow from 14. *65 Butler Road, Harrow HA1 4DS* M: 07957-247239 E: rodeagreen@gmail.com

GREEN, Rodney William. b 52. **d** 93 **p** 94. OLM Flixton St Jo *Man* from 93. *85 Arundel Avenue, Flixton, Manchester M41 6MG* T: 0161-748 7238

GREEN, Roger Thomas. b 43. Oak Hill Th Coll. **d** 79 **p** 80. C Paddock Wood *Roch* 79-83; R High Halstow w All Hallows and Hoo St Mary 83-89; Chapl HM Pris Brixton 89-90; Chapl HM Pris Standford Hill 90-94; Chapl HM Pris Swaleside 94-99; Chapl HM Pris Roch 99-03; Chapl HM Pris Blantyre Ho 03; Chapl HM Pris Brixton 03-06; rtd 06; PtO *Sarum* from 11. *30 Anvil Crescent, Broadstone BH18 9DY* E: rogert.green@btinternet.com

GREEN (née JARMAN), Mrs Rosemary Susan. b 44. SAOMC 99. **d** 01 **p** 02. OLM Bradfield and Stanford Dingley *Ox* 01-14; PtO from 14. *1 Buscot Copse, Bradfield, Reading RG7 6JB* T: 0118-974 4640 F: 974 4910 E: rosegreen.buscot@gmail.com

GREEN, Ruth. b 54. RGN 76. New Coll Edin BD 11. **d** 11 **p** 12. C Edin St Pet 11-14; R Edin St Dav from 14. *30/2 Mayfield Gardens, Edinburgh EH9 2BZ* T: (01316) 292018 M: 07941-552768 E: curate@stpetersedinburgh.org

GREEN, Ruth Valerie. *See* JAGGER, Ruth Valerie

GREEN, Ryan Albert. b 77. Nottm Univ BA 99. St Steph Ho Ox MTh 05. **d** 05 **p** 06. C The Cookhams *Ox* 05-09; R Swanbourne w Mt Claremont Australia from 09. *The Rectory, Shenton Road, Swanbourne, Perth WA 6010, Australia* E: rev_green@hotmail.co.uk

GREEN, Sidney Leonard. b 44. K Coll Lon MTh 86 Montessori DipEd 84. Oak Hill Th Coll BD 72. **d** 72 **p** 73. C Skelmersdale St Paul *Liv* 72-74; C Denton Holme *Carl* 74-76; In Bapt Min 76-85; Chapl Qu Eliz Gr Sch Blackb 85-91; Chapl Epsom Coll 91-01; P-in-c Sway *Win* 01-03; V 03-04; rtd 04; Australia from 04; Asst Min Adelaide H Trin 05; R Adelaide St Luke 06; Chapl Kensington St Matt from 07. *Bethany, 31 Maesbury Circuit, Sturt, Adelaide SA 5047, Australia* T: (0061) (8) 8358 1406 E: sandjgreen@adam.com.au

GREEN, Ms Stella Louise. b 61. Kent Univ BA 84 Cardiff Univ MTh 05. St Mich Coll Llan 01. **d** 03 **p** 04. C Stamford Hill St Thos *Lon* 03-06; R Horsford, Felthorpe and Hevingham *Nor* 06-10; Chapl Norfolk and Nor Univ Hosp NHS Trust from 10. *41 Notykin Street, Norwich NR5 9DN* T: (01603) 749836 *or* 287470 E: stella.green@nnuh.nhs.uk

GREEN, Steven Douglas. b 57. Univ of Wales BA 97. Sarum & Wells Th Coll 81. **d** 82 **p** 83. C Hawarden *St As* 82-86; V Mostyn 86-93; V Ffynnongroew 86-93; V Mostyn w Ffynnongroyw 93-99; R Trefnant w Tremeirchion 99-01; R Cefn w Trefnant w Tremeirchion 01-07; V Shotton from 07; Warden of Readers from 10. *The Vicarage, Chester Road East, Shotton, Deeside CH5 1QD* T: (01244) 836991 E: sdgreen1957@gmail.com

GREEN, Canon Susan Denise. b 66. TCD BA 89 HDipEd 90. **d** 92 **p** 93. C Antrim All SS *Conn* 92-95; Dioc Youth Officer (Cashel) *C & O* 95-00; Chapl Adelaide and Meath Hosp Dublin 00-09; Chapl Kilkenny Coll *C & O* from 10; Can Ossory Cathl from 13. *The Rectory, Tullow, Co Carlow, Republic of Ireland* T/F: (00353) (59) 915 1481 M: 87-262 0054 E: s2011green@gmail.com

GREEN, Mrs Susan Margaret. b 54. Univ of Wales (Abth) BSc 75. SWMTC 92. **d** 95 **p** 96. NSM Wiveliscombe w Chipstable, Huish Champflower etc *B & W* 95-05; R Blackdown 05-14; C Trull w Angersleigh 05-14; rtd 14. *Flat 3, 6 Nelson Gardens, Plymouth PL1 5RH* E: suegreen@summit.me.uk

GREEN, Susannah Ruth. *See* THORP, Susannah Ruth

GREEN, Canon Trevor Geoffrey Nash. b 45. BA. Oak Hill Th Coll 81. **d** 84 **p** 85. C Stalybridge H Trin and Ch Ch *Ches* 84-89; V 89-96; V Lache cum Saltney 96-10; Hon Can Ches Cathl 08-10; rtd 10; PtO *Ches* from 10; *Man* from 13. *27 Winchester Road, Dukinfield SK16 5DH* T: 0161-304 7796 M: 07837-424038 E: trevlaine10@aol.co.uk

GREEN, Trevor Howard. b 37. Sarum & Wells Th Coll 72. **d** 74 **p** 75. C Bloxwich *Lich* 74-77; C Willenhall St Steph 77-79; P-in-c 79-80; V 80-82; V Essington 82-90; V Bishopswood and Brewood 90-02; P-in-c Coven 00-02; RD Penkridge 94-01; rtd 02; PtO *Lich* from 02. *113 Stafford Street, Cannock WS12 2EN* T: (01543) 271159

GREEN, Mrs Veronica Gale. b 62. All SS Cen for Miss & Min 12. **d** 14 **p** 15. C Bunbury and Tilstone Fearnall *Ches* from 14. *Park View Cottage, Nantwich Road, Broxton, Chester CH3 9JH* T: (01829) 782281 M: 07928-792337 E: veronicaron838@aol.com

GREEN, William. b 44. Newc Univ BA 66 DipEd 67 MA 77. NOC 87. **d** 90 **p** 91. NSM Utley *Bradf* 90-97; P-in-c Scarborough St Jas w H Trin *York* 97-00; V Thornton St Jas

Bradf 00-06; rtd 07; PtO *Leeds* from 07. *105 Shann Lane, Keighley BD20 6DY* T: (01535) 669360
E: billalice@tiscali.co.uk

GREEN OF HURSTPIERPOINT, Preb the Lord (Stephen Keith). b 48. Ex Coll Ox BA 69 Mass Inst of Tech MSc 75. NOC 84. d 87 p 88. NSM St Jo Cathl Hong Kong 87-93; PtO *Lon* from 93; Preb St Paul's Cathl from 07. *House of Lords, London SW1A 0PW*

GREENALL, Canon Ronald Gilbert. b 41. St Aid Birkenhead 61. d 64 p 65. C Adlington *Blackb* 64-67; C Ribbleton 67-69; R Coppull St Jo 69-84; V Garstang St Thos 84-99; RD Garstang 89-96; Hon Can Blackb Cathl 95-99; rtd 99; PtO *Blackb* from 99. *40 Duckworth Drive, Catterall, Preston PR3 1YS* T: (01995) 606135

GREENE, Colin John David. b 50. QUB BA 73 Fitzw Coll Cam MA 75 Nottm Univ PhD. St Jo Coll Nottm 78. d 80 p 81. NSM Sandiacre *Derby* 80-81; C Loughborough Em *Leic* 81-84; V Thorpe Acre w Dishley 84-89; Evang Tr Consultant Bible Soc 89-91; Tutor Trin Coll Bris 91-95; Th Consultant Bible Soc and Springdale Coll 95-96; Hd Th and Public Policy Bible Soc 96-03; Dean Th and Prof Seattle Pacific Univ USA 03-05; Prof Seattle Sch of Th and Psychology 05-08; Research Prof New York Th Sem from 11; Progr Ldr Sarum Coll from 11; P-in-c Marnhull *Sarum* 11-13; R 13-15; rtd 15. *21A Upton Way, Broadstone BH18 9LT* E: colin.greeneuk@gmail.com

GREENE, Ms Rachel Elizabeth. b 78. Virginia Univ BA 01 Peterho Cam MPhil 04. Westcott Ho Cam 05 Yale Div Sch 06. d 08 p 09. C Sturminster Newton, Hinton St Mary and Lydlinch *Sarum* 08-11; C Ox St Mary V w St Cross and St Pet 11-13; Chapl Trin Coll Cam from 14. *8 South Green Road, Cambridge CB3 9JP* E: rachelegreene@gmail.com *or* reg40@cam.ac.uk

GREENE, Richard Francis. b 47. TCD BAI 70 BA 70 MA 86 AMIMechE. CITC 03. d 06 p 07. NSM Waterford w Killea, Drumcannon and Dunhill *C & O* 06-10; NSM New w Old Ross, Whitechurch, Fethard etc 10-11; P-in-c from 11; rtd 14. *Shallon, 2 Pleasant Avenue, Mount Pleasant, Waterford, Republic of Ireland* M: 87-825 0418 T: (00353) (51) 878477
E: rev.greene@gmail.com

GREENE, Valerie. b 45. Sheff Univ MA 04. Linc Th Coll 09. d 11 p 12. OLM Kirkby Laythorpe *Linc* from 11. *68 Church Lane, Kirkby-la-Thorpe, Sleaford NG34 9NU* T: (01529) 413148
E: val.greene@btinternet.com

GREENER, The Very Revd Jonathan Desmond Francis. b 61. Trin Coll Cam BA 83 MA 87. Coll of Resurr Mirfield 89. d 91 p 92. C S'wark H Trin w St Matt 91-94; Bp's Dom Chapl *Truro* 94-96; V Brighton Gd Shep Preston *Chich* 96-03; Adn Pontefract *Wakef* 03-07; Dean Wakef *Leeds* from 07. *The Deanery, 1 Cathedral Close, Wakefield WF1 2DP* T: (01924) 239308 *or* 373923 F: 215054 E: jonathan.greener@wakefield-cathedral.org.uk

GREENER, Mrs Yvonne. b 59. St Cuth Soc Dur BA 99 Ox Brookes Univ MA 12. Ripon Coll Cuddesdon. d 12 p 13. C N Shields *Newc* from 12. *St Augustine's Vicarage, 51 Drummond Terrace, North Shields NE30 2AW* T: 0191-258 3768
E: ygreener2002@yahoo.co.uk

GREENFIELD, Diana Marion. b 71. NTMTC. d 10 p 11. C Glastonbury w Meare *B & W* from 10; C Street w Walton from 13; Adv on New Relig Movements etc from 15. *25 Brookfield Way, Street BA16 0UE* T: (01458) 446838
E: dmgreenfield@me.com

GREENFIELD, Judith Frances. b 44. d 10. NSM Hove St Jo *Chich* from 10. *Flat 2, 117 St George's Road, Brighton BN2 1EA*

GREENFIELD, Canon Martin Richard. b 54. Em Coll Cam MA 75. Wycliffe Hall Ox MA 78. d 79 p 80. C Enfield Ch Ch Trent Park *Lon* 79-83; CMS 84-94; Nigeria 85-94; Hon Can Aba from 89; C Langdon Hills *Chelmsf* 94-95; R Brampton *Ely* 95-13; RD Huntingdon 99-04; P-in-c Sanderstead *S'wark* from 13. *The Rectory, 1 Addington Road, South Croydon CR2 8RE* T: (020) 8657 1366 E: rector@sanderstead-parish.org.uk

GREENHALGH, Harry. b 54. d 11 p 13. NSM Winwick *Liv* from 11. *13 Blair Avenue, Hindley Green, Wigan WN2 4HQ*

GREENHALGH, Canon Ian Frank. b 49. Wycliffe Hall Ox 74. d 77 p 78. C Parr *Liv* 77-80; V Wigan St Barn Marsh Green 80-84; Chapl RAF 84-04; RD Ewecross *Bradf* 05-14; AD *Leeds* from 14; RD Bowland *Bradf* 14; AD *Leeds* from 14; Hon Can Bradf Cathl from 11. *The Vicarage, Clapham Road, Austwick, Lancaster LA2 8BE* T: (01524) 251313
E: ian.greenhalgh@bradford.anglican.org

GREENHALGH, Philip Adrian. b 52. Dur Univ MA 05. Ian Ramsey Coll Brasted 75 Wycliffe Hall Ox 76. d 79 p 80. C GT Clacton *Chelmsf* 79-82; P-in-c Stalmine *Blackb* 82-86; Rep Leprosy Miss E Anglia 86-87; Area Org CECS 88-90; NSM Alston Team *Newc* 90-92; NSM Chulmleigh *Ex* 92-93; NSM

Chawleigh w Cheldon 92-93; NSM Wembworthy w Eggesford 92-93; P-in-c Gilsland w Nether Denton *Carl* 93-95; V Millom 95-00; P-in-c Heatherycleugh *Dur* 00-04; P-in-c Westgate 00-04; P-in-c St John in Weardale 00-04; P-in-c Stanhope w Frosterley 02-04; P-in-c Eastgate w Rookhope 02-04; R Upper Weardale 04-07; AD Stanhope 00-07; R Bewcastle, Stapleton and Kirklinton etc *Carl* from 07; RD Brampton 12-15. *Priory Cottage, Lanercost, Brampton CA8 2HQ* T: (01697) 742846

GREENHALGH, Mrs Rosalyn. b 61. S Bank Poly BSc 83. WEMTC 09. d 12 p 13. C Cheltenham St Mark *Glouc* from 12. *50 Robert Burns Avenue, Cheltenham GL51 6NT* T: (01242) 244440 M: 07581-235524 E: ros.greenhalgh@btinternet.com

GREENHALGH, Stephen. b 53. Man Univ MA 99. Lon Bible Coll BA 81. d 81 p 82. C Horwich H Trin *Man* 81-84; C Horwich 84-85; Chapl RAF 85-89; PtO *Blackb* 96-01; *Carl* 01-07; *Man* from 07. *2 Old Chapel Lane, Levens, Kendal LA8 8PX* T: (01539) 737856

GREENHAM (née MORTIMER), Mrs Helen Teän. b 69. Leeds Univ BA 91 Univ of Wales (Swansea) PGCE 92. Ripon Coll Cuddesdon 06. d 08 p 09. C Bridgnorth, Tasley, Astley Abbotts, etc *Heref* 08-11; TV Solihull *Birm* from 11. *St Helen's House, 6 St Helen's Road, Solihull B91 2DA* T: 0121-704 2878 M: 07720-543885 E: helen.greenham@gmail.com

GREENHILL, Anthony David. b 39. Bris Univ BSc 59. Tyndale Hall Bris 61. d 63 p 64. C Southsea St Jude *Portsm* 63-65; India 65-78; C Kinson *Sarum* 78-81; V Girlington *Bradf* 81-97; C Platt Bridge *Liv* 97-00; rtd 00; PtO *Bradf* 01-05; *Man* from 05. *65 Lymbridge Drive, Blackrod, Bolton BL6 5TH* T: (01204) 696509 E: admp@greenhill.me.uk

GREENHOUGH, Alan Kenneth. b 40. St D Coll Lamp. d 66 p 67. C Allestree *Derby* 66-70; C Ilkeston St Mary 70-73; V Bradwell 73-85; R Twyford w Guist w Bintry w Themelthorpe etc *Nor* 85-95; P-in-c Stibbard 94-95; R Twyford, Guist, Bintree, Themelthorpe etc 95-05; rtd 05. *10 Newton Close, Metheringham, Lincoln LN4 3EQ* T: (01526) 328642

GREENHOUGH, Andrew Quentin. b 68. E Lon Poly BSc 89. Wycliffe Hall Ox BTh 94. d 94 p 95. C Partington and Carrington *Ches* 94-98; C Davenham 98-05; P-in-c Moulton 01-05; V New Ferry from 05. *St Mark's Vicarage, New Chester Road, Wirral CH62 1DG* T: 0151-645 2638
E: andy@macvicar.org.uk

GREENHOUGH, Arthur George. b 30. Fitzw Ho Cam BA 52 MA 56. Tyndale Hall Bris 55. d 57 p 58. C Wakef St Andr 57-63; R Birkin w Haddlesey *York* 63-85; RD Selby 77-84; P-in-c Hambleton 84-85; R Haddlesey w Hambleton and Birkin 85-00; rtd 01; PtO *York* from 01. *4 Sandway Drive, Camblesforth, Selby YO8 8JX* T: (01757) 617347

GREENHOUGH, Geoffrey Herman. b 36. Sheff Univ BA 57 Lon Univ BD 71. St Jo Coll Nottm 74. d 75 p 76. C Cheadle Hulme St Andr *Ches* 75-78; R Tilston and Shocklach 78-82; V Hyde St Geo 82-87; V Pott Shrigley 87-00; rtd 00; PtO *Ches* from 01. *9 Spey Close, Winsford CW7 3BP* T: (01606) 556275
E: ghgreenhough@uwclub.net

GREENISH, Brian Vivian Isitt. b 20. LRCP MRCS Lon Univ MB BS. d 89 p 89. NSM Bedford St Pet w St Cuth *St Alb* 89-91; PtO 91-08. *Address temp unknown*

GREENLAND, Martin. b 65. Warwick Univ BSc 87. Westcott Ho Cam 94. d 97 p 98. C Scarborough St Martin *York* 97-00; TV Bramley and Ravenfield w Hooton Roberts etc *Sheff* 00-04; V Ravenfield, Hooton Roberts and Braithwell 04-08; R Acle w Fishley, N Burlingham, Beighton w Moulton *Nor* 08-15; R Acle and Bure to Yare from 15. *The Rectory, Norwich Road, Acle, Norwich NR13 3BU* T: (01493) 750393
E: rector@aclechurch.plus.com

GREENLAND, Paul Howard. b 59. Bath Univ BA 80 ACA 85. Trin Coll Bris 98. d 00 p 01. C Caverswall and Weston Coyney w Dilhorne *Lich* 00-03; P-in-c Chelmsf St Andr 03-05; V from 05. *The Vicarage, 88 Chignal Road, Chelmsford CM1 2JB* T/F: (01245) 496722 M: 07811-539328
E: paulhgreenland@care4free.net

GREENLAND, Roy Wilfrid. b 37. St Steph Ho Ox 71. d 73 p 74. C Wanstead St Mary *Chelmsf* 73-76; V Harlow St Mary Magd 76-83; P-in-c Huntingdon All SS w St Jo *Ely* 83-84; P-in-c Huntingdon St Barn 83-84; P-in-c Huntingdon St Mary w St Benedict 83-84; Bermuda 84-89; V Northampton St Alb *Pet* 89-92; R Waldron *Chich* 92-02; rtd 02; PtO *Pet* 05-07; Cov from 08. *7 Margetts Close, Kenilworth CV8 1EN* T: (01926) 852560

GREENMAN, David John. b 35. Lon Univ BA 59. Oak Hill Th Coll 57. d 61 p 62. C Wandsworth St Steph *S'wark* 61-63; C Bishopwearmouth St Gabr *Dur* 63-66; C-in-c Bedgrove CD *Ox* 66-74; P-in-c Macclesfield Ch Ch *Ches* 74-77; V 77-81; P-in-c Glouc All SS 81-85; V Glouc St Jas 81-85; V Bare *Blackb* 85-91; V Market Lavington and Easterton *Sarum* 91-99; rtd 99; PtO *Sarum* from 00; *Win* from 00. *3 Bure Lane, Christchurch BH23 4DJ* T: (01425) 241034

GREENMAN (née CHESTER), Mrs Irene Mary. b 51. Dioc OLM tr scheme 97. **d** 99 **p** 00. OLM Cornholme *Wakef* 99-00; OLM Cornholme and Walsden 00-11. *8 Glenview Street, Cornholme, Todmorden OL14 8LT* T/F: (01706) 817296
E: revgreenman@aol.com

GREENSLADE, Canon Gillian Carol. b 43. Leic Univ BA 64 Essex Univ MA 78 Nottm Univ PGCE 65. EAMTC 93. **d** 96 **p** 97. NSM Dovercourt and Parkeston w Harwich *Chelmsf* 96-00; NSM Colchester, New Town and The Hythe 00-02; R Broxted w Chickney and Tilty etc 02-08; Hon Can Chelmsf Cathl 07-08; rtd 08; Adv for Women's Min (Colchester Area) *Chelmsf* 05-08; PtO from 08. *24 Quayside Court, The Quay, Harwich CO12 3HH* T: (01255) 552055
E: gcgreenslade@googlemail.com

GREENSLADE, Timothy Julian. b 63. St Jo Coll Ox BA 86. Oak Hill Th Coll BA 95. **d** 95 **p** 96. C Broadwater *Chich* 95-99; TV Radipole and Melcombe Regis *Sarum* from 99. *The Vicarage, 106 Spa Road, Weymouth DT3 5ER* T: (01305) 771938
E: the.greenslades@tiscali.co.uk

GREENSMITH, Mrs Sharon Suzanne. **d** 14 **p** 15. NSM Clayton *Lich* from 14. *17 Beechwood Close, Newcastle ST5 4EL* T: (01782) 717827 E: sharon116@btinternet.com

GREENSTREET, Mark George. b 68. St Jo Coll Dur BA 97. Cranmer Hall Dur 94. **d** 97 **p** 98. C St Alb St Pet *St Alb* 97-99; C Stevenage St Hugh and St Jo 99-01; C Dorridge *Birm* 01-04; V Halton *Ches* 04-09; I Seapatrick *D & D* 09-12; I Urney w Sion Mills *D & R* from 12. *112 Melmount Road, Sion Mills, Strabane BT82 9PY* T: (028) 8165 8835
E: mark-greenstreet@lineone.net

GREENWAY, John. b 32. Bps' Coll Cheshunt 68 Qu Coll Birm 69. **d** 69 **p** 70. C Luton Ch Ch *St Alb* 69-74; C Pulloxhill w Flitton 75-76; P-in-c Marston Morteyne 76-79; P-in-c Lidlington 77-79; P-in-c Marston Morteyne w Lidlington 80-81; R 81-97; rtd 97; PtO *Portsm* from 98. *73 Northmore Road, Locks Heath, Southampton SO31 6ZW* T: (01489) 886791

GREENWAY, John Michael. b 34. **d** 96 **p** 97. OLM Gt Yarmouth *Nor* 96-04; PtO from 04. *17 Hamilton Road, Great Yarmouth NR30 4ND* T: (01493) 853558
E: john.greenway3@ntlworld.com

GREENWELL, Christopher. b 49. Linc Th Coll 79. **d** 81 **p** 82. C Scarborough St Martin *York* 81-84; V S Bank 84-89; R Bolton by Bowland w Grindleton *Bradf* 89-92; V Nether Hoyland St Andr *Sheff* 92-96; V Kirkleatham *York* 96-07; rtd 07. *79 Hillshaw Park Way, Ripon HG4 1JU* T: (01765) 600467
E: chris@greenwell49.wanadoo.co.uk

GREENWELL, Canon Paul. b 60. Magd Coll Ox BA 81 MA 85. St Steph Ho Ox 82. **d** 85 **p** 86. C Hendon and Sunderland *Dur* 85-88; Min Can and Prec Ripon Cathl 88-93; Chapl Univ Coll of Ripon and York St Jo 88-93; V Hunslet St Mary *Ripon* 93-02; Chapl Harrogate and Distr NHS Foundn Trust 02-08; Chapl St Mich Hospice Harrogate 02-08; Convenor Dioc Adv Gp for Chr Healing *Ripon* 03-08; Can Res Ripon Cathl from 08; Chapl MU from 09. *St Wilfrid's House, Minster Close, Ripon HG4 1QP* T: (01765) 600211 E: canonpaul@riponcathedral.org.uk

GREENWOOD, Caroline Elizabeth. b 63. Lanc Univ BSc 85 Open Univ BSc 96 Trent Poly PGCE 88. St Jo Coll Nottm MTh 14. **d** 14 **p** 15. C Hillock and Unsworth *Man* from 14. *St Andrew's House, Mersey Drive, Whitefield, Manchester M45 8LA* T: 0161-767 8304 M: 07771-858404
E: karis1763@gmail.com

GREENWOOD, Claire. *See* GREENWOOD, Helen Claire

GREENWOOD, David. **d** 15 **p** 15. C Kincardine O'Neil *Ab* from 14; C Banchory from 14. *Gardener's Cottage, Kincardine, Kincardine O'Neil, Aboyne AB34 5AE* T: (01339) 884060
E: dngreenwood@gmail.com

GREENWOOD, David. *See* GREENWOOD, Norman David

GREENWOOD, Elizabeth. *See* GREENWOOD, Margaret Elizabeth

GREENWOOD, Canon Gerald. b 33. Leeds Univ BA 57 Sheff Poly MSc 81 Surrey Univ Hon MA 93. Linc Th Coll 57. **d** 59 **p** 60. C Rotherham *Sheff* 59-62; V Elsecar 62-70; V Wales 70-77; P-in-c Thorpe Salvin 74-77; Dioc Sch Officer 77-84; P-in-c Bramley and Ravenfield 77-78; P-in-c Hooton Roberts 77-78; R 78-84; Hon Can Sheff Cathl 80-84; Dioc Dir of Educn 81-84; Hon Can S'wark Cathl 84-97; Dir of Educn 84-97; rtd 97; PtO *Cant* from 97. *Home Farm Cottage, Westmarsh, Canterbury CT3 2LW* T: (01304) 812160

GREENWOOD, Helen Claire. b 54. Cranmer Hall Dur 05. **d** 06 **p** 07. C Willington *Newc* 06-10; V Marden w Preston Grange 10-13; V Billy Mill 10-13; rtd 13; Hon C Barnoldswick w Bracewell *Leeds* from 14. *24 Upper Union Street, Skipton BD23 2NN* E: hcgreenwood@yahoo.com

GREENWOOD, Ian Richard. b 74. Liv Hope BEd 96. St Jo Coll Nottm MTh 09. **d** 09. C Burscough Bridge *Liv* 09-13; P-in-c Aigburth 13-14; V from 14. *St Anne's Vicarage, 389 Aigburth Road, Liverpool L17 6BH* T: 0151-727 1101 M: 07840-829956
E: reviangreenwood@gmail.com

GREENWOOD, James Peter. b 61. Univ Coll Lon BSc 83 St Jo Coll Dur BA 90 RIBA 87. Cranmer Hall Dur 88. **d** 91 **p** 92. C Belper *Derby* 91-94; CMS Pakistan 95-01; V Islamabad St Thos 95-00; V Silsden *Bradf* 01-09; Dioc Spirituality Adv 05-09; RD S Craven 07-09; P-in-c Gillingham and Milton-on-Stour *Sarum* from 09. *The Rectory, High Street, Gillingham SP8 4AJ* T: (01747) 822435 *or* 821598

GREENWOOD, John Newton. b 44. St Chad's Coll Dur BA 69. **d** 70 **p** 71. C Hartlepool H Trin *Dur* 70-72; LtO from 72; Hd Master Archibald Primary Sch Cleveland 84-97; Asst Chapl HM Pris Holme Ho from 99; PtO *Dur* from 13. *1 Brae Head, Eaglescliffe, Stockton-on-Tees TS16 9HP* T: (01642) 783200

GREENWOOD, Leslie. b 37. Dur Univ BA 59. Cranmer Hall Dur. **d** 61 **p** 62. C Birstall *Wakef* 61-63; C Illingworth 64-70; Chapl H Trin Sch Halifax 64-89; V Charlestown *Wakef* 70-91; TV Upper Holme Valley 91-97; PtO *Leeds* from 97; rtd 00. *2 Trenance Gardens, Greetland, Halifax HX4 8NN* T/F: (01422) 373926 E: kyandles@aol.com

GREENWOOD, Mrs Margaret Elizabeth. b 34. St Mary's Coll Chelt TCert 65 Surrey Univ MA 93. St Mich Ho Ox 60. **d** 00. NSM Shepperton *Lon* 00-01; NSM Whitton SS Phil and Jas 01-04; PtO from 04. *Bundoran Cottage, Vicarage Lane, Staines TW18 1UE* T: (01784) 458115
E: elizabethgreenwood@btinternet.com

GREENWOOD, Canon Michael Eric. b 44. Oak Hill Th Coll 78. **d** 80 **p** 81. C Clubmoor *Liv* 80-83; V Pemberton St Mark Newtown 83-94; V Grassendale 94-00; V Ashton-in-Makerfield St Thos 00-09; Hon Can Liv Cathl 08-09; rtd 09. *1 Fardon Close, Wigan WN3 6SN* E: mikeg@tinyonline.co.uk

GREENWOOD, Norman David. b 52. Edin Univ BMus 74 Lon Univ BD 78 Nottm Univ MPhil 90. Oak Hill Th Coll 76. **d** 78 **p** 79. C Gorleston St Andr *Nor* 78-81; SAMS 81-83; C Cromer *Nor* 83-84; R Appleby Magna and Swepstone w Snarestone *Leic* 84-94; P-in-c Chesterfield H Trin *Derby* 94-95; P-in-c Chesterfield Ch Ch 94-95; R Chesterfield H Trin and Ch Ch 95-99; V S Ramsey St Paul *S & M* 99-12; Dir Voc and Tr 01-12; RD Ramsey 08-11; Chapl HM Pris Is of Man 05-12; Hon Can St German's Cathl 09-12; Chapl St Pet Viña del Mar Chile from 12. *Casilla 676 (Central), Viña del Mar, Chile*

GREENWOOD, Peter. *See* GREENWOOD, James Peter

GREENWOOD, Canon Robin Patrick. b 47. St Chad's Coll Dur BA 68 MA 71 Birm Univ PhD 92. **d** 70 **p** 71. C Adel *Ripon* 70-73; Min Can and Succ Ripon Cathl 73-78; V Leeds Halton St Wilfrid 78-86; Dioc Can Res Glouc Cathl 86-95; Dioc Missr and Dir Lay and Post-Ord Tr 86-95; Dir of Min and Hon Can Chelmsf Cathl 95-00; Prov Officer for Min Ch in Wales 01-05; Hon C Canton St Jo *Llan* 02-05; V Monkseaton St Mary *Newc* 05-13; rtd 13. *24 Upper Union Street, Skipton BD23 2NN*

GREENWOOD, Roy Douglas. b 27. Tyndale Hall Bris 58. **d** 60 **p** 61. C Ox St Matt 60-62; V Ulpha *Carl* 62-63; V Seathwaite w Ulpha 63-72; P-in-c Haverthwaite 72-74; C Ulverston St Mary w H Trin 74-78; V Egton w Newland 78-86; Assoc Chapl Palma de Mallorca *Eur* 86-95; rtd 95. *La Finquita, Apartado 78, 07460 Pollenca (Illes Balears), Spain* T: (0034) 971 530 966

GREENWOOD, Sharon. b 44. **d** 07 **p** 08. NSM Welling *S'wark* from 07. *44 Honiton Road, Welling DA16 3LE* T: (020) 8854 3541 E: sharon.greenwood44@tiscali.co.uk

GREENWOOD-HAIGH, Mrs Lesley Karen. b 61. Leeds Univ MHSc 07. St Jo Coll Nottm 10. **d** 12 **p** 13. C Almondbury w Farnley Tyas *Leeds* from 12. *50 Longcroft, Huddersfield HD5 8XW* T: (01484) 421652 M: 07596-317876
E: lesleygh@hotmail.co.uk

GREER, Eric Gordon. b 52. Pepperdine Univ BA 74. Princeton Th Sem MDiv 80. **d** 93 **p** 94. C Southgate St Andr *Lon* 93-96; C Camden Square St Paul 96-00; V Grange Park St Pet from 00. *The Vicarage, Langham Gardens, London N21 1DN* T: (020) 8360 2294 E: egreer@talk21.com

GREEVES, Roger Derrick. b 43. TCD BA 66 MA 70 Fitzw Coll Cam BA 68 MA 73. Westcott Ho Cam 98. **d** 98 **p** 99. In Methodist Ch 68-98; NSM Cam St Edw *Ely* 98-00; Chapl Oakington Immigration Reception Cen 00-01; Chapl Peterho Cam 00-01; Dean Clare Coll Cam 01-08; rtd 08; PtO *Ely* from 08; *Eur* from 15. *The Cart Lodge, 5 Home Farm, 89 High Street, Harston, Cambridge CB22 7PZ* M: 07817-032301 T: (01223) 977988 E: rdg20@cam.ac.uk

GREGG, David William Austin. b 37. Lon Univ BD 66 Bris Univ MA 69. Tyndale Hall Bris 63. **d** 68 **p** 69. C Barrow St Mark *Carl* 68-71; P-in-c Lindal w Marton 71-75; Communications Sec Gen Syn Bd for Miss and Unity 76-81; Prin Romsey Ho Coll Cam 81-88; V Haddenham w Cuddington, Kingsey etc Ox 88-96; P-in-c Newton Longville w Stoke Hammond and Whaddon 96-02; rtd 03; PtO *Carl* from 03. *Lowick Farm House, Lowick Green, Ulverston LA12 8DX* T: (01229) 885258

GREGORY, Alan Paul Roy. b 55. K Coll Lon BD 77 MTh 78 Emory Univ Atlanta PhD 94 AKC 77. Ripon Coll Cuddesdon 78. **d** 79 **p** 80. C Walton-on-Thames *Guildf* 79-82;

Lect Sarum & Wells Th Coll 82-88; Dir Studies 85-88; Assoc R Atlanta St Patr USA 88-94; R Athens Em 94-95; Assoc Prof Ch Hist Episc Th Sem of the SW 95-04; Academic Dean and Prof Ch Hist 04-12; P-in-c Stannington Newc 12-14; Dioc CMD Officer 12-14; Prin SEITE from 14; PtO S'wark from 14. SEITE, Hf17 Hepworth Building, Canterbury Christ Church University, North Holmes Rd, Canterbury CT1 1QU   T: (01227) 471120
M: 07969-335562   E: principal@seite.co.uk or
alan@scrivenersgloom.com

GREGORY, Andrew Forsythe. b 71. St Jo Coll Dur BA 92. Wycliffe Hall Ox BA 96 MA 00 DPhil 01. **d** 97 **p** 98. C E Acton St Dunstan w St Thos Lon 97-99; Asst Chapl Keble Coll Ox 97-99; Chapl Linc Coll Ox 99-03; Research Fell Keble Coll Ox 03-05; Chapl and Fell Univ Coll Ox from 05. University College, High Street, Oxford OX1 4BH   T: (01865) 276663
E: andrew.gregory@theology.ox.ac.uk

GREGORY, Brian. b 43. BEM 14. Trin Coll Bris. **d** 82 **p** 83. C Burscough Bridge Liv 82-85; V Platt Bridge 85-92; V Ben Rhydding Bradf 92-06; rtd 06; PtO Leeds from 07; Blackb from 15. 6 Hawthorn Close, Hesketh Bank, Preston PR4 6EP
T: (01772) 812234   E: gregory.brian@btinternet.com

✢**GREGORY, The Rt Revd Clive Malcolm.** b 61. Lanc Univ BA 84 Qu Coll Cam BA 87 MA 89 Warwick Univ Hon MA 99. Westcott Ho Cam 85. **d** 88 **p** 89 **c** 07. C Margate St Jo Cant 88-92; Chapl Warw Univ Cov 92-98; TR Cov E 98-07; Area Bp Wolverhampton Lich from 07. 61 Richmond Road, Wolverhampton WV3 9JH   T: (01902) 824503   F: 824504
E: bishop.wolverhampton@lichfield.anglican.org

GREGORY, Ms Elizabeth Louise Annunciata. b 83. UWE LLB 05 Univ of Wales (Swansea) MA 07 Lucy Cavendish Coll Cam BA 11. Westcott Ho Cam 09. **d** 12 **p** 13. C Sole Bay St E 12-15; R Filton Bris from 15. The Rectory, Rectory Lane, Filton, Bristol BS34 7BE   M: 07528-518968   T: (0117) 979 1128
E: elizabeth.gregory@talk21.com

GREGORY, Graham. b 36. Open Univ BA 78. Tyndale Hall Bris 63. **d** 66 **p** 67. C Wandsworth St Mich S'wark 66-71; C Hastings Em and St Mary in the Castle Chich 71-75; V Douglas St Ninian S & M 75-91; Dioc Youth Officer 78-88; Chapl HM Pris Douglas 82-86; RD Douglas S & M 86-91; V Wollaton Park S'well 91-95; V Lenton Abbey 91-95; rtd 95; PtO York 98-09. 53 Brockfield Park Drive, York YO31 9EL

GREGORY, Ian Peter. b 45. Open Univ BA 82 Rolle Coll PGCE 92. Bernard Gilpin Soc Dur 66 Chich Th Coll 67. **d** 70 **p** 71. C Tettenhall Regis Lich 70-73; C Shrewsbury H Cross 73-76; P-in-c Walsall St Mary and All SS Palfrey 76-80; R Petrockstowe, Petersmarland, Merton, Meeth etc Ex 80-87; TV Ex St Thos and Em 87-91; Hon C S Wimbledon All SS S'wark 94-00; rtd 10. 20 Etonhurst Close, Exeter EX2 7QZ
T: (01392) 447548   M: 07598-984623
E: revipg@btinternet.com

GREGORY, John Frederick. b 33. Glouc Sch of Min 75. **d** 78 **p** 78. NSM S Cerney w Cerney Wick Glouc 78-81; NSM Coates, Rodmarton and Sapperton etc 81-88; P-in-c Kempsford w Welford 88-98; rtd 98; PtO B & W from 99. 22 Jury Road, Dulverton TA22 9DU   T: (01398) 323587

GREGORY, Judith Rosalind. See GAVIN, Judith Rosalind

GREGORY, Canon Mary Emma. b 70. Birm Univ BA 92 St Jo Coll Dur BA 04 MA 06. Cranmer Hall Dur 02. **d** 05 **p** 06. C Hatfield Sheff 05-08; R Kirk Sandall and Edenthorpe from 08; Dean of Women's Min from 13; Hon Can Sheff Cathl from 14; TV Ashby-de-la-Zouch and Breedon on the Hill Leic from 15. The Rectory, 31 Doncaster Road, Kirk Sandall, Doncaster DN3 1HP   T: (01302) 882861   M: 07734-052524
E: mary.gregory@sheffield.anglican.org or
revmarygregory@aol.co.uk

GREGORY, Nathan James. b 82. Wycliffe Hall Ox. **d** 11 **p** 12. C Fair Oak Win 11-15; Asst Chapl Tervuren Eur from 15. Lindenberg 11, 3080 Tervuren, Belgium
E: n.j.gregory@talk21.com

GREGORY, Peter. b 35. Cranmer Hall Dur 59. **d** 62 **p** 63. C Pennington Man 62-65; C N Ferriby York 65-68; V Tonge Fold Man 68-72; V Hollym w Welwick and Holmpton York 72-77; P-in-c Foston w Flaxton 77-80; P-in-c Crambe w Whitwell and Huttons Ambo 77-80; R Whitwell w Crambe, Flaxton, Foston etc 81-94; rtd 94; PtO York from 13. 6 High Terrace, Northallerton DL6 1BG   T: (01609) 776956

GREGORY, Richard Branson. b 33. Fitzw Ho Cam BA 58 MA 62. Sarum Th Coll 58 Ridley Hall Cam 59. **d** 60 **p** 61. C Sheff St Cuth 60-62; Asst Chapl Leeds Univ Ripon 62-64; V Yeadon St Jo Bradf 64-71; R Keighley 71-74; TR Keighley St Andr 74-82; Hon Can Bradf Cathl 71-82; RD S Craven 71-73 and 78-82; P-in-c Broadmayne, W Knighton, Owermoigne etc Sarum 82-85; R 85-98; rtd 98; PtO Sarum from 98. 2 Huish Cottages, Sydling, Dorchester DT2 9NS   T: (01300) 341835

GREGORY, Canon Stephen Simpson. b 40. Nottm Univ BA 62 CertEd 63. St Steph Ho Ox. **d** 68 **p** 69. C Aldershot St Mich Guildf 68-71; Chapl St Mary's Sch Wantage 71-74; R Edgefield Nor 74-88; R Holt 74-94; R Holt w High Kelling 94-95; RD Holt 79-84 and 93-95; Hon Can Nor Cathl 94-95; V Prestbury Glouc 95-03; P-in-c Pittville All SS 99-03; TR Prestbury and All SS 03-06; RD Cheltenham 00-05; Hon Can Glouc Cathl 04-06; rtd 06; PtO Nor from 08. Mulberry Cottage, Balfour Road, West Runton, Cromer NR27 9QJ   T: (01263) 838049

GREGORY, Timothy Stephen. b 48. Sheff City Coll of Educn CertEd 70. NOC 96. **d** 99 **p** 00. NSM Deepcar Sheff 99-06; NSM Ecclesfield Deanery 06-14; PtO Sheff from 15. 33 St Margaret Avenue, Deepcar, Sheffield S36 2TE   T: 0114-288 4198
E: t.gregory@tiscali.co.uk or
tim.gregory@sheffield.anglican.org

GREGORY-SMITH, Hew Quentin. b 69. Univ of Wales (Abth) BSc 93. St Mich Coll Llan 98. **d** 01 **p** 02. C Pembroke Gp St D 01-04; C Henfynyw w Aberaeron and Llanddewi Aberarth etc 04-07; P-in-c Llanllwchaearn and Llanina 07-10. Brynawelon, New Cross, Aberystwyth SY23 4LY

GREGSON (née ROBERTSON), Mrs Fiona Jane Robertson. b 76. Birm Univ BA 98. Wycliffe Hall Ox BA 05 MA 10. **d** 06 **p** 07. C Aston SS Pet and Paul Birm 06-08; C Aston St Jas 06-08; C Nechells 06-08; C Aston and Nechells 08-10; P-in-c Girlington Bradf 10-13; V 13; C Manningham 10-12; PtO Birm from 14. 25 White Field Avenue, Birmingham B17 9AJ
T: 0121-686 1148   M: 07958-494560
E: fionajanerobertson@yahoo.co.uk

GREGSON, Gillian Amy. b 33. Westmr Coll Ox BTh 02 CQSW 78. **d** 98 **p** 99. OLM Coulsdon St Jo S'wark 98-05; PtO from 05. 21 Canons Hill, Coulsdon CR5 1HB   T: (01737) 479689
E: gillgregson21@gmail.com

GREGSON, Peter John. b 36. Univ Coll Dur BSc 61. Ripon Hall Ox 61. **d** 63 **p** 64. C Radcliffe St Thos Man 63-65; C Baguley 65-67; Chapl RN 68-91; V Ashburton w Buckland in the Moor and Bickington Ex 91-01; RD Moreton 95-98; rtd 01; PtO Sarum 01-11; Blackb from 11. 26 Astley Road, Chorley PR7 1RR
T: (01257) 247999

GREIFF, Andrew John. b 64. Huddersfield Univ BA 98 Leeds Univ PGCE 99 St Jo Coll Dur BA 05. Cranmer Hall Dur 03. **d** 05 **p** 06. C Pudsey St Lawr and St Paul Bradf 05-08; P-in-c Thornton St Jas 08-12; P-in-c Fairweather Green 08-12; TV Shelf w Buttershaw St Aid Leeds from 12. 80 Carr House Road, Halifax HX3 7RJ   T: (01274) 671576 or 676335
E: andrew.greiff667@gmail.com

GREIG, George Malcolm. b 28. CA 53 St Andr Univ BD 95. LNSM course 75. **d** 81 **p** 82. NSM Dundee St Mary Magd Bre 81-84; NSM Dundee St Jo 82-84; P-in-c Dundee St Ninian 84-85; Chapl St Paul's Cathl Dundee 85-98; rtd 98; Hon C Dundee St Salvador Bre from 98. 61 Charleston Drive, Dundee DD2 2HE   T: (01382) 566709   E: gmg28@btinternet.com

GREIG, Martin David Sandford. b 45. Bris Univ BSc 67. St Jo Coll Nottm 72. **d** 75 **p** 76. C Keresley and Coundon Cov 75-79; C Rugby 79-83; TV 83-86; V Cov St Geo 86-93; TV Southgate Chich 93-01; R Maresfield 01-06; P-in-c Nutley 01-06; rtd 06. Bodawen, Llangrannog, Llandysul SA44 6SH
T: (01239) 654257   E: mg@bodawen.org.uk

GREIG, Michael Lawrie Dickson. b 48. All Nations Chr Coll 78 St Jo Coll Nottm 94. **d** 96 **p** 97. C Hunningham Cov 96-00; C Wappenbury w Weston under Wetherley 96-00; C Offchurch 96-00; C Long Itchington and Marton 96-00; P-in-c Napton-on-the-Hill, Lower Shuckburgh etc 00-13; P-in-c Priors Hardwick, Priors Marston and Wormleighton 09-13; rtd 13; PtO Cov from 13; Ox from 14. Owl Cottage, 21 Lenborough Road, Buckingham MK18 1DH   T: (01280) 309025   E: mg@biggles99.freeserve.co.uk

GREIG, Philip. b 76. Ox Brookes Univ BA 02. Ridley Hall Cam 09. **d** 11 **p** 12. C Chartham Cant 11-14; C Cant All SS from 14. Glebe House, Military Road, Canterbury CT1 1PA
M: 07411-936354   E: revphilgreig@me.com

GRENFELL, James Christopher. b 69. Qu Coll Ox BA 93 MA 96 MPhil 95 Ox Univ DPhil 00. Westcott Ho Cam 98. **d** 00 **p** 01. C Kirkby Liv 00-03; P-in-c Sheff Manor 03-06; TR 06-09; P-in-c Ranmoor 09-13; AD Hallam 12-13; PtO Portsm from 13. 313 Havant Road, Farlington, Portsmouth PO6 1DD
E: jamescgrenfell@gmail.com

GRENFELL, The Ven Joanne Woolway. b 72. Oriel Coll Ox BA 93 DPhil 97 Univ of BC MA 94. Westcott Ho Cam 98. **d** 00 **p** 01. C Kirkby Liv 00-03; Jt P-in-c Sheff Manor 03-06; Can Res Sheff Cathl 06-13; Dioc Dir of Ords 06-13; Dean of Women's Min 08-13; Adn Portsdown Portsm from 13. 313 Havant Road, Farlington, Portsmouth PO6 1DD   M: 07833-430140
E: joanne.grenfell@portsmouth.anglican.org

GRENHAM-THOMPSON, Mrs Sharon Carmel. b 66. Reading Univ LLB 87 Solicitor 92. Trin Coll Bris 94 SAOMC 96. **d** 98 **p** 00. C Buckingham Ox 98-00; C Milton Keynes 00-02; Miss Adv USPG Lon, Ox and St Alb 02-03; NSM Wilshamstead and Houghton Conquest St Alb 03-04; Chapl Oakhill Secure Tr

Cen 04-05; PtO *St Alb* from 04; Asst Chapl HM Pris Woodhill 08-11; Chapl HM Pris Bedf from 11. *HM Prison Bedford, St Loyes Street, Bedford MK40 1HG* T: (01234) 373000
E: sharongrenham-thompson@hmps.gsi.gov.uk

GRESHAM, Karen Louise. *See* SMEETON, Karen Louise

GRETTON, Tony Butler. b 29. St Jo Coll Dur BA 53. **d** 54 **p** 55. C W Teignmouth *Ex* 54-57; R Norton Fitzwarren *B & W* 57-68; rtd 68; Chapl Glouc Docks Mariners' Ch 73-92; P-in-c Brookthorpe w Whaddon 79-82; Hon C The Edge, Pitchcombe, Harescombe and Brookthorpe 82-89; PtO from 89. *18 Clover Drive, Hardwicke, Gloucester GL2 4TG*
T: (01452) 721505

GRETTON-DANN, Judith Adrienne. b 75. St Andr Univ MSci 97 PhD 01. St Mich Coll Llan 12. **d** 14 **p** 15. NSM Chesterton Gd Shep *Ely* from 14. *45 Darwin Drive, Cambridge CB4 3HQ*
T: (01223) 750013 M: 07900-523959
E: goodshepherdcurate@gmail.com

GREW, Nicholas David. b 52. Surrey Univ BSc 74 MSc 75. Wycliffe Hall Ox 93. **d** 95 **p** 96. C Biddulph *Lich* 95-99; P-in-c Knaphill *Guildf* 99-00; V Knaphill w Brookwood from 00. *Trinity House, Trinity Road, Knaphill, Woking GU21 2SY*
T: (01483) 473489 E: nickthevic@talktalk.com *or* nickthevic@knaphillchurch.co.uk

GREW, Richard Lewis. b 32. Clare Coll Cam BA 54 MA 58. Wycliffe Hall Ox 67. **d** 68 **p** 70. C Repton *Derby* 68-73; Asst Chapl Repton Sch Derby 74-93; LtO *Derby* 73-93; rtd 93; PtO *Sarum* 94-07. *5 Priory Gardens, Spetisbury, Blandford Forum DT11 9DS* T: (01258) 857613 E: richard@grew5.plus.com

GREW, Timothy Richard. b 65. SS Coll Cam MA 88. WEMTC 03. **d** 06 **p** 07. NSM Cheltenham H Trin and St Paul *Glouc* 06-10; TV from 10. *208 Prestbury Road, Cheltenham GL52 3ER* T: (01242) 321473
E: tim.grew@trinitycheltenham.com

GREY, Andrew James. b 76. St Chad's Coll Dur BA 99 MA 00. Oak Hill Th Coll 03. **d** 08 **p** 09. C Harold Wood *Chelmsf* 08-14; LtO from 14. *14 Doddinghurst Road, Brentwood CM15 9EH* T: (01277) 217367 E: andrew.grey@immanuelbrentwood.org

GREY, Mrs Nicola Jane Francis. b 61. **d** 13 **p** 14. C Burton St Chad *Lich* from 13. *Scarista House, School Lane, Church Leigh, Leigh, Stoke-on-Trent ST10 4SR* T: (01889) 502243
E: nickygrey@totalise.co.uk

GREY, Richard Thomas. b 50. TD 94 QVRM 06. St D Coll Lamp BA 73 Ripon Hall Ox 73. **d** 75 **p** 76. C Blaenavon w Capel Newydd *Mon* 75-77; Ind Chapl 77-02; C Newport St Paul 77-80; CF (TA) from 78; Chapl Aberbargoed Hosp 80-88; V Bedwellty *Mon* 80-88; R Llanwenarth Ultra 88-92; R Govilon w Llanfoist w Llanelen 92-02; RD Abergavenny 98-02; V Brynmawr *S & B* 02-09. *Rivendell, Cefn Rhoss, Tredegar NP22 3PA* E: richard.t.grey@btinternet.com

GREY, Canon Roger Derrick Masson. b 38. AKC 61. **d** 62 **p** 63. C Darlington H Trin *Dur* 62-63; C Bishopwearmouth St Mich 63-67; V Mabe *Truro* 67-70; Dioc Youth Chapl 67-70; Youth Chapl *Glouc* 70-77; V Stroud H Trin 77-82; Dioc Can Res Glouc Cathl 82-03; Dir of Educn 82-94; Bp's Chapl 94-03; rtd 03; Clergy Widows' Officer (Glouc Adnry) from 03; PtO from 04. *12 Buckingham Close, Walton Cardiff, Tewkesbury GL20 7QB*
T: (01684) 275742

GREY, Stephen Bernard. b 56. Linc Th Coll 86. **d** 88 **p** 89. C Worsley *Man* 88-93; V Bamford 93-04; P-in-c Rochdale St Geo w St Alb 99-04; P-in-c Preesall *Blackb* 04-05; P-in-c Hambleton w Out Rawcliffe 04-05; V Waterside Par 05-10; P-in-c Garstang St Thos 10-13; V from 13. *St Thomas's Vicarage, Church Street, Garstang, Preston PR3 1PA* T: (01995) 602192 M: 07910-854911 E: revsbgrey@btinternet.com

GREY-SMITH, Donald Edward. b 31. ACT ThL 64. **d** 64 **p** 65. Australia 64-68 and from 71; W Germany 68-69; C Weeke *Win* 69-71; rtd 96. *6/317 Military Road, Semaphore Park SA 5019, Australia* T: (0061) (8) 8449 4420

GRIBBEN, John Gibson. b 44. K Coll Lon BD 75 QUB MTh 81. CITC 73. **d** 75 **p** 76. C Dunmurry *Conn* 75-78; CR from 79; LtO *Leeds* from 83; rtd 09. *House of the Resurrection, Stocks Bank Road, Mirfield WF14 0BN* T: (01924) 483339
E: jgribben@mirfield.org.uk

GRIBBIN, Canon Bernard Byron. b 35. Bradf Univ MPhil 84. St Aid Birkenhead 58. **d** 60 **p** 61. C Maghull *Liv* 60-63; C Prescot 63-65; V Denholme Gate *Bradf* 65-71; V Bankfoot 71-79; Dioc Stewardship Adv 79-86; Prec and Chapl Choral Ches Cathl 86-91; V Ringway 91-96; Dioc Tourism Officer 91-96; Hon Can Ches Cathl 91-96; rtd 96; PtO *Leeds* from 96. *5 Heather Court, Ilkley LS29 9TZ* T: (01943) 816253

GRIBBLE, Malcolm George. b 44. Chu Coll Cam BA 67 MA 71. Linc Th Coll 79. **d** 81 **p** 82. C Farnborough *Roch* 81-84; V Bostall Heath 84-90; V Bexleyheath Ch Ch 90-02; P-in-c Hever, Four Elms and Mark Beech 02-06; R 06-09; rtd 10. *26 Neville Road, Tewkesbury GL20 5ED* T: (01684) 290641
E: m@griblog.net

GRICE, Charles. b 24. MBE 83. **d** 58 **p** 59. C Stocksbridge *Sheff* 58-61; R Armthorpe 61-66; Ind Missr 66-69; Ind Chapl 69-76; V Tinsley 69-73; V Oughtibridge 73-76; Gen Sec Ch Lads' and Ch Girls' Brigade 77-91; R Braithwell w Bramley *Sheff* 88-91; rtd 89; PtO *Sheff* from 89. *57 Deepdale Road, Rotherham S61 2NR* T: (01709) 557551

GRICE, Canon David Richard. b 32. Keble Coll Ox BA 55 MA 59. St Steph Ho Ox 55. **d** 57 **p** 58. C Leeds St Aid *Ripon* 57-61; C Middleton St Mary 61-62; V Woodlesford 62-69; V Leeds St Wilfrid 69-78; TR Seacroft 78-93; Hon Can Ripon Cathl 92-99; P-in-c Thorner 93-95; V 95-99; rtd 99; PtO *Leeds* from 00. *15 Mead Road, Leeds LS15 9JR* T: 0113-260 4371 E: david@grice12.freeserve.co.uk

GRICE, John William Rupert. b 84. Wolv Univ BA 05. St Jo Coll Nottm 09. **d** 12 **p** 13. C Wellington All SS w Eyton *Lich* from 12. *11 Rushbury Road, Wellington, Telford TF1 3NT*
M: 07815-817095 E: revjohngrice@gmail.com

GRIDLEY, Miss Susan Mary. b 49. EAMTC 94. **d** 97 **p** 98. NSM Doddinghurst and Mountnessing *Chelmsf* 97-03; PtO *Bradf* 03-04; *Chelmsf* from 06. *7 Thracian Close, Colchester CO2 9RN* T: (01206) 548766

GRIER, James Emerson. b 74. St Pet Coll Ox BA 95 MA 01. Wycliffe Hall Ox 96. **d** 98 **p** 99. C Ox St Andr 98-02; C Harborne Heath *Birm* 02-07; TV Pinhoe and Broadclyst *Ex* 07-12; Dioc Youth Adv 07-12; Ldr Unlimited Ch from 12. *St Thomas's Rectory, 57 Cowick Street, Exeter EX4 1HR*
E: james.grier@exeter.anglican.org

GRIERSON, Peter Stanley. b 42. Lon Univ BD 68 Leeds Univ MPhil 74. Linc Th Coll 68. **d** 69 **p** 70. C Clitheroe St Mary *Blackb* 69-71; C Aston cum Aughton *Sheff* 71-74; V Preston St Jude w St Paul *Blackb* 74-81; V Blackb St Luke w St Phil 89-97; RD Blackb 91-97; V Burnley St Matt w H Trin 97-02; PtO *Bradf* 03-13; *Blackb* from 13. *21 Fosbrooke House, 8 Clifton Drive, Lytham St Annes FY8 5RQ* T: (01253) 667014
E: olwen62@sky.com

GRIEVE, David Campbell. b 51. St Jo Coll Dur BA 74. Wycliffe Hall Ox 74. **d** 76 **p** 77. C Upton (Overchurch) *Ches* 76-80; C Selston *S'well* 80-82; V Pelton *Dur* 82-89; rtd 89; PtO *Dur* from 04. *The Rectory, 107 Front Street, Cockfield, Bishop Auckland DL13 5AA* T: (01388) 718447
E: davidgrieve@cix.co.uk

GRIEVE (née PIERSSENÉ), Canon Frances Jane. b 55. St Jo Coll Dur BA 76. Cranmer Hall Dur 99. **d** 01 **p** 02. C Barnard Castle w Whorlton *Dur* 01-05; P-in-c Cockfield 05-14; R 14-15; P-in-c Lynesack 05-14; V 14-15; P-in-c Evenwood 09-14; V 14-15; Adv for Women's Min from 10; Hon Can Dur Cathl from 10; P-in-c Wheatley Hill and Wingate w Hutton Henry from 15; AD Easington from 15. *The Old Vicarage, The Village, Castle Inn, Hartlepool TS27 4SL* E: jane.grieve@durham.anglican.org

GRIEVE, Mrs Judith Margaret. b 52. Goldsmiths' Coll Lon CertEd 73. NEOC 91. **d** 94 **p** 96. NSM Choppington *Newc* 94-99; P-in-c Woodhorn w Newbiggin 99-06; V 06-10; V Whorlton from 10; Chapl All SS Coll Newc from 10. *St John's Vicarage, Whorlton, Westerhope, Newcastle upon Tyne NE5 1NN* T: 0191-286 9648 E: church_point@mail.com

GRIEVES, Anthony Michael. b 47. St Alb Minl Tr Scheme 81. **d** 84 **p** 85. NSM Stevenage St Mary Shephall *St Alb* 84-86; NSM Stevenage St Mary Shephall w Aston 86-95; PtO from 95. *27 Falcon Close, Stevenage SG2 9PG* T: (01438) 727204

GRIFFIN, Alan Howard Foster. b 44. TCD BA 66 MA 69 Peterho Cam PhD 71. Sarum & Wells Th Coll 75. **d** 78 **p** 79. Lect Ex Univ 78-01; Asst to Lazenby Chapl 78-92; Sub-Warden Duryard Halls 78-81; Warden 81-84; Sen Warden 84-98; PtO *Ex* 92-98; C Heavitree w Ex St Paul 98-01; Ex Campus Chapl Plymouth Univ 98-01; R St Andr-by-the-Wardrobe w St Ann, Blackfriars *Lon* 01-11; R St Jas Garlickhythe w St Mich Queenhithe etc 01-11; CME Officer Two Cities Area 01-08; rtd 11. *24 Cinnamon Street, London E1W 3NJ*
E: a.h.f.griffin@gmail.com

GRIFFIN, Christopher Donald. b 59. Reading Univ BA 80 CertEd 81. Wycliffe Hall Ox 82. **d** 85 **p** 86. C Gerrards Cross *Ox* 85-88; Chapl Felsted Sch 88-98; Chapl Sedbergh Sch 98-06; Ho Master from 00. *Sedbergh School, Sedbergh LA10 5HG*
T: (01539) 620535

GRIFFIN, Eugene Thomas. **d** 13 **p** 14. C Castleknock and Mulhuddart w Clonsilla *D & G* from 14. *Kilbride, Main Street, Castleknock, Dublin 15, Republic of Ireland* M: (00353) 86-382 6646 E: eugenethomasgriffin@gmail.com

GRIFFIN, Gerald Albert Francis. b 31. Qu Coll Birm 74. **d** 77 **p** 78. NSM Bushbury *Lich* 77-83; Ind Chapl *Dur* 83-88; Chapl HM Pris Man 88-89; Chapl HM Pris Featherstone 89-93; C Toxteth St Philemon w St Gabr and St Cleopas *Liv* 93-96; rtd 96; NSM W Bromwich *Lich* 00-10. *7 Chartwell Drive, Bushbury, Wolverhampton WV10 8JL* T: (01902) 836414
E: revgerrygriffinhome@msn.com

GRIFFIN, Harold Rodan Bristow. b 12. Jes Coll Cam BA 33 LLB 34 MA 43. Ridley Hall Cam 43. **d** 45 **p** 46. C Kirby Moorside w Gillamoor *York* 45-49; C Linthorpe 49-52; C Boylestone *Derby* 52; R Hulland, Atlow and Bradley 52-61; V Framsden *St E* 61-71; R Helmingham 61-71; rtd 77; PtO *Ely* 91-99. *Highlands, Fitzgerald Road, Woodbridge IP12 1EN* T: (01394) 383090

GRIFFIN, Joan Angela. b 35. Qu Coll Birm 82. dss 85 **d** 92 **p** 94. Moseley St Mary *Birm* 85-05; NSM 92-05; Chapl Univ Hosp Birm NHS Trust 95-02; Chapl Priory Hosp Birm from 02; PtO *Birm* from 08. *389 Wake Green Road, Birmingham B13 0BH* T: 0121-777 8772

GRIFFIN, Canon Joseph William. b 48. St Mich Coll Llan 70. **d** 74 **p** 75. C Killay *S & B* 74-78; C Swansea St Thos and Kilvey 78-81; V Troedrhiwgarth *Llan* 81-91; V Llanrhidian w Llanmadoc and Cheriton *S & B* 91-99; RD Gower 94-99; V Swansea St Nic 99-04; RD Swansea 02-04; P-in-c SW Gower 04-05; R 05-15; AD Gower 11-14; Hon Can Brecon Cathl 98-01; Can Res 01-11; Can Treas 11-15; rtd 15; PtO *S & B* from 15. *25 Maes-y-Coed, Gorseinon, Swansea SA4 6RN* T: (01792) 410321 E: joe.griffin3@hotmail.co.uk

GRIFFIN, Judith. b 59. Wycliffe Hall Ox. **d** 12 **p** 12. C Onslow Square and S Kensington St Aug *Lon* 12-15; Chapl Guy's and St Thos' NHS Foundn Trust from 15. *Address temp unknown* E: judith.griffin007@gmail.com

GRIFFIN, Keith. b 66. Nottm Trent Univ BA 88. Cranmer Hall Dur BA 94. **d** 95 **p** 96. C Gedling *S'well* 95-98; V Barkingside St Geo *Chelmsf* 99-02; TV Upper Holme Valley *Leeds* from 02. *The Vicarage, 3 Vicarage Meadows, Holmfirth HD9 1DZ* T: (01484) 682644 E: revdkg@tiscali.co.uk

GRIFFIN, Malcolm Roger. b 46. Goldsmiths' Coll Lon TCert 67 Open Univ BA 73. S'wark Ord Course. **d** 83 **p** 84. NSM Romford St Andr *Chelmsf* 83-87; NSM Romford St Jo 87-00; P-in-c 98-00; NSM Gt Ilford St Alb 91-97; PtO 97-98; P-in-c Cratfield w Heveningham and Ubbeston etc *St E* 00-02; Dioc Dir of Educn 05-06; PtO *Nor* 02-08; *St E* 02-05 and 06-08; *Nor* from 15. *4 Old Forge Court, Brockdish, Diss IP21 4JE* T: (01379) 669252 E: bothgriffins@waitrose.com

GRIFFIN, Mark Richard. b 68. Trin Coll Bris BA 93. Westcott Ho Cam 94. **d** 96 **p** 97. C Walmer *Cant* 96-00; V Wingham w Elmstone and Preston w Stourmouth 00-07; V Sevenoaks St Luke *Roch* from 07; RD Sevenoaks from 11. *St Luke's House, 30 Eardley Road, Sevenoaks TN13 1XT* T: (01732) 452462 E: revd.mark.griffin@talk21.com

GRIFFIN, Michael John. b 59. **d** 01 **p** 01. C Kirkdale St Lawr *Liv* 01-02; P-in-c 02-05; V from 05. *81 Rawcliffe Road, Liverpool L9 1AN* T: 0151-523 6968 E: mike.j.griffin@amserve.net

GRIFFIN, Niall Paul. b 37. TCD BA 61 Div Test 61. **d** 61 **p** 62. C Newtownards *D & D* 61-63; C Arm St Mark w Aghavilly 63-64; C Cross Roads Jamaica 64-66; C Lurgan Ch the Redeemer *D & D* 66-69; Chapl RAF 69-84; Missr Chr Renewal Cen *D & D* 84-89; Nat Dir (Ireland) SOMA UK 89-07; rtd 07. *7 Cloughmore Park, Rostrevor, Newry BT34 3AX* T/F: (028) 4173 8959 E: nandg@griffin.go-plus.net

GRIFFIN, Nicholas Philip. b 84. Moorlands Coll BA 06. Wycliffe Hall Ox 09. **d** 11 **p** 12. C Frome H Trin *B & W* 11-15; Chapl Univ of St Mark and St Jo *Ex* from 15. *The Oaks, University of St Mark and St John, Derriford Road, Plymouth PL6 8BH* M: 07947-672547 E: ngriffin84@gmail.com

GRIFFIN, Nigel Robert. b 50. Univ of Wales (Lamp) BA 71. Ripon Hall Ox 71. **d** 73 **p** 74. C Burry Port and Pwll *St D* 73-77; C Carmarthen St Pet 77-79; Youth Chapl 79-86; V Whitland and Kiffig 80-89; Warden of Ords 86-91; V Llangunnor w Cwmffrwd 89-92; RD Carmarthen 91-92; R Aberporth w Tremain and Blaenporth 92-95; R Aberporth w Tremain w Blaenporth and Betws Ifan 95-96; Chapl Morriston Hosp/Ysbyty Treforys NHS Trust 96-99; Chapl Swansea NHS Trust from 99. *Morriston Hospital, Heol Maes Eglwys, Cwmrhydyceirw, Swansea SA6 8EL* T: (01792) 702222

GRIFFIN, The Very Revd Victor Gilbert Benjamin. b 24. MRIA TCD BA 46 MA 57 Hon DD 92. CITC 47. **d** 47 **p** 48. C Londonderry St Aug *D & R* 47-51; C Londonderry Ch Ch 51-57; I 57-68; Preb Howth St Patr Cathl Dublin 62-68; Dean St Patr Cathl Dublin 68-91; rtd 91. *7 Tyler Road, Limavady BT49 0DW* T: (028) 7176 2093

GRIFFISS, Helen Mary. b 48. Univ of Wales (Ban) CertEd 69 K Alfred's Coll Win MA 98. STETS 97. **d** 00 **p** 01. Miss Adv USPG Bris, Sarum and Win 00-03; NSM Bransgore *Win* 00-03; C Milton 04-06; P-in-c Mudeford 06-09; V from 09. *All Saints' Vicarage, 22 Kestrel Drive, Christchurch BH23 4DE* T: (01425) 276267 E: revhelen@4afairworld.co.uk

GRIFFITH, Benedict Lloyd Thomas. b 64. Trin Coll Carmarthen BA 86. Ripon Coll Cuddesdon 04. **d** 06 **p** 07. C Kempston Transfiguration *St Alb* 06-09; V Upper Wye *S & B* 09-14; P-in-c

Erwood Gp w Painscastle Gp from 14. *Trefechan, Aberedw, Builth Wells LD2 3UH* T: (01982) 560615 M: 07960-947137 E: benedictgriffith@sky.com

GRIFFITH, The Ven David Vaughan. b 36. St D Coll Lamp BA 60. Lich Th Coll 60. **d** 62 **p** 63. C Llanfairfechan *Ban* 62-66; C Dolgellau 66-70; R Llanfair Talhaiarn *St As* 70-82; R Llanfairtalhaiarn and Llansannan 82-85; P-in-c Llangernyw and Gwytherin 77-85; V Colwyn 85-98; Warden of Readers 91-99; Can Cursal St As Cathl 95-98; P-in-c Berriew and Manafon 98-99; V 99-02; Preb St As Cathl and Adn Montgomery 98-02; rtd 02; PtO *St As* from 09. *1 Bishop's Walk, St Asaph LL17 0SU* T: (01745) 582903

GRIFFITH, Frank Michael. b 24. Bris Univ BSc 50. St Aid Birkenhead 58. **d** 60 **p** 61. C Leamington Priors H Trin *Cov* 60-63; C Stratford-on-Avon w Bishopton 63-67; V Rounds Green *Birm* 67-70; R Barford *Cov* 70-78; V Wasperton 70-78; RD Stratford-on-Avon 77-78; R Barford w Wasperton and Sherbourne 78-89; RD Fosse 79-87; rtd 90; PtO *Cov* from 90. *Wusi, Armscote Road, Tredington, Shipston-on-Stour CV36 4NP* T: (01608) 661621 E: michaelgriffith1@btinternet.com

GRIFFITH, Glyn Keble Gethin. b 37. St D Coll Lamp BA 59. Ridley Hall Cam 67. **d** 69 **p** 70. C Derby St Aug 69-72; C Coity w Nolton *Llan* 72-75; P-in-c Heage *Derby* 75-81; V Allestree St Nic 81-92; R Wilne and Draycott w Breaston 92-01; rtd 01; PtO *Mon* from 02; *Heref* from 02; *Glouc* from 04. *3 Cornford Close, Osbaston, Monmouth NP25 3NT* T: (01600) 719740

GRIFFITH, Canon John Vaughan. b 33. St D Coll Lamp 53. **d** 58 **p** 59. C Holyhead w Rhoscolyn *Ban* 58-63; R Maentwrog w Trawsfynydd 63-68; Chapl RAF 68-72; V Winnington *Ches* 72-76; V Northwich St Luke and H Trin 76-81; V Sandiway 81-98; Dioc Communications Officer 84-86; Ed *Chester Diocesan News* 84-92; Hon Can Ches Cathl 89-98; rtd 98; PtO *Ches* from 99. *41 Moss Lane, Cuddington, Northwich CW8 2PT*

GRIFFITH, Justin David. b 48. Imp Coll Lon BScEng 74 Cranfield Inst of Tech MSc 89. NEOC 03. **d** 06 **p** 07. NSM N Ferriby *York* 06-09; NSM Broad Blunsdon and Highworth w Sevenhampton and Inglesham etc *Bris* 10-14; CF (ACF) 09-14; New Zealand from 14. *Address temp unknown* E: j@swanland.co.uk

GRIFFITH, Michael. *See* GRIFFITH, Frank Michael

GRIFFITH, Sandra. b 44. Open Univ BA 94. EAMTC 01. **d** 04 **p** 05. NSM The Ortons, Alwalton and Chesterton *Ely* 04-06; NSM Sawtry and Glatton 06-11; Asst Chapl Hinchingbrooke Health Care NHS Trust from 05. *40 Chesinhale, Orton Waterville, Peterborough PE2 5FP* T: (01733) 686042 E: sandra@revgriffith.com

GRIFFITH, Stephen. *See* GRIFFITH, William Stephen

GRIFFITH, Steven Ellsworth. b 63. Univ of Wales BTh 91. St Steph Ho Ox. **d** 87 **p** 88. C Holyhead w Rhoscolyn w Llanfair-yn-Neubwll *Ban* 87-90; CF 90-08; Sen C 08-13; PtO *S & B* 12-13; Min Can Brecon Cathl 13-15; PV Brecon Cathl from 15; P-in-c Brecon St Mary from 14. *The Clergy House, The Cathedral Close, Brecon LD3 9DP* M: 07540-609029 T: (01874) 622044 E: frstevengriffith@outlook.com

GRIFFITH, Mrs Wendy Margaret. b 41. **d** 01 **p** 02. NSM Sixpenny Handley w Gussage St Andrew etc *Sarum* 01-08; NSM Somerton w Compton Dundon, the Charltons etc *B & W* 08-14; PtO from 14. *The Parsonage, George Street, Charlton Adam, Somerton TA11 7AS* T: (01458) 224087 M: 07720-942996

GRIFFITH, William Stephen. b 50. MBE 02. Univ of Wales (Ban) BA 71 FRAS 92. Westcott Ho Cam 71. **d** 73 **p** 74. C Llandudno *Ban* 73-76; C Calne and Blackland *Sarum* 76-78; P-in-c Broadwindsor w Burstock and Seaborough 78-79; TV Beaminster Area 79-81; PtO 81-83; Chapl St Pet Sch York 83-87; C Leeds St Pet *Ripon* 87; Chapl Bearwood Coll Wokingham 87-92; CMS Jordan 92-95; Sen Chapl Univ of Wales (Cardiff) *Llan* 95-96; Chapl Damascus 96-02; P-in-c Yerevan, Baku and Tbilisi *Eur* 03; V Denton *Newc* 04-08; TV Mortlake w E Sheen *S'wark* from 09. *17 Sheen Gate Gardens, London SW14 7PD* T: (020) 8876 5002 M: 07729-278294 E: haywales@hotmail.com

GRIFFITH-JONES, David Laugharne. b 79. Pemb Coll Cam MA 06. Wycliffe Hall Ox BTh 12. **d** 12 **p** 13. C Toxteth St Philemon w St Gabr and St Cleopas *Liv* from 12. *2 Steble Street, Liverpool L8 6QH* M: 07775-563126 E: dave_gj@hotmail.com

GRIFFITH-JONES, Robin Guthrie. b 56. New Coll Ox BA 78 Ch Coll Cam BA 88. Westcott Ho Cam 86. **d** 89 **p** 90. C Cantril Farm *Liv* 89-92; Chapl Linc Coll Ox 92-99; Master of The Temple from 99. *The Master's House, Temple, London EC4Y 7BB* T: (020) 7353 8559 E: master@templechurch.com

GRIFFITHS, Ainsley. *See* GRIFFITHS, John Mark Ainsley

GRIFFITHS, Alan Charles. b 46. Dur Univ BA 67. Cranmer Hall Dur 66. **d** 69 **p** 70. C Leic H Apostles 69-72; LtO *York* 73-77; V Lea Hall *Birm* 77-87; Asst Dir of Educn *Sheff* 87-92; V W Bessacarr 92-02; V Conisbrough 02-13; rtd 13; PtO *Sheff* 13-14; P-in-c Barnburgh w Melton on the Hill etc from 14. *The Rectory, Fox Lane, Barnburgh, Doncaster DN5 7ET* T: (01709) 891812 E: alan.c.griffiths@btinternet.com

GRIFFITHS, Alec. b 42. St Chad's Coll Dur BA 63. **d** 65 **p** 66. C Glas St Ninian 65-68; C Greenock 68-72; R Glas H Cross 72-79; V Birchencliffe *Wakef* 79-83; Chapl Kingston Hosp Surrey 83-99; rtd 99; PtO *S'wark* 99-00; Hon C W Acton St Martin and Ealing All SS *Lon* 00-10. *Room 24, Moorburn Manor Nursing Home, 31 Moorburn Road, Largs KA30 9JB* T: (01475) 687177 M: 07903-372561 E: alec.griffiths@btopenworld.com

GRIFFITHS, Aled. *See* GRIFFITHS, William David Aled

GRIFFITHS, Andrew Taylor. b 68. Jes Coll Ox BA 92 MA 96. Cranmer Hall Dur 98. **d** 00 **p** 01. C Paris St Mich *Eur* 00-04; C Galleywood Common *Chelmsf* 04-05; V from 05; RD Chelmsf S from 07; C Moulsham St Luke from 13; C Moulsham St Jo from 13; C Widford from 13. *Galleywood Vicarage, 450 Beehive Lane, Chelmsford CM2 8RN* T: (01245) 353922 M: 07969-605059 E: aggalleywood@yahoo.co.uk

GRIFFITHS, Beatrice Mary. b 29. Chelsea Coll Lon CertEd 60. Westcott Ho Cam 85. **dss** 86 **d** 87 **p** 94. W Bridgford *S'well* 86-87; NSM Wilford Hill 87-99; rtd 99; PtO *S'well* from 99. *7 Stella Avenue, Tollerton, Nottingham NG12 4EX* T: 0115-937 4155

GRIFFITHS, Benjamin David. b 78. Ches Univ MA 14. St Jo Coll Nottm BA 12. **d** 13 **p** 14. C Brampton St Thos *Derby* from 13. *6 Westfield Close, Chesterfield S40 3RS* T: (01246) 569142 M: 07813-285445 E: revbengriffiths@gmail.com

GRIFFITHS, Brian John. b 45. Brunel Univ PhD 82. **d** 05 **p** 06. OLM Iver *Ox* 05-14; PtO from 14; *Win* from 11. *7 Benton Drive, Chinnor OX39 4DP* T: (01844) 355953

GRIFFITHS, Caroline. *See* PRINCE, Caroline Heidi Ann

GRIFFITHS, Christopher Rhys. b 82. Leeds Univ BA 06 Anglia Ruskin Univ MA 14. Westcott Ho Cam 10. **d** 13 **p** 14. C Wimbledon *S'wark* from 13. *9 Thornton Road, London SW19 4NE* E: revdchrisgriffiths@gmail.com

GRIFFITHS (*née* MITCHELL), **Mrs Clare Elizabeth.** b 68. **d** 01 **p** 02. C Caerleon w Llanhennock *Mon* 01-03; Chapl Malvern Girls' Coll 03-06; C Gt Malvern St Ch *Worc* 06-12; TV Worc SE from 12. *11 Jasmine Close, Worcester WR5 3LU*

GRIFFITHS, Colin Lindsay. b 50. ACT 75. **d** 79 **p** 80. C Adelaide St Jo Australia 79-81; C Masite Lesotho 82-83; P-in-c Maseru St Jo 84; Chapl St Mich Priory Melbourne Australia 85-87; Prior 87-90; P-in-c Port Augusta 90-95; P-in-c Point Pearce Min Distr 95-96; Assoc P Thornbury 97-98; R Alice Springs and Can Ch Ch Cathl Darwin 99-05; Dioc Admin N Territory 00-05; PtO *Ox* from 06; Prov SSM in Eur from 10. *The Well, Newport Road, Willen, Milton Keynes MK15 9AA* T: (01908) 231986 E: cgcolgrif10@gmail.com

GRIFFITHS, Canon David. b 38. St Mich Coll Llan. **d** 67 **p** 68. C Llangollen *St As* 67-71; C Rhyl w St Ann 71-74; V Kerry 74-77; V Kerry and Llanmerewig 77-82; R Caerwys and Bodfari 82-87; V Gresford 87-97; V Gresford w Holt 97-03; RD Wrexham 97-01; C Llan as Cathl 01-03; Can St As Cathl 98-03; rtd 03; PtO *St As* from 09. *16 Heol-y-Wal, Bradley, Wrexham LL11 4BY* T: (01978) 751416

GRIFFITHS, David Bruce. b 44. Sussex Univ BA 69 Hull Univ MA 83. Linc Th Coll. **d** 82 **p** 83. C Springfield All SS *Chelmsf* 82-84; TV Horwich *Man* 84-92; V Heaton Ch Ch 92-03; P-in-c Ainsworth 03-09; rtd 09; PtO *Man* from 09. *Woodford, Mill Lane, Horwich, Bolton BL6 6AQ* T: (01204) 469621 E: dandbgriffiths@googlemail.com

GRIFFITHS, David John. b 53. St Jo Coll Nottm BTh 93. **d** 94 **p** 95. C Retford St Sav *S'well* 94-96; NSM Thwaites Brow *Bradf* 96-98; P-in-c Oakenshaw cum Woodlands 98-03; V Buttershaw St Paul 03-10; V Silsden *Leeds* from 10; Asst Chapl Airedale NHS Foundn Trust from 96. *The Vicarage, Briggate, Silsden, Keighley BD20 9JS* T: (01535) 652204 E: david.griffiths@bradford.anglican.org

GRIFFITHS, David Mark. b 59. Kent Univ BA 80. Chich Th Coll 81. **d** 83 **p** 84. C Clydach *S & B* 83-84; C Llwynderw 84-88; V Swansea St Nic 88-98; Chapl Swansea Inst of HE 88-98; V Swansea St Gabr from 98; Chapl Swansea NHS Trust from 98. *St Gabriel's Vicarage, Bryn Road, Brynmill, Swansea SA2 0AP* T: (01792) 464011 E: mark.griffiths35@btinternet.com

GRIFFITHS, David Mark. b 41. Univ of Wales (Cardiff) BA 67 CertEd 71. St Mich Coll Llan 92. **d** 94 **p** 95. C Llwynderw *S & B* 94-96; R Llanbadarn Fawr, Llandegley and Llanfihangel etc 96-02; P-in-c Slebech and Uzmaston w Boulston *St D* 02-06; rtd 06. *17 Catherine's Gate, Merlins Bridge, Haverfordwest SA61 1NB* T: (01437) 783950 M: 07811-647910 E: markgriffiths16@btopenworld.com

GRIFFITHS, David Percy Douglas. b 25. St Mich Coll Llan. **d** 78 **p** 79. C Betws w Ammanford *St D* 78-80; V Llanarth w Mydroilyn, Capel Cynon, Talgarreg etc 80-84; V Llanarth and Capel Cynon w Talgarreg etc 84-86; V Newcastle Emlyn w Llandyfriog and Troed-yr-aur 86-95; rtd 95. *The Poplars, Ebenezer Street, Newcastle Emlyn SA38 9BS* T: (01239) 711448

GRIFFITHS, David Rowson Hopkin. b 38. Oak Hill Th Coll 59. **d** 62 **p** 63. C Barrow St Mark *Carl* 62-65; OMF Internat 66-09; Japan 66-88; Philippines 88-09; rtd 03. *4 Warwick Place, West Cross, Swansea SA3 5JG* T: (01792) 402885

GRIFFITHS, Dorothy Anastasia de Jaegher. **d** 14 **p** 15. NSM Cheltenham St Mary w St Matt and St Luke *Glouc* from 14. *Address temp unknown*

GRIFFITHS, Ms Elizabeth Leigh. b 61. St Hugh's Coll Ox BA 83 MA 87 Warwick Univ PGCE 84. Ripon Coll Cuddesdon 96. **d** 98 **p** 99. C Bettws *Mon* 98-99; C Maindee Newport 99-01; TV Cen Swansea and Dioc Chapl Tertiary Educn *S & B* 01-03; C St Martin-in-the-Fields *Lon* 03-09; Dir Past Studies ERMC and Nor Dioc Min Course 09-10; Dir Past Studies and Vice Prin ERMC 10-11; V Cardiff City Par *Llan* 11-12; Dioc Dir of Ords 12; TV Basingstoke *Win* from 14. *219 Paddock Road, Basingstoke RG22 6QP* T: (01256) 352682 E: lizg.stpeter@btinternet.com

GRIFFITHS, Eric. b 33. **d** 02 **p** 04. NSM St Andr-by-the-Wardrobe w St Ann, Blackfriars *Lon* 02-08; NSM St Jas Garlickhythe w St Mich Queenhithe etc 02-08; rtd 08. *The Charterhouse, Charterhouse Square, London EC1M 6AN* T: (020) 7490 1025 E: egcharterhouse@yahoo.co.uk

GRIFFITHS, Garrie Charles. b 53. St Jo Coll Nottm. **d** 77 **p** 78. Canada 77-78; C Stalybridge H Trin and Ch Ch Ches 78-81; C Moreton 81-84; V Godley cum Newton Green 84-89; V Bayston Hill *Lich* 89-01; TR Mildenhall *St E* 01-04; V Hadfield *Derby* 04-10; RD Glossop 06-10; V Youlgreave, Middleton, Stanton-in-Peak etc from 10; Spiritual Dir Adv from 13. *The New Vicarage, Conksbury Lane, Youlgrave, Bakewell DE45 1WR* T: (01629) 630409 E: ggriffiths787@btinternet.com *or* ggriffiths787@gmail.com

GRIFFITHS, Gerald Brian. b 41. Open Univ BA 88. SEITE 97. **d** 00 **p** 01. NSM Cliftonville *Cant* 00-03; TV St Laur in Thanet 04-09; rtd 09; Chapl Costa Blanca *Eur* 10-12; PtO *Cant* from 13. *11 Wellesley Court, Ramsgate CT11 8NU* T: (01843) 850229 E: gbgriffiths41@gmail.com

GRIFFITHS, Gerald Lewis. b 38. Westmr Coll Ox MTh 97. Qu Coll Birm. **d** 88 **p** 89. C Wrexham *St As* 88-91; TV 91-95; R Hope 95-00; rtd 00. *10 Ryder Close, Wrexham LL13 9GS* T: (01978) 355244

GRIFFITHS, Gordon John. b 31. Univ of Wales (Cardiff) BA 53. *S'wark* Ord Course 72. **d** 75 **p** 76. NSM Sutton New *S'wark* 75-78; Asst Chapl Eastbourne Coll 78-81; PtO *Chich* from 81. *15 Buckhurst Close, Willingdon, Eastbourne BN20 9EF* T: (01323) 505547

GRIFFITHS, Griff. *See* GRIFFITHS, Stephen David

GRIFFITHS, Harvey Stephen. b 35. Linc Coll Ox BA 58 MA 62. Linc Th Coll 62. **d** 62 **p** 63. C Frodingham *Linc* 62-65; C Darlington St Cuth *Dur* 65-70; Chapl RN 70-92; P-in-c Southwick w Boarhunt *Portsm* 92-05; rtd 05; PtO *Portsm* from 05. *27 Burnham Wood, Fareham PO16 7UD* T: (01329) 232915 M: 07747-093365 E: harvey@hsgriffiths.fsnet.co.uk

GRIFFITHS, Hugh. b 44. Nottm Univ BEd 78. Clifton Th Coll 69. **d** 71 **p** 72. C Mansfield SS Pet and Paul *S'well* 71-77; NSM Stockport St Geo *Ches* 08-09; rtd 09; PtO *Ches* from 09. *1 Heath Crescent, Stockport SK2 6JN* T: 0161-285 9772 E: hughgriffiths@hotmail.co.uk

GRIFFITHS, James Brian. b 69. Oak Hill Th Coll 13. **d** 15. C Gabalfa *Llan* from 15. *27 Pen-y-Bryn Road, Gabalfa, Cardiff CF14 3LG* E: j.b.griffiths69@gmail.com

GRIFFITHS, Mrs Jean Rose. b 36. Avery Hill Coll TCert 56. *S'wark* Ord Course 93. **d** 95 **p** 96. NSM Charlton *S'wark* 95-03; Asst Chapl HM Pris Brixton 95-03; Chapl 03-04; rtd 04; PtO *S'wark* from 04. *32 Weyman Road, London SE3 8RY* T: (020) 8319 8676 *or* 8588 6051 E: jean.peter@talktalk.net

GRIFFITHS, John. b 57. Coll of Ripon & York St Jo BEd 83. LCTP 12. **d** 14 **p** 15. C Heart of Eden *Carl* from 14. *92 Rivington Park, Appleby-in-Westmorland CA16 6HU* M: 07984-895722 T: (017683) 52894 E: johntherev@btinternet.com

GRIFFITHS, John Alan. b 48. CPsychol AFBPsS Univ of Wales BSc 72 Cape Town Univ MSc 76. St Mich Coll Llan 87. **d** 89 **p** 90. C Neath w Llantwit *Llan* 89-93; V Roath St German 93-95. *All Pine Grange, Bath Road, Bournemouth BH1 2PF* T: (01202) 314120

GRIFFITHS, John Gareth. b 44. Lich Th Coll 68. **d** 71 **p** 72. C Shotton *St As* 71-73; C Rhyl w St Ann 73-76; V Llanasa 76-95; RD Holywell 89-95; V Rhuddlan 95-10; rtd 10; PtO *St As* from 10. *13 Llwyn Harlech, Bodelwyddan, Rhyl LL18 5WG* T: (01745) 539955

GRIFFITHS, John Mark Ainsley. b 68. Man Univ BSc 90 MSc 91 PGCE 92. Ripon Coll Cuddesdon BA 97. **d** 98 **p** 99. Min Can Bangor *Ban* 98-01; P-in-c Denio w Abererch 01-02; V 02-05; Chapl Univ of Wales (Trin St Dav) from 05. *University of Wales Trinity St David, Carmarthen Campus, Carmarthen SA31 3EP* T: (01267) 676607 E: ainsley.griffiths@trinitysaintdavid.ac.uk

GRIFFITHS, Mrs Linda Betty. b 48. Trin Coll Carmarthen CertEd 69 Gwent Coll of HE BEd 96 Open Univ MA 97. Mon Dioc Tr Scheme 05. **d** 06 **p** 11. NSM Newbridge *Mon* 06-10; NSM Risca 10-13; NSM Lower Islwyn from 13. *19 Cromwell Road, Risca, Newport NP11 7AF* T: (01495) 270455 E: griff.l@btinternet.com

GRIFFITHS, Malcolm. b 47. St Alb Minl Tr Scheme. **d** 82 **p** 83. NSM Hemel Hempstead *St Alb* 82-86; C 86-87; TV Liskeard, St Keyne, St Pinnock, Morval etc *Truro* 87-96; V Landrake w St Erney and Botus Fleming 96-12; rtd 12. *12 Lowertown Close, Landrake, Saltash PL12 5DG*

GRIFFITHS, Margaret. *See* MacLACHLAN, Margaret

GRIFFITHS, Mrs Margarett. b 29. ATCL 47 LRAM 48. CA Tr Coll 50. **dss** 81 **d** 87. Par Dn Ashford *Cant* 87-89; rtd 89. *39 Newington Way, Craven Arms SY7 9PS* T: (01588) 673848

GRIFFITHS, Mark. *See* GRIFFITHS, David Mark

GRIFFITHS, Mark. b 68. Nottm Univ PhD 09. St Jo Coll Nottm 04. **d** 07 **p** 08. C Stoke Poges *Ox* 07-10; P-in-c Warfield from 10. *The Vicarage, Church Lane, Warfield, Bracknell RG42 6EE* T: (01344) 882228 E: revmarkgriff@sky.com

GRIFFITHS, Canon Martyn Robert. b 51. Nottm Univ BTh 74 St Martin's Coll Lanc PGCE 75. Kelham Th Coll 70. **d** 74 **p** 75. C Kings Heath *Birm* 74-77; C-in-c Elmdon Heath CD 77-79; TV Solihull 79-81; Asst Admin Shrine of Our Lady of Walsingham 81-85; V Oldham St Steph and All Martyrs *Man* 85-89; TR Swinton and Pendlebury 89-98; Hon Can Man Cathl 96-98; R Preston St Jo and St Geo *Blackb* 98-05; Hon Can Blackb Cathl 00-05; R Henley w Remenham *Ox* from 05. *St Mary's Rectory, Hart Street, Henley-on-Thames RG9 2AU* T/F: (01491) 577340 E: rector.hwr@btinternet.com

GRIFFITHS, Meirion. b 38. Clifton Th Coll 63. **d** 66 **p** 67. C Upper Holloway St Pet *Lon* 66-68; C Taunton St Jas *B & W* 68-70; C Radipole *Sarum* 70-74; R Chich St Pancras and St Jo 74-82; R Corwen and Llangar *St As* 82-88; RD Edeyrnion 82-88; C Albany Australia 88; R Collie 89-93; P-in-c Maddington 97-00; rtd 00. *27 Coachwood Way, Maddington WA 6109, Australia* T: (0061) (8) 9459 2920 F: 9452 2720 E: meirion4@aol.com

GRIFFITHS, Michael James. b 76. St Mellitus Coll. **d** 15. C Yateley *Win* from 15. *24 Frogmore Park Drive, Blackwater, Camberley GU17 0PG* T: (01276) 505003 E: mike.griffiths@psalmdrummers.com

GRIFFITHS, Neil Timothy. b 62. Portsm Poly BSc 84 De Montfort Univ MSc 01. Qu Coll Birm 12. **d** 14 **p** 15. C Broom Leys *Leic* from 14. *26 Harker Drive, Coalville LE67 4GG* M: 07879-620041 E: neilgriffiths01@btinternet.com

GRIFFITHS, Neville. b 39. Univ of Wales BA 63. St D Coll Lamp LTh 66. **d** 66 **p** 67. C Newport St Mark *Mon* 66-68; C Cardiff St Jo *Llan* 68-70; Chapl Greystoke Coll Carl 70-76; C Greystoke w Matterdale *Carl* 70-75; TV Greystoke, Matterdale and Mungrisdale 75-76; Chapl Grey Coll Dur 76-81; C Croxdale *Dur* 76-81; R Didsbury Ch Ch *Man* 81-83; P-in-c Lowther and Askham *Carl* 83-84; R 84-88; V Guernsey St Matt *Win* 88-93; R Guernsey St Pierre du Bois 93-02; R Guernsey St Philippe de Torteval 93-02; Vice-Dean Guernsey 99-02; rtd 03; PtO *Dur* from 02. *6 Howlcroft Villas, Neville's Cross, Durham DH1 4DU* T: 0191-386 4778

GRIFFITHS, Nigel Timothy. b 64. Wycliffe Hall Ox 13. **d** 15. C Southborough St Pet w Ch Ch and St Matt etc *Roch* from 15. *54 Holden Park Road, Tunbridge Wells TN4 0EP* M: 07879-427944 E: nigegriffiths@hotmail.com

GRIFFITHS, Mrs Pamela Verley. **d** 07 **p** 10. NSM Ebbw Vale *Mon* 07-13; NSM Upper Ebbw Valleys from 13. *3 Ivy Close, Rassau, Ebbw Vale NP23 5SJ* T: (01495) 303926 F: 210433

GRIFFITHS, Paul Edward. b 48. St Jo Coll Nottm 86. **d** 88 **p** 89. C Ipswich St Andr *St E* 88-92; P-in-c Tollerton *S'well* 92-00; P-in-c Plumtree 95-97; Ind Chapl and Dioc Adv on Ind Soc 97-00; V Hellesdon *Nor* 00-13; rtd 13; PtO *Leic* 13-15. *5 Rowan Close, Bingham, Nottingham NG13 8GL* T: (01949) 838186 E: revgriffiths@btinternet.com

GRIFFITHS, Ms Paula Whitmore Llewellyn. b 49. LMH Ox BA 71 MA 75 Anglia Ruskin Univ BA 09. Westcott Ho Cam 08. **d** 09 **p** 10. NSM Saffron Walden and Villages *Chelmsf* from 09. *Greatford Cottage, Stocking Green, Radwinter, Saffron Walden CB10 2SS* E: paula.greatford@btinternet.com

GRIFFITHS, Percy. *See* GRIFFITHS, David Percy Douglas

GRIFFITHS, Richard Barré Maw. b 43. CCC Ox BA 65 MA 69 St Jo Coll Dur BA 71. Cranmer Hall Dur. **d** 71 **p** 72. C Fulwood *Sheff* 71-74; Hon C Sheff St Jo 74-76; Fell Dept of Bibl Studies Sheff Univ 74-76; C Fulham St Matt *Lon* 76-78; P-in-c 78-83;

R Chich St Pancras and St Jo 83-09; rtd 09. *24 Beechcroft, Humshaugh, Hexham NE46 4ON* E: richardgriff@clara.co.uk

GRIFFITHS, Prof Richard Mathias. b 35. K Coll Cam BA 57 MA 61 PhD 62 BNC Ox MA 66 FIL 91 FKC 95. Ox Min Course 89 SAOMC 96. **d** 97 **p** 98. Prof French K Coll Lon 90-00; NSM W Woodhay w Enborne, Hampstead Marshall etc *Ox* 97-00; NSM Llantrisant *Llan* 01-02; NSM Penarth and Llandough from 03. *Waltham House, Bradford Place, Penarth CF64 1AG* T: (029) 2070 7828 F: 2070 9699

GRIFFITHS, The Ven Robert Herbert. b 53. Chich Th Coll 75. **d** 76 **p** 77. C Holywell *St As* 76-80; CF (TA) 79-87; P-in-c Gyffylliog *St As* 80-84; V Llanfair Dyffryn Clwyd 80-84; V Llanfair DC, Derwen, Llanelidan and Efenechtyd 84-88; Asst Dioc Youth Chapl 81-86; Dioc Youth Chapl 86-91; PV St As and Tremeirchion w Cefn 88-97; Chapl H M Stanley Hosp 88-97; Bp's Visitor and Dioc RE Adv *St As* 88-93; Chapl Glan Clwyd Distr Gen Hosp 93-97; V Llanrhos *St As* 97-09; TR Rhos-Cystennin 09-14; R Llandegla and Bryneglwys from 14; Can St As Cathl from 98; AD Llanrwst 01-09; Chapl NW Wales NHS Trust from 97; Adn Wrexham *St As* from 14. *The Rectory, Llandegla, Wrexham LL11 3AW* T: (01978) 790362 E: archdeacon.wrexham@churchinwales.org.uk

GRIFFITHS, Robert James. b 52. Nottm Univ BTh 82. St Jo Coll Nottm 79. **d** 82 **p** 83. C Kettering St Andr *Pet* 82-85; C Collier Row St Jas and Havering-atte-Bower *Chelmsf* 86-89; R High Ongar w Norton Mandeville 89-97; R Ilmington w Stretton-on-Fosse etc *Cov* 97-99; V Newport *Chelmsf* 99-03; V Newport and Widdington 03-06; PtO *Ely* 09-10; R Horringer *St E* 10-15; rtd 15. *The Rectory, Manor Lane, Horringer, Bury St Edmunds IP29 5PY* T: (01284) 735946 E: r.griffiths45@btinternet.com

GRIFFITHS, Canon Roger. b 46. Trin Coll Bris 70. **d** 74 **p** 75. C Normanton *Derby* 74-77; C Bucknall and Bagnall *Lich* 77-80; TV 80-83; TV Aberystwyth *St D* 83-86; R Letterston w Llanfair Nant-y-Gof etc 86-13; Hon Can St D Cathl 10-13; rtd 13. *7 Aintree Close, Leegomery, Telford TF1 6UY* E: groger6@aol.com

GRIFFITHS, Roger Michael. b 47. Wycliffe Hall Ox 83. **d** 86 **p** 87. Min Can St D Cathl 86-88; V Pen-boyr 88-94; V Fishguard w Llanychar and Pontfaen w Morfil etc 94-03. *Nevern Cottage, 10 Feidr Gongol, Fishguard SA65 9BA* T: (01348) 218073 E: roger@rogriff.freeserve.co.uk

GRIFFITHS, Sarah. *See* BICK, Sarah

GRIFFITHS, Shane Owen. b 63. Ripon Coll Cuddesdon 01. **d** 04 **p** 04. C Icknield *Ox* 04-07; P-in-c Mullion *Truro* from 07; P-in-c Cury and Gunwalloe from 07. *The Vicarage, Nansmellyon Road, Mullion, Helston TR12 7DH* T: (01326) 240325 E: shaneowengriffiths@yahoo.co.uk

GRIFFITHS, The Ven Shirley Thelma. b 48. Univ of Wales (Ban) CertEd 69 Open Univ BA 83 Coll of Ripon & York St Jo MA 01. St Deiniol's Hawarden 79. **d** 82 **p** 95. NSM Dyserth and Trelawnyd and Cwm *St As* 82-91; RE Officer 89-95; Min Can St As Cathl 91-95; P-in-c The Cowtons *Ripon* 95-02; RE Adv 95-02; V Abergele *St As* 02-08; V Abergele and St George 08-10; Adn Wrexham 10-13; R Llandegla 10-11; R Bryneglwys 11; R Llandegla and Bryneglwys 11-13; rtd 13; PtO *Dur* from 14. *The Gables, 22 Greenways, Sunnybrow, Crook DL15 0LX* T: (01388) 747035 E: shirleygriffiths@gmail.com

GRIFFITHS, Simon Mark. b 62. Ch Ch Coll Cant BA 84 Kent Univ MA 95. Chich Th Coll. **d** 87 **p** 88. C Cardiff St Jo *Llan* 87-91; Sub Chapl HM Pris Cardiff 87-91; Chapl and Succ Roch Cath 91-96; Chapl Univ Coll Chich 96-01; V Sheff St Matt 01-11; TR Cen Swansea *S & B* from 11. *St Barnabas' Vicarage, 57 Sketty Road, Swansea SA2 0EN* T: (01792) 298002 E: frsimongriffiths@gmail.com

GRIFFITHS, Stephen David (Griff). b 70. Oak Hill Th Coll BA 96 Trin Coll Bris. **d** 00 **p** 01. C Cranleigh *Guildf* 00-04; TV Thetford *Nor* 04-10; Chapl Cam Univ Hosps NHS Foundn Trust from 10. *89 Sycamore Drive, Bury St Edmunds IP32 7PW* T: (01842) 755769 M: 07592-800259 E: revgriff@sky.com

GRIFFITHS, Stephen Mark. b 67. Nottm Univ BTh 93 PhD 00. St Jo Coll Nottm 90. **d** 93 **p** 94. C Glascote and Stonydelph *Lich* 93-96; P-in-c Stratford New Town St Paul *Chelmsf* 96-02; P-in-c Steeple Bumpstead and Helions Bumpstead 02-05; Tutor Ridley Hall Cam 01-09; TR Linton *Ely* 09-14; V Enfield St Andr *Lon* from 14. *Enfield Vicarage, 36 Silver Street, Enfield EN1 3EG* M: 07905-861234 E: revd.steve@hotmail.com

GRIFFITHS, Stephen Robert. b 78. Oak Hill Th Coll BA 00 Anglia Poly Univ MA 05. Ridley Hall Cam 02. **d** 04 **p** 05. C Normanton *Derby* 04-08; P-in-c Moresby *Carl* 08-13; RD Calder 12-13; TR Cherwell Valley *Ox* from 13; AD Bicester and Islip from 14. *104 Camp Road, Upper Heyford, Bicester OX25 5AG* T: (01869) 233249 E: steph78griff@hotmail.com

GRIFFITHS, Mrs Susan Angela. b 61. St Jo Coll Nottm BTh 94. **d** 94 **p** 95. C Ingrow w Hainworth *Bradf* 94-98; V Wyke 98-03;

C Buttershaw St Paul 03-10; C Silsden *Leeds* from 10; RD S Craven *Bradf* 10-14; AD Keighley *Leeds* from 14. *The Vicarage, Briggate, Silsden, Keighley BD20 9JS* T: (01535) 652204
E: susan.griffiths@bradford.anglican.org

GRIFFITHS, Canon Sylvia Joy. b 50. Gipsy Hill Coll of Educn CertEd 71. St Jo Coll Nottm 85. **dss** 86 **d** 87 **p** 94. Woodthorpe *S'well* 86-90; Par Dn 87-90; Min Bestwood/Rise Park LEP 90-94; Team Dn Bestwood 90-94; TR 94-99; P-in-c Sherwood 99-01; V from 01; Hon Can S'well Minster 04-11. *St Martin's Vicarage, Trevose Gardens, Sherwood, Nottingham NG5 3FU* T: 0115-960 7547
E: sylvia.griffiths@homecall.co.uk

GRIFFITHS, Canon Tudor Francis Lloyd. b 54. Jes Coll Ox BA 76 MA 81 Wycliffe Hall Ox BA 78 MA 81 Leeds Univ PhD 99. Wycliffe Hall Ox 76. **d** 79 **p** 80. C Brecon w Battle *S & B* 79-81; Min Can Brecon Cathl 79-81; C Swansea St Mary w H Trin 81-83; R Llangattock and Llangynidr 83-88; CMS Uganda 89-95; C Newton St Pet *S & B* 96; Dioc Missr *Mon* 96-03; V Goldcliffe and Whitson and Nash 96-98; TV Magor 98-03; TR Hawarden *St As* 03-11; Can Cursal St As Cathl 05-08; Chan St As Cathl 08-11; R Cheltenham St Mary w St Matt *Glouc* 11-12; R Cheltenham St Mary w St Matt and St Luke from 12; AD Cheltenham from 11; Hon Can Glouc Cathl from 13. *38 Sydenham Villas Road, Cheltenham GL52 6DZ* T: (01242) 234470 M: 07718-906066 E: tudorg@stmstm.org.uk

GRIFFITHS, Canon William David Aled. b 52. Univ of Wales (Abth) BA 74 Man Univ AHA 77. St Mich Coll Llan. **d** 82 **p** 84. C Carmarthen St Pet *St D* 83-87; Asst Warden of Ords 84-91; Warden of Ords 91-07; V Llansadwrn w Llanwrda and Manordeilo 87-92; V Llangunnor w Cwmffrwd 92-13; Can St D Cathl 01-13; rtd 13; PtO *St D* from 14. *55 Glynderi, Tanerdy, Carmarthen SA31 2EX* T: (01267) 242849

GRIFFITHS, William David Maldwyn. b 23. St D Coll Lamp BA 47. **d** 50 **p** 51. C Cardigan *St D* 50-54; C Henfynyw w Aberaeron 54-57; P-in-c Llechryd 57-59; V Mathri, St Edrens and Llanrheithan 59-67; V Llanfihangel Genau'r Glyn 67-88; V Llanfihangel Genau'r-glyn and Llangorwen 89; RD Llanbadarn Fawr 87-89; rtd 89. *Bro Enlli, Lower Regent Street, Aberaeron SA46 0HZ* T: (01545) 570176

GRIFFITHS, William Thomas Gordon. b 48. York Univ BA 70 Fitzw Coll Cam BA 79. Ridley Hall Cam 78. **d** 80 **p** 81. C Dulwich St Barn *S'wark* 80-83; C Egglescliffe *Dur* 83-85; Ind Chapl 85-90; V Stockton St Jas 90-98; NSM Leamington Hastings and Birdingbury *Cov* 98-03; NSM Grandborough w Willoughby and Flecknoe 98-03; NSM Leam Valley 03-06; PtO from 06. *24 Park Road, Rugby CV21 2QH* T: (01788) 547815

GRIGG, Mrs Deborah Ann. b 56. R Holloway Coll Lon BA 79 Kingston Poly PGCE 80. SWMTC 09. **d** 12 **p** 14. C Liskeard and St Keyne *Truro* 12-13; C Bodmin w Lanhydrock and Lanivet from 13. *Rose Veanoad, North Pool Road, Redruth TR15 3JQ* T: (01209) 213401 E: deborahgrigg@hotmail.com

GRIGG, Robin Harold. b 44. **d** 07 **p** 08. NSM St Mewan w Mevagissey and St Ewe *Truro* from 07; Chapl R Cornwall Hosps Trust 07-11. *Higher Polstreath, School Hill, Mevagissey, St Austell PL26 6TH* T: (01726) 843708
E: robingrigg124@btinternet.com

GRIGG, Simon James. b 61. Warwick Univ BA 82 MA 83 Southn Univ BTh 90. Chich Th Coll 87. **d** 90 **p** 91. C Cowley St Jas *Ox* 90-94; C W Hampstead St Jas *Lon* 94-95; V Munster Square Ch Ch and St Mary Magd 95-96; R Covent Garden St Paul from 06. *Flat 3, 35 Craven Street, London WC2N 5NF* T: (020) 7836 5221 M: 07958-472568 E: simon.grigg@btopenworld.com

GRIGG, Canon Terence George. b 34. Kelham Th Coll 54. **d** 59 **p** 60. C Brookfield St Anne, Highgate Rise *Lon* 59-62; Chapl Lee Abbey 63-66; Chapl and Lect St Luke's Coll Ex 66-70; V Stainton-in-Cleveland *York* 70-83; R Cottingham 83-04; rtd 04; Can and Preb York Minster from 90; Hon Can Koforidua from 84; Hon Can Ho from 06. *The Canon's House, 14 Grove Street, Norton, Malton YO17 9BG* T: (01653) 691157

GRIGGS, Alan Peter. b 34. St Jo Coll Nottm. **d** 15. NSM Derby St Barn from 15. *4 Ravenscourt Road, Derby DE22 4DL*
T: (01332) 361534 E: alan@stbd.org.uk

GRIGGS, Canon Alan Sheward. b 33. Trin Hall Cam BA 56 MA 60. Westcott Ho Cam 58. **d** 60 **p** 61. C Arnold *S'well* 60-63; Succ S'wark Cathl 63-66; Ind Chapl 66-71; C Leeds H Trin *Ripon* 71-81; V 81-90; Soc and Ind Adv 71-81; Hon Can Ripon Cathl 84-98; Soc Resp Officer 91-98; rtd 98; PtO *Leeds* from 98. *32 St Chad's Avenue, Leeds LS6 3QF* T: 0113-275 8100 E: alan@alangriggs.freeserve.co.uk

GRIGGS, Mrs Anthea Mary. b 37. Homerton Coll Cam TCert 57 New Coll Edin BA 86. SAOMC. **d** 00 **p** 01. NSM Sunningdale *Ox* 00-05; LtO *Edin* from 06. *8/1 Rattray Drive, Edinburgh EH10 5TH* T: 0131-447 2448 E: antheagriggs@me.com

✠**GRIGGS, The Rt Revd Ian Macdonald.** b 28. Trin Hall Cam BA 52 MA 56. Westcott Ho Cam. **d** 54 **p** 55 **c** 87. C Portsea

St Cuth *Portsm* 54-59; Dioc Youth Chapl *Sheff* 59-64; Bp's Dom Chapl 59-64; V Sheff St Cuth 64-71; V Kidderminster St Mary *Worc* 71-82; Hon Can Worc Cathl 77-84; TR Kidderminster St Mary and All SS, Trimpley etc 82-84; Preb Heref Cathl 84-94; Adn Ludlow 84-87; P-in-c Tenbury St Mich 84-87; Suff Bp Ludlow 87-94; rtd 94; Hon Asst Bp Carl from 94. *Rookings, Patterdale, Penrith CA11 0NP* T: (01768) 482064
E: ian.griggs@virgin.net

GRIGOR, Miss Alice Moira (Tirsh). b 49. Ripon Coll Cuddesdon 94. **d** 96 **p** 97. C Curry Rivel w Fivehead and Swell *B & W* 96-98; C Nailsea Ch Ch w Tickenham 98-00; TV Ross *Heref* 00-06; P-in-c Quinton and Welford w Weston *Glouc* 06-14; C Pebworth, Dorsington, Honeybourne etc 11-14; V Quinton, Welford, Weston and Marston Sicca 14-15; rtd 15. *Address temp unknown* E: tirshgrigor@hotmail.co.uk

GRIGOR, David Alexander. b 29. St Aid Birkenhead 51. **d** 54 **p** 55. C Hengrove *Bris* 54-57; C Marshfield w Cold Ashton 57-60; V Newport *Ex* 60-67; V Paignton St Paul Preston 67-73; R Rio de Janeiro Ch Ch Brazil 73-74; Hon C Heavitree *Ex* 74-77; Chapl Ex Sch 74-77; Chapl Brighton Coll 77-89; Chapl Warminster Sch 89-93; rtd 93; PtO *Win* 02-06; *Portsm* 03-06. *42 Russell Crescent, Wollaton, Nottingham NG8 2BQ* T: 0115-928 9036

GRIGSBY, Peter Edward. b 31. Magd Coll Cam MA 56 CertEd 56. NEOC 85. **d** 88 **p** 89. NSM Haxby w Wigginton *York* 88-90; C Brayton 90-92; TV 92-97; rtd 97; PtO *Chich* 98-01 and from 04. *4 The Hop Garden, South Harting, Petersfield GU31 5QL* T: (01730) 825295

GRIGSON, Preb Richard John Stephen. b 60. Man Univ BA 83. Qu Coll Birm 86. **d** 88 **p** 89. C W Bromwich St Fran *Lich* 88-92; V Smallthorne 92-14; P-in-c Brown Edge 05-14; V Stafford St Mary and Marston from 14; V Stafford St Chad from 14; Preb Lich Cathl from 11. *The Vicarage, Victoria Terrace, Stafford ST16 3HA*
E: richard.grigson@lichfield.anglican.org

GRIMASON, The Very Revd Alistair John. b 57. CITC 76. **d** 79 **p** 80. C Belfast H Trin *Conn* 79-82; C Dublin Drumcondra w N Strand *D & G* 82-84; I Navan w Kentstown, Tara, Slane, Painestown etc *M & K* 84-91; Dioc Youth Officer (Meath) 90-94; Dioc Info Officer (Meath) 90-96; I Tullamore w Durrow, Newtownfertullagh, Rahan etc 91-00; Preb Tipper St Patr Cathl Dublin 91-00; Can Meath *M & K* 92-00; Chan Kildare Cathl 98-00; Dean Tuam *T, K & A* from 00; I Tuam w Cong and Aasleagh from 00; Dioc Communications Officer from 10; Dean Killala from 13; Dean Achonry from 13. *Deanery Place, Cong, Claremorris, Co Mayo, Republic of Ireland* T: (00353) (94) 954 6909 M: 85-282 1073 E: deantuam@hotmail.com

GRIME, William John Peter. b 38. St Jo Coll Ox BA 60 MA 66. Cuddesdon Coll 69. **d** 70 **p** 71. C Blackb St Jas 70-74; Chapl St Martin's Coll of Educn 74-77; V Seascale *Carl* 77-78; P-in-c Irton w Drigg 77-78; V Seascale and Drigg 78-05; rtd 05; PtO *York* 05-08. *Bridge House, Snape, Bedale DL8 2SZ* T: (01677) 470077 E: wjpgrime@gmail.com

GRIMLEY, The Very Revd Robert William. b 43. Ch Coll Cam BA 66 MA 70 Wadh Coll Ox BA 68 MA 76 UWE Hon DLitt 04 Bris Univ Hon LLD 09. Ripon Hall Ox 66. **d** 68 **p** 69. C Radlett *St Alb* 68-72; Chapl K Edw Sch Birm 72-84; Hon C Moseley St Mary *Birm* 72-84; V Edgbaston St Geo 84-97; Dean Bris 97-09; rtd 09; PtO *Ox* from 10. *88 Old High Street, Headington, Oxford OX3 9HW* T: (01865) 308219
E: robertgrimley88@gmail.com

GRIMSBY, Suffragan Bishop of. See COURT, The Rt Revd David Eric

GRIMSDALE, Mrs Margaret. b 24. SRN 48. Gilmore Course 80. **dss** 82 **d** 87. Stoke Poges *Ox* 82-88; Hon Par Dn 87-88; Hon Par Dn Burrington and Churchill *B & W* 88-90; rtd 90; PtO *B & W* 90-94. *Widecombe House, Barrington Road, Torquay TQ1 2QJ* T: (01803) 298692

GRIMSTER, Barry John. b 49. Ex Univ BA 70. Trin Coll Bris 72. **d** 74 **p** 75. C S Lambeth St Steph *S'wark* 74-77; C New Malden and Coombe 77-82; P-in-c Deptford St Jo 82-84; V Deptford St Jo w H Trin 84-89; V Woking St Pet *Guildf* 89-01; TR 02-13; rtd 13. *16 Littlefield, Bishopsteignton, Teignmouth TQ14 9SG* T: (01626) 870921 E: bjay1@onetel.com

GRIMWOOD, Andrew Stuart. b 68. Ex Univ BA 89. St Mich Coll Llan BD 97. **d** 98 **p** 99. C Llangynwyd w Maesteg *Llan* 98-01; P-in-c Rhyl w St Ann *St As* 01-04; R Llanllwchaiarn and Newtown w Aberhafesp 04-13; AD Cedewain 08-13; V Rhyl w St Ann from 13. *18B Dyserth Road, Rhyl LL18 4DP* T: (01745) 797196 E: andygrimwood@live.co.uk or vicar@parishofrhyl.co.uk

GRIMWOOD, Canon David Walter. b 48. Lon Univ BA 70 K Coll Lon BD 73 AKC 73. **d** 74 **p** 75. C Newc St Geo 74-78; C Whorlton 78-80; TV Totton *Win* 80-93; Adv to Coun for Soc Resp Roch and Cant 93-02; Chief Exec Ch in Soc Roch

and Cant 02-09; Hon Can Roch Cathl 97-09; PtO *Cant* from 09; *Roch* from 12. *56 Postley Road, Maidstone ME15 6TR* T: (01622) 764625 M: 07960-369681
E: d.grimwood@zedakah.co.uk

GRINDELL, James Mark. b 43. Nottm Univ BA 66 Bris Univ MA 69. Wells Th Coll 66. **d** 68 **p** 69. C Bushey Heath *St Alb* 68-72; C Ex *St Dav* 72-74; Chapl St Audries Sch W Quantoxhead 74-83; Chapl Berkhamsted Colleg Sch Herts 83-86; Chapl Denstone Coll Uttoxeter 86-91; Chapl Portsm Gr Sch and Hon Chapl Portsm Cathl 91-03; rtd 03. *6A Victoria Place, Ryde PO33 2PX* E: jmgrindell@yahoo.co.uk

GRINDROD (née UTTIN), Suzanne. b 72. Trin Coll Bris 09. **d** 11 **p** 12. C Lydney *Glouc* 11-15; P-in-c Ashchurch and Kemerton from 15. *2 Abbey Lodge, Church Street, Tewkesbury GL20 5SR* E: revsuttin@hotmail.co.uk

GRINHAM, Julian Clive. b 39. Birkbeck Coll Lon BA 65. Oak Hill Th Coll 79. **d** 81 **p** 82. C Blackb Ch Ch w St Matt 81-83; Nat Sec Pathfinders CPAS 83-89; Dir CYPECS 89-94; V Normanton *Derby* 94-00; rtd 00; PtO *Nor* from 01. *85 Gwyn Crescent, Fakenham NR21 8NE* T: (01328) 853068
E: jcgrinham@btinternet.com

GRINSELL, Robert Paul. b 62. Ch Ch Coll Cant BA 86 PGCE 89. Trin Coll Bris MA 03. **d** 03 **p** 04. C Folkestone St Jo *Cant* 03-07; P-in-c Hawkinge from 07. *The Rectory, 78 Canterbury Road, Hawkinge, Folkestone CT18 7BP* T: (01303) 893215
E: robgrinsell@tiscali.co.uk

GRINSTED, Richard Anthony. b 43. Leic Univ BSc 65. Oak Hill Th Coll 67. **d** 70 **p** 71. C Egham *Guildf* 70-73; C Woodford Wells *Chelmsf* 73-76; P-in-c Havering-atte-Bower 76-84; R Ditton *Roch* 84-94; R Chulmleigh *Ex* 94-96; R Chawleigh w Cheldon 94-96; R Wembworthy w Eggesford 94-96; R Chulmleigh, Chawleigh w Cheldon, Wembworthy etc 96-00; rtd 00. *Stone House, Village Road, Christow, Exeter EX6 7NF* T: (01647) 252653

GRISCOME, David. b 47. Oak Hill Th Coll BA 88 TCD Div Sch 89. **d** 89 **p** 90. C Glendermott *D & R* 89-91; I Clondehorkey w Cashel 91-95; I Mevagh w Glenalla 91-95; Bp's C Calry *K, E & A* 95-97; I 97-00; Dean Elphin and Ardagh 99-04; I Sligo w Knocknarea and Rosses Pt 99-04; PtO *Cant* 04-06; I Convoy w Monellan and Donaghmore *D & R* 06-13; Bp's Dom Chapl 07-13; rtd 13. *Keida, 15 Birchill Upper, Creeslough, Letterkenny, Co Donegal, Republic of Ireland* T: (00353) (74) 913 8395 E: keida@eircom.net

✠**GRISWOLD, The Most Revd Frank Tracy.** b 37. Harvard Univ AB 59 Oriel Coll Ox BA 62 MA 66. Gen Th Sem NY 59 Hon DD 85 Seabury-Western Th Sem Hon DD 85. **d** 62 **p** 63 **c** 85. C Bryn Mawr Redeemer USA 63-67; R Yardley St Andr 67-74; R Philadelphia St Martin-in-the-Fields 74-85; Bp Coadjutor Chicago 85-87; Bp Chicago 87-97; Presiding Bp 98-06; rtd 06. *Episcopal Church Center, 815 Second Avenue, New York, NY 10017, USA* T: (001) (212) 716 6276 *or* 867 8400
F: 490 3298 E: pboffice@episcopalchurch.org

GROARKE, The Ven Nicola Jane. b 62. Lanc Univ BA 84. Ridley Hall Cam. **d** 00 **p** 01. C Balham Hill Ascension *S'wark* 00-08; V Canonbury St Steph *Lon* 08-14; Adn Dudley *Worc* from 14. *15 Worcester Road, Droitwich WR9 8AA* T/F: (01905) 773301
E: ngroarke@cofe-worcester.org.uk

GROEPE, Canon Thomas Matthew Karl. b 51. St Pet Coll Natal 76. **d** 78 **p** 79. S Africa 78-83 and from 88; Hon C Waterloo St Jo w St Andr *S'wark* 83-88. *PO Box 1932, Cape Town, 8000 South Africa* T/F: (0027) (21) 465 4946 T: 461 9566
E: karlgroepe@mweb.co.za

GROOCOCK, Christopher John. b 59. Cardiff Univ MTh 12. St Jo Coll Nottm LTh 92. **d** 92 **p** 93. C Shawbury *Lich* 92-95; V Hengoed w Gobowen 95-00; CF from 00. *c/o MOD Chaplains (Army)* F: 381824 T: (01264) 383430

GROOCOCK, Craig Ronald. WMMTC 03. **d** 05 **p** 06. C Kenilworth St Nic *Cov* 05-08; P-in-c Harbury and Ladbroke from 08; AD Southam from 11. *The Rectory, 2 Vicarage Lane, Harbury, Leamington Spa CV33 9HA* T: (01926) 612377 M: 07811-395169 E: craiggroocock@aol.com

GROOM, Mrs Susan Anne. b 63. Univ of Wales BA 85 Hughes Hall Cam MPhil 86 Lon Bible Coll MA 94 Open Univ MPhil 00. St Jo Coll Nottm 94. **d** 96 **p** 97. C Harefield *Lon* 96-99; C Eastcote St Lawr *S'wark* 99-01; P-in-c Yiewsley 01-03; V 03-07; Dir Lic Min Kensington Area 07-09; P-in-c Henlow and Langford *St Alb* from 09; Asst Dir of Ords 09-11; Dir of Ords from 11. *The Vicarage, 65 Church Street, Langford, Biggleswade SG18 9QT* T: (01462) 700248

GROOMBRIDGE, Jeremy Carl. b 55. SEITE 13. **d** 15. NSM Sanderstead *S'wark* from 15. *Address temp unknown*

GROOMBRIDGE, Mrs Sonia Elizabeth. b 58. NTMTC. **d** 12 **p** 13. OLM Hornchurch St Andr *Chelmsf* from 12. *300 Goodwood Avenue, Hornchurch RM12 6DH*

GROSSCURTH, Stephen. b 55. Sarum & Wells Th Coll 81. **d** 84 **p** 85. C Southport H Trin *Liv* 84-87; C Amblecote *Worc* 87-89;

V Walton St Jo *Liv* 89-95; Chapl Univ Hosp of S Man NHS Foundn Trust 95-12; rtd 12. *68 Lincoln Close, Woolston, Warrington WA1 4LU* T: (01925) 821124

GROSSE, Anthony Charles Bain. b 30. Oak Hill Th Coll 58. **d** 61 **p** 62. C Chislehurst Ch Ch *Roch* 61-65; C Washfield *Ex* 65-71; TV Washfield, Stoodleigh, Withleigh etc 71-73; R Hemyock 73-86; P-in-c Clayhidon 76-86; R Hemyock w Culm Davy and Clayhidon 87-93; R Hemyock w Culm Davy, Clayhidon and Culmstock 93-96; rtd 96; PtO *Ex* from 98. *17 Frog Street, Bampton, Tiverton EX16 9NT* T: (01398) 331981
E: acgrosse@btinternet.com

GROSSE, Peter George. b 43. St Steph Ho Ox 02. **d** 03 **p** 04. NSM Reading St Matt *Ox* 03-06; NSM Tilehurst St Geo and St Mary 06-12; PtO from 12. *18 Rangewood Avenue, Reading RG30 3NN* T: 0118-959 4573
E: revdpetergrosse@talktalk.net

GROSSE, Richard William. b 52. Solicitor 77 Mid Essex Tech Coll LLB 73. Ridley Hall Cam 86. **d** 88 **p** 89. C Soham *Ely* 88-91; C Bedale *Ripon* 91-93; C-in-c Thornton Watlass w Thornton Steward 91-93; V Barton and Manfield w Cleasby 93-95; V Barton and Manfield and Cleasby w Stapleton 95-99; R Keelby Gp *Linc* 99-04; R Callander *St And* from 04; R Aberfoyle from 04. *St Mary's Rectory, Main Street, Aberfoyle, Stirling FK8 3UJ* T/F: (01877) 382887
E: richard_grosse@hotmail.com

GROSU, Iosif. b 60. Iasi Univ BTh 92. RC Inst Iasi. **d** 89 **p** 89. In RC Ch 89-93; C Darlington St Cuth *Dur* 96-99; C Stockton St Jo and Stockton St Jas 99-02; TV Che the K 02-08; P-in-c Purston cum S Featherstone *Wakef* 08-09; P-in-c Featherstone 08-09; V Leeds from 09. *St Thomas's House, 32 Victoria Street, Featherstone, Pontefract WF7 5EZ* T: (01977) 792280
E: iosifgrosu@btinternet.com

GROSVENOR, Royston Johannes Martin. b 47. K Coll Lon BD 70 AKC. **d** 71 **p** 72. C Pontesbury I and II *Heref* 71-75; C Bishopston *Bris* 75-79; P-in-c Croydon St Pet S End *Cant* 79-81; V Croydon St Pet 81-84; V *S'wark* 85-87; R Merstham and Gatton 87-97; V Tidenham w Beachley and Lancaut *Glouc* 97-11; P-in-c St Briavels w Hewelsfield 05-11; AD Forest S 04-09; rtd 11. *75 King's Drive, Bishopston, Bristol BS7 8JQ* T: 0117-924 7919
E: royston.grosvenor@hotmail.co.uk

GROVE, Lynn. b 43. Lon Univ MB, BS 67. Cranmer Hall Dur 03. **d** 04 **p** 05. NSM Pickering w Lockton and Levisham *York* 04-11; NSM Helmsley from 12; NSM Upper Ryedale from 12. *The Rectory, Old Byland, York YO62 5LG* T: (01439) 798905
E: lynngrove43@hotmail.com *or* revlynn625@gmail.com

GROVER, Wilfrid John. b 29. Lich Th Coll 55. **d** 58 **p** 59. C Northampton St Alb *Pet* 58-61; C Boyne Hill *Ox* 61-65; V Cookham 65-85; RD Maidenhead 82-85; Warden Christchurch Retreat Ho *Glouc* 85-93; rtd 89; Hon C Jedburgh *Edin* from 93. *5 The Stables, Buccleuch Chase, St Boswells, Melrose TD6 0HE* T: (01835) 824435

GROVES, Caroline Anne. b 41. **d** 05 **p** 06. OLM Norbiton *S'wark* 05-11; PtO from 11. *16 Beaufort Road, Kingston upon Thames KT1 2TQ* T: (020) 8549 1585 E: sicaro@blueyonder.co.uk

GROVES, Elizabeth Ann. b 36. Bp Otter Coll 94. **d** 97 **p** 09. NSM Soberton w Newtown *Portsm* 97-01; NSM Botley, Durley and Curdridge 01-06; NSM Wickham 06; NSM Shedfield and Wickham 07-12; rtd 12; PtO *Portsm* from 12. *54 Privett Road, Gosport PO12 3SU* T: (023) 9258 6168
E: akeagroves@aol.com

GROVES, James Alan. b 32. CCC Cam BA 58 MA 62. Wells Th Coll 58. **d** 60 **p** 61. C Milton next Gravesend Ch Ch *Roch* 60-64; C Beckenham St Jas 64-66; V Orpington St Andr 66-98; rtd 98; PtO *Chich* from 98. *9 Wykeham Road, Hastings TN34 1UA* T: (01424) 200839

GROVES, Preb Jill. b 61. Univ Coll Lon BSc 82. St Jo Coll Nottm MA 93. **d** 93 **p** 94. C Tenbury Wells *Heref* 93-98; P-in-c Hope Bowdler w Eaton-under-Heywood 98-11; P-in-c Cardington 98-11; P-in-c Rushbury 98-11; Asst Chapl St Mich Hospice Hereford from 11; Preb Heref Cathl from 09. *St Michael's Hospice, Bartestree, Hereford HR1 4HA* T: (01432) 851000
E: jill@grovesfamily.org.uk

GROVES, Justin Simon John. b 69. Lon Bible Coll BA 93. Ridley Hall Cam 00. **d** 02 **p** 03. C Glouc St Cath 02-05; C Newport St Paul *Mon* 05-07; P-in-c from 07. *52 Oakfield Road, Newport NP20 4LX* T: (01633) 419775 E: revgrooves@hotmail.com

GROVES, Margaret Ann. b 49. Nottm Univ BEd 71 BPhil 88. EMMTC 95. **d** 98 **p** 99. NSM Farnsfield *S'well* from 98; NSM Bilsthorpe from 98. *Churchill House, Church Hill, Bilsthorpe, Newark NG22 8RU* T: (01623) 870679

GROVES, Peter John. b 70. New Coll Ox BA 92 MA 96 DPhil 96. Westcott Ho Cam 95. **d** 97 **p** 98. C Leigh-on-Sea St Marg *Chelmsf* 97-99; Lib Pusey Ho 99-01; Asst Chapl and Tutor Keble Coll Ox 01-02; Chapl and Fell BNC Ox 02-06; Hon C

Ox St Mary Magd 01-04; P-in-c 05-13; V from 13. *15 Beaumont Street, Oxford OX1 2NA* T: (01865) 247836
E: peter.groves@theology.ox.ac.uk

GROVES, Canon Philip Neil. b 62. Man Univ BA 84 Birm Univ PhD 10. St Jo Coll Nottm 86. **d** 88 **p** 89. C Holbeck *Ripon* 88-91; CMS 91-99; Lect St Phil Th Coll Kongwa Tanzania 93-98; Hon Can Mpwampwa from 98; TV Melton Mowbray *Leic* 99-05; Listening Process Facilitator on Human Sexuality Angl Communion 06-09; Project Dir for Continuing Indaba from 09. *Anglican Communion Office, 16 Tavistock Crescent, London W11 1AP* T: (020) 7313 3917
E: phil.groves@anglicancommunion.org

GROVES, Robert John. b 42. Trin Coll Bris 74. **d** 76 **p** 77. C Norwood St Luke *S'wark* 76-79; P-in-c Clapham Park All SS 79-86; V Anerley *Roch* 86-95; TV Canford Magna *Sarum* 95-98; TR Tollington *Lon* 98-02; rtd 02; PtO *Cant* 02-09; *Roch* from 02. *23 Ramsay Hall, 9-13 Byron Road, Worthing BN11 3HN*
E: bob_groves@lineone.net

GROWNS, John Huntley. b 28. Chich Th Coll 57. **d** 60 **p** 61. C Hayes St Mary *Lon* 60-64; C Addlestone *Guildf* 64-67; C-in-c Kempston Transfiguration CD *St Alb* 67-74; R Stevenage St Geo 74-82; R Felpham w Middleton *Chich* 82-88; P-in-c Westmill w Gt Munden *St Alb* 88-89; P-in-c Westmill 89-93; Dioc Stewardship Adv 88-93; rtd 93; PtO *Chich* 93-04; *St Alb* 93-00. *5 Little London Gardens, Ely CB6 1BF* T: (01353) 772794

GRUBB, Greville Alexander (Alex). b 36. Saltley Tr Coll Birm CertEd 60. St Jo Coll Nottm 72. **d** 74 **p** 75. C Rushden w Newton Bromswold *Pet* 74-77; Chapl St D Coll Llandudno 77-89; Chapl Casterton Sch Lancs 90-96; rtd 96; PtO *Blackb* 96-11; *Leeds* from 02; *Chich* from 15. *5 Cambridge Lodge, 10 Southey Road, Worthing BN11 3HT* T: (01903) 368580

GRUMBALL, Kevin. b 67. St Steph Ho Ox. **d** 11 **p** 12. NSM Temple Grafton w Binton *Cov* 11-15; NSM Exhall w Wixford 11-15; NSM Salford Priors 11-15; NSM Heart of England from 15. *Stone Croft, Ardens Grafton, Alcester B49 6DR*

GRUNDY, Anthony Brian. b 36. Pemb Coll Cam BA 62 MA 87. Ridley Hall Cam 61. **d** 63 **p** 64. C Hatcham St Jas *S'wark* 63-66; C Margate H Trin *Cant* 66-68; C Brixton Hill St Sav *S'wark* 68-70; V Assington *St E* 70-76; TV Much Wenlock w Bourton *Heref* 76-81; TV Wenlock 81-82; TR 82-88; RD Condover 86-88; R Burghfield *Ox* 88-02; rtd 02; PtO *Chich* from 03. *18 Victoria Court, Henley-on-Thames RG9 1XG*

GRUNDY, Christopher John. b 49. ACA 72. Trin Coll Bris 74. **d** 77 **p** 78. C Maidstone St Luke *Cant* 77-81; Argentina 81-82; Chile 82-84; PtO *Guildf* 84-96; NSM Guildf Ch Ch w St Martha-on-the-Hill 96-99; C Shere, Albury and Chilworth 99-06; TV Drypool *York* 06-12; rtd 12. *The Lyttons, Elstead Road, Seale, Farnham GU10 1HZ* E: chris@grundy.org.uk

GRUNDY, David. *See* GRUNDY, Julian David

GRUNDY, Judith Michal Towers Mynors. b 54. Lady Spencer Chu Coll of Educn CertEd 76 Ox Univ BEd 77. Trin Coll Bris 85. **d** 93 **p** 94. NSM Kensal Rise St Mark and St Martin *Lon* 93-95; NSM Snettisham w Ingoldisthorpe and Fring *Nor* 95-04; R Denver and Ryston w Roxham and W Dereham etc *Ely* from 04. *The Rectory, Ryston Road, Denver, Downham Market PE38 0DP* T: (01366) 383226
E: judith.grundy@ely.anglican.org

GRUNDY, Julian David. b 60. St Andr Univ MA 83. Trin Coll Bris BA 88. **d** 89 **p** 90. C Lancaster St Thos *Blackb* 89-92; C Kensal Rise St Mark and St Martin *Lon* 92-95; R Snettisham w Ingoldisthorpe and Fring *Nor* 95-03; PtO *Ely* from 08. *The Rectory, Ryston Road, Denver, Downham Market PE38 0DP* T: (01366) 383224 E: dave@grundyd.fslife.co.uk

GRUNDY, Canon Malcolm Leslie. b 44. Open Univ BA 76 Leeds Univ PhD 14. St Boniface Warminster AKC 68. **d** 69 **p** 70. C Doncaster St Geo *Sheff* 69-72; Ind Chapl 72-80; Dir of Educn *Lon* 80-86; TR Huntingdon *Ely* 86-91; Hon Can Ely Cathl 88-94; Dir Avec 91-94; Adn Craven *Bradf* 94-05; Dir Foundn for Ch Leadership 05-09; rtd 09; PtO *York* from 09. *11 Givendale Grove, York YO10 3QF* M: 07950-816641
T: (01904) 422999 E: mlgweg@gmail.com

GRUNDY, Paul. b 55. BD 77 AKC. Linc Th Coll 79. **d** 80 **p** 81. C Ryhope *Dur* 80-82; C Ferryhill 82-85; TV Cramlington *Newc* 85-87; TV Swinton and Pendlebury *Man* 87-90; V Wingate Grange *Dur* 90-95; R Willington and Sunnybrow 95-07; P-in-c Usworth 07-09; R 09-13; rtd 13; PtO *Dur* from 13. *14 Kellsway, Gateshead NE10 8NB*

GRÜNEBERG, Keith Nigel. *See* BEECH-GRÜNEBERG, Keith Nigel

GRÜNEWALD, Gottfried Johannes. b 38. Loyola Univ Chicago MPS 92. Th Faculty Frankfurt 66. **d** 69 **p** 69. Denmark 70-95; C Dunbar *Edin* 95-97; R Dollar *St And* 98-05; rtd 05. *Teglparken 8, 8860 Ulstrup, Denmark* T: (0045) 864 6341
E: grunewald@email.dk

GRYLLS, Canon Catherine Anne. b 70. **d** 00 **p** 01. C Hall Green St Pet *Birm* 00-04; P-in-c Balsall Heath St Paul 04-07; P-in-c Edgbaston SS Mary and Ambrose 04-07; P-in-c Balsall Heath and Edgbaston SS Mary and Ambrose 07-08; V from 08; AD Moseley from 13; Hon Can Birm Cathl from 15. *St Ambrose Vicarage, 15 Raglan Road, Birmingham B5 7RA* T: 0121-440 2196 E: gryllsc@btinternet.com

GRYLLS, Canon Michael John. b 38. Qu Coll Cam BA 62 MA 66. Linc Th Coll 62. **d** 64 **p** 65. C Sheff Gillcar St Silas 64-67; C-in-c Dunscroft CD 67-70; V Herringthorpe 70-78; V Amport, Grateley, Monxton and Quarley *Win* 78-89; RD Andover 85-89; V Whitchurch w Tufton and Litchfield 89-03; Hon Can Win Cathl 01-03; rtd 03; PtO *Worc* from 04. *41 Church Street, Evesham WR11 1DY* T: (01386) 442086

GUBBINS, Andrew Martin. b 65. York Univ BA 86 Keele Univ 93. St Jo Coll Nottm LTh 93. **d** 96 **p** 97. C Harrogate St Mark *Ripon* 96-00; P-in-c Osmondthorpe St Phil 00-03; V Leeds All SS w Osmondthorpe 03-09; P-in-c Chippenham St Pet *Bris* from 09. *St Peter's Vicarage, 32 Lords Mead, Chippenham SN14 0LL* T: (01249) 448530
E: gubbinsrevs@sky.com

GUBBINS (née O'BRIEN), Mrs Mary. b 68. Leeds Univ BSc 90. St Jo Coll Nottm BTh 93. **d** 94 **p** 95. C Middleton St Mary *Ripon* 94-96; C Bilton 96-99; PtO 99-09. *St Peter's Vicarage, 32 Lords Mead, Chippenham SN14 0LL* T: (01249) 448530

GUDGEON, Canon Michael John. b 40. Qu Coll Cam BA 63 MA 67. Chich Th Coll 65. **d** 66 **p** 67. C Kings Heath *Birm* 66-72; Asst Chapl K Edw Sch Birm 69-72; Chapl and Tutor Cuddesdon Coll 72-75; V Hawley H Trin *Guildf* 75-80; V Minley 75-80; Adult Educn Adv *Chich* 80-87; Can Res Portsm Cathl 87-90; Dioc Dir of Educn 87-90; V Hove St Thos *Chich* 90-93; TV Hove 93-94; Bp's Chapl *Eur* 94-98; Dir of Ords 94-97; Can Gib Cathl 96-06; P-in-c Worthing St Andr *Chich* 98-05; rtd 05. *11 Gloucester Road, Littlehampton BN17 7BT* T: (01903) 739682 E: michaelgudgeon@aol.com

✠**GUERRERO, The Rt Revd Orlando.** b 45. Episc Sem of Ecuador. **p** 80 **c** 95. P Puerto la Cruz H Trin 80-93; Interim P Caracas St Mary 80-84; Bp Venezuela from 95. *Apartado 49-143, Avenida Caroní 100, Colinas de Bello Monte, Caracas 1042-A, Venezuela* T: (0058) (2) 753 0723 F: 751 3180

GUEST, David. b 41. Dur Univ BA 62. Coll of Resurr Mirfield 70. **d** 72 **p** 73. C Horsforth *Ripon* 72-75; C Richmond 75-76; C Richmond w Hudswell 76-78; R Middleham 78-81; R Middleham and Coverham w Horsehouse 81-86; V W Rainton and E Rainton *Dur* 86-03; RD Houghton 92-94 and 96-97; rtd 03; PtO *Leeds* from 03. *Lindisfarne, 3 New Croft, Horsforth, Leeds LS18 4TD* T: 0113-258 0521

GUEST, David Andrew. b 61. Chich Th Coll BTh 92. **d** 92 **p** 93. C Prenton *Ches* 92-94; C Ches H Trin 94-97; Assoc P Douglas All SS and St Thos *S & M* 97-00; Dioc Communications Officer 97-00; Relig Adv Manx Radio 97-00; Bp's Dom Chapl *S & M* 98-00; Dioc Communications Officer *Chich* 00-09; C Hove 00-03; C Southwick 03-09; P-in-c Heathfield 09-13; V from 13. *The Vicarage, Old Heathfield, Heathfield TN21 9AB* T: (01435) 862457 E: davidguest731@btinternet.com

GUEST, Derek William. b 55. NOC 90. **d** 93 **p** 94. C Cheadle Hulme St Andr *Ches* 93-99; V from 99. *2 Orrishmere Road, Cheadle Hulme, Cheadle SK8 5HP* T: 0161-486 9306
E: revdguest@yahoo.co.uk

GUEST, Ernest Anthony. b 64. NTMTC 99. **d** 02 **p** 03. C Gt Ilford St Jo *Chelmsf* 02-05; V Barkingside St Laur 05-13; P-in-c Tye Green w Netteswell from 13. *The Rectory, Tawney Road, Harlow CM18 6QR* T: (01279) 432626 M: 07810-516356
E: ernie@ernieguest.fsnet.co.uk

GUEST, Canon Helen. b 54. Totley Thornbridge Coll CertEd 75 Nottm Univ MA 02. EMMTC 99. **d** 02 **p** 03. NSM Brimington *Derby* 02-05; C Hatton 05-07; P-in-c Killamarsh 07-13; C Barlborough and Renishaw 07-13; R Killamarsh and Renishaw from 13; RD Bolsover and Staveley from 11; Hon Can Derby Cathl from 12. *The Rectory, Sheepcote Road, Killamarsh, Sheffield S21 1DU* T: 0114-248 2769
E: revsguest@btinternet.com *or* revshmguest@gmail.com

GUEST, John. b 36. Trin Coll Bris 59. **d** 61 **p** 62. C Barton Hill St Luke w Ch Ch *Bris* 61-64; C Liv St Sav 65-66; V Hoxton from 66; rtd 01. *30 Myrtle Hill Road, Sewickley PA 15143-8700, USA* T: (001) (412) 741 6445

GUEST, John Andrew Kenneth. b 55. Univ of Wales (Lamp) BA 78. Wycliffe Hall Ox 78. **d** 80 **p** 81. C Eastwood *S'well* 80-84; TV Toxteth St Philemon w St Gabr and St Cleopas *Liv* 84-89; C Cranham Park *Chelmsf* 89-93; P-in-c Stanford-le-Hope w Mucking 93-03; R from 03. *The Rectory, The Green, Stanford-le-Hope SS17 0EP* T: (01375) 672271
E: gof4god@aol.com

GUEST, Matthew William. b 83. Oak Hill Th Coll 12. **d** 15. C Wharton *Ches* from 15. *2 Beaulieu Avenue, Winsford CW7 3AR* M: 07793-075907 E: mattwguest@outlook.com

GUEST, Michael. b 52. EMMTC. **d** 99 **p** 00. NSM Heath *Derby* 99-07; NSM Killamarsh and Barlborough and Renishaw 07-13. *The Rectory, Sheepcote Road, Killamarsh, Sheffield S21 1DU* T: 0114-248 2769 E: revsguest@btinternet.com *or* revshmguest@gmail.com

GUEST, Mrs Sharon Michelle. b 62. St Jo Coll Nottm. **d** 12 **p** 13. C Chigwell and Chigwell Row *Chelmsf* from 12. *The Rectory, Tawney Road, Harlow CM18 6QR* T: (01279) 432626 E: sharon@ernieguest.fsnet.co.uk

GUEST, Canon Simon Llewelyn. b 56. Univ of Wales (Lamp) BA 78 CertEd 79. St Mich Coll Llan 83. **d** 85 **p** 86. C Bassaleg *Mon* 85-88; C Cwmbran 88-89; TV 89-91; V Raglan w Llandenny and Bryngwyn 91-05; V Rockfield and Dingestow Gp from 05; AD Raglan-Usk 01-05; AD Monmouth 06-13; Can St Woolos Cathl from 12. *The Vicarage, Dingestow, Monmouth NP25 4DY* T: (01600) 740206

GUEST-BLOFELD, Thomas. b 35. St D Coll Lamp BA 59. Cranmer Hall Dur 59. **d** 62 **p** 63. C Maltby *Sheff* 62-63; C Goole 63-66; C Pocklington w Yapham-cum-Meltonby, Owsthorpe etc *York* 67-68; C Ely 68-70; C Pemberton St Jo *Liv* 70-72; V Walton St Jo 72-74; V Barkisland w W Scammonden *Wakef* 74-80; V Smallbridge *Man* 80-82; C Irlam 83-86; r-d 87. *234 M005, Tambon Maesai, Amphoe Mueang, Phayao 56000, Thailand* T: (0066) (8) 7184 3624

GUILDFORD, Bishop of. *See* WATSON, The Rt Revd Andrew John

GUILDFORD, Dean of. *See* GWILLIAMS, The Very Revd Dianna Lynn

GUILFORD, John Edward. b 50. S & M Dioc Tr Inst 94. **d** 99 **p** 00. OLM Lonan *S & M* 99-12; OLM Laxey 99-12; OLM Onchan, Lonan and Laxey from 12. *Tremissary House, Strathallan Road, Douglas, Isle of Man IM2 4PN* T/F: (01624) 672001 M: 07624-494274 E: revjohnnyg@manx.net

GUILLAN, Miss Barbara Doris. b 19. S'wark Ord Course 45. **d** 87. NSM St Stythians w Perranarworthal and Gwennap *Truro* 87-89; rtd 89; PtO *Truro* 89-94. *St Cecilia's Nursing Home, 1 Hitchen Lane, Shepton Mallet BA4 5TZ* T: (01749) 342809

GUILLE, The Very Revd John Arthur. b 49. Southn Univ BTh 79. Sarum & Wells Th Coll 73. **d** 76 **p** 77. C Chandler's Ford *Win* 76-80; P-in-c Bournemouth St Jo 80-84; P-in-c Bournemouth St Mich 83-84; V Bournemouth St Jo w St Mich 84-89; R Guernsey St Andr 89-99; Adn Win 99-07; Can Res Win Cathl 99-07; Dean S'well 07-14; rtd 14; PtO *Win* from 14. *Pelerins, La Planque Road, St Martin, Guernsey GY4 6TH* T: (01481) 237168

GUILLEBAUD, Mrs Jette Margaret (Maggie). b 48. Ex Univ BA 70 UWE Hon MA 98 FRSA 95. Ripon Coll Cuddesdon 03. **d** 05 **p** 06. NSM Sarum Cathl 05-12; Asst Chapl Sarum Coll 10-12; Chapl Ch Ho *Sarum* from 12. *The Dovecote, Mount Sorrel, Broad Chalke, Salisbury SP5 5HQ* T: (01722) 781281 *or* 411922 M: 07985-576739 E: maggieguillebaud@gmail.com

GUILLEBAUD, Canon Margaret Jean. b 43. MBE 03. Edin Univ BSc 66. Cranmer Hall Dur 79. **dss** 80 **d** 87 **p** 94. New Malden and Coombe *S'wark* 80-84; Carlton Colville w Mutford and Rushmere *Nor* 84-91; Par Dn 87-91; Par Dn Rodbourne Cheney *Bris* 91-94; C 94-95; CMS Rwanda 95-08; rtd 08; PtO *Birm* from 08; Can Res Byumba from 10. *7 Poplar Road, Dorridge, Solihull B93 8DD* T: (01564) 770113 E: mguillebaud@gmail.com

GUILLEMIN, Thierry Jean-Louis. b 62. Coll of Resurr Mirfield 08. **d** 01 **p** 01. In RC Ch 01-07; PtO *Wakef* 08-09; C Heckmondwike 09-11; C Liversedge w Hightown 09-11; P-in-c Wibsey St Paul *Leeds* from 11; C Shelf w Buttershaw St Aid from 11. *St Paul's Vicarage, 42A Wibsey Park Avenue, Bradford BD6 3QA* T: (01274) 690832 *or* 676359 M: 07778-577008 E: t.guillemin@btinternet.com

GUINNESS, Alexander. *See* GUINNESS, Graham Alexander

GUINNESS, Christopher Paul. b 43. Lon Coll of Div 64. **d** 67 **p** 68. C Farnborough *Guildf* 67-70; C Tulse Hill H Trin *S'wark* 70-74; C Worting *Win* 74-78; P-in-c S Lambeth St Steph *S'wark* 78-89; V 89-91; RD Lambeth 86-90; C Ches Square St Mich w St Phil *Lon* 91-97; Living Waters Trust 98-00; Chapl Ealing Hosp NHS Trust 00-01; Chapl Hammersmith Hosps NHS Trust 01-08; Chapl Imp Coll Healthcare NHS Trust 08-10; rtd 10. *Ashley Cottage, Station Road, Sway, Lymington SO41 6AA* T: (01590) 682463 E: christopherguinness@hotmail.co.uk

GUINNESS, Canon Garry Grattan. b 40. Em Coll Cam BA 64 MA 68. Ridley Hall Cam 64. **d** 66 **p** 67. C Wallington *S'wark* 66-69; C St Marylebone All So w SS Pet and Jo *Lon* 69-72; P-in-c Clifton H Trin, St Andr and St Pet *Bris* 72-79; V Watford St Luke *St Alb* 79-90; TR Worthing Ch the King *Chich* 90-05; Hon Can Kigeme from 02; rtd 05. *37 Stowell Crescent, Wareham BH20 4PT* T: (01929) 550215 E: gguinness@talktalk.net

GUINNESS, Graham Alexander. b 60. Edin Th Coll 82. **d** 85 **p** 86. Dioc Youth Chapl *Mor* 85-88; C Elgin w Lossiemouth 85-88; Asst P Glas St Ninian 88-90; R Tighnabruaich *Arg*

90-91 and 94-99; R Dunoon 90-99; Miss to Seamen 90-99; R Fort William *Arg* from 99. *St Andrew's Rectory, Parade Road, Fort William PH33 6BA* T/F: (01397) 702979 E: ftwilliam@argyll.anglican.org *or* alexinness@ymail.com

GUINNESS, Canon Peter Grattan. b 49. Man Univ BSc 71 CertEd 73. St Jo Coll Nottm 80. **d** 82 **p** 83. C Normanton *Wakef* 82-87; V Fletchamstead *Cov* 87-91; V Lancaster St Thos *Blackb* 91-10; Hon Can Blackb Cathl 04-10; P-in-c Gillingham St Mark *Roch* 10-14; rtd 14. *56 Malvern Road, Gillingham ME7 4BB* E: peter.guinness@yahoo.co.uk

GUINNESS, Canon Robin Gordon. b 38. St Jo Coll Cam MA 61. Ridley Hall Cam 63. **d** 63 **p** 64. C Bedworth *Cov* 63-66; CMS 66-68; Canada from 68. *1243-109 Front Street East, Toronto ON M5A 4P7, Canada* E: rguinnness@primus.ca

GUINNESS, Sarah. b 76. Cant Ch Ch Univ Coll BSc 98. STETS 11. **d** 14 **p** 15. C Buckhurst Hill *Chelmsf* from 14. *71 Chestnut Avenue, Buckhurst Hill IG9 6EP* E: sarah.guinness@yahoo.co.uk

GUISE, John Christopher. b 29. Cheltenham & Glouc Coll of HE MA 94 MRPharmS 51. WMMTC 80. **d** 83 **p** 84. NSM Alfrick, Lulsley, Suckley, Leigh and Bransford *Worc* 83-94; NSM Martley and Wichenford, Knightwick etc 94-00; PtO from 00. *Marsh Cottage, Leigh, Worcester WR6 5LE* T: (01886) 832336

GUISE, Stephen. b 48. Win Sch of Art BA 75. Chich Th Coll 85. **d** 87 **p** 88. C Bexhill St Pet *Chich* 87-90; TV Haywards Heath St Wilfrid 90-94; V Kirdford 94-97; Chapl Community of Servants of the Cross 97-01; P-in-c Amberley w N Stoke and Parham, Wiggonholt etc *Chich* 99-03; TV Bridport *Sarum* 03-07; rtd 07; PtO *Chich* 07-09; P-in-c Sidlesham from 09. *The Vicarage, Church Farm Lane, Sidlesham, Chichester PO20 7RE* T: (01243) 641237

GUITE, Ayodeji Malcolm. b 57. Pemb Coll Cam BA 80 MA 84 Newc Poly PGCE 82 Dur Univ PhD 93. Ridley Hall Cam 88. **d** 90 **p** 91. C Ely 90-93; TV Huntingdon 93-98; Chapl Anglia Poly Univ 98-03; Chapl Girton Coll Cam from 03. *Girton College, Cambridge CB3 0JG* T: (01223) 338999 E: mg320@cam.ac.uk

GUITE, Mrs Frances Clare. b 56. Leeds Univ BA 08. Coll of Resurr Mirfield 06. **d** 08 **p** 09. C Westleigh St Pet *Man* 08-11; C Westleigh St Paul 09-11; P-in-c Castleton Moor from 11. *St Martin's Vicarage, Vicarage Road North, Rochdale OL11 2TE* T: (01706) 632353 M: 07791-328624 E: francesguite@yahoo.co.uk

GUITE, Canon Margaret Ann. b 53. Girton Coll Cam BA 74 MA 78 St Jo Coll Dur PhD 81. Cranmer Hall Dur 75. **dss** 79 **d** 87 **p** 94. Warlingham w Chelsham and Farleigh *S'wark* 79-82; Cherry Hinton St Jo *Ely* 82-86; Tutor Westcott Ho Cam 82-90; Tutor Wesley Ho Cam 87-90; NSM Ely 90-93; NSM Chettisham 90-93; NSM Prickwillow 90-93; NSM Huntingdon 93-99; V Fenstanton 99-06; V Hilton 99-06; RD Huntingdon 05-06; P-in-c Cambridge St Mark 06-15; TV Linton from 15; Hon Can Ely Cathl from 04. *The Rectory, 11A Joiners Road, Linton CB21 4NP* T: (01223) 327621 E: margaret.guite@ntlworld.com

GUIVER, Paul Alfred (George). b 45. St Chad's Coll Dur BA 68. Cuddesdon Coll 71. **d** 73 **p** 74. C Mill End and Heronsgate w W Hyde *St Alb* 73-76; P-in-c Bishop's Frome *Heref* 76-82; P-in-c Castle Frome 76-82; P-in-c Acton Beauchamp and Evesbatch w Stanford Bishop 76-82; CR from 85; Superior CR from 02; LtO from 85. *House of the Resurrection, Stocks Bank Road, Mirfield WF14 0BN* T: (01924) 483301 F: 490489 E: gguiver@mirfield.org.uk

GUIVER, Roger William Antony. b 53. Edin Univ MA 75 St Chad's Coll Dur BA 78. Coll of Resurr Mirfield. **d** 82 **p** 83. C Rekendyke *Dur* 82-85; Chapl Middlesbrough Gen Hosp 85-91; Chapl S Tees Acute Hosps NHS Trust 92-93; P-in-c Middlesbrough St Columba w St Paul *York* 85-94; V Acomb Moor 94-97; V Middlesbrough St Thos 97-00. *Swang Farm, Glaisdale, Whitby YO21 2QZ* T: (01947) 897210

GULL, William John. b 42. Ripon Hall Ox 63. **d** 65 **p** 66. C Worksop Priory *S'well* 65-69; C Newark St Mary 69-71; P-in-c Mansfield St Lawr 71-77; V 77-78; Chapl HM YOI Lowdham Grange 78-90; R Lambley *S'well* 78-91; V Sneinton St Cypr 91-99; rtd 99; PtO *S'well* from 03. *37 Hazel Grove, Mapperley, Nottingham NG3 6DQ* T: 0115-920 8071 E: wjgull@btopenworld.com

GULLAND, John Robertson. b 46. Open Univ BA 76 Chelsea Coll Lon MA 82 Avery Hill Coll CertEd 70 ACIB. Oak Hill Th Coll 88. **d** 90 **p** 91. NSM Woodside Park St Barn *Lon* 90-92; LtO *S & M* 91-09; NSM Castletown 92-09; Chapl K Wm's Coll Is of Man 92-09; P-in-c Corfu *Eur* 09-12; PtO *S & M* from 13; Dir Studies from 14. *3 Snaefell House, Promenade, Port Erin, Isle of Man IM9 6LE* T: (01624) 834548 E: gulland@talk21.com

GULLIDGE, Philip Michael Nowell. b 60. Univ of Wales (Swansea) BSc 82 Univ of Wales (Cardiff) BD 93. St Mich Coll Llan 90. **d** 93 **p** 94. C Neath w Llantwit *Llan* 93-97; V Treharris w Bedlinog 97-03; V Treharris, Trelewis and Bedlinog 04-08; V Llantwit Fardre from 08. *The Vicarage, Church Village, Pontypridd CF38 1EP* T: (01443) 202538
E: philipgullidge@aol.com

GULLIFORD, Mrs Susan Diane. b 49. W Midl Coll of Educn BEd 86. WMMTC 97. **d** 00 **p** 01. NSM Tettenhall Regis *Lich* 00-02; C Wednesfield 02-04; PtO 04-11. *2 James Street, Willenhall WV13 1SS* E: sue.gulliford@btinternet.com

GULLIFORD, Canon William Douglas FitzGerald. b 69. Selw Coll Cam BA 91 MA 95. Westcott Ho Cam. **d** 94 **p** 95. C Banstead *Guildf* 94-97; C Wilton Place St Paul *Lon* 97-00; Chapl Guildhall Sch of Music and Drama 97-01; P-in-c St Dunstan in the West 00-08; V 08-12; Gen Sec Angl and E Churches Assn 00-05; Bp's Chapl *Lon* 00-02; R St Mary le Strand w St Clem Danes 02-08; Bp's Chapl for E Orthodox Affairs 02-12; V Regent's Park St Mark from 12; Dioc Dir of Ords *Eur* from 03; Hon Can from 12. *St Mark's Vicarage, 4 Regent's Park Road, London NW1 7TX* T: (020) 7485 6340
E: william.gulliford@london.anglican.org

GULLY, Mrs Carol Glenys. b 57. Coll of Ripon & York St Jo BEd 79. NOC 02. **d** 05 **p** 06. NSM Castleton Moor *Man* 05-09; NSM Kirkholt 09-10; Asst Chapl Pennine Acute Hosps NHS Trust 08-10; PtO *Portsm* 10-11; NSM Portsea St Cuth from 11; Asst Chapl Portsm Hosps NHS Trust 12-13; Chapl The Rowans Hospice from 13. *The Rectory, 27 Farlington Avenue, Cosham, Portsmouth PO6 1DF* T: (023) 9237 5145 *or* 9225 0001
E: revdcarolggully@gmail.com

GULLY, Paul David. b 59. Shoreditch Coll Lon BEd 81. Trin Coll Bris BA 95. **d** 95 **p** 96. C Radcliffe *Man* 95-99; TV New Bury 99-05; V Oakenrod and Bamford 05-10; R Farlington *Portsm* from 10. *The Rectory, 27 Farlington Avenue, Cosham, Portsmouth PO6 1DF* T: (023) 9237 5145
E: paul@farlingtonparish.co.uk

GULVIN, Philip Christopher. b 53. BSc 76. St Jo Coll Nottm 82. **d** 85 **p** 86. C Northwood H Trin *Lon* 85-89; TV Sanderstead All SS *S'wark* 89-96; V Croydon St Matt 96-99; C W Wickham St Fran 99-02; C W Wickham St Fran and St Mary 02-04; rtd 04. *2 Ellis Close, Five Oak Green, Tonbridge TN12 6PQ*
E: gulvins@tiscali.co.uk

GUMBEL, Jonathan Philip. b 82. Oriel Coll Ox BA 05. NTMTC 07. **d** 09 **p** 10. C Brighton St Pet *Chich* from 09. *112 Islingword Road, Brighton BN2 9SG*
E: jonny@stpetersbrighton.org

GUMBEL, Nicholas Glyn Paul. b 55. Trin Coll Cam MA 76. Wycliffe Hall Ox MA 86. **d** 86 **p** 87. C Brompton H Trin w Onslow Square St Paul *Lon* 86-05; V 05-11; V Onslow Square and S Kensington St Aug from 11. *Holy Trinity Vicarage, 73 Princes Gate Mews, London SW7 2PP* T: (020) 7052 0263 *or* 7052 0264 F: 7589 3390
E: roslyn.dehaan@htb.org.uk

GUNASEKERA, Nilanka Keith (Kit). b 72. Ridley Hall Cam 04. **d** 06 **p** 07. C Brentford *Lon* 06-09; P-in-c Clapham St Jas *S'wark* from 09. *The Vicarage, 8A West Road, London SW4 7DN* M: 07968-591695 E: kit_gunasekera@yahoo.co.uk

GUNDERSON, Ross. b 79. Westcott Ho Cam 13. **d** 15. C Dulwich St Barn *S'wark* from 15. *70 Frankfurt Road, London SE24 9NY* T: (020) 8693 1524 M: 07962-274381
E: gunderson_ross@hotmail.com

GUNN, Jeffrey Thomas. b 47. St Chad's Coll Dur BA 77 Kent Univ MA 95. Coll of Resurr Mirfield 77. **d** 79 **p** 80. C Prestbury *Glouc* 79-82; P-in-c Coldham, Elm and Friday Bridge *Ely* 82-87; V Larkfield *Roch* 87-94; P-in-c Leybourne 87-94; V Petts Wood 94-99; Dean Ballarat Australia 99-04; V Eastbourne St Sav and St Pet *Chich* from 05; RD Eastbourne from 10. *St Saviour's Vicarage, Spencer Road, Eastbourne BN21 4PA* T: (01323) 722317

GUNN, Robert. b 35. Oak Hill Th Coll 59. **d** 62 **p** 63. C Upper Holloway St Jo *Lon* 62-66; C Woking St Jo *Guildf* 66-69; Scripture Union 69-71; R Necton w Holme Hale *Nor* 71-77; V Tottenham St Jo *Lon* 77-81; V Gt Cambridge Road St Jo and St Jas 82-85; V Luton St Fran *St Alb* 85-90; Chapl Luton Airport 90-95; rtd 95; PtO *St Alb* 95-15. *95 Edgewood Drive, Luton LU2 8ER* T: (01582) 416151

GUNN-JOHNSON, The Ven David Allan. b 49. Lambeth STh 85 MA 95. St Steph Ho Ox 79. **d** 81 **p** 82. C Oxhey St Matt *St Alb* 81-84; C Cheshunt 84-88; TR Colyton, Southleigh, Offwell, Widworthy etc *Ex* 88-03; RD Honiton 90-96; Preb Ex Cathl 99-03; Adn Barnstaple 03-14; Warden of Readers 04-14; rtd 14. *12 Hylton Gardens, Exeter EX4 2QE*

GUNNER, Canon Laurence François Pascal. b 36. Keble Coll Ox BA 59 MA 63. Wells Th Coll 59. **d** 61 **p** 62. C Charlton Kings St Mary *Glouc* 61-65; C Hemel Hempstead *St Alb* 65-69; Hd RE Adeyfield Secondary Modern Sch 67-69; Chapl Bloxham Sch 69-86; Chapl Tudor Hall Sch 70-84; Sen Chapl Marlborough Coll 86-96; Can Windsor 96-06; Can Steward 97-06; rtd 06; LtO *Mor* from 07. *Contin Mains, Contin, Strathpeffer IV14 9ES* T/F: (01997) 421996 M: 07836-369729
E: laurence@gunner.co.uk

GUNNER, Mrs Susanna Mary. b 58. St Jo Coll Dur BA 80 Anglia Ruskin Univ MA 10 SS Coll Cam PGCE 81. ERMC 05. **d** 08 **p** 09. Dioc Lay Development and Tr Co-ord *Nor* from 07; C N Walsham and Edingthorpe 08-11; NSM from 13. *36 Vicarage Street, North Walsham NR28 9DQ* T: (01692) 405501 *or* (01603) 882336
E: susanna.gunner@dioceseofnorwich.org

GUNSTONE, Canon John Thomas Arthur. b 27. St Chad's Coll Dur BA 48 MA 55. Coll of Resurr Mirfield 50. **d** 52 **p** 53. C Walthamstow St Jas Gt *Chelmsf* 52-53; C Forest Gate St Edm 53-58; C-in-c Rush Green St Aug CD 58-71; Chapl Barn Fellowship Winterborne Whitechurch 71-75; Tutor Sarum & Wells Th Coll 71-75; Sec Gtr Man Co Ecum Coun 75-92; LtO *Man* 75-80; Hon Can Man Cathl 80-92; rtd 92; PtO *Man* from 03. *12 Deneford Road, Didsbury, Manchester M20 2TD* T: 0161-434 8351

GUNTER, Timothy Wilson. b 37. Leeds Univ BA 59 St Jo Coll Cam BA 62 MA 66. Ridley Hall Cam 59. **d** 62 **p** 63. C Beverley Minster *York* 62-65; C Hornsea and Goxhill 65-70; V Silsden *Bradf* 70-80; V Sunninghill *Ox* 80-03; rtd 03; PtO *Worc* from 04. *2 Hillstone Court, Victoria Road, Malvern WR14 2TE* T: (01684) 899377 E: gunters@gmail.com

GURD, Brian Charles (Simon). b 44. Sarum & Wells Th Coll 72. **d** 74 **p** 75. OSP from 67; LtO *Win* 74-82; Prior Alton Abbey 79-82; C Shepherd's Bush St Steph w St Thos *Lon* 82-84; NSM Willesborough *Cant* 85-87; V Bethersden w High Halden 87-95; R Etchingham and V Hurst Green *Chich* 95-97; V Langney 97-01; R Yarm *York* 01-10; rtd 10. *Barley Cottage, Main Street, Beckley, Rye TN31 6RS* T: (01797) 260244
E: simongurd@btinternet.com

GURDON, Mrs June Mary. b 38. Sarum Th Coll 83. **dss** 85 **d** 87 **p** 94. Jersey St Sav *Win* 85-86; Jersey St Mary 86-88; Par Dn 87-88; Par Dn Jersey St Brelade 88-94; C 94-00; rtd 00; PtO *Win* 00-14. *Dower House Alfriston, La Route d'Ebenezer, Trinity, Jersey JE3 3EH* T: (01534) 863245 M: 07797-736280

GURNER (formerly RAVEN), Mrs Margaret Ann. b 54. Westmr Univ BSc 76 City Univ MSc 87. Ridley Hall Cam 03. **d** 05 **p** 06. C Woodhall Spa Gp *Linc* 05-08; P-in-c Cheveley *Ely* 08-12; P-in-c Wood Ditton w Saxon Street 08-12; P-in-c Kirtling 08-12; P-in-c Ashley w Silverley 08-12; rtd 12. *Wilderness, Church Street, Lopen, South Petherton TA13 5JX* T: (01460) 249253 E: revgurner@btinternet.com

GURNEY, Miss Ann. b 27. Lambeth STh 92. Gilmore Ho 45. **dss** 54 **d** 87 **p** 94. Lewisham St Jo Southend *S'wark* 54-56; Warden Berridge Ho Coll of Educn 56-59; Prin Gilmore Ho 59-70; Bp's Adv for Lay Min *Lon* 70-87; rtd 87; Hon C Eltham H Trin *S'wark* from 98. *3 Brecon Court, Greenacres, London SE9 5BG* T: (020) 8850 4083

GURNEY, Canon Dennis Albert John. b 31. OBE 02. Lon Coll of Div. **d** 67 **p** 68. C Boscombe St Jo *Win* 67-69; V Hurstbourne Tarrant and Faccombe 70-77; R Jersey St Ouen w St Geo 77-84; Hon Chapl Miss to Seafarers from 84; Chapl ICS UAE 84-01; Can Bahrain 98; rtd 01; PtO *Ex* from 02; *B & W* from 02. *3 Stevens Cross Close, Sidford, Sidmouth EX10 9QJ* T: (01395) 515362 M: 07789-111226
E: d.gurney123@btinternet.com

GURNEY, Jean Elizabeth. *See* MAYHEW, Jean Elizabeth

GURNEY, Nicholas Peter. b 69. St Jo Coll Nottm 09. **d** 11 **p** 12. C Ashby-de-la-Zouch and Breedon on the Hill *Leic* 11-14; V Boulton *Derby* from 14. *The Vicarage, 1 St Mary's Close, Alvaston, Derby DE24 0GF* M: 07841-842540
E: revnickcofe@live.com

GURR, Mrs Mary Sandra. b 42. SAOMC 95. **d** 98 **p** 99. C Easthampstead *Ox* 98-02; TV High Wycombe 02-09; rtd 09; Chapl Pipers Corner Sch from 04; Chapl to the Homeless *Ox* from 11. *12 Navigation Way, Oxford OX2 6XW* T: (01865) 552010 E: mary.gurr1@btinternet.com

GURR, Stephen John. b 72. Kent Univ BA 94. Trin Coll Bris MLitt 97. **d** 97 **p** 98. C Ore St Helen and St Barn *Chich* 97-00; C Goring-by-Sea 00-03; V Findon w Clapham and Patching 03-06; Chapl St Barn Ho Worthing from 07; Chapl Chestnut Tree Ho Arundel from 07; PtO *Chich* from 07. *c/o St Barnabas House, Titnore Lane, Worthing BN12 6NZ*
E: stephen.gurr@stbh.org.uk

GUSSMAN, Canon Robert William Spencer Lockhart. b 50. Ch Ch Ox BA 72 MA 76. Coll of Resurr Mirfield BA 74. **d** 75 **p** 76. C Pinner *Lon* 75-79; C Northolt St Jos 79-81; P-in-c Sutton *Ely* 81-82; V 82-89; P-in-c Witcham w Mepal 81-82; R 82-89;

RD Ely 86-89; V Alton St Lawr *Win* 89-02; Hon Can Win Cathl 99-02; rtd 02; PtO *Win* 02-10. *6A Patrick's Close, Liss GU33 7ER* T: (01730) 893545

GUTHRIE, Adrian Malcolm. b 57. Goldsmiths' Coll Lon BEd 80. Wycliffe Hall Ox 01. **d** 03 **p** 04. C Ickenham *Lon* 03-05; R 05-13; R Alcester Minster *Cov* from 13. *St Nicholas' Rectory, Old Rectory Garden, Alcester B49 5DB*
E: adrianmguthrie@gmail.com

GUTHRIE, Preb Nigel. b 60. Bris Univ BA 82 LRAM 78 ARCO 80 ARCM 81. Ripon Coll Cuddesdon BA 87 MA 91. **d** 88 **p** 89. C Cov St Jo 88-91; Chapl Cov Cathl 91-94; V Chellaston *Derby* 94-02; RD Melbourne 99-02; R Crediton, Shobrooke and Sandford etc *Ex* from 02; Preb Ex Cathl from 10. *The Rectory, Church Street, Crediton EX17 2AQ* T: (01363) 772669 *or* 773226 E: rev.guthrie@btinternet.com

GUTSELL, Canon David Leonard Nicholas. b 35. Sheff Univ BA 59. ALCD 61. **d** 61 **p** 62. C Clapham Common St Barn *S'wark* 61-65; V Upper Tulse Hill St Matthias 65-76; RD Clapham and Brixton 74-75; V Patcham *Chich* 76-93; Can and Preb Chich Cathl 89-00; V Polegate 93-00; rtd 00; C Peacehaven and Telscombe Cliffs *Chich* 01-05; C Southease 01-05; C Piddinghoe 01-05; PtO from 05. *6 Solway Avenue, Brighton BN1 8UJ* T: (01273) 554434
E: davidgutsell@googlemail.com

GUTSELL, Eric Leslie. b 44. Goldsmiths' Coll Lon TCert 65. Ox NSM Course 79. **d** 82 **p** 83. NSM Gt Faringdon w Lt Coxwell *Ox* 82-88; NSM Shrivenham w Watchfield and Bourton 82-99; Asst Chapl HM Pris Wormwood Scrubs 99-00; Chapl HM Pris Coldingley 00-03; Chapl HM Pris Erlestoke 03-04; rtd 04; PtO *Ox* from 05. *54 Folly View Road, Faringdon SN7 7DH* T: (01367) 240886
E: ericgutsell@virgin.net

GUTTERIDGE, David Frank. b 39. Man Univ BSc 61 Lon Inst of Educn PGCE 62 DipEd 67 Birkbeck Coll Lon MSc 73. WMMTC 82. **d** 85 **p** 87. NSM Droitwich *Worc* 85-87; NSM Droitwich Spa 87-93; C Shrawley, Witley, Astley and Abberley 93-98; Chapl Abberley Hall Sch *Worc* 93-97; Dioc Tertiary Educn Officer *Worc* 97-99; NSM Ombersley w Doverdale 98-99; TV Malvern Link w Cowleigh 99-02; rtd 02. *79 Tan House Lane, Malvern WR14 1LQ* T: (01886) 833578
M: 07962-129241 E: david@mlwc.co.uk

GUTTERIDGE, John. b 34. Oak Hill Th Coll 60. **d** 63 **p** 64. C Deptford St Luke *S'wark* 63-66; C Southgate *Chich* 66-70; P-in-c Brixton Road Ch Ch *S'wark* 70-73; P-in-c Manuden w Berden *Chelmsf* 73-76; Distr Sec (N Lon, Herts and Essex) BFBS 76-82; Hon C Walthamstow St Gabr *Chelmsf* 79-82; V 82-95; Chapl Thorpe Coombe Psycho-Geriatric Hosp 83-95; rtd 95; PtO *Chelmsf* 95-12. *52 Hatch Road, Pilgrims Hatch, Brentwood CM15 9PX* T: (01277) 375401
E: john_gutteridge@hotmail.com

GUTTERIDGE, John Philip. b 52. QUB BA 74. Chich Th Coll 75. **d** 78 **p** 79. C Leeds St Aid *Ripon* 78-82; C Manston 82-85; P-in-c Beeston Hill H Spirit 85-00; PtO *Leeds* from 03. *4 Amberton Garth, Leeds LS8 3JW*

GUTTRIDGE (née EVANS), Mrs Frances Margaret Bethan. b 54. Reading Univ BSc 75 Univ of Wales (Cardiff) PGCE 76. STETS. **d** 00 **p** 01. C Weston-super-Mare St Andr Bournville *B & W* 00-04; V 04-09; C Watchet and Williton from 09. *The Vicarage, 47A Brendon Road, Watchet TA23 0HU*
T: (01984) 631103 M: 07778-137454
E: bethanguttridge@hotmail.com

GUTTRIDGE, John William. b 54. Surrey Univ BSc 75 Cardiff Coll of Educn PGCE 76 MRSC 95. STETS 08. **d** 11 **p** 12. NSM Aisholt, Enmore, Goathurst, Nether Stowey etc *B & W* 11-15; PtO from 15. *The Vicarage, 47A Brendon Road, Watchet TA23 0HU* T: (01984) 631228 M: 07813-350710
E: jwguttridge@hotmail.com

GUY, Mrs Alison. b 43. CQSW 69. WMMTC 95. **d** 98 **p** 99. NSM Minchinhampton *Glouc* 98-04; C Bisley, Chalford, France Lynch, and Oakridge 04-08. *7 Tooke Road, Minchinhampton, Stroud GL6 9DA* T: (01453) 883906
E: alisonguy@metronet.co.uk

GUY, Ian Towers. b 47. Newc Univ MB, BS 70 MSc 89 MRCGP. NEOC. **d** 83 **p** 84. NSM Saltburn-by-the-Sea *York* 83-88; NSM Skelton w Upleatham 88-92; PtO from 92. *14 North Terrace, Skelton-in-Cleveland, Saltburn-by-the-Sea TS12 2ES*
T: (01287) 650309 M: 07092-298033 E: iantguy@mac.com

GUY, John Richard. *See* MORGAN-GUY, John Richard

GUY, Kate Anne. b 26. **d** 88 **p** 94. OLM Welton *Linc* 88-92; OLM Welton and Dunholme w Scothern 92-96; PtO 96-02. *Address temp unknown*

GUY, Peter-John. b 71. Bournemouth Univ BA 93. Oak Hill Th Coll BA 03. **d** 03 **p** 04. C Eastbourne All So *Chich* 03-07; C Lindfield 07-11; V Horam from 11. *The Vicarage, Horebeech Lane, Horam, Heathfield TN21 0DT* T: (01435) 813372
E: pjgerdaguy@hotmail.com

GUY, Simon Edward Walrond. b 39. St Andr Univ MA 61. St D Coll Lamp LTh 67. **d** 67 **p** 68. C Bris St Mary Redcliffe w Temple etc 67-68; C Knowle St Martin 68-71; C Bishopston 71-75; V Westwood *Sarum* 75-81; TV Melksham 81-82; TV Wednesfield *Lich* 82-90; R Heaton Moor *Man* 90-02; P-in-c Heaton Norris Ch w All SS 99-01; TV Heatons 02-04; rtd 04. *1 Holley Close, Exminster, Exeter EX6 8SS*
T: (01392) 823084 E: sewguy@supanet.com

GUYMER, Canon Raymond John. b 41. AKC 64. St Boniface Warminster. **d** 65 **p** 66. C W Bromwich All SS *Lich* 65-70; Chapl HM Pris Wormwood Scrubs 70-71 and 84-93; Chapl HM Borstal Portland 71-78; Chapl HM Youth Cust Cen Hollesley Bay Colony 78-84; Chapl HM Pris Win 93-01; Hon C Upper Itchen *Win* 02-06; Hon Can Win Cathl 99-06; rtd 06. *16 St Mary's Gardens, Hilperton Marsh, Trowbridge BA14 7PG* T: (01225) 751063

GUZEK, Mrs Bridget Louise. b 47. York Univ BA 70 Keswick Hall Coll PGCE 79. STETS 05. **d** 08 **p** 09. NSM E Clevedon w Clapton in Gordano etc *B & W* 08-12; P-in-c St Buryan, St Levan and Sennen *Truro* 12-13; C St Stythians w Perranarworthal and Gwennap from 14; C Chacewater w St Day and Carharrack from 14; C Feock from 14; C Devoran from 14. *The Vicarage, 2 Old Vicarage Close, Stithians, Truro TR3 7DZ* E: blguzek@gmail.com

GWILLIAM, Christopher. b 44. St Chad's Coll Dur BA 65. **d** 67 **p** 68. C Chepstow *Mon* 67-70; C Risca 70-72; V Cwmtillery 72-75; V Hartlepool St Oswald *Dur* 75-82; Relig Progr Producer Radio Tees 82-87; C Stockton w St Jo *Dur* 82-83; R Longnewton w Elton 83-87; Relig Progr Producer Radio Nottm *S'well* 87-93; Relig Progr Producer BBC Network Radio 93-95; rtd 04. *Les Perreaux, 71140 Maltat, France* T: (0033) 3 85 84 87 57
E: christopher.gwilliam@googlemail.com

GWILLIAMS, The Very Revd Dianna Lynn. b 57. California Univ BA 78 K Coll Lon MA 01. S'wark Ord Course 89. **d** 92 **p** 94. NSM Peckham St Sav *S'wark* 92-97; C Dulwich St Barn 97-99; V 99-13; P-in-c Peckham St Sav 07-11; AD Dulwich 05-12; Dean of Women's Min 09-12; Chapl Alleyn's Foundn Dulwich 99-13; Hon Can S'wark Cathl 06-13; Dean Guildf from 13. *The Deanery, Cathedral Close, Guildford GU2 7TL* F: 303350 T: (01483) 547860
E: dean@guildford-cathedral.org

GWILLIM, Allan John. b 51. Coll of Resurr Mirfield 87. **d** 89 **p** 90. C Skerton St Luke *Blackb* 89-94; P-in-c Ellel 94-98; V Fleetwood St Pet 98-06; V Leyland St Jas 06-08; V Ocker Hill *Lich* from 08; RD Wednesbury from 13. *St Mark's Vicarage, Ocker Hill Road, Tipton DY4 0UT* T: 0121-556 0678
E: allan.gwillim@btinternet.com

GWILT, Stephen Gary. b 59. **d** 88 **p** 89. S Africa 88-94; Chapl Glouc Docks Mariners' Ch 95-00; C Moreton *Ches* 00-03; R High Halstow w All Hallows and Hoo St Mary *Roch* from 03. *The Rectory, 2 Cooling Road, High Halstow, Rochester ME3 8SA* T: (01634) 250637

GWINN, Brian Harvey. b 35. MIQA 75. St Alb Minl Tr Scheme 83. **d** 86 **p** 87. NSM Wheathampstead *St Alb* 86-88; Ind Chapl 88-95; RD Hatfield 93-95; P-in-c Watton at Stone 95-99; P-in-c Bramfield w Stapleford and Waterford 96-99; R Bramfield, Stapleford, Waterford etc 99-01; rtd 01; PtO *St Alb* from 01. *18 Kingfisher Close, Wheathampstead, St Albans AL4 8JJ* T: (01582) 629903 M: 07966-469754
E: gwinns@ntlworld.com

GWINNETT, Clifton Harry. b 57. Cranmer Hall Dur 08. **d** 10 **p** 11. C Golcar and Longwood *Wakef* 10-13; V Thornton St Jas Leeds from 13. *The Vicarage, Thornton Road, Thornton, Bradford BD13 3AB* M: 07817-526342 E: harry@james4u.org

GWYN-THOMAS, James John. b 82. Ex Univ BA 03. Wycliffe Hall Ox BTh 13. **d** 13 **p** 14. C Leyland St Andr *Blackb* from 13. *1 Bridgewater Drive, Buckshaw Village, Chorley PR7 7EU* T: (01772) 456494 M: 07988-66360
E: jamesgwynthomas@gmail.com

GWYNN, Mrs Fiona Jane. b 67. SCRTP 12. **d** 15. OLM Haslemere and Grayswood *Guildf* from 15. *The Gables, Park Close, Grayswood, Haslemere GU27 2DT* T: (01428) 654728
E: gwynnfamily@sky.com

GWYNN, Phillip John. b 57. Univ of Wales (Lamp) BA 87 MA 04. St Mich Coll Llan 87. **d** 89 **p** 90. C Clydach *S & B* 89-93; V Swansea St Thos and Kilvey 93-00; Hon Chapl Miss to Seafarers 93-00; V Tycoch *S & B* from 00; AD Clyne from 12; Chapl Swansea NHS Trust from 00. *The Vicarage, 26 Hendrefoilan Road, Swansea SA2 9LS* T/F: (01792) 204476 M: 07946-351787 E: phillip@gwynn.org.uk

GWYNNE, Robert Durham. b 44. Qu Coll Birm 67. **d** 70 **p** 72. C N Hammersmith St Kath *Lon* 70-75; C Ramsey *Ely* 76-78; TV Old Brumby *Linc* 78-81; P-in-c Goxhill and Thornton Curtis 81-83; C Edmonton All SS w St Mich *Lon* 83-84; rtd 86. *127 Eastfield Road, Louth LN11 7AS* T: (01507) 600966

GWYTHER, Canon Geoffrey David. b 51. St D Coll Lamp. **d** 74 **p** 75. C Pembroke Dock *St D* 74-77; C Milford Haven 77-81; V Llawhaden w Bletherston and Llanycefn 81-88; R Prendergast w Rudbaxton from 88; AD Daugleddau 01-12; Can St D Cathl from 01; Treas from 14. *Prendergast Rectory, 5 Cherry Grove, Haverfordwest SA61 2NT* T: (01437) 762625

GWYTHER, Ronald Lloyd. b 23. Lon Univ BA 85 Southn Univ MA 97. St Fran Coll Brisbane ThL 47. **d** 47 **p** 48. Australia 48-50; PtO *Ox* 50-51; Australia 51-56; C Broadstairs *Cant* 56-60; R Pinxton *Derby* 60-73; CF (TA) 71-88; V Swanley St Mary *Roch* 73-89; rtd 89; PtO *Portsm* 89-13. *c/o Mrs E Eyre, Box Cottage, The Street, Bethersden, Ashford TN26 3AD*

GYLE, Alan Gordon. b 65. Aber Univ MA 87 Ox Univ BA 91 Univ of E Lon MA 09 FRSA 99. St Steph Ho Ox. **d** 92 **p** 93. C Acton Green *Lon* 92-94; Min Can, Succ and Dean's V Windsor 94-99; Chapl Imp Coll and R Coll of Art 99-04; P-in-c Wilton Place St Paul *Lon* 01-03; V from 03; PV Westmr Abbey from 07; Dir Development Two Cities Area *Lon* 08-12. *St Paul's Vicarage, 32 Wilton Place, London SW1X 8SH* T/F: (020) 7201 9990 T: 7201 9999 E: alan@stpaulsknightsbridge.org

GYLES, Ms Sonia. b 76. TCD BTh 01. CITC 98. **d** 01 **p** 02. C Taney *D & G* 01-04; I Dublin Sandford w Milltown from 04; Chan V St Patr Cathl Dublin 01-07. *The Rectory, Sandford Close, Ranelagh, Dublin 6, Republic of Ireland* T: (00353) (1) 497 2983 E: sandford@dublin.anglican.org

H

HAARHOFF, Preb Robert Russell. b 46. St Paul's Coll Grahamstown 89 Th Ext Educn Coll 91. **d** 90 **p** 91. Harare Cathl Zimbabwe 91-94; I Makonde 94-02; P-in-c Astley, Clive, Grinshill and Hadnall *Lich* from 02; RD Wem and Whitchurch 08-13; Preb Lich Cathl from 11. *The Vicarage, Shrewsbury Road, Hadnall, Shrewsbury SY4 4AG* T: (01939) 210241 E: robhaarhoff@tiscali.co.uk

HABERSHON, Kenneth Willoughby. b 35. MBE 01. New Coll Ox BA 57 MA 60. Wycliffe Hall Ox 57. **d** 59 **p** 60. C Finchley Ch Ch *Lon* 59-66; Sec CYFA 66-74; CPAS Staff 74-90; Hon C Slaugham *Chich* 84-10; Hon C Slaugham and Staplefield Common from 10; Ldr Mayfield CYFA 90-00; rtd 00; Sec Ch Patr Trust 90-07; Sec Peache Trustees 90-11. *Truckers Ghyll, Horsham Road, Handcross, Haywards Heath RH17 6DT* T: (01444) 400274 E: kandmhab@btopenworld.com

✠**HABGOOD, The Rt Revd and Rt Hon Lord (John Stapylton).** b 27. PC 83. K Coll Cam BA 48 MA 51 PhD 52 Dur Univ Hon DD 75 Cam Univ Hon DD 84 Aber Univ Hon DD 88 Huron Coll Hon DD 90. Cuddesdon Coll 53. **d** 54 **p** 55 **c** 73. C Kensington St Mary Abbots w St Geo *Lon* 54-56; Vice-Prin Westcott Ho Cam 56-62; R Jedburgh *Edin* 62-67; Prin Qu Coll Birm 67-73; Hon Can Birm Cathl 71-73; Bp Dur 73-83; Abp York 83-95; rtd 95. *18 The Mount, Malton YO17 7ND*

HABGOOD, Simon. *See* LAWRENCE, Simon Peter

HABGOOD, Stephen Roy. b 52. Open Univ MBA 95 Fitzw Coll Cam MSt 01. St Mich Coll Llan 75. **d** 77 **p** 78. C Whitchurch *Llan* 77-80; PtO *Worc* 85-91. *Yew Tree Cottage, Wharf Road, Gnosall, Stafford ST20 0DA* T: (01785) 824244

HABIBY, Canon Samir Jamil. b 33. Phillips Univ BA 55 MA 56. Ch Div Sch of Pacific MDiv 58 Episc Th Sem Kentucky DD. **d** 58 **p** 59. R Hinesville St Phil USA 58-98; P-in-c Lausanne *Eur* 98-04; rtd 04. *24 Sawyers Crossing Road, Swanzey NH 03446, USA* T/F: (001) (603) 357 8778

HACK, Arthur John. b 52. Bris Univ BEd 75 St Paul's Coll Chelt CertEd 74. **d** 08 **p** 09. NSM Alstonfield, Butterton, Ilam etc *Lich* 08-13; Warden Dovedale Ho 89-13; NSM Watershed *Lich* from 13. *Dovedale House, Ilam, Ashbourne DE6 2AZ* T: (01335) 350365 M: 07749-294386 E: warden@dovedalehouse.org.uk

HACK, Canon Rex Hereward. b 28. ACA 56 FCA 67 Pemb Coll Cam BA 50 MA 56. Ripon Hall Ox 58. **d** 59 **p** 60. C Ashton-upon-Mersey St Mary Magd *Ches* 59-62; C Ellesmere Port 62-65; V Norton Cuckney *S'well* 65-69; V Bramhall *Ches* 69-93; RD Cheadle 87-92; Hon Can Ches Cathl 90-93; rtd 93; PtO *Ches* from 93. *Marshmead, 8A Pownall Avenue, Bramhall, Stockport SK7 2HE* T: 0161-439 0300

✠**HACKER, The Rt Revd George Lanyon.** b 28. Ex Coll Ox BA 52 MA 56. Cuddesdon Coll 52. **d** 54 **p** 55 **c** 79. C Bris St Mary Redcliffe w Temple 54-59; Chapl St Boniface Coll Warminster 59-64; V Bishopwearmouth Gd Shep *Dur* 64-71; R Tilehurst St Mich *Ox* 71-79; Suff Bp Penrith *Carl* 79-94; Hon Can Carl Cathl 79-94; Episc Adv for the Angl Young People's Assn 87-94; rtd 94; Hon Asst Bp Carl from 94. *Keld House, Milburn, Penrith CA10 1TW* T: (01768) 361506 E: bishhack@btopenworld.com

HACKER HUGHES, Katherine Lucy. b 61. York Univ BA 81. Westcott Ho Cam 90. **d** 92 **p** 94. Par Dn S Woodham Ferrers *Chelmsf* 92-94; C 94-95; NSM Maldon All SS w St Pet 95-98; Chapl Chelmsf Cathl 98-01; P-in-c Gt Waltham w Ford End 01-05; Adv relationship and family issues (Bradwell Area) 01-03; PtO from 05; Chapl Mid-Essex Hosp Services NHS Trust 06-07; Chapl Farleigh Hospice 07-14; P-in-c Newington St Paul *S'wark* from 14. *St Paul's Vicarage, Lorrimore Square, London SE17 3QU* T: (020) 7735 3506 E: katyhh@hotmail.co.uk

HACKETT, Bryan Malcolm. b 66. Magd Coll Ox BA 88 MA 93 Cam Univ BA 92 MA 03. Westcott Ho Cam 90. **d** 93 **p** 94. C Willington *Newc* 93-97; TV Radcliffe *Man* 97-03; P-in-c Prestwich St Mary 03-12; C Prestwich St Marg and Prestwich St Gabr 10-12; V Baguley 12-15. *Address temp unknown* E: bryan.hackett@btinternet.com

HACKETT, Canon Frank James. b 33. Birm Univ MA 77 AMIMechE 68 MBIM 72 MIIM 79. Bps' Coll Cheshunt 62. **d** 64 **p** 65. C Feltham *Lon* 64-69; Ind Chapl *Lich* 69-73; Ind Chapl Port of Lon *Chelmsf* 73-98; P-in-c N Ockendon 79-93; Hon Can Chelmsf Cathl 93-98; Ind Chapl 93-98; rtd 98; PtO *Lon* 98-02 and from 05; *Chelmsf* from 99. *11 Fairfield Avenue, Upminster RM14 3AZ* T: (01708) 221461

HACKETT, Glyndwr. *See* HACKETT, Ronald Glyndwr

HACKETT, John Nigel. b 32. Trin Hall Cam BA 55 MA 59. Ely Th Coll. **d** 59 **p** 60. C Handsworth St Mary *Birm* 59-66; V Handsworth St Jas 66-82; P-in-c Balsall Common 82-83; V 83-95; PtO *B & W* from 96; rtd 97. *Honeymead, Duck Lane, Kenn, Clevedon BS21 6TP* T: (01275) 876591

HACKETT, Peter Edward. b 25. Magd Coll Ox BA 48 MA 51 ALCD 60. **d** 60 **p** 61. C Lenton *S'well* 60-62; C Attenborough w Bramcote 62-63; V Lenton Abbey 63-67; R Acton Beauchamp and Evesbatch w Stanford Bishop *Heref* 67-71; V Choral Heref Cathl 72-76; P-in-c St Weonards w Orcop 76-79; P-in-c Tretire w Michaelchurch and Pencoyd 76-79; P-in-c Garway 76-79; P-in-c Welsh Newton w Llanrothal 77-79; V Rounds Green *Birm* 79-87; C Sutton Coldfield H Trin 87-90; rtd 90; NSM Shipton Moyne w Westonbirt and Lasborough *Glouc* 91-94; PtO *Birm* 94-99; *Worc* 94-99; *Heref* 00-09. *31 Capel Court, The Burgage, Prestbury, Cheltenham GL52 3EL* T: (01242) 520348

HACKETT, The Ven Ronald Glyndwr. b 47. Hatf Coll Dur BA 70. Cuddesdon Coll 70. **d** 72 **p** 73. C Pembroke St Mary w St Mich *St D* 72-75; C Bassaleg *Mon* 75-78; V Blaenavon w Capel Newydd 78-84; Chapl R Gwent Hosp 84-90; V Newport St Paul *Mon* 84-90; V Newport Ch Ch 90-01; Adn Mon 01-08; R Mamhilad and Llanfihangel Pontymoile 01-03; R Mamhilad w Monkswood and Glascoed Chapel 03-08; Adn Newport 08-12; rtd 12. *71 Castle Lea, Caldicot NP26 4PJ*

HACKETT, Victoria Anne. b 52. St Gabr Coll Lon CertEd 73 Open Univ BA 91. SEITE 97. **d** 00 **p** 01. NSM Earlsfield St Andr *S'wark* 00-14; PtO *St D* from 14. *Gelli Aur, Bryn Road, Lampeter SA48 7EE* T: (01570) 421683 E: v.ah@btopenworld.com

HACKING, Philip Henry. b 31. St Pet Hall Ox BA 53 MA 57. Oak Hill Th Coll 53. **d** 55 **p** 56. C St Helens St Helen *Liv* 55-58; C-in-c Edin St Thos 59-68; V Fulwood *Sheff* 68-97; rtd 97; PtO *Sheff* from 98. *61 Sefton Court, Sefton Road, Sheffield S10 3TP* T: 0114-230 4324 E: philiphacking@fulwood-s10.me.uk

HACKING, Rodney Douglas. b 53. K Coll Lon BD 74 AKC 74 Man Univ MA 83. St Aug Coll Cant 75. **d** 76 **p** 78. C Byker St Mich *Newc* 76-77; C Eltham St Jo *S'wark* 77-79; Ind Chapl *Ripon* 80-85; R Upwell St Pet and Outwell *Ely* 85-88; Vice Prin S Dios Minl Tr Scheme 89-93; V Bolton-le-Sands *Blackb* 93-97; In Orthodox Ch 01-03; R The Wainfleet Gp *Linc* 03-06; rtd 06. *135 The Close, Salisbury SP1 2EY* T: (01722) 417289 E: rdnyhacking@aol.com

HACKING, Stuart Peter. b 60. St Pet Coll Ox BA 82 MA. Oak Hill Th Coll 83. **d** 85 **p** 86. C Shipley St Pet *Bradf* 85-88; C Darfield *Sheff* 88-91; V Thornton St Jas *Bradf* 91-00; P-in-c Frizinghall St Marg 00-12; Chapl Immanuel Coll from 00. *33 Cyprus Gardens, Idle, Bradford BD10 8JF* T: (01274) 616473 *or* 425900 E: stuart.hacking@btinternet.com

HACKL, Aileen Patricia. b 41. Wycliffe Hall Ox 00. **d** 01 **p** 02. C Vienna *Eur* 01-09; NSM 09-11; rtd 11. *Hardtmuthgasse 28/3/20, A-1100 Vienna, Austria* T/F: (0043) (1) 600 3083 E: aileen_hackl@hotmail.com

HACKNEY, Archdeacon of. Vacant

HACKSHALL, Brian Leonard. b 33. K Coll Lon BD 53 AKC 53. **d** 57 **p** 58. C Portsea St Mary *Portsm* 57-62; C Westbury-on-Trym St Alb *Bris* 62-64; V Avonmouth St Andr 64-71; Miss to Seamen 71-79; C Crawley *Chich* 79; TV 79-98; Ind Chapl 89-98; rtd 98. *5 St Michael Street, Brecon LD3 9AB* T: (01874) 611319

HACKWOOD, Canon Paul Colin. b 61. Huddersfield Poly BSc 84 Bradf Univ MBA 05. Qu Coll Birm 86. **d** 89 **p** 90. C Horton *Bradf* 89-93; Soc Resp Adv *St Alb* 93-97; V Thornbury *Bradf* 97-05; Adn Loughborough *Leic* 05-09; Can Res Leic Cathl 07-15; Hon Can Leic Cathl from 15. *Church View Farm, Church Lane, Osgathorpe, Loughborough LE12 9SY* T: 0116-239 6533 E: paul.hackwood@leccofe.org

HADDEN, Timothy. b 48. Brighton Poly BSc 72 Surrey Univ MSc 75. **d** 05 **p** 06. OLM Watling Valley *Ox* from 05. *13 Weavers Lane, Oakridge Park, Milton Keynes MK14 6FQ* M: 07889-614386 E: tim@willetts13.freeserve.co.uk

HADDOCK, Malcolm George. b 27. Univ of Wales (Cardiff) BA 56 CertEd 73. St Deiniol's Hawarden 87. **d** 80 **p** 81. NSM Newport Ch Ch *Mon* 80-85; NSM Risca 85-87; C 87-89; C Caerleon 89-96; rtd 96; LtO *Mon* from 96. *48 Cambria Close, Caerleon, Newport NP18 1LF* T: (01633) 422960

HADDON-REECE (née STREETER), Mrs Christine Mary. b 50. St Jo Coll Nottm BTh 81 LTh 81. **dss** 83 **d** 87 **p** 94. Par Dn Stranton *Dur* 87-90; Par Dn Lastingham w Appleton-le-Moors, Rosedale etc *York* 90-94; C 94-97; V Topcliffe, Baldersby w Dishforth, Dalton etc 97-08; V Middle Esk Moor from 08. *St Hilda's Vicarage, Egton, Whitby YO21 1UT* T: (01947) 895315 E: c.haddonreece@btinternet.com

HADLEY, Ann Elizabeth Mary. *See* EVANS, Ann Elizabeth Mary

HADFIELD, Prof Brigid. b 50. Edin Univ LLB 72 QUB LLM 77 Essex Univ PhD 03. EAMTC 02. **d** 03 **p** 04. NSM Wivenhoe *Chelmsf* 03-06; NSM Shrub End 06-11; P-in-c Harston w Hauxton and Newton *Ely* from 11. *The Vicarage, Church Street, Harston, Cambridge CB22 7NP* T: (01223) 871305

HADFIELD, Christopher John Andrew Chad. b 39. Jes Coll Cam BA 61. Wells Th Coll 63. **d** 65 **p** 66. C Wigton w Waverton *Carl* 65-68; Teacher Newlands Sch Seaford 70-06; LtO *Mor* from 92; PtO *Chich* from 96. *15 The Fridays, East Dean, Eastbourne BN20 0DH* T: (01323) 422050

HADFIELD, David William. b 53. Newc Univ BA 74 MA 76 PhD 83 Barrister 82 Solicitor 88. SEITE 10. **d** 13 **p** 14. NSM E Grinstead St Mary *Chich* from 13. *Highgate House, Tomtits Lane, Forest Row RH18 5AT* T: (01342) 823105 M: 07526-792889 E: revdhad@gmail.com

HADFIELD, Derek. b 34. **d** 01 **p** 02. OLM Folkestone H Trin w Ch Ch *Cant* 01-04; OLM Sandgate St Paul w Folkestone St Geo 01-04; rtd 04; PtO *Cant* 04-11; *York* from 11. *Mon Abri, South Duffield Road, Osgodby, Selby YO8 5HW* T: (01757) 705940 E: dhaddy49@tiscali.co.uk

HADFIELD, Douglas. b 22. K Coll Cam BA 44 MA 49. St Jo Coll Nottm 84. **d** 88 **p** 89. NSM Lenzie *Glas* 88-92; rtd 92; PtO *Glas* from 92; *Pet* from 94. *8 Church Street, Helmdon, Brackley NN13 5QJ* T: (01295) 760679 E: douglas.hadfield@firelight.co.uk

HADFIELD, Graham Francis. b 48. Bris Univ BSc 69. Cranmer Hall Dur 69. **d** 73 **p** 74. C Blackpool St Thos *Blackb* 73-76; CF 76-99; Asst Chapl Gen 99-04; QHC 02-04; P-in-c Nottingham St Jude *S'well* 04-11; V 11-12; rtd 12; PtO *Chelmsf* from 13. *22 Coast Road, West Mersea, Colchester CO5 8LH* T: (01206) 382458 E: graham@hadf48.fsnet.co.uk

HADFIELD, Jonathan Benedict Philip John. b 43. Lon Univ BA 64 Jes Coll Cam BA 67 MA 72. Edin Th Coll 66. **d** 68 **p** 69. C Fort William *Arg* 68-70; Chapl K Sch Glouc and Hon Min Can Glouc Cathl 70-03; rtd 03. *36 Corsend Road, Hartpury, Gloucester GL19 3BP*

HADFIELD, Norman. b 39. Doncaster Coll of Educn TEng 78. St Mich Coll Llan 89 Llan Dioc Tr Scheme 83. **d** 86 **p** 87. NSM Ferndale w Maerdy *Llan* 86-90; C Llanbradach w Cowbridge and Llandough etc 90-92; V Resolven w Tonna 92-04; RD Neath 01-03; rtd 04; PtO *Llan* from 04. *42 Lakeside, Cwmdare, Aberdare CF44 8AX* T: (01685) 872764

HADJIOANNOU, John. b 56. Ch Coll Cam BA 78 MA 81. SAOMC 95. **d** 97 **p** 98. C Linslade *Ox* 97-00; V Kinsley w Wragby *Leeds* from 00; P-in-c Felkirk *Wakef* 05-12. *Kinsley Vicarage, Wakefield Road, Fitzwilliam, Pontefract WF9 5BX* T: (01977) 610497 E: john@minster.co.uk

HADLEY, Ann. *See* HADLEY, Elizabeth Ann

HADLEY, Charles Adrian. b 50. Trin Coll Cam BA 71 MA 75. Cuddesdon Coll 73. **d** 75 **p** 76. C Hadleigh w Layham and Shelley *St E* 75-78; C Bracknell *Ox* 78-82; R Blagdon w Compton Martin and Ubley *B & W* 82-92; RD Chew Magna 88-92; R Somerton w Compton Dundon, the Charltons etc 92-04; Chapl Ex Univ 04-10; Chemin Neuf Community Israel 10-15; Hon C Storrington *Chich* from 15. *28 Meadowside, Storrington, Pulborough RH20 4EG* T: (01903) 740787 E: charles.felicity@gmail.com

HADLEY, David Charles. b 42. **d** 02 **p** 03. NSM Kenley *S'wark* 02-13; NSM Purley St Barn 08-13; PtO from 13. *21 Park Road, Kenley CR8 5AQ* T: (020) 8763 6206 E: dchadley@btinternet.com

HADLEY, Preb Elizabeth Ann. b 33. St Jo Coll Nottm 80. **dss** 81 **d** 87 **p** 94. Aspley *S'well* 81-85; Stone St Mich w Aston St Sav *Lich* 85-92; Par Dn 87-92; P-in-c Myddle 92-97; R 97-99; P-in-c Broughton 92-97; V 97-99; Dioc Voc Officer 92-99; Preb Lich Cathl 97-99; rtd 99; P-in-c Harvington *Worc* 99-00; PtO from 00. *6 Peninsular Road, Norton, Worcester WR5 2SE* T: (01905) 353710 E: annhadley@go-plus.net

HADLEY, Mrs Georgina Ann Lacy. b 53. De Montfort Univ BA 96 PGCE 97. Linc Sch of Th and Min 12. **d** 13 **p** 14. C Retford Area *S'well* from 13. *43 Great North Road, Sutton on Trent, Newark NG23 6PL* M: 07811-393920 T: (01636) 821780 E: georgie.hadley@yahoo.co.uk

HADLEY, Canon John Spencer Fairfax. b 47. Ch Ch Ox BA 70 MA 73. Coll of Resurr Mirfield BA 72. **d** 73 **p** 74. C Stoke Newington St Mary *Lon* 73-77; C High Wycombe *Ox* 77-81; TV 82-87; P-in-c Clifton St Paul *Bris* 87-91; Sen Chapl Bris Univ 87-91; Chapl Hengrave Hall Ecum Cen 91-94; Ecum Assoc Min Chelsea Methodist Ch 94-97; Hon C Chelsea St Luke and Ch Ch *Lon* 94-97; Chapl Westcott Ho Cam 97-02; P-in-c Horfield H Trin *Bris* 02-15; R from 15; Hon Can Bris Cathl from 12. *Horfield Rectory, Wellington Hill, Bristol BS7 8ST* T: 0117-924 6185 E: john-hadley@tiscali.co.uk

HADLEY, Stuart James. b 55. K Coll Lon BD 76 AKC 76. St Steph Ho Ox 77. **d** 78 **p** 79. C Mansfield St Mark *S'well* 78-82; V Cowbit *Linc* 82-86; PtO 86-88; NSM W w E Allington and Sedgebrook 88-95; NSM Saxonwell 95-96; NSM Woolsthorpe 88-95; NSM Harlaxton Gp 95-96; PtO 97-99; NSM Barkston and Hough Gp from 99. *35 Wensleydale Close, Grantham NG31 8FH* T: (01476) 575854 E: hadleystuart@hotmail.com

HADLOW, Mrs Jennifer Lesley. b 48. **d** 01 **p** 02. OLM Reculver and Herne Bay St Bart and Hoath *Cant* from 01. *2 Hicks Forstal Cottages, Hicks Forstal Road, Hoath, Canterbury CT3 4NA* T: (01227) 711516 E: jennyhadlow@hotmail.com

HAGAN, Canon Kenneth Raymond. b 40. Fairfax Univ Australia BA 97. St Jo Coll Morpeth 62. **d** 64 **p** 65. C Charlestown Australia 64-69; C Cessnock 69-70; R E Pilbara 70-75; C Portsea St Mary *Portsm* 75-78; P-in-c Wolvey, Burton Hastings and Stretton Baskerville *Cov* 78-81; P-in-c Withybrook w Copston Magna 78-81; P-in-c Shilton w Ansty 78-81; OCM 78-81; Dir St Mungo Community 82-88; R Hamilton Australia 89-98; R Portland 98-05; Can Ballarat from 99; rtd 05; P-in-c Heveningham *St E* 04-07. *35B Narrunga Avenue, Buff Point NSW 2262, Australia* T: (0061) (2) 4399 3523

HAGAN, Matthew Henry. b 59. TCD MPhil 09. CITC. **d** 06 **p** 07. NSM Derryloran *Arm* 06-10; P-in-c Tynan w Middletown and Aghavilly 10-12; Bp's C 12-13; I from 13. *The Rectory, 16 Derryhaw Road, Tynan, Armagh BT60 4SS* T: (028) 3756 8619 M: 07778-038454 E: mhhagan@hotmail.com

HAGAN-PALMER, David Edward. b 66. UEA BSc 88 PGCE 96. ERMC 10. **d** 13 **p** 14. C Lowestoft St Marg *Nor* 13-14; C Drayton from 14; C Taverham from 14. *6 Cricket Close, Drayton, Norwich NR8 6YA* M: 07880-660900 E: revdavepalmer@gmail.com

HAGENBUCH, Mrs Andrea. b 63. STETS 05. **d** 08 **p** 09. C Corfe Castle, Church Knowle, Kimmeridge etc *Sarum* 08-12; V Stour Vale from 12. *The Vicarage, Kington Magna, Gillingham SP8 5EW* T: (01747) 838494 E: stephenhagenbuch@hotmail.com

HAGGAN, David Anthony. b 25. QUB LLB 49 Barrister-at-Law 70. *S'wark* Ord Course 87. **d** 89 **p** 90. NSM Reigate St Mary *S'wark* 89-05; PtO from 05. *2 Fairford Close, Reigate RH2 0EY* T: (01737) 246197

HAGGIS, Richard. b 66. Ch Ch Ox BA 88 MA 95 Nottm Univ MA 95. Linc Th Coll. **d** 95 **p** 96. C Romford St Edw *Chelmsf* 95-98; Chapl Trin Coll Cam 98-00; C St Giles-in-the-Fields *Lon* 00-03; C Upper Chelsea H Trin 04-06. *Flat 5, 14-16 Mather Road, Barton-Upon-Bayswater, Oxford OX3 9PG* M: 07788-704044 T: (01865) 750068 E: rh.giles@btopenworld.com

HAGGIS, Timothy Robin. b 52. New Coll Ox BA 75 MA 79. St Jo Coll Nottm. **d** 82 **p** 83. C Chilwell *S'well* 82-86; TV Hucknall

Torkard 86-94; Chapl Trent Coll Nottm 94-11; rtd 11. *86 Trowell Grove, Long Eaton, Nottingham NG10 4BB* T: 0115-972 9589 E: timhaggis@hotmail.co.uk

HAGON, Roger Charles. b 58. Nottm Univ BA 80. St Steph Ho Ox 82. d 85 p 86. C Charlton St Luke w H Trin *S'wark* 85-88; C St Helier 88-95; V Kenley 95-10; P-in-c Purley St Barn 01-10; V Addiscombe St Mildred from 10. *St Mildred's Vicarage, Sefton Road, Croydon CR0 7HR* T: (020) 8676 1569
E: vicar@stmildredschurch.org.uk

HAGUE, David Hallett. b 59. Univ Coll Lon BScEng 81 MSc 82. Ridley Hall Cam 91. d 93 p 94. C Luton St Mary *St Alb* 93-96; V Stevenage St Pet Broadwater 96-09; P-in-c Romford Gd Shep *Chelmsf* 09-14; V from 14; AD Havering from 14. *Good Shepherd Vicarage, 97 Collier Row Lane, Romford RM5 3BA* T: (01708) 753395 E: vicargs@thegoodshepherd.co.uk

HAHNEMAN, Geoffrey Mark. b 54. Baylor Univ (USA) BA 77 Virginia Th Sem MDiv 80 Ox Univ DPhil 87. d 80 p 80. C Boston Advent USA 80-84; Hon C Ox St Mary Magd 85-87; Asst Chapl Brussels *Eur* 87-90; Can Minneapolis Cathl USA 90-94; R Portsmouth Trin Ch 95-00; R Bridgeport St Jo from 05. *154 Jackman Avenue, Fairfield CT 06825-1724, USA* T: (001) (203) 362 0890 *or* 335 2528
E: rector@saintjohnbridgeport.org

HAIG, Alistair Matthew. b 39. K Coll Lon BD 63 AKC 63. d 64 p 65. C Forest Gate St Edm *Chelmsf* 64-67; C Laindon w Basildon 67-71; V S Woodham Ferrers 71-78; P-in-c Bath H Trin *B & W* 78-83; R 83-89; R Bocking St Mary *Chelmsf* 89-95; Dean Bocking 89-95; rtd 00. *17 Maidenburgh Street, Colchester CO1 1UB* T: (01206) 795275

HAIG, Canon Andrew Livingstone. b 45. Keble Coll Ox BA 67. Coll of Resurr Mirfield 67. d 69 p 70. C Elton All SS *Man* 69-75; R Brantham *St E* 75-76; R Brantham w Stutton 76-82; RD Samford 81-82; P-in-c Haverhill 82; TR Haverhill w Withersfield, the Wrattings etc 82-90; RD Clare 84-87; Chapl Qu Eliz Hosp King's Lynn 90-10; Hon Can Nor Cathl 07-10; rtd 10; PtO Nor from 10; *Ely* from 13. *46 Elvington, King's Lynn PE30 4TA* T: (01553) 761389
E: bandahaig@yahoo.co.uk

HAIG, Canon Murray Nigel Francis. b 39. Univ of Wales (Lamp) BA 62. Kelham Th Coll 62. d 66 p 67. C Felixstowe St Jo *St E* 66-72; C Morpeth *Newc* 72-74; V Byker St Mich 74-79; V Byker St Mich w St Lawr 79-81; I Benwell St Jas 81-85; TR Benwell 85-91; TR Cramlington 91-97; Hon Can Newc Cathl 95-05; P-in-c Alnwick 97-98; V 98-05; rtd 05. *4 Farm Well Place, Prudhoe NE42 5FB* T: (07801) 495616
E: d.haig@abbeyfield.com

HAIGH, Alan Bernard. b 42. NEOC 87. d 90 p 91. NSM Thorner *Leeds* from 90. *4 The Paddock, Thorner, Leeds LS14 3JB* T: 0113-289 2870

HAIGH, Nicholas James. b 71. Sheff Univ BA 00 St Jo Coll Dur MA 04. Cranmer Hall Dur 02. d 04 p 05. C Bredbury St Mark *Ches* 04-06; P Missr Huddersfield *Wakef* 06-09; C Crookes St Thos *Sheff* 09-15; V Haydock St Mark *Liv* from 15. *The Vicarage, 2 Stanley Bank Road, St Helens WA11 0UW* M: 07876-782888 T: (01744) 602641
E: nickhaigh@breathemail.net *or* info@stmarkshaydock.org

HAIGH, Nicolas Peter. b 57. Teesside Poly BEd 84. Ripon Coll Cuddesdon 07. d 09 p 10. C Eastbourne St Mary *Chich* 09-12; P-in-c Fernhurst 12-14; V from 14. *The Vicarage, Church Road, Fernhurst, Haslemere GU27 3HZ* T: (01428) 652229 M: 07966-187349 E: nickhaigh95@hotmail.com

HAIGH, Richard Michael Fisher. b 30. Dur Univ BA 57. Cranmer Hall Dur 57. d 59 p 60. C Stanwix *Carl* 59-62; CMS India 63-67; 68-70; R Salford St Clem w St Cypr Ordsall *Man* 71-75; R Holcombe 75-85; V Unsworth 85-93; R Brough w Stainmore, Musgrave and Warcop *Carl* 93-97; rtd 97; PtO *Carl* from 98. *21 Templand Park, Allithwaite, Grange-over-Sands LA11 7QS* T: (015395) 32312

HAIGH, Samuel Edward. b 85. Anglia Ruskin Univ BA 11. Ridley Hall Cam 08. d 11 p 12. C Wootton *St Alb* 11-14; C Tollington *Lon* from 14. *Emmanuel Vicarage, 145 Hornsey Road, London N7 6DU* M: 07429-022977 T: (020) 3759 8879
E: revhaigh@me.com

HAILES, Derek Arthur. b 38. Coll of Resurr Mirfield. d 82 p 83. C Sneinton St Cypr *S'well* 82-84; V Kneesall w Laxton 84-85; P-in-c Wellow 84-85; V Kneesall w Laxton and Wellow 85-88; V Sneinton St Steph w St Alb 88-95; P-in-c Bury H Trin *Man* 95-03; rtd 03; PtO *S'well* from 05. *14 Manor Road, Carlton, Nottingham NG4 3AY* T: 0115-987 3314

HAILS, Canon Brian. b 33. JP 71. ACMA 62 FCMA 76. NEOC 77. d 81 p 82. NSM Harton *Dur* 81-87; Ind Chapl 87-99; Hon Can Dur Cathl 93-99; TR Sunderland 96-99; rtd 99; PtO *Dur* from 99. *The Coach House, Church Lane, Whitburn, Sunderland SR6 7JL* T: 0191-529 5297
E: canon-hails@ukonline.co.uk

HAINE, Mrs Joanne Elizabeth. b 78. RMN 00. St Jo Coll Nottm 13. d 15. C Dorchester and the Winterbournes *Sarum* from 15. *10 Teves Road, Dorchester DT1 2HD*
M: 07530-255684 E: revjohaine@gmail.com

HAINES, Andrew Philip. b 47. LSE BSc 68. Oak Hill Th Coll 84. d 87 p 88. C Enfield Ch Ch Trent Park *Lon* 87-91; V Hillmorton *Cov* 91-12; rtd 12; PtO *Cov* from 12. *69 Waverley Road, Kenilworth CV8 1JL* T: (01926) 855518
E: revaph@btinternet.com *or* andrew@haines.uk.com

HAINES, Daniel Hugo. b 43. TD 89. Lon Univ BDS 68 MRCS 73. d 79 p 84. Hon C Bhunya Swaziland 79-80; Hon C Falkland Is 80-82; Hon C Hatcham St Cath *S'wark* 84-99; PtO 99-14. *56 Vesta Road, London SE4 2NH* T: (020) 7635 0305
E: 113270.506@compuserve.com

HAINES, Stephen Decatur. b 42. Freiburg Univ MA 68 Fitzw Coll Cam BA 70 MA 74. d 71 p 72. C Fulham St Dionis *Lon* 71-76; C Finchley St Mary 76-78; Hon C Clapham Old Town *S'wark* 83-87; Hon C Clapham Team 87-88; Hon C Camberwell St Giles w St Matt 88-94; Hon Chapl S'wark Cathl 92-11. *3 Lyndhurst Square, London SE15 5AR* T: (020) 7703 4239

HAINSWORTH, Richard John. b 79. Jes Coll Cam BA 01 MA 03. St Mich Coll Llan 04. d 06 p 07. C Newtown w Llanllwchaiarn w Aberhafesp *St As* 06-07; C Llanllwchaiarn and Newtown w Aberhafesp 07-08; C Wrexham 08-09; TV 09-14; V Northop from 14; Dioc Dir for Exploring Faith from 14. *The Vicarage, Sychdyn Road, Northop, Mold CH7 6AW* T: (01352) 840842 M: 07886-117922
E: rich_hainsworth@yahoo.co.uk

HAIR, James Eric. b 48. Lon Univ BA 69 MPhil 92. St Steph Ho Ox 69. d 72 p 73. C Fishponds St Jo *Bris* 72-75; C Bushey *St Alb* 75-79; P-in-c Lake *Portsm* 79-81; V 81-88; P-in-c Shanklin St Sav 79-81; V 81-88; TV Totton *Win* 88-95; C Portchester *Portsm* 96-97; Community Mental Health Chapl Portsm Health Care NHS Trust 97-00; Community Portsm Hosps NHS Trust 01-02; Community Mental Health Chapl Hants Partnership NHS Trust 02-13; Chapl Team Ldr E Hants Primary Care Trust 99-13; Asst to RD Fareham *Portsm* 97-99; Dioc Adv for Mental Health from 12; PtO *Win* 09-14. *26 Bayly Avenue, Fareham PO16 9LD*

HAKE, Darren Mark. b 73. Plymouth Univ BSc 01 Lanc Univ MRes 02 FGS 01. Wycliffe Hall Ox 09. d 11 p 12. C Wembdon *B & W* 11-14. *8 King's Drive, Bridgwater TA6 4FP* M: 07545-379112 E: markh@sgw.org.uk

HAKE (née JACKSON), Mrs Ruth Victoria. b 78. MBE 11. Univ Coll Dur BA 99 Fitzw Coll Cam BA 01 MA 05. Ridley Hall Cam 99. d 02 p 03. C York St Mich-le-Belfrey 02-05; CF(V) 04-05; Chapl RAF from 05. *Chaplaincy Services (RAF), HQ Air Command, RAF High Wycombe HP14 4UE* T: (01494) 496800 F: 496343

HALAHAN, Maxwell Crosby. b 30. Lon Univ BSc 52 Southn Univ CertEd 78. Westcott Ho Cam 54. d 56 p 57. C Forton *Portsm* 56-60; C Liv Our Lady and St Nic 60-62; Dom Chapl to Bp Nassau and the Bahamas 62-64; C Widley w Wymering *Portsm* 64-66; C-in-c Cowes St Faith CD 66-70; V Cowes St Faith 70-77; Hon C Portsea St Sav 77-84; rtd 84; PtO *Portsm* 84-94. *4 Coach House Mews, Old Canal, Southsea PO4 8HD*

HALBERT, Mrs Elizabeth Mary. b 58. Liv Hope BA 97 PGCE 98. d 06 p 07. OLM Sefton and Thornton *Liv* 06-11; OLM Sefton, Thornton and Crosby 11-13. *15 Third Avenue, Crosby, Liverpool L23 5SA* T: 0151-281 1390 E: lizhalbert1000@msn.com

HALE, Antony Jolyon (Jon). b 56. Newc Univ BA 79 MRTPI 89. Sarum & Wells Th Coll 86. d 88 p 89. C Monkseaton St Mary *Newc* 88-92; P-in-c Tandridge *S'wark* 92-97; C Oxted 92-97; C Oxted and Tandridge 97-98; V Crawley Down All SS *Chich* from 98. *The Vicarage, Vicarage Road, Crawley Down, Crawley RH10 4JJ* T: (01342) 714922 E: aj@jkcahale.plus.com

HALE, David Nigel James. b 43. SEITE 00. d 03 p 04. NSM Aylesham w Adisham *Cant* 03-12; NSM Nonington w Wymynswold and Goodnestone etc 03-12; NSM Canonry 12-13; rtd 14; PtO *Cant* from 14. *Chilton House, 43 The Street, Ash, Canterbury CT3 2EN* T: (01304) 813161 *or* (01843) 862991 E: halenigelval@hotmail.com

HALE, Jon. *See* HALE, Antony Jolyon

HALE, Canon Keith John Edward. b 53. Sheff Poly BSc 75. St Jo Coll Nottm MA 94. d 91 p 92. C Greasbrough *Sheff* 91-94; P-in-c Tankersley 94-95; R Tankersley, Thurgoland and Wortley from 95; Ind Chapl 96-01; Bp's Rural Adv from 01; AD Tankersley from 07; Hon Can Sheff Cathl from 10. *The Rectory, 9 Chapel Road, Tankersley, Barnsley S75 3AR* T: (01226) 744140 E: revkeith.hale@virgin.net

HALE (née McKAY), Mrs Margaret McLeish (Greta). b 37. RN 76. WEMTC 92. d 95 p 96. OLM Bream *Glouc* 95-01; NSM 01-04; NSM Newland and Redbrook w Clearwell 04-06; NSM Coleford, Staunton, Newland, Redbrook etc from 06. *Address temp unknown* E: gretahale@hotmail.com

369

HALE, Nigel. *See* HALE, David Nigel James

HALE, Roger Anthony. b 41. MCIH 85. Brasted Th Coll 68 Oak Hill Th Coll 70. **d** 72 **p** 73. C Blackb Sav 72-75; C Burnley St Pet 75-77; Chapl Burnley Gen Hosp 75-77; V Fence in Pendle *Blackb* 77-82; Chapl Lancs Ind Miss 77-82; NSM Tottenham St Mary *Lon* 88-91; R Cheddington w Mentmore and Marsworth *Ox* 91-06; rtd 06; PtO *Ox* from 06. *Chiltern House, 12 High Street, Cheddington, Leighton Buzzard LU7 0RQ* T: (01296) 668114 E: rogertherector@yahoo.co.uk

HALES, Peter John. b 45. Open Univ BSc 02. ERMC 08. **d** 08 **p** 09. C Coutances *Eur* 08-09; P-in-c 09-14. *4 rue le Mascaret, 50220 Précey, France* T: (0033) 2 33 58 86 76 F: 6 87 53 20 13 E: halesphx2@aol.com

HALES, Sandra Louise. Lon Univ BSc 94 Univ Coll Lon MSc 96 TCD BTh 02 RGN. CITC. **d** 02 **p** 03. C Lucan w Leixlip *D & G* 02-06; I Celbridge w Straffan and Newcastle-Lyons 06-14; rtd 14. *Railway Road, Killeshandra, Co Cavan, Republic of Ireland* E: slhales@eircom.net

HALEY, Thomas Arthur. b 52. NTMTC 98. **d** 98 **p** 99. NSM Old Ford St Paul and St Mark *Lon* 98-02; NSM Hackney Marsh from 02; TV from 07. *All Souls' Vicarage, 44 Overbury Street, London E5 0AJ* T: (020) 8525 2863 E: tomarcie@aol.com

HALFORD, David John. b 47. JP 84. Didsbury Coll Man CertEd 69 Open Univ BA 75 DipEd 86 Man Univ MEd 79 ACP 72. **d** 96 **p** 97. OLM Royton St Anne *Man* 96-12; NSM Leesfield from 12. *Address temp unknown*

HALFORD, Nicola Jane. b 80. TCD Div Sch MTh 12. **d** 11 **p** 12. C Athy w Kilberry, Fontstown and Kilkea *D & G* 11-12; C Wexford and Kilscoran Union *C & O* from 12. *The Rectory, Killinick, Co Wexford, Republic of Ireland* T: (00353) (53) 915 8764 M: 87-123 3338 E: revnicolahalford@gmail.com

HALFPENNY, Brian Norman. b 36. CB 90. St Jo Coll Ox BA 60 MA 64. Wells Th Coll 60. **d** 62 **p** 63. C Melksham *Sarum* 62-65; Chapl RAF 65-83; Sen Chapl RAF Coll Cranwell 82-83; Asst Chapl-in-Chief RAF 83-88; Chapl-in-Chief RAF 88-91; QHC 85-91; Can and Preb Linc Cathl 89-91; TR Redditch, The Ridge *Worc* 91-01; rtd 01; PtO *Glouc* from 02. *80 Roman Way, Bourton-on-the-Water, Cheltenham GL54 2EW* T: (01451) 821589

HALIFAX, Archdeacon of. *See* DAWTRY, The Ven Anne Frances

HALKES, Canon John Stanley. b 39. SWMTC 87. **d** 90 **p** 91. NSM St Buryan, St Levan and Sennen *Truro* 90-92; P-in-c Lanteglos by Fowey 92-04; P-in-c Lansallos 03-04; Hon Can Truro Cathl 03-08; rtd 04. *Reading Room Cottage, Mixton Farm, Lerryn, Lostwithiel PL22 0QE*

HALL, Canon Alfred Christopher. b 35. Trin Coll Ox BA 58 MA 61. Westcott Ho Cam 58. **d** 61 **p** 62. C Frecheville *Derby* 61-64; C Dronfield 64-67; V Smethwick St Matt *Birm* 67-70; V Smethwick St Matt w St Chad 70-75; Can Res Man Cathl 75-83; Hon Can Man Cathl 83-90; Dioc Adult Educn Officer 75-83; Dioc World Development Officer 76-88; V Bolton St Pet 83-90; Co-ord Chr Concern for One World 90-00; rtd 96; Hon Can Ch Ch *Ox* 00-01; PtO from 03. *The Knowle, Philcote Street, Deddington, Banbury OX15 0TB* T: (01869) 338225 F: 337766 E: achall@globalnet.co.uk

HALL, Andrew David. b 62. Mattersey Hall MA 09 St Jo Coll Dur MATM 12. Cranmer Hall Dur 10. **d** 12 **p** 13. C Brighouse and Clifton *Leeds* from 12. *35 Robin Hood Way, Brighouse HD6 4LA* T: (01484) 719255 M: 07507-561216 E: 1andrewdavidhall@gmail.com

HALL, Andrew John. **d** 14 **p** 15. C Cheltenham St Mary w St Matt and St Luke *Glouc* from 14. *Address temp unknown*

HALL, Mrs Ann Addington. b 34. Ex Univ CertEd 71. SWMTC 82. **dss** 85 **d** 87 **p** 94. Ex St Mark 85-90; Hon Par Dn 87-90; PtO 90-02; NSM Cen Ex 92-10; rtd 10. *5 Harringcourt Road, Exeter EX4 8PQ* T: (01392) 278717

HALL, Barry George. b 38. Solicitor 62. Oak Hill Th Coll 78. **d** 81 **p** 82. NSM Stock Harvard *Chelmsf* 81-90; NSM W Hanningfield 90-02; P-in-c 93-02; PtO from 02. *Harvard Cottage, Swan Lane, Stock, Ingatestone CM4 9BQ* T: (01277) 840387

HALL, Brian. b 59. Aston Tr Scheme 90 Oak Hill Th Coll 92. **d** 94 **p** 95. C Mansfield St Jo *S'well* 94-96; C Skegby 96-99; P-in-c Sutton in Ashfield St Mich 99-04; R Carlton-in-the-Willows from 04. *St Paul's Rectory, Church Street, Nottingham NG4 1BJ* T: 0115-961 1644 E: revbhall@aol.com

HALL, Canon Brian Arthur. b 48. Ex Univ BEd 70. Cuddesdon Coll 73. **d** 75 **p** 76. C Hobs Moat *Birm* 75-79; V Smethwick 79-93; R Handsworth St Mary 93-13; AD Handsworth 99-05 and 06-08; Hon Can Birm Cathl 05-13; rtd 13; PtO *Birm* from 13. *97 Perry Hill Road, Oldbury B68 0AH* E: brian.a.hall@btinternet.com

HALL, Mrs Carolyn Ruth. **d** 08 **p** 09. NSM Builth and Llanddewi'r Cwm w Llangynog etc *S & B* 08-11; NSM Builth Deanery from 11. *Coedmor, Broadway, Llandrindod Wells LD1 5HT* T: (01597) 829637 E: nigeldhall@hotmail.com

HALL, Ms Christine Beryl. b 52. Southn Univ BSc 73 Leeds Univ MA 06. NTMTC BA 08. **d** 08 **p** 09. NSM Stepney St Dunstan and All SS *Lon* 08-13; NSM St Jo on Bethnal Green from 13; Chapl Guy's and St Thos' NHS Foundn Trust from 08; Chapl Lon Fire Brigade from 08. *15 Lidfield Road, London N16 9NA* T: (020) 7254 9185 E: christine.b.hall@btinternet.com

HALL, Canon Christine Mary. b 45. K Coll Lon BD 67 MPhil 86. **d** 87. NSM Bickley *Roch* 87-92; Vice-Prin Chich Th Coll 92-94; LtO *Chich* 95-03; Can and Preb Chich Cathl from 15; PtO *Portsm* from 15. *The Old School, East Marden, Chichester PO18 9JE* T: (01243) 535244 E: dcnchall@eastmarden.net

HALL, Christopher. *See* HALL, Alfred Christopher

HALL, Darryl Christopher. b 69. Cranmer Hall Dur 07. **d** 09 **p** 10. C Knaresborough *Ripon* 09-13; V Upper Nidderdale *Leeds* from 13. *The New Vicarage, New Church Street, Pateley Bridge, Harrogate HG3 5LQ* M: 07792-419982 E: horlix@aol.com

HALL, David Anthony. b 43. Reading Univ BA 66. Qu Coll Birm 79. **d** 81 **p** 82. C Norton *St Alb* 81-85; TV Hitchin 85-93; P-in-c Bidford-on-Avon *Cov* 93; V 93-08; RD Alcester 05-08; rtd 08; PtO *Cov* from 09. *1 Abbey Close, Alcester B49 5QW* T: (01789) 763252 E: davidahall@onetel.com

HALL, David Martin. b 66. Greenwich Univ BA 89. Oak Hill Th Coll BA 00. **d** 00 **p** 01. C Bebington *Ches* 00-03; P-in-c Danehill *Chich* 03-05; V 05-12; RD Uckfield 11-12; V Chorleywood Ch Ch *St Alb* from 12. *Christ Church Vicarage, Rickmansworth Road, Chorleywood, Rickmansworth WD3 5SG* T: (01923) 282149 *or* 284325 E: david.andmaryhall@tiscali.co.uk

HALL, Denis. b 43. Lon Coll of Div 65. **d** 69 **p** 70. C Netherton *Liv* 69-71; C Roby 72-75; V Wigan St Steph 75-90; V Newton-le-Willows 90-13; rtd 13. *39 Tracy Drive, Newton-le-Willows WA12 8PX* E: allsaints@3tc4u.net

HALL, Derek. *See* HALL, John Derek

HALL, Derek Guy. b 26. Tyndale Hall Bris 50. **d** 51 **p** 52. C Preston All SS *Blackb* 51-54; C Halliwell St Pet *Man* 54-56; C-in-c Buxton Trin Prop Chpl *Derby* 56-58; V Blackb St Jude 58-67; R Fazakerley Em *Liv* 67-74; TR 74-81; V Langdale *Carl* 81-86; rtd 86; PtO *Carl* from 86. *14 Gale Park, Ambleside LA22 0BN* T: (01539) 433144

HALL, Diana Mary. **d** 14. C St Andrews St Andr *St And* from 14. *Address temp unknown*

HALL, Canon Elaine Chegwin. b 59. Liv Univ MTh 01 RGN 82. NOC 94. **d** 97 **p** 98. C Frankby w Greasby *Ches* 97-01; V Stretton and Appleton Thorn 01-13; RD Gt Budworth 03-10; V Stockport St Geo from 13; Hon Can Ches Cathl from 12. *17 Frewland Avenue, Stockport SK3 8TZ* E: petera.hall@care4free.net

HALL, Elizabeth. *See* SNOWDEN, Elizabeth

HALL, Fiona Myfanwy Gordon. b 63. Regents Th Coll BA 95 Anglia Ruskin Univ MA 04 Roehampton Inst PGCE 96. Ridley Hall Cam 02. **d** 04 **p** 05. C Maybush and Southampton St Jude *Win* 04-07; Asst Chapl R Berks NHS Foundn Trust 08-12; TV Dorchester *Sarum* 12-14; TV Dorchester and the Winterbournes from 14. *St George's Vicarage, 59 High Street, Dorchester DT1 1LB* T: (01305) 262394 E: revfionahall@yahoo.co.uk

HALL, Frances. *See* SHOESMITH, Judith Frances

HALL, Geoffrey Hedley. b 33. Bris Univ BA 55. St Steph Ho Ox 63. **d** 65 **p** 66. C Taunton H Trin *B & W* 65-67; CF 67-80; Sen CF 80-86; P-in-c Ambrosden w Arncot and Blackthorn *Ox* 72-75; V Barnsley St Edw *Wakef* 86-98; rtd 98; PtO *St And* from 98; *Bre* from 99. *Montana Villa, 39 Haisan Crescent, Perth PH2 7XD* T: (01738) 636802 M: 07803-578499 E: geoffreyhall@blueyonder.co.uk

HALL, George Richard Wyndham. b 49. Ex Univ LLB 71. Wycliffe Hall Ox BA 74 MA 78. **d** 75 **p** 76. C Walton H Trin *Ox* 75-79; C Farnborough *Guildf* 79-84; Bp's Chapl *Nor* 84-87; R Saltford w Corston and Newton St Loe *B & W* 87-14; Chapl Bath Coll of HE 88-90; RD Chew Magna *B & W* 97-03; rtd 14; PtO *Carl* from 15. *45 Howard Park, Greystoke, Penrith CA11 0TU* T: (01768) 483394 E: revrichardhall45@gmail.com

HALL, Canon George Rumney. b 37. LVO 99 CVO 03. Westcott Ho Cam 60. **d** 62 **p** 63. C Camberwell St Phil *S'wark* 62-65; C Waltham Cross *St Alb* 65-67; R Buckenham w Hassingham and Strumpshaw *Nor* 67-74; Chapl St Andr Hosp Thorpe 67-72; Chapl HM Pris Nor 72-74; Chapl St Andr Hosp Thorpe 72-74; V Wymondham *Nor* 74-87; RD Humbleyard 86-87; R Sandringham w W Newton 87-94; P-in-c Flitcham 87-94; P-in-c Wolferton w Babingley 87-94; R Sandringham w W Newton and Appleton etc 95-03; P-in-c Castle Rising 87-03; P-in-c Hillington 87-03; Hon Can Nor Cathl 87-03; RD Heacham and Rising 89-01; Dom Chapl to The Queen 87-03; Chapl to The Queen 03-07; r-d 03; PtO *Nor* from 03. *Town Farm Cottage, 95 Lynn Road, Great Bircham, King's Lynn PE31 6RJ* T: (01485) 576134 M: 07889-627940 E: george_hall@btinternet.com

HALL, Mrs Gillian Louise. b 45. Univ of Wales (Ban) MPhil 06. NOC 87. **d** 90 **p** 94. NSM Earby *Bradf* 90-96; NSM Gisburn 96-01; NSM Hellifield 96-01; PtO 01-02; Chapl Airedale NHS Trust 02-04; PtO *Leeds* from 05. *Mitton House, Lothersdale, Keighley BD20 8HR* T: (01535) 636144
E: gill@hesslelodge.freeserve.co.uk

HALL, Gillian Mary. b 58. Linc Sch of Th and Min. **d** 12 **p** 13. NSM Bilborough w Strelley *S'well* from 12. *30 Parkside, Nottingham NG8 2NN* T: 0115-943 0881
E: gillhall30@gmail.com

HALL, Harry. b 41. Open Univ BA 93. Chich Th Coll 91. **d** 91 **p** 92. C Boston *Linc* 91-92; C Bourne 92-94; P-in-c Sutterton w Fosdyke and Algarkirk 94-97; R Sutterton, Fosdyke, Algarkirk and Wigtoft 97-99; V Barnsley St Edw *Wakef* 99-05; Chapl ATC 99-05; I Ardstraw w Baronscourt, Badoney Lower etc *D & R* 05-10; rtd 10. *18 Kings Road, Metheringham, Lincoln LN4 3HT* T: (01526) 320308 E: slk248@hotmail.com

HALL, Miss Helen Constance Patricia Mary. b 77. Peterho Cam BA 99 MA 03 St Jo Coll Dur BA 05 Solicitor 02. Cranmer Hall Dur 03. **d** 06 **p** 07. C Maindee Newport *Mon* 06-09; P-in-c Newport St Andr from 09. *The Vicarage, 1 Brookfield Close, Newport NP19 4LA* T: (01633) 677775 M: 07919-538077
E: bititt@yahoo.co.uk

HALL, Canon Hubert William Peter. b 35. Ely Th Coll 58. **d** 60 **p** 61. C Louth w Welton-le-Wold *Linc* 60-62; C Gt Grimsby St Jas 62-69; C Gt Grimsby St Mary and St Jas 69-71; Hon Chapl Miss to Seafarers 71-01; V Immingham *Linc* 71-01; RD Haverstoe 86-01; Can and Preb Linc Cathl 89-01; rtd 01; PtO *Linc* from 01. *6 Abbey Rise, Barrow-upon-Humber DN19 7TF* T: (01469) 531504 E: hwphall@talktalk.net

HALL, Ian Alfred. b 60. Sheff Univ BA 96. Ushaw Coll Dur 81 NOC 98. **d** 85 **p** 86. C Whitkirk *Ripon* 99-02; TV Swinton and Pendlebury *Man* 02-09; P-in-c Winton from 09; P-in-c Barton w Peel Green from 14. *Winton Vicarage, Albany Road, Eccles, Manchester M30 8FE* T: 0161-788 8991
E: carolian86@yahoo.com

HALL, Canon James Robert. b 24. TCD BA 48 MA 54. **d** 49 **p** 50. C Seagoe *D & D* 49-51; C Lisburn Ch Ch *Conn* 51-59; I Belfast St Mich 59-66; I Finaghy 66-89; Can Belf Cathl 82-89; rtd 89. *3 Coachman's Way, Hillsborough BT26 6HQ* T: (028) 9268 9678

HALL, Mrs Jane Daphne. b 60. Trent Poly BA 92 Solicitor 93. **d** 09 **p** 10. NSM Clopton w Otley, Swilland and Ashbocking *St E* 09-13; NSM Carlford from 13. *Countryside, Gibraltar Road, Otley, Ipswich IP6 9LL* T: (01473) 785251
E: alltthealls@tiscali.co.uk

HALL, Jeffrey Ernest. b 42. Linc Th Coll 73. **d** 75 **p** 76. C Brampton St Thos *Derby* 75-78; C Whittington and New Whittington 78-81; TV Riverside *Ox* 81-90; Ind Chapl Slough Deanery 81-89; R Anstey *Leic* 90-97; TR Hugglescote w Donington, Ellistown and Snibston 97-08; rtd 08; PtO *Sarum* from 10. *21 Woodsage Drive, Gillingham SP8 4UE* T: (01747) 823480 M: 07876-540343 E: jeffreyhall123@btinternet.com

HALL, Jennifer. *See* HALL, Margaret Jennifer

HALL, The Ven John Barrie. b 41. Sarum & Wells Th Coll 82. **d** 84 **p** 85. Chapl St Edward's Hosp Cheddleton 84-88; C Cheddleton *Lich* 84-88; V Rocester 88-94; V Rocester and Croxden w Hollington 94-98; RD Uttoxeter 91-98; Adn Salop 98-11; V Tong 98-11; P-in-c Donington 98-00; rtd 11; PtO *Lich* 11-13; Hon C Hanbury, Newborough, Rangemore and Tutbury 13; PtO from 13. *16 Mill House Drive, Cheadle, Stoke-on-Trent ST10 1XL* T: (01538) 750628
E: j.hall182@btinternet.com

HALL, John Bruce. b 33. Covenant Th Sem St Louis MTh 80 DMin 85. ALCD 60. **d** 60 **p** 61. C Kingston upon Hull H Trin *York* 60-67; C Beverley Minster 67-68; V Clapham Park St Steph *S'wark* 68-76; R Tooting Graveney St Nic 76-03; rtd 03; PtO *S'wark* from 03. *44 Mayford Road, London SW12 8SD* T: (020) 8673 6869
E: jbewhall@johnbhall.plus.com

HALL, John Charles. b 46. Hull Univ BA 71 Spurgeon's Coll MTh 05. Ridley Hall Cam 71. **d** 73 **p** 74. C Bromley Common St Aug *Roch* 73-77; C Westbury-on-Trym St Alb *Bris* 78-80; Oman 80-82; C-in-c Bishop Auckland Woodhouse Close CD *Dur* 82-90; P-in-c Gt and Lt Glemham, Blaxhall etc *St E* 90-91; P-in-c Rodney Stoke w Draycott *B & W* 91-01; Dioc Ecum Officer 91-01; V Southmead *Bris* 01-11; rtd 11. *8 Ridgeway Close, West Harptree, Bristol BS40 6EF* M: 07771-848412 T: (01761) 221881
E: sarasgarden@hotmail.co.uk

HALL, John Curtis. b 39. CEng 73 MIMechE 73. Coll of Resurr Mirfield 80. **d** 82 **p** 83. C Pet Ch Carpenter 82-86; TV Heavitree w Ex St Paul 86-93; R Bow w Broad Nymet 93-04; V Colebrooke 93-04; R Zeal Monachorum 93-04; RD Cadbury 97-02; rtd 04. *37 Lawn Drive, Chudleigh, Newton Abbot TQ13 0LS* T: (01626) 853245

HALL, Canon John Derek. b 25. St Cuth Soc Dur BA 50. Linc Th Coll 50. **d** 52 **p** 53. C Redcar *York* 52-54; C Newland St Jo 54-57; V Boosbeck w Moorsholm 57-61; V Middlesbrough St Oswald 61-68; Chapl St Luke's Hosp Middlesbrough 61-67; V York St Chad 68-90; Chapl Bootham Park Hosp 68-85; Can and Preb York Minster 85-90; rtd 90; Chapl Castle Howard 90-02; PtO *York* from 98. *25 Fairfields Drive, Skelton, York YO30 1YP* T: (01904) 470978

HALL, Canon John Edmund. b 49. Open Univ BA 84 Birm Univ MPhil 05 Warwick Univ PhD 06 CQSW 76. Trin Coll Bris BA 89. **d** 89 **p** 90. C Winchmore Hill St Paul *Lon* 89-92; V Edmonton St Aldhelm 92-01; Dir Soc Resp *Cov* 01-10; Dir Interfaith Relns and Dir St Phil Cen *Leic* 10-14; Hon Can Leic Cathl 10-14; rtd 14. *7 Riverside View, Ottery St Mary EX11 1YA*

HALL, Canon John Kenneth. b 32. Qu Coll Birm 61. **d** 63 **p** 64. C Ilminster w Whitelackington *B & W* 63-66; P-in-c Mackworth St Fran *Derby* 66-69; V Blackford *B & W* 69-76; R Chapel Allerton 69-76; New Zealand from 77; Can St Pet Cathl Waikato 85-91; rtd 93. *24 Pohutukawa Drive, RD 1, Katikati 3177, New Zealand* T/F: (0064) (7) 863 4465
E: gee.jay@paradise.net.nz

HALL, John MacNicol. b 44. Glas Univ BSc 65 MB, ChB 69 St Jo Coll Cam BA 73 MA 76 Nottm Univ MTh 88 MSc 93 MRCGP 75. Westcott Ho Cam 71. **d** 86 **p** 86. NSM Clarendon Park St Jo w Knighton St Mich *Leic* 86-89; PtO *Ely* 89-91; St Alb 90-92; *Birm* 91-00 and from 02. *85 Galton Road, Smethwick B67 5JX* T: 0121-434 3957

HALL, Canon John Michael. b 62. Leeds Univ BA. Coll of Resurr Mirfield 83. **d** 86 **p** 87. C Ribbleton *Blackb* 86-89; C Carnforth 89-92; V Lt Marsden 92-98; V Lt Marsden w Nelson St Mary 98; V Warton St Oswald w Yealand Conyers 98-08; AD Tunstall 05-08; P-in-c Fleetwood St Pet 08-11; V 11-14; P-in-c Fleetwood St Dav 08-14; V Fleetwood St Pet and St Dav from 14; Hon Can Bloemfontein Cathl from 01; Hon Can Blackb Cathl from 09. *The Vicarage, 49 Mount Road, Fleetwood FY7 6QZ* T: (01253) 876176 E: johnbloem@aol.com

HALL, John Michael. b 47. BD. Oak Hill Th Coll 68. **d** 73 **p** 74. C Walthamstow St Mary w St Steph *Chelmsf* 73-76; C Rainham 76-79; P-in-c Woodham Mortimer w Hazeleigh 79-93; P-in-c Woodham Walter 79-93; Ind Chapl 79-93; R Fairstead w Terling and White Notley etc 93-13; RD Witham 01-07; rtd 13; PtO *Ely* from 15. *43 Northwold, Ely CB6 1BG* T: (01353) 969089 E: rev.johnhall@tiscali.co.uk

HALL, The Very Revd John Robert. b 49. St Chad's Coll Dur BA 71 Roehampton Univ Hon DD 07 Ches Univ Hon DTheol 08 FRSA 02 Hon FCollT 09. Cuddesdon Coll 72. **d** 75 **p** 76. C Kennington St Jo *S'wark* 75-78; P-in-c S Wimbledon All SS 78-84; V Streatham St Pet 84-92; Dioc Dir of Educn *Blackb* 92-98; Hon Can Blackb Cathl 92-94 and 98-02; Can Res Blackb Cathl 94-98; Gen Sec Nat Soc 98-06; Gen Sec C of E Bd of Educn 98-02; Chief Educn Officer and Hd Educn Division Abps' Coun 03-06; Hon C S Norwood St Alb *S'wark* 03-06; Dean Westmr from 06. *The Deanery, Dean's Yard, London SW1P 3PA* T: (020) 7654 4801 F: 7654 4883
E: john.hall@westminster-abbey.org

HALL, Canon John Terence Peter. b 67. St Jo Coll Dur BA 98. Cranmer Hall Dur. **d** 98 **p** 99. C Towcester w Easton Neston *Pet* 98-01; P-in-c Blakesley w Adstone and Maidford etc 01-07; C Greens Norton w Bradden and Lichborough 06-07; R Lambfold 07-11; RD Towcester 09-11; P-in-c Irthlingborough 11-12; P-in-c Gt w Lt Addington and Woodford 11-12; R Irthlingborough, Gt Addington, Lt Addington etc from 13; Warden of Readers from 14; Can Pet Cathl from 10. *The Rectory, 79 Finedon Road, Irthlingborough, Wellingborough NN9 5TY* T: (01933) 650278
E: canon.johnhall@gmail.com *or* fr.john@nenecrossings.org.uk

HALL, Jonathan. b 62. Ch Ch Coll Cant BA 83 MCIPD 94. STETS BTh 99. **d** 99 **p** 00. C Weymouth H Trin *Sarum* 99-03; R Whippingham w E Cowes *Portsm* 03-10; RD W Wight 07-10; Chapl Burrswood Chr Hosp *Roch* from 10; PtO *Portsm* from 14. *Burrswood Hospital, Burrswood, Groombridge, Tunbridge Wells TN3 9PY* T: (01892) 863637

HALL, Judith Frances. *See* SHOESMITH, Judith Frances

HALL, The Very Revd Kenneth Robert James. b 59. St Jo Coll Nottm 95. **d** 98 **p** 99. NSM Derryloran *Arm* 98-02; C Drumglass w Moygashel 02-03; C Brackaville w Donaghendry and Ballyclog 03-04; I 04-10; Dean Clogh from 10; I Enniskillen from 10. *St Macartin's Deanery, 13 Church Street, Enniskillen BT74 7DW* T: (028) 6632 2465 or 6632 2917
E: krjhall@btinternet.com

HALL, Keven Neil. b 47. Auckland Univ BSc PhD 74. K Coll Lon BD AKC 79. **d** 79 **p** 80. New Zealand 79-87; NSM Shepherd's Bush St Steph w St Thos *Lon* 91-95 and 98-00; NSM W Acton St Martin 96-98; Asst Chapl NW Lon Hosp NHS Trust 00-07;

Chapl Nat Soc for Epilepsy 91-03. *Flat B, Rutland House, 30 Greencroft Gardens, London NW6 3LT* M: 07930-353717 E: kevenhall@hotmail.com

HALL, Leslie. b 37. Man Univ BSc 59. EMMTC 83. d 86 p 87. NSM Freiston w Butterwick and Benington *Linc* 86-02; PtO 02-05; Dioc NSM Officer 94-97. *29 Brand End Road, Butterwick, Boston PE22 0ET* T: (01205) 760375

HALL, Mrs Lilian Evelyn Mary. b 42. SWMTC 02. d 05 p 06. NSM Ludgvan, Marazion, St Hilary and Perranuthnoe *Truro* 05-11; C Barkston and Hough Gp *Linc* from 11. *The Rectory, Barkston Road, Marston, Grantham NG32 2HN* T: (01400) 251590 E: johnandlily.hall@btinternet.com

HALL, Mrs Linda Charlotte. b 50. Cam Inst of Educn CertEd 72. St Alb Minl Tr Scheme 85 Oak Hill Th Coll 91. d 92 p 94. NSM St Alb St Steph *St Alb* 92-98; NSM Sandridge 98-99; C Ipswich All Hallows *St E* 99-00; PtO 01; TV Cwmbran *Mon* 01-08; P-in-c Maesglas and Duffryn from 08. *The Vicarage, Old Cardiff Road, Newport NP20 3AT* T: (01633) 815738 E: rev.linda.chall@gmail.com

HALL, Margaret Jennifer. b 44. Univ Coll Lon BSc 67 Brunel Univ MA 83. Trin Coll Bris 10. d 12 p 13. OLM Stoke Bishop *Bris* from 12. *Dial Cottage, 34 Julian Road, Bristol BS9 1JY* T: 0117-968 5959 E: mjenniferhall@btinternet.com

HALL, Mrs Marigold Josephine. b 29. Linc Th Coll 81. dss 83 d 87. Chapl Asst Hellesdon Hosp Nor 83-94; Nor St Pet Parmentergate w St Jo 83-87; C 87-94; rtd 90; PtO *Nor* from 94. *36 Cavendish House, Recorder Road, Norwich NR1 1BW* T: (01603) 625933

HALL, Ms Melanie Jane. b 55. Ex Univ BA 78. Ripon Coll Cuddesdon 01. d 03 p 04. C Stepney St Dunstan and All SS *Lon* 03-06; rtd 06. *9 Jephson House, Doddington Grove, London SE17 3TF* M: 07848-440078 E: melanie.jh@btopenworld.com

HALL, Michael Alan. b 76. Univ of Wales (Lamp) BA 98. Ripon Coll Cuddesdon 99. d 01 p 02. C Wellington Ch Ch *Lich* 01-05; V Chelmsf All SS 05-14; P-in-c Gt Burstead w Ramsden Crays from 14. *The Vicarage, 111 Church Street, Billericay CM11 2TR* T: (01277) 632060 E: revd.michael@btinternet.com

HALL, Canon Michael Anthony. b 41. St Paul's Coll Grahamstown LTh 64. d 64 p 65. C E London St Alb S Africa 65-67; C Queenstown St Mich 67-69; R Port Elizabeth All SS 70-78; R E London All SS 78-81; R Queenstown St Mich w Tarkastad St Mary 81-91; Adn Aliwal N 81-01; R Barkly E St Steph 91-01; P-in-c Dordrecht St Aug 91-02; Hon Can Grahamstown from 01; P-in-c Lapford, Nymet Rowland and Coldridge *Ex* 01-03; TV N Creedy 03-11; rtd 11. *10 Blagdon Rise, Crediton EX17 1EN* T: (01363) 774023 M: 07751-798670 E: micksandhall@btopenworld.com

HALL, Michael Edward. b 32. Fitzw Ho Cam BA 57 MA 61. Ridley Hall Cam 68. d 69 p 70. C Aspley *S'well* 69-73; P-in-c Bulwell St Jo 73-75; V 75-81; P-in-c Tyler's Green *Ox* 81-90; V 90-00; rtd 00. *5 Hawkings Meadow, Marlborough SN8 1UR* T: (01672) 511713

HALL, Murray. b 34. K Coll Lon. d 61 p 62. C Eaton *Nor* 61-64; C Shalford *Guildf* 64-67; V Oxshott 67-72; P-in-c Runham *Nor* 72-80; R Filby w Thrigby w Mautby 72-80; P-in-c Stokesby w Herringby 72-80; R Filby w Thrigby, Mautby, Stokesby, Herringby etc 80-94; rtd 94; PtO *Nor* 94-07. *64 Nursery Close, Acle, Norwich NR13 3EH* T: (01493) 751287

HALL, Nicholas Charles. b 56. d 86 p 87. C Hyde St Geo *Ches* 86-89; C Cheadle 89-91; NSM from 91. *58 Warren Avenue, Cheadle SK8 1ND* T: 0161-491 6758 F: 491 0285 E: nick@domini.org

HALL, Canon Nigel David. b 46. Univ of Wales (Cardiff) BA 67 BD 76 Lon Univ CertEd 68. St Mich Coll Llan 73. d 76 p 77. C Cardiff St Jo *Llan* 76-81; R Llanbadarn Fawr, Llandegley and Llanfihangel etc *S & B* 81-95; RD Maelienydd 89-95; V Builth and Llanddewi'r Cwm w Llangynog etc 95-11; Can Brecon Cathl 94-11; Prec Brecon Cathl 99-00; Treas Brecon Cathl 00-11; Chan Brecon Cathl 04-11; AD Builth 04-11; rtd 11; PtO *S & B* from 11. *Coedmor, Broadway, Llandrindod Wells LD1 5HT* T: (01597) 829637

HALL (née WANSTALL), Canon Noelle Margaret. b 53. Wolfs Coll Cam BEd 76. Sarum & Wells Th Coll 84. dss 86 d 87 p 94. Hythe *Cant* 86-89; Par Dn 87-89; Par Dn Reculver and Herne Bay St Bart 89-94; C 94-95; Dioc Adv in Women's Min 92-99; Asst Dir Post-Ord Tr 94-97; P-in-c Sittingbourne St Mary 95-00; P-in-c Cant St Martin and St Paul 00-02; R from 02; P-in-c Blean 07-09; P-in-c Cant All SS from 14; AD Cant 05-11; Hon Can Cant Cathl from 96. *The Rectory, 13 Ersham Road, Canterbury CT1 3AR* T: (01227) 462686 or T/F: 768072 E: noelle@thinker117.freeserve.co.uk

HALL, Peter. See HALL, Hubert William Peter

HALL, Canon Peter Douglas. b 60. Oak Hill Th Coll BA 92. d 92 p 93. C Bromyard *Heref* 92-96; C Dorridge *Birm* 96-01;

V Fareham St Jo *Portsm* 01-13; P-in-c Crookhorn from 13; C Purbrook from 13; C Portsdown from 13; Hon Can Portsm Cathl from 15. *The Vicarage, 87 Perseus Place, Waterlooville PO7 8AW* T: (023) 9225 1520 E: revpdhall@btinternet.com or vicar@cogs.org.uk

HALL, Philip Edward Robin. b 36. Oak Hill Th Coll 64. d 67 p 68. C Ware Ch Ch *St Alb* 67-70; C Rayleigh *Chelmsf* 70-73; R Leven w Catwick *York* 73-85; P-in-c Mayfield *Lich* 85-95; P-in-c Ilam w Blore Ray and Okeover 89-95; Res Min Canwell 95-01; Res Min Hints 95-01; Res Min Drayton Bassett 95-01; rtd 01; PtO *Sheff* from 01; *Derby* 02-13. *45 St Alban's Road, Sheffield S10 4DN* T: 0114-229 5032

HALL, Richard. See HALL, George Richard Wyndham

HALL, Richard Alexander Bullock. b 71. Ex Univ BA 93 Edin Univ MTh 95 BD 98. TISEC 95. d 98 p 99. C Boxmoor St Jo *St Alb* 98-01; CF 01-09; Hon Min Can Ripon Cathl 06-09; P-in-c Kirkby Stephen w Mallerstang etc *Carl* 09-11; CF from 11. *c/o MOD Chaplains (Army)* F: 381824 T: (01264) 383430 E: richard.moonhall@btinternet.com

HALL, Robert Arthur. b 35. Lon Univ BSc 66. NW Ord Course 74. d 77 p 78. C York St Paul 77-79; R Elvington w Sutton on Derwent and E Cottingwith 79-82; Chapl Tiffield Sch Northants 82-84; V Bessingby and Carnaby *York* 84-88; V Fulford 88-00; P-in-c York St Denys 97-00; rtd 00; PtO *York* from 00. *11 Almond Grove, Filey YO14 9EH* T: (01723) 518355 E: robertandjune@cwctv.net

HALL, Robert Stainburn. b 72. Qu Coll Cam BA 93. St Steph Ho Ox 96. d 98 p 99. C Worc SE 98-01; TV Halas 01-10; P-in-c from 10. *St Margaret's Vicarage, 55 Quarry Lane, Halesowen B63 4PD* T: 0121-550 8744

HALL, Canon Roger John. b 53. MBE 97. Linc Th Coll. d 84 p 85. C Shrewsbury St Giles w Sutton and Atcham *Lich* 84-87; CF 87-07; Warden Amport Ho 98-01; Chapl Guards Chpl Lon 01-03; Asst Chapl Gen 03-07; Dir Ords 98-02 and Warden of Readers 98-07; QHC 06-07; Dep P in O from 07; Chapl St Pet-ad-Vincula at HM Tower of Lon from 07; Can Chpls R from 12; Chapl Bacon's Coll from 07. *The Chaplain's Residence, HM Tower of London, London EC3N 4AB* T: (020) 3166 6796 E: roger.hall@hrp.org.uk

HALL, Ronald Cecil. b 20. St Aid Birkenhead 63. d 65 p 66. C Tamworth *Lich* 65-69; R Talke 69-74; V Birstwith *Ripon* 74-90; P-in-c Thornthwaite w Thruscross and Darley 76-77; rtd 90. *Wickham House, Kingsmead, Farm Road, Bracklesham Bay, Chichester PO20 8JU* T: (01243) 671190

HALL, Mrs Rosalyn. b 58. NEOC 04. d 07 p 08. C Washington *Dur* 07-11; V Hartlepool H Trin from 11. *Holy Trinity Vicarage, Davison Drive, Hartlepool TS24 9BX* T: (01429) 869618 M: 07985-134577 E: rosalyn44@hotmail.com

HALL, Sandra June. b 58. Westcott Ho Cam. d 10 p 11. C Cuckfield *Chich* 10-15; P-in-c Itchingfield w Slinfold from 15. *The Rectory, The Street, Slinfold, Horsham RH13 0RR* T: (01403) 790197 M: 07817-056986

HALL, Sonia Winifred. See RUDD, Sonia Winifred

HALL, Stephen Philip. b 56. Ripon Coll Cuddesdon. d 84 p 85. C Camberwell St Giles *S'wark* 84-88; Chapl Brighton Poly *Chich* 88-92; TV Bicester w Bucknell, Caversfield and Launton *Ox* 92-02; Sub Chapl HM Pris Bullingdon 92-02; TV Southampton (City Cen) *Win* 02-12; V Lewisham St Mary *S'wark* from 12. *48 Lewisham Park, London SE13 6QZ* T: (020) 8690 2682

HALL, Prof Stuart George. b 28. New Coll Ox BA 52 MA 55 BD 72. Ripon Hall Ox 53. d 54 p 55. C Newark w Coddington *S'well* 54-58; Tutor Qu Coll Birm 58-62; Lect Th Nottm Univ 62-73; Sen Lect 73-78; Prof Ecclesiastical Hist K Coll Lon 78-90; PtO *St Alb* 80-86; *S'wark* 86-90; R Pittenweem *St And* 90-98; R Elie and Earlsferry 90-98; rtd 93. *Hopedene, 15 High Street, Elie, Leven KY9 1BY* T/F: (01333) 330145 E: sgh1@st-andrews.ac.uk

HALL, Thomas Bartholomew Berners. b 39. St Fran Coll Brisbane 63 ThL 65. d 65 p 66. C Townsville Cathl Australia 65-66; C Rockhampton Cathl 66-69; P-in-c Emerald 69-70; R 70-75; P-in-c Whitehawk *Chich* 75-82; V Inglewood and Texas Australia 82-89; V Pine Rivers S 85-89; R Strathpine from 89. *6 Gladdon Street, Bald Hills QLD 4036, Australia* T: (0061) 42-871 1719 E: tombbhall@aanet.com.au

HALL, Timothy Patrick. b 65. Bucks Coll of Educn BSc 87 Oak Hill Th Coll BA 93. Trin Coll Bris 99. d 01 p 02. C Kingsnorth and Shadoxhurst *Cant* 01-04; P-in-c Crowfield w Stonham Aspal and Mickfield *St E* 04-12; P-in-c Coddenham w Gosbeck and Hemingstone w Henley 04-12; RD Bosmere 07-08; V Sheppey *Cant* from 12. *The Vicarage, Vicarage Road, Minster-on-Sea, Sheerness ME12 2HE* E: tph@tesco.net

HALL, Timothy Robert. b 52. Dur Univ BA 74. St Jo Coll Nottm LTh 87. d 87 p 88. C Hawarden *St As* 87-89; Chapl St D Coll Llandudno from 90. *Woodpecker Cottage, St David's College, Llandudno LL30 1RD* T: (01492) 581224

HALL, William. b 34. Hull Univ BSc(Econ) 56. NEOC 89. **d** 92 **p** 93. NSM Bishopwearmouth St Nic *Dur* 92-01; rtd 01. *31 Nursery Road, Silksworth Lane, Sunderland SR3 1NT* T: 0191-528 4843

HALL, Canon William Cameron. b 40. K Coll Lon 60. **d** 65 **p** 66. C Thornaby on Tees St Paul *York* 65-68; Chapl to Arts and Recreation *Dur* 68-05; V Grindon 71-80; Hon Can Dur Cathl from 84; Sen Chapl Actors' Ch Union 89-04; Hon Sen Research Fell Sunderland Univ *Dur* from 98; Hon Fell St Chad's Coll Dur from 09; PtO *Dur* from 07. *41 Ellerby Mews, Thornley, Durham DH6 3FB* T: (01429) 820869 E: billhalluk@yahoo.co.uk

HALL-MATTHEWS, Preb John Cuthbert Berners. b 33. Univ of Qld BA 55 K Coll Lon PGCE 65. Coll of Resurr Mirfield 58. **d** 60 **p** 61. C Woodley St Jo the Ev *Ox* 63-65; C Is of Dogs Ch Ch and St Jo w St Luke *Lon* 63-65; Asst Chapl Ch Hosp Horsham 65-72; Chapl R Hosp Sch Holbrook 72-75; V Tupsley *Heref* 75-90; P-in-c Hampton Bishop and Mordiford w Dormington 77-90; RD Heref City 84-90; Preb Heref Cathl 85-90; TR Wolverhampton *Lich* 90-98; TR Cen Wolverhampton 98-02; Preb Lich Cathl 01-02; rtd 02. *Hillcrest, Corvedale Road, Halford, Craven Arms SY7 9BT* T: (01588) 672706 E: jotricia@hall-matthews.freeserve.co.uk

HALL-THOMPSON, Colin Lloyd. b 51. JP . TCD. **d** 84 **p** 85. C Dublin Rathfarnham *D & G* 84-86; Bp's C Clonmel Union C, C & R 86-91; Chapl Fort Mitchel Pris 86-91; Chapl Port of Cork 86-89; I Kilbride *Conn* 91-03; I Ballymacarrett *D & G* 03-09; Hon Chapl Miss to Seafarers 91-09; Sen Chapl from 09. *7A Wilshere Drive, Belmont, Belfast BT4 2GP* T: (028) 9022 3910 *or* 9075 1131 M: 07984-571220 E: colin.hall-thompson@mtsmail.org

HALLAM, Mrs Janet Kay. b 59. EN(G) 79 RGN 01. STETS 05. **d** 08 **p** 13. NSM Newport St Jo *Portsm* from 08; NSM Newport St Thos from 08; Chapl Isle of Wight NHS Primary Care Trust from 13. *Maranatha, 10 Broadwood Lane, Newport PO30 5NE* T: (01983) 529973 M: 07955-381319 E: jezjanet@btinternet.com

HALLAM, Lawrence Gordon. b 31. Lich Th Coll 61. **d** 63 **p** 64. C Brighton St Martin *Chich* 63-68; R Cocking w Bepton 68-71; V Eastbourne Ch Ch 71-84; V Bexhill St Barn 84-87; rtd 87; PtO *Chich* 87-92. *18 Eaton Court, Eaton Gardens, Hove BN3 3PL* T: (01273) 772328

HALLAM, Mrs Marilyn. b 61. **d** 03 **p** 04. NSM Hayes *Roch* from 03. *83 Pickhurst Rise, West Wickham, Bromley BR4 0AE* T: (020) 8777 2246 E: lyn.hallam@diocese-rochester.org

HALLAM, Nicholas Francis. b 48. Univ Coll Ox BA 71 MA 81 Glas Univ PhD 76 MB, ChB 81 FRCPath 00. Ox NSM Course 84. **d** 87 **p** 88. NSM Ox St Clem 87-93; NSM Balerno *Edin* 93-05; NSM Hawkshead and Low Wray w Sawrey and Rusland etc *Carl* from 06; NSM Ambleside w Brathay 06-10; NSM Loughrigg from 10. *Wetherlam, Hawkshead, Ambleside LA22 0NR* T: (01539) 436069 E: nick.hallam@uwclub.net

HALLAM, Canon Peter Hubert. b 33. MBE 98. Trin Hall Cam BA 56 MA 60. Westcott Ho Cam 56. **d** 58 **p** 59. C Heyhouses on Sea *Blackb* 58-62; Asst Chapl and Tutor St Bede Coll Dur 62-67; V Briercliffe *Blackb* 67-98; Hon Can Blackb Cathl 92-98; rtd 98; PtO *Blackb* from 02. *174 Briercliffe Road, Burnley BB10 2NZ* T: (01282) 441070

HALLAM, Stuart Peter. b 66. St Martin's Coll Lanc BA 92 Wolfs Coll Cam BTh 99. Westcott Ho Cam 96. **d** 99 **p** 00. C Battersea St Mary *S'wark* 99-02; Chapl RN from 02. *Royal Naval Chaplaincy Service, Mail Point 1-2, Leach Building, Whale Island, Portsmouth PO2 8BY* T: (023) 9262 5055 F: 9262 5134 E: revhallam@aol.com

✠**HALLATT, The Rt Revd David Marrison.** b 37. Southn Univ BA 59 St Cath Coll Ox BA 62 MA 66. Wycliffe Hall Ox 59. **d** 63 **p** 64 **c** 94. C Maghull *Liv* 63-67; PC Totley *Derby* 67-75; R Didsbury St Jas *Man* 75-80; R Barlow Moor 76-80; TR Didsbury St Jas and Em 80-89; Adn Halifax *Wakef* 89-94; Area Bp Shrewsbury *Lich* 94-01; Asst Bp Sheff 01-10; rtd 02; Hon Asst Bp Sarum from 11; PtO *Win* 11-15. *10 St Nicholas Hospital, St Nicholas Road, Salisbury SP1 2SW* T: (01722) 413360 E: david.hallatt@btopenworld.com

HALLATT, John Leighton. b 34. St Pet Coll Ox BA 58 MA 62. Wycliffe Hall Ox 58. **d** 60 **p** 61. C Ipswich St Jo *St E* 60-63; C Warrington St Paul *Liv* 63-66; V Wadsley *Sheff* 66-72; V Hindley St Pet *Liv* 72-75; Area Sec (Scotland and Dios Newc and Dur) CMS 75-83; N Sec CMS 78-83; TR Cramlington *Newc* 83-90; V Monkseaton St Mary 90-99; rtd 99; PtO *Newc* from 99. *16 Eastfield Avenue, Whitley Bay NE25 8LT* T: 0191-252 9518

HALLETT, Miss Caroline Morwenna. b 51. Nottm Univ BSc 72 PGCE 74 Univ of Wales (Ban) BTh 05. EAMTC 03. **d** 05 **p** 06. C Sole Bay *St E* 05-09; P-in-c Acton w Gt Waldingfield from 09. *The Vicarage, Melford Road, Acton, Sudbury CO10 0BA* T: (01787) 377287 E: revhallett@yahoo.co.uk

HALLETT, Howard Adrian. b 43. Man Univ MPhil 90. Oak Hill Th Coll BA 81. **d** 81 **p** 82. C Walshaw Ch Ch *Man* 81-84; V Stoke sub Hamdon *B & W* 84-99; RD Ivelchester 91-95; V Kea *Truro* 99-05; rtd 05; PtO *Truro* from 05. *Address temp unknown*

HALLETT, Keith Philip. b 37. Tyndale Hall Bris 61. **d** 64 **p** 65. C Higher Openshaw *Man* 64-68; C Bushbury *Lich* 68-71; P-in-c Drayton Bassett 71-72; R 72-90; V Fazeley 71-90; P-in-c Hints 78-83; V 83-90; C-in-c Canwell CD 78-83; V Canwell 83-90; RD Tamworth 81-90; P-in-c Buckhurst Hill *Chelmsf* 90-93; TR 93-02; rtd 02; PtO *B & W* from 03. *46 Balmoral Way, Worle, Weston-super-Mare BS22 9AL* T: (01934) 413711 E: keithkph@talktalk.net

HALLETT, Peter. b 49. Bath Univ BSc 72. Oak Hill Th Coll. **d** 76 **p** 77. C Brinsworth w Catcliffe *Sheff* 76-79; P-in-c Doncaster St Jas 80-81; V 81-86; R Henstridge and Charlton Horethorne w Stowell *B & W* 86-07; P-in-c Abbas and Templecombe w Horsington 06-07; R Abbas and Templecombe, Henstridge and Horsington from 07. *The Vicarage, Church Street, Henstridge, Templecombe BA8 0QE* T/F: (01963) 362266 E: halatvic@gmail.com

HALLETT, Peter Duncan. b 43. CCC Cam BA 66 MA 68. Westcott Ho Cam 69. **d** 71 **p** 72. C Sawston *Ely* 71-73; C Lyndhurst and Emery Down *Win* 73-78; C Skegness and Winthorpe *Linc* 78-80; P-in-c Samlesbury *Blackb* 80-91; Asst Dir RE 80-00; C Leyland St Ambrose 91-94; V Lostock Hall 00-09; P-in-c Farington Moss 03-09; V Lostock Hall and Farington Moss 09; rtd 09; PtO *Blackb* from 09. *31 Southworth House, Larmenier Retirement Village, Preston New Road, Blackburn BB2 7AL*

HALLETT, Raymond. b 44. EMMTC 85. **d** 88 **p** 89. NSM Hucknall Torkard *S'well* 88-01; NSM Basford St Leodegarius 01-03. *26 Nursery Close, Hucknall, Nottingham NG15 6DQ* T: 0115-953 7677

HALLIDAY, Christopher Norton Robert. b 48. Bradf Univ PhD 99. NOC 82. **d** 85 **p** 86. C Davyhulme St Mary *Man* 85-87; Lect Bolton St Pet 87-90; I Rathdrum w Glenealy, Derralossary and Laragh *D & G* 90-00; R Valley Lee St Geo USA 00-05; PtO *Man* 07-08; TR Saddleworth from 08. *Lydgate Vicarage, Stockport Road, Lydgate, Oldham OL4 4JJ* T: (01457) 872117 E: frchristopher@waitrose.com

HALLIDAY, Mrs Diana Patricia. b 40. ALA 66. NOC 89. **d** 92 **p** 94. NSM Burley in Wharfedale *Bradf* 92-95; NSM Harden and Wilsden 95-97; P-in-c Cullingworth 97-05; Chapl Airedale NHS Foundn Trust 04-11; PtO *Leeds* from 11. *8 Malham Court, Silsden, Keighley BD20 0QB* T: (01535) 656777 E: di.halliday@bradford.anglican.org

HALLIDAY, Edwin James. b 35. NW Ord Course 70. **d** 73 **p** 74. C New Bury *Man* 73-76; V Bolton St Phil 76-82; Dioc Communications Officer 82-88; V Radcliffe St Thos and St Jo 82-90; R Gt Lever 90-02; rtd 02; PtO *Man* from 02. *8 Oxford Close, Farnworth, Bolton BL4 0NF* T: (01204) 792347

HALLIDAY, Geoffrey Lewis. b 40. Lon Coll of Div LTh 66. **d** 66 **p** 67. C W Bridgford *S'well* 66-72; V Woodborough 72-78; P-in-c St Dav Bermuda 78-80; V Rampton *S'well* 80-81; P-in-c Laneham 80-81; P-in-c Treswell and Cottam 80-81; V Rampton w Laneham, Treswell and Cottam 81-85; V Attenborough 85-88; PtO *Derby* 91-92; NSM Ilkeston St Mary 92-03; rtd 03; PtO *Derby* from 03. *Frog Hollow, 323 Heanor Road, Ilkeston DE7 8TN* T: 0115-930 8607 M: 07799-111093 E: fayandgeoff@froghollow.f9.co.uk

HALLIDAY, Jean Douglas. b 47. NTMTC 99. **d** 01 **p** 02. NSM Forest Gate Em w Upton Cross *Chelmsf* 01-02; NSM E Ham w Upton Park and Forest Gate 02-05; NSM Becontree S 05-09; P-in-c Margaretting w Mountnessing and Buttsbury from 09; Dioc Child Protection Adv from 05. *The Vicarage, Penny's Lane, Margaretting, Ingatestone CM4 0HA* T: (01277) 354359 E: jhalliday@chelmsford.anglican.org

HALLIDAY, Louisa. b 42. Open Univ BA 77 BA 94. STETS. **d** 00 **p** 01. NSM Wylye and Till Valley *Sarum* 00-09; rtd 09. *Station House, Great Wishford, Salisbury SP2 0PA* T: (01722) 790618 E: louisahalliday@rocketmail.com

HALLIDAY, Paula Patricia. *See* ROBINSON, Paula Patricia

✠**HALLIDAY, The Rt Revd Robert Taylor.** b 32. Glas Univ MA 54 BD 57. Edin Th Coll 55. **d** 57 **p** 58 **c** 90. C St Andrews St Andr *St And* 57-60; C Glas St Marg 60-63; Lect NT Edin Th Coll 63-74; R Edin H Cross 63-83; Tutor Edin Univ 69-71; Can St Mary's Cathl 73-83; R St Andrews St Andr *St And* 83-90; Tutor St Andr Univ 84-90; Bp Bre 90-96; rtd 96; LtO *Edin* from 97; NSM Edin Ch Ch 97-09; NSM Edin St Pet from 09. *28 Forbes Road, Edinburgh EH10 4ED* T: 0131-221 1490

HALLIGAN, Adrian Ronald. b 69. Ulster Univ MSc 96 PGCE 05. CITC 06. **d** 11. NSM Antrim All SS *Conn* 11-14; NSM Skerry w Rathcavan and Newtowncrommelin from 14. *35 Castle Manor, Ballynure, Ballyclare BT39 9GW* T: (028) 9334 2572 M: 07846-451932 E: adrian.halligan@sky.com

HALLISSEY, Catherine Jane. d 14. Kilternan *D & G* 14-15; C Taney from 15. *Address temp unknown*

HALLIWELL, Christopher Eigil. b 57. Newc Univ BA 78. Trin Coll Bris 89. **d** 91 **p** 92. C Mildenhall *St E* 91-94; R Wrentham w Benacre, Covehithe, Frostenden etc 94-97; TV Sileby, Cossington and Seagrave *Leic* 97-01; V Preston St Cuth *Blackb* 01-12; V Grimsargh from 12; Rural and Environmental Officer from 11. *Starch Hall Farm, Gallows Lane, Ribchester, Preston PR3 3XX* T: (01254) 820430

HALLIWELL, Ivor George. b 33. St Cath Coll Cam BA 57 MA 60. Wells Th Coll 58. **d** 60 **p** 60. C Hanworth St Geo *Lon* 60-62; C Willenhall *Cov* 62-65; C-in-c Whitley St Jas *CD* 65-68; V Whitley 68-72; V Corton *Nor* 72-77; P-in-c Hopton 72-74; V 74-77; Asst Chapl HM Pris Pentonville 77; Chapl HM Pris Ex 77-83; Chapl HM Pris Wakef 83-85; P-in-c Bickington *Ex* 85-87; P-in-c Ashburton w Buckland-in-the-Moor 85-87; V Ashburton w Buckland in the Moor and Bickington 87-90; Chapl HM Pris Channings Wood 90-97; LtO *Ex* 90-97; rtd 97; PtO *Ex* from 97. *Anastasis, Avenue Road, Bovey Tracey, Newton Abbot TQ13 9BQ* T: (01626) 834899 E: ivor@ivorhalliwell.com

HALLIWELL, Canon Michael Arthur. b 28. St Edm Hall Ox BA 50 MA 53. Ely Th Coll 52. **d** 54 **p** 55. C Welling *S'wark* 54-57; C Bournemouth St Alb *Win* 57-59; Asst Gen Sec C of E Coun on Foreign Relns 59-62; C St Dunstan in the West *Lon* 60-62; Chapl Bonn w Cologne *Eur* 62-67; Chapl RAF 66-67; V Croydon St Andr *Cant* 67-71; R Jersey St Brelade *Win* 71-96; Chapl HM Pris Jersey 75-80; Vice-Dean Jersey *Win* 85-99; Tutor S Dios Minl Tr Scheme 92-96; rtd 96; Hon C Jersey Grouville *Win* 96-99; Hon Can Win Cathl 98-99; PtO from 99. *1 Alliance Cottages, Awbridge Hill, Romsey SO51 0HF* T: (01794) 830395 E: halliwells@jerseymail.co.uk

HALLOWS, John Martin. b 50. Birm Univ BA 78 Lon Univ PGCE 82 E Lon Univ MSc 93. Oak Hill Th Coll 92. **d** 94 **p** 95. C Boxmoor St Jo *St Alb* 94-98; TV Bracknell *Ox* 98-01; V Barrowford and Newchurch-in-Pendle *Blackb* from 01. *St Thomas's Vicarage, Wheatley Lane Road, Barrowford, Nelson BB9 6QS* T/F: (01282) 613206 E: jhallows@tiscali.co.uk

HALLS, Canon Peter Ernest. b 38. Bris Univ BA 62. Tyndale Hall Bris 59. **d** 64 **p** 65. C Blackb St Barn 64-67; C Bromley Ch Ch *Roch* 67-70; V Halvergate w Tunstall *Nor* 70-79; V Freethorpe w Wickhampton 71-79; P-in-c Beighton and Moulton 77-79; V Tuckswood 79-90; RD Nor S 86-90; R Brooke, Kirstead, Mundham w Seething and Thwaite 90-03; RD Depwade 91-97 and 01-03; Hon Can Nor Cathl 99-03; rtd 03; PtO *Nor* from 03. *1 Church Farm Close, Weston Longville, Norwich NR9 5JY* T: (01603) 880835

HALLS, Susan Mary. *See* HEMSLEY HALLS, Susan Mary

HALLSWORTH, Peter Michael. b 59. Nottm Univ BSc 81 PGCE 82 York St Jo Univ MA 05. Wilson Carlile Coll 00. **d** 12 **p** 13. C Bridlington Quay Ch Ch *York* from 12. *40 Georgian Way, Bridlington YO15 3TB* T: (01262) 677871 M: 07772-549088 E: petermhallsworth@gmail.com

HALMSHAW, Mrs Stella Mary. b 36. Brighton Coll of Educn TCert 57. St Alb Minl Tr Scheme 81. **dss** 84 **d** 87 **p** 96. Radlett *St Alb* 84-01; Par Dn 87-93; Hon C 93-01; Chapl Herts Univ 93-96; rtd 96; NSM Wittersham w Stone and Ebony *Cant* 01-12; PtO from 13. *Orchard Field House, Grove Lane, Iden, Rye TN31 7PX* T: (01797) 280435

HALSALL, Graham. b 61. Sheff Univ BA 82 Westmr Coll Ox PGCE 84. St Steph Ho Ox MTh 00. **d** 00 **p** 01. C Preston St Jo and St Geo *Blackb* 00-02; C Torrisholme 02-04; P-in-c Bamber Bridge St Sav 04-12; V from 12. *St Saviour's Vicarage, Church Road, Bamber Bridge, Preston PR5 6AJ* T: (01772) 335374 E: graham@halsall4461.freeserve.co.uk

HALSALL, Mrs Isobel Joan. b 47. Liv Univ CertEd 71. **d** 94 **p** 95. OLM Walshaw Ch Ch *Man* 94-05; NSM Cockermouth Area *Carl* 05-13; rtd 13. *1 London Head, Santon Bridge, Holmrook CA19 1UY* E: isobel@cateam.org.uk

HALSEY, Anthony Michael James. b 35. K Coll Cam BA 56 MA 62 Solicitor 64. St Jo Coll Nottm 73. **d** 75 **p** 76. C Derby St Werburgh 75-77; Chapl Canford Sch 78-87; TV Sanderstead All SS *S'wark* 87-89; PtO *Portsm* from 89; rtd 00. *Woodlands, South Road, Liphook GU30 7HS* T: (01428) 724459 E: halseys@southroad.fsbusiness.co.uk

HALSEY, Brother John Walter Brooke. b 33. Cam Univ BA 57. Westcott Ho Cam 61. **d** 61 **p** 62. C Stocksbridge *Sheff* 61-65; Community of the Transfiguration Midlothian from 65; Ind Chapl Edin 65-69. *Hermitage of the Transfiguration, 23 Manse Road, Roslin EH25 9LF* T: 0131-440 3028

HALSON, Bryan Richard. b 32. Jes Coll Cam BA 56 MA 60 Liv Univ MA 72 Geneva Univ 59. Ridley Hall Cam 57. **d** 59 **p** 60. C Coulsdon St Andr *S'wark* 59-62; LtO *Ches* 63-68; Tutor St Aid Birkenhead 63-65; Sen Tutor 65-68; Vice-Prin 68-69; Lect Alsager Coll of Educn 69-72; Prin Lect Crewe and Alsager Coll of HE 72-90; PtO *Ches* from 97. *1 Victoria Mill Drive, Willaston, Nantwich CW5 6RR*

HALSTEAD, James. b 74. Nottm Univ BA 97. Oak Hill Th Coll MTh 09. **d** 09 **p** 10. C Gee Cross *Ches* 09-12; V Mottram in Longendale from 12. *The Vicarage, 30A Broadbottom Road, Mottram, Hyde SK14 6JB* E: jameshalstead@mac.com

HALSTEAD, Stuart. NTMTC 02. **d** 05 **p** 06. C Houghton Regis *St Alb* 05-08; C Kilburn St Aug w St Jo *Lon* 08-10; P-in-c Gt Ilford St Alb *Chelmsf* 10-14; V from 14. *The Vicarage, 99 Albert Road, Ilford IG1 1HS* T: (020) 8478 2031 E: stuart.halstead@btinternet.com

HALTON, Tony James. b 66. Dundee Univ BSc 88 City Univ MSc 01 RGN 94. NTMTC BA 06. **d** 06 **p** 07. NSM W Hendon St Jo *Lon* from 06. E: tonyjhalton@hotmail.com

HAM, Mark Peter. b 65. Sheff Univ BA 86 Birkbeck Coll Lon MSc 96 Ox Brookes Univ BA 15. Ripon Coll Cuddesdon BA 15. **d** 14. C Staplehurst *Cant* 14-15; C The Six from 15. *The Vicarage, 15 Oak Lane, Upchurch, Sittingbourne ME9 7AT* M: 07790-430805 T: (01634) 360794 E: m.ham904@gmail.com

HAM, Robin Peter. b 84. St Aid Coll Dur BA 07. Oak Hill Th Coll MA 15. **d** 15. C S Barrow *Carl* from 15. *33 Holebeck Road, Barrow-in-Furness LA13 0HR* M: 07828-333106 E: robinpeterham@gmail.com

✤**HAMBIDGE, The Most Revd Douglas Walter.** b 27. Lon Univ BD 58. ALCD 53 Angl Th Coll (BC) DD 70. **d** 53 **p** 54 **c** 69. C Dalston St Mark w St Bart *Lon* 53-56; R Cassiar Canada 56-58; R Smithers 58-64; R Fort St John 64-69; Can Caledonia 65-69; Bp Caledonia 69-80; Bp New Westmr 80; Abp New Westmr and Metrop BC Canada 81-93; Prin St Mark's Th Coll Dar es Salaam 93-95; Asst Bp Dar-es-Salaam 93-95; Chan Vancouver Sch of Th Canada from 95. *1621 Golf Club Drive, Delta BC V4M 4E6, Canada* T: (001) (604) 948 1931 E: hambidge@vst.edu

HAMBIDGE, John Robert. b 29. Birm Univ MA 02. Sarum Th Coll. **d** 55 **p** 56. C Tynemouth H Trin W Town *Newc* 55-57; C Middlesbrough St Jo the Ev *York* 58-63; C Clerkenwell H Redeemer w St Phil *Lon* 63-64; C Richmond St Mary *S'wark* 64-66; V Richmond St Jo 66-76; R Swanscombe *Roch* 76-84; V Aberedw w Llandeilo Graban and Llanbadarn etc *S & B* 84-91; P-in-c Sibson w Sheepy and Ratcliffe Culey *Leic* 91-94; P-in-c Orton-on-the-Hill w Twycross etc 92-94; R The Sheepy Gp 95-97; rtd 97; PtO *Lich* from 99. *99 Elizabeth Drive, Tamworth B79 8DE* T: (01827) 61526 E: john@hambidge.com

HAMBLIN, Derek Gordon Hawthorn. b 35. SWMTC 94. **d** 96 **p** 97. NSM S Brent and Rattery *Ex* 96-01; Chapl Larnaca Cyprus 01-02; Asst Chapl Dubai UAE 03-04; PtO *Ex* from 04. *2 Brookwood Close, South Brent TQ10 9DH* T: (01364) 72388 or (00357) (24) 620455 E: derekthecleric1@aol.com

HAMBLIN, Mrs Karen Elizabeth. b 59. St Mary's Coll Dur BA 80 Homerton Coll Cam PGCE 82. St Jo Coll Nottm 05. **d** 07 **p** 08. C Long Eaton St Jo *Derby* 07-11; TV N Wingfield, Clay Cross and Pilsley from 11; RD Chesterfield from 15. *The New Vicarage, Morton Road, Pilsley, Chesterfield S45 8EF* T: (01773) 590529 M: 07711-664649 E: andrew.hamblin1@virgin.net or khstmarys@gmail.com

HAMBLIN, Canon Roger Noel. b 42. Ripon Hall Ox 67. **d** 70 **p** 71. C Scotforth *Blackb* 70-73; C Altham w Clayton le Moors 73-76; V Cockerham w Winmarleigh 76-87; V Cockerham w Winmarleigh and Glasson 87-00; P-in-c Wray w Tatham and Tatham Fells 00-03; V E Lonsdale 03-09; Agric Chapl 01-09; Hon Can Blackb Cathl 04-09; rtd 09; PtO *Blackb* from 09. *Wycoller, School Lane, Pilling, Preston PR3 6AA* T: (01253) 790555 E: rogerhamblin@yahoo.co.uk

HAMBLING, Paul Gary. b 73. St Steph Ho Ox 05. **d** 07 **p** 08. C Woodbridge St Mary *St E* 07-10; TV Merton Priory *S'wark* 10-15; R Melton and Ufford *St E* from 15. *Melton Rectory, Station Road, Melton, Woodbridge IP12 1PX* E: vicarpaul@yahoo.co.uk

HAMBORG, Canon Graham Richard. b 52. Bris Univ BSc 73 Nottm Univ BA 76 MTh 77. St Jo Coll Nottm 74. **d** 77 **p** 78. C Tile Cross *Birm* 77-80; C Upton cum Chalvey *Ox* 80-82; TV 82-86; V Ruscombe and Twyford 86-04; AD Sonning 03-04; CME Adv *Chelmsf* 04-12; Ord Min Development Adv from 12; C Gt Baddow from 04; C Lt Baddow from 05; Hon Can Chelmsf Cathl from 12. *The Rectory, Colam Lane, Little Baddow, Chelmsford CM3 4SY* T: (01245) 222454 E: revghamborg@hotmail.com

HAMBORG, Peter Graham. b 79. BMus 00. Trin Coll Bris BA 09. **d** 10 **p** 11. C Fulwood Ch Ch *Blackb* 10-14; V Lea from 14; V Preston Em from 14. *45 Abingdon Drive, Ashton-on-Ribble, Preston PR2 1EY* M: 07771-993004 T: (01772) 726987

HAMBROOK, Peter John. b 37. **d** 01 **p** 02. OLM Gt Mongeham w Ripple and Sutton by Dover *Cant* 01-04; OLM Deal St Leon w St Rich and Sholden etc 04-10; OLM Ringwould w Kingsdown and Ripple etc 05-10; PtO from 11. *4 Brewery Cottages, Northbourne Road, Great Mongeham, Deal CT14 0HA* T: (01304) 364457 E: peter@4brewerycotts.fsnet.co.uk

HAMEL COOKE, Ian Kirk. b 17. Birm Univ BA 39. Chich Th Coll 39. **d** 41 **p** 42. C Bedminster St Fran *Bris* 41-43; C Alton All SS *Win* 43-48; V N Baddesley 48-55; R Hartest w Boxted *St E* 55-63; V Addlestone *Guildf* 63-75; R Tittleshall w Godwick and Wellingham *Nor* 75-76; R Tittleshall w Godwick, Wellingham and Weasenham 76-82; rtd 82; PtO *Nor* 82-09. *31 Hawthorn Road, Godalming GU7 2NE* T: (01483) 429166

HAMER, David Handel. b 41. Cape Town Univ BA 61 Trin Coll Ox BA 66. Coll of Resurr Mirfield 62. **d** 66 **p** 67. C Claremont S Africa 66-70; Chapl St Paul's Coll Grahamstown 70-73; Chapl Blundell's Sch Tiverton 73-01; rtd 01. *Jaspers Green, Uplowman, Tiverton EX16 7DP* T: (01884) 829130

HAMER, Irving David. b 59. **d** 84 **p** 85. C Newton Nottage *Llan* 84-88; C Roath 88-90; V Llansawel, Briton Ferry 90-00; V Roath St Martin from 00; Miss to Seafarers from 94. *St Martin's Vicarage, Strathnairn Street, Roath, Cardiff CF24 3JL* T: (029) 2048 2295 E: fr.irving.hamer@ntlworld.com

HAMER, Mrs Jeanette Estelle. b 55. Wall Hall Coll Aldenham CertEd 76. SNWTP 10. **d** 12 **p** 13. NSM Douglas St Geo *S & M* 12-14; NSM Douglas St Geo and All SS from 15. *15 Faaie Ny Cabbal, Kirk Michael, Isle of Man IM6 2HS* T/F: (01624) 877814 M: 07624-462251 E: manxmiffy55@gmail.com

HAMER, Penelope Ann. *See* WEST, Penelope Ann

HAMER, Canon Val. b 52. Leeds Univ BA 74. S'wark Ord Course 83. **dss** 86 **d** 87 **p** 94. Warlingham w Chelsham and Farleigh *S'wark* 86-88; Par Dn 87-88; Par Dn Caterham 88-94; C 94-96; RD 95-96; Sub Chapl HM Pris Wandsworth 88-95; V Addiscombe St Mildred *S'wark* 96-02; Ldr Post Ord Tr Croydon Area 94-99; Can Res and Chan Heref Cathl 02-08; Dioc Missr and P-in-c Coychurch, Llangan and St Mary Hill *Llan* 08-12; rtd 12. *Noddfa Fach, 126 West Hill Road, St Leonard's-on-Sea TN38 0AY* T: (01424) 254564

HAMES, Daniel Lewis. b 84. Leic Univ BSc 06. Wycliffe Hall Ox BA 11 MSt 12. **d** 15. NSM Ox St Aldate w H Trin from 15. *19 Percy Street, Oxford OX4 3AA* E: danielhames@gmail.com

✠HAMID, The Rt Revd David. b 55. McMaster Univ Ontario BSc 78. Trin Coll Toronto MDiv 81 Hon DD 05. **d** 81 **p** 82 **c** 02. C Burlington St Chris Canada 81-83; R Burlington St Jo 83-87; Miss Co-ord Gen Syn of Angl Ch of Canada 87-96; Hon Can Santo Domingo 93-02; Dir Ecum Affairs ACC 96-02; Suff Bp Eur from 02; Hon Asst Bp Roch 03-11; Hon C Orpington St Andr 03-09. *14 Tufton Street, London SW1P 3QZ* T: (020) 7898 1160 F: 7898 1166
E: david.hamid@churchofengland.org

HAMIL, Sheila. b 49. Northd Coll of Educn TCert 71. NEOC 92. **d** 95 **p** 98. NSM Wallsend St Luke *Newc* 95-97; NSM Long Benton St Mary 97-02; NSM Willington 02-06; rtd 06; PtO *Newc* from 06. *5 Kings Road, Wallsend NE28 7QT* T: 0191-287 3449 E: sheila@sheilahamil.co.uk

HAMILL-STEWART, Simon Francis. b 32. Pemb Coll Cam BA 56. NOC 77. **d** 80 **p** 81. NSM Neston *Ches* 80-83; C 83-86; V Over St Jo 86-00; Dioc Ecum Officer 92-00; rtd 00; PtO *Ches* 00-01 and from 04; C Middlewich w Byley 01-03. *87 Warmingham Lane, Middlewich CW10 0DJ* T: (01606) 737329

HAMILTON, Graham. *See* HAMILTON, William Graham

HAMILTON, John Frederick. b 57. Leeds Univ BA 78. Edin Th Coll 78. **d** 80 **p** 81. C Whitkirk *Ripon* 80-83; C Leeds Belle Is St Jo and St Barn 83-86; V Oulton w Woodlesford 86-94; V Cookridge H Trin *Leeds* from 94. *Cookridge Vicarage, 53 Green Lane, Cookridge, Leeds LS16 7LW* T: 0113-267 4921 F: 261 2102 M: 07780-677341 E: sulaco57@btopenworld.com

HAMILTON, John Hans Patrick. b 44. K Coll Lon BD 66 AKC 67 Lon Univ DipAdEd 76 FCMI 96. St Boniface Warminster 66. **d** 67 **p** 68. C Cleobury Mortimer w Hopton Wafers *Heref* 67-69; C Sanderstead All SS *S'wark* 69-73; V Battersea St Mary-le-Park 73-75; PtO *Ely* 75-90; Dir of Educn *Derby* 90-95; P-in-c Cliddesden and Ellisfield w Farleigh Wallop etc *Win* 95-00; PtO 00-03; P-in-c Dungeon Hill and The Caundles w Folke and Holwell *Sarum* 03-07; TR Wylye and Till Valley 07-11; rtd 11. *Hillview, Duck Street, Tisbury, Salisbury SP3 6LJ* T: (01722) 790117
E: johnhamilton365@gwa.1.com

HAMILTON, John Nicholas. b 49. Trin Coll Cam BA 71 MA 75. Ridley Hall Cam 72. **d** 75 **p** 76. C Ealing Dean St Jo *Lon* 75-79; C Stoughton *Guildf* 79-83; R Denton St Lawr *Man* 83-88; R The Sherbornes w Pamber *Win* from 88. *The Rectory, Vyne Road, Sherborne St John, Basingstoke RG24 9HX* T: (01256) 850434 E: jt77hamilton@waitrose.com

HAMILTON, Nigel John. *See* TABER-HAMILTON, Nigel John

HAMILTON, Canon Noble Ridgeway. b 23. TD 66. TCD BA 45 MA 49. **d** 47 **p** 48. C Dundela St Mark *D & D* 47-51; C Holywood 51-55; I Belfast St Clem 55-61; I Seapatrick 61-89; Can Dromore Cathl 66-89; Prec 75-84; Chan 84-89; rtd 89; LtO *D & D* from 90. *67 Meadowvale, Waringstown, Craigavon BT66 7RL* T: (028) 3888 2064

HAMILTON, Paul Stuart. b 69. Univ of Wales (Ban) BTh 02. EAMTC. **d** 02 **p** 03. C Hawkwell *Chelmsf* 02-06; V Ingrave St Nic and St Steph from 06; AD Brentwood from 15. *The Rectory, Thorndon Gate, Ingrave, Brentwood CM13 3RG* T: (01277) 812452 E: psh@btinternet.com

HAMILTON, Sarah Louise. *See* BRUSH, Sarah Louise

HAMILTON, Wayne. b 65. **d** 13 **p** 14. NSM Ladywood St Jo and St Pet *Birm* from 13. *249 Sutton Road, Walsall WS5 3AR* T: (01922) 634530 M: 07771-642751
E: waneham@aol.com

HAMILTON, William Graham. b 63. New Coll Ox BA 86. Wycliffe Hall Ox BA 95. **d** 95 **p** 96. C Ivybridge w Harford *Ex* 95-99; V Bovey Tracey SS Pet, Paul and Thos w Hennock from 99. *The Vicarage, Coombe Cross, Bovey Tracey, Newton Abbot TQ13 9EP* T: (01626) 833813 E: pptbovey@mac.com

HAMILTON, William Joseph Taylor. b 40. Univ Coll Ches MTh 00. **d** 97 **p** 98. NSM Ches 97-02; C Thurlestone, S Milton, W Alvington etc *Ex* 02-07; rtd 07; PtO *Ches* from 07. *51 Vincent Drive, Chester CH4 7RQ* T: (01244) 428457
E: william-hamilton3@sky.com

HAMILTON-BROWN, James John. b 35. Lon Univ BSc 59. Ridley Hall Cam 59. **d** 61 **p** 62. C Attenborough w Bramcote *S'well* 61-67; V Bramcote 67-76; R and D Officer Abps' Coun on Evang 76-79; LtO *Sarum* 76-81 and 91-95; TR Dorchester 81-91; Sec Par and People 91-95; P-in-c Tarrant Valley *Sarum* 95-99; C Tollard Royal w Farnham, Gussage St Michael etc 99-00; rtd 00; PtO *Sarum* from 00. *April Cottage, West Street, Winterborne Stickland, Blandford Forum DT11 0NT* T: (01258) 880627 E: jumperhb@btinternet.com

HAMILTON-GREY, Mrs Deborah. b 66. Birm Univ BA 99 MA 03 Sheff Univ BA 14. Coll of Resurr Mirfield 12. **d** 14 **p** 15. C Diss *Nor* 14-15; C Watton from 15. *44 Jubilee Road, Watton, Thetford IP25 6BJ* M: 07896-658373
E: deborah.hamiltongrey@gmail.com

HAMILTON-MANON, Phillipp Robert Christian. b 49. BA 88. St Steph Ho Ox 89. **d** 90 **p** 91. C Norton St Mary *Dur* 90-94; P-in-c Cleadon Park 94-95; V 95-97; TV Lewes All SS, St Anne, St Mich and St Thos *Chich* 97-00; R Lewes St Anne 00-10; R Lewes St Anne and St Mich and St Thos etc 10-12; rtd 12. *11 Cameron Close, Hailsham BN27 3WF* T: (01323) 441908
E: hamilton-manon@aol.com

HAMLET, Paul Manning. b 42. Open Univ BA 81 Ex Univ MEd 96 Univ of Wales (Lamp) MTh 04 PhD 12 Lambeth STh 84 FCollP 96. Kelham Th Coll 61. **d** 66 **p** 67. C Rumboldswyke *Chich* 66-69; C Ely 69-73; Hon C Ipswich St Bart *St E* 73-84; Chapl Wellington Sch Somerset 84-94; Chapl Ipswich Sch 94-02; CF (TAVR) 88-99; CF (ACF) 99-09; rtd 02; PtO *St E* from 02. *5 Wincanton Close, Ipswich IP4 3EE* T: (01473) 724413
E: paul.hamlet@btopenworld.com

HAMLETT, David. b 50. All SS Cen for Miss & Min 13. **d** 15. OLM Ince Ch Ch w Wigan St Cath *Liv* from 15. *17 Woodedge, Ashton-in-Makerfield, Wigan WN4 9JY* T: (01942) 740812 M: 07972-577801

HAMLEY, Mrs Isabelle Maryvonne. b 75. Orléans Univ BA 95 MA 96 Birm Univ BA 03. St Jo Coll Nottm 09. **d** 11 **p** 12. C W Bridgford *S'well* 11-12; C Wilford Hill 12-14; C Edwalton from 14. *The Vicarage, Village Street, Edwalton, Nottingham NG12 4AB* M: 07850-402321
E: isabellehamley@yahoo.co.uk

HAMMERSLEY, Peter Angus Ragsdale. b 35. Linc Th Coll 74. **d** 76 **p** 77. C Stafford *Lich* 76-79; P-in-c W Bromwich St Andr 79-83; V 83-88; P-in-c W Bromwich Ch Ch 85-88; V Streetly 88-98; RD Walsall 90-98; C Ledbury *Heref* 98-00; Team Chapl W Heref 98-01; Asst TV Ledbury *Heref* 01-04; PtO from 04. *15 Pound Close, Tarrington, Hereford HR1 4AZ* T: (01432) 890609

HAMMERSLEY, Susan. b 67. Nottm Univ BA 90. Ripon Coll Cuddesdon BA 07. **d** 07 **p** 08. C Ecclesfield *Sheff* 07-10; C Sheff St Mark Broomhill 10-15; V from 15. *9 Betjeman Gardens, Sheffield S10 3FW* T: 0114-327 6908
E: suehammersley@tiscali.co.uk *or* sue.hammersley@sheffield.anglican.org

HAMMETT, The Ven Barry Keith. b 47. CB 06. Magd Coll Ox BA 71 MA 74. St Steph Ho Ox 71. **d** 74 **p** 75. C Plymouth St Pet *Ex* 74-77; Chapl RN 77-02; Chapl of the Fleet and Adn for the RN 02-06; Dir Gen Naval Chapl Service 02-06; Hon Can Portsm Cathl 02-06; Can Gib Cathl 03-06; rtd 06; QHC from 99; PtO *Portsm* 07-15. *3 Carriage Crescent, Witney OX28 4DR*

HAMMILL, Anthony Lawrence. b 71. Linc Coll Ox BA 92 MA 97 Univ Coll Lon MSc 95 Anglia Ruskin Univ MA 08 Fitzw Coll Cam MPhil 08. Ridley Hall Cam 05. **d** 08 **p** 09. C Chalk *Roch* 08-11; C Tonbridge SS Pet and Paul from 11. *13 Dry Hill Park Crescent, Tonbridge TN10 3BJ*
E: anthony.hammill@diocese-rochester.org

HAMMOND, Andrew Charles Raphael. b 63. Clare Coll Cam BA 86 K Coll Cam MPhil 07 LRAM 91. Westcott Ho Cam 05. **d** 07 **p** 08. C St John's Wood Lon 07-09; Min Can and Succ St Paul's Cathl 09-12; V Willesden St Mary 12-15. *110 Ellesmere Road, London NW10 1JS* M: 07884-185207
E: andrewch007@googlemail.com

HAMMOND, Mrs Barbara Watson. b 33. Lanc Univ MA 79 Bp Otter Coll TCert 53 ACP 70. S'wark Ord Course 89. **d** 92 **p** 94. NSM Upper Norwood St Jo S'wark 92-94; Hon C Spring Park All SS 94-97; PtO 97-02; *Portsm* from 98. *28 Church Path, Emsworth PO10 7DP* T: (01243) 370531
E: barbarawh@virginmedia.com

HAMMOND, Canon Brian Leonard. b 31. Bris Univ BSc 54. Wells Th Coll 56. **d** 58 **p** 59. C Clapham H Trin S'wark 58-62; V Walworth All SS and St Steph 62-72; V S Merstham 72-87; RD Reigate 80-86; Hon Can S'wark Cathl 83-97; V Spring Park All SS 87-97; rtd 97; PtO S'wark 97-02; *Portsm* from 98; *Chich* from 05. *28 Church Path, Emsworth PO10 7DP*
T: (01243) 370531 M: 07802-482974
E: brianbr2811@virginmedia.com

HAMMOND, Carolyn John-Baptist. b 64. St Jo Coll Ox MA 90 Univ Coll Ox DPhil 93 CCC Cam BA 97 MA 02. Westcott Ho Cam 95. **d** 98 **p** 99. C Gamlingay w Hatley St George and E Hatley *Ely* 98-99; C Gamlingay and Everton 99-01; R 01-05; Dean G&C Coll Cam from 05. *Gonville and Caius College, Trinity Street, Cambridge CB2 1TA* T: (01223) 332400
F: 332336 E: cjbh2@cam.ac.uk or dean@cai.cam.ac.uk

HAMMOND, David Geoffrey. b 80. Glos Univ BA 02. Cranmer Hall Dur 02. **d** 04 **p** 05. NSM Preston-on-Tees and Longnewton *Dur* 04-06; C 06-08; Pioneer Missr and P-in-c Nottingham St Sav S'well 08-11; V 11-15; P-in-c Westwood *Cov* from 15; P-in-c Charing from 15. *St John's Vicarage, 5 Featherbed Lane, Coventry CV4 7DD* M: 07939-464095

HAMMOND, Diana Mary. b 46. **d** 99 **p** 00. OLM Bishopstrow and Boreham *Sarum* 99-04; OLM Upper Wylye Valley from 04. *123A Park Lane, Heytesbury, Warminster BA12 0HE* T: (01985) 841185 E: roger.hammond12@virginmedia.com

HAMMOND, Kathryn Mary. b 49. JP . LCTP 07. **d** 08 **p** 09. NSM Linton in Craven and Burnsall w Rylstone *Bradf* 08-11; NSM Adbaston, High Offley, Knightley, Norbury etc *Lich* from 11. *Church House, Newport Road, Woodseaves, Stafford ST20 0NP* T: (01785) 284648 E: ckham@tiscali.co.uk

HAMMOND, Canon Lindsay John. b 57. Southn Univ BA 83. Sarum & Wells Th Coll 84. **d** 86 **p** 87. C Ashford *Cant* 86-90; V Appledore w Brookland, Fairfield, Brenzett etc 90-03; P-in-c Wittersham w Stone and Ebony 95-03; RD S Lympne 95-01; P-in-c Westwell and Hothfield 03-11; P-in-c Charing w Charing Heath and Lt Chart 06-11; AD Ashford 09-11; V Tenterden and Smallhythe from 11; Hon Min Can Cant Cathl 93-08; Hon Can Cant Cathl from 08; AD Romney and Tenterden from 13. *The Vicarage, Church Road, Tenterden TN30 6AT* T: (01580) 761951
E: lindsayhammond@hotmail.co.uk

HAMMOND, Martin James. b 62. St Jo Coll Nottm 03. **d** 05 **p** 06. C Walmley *Birm* 05-08; C Erdington 08-09; TV Bedworth *Cov* from 09; Chapl Geo Eliot Hosp NHS Trust Nuneaton from 14. *2 Bryony Close, Bedworth CV12 0GG* T: (024) 7664 4693
E: revmartinh@blueyonder.co.uk

HAMMOND, Michael John. b 36. St Jo Coll Dur BA 57 MA 65. NW Ord Course 73. **d** 76. NSM Formby St Pet *Liv* 76-80; Sen Lect Nor City Coll 86-01; Lect Guon Inst of HE Italy 01-06; rtd 06; PtO *Nor* from 09. *7 Friars Quay, Norwich NR3 1ES* T: (01603) 614969

HAMMOND, Peter Clark. b 27. Linc Coll Ox BA 49 MA 53. Wells Th Coll 51. **d** 52 **p** 53. C Willesborough *Cant* 52-55; C Croydon St Jo 55-59; R Barham 60-66; V Walmer 66-85; V Rolvenden 85-89; rtd 89; PtO *Ely* from 89. *19 Hardwick Street, Cambridge CB3 9JA* T: (01223) 467425

HAMPEL, Canon Michael Hans Joachim. b 67. Univ Coll Dur BA 89 St Chad's Coll Dur MA 02 FRSA 02. Westcott Ho Cam 90. **d** 93 **p** 94. C Whitworth w Spennymoor *Dur* 93-97; Min Can, Prec and Sacr Dur Cathl 97-02; Sen Tutor St Chad's Coll Dur 02-04; Can Res St E Cathl 04-11; Sub Dean 08-11; Can Res and Prec St Paul's Cathl from 11. *1 Amen Court, London EC4M 7BU* T: (020) 7248 1817 F: 7246 3104
E: michael.hampel@dunelm.org.uk

HAMPSON, Claude Eric. b 25. Rhodes Univ BA 49. St Paul's Coll Grahamstown LTh 50. **d** 50 **p** 51. C Pietermaritzburg Cathl S Africa 50-54; C Greenford H Cross *Lon* 54-58; Sec Fellowship of SS Alb and Sergius 58-60; Brotherhood of St Barn Australia 60-66; R Mt Isa and Adn of the W 67-74; P-in-c Mekong Vietnam 74-75; V Kilburn St Aug w St Jo *Lon* 75-77; R Branxton Australia 77-82; rtd 85. *17/250 Jersey Road, Woollahra NSW 2025, Australia* T: (0061) (2) 9327 8215

HAMPSON, David. b 46. Chich Th Coll 69. **d** 72 **p** 73. C Penrith *Carl* 72-78; V Crosscrake 78-95; V Crosscrake and Preston

Patrick 95; P-in-c Arnside 95-97; rtd 97. *81 Rectory Road, Ashton-in-Makerfield, Wigan WN4 0QD* T: (01942) 728760

HAMPSON, Miss Judith Elizabeth. b 50. I M Marsh Coll of Physical Educn Liv BEd 72 Open Univ BA 89. Ripon Coll Cuddesdon 90. **d** 92 **p** 94. C Alnwick *Newc* 92-96; R Allendale w Whitfield 96-05; V Haydon Bridge and Beltingham w Henshaw 05-13; rtd 13. *5 St Aidan's Terrace, Trimdon Station TS29 6BT* T: (01429) 551022 E: rev.jude@dsl.pipex.com

HAMPSON, Michael John. b 67. Jes Coll Ox BA 88. Ripon Coll Cuddesdon 88. **d** 91 **p** 92. C W Burnley All SS *Blackb* 91-93; C Harlow St Mary Magd *Chelmsf* 93-00; V Church Langley 00-04; PtO *Blackb* 10-12; V Hornby w Claughton and Whittington etc from 12. *Station House, Arkholme, Carnforth LA6 1AZ* T: (015242) 21722 M: 07712-477003
E: michael.hampson.mobile@googlemail.com

HAMPSON, Robert Edward. b 58. LSE BSc 80 Heythrop Coll Lon BA 91 MTh 93. Ridley Hall Cam. **d** 97 **p** 98. C Chingford SS Pet and Paul *Chelmsf* 97-01; V Wanstead H Trin Hermon Hill from 01. *Holy Trinity Vicarage, 185 Hermon Hill, London E18 1QQ* T: (020) 8530 3029
E: roberthampson@btopenworld.com

HAMPSTEAD, Archdeacon of. *See* MILLER, The Ven Luke Jonathan

HAMPTON, Alison Jean. b 61. St Mary's Coll Twickenham BA 98. SEITE 98. **d** 01 **p** 02. C Notting Dale St Clem w St Mark and St Jas *Lon* 01-04; P-in-c Burrough Hill Pars *Leic* 04-06; Chapl Brooksby Melton Coll 04-06; P-in-c Husbands Bosworth w Mowsley and Knaptoft etc *Leic* 06-09; P-in-c Arnesby w Shearsby and Bruntingthorpe 06-09; R Hexagon 09-10; PtO *Cov* 10-11; Chapl Shakespeare Hospice 11-13; Dominican Republic 13-15; V Millfield St Mark and Pallion St Luke *Dur* from 15. *The Vicarage, St Mark's Terrace, Sunderland SR4 7BN* E: alijhampton@gmail.com

HAMPTON, Canon Carla Irene. b 47. ARCM 67 GRSM 68. NTMTC 96. **d** 99 **p** 00. Asst Chapl Mid-Essex Hosp Services NHS Trust 98-02; Chapl Team Ldr 02-04; NSM Chelmsf St Andr 99-04; NSM Gt and Lt Leighs and Lt Waltham 04-06; P-in-c Gt Waltham w Ford End 06-10; V 10-12; rtd 12; RD Chelmsf N 07-14; Hon Can Chelmsf Cathl from 08. *37 Timsons Lane, Chelmsford CM2 6AF* M: 07850-913452
E: revcarlahampton@gmail.com

HAMPTON, Canon John Waller. b 28. Linc Coll Ox BA 51 MA 58. Westcott Ho Cam 51. **d** 53 **p** 54. C Rugby St Andr *Cov* 53-56; Chapl St Paul's Sch Hammersmith 56-65; Chapl St Paul's Girls' Sch Hammersmith 60-65; V Gaydon w Chadshunt *Cov* 65-69; Asst Dir RE 65-70; C-in-c Warwick St Nic 69-75; Fell Qu Coll Birm 75-76; P-in-c Wetton *Lich* 76-82; P-in-c Alstonfield 76-82; P-in-c Sheen 76-80; RD Alstonfield 80-82; P-in-c Butterton 80-82; P-in-c Warslow and Elkstones 80-82; P-in-c Broadway *Worc* 82-91; V 91-93; RD Evesham 87-93; Hon Can Worc Cathl 88-93; rtd 93; PtO *Ab* from 93. *29 Midmar Gardens, Edinburgh EH10 6DY*
T: 0131-447 3520

HAMPTON, Stephen William Peter. b 72. Magd Coll Cam BA 93 MA 97 Ex Coll Ox MSt 99 DPhil 02. Wycliffe Hall Ox BA 95 MA 98. **d** 96 **p** 97. C St Neots *Ely* 96-98; Chapl and Fell Ex Coll Ox 98-03; Sen Tutor St Jo Coll Dur 04-07; Hon Min Can Dur Cathl 05-07; Fell and Dean Peterho Cam from 07. *Peterhouse, Cambridge CB2 1RD* T: (01223) 338217 F: 337578
E: swph2@cam.ac.uk

HANAWAY, Peter Louis. b 47. Open Univ BA 85 Middx Univ BA 02. NTMTC 99. **d** 02 **p** 03. NSM Westmr St Matt *Lon* from 02. *St Matthew's House, 20 Great Peter Street, London SW1P 2BU* T: (020) 7222 3704 M: 07947-722214
E: peter.hanaway@cwctv.com *or* fr.peter@stmw.org

HANCE, Mrs Joy. b 47. Cam Inst of Educn. SAOMC 99. **d** 02 **p** 03. NSM Cherbury w Gainfield *Ox* 02-14; C Witney from 14. *1 Grangers Place, Witney OX28 4BS* T: (01993) 707935
M: 07752-187014 E: joysmail@talk21.com

HANCE, Mrs Marion. b 49. **d** 01 **p** 02. OLM Cheddington w Mentmore and Marsworth *Ox* 01-08; NSM Quantock Coast *B & W* 08-13; rtd 13. *Shardloes, Staple Lane, West Quantoxhead, Taunton TA4 4DE* E: marionhance@yahoo.co.uk

HANCE, Canon Stephen John. b 66. Portsm Poly BSc 89 Nottm Univ BTh 92 MA 93. St Jo Coll Nottm 90. **d** 93 **p** 94. C Southsea St Jude *Portsm* 93-96; TV Tollington *Lon* 96-99; V Balham Hill Ascension *S'wark* 99-13; Can Res S'wark Cathl from 13. *483A Southwark Park Road, London SE16 2JP*
E: stephen.hance@btinternet.com

HANCOCK, Christopher David. b 54. Qu Coll Ox BA 75 MA 80 St Jo Coll Dur BA 78 PhD 84. Cranmer Hall Dur. **d** 82 **p** 83. C Leic H Trin w St Jo 82-85; Chapl Magd Coll Cam 85-88; USA 88-94; V Cambridge H Trin *Ely* 94-02; Dean Bradf 02-04. *3 College Farm Cottages, Garford, Abingdon OX13 5PF* T: (01865) 392804 E: chancock@btinternet.com

HANCOCK, Dorothy Myfanwy. *See* WOFFENDEN, Dorothy Myfanwy

HANCOCK, Mrs Eleanor Mary Catherine. b 55. Huddersfield Univ CertEd 91. CBDTI. **d** 05 **p** 06. C Carl H Trin and St Barn 05-08; P-in-c from 08. *Sandsfield Vicarage, 104 Housesteads Road, Carlisle CA2 7XG* T/F: (01228) 527106
M: 07763-482542 E: eleanor.hancock@sky.com

HANCOCK, Miss Gillian. b 59. St Jo Coll Nottm 05. **d** 07 **p** 08. C Iffley *Ox* 07-11; Chapl Mary Ann Evans Hospice from 11. *Mary Ann Evans Hospice, Eliot Way, Nuneaton CV10 7QL*
T: (024) 7686 5440 M: 07919-064612
E: gillhancock@btinternet.com

HANCOCK, Mrs Helen Margaret. b 62. Rob Coll Cam MA 85. SEITE 06. **d** 09 **p** 10. NSM New Malden and Coombe *S'wark* 09-11; C Surbiton St Andr and St Mark 11-12; P-in-c Surbiton St Matt 12-14; TR from 14. *The Vicarage, 20A Kingsdowne Road, Surbiton KT6 6JZ* T: (020) 8942 6987
E: helenccnm@gmail.com *or* teamrector@tolworthtm.org

HANCOCK, Ivor Michael. b 31. Lon Univ BD 60. Linc Th Coll 65. **d** 66 **p** 67. C Havant *Portsm* 66-69; V Gosport Ch Ch 69-76; P-in-c Southend St Alb *Chelmsf* 76-80; V Hawley H Trin *Guildf* 80-96; V Minley 80-96; RD Aldershot 83-88; rtd 96; PtO *Ox* from 98. *4 Meachen Court, Palmer School Road, Wokingham RG40 1TJ*

HANCOCK, Canon John Clayton. b 36. Dur Univ BA 58. Cranmer Hall Dur. **d** 60 **p** 61. C Newbarns w Hawcoat *Carl* 60-65; V Church Coniston 65-76; R Torver 66-76; P-in-c Heversham 76-77; V 77-93; V Heversham and Milnthorpe 93-05; Hon Can Carl Cathl 98-05; rtd 05; P-in-c Levens *Carl* 04-06; PtO from 06. *Fairfield, Sandside, Milnthorpe LA7 7HW*
T: (015395) 63659 E: jandmhan@btinternet.com

HANCOCK, John Llewellyn. d 14 **p** 15. NSM Llanstadwel *St D* from 14. *Mill House, Llanstadwell, Milford Haven SA73 1EG*
T: (01646) 600610

HANCOCK, John Martin. b 55. Ealing Coll of Educn BA 78. Wycliffe Hall Ox 97. **d** 99 **p** 00. C Bedford St Jo and St Leon *St Alb* 99-04; V Old Hill H Trin *Worc* 04-12; P-in-c Hengrove *Bris* from 12; P-in-c Whitchurch 12-15; V Whitchurch St Nic from 15. *3 Church Meadows, Whitchurch, Bristol BS14 0BS*
T: (01275) 892469 E: martin@hancocks.plus.com

HANCOCK, Canon John Mervyn. b 38. St Jo Coll Dur BA 61 MA 70 Hertf Coll Ox BA 63 MA 66. Cranmer Hall Dur 63. **d** 64 **p** 65. C Bishopwearmouth St Gabr *Dur* 64-67; V Hebburn St Jo 67-87; RD Jarrow 83-92; V S Westoe 87-03; C-in-c S Shields St Aid w St Steph 92-95; Hon Can Dur Cathl 88-03; rtd 03; PtO *Dur* from 04; C Chilton Moor 07-08. *9 Railway Cottages, Dubmire, Houghton le Spring DH4 6LE* T: 0191-385 7491
E: kda77@dial.pipex.com

HANCOCK, Malcolm James. b 50. Leeds Univ MA 02 AGSM 73. Sarum & Wells Th Coll 85. **d** 87 **p** 88. C Sandhurst *Ox* 87-90; P-in-c Bradbourne and Brassington *Derby* 90-92; TV Wirksworth 92-95; V Tunbridge Wells K Chas *Roch* 95-02; R Beckenham St Geo 02-10; Asst Chapl Lewisham Healthcare NHS Trust 10-11; Chapl from 11. *University Hospital Lewisham, Lewisham High Street, London SE13 6LH* T: (020) 8333 3000
E: malcolm.j.hancock@btinternet.com

HANCOCK, Martin. *See* HANCOCK, John Martin

HANCOCK, Mrs Mary. b 52. Imp Coll Lon BSc 73 ARCS 73. Ridley Hall Cam 04. **d** 07 **p** 08. C Fen Orchards *Ely* 07-11; P-in-c Sutton from 11; P-in-c Witcham w Mepal from 11. *The Vicarage, 7 Church Lane, Sutton, Ely CB6 2RQ* T: (01353) 778722 E: mhancock@waitrose.com

HANCOCK, Ms Mary Joy. b 40. Auckland Univ BA 61 Auckland Teachers' Coll PGCE 62 Man Univ CQSW 69. S'wark Ord Course 91. **d** 94 **p** 95. NSM Merton St Mary S'wark 94-01; NSM Colliers Wood Ch 01-06; NSM Upper Tooting H Trin w St Aug 06-12; PtO from 12. *55 Huntspill Street, London SW17 0AA* T: (020) 8946 8984

HANCOCK, Nigel John. b 35. K Coll Cam BA 63 MA 67. EAMTC 86. **d** 89 **p** 91. NSM Cambridge St Mary Less *Ely* 89-00; PV St Jo Coll Cam 99-95; PtO *Ely* from 00. *5 Atherton Close, Cambridge CB4 2BE* T: (01223) 355828

HANCOCK, Preb Paul. b 43. AKC 66. **d** 67 **p** 68. C Wednesbury St Paul Wood Green *Lich* 67-70; C Rugeley 70-73; V Rickerscote 73-75; R Blisland w St Breward *Truro* 75-78; V Mansfield St Lawr *S'well* 78-82; P-in-c Charleton *Ex* 82-83; P-in-c E Portlemouth, S Pool and Chivelstone 82-83; R Charleton w Buckland Tout Saints etc 83-95; RD Woodleigh 88-95; P-in-c Plymouth Crownhill Ascension 95-99; V 99-09; Preb Ex Cathl 03-09; rtd 09. *27 Paddock Drive, Ivybridge PL21 0UB* T: (01752) 690655 E: hazelnut33@aol.com

HANCOCK, Paul David. Oak Hill Th Coll. **d** 10 **p** 11. C Buxton Trin Prop Chpl *Derby* from 10. *24 Bath Road, Buxton SK17 6HH*
T: (01298) 23104 *or* 767551 M: 07816-409476
E: paulhancock2001@hotmail.com

✠**HANCOCK, The Rt Revd Peter.** b 55. Selw Coll Cam BA 76 MA 79. Oak Hill Th Coll BA 80. **d** 80 **p** 81 **c** 10. C Portsdown *Portsm* 80-83; C Radipole and Melcombe Regis *Sarum* 83-87;

V Cowplain *Portsm* 87-99; Adn The Meon 99-10; RD Havant 93-98; Hon Can Portsm Cathl 97-10; Dioc Dir Miss 03-06; Suff Bp Basingstoke *Win* 10-14; Bp B & W from 14. *The Palace, Wells BA5 2PD* T: (01749) 672341 F: 679355
E: bishop@bathwells.anglican.org

HANCOCK, Peter Thompson. b 31. G&C Coll Cam BA 54 MA 58. Ridley Hall Cam 54. **d** 56 **p** 57. C Beckenham Ch Ch *Roch* 56-59; Chapl St Lawr Coll Ramsgate 59-62; Chapl Stowe Sch 62-67; Asst Chapl and Lect Br Embassy Ch Paris *Eur* 67-70; V Walton H Trin *Ox* 70-80; Canada 80-84; V Northwood H Trin *Lon* 84-94; rtd 94; PtO *Ox* 09-07; *Guildf* from 07. *High Lawns, Woodhouse Lane, Holmbury St Mary, Dorking RH5 6NN*
T: (01483) 205430

HANCOCK, Canon Richard Manuel Ashley. b 69. LRPS 02. Linc Th Coll 94 Westcott Ho Cam 95. **d** 97 **p** 98. C Didcot St Pet *Ox* 97-00; P-in-c Shrivenham w Watchfield and Bourton 00-03; V Shrivenham and Ashbury from 03; AD Vale of White Horse 05-12; Hon Can Ch Ch from 12. *St Andrew's Vicarage, Shrivenham, Swindon SN6 8AN* T: (01793) 780183
E: vicar@standrews-shrivenham.fsnet.co.uk

HANCOCK, Ms Vittoria Ruth. b 74. Univ of Wales (Ban) BSc 95 BD 99. Cranmer Hall Dur 91. **d** 01 **p** 02. C Llanberis w Llanrug *Ban* 01-03; C Llanberis, Llanrug and Llandinorwig 03-04; C Dolgellau w Llanfachreth and Brithdir etc 04-05; Chapl St As Cathl and Dioc Evang Officer 06-12; P-in-c Ballater *Ab* from 14; P-in-c Aboyne from 14. *23 Main Street, Port William, Newton Stewart DG8 9QH*

HANCOCKS, Graeme. b 58. Univ of Wales (Ban) BD 79 Oslo Univ 87. Linc Th Coll 79. **d** 81 **p** 82. C Denbigh and Nantglyn *St As* 81-84; Asst Chapl Oslo St Edm *Eur* 84-88; Chapl Stockholm 88-89; Chapl Marseille w St Raphaël, Aix-en-Provence etc 89; Chapl Gothenburg w Halmstad, Jönköping etc 90-93; Chapl Southn Univ Hosps NHS Trust 93-98; Chapl Trafford Healthcare NHS Trust 98-02; Chapl Leeds Teaching Hosps NHS Trust 02-09; rtd 09; PtO *Leeds* from 09. *7 Woodfield Road, Cullingworth, Bradford BD13 5JL* T: (01535) 271551

HANCOX, Ms Sarah Anne. b 85. Edin Univ BD 07. Cranmer Hall Dur 09. **d** 11 **p** 12. C Kirk Sandall and Edenthorpe *Sheff* 11-14; P-in-c Methley w Mickletown *Leeds* 14-15; P-in-c Oulton w Woodlesford 14-15; TV Rothwell, Lofthouse, Methley etc from 15. *The Rectory, Church Side, Methley, Leeds LS26 9BJ* E: hancoxsa@gmail.com

HAND, Michael. *See* HAND, Peter Michael

HAND, Michael Anthony (Tony). b 63. York Univ BA 84 DipCOT 88 SROT. St Jo Coll Nottm MA 95. **d** 95 **p** 96. C Lutterworth w Cotesbach *Leic* 95-98; C Lutterworth w Cotesbach and Bitteswell 99-01; V Acomb H Redeemer *York* from 01; Chapl Manor Sch from 01. *The Vicarage, 108 Boroughbridge Road, York YO26 6AB* T: (01904) 798593
E: tony@holyredeemeryork.com

HAND, Canon Nigel Arthur. b 54. St Jo Coll Nottm. **d** 84 **p** 85. C Birm St Luke 84-88; C Walton H Trin *Ox* 88-89; TV 89-97; C Selly Park St Steph and St Wulstan *Birm* 97-04; P-in-c Selly Park Ch Ch 04-08; AD Moseley 04-07; Can Res Birm Cathl from 08. *12 Nursery Drive, Handsworth, Birmingham B20 2SW*
E: nigelhand@me.com

HAND, Peter Michael. b 42. Univ Coll Ox BA 63 Lon Univ BSc 75. Sarum & Wells Th Coll 77. **d** 80 **p** 81. NSM Shaston *Sarum* 80-81; C Tisbury 81-83; C Glastonbury St Jo w Godney *B & W* 83-84; C Glastonbury w Meare, W Pennard and Godney 84-87; V High Littleton 87-99; RD Midsomer Norton 92-98; R Winford w Felton Common Hill 99-07; Warden of Readers Bath Adnry 98-06; rtd 07; TV Winchcombe *Glouc* 10-13. *27 Stancombe View, Winchcombe, Cheltenham GL54 5LE*
T: (01242) 609575 E: anne_michael_hand@yahoo.co.uk

HAND, Philip Ronald. b 53. Spurgeon's Coll BA 78. **d** 03 **p** 04. NSM Southampton (City Cen) *Win* from 03. *52 Cranbury Avenue, Southampton SO14 0LT* T: (023) 8049 4490

HANDCOCK, Mrs Alison Dawn. b 66. STETS 12. **d** 15. C Preston Plucknett *B & W* from 15. *31 Primrose Lane, Yeovil BA21 5SH*
T: (01935) 414238 E: alison.handcock@btinternet.com

✠**HANDFORD, The Rt Revd George Clive.** b 37. CMG 07. Hatf Coll Dur BA 61. Qu Coll Birm 61. **d** 63 **p** 64 **c** 90. C Mansfield SS Pet and Paul *S'well* 63-67; Lebanon 67-74; Dean Jerusalem 74-78; UAE 78-83; Adn Gulf 78-83; V Kneesall w Laxton *S'well* 83-84; P-in-c Wellow 83-84; RD Tuxford and Norwell 83-84; Adn Nottingham 84-90; Suff Bp Warw *Cov* 90-96; Bp Cyprus and the Gulf 96-07; Pres Bp Episc Ch Jerusalem and Middle E 02-07; rtd 07; Hon Asst Bp Ripon and Leeds 07-14. *Wayside, 1 The Terrace, Kirby Hill, Boroughbridge, York YO51 9DQ*
T: (01423) 325406 E: gchandford@gmail.com

HANDFORTH, Canon Richard Brereton. b 31. St Pet Coll Ox BA 55 MA 60. Westcott Ho Cam 63. **d** 64 **p** 65. C Hornchurch St Andr *Chelmsf* 64-65; Warden St Steph Coll Hong Kong 65-73; Chapl CMS Fellowship Ho Chislehurst 73-75; Hon C

Chislehurst St Nic *Roch* 73-75; Home Educn Sec CMS 75-83; V Biggin Hill *Roch* 83-88; Inter-change Adv CMS 88-96; Hon C Plaistow St Mary *Roch* 95-04; Hon Can Lagos from 95; rtd 96; PtO *Roch* from 01. *1 Bromley College, London Road, Bromley BR1 1PE* T: (020) 8460 0238
E: r.handforth1@btinternet.com

HANDLEY, The Ven Anthony Michael. b 36. Selw Coll Cam BA 60 MA 64. Chich Th Coll 60. **d** 62 **p** 63. C Thorpe St Andr *Nor* 62-66; C Gaywood, Bawsey and Mintlyn 66-72; V Hellesdon 72-81; RD Nor N 80-81; Adn Nor 81-93; Adn Norfolk 93-02; rtd 02; PtO *Nor* from 02. *25 New Street, Sheringham NR26 8EE* T: (01263) 820928
E: amhandley@yahoo.co.uk

HANDLEY, Dennis Francis. b 57. MIE 79 TEng(CEI) 80. Coll of Resurr Mirfield 82. **d** 85 **p** 86. C Headingley *Ripon* 85-88; C Rothwell 88-92; V Liversedge *Wakef* 92-97; V Ripponden and Barkisland w W Scammonden 97-06; TR Almondbury w Farnley Tyas 06-14; Dioc Rural Officer 04-14; V Berwick H Trin and St Mary *Newc* from 14. *The Vicarage, Parade, Berwick-upon-Tweed TD15 1DF* T: (01289) 306136 E: dennis@ntlworld.com

HANDLEY, John. b 38. Oak Hill Th Coll. **d** 83 **p** 84. C Witton w Brundall and Braydeston *Nor* 83-86; R Reedham w Cantley w Limpenhoe and Southwood 86-93; P-in-c E w W Harling and Bridgham w Roudham 93-95; R E w W Harling, Bridgham w Roudham, Larling etc 95-05; P-in-c Garboldisham w Blo' Norton, Riddlesworth etc 94-96; RD Thetford and Rockland 95-98; rtd 05; PtO *Nor* from 05. *6 Barton Close, Swaffham PE37 7SB* T: (01760) 336328 E: john.handley@hotmail.co.uk

HANDLEY, Mrs Kathryn Emma. b 70. **d** 14 **p** 15. C Bredbury St Mark *Ches* from 14. *1 Kennett Drive, Bredbury, Stockport SK6 2GA* T: 0161-430 8516 E: kehandley@btinternet.com

HANDLEY, Michael. *See* HANDLEY, Anthony Michael

HANDLEY, Timothy John. b 63. St Steph Ho Ox 94. **d** 96 **p** 97. C St Marychurch *Ex* 96-98; PtO *Cant* 06-10. *All Saints' House, Churchview Road, Twickenham TW2 5BX* T: (020) 8894 3580

HANDLEY MACMATH, Terence. b 59. Goldsmiths' Coll Lon BA 80 K Coll Cam MA 98. Westcott Ho Cam 91. **d** 94 **p** 95. NSM Southwold *St E* 94-95; PtO *St Alb* 96-99; C St Alb St Pet 99-05; V Harrow Weald All SS *Lon* 05-07; Chapl R Free Hampstead NHS Trust 07-09; Chapl R Brompton and Harefield NHS Trust from 09. *Harefield Hospital, Hill End Road, Harefield, Uxbridge UB9 6JH* T: (01895) 823737
E: terencehandleymacmath@googlemail.com

HANDY, Miss Laura Jane. b 82. Regents Th Coll BA 13. St Mellitus Coll 13. **d** 15. C Droitwich Spa *Worc* from 15. *6 Riverside Way, Droitwich WR9 8UP* T: (01905) 774874 M: 07921-524394 E: revlaurahandy@gmail.com

HANDY, Thomas. b 79. Ex Univ BA 02 Bris Univ PGCE 05. Trin Coll Bris MA 09. **d** 09 **p** 10. C Shepton Mallet w Doulting *B & W* 09-12; R S Petherton w The Seavingtons 12-14; C Kingsbury Episcopi w E Lambrook, Hambridge etc 13-14; R S Petherton w The Seavingtons and The Lambrooks from 14. *The Rectory, Hele Lane, South Petherton TA13 5DY* T: (01460) 249443 E: revdtomhandy@hotmail.com

HANFORD, Canon William Richard. b 38. Keble Coll Ox BA 60 MA 64 Lon Univ BD 66 Univ of Wales LLM 95. St Steph Ho Ox 60. **d** 63 **p** 64. C Roath St Martin *Llan* 63-66; C Llantwit Major 67-68; PV Llan Cathl 68-72; Chapl RN 72-76; Hon Chapl Gibraltar Cathl 74-76; Hon C Eastbourne St Sav and St Pet *Chich* 76-77; C Brighton St Pet 77-78; Can Res and Prec Guildf Cathl 78-83; Hon Can Guildf Cathl 03-09; V Ewell 83-09; Tutor and Lect Chich Th Coll 79-86; rtd 09; PtO *Guildf* from 09; *Llan* from 09. *15 Austin Avenue, Laleston, Bridgend CF32 0LG* T: (01656) 656892 *or* (020) 8786 0552
E: wrhanford@btinternet.com

HANKE, Mrs Hilary Claire. b 53. Qu Coll Birm BTheol 93. **d** 93 **p** 94. C Kempsey and Severn Stoke w Croome d'Abitot *Worc* 93-97; TV Wordsley 97-99; Convenor for Women's Min 98-05; P-in-c Reddal Hill St Luke 01-08; V 08-12; RD Dudley 04-10; Hon Can Worc Cathl 98-12; P-in-c Upholland *Liv* from 12. *The Rectory, 1A College Road, Upholland, Skelmersdale WN8 0PY* T: (01695) 622936 E: hchanke@btinternet.com

HANKEY, Miss Dorothy Mary. b 38. CertEd 65. Trin Coll Bris 75. **dss** 78 **d** 87 **p** 94. Wigan St Jas w St Thos *Liv* 78-84; Middleton *Man* 84-85; Litherland Ch Ch *Liv* 85-89; Par Dn 87-89; Par Dn Blackpool St Mark *Blackb* 89-94; C 94-95; C Blackpool St Paul 95-98; rtd 98; PtO *Blackb* from 98. *89 Rutland Avenue, Poulton-le-Flyde FY6 7RX* T: (01253) 890635

HANKEY, Rupert Christopher Alers. b 60. Sheff Univ LLB 82. Wilson Carlile Coll 86 St Jo Coll Nottm MTh 06. **d** 07 **p** 08. C Bedford St Jo and St Leon *St Alb* 07-11; V Sidcup St Andr *Roch* from 11. *The Vicarage, St Andrew's Road, Sidcup DA14 4SA* T: (020) 8300 4712 M: 07539-319545 E: rupert3@tesco.net

HANKINS, Clifford James. b 24. Chich Th Coll 70. **d** 72 **p** 73. C Henfield *Chich* 72-76; V Fernhurst 76-84; V Mithian w

Mount Hawke *Truro* 84-89; rtd 89; Hon C W Wittering and Birdham w Itchenor *Chich* from 90. *c/o C J Hankins Esq, 48 Windmill Court, East Wittering, Chichester PO20 8RJ*

HANKS, John Martin. b 57. St Chad's Coll Dur BA 80 Univ of Wales (Cardiff) LLM 94 Selw Coll Cam PGCE 82. St Steph Ho Ox 10. **d** 12. NSM Ox St Barn and St Paul from 12; NSM Ox St Thos from 12; Chapl to Suff Bp Ebbsfleet (PEV) *Cant* 12-13. *50 Thames Street, Oxford OX1 1SU* E: john@hanksox.com

HANLEY, Máirt Joseph. b 74. Univ Coll Ches BA 95. CITC BTh 03. **d** 03 **p** 04. NSM Tralee w Kilmoyley, Ballymacelligott etc *L & K* 03-11; Bp's C Kilcolman w Kiltallagh, Killorglin, Knockane etc 11-15; I Baltinglass w Ballynure etc *C & O* from 15. *The Rectory, Baltinglass, Co Wicklow, Republic of Ireland* M: (00353) 87-619 4733 E: rev.hanley@gmail.com

HANLON, Michael James. b 50. St Jo Coll Nottm 96. **d** 98 **p** 99. C Tamworth *Lich* 98-00; C Melbourne St Jo Australia from 00. *25 The Eyrie, Lilydale Vic 3140, Australia* T: (0061) (3) 9739 5235 *or* 9739 3541 E: mikeruth@alphalink.com.au

HANLON, Thomas Kyle. b 72. QUB BA 94 TCD BTh 97. **d** 97 **p** 98. C Bangor St Comgall *D & D* 97-00; I Dromore *Clogh* 00-06; I Fivemiletown from 06; Chapl to Bp Clogh from 03. *St John's Rectory, 160 Ballagh Road, Fivemiletown BT75 0QP* T: (028) 8952 1030 *or* 8952 2422
E: fivemiletown@clogher.anglican.org

HANMER, Sister Phoebe Margaret. b 31. Edin Univ MA 54. **d** 96 **p** 97. NSM Brakpan S Africa 96-00; NSM Actonville 00-03; PtO Ox 99-00; *Birm* from 04. *Address temp unknown*

HANMER, Canon Richard John. b 38. Peterho Cam BA 61 MA 65. Linc Th Coll 62. **d** 64 **p** 65. C Sheff St Swithun 64-69; Bp's Chapl Nor 69-73; V Cinderhill *S'well* 73-81; V Eaton *Nor* 81-94; Dioc Chapl MU 91-04; Hon Can Nor Cathl 93-94; Can Res Nor Cathl 94-04; P-in-c Nor St Mary in the Marsh 94-04; rtd 04; PtO *Nor* from 04. *18 Quebec Road, Dereham NR19 2DR* T: (01362) 655092

HANNA, Miss Elizabeth. b 50. QUB BA 73 Lon Bible Coll BA 79 Milltown Inst Dub MA 01. CITC 99. **d** 01 **p** 02. C Bangor Abbey *D & D* 01-04; I Magherally w Annaclone 04-08; I Belfast St Nic *Conn* from 08. *St Nicolas' Rectory, 15 Harberton Park, Belfast BT9 6TW* T: (028) 9066 7753 M: 07801-946909 *or* T/F: 9068 2924 E: hannamanor15@btinternet.com

HANNA, Isaac James. b 70. York St Jo Coll MA 03. CITC 07. **d** 08 **p** 09. Bp's C Dungiven w Bovevagh *D & R* 08-10; I Maghera w Killelagh 10-15; I Drumcliffe w Lissadell and Munninane *K, E & A* from 15. *The Rectory, Drumcliffe, Co Sligo, Republic of Ireland* T: (00353) (71) 916 3125

HANNA, John. b 44. Lon Bible Coll BA 83. Westcott Ho Cam 86. **d** 87 **p** 88. C Denton Ch Ch *Man* 87-91; V Higher Walton *Blackb* 91-98; C Marple All SS *Ches* 98-02; TV Burrington, Chawleigh, Cheldon, Chulmleigh etc *Ex* 02-09; RD S Molton 03-09; rtd 09; PtO *S & B* 10-12; P-in-c Beguildy and Heyope and Llangynllo and Bleddfa from 12. *Victoria House, Victoria Road, Knighton LD7 1BD* T: (01547) 529296

HANNA, Patricia Elizabeth. *See* McGEE HANNA, Patricia Elizabeth

HANNA, Peter Thomas. b 45. ACII 66 GIFireE 75. CITC 85. **d** 88 **p** 89. NSM Cork St Fin Barre's Union *C, C & R* 88-95; Min Can Cork Cathl from 92; Dioc Info Officer 94-95; Aux Min Cork St Luke Union 95-00; Aux Min Kinsale Union 00-04; Aux Min Douglas Union w Frankfield from 04. *Mount Windsor, Farnahoe, Inishannon, Co Cork, Republic of Ireland* T/F: (00353) (21) 477 5470 E: peterhanna7@vodafone.ie

HANNA, Canon Robert Charles. b 49. Oak Hill Th Coll 75. **d** 77 **p** 78. C Coleraine *Conn* 77-82; I Convoy w Monellan and Donaghmore *D & R* 82-94; Can Raphoe Cathl 88-94; I Drumcliffe w Kilnasoolagh *L & K* from 94; Can Limerick, Killaloe and Clonfert Cathls from 00; Chan from 04. *St Columba's Rectory, Bindon Street, Ennis, Co Clare, Republic of Ireland* T: (00353) (65) 682 0109 M: 086-6216 7040 E: bobhanna@eircom.net

HANNA, Steven John. b 70. Oak Hill Th Coll BA 02. **d** 02 **p** 03. C Dagenham *Chelmsf* 02-07; V Becontree St Elisabeth from 07. *St Elisabeth's Vicarage, Hewett Road, Dagenham RM8 2XT* T: (020) 8517 0355 E: vicar@st-elisabeths.org.uk

HANNAFORD, Prof Robert. b 53. Ex Univ BEd 76 MA 78 PhD 87. St Steph Ho Ox 78. **d** 80 **p** 81. C Ex St Jas 80-83; Chapl Ex Univ 83-88; Tutor St Steph Ho Ox 89-92; Sen Lect Cant Ch Ch Univ Coll 92-99; Prof Chr Th Univ Coll Chich 99-01; Hon C Bury w Houghton and Coldwaltham and Hardham *Chich* 99-01; Th Consultant Bp Horsham 99-01; Can and Preb Chich Cathl from 00; Prof Th St Martin's Coll Lanc 02-05; Dean of Faculty 05-07; Dean of Faculty Cumbria Univ *Carl* from 07; Hon C Tunstall w Melling and Leck *Blackb* 02-03; Hon C E Lonsdale from 03. *The Vicarage, Church Lane, Tunstall, Carnforth LA6 2RQ* T: (015242) 74376
E: rhannaford@ucsm.ac.uk

HANNAH, Darrell Dale. b 62. Grand Canyon Univ BA 85 S Bapt Th Sem MDiv 89 Regent Coll Vancouver ThM 92 Magd Coll Cam PhD 96. WMMTC 00. **d** 03 **p** 03. NSM Edgbaston St Geo *Birm* 03-04; NSM Iffley *Ox* 04-07; NSM Earley St Pet 07-08; R Ascot Heath from 08. *All Saints' Rectory, London Road, Ascot SL5 8DQ* T: (01344) 621200 E: drddhannah@yahoo.co.uk

HANNAH, Kimberley Victoria. *See* WILLIAMS, Kimberley Victoria

HANNAM, Robert Stephen. b 46. CertEd 69. **d** 05 **p** 06. NSM Rastrick St Matt *Wakef* 05-08; NSM Rastrick *Leeds* from 08. *33 Lyndhurst Road, Brighouse HD6 3RX* T: (01484) 716053 E: stephnr.hannam@btinternet.com

HANNEN, Robert John. *See* DAVIES-HANNEN, Robert John

✠**HANNON, The Rt Revd Brian Desmond Anthony.** b 36. TCD BA 59 MA 62. TCD Div Sch Div Test 61. **d** 61 **p** 62 **c** 86. C Clooney *D & R* 61-64; I Desertmartin 64-69; I Londonderry Ch Ch 69-82; I Enniskillen *Clogh* 82-86; Preb Clogh Cathl 82-84; Dean Clogh 85-86; Bp Clogh 86-01; rtd 01. *Drumconnis Top, 202 Mullaghmeen Road, Ballinamallard, Enniskillen BT94 2DZ* T: (028) 6638 8557 F: 6638 8086 E: bdah@btinternet.com

HANNY, Mrs Annette Elizabeth. b 49. Keele Univ MA 95. WMMTC 02. **d** 05 **p** 06. NSM Oldbury, Langley and Londonderry *Birm* 05-12; Chapl Sandwell Mental Health NHS and Social Care Trust from 10. *93 St Mary's Road, Smethwick B67 5DG* T: 0121-420 2858 M: 07970-841662 E: annette.hanny@hotmail.com *or* annette.hanny@hobtpct.nhs.uk

HANOVA, Petra. *See* ELSMORE, Petra

HANSELL, Anupama. *See* KAMBLE-HANSELL, Anupama

HANSELL, Peter Michael. b 76. Selw Coll Cam BA 97 MA 01 MPhil 99 PhD 02. Qu Coll Birm 03. **d** 05 **p** 06. C Moseley St Mary *Birm* 05-07; C Moseley St Mary and St Anne 07-09; Reader Initial Tr Adv *Cov* 09-10; R Bure Valley *Nor* 10-13; Chapl Trent Coll Nottm 13-14; Chapl Clifton Coll Bris from 14. *7 Worcester Terrace, Bristol BS8 3JW* M: 07875-640575 E: revd.pmh@btinternet.com

HANSEN, Mrs Moira Jacqueline. b 55. K Coll Lon BSc 76. Oak Hill Th Coll BA 88. **d** 88 **p** 96. Par Dn Finchley Ch Ch *Lon* 88-91; Par Dn Broadwater *Chich* 91-94; Chapl Oak Hill Th Coll 94-00; P-in-c Stanton *St E* 00-04; P-in-c Hopton, Market Weston, Barningham etc 04-06; R Stanton, Hopton, Market Weston, Barningham etc 04-06; rtd 06. *49 Turnstone Drive, Bury St Edmunds IP32 7GT*

HANSFORD, Gordon John. b 40. Southn Univ BSc 61. Trin Coll Bris 77. **d** 79 **p** 80. C Ex St Leon w H Trin 79-82; C Shirley *Win* 82-87; R Landcross, Littleham, Monkleigh etc *Ex* 87-96; TV Bideford, Northam, Westward Ho!, Appledore etc 96-99; P-in-c Monkleigh 96-99; RD Hartland 96-99; V Paul *Truro* 99-07; rtd 07. *14 Chilpark, Fremington, Barnstaple EX31 3BY* E: hansford@tinyworld.co.uk

HANSFORD, Ruth Patricia. b 68. K Coll Lon BSc 90 Surrey Univ MSc 96 Sch of Pharmacy Lon PhD 00. Trin Coll Bris BA 02. **d** 03 **p** 04. C Parkham, Alwington, Buckland Brewer etc *Ex* 03-07; P-in-c Hatherleigh, Meeth, Exbourne and Jacobstowe 07-11; TV Okehampton, Inwardleigh, Belstone, Sourton etc from 12; RD Okehampton from 12. *The Rectory, Hatherleigh, Okehampton EX20 3JY* T: (01837) 810314 M: 07718-765936 E: maggiethecat@waitrose.com

HANSON, Dale Robert. b 57. Fitzw Coll Cam BA 78 MA 81 Univ of BC MA 80. Ridley Hall Cam 81. **d** 84 **p** 85. C Much Woolton *Liv* 84-87; Assoc Min Kowloon St Andr Hong Kong 87-91; TV Billingham St Aid *Dur* 91-95; C Dur St Nic 95-98; V 98-07; C Kowloon St Andr Hong Kong from 07. *St Andrew's Church, 138 Nathan Road, Tsim Sha Tsui, Kowloon, Hong Kong, China* T: (00852) 2367 1478 F: 2367 6562 E: dale@standrews.org.hk

HANSON, David John. b 59. All SS Cen for Miss & Min. **d** 14 **p** 15. C Chadderton Ch Ch *Man* from 14. *23 Lindale Avenue, Chadderton, Oldham OL9 9DW*

HANSON, Edward William. b 51. Salem State Coll (USA) BA 73 Tufts Univ MA 78 Boston Coll PhD 92 Episc Div Sch MDiv 00. Ripon Coll Cuddesdon 00. **d** 01 **p** 02. C Linc St Botolph and Linc St Pet-at-Gowts and St Andr 01-04; P-in-c Orsett and Bulphan and Horndon on the Hill *Chelmsf* 04-06; R 06-14; RD Thurrock 08-11; rtd 14. *14 Erncroft Way, Twickenham TW1 1DA* E: ed.hanson@alumni.tufts.edu

HANSON, Keith. b 59. Cranmer Hall Dur 99. **d** 01 **p** 02. C Armley w New Wortley *Ripon* 01-04; C Whitkirk 04-06; P-in-c Illingworth *Wakef* 06-09; Chapl H Trin Sch Halifax 06-09; P-in-c Harlaxton Gp *Linc* from 09. *The Rectory, 6 Rectory Lane, Harlaxton, Grantham NG32 1HD* T: (01476) 594608 E: revkeef@hotmail.com

HANSON, Mrs Margaret Patricia. b 45. Ripon Coll Cuddesdon 04. **d** 05 **p** 06. NSM Ifield *Chich* 05-15; rtd 15. *Birch Cottage, 7 Barnwood, Crawley RH10 7TH* T: (01293) 535569 E: margaret.hanson1@tesco.net

HANSON, Michael Beaumont. b 49. Univ Coll Ox MA 70 PGCE 71. NOC 81. **d** 84 **p** 85. Chapl Leeds Gr Sch 84-99; Hon C Leeds St Geo *Ripon* 84-99; rtd 99; PtO *Carl* from 99. *5 The Crofts, Crosby, Maryport CA15 6SP* T: (01900) 816630 E: mikeandchristinehanson@sky.com

HANSON, Peter Richard. b 45. ARCM. Chich Th Coll 72. **d** 75 **p** 76. C Forest Gate St Edm *Chelmsf* 75-79; C Chingford SS Pet and Paul 79-81; V Leytonstone H Trin and St Aug Harrow Green 81-86; Dep Chapl HM Pris Wandsworth 86-88; Chapl HM Pris Lewes 88-91; rtd 91; PtO *Chich* from 91. *Flat 2, 39 St Anne's Crescent, Lewes BN7 1SB* T: (01273) 471714

HANSON, Philip Arthur. b 46. Loughb Univ BTech 69 City Univ MSc 73 St Jo Coll Nottm MA 04 CEng 72 FRSA 96. Qu Coll Birm MA 12. **d** 12 **p** 13. NSM Claverdon w Preston Bagot *Cov* from 12. *Lion Hill Cottage, Station Road, Claverdon, Warwick CV35 8PE* T: (01926) 843421 M: 07879-400947 E: phil@philiphanson.net

HANSON, Robert Arthur. b 35. Keele Univ BA 57. St Steph Ho Ox 57 St Mich Coll Llan 59. **d** 60 **p** 61. C Longton St Mary and St Chad *Lich* 60-65; Chapl St Mary's Cathl *Edin* 65-69; R Glas St Matt 69-79; R Paisley H Trin 79-87; V Walsall St Andr *Lich* 87-93; PtO *Worc* 94-97; C Kentish Town *Lon* 97-01; Hon C 02-06; rtd 02; PtO *Lon* from 06. *7B Fraser Regnart Court, Southampton Road, London NW5 4HU* T: (020) 7284 3634 M: 07951-154384 E: bob.hanson@btinternet.com

HANSON, Timothy David. b 68. Oak Hill Th Coll BA 95. **d** 95 **p** 96. C Boscombe St Jo *Win* 95-00; V Wharton *Ches* from 00. *The Vicarage, 165 Crook Lane, Winsford CW7 3DR* T: (01606) 593215 *or* 861860 E: tiohanson@aol.com

HANWELL, David John. b 46. Leic Univ CertEd 74 UEA BEd 94. **d** 98 **p** 99. OLM Mundford w Lynford, Cranwich and Ickburgh w Langford *Nor* 98-04; OLM Cockley Cley w Gooderstone 99-04; P-in-c 04-13; OLM Gt and Lt Cressingham w Threxton 99-04; C 04-13; OLM Hilborough w Bodney 99-04; C 04-13; OLM Oxborough w Foulden and Caldecote 99-04; C 04-13; rtd 13; PtO *Nor* from 15. *Cherry Tree Cottage, Back Lane, Castle Acre, King's Lynn PE32 2AR* T: (01760) 755812 E: david.hanwell@btopenworld.com

HAOKIP (*formerly* YAM), Canon David Tongkhoyam. b 60. Serampore Univ BTh 89 Madras Univ MDiv 92. H Cross Coll Rangoon. **d** 84 **p** 85. Burma 83-93; Hon Can Sittwe from 09; India 93-95; Korea 96-97; PtO *S'wark* 99; TV Southampton (City Cen) *Win* 00-05; V E Ham St Geo *Chelmsf* from 05. *The Vicarage, Buxton Road, London E6 3NB* T: (020) 8472 2111 M: 07817-702358 E: dthaokip1@yahoo.co.uk

HAPGOOD-STRICKLAND, Canon Peter Russell. b 57. St Steph Ho Ox BA 83. **d** 83 **p** 84. C Ashford *Cant* 83-86; C Sheerness H Trin w St Paul 86-90; V Blackb St Thos w St Jude 90-97; P-in-c Burnley St Andr w St Marg 97; V Burnley St Andr w St Marg and St Jas from 98; P-in-c Burnley St Mark from 14; Hon Can Blackb Cathl from 05. *St Andrew's Vicarage, 230 Barden Lane, Burnley BB10 1JD* T: (01282) 423185 E: hapgoodstrickland@btinternet.com

HARARE, Bishop of. *See* GANDIYA, The Rt Revd Chad Nicholas

HARBAGE, Matthew Michael. b 86. York Univ MMath 10 Cam Univ BTh 15. Westcott Ho Cam 12. **d** 15. C Louth *Linc* from 15. *The Rectory, Church Lane, Legbourne, Louth LN11 8LN* E: mharbage@hotmail.com

HARBIDGE, The Ven Adrian Guy. b 48. St Jo Coll Dur BA 70. Cuddesdon Coll 73. **d** 75 **p** 76. C Romsey *Win* 75-80; V Bournemouth St Andr 80-86; V Chandler's Ford 86-99; RD Eastleigh 93-99; Adn Bournemouth 99-10; P-in-c Seale, Puttenham and Wanborough *Guildf* from 10. *The Rectory, Elstead Road, Seale, Farnham GU10 1JA* T: (01252) 783057 E: rector@spw.org.uk

HARBORD, Canon Paul Geoffrey. b 56. JP 99. Keble Coll Ox BA 78 MA 86. Chich Th Coll 81. **d** 83 **p** 84. C Rawmarsh w Parkgate *Sheff* 83-86; C Doncaster St Geo 86-90; C-in-c St Edm Anchorage Lane CD 90-95; V Masbrough 95-03; Bp's Chapl from 03; Hon Can Sheff Cathl from 07. *4 Clarke Drive, Sheffield S10 2NS* T: 0114-266 1932 *or* 230 2170 M: 07898-485428 E: geoffrey.harbord@sheffield.anglican.org

HARBORD, Philip James. b 56. St Cath Coll Ox BA 77. Cranmer Hall Dur 78. **d** 80 **p** 81. C Enfield St Andr *Lon* 80-83; CMS Pakistan 84-88; C Clay Hill St Jo and St Luke *Lon* 88-91; Chapl Wexham Park Hosp Slough 91-92; Chapl Upton Hosp Slough 91-92; Chapl Heatherwood and Wexham Park Hosps NHS Trust 92-95; Chapl Leic Gen Hosp NHS Trust 95-98; Chapl Fosse Health NHS Trust 98-99; Chapl Leics and Rutland Healthcare NHS Trust 99-01; P-in-c Cosby *Leic* 01-07; P-in-c Whetstone 03-07; rtd 07. *47 Maple Avenue, Blaby, Leicester LE8 4AT* T: 0116-277 6522 E: philipjharbord@btinternet.com

HARBRIDGE, Philip Charles Anthony. b 65. K Coll Lon LLB 88 AKC 88 Ch Coll Cam BA 98 MA 02. Westcott Ho Cam. **d** 99 **p** 00. C Hampton All SS *Lon* 99-02; Chapl Ch Coll Cam 02-07;

Chapl Millfield Sch Somerset from 07. *Millfield School, Street BA16 0YD* T: (01458) 442291 E: pch@millfieldschool.com

HARCOURT, Canon Giles. b 36. Westcott Ho Cam 68. **d** 71 **p** 72. C Bishopwearmouth St Mich w St Hilda *Dur* 71-73; C Fishponds St Mary *Bris* 73-75; Bp's Dom Chapl *S'wark* 75-78; LtO 78-79; V S Wimbledon H Trin and St Pet 79-88; V Greenwich St Alfege 88-04; Hon Chapl RN Coll Greenwich 89-99; RD Greenwich Thameside *S'wark* 94-98; Boro Dean Greenwich 94-98; Hon Can S'wark Cathl 96-04; rtd 05; PtO *Chich* from 05. *1A Trinity Trees, Eastbourne BN21 3LA* T: (01323) 638790

HARCOURT, Paul George. b 67. Em Coll Cam BA 88 MA 92. Wycliffe Hall Ox BA 91. **d** 92 **p** 93. C Moreton *Ches* 92-95; C Woodford Wells *Chelmsf* 95-00; V from 00; AD Redbridge 10-14. *All Saints' Vicarage, 4 Inmans Row, Woodford Green IG8 0NH* T: (020) 8504 0266 F: 8504 9640 E: pharcourt@btconnect.com

HARCOURT-NORTON, Michael Clive. *See* NORTON, Michael Clive Harcourt

HARDACRE (née BROOKFIELD), Mrs Patricia Anne. b 50. St Mary's Coll Dur BA 72 St Jo Coll Dur MA 74. Cranmer Hall Dur. **dss** 84 **d** 87 **p** 94. Par Dn Acomb St Steph and St Aid *York* 87-94; C 94-96; TV Preston Risen Lord *Blackb* 96-07; rtd 07; PtO *Blackb* from 07. *17 Fairfield Drive, Clitheroe BB7 2PE* T: (01200) 429341 E: anne@hipporage.fsnet.co.uk

HARDCASTLE, Ian Kenneth Dalton. b 56. Auckland Univ BE 78 ME 80. St Jo Coll Nottm MTh 04. **d** 04 **p** 05. C Denton Holme *Carl* 04-09; V Whangaparaoa Peninsular New Zealand from 09. *3/39 Wade River Road, Whangaparaoa 0932, New Zealand* T: (0064) (9) 424 0939 E: vicar@ststephenswgp.org.nz

HARDCASTLE, Nigel John. b 47. Reading Univ BSc 68. Qu Coll Birm. **d** 72 **p** 73. C Weoley Castle *Birm* 72-75; C Handsworth St Andr 75-78; V Garretts Green 78-86; Exec Sec Ch Computer Project BCC 86-89; R Emmer Green Ox 89-99; V Reading St Luke w St Bart 99-12; rtd 12; PtO *Ox* from 13. *67 Dunstall Close, Tilehurst, Reading RG31 5AY* T: 0118-943 1258 E: nigel@hardcastle33.fsnet.co.uk

HARDCASTLE, Roger Clive. b 52. Southn Univ BSc 73. Qu Coll Birm. **d** 78 **p** 79. C Walton St Mary *Liv* 78-82; V Pemberton St Fran Kitt Green 82-94; TV Padgate 94-96; V Birchwood 96-06; rtd 06. *15 Ullswater Avenue, Orrell, Wigan WN5 8PF* T: (01942) 513568 E: rhardcastle@btopenworld.com

HARDIE, John Blair. b 16. MBE 46. LDS FDS MRCS 38 MRCSE 66. Edin Th Coll 73. **d** 76 **p** 76. Chapl St Paul's Cathl Dundee 76-86; rtd 86; Hon C Carnoustie *Bre* from 86. *4 Lammerton Terrace, Dundee DD4 7BW* T: (01382) 860836

HARDIE, Canon Stephen. b 41. AKC 67. **d** 68 **p** 69. C Roxbourne St Andr *Lon* 68-73; C Colchester St Mary V *Chelmsf* 73-76; R Wivenhoe 76-92; TR Dovercourt and Parkeston 92-96; P-in-c Harwich 92-96; R Dovercourt and Parkeston w Harwich 96-04; TR Harwich Peninsula 04-05; P-in-c Ramsden Crays w Ramsden Bellhouse 02-05; RD Harwich 97-04; Hon Can Chelmsf Cathl 02-05; rtd 05; PtO *St E* from 06; *Nor* from 09. *The Croft, 2 Lowestoft Road, Worlingham, Beccles NR34 7EH* T: (01502) 711625

HARDING, Alan. b 45. St Jo Coll Ox BA 67 MA 73 Pemb Coll Ox DPhil 92. Oak Hill NSM Course 89. **d** 93 **p** 94. NSM Lt Heath *St Alb* 93-99; P-in-c S Mymms and Ridge 99-05; PtO *St E* 05-08; NSM S Hartismere 08-13; PtO *St Alb* from 05; *St E* from 13. *The Old Guildhall, Mill Street, Gislingham, Eye IP23 8JT* T: (01379) 783361 E: alansharon.harding@googlemail.com

HARDING, Alec James. b 61. St Andr Univ MA 83 DTh. Cranmer Hall Dur 86. **d** 89 **p** 90. C Thirsk *York* 89-93; TV Heref St Martin w St Fran 93-95; TV Heref S Wye 95-00; V Barnard Castle w Whorlton *Dur* from 00; AD Barnard Castle from 03. *The Vicarage, Parson's Lonnen, Barnard Castle DL12 8ST* T: (01833) 637018 E: alec.harding@durham.anglican.org

HARDING, Mrs Allison Joan. b 65. Sheff Univ BA 96 Northumbria Univ BSc 04. Cranmer Hall Dur 11. **d** 13 **p** 14. C Benwell *Newc* 13-15; C Benwell and Scotswood from 15. *14 Bentinck Road, Newcastle upon Tyne NE4 6UU* T: 0191-421 3587 M: 07977-122020 E: allisonjamie@live.co.uk

HARDING, Andrew Barry. b 66. Westcott Ho Cam 97. **d** 99 **p** 00. C Rainham *Roch* 99-03; V Hoo St Werburgh 03-11; CF from 11. *c/o MOD Chaplains (Army)* F: 381824 T: (01264) 383430 E: ardy@abh123.freeserve.co.uk

HARDING, Benjamin Lee. b 75. Bris Univ BA 97. Trin Coll Bris BA 07. **d** 07. C Cullompton, Willand, Uffculme, Kentisbeare etc *Ex* 07-12; C Brampton St Thos *Derby* 12-14; Chapl Lyon *Eur* from 14. *38 chemin de Taffignon, Sainte-Foy-lès-Lyon, 69110 Lyon, France* E: benlharding@btinternet.com

HARDING, Canon Brenda Kathleen. b 39. Bedf Coll Lon BA 60 K Coll Lon BD 62 Lon Inst of Educn PGCE 65. St Deiniol's Hawarden 91. **d** 92 **p** 94. NSM Lancaster Ch Ch *Blackb* 92-13; Acting Vice-Prin CBDTI 04-05; Hon Can Blackb Cathl 05-13;

rtd 13; PtO *Blackb* from 13. *14 Ascot Close, Lancaster LA1 4LT* T: (01524) 66071 E: brenda.harding@cumbria.ac.uk

HARDING, Canon Brian Edward. b 38. ALCD 65. **d** 65 **p** 66. C Chislehurst Ch Ch *Roch* 65-68; P-in-c Baxenden *Blackb* 68-70; V 70-88; V Douglas 88-07; Hon Can Blackb Cathl 96-07; rtd 07. *8 Lon Eirlys, Prestatyn LL19 9JZ* T: (01745) 851615 E: bnbharding@tiscali.co.uk

HARDING, Carl Julius. b 64. St Jo Coll Dur BA 15. Cranmer Hall Dur 12. **d** 15. C Stanwix *Carl* from 15. *54 Eden Street, Carlisle CA3 9LH* M: 07961-862956 T: (01228) 524436 E: carljharding@gmail.com

HARDING, Mrs Christine Joan. b 54. St Mellitus Coll. **d** 11 **p** 12. NSM Chadwell Heath *Chelmsf* from 11. *69 Eric Road, Romford RM6 6JH* T: (020) 8599 6174

HARDING, Clifford Maurice. b 22. Leeds Univ BA 47. Coll of Resurr Mirfield 46. **d** 48 **p** 49. C Tonge Moor *Man* 48-54; Nyasaland 54-56; CF 56-59; V Oldham St Jo *Man* 59-65; LtO *Blackb* 65-87; rtd 87; PtO *Blackb* 87-11. *31 Riley Avenue, Lytham St Annes FY8 1HZ* T: (01253) 725138

HARDING, Mrs Elise. b 44. RGN 65. STETS 07. **d** 10 **p** 11. NSM Wimborne Minster *Sarum* from 10; NSM Witchampton, Stanbridge and Long Crichel etc from 15; NSM Horton, Chalbury, Hinton Martel and Holt St Jas from 15. *The Beaches, 22 Middlehill Road, Wimborne BH21 2SD* T: (01202) 884775 E: fur_elise_h@yahoo.co.uk

HARDING, Elizabeth. *See* BUNKER, Elizabeth

HARDING, James. b 77. Liv Univ BA 01 MA 02 PhD 06. SNWTP 09. **d** 11 **p** 12. Chapl Liv Univ 11-13; Chapl Liv Jo Moores Univ 11-13; Tutor St Mellitus Coll *Lon* from 13; C Springfield H Trin *Chelmsf* 13-15; Public Preacher from 15. *St Mellitus College, 24 Collingham Road, London SW5 0LX* T: (020) 7052 0573 M: 07545-451542

HARDING, James Alexander. b 78. Trin Coll Bris BA 11. **d** 11 **p** 12. C Fulham Ch Ch *Lon* from 11. *55 Clancarty Road, London SW6 3AH* M: 07956-222940 E: hardingjamesa@gmail.com

HARDING, James Owen Glyn. b 42. Sussex Univ BA 65. NEOC 04. **d** 06 **p** 07. NSM Acomb H Redeemer *York* 06-12; PtO from 12. *63 Station Road, Upper Poppleton, York YO26 6PZ* T: (01904) 784495 E: jim2sal65@yahoo.co.uk

HARDING, John Stuart Michael. b 45. St Jo Coll Nottm 79. **d** 81 **p** 82. C Clifton *S'well* 81-87; V Broxtowe 87-98; PtO *Chelmsf* 98-01; M & K 01-02; rtd 07. *Greystone Farm, 9 Liscable Road, Newtownstewart BT78 4EF*

HARDING, Lesley Anne. *See* ATKINS, Lesley Anne

HARDING, Mrs Marion. b 33. Gilmore Course 75. **dss** 85 **d** 87 **p** 94. Hertford St Andr *St Alb* 85-87; Par Dn 87-93; rtd 93; NSM Lt Amwell *St Alb* 93-97; PtO from 97. *41 Calton Avenue, Hertford SG14 2ER*

HARDING, Mrs Mary Elizabeth. b 46. SRN 67. STETS 97. **d** 00 **p** 01. NSM Shaftesbury *Sarum* 00-13; Chapl Westmr Memorial Hosp Shaftesbury 02-13; rtd 13. *Greenacres, Boxfield Road, Axminster EX13 5LD* T: (01297) 32155 E: mary.harding617@btinternet.com

HARDING, Michael Anthony John. b 37. Brasted Th Coll 67 Sarum Th Coll 68. **d** 71 **p** 72. C Forest Hill Ch Ch *S'wark* 71-72; C Catford St Laur 72-74; C Leominster *Heref* 74-77; R Neenton and V Ditton Priors 77-86; P-in-c Aston Botterell w Wheathill and Loughton 77-86; P-in-c Burwarton w N Cleobury 77-86; R Ditton Priors w Neenton, Burwarton etc 86-94; V E Budleigh w Bicton and Otterton *Ex* 94-03; rtd 03; PtO *Sarum* from 03. *The Beaches, 22 Middlehill Road, Wimborne BH21 2SD* T: (01202) 884775 E: michaelharding@talktalk.net

HARDING, Preb Michael David. b 38. Man Univ BA 61. Lich Th Coll 61. **d** 63 **p** 64. C Hednesford *Lich* 63-67; C Blurton 67-70; V Newcastle St Paul 70-99; RD Newcastle 87-97; Preb Lich Cathl 89-99; rtd 99; PtO *Lich* from 00. *7 Staines Court, Stone ST15 8XF* T: (01785) 811737 E: mdharding@argonet.co.uk

HARDING, Peter Gordon. b 45. Lon Univ BA 70 Open Univ BA 88 MA 90. Cranmer Hall Dur 77. **d** 79 **p** 80. C Kirkheaton *Wakef* 79-82; NSM New Sleaford *Linc* 90-00. *77 The Drove, Sleaford NG34 7AS* T: (01529) 306055 E: peter@harding67.plus.com

HARDING, Mrs Ren Elaine Lois. b 56. Glos Univ BA 05. Trin Coll Bris MA 07. **d** 07 **p** 08. C Rainham *Roch* 07-11; V Joydens Wood St Barn from 11. *The Vicarage, 6 Tile Kiln Lane, Bexley DA5 2BB* T: (01322) 528923 M: 07836-644782 E: renharding@hotmail.com

HARDING, Richard Michael. b 42. St Alb Minl Tr Scheme 80. **d** 83 **p** 84. C Pershore w Pinvin, Wick and Birlingham *Worc* 83-86; V Longdon, Castlemorton, Bushley, Queenhill etc 86-95; P-in-c Catshill and Dodford 95-97; V 97-02; P-in-c Stokenham w Sherford and Beesands, and Slapton *Ex* 02-05; R 05-09; R Stokenham, Slapton, Charleton w Buckland etc 09-10; rtd 10; PtO *Portsm* from 10. *7 West View, Victoria Road, Yarmouth PO41 0QW*

HARDING, Richard Warrington. b 60. Trin Coll Bris 05. **d** 07 **p** 08. C Broadway w Wickhamford *Worc* 07-09; C Old Hill H Trin 09-11; TV Ipsley from 11. *Matchborough Vicarage, Winward Road, Redditch B98 0SX* T: (01527) 523768

HARDING, Rolf John. b 22. Oak Hill Th Coll 41 Lon Coll of Div 46. **d** 49 **p** 50. C Sydenham H Trin *S'wark* 49-52; C Harold Wood *Chelmsf* 52-53; Min Harold Hill St Paul CD 53-61; V Coopersale 61-91; Chapl St Marg Hosp Epping 73-91; Chapl W Essex HA 86-91; rtd 91; PtO *B & W* 91-05; Asst Chapl R United Hosp Bath NHS Trust 92-94. *11 Westbrook Park, Weston, Bath BA1 4DP* T: (01225) 484968

HARDINGHAM, Paul David. b 52. Lon Univ BSc 74 Fitzw Coll Cam BA 77. Ridley Hall Cam 75. **d** 78 **p** 79. C Cambridge St Martin *Ely* 78-81; C Jesmond Clayton Memorial *Newc* 81-88; C Harborne Heath *Birm* 88-91; R Ipswich St Matt *St E* 91-04; V Halliwell St Pet *Man* from 04. *St Peter's Vicarage, 1 Sefton Road, Bolton BL1 6HT* T: (01204) 848567 E: paul@hardingham60.freeserve.co.uk

HARDINGHAM, Paul Ernest. b 57. **d** 06 **p** 07. OLM Gosberton, Gosberton Clough and Quadring *Linc* from 06; OLM Glen Gp from 07. *23 Lowgate, Gosberton, Spalding PE11 4NL* T: (01775) 840803

HARDINGHAM, Timothy Kenneth. b 49. G&C Coll Cam BA 70. ERMC 08. **d** 11 **p** 12. NSM Saffron Walden and Villages *Chelmsf* from 11. *Steading, West End, Wendens Ambo, Saffron Walden CB11 4UJ* T: (01799) 542874 M: 07894-537990 E: tim@hardingham.net

HARDISTY, Gloria. b 62. **d** 10 **p** 11. NSM Thornton St Jas *Leeds* from 10. *1 Wembley Avenue, Thornton, Bradford BD13 3BY* T: (01274) 833280 E: john-hardisty@sky.com

HARDMAN, Bryan Edwin. b 29. Lon Univ BD 60 Selw Coll Cam PhD 64 K Coll Lon MTh 75. Moore Th Coll Sydney. **d** 55 **p** 55. C Hurstville Australia 55-60; PtO *Ely* 60-65; V Cambridge St Andr Less 65-68; Prin Bible Coll of S Australia 68-83; Prin Karachi Dioc Sem Pakistan 83-86; Prin Discipleship Tr Cen Singapore 87-94; Nat Dir Interserve Korea 94-97; Visiting Prof Tyndale Univ Canada 99-00; rtd 01; LtO Adelaide from 06. *197 Kappler Court, 1215 Grand Junction Road, Hope Valley, SA 5090, Australia* T: (0061) (8) 8265 6494 E: hardmanbryan@gmail.com

HARDMAN, The Ven Christine Elizabeth. b 51. Lon Univ BSc(Econ) 73. St Alb Minl Tr Scheme 81. **dss** 84 **d** 87 **p** 94. Markyate Street *St Alb* 84-88; Par Dn 87-88; Tutor St Alb Minl Tr Scheme 88-91; Course Dir 91-96; C Markyate Street *St Alb* 94-96; V Stevenage H Trin 96-01; RD Stevenage 99-01; Adn Lewisham *S'wark* 01-08; Adn Lewisham and Greenwich 08-12; rtd 12; NSM S'wark Cathl from 12; PtO *St Alb* from 13. *9 Foster Close, Stevenage SG1 4SA* T: (01438) 230611 E: christine.elizabeth.hardman@gmail.com

HARDMAN, Geoffrey James. b 41. Birm Univ BA 63. NOC 77. **d** 80 **p** 81. NSM Latchford St Jas *Ches* 80-93; NSM Haydock St Jas *Liv* from 94. *48 Denbury Avenue, Stockton Heath, Warrington WA4 2BW* T: (01925) 264064 E: geoff@ghardman.freeserve.co.uk

HARDMAN, Mrs Pamela. b 39. **d** 01 **p** 02. NSM Bramhall *Ches* 01-07; NSM Prestbury 07-12; rtd 12. *38 Deva Close, Poynton, Stockport SK12 1HH* T: (01625) 877936 E: pamela.prestbury@yahoo.co.uk

HARDMAN, Canon Peter George. b 35. Man Univ BSc 56. Ridley Hall Cam 58. **d** 60 **p** 61. C Oldham St Paul *Man* 60-63; NW England Area Sec SCM 63-64; NW England Area Sec CEM 64-67; Asst Chapl Marlborough Coll 67-72; Chapl 72-79; P-in-c Wareham *Sarum* 79-80; TR 80-00; Chapl Wareham Hosp 80-92; Chapl Dorset HealthCare University NHS Foundn Trust 92-00; Can and Preb Sarum Cathl 87-00; RD Purbeck 89-99; rtd 00; PtO *Sarum* from 00; *B & W* from 02. *55 Palairet Close, Bradford-on-Avon BA15 1US* T: (01225) 867198 E: peterhardman@onetel.com

HARDS, Mrs Valerie Joy. b 51. STETS. **d** 08 **p** 09. NSM Whippingham w E Cowes *Portsm* 08-12; NSM Binstead from 12; NSM Havenstreet St Pet from 12. *Dallimores, Barton Estate, East Cowes PO32 6NR* T: (01983) 883943

HARDWICK, Christopher George. b 57. Open Univ BA 94 Birm Univ MA 96 PhD 00 ACIB 79. Ripon Coll Cuddesdon 90. **d** 92 **p** 93. C Worc SE 92-95; R Ripple, Earls Croome w Hill Croome and Strensham 95-00; R Upton-on-Severn, Ripple, Earls Croome etc 00-05; RD Upton 97-05; Hon Can Worc Cathl 03-05; Dean Truro 05-11; R Truro St Mary 05-11; P-in-c Pyworthy, Pancrasweek and Bridgerule *Ex* 11-15; P-in-c Tavistock and Gulworthy 15; V Tavistock, Gulworthy and Brent Tor from 15. *The Rectory, 5A Plymouth Road, Tavistock PL19 8AU* T: (01822) 615648

HARDWICK, Mrs Daphne Anne. b 45. Reading Univ BA 97 SRN 67 SCM 69 HVCert 79. Trin Coll Bris 10. **d** 12 **p** 13. OLM Swindon Ch Ch *Bris* from 12. *6 St Margaret's Road, Swindon SN3 1RU* T: (01793) 693721 M: 07881-281843 E: daphne@christchurchswindon.co.uk

HARDWICK, Canon Graham John. b 42. Qu Coll Birm 68. **d** 70 **p** 71. C Watford St Mich *St Alb* 70-73; C N Mymms 73-75; Youth Officer Cov Cathl 75-81; Chapl Lanchester Poly 76-81; V Nuneaton St Nic 81-95; Ind Chapl and P-in-c New Bilton 95-07; Hon Can Cov Cathl 04-07; rtd 08; PtO *Cov* from 08. *150 Pytchley Road, Rugby CV22 5NG* T: (01788) 544011 F: 333256 E: revgjh@btinternet.com

HARDWICK, John Audley. b 28. Em Coll Cam BA 51 MA 55. Westcott Ho Cam 51. **d** 53 **p** 54. C Selby Abbey *York* 53-56; Chapl St Edm Sch Hindhead 56-60; Chapl Aysgarth Sch 60-62; Chapl St Edm Sch Hindhead 62-86; Asst Hd Master 73-90; rtd 93; PtO *Ches* 95-09. *8 Kingstone Court, Wards Road, Chipping Norton OX7 5BP*

HARDWICK, The Ven Robert. b 56. St Jo Coll Nottm 91. **d** 93 **p** 94. C Beeston *S'well* 93-97; V Scawby, Redbourne and Hibaldstow *Linc* 97-01; RD Yarborough 00-01; R Swift Current Canada from 01; Adn Swift Current from 02. *731 North Hill Drive, Swift Current SK S9H 1X4, Canada* T: (001) (306) 773 8871 E: rob.hardwick@shaw.ca

HARDWICK, Canon Susan Frances. b 44. Warwick Univ BA 81. Qu Coll Birm 82. **dss** 85 **d** 87 **p** 94. Chilvers Coton w Astley *Cov* 85-91; C 87-91; Dioc Disabilities Officer 91-96; Chapl Hereward Coll 91-96; Chapl FE Colls *Cov* 94-09; Hon C New Bilton 96-98; FE Field Officer Team Co-ord (W Midl) 97-09; Chapl Rainsbrook Secure Tr Cen 99-09; Hon Can Cov Cathl 04-09; rtd 09; PtO *Cov* from 09. *150 Pytchley Road, Rugby CV22 5NG* T: (01788) 544011 F: 333256 E: revgjh@btinternet.com

HARDWICKE, Stephen Michael. b 57. Herts Coll BA 85 Lon Bible Coll MA 87 K Coll Lon MTh 92. Westcott Ho Cam 93. **d** 95 **p** 96. C Leagrave *St Alb* 95-01; P-in-c Cowley *Lon* 01-03; R from 03. *St Laurence Rectory, Church Road, Cowley, Uxbridge UB8 3NB* T/F: (01895) 232728 E: stevehardwicke660@hotmail.com

HARDY, Alison Jane. b 60. **d** 14 **p** 15. C Stratton and Launcells *Truro* from 14; C Bude Haven and Marhamchurch from 14. *Newfield, Brook Drive, Bude EX23 8NY* T: (01288) 488308 E: reverendalisonhardy@gmail.com

HARDY, Ms Alison Jane. b 61. St Anne's Coll Ox BA 82 MA 96. NOC 92. **d** 95 **p** 96. C Flixton St Mich *Man* 95-98; Lect Bolton St Pet 98-00; P-in-c Irlam 00-05; R Stand from 05; AD Radcliffe and Prestwich from 13. *Stand Rectory, 32 Church Lane, Whitefield, Manchester M45 7NF* T: 0161-766 2619 E: alisonhardy@fsmail.net

HARDY, Anthony. b 36. **d** 86 **p** 87. NSM Malden St Jas *S'wark* 86-06; PtO 06-10. *48 Blake's Lane, New Malden KT3 6NR* T: (020) 8949 0703 E: aehardy@waitrose.com

HARDY, Anthony William. b 56. Man Univ BEd 79 MEd 86 Open Univ BSc 00. St Jo Coll Nottm LTh 88. **d** 88 **p** 89. C Pennington *Man* 88-91; V Eccleston St Luke *Liv* 91-00; Min Consultant CPAS 00-09; Dioc Evang *Liv* 00-02; Can Ev Man Cathl 09-14; R Whalley Range St Edm and Moss Side etc from 14. *St Edmund's Rectory, 1 Range Road, Manchester M16 8FS* T: 0161-226 4554 E: tonybillhardy@gmail.com *or* stedsandstjames@gmail.com

HARDY, Canon Brian Albert. b 31. St Jo Coll Ox BA 54 MA 58. Westcott Ho Cam 55. **d** 57 **p** 58. C Rugeley *Lich* 57-62; Chapl Down Coll Cam 62-66; C-in-c Livingston Miss *Edin* 66-74; Preb Heref Cathl 74-78; Ch Planning Officer Telford 74-78; RD Telford Severn Gorge 75-78; Chapl Edin Th Coll 78-82; Chapl Edin R Infirmary 82-86; R Edin St Columba 82-91; Dean Edin 86-91; Hon Can St Mary's Cathl from 91; R St Andrews All SS *St And* 91-96; rtd 96; LtO *Edin* from 10. *3/3 Starbank Road, Edinburgh EH5 3BN* T: 0131-551 6783 E: brian.hardy10@btinternet.com

HARDY, Christopher Richard. b 52. R Holloway Coll Lon BMus 77 Southn Univ BTh 90. Chich Th Coll 87. **d** 90 **p** 91. C Kenton *Lon* 90-95; V E Finchley All SS from 95. *All Saints' Vicarage, Twyford Avenue, London N2 9NH* T/F: (020) 8883 9315 M: 07785-728272 E: christopherhardy@btinternet.com

HARDY, Miss Janet Frances. b 59. Newc Univ BA 81 CertEd 82. Trin Coll Bris 87. **d** 89 **p** 94. Par Dn Sheff St Paul 89-92; Team Dn Gt Snaith 92-94; TV 94-96; V Pitsmoor Ch Ch 96-01; V Thorpe Hesley 01-14; Dioc Ecum Officer 11-14; V Barmby Moor Gp *York* from 14. *The Vicarage, St Helen's Square, Barmby Moor, York YO42 4HF* T: (01759) 307042

HARDY, John Christopher. b 61. St Jo Coll Dur BA 83 Dur Univ MA 95 New Coll Edin BD 92 Ox Univ MLitt 00. Aston Tr Scheme 87 Coates Hall Edin 89. **d** 92 **p** 93. C Walker *Newc* 92-95; Fell Chapl Magd Coll Ox 95-98; TV Benwell *Newc* 98-03; R Alston Moor 03-08; R Newmarket St Mary w Exning St Agnes *St E* from 08. *The Rectory, 21 Hamilton Road, Newmarket CB8 0NY* T: (01638) 660729

HARDY, Canon John Lewis Daniel. b 26. St Chad's Coll Dur BA 51. **d** 52 **p** 53. C Hucknall Torkard *S'well* 52-58; V Harworth 58-65; V Sutton in Ashfield St Mary 65-85;

R Keyworth 85-93; P-in-c Stanton-on-the-Wolds 85-93; RD
S Bingham 91-93; Hon Can S'well Minster 92-93; rtd 93; PtO
S'well from 93. *c/o M J Hardy Esq, 93 Belmont Road, St Andrews,
Bristol BS6 5AR*

HARDY, Joseph. b 42. RMN 64. CA Tr Coll 68. **d** 05 **p** 05.
C Tralee w Kilmoyley, Ballymacelligott etc *L & K* 05-12; rtd 12.
18 Woodlee, Monavally, Tralee, Co Kerry, Republic of Ireland
T: (00353) (66) 712 6733 M: 87-240 0914

HARDY, Mrs Lesley Anne. b 53. Nottm Univ BA 75 St Luke's
Coll Ex PGCE 76. **d** 05 **p** 06. OLM Lydd *Cant* 05-09; NSM
Barham Downs from 09. *The Rectory, The Street, Barham,
Canterbury CT4 6PA* T: (01227) 831340

HARDY, Michael Frederick Bryan. b 36. Selw Coll Cam BA 60
MA 64. Linc Th Coll 60. **d** 62 **p** 63. C Pontefract St Giles
Wakef 62-66; C Lightcliffe 66-69; V Hightown 69-78; V Birkby
78-85; C Boultham *Linc* 88-89; V Misterton and W Stockwith
S'well 89-01; rtd 01; PtO S'well from 01. *23 Anderson Way, Lea,
Gainsborough DN21 5EF* T: (01427) 614468

HARDY, Michael Henry. b 33. Qu Coll Birm 85. **d** 86 **p** 87.
C Leic St Jas 86-88; R Arnesby w Shearsby and Bruntingthorpe
88-94; RD Guthlaxton 1 91-94; TV Bradgate Team 94-99;
rtd 99; PtO *Leic* 99-12; *Pet* from 99. *14 Dean's Street,
Oakham LE15 6AF* T: (01572) 722591

HARDY, Miss Pauline. b 41. CertEd. Linc Th Coll 85. **d** 87 **p** 94.
Par Dn Walsall Wood *Lich* 87-89; Par Dn Buckingham *Ox*
89-93; C Buckingham w Radclive cum Chackmore 93-97;
C Nash w Thornton, Beachampton and Thornborough 96-97;
C Buckingham 97-03; C Watling Valley 03-06; rtd 06.
32 Campbell Road, Plymouth PL9 9UE
E: pauline@revhardy.plus.com

⛪**HARDY, The Rt Revd Robert Maynard.** b 36. CBE 01. Clare
Coll Cam BA 60 MA 64 Hull Univ Hon DD 92. Cuddesdon
Coll 60. **d** 62 **p** 63 **c** 80. C Langley St Aid CD *Man* 62-64;
C Langley All SS and Martyrs 64-65; Chapl and Lect Th Selw
Coll Cam 65-72; V Boreham Wood All SS *St Alb* 72-75; Dir
St Alb Minl Tr Scheme 75-80; P-in-c Aspley Guise *St Alb* 75-79;
P-in-c Husborne Crawley w Ridgmont 76-79; R Aspley Guise w
Husborne Crawley and Ridgmont 80; Suff Bp Maidstone *Cant*
80-87; Bp Linc 87-01; Bp HM Pris 85-01; rtd 01; Hon
Asst Bp Carl from 01. *Carleton House, Back Lane, Langwathby,
Penrith CA10 1NB* T: (01768) 881210

HARDY, Sam Richard Ian. b 71. Wall Hall Coll Aldenham
BEd 95 Open Univ MA 00. Wycliffe Hall Ox BTh 04. **d** 04.
C Parr *Liv* 04-05. *Knarrside, Woodhead Road, Tintwistle, Glossop
SK13 1JX* E: sam.hardy@tiscali.co.uk

HARDY, Stephen John Arundell. b 49. SEITE 95. **d** 97 **p** 98.
NSM Marden *Cant* 97-00; P-in-c Lydd 00-09; AD Romney
03-08; P-in-c Barham w Bishopsbourne and Kingston 09-12;
C Nonington w Wymynswold and Goodnestone etc 11-12;
P-in-c Barham Downs from 12; AD E Bridge from 11; AD
W Bridge 11-14. *The Rectory, The Street, Barham, Canterbury
CT4 6PA* T: (01227) 831340 E: stephenhardy1@mac.com

HARE, Christopher Sumner. b 49. Solicitor 73. WEMTC 92.
d 95 **p** 96. NSM Saltford w Corston and Newton St Loe *B & W*
95-01; P-in-c Timsbury and Priston 01-10; R Timsbury w
Priston, Camerton and Dunkerton 10-12; Bp's Officer for
Ord NSM (Bath Adnry) 07-08; RD Midsomer Norton 07-12;
rtd 12. *Cuckoo Hill, 61 Packsaddle Way, Frome BA11 2RW*
T: (01373) 469788 M: 07779-825348

HARE, David. b 46. Qu Coll Birm 81. **d** 83 **p** 83. SSF 67-94; Bp's
Dom Chapl *Birm* 83-87; V Handsworth St Mich 87-97;
R Newton Regis w Seckington and Shuttington 97-03; rtd 03;
PtO *Birm* 03-12. *34 The Charters, Lichfield WS13 7LX*
E: dandjhare@hallgreen118.fsnet.co.uk

HARE, Michael John. b 41. Lon Univ MD 71 Cam Univ MA 77.
EAMTC 00. **d** 02 **p** 03. NSM E Leightonstone *Ely* 02-06; NSM
Buckworth and Alconbury cum Weston 04-06; PtO *St E* 06-09;
NSM Woodbridge St Mary from 09. *The Q Tower, 14 South Hill,
Felixstowe IP11 2AA* T: (01394) 670264 E: hare@waitrose.com

HARE, Richard William. b 66. Bris Univ BSc 88 PhD 94.
Cranmer Hall Dur BA 95. **d** 95 **p** 96. C Coulsdon St Jo *S'wark*
95-98; C Coventry Caludon *Cov* 98-99; TV 99-07; AD Cov
E 01-07; TR Bedworth from 07; AD Nuneaton from 12. *The
Rectory, 1 Linden Lea, Bedworth CV12 8UD* T: (024) 7631 0219
E: thehares@ic24.net

HARE (née CALDWELL), Mrs Sarah Louise. b 75. St Jo Coll
Nottm 11. **d** 13 **p** 14. C Bishop's Castle w Mainstone, Lydbury
N etc *Heref* from 13. *The Vicarage, Lydbury North SY7 8AU*
T: (01588) 680147 M: 07709-056177 E: sarah.hare@aol.co.uk

HARES, David Ronald Walter. b 40. Qu Coll Cam BA 63 MA 67
CertEd. Westcott Ho Cam 64. **d** 66 **p** 67. C Cannock *Lich*
66-69; Chapl Peterho Cam 69-72; Asst Master Chesterton
Sch Cam 72-74; V Kesgrave *St E* 74-98; R Lt Barningham,
Blickling, Edgefield etc *Nor* 98-05; rtd 05; PtO *Nor* from 05.
17 Trory Street, Norwich NR2 2RH T: (01603) 626392
E: david.hares@gmail.com

HARFORD, Julian Gray. b 29. Univ Coll Ox BA 52 MA 59 Lon
Univ PGCE 58. Qu Coll Birm. **d** 64 **p** 65. C W End *Win* 64-67;
C Chearsley w Nether Winchendon Ox 67-77; C Chilton All
SS 72-77; R Westbury w Turweston, Shalstone and Biddlesden
77-86; C Chenies and Lt Chalfont 86-87; C Chenies and
Lt Chalfont, Latimer and Flaunden 87-95; rtd 95; PtO *Sarum*
from 95; *Ox* from 11. *49 Dove Court, Faringdon SN7 7AB*
T: (01367) 243790

HARFORD, The Ven Michael Rivers Dundas. b 26. Trin
Coll Cam BA 49 MA 51. Westcott Ho Cam 50. **d** 52 **p** 53.
C Ashton-on-Ribble St Andr *Blackb* 52-55; PtO *Edin* 55-56;
C Singapore Cathl and Chapl Univ of Malaya Malaya 56-60;
C Kaula Lumpur St Mary 60-62; V Kuala Lumpur St Mary
Malaysia 62-66; V Childwall St Dav *Liv* 66-71; R Katanning
Australia 71-76; Adn Albany 76-79; R Bicton and Attadale
Australia 79-86; R Guildford 86-91; Adn Swan 86-89;
Adn Mitchell Australia 90-91; rtd 91. *Unit 12, 18 Bridges Road,
Melville WA 6156, Australia* T: (0061) (8) 9319 1538
M: 410-566896 E: venmike@optusnet.com.au

HARFORD, Paul Roger. b 83. York Univ BA 04 Selw Coll Cam
BA 09. Ridley Hall Cam 07. **d** 10 **p** 11. C Stokesley w Seamer
York 10-13; R Bishop Thornton, Burnt Yates, Markington
etc *Leeds* from 13. *The Vicarage, Westerns Lane, Markington,
Harrogate HG3 3PB* E: revpaulharford@gmail.com

HARFORD, Timothy William. b 58. Nottm Univ BTh 89.
Linc Th Coll 86. **d** 89 **p** 90. C Minehead *B & W* 89-93;
R Knebworth *St Alb* 93-03; Children's Soc 03-09; Hd Donor
Care and Fund-raising Depaul UK 10-14; Dir Fund-raising and
Communications United Soc from 14. *Us, Harling House,
47-51 Great Suffolk Street, London SE1 0BS* T: (020) 7921 2200
or 660300 F: 665658
E: alan.hargrave@cathedral.ely.anglican.org

HARGER, Robin Charles Nicholas. b 49. BTh. Sarum & Wells Th
Coll 78. **d** 81 **p** 82. C Charlton Kings St Mary *Glouc* 81-85;
C Folkestone St Mary and St Eanswythe *Cant* 85-89; TV
Langley and Parkfield *Man* 89-95; TV Bournemouth Town
Cen *Win* 95-12; rtd 12. *Address temp unknown*
E: robin.cn.harger@gmail.com

HARGRAVE, Canon Alan Lewis. b 50. Birm Univ BSc 73 PhD 77.
Ridley Hall Cam 87. **d** 89 **p** 90. C Cambridge H Trin w St Andr
Gt *Ely* 89-92; C Cambridge H Trin 92-93; C-in-c Fen Ditton
93-94; V Cambridge H Cross 94-04; Can Res Ely Cathl from
04. *Powchers Hall, The College, Ely CB7 4DL* T: (01353) 660304
or 660300 F: 665658
E: alan.hargrave@cathedral.ely.anglican.org

HARGRAVES, Mrs Christobel Mary Kathleen. b 58. Man Poly
BSc 79 Open Univ MBA RGN 83. SAOMC 03. **d** 06 **p** 07.
C Goring and Streatley w S Stoke *Ox* 06-09; R Shelswell 09-14;
AD Bicester and Islip 13-14; PtO *S & B* from 15. *Pye Corner,
Llangunilo, Knighton LD7 1ST* T: (01547) 550311
E: chris.hargraves@psaconnect.com

HARGREAVE, James David. b 44. K Coll Lon BA 66 Lon Univ
PGCE 68 ALCM 89 LTCL 90. Coll of Resurr Mirfield 70.
d 73 **p** 74. C Houghton le Spring *Dur* 73-77; C Gateshead
St Cuth w St Paul 77-79; V Trimdon 79-87; C-in-c Stockton
Green Vale H Trin CD 87-94; V Hedon w Paull *York* 94-02;
rtd 02. *1 The Avenue, Crescent Street, Cottingham HU16 5QT*
T: (01482) 844297

HARGREAVES, Andrew David. b 74. Homerton Coll Cam
BEd 97. Trin Coll Bris BA 08. **d** 08 **p** 09. C Shirley *Win*
08-12; V Whitfield *Derby* from 12. *The Vicarage, 16 Scotty Brook
Crescent, Glossop SK13 8UG* T: (01457) 866022
M: 07801-062986 E: adhargreaves@btinternet.com or
andrew@glossop.com

HARGREAVES, Arthur Walsh. b 34. Man Univ MB, ChB FRCSE
FRCS FRCSGlas. St Deiniol's Hawarden 89. **d** 90 **p** 91. NSM
Baguley *Man* 90-04; rtd 04; PtO *Man* 04-08. *33 Chelford Road,
Knutsford WA16 8NN* T: (01565) 654343

HARGREAVES, John. b 43. St Jo Coll Nottm 86. **d** 88 **p** 89.
C Werneth *Man* 88-91; TV Rochdale 91-96; C Man Gd Shep
96-97; PtO *Liv* 96-97; C Manchester Gd Shep and St Barn *Man*
97-98; rtd 98; PtO *Man* 06-08. *Water House, Wyebank, Bakewell
DE45 1BH* M: 07922-004930 E: johnatbakewell@gmail.com

HARGREAVES, John Rodney. b 36. Open Univ BA 74. Didsbury
Methodist Coll 59 St Deiniol's Hawarden 74. **d** 75 **p** 75. In
Methodist Ch 63-74; C Pontypool *Mon* 75-77; C Llanedeyrn
77-79; Chapl HM Pris Aylesbury 79-83; Sen Chapl HM Pris
Stafford 83-88; Asst Chapl Gen of Pris (N) 88-90; Asst
Chapl Gen of Pris 90-96; R Stone St Mich and St Wulfad w
Aston St Sav *Lich* 96-01; rtd 01; Master St Jo Hosp Lich 01-04;
PtO from 04. *217 Newcastle Road, Stone ST15 8LF*
T: (01785) 814765 E: jrhargreaves@easynet.co.uk

HARGREAVES, John Wilson. b 46. Aber Univ BScForII 67.
Westcott Ho Cam 84. **d** 86 **p** 87. C Rugby *Cov* 86-90;
TV Daventry, Ashby St Ledgers, Braunston etc *Pet* 90-97;
Chapl Daventry Tertiary Coll 94-97; P-in-c Pinxton *Derby*
97-01; R 01-02; TR E Scarsdale 02-11; rtd 11. *66 Bishopton
Lane, Ripon HG4 2QN* T: (01765) 609413
E: jwh100@btinternet.com

HARGREAVES, Julia Gay. b 61. EMMTC 04. **d** 07 **p** 08. NSM Glenfield *Leic* 07-08; NSM Upper Soar 08-11; TV Bosworth and Sheepy Gp from 11; C Nailstone and Carlton w Shackerstone from 11. *The Rectory, Church Lane, Sheepy Magna, Atherstone CV9 3QS* T: (01827) 881389
E: julia.hargreaves@btinternet.com

HARGREAVES, Ms Marise. b 60. Leeds Univ BA 81. Cranmer Hall Dur 82. **dss** 85 **d** 94 **p** 95. Yeadon St Jo *Bradf* 85-87; NSM Bradf St Clem 94-96; NSM Buttershaw St Paul 96-00; C Eccleshill 00-03; PtO 03-09; Chapl Derby Hosps NHS Foundn Trust from 09. *Chaplaincy, Royal Derby Hospital, Uttoxeter Road, Derby DE22 3NE* T: (01332) 340131
E: ma6591@hotmail.com

HARGREAVES, Mark Kingston. b 63. Oriel Coll Ox BA 85 MA 89 Rob Coll Cam PhD 91 W Lon Inst of HE PGCE 86. Ridley Hall Cam 87. **d** 91 **p** 92. C Highbury Ch Ch w St Jo and St Sav *Lon* 91-94; C Ealing St Steph Castle Hill 94-97; C Notting Hill St Jo and St Pet 97-02; V Notting Hill St Pet from 03; AD Kensington 06-11. *48 Ladbroke Road, London W11 3NW* T: (020) 7221 9841
E: mark@stpetersnottinghill.org.uk

HARGREAVES-STEAD, Terence Desmond. b 32. Edin Th Coll 60. **d** 63 **p** 64. C Walney Is *Carl* 63-66; Chapl Withington Hosp Man 66-72; V Westleigh St Paul *Man* 72-06; Chapl Wigan and Leigh Health Services NHS Trust 96-01; Chapl Wrightington Wigan and Leigh NHS Trust 01-06; rtd 07; PtO *Man* from 08. *4 Hartford Green, Westhoughton, Bolton BL5 2GL* T: (01942) 859929

HARINGTON, Roger John Urquhart. b 48. Trin Hall Cam BA 70 MA 71. Coll of Resurr Mirfield 72. **d** 75 **p** 76. C Liv Our Lady and St Nic w St Anne 75-78; Asst Chapl Leeds Univ and Poly *Ripon* 78-81; TV Moor Allerton 81-86; Dioc Drama Adv (Jabbok Theatre Co) 86-95; V Leeds Gipton Epiphany 95-02. *21 Spencer Place, Leeds LS7 4DQ* T: 0113-240 0769
E: jabbok@gn.apc.org

HARKER, Harold Aidan. b 35. **d** 82 **p** 83. OSB from 53; C Reading St Giles *Ox* 82-83; LtO 83-87; C Halstead St Andr w H Trin and Greenstead Green *Chelmsf* 87-89; P-in-c Belchamp St Paul 89-97; R Belchamp Otten w Belchamp Walter and Bulmer etc 97-00; rtd 00; LtO *Chelmsf* from 00. *38 Sheppard's College, London Road, Bromley BR1 1PE* T: (020) 8464 1206

HARKER, Ian. b 39. Dur Univ BA 61. Lich Th Coll Moray Ho Edin 66. **d** 63 **p** 64. C Knottingley *Wakef* 63-66; PtO 66-70; C Notting Hill *Lon* 70-75; Chapl Newc Univ 75-83; Master Newc St Thos Prop Chpl 75-83; PtO *Chelmsf* 99-01; C Plaistow and N Canning Town 01; C Loughton St Jo 01-02; V Leytonstone H Trin and St Aug Harrow Green 02-11; rtd 11; PtO *Chelmsf* 11-13; *Cant* from 14. *70 Sturry Hill, Canterbury CT2 0NH* T: (01227) 711247 E: harkatvic@aol.com

HARKER, John Hadlett. b 37. Dur Univ BSc 59 Newc Univ PhD 67 CEng MIChemE 64 MInstE 64 CChem MRSC 65 FIChemE 80. NEOC 81. **d** 84 **p** 85. C Earsdon *Newc* 84-87; P-in-c Long Horsley 87-91; V Bassenthwaite, Isel and Setmurthy *Carl* 91-94; TR Howden *York* 94-96; P-in-c Willerby w Ganton and Folkton 96-98; rtd 98; PtO *Newc* 98-01 and 04-13; Hon C Newc St Geo and St Luke 01-04. *62 Priory Lane, Grange-over-Sands LA11 7BJ* E: harker@thestell.freeserve.co.uk

HARKER, Stephan John. b 47. Em Coll Cam BA 68 MA 72. Westcott Ho Cam 70. **d** 72 **p** 73. C Marton *Blackb* 72-76; C Preston St Matt 76-79; C Fleetwood St Pet 79-80; Sen Chapl Charterhouse Sch Godalming 81-07; Chapl from 07. *Firview, 63 Peperharow Road, Godalming GU7 2PL* T: (01483) 422155
E: sjh@charterhouse.org.uk

HARKIN, Canon John Patrick. b 53. Oak Hill Th Coll 87. **d** 89 **p** 90. C Wisley w Pyrford *Guildf* 89-93; P-in-c Mickleham 93-98; Chapl Box Hill Sch Surrey 93-98; R Jersey St Ouen w St Geo *Win* 98-10; Vice-Dean Jersey 01-10; P-in-c Andover 10-11; V from 11; RD from 10; Hon Can Win Cathl from 09. *St Mary's Vicarage, Church Close, Andover SP10 1DP* T: (01264) 362268 E: harkin12@btinternet.com

HARKIN, Terence James. b 46. Lon Bible Coll BA 82 New Coll Edin MTh 94. **d** 95 **p** 96. In Bapt Min 86-95; C Edin H Cross 95-96; C S Queensferry 95-96; P-in-c from 96; R Edin Clermiston Em from 09. *6 Wellhead Close, South Queensferry EH30 9WA* T: 0131-319 1099 *or* 331 1958
E: tjharkin@priorychurch.com

HARKINS, James Robert. b 27. Minnesota Univ BA 49. Seabury-Western Th Sem MTh 53. **d** 52 **p** 52. USA 52-60, 72-79 and 91-93; Colombia 60-72; Dominica 79-85; Venezuela 85-91; Chapl Venice w Trieste *Eur* 94-99; P-in-c Menton 99-01; rtd 01. *69 Main Street Apt 201, North Adams MA 01247-3427, USA*

HARKNETT, David Philip. b 74. St Pet Coll Ox BA 97. Oak Hill Th Coll BA 03. **d** 03 **p** 04. C Radipole and Melcombe Regis *Sarum* 03-07; TV Melbury from 07. *The Vicarage, Corscombe, Dorchester DT2 0NU* T: (01935) 891247
E: melburyvicar@btinternet.com

HARKNETT, Linda. b 48. Open Univ BA 81 Croydon Coll CertEd 92. SEITE 97. **d** 00 **p** 01. NSM Sutton St Nic *S'wark* 00-03; Chapl Epsom and St Helier NHS Trust 00-03; Chapl Whitelands Coll Roehampton Univ *S'wark* 03-07; Dioc FE and HE Chapl Officer 03-07; P-in-c Headley w Box Hill *Guildf* from 07. *The Rectory, Church Lane, Headley, Epsom KT18 6LE* T: (01372) 377327 M: 07796-903167
E: lindaharknett@gmail.com

HARLAND, Brenda. b 49. **d** 08. NSM Thatcham *Ox* from 08. *St Mary's Church Office, Church Gate, Thatcham RG19 3PN* T: (01635) 862277 E: brenda.harland@ntlworld.com

HARLAND, Canon Harold William James. b 35. Hertf Coll Ox BA 59 MA 63. Clifton Th Coll 59. **d** 61 **p** 62. C Reigate St Mary *S'wark* 61-64; C Farnborough *Guildf* 64-68; V Walmley *Birm* 68-74; V Bromley Ch Ch *Roch* 74-86; V Folkestone St Jo *Cant* 86-00; Dir Post-Ord Tr 93-97; Hon Can Cant Cathl 94-00; rtd 00; PtO *Cant* from 00. *121 Station Road West, Canterbury CT2 8DE* T: (01227) 764699
E: harlandh992@aol.com

HARLE, Michael Richardson. b 58. BA 80 Man Univ MBM 91. **d** 11 **p** 12. NSM Claygate *Guildf* from 11. *1 The Green, Claygate, Esher KT10 0JL* T: (01372) 463898 M: 07788-160040
E: mikeharle@btinternet.com

HARLEY, Brother Brian Mortimer. b 25. K Coll Lon 48. **d** 53 **p** 54. C Bris St Agnes w St Simon 53-56; LtO *Sarum* 56-62; SSF from 56; Chapl St Fran Sch Hooke 58-61; Papua New Guinea 61-79; Australia from 87; Min Gen SSF from 91. *The Hermitage of St Bernadine, PO Box 46, Stroud NSW 2425, Australia* T: (0061) (2) 4994 5372

HARLEY, Canon Brian Nigel. b 30. Clare Coll Cam BA 53 MA 57. Cuddesdon Coll 53. **d** 55 **p** 56. C Basingstoke *Win* 55-60; TV 71-73; TR 73-80; C W End 60-61; C-in-c Southn St Chris Thornhill CD 61-71; V Eastleigh 80-93; RD 85-93; rtd 93; PtO *Win* 93-13; Bp's Dom Chapl 94-96. *18 Phillimore Road, Southampton SO16 2NR* T: (023) 8055 1049

HARLEY, Mrs Carol Anne. b 46. **d** 00 **p** 01. OLM Tettenhall Wood and Perton *Lich* from 00. *27 Tyrley Close, Compton, Wolverhampton WV6 8AP* T: (01902) 755316
E: allynharley@lineone.net

HARLEY, Christopher David. b 41. Selw Coll Cam BA 63 MA 69 Bris Univ PGCE 64 Columbia Bible Sem DMin 92 Utrecht Univ PhD 02. Clifton Th Coll 64. **d** 66 **p** 67. C Finchley Ch Ch *Lon* 66-69; Hon C 75-78; Ethiopia 70-75; Hd of UK Miss CMJ 75-78; Lect All Nations Chr Coll Ware 78-85; Prin 85-93; Chmn Lon Inst of Contemporary Christianity 88-89; Chmn CMJ 89-90; Crosslinks 93-06; Gen Dir OMF Internat 93-05; NSM Bromley Ch Ch *Roch* 93-96; NSM Singapore 96-06; rtd 06; PtO *Ex* from 06. *12 Harrington Drive, Exeter EX4 8PD* T: (01392) 460457 E: cdrkharley@gmail.com

HARLEY, David Bertram. b 22. Down Coll Cam BA 50 MA 55. Westcott Ho Cam 55. **d** 56 **p** 58. Asst Master Bedford Sch 50-58; C Biddenham *St Alb* 56-58; Chapl Stamford Sch 58-87; rtd 87; Confrater Browne's Hosp Stamford 87-11; LtO *Linc* 59-94; PtO 94-15. *Whitchurch House, Whitchurch, Ross-on-Wye HR9 6BZ* T: (01600) 890489

HARLEY, The Ven Michael. b 50. AKC 73 Ch Ch Coll Cant CertEd 74 Lambeth STh 92 Kent Univ MPhil 95. St Aug Coll Cant 74. **d** 75 **p** 76. C Chatham St Wm *Roch* 75-78; C-in-c Weeke *Win* 78-81; V Southampton St Mary Extra 81-86; V Hurstbourne Tarrant, Faccombe, Vernham Dean etc 86-99; ACORA Link Officer 91-94; Dioc Rural Officer 95-97; RD Andover 95-99; V Chandler's Ford 99-09; Tutor STETS 03-06; Hon Can Win Cathl 06-09; Adn Win from 09; P-in-c Win St Cross w St Faith and Master St Cross Hosp 09-11. *22 St John's Street, Winchester SO23 0HF* T: (01962) 869442
E: michael.harley@winchester.anglican.org

HARLEY, Nigel. *See* HARLEY, Brian Nigel

HARLEY, Peter David. b 59. Sheff Univ BSc 82 Warwick Univ MBA 86. **d** 09 **p** 10. OLM Horwich and Rivington *Man* 09-14; OLM Blackrod 11-14. *6 Barford Grove, Lostock, Bolton BL6 4NQ* T: (01204) 694611 E: peter.harley@talktalk.net

HARLEY, Canon Robert Patterson. b 53. St Andr Univ MA 75 Cam Univ CertEd 76 Glas Univ PhD 89 Edin Univ BD 97. **d** 97 **p** 98. C Edin St Thos 97-00; Chapl Lothian Univ Hosps NHS Trust 98-00; P-in-c Kirriemuir *St And* from 00; Can St Ninian's Cathl Perth from 08. *128 Glengate, Kirriemuir DD8 4JG* T: (01575) 575515 E: robert.harley@gmx.co.uk

HARLEY, Roger Newcomb. b 38. Ely Th Coll 61. **d** 64 **p** 65. C Plymouth St Pet *Ex* 64-66; C Heston *Lon* 66-69; C Maidstone All SS w St Phil and H Trin *Cant* 69-73; R Temple Ewell w Lydden 73-79; P-in-c Shirley St Geo 79-81; V 81-84; V Croydon H Sav *S'wark* 85-95; V Forest Row *Chich* 95-03; rtd 03; PtO *Cant* from 03. *7 Roman Way, St Margarets-at-Cliffe, Dover CT15 6AH* T: (01304) 851720
E: rogerharley@btinternet.com

HARLING, Timothy Charles. b 80. Fitzw Coll Cam BA 04. Westcott Ho Cam 02. **d** 05 **p** 06. C Romsey *Win* 05-09; Chapl HM Pris Peterborough 09-13; Chapl Qu Coll Cam from 13. *Queens' College, Silver Street, Cambridge CB3 9ET* T: (01223) 335511 E: tch42@cam.ac.uk

HARLOW, Antony Francis. b 24. Pemb Coll Cam BA 50 MA 55. Oak Hill Th Coll 84. **d** 85 **p** 86. NSM Watford St Luke *St Alb* 85-86; CMS 86-91; Uganda 86-91; PtO *St Alb* 90-98; NSM Watford St Pet 92-96; PtO *B & W* from 98. *16 Derham Court, High Street, Yatton, Bristol BS49 4DW* T: (01934) 832651 M: 07884-222819

HARLOW, Kathryn. b 78. Southn Univ BSc 99. Wycliffe Hall Ox BTh 07. **d** 07 **p** 08. C Folkestone St Jo *Cant* 07-11. *10 Barrons Way, Comberton, Cambridge CB23 7EQ* E: rev_kathryn@hotmail.co.uk

HARLOW, Mark Jonathan. b 80. Man Univ BSc 01 K Coll Lon MA 10. Ridley Hall Cam 11. **d** 14 **p** 15. C Leeds St Geo from 14. *St Peter's Vicarage, 15 Parkside Green, Leeds LS6 4NY* T: 0113-278 3800 M: 07725-625900 E: mark.harlow@stgeorgesleeds.org.uk

HARLOW, Richard John St Clair. b 63. Cam Univ BA 85 MA 88. Cranmer Hall Dur 87. **d** 89 **p** 90. C Basford w Hyson Green *S'well* 89-94; C Mansfield SS Pet and Paul 94-97; TV Newark 97-01; Chapl Brighton and Sussex Univ Hosps NHS Trust 01-10; Lead Chapl Sussex Partnership NHS Foundn Trust 10-13; Chapl St Pet and St Jas Hospice N Chailey 02-05; R Tadley w Pamber Heath and Silchester *Win* from 13. *The Rectory, The Green, Tadley RG26 3PB* M: 07875-969128 E: richard73harlow@aol.com

HARLOW, Archdeacon of. *See* WEBSTER, The Ven Martin Duncan

HARMAN, Karin. *See* VOTH HARMAN, Karin

HARMAN, Kathleen Joyce. b 49. **d** 03 **p** 04. C Llangynwyd w Maesteg *Llan* 03-08; R Dowlais and Penydarren from 08. *The Rectory, Gwernllwyn Road, Dowlais, Merthyr Tydfil CF48 3NA* T: (01685) 722118

HARMAN, Canon Leslie Davies. b 46. Nottm Univ BTh 76. St Jo Coll Nottm LTh 75. **d** 76 **p** 77. C Wandsworth All SS *S'wark* 76-78; C Godstone 78-82; V Thorncombe w Winsham and Cricket St Thomas *B & W* 82-87; TV Hitchin *St Alb* 87-95; V Royston 95-11; RD Buntingford 96-01; Hon Can St Alb 09-11; rtd 11. *1 Berry Meadow, Kingsteignton, Newton Abbot TQ12 3BL* T: (01626) 351757

HARMAN, Michael John. b 48. Chich Th Coll 71. **d** 74 **p** 75. C Blackpool St Steph *Blackb* 74-79; Chapl RN 79-06; rtd 06; PtO *Ex* 06-08; *Truro* from 06; P-in-c Wembury *Ex* 08-14. *18 Furzeacre Close, Plymouth PL7 5DZ* T: (01752) 338910 M: 07836-377820 E: revmikeharman@blueyonder.co.uk

HARMAN, Theodore Allan. b 27. Linc Coll Ox BA 52 MA 56 Hatf Coll Dur MA 90. Wells Th Coll 52. **d** 54 **p** 55. C Hawkshead and Low Wray *Carl* 54-55; C Kirkby Stephen w Mallerstang 55-57; Asst Chapl Sedbergh Sch 57-84; Sen Chapl 84-87; Tutor Hatf Coll Dur from 88; Admissions Tutor 89-90; Lib and Coll Officer 91-02; Acting Chapl 99-00; Fell from 00; PtO *Dur* from 88. *2 Palmers Close, Church Street Head, Durham DH1 3DN* T: 0191-386 7213 F: 334 3101 E: theoharman@gmail.com

HARMER, Timothy James. b 47. Birm Univ CertEd 68. St Jo Coll Nottm BA 95. **d** 95 **p** 96. C Studley *Cov* 95-98; V Tanworth *Birm* 98-05; P-in-c Helsington *Carl* 05-12; P-in-c Underbarrow 05-12; RD Kendal 08-12; rtd 12; PtO *Carl* 12-13; P-in-c Church Coniston from 13; P-in-c Torver from 13. *New Vicarage, Yewdale Road, Coniston LA21 8DX* T: (015394) 41171 E: tharmer246@btinternet.com

HARMON, Michael Edgar. b 54. Birm Univ BEd 76. Wycliffe Hall Ox 10. **d** 12 **p** 13. NSM Aston and Nechells *Birm* 12-15; R Chelmsley Wood from 15. *The Vicarage, Pike Drive, Birmingham B37 7US* M: 07900-405455 E: harmon.mike2@gmail.com

HARMSWORTH, Canon Roger James. b 46. Univ of W Ontario BA 87. Huron Coll Ontario MDiv 90. **d** 90 **p** 90. Canada 90-96; I Maryborough w Dysart Enos and Ballyfin *C & O* 96-01; I Killanne w Killegney, Rossdroit and Templeshanbo from 01; Treas Ferns Cathl 03-04; Chan from 04. *The Rectory, Clonroche, Enniscorthy, Co Wexford, Republic of Ireland* T/F: (00353) (53) 924 4180 E: precentor.1@hotmail.com

HARNDEN, Peter John. b 63. Coll of Resurr Mirfield 96. **d** 98 **p** 99. C Staplehurst *Cant* 98-02; V Tokyngton St Mich *Lon* 02-11; P-in-c Benhilton *S'wark* 11-15; V from 15. *All Saints' Vicarage, All Saints' Road, Sutton SM1 3DA* T: (020) 8644 9070 E: allsaintsbenhilton@btconnect.com

HARNEY, Janice. b 56. **d** 02 **p** 03. OLM Pennington *Man* 02-06; PtO 06-11; NSM Astley, Tyldesley and Mosley Common from 11. *29 Green Lane, Leigh WN7 2TL* T/F: (01942) 671481 M: 07811-764355 E: jan.harney@btinternet.com

HARNISH, Robert George. b 64. Univ of Ottawa BSc 87 Worc Coll Ox DPhil 90 MA 92. Wycliffe Hall Ox 93. **d** 93 **p** 94. C Chinnor w Emmington and Sydenham etc *Ox* 93-95; Chapl and Dean of Div New Coll Ox 96-01; Chapl Eliz Coll Guernsey from 01. *11 Saumarez Street, St Peter Port, Guernsey GY1 2PT* T: (01481) 713298 *or* 726544

HARONSKI, Boleslaw. b 46. Pemb Coll Ox BA 68 MA 72 DPhil 73. St Mich Coll Llan 80 Westcott Ho Cam 82. **d** 82 **p** 83. C Maindee Newport *Mon* 82-85; V Llanishen w Trellech Grange and Llanfihangel etc 85-89; V Blackwood 89-92; rtd 11. *Tir Llandre, Llanarthney, Carmarthen SA32 8JE*

✠HARPER, The Rt Revd Alan Edwin Thomas. b 44. OBE 96. Leeds Univ BA 65. CITC 75. **d** 78 **p** 79 **c** 02. C Ballywillan *Conn* 78-80; I Moville w Greencastle, Upper Moville etc *D & R* 80-82; I Londonderry Ch Ch 82-86; I Belfast Malone St Jo *Conn* 86-02; Preb St Audoen St Patr Cathl Dublin 90-01; Adn Conn 96-02; Prec Belf Cathl 96-02; Bp Conn 02-07; Abp Arm 07-12; rtd 12. *Forth Cottage, 67 Lisnacroppan Road, Rathfriland, Newry BT61 5NZ* T: (028) 4065 1649 M: 07713-954758 E: a.e.t.harper@gmx.com

HARPER, Canon Alan Peter. b 50. Man Univ BA 73 FCA 83. Ripon Coll Cuddesdon 86. **d** 88 **p** 89. C Newport w Longford and Chetwynd *Lich* 88-91; P-in-c Wilnecote 91-94; V 94-98; V Codsall 98-07; Preb Lich Cathl 02-07; RD Penkridge 06-07; Bp's Dom Chapl *Derby* 07-11; P-in-c Mackworth All SS from 11; P-in-c Kirk Langley from 11; P-in-c Mugginton and Kedleston from 11; Hon Can Derby Cathl from 12. *The Vicarage, 4 Church Lane, Kirk Langley, Ashbourne DE6 4NG* T: (01332) 825667 E: revd.alan8@btinternet.com

HARPER, Barry. *See* HARPER, Malcolm Barry

HARPER, Canon Brian John. b 61. Liv Univ BA 82. CITC. **d** 85 **p** 86. C Portadown St Columba *Arm* 85-88; C Drumglass w Moygashel 88-89; I Errigle Keerogue w Ballygawley and Killeshil 89-93; I Mullavilly 93-12; I Magheracross *Clogh* from 12; Can Clogh Cathl from 14. *27 Craghan Road, Ballinamallard, Enniskillen BT94 2BT* T: (028) 6638 8238 M: 07898-743545 E: magheracross@btinternet.com

HARPER, Clive Stewart. b 35. FCIS 71. Ridley Hall Cam 80. **d** 82 **p** 83. C Bromyard *Heref* 82-85; P-in-c Bredenbury and Wacton w Grendon Bishop 85-89; P-in-c Edwyn Ralph and Collington w Thornbury 85-89; P-in-c Pencombe w Marston Stannett and Lt Cowarne 85-89; R Bredenbury w Grendon Bishop and Wacton etc 89-92; R Bilton *Cov* 92-02; rtd 02; Hon C Churchover w Willey *Cov* 02-05; PtO from 05. *Kairos, 18 Whimbrel Close, Rugby CV23 0WG* T: (01788) 541041 E: harperclival@btinternet.com

HARPER, David Laurence. b 51. Qu Coll Cam BA 73 MA 77 PhD 78. Wycliffe Hall Ox BA 80. **d** 80 **p** 81. C Mansfield SS Pet and Paul *S'well* 80-84; C Wollaton 84-87; V Brinsley w Underwood 87-94; R Bingham from 94; AD 00-03; AD E Bingham 03-07. *The Rectory, Bingham, Nottingham NG13 8DR* T: (01949) 837335 E: dl.harper@btopenworld.com

HARPER, Canon Geoffrey Roger. b 57. Jes Coll Cam BA 79 MA 83. St Jo Coll Nottm 81. **d** 84 **p** 85. C Belper *Derby* 84-87; C Birstall and Wanlip *Leic* 87-90; TV Tettenhall Regis *Lich* 90-97; C Aldridge 97-02; PtO 02-07; Chapl Douglas MacMillan Hospice Stoke-on-Trent 04-07; C W Bromwich Gd Shep w St Jo *Lich* 07-09; PtO *Derby* 09-10; P-in-c Burton Joyce w Bulcote and Stoke Bardolph *S'well* 10-11; V from 11; Hon Can W Ankole from 05. *The Vicarage, 9 Chestnut Grove, Burton Joyce, Nottingham NG14 5DP* T: 0115-931 2109 M: 07954-409635 E: harperrog@googlemail.com

HARPER, Gordon. b 32. Oak Hill Th Coll 64. **d** 66 **p** 67. C Halliwell St Pet *Man* 66-71 and 84-99; P-in-c Brinsworth *Sheff* 71-75; V Brinsworth w Catcliffe 76-84; rtd 99; PtO *Man* 99-13. *15 New Church Road, Bolton BL1 5QP* T: (01204) 849413

HARPER, Gordon William Robert. b 48. Wellington Univ (NZ) BA 70 St Chad's Coll Dur BA 74 Nottm Univ PhD 89. Coll of Resurr Mirfield 74. **d** 75 **p** 76. C Battyeford *Wakef* 75-76; New Zealand 76-80; P-in-c Byers Green *Dur* 80-83; V Evenwood 83-89; R Wolviston 89-00; V Billingham St Mary 97-01; P-in-c Winlaton 01-06; R 06-13; rtd 13; PtO *Dur* from 13. *66 Rochester Road, Durham DH1 5QD* T: 0191-383 1348 E: drgwr&jharper@westbill.freeserve.co.uk

HARPER, Ian. b 51. AKC 78. Oak Hill Th Coll 79. **d** 80 **p** 81. C Sidcup St Jo *Roch* 80-83; C Bushey *St Alb* 83-87; TV Thamesmead *S'wark* 87-92; TR N Lambeth 92-00; V Homerton St Luke *Lon* 00-10; AD Hackney 04-09; V Ladywood St Jo and St Pet *Birm* from 10; AD Cen Birm from 12. *St John's Vicarage, Darnley Road, Birmingham B16 8TF* T: 0121-454 0973 E: harper-il@sky.com

HARPER, James. b 35. St Luke's Coll Ex TDip 57. SWMTC. **d** 90 **p** 91. NSM Pendeen w Morvah *Truro* 90-97; PtO *Win* from 09. *1 Millstream Mews, 50 Beaconsfield Road, Christchurch BH23 1QT* T: (01202) 477138

HARPER, John Anthony. b 46. AKC 69. **d** 70 **p** 71. C Pet St Mary Boongate 70-73; C Abington 73-75; V Grendon w Castle Ashby 75-82; Asst Dioc Youth Chapl 75-82; R Castor w Sutton and Upton *Pet* 82-94; TV Riverside *Ox* 94-04; V Meppershall and Shefford *St Alb* 04-11; RD Shefford 08-10; RD Ampthill and Shefford 11; rtd 11; PtO *Ely* from 12; *Pet* from 12. *54 Chapel Street, Yaxley, Peterborough PE7 3LN* T: (01733) 688923 E: revjohnharper@talktalk.net

HARPER, Joseph Frank. b 38. Hull Univ BA 60 MA 86 MPhil 98 Dur Univ PhD 10. Linc Th Coll 80. **d** 81 **p** 82. C Preston St Cuth *Blackb* 81-83; C Lancaster St Mary 83-87; V Bamber Bridge St Aid 87-92; V Kinsley w Wragby *Wakef* 92-99; R Newhaven *Chich* 99-04; rtd 04; PtO *Dur* from 04. *30 Greenways, Consett DH8 7DE* T: (01207) 590962 E: j925harper@btinternet.com

HARPER, Ms Lisa Rae. b 67. Cranmer Hall Dur 13. **d** 15. C Cen Telford *Lich* from 15. *32 Viscount Avenue, Telford TF4 3SW* M: 07808-924223 E: lisataraharper@yahoo.co.uk

HARPER, Canon Malcolm Barry. b 37. Dur Univ BSc 59. Wycliffe Hall Ox 59. **d** 61 **p** 62. C Harold Wood *Chelmsf* 61-65; C Madeley *Heref* 65-68; V Slaithwaite w E Scammonden *Wakef* 68-75; V Walmley *Birm* 75-03; Hon Can Birm Cathl 96-03; rtd 03; PtO *Birm* from 03. *1 Welcombe Drive, Sutton Coldfield B76 1ND* T: 0121-351 3990 E: canonbarryharper@tiscali.co.uk

HARPER, Mrs Margaret. b 51. Nottm Coll of Educn TCert 73 Nottm Univ BEd 74. SAOMC 98. **d** 01 **p** 02. C Slough *Ox* 01-05; P-in-c Leeds St Cypr Harehills *Ripon* 05-09; P-in-c Burmantofts St Steph and St Agnes 05-09; TV Ely 09-14; rtd 14. *11 Greenacre Way, Bishops Cleeve, Cheltenham GL52 8SQ* T: (01242) 679850 E: margaretharper@waitrose.com

HARPER, Martin Nigel. b 48. Cant Ch Ch Univ Coll PGCE 95 FRICS 88. S Dios Minl Tr Scheme 82. **d** 85 **p** 86. NSM St Leonards Ch Ch and St Mary *Chich* 85-93; NSM Rye 94-95; R Brede w Udimore 08-14; R Brede w Udimore and Beckley and Peasmarsh from 14. *The Rectory, Brede Hill, Brede, Rye TN31 6HG* T: (01424) 883408 M: 07760-197954 E: martin.harper@tiscali.co.uk

HARPER, Canon Maurice. b 20. St Steph Ho Ox 60. **d** 62 **p** 63. C Upminster *Chelmsf* 62-67; V Gt Ilford St Mary 67-71; R Upminster 71-85; RD Havering 80-85; Hon Can Chelmsf Cathl 84-85; rtd 85; PtO *Chelmsf* from 85; *Nor* from 85; *Chich* from 05. *30 Cookham Dene, Buckhurst Road, Bexhill-on-Sea TN40 1RU* T: (01424) 222189 E: canonmauriceharper@o2.co.uk

HARPER, Michael Sydney. b 36. Portsm Dioc Tr Course 86. **d** 87. NSM Leigh Park St Clare *Portsm* 87-88; NSM Warren Park 88-05; NSM Leigh Park 96-05; rtd 05; PtO *Portsm* from 07. *17 Hampage Green, Warren Park, Havant PO9 4HJ* T: (023) 9245 4275 E: michael_harper06@btinternet.co.uk

HARPER, Richard Michael. b 53. Lon Univ BSc 75 Univ of Wales PhD 78. St Steph Ho Ox BA 80 MA 87. **d** 81 **p** 82. C Holt *Nor* 81-84; C-in-c Grahame Park St Aug CD *Lon* 84-88; Sub-Warden and Dir Studies St Mich Coll Llan 88-93; Lect Ch Hist Univ of Wales (Cardiff) 88-93; R St Leonards Ch Ch and St Mary *Chich* 94-03; RD Hastings 02-03; V Weymouth St Paul *Sarum* from 03. *St Paul's Vicarage, 58 Abbotsbury Road, Weymouth DT4 0BJ* T: (01305) 778821 E: frrharper@btinternet.com

HARPER, Roger. *See* HARPER, Geoffrey Roger

HARPER, Roger. b 43. Man Univ BSc 64 FCA 80. Local Minl Tr Course 84. **d** 87 **p** 88. NSM Onchan *S & M* 87-97; NSM Douglas St Geo 97-06. *The Barns, Strawberry Fields, Croit-e-Caley, Colby, Isle of Man IM9 4BZ* T: (01624) 842466

HARPER, Canon Rosemary Elizabeth. b 55. Birm Univ BA 76 ARCM 75 LRAM 78. NTMTC 96. **d** 99 **p** 00. C Amersham *Ox* 99-03; P-in-c Gt Missenden w Ballinger and Lt Hampden 03-07; V from 07; Chapl to Bp Buckingham from 06; Hon Can Ch Ch from 11. *The Rectory, Church Street, Amersham HP7 0BD* T: (01494) 728988 E: rosie51619@aol.com

HARPER, Thomas Reginald. b 31. Dur Univ BA 57 MA 67. **d** 58 **p** 59. C Corbridge w Halton *Newc* 58-60; C Byker St Mich 60-62; V Ushaw Moor *Dur* 62-67; Asst Chapl HM Pris Dur 62-67; N Sec CMS 67-74; V Thornthwaite *Carl* 74-75; V Thornthwaite cum Braithwaite and Newlands 76-90; TV Bellingham/Otterburn Gp *Newc* 90-91; TV N Tyne and Redesdale 91-92; TR 92-98; RD Bellingham 93-98; rtd 98; PtO *Carl* from 98. *Dunelm, Old Lake Road, Ambleside LA22 0DH* T: (015394) 33556

HARPER, Timothy James Lincoln. b 54. Lon Univ BMus 76 MA 96 CertEd LRAM. Wycliffe Hall Ox 84. **d** 86 **p** 87. C Morden *S'wark* 86-90; V Deptford St Pet 90-97; R Amersham *Ox* from 97. *The Rectory, Church Street, Amersham HP7 0DB* T: (01494) 724426 or 729380 F: 08701-639596 E: harpervic@yahoo.co.uk

HARPHAM, Mrs Diana Joan. b 44. MCSP 66. St Alb Minl Tr Scheme 94. **d** 98 **p** 99. NSM Harrold and Carlton w Chellington *St Alb* 98-01; NSM Bromham w Oakley and Stagsden 01-15; PtO from 15. *The Old Police House, 40 Stagsden Road, Bromham, Bedford MK43 8PT* T: (01234) 823222 F: 825577 E: di@harpham.com

HARRATT, James Michael. b 87. Univ of Wales (Ban) BSc 08. Ripon Coll Cuddesdon BA 14. **d** 15. C Rainham *Roch* from 15. *123 Station Road, Rainham, Gillingham ME8 7SP* T: (01634) 362921 M: 07969-293648 E: jharratt@outlook.com

HARRATT, Philip David. b 56. Magd Coll Ox BA 79 MA 83. Ripon Coll Cuddesdon 82. **d** 85 **p** 86. C Ewyas Harold w Dulas, Kenderchurch etc *Heref* 85-88; V Chirbury 88-09; V Marton 88-09; V Trelystan w Leighton 88-09; P-in-c Middleton 02-09; RD Pontesbury 01-08; Preb Heref Cathl 03-09; V Embleton w Rennington and Rock *Newc* from 09. *The Vicarage, Embleton, Alnwick NE66 3UW* T: (01665) 576660 E: philipharratt@mypostoffice.co.uk

HARREX, David Brian. b 54. Trin Coll Bris 87. **d** 89 **p** 90. C Bedminster St Mich *Bris* 89-93; V Pilning w Compton Greenfield 93-00; RD Westbury and Severnside 97-99; AD Bris W 99-00; TR Yate New Town 00-12; C Frampton Cotterell and Iron Acton 07-12; Hon Can Bris Cathl 10-12; TV Yatton Moor *B & W* from 12. *The Rectory, 1 Millier Road, Cleeve, Bristol BS49 4NL* T: (01934) 833152 M: 07798-830172 E: davidharrex@hotmail.com

HARRIES, John Edward. b 60. Bris Univ BSc 81 PhD 84. Wycliffe Hall Ox 94. **d** 96 **p** 97. C Hyde St Geo *Ches* 96-00; P-in-c Walton 00-15; C Latchford St Jas 00-15; Chapl Sir Thos Boteler High Sch 03-15; V Sutton, Wincle, Wildboarclough and Bosley *Ches* from 15. *The Vicarage, Wincle, Macclesfield SK11 0QH* E: stjohnswalton@btinternet.com

HARRIES, Mrs Judith Janice. b 43. SRN 67 Trin Coll Bris BA 93 Bris Univ PGCE 94. WEMTC 99. **d** 01 **p** 02. NSM Bath St Sav w Swainswick and Woolley *B & W* 01-03; Hon C Farmborough, Marksbury and Stanton Prior 03-08; PtO from 09. *19 Victoria Buildings, Bath BA2 3EH* T: (01225) 332418 E: judithharries@btinternet.com

HARRIES, Malcolm David. b 44. BA 99. Oak Hill Th Coll 94. **d** 96 **p** 97. C Rock Ferry *Ches* 96-00; P-in-c Godley cum Newton Green 00-14; rtd 14. *17 Barnes Court, Durham Avenue, Woodford Green IG8 7NJ* E: malcolmharries2@btinternet.com

✠**HARRIES OF PENTREGARTH, The Rt Revd Lord (Richard Douglas).** b 36. Selw Coll Cam BA 61 MA 65 Lon Univ Hon DD 94 FKC 83 FRSL 96. Cuddesdon Coll 61. **d** 63 **p** 64 **c** 87. C Hampstead St Jo *Lon* 63-69; Chapl Westf Coll Lon 67-69; Tutor Wells Th Coll 69-71; Warden Sarum & Wells Th Coll 71-72; V Fulham All SS *Lon* 72-81; Dean K Coll Lon 81-87; Consultant to Abps Cant and York on Inter-Faith Relns 86-06; Bp Ox 87-06; rtd 06; Asst Bp S'wark from 06; Hon Prof Th K Coll Lon from 06. *House of Lords, London SW1A 0PW* E: harriesr@parliament.uk

HARRINGTON, Christopher Robert. b 57. Wilson Carlile Coll 99 ERMC 06. **d** 08 **p** 09. C Middle Rasen Gp *Linc* 08-12; P-in-c Heckington Gp 12-13; P-in-c Helpringham w Hale 12-13; R Heckington and Helpringham Gp from 13. *The Rectory, 10 Cameron Street, Heckington, Sleaford NG34 9RW* T: (01529) 460904 E: c.r.harrington@btinternet.com

HARRINGTON, John Christopher Thomas. b 43. Qu Coll Birm 71. **d** 74 **p** 75. C Northampton St Mich *Pet* 74-76; C Paston 76-79; R Doddington *Ely* 79-82; R Benwick St Mary 79-82; R Doddington w Benwick 82-83; CF (TA) 75-85; Chapl Doddington Co Hosp 79-83; V Eastbourne St Mich *Chich* 83-02; R Selsey 02-11; Chapl RNLI 03-11; rtd 11; Custos St Mary's Hosp Chich from 11. *12 St Martin's Square, Chichester PO19 1NR* T: (01243) 778987 E: jctharrington@tiscali.co.uk

HARRIS, Mrs Alison Ann. b 54. Univ of Wales (Abth) BA 75 Westmr Coll Ox PGCE 76 Ches Univ MTh 07. Qu Coll Birm 07. **d** 08 **p** 09. C Neston *Ches* 08-12; V Witton from 12. *The Vicarage, 61 Church Road, Northwich CW9 5PB* T: (01606) 42943 M: 07969-005978 E: alisonannharris@hotmail.co.uk

HARRIS, Arthur Emlyn Dawson. b 27. Ex Univ BSc 47. S'wark Ord Course 83. **d** 86 **p** 87. NSM Frant w Eridge *Chich* 86-87; P-in-c Withyham St Mich 87-95; rtd 95; PtO *Sarum* 96-07. *53A The Close, Salisbury SP1 2EL* T: (01722) 339886 E: closecelts@aol.com

HARRIS, Bernard Malcolm. b 29. Leeds Univ BA 54. Coll of Resurr Mirfield 54. **d** 56 **p** 57. C Shrewsbury St Chad *Lich* 56-60; C Porthill 60-61; V Birches Head 61-66; V W Bromwich St Jas 66-78; V Sedgley All SS 78-93; rtd 93; PtO *Worc* from 93; *Lich* from 09. *6 Beacon Lane, Sedgley, Dudley DY3 1NB* T: (01902) 663134 E: bernard.harris@care4free.co.uk

HARRIS, Brian. *See* HARRIS, Reginald Brian

HARRIS, Brian. b 33. Man Univ BSc. Qu Coll Birm 79. **d** 80 **p** 81. C Lich St Chad 80-81; PtO *Ches* 82-87; NSM Warburton 87-88; P-in-c 88-92; R Gt and Lt Casterton w Pickworth and

Tickencote *Pet* 92-98; RD Barnack 94-98; rtd 98; PtO *Pet* 99-07; *St Alb* 06-07; *Ches* from 10. *16 Westminster Green, Chester CH4 7LE* T: (01244) 675824 E: meadowbrook@waitrose.com

HARRIS, Brian William. b 38. K Coll Lon BD 61 AKC 61. St Boniface Warminster 61. **d** 62 **p** 63. C Liversedge *Wakef* 62-65; C Kirkby *Liv* 65-70; V Dalton 70-79; V Aberford w Saxton *York* 79-91; V Hemingbrough 91-95; rtd 95; PtO *York* from 95; Dom Chapl to Bp Selby 95-03; Rtd Clergy and Widows Officer (York Adnry) from 99. *2 Furness Drive, Rawcliffe, York YO30 5TD* T: (01904) 638214 E: harrischap@ntlworld.com

HARRIS, Catherine Elizabeth. *See* EDMONDS, Catherine Elizabeth

HARRIS, David Anthony. b 68. **d** 96. Canada 96-11; R Reading St Giles *Ox* from 11. *St Giles's Rectory, Church Street, Reading RG1 2SB* T: 0118-957 2831 E: sgiles.vicar@gmail.com

HARRIS, David Rowland. b 46. Ch Ch Ox BA 69 MA 72. Wycliffe Hall Ox 70. **d** 73 **p** 74. C Virginia Water *Guildf* 73-76; C Clifton Ch Ch w Em *Bris* 76-79; Scripture Union 79-85; V Bedford Ch Ch *St Alb* 85-99; R Ex St Leon w H Trin 99-12; rtd 12; P-in-c Ilsington *Ex* from 12. *The Vicarage, Ilsington, Newton Abbot TQ13 9RW* T: (01364) 661781 E: dandsharris@hotmail.com

HARRIS, Derrick William. b 21. **d** 63 **p** 64. C Birkdale St Jo *Liv* 63-67; V Billinge 67-81; V Walton *Ches* 81-87; rtd 88; PtO *Ches* from 88; *Liv* from 88. *3 Melrose Avenue, Southport PR9 9UY* T: (01704) 213828

HARRIS, Mrs Elaine Sarah. b 43. SWMTC 02. **d** 03 **p** 04. NSM Dyffryn *Llan* 03-06; P-in-c Penyfai 06-12; rtd 12. *15 Neath Road, Fforest Goch, Pontardawe, Swansea SA8 3JB* T: (01656) 651719 E: revel07@hotmail.com

HARRIS, Ernest John. b 46. QUB BD 75. **d** 75 **p** 76. C Lisburn Ch Ch *Conn* 75-78; C Coleraine 78-83; I Belfast St Kath 83-90; I Ballinderry 90-11; Preb Conn Cathl 06-11; rtd 11. *10 Little Wenham, Moira, Craigavon BT67 0NN* M: 07842-114854

HARRIS, Geoffrey Daryl. b 39. Open Univ BA 83. St Aid Birkenhead 63. **d** 66 **p** 67. C Eston *York* 66-70; C Iffley *Ox* 70-75; V Bubwith *York* 75-78; V Bubwith w Ellerton and Aughton 78-79; P-in-c Stillingfleet w Naburn 79-80; R Escrick and Stillingfleet w Naburn 80-95; Chapl Qu Marg Sch York 83-94; Hon C Okehampton w Inwardleigh, Bratton Clovelly etc *Ex* 96-99; P-in-c Ashwater, Halwill, Beaworthy, Clawton etc 99-01; R 01-03; rtd 03; C Okehampton w Inwardleigh, Bratton Clovelly etc *Ex* 07-11. *The Old Barnsite, 7 Crossley Moor Road, Kingsteignton, Newton Abbot TQ12 3LE* E: the.harrisclan1@tinyonline.co.uk

HARRIS, Harriet Anne. b 68. Oriel Coll Ox BA 90 New Coll Ox DPhil 94. St Steph Ho Ox. **d** 00 **p** 01. C Ox St Mary V w St Cross and St Pet 00-06; Chapl Wadham Coll 00-10; Chapl Edin Univ from 10; NSM St Mary's Cathl from 10. *Chaplaincy Centre, The University of Edinburgh, 1 Bristo Square, Edinburgh EH8 9AL* T: 0131-650 2595 M: 07896-244792 E: h.harris@ed.ac.uk

HARRIS, James. b 54. CITC 99. **d** 02 **p** 03. Aux Min Ballybeen *D & D* 02-05; C Belfast St Brendan from 05. *8 Grangewood Avenue, Dundonald, Belfast BT16 1GA* T: (028) 9050 6074 M: 07761-066421 E: jimmy.harris@dsdni.gov.uk

HARRIS, James. b 78. Ox Min Course 12. **d** 15. NSM Stoke Bishop *Bris* from 15. *Address temp unknown*

HARRIS, Canon James Nigel Kingsley. b 37. St D Coll Lamp BA 60. Sarum Th Coll. **d** 62 **p** 63. C Painswick *Glouc* 62-65; C Glouc St Paul 65-67; V Slad 67-77; V Cam 77-78; P-in-c Stinchcombe 77-78; V Cam w Stinchcombe 78-82; V Stonehouse 82-02; Chapl Glos R Hosp NHS Trust 92-02; rtd 02; Hon Can Antsiranana Madagascar from 00; PtO *Glouc* from 03. *14 Shalford Close, Cirencester GL7 1WG* T: (01285) 885641

HARRIS, James Philip. b 59. Westf Coll Lon BA 82 Cardiff Univ MPhil 12 Univ of Wales PGCE 97. St Mich Coll Llan BD 86. **d** 86 **p** 87. C Newport St Paul *Mon* 86-89; C Bedwellty 89-91; V Newport St Matt 91-96; Chapl Univ of Wales Inst Cardiff *Llan* 97-99; Chapl Glam Univ 99-03; V Gwernaffield and Llanferres *St As* 03-09; Dioc Dir of Ords 03-09; V Bwlchgwyn and Minera *St As* 09-10; V Minera w Coedpoeth and Bwlchgwyn 10-14; V Minera w Coedpoeth from 14; AD Alyn from 12. *The Vicarage, Church Road, Minera, Wrexham LL11 3DA* T: (01978) 753133 M: 07757-595154 E: jamespharris03@aol.com

HARRIS, Jeremy David. b 63. Leeds Metrop Univ MA 00 Univ of Wales (Lamp) BA 04 Cardiff Univ MPhil 07 FCCA 92. St Mich Coll Llan 05. **d** 07 **p** 08. C Monmouth w Overmonnow etc *Mon* 07-09; C Magor 09-10; TV 10-12; TR from 12; AD Netherwent from 14. *The Rectory, Redwick Road, Magor, Caldicot NP26 3GU* M: 07710-410950 E: jeremydharris@hotmail.com

HARRIS, Jeremy Michael. b 64. St Steph Ho Ox BTh 93. **d** 93 **p** 94. C Newport St Julian *Mon* 93-95; C Ebbw Vale 95-97; TV 97-98; Dioc Youth Chapl 96-98; TV Bracknell *Ox* 98-05; V Boyne Hill from 05. *The Vicarage, Westmorland Road, Maidenhead SL6 4HB* T: (01628) 626921

HARRIS, The Very Revd John. b 32. Univ of Wales (Lamp) BA 55. Sarum Th Coll 55. **d** 57 **p** 58. V Pontnewynydd *Mon* 57-60; C Bassaleg 60-63; V Penmaen 63-69; V Newport St Paul 69-84; RD Newport 77-93; V Maindee Newport 84-93; Can St Woolos Cathl 84-93; Dean Brecon *S & B* 93-98; V Brecon St Mary and Battle w Llanddew 93-98; rtd 98; LtO *Mon* from 98. *40 Mounton Drive, Chepstow NP16 5EH* T: (01291) 621233

HARRIS, Canon John. b 45. St Steph Ho Ox 72. **d** 75 **p** 76. C Wanstead St Mary *Chelmsf* 75-84; V Penponds *Truro* 84-91; V St Gluvias 91-12; RD Carnmarth S 00-12; Hon Can Truro Cathl 01-12; rtd 12. *The Anchorage, 2 Penlee View Terrace, Penzance TR18 4HY* T: (01736) 365119

HARRIS, John. b 54. Leeds Univ BSc 75. St Jo Coll Nottm LTh 86. **d** 86 **p** 87. C S Ossett *Wakef* 86-90; V Moldgreen 90-97; P-in-c S Ossett 97-04; V 04-10; P-in-c Luddenden w Luddenden Foot 10-13; rtd 13. *68 Springwood Drive, Halifax HX3 0TQ*

HARRIS, John Brian. b 53. Hertf Coll Ox BA 76. Ripon Coll Cuddesdon 87. **d** 89 **p** 90. C Witton *Ches* 89-93; R Thurstaston 93-99; V Stockton Heath 99-04; P-in-c Gt Saughall 04-12; P-in-c Lostock Gralam from 12. *The Vicarage, 61 Church Road, Northwich CW9 SPB* E: brian@jbharris.fsnet.co.uk

HARRIS, John Stuart. b 29. Hertf Coll Ox BA 52 MA 56. Wells Th Coll 52. **d** 54 **p** 55. C Epsom St Martin *Guildf* 54-58; C Guildf H Trin w St Mary 58-63; R Bentley 63-72; V Milford 72-87; R Walton-on-the-Hill 87-98; Dioc Ecum Officer 87-92; rtd 98; PtO *Roch* from 00. *6 Pearse Place, Lamberhurst, Tunbridge Wells TN3 8EJ* T: (01892) 890582

HARRIS, Mrs Judith Helen. b 42. Chelsea Coll Lon TCert 64 Westmr Coll Ox MTh 03. St Alb Minl Tr Scheme 83. **dss** 86 **d** 87 **p** 94. Leagrave *St Alb* 86-87; Hon Par Dn 87-91; Team Dn Dunstable 91-94; TV 94-03; rtd 03; PtO *Truro* from 03. *Belmont, Fore Street, Porthleven, Helston TR13 9HN* T: (01326) 563090 E: revdjhharris@ntlworld.com

HARRIS, Canon Kenneth. b 28. NW Ord Course 70. **d** 72 **p** 73. NSM Upton Ascension *Ches* 72-77; NSM Eccleston and Pulford 77-80; P-in-c Hargrave 80-81; V 81-94; Exec Officer Dioc Bd for Soc Resp 84-94; Hon Can Ches Cathl 91-94; rtd 94; PtO *Ches* 94-96 and from 00; P-in-c Ashton Hayes 96-98; P-in-c Alvanley 98-99. *1 Chapel Green Mews, Grub Lane, Kelsall, Tarporley CW6 0QU* T: (01829) 751880

HARRIS, Lawrence Rex Rowland. b 35. St Cath Coll Cam BA 59 MA 63. Ely Th Coll. **d** 61 **p** 62. C Carrington *S'well* 61-63; Chapl Rampton Hosp Retford 63-66; V Sturton w Littleborough *S'well* 66-71; V Bole w Saundby 66-71; R Clowne *Derby* 71-04; RD Bolsover and Staveley 81-86; rtd 04; PtO *Derby* from 04. *131 North Road, Clowne, Chesterfield S43 4PQ*

HARRIS, Linda Margaret. b 55. Man Univ BSc 76 UMIST MSc 78 Birkbeck Coll Lon MSc 98. Wycliffe Hall Ox 03. **d** 05 **p** 06. C Cannock *Lich* 05-08; P-in-c Hatch Warren and Beggarwood *Win* 08-13; V Birchwood *Linc* from 13. *St Luke's Vicarage, 78 Jasmin Road, Lincoln LN6 0YR* E: revlinda@btinternet.com

HARRIS, Margaret Claire (Sister Margaret Joy). b 53. RGN 85 Homerton Coll Cam BEd 78. Ridley Hall Cam 90. **d** 92. Par Dn Stevenage All SS Pin Green *St Alb* 92-93; C 93-95; CSMV 95-99; OSB from 99. *St Mary's Abbey, 52 Swan Street, West Malling ME19 6JX* T: (01732) 843309

HARRIS, Mark Andrew. b 69. Heythrop Coll Lon BD 92 K Coll Lon MA 05 Jes Coll Cam PhD 12. Ridley Hall Cam 06. **d** 10 **p** 11. C Meopham w Nurstead *Roch* 10-13; C Blockhouse Bay New Zealand from 13. *4 Heaphy Street, Blockhouse Bay, Auckland 0600, New Zealand* E: mark@cots.org.nz

HARRIS, Mark Jonathan. b 55. St Cath Coll Cam BA 88 MA 92 PhD 92. Ripon Coll Cuddesdon BA 01 MA 05. **d** 02 **p** 03. C Cowley St Jas *Ox* 02-04; Chapl Oriel Coll Ox 04-10; Can and Vice Provost St Mary's Cathl Edin 10-12; Lect Edin Univ from 12; LtO from 14. *University Divinity Faculty, New College, Mound Place, Edinburgh EH1 2LX* M: 07813-676892 E: viceprovost@cathedral.net

HARRIS, Martin John. b 54. Trin Coll Cam BA 76 MA. Wycliffe Hall Ox 82. **d** 85 **p** 86. C Lindfield *Chich* 85-88; C Galleywood Common *Chelmsf* 88-91; V Southchurch Ch 91-08; RD Southend 00-05; TR Harlow Town Cen w Lt Parndon from 08; RD Harlow from 09. *The Rectory, 43 Upper Park, Harlow CM20 1TW* T: (01279) 411100 or 434243 E: martin.harris@messages.co.uk

HARRIS, Mary Noreen Cecily. *See* SOKANOVIC, Mary Noreen Cecily

HARRIS, Michael. b 34. St Mark & St Jo Coll Lon CertEd 56 ACP 65 MIL 76. Qu Coll Birm. **d** 83 **p** 84. NSM Bournville *Birm* 83-90; NSM Stirchley 90-96; Chapl Univ of Cen England in Birm 92-99; Dean NSMs 96-99; rtd 00; PtO *Birm* 00-12; *Cov* from 00. *33 Bosley Close, Shipston-on-Stour CV36 4QA* T/F: (01608) 661672　M: 07811-489713 E: mike.harris@pikkle.net

HARRIS, Michael Andrew. b 53. Ian Ramsey Coll Brasted 74 Trin Coll Bris 75. **d** 78 **p** 79. C St Paul's Cray St Barn *Roch* 78-82; C Church Stretton *Heref* 82-87; Res Min Penkridge w Stretton *Lich* 87-90; Res Min Penkridge Team 90-92; V Amington *Birm* 92-15; AD Polesworth 07-14; V Highley w Billingsley, Glazeley etc *Heref* from 15. *The Rectory, Church Street, Highley, Bridgnorth WV16 6NA* E: mikeharassed@gmail.com

HARRIS, Nicholas Bryan. b 60. Down Coll Cam BA 81 MA 85. Ridley Hall Cam 82. **d** 85 **p** 86. C Walney Is *Carl* 85-88; C S'wark Ch 88-92; PtO *Chich* 92-08. *Wheelwrights, High Street, Fairwarp, Uckfield TN22 3BP* E: box534@yahoo.co.uk

HARRIS, Owen. b 50. Univ of Wales (Swansea) BSc(Econ) 71 PGCE 72. St Mich Coll Llan. **d** 94 **p** 95. C Bassaleg *Mon* 94-98; TV Cwmbran 98-01; V Maindee Newport 01-02; rtd 02. *130 Lighthouse Park, St Brides Wentlooge, Newport NP10 8SU* T: (01633) 681522

✠**HARRIS, The Rt Revd Patrick Burnet.** b 34. Keble Coll Ox BA 58 MA 63. Clifton Th Coll 58. **d** 60 **p** 61 **c** 73. C Ox St Ebbe w St Pet 60-63; SAMS 63-81; Adn N Argentina 70-73; Bp N Argentina 73-80; R Kirkheaton *Wakef* 81-85; Asst Bp Wakef 81-85; Sec C of E Partnership for World Miss 86-88; Asst Bp Ox 86-88; Bp S'well 88-99; rtd 99; Asst Bp Linc 99-05; Asst Bp Eur from 99; Hon Asst Bp Glouc from 05. *Apartment B, Ireton House, Pavilion Gardens, Cheltenham GL50 2SR* T: (01242) 231376 E: pandvharris@blueyonder.co.uk

HARRIS, Canon Paul. b 55. St Paul's Coll Chelt BEd 79. Oak Hill Th Coll 82. **d** 84 **p** 85. C Billericay and Lt Burstead *Chelmsf* 84-87; TV Cheltenham St Mary, St Matt, St Paul and H Trin *Glouc* 87-93; V Bitterne *Win* 93-97; UK Evang Co-ord Evang Alliance 97-02; C Portswood Ch Ch *Win* 02-04; TR Cheltenham St Mark *Glouc* 04-11; Hon Can Glouc Cathl 09-11; rtd 11; PtO *Win* 12-15. *Anchor House, 119 Parkwood Road, Bournemouth BH5 2BT* E: harrisrevpaul@blueyonder.co.uk

HARRIS, Paul Ian. b 45. MSc. Qu Coll Birm. **d** 82 **p** 83. C The Quinton *Birm* 82-86; V Atherstone *Cov* 86-13; rtd 13; PtO *Cov* from 13; *Leic* from 13. *31 Woodside, Ashby-de-la-Zouch LE65 2NJ* T: (01530) 589873 E: paulih@ntlworld.com

HARRIS, Paul Michael. b 58. Chelsea Coll Lon BSc 79 Oak Hill Th Coll BA 89 Bath Coll of HE CertEd 82 Open Univ BA 04 MA 14. **d** 89. C Finchley Ch Ch *Lon* 89-90; Asst Master St Luke's Sch W Norwood 90-91; Master and Asst Chapl Brent Internat Sch Philippines 91-92; Volunteer Miss Movement Sunningdale 93-94; Past Asst St Joseph's RC Ch Dorking 94-95; Form Master Merton Court Prep Sch Sidcup 95-97; Asst Master Clewborough Ho Prep Sch Camberley 98-01; Teacher St Nic Sch for Girls Church Crookham 01-02; Culford Sch Bury St Edmunds 02-04; Teacher St Marg Prep Sch Calne 05-07. *Maes-yr-Haf, 4 Penllain, Penparc, Cardigan SA43 1RJ* T: (01239) 613797 E: paul.harris.007@hotmail.com

HARRIS, Peter Dudley. b 44. Sir John Cass Coll Lon BSc 72 MA 77. **d** 13 **p** 14. NSM Hanger Hill Ascension and W Twyford St Mary *Lon* from 13. *91 Ashbourne Road, London W5 3DH* T: (020) 8997 7852　M: 07944-576375 E: pete@richard-rose.co.uk

HARRIS, Peter Frank. b 43. WMMTC 89. **d** 92 **p** 93. NSM Lich Ch Ch 92-96; NSM Ogley Hay 96-00; NSM Rushall 00-03; PtO from 03. *94 Ogley Hay Road, Burntwood WS7 2HU* T: (01543) 319163

HARRIS, Peter Malcolm. b 52. Em Coll Cam BA 74 MA 79. Trin Coll Bris. **d** 80 **p** 81. C Upton (Overchurch) *Ches* 80-83; Crosslinks from 83; Portugal 93-97; France from 97. *rue de Meunier 4, Ribet, 13990 Fontvieille, France* M: 8 77 35 61 53 E: harris@crosslinks.org

HARRIS, Peter Samuel. b 68. Dundee Univ BA 98 St Jo Coll Dur BA 04. Cranmer Hall Dur 02. **d** 04 **p** 05. C Walton and Trimley St E 04-07; R Dalkeith *Edin* from 07; R Lasswade from 07. *The Rectory, 7 Ancrum Bank, Dalkeith EH22 3AY* T: 0131-663 7000 E: revpharris@googlemail.com

HARRIS, Raymond. b 36. Nottm Univ BA 58. Lich Th Coll 58. **d** 60 **p** 61. C Clifton St Fran *S'well* 60-63; C Davyhulme St Mary *Man* 63-66; V Bacup Ch Ch 66-82; R Dunsby w Dowsby *Linc* 82-87; R Rippingale 82-87; R Rippingale Gp 87-94; rtd 94. *2 The Bungalow, Swaton Lane, Swaton, Sleaford NG34 0JU* T: (01529) 421343

HARRIS, Canon Raymond John. b 29. Leeds Univ BA 51. Coll of Resurr Mirfield 51. **d** 53 **p** 54. C Workington St Mich *Carl* 53-59; V New Swindon St Barn Gorse Hill *Bris* 59-94; Hon Can

Bris Cathl 80-94; RD Cricklade 82-88; rtd 94; PtO *Glouc* from 94. *c/o P Goodchild Esq, 20 Rodney Road, West Bridgford, Nottingham NG2 6JJ*

HARRIS, Rebecca Jane. See SWYER, Rebecca Jane

HARRIS (née LEE), Mrs Rebecca Susan. b 62. Man Univ BA 85. Trin Coll Bris 93. **d** 95 **p** 96. C Cirencester *Glouc* 95-99; TV Gt Chesham *Ox* 99-11; V Creech St Michael and Ruishton w Thornfalcon *B & W* from 11. *The Rectory, Creech St Michael, Taunton TA3 5PP* E: harrisrs211@btinternet.com

HARRIS, The Ven Reginald Brian. b 34. Ch Coll Cam BA 58 MA 61. Ridley Hall Cam. **d** 59 **p** 60. C Wednesbury St Bart *Lich* 59-61; C Uttoxeter w Bramshall 61-64; V Bury St Pet *Man* 64-70; V Walmsley 70-80; RD 70-80; Adn Man 80-98; Can Res Man Cathl 80-98; rtd 98; PtO *Derby* from 98. *9 Cote Lane, Hayfield, High Peak SK22 2HL* T: (01663) 746321 E: aandbharris@btinternet.com

HARRIS, Robert. See WYNFORD-HARRIS, Robert William

HARRIS, Robert Douglas. b 57. Ex Univ BEd 80 Bris Univ MEd 96. Chich Th Coll 80. **d** 82 **p** 83. C Portsea St Mary *Portsm* 82-87; V Clevedon St Jo *B & W* 87-92; R Felpham w Middleton *Chich* 92-99; R Felpham 99-04; RD Arundel and Bognor 98-04; P-in-c Southwick 04-06; R 06-10; RD Hove 09-10; P-in-c Ilfracombe, Lee, Woolacombe, Bittadon etc *Ex* from 10. *The Vicarage, St Brannock's Road, Ilfracombe EX34 8EG* T: (01271) 863467 E: robdharris@btinternet.com

HARRIS, Robert James. b 45. Nottm Univ MA 02 ALCD 73. St Jo Coll Nottm 69. **d** 72 **p** 73. C Sheff St Jo 72-76; C Goole 76-78; V Bramley and Ravenfield 78-91; P-in-c Boulton *Derby* 91-99; RD Melbourne 96-99; P-in-c Hazlewood 99-02; P-in-c Hazlewood and Milford 02-05; V Hazelwood, Holbrook and Milford 05-10; rtd 10. *13 Mill Close, Findern, Derby DE65 6AP* T: (01283) 703024 E: robert@kneetinnit.fsnet.co.uk *or* jrjubilate@btinternet.com

HARRIS, Mrs Ruth. b 60. Hull Univ BA 82 Liv Univ MArAd 84. NOC 01. **d** 04 **p** 05. C Kinsley w Wragby *Wakef* 04-07; C Felkirk 05-07; P-in-c Wrenthorpe *Leeds* from 07. *The Vicarage, 121 Wrenthorpe Road, Wrenthorpe, Wakefield WF2 0JS* T: (01924) 373758 E: wrenvic121@talktalk.net

HARRIS, Sian Elizabeth. b 54. Kingston Poly BSocSc 75. WEMTC 03. **d** 06 **p** 07. NSM Leominster *Heref* 06-09; Chapl St Mich Hospice Hereford 09-11; TV Tenbury *Heref* from 11. *The Rectory, Burford, Tenbury Wells WR15 8HG* T: (01584) 819792 M: 07866-492863 E: sianharris@f2s.com

HARRIS, Stephen Mark. b 63. Mansf Coll Ox BA 85 Lon Business Sch MBA 95 Cam Univ BTh 11 Solicitor 86. Ridley Hall Cam 09. **d** 11 **p** 12. NSM Trumpington *Ely* from 11. *6 Aberdeen Square, Cambridge CB2 8BZ* M: 07971-818394 E: steve16copperfields@msn.com

HARRIS, Suzanne Sarah. CITC. **d** 09 **p** 10. NSM Dublin Booterstown *D & G* from 09. *Caneel, 3 Belmont Green, Blackrock, Co Dublin, Republic of Ireland* M: (00353) 87-935 4869 E: curate.booterstown@dublin.anglican.org

HARRIS, Thomas William. b 54. Univ of Wales (Lamp) MA 04 AKC 76. Linc Th Coll 77. **d** 78 **p** 79. C Norton Woodseats St Chad *Sheff* 78-81; V Barnby Dun 81-91; P-in-c Kirk Bramwith and Fenwick 81-85; Chapl RN 91-94; R Draycot *Bris* 94-02; P-in-c Cawston w Booton and Brandiston etc *Nor* 02-12; Chapl Norfolk and Nor Univ Hosp NHS Trust 02-07; Chapl Cawston Park Hosp 07-12; P-in-c Gt w Lt Massingham, Harpley, Rougham etc *Nor* 12-13; rtd 13; PtO *Nor* from 14. *Blake House, The Common, Hanworth, Norwich NR11 7HP* T: (01263) 761570 E: revtomharris@gmail.com

HARRIS, William Edric Mackenzie. b 46. Sarum & Wells Th Coll 72. **d** 75 **p** 76. C Langney *Chich* 75-79; C Moulsecoomb 80-81; TV 81-85; R W Grinstead from 85. *The Rectory, Steyning Road, West Grinstead, Horsham RH13 8LR* T: (01403) 710339 E: williammemharris@gmail.com

HARRIS, William Fergus. b 36. CCC Cam BA 59 MA 63 Edin Univ DipEd 70. Yale Div Sch 59 Westcott Ho Cam 60. **d** 62 **p** 63. C St Andrews St Andr *St And* 62-64; Chapl Edin Univ 64-71; R Edin St Pet 71-83; R Perth St Jo *St And* 83-90; Hon C 90-08; rtd 90; Prov Archivist 91-02; LtO *St And* from 08. *35 St Mary's Drive, Perth PH2 7BY* T: (01738) 621379 E: ruth.harris1@tesco.net

HARRIS-EVANS, William Giles. b 46. AKC 68. Bangalore Th Coll. **d** 70 **p** 71. C Clapham H Trin *S'wark* 70-74; Sri Lanka 75-78; V Benhilton *S'wark* 78-86; TR Cov E 86-93; TR Brighouse and Clifton *Wakef* 93-99; V Petersfield and R Buriton *Portsm* 99-10; rtd 10; PtO *Portsm* from 11. *11 Great Southsea Street, Southsea PO5 3BY* E: wgh-evans12@tiscali.co.uk

HARRIS-WHITE, John Emlyn. b 34. St Aid Birkenhead 59. **d** 62 **p** 63. C Cricklade w Latton *Bris* 62-63; C Kingswood 63-66; C Ashton-on-Ribble St Andr *Blackb* 66-69; V Heyhouses 69-71; Chapl Roundway Hosp Devizes 71-77; Chapl R Variety Children's Hosp and K Coll Hosp Lon 77-89; Chapl Belgrave

Hosp Lon 77-89; Regional Community Relns Co-ord 89-93; rtd 94; Hon C Folkestone St Pet *Cant* 97-01. *40 Tippet Knowes Road, Winchburgh, Broxburn EH52 6UL*

HARRISON, Alastair Lee. b 22. ALCD 51. **d** 51 **p** 52. C Stoke Damerel *Ex* 51-54; Chapl RAF 54-67; Chapl Miss to Seamen 67-77; LtO *D & G* 77-83; *M & K* 77-83; C Dublin St Ann and St Steph *D & G* 83-92; rtd 92. *8 Grosvenor Place, Rathgar, Dublin 6, Republic of Ireland* T: (00353) (1) 497 6053

HARRISON, Alison Edwina. *See* HART, Alison Edwina

HARRISON, Mrs Barbara Ann. b 41. Man Univ BA 63 Leic Univ CertEd 64. EMMTC 85. **d** 88 **p** 94. C Immingham *Linc* 88-94; P-in-c Habrough Gp 94-99; V 99-01; rtd 02; PtO *Linc* from 02. *3 Windsor Mews, Louth LN11 9AY* T: (01507) 610015

HARRISON, Canon Barbara Anne. b 34. Westf Coll Lon BA 56 CertEd 57 Hull Univ MA 85. Linc Th Coll 76. **dss** 79 **d** 87 **p** 94. Chapl York Univ 80-88; Team Dn Sheff Manor 88-93; Par Dn Holts CD *Man* 93-94; C-in-c 94-98; Dioc UPA Officer 93-98; Chapl Rochdale Healthcare NHS Trust 98-02; Chapl Pennine Acute Hosps NHS Trust 02-04; C Bury Ch King *Man* 98-01; C Bury St Paul 98-04; P-in-c Kirkholt 01-04; Hon Can Man Cathl 02-04; rtd 04; PtO *Man* from 04. *66 Gainsborough Drive, Rochdale OL11 2QT* T: (01706) 639872

HARRISON, Brian John. b 35. FCP. Glouc Sch of Min 83. **d** 86 **p** 89. NSM Broseley w Benthall *Heref* 86-93; PtO 94-97. *17 Hafren Road, Little Dawley, Telford TF4 3HJ* T: (01952) 591891

HARRISON, Bruce. b 49. Linc Th Coll 86. **d** 88 **p** 89. C Syston *Leic* 88-90; C Whitby *York* 90-93; V Glaisdale 93-99; R Brotton Parva 99-04; V Coatham and Dormanstown 04-08; Chapl Tees and NE Yorks NHS Trust 04-07; rtd 08; PtO *York* from 08. *St Peter's Vicarage, 66 Aske Road, Redcar TS10 2BP* T: (01642) 489842 *or* 484833 E: bruce.harrison@live.co.uk

HARRISON, Bruce Mountford. b 49. AKC 71. **d** 72 **p** 73. C Hebburn St Cuth *Dur* 72-75; C Bethnal Green St Jo w St Simon *Lon* 75-77; P-in-c Bethnal Green St Bart 77-78; TV Bethnal Green St Jo w St Bart 78-80; C-in-c Pennywell St Thos and Grindon St Oswald CD *Dur* 80-85; V Sunderland Pennywell St Thos 85-90; V Gateshead St Helen 90-14; rtd 14. *18 Salkeld Road, Gateshead NE9 5UD*

HARRISON, Mrs Caroline Jane. b 74. Bradf Univ BSc 01. Ripon Coll Cuddesdon 14. **d** 15. C Royston *Leeds* from 15; C Felkirk from 15. *Felkirk Vicarage, George Street, South Hiendley, Barnsley S72 9BX* M: 07939-027572 E: carolinejaneharrison@aol.com

HARRISON, Sister Cécile. b 29. Bp Lonsdale Coll TCert 51. St Steph Ho Ox 97. **d** 97 **p** 97. CGA from 66; LtO *Eur* from 97. *38 Green Park Way, Chillington, Kingsbridge TQ7 2HY* E: cga.prasada@wanadoo.fr

HARRISON, Christine Amelia. b 47. STETS 94. **d** 98 **p** 99. NSM Goldsworth Park *Guildf* 98-12; rtd 12. *2 Abercorn Way, Woking GU21 3NY* T: (01483) 750645 E: revchrissie@btinternet.com

HARRISON, Christopher Dennis. b 57. Clare Coll Cam BA 79 BA 86. Westcott Ho Cam 84. **d** 87 **p** 88. C Camberwell St Geo *S'wark* 87-92; V Forest Hill 92-96; P-in-c Fenny Bentley, Kniveton, Thorpe and Tissington *Derby* 96-98; P-in-c Parwich w Alsop-en-le-Dale 96-98; R Fenny Bentley, Thorpe, Tissington, Parwich etc 98-09; RD Ashbourne 98-09; P-in-c Nottingham All SS, St Mary and St Pet *S'well* 09-11; R from 11. *24 Pelham Crescent, Nottingham NG7 1AW* T: 0115-941 8927 E: christopher.d.harrison@btinternet.com

HARRISON, Christopher Joseph. b 38. AKC 61 Hull Univ CertEd 68. Bris Univ BEd 75. **d** 62 **p** 63. C Bottesford *Linc* 62-67; C Elloughton *York* 67-68; Asst Master Bishop's Cleeve Primary Sch 68-74; Sen Master 74-78; Dep Hd 78-96; P-in-c Farmington *Glouc* 69-73; C Tredington w Stoke Orchard and Hardwicke 74-86; rtd 96; PtO *Glouc* from 87. *Appledore, 93 Stoke Road, Bishops Cleeve, Cheltenham GL52 8RP* T: (01242) 673452

HARRISON, Crispin. *See* HARRISON, Michael Burt

HARRISON, David Daniel. b 62. St Paul's Coll Chelt BA 84 Leeds Univ MA 85 Westmr Coll Ox PGCE 88. Westcott Ho Cam 03. **d** 05 **p** 06. C Beckenham St Geo *Roch* 05-09; P-in-c Woodnesborough w Worth and Staple *Cant* 09-12; PtO *St E* from 13. *16 Priory Road, Felixstowe IP11 7NE* T: (01394) 276380 E: ddh25@btinternet.com

HARRISON, David Henry. b 40. Tyndale Hall Bris 65. **d** 68 **p** 69. C Bolton St Paul *Man* 68-72; V Bircle 72-83; V Southport SS Simon and Jude *Liv* 83-91; TR Fazakerley Em 91-99; V Toxteth Park Ch Ch and St Mich w St Andr 99-05; rtd 05; PtO *Blackb* from 06. *55 The Oval, Shevington, Wigan WN6 8EN* T: (01257) 400084 E: getrevdave@hotmail.com

HARRISON, David Samuel. b 44. Univ of Wales (Ban) BSc 67. St Mich Coll Llan 68. **d** 70 **p** 71. C Canton St Jo *Llan* 70-74; C Witton *Ches* 74-78; V Sutton St Geo 78-96; P-in-c Henbury 96-01; V 01-06; rtd 06; PtO *Ches* from 07. *50 Cherryfields Road, Macclesfield SK11 8RF* T: (01625) 268460

HARRISON, Dawn Michelle. b 78. Edge Hill Coll of HE BSc 99 St Jo Coll Dur BA St Martin's Coll Lanc PGCE 01. Cranmer Hall Dur 07. **d** 10 **p** 11. C S Widnes *Liv* 10-14; TV Upholland from 14; PtO *Man* from 13. *The Vicarage, 158 Back Lane, Birleywood, Skelmersdale WN8 9BX* M: 07786-365193 E: dawnmharrison@hotmail.co.uk

HARRISON, Miss Doreen. b 32. Leeds Univ BA 53 PGCE 54 Lanc Univ MLitt 78 MA(Ed) 79. **d** 92 **p** 94. C Ambleside w Brathay *Carl* 92-96; Asst P Colton 96-01; P-in-c 01-02; Asst P Rusland 96-01; P-in-c 01-02; Asst P Satterthwaite 96-01; P-in-c 01-02; rtd 02; PtO *Carl* from 02. *Fox How, Ambleside LA22 9LL* T: (015394) 33021

HARRISON, Fred Graham. b 41. Lon Univ BSc 62. Ridley Hall Cam 80. **d** 82 **p** 83. C Lenton *S'well* 82-85; V Ruddington 85-04; rtd 04; PtO *Ches* from 05. *18 Holly Bank, Hollingworth, Hyde SK14 8QL* T: (01457) 765955 E: fg.harrison@virgin.net

HARRISON, Guy Patrick. b 58. Ox Univ MTh 99 MBACP 04. Sarum & Wells Th Coll 92. **d** 94 **p** 95. C Wimborne Minster and Holt *Sarum* 94-96; C Wimborne Minster 96-97; Chapl Dorothy House Hospice Winsley 97-01; Chapl Stoke Mandeville Hosp NHS Trust 01-02; Chapl Team Ldr 02-05; Team Ldr and Bereavement Service Manager Bucks Hosps NHS Trust 05-07; Hd Spiritual and Past Care W Lon Mental Health NHS Trust 07-12; Hd Spiritual and Past Care Ox Health NHS Foundn Trust from 12. *Littlemore Mental Health Centre, Sandford Road, Littlemore, Oxford OX4 4XN* T: 08452-191145 M: 07786-843878 E: guy.harrison@oxfordhealth.nhs.uk

HARRISON, Ian David. b 45. Imp Coll Lon BSc 66. Oak Hill Th Coll 93. **d** 96 **p** 97. NSM Tunbridge Wells St Jo *Roch* 96-99; P-in-c Chiddingstone w Chiddingstone Causeway 99-10; rtd 10; PtO *Roch* from 10. *3 Brunswick Terrace, Tunbridge Wells TN1 1TR* T: (01892) 871639 E: ian.harrison.tw@gmail.com

HARRISON, Joanne Elizabeth. b 47. SAOMC. **d** 05 **p** 06. NSM Wokingham St Paul *Ox* 05-10; PtO 10-14. *25 Harvard Road, Owlsmoor, Sandhurst GU47 0XB* T: (01276) 34409

HARRISON, John. *See* HARRISON, Steven John

HARRISON, Canon John. b 49. Fitzw Coll Cam BA 71 MA 74. Westcott Ho Cam 74. **d** 77 **p** 78. C Nunthorpe *York* 77-81; C Acomb St Steph and St Aid 81-83; V Heptonstall *Wakef* 83-91; R Stamford Bridge Gp *York* 91-02; V Easingwold w Raskelf 02-14; RD Easingwold 05-14; Can and Preb York Minster 10-14; rtd 14; PtO *York* from 14. *24 The Manor Beeches, Dunnington, York YO19 5PX*

HARRISON, John Christopher. b 69. Liv Univ BA 90 MSc 98 Liv Jo Moores Univ PhD 06. SNWTP 07. **d** 10 **p** 11. NSM Hoylake *Ches* from 10. *St Hildeburgh's Church, Stanley Road, Hoylake, Wirral CH47 1HL* M: 07834-262166 E: j.c.harrison@ljmu.ac.uk

HARRISON, John Northcott. b 31. St Jo Coll Cam BA 54. Westcott Ho Cam 54. **d** 56 **p** 57. C Moor Allerton *Ripon* 56-59; C Bedale 59-61; V Hudswell w Downholme 61-64; Youth Chapl *Dur* 64-68; V Auckland St Andr and St Anne 68-76; Community Chapl Stockton-on-Tees 76-83; TR Southampton (City Cen) *Win* 83-88; V Bris Ch the Servant Stockwood 88-96; RD Brislington 89-95; Chapl St Brendan's Sixth Form Coll 90-96; rtd 96; PtO *B & W* 96-12; *Bris* 96-12. *3 Dulverton Hall, Esplanade, Scarborough YO11 2AR* T: (01723) 449828

HARRISON, Josephine Mary. b 42. **d** 97 **p** 98. NSM Yatton Keynell *Bris* 97-99; NSM By Brook 99-01; PtO *B & W* 01-02 and from 07; NSM Wellington and Distr 02-07. *14 Four Acre Mead, Bishops Lydeard, Taunton TA4 3NW* T: (01823) 433572

HARRISON, Mrs Kathryn Maxine. b 70. Ox Min Course 13. **d** 15. C New Windsor *Ox* from 15. *30 Devereux Road, Windsor SL4 1JJ* M: 07794-113782 E: mail.kmh22@gmail.com

HARRISON, Keith. *See* HARRISON, Peter Keith

HARRISON, Canon Lyndon. b 47. St Mich Coll Llan 91. **d** 93 **p** 94. C Ebbw Vale *Mon* 93-96; TV 96-01; TV Caldicot 01-05; TR 05-14; Can St Woolos Cathl 12-14; rtd 14; PtO *Mon* from 14. *14 Swallow Drive, Caldicot NP26 5RD* T: (01291) 430041

HARRISON, Mrs Marion Jeanne. b 56. SAOMC 04. **d** 07 **p** 08. C Watercombe *Sarum* 07-11; P-in-c Lt Barningham, Blickling, Edgefield etc *Nor* 11-15; C from 15; P-in-c Barningham w Matlaske w Baconsthorpe etc from 15. *The Rectory, The Street, Itteringham, Norwich NR11 7AX* T: (01263) 587977 M: 07932-521776 E: marion681@btinternet.com

HARRISON, Martin. b 58. Bris Univ BA 89 DCR(R) 78. Trin Coll Bris BA 89. **d** 89 **p** 90. C Heworth H Trin *York* 89-94; Chapl York Distr Hosp 89-94; P-in-c Skelton w Shipton and Newton on Ouse *York* R 95-01; V Strensall from 01; RD Easingwold 00-05. *The Vicarage, 10 York Road, Strensall, York YO32 5UN* T: (01904) 490683 E: vicar@strensallstmarys.org.uk *or* martinharrison2@btinternet.com

HARRISON, Matthew Henry. b 64. Univ Coll Dur BA 85 Union Th Sem (NY) STM 93. St Steph Ho Ox BA 88 MA 92. **d** 89 **p** 90.

C Whickham *Dur* 89-92; C Owton Manor 93-95; USA 92-93; Asst Chapl Paris St Geo *Eur* 95-02; PtO 02-04; C Paddington St Jas *Lon* 04-07; Chapl Paris St Geo *Eur* from 07. *St George, 7 rue Auguste-Vacquerie, 75116 Paris, France* T: (0033) (1) 47 20 22 51 E: office@stgeorgesparis.com

HARRISON, Maureen. b 39. **d** 08 **p** 09. OLM Sutton *Liv* 08-13; rtd 13. *89 Farndon Avenue, Sutton Manor, St Helens WA9 4DN* E: maureen.harrison@talktalk.net

HARRISON, Michael Anthony. b 48. Westhill Coll Birm CertCYW 72 Huddersfield Poly CertEd 88 Leeds Poly BA 91 Leeds Univ MA 98. NOC 94. **d** 97 **p** 98. NSM Thornhill and Whitley Lower *Wakef* 97-99; TV Wrexham *St As* 99-03; V Ruabon 03-11; rtd 11; PtO *St As* from 11; *Ban* from 12. *15 Vicarage Gardens, Llandudno LL30 1RG* E: whernside@aol.com

HARRISON, Michael Burt (Crispin). b 36. Leeds Univ BA 59 Trin Coll Ox BA 62 MA 66. Coll of Resurr Mirfield 59. **d** 63 **p** 64. C W Hartlepool St Aid *Dur* 63-64; C Middlesbrough All SS *York* 64-66; LtO *Wakef* 67-69 and 78-87 and 97-02; *Leeds* from 06; CR from 68; S Africa 69-78 and 87-97 and 03-06; Registrar Coll of the Resurr Mirfield 78-84; Vice-Prin 84-87; Superior CR 97-02. *Community of the Resurrection, Stocks Bank Road, Mirfield WF14 0BN* T: (01924) 483337 E: charrison@mirfield.org.uk

HARRISON, Canon Michael Robert. b 63. Selw Coll Cam BA 84 K Coll Lon PhD 97 Bradf Univ MA 99. Ripon Coll Cuddesdon BA 89 Union Th Sem (NY) STM 90. **d** 90 **p** 91. C S Lambeth St Anne and All SS *S'wark* 90-94; Bp's Chapl to Students *Bradf* 94-98; Chapl Bradf Univ 94-98; Chapl Bradf and Ilkley Community Coll 94-98; V Eltham H Trin *S'wark* 98-06; RD Eltham and Mottingham 05-06; Dir Min and Miss *Leic* from 06; Hon Can Leic Cathl from 06. *11 Paterson Drive, Woodhouse Eaves, Loughborough LE12 8RL* T: (01509) 891670 E: mikeharrison7@hotmail.com

HARRISON, Canon Noel Milburn. b 27. Leeds Univ MPhil 75 PhD 80. St Aid Birkenhead 54. **d** 57 **p** 58. C Doncaster St Jas *Sheff* 57-60; Chapl Yorkshire Res Sch for Deaf Doncaster 60-68; C Woodlands *Sheff* 60-62; Chapl to the Deaf 60-68; Hd Master Elmete Hall Sch Leeds 68-84; Hon C Whitgift w Adlingfleet and Eastoft *Sheff* 83-84; Hon C Abbeydale St Jo 84-86; Dioc Dir of Educn 84-94; R Tankersley 86-94; Hon Can Sheff Cathl 88-94; rtd 94; PtO *Sheff* from 94; *Linc* 95-99. *Aidan House, 118 High Street, Crowle, Scunthorpe DN17 4DR*

HARRISON, Mrs Nona Margaret. b 50. Open Univ BA 80. S Dios Minl Tr Scheme 92. **d** 95 **p** 96. NSM E w W Wellow and Sherfield English *Win* 95-99; NSM Barton Stacey and Bullington etc 99; NSM Hurstbourne Priors, Longparish etc 00-08; PtO from 08. *5 Chichester Close, East Wellow, Romsey SO51 6EY* T: (01794) 323154

HARRISON, Oliver. b 71. SS Paul & Mary Coll Cheltenham BA 93. St Jo Coll Nottm MA 95. **d** 97 **p** 98. Asst Chapl The Hague *Eur* 97-00; C Walmley *Birm* 00-04; C-in-c Grove Green LEP *Cant* 04-08; V Wilnecote *Lich* from 08. *The Vicarage, 64 Glascote Lane, Wilnecote, Tamworth B77 2PH* T: (01827) 260560 E: oliver.harrison@tiscali.co.uk

HARRISON, Miss Patricia Mary. b 35. St Kath Coll Lon CertEd 65 Open Univ BA 74. St Mich Ho Ox IDC 59. **dss** 85 **d** 87 **p** 94. NSM Nunthorpe *York* 85-98; rtd 98; PtO *York* from 98. *22 Lamonby Close, Nunthorpe, Middlesbrough TS7 0QG* T: (01642) 313524

HARRISON, Paul Graham. b 53. Univ of Wales (Lamp) MA 10. Sarum & Wells Th Coll 76. **d** 79 **p** 80. C Brixham w Churston Ferrers *Ex* 79-82; C Portsea N End St Mark *Portsm* 82-87; V Tiverton St Andr *Ex* 87-94; Chapl Tiverton and Distr Hosp 90-94; P-in-c Astwood Bank *Worc* 94-05; TV Redditch Ch the K 05-08; P-in-c Churchill-in-Halfshire w Blakedown and Broome from 08; Chapl to Deaf People 94-08; Dioc Adv for Disability Issues 03-08; RD Stourbridge from 13; PtO *Cov* from 94. *The Rectory, 5 Mill Lane, Blakedown, Kidderminster DY10 3ND* T: (01562) 700144 E: p.g.harrison@btinternet.com *or* dda@cofe-worcester.org.uk

HARRISON, Paul Thomas. b 57. Nor Sch of Art BA 80 Leic Poly PGCE 88 Coll of Ripon & York St Jo MA 99. Qu Coll Birm 95. **d** 97 **p** 98. C Northallerton w Kirby Sigston *York* 97-01; TV Usworth *Dur* 01-05; V Dalton le Dale and New Seaham from 05. *The Vicarage, 269 Station Road, Seaham SR7 0BH* T: 0191-581 3270

HARRISON, Mrs Penelope Ann. b 58. St Andr Univ MA 79. Qu Coll Birm MA 09. **d** 09 **p** 10. C Hamstead St Paul *Birm* 09-13; V Marston Green from 13. *The Vicarage, 32 Elmdon Road, Marston Green, Birmingham B37 7BT* M: 07722-446222 E: penny_h123@hotmail.com

HARRISON, Peter. *See* HARRISON, Robert Peter

HARRISON, Peter Keith. b 44. Open Univ BA 85. St Aid Birkenhead. **d** 68 **p** 69. C Higher Bebington *Ches* 68-71;

C Walmsley *Man* 71-74; V Lumb in Rossendale 74-79; V Heywood St Marg 79-87; V Hey 87-95; AD Saddleworth 93-95; Chapl Athens w Kifissia *Eur* 95-98; V Aston Cantlow and Wilmcote w Billesley *Cov* 98-02; V W Burnley All SS *Blackb* 02-09; rtd 09; PtO *Blackb* from 09. *57 West Cliffe, Lytham St Annes FY8 5DR* T: (01253) 735128 E: harrison.ssc@virgin.net

HARRISON, The Ven Peter Reginald Wallace. b 39. Selw Coll Cam BA 62. Ridley Hall Cam 62. **d** 64 **p** 65. C Barton Hill St Luke w Ch Ch *Bris* 64-69; Chapl Greenhouse Trust 69-77; Dir Northorpe Hall Trust 77-84; TR Drypool *York* 84-98; AD E Hull 88-98; Adn E Riding 98-06; Can and Preb York Minster 94-06; rtd 06; PtO *York* from 06. *10 Priestgate, Sutton-on-Hull, Hull HU7 4QR* T: (01482) 797110 E: peter@harrisons.karoo.co.uk

HARRISON, Canon Philip Hubert. b 37. Sarum & Wells Th Coll 77. **d** 79 **p** 80. C Wymondham *Nor* 79-83; V Watton w Carbrooke and Ovington 83-92; R Drayton w Felthorpe 92-02; Hon Can Nor Cathl 99-02; rtd 02; PtO *Nor* from 02. *The Fairstead, 1 Back Street, Horsham St Faith, Norwich NR10 3JP* T: (01603) 893087 E: harrison-thewarren@talktalk.net

HARRISON, Phillip Roger Neil. b 74. Trin Coll Bris 12. **d** 15. C Gtr Corsham and Lacock *Bris* from 15. *The Vicarage, Wadswick Lane, Neston, Corsham SN13 9TA* E: phillip_harrison@blueyonder.co.uk

HARRISON, Mrs Rachel Elizabeth. b 53. NEOC 98. **d** 01 **p** 02. C Skelton w Upleatham *York* 01-04; P-in-c New Marske 04-06; V 06-12; P-in-c Wilton 04-06; V 06-12; V Redcar from 12; Ind Chapl from 04; RD Guisborough from 13. *St Peter's Vicarage, 66 Aske Road, Redcar TS10 2BP* T: (01642) 489842 *or* 490700 E: rachelhere@hotmail.com

HARRISON, Richard Kingswood. b 61. Linc Coll Ox BA 83 MA 88 Leeds Univ BA 90. Coll of Resurr Mirfield 88. **d** 91 **p** 92. C Reading St Giles *Ox* 91-93; Asst Chapl Merchant Taylors' Sch Northwood 93-96; Chapl Ardingly Coll 96-02; R Shill Valley and Broadshire *Ox* 02-04; Chapl Uppingham Sch 04-09; Chapl Lancing Coll from 09. *Ladywell House, Lancing College, Lancing BN15 0RW* T: (01273) 465961

HARRISON, Robert Peter. b 28. Chich Th Coll. **d** 60 **p** 61. C Ealing Ch the Sav *Lon* 60-64; C Hammersmith SS Mich and Geo White City Estate CD 64-66; P-in-c Fulham St Pet 66-73; V 73-94; rtd 94; PtO *Chich* from 94. *8 Broadwater Way, Worthing BN14 9LP* T: (01903) 217073

HARRISON, Robert William. b 62. Mansf Coll Ox BA 84. Qu Coll Birm 87. **d** 89 **p** 90. C Sholing *Win* 89-93; Communications Adv to Bp Willesden *Lon* 93-97; C Cricklewood St Gabr and St Mich 93-97; V Hillingdon St Jo 97-15; V Neasden St Cath w St Paul from 15. *60 Chartwell Court, 151 Brook Road, London NW2 7DW* E: rob.harrison@london.anglican.org

HARRISON, Rodney Lovel Neal. b 46. MBE 87. Dur Univ BA 67. Ripon Coll Cuddesdon 93. **d** 95 **p** 96. C N w S Wootton *Nor* 95-98; P-in-c Gt and Lt Bedwyn and Savernake Forest *Sarum* 98-02; TV Savernake 02-11; rtd 11; PtO *Heref* from 12. *55 Browning Road, Ledbury HR8 2GA* T: (01531) 633360 E: rodney@rodneyandjenny.plus.com

HARRISON, Rosemary Jane. b 53. Bradf Coll of Educn CertEd 76. Trin Coll Bris 83. **d** 87 **p** 94. NSM Southway *Ex* 87-89; NSM Kinson *Sarum* 89-96. *28 First Avenue, Havant PO9 2QN* T: (023) 9245 5226

HARRISON, Miss Ruth Margaret. b 33. BEM 85. FRSA 94. Ripon Coll Cuddesdon 02. **d** 02 **p** 03. NSM Baddiley and Wrenbury w Burleydam *Ches* 02-08; PtO from 08. *2 Heywood Cottages, Heywood Lane, Audlem, Crewe CW3 0EX* T: (01270) 812010

HARRISON, Shirley Ann. b 56. Leic Univ BA 76. NOC 02. **d** 05 **p** 06. C Saddleworth *Man* 05-08; P-in-c Denton Ch Ch 08-11; TV Redruth w Lanner and Treleigh *Truro* from 11. *1 Wheal Uny, Trewirgie Hill, Redruth TR15 2TD* T: (01209) 211100 M: 07584-416903 E: bluebetty@btinternet.com

HARRISON, Steven John. b 47. Univ of Wales (Abth) BSc 68 PhD 74 FRMetS 74. St And Dioc Tr Course 87. **d** 90 **p** 91. NSM Alloa *St And* 90-94; NSM Bridge of Allan 94-02; NSM Spittal *Newc* 02-10; NSM Scremerston 02-10; P-in-c 06-10; rtd 10. *East Cottage, Plunderheath, Haydon Bridge, Hexham NE47 6JU* T: (01434) 684994 E: johnandaveril@aol.com

HARRISON-SMITH, Ms Fiona Jane. b 74. Huddersfield Univ BMus 96 Ox Brookes Univ BA 03 Leeds Univ MA 07. Coll of Resurr Mirfield 05. **d** 07 **p** 08. C Redcar *York* 07-11; TV Seacroft *Leeds* from 11. *St James Vicarage, 47 St James Approach, Leeds LS14 6JJ* M: 07709-914786 E: fharrisonsmith@btinternet.com

HARRISON-WATSON, Carole. *See* FORD, Carole

HARRISSON, John Anthony Lomax. b 47. Ex Univ BA 72. Qu Coll Birm 72. **d** 74 **p** 75. C Loughton St Jo *Chelmsf* 74-81; V Chingford St Anne 81-98; TV Aldrington *Chich* 98-04;

TV Golden Cap Team *Sarum* 04-09; rtd 09. *82 Chestnut Way, Honiton EX14 2XF* E: john@jharrisson.wanadoo.co.uk

HARROLD, Canon Jeremy Robin. b 31. Hertf Coll Ox BA 54 BSc 56 MA 58. Wycliffe Hall Ox. **d** 59 **p** 60. C Rushden *Pet* 59-61; Bp's Chapl *Lon* 61-64; Australia 64-67; V Harlesden St Mark *Lon* 67-72; V Hendon St Paul Mill Hill 72-84; V Stowmarket *St E* 84-96; RD 90-96; Hon Can St E Cathl 94-96; rtd 96; PtO *St E* from 96. *18 Wilkinson Way, Woodbridge IP12 1SS* T: (01394) 380127

HARRON, Canon Gareth Andrew. b 71. QUB BA 92. CITC BTh 95. **d** 95 **p** 96. C Willowfield *D & D* 95-98; C Dromore Cathl 98-02; I Magheralin w Dollingstown from 02; Can Dromore Cathl from 12. *The Rectory, 12 New Forge Road, Magheralin, Craigavon BT67 0QJ* T: (028) 9261 1273
E: garethharron@btinternet.com

HARRON, James Alexander. b 37. GIMechE 61. St Aid Birkenhead 63. **d** 65 **p** 66. C Willowfield *D & D* 65-69; I Desertmartin *D & R* 69-80; Dep Sec BCMS (Ireland) 80-84; I Aghalee *D & D* 84-03; Preb Dromore Cathl 02-03; Chapl HM Pris Maghaberry 86-03; rtd 03. *8 Churchill Avenue, Lurgan, Craigavon BT66 7BW* T/F: (028) 3834 6543

HARROP, Mrs Eileen Khean Geok. b 59. Ridley Hall Cam. **d** 12 **p** 13. C Tenterden and Smallhythe *Cant* from 12; C Rother and Oxney from 13. *The Vicarage, Ashford Road, St Michael's, Tenterden TN30 6PY* T: (01580) 441069
E: ekgharrop@gmail.com

HARROP, Stephen Douglas. b 48. St Jo Coll York CertEd 74 Man Univ DipAdEd 90. Edin Th Coll 77. **d** 79 **p** 82. C Middlesbrough St Martin *York* 79-80; C Cayton w Eastfield 80-81; C Oldham *Man* 82-84; V Oldham St Barn 84-89; P-in-c Em Ch Hong Kong 89-93; Ind Chapl and TV Kidderminster St Mary and All SS w Trimpley etc *Worc* 93-95; Chapl Kidderminster Coll 93-95; Sandwell Chs Link Officer *Birm* 95-96; Dep Chapl HM Pris Brixton 96-97; Chapl Taichung St Jas Taiwan 97-98; R Lower Merion St Jo USA 98-99; R Essington *Lich* 99-03; PtO *Man* 03-04 and 09-13; C Elton St Steph 04-05; P-in-c 05-08; Chapl HM Pris Forest Bank 08-13; P-in-c Petton w Cockshutt, Welshampton and Lyneal etc *Lich* from 13. *The Rectory, Cockshutt, Ellesmere SY12 0JQ* E: steph60en@aol.com

HARRY, Bruce David. b 40. JP 77. Culham Coll Ox CertEd 60. NOC 83. **d** 86 **p** 87. NSM Liscard St Thos *Ches* 86-91; NSM Eastham 91-94; C New Brighton St Jas 94-96; C New Brighton Em 94-96; C New Brighton St Jas w Em 96-98; NSM 98-02; NSM New Brighton All SS 98-02; P-in-c 02-03; PtO from 03. *21 Sandymount Drive, Wallasey CH45 0LJ* T: 0151-639 7232

HART (formerly HARRISON), Mrs Alison Edwina. b 53. Newc Univ BEd 75. Linc Th Coll 84. **dss** 86 **d** 87 **p** 94. Loughborough Em *Leic* 86-89; Par Dn 87-89; C Stockton *Dur* 89-92; P-in-c Lynesack and Cockfield 92-95; P-in-c Ebchester 95-96; R Newc 96-97; V Medomsley 96-97; V Newc H Cross 97-01; P-in-c Ulgham and Widdrington 01-06; P-in-c Beckermet St Jo and St Bridget w Ponsonby *Carl* 06-10; rtd 10. *1 Braeval, Carrbridge PH23 3AA* E: coolingsteam@yahoo.co.uk

HART, Allen Sydney George. b 38. Chich Th Coll 64. **d** 67 **p** 68. C N Wembley St Cuth *Lon* 67-71; C W Bromwich All SS *Lich* 71-74; TV Hucknall Torkard *S'well* 74-80; V Annesley Our Lady and All SS 80-86; V Bilborough St Jo 86-99; RD Nottingham W 94-99; P-in-c Clarborough w Hayton 99-03; Asst Chapl HM Pris Ranby 99-03; rtd 03; PtO *S'well* from 03. *3 Castleton Close, Hucknall, Nottingham NG15 6TD* T: 0115-955 2067
E: a.hart557@ntlworld.com

HART, André Hendrik. b 62. Cape Town Univ BA 86. St Steph Ho Ox 89. **d** 91 **p** 92. C Newbold w Dunston *Derby* 91-95; P-in-c Clifton and Norbury w Snelston 95-02; Chapl S Derbyshire Community Health Services NHS Trust 95-01; Chapl Derbyshire Mental Health Services NHS Trust 01-02; V Westbury-on-Trym H Trin *Bris* from 02. *Holy Trinity Vicarage, 44 Eastfield Road, Westbury-on-Trym, Bristol BS9 4AG* T: 0117-962 1536 *or* 950 8644

HART, Anthony. b 35. St Mich Coll Llan 77. **d** 79 **p** 80. NSM Jersey St Helier *Win* 79-81; C Heref All SS 81-82; C Kingstone 82-84; C Eaton Bishop 82-84; C Clehonger 82-84; R Sutton St Nicholas w Sutton St Michael 84-88; R Withington w Westhide 84-88; R Jersey St Mary *Win* 88-01; rtd 01; PtO *Win* from 02. *Villa Rapallo, Mont de la Trinite, St Helier, Jersey JE2 4NJ* T: (01534) 739146 M: 07797-750435 E: hart@localdial.com

HART, Colin Edwin. b 45. Leeds Univ BA 66 PGCE 67 MPhil 89 Fitzw Coll Cam BA 73 MA 77 K Coll Lon MTh 76 Man Univ PhD 98. Trin Coll Bris 74. **d** 74 **p** 75. C Ware Ch Ch *St Alb* 74-78; TV Sheff Manor 78-80; V Wombridge *Lich* 80-87; Lect St Jo Coll Nottm 87-01; Public Preacher *S'well* 87-01; Hon C Chilwell 87-91; Hon C Trowell 91-01; PtO *Ches* from 09. *47 Deveraux Drive, Wallasey CH44 4DG* T: 0151-630 0749
E: ceh2397@gmail.com

HART, Dagogo. b 50. Birm Bible Inst 77. **d** 82 **p** 83. Nigeria 82-00; C St Cypr Niger Delta 82-88; V 93-96; Chapl to Bp 83-88; Res Min Niger Delta Ch Ch 89-92; Can Res St Steph Cathl Niger Delta 97-00; C W Bromwich St Jas w St Paul *Lich* 01-06; V from 06. *3 Tiverton Drive, West Bromwich B71 1DA* T: 0121-553 0601

HART, David. b 48. Edge Hill Coll of HE BEd 80 Liv Univ MEd 87 Ches Coll of HE BPhil 94. NOC 91. **d** 94 **p** 95. NSM Ashton-in-Makerfield St Thos *Liv* 94-02; NSM Wigan W Deanery 02-05. *12 Ratcliffe Road, Aspull, Wigan WN2 1YE* T: (01942) 832918

HART, David Alan. b 54. Rhodes Univ BTh 86 MTh 89 PhD 92 Bournemouth Univ DEd 08. **d** 81 **p** 82. R Auckland Park St Pet S Africa 82-86; Sub Dean Kimberley Cathl 86-90; Chapl Cape Town Univ 90-94; NSM Cape Town Cathl 94-98; Chapl Bournemouth and Poole Coll of FE *Sarum* 99-06; Co-ord of IME 07-11; Vice Prin Sarum OLM Scheme 07-11; Asst Dioc Dir of Ords 07-11; rtd 11; PtO *Sarum* from 11; P-in-c Menton *Eur* from 14. *St John, 31 avenue Carnot, 06500 Menton, France* T/F: (0033) 4 93 57 20 25
M: 07521-741534 E: dhart.home@gmail.com

HART, David Alan. b 54. Keble Coll Ox BA 75 MPhil 78 Union Th Sem (NY) STM 79 Derby Univ PhD 06. Westcott Ho Cam 83. **d** 83 **p** 84. Asst Chapl Gresham's Sch Holt 83-84; Chapl Nor Sch 84-85; Chapl Shrewsbury Sch 85-87; Chapl St Jo Coll Sch Cam 87-88; C Camberwell St Giles w St Matt *S'wark* 88-90; Chapl Loughb Univ *Leic* 90-97; Chapl Roehampton Inst *S'wark* 97-98; Relig and Past Services Development Co-ord Derby Univ 98-02; Sen Lect Win Univ 03-05; PtO S Kerala India from 05. *TC 50/312(4), Rose Gardens, S Karamana PO, Trivandrum, Kerala, 695 002, India*
E: hart.da@gmail.com

HART, David John. b 58. K Coll Lon BD 80. St Mich Coll Llan 83. **d** 85 **p** 86. C Denbigh and Nantglyn *St As* 85-88; Chapl RAF 88-89; C Llanrhos *St As* 89-91; V Rhosllannerchrugog 91-01; PtO *Lich* from 11. *11 Cilcoed, Chirk, Wrexham LL14 5BX*

HART, David Maurice. b 35. Univ Coll Dur BSc 57. Clifton Th Coll 59. **d** 61 **p** 62. C Bolton St Paul *Man* 61-64; C Hamworthy *Sarum* 64-70; R W Dean w E Grimstead 70-81; R Farley w Pitton and W Dean w E Grimstead 81-90; V Steeple Ashton w Semington and Keevil 90-03; rtd 03. *9 Field Close, Westbury BA13 3AG* T: (01373) 827912 E: dmhart@fish.co.uk

HART, Debbie. *See* HORE, Debbie

HART, Canon Dennis Daniel. b 22. Linc Th Coll 45. **d** 48 **p** 49. C Abbots Langley *St Alb* 48-49; C Bedford St Paul 49-53; CF 53-55; V St Alb St Sav *St Alb* 55-92; Hon Can St Alb 79-92; RD St Alb 84-90; rtd 92. *Grace Muriel House, 104 Tavistock Avenue, St Albans AL1 2NW* T: (01727) 815829

HART, Dennis William. b 30. JP. Open Univ BA. Oak Hill Th Coll 75. **d** 78 **p** 79. NSM Clacton St Paul *Chelmsf* 78-04; PtO 04-07. *Maranatha, 15 Albert Gardens, Clacton-on-Sea CO15 6QN* T: (01255) 431794

HART, Edwin Joseph. b 21. Oak Hill Th Coll 56. **d** 58 **p** 59. C Harlow New Town w Lt Parndon *Chelmsf* 58-60; C-in-c Cranham Park St Luke CD 61-69; V Cranham Park 69-71; R Markfield *Leic* 71-89; rtd 89; PtO *Leic* from 89. *c/o Ms G Gordon, 1 Meadow Lane, Markfield LE67 9WT*

HART, Geoffrey Robert. b 49. TISEC 93. **d** 95 **p** 96. P-in-c Edin St Salvador 96-98; C Edin St Cuth 96-98; LtO 98-00; TV Edin St Marg 00-04; NSM Edin St Dav 04-09; P-in-c Edin St Marg 09-13; rtd 13. *27 Links View, Port Seton, Prestonpans EH32 0EZ* T: (01875) 811147 M: 07963-463551
E: geoff@geoffhart.co.uk *or* geoff@stmegs.co.uk

HART, Canon Gillian Mary. b 57. Sheff City Poly BA 79. Carl Dioc Tr Inst 92. **d** 95 **p** 96. C Burgh-by-Sands and Kirkbampton w Kirkandrews etc *Carl* 95-99; C Aikton 95-99; C Orton St Giles 95-99; Dioc Youth Officer 99-03; Chapl St Martin's Coll Carl 99-03; R Barony of Burgh *Carl* 03-10; TR Maryport, Netherton and Flimby 10-15; P-in-c Brigham, Gt Broughton and Broughton Moor 14-15; Adv for Women in Min from 08; Hon Can Carl Cathl from 10; P-in-c Eskdale, Irton, Muncaster and Waberthwaite from 15. *2 Smithy Banks, Holmrook CA19 1TP* T: E: hart.gill@btopenworld.com

HART, Graham Cooper. b 36. S Dios Minl Tr Scheme 88. **d** 91 **p** 92. NSM Filton *Bris* 91-93; NSM Downend 93-01. *11 West Hill, Portishead, Bristol BS20 6LQ* T: (01275) 840363

HART, James. b 53. Dur Univ BA 75 DipEd 76 Lon Univ BD 96 MIL 84. Oak Hill Th Coll 86. **d** 88 **p** 89. C Starbeck *Ripon* 88-90; SAMS Argentina 90-96; R Buenos Aires St Sav 91-95; Chapl Bishop's Stortford Coll 96-00; Chapl Felsted Sch 00-06; P-in-c Steeple Bumpstead and Helions Bumpstead *Chelmsf* 06-11; Dioc FE Officer 00-11; rtd 12. *9 Margetts Close, Kenilworth CV8 1EN* M: 07764-500662
E: james@harthome.org

HART, Jane Elizabeth. *See* WARHURST, Jane Elizabeth

HART, John Peter. b 39. Bris Sch of Min 80. **d** 84 **p** 85. NSM Malmesbury w Westport and Brokenborough *Bris* 84-88; C Yatton Moor *B & W* 89-90; V Bridgwater H Trin 90-96; Chapl HM Pris The Mount 96-01; P-in-c Sarratt *St Alb* 96-04; P-in-c Chipperfield St Paul 01-04; rtd 04; PtO *Pet* from 05. *4 Waverley Gardens, Stamford PE9 1BH* T: (01780) 754756

HART, Julia Lesley. b 43. **d** 08 **p** 09. NSM Nettleham *Linc* 08-12; NSM Linc St Mary-le-Wigford w St Benedict from 12; NSM Linc St Botolph from 12; NSM Linc St Pet-at-Gowts and St Andr from 12. *Shrewsbury Cottage, Nettleham Lane, Scothern, Lincoln LN2 2TY* T: (01673) 862426
E: jldf.hart@btinternet.com

HART, Mark. b 61. Chu Coll Cam BA 82 Cam Univ MA 86 PhD 86. Trin Coll Bris BA 98. **d** 98 **p** 99. C Bromborough *Ches* 98-02; V Plemstall w Guilden Sutton from 02; RD *Ches* 09-13. *41 Oaklands, Guilden Sutton, Chester CH3 7HE* T: (01244) 300306 E: markhart61@gmail.com

HART, Canon Michael Anthony. b 50. AKC 71. St Aug Coll Cant 72. **d** 73 **p** 74. C Southwick St Columba *Dur* 73-76; C Hendon St Alphage *Lon* 76-78; P-in-c Eltham Park St Luke *S'wark* 78-83; V 83-85; R Newington St Mary 85-96; P-in-c Camberwell St Mich w All So w Em 85-96; RD S'wark and Newington 93-96; P-in-c Chaldon 96-97; P-in-c Caterham 96-97; TR 98-05; RD 98-05; Hon Can S'wark Cathl 01-05 and 10-15; Can Missr 05-10; TR Catford (Southend) and Downham 10-15; rtd 15; PtO *S'wark* from 15. *1 High Beeches, Worthing BN11 4TJ* E: michael.hart@southwark.anglican.org

HART, Preb Michael Stuart. b 39. Univ of Wales (Lamp) BA 61 Lanc Univ MA 72. Wycliffe Hall Ox 61. **d** 63 **p** 64. C W Bromwich St Jas *Lich* 63-66; C Tarrington w Stoke Edith *Heref* 66-67; C Putney St Mary *S'wark* 67-70; V Accrington St Mary *Blackb* 70-82; RD Accrington 76-82; Hon Can Blackb Cathl 81-91; V Walton-le-Dale 82-91; TR Heavitree w Ex St Paul 91-02; P-in-c Ex St Mary Steps 01-02; TR Heavitree and St Mary Steps 02-07; P-in-c Exwick 05-07; Preb Ex Cathl 02-07; rtd 07; P-in-c Bath H Trin *B & W* 09-11; PtO from 11. *New Breezes, Camrose, Haverfordwest SA62 6JG* M: 07786-516076
E: m.hart254@btinternet.com

HART, Mrs Mildred Elizabeth. b 49. **d** 10 **p** 11. OLM Len Valley *Cant* 10-14; NSM from 14. *15 Mercer Drive, Harrietsham ME17 1AY* T: (01622) 859753 E: millie.hart@uwclub.net

HART, Mrs Pauline Jayne. b 58. St Mellitus Coll 13. **d** 15. OLM Alresford and Frating w Thorrington *Chelmsf* from 15. *Leigh House, 52 The Avenue, Wivenhoe, Colchester CO7 9AH*

HART, Peter. *See* HART, John Peter

HART, Preb Peter Osborne. b 57. St Jo Coll Nottm. **d** 92 **p** 93. C Shipley St Pet *Bradf* 92-97; TV Walsall *Lich* 97-03; TV Cannock 03-09; TV Cannock and Huntington 09-10; V from 10; V Hatherton from 10; Preb Lich Cathl from 13. *The Rectory, 11 Sherbrook Road, Cannock WS11 1HJ* T: (01543) 579660

HART, Peter William. b 60. Liv Univ BA 82 Université de Haute Normandie MèsL 84 Univ of Wales (Swansea) MPhil 92. Sarum & Wells Th Coll 86. **d** 88 **p** 89. C Llansamlet *S & B* 88-89; C Sketty 89-92; P-in-c Warndon St Nic *Worc* 92-97; R Berkhamsted St Mary *St Alb* 97-04; V Kew St Phil and All SS w St Luke *S'wark* from 04; Ecum Adv Kingston Area from 05. *St Philip's Vicarage, 70 Marksbury Avenue, Richmond TW9 4JF* T: (020) 8392 1425 *or* 8332 1324 E: pwhart1@aol.com

HART, Robert William. b 76. R Holloway & Bedf New Coll Lon BSc 97 Leeds Univ BA 01 MA 04. Coll of Resurr Mirfield 99. **d** 02 **p** 03. C Haydock St Jas *Liv* 02-06; R Hemsworth *Leeds* from 06. *The Rectory, 3 Church Close, Hemsworth, Pontefract WF9 4SJ* T: (01977) 610507
E: frrobert@parishofhemsworth.org.uk

HART, Ronald George. b 46. BSc CQSW 77. Sarum & Wells Th Coll. **d** 85 **p** 86. C Sittingbourne St Mich *Cant* 85-88; C Walton H Trin *Ox* 88-89; TV 89-96; R Broughton Gifford, Gt Chalfield and Holt *Sarum* 96-05; Chapl UWE *Bris* 05-07; C Mangotsfield 06-07; R Vale of White Hart *Sarum* 07-11; rtd 11. *Lavenders, 6 Squarey Close, Downton, Salisbury SP5 3LQ* T: (01725) 514772 E: ronhart1@yahoo.co.uk

HART, Mrs Sheila Elizabeth. b 49. ERMC. **d** 08 **p** 09. NSM Whinlands *St E* from 08. *3 Keats Close, Saxmundham IP17 1WJ* T: (01728) 602456 E: sheila.hart@tesco.net

HART, Tony. b 36. CCC Cam BA 59 MA 63. Cuddesdon Coll 59. **d** 61 **p** 62. C Middlesbrough All SS *York* 61-64; Bp's Dom Chapl *Dur* 64-67; Hon Chapl 67-72; C Owton Manor CD *Dur* 67-70; V Harton Colliery 70-71; TR S Shields All SS 71-83; RD Jarrow 77-83; Can Res Dur Cathl 83-92; V Easingwold w Raskelfe *York* 92-01; RD Easingwold 97-00; rtd 01; PtO *Newc* from 02. *13 Stobhill Villas, Morpeth NE61 2SH* T: (01670) 519017

HART, Prof Trevor Andrew. b 61. St Jo Coll Dur BA 82 Aber Univ PhD 89. **d** 88 **p** 88. NSM Bieldside *Ab* 88-95; NSM St Andrews St Andr *St And* 95-13; R from 13; Prof Div St Mary's Coll St Andr Univ from 95; Prin St Mary's

Coll 01-06. *5 Pipland Farm Steading, St Andrews KY16 8NL* M: 07545-322259 E: tah@st-andrews.ac.uk

HART, Mrs Valerie Mary. b 44. Sheff Univ MEd 89 Wolv Univ MSc 95 Nottm Univ MA 08 RSCN. EMMTC 06. **d** 08 **p** 09. NSM Derby St Andr w St Osmund 08-12; P-in-c Ambergate and Heage from 12. *6 Calder Close, Allestree, Derby DE22 2SH* T: (01332) 550313

HARTE, Matthew Scott. b 46. TCD BA 70 MA 74. CITC 71. **d** 71 **p** 72. C Bangor Abbey *D & D* 71-74; C Ballynafeigh St Jude 74-76; I Ardara w Glencolumbkille, Inniskeel etc *D & R* 76-98; I Dunfanaghy, Raymunterdoney and Tullaghbegley 98-13; Adn Raphoe 83-13; Preb Howth St Patr Cathl Dublin 07-13; rtd 13. *Largymore, Kilcar, Co Donegal, Republic of Ireland* T: (00353) (74) 973 8434 M: 87-756 5081
E: msharte1@eircom.net

HARTER, Andrew Michael Hatfeild. b 44. K Coll Cam BA 66 MA 69. Ripon Coll Cuddesdon 12. **d** 13 **p** 14. NSM Grosmont and Skenfrith and Llangattock etc *Mon* from 13. *The Rectory, Grosmont, Abergavenny NP7 8LW* T: (01981) 241172
E: andrew@harter.co.uk

HARTERINK, Mrs Joy Frances. b 49. Essex Univ BA 71 Hughes Hall Cam CertEd 72 Lon Univ MSc 87. Oak Hill NSM Course 89. **d** 92 **p** 94. NSM Richmond H Trin and Ch Ch *S'wark* 92-05; Chapl Richmond Coll 97-01; PtO *Guildf* from 05. *9 Eastmead, Woking GU21 3BP* T: (01483) 751179
E: joyharterink@yahoo.com

HARTILL, Gary. **d** 14 **p** 15. OLM W Bromwich St Fran *Lich* from 14. *34 Rydding Lane, West Bromwich B71 2HA* T: 0121-505 3954 E: father.gary@outlook.com

HARTLAND, Ian Charles. b 49. K Coll Lon BD 72 AKC 72 PGCE 73 MTh 76. Sarum & Wells Th Coll 83. **d** 84 **p** 85. C Orpington All SS *Roch* 84-87; Sen Lect Ch Ch Coll Cant 87-95; Adv RE Kent Coun 96-04; HMI of Schs from 04. *Ivy Lodge, 4 The Terrace, Canterbury CT2 7AJ* T: (01227) 472836 E: ian.hartland@ofsted.gov.uk

HARTLAND, Michael. b 58. **d** 08. NSM Sutton *S'wark* 08-10; PtO 10-11. *Address temp unknown*
E: mandjhartland@blueyonder.co.uk

HARTLAND (née CLARKE), Mrs Rachel Frances. b 69. Univ of Wales (Abth) BSc 90. Ox Min Course 12. **d** 14 **p** 15. NSM Old Basing and Lychpit *Win* from 14. *Ramtops, 26 Cornfields, Yateley GU46 6YT* E: ramtopsrac@yahoo.co.uk

HARTLESS, Berengaria Isabella de la Tour. b 52. Univ of Wales (Cardiff) BSc 74 Goldsmiths' Coll Lon PGCE 76 Liv Univ MA 03 K Coll Lon DThMin 15. Ox Min Course 90. **d** 93 **p** 94. Par Dn High Wycombe *Ox* 93-94; C 94-97; P-in-c Seer Green and Jordans 97-00; OLM Tr Officer (Bucks) 97-00; Dioc Prin of OLM from 00; Dir of IME (2) from 11; PtO *Cov* from 10. *Lloyd's House, Banbury Street, Kineton, Warwick CV35 0JS* T: (01926) 642975

HARTLEY, Mrs Anne Theresa. b 52. St Cuth Soc Dur BSc 74 Worc Coll of Educn PGCE 75. **d** 03 **p** 04. OLM Wychwood *Ox* from 03. *The Old House, Upper Milton, Milton-under-Wychwood, Chipping Norton OX7 6EX* T: (01993) 830160 M: 07976-025101 E: anne@thartley.net

HARTLEY, Brian. b 41. NOC 82. **d** 85 **p** 86. NSM Royton St Paul *Man* 85-91; NSM Oldham St Steph and All Martyrs 91-94; TV E Farnworth and Kearsley 94-97; TR New Bury 97-06; P-in-c Gt Lever 03-06; AD Farnworth 98-05; rtd 06; PtO *Man* from 06. *21 Penryn Avenue, Royton, Oldham OL2 6JR* T: (01706) 849132 E: brian_hartley@tiscali.co.uk

HARTLEY, Christopher Neville. b 56. Hull Univ BA 82 SS Paul & Mary Coll Cheltenham PGCE 84. SNWTP 08. **d** 10 **p** 11. OLM Man Victoria Park from 10. *8 Bronte Street, Manchester M15 6QL* T: 0161-232 0644 M: 07783-932386
E: christopherhartley@ymail.com

HARTLEY, Colin Redfearn. b 60. Cant Ch Ch Univ Coll BA 98. Ridley Hall Cam 02. **d** 04 **p** 05. C Herne Bay Ch Ch *Cant* 04-08; TV Langley Marish *Ox* from 08. *Christ the Worker Vicarage, Parlaunt Road, Slough SL3 8BB* T: (01753) 596722 E: rev.hartley@btinternet.com

HARTLEY, Daniel George. b 73. Leeds Univ BA 95. Coll of Resurr Mirfield 96. **d** 99 **p** 00. C Richmond w Hudswell *Ripon* 99-03; Chapl HM YOI Deerbolt 03-10; V Ecclesfield *Sheff* 11-15; P-in-c Thurlestone, S Milton, W Alvington etc *Ex* from 15. *The Rectory, Thurlestone, Kingsbridge TQ7 3LF*

HARTLEY, Denis. b 54. NTMTC BA 07. **d** 07 **p** 15. NSM Wood Green St Mich w Bounds Green St Gabr etc *Lon* 07-12; Chapl HM Pris Thameside from 12. *HM Prison Thameside, Griffin Manor Way, London SE28 0FJ* T: (020) 8317 9777 M: 07957-227764 E: dhart74802@blueyonder.co.uk

HARTLEY, Dianna Lynn. *See* GWILLIAMS, Dianna Lynn

HARTLEY, Graeme William. b 68. Ripon Coll Cuddesdon 05. **d** 07 **p** 08. C Sherborne w Castleton, Lillington and Longburton *Sarum* 07-10; V Milborne Port w Goathill etc *B & W* 10-13. *Address temp unknown* E: revd.graeme@gmail.com

✠**HARTLEY, The Rt Revd Helen-Ann Macleod.** b 73. St Andr Univ MTheol 95 Princeton Th Sem ThM 96 Worc Coll Ox MPhil 00 DPhil 05. SAOMC 03. **d** 05 **p** 06 **c** 14. C Wheatley *Ox* 05-07; C Littlemore 07-12; Lect Ripon Coll Cuddesdon 05-12; Tutor 09-12; Tutor St Jo Coll Auckland New Zealand 12-14; Bp Waikato from 14. *PO Box 21, Hamilton 3240, New Zealand* T: (0064) (7) 857 0020
E: bishop@waikatoanglican.org.nz

HARTLEY, John Peter. b 56. Cam Univ BA 78 Leeds Univ PhD 82 Dur Univ BA 84. Cranmer Hall Dur 82. **d** 85 **p** 86. C Spring Grove St Mary *Lon* 85-88; C Bexleyheath St Pet *Roch* 88-91; P-in-c Hanford *Lich* 91-00; Faith in the City Officer (Potteries) 91-00; V Eccleshill *Leeds* from 00. *The Vicarage, 2 Fagley Lane, Bradford BD2 3NS* T: (01274) 636403 M: 07811-915320
E: john.hartley@bradford.anglican.org

HARTLEY, Canon John William. b 47. St Jo Coll Dur BA 69. Linc Th Coll 70. **d** 72 **p** 73. C Poulton-le-Fylde *Blackb* 72-76; C Lancaster St Mary 76-79; V Barrowford 79-87; V Salesbury 87-11; AD Whalley 01-11; Hon Can Blackb Cathl 09-11; rtd 11. *14 Beech Mount, Ramsgreave, Blackburn BB1 9BP* T: (01254) 243700 E: john.hartley828@btinternet.com

HARTLEY, Julian John. b 57. Oak Hill Th Coll BA 85. **d** 85 **p** 86. C Eccleston Ch Ch *Liv* 85-89; V Goose Green 89-00; P-in-c Mosley Common *Man* 00-06; TV Astley, Tyldesley and Mosley Common from 06. *St John's Vicarage, Mosley Common Road, Worsley, Manchester M28 1AN* T: 0161-790 2957 F: 799 0314 E: rev.hartley@hartley.me.uk

HARTLEY, Martin John Edward. b 67. Ridley Hall Cam 11. **d** 13 **p** 14. C Newton Flotman, Swainsthorpe, Tasburgh, etc *Nor* from 13. *The New Rectory, Church Hill, Tasburgh, Norwich NR15 1NB* M: 07876-643560 E: mjehartley@gmail.com

HARTLEY, Michael Leslie. b 56. Leeds Univ BSc 77. Ripon Coll Cuddesdon 87. **d** 89 **p** 90. C Standish *Blackb* 89-93; V Bamber Bridge St Aid 93-98; TR Colne and Villages 98-08; P-in-c Warton St Paul from 08; Dioc Ecum Officer from 08. *The Vicarage, Church Road, Warton, Preston PR4 1BD* T: (01772) 632227 E: blackburndeo@googlemail.com

HARTLEY, Canon Nigel John. b 48. Portsm Poly BA 70. St Jo Coll Nottm. **d** 83 **p** 84. C Ipswich St Marg *St E* 83-86; P-in-c Hintlesham w Chattisham 86-95; Dioc Radio Officer 86-95; P-in-c Gt Finborough w Onehouse, Harleston, Buxhall etc 95-04; RD Stowmarket 96-99; V Aldeburgh w Hazlewood 04-14; RD Saxmundham 05-12; Hon Can St E Cathl 10-14; rtd 14; PtO *St E* from 14. *Sheppens, Newham Lane, Steyning BN44 3LR* E: nigel.hartley2@btinternet.com

HARTLEY, Paul. b 51. Nottm Univ BTh 88. Linc Th Coll 85. **d** 88 **p** 89. C Clitheroe St Mary *Blackb* 88-91; TV Guiseley w Esholt *Bradf* 91-97; R Ackworth *Leeds* from 97. *The Rectory, Cross Hill, Ackworth, Pontefract WF7 7EJ* T: (01977) 602751
E: rev.paulhartley@yahoo.co.uk

HARTLEY, Canon Peter. b 44. St Cath Coll Cam BA 66 MA 69 Avery Hill Coll PGCE 67. Sarum & Wells Th Coll 77. **d** 78 **p** 79. C Hon C Freemantle *Win* 78-79; Chr Educn Officer *Pet* 79-81; Dir of Educn 81-90; Dir Coun of Educn and Tr *Chelmsf* 90-09; Hon Can Chelmsf Cathl 92-09; rtd 09; PtO *Nor* from 04. *3 St Mary's Lane, Langham, Holt NR25 7AF* T: (01328) 830624 E: peter.hartley49@btinternet.com

HARTLEY, Peter Mellodew. b 41. Qu Coll Cam BA 63 MA 66 Lon Univ MSc 71 FICE. S'wark Ord Course 80. **d** 83 **p** 84. NSM Salfords *S'wark* 83-97; Chapl Surrey and Sussex Healthcare NHS Trust 97-02; rtd 02; PtO *Chich* from 00; *S'wark* from 02; *Eur* from 05. *Old Timbers, North Lane, West Hoathly, East Grinstead RH19 4QF* T: (01342) 811238
E: petermhartley@btinternet.com

HARTLEY (née ARCHER), Sarah Elizabeth. b 66. Charing Cross Hosp Medical Sch MB, BS 89 Heythrop Coll Lon MA 03 MRCGP 95. Ripon Coll Cuddesdon BA 99 MA 07. **d** 00 **p** 01. C Dulwich St Barn *S'wark* 00-03; C Shepherd's Bush St Steph w St Thos *Lon* 03-07; PV Westmr Abbey from 07; PtO *Lon* 07-08; *B & W* 08-11; NSM Bath Abbey w St Jas from 11. *Glen Gilda, St Saviour's Road, Bath BA1 6RN* M: 07717-718569
E: searcher@doctors.org.uk

HARTLEY, Stewart John Ridley. b 47. St Jo Coll Nottm 78. **d** 80 **p** 81. C Altham w Clayton le Moors *Blackb* 80-84; P-in-c Nelson St Phil 84-91; V 91-98; V Gt Marsden w Nelson St Phil 99-03; Hon Can Blackb Cathl 99-03; V Bermondsey St Anne and St Aug *S'wark* 03-12; V Bermondsey St Jas w Ch Ch and St Crispin 03-12; rtd 12. *8 Weston Park View, Leeds LS21 2DU* E: stewarthartley@btinternet.com

HARTLEY, Susan Mary. b 49. Newc Univ MB, BS 73 MRCGP 77. SEITE 99. **d** 02 **p** 03. NSM Spitalfields Ch Ch w All SS *Lon* 02-07; NSM Hainault *Chelmsf* from 07; Asst Chapl St Joseph's Hospice Hackney from 06. *272 New North Road, Ilford IG6 3BT* T: (020) 8500 4592 E: suemhartley@btinternet.com

HARTMAN, Mrs Jill Norma. b 57. Cen Sch of Art London BA 80. SEITE 08. **d** 11. NSM Upper St Leonards St Jo *Chich* from 11. *21 Nelson Road, Hastings TN34 3RX* T: (01424) 716126 M: 07952-950316

HARTNELL, Canon Bruce John. b 42. Ex Univ BA 64 Linacre Coll Ox BA 66 MA. Ripon Hall Ox 64. **d** 66 **p** 67. C S Stoneham *Win* 66-69; Chapl and Tutor Ripon Hall Ox 69-74; V Knowl Hill w Littlewick *Ox* 74-78; Chapl Southn Univ *Win* 78-83; V Sholing 83-07; AD Southampton 93-01; Hon Can Win Cathl 93-07; rtd 07; PtO *Win* from 07. *9 Ash Close, Southampton SO19 5SD* T: (023) 8090 5420
E: bruce.hartnell@ukgateway.net

HARTNELL, Graham Philip. b 50. **d** 08 **p** 08. NSM Flackwell Heath *Ox* 08-15. *36 Whinneys Road, Loudwater, High Wycombe HP10 9RL* T: (01494) 521783 E: g.hartnell@talktalk.net

HARTOPP, Mrs Penelope Faye. b 55. Ripon Coll Cuddesdon. **d** 03 **p** 04. C Studley *Cov* 03-04; C Cov E 04-07; TV Godalming *Guildf* 07-11; V Over St Chad *Ches* 11-15; C Budleigh Salterton, E Budleigh w Bicton etc *Ex* from 15. *The Vicarage, 4A West Hill Lane, Budleigh Salterton EX9 6AA* M: 07884-314752 T: (01395) 446269
E: penniehartopp@googlemail.com

HARTREE, Steven John. b 45. FFA 78. WEMTC 96. **d** 99 **p** 00. NSM Highbridge *B & W* 99-03; P-in-c Tintinhull w Chilthorne Domer, Yeovil Marsh etc 03-09; rtd 09; PtO *B & W* from 10. *Chestnuts, Chestnut Lane, Bleadon, Weston-super-Mare BS24 0QD* T: (01934) 811849 M: 07899-660422
E: stevenhartree194@btinternet.com

HARTRIDGE, James Bernard Robertson. b 44. Open Univ BSc 01. S Dios Minl Tr Scheme 89. **d** 92 **p** 93. C Portsea St Cuth *Portsm* 92-95; In RC Ch 96-09; PtO *Portsm* from 10; *Win* from 13. *15 Hundred Acres, Wickham, Fareham PO17 6JB* T: (01329) 833206 E: revjhartridge@rocketmail.com

HARTROPP, Andrew James. b 59. Southn Univ BSc 80 PhD 85 K Coll Lon PhD 03. Oak Hill Th Coll BA 95. **d** 98 **p** 99. C Watford *St Alb* 98-01; C Watford Ch Ch 01-08; Teacher Henrietta Barnett Sch 01-06; NSM White Waltham w Shottesbrooke and Waltham St Lawrence *Ox* 08-12; Research Tutor Ox Cen for Miss Studies from 12. *Oxford Centre for Mission Studies, St Philip and St James Church, Woodstock Road, Oxford OX2 6HR* T: (01865) 556071
E: a.hartropp@btinternet.com

HARTSHORNE, Mrs Kim. b 68. Ox Min Course 12. **d** 15. C Tetbury, Beverston, Long Newnton etc *Glouc* from 15. *Sycamore House, Upper Up, South Cerney, Cirencester GL7 5US* T: (01285) 862051 E: kimjhartshorne@yahoo.co.uk

HARTWELL, Mrs Jeanette May. b 65. Aston Univ BSc 88. Qu Coll Birm BA 07. **d** 07 **p** 08. C Brereton and Rugeley *Lich* 07-10; TV Smestow Vale from 10. *The Vicarage, School Road, Trysull, Wolverhampton WV5 7HR* T: (01902) 896650

HARVEY, Alan Douglas. b 25. FRSH 82. Melbourne Coll of Div 78. **d** 79 **p** 81. Australia 79-86; PtO *Ely* 86-87; V Wiggenhall St Germans and Islington 88-95; V Wiggenhall St Mary Magd 88-95; rtd 95; PtO *Cant* 95-14. *17 Bay View Road, Broadstairs CT10 2EA* T: (01843) 862794

HARVEY, Anne. See HARVEY, Ruth Anne

HARVEY, Canon Anthony Ernest. b 30. Worc Coll Ox BA 53 MA 56 DD 83. Westcott Ho Cam 56. **d** 58 **p** 59. C Chelsea Ch Ch *Lon* 58-62; Ch Ch Ox 62-69; Warden St Aug Coll Cant 69-75; Lect Th Ox Univ 76-82; Chapl Qu Coll Ox 77-82; Can and Lib Westmr Abbey 82-99; Sub-Dean and Adn Westmr 87-99; rtd 99; PtO *Glouc* from 00. *Mendelssohn Cottage, Broadway Road, Willersey, Broadway WR12 7BH* T: (01386) 859260

HARVEY, Anthony Peter. b 42. Birm Univ BSc 63 MSc 64. Wycliffe Hall Ox 79. **d** 81 **p** 82. C Stoke Damerel *Ex* 81-84; Canada 84-90; Chapl HM YOI Deerbolt 91-92; Chapl HM Pris Wakef 92-95; Chapl HM Pris Kirkham 95-01; rtd 07. *570-20th Avenue #5, Deux Montagnes QC J7R 7E9, Canada* T: (001) (450) 974 4358

HARVEY, Brian. b 51. Hatf Poly BA 74. St As Minl Tr Course 02. **d** 05 **p** 06. NSM Cilcain and Nannerch and Rhydymwyn *St As* 05-09; P-in-c 06-09; R Flint from 09; P-in-c Bagillt from 13. *The Rectory, Allt Goch, Flint CH6 5NF* T: (01352) 733274
E: brianharvey@mac.com

HARVEY, Carol Richmond. b 47. NUU BA 89. CITC 03. **d** 06 **p** 07. NSM Carnmoney *Conn* from 06. *26 Larne Road, Carrickfergus BT38 7DX* T: (028) 9335 1654
E: carolrharvey@hotmail.com

HARVEY, Christopher John Alfred. b 41. S'wark Ord Course 66. **d** 69 **p** 70. C Grays Thurrock *Chelmsf* 69-73; C Gt Baddow 73-75; V Berechurch St Marg w St Mich 75-94; R Tendring and Lt Bentley w Beaumont cum Moze 94-00; P-in-c Alresford *Chelmsf* 00-08; rtd 08; PtO *Chelmsf* from 08. *Bethel, 9 Laburnum Crescent, Kirby Cross, Frinton-on-Sea CO13 0QQ* T: (01255) 678649 E: chris.anne@tiscali.co.uk

HARVEY, The Ven Cyril John. b 30. Univ of Wales (Lamp) BA 51. Coll of Resurr Mirfield 51. **d** 53 **p** 54. C Caerau w Ely *Llan* 53-57; C Milford Haven *St D* 57-61; V Castlemartin and

Warren 61-65; R Begelly w Ludchurch and Crunwere 65-73; V Haverfordwest St Martin w Lambston 73-88; Can St D Cathl from 85; R Tenby 88-96; Adn St D 91-96; rtd 96. *5 Paxton Court, White Lion Street, Tenby SA70 7ET*
E: johnofwales@hotmail.co.uk

HARVEY, Canon Debra Eileen. b 54. SWMTC. **d** 94 **p** 95. NSM Camborne *Truro* 94-11; Chapl w Deaf People from 94; Hon Can Truro Cathl from 03. *Ankorva Salow, Tehidy Road, Camborne TR14 0NA* T: (01209) 716282 M: 07774-975268 F and minicom as telephone E: debbieharvey127@me.com

HARVEY, Desmond Victor Ross. b 37. QUB BA 59. Princeton Th Sem ThM 63 Fuller Th Sem California DMin 93 St Mich Coll Llan 95. **d** 95 **p** 96. Presbyterian Min 65-95; C Cwmbran *Mon* 95-97; TV 97; PtO from 97; OCM from 98. *Mallory, Llanmaes, Llantwit Major CF61 2XR* T/F: (01446) 792753

HARVEY, Ian Malcolm. b 51. **d** 03 **p** 04. NSM Burnie Australia 03-07; NSM Filwood Park *Bris* 07-09; C S Barrow *Carl* 09-11; Australia from 11. *34 Old Surrey Road, Burnie TAS 7320, Australia* T: (0061) (3) 6431 6317
E: imharvey@bigpond.net.au

HARVEY, James. See HARVEY, Thomas James

HARVEY, John. b 30. S'wark Ord Course. **d** 65 **p** 66. C Lewisham St Jo Southend *S'wark* 65-73; V Bellingham St Dunstan 73-78; TV Bourne Valley *Sarum* 78-81; TR 81-87; R Kilkhampton w Morwenstow *Truro* 87-90; rtd 90; PtO *Roch* 90-99. *4 Ramsay Hall, 9-13 Byron Road, Worthing BN11 3HN*

HARVEY, John Christopher. b 65. Univ of Wales (Lamp) BA 86 Nottm Univ BTh 89. Linc Th Coll 86. **d** 89 **p** 90. C Dwygyfylchi *Ban* 89-93; V Llangrannog w Llandysiliogogo w Penbryn *St D* 93-02; RD Glyn Aeron 99-02; P-in-c Llangystennin *St As* 02-04; R 04-09; V Meliden and Gwaenysgor from 09; Dioc Voc Adv from 08. *The Vicarage, Ffordd Penrhwylfa, Prestatyn LL19 8HN* T: (01745) 856220

HARVEY, Canon John Mark. b 64. QUB BEd 87 TCD BTh 93. CITC 90. **d** 93 **p** 94. C Portadown St Columba *Arm* 93-96; I Monaghan w Tydavnet and Kilmore *Clogh* 96-01; Dioc Communications Officer 97-00; Miss Officer (Ireland) CMS 01-05; I Ballybeen *D & D* from 05; Preb Down Cathl from 15. *1 Grahamsbridge Road, Dundonald, Belfast BT16 2DB* T: (028) 9048 0834 M: 07966-332310
E: rector@stmarysballybeen.com *or* harveys@homecall.co.uk

HARVEY, Lt Col John William Arthur. b 43. Guildf Dioc Min Course 98. **d** 01 **p** 02. OLM Aldershot St Aug *Guildf* 01-13; PtO from 13. *59 Knoll Road, Fleet GU51 4PT* T: (01252) 622793
E: father.john@talktalk.net

HARVEY, Jonathan Bromley. b 72. BSc BA PGCE. St Mellitus Coll. **d** 14 **p** 15. C Eastleigh *Win* from 14. *St Francis House, Nightingale Avenue, Eastleigh SO50 9JH* M: 07515-287108 T: (023) 8019 1254 E: jonoharvey@hotmail.com *or* jono@sttoms.com

HARVEY, Lance Sydney Crockford. b 25. Ridley Hall Cam 67. **d** 69 **p** 70. C Mortlake w E Sheen *S'wark* 69-74; P-in-c Woolwich St Thos 75-86; V Lee Gd Shep w St Pet 86-92; RD E Lewisham 87-91; rtd 92; PtO *Truro* 92-06. *17 Lariggan Road, Penzance TR18 4NJ*

HARVEY, Lincoln. b 69. Univ of Wales (Swansea) BA 92 K Coll Lon MA 01 PhD 08. **d** 09 **p** 10. NSM St John-at-Hackney *Lon* 09-12; NSM Fulham St Andr from 12; Tutor SEITE 06-10; Tutor St Mellitus Coll *Lon* from 10. *St Mellitus College, St Paul's Church, Onslow Square, London SW7 3NX* M: 07855-866823
E: lincoln.harvey@stmellitus.org

HARVEY, Margaret Claire. b 41. Univ of Wales (Abth) BA 62 DipEd 63 Lon Univ BD 68. Dalton Ho *Bris* 66. **dss** 68 **d** 80 **p** 97. Flint *St As* 68-74; Lect Trin Coll Bris 74-80; Connah's Quay *St As* 79-80; C 80-86; Bp's Adv for Continuing Clerical Educn 86-98; Hon C Corwen and Llangar 86-87; Dn-in-c Bryneglwys 87-97; P-in-c 97-02; rtd 02; PtO *St As* from 09. *Coleg y Groes, The College, London Road, Corwen LL21 0DR* T: (01490) 412169 E: colegygroes@talk21.com

HARVEY, Mark. See HARVEY, John Mark

HARVEY, Murray Alexander. b 63. Univ of Qld BA 85 Deakin Univ Australia DHSc 03 MAPsS 87. St Fran Coll Brisbane BTh 91. **d** 91 **p** 92. C Milton Australia 92-93; C Stafford 94-95; P-in-c Tamborine Mt St Geo 95-02; V Glen Gp *Linc* 02-11; R Clayfield Australia from 11. *The Rectory, 56 Bellevue Terrace, Clayfield QLD 4011, Australia* T: (0061) (7) 3862 1411
E: revmharvey@stmarksclayfield.org

HARVEY, Canon Norman Roy. b 43. Nottm Univ DipAE 86. Wycliffe Hall Ox 66. **d** 69 **p** 70. C Clay Cross *Derby* 69-72; C Dronfield 72-76; TV 76-79; P-in-c Rowsley 79-89; Dioc Youth Officer 79-83; Dioc Adv in Adult and Youth Educn 83-89; TR Eckington w Handley and Ridgeway 89-01; R Eckington and Ridgeway 01-08; RD Bolsover and Staveley 00-05; Hon Can Derby Cathl 00-08; rtd 08; PtO *Derby* 08-13; *Sheff* 09-11. *62 Parklands View, Aston, Sheffield S26 2GW* T: 0114-287 2243 E: norman.harvey2@btopenworld.com

HARVEY, Oliver Paul. b 33. Magd Coll Ox BA 55 MA 59. Cuddesdon Coll 57. **d** 59 **p** 60. C S Norwood St Mark *Cant* 59-61; C Hythe 61-64; Zambia 64-71; Chapl Cant Coll of Tech 71-77; Hon C Cant St Martin and St Paul 73-77; Chapl K Sch Roch 77-88; C Roch 88-90; V Gillingham St Mary 90-00; RD Gillingham 98-00; rtd 00; PtO *Roch* 00-03; *B & W* from 05. *11 Henley Road, Taunton TA1 5BN* T: (01823) 272825

HARVEY, Miss Pamela Betty. b 33. Dalton Ho Bris IDC 59. **dss** 68 **d** 87 **p** 95. Hon C Glenfield *Leic* 95-04; PtO from 04. *72 Chestnut Road, Glenfield, Leicester LE3 8DB* T: 0116-232 2959 E: pam.harvey@ukgateway.net

HARVEY, Mrs Patricia Ann. b 45. Qu Coll Birm. **dss** 82 **d** 87 **p** 94. Gospel Lane St Mich *Birm* 82-85; Exhall *Cov* 85-87; C 87-89; Team Dn Droitwich Spa *Worc* 89-94; TV 94-97; P-in-c Finstall 97-00; V 00-02; rtd 02; PtO *Heref* from 02; *Worc* from 04. *27 Ropewalk Avenue, Leominster HR6 8LY* E: patricia.harvey3@virgin.net

HARVEY, Canon Patrick Arnold. b 58. TCD BA MA. CITC 82. **d** 85 **p** 86. C Bandon Union *C, C & R* 85-88; Dean's V Limerick St Mich *L & K* 88-91; Dioc Info Officer 88-91; I Abbeyleix w Ballyroan etc *C & O* from 91; Can Ossory Cathl from 97; Can St Patr Cathl Dublin from 13; Can Ferns Cathl from 14. *The Rectory, Abbeyleix, Portlaoise, Co Laois, Republic of Ireland* T/F: (00353) (57) 873 1243 E: patrickharveyone@gmail.com

HARVEY, Paul. See HARVEY, Oliver Paul

HARVEY, Robert Martin. b 30. S'wark Ord Course 69. **d** 70 **p** 71. C Sutton New Town St Barn *S'wark* 70-75; C Leatherhead *Guildf* 76-78; V Wadworth w Loversall *Sheff* 78-96; RD W Doncaster 94-97; rtd 96; PtO *Sheff* 96-13. *58 Thomson Avenue, Doncaster DN4 0NU* T: (01302) 857599

HARVEY, Robin Grant. b 43. Clare Coll Cam BA 64 MA 68 Univ of NSW PhD 74. Linc Th Coll 85. **d** 87 **p** 88. C Keynsham *B & W* 87-91; R E w W Harptree and Hinton Blewett 91-97; Chapl Surrey Univ *Guildf* 98-02; P-in-c Cuddington 02-07; V 07-08; rtd 08; PtO *B & W* from 09. *21 St Cadoc House, Temple Street, Keynsham, Bristol BS31 1HD* T: 0117-986 2295
E: rgharvey.194@btinternet.com

HARVEY, Canon Roland. b 68. St Jo Coll Nottm 99. **d** 01 **p** 02. C Skelmersdale St Paul *Liv* 01-05; P-in-c Pemberton St Fran Kitt Green 05-12; P-in-c Garston 12-14; V from 14; AD Liv S from 14; Hon Can Liv Cathl from 14. *St Michael's Vicarage, 49 Harbour Drive, Liverpool L19 8AB* M: 07817-901455 T: 0151-345 7475 E: rolandharvey68@gmail.com

HARVEY, Ruth Anne. b 59. Leic Univ MB, ChB 83 Open Univ BA 02. St Mellitus Coll BA 12. **d** 13 **p** 14. NSM Broomfield *Chelmsf* from 13. *Ladyhope House, Mill Lane, Broomfield, Chelmsford CM1 7BQ* E: rev.anneharvey@gmail.com

HARVEY, Simon John. b 63. Trin Coll Bris BA 00. **d** 00 **p** 01. C Walsall St Paul *Lich* 00-03; TV Oadby *Leic* 03-10; Warden of Readers 05-10; V Islington St Mary *Lon* from 10. *St Mary's Church, Upper Street, London N1 2TX* T: (020) 7226 3400
E: simonharvey@stmaryislington.org

HARVEY, Canon Steven Charles. b 58. Reading Univ BA 79 Cam Univ PGCE 80 Ox Univ BA 83 MA 88. Ripon Coll Cuddesdon 81. **d** 84 **p** 85. C Oldham *Man* 84-87; Chapl and Hd RS St Pet Sch York 87-96; Sen Dep Hd Kingswood Sch Bath 96-03; Educn Officer and Sen Provost Woodard Corp 03-06; PtO *B & W* 96-03; *Lich* 03-06; Hd Master Bury Gr Sch 06-13; PtO *Blackb* 06-13; *Man* 06-13; Can Res Newc Cathl from 13. *2A Holly Avenue, Jesmond, Newcastle upon Tyne NE2 2PY* T: 0191-281 5790
E: steven.harvey@stnicholascathedral.co.uk

HARVEY, Mrs Susan Esther. b 44. **d** 11 **p** 12. OLM Sherston Magna, Easton Grey, Luckington etc *Bris* from 11; OLM Hullavington, Norton and Stanton St Quintin from 15. *55 The Tarters, Sherston, Malmesbury SN16 0NT* T: (01666) 840696

HARVEY, Thomas James. b 71. Nottm Univ BA 92 Leic Univ MA 96 DipSW 96. Cranmer Hall Dur 09. **d** 11 **p** 12. C Cramlington *Newc* 11-14; P-in-c Felton from 14; P-in-c Longframlington w Brinkburn from 14. *The Vicarage, 1 Benlaw Grove, Felton, Morpeth NE65 9NG* T: (01670) 787263
M: 07722-405253 E: james.harvey@live.com

HARVEY, Mrs Verity Margaret. b 48. Bris Univ BA 69 Saltley Tr Coll Birm DipEd 70. SAOMC 99. **d** 02 **p** 03. NSM Radlett *St Alb* 02-05; NSM Bushey 05-11; Chapl Herts Partnership NHS Foundn Trust from 10. *28 Field Road, Watford WD19 4DR* T: (01923) 492863

HARVEY, Wendy Marion. b 46. SEITE 06. **d** 09 **p** 10. NSM Hurst Green *S'wark* 09-14; NSM Limpsfield and Tatsfield from 14; Chapl HM Pris Downview from 11; PtO *Lon* from 14. *HM Prison Downview, Sutton Lane, Sutton SM2 5PD* T: (020) 8196 6300 M: 07973-428683 E: wendy.harvey@hmps.gsi.gov.uk *or* wendyharvey@talktalk.net

HARVEY-NEILL, Nicola Lisa Jane. b 69. QUB BD 91 TCD MPhil 95. CITC BTh 94. **d** 95 **p** 96. Dioc C *T, K & A* 95-96; C Galway w Kilcummin 96-97; Dioc Youth Adv (Limerick) *L & K* 97-01; Chapl Villier's Sch Limerick 98-01; Chapl Limerick Univ 98-01; PtO 01-15. *The Rectory, Maynooth Road, Celbridge, Co Kildare, Republic of Ireland* M: (00353) 87-250 0570 E: nickihn@eircom.net *or* smneill@iol.ie

HARVIE, Robert. b 53. **d** 04 **p** 05. OLM Godalming *Guildf* from 04. *4 Bargate Court, Godalming GU7 2NA* T: (01483) 414378 E: robert.harvie@btinternet.com

HARWOOD, Ann Jane. *See* CLARKE, Ann Jane

HARWOOD, Anna Charlotte. b 75. Ripon Coll Cuddesdon. **d** 11 **p** 12. C Ruscombe and Twyford w Hurst *Ox* 11-14; C Wokingham All SS from 14. *69 Bishop's Drive, Wokingham RG40 1WA*

HARWOOD, Christopher Mark. b 82. **d** 14 **p** 15. C Poole *Sarum* from 14. *14 Emerson Road, Poole BH15 1QT* M: 07813-782801 E: harwood.chris@hotmail.co.uk

HARWOOD (formerly SOUTH), Mrs Gillian. b 51. NEOC 87. **d** 90 **p** 94. C Rothbury *Newc* 90-93; C Morpeth 93-97; V Amble 97-06; Chapl Northumbria Healthcare NHS Foundn Trust 06-15; rtd 15. *7 Hedgerow Mews, Fallowfield, Ashington NE63 8LH* T: (01670) 810478 E: gillian.harwood@sky.com

HARWOOD, Canon John Rossiter. b 26. Selw Coll Cam BA 51 MA 55. Wycliffe Hall Ox 51. **d** 53 **p** 54. C Handsworth St Mary *Birm* 53-55; Tutor Trin Coll Umuahia Nigeria 57-64; Warden Minl Tr Cen Freetown Sierra Leone and Bp's Dom Chapl 64-67; Home Educn Sec CMS 67-75; V Cheltenham Ch Ch *Glouc* 75-91; RD Cheltenham 84-89; Hon Can Glouc Cathl 85-91; rtd 91; PtO *Ex* 91-99; *Chich* from 00; *Portsm* from 00. *8 Kingsey Avenue, Emsworth PO10 7HP* T: (01243) 372215

HARWOOD, Mary Ann. b 46. Cam Inst of Educn CertEd 68. Ox Min Course 04. **d** 07 **p** 08. NSM Burghfield *Ox* 07-10; NSM W Downland from 10. *The Rectory, Main Street, Chaddleworth, Newbury RG20 7EW* T: (01488) 638566 M: 07721-437316 E: maryharwood695@btinternet.com

HARWOOD, Peter James. b 64. Birm Univ MB 88 ChB 88 K Coll Lon MA 02. Wycliffe Hall Ox BA 93 MA 98. **d** 94 **p** 95. C Cov H Trin 94-97; C Kensington St Barn *Lon* 97-02; V Woking Ch Ch *Guildf* from 02; Chapl Woking Hospice from 02. *Christ Church Vicarage, 10 Russetts Close, Woking GU21 4BH* T: (01483) 762100 E: peter.harwood@christchurchwoking.org

HASELHURST (née STERLING), Mrs Anne. b 51. Macalester Coll (USA) BA 73. EAMTC 89. **d** 92 **p** 94. Par Dn Bury St Edmunds St Jo *St E* 92-94; C 94-95; V Fordham St Pet *Ely* 95-06; P-in-c Kennett 95-06; P-in-c Isleham 05-06; R Cupar *St And* from 06; R Ladybank from 06. *13 Robertson Road, Cupar KY15 5YR* T: (01334) 652982 E: annehaselhurst@talktalk.net

HASELOCK, Canon Jeremy Matthew. b 51. York Univ BA 73 BPhil 74. St Steph Ho Ox BA 82 MA 86. **d** 83 **p** 84. C Pimlico St Gabr *Lon* 83-86; C Paddington St Jas 86-88; Bp's Dom Chapl *Chich* 88-91; P-in-c Boxgrove 91-94; V 94-98; Dioc Adv on Liturgy 91-98; Can and Preb Chich Cathl 94-98; Can Res and Prec Nor Cathl from 98; Chapl to The Queen from 13. *34 The Close, Norwich NR1 4DZ* T: (01603) 619169 F: 766032 E: precentor@cathedral.org.uk

HASKETT, Mrs Fiona Ann. b 55. SEITE 01. **d** 04 **p** 05. NSM Leigh *Roch* 04-09; V Whittington w Weeford and Hints *Lich* 09-15; V Headcorn and The Suttons *Cant* from 15. *The Vicarage, 64 Oak Lane, Headcorn, Ashford TN27 9TB* E: fiona.haskett@btopenworld.com

HASKETT, Stephen Ian. b 78. Cranmer Hall Dur. **d** 13 **p** 14. C Anchorsholme *Blackb* from 13. *2 Norman Close, Thornton-Cleveleys FY5 3UA* M: 07890-248917 E: stephen_haskett@sky.com

HASKINS, Thomas. b 41. TCD BA 72. CITC 71. **d** 73 **p** 74. C Larne and Inver *Conn* 73-78; C Antrim All SS 78-83; I Belfast St Mark 83-90; I Dublin Clontarf *D & G* 90-02; I Dublin St Ann and St Steph 02-08; Can Ch Ch Cathl Dublin 99-08; rtd 08. *7 Gorse Haven, Coolboy, Tinahely, Co Wicklow, Republic of Ireland* T: (00353) (402) 34997 E: tomhaskins2@gmail.com

HASLAM, Andrew James. b 57. Univ Coll Dur BSc 78 Coll of Ripon & York St Jo PGCE 79 Lambeth STh 84. Trin Coll Bris 80. **d** 83 **p** 84. C Leyland St Andr *Blackb* 83-86; C Hartford *Ches* 86-88; V Grimsargh *Blackb* 88-98; V St Helens St Mark *Liv* 98-05; V Birkenhead Ch Ch *Ches* 05-13. *Address temp unknown*

HASLAM, James Robert. b 31. Open Univ BA 74. Bps' Coll Cheshunt 55. **d** 57 **p** 58. C Penwortham St Mary *Blackb* 57-63; V Cockerham 63-74; V Cockerham w Winmarleigh 74-76; V Gt Harwood St Bart 76-88; V Fairhaven 88-95; rtd 95; PtO *Blackb* from 95. *5 Willow Trees Drive, Blackburn BB1 8LB* T: (01254) 697092

HASLAM, Mrs Jane. b 70. Leeds Poly BA 92. Trin Coll Bris BA 97. **d** 97 **p** 98. C Minehead *B & W* 97-00; PtO *Newc* 00-03; C Balkwell 03-04; P-in-c Purton *Bris* 04-10; R Alfred Jewel *B & W* from 10. *The New Rectory, Cliff Road, North Petherton, Bridgwater TA6 6NY* T: (01278) 662429 E: revjane.haslam@hotmail.co.uk

HASLAM, John Gordon. b 32. Birm Univ LLB 53. Qu Coll Birm 75. **d** 77 **p** 77. Hon C Bartley Green *Birm* 77-79; Hon C Moseley St Mary 79-96; Chapl to The Queen 89-02; PtO *Heref* from 97. *16 Mill Street, Ludlow SY8 1BE* T/F: (01584) 876663

HASLAM, Michael Henry. b 72. Buckingham Univ BA 93. Trin Coll Bris BA 94 MA 94. **d** 97 **p** 98. C Minehead *B & W* 97-00; Chapl Newc Univ 00-04; C Purton and Dioc Ecum Officer *Bris* 04-06; P-in-c N Swindon St Andr 06-09; NSM Alfred Jewel *B & W* from 10. *The New Rectory, Cliff Road, North Petherton, Bridgwater TA6 6NY* T: (01278) 662429 M: 07530-677493 E: mike.haslam@hotmail.co.uk *or* mhaslam@thetauntonacademy.com

HASLAM, Robert John Alexander. b 34. CCC Cam BA 58. Coll of Resurr Mirfield 58. **d** 60 **p** 61. C Rawmarsh w Parkgate *Sheff* 60-66; PtO *Edin* 66-73; *Carl* 73-77; P-in-c Peebles *Edin* 77-81; V Darnall *Sheff* 81-85; Hon C Bermondsey St Hugh CD *S'wark* 86-88; R Clydebank *Glas* 88-98; Chapl Málaga *Eur* 98-03. *Flat 1/1, 134 Fergus Drive, Glasgow G20 6AT* T: 0141-945 4132

HASLER, Canon John Joseph. b 45. Univ of Wales (Cardiff) MPhil 99. Qu Coll Birm 89. **d** 90 **p** 91. C Horfield H Trin *Bris* 90-93; V Bris St Andr Hartcliffe 93-01; V Bris Lockleaze St Mary Magd w St Fran 01-15; AD City 03-06; Hon Can Bris Cathl 08-15; rtd 15. *Address withheld by request* E: joehasler@btinternet.com

HASLER, Kevin John. b 56. RGN 80 RMN 80. St Mich Coll Llan 03. **d** 06 **p** 07. NSM Raglan w Llandenny and Bryngwyn *Mon* 06-08; P-in-c Llangwm Uchaf and Llangwm Isaf w Gwernesney etc 08-12; PtO 13-15; V Usk and Gwehelog w Llantrisant w Llanllowell from 15. *The Vicarage, 10 Cassia Drive, Usk NP15 1TZ* M: 07836-795753 E: kevin@hasler.org.uk *or* kevin@deanery.info

HASSALL, Mrs Elizabeth Claire. b 80. R Holloway Coll Lon BSc 01. Trin Coll Bris BA 08. **d** 09 **p** 10. C Bempton w Flamborough, Reighton w Speeton *York* 09-13; V Coxwold and Husthwaite from 13; R Crayke w Brandsby and Yearsley from 13; RD Easingwold from 14. *The Rectory, Church Hill, Crayke, York YO61 4TA* T: (01347) 822809 E: revliz@trundlebug.co.uk

HASSALL, William Edwin. b 41. St Jo Coll Nottm 75. **d** 77 **p** 78. C Wellington w Eyton *Lich* 77-80; C Farewell 80-82; V 82-93; C Gentleshaw 80-82; V 82-93; P-in-c Cheddleton 93-94; PtO 97-09; Asst Chapl Birm Heartlands and Solihull NHS Trust 98-01; Chapl Team Ldr 01-06; rtd 06; PtO *Birm* from 06; C Hatherton *Lich* from 09. *17 Bradwell Lane, Rugeley WS15 4RW* T: (01543) 670739

HASSAN, Brian Joseph. b 67. CITC 05. **d** 08 **p** 09. NSM Clooney w Strathfoyle *D & R* 08-09; NSM Faughanvale from 09. *59 Newton Road, Limavady BT49 0UD* T: (028) 7776 6281 M: 07828-668342 E: brian.hassan2@btinternet.com

HASSELL, Christopher John. b 90. St Jo Coll Nottm BA 13. **d** 13 **p** 14. C Aldridge *Lich* from 13. *5 Whetstone Lane, Aldridge, Walsall WS9 8PB* M: 07875-307927 E: chrishassell@outlook.com

HASSELL, David Edwin. b 38. WMMTC 87. **d** 90 **p** 91. NSM Worc SE 90-93; C Abberton, Naunton Beauchamp and Bishampton etc 93-94; P-in-c 94; R Abberton, The Flyfords, Naunton Beauchamp etc 94-04; rtd 04; PtO *Worc* from 04. *14 Napleton Lane, Kempsey, Worcester WR5 3PT* T: (01905) 828096 E: davidhassellrev@aol.com

HASTE, James Victor William. b 36. St Mich Th Coll Crafers 64. **d** 68 **p** 70. C Ormond Australia 68-69; C Roehampton H Trin *S'wark* 70-72; P-in-c Boroko Papua New Guinea 72-76; Sec ABM Vic Australia 76-81; I Armadale w Hawksburn 81-86; I Vermont 86-89; Inter-Ch Trade and Ind Chapl 89-99; rtd 01; LtO The Murray Australia 99-05; PtO Melbourne from 05. *17 Park View Drive, Aspendale Vic 3195, Australia* T: (0061) (3) 9588 2805 M: 407-044086 E: baha@picknowl.com.au

HASTED, Marcus Arthur David. b 35. Qu Coll Birm 63. **d** 66 **p** 67. C Woodchurch *Ches* 66-69; C W Kirby St Bridget 69-72; V Farndon 72-76; V Farndon and Coddington 76-79; PtO 98-00 and from 02; NSM Liscard St Mary w St Columba 00-02. *62 South Road, West Kirby, Wirral CH48 3HQ* T: 0151-625 0428

HASTEY, Erle. b 44. St Mich Coll Llan 66. **d** 68 **p** 69. C Pontefract St Giles *Wakef* 68-71; C Almondbury 71-74; V Purlwell 74-79; P-in-c Batley Carr 76-79; V Ynyshir *Llan* 79-86; V Tylorstown w Ynyshir 86-87; V Tonyrefail w Gilfach Goch 87-97; P-in-c Llandyfodwg 87-97; V Tonyrefail w Gilfach Goch and Llandyfodwg 97-99; V Pyle w Kenfig 99-04; rtd 04; PtO *Llan* from 04. *2 Cambray Close, Porthcawl CF36 3PY* T: (01656) 783935

HASTIE-SMITH, Timothy Maybury. b 62. Magd Coll Cam MA 84. Wycliffe Hall Ox 85. **d** 88 **p** 89. C Ox St Ebbe w H Trin and St Pet 88-91; Chapl Stowe Sch 91-98; Hd Master Dean

Close Sch Cheltenham 98-08; TV S Cotswolds *Glouc* from 08. *The Parsonage, High Street, Kempsford, Fairford GL7 4ET* T: (01285) 810773 E: tim.hastie-smith@hotmail.com

HASTINGS, David Kerr. b 40. St Luke's Coll Ex CertEd 63. Ox NSM Course 84. **d** 87 **p** 88. Hd Master St Edburg's Sch Bicester 82-89; Asst Chapl HM Pris Grendon and Spring Hill 87-89; NSM Bicester w Bucknell, Caversfield and Launton *Ox* 87-89; Chapl HM Pris Reading 90-92; P-in-c St Wishford *Sarum* 92; P-in-c S Newton 92; P-in-c Stapleford w Berwick St James 92; P-in-c Winterbourne Stoke 92; R Lower Wylye and Till Valley 92-95; Chapl HM Pris Ex 96-01; PtO from 01; rtd 01. *26 Hoopern Street, Exeter EX4 4LY* T: (01392) 498233

HASTINGS, The Ven Gary Lea. b 56. NUU BA 82 MA 87 TCD BTh 93. CITC 90. **d** 93 **p** 94. C Galway w Kilcummin *T, K & A* 93-95; I Aughaval w Achill, Knappagh, Dugort etc 95-09; I Galway w Kilcummin from 09; Dom Chapl to Bp Tuam 94-12; Can Tuam Cathl from 00; Adn Tuam from 06; Can St Patr Cathl Dublin from 10; Can Killala Cathl from 13. *The Rectory, Taylor's Hill, Galway, Republic of Ireland* T: (00353) (91) 521914 E: gryh@me.com

HASTROP, Paul. b 39. Wells Th Coll 70. **d** 72 **p** 73. C Parkstone St Osmund *Sarum* 72-75; C Parkstone St Pet w Branksea and St Osmund 75-76; C Penzance St Mary w St Paul *Truro* 76-79; V St Blazey 79-87; V Bournemouth St Pet w St Swithun, H Trin etc *Win* 87-94; TV Thornaby on Tees *York* 94-96; P-in-c Portsea St Sav *Portsm* 96-03; rtd 03; Hon C Paignton St Jo *Ex* 05-06; PtO *Win* from 05; *Portsm* 08-13. *22 Ladysmith Close, Christchurch BH23 3DR* T: (01202) 476278 E: fr.paulhastrop@yahoo.co.uk

HASTWELL, James Sydney. b 37. Roch Th Coll 67. **d** 69 **p** 70. C Croydon St Aug *Cant* 69-73; C Hurstpierpoint *Chich* 73-75; P-in-c Twineham 76; P-in-c Sayers Common 76; P-in-c Albourne 76; R Albourne w Sayers Common and Twineham 76-88; V Forest Row 88-94; rtd 97; PtO *Chich* 97-09; *Nor* from 11. *36 Broad Reaches, Ludham, Great Yarmouth NR29 5PD* T: (01692) 678574 E: jen-jim@hotmail.co.uk

HASWELL, Jeremy William Drake. b 60. Ridley Hall Cam. **d** 08 **p** 09. C St Alb St Paul *St Alb* 08-13; PtO from 13. *46 Brampton Road, St Albans AL1 4PT* T: (01727) 847236 M: 07717-762539 E: revjhas@gmail.com

HATCH, Canon George Andrew. b 29. Leeds Univ BA. Coll of Resurr Mirfield 51. **d** 53 **p** 54. C S Farnborough *Guildf* 53-55; Windward Is 55-63; R St Mary Barbados 63-73; Assoc Dir Chr Action Development 73-83; R St Jas 83-94; rtd 94. *St James, Barbados* T: (001809) 432 0700

HATCHER, Mark. b 54. **d** 12 **p** 13. NSM Brockley Hill St Sav *S'wark* from 12. *Gloucester Circus, London SE10 8RY* T: (020) 8923 4969

HATCHETT, Michael John. b 49. Enfield Coll BSc 72 K Coll Lon BD 77 AKC 77. Linc Th Coll 77. **d** 78 **p** 79. C Halstead St Andr w H Trin and Greenstead Green *Chelmsf* 78-81; C Greenstead 81-85; V Gt Totham 85-01; R Gt Totham and Lt Totham w Goldhanger 01-06; RD Witham 96-01; Chapl MU 04-06; Dioc Melton and Ufford *St E* 06-15; rtd 15; PtO *St E* from 15. *The Vicarage, 6 Rectory Road, Hollesley, Woodbridge IP12 3JS* T: (01394) 412052 E: mikehatchett2004@yahoo.co.uk

HATCHETT, Mrs Ruth Merrick. b 54. K Coll Lon BD 77 AKC 77 Open Univ BA 92. EAMTC 03. **d** 05 **p** 06. NSM Tolleshunt Knights w Tiptree and Gt Braxted *Chelmsf* 05-06; NSM Melton and Ufford *St E* 06-10; TV Wilford Peninsula from 10. *The Vicarage, 6 Rectory Road, Hollesley, Woodbridge IP12 3JS* T: (01394) 412052 E: ruth.hatchett@yahoo.com

HATCHMAN, Ms Elizabeth Mary. b 63. St Andr Univ MA 85. Selly Oak Coll Qu Coll Birm BD 92. **d** 93 **p** 94. C Aston SS Pet and Paul *Birm* 93-96; C Rowley Regis 96-00; Chapl St Geo Post 16 Cen 00-04; PtO 05-06. *21 Westfield Road, Birmingham B14 7SX* T: 0121-441 2711

HATFIELD, Rebecca Alison. *See* LUMLEY, Rebecca Alison

HATHAWAY, Canon David Alfred Gerald. b 48. St Mich Coll Llan. **d** 72 **p** 73. C Newport St Julian *Mon* 72-74; P-in-c Oakham w Hambleton and Egleton *Pet* 74-77; V Newport St Matt *Mon* 77-83; CF (TA) from 78; V Abertillery *Mon* 83-88; V Rumney 88-14; Hon Can St Woolos Cathl 91-05; Can St Woolos Cathl 05-14; rtd 14. *184 Moorland Road, Cardiff CF24 2LR*

HATHAWAY, John Albert. b 24. Sarum Th Coll 59. **d** 60 **p** 61. C Fleet *Guildf* 60-64; C Cowley St Jas *Ox* 64-66; V Holmwood *Guildf* 66-71; V Westborough 71-74; V Newmarket All SS *St E* 74-82; V Acton w Gt Waldingfield 82-85; R W Downland *Sarum* 85-90; rtd 90; PtO *Sarum* 94-10. *15 Stuart Court, High Street, Kibworth, Leicester LE8 0LR* T: 0116-279 2447

HATHAWAY, Martin Charles. b 48. St Jo Coll Nottm 93. **d** 95 **p** 96. C Weddington and Caldecote *Cov* 95-99; V Potters Green 99-04; C The Heyfords w Rousham and Somerton *Ox* 04-05; C Fritwell w Souldern and Ardley w Fewcott

04-05; TV Dunstable *St Alb* 05-13; rtd 13. *61 Symington Way, Market Harborough LE16 7XA* E: revd.martinhathaway@tiscali.co.uk

HATHAWAY, Vivienne Ann. b 57. Bucks Chilterns Univ Coll BSc 96. Westcott Ho Cam 00. **d** 02 **p** 03. C Bp's Hatfield *St Alb* 02-05; C Bp's Hatfield, Lemsford and N Mymms 05-07; P-in-c Stevenage St Mary Shephall w Aston 07-14; V from 14. *St Mary's Vicarage, 148 Hydean Way, Shephall, Stevenage SG2 9YA* T: (01438) 351963 E: vivienne@vhathaway.freeserve.co.uk

HATHERLEY, Peter Graham. b 46. Univ of Wales (Cardiff) BSc 67 PhD 70. St Mich Coll Llan 70. **d** 72 **p** 73. C Ystrad Mynach *Llan* 72-75; Hon C Tonyrefail 75-84; Hon C Tonyrefail w Gilfach Goch 85-88; PtO from 88. *Ty Tegeirianau, The Derwen, Bridgend CF35 6HD* T: (01656) 662196

HATHORNE (née MARSH), Mrs Carol Ann. b 44. W Midl Coll of Educn BA 83. WMMTC 88. **d** 91 **p** 94. Par Dn Wednesbury St Paul Wood Green *Lich* 91-93; NSM Pensnett *Worc* 93-97; TV Cannock *Lich* 97-01; NSM Willenhall H Trin 05-11; NSM Bentley Em and Willenhall H Trin 11-12; PtO from 12. *St Chad's Vicarage, 8 Cumberland Road, Bilston WV14 6LT* E: hathorne@btinternet.com

HATHORNE, Mark Stephen. b 51. Boston Univ MDiv 76. **d** 00 **p** 00. C Willenhall H Trin *Lich* 00-01; TV 01-06; TR 06-11; P-in-c Bentley 06-09; TR Bentley Em and Willenhall H Trin 11-13; TV Bilston from 13. *St Chad's Vicarage, 8 Cumberland Road, Bilston WV14 6LT* E: m.s.hathorne@virgin.net

HATHWAY, Ross Arthur. b 56. Moore Th Coll Sydney BTh 86. **d** 86 **p** 87. C Tamworth St Pet Australia 87-88; C Corby St Columba *Pet* 89-92; R Trull w Angersleigh *B & W* 92-02; R Kellyville St Steph Australia from 03. *45 President Road, Kellyville NSW 2155, Australia* T: (0061) (2) 9629 6255 E: kellyvilleanglican@bigpond.com

HATREY, David Nigel. b 57. SS Mark & Jo Univ Coll Plymouth CertEd 79 BEd 90 Ex Univ MA 01. SWMTC 90. **d** 93 **p** 94. NSM S Hill w Callington *Truro* 93-01; Hon C Street w Walton *B & W* from 01. *Pilgrims Way, Chilton Polden Hill, Edington, Bridgwater TA7 9AL* T: (01278) 723616 E: hatreys@micehouse.fsnet.co.uk

HATTAN, Jeffrey William Rowland. b 49. Cranmer Hall Dur 83. **d** 85 **p** 86. C Eston w Normanby *York* 85-89; TV 89-95; V Hunmanby w Muston 95-15; rtd 15. *Address temp unknown* E: revjeff.hattan@yahoo.co.uk

HATTAWAY, Judith Helen Alison. b 53. Kent Univ BA 79 PGCE 80 Liv Univ MA 02 MBACP 00. STETS 07. **d** 10 **p** 11. NSM Hurst *Ox* 10-11; Asst Chapl Broadmoor Hosp Crowthorne 10-11; NSM Frimley *Guildf* 11-14; Asst Chapl Frimley Park Hosp NHS Foundn Trust 11-12; Lead Chapl 12-14; NSM Wokingham St Paul *Ox* from 15. *15 Rayner Drive, Arborfield, Reading RG2 9FB* T: 0118-976 1197 M: 07798-723232 E: judihattaway@mac.com

HATTON, Jane Elizabeth. b 53. SAOMC 95. **d** 98 **p** 99. NSM Stevenage St Pet Broadwater *St Alb* 98-04; Asst Chapl E and N Herts NHS Trust from 04. *2 Dancote, Park Lane, Knebworth SG3 6PB* T: (01438) 811039 E: janehatton@dial.pipex.com

HATTON, Jeffrey Charles. b 49. K Coll Lon BD 70 Bris Univ MA 72. Westcott Ho Cam 72 Episc Th Sch Cam Mass 73. **d** 74 **p** 75. C Nor St Pet Mancroft 74-78; C Earlham St Anne 78-79; Relig Broadcasting Asst IBA 79-82; Hon C Kensington St Barn *Lon* 79-84; Hon C Fulham All SS 85-89; R Win All SS w Chilcomb and Chesil 89-94; Dioc Communications Officer 89-94; P-in-c Salisbury St Thos and St Edm *Sarum* 94-99; R 99-05; rtd 05; Hon C Chalke Valley *Sarum* 06-11; Hon C E Coker w Sutton Bingham and Closworth *B & W* 11-13; Hon C W Coker w Hardington Mandeville, E Chinnock etc 11-13; Hon C Coker Ridge 13-15. *The Vicarage, East Coker, Yeovil BA22 9JG* T: (01935) 862125 E: charles.hatton51@btinternet.com

HATTON, Michael Samuel. b 44. St Jo Coll Dur BA 72. Cranmer Hall Dur. **d** 74 **p** 75. C Dudley St Jas *Worc* 74-75; C N Lynn w St Marg and St Nic *Nor* 75-77; C Walsall Wood *Lich* 78-79; Min Shelfield St Mark CD 79-89; V Middleton St Cross *Ripon* 89-97; V Ingol *Blackb* 97-11; rtd 11; PtO *Blackb* from 11. *7 Laurel Avenue, Euxton, Chorley PR7 6AY* T: (01257) 274584 E: m.hatton719@btinternet.com

HATTON, Trevor. b 55. Oak Hill Th Coll BA 86. **d** 86 **p** 87. C Chilwell *S'well* 86-90; R Trowell 90-95; Chapl Nottm Trent Univ 95-99; P-in-c Nottingham St Nic 99-02; R 02-07; rtd 07. *53 Ashchurch Drive, Nottingham NG8 2RB* E: trev_ali@talk21.com

HATTON, Mrs Vivienne Gloria. b 57. Birm Univ BA 03. St Jo Coll Nottm MA 06. **d** 06 **p** 07. C Wednesfield Heath *Lich* 06-09; V Chasetown 09-13; P-in-c Shenstone and Stonnall 13-14; V Stainton w Hilton *York* from 14; V Brookfield from 14. *The Vicarage, Low Lane, Middlesbrough TS5 8EF* E: vivhatton@gmx.com

HATWELL, Timothy Rex. b 53. Oak Hill Th Coll BA 85. **d** 85 **p** 86. C Tonbridge St Steph *Roch* 85-90; V Cudham and Downe 90-07; V Falconwood 07-15; R Ightham from 15. *The Rectory, Bates Hill, Ightham, Sevenoaks TN15 9BG* M: 07799-601546 T: (01732) 886827
E: revtim.hatwell@gmail.com

HAUGH, Geoffrey Norman. **d** 13 **p** 14. Ballymore *Arm* 13-14; C Holywood *D & D* from 14. *51 Princess Gardens, Holywood BT18 0PN* M: 07568-364573 T: (028) 9029 3864
E: geoff_karen@hotmail.co.uk *or* revghaugh@hotmail.com

HAUGHTON, Peter Steele. b 57. K Coll Lon BD 84 MA 90. Westcott Ho Cam 84. **d** 86 **p** 87. C Cheam Common St Phil *S'wark* 86-90; Chapl Lon Univ Medical Schs 90-94; Educn Adv 94-95; P-in-c Kingston Vale St Jo 95-03; Adv in Ethics and Law K Coll Lon 03-13; PtO *Win* 03-13; C Southampton (City Cen) from 13. *95 Bullar Road, Southampton SO18 1GT* M: 07815-803920 E: peter.haughton@btinternet.com

HAUGHTY, Miss Rebecca Mary. b 69. Coll of Resurr Mirfield 09. **d** 11 **p** 12. C Pocklington Wold and Londesborough Wold *York* 11-15; V Coatham and Dormanstown from 15. *9 Blenheim Terrace, Redcar TS10 1QP* M: 07518-412149
E: r.haughty@btinternet.com

HAVARD, David William. b 56. Man Univ BA 84. Qu Coll Birm 84. **d** 85. C Man Clayton St Cross w St Paul 85-88; Canada 88-02; PtO *Sheff* from 03. *35 Roe Lane, Sheffield S3 9AL* T: 0114-272 9695 E: deacondave@onetel.com

HAVELL, Edward Michael. b 38. Dur Univ BA 65. Ridley Hall Cam 66. **d** 68 **p** 69. C Ecclesall *Sheff* 68-71; C Roch St Justus 71-74; P-in-c Holbeach Hurn *Linc* 74-75; C Hollington St Jo *Chich* 75-85; TV Rye 85-92; C E Dereham and Scarning *Nor* 92; rtd 93; PtO *Chich* from 99. *4 Gammons Way, Sedlescombe, Battle TN33 0RQ* T: (01424) 870864

HAVENS, Mrs Anita Sue. b 44. Univ of Mass BSEd 67 Clark Univ (USA) MA 72 Hughes Hall Cam BA 79. Cranmer Hall Dur MA 83. **dss** 84 **d** 87 **p** 94. Gateshead Hosps 84-87; Par Dn Cen Telford *Lich* 87-90; Ind Chapl 87-90; *Liv* 90-96; TV Man Whitworth 96-99; Chapl Man Univ 96-99; R Birch St Agnes w Longsight St Jo w St Cypr 99-01; rtd 01; PtO *Carl* from 03. *Stone Cottage, Kirkby Thore, Penrith CA10 1UE* T: (01768) 362682 E: sue.havens@lineone.net

HAVEY, Kenneth Richard. b 61. St Steph Ho Ox 95. **d** 97 **p** 98. C Corringham *Chelmsf* 97-98; C Leigh St Clem 98-02; R 02-13; P-in-c Hockley from 13. *The Vicarage, 6A Silvertree Close, Hockley SS5 4SP* T: (01702) 203668
E: kenneth.havey@btinternet.com

HAVILAND, Canon Andrew Mark James. b 65. Leeds Univ BEd 87. STETS 02. **d** 05 **p** 06. NSM N Holmwood *Guildf* 05-08; Chapl Bryanston Sch from 08; Can and Preb Sarum Cathl from 15. *Bryanston School, Blandford DT11 0PX* T: (01258) 452411 M: 07855-823255 E: amh@bryanston.co.uk

HAVILAND, Edmund Selwyn. b 24. K Coll Cam BA 49 MA 51. Wells Th Coll 49. **d** 51 **p** 52. C St Helier *S'wark* 51-55; C-in-c Bermondsey St Hugh CD 55-58; V Ockbrook *Derby* 58-68; V E Peckham *Roch* 68-78; R E Peckham and Nettlestead 78-84; S Africa 84-85; Dep Chapl HM Pris Brixton 85-89; rtd 89; PtO *Guildf* from 89. *Hill Farm, Thursley, Godalming GU8 6QQ* T: (01252) 702115

HAWES, Canon Andrew Thomas. b 54. Sheff Univ BA 77 Em Coll Cam MA 79. Westcott Ho Cam 77. **d** 80 **p** 81. C Gt Grimsby St Mary and St Jas *Linc* 80-84; P-in-c Gedney Drove End 84-86; P-in-c Sutton St Nicholas 84-86; V Lutton w Gedney Drove End, Dawsmere 86-89; V Edenham w Witham on the Hill 89-00; V Edenham w Witham on the Hill and Swinstead from 00; RD Beltisloe 97-13; Can and Preb Linc Cathl from 09. *The Vicarage, Church Lane, Edenham, Bourne PE10 0LS* T/F: (01778) 591358

HAWES, The Ven Arthur John. b 43. UEA BA 86. Chich Th Coll 65. **d** 68 **p** 69. C Kidderminster St Jo *Worc* 68-72; P-in-c Droitwich 72-76; R Alderford w Attlebridge and Swannington *Nor* 76-92; Chapl Hellesdon and David Rice Hosps and Yare Clinic 76-92; RD Sparham *Nor* 81-91; Mental Health Act Commr 86-94; Hon Can Nor Cathl 88-95; TR Gaywood 92-95; Adn Linc and Can and Preb Linc Cathl 95-08; rtd 08; PtO *S'wark* from 09; *Nor* from 12. *29 Market Street, Shipdham, Thetford IP25 7LY* T: (01362) 822441 M: 07803-249834
E: arthur.hawes@yahoo.co.uk

HAWES, Canon Joseph Patricius. b 65. St Chad's Coll Dur BA 87 K Coll Lon MA 12. St Steph Ho Ox 88. **d** 91 **p** 92. C Clapham Team *S'wark* 91-96; P-in-c Barnes St Mich 96-97; TV Barnes 97-03; V Fulham All SS *Lon* from 03; Hon Can Gaborone Botswana from 11. *All Saints' Vicarage, 70 Fulham High Street, London SW6 3LG* T: (020) 7371 5202 or 7736 6301
E: vicar@allsaints-fulham.org.uk

HAWES, Mrs Joy Elizabeth. b 58. STETS 12. **d** 15. NSM Wedmore w Theale and Blackford *B & W* from 15. *Glencoe, Fishers Hill, Glastonbury BA6 8AH* E: therevjoy@gmail.com

HAWES, Mary Elizabeth. b 56. SEITE 94. **d** 00 **p** 01. Dioc Children's Adv *Lon* 98-06; Nat Children's Adv Abps' Coun 06-12; Nat Going for Growth (Children and Youth) Adv from 12; NSM Streatham St Leon *S'wark* 00-11; NSM Teddington St Mary w St Alb *Lon* from 11. *47 Traherne Lodge, 64 Walpole Road, Teddington TW11 8PW* T: (020) 7898 1504
E: mary.hawes@churchofengland.org

HAWES, Michael Rowell. b 31. AKC 61. **d** 62 **p** 63. C Epsom St Martin *Guildf* 62-65; Chapl RAF 65-86; R Newnham w Nately Scures w Mapledurwell etc *Win* 86-97; rtd 97; PtO *Win* 97-09. *7 Holly Lane, Ashley, New Milton BH25 5RF* T: (01425) 620698

HAWES, Ms Rachel. b 54. St Hugh's Coll Ox BA 76 MA 80. STETS 05. **d** 07 **p** 08. NSM Kensington St Mary Abbots w Ch Ch and St Phil *Lon* 07-10; NSM Notting Hill St Jo from 10; P-in-c St Martin Ludgate from 14. *26 Talbot Road, London W2 5LJ* T: (020) 7792 3909 *or* 7329 2702 M: 07768-875590
E: rachel.hawes@lawcol.co.uk

HAWKEN, Andrew Robert. b 58. K Coll Lon BD 81 AKC 81. St Steph Ho Ox 83. **d** 85 **p** 86. C Ex St Dav 85-88; TV Witney *Ox* 88-93; V Benson 93-10; AD Aston and Cuddesdon 02-07; Hon Can Ch Ch 09-10; Chapl Midi-Pyrénées and Aude *Eur* from 10. *Le Presbytère, St Gervais, 82190 Touffailles, France* T: (0033) (5) 63 95 78 24
E: andrew.hawken@ntlworld.com

HAWKEN, Rosalind Mary. b 56. York Univ BA 77 Univ of Wales (Cardiff) BTh 02. St Mich Coll Llan 99. **d** 02 **p** 03. C Swansea St Thos and Kilvey *S & B* 02-03; C Gorseinon 03-07. *Society of the Sacred Cross, Tymawr Convent, Lydart, Monmouth NP25 4RN* T: (01600) 860244

HAWKER, The Ven Alan Fort. b 44. Hull Univ BA 65. Clifton Th Coll 65. **d** 68 **p** 69. C Bootle St Leon *Liv* 68-71; C Fazakerley Em 71-73; V Goose Green 73-81; TR Southgate *Chich* 81-98; Can and Preb Chich Cathl 91-98; RD E Grinstead 94-98; Hon Can Bris Cathl 98-10; Adn Swindon 98-99; Adn Malmesbury 99-10; rtd 10; PtO *Cov* from 11. *21 Paddocks Close, Wolston, Coventry CV8 3GW* T: (024) 7654 4021
E: alanandjen68@gmail.com

HAWKER, Alan John. b 53. K Coll Lon BD 76 AKC 76. Sarum & Wells Th Coll 77. **d** 78 **p** 79. C Coleford w Staunton *Glouc* 78-81; C Up Hatherley 81-84; V Plymouth St Jas Ham *Ex* 84-92; TV Worc SE 92-99; TR Leic Presentation 99-02; P-in-c Leic St Chad 02-03; PtO 09-10; NSM Eyres Monsell 10-11; R Narborough and Huncote from 11. *The Rectory, 15 Church View, Narborough, Leicester LE9 5GY* T: 0116-275 0388 E: a.hawker87@btinternet.com

HAWKER, Brian Henry. b 34. AKC 61. St Boniface Warminster 61. **d** 62 **p** 63. C Hemel Hempstead *St Alb* 62-66; R Stone w Hartwell w Bishopstone *Ox* 66-69; Chapl St Jo Hosp 66-69; V W Wycombe *Ox* 69-72; Past Consultant Clinical Th Assn 72-83; Past Consultant 83-94; Public Preacher *S'well* 72-76; PtO *B & W* 76-83; *Truro* 83-90; rtd 94; PtO *Leic* from 99. *12 Burfield Avenue, Loughborough LE11 3AZ* T: (01509) 261439

HAWKER, Canon Peter John. b 37. OBE 96. Ex Univ BA 59. Wycliffe Hall Ox 69. **d** 70 **p** 71. Asst Chapl Berne *Eur* 70-76; Chapl Berne w Neuchâtel 76-89; Adn Switzerland 86-04; Chapl Zürich w St Gallen, Baden and Zug 90-00; Can Brussels Cathl 86-04; rtd 04. *Schulgasse 10, 3280 Murten, Switzerland* T: (0041) (26) 670 6221 F: 670 6219 E: phawker@bluewin.ch

HAWKES, Mrs Cecilia Mary (Cilla). b 48. Reading Univ BSc 69 Canley Coll of Educn DipEd 71. EAMTC 99. **d** 02 **p** 03. NSM Takeley w Lt Canfield *Chelmsf* 02-10; NSM Stebbing and Lindsell w Gt and Lt Saling from 10; Voc Officer Colchester Area from 08; RD Dunmow and Stansted from 10. *Greenfields, Felsted, Dunmow CM6 3LF* T/F: (01371) 856480
E: cilla@hawkesfarming.co.uk

HAWKES, Mrs Elisabeth Anne. b 56. GRNCM 78 PGCE 80 Kent Univ MA 97. Linc Th Coll 86. **d** 88 **p** 97. Hon Par Dn Finham *Cov* 88-90; Hon Par Dn Bexhill St Pet *Chich* 90-97; Asst to RD Oundle *Pet* 97-98; NSM 98-00; NSM Benefield and Southwick w Glapthorn 99-00; PtO *Cant* 00-04; Hon Min Can Cant Cathl 03-12; NSM Reculver and Herne Bay St Bart 04-12; NSM St Nicholas at Wade w Sarre and Chislet w Hoath 04-12; Dioc Adv in Liturgy 04-12; NSM Wykeham *Ox* from 12. *The New Rectory, Sibford Gower, Banbury OX15 5RW* T: (01295) 780555
E: revlizhawkes@gmail.com

HAWKES, Mrs Helen Vanda. b 50. Surrey Univ BA 01. STETS 98. **d** 01 **p** 02. NSM N Hayling St Pet and Hayling Is St Andr *Portsm* 01-05; NSM Bedhampton 05-11; rtd 11; PtO *Portsm* from 11. *67 East Lodge Park, Farlington, Portsmouth PO16 1BZ* T: (023) 9221 9005 M: 07719-828113
E: vanda.hawkes@btinternet.com

HAWKES, Keith Andrew. b 28. Oak Hill Th Coll 72. **d** 74 **p** 75. C Gt Yarmouth *Nor* 74-77; C-in-c Bowthorpe CD 77; Chapl Düsseldorf *Eur* 77-83; TV Quidenham *Nor* 83-88; TR 88-90; RD Thetford and Rockland 86-90; R Wickmere w Lt Barningham,

Itteringham etc 90-96; Dioc Rural Officer 90-94; P-in-c Saxthorpe w Corpusty, Blickling, Oulton etc 94-96; R Lt Barningham, Blickling, Edgefield etc 96-98; Bp's Chapl 98; rtd 98; PtO *Nor* 98-00 and from 04; P-in-c Guiltcross 00-03; Chapl Norwich Primary Care Trust 00-02; Chapl Riddlesworth Hall Sch *Nor* from 04. *Peel Cottage, West Church Street, Kenninghall, Norwich NR16 2EN* T/F: (01953) 888533
E: revkahawkes@aol.com

HAWKES, Martyn John. b 71. Nottm Univ BA 94 St Jo Coll Dur BA 01. Cranmer Hall Dur 99. **d** 02 **p** 03. C Is of Dogs Ch Ch and St Jo w St Luke *Lon* 02-05; C Brownswood Park and Stoke Newington St Mary 05-11; V Aldersbrook *Chelmsf* from 11. *St Gabriel's Vicarage, 12 Aldersbrook Road, London E12 5HH* T: (020) 8989 0315 E: mj_hawkes@yahoo.co.uk

HAWKES, Nigel Anthony Robert. b 59. UEA BSc 80 Edin Univ MSc 82. Ripon Coll Cuddesdon 00. **d** 02 **p** 03. C Chase *Ox* 02-04; C Chipping Norton 04-05; TV Dorchester 05-11; P-in-c Wheatley 11-14; V Albury w Tiddington, Holton, Waterperry, Waterstock and Wheatley from 14. *The Vicarage, 18 London Road, Wheatley, Oxford OX33 1YA* T: (01865) 872224
E: vicar.wheatley@gmail.com

HAWKES, Ronald Linton. b 54. St Jo Coll York CertEd 75 Leeds Univ BEd 76 Kent Univ MA 96. Linc Th Coll 85. **d** 87 **p** 88. C Finham *Cov* 87-90; TV Bexhill St Pet *Chich* 90-97; V Oundle *Pet* 97-00; P-in-c Benefield and Southwick w Glapthorn 99-00; Dir Post-Ord Tr 98-00; Chapl St Edm Sch *Cant* 00-03; V Reculver and Herne Bay St Bart *Cant* 03-12; P-in-c Hoath H Cross 04-12; AD Reculver *Cant* 06-12; Hon Min Can *Cant* Cathl 01-12; R Wykeham *Ox* from 12. *The New Rectory, Sibford Gower, Banbury OX15 5RW* T: (01295) 780555
E: reverendronald1954@gmail.com

HAWKES, Vanda. *See* HAWKES, Helen Vanda

HAWKETT, Graham Kenneth. b 20. Bps' Coll Cheshunt 61. **d** 63 **p** 64. C Farncombe *Guildf* 63-67; V Wyke 67-85; r-d 85; PtO *Guildf* from 85. *Bede House, Beech Road, Haslemere GU27 2BX* T: (01428) 656430

HAWKEY, James Douglas Thomas. b 79. Girton Coll Cam BA 01 MA 05 Selw Coll Cam MPhil 02 PhD 08. Westcott Ho Cam 03 St Thos Aquinas Pontifical Univ Rome 06. **d** 07 **p** 08. C Portsea St Mary *Portsm* 07-10; Min Can and Sacr Westmr Abbey from 10; Prec Westmr Abbey 13-15; Dean Clare Coll Cam from 15. *Clare College, Cambridge CB2 1TL* M: 07792-908026 T: jdth2@cam.ac.uk

HAWKINGS, Timothy Denison. b 55. Ex Univ BA 78. St Jo Coll Nottm BA 80. **d** 81 **p** 82. C Penn *Lich* 81-85; TV Stafford 85-94; TR Stratton St Margaret w S Marston etc *Bris* 94-05; P-in-c Axbridge w Shipham and Rowberrow *B & W* 05-11; R from 11; P-in-c Mark w Allerton 08-10; RD Axbridge 08-14. *The Rectory, Cheddar Road, Axbridge BS26 2DL* T: (01934) 732261 E: revhawkings@googlemail.com

HAWKINS, The Very Revd Alun John. b 44. K Coll Lon BA 66 AKC 66 Univ of Wales (Ban) BD 81. St Deiniol's Hawarden 78. **d** 81 **p** 82. C Dwygyfylchi *Ban* 81-84; R Llanberis 84-89; Tutor Ban Dioc NSM Course 85-90; Dir of Ords *Ban* 86-90; V Knighton and Norton *S & B* 89-93; Chapl Knighton Hosp 89-93; TR Bangor *Ban* 93-06; Adult Educn Officer 93-11; Sec Dioc Bd of Miss 93-11; Can Res and Can Missr Ban Cathl 93-00; Adn Ban 00-04; Dean Ban 04-11; rtd 11; PtO *Ban* from 11. *9 Cil y Craig, Llanfairpwllgwyngyll LL61 5NZ* T: (01248) 717403

HAWKINS, Andrew Robert. b 40. St Andr Univ BSc 64. St Chad's Coll Dur BA 68. **d** 69 **p** 70. C Sutton St Nic *S'wark* 69-73; C Wimbledon 73-77; TV Cramlington *Newc* 77-81; R Clutton w Cameley *B & W* 81-89; Chapl City of Bath Coll of FE from 89; PtO *B & W* from 90. *18 Wally Court Road, Chew Stoke, Bristol BS40 8XN* T: (01275) 332422 M: 07867-937529 E: andrewr.hawkins@virgin.net

HAWKINS (née BRAZIER), Mrs Annette Michaela. b 59. Brighton Univ BEd 95 Homerton Coll Cam BTh. Ridley Hall Cam 07. **d** 09 **p** 10. C Ore St Helen and St Barn *Chich* from 09. *4 Gresham Way, St Leonards-on-Sea TN38 0NU* M: 07900-332791 E: annette@jhbd.co.uk

HAWKINS, Canon Bruce Alexander. b 44. Qu Coll Ox BA 66 MA 71. Sarum Th Coll 66. **d** 68 **p** 69. C Epsom St Martin *Guildf* 68-71; Dioc Youth Chapl *Cant* 72-81; Hon Min Can Cant Cathl 75-99; Dep Dir of Educn 81-86; V Walmer 86-05; RD Sandwich 94-00; Hon Can Cant Cathl 99-05; rtd 05; PtO *Cant* from 05. *88 The Gateway, Dover CT16 1LQ* T: (01304) 240820

HAWKINS, Mrs Christine Ann. b 56. SEITE 98. **d** 01 **p** 02. NSM Epping Distr *Chelmsf* 01-02; C Woodford St Mary w St Phil and St Jas 02-05; P-in-c Hatfield Broad Oak and Bush End 05-07; Ind Chapl Harlow 05-07; Chapl Princess Alexandra Hosp NHS Trust 07-14; TV Louth *Linc* from 15. *The Vicarage, Little Lane, Louth LN11 9DU* E: cah56@sky.com

HAWKINS, Canon Clive Ladbrook. b 53. St Pet Coll Ox BA 76 MA 79. Trin Coll Bris 80. **d** 82 **p** 83. C Win Ch Ch 82-86; R Eastrop from 86; AD Basingstoke 00-08; Hon Can Win Cathl from 05. *Eastrop Rectory, 2A Wallis Road, Basingstoke RG21 3DW* T: (01256) 355507 or 464249
E: clive.hawkins@stmarys-basingstoke.org.uk

✠**HAWKINS, The Rt Revd David John Leader.** b 49. Nottm Univ BTh 73. St Jo Coll Nottm 69 ALCD 73. **d** 73 **p** 74 **c** 02. C Bebington *Ches* 73-76; Nigeria 76-82; C Ox St Aldate w St Matt 83-86; V Leeds St Geo *Ripon* 86-99; TR 99-02; Area Bp Barking *Chelmsf* 02-14; rtd 14. *3 Princes Drive, Skipton BD23 1HN*

HAWKINS, David Kenneth Beaumont. b 36. Em Coll Saskatoon LTh 63. **d** 63 **p** 64. C Northminster Canada 63-69; C Belleville Ch Ch 69-71; I Wellington 71-79; I Barriefield w Pittsburgh 80-85; C St Alb St Paul *St Alb* 85-87; C Hednesford *Lich* 87-92; R Buildwas and Leighton w Eaton Constantine etc 92-95; TV Wrockwardine Deanery 95-01; rtd 01. *PO Box 454, 131 Westwind Crescent, Wellington ON K0K 3L0, Canada*
T: (001) (613) 399 5666 E: rowenadavid@sympatico.ca

HAWKINS, Mrs Dorothy. b 56. RGN 77 RM 79. All SS Cen for Miss & Min 07. **d** 14 **p** 15. OLM Worsley *Man* from 14. *4 Ryecroft Lane, Worsley, Manchester M28 2PN* T: 0161-794 5072 E: dh89@btinternet.com

HAWKINS, James Reginald. b 39. Ex Univ BA 61 Hull Univ MA 00. Westcott Ho Cam 61. **d** 63 **p** 64. C Cannock *Lich* 63-66; C Wem 66-67; C Cheddleton 67-69; R Yoxall 69-77; R The Quinton *Birm* 77-84; V Bosbury w Wellington Heath etc *Heref* 84-96; P-in-c Ancaster Wilsford Gp *Linc* 96-99; R 99-04; RD Loveden 97-03; rtd 04. *14 Pound Pill, Corsham SN13 9JA* T: (01249) 715353
E: james.hawkins39@btopenworld.com

HAWKINS, John Colin. b 50. SEITE 97. **d** 00 **p** 01. NSM W Wickham St Jo *S'wark* 00-04; P-in-c Burwash Weald *Chich* 04-11; PtO from 11. *Bell Cottage, Vinehall Road, Mountfield, Robertsbridge TN32 5JN* E: john.c.hawkins@btinternet.com

HAWKINS, Preb John Edward Inskipp. b 63. K Coll Lon BD 85. Qu Coll Birm 86. **d** 88 **p** 89. C Birchfield *Birm* 88-92; C Poplar *Lon* 92-93; TV 93-99; V W Hendon St Jo from 99; P-in-c Colindale St Matthias from 07; AD W Barnet 04-09; Preb St Paul's Cathl from 13. *St John's Vicarage, Vicarage Road, London NW4 3PX* T/F: (020) 8202 8606
E: jeih.stj@aladdinscave.net

HAWKINS, Jonathan Desmond. b 53. FRICS 93. Ox Min Course 04. **d** 07 **p** 08. NSM Walton H Trin *Ox* 07-09; NSM Southcourt 09-10; NSM Haddenham w Cuddington, Kingsey etc from 10. *Croft End, 1A White Hart Lane, Haddenham, Aylesbury HP17 8BB* M: 07976-281699 T: (01844) 299429
E: jon@jdhawkins.co.uk

HAWKINS, Nicholas Milner. b 45. Univ of Wales (Swansea) BA 69 MSc 71. **d** 01 **p** 05. Par Dn Dingestow and Llangovan w Penyclawdd etc *Mon* 01-02; PtO *Ban* 02-03; NSM Nefyn w Tudweiliog w Llandudwen w Edern 03-08; P-in-c Botwnnog w Bryncroes w Llangwnnadl w Penllech 08-12; rtd 12; C Dawlish *Ex* 12-15; C Kenton, Mamhead, Powderham, Cofton and Starcross 12-15; C Dawlish, Cofton and Starcross from 15; C Exminster, Kenn, Kenton w Mamhead, and Powderham from 15. *The Rectory, 1 Staplake Rise, Starcross, Exeter EX6 8SJ* T: (01626) 899166 M: 07870-264385
E: rev.starcross@gmail.com

HAWKINS, Noel. b 46. St Jo Coll Nottm 82. **d** 84 **p** 85. C Worksop St Jo *S'well* 84-86; C Wollaton Park 86-89; TV Billericay and Lt Burstead *Chelmsf* 89-95; TV Keynsham *B & W* 95-00; V Brislington St Chris and St Cuth *Bris* 00-08; V Brislington St Chris 08-12; P-in-c Hengrove 06-12; rtd 12. *17 White Horse Drive, Frome BA11 2DA* T: (01373) 451305
E: henbriznl@gmail.com

HAWKINS, Canon Patricia Sally. b 59. LMH Ox BA 80 MA 84 Ex Univ BPhil 85 Ox Univ BTh 04 CQSW 85. St Steph Ho Ox 99. **d** 01 **p** 02. C Stafford *Lich* 01-04; V Oxley 04-14; AD Wolverhampton 08-11; RD Wulfrun 11-14; Preb Lich Cathl 09-14; Can Res Lich Cathl from 14. *23 The Close, Lichfield WS13 7LD* T: (01543) 306142 E: pat.hawkins@lichfield-cathedral.org

HAWKINS, Paul Henry Whishaw. b 46. Ex Coll Ox BA 68 MA 74 SS Coll Cam MA 84. St Steph Ho Ox 70. **d** 72 **p** 73. C Fawley *Win* 72-75; C Ealing St Steph Castle Hill *Lon* 75-77; P-in-c Dorney *Ox* 77-78; TV Riverside 78-81; Chapl SS Coll Cam 82-87; V Plymstock *Ex* 87-97; RD Plymouth Sutton 91-96; TR Plymstock and Hooe 97-00; Preb Ex Cathl 98-00; P-in-c St Pancras w St Jas and Ch Ch *Lon* 00-02; V 02-11; rtd 11. *Hall Floor Flat, 9 Buckingham Place, Clifton, Bristol BS8 1LJ*

HAWKINS, Peter Edward. b 35. Leeds Univ BA 60. Coll of Resurr Mirfield 60. **d** 62 **p** 63. C Forest Gate St Edm *Chelmsf* 62-65; C Sevenoaks St Jo *Roch* 65-68; Chapl Metrop Police

Cadet Corps Tr Sch 68-73; P-in-c Knowle H Nativity *Bris* 73; TV Knowle 73-79; V Westbury-on-Trym H Trin 79-87; TR Solihull *Birm* 87-96; Hon Can Birm Cathl 92-96; rtd 00. *Back Street Cottage, 15 St Andrew's Road, Stogursey, Bridgwater TA5 1TE* T/F: (01278) 733635 E: peh.stogursey@tiscali.uk

HAWKINS, Peter Michael. b 38. Kelham Th Coll 58. **d** 63 **p** 64. Ox Miss to Calcutta India 63-64; C Calcutta Cathl 64-66; C-in-c Kidderpore 66-68; V Asansol w Burnpur 68-69; C Manningham St Paul and St Jude *Bradf* 70-72; C Bradf Cathl 72-75; V Allerton 75-90; V Pet H Spirit Bretton 90-07; P-in-c Marholm 90-95; rtd 07. *Le Pavillon, Mané Gouélo, RD 765, 56690 Landaul, France* T: (0033) 2 97 59 90 83 M: 6 48 42 78 70 E: peterhawkins@sfr.fr

HAWKINS, Mrs Rachel Ann. b 76. Trin Coll Bris 09. **d** 11 **p** 12. C Long Eaton St Jo *Derby* 11-15; V Rushden St Pet from 15. *St Peter's Vicarage, 12 Kensington Close, Rushden NN10 6RR* M: 07930-827203 E: revrach@email.co.uk

HAWKINS, Richard Randal. b 39. **d** 65 **p** 66. C Bushbury *Lich* 65-68; C Woodford St Mary *Chelmsf* 68-71; S Africa from 71; rtd 04. *7 Chapter Close, 6 Taunton Road, Pietermaritzburg, 3201 South Africa*

✠**HAWKINS, The Rt Revd Richard Stephen.** b 39. Ex Coll Ox BA 61 MA 65 Ex Univ BPhil 76. St Steph Ho Ox 61. **d** 63 **p** 64 **c** 88. C Ex St Thos 63-66; C Clyst St Mary 66-75; TV Clyst St George, Aylesbeare, Clyst Honiton etc 75-78; TV Cen Ex 78-81; Bp's Officer for Min and Jt Dir Ex and Truro NSM Scheme 78-81; Dioc Dir of Ords 79-81; Adn Totnes 81-88; P-in-c Oldridge and Whitestone 81-87; Suff Bp Plymouth 88-96; Suff Bp Crediton 96-04; rtd 04; Hon Asst Bp Ex from 05. *3 Westbrook Close, Exeter EX4 8BS* T: (01392) 462622

HAWKINS, Canon Richard Whishaw. b 51. Coll of Resurr Mirfield 93. **d** 95 **p** 96. C Weymouth H Trin *Sarum* 95-99; P-in-c Hey *Man* 99-06; TR Medlock Head from 06; AD Saddleworth 03-09; Hon Can Man Cathl from 12. *St John's Vicarage, 1 Owen Fold, Oldham OL4 3DT* T: 0161-626 3630 E: richard.hawkins107@ntlworld.com

HAWKINS, Roger David William. b 33. K Coll Lon BD 58 AKC 58. **d** 59 **p** 60. C Twickenham St Mary *Lon* 59-61; C Heston 61-64; C Dorking w Ranmore *Guildf* 64-65; V Mitcham St Mark *S'wark* 65-74; V Redhill St Matt 74-91; P-in-c Warlingham w Chelsham and Farleigh 91-97; TR 97-98; rtd 98; PtO *Guildf* from 11. *The College of St Barnabas, Blackberry Lane, Lingfield RH7 6NJ*

HAWKINS, Roger Julian. b 32. Ripon Hall Ox 59. **d** 61 **p** 62. C-in-c Newall Green CD *Man* 61-63; Chapl RAF 63-67; R Mawgan in Pyder *Truro* 67-75; R Lanteglos by Camelford w Advent 75-78; R Newmarket St Mary *St E* 78-85; P-in-c Coltishall w Gt Hautbois *Nor* 85-87; R Coltishall w Gt Hautbois and Horstead 87-90; Chapl Whiteley Village *Guildf* 90-94; rtd 97; PtO *Win* 01-02; *Sarum* 02-08; *Nor* from 10. *3 Norman Cockaday Court, Holt NR25 6JA* T: (01263) 710004

HAWKINS, Steven Andrew. b 51. Nottm Univ BEd 75 Open Univ BSc 91 Bris Poly AdEd 90. STETS 95. **d** 98 **p** 99. C Horfield H Trin *Bris* 98-02; V Brislington St Anne 02-08; P-in-c Knowle St Martin 08-13; V 13-15; rtd 15. *130 Charlton Mead Drive, Bristol BS10 6LH* M: 07929-485006 T: 0117-914 4630 E: sh1951@outlook.com

HAWKINS, Susan. b 47. Doncaster Coll of Educn CertEd 69 Ches Coll of HE BTh 99. NOC 95. **d** 99 **p** 00. NSM Prestbury *Ches* 99-02; P-in-c Marthall and Chapl David Lewis Cen for Epilepsy 02-09; rtd 09; PtO *Ches* from 09. *3 Thorne Close, Prestbury, Macclesfield SK10 4DE* T: (01625) 829833 E: suehawkins03@virginmedia.com

HAWKINS, Timothy St John. b 59. CCC Ox BA 82. Trin Coll Bris BA 87. **d** 87 **p** 88. C Cheltenham St Mary, St Matt, St Paul and H Trin *Glouc* 87-90; C Cowplain *Portsm* 90-94; V Pennycross *Ex* 94-96; P-in-c St Keverne *Truro* 96-05; P-in-c Gulval and Madron from 05. *The Vicarage, Church Road, Madron, Penzance TR20 8SW* T: (01736) 360992 E: revtimhawkins@hotmail.co.uk

HAWKSWORTH, Maldwyn Harry. b 45. Aston Univ CertEd 74. St Jo Coll Nottm 87. **d** 89 **p** 90. C Penn *Lich* 89-94; TV Bloxwich 94-09; Local Min Adv (Wolverhampton) 09-15; Local Par Development Adv Wolverhampton Area 10-15; P-in-c Yoxall from 09. *The Rectory, Savey Lane, Yoxall, Burton-on-Trent DE13 8PD* T: (01543) 473202

HAWKSWORTH, Peter John Dallas. b 54. St Jo Coll Ox BA 75 MA 79 Solicitor 79. Sarum & Wells Th Coll 89. **d** 91 **p** 92. C Warminster St Denys, Upton Scudamore etc *Sarum* 91-95; P-in-c Salisbury St Mark 95-99; V 99-05; RD Salisbury 03-05; PtO from 07. *6 Newton Rise, Swanage BH19 2QP* E: onehundredkilos@btinternet.com

HAWLEY, Canon Anthony Broughton. b 41. St Pet Coll Ox BA 67 MA 71. Westcott Ho Cam 67. **d** 69 **p** 70. C Wolverhampton St Pet *Lich* 69-72; C-in-c Bermondsey St Hugh CD *S'wark* 73-84; Hon PV S'wark Cathl 83-84;

TR Kirkby *Liv* 84-02; AD Walton 93-02; Hon Can Liv Cathl 96-02; Can Res Liv Cathl 02-11; rtd 11; PtO *Sarum* from 12. *Pimlico Cottage, Black Lane, Lover, Salisbury SP5 2PQ* T: (01794) 390607 E: anthony@hawley77.freeserve.co.uk

HAWLEY, Georgina. b 45. **d** 01 **p** 02. Australia 01-02 and from 07; NSM Chippenham St Pet *Bris* 02-03; PtO 03-07. *32A Wishart Street, Gwelup WA 6018, Australia* T: (0061) (8) 9446 4021 E: georginahawley@hotmail.co.uk

HAWLEY, The Ven John Andrew. b 50. K Coll Lon BD 71 AKC 71. Wycliffe Hall Ox 72. **d** 74 **p** 75. C Kingston upon Hull H Trin *York* 74-77; C Bradf Cathl Par 77-80; V Woodlands *Sheff* 80-91; TR Dewsbury *Wakef* 91-02; Hon Can Wakef Cathl 98-02; Adn Blackb 02-15; rtd 15. *35 Woodland Avenue, Goole DN14 6QT* M: 07980-945035 T: (01405) 762678 E: john.hawley627@gmail.com

HAWLEY, William David Llewellyn. b 41. Univ of W Aus BCom 77 Murdoch Univ Aus BD 94. **d** 92 **p** 95. Hon C Bullcreek w Bateman Australia 92-94; Hon C Kwinana 94-95; Dioc Registrar 95-98; Assoc P Spearwood w Hilton 95-98; R Hilton 98-00; TV By Brook *Bris* 01-07; C Colerne w N Wraxall 06-07; rtd 07. *32A Wishart Street, Gwelup WA 6018, Australia* T: (0061) (8) 9446 4021

HAWNT, John Charles Frederick. b 30. Westwood Cen Zimbabwe 72. **d** 75 **p** 76. Zimbabwe 75-81; C Rugby *Cov* 81-85; R Lydeard St Lawrence w Brompton Ralph etc *B & W* 85-00; rtd 00. *39 St Andrew Road, Houghton, Johannesburg, 2198 South Africa* T: (0027) (11) 487 3259

HAWORTH (née ARMSTRONG), Fiona Heather. b 65. Reading Univ BSc 86 Nottm Univ PhD 90. St Jo Coll Nottm BTh 94. **d** 97 **p** 98. C Sutton in Ashfield St Mary *S'well* 97-02; TV Kidderminster St Mary and All SS w Trimpley etc *Worc* 02-09; Chapl Worc Univ from 09. *University of Worcester, Henwick Grove, Worcester WR2 6AJ* T: (01905) 542327 E: f.haworth@worc.ac.uk

HAWORTH, Julie. b 59. St Mich Coll Llan. **d** 09. C Wigan All SS and St Geo *Liv* 09-13; C Wigan St Anne 13-15; C Wigan All SS from 15. *63 Kendal Street, Wigan WN6 7DJ* T: (01942) 733209 E: je.haworth@yahoo.co.uk

HAWORTH, Mark Newby. b 50. Aber Univ BSc 73 MICFor 81. Westcott Ho Cam 88. **d** 90 **p** 91. C Cherry Hinton St Andr *Ely* 90-93; C Teversham 90-93; P-in-c Swaffham Bulbeck and Swaffham Prior w Reach 93-94; V 94-02; Sub Warden of Readers 95-02; RD Fordham 96-02; Chapl Framlingham Coll and Brandeston Hall Sch 03; Chapl to Bp Pet 03-05; TR Pendleton *Man* 05-09; P-in-c Lower Kersal 06-09; TR Salford All SS 09-12; Borough Dean Salford 10-12; R Rochdale 12-13; Hon Can Man Cathl 12-13; TR Bury St Edmunds All SS w St Jo and St Geo *St E* from 13; P-in-c Lark Valley from 14; RD Thingoe from 14. *The Rectory, 59 Bennett Avenue, Bury St Edmunds IP33 3JJ* T/F: (01284) 755374 M: 07932-160009 E: father.mark@virgin.net *or* rectornorthburyteam@btinternet.com

HAWORTH, Paul. b 47. G&C Coll Cam BA 68 MA 72. Westcott Ho Cam 75. **d** 78 **p** 79. C Hornchurch St Andr *Chelmsf* 78-81; C Loughton St Mary and St Mich 81-88; TV Waltham H Cross 88-92; TR Becontree S 92-00; P-in-c S Woodham Ferrers 00-11; rtd 11; PtO *Chelmsf* from 11. *17 Ember Way, Burnham-on-Crouch CM0 8TJ* E: onthemat@btconnect.com

HAWORTH, Stanley Robert. b 48. St Jo Coll Dur BA 69. Sarum & Wells Th Coll 71. **d** 73 **p** 74. C Skipton H Trin *Bradf* 73-76; C Bradf Cathl 76-78; C Grantham *Linc* 78; TV 78-82; V Deeping St James 82-96; V Middlewich w Byley *Ches* 96-01; P-in-c Forcett and Aldbrough and Melsonby *Ripon* 01-12; AD Richmond 08-12; rtd 12; PtO *Pet* from 12. *45 Finedon Road, Irthlingborough, Wellingborough NN9 5TY* T: (01933) 653798 E: stantherevman@hotmail.com

HAWORTH, Stuart. b 43. **d** 94 **p** 95. OLM Bradshaw *Man* 94-01; OLM Turton Moorland 01-08; rtd 08; PtO *Man* from 08. *39 Patterdale Road, Bolton BL2 3LX* T: (01204) 384006

HAWRISH, Mary-Beth Louise Ladine. b 66. **d** 09 **p** 10. OLM Oxshott *Guildf* from 09. *Cedar House, Sandy Lane, Cobham KT11 2EP* T: (01932) 864695 E: mhawrish@yahoo.co.uk

HAWTHORN, The Ven Christopher John. b 36. Qu Coll Cam BA 60 MA 64. Ripon Hall Ox 60. **d** 62 **p** 63. C Sutton St Jas *York* 62-66; V Kingston upon Hull St Nic 66-72; V E Coatham 72-79; V Scarborough St Martin 79-91; RD Scarborough 82-91; Can and Preb York Minster 87-01; Adn Cleveland 91-01; rtd 01; PtO *York* from 01. *43 Barley Rise, Strensall, York YO32 5AB* T: (01904) 492060

HAWTHORN, David. b 63. Chich Th Coll 87. **d** 90 **p** 91. C Hartlepool H Trin *Dur* 90-94; C Middlesbrough All SS *York* 94-95; P-in-c Thornaby on Tees 95-96; V S Thornaby 96-02; P-in-c Brighton Annunciation *Chich* 02-04; V Hollinwood and Limeside *Man* from 04. *St Margaret's Vicarage, 61 Chapel Road, Oldham OL8 4QQ* T/F: 0161-681 4541 E: hawthorn@supanet.com

HAWTHORN, Philip Alan. b 58. Essex Univ BSc 79. Ripon Coll Cuddesdon 05. **d** 07 **p** 08. C Hardington Vale *B & W* 07-10; P-in-c Charlcombe w Bath St Steph from 10. *The Rectory, Richmond Place, Bath BA1 5PZ* T: (01225) 466114 M: 07973-350560 E: philiphawthorn@btinternet.com

HAWTHORNE, John William. b 32. St Aug Coll Cant 74. **d** 77 **p** 78. C Boxley *Cant* 77-80; P-in-c Otham 80-82; P-in-c Langley 80-82; R Otham w Langley 82-83; TR Preston w Sutton Poyntz, Littlemoor etc *Sarum* 83-87; R Tetbury w Beverston *Glouc* 87-01; rtd 01; PtO *Ex* from 02; *Sarum* from 06; *Bris* from 14. *19 Long Street, Devizes SN10 1NN* T: (01380) 728056 E: j.hawthorne146@btinternet.com

HAWTHORNE, Canon William James (Jim). b 46. MBE 01. TCD 66 Ch of Ireland Tr Coll 66. **d** 69 **p** 70. C Gilnahirk *D & D* 69-72; Asst Chapl Miss to Seamen 72-76; C Boultham *Linc* 76-78; C Bracebridge Heath 78-90; Dioc Adv for Relig Broadcasting 80-90; Chapl Palma de Mallorca *Eur* 90-01; P-in-c Menorca 97-98; Can Gib Cathl 97-01; rtd 01. *16-08 Victoria Centre, Milton Street, Nottingham NG1 3PL* T: 0115-840 7913 E: williamjameshawthorne@hotmail.com

HAWTHORNE-STEELE, Isobel. **d** 14. Ahoghill w Portglenone *Conn* from 14. *16 Gorman Close, Greenisland, Carrickfergus BT38 8GA* T: (028) 9086 9410 M: 07788-553376 E: i.hawthorne@ulster.ac.uk

✠**HAWTIN, The Rt Revd David Christopher.** b 43. Keble Coll Ox BA 65 MA 70. Wm Temple Coll Rugby 65 Cuddesdon Coll 66. **d** 67 **p** 68 **c** 99. C Pennywell St Thos and Grindon St Oswald CD *Dur* 67-71; C Stockton St Pet 71-74; C-in-c Leam Lane CD 74-79; R Washington 79-88; Dioc Ecum Officer 88-91; Adn Newark *S'well* 92-99; Suff Bp Repton *Derby* 99-06; rtd 06; Hon Asst Bp Sheff from 07. *162 Greenhill Avenue, Sheffield S8 7TF* T: 0114-274 0006

HAY, David Frederick. b 38. Pemb Coll Ox BA 62 MA 67. Qu Coll Birm 82. **d** 84 **p** 85. C Prenton *Ches* 84-88; V Stockport St Sav 88-96; P-in-c Gt Saughall 96-03; rtd 03; PtO *Ches* from 04; Hon Min Can Ches Cathl from 04; PtO *St As* from 09. *2 Moel View Road, Buckley CH7 2BT* T: (01244) 541342 E: dfhay@talktalk.net

HAY, Ian Gordon. b 52. Dundee Univ MA 73 Edin Univ BD 76 CertEd 84. Edin Th Coll 73. **d** 76 **p** 77. C Dumfries *Glas* 76-79; Dioc Chapl *Bre* 79-81; R Brechin 81-85; Asst Chapl H Trin Sch Halifax 85-88; Dioc Youth Officer *Carl* 89-98; Sen Development Worker Youth Link Scotland from 98. *The Ross House, Pittendreich, Kinross KY13 9HD* T: (01592) 840820 E: youthlink-scot@sol.co.uk

HAY, Jack Barr. b 31. Bps' Coll Cheshunt 57. **d** 60 **p** 61. C Byker St Ant *Newc* 60-63; C Killingworth 63-68; V Cowgate 68-77; V Woodhorn w Newbiggin 77-96; rtd 96; PtO *Newc* from 96. *7 Glebelands, Corbridge NE45 5DS* T: (01434) 632979

HAY, Joanna Jane Louise. *See* DOBSON, Joanna Jane Louise

HAY, John. b 45. CITC 77. **d** 79 **p** 80. C Newtownards *D & D* 79-81; I Galloon w Drummully *Clogh* 81-89; I Donacavey w Barr 89-03; Can Clogh Cathl 91-03; Dean Raphoe *D & R* 03-13; I Raphoe w Raymochy and Clonleigh 03-13; rtd 13. *85 Corbally Road, Fintona, Omagh BT78 2JP* T: (028) 8284 0377 M: 07909-530084 E: johnhayfintona@btinternet.com

HAY, John. b 43. St D Coll Lamp 63. **d** 67 **p** 68. C Ynyshir *Llan* 67-70; C Cardiff St Mary and St Steph w St Dyfrig etc 70-74; V Llanwynno 74-78; P-in-c Weston-super-Mare All SS *B & W* 78-80; TV Weston-super-Mare Cen Par 80-85; P-in-c Handsworth St Mich *Birm* 85-86; NSM Eastbourne St Sav and St Pet *Chich* 88-91; V Buckley *St As* 91-96; P-in-c Ardwick St Benedict *Man* 96-99; C Hollinwood and Oldham St Chad Limeside 99-01; rtd 01; Hon C Hampden Park and The Hydnye *Chich* 09-12. *20 Fenners Court, Cambridge Road, Worthing BN11 1XR*

HAY, Miss Lesley Jean Hamilton. b 48. St Andr Univ MA 71. Westcott Ho Cam 04 Yale Div Sch 05. **d** 06 **p** 07. C Shrivenham and Ashbury *Ox* 06-08; C Bethany USA 08; Asst R Hamden 08-10; R Mentone St Jos from 10. *PO Box 161, Mentone AL 35984-0161, USA* T: (001) (256) 634 4476 E: lesleyhay@yahoo.co.uk

HAY, Margaret Ann. b 47. Brunel Univ BTech 71 W Sussex Inst of HE PGCE 95. STETS 02. **d** 05 **p** 06. NSM Elson *Portsm* from 05. *Bodinnick, 12 Longwater Drive, Gosport PO12 2UP* T: (023) 9234 3303

HAY, Mark Alastair. b 71. St Martin's Coll Lanc BA 94. Trin Coll Bris 11. **d** 14 **p** 15. C Longfleet *Sarum* from 14. *32 Linthorpe Road, Poole BH15 2JS* M: 07792-405805 T: (01202) 677573 E: mark.hay@smlpoole.org.uk

HAY, Canon Nicholas John. b 56. Sheff Poly BSc 85. St Jo Coll Nottm 85. **d** 88 **p** 89. C Blackb Redeemer 88-91; C Hellesdon *Nor* 91-95; R Widford *Chelmsf* 95-01; Sen Chapl HM Pris Ashfield 01-09; C Bedminster *Bris* from 09; C Whitchurch 09-15; V Whitchurch St Aug from 15; Hon Can Bris Cathl

from 09. *St Paul's Vicarage, 2 Southville Road, Bristol BS3 1DG* M: 07534-249338 T: 0117-971 1465 E: nickthevichay@googlemail.com

HAY, Richard. b 42. CMG 92. Ball Coll Ox BA 63. Cranmer Hall Dur 94. **d** 96 **p** 97. C Hastings St Clem and All SS *Chich* 96-99; V Addlestone *Guildf* 99-07; RD Runnymede 02-07; rtd 07; PtO *Guildf* from 07. *15 Fox Close, Woking GU22 8LP* T: (01932) 343585 E: richard.hay3@btinternet.com

HAYCOCK, Edward. b 60. **d** 09 **p** 10. OLM Adbaston, High Offley, Knightley, Norbury etc *Lich* 09-13; PtO from 13. *390 New Inn Lane, Stoke-on-Trent ST4 8BW* T: (01782) 641867

HAYCRAFT, Roger Brian Norman. b 43. Oak Hill Th Coll 69. **d** 73 **p** 74. C Belsize Park *Lon* 73-76; C Yardley St Edburgha *Birm* 76-79; V Hornchurch H Cross *Chelmsf* 79-03; rtd 03; PtO *Chelmsf* from 04. *12 Hannards Way, Hainault IG6 3TB* T: (020) 8501 1718

HAYDAY, Canon Alan Geoffrey David. b 46. Kelham Th Coll 65. **d** 69 **p** 70. C Evington *Leic* 69-72; C Spalding St Mary and St Nic *Linc* 72-78; V Cherry Willingham w Greetwell 78-86; RD Lawres 84-86; TR Brumby 86-02; RD Manlake 93-99; Can and Preb Linc Cathl 00-02; Dean St Chris Cathl Bahrain 02-09; Hon Can Bahrain from 09; rtd 09. *22 Kestral Drive, Louth LN11 0GE* T: (01507) 600877 M: 07709-873224 E: windhover22@live.co.uk

HAYDEN, Carol Toni. b 64. Leeds Univ BA 05. NOC 02. **d** 05 **p** 06. NSM Ainsworth *Man* 05-09; NSM Bury St 09-11; TV Radcliffe from 11. *38 Launceston Road, Radcliffe, Manchester M26 3UN* T: 0161-725 9065 M: 07866-995567 E: c_hayden1@sky.com

HAYDEN, The Ven David Frank. b 47. Lon Univ BD 71. Tyndale Hall Bris 67. **d** 71 **p** 72. C Silverhill St Matt *Chich* 71-75; C Galleywood Common *Chelmsf* 75-79; R Redgrave cum Botesdale w Rickinghall *St E* 79-84; RD Hartismere 81-84; V Cromer *Nor* 84-02; P-in-c Gresham 84-98; Chapl Cromer and Distr Hosp Norfolk 84-94; Chapl Norfolk and Nor Health Care NHS Trust 94-00; Chapl Fletcher Hosp Norfolk 85-00; RD Repps *Nor* 95-02; Hon Can Nor Cathl 96-12; Adn Norfolk 02-12; rtd 12; PtO *Nor* from 12. *Church Farm House, Church Lane, Lowestoft NR32 3JN* T: (01502) 456001 E: davidf.hayden@gmail.com

HAYDEN, Eric Henry Ashmore. b 26. ACII 65. Sarum & Wells Th Coll 71. **d** 73 **p** 74. C Horsham *Chich* 73-78; V Cuckfield 78-92; rtd 92; P-in-c Tilshead, Orcheston and Chitterne *Sarum* 92-97; PtO *Ox* 98-08; *Sarum* 98-08; *Chich* from 09. *3 Heather Bank, Haywards Heath RH16 1HY* T: (01444) 412169

✠**HAYDEN, The Rt Revd John Donald.** b 40. Lon Univ BD 62. Tyndale Hall Bris 63. **d** 65 **p** 66 **c** 03. C Macclesfield Ch Ch *Ches* 65-68; C H Spirit Cathl Dodoma Tanzania 68-69; V Moshi 70-77; Home Sec USCL 77-83; TV Ipswich St Mary at Stoke w St Pet *St E* 83-94; P-in-c Bury St Edmunds St Mary 94-99; V 99-04; Asst Bp Mt Kilimanjaro from 04; Hon Asst Bp Ches from 08. *45 Birkenhead Road, Meols, Wirral CH47 5AF* T: 0151-632 0448 E: johndhayden@gmail.com

HAYDEN, Canon Mark Joseph James. b 68. St Thos Aquinas Pontifical Univ Rome BD 93. H Cross Coll Clonliffe 86. **d** 92 **p** 93. In RC Ch 92-99; C Monkstown *D & G* 99-01; I Gorey w Kilnahue, Leskinfere and Ballycanew *C & O* from 01; Can Treas Ferns Cathl from 07. *The Rectory, The Avenue, Gorey, Co Wexford, Republic of Ireland* T/F: (00353) (53) 942 1383 E: gorey@ferns.anglican.org

HAYDOCK, Canon Alan. b 41. Kelham Th Coll 60. **d** 65 **p** 66. C Rainworth *S'well* 65-68; C Hucknall Torkard 68-71; TV 71-74; V Bilborough St Jo 74-80; R E Bridgford 80-82; R E Bridgford and Kneeton 82-06; RD Bingham 84-94; Hon Can S'well Minster 86-06; rtd 06. *29 The Teasels, Bingham, Nottingham NG13 8TY* T: (01949) 875805 M: 07944-569661

HAYDON, Keith Frank. b 46. Southdon Coll 73. **d** 75 **p** 76. C De Beauvoir Town St Pet *Lon* 75-77; C Wells St Thos w Horrington *B & W* 77-80; TV Weston-super-Mare Cen Par 80-84; TV Cowley St Jas *Ox* 84-87; TR 87-95; V Walsingham, Houghton and Barsham *Nor* 95-96; P-in-c 96-99; rtd 01; C Sutton on Plym *Ex* 09-11; C Plymouth St Simon and St Mary 09-11; P-in-c Sutton-on-Plym, Plymouth St Simon and St Mary from 11; P-in-c Plymouth St Gabr from 11. *Address withheld by request*

HAYES, Brian Richard Walker. b 33. Qu Coll Birm 81. **d** 83 **p** 84. C Cheadle Hulme All SS *Ches* 83-87; C Sheff St Cecilia Parson Cross 87-88; C Sheff St Leon Norwood 88-91; V Gazeley w Dalham, Moulton and Kentford *St E* 91-02; P-in-c Higham Green 98-02; rtd 02; Hon C W Felton *Lich* 02-07; PtO 07-10. *8 Lutton Close, Oswestry SY11 2GZ* E: brianhayes@cwcom.net

HAYES, Bruce John. b 75. UCD BA 97 TCD BTh 01. CITC 98. **d** 01 **p** 02. C Cregagh *D & D* 01-04; I Abbeystrewry Union *C, C & R* 04-13; Warden of Readers 08-13; I Dalkey St Patr *D & G* from 13. *The Rectory, Barnacoille Park, Church Road, Dalkey, Co Dublin, Republic of Ireland* T: (00353) (1) 280 3369 M: 86-232 7349 E: brucejohnhayes@gmail.com

HAYES, Carmen Miranda. b 61. TCD BTh 08. **d** 08 **p** 09. C Portadown St Mark *Arm* 08-11; I Kilcronaghan w Draperstown and Sixtowns *D & R* from 11; Bp's Dom Chapl from 12. *Kilcronaghan Rectory, 12 Rectory Road, Tobermore, Magherafelt BT45 5QP* T: (028) 7962 8823 M: 07907-579913 E: carmenmirandahayes@hotmail.com

HAYES, Christopher John. b 64. Univ of Wales BN Leeds Univ MA RGN. Cranmer Hall Dur. **d** 96 **p** 97. C Burton Fleming w Fordon, Grindale etc *York* 96-99; R Buckrose Carrs 99-06; P-in-c Weaverthorpe w Helperthorpe, Luttons Ambo etc 03-06; C Heworth Ch Ch 06-07; PtO from 11; Chapl York Teaching Hosp NHS Foundn Trust from 13. *9 Hunters Way, Norton, Malton YO17 9EG* E: cjhayes@dunelm.org.uk

HAYES, David Malcolm Hollingworth. b 42. K Coll Lon BD 68 AKC 68 MPhil 97. **d** 69 **p** 70. C Upper Teddington SS Pet and Paul *Lon* 69-70; C Ruislip St Martin 70-75; P-in-c Ludford *Heref* 75-80; P-in-c Ashford Carbonell w Ashford Bowdler 75-80; V Eastcote St Lawr *Lon* 80-90; R Cant St Pet w St Alphege and St Marg etc 90-07; P-in-c Blean 03-07; Master Eastbridge Hosp 90-07; Guardian of the Greyfriars 97-07; rtd 07; PtO *Sarum* from 07. *Forge Cottage, 3 North Row, Warminster BA12 9AD* T: (01985) 212929 E: dmhforge@btinternet.com

HAYES, David Roland Payton. b 37. Hertf Coll Ox BA 62 MA 66. Coll of Resurr Mirfield 62. **d** 64 **p** 65. C Woodley St Jo the Ev *Ox* 64-67; C Emscote *Cov* 67-69; C Farnham Royal *Ox* 69-75; P-in-c 75-78; P-in-c Newport Pagnell 78-79; P-in-c Lathbury 78-79; R Newport Pagnell w Lathbury 79-85; R Newport Pagnell w Lathbury and Moulsoe 85-86; P-in-c 86-87; RD Newport 80-85; Chapl Renny Lodge Hosp 85-87; P-in-c Bucknell w Buckton, Llanfair Waterdine and Stowe *Heref* 87-91; V Bucknell w Chapel Lawn, Llanfair Waterdine etc 91-94; RD Clun Forest 91-94; P-in-c Presteigne w Discoed, Kinsham and Lingen 94-00; R Presteigne w Discoed, Kinsham, Lingen and Knill 00-01; rtd 01; PtO *Heref* from 01. *3 Redcar Avenue, Hereford HR4 9TJ* T: (01432) 261466

HAYES, David Thomas. b 70. Leeds Univ BA 09. NOC. **d** 09 **p** 10. NSM Leeds Belle Is St Jo and St Barn *Ripon* 09-12; NSM Aberford w Micklefield *York* from 12; NSM Sherburn in Elmet w Saxton from 12. *15 Windsor Mount, Leeds LS15 7DD* M: 07739-364755 E: dandh.whitkirk.uk@lineone.net

HAYES, Denise Angela. b 62. NOC 02. **d** 05 **p** 06. C Ashton-in-Makerfield St Thos *Liv* 05-10; P-in-c Litherland St Phil 10-14; P-in-c Pemberton St Fran Kitt Green 14-15; V from 14; P-in-c Marsh Green 14-15; V from 15. *St Francis's Vicarage, 42-44 Sherborne Road, Orrell, Wigan WN5 0JA* M: 07736-523168 E: denisehayes4@aol.com

HAYES, Helen. b 45. **d** 10 **p** 11. NSM Bradgate Team *Leic* 10-13; Pioneer P among homeless in W Leic from 13. *32 Hawthorne Drive, Thornton, Leicester LE67 1AW* T: (01530) 231401

HAYES, Canon John Henry Andrew. b 52. BSc. Wycliffe Hall Ox 82. **d** 84 **p** 85. C Moreton *Ches* 84-87; R Barrow 87-94; Bp's Chapl 87-94; P-in-c Runcorn St Mich 94-04; P-in-c Runcorn All SS 94-05; P-in-c Runcorn H Trin 04-05; V Runcorn All SS w H Trin 05-15; Hon Can Ches Cathl 08-15; rtd 15. *Crosbies Cottage, Buxworth, High Peak SK23 7NE* E: revjohnhayes@ntlworld.com

HAYES, Mrs Marion Anne. b 51. Cranmer Hall Dur 04. NOC 02. **d** 05 **p** 06. NSM Runcorn All SS w H Trin *Ches* 05-15; rtd 15. *Crosbies Cottage, Buxworth, High Peak SK23 7NE* E: marion.hayes@hotmail.co.uk

HAYES, Michael Gordon William. b 48. St Cath Coll Cam BA 69 MA 73 PhD 73. Ridley Hall Cam 73. **d** 75 **p** 76. C Combe Down w Monkton Combe *B & W* 75-78; C Cambridge H Trin *Ely* 78-81; V Bathampton *B & W* 81-88; V Clevedon St Andr and Ch Ch 88-95; C Belper *Derby* 95-00; P-in-c Drayton in Hales *Lich* 00-07; RD Hodnet 01-06; P-in-c Chilton Cantelo, Ashington, Mudford, Rimpton etc *B & W* 07-13; rtd 13. *10 Paddock Close, Creech St Michael, Taunton TA3 5DZ* T: (01823) 444766 E: mhhayes.7@btinternet.com

HAYES, Michael John. b 52. Lanc Univ BA 73. Coll of Resurr Mirfield 75. **d** 78 **p** 79. C Notting Hill *Lon* 78-81; C-in-c Hammersmith SS Mich and Geo White City Estate CD 81-88; PtO 98-00; NSM Norwood St Mary 00-03; Chapl Heart of Kent Hospice 05-12; P-in-c Burham and Wouldham *Roch* from 12. *22 Ridley Road, Rochester ME1 1UL* M: 07964-697556 E: mikejhayes@hotmail.com

HAYES, Mrs Miranda Jane. b 57. STETS BA 06. **d** 06 **p** 07. C Dorking w Ranmore *Guildf* 06-10; P-in-c Earls Barton *Pet* from 10; RD Wellingborough from 15. *The Vicarage, 7 High Street, Earls Barton, Northampton NN6 0JG* T: (01604) 810447 E: mail@mirandahayes.org

HAYES, Peter Rowland. b 53. Melbourne Coll of Div BD 82 MMin 05. **d** 82 **p** 83. C Hamilton Australia 82-83; R Wongan Hills w Dalwallinu 84-87; R Kwinana 87-91; CF 91-09; P-in-c

Lurgashall *Chich* from 14; P-in-c N Chapel w Ebernoe from 14. *The Rectory, Northchapel, Petworth GU28 9HP* E: rowls3613@gmail.com

HAYES, Richard. b 39. K Coll Lon BD 68 AKC 68. **d** 69 **p** 70. C Dartford H Trin *Roch* 69-72; C S Kensington St Steph *Lon* 72-76; V Ruislip Manor St Paul 76-82; V Ealing St Pet Mt Park 82-91; R St Edm the King and St Mary Woolnoth etc 91-99; rtd 99; PtO *Lich* 99-04; *Heref* from 00; Hon C Shrewsbury St Alkmund *Lich* 04-07; Hon C Shrewsbury St Chad, St Mary and St Alkmund 07-15; PtO from 15; OCM from 09. *26 St John's Hill, Shrewsbury SY1 1JJ* T: (01743) 244668 E: l.r.hayes@btinternet.com

HAYES, Richard Henry. b 65. St Jo Coll Nottm 89. **d** 92 **p** 93. C Southborough St Pet w Ch Ch and St Matt *Roch* 92-95; C Downend *Bris* 95-97; V Gravesend St Mary *Roch* 97-02; R Clymping and Yapton w Ford *Chich* from 02. *The Rectory, St Mary's Meadow, Yapton, Arundel BN18 0EE* T: (01243) 552962 M: 07944-804933 E: hayesrev@supanet.com

HAYES, Canon Rosemarie Eveline. b 51. Brighton Coll of Educn CertEd 72. NOC 88. **d** 91 **p** 94. Par Dn Manston *Ripon* 91-94; C 94-95; C Beeston 95-00; V Horsforth 00-11; P-in-c Kirkstall 06-11; TR Abbeylands 11-12; P-in-c Kippax w Allerton Bywater *Leeds* from 12; P-in-c Swillington from 12; Hon Can Ripon Cathl from 10. *The Rectory, Church Lane, Kippax, Leeds LS25 7HF* T: 0113-286 2710 E: rosemariehayes@live.co.uk

HAYES, Sarah Caroline. b 61. Man Univ BA 84 Solicitor 90. St Jo Coll Nottm 05 Qu Coll Birm 07. **d** 09 **p** 10. NSM Hall Green St Pet *Birm* 09-13; NSM Edgbaston St Germain from 13. *25 Valentine Road, Birmingham B14 7AN* T: 0121-441 1264 M: 07891-136654 E: sarahhayes2@me.com

HAYES, Sarah Elizabeth. b 63. Ch Coll Cam BA 85 MA 89. Wycliffe Hall Ox 08. **d** 10 **p** 11. C Chipping Campden w Ebrington *Glouc* 10-13; V Horsell *Guildf* from 13. *The Vicarage, Wilson Way, Woking GU21 4QJ* M: 07878-455644 E: sarah@sehayes.co.uk

HAYES, Stephen Anthony. b 57. St Jo Coll Dur BA 80 S Bank Univ PGCE 96. SAOMC 97. **d** 99 **p** 00. NSM Kingham w Churchill, Daylesford and Sarsden *Ox* 99-01; NSM Chipping Norton 01-06; Chapl Kingham Hill Sch from 99-06; Teacher Arnold Lodge Sch Leamington Spa from 06. *9 Hastings Hill, Churchill, Chipping Norton OX7 6NA* T: (01608) 658267 E: hayesfamily@freeuk.com

HAYES, Timothy James. b 62. **d** 89 **p** 90. C Lache cum Saltney *Ches* 89-94; P-in-c Dukinfield St Jo 94-99; V from 99. *37 Harold Avenue, Dukinfield SK16 5NH* T: 0161-308 4708 E: revtimhayes@hotmail.com

HAYHOE, Geoffrey John Stephen. b 57. Portsm Univ BSc 00. Qu Coll Birm 01. **d** 03 **p** 04. C Felixstowe St Jo *St E* 03-06; V Geraldine New Zealand from 06. *The Parish Office, 77 Talbot Street, Geraldine 7930, New Zealand* T: (0064) (3) 693 9691 E: john@hayhoe.net

HAYLER, Mrs Lynn Christina. b 64. **d** 14 **p** 15. C S Cotswolds *Glouc* from 14. *5 Pips Field Way, Fairford GL7 4FG* E: lynnhayler@hotmail.co.uk

HAYLER, Peter John. b 65. R Holloway Coll Lon BSc 87 Univ of Wales (Cardiff) MPhil 01. Wilson Carlile Coll 89 St Mich Coll Llan 99. **d** 00 **p** 04. C Pontnewydd *Mon* 00-03; C Magor 03-06; TV 06-09; C Cambridge Gt St Mary w St Mich *Ely* from 09; Chapl Univ Staff Cam from 09. *35 Pakenham Close, Cambridge CB4 1PW* T: (01223) 510595 *or* 741718 E: pjhayler@virginmedia.com *or* pjh89@cam.ac.uk

HAYLES, Graham David. b 39. Clifton Th Coll 64. **d** 67 **p** 68. C Gipsy Hill Ch Ch *S'wark* 67-70; C Heatherlands St Jo *Sarum* 70-74; V W Streatham St Jas *S'wark* 74-90; TR Hinckley H Trin *Leic* 90-03; rtd 03; PtO *S'wark* 04-14. *19 Park Road, Redhill RH1 1BT* T: (01737) 761732

HAYLETT, David William. b 44. **d** 05 **p** 06. OLM Dorchester *Ox* from 05. *8 Westfield Road, Long Wittenham, Abingdon OX14 4RF* T: (01865) 407382 E: familyhaylett@yahoo.com

HAYLOCK, Mrs Jill Caroline. b 54. ERMC 12. **d** 15. OLM Loddon, Sisland, Chedgrave, Hardley and Langley *Nor* from 15. *Lodge Farm, Sisland, Norwich NR14 6EE* T: (01508) 520248 E: jillhaylock@aol.com

HAYMAN, Mrs Audrey Doris. b 41. St Mary's Coll Chelt 61 Bris Univ CertEd 61 Cov Coll of Educn 65. Glouc Sch of Min 88. **d** 91 **p** 94. NSM Matson *Glouc* 91-98; P-in-c Falfield w Rockhampton 98-02; P-in-c Oldbury-on-Severn 98-02; PtO 02-04; NSM Barnwood from 04. *32 Corncroft Lane, Matson, Gloucester GL4 6XU* T: (01452) 411786 E: audrey.hayman@gmail.com

HAYMAN, Canon Robert Fleming. b 31. Princeton Univ BA 53. Gen Th Sem (NY) MDiv 56. **d** 56 **p** 56. USA 56-88; I Drumcliffe w Lissadell and Munninane *K, E & A* 88-92; Preb Elphin Cathl 88-92; rtd 92. *1102 East Boston Street, Seattle WA 98102-4128, USA* T: (001) (206) 860 7565

HAYNES, Anthony. *See* HAYNES, Michael Anthony Richard

HAYNES, Miss Catherine Mary. b 68. Man Univ BA 90 Win Univ MA 11. St Mich Coll Llan BD 95. **d** 96 **p** 97. C Llantwit Major *Llan* 96-99; C Coity w Nolton 99-01; Dioc Children's Officer 99-01; P-in-c Llangammarch w Llanganten and Llanlleonfel etc *S & B* 01-03; P-in-c Irfon Valley 03-06; R 06-10; V Blaenau Irfon 06-10; Dioc Dir of Educn 02-08; Chapl Haberdashers' Monmouth Sch for Girls from 12; C Monmouth w Overmonnow etc *Mon* from 14; Dioc Children's Adv from 14. *St Thomas's Vicarage, St Thomas Square, Monmouth NP25 5ES* T: (01600) 715159
E: revcmhaynes@btinternet.com

HAYNES, Clifford. b 33. Cam Univ MA 60. Linc Th Coll 80. **d** 82 **p** 83. C Lightcliffe *Wakef* 82-85; V Bradshaw 85-98; rtd 98; PtO *Carl* from 98. *East Lyn, Lazonby, Penrith CA10 1BX*
T: (01768) 897018

HAYNES (née RYDER), Mrs Jennifer Ann. b 40. Bath Spa Univ Coll BSc 99. **d** 04 **p** 06. OLM Potterne w Worton and Marston *Sarum* 04-06; OLM Southbroom 06-14; PtO from 14. *9 Cranesbill Road, Devizes SN10 2TJ* T: (01380) 738536
E: jennifer.a.haynes@hotmail.com

HAYNES, Canon John Richard. b 35. Ely Th Coll 60. **d** 63 **p** 64. C Bollington St Jo *Ches* 63-67; C Ches St Jo 67-68; C Davenham 68-70; Rhodesia 70-80; Zimbabwe 80-90; Sub-Dean Bulawayo Cathl 78-83; Hon Can Matabeleland from 90; V Bishop's Stortford *St Alb* 90-00; rtd 00; PtO *B & W* 01-10; *York* from 11. *33 Dulverton Hall, Esplanade, Scarborough YO11 2AR* T: (01723) 341530

HAYNES, John Stanley. b 30. WMMTC. **d** 82 **p** 83. NSM Westwood *Cov* 82-84; C Radford Semele and Ufton 84-85; V 85-95; rtd 95; PtO *Cov* from 95. *64 Rugby Road, Cubbington, Leamington Spa CV32 7JF* T: (01926) 330016

HAYNES, Michael Anthony Richard (Tony). b 47. Heythrop Coll Lon MA 95 Univ of Wales (Cardiff) LLM 03. NTMTC 98. **d** 00 **p** 01. NSM Tottenham St Paul *Lon* 00-05; Hon C W Green Ch Ch w St Pet from 05. *Christ Church Vicarage, Waldeck Road, London N15 3EP* T: (020) 8889 9677
E: tony.haynes@blueyonder.co.uk

HAYNES, Canon Michael Thomas Avery. b 32. AKC 61. St Boniface Warminster 61. **d** 62 **p** 63. C Hebden Bridge *Wakef* 62-64; C Elland 64-68; V Thornhill Lees 68-82; V Lindley 82-97; Hon Can Wakef Cathl 82-97; rtd 97; PtO *Leeds* from 97. *Longwood Edge Cottage, 86 Lamb Hall Road, Huddersfield HD3 3TJ*

HAYNES, The Very Revd Peter. b 25. Selw Coll Cam BA 49 MA 54. Cuddesdon Coll 50. **d** 52 **p** 53. C Stokesley *York* 52-54; C Hessle 54-58; V Drypool St Jo 58-63; Asst Dir RE *B & W* 63-70; Youth Chapl 63-70; V Glastonbury St Jo 70-72; V Glastonbury St Jo w Godney 72-74; Adn Wells, Can Res and Preb Wells Cathl 74-82; Dean Heref and V Heref St Jo 82-92; rtd 92; PtO *B & W* 92-04; *Heref* 05-09. *5 St John Street, Hereford HR1 2NB*

HAYNES, Peter Nigel Stafford. b 39. Hertf Coll Ox BA 62 MA 66. Cuddesdon Coll 62. **d** 64 **p** 65. C Norwood All SS *Cant* 64-68; C Portsea N End St Mark *Portsm* 68-72; Asst Chapl Brussels *Eur* 72-76; TV Hanbury *Ox* 76-80; Asst Sec (Internat Affairs) Gen Syn Bd Soc Resp 80-85; P-in-c E Peckham and Nettlestead *Roch* 85-92; R Bredgar w Bicknor and Frinsted w Wormshill etc *Cant* 92-99; rtd 99. *1 Vesper Cottage, Cage Lane, Smarden, Ashford TN27 8QD* T: (01233) 770367

HAYNES, Spencer Malcolm. b 46. Sarum & Wells Th Coll 93. **d** 93 **p** 94. C Devonport St Budeaux *Ex* 93-96; TV Tedburn St Mary, Whitestone, Oldridge etc 96-97; rtd 11. *Leander, 23 Silverdale, Silverton, Exeter EX5 4JF* T: (01392) 860885
E: mhaynes@allotment.eclipse.co.uk

HAYNES, Stuart Edward. b 69. Edge Hill Coll of HE BA 91. SNWTP 07. **d** 10 **p** 11. NSM Ormskirk *Liv* from 10. *11 Fairfield Close, Ormskirk L39 1RN* M: 07534-218122
E: stuart.haynes@liverpool.anglican.org

HAYNES, Valerie Elizabeth Mary-Benedict. b 53. Cant Ch Ch Univ BA 09. St Steph Ho Ox 03. **d** 05 **p** 06. C Sheerness H Trin w St Paul *Cant* 05-09; PtO 09-10; P-in-c Skelton w Upleatham *York* 10-14; R from 14; P-in-c Boosbeck and Lingdale 10-14; V from 14. *2 Nidderdale, Skelton-in-Cleveland, Saltburn-by-the-Sea TS12 2FY* T: (01287) 654040 M: 07803-798475
E: revhaynes@btinternet.com

HAYNS, Mrs Clare Julia Yates. b 69. Warwick Univ BA 91 R Holloway Coll Lon MSc 95 DipSW 95. Ripon Coll Cuddesdon 08. **d** 11 **p** 12. C Blenheim *Ox* 11-15. *Rectory Farm House, 2 Church Street, Bladon, Woodstock OX20 1RS* M: 07801-930702 E: clare@hayns.com

HAYSMORE, Geoffrey Frederick. b 39. Bps' Coll Cheshunt 63. **d** 66 **p** 67. C St Marylebone St Mark w St Luke *Lon* 66-69; C Stockton St Chad *Dur* 69-72; C-in-c Town End Farm CD 72-77; PtO *York* from 95; rtd 01. *139 Lambton Road, Middlesbrough TS4 2ST* T: (01642) 275259

HAYTER, Mark Harrison George. b 49. Newc Univ BA 72. WEMTC 10. **d** 12 **p** 13. NSM St Weonards *Heref* 12-14; C Nadder Valley *Sarum* from 14. *Address temp unknown*
E: haytermhg@btinternet.com

HAYTER, Mary Elizabeth. *See* BARR, Mary Elizabeth

HAYTER, Canon Raymond William. b 48. Oak Hill Th Coll 74. **d** 77 **p** 78. C Bermondsey St Jas w Ch Ch *S'wark* 77-80; C Sydenham H Trin 81-83; Asst Chapl HM Pris Brixton 83-84; Chapl HM Youth Cust Cen Stoke Heath 84-88; Chapl HM Pris Maidstone 88-91; CF 91-08; Chapl HM Pris Standford Hill 08-11; Min Can St Woolos Cathl 11-14; Can Pastor from 14. *Canon's House, Stow Hill, Newport NP20 4EA*

HAYTER, Sandra. *See* RAILTON, Sandra

HAYTON, John Anthony. b 45. TD 81. Heythrop Coll Lon MA 00 ACII 70. Oak Hill Th Coll 93. **d** 96 **p** 97. NSM St Alb St Mich *St Alb* from 96; OCM 02-08. *89 Harpenden Road, St Albans AL3 6BY* T: (01727) 761719 *or* 835037 F: 811744
E: john.hayton@ntlworld.com

HAYTON, Mark William. b 59. St Steph Ho Ox 85. **d** 88 **p** 89. C Sittingbourne St Mich *Cant* 88-91; C Kennington 91-94; R Broadstairs 94-07; RD Thanet 96-01; P-in-c Folkestone Trin 07-11; V 11-14; AD Elham 11-14; V Fleet *Guildf* from 14. *The Vicarage, Branksomewood Road, Fleet GU51 4JU* T: (01252) 219281 E: markhayton@supanet.com

HAYTON, Norman Joseph Patrick. b 32. MRICS 57. Sarum Th Coll 69. **d** 71 **p** 72. C Lytham St Cuth *Blackb* 71-74; V Wesham 74-79; V Chorley St Geo 79-80; NSM Kells *Carl* 84-85; P-in-c Flimby 85-90; V Barrow St Jas 90-94; TV Egremont and Haile 94-97; P-in-c Distington 97-00; rtd 00; P-in-c Charnock Richard *Blackb* 01-05; PtO *Ches* 05-11; *Derby* 11-13; *Leic* from 13. *1 Stuart Court, High Street, Kibworth, Leicester LE8 0LR* T: 0116-279 1568
E: normanhayton@hotmail.com

HAYWARD, Canon Christopher Joseph. b 38. TCD BA 63 MA 67. Ridley Hall Cam 63. **d** 65 **p** 66. C Hatcham St Jas *S'wark* 65-69; Warden Lee Abbey Internat Students' Club Kensington 69-74; Chapl Chelmsf Cathl 74-77; P-in-c Darlaston All SS *Lich* 77-83; Ind Chapl 77-83; Can Res Bradf Cathl 83-92; Sec Bd Miss 83-92; R Linton in Craven *Bradf* 92-03; P-in-c Burnsall w Rylstone 97-03; RD Skipton 93-98; Hon Can Bradf Cathl 92-03; rtd 03; PtO *Leeds* from 04. *12 Ron Lawton Crescent, Burley in Wharfedale, Ilkley LS29 7ST* T: (01943) 865261 E: chris.hayward@bradford.anglican.org

HAYWARD, Jane. *See* HAYWARD, Pamela Jane

HAYWARD, Jeffrey Kenneth. b 47. St Jo Coll Nottm BTh 74. **d** 74 **p** 75. C Stambermill *Worc* 74-77; C Woking St Jo *Guildf* 77-83; V Springfield H Trin *Chelmsf* 83-98; Chapl HM Pris Chelmsf 86-00; Area RD Chelmsf 86-88; RD Chelmsf 88-93; RD Chelmsf N 93-95; Hon Can Chelmsf Cathl 93-98; Chapl HM Pris Wakef 00-05; Chapl HM Pris Long Lartin 05-12; rtd 12; PtO *Chelmsf* from 14. *4 Durham Close, Great Bardfield, Braintree CM7 4UA* T: (01371) 810827

HAYWARD, Mrs Jennifer Dawn. b 38. WMMTC 85. **d** 88 **p** 94. NSM Gt Malvern St Mary *Worc* 88-90; NSM Gt Malvern Ch Ch 88-90; Par Dn 90-94; C 94-96; TV Wirksworth *Derby* 96-04; rtd 04; PtO *Worc* from 04. *26 Barley Crescent, Long Meadow, Worcester WR4 0HW* T: (01905) 29545 M: 07963-089437
E: revjenniehayward@gmail.com

HAYWARD, John Andrew. b 63. Nottm Univ BTh 89 MHCIMA 83. Linc Th Coll 86. **d** 89 **p** 90. C Seaford w Sutton *Chich* 89-92; C St Pancras H Cross w St Jude and St Pet *Lon* 92-95; V Kentish Town St Martin w St Andr 95-08; AD S Camden 05-08; V Merton St Mary *S'wark* from 08. *The Vicarage, 3 Church Path, London SW19 3HJ* T: (020) 8543 6192
E: vicar@stmarysmerton.org.uk

HAYWARD, Preb John Talbot. b 28. Selw Coll Cam BA 52 MA 56. Wells Th Coll 52. **d** 54 **p** 55. C S Lyncombe *B & W* 54-58; R Lamyatt 58-71; V Bruton w Wyke Champflower and Redlynch 58-71; RD Bruton 62-71; P-in-c Weston-super-Mare St Jo 71-75; Preb Wells Cathl 73-03; TR Weston-super-Mare Cen Par 75-92; rtd 92; PtO *B & W* from 92. *5 Chelswood Avenue, Weston-super-Mare BS22 8QP* T: (01934) 628431

HAYWARD, Martin. b 45. WMMTC 07. **d** 07 **p** 08. Dir Internat Min *Cov* 07-08; NSM Cov St Fran N Radford 07-12; Dean's V Cov Cathl 10-12; rtd 12; PtO *S'wark* from 12. *31 Waterside Court, Millpond Place, Carshalton SM5 2JT*
T: (020) 8652 0551 M: 07917-182579
E: martin.hayward12@sky.com

HAYWARD, Ms Pamela Jane. b 52. RGN 82. Westcott Ho Cam 84. **d** 87 **p** 94. Par Dn Northampton St Mary *Pet* 87-90; Par Dn Bris St Mary Redcliffe w Temple etc 90-94; V Eastville St Anne w St Mark and St Thos 96-13; rtd 13. *18 Tilley Hill Close, Oundle, Peterborough PE8 4PU*
E: janehayward266@btinternet.com

HAYWARD, Peter Noel. b 26. Leeds Univ BA 48 BD 78. Coll of Resurr Mirfield 48. **d** 50 **p** 51. C S Elmsall *Wakef* 50-56; C Sheldon *Birm* 56-60; C-in-c Garretts Green CD 60-69;

V Garretts Green 69-70; V N Cave w Cliffe *York* 70-00; R Hotham 70-00; RD Howden 78-86; P-in-c Newbald 97-00; rtd 00; PtO *Carl* from 00. *The Old Chapel, Allonby, Maryport CA15 6QH* T: (01900) 881466

HAYWARD, Mrs Sarah Lynn. b 77. St Mary's Coll Strawberry Hill BA 99. St Jo Coll Nottm MTh 06. d 08 p 09. C Dibden *Win* 08-13; P-in-c Braintree St Paul *Chelmsf* from 13. *The Vicarage, Hay Lane South, Braintree CM7 3DY* T: (01376) 325095 M: 07828-046193 E: sarah.hayward@talktalk.net

HAYWARD, Timothy David Mark. b 78. St Andr Univ MTheol 00. Westcott Ho Cam 07. d 09 p 10. C Buckden w the Offords *Ely* 09-12; V Bunbury and Tilstone Fearnall *Ches* from 12. *The New Vicarage, Vicarage Lane, Bunbury, Tarporley CW6 9PE* T: (01829) 261511 M: 07988-994481 E: timhayward@hotmail.co.uk

HAYWARD-WRIGHT, Mrs Diane. b 51. WEMTC 06. d 09 p 10. NSM Inkberrow w Cookhill and Kington w Dormston *Worc* from 09. *1 Church Drive, Cookhill, Alcester B49 5JH* T: (01527) 892727 M: 07815-520107 E: diane@shopwright.co.uk

HAYWOOD, James William. b 36. Chich Th Coll 69. d 73 p 74. C Leeds Halton St Wilfrid *Ripon* 73-76; C Workington St Jo *Carl* 76-78; V Clifton 78-84; P-in-c Barrow St Jas 84-85; V 85-89; V Crosby Ravensworth 89-94; R Asby 89-94; V Bolton 89-94; rtd 98. *19 Bramham Road, Whitwood, Castleford WF10 5PA*

HAYWOOD, Preb Keith Roderick. b 48. Oak Hill Th Coll 84. d 86 p 87. C Fazeley *Lich* 86-90; TV Leek and Meerbrook 90-01; Acting TR Hanley H Ev 01-03; TR 03-13; Preb Lich Cathl 07-13; rtd 13; PtO *Lich* from 14. *135 Chase Road, Burntwood WS7 0EB* E: keithrhaywood@gmail.com

HAZEL, Sister. *See* SMITH, Hazel Ferguson Waide

HAZELL, The Ven Frederick Roy. b 30. Fitzw Ho Cam BA 53 MA 59. Cuddesdon Coll 54. d 56 p 57. C Ilkeston St Mary *Derby* 56-59; C Heanor 59-62; V Marlpool 62-63; Chapl Univ of W Indies 63-66; C St Martin-in-the-Fields *Lon* 66-68; V Croydon H Sav *Cant* 68-84; RD Croydon 72-77; Hon Can Cant Cathl 73-84; P-in-c Croydon H Trin 77-80; Adn Croydon *S'wark* 84-93; rtd 93; P-in-c Chard, Furnham w Chaffcombe, Knowle St Giles etc *B & W* 95-99; P-in-c Tardebigge *Worc* 00-03; PtO *Birm* 00-11; *Worc* 04-11. *27 Ramsay Hall, 9-13 Byron Road, Worthing BN11 3HN* T: (01903) 217108

HAZELL, Thomas Jeremy. b 35. Bris Univ LLB 56 PhD 01. St D Coll Lamp 56. d 58 p 59. C Newport St Paul *Mon* 58-61; C Derby St Jo 61-64; V Arksey *Sheff* 64-69; Sen Student Cllr Univ of Wales (Cardiff) *Llan* 69-89; rtd 95. *Castlewood Barn, Ponde, Llandefalle, Brecon LD3 0NR* T: (01874) 754030

HAZELTON, Michael John. b 53. UEA BA 76 Bedf Coll Lon PhD 81 Heythrop Coll Lon BD 89. d 90 p 91. Asst Chapl Helsinki *Eur* 94-95; Asst Chapl Zürich w Winterthur 95-98; R Mablethorpe w Trusthorpe *Linc* 98-02; R Saxonwell 02-05; V Danby w Castleton and Commondale *York* from 05; V Westerdale from 05; V Moorsholm from 09. *The Vicarage, Yall Flats Lane, Danby, Whitby YO21 2NQ* T: (01287) 660388 E: mjh_uk@hotmail.com

HAZELWOOD, Ms Jillian. b 32. Bp Otter Coll CertEd 52 St Alb Minl Tr Scheme 82. d 87 p 94. NSM Wheathampstead *St Alb* 87-02; PtO from 02. *14 Butterfield Road, Wheathampstead, St Albans AL4 8PU* T/F: (01582) 833146

HAZLEHURST, Anthony Robin. b 43. Man Univ BSc 64. Tyndale Hall Bris 65. d 68 p 69. C Macclesfield Ch Ch *Ches* 68-71; C Bushbury *Lich* 71-75; P-in-c New Clee *Linc* 75-85; TV Deane *Man* 85-96; V Harwood 96-07; rtd 07; PtO *Man* from 07. *1 Maybury Close, Ramsbottom, Bury BL0 9WG* T: (01706) 281661 E: robinhaz@btinternet.com

HAZLEHURST, David. b 32. Liv Univ BSc 54. St Steph Ho Ox 55. d 57 p 58. C Sheff Arbourthorne 57-59; C Doncaster Ch Ch 59-61; C W Wycombe *Ox* 61-63; P-in-c Collyhurst St Jas *Man* 66-67; V Blackrod 67-79; V Halliwell St Marg 79-84; R Sutton St Nic *S'wark* 84-94; rtd 94; PtO *S'wark* 95-13; *Guildf* 95-99. *Cullum Welch Court (Nursing), Morden College, 19 St Germans Place, London SE3 0PW* T: (020) 8463 8454

HAZLEHURST, David John Benedict (Benny). b 63. Trin Coll Bris 88. d 91 p 92. C Plumstead St Jo w St Jas and St Paul *S'wark* 91-98; Estates Outreach Worker (S'wark Adnry) 98-02; V Brixton Road Ch Ch 02-05; R Puddletown, Tolpuddle and Milborne w Dewlish *Sarum* 05-11; PtO 11-13; Asst Chapl HM Pris Dorchester 12-13; Asst Chapl HM YOI Portland from 13. *HM Young Offender Institution, The Grove, Grove Road, Portland DT5 1DL* T: (01305) 715600 M: 07788-426090 E: benny@somail.it

HAZLEHURST, Robin. *See* HAZLEHURST, Anthony Robin

HAZLETT, Stephen David. b 56. TCD BTh 88. CITC 85. d 88 p 89. C Ballywillan *Conn* 88-90; I Rathcoole 90-95; I Dunluce 95-00; Ind Chapl *Dur* 00-12; TV Sunderland 00-07; Chapl Sunderland Minster 07-12; Chapl Rotterdam w Schiedam Miss to Seafarers *Eur* from 12; Hon C Rotterdam from 12. *Jan Steenstraat,*

3117 TC Schiedam, The Netherlands M: 07900-231360 E: stephen.hazlett@lineone.net

HAZLEWOOD, Canon Andrew Lord. b 54. Essex Univ BSc 76. Wycliffe Hall Ox. d 82 p 83. C Leckhampton SS Phil and Jas w Cheltenham St Jas *Glouc* 82-85; C Waltham H Cross *Chelmsf* 85-89; R Pedmore *Worc* 89-15; P-in-c Wollaston 09-13; RD Stourbridge 07-13; Hon Can Worc Cathl 10-15; rtd 15. *Address temp unknown* T: (01562) 884856 *or* 887287 E: andrewhazlewood@gmail.com

HAZLEWOOD, David Paul. b 47. Sheff Univ MB, ChB 70 Campion Hall Ox BA 72 MA 77. Wycliffe Hall Ox 70. d 73 p 74. C Chapeltown *Sheff* 73-75; Singapore 76; Indonesia 76-88; R Ipswich St Helen *St E* 88-97; V Shirley *Win* 97-11; rtd 11; PtO *Llan* 11-14. *7 Hanson Road, Liskeard PL14 3NT* T: (01579) 324848 E: david.hazlewood@ukgateway.net

HAZLEWOOD, William Peter Guy. b 71. De Montfort Univ BA 97. St Steph Ho Ox BTh 01. d 01 p 02. C Knowle H Nativity and Easton All Hallows *Bris* 01-04; P-in-c Iver Heath *Ox* 04-08; R 08-11; P-in-c Dartmouth and Dittisham *Ex* from 11. *The Vicarage, 79 Seymour Drive, Dartmouth TQ6 9GE* T: (01803) 414767 E: frwill@hazlewoodhq.co.uk

HEAD, David Nicholas. b 55. Pemb Coll Cam BA 77 MA 81 Westmr Coll of Educn MTh 01. Westcott Ho Cam 78. d 81 p 82. C Surbiton St Andr and St Mark *S'wark* 81-84; C St Marylebone w H Trin *Lon* 84-89; TV Clapham Team *S'wark* 89-96; Chapl Trin Hospice Lon 89-96; Chapl Princess Alice Hospice Esher 96-03; R Lyng, Sparham, Elsing, Bylaugh, Bawdeswell etc *Nor* 03-14; RD Sparham 13-14; R Aylmerton, Runton, Beeston Regis and Gresham from 14. *The Rectory, Cromer Road, West Runton, Cromer NR27 9QT* T: (01263) 838773 E: david@davidhead.plus.com

HEAD, Canon Derek Leonard Hamilton. b 34. ALCD 58. d 58 p 59. C Bexleyheath Ch Ch *Roch* 58-61; C Wisley w Pyrford *Guildf* 61-66; C-in-c Ewell St Paul Howell Hill CD 66-73; R Headley All SS 73-81; TR 81-82; RD Farnham 80-82; V Chertsey 82-99; Hon Can Guildf Cathl 83-99; RD Runnymede 88-93; Dir Post-Ord Tr 90-94; rtd 99; PtO *Win* from 00. *9 Tangmere Close, Mudeford, Christchurch BH23 4LZ* T: (01425) 276545 E: headd@onetel.com

HEAD, Canon Ivan Francis. b 53. Univ of W Aus BA 75 Glas Univ PhD 85. Melbourne Coll of Div BD 78. d 79 p 79. Australia 79-81 and from 85; C Uddingston *Glas* 81-85; C Cambuslang 81-85; Dir Angl Inst Theol Perth 85-91; Warden Ch Coll Tasmania Univ 91-94; Warden St Paul's Coll Sydney Univ from 95. *St Paul's College, University of Sydney NSW 2006, Australia* T: (0061) (2) 9550 7444 *or* 9557 1447 F: 9519 7244 E: ihead@mail.usyd.edu.au

HEAD, Peter Ernest. b 38. Lon Univ BSc 59. Ridley Hall Cam 61. d 63 p 64. C Fulwood *Sheff* 63-66; C Belper *Derby* 66-68; Hd RE Shoeburyness Sch Southend-on-Sea 69-74; Hd RE Bilborough Coll 74-79; Public Preacher *S'well* 74-79; NSM Bramcote 74-79; Vice-Prin Totton Coll Southn 79-93; Hon C Hordle *Win* 94-02; rtd 03; PtO *Win* from 02. *44 Lentune Way, Lymington SO41 3PF* T/F: (01590) 678097 E: peter_head@bigfoot.com

HEADING, Margaret Anne. b 66. Leeds Univ BSc 88 Man Univ PhD 91 Aston Univ PGCE 99. Wycliffe Hall Ox BA 01. d 02 p 03. C Fletchamstead *Cov* 02-05; V Ingleby Greenhow, Bilsdale Priory etc *York* from 05. *3 Holmemead, Great Broughton, Middlesbrough TS9 7HQ* T: (01642) 710045 E: anne.heading@tesco.net

HEADING, Canon Richard Vaughan. b 43. Lon Univ BSc 65 ARCS 65. Coll of Resurr Mirfield 66. d 68 p 69. C Heref St Martin 68-75; P-in-c Birches Head and Northwood *Lich* 75-77; TV Hanley H Ev 77-82; V Heref H Trin 82-92; TR Bedminster *Bris* 92-08; AD Bris S 01-06; Hon Can Bris Cathl 01-08; rtd 08; PtO *Worc* from 09. *18 Timberdine Avenue, Worcester WR5 2BD* T: (01905) 360998 E: richard.heading@gmx.co.uk

HEADLAND, James Frederick. b 20. Clifton Th Coll 51. d 53 p 54. C Barnsbury St Andr *Lon* 53-55; C Spitalfields Ch Ch w All SS 55-57; V Upper Tulse Hill St Matthias *S'wark* 57-65; R Church Pulverbatch *Heref* 65-81; P-in-c Smethcott w Woolstaston 65-81; R Reedham w Cantley w Limpenhoe and Southwood *Nor* 81-86; rtd 86; PtO *Heref* 86-13; *Lich* 88-00. *3 Ashford Avenue, Pontesbury, Shrewsbury SY5 0QN* T: (01743) 790565

HEADLEY, Miss Carolyn Jane. b 50. K Coll Lon MA 94 MCSP 71. Oak Hill Th Coll BA 83. dss 83 d 87 p 94. Kensal Rise St Mark and St Martin *Lon* 83-87; Par Dn Uxbridge 87-90; Team Dn 90-92; Warden of Readers (Willesden Area) 88-92; Tutor Wycliffe Hall Ox 94-05; P-in-c W Meon and Warnford *Portsm* 05-07; Chapl Portsm Hosps NHS Trust 07-11; Chapl Team Ldr 11-13; PtO *Portsm* 13-14; Chapl Epsom and St Helier Univ Hosps NHS Trust 14; PtO *S'wark* from 15. *17 Hawkwood Rise, Bookham, Leatherhead KT23 4JS* T: (01372) 456330 M: 07777-617516 E: carolynheadley@btinternet.com

HEAGERTY, Alistair John. b 42. MBE 86. Oriel Coll Ox BA 63 MA 67. Lon Coll of Div BD 68. **d** 68 **p** 69. C Margate H Trin *Cant* 68-72; CF 72-97; Chapl R Memorial Chpl Sandhurst 92-97; TV Kingswood *Bris* 97-08; rtd 08. *44 Ferney Road, East Barnet, Barnet EN4 8LF* T: (020) 3234 1003
E: alistair@heagerty.freeserve.co.uk

HEAK, Philip George. b 70. QUB BA 92. CITC BTh 95. **d** 95 **p** 96. C Ballymacash *Conn* 95-98; C Galway w Kilcummin *T, K & A* 98-00; Dioc Youth Officer (Cashel) *C & O* 00-06; I Naas w Kill and Rathmore *M & K* from 06. *15 Spring Gardens, Naas, Co Kildare, Republic of Ireland* T: (00353) (45) 897206 M: 86-817 2356 E: pheak@eircom.net

HEAL, David Walter. b 37. Ox Univ MA 63. Trin Coll Carmarthen 87. **d** 90 **p** 91. NSM Henfynyw w Aberaeron and Llanddewi Aberarth *St D* 90-96; Hon Asst Chapl Algarve *Eur* 96-98; Chapl Madeira 98-03; rtd 03; PtO *St D* from 04. *Cae Gwair Bach, Llanon SY23 5LZ* T: (01974) 202596

HEAL, Miss Felicity Joan. b 42. Portsm Dioc Tr Course 89. **d** 92. NSM Bramshott and Liphook *Portsm* 92-95; NSM Blendworth w Chalton w Idsworth 95-97; PtO from 97. *25 College Street, Petersfield GU31 4AG* T: (01730) 260410 M: 07712-249608
E: fj.heal@ntlworld.com

HEALD, William Roland. b 40. St Jo Coll Auckland 72. **d** 74 **p** 75. C Howick New Zealand 74; C Kaitaia 75; C Auckland St Paul Symonds Street 76-78; C Bournville *Birm* 78-79; V Henderson New Zealand 79-82; V S Kensington St Luke *Lon* 93-07; rtd 07; V Kaitaia New Zealand 07-13. *408/42 Herd Road, Hillsborough, Auckland 1042, New Zealand*
E: bill.heald@virgin.net

HEALE, Nicholas James. b 67. St Cath Coll Ox BA 89 DPhil 95 Leeds Univ BA 94. Coll of Resurr Mirfield 95. **d** 95 **p** 96. C Syston *Leic* 95-99; V Blackpool St Mich *Blackb* 99-10; P-in-c Skerton St Chad 10-15; V from 15. *St Chad's Vicarage, 1 St Chad's Drive, Lancaster LA1 2SE* T: (01524) 63816

HEALE, Walter James Grenville. b 40. Wycliffe Hall Ox 77. **d** 79 **p** 80. C Walsall *Lich* 79-82; TV Marfleet *York* 82-89; TR 89-94; R Easington w Skeffling, Kilnsea and Holmpton 94-05; P-in-c Owthorne and Rimswell w Withernsea 00-05; rtd 05; P-in-c Easington w Skeffling, Kilnsea and Holmpton *York* 05-06; PtO from 06. *18 Sloe Lane, Beverley HU17 8ND* T: (01482) 865915

HEALES, Canon John. b 48. K Coll Lon BD 71 AKC 71 PGCE 72. St Mich Coll Llan 75. **d** 76 **p** 77. C Cwmbran *Mon* 76-78; Chapl Rendcomb Coll Cirencester 78-82; Chapl Mon Sch 84-88; V Penhow, St Brides Netherwent w Llandavenny etc *Mon* 88-14; Hon Can St Woolos Cathl 11-14; rtd 14. *26 The Paddocks, Undy, Caldicot NP26 3TD* T: (01633) 881655

HEALEY, Mrs Hilary Louise. b 51. RSCN 73 SRN 73. STETS 10. **d** 13 **p** 14. NSM Ampfield, Chilworth and N Baddesley *Win* from 13. *178 Oliver's Battery Road South, Winchester SO22 4LF* T: (01962) 865923 M: 07443-437472
E: hilary.healey@ntlworld.com

HEALEY, James Christopher. b 44. Linc Th Coll 84. **d** 86 **p** 87. C Boultham *Linc* 86-90; TV Gt Grimsby St Mary and St Jas 90-91; I Narraghmore and Timolin w Castledermot etc *D & G* 91-93; I New Ross *C & O* 93-97; Dean Lismore 97-99; I Lismore w Cappoquin, Kilwatermoy, Dungarvan etc 97-99; Chan Cashel Cathl 97-99; Prec Waterford Cathl 97-99; Can Ossory Cathl 97-99; I Arvagh w Carrigallen, Gowna and Columbkille *K, E & A* 99-02; P-in-c Winthorpe and Langford w Holme S'well 02-03; R Coddington and Winthorpe and Langford w Holme 03-05; rtd 05. *12 Ridgeway, Nettleham, Lincoln LN2 2TL* T: (01522) 753622

HEALEY, Michael Harry Edmund. b 74. Mansf Coll Ox MA 01 Leeds Univ BA 03. Coll of Resurr Mirfield 01. **d** 04 **p** 05. C Norton *Sheff* 04-07; P-in-c Beighton from 07. *The Vicarage, 27 Tynker Avenue, Beighton, Sheffield S20 1DX* T: 0114-248 7635 E: mhehealey@hotmail.com

HEALY (née THOROLD), Mrs Alison Susan Joy. b 59. St Jo Coll Dur BA 80. Ripon Coll Cuddesdon 97 SEITE 03. **d** 06 **p** 07. NSM Shooters Hill Ch Ch *S'wark* 06-11; PtO 12-13; R Brant Broughton and Beckingham *Linc* from 13; R Leadenham from 13; R Welbourn from 13; P-in-c Caythorpe from 13. *The Rectory, Church End, Fulbeck Road, Leadenham, Lincoln LN5 0PX* M: 07962-318728 E: vicardancer@supanet.com

HEANEY, Eileen. b 59. **d** 11 **p** 12. NSM Burscough Bridge *Liv* 11-13; NSM Scarisbrick from 13. *473 Southport Road, Scarisbrick, Ormskirk L40 9RF*

HEANEY, Canon James Roland. b 59. **d** 85 **p** 86. C Ballynafeigh St Jude *D & D* 85-88; C Lisburn Ch Ch Cathl 88-90; I Dungannon w Redcross and Conary *D & D* from 90; Can Ch Ch Cathl Dublin from 05. *The Rectory, Redcross, Co Wicklow, Republic of Ireland* T/F: (00353) (404) 41637
E: rolyheaney@gmail.com

HEANEY, Michael Roger. b 43. TCD BA 66 HDipEd 67 MA 69. CITC 74. **d** 76 **p** 77. Chapl St Columba's Coll Dub 76-09; rtd 09. *Montana, Scholarstown Road, Dublin 16, Republic of Ireland* T: (00353) (1) 493 1167 M: 86-265 1791
E: revmheaney@gmail.com

HEANEY, Robert Stewart. b 40. **d** 01 **p** 02. C Dunboyne Union *M & K* 01-04; PtO *Ox* from 05; Sen Lect St Jo Univ Tanzania 10-12; Asst Prof Virginia Th Sem USA from 13; Dir Cen for Angl Communion Studies from 13. *Virginia Theological Seminary, 3737 Seminary Road, Alexandria, VA 22304, USA* T: (001) (703) 370 6600 E: robert.s.heaney@gmail.com

HEANEY, Samuel Stewart. b 44. Open Univ BA 79 Ulster Univ BEd 83 Lon Univ BD 93 QUB MPhil 99. St Deiniol's Hawarden 92. **d** 92 **p** 93. In Presbyterian Ch 85-92; C Knockbreda *D & D* 92-96; I Belfast H Trin and St Silas *Conn* 96-02; I Ballyrashane w Kildollagh 02-09; rtd 09. *3 Edgewood Court, Antrim BT41 4PG* T: (028) 9446 1076
E: stewartheaney@yahoo.co.uk

HEANEY, Timothy Daniel. b 59. Trin Coll Bris BA 04. **d** 04 **p** 05. C Dursley *Glouc* 04-08; P-in-c Paul *Truro* 08-12; Assoc Chapl Dubai and Sharjah w N Emirates from 12. *PO Box 7415, Dubai, UAE* T: (00971) (4) 336 4899 M: (5) 6114 0231
E: tim@heaney.org.uk *or* htchaplain@holytrinity.ae

HEANEY, Wendy Anne. b 42. St Alb Minl Tr Scheme 90. **d** 95 **p** 96. NSM Clifton and Southill *St Alb* 95-99; Asst Chapl HM Pris Bedf 95-99; Chapl 99-02; LtO *St Alb* 99 02; PtO *St Alb* from 03. *34 Meadow Way, Letchworth Garden City SG6 3JB* T: (01462) 641303

HEAP, David Leonard. b 58. Man Univ BA 79. Cranmer Hall Dur 82. **d** 85 **p** 86. C Clitheroe St Jas *Blackb* 85-88; C Blackb St Gabr 88-92; V Bare from 92. *St Christopher's Vicarage, 12 Elm Grove, Morecambe LA4 6AT* T: (01524) 411363
E: davidheap@readingroom.freeserve.co.uk

HEAPS, Richard Peter. b 35. Bernard Gilpin Soc Dur 58 Qu Coll Birm 58. **d** 61 **p** 62. C Castle Bromwich SS Mary and Marg *Birm* 61-65; C-in-c Erdington St Chad CD 65-70; V Nechells 70-81; RD Aston 75-81; V Marston Green 81-86; P-in-c Shrawley and Witley w Astley *Worc* 86-92; R Shrawley, Witley, Astley and Abberley 92-01; rtd 01; PtO *Worc* from 01. *9 Timberdyne Close, Rock, Kidderminster DY14 9RT* T: (01299) 832376

HEARD, James Barrie. b 66. Brunel Univ BA 98 K Coll Lon MA 01. Ridley Hall Cam 03. **d** 06 **p** 07. C Fulham All SS *Lon* 06-09; C Chelsea St Luke and Ch Ch 09-13; P-in-c Holland Park from 13. *2 Aubrey Walk, London W8 7JG* M: 07867-508919

HEARD, Richard Adrian. b 72. Univ of Wales (Swansea) BSc 94 Hull Univ PGCE 96. St Jo Coll Nottm 06. **d** 08 **p** 09. C Hackenthorpe *Sheff* 08-11; V Hexthorpe from 11. *The Vicarage, 39 Sturton Close, Doncaster DN4 7JG* T: (01302) 953342 M: 07818-850347 E: rev.richardheard@yahoo.co.uk

HEARD, Stephen Edward. b 53. NTMTC 02. **d** 04 **p** 08. NSM Bush Hill Park St Mark *Lon* from 04; NSM Bush Hill Park St Steph from 13; Parliamentary Chapl to Bp Lon from 07. *Old Deanery, Dean's Yard, London EC4V 5AA* T: (020) 7638 9501 *or* 7248 6233 M: 07939-263657
E: stephen.heard3@btinternet.com

HEARL, Maria Christina. b 47. New Hall Cam BA 69 Ex Univ MA 98 PhD 07 PGCE 70. SWMTC 03. **d** 07 **p** 08. NSM Ex St Dav 07-13; PtO *B & W* 13-15; NSM Wellington and Distr from 15. *16 Twyford Place, Tiverton EX16 6AP* T: (01884) 256380 E: rev.maria@stdavidschurchexeter.org.uk

HEARN, John Henry. b 49. Trin Coll Bris. **d** 82 **p** 83. C Epsom Common Ch Ch *Guildf* 82-85; C Ringwood *Win* 85-88; Chapl Basingstoke Distr Hosp 88-91; Chapl Luton and Dunstable Hosp 91-96; C Ampthill w Millbrook and Steppingley *St Alb* 96-99; P-in-c Wymington w Podington 99-03; V W Acklam *York* 03-14; rtd 14; PtO *Dur* from 14. *18 Thurso Close, Stockton-on-Tees TS19 7JD* E: john.hearn@tesco.net

HEARN, Jonathan. b 58. Leeds Univ BA 81 GradIPM 85. Westcott Ho Cam 89. **d** 91 **p** 92. C Tuffley *Glouc* 91-94; C Milton *Win* 94-02; P-in-c Warwick St Paul *Cov* 02-03; TV Warwick from 03. *St Paul's Vicarage, 33 Stratford Road, Warwick CV34 6AS* T: (01926) 419814

HEARN, Canon Peter Brian. b 31. St Jo Coll Dur 52. **d** 55 **p** 56. C Frodingham *Linc* 55-59; R Belton SS Pet and Paul 59-64; PC Manthorpe w Londonthorpe 59-64; V Billingborough 64-73; V Sempringham w Pointon and Birthorpe 64-73; V Flixborough w Burton upon Stather 73-96; RD Manlake 87-93; Can and Preb Linc Cathl 92-01; rtd 96; PtO *Linc* from 01. *7 St Andrews Drive, Burton-upon-Stather, Scunthorpe DN15 9BY* T: (01724) 720510

HEARN, Stephen Isaac Raphael. b 79. Linc Coll Ox BA 04 MA 08. St Steph Ho Ox 06 MPhil 12. Ven English Coll Rome 08. **d** 09 **p** 10. C Market Deeping *Linc* 09-11; Fell and Chapl Ex Coll Ox 11-13. *Address temp unknown*
E: stephen.hearn@lincoln.oxon.org

HEARN, Trevor. b 36. Sarum Th Coll 61. **d** 64 **p** 65. C Hounslow St Steph *Lon* 64-67; Miss to Seafarers 67-01; UAE 92-01; rtd 01; PtO *Bris* from 01. *37 Elberton Road, Bristol BS9 2PZ* T: 0117-983 6526 E: tandv@hearn3136.fsnet.co.uk

HEARTFIELD, Canon Peter Reginald. b 27. Chich Th Coll 61. **d** 63 **p** 64. C Hurstpierpoint *Chich* 63-67; V Brighton St Alb Preston 67-73; Chapl Kent and Cant Hosp 73-92; Chapl Nunnery Fields Hosp Cant 73-92; Six Preacher Cant Cathl 79-84; Hon Can Cant Cathl 84-92; rtd 92; PtO *Cant* from 00; Chapl St Jo Hosp Cant from 10. *1 St John's House, 40 Northgate, Canterbury CT1 1BE* T: (01227) 451621 E: prheartfield@btinternet.com

HEASLIP, Eoghan. b 76. St Mellitus Coll. **d** 11 **p** 12. C Worc City 11-14. *1 Willowfield Avenue, Goatstown Road, Clonskeagh, Dublin 14, Republic of Ireland*

HEATH, Mrs Cynthia Grace. b 46. St Mark & St Jo Coll Lon TCert 68 Open Univ BA 85 ARCM 66 GRSM 68. WMMTC 94. **d** 97 **p** 98. NSM Penkridge *Lich* 97-00; TV 00-07. *2 Hall Farm Road, Brewood, Stafford ST19 9EZ* T: (01902) 850175 E: cynthgren@btinternet.com

HEATH, Henry. b 40. FCII 77. Oak Hill Th Coll 77. **d** 80 **p** 81. NSM Lexden *Chelmsf* 80-86; C Colne Engaine 86; NSM Halstead St Andr w H Trin and Greenstead Green 86-90; NSM W w E Mersea 90-95; R Stanway 95-02; rtd 02; PtO *Chelmsf* 02-05; P-in-c Wormingford, Mt Bures and Lt Horkesley 05-12; PtO *St E* from 13. *The Mews, Hill House, High Street, Long Melford, Sudbury CO10 9BD* M: 07885-306699 E: hillhousemews@aol.com

HEATH, Mrs Janet. b 46. EMMTC 89. **d** 91 **p** 94. Par Dn Rainworth *S'well* 91-94; C 94-96; C Mansfield Woodhouse 96-99; rtd 00; PtO *S'well* from 00. *17 The Hollies, Sherwood Park, Rainworth, Mansfield NG21 0FZ* T: (01623) 490422 E: janheath@supanet.com

HEATH, John Henry. b 41. Chich Th Coll 69. **d** 71 **p** 72. C Crediton *Ex* 71-74; C Tavistock and Gulworthy 74-76; C Brixham 76-77; C Brixham w Churston Ferrers 77-79; R Bere Ferrers 79-85; P-in-c Moretonhampstead, N Bovey and Manaton 85-88; R 88-93; P-in-c Lifton 93-99; P-in-c Kelly w Bradstone 93-99; P-in-c Broadwoodwidger 93-99; R Lifton, Broadwoodwidger, Coryton, Stowford etc 99-01; V Lifton, Broadwoodwidger, Stowford etc 01-03; rtd 03; PtO *Heref* 04-10. *30 Wye Way, Hereford HR1 2NP*

HEATH, Julie Ann. b 62. Nottm Univ BA 09. EMMTC. **d** 06 **p** 07. NSM Kegworth, Hathern, Long Whatton, Diseworth etc *Leic* 06-08; Workplace Chapl 08-14; Chapl Leic Univ 09-13; Chapl Leic Cathl 12-14; PtO from 14. *Fairmount House, 87 Leicester Road, Ashby-de-la-Zouch LE65 1DD* M: 07801-467348 E: julieannheath@pottersmaze.co.uk

HEATH, Martin Jonathan. b 68. St Jo Coll Nottm 07. **d** 09 **p** 10. C Gt Wyrley *Lich* 09-12; C Harlescott from 12. *Emmanuel Vicarage, Mount Pleasant Road, Shrewsbury SY1 3HY* T: (01743) 350907 M: 07847-370572 E: martinjheath@talktalk.net

HEATH, Robert John. b 54. Worc Coll of Educn BEd 75 Wolv Univ MA 11 Worc Univ BA 12. Qu Coll Birm 10. **d** 13 **p** 14. Sen Lect Wolv Univ *Lich* from 06; NSM Heath Hayes from 13. *6 Shugborough Way, Cannock WS11 7YT* T: (01543) 275079 M: 07930-640642 E: robert.heath@zen.co.uk

HEATH, Mrs Wendy Hillary. b 47. WMMTC 95. **d** 98 **p** 99. NSM Rugeley *Lich* 98-99; C 00-01; P-in-c Brereton 01-06; TV Brereton and Rugeley 06-12; rtd 12; Hon C Essington *Lich* from 12. *The Vicarage, 21 Wolverhampton Road, Essington, Wolverhampton WV11 2BX* E: wen_heath@hotmail.com

HEATH-WHYTE, David Robert. b 68. Fitzw Coll Cam BA 89. Wycliffe Hall Ox BTh 98. **d** 98 **p** 99. C Gt Chesham *Ox* 98-02; V Frogmore *St Alb* 02-14; TR Morden *S'wark* from 14. *The Rectory, London Road, Morden SM4 5QT* T: (020) 8648 3920 E: david.hw@hotfrog.info

HEATHCOTE, Warwick Geoffrey. b 46. Th Ext Educn Coll 97. **d** 00 **p** 01. C Grahamstown Cathl S Africa 00-03; C Cirencester *Glouc* 03-09; P-in-c Stratton, N Cerney, Baunton and Bagendon 09-14; P-in-c Rendcomb 09-14; R Churn Valley from 14. *The Rectory, 94 Gloucester Road, Stratton, Cirencester GL7 2LJ* T: (01285) 655199 E: warwick.heathcote@btinternet.com

HEATHER, Dennis Eric. b 34. **d** 98 **p** 99. OLM Hook *S'wark* 98-05; PtO from 05. *276 Hook Road, Chessington KT9 1PF* T: (020) 8397 0063

HEATHER, Mark Duncan Grainger. b 62. Leic Poly LLB 83 Leeds Univ BA 99. Coll of Resurr Mirfield 97. **d** 99 **p** 00. C Leeds St Aid *Ripon* 99-03; V Leeds Halton St Wilfrid 03-10; Bp's Chapl *Guildf* from 10. *59 Brookside, Jacob's Well, Guildford GU4 7NS* T: (01483) 566082 *or* 590500 F: 590501 E: mark.heather@cofeguildford.org.uk

HEATHER, Mrs Sally Patricia. b 51. Avery Hill Coll BEd 73. STETS 99. **d** 02 **p** 03. NSM Michelmersh and Awbridge and Braishfield etc *Win* 02-06; TV Basingstoke 06-11; rtd 11;

PtO *Win* from 11. *8 Sparkford Road, Winchester SO22 4NL* T: (01962) 622550 E: spheather@gmail.com

HEATHFIELD, The Ven Simon David. b 67. Birm Univ BMus 88 Fitzw Coll Cam BTh 99. Ridley Hall Cam 96. **d** 99 **p** 00. C Heswall *Ches* 99-02; Voc and Min Adv CPAS 02-05; TR Walthamstow *Chelmsf* 06-14; AD Waltham Forest 12-14; Adn Aston *Birm* from 14. *34 Chattock Avenue, Solihull B91 2QX* E: simonh@birmingham.anglican.org

HEATLEY, Cecil. *See* HEATLEY, William Cecil

HEATLEY, David Henry. b 50. Kent Univ BA 72. Qu Coll Birm 86. **d** 88 **p** 89. C Liss *Portsm* 88-91; V Newchurch and Arreton 91-99; R Greatham w Empshott and Hawkley w Prior's Dean 99-13; Dioc Rural Officer 98-13; rtd 13; PtO *Portsm* from 14. *1 Osborne Chase, Cowes PO31 7FA* T: (01983) 290567 E: dhheatley@aol.com

HEATLEY, Canon William Cecil. b 39. QUB BA 61. Ridley Hall Cam 62. **d** 64 **p** 65. C Ballymacarrett St Patr *D & D* 64-69; C Herne Hill St Paul *S'wark* 69-74; TV Sanderstead All SS 75-82; P-in-c Peckham St Sav 82-87; V 87-07; RD Dulwich 97-02; Hon Can S'wark Cathl 01-07; rtd 07; PtO *S'wark* from 07; *Roch* from 07. *37 Bromley College, London Road, Bromley BR1 1PE* T: (020) 8460 9505 E: cecilheatley@yahoo.com

HEATON, Alan. b 36. K Coll Lon BD 64 AKC 64 Nottm Univ MTh 76. **d** 65 **p** 66. C Stockton St Chad *Dur* 65-68; C Englefield Green *Guildf* 68-70; C Winlaton *Dur* 70-74; Chapl Derby Lonsdale Coll 74-79; V Alfreton 79-87; RD 81-86; TR Clifton *S'well* 87-93; P-in-c Rolleston w Fiskerton, Morton and Upton 93-96; rtd 97; PtO *Liv* from 97. *29 The Parchments, Newton-le-Willows WA12 0DX* T: (01925) 292209 E: a.ms-heaton@tiscali.co.uk

HEATON, Sister Elizabeth Ann. b 65. Bath Coll of HE BSc 87. Ripon Coll Cuddesdon 98. **d** 00 **p** 01. C Lostwithiel, St Winnow w St Nectan's Chpl etc *Truro* 00-03; CSF from 03; PtO *B & W* 03-10; *Linc* 10-12; C Branston w Nocton and Potterhanworth 12-15; C Metheringham w Blankney and Dunston 12-15. *The Community of St Francis, San Damiano, 38 Drury Street, Metheringham, Lincoln LN4 3EZ* T: (01526) 321115 E: lizcsf@franciscans.org.uk

HEATON, Joseph Anthony Turnley. b 70. Univ of Wales (Abth) BSc 91 PhD 95 St Jo Coll Dur BA 08. Cranmer Hall Dur 06. **d** 08 **p** 09. C Ribbesford w Bewdley and Dowles *Worc* 08-11; P-in-c Rushen *S & M* 11-13; V from 13. *Rushen Vicarage, Barracks Road, Port St Mary, Isle of Man IM9 5LP* T: (01624) 832275 E: rev.joeheaton@gmail.com

HEATON, Julian Roger. b 62. LSE BSc(Econ) 83. St Steph Ho Ox BA 86 MA 92. **d** 87 **p** 88. C Stockport St Thos w St Pet *Ches* 87-90; Chapl Asst Qu Medical Cen and Univ Hosp Nottm 90-92; V Knutsford St Cross *Ches* 92-01; P-in-c Altrincham St Jo 01-05; Voc Officer (Macclesfield Adnry) 01-05; V Sale St Anne from 05; RD Bowdon from 12. *St Anne's Vicarage, Church Road West, Sale M33 3GD* T: 0161-973 4145 E: julian.heaton@talktalk.net

HEATON, Nicholas Mark. b 70. Leeds Metrop Univ BEd 92 Ches Coll of HE BTh 04. NOC 01. **d** 04 **p** 05. C Linthorpe *York* 04-08; TV Morley *Wakef* 08-10; TV Upper Holme Valley *Leeds* from 10. *The Vicarage, Ashgrove Road, Holmfirth HD9 3JR* T: (01484) 683593 E: nickheaton2@sky.com

HEATON, Timothy. b 59. STETS 08. **d** 08 **p** 10. NSM Upper Stour *Sarum* 08-11; NSM Gillingham and Milton-on-Stour from 11. *Grange Cottage, Chaffeymoor, Bourton, Gillingham SP8 5BY* T: (01747) 840936 E: tim4heaton@yahoo.co.uk

HEAVER, Derek Cyril. b 47. St Jo Coll Nottm BTh 69. **d** 73 **p** 74. C Win Ch Ch 73-77; CF 77-02; rtd 02. *Orchard Cottage, 2 Myrtle Close, Puncknowle, Dorchester DT2 9EH* T/F: (01308) 898466 E: delsaun@eurobell.co.uk

HEAVISIDES, Canon Neil Cameron. b 50. Selw Coll Cam BA 72 MA 76 Ox Univ BA 74 MA 85. Ripon Hall Ox 72. **d** 75 **p** 76. C Stockton St Pet *Dur* 75-78; Succ S'wark Cathl 78-81; V Seaham w Seaham Harbour *Dur* 81-88; P-in-c Edington and Imber, Erlestoke and E Coulston *Sarum* 88-89; R 89-93; Can Res Glouc Cathl from 93. *7 College Green, Gloucester GL1 2LX* T: (01452) 523987 E: nheavisides@gloucestercathedral.org.uk

HEAWOOD, Canon Alan Richard. b 32. G&C Coll Cam BA 54 MA 58. Union Th Sem (NY) BD 56 Ripon Hall Ox 56. **d** 57 **p** 58. C Horwich H Trin *Man* 57-59; C Weaste 59-60; C Beverley Minster *York* 60-62; Chapl and Lect St Pet Coll Saltley 62-65; R Hockwold w Wilton *Ely* 65-72; R Weeting 65-72; V Melbourn 72-80; V Meldreth 72-80; P-in-c Teversham 80-90; Adult Educn Sec 80-89; Dir of Educn 80-98; Hon Can Ely Cathl 80-98; rtd 98; PtO *Ely* from 98. *10 Westberry Court, Grange Road, Cambridge CB3 9BG* T: (01223) 460088 E: btalan@heawood9.plus.com

HEAZELL, Pamela Fletcher. b 50. NTMTC 96. **d** 99 **p** 00. NSM Hayes St Nic CD *Lon* 99-01; NSM N Greenford All Hallows 01-04; P-in-c 04-08; V from 08. *72 Horsenden Lane North, Greenford UB6 0PD* T: (020) 8933 7700 E: pfheazell@aol.com

HEBBERN, Geoffrey Alan. b 43. MBE 98. **d** 05 **p** 06. NSM Radipole and Melcombe Regis *Sarum* from 05; Asst Chapl HM Pris The Verne from 05. *11 Hawthorn Close, Weymouth DT4 9UG* T/F: (01305) 772205 E: ghebbern@hotmail.com

HEBBLETHWAITE, Canon Brian Leslie. b 39. Magd Coll Ox BA 61 MA 67 Magd Coll Cam BA 63 MA 68 BD 84. Westcott Ho Cam 62. **d** 65 **p** 66. C Elton All SS *Man* 65-68; Chapl Qu Coll Cam 68; Dean of Chpl and Fell 69-94; Asst Lect Div Cam Univ 73-77; Lect 77-99; Can Th Leic Cathl 82-00; rtd 99; PtO *Ely* from 02. *The Old Barn, 32 High Street, Stretham, Ely CB6 3JQ* T: (01353) 648279 M: 07740-307568 E: blh1000@cam.ac.uk

HEBBLEWHITE, David Ernest. b 52. Hull Univ BA 81 Nottm Univ MA 82 CQSW 82. St Jo Coll Nottm MA 95. **d** 97 **p** 98. C Melton Mowbray *Leic* 97-00; TV Cannock *Lich* 00-07; P-in-c Countesthorpe w Foston *Leic* from 07; Warden of Ev from 10. *The Vicarage, 102 Station Road, Countesthorpe, Leicester LE8 5TB* T: 0116-278 4442 or 277 8643

HEBBORN, Roy Valentine Charles. b 28. S Dios Minl Tr Scheme 83. **d** 86 **p** 87. NSM Lewes All SS, St Anne, St Mich and St Thos *Chich* 86-00; NSM Lewes St Anne 00-01; rtd 01; PtO *Chich* from 03. *27 Greater Paddock, Ringmer, Lewes BN8 5LH* T: (01273) 812005 E: roy.hebborn@connectfree.co.uk

HEBDEN, Canon Cynthia Margaret. b 47. Univ of Wales (Ban) BTh 94. **d** 94 **p** 97. NSM Llanfairpwll w Penmynydd *Ban* 94-95; C Twrcelyn Deanery 95-96; C Knighton St Mary Magd *Leic* 96-99; P-in-c Higham-on-the-Hill w Fenny Drayton and Witherley 99-02; P-in-c Stoke Golding w Dadlington 01-02; R Fenn Lanes Gp 02-03; V Shepshed and Oaks in Charnwood from 03; RD Akeley E 06-11; Hon Can Leic Cathl from 13. *1 Charles Hall Close, Shepshed, Loughborough LE12 9UP* T: (01509) 506791 or 502255 E: cynthia.hebden47@gmail.com

HEBDEN, John Percy. b 18. Sheff Univ 46 Lon Univ 67. St Aid Birkenhead 58. **d** 60 **p** 60. C Skipton H Trin *Bradf* 60-62; R Kirby Misperton *York* 63-67; V Laxey *S & M* 70-83; V Lonan 80-83; rtd 84; Hon C Douglas St Geo and St Barn *S & M* 84-95. *Begra, Clayhead Road, Baldrine, Isle of Man IM4 6DN* T: (01624) 861296

HEBDEN, Keith Oliver. b 76. Univ of Wales (Ban) BD 98 MTh 00 Warwick Univ PGCE 01 Birm Univ PhD 08. Qu Coll Birm 07. **d** 09 **p** 10. C Matson *Glouc* 09-12; C Mansfield SS Pet and Paul S'well from 12; C Mansfield St Mark from 12. *St Mark's Vicarage, Nottingham Road, Mansfield NG18 1BP* E: keithhebden@gmail.com

HEBER, Andrew John. b 63. Nottm Univ BA 86 MA 89 CQSW 89. Trin Coll Bris BA 99. **d** 99 **p** 00. C Parr *Liv* 99-03; TV Kirkby 03-12; R Clogherny w Seskinore and Drumnakilly *Arm* from 12. *The Rectory, 96 Church Road, Sixmilecross, Omagh BT79 0SA* T: (028) 8075 8570 E: andy.heber@googlemail.com

HEBER PERCY, Canon Christopher John. b 41. St Jo Coll Cam BA 64 MA 68. Wells Th Coll 66. **d** 68 **p** 69. C Leigh St Mary *Man* 68-71; Asst Ind Chapl 71-80; P-in-c Oldham St Andr 75-78; TV Oldham 78-80; Ind Chapl *Win* 80-90; N Humberside Ind Chapl *York* 90-06; AD E Hull 98-06; Can and Preb York Minster 05-06; rtd 06. *59 Swarcliffe Road, Harrogate HG1 4QZ* T: (01423) 884076 E: percy@lindisandchris.karoo.co.uk

HECTOR, Noel Antony. b 61. Sheff Univ LLB 83 Barrister-at-Law 84. Oak Hill Th Coll BA 91. **d** 91 **p** 92. C Rodbourne Cheney *Bris* 91-92; C Bris St Mary Redcliffe w Temple etc 92-95; R Wrington w Butcombe *B & W* 95-03; R E Clevedon w Clapton in Gordano etc from 03; Chapl N Bris NHS Trust from 03; RD Portishead *B & W* from 10. *The Rectory, All Saints' Lane, Clevedon BS21 6AU* T/F: (01275) 873257 E: eastcleveub@blueyonder.co.uk

HEDDERLY, Katherine. b 63. St Hugh's Coll Ox BA 85 MA 94. NTMTC BA 06. **d** 06 **p** 07. C Bedford Park *Lon* 06-09; C St Martin-in-the-Fields from 09. *Flat 2, 6 St Martin's Place, London WC2N 4JH*

HEDDLE, Duncan. b 34. Wadh Coll Ox BA 57 MA 61 DPhil 64. **d** 86 **p** 86. Chapl Aber Univ *Ab* from 86; P-in-c Bucksburn from 90. *2 Douglas Place, High Street, Aberdeen AB24 3EA* T: (01224) 485975 or 272888 E: d.heddle@abdn.ac.uk

HEDGECOCK, Jonathan James. b 64. Imp Coll Lon BScEng 86 Ban Univ BTh 09 CEng MIET 89. OLM Guildf H Trin w St Mary from 07. *8 Foxglove Gardens, Guildford GU4 7ES* T: (01483) 502199 M: 07785-766631 E: jonathanjhedgecock@hotmail.com

HEDGER, Canon Graham. b 57. Lon Bible Coll BA 79. Ridley Hall Cam 81. **d** 83 **p** 84. C Walton St E 83-86; TV Mildenhall 86-91; R Swainsthorpe w Newton Flotman *Nor* 91-94; Dioc Evang Officer 91-94; PtO *St E* 95-99; Bp's Chapl and Liaison Officer 99-07; Bp's Policy and Liaison Officer 07-11; P-in-c

Clopton w Otley, Swilland and Ashbocking 09-12; Asst Dioc Sec from 10; Hon Can St E Cathl from 04. *14 St Peter's Close, Charsfield, Woodbridge IP13 7RG* T: (01473) 277042 E: graham@stedmundsbury.anglican.org

HEDGES, Mrs Anne Violet. b 53. Ripon Coll Cuddesdon 87. **d** 89 **p** 94. C Thetford *Nor* 89-94; P-in-c Garboldisham w Blo' Norton, Riddlesworth etc 94-97; R Guiltcross 97-00; Chapl Riddlesworth Hall Sch Nor 93-00; Dep Chapl HM Pris Leeds 00-01; Chapl HM Pris Leic 01-05; Chapl HM Pris Highpoint 05-09; Chapl HM Pris Bure from 09. *HM Prison Bure, Jaguar Drive, Scottow, Norwich NR10 5GB* T: (01603) 326180 E: anne.hedges@hmps.gsi.gov.uk

HEDGES, Ian Charles. b 55. Sarum & Wells Th Coll 79. **d** 82 **p** 83. C Chessington *Guildf* 82-85; C Fleet 85-90; Dioc Adv on Homelessness from 87; V S Farnborough from 90; Tr Officer for Past Assts 91-00. *The Vicarage, 1 St Mark's Close, Farnborough GU14 6PP* T: (01252) 544711 E: smarksfbro@btinternet.com

HEDGES, The Very Revd Jane Barbara. b 55. St Jo Coll Dur BA 78. Cranmer Hall Dur 78. **dss** 80 **d** 87 **p** 94. Fareham H Trin *Portsm* 80-83; Southampton (City Cen) *Win* 83-87; Par Dn 87-88; Dioc Stewardship Adv *Portsm* 88-93; Can Res Portsm Cathl 93-01; P-in-c Honiton, Gittisham, Combe Raleigh, Monkton etc *Ex* 01-03; TR 03-06; RD Honiton 03-06; Can Steward Westmr Abbey 06-14; Dean Nor from 14. *The Deanery, The Close, Norwich NR1 4EG* T: (01603) 218300 E: dean@cathedral.org.uk

HEDGES, Mrs Jane Rosemary. b 44. RGN 65. S Dios Minl Tr Scheme 86. **d** 89 **p** 94. NSM Gillingham *Sarum* 89-04; NSM Gillingham and Milton-on-Stour 04-08; Lic to RD Blackmore Vale 08-12. *Dene Hollow, Wyke Road, Gillingham SP8 4NG* T: (01747) 822812 E: denehollow@msn.com

HEDGES, John Michael Peter. b 34. Leeds Univ BA 60. Ripon Hall Ox 60. **d** 61 **p** 62. C Weaste *Man* 61-65; V Ashton St Pet 65-74; C Easthampstead *Ox* 74-85; V Tilehurst St Geo 85-91; C Thatcham 91-94; TV 94-99; rtd 99; PtO *Ox* from 99. *39 Mallard Way, Grove, Wantage OX12 0QG* T: (01235) 766834

HEDLEY, Charles John Wykeham. b 47. R Holloway Coll Lon BSc 69 PhD 73 Fitzw Coll Cam BA 75 MA 79. Westcott Ho Cam 73. **d** 76 **p** 77. C Chingford St Anne *Chelmsf* 76-79; C St Martin-in-the-Fields *Lon* 79-84 and 85-86; P-in-c 84-85; Chapl Ch Coll Cam 86-90; TR Gleadless *Sheff* 90-99; R Westmr St Jas *Lon* 99-09; rtd 09. *95 Brighton Belle, 2 Stroudley Road, Brighton BN1 4ZD* E: chequal@googlemail.com

HEDLEY, Mrs Julia Margaret. b 56. Goldsmiths' Coll Lon BA 78 Bedf Coll Lon MSc 85 Liv Univ MTh 03 SRN 80. NOC 97. **d** 00 **p** 01. C Altrincham St Geo *Ches* 00-04; PV Ches Cathl 04-07; Bps' Dom Chapl *B & W* 07-13; NSM Kensington St Mary Abbots w Ch Ch and St Phil *Lon* from 13. *4 Kensington Church Court, London W8 4SP* T: (020) 3686 1513 E: julia.hedley@stmaryabbotschurch.org

HEDLEY, William Clifford. b 35. Tyndale Hall Bris 65. **d** 67 **p** 68. C Hensingham *Carl* 67-69; C Rainhill *Liv* 69-71; C St Helens St Helen 71-73; V Low Elswick *Newc* 73-81; V Kingston upon Hull St Aid Southcoates *York* 81-87; TV Heworth H Trin 87-94; V Norton juxta Malton 94-97; C Newburn *Newc* 97-01; rtd 01; PtO *Dur* from 01. *21 Laburnum Grove, Sunniside, Newcastle upon Tyne NE16 5LY* T: 0191-488 2908

HEDWORTH, Paul Simon James. b 56. Worc Coll of Educn BEd 78. Qu Coll Birm BA(Theol) 84. **d** 04 **p** 05. NSM Bacup and Stacksteads *Man* 04-06; Chapl Qu Eliz Gr Sch Blackb 98-06; Chapl Bromsgrove Sch from 06. *Bromsgrove School, Worcester Road, Bromsgrove B61 7DU* T: (01527) 579679 M: 07966-503194 E: hedworthfamily@yahoo.co.uk

HEELEY, Mrs Janet. b 45. **d** 00 **p** 01. OLM Lich St Chad 00-10; rtd 10; PtO *Lich* from 10. *43 High Grange, Lichfield WS13 7DU* T: (01543) 251600 E: janet.heeley@talktalk.net

HEELEY, Robert Francis. b 54. NOC 06. **d** 08 **p** 09. NSM Hadfield *Derby* 08-12; NSM Charlesworth and Dinting Vale 12-14; NSM Dinting Vale from 14. *3 Chesham Close, Hadfield, Glossop SK13 1QX* T: (01457) 855541 E: rob.heeley@uwclub.net

HEELEY, Mrs Ruth Mary. b 41. Qu Coll Birm 04. **d** 06 **p** 07. NSM Halas *Worc* 06-11; rtd 11; PtO *Worc* from 11. *4 Cherry Tree Lane, Halesowen B63 1DU* T: 0121-550 7622 E: ruthmh@hotmail.co.uk

HEENAN, Vivienne Mary. b 48. Univ of Wales (Abth) BA 70 SS Paul & Mary Coll Cheltenham PGCE 90. STETS 03. **d** 06 **p** 07. NSM Whitwell and Niton *Portsm* 06-11; NSM Ventnor St Cath 11-13; NSM Ventnor H Trin 11-13; NSM Bonchurch 11-13; PtO from 13. *Dolphins House, Boxers Lane, Niton, Ventnor PO38 2BH* T/F: (01983) 730352 M: 07740-780767 E: vivienne.heenan@tiscali.co.uk

HEFFER, William John Gambrell. b 30. AKC 55. **d** 56 **p** 57. C Biggleswade *St Alb* 56-59; C Clacton St Jas *Chelmsf* 59-61;

V Langford *St Alb* 61-67; V Luton All SS 67-73; P-in-c Eaton Socon 73-75; V 75-77; LtO 78-81; R Wingrave w Rowsham, Aston Abbotts and Cublington *Ox* 81-88; R Wilden w Colmworth and Ravensden *St Alb* 88-91; C Leighton Buzzard w Eggington, Hockliffe etc 91-94; rtd 94; PtO *St Alb* 94-00 and from 01; *Ox* 97-01; P-in-c Empingham and Exton w Horn w Whitwell *Pet* 00-01. *Domus, 35 Pebblemoor, Edlesborough, Dunstable LU6 2HZ* T: (01525) 220618

HEFFERNAN, Anna Elizabeth. See LINDSEY, Anna Elizabeth

HEGARTY, Ms Bernadette Grace. b 58. Man Poly BA 81 Leeds Univ BA 11 CQSW 90. Coll of Resurr Mirfield 09. **d** 11 **p** 12. C High Harrogate St Pet *Leeds* 11-14; V Bow Common *Lon* from 14. *St Paul's Vicarage, Leopold Street, London E3 4LA* E: bhgrace@hotmail.co.uk

HEGEDUS, Frank Michael. b 48. St Louis Univ BA 71 Michigan State Univ MA 76 Univ of St Thos St Paul MBA 84. Colgate-Rochester Div Sch DMin 80. **d** 74 **p** 74. P-in-c St Paul St Paul's-on-the-Hill USA 87-89; P-in-c Northfields All SS & Dundas H Cross 88-90; R Farmington Advent 89-96; Asst P Orange Trin Ch 97-98; P-in-c Norwalk St Fran 98-99; NSM Budapest *Eur* 99-01; Asst P Huntington Beach St Wilfrid USA 01-02; P-in-c Redlands Trin Ch 02-03; P-in-c Plymouth St Jo 04-05; P-in-c El Cajon St Alb 05-08; P-in-c Del Mar St Pet 08-09; P-in-c El Centro St Pet and St Paul 09; P-in-c Episc Ch in Almaden San Jose 09-10; P-in-c Budapest *Eur* from 11. *1117 Budapest, Szerémi út 7/A - 603, Hungary* T: (0036) (20) 269 5161 E: anglicanbudapest@gmail.com

HEIGHT (formerly WATKINS), Susan Jane. b 58. Qu Coll Birm. **d** 01 **p** 02. C Edgbaston St Germain *Birm* 01-05; TV Salter Street and Shirley 05-11; P-in-c N Dulwich St Faith *S'wark* from 11. *110 Fawnbrake Avenue, London SE24 0BZ* E: susan_height@yahoo.co.uk

HEIGHTON, George. b 55. Qu Coll Birm 08. **d** 11 **p** 12. NSM Bilton *Cov* 11-14; C Willenhall from 14; C Whitley from 14. *St James's Church Vicarage, Abbey Road, Coventry CV3 4BG* F: (01788) 815514 T: (024) 7630 1978 M: 07730-009098 E: revgeorgeh@outlook.com

HEIGHTON, Miss Janet Elizabeth. b 67. Leeds Poly BSc 92. Ripon Coll Cuddesdon. **d** 00 **p** 01. C Leeds Gipton Epiphany *Ripon* 00-04; P-in-c 04-07; TV Upholland *Liv* 07-14; V Rainford from 14. *1 Tudor Close, Rainford, St Helens WA11 8SD* E: revjanet.rainford@ad.com

HEIL, Janet. b 53. Liv Univ BEd 75 St Jo Coll Dur BA 84. Cranmer Hall Dur. **dss** 85 **d** 87 **p** 94. Ashton Ch Ch *Man* 85-91; Par Dn 87-91; Par Dn Scotforth *Blackb* 91-94; C 94-95; V Gt Harwood St Bart 95-06; P-in-c Gt Harwood St Jo 02-06; Hon Can Blackb Cathl 04-06; Chapl Oslo w Bergen, Trondheim and Stavanger *Eur* 06-13; rtd 13. *4 Hornby Court, Beaumont Park, Lancaster LA1 2LB* E: janetheil@btinternet.com

HEININK, Mrs Jennifer Ann. b 54. K Coll Lon BD 75 Sarum Coll MA 10. St Mellitus Coll 13. **d** 14 **p** 15. OLM Cranham Park *Chelmsf* from 14. *14 Grosvenor Gardens, Upminster RM14 1DJ* T: (01708) 227374 E: jennyheinink@hotmail.com

HEINZE, Canon Rudolph William. b 31. Concordia Coll (USA) BSc 56 CertEd 56 De Paul Univ (USA) MA 59 Univ of Iowa PhD 65. **d** 86 **p** 87. NSM London Colney St Pet *St Alb* 86-98; Lect Oak Hill Th Coll 86-98; Sen Tutor 88-94; Vice-Prin 94-97; Visiting Scholar from 99; Hon Can Port Sudan from 94; Hon Prof Middx Univ *Lon* from 98. *1714D Lakecliffe Drive, Wheaton IL 60187-8368, USA* T: (001) (630) 588 8954 E: revrudi@aol.com

HEITZMANN, Pamela. See BARRIE, Pamela

HELEN, Sister. See LODER, Helen

HELEN JULIAN, Sister. See ENGLISH, Helen Margaret

HELEY, John. b 28. Lon Univ BA 72. Bps' Coll Cheshunt 54. **d** 56 **p** 57. C Claremont St Sav S Africa 57-61; C Wimborne Minster *Sarum* 61-62; V Narborough w Narford *Nor* 62-67; R Pentney St Mary Magd w W Bilney 62-67; V Catton 67-69; LtO *Ox* 69-72; R E w W Rudham *Nor* 72-75; P-in-c Houghton 72-74; V 74-75; V Hunstanton St Edm 75-82; V Hunstanton St Edm w Ringstead 82-83; rtd 88. *24 Kestrel Close, Burnham Market, King's Lynn PE31 8EF* T: (01328) 730036

HELLARD, Dawn Yvonne Lorraine. b 47. St Mich Coll Llan 89. **d** 91 **p** 97. C Llantwit Major *Llan* 91-95; TV Cowbridge 95-05; rtd 05; PtO *Llan* from 05. *10 Maes Lloi, Aberthin, Cowbridge CF71 7HA* T: (01446) 772460

HELLEWELL, John. b 63. Bris Univ BSc 86 BTh 93 Nottm Univ MA 94. St Jo Coll Nottm 93. **d** 94 **p** 95. C Greasbrough *Sheff* 94-98; P-in-c High Hoyland, Scissett and Clayton W *Wakef* 98-04; V Mount Pellon 04-09; V Halifax St Aug and Mount Pellon *Leeds* from 09; Warden of Readers *Wakef* 04-12. *The Vicarage, Church Lane, Halifax HX2 0EF* T: (01422) 365027 E: revjhell@blueyonder.co.uk

HELLICAR, Hugh Christopher. b 37. Qu Coll Birm 69. **d** 70 **p** 71. C Bromyard *Heref* 70-73; C Bishop's Castle w Mainstone

73-75; PtO *S'wark* 77-85; *Chich* 83-93; NSM Hove 93-98; rtd 02. *74 Marina, St Leonards-on-Sea TN38 0BJ* T: (01424) 444072

HELLIER, Jeremy Peter. b 53. K Coll Lon BD 75 AKC 75. St Aug Coll Cant 75. **d** 76 **p** 77. C Walton *St E* 76-79; C Ipswich St Fran 79-80; C Wolborough w Newton Abbot *Ex* 80-82; CF 82-84; R Pendine w Llanmiloe and Eglwys Gymyn w Marros *St D* 84-89; TR Widecombe-in-the-Moor, Leusdon, Princetown etc *Ex* 89-94; CF (TAVR) 90-03; RD Moreton *Ex* 91-94; Chapl and Hd RE Wellington Sch Somerset from 94; Hon Chapl Miss to Seafarers from 02. *Wellington School, Wellington TA21 8NT* T: (01823) 668827 or 668837 F: 668844 M: 07971-588184 E: jeremyhellier@hotmail.com

HELLINGS, Mrs Tara Charmian Lashmar. b 68. Ch Ch Ox MA 90. STETS 06. **d** 09 **p** 10. NSM Alton *Win* 09-12; Chapl Alton Coll 11-12; V Crondall and Ewshot *Guildf* from 12. *The Vicarage, Farm Lane, Crondall, Farnham GU10 5QE* M: 07932-184873 E: tartzhellings@yahoo.co.uk

HELLIWELL, Judith Hazel. See KENWORTHY, Judith Hazel

HELLMUTH, Miss Lynn Margaret. b 61. Lon Bible Coll BA 82 Birm Univ PGCE 83. Wycliffe Hall Ox 00. **d** 02 **p** 03. C Twickenham Common H Trin *Lon* 02-05; TV Crawley *Chich* 05-08; V Stoneleigh *Guildf* from 08. *The Vicarage, 59 Stoneleigh Park Road, Epsom KT19 0QU* T: (020) 8393 3738 E: lynnhellmuth@yahoo.co.uk

HELLYER, Stephen John. b 56. St Cath Coll Cam BA 77 MA 81. Wycliffe Hall Ox 82. **d** 84 **p** 85. C Plymouth St Andr w St Paul and St Geo *Ex* 84-88; Chapl Lee Abbey 88-89; Lon and SE Consultant CPAS 90-94; C Nottingham St Nic *S'well* 94-98; P-in-c Ox St Matt 98-10; R from 10. *St Matthew's Vicarage, Marlborough Road, Oxford OX1 4LW* T: (01865) 243434 M: 07811-001712 E: stevejohnhellyer@yahoo.co.uk

HELM, Alistair Thomas. b 53. Aston Univ BSc 75. EAMTC 88. **d** 91 **p** 92. NSM Leic St Jas 91-95; NSM Humberstone 95-04; NSM Emmaus Par Team 04-12; NSM Giggleswick and Rathmell w Wigglesworth *Bradf* 09-12; NSM Settle 09-12; P-in-c Manningham 12-13; V *Leeds* from 13. *The Rectory, 63 St Paul's Road, Manningham, Bradford BD8 7LS* T: (01274) 482495 M: 07799-381368 E: alistair.helm@btinternet.com

HELM, Catherine Mary. b 64. St Martin's Coll Lanc BEd 86. St Jo Coll Nottm 03. **d** 05 **p** 06. C Heswall *Ches* 05-09; V Burton and Shotwick from 09. *The Vicarage, Vicarage Lane, Burton, Neston CH64 5TJ* T: 0151-353 0453 E: chelm@shotwick.org.uk

HELM, Nicholas. b 57. Surrey Univ BSc 81. St Jo Coll Nottm 85. **d** 88 **p** 89. C Old Ford St Paul w St Steph and St Mark *Lon* 88-92; TV Netherthorpe *Sheff* 92-93; V Sheff St Bart 93-98; Bp's Chapl 99-03; Bp's Adv in Spirituality 99-09; Chapl Whirlow Grange Conf Cen Sheff 99-09; CMD Officer *Heref* from 10. *Diocese of Hereford, 8-9 The Business Quarter, Eco Park Road, Ludlow SY8 1FD* T: (01584) 871082 E: n.helm@hereford.anglican.org

HELMS, David Clarke. b 50. Boston Univ BA 72. Yale Div Sch MDiv 77. **d** 77 **p** 77. USA 77-88; Ind Chapl *Worc* 88-97; Ind Chapl Teesside *York* 97-02; Dir Workplace Min for Ch in Soc *Roch* 05-12; P-in-c Dartford St Alb from 12. *3 Royal Oak Terrace, Gravesend DA12 1JU* M: 07957-193816

HEMING, Douglas. b 75. Bradf Univ BA 99 K Coll Lon MA 02 Ox Univ MTh 12. **d** 12 **p** 13. C Ashley and Mucklestone and Broughton and Croxton *Lich* from 12. *28 Burntwood View, Loggerheads, Market Drayton TF9 4GZ* T: (01630) 672430 E: doug.heming@yahoo.co.uk

HEMING, Mrs Zoe Norah. b 76. **d** 14 **p** 15. Lic to RD Hodnet *Lich* from 14. *28 Burntwood View, Loggerheads, Market Drayton TF9 4GZ* T: (01630) 672430 E: hemingzoe@yahoo.co.uk

HEMINGRAY, Raymond. b 47. Leeds Univ LLB 68 Solicitor 71. ERMC 04. **d** 07 **p** 08. Dioc Registrar *Pet* 74-14; NSM Castor w Sutton and Upton w Marholm 07-15; NSM Castor w Upton and Stibbington and Water Newton, Marholm and Sutton from 15; PtO *Ely* from 11. *4 Holywell Way, Peterborough PE3 6SS* T: (01733) 262523 E: rh@raymondhemingray.co.uk

HEMINGWAY, Peter. b 32. S'wark Ord Course 72. **d** 75 **p** 76. NSM Belmont *S'wark* 75-79; C Herne Hill St Paul 79-81; V Headstone St Geo *Lon* 81-92; V N Harrow St Alb 87-02; rtd 02. *Chelmerton, 138 Winthrope Road, Bury St Edmunds IP33 3XW* T: (01284) 705070

HEMMING, Andrew Martyn. b 56. Bath Univ BSc 78. STETS 08. **d** 11 **p** 12. NSM Axbridge w Shipham and Rowberrow *B & W* 11-14; NSM Wrington w Butcombe and Burrington from 14. *Eleuthera, Garston Lane, Blagdon, Bristol BS40 7TF* T: (01761) 462582 M: 07584-124198 E: andrewmhemming@btinternet.com

HEMMING, Terry Edward. b 47. Calvin Coll Michigan MA 84. S Dios Minl Tr Scheme 88. **d** 90 **p** 91. NSM E Win 90-09; Chapl St Swithun's Sch Win 95-07; NSM Hurstbourne Priors,

Longparish etc *Win* from 09. *St Nicholas House, Longparish, Andover SP11 6PG* T: (01264) 720215
E: revhemm@yahoo.co.uk

HEMMING-CLARK, Stanley Charles. b 29. Peterho Cam BA 52 MA 56. Ridley Hall Cam 52. **d** 54 **p** 55. C Redhill H Trin *S'wark* 54-56; C Woking St Jo *Guildf* 56-59; V Crockenhill All So *Roch* 59-97; rtd 97; PtO *Guildf* from 97. *St Anthony's, 22 Ashcroft, Shalford, Guildford GU4 8JT* T: (01483) 568197

HEMMINGS, Ms Jane Marie. b 68. Lon Univ BD 91 AKC 91 Heythrop Coll Lon MTh 95 Southn Univ PGCE 08. NTMTC 01. **d** 03 **p** 04. C Bishop's Waltham *Portsm* 03-08; NSM 07-08; C Upham 03-08; NSM 07-08; NSM Akeman *Ox* 08-12; R from 12. *The Rectory, Troy Lane, Kirtlington, Kidlington OX5 3HA* T: (01869) 350224 E: akemanbenefice@gmail.com

HEMMINGS, Keith. b 43. **d** 97. Par Dn Bedwellty *Mon* 97-05; Par Dn Bedwellty w New Tredegar 05-06; PtO from 06. *Penydarren, Park Drive, Bargoed CF81 8PJ* T: (01443) 830662

HEMMINGS, Roy Anthony. b 48. Univ of Wales (Cardiff) BD 85 MTh 00. St Mich Coll Llan 82. **d** 86 **p** 87. C Rhyl w St Ann *St As* 86-90; CF 90-08; V Maybush and Southampton St Jude *Win* from 08. *Maybush Vicarage, Sedbergh Road, Southampton SO16 9HJ* T: (023) 8070 3443 M: 07710-774431
E: padreroy48@aol.com

HEMP, Mrs Julia. b 61. Reading Univ BA 82. ERMC 10. **d** 13 **p** 14. C Earlham *Nor* from 13. *St Mary's Vicarage, Douglas Haig Road, Norwich NR5 8LD* M: 07702-665000
E: julia5454@googlemail.com

HEMPHILL, John James. b 44. TCD BA 68 MA 72. Oak Hill Th Coll 71. **d** 73 **p** 74. C Dundonald *D & D* 73-78; I Balteagh w Carrick *D & R* 78-02; I Ballyhalbert w Ardkeen *D & D* from 02. *Ballyeasboro Rectory, 187 Main Road, Portavogie, Newtownards BT22 1DA* T: (028) 4277 1234 M: 07890-012843

HEMSLEY, David Ridgway. b 36. AKC 61. **d** 61 **p** 62. C Penhill *Bris* 61-64; C Highworth w Sevenhampton and Inglesham etc 64-66; C Surbiton St Andr *S'wark* 67-70; P-in-c Tingewick w Water Stratford *Ox* 70-75; P-in-c Radclive 72-75; PM N Marston w Granborough etc 75-81; P-in-c Quainton *Ox* 75-81; TV Schorne 81-90; P-in-c Lt Missenden 90-93; V 93-01; rtd 01; PtO *Ox* from 03; AD Buckingham 09-10. *27 Overn Avenue, Buckingham MK18 1LG* T: (01280) 814636

HEMSLEY HALLS, Susan Mary. b 59. Cranmer Hall Dur 93. **d** 95 **p** 96. C Wilnecote *Lich* 95-00; P-in-c Attenborough *S'well* 00-11; V 11-13; Dioc Chapl amongst Deaf People 00-12; Dioc Dir of Ords from 12. *Address temp unknown*
E: suehh@southwell.anglican.org

HEMSTOCK, Canon Julian. b 51. Trent Poly BSc 74 CEng MIProdE. Sarum & Wells Th Coll 89. **d** 91 **p** 92. C Carrington *S'well* 91-94; C Basford St Aid 94-97; Asst Chapl Qu Medical Cen Nottm Univ Hosp NHS Trust 97-03; Chapl from 03; Hon Can *S'well* Minster from 13. *Queen's Medical Centre University Hospital, Derby Road, Nottingham NG7 2UH* T: 0115-924 9924 ext 43799 E: julian.hemstock@qmc.nhs.uk

HEMSTOCK, Mrs Pat. b 51. Sarum & Wells Th Coll 89. **d** 91 **p** 95. Par Dn Carrington *S'well* 91-94; Par Dn Basford St Aid 94-95; C 95-97; P-in-c 97-05; V Calverton from 05. *The Vicarage, Crookdole Lane, Calverton, Nottingham NG14 6GF* T: 0115-965 2552 E: pat.hemstock@btinternet.com

HEMSWORTH, John Alan. b 45. FGA 67. **d** 02 **p** 03. OLM Droylsden St Andr *Man* 02-10; P-in-c from 10; C Droylsden St Martin from 13. *St Andrew's Rectory, Merton Drive, Droylsden, Manchester M43 6BH* T: 0161-370 3242
E: john.hemsworth@ntlworld.com

HENDERSON, Canon Alastair Roy. b 27. BNC Ox BA 51 MA 54. Ridley Hall Cam 52. **d** 54 **p** 55. C Ex St Leon w H Trin 54-57; Travelling Sec IVF 57-60; C St Mary le Bow w St Pancras Soper Lane etc *Lon* 58-60; V Barton Hill St Luke w Ch Ch *Bris* 60-68; P-in-c Bris St Phil and St Jacob w Em 67-68; V Stoke Bishop 68-92; Lect Clifton Th Coll 69-71; Lect Trin Coll Bris 71-73; RD Westbury and Severnside *Bris* 73-79; Hon Can Bris Cathl 80-92; rtd 92; PtO *Ex* from 92. *3 Garden Court, Cricketfield Lane, Budleigh Salterton EX9 6PN* T: (01395) 446147

HENDERSON, Andrew Douglas. b 36. Trin Coll Cam BA 60 MA 64 Liv Univ DASS 65 MBASW. Cuddesdon Coll 60. **d** 62 **p** 63. C Newington St Paul *S'wark* 62-64; Hon C Camberwell St Luke 65-80; PtO *Lon* 85-06; *Chich* from 06. *4 Western Terrace, Brighton BN1 2LD* T: (01273) 327829

HENDERSON, Ashley. *See* HENDERSON, Peter Ashley
HENDERSON, Colin. *See* HENDERSON, Francis Colin
HENDERSON, Daniel Thomas. b 81. Nottm Univ BSc 03. Oak Hill Th Coll BTh 10. **d** 10 **p** 11. C Hailsham *Chich* 10-14; C Hove St Andr from 14. *St Andrew's Vicarage, 17 Vallance Gardens, Hove BN3 2DB* M: 07734-928877
E: dan-henderson@hotmail.co.uk

HENDERSON, David. *See* HENDERSON, Robert David Druitt
HENDERSON, David. b 35. Oak Hill NSM Course. **d** 83 **p** 84. NSM Rush Green *Chelmsf* 83-00; PtO from 00. *Le Strange*

Cottages, 2-8 Hunstanton Road, Heacham, King's Lynn PE31 7HH T: (01485) 572150

HENDERSON, Mrs Elizabeth. b 42. CITC 96. **d** 99 **p** 00. C Ballymacash *Conn* 99-00; C Finaghy 00-15; Asst Chapl Belfast City Hosp Health and Soc Services Trust 99-05; Asst Chapl Down Lisburn Health and Soc Services Trust 05-15; rtd 15. *39 Garvey Court, Lisburn BT27 4DG* T: (028) 9260 7146
E: lilabethenderson@yahoo.com

HENDERSON, Francis Colin. b 35. St Cath Coll Cam BA 59 MA 63. Cuddesdon Coll 60. **d** 62 **p** 63. C Croydon St Jo *Cant* 62-67; V Westwood *Cov* 67-75; V Chilvers Coton w Astley 75-80; P-in-c Wolston 80; P-in-c Church Lawford w Newnham Regis 80; V Wolston and Church Lawford 80-85; USA from 85; rtd 00. *1364 Katella Street, Laguna Beach CA 92651-3247, USA* T: (001) (949) 497 2239 E: echenderson@earthlink.net

HENDERSON, Janet. b 57. St Jo Coll Dur BA 88 RGN 82. Cranmer Hall Dur 85. **d** 88 **p** 94. Par Dn Wisbech SS Pet and Paul *Ely* 88-90; Par Dn Bestwood *S'well* 90-93; Tutor St Jo Coll Nottm 92-97; Lect Worship 93-97; NSM Bramcote *S'well* 94-97; Lect Worship and Tutor Ridley Hall Cam 97-01; Dir Studies 00-01; P-in-c Nuthall *S'well* 01-07; Dean of Women's Min 01-07; AD Beeston 06-07; Hon Can *S'well* Minster 03-07; Adn Richmond *Ripon* 07-13; Hon Can Ripon Cathl 11-13; Dioc Adv for NSM 11-13; Dean Llan 13; V Llandaff 13; Chapl St Mich Hospice Harrogate from 13. *Crimple House, Hornbeam Park Avenue, Harrogate HG2 8QL* T: (01423) 879687 F: 872654

HENDERSON, Mrs Janet Elizabeth. b 53. N Lon Poly BSc 75. Ripon Coll Cuddesdon 05. **d** 06 **p** 07. NSM Ellesborough, The Kimbles and Stoke Mandeville *Ox* 06-09; R from 09. *The Rectory, 28A Risborough Road, Stoke Mandeville, Aylesbury HP22 5UT* T: (01296) 612855 E: brook-farm@supanet.com

HENDERSON, Judith Ann. b 37. **d** 89 **p** 94. NSM Sheringham *Nor* 89-92; NSM Brampton St Thos *Derby* 92-00; PtO *Sarum* from 00. *Blackmore House, Stone Lane, Wimborne BH21 1HD* T: (01202) 881422

✠**HENDERSON, The Rt Revd Julian Tudor.** b 54. Keble Coll Ox BA 76 MA 81. Ridley Hall Cam 77. **d** 79 **p** 80 **c** 13. C Islington St Mary *Lon* 79-83; V Hastings Em and St Mary in the Castle *Chich* 83-92; V Claygate *Guildf* 92-05; RD Emly 96-01; Adn Dorking 05-13; Hon Can Guildf Cathl 02-13; Bp Blackb from 13. *Bishop's House, Ribchester Road, Clayton le Dale, Blackburn BB1 9EF* T: (01254) 248234 F: 246668
E: bishop@bishopofblackburn.org.uk

HENDERSON, Nicholas Paul. b 48. Selw Coll Cam BA 73 MA 77 Univ of Wales (Lamp) PhD 09. Ripon Hall Ox 73. **d** 75 **p** 76. C St Alb St Steph *St Alb* 75-78; Warden J F Kennedy Ho Cov Cathl 78-79; C Bow w Bromley St Leon *Lon* 79-85; P-in-c W Acton St Martin 85-96; V from 96; P-in-c Ealing All SS 89-95; V from 96. *The Parishes Office, 25 Birch Grove, London W3 9SP* T: (020) 8992 2333 *or* 8248 0608 F: 8993 5812
E: nicholashenderson@btinternet.com

HENDERSON, Olive Elizabeth. b 48. St Jo Coll Nottm. **d** 97 **p** 98. Aux Min Tallaght *D & G* 97-99; P-in-c Moviddy Union *C, C & R* 99-01; P-in-c Rathdrum w Glenealy, Derralossary and Laragh *D & G* 01-04; C 04-07; I 07-08; I Killeshin w Cloydagh and Killabban *C & O* 08-10; Chapl Kingston Coll Mitchelstown 10-12; I Donoughmore and Donard w Dunlavin *D & G* 12-14; rtd 14. *Strathmore, Grangemellon, Athy, Co Kildare, Republic of Ireland* M: (00353) 87-218 1891
E: oliveernest@hotmail.com

HENDERSON, Patrick James. b 57. R Holloway Coll Lon BA 78 Surrey Univ PGCE 01. St Steph Ho *Ox* 83. **d** 86 **p** 87. C Hornsey St Mary w St Geo *Lon* 86-90; V Whetstone St Jo 90-95; In RC Ch 95-01; PtO *Lon* 01-02; C Hornsey H Innocents 02-07; C Stroud Green H Trin 02-04; P-in-c 04-07; V from 07; C Hornsey H Innocents from 07; C Harringay St Paul from 10; Chapl Greig City Academy from 02. *Holy Trinity Vicarage, Granville Road, London N4 4EL* T: (020) 8340 2051 M: 07947-714893 E: pjhenderson2001@yahoo.co.uk

HENDERSON, Peter Ashley. b 59. St Martin's Coll Lanc PGCE 00. CBDTI 02. **d** 05 **p** 06. NSM Arnside *Carl* 05-08; NSM Kendal H Trin from 08. *2 Lowther Park, Kendal LA9 6RS* T: (01539) 736079 E: janash@btinternet.com

HENDERSON, Richard. b 69. St Jo Coll Nottm 04. **d** 06 **p** 07. C Beccles St Mich and St Luke *St E* 06-09; TV Sole Bay from 09. *The Rectory, 45 Wangford Road, Reydon, Southwold IP18 6PZ* T: (01502) 722192 E: richhenderson@btinternet.com

✠**HENDERSON, The Rt Revd Richard Crosbie Aitken.** b 57. Magd Coll Ox MA 84 DPhil 84. St Jo Coll Nottm 83. **d** 86 **p** 87 **c** 98. C Chinnor w Emmington and Sydenham etc *Ox* 86-89; I Abbeystrewry Union *C, C & R* 89-95; I Ross Union 95-98; Dean Ross 95-98; Chan Cork Cathl 95-98; Bp T, K & A 98-11; TV Heart of Eden *Carl* 11-12; Hon Asst Bp Carl from 11. *Tralispean, Skibbereen, Co Cork, Republic of Ireland*
E: rcah57@gmail.com

HENDERSON, Robert. b 43. TCD 66 Lambeth STh 94. **d** 69 **p** 70. C Drumglass *Arm* 69-72; Chapl Miss to Seamen 72-77; Sen Chapl Mombasa Kenya 77-78; I Mostrim w Granard, Clonbroney, Killoe etc *K, E & A* 78-82; I Belfast St Matt *Conn* 82-92; I Kilroot and Templecorran 92-98; rtd 98. *39 Garvey Court, Lisburn BT27 4DG* T: (028) 9260 7146
E: robcleric@yahoo.com

HENDERSON, Robert David Druitt. b 41. St Edm Hall Ox MA 64 Brunel Univ MA 77 K Alfred's Coll Win PGCE 88. **d** 03 **p** 04. OLM Wylye and Till Valley *Sarum* 03-10; rtd 10. *Orchard House, Salisbury Road, Steeple Langford, Salisbury SP3 4NQ* T: (01722) 790388 E: henderson.family@virgin.net

HENDERSON, Mrs Shirley Claire. b 49. Surrey Univ BA 02. Bp Otter Coll 94. **d** 96 **p** 02. NSM Gatcombe, Chale and Shorwell w Kingston *Portsm* 96-00; NSM Whitwell, Niton and St Lawrence 00-03; P-in-c Shedfield 03-06; R Shedfield and Wickham 07; TV Parkham, Alwington, Buckland Brewer etc *Ex* 07-12; TR 12-15; RD Hartland 09-15; rtd 15. *6 Town Meadows, Woolsery, Bideford EX39 5TS*
E: shirley.1949@hotmail.co.uk

HENDERSON, Terry James. b 45. St Deiniol's Hawarden 76. **d** 77 **p** 77. C Wrexham *St As* 77-79; Wilson Carlile Coll of Evang 79-81; TV Langtree *Ox* 81-87; P-in-c Aston Cantlow and Wilmcote w Billesley *Cov* 87-90; V 90-97; V St Peter-in-Thanet *Cant* 97-02; R Elmley Castle w Bricklehampton and Combertons *Worc* 02-12; V Teddington, Alstone etc 09-12; rtd 12; PtO *Cov* from 13. *8 Birdhaven Close, Banbury Road, Lighthorne, Warwick CV35 0BE*
E: terryhenderson15@gmail.com

HENDERSON, William Ernest. b 53. CEng 81 MICE 81 Southn Univ BSc 75. St Jo Coll Nottm 87. **d** 89 **p** 90. C Win Ch Ch 89-93; V Stanley *Leeds* from 93. *The Vicarage, 379 Aberford Road, Stanley, Wakefield WF3 4HE* T: (01924) 822143 *or* 835746 E: billh@stpeters-stanley.org.uk

HENDERSON SMITH, Mrs Judith Hazel. b 55. De Montfort Univ BSc 00 Nottm Univ MA 11. EMMTC 08. **d** 11 **p** 12. NSM Alvaston *Derby* 11-15; NSM Sawley from 15; Jt Dioc Ecum Officer from 12. *42 Charlton Avenue, Long Eaton, Nottingham NG10 2BX* T/F: 0115-946 0395 M: 07810-580340
E: jhhs91@hotmail.com

HENDRICKSE, Canon Clarence David. b 41. Nottm Univ PGCE 73 CEng MIMechE 71. St Jo Coll Nottm 71. **d** 74 **p** 75. C St Helens St Helen *Liv* 74-76; C Netherley Ch Ch CD 76-77; TV 78-87; V Liv Ch Ch Norris Green 87-93; V Eccleston Ch Ch 93-06; Hon Can Liv Cathl 96-06; rtd 06; PtO *Carl* from 09. *Highfield, 17 Meadow Road, Windermere LA23 2EU* T: (015394) 43058 E: canon.clarence.hendrickse@talktalk.net

HENDRY, Felicity Ann. b 65. **d** 10 **p** 11. NSM Crawley *Chich* 10-15; NSM Tadworth *S'wark* from 15. *21 East Park, Crawley RH10 6AN*

HENDRY, Mrs Helen Clare. b 58. Lanc Univ BA 79 Cam Univ PGCE 80. Reformed Th Sem Mississippi MA 85 Oak Hill Th Coll 94. **d** 95. Locat Oak Hill Th Coll 86-08; NSM Muswell Hill St Jas w St Matt *Lon* from 95. *44 The Grove, London N13 5JR* T: (020) 8882 2186 *or* 8883 6277
E: clare.hendry@st-james.org.uk

HENDRY, Leonard John. b 34. St D Coll Lamp 65. **d** 68 **p** 69. C Minchinhampton *Glouc* 68-71; C Bishop's Cleeve 71-74; V Cheltenham St Mich 74-78; V Horsley and Newington Bagpath w Kingscote 78-82; Chapl Salonika *Eur* 82-91; rtd 94. *Stratigi 34, Pilea, 543 52 Salonika, Greece* T: (0030) (231) 091 8557

HENDRY, Malcolm Graham. b 54. **d** 13 **p** 14. NSM Wrose *Leeds* 13-14; C Shipley St Paul *Bradf* from 15. *St Paul's Church House, 35 Scarborough Road, Shipley BD18 3DW* T: (01274) 599043 M: 07545-073075 E: hendrymgh@virginmedia.com

HENDY, Canon Graham Alfred. b 45. St Jo Coll Dur BA 67 MA 75 Fitzw Coll Cam CertEd Univ of Wales (Lamp) MTh 03 MPhil 07. Sarum Th Coll 67. **d** 70 **p** 71. C High Wycombe *Ox* 70-75; TV 75-78; R Upton cum Chalvey 78-83; TR 83-90; R S Walsham and Upton *Nor* 90-97; Dioc Lay Tr Officer 90-97; Can Res S'well Minster 97-02; R Upper Itchen *Win* 02-08; rtd 08; PtO *B & W* from 09. *74 Bath Road, Wells BA5 3LJ* T: (01749) 677003 E: grahamhendy@dunelm.org.uk

HENEY, William Butler. b 22. Potchefstroom Univ BA 99. CITC. **d** 60 **p** 61. C Seagoe *D & D* 60-63; I Carrickmacross *Clogh* 64-73; I Newbridge w Carnalway and Kilcullen *M & K* 73-95; Treas Kildare Cathl 81-86; Can Kildare Cathl 81-95; Adn Kildare 86-94; rtd 95; Chapl Mageough Home *D & G* from 96. *14 Trees Road, Mount Merrion, Blackrock, Co Dublin, Republic of Ireland* T: (00353) (1) 288 9773

HENGIST, Barry. b 59. N Lon Poly BA 88. Ripon Coll Cuddesdon 07. **d** 09 **p** 10. C Weybridge *Guildf* 09-13; P-in-c Shirley St Geo *S'wark* from 13. *St George's Vicarage, Elstan Way, Croydon CR0 7PR* T: (020) 8654 8747 M: 07947-068209
E: barryhengist@gmail.com

HENIG, Martin Edward. b 42. St Cath Coll Cam BA 63 MA 66 Worc Coll Ox DPhil 72 DLitt 98 FSA 75. St Steph Ho Ox 08. **d** 10 **p** 11. NSM Osney Ox from 10. *16 Alexandra Road, Oxford OX2 0DB* T: (01865) 241118 *or* 278265
E: martin.henig@arch.ox.ac.uk

HENLEY, Claud Michael. b 31. Keble Coll Ox BA 55 MA 59. Chich Th Coll 55. **d** 57 **p** 58. C Cowley St Jas *Ox* 57-60; C Wetherby *Ripon* 60-63; C Brighton St Pet *Chich* 63-69; V Brighton St Jo 69-75; V New Groombridge 75-96; rtd 96; PtO *Chich* from 97. *12 Barn Stables, De Montfort Road, Lewes BN7 1ST* T: (01273) 472467

HENLEY, Canon David Edward. b 44. Sarum & Wells Th Coll 69. **d** 72 **p** 73. C Fareham H Trin *Portsm* 72-76; C-in-c Leigh Park St Clare CD 76-78; R Freshwater 78-87; RD W Wight 83-87; R Meonstoke w Corhampton cum Exton 87-02; R Droxford 87-02; RD Bishop's Waltham 93-98; Hon Can Portsm Cathl 96-02; TR Chalke Valley *Sarum* 02-14; RD Chalke 07-12; rtd 14. *2 Beauchamp Gardens, Hatch Beauchamp, Taunton TA3 6SD* T: (01823) 481562
E: david.henley257@btinternet.com

HENLEY, Dean. b 64. St Chad's Coll Dur BA 93. Westcott Ho Cam 95. **d** 95 **p** 96. C Farncombe *Guildf* 95-99; TV Hale w Badshot Lea 99-06; R Campton, Clophill and Haynes *St Alb* from 06. *The Rectory, 4A North Lane, Haynes, Bedford MK45 3PW* T: (01234) 381235 E: deanhenley@waitrose.com

HENLEY, James Andrew. d 15. C Newport St Paul *Mon* from 15. *19 Jamaica Circle, Coedkernew, Newport NP10 8AB*
E: james.henley@gmail.com

HENLEY, John Francis Hugh. b 48. SS Mark & Jo Coll Chelsea CertEd 69. St Mich Coll Llan. **d** 82 **p** 83. C Griffithstown *Mon* 82-85; V St Hilary Greenway 85-90; P-in-c Fulham St Etheldreda w St Clem *Lon* 90-11; V from 11. *St Etheldreda's Vicarage, Doneraile Street, London SW6 6EL* T: (020) 7736 3809

HENLEY, Michael. *See* HENLEY, Claud Michael

HENNEBRY, Ian James. b 63. Cranmer Hall Dur. **d** 09 **p** 11. Argentina 09-10; C Bedlington *Newc* from 10. *St John's Vicarage, North View, Bedlington NE22 7ED* T: (01670) 822309
E: ihennebry@bedeacademy.org.uk

HENNING, Mrs Judy. b 49. Portsm Univ MSc 99. S Dios Minl Tr Scheme 85. **d** 88 **p** 97. C Catherington and Clanfield *Portsm* 88-91; C Leigh Park 91-92; PtO 94-96; Min in Whiteley and Asst to RD Fareham 96-99; C-in-c Whiteley CD 99-04; P-in-c Old Cleeve, Leighland and Treborough *B & W* 04-06; R 06-11; P-in-c Rainham *Roch* 11-13; V from 13. *The Vicarage, 80 Broadview Avenue, Gillingham ME8 9DE* T: (01634) 362874
E: judy.henning@btinternet.com

HENNINGS, John Richard. b 58. Sheff Univ BA 80. Spurgeon's Coll BA 87. **d** 07 **p** 08. SSF from 05; PtO *Ripon* 09-10; *Sheff* 10-11. *The Friary, Hilfield, Dorchester DT2 7BE* T: (01300) 341345 E: johnssf@franciscans.org.uk

HENRY, Cornelius Augustus. b 70. K Coll NY BA 92 Heythrop Coll Lon MA 06. NTMTC 07. **d** 09 **p** 10. C Hornchurch St Andr *Chelmsf* 09-13; V Forest Gate St Sav and St Jas from 13. *St Saviour's Rectory, Sidney Road, London E7 0EF* T: (020) 8534 6109 E: revcahenry@gmail.com

HENRY, Miss Jacqueline Margaret. b 40. Open Univ BA 82. Trin Coll Bris 77. **dss** 83 **d** 87 **p** 94. Par Dn The Lye and Stambermill *Worc* 87-89; Educn Chapl 89-93; C Tolleshunt Knights w Tiptree and Gt Braxted *Chelmsf* 94-97; Chapl amongst Deaf People 94-97; TV Stantonbury and Willen *Ox* 97-02; rtd 02; PtO *Cant* 02-09; *Roch* from 09. *114 Maidstone Road, Rochester ME1 3DT* T: (01634) 829183

HENRY, Peter. b 49. BTh. St Jo Coll Nottm. **d** 84 **p** 85. C Sinfin Moor and Blagreaves St Andr CD *Derby* 84-89; V Guernsey St Jo *Win* 89-97; P-in-c Sawley *Derby* 97-01; R 01-06; rtd 06. *5 Les Casquets, Amherst Road, St Peter Port, Guernsey GY1 2DH* T: (01481) 715699

HENRY, Canon Stephen Kenelm Malim. b 37. Brasted Th Coll 58 Bps' Coll Cheshunt 60. **d** 62 **p** 63. C Leic St Phil 62-67; CF 67-70; V Woodhouse *Wakef* 70-01; Hon Can Wakef Cathl 00-01; rtd 01; PtO *Leeds* from 01. *1 Yorkstone, Crosland Moor, Huddersfield HD4 5NQ* T: (01484) 644807
E: mandsmalim64@btinternet.com

HENRY HOLLAND, Miss Anne. b 56. **d** 12 **p** 13. NSM Ludgvan, Marazion, St Hilary and Perranuthnoe *Truro* from 12. *Seawards, Perranuthnoe, Penzance TR20 9NF* T: (01736) 710820 M: 07768-166309 E: missanniehenry@hotmail.com

HENSHALL, Keith. *See* HENSHALL, Ronald Keith

✠**HENSHALL, The Rt Revd Michael.** b 28. St Chad's Coll Dur BA 54. **d** 56 **p** 57 **c** 76. C Sewerby w Marton *York* 56-59; C Bridlington Quay H Trin 56-59; C-in-c Micklehurst CD *Ches* 59-62; V Micklehurst 62-63; V Altrincham St Geo 63-76; Hon Can Ches Cathl 72-76; Suff Bp Warrington *Liv* 76-96; rtd 96; PtO *Liv* 96-03; *York* 96-99; Hon Asst Bp York from 99. *28 Hermitage Way, Sleights, Whitby YO22 5HG* T: (01947) 811233

HENSHALL, The Very Revd Nicholas James. b 62. Wadh Coll Ox BA 84 MA 88. Ripon Coll Cuddesdon 85. **d** 88 **p** 89. C Blyth St Mary *Newc* 88-92; V Scotswood 92-02; Can Res Derby Cathl 02-08; V High Harrogate Ch Ch *Ripon* 08-14; Dean Chelmsf from 14. *3 Harlings Grove, Chelmsford CM1 1YQ* T: (01245) 294492
E: nicholas.henshall@chelmsfordcathedral.org.uk

HENSHALL, Ronald Keith. b 54. Loughb Coll of Educn CertEd 76. Chich Th Coll 87. **d** 89 **p** 90. C Ribbleton *Blackb* 89-92; TV 95-98; P-in-c Charlestown and Lowland St Kitts-Nevis 92-95; V Ellel w Shireshead *Blackb* 98-02; Cyprus 02-05; Chapl R Alexandra and Albert Sch Reigate 05-06; P-in-c Lerwick and Burravoe *Ab* 06-10; V Holme-in-Cliviger w Worsthorne *Blackb* from 10. *The Vicarage, Gorple Road, Worsthorne, Burnley BB10 3NN* T: (01282) 428478
E: keithhenshall@btinternet.com

HENSHAW, Nicholas Newell. b 49. Rhodes Univ BA 72. Cuddesdon Coll 73. **d** 75 **p** 76. C Beaconsfield *Ox* 75-78; Chapl Wellington Coll Berks 78-80; C Pimlico St Pet w Westmr Ch Ch *Lon* 80-82; Chapl Sevenoaks Sch from 82; Hon C Sevenoaks St Nic *Roch* from 82; PtO *St E* from 08. *Sevenoaks School, High Street, Sevenoaks TN13 1HU* T: (01732) 455133

HENSON, Carolyn. b 44. Bedf Coll Lon BA 65 Nottm Univ MTh 88 PhD 97 Solicitor 75. EMMTC 82. **dss** 85 **d** 87 **p** 94. Braunstone *Leic* 85-89; Par Dn 87-89; Adult Educn and Tr Officer *Ely* 89-91; NSM Sutton and Witcham w Mepal 89-95; Chapl Gt Ormond Street Hosp for Children NHS Trust 95-96; NSM Cainscross w Selsley *Glouc* 96-97; Vice Prin EMMTC *S'well* 97-01; R Morley w Smalley and Horsley Woodhouse *Derby* 02-05; rtd 05; Chapl St Mich Hospice Harrogate from 09. *Ryedale View, Scagglethorpe, Malton YO17 8DY* T: (01944) 758283 E: carolyn.henson@virgin.net

HENSON, Joanna. b 62. **d** 06 **p** 07. NSM Egton-cum-Newland and Lowick and Colton *Carl* 06-12; rtd 12. *Woodside Cottage, Colton, Ulverston LA12 8HE* T: (01229) 861800
E: joannahenson@aol.com

HENSON, John David. b 49. EMMTC. **d** 00 **p** 01. NSM Beckingham w Walkeringham *S'well* 00-02; NSM Gringley-on-the-Hill 00-02; NSM Misterton and W Stockwith 02-05; C 06-07; C Beckingham w Walkeringham and Gringley 06-07; P-in-c Beckingham and Walkeringham and Misterton etc 07-11; V 11-15; Asst Chapl HM Pris Whatton 00-05; V Beckingham, Walkeringham, Misterton, W Stockwith, Clayworth and Gringley-on-the-Hill *S'well* from 15; Sen Police Chapl from 03. *The Vicarage, 4 Church Lane, Misterton, Doncaster DN10 4AL* T: (01427) 890270
E: jd.henson@btinternet.com

HENSON, Canon John Richard. b 40. Selw Coll Cam BA 62 MA 66. Ridley Hall Cam 62. **d** 65 **p** 66. C Ollerton *S'well* 65-68; Univs Sec CMS 68-73; Chapl Scargill Ho 73-78; V Shipley St Paul *Bradf* 78-83; TR Shipley St Paul and Frizinghall 83-91; V Ilkeston St Mary *Derby* 91-99; V Mickleover St Jo 99-05; Dioc Ecum Officer 96-05; Hon Can Derby Cathl 00-05; rtd 05; PtO *Derby* from 05. *6 Ganton Close, Nottingham NG3 3ET* E: john.henson3@ntlworld.com

HENSON, Shaun Christopher. b 64. E Nazarene Coll (USA) BA 94 Duke Univ (USA) MDiv 98 Regent's Park Coll Ox DPhil 07. Duke Div Sch. **d** 04 **p** 05. C Blenheim *Ox* from 04; Chapl St Hugh's Coll Ox from 07. *St Hugh's College, St Margarets Road, Oxford OX2 6LE, or 19 Park Close, Bladon, Woodstock OX20 1RN* T: (01865) 274955 M: 07795-547555
E: shaun.henson@st-hughs.ox.ac.uk

HENSTRIDGE, Edward John. b 31. Ex Coll Ox BA 55 MA 59 FCIPD 77. Wells Th Coll 55. **d** 57 **p** 58. C Milton *Portsm* 57-62; V Soberton w Newtown 62-69; LtO *Derby* 69-71; PtO *Guildf* 72-84 and from 02; LtO 84-02; Bp's Officer for NSMs 97-01. *Hunters Moon, Lower Ham Lane, Elstead, Godalming GU8 6HQ* T: (01252) 702272 E: johnhn@globalnet.co.uk

HENTHORNE, Thomas Roger. b 30. EAMTC. **d** 79 **p** 80. Hd Master St Mary's Sch St Neots 67-93; NSM St Neots *Ely* 79-04; PtO from 04. *Stapeley, 45 Berkley Street, Eynesbury, St Neots PE19 2ND* T: (01480) 472548
E: roger.henthorne@uwclub.net

HENTON, John Martin. b 48. AKC 71 St Luke's Coll Ex DipEd 72. St Aug Coll Cant 74. **d** 74 **p** 75. C Woolwich St Mary w H Trin *S'wark* 74-77; C Cotham St Mary *Bris* 77-78; C Cotham St Sav w St Mary 78-80; R Filton 80-87; Chapl Ex Sch and St Marg Sch 87-91; V Ex St Dav 91-09; rtd 09. *Upexe Cottage, Upexe, Exeter EX5 5ND* T: (01392) 860038
E: j.henton@tesco.net

HENWOOD, Mrs Gillian Kathleen. b 56. ABIPP 81 Lanc Univ MA 97. CBDTI 94. **d** 97 **p** 98. NSM Whitechapel w Admarsh-in-Bleasdale *Blackb* 97-00; NSM Fellside Team 00-01; Rural Chapl 00-03; Bp's Adv for Leisure and Tourism 01-03; C Westmr St Jas *Lon* 03-04; V Nunthorpe *York* 04-09; P-in-c Riding Mill *Newc* 09-10; Chapl Shepherd's Dene Retreat Ho 09-10; Adv for Spirituality and Spiritual Direction 09-10;

P-in-c Ribchester w Stidd *Blackb* 10-11; R from 11. *The Rectory, Riverside, Ribchester, Preston PR3 3XS* T: (01254) 878352
E: gillhenwood@hotmail.com

HENWOOD, Martin John. b 58. DL 05. Glas Univ BD 81. Ripon Coll Cuddesdon. **d** 85 **p** 86. C Dartford H Trin *Roch* 85-88; C St Martin-in-the-Fields *Lon* 88-93; V Dartford H Trin *Roch* from 93. *The Vicarage, High Street, Dartford DA1 1RX* T: (01322) 222782

HENWOOD, Canon Peter Richard. b 32. St Edm Hall Ox BA 55 MA 69. Cuddesdon Coll 56. **d** 57 **p** 58. C Rugby St Andr *Cov* 57-62; C-in-c Gleadless Valley CD *Sheff* 62-71; V Plaistow St Mary *Roch* 71-97; RD Bromley 79-96; Hon Can Roch Cathl 88-97; rtd 97; PtO *Cant* 99-14. *Wayside, 1 Highfield Close, Sandling Road, Saltwood, Hythe CT21 4QP* T: (01303) 230039

HENWOOD (née OAKLEY), Mrs Susan Mary. b 55. Salford Univ BSc 76. St Jo Coll Nottm 84. **d** 87 **p** 94. Par Dn Armthorpe *Sheff* 87-91; C Howell Hill *Guildf* 91-97; PtO *Cov* 02-04; NSM Bidford-on-Avon 04-15; NSM Heart of England from 15. *24 High Street, Bidford-on-Avon, Alcester B50 4BU* T: (01789) 490630

HEPBURN, Julia Mary. b 61. St Andr Univ BSc 82 Man Univ MB, ChB 85. Linc Sch of Th and Min 04. **d** 12 **p** 13. OLM Spring Line Gp *Linc* from 12; OLM Owmby Gp from 12. *Garden House, Burton, Lincoln LN1 2RD* T: (01522) 526120
E: julia@owmbygroup.co.uk

HEPPER, Christopher Michael Alan. b 55. Wolv Univ BSc 78. St Jo Coll Nottm 90. **d** 92 **p** 93. C High Harrogate Ch Ch *Ripon* 92-95; Bp's Dom Chapl 95-99; Dioc Communications Officer 95-97; NSM Ripon H Trin 98-99; P-in-c Poitou-Charentes *Eur* 99-11; P-in-c Leyburn w Bellerby *Leeds* from 11; AD Wensley from 13. *The Vicarage, I'Anson Close, Leyburn DL8 5LF* T/F: (01969) 622251 E: revmichael@btinternet.com

HEPPER, William Raymond. b 62. Kingston Poly BA 83. Trin Coll Bris BA 98. **d** 98 **p** 99. C Spring Grove St Mary *Lon* 98-01; CMS Egypt 01-04; NSM Greenford H Cross *Lon* 05-08; PtO from 08. *12A Medway Drive, Perivale, Greenford UB6 8LN* T: (020) 8997 4953 E: williamhepper@hotmail.com

HEPTINSTALL, Canon Lillian. b 49. EMMTC 99. **d** 02 **p** 03. NSM Chilwell *S'well* 02-15; Hon Can S'well Minster 12-15; rtd 15. *8 Cranston Road, Bramcote, Nottingham NG9 3GU* T: 0115-916 4588 E: heptinstall@ntlworld.com

HEPTINSTALL, Mrs Susan Margaret. b 56. Yorks Min Course 08. **d** 10 **p** 11. NSM Halifax St Aug and Mount Pellon *Leeds* from 10. *26 Sandbeds Road, Pellon, Halifax HX2 0JF* T: (01422) 341436 M: 07510-510359 E: vicarsue@gmail.com

HEPWORTH, Canon Ernest John Peter. b 42. K Coll Lon BD 65 AKC 65 Hull Univ MA 87. **d** 66 **p** 67. C Headingley *Ripon* 66-69; Asst Chapl St Geo Hosp Lon 69-71; C Gt Grimsby St Mary and St Jas *Linc* 71-72; TV 72-74; V Crosby 74-80; V Barton upon Humber 80-04; RD Yarborough 86-92; Can and Preb Linc Cathl 94-04; rtd 04. *63 Ferriby Road, Barton-upon-Humber DN18 5LQ* T: (01652) 661363 E: ehep01@aol.com

HEPWORTH, Michael David Albert. b 37. Em Coll Cam BA 59 MA 63 Lon Inst of Educn PGCE 60. Ridley Hall Cam 65. **d** 67 **p** 68. C Eastbourne All SS *Chich* 67-69; Teacher Eastbourne Coll 67-69; Asst Chapl Bedford Sch 69-72; Chapl 72-83; Hd Master Birkdale Sch 83-98; PtO *Sheff* 83-09; *Derby* 83-09; *Guildf* from 10. *6 Elm Gardens, Claygate, Esher KT10 0JS* T: (01372) 466651 E: michaelhepworth@talktalk.net

HERAPATH, Jonathan James. b 67. Westmr Coll Ox BTh 96 Ox Brookes Univ PGCE 02. St Steph Ho Ox MTh 06. **d** 05 **p** 06. C Cowley St Jo *Ox* 05-07; Chapl SS Helen and Kath Sch Abingdon 07-10; Chapl Wadh Coll Ox 10-12; PtO *Portsm* from 12. *The Rectory, Rectory Lane, Brighstone, Newport PO30 4QH* T: (01983) 740267 M: 07745-405150
E: jonathanherapath@gmail.com

HERBERT, Christopher John. b 37. Dur Univ BA 60. Cranmer Hall Dur 60. **d** 62 **p** 63. C Huyton Quarry *Liv* 62-65; C Rainford 65-68; V Impington *Ely* 68-78; RD N Stowe 76-78; V Gt Shelford 78-97; RD Shelford 80-85; rtd 97. *North Place, Crown Street, Great Bardfield, Braintree CM7 4ST* T: (01371) 810516

✠**HERBERT, The Rt Revd Christopher William.** b 44. Univ of Wales (Lamp) BA 65 Bris Univ PGCE 65 Leic Univ MPhil 02 PhD 08 Herts Univ Hon DLitt 03. Wells Th Coll 65. **d** 67 **p** 68 **c** 95. C Tupsley *Heref* 67-71; Dioc RE Adv 71-76; Dioc Dir RE 76-81; Preb Heref Cathl 76-81; V Bourne *Guildf* 81-90; Hon Can Guildf Cathl 85-95; Adn Dorking 90-95; Bp St Alb *St Alb* 95-09; rtd 09; Hon Asst Bp Guildf from 09; Hon Asst Bp Win from 09; Hon Asst Bp Chich 10-14. *1 Beacon Close, Wrecclesham, Farnham GU10 4PA* T: (01252) 795600
E: cherbert@threeabbeys.org.uk

HERBERT, Clair Geoffrey Thomas. b 36. Tyndale Hall Bris 61. **d** 64 **p** 65. C Nottingham St Sav *S'well* 64-67; C Harwell *Ox* 67-70; C Chilton All SS 67-70; V Bucklebury w Marlston 70-80; Chapl Brighton Coll Jun Sch 80-83; Hon C Upton

(Overchurch) *Ches* 85-86; C 86-88; V Collier Row St Jas and Havering-atte-Bower *Chelmsf* 88-01; rtd 01; PtO *Leeds* from 01. *24 Birstwith Grange, Birstwith, Harrogate HG3 3AH* T: (01423) 771315 E: geoffnval@vwclub.net

HERBERT, Clare Marguerite. b 54. St Hild Coll Dur BA 76 New Coll Edin MTh 78. Linc Th Coll 79. **dss 81 d** 87 **p** 94. Clifton St Paul and Asst Chapl Bris Univ 81-84; Hon Par Dn Bris St Mary Redcliffe w Temple etc 87-90; Dioc Past Care Adv *Lon* 92-95; Hon C Clapham Team *S'wark* 94-96; C St Martin-in-the-Fields *Lon* 96-98; R Soho St Anne w St Thos and St Pet 98-07; Dean of Women's Min Two Cities Area 01-07; Nat Co-ord Inclusive Ch 07-10; Lect St Martin-in-the-Fields *Lon* 10-14; rtd 14; Tutor SEITE from 13; PtO *S'wark* from 14. *37 Sydenham Hill, London SE26 6SH* M: 07504-577210 T: (020) 8761 3616 E: herbert.clare@googlemail.com

HERBERT, Canon David Alexander Sellars. b 39. Bris Univ BA 60. St Steph Ho Ox 65. **d** 67 **p** 68. C St Leonards Ch Ch *Chich* 67-81; V Bickley *Roch* 81-09; Hon Can Roch Cathl 92-09; rtd 09. *54 High Street, Chislehurst BR7 5AQ* M: 07748-997586 T: (020) 8467 5230 E: fatherdavidherbert@btinternet.com

HERBERT, Canon David Roy. b 51. K Coll Lon BD 73 AKC 73 Ches Univ MTh 12. **d** 74 **p** 75. C Sheff St Aid w St Luke 74-75; C Sheff Manor 75-78; TV Gleadless Valley 78-83; TV Ellesmere Port *Ches* 83-93; V Tarvin 93-09; Continuing Minl Tr Officer 03-09; CMD Officer and IME (4-7) Officer from 09; Hon Can Ches Cathl from 08. *25 Blackstairs Road, Ellesmere Port CH66 1TX* T: 0151-356 4554 E: david.herbert@chester.anglican.org

HERBERT, Mrs Denise Bridget Helen. b 42. Win Univ MA 11 SRN 72 SCM 74. Ripon Coll Cuddesdon. **d** 95 **p** 96. C Ocean View S Africa 95-97; C Grahamstown Cathl 97-99; Sub-Dean 99-00; R Jedburgh *Edin* 00-08; rtd 08; R Newport-on-Tay St And from 09. *43 Bridiewell Gardens, Gauldry, Newport-on-Tay DD6 8RY* T: (01382) 330411 E: dbh.herbert@btinternet.com

HERBERT, Geoffrey. See HERBERT, Clair Geoffrey Thomas

HERBERT, Geoffrey William. b 38. Ox Univ MA 62 Birm Univ PhD 72. Qu Coll Birm 80. **d** 82 **p** 83. C Hall Green Ascension *Birm* 82-85; R Sheldon 85-95; rtd 95; PtO *Birm* from 95; Co-ord for Spiritual Direction 00-05. *28 Lulworth Road, Birmingham B28 8NS* T: 0121-777 2684 E: gandjherbert@tesco.net

HERBERT, Graham Victor. b 61. St Jo Coll Nottm BA 02. **d** 02 **p** 03. C Strood St Nic w St Mary *Roch* 02-06; P-in-c Grain w Stoke 06-09; R Milton next Gravesend w Denton from 09. *The Rectory, Church Walk, Gravesend DA12 2QU* T: (01474) 533434 E: graham.herbert@diocese-rochester.org

HERBERT, Ian Charles. b 65. Trin Coll Bris 10. **d** 12 **p** 13. C Haddenham w Cuddington, Kingsey etc *Ox* from 12. *2 Church Close, Cuddington, Aylesbury HP18 0AT* E: ian.herbert@yahoo.co.uk

HERBERT, Jonathan Patrick. b 62. Bris Univ BA 86. Linc Th Coll 86. **d** 88 **p** 89. C Kirkby *Liv* 88-91; TV Blakenall Heath *Lich* 91-96; Pilsdon Community 96-10. *The Friary, Hilfield, Dorchester DT2 7BE* T: (01300) 341345 E: jonathanherbert1@hotmail.co.uk

HERBERT, Malcolm Francis. b 53. K Coll Lon BD 74 AKC 74 Glos Univ PhD 11 St Mary's Coll Chelt CertEd 75. Trin Coll Bris 76. **d** 77 **p** 78. C Wotton-under-Edge w Ozleworth and N Nibley *Glouc* 77-79; C Milton B A W 79-80; C Worle 80-85; V Woking Ch Ch *Guildf* 86-02; RD Woking 94-99; Dioc Dir of Ords *Bris* 02-07; C Kington St Michael and Chippenham St Paul w Hardenhuish etc 02-05; C Chippenham St Pet 05-07; Hon Can Bris Cathl 05-07; V Hounslow H Trin w St Paul and St Mary *Lon* 07-13; rtd 13. *Address temp unknown* E: malcolm.herbert2@btopenworld.com

HERBERT, Michael. b 35. Nottm Univ BA 57. St D Coll Lamp 59. **d** 61 **p** 62. C Paston *Pet* 61-65; C Northampton All SS w St Kath 65-67; R Sutton w Upton 67-72; Asst Youth Chapl 67-72; Ind Chapl 72-84; P-in-c Pitsford 79-84; Ind Chapl *Worc* 84-01; TV Redditch, The Ridge 84-01; Chapl NE Worcs Coll 86-01; rtd 01; PtO *Worc* from 01. *33 Abbey Road, Redditch B97 4BL* T/F: (01527) 69975 E: rev.mike.herbert@fsmail.net

HERBERT, Peter David. b 83. Pemb Coll Cam BA 05 MSci 05 MA 08 Herts Univ PhD 12. Oak Hill Th Coll BA 13. **d** 13 **p** 14. C Cromer *Nor* from 13. *18 Vicarage Road, Cromer NR27 9DQ* T: (01263) 514990 E: revpeterherbert@gmail.com

HERBERT, Canon Ronald. b 53. Worc Coll Ox BA 75 MA 80 Lon Univ BD 78 W Kentucky Univ MA 79. Oak Hill Th Coll 75. **d** 79 **p** 80. C Welling *Roch* 79-89; V Falconwood 89-90; V Beacontree St Mary *Chelmsf* 90-07; Hon Can Chelmsf Cathl 02-07; V Stonebridge St Mich *Lon* from 07. *St Michael's Vicarage, Hillside, London NW10 8LB* T: (020) 8965 7443 E: ronald.herbert@virgin.net

HERBERT, Mrs Rosemary. b 44. Westf Coll Lon BSc 65. Qu Coll Birm 81. **dss** 85 **d** 87. Malvern Link w Cowleigh *Worc* 85-91; Hon Par Dn 87-91; NSM Malvern H Trin and St Jas from 91. *4 Cedar Avenue, Malvern WR14 2SG* T: (01684) 572497

HERBERT, Stephen Edward. b 54. Hastings Coll Nebraska BA 76 Bemidji State Univ MA 81. Seabury-Western Th Sem MDiv 87. **d** 87 **p** 87. V Lake City Grace Ch USA 87-90; Asst P Vancouver St Jas Canada 90-00; TV Wythenshawe *Man* 00-06; TR 06-09; P-in-c Byker St Martin *Newc* from 09; P-in-c Byker St Mich w St Lawr from 09; P-in-c Byker St Ant from 12. *St Martin's Vicarage, 152 Roman Avenue, Newcastle upon Tyne NE6 2RJ* T: 0191-265 5931 E: stephenherbert152@btinternet.com

HERBERT, Canon Timothy David. b 57. Man Univ BA 78 MPhil 88 PhD 04. Ridley Hall Cam 79. **d** 81 **p** 82. C Macclesfield St Mich *Ches* 81-85; V Wharton 85-93; Asst CME Officer 90-93; P-in-c Thanington *Cant* 93-98; Dir of Ords 93-98; Dir Dioc Tr Inst *Carl* 99-14; C Cotehill and Cumwhinton 99-00; C Scotby and Cotehill w Cumwhinton 00-14; P-in-c Aspatria w Hayton and Gilcrux from 14; Hon Can Carl Cathl from 99. *The Vicarage, King Street, Aspatria, Wigton CA7 3AL* T: (016973) 22712 E: therbert@globalnet.co.uk

✠**HERD, The Rt Revd William Brian.** b 31. Clifton Th Coll 55. **d** 58 **p** 59 **c** 76. C Wolverhampton St Luke *Lich* 58-61; Uganda 61-77; Adn Karamoja 70-75; Bp Karamoja 76-77; Deputation Sec (Ireland) BCMS 77-89; C Harrow Trin St Mich *Lon* 89-93; V Gresley *Derby* 93-98; rtd 98; PtO *Sarum* from 98. *Karibu, 13 Ambleside, Weymouth DT3 5HH* T: (01305) 770257

HEREFORD, Archdeacon of. See BENSON, The Ven George Patrick

HEREFORD, Bishop of. See FRITH, The Rt Revd Richard Michael Cokayne

HEREFORD, Dean of. See TAVINOR, The Very Revd Michael Edward

HEREWARD, John Owen. b 53. Lon Univ MB, BS 77 FRCSE 82. Ridley Hall Cam 89. **d** 91 **p** 92. C W Ealing St Jo w St Jas *Lon* 91-95; P-in-c Hanwell St Mellitus w St Mark 95-10; V 10-13; Dir Post-Ord Tr 97-05; AD Ealing 98-03; R St Breoke and Egloshayle *Truro* from 13. *8 Winwell Field, Wadebridge PL27 6UJ* E: johnhereward@hotmail.com

HERKES, Richard Andrew. b 54. Kent Univ BA 75. STETS 99. **d** 02 **p** 03. NSM Polegate *Chich* from 02. *31 Wannock Lane, Eastbourne BN20 9SB* T: (01323) 488328 E: rherkes@hotmail.com

HERKLOTS, Canon John Radu. b 31. Trin Hall Cam BA 53 MA 61. Westcott Ho Cam 54. **d** 55 **p** 56. C Attercliffe w Carbrook *Sheff* 55-60; C Stoke Damerel *Ex* 60-65; V Devonport St Bart 65-72; V Denmead *Portsm* 72-97; RD Havant 82-87; Hon Can Portsm Cathl 86-97; rtd 97; PtO *Heref* 97-02; *Portsm* from 03. *14 Derwent Road, Lee-on-the-Solent PO13 8JG* T: (023) 9255 2652

HERON, David George. b 49. AKC 72. **d** 73 **p** 74. C Stockton St Chad *Dur* 73-77; C Beamish 77-81; R Willington and Sunnybrow 81-95; V Dipton and Leadgate 95-11; rtd 11. *31 Hill Top, Stanley DH9 0UZ* E: fatherheron@talktalk.net

HERON, George Dobson. b 34. TD. Cranmer Hall Dur 58. **d** 61 **p** 62. C Benfieldside *Dur* 61-65; C Winlaton 65-68; V Dunston St Nic 68-77; P-in-c Dunston Ch Ch 74-77; V Dunston 77-82; V Gateshead St Helen 82-89; rtd 94; PtO *Dur* 94-96; *Newc* from 94. *36 Woodlands Road, Shotley Bridge, Consett DH8 0DE* T: (01207) 507733

HERON, Nicholas Peter. b 60. Man Univ BA 81 Southn Univ BTh 86. Sarum & Wells Th Coll. **d** 84 **p** 85. C Brinnington w Portwood *Ches* 84-87; Chapl RAF 87-14; P-in-c Wem *Lich* from 14; P-in-c Lee Brockhurst from 14. *The Rectory, Ellesmere Road, Wem, Shrewsbury SY4 5TU*

HERON, Simon Alexander. b 68. Ridley Hall Cam 05. **d** 07 **p** 08. C Frindsbury w Upnor and Chattenden *Roch* 07-11; P-in-c Lawford *Chelmsf* from 11. *The Rectory, Church Hill, Lawford, Manningtree CO11 2JX* T: (01206) 392659 E: simon.heron@mac.com

HERRICK, Canon Andrew Frederick. b 58. Univ of Wales (Lamp) BA 80. Wycliffe Hall Ox 80. **d** 82 **p** 83. C Aberystwyth St D 82-85; P-in-c Llangeitho and Blaenpennal w Betws Leucu etc 85-86; R 86-88; Youth Chapl 86-88; R Aberporth w Tremain and Blaenporth 88-91; Succ St D Cathl 91-94; V Betws w Ammanford 94-00; TV Aberystwyth from 00; Hon Can St D Cathl from 14. *The Vicarage, Piercefield Lane, Penparcau, Aberystwyth SY23 1RX* T: (01970) 617819 E: andyherrick101@gmail.com

HERRICK, Canon David William. b 52. Middx Poly BSc 73. St Jo Coll Nottm 79. **d** 82 **p** 83. C Ipswich St Matt *St E* 82-85; C Nor St Pet Mancroft w St Jo Maddermarket 85-88; V Bury St Edmunds St Geo *St E* 88-96; P-in-c Gt Barton 96-99; Dir Studies Dioc Min Course 99-12; Vice Prin 04-12; Lay Min Tr Officer from 12; Dioc Warden of Readers and Lic Lay Min from

14; PtO *Sarum* from 13; Hon Can St E Cathl from 13. *Diocesan Office, St Nicholas Centre, 4 Cutler Street, Ipswich IP1 1UQ* T: (01473) 298500 *or* (01202) 882340
E: david.herrick@cofesuffolk.org

HERRICK (*formerly* COWLEY), Mrs Jean Louie Cameron. b 39. Sarum Dioc Tr Coll CertEd 59. SAOMC 94. **d** 96 **p** 97. NSM Chorleywood Ch Ch *St Alb* 96-02; NSM Hermitage *Ox* 02-05; PtO *Glouc* from 05. *52 Cambrian Road, Walton Cardiff, Tewkesbury GL20 7RP* T: (01684) 295598
E: jean.herrick@tesco.net

HERRICK (*née* RENAUT), Canon Vanessa Anne. b 58. York Univ BA 80 Fitzw Coll Cam MA 96 LTCL 75. St Jo Coll Nottm 80 Ridley Hall Cam 94. **d** 96 **p** 97. C St E Cathl Distr 96-99; Chapl Fitzw Coll Cam 99-02; Fell 01-02; Tutor Ridley Hall Cam 99-02; Dir Min and Vocation *Ely* 03-12; Hon Can Ely Cathl 03-12; R Wimborne Minster *Sarum* from 12; P-in-c Witchampton, Stanbridge and Long Crichel etc from 15; P-in-c Horton, Chalbury, Hinton Martel and Holt St Jas from 15; Can and Preb Sarum Cathl from 14. *The Rectory, 17 King Street, Wimborne BH21 1DZ* T: (01202) 882340
E: rector@wimborneminster.org.uk

HERRINGTON, Philip. b 75. St Mellitus Coll. **d** 12 **p** 13. C Enfield Ch Ch Trent Park *Lon* from 12. *2 Chalk Lane, Cockfosters, Barnet EN4 9JQ* M: 07887-706734
E: philherrington181@gmail.com

HERROD, Canon Kathryn. b 59. Warwick Univ BSc 80 Matlock Coll of Educn PGCE 81. St Jo Coll Nottm MA 97. **d** 97 **p** 98. C Wollaton *S'well* 97-01; R Warsop 01-10; TR Hucknall Torkard from 10; Dean of Women's Min from 15; Hon Can S'well Minster from 11. *The Rectory, Annesley Road, Hucknall, Nottingham NG15 7DE* T: 0115-964 1499
E: revkathryn@aol.com

HERRON, Robert Gordon John. b 36. MCIPD 75. Wycliffe Hall Ox 65. **d** 77 **p** 78. C Ditton St Mich *Liv* 77-80; C W Kirby St Bridget *Ches* 80-82; R Gorton Our Lady and St Thos *Man* 82-00; rtd 00; PtO *Ches* from 10. *The Gables, 13 West Road, Bowdon, Altrincham WA14 2LD*

HERTFORD, Archdeacon of. See JONES, The Ven Trevor Pryce

HERTFORD, Suffragan Bishop of. See BEASLEY, The Rt Revd Noel Michael Roy

HERTH, Daniel Edwin. b 36. Xavier Univ Cincinnati BS 58. Ch Div Sch of Pacific MDiv 83. **d** 83 **p** 84. C Oakland St Paul USA 83-86; R Alameda Ch 86-97; NSM Gt and Lt Ouseburn w Marton cum Grafton etc *Ripon* 98-01; Chapl HM YOI Wetherby from 99. *The Garden House, 32 Mallorie Park Drive, Ripon HG4 2QF* T/F: (01765) 602558 M: 07779-379420
E: danieleherthsr@hotmail.com

HERVÉ, Canon John Anthony. b 49. TD 94. Open Univ BA 81 Wolv Univ PGCE 95. Lich Th Coll 70. **d** 73 **p** 74. C Middlesbrough All SS *York* 73-76; CF 76-81; CF (TAVR) 81-08; P-in-c Handsworth St Andr *Birm* 81-86; Hon C Cowley St Jo *Ox* 86-90; Tutor St Steph Ho Ox 86-90; V Sparkbrook St Agatha w Balsall Heath St Barn *Birm* 90-14; P-in-c Highgate 05-10; Hon Can Birm Cathl 05-14; rtd 14. *29 Lytton House, St Luke's Road South, Torquay TQ2 5PA* T: (01803) 295887

HERVEY, Mrs Mary Diana. b 41. St Hugh's Coll Ox BA 63. St And Dioc Tr Course 83 TISEC 96. **d** 92 **p** 94. Par Dn Cupar *St And* 92-94; Asst Chapl St Andr Univ 94-97; Asst P Cen Fife Team 94-97; C Ulverston St Mary w H Trin *Carl* 97-00; P-in-c Barrow St Jo 00-06; rtd 06; PtO *Carl* from 08; *Leeds* from 11. *Norihamar, Baltasound, Unst, Shetland ZE2 9DS*
T: (01957) 711331 E: revdih@aol.com

HESELTINE, Mrs Barbara Joan. b 42. Keele Univ BA 65. S'wark Ord Course 85. **d** 88 **p** 94. NSM Addington *S'wark* 88-98; PtO *Truro* 98-02; NSM Feock 02-13; rtd 13. *The Lodge, Penpol, Devoran, Truro TR3 6NA* T/F: (01872) 870039
M: 07767-264060 E: barbara.heseltine@tiscali.co.uk

HESELWOOD, Eric Harold. b 43. Oak Hill Th Coll 84. **d** 86 **p** 87. C Farnborough *Roch* 86-88; V Biggin Hill 88-96; V Orpington All SS 96-98; V Bromley Common St Aug 98-05; rtd 05; PtO *Roch* 06-08; P-in-c Cudham and Downe from 08. *34 Victoria Gardens, Biggin Hill, Westerham TN16 3DJ* T/F: (01959) 509131 E: eric.heselwood@ntlworld.com

HESFORD-LOCKE, Richard Nigel. b 61. Coll of Resurr Mirfield 92. **d** 94 **p** 95. C Middlesbrough Ascension *York* 94-97; C Paignton St Jo *Ex* 97-98; rtd 98. *2 Windyhill Drive, Bolton BL3 4TH*

HESKETH, Derrick. **d** 12 **p** 13. OLM Blackwell w Tibshelf *Derby* from 12. *61 Peveril Road, Tibshelf, Alfreton DE55 5LR*
T: (01773) 872146 E: derrickhesketh61@btinternet.com

HESKETH, Canon Philip John. b 64. K Coll Lon BD 86 AKC 86 PhD 94. Ripon Coll Cuddesdon 92. **d** 94 **p** 95. C Bearsted w Thurnham *Cant* 94-98; V Chatham St Steph *Roch* 98-05; Can Res Roch Cathl from 05. *East Canonry, Kings Orchard, Rochester ME1 1TG* T: (01634) 841491 *or* 843366
E: canonpastor@rochestercathedral.org

HESKETH, The Ven Ronald David. b 47. CB 04. Bede Coll Dur BA 68 FRGS 02. Ridley Hall Cam 69 St Mich Coll Llan 71. **d** 71 **p** 72. C Southport H Trin *Liv* 71-74; Asst Chapl Miss to Seamen 74-75; Chapl RAF 75-98; Command Chapl RAF 98-01; Chapl-in-Chief RAF 01-06; Can and Preb Linc Cathl 01-06; Voc Officer *Worc* 06-11; Co-ord Chapl W Mercia Police from 09; QHC from 01. *Whistledown, Twyning Green, Twyning, Tewkesbury GL20 6DQ* T: (01684) 299773
E: ron@hesketh.org.uk

HESKINS, Georgiana Mary. b 48. K Coll Lon BD 81 AKC 81 MTh 93. Westcott Ho Cam 81. **dss** 83 **d** 87 **p** 94. Cobbold Road St Sav w St Mary *Lon* 83-85; St Botolph Aldgate w H Trin Minories 85-87; Par Dn 87; PtO *S'wark* 88-93; Par Dn Kidbrooke St Jas 93-95; Tutor S'wark Ord Course 93-94; Tutor SEITE 94-98; Teacher Eltham Coll 98-02; Asst Chapl Qu Eliz Hosp NHS Trust 03-11; Asst Chapl S Lon Healthcare NHS Trust from 11; Hon Chapl S'wark Cathl from 95. *4 Roupell Street, London SE1 8SP* T: (020) 7642 1161 M: 07776-122350
E: georgiana@lineone.net

HESKINS, Canon Jeffrey George. b 55. Heythrop Coll Lon MA 94 Princeton Th Sem DMin 00 AKC 78. Chich Th Coll 80. **d** 81 **p** 82. C Primrose Hill St Mary w Avenue Road St Paul *Lon* 81-85; Enfield Deanery Youth Officer 85-88; C Enfield Chase St Mary *Lon* 85-88; TV Kidbrooke St Jas *S'wark* 88-95; R Charlton St Luke w H Trin 95-02; P-in-c Old Charlton St Thos 02; R Charlton 02-07; Dioc Dir of Ords *Linc* from 07; Min Can and PV Linc Cathl 08-10; Dir IME 4-7 from 10; Can and Preb Linc Cathl from 10. *Church House, The Old Palace, Lincoln LN2 1PU* T: (01522) 504029 F: 504051
E: jeffrey.heskins@lincoln.anglican.org

HESLAM, Peter Somers. b 63. Hull Univ BA 89 Keble Coll Ox DPhil 94 Trin Coll Cam BA 96 MA 01. Ridley Hall Cam 93. **d** 96 **p** 97. C Huntingdon *Ely* 96-99; Min Stukeley Meadows LEP 99; Dir Studies EAMTC 99-00; Tutor Ridley Hall Cam 99-05; Dir Capitalism Project Lon Inst of Contemporary Chr 00-04; Fell Faculty of Div Cam Univ from 05; Hon C Cherry Hinton St Jo *Ely* from 00. *Glebe House, 64A Glebe Road, Cambridge CB1 7SZ* T: (01223) 722822 E: psh20@cam.ac.uk

HESLOP, Alan. See HESLOP, James Alan

HESLOP, Andrew James. b 66. Man Univ BA 87 PGCE 88. **d** 03 **p** 04. OLM Turton Moorland *Man* from 03; Chapl Wrightington Wigan and Leigh NHS Trust 07-10; Chapl Springhill Hospice 10-14; Chapl Salford R NHS Foundn Trust from 14; PtO *Blackb* from 07. *The Chaplaincy, Salford Royal NHS Foundation Trust, Stott Lane, Salford M6 8HD*
T: 0161-789 7373

HESLOP, Caroline Susan. See WILSON, Caroline Susan

HESLOP, David Anthony. b 45. BSc DipEd MTh Birm Univ MLitt 97. St Jo Coll Nottm 81. **d** 83 **p** 84. C Willenhall H Trin *Lich* 83-86; V Gresley *Derby* 86-92; V Marston on Dove w Scropton 92-95; Chapl Derby Univ 95-99; V Castle Donington and Lockington cum Hemington *Leic* 99-03; Chapl E Midl Airport 99-03; Prin OLM and Integrated Tr *Sarum* 03-07; Co-ord for Learning and Discipleship 07-10; rtd 11; Dir of Ords (Berks) *Ox* 11-13. *48 Badgers Way, Sturminster Newton DT10 1EP* T: (01258) 268437 E: revdave@heslops.co.uk

HESLOP, Harold William. b 40. Leeds Univ BA 62 Open Univ BA 72. Ox NSM Course 75. **d** 78 **p** 79. NSM Stoke Mandeville *Ox* 78-91; NSM Wendover 82-00; NSM Ellesborough, The Kimbles and Stoke Mandeville 91-94. *Farmside House, 42 Beechburn Park, Crook DL15 8NA* T: (01388) 765903

HESLOP, James Alan. b 37. Codrington Coll Barbados 61. **d** 64 **p** 65. C Bartica Guyana 64-68; P-in-c Long Is Nussau Bahamas 68-71; C Ch Ch Cathl 71-72; C Haxby w Wigginton *York* 72-74; TV 74-76; V York St Olave w St Giles 76-87; V Northampton All SS w St Kath *Pet* 87-88; R Felpham w Middleton *Chich* 88-92; TR Howden *York* 92-94; Warden Coll of St Barn Lingfield 94-95; Warden Morley Retreat and Conf Ho Derby 95-98; R Kirkbride and V Lezayre St Olave Ramsey *S & M* 98-99; P-in-c Woburn w Eversholt, Milton Bryan, Battlesden etc *St Alb* 99-03; rtd 03; Chapl Soc of St Marg 04-05; P-in-c Pau *Eur* 05-06. *1 Coniston Close, Bognor Regis PO22 8ND*
T: (01243) 869499

HESLOP, Michael Andrew. b 47. Trin Coll Bris 73. **d** 76 **p** 77. C Burmantofts St Steph and St Agnes *Ripon* 76-80; V Thorpe Edge *Bradf* 80-87; TV Penrith w Newton Reigny and Plumpton Wall *Carl* 87-91; V Silloth 91-01; V Kettlewell w Conistone, Hubberholme etc *Bradf* 01-07; PtO *Carl* from 07. *8 Lowscales Drive, Cockermouth CA13 9DR* T: (01900) 829542

HESLOP, Neil. b 73. Sunderland Univ BSc 95 MSc 03 Sheff Univ BA 15. Coll of Resurr Mirfield 13. **d** 15. C Fenham St Jas and St Basil *Newc* from 15. *32 Auburn Gardens, Newcastle upon Tyne NE4 9XP* M: 07847-415360 E: n.heslop@yahoo.com

HESS, Paul Austin. b 67. Cape Town Univ BA 89. St Bede's Coll Umtata. **d** 93 **p** 93. C Matroosfontein S Africa 92-94; NSM Eythorne and Elvington w Waldershare etc *Cant* 95-96;

C Storrington *Chich* 96-99; Chapl Hurstpierpoint Coll 99-05; Chapl Eton Coll from 05. *Eton College, Windsor SL4 6DW* T: (01753) 671161 E: pahess@tiscali.co.uk

HETHERINGTON, Andrew. b 50. Sheff Univ BSc 71. Wycliffe Hall Ox 71. **d** 74 **p** 75. C Leic H Trin w St Jo 74-78; C Leic H Apostles 78-82; V Bootle St Mary w St Paul *Liv* 82-93; TR W Swindon and the Lydiards *Bris* 93-01; P-in-c Chebsey, Ellenhall and Seighford-with-Creswell *Lich* 01-06; V Chebsey, Creswell, Ellenhall, Ranton etc 06-15; rtd 15. *67 Maliston Road, Great Sankey, Warrington WA5 1JS* E: andrewhetherington@btinternet.com

HETHERINGTON, Mrs Charlotte Elizabeth. b 52. Girton Coll Cam BA 74 Maria Grey Coll Lon PGCE 75 Heythrop Coll Lon MA 02. SAOMC 95. **d** 98 **p** 99. NSM Stratfield Mortimer and Mortimer W End etc *Ox* 98-04; C Portsea St Mary *Portsm* from 04. *Flat 10, 1 Bill Sargent Crescent, Portsmouth PO1 4JP* T: (023) 9282 6892 E: charlottehetherington@hotmail.com

HETHERINGTON, Mrs Glynis Catherine. b 48. EMMTC 93. **d** 93 **p** 94. NSM E and W Leake, Stanford-on-Soar, Rempstone etc *S'well* 93-99; R 99-13; rtd 13; PtO *Leic* from 14. *1 Hollytree Close, Hoton, Loughborough LE12 5SE* T: (01509) 880760 E: revd.glynis@btinternet.com

HETHERINGTON, John Carl. b 52. Hull Univ BTh 93. Linc Th Coll 82. **d** 84 **p** 85. C Crosby *Linc* 84-88; TV Cleethorpes 88-93; Chapl RAF 93-07; R Monk Fryston and S Milford *York* from 07. *The Rectory, Main Street, Hillam, Leeds LS25 5HH* T: (01977) 682357 *or* 680788 M: 07903-450228 E: hetherington556@btinternet.com

HETHERINGTON, Mrs Rachel Marie. b 65. ERMC 05. **d** 08 **p** 12. NSM Northampton Ch Ch *Pet* 08-11; NSM Northampton H Sepulchre w St Andr and St Lawr 08-11; NSM Northampton St Mich w St Edm 08-11; NSM Northampton H Trin and St Paul 08-11; Asst Chapl St Andr Healthcare from 11; C Kingsthorpe *Pet* from 12. *13 Woodrush Way, Moulton, Northampton NN3 7HU* T: (01604) 459864 E: rh10@ntlworld.com

HETLING, William Maurice. b 37. AKC 61. **d** 62 **p** 63. C Eltham St Barn *S'wark* 62-66; C Horley 66-71; C Kingston Jamaica 71-72; R Highgate 72-73; P-in-c Porus 74-75; C-in-c Farnham Royal S CD *Ox* 75-78; TV W Slough 78-80 and 88-91; TR 80-88; TV Parkstone St Pet w Branksea and St Osmund *Sarum* 91-96; P-in-c Reading St Barn *Ox* 96-99; rtd 99; PtO *Chich* 99-06. *12 Manor Close, Storrington, Pulborough RH20 4LF*

HEWERDINE, Mark Richard. b 77. Man Univ BA 99. Qu Coll Birm MA 13. **d** 13 **p** 14. C W Didsbury and Withington St Chris *Man* from 13. *70 Ashford Road, Manchester M20 3EH* T: 0161-448 9421 M: 07772-538491 E: markhewerdine@gmail.com

HEWES, John. b 29. Nottm Univ BA 50. Chich Th Coll 79. **d** 81 **p** 82. C Buckland in Dover w Buckland Valley *Cant* 81-84; P-in-c Elmsted w Hastingleigh 84-89; P-in-c Crundale w Godmersham 84-89; RD W Bridge 88-89; R Lydd 89-95; RD S Lympne 89-95; rtd 95; PtO *Cant* from 95. *Brambledown, Tamley Lane, Hastingleigh, Ashford TN25 5HW* T: (01233) 750214

HEWES, Timothy William. b 50. Sheff Univ BDS 74. SAOMC 98. **d** 01. NSM Abingdon *Ox* 01-14; NSM Sutton Courtenay w Appleford from 14. *55 Lower Radley, Abingdon OX14 3AY* T: (01235) 523963 M: 07771-880117 E: tim@rdlf.uninet.co.uk

HEWETSON, The Ven Christopher. b 37. Trin Coll Ox BA 60 MA 64. Chich Th Coll 67. **d** 69 **p** 70. C Leckhampton St Pet *Glouc* 69-71; C Wokingham All SS *Ox* 71-73; V Didcot St Pet 73-82; R Ascot Heath 82-90; RD Bracknell 86-90; P-in-c Headington Quarry 90-94; Hon Can Ch Ch 92-94; RD Cowley 94; Adn Ches 94-02; rtd 02; Bp's Adv for Spirituality *Ex* 03-07; PtO *Ches* from 05; B & W from 09. *1 Swan Hill Court, Swan Hill, Shrewsbury SY1 1NP* E: christopher.hewetson@sky.com

HEWETSON, Canon Robin Jervis. b 39. AKC 63 K Coll Lon MA 93. **d** 64 **p** 65. C Thorpe St Andr *Nor* 64-67; C E Dereham w Hoe 67-69; TV Mattishall w Mattishall Burgh 69-72; R Ingham w Sutton 72-78; R Catfield 75-78; R Taverham w Ringland 78-89; P-in-c Marsham 89-92; P-in-c Burgh 89-92; Dioc Ecum Officer 89-04; Exec Officer Norfolk Ecum Coun 89-04; R Marsham w Burgh-next-Aylsham *Nor* 92-04; Hon Can Nor Cathl 01-04; rtd 04; PtO *Nor* from 04. *83 Soame Close, Aylsham, Norwich NR11 6JF* T: (01263) 734325 E: robin.hewetson@googlemail.com

HEWETSON, Canon Valerie Patricia. b 44. St Mary's Coll Dur BSc 66 MSc 70 Leeds Univ MA 75. Linc Th Coll 89. **d** 91 **p** 94. C Kingston upon Hull St Nic *York* 91-94; V Barmby Moor w Allerthorpe, Fangfoss and Yapham 94-98; V Barmby Moor Gp 98-10; RD S Wold 01-06; Can and Preb York Minster 01-10; rtd 10. *27 Briarsfield, Barmby Moor, York YO24 4HN* T: (01759) 303816 E: valerie.hewetson@btinternet.com

HEWETT, Andrew David. b 63. Univ of Wales (Lamp) BA. Chich Th Coll 84. **d** 86 **p** 87. C Caldicot *Mon* 86-90; Chapl RAF from 90. *Chaplaincy Services (RAF), HQ Air Command, RAF High Wycombe HP14 4UE* T: (01494) 496800 F: 496343

HEWETT, Canon Roger Leroy. b 45. St Mich Coll Llan 93. **d** 95 **p** 96. C Whitchurch *Llan* 95-98; R Blaina and Nantyglo *Mon* 98-10; AD Blaenau Gwent 05-10; Can St Woolos Cathl 08-10; rtd 10; PtO *St D* from 10; *Mon* from 12. *27 Maenor Helig, Burry Port SA16 0TU* T: (01554) 834595 E: roger.hewett@tiscali.co.uk

HEWISH, Mrs Lesley Gillian. b 60. Trin Coll Bris 08. **d** 10 **p** 11. C Tetbury, Beverston, Long Newnton etc *Glouc* 10-13; Chapl HM Pris Eastwood Park from 13. *HM Prison Eastwood Park, Falfield, Wotton-under-Edge GL12 8DB* T: (01454) 382100 M: 07876-775290 E: lesley.hewish1@virgin.net

HEWISON, Alan Stuart. b 30. SS Mark & Jo Univ Coll Plymouth BEd 82. K Coll Lon. **d** 57 **p** 58. C S Mymms K Chas *Lon* 57-60; C Bourne *Guildf* 60-63; Chapl RN 63-79; PtO *Ex* from 79; rtd 95. *8 Hazelwood Crescent, Plymouth PL9 8BL*

HEWITSON, John Kenneth. b 48. Curtin Univ Aus BA Flinders Univ Aus MA 96. Adelaide Coll of Div ThL 70 ACT ThSchol 83. **d** 71 **p** 72. C Swindon Ch Ch *Bris* 71-74; C Spearwood Australia 74-76; R Balga 76-77; Chapl Royal Perth Hosp 79-83; R Lockridge 83-86; R Eliz 92-97; Chapl Trin Coll 93-98; Chapl Kormilda Coll Darwin from 99; R Freds Pass from 00. *PO Box 346, Humpty Doo NT 0836, Australia* T: (0061) (8) 8983 3947 F: 8983 3951 E: jah@octa4.net.au

HEWITT, Caroline Doris. b 62. All SS Cen for Miss & Min 12. **d** 15. C Salford All SS *Man* from 15. *Address temp unknown*

HEWITT, Christopher James Chichele (Chich). b 45. Witwatersrand Univ BSc 68 UNISA BA 78 MTh 92 LTCL 69. St Paul's Coll Grahamstown. **d** 78 **p** 79. S Africa 78-99; Chapl St Paul's Coll Grahamstown 84-86; Warden 86-92; Can Grahamstown Cathl 88-93; Chan 92; Sub-Dean 93; Dean and Adn Grahamstown 93-98; USA 99; TR Radcliffe *Man* 00-09; AD Radcliffe and Prestwich 02-09; P-in-c Swinton H Rood 09-13; V 13-14; C Worsley 13-14; rtd 14; PtO *Man* from 14. *79 Long Lane, Bolton BL2 6EU* E: chich@rink-hewitt.co.uk

HEWITT, Christopher William. b 63. Nottm Trent Univ BEng 98 PGCE 05 Linc Univ BA 14 CEng 01 MIET 01. Linc Sch of Th and Min 10. **d** 15. C Barlings *Linc* from 15; C S Lawres Gp from 15. *The Rectory, Reepham Road, Fiskerton, Lincoln LN3 4EZ* T: (01522) 754924 M: 07853-277065 E: cwhewitt@btinternet.com

HEWITT, Colin Edward. b 52. Man Poly BA 80 Em Coll Cam BA 82 MA 86 Maryvale Inst PGCE 08. Westcott Ho Cam 81. **d** 83 **p** 84. C Radcliffe St Thos and St Jo *Man* 83-84; C Langley and Parkfield 84-86; R Byfield w Boddington *Pet* 86-89; R Byfield w Boddington and Aston le Walls 89-91; Chapl RAF 91-09; V Brentwood St Thos *Chelmsf* from 09. *The Vicarage, 91 Queen's Road, Brentwood CM14 4EY* T: (01277) 225700 M: 07704-495001 E: fathercolin@live.co.uk

HEWITT, David Warner. b 33. Selw Coll Cam BA 56 MA 60. Wells Th Coll 57. **d** 59 **p** 60. C Longbridge *Birm* 59-61; C Sheldon 61-64; V Smethwick Old Ch 64-70; V Smethwick 70-78; P-in-c Littlehampton St Jas *Chich* 78-85; P-in-c Wick 78-85; V Littlehampton St Mary 78-85; TR Littlehampton and Wick 86-89; PtO *Eur* from 95; rtd 98; Hon Asst Chapl Gtr Athens *Eur* 00-03; PtO *Chelmsf* from 07. *18 Orchard Close, Weaverhead Lane, Thaxted, Dunmow CM6 2JX* T: (01371) 830591 E: tangulls1@mac.com

HEWITT, Canon Francis John Adam. b 42. St Chad's Coll Dur BA 64. **d** 66 **p** 67. C Dewsbury Moor *Wakef* 66-69; C Huddersfield St Jo 69-73; V King Cross 73-81; V Lastingham w Appleton-le-Moors, Rosedale etc *York* 81-94; RD Helmsley 85-94; V Pickering 94-95; V Pickering w Lockton and Levisham 95-07; RD Pickering 94-06; rtd 07; PtO *York* from 07; Can and Preb York Minster from 97. *Michaelmas Cottage, 3 Lime Chase, Kirkbymoorside, York YO62 6BX* T: (01751) 430322 E: fandb.michaelmas1@btinternet.com

HEWITT, Canon Garth Bruce. b 46. St Jo Coll Dur BA 68. Lon Coll of Div LTh 70. **d** 70 **p** 71. C Maidstone St Luke *Cant* 70-73; Staff Evang CPAS 73-79; Hon C W Ealing St Jo w St Jas *Lon* 73-81; Dir Amos Trust 88-96; World Affairs Adv *Guildf* 94-96; Regional Co-ord (Lon and SE) Chr Aid from 96; PtO *S'wark* 96-04; P-in-c All Hallows Lon Wall 97-99; V from 99; Hon Can Jerusalem from 06. *Christian Aid, All Hallows on the Wall, 83 London Wall, London EC2M 5ND* T: (020) 7496 1680 *or* 7588 2638 F: 7496 1684 E: ghewitt@christian-aid.org

HEWITT, Geoffrey Williams. b 48. Leeds Univ BA 69. Wells Th Coll 70. **d** 72 **p** 73. C Heywood St Luke *Man* 72-74; Ind Chapl 74-77; P-in-c Hulme St Geo 74-77; R Mamhilad and Llanfihangel Pontymoile *Mon* 77-80; Ind Chapl 77-80; V Arthog w Fairbourne *Ban* 80-87; R Llangelynnin w Rhoslefain 87; R Llangelynnin w Rhoslefain and Arthog etc 88-89; TV Bangor 89-94; Dioc Soc Resp Officer 89-02;

P-in-c Pentir 94-02; Hon Can Ban Cathl 99-02; RD Ogwen 00-02; P-in-c Draycot *Bris* 02-13; rtd 13. *1 Shapway Road, Evercreech, Shepton Mallet BA4 6JT* T: (01749) 831399 M: 07950-497580 E: geoffrey@revhewitt.freeserve.co.uk

HEWITT, Guy Arlington Kenneth. b 67. Univ of W Indies BSc 92 MSc 94. SEITE 00. d 04 p 05. C Ch Ch Barbados 04-06; P-in-c Ruby H Trin 06-07; C Ch Ch 07-08. *33 Tino Terrace, Warners, Christ Church BB15104, Barbados* T: (001) (246) 437 6569 M: 435 6052 E: guyhewitt@gmail.com

HEWITT, John Kaffrell. b 34. St Aid Birkenhead 60. d 63 p 64. C Woking Ch Ch *Guildf* 63-66; P-in-c Sudbury w Ballingdon and Brundon *St E* 66-70; V 70-80; V Portsdown *Portsm* 80-96; rtd 96; PtO *Win* from 97. *45 Knowland Drive, Milford-on-Sea, Lymington SO41 0RH* T: (01590) 644473

HEWITT, Kenneth Victor. b 30. Lon Univ BSc 49 CertEd 51 MSc 53. Cuddesdon Coll 60. d 62 p 63. C Maidstone St Martin *Cant* 62-64; C Croydon St Mich 64-67; P-in-c S Kensington St Aug *Lon* 67-73; V 73-95; Asst Chapl Lon Univ 67-73; rtd 95; PtO *Roch* from 95. *41 Bromley College, London Road, Bromley BR1 1PE* T: (020) 8464 0014

HEWITT, Michael David. b 49. K Coll Lon BD 79 AKC 79 CertEd. Qu Coll Birm 79. d 80 p 81. C Bexleyheath Ch Ch *Roch* 80-84; C Buckland in Dover w Buckland Valley *Cant* 84-89; R Ridgewell w Ashen, Birdbrook and Sturmer *Chelmsf* 89-13; rtd 13. *22 Bromley College, London Road, Bromley BR1 1PE*

HEWITT, Patrick. *See* HEWITT, William Patrick

HEWITT, Paul Stephen Patrick. b 59. TCD BA 82 MA 87. CITC 83. d 86 p 87. C Ballymacash *Conn* 86-89; C Ballymena w Ballyclug 89-91; I Glencraig *D & D* 91-12. *18A Old Cultra Road, Holywood BT18 0AE* T: (028) 9042 1847 E: paulsphewitt@btconnect.com

HEWITT, Robert Samuel. b 51. QUB BSc 73. CITC 77. d 80 p 81. C Dundela St Mark *D & D* 80-84; R Donaghadee 84-92. *3 The Trees, New Road, Donaghadee BT21 0EJ* T: (028) 9188 2594

HEWITT, Simon. b 76. Brunel Univ BSc 99 Birkbeck Coll Lon MA 08 PhD 12. St Steph Ho Ox BA 01 MA 04. d 02 p 05. C Warren Park and Leigh Park *Portsm* 02-04; C Walthamstow St Sav *Chelmsf* 04-08; PtO *Lon* 11-12; C Colindale St Matthias from 12; C W Hendon St Jo from 12. *St Matthias' Vicarage, 48 Rushgrove Avenue, London NW9 6QY* E: frsimonhewitt@hotmail.co.uk

HEWITT, Stephen Wilkes. b 49. Fitzw Coll Cam MA 71. St Jo Coll Nottm 88. d 90 p 91. C Eaton *Nor* 90-93; V Warwick St Paul *Cov* 93-01; PtO *Newc* 01-02; P-in-c High Spen and Rowlands Gill *Dur* 02-05; V 05-09; TR Cramlington *Newc* 09-14; rtd 15. *54 Prior Road, Tweedmouth, Berwick-upon-Tweed TD15 2EH* E: sandshewitt@hotmail.com

HEWITT, Timothy James. b 67. St D Coll Lamp BD 88. Ripon Coll Cuddesdon 89. d 91 p 92. C Milford Haven *St D* 91-94; C Llanelli 94-96; P-in-c Llan-non 96-97; V Clydach *S & B* 98-07; V Ystalyfera from 07; Dioc Voc Adv from 07. *The Vicarage, Glan yr Afon Road, Ystalyfera, Swansea SA9 2EP* T: (01639) 842257 E: revtimothyhewitt@btinternet.com

HEWITT, William Patrick. b 48. Nottm Univ BTh 79. Linc Th Coll 75. d 79 p 80. C Workington St Jo *Carl* 79-83; V Flookburgh 83-87; V Barrow St Matt 87-90; V Lowick and Kyloe w Ancroft *Newc* 90-96; R Ford and Etal 90-96; RD Norham 91-96; I Fanlobbus Union *C, C & R* 96-07; I Bandon Union 07-10; I Youghal Union 10-13; Can Cork Cathl 00-13; Can Cloyne Cathl 00-13; rtd 13. *1 Tir Celyn, Margam, Port Talbot SA13 2UZ* E: wphewitt@gmail.com

HEWITT-HORSMAN, Simon. *See* HEWITT, Simon

HEWLETT, Mrs Caroline Joan. b 68. Coll of Ripon & York St Jo BEd 92 St Jo Coll Dur BA 01. Cranmer Hall Dur 99. d 01 p 02. C Leeds St Geo *Ripon* 01-04; C Aldborough w Boroughbridge and Roecliffe 04-06; Chapl Leeds Combined Court Cen 03-06; V Swaledale *Leeds* from 06. *The Vicarage, Reeth, Richmond DL11 6TR* T: (01748) 884706 M: 07866-750211 E: carolinehewlett@hotmail.com

HEWLETT, David Bryan. b 49. Bris Univ BEd 72. Qu Coll Birm 77. d 79 p 80. C Ludlow *Heref* 79-81; TV 81-84; V Marden w Amberley and Wisteston 84-92; Lect Glouc Sch for Min 84-92; Field Officer for Lay Min *Heref* 84-91; CME Officer 86-92; Dir Post-Ord Tr 91-92; Hd Master St Fran Sch Pewsey 92-94; Co-ord Chapl Frenchay Healthcare NHS Trust Bris 94-99; Chapl N Bris NHS Trust 99-00; Dir Past Studies OLM Scheme and CME Adv *Linc* 00-04; Par Development Adv (South) 00-04; R Pontesbury I and II *Heref* 04-08; V Corbridge w Halton and Newton Hall *Newc* from 08; AD Corbridge from 09. *The Vicarage, Greencroft Avenue, Corbridge NE45 5DW* T: (01434) 632128 E: david.hewlett3@btopenworld.com

HEWLETT, Canon David Jonathon Peter. b 57. Dur Univ BA 79 PhD 83. Ridley Hall Cam 82. d 83 p 84. C New Barnet St Jas *St Alb* 83-86; Lect CITC 86-90; P-in-c Feock *Truro* 91-95; Jt Dir SWMTC 91-95; Prin 95-03; Adv Local Ord Min 91-95; Hon

Can Truro Cathl 01-03; Prin Qu Coll Birm from 03; Hon Can Birm Cathl from 14. *71 Farquhar Road, Edgbaston, Birmingham B15 2QP* T: 0121-452 2612 *or* 452 2603 F: 454 8171 E: d.hewlett@queens.ac.uk

HEWLETT, Guy Edward. b 59. Thames Poly CertEd 89 Open Univ BA 90. Oak Hill Th Coll 96. d 96 p 97. NSM Sudbury St Andr *Lon* 96-99; C Harrow Trin St Mich 99-05; V Harrow Weald St Mich 05-13; Chapl Worcs Acute Hosps NHS Trust from 13. *Worcestershire Royal Hospital, Charles Hastings Way, Worcester WR5 1DD* T: (01905) 763333 E: guy.saintmikes@gmail.com

HEWLETT-SMITH, Peter Brian. b 40. OBE 87. Ripon Coll Cuddesdon 06. d 06. NSM Heckfield w Mattingley and Rotherwick *Win* 06-07; NSM Whitewater 07-10; PtO from 10. *10 Winchfield Court, Pale Lane, Winchfield, Hook RG27 8SP* T: (01252) 842163 M: 07799-404206 E: peter.hewlettsmith@gmail.com

HEWLINS, Pauline Elizabeth. *See* SEAMAN, Pauline Elizabeth

HEWSON, Douglas Peter. b 43. d 12 p 13. OLM Milford *Guildf* from 12. *Meijendel, Sandy Lane, Milford, Godalming GU8 5BL* T: (01483) 425131 E: peter_hewson@sky.com

HEWSON, Mrs Mandy Carol. b 61. Anglia Ruskin Univ BSc 05. St Mellitus Coll BA 11. d 11 p 13. NSM E Springfield *Chelmsf* from 11. *33 Meon Close, Chelmsford CM1 7QG* T: (01245) 287710 E: mandy@hewson67.fsnet.co.uk

HEWSON, Mrs Rose Raylene. b 51. SAOMC 96. d 99 p 00. NSM High Wycombe *Ox* 99-02; NSM Burnham w Dropmore, Hitcham and Taplow 02-08; NSM Hitcham 08-10; rtd 10. *11 Hammerwood Road, Ashurst Wood, East Grinstead RH19 3TJ* T: (01342) 319027 E: rosie@hewsons.net

HEWSON, Thomas Robert. b 45. Man Univ BA 66. S'wark Ord Course 85. d 89 p 90. C Chinnor w Emmington and Sydenham etc *Ox* 89-92; TV Burnham w Dropmore, Hitcham and Taplow 92-08; V Hitcham 08-10; rtd 10. *11 Hammerwood Road, Ashurst Wood, East Grinstead RH19 3TJ* T: (01342) 319027 E: trh@hewsons.net

HEYCOCKS, Christian John. b 71. Univ of Wales (Ban) BA 93 MA 96. Westcott Ho Cam 94 CITC 97. d 97 p 98. C Rhyl w St Ann *St As* 97-00; Chapl RN 00-06; Chapl Univ Staff Cam and C Cambridge Gt St Mary w St Mich *Ely* 06-09; V Sheringham *Nor* from 09; RD Repps from 14. *The Vicarage, 10 North Street, Sheringham NR26 8LW* T: (01263) 822089 E: rev.heycocks15@btinternet.com

HEYES, Andrew Robin. b 61. Man Univ BA 93. St Steph Ho Ox 93. d 95 p 96. C Tonge Moor *Man* 95-00; V Glodwick 00-06; R Tampa St Clem USA from 06. *3817 Beneraid Street, Land o' Lakes FL 34638, USA* T: (001) (813) 995 5364 E: aheyes@tampabay.rr.com

HEYES, Robert John. b 46. STETS 00. d 03 p 04. NSM Bramley and Grafham *Guildf* 03-08; NSM Shamley Green 08-11; rtd 11. *Juniper Cottage, 22 Eastwood Road, Bramley, Guildford GU5 0DS* T: (01483) 893706 F: 894001 E: bobheyes@onetel.net

HEYGATE, Stephen Beaumont. b 48. Loughb Univ BSc 71 CQSW 73 PhD 89. St Jo Coll Nottm 86. d 88 p 89. C Aylestone St Andr w St Jas *Leic* 88-90; V Cosby 90-00; V Evington 00-11; P-in-c Leic St Phil 00-04; rtd 12; PtO *Leic* from 12; Bp's Adv for Healing and Deliverance from 04. *4 Gapstile Close, Desborough, Kettering NN14 2TZ* T: (01536) 764106 E: stephenheygate@btinternet.com

HEYHOE, Jonathan Peter. b 53. Man Univ BA 75. Trin Coll Bris 77. d 80 p 81. C Woking St Pet *Guildf* 80-83; C Heatherlands St Jo *Sarum* 83-91; Chr Renewal Cen Rostrevor 91-95; PtO *D & D* 91-97; I Ballybay w Mucknoe and Clontibret *Clogh* 98-11; Preb Clogh Cathl 06-11; rtd 11. *11 Rowallon, Warrenpoint, Newry BT34 3TR* T: (028) 4175 4659 M: (00353) 87-418 1427 E: jheyhoe@iol.ie

HEYN, Lucinda Jane. b 68. Ripon Coll Cuddesdon 07. d 10 p 11. C Goring and Streatley w S Stoke *Ox* 10-14; TV Hermitage from 14; Bp's Adv for Women in Ord Min from 14. *The Rectory, 8 Yew Tree Mews, High Street, Compton, Newbury RG20 6NQ* T: (01491) 871970 E: luci_heyn@hotmail.co.uk

HEYWARD, Daniel James. b 74. Ex Univ BA 97 MCIPD. Wycliffe Hall Ox 09. d 11 p 12. C Reading Greyfriars *Ox* 11-15; C Bris St Phil and St Jacob w Em from 15. *City Rectory, Apartment 8, 10 Unity Street, Bristol BS1 5HH* M: 07508-346550 E: daniel_heyward@hotmail.com

HEYWOOD, Mrs Anne Christine. b 44. Sarum Th Coll. d 97 p 98. C Talbot Village *Sarum* 97-01; TV Shaston 01-09; rtd 10. *26 Casterbridge Way, Gillingham SP8 4FG* T: (01747) 825259 E: ac.heywood@virgin.net

HEYWOOD, Anthony. *See* HEYWOOD, Richard Anthony

HEYWOOD, David Stephen. b 55. Selw Coll Cam BA 76 MA 80 SS Hild & Bede Coll Dur 89. Cranmer Hall Dur 80. d 86 p 87. C Cheltenham St Luke and St Jo *Glouc* 86-90; TV Sanderstead All SS *S'wark* 90-98; V Edensor *Lich* 98-03; Deanery and Min Development Officer 03-06; Lect Past Th

Ripon Coll Cuddesdon from 06. *3 College Field, Cuddesdon, Oxford OX44 9HL* T: (01865) 874974 *or* 877444
E: david.heywood@ripon-cuddesdon.ac.uk

HEYWOOD, Deiniol John Owen. *See* KEARLEY-HEYWOOD, Deiniol John Owen

HEYWOOD, Geoffrey Thomas. b 26. St Mich Coll Llan 60. **d** 62 **p** 63. C Porthmadog *Ban* 62-64; C Llandudno 64-67; V Caerhun w Llangelynin w Llanbedr-y-Cennin 67-74; Asst Chapl HM Pris Liv 74-75; Chapl HM Pris Ex 75-77; Chapl HM Pris Wakef 77-79; Chapl HM YOI Eastwood Park 79-90; Chapl HM Pris Leyhill 79-90; rtd 90; PtO *Glouc* 94-05. *5 Meadow Road, Leyhill, Wotton-under-Edge GL12 8HW*

HEYWOOD, Mrs Margaret Anne (Meg). b 52. Luton Coll of HE BSc 81. EMMTC 04. **d** 07 **p** 07. Chapl Ox Min Course from 06; NSM Ox St Clem 07-08; NSM Thame 09-10; PtO from 11. *3 College Field, Cuddesdon, Oxford OX44 9HL* T: (01865) 874974 E: meg_heywood@hotmail.com

HEYWOOD, Michael Herbert. b 41. Liv Univ BSc 63. Clifton Th Coll 63. **d** 65 **p** 66. C Low Elswick *Newc* 65-68; C St Helens St Mark *Liv* 68-75; Leprosy Miss Area Org NE and Cumbria 75-85; S Lon, Surrey and Berks 85-91; Internat Publicity and Promotional Co-ord 91-01; Hon C New Malden and Coombe *S'wark* from 06. *9 Dryburn Road, Durham DH1 5AJ* T: 0191-386 0087 E: biddyandmike@lineone.net

HEYWOOD, Peter. b 46. Cranmer Hall Dur 72. **d** 75 **p** 76. C Blackley St Andr *Man* 75-78; C Denton Ch Ch 78-80; V Constable Lee 80-01; rtd 01; PtO *Man* from 01. *3 Brockclough Road, Rossendale BB4 9LG* T: (01706) 212297

HEYWOOD, Richard Anthony. b 77. St Jo Coll Dur BA 99. Oak Hill Th Coll 04. **d** 07 **p** 08. C Lt Shelford *Ely* 07-11; TV Thetford *Nor* from 11. *44 Nunsgate, Thetford IP24 3EL* M: 07804-671405 E: tony.heywood@talk21.com

HEZEL, Adrian. b 43. Chelsea Coll Lon BSc 64 PhD 67. NOC 78. **d** 81 **p** 82. NSM Mirfield *Wakef* 81-89; C 89-90; V Shelley and Shepley 90-99; V Hoylake *Ches* 99-08; rtd 08; PtO *Ches* from 09. *17 West Drive, Neston CH64 0SA* T: 0151-336 3773 E: ahezel@btinternet.com

HIBBARD, John. b 42. **d** 03 **p** 04. NSM Stewkley w Soulbury and Drayton Parslow *Ox* 03-06; PtO 06-08 and from 11; NSM Fenny Stratford 08-11. *Chapel Gate, 6 Nearton End, Swanbourne, Milton Keynes MK17 0SL* T: (01296) 720449

HIBBERD, Brian Jeffery. b 35. Fitzw Coll Cam MA 62 Southn Univ MA 84. Ridley Hall Cam 58. **d** 60 **p** 61. C Cambridge H Trin *Ely* 60-63; C Doncaster St Mary *Sheff* 63-66; Asst Master Price's Sch Fareham 66-69; Warblington Sch Havant 69-71; Hd Soc and RS Carisbrooke High Sch 71-84; Distr Health Promotion Officer Is of Wight 84-88; SW Herts 88-90; Hd RS Goffs Sch Cheshunt 90-95; rtd 95; Teacher Qu Sch Bushey 95-97; Teacher R Masonic Sch for Girls Rickmansworth 97-00; Hon C Abbots Langley *St Alb* 00-01; PtO from 01. *50 Rosehill Gardens, Abbots Langley WD5 0HF* T: (01923) 267391

HIBBERD, John. b 60. Wadh Coll Ox MA 82. Trin Coll Bris BA 89. **d** 89 **p** 90. C Northolt St Mary *Lon* 89-92; C-in-c Southall Em CD 92-94; Min of Miss Through Faith Miss *Ely* 95-14; Miss Development Adv Sheff and Rotherham Adnry from 14. *14 Hollingswood Way, Sunnyside, Rotherham S66 3ZN* T: (01709) 700351 E: jhibberd14@btinternet.com

HIBBERD, John Charles. b 38. Bernard Gilpin Soc Dur 62 Chich Th Coll 63. **d** 66 **p** 67. C W Drayton *Lon* 66-70; C Noel Park St Mark 70-72; C Ealing St Steph Castle Hill 72-75; V Gunnersbury St Jas 75-84; V Whitton SS Phil and Jas 84-86; Finance and Trust Sec Lon Dioc Fund 87-98; PtO *Lon* 87-98; rtd 98. *18 Pursley Close, Sandown PO36 9QP* T: (01983) 401036

HIBBERT, Miss Anne Mary Elizabeth. Southn Univ BA 81. Trin Coll Bris 81. dss 83 **d** 87 **p** 94. Muswell Hill St Jas w St Matt *Lon* 83-86; Leic H Trin w St Jo 86-87; Par Dn 87-90; PtO *Cov* from 90; Evang Co-ord and Adv CPAS 90-98; Churches Millennium Exec 98-99; Miss and Spirituality Adv BRF 99-03; Dir Well Chr Healing Cen from 03. *The Well Christian Healing Centre, PO Box 3407, Leamington Spa CV32 6ZH* T: (01926) 888003 M: 07973-563667 E: anne@wellhealing.org

HIBBERT, Canon Peter John. b 43. Hull Univ BA 71 Lon Univ CertEd 72 MA 79. Sarum & Wells Th Coll 85. **d** 88 **p** 89. C Newsome and Armitage Bridge *Wakef* 88-92; P-in-c Newton Flowery Field *Ches* 92-00; P-in-c Hyde St Thos 97-00; V Handsworth St Jas *Birm* 00-08; P-in-c Altarnon w Bolventor, Laneast and St Clether *Truro* 08-09; P-in-c Micklehurst *Ches* 09-13; P-in-c Hyde St Thos from 10; Hon Can Ches Cathl from 11. *203 Petersburg Road, Stockport SK3 9RA* E: hibbert631@btinternet.com

HIBBERT, Prof Peter Rodney. b 53. Man Univ LLB 74 Nottm Univ MA 99 Solicitor 77. EMMTC 96. **d** 99 **p** 00. C Knighton St Mary Magd *Leic* 99-01; PtO 01-12; *Birm* from 03; *Leic* from 15. *Grange Cottage, 37 Rushes Lane, Lubenham, Market Harborough LE16 9TN* T: (01858) 433174 E: for.peter@hotmail.com

HIBBERT, Canon Richard Charles. b 62. Trin Coll Bris BA 93. **d** 96 **p** 97. C Luton St Mary *St Alb* 96-00; V Bedford Ch Ch from 00; RD Bedford from 10; Hon Can St Alb from 13. *Christ Church Vicarage, 115 Denmark Street, Bedford MK40 3TJ* T/F: (01234) 359342 E: vicar@christchurchbedford.org.uk

HIBBINS, Neil Lance. b 60. St Anne's Coll Ox BA 82 MA 87. St Mich Coll Llan 83. **d** 85 **p** 86. C Griffithstown *Mon* 85-87; C Pontypool 87-88; TV 88-92; Walsall Hosps NHS Trust 92-96; Asst Chapl Manor Hosp Walsall 92-96; R Norton Canes *Lich* from 96. *The Rectory, 81 Church Road, Norton Canes, Cannock WS11 9PQ* T: (01543) 278969 E: neil_hibbins@lycos.com

HIBBS, Peter Wilfred. b 56. NOC 05. **d** 08 **p** 09. NSM Gt Snaith *Sheff* from 08. *Peveril, High Street, Snaith, Goole DN14 9HJ* T: (01405) 862517 M: 07885-348498 E: peter.hibbs@sheffield.anglican.org

HICHENS, Anthony. b 29. AKC 59. **d** 60 **p** 61. C Ashford St Hilda *Lon* 60-64; C Leeds St Wilfrid *Ripon* 64-66; V Waramuri Guyana 67-75; P-in-c Stratton Audley w Godington *Ox* 76-83; P-in-c Finmere w Mixbury 76-78; P-in-c Fringford w Hethe and Newton Purcell 78-83; R Stratton Audley and Godington, Fringford etc 83-95; rtd 95; PtO *Pet* 95-07. *St John's Home, St Mary's Road, Oxford OX4 1QE* T: (01865) 247725

HICKEN, Kathryn Elizabeth. b 69. Moorlands Coll BA 10. St Mellitus Coll 11. **d** 13 **p** 14. C Holdenhurst and Iford *Win* from 13. *19 Colemore Road, Bournemouth BH7 6RZ* T: (01202) 419047 M: 07590-211015 E: kathy.iford@icloud.com

HICKES, Roy Edward. b 31. St Aid Birkenhead 56. **d** 59 **p** 60. C New Bury *Man* 59-63; C Wyther *Ripon* 63-65; R Oldham St Andr *Man* 65-69; V Smallbridge 69-79; R Winford *B & W* 79-81; R Winford w Felton Common Hill 81-88; RD Chew Magna 85-88; Chapl Costa Blanca *Eur* 88-92; rtd 92; PtO *Bris* from 92; *B & W* 92-97 and from 98; Hon C Wrington w Butcombe 97-98. *17 Haycombe, Bristol BS14 0AJ* T: (01275) 544750 M: 07870-624903 E: royhickes@blueyonder.co.uk *or* randwhickes@blueyonder.co.uk

HICKISH, James Rupert. b 66. Warwick Univ BA 89. ERMC 09. **d** 12 **p** 13. NSM Ely from 12. *The Old Chapel, Butchers Row, Ely CB7 4NA* T: (01353) 662684 E: hickishes@btinternet.com

HICKLING, John. b 34. Handsworth Coll Birm 56. Launde Abbey 69. **d** 69 **p** 70. In Methodist Ch 59-69; C Melton Mowbray w Thorpe Arnold *Leic* 69-71; TV 71-75; R Waltham on the Wolds w Stonesby and Saltby 75-84; R Aylestone St Andr w St Jas 84-93; R Husbands Bosworth w Mowsley and Knaptoft etc 93-96; rtd 96; PtO *Leic* from 99. *28 Oxford Drive, Melton Mowbray LE13 0AL* T: (01664) 560770

HICKMAN, John William. b 38. Barrister-at-Law (Middle Temple) 69 Qu Coll Cam LLM 81. Oak Hill Th Coll 92. **d** 95 **p** 96. NSM Sevenoaks St Nic *Roch* 95-98; P-in-c Stedham w Iping *Chich* 98-04; rtd 04; PtO *Chich* from 05. *Bywood, Selham Road, West Lavington, Midhurst GU29 0EG* T: (01730) 810821

HICKS, Miss Barbara. b 42. Cranmer Hall Dur BA 71. dss 85 **d** 87 **p** 94. Par Dn Sheff St Jo 87-94; C 94-02; Chapl Shrewsbury Hosp 96-02; rtd 02; PtO *Sheff* from 06. *87 Underwood Road, Sheffield S8 8TG* T: 0114-255 8087

HICKS, Clive Anthony. b 58. Man Univ BA 79 Bris Univ PhD 88. Coll of Resurr Mirfield 09. **d** 11 **p** 12. C Budbrooke *Cov* 11-14; V Ossett and Gawthorpe *Wakef* from 14. *The Vicarage, 12 Fearnley Avenue, Ossett WF5 9ET* M: 07804-792307 E: cliveahicks@gmail.com

HICKS, Ms Eunice. b 41. Trin Coll Bris BA 00. WEMTC 01. **d** 01 **p** 02. NSM Chew Magna w Dundry and Norton Malreward *B & W* 01-06; NSM Rowledge and Frensham *Guildf* 06-10; rtd 10; PtO *B & W* from 11. *7 Partis College, Bath BA1 3QD* T: (01225) 336413 M: 07799-178833 E: reveunice@hickshome.co.uk

HICKS, Hazel Rebecca. b 54. Open Univ BA 92. CITC 05. **d** 08 **p** 09. NSM Annagh w Drumaloor, Cloverhill and Drumlane *K, E & A* 08-11; P-in-c Arvagh w Carrigallen, Gowna and Columbkille from 11. *Garvary Lodge, 49 Teemore Road, Derrylin, Enniskillen BT92 9QB* T: (028) 6774 8422 M: 07770-852362 E: hazel6004@yahoo.co.uk

HICKS, Miss Joan Rosemary. b 60. Homerton Coll Cam BEd 83. Westcott Ho Cam 87. **d** 90 **p** 94. C Wendover *Ox* 90-95; C Earley St Pet 95-98; P-in-c Beech Hill, Grazeley and Spencers Wood 98-05; P-in-c Cox Green from 05. *The Vicarage, 9 Warwick Close, Maidenhead SL6 3AL* T: (01628) 622139 E: joanhicks@compuserve.com

HICKS, John Michael. b 67. Crewe & Alsager Coll BA 89 K Coll Lon MA 01 K Alfred's Coll Win PGCE 90. NTMTC 02. **d** 05 **p** 06. NSM Grosvenor Chpl *Lon* 05-09; NSM Westmr St Steph w St Jo from 09. *167 John Ruskin Street, London SE5 0PQ* T: (020) 7641 5930 M: 07971-670092 E: frhicks@me.com

HICKS (née HODGSON), Julia Ruth. b 66. Somerville Coll Ox BA 88 UEA PGCE 89. Westcott Ho Cam 06. d 08 p 09. C Bridgwater St Mary and Chilton Trinity *B & W* 08-11; R Merriott w Hinton, Dinnington and Lopen from 11. *The Rectory, Church Street, Merriott TA16 5PS* T: (01460) 76406 E: juliahicks1@gmail.com

HICKS, Richard Barry. b 32. Dur Univ BA 55. Sarum Th Coll 59. d 61 p 62. C Wallsend St Luke *Newc* 61-64; C Tynemouth Ch 64-69; V Tynemouth St Jo 69-75; V Prudhoe 75-82; TV Swanborough *Sarum* 82-86; R Hilperton w Whaddon and Staverton etc 86-97; rtd 97; PtO *Newc* from 97; *Carl* from 98. *Lane House, Sawmill Lane, Brampton CA8 1DA* T: (016977) 2156 E: richard@hicksfam.force9.co.uk

HICKS, Robert Buxton. b 66. Ex Univ BSc 90. Westcott Ho Cam 06. d 08 p 09. C Bridgwater St Fran *B & W* 08-11; C Merriott w Hinton, Dinnington and Lopen from 11. *The Rectory, Church Street, Merriott TA16 5PS* T: (01460) 76406 E: bobhicks66@googlemail.com

HICKS, Mrs Valerie Joy. b 47. SRN 69. Cant Sch of Min 82. dss 85 d 87 p 94. Roch 85-89; Hon Par Dn 87-89; Par Dn Thatcham *Ox* 89-93; Team Dn Aylesbury 93-94; TV 94-00; P-in-c Dordon *Birm* 00-09; V 09-10; Dioc Chapl MU 01-06; rtd 10; PtO *Birm* from 10; *Lich* from 11. *12 Rocklands Crescent, Lichfield WS13 6DH* E: val@hicksres.plus.com

HICKS, Canon William Trevor. b 47. Hull Univ BA 68 Fitzw Coll Cam BA 70 MA 74. Westcott Ho Cam 68. d 70 p 71. C Cottingham *York* 70-73; C Elland *Wakef* 73-76; V Walsden 76-81; V Knottingley 81-92; R Castleford All SS 92-96; P-in-c Womersley and Kirk Smeaton 94-00; RD Pontefract 94-99; V Bolsover *Derby* 00-11; RD Bolsover and Staveley 05-11; Hon Can Derby Cathl 07-11; rtd 11. *18 Spittal Green, Bolsover, Chesterfield S44 6TP* T: (01246) 827856 E: wtrevorhicks@gmail.com *or* trevorhicks1@aol.com

HICKSON, Gordon Crawford Fitzgerald. b 51. CCC Cam MA 76. d 06 p 07. NSM Ox St Aldate 06-10; PtO 10-11; NSM Cowley St Jas from 11. *31 Orchard Road, Oxford OX2 9BL* T: (01865) 862981 M: 07713-688079

HIDDEN, Jonathan Martin. b 79. Portsm Univ BSc 00. Wycliffe Hall Ox BTh 13. d 13 p 14. C Guildf Ch Ch w St Martha-on-the-Hill from 13. *2 Ivor Close, Guildford GU1 2ET* M: 07790-018645 E: jonhidden@yahoo.co.uk

HIDE, Timothy John. b 71. Roehampton Inst BA 95. St Steph Ho Ox 97. d 99 p 00. C Woodford St Mary w St Phil and St Jas *Chelmsf* 99-01; C Upminster 01-05; Asst P Forest Gate Em w Upton Cross 05-06; PtO 06-08; TV Canvey Is 08-12; P-in-c Beckenham St Barn *Roch* from 12. *St Barnabas' Vicarage, Oakhill Road, Beckenham BR3 6NG* T: (020) 8650 3332 M: 07857-262826 E: tim.hide@stbarnabasbeckenham.org

HIDER, David Arthur. b 46. Lon Univ BSc 67. Sarum & Wells Th Coll 86. d 89 p 90. NSM Southbourne w W Thorney *Chich* 89-91; C Goring-by-Sea 91-94; P-in-c Peacehaven and Telscombe Cliffs 94-99; V 99-09; P-in-c Telscombe w Piddinghoe and Southease 94-99; V Telscombe Village 99-09; V Piddinghoe 99-09; V Southease 99-09; rtd 09; PtO *Chich* from 09. *4 Guildford Close, Emsworth PO10 8LW* T: (01243) 377636 E: revd_d_hider@msn.com

HIDER, Mrs Melanie Anne. b 53. UEA BA 91 Homerton Coll Cam PGCE 92. d 06 p 07. OLM Nor Lakenham St Alb and St Mark from 06. *10 Brian Avenue, Norwich NR1 2PH* T: (01603) 622373 E: melaniehider@beemerz.co.uk

HIGGINBOTTOM, Richard. b 48. Lon Univ BD 74. Oak Hill Th Coll. d 74 p 75. C Kenilworth St Jo *Cov* 74-77; C Finham 77-79; P-in-c Attleborough 79-81; V 81-84; Asst Chapl HM Pris Brixton 84-85; Chapl HM Pris Roch 85-92; Camp Hill 92-00; HM YOI Dover 00-03; rtd 03; PtO *Cant* 03-07; *Cov* from 09. *c/o Crockford, Church House, Great Smith Street, London SW1P 3AZ* M: 07779-775081

HIGGINBOTTOM, Richard William. b 51. Man Univ BA 73 MA 75. Edin Th Coll 83. d 85 p 86. C Knighton St Mary Magd *Leic* 85-87; C Northleach w Hampnett and Farmington *Glouc* 87-89; V Hayfield *Derby* 89-93; CPAS Min Adv for Scotland 93-08; Community Development Officer Tulloch NET 08-14; rtd 14. *Caberfeidh, 2 Highfield Place, Bankfoot, Perth PH1 4AX* T: (01738) 787429 M: 07548-209922 E: richwhigg@gmail.com

HIGGINS, Anthony Charles. b 46. d 97 p 98. OLM Swanage and Studland *Sarum* from 97. *The Old School House, School Lane, Studland, Swanage BH19 3AJ* T: (01929) 450691 E: revtonyhiggins@btinternet.com

HIGGINS, Bernard. b 42. Leic Poly BPharm 63 PhD 66 MRPharmS 68. St Jo Coll Nottm 89. d 91 p 92. C Stockport St Geo *Ches* 91-94; C Stockport SW 94-95; P-in-c Dunham Massey St Marg and St Mark 95-98; V 98-00; rtd 00; PtO *Blackb* 01-11; *Carl* 01-13; *Leic* from 15. *20 Kingfisher Close, Great Glen, Leicester LE8 9DG* T: 0116-259 2624 E: bclhigg@btinternet.com

HIGGINS, Charles Christopher. b 90. Ex Univ BA 12 MA 13 Magd Coll Cam MPhil 15. Ridley Hall Cam 13. d 15. C Rugby W *Cov* from 15. *77 Mellish Road, Rugby CV22 6BB* T: (01788) 560168 M: 07925-715696 E: charles.higgins90@gmail.com

HIGGINS (née JAMIESON), Mrs Emma Victoria. b 89. Edin Univ MA 12 Fitzw Coll Cam MPhil 15. Ridley Hall Cam 13. d 15. C Rugby W *Cov* from 15. *77 Mellish Road, Rugby CV22 6BB* T: (01788) 560168 M: 07843-878636 E: emmavjamieson@gmail.com

HIGGINS, Canon Godfrey. b 39. St Chad's Coll Dur BA 61 DipEd 63. d 63 p 64. C Brighouse *Wakef* 63-66; C Huddersfield St Jo 66-68; R High Hoyland w Clayton W 68-75; V Marsden 75-83; V Pontefract St Giles 83-04; Hon Can Wakef Cathl 93-04; rtd 04; PtO *Leeds* from 05. *2 Holme View, Ilkley LS29 9EL* T: (01943) 603861 E: godfreyhiggins@yahoo.co.uk

HIGGINS, Canon John Leslie. b 43. Open Univ BA 79 Birm Univ MEd 89 PhD 07 CQSW 75. Lich Th Coll 64. d 66 p 67. C Sale St Anne *Ches* 66-69; C Bredbury St Mark 69-72; V Wharton 72-74; Hon C Annan and Lockerbie *Glas* 75-79; V Coseley Ch Ch *Lich* 79-89; R Arthuret *Carl* 89-96; Soc Resp Officer and Child Protection Co-ord 96-00; C Brampton and Farlam and Castle Carrock w Cumrew 96-00; Hon Can Carl Cathl 96-00; Hon C Annan *Glas* 00-12; Child Protection Adv and Researcher Abps' Coun 00-03; PtO *Carl* from 01; *Eur* 09-12; P-in-c Ankara 12-15. *Green Croft Cottage, The Haggs, Ecclefechan, Lockerbie DG11 3ED* T: (01576) 300796 F: 300790 M: 07867-505644 E: john-higgins@vodafoneemail.co.uk

HIGGINS, Canon Kenneth. b 56. TCD BTh 93. CITC 90. d 93 p 94. C Cregagh *D & D* 93-96; Bp's C Movilla 96-01; I 01-09; I Belfast St Donard from 09; Can Down Cathl from 06; Treas Down Cathl from 12. *St Donard's Rectory, 421 Beersbridge Road, Belfast BT5 5DU* T: (028) 9065 2321 M: 07986-866690 E: revkenhiggins@hotmail.com

HIGGINS, The Very Revd Michael John. b 35. OBE 03. Birm Univ LLB 57 G&C Coll Cam LLB 59 PhD 62. Ridley Hall Cam 63. d 65 p 65. C Ormskirk *Liv* 65-67; Selection Sec ACCM 67-74; Hon C St Marylebone St Mark w St Luke *Lon* 69-74; P-in-c Woodlands *B & W* 74-80; V Frome St Jo 74-80; TR Preston St Jo *Blackb* 80-91; Dean Ely 91-03; rtd 03; PtO *Ely* from 05. *Twin Cottage, North Street, Great Dunham, King's Lynn PE32 2LR* T: (01328) 701058 E: michaelj.higgins@btinternet.com

HIGGINS, Natasha Caroline. *See* WOODWARD, Natasha Caroline

HIGGINS, Richard Ellis. b 63. Univ of Wales BA 84. St Mich Coll Llan 86. d 89 p 90. C Bargoed and Deri w Brithdir *Llan* 89-92; Zimbabwe 92-94; V Penmaen and Crumlin *Mon* 94-99; Chapl Glan Hafren NHS Trust 94-99; V Rhymney *Mon* 99-02; Chapl Pet Hosps NHS Trust from 03. *Chaplaincy Services, Peterborough Hospital NHS Trust, Thorpe Road, Peterborough PE3 6DA* T: (01733) 874345 E: richard.higgins@pbh-tr.nhs.uk

HIGGINS, Rupert Anthony. b 59. Man Univ BA 80. Wycliffe Hall Ox 82. d 85 p 86. C Plymouth St Andr w St Paul and St Geo *Ex* 85-90; C-in-c St Paul 88-90; Assoc V Clifton Ch Ch w Em *Bris* 90-95; V S Croydon Em *S'wark* 95-02; C Langham Place All So *Lon* 02-05; P-in-c Clifton Ch Ch w Em *Bris* 05-09; Asst Vacancy Development Adv Strategy Support 09-10; V Talbot Village *Sarum* from 10. *The Vicarage, 20 Alton Road, Bournemouth BH10 4AE* T: (01202) 939799 E: rupert.higgins@gmail.com

HIGGINS, Mrs Sheila Margaret. b 46. STETS 09. d 10 p 11. NSM Aldingbourne, Barnham and Eastergate *Chich* from 10. *2 Orchard Terrace, The Street, Walberton, Arundel BN18 0PH* T: (01243) 553901 M: 07884-495916 E: smhandaway@tiscali.co.uk

HIGGINS, Canon Timothy John. b 45. Bris Univ BEd 70 Lanc Univ MA 74. Cranmer Hall Dur. d 79 p 80. C Northampton All SS w St Kath *Pet* 79-82; V Whitton St Aug *Lon* 82-90; AD Hampton 86-90; TR Aylesbury *Ox* 90-06; RD 94-04; Hon Can Ch Ch 00-06; Can Res Bris Cathl 06-14; P-in-c City of Bris 06-08; P-in-c Bris St Steph w St Jas and St Jo w St Mich etc 08-14; rtd 14; PtO *Ban* from 15. *Cae Helyg, Tudweiliog, Pwllheli LL53 8PB* T: (01758) 770303

HIGGINSON, Andrew John. b 62. Bradf Univ BTech 85. Trin Coll Bris 02. d 04 p 05. C Quarrington w Old Sleaford *Linc* 04-08; C Silk Willoughby 04-08; P-in-c Freiston, Butterwick w Bennington, and Leverton from 08. *The Rectory, Butterwick Road, Freiston, Boston PE22 0LF* T: (01205) 760480 E: andrewj.higginson@btopenworld.com

HIGGINSON (née BROOKS), Hannah Victoria. b 90. d 14 p 15. C Finchampstead and California *Ox* from 14. *43 McCarthy Way, Finchampstead, Wokingham RG40 4UA* M: 07976-309668 E: hannahbrooks1990@gmail.com

HIGGINSON, Richard Andrew. b 53. St Jo Coll Cam BA 74 Man Univ PhD 82. EAMTC 02. d 04 p 05. NSM Cambridge St Phil

Ely 04-11; Dir of Studies Ridley Hall Cam from 05. *15 Guest Road, Cambridge CB1 2AL* T: (01223) 315667 *or* 741074 E: rah41@cam.ac.uk

HIGGINSON, Stanley. b 53. **d** 08 **p** 09. NSM Wigan St Mich *Liv* 08-15; TV Wigan All SS from 15. *12 Clifton Crescent, Wigan WN1 2LB* T: (01942) 235900 E: stanley.higginson33@yahoo.co.uk

HIGGON, David. b 49. Univ of Wales (Swansea) BA 75 Birm Univ MBA 96 Nottm Univ MA 99. EMMTC 96. **d** 00 **p** 01. NSM Crich and S Wingfield *Derby* 00-04; Chapl HM Pris Dovegate 04-05; PtO *Derby* 05-07; Chapl HM Pris Ranby 07-11; NSM Crich and S Wingfield *Derby* from 11. *67 Main Road, Morton, Alfreton DE55 6HH* T: (01773) 872332 E: dhiggon@btopenworld.com

HIGGOTT, Bryn Graham. b 54. Birm Poly BA 76 Solicitor 79. NEOC 03. **d** 06 **p** 07. NSM Thirsk *York* 06-08. *19 Main Street, Mawsley, Kettering NN14 1GA* E: bghiggott@gmail.com

HIGGS, Andrew Richard Bowen. b 53. Man Univ BSc 75. St Jo Coll Nottm 81. **d** 85 **p** 86. C Droylsden St Mary *Man* 85-88; C Harlow Town Cen w Lt Parndon *Chelmsf* 88-95; TV 95-02; Chapl Princess Alexandra Hosp NHS Trust 96-02; R Stifford *Chelmsf* from 02. *The Rectory, High Road, North Stifford, Grays RM16 5UE* T: (01375) 372733 E: andy@higgs4a.fsnet.co.uk

HIGGS, Michael John. b 53. Sarum & Wells Th Coll 76. **d** 80 **p** 81. C Cant St Martin and St Paul 80-84; C Maidstone St Martin 84-88; R Egerton w Pluckley 88-03; rtd 03. *8 Robinsons Mill, Mellis, Eye IP23 8DW* T: (01379) 783926

HIGGS, Owen Christopher Goodwin. b 63. St Anne's Coll Ox BA 84 MA 88. St Steph Ho Ox 90. **d** 93 **p** 94. C Teddington St Mark and Hampton Wick *Lon* 93-96; C Lon Docks St Pet w Wapping St Jo 96-00; V Petts Wood *Roch* 00-09; V Bickley 09-14; V Pimlico St Gabr *Lon* from 14. *St Gabriel's Vicarage, 30 Warwick Square, London SW1V 2AD* T: (020) 7834 7520 E: owen.higgs930@btinternet.com

HIGHAM, Gerald Norman. b 40. St Aid Birkenhead 64. **d** 68 **p** 69. C Garston *Liv* 68-71; C Blundellsands St Nic 71-73; V Bolton All So w St Jas *Man* 73-78; V Tonge w Alkrington 78-84; P-in-c Edenfield 84-86; P-in-c Stubbins 84-86; V Edenfield and Stubbins 86-03; rtd 03; PtO *Blackb* from 03. *71 Cherry Tree Way, Rossendale BB4 4JZ* T: (01706) 210143 E: revg.higham@rotary1280.org

HIGHAM, Canon Jack. b 33. Linc Coll Ox BA 56 MA 60 Union Th Sem (NY) STM 61. Qu Coll Birm 58. **d** 60 **p** 61. C Handsworth *Sheff* 60-64; V Handsworth Woodhouse 64-70; USA 70-78; R Stoke Bruerne w Grafton Regis and Alderton *Pet* 78-83; RD Towcester 82-83; Can Res, Chan and Lib Pet Cathl 83-03; rtd 03; PtO *S'well* from 04. *44 Alma Hill, Kimberley, Nottingham NG16 2JF* T: 0115-938 6063

HIGHAM, John Leonard. b 39. Wycliffe Hall Ox 62. **d** 65 **p** 66. C Prescot *Liv* 65-71; V Hollinfare 71-74; Adult and Youth Service Adv Knowsley 74-76; TV Padgate *Liv* 76-84; V Farnworth 84-89; TR Sutton 89-02; rtd 02; PtO *Liv* from 03. *86 Ormskirk Road, Rainford, St Helens WA11 8DB*

HIGHAM (née ANNS), Canon Pauline Mary. b 49. Bris Univ BEd 71. EMMTC 87. **d** 90 **p** 94. Par Dn Wirksworth w Alderwasley, Carsington etc *Derby* 90-92; Par Dn Lt Berkhamsted and Bayford, Essendon etc *St Alb* 92-94; C 94-96; P-in-c 96-05; R from 05; Jt RD Hertford and Ware 05-15; Hon Can *St Alb* from 06. *1 Little Berkhamsted Lane, Little Berkhamsted, Hertford SG13 8LU* T: (01707) 875940 F: 875289

HIGHTON, Philip William. b 70. Liv Univ BSc 91 Nottm Univ MSc 92. Oak Hill Th Coll BA 05. **d** 05 **p** 06. C Knutsford St Jo and Toft *Ches* 05-09; V Cheadle All Hallows 09-14; NSM Hartford from 14; Chapl Hartford C of E High Sch from 14. *9 Blenheim Close, Northwich CW9 8FB* T: (01606) 810685 E: phil@stjameshartford.org

HIGHTON, William James. b 31. St Deiniol's Hawarden. **d** 82 **p** 83. Hon Thornton Hough *Ches* 82-84; C Cheadle 84-88; V Walton 88-99; rtd 99; PtO *Carl* from 01. *15 Mowbray Drive, Burton-in-Kendal, Carnforth LA6 1NF* T: (01524) 782073

HIGHWAY, Andrew David Carnell. b 67. St Mich Coll Llan 09. **d** 12 **p** 13. NSM Llanishen *Llan* 12-15. *30 Heol Erwin, Cardiff CF14 6QR* M: 07969-757742 E: a.highway30@btinternet.com

HIGMAN, John Charles. b 62. Plymouth Poly BSc 84 Ex Univ BTh 09 MRSC 01. SWMTC 03. **d** 06 **p** 07. NSM Peter Tavy, Mary Tavy and Brent Tor *Ex* 06-15; R Peter Tavy and Mary Tavy from 15. *Balwynd, Bal Lane, Mary Tavy, Tavistock PL19 9PE* T: (01822) 810431 E: higman687@btinternet.com

HIGTON, Anthony Raymond. b 42. Lon Sch of Th BD 65. Oak Hill Th Coll 65. **d** 67 **p** 68. C Newark Ch Ch *S'well* 67-69; C Cheltenham St Mark *Glouc* 70-75; R Hawkwell *Chelmsf* 75-99; Gen Dir CMJ 99-05; R Jerusalem Ch Ch Israel 03-06; R N w S Wootton *Nor* 06-09; rtd 09; PtO *Ely* from 09; *Nor* from 09. *17 Church View, Marham, King's Lynn PE33 9HW* T: (01760) 338342 M: 07815-891582 E: tony@higton.info

HILARY, Sister. *See* JORDINSON, Vera

HILBORN, David Henry Kyte. b 64. Nottm Univ BA 85 PhD 94 Mansf Coll Ox MA 88. **d** 02 **p** 02. C Acton St Mary *Lon* 02-06; Dir Studies NTMTC 06-09; Dir 09-11; Asst Dean St Mellitus Coll *Lon* 09-11; Prin St Jo Coll Nottm from 11. *St John's College, Chilwell Lane, Bramcote, Nottingham NG9 3DS* T: 0115-925 1114 F: 943 6438

HILBORN, Mrs Mia Alison Kyte. b 63. City Univ BSc 84 Mansf Coll Ox MA 87. **d** 02 **p** 02. Chapl Team Ldr Guy's and St Thos' NHS Foundn Trust from 01; NSM N Lambeth *S'wark* from 02. *Guy's & St Thomas' NHS Foundation Trust, St Thomas Street, London SE1 9RT* T: (020) 7188 5588 M: 07740-779585 E: mia.hilborn@gstt.nhs.uk

HILDITCH, Canon Janet. b 59. St Andr Univ MTheol 81 PhD 87. NOC 92. **d** 94 **p** 95. C Kirkholt *Man* 94-98; Chapl Rochdale Healthcare NHS Trust 97-98; Chapl N Man Health Care NHS Trust 98-00; Chapl Tameside and Glossop Acute Services NHS Trust from 00; Hon Can Man Cathl from 04. *Tameside General Hospital, Fountain Street, Ashton-under-Lyne OL6 9EW* T: 0161-331 6000

HILDRED, David. b 61. Bath Univ BSc 83 CertEd 83. Wycliffe Hall Ox 86. **d** 89 **p** 90. C Westcliff St Mich *Chelmsf* 89-92; C Rayleigh 92-96; V Sidcup St Andr *Roch* 96-10; AD Sidcup 03-08; R Darfield *Sheff* from 10. *The Rectory, Church Street, Darfield, Barnsley S73 9JX* T: (01226) 752236 E: david.hildred@talktalk.net

HILDRETH, Sarah Frances. b 72. St Mich Coll Llan BTh 05. **d** 05 **p** 06. C Hawarden *St As* 05-08; V Bagillt 08-12; P-in-c Mostyn 08-12; R Llanrwst, Llanddoged w Capel Garmon etc from 12; PtO *Ban* from 14. *The Rectory, Llandoged Road, Llanrwst LL26 0DW* T: (01492) 640032 M: 07752-261931 E: revsarah3005@btinternet.com

HILDRETH, Steven Marcus. b 47. Leeds Univ LLB 69 Solicitor 78. SNWTP 08. **d** 11 **p** 12. NSM Ches St Paul 11-14; rtd 15; PtO *Ches* from 15. *3 Field Close, Tarvin, Chester CH3 8DL* T: (01829) 749303 E: shildr1027@aol.com

HILES, Janet Rita. b 39. SAOMC 96. **d** 98 **p** 99. OLM Dorchester *Ox* 98-03; rtd 03; PtO *Portsm* 04-11; *Ox* from 11. *30 Evenlode Drive, Berinsfield, Wallingford OX10 7NY* E: chrishiles@4thenet.co.uk

HILES, John Michael. b 32. Qu Coll Cam BA 57 MA 61. Sarum Th Coll 57. **d** 59 **p** 60. C Clifton St Jas *Sheff* 59-62; V Bramley St Fran 62-69; Hon C Holmfirth *Wakef* 69-89; Hon C Upper Holme Valley 89-91; LtO 91-97; PtO 97-03; *Sarum* from 03. *22 Oldfield Road, Bishopdown, Salisbury SP1 3GQ* T: (01722) 349951 E: mike.hiles@btinternet.com

HILL, Mrs Anne Doreen. b 40. **d** 88 **p** 94. Par Dn Bexleyheath St Pet *Roch* 88-90; Sub Chapl HM Pris Belmarsh 91-96; Dep Chapl 96-99; Hon C Lee St Mildred *S'wark* 93-04; rtd 04; PtO *Sarum* 05-08. *St Mary's Road, Poole BH15 2LL* T: (01202) 666076 E: adhill40@hotmail.com

HILL, Barry Leon. b 79. Wycliffe Hall Ox BTh 05. **d** 05 **p** 06. C Loughborough Em and St Mary in Charnwood *Leic* 05-09; Dioc Miss Enabler from 09. *1 Old Vicarage Mews, Sileby, Loughborough LE12 7FZ* E: barry@hill-home.co.uk

HILL, Mrs Carol. b 52. SCRTP 13. **d** 15. OLM Bicester w Bucknell, Caversfield and Launton *Ox* from 15. *Address temp unknown*

HILL, Canon Charles Bernard. b 50. Sheff Univ BA 71 Qu Coll Ox DPhil 76. Cant Sch of Min 91. **d** 94 **p** 95. NSM Sandgate St Paul w Folkestone St Geo *Cant* 94-98; NSM Folkestone H Trin w Ch Ch 98-04; Eur Sec Coun for Chr Unity 99-08; PtO *Eur* from 03; Can Gib Cathl 03-08; P-in-c Benenden *Cant* 08-10; P-in-c Sandhurst w Newenden 08-10; P-in-c Benenden and Sandhurst 10-13; rtd 13; PtO *Cant* from 14. *18 Audley Road, Folkestone CT20 3QA* T: (01303) 253861 E: cbhill18@hotmail.com

HILL, Charles Merrick. b 52. Strathclyde Univ BA 74. Qu Coll Birm. **d** 80 **p** 81. C Silksworth *Dur* 80-83; C Stockton St Pet 83-85; TV Southampton (City Cen) *Win* 85-87; V Portsea St Geo *Portsm* 87-94; P-in-c Bodenham w Hope-under-Dinmore, Felton etc *Heref* 94-04; P-in-c Hellingly and Upper Dicker *Chich* 04-05; V 05-14; P-in-c Blacklands Hastings Ch Ch and St Andr from 14. *1 Henderson Close, Hastings TN34 2DU* M: 07816-391951 E: charles.hill14@tiscali.co.uk

HILL, Charles Winston. b 78. Lanc Univ BA 99. St Steph Ho Ox 00. **d** 03 **p** 04. C Lt Marsden w Nelson St Mary *Blackb* 03-04; C Blackb St Thos w St Jude 04-07; C Blackb St Mich w St Jo and H Trin 04-07; Chapl HM Pris Preston 07-08; Chapl HM Pris Hindley 08-09; P-in-c Burnley St Mark *Blackb* 09-10; P-in-c W Burnley All SS 09-10; C 12-15; V from 12. *All Saints House, Padiham Road, Burnley BB12 6PA* T: (01282) 775629 E: judopriest@orange.net

HILL, Christopher David. b 84. Moorlands Coll BA 07. St Mellitus Coll BA 12. **d** 12 **p** 13. C Cricklewood St Gabr and St Mich *Lon* 12-15; R Northolt St Mary from 15. *The Rectory, Ealing Road, Northolt UB5 6AA* E: chris.hill@northolt.org

✠**HILL, The Rt Revd Christopher John.** b 45. KCVO 14. K Coll Lon BD 67 AKC 67 MTh 68. **d** 69 **p** 70 **c** 96. C Tividale *Lich* 69-73; C Codsall 73-74; Abp's Asst Chapl on Foreign Relns *Cant* 74-81; ARCIC from 74; Sec 74-90; Abp's Sec for Ecum Affairs *Cant* 82-89; Hon Can Cant Cathl 82-89; Chapl to The Queen 87-96; Can Res and Prec St Paul's Cathl 89-96; Select Preacher Ox Univ 90; Area Bp Stafford *Lich* 96-04; Bp Guildf 04-13; rtd 13; Hon Asst Bp Glouc from 14; Clerk of the Closet 05-14. *Hillview, West End, Ruardean GL17 9TP*
T: (01594) 541831 E: christopher.j.hill@outlook.com

HILL, Christopher Murray. b 57. Lanchester Poly Cov BA 78. Ox Min Course 05. **d** 07 **p** 08. NSM Warfield *Ox* 07-11; C 11-13; P-in-c Ely from 13. *The Vicarage, St Mary's Street, Ely CB7 4HF*
T: (01353) 662308 M: 07788-206361
E: revchill@hotmail.com *or* revchill@elyparishchurch.org.uk

HILL, The Ven Colin. b 42. Leic Univ BSc 64 Open Univ PhD 88. Ripon Hall Ox 64. **d** 66 **p** 67. C Leic Martyrs 66-69; C Braunstone 69-71; Lect Ecum Inst Thornaby Teesside 71-72; V Worsbrough St Thos and St Jas *Sheff* 72-78; Telford Planning Officer *Lich* 78-96; RD Telford and Telford Severn Gorge *Heref* 80-96; Preb Heref Cathl 83-96; Can Res Carl Cathl 96-04; Dioc Sec 96-04; Adn W Cumberland 04-08; rtd 08; PtO *Carl* from 09. *1A Briery Bank, Arnside, Carnforth LA5 0HW*
T: (01524) 762629

HILL, Canon Colin Arnold Clifford. b 29. OBE 96. Bris Univ 52 Univ of Wales (Ban) MPhil 03. Ripon Hall Ox 55. **d** 57 **p** 58. C Rotherham *Sheff* 57-61; V Brightside St Thos 61-64; R Easthampstead *Ox* 64-73; Chapl RAF Coll Bracknell 68-73; V Croydon St Jo *Cant* 73-84; V S'wark 85-94; Chapl Abp Whitgift Foundn 73-94; Hon Can Cant Cathl 75-84; Hon Can S'wark Cathl 85-94; Chapl to The Queen 90-99; rtd 94; PtO *Ox* from 11. *Silver Birches, 70 Preston Crowmarsh, Wallingford OX10 6SL* T/F: (01491) 836102
E: colin.sb@btopenworld.com

HILL, David Rowland. b 34. Lon Univ BSc 55. Qu Coll Birm. **d** 59 **p** 60. C Upper Tooting H Trin *S'wark* 59-61; C Cheam 61-63; C Richmond St Mary 63-68; V Sutton St Nicholas *Linc* 68-82; V Pinchbeck 82-99; rtd 99; PtO *Linc* 99-02 and from 05; *Pet* 04-11. *24 London Road, Spalding PE11 2TA*
T: (01775) 768912 E: revdandj.hill@virgin.net

HILL, David Royston. b 68. Westmr Coll Ox BTh 96. ERMC 04. **d** 06 **p** 07. C Dereham and Distr *Nor* 06-09; R Quidenham Gp 09-14; R Upper St Leonards St Jo *Chich* from 14; CF(V) from 09. *St John's Rectory, 53 Brittany Road, St Leonards-on-Sea TN38 0RD* M: 07827-815247 T: (01424) 423367
E: david.hill007@btinternet.com

HILL, Derek Stanley. b 28. AKC 53. **d** 53 **p** 54. C Rushmere *St E* 53-55; S Africa 55-57; C Boreham Wood All SS *St Alb* 57-59; V Crowfield *St E* 59-67; P-in-c Stonham Aspal 59-61; R 61-67; V Bury St Edmunds St Geo 67-73; P-in-c Ampton w Lt Livermere and Ingham 68-73; V Gazeley w Dalham 73-75; P-in-c Lidgate w Ousden 73-74; P-in-c Gt Bradley 74-78; V Gazeley w Dalham and Moulton 75-78; V Gt Barton 78-86; V Bury St Edmunds All SS 86-93; rtd 93; PtO *St E* from 93. *Whinwillow, 38 Maltings Garth, Thurston, Bury St Edmunds IP31 3PP* T: (01359) 230770

HILL, Elizabeth Jayne Louise. See DAVENPORT, Elizabeth Jayne Louise

HILL, Eugene Mark. b 48. Univ of Wales (Lamp) BA 71. Sarum Th Coll 71. **d** 73 **p** 74. C Sutton St Nic *S'wark* 73-77; Hon C 77-80; Asst Chapl Em Sch Wandsworth 77-87; Chapl 87-04; Hon C St Helier *S'wark* 83-84; Hon C Caterham 84-98; Dir Chr Studies Course 85-04; PtO 98-07 and from 10; Hon C Croydon St Jo 07-10. *20A Haling Park Road, South Croydon CR2 6NE*
T: (020) 8688 1387 M: 07771-708893
E: eugenemarkhill@btinternet.com

HILL, Geoffrey Lionel. b 45. WEMTC 96. **d** 03 **p** 04. OLM Thornbury and Oldbury-on-Severn w Shepperdine *Glouc* 03-06; PtO Cyprus and the Gulf from 07. *4 Kalamionas Villas, Vasilikon Anavargos, 8025 Paphos, Cyprus* T: (00357) (26) 910123 E: gl.hill@cytanet.com

HILL, Giles. See HILL, Michael John Giles

HILL, Canon Gillian Beryl. b 53. Open Univ BA 86 Portsm Univ PhD 06. S Dios Minl Tr Scheme 87. **d** 90 **p** 94. NSM Southsea St Jude *Portsm* 90-95; C Southsea St Pet 95-01; V Catherington and Clanfield from 01; Hon Can Portsm Cathl from 03. *The Vicarage, 330 Catherington Lane, Catherington, Waterlooville PO8 0TD* T: (023) 9259 3228 *or* 9259 3139
E: gillhillsrd.freeserve.co.uk

HILL, Ian Maxwell. b 60. Loughb Univ BSc 81 MCIT 85. EMMTC 92. **d** 95 **p** 96. NSM Thurnby Lodge *Leic* 95-00; NSM Thurmaston 00-08; NSM Fosse from 08. *2 Shady Ash, 4 Sturrock Close, Thurnby, Leicester LE7 9QP* T: 0116-243 1609

HILL, Ian Richard. b 69. Wycliffe Hall Ox 04. **d** 06 **p** 07. C Fareham St Jo *Portsm* 06-09; P-in-c Aspenden, Buntingford

and Westmill *St Alb* 09-13; R from 13. *The Vicarage, Vicarage Road, Buntingford SG9 9BH* T: (01763) 271552
E: ian@iansarahhill.co.uk

HILL, James. See HILL, Kenneth James

HILL, James Aidan Stuart. b 75. Ridley Hall Cam 06. **d** 09 **p** 10. C Cov H Trin 09-13; Asst Chapl Amsterdam w Den Helder and Heiloo *Eur* from 13. *Van Reigersbergenstraat 322, 1052 WT Amsterdam, The Netherlands* E: jamesincitycentre@gmail.com *or* james@christchurch.nl

HILL, James Alexander Hart. b 82. K Coll Lon BA 05. St Steph Ho Ox 05. **d** 07 **p** 08. C Tottenham St Paul *Lon* 07-11; C Tottenham St Benet Fink 10-11; P-in-c from 11; P-in-c Tottenham St Phil from 14. *St Benet Fink Vicarage, Walpole Road, London N17 6BH* T: (020) 8888 4541
E: frjameshill@hotmail.co.uk

HILL, Mrs Janice. Sheff Univ BEd 79 Nottm Univ MA 10. St Jo Coll Nottm 05. **d** 07 **p** 08. C Formby H Trin *Liv* 07-10; TV N Meols 10-14. *15 Rothwell Drive, Southport PR8 2SB*
T: (01704) 572676 E: janicehill.htc@gmail.com

HILL, Mrs Jennifer Clare. b 50. City Univ BSc 71 FBCO 72. EMMTC 94. **d** 97 **p** 98. NSM Bottesford and Muston *Leic* 97-98; C Glen Parva and S Wigston 98-01; C Walsall Wood *Lich* 01-08; V Shelfield and High Heath 08-10; RD Walsall 05-10; TV Hemel Hempstead *St Alb* 10-13; TR from 13; Dioc Adv for Women's Min from 11. *The Rectory, High Street, Hemel Hempstead HP1 3AE* T: (01442) 265272
E: jennyhill@pawstime.co.uk

HILL, Mrs Jennifer Susan. b 50. Ex Univ BTh 06 ALCM 71 LLCM 72 Gipsy Hill Coll of Educn CertEd 75. SWMTC 03. **d** 06 **p** 07. C St Mewan w Mevagissey and St Ewe *Truro* 06-09; R W Buckrose *York* 09-14; rtd 14. *7B Newton Street, Whitby YO21 1QX* T: (01947) 820543
E: jenny@primrosemusic.btinternet.com

HILL, Jonathan Carey. b 68. St Jo Coll Nottm 12. **d** 14 **p** 15. C Cheylesmore *Cov* from 14. *264 Daventry Road, Coventry CV3 5HL* M: 07810-652011
E: jonathan.carey.hill@gmail.com

HILL, Mrs Judith Anne. b 47. RGN 68. STETS 99. **d** 02 **p** 03. OLM Wool and E Stoke *Sarum* 02-12; rtd 12; PtO *Sarum* from 12. *9 High Street Close, Wool, Wareham BH20 6BW*
T: (01929) 462888 E: reverendjudy@talktalk.net

HILL, Kenneth James. b 43. Leic Univ BA 64 Lon Univ BD 68. Oak Hill Th Coll 65. **d** 69 **p** 70. C Southall Green St Jo *Lon* 69-72; C Blackheath Park St Mich *S'wark* 72-75; C Bath Abbey w St Jas *B & W* 75-83; P-in-c Bath St Mich w St Paul 75-82; R 82-83; R Huntspill 83-91; Omega Order 91-98; PtO *B & W* 91-98; *Bris* 91-98; C Somerton w Compton Dundon, the Charltons etc *B & W* 98-07; rtd 07; PtO *B & W* from 08. *14 White Horse Road, Winsey, Bradford-on-Avon BA15 2JZ*
T: (01225) 864119 E: kjhill23@btinternet.com

HILL, Mrs Laura Michelle. b 72. Qu Coll Birm BA 12. **d** 12 **p** 13. C Bridgnorth, Tasley, Astley Abbotts, etc *Heref* from 12. *41 Innage Lane, Bridgnorth WV16 4HS* T: (01746) 768027
M: 07540-066785 E: lauralollipop1972@btinternet.com

HILL, Laurence Bruce. b 43. Open Univ BA 97. AKC 67. **d** 69 **p** 70. C Feltham *Lon* 69-72; C-in-c Hampstead St Stephen 72-77; V Finchley H Trin 77-10; rtd 10. *49 Abbots Gardens, London N2 0JG* T: (020) 8444 0510 E: lorenzohill@yahoo.co.uk

HILL, Mrs Leonora Anne. b 59. Bath Univ BSc 81 Westmr Coll Ox PGCE 93. Ox Min Course 05. **d** 08 **p** 09. C Charlton Kings St Mary *Glouc* 08-12; R Ridgeway *Ox* from 12. *Ridgeway Rectory, Warborough Road, Letcombe Regis, Wantage OX12 9LD*
M: 07867-420234 T: (01235) 760112
E: revd.lahill@btinternet.com

HILL, Malcolm Crawford. b 43. Oak Hill Th Coll 68. **d** 71 **p** 72. C Maidstone St Luke *Cant* 71-74; C Longfleet *Sarum* 74-79; V Bexleyheath St Pet *Roch* 79-90; V Lee St Mildred *S'wark* 90-04; rtd 04; PtO *Sarum* from 05. *44 St Mary's Road, Poole BH15 2LL* T: (01202) 666076 E: adhill40@hotmail.com

HILL, Mrs Marjorie Ann. b 38. MCSP 60. St Jo Coll Nottm 92. **d** 94 **p** 95. C Hull St Martin w Transfiguration *York* 94-99; P-in-c Willerby w Ganton and Folkton 99-03; rtd 03; PtO *York* 03-06 and from 10; P-in-c Sigglesthorne w Nunkeeling and Bewholme 06-09; RD N Holderness 07-08. *40 Potterdale Drive, Little Weighton, Cottingham HU20 3UX* T: (01482) 840544
E: marjoriehill28@googlemail.com

HILL, Mark. See HILL, Eugene Mark

HILL, Martyn William. b 43. Man Univ BSc 64 Univ of Wales (Ban) PhD 70 MInstP 68 CPhys 85. Westcott Ho Cam 90. **d** 92 **p** 93. C Horninglow *Lich* 92-95; TV Hawarden *St As* 95-00; V Bistre 00-05; rtd 05; PtO *St As* from 05. *Llys Penmaen, Penmaenpool, Dolgellau LL40 1YD* T: (01391) 423305
M: 07835-238522 E: machillpenmaen@aol.com

HILL, Matthew Anthony Robert. b 71. Leeds Univ BA 93 Univ of Wales (Cardiff) BD 96. St Mich Coll Llan 94. **d** 97 **p** 98. C Cardiff St Jo *Llan* 97-00; Min Can Llan Cathl 00-04; P-in-c

Dowlais and Penydarren 04-05; R 05-07; Chapl Univ of Wales (Trin St Dav) *St D* 07-13; P-in-c Llanfihangel Ystrad and Cilcennin w Trefilan etc from 13. *Ystrad Vicarage, Felinfach, Lampeter SA48 8AE* T: (01570) 471241
E: matthewhill@churchinwales.org.uk

✠HILL, The Rt Revd Michael Arthur. b 49. Ridley Hall Cam 74. d 77 p 78 c 98. C Addiscombe St Mary *Cant* 77-81; C Slough *Ox* 81-83; P-in-c Chesham Bois 83-90; R 90-92; RD Amersham 89-92; Adn Berks 92-98; Area Bp Buckingham 98-03; Bp Bris from 03. *Bishop's Office, 58A High Street, Winterbourne, Bristol BS36 1JQ* T: (01454) 777728 E: bishop@bristoldiocese.org

HILL, The Rt Revd Michael John Giles. b 43. S Dios Minl Tr Scheme 82. d 84 p 86. Community of Our Lady and St John from 67; Abbot from 90; PtO *Win* 84-92 and from 13; Public Preacher 92-13; PtO *Portsm* from 04; Hon Can Win Cathl from 15. *Abbey of Our Lady and St John, Abbey Road, Beech, Alton GU34 4AP* T: (01420) 562145 or 563575 F: 561691

HILL, Miss Naomi Jean. b 75. Coll of Ripon & York St Jo BA 96. Wycliffe Hall Ox BTh 06. d 06 p 07. C Northampton St Giles *Pet* 06-10; C Nottingham St Nic *S'well* 10-14; C Sneinton St Chris w St Phil 10-14; P-in-c from 14; C Nottingham St Ann w Em from 14. *St Christopher's Vicarage, 180 Sneinton Boulevard, Nottingham NG2 4GL* M: 07855-060410
E: naomi.hill3@ntlworld.com

HILL, Nora. b 47. Univ of Wales BA 95 PGCE 97. St Mich Coll Llan 00. d 03 p 04. NSM Llandogo w Whitebrook Chpl and Tintern Parva *Mon* from 03. *3 Warwick Close, Chepstow NP16 5BU* T: (01291) 626784

HILL, Patricia Frances. b 49. RGN 90. SEITE 96. d 99 p 00. NSM Hythe *Cant* 99-01; Asst Chapl E Kent Hosps NHS Trust 99-00; Team Ldr Chapl from 01; NSM Saltwood *Cant* 10-13; NSM Aldington w Bonnington and Bilsington etc 10-13; NSM Lympne and Saltwood from 13. *Springville, Sandling Road, Saltwood, Hythe CT21 4QJ* T: (01303) 266649 *or* (01233) 633331 ext 88381 E: patricia.hill@ekht.nhs.uk

HILL, Peppie. *See* HILL, Stephanie Jane

✠HILL, The Rt Revd Peter. b 50. Man Univ BSc 71 Nottm Univ MTh 90. Wycliffe Hall Ox 81. d 83 p 84 c 14. C Porchester *S'well* 83-86; V Huthwaite 86-95; P-in-c Calverton 95-04; RD S'well 97-01; Dioc Chief Exec 04-07; Adn Nottingham 07-14; Hon Can S'well Minster 01-07; Area Bp Barking *Chelmsf* from 14. *Barking Lodge, 35A Verulam Avenue, London E17 8ES* T: (020) 8509 7377 E: b.barking@chelmsford.anglican.org

HILL, Canon Peter. b 36. AKC 60. St Boniface Warminster 60. d 61 p 62. C Gt Berkhamsted *St Alb* 61-67; R Bedford St Mary 67-69; P-in-c 69-70; V Goldington 69-79; V Biggleswade 79-90; RD 80-85; Hon Can St Alb 85-90; V Holbeach *Linc* 90-01; RD Elloe E 94-99; P-in-c The Suttons w Tydd 99-01; r-d 01; PtO *Nor* 01-12; *Ely* from 06. *40 Walnut Tree Crescent, Fenstanton, Huntingdon PE28 9LE* T: (01480) 461005

HILL, Peter. d 14 p 15. NSM Bicester w Bucknell, Caversfield and Launton *Ox* from 14. *25 Shaw Close, Bicester OX26 2FN*
E: peterghill@hotmail.com

HILL, Canon Richard Brian. b 47. Dur Univ BA 68. Cranmer Hall Dur 68 Westcott Ho Cam 70. d 71 p 72. C Cockermouth All SS w Ch Ch *Carl* 71-74; C Barrow St Geo w St Luke 74-76; V Walney Is 76-83; Dir of Clergy Tr 83-90; P-in-c Westward, Rosley-w-Woodside and Welton 83-90; V Gosforth All SS *Newc* 90-03; rtd 05; Hon Can Newc Cathl from 05; Chapl St Mary Magd and H Jes Trust from 06; Asst Dioc Ecum Officer *Newc* from 08. *56 St Mary Magdalene Hospital, Claremont Road, Newcastle upon Tyne NE2 4NN* T: 0191-261 2648
E: r.b.hill@lineone.net

HILL, Richard Hugh Oldham. b 52. CCC Ox BA 74 BA 77 MA 78. Wycliffe Hall Ox 75. d 78 p 79. C Harold Wood *Chelmsf* 78-81; C Hampreston *Sarum* 81-86; TV N Ferriby *York* 86-97; V Swanland 97-08; R Church Stretton *Heref* from 08; RD Condover from 11. *The Rectory, Ashbrook Meadow, Carding Mill Valley, Church Stretton SY6 6JF* T: (01694) 722585

HILL, Robert Arthur. b 59. Trent Poly BSc 83 Open Univ BA 93. ACT 96. d 01 p 02. Sen Chapl Miss to Seafarers Australia 95-03; C Kettering SS Pet and Paul 03-08; Soc Resp Adv 08-15. *19 Greenhill Road, Kettering NN15 7LW* T/F: (01536) 523603
E: robert.hill@peterborough-diocese.org.uk

HILL, Robert Joseph. b 45. Oak Hill Th Coll BA 81. d 81 p 82. C W Derby St Luke *Liv* 81-84; P-in-c Devonport St Mich *Ex* 84-97; Chapl Morden Coll Blackheath 97-99; TV Manningham *Bradf* 99-04; P-in-c Davyhulme Ch Ch *Man* 04-13; rtd 13. *52 Wellfield Road, Stockport SK2 6AT* T: 0161-456 2450
E: rjandh@gmail.com

HILL, Robin. b 35. Cranmer Hall Dur 59. d 62 p 63. C Aspley *S'well* 62-65; V Mansfield St Aug 65-71; R Hulland, Atlow and Bradley *Derby* 71-76; R Nollamara Australia 76-82; R Armadale 82-86; P-in-c Alkmonton, Cubley, Marston Montgomery etc *Derby* 86-93; P-in-c Ticknall, Smisby and Stanton-by-Bridge 93-99; P-in-c Barrow-on-Trent w Twyford and Swarkestone

---

94-99; rtd 99; Assoc P Fremantle Australia 99-05. *10/31 Pakenham Street, Freemantle WA 6160, Australia*
T: (0061) (8) 9336 4663

HILL, Rodney Maurice. b 44. Leeds Univ BA 67 FCIPD. Ripon Coll Cuddesdon 04. d 05 p 06. NSM N Hinksey and Wytham *Ox* 05-10; NSM Osney 10-12; PtO from 12. *13 Hobson Road, Oxford OX2 7JX* T: (01865) 426804
E: rodneymauricehill@hotmail.com

HILL, Canon Roger Anthony John. b 45. Liv Univ BA 67 Linacre Coll Ox BA 69 MA. Ripon Hall Ox 67. d 70 p 71. C St Helier *S'wark* 70-74; C Dawley Parva *Lich* 74-75; C Cen Telford 76-77; TV 77-81; TR 81-88; TR Newark *S'well* 88-02; RD 90-95; Hon Can S'well Minster 98-02; R Man St Ann 02-07; AD Hulme 05-07; Bp's Missr 07-11; Hon Can Man Cathl 02-11; rtd 11; PtO *Man* from 11; Chapl to The Queen 01-15. *4 Four Stalls End, Littleborough OL15 8SB* T: (01706) 374719
E: hillraj@googlemail.com

HILL, Simon George. b 53. Reading Univ BSc 75 MSc 78 Lon Univ DMin 10. S'wark Ord Course 80. d 83 p 84. NSM Croydon St Aug *Cant* 83-84; Swaziland 84-86; Fiji 86-88; NSM Croydon St Aug *S'wark* 88-90; Tanzania 90-94; Uganda 94-96; Swaziland 96-98; PtO *S'wark* 99-02; *Chich* 99-02; P-in-c Cockfield w Bradfield St Clare, Felsham etc *St E* 02-04; R Bradfield St Clare, Bradfield St George etc 04-11; RD Lavenham 09-11; V Copthorne *Chich* from 11. *The Vicarage, Church Road, Copthorne, Crawley RH10 3RD* T: (01342) 712063 M: 07747-022903 E: mlima001@btinternet.com

HILL, Preb Simon James. b 64. Sheff Univ BA 85 Ex Univ PGCE 88 Bris Univ MA 09. Ripon Coll Cuddesdon 84. d 95 p 96. C Manston *Ripon* 95-98; TV Dorchester *Ox* 98-03; Dir Berinsfield Progr Ripon Coll Cuddesdon 98-03; R Backwell w Chelvey and Brockley *B & W* 03-10; Dioc Dir of Clergy Development from 10; Preb Wells Cathl from 14. *87 Hawthorn Crescent, Yatton, Bristol BS49 4RG* T: (01934) 832907
or (01749) 685107 E: simon.hill@bathwells.anglican.org

HILL, Stephanie Jane (Peppie). b 67. K Coll Lon LLB 88. Wycliffe Hall Ox BTh 05. d 05 p 15. C Loughborough Em and St Mary in Charnwood *Leic* 05-06; NSM Leic H Trin w St Jo from 14. *1 Old Vicarage Mews, Sileby, Loughborough LE12 7FZ*
E: pep@hill-home.co.uk

HILL, Stuart Graeme. b 64. Ripon Coll Cuddesdon BTh 97. d 97 p 98. C Usworth *Dur* 97-99; C Monkwearmouth 99-01; TV 01-06; V Upper Derwent *York* from 06. *The Vicarage, 4 Cayley Lane, Brompton-by-Sawdon, Scarborough YO13 9DL* T: (01723) 859694 E: revd.stuarthill@icloud.com

HILL (formerly SAYERS), Susan. b 46. Bp Otter Coll Chich BEd 69 Middx Univ BA 02. NTMTC 99. d 02 p 03. NSM Southend *Chelmsf* 02-12; TV 05-12; Asst Chapl HM Pris Bullwood Hall 02-06; rtd 12; PtO *Chelmsf* from 13. *17 Claremont Close, Westcliff-on-Sea SS0 7UA* T: (01702) 431843 M: 07765-857320 E: susansayers@yahoo.com

HILL, Walter Henry. d 06 p 07. Aux Min Cloyne Union *C, C & R* 06-14; NSM Fermoy Union from 14. *Quetta, Glenatore, Conna, Co Cork, Republic of Ireland* M: (00353) 87-629 6545
E: whill911@gmail.com

HILL, William. b 44. Man Univ BSc 66 CEng 73 MICE 73. SEITE 97. d 98 p 99. NSM Farnham *Guildf* 98-01; P-in-c Smallburgh w Dilham w Honing and Crostwight *Nor* 01-05; rtd 05; PtO *Nor* from 05; RD St Benet 07-12. *65 New Road, Hethersett, Norwich NR9 3HJ* T: (01603) 812220
E: revd.william.hill@btinternet.com

HILL-BROWN, Rachel Judith. b 65. Westmr Coll Ox BEd 88. St Jo Coll Nottm MTh 07. d 07 p 09. C Knowle *Birm* 07-10; C Tanworth 10-11; Hon C Dorridge from 11; Hon Chapl Birm Children's Hosp NHS Trust from 11. *54 Glendon Way, Dorridge, Solihull B93 8SY* T: (01564) 772472
E: rhillbrown@googlemail.com

HILL-BROWN, Timothy Duncan. b 65. Westmr Coll Ox BA 87. Wycliffe Hall Ox 91. d 93 p 94. C Sparkhill w Greet and Sparkbrook *Birm* 93-97; C Sutton Coldfield H Trin 97-99; P-in-c Short Heath 99-00; V 00-06; V Dorridge from 06; AD Shirley from 12. *54 Glendon Way, Dorridge, Solihull B93 8SY* T: (01564) 772472 E: duncan@ukonline.co.uk

HILLARY, Leslie Tyrone James. b 59. Cranmer Hall Dur 84. d 87 p 88. C Middlesbrough All SS *York* 87-89; C Stainton-in-Cleveland 89-91; CF from 91. *c/o MOD Chaplains (Army)* F: 381824 T: (01264) 383430 E: lthillary@hotmail.com

HILLAS, Canon Patricia Dorothy. b 66. E Lon Univ BA 91 Middx Univ BA 02. NTMTC 98. d 02 p 03. C Kensal Rise St Mark and St Martin *Lon* 02-05; V Northolt Park St Barn 05-14; Can Pastor St Paul's Cathl from 14. *2 Amen Court, London EC4M 7BU* M: 07894-219366 T: (020) 7246 8378
E: mountainskies@btinternet.com

HILLEBRAND, Frank David. b 46. AKC 68. St Boniface Warminster 68. d 69 p 70. C Wood Green St Mich *Lon* 69-72; C Evesham *Worc* 72-75; V Worc H Trin 75-80; V Kidderminster

St Jo 80-90; TR Kidderminster St Jo and H Innocents 90-91; TV High Wycombe *Ox* 91-95; TR 95-00; Team Chapl Portsm Hosps NHS Trust 00-06; rtd 06; PtO *Portsm* 07-13. *40 Woodfield Park Road, Emsworth PO10 8BG* T: (01243) 378846
E: frankandsue68@btinternet.com

HILLEL, Laurence Christopher Francis. b 54. Bris Univ BA 76 Sheff Univ PGCE 78 SOAS Lon MA 84. Cuddesdon Coll 98. d 98 p 99. C Pinner *Lon* 98-00; Chapl Bp Ramsey Sch 01-14; Inter Faith Adv Willesden Area *Lon* from 14; NSM Eastcote St Lawr 01-04; NSM Brondesbury St Anne w Kilburn H Trin from 04. *49 Keslake Road, London NW6 6DH* T: (020) 8969 9063 M: 07801-286819 E: revhillel@aol.com

HILLER, Ms Frances. b 53. Greenwich Univ BA 93. NTMTC 07. d 09. Chapl to Suff Bp Eur from 09; PtO *S'wark* from 09. *14 Tufton Street, London SW1P 3QZ* T: (020) 7898 1161
E: frances.hiller@churchofengland.org

HILLIAM, Mrs Cheryl. b 49. EMMTC. d 94 p 95. C Linc St Faith and St Martin w St Pet 94-98; P-in-c S Ormsby Gp from 98. *The Rectory, South Ormsby, Louth LN11 8QT* T: (01507) 480236

HILLIARD, David. b 54. TCD BTh 91. CITC 88. d 91 p 92. C Holywood *D & D* 91-94; C Seagoe 94-96; I Tartaraghan w Diamond *Arm* from 96. *The Rectory, 5 Tarthlogue Road, Portadown BT62 1RB* T/F: (028) 3885 1289
E: tartaraghan@armagh.anglican.org

HILLIARD, George Percival St John. b 45. TCD BA 67. d 69 p 70. C Seapatrick *D & D* 69-73; C Carrickfergus *Conn* 73-76; I Fanlobbus Union *C, C & R* 76-85; Dean Cloyne 85-02; Prec Cork Cathl 85-02; I Cloyne Union 85-02; Chapl Univ Coll Cork 02-10; Can Cork and Cloyne Cathls 02-10; rtd 11; PtO *Nor* from 11. *13 Rose Lane, Botesdale, Diss IP22 1DJ* T: (01379) 890085 M: (00353) 86-191 7644
E: gchilliard@hotmail.com

HILLIARD, Ms Lorelli Alison. b 60. St Mary's Coll Dur BSc 82 Dur Univ MA 07. Cranmer Hall Dur 04. d 06 p 07. C Drypool *York* 06-10; P-in-c St Marsden w Nelson St Phil *Blackb* 10-13; V from 13. *St Philip's Vicarage, 1 Victory Close, Nelson BB9 9ED* T: (01282) 697011 E: lorelli.hilliard@googlemail.com

HILLIARD, Martin. b 45. TCD BA 69 BTh 08. CITC 05. d 08 p 09. C Larne and Inver and Glynn w Raloo *Conn* 08-11; I Kells Gp *C & O* from 11. *The Priory, Kells, Co Kilkenny, Republic of Ireland* T: (00353) (56) 772 8367 M: 86-108 7432
E: revmartinhilliard@gmail.com

HILLIARD, Robert Godfrey. b 52. Portsm Univ BA(Ed) 97 MA 03. St Mich Coll Llan 72. d 75 p 76. C Whitchurch *Llan* 75-80; Chapl RNR 77-80; Chapl RN 80-06; Hon Chapl Portsm Cathl 03-06; Chapl Bradfield Coll Berks 06-12; C Cobham and Stoke D'Abernon *Guildf* from 13. *The Rectory, Blundel Lane, Stoke D'Abernon, Cobham KT11 2SE* T: (01932) 868428
M: 07786-257395 E: godfreyhilliard@hotmail.co.uk

HILLIARD, Russell Baston. b 57. Univ of N Carolina BA 82 Zürich Univ Lic 89 Vanderbilt Univ (USA) PhD 95. St Jo Coll Nottm 01. d 03 p 04. C Zürich *Eur* 03-06; PtO 06-09; Asst Chapl Basle from 09. *Rebweg 12, 8309 Nürensdorf, Switzerland* T/F: (0041) (44) 836 9245 M: 79-501 4904
E: r.hilliard@anglicanbasel.ch

HILLIER, Andrew. b 68. RGN 92. SWMTC 99. d 02 p 03. C Castle Cary w Ansford *B & W* 02-05; Chapl RN 05-12. *5 Burton Close, Curry Rivel, Langport TA10 0AF*
E: andrewhillier@bigfoot.com

HILLIER, Derek John. b 30. Sarum Th Coll 61. d 63 p 64. C Salisbury St Mark *Sarum* 63-65; C Weymouth H Trin 65-66; R Caundle Bishop w Caundle Marsh and Holwell 66-75; R The Caundles and Holwell 75-81; R The Caundles w Folke and Holwell 81-02; P-in-c Pulham 70-78; rtd 02; PtO *Sarum* from 02; *B & W* from 02. *Sarum House, Bishop's Caundle, Sherborne DT9 5ND* T/F: (01963) 23243

HILLIER, John Frederick. b 43. ARIBA 67. d 01 p 02. OLM Merton St Mary *S'wark* 01-06; PtO *St Alb* 07; NSM Sandridge 07-13; rtd 13; PtO *St Alb* 13; *Ely* from 14. *70 Royal Way, Trumpington, Cambridge CB2 9AX* M: 07802-646374

HILLIER (née CHAPMAN), Mrs Linda Rosa. b 54. Middx Univ BA 04. NTMTC 01. d 04 p 05. C W Drayton *Lon* 04-07; Faith and Work Development Officer Slough *Ox* 07-13; NSM Upton cum Chalvey from 12. *79 Torbay Road, Harrow HA2 9QG* T: (020) 8864 5728 E: lindarosahillier@msn.com

HILLIER, Ms Marilyn Jean. b 51. Ches Coll of HE CertEd 73. NTMTC BA 08. d 08 p 09. NSM Gt Parndon *Chelmsf* 08-12; PtO from 13. *23 Chapel Hill, Stansted CM24 8AD* T: (01279) 813833 E: lynhillier@btinternet.com

HILLIER, The Ven Michael Bruce. b 49. St Barn Coll Adelaide ThD 73. d 74 p 75. C Plympton Australia 74-76; Assoc P Walkerville 76-80; C Tewkesbury w Walton Cardiff *Glouc* 81-86; Australia from 86; P-in-c Whyalla from 94; Adn Eyre Peninsula from 01. *37 Wood Terrace, PO Box 244, Whyalla SA 5600, Australia* T: (0061) (8) 8644 0391 F: 8644 0657
E: mjhillier@ozemail.com.au

HILLIER, Timothy John. b 55. Westmr Coll Ox CertEd 77. Oak Hill Th Coll 94. d 96 p 97. C Chertsey *Guildf* 96-00; V 00-04; V Chertsey, Lyne and Longcross from 04; RD Runnymede 07-13. *The Vicarage, London Street, Chertsey KT16 8AA* T/F: (01932) 563141 E: tim.hillier@o2.co.uk

HILLMAN, Clive Ralph. b 71. York Univ BSc 92. St Steph Ho Ox BA 93. d 96 p 97. C Kingston upon Hull St Alb *York* 96-00; TV Ifield *Chich* 00-02; Chapl St Jo Coll Cam 02-06; V Betws-y-Coed and Capel Curig w Penmachno etc *Ban* 06-13; P-in-c Leigh St Clem *Chelmsf* from 14. *The Rectory, 80 Leigh Hill, Leigh-on-Sea SS9 1AR* T: (01702) 475967
E: clivehillman@btinternet.com

HILLMAN, John Anthony. b 32. St Chad's Coll Dur BA 53. St Mich Coll Llan 54. d 55 p 56. C Llangollen *St As* 56-60; C Silvertown S Africa 60-64; P-in-c Matroosfontein 64-72; R Noorder Paarl 72-75; R Durbanville 75-80; R Somerset W 80-86; TV Wolstanton *Lich* 86-91; P-in-c E Goscote w Ratcliffe and Rearsby *Leic* 91-93; TV Syston 93-98; rtd 98; PtO *St As* 09-13. *7 Hafod Road West, Penrhyn Bay, Llandudno LL30 3PN* T: (01492) 541374

HILLMAN, Jonathan. b 68. Man Univ BEng 90. Ridley Hall Cam. d 00 p 01. C N Wingfield, Clay Cross and Pilsley *Derby* 00-03; TV Cove St Jo *Guildf* 03-10; R Windlesham from 10. *The Rectory, Kennel Lane, Windlesham GU20 6AA* T: (01276) 472363 E: rector@windleshamchurch.org.uk

HILLMAN, Sarah Catherine. b 68. Selw Coll Cam BA 90 MA 94. St Jo Coll Nottm MA 05. d 03 p 04. C Sandy *St Alb* 03-06; P-in-c Barkway, Reed and Buckland w Barley 06-11; P-in-c Puddletown, Tolpuddle and Milborne w Dewlish *Sarum* 11-15; R from 15. *The Vicarage, The Square, Puddletown, Dorchester DT2 8SL* T: (01305) 848784 E: sarah.c.hillman@tesco.net

HILLS, Alan Arthur. b 49. Sussex Univ BA 73 Ches Coll of HE MEd 94. d 09 p 10. OLM Ashton Ch Ch *Man* from 09. *41 Bollington Road, Stockport SK4 5ER* T: 0161-432 2964 F: 477 7459 M: 07752-162333 E: alan@cahills.co.uk

HILLS, Mrs Christine Ann. b 54. NTMTC BA 05. d 05 p 06. C Romford Gd Shep *Chelmsf* 05-08; C Blackmore and Stondon Massey 08-10; P-in-c Mistley w Manningtree and Bradfield from 10. *The Rectory, 21 Malthouse Road, Manningtree CO11 1BY* T: (01206) 392200 E: chris-hills@ntlworld.com

HILLS, Elaine. b 45. RN 67. Mon Dioc Tr Scheme 02. d 04 p 08. NSM Caerleon w Llanhennock *Mon* 04-09; NSM Caerleon and Llanfrechfa from 09. *6 Anthony Drive, Caerleon, Newport NP18 3DS* T: (01633) 421248 M: 07967-349096
E: rev.elaine@btinternet.com

HILLS, James Luke. b 84. Ex Univ MEng 06. Oak Hill Th Coll BA 14. d 14 p 15. C Kea *Truro* from 14. *Nancemere House, 169 Treffry Road, Truro TR1 1UF* M: 07736-316145
E: jameshills@gmail.com

HILLS, Jonathan Mark. b 84. Trin Coll Bris BA 10. d 10 p 11. C Churchdown *Glouc* 10-13. *PO Box 321, Mason TX 76856, USA* T: (001) (325) 347 2139 E: jjhills@gmail.com

HILLS, Kenneth Hugh. b 30. Univ of NZ BCom 54. Ripon Hall Ox 55. d 57 p 58. C Handsworth St Mary *Birm* 57-59; V Wanganui Paroch Distr New Zealand 59-61; V Porirua 67-74; Ind Chapl *Birm* 67-74; Chapl Aston Univ 74-82; rtd 91; Community Member Cluny Hill Coll 93-00. *2 O'Neills Place, Church Road, Holywood BT18 9BU* T: (028) 9042 1545
E: ken.hills@findhorn.org or k_h@onetel.com

HILLS, Lee Anthony. b 74. St Jo Coll Nottm 04. d 06. Deanery Missr *Birm* 06-08. *23 Jubilee Gardens, Birmingham B23 5HS* T: 0121-382 6887 M: 07796-137423 E: lee@djvicar.co.uk

HILLS, Michael John. b 58. MBE 09. BA 82. Westcott Ho Cam 87. d 88 p 89. C Workington St Jo *Carl* 88-91; C Gosforth All SS *Newc* 91-93; TV Seaton Hirst 93-98; Chapl RN from 98. *Royal Naval Chaplaincy Service, Mail Point 1-2, Leach Building, Whale Island, Portsmouth PO2 8BY* T: (023) 9262 5055 F: 9262 5134 E: revmikehills@hotmail.com

HILLS, Michael Rae Buchanan. b 52. Univ of Wales (Lamp) BA 81 Ex Univ BPhil 83. St Steph Ho Ox 92. d 94 p 95. C Kingston upon Hull St Nic *York* 94-97; V Newington w Dairycoates 97-03; P-in-c 03-06; P-in-c Kingston upon Hull St Nic 05-06; N Humberside Ind Chapl 03-06; Sen Chapl 07-13; Hon C Newington w Dairycoates 07-08; P-in-c Kingston upon Hull St Mary 08-13; P-in-c Stranraer from 14; P-in-c Portpatrick from 14; P-in-c Challoch *Glas* from 14; P-in-c Stranraer from 14. *Glenview, Glenjorrie Avenue, Glenluce, Newton Stewart DG8 0QW-ql; E: vicar@kanga.karoo.co.uk*

HILLS, Michael William John. b 54. Univ of Wales (Lamp) BA 84. Westcott Ho Cam 85. d 87 p 88. C Reddish *Man* 87-91; V Bolton St Phil 91-00; V Northampton St Mich w St Edm *Pet* from 00; P-in-c Northampton H Sepulchre w St Andr and St Lawr 04-07; V from 07. *The Vicarage, 94 St Georges Avenue, Northampton NN2 6JF* T: (01604) 230316 or 717855
F: 635673 E: mickhills@btconnect.com

HILLS, Richard Leslie. b 36. MBE 15. Qu Coll Cam BA 60 MA 63 UMIST PhD 68 FMA 83. St Deiniol's Hawarden 85. **d** 87 **p** 88. C Urmston *Man* 87-89; C Gt Yarmouth *Nor* 89-90; NSM Mottram in Longdendale *Ches* 90-01; PtO from 01. *261 Broadbottom Road, Mottram, Hyde SK14 6HY* T: (01457) 763104

HILLS, Roger Malcolm. b 42. Oak Hill Th Coll 83. **d** 86 **p** 87. NSM Mill Hill Jo Keble Ch *Lon* 86-98; NSM Mill Hill St Mich 86-98; PtO 98-00; V Queensbury All SS 00-07; rtd 07; PtO *Lon* from 08. *22 Sefton Avenue, London NW7 3QD* T: (020) 8959 1931 E: roger.hills2@btinternet.com

HILLS, Canon Sarah Ann St Leger. b 65. Sheff Univ MB, ChB 89 Leeds Univ MA 07. NOC 04. **d** 07 **p** 08. C Millhouses H Trin *Sheff* 07-10; PtO 10-11; Hon C Sheff St Pet and St Oswald 11-14; Bp's Adv in Past Care and Reconciliation 13-14; Can for Reconciliation Min Cov Cathl from 14. *Coventry Cathedral, 1 Hill Top, Coventry CV1 5AB* T: (024) 7652 1200 M: 07557-054641

HILLS, Stephen Alan. b 59. Sheff Univ BA 81. Ridley Hall Cam 97. **d** 99 **p** 00. C Southborough St Pet w Ch Ch and St Matt etc *Roch* 99-02; TV from 02. *The Rectory, Rectory Drive, Bidborough, Tunbridge Wells TN3 0UL* T: (01892) 528081 E: stephen.hills@diocese-rochester.org

HILLYER, Charles Norman. b 21. Lon Univ BD 48 Lambeth STh 67. ALCD 48. **d** 48 **p** 49. C Finchley Ch Ch *Lon* 48-51; C New Malden and Coombe *S'wark* 51-54; V Hanley Road St Sav w St Paul *Lon* 54-59; Chapl City of Lon Maternity Hosp 54-59; V Ponsbourne *St Alb* 59-70; Chapl Tolmers Park Hosp 59-70; Lib Tyndale Ho Cam 70-73; Org Ed UCCF 73-79; Sec Tyndale Fellowship Bibl Research Cam 73-75; P-in-c Hatherleigh *Ex* 79-81; V 81-86; rtd 86; PtO *Sarum* 89-03; *Leic* from 03. *c/o Mrs J V H White, 3 Little Cloister, London SW1P 3PL* E: norman.hillyer@btinternet.com

HILTON, Mrs Barbara Anne. b 59. Lindisfarne Regional Tr Partnership BA 14. **d** 14 **p** 15. C Heighington and Darlington St Matt and St Luke *Dur* from 14. *1 Manor Court, Heighington Village, Newton Aycliffe DL5 6TL* M: 07456-082231 E: barbara17hilton@yahoo.co.uk

HILTON, Clive. b 30. K Coll Lon 54. **d** 58 **p** 59. C Wythenshawe Wm Temple Ch CD *Man* 58-61; C Newton Heath All SS 61-62; C-in-c Oldham St Chad Limeside CD 62-65; V Oldham St Chad Limeside 65-70; P-in-c Gravesend H Family *Roch* 70-71; R Killamarsh *Derby* 71-88; R Broughton w Loddington and Cransley etc *Pet* 88-91; rtd 92; PtO *Man* 92-95; *Pet* from 98; *Ches* 95-99; *Linc* from 98; *Ely* 05-08. *73A Tattershall Drive, Market Deeping, Peterborough PE6 8BZ* T: (01778) 346217

HILTON, Canon Ian Anthony. b 57. St Jo Coll Nottm 83. **d** 86 **p** 87. C Nottingham St Sav *S'well* 86-90; C Aspley 90-97; P-in-c Colchester, New Town and The Hythe *Chelmsf* 97-02; R from 02; RD Colchester 06-14; Hon Can Chelmsf Cathl from 12. *The Rectory, 24 New Town Road, Colchester CO1 2EF* T: (01206) 618652 *or* 512845 E: ian.hilton@talktalk.net

HILTON, John. b 49. Ex Univ BA 70. Cuddesdon Coll 71. **d** 73 **p** 74. C W Derby St Jo *Liv* 73-79; V Orford St Andr 79-96; V Leeds St Wilfrid 96-14; rtd 14; PtO *Man* from 15. *42 College Avenue, Oldham OL8 4DS* T: 0161-624 9172 E: john@the-oak-403.demon.co.uk

HILTON-TURVEY, Geoffrey Michael. b 34. Oak Hill Th Coll 80. **d** 81 **p** 82. C Bispham *Blackb* 81-85; V Inskip 85-99; rtd 99; PtO *Heref* from 00. *20 Cralves Mead, Tenbury Wells WR15 8EX* T: (01584) 811153 E: gmh-t@gmh-t.freeserve.co.uk

HILTON-TURVEY, Keith Geoffrey Michael. b 59. Oak Hill Th Coll BA 03. **d** 03 **p** 04. C S Mimms Ch Ch *Lon* 03-09; P-in-c Cricklewood St Pet from 09. *St Peter's Vicarage, 5 Farm Avenue, London NW2 2EG* T: (020) 8438 8903 E: kht@fideste.freeserve.co.uk

HINA, Christine Magdeleine. b 66. SAOMC. **d** 01 **p** 02. C Stevenage St Hugh and St Jo *St Alb* 01-06; C Stevenage St Nic and Graveley 06-12; TV Elstree and Borehamwood from 12. *Holy Cross Vicarage, 1 Warren Grove, Borehamwood WD6 2QU* T: (020) 8953 2183 E: christine.hina@hotmail.co.uk

HINCHCLIFFE, Garry Anthony Frank. b 68. New Coll Edin BD 94. Edin Th Coll 90. **d** 94 **p** 95. C Dumfries *Glas* 94-97; P-in-c Motherwell and Wishaw 97-00; V Hampsthwaite and Killinghall *Ripon* 00-04; V Hampsthwaite and Killinghall and Birstwith 04-13; TR Knaresborough *Leeds* from 13; P-in-c Nidd *Ripon* from 14. *The Rectory, High Bond End, Knaresborough HG5 9BT* T: (01423) 202092 E: garry.hinchcliffe@btinternet.com

HINCKLEY, Paul Frederick. b 61. Cranfield Inst of Tech MSc 85. Ridley Hall Cam 92. **d** 94 **p** 95. C Ovenden *Wakef* 94-99; TV Billericay and Lt Burstead *Chelmsf* 99-06; R Yateley *Win* 06-10; TV Gt Marlow w Marlow Bottom, Lt Marlow and Bisham *Ox* 10-13; TV Stoke Gifford *Bris* from 13. *106 Cooks Close, Bradley Stoke, Bristol BS32 0BB* T: (01454) 880065 E: paul@ctkchurch.org.uk

⊹**HIND, The Rt Revd John William.** b 45. Leeds Univ BA 66 Lambeth DD 09. Cuddesdon Coll 70. **d** 72 **p** 73 **c** 91. C Catford (Southend) and Downham *S'wark* 72-76; V Forest Hill Ch Ch 76-82; P-in-c Forest Hill St Paul 81-82; Prin Chich Th Coll 82-91; Wiccamical Preb Chich Cathl 82-91; Area Bp Horsham 91-93; Bp Eur 93-01; Asst Bp Chich 93-01; Bp Chich 01-12; rtd 12; Hon Asst Bp Portsm from 12. *1 Stanley Road, Emsworth PO10 7BD* E: john@hind.org.uk

HIND, Canon Ruth Elizabeth. b 71. Cen Lancs Univ BA 93 Huddersfield Univ PGCE 13. St Jo Coll Nottm MTh 01. **d** 02 **p** 03. C Caldbeck, Castle Sowerby and Sebergham *Carl* 02-06; V Hutton Cranswick w Skerne, Watton and Beswick *York* 06-11; RD Harthill 10-11; P-in-c Kirklington w Burneston and Wath and Pickhill *Leeds* 11-15; Can Res Ripon Cathl from 15. *St Peter's House, Minster Close, Ripon HG4 1QP* T: (01765) 604108 E: ruthhind@gmail.com *or* canonruth@riponcathedral.org.uk

HINDER, Richard Alan. b 46. Birm Univ BSc 67 CCC Cam PhD 71 FRAS 70 CEng 82 FIEE 80. S'wark Ord Course 04. **d** 07 **p** 08. NSM Croydon St Matt *S'wark* from 07. *18 Mapledale Avenue, Croydon CR0 5TB* T: (020) 8123 5256 E: richard@richardhinder.com

HINDLE (formerly PARKER), Anne Margaret. b 57. Leeds Univ BSc 78. EAMTC 96. **d** 99 **p** 00. C Greenstead w Colchester St Anne *Chelmsf* 99-04; TV 04-08; P-in-c Kingsley and Foxt-w-Whiston *Lich* 08-10; R Kingsley and Foxt-w-Whiston and Oakamoor etc 10-11; P-in-c Clifton and Southill *St Alb* 11-15; R from 15. *The Rectory, 8 Rectory Close, Clifton, Shefford SG17 5EL* T: (01462) 850150 M: 07738-230985 E: anne.hindle@hotmail.co.uk *or* revanne@cliftonbeds.co.uk

HINDLE, Miss Penelope Jane Bowyn. b 45. Trin Coll Bris 76. **dss** 84 **d** 87 **p** 94. Par Dn Stoneycroft All SS *Liv* 87-89; Asst Chapl Broadgreen Hosp Liv 87-89; Asst Chapl R Free Hosp Lon 89-93; Chapl N Herts NHS Trust 93-00; Chapl E and N Herts NHS Trust 00-02; rtd 02; PtO *B & W* from 07. *Cleeve House, Level Lane, Charlton Horethorne, Sherborne DT9 4NN* T: (01963) 220055 E: jane.hindle@btinternet.com

HINDLEY, Canon Andrew David. b 59. Univ of Wales (Lamp) BA. Sarum & Wells Th Coll. **d** 82 **p** 83. C Huddersfield St Pet *Wakef* 82-84; C Huddersfield St Pet and All SS 84-86; P-in-c Holmfield 86-91; R Ribchester w Stidd *Blackb* 91-96; Bp's Adv for Leisure and Tourism 91-96; Chapl Ribchester Hosp from 91; Can Res Blackb Cathl from 96. *22 Billinge Avenue, Blackburn BB2 6SD* T: (01254) 261152 *or* 51491 F: 689666 E: andrew.hindley@blackburn.anglican.org

HINDLEY, Canon Anthony Talbot. b 41. Bernard Gilpin Soc Dur 61 Oak Hill Th Coll 62. **d** 66 **p** 67. C Stoke next Guildf St Jo 66-69; C Eldoret Kenya 70-72; V Menengai 72-78; C Redhill H Trin *S'wark* 78-79; P-in-c Eastbourne All So *Chich* 79-83; V 83-86; V S Malling 86-98; R Wainford *St E* 98-06; RD Beccles and S Elmham 00-03; Hon Can St E Cathl 05-06; rtd 06; PtO *St E* 07-13; *Nor* 07-13. *19 Thorne Park Road, Torquay TQ2 6RU* T: (01803) 445885 M: 07766-546601 E: anthonyhindley1@gmail.com

HINDLEY, John Philip Talbot. b 76. Ex Univ BA 96 Oak Hill Th Coll BA 01. **d** 01 **p** 02. C Astley Bridge *Man* 01-04; Assoc Miss Partner Crosslinks from 04. *40 Mill Road, Frettenham, Norwich NR12 7LQ* T: (01603) 737974 M: 07790-007390 E: john@theplant.net

HINDLEY, Michael Alexander. b 72. Man Metrop Univ BA 94. Wycliffe Hall Ox BTh 05. **d** 05 **p** 06. C Clubmoor *Liv* 05-09; TV Fazakerley Em from 09. *Emmanuel Rectory, Higher Lane, Liverpool L9 9DJ* T: 0151-525 5229 M: 07980-912768 E: revd.mike@btinternet.com

HINDLEY, Roger Dennis. b 48. Birm Univ BA 70 Ox Univ BA 77 MA 83. Ripon Coll Cuddesdon 75 Qu Coll Birm 77. **d** 78 **p** 79. C Rubery *Birm* 78-81; C Henbury *Bris* 81-83; V Erdington St Chad *Birm* 83-89; V Hill 89-05; AD Sutton Coldfield 96-02; Hon Can Birm Cathl 00-05; TR Willington *Newc* 05-11; rtd 11; PtO *Lich* from 11. *29 Thacker Drive, Lichfield WS13 6NS* T: (01543) 253686 E: rdhindley@yahoo.co.uk

HINDS, Francis. b 73. Bath Univ BSc 96 Edge Hill Coll of HE PGCE 98. Wycliffe Hall Ox 96. **d** 08 **p** 09. C Haydock St Mark *Liv* 08-12; Dir Pioneer Min 08-12; Pioneer Min Wigan from 12. *St Anne's Vicarage, 154 Beech Hill Avenue, Wigan WN6 7TA* M: 07736-176826

HINDS, Kenneth Arthur Lancelot. b 30. K Coll Lon BA 00 Birkbeck Coll Lon MA 04. Bps' Coll Cheshunt. **d** 64 **p** 65. C Sawbridgeworth *St Alb* 64-67; C Gt Berkhamsted 67-71; V Boreham Wood St Mich 71-75; Trinidad and Tobago 75-79; P-in-c Gt Ilford St Luke *Chelmsf* 79-81; V 81-95; rtd 95; PtO *Chelmsf* from 95. *214 Aldborough Road South, Ilford IG3 8HF* T: (020) 8598 2963 E: frkalhinds@ntlworld.com

HINE, John Victor. b 36. Open Univ BA 82. Carl Dioc Tr Course 85. **d** 88 **p** 89. NSM Dean *Carl* 88-92; NSM Clifton 88-92; C Millom 92-94; P-in-c Gt Broughton and Broughton Moor 94-02; P-in-c Brigham 99-02; rtd 02; PtO *Carl* from 02. *4 The Paddocks, Thursby, Carlisle CA5 6PB* T: (01228) 712704 E: hine.hine@virgin.net

HINE, Keith Ernest. b 50. Bradf Univ BA Leeds Univ CertEd. NOC 89. **d** 89 **p** 90. C Wilmslow *Ches* 89-94; V Bowdon 94-08; R Tarporley 08-14; C Acton and Worleston, Church Minshull etc 10-14; RD Malpas 10-14; rtd 14. *Address temp unknown* E: kehine@btinternet.com

HINE, Patrick Lewis. b 45. **d** 06 **p** 07. OLM Horfield H Trin *Bris* from 06. *16 Red House Lane, Bristol BS9 3RZ* T: 0117-962 3861 E: patrick.hine@horfieldparishchurch.org.uk

HINES, Mrs Ashley Jane. b 64. Qu Coll Birm 11. **d** 14 **p** 15. OLM Horninglow *Lich* from 14. *24 Church View, Burton-on-Trent DE13 0NQ* T: (01283) 563115 E: ashleyhines1964@hotmail.com

HINES, Richard Arthur. b 49. Imp Coll Lon MSc 73 PhD 76 K Coll Lon MTh 89. Oak Hill Th Coll 82. **d** 84 **p** 85. C Mile Cross *Nor* 84-87; Lect Oak Hill Th Coll 87-97; Vice-Prin NTMTC 94-97; R Happisburgh, Walcott, Hempstead w Eccles etc *Nor* 97-07; C Bacton w Edingthorpe w Witton and Ridlington 04-07; R Bacton, Happisburgh, Hempstead w Eccles etc 07; R Falkland Is 07-14; rtd 14; P-in-c Aberdeen St Jas *Ab* from 15. *95 Gray Street, Aberdeen AB10 6JH* T: (01224) 212681 M: 07933-198943 E: richard.hines@outlook.com

HINEY, Thomas Bernard Felix. b 35. MC 61. Open Univ BA 07. Ridley Hall Cam 67. **d** 69 **p** 70. C Edgbaston St Aug *Birm* 69-71; CF 71-91; Chapl R Hosp Chelsea 91-01; Chapl Mercers' Coll Holborn 99-01; rtd 01. *7B Dagmar Road, Exmouth EX8 2AN* T: (01395) 270688 E: thiney@onetel.net

HINEY, Thomas Robert Cornelius. b 70. Edin Univ MA 92 St Jo Coll Dur MA 11. Cranmer Hall Dur 09. **d** 11 **p** 12. C Dewsbury *Leeds* 11-14; CF from 14. *c/o MOD Chaplains (Army)* F: 381824 T: (01264) 383430 E: trchiney@gmail.com

HINGE, Derek Colin. b 36. Imp Coll Lon BSc 58 CChem 60 MRSC 60. St Alb Minl Tr Scheme 84. **d** 88 **p** 89. NSM Bishop's Stortford St Mich *St Alb* 88-08; PtO from 08. *12 Avenue Road, Bishop's Stortford CM23 5NU* T: (01279) 652173 E: derek.hinge@btinternet.com

HINGLEY, Christopher James Howard. b 48. Trin Coll Ox BA 69 MA 71. Wycliffe Hall Ox 81. **d** 80 **p** 81. C St Jo Cathl Bulawayo Zimbabwe 80-81; C Hillside Ascension 82-84; Tutor Wycliffe Hall Ox 84-88; Chapl Whitesone Sch Bulawayo Zimbabwe 89-04; Headmaster Petra High Sch 04-06; R Petra Schs Bulawayo from 06. *Whitestone School, Private Bag 4, Bulawayo, Zimbabwe* E: hingley@yoafrica.com

HINGLEY (née EDWARDS), Canon Helen. b 55. Natal Univ BSW 75. St Steph Ho Ox 94. **d** 96 **p** 97. C Gravelly Hill *Birm* 96-01; TV Cen Wolverhampton *Lich* 01-05; P-in-c Hamstead St Bernard *Birm* 05-08; V 08-14; AD Handsworth 08-11; Hon Can Birm Cathl 11-14; rtd 14; PtO *Birm* from 14. *4 Adrian Croft, Birmingham B13 9YF* T: 0121-777 2171 E: h.hingley@btinternet.com

HINGLEY, Robert Charles. b 46. Ball Coll Ox BA 69 MA 74 Birm Univ CertEd 73. Qu Coll Birm 70. **d** 73 **p** 74. C Charlton St Luke w H Trin *S'wark* 73-76; Asst Warden Iona Abbey 76-77; TV Langley Marish *Ox* 77-83; V Balsall Heath St Paul *Birm* 83-90; PtO 90-91; V Birm St Luke 91-96; LtO 96-05; Hon C Hamstead St Bernard 05-14; rtd 14; PtO *Birm* from 14; *Lich* from 01. *4 Adrian Croft, Birmingham B13 9YF* T: 0121-777 2171 E: rob.hingley@btinternet.com

HINGLEY, Roderick Stanley Plant. b 51. St Chad's Coll Dur BA 72. St Steph Ho Ox 74. **d** 75 **p** 76. C Lower Gornal *Lich* 75-79; C Tividale 79-82; C Broseley w Benthall *Heref* 82-84; C Wanstead St Mary *Chelmsf* 84-92; V Romford St Alb from 92. *St Alban's Vicarage, 3 Francombe Gardens, Romford RM1 2TH* T: (01708) 473580

HINGSTON, Barry David. b 63. LSE BSc(Econ) 84. NTMTC BA 08. **d** 08 **p** 09. C Ealing St Paul *Lon* 08-12; P-in-c Greenhill St Jo 12-14; V from 14. *11 Flambard Road, Harrow HA1 2NB* T: (020) 8907 7956 M: 07710-359483 E: barryhingston@btinternet.com *or* barry@stjohnsharrow.org

HINKLEY, Maureen. b 41. **d** 04. NSM Hollington St Jo *Chich* from 04. *8 Wadhurst Close, St Leonards-on-Sea TN37 7AZ* T: (01424) 754872 E: hinkley872@btinternet.com

HINKS, David John. b 63. STETS 04. **d** 07 **p** 08. C Cowes H Trin and St Mary *Portsm* 07-11; C Asst to Adn Is of Wight 11-12; C Alton *Win* from 12. *All Saint's Vicarage, Queens Road, Alton GU34 1HU* T: (01420) 83458 M: 07766-355196 E: julie@hinks42.freeserve.co.uk

HINKS, Margaret Anne. b 47. Birm Univ MB, ChB 65. Qu Coll Birm 08. **d** 10 **p** 11. NSM Birm St Geo 10-14; NSM Hampton-in-Arden w Bickenhill from 14. *29 Birchy Close, Shirley, Solihull B90 1QL* T: (01564) 829088 E: annehinks@uwclub.net

HINKS (née CHAMBERS), Mrs Marion Patricia. b 48. Univ of Wales BDS 72. SWMTC 97. **d** 97 **p** 98. NSM Plymstock and Hooe *Ex* from 97. *52 Southland Park Road, Wembury, Plymouth PL9 0HQ* T: (01752) 862439 M: 07889-291228 E: marion@southlandpark.freeserve.co.uk

HINKSMAN, Adrian James Terence. b 43. Open Univ BA 76. SAOMC 96. **d** 99 **p** 00. NSM Hemel Hempstead *St Alb* 99-02; Dioc CME Officer and NSM St Alb St Mary Marshalswick 02-07; rtd 07; NSM King's Walden and Offley w Lilley *St Alb* 07-12; PtO from 12. *33 Sycamore Close, St Ippolyts, Hitchin SG4 7SN* T: (01462) 458260 E: adrian_hinksman@hotmail.com

HINKSMAN, Barrie Lawrence James. b 41. K Coll Lon BD 64 AKC 64 Birm Univ PhD 02. St Boniface Warminster 64. **d** 65 **p** 66. C Crosby *Linc* 65-67; Ecum Development Officer Scunthorpe Coun of Chs 67-69; C Chelmsley Wood *Birm* 69-72; TV 72-75; P-in-c Offchurch *Cov* 75-79; Dioc Lay Tr Adv 75-79; PtO 89-90; Hon Chapl Cov Cathl 90-01; PtO *Birm* from 01; Hon Sen Fell Warw Univ *Cov* from 02. *c/o Crockford, Church House, Great Smith Street, London SW1P 3AZ*

HINSLEY, Robert Charles. b 77. Univ of Wales (Abth) BTh 98 St Jo Coll Dur MATM 06. Cranmer Hall Dur 03. **d** 05 **p** 06. C Carlton-in-Lindrick and Langold w Oldcotes *S'well* 05-08; P-in-c Felixstowe St Jo *St E* 08-14; RD Colneys 11-14; TR Ipswich St Mary at Stoke w St Pet and St Fran from 14. *The Rectory, 1 Salmet Close, Ipswich IP2 9BA* E: roberthinsley@tiscali.co.uk

HINTON, Mrs Frances Mary. b 43. EN(G) 85. EMMTC 89. **d** 92 **p** 94. Par Dn Hornsey Rise Whitehall Park Team *Lon* 92-94; C 94-97; C Upper Holloway 97; TV Barking St Marg w St Patr *Chelmsf* 97-04; rtd 04. *5 Little Thorpe Lane, Thorpe-on-the-Hill, Lincoln LN6 9BL* T: (01522) 688886

HINTON, Geoffrey. b 34. Bede Coll Dur BA 56 Em Coll Cam MA 67 Sussex Univ PGCE 72. Ridley Hall Cam 58. **d** 60 **p** 61. C Cheltenham St Mary *Glouc* 60-61; C Beverley Minster *York* 61-65; C Newark St Mary *S'well* 70-71; rtd 99. *1 Northmoor Place, Oxford OX2 6XB* T: (01865) 510267

HINTON, James William. b 63. Cov Poly BSc 84 Leeds Univ PGCE 86. St Jo Coll Nottm 00. **d** 02 **p** 03. C Thornbury *Bradf* 02-05; P-in-c Bowling St Steph *Leeds* 05-15; C Lt Horton from 05; P-in-c Bankfoot 09-15; V Bankfoot and Bowling St Steph from 15. *St Stephen's Vicarage, 48 Newton Street, Bradford BD5 7BH* T: (01274) 720784 or 391537 E: jimmy.hinton@bradford.anglican.org

HINTON, Michael Ernest. b 33. K Coll Lon 53 St Boniface Warminster 56. **d** 57 **p** 58. C Babbacombe *Ex* 57-60; S Africa 60-66; P-in-c Limehouse St Pet *Lon* 66-68; R Felmingham *Nor* 68-72; R Suffield 68-72; P-in-c Colby w Banningham and Tuttington 68-72; Bahamas 72-76; P-in-c Mylor w Flushing *Truro* 76-77; V 77-80; R The Deverills *Sarum* 82-87; Bermuda 87-89; Virgin Is 89-91; Chapl Sequoian Retreat and Conf Progr from 91; rtd 98; PtO *St E* 00-01; *Ex* from 02. *Le Petit Pain, St Ann's Chapel, Kingsbridge TQ7 4HQ* T: (01548) 810124 E: lacton.int@virgin.net

HINTON, Michael George. b 27. Mert Coll Ox BA 48 MA 51 Reading Univ PhD 59. S Dios Minl Tr Scheme 81. **d** 83 **p** 84. NSM Weston-super-Mare St Paul *B & W* 83-85; NSM Sibertswold w Coldred *Cant* 85-87; NSM Eythorne and Elvington w Waldershare etc 87-95; PtO from 95. *212 The Gateway, Dover CT16 1LL* T/F: (01304) 204198 E: michael@hintonm.demon.co.uk

HINTON, Paul Robin George. b 64. St Jo Coll Dur BA 86. Qu Coll Birm BA 05. **d** 05 **p** 06. C Rowley Regis *Birm* 05-09; V Warley Woods from 09. *St Hilda's Vicarage, Abbey Road, Smethwick, Warley B67 5NQ* T: 0121-429 1384 F: 420 2386 M: 07777-603188 E: revpaulhinton@btinternet.com

HINTON, Robert Matthew. b 69. Lanc Univ BA 91. Cranmer Hall Dur BA 97. **d** 97 **p** 98. C Lache cum Saltney *Ches* 97-99; C Cheadle Hulme St Andr 99-02; V Hale Barns w Ringway 02-09; Ind Chapl *Ripon* 09-13; V Beckenham Ch Ch *Roch* from 13; AD Beckenham from 15. *Christ Church Vicarage, 18 Court Downs Road, Beckenham BR3 6LR* T: (020) 8650 3487 E: revrobhinton@hotmail.com

HIPKINS, Leslie Michael. b 35. Univ Coll Dur BA 57 ACIS 60. Oak Hill Th Coll 78 Westcott Ho Cam 89. **d** 81 **p** 82. NSM Halstead St Andr w H Trin and Greenstead Green *Chelmsf* 81-87; C Tolleshunt Knights w Tiptree and Gt Braxted 87-89; P-in-c Cratfield w Heveningham and Ubbeston etc *St E* 89-00; rtd 00; PtO *St E* 01-11; *Nor* from 12. *72 Clarendon Road, Norwich NR2 2PW* T: (01603) 663100

HIPPISLEY-COX, Stephen David. b 63. Sheff Univ BSc 85 PhD 92 Peterho Cam BA 98. Westcott Ho Cam 96. **d** 99 **p** 00. C Ollerton w Boughton *S'well* 99-02; NSM Wilford Hill 02-07; P-in-c Willoughby-on-the-Wolds w Wysall and Widmerpool 07-11; V from 11. *The Rectory, Keyworth Road, Wysall, Nottingham NG12 5QQ* T: (01509) 889706 E: s.d.hippisley.cox@gmail.com

HIRD, Matthew. b 83. Jes Coll Ox BA 04. St Jo Coll Nottm MA 09. **d** 09 **p** 10. C Penn *Lich* 09-13; V Wolverhampton St Matt from 13. *St Matthew's Vicarage, 14 Sydenham Road, Wolverhampton WV1 2NY* E: matthew_hird@hotmail.com

HIRONS, Malcolm Percy. b 36. Oriel Coll Ox BA 59 MA 62. Wycliffe Hall Ox 59. **d** 61 **p** 62. C Edgbaston St Aug *Birm* 61-64; Chapl Warw Sch 64-65; C Beverley Minster *York* 65-69; V Barnby upon Don *Sheff* 69-80; P-in-c Kirk Bramwith 75-80; P-in-c Fenwick 75-80; V Norton Woodseats St Paul 80-98; rtd 98; PtO *Nor* from 98. *Broome Lodge, 8 Lincoln Square, Hunstanton PE36 6DL* T: (01485) 532385

HIRST, Alan. b 44. CQSW 74. Linc Th Coll 79. **d** 81 **p** 82. C Newton Heath All SS *Man* 81-84; Chapl to the Deaf 84-88; V Oldham St Chad Limeside 88-91; Dep Chapl HM Pris Liv 91-92; Chapl HM Pris Ranby 92-96 and 00-07; Chapl HM Pris Wakef 96-99; NSM Retford *S'well* 07-10; PtO from 10. *8 Maple Drive, Elkesley, Retford DN22 8AX*

HIRST, Anthony Melville (Anthony Mary). b 50. Cuddesdon Coll 74. **d** 77 **p** 78. C S Gillingham *Roch* 77-80; C Coity w Nolton *Llan* 80-83; OSB from 81; R Hallaton w Horninghold, Allexton, Tugby etc *Leic* 83-90; R Arthog w Fairbourne w Llangelynnin w Rhoslefain *Ban* 90-97; R Montgomery and Forden and Llandyssil *St As* 97-04; P-in-c S Ashford St Fran *Cant* from 09; P-in-c S Ashford Ch Ch from 09. *Christ Church Vicarage, 112 Beaver Road, Ashford TN23 7SR* T: (01233) 620600 E: ahirst@avnet.co.uk

HIRST, Mrs Carol Anne. b 46. Yorks Min Course 06. **d** 09 **p** 10. NSM Ripponden *Leeds* from 09; NSM Barkisland w W Scammonden from 09. *86 Crow Wood Park, Halifax HX2 7NR* T: (01422) 363095 M: 07977-210297 E: carolhirst1@btinternet.com

HIRST, David William. b 37. Man Univ BA 78. Brasted Th Coll 59 Man Univ BA 78. Brasted Th Coll 59 St Aid Birkenhead 61. **d** 63 **p** 64. C Clayton *Man* 63-64; C Bury St Jo 64-66; C Wythenshawe Wm Temple Ch 67-70; V Oldham St Chad Limeside 70-79; V Friezland 79-91; R Ashton St Mich 91-95; Chapl HM Pris Buckley Hall 95-00; Chapl HM Pris Wolds 00-02; rtd 02; PtO *Blackb* from 09. *8 Priory Mews, Lytham St Annes FY8 4FT* M: 07833-353837

HIRST, Canon Godfrey Ian. b 41. Univ of Wales (Lamp) BA 63 MBIM. Chich Th Coll 63. **d** 65 **p** 66. C Brierfield *Blackb* 65-68; Ind Chapl *Liv* 68-71; TV Kirkby 71-75; Ind Chapl *Blackb* 75-94; P-in-c Treales 75-87; Hon Can Blackb Cathl 83-87 and 94-06; Can Res Blackb Cathl 87-94; V Lytham St Cuth 94-06; AD Kirkham 98-06; rtd 06; PtO *Blackb* from 06. *11 Arundel Road, Lytham St Annes FY8 1AF* T: (01253) 732474 M: 07885-118331 E: ghirst1@compuserve.com

HIRST, John Adrian. b 49. St Jo Coll Nottm BTh 78. **d** 78 **p** 79. C Chaddesden St Mark *Glouc* 78-84; TV 84-85; V Swan *Ox* 85-89; R Denham 89-15; rtd 15; PtO *Ox* from 15. *15 Riverview, Flackwell Heath, High Wycombe HP10 9AT* E: adrian@hirst54.freeserve.co.uk

HIRST, Canon Judith. b 54. St Mary's Coll Dur BA 76 LMH Ox PGCE 77 Hull Univ MA 86 St Jo Coll Dur BA 94. Cranmer Hall Dur 91. **d** 94 **p** 95. Bp's Adv in Past Care and Counselling *Dur* 94-00; C Dur St Oswald 94-00; Dir Min Formation Cranmer Hall Dur 00-07; Local Min Development Officer Dur and *Newc* 07-11; Local Ch Growth and Development Adv (Missr) *Dur* from 11; NSM Dur St Marg and Neville's Cross St Jo from 12; Hon Can Dur Cathl from 11. *5 Beechways, Durham DH1 4LG* T: 0191-370 9505 E: judy.hirst@durham.anglican.org

HIRST, Margaret. *See* FOSSEY, Margaret

HIRST, Mrs Rachel Ann. b 58. Portsm Poly BA 79 Hull Univ PGCE 81 ACII 85. NEOC 99. **d** 02 **p** 03. NSM Clifton *York* 02-04; C 04-06; Par Development and Tr Officer (York Adnry) 06-11; V Norton juxta Malton from 11; RD S Ryedale from 13. *The Vicarage, 80 Langton Road, Norton, Malton YO17 9AE* T: (01653) 699222 M: 07896-204121 E: rachel.hirst40@googlemail.com

HISCOCK, Donald Henry. b 26. St Mich Th Coll Crafers 50 ACT ThL 56. **d** 53 **p** 54. Australia 53 and from 65; SSM 54-82; C Averham w Kelham *S'well* 56-58; LtO 58-59; S Africa 59-60; Basutoland 60-61; rtd 92. *12 Charsley Street, Willagee WA 6156, Australia* T: (0061) (8) 9314 5192

HISCOCK, Gary Edward. b 43. Oak Hill Th Coll BA 90. **d** 90 **p** 91. C Cheltenham St Luke and St Jo *Glouc* 90-94; C Hardwicke, Quedgeley and Elmore w Longney 95-96; rtd 96. *25 Bournside Road, Cheltenham GL51 3AL* T: (01242) 513002

HISCOCK, Phillip George. b 47. Southn Univ CertEd 68 MPhil 90 MCIPD 83. STETS 95. **d** 98 **p** 99. NSM Portchester and Chapl Portsm Docks 98-02; Chapl Dunkirk Miss to Seafarers *Eur* 02-08; C Alverstoke *Portsm* 08-15; rtd 15; PtO *Portsm* from 15. *36 Gomer Lane, Gosport PO12 2SA* T/F: (023) 9234 6881 M: 07830-362149 E: phillip.hiscock@ntlworld.com

HISCOCKS, Nicholas Robin Thomas. b 75. Keble Coll Ox BA 96 MA 01 Anglia Poly Univ MA 01. Ridley Hall Cam 99. **d** 01 **p** 02. C Bromley Ch Ch *Roch* 01-11; V Westbourne Ch Ch Chpl *Win* from 11. *134 Alumhurst Road, Bournemouth BH4 8HU* T: (01202) 767881 E: nick@christchurchwestbourne.com

HISCOX, Miss Denise. b 47. Lon Univ TCert 68 Lanchester Poly Cov BSc 78. WMMTC 98. **d** 01 **p** 02. NSM Cov St Mary 01-05; NSM Leamington Priors All SS 05-07; NSM Leamington Spa H Trin and Old Milverton 05-07; PtO 07-08; NSM Willenhall 08-10. *48 Wainbody Avenue North, Coventry CV3 6DB* T: (024) 7641 1034 E: denise@dhiscox.co.uk

HISCOX, Jonathan Ronald James. b 64. Qu Coll Birm 87. **d** 89 **p** 90. C Wiveliscombe *B & W* 89-93; P-in-c Donyatt w Horton, Broadway and Ashill 93-94; TV Ilminster and Distr 94-02; R Rowde and Bromham *Sarum* 02-10. *58 Sadlers Mead, Chippenham SN15 3PL*

HISLOP, Martin Gregory. b 55. Jas Cook Univ Townsville BA 78 Univ of S Aus MEd 88. **d** 92 **p** 93. C N Mackay St Ambrose Australia 92-93; Dir Studies St Barn Coll of Min 93-94; Chapl Ballarat Univ 95-98; Asst Chapl St Mich Gr Sch 98; Assoc P E St Kilda 98; C Kingston St Luke *S'wark* 00-01; P-in-c 01-05; V from 05. *St Luke's Vicarage, 4 Burton Road, Kingston upon Thames KT2 5TE* T: (020) 8546 4064 E: mhislop@btinternet.com

HISLOP, Mrs Patricia Elizabeth. b 42. Heythrop Coll Lon MA 03. **d** 08 **p** 09. OLM Bramley *Guildf* 08-12; PtO from 12; Birtley Ho Bramley from 12. *2 Napper Place, Cranleigh GU6 8DG* T: (01483) 274359 E: patricia.hislop@phrh.co.uk

HITCH, Canon Kim William. b 54. Leic Univ BSc 75 K Coll Lon MA 94 Birm Univ MPhil 08. Trin Coll Bris 76. **d** 78 **p** 79. C Becontree St Mary *Chelmsf* 78-80; C Huyton Quarry *Liv* 80-83; V Hatcham St Jas *S'wark* 83-91; TR Kidbrooke 91-02; R Kidbrooke St Jas from 02; Lewisham Adnry Ecum Officer 03-06; Dir Ords (Woolwich Area) 05-12; AD Charlton from 06; Hon Can S'wark Cathl from 08; Dioc Voc Adv from 12; Dir Ords Woolwich Area from 13. *St James's Rectory, 62 Kidbrooke Park Road, London SE3 0DU* T: (020) 8856 3438 E: k.w.hitch@btinternet.com

HITCHCOCK, David. b 37. MCIEH. S'wark Ord Course 70. **d** 73 **p** 74. NSM Milton next Gravesend Ch Ch *Roch* 73-94; NSM Chalk 96-98; CF (ACF) from 79; PtO *Lon* 93-02; NSM St Andr-by-the-Wardrobe w St Ann, Blackfriars 02-09; NSM St Jas Garlickhythe w St Mich Queenhithe etc 02-09. *148 Old East Road, Gravesend DA12 1PF* T: (01474) 361091 E: hitch5@btinternet.com

HITCHEN, Carol Ann. *See* CLOSE, Carol Ann

HITCHEN, Lisa Jan. *See* MACINNES, Lisa Jan

HITCHENS (née GREEN), Mrs Catherine Isabel. b 48. Cant Sch of Min 89. **d** 92 **p** 94. C Willesborough *Cant* 92-96; Sen Asst P E Dereham and Scarning *Nor* 96-97; Asst Chapl HM Pris Wayland 96-97; Chapl HM Pris Leic 97-00; Chapl HM YOI Castington 00-02; Chapl HM Pris Cant 02-12; rtd 12. *12 Maylam Gardens, Sittingbourne ME10 1GB* T: (01795) 436353 E: cathandfred@hotmail.co.uk

HITCHINER, Mrs Elizabeth Ann. b 59. Birm Univ BSc 80. WEMTC 03. **d** 06 **p** 07. NSM Cagebrook *Heref* from 06. *Dunan House, Clehonger, Hereford HR2 9SF* T: (01432) 355980

HITCHINER, Sally Ann. b 80. Wycliffe Hall Ox. **d** 09 **p** 10. C W Ealing St Jo w St Jas *Lon* 09-12; Chapl Brunel Univ from 12. *The Meeting House, Brunel University, Uxbridge UB8 3PH* T: (01895) 266460 M: 07761-661529 E: sally.hitchiner@brunel.ac.uk

HITCHING, His Honour Judge Alan Norman. b 41. Ch Ch Ox BA 62 MA 66 BCL 63 Barrister-at-Law (Middle Temple) 64. **d** 01 **p** 02. NSM High Ongar w Norton Mandeville *Chelmsf* 01-06; PtO from 06. *9 Monkhams Drive, Woodford Green IG8 0LG* T: (020) 8504 4260 E: anhitching@btinternet.com

HITCHINS, Graham Edward David. b 54. S Dios Minl Tr Scheme 91. **d** 94 **p** 95. C Bishop's Waltham *Portsm* 94-97; C Upham 94-97; C Honiton, Gittisham, Combe Raleigh, Monkton etc *Ex* 97-98; TV 98-03; Chapl RN 03-10; R Burnham Gp of Par *Nor* from 09; Corps Chapl Sea Cadet Corps from 10. *The Rectory, The Pound, Burnham Market, King's Lynn PE31 8UL* E: revdgrahamhitchins@hotmail.com

HITCHMAN, Keith John. b 62. Middx Univ BSc 90. Trin Coll Bris BA 95. **d** 95 **p** 96. C Bestwood *S'well* 95-99; Chapl Glos Univ 99-04; C Cheltenham St Mary, St Matt, St Paul and H Trin *Glouc* 04-07; TV Cheltenham H Trin and St Paul 07-10; Pioneer Min River in the City *Liv* from 10. *499 Mather Avenue, Liverpool L19 4TF*

HITCHMOUGH, William. b 30. NOC. **d** 81 **p** 82. NSM Penketh *Liv* 81-83; Chapl Warrington Distr Gen Hosp 83-99; PtO *Liv* 83-03; *Guildf* 00-09. *4 Rex Court, Haslemere GU27 1LJ* T: (01428) 661504

HIZA, Douglas William. b 38. Richmond Univ Virginia BA 60 MDiv 63 Mankato State Univ MS 70. Virginia Th Sem 60. **d** 63 **p** 64. C Calvary Cathl Sioux Falls USA 63-65; V Sioux Falls Gd Shep 65-66; V Vermillion St Paul 66-69; V New Ulm St Pet 71-80; Chapl Mankato State Univ 74-80; Chapl Hackney Hosp Gp Lon 80-95; Chapl Homerton Hosp Lon 80-95; PtO *Lon* 96-04; Hon C Smithfield St Bart Gt 04-06; PtO from 06; *S'wark* from 06. *10 Meynell Crescent, London E9 7AS* T: (020) 8985 7832 *or* 7253 3107 E: general@joanhudson.co.uk

HOAD, Anne Elizabeth. b 42. Bris Univ BA 63. **dss** 69 **d** 94 **p** 95. Asst Chapl Imp Coll *Lon* 69-74; S'wark Lay Tr Scheme 74-77; Brixton St Matt *S'wark* 77-80; Charlton St Luke w H Trin 80-94; Project Worker Community of Women and Men 88-91; Voc Adv Lewisham from 91; Asst Chapl Lewisham Hosp *S'wark* 92-03; Hon C Lee Gd Shep w St Pet 94-03; C 03-10; rtd 10; PtO *S'wark* from 11. *14 Silk Close, London SE12 8DL* T: (020) 8297 8761 E: hoadanne@yahoo.co.uk

HOAD, Miss Rosemary Claire. b 60. Cranmer Hall Dur 92. **d** 94 **p** 95. C Epsom St Martin *Guildf* 94-97; TV Brentford *Lon* 97-05; V Spring Grove St Mary from 05. *St Mary's Vicarage, Osterley Road, Isleworth TW7 4PW* T: (020) 8560 3555 E: rosemary.hoad@dsl.pipex.com

HOAD, Mrs Shona Mary. b 66. Newc Univ BA 88. STETS 07. **d** 10 **p** 11. C Dorking St Paul *Guildf* 10-14; V Atworth w Shaw and Whitley *Sarum* from 14. *The Vicarage, Corsham Road, Shaw, Melksham SN12 8EH* T: (01225) 793536 E: shona@boasw.org

HOARE, Carol. b 46. Lon Univ BA 68 Birm Univ CertEd 69. Qu Coll Birm 86 WMMTC 86. **d** 91 **p** 94. NSM Curdworth *Birm* 91-00; PtO from 00. *14 Elms Road, Sutton Coldfield B72 1JF* T: 0121-354 1117 E: c.hoare@btinternet.com

HOARE, David Albert Sylvester. b 47. **d** 95. C Gibraltar Cathl 95-00. *3 Governor's Lane, Gibraltar*

HOARE, Canon David Marlyn. b 33. Bps' Coll Cheshunt 60. **d** 63 **p** 64. C Ampthill w Millbrook and Steppingley *St Alb* 63-67; C Bushey 67-70; V Harlington 70-76; V Oxhey All SS 76-81; V Hellesdon *Nor* 81-98; Hon Can Nor Cathl 95-98; rtd 98; PtO *Nor* from 98. *42 Starling Close, Aylsham, Norwich NR11 6XG* T: (01263) 734565 E: dmhoare@supanet.com

HOARE, Diana Charlotte. Kent Univ BA 78. WEMTC 02. **d** 05 **p** 06. C Bishop's Castle w Mainstone, Lydbury N etc *Heref* 05-09; P-in-c Bucknell w Chapel Lawn, Llanfair Waterdine etc 09-14; V Middle Marches 14-15; rtd 15. *Address temp unknown* E: diana@stonescribe.com

HOARE (née CULLING), Elizabeth Ann. b 58. St Mary's Coll Dur BA 76 St Jo Coll Dur PhD 87 Rob Coll Cam BA 88 PGCE 80. Ridley Hall Cam 86. **d** 89 **p** 94. Par Dn S Cave and Ellerker w Broomfleet *York* 89-92; Tutor Cranmer Hall Dur 93-95; P-in-c Cherry Burton *York* 95-00; Abp's Sen Adv on Rural Affairs 95-98; Spiritual Dir York Angl Cursillo 98-00; Chapl Bp Burton Coll *York* 95-00; PtO *York* 01-02; NSM Cowesby 02-07; NSM Felixkirk w Boltby 02-07; NSM Kirkby Knowle 02-07; NSM Leake w Over and Nether Silton and Kepwick 02-07; Tutor and Lect Cranmer Hall Dur 02-07; Tutor Wycliffe Hall Ox from 07. *Wycliffe Hall, 54 Banbury Road, Oxford OX2 6PW* T: (01865) 274200 *or* 873412 E: eahoare@googlemail.com

HOARE, Janet Francis Mary. *See* MILES, Janet Francis Mary

HOARE, Patrick Gerard. *See* GERARD, Patrick Hoare

HOARE, Patrick Reginald Andrew Reid (Toddy). b 47. TD 80 and Bar 88. Hull Univ MA 90. Wycliffe Hall Ox 77. **d** 80 **p** 81. C Guisborough *York* 80-83; P-in-c Felixkirk w Boltby 83-07; P-in-c Kirkby Knowle 83-07; P-in-c Leake w Over and Nether Silton and Kepwick 83-07; P-in-c Cowesby 83-07; Chapl Yorks Agric Soc 92-09; CF (TA) 82-99; rtd 07; PtO *Ox* from 07. *Pond Farm House, Holton, Oxford OX33 1PY* T: (01865) 873412 E: toddy100@btinternet.com

HOARE, Roger John. b 38. Tyndale Hall Bris 63. **d** 66 **p** 67. C Stoughton *Guildf* 66-70; C Chesham St Mary *Ox* 70-73; V Bath St Bart *B & W* 73-83; V Gt Faringdon w Lt Coxwell *Ox* 83-89; Deputation Appeals Org (NE Lon) Children's Soc 89-93; P-in-c Lambourne w Abridge and Stapleford Abbotts *Chelmsf* 93-03; Ind Chapl 93-03; rtd 03; PtO *Chelmsf* from 04. *44 Anchor Road, Tiptree, Colchester CO5 0AP* T: (01621) 817236 E: randdh@btinternet.com

✠HOARE, The Rt Revd Rupert William Noel. b 40. Trin Coll Ox BA 61 MA 66 Fitzw Ho Cam BA 64 MA 84 Birm Univ PhD 73. Kirchliche Hochschule Berlin 61 Westcott Ho Cam 62. **d** 64 **p** 65 **c** 93. C Oldham St Mary w St Pet *Man* 64-67; Lect Qu Coll Birm 68-72; Can Th Cov Cathl 70-76; R Man Resurr 72-78; Can Res Birm Cathl 78-81; Prin Westcott Ho Cam 81-93; Area Bp Dudley and Hon Can Worc Cathl 93-00; Dean Liv 00-07; rtd 07; Hon Asst Bp Man from 08. *14 Shaw Hall Bank Road, Greenfield, Oldham OL3 7LD* T: (01457) 820375

HOARE, Canon Simon Gerard. b 37. AKC 61. **d** 62 **p** 63. C Headingley *Ripon* 62-65; C Adel 65-68; R Spofforth 68-71; R Spofforth w Kirk Deighton 71-77; V Rawdon *Bradf* 77-85; Hon Can Bradf Cathl 85-02; R Carleton and Lothersdale

85-02; Dioc Ecum Officer 85-94; rtd 02; PtO *Leeds* from 02. *Skell Villa, 20 Wellington Street, Ripon HG4 1PH* T: (01765) 692187 E: sghoare@talktalk.net

HOARE, Toddy. *See* HOARE, Patrick Reginald Andrew Reid

HOARE, Mrs Valerie Mary. b 54. Ex Univ BTh 07. SWMTC 04. **d** 07 **p** 08. NSM Chard St Mary *B & W* 07-10; C Chard St Mary w Combe St Nicholas, Wambrook etc 10-14; NSM Ilminster and Whitelackington from 15. *Nyleve, Church Lane, Horton, Ilminster TA19 9RN* T: (01460) 54542 E: cherrybrook@hotmail.co.uk

HOBBINS, Mrs Susan. b 47. Birm Univ CertEd 68. STETS 04. **d** 07 **p** 08. NSM Hatherden w Tangley, Weyhill and Penton Mewsey *Win* 07-09; NSM Pastrow 09-13; rtd 13; PtO *Win* from 13. *Rose Cottage, Upton, Andover SP11 0JP* T: (01264) 736166 E: suehobbins@yahoo.com

HOBBS, Mrs Alison Clare. b 58. Imp Coll Lon BSc 80. Lindisfarne Regional Tr Partnership 09. **d** 12 **p** 13. NSM Brancepeth *Dur* from 12. *Brancepeth Castle, Brancepeth, Durham DH7 8DF* T: 0191-378 9670 M: 07504-489089 E: alison@brancepethcastle.org.uk

HOBBS, Andrew David. b 76. Hull Univ BA 97 Moorlands Coll MA 11. Trin Coll Bris 11. **d** 13. C Bromley Common St Aug *Roch* from 13. *20 Bromley Common, Bromley BR2 9PD* E: adhobbs@hotmail.co.uk

HOBBS (formerly DUFFUS), Mrs Barbara Rose. b 51. EMMTC 95. **d** 98 **p** 99. C Linc St Faith and St Martin w St Pet 98-00; C Grantham 00-02; P-in-c Brothertoft Gp 02-04; Mental Health Chapl SE Lincs 02-04; P-in-c Hastings St Clem and All SS *Chich* 04-08; rtd 08; PtO *Chich* from 08. *Courtyard Cottage, Main Road, Westfield, Hastings TN35 4QE* T: (01424) 756479 M: 07724-410292 E: barbara.r.hobbs@googlemail.com

HOBBS, Basil Ernest William. b 22. St Chad's Coll Dur BA 49. **d** 51 **p** 52. C Mitcham St Mark *S'wark* 51-54; CF 54-68; Hon C Paddington H Trin w St Paul *Lon* 70-72; Asst Chapl St Mary's Hosp Praed Street Lon 69-72; Novice CR 72-74; Past Consultant Clinical Th Assn 74-84; LtO *S'well* 74-83; Chapl HM Pris Nottm 81-84; Hon C Nottingham St Andr *S'well* 83-84; C 84-86; TV Clifton 86-87; rtd 87; PtO *S'well* 87-00; *Leic* 99-12. *c/o Mrs S M Davies, 2 Woodward Close, Tetbury GL8 8LJ*

HOBBS, Christopher Bedo. b 61. Jes Coll Cam BA 83 BTh 90. Ridley Hall Cam 88. **d** 91 **p** 92. C Langham Place All So *Lon* 91-95; C Hull St Jo Newland *York* 95-00; V Selly Park St Steph and St Wulstan *Birm* from 00. *18 Selly Wick Road, Selly Park, Birmingham B29 7JA* T: 0121-472 0050 *or* 472 8253

HOBBS, Christopher John Pearson. b 60. Sydney Univ BA 82 K Coll Lon BD 89 AKC 89. Wycliffe Hall Ox 89. **d** 91 **p** 92. C S Mimms Ch Ch *Lon* 91-94; C Jesmond Clayton Memorial *Newc* 94-97; V Oakwood St Thos *Lon* from 97. *St Thomas's Vicarage, 2 Sheringham Avenue, London N14 4UE* T: (020) 8360 1749 *or* T/F: 8245 9152 E: christopher.hobbs@blueyonder.co.uk

HOBBS, Edward Quincey. b 74. Bris Univ BSc 95. Wycliffe Hall Ox BA 99. **d** 00 **p** 01. C Stapenhill w Cauldwell *Derby* 00-03; C Newbury *Ox* 03-08; C Brompton H Trin w Onslow Square St Paul *Lon* 08-09; P-in-c Cullompton, Willand, Uffculme, Kentisbeare etc *Ex* from 09. *Windyridge, 10 Willand Road, Cullompton EX15 1AP* E: eqhobbs@gmail.com

HOBBS, Ian. *See* HOBBS, Kenneth Ian

HOBBS, James. b 42. K Alfred's Coll Win CertEd 64 Open Univ BA 89 Hull Univ MA 94 Win Univ BUniv 15. Linc Th Coll 66. **d** 68 **p** 69. C Moseley St Mary *Birm* 68-73; V Kingstanding St Mark 73-77; R Rushbrooke *St E* 77-78; R Bradfield St Geo w Rushbrooke 77-78; R Bradfield St Geo 78-80; P-in-c Bradfield St Clare 77-80; P-in-c Felsham w Gedding 77-80; R Bradfield St George w Bradfield St Clare etc 80-84; P-in-c Gt and Lt Whelnetham 84-85; R Gt and Lt Whelnetham w Bradfield St George 85-90; Ecum Chapl for F&HE Grimsby *Linc* 90-97; Chapl Lincs and Humberside Univ (Grimsby Campus) 90-97; Gen Preacher 92-97; V Ingham w Cammeringham w Fillingham 97-01; R Aisthorpe w Scampton w Thorpe le Fallows etc 97-01; P-in-c N w S Carlton 97-01; P-in-c Burton by Linc 97-01; rtd 01; PtO *Linc* 01-04; *Chich* from 04. *Courtyard Cottage, Main Road, Westfield, Hastings TN35 4QE* T: (01424) 756479 M: 07726-302341 E: hobbs.jim1@gmail.com

HOBBS, Jason Michael. b 74. Northumbria Univ BSc 97 Sunderland Univ BA 00. TISEC 07. **d** 10 **p** 11. C Aberdeen St Mary *Ab* from 10. *21 Wallfield Place, Aberdeen AB25 2JR* T: (01224) 641621 M: 07446-113014 E: jhobbs10@gmail.com

HOBBS, Mrs Joan Rosemary. b 39. Chelsea Coll Lon TDip 61. WEMTC 97. **d** 00 **p** 01. NSM Cheltenham St Mary, St Matt, St Paul and H Trin *Glouc* 00-02; PtO 02-04; NSM Brimpsfield w Birdlip, Syde, Daglingworth etc 04-09; rtd 10; PtO *Glouc* from 10. *Manor Farmhouse, Woodmancote, Cirencester GL7 7EF* T/F: (01285) 831244 E: joan@hobbsjr.fsnet.co.uk

HOBBS, John Antony. b 36. S Dios Minl Tr Scheme. **d** 87 **p** 88. NSM Crowborough *Chich* from 87. *May Cottage, Alice Bright Lane, Crowborough TN6 3SQ* T: (01892) 653909

HOBBS, Kenneth Brian. b 47. Sussex Univ BA 68 Lon Inst of Educn PGCE 70. NTMTC 98. **d** 98 **p** 99. NSM Howell Hill *Guildf* 98-01; NSM Shere, Albury and Chilworth 01-11; rtd 11; PtO *Guildf* from 11. *5 Burdon Park, Cheam SM2 7PS* T: (020) 8643 7878 E: hobbs@farleygreen.net

HOBBS, Kenneth Ian. b 50. Oak Hill Th Coll 74. **d** 77 **p** 78. C Southborough St Pet w Ch Ch and St Matt *Roch* 77-80; C Hoole *Ches* 80-84; V Barnston 84-95; P-in-c Bedworth *Cov* 95; TR 95-01; RD Nuneaton 00-01; TR Radipole and Melcombe Regis *Sarum* 01-15; RD Weymouth and Portland 08-12; rtd 15. *4 Daryl Road, Wirral CH60 5RD* E: kijahobbs@gmail.com

HOBBS, Leslie Robert. b 42. Sussex Univ BA 64 Lon Bible Coll BD 67. EAMTC 02. **d** 02 **p** 03. NSM Somerleyton, Ashby, Fritton, Herringfleet etc *Nor* 02-09; R 09-12; rtd 12; PtO *Nor* from 13. *Nether End Cottage, Blacksmiths Loke, Lound, Lowestoft NR32 5LS* T: (01502) 732536 E: hobbsnec@btinternet.com

HOBBS, Preb Maureen Patricia. b 54. Surrey Univ BSc 76. Westcott Ho Cam 95. **d** 97 **p** 98. C Shrewsbury St Chad w St Mary *Lich* 97-01; R Baschurch and Weston Lullingfield w Hordley 01-09; P-in-c Pattingham w Patshull 09-14; V from 14; RD Trysull from 09; Dioc Adv for Women in Min 04-11; Preb Lich Cathl from 12. *The Vicarage, 20 Dartmouth Avenue, Pattingham, Wolverhampton WV6 7DP* T: (01902) 700257 E: hobbsmaureen@yahoo.co.uk

HOBBS, Michael Bedo. b 30. Fitzw Ho Cam BA 58 MA 62. Clifton Th Coll 58. **d** 60 **p** 61. C Southsea St Jude *Portsm* 60-63; Paraguay 63-65; Argentina 65-67; V Potters Green *Cov* 68-75; Distr Sec BFBS 75-82; R Plaxtol *Roch* 82-96; Dioc Miss Audits Consultant 90-96; rtd 96; PtO *Sarum* from 96. *Falcons, Barkers Hill, Semley, Shaftesbury SP7 9BH* T: (01747) 828920

HOBBS, Mrs Nicola. b 77. **d** 14. **p** 15. C Broughton w Loddington and Cransley etc *Pet* from 14. *15 Loddington Way, Mawsley, Kettering NN14 1GE* E: revnicki@familyhobbs.org.uk

HOBBS, Mrs Sarah Kathleen. b 72. Liv Univ BA 94 UMIST BSc 98 PGCE 95. Wycliffe Hall Ox BA 05. **d** 05 **p** 06. C W Ealing St Jo w St Jas *Lon* 05-08; V Blockhouse Bay New Zealand from 08. *429A Blockhouse Bay Road, Blockhouse Bay, Auckland 0600, New Zealand* T: (0064) (9) 627 8779 E: sarah@churchofthesaviour.org.nz

HOBBS, Sarah May. b 47. WEMTC 01. **d** 04 **p** 05. NSM Westbury-on-Severn w Flaxley, Blaisdon etc *Glouc* 05-14; NSM Abenhall w Mitcheldean 11-14; NSM Huntley and Longhope, Churcham and Bulley 12-14; rtd 14. *Folly Cottage, Adsett Lane, Adsett, Westbury-on-Severn GL14 1PQ* T: (01452) 760337 E: shobbs001@btinternet.com

HOBBS, Susan May. b 15. NSM Pontnewydd *Mon* from 15. *5 Picton Walk, Fairwater, Cwmbran NP44 4QW* T: (01633) 679055 E: s.hobbs47@ntlworld.com

HOBDAY, Hannah Elizabeth. b 80. Jes Coll Ox BA 03 Cam Univ BA 06. Ridley Hall Cam 04. **d** 07 **p** 08. C Margate H Trin *Cant* 07-09; C Cliftonville 07-09; Hon C Chesterton St Geo *Ely* from 09. *9 Hertford Street, Cambridge CB4 3AE* T: (01223) 748872 M: 07792-923575 E: hannah.hobday@googlemail.com

HOBDAY, Peter Hugh Francis. b 34. IEng 90. Oak Hill NSM Course 99. **d** 00 **p** 01. NSM Perivale *Lon* 00-05; PtO 05-07; *Pet* from 07. *48 Juniper Close, Towcester NN12 6XP* T: (01327) 359045 M: 07778-007370 E: petehobday126@btinternet.com

HOBDAY, Philip Peter. b 81. Ex Coll Ox BA 02 MA 09 Fitzw Coll Cam BA 05 MA 09 Nottm Univ MA 14. Ridley Hall Cam 03. **d** 06 **p** 07. C St Peter-in-Thanet *Cant* 06-09; Chapl Cant Ch Ch Univ 06-09; Chapl and Fell Magd Coll Cam from 09. *Magdalene College, Cambridge CB3 0AG* T: (01223) 332129 M: 07894-219629 E: pph21@cam.ac.uk

HOBDEN, Canon Brian Charles. b 38. Oak Hill Th Coll 63. **d** 66 **p** 67. C S Lambeth St Steph *S'wark* 66-70; C Cheadle *Ches* 70-76; R Brandon USA 76-87; C Portsm St Jo 87-98; R Mesilla Park St Jas from 98; rtd 03. *3160 Executive Hills Road, Las Cruces NM 88011-4724, USA* T: (001) (505) 521 9435 F: 526 4821 E: stjames@lascruces.com

HOBDEN, Christopher Martin. b 49. Lon Univ BSc 71. Oak Hill Th Coll 80. **d** 87 **p** 88. NSM St Marylebone All So w SS Pet and Jo *Lon* 87-88; NSM Langham Place All So 88-95. *10 Kent Terrace, London NW1 4RP*

HOBDEN, David Nicholas. b 54. K Coll Lon BD 76 AKC 76 Cam Univ PGCE. Ripon Coll Cuddesdon 77. **d** 78 **p** 79. C Marlborough *Sarum* 78-80; C Salisbury St Thos and St Edm 81-85; V Shalford *Guildf* 85-99; Asst Chapl R Surrey Co Hosp NHS Trust 99-00; Sen Chapl from 00. *Department of Pastoral Care, Royal Surrey County Hospital, Egerton Road, Guildford GU2 5XX* T: (01483) 406835 or 571122 E: cmhobden@aol.com *or* dhobden@nhs.net

HOBDEN, Geoffrey William. b 46. Trin Coll Bris 80. **d** 82 **p** 83. C Ex St Leon w H Trin 82-86; V Weston-super-Mare Ch Ch *B & W* 86-06; V Weston super Mare Ch Ch and Em 06-11; RD Locking 93-99; rtd 11; PtO *B & W* from 11. *21 Burrington Avenue, Weston-super-Mare BS24 9LP* T: (01934) 707981 E: hobdenshouse@gmail.com

HOBLEY, Ms Susan Elizabeth. b 51. Newc Univ BA 74 Dur Univ PGCE 75. NEOC 98. **d** 01 **p** 02. NSM Millfield St Mark and Pallion St Luke *Dur* 01-05; C Sheff St Mark Broomhill 05-09; V Wath-upon-Dearne from 09. *The Vicarage, Church Street, Wath-upon-Dearne, Rotherham S63 7RD* T: (01709) 872299 E: sue.hobley@sheffield.anglican.org

HOBROUGH, Mrs Margaret Edith. b 40. OBE 97. Man Univ BA 63 Newc Univ MEd 75 K Coll Lon MTh 80 FRSA 94. STETS 01. **d** 03 **p** 04. NSM Godalming *Guildf* 03-05; NSM Warkworth and Acklington *Newc* from 05. *3 St Lawrence Terrace, Warkworth, Morpeth NE65 0XE* T: (01665) 711203 E: margarethobrough@v21.me.uk

HOBSON, Alexander. *See* HOBSON, John Alexander

HOBSON, Anthony Peter. b 53. St Jo Coll Cam BA 74. St Jo Coll Nottm 75. **d** 77 **p** 78. C Brunswick *Man* 77-82; R Stretford St Bride 82-92; TR Hackney Marsh *Lon* 92-00; V Leic Martyrs 00-08; Dir St Martin's Ho from 09; PtO from 15. *4 Church Road, Aylestone, Leicester LE2 8LB* T: 0116-283 3251 E: petehobson@me.com *or* pete.hobson@leccofe.org

HOBSON, Barry Rodney. b 57. Open Univ BA 98. Wilson Carlile Coll 82 EAMTC 97. **d** 98 **p** 99. C Warboys w Broughton and Bury w Wistow *Ely* 98-01; P-in-c Roxwell *Chelmsf* 01-07; RD Chelmsf N 06-07; V Hornchurch St Andr from 07. *The Vicarage, 222 High Street, Hornchurch RM12 6QP* T: (01708) 454594 *or* 441571 E: b.hobson@btinternet.com

HOBSON, Jeremy Graeme. b 71. Lon Univ BMedSci 95 MB, BS 96. Oak Hill Th Coll BA 03. **d** 03 **p** 04. C Eastbourne H Trin *Chich* 03-07; C Clerkenwell St Jas and St Jo w St Pet *Lon* 07-08; Lic to AD Islington 08-13; C Clerkenwell St Mark from 13. *193A Liverpool Road, London N1 0RF* T: (020) 7251 1190 E: thehobsons@onetel.com

HOBSON, John Alexander (Alex). b 70. LMH Ox BA 91 MA 02 York Univ MA 94. Wycliffe Hall Ox BA 01. **d** 02 **p** 03. C Aynho and Croughton w Evenley etc *Pet* 02-05; Chapl RAF from 05. *Chaplaincy Services (RAF), HQ Air Command, RAF High Wycombe HP14 4UE* T: (01494) 496800 F: 496343

HOBSON, Canon Patrick John Bogan. b 33. MC 53. Magd Coll Cam BA 56 MA 60 Ox Brookes Univ BA 08. S'wark Ord Course 75 Qu Coll Birm 77. **d** 79 **p** 80. C St Jo in Bedwardine *Worc* 79-81; R Clifton-on-Teme, Lower Sapey and the Shelsleys 81-88; TR Waltham H Cross *Chelmsf* 88-98; Hon Can Chelmsf Cathl 95-98; rtd 98. *24 Cunliffe Close, Oxford OX2 7BL* T/F: (01865) 556206 E: patrick.hobson@btinternet.com

HOBSON, Peter. *See* HOBSON, Anthony Peter

HOBSON, Mrs Yvonne Mary. b 45. Ex Univ BTh 03. SWMTC 00. **d** 03 **p** 04. C St Illogan *Truro* 03-06; C Paul 06-10; rtd 10. *8 Donnington Road, Penzance TR18 4PQ* T: (01736) 364354 E: yvonnehobson@btinternet.com

HOCKEN, Glen Rundle. b 59. Kent Univ BA 80 Southlands Coll Lon PGCE 90 ACA 84. Wycliffe Hall Ox 90. **d** 92 **p** 93. C Cogges *Ox* 92-94; C Cogges and S Leigh 94-96; C Boldmere *Birm* 96-99; TV Southgate *Chich* 99-06; Chapl HM Pris Lewes 06-13; Chapl St Pet and St Jas Hospice N Chailey 05-13; Chapl HM Pris Onley from 13. *HM Prison Onley, Willoughby, Rugby CV23 8AP* T: (01788) 523400

HOCKEY, Ms Christine Helen. St Mich Coll Llan. **d** 09 **p** 10. NSM Maindee Newport *Mon* from 09. *134 Christchurch Road, Newport NP19 7SB* T: (01633) 768900

HOCKEY (née LOOMES), Gaenor Mary. b 65. Hull Univ BA 92 RGN 86. St Jo Coll Nottm MPhil 93. **d** 96 **p** 97. C Charles w Plymouth St Matthias *Ex* 96-00; C Devonport St Aubyn 00-05; PtO 05-06; P-in-c Seer Green and Jordans *Ox* 06-13; R Yeovil H Trin w Barwick *B & W* from 13. *Holy Trinity Vicarage, 24 Turners Barn Lane, Yeovil BA20 2LW* T: (01935) 423774 E: rev.gaenor@btinternet.com

HOCKEY, Paul Henry. b 49. Oak Hill Th Coll BA 86. **d** 86 **p** 87. C Dalton-in-Furness *Carl* 86-89; R Clifton, Brougham and Cliburn 89-94; V Fremington *Ex* 94-10; R Fremington, Instow and Westleigh 10-14; RD Barnstaple 07-14; rtd 14. *51 Chestnut Drive, Willand, Cullompton EX15 2SJ* E: paulhockey@talktalk.net

HOCKING, Paul Frederick. b 43. Chich Th Coll 84. **d** 86 **p** 87. C Whitton and Thurleston w Akenham *St E* 86-89; V Ipswich All Hallows 89-91; P-in-c Gt Cornard 91-98; V 98; P-in-c Woolpit w Drinkstone 98-03; R 03-05; rtd 05; PtO *St E* from 05. *22111 Town Walk Drive, Hamden CT 06518-3759, USA* E: paulfhocking@gmail.com

HOCKLEY, Paul William. b 47. Chu Coll Cam BA 68 MA 72 Nottm Univ BA 73. St Jo Coll Nottm 71. **d** 74 **p** 75.

C Chatham St Phil and St Jas *Roch* 74-78; C Tunbridge Wells St Jo 78-81; V Penketh *Liv* 81-14; TV Warrington W 14-15; r-d 15. *76 Vale Road, Poole BH14 9AU* T: (01202) 730626
E: hockleys@ntlworld.com

HOCKLEY, Miss Tanya. b 89. Cardiff Univ BA 10 Anglia Ruskin Univ MA 14. Westcott Ho Cam 12. **d** 14 **p** 15. C Stone Cross St Luke w N Langney *Chich* from 14. *11 Shipley Mill Close, Stone Cross, Pevensey BN24 5PY* M: 07971-442264
E: tanyahockley1989@hotmail.co.uk

HOCKNULL, Canon Mark Dennis. b 63. Surrey Univ BSc 85 Univ Coll Lon PhD 89 St Jo Coll Dur BA 93. Cranmer Hall Dur 91. **d** 94 **p** 95. C Prenton *Ches* 94-96; C Runcorn All SS and Runcorn St Mich 96-99; V Gt Meols 99-05; CME Officer *Linc* 05-09; Lic Preacher 05-09; Can Res and Chan Linc Cathl from 09; Hd of Min Tr (Dioc Min Course) from 09. *The Chancery, 12 Eastgate, Lincoln LN2 1QG* T: (01522) 561633 *or* 504025 E: mark.hocknull@lincoln.anglican.org

HOCKRIDGE, Joan. b 25. Girton Coll Cam BA 47 MA 50. St Steph Ho Ox 82. **dss** 83 **d** 87 **p** 94. Ealing Ascension Hanger Hill *Lon* 83-88; Hon C 87-88; Hon C Hanger Hill Ascension and W Twyford St Mary 88-92; Hon C Hillingdon St Jo 92-95; PtO 95-00. *Address temp unknown*

HODDER, Anthony Mark. b 56. Univ of Wales (Newport) CertEd 00 FCCA 90. Ridley Hall Cam 08. **d** 11 **p** 13. C Heref S Wye 11-12; C Ledbury from 12. *21 Biddulph Way, Ledbury HR8 2HP* M: 07977-063294 E: tony.hodder@gmail.com

HODDER, Christopher John. b 75. Huddersfield Univ BA 96. St Jo Coll Nottm BTh 00. **d** 01 **p** 02. C Loughborough Em and St Mary in Charnwood *Leic* 01-05; Chapl Derby Univ and Derby Cathl 05-10; P-in-c Wilford Hill *S'well* 10-11; V from 11. *The Parsonage, Boundary Road, West Bridgford, Nottingham NG2 7BD* M: 07833-592800

HODDER, John Kenneth. b 45. Edin Univ MA 68. Cuddesdon Coll 71. **d** 73 **p** 74. C Kibworth Beauchamp *Leic* 73-76; C Whittlesey *Ely* 76-80; R Downham 80-87; P-in-c Coveney 80-81; R 81-87; R Nunney and Witham Friary, Marston Bigot etc *B & W* 87-10; rtd 10; PtO *B & W* from 10. *95 Nunney Road, Frome BA11 4LF* T: (01373) 466063
E: hodderhodder@btinternet.com

HODDER, Trevor Valentine. b 31. Bps' Coll Cheshunt 65. **d** 67 **p** 68. C Oxhey All SS *St Alb* 67-70; C Digswell 70-73; V Chelmsford St Anne *Chelmsf* 74-96; rtd 96; PtO *Chelmsf* from 00. *30 Drury Road, Colchester CO2 7UX* T: (01206) 766480

HODGE, Albert. b 40. NOC 84. **d** 87 **p** 88. C Huyton St Geo *Liv* 87-89; P-in-c Widnes St Paul 89-97; Chapl Halton Coll of FE 89-97; C Linton in Craven and Burnsall w Rylstone *Bradf* 97-05; rtd 05; PtO *Man* from 06. *Sunnyhurst, 50 Sandfield Road, Bacup OL13 9PD* T: (01706) 873285
E: sergeant1832@aol.com

HODGE, Anthony Charles. b 43. AKC 66. **d** 67 **p** 68. C Carrington *S'well* 67-69; C Bawtry w Austerfield 69-72; C Misson 69-72; Grenada 72-74; Trinidad and Tobago 74-76; V Tuckingmill *Truro* 76-78; V Worksop St Paul *S'well* 78-81; P-in-c Patrington w Hollym, Welwick and Winestead *York* 81-86; R 86-88; V York St Olave w St Giles 88-08; V York St Helen w St Martin 97-08; Chapl York Coll for Girls 88-96; rtd 08; P-in-c Duloe, Herodsfoot, Morval and St Pinnock *Truro* 08-14. *3 Tower Hill Gardens, Rhind Street, Bodmin PL31 2FD* T: (01208) 892929 M: 07717-877430 E: achodge@live.co.uk

HODGE, Colin. b 39. Sarum & Wells Th Coll. **d** 83 **p** 84. NSM Wareham *Sarum* 84-87; C Parkstone St Pet w Branksea and St Osmund 87-89; V Lilliput 89-00; rtd 00; PtO *Sarum* from 01. *35 Stowell Crescent, Wareham BH20 4PT* T: (01929) 553222
E: colin.hodge2@btinternet.com

HODGE, Canon Michael Robert. b 34. Pemb Coll Cam BA 57 MA 61. Ridley Hall Cam 57. **d** 59 **p** 60. C Harpurhey Ch Ch *Man* 59; C Blackpool St Mark *Blackb* 59-62; V Stalybridge Old St Geo *Man* 62-67; R Cobham w Luddesdowne and Dode *Roch* 67-81; Hon Can Roch Cathl 81-99; R Bidborough 81-99; rtd 99; Hon C Chale *Portsm* 99-06; Hon C Gatcombe 99-06; Hon C Shorwell w Kingston 99-06; Asst to RD W Wight 99-06; PtO from 06. *Braxton Cottage, Halletts Shute, Norton, Yarmouth PO41 0RH* T/F: (01983) 761121 M: 07941-232983 E: michael.hodge.1954@pem.cam.ac.uk

HODGE, Nigel John. b 61. BTh 83 Open Univ BSc 97 MSB 98. St Mich Coll Llan 83. **d** 85 **p** 86. C Mynyddislwyn *Mon* 85-87; C Machen 87-89; TV Ebbw Vale 89-91; V Abercarn 91-98; LtO from 99. *Address temp unknown*

HODGES, Christina Caroline. *See* FFRENCH-HODGES, Christina Caroline

HODGES, Edward Rhys John. b 90. Ex Univ BA 12. St Mellitus Coll 13. **d** 15. C Onslow Square and S Kensington St Aug *Lon* from 15. *Holy Trinity Brompton, Ennismore Gardens Mews, London SW7 1JA* M: 07595-308359 T: (020) 7052 0458
E: ed.hodges@htb.org

HODGES, Ian Morgan. b 72. Glam Univ BSc 95 Cam Univ BTh(Min) 05. Ridley Hall Cam. **d** 05 **p** 06. C Llantrisant *Llan* 05-11; R Llanilid w Pencoed from 11. *60 Coychurch Road, Pencoed, Bridgend CF35 5NA* T: (01656) 860337
E: revian@lphparish.org.uk

HODGES, Mrs Jane Anne Christine. b 62. Leeds Univ BA 84. SEITE 06. **d** 09 **p** 10. C Poplar *Lon* 09-11; TV from 11. *164 St Leonard's Road, London E14 6PW*
E: revjanehodges@hotmail.com

HODGES, Jasper Tor. b 62. Leeds Univ BSc 84 Sheff Univ MEng 85 Lon Univ PGCE 87. Trin Coll Bris BA 94. **d** 94 **p** 95. C Holbeck *Ripon* 94-97; C Ealing St Steph Castle Hill *Lon* 97-04; V Arbourthorne and Norfolk Park *Sheff* from 04. *St John's Vicarage, 91 Manor Oaks Road, Sheffield S2 5EA* E: vicar@thebeaconchurch.net

HODGES, Keith Michael. b 53. Southn Univ BTh 82 Heythrop Coll Lon MA 04. Chich Th Coll 77. **d** 80 **p** 81. C Sydenham St Phil *S'wark* 80-84; PtO 85; C Leatherhead *Guildf* 86-89; V Aldershot St Aug from 89. *St Augustine's Vicarage, Holly Road, Aldershot GU12 4SE* T: (01252) 320840
E: father.keith@ntlworld.com

HODGES, Mrs Laura. b 53. SAOMC 01. **d** 04 **p** 05. NSM Abingdon *Ox* 04-12; PtO from 12; Chapl SW Oxon Primary Care Trust 07-11. *38 Baker Road, Abingdon OX14 5LW* T: (01235) 527654 E: laura.hodges@btinternet.com

HODGES, Miss Stefanie Margaret. b 54. Trin Coll Bris 93. **d** 97 **p** 98. C Croydon Ch Ch *S'wark* 97-99; C Sutton St Nic 99-02; TV Mildenhall *St E* 02-08; TR Westborough *Guildf* from 08. *St Francis's Vicarage, Beckingham Road, Guildford GU2 8BU* T: (01483) 546412 E: stefanie@mhodges.co.uk

HODGES, Mrs Valerie Irene. b 44. **d** 06. NSM Newbridge *Mon* 06-14; NSM Lower Islwyn from 14. *Ty-Pwll House, The Pant, Newbridge, Newport NP11 5GF* T: (01495) 244676
E: val.hodges@btinternet.com

HODGETT, Ms Tina Elizabeth. b 64. Leic Univ MBA 05 Sheff Univ PGCE 90 St Mary's Coll Dur BA 88. Ridley Hall Cam 06. **d** 08 **p** 09. C Bestwood Em w St Mark *S'well* 08-11; TV Portishead *B & W* from 11. *110 Brampton Way, Portishead, Bristol BS20 6YT* M: 07759-909106
E: pilgrim@portisheadparish.co.uk

HODGETTS, Alan Paul. b 54. Birm Poly BSc 78 Heythrop Coll Lon MA 96. St Steph Ho Ox 79. **d** 82 **p** 83. C Perry Barr *Birm* 82-85; C Broseley w Benthall *Heref* 85-87; V Effingham w Lt Bookham *Guildf* 87-96; R Merrow 96-06; Chapl HM Pris Woodhill from 06. *The Chaplaincy Department, HM Prison Woodhill, Tattenhoe Street, Milton Keynes MK4 4DA* T: (01908) 722000 ext 2097
E: alan.hodgetts@hmps.gsi.gov.uk

HODGETTS, Colin William John. b 40. St D Coll Lamp BA 61. Ripon Hall Ox 61. **d** 63 **p** 64. C Hackney St Jo *Lon* 63-68; Hon C St Martin-in-the-Fields 70-76; C Creeksea w Althorne *Chelmsf* 76-79; PtO *Ex* 84-03; C Parkham, Alwington, Buckland Brewer etc 03-07; AD Gambela Ethiopia 11-12; rtd 12; PtO *Ex* from 12. *Quincecote, Hartland, Bideford EX39 6DA* T: (01237) 441426 E: colin@hodgetts.me.uk

HODGETTS, Harry Samuel. b 30. Chich Th Coll 63. **d** 65 **p** 66. C Harton Colliery *Dur* 65-68; C Penzance St Mary *Truro* 68-70; V Penwerris 70-79; V Kettering St Mary *Pet* 79-94; rtd 95; PtO *Win* 03-09. *The Flat, Etal Manor, Etal, Cornhill-on-Tweed TD12 4TL* T: (01890) 820378

HODGINS, Miss Kylie Anne. b 68. SEITE 98 Ridley Hall Cam 00. **d** 02 **p** 03. C Histon and Impington *Ely* 02-07; Chapl Sherborne Sch for Girls 07-08; P-in-c Cottenham *Ely* from 08; P-in-c Rampton from 09. *The Rectory, 6 High Street, Cottenham, Cambridge CB24 8SA* T: (01954) 250454
E: kylie@gumnut.me.uk *or* rector@allsaintscottenham.org.uk

HODGINS, Philip Arthur. b 57. Lanc Univ BA 78 Bradf Univ MBA 90 MCIPD 92. Linc Th Coll 82. **d** 85 **p** 86. C Norton *Ches* 85-88; C Whitkirk *Ripon* 88-89; PtO *Bradf* 89-90; *Chich* 91-02; Hon C Chiddingly w E Hoathly 02-04; P-in-c 04-09; R from 09; RD Uckfield 06-11. *The Rectory, Rectory Close, East Hoathly, Lewes BN8 6EG* T: (01825) 840270
E: philhodgins@btinternet.com

HODGKINS, Christopher Thomas Alan. b 73. Westcott Ho Cam. **d** 13 **p** 14. C G7 Benefice *Cant* from 13. *The Vicarage, 8 Glebeland, Egerton, Ashford TN27 9DH* T: (01233) 756731
E: ctahodgkins@hotmail.co.uk

HODGKINSON, Mrs Jennifer Mary. b 57. **d** 12 **p** 13. OLM Cromer *Nor* from 12. *29 Fulcher Avenue, Cromer NR27 9SG* T: (01263) 510153 E: jenniehodgkinson@supanet.com

HODGKINSON, Canon John. b 27. Trin Hall Cam BA 51 MA 55. Linc Th Coll 51. **d** 53 **p** 54. C Penrith St Andr *Carl* 53-56; C Linc St Nic w St Jo Newport 56-58; C-in-c Lin St Jo Bapt CD 58-63; V Linc St Jo 63-66; R Old Brumby 66-71; V Kendal H Trin *Carl* 71-90; Hon Can Carl Cathl 84-90; rtd 90; PtO *Carl* from 90. *Boxtree Barn, Levens, Kendal LA8 8NZ* T: (015395) 60806 E: boxtreebarn@hotmail.com

HODGKINSON, John David. b 57. Birm Univ BA 78 Edin Univ BD 89. Edin Th Coll 86. **d** 89 **p** 90. C Darwen St Cuth w Tockholes St Steph 92-94; R Harrington *Carl* 94-00; V Walney Is 00-12; TV N Barrow from 12. *St Francis House, 158 Schneider Road, Barrow-in-Furness LA14 5ER* T: (01229) 833051

HODGSON, Ms Amanda Jane. b 66. Westmr Coll Ox BA 88 Heythrop Coll Lon MA 99. Westcott Ho Cam 94. **d** 96 **p** 97. C Epping Distr *Chelmsf* 96-01; TV Wythenshawe *Man* 01-07; R Streatham St Leon *S'wark* from 07; Adv for Women's Min Kingston Area from 12. *The Rectory, 1 Becmead Avenue, London SW16 1UH* T: (020) 8769 4366
E: rectorstleonards@btinternet.com

HODGSON, Anthony Owen Langlois. b 35. Ripon Hall Ox 60. **d** 62 **p** 63. C Stiffkey w Morston and Blakeney w Lt Langham *Nor* 62-65; C Paddington Ch Ch *Lon* 66-70; Area Sec (Beds & Cambs) Chr Aid 70-74; (Herts & Hunts) 70-73; (Rutland & Northants) 73-74; V Gt w Lt Gidding and Steeple Gidding *Ely* 77-81; Warden Dovedale Ho 81-89; P-in-c Ilam w Blore Ray and Okeover *Lich* 81-89; Dir Chr Rural Cen 89-91; C Checkley and Stramshall 91-97; TV Uttoxeter Area 97-00; rtd 00. *9 Trent House, Station Road, Oundle, Peterborough PE8 4DE* T: (01832) 275343 E: hodgsons@phonecoop.coop

HODGSON, Antony Robert. b 66. Dundee Univ MA 88 Jes Coll Cam BA 92 MA 96 Lanc Univ MA 04 K Coll Lon MPhil 10 AKC 10 Lambeth PhD 15 FSAScot 15. Westcott Ho Cam 90 Ven English Coll Rome 92. **d** 93 **p** 94. C Chorley St Geo *Blackb* 93-96; C Lytham St Cuth 96-99; V St Annes St Marg from 99. *St Margaret's Vicarage, 24 Chatsworth Road, Lytham St Annes FY8 2JN* T: (01253) 722329

HODGSON, Barbara Elizabeth. b 46. N Riding Coll of Educn BEd 85. NEOC 06. **d** 08 **p** 09. NSM Bridlington Em *York* 08-11; NSM Burton Fleming w Fordon, Grindale etc from 11. *The Vicarage, Back Street, Burton Fleming, Driffield YO25 3PD* T: (01262) 470873 M: 07907-593234
E: vidara1972@talktalk.net

HODGSON, Canon David George. b 54. Coll of Resurr Mirfield. **d** 82 **p** 83. C Stainton-in-Cleveland *York* 82-87; R Loftus 87; P-in-c Carlin How w Skinningrove 87; R Loftus and Carlin How w Skinningrove 87-93; V Middlesbrough Ascension from 93; P-in-c S Bank 03-07; RD Middlesbrough 98-05; Can and Preb York Minster from 01. *The Ascension Vicarage, Penrith Road, Middlesbrough TS3 7JR* T: (01642) 244857
E: dhodgson199@btinternet.com

HODGSON, Canon David Peter. b 56. Fitzw Coll Cam BA 77 MA 81 Nottm Univ BA 82 MTh 85. St Jo Coll Nottm 80. **d** 83 **p** 84. C Guiseley w Esholt *Bradf* 83-86; Asst Chapl Loughb Univ *Leic* 86-89; P-in-c Hatfield Broad Oak *Chelmsf* 89-90; P-in-c Bush End 89-90; R Hatfield Broad Oak and Bush End 90-97; Ind Chapl Harlow 89-97; R Wokingham All SS *Ox* from 97; AD Sonning 04-13; Hon Can Ch Ch from 09. *The Rectory, 2A Norreys Avenue, Wokingham RG40 1TU* T: 0118-979 2999 E: david@allsaints.prestel.co.uk

HODGSON, Gary Stuart. b 65. Ridley Hall Cam 95. **d** 98 **p** 99. C S Ossett *Wakef* 98-01; V Kirkburton 01-07; Chapl Huddersfield Univ and Hon C Fixby and Cowcliffe 07-09; P-in-c Cottingley *Bradf* 09-14; V Cottingley *Leeds* from 14; AD Airedale *Leeds* from 14. *St Michael's Vicarage, 81 Littlelands, Bingley BD16 1AL* T: (01274) 560761 E: gshodgson@sky.com

HODGSON, George. b 36. Qu Coll Birm 75. **d** 78 **p** 79. NSM Wordsley *Lich* 78-93; NSM *Worc* from 93; PtO 84-93. *1 Newfield Drive, Kingswinford DY6 8HY* T: (01384) 292543 M: 07811-753160 E: hodgson@talktalk.net

HODGSON, Mrs Helen Mary. b 66. NOC 01. **d** 04 **p** 05. C Emley and Flockton cum Denby Grange *Wakef* 04-05; NSM Kirkburton 05-07; Asst to RD Huddersfield 07-09; LtO *Bradf* 09-11; Hon C Thwaites Brow 11-12; C Bingley All SS *Leeds* 12-15; C Cottingley from 15. *St Michael's Vicarage, 81 Littlelands, Bingley BD16 1AL* T: (01274) 560761 E: hmhodgson@sky.com

HODGSON, John. b 35. St Jo Coll Cam MA 62 Lon Univ BD 61. St Deiniol's Hawarden 80. **d** 81 **p** 82. Hon C Padiham *Blackb* 81-84; C W Burnley All SS 85-87; V 87-95; rtd 95; PtO *Worc* 95-02; *Glouc* 98-02; *Win* from 12. *33 Ticonderoga Gardens, Southampton SO19 9HB* T: (023) 8043 2895

HODGSON, Julia Ruth. *See* HICKS, Julia Ruth

HODGSON, Kenneth Jonah. b 36. Open Univ BA 79 CQSW 89. Oak Hill Th Coll. **d** 69 **p** 70. C Rainford *Liv* 69-72; C Fazakerley Em 72-74; TV 74-78; Soc Worker 78-96; CF 79-82; rtd 00; C Wallasey St Hilary *Ches* 01-03; PtO from 03. *134 Rake Lane, Wallasey, Merseyside CH45 1JW* T/F: 0151-639 2980 E: kennethjhodgson@talktalk.net

HODGSON, The Ven Thomas Richard Burnham. b 26. FRMetS 88. Lon Coll of Div BD 52 ALCD 52. **d** 52 **p** 53. C Crosthwaite Kendal *Carl* 52-55; C Stanwix 55-59; V Whitehaven St Nic 59-65; R Aikton 65-67; Bp's Dom Chapl and V Raughton Head w Gatesgill 67-73; Dir of Ords 70-74; Hon Can Carl Cathl 72-91; V Grange-over-Sands 73-79; RD Windermere 76-79; Adn W Cumberland 79-91; V Mosser 79-83; rtd 91; PtO *Carl* from 91. *58 Greenacres, Wetheral, Carlisle CA4 8LD* T: (01228) 561159

HODKINSON, George Leslie. b 48. Qu Coll Birm 86. **d** 88 **p** 89. C Hall Green St Pet *Birm* 88-91; TV Solihull 91-96; P-in-c Billesley Common 96-00; V 00-05; AD Moseley 01-02; rtd 05; Chapl Countess of Chester Hosp NHS Foundn Trust from 05; Chapl Cheshire and Wirral Partnerships NHS Trust from 05. *2 Birch Close, Four Crosses, Llanymynech SY22 6NH* T: (01691) 839946 *or* (01244) 364543

HODSON, Gordon George. b 35. St Chad's Coll Dur BA 59. **d** 60 **p** 61. C Tettenhall Regis *Lich* 60-64; C Rugeley 64-68; V Shrewsbury St Mich 68-74; V Kinnerley w Melverley 74-87; P-in-c Knockin w Maesbrook 75-87; P-in-c Chebsey 87-91; P-in-c Seighford, Derrington and Cresswell 87-91; V Chebsey, Ellenhall and Seighford-with-Creswell 91-00; rtd 00; PtO *Lich* from 01. *27 Oak Drive, Oswestry SY11 2RU* T: (01691) 662849

HODSON, Henry Charles. b 55. Magd Coll Ox MA 77. Ox Min Course 10. **d** 12. NSM Taunton St Andr *B & W* 12-13. *Preston Farm, Lydeard St Lawrence, Taunton TA4 3QQ* T: (01984) 656891 M: 07979-756327
E: revd.charles.hodson@gmail.com

HODSON, Keith. b 53. Hatf Coll Dur BA 74. Wycliffe Hall Ox 77. **d** 80 **p** 81. C Ashton-upon-Mersey St Mary Magd *Ches* 80-84; C Polegate *Chich* 84-92; V Baddesley Ensor w Grendon *Birm* 92-08; R Beckbury, Badger, Kemberton, Ryton, Stockton etc *Lich* from 08; RD Edgmond and Shifnal from 10. *The Rectory, Beckbury, Shifnal TF11 9DG* T: (01952) 750474 E: keithhodson@talk21.com

HODSON, Miss Margaret Christina. b 39. Linc Th Coll 88. **d** 90 **p** 94. Par Dn Old Trafford St Jo *Man* 90-94; C 94-95; P-in-c Calderbrook and Shore 95-01; rtd 01. *53 Lon Thelwal, Benllech, Tyn-y-Gongl LL74 8QH* T: (01248) 852990

HODSON, Mrs Margot Rosemary. b 60. Bris Univ BSc 82 PGCE 83 Ox Brookes Univ BA 06. All Nations Chr Coll 87 SAOMC 99. **d** 01 **p** 02. C Grove Ox 01-04; Chapl Jes Coll Ox 04-09; P-in-c Haddenham w Cuddington, Kingsey etc Ox from 09. *Parish Office, St Mary's Centre, Station Road, Haddenham, Aylesbury HP17 8AH* T: (01844) 291244
E: vicar@haddenhamstmarys.org

HODSON, Canon Raymond Leslie. b 42. St Chad's Coll Dur BSc 64. **d** 66 **p** 67. C Adlington *Blackb* 66-68; C Cleveleys 68-72; V Ewood 72-77; V Nazeing *Chelmsf* 77-84; R Ampthill w Millbrook and Steppingley *St Alb* 84-95; Chapl Madrid *Eur* 95-04; Can Gib Cathl 02-04; rtd 04. *Los Alcazares 3, 03726 Benitachell (Alicante), Spain* M: 607 706 904
E: m2813341g@yahoo.co.uk

HODSON, Trevor. b 57. Sheff Univ BA 78 Padgate Coll of Educn PGCE 79 Leeds Univ MA 06. NOC 04. **d** 06 **p** 07. NSM Broadheath *Ches* 06-13; NSM Latchford Ch Ch from 13. *40 Riversdale, Woolston, Warrington WA1 4PZ* T: (01925) 811952 E: t.hodson@lathom.lancs.sch.uk

HOEY, David Paul. b 57. QUB BD 79. CITC 79. **d** 81 **p** 82. C Belfast Whiterock *Conn* 81-83; C Portadown St Mark *Arm* 83-84; I Cleenish w Mullaghdun *Clogh* 84-90; I Magheracross 90-03; Dir of Ords 91-03; Can Clogh Cathl 95-03; Min Consultant for Ireland CPAS 03-11; Dioc Par Development Officer and P-in-c Clondevaddock w Portsalon and Leatbeg *D & R* from 11. *Tamney Rectory, Letterkenny, Co Donegal, Republic of Ireland* T: (00353) (74) 919 2811
E: dphoey@eircom.net

HOEY, Raymond George. b 46. TCD BA 70 MA. **d** 72 **p** 73. C Portadown St Mark *Arm* 72-78; I Camlough w Mullaglass 78-14; Dom Chapl to Abp *Arm* 86-14; Adn *Arm* 92-14; rtd 14. *252A Armagh Road, Newry BT35 6NL*
E: rghoey@btinternet.com

HOEY, William Thomas. b 32. CITC 64. **d** 66 **p** 67. C Belfast St Mary *Conn* 66-68; C Lisburn Ch Ch 69-72; I Ballinderry 72-78; I Belfast St Simon w St Phil 78-02; rtd 02. *11 Carnshill Court, Belfast BT8 6TX* T: (028) 9079 0595

HOFBAUER, Canon Andrea Martina. b 71. Johannes Gutenberg Univ Mainz Ox Univ MTh 04. St Steph Ho Ox 00. **d** 02 **p** 03. C Teignmouth, Ideford w Luton, Ashcombe etc *Ex* 02-05; Chapl Ex Univ 05-09; Tutor SWMTC 05-09; PV Ex Cathl 06-09; Prec Wakef Cathl from 09. *4 Cathedral Close, Wakefield WF1 2DP* T: (01924) 200191 *or* 373923
E: andi.hofbauer@wakefield-cathedral.org.uk

HOFFMANN, Jonathan Mark. b 60. Cranmer Hall Dur 95. **d** 97 **p** 99. C Eaton *Nor* 97-98; C Horsell *Guildf* 98-02; V Aston cum Aughton w Swallownest and Ulley *Sheff* 02-06; P-in-c Freshford, Limpley Stoke and Hinton Charterhouse *B & W* 06-14. *40 Park Street, Bath BA1 2TD*

HOFFMANN, Miss Rosalind Mary. b 49. **d** 10 **p** 11. OLM Loddon, Sisland, Chedgrave, Hardley and Langley *Nor* from 10. *Oakhurst, Briar Lane, Hales, Norwich NR14 6SY* T: (01508) 548200 E: ros@hoffman2011.plus.com

HOFREITER, Christian. b 75. Wycliffe Hall Ox BA 08 MA 12 Keble Coll Ox MSt 09 Innsbruck Univ MPhil 01. Ox Min Course 09. **d** 10 **p** 10. NSM Ox St Aldate from 10. *39 Alan Bullock Close, Oxford OX4 1AU* M: 07771-781130 E: chofreiter@gmail.com

HOGAN, Edward James Martin. b 46. Trin Coll Bris. **d** 85 **p** 86. C St Austell *Truro* 85-88; V Gt Broughton and Broughton Moor *Carl* 88-94; V St Stythians w Perranarworthal and Gwennap *Truro* 94-10; RD Carnmarth N 03-08; rtd 10; PtO *Heref* from 15. *444 Buckfield Road, Leominster HR6 8SD* T: (01568) 620064 E: martin@houseofhogan.org *or* martinhogan@me.com

HOGAN, Miss Jennie. b 75. Goldsmiths' Coll Lon BA 99 Fitzw Coll Cam BA 03. Westcott Ho Cam 01. **d** 04 **p** 05. C Westmr St Steph w St Jo *Lon* 04-07; C All Hallows by the Tower etc 07-09; Chapl Chelsea Coll from 07; Chapl Lon Goodenough Trust from 09. *William Goodenough House, 35 Mecklenburgh Square, London WC1N 2AN* M: 07515-486806 E: jennie@goodenough.ac.uk

HOGARTH, Alan Francis. b 58. Oak Hill Th Coll BA 89. **d** 89 **p** 90. C Felixstowe SS Pet and Paul *St E* 89-93; R Beckington w Standerwick, Berkley, Rodden etc *B & W* 93-04; P-in-c Basildon w Aldworth and Ashampstead *Ox* 04-08; P-in-c Heapey and Withnell *Blackb* 08-12; V from 12. *34 Kittiwake Road, Heapey, Chorley PR6 9BA* T: (01257) 231868 E: alan.hogarth@gmail.com

HOGARTH, Joseph. b 32. Edin Th Coll 65. **d** 67 **p** 67. C Walney Is *Carl* 67-71; V Whitehaven St Jas 71-76; V Millom H Trin w Thwaites 76-82; V Maryport 82-91; V Consett *Dur* 91-97; rtd 97; PtO *Roch* from 99. *56A Bexley Lane, Dartford DA1 4DD* T: (01322) 526733

HOGARTH, Peter Robert. b 61. Bath Univ MSc 97. Trin Coll Bris BA 01. **d** 01 **p** 02. C Martock w Ash *B & W* 01-04; Asst Chapl Oslo w Bergen, Trondheim and Stavanger *Eur* from 04. *dragabergveien 11, 4085 Hundvåg, Stavanger, Norway* T: (0047) 5155 5488 E: revpastorpete@yahoo.co.uk

HOGARTH MORGAN, Anthony. *See* MORGAN, Anthony Hogarth

HOGG, Mrs Ann Grant. b 46. St Andr Univ MA 68 Hughes Hall Cam PGCE 70. NOC 99. **d** 02 **p** 03. NSM Bromborough *Ches* 02-04; PtO *St Alb* 04-05; NSM Watford Ch Ch 05-06; NSM Aldenham, Radlett and Shenley 06-12; rtd 12. *Craigwood, Brae Street, Dunkeld PH8 0BA* T: (01350) 727053 E: angrho@btinternet.com

HOGG, Anthony. b 42. Univ of Wales (Lamp) BA 63. Linc Th Coll 64 Chich Th Coll 78. **d** 78 **p** 79. NSM Ridgeway *Ox* 78-86; NSM W w E Hanney 86-88; Hd Master New Coll Sch Ox 88-89; C Ridgeway *Ox* 90-91; P-in-c Hanney, Denchworth and E Challow 91-92; V 92-11; rtd 11. *11 Beckett House, Wallingford Street, Wantage OX12 8AZ* T: (01235) 799240 E: victory@ukgateway.net

HOGG, Matthew. b 79. **d** 08 **p** 09. C Brompton H Trin w Onslow Square St Paul *Lon* 08-10; C Hammersmith St Paul 10-11; P-in-c Fulham St Alb w St Aug 11-13; V from 13. *St Alban's Vicarage, 4 Margravine Road, London W6 8HJ* T: (020) 7610 2151 E: matt@stalbansfulham.org

HOGG, Neil Richard. b 46. BSc 69. Ridley Hall Cam 82. **d** 84 **p** 85. C Bingham *S'well* 84-87; TV Bushbury *Lich* 87-00; V Worksop St Jo *S'well* 00-11; rtd 11. *4 Lowick, York YO24 2RF* M: 07585-816697 E: hogg350@btinternet.com

HOGG, William John. b 49. New Coll Ox MA 71 Lon Univ CertEd 72 Crewe & Alsager Coll MSc 88. Edin Th Coll 86. **d** 88 **p** 89. C Oxton *Ches* 88-93; R Bromborough 93-04; P-in-c Radlett *St Alb* 04-05; TR Aldenham, Radlett and Shenley 05-12; rtd 12. *Craigwood, Brae Street, Dunkeld PH8 0BA* T: (01350) 727053 E: wijoho@aol.com

HOGG, William Ritson. b 47. Leeds Univ BSc 69. Qu Coll Birm. **d** 72 **p** 73. C Bordesley St Oswald *Birm* 72-76; TV Seacroft *Ripon* 76-82; V Hunslet St Mary 82-88; V Catterick 88-97; rtd 07. *c/o Crockford, Church House, Great Smith Street, London SW1P 3AZ* E: bill.denise@yahoo.co.uk

HOGGARD, Mrs Jean Margaret. b 36. NW Ord Course 76. dss 79 **d** 87 **p** 94. Northowram *Wakef* 79-94; Par Dn 87-94; C Ovenden 94-00; rtd 00; PtO *Leeds* from 01. *13 Joseph Avenue, Northowram, Halifax HX3 7HJ* T: (01422) 201475

HOGGER-GADSBY, Alison. **d** 14 **p** 15. C Coventry Caludon *Cov* from 14; Chapl K Henry VIII Sch Cov from 15. *St Margaret's Vicarage, 18 South Avenue, Coventry CV2 4DR* M: 07788-593805 E: alison.hogger@gmail.com

HOGGER, Clive Duncan. b 35. Sheff Univ BA 92. Ridley Hall Cam 06. **d** 08 **p** 09. C Fletchamstead *Cov* 08-11; TV Cov E from 11; AD from 14. *St Margaret's Vicarage, 18 South Avenue, Coventry CV2 4DR* T: (024) 7665 1642 E: rev2b@tiscali.co.uk

HOGWOOD, Brian Roy. b 38. Bps' Coll Cheshunt. **d** 65 **p** 92. NSM Thetford *Nor* 91-93; Hon C 93-09; Chapl Addenbrooke's NHS Trust 98-99. *31 Byron Walk, Thetford IP24 1JX* T: (01842) 753915

HOLBEN, Bruce Frederick. b 45. STETS 99. **d** 02 **p** 03. NSM W Wittering and Birdham w Itchenor *Chich* from 02. *3 Elmstead Gardens, West Wittering, Chichester PO20 8NG* T: (01243) 514129 M: 07940-759060

HOLBIRD, Thomas James. b 79. Leeds Univ BSc 00 Cam Univ BTh 11. Ridley Hall Cam 08. **d** 11 **p** 12. C Gerrards Cross and Fulmer *Ox* 11-15; C Brighton St Pet *Chich* from 15. *45 Hollingbury Park Avenue, Brighton BN1 7JQ* M: 07870-682853 T: (01273) 553246 E: tomh@stpetersbrighton.org

HOLBROOK, Canon Barbara Mary. b 58. Nottm Trent Univ BA 94 Nottm Univ MA 04. EMMTC 02. **d** 04 **p** 05. C Chesterfield H Trin and Ch Ch *Derby* 04-08; P-in-c Kimberley *S'well* 08-15; P-in-c Nuthall 08-15; R Kimberley and Nuthall from 15; Hon Can S'well Minster from 13. *The Rectory, 1 Eastwood Road, Kimberley, Nottingham NG16 2HX* T: 0115-938 3565 M: 07766-732514

HOLBROOK, Colin Eric Basford. *See* BASFORD HOLBROOK, Colin Eric

✠**HOLBROOK, The Rt Revd John Edward.** b 62. St Pet Coll Ox BA 83 MA 87. Ridley Hall Cam 82. **d** 86 **p** 87 **c** 11. C Barnes St Mary *S'wark* 86-89; C Bletchley *Ox* 89-93; C N Bletchley CD 89-93; V Adderbury w Milton 93-02; RD Deddington 00-02; R Wimborne Minster *Sarum* 02-11; P-in-c Witchampton, Stanbridge and Long Crichel etc 02-11; P-in-c Horton, Chalbury, Hinton Martel and Holt St Jas 06-11; RD Wimborne 04-11; Chapl S and E Dorset Primary Care Trust 02-11; Can and Preb Sarum Cathl 06-11; Suff Bp Brixworth *Pet* from 11; Can Pet Cathl from 11. *Orchard Acre, 11 North Street, Mears Ashby, Northampton NN6 0DW* T: (01733) 562492 E: bishop.brixworth@peterborough-diocese.org.uk

HOLCOMBE, Canon Graham William Arthur. b 50. Open Univ BA 99. St Mich Coll Llan. **d** 80 **p** 81. C Neath w Llantwit *Llan* 80-84; Asst Youth Chapl 81-84; PV Llan Cathl 84-86; V Pentyrch 86-00; V Pentyrch w Capel Llanilltterne 00-02; Can Llan Cathl 02-14; Can Res from 14. *1 White House, Cathedral Green, Llandaff, Cardiff CF5 2EB* T: (029) 2056 9521

HOLDAWAY, Mark Daniel James. b 78. Selw Coll Cam BA 99 MA 02. Oak Hill Th Coll BA 07. **d** 07 **p** 08. C Bury St Edmunds St Mary *St E* 07-11; R Kirby-le-Soken w Gt Holland *Chelmsf* from 11. *The Rectory, 10 Thorpe Road, Kirby Cross, Frinton-on-Sea CO13 0LT* T: (01255) 675997 E: mdjholdaway@gmail.com

HOLDAWAY, Canon Stephen Douglas. b 45. Hull Univ BA 67. Ridley Hall Cam 67. **d** 70 **p** 71. C Southampton Thornhill St Chris *Win* 70-73; C Tardebigge *Worc* 73-78; Ind Chapl 73-78; *Linc* 78-93; Co-ord City Cen Group Min 81-93; TR Louth *Linc* 93-11; RD Louthesk 95-11; rtd 11; Can and Preb Linc Cathl from 00. *36 Wesley Way, Horncastle LN9 6RY* E: stephen.holdaway@btinternet.com

HOLDEN, Christopher Charles. b 54. **d** 11 **p** 12. OLM Codnor *Derby* from 11; OLM Horsley and Denby from 11. *62 Waingroves Road, Waingroves, Ripley DE5 9TD* T: (01773) 746411 E: cholden123@aol.com

HOLDEN, Christopher Graham. b 78. Lanc Univ BA 06. Westcott Ho Cam 07. **d** 09 **p** 10. C Carnforth *Blackb* 09-12; V Torrisholme from 12. *The Ascension Vicarage, 63 Michaelson Avenue, Morecambe LA4 6SF* T: (01524) 413144 M: 07790-202429 E: wilfridcgh@hotmail.com

HOLDEN, Geoffrey. b 26. FCII 54. Oak Hill Th Coll 57. **d** 59 **p** 60. C Crookes St Thos *Sheff* 59-61; C Belper *Derby* 61-63; C Woking St Jo *Guildf* 63-66; R Bath St Mich w St Paul *B & W* 66-73; Chapl Bath Gp Hosps 73-91; rtd 91; PtO *B & W* from 91. *32 Crescent Gardens, Bath BA1 2NB* T: (01225) 427933

HOLDEN, Jack Crawford (Simon). b 30. Leeds Univ BA 59. Coll of Resurr Mirfield 59. **d** 61 **p** 61. C Middlesbrough All SS *York* 61-64; LtO *Wakef* 65-69; *Leeds* from 98; CR from 67; Asst Chapl Univ Coll Lon 69-74; rtd 98. *House of the Resurrection, Stocks Bank Road, Mirfield WF14 0BN* T: (01924) 494318

HOLDEN, Canon John. b 33. MBE 76. Sheff Univ MA 02 ACMA 62. Ridley Hall Cam 65 Selly Oak Coll 71. **d** 67 **p** 68. C Flixton St Jo CD *Man* 67-71; Lostock 71-75; V Aston SS Pet and Paul *Birm* 75-87; RD Aston 86-87; Hon Can Birm Cathl 86-87; R Ulverston St Mary w H Trin *Carl* 87-98; RD Furness 90-94; Hon Can Carl Cathl 91-94; rtd 98; PtO *Carl* from 98; *Heref* from 99. *3 Alison Road, Church Stretton SY6 7AT* T: (01694) 724167

HOLDEN, John Norman. b 35. Heythrop Coll Lon MA 97. Oak Hill Th Coll 91. **d** 95 **p** 96. NSM Codicote *St Alb* 95-96; PtO from 96; *Ely* from 00. *4 Chapel Row, Shay Lane, Upper Dean, Huntingdon PE28 0LU* T: (01234) 708928

HOLDEN, Mark Noel. b 61. Collingwood Coll Dur BA 82 Birm Univ MA 95 Edin Univ CQSW 85 Warwick Univ TCert 93. Qu Coll Birm 93. **d** 95 **p** 96. C Brumby *Linc* 95-99; P-in-c Wragby 99-00; R Wragby Gp from 00; RD Horncastle from 15. *The Vicarage, Church Street, Wragby, Lincoln LN8 5RA* T: (01673) 857825

HOLDEN, Norman. See HOLDEN, John Norman

HOLDEN, Paul Edward. b 53. BSc 75 CEng 79 MIM MIBF. Trin Coll Bris 82. **d** 86 **p** 87. C Harpurhey Ch Ch *Man* 86-88; C Harpurhey St Steph 88-93; Sen Min Harpurhey LEP 88-93. *2 Baywood Street, Harpurhey, Manchester M9 5XJ* T: 0161-205 2938

HOLDEN, Richard Gary. **d** 04 **p** 05. C Louth *Linc* 04-07; P-in-c Clee from 07; P-in-c Cleethorpes St Aid from 07. *Old Clee Vicarage, 202 Clee Road, Grimsby DN32 8NG* T: (01472) 581570 E: revrichard.holden@btinternet.com

HOLDEN, Mrs Rita. b 45. SAOMC 98. **d** 01 **p** 03. OLM Burghfield *Ox* 01-02; NSM Droitwich Spa *Worc* from 02. *40 Nightingale Close, Droitwich WR9 7HB* T: (01905) 772787 M: 07814-621389 E: rita.openv@btinternet.com

HOLDEN, Simon. See HOLDEN, Jack Crawford

HOLDER, Adèle Claire. See REES, Adèle Claire

HOLDER, John William. b 41. Chester Coll CertEd 61 Open Univ MA 73 Bath Univ MEd 85. Trin Coll Bris MA 94. **d** 87 **p** 88. C Brockworth *Glouc* 87-91; P-in-c Avening w Cherington 91-95; V Cinderford St Jo 95-05; P-in-c Lydbrook 99-03; P-in-c Coberley, Cowley, Colesbourne and Elkstone 05-13; Hon Can Glouc Cathl 03-13; rtd 13. *8 Elmfield Road, Seaton EX12 2EG* T: (01297) 24351 E: canon.john@holder-net.co.uk

HOLDER, Rodney Dennis. b 50. Trin Coll Cam BA 71 MA 75 Ch Ch Ox MA 75 DPhil 78 FRAS 75 CPhys 91 MInstP 91 CMath 95 FIMA 95. Wycliffe Hall Ox BA 96. **d** 97 **p** 98. C Long Compton, Whichford and Barton-on-the-Heath *Cov* 97-01; C Wolford w Burmington 97-01; C Cherington w Stourton 97-01; C Barcheston 97-01; PtO 01-02; P-in-c The Claydons *Ox* 02-05; Course Dir Faraday Inst for Science and Relig from 06. *The Faraday Institute, St Edmund's College, Cambridge CB3 0BN* T: (01223) 741284 *or* 363347 E: drandmrsr.holder@virginmedia.com

HOLDING (formerly SMITH), Mrs Georgina Leah. b 83. Nottm Univ BA 05. Ripon Coll Cuddesdon 07. **d** 10 **p** 11. C Gt and Lt Coates w Bradley *Linc* 10-14; TV Brereton and Rugeley *Lich* from 14. *The Vicarage, 72 Main Road, Rugeley WS15 1DU* E: rev.georgesmith@hotmail.co.uk

HOLDING, Kenneth George Frank. b 27. Sarum & Wells Th Coll 75. **d** 77 **p** 78. C Bexley St Mary *Roch* 77-80; Min Joydens Wood St Barn CD 80-85; R Mereworth w W Peckham 85-92; rtd 92; PtO *York* 92-04; P-in-c Willerby w Ganton and Folkton from 04. *Willerby Vicarage, Wains Lane, Staxton, Scarborough YO12 4SF* T: (01944) 710364

HOLDRIDGE, The Ven Bernard Lee. b 35. Lich Th Coll 64. **d** 67 **p** 68. C Swinton *Sheff* 67-71; V Doncaster St Jude 71-81; R Rawmarsh w Parkgate 81-88; RD Rotherham 86-88; V Worksop Priory *S'well* 88-94; Adn Doncaster *Sheff* 94-01; rtd 01; PtO *Sheff* 01-06; *Guildf* from 06. *35 Denehyrst Court, York Road, Guildford GU1 4EA* T: (01483) 570791

HOLDSTOCK, Adrian Charles. b 51. Peterho Cam BA MA 75 Nottm Univ MA 03 CEng MIMechE MCMI. EMMTC 00. **d** 03 **p** 04. NSM Bosworth and Sheepy Gp *Leic* 03-12; NSM Nailstone and Carlton w Shackerstone 07-12; P-in-c Pet St Mark and St Barn from 12; Asst Dir Ords from 14. *The Vicarage, 82 Lincoln Road, Peterborough PE1 2SN* M: 07792-452669 E: adrian@galileecoaching.co.uk

HOLDSWORTH, Ian Scott. b 52. Sheff Poly BA 75. Oak Hill Th Coll BA 81. **d** 81 **p** 82. C Denham *Ox* 81-84; P-in-c S Leigh 84-89; P-in-c Cogges 84-88; V 88-89; PtO *Pet* 95; NSM Brackley St Pet w St Jas 96-99; P-in-c Northampton St Mary 99-04; V from 04. *St Mary's Vicarage, Towcester Road, Northampton NN4 9EZ* T: (01604) 761104 M: 07912-639980 E: ianholdworth@aol.com

HOLDSWORTH, The Ven John Ivor. b 49. Univ of Wales (Abth) BA 70 Univ of Wales (Cardiff) BD 73 MTh 75. St Mich Coll Llan 70. **d** 73 **p** 74. C Newport St Paul *Mon* 73-77; CF (TAVR) 75-90; V Abercrâf and Callwen *S & B* 77-86; Bp's Chapl for Th Educn 80-97; V Gorseinon 86-97; Hon Lect Th Univ of Wales (Swansea) 88-96; Prin and Warden St Mich Coll Llan 97-03; Lect Th Univ of Wales (Cardiff) *Llan* 97-03; Adn St D and V Steynton *St D* 03-10; Adn Cyprus, Chapl Larnaca and Exec Adn Cyprus and Gulf from 10. *15 Odyssea Androutsou, CY-7104 Aradippou, Cyprus* T: (00357) (22) 671220 E: archdeaconjohn@yahoo.co.uk

HOLDSWORTH, The Very Revd Kelvin. b 66. Man Poly BSc 89 St Andr Univ BD 92 Edin Univ MTh 96. TISEC 95. **d** 97 **p** 98. Prec St Ninian's Cathl Perth 97-00; R Bridge of Allan 00-06; Chapl Stirling Univ 00-06; Provost St Mary's Cathl from 06;

R Glas St Mary from 06. *300 Great Western Road, Glasgow G4 9JB* T: 0141-530 8643 E: kelvin@thurible.net *or* provost@thecathedral.org.uk

HOLE, Alice. **d** 12 **p** 13. NSM Brixton St Matt w St Jude *S'wark* from 12. *19 Wolfington Road, London SE27 0JF* M: 07557-048236 T: (020) 8670 6902 E: Alice.hole@btinternet.com

HOLE, The Very Revd Derek Norman. b 33. De Montfort Univ Hon DLitt 99 Leic Univ Hon LLD 05. Linc Th Coll 57. **d** 60 **p** 61. C Knighton St Mary Magd *Leic* 60-62; S Africa 62-64; C Kenilworth St Nic *Cov* 64-67; R Burton Latimer *Pet* 67-73; V Leic St Jas 73-92; Hon Can Leic Cathl 83-92; RD Christianity S 83-92; Provost Leic 92-99; Chapl to The Queen 85-93; rtd 99; PtO *Leic* from 00. *25 Southernhay Close, Leicester LE2 3TW* T: 0116-270 9988 E: dnhole@btinternet.com

HOLE, Toby Kenton. b 72. Dur Univ BA 94 MA 95 Cam Univ BTh 06. Ridley Hall Cam 03. **d** 06 **p** 07. C Islington St Mary *Lon* 06-10; V Woodseats St Chad *Sheff* from 10; AD Ecclesall from 14. *St Chad's Vicarage, 9 Linden Avenue, Sheffield S8 0GA* T: 0114-274 9302 *or* 274 5086 M: 07906-312998 E: toby.hole@gmail.com *or* toby.hole@sheffield.anglican.org

HOLFORD, Andrew Peter. b 62. Nottm Univ BSc 84. Cranmer Hall Dur 87. **d** 90 **p** 91. C Waltham Cross *St Alb* 90-93; C Northampton St Benedict *Pet* 93-95; V Pet Ch Carpenter 95-04; TR Baldock w Bygrave and Weston *St Alb* 04-13; R Baldock w Bygrave from 13. *The Rectory, 9 Pond Lane, Baldock SG7 5AS* T: (01462) 896273 E: 2008luddite@googlemail.com

HOLFORD, Canon John Alexander. b 40. Chich Th Coll 65. **d** 67 **p** 68. C Cottingley *Bradf* 67-71; C Baildon 71-73; P-in-c Bingley H Trin 73-74; V 74-86; V Woodhall 86-93; C Shelf 93-94; TV Shelf w Buttershaw St Aid 94-99; rtd 99; P-in-c Embsay w Eastby *Bradf* 99-04; Hon Can Bradf Cathl 03-04; PtO *Leeds* from 04. *3 Wheelwrights Court, Hellifield, Skipton BD23 4LX* T: (01729) 851740 E: john.holford@bradford.anglican.org

HOLFORD, Margaret Sophia. b 39. SAOMC 95. **d** 98 **p** 99. NSM Stevenage St Andr and St Geo *St Alb* 98-03; NSM Ickleford w Holwell 03-05; NSM Holwell, Ickleford and Pirton from 05. *Icknield House, Westmill Lane, Ickleford, Hitchin SG5 3RN* T: (01462) 432794 F: 436618

HOLGATE, Canon David Andrew. b 54. Cape Town Univ BA 77 Port Eliz Univ BA 89 Rhodes Univ MTh 90 PhD 94. All Nations Chr Coll 80. **d** 82 **p** 84. C Uitenhage St Kath S Africa 82-84; Asst P Port Elizabeth St Hugh 84-87; P-in-c Somerset E All SS 88-89; St Paul's Coll Grahamstown 90-93; CME Officer *Chelmsf* 93-96; P-in-c Felsted 93-96; V Felsted and Lt Dunmow 96-97; Dean of Studies STETS 97-14; Vice-Prin 01-11; Prin 11-14; Can Res Man Cathl from 14. *3 Booth Clibborn Court, Salford M7 4PJ* E: daholgate@googlemail.com

✠**HOLLAND, The Rt Revd Alfred Charles.** b 27. St Chad's Coll Dur BA 50. **d** 52 **p** 53 **c** 70. C W Hackney St Barn *Lon* 52-54; R Scarborough Australia 55-70; asst Bp Perth 70-77; Bp Newcastle 78-92; rtd 92; Bp Jerusalem 93-94; Australia from 94. *21 Sullivan Crescent, Wanniassa ACT 2903, Australia* T: (0061) (2) 6231 8368 E: acjmholland@bigpond.com

✠**HOLLAND, The Rt Revd Edward.** b 36. AKC 64. **d** 65 **p** 66 **c** 86. C Dartford H Trin *Roch* 65-69; C Mill Hill Jo Keble Ch *Lon* 69-72; Prec Gib Cathl 72-74; Chapl Naples Ch Ch 74-79; Chapl Bromley Hosp 79-86; V Bromley St Mark *Roch* 79-86; Suff Bp Eur 86-95; Dean Brussels 86-95; Area Bp Colchester *Chelmsf* 95-01; rtd 01; Hon Asst Bp Lon from 02; Hon Asst Bp Eur from 02. *37 Parfrey Street, London W6 9EW* T: (020) 8746 3636 E: ed.holland@uwclub.net

HOLLAND, Geoffrey. See HOLLAND, William Geoffrey Bretton

HOLLAND, Mrs Gillaine. b 67. Kent Inst of Art & Design BA 89. STETS 05. **d** 08 **p** 09. C Epsom St Martin *Guildf* 08-09; C Woking St Mary 09-12; Asst Chapl HM Pris Send 11-12; Chapl St Columba's Retreat and Conf Cen from 12. *St Columba's House, Maybury Hill, Woking GU22 8AB* T: (01483) 713006 M: 07969-067116 E: chaplain@stcolumbashouse.org.uk

HOLLAND, Glyn. b 59. Hull Univ BA Bris Univ CertEd. Coll of Resurr Mirfield 83. **d** 85 **p** 86. C Brayton St Martin *Wakef* 85-89; V Ferrybridge 89-96; Chapl Pontefract Gen Infirmary 89-96; V Middlesbrough All SS *York* from 96. *All Saints' Vicarage, 14 The Crescent, Middlesbrough TS5 6SQ* T: (01642) 820304

HOLLAND, Jesse Marvin Sean. b 66. Westmr Coll Ox MTh 03. Oak Hill Th Coll BA 97. **d** 98 **p** 99. C Thundersley *Chelmsf* 98-02; P-in-c Tedburn St Mary, Whitestone, Oldridge etc *Ex* 02-06; V Buller New Zealand 06-08; P-in-c Lyneham w Bradenstoke *Sarum* 08-10; Chapl RAF from 10. *Chaplaincy Services (RAF), HQ Air Command, RAF High Wycombe HP14 4UE* T: (01494) 496800 F: 496343 E: revdjmsholland@aol.com

HOLLAND, John Stuart. b 52. Sarum & Wells Th Coll 77. **d** 80 **p** 81. C Wylde Green *Birm* 80-83; C Swanage and Studland *Sarum* 83-85; P-in-c Handley w Pentridge 85-88; TV Preston w

Sutton Poyntz, Littlemoor etc 88-95; P-in-c Failsworth St Jo *Man* 95-01; V Ashton Ch Ch 01-07; P-in-c Carbis Bay w Lelant *Truro* 07-10; P-in-c Towednack and Zennor 08-10; P-in-c Oswaldtwistle Immanuel and All SS *Blackb* 10-12; P-in-c Oswaldtwistle St Paul 10-12; V Oswaldtwistle from 12; AD Accrington from 14. *The Vicarage, 29 Mayfield Avenue, Oswaldtwistle, Accrington BB5 3AA* T: (01254) 231038 M: 07718-483817 E: vicar-cbl@fsmail.net

HOLLAND, Lesley Anne. *See* LEON, Lesley Anne

HOLLAND, Mrs Linda. b 48. Sarum & Wells Th Coll 91. **d** 93 **p** 94. Par Dn Queensbury All SS *Lon* 93-94; C 94-96; C Enfield St Jas 96-01; V Coney Hill *Glouc* 01-10; rtd 10. *1 Ann Edwards Mews, Abbeydale, Gloucester GL4 4FG* T: (01452) 537493 E: revlynneholland@hotmail.com

HOLLAND, Matthew Francis. b 52. Lon Univ BA 73. Qu Coll Birm. **d** 79 **p** 80. C Ecclesall *Sheff* 79-83; TV Gleadless Valley 83-86; TR 86-88; V Sheff Gillcar St Silas 88-92; V Sheff St Silas Broomhall 92-98; V Southsea St Simon *Portsm* 98-15; rtd 15. *6 Rifts Avenue, Saltburn-by-Sea TS12 1QE* T: (01287) 624915 E: matthew758@btinternet.com

HOLLAND, Paul William. b 55. Coll of Resurr Mirfield 78. **d** 80 **p** 81. C Parkstone St Pet w Branksea and St Osmund *Sarum* 80-83; CR 85-93; Asst Chapl Musgrove Park Hosp 93; Asst Chapl St Helier Hosp Carshalton 93-96; C Croydon St Jo *S'wark* 96-04; TV Barnes 04-15; rtd 15. *Flat 3, 1 Coburg Terrace, Sidmouth EX10 8NH* M: 07984-746436 E: pauhold@mac.com

HOLLAND, Peter Christie. b 36. St Andr Univ BSc 60. Cranmer Hall Dur 60. **d** 62 **p** 63. C Darlington St Jo *Dur* 62-64; C Bishopwearmouth Ch Ch 64-69; V Tudhoe 69-77; V New Seaham 77-89; V Totternhoe, Stanbridge and Tilsworth *St Alb* 89-01; rtd 02; PtO *Dur* from 02. *Bracken Ridge, Woodland, Bishop Auckland DL13 5RH* T: (01388) 718881 E: hollandpeter90@supanet.com

HOLLAND, Simon Geoffrey. b 63. MHCIMA 83. Trin Coll Bris BA. **d** 91 **p** 92. C Reigate St Mary *S'wark* 91-95; Chapl Lee Abbey 95-99; C Guildf St Sav 99-07; P-in-c Bath Walcot *B & W* 07-15; R from 15. *Swallowgate, Lansdown Road, Bath BA1 5TD* T: (01225) 334748 E: simongh10@gmail.com

HOLLAND, Canon Simon Paul. b 56. Westcott Ho Cam 79. **d** 81 **p** 82. C Uckfield *Chich* 81-84; TV Lewes All SS, St Anne, St Mich and St Thos 84-88; TR 88-91; R Glas St Matt 91-95; P-in-c Glas St Kentigern 95-96; R Aldingbourne, Barnham and Eastergate *Chich* 96-12; R Chich St Paul and Westhampnett from 12; Can and Preb Chich Cathl from 10. *The Rectory, Tower Close, Chichester PO19 1QN* T: (01243) 779089 E: simonholland578@btinternet.com

HOLLAND, Mrs Tessa Christine. b 59. Hull Univ BA 81 Heythrop Coll Lon MA 12. STETS 00. **d** 03 **p** 04. NSM Storrington *Chich* 03-05; NSM Pulborough 05-07; LtO from 07. *Wild Fortune, Sandgate Lane, Storrington, Pulborough RH20 3HJ* T: (01903) 740487 E: wildfortune@btinternet.com

HOLLAND, William Geoffrey Bretton. b 36. Magd Coll Cam BA 59 MA 63. Westcott Ho Cam 61. **d** 63 **p** 64. C Cannock *Lich* 63-66; C Paddington Ch Ch *Lon* 66-69; Chapl Magd Coll Cam 69-73; V Twyford *Win* 74-78; V Twyford and Owslebury and Morestead 78-84; Chapl Twyford Sch Win 84-90; rtd 01. *16 Southgate Villas, St James Lane, Winchester SO23 9SG* T: (01962) 842802

HOLLANDS, Derek Gordon. b 45. Brasted Th Coll Chich Th Coll 72. **d** 74 **p** 75. C Banstead *Guildf* 74-77; C Cranleigh 77-79; C Haywards Heath St Wilfrid *Chich* 79-80; TV 80-82; Chapl Hillingdon Area HA 82-86; Chapl W Suffolk Hosp Bury St Edm 86-95; Pres Coll Health Care Chapls 92-94; Sen Chapl R Cornwall Hosps Trust 95-98; rtd 99. *The Cedars, 59 Hardwick Lane, Bury St Edmunds IP33 2RB* T: (01284) 386196 E: derek.hollands@tesco.net

HOLLANDS, Percival Edwin Macaulay. b 36. Edin Th Coll 57. **d** 60 **p** 61. C Greenock *Glas* 60-64; C Aberdeen St Mary *Ab* 64-65; P-in-c Aberdeen St Clem 65-68; R Cruden Bay 68-70; CF 70-82; C Ribbleton *Blackb* 82-83; TV 83-88; C Penwortham St Mary 88-92; V Farington 92-98; rtd 98; PtO *Nor* from 00. *30 Teasel Road, Attleborough NR17 1XX* T: (01953) 457372

HOLLANDS, Ray Leonard. b 42. MRICS 02 MASI MRSPH MCIOB. S'wark Ord Course 68. **d** 71 **p** 72. NSM Hanworth All SS *Lon* 71-77 and 85-91 and 95-98 and 02-03; NSM Hanworth St Geo 77-85; NSM Marshwood Vale *Sarum* 81-91; NSM Upper Sunbury St Sav *Lon* 98-01; rtd 03. *Yew Tree Cottage, Marshwood, Bridport DT6 5QF* T: (01297) 678566 E: rlh.ltd@virgin.net

HOLLETT, Catherine Elaine. *See* DAKIN, Catherine Elaine

HOLLEY, Paul Robert. b 65. Cranmer Hall Dur 91. **d** 94 **p** 95. C Tonge w Alkrington *Man* 94-98; P-in-c Salford St Phil w St Steph 98-00; P-in-c Salford Sacred Trin 99-00; R Salford Sacred Trin and St Phil 00-03; P-in-c La Côte *Eur* 03-10; PtO from 10; Hon C S Dulwich St Steph *S'wark* 12-14; P-in-c Colbury *Win* from 14. *The Vicarage, Deerleap Lane, Totton, Southampton SO40 7EH* E: paul.holley@anglicanhealth.org

HOLLIDAY, Canon Andrew. b 62. St Steph Ho Ox 89. **d** 92 **p** 93. C Marton *Blackb* 92-95; C Poulton-le-Fylde 95-97; V Leyland St Jas 97-04; AD Leyland 02-04; P-in-c Darwen St Pet w Hoddlesden 04-10; V Darwen St Pet 10-11; R Standish from 11; Chapl MU from 12; Hon Can Blackb Cathl from 12. *The Rectory, 13 Rectory Lane, Standish, Wigan WN6 0XA* T: (01257) 421396 E: andrew.holliday@tesco.net

HOLLIDAY, Canon Peter Leslie. b 48. FCA 79 Birm Univ BCom 70 MA 92. Qu Coll Birm 81. **d** 83 **p** 84. C Burton *Lich* 83-87; P-in-c Longdon 87-93; PV and Subchanter Lich Cath 87-93; R Stratford-on-Avon w Bishopton *Cov* 93-00; Dir St Giles Hospice Lich from 00; Chan's V Lich Cathl 02-13; Can Custos Lich Cathl from 13; QHC from 15. *St Giles Hospice, Fisherwick Road, Lichfield WS14 9LH* T: (01543) 432031 E: plh@clara.net

HOLLIDAY, William. b 33. Qu Coll Cam BA 56 MA 60 McGill Univ Montreal BD 58 LTh 58. Montreal Dioc Th Coll 56 Linc Th Coll 58. **d** 58 **p** 59. C Stanningley St Thos *Ripon* 58-63; C Romaldkirk 63-64; India 64-77; V Thwaites Brow *Bradf* 77-86; RD S Craven 82-86; P-in-c Horton 86-98; P-in-c Bradf St Oswald Chapel Green 91-98; RD Bowling and Horton 95-98; rtd 98; PtO *Leeds* from 99. *61 Woodside Crescent, Bingley BD16 1RE* T: (01274) 568413

HOLLIDAY, William John. b 49. Middleton St Geo Coll of Educn TCert 72. CBDTI 05. **d** 07 **p** 08. NSM Kendal St Thos *Carl* 07-12; TV Loughrigg 12-13; rtd 13. *2 Michaelson Road, Kendal LA9 5JQ* T: (01539) 730701 E: billholliday@googlemail.com

HOLLIMAN, The Ven John James. b 44. St D Coll Lamp BA 66. **d** 67 **p** 68. C Tideswell *Derby* 67-71; CF 71-99; Dep Chapl Gen and Adn for the Army 96-99; QHC 94-99; V Funtington and Sennicotts *Chich* 99-09; R W Stoke 99-09; RD Westbourne 04-09; rtd 09. *3 Littledown, Shaftesbury SP7 9HD* T: (01747) 853637

HOLLIN, Ian. b 40. Open Univ BA 76 DCC 91. Sarum Th Coll 67. **d** 70 **p** 71. C Lancaster Ch Ch *Blackb* 70-72; C S Shore H Trin 72-75; C Marton Moss 72-75; V Morecambe St Lawr 75-78; V Blackpool St Mary 78-83; PV and Succ Ex Cathl 83-87; Counsellor Coun for Chr Care and TV 87-91; Admin Boniface Cen Ex 91-93; TV Maltby *Sheff* 93-96; R Handsworth 96-08; rtd 08; PtO *Blackb* from 08. *30 Sumpter Croft, Penwortham, Preston PR1 9UJ* T: (01772) 749806

HOLLINGHURST, Mrs Anne Elizabeth. b 64. Trin Coll Bris BA 96 Hughes Hall Cam MSt 10. **d** 96 **p** 97. C Nottingham St Sav *S'well* 96-99; Chapl Derby Univ and Derby Coll 99-05; Bp's Dom Chapl and Can Res Man Cathl 05-10; V St Alb St Pet *St Alb* from 10. *The Vicarage, 23 Hall Place Gardens, St Albans AL1 3SB* T: (01727) 851464 E: annehollinghurst@hotmail.co.uk

HOLLINGHURST, Preb Stephen. b 59. St Jo Coll Nottm 81. **d** 83 **p** 84. C Hyde St Geo *Ches* 83-86; C Cropwell Bishop w Colston Bassett, Granby etc *S'well* 86-90; R Pembridge w Moor Court, Shobdon, Staunton etc *Heref* 90-02; R Presteigne w Discoed, Kinsham, Lingen and Knill from 02; RD Kington and Weobley 95-02 and 07-12 and from 14; Preb Heref Cathl from 08. *The Rectory, St David's Street, Presteigne LD8 2BP* T: (01544) 267777 E: steve.hollinghurst@lineone.net

HOLLINGHURST, Stephen Patrick. b 63. Hull Univ BA 84. Trin Coll Bris BA 93 MA 93. **d** 96 **p** 97. C Nottingham St Sav *S'well* 96-99; Chapl Nottm Trent Univ 99-03; Researcher CA from 03; PtO *Derby* 00-04; Chapl Derby Cathl 04-05. *The Vicarage, 23 Hall Place Gardens, St Albans AL1 3SB*

HOLLINGS, Ms Daphne. b 46. WMMTC 02. **d** 05 **p** 06. NSM Adbaston, High Offley, Knightley, Norbury etc *Lich* 05-09; C Edstaston, Fauls, Prees, Tilstock and Whixall 09-15; C Whitchurch 13-15; rtd 15. *Nythfa, County Road, Penygroes, Caernarfon LL54 6EY* E: daphne.hollings785@btinternet.com

HOLLINGS, Miss Patricia Mary. b 39. CertEd 59. S'wark Ord Course 84. **d** 87. Par Dn Wyke *Bradf* 87-94; C 94-96; rtd 96; PtO *Bradf* 96-10; *Leeds* from 10. *1 Greenacre Way, Wyke, Bradford BD12 9DJ* T: (01274) 677439

HOLLINGS, Robert George. b 48. St Jo Coll Nottm. **d** 94 **p** 95. C Cotmanhay *Derby* 94-97; TV Godrevy *Truro* 97-02; V Newhall *Derby* 02-12; rtd 12; P-in-c Six Pilgrims *B & W* 12-13; PtO from 15. *2 Meadow View, Rolleston-on-Dove, Burton-on-Trent DE13 9AN* E: bobandjacqui@btinternet.com

HOLLINGSHURST, Christopher Paul. b 63. St Chad's Coll Dur BA 85 Westmr Coll Ox PGCE 86 Anglia Poly Univ MA 04. Ridley Hall Cam 96. **d** 99 **p** 00. C Bourn and Kingston w Caxton and Longstowe *Ely* 99-00; C Papworth 00-03; V Hook *S'wark* 03-14; Voc Adv Wandsworth Adnry 09-12; Dioc Voc Adv 12-13; Dir Ords Kingston Area 13-14; P-in-c W Byfleet *Guildf* from 14. *3 Clare Close, West Byfleet KT14 6RD*

HOLLINGSWORTH, Geoffrey. b 53. MCIPD 85. NOC 86. **d** 86 **p** 87. C Thorne *Sheff* 86-89; V Rawcliffe 89-96; V Airmyn, Hook and Rawcliffe 96-09; P-in-c Pocklington and Owsthorpe and Kilnwick Percy etc *York* 09-10; P-in-c Burnby 09-10; P-in-c

Londesborough 09-10; P-in-c Nunburnholme and Warter and Huggate 09-10; P-in-c Shiptonthorpe and Hayton 09-10; R Pocklington Wold from 10; R Londesborough Wold from 10. *The Rectory, 29 The Balk, Pocklington, York YO42 2QQ* T: (01759) 302133 *or* 306045
E: geoff.holly145@btinternet.com

HOLLINGSWORTH, James William. b 69. Southn Univ BA 91 SS Coll Cam BA 96. Aston Tr Scheme 92 Ridley Hall Cam 94. **d** 97 **p** 98. C Mildenhall *St E* 97-01; R Barcombe *Chich* from 01. *The Rectory, 1 The Grange, Barcombe, Lewes BN8 5AT* T: (01273) 400260 E: james@barcombe.net

HOLLINGSWORTH, Preb Paula Marion. b 62. Van Mildert Coll Dur BSc 83 Univ of Wales (Lamp) MA 08. Trin Coll Bris BA 91. **d** 91 **p** 94. C Keynsham *B & W* 91-95; C Balsall Heath St Paul *Birm* 95-98; Tutor Crowther Hall CMS Tr Coll Selly Oak 95-01; P-in-c Houghton-on-the-Hill, Keyham and Hungarton *Leic* 01-10; Bp's Adv for CME 01-04; P-in-c Westbury sub Mendip w Easton *B & W* 10-12; V from 12; V Priddy from 12; Sub-Dean and Preb Wells Cathl from 14; Dean of Women's Min from 15. *The Vicarage, Crow Lane, Westbury sub Mendip, Wells BA5 1HB* T: (01749) 870293 M: 07909-631977
E: pmhollingsworth@btinternet.com

HOLLINS, Mrs Beverley Jayne. b 68. Univ of Wales (Abth) BLib 90. SAOMC 00. **d** 03 **p** 04. C Milton Keynes *Ox* 03-06; LtO 06-07; Newport Deanery Development Facilitator 07-12; P-in-c Hardingstone and Piddington w Horton *Pet* from 12. *The Vicarage, 29 Back Lane, Hardingstone, Northampton NN4 6BY* T: (01604) 945818 E: beverley.hollins@gmail.com

HOLLINS, John Edgar. b 35. St Jo Coll Cam BA 58 MA 62. Oak Hill Th Coll 58. **d** 60 **p** 61. C Whalley Range St Edm *Man* 60-63; C Highbury Ch Ch *Lon* 63-66; C St Alb St Paul *St Alb* 66-71; Hon C Halliwell St Paul *Man* 71-72; C Ravenhill St Jo 72-73; PtO *Birm* 79-81; V Millbrook *Ches* 81-89; rtd 89; PtO *Truro* from 89. *3 Victoria Close, Liskeard PL14 3HU* T: (01579) 349963

HOLLINS (*formerly* SHIPP), Patricia Susan. b 54. Univ of Wales BA 76. St Paul's Coll Grahamstown 77 Linc Th Coll 81. **d** 83 **p** 94. C Cyncoed *Mon* 83-87; Par Dn Lawrence Weston *Bris* 89-91; Par Dn Henbury 91-94; V Longwell Green 94-99; Hon Can Bris Cathl 97-99; Chapl Mt Vernon and Watford Hosps NHS Trust 99-00; Sen Co-ord Chapl W Herts Hosps NHS Trust 00-04; Lead Chapl (E) Caring for the Spirit NHS Project 04-09; P-in-c Boxley w Detling *Cant* 09-14; AD N Downs 09-14; Chapl Cam St Edw Ely 14-15; Lead Chapl Qu Eliz Hosp King's Lynn NHS Foundn Trust from 15. *Queen Elizabeth Hospital, Gayton Road, King's Lynn PE30 4ET* M: 07918-671476 T: (01553) 613441 E: s.hollins@qehkl.nhs.uk *or* susan.hollins.sh@gmail.com

HOLLIS, Anthony Wolcott Linsley. b 40. McGill Univ Montreal BA 61 Long Is Univ MA 76. Gen Th Sem NY MDiv 64. **d** 64 **p** 65. V Lonaconing St Pet USA 66-67; Chapl US Army 67-79; R Sherwood Ch Cockeysville 79-92; R St George St Pet Bermuda 92-02; rtd 02; USA from 02. *712 Murdock Road, Baltimore MD 21212, USA*

HOLLIS, The Ven Arnold Thaddeus. b 33. JP 87. Stockton State Coll New Jersey BA 74 NY Th Sem MDiv 74 STM 76 DMin 78. Codrington Coll Barbados 56. **d** 59 **p** 60. C Wakef St Jo 60-62; Br Guiana 62-64; P-in-c Horbury Bridge *Wakef* 64-66; C Loughton St Jo *Chelmsf* 66-69; USA 69-77; Hon Chapl RN Bermuda from 77; Chapl HM Pris from 77; Chapl Miss to Seafarers from 90; Hon Can Bermuda Cathl from 87; Adn Bermuda 96-03; rtd 03. *3 Middle Road, Sandys SB 02, Bermuda* T: (001441) 234 0834 *or* 234 2025 F: 234 2723 E: athol@logic.bm

HOLLIS, Derek. b 60. Loughb Univ BA 82. Cranmer Hall Dur 83. **d** 86 **p** 87. C Evington *Leic* 86-89; C Arnold *S'well* 89-93; V Beckingham w Walkeringham 93-03; P-in-c Gringley-on-the-Hill 95-03; V Beckingham w Walkeringham and Gringley 03-05; P-in-c Elston w Elston Chapelry 05-11; P-in-c E Stoke w Syerston 05-11; P-in-c Shelton 05-11; P-in-c Sibthorpe 05-11; P-in-c Staunton w Flawborough 05-11; P-in-c Kilvington 05-11; Hon Chapl Miss to Seafarers 03-04; Bp's Adv on Rural Affairs *S'well* 04-11; V Stourhead *St E* from 11. *The Rectory, Mill Road, Kedington, Haverhill CB9 7NN* E: rectorofkedington@hotmail.co.uk

HOLLIS, Mrs Lorna Mary. b 40. Cranmer Hall Dur 05. **d** 06 **p** 07. NSM Scarborough St Jas w H Trin *York* from 06; Asst Chapl Scarborough and NE Yorks Healthcare NHS Trust 06-12; Asst Chapl York Teaching Hosp NHS Foundn Trust from 12. *30 Hartford Court, Filey Road, Scarborough YO11 2TP* T: (01723) 351395 E: mary.hollis3@btinternet.com

HOLLIS, Rebecca Catherine. *See* MATHEW, Rebecca Catherine

HOLLIS, Timothy Knowles. b 28. RN Coll Dartmouth 45. St Steph Ho Ox 54. **d** 58 **p** 59. C Oatlands *Guildf* 58-60; C Crawley *Chich* 60-63; C Sotterley w Willingham *St E* 63-69; C Sotterley, Willingham, Shadingfield, Ellough etc 69;

R 69-76; Gen Sec L'Arche UK 77-93; rtd 93; PtO *Chich* 93-02; *Glouc* from 03. *9 Abbots Court Drive, Twyning, Tewkesbury GL20 6JJ* T: (01684) 274903

HOLLIS, Mrs Valerie Elizabeth. b 40. Maria Grey Coll Lon CertEd 61. St Alb Minl Tr Scheme 89. **d** 92 **p** 94. NSM Kempston Transfiguration *St Alb* 92-06; NSM Officer Bedford Adnry 06-10; PtO from 06. *33 Silverdale Street, Kempston, Bedford MK42 8BE* T: (01234) 853397
E: nsmobeds@stalbans.anglican.org

HOLLOWAY, Canon David Dennis. b 43. Lich Th Coll 65. **d** 68 **p** 69. C Cricklade w Latton *Bris* 68-71; C Bris St Agnes and St Simon w St Werburgh 71-74; V Bitton 74-78; TV E Bris 78-80; P-in-c Tormarton w W Littleton 80-83; Dioc Ecum Officer 83-93; Hon C Bris St Mich 89-93; V Horfield St Greg 93-00; RD Horfield 97-99; Chapl St Monica Home Westbury-on-Trym 00-07; Hon Can Bris Cathl 92-07; rtd 07. *76 Marsworth Road, Pitstone, Leighton Buzzard LU7 9AS* T: (01296) 662765 M: 07974-648556

HOLLOWAY, David Ronald James. b 39. Univ Coll Ox BA 62 MA 66. Ridley Hall Cam 65. **d** 67 **p** 68. C Leeds St Geo *Ripon* 67-71; Tutor Wycliffe Hall Ox 71-72; V Jesmond Clayton Memorial *Newc* from 73. *7 Otterburn Terrace, Newcastle upon Tyne NE2 3AP* T: 0191-281 2001 *or* 281 2139

HOLLOWAY, Graham Edward. b 45. Chich Th Coll 69. **d** 72 **p** 73. C W Drayton *Lon* 72-75; P-in-c Hawton *S'well* 75-80; V Ladybrook 80-85; P-in-c Babworth 85-87; R Babworth w Sutton-cum-Lound 87-97; RD Retford 88-93; C Mansfield Woodhouse 97-04; P-in-c Mansfield St Aug 04-12; P-in-c Pleasley Hill 04-12; rtd 12. *6 Aylesbury Way, Forest Town, Mansfield NG19 0GJ* E: padreg@btinternet.com

HOLLOWAY, Keith Graham. b 45. Linc Coll Ox BA 67. Cranmer Hall Dur. **d** 73 **p** 74. C Gt Ilford St Andr *Chelmsf* 73-78; Hon C Squirrels Heath 78-80; Min Chelmer Village CD 80-87; V E Springfield 87-89; P-in-c Gt Dunmow 89-96; R Gt Dunmow and Barnston 96-02; R Upper Colne 02-10; rtd 10; PtO *Chelmsf* from 10. *5 Martens Meadow, Braintree CM7 3LB* T: (01376) 334976 E: kanddway@aol.com

HOLLOWAY, Michael Sinclair. b 50. UEA BSc 74 Southn Univ PGCE 75. STETS 99. **d** 02 **p** 03. NSM Catherington and Clanfield *Portsm* 02-07; C Bishop's Cleeve *Glouc* 07-08; TV Bishop's Cleeve and Woolstone w Gotherington etc 08-13; V Painswick, Sheepscombe, Cranham, The Edge etc from 13. *The Vicarage, Orchard Mead, Painswick, Stroud GL6 6YD* E: revmike.sh@btinternet.com

✠**HOLLOWAY, The Rt Revd Prof Richard Frederick.** b 33. Lon Univ BD 63 NY Th Sem STM 68 Strathclyde Univ DUniv 94 Aber Univ Hon DD 95 Napier Univ Edin DLitt 00 Glas Univ DD 01 FRSE 95. Edin Th Coll 58. **d** 59 **p** 60 **c** 86. C Glas St Ninian 59-63; P-in-c Glas St Marg 63-68; R Edin Old St Paul 68-80; R Boston The Advent MA USA 80-84; V Ox St Mary Magd 84-86; Bp Edin 86-00; Primus 92-00; rtd 00; Gresham Prof of Div 97-01. *6 Blantyre Terrace, Edinburgh EH10 5AE* T: 0131-446 0696 M: 07710-254500
E: richard@docholloway.org.uk

HOLLOWAY, Simon Anthony. b 50. Sussex Univ BSc 72 Univ of Wales MA 03. Trin Coll Bris 76. **d** 79 **p** 81. C Bushbury *Lich* 79-81; C Castle Church 81-84; P-in-c Sparkbrook Ch Ch *Birm* 84-91; V 91-02; AD Bordesley 92-99; TV Horley *S'wark* 02-11; Chapl SE Cyprus 11-14; P-in-c Kilmington, Stockland, Dalwood, Yarcombe etc *Ex* from 14. *The Vicarage, Whitford Road, Kilmington, Axminster EX13 7RF* M: 07986-274393 E: simonholloway55@yahoo.co.uk

HOLLOWOOD, Christopher George. b 54. K Alfred's Coll Win BEd 76 Open Univ MA 97. Ripon Coll Cuddesdon 83. **d** 86 **p** 87. C Tupsley *Heref* 86-89; R Much Birch w Lt Birch, Much Dewchurch etc 89-92; Hd RS Haywood High Sch Heref 92-97; Sen Teacher St Aug Upper Sch Ox 97-00; Dep Hd N Bromsgrove High Sch 00-02; Headmaster Bp Llan Ch in Wales High Sch Cardiff from 02. *170 Kings Road, Cardiff CF11 9DG* T: (029) 2056 2485 E: c.hollowood@ntlworld.com

HOLLOWOOD, Graham. b 56. Anglia Ruskin Univ MA 07. St Steph Ho Ox 97. **d** 99 **p** 00. C Newport St Julian *Mon* 99-02; V Newport All SS 02-08; V Glodwick *Man* from 08; AD Oldham E from 14. *St Mark's Vicarage, 1 Skipton Street, Oldham OL8 2JF* T/F: 0161-624 4964 M: 07748-106718
E: graham.hollowood@virgin.net

HOLLYWELL, Mrs Catherine Ann Mary. b 62. Qu Coll Birm 12. **d** 15. C Derby St Jo from 15. *St Werburgh's Vicarage, Gascoigne Drive, Spondon, Derby DE21 7GL* M: 07506-742810
E: chollywell@btinternet.com

HOLLYWELL, Julian Francis. b 70. Liv Univ BSc 91 Leeds Univ MA 05. NOC 03. **d** 05 **p** 06. C W Didsbury and Withington St Chris *Man* 05-08; V Spondon *Derby* from 08; RD Derby N from 10. *St Werburgh's Vicarage, Gascoigne Drive, Spondon, Derby DE21 7GL* T: (01332) 673573 M: 07963-420564
E: fatherjulian@btinternet.com

HOLMAN, Francis Noel. b 37. Sarum Th Coll 62. **d** 65 **p** 66. C Weston Favell *Pet* 65-68; C Eckington *Derby* 68-71; Asst Chapl St Thos Hosp Lon 72-77; Chapl Hope Hosp Salford 77-02; Chapl Salford R Hosp 77-93; Chapl Ladywell Hosp 77-99; Chapl Man and Salford Skin Hosp 88-94; rtd 02; PtO *Man* from 03. *90 Rocky Lane, Eccles, Manchester M30 9LY* T: 0161-707 1180

HOLMAN, Geoffrey Gladstone. b 32. AKC 56. **d** 57 **p** 58. C Eltham St Barn *S'wark* 57-60; CF 60-73; Dep Asst Chapl Gen 73-80; Asst Chapl Gen 80-84; QHC 82-84; V Wetwang and Garton-on-the-Wolds w Kirkburn *York* 84-92; RD Harthill 87-92; rtd 92; P-in-c Askham Bryan *York* 93-01; PtO from 01. *3 Westholme Drive, York YO30 5TH* T: (01904) 624419 E: samegus@virginmedia.com

HOLMAN, Mrs Lesley Anita. b 50. SWMTC 11. **d** 14. NSM Littleham-cum-Exmouth w Lympstone *Ex* from 14. *6 Dukes Close, Otterton, Budleigh Salterton EX9 7EY* T: (01395) 567255 E: lesley.holman@btinternet.com

HOLMDEN, Miss Maria Irene. b 50. Trent Poly TCert 72 BEd 73. Oak Hill Th Coll 90. **d** 92 **p** 94. Par Dn Stratford St Jo and Ch Ch w Forest Gate St Jas *Chelmsf* 92-94; C Hadley and All SS 96-01; V from 01. *All Saints' Vicarage, 47 Melbourne Road, London E10 7HF* T: (020) 8558 8139 E: mholmden@tiscali.co.uk

HOLME, Thomas Edmund. b 49. Selw Coll Cam BA 71 MA 75. Coll of Resurr Mirfield 71. **d** 73 **p** 74. C Wyther *Ripon* 73-76; C Wimbledon S'wark 76-78; TV 78-79; V Bermondsey St Anne 79-81; V Stamford Baron *Pet* 83-89; P-in-c Tinwell 83-89; Hon Min Can Pet Cathl 84-89; Prec Worc Cathl 89-95; P-in-c Penshurst and Fordcombe *Roch* 95-05; R from 05. *The Rectory, High Street, Penshurst, Tonbridge TN11 8BN* T: (01892) 870316

HOLMES, Andrew Keith. b 69. Univ of Wales BEng 93. St Mich Coll Llan BTh 96. **d** 96 **p** 97. C Clydach *S & B* 96-97; C Swansea St Thos and Kilvey 98-00; P-in-c New Radnor and Llanfihangel Nantmelan etc 00-03; V Penrhiwceiber, Matthewstown and Ynysboeth *Llan* from 03; Voc Adv from 13. *The Vicarage, Penrhiwceiber, Mountain Ash CF45 3YF* T: (01443) 473716 E: frandrew@penrhiwceiber.plus.com

HOLMES (née PLATT), Mrs Anne Cecilia. b 46. Birm Univ BA 67 Anglia Ruskin Univ MA 09 Ox Univ DipEd 68 MInstGA 96. SAOMC 99. **d** 02 **p** 03. Chapl Headington Sch 02-04; Asst Chapl Oxon & Bucks Mental Health Partnership NHS Trust 04-09; NSM Marston w Elsfield *Ox* 02-12; PtO from 12. *Trinity Cottage, 27 Mill Street, Eynsham, Witney OX29 4JX* T: (01865) 881397 M: 07831-254727 E: administrator@acholmes.demon.co.uk

HOLMES, Anthony David Robert. b 38. Oak Hill Th Coll 75. **d** 77 **p** 78. C Iver *Ox* 77-81 and 00-05; V Bucklebury w Marlston 81-00; rtd 05; PtO *Ox* from 11. *16 Lawrence Close, Aylesbury HP20 1DY* T: (01296) 398945

HOLMES, Brian. b 41. NEOC 92. **d** 95 **p** 96. NSM Darlington St Matt and St Luke *Dur* 95-98; V 98-08; rtd 08; PtO *Dur* from 08. *2 Christchurch Close, Darlington DL1 2YL* T: (01325) 482255 E: revbholmes@tiscali.co.uk

HOLMES (née KENYON), Caroline Elizabeth. b 40. SRN 62. NOC 04. **d** 05 **p** 06. NSM Hale and Ashley *Ches* 05-10; PtO from 10. *1 Broomfield House, 134 Hale Road, Hale, Altrincham WA15 9HJ* T: 0161-233 0761 E: caroline.holmes@btinternet.com

HOLMES, Clive Horace. b 31. Ox NSM Course. **d** 83 **p** 84. NSM Cumnor *Ox* 83-98; PtO from 98. *108 New Road, East Hagbourne, Didcot OX11 9JZ* T: (01235) 811996

HOLMES, Craig Walter. b 72. Southn Univ BSc 95 R Holloway & Bedf New Coll Lon PhD 01 Fitzw Coll Cam BA 03 MA 07 CCC Cam MPhil 04. Ridley Hall Cam 01. **d** 07 **p** 08. C Egham *Guildf* 07-10; V Hanworth St Rich *Lon* from 10. *St Richard's Vicarage, 35 Forge Lane, Feltham TW13 6UN* T: (020) 8893 4935 E: craigholmes@strichardshanworth.org

HOLMES (formerly WARD), Mrs Elizabeth Joyce. b 42. Open Univ BA. WEMTC 04. **d** 06 **p** 07. OLM Painswick, Sheepscombe, Cranham, The Edge etc *Glouc* 06-11; rtd 11. *Arbour Cottage, Mount Hawke, Truro TR4 8EE* T: (01209) 890388

HOLMES, Frank. b 22. NW Ord Course 75. **d** 78 **p** 79. NSM Hyde St Geo *Ches* 78-81; C Poynton 81-87; rtd 87; PtO *Ches* from 87. *277 Stockport Road, Marple, Stockport SK6 6ES* T: 0161-449 9289

HOLMES, Geoffrey Robert. b 67. Nottm Univ BSc 89. Ridley Hall Cam BA 92. **d** 93 **p** 94. C Clifton St Jas *Sheff* 93-98; V Worsbrough St Thos and St Jas 98-05. *16 Vernon Road, Worsbrough, Barnsley S70 5BD* E: geoffrey.r.holmes@tesco.net

HOLMES, Grant Wenlock. b 54. St Steph Ho Ox BA 78 MA 83. **d** 79 **p** 80. C Benhilton *S'wark* 79-82; C-in-c S Kenton Annunciation CD *Lon* 82-86; Tutor Chich Th Coll 86-87; Bp's Dom Chapl *Chich* 86-88; V Mayfield 88-99; P-in-c Mark Cross 97-99; Asst Chapl Lewisham Hosp NHS Trust 99-01; Lead

Chapl Kingston Hosp NHS Trust Surrey 01-14; Hon C Barnes *S'wark* 01-06; V St Alb St Mary Marshalswick *St Alb* from 14. *The Old Rectory, Sumpter Yard, Holywell Hill, St Albans AL1 1BY* T: (01727) 890260 E: wenlockholmes@gmail.com

HOLMES, Gregory Thomas. b 73. Open Univ MSc 04 Cam Univ BTh 11. Ridley Hall Cam 09. **d** 11 **p** 12. C Fareham St Jo *Portsm* 11-14; V Nelson Victory Community Ch New Zealand from 14. *Victory Anglican Community Church, 238 Vanguard Street, Nelson South, 7010 New Zealand* E: revgtholmes@gmail.com

HOLMES, Jane Margaret. b 57. Ridley Hall Cam 05. **d** 07 **p** 08. C Stamford Ch Ch *Linc* 07-11; P-in-c Gayton, Gayton Thorpe, E Walton, E Winch etc *Nor* 11-15; P-in-c Grimston, Congham and Roydon 14-15; P-in-c Gt w Lt Massingham, Harpley, Rougham etc 14-15; TR Ashwicken w Leziate, Bawsey etc from 15. *The Rectory, Grimston Road, Gayton, King's Lynn PE32 1QA* T: (01553) 636227 E: jmh200@btinternet.com

HOLMES, Mrs Janet Ellen. b 61. Wolv Univ BSc 95 RCN MSc 99 RGN 83. Qu Coll Birm MA 09. **d** 09 **p** 10. C Hadley and Wellington Ch Ch *Lich* 09-12; C Cen Telford 11-12; TV from 12; Chapl Severn Hospice from 15. *Sutton Bank Farm, Sutton, Newport TF10 8DD* T: (01952) 813658 E: janeteholmes@btinternet.com

HOLMES, Canon John Robin. b 42. Leeds Univ BA 64. Linc Th Coll 64. **d** 66 **p** 67. C Wyther *Ripon* 66-69; C Adel 69-73; V Beeston Hill St Luke 73-76; V Holbeck 76-86; RD Armley 82-86; V Manston 86-93; Hon Can Ripon Cathl 89-98; Dioc Missr 93-98; Can Missr *Wakef* 98-07; rtd 07. *31 Detroit Avenue, Leeds LS15 8NU* T: 0113-264 2667 M: 07712-044364 E: canon.john@sky.com

HOLMES, Jonathan Michael. b 49. Qu Coll Cam BA 70 MA 74 VetMB 73 PhD 78 MRCVS 73. Ridley Hall Cam 87. **d** 88 **p** 89. Chapl Qu Coll Cam 88-13; Dean of Chpl 94-14; rtd 14; PtO *Ely* from 15. *Queens' College, Cambridge CB3 9ET* T: (01223) 335545 F: 335522 E: jmh38@cam.ac.uk

HOLMES, Lisa. b 65. **d** 13 **p** 14. OLM Ray Valley *Ox* from 13. *Holly Tree Cottage, Merton Road, Ambrosden, Bicester OX25 2LZ* T: (01869) 240435

HOLMES, Nigel Peter. b 48. Nottm Univ BTh 72 Lanc Univ CertEd 72 Lon Univ BD 76 Sheff Univ MEd 84. Kelham Th Coll. **d** 72 **p** 73. C Barrow St Matt *Carl* 72-75; C Derby St Bart 75-78; P-in-c Gt Barlow 78-84; V Carl St Herbert w St Steph 84-91; V Keswick St Jo 91-94; V Mexborough *Sheff* 94-97; P-in-c Nether Hoyland St Pet 97-98; P-in-c Nether Hoyland St Andr 97-98; V Hoyland 98-07; AD Tankersley 04-07; V Monk Bretton *Wakef* 07-09; rtd 09. *6 The Signals, Widdrington, Morpeth NE61 5QU* E: paxlives@btinternet.com

HOLMES, Mrs Patricia Ann. b 52. Bris Univ BA 89 MA 90. NOC 96. **d** 97 **p** 98. C Almondbury w Farnley Tyas *Wakef* 97-00; V Northowram *Leeds* 00-14; rtd 14. *17 Palatine Avenue, Lancaster LA1 4HD* E: patriciaholmes@sky.com

HOLMES, Peter Anthony. b 55. Univ of Wales (Ban) BA 77 Brighton Poly CertEd 78. Trin Coll Bris. **d** 88 **p** 89. C Croydon Ch Ch *S'wark* 88-93; V Norbiton from 93; RD Kingston 97-00. *The Vicarage, 21 Wolsey Close, Kingston upon Thames KT2 7ER* T: (020) 8942 8330 *or* 8546 3212 E: revdrock@yahoo.co.uk

HOLMES, Prof Peter Geoffrey. b 32. Bris Univ BSc 59 MSc 69 Leic Univ PhD 74 CEng FIEE. St Deiniol's Hawarden 74. **d** 76 **p** 77. NSM Glen Parva and S Wigston *Leic* 76-02; Prof Nottm Poly 85-92; Prof Nottm Trent Univ 92-96; rtd 02; PtO *Leic* from 02. *19 Windsor Avenue, Glen Parva, Leicester LE2 9TQ* T: 0116-277 4534 E: peterholmes@iee.org

HOLMES, Peter John. b 41. Reading Univ TCert 63 Open Univ BA 76 K Coll Lon BA 96 AKC 96 MA 97 Glas Univ PhD 02. St Steph Ho Ox 03. **d** 04 **p** 05. NSM Beaconsfield *Ox* 04-08; PtO 08-10; *Pet* from 11. *14 Bayley Close, Uppingham, Oakham LE15 9TG* T: (01572) 821834 E: peterholmes734@gmail.com *or* p.holmes4@me.com

HOLMES, Roger Cockburn. b 46. Jes Coll Ox BA 70 MA 84 Edin Univ BD 76. Edin Th Coll 73. **d** 84 **p** 85. Canada 84-88; R Ditchingham w Pirnough *Nor* 88-90; R Hedenham 88-90; R Broome 88-90; R Ditchingham, Hedenham and Broome 90-93; V Helmsley *York* 93-97; PtO *Wakef* 07. *1 Bishopgate, Howden, Goole DN14 7AD* T: (01430) 430880 E: fatherholmes@hotmail.com

HOLMES, Roy Grant. b 37. Ox NSM Course 83. **d** 86 **p** 87. NSM Wokingham St Paul *Ox* from 86. *58 Copse Drive, Wokingham RG41 1LX* T: 0118-978 4141

HOLMES, Stephen. b 54. St Andr Univ MTheol 84. Chich Th Coll 84. **d** 86 **p** 87. C Croydon St Jo *S'wark* 86-89; C Tewkesbury w Walton Cardiff *Glouc* 89-92; P-in-c Bournemouth St Luke *Win* 92-94; V 94-10; P-in-c N Stoneham and Bassett 10-15; rtd 15. *Address temp unknown*

HOLMES, Stephen John. b 50. CertEd 72. Trin Coll Bris 81 Sarum & Wells Th Coll 88. **d** 89 **p** 90. C Skegness and

Winthorpe *Linc* 89-93; P-in-c Mablethorpe w Trusthorpe 93-97; V Hadleigh St Barn *Chelmsf* 97-07; R Gt and Lt Leighs and Lt Waltham 07-14; rtd 14. *105 Grand Parade, Leigh-on-Sea SS9 1DW* E: familyholmes@hotmail.co.uk

HOLMES, Stephen Mark. b 65. St Andr Univ MA 87 Pontifical Univ Maynooth BD 04 Edin Univ PhD 13 CCC Cam PGCE 88 FSAScot 98. TISEC 11. d 04 p 04. In RC Ch 04-08; NSM Edin Old St Paul 12-14; P-in-c Edin St Marg 13-14; C Edin St Jo from 14. *11A Cornwall Street, Edinburgh EH1 2EQ* T: 0131-229 7565 M: 07584-091870 E: stephenmholmes@gmail.com

HOLMES, Susan. b 46. Hull Univ LLB 68 Univ of Wales LLM 00. d 06 p 07. NSM Scotby and Cotehill w Cumwhinton *Carl* 06-11; rtd 11. *Woodside, Great Corby, Carlisle CA4 8LL* T: (01228) 560617 E: susan@gtcorby.plus.com

HOLMES, Trevor. d 13. NSM Julianstown and Colpe w Drogheda and Duleek *M & K* from 13. *Address temp unknown*

HOLMES, William John. b 49. d 97 p 98. Aux Min Billy w Derrykeighan *Conn* 97-02; Aux Min Ballymoney w Finvoy and Rasharkin 02-14; NSM Killowen *D & R* from 14. *14 Glenlough Park, Coleraine BT52 1TY* T: (028) 7035 5993

HOLMYARD, Deborah. *See* FRAZER, Deborah

HOLNESS, Edwin Geoffrey Nicholas. b 39. RGN. Sarum Th Coll 68. d 71 p 72. C Upper Beeding and Bramber w Botolphs *Chich* 71-74; C Munster Square St Mary Magd *Lon* 74-75; PtO *Chich* 75-76 and 77-99; C Brighton Annunciation 76-77; Chapl Brighton Hosp Gp 77-94; Chapl R Sussex Co Hosp Brighton 77-94; P-in-c Southwick St Pet *Chich* 99-02; rtd 02. *41 Wivelsfield Road, Saltdean, Brighton BN2 8FP* T: (01273) 307025

HOLROYD, John Richard. b 54. Liv Univ BA 75 PGCE 77. Wycliffe Hall Ox 78. d 81 p 82. C Gt Stanmore *Lon* 81-84; Min Can, V Choral and Prec St E Cathl 84-89; TV Wolverton *Ox* 89-96; P-in-c Maidenhead St Luke 96-10; P-in-c Cotham St Sav w St Mary and Clifton St Paul *Bris* 10-14; V from 14. *12 Belgrave Road, Bristol BS8 2AB* T: 0117-973 1564 E: richardholroyd@mac.com

HOLROYD, Stephen Charles. b 56. UEA BA 79. St Jo Coll Nottm 84. d 87 p 88. C Barton Seagrave w Warkton *Pet* 87-91; V Eye 91-97; V Silsoe, Pulloxhill and Flitton *St Alb* 97-14; P-in-c The Stodden Churches from 14. *Stodden Rectory, High Street, Upper Dean, Huntingdon PE28 0ND* E: stephenholroyd@btinternet.com

HOLT, Mrs Claire Frances. b 66. Bris Univ BSc 88 Kingston Poly PGCE 89. STETS 02. d 05 p 06. C N Farnborough *Guildf* 05-12; P-in-c Tongham 12-14; V from 14. *The Vicarage, Poyle Road, Tongham, Farnham GU10 1DU* T: (01252) 782790 E: clairefholt@hotmail.com *or* claire@stpaulstongham.org.uk

HOLT, Canon David. b 44. St Jo Coll Dur BSc 67. d 70 p 71. C Blackley St Pet *Man* 70-73; C Radcliffe St Thos 73-74; C Radcliffe St Thos and St Jo 74-75; V Ashton St Pet 75-79; Dioc Youth Officer *Guildf* 80-85; V Bagshot 85-97; RD Surrey Heath 92-97; V Fleet 97-03; RD Aldershot 98-03; Hon Can Guildf Cathl 99-03; rtd 03; PtO *Guildf* from 03. *62 Lynwood Drive, Mytchett, Camberley GU16 6BY* T: (01276) 507538 M: 07974-354411 E: david.holt10@ntlworld.com

HOLT, Canon Douglas Robert. b 49. MA. Ridley Hall Cam. d 82 p 83. C Cambridge St Barn *Ely* 82-84; P-in-c 84-86; V 86-91; V Ealing St Mary *Lon* 91-98; Dioc Dir Strategy Support *Bris* 98-09; Can Res Bris Cathl 98-10; Hon Can and Dioc Dir Strategy Support 10-14; rtd 14; PtO *Bris* from 14; P-in-c Hove St Jo *Chich* from 14. *The Vicarage, 119 Holland Road, Hove BN3 1JS* T: (01273) 723029 E: douglas.holt49@gmail.com

HOLT, Francis Thomas. b 38. Edin Th Coll 79. d 81 p 82. C Cullercoats St Geo *Newc* 81-83; C Ponteland 83-86; Chapl Worc Coll of HE 86-89; R Worc St Clem 86-93; V Finstall 93-96; Chapl Menorca *Eur* 96-97; rtd 98; PtO *Worc* 97-13. *34 Meadow Grange, Berwick-upon-Tweed TD15 1NW*

HOLT, Jack Derek. b 38. Trin Coll Bris 71. d 73 p 74. C Daubhill *Man* 73-76; P-in-c Thornham w Gravel Hole 76-79; V 79-83; R Talke *Lich* 83-93; V Cotmanhay *Derby* 93-03; Chapl Derbyshire Mental Health Services NHS Trust 93-03; rtd 03; PtO *Lich* from 03. *31 Hatherton Close, Newcastle ST5 7SN* T: (01782) 560845

HOLT, James Edward. b 49. St Martin's Coll Lanc BA 94 PGCE 95. NOC 99. d 02 p 04. NSM Holme-in-Cliviger w Worsthorne *Blackb* 02-03; NSM Whalley 03-12; NSM W Pendleside from 12. *15 Wheatley Close, Fence, Burnley BB12 9QH* T: (01282) 778319 E: jimeholt@btinternet.com

HOLT, Mrs Lucinda Jane. b 65. Open Univ BSc 00. Wycliffe Hall Ox 01. d 03 p 04. C Newton Longville and Mursley w Swanbourne etc *Ox* 03-06; TV Riverside 06-08; V Eton w Eton Wick, Boveney and Dorney 08-13; R Poole *Sarum* from 13. *The Rectory, 10 Poplar Close, Poole BH15 1LP* T: (01202) 672694 E: revlucy@tiscali.co.uk

HOLT, Michael. b 38. Univ of Wales (Lamp) BA 61. St D Coll Lamp. d 63 p 64. C Stand *Man* 63-69; V Bacup St Jo 69-03;

AD Rossendale 98-00; rtd 03; PtO *Man* from 03. *22 Windermere Road, Bacup OL13 9DN* T: (01706) 877976

HOLT, Shirley Ann. d 98 p 99. OLM High Oak, Hingham and Scoulton w Wood Rising *Nor* 98-14; PtO from 14. *Westfield, 59 Church Lane, Wicklewood, Wymondham NR18 9QH* T: (01953) 603668 E: saholt@talk21.com

HOLT, Stephen Richard. b 64. Leeds Univ BA 11. Coll of Resurr Mirfield 09. d 11 p 12. C Gt Grimsby St Mary and St Jas *Linc* 11-14; C Boston from 14. *St Thomas's Vicarage, 2 Linley Drive, Boston PE21 7EJ* M: 07984-543892

HOLT, Stuart Henry. b 57. Bath Coll of HE BEd 78. Ridley Hall Cam 84. d 87 p 88. C Locks Heath *Portsm* 87-90; Chapl RAF 90-91; C Worthing St Geo *Chich* 91-93; C Portchester *Portsm* 93-95; PtO 02-03; P-in-c Soberton w Newtown 03-09; R Meon Bridge 09-15; AD Bishop's Waltham 09-14; P-in-c Fawley *Win* from 15. *The Rectory, 1 Sherringham Close, Fawley, Southampton SO45 1SQ* T: (023) 8089 3552 E: stuart.holt2@btopenworld.com

HOLT, Susan Mary. b 45. Coll of Ripon & York St Jo MA 98. NOC 97. d 97 p 98. NSM Longwood *Wakef* 97-00; NSM Liversedge w Hightown 00-12; NSM Heckmondwike (w Norristhorpe) and Liversedge *Leeds* from 12; NSM Hartshead, Hightown, Roberttown and Scholes from 12. *229/231 Stainland Road, Holywell Green, Halifax HX4 9AJ* T: (01422) 376481 E: susan@micromundi.net

✣**HOLTAM, The Rt Revd Nicholas Roderick.** b 54. Collingwood Coll Dur BA 75 K Coll Lon BD 78 AKC 78 FKC 05 Dur Univ MA 89 Hon DCL 05. Westcott Ho Cam 78. d 79 p 80 c 11. C Stepney St Dunstan and All SS *Lon* 79-83; Tutor Linc Th Coll 83-88; V Is of Dogs Ch Ch and St Jo w St Luke *Lon* 88-95; V St Martin-in-the-Fields 95-11; Bp Sarum from 11. *South Canonry, 71 The Close, Salisbury SP1 2ER* T: (01722) 334031 F: 413112 E: bishop.salisbury@salisbury.anglican.org

HOLTH, Oystein Johan. b 31. Open Univ BA 75. AKC 54. d 54 p 55. C Greenford H Cross *Lon* 54-56; Br N Borneo and Sarawak 56-63; E Malaysia 63-67; Chapl OHP and St Hilda's Sch Whitby 67-75; P-in-c Pimlico St Barn *Lon* 75-97; Ind Chapl 75-97; rtd 97; PtO *Lon* from 97. *13 Dollis Park, London N3 1HJ* T: (020) 8346 8131 E: steinandclare@holth.de

HOLY, Ravi. b 69. K Coll Lon MA 09. Trin Coll Bris BA 05. d 05 p 06. C Battersea St Luke *S'wark* 05-09; P-in-c Wye w Brook and Hastingleigh etc *Cant* 10-14; V Wye from 14. *The Vicarage, Cherry Garden Crescent, Wye, Ashford TN25 5AS* T: (01233) 812450 M: 07930-401963 E: raviholy@aol.com

HOLYER, Vincent Alfred Douglas. b 28. Ex Univ BA 54. Oak Hill Th Coll d 56 p 57. C Bethnal Green St Jas Less *Lon* 56-58; C Braintree *Chelmsf* 58-61; V Islington All SS *Lon* 61-65; R St Ruan w St Grade *Truro* 65-85; V Constantine 85-91; rtd 91; PtO *Truro* from 91. *32 Valley Gardens, Illogan, Redruth TR16 4EE* T: (01209) 211509

HOLZAPFEL, Mrs Christine Anne. b 53. Ex Univ BA 74 PGCE 75. WMMTC 04. d 07 p 08. C Worc SE 07-10; P-in-c Finstall 10-12; C Catshill and Dodford 10-12; TV Bromsgrove 12-14; TR from 14; V Dodford from 14. *The Vicarage, 15 Finstall Road, Bromsgrove B60 2EA* T: (01527) 579561 M: 07749-898698 E: cherrytree@tesco.net

HOLZAPFEL, Peter Rudolph. b 51. St Jo Coll Nottm 84. d 86 p 87. C St Jo in Bedwardine *Worc* 86-89; R Kempsey and Severn Stoke w Croome d'Abitot 99-11; rtd 11; PtO *Birm* from 12. *The Vicarage, 15 Finstall Road, Bromsgrove B60 2EA* T: (01527) 579561 E: cherrytree@tesco.net

HOMDEN, Peter David. b 56. Moorlands Coll BA 06. STETS 07. d 09 p 10. C Heatherlands St Jo *Sarum* from 09. *72 Alexandra Road, Poole BH14 9EW* M: 07841-699094 T: (01202) 241437 E: homdenhome@virginmedia.com

HOMEWOOD, Michael John. b 33. Wells Th Coll 69. d 71 p 72. C Ilfracombe H Trin *Ex* 71-72; C Ilfracombe, Lee and W Down 72-75; P-in-c Woolacombe 76-78; TV Ilfracombe, Lee, W Down, Woolacombe and Bittadon 78-82; TR S Molton w Nymet St George, High Bray etc 82-97; RD S Molton 93-95; rtd 97; PtO *Sarum* 97-13; *Cant* from 13. *1 Orlestone View, Hamstreet, Ashford TN26 2LB* T: (01233) 879511

HOMEWOOD, Peter Laurence de Silvie. b 58. Oriel Coll Ox BA 80 MA 84. St Steph Ho Ox 90. d 92 p 93. C Ruislip St Martin *Lon* 92-96; R Hayes St Mary from 96; P-in-c Hayes St Anselm 03-07. *The Rectory, 170 Church Road, Hayes UB3 2LR* T: (020) 8573 2470 E: peter@hayes-rectory.demon.co.uk

HOMFRAY, Kenyon Lee James. b 55. TCD BTh 99 MA 03 Univ of Wales (Cardiff) LLM 02. CITC 96. d 99 p 00. C Convoy w Monellan and Donaghmore *D & R* 99-02; I 02-05; I Bunclody w Kildavin, Clonegal and Kilrush *C & O* 05-11; rtd 12. *Garrankyle, Cloneen, Fethard, Co Tipperary, Republic of Ireland* E: homfrayk@eircom.net

HONES, Simon Anthony. b 54. Sussex Univ BSc 75. Qu Coll Birm. d 79 p 80. C Win Ch Ch 79-82; C Basing 82-88; Min

Chineham CD 88-90; V Surbiton St Matt *S'wark* 90-08; TR 08-11; P-in-c Marchwood *Win* from 11. *St John's Vicarage, Vicarage Road, Marchwood, Southampton SO40 4SX* T: (023) 8086 1496 E: simon.hones@btinternet.com

HONEY, Mrs Elizabeth Katherine. b 81. Keble Coll Ox MA 07. Wycliffe Hall Ox 06. **d** 09 **p** 10. C Furze Platt *Ox* 09-13; Pioneer Min *Derby* from 13. *119 Francis Street, Derby DE21 6DE* T: (01332) 299110 M: 07883-470158 E: revhoney@live.co.uk *or* benandbethderby@gmail.com

HONEY, Canon Frederick Bernard. b 22. Selw Coll Cam BA 48 MA 72. Wells Th Coll 48. **d** 50 **p** 51. C S'wark St Geo 50-52; C Claines St Jo *Worc* 52-55; V Wollaston 55-87; RD Stourbridge 72-83; Hon Can Worc Cathl 75-87; rtd 87. *38 Park Farm, Bourton-on-the-Water, Cheltenham GL54 2HF* T: (01451) 822218

HONEY, Canon Thomas David. b 56. Lon Univ BA 78. Ripon Coll Cuddesdon 80. **d** 83 **p** 84. C Mill End and Heronsgate w W Hyde *St Alb* 83-86; C Stepney St Dunstan and All SS *Lon* 86-89; TV High Wycombe *Ox* 89-95; P-in-c Headington Quarry 95-07; Can Res and Treas Ex Cathl 07-10; V Ex St Dav from 10. *St David's Vicarage, 95 Howell Road, Exeter EX4 4LH* T: (01392) 686000 E: vicar@stdavidschurchexeter.org.uk

HONEYMAN, Jennifer Mary. See LANE, Jennifer Mary

HONG KONG ISLAND, Bishop of. See KWONG KONG KIT, Peter

HONG KONG SHENG KUNG HUI, Archbishop of. See KWONG KONG KIT, The Most Revd Peter

HONNOR, Jonathan Michael Bellamy. b 62. Leeds Univ BA 84 Cant Ch Ch Univ Coll PGCE 89. Stavanger Sch of Miss and Th 98. **d** 00 **p** 00. Norway 00-03; C Leigh Park and Warren Park *Portsm* 03-08; P-in-c Aylesham w Adisham *Cant* 08-12; P-in-c Aylesham w Adisham and Nonington 12-13. *Address temp unknown*

HONNOR, Mrs Marjorie Rochefort. b 27. Birm Univ BA 48. Cranmer Hall Dur 79. **dss** 81 **d** 87 **p** 94. Church Oakley and Wootton St Lawrence *Win* 81-87; Par Dn 87-89; rtd 89; PtO *Win* 98-13. *15 Kernella Court, 51-53 Surrey Road, Bournemouth BH4 9HS* T: (01202) 761021

HONOR MARGARET, Sister. See McILROY, Honor Margaret

HONOUR, Colin Reginald. b 44. Lanc Univ CertEd 69 Man Univ AdDipEd 75 Newc Univ MEd 80. NOC 88. **d** 91 **p** 92. NSM Walmsley *Man* 91; C Middleton 92-94; R Holcombe 94-01; P-in-c Hawkshaw Lane 99-01; P-in-c Aldingham, Dendron, Rampside and Urswick *Carl* 01-03; R 03-09; rtd 09; PtO *Carl* from 10. *1 Crow Wood, Heversham, Milnthorpe LA7 7ER* T: (015395) 64357 E: cnchonour@btinternet.com

HONOUR, Derek Gordon. b 59. Bath Univ BSc 84. St Jo Coll Nottm. **d** 89 **p** 90. C High Wycombe *Ox* 89-91; C Brightside w Wincobank *Sheff* 91-94; P-in-c Dawley St Jerome *Lon* 94-01; C Derby St Alkmund and St Werburgh 01-05; V Stoke Hill *Guildf* 05-09; P-in-c Derby St Barn 09-13; V from 13. *St Barnabas' Vicarage, 122 Radbourne Street, Derby DE22 3BU* T: (01332) 342553 E: derekhonour@compuserve.com *or* dghonour@ad.co.uk

HONOUR, Canon Joanna Clare. b 61. Westmr Coll Ox BEd 83. St Jo Coll Nottm 86. **d** 89 **p** 94. Par Dn High Wycombe *Ox* 89-91; Par Dn Brightside w Wincobank *Sheff* 91-94; C 94; Dep Chapl HM Pris Wandsworth 95-97; Chapl HM Pris The Mount 97; NSM Dawley St Jerome *Lon* 96-01; Chapl HM Pris Foston Hall 01-05; Chapl HM Pris Coldingley 06-09; Chapl HM Pris Whatton from 09; Hon Can S'well Minster from 15. *HM Prison Whatton, New Lane, Whatton, Nottingham NG13 9FQ* T: (01949) 803200 F: 803201 E: jo.honour@hmps.gsi.gov.uk

HONOUR, Jonathan Paul. b 68. Ox Brookes Univ BSc 90 Greenwich Univ PGCE 91. St Jo Coll Nottm MA 98. **d** 99 **p** 00. C Tonbridge St Steph *Roch* 99-03; TV Woodley *Ox* 03-08; V Guernsey H Trin from 08. *Holy Trinity Vicarage, Brock Road, St Peter Port, Guernsey GY1 1RS* T: (01481) 724382 M: 07752-241255 E: jonhonour@googlemail.com

HOOD, Christopher Alan. b 69. Portsm Poly BA 92 UEA PGCE 93. Ridley Hall Cam 13. **d** 15. C Haughley w Wetherden and Stowupland *St E* from 15. *1 Church View, Haugley, Stowmarket IP14 3NU* M: 07584-291148 E: chrishood@live.co.uk

HOOD, Mrs Doreen. b 38. Open Univ BA 90 SRN 59 RFN 61. NEOC 90. **d** 93 **p** 94. NSM Cullercoats St Geo *Newc* 93-99; NSM Monkseaton St Pet 99-00; P-in-c Newc St Hilda 00-03; rtd 03. *24 Keswick Drive, North Shields NE30 3EW* T: 0191-253 1762

HOOD, Mrs Elizabeth Mary. b 57. Ex Univ BA 79. ERMC 05. **d** 08 **p** 09. C Boxmoor St Jo *St Alb* 08-12; TV Langelei from 12; AD Hemel Hempstead from 14. *The Vicarage, 14 Pancake Lane, Hemel Hempstead HP2 4NB* T: (01442) 264860 E: lizziehood@aol.com

HOOD, Miss Jennifer Louise. St Mich Coll Llan. **d** 10 **p** 11. C Glanogwen and Llanllechid w St Ann's and Pentir *Ban* 10-13; Chapl Salford R NHS Foundn Trust from 14. *Salford Royal NHS Foundation Trust, Hope Hospital, Stott Lane, Salford M6 8HD* T: 0161-789 7373 E: jenniferhood.7@hotmail.co.uk

HOOD, Mrs Linda. b 47. Leeds Univ BA 68. St Jo Coll Nottm 07. **d** 09 **p** 10. NSM Chase Terrace *Lich* from 09. *13 Mossbank Avenue, Burntwood WS7 4UN* T: (01543) 301728 M: 07786-987114 E: linda.hood@stjohnscommunitychurch.org.uk

HOOD, Peter Michael. b 47. Sheff Univ BSc 68. Wycliffe Hall Ox 70. **d** 73 **p** 74. C Soundwell *Bris* 73-76; P-in-c Walcot St Andr CD 76-77; TV Swindon St Jo and St Andr 77-80; V Esh and Hamsteels *Dur* 80-88; V Stockton St Paul 88-00; P-in-c Herrington 00-05; P-in-c 00-05; P-in-c Shiney Row 00-05; R Herrington, Penshaw and Shiney Row 05-07; Lic to Adn Sunderland and Houghton Deanery 07-12; rtd 12; PtO *Dur* from 12. *1 Victory Street East, Hetton le Hole, Houghton le Spring DH5 9DN* T: 0191-526 9187 E: peter.hood@rohlfinghood.freeserve.co.uk

HOOD, Stephen William. **d** 13 **p** 14. NSM New Milverton *Cov* from 13. *Millbrook House, Wasperton, Warwick CV35 8EB*

HOOD, Canon Thomas Henry Havelock. b 24. Chich Th Coll 51. **d** 54 **p** 55. C Stella *Dur* 54-57; Australia from 57; Hon Can Brisbane from 88; rtd 93. *18 Moonyean Street, Bellbird Park Qld 4300, Australia* T: (0061) (7) 3288 5106 E: havelock@gil.com.au

HOOGERWERF, John Constant. b 50. Bris Poly BA 85 MCIH 86. Oscott Coll (RC) 68. **d** 73 **p** 74. In RC Ch 73-84; NSM Davyhulme Ch Ch *Man* 84-93; PtO *Heref* 93-04; NSM Mold *St As* 04; LtO 04-10. *2 Llys y Foel, Mold CH7 1EX* T: (01352) 750701

HOOK, Canon Ian Kevin. b 57. Trin Coll Bris 93. **d** 95 **p** 96. C Dalton-in-Furness *Carl* 95-98; C Newbarns w Hawcoat 98-01; V Barrow St Mark from 01; RD Barrow 06-11; Hon Can Carl Cathl from 10. *St Mark's Vicarage, Rawlinson Street, Barrow-in-Furness LA14 1BX* T: (01229) 820405 E: ianhook@dsl.pipex.com

HOOK (née KAMINSKI), Mrs Julia Ann. b 55. WEMTC 07. **d** 10 **p** 11. TV Winchcombe *Glouc* from 10; TV from 14. *18 Ratcliff Lawns, Southam, Cheltenham GL52 3PA* T: (01242) 519346 M: 07715-953076 E: julia.hook@btinternet.com

HOOK, Neil. b 73. Univ of Wales (Swansea) BA 94 Univ of Wales (Cardiff) BD 96. St Mich Coll Llan 94. **d** 97 **p** 98. C Brecon St Mary and Battle w Llanddew *S & B* 97-99; Min Can Brecon Cathl 97-99; P-in-c Llanllyr-yn-Rhos w Llanfihangel Helygen 99-00; V Upper Wye 00-05; P-in-c Trallwng w Bettws Penpont w Aberyskir etc 05-09; P-in-c Cynog Honddu 08-09; V Dan yr Eppynt 10-12; V Builth and Llanddewi'r Cwm w Llangynog etc 12-15; V Buallt from 15. *The Vicarage, 1 North Road, Builth Wells LD2 3BT* T: (01982) 552355 E: hrhooky@gmail.com

HOOKWAY, John Leonard Walter. b 73. St Jo Coll Dur BSc 95. St Jo Coll Nottm MTh 04. **d** 04 **p** 05. C St Alb St Paul *St Alb* 04-07; C Howell Hill w Burgh Heath *Guildf* 07-11; V Ware Ch Ch *St Alb* from 11. *The Vicarage, 15 Hanbury Close, Ware SG12 7BZ* T: (01920) 463165 E: vicar@christchurchware.co.uk

HOOLE, Charles. b 33. St Aid Birkenhead 61. **d** 63 **p** 64. C Skerton St Luke *Blackb* 63-65; P-in-c Preston St Jas 65-69; V Lostock Hall 69-73; Chapl HM Pris Featherch 74-75; V St Annes St Marg *Blackb* 75-81; V S Shore St Pet 81-92; C Laneside 92-94; rtd 95; PtO *Blackb* 95-11. *32 Hanover Crescent, Blackpool FY2 9DL* T: (01253) 353564

HOOPER, Preb Derek Royston. b 33. St Edm Hall Ox BA 57 MA 65. Cuddesdon Coll 57. **d** 59 **p** 60. C Gt Walsingham *Nor* 59-62; C Townstall w Dartmouth *Ex* 62-65; V Lynton and Brendon 65-69; C Littleham w Exmouth 70-72; TV 72-79; R Wrington w Butcombe *B & W* 79-94; Preb Wells Cathl 93-94; rtd 94; PtO *Ex* from 95; *B & W* 95-00. *23 Dagmar Road, Exmouth EX8 2AN* T: (01395) 272831

HOOPER, Geoffrey Michael. b 39. MBE 00. Univ of Wales (Ban) MA 07. K Coll Lon 61. **d** 66 **p** 67. C Chesterfield St Mary and All SS *Derby* 66-69; Chapl RAF 69-74; P-in-c Hook Norton w Swerford and Wigginton *Ox* 74-80; P-in-c Gt Rollright 75-80; R Hook Norton w Gt Rollright, Swerford etc 80-82; Warden Mansf Ho Univ Settlement Plaistow 82-00; Dir 86-00; rtd 03; PtO *Ban* from 09. *2 Mount Pleasant, Corris, Machynlleth SY20 9RL* T: (01654) 761392 M: 07740-467426 E: geoffrey.hooper678@btinternet.com

HOOPER, Ian. b 44. St Jo Coll York CertEd 67. Trin Coll Bris. **d** 88 **p** 89. C Martlesham w Brightwell *St E* 88-92; R Pakenham w Norton and Tostock 92-09; RD Ixworth 03-09; rtd 09; PtO *St E* from 09; Dioc Retirement Officer from 10. *26 Drake Close, Stowmarket IP14 1UP* T: (01449) 770179 E: ianavrilhooper126@btinternet.com

✠HOOPER, The Rt Revd Michael Wrenford. b 41. Univ of Wales (Lamp) BA 63. St Steph Ho Ox 63. **d** 65 **p** 66 **c** 02. C Bridgnorth St Mary *Heref* 65-70; P-in-c Habberley 70-78; R 78-81; V Minsterley 70-81; RD Pontesbury 75-80; Preb Heref Cathl 81-02; V Leominster 81-85; TR 85-97; P-in-c Eyton 81-85; RD Leominster 81-97; P-in-c Eye, Croft w Yarpole and Lucton 91-97; Adn Heref 97-02; Suff Bp Ludlow 02-09; Adn Ludlow 02-09; rtd 09. *6 Avon Drive, Eckington, Pershore WR10 3BU* T: (01386) 751589
E: bishopmichael@btinternet.com

HOOPER, The Ven Paul Denis Gregory. b 52. Man Univ BA 75 Ox Univ BA 80 MA 87. Wycliffe Hall Ox 78. **d** 81 **p** 82. C Leeds St Geo *Ripon* 81-84; Dioc Youth Officer 84-87; Bp's Dom Chapl 87-95; Dioc Communications Officer 87-97; V Harrogate St Mark 95-09; AD Harrogate 05-09; Dir Clergy Development 09-12; Adn Leeds from 12; Hon Can Ripon Cathl from 08. *2 Wike Ridge Avenue, Leeds LS17 9NL*
E: paul.hooper@westyorkshiredales.anglican.org

HOOPER, Peter George. b 62. BSc PhD. EMMTC. **d** 06 **p** 07. C Melton Mowbray *Leic* 06-10; TR Bradgate Team 10-15; R Groby and Ratby from 15; R Peckleton from 15; Dioc Rural Officer from 11; AD Sparkenhoe E from 11. *23 Ferndale Drive, Ratby, Leicester LE6 0LH* T: 0116-239 4606

HOOPER, Sydney Paul. b 46. QUB BA 68 Lanc Univ CertEd 69. **d** 85 **p** 87. NSM Killaney w Carryduff *D & D* 85-91; LtO from 91; NSM Belfast St Chris 01-02; NSM Ballymacarrett 03-11; NSM Belfast St Donard from 11. *26 Manse Park, Carryduff, Belfast BT8 8RX* T: (028) 9081 5607 *or* 9056 6289

HOOTON, David James. b 50. St Kath Coll Liv CertEd 73. NOC 83. **d** 86 **p** 87. NSM Pemberton St Mark Newtown *Liv* 86-89; C Ashton-in-Makerfield St Thos 89-92; V Bryn 92-14; rtd 14. *Address temp unknown*

HOPE, Charles Henry. b 64. Regent's Park Coll Ox BA 87 MA 90 St Jo Coll Dur BA 90 FRGS 82. Cranmer Hall Dur. **d** 90 **p** 91. C Tynemouth St Jo *Newc* 90-94; V 94-03; P-in-c Prudhoe 03-07; V from 07; CF(V) from 94. *The Vicarage, 5 Kepwell Court, Prudhoe NE42 5PE* T: (01661) 836059 M: 07884-070619
E: charleshope@btopenworld.com

HOPE, Colin Frederick. b 49. St Mich Coll Llan 73. **d** 76 **p** 77. C Warrington St Elphin *Liv* 76-80; V Newton-le-Willows 80-84; CSWG from 84; LtO *Chich* from 88. *The Monastery, Crawley Down, Crawley RH10 4LH* T: (01342) 712034

HOPE, Edith. b 43. Lanc Univ MA 86 SRN 64 SCM 66. Wycliffe Hall Ox 89. **d** 91 **p** 94. Par Dn Droylsden St Mary *Man* 91-94; Par Dn Ecclesall *Sheff* 94; C from 01; V Crosspool 01-08; rtd 08. *46 Gisborne Road, Sheffield S11 7HB* T: 0114-263 1230
E: edithhope@btinternet.com

HOPE, Robert. b 36. Dur Univ BSc 61. Clifton Th Coll 61. **d** 63 **p** 64. C Woking St Mary *Guildf* 63-66; C Surbiton Hill Ch Ch *S'wark* 66-68; Th Students' Sec IVF 68-71; Hon C Wallington *S'wark* 69-71; C Ox St Ebbe w St Pet 71-74; V Walshaw Ch Ch *Man* 74-87; TR Radipole and Melcombe Regis *Sarum* 87-93; rtd 93; PtO *St D* from 93. *1A Swiss Valley, Felinfael, Llanelli SA14 8BS* T: (01554) 759199

HOPE, Canon Susan. b 49. St Jo Coll Dur BA 83 Sheff Univ MA 04. Cranmer Hall Dur 80. **dss** 83 **d** 87 **p** 94. Boston Spa *York* 83-86; Brightside w Wincobank *Sheff* 86-97; Par Dn 87-89; Dn-in-c 89-94; V 94-97; V Chapeltown 97-02; Dioc Missr 02-07; RD Tankersley 00-02; Hon Can Sheff Cathl 00-09; Dir Tr Wilson Carlile Coll of Evang 07-08; P-in-c Shipley St Paul *Bradf* 09-14; V Leeds from 14; Dioc Adv in Evang from 09; Six Preacher Cant Cathl 99-09; Hon Can Bradf Cathl from 12. *31 South Edge, Shipley BD18 4RA* T: (01274) 583652 M: 07736-774937 E: shope12443@aol.com

HOPE-BELL, Mrs Vanessa Anne. b 45. TCD BA 67 Univ of Wales (Swansea) MEd 98. **d** 14 **p** 15. NSM Catheiniog *St D* from 14. *The Mill House, Llansadwrn, Llanwrda SA19 8LW* T: (01550) 777239 E: v.hopebell@btinternet.com

✠HOPE OF THORNES, The Rt Revd and Rt Hon Lord (David Michael). b 40. PC 91 KCVO 95. Nottm Univ BA 62 Linacre Ho Ox DPhil 65 Hon FGCM 94. St Steph Ho Ox 62. **d** 65 **p** 66 **c** 85. C W Derby St Jo *Liv* 65-67 and 68-70; Chapl Bucharest *Eur* 67-68; V Orford St Andr *Liv* 70-74; Prin St Steph Ho Ox 74-82; V St Marylebone All SS *Lon* 82-85; Master of Guardians Shrine of Our Lady of Walsingham 82-93; Bp Wakef 85-91; Bp Lon 91-95; Dean of HM Chpls Royal and Prelate of OBE 91-95; Abp York 95-05; rtd 05; P-in-c Ilkley St Marg *Bradf* 05-06; Hon Asst Bp Bradf 05-14; Hon Asst Bp Eur 07-12; Hon Asst Bp Blackb from 08. *35 Hammerton Drive, Hellifield, Skipton BD23 4LZ* E: dmhhellifield@gmail.com

HOPEWELL, Canon Jeffery Stewart. b 52. Leic Univ BA 75 ACA 79. EMMTC 82. **d** 85 **p** 86. NSM Houghton on the Hill w Keyham *Leic* 85-88; NSM Houghton-on-the-Hill, Keyham and Hungarton 88-91; C Syston 91-93; TV 93-97; Bp's Ecum Adv 91-97; P-in-c Wymeswold and Prestwold w Hoton 97-04;

V Old Dalby, Nether Broughton, Saxelbye etc 04-15; Dioc Ecum Officer 03-06; Hon Can Leic Cathl 14-15; rtd 15; PtO *Leic* from 15. *23 Weare Close, Billesdon, Leicester LE7 9DY* T: 0116-259 9760 E: jshopewell@btinternet.com

HOPKIN, David James. b 67. Birm Univ BTh 94 Univ of Wales MA 14. Ripon Coll Cuddesdon 98. **d** 99 **p** 00. C Wickford and Runwell *Chelmsf* 99-02; TV Penistone and Thurlstone *Wakef* 02-06; TR 06-14; TR *Sheff* from 14. *The Vicarage, Shrewsbury Road, Penistone, Sheffield S36 6DY* T: (01226) 370954 *or* 370006 E: david.hopkin@sheffield.org

HOPKINS, Mrs Angela Joan. b 42. Bp Otter Coll Chich CertEd 64. S Dios Minl Tr Scheme 92. **d** 95 **p** 96. NSM Kingsbury H Innocents *Lon* 95-13; PtO from 13. *3 Regal Way, Harrow HA3 0RZ* T: (020) 8907 1045
E: ahopkins762@btinternet.com

HOPKINS, Miss Barbara Agnes. b 28. Lon Univ BSc 60 Imp Coll Lon MPhil 67. St Alb Minl Tr Scheme 82. **dss** 85 **d** 87. Bedford All SS *St Alb* 85-86; Chapl Asst Bedf Gen Hosp 86-88; Bedford St Mich *St Alb* 86-88; Hon Par Dn 87-88; Chapl Asst N Lincs Mental Health Unit 89-91; rtd 91; PtO *Linc* 93-95. *6 Olsen Court, Olsen Rise, Lincoln LN2 4UZ* T: (01522) 513359

HOPKINS, Brenda Alison. b 63. St Martin's Coll Lanc BA 95 Anglia Poly Univ MA 97. Westcott Ho Cam 95. **d** 97 **p** 98. C Camberwell St Geo *S'wark* 97-00; Chapl Nor City Coll of F&HE 00-03. *Rose Tree Cottage, The Green, Stokesby, Great Yarmouth NR29 3EX* E: bhopkins@ccn.ac.uk

HOPKINS, Christopher Freeman. b 41. Dur Univ BA 63. Wells Th Coll 63. **d** 65 **p** 66. C Spring Park *Cant* 65-69; C Mafeking S Africa 69-70; R Potchefstroom 70-78; LtO Botswana 78-81; R Beckley and Peasmarsh *Chich* 81-12; rtd 12. *Green Leas, Udimore Road, Broad Oak, Rye TN31 6DG* T: (01424) 883024 E: fr-christopher_hopkins@bigfoot.com

HOPKINS, Christopher John. b 61. Trin Coll Bris 11. **d** 13 **p** 14. C Somerton w Compton Dundon, the Charltons etc *B & W* from 13. *Greenbank House, 42 High Street, Street BA16 0EQ* T: (01458) 448250

HOPKINS, Gillian Frances. b 55. Bedf Coll Lon BA 76 SS Mark & Jo Univ Coll Plymouth PGCE 77 Cam Inst of Educn MA 91. NTMTC BA 07. **d** 07 **p** 08. C Wickford and Runwell *Chelmsf* 07-10; TV Waltham H Cross from 10. *15 Deer Park Way, Waltham Abbey EN9 3YN* E: gill_hopkins@yahoo.co.uk

HOPKINS, Henry Charles. b 46. RD 87. Edin Th Coll 65. **d** 71 **p** 72. C Dundee St Salvador *Bre* 71-74; C Dundee St Martin 71-74; Chapl RNVR 72-81; R Monifieth *Bre* 74-78; Chapl Miss to Seamen Kenya 78-85; Singapore 85-92; Offg Chapl NZ Defence Force 89-92; Chapl Miss to Seamen Teesside 92-94; V Middlesbrough St Thos *York* 94-97; V N Thornaby from 97. *St Paul's Vicarage, 60 Lanehouse Road, Thornaby, Stockton-on-Tees TS17 8EA* T/F: (01642) 868086
E: harry.hopkins@ntlworld.com

HOPKINS, Hugh. b 33. TCD BA. **d** 62 **p** 63. C Ballymena w Ballyclug *Conn* 62-64; C Belfast Ch Ch 64-67; I Ballintoy 67-72; I Belfast St Ninian 72-81; I Mossley 81-86; I Ballywillan 86-96; Can Belf Cathl 94-96; rtd 96. *2 Bush Gardens, Ballyness, Bushmills BT57 8AE* T: (028) 2073 2981

HOPKINS, Ian Richard. b 70. Collingwood Coll Dur BA 92 Ox Univ BTh 00. **d** 00 **p** 01. C Edin St Thos 00-04; I 04-13; C Haydock St Mark *Liv* from 13. *11 Wagon Lane, Haydock, St Helens WA11 0HZ* T: (01744) 302265
E: info@stmarkshaydock.com

HOPKINS, John Dawson. b 39. Chich Th Coll 85. **d** 87 **p** 88. C Walker *Newc* 87-89; C Newc St Fran 89-92; V Horton 92-00; rtd 00; PtO *Newc* from 01. *Amen Cottage, 31 High Fair, Wooler NE71 6PA* T: (07790) 915763

HOPKINS, Kenneth Victor John. b 45. Univ Coll Lon BA 66 Lon Univ BD 69 Hull Univ PhD 84. Tyndale Hall Bris 66. **d** 69 **p** 70. C S Mimms Ch Ch *Lon* 69-72; C Branksome St Clem *Sarum* 72-75; P-in-c Trowbridge St Thos 75-76; V 76-81; R Wingfield w Rowley 76-81; Chapl and Lect NE Surrey Coll of Tech 81-84; Hd Student Services Essex Inst of HE 84-88; Kingston Poly 88-92; Kingston Univ 92-98; Dean of Students 98-03; Pro Vice-Chan 04-06; rtd 06. *Quarry Cottage, Duke Street, Withington, Hereford HR1 3QD* T: (01432) 850933
E: ken_hopkins@dsl.pipex.com

HOPKINS, Lionel. b 48. MBE 14. Open Univ BA 82. St D Coll Lamp. **d** 71 **p** 72. C Llandeilo Tal-y-bont *S & B* 71-74; C Morriston 74-78; P-in-c Waunarlwydd 78-80; V 80-86; Youth Chapl 84-86; V Llangyfelach 86-96; P-in-c Swansea Ch Ch 96-00; Chapl HM Pris Swansea 96-13; rtd 13. *1051 Llangyfelach Road, Tirdeunaw, Swansea SA5 7HY*

HOPKINS, Mark James. b 86. Fitzw Coll Cam MA 10. Trin Coll Bris 10. **d** 13 **p** 14. C Warley Woods *Birm* from 13. *21 Upper St Mary's Road, Smethwick B67 5JR* M: 07745-805478 E: revmarkhopkins@gmail.com

HOPKINS, Neil James. b 72. Brunel Univ BTh 97 MTh 01. Trin Coll Bris 10. **d** 12 **p** 13. C Portswood Ch Ch *Win* from 12. *6 Royston Close, Southampton SO17 1TB* T: (023) 8058 3880 M: 07557-908383 E: neiljuleshopkins@me.com *or* neil.hopkins@highfield.org.uk

HOPKINS, Miss Patricia Mary. b 46. Kingston Poly BEd 78. Trin Coll Bris 83. **dss** 85 **d** 87 **p** 94. Gorleston St Andr *Nor* 85-88; C 87-88; C Woking St Jo *Guildf* 88-90; Team Dn Barnham Broom *Nor* 90-94; TV 94-97; V Otford *Roch* 97-07; rtd 07; PtO *Nor* from 08. *Hill Cottage, Broomhill, East Runton, Cromer NR27 9PF* T: (01263) 512338 E: popkins@greenbee.net

HOPKINS, Peter. b 54. Nottm Univ BSc 75 Imp Coll Lon MSc 79. Oak Hill Th Coll BA 86. **d** 86 **p** 87. C Gee Cross *Ches* 86-90; R Gt Gonerby *Linc* 90-95; R Barrowby and Gt Gonerby from 95; RD Grantham 01-09. *The Rectory, 7 Long Street, Great Gonerby, Grantham NG31 8LN* T: (01476) 565737 E: peterhoppy@worldonline.co.uk

HOPKINS, Richard Clive John. b 74. Nottm Univ BA 95 Ex Univ PGCE 97. Wycliffe Hall Ox BTh 02. **d** 02 **p** 03. C Duffield *Derby* 02-05; C Duffield and Lt Eaton 05-06; P-in-c Sileby, Cossington and Seagrave *Leic* 06-09; R from 09. *The Rectory, 11 Mountsorrel Lane, Sileby, Loughborough LE12 7NF* T: (01509) 812493 E: rectorscs@btinternet.com

HOPKINS, Robert James Gardner. b 42. Bris Univ BSc 64 ACA 76 FCA 81. St Alb Minl Tr Scheme. **d** 79 **p** 80. NSM Chorleywood Ch Ch *St Alb* 79-83; NSM Parr Mt *Liv* 83-97; NSM Crookes St Thos *Sheff* 97-09; NSM Philadelphia St Thos 09-15; PtO from 15; Dir Angl Ch Planting Initiatives from 92; Missr Fresh Expressions from 05. *70 St Thomas Road, Sheffield S10 1UX* T: 0114-267 8266 *or* 278 9378 E: hopkins.the@gmail.com

HOPKINS, Victor John. b 44. UEA LLB 82. CBDTI 06. **d** 07 **p** 08. NSM Sedbergh, Cautley and Garsdale *Bradf* 07-12; NSM *Carl* 12-14; PtO *St E* from 15; *Pet* from 15. *94 Chediston Street, Halesworth IP19 8BJ* T: (01986) 875934 E: csninefour@btinternet.com

HOPKINSON, The Ven Barnabas John. b 39. Trin Coll Cam BA 63 MA 67. Linc Th Coll 63. **d** 65 **p** 66. C Langley All SS and Martyrs *Man* 65-67; C Cambridge St St Mary w St Mich *Ely* 67-71; Asst Chapl Charterhouse Sch Godalming 71-75; P-in-c Preshute *Sarum* 75-76; TV Marlborough 76-81; RD 77-81; TR Wimborne Minster and Holt 81-86; Can and Preb Sarum Cathl 83-04; RD Wimborne 85-86; Adn Sarum 86-98; P-in-c Stratford sub Castle 87-98; Adn Wilts 98-04; rtd 04; PtO *B & W* from 09. *Tanners Cottage, 22 Frog Street, Bampton, Tiverton EX16 9NT* T: (01398) 331611 E: barneyesme@onetel.net

HOPKINSON, Benjamin Alaric. b 36. Trin Coll Ox BA 59. Chich Th Coll 59. **d** 61 **p** 62. C Pallion *Dur* 61-66; Rhodesia 66-67; Botswana 67-74; Hon C Sherwood *S'well* 74-77; Hon C Carrington 74-77; V Lowdham 77-85; R Whitby *York* 85-95; Miss to Seafarers from 85; V Stainton w Hilton *York* 95-01; Chapl Cleveland Constabulary 95-01; rtd 01; PtO *Newc* from 01. *1 Watershaugh Road, Warkworth, Morpeth NE65 0TT* T/F: (01665) 714213 E: dumela@dial.pipex.com

HOPKINSON, Colin Edward. b 57. BA LLB. Ridley Hall Cam. **d** 84 **p** 85. C Chadwell *Chelmsf* 84-87; C Canvey Is 87-90; P-in-c E Springfield 90-98; RD Chelmsf N 95-99; R Langdon Hills from 98. *The Rectory, 105A Berry Lane, Langdon Hills, Basildon SS16 6AN* T: (01268) 542156 E: cchopkinson@aol.com

HOPKINSON, David John. b 47. Ox NSM Course. **d** 79 **p** 80. NSM Wardington *Ox* 79; Hon C Didcot St Pet 80-83; C Headingley *Ripon* 83-87; P-in-c Leeds All So 87-91; R Middleton Tyas w Croft and Eryholme 91-95; V Leeds Belle Is St Jo and St Barn 95-98; rtd 98; PtO *Ripon* 98-06; *Leeds* from 07. *11 Old Well Head, Halifax HX1 2BN* T: (01422) 361226

HOPKINSON, William Humphrey. b 48. Lon Univ BSc 69 Dur Univ MA 78 Nottm Univ MPhil 84 Man Poly MSc 90 California State Univ MEd 00 ARIC 73. Cranmer Hall Dur. **d** 77 **p** 78. C Normanton *Derby* 77-80; C Sawley 80-82; V Birtles *Ches* 82-87; Dir Past Studies NOC 82-94; Dir Course Development 90-94; CME Officer *Ches* 87-94; P-in-c Tenterden St Mich *Cant* 94-96; Dir Min and Tr 94-02; Hon Can Cant Cathl 01-02; PtO 03-06; World Faith Manager Harmondsworth Immigration Removal Cen 03-05; Registrar Lon Academy of HE 05-06; Manager Independent Newham Users Forum 07; Asst Prof California State Univ USA from 07; rtd 13. *91 Chobham Road, London E15 1LX* M: 07057-111933 E: bill@bhopkinson.co.uk

HOPLEY, David. b 37. Wells Th Coll 62. **d** 65 **p** 66. C Frome St Jo *B & W* 65-68; R Staunton-on-Arrow w Byton and Kinsham *Heref* 68-81; P-in-c Lingen 68-81; P-in-c Aymestrey and Leinthall Earles w Wigmore etc 72-81; R Buckland Newton, Long Burton etc *Sarum* 81-02; rtd 02; PtO *B & W* from 07. *Sunnyside, Clatworthy, Taunton TA4 2EH* T: (01984) 623842

HOPLEY, Gilbert. b 40. Univ of Wales (Ban) BA 62. St D Coll Lamp LTh 65. **d** 65 **p** 66. C St As and Tremeirchion 65-73; Warden Ch Hostel Ban 73-76; Chapl Univ of Wales (Ban) 73-76; V Meifod and Llangynyw *St As* 76-79; Chapl St Marg Sch Bushey 79-87; Hd Master St Paul's Cathl Choir Sch 87-97. *73 The Larches, London N13 5QD*

HOPPER, Peter Edward. b 60. **d** 99 **p** 00. OLM Bermondsey St Mary w St Olave, St Jo etc *S'wark* 99-05. *56 Reverdy Road, London SE1 5QD* T: (020) 7237 1543 *or* 7525 1831 E: phopper@phopper.screaming.net

HOPPER, Peter John. b 37. Univ Coll Dur BSc 59 Lon Univ PGCE 60. NOC 89. **d** 91 **p** 91. C Aston cum Aughton and Ulley *Sheff* 91-93; C Aston cum Aughton w Swallownest, Todwick etc 93-94; P-in-c Braithwell w Bramley 94-95; TV Bramley and Ravenfield w Hooton Roberts etc 95-00; rtd 00; PtO *Worc* from 00. *21 Hornsby Avenue, Worcester WR4 0PN* T: (01905) 731618 E: peterjhopper@supanet.com

HOPPER, Canon Robert Keith. b 45. Cranmer Hall Dur 74. **d** 77 **p** 78. C Oxclose *Dur* 77-80; C Hebburn St Jo 80-82; V Lobley Hill 82-04; P-in-c Marley Hill 02-04; V Hillside from 04; Hon Can Dur Cathl from 09. *All Saints' Vicarage, Rowanwood Gardens, Gateshead NE11 0DP* T/F: 0191-460 4409 M: 07960-754744 E: canonbob@durham.uk.net

HOPPERTON, Thomas. b 33. Chich Th Coll 71. **d** 73 **p** 74. C Cheam *S'wark* 73-89; P-in-c St Alb 76-89; P-in-c Rotherhithe St Kath w St Barn 89-92; P-in-c S Bermondsey St Bart 91-92; P-in-c Bermondsey St Kath w St Bart 92; V 92-01; rtd 01; PtO *York* 03-11. *8 Croft Heads, Sowerby, Thirsk YO7 1ND* T: (01845) 524210 E: fathertom21@aol.com

HOPTHROW, Mrs Elizabeth Rosemary Gladys. b 45. **d** 01 **p** 02. NSM Aylesham w Adisham *Cant* 01-04; NSM Nonington w Wymynswold and Goodnestone etc 01-04; NSM Barham w Bishopsbourne and Kingston 04-11; Chapl Pilgrims Hospice Cant 01-11; PtO *Cant* from 11. *146 The Street, Kingston, Canterbury CT4 6JQ* T: (01227) 830070 *or* 812610 M: 07977-754920 E: lizziehopthrow@quista.net

HOPWOOD, Adrian Patrick. b 37. N Lon Poly BSc 61 CBiol MSB MCIWEM. Ox Min Course 87. **d** 90 **p** 91. NSM Chesham Bois *Ox* 90-93; NSM Amersham 93-95; NSM Ridgeway 95-05; rtd 05; PtO *B & W* from 06. *15 Waverley, Somerton TA11 6SH* T: (01458) 274527 E: adrian@proceff.f9.co.uk

HOPWOOD OWEN, Mrs Karen. b 58. Padgate Coll of Educn CertEd 79 St Martin's Coll Lanc DASE 90. **d** 95 **p** 96. OLM Peel *Man* 95-99; OLM Walkden and Lt Hulton 99-13; TV Worsley from 13. *8 Landrace Drive, Worsley, Manchester M28 1UY* M: 07964-663225 E: karen.h.owen@ntlworld.com

HORAN, Joan Anne. b 53. BA 74 DipEd 75. **d** 05 **p** 06. Australia 05-09; R Grimshoe *Ely* from 09. *The Rectory, 7 Oak Street, Feltwell, Thetford IP26 4DD* T: (01842) 828034 E: joanhoran123@btinternet.com

HORAN, John Champain. b 52. WMMTC 95. **d** 98 **p** 99. NSM Leckhampton SS Phil and Jas w Cheltenham St Jas *Glouc* 98-08; Dioc Communications Officer 01-02. *38 Leckhampton Road, Cheltenham GL53 0BB* T: (01242) 235370 E: horan.jc@btinternet.com

HORBURY, Prof William. b 42. Oriel Coll Ox BA 64 MA 67 Clare Coll Cam BA 66 PhD 71 DD 00 FBA 97. Westcott Ho Cam 64. **d** 69 **p** 70. Fell Clare Coll Cam 68-72; CCC Cam from 78; R Gt w Lt Gransden *Ely* 72-78; Lect Div Cam Univ 84-98; Prof Jewish and Early Chr Studies from 98; P-in-c Cambridge St Botolph *Ely* from 90. *5 Grange Road, Cambridge CB3 9AS* T: (01223) 363529 F: 462751 E: wh10000@cam.ac.uk

HORDER, Mrs Catharine Joy. b 51. Battersea Coll of Educn CertEd 72 UWE BA 98. S Dios Minl Tr Scheme 02. **d** 95 **p** 96. C Burrington and Churchill *B & W* 95-00; TV Yatton Moor 00-11; rtd 11. *The Sanctuary, Bridford, Exeter EX6 7HS* T: (01647) 252750 E: cathy.horder@btinternet.com

HORDER, Peter Alan Trahair. b 43. **d** 97 **p** 98. OLM Madron *Truro* 97-01; OLM Gulval 99-01; OLM Gulval and Madron 01-13; rtd 13. *Kourion, 38 Boscathnoe Way, Heamoor, Penzance TR18 3JS* T: (01736) 360813

HORDERN, Peter John Calveley. b 35. Jes Coll Cam BA 59 MA 64 McMaster Univ Ontario PhD 72. Linc Th Coll 59. **d** 61 **p** 62. C Billingham St Aid *Dur* 61-65; Canada from 65; rtd 00. *346 Aberdeen Avenue, Brandon MB R7A 1N4, Canada* T: (001) (204) 727 3324

HORE (formerly HART), Debbie. b 56. **d** 11. NSM St Marylebone St Paul *Lon* from 11. *18C Chesham Flats, Brown Hart Gardens, London W1K 6WP* M: 07985-649120 E: deacondebs@gmail.com

HORE, Leslie Nicholas Peter. b 40. SWMTC 99. **d** 02 **p** 03. OLM Treverbyn *Truro* 02-10; rtd 10. *Tremore, Hallaze Road, Penwithick, St Austell PL26 8YW* T: (01726) 851750 E: peterhore@hotmail.co.uk

HORLESTON, Kenneth William. b 50. Oak Hill Th Coll BA 86. **d** 86 **p** 87. C Wednesfield Heath *Lich* 86-89; V Blagreaves *Derby* 89-00; P-in-c Horsley 00-02; P-in-c Denby 00-02;

V Horsley and Denby 02-10; C Morley w Smalley and Horsley Woodhouse 06-07; rtd 10. *11 Pegasus Way, Hilton, Derby DE65 5HW* T: (01283) 735600 E: kenhorleston@tiscali.co.uk *or* kwh@gmx.co.uk

HORLOCK, Andrew John. b 51. Bath Univ BSc 74 Open Univ MPhil 89 Nottm Univ PhD 99. Ridley Hall Cam 03. **d** 05 **p** 06. C Crich and S Wingfield *Derby* 05-08; P-in-c Lugano *Eur* 08-15; rtd 15. E: andyhorlock@hotmail.com

HORLOCK, The Very Revd Brian William. b 31. OBE 78. Univ of Wales (Lamp) BA 55. Chich Th Coll 55. **d** 57 **p** 58. C Chiswick St Nic w St Mary *Lon* 57-61; C Witney *Ox* 61-62; V N Acton St Gabr *Lon* 62-68; Chapl Oslo w Bergen, Trondheim and Stavanger *Eur* 68-89; RD Scandinavia 75-79; Adn 80-89; Hon Can Brussels Cathl 80-89; Dean Gib 89-98; Chapl Gib 89-98; rtd 98; PtO *Eur* from 98; Hon C R Wootton Bassett *Sarum* from 98. *1 Richard's Close, Royal Wootton Bassett, Swindon SN4 7LE* T: (01793) 848344 F: 848378

HORLOCK, Louise Frances. b 49. **d** 10 **p** 11. NSM Hampreston *Sarum* from 10. *35 Award Road, Wimborne BH21 7NT* T: (01202) 855356 E: lhorlock@hotmail.co.uk

HORLOCK, Peter Richard. b 76. UWE BA 97. Oak Hill Th Coll BA 04. **d** 04 **p** 05. C Rusholme H Trin *Man* 04-12; Missr to Business Community from 12; C Man St Ann from 12. *63 Burnside Drive, Burnage, Manchester M19 2NA* M: 07890-860022 Alt E-mail pete@ministry2business.co.uk *or* petehorlock@googlemail.com

HORLOCK, Timothy Edward. b 72. Anglia Poly Univ BSc 94 Bath Univ PGCE 96. Ridley Hall Cam 05. **d** 07 **p** 08. C Bedford Ch Ch *St Alb* 07-10; P-in-c Stevenage St Pet Broadwater 10-14; V from 14; RD Stevenage from 13. *St Peter's House, 1 The Willows, Stevenage SG2 8AN* M: 07787-968843 T: (01438) 221024 E: alextim_horlock@hotmail.com *or* vicar@stpeter-stevenage.co.uk

HORN, Colin Clive. b 39. CEng MIMechE FEI. Cant Sch of Min. **d** 83 **p** 84. NSM Yalding w Collier Street *Roch* 83-91; V Kemsing w Woodlands 91-98; RD Shoreham 94-98; rtd 99; PtO *B & W* from 00. *Saw Mill Cottage, Leigh Street, Leigh upon Mendip, Radstock BA3 5QQ* T/F: (01373) 812736 M: 07885-523190 E: colinhorn@hotmail.com

HORN, David Henry. *See* RANDOLPH-HORN, David Henry

HORNBY (née CHRISTIAN), Mrs Helen. b 47. K Coll Lon BA 68 AKC 68 Lon Inst of Educn PGCE 69. Cranmer Hall Dur 00. **d** 02 **p** 03. C Briercliffe *Blackb* 02-07; C Blackpool St Jo 07-11; C Layton and Staining 11-12; rtd 12. *2 Arnside Avenue, Lytham St Annes FY8 3SA* T: (01253) 711215 E: revhelenhornby@yahoo.co.uk

HORNBY, Matthew. b 75. **d** 13 **p** 14. C S Barrow *Carl* from 13. *The Vicarage, 98A Roose Road, Barrow-in-Furness LA13 9RL* M: 07903-136128 T: (01229) 877755 E: hornbymatt@gmail.com

HORNE, Brian Edward. b 37. Lon Univ BSc 62 PhD 78 CEng 68 MRAeS 68 MIET 68 EurIng 92. WEMTC 92. **d** 95 **p** 96. OLM Cheltenham St Mark *Glouc* 95-12; rtd 12. *87A Rowanfield Road, Cheltenham GL51 8AF* T: (01242) 236786 E: lynbrihorne@btinternet.com

HORNE, Mona Lyn Denison. b 38. Gipsy Hill Coll of Educn TCert 58. WEMTC 98. **d** 99 **p** 00. OLM Cheltenham St Mark *Glouc* 99-12; rtd 12. *87A Rowanfield Road, Cheltenham GL51 8AF* T: (01242) 236786 E: lynbrihorne@btinternet.com

HORNE, Simon Timothy. b 62. Ball Coll Ox BA 86 MA 90 Birm Univ PhD 99 RN(MH) 89. Qu Coll Birm BD 94. **d** 95 **p** 96. C Basingstoke *Win* 95-99; C Fordingbridge 99-01; TV Fordingbridge and Breamore and Hale etc from 01. *29 Shaftesbury Street, Fordingbridge SP6 1JF* M: 07502-146758 E: simon.horne31@googlemail.com

HORNER, Eric. b 43. EMMTC 87. **d** 90 **p** 91. C Boultham *Linc* 90-93; P-in-c Frampton w Kirton in Holland 93-97; V Kirton in Holland 97-04; rtd 05. *24 Hurn Close, Ruskington, Sleaford NG34 9FE* T: (01526) 834043 E: erichorner04@aol.com

HORNER, Graham. b 57. Grey Coll Dur BSc 78 ACA 81. St Jo Coll Nottm 93. **d** 93 **p** 94. C Longdon-upon-Tern, Rodington, Uppington etc *Lich* 93-95; C Wrockwardine Deanery 95-96; TV 96-02; TR 02-07; RD Wrockwardine 02-07; V Gt Wyrley from 07. *The Vicarage, 1 Cleves Crescent, Cheslyn Hay, Walsall WS6 7LR* T: (01922) 414309 E: horner314@btinternet.com

HORNER, Ian. **d** 13 **p** 14. C Bailieborough w Knockbride, Shercock and Mullagh *K, E & A* from 14. *The Rectory, Bailieborough, Co Cavan, Republic of Ireland* M: 87-622 3609 T: (00353) (42) 967 5822 E: ianewhorner@gmail.com

HORNER, John Henry. b 40. Leeds Univ BA 62 Middx Poly MA 87. Oak Hill Th Coll 76. **d** 79 **p** 80. NSM Datchworth w Tewin *St Alb* 79-85; NSM Ware St Mary 85-91; C S Ashford Ch Ch *Cant* 91-94; C Bp's Hatfield *St Alb* 94-99; V Sandridge 99-02; rtd 02; P-in-c Broxbourne w Wormley *St Alb* 03-04. *41 St Leonard's Road, Hertford SG14 3JW* T: (01992) 423725 E: john.horner1@ntlworld.com

HORNER, Richard Murray. b 61. Dur Univ BSc 83. NTMTC 93. **d** 96 **p** 97. C Sherborne w Castleton and Lillington *Sarum* 96-99; Chapl Rugby Sch from 99. *Tudor House, 4 Horton Crescent, Rugby CV22 5DL* T: (01788) 544939

HORNER, Sally. b 68. City Univ BSc 94. Westcott Ho Cam 06. **d** 08 **p** 09. C Peckham St Jo w St Andr *S'wark* 08-12; Chapl Notts Healthcare NHS Trust 12-15; Chapl W Lon Mental Health NHS Trust from 15; PtO *S'wark* from 15. *West London Mental Health NHS Trust, Uxbridge Road, Southall UB1 3EU* T: (020) 8354 8354 E: sallyhorner770@btinternet.com

HORNSBY, William John. b 49. RIBA 79. SEITE 98. **d** 01 **p** 02. C Faversham *Cant* 01-04; C Preston next Faversham, Goodnestone and Graveney 02-04; P-in-c Newington w Hartlip and Stockbury 04-07; P-in-c Iwade and Upchurch w Lower Halstow 05-07; PtO 07-08; V Goudhurst w Kilndown 08-12; AD Weald 10-12; rtd 12; PtO *Cant* from 12. *25 Manwood Avenue, Canterbury CT2 7AH* T: (01227) 454605 E: billhornsby@btinternet.com

HOROBIN, Timothy John. b 60. St Jo Coll Nottm 92. **d** 94 **p** 95. C Nelson St Phil *Blackb* 94-96; P-in-c Blackpool St Paul 98-00; PtO 05-06; LtO 06-10; P-in-c Lower Darwen St Jas 10-11; V from 11. *The Vicarage, Stopes Brow, Lower Darwen, Darwen BB3 0QP* T: (01254) 53898 M: 07811-074063 E: tim.horobin@blackburn.anglican.org

HORREX, Mrs Gay Lesley. b 42. **d** 96 **p** 97. OLM Walton-on-Thames *Guildf* 96-07; rtd 07; P-in-c Blackpool St Paul 98-00; PtO 05-06; LtO 06-10; P-in-c Blackpool St Paul 98-00; PtO 05-06; LtO 06-10; P-in-c Lower Darwen St Jas 10-11; PtO *Portsm* from 08. *25 Pine Walk, Liss GU33 7AT* T: (01730) 893827 E: glhorrex@homecall.co.uk

HORROCKS, Judith Anne. b 53. Univ of Calgary BSc 76 Keele Univ MA 99. St Jo Coll Nottm. **dss** 82 **d** 87 **p** 94. Denton Ch Ch *Man* 82-85; Whalley Range St Edm 85-97; Par Dn 87-97; C 94-97; Chapl Man R Infirmary 88-90; Chapl Christie Hosp NHS Trust Man 95-03; Chapl S Man Univ Hosps NHS Trust 98-03; Lic Preacher *Man* 97-03; Hon Can Man Cathl 02-03; Multifaith Chapl Co-ord Sheff Hallam Univ 03-05; Chapl St Ann's Hospice Manchester 05-09; Lect Bolton St Pet *Man* 09-11; Lect Bolton St Pet w St Phil 11-14; Ch in Sch Development Officer from 14; Lic Preacher from 14. *Five Saints Rectory, 130A Highfield Road, Farnworth, Bolton BL4 0AJ* T: (01204) 572334 M: 07725-957219 F: 08709-138446 E: lecturer@boltonparishchurch.co.uk

HORROCKS, Oliver John. b 30. Clare Coll Cam BA 53 MA 57. Westcott Ho Cam 53. **d** 55 **p** 56. C Moss Side Ch Ch *Man* 55-58; C Arnold *S'well* 58-60; R Ancoats *Man* 60-67; R Barthomley *Ches* 67-96; rtd 96; PtO *Ches* from 98. *36 Station Road, Alsager, Stoke-on-Trent ST7 2PD* T: (01270) 877284

HORROCKS, Robert James. b 56. Grey Coll Dur BSc 78. St Jo Coll Nottm. **d** 82 **p** 83. C Denton Ch Ch *Man* 82-85; R Whalley Range St Edm 85-97; P-in-c Bolton St Paul w Em 97-06; P-in-c Daubhill 05-06; TR New Bury w Gt Lever from 06. *Five Saints Rectory, 130A Highfield Road, Farnworth, Bolton BL4 0AJ* T: (01204) 572334 F: 08709-138446 E: revbobhorrocks@yahoo.co.uk

HORSEMAN, Christopher Michael. b 54. Bris Sch of Min 84 Trin Coll Bris 87. **d** 88 **p** 89. C Weston-super-Mare Cen Par *B & W* 88-92; TV Yatton Moor 92-02; NSM 02-08. *6 Westaway Park, Yatton, Bristol BS49 4JU* T: (01934) 834537 E: cfhors@globalnet.co.uk

HORSEMAN, Colin. b 46. Lon Coll of Div ALCD 69 BD 70 STh 75. **d** 70 **p** 71. C Higher Openshaw *Man* 70-74; C Darfield *Sheff* 75-78; V Stainforth 78-88; V Heeley 88-95; P-in-c Ducklington *Ox* 95-99; P-in-c Gt Horkesley *Chelmsf* 99-02; P-in-c W Bergholt 00-02; R W Bergholt and Gt Horkesley 02-12; RD Dedham and Tey 03-08; rtd 12. *14 Leslie Drive, Amble, Morpeth NE65 0PX* E: horsemancolin61@gmail.com

HORSEY, Maurice Alfred. b 30. ACIB. S'wark Ord Course 61. **d** 64 **p** 65. C Oxhey All SS *St Alb* 64-67; C Coulsdon St Jo *S'wark* 67-71; P-in-c Champion Hill St Sav 71-76; Hon C Lewisham St Swithun 84-86; P-in-c Woolwich St Thos 86-90; R 90-94; rtd 94; Chapl Costa del Sol W *Eur* 94-98; PtO from 99. *6/47 Marina de Casares, 29690 Casares (Malaga), Spain* T: (0034) 952 892 166 E: dorothy@tesal.es

HORSEY, Stanley Desmond. b 20. Ely Th Coll 46. **d** 49 **p** 50. C S Clevedon *B & W* 49-51; C Leigh-on-Sea St Marg *Chelmsf* 51-53; C Barbourne *Worc* 53-55; V Edgbaston St Jas *Birm* 55-60; V Brighton St Martin *Chich* 60-67; V Hove St Barn 67-77; V Hove St Barn and St Agnes 77-85; rtd 85; PtO *Chich* from 85. *27A Amesbury Crescent, Hove BN3 5RD* T: (01273) 732081

HORSFALL, Andrew Stuart. b 64. Qu Coll Birm 93. **d** 06 **p** 06. Methodist Min 95-06; Chapl E Lancs Hosps NHS Trust 05-09; Chapl Co-ord from 09; NSM Feniscowles *Blackb* 06-07; Hon C Accrington Ch the King 11-12. *Royal Blackburn Hospital, Haslingden Road, Blackburn BB2 3HH* T: (01254) 263555 *or* (01282) 832853 E: andrew.horsfall@elht.nhs.uk *or* revhors@aol.com

HORSFALL, David John. b 55. Bris Poly BA 77. St Jo Coll Nottm 87. **d** 89 **p** 90. C Chaddesden St Mary *Derby* 89-92; V Swadlincote 92-11; RD Repton 99-09; R Chesterfield H Trin and Ch Ch from 11. *Holy Trinity Rectory, 31 Newbold Road, Chesterfield S41 7PG* T: (01246) 220860
E: djhorsfall@hotmail.com

HORSFALL, Mrs Deborah. b 66. Sheff Univ BA 14. Yorks Min Course 11. **d** 14 **p** 15. C S Ossett *Leeds* from 14. *6 Sunnybank Street, Ossett WF5 8PE* M: 07834-788618
E: revdhorsfall@gmail.com

HORSFALL, Keith. b 39. Tyndale Hall Bris 62. **d** 65 **p** 66. C Walton Breck *Liv* 65-68; C Fazakerley Em 68-70; C Mile Cross *Nor* 70-73; V Gayton 73-80; TR Parr *Liv* 80-90; V Leyland St Andr *Blackb* 90-00; P-in-c Willand *Ex* 00-01; TV Cullompton, Willand, Uffculme, Kentisbeare etc 01-05; rtd 05; PtO *Nor* from 13. *Honeycroft, 9 Sporle Road, Swaffham PE37 7HL* T: (01760) 723112 E: horsfall@xalt.co.uk

HORSHAM, Archdeacon of. *See* WINDSOR, The Ven Julie Fiona

HORSHAM, Area Bishop of. *See* SOWERBY, The Rt Revd Mark Crispin Rake

HORSINGTON, Timothy Frederick. b 44. Dur Univ BA 66. Wycliffe Hall Ox 67. **d** 69 **p** 70. C Halewood *Liv* 69-72; C Farnworth 72-75; C-in-c Widnes St Jo 72-75; P-in-c Llangarron w Llangrove *Heref* 75-82; P-in-c Whitchurch w Ganarew 77-82; R Llangarron w Llangrove, Whitchurch and Ganarew 83-84; R Highclere and Ashmansworth w Crux Easton *Win* 84-09; rtd 09; PtO *B & W* from 12; *Win* from 12. *27 Arlington Close, Yeovil BA21 3TB* T: (01935) 410731
E: timhorsington@timicomail.co.uk

HORSLEY, Canon Alan Avery. b 36. St Chad's Coll Dur BA 58 Pacific States Univ MA 84 PhD 85. Qu Coll Birm 58. **d** 60 **p** 61. C Daventry *Pet* 60-63; C Reading St Giles *Ox* 63-64; C Wokingham St Paul 64-66; V Yeadon St Andr *Bradf* 66-71; R Heyford w Stowe Nine Churches *Pet* 71-78; RD Daventry 76-78; V Oakham w Hambleton and Egleton 78-81; V Oakham, Hambleton, Egleton, Braunston and Brooke 81-86; Can Pet Cathl 79-86; V Lanteglos by Fowey *Truro* 86-88; Provost St Andr Cathl Inverness 88-91; R Inverness St Andr 88-91; P-in-c Culloden St Mary-in-the-Fields 88-91; P-in-c Strathnairn St Paul 88-91; V Mill End and Heronsgate w W Hyde *St Alb* 91-01; RD Rickmansworth 00-01; rtd 01; PtO *Pet* from 03. *3 Leicester Terrace, Northampton NN2 6AJ* T: (01604) 628868 E: canonalanahorsley@gmail.com

HORSLEY, Amelia Mary Elizabeth. b 69. K Alfred's Coll Win BEd 91. St Jo Coll Nottm MA 97. **d** 98 **p** 99. C Southampton Maybush St Pet *Win* 98-01; Teacher Mansel Infant Sch Southampton 01; Teacher Highfields Primary Sch Leic from 01; Dep Hd from 05. *95 Aylestone Drive, Leicester LE2 8SB* T: 0116-283 7710 E: amehorsley@aol.com

HORSLEY, Peter Alec. b 56. Leeds Metrop Univ CertEd 98. Cranmer Hall Dur 99. **d** 01 **p** 02. C Acomb St Steph and St Aid *York* 01-05; P-in-c Wheldrake w Thorganby 05-08; R Derwent Ings 08-11; V Acomb St Steph and St Aid 11-15; rtd 15; PtO *York* from 15. *38 Campbell Avenue, Holgate, York YO24 4LA* T: (01904) 799095 E: peterhorsley@tiscali.co.uk

HORSMAN, Andrew Alan. b 49. Otago Univ BA 70 Man Univ MA 72 PhD 75. St Steph Ho Ox BA 80 MA 87. **d** 81 **p** 82. C Hillingdon All SS *Lon* 81-84; C Lt Stanmore St Lawr 84-87; TV Haxby w Wigginton *York* 87-98; V Acomb Moor 98-15; P-in-c York All SS N Street 03-15; rtd 15. *Address temp unknown* E: andrew@horsmanz.plus.com

HORSWELL, Kevin George. b 55. Jes Coll Cam BA 77 MA 81 Nottm Univ BA 81. St Jo Coll Nottm 79. **d** 82 **p** 83. C Bootle Ch Ch *Liv* 82-86; Chapl LMH Ox 86-91; C Ox St Giles and SS Phil and Jas w St Marg 86-91; R Dodleston *Ches* 91-00; R Llanaber w Caerdeon *Ban* from 00; AD Ardudwy from 12. *The Rectory, Mynach Road, Barmouth LL42 1RL* T: (01341) 280516

HORTA, Nelson Pinto. b 40. Lisbon Univ Lic 80 Catholic Univ of Portugal LicTh 92. **d** 65 **p** 69. V Setúbal H Spirit Portugal 69-71; V Lisbon St Paul 71-96; Asst Chapl Gtr Lisbon *Eur* 97-00. *Quinta da Cerieira, rua C, Lote 261, Vale de Figueira-Sobreda, 2800 Almada, Portugal* M: (00351) (1) 295 7943

HORTON, Anne. *See* HORTON, Roberta Anne

HORTON, David Harold. b 49. St Jo Coll Dur BA 72. NEOC 82. **d** 86 **p** 87. C Enfield St Jas *Lon* 86-90; Min Joydens Wood St Barn CD *Roch* 90-93; V Joydens Wood St Barn 93-99; P-in-c Rosherville 99-04; rtd 04; PtO *Roch* from 09. *5B Hawes Road, Bromley BR1 3JS* T: (020) 8466 9211
E: davidhhorton@gmail.com

HORTON, Jane. *See* HORTON, Margaret Jane

HORTON, Canon Jeremy Nicholas Orkney. b 44. Cranmer Hall Dur 64. **d** 68 **p** 69. C Dalton-in-Furness *Carl* 68-70; C Penrith 70-73; V Hudswell w Downholme and Marske *Ripon* 73-75; R Middleton Tyas and Melsonby 75-81; P-in-c Croft 78-81; P-in-c Eryholme 78-81; V Wortley-de-Leeds 81-93; V Middleton St Mary 93-98; RD Armley 96-98; V Kirby-on-the-

Moor, Cundall w Norton-le-Clay etc 98-09; Jt AD Ripon 01-04; Hon Can Ripon Cathl 01-09; rtd 09. *4 Downes Court, 70A South Street, Leominster HR6 8GB* T: (01568) 610040 M: 07527-209028 E: nickhorton199@btinternet.com

HORTON, John. b 49. STETS 05. **d** 07 **p** 08. NSM Exhall *Cov* 07-11; NSM Stourdene Gp from 11. *The Vicarage, New Road, Alderminster, Stratford-upon-Avon CV37 8PE*
E: john@horton6677.freeserve.co.uk

HORTON, John Ward. b 27. Leeds Univ BA 50. Coll of Resurr Mirfield 50. **d** 52 **p** 53. C Balkwell CD *Newc* 52-55; C E Coatham *York* 55-58; C-in-c Acomb Moor CD 58-71; V Acomb Moor 71-93; rtd 93; PtO *Newc* from 93. *39 Billy Mill Lane, North Shields NE29 8BZ* T: 0191-296 4082

HORTON, Mrs Joy. b 52. CertEd 73 Kent Univ MA 98. SEITE 94. **d** 97 **p** 98. C Dartford St Edm *Roch* 97-01; Chapl Bromley Hosps NHS Trust 01-02; C Erith St Jo *Roch* 02-03; PtO 03-04; Chapl Burrswood Chr Cen 04-08; PtO *St E* from 09. *3 Furze Close, Thurston, Bury St Edmunds IP31 3PR* T: (01359) 230649

HORTON, Mrs Margaret Jane. b 60. ARCM 83. Ripon Coll Cuddesdon 13. **d** 15. C Truro St Mary from 15. *11 Brunel Court, Truro TR1 3AE* M: 07808-331463
E: janehorton@trurocathedral.org.uk

HORTON, Melanie Jane. b 64. Birm Poly LLB 85 Solicitor 86. Ripon Coll Cuddesdon BA 95. **d** 96 **p** 97. C Lich St Chad 96-00; Chapl R Masonic Sch for Girls Rickmansworth 00-03; Chapl St Edm Sch Cant 03-08; R Colwall w Upper Colwall and Coddington *Heref* from 08. *The Rectory, Walwyn Road, Colwall, Malvern WR13 6EG* T: (01684) 540330 M: 07748-842825
E: colwallrector@tiscali.co.uk

HORTON, Michael John. b 56. St Jo Coll Cam BA 80 MA 83 Univ of Wales (Swansea) PGCE 83. Wycliffe Hall Ox BA 88 MA 92. **d** 89 **p** 90. C Northallerton w Kirby Sigston *York* 89-92; C Ulverston St Mary w H Trin *Carl* 92-94; V Lightwater *Guildf* 94-04; Chapl Wrekin Coll Telford from 04. *Five Gables, Prospect Road, Wellington, Telford TF1 3BE* T: (01952) 415059
E: michael@hortonfamily.co.uk *or* mjhorton@wrekincollege.ac.uk

HORTON, Nicholas. *See* HORTON, Jeremy Nicholas Orkney

HORTON, Ralph Edward. b 41. S'wark Ord Course 75. **d** 78 **p** 79. C Streatham St Leon *S'wark* 78-81; TV Catford (Southend) and Downham 81-88; V Ashford St Matt *Lon* 88-12; rtd 12. *12 Convent Fields, Sidmouth EX10 8QR*

HORTON, Canon Roberta Anne. b 44. Leic Univ BSc 66 CertEd 67 Nottm Univ BCombStuds 82. Linc Th Coll 79. **dss** 82 **d** 87 **p** 94. Cambridge St Jas *Ely* 82-86; Beaumont Leys *Leic* 86-91; Par Dn 87-91; Dioc Dir of Tr 91-00; P-in-c Swithland 94-99; R Woodhouse, Woodhouse Eaves and Swithland 00-14; Hon Can Leic Cathl 94-14; rtd 14; PtO *Leic* from 14. *8B Copeland Road, Birstall, Leicester LE4 3AA* E: rahorton@outlook.com

HORTON, Simon James. b 65. **d** 12 **p** 13. C Goring-by-Sea *Chich* from 12. *19 Angus Road, Goring-by-Sea, Worthing BN12 4BL*

HORTON, Mrs Wilma Alton. b 46. **d** 06 **p** 07. OLM Alford w Rigsby *Linc* 06-14; PtO *York* from 14. *15 Bay Crescent, Filey YO14 0AP* E: malc.horton@btinternet.com

HORWELL, Elizabeth. b 54. Southn Univ BSc 76 Essex Univ MA 77 Birm Univ PhD 84 Wolv Univ PGCE 94. ERMC 4. **d** 07 **p** 08. C Wanstead St Mary w Ch Ch *Chelmsf* 07-11; R from 11. *The Rectory, 37 Wanstead Place, London E11 2SW* T: (020) 3556 4853 M: 07835-450837
E: ehorwell@hotmail.com *or* lizhorwell@parishofwanstead.org

HORWOOD, Graham Frederick. b 34. Univ of Wales (Cardiff) BA 55. Coll of Resurr Mirfield 55. **d** 57 **p** 58. C Llantrisant *Llan* 57-61; C Roath St Sav 61-62; C Roath 62-66; V Clydach Vale 66-77; V Canton St Luke 77-99; rtd 99. *26 Heol-yr-Onnen, Llanharry, Pontyclun CF72 9NJ* T: (01443) 225777
E: ghorwood@freeuk.com

HORWOOD, Mrs Juliet Joy. b 51. Ex Univ BSc 73. SWMTC 09. **d** 11. NSM Topsham and Wear *Ex* from 11. *20 Higher Shapter Street, Topsham, Exeter EX3 0AW* T: (01392) 875558
E: juliet_horwood@yahoo.co.uk

HOSKIN, Brian. *See* HOSKIN, Henry Brian

HOSKIN, Canon David William. b 49. Hatf Coll Dur BSc 71. Wycliffe Hall Ox 72. **d** 75 **p** 76. C Bridlington Priory *York* 75-78; C Rodbourne Cheney *Bris* 78-79; C Bebington *Ches* 79-82; R Lockington and Lund and Scorborough w Leconfield *York* 82-88; V Beverley St Mary 88-10; RD Beverley 97-07; Can and Preb Minster 05-10; rtd 10. *24 Chestnut Avenue, Driffield YO25 6SH* T: (01377) 538172 E: david@hoskin.eu

HOSKIN, Henry Brian. b 32. NW Ord Course 72. **d** 75 **p** 76. NSM Chesterfield SS Aug *Derby* 75-79; NSM Bolsover 79-83; NSM Old Brampton and Loundsley Green 83-88; P-in-c Gt Barlow 88-94; rtd 97; PtO *Derby* from 97. *25 Barn Close, Chesterfield S41 8BD* T: (01246) 201550

HOSKING, Suzanne Elizabeth. b 68. Wycliffe Hall Ox 07. **d** 10 **p** 11. C St Merryn and St Issey w St Petroc Minor *Truro* 10-14; P-in-c Carbis Bay w Lelant from 14. *The Vicarage, Porthrepta Road, Carbis Bay, St Ives TR26 2LD* T: (01736) 796206 E: sehosking@hotmail.com

HOSKINS, Hugh George. b 46. S Dios Minl Tr Scheme. **d** 84 **p** 85. NSM Hilperton w Whaddon and Staverton etc *Sarum* 84-87; C Calne and Blackland 87-90; R W Lavington and the Cheverells 90-97; TR Upper Wylye Valley 97-04; RD Heytesbury 00-03; TR Pewsey and Swanborough 04-10; P-in-c Upavon w Rushall and Charlton 07-10; TR Vale of Pewsey 10-11; rtd 11; PtO *Sarum* from 11. *42 St Mary's Close, Hilperton Marsh, Trowbridge BA14 7PW* T: (01225) 781579 E: h.hoskins123@btinternet.com

HOSKINS, John Paul. b 74. Univ Coll Dur BA 95 MA 96 MLitt 07 Trin Coll Cam BA 99 MA 04 Ox Univ MTh 10. Westcott Ho Cam 97 Ripon Coll Cuddesdon 05. **d** 07 **p** 08. C Bakewell *Derby* 07-11; Bp's Chapl *Glouc* from 11; Min Can Glouc Cathl from 13. *2 College Green, Gloucester GL1 2LR* T: (01452) 835513 F: 308324 E: jphoskins@glosdioc.org.uk

HOSKINS, Preb Rosemary Anne. b 56. Surrey Univ BA 03. Wesley Coll Bris 99 STETS 01. **d** 02 **p** 03. NSM Camelot Par *B & W* 02-06; NSM Cam Vale from 06; Warden of Readers Wells Adnry 05-09; RD Bruton and Cary from 10; Preb Wells Cathl from 09. *Springfields, Weston Bampfylde, Yeovil BA22 7HZ* T: (01963) 440026 E: revroseanne@gmail.com

HOTCHEN, Stephen Jeffrie. b 50. Bradf Coll of Educn. Linc Th Coll 85. **d** 87 **p** 88. C Morpeth *Newc* 87-90; TV High Wycombe *Ox* 90-91; R Dingwall and Strathpeffer *Mor* 91-94; V Rickerscote *Lich* 94-04; R Aylmerton, Runton, Beeston Regis and Gresham *Nor* 04-07; P-in-c Altofts *Wakef* 07-13; P-in-c Badsworth *Leeds* from 13; Dioc Adv on Disability Issues from 13; Chapl Princess of Wales Hospice from 13. *The Rectory, Main Street, Badsworth, Pontefract WF9 1AF* T: (01977) 643642 *or* 708868 M: 07976-387199 E: stephenhotchen@btinternet.com

HOTCHIN, Mrs Hilary Moya. b 52. Birm Univ CertEd 73. WMMTC 85. **d** 88 **p** 94. NSM Redditch St Steph *Worc* 88-91; Par Dn Handsworth *Sheff* 91-94; C 94-96; TV Maltby 96-98; NSM Marfleet *York* 06-08; NSM Sutton St Mich from 08. *8 Whisperwood Way, Bransholme, Hull HU7 4JT* T: (01482) 828015 E: hotchin@hotchin.karoo.co.uk

HOUGH, Adrian Michael. b 59. Hertf Coll Ox BA 80 MA 84 DPhil 84 MRSC LRPS. Ripon Coll Cuddesdon BA 91. **d** 92 **p** 93. C Martley and Wichenford, Knightwick etc *Worc* 92-96; Asst P Evesham Deanery 96-97; V Badsey w Aldington and Offenham and Bretforton 97-04; C Lerwick and Burravoe *Ab* 04-05; PtO *Worc* 05-06; Bp's Chapl and Asst *Ex* 06-11; Episc V and Chapl from 11; Dir IME 4-7 from 08. *96 Old Tiverton Road, Exeter EX4 6LD* T: (01392) 214867 *or* 272362 E: adrian.amhough@btinternet.com

HOUGH, Miss Carole Elizabeth. b 59. Lon Hosp SRN 81. St Jo Coll Nottm 87. **d** 91 **p** 94. C Beoley *Worc* 91-95; Asst Chapl Addenbrooke's NHS Trust 95-98; Chapl Milton Keynes Hosp NHS Foundn Trust 98-09; Chapl Milton Keynes Primary Care Trust 98-09; Chapl St Jo Hospice Moggerhanger 10-12; Chapl Florence Nightingale Hospice from 13. *28 Pettigrew Close, Walnut Tree, Milton Keynes MK7 7LL* T: (01296) 332600

HOUGH, Michael Jeremy. b 61. Wilson Carlile Coll. Oak Hill Th Coll 00. **d** 02 **p** 03. C Redhill H Trin *S'wark* 02-06; P-in-c Woodmansterne 06-11; R 11-13; V Redhill H Trin from 13. *4 Carlton Road, Redhill RH1 2BX* T: (01737) 773816 M: 07872-525144 E: mick@htredhill.com

HOUGH, Peter George. b 40. Dur Univ BA 62. Wells Th Coll 62. **d** 64 **p** 65. C Stocking Farm CD *Leic* 64-68; V Leic St Aid 68-76; V Knutton *Lich* 76-05; P-in-c Silverdale and Alsagers Bank 93-94; V Alsagers Bank 01-05; rtd 05. *2 Station Road, Keele, Newcastle ST5 5AH* T: (01782) 624282

HOUGH, Sharron Lesley. b 54. **d** 01 **p** 02. OLM Willenhall H Trin *Lich* 01-05; C Bentley 05-09; P-in-c 09-11; TV Bentley Em and Willenhall H Trin from 11. *10 Pineneedle Croft, Willenhall WV12 4BY* T: (01902) 410458

HOUGH, Wendy Lorraine. b 63. Trin Coll Bris BA 94 LLAM 81. Cranmer Hall Dur 98. **d** 00 **p** 01. C The Hague *Eur* 00-03; Asst Chapl Berne w Neuchâtel 05-07; C Bris St Mary Redcliffe w Temple etc 07-14; Chapl St Mary Redcliffe and Temple Sch 07-14; Cyprus from 14. *Diocesan Office, PO Box 22075, 1517 Nicosia, Cyprus* T: (0090) (392) 815 4329

HOUGHTON, Christopher Guy. b 64. W Surrey Coll of Art & Design BA 86. Oak Hill Th Coll BA 89. **d** 89 **p** 90. C Mossley Hill St Matt and St Jas *Liv* 89-92; C Ashton-in-Makerfield St Thos 92-95; C Southport St Phil and St Paul 95-96; Chapl Chorley and S Ribble NHS Trust 96-01; rtd 01; PtO *Blackb* from 03. *35 Deerfold, Chorley PR7 1UD*

HOUGHTON, David John. b 47. Edin Univ BSc(Econ) 68. Cuddesdon Coll 69. **d** 71 **p** 72. C Prestbury *Glouc* 71-74; Prec

Gib Cathl 74-76; Chapl Madrid 76-78; C Croydon St Jo *Cant* 78-80; Chapl Warw Sch 80-85; P-in-c Isleworth St Fran *Lon* 85-90; USA 90-91; TV Clapham Team *S'wark* 91-01; RD Clapham 93-01; V Clapham H Spirit 02; Chapl Paris St Geo *Eur* 02-07; P-in-c Surbiton St Andr and St Mark *S'wark* 07-10; V 10-12; AD Kingston 09-12; rtd 12; PtO *S'wark* from 14. *2 Milton Drive, Tunbridge Wells TN2 3DE* T: (01892) 541988 E: houghton308@btinternet.com

HOUGHTON, Mrs Evelyn Mabel. b 44. Stockwell Coll of Educn TCert 65. Oak Hill NSM Course 92. **d** 94 **p** 95. NSM Bedford St Jo and St Leon *St Alb* 94-98; C Reading St Agnes w St Paul Ox 98-02; C Reading St Agnes w St Paul and St Barn 02-10; rtd 10; PtO *St Alb* from 10. *1 Peashill Lane, Great Barford, Bedford MK44 3HG* T: (01234) 871915 E: evehoughton@dsl.pipex.com

HOUGHTON, Canon Geoffrey John. b 59. Ridley Hall Cam 87. **d** 90 **p** 91. C Sholing *Win* 90-94; P-in-c Jersey All SS 94-99; V 99-09; P-in-c Jersey St Simon 94-99; V 99-09; P-in-c Jersey H Trin 05-06; R from 06; Vice-Dean Jersey from 99; Hon Chapl Jersey Hospice from 96; Hon Can Win Cathl from 11. *Holy Trinity Rectory, La Rue du Presbytere, Trinity, Jersey JE3 5JB* T/F: (01534) 861110 E: geoffhoughton@jerseymail.co.uk *or* gjh@super.net.uk

HOUGHTON, Graham. *See* HOUGHTON, Peter Graham

HOUGHTON, Hugh Alexander Gervase. b 76. St Jo Coll Cam BA 97 MPhil 98 MA 01 Leeds Univ BA 02 Birm Univ PhD 06. Coll of Resurr Mirfield 00. **d** 03 **p** 04. NSM Weoley Castle *Birm* 03-06; NSM Headington Quarry Ox 06-09; PtO *Birm* from 09; Research Fell Birm Univ from 06. *The Vicarage, 18 Pineapple Grove, Birmingham B30 2TJ* T: 0121-443 1371 E: h.a.g.houghton@bham.ac.uk

HOUGHTON, Ian David. b 50. Lanc Univ BA 71 Newc Univ CertEd 74. Sarum & Wells Th Coll 80. **d** 82 **p** 83. C Newc St Geo 82-85; Chapl Newc Poly 85-92; Chapl Northumbria Univ 92-95; Master Newc St Thos Prop Chpl 90-95; Ind Chapl Black Country Urban Ind Miss *Lich* 95-04; Res Min Bilston 95-04; Chapl Pet City Cen 04-08; C Pet St Jo 04-08; P-in-c Osmotherley w Harlsey and Ingleby Arncliffe *York* 08-09; V from 09; P-in-c Leake w Over and Nether Silton and Kepwick 08-09; V from 09; P-in-c Felixkirk w Boltby 08-09; V from 09; P-in-c Kirkby Knowle 08-09; V from 09; P-in-c Cowesby 08-09; R from 09; RD Mowbray from 14. *Leake Vicarage, Knayton, Thirsk YO7 4AZ* T: (01845) 537277 E: ian.houghton@tiscali.co.uk

HOUGHTON, Josephine Elizabeth Mayer. b 80. Birm Univ BA 01 PhD 07. St Steph Ho Ox BA 09. **d** 09 **p** 10. C Handsworth St Andr *Birm* 09-13; P-in-c Stirchley from 13. *The Vicarage, 18 Pineapple Grove, Birmingham B30 2TJ* T: 0121-443 1371 E: josephine@houghtons.org.uk

HOUGHTON, Peter Graham. b 51. St Jo Coll Nottm 85. **d** 87 **p** 88. C Toxteth Park St Clem *Liv* 87-91; Chapl Winwick Hosp Warrington 91-92; Chapl Warrington Community Health Care NHS Trust 93-98; Chapl HM Pris Styal 98-01; Asst Chapl St Helens and Knowsley Hosps NHS Trust 03-04; rtd 04; PtO *Liv* from 04. *10 Burlington Drive, Great Sankey, Warrington WA5 8AB* T: (01925) 711451

HOUGHTON, Prof Peter John. b 47. Chelsea Coll Lon BPharm 68 PhD 73 Cant Ch Ch Univ MA 13 FRPharmS 94 FRSC 95 CChem 95. Dioc OLM tr scheme 05. **d** 08 **p** 09. NSM Balham Hill Ascension *S'wark* 08-12; PtO 12-13; NSM Heref S Wye from 13. *The Lodge, Ballingham, Hereford HR2 6NN* T: (01432) 840443 F: 352412 M: 07734-747688 E: peter.houghton@kcl.ac.uk

HOUGHTON, Mrs Rosemary Margaret Anne. b 46. **d** 00 **p** 01. OLM Earlham *Nor* from 00. *74 St Mildred's Road, West Earlham, Norwich NR5 8RS* T: (01603) 502752 M: 07808-774811 E: rosemary.houghton@ntlworld.com

HOUGHTON, Mrs Susan Jeanette. b 39. Qu Mary Coll Lon BSc 61 Nottm Univ PGCE 62. WMMTC 98. **d** 99 **p** 00. OLM Dursley *Glouc* 99-02; rtd 02; NSM Offwell, Northleigh, Farway, Cotleigh etc *Ex* 02-09. *2 Combewater Cottages, Wilmington, Honiton EX14 9SQ* T: (01404) 831887 E: sue.houghton2@btinternet.com

HOUGHTON, Thomas. b 17. NW Ord Course 71. **d** 74 **p** 75. NSM Newcastle w Butterton *Lich* 74-82; PtO from 82. *Madeley Manor Nursing Home, Heighley Castle Way, Madeley, Crewe CW3 9HF* T: (01782) 750610

HOULDEN, Prof James Leslie. b 29. Qu Coll Ox BA 52 MA 56. Cuddesdon Coll 53. **d** 55 **p** 56. C Hunslet St Mary and Stourton *Ripon* 55-58; Tutor Chich Th Coll 58-59; Chapl 59-60; Chapl Trin Coll Ox 60-70; Prin Cuddesdon Coll 70-75; Prin Ripon Coll Cuddesdon 75-77; V Cuddesdon Ox 70-77; Hon Can Ch Ch 76-77; Sen Lect NT Studies K Coll Lon 77-87; Prof Th 87-94; rtd 94; PtO *S'wark* 94-99; *Birm* 99-12. *5 The Court, Fen End Road West, Knowle, Solihull B93 0AN* T: (01564) 777138 E: leslie.houlden@btopenworld.com

HOULDERSHAW, Michelle Louise. b 67. **d** 12 **p** 13. OLM Brothertoft Gp *Linc* from 12; OLM Sibsey w Frithville from 12. *Sheaf House, Main Road, Holland Fen, Lincoln LN4 4QH* T: (01205) 280094 M: 07986-433358 E: michelle@sheafhf.com

HOULDING, Preb David Nigel Christopher. b 53. AKC 76. **d** 77 **p** 78. C Hillingdon All SS *Lon* 77-81; C Holborn St Alb w Saffron Hill St Pet 81-85; V Hampstead St Steph w All Hallows from 85; AD N Camden 01-02; Preb St Paul's Cathl from 04. *All Hallows' House, 52 Courthope Road, London NW3 2LD* T: (020) 7267 7833 or 7267 6317 F: 7267 6317 M: 07710-403294 E: fr.houlding@lineone.net

HOULT, Roy Anthony. b 35. AKC 58. **d** 59 **p** 60. C Walton St Mary *Liv* 59-63; Canada from 63; Hon Can Koot 75-79. *381 Huron Street, Toronto ON M5S 2G5, Canada*

HOULTON, David Andrew. b 58. Bradf Univ BEng 80 MPhil 86 Wycliffe Hall Ox BTh 11 CEng 90 EurIng 90 FIChemE 98 SOSc 13. Wycliffe Hall Ox 07. **d** 09 **p** 10. C Old Trafford St Bride *Man* 09-12; NSM Stoke Bishop *Bris* 12-13; V Gargrave w Coniston Cold *Leeds* from 13; Rural Adv from 13. *The Vicarage, Church Lane, Gargrave, Skipton BD23 3NQ* T: (01756) 748468 M: 07766-235952 E: david.houlton@wycliffe.oxon.org

HOULTON, Heather Joy. b 61. Bradf Univ BA 83 Open Univ MA 03. Trin Coll Bris MA 14. **d** 13 **p** 14. C Linton in Craven *Leeds* from 13; C Burnsall w Rylstone from 13. *The Vicarage, Church Lane, Gargrave, Skipton BD23 3NQ* T: (01756) 748468 E: heatherjoyhoulton@gmail.com

HOULTON, Neil James. b 54. STETS 04. **d** 07 **p** 08. NSM Pokesdown St Jas *Win* 07-10; NSM Boscombe St Andr from 10; P-in-c from 12. *3 Wilfred Road, Bournemouth BH5 1NB* T: (01202) 462476 E: neil.houlton@ntlworld.com

HOUNSELL, Mrs Susan Mary. b 49. STETS BA 10. **d** 07 **p** 08. NSM W Monkton *B & W* 07-11; NSM W Monkton w Kingston St Mary, Broomfield etc 11-13; rtd 13. *33 Home Orchard, Hatch Beauchamp, Taunton TA3 6TG* T: (01823) 480545 E: susanhounsell@tiscali.co.uk

HOUSE, Graham Ivor. b 44. Oak Hill Th Coll BA 80. **d** 80 **p** 81. C Ipswich St Jo *St E* 80-84; V Ipswich St Andr 84-00; R Monks Eleigh w Chelsworth and Brent Eleigh etc 00-03; rtd 03; PtO *St E* from 03. *6 Through Duncans, Woodbridge IP12 4EA* T: (01394) 386066 M: 07966-169372

HOUSE, Jack Francis. b 35. Bris Univ BEd 70 Lon Univ MA 80 Univ of Wales MTh 94. Bris & Glouc Tr Course 79. **d** 80 **p** 81. NSM Bedminster *Bris* 80-92; PtO 92-94; NSM Knowle H Nativity 94-03; NSM Easton All Hallows 98-03; NSM Brislington St Anne 03-05; rtd 05; PtO *Bris* from 05. *48 Hendre Road, Bristol BS3 2LR* T: 0117-966 1144 E: rhouse3766@virginmail.com

HOUSE, Mrs Janet. b 45. UEA BA 67 Keswick Hall Coll PGCE 68 Sussex Univ MA 80. Ripon Coll Cuddesdon 93. **d** 95 **p** 96. C Swindon Ch Ch *Bris* 95-99; TV Worc SE 99-06; rtd 06; PtO *Nor* from 06. *11 Caernarvon Road, Norwich NR2 3HZ* T: (01603) 762259 E: jhouse@waitrose.com

HOUSE, Simon Hutchinson. b 30. Peterho Cam BA 65 MA 67. Cuddesdon Coll 61. **d** 64 **p** 65. C Sutton St Jas *York* 64-67; C Acomb St Steph and St Aid 67-69; V Allestree St Nic *Derby* 69-81; RD Duffield 74-81; V Bitterne Park *Win* 81-91; rtd 91; PtO *Win* 91-12. *22 Stanley Street, Southsea PO5 2DS* T: (023) 9283 8592

HOUSE, Vickery Willis. b 45. Kelham Th Coll. **d** 69 **p** 70. C Crediton *Ex* 69-76; TV Sampford Peverell, Uplowman, Holcombe Rogus etc 76-81; R Berwick w Selmeston and Alciston *Chich* 81-90; Chapl Ardingly Coll 90-94; V Brighton St Bart *Chich* 94-10; rtd 10. *1 Jessamine Cottages, Brighton Road, Handcross, Haywards Heath RH17 6BU* T: (01444) 401496 E: vic4khouse@hotmail.com

HOUSEMAN, Patricia Adele. *See* CAMPION, Patricia Adele

HOUSLEY, Andrew Arthur. b 67. Wilson Carlile Coll 91 Ridley Hall Cam 00. **d** 02 **p** 03. C Ormskirk *Liv* 02-06; V Litherland St Phil 06-09; R Aughton St Mich and Bickerstaffe from 09. *The Rectory, 10 Church Lane, Aughton, Ormskirk L39 6SB* T: (01695) 423204 E: andrew.housley67@gmail.com

HOUSMAN, Arthur Martin Rowand. b 53. MA CertEd. Trin Coll Bris 81. **d** 83 **p** 84. C Croydon Ch Ch Broad Green *Cant* 83-84; C Croydon Ch Ch *S'wark* 85-87; TV Stratton St Margaret w S Marston etc *Bris* 87-93; Chapl Peterhouse Sch Zimbabwe 93-98; Chapl Nor Sch 98-07; Hon PV Nor Cathl 98-07; Hon C Raveningham Gp from 08. *Orchards, Beccles Road, Raveningham, Norwich NR14 6NW* T: (01508) 548322 M: 07790-944860 E: orchardsone@uwclub.net

HOUSTON, Canon Arthur James. b 54. Trin Coll Bris BA 87. **d** 87 **p** 88. C Chatham St Phil and St Jas *Roch* 87-91; I Carrigaline Union *C, C & R* 91-99; Can Cork Cathl 95-99; Can Ross Cathl 95-99; Dir of Ords 96-99; V Margate H Trin *Cant* 99-08; P-in-c Maidstone St Paul 08-10; AD Thanet 02-08;

AD Maidstone 08-10; P-in-c Minster-in-Sheppey 10-12; C Eastchurch w Leysdown and Harty 10-12; C Sheerness H Trin w St Paul 10-12; Min Parkwood CD from 12; C Maidstone St Luke 12-15; P-in-c Maidstone St Faith from 15; Hon Can Cant Cathl from 03. *11 Maidstone Road, Lenham, Maidstone ME17 2QH* T: (01622) 858020 E: arthurjhouston@googlemail.com

HOUSTON, David William James. b 52. Th Ext Educn Coll. **d** 93 **p** 95. C Lyttelton S Africa 93-96; R Sabie w Lydenburg 96-00; P-in-c Elmsted w Hastingleigh *Cant* 00-06; P-in-c Petham and Waltham w Lower Hardres etc 00-06; V Stone Street Gp 06; R Southfleet *Roch* from 06. *The Rectory, Hook Green Road, Southfleet, Gravesend DA13 9NQ* T: (01474) 833252 E: david@houstonclan.net

HOUSTON, Edward Davison. b 31. TCD BA 56. **d** 57 **p** 58. C Conwall Union *D & R* 57-59; India 59-88; V Whittlebury w Paulerspury *Pet* 89-01; P-in-c Wicken 89-01; rtd 01; PtO *Pet* from 01. *38 Meadow Street, Market Harborough LE16 7JZ* T: (01858) 433309

HOUSTON, Helen Sarah. b 70. Bris Univ BA 91. St Jo Coll Nottm MA 95. **d** 95 **p** 96. C Bourne *Guildf* 95-98; PtO *Bris* 98-99; Hon C Chippenham St Pet 99-00; C Ballyholme *D & D* 02-04; C Stretton and Appleton Thorn *Ches* 04-05; Asst to RD Gt Budworth 05; Chapl St Rocco's Hospice 05-11; Hon C Stockton Heath *Ches* 08-11; Chapl Rossall Sch Fleetwood 11-12; Chapl St Geo Sch Blackpool from 12. *St George's School, Cherry Tree Road, Blackpool FY4 4PH* T: (01253) 316725 E: helen.davehouston@btinternet.com

HOUSTON, Kenneth. *See* HOUSTON, Samuel Kenneth

HOUSTON, Maurice Iain. b 48. TISEC 99. **d** 02 **p** 03. C Edin Old St Paul 02-05; R Melrose 05-13; R Edin St Cuth from 13. *6 Westgarth Avenue, Edinburgh EH13 0BD* T: 0131-441 6949 M: 07543-849248 E: mauriceihouston@me.com

HOUSTON, Michael Alexander. b 46. Lanc Univ MA 92. Linc Th Coll 86. **d** 88 **p** 89. C Longton *Blackb* 88-91; C Woughton Ox 91-92; TV 92-98; TR 98-99; TR Gd Shep TM *Carl* 99-07; rtd 07; PtO *Carl* from 08. *3 Flakebridge Cottages, Flakebridge, Appleby-in-Westmorland CA16 6JZ* E: michael.eastwing@btinternet.com

HOUSTON, Michael James. b 41. Dub Bible Coll St Jo Coll Nottm. **d** 95 **p** 97. Aux Min *D & D* 95-99; P-in-c Ballyphilip w Ardquin 99-07; Chapl Kyrenia St Andr Cyprus 07-10. *Milltown Cottage, 12 Kearney Road, Portaferry, Newtownards BT22 1QF* T: (028) 4272 9997 M: 07547-128350 E: office@milltowncottage.org.uk

HOUSTON, Prof Samuel Kenneth. b 43. QUB BSc 64 PhD 67 FIMA 73 MILT. CITC 81. **d** 85 **p** 86. NSM Belfast St Jas w St Silas *Conn* 85-91; NSM Belfast St Andr from 91; Prof Mathematical Studies Ulster Univ from 96. *29 North Circular Road, Belfast BT15 5HB* T: (028) 9077 1830 or 9036 6953 F: 9036 6859 M: 07929-725319 E: skhouston43@gmail.com

HOUSTON, Canon William Paul. b 54. QUB BSSc 76 TCD BTh 78. CITC 78. **d** 81 **p** 82. C Carrickfergus *Conn* 81-83; C Bangor St Comgall *D & D* 83-86; I Gilford 86-90; I Carnalea 90-99; I Clondalkin w Rathcoole *D & G* 99-09; I Castleknock and Mulhuddart w Clonsilla from 09; Min Can St Patr Cathl Dublin 00-14; Can St Patr Cathl Dublin from 14. *The Rectory, 12 Hawthorn Lawn, Castleknock, Dublin 15, Republic of Ireland* T: (00353) (1) 821 3083

HOVENDEN, Gerald Eric. b 53. York Univ BA 75 Ox Univ MA 85. Wycliffe Hall Ox 78. **d** 81 **p** 82. C Pitsmoor w Ellesmere *Sheff* 81-85; Chapl Lyon w Grenoble and St Etienne *Eur* 85-90; TV S Gillingham *Roch* 90-98; TR Southborough St Pet w Ch Ch and St Matt etc from 98. *The Vicarage, 86 Prospect Road, Southborough, Tunbridge Wells TN4 0EG* T: (01892) 528534 or T/F: 513680 E: gerald.hovenden@diocese-rochester.org

HOVEY, Richard Michael. b 58. Imp Coll Lon BScEng 79 Cranfield Inst of Tech MBA 84 CEng 83 MIET 83 EurIng 92. Cranmer Hall Dur 93. **d** 95 **p** 96. C Cheddar *B & W* 95-99; TV Gtr Corsham *Bris* 99-01; TV Gtr Corsham and Lacock 01-05; S Team Ldr CMS from 05. *80 High Street, Corsham SN13 0HF* T: (01249) 715407 E: crockford@richardhovey.co.uk

HOVIL, Jeremy Richard Guy. b 65. K Coll Lon BSc 86 Spurgeon's Coll Lon MTh 99 Stellenbosch Univ ThD 05. Wycliffe Hall Ox BTh 95. **d** 95 **p** 96. C Kensington St Barn *Lon* 95-99; Crosslinks Uganda 00-07; Field Dir Trust in Chr S Africa from 07. *11 Upper Towers Road, Muizenberg, Cape Town, 7945 South Africa* T: (0027) (21) 788 3313 M: 76-120 5888 E: jem@trustinchrist.org

HOVIL, Richard Guy. b 29. Ex Coll Ox BA 51 MA 57. Ridley Hall Cam. **d** 55 **p** 56. C Finchley Ch Ch *Lon* 55-58; Staff Worker Scripture Union 58-71; Chapl Monkton Combe Sch Bath 71-83; V Fremington *Ex* 83-94; rtd 94; PtO *Sarum* from 94. *37 Upper Marsh Road, Warminster BA12 9PN* T: (01985) 214337 E: richard.hovil@sky.com

HOW, Gillian Carol. *See* BUNCE, Gillian Carol

HOWARD, Alan James. b 45. Bris Univ BA 69. Clifton Th Coll. d 71 p 72. C Welling *Roch* 71-74; C Cromer *Nor* 74-78; V Sidcup St Andr *Roch* 78-86; V Leyton St Cath *Chelmsf* 86-93; V Leyton St Cath and St Paul 93-00; rtd 05. *4 Bower Close, Romford RM5 3SR* T: (01708) 760905

HOWARD, Andrew. b 63. Man Univ BA 95 Leeds Univ MA 97. Coll of Resurr Mirfield 95. d 97 p 98. C Worksop Priory *S'well* 97-01; V Hemlington *York* 01-05; Chapl Teesside Univ 05-13; C Middlesbrough St Jo the Ev and Middlesbrough St Columba w St Paul 05-13; V Cantley *Sheff* from 13. *St Wilfrid's Vicarage, 200 Cantley Lane, Doncaster DN4 6PA* T: (01302) 285316
E: fatherahoward@gmail.com

HOWARD, Arthur Calvin. b 60. Leeds Univ LLB 82 Barrister 83. Wycliffe Hall Ox 00. d 03 p 04. C Heswall *Ches* 03-04; C Weston 04-07; Chapl E Lancs Hospice 09-11; C Bispham *Blackb* 11-13; V Copp w Inskip from 13. *St Peter's Vicarage, Preston Road, Inskip, Preston PR4 0TT*
E: calvina.howard@googlemail.com

HOWARD, Charles William Wykeham. b 52. Southn Univ BTh 81. Sarum & Wells Th Coll 76. d 79 p 80. C St Mary-at-Latton *Chelmsf* 79-82; Chapl RN 82-06; Chapl Midi-Pyrénées and Aude *Eur* 06-09; V Funtington and Sennicotts *Chich* 10-15; R W Stoke 10-15; R Funtington and W Stoke w Sennicotts from 15. *The Vicarage, Church Lane, Funtington, Chichester PO18 9LH* T: (01243) 575127 E: ch@scwwh.com

HOWARD, Clive Eric. b 65. Oak Hill Th Coll BA 99. d 99 p 00. C Chipping Sodbury and Old Sodbury *Glouc* 99-03; V Tipton St Matt *Lich* 03-13; RD Wednesbury 12-13; V Woodbridge St Jo and Bredfield *St E* from 13. *The Vicarage, St John's Hill, Woodbridge IP12 1HS* T: (01394) 382083
E: clive.howard65@gmail.com

HOWARD, Daniel James. b 71. Nottm Univ BA 94. Oak Hill Th Coll 04. d 06 p 07. C Deane *Man* 06-09; V Thornton Hough *Ches* from 09. *All Saints' Vicarage, Raby Road, Thornton Hough, Wirral CH63 1JP* T: 0151-336 3429 *or* 336 1654
E: vicar@allsaintsth.org.uk

HOWARD, Daniel Thomas. b 90. Liv Hope Univ BA 11. St Steph Ho Ox MSt 13. d 14 p 15. C Anfield St Columba *Liv* from 14. *9 Hilary Close, Liverpool L4 7TR*
E: fr.danielhoward@gmail.com

HOWARD, David John. b 47. Brasted Th Coll 68 Ripon Hall Ox 70. d 72 p 73. C Benchill *Man* 72-75; C Sedgley All SS *Lich* 75-77; C-in-c Lostock CD *Man* 77-85; V Lt Hulton 85-88; PtO 90-91; C E and W Leake, Stanford-on-Soar, Rempstone etc *S'well* 91-94; P-in-c Bilborough w Strelley 94-98; Chapl HM YOI Werrington Ho 98-03; Chapl HM Pris Drake Hall 03-14; rtd 14; PtO *Lich* from 14. *c/o Crockford's Clerical Directory, Church House, Great Smith Street, London SW1P 3AZ*
E: davidjohnhoward@virginmedia.com

HOWARD, David John. b 51. Lon Univ BSc 73. Oak Hill Th Coll 74. d 77 p 78. C Radipole and Melcombe Regis *Sarum* 77-83; R Tredington and Darlingscott w Newbold on Stour *Cov* 83-90; P-in-c Binley 90-94; V 94-04; RD Cov E 95-99; V Potterne w Worton and Marston *Sarum* from 04. *The Vicarage, 4 Rookes Lane, Potterne, Devizes SN10 5NF* T: (01380) 723189 E: dahoward@waitrose.com

HOWARD, Mrs Erika Kathryn. b 49. SRN 70 SCM 72 FRSA. S Dios Minl Tr Scheme 88. d 91 p 94. NSM New Shoreham and Old Shoreham *Chich* 91-94; C Kingston Buci 94-03; V Sompting from 03. *The Vicarage, West Street, Sompting, Lancing BN15 0AP* T: (01903) 234511
E: rev.erikahoward@ntlworld.com

HOWARD, Canon Francis Curzon. b 27. St Aid Birkenhead 54. d 57 p 58. C Claughton cum Grange *Ches* 57-60; C Cheltenham St Paul *Glouc* 60-62; V Sheff St Barn 62-65; R Sandys Bermuda 65-71; Asst P Westfield Atonement USA 71-76; R Tariffville 76-98; rtd 98; Hon Can Kaduna from 95. *PO Box 423, Simsbury CT 06070-0423, USA* T: (001) (860) 658 1897

HOWARD, Frank Thomas. b 36. Lon Univ BSc 57. Bps' Coll Cheshunt 59. d 61 p 62. C Macclesfield St Mich *Ches* 61-64; C Claughton cum Grange 64-66; V Lache cum Saltney 66-76; R Stanton *St E* 76-97; RD Ixworth 79-85; P-in-c Hempnall Nor 97-01; rtd 01; PtO *Nor* from 01. *55 Heywood Avenue, Diss IP22 4DN* T: (01379) 640819 E: fandrhoward@hotmail.com

HOWARD, Geoffrey. b 30. Barrister-at-Law 83 Lon Univ LLB 77. EMMTC. d 85 p 86. NSM Barton *Ely* 85-87; NSM Coton 85-87; C W Walton 87-92; TV Daventry, Ashby St Ledgers, Braunston etc *Pet* 92-97; rtd 97; PtO *Ely* 97-00 and from 07. *11 Porson Court, Porson Road, Cambridge CB2 8ER* T: (01223) 300738 E: geoffreyhoward@btinternet.com

HOWARD, Geoffrey. b 45. St Jo Coll Dur BA 68. Cranmer Hall Dur 67. d 71 p 72. C Cheetham Hill *Man* 71-74; C Denton Ch Ch 74-77; V Newchurch St Ambrose 77-91; TR Pendleton St Thos w Charlestown 91-94; AD Salford 86-94; PtO from 04. *20 May Road, Swinton, Manchester M27 5FR* T: 0161-950 7778 E: geoffrey.howard@ntlworld.com

HOWARD, Canon George Granville. b 47. Trin Coll Bris. d 88 p 89. C Downend *Bris* 88-92; V Clifton H Trin, St Andr and St Pet 92-99; Bp's Officer for Miss and Evang 92-99; V W Streatham St Jas *S'wark* 99-12; P-in-c Streatham St Paul 10-12; TR Furzedown 12; AD Tooting 02-07; Hon Can S'wark Cathl 10-12; rtd 12; PtO *St E* from 13. *1 Old Stable Yard, Bury St Edmunds IP33 1SU* T: (01284) 701203
E: george.g_howard@btinternet.com

HOWARD, George Victor Richard. b 69. Northn Univ MBA 06. Ripon Coll Cuddesdon 07. d 09 p 10. C Iver *Ox* 09-14; PtO from 14. *St Leonards House, St Leonards Walk, Iver SL0 9DD*-ql; E: georgehoward01@btinternet.com

HOWARD, John. *See* HOWARD, Nicolas John

HOWARD, Canon John Robert. b 60. NUI BA HDipEd. d 84 p 85. C Donaghcloney w Waringstown *D & D* 84-88; I Belfast St Ninian *Conn* 88-94; Bp's Dom Chapl 88-94; Chapl Ulster Univ 88-94; I Annahilt w Magherahamlet *D & D* from 94; Chapl HM Pris Maghaberry from 96; Can Dromore Cathl from 06; Chan Dromore Cathl from 12. *Annahilt Rectory, 15 Ballykeel Road, Hillsborough BT26 6NW* T: (028) 9263 8218 E: jrobert.howard@btinternet.com

HOWARD, Mrs Judith Marion. b 46. WEMTC 98. d 01 p 02. NSM Glouc St Jas and All SS 01-10; NSM Glouc St Jas and All SS and Ch Ch from 10. *Paulmead, Wells Road, Bisley, Stroud GL6 7AG* T: (01452) 770776 E: judy.howard@homecall.co.uk

HOWARD, Keith. b 55. St Jo Coll Nottm 81. d 84 p 85. C Llanidloes w Llangurig *Ban* 84-87; R Llansantffraid Glan Conwy and Eglwysbach *St As* 87-00; V Heapey and Withnell *Blackb* 00-07; V Hooton *Ches* from 07. *Hooton Vicarage, Chester Road, Childer Thornton, Ellesmere Port CH66 1QF* T: 0151-339 2020 E: stpaulschurch.hooton@virgin.net

HOWARD, Martin John Aidan. b 68. Lon Univ BA 90 Open Univ MA 96. St Jo Coll Nottm MA 97. d 97 p 98. C Billericay and Lt Burstead *Chelmsf* 97-01; TV Kinson *Sarum* 01-06; TV Hampreston 06-08; TR 08-14. *Address temp unknown*

HOWARD, Canon Michael Charles. b 35. Selw Coll Cam BA 58 MA 63 CQSW 72. Wycliffe Hall Ox 58. d 60 p 61. C Stowmarket *St E* 60-64; CMS Nigeria 64-71; Hon Can Ondo 70-71; Hon C Southborough St Pet w Ch Ch and St Matt *Roch* 72-73; PtO *Ox* from 73; rtd 00. *17 Milton Road, Bloxham, Banbury OX15 4HD* T: (01295) 720470

HOWARD, Michael John. b 51. Redland Coll of Educn CertEd 74 Open Univ BA 78. d 09 p 10. OLM Ness Gp *Linc* from 09. *East Dean House, East End, Langtoft, Peterborough PE6 9LP* T: (01778) 349576 E: michaelj.howard@virgin.net

HOWARD, Natalie Delia. b 51. St Mich Coll Llan 99. d 02 p 03. NSM Magor *Mon* 02-14; rtd 14; PtO *Mon* from 14. *8 The Meadows, Magor, Caldicot NP26 3LA* T: (01633) 881714

HOWARD, Nicolas John. b 61. Nottm Univ BTh 90. Aston Tr Scheme 85 Linc Th Coll 87. d 90 p 91. C Bracknell *Ox* 90-94; P-in-c Oldham St Chad Limeside *Man* 94-96; PtO *Birm* 96-99. *11 Chesterfield Court, Middleton Hall Road, Birmingham B30 1AF* T: 0121-459 4975

HOWARD, Norman. b 26. AKC 57. St Boniface Warminster 57. d 58 p 59. C Friern Barnet St Jas *Lon* 58-62; Jamaica 62-69; USA from 69; rtd 91. *766 Lake Forest Road, Clearwater FL 33765-2231, USA* T: (001) (813) 799 3929

HOWARD, Paul David. b 47. Lanchester Poly Cov BA 69. St Jo Coll Nottm 74. d 77 p 78. C Bedworth *Cov* 77-83; V Newchapel *Lich* 83-93; V Stretton w Claymills 93-04; P-in-c Talke 04-10; R 10-13; PtO *Lich* from 13. *29 Essington Way, Stoke-on-Trent ST6 5GB* E: paulhoward510@tiscali.co.uk

HOWARD, Canon Peter Leslie. b 48. Nottm Univ BTh 77 Birm Univ MA 80 Leeds Univ MEd 91. St Jo Coll Nottm LTh 77. d 77 p 78. C Gospel Lane St Mich *Birm* 77-81; P-in-c Nechells 81-85; V Stanley *Wakef* 85-92; P-in-c Nor Heartsease St Fran from 92; from 15; Dioc UPA/CUF Link Officer from 02; Hon Can Nor Cathl from 10; RD Nor E 06-14. *The Office, St Francis's Vicarage, 100 Rider Haggard Road, Norwich NR7 9UQ* T: (01603) 702799 E: plhoward@btinternet.com

HOWARD, Robert. *See* HOWARD, John Robert

HOWARD, Canon Robert Weston (Robin). b 28. Pemb Coll Cam BA 49 MA 53. Westcott Ho Cam 51. d 53 p 54. C Bishopwearmouth St Mich *Dur* 53-56; C Cambridge Gt St Mary w St Mich *Ely* 56-60; Hong Kong 60-66; V Prenton *Ches* 66-75; RD Frodsham 74-82; P-in-c Dunham-on-the-Hill 75-77; V Helsby and Ince 75-77; V Helsby and Dunham-on-the-Hill 77-82; Hon Can Ches Cathl 78-82; V Moseley St Mary *Birm* 82-88; V Chalke Valley W *Sarum* 88-93; rtd 93; PtO *St D* 93-08; *Heref* 93-08; Ox from 08. *4 Hitchmans Drive, Chipping Norton OX7 5BG* T: (01608) 641248

HOWARD, Ronald. b 40. AMIBF 65 AMICME 01. Cranmer Hall Dur 86. d 88 p 89. C Baildon *Bradf* 88-92; P-in-c Sutton 92-96; P-in-c St Tudy w St Mabyn and Michaelstow *Truro* 96-00; P-in-c Keyingham w Ottringham, Halsham and Sunk Is *York*

00-03; R 03-08; RD S Holderness 04-06; rtd 08; PtO *York* from 08. *Silver Gates, Withernsea Road, Hollym, Withernsea HU19 2QH*   T: (01964) 611270
E: ronaldhoward146@btinternet.com

HOWARD, Simon Charles. b 60. Birm Univ BA 81. Ridley Hall Cam 90. **d** 92 **p** 93. C Cambridge St Martin *Ely* 92-96; Chapl St Bede's Sch Cam 92-96; P-in-c Earley Trin *Ox* 96-05; P-in-c Ruscombe and Twyford 05-12; V Ruscombe and Twyford w Hurst from 12. *The Vicarage, Ruscombe, Reading RG10 9UD*   T: 0118-934 1092 *or* 934 1685   E: revsimon@lineone.net

HOWARD, Ms Susan. b 65. Lanc Univ BA 86. Ripon Coll Cuddesdon 88. **d** 91 **p** 94. C Ditton St Mich *Liv* 91-94; C Kirkby 94-97; Adv for Youth and Young Adults *Man* 97-00; Governor HM Pris Styal from 01. *HM Prison, Styal, Wilmslow SK9 4HR*   T: (01625) 532141

HOWARD, Thomas Norman. b 40. St Aid Birkenhead 64. **d** 67 **p** 68. C Farnworth and Kearsley *Man* 67-70; C Prestwich St Marg 70-73; V Heyside 73-85; Warden Lamplugh Ho Angl Conf Cen 85-90; Hon C Langtoft w Foxholes, Butterwick, Cottam etc *York* 85-87; C 87-90; V Fence and Newchurch-in-Pendle *Blackb* 90-00; Dioc Ecum Officer 90-95; rtd 00; Hon C Stalybridge H Trin and Ch Ch *Ches* 01-03; PtO from 03. *36 Bridgeside, Carnforth LA5 9LF*   T: (01524) 736552

HOWARD, William Alfred. b 47. St Jo Coll Dur BA 69. Wycliffe Hall Ox 74. **d** 77 **p** 79. C Norbiton *S'wark* 77-80; C Mile Cross *Nor* 80-84; R Grimston, Congham and Roydon 84-13; Chapl Norfolk Constabulary 00-13; rtd 13; PtO *Cov* from 14. *21 Daniell Road, Wellesbourne, Warwick CV35 9UD* E: william.howard@dunelm.org.uk

HOWARD-COWLEY, Joseph Charles. b 27. Trin Coll Cam BA 53 MA 56. Wells Th Coll 53. **d** 55 **p** 56. C Newmarket All SS *St E* 55-58; Chapl Aycliffe Approved Sch Co Dur 58-61; V Aldringham *St E* 61-86; rtd 86; PtO *St E* 86-93; *Truro* 93-03. *36 Bath Road, Royal Wootton Bassett, Swindon SN4 7DF*

HOWARD JONES, Preb Raymond Vernon. b 31. AKC 54. **d** 55 **p** 56. C Hutton *Chelmsf* 55-58; CF 58-62; V Walpole St Andrew *Ely* 62-64; Chapl St Crispin's Hosp Northampton 64-70; V Brockhampton w Fawley *Heref* 70-86; V Fownhope 70-86; RD Heref Rural 77-81; Preb Heref Cathl 81-97; Communications Adv and Bp's Staff Officer 86-97; rtd 97; PtO *Heref* from 97. *Kingfishers, Breinton, Hereford HR4 7PP* T: (01432) 279371

HOWARTH, David Alexander. b 81. Wycliffe Hall Ox BTh 14. **d** 14. C Bromley Ch Ch *Roch* from 14. *56 Heathfield Road, Bromley BR1 3RW*   M: 07740-361097
E: dahowarth1@gmail.com

HOWARTH, Delphine. *See* HOWARTH, Victoria Elizabeth Delphine

HOWARTH, Mrs Henriette. b 66. Utrecht Univ MTh 94. Wycliffe Hall Ox 91. **d** 04 **p** 05. C Sparkbrook Ch Ch *Birm* 04-05; C Springfield 05-09; PtO 09-11; Chapl St Mich C of E Academy 11-14; NSM Peckham All SS *S'wark* 12-14. *7 Delaunay House, 8 Burnett Street, Bradford BD1 5BJ*
E: hentob@tiscali.co.uk

HOWARTH, Michael Scott. b 42. SNWTP. **d** 13 **p** 14. NSM Dearnley *Man* 13-14; NSM Dearnley, Wardle and Smallbridge from 14. *5 Starfield Avenue, Littleborough OL15 0NG*   T: (01706) 371544   M: 07977-164848   E: michael.howarth@zen.co.uk

HOWARTH, Miles. b 58. **d** 08 **p** 09. OLM Failsworth St Jo *Man* 08-12; Spiritual Care Co-ord Dr Kershaw's Hospice Oldham from 11; NSM Kirkholt *Man* 12-14; P-in-c Denton Ch Ch from 14; C Audenshaw St Steph from 14; C Denton St Lawr from 14; C Haughton St Anne from 14. *15 Grimshaw Street, Failsworth, Manchester M35 0DF*   T: 0161-688 7710
M: 07718-326321   E: miles@howarth8023.freeserve.co.uk

HOWARTH, Robert Francis Harvey. b 31. S'wark Ord Course 71. **d** 72 **p** 73. C St Marylebone All So w SS Pet and Jo *Lon* 72-73; C St Helen Bishopsgate w St Martin Outwich 73-78; V Harlow St Mary and St Hugh w St Jo the Bapt *Chelmsf* 78-88; P-in-c Victoria Docks Ascension 88-96; rtd 96; PtO *Chelmsf* from 12. *14 Quinlan Court, 78 Mill Lane, Danbury, Chelmsford CM3 4HX*   T: (01245) 698142

HOWARTH, Canon Ronald. b 26. TCD BA 51 MA 54. Linc Th Coll 50. **d** 52 **p** 53. C Gannow *Blackb* 52-55; Chapl Victory Coll Ikare Nigeria 55-60; Chapl St Paul's Abeokuta 60-66; Chapl Egbado Coll Ilaro 66-84; Vice Prin 75-84; P-in-c Ilaro All So 84-86; Bp's Sec and P-in-c Abeokuta St Paul 86-89; Hon Can Abeokuta 83-86; Canon from 86; rtd 91. *c/o Mrs H Howarth Downey, 35 Alford Road, West Bridgford, Nottingham NG2 6GJ*

✠**HOWARTH, The Rt Revd Toby Matthew.** b 62. Yale Univ BA 86 Birm Univ MA 91 Free Univ of Amsterdam PhD 01. Wycliffe Hall Ox 89. **d** 92 **p** 93 **c** 14. C Derby St Aug 92-95; Crosslinks India 95-00; The Netherlands 00-02; Vice Prin and Tutor Crowther Hall CMS Tr Coll Selly Oak 02-04; P-in-c Springfield *Birm* 04-11; Bp's Adv on Inter-Faith Relns

05-11; Abp's Sec for Internat and Inter-Relig Relns *Cant* 11-14; Suff Bp Bradf *Leeds* from 14. *Bradford Cathedral, 1 Stott Hill, Bradford BD1 4EH*
E: bishop.toby@westyorkshiredales.anglican.org

HOWARTH, Victoria Elizabeth Delphine. b 53. **d** 11 **p** 12. OLM Penkridge *Lich* from 11. *Lower Farm House, Bednall, Stafford ST17 0SA*   T: (01785) 714527   E: delphine.howarth@ifdev.net

HOWAT, Jeremy Noel Thomas. b 35. Em Coll Cam BA 59 MA 62. Ridley Hall Cam 59. **d** 63 **p** 64. C Sutton *Liv* 63-65; C Kirk Ella *York* 65-66; C Bridlington Quay Ch Ch 66-69; R Wheldrake 69-78; Dioc Youth Officer 69-74; SAMS Argentina 78-81; 90-97; P-in-c Newton upon Ouse *York* 81-82; V Shipton w Overton 81-82; P-in-c Skelton by York 81-82; R Skelton w Shipton and Newton on Ouse 82-89; C Elloughton and Brough w Brantingham 97-99; rtd 99; PtO *York* from 00. *18 Petersway, York YO30 6AR*   T: (01904) 628946   E: nowell@ntlworld.com

HOWDEN, Canon John Travis. b 40. RIBA 62. Sarum Th Coll 66. **d** 69 **p** 70. C S Gillingham *Roch* 69-72; C Banbury *Ox* 72-73; LtO *York* 73-74; Hon C Hull St Jo Newland 74-81; Hon C Stock Harvard *Chelmsf* 82-86; R Doddinghurst and Mountnessing 86-91; P-in-c Pleshey 91-00; Warden Pleshey Retreat Ho 91-00; R Wickham Bishops w Lt Braxted *Chelmsf* 00-05; Hon Can Chelmsf Cathl 97-05; rtd 05; PtO *Chelmsf* from 05. *12A Back Road, Writtle, Chelmsford CM1 3PD*   T: (01245) 422023   E: johnhowden@talktalk.net

HOWDLE, Glyn. b 50. Bp Lonsdale Coll BEd 72. St Alb Minl Tr Scheme 90. **d** 01 **p** 02. NSM Aspenden, Buntingford and Westmill *St Alb* 01-11; PtO from 11. *33 Cappell Lane, Stanstead Abbotts SG12 8BU*   M: 07507-541884   T: (01920) 739162
E: glynhowdle@gmail.com

HOWE, Canon Alan Raymond. b 52. Nottm Univ BTh 79. St Jo Coll Nottm 76. **d** 80 **p** 81. C Southsea St Simon *Portsm* 80-83; C Bexleyheath St Pet *Roch* 83-86; TV Camberley St Paul *Guildf* 86-93; P-in-c Mansfield St Jo *S'well* 93-96; P-in-c Wollaton Park 96-02; V 02-05; AD Nottingham W 99-05; V Chilwell from 05; P-in-c Lenton Abbey from 09; Hon Can S'well Minster from 11. *Christ Church Vicarage, 8 College Road, Beeston, Nottingham NG9 4AS*   T: 0115-925 7419   E: ar.howe1@ntlworld.com

HOWE, Anthony Graham. b 72. Qu Coll Ox BA 93 MA 99. St Steph Ho Ox BA 00. **d** 01 **p** 02. C Newbury *Ox* 01-04; Dioc Communications Officer *Wakef* 04-05; C Athersley and Monk Bretton 05-06; V Staincliffe and Carlinghow *Leeds* from 06. *The Vicarage, Staincliffe Hall Road, Batley WF17 7QX*   T: (01924) 473343   M: 07795-095157
E: fatherhowe@tiscali.co.uk

HOWE, Brian Moore. b 48. **d** 10 **p** 11. NSM Ballymoney w Finvoy and Rasharkin *Conn* from 10. *10 Station Road, Portstewart BT55 7DA*   T: (028) 7083 1848   M: 07712-069600
E: brianmoorehowe@gmail.com

HOWE, Charles. b 30. Lon Univ BD 65 Open Univ BA 79. Tyndale Hall Bris 55. **d** 58 **p** 59. C Willowfield *D & D* 58-60; C Derryloran *Arm* 60-64; C Belfast St Bart *Conn* 64-65; I Tullyaughnish w Kilmacrennan and Killygarvan *D & R* 65-72; I Londonderry St Aug 73-95; Can Derry Cathl 85-95; Dioc Org and Tutor for Aux Min 93-95; rtd 95. *43 Ashburn Avenue, Londonderry BT47 5QE*   T: (028) 7131 2305
E: charleshowe1@hotmail.com

HOWE, Canon David Randall. b 24. St Jo Coll Cam BA 51 MA 55. Wells Th Coll 51. **d** 53 **p** 54. C Basingstoke *Win* 53-59; V Rotherwick, Hook and Greywell 59-70; R Bossington w Broughton 70-81; R Broughton w Bossington and Mottisfont 81-86; R Broughton, Bossington, Houghton and Mottisfont 86-89; Hon Can Win Cathl 87-89; rtd 89; PtO *Win* 89-05; *Sarum* 89-05; *Ox* from 06. *Easter Cottage, 36 Britwell Road, Burnham, Slough SL1 8AG*   T: (01628) 603046

HOWE, Miss Frances Ruth. b 28. ACIB 67. Cranmer Hall Dur IDC 80. **dss** 80 **d** 87 **p** 94. Newc St Andr 80-82; Chapl Asst R Victoria Infirmary Newc 80-87; Chapl Wylam and Fleming Ch Hosp 82-87; Chapl St Oswald's Hospice Newc 86-92; C Newc Epiphany 87-90; rtd 92; Hon C Delaval Newc 92-98; PtO from 98. *18 Mason Avenue, Whitley Bay NE26 1AQ*   T: 0191-252 5163

HOWE, The Ven George Alexander. b 52. St Jo Coll Dur BA 73. Westcott Ho Cam 73. **d** 75 **p** 76. C Peterlee *Dur* 75-79; C Norton St Mary 79-81; V Hart w Elwick Hall 81-85; R Sedgefield 85-91; RD 89-91; V Kendal H Trin *Carl* 91-00; RD Kendal 94-00; Hon Can Carl Cathl 94-15; Adn Westmorland and Furness 00-11; Bp's Adv for Ecum Affairs 01-11; Bp's Chapl and Chief of Staff and Dioc Dir of Ords 11-15; rtd 15. *29 Forge Bank, Bosbury, Ledbury HR8 1QU*   M: 07879-452763   E: gahowe@hotmail.co.uk

HOWE, Canon John. b 36. Ex Coll Ox BA 58 MA 63. St Steph Ho Ox 58. **d** 61 **p** 62. C Horninglow *Lich* 61-64; C Sedgley All SS 64-66; V Ocker Hill 66-73; V Gnosall 73-79; P-in-c Hoar Cross 79-82; Preb Lich Cathl 83-88; V Hoar Cross w Newchurch

83-88; Can Res Lich Cathl 88-96; Master St Jo Hosp Lich 96-00; rtd 00; PtO *Lich* 01-11. *9 Cherry Street, The Leys, Tamworth B79 7ED* T: (01827) 57817

HOWE, Nicholas Simon. b 60. Man Univ BA 81 K Coll Lon MTh 85. Ridley Hall Cam 86. **d** 88 **p** 89. C Lich St Chad 88-92; TV Leeds City *Ripon* 92-01; Dioc Dir of Ords and Post-Ord Tr *Sheff* 01-06; Chapl Sheff Cathl 01-06; Can Res Sheff Cathl 03-06; Chapl Stockholm w Gävle and Västerås *Eur* from 06. *Västerlånggatan 31, 11129 Stockholm, Sweden* T/F: (0046) (8) 663 8248 E: anglican.church@chello.se

HOWE, Canon Rex Alan. b 29. Ch Coll Cam BA 53 MA 57. Coll of Resurr Mirfield 53. **d** 55 **p** 56. C Barnsley St Pet *Wakef* 55-57; C Helmsley *York* 57-60; V Middlesbrough St Martin 60-67; V Redcar 67-73; V Kirkleatham 67-73; RD Guisborough 67-73; Dean Hong Kong 73-76; Adn Hong Kong 75-76; TR Grantham *Linc* 77-85; RD 78-85; Can and Preb Linc Cathl 81-85; V Canford Cliffs and Sandbanks *Sarum* 85-94; RD Poole 92-94; rtd 94; PtO *Sarum* from 94. *2 St Nicholas Hospital, 5 St Nicholas Road, Salisbury SP1 2SW* T: (01722) 326677

HOWE, Roy William. b 38. ALCD 67. **d** 66 **p** 67. C Bradf Cathl 66-70; C Barnoldswick w Bracewell 70-72; V Yeadon St Jo 72-79; P-in-c Bainton *York* 79-86; P-in-c Middleton-on-the-Wolds 79-86; P-in-c N Dalton 79-86; RD Harthill 81-87; C Watton w Beswick and Kilnwick 82-86; R Bainton w N Dalton, Middleton-on-the-Wolds etc 86-87; TV Penrith w Newton Reigny and Plumpton Wall *Carl* 87-92; Dioc Chapl to Agric and Rural Life 87-92; V Cornhill w Carham *Newc* 92-98; V Branxton 92-98; P-in-c Coddenham w Gosbeck and Hemingstone w Henley *St E* 98-03; rtd 03; PtO *St E* from 04. *Ballaclague, 2 Halvasso Vean, Longdowns, Penryn TR10 9DN* T: (01209) 860552

HOWE, Ruth. *See* HOWE, Frances Ruth

HOWE, William Ernest. b 25. MRICS 51. Westcott Ho Cam 68. **d** 70 **p** 71. C Anston *Sheff* 70-73; V 84-92; C Woodsetts 70-73; V Greasbrough 73-84; rtd 92; PtO *Sheff* from 92; *S'well* from 97. *21 Broad Bridge Close, Kiveton Park, Sheffield S26 6SL* T: (01909) 779779

HOWELL, Andrew John. b 44. Clifton Th Coll 68. **d** 71 **p** 72. C Halliwell St Pet *Man* 71-77; V Facit 77-95; P-in-c Wardle and Smallbridge 95-13; rtd 13; PtO *Man* from 13. *21 Bateman Avenue, Rochdale OL12 9ST* T: (01706) 375082 E: a.howell554@btinternet.com

HOWELL, Brian. b 43. MBE 99. Newc Univ MA 95. Cranmer Hall Dur 11. **d** 11 **p** 12. NSM Blaydon and Swalwell *Dur* from 11; PtO from 14. *Hillcroft House, Sourmilk Hill Lane, Gateshead NE9 5RU* T: 0191-482 3158 M: 07710-000654 E: b_howell2004@yahoo.co.uk

HOWELL, David. b 29. Clifton Th Coll 56. **d** 59 **p** 60. C Tipton St Martin *Lich* 59-62; V W Bromwich St Paul 62-71; V Deptford St Jo *S'wark* 71-81; Dir and Chapl Home of Divine Healing Crowhurst 81-89; rtd 90; Dir Ch Coun for Health and Healing 91-93; Hon Dioc Adv on Health and Healing *B & W* 93-00; PtO from 01. *60 Andrew Allan Road, Rockwell Green, Wellington TA21 9DY* T: (01823) 664529 E: revshowell@waitrose.com

HOWELL (formerly WILLIAMS), David Paul. b 61. Coll of Resurr Mirfield 91. **d** 93 **p** 94. C Leic St Aid 93-97; P-in-c Edvin Loach w Tedstone Delamere etc *Heref* from 97. *The Rectory, Whitbourne, Worcester WR6 5RP* T: (01886) 821285

HOWELL, Geoffrey Peter. b 52. Selw Coll Cam BA 75 MA 78 Leeds Univ MA 01 K Alfred's Coll Win PGCE 77 LTCL 82. Cranmer Hall Dur 85. **d** 87 **p** 88. C Hartlepool St Luke *Dur* 87-90; TV Burford I, Nash and Boraston *Heref* 90-94; TV Whitton w Greete and Hope Bagot 90-94; TV Burford III w Lt Heref 90-94; TV Tenbury Wells 90-94; P-in-c Cradley w Mathon and Storridge 94-97; Succ Heref Cathl 97-99; Chapl Heref Cathl Jun Sch 97-99; PtO *Heref* from 99; Min Can St Woolos Cathl 02-10; TV Monkton *St D* from 10. *The Vicarage, 13 Reginald Close, Hundleton, Pembroke SA71 5RZ* T: (01646) 687459 E: gphowell@btinternet.com

HOWELL, Mrs Heather Ellen. b 40. Bp Otter Coll Chich TCert 60 Sussex Univ BA 83. Ripon Coll Cuddesdon 00. **d** 01 **p** 02. NSM Newhaven *Chich* 01-06; P-in-c Fletching 06-11; rtd 11. *1 Rookery Way, Seaford BN25 2SA* T: (01323) 873643 E: heather.howell@tiscali.co.uk

HOWELL, Mrs Pamela Isobel Anne. b 62. Sheff Univ LLB 84 Solicitor 87. Qu Coll Birm 09. **d** 12 **p** 13. C Whitnash *Cov* from 12. *10 Launce Grove, Heathcote, Warwick CV34 6EH* T: (01926) 337609 E: revpamhowell@st-margc.co.uk

HOWELL, Roger Brian. b 43. ALCD 67. **d** 67 **p** 68. C Battersea Park St Sav *S'wark* 67-71; C Southgate *Chich* 71-76; V Pendeen and P-in-c Sancreed *Truro* 76-81; V Bedgrove *Ox* 81-91; R Purley 91-08; RD Bradfield 94-04; rtd 08; PtO *Ox* from 08. *246 Burwell Meadow, Witney OX28 5JJ* T: (01993) 706893 E: rbh@bradean.fsnet.co.uk

HOWELL, Ronald William Fullerton. b 51. Man Univ BA 72 CertEd Ox Univ BA 78 MA. Ripon Coll Cuddesdon 76. **d** 79

p 80. C Newc St Fran 79-81; C Warmsworth *Sheff* 81-82; Dioc Educn Officer 82-85; V Millhouses H Trin 85-93; R Thornhill and Whitley Lower *Wakef* 93-96. *11 Hartington Road, Aldeburgh IP15 5HD* T: (01728) 453000

HOWELL, Simon Gordon. b 63. Sheff Univ BMus 84 Bath Coll of HE PGCE 85 Anglia Ruskin Univ MA 07 ACII 90. Ridley Hall Cam 00. **d** 03 **p** 04. C Northwood Em *Lon* 03-06; TV Keynsham *B & W* 06-14; Bp's Inter Faith Officer 10-14; TV Stroud Team *Glouc* from 14. *Holy Trinity Vicarage, 10 Bowbridge Lane, Stroud GL5 2JW* M: 07971-582332 T: (01453) 350387 E: revsimonhowell@blueyonder.co.uk

HOWELL-JONES, Canon Peter. b 62. Huddersfield Poly BMus 84 Bretton Hall Coll PGCE 85. St Jo Coll Nottm 90 MA 96. **d** 93 **p** 94. C Walsall *Lich* 93-98; V Boldmere *Birm* 98-05; Can Res Birm Cathl 05-11; Bp's Adv for Miss 05-11; Asst Dean 07-11; Vice-Dean and Can Res Ches Cathl from 11. *5 Abbey Street, Chester CH1 2JF* T: (01244) 500968 M: 07435-969256 E: vice.dean@chestercathedral.com

HOWELLS, Chan Arthur Glyn. b 32. Univ of Wales (Lamp) BA 54. St Mich Coll Llan 54. **d** 56 **p** 57. C Oystermouth *S & B* 56-58; C Llangyfelach 58-64; R Llandefalle and Llyswen w Boughrood etc 64-69; Youth Chapl 67-71; V Landore 70-80; Dioc Missr 80-89; Can Brecon Cathl 80-89; Can Tres Brecon Cathl 89-94; Dir St Mary's Coll Swansea 82-89; V Swansea St Jas *S & B* 89-98; Chan Brecon Cathl 94-98; RD Swansea 96-98; rtd 98. *2 Lilliput Lane, West Cross, Swansea SA3 5AQ* T: (01792) 402123

HOWELLS, David. b 55. Grey Coll Dur BA 78. Ripon Coll Cuddesdon 79. **d** 81 **p** 82. C Birtley *Dur* 81-84; Canada from 84. *5551 West Saanich Road, Victoria BC V9E 2G1, Canada* E: smaaac@telus.net

HOWELLS (formerly SMITHAM), Mrs Elizabeth Ann. b 62. St D Coll Lamp BA 90 Univ of Wales (Lamp) MA 04. St Mich Coll Llan. **d** 92 **p** 97. C Llangiwg *S & B* 92-94; C Morriston 94-98; P-in-c Llanfair-is-gaer and Llanddeiniolen *Ban* 98-00; V 00-03; V Llanddeiniolen w Llanfair-is-gaer etc 03-04; V Clydau w Egremont and Llanglydwen *St D* 04-06; P-in-c Llanpumsaint w Llanllawddog 06-08; V Llanilar w Rhostie and Llangwyryfon etc 09-10; V Llandybie from 10. *77 Kings Road, Llandybie, Ammanford SA18 2TL* T: (01269) 850337

HOWELLS, Euryl. b 60. Univ of Wales (Cardiff) BD 93. St Mich Coll Llan 90. **d** 93 **p** 94. C Deanery of Emlyn *St D* 93-97; V Llangeler w Pen-Boyr 97-03; P-in-c Tre-lech a'r Betws w Abernant and Llanwinio 03-06; Chapl Carmarthenshire NHS Trust 06-08; Chapl R Devon and Ex NHS Foundn Trust 08-09; V Grwp Bro Ystwyth a Mynach *St D* 09-10; PtO from 10; Sen Chapl Hywel Dda Health Bd from 11. *Chaplaincy Office, Glangwili Hospital, Dolgwili Road, Carmarthen SA31 2AF* T: (01267) 227563 E: euryl.howells@virgin.net

HOWELLS, Garfield Edwin. b 18. K Coll Lon 53 St Boniface Warminster 53. **d** 54 **p** 55. C Sanderstead All SS *S'wark* 54-57; CF 57-60; R Kingsdown *Roch* 60-64; Australia from 64; rtd 83. *301/17 Hefron Street, Rockingham WA 6168, Australia* T: (0061) (8) 9592 8337

HOWELLS, Gordon. b 39. Univ of Wales (Cardiff) BSc 61 DipEd 62. Ripon Coll Cuddesdon 86. **d** 88 **p** 89. C Atherstone *Cov* 88-89; C Lillington 89-92; R Clymping and Yapton w Ford *Chich* 92-97; P-in-c Rackheath and Salhouse *Nor* 97-04; Chapl among Deaf People 97-04; rtd 04; PtO *St As* from 09; *Ban* from 14. *53 Abbey Road, Rhos on Sea, Colwyn Bay LL28 4NR* T: (01492) 525899 E: g.howells.norwich@virgin.net

HOWELLS, Richard Grant. b 62. Univ of Wales (Lamp) BA 83. Westcott Ho Cam 83 and 92. **d** 93 **p** 94. NSM Harston w Hauxton and Newton *Ely* 93-15; NSM Nar Valley *Nor* from 15. *Church Farm House, South Acre, King's Lynn PE32 2AD* T: (01223) 871902 E: rhowells@harvardup.co.uk

HOWELLS, Mrs Sandra June. b 52. FBDO 77. Mon Dioc Tr Scheme 90. **d** 93 **p** 97. NSM Caerwent w Dinham and Llanfair Discoed etc *Mon* 93-97; C Griffithstown 97-00; V Penallt and Trellech 00-07; V Trellech and Penallt from 07. *The Vicarage, Penallt, Monmouth NP25 4SE* T: (01600) 716622

HOWES, Alan. b 49. Chich Th Coll 76. **d** 79 **p** 80. C Bilborough St Jo *S'well* 79-82; TV Newark w Hawton, Cotham and Shelton 82-89; TV Newark 89-94; P-in-c Coseley St Chad *Worc* 94-96; V from 96. *St Chad's Vicarage, 3 Oak Street, Coseley, Bilston WV14 9TA* T: (01902) 882285 M: 07941-284048 E: alan@heavensdoor.co.uk

HOWES, David. b 30. Open Univ BA 75. Roch Th Coll 62. **d** 64 **p** 65. C Highweek *Ex* 64-67; C Clyst St George 67-71; P-in-c Woolfardisworthy w Kennerleigh 71-72; P-in-c Washford Pyne w Puddington 71-72; TR N Creedy 72-73; PtO 74-77; C Walworth *S'wark* 77-78; P-in-c Roundshaw LEP 78-83; R S'wark St Geo 83-90; P-in-c Coseley St Jude 84-90; P-in-c Risley *Derby* 90-93; Bp's Ind Adv 90-93; rtd 93; PtO *Derby* 93-00; *S'well* 95-00; *Win* 01-13; *Lich* 13-14. *41 Sutton Road, Shrewsbury SY2 6DL*

HOWES, Miss Judith Elizabeth. b 44. SRN RSCN. Ripon Coll Cuddesdon 83. **d** 89 **p** 94. Par Dn Ex St Sidwell and St Matt 89-92; Par Dn Brixham w Churston Ferrers and Kingswear 92-94; C 94-95; TV E Darlington *Dur* 95-97; TR 97-02; P-in-c Washington 02-04; P-in-c S Shields St Simon 04-08; C Hedworth 04-08; rtd 08; PtO *Dur* from 08. *25 Firtree Avenue, Harraton, Washington NE38 9BA*

HOWES, Mrs Kathleen Valerie. b 44. Surrey Univ BA 05. STETS 03. **d** 05 **p** 06. NSM Droxford and Meonstoke w Corhampton cum Exton *Portsm* 05-08; NSM Cosham 08-09; NSM Bath St Sav w Swainswick and Woolley *B & W* 09-11; rtd 11; PtO *Lich* from 13. *41 Sutton Road, Shrewsbury SY2 6DL* E: valerie.howes@btinternet.com

HOWES, Canon Norman Vincent. b 36. AKC 61. **d** 62 **p** 63. C Radford *Cov* 62-66; V Napton on the Hill 66-72; V Exhall 72-83; R Walton d'Eiville and V Wellesbourne 83-03; RD Fosse 87-93; Hon Can Cov Cathl 89-03; rtd 03; PtO *Cov* from 03. *Harwood, Bottom Street, Northend, Southam CV47 2TH* T: (01295) 770303 E: howes.howes@btinternet.com

HOWES, Valerie. *See* HOWES, Kathleen Valerie

HOWES, William John Lawrence. b 46. EAMTC. **d** 00 **p** 01. NSM Lexden *Chelmsf* 00-04; NSM Coggeshall w Markshall 04-11; rtd 11; PtO *Chelmsf* from 12. *26 Westfield Drive, Coggeshall, Colchester CO6 1PU* T/F: (01376) 561826 M: 07718-048574 E: frbill_105@fsmail.net

HOWETT, Miss Amanda Jane. b 68. Reading Univ BA 91 Birm Univ MPhil 08 Cam Univ BTh 11. Ridley Hall Cam 09. **d** 11 **p** 12. C Boldmere *Birm* 11-15; C Birm St Luke from 15. *27-29 Bradshaw Close, Birmingham B15 2DD*

HOWITT, Mrs Barbara Gillian. b 39. K Coll Lon BD 60 PGCE 61 MA 95. EAMTC 99. **d** 00 **p** 01. NSM Longthorpe *Pet* 00-09; rtd 09; PtO *Pet* from 09. *8 Wakerley Drive, Orton Longueville, Peterborough PE2 7WF* T: (01733) 391092 E: barbara@bhowitt.wanadoo.co.uk

HOWITT, Ivan Richard. b 56. Kent Univ BA 81. Sarum & Wells Th Coll 83. **d** 85 **p** 86. C Herne Bay Ch Ch *Cant* 85-87; C St Laur in Thanet 87-90; R Owmby and Normanby w Glentham *Linc* 90-91; P-in-c Spridlington w Saxby and Firsby 90-91; R Owmby Gp 91-99; RD Lawres 96-99; Chapl Hull Miss to Seafarers 99-03; V Hedon w Paull *York* 03-09; P-in-c Sand Hutton 09-12; P-in-c Whitwell w Crambe and Foston 09-12; R Harton 12-13; rtd 13; PtO *York* from 14. *40 Clipson Crest, Barton-upon-Humber DN18 5GW* T: (01652) 781491 M: 07739-316019 E: ivan.howitt@btinternet.com

HOWITT, John Leslie. b 28. Lon Coll of Div 60. **d** 62 **p** 63. C Attenborough w Bramcote *S'well* 62-66; Chapl Rampton Hosp Retford 66-71; P-in-c Treswell and Cottam *S'well* 68-71; Chapl HM Pris Cardiff 71-75; Chapl HM Youth Cust Cen Dover 75-79; Chapl HM Pris Dartmoor 79-83; Chapl HM Pris Cant 83-87; Chapl HM Det Cen Aldington 83-87; PtO *Cant* 87-88; V Shobnall *Lich* 88-94; rtd 94; PtO *Chich* from 94. *7 Wish Court, Ingram Crescent West, Hove BN3 5NY* T: (01273) 414535

HOWITZ (formerly TEDD), Christopher Jonathan Richard. b 74. Ch Ch Ox MEng 96. Oak Hill Th Coll BA 00. **d** 00 **p** 01. C Harpurhey Ch Ch *Man* 00-04; P-in-c Higher Openshaw 05-12; Co-Chapl Oman from 12. *PO Box 1982, Ruwi 112, Sultanate of Oman* E: cjhowitz@hotmail.com

HOWLAND, David John. b 55. SEITE 12. **d** 15. NSM Horsted Keynes *Chich* from 15. *13 Holtye Avenue, East Grinstead RH19 3EG* T: (01342) 313094 E: david@davidhowland.co.uk

HOWLES, Kenneth. b 56. Oak Hill Th Coll 91. **d** 93 **p** 94. C Leyland St Andr *Blackb* 93-96; C Livesey 96-97; C Ewood 96-97; P-in-c 97-99; V 99-03; P-in-c Blackb Sav 01-03; V Chorley St Jas 03-10; rtd 10. *20 Waverley Drive, Tarleton, Preston PR4 6XX* T: (01772) 815752 E: kenhowles@btinternet.com

HOWLETT, Mrs Elizabeth Mary. b 58. Southn Univ BA 80. WMMTC 99. **d** 01 **p** 02. C Salter Street and Shirley *Birm* 01-04; Bp's Adv for Lay Adult Educn and Tr from 04. *6 Greenside, Shirley, Solihull B90 4HH* T: (01564) 702233 E: liz@birmingham.anglican.org

HOWLETT, Richard Laurence. b 56. Kent Univ BA 79. Trin Coll Bris. **d** 94 **p** 95. C Louth *Linc* 94-98; R Marston Morteyne w Lidlington *St Alb* 98-05; V Goldington from 05. *St Mary's Vicarage, Church Lane, Goldington, Bedford MK41 0AP* T: (01234) 355024 E: richard@revhowlett.fslife.co.uk

HOWLETT, Mrs Susannah Elizabeth. b 62. RGN 84. St Mellitus Coll BA 14. **d** 14 **p** 15. NSM Boreham *Chelmsf* from 14. *4 Willow Close, Chelmsford CM1 7AY* T: (01245) 441390 E: sue_howlett@hotmail.co.uk

HOWLETT, Victor John. b 43. S Dios Minl Tr Scheme 90. **d** 93 **p** 94. NSM Bris St Andr w St Bart 93-95; NSM Bishopston and Bris St Matt and St Nath 95-96; C Gtr Corsham 96-99;

V Wick w Doynton and Dyrham 99-05; AD Kingswood and S Glos 02-05; P-in-c Stratton St Margaret w S Marston etc 05-10; rtd 10. *11 Moor Park, Neston, Corsham SN13 9YJ* T: (01225) 819954 E: victorhowlett@hotmail.co.uk

HOWMAN, Anne Louise. b 43. Ex Univ BA 97. SWMTC 97. **d** 99 **p** 00. NSM Ex St Dav 99-02; C Salcombe and Malborough w S Huish 02-07; rtd 08. *28 Sentrys Orchard, Exminster, Exeter EX6 8UD* E: alhow@btinternet.com

HOWORTH, Andrew John. **d** 15. NSM Addingham *Leeds* from 15. *75 Silverdale Drive, Guiseley, Leeds LS20 8BE* T: (01943) 879267 E: andrew.howorth@nhs.net

HOWORTH, Sister Rosemary. b 44. Newnham Coll Cam MA. Westcott Ho Cam. **d** 98 **p** 99. NSM Derby St Andr w St Osmund 98-10; NSM Morley w Smalley and Horsley Woodhouse 10-14; NSM Loscoe 10-13; NSM Morley and Smalley 14; PtO from 14. *The Convent of the Holy Name, Morley Road, Oakwood, Derby DE21 4QZ* T: (01332) 671716 E: rosemarychn@yahoo.co.uk

HOWSE, Martin David. b 58. St Steph Ho Ox 97. **d** 99 **p** 00. C Colchester St Jas and St Paul w All SS etc *Chelmsf* 99-03; V Rush Green from 03. *St Augustine's Vicarage, 78 Birkbeck Road, Romford RM7 0QP* T: (01708) 741460 F: 732093 M: 07770-928167 E: martin.howse@virgin.net

HOWSON, Christopher Stewart. b 69. Bradf Univ BA 94 St Jo Coll Dur BA 02 CQSW 94. Cranmer Hall Dur 99. **d** 02 **p** 03. C Tong *Bradf* 02-05; Miss P Bradf Adnry 05-12; Chapl Sunderland Univ *Dur* from 12; Hon C Sunderland Minster from 12. *2 Thornhill Terrace, Sunderland SR2 7JL* E: chrishowson@yahoo.com

HOWSON, Edwin. b 51. ERMC. **d** 13 **p** 14. NSM St Osyth *Chelmsf* 13-15; NSM St Osyth and Great Bentley from 15. *Little Kings, 41 High Street, Brightlingsea, Colchester CO7 0AQ* T: (01206) 308039

HOWSON, James Edward. b 62. Ridley Hall Cam 97 EAMTC 98. **d** 00 **p** 01. C Cogges and S Leigh *Ox* 00-05; PtO 05-06; *Eur* 05-06; P-in-c Kiev 06-08; R Alfriston w Lullington, Litlington and W Dean *Chich* 09-14; PtO *Pet* from 14. *14 Bentley Close, Northampton NN3 5JS* E: jameshowson@rocketmail.com

HOY, Michael John. b 30. Reading Univ BSc 52. Oak Hill Th Coll 57. **d** 59 **p** 60. C Worthing St Geo *Chich* 59-62; C Tulse Hill H Trin *S'wark* 62-66; R Danby Wiske w Yafforth and Hutton Bonville *Ripon* 66-76; V Camelsdale *Chich* 76-87; V Gt Marsden *Blackb* 87-96; rtd 96. *35 Hardwick Park, Banbury OX16 1YF* T: (01295) 268744

HOY, Stephen Anthony. b 55. Leeds Poly BA 76. Linc Th Coll 92. **d** 94 **p** 95. C Glen Parva and S Wigston *Leic* 94-98; V Linc St Jo from 98. *St John's Vicarage, 102 Sudbrooke Drive, Lincoln LN2 2EF* T: (01522) 525621 E: fr-stephen@stjohnthebaptistparishchurch.org.uk

HOYAL, Richard Dunstan. b 47. Ch Ch Ox BA 67 MA 71 BA 78. Ripon Coll Cuddesdon 76. **d** 79 **p** 80. C Stevenage St Geo *St Alb* 79-83; V Monk Bretton *Wakef* 83-89; V Ilkley St Marg *Bradf* 89-04; Dir of Ords 96-04; Hon Can Bradf Cathl 03-04; P-in-c Clifton All SS w St Jo *Bris* 04-12; P-in-c Easton All Hallows 04-12; P-in-c Bris Ch Ch w St Ewen, All SS and St Geo 09-12; rtd 12. *15 Garland Close, Petworth GU22 0QZ* E: richardhoyal@btinternet.com

HOYLAND, John Gregory. b 50. Sussex Univ BEd 73. Wycliffe Hall Ox 75. **d** 78 **p** 79. C Pudsey St Lawr *Bradf* 78-81; P-in-c Long Preston 81-84; V Long Preston w Tosside 84; CPAS Staff 85-87; Chapl York St Jo Coll 87-01; Lect York St Jo Univ from 01; PtO *York* from 01. *18 Caxton Avenue, York YO26 5SN* T: (01904) 784140 or 876533

HOYLE, David Fredric. b 46. Lon Bible Coll. **d** 02 **p** 03. NSM Northwood Em *Lon* 00-05; PtO *Win* from 11. *23 Cranleigh Gardens, Bournemouth BH6 5LE* T: (01202) 386305 E: david.f.hoyle@lineone.net

HOYLE, The Very Revd David Michael. b 57. CCC Cam BA 80 MA 83 PhD 91. Ripon Coll Cuddesdon 84. **d** 86 **p** 87. C Chesterton Gd Shep *Ely* 86-88; Chapl and Fell Magd Coll Cam 88-91; Dean and Fell 91-95; V Southgate Ch Ch *Lon* 95-02; Dir Post-Ord Tr Edmonton Area 00-02; Dioc Officer for Min *Glouc* 02-10; Dioc Can Res Glouc Cathl 02-10; Dean Bris from 10. *20 Charlotte Street, Bristol BS1 5PZ* T: 0117-926 4879 E: dean@bristol-cathedral.co.uk

HOYLE, Philip James. b 77. St Mellitus Coll. **d** 13 **p** 14. C Shepherd's Bush St Steph w St Thos *Lon* from 13. *60 Sundew Avenue, London W12 0RR* M: 07989-969257 E: holyus@hotmail.com

HOYLE, Stephen Jonathan. b 64. Leeds Univ BA 87. Ripon Coll Cuddesdon 88. **d** 90 **p** 91. C Lt Stanmore St Lawr *Lon* 90-93; C Lon Docks St Pet w Wapping St Jo 93-96; PtO 01-02; TV Withycombe Raleigh *Ex* from 02. *St John's Vicarage, 3 Diane Close, Exmouth EX8 5QG* T: (01395) 270094

HOYTE, David Anthony. St Mellitus Coll BA 15. **d** 15. OLM Forest Gate All SS *Chelmsf* from 15. *89 Warner Place, London E2 7DB*

HRYZIUK, Petro. b 57. Lanc Univ BEd 80 Open Univ MA 95. St Jo Coll Nottm 89. **d** 90 **p** 91. C Huyton St Geo *Liv* 90-93; C Goose Green 93-96; C Wavertree H Trin 96-98; TV Maghull 98-05; Chapl Shrewsbury and Telford NHS Trust 05-13; Lead Chapl from 13. *Chaplaincy Department, Royal Shrewsbury Hospital, Mytton Oak Road, Shrewsbury SY3 8XQ* T: (01743) 261000 E: petroh@hotmail.com

HUARD, The Ven Geoffrey Robert. b 43. N Bapt Th Sem Illinois DMin 95. Clifton Th Coll 65. **d** 70 **p** 71. C Barking St Marg *Chelmsf* 70-73; C Everton St Ambrose w St Tim *Liv* 73-74; C Everton St Pet 74-76; R Redfern and Waterloo Australia 76-78; R S Sydney St Sav 78-89; Adn Sydney and Cumberland 89-93; Adn Liverpool Australia 93-08; C-in-c Cabramatta 97-99; R Chester Hill w Sefton 01-03; R Bankstown from 03. *34 Wigram Road, Austinmer NSW 2515, Australia* T: (0061) (2) 4268 4243 M: 43-995 1571 E: gchuard@smartchat.net.au

HUBAND, Richard William. b 39. Trin Coll Cam BA 62 MA 66. Qu Coll Birm 76. **d** 78 **p** 79. C Norton *St Alb* 78-81; R Aspley Guise w Husborne Crawley and Ridgmont 81-91; V Elstow 91-03; rtd 03. *5 Shooters Paddock, Layton Lane, Shaftesbury SP7 8AB* T: (01747) 854741

HUBBARD, David Harris. b 33. St Pet Hall Ox BA 57 MA 61 K Coll Lon MTh 88. Ridley Hall Cam 59. **d** 60 **p** 61. C Dalston St Mark w St Bart *Lon* 60-63; C Stoke Newington St Olave 63-67; Hon C 67-68; Asst Master Dalston Sch 67-75; Hon C Hornsey Ch Ch *Lon* 69-70; V 70-82; AD W Haringey 78-85; V Highgate All SS 82-02; rtd 02; Hon C W Hampstead St Cuth *Lon* 02-04; PtO from 04. *35 Sheppards College, London Road, Bromley BR1 1PF* T: (020) 8695 7477

HUBBARD, Mrs Gillian Carol. b 63. RGN 84. WEMTC 05. **d** 08 **p** 09. NSM Glouc St Paul and St Steph 08-12; P-in-c Mow Cop *Lich* from 12. *The Vicarage, 5 Congleton Road, Mow Cop, Stoke-on-Trent ST7 3PJ* T: (01782) 515077 M: 07525-039323 E: gillyhubbard@hotmail.co.uk

HUBBARD, Haynes Quinton. b 68. Dalhousie Univ BA 89. Wycliffe Coll Toronto MDiv 95. **d** 96 **p** 96. C Elora Canada 96-99; R Dunville 99-07; Sen Chapl Algarve *Eur* 07-12; Canada from 12. *Address temp unknown*

HUBBARD, Ian Maxwell. b 43. Surrey Univ BEd 84 Goldsmiths' Coll Lon MA 86 FCollP 83 ACP 83. Sarum & Wells Th Coll 69. **d** 73 **p** 74. Hon C S'wark H Trin w St Matt 73-78; Hon C Camberwell St Mich w All So w Em 78-87; Hon C Dulwich St Barn 87-90; C Battersea St Mary 90-92; V Winscombe *B & W* 92-98; TR Yatton Moor 98-13; RD Portishead 02-10; rtd 13. *38 Wemberham Lane, Yatton, Bristol BS49 4BP* T: (01934) 835859 E: ian.hubbard@gmail.com

HUBBARD, Ms Judith Frances. b 49. St Alb Minl Tr Scheme 79. dss 82 **d** 87 **p** 94. Hemel Hempstead *St Alb* 82-86; Longden and Annscroft w Pulverbatch *Heref* 86-87; Hon C 87-91; Vice Prin WEMTC 91-97; Acting Prin 94-95; Hon C Leominster *Heref* 94-97; Cathl Chapl and Visitors' Officer 97-02; I Kinneigh Union *C, C & R* 02-09; Warden of Readers 05-08; P-in-c Frampton on Severn, Arlingham, Saul etc *Glouc* 09-10; rtd 10. *Moorcott, Upper Ivington, Leominster HR6 0JN* T: (01568) 720311 E: judithfrances@gmail.com

HUBBARD, Julian Richard Hawes. b 55. Em Coll Cam BA 76 MA 81. Wycliffe Hall Ox BA 80 MA 85. **d** 81 **p** 82. C Fulham St Dionis *Lon* 81-84; Chapl Jes Coll and Tutor Wycliffe Hall Ox 84-89; Selection Sec ACCM 89-91; Sen Selection Sec ABM 91-93; V Bourne *Guildf* 93-99; P-in-c Tilford 97-99; RD Farnham 96-99; Can Res Guildf Cathl and Dir Minl Tr 99-05; Adn Ox and Can Res Ch Ch 05-11; Dir Min Division Abps' Coun from 11. *Church House, Great Smith Street, London SW1P 3AZ* T: (020) 7898 1390 F: 7898 1421 E: julian.hubbard@churchofengland.org

HUBBARD, Laurence Arthur. b 36. Qu Coll Cam BA 60 MA 64. Wycliffe Hall Ox 60 CMS Tr Coll Chislehurst 65 CMS Tr Coll Selly Oak 93. **d** 62 **p** 63. C Widcombe *B & W* 62-65; CMS Kenya 66-73; V Pype Hayes *Birm* 73-79; P-in-c Norwich-over-the-Water Colegate St Geo *Nor* 79-85; P-in-c Nor St Aug w St Mary 79-85; CMS 85-97; Area Sec *Cant* and *Roch* 85-93; Chapl Damascus, Syria 93-97; Miss to Seamen Aqaba, Jordan 97-00; rtd 00; PtO *Glouc* from 01. *31 Saddlers Road, Quedgeley, Gloucester GL2 4SY* T: (01452) 728061

HUBBARD, Peter James. b 72. York Univ BA 93 Nottm Univ PGCE 97. Trin Coll Bris BA 03. **d** 04 **p** 05. C Hinckley H Trin *Leic* 04-08; R Karrinyup Australia 08-12; C Meole Brace *Lich* from 12; Chapl Prestfelde Sch Shrewsbury from 12. *2 Perivale Close, Meole Brace, Shrewsbury SY3 6DH* T: (01743) 233671 M: 07951-444269 E: peterhubbard1972@hotmail.com

HUBBARD, Roy Oswald. b 32. Lich Th Coll 62. **d** 64 **p** 65. C Baswich *Lich* 64-68; P-in-c Ash 68-70; V Stevenage St Pet Broadwater *St Alb* 71-78; V Flitwick 78-90; RD Ampthill 87-90;

R Sharnbrook and Knotting w Souldrop 90-96; rtd 96; PtO *St Alb* from 96; *Pet* from 96. *11 Cowslip Close, Rushden NN10 0UD* T: (01933) 419210 E: roynpam11@gmail.com

HUBBLE, Canon Raymond Carr. b 30. Wm Temple Coll Rugby 60. **d** 61 **p** 62. C Newbold w Dunston *Derby* 61-64; Chapl RAF 64-80; Asst Chapl-in-Chief RAF 80-85; QHC 84-85; P-in-c Odiham w S Warnborough and Long Sutton *Win* 85; P-in-c Odiham 85-86; V 86-95; RD 88-95; Hon Can Win Cathl 94-95; rtd 95; PtO *Win* from 95. *Dormers, Centre Lane, Everton, Lymington SO41 0JP*

HUBBLE, Canon Trevor Ernest. b 46. Bernard Gilpin Soc Dur 69 Chich Th Coll 70. **d** 76 **p** 77. C Eltham St Barn *S'wark* 76-79; C St Agnes Mission Teyateyameng Lesotho 80-81; R Quthing H Trin 81-85; Adn S Lesotho 84-87; Warden Angl Tr Cen and Dir Chr Educn 85-87; Co-ord of Tr for Lay Min S Africa 87-89; R Matatiele St Steph 89-00; Adn Matatiele 91-00; V Gen Umzimvubu 95-00; Shared Min Tr Officer *Dur* 00-07; C Esh, Hamsteels, Langley Park and Waterhouses 00-07; Warden Lee Abbey Internat Students' Club Kensington 07-13; rtd 13; PtO *Portsm* from 14. *24 Jute Close, Fareham PO16 8EZ*

HUCKETT, Andrew William. b 50. AKC 72. St Aug Coll Cant 72. **d** 73 **p** 74. C Chipping Sodbury and Old Sodbury *Glouc* 73-76; Miss to Seafarers 76-14; Chapl Flushing 76-79; Chapl Teesside 79-82; Chapl Lagos Nigeria 82-85; Chapl Mombasa Kenya 85-86; Chapl Milford Haven 86-92; Chapl Medway Ports 92-03; Staff Chapl and Chapl Thames/Medway 03-05; Chapl Southampton 05-14; rtd 14; PtO *Cant* from 14. *24 Chegworth Gardens, Tunstall, Sittingbourne ME10 1RH* M: 07836-261324 E: andrewhuckett@outlook.com

HUCKLE, John Walford (Wally). b 39. EMMTC. **d** 89 **p** 90. C Nottingham St Pet and St Jas *S'well* 89-00; Commercial Chapl Nottingham City Cen 89-00; Dioc Adv on Ind Soc *S'well* 96-97; rtd 00; PtO *S'well* from 00. *6 Lime Close, Radcliffe-on-Trent, Nottingham NG12 2DF* T: 0115-933 2278 E: wally.huckle@ntlworld.com

HUCKLE, Peter. b 46. Ox Univ Inst of Educn CertEd 69 Auckland Univ DipEd 71. Educn for Min (NZ). **d** 90 **p** 91. New Zealand 90-91; Hon C N Walsham w Antingham *Nor* 91-92; C Gt Yarmouth 92-94; TV 94-96; Min Can and Chapl St Paul's Cathl 96-97; Asst Chapl Athens and PtO *Eur* 97; SSJE from 97; Superior from 02. *Address withheld by request* T: (01760) 788014 E: superior@ssje.org.uk

HUCKLE, Stephen Leslie. b 48. Ch Ch Ox BA 70 BA 72 MA 74. Coll of Resurr Mirfield 73. **d** 75 **p** 76. C Wednesbury St Paul Wood Green *Lich* 75-78; C Aylesbury *Ox* 78-85; C Farnham Royal w Hedgerley 85-88; V Fenny Stratford 88-96; V Stirchley *Birm* 98-05; P-in-c Kempston All SS *St Alb* 05-15; V from 15; P-in-c Biddenham 05-15; V from 15. *The Vicarage, Church End, Kempston, Bedford MK43 8RH* T: (01234) 852241

HUCKLE, Walford. See HUCKLE, John Walford

HUDD, Philip Simon. b 68. Westmr Coll Ox BA 90 Lanc Univ MA 06. Westcott Ho Cam 91. **d** 93 **p** 94. C Kirkby *Liv* 93-97; TV 97-99; V Lancaster Ch Ch *Blackb* from 99; AD Lancaster 04-10. *Christ Church Vicarage, 1 East Road, Lancaster LA1 3EE* T: (01524) 34430 E: p.hudd@uwclub.net

HUDDERSFIELD, Suffragan Bishop of. See GIBBS, The Rt Revd Jonathan Robert

HUDDLESON, Robert Roulston. b 32. QUB BA 55 TCD Div Test 57. **d** 57 **p** 58. C Ballymena w Ballyclug *Conn* 57-59; C Belfast St Pet and St Jas 59-63; Ethiopia 65-69; Exec Asst WCC Geneva 69-75; Dep Sec Gen Syn Bd for Miss and Unity 75-81; Admin Sec *Dur* 81-86; Dioc Sec *Ex* 86-97; rtd 97; PtO *Ex* from 97. *6 Newton Court, Bampton, Tiverton EX16 9LG* T: (01398) 331412

HUDDLESTON, Geoffrey Roger. b 36. TCD BA 63 MA 67. Ridley Hall Cam 63. **d** 65 **p** 66. C Tonbridge SS Pet and Paul *Roch* 65-69; Chapl RAF 69-85; V Lyonsdown H Trin *St Alb* 85-00; RD Barnet 94-99; rtd 00; PtO *Lich* from 01. *The Granary, Bellamour Lodge Farm, Colton Road, Colton, Rugeley WS15 3NZ* T: (01889) 574052

HUDDLESTON, Mark Geoffrey. b 68. Bath Univ BSc 90. Wycliffe Hall Ox 06. **d** 08 **p** 09. C Heigham H Trin *Nor* 08-12; C Arborfield w Barkham *Ox* from 12. *Church Office, The Rectory, Church Lane, Arborfield, Reading RG2 9HZ* T: 0118-976 2186 E: mark@abch.org.uk

HUDGHTON, John Francis. b 56. BA. Cranmer Hall Dur 81. **d** 83 **p** 84. C Stockport St Geo *Ches* 83-85; C Witton 85-87; C Stockport St Alb Hall Street 87-90; V Thornton-le-Moors w Ince and Elton 90-95; Chapl RAF 95-01; P-in-c Burnby *York* 01-03; P-in-c Londesborough 01-03; P-in-c Nunburnholme and Warter and Huggate 01-03; P-in-c Shiptonthorpe and Hayton 01-03; TR Buxton w Burbage and King Sterndale *Derby* from 03; RD Buxton 11-14. *The Rectory, 7 Lismore Park, Buxton SK17 9AU* T: (01298) 22151 E: rectorofbuxton@hotmail.com

HUDSON, Andrew Julian. b 57. Cranmer Hall Dur 93. **d** 93 **p** 94. C Moldgreen *Wakef* 93-97; P-in-c Lundwood 97-01; V Dodworth 01-04; Ind Chapl *Chelmsf* from 04; C Aveley

and Purfleet 04-13; TV Mardyke from 13. *St Stephen's Vicarage, London Road, Purfleet RM19 1QD* T: (01708) 891242
M: 07989-988496 E: hudsona6@aol.com

HUDSON, Anthony George. b 39. NOC. **d** 84 **p** 85. C Harrogate St Mark *Ripon* 84-87; P-in-c Hampsthwaite 87-94; P-in-c Killinghall 87-94; P-in-c Hampsthwaite and Killinghall 94-96; V 96-99; rtd 99; PtO *Leeds* from 00. *26 Beckwith Crescent, Harrogate HG2 0BQ* T: (01423) 858740

HUDSON, Brainerd Peter de Wirtz Goodwin. *See* GOODWIN HUDSON, Brainerd Peter de Wirtz

HUDSON, Charles Edward Cameron. b 73. Univ Coll Ox BA 94 MA 08. Wycliffe Hall Ox BA 07. **d** 08 **p** 09. C St Margaret's-on-Thames *Lon* 08-11; R Broxbourne w Wormley *St Alb* from 11. *The Vicarage, Churchfields, Broxbourne EN10 7AU* T: (01992) 444117 E: bwparishoffice@btinternet.com

HUDSON, Christopher John. b 45. Bedf Coll Lon BSc 68 MCIH 73. Cranmer Hall Dur. **d** 77 **p** 78. C Bath Weston St Jo *B & W* 77-80; Youth Chapl 77-80; P-in-c Baltonsborough w Butleigh and W Bradley 80-84; V 84-87; P-in-c Shirwell w Loxhore *Ex* 87-89; P-in-c Kentisbury, Trentishoe, E Down and Arlington 88-89; TR Shirwell, Loxhore, Kentisbury, Arlington, etc 90-91; P-in-c Trentishoe 90-91; RD Shirwell 88-91; R Huntspill *B & W* 91-94; rtd 01; PtO *B & W* from 98; Ex from 06. *Achray, 5 Conigar Close, Hemyock, Cullompton EX15 3RE* T: (01823) 680170
E: revchris@mhbruton.eclipse.co.uk

HUDSON, John. *See* HUDSON, Reginald John

HUDSON, John. b 51. Oak Hill Th Coll 84. **d** 86 **p** 87. C Leyland St Andr *Blackb* 86-89; V Coppull from 89; P-in-c Coppull St Jo 10-11; R from 11. *The Vicarage, 209 Chapel Lane, Coppull, Chorley PR7 4NA* T: (01257) 791218
E: saintjohns824@btinternet.com

HUDSON, Canon John Leonard. b 44. AKC 66. St Boniface Warminster 66. **d** 67 **p** 68. C Dodworth *Wakef* 67-70; Prec Wakef Cathl 70-73; V Ravensthorpe 73-80; V Royston 80-09; P-in-c Carlton 90-09; RD Barnsley 93-04; Hon Can Wakef Cathl 97-09; rtd 09; PtO *Leeds* from 09; *York* from 10. *Millbank Cottage, Thorpe Bassett, Malton YO17 8LU* T: (01944) 718518 E: j.hudson93@btinternet.com

HUDSON, John Peter. b 42. AKC 64. St Boniface Warminster 64. **d** 65 **p** 66. C S Shields St Hilda w St Thos *Dur* 65-68; Chapl RN 68-84; V Mellor *Blackb* 84-07; rtd 07; PtO *Blackb* from 07. *Hazel Mount, Bailrigg Lane, Bailrigg, Lancaster LA1 4XP* T: (01524) 848693
E: jpeterhudson@btinternet.com

HUDSON, Prof John Richard Keith. b 35. St Pet Coll Ox BA 60 MA 64 State Univ NY PhD 83. Linc Th Coll 60. **d** 62 **p** 63. C Tettenhall Wood *Lich* 62-65; Chapl and Lect Bp Grosseteste Coll Linc 65-71; Staff Officer Gen Syn Bd of Educn 72-73; Lect Riverina Coll of Advanced Educn Wagga Australia 73-74; Lect Mt Gravatt Coll of Advanced Educn 74-79; Master and Chapl Yardley Court Sch Tonbridge 79-82; Teaching Asst State Univ NY USA 82-83; Asst Prof Louisiana State Univ Alexandria 83-85; Asst R Alexandria St Jas 84-85; R Camden St Paul Delaware 85-05; Prof Wesley Coll Dover 85-92; Chapl Delaware Hospice 92-96; rtd 01. *1300 Morris Avenue, Villanova PA 19085-2131, USA* T: (001) (610) 525 3131
E: jrkh65@msn.com

HUDSON, John Stephen Anthony. b 49. S Dios Minl Tr Scheme 85 Chich Th Coll 86. **d** 88 **p** 89. C Horsham *Chich* 88-91; TV Littlehampton and Wick 91-15; rtd 15. *166 Little Breach, Chichester PO19 5UA* T: (01243) 931557
E: stephen.hudson@outlook.com

HUDSON, Peter. *See* HUDSON, John Peter

HUDSON, Peter. b 66. **d** 03 **p** 04. OLM Deptford St Paul *S'wark* 03-07; NSM Lewisham St Steph and St Mark from 07. *7A Blackheath Rise, London SE13 7PN* T: (020) 8318 0483
M: 07908-640369 E: frpeter@sky.com

HUDSON, Philip Howard. b 50. St Steph Ho Ox 89. **d** 91 **p** 92. C Poulton-le-Fylde *Blackb* 91-95; V Blackpool St Wilfrid 95-14; rtd 14. *207 Hornby Road, Blackpool FY1 4JA*

HUDSON, Reginald John. b 47. FRSA CertSS. Linc Th Coll. **d** 83 **p** 84. C Merton St Mary *S'wark* 83-86; C Kirk Ella *York* 86-88; P-in-c Lenborough *Ox* 88-93; V 93-03; P-in-c Tingewick w Water Stratford, Radclive etc 89-93; P-in-c Water Stratford 93-00; P-in-c Reading St Matt 03-10; rtd 11. *La Columbine, route d'Orbec, 61120 Canapville, France* T: (0033) (2) 33 67 03 21 E: rjhfootsteps@virginmedia.com

HUDSON, Robert Antony. b 82. York Univ BA 04. Wycliffe Hall Ox BA 09. **d** 10 **p** 11. C Elburton *Ex* 10-14; C Harold Wood *Chelmsf* from 14. *8 Archibald Road, Romford RM3 0RH*
T: (01708) 348406 M: 07799-600147
E: roberthudson79@btinternet.com

HUDSON, Stephen. *See* HUDSON, John Stephen Anthony

HUDSON, Trevor. b 32. Dur Univ BA 56. Cranmer Hall Dur. **d** 58 **p** 59. C Doncaster St Mary *Sheff* 58-62; C Attercliffe

62-64; V Stannington 64-79; V Abbeydale St Jo 79-88; V Worsbrough St Mary 88-95; rtd 95; PtO *Sheff* from 95. *Spring Villa Garden, 136A Langsett Road South, Oughtibridge, Sheffield S35 0HA* T: 0114-286 3559

HUDSON, Walter Gerald. b 29. **d** 95 **p** 96. Hon C Eccleston Park *Liv* 95-99; PtO from 99. *31 Springfield Lane, Eccleston, St Helens WA10 5EW* T: (01744) 24919

HUDSON, Wilfred. b 23. St Jo Coll Dur BA 49. **d** 51 **p** 52. C Doncaster St Mary *Sheff* 51-56; V Brampton Bierlow 56-64; V Anston 64-74; V Woodsetts 64-74; V Sharrow St Andr 74-88; rtd 88; PtO *Sheff* from 88. *c/o P W Hudson Esq, 45 Middleton Avenue, Dinnington, Sheffield S25 2QP*

HUDSON-WILKIN, Preb Rose Josephine. b 61. WMMTC 89. **d** 91 **p** 94. Par Dn Wolverhampton St Matt *Lich* 91-94; C 94-95; C W Bromwich Gd Shep w St Jo 95-98; Black Anglican Concern 95-98; V Dalston H Trin w St Phil and Haggerston All SS *Lon* 98-14; P-in-c St Mary at Hill w St Andr Hubbard etc from 14; Chapl to The Queen from 08; Chapl to Speaker of Ho of Commons from 10; PV Westmr Abbey from 10; Preb St Paul's Cathl from 13. *14 Hide Place, London SW1P 4NJ* T: (020) 7626 4184 E: revdrose@aol.com *or* revrose@stmary-at-hill.org

HUDSPETH, Ralph. b 46. **d** 06 **p** 07. NSM Ripley w Burnt Yates *Ripon* 06-12; NSM Lower Wharfedale *Leeds* from 12. *10 Winksley Grove, Harrogate HG3 2SZ* T: (01423) 561918
M: 07810-631826 E: ralphhudspeth@hotmail.com

HUDSPITH, Colin John. b 46. Nottm Univ BA 67. SWMTC 93. **d** 96 **p** 97. C Pilton w Ashford *Ex* 96-97; C Barnstaple 97-99; C Shirwell, Loxhore, Kentisbury, Arlington, etc 99-00; TV 00-11; rtd 11. *Brackendale, Heanton, Barnstaple EX31 4DG* T: (01271) 813547

HUDSPITH, Mrs Susan Mary. b 49. St Alb Minl Tr Scheme 79. **dss** 82 **d** 87 **p** 94. Luton St Chris Round Green *St Alb* 82-92; Par Dn 87-88; NSM 88-92; PtO 92-94 and 00-05; NSM Luton St Mary 94-00; NSM Stevenage St Pet Broadwater 05-08; PtO from 08. *15 Waverley Close, Stevenage SG2 8RU* T: (01438) 725030 E: geoff-sue.hudspith@virgin.net

HUGGETT, David John. b 34. Lon Univ BSc 56 Southn Univ PhD 59. Clifton Th Coll 64. **d** 67 **p** 68. C Heatherlands St Jo *Sarum* 67-70; C Cambridge St Sepulchre *Ely* 70-73; C Cambridge H Sepulchre w All SS 73; R Nottingham St Nic *S'well* 73-92; Cyprus 93-99; rtd 99; PtO *Win* from 08. *101 Admirals Walk, West Cliff Road, Bournemouth BH2 5HF* T: (01202) 558199

HUGGETT, John Victor James. b 39. Dur Univ BA 64. Tyndale Hall Bris 64. **d** 66 **p** 67. C Hailsham *Chich* 66-69; C Worthing St Geo 69-71; C Woking St Pet *Guildf* 71-73; C Buckhurst Hill *Chelmsf* 73-76; V Meltham Mills *Wakef* 76-78; V Wilshaw 76-78; rtd 79; Jt Ldr Breath Fellowship from 79; PtO *Wakef* 79-84; *Roch* from 84. *Breath Ministries, 3 Cannon House, St John's Close, Tunbridge Wells TN4 9GE* T: (01892) 512520
E: cjphuggett@yahoo.co.uk

HUGGETT, Kevin John. b 62. St Jo Coll Dur BA 83. Trin Coll Bris 88. **d** 91 **p** 92. C Gt Ilford St Andr *Chelmsf* 91-94; Regional Manager for Uganda and Sudan CMS 94-01; Hon C Tonbridge SS Pet and Paul *Roch* 98-01; Chapl Lanc Univ *Blackb* from 01. *11 Alderman Road, Lancaster LA1 5FW* T: (01524) 843091
or 594082 *or* 594071 E: k.huggett@lancaster.ac.uk

HUGGETT, Michael George. b 38. Bris Univ BA 60 Birm Univ CertEd 61. EMMTC 85. **d** 88 **p** 89. C Sawley *Derby* 88-92; C Chaddesden St Phil 92-93; P-in-c Alkmonton, Cubley, Marston Montgomery etc 93-99; R 99-04; rtd 04. *12 Murray Road, Mickleover, Derby DE3 9LE* T: (01332) 511259
E: m.huggett152@btinternet.com

HUGGINS, Jonathan Paul (John). b 59. Leeds Univ BSc 80 Bris Univ PhD 83. SEITE 12. **d** 14 **p** 15. C Kingsdown and Creekside *Cant* from 14. *The Vicarage, Vicarage Lane, Selling, Faversham ME13 9RD* T: (01227) 752027
E: john.p.huggins1@gmail.com

HUGGINS, Stephen David. b 53. Sussex Univ BEd 75 K Coll Lon MA 80 Leic Univ DipEd 79. STETS. **d** 01 **p** 02. NSM Bexhill St Aug *Chich* 01-02; NSM Sedlescombe w Whatlington 02-07; P-in-c Turners Hill 07-09; Angl Chapl Worth Sch 07-09; TV Bexhill St Pet *Chich* from 09. *20 Glassenbury Drive, Bexhill-on-Sea TN40 2NY* E: frshuggins@aol.com

HUGHES, Canon Adrian John. b 57. Newc Univ BA 78 St Jo Coll Dur BA 82. Cranmer Hall Dur 80. **d** 83 **p** 84. C Shard End *Birm* 83-86; TV Solihull 86-90; TV Glendale Gp *Newc* 90-94; P-in-c Belford 94-95; V Belford and Lucker 95-06; V Ellingham 95-02; AD Bamburgh and Glendale 97-06; Asst Dioc Dir of Ords 98-06; V Cullercoats St Geo from 06; AD Tynemouth 09-14; Hon Can Newc Cathl from 05. *St George's Vicarage, 1 Beverley Gardens, North Shields NE30 4NS* T: 0191-252 1817
E: revajh@btinternet.com

HUGHES, Canon Alan. b 46. TD MBE 14. Edin Th Coll 71. **d** 74 **p** 75. C Edin St Cuth 74-76; P-in-c Wester Hailes St Luke

76-78; C Marske in Cleveland *York* 78-81; V New Marske 81-84; V Kirkbymoorside w Gillamoor, Farndale etc 84-94; CF 84-94; V Berwick H Trin and St Mary *Newc* 94-13; Hon Can Newc Cathl 08-13; rtd 13. *Middle Eden, Wark, Cornhill-on-Tweed TD12 4RE* T: (01890) 885854 M: 07941-757412 E: skypilot60@btinternet.com

HUGHES, Albert William. b 48. S Dios Minl Tr Scheme 90. **d** 92 **p** 93. Community of Our Lady and St John 70-13; Prior 90-10; Abbot 10-13; rtd 13; PtO *Win* 96-14. *Address temp unknown*

HUGHES, The Ven Alexander James. b 75. Greyfriars Ox BA 97 MA 04 St Edm Coll Cam MPhil 99 PhD 11. Westcott Ho Cam 98. **d** 00 **p** 01. C Headington Quarry *Ox* 00-03; Bp's Dom Chapl *Portsm* 03-08; P-in-c Portsea St Luke 08-13; P-in-c Southsea St Pet 08-13; V Southsea St Luke and St Pet 13-14; Adn Cam *Ely* from 14; Hon Can Ely Cathl from 14. *1A Summerfield, Cambridge CB3 9HE* T: (01223) 350424 E: archdeacon.cambridge@ely.anglican.org

HUGHES, Allan Paul. b 45. Open Univ BA 91 Glam Coll of Educn CertEd 69. Abp's Sch of Min 01. **d** 02 **p** 03. Chapl St Olave's Sch York 02-05; NSM Skelton w Shipton and Newton on Ouse *York* 02-03; Asst to RD Easingwold 03-04; NSM York All SS Pavement w St Crux and St Mich 04-12; NSM York St Denys 04-12; rtd 12; PtO *York* from 12; Asst Dioc Dir of Ords from 10. *2 Burtree Avenue, Skelton, York YO30 1YT* T: (01904) 471521 E: revd_al@hotmail.co.uk

HUGHES, Andrew Karl William. b 58. St Steph Ho Ox 07 WEMTC 08. **d** 08 **p** 09. NSM N Cheltenham *Glouc* 08-09; C W Bromwich St Fran *Lich* 09-11; P-in-c Weston super Mare All SS and St Sav *B & W* from 11. *The Vicarage, 46 Manor Road, Weston-super-Mare BS23 2SU* T: (01934) 204217 E: fatherandrew@sky.com

HUGHES, Andrew Terrell. b 29. Bris Univ BA 56 DipEd. Coll of Resurr Mirfield 64. **d** 66 **p** 67. C Weston-super-Mare St Sav *B & W* 66-70; C Yeovil St Jo w Preston Plucknett 70-73; TV Yeovil 73-83; R Wincanton 83-88; rtd 89; PtO *Sarum* from 89. *2 Cove Street, Weymouth DT4 8TS* T: (01305) 778639 E: andauhughes@googlemail.com

HUGHES, Miss Angela Mary. b 52. Avery Hill Coll CertEd 75. St Steph Ho Ox 90. **d** 92 **p** 94. Par Dn Kidderminster St Mary and All SS w Trimpley etc *Worc* 92-94; C 94-96; P-in-c Gilmorton w Peatling Parva and Kimcote etc *Leic* 96-01; RD Guthlaxton II 99-01; R Wyberton *Linc* 01-09; V Frampton 01-09; RD Holland W 04-09; R Carnoustie and Monifieth *Bre* 09-13; P-in-c Clipston w Naseby and Haselbech w Kelmarsh *Pet* from 13. *The Rectory, 18 Church Lane, Clipston, Market Harborough LE16 9RW* T: (01858) 525342 E: ahughes@webleicester.co.uk

HUGHES, Arthur John. b 41. MCIOB 71 MRICS 78. WEMTC 03. **d** 05 **p** 06. NSM Church Stretton *Heref* from 05. *Jacey, 4 Lawley Close, Church Stretton SY6 6EL* T: (01694) 722582 E: jonhughes@uwclub.net

HUGHES, Arthur Lewis. b 36. St Deiniol's Hawarden 65. **d** 68 **p** 69. C Holywell *St As* 68-71; Lect Watford St Mary *St Alb* 71-73; C Watford 73-75; V Thornton in Lonsdale w Burton in Lonsdale *Bradf* 75-84; V Daubhill *Man* 84-89; V Castle Town *Lich* 89-00; Chapl Staffs Univ 91-00; rtd 00; PtO *Ches* 00-04; *Pet* from 05. *31 Hunt Close, Towcester NN12 7AD* T: (01327) 358257

HUGHES, Benjamin John. b 65. Golds Coll Lon BEd 91 Lon Metrop Univ MA 08. Cranmer Hall Dur BTh 97. **d** 99 **p** 00. NSM Fulham St Matt *Lon* 99-03; Chapl RN 03; PtO *Lon* from 04; S'wark 08-13; NSM Herne Hill *Lon* from 13. *101 Herne Hill Road, London SE24 0AD* E: benbassforty@yahoo.co.uk

HUGHES, Bernard Patrick. b 35. Oak Hill Th Coll. **d** 65 **p** 66. C Fulham St Matt *Lon* 65-69; Chapl St Steph Hosp Lon 69-89; Chapl St Mary Abbots Hosp Lon 69-97; Chapl Chelsea and Westmr Hosp Lon 89-94; Chapl Westmr Children's Hosp Lon 89-94; Sen Chapl Chelsea and Westmr Hosp NHS Foundn Trust 94-97; rtd 97; PtO *Bris* from 97; *Sarum* from 97. *Charis, 6 Priory Park, Bradford-on-Avon BA15 1QU* T: (01225) 868679

HUGHES, Miss Carol Lindsay. b 51. Cam Inst of Educn CertEd 72 Nottm Univ BEd 86. Trin Coll Bris 91. **d** 93 **p** 94. C Ilkeston St Mary *Derby* 93-97; P-in-c Langley Mill 97-02; V 02-06; P-in-c Oakwood 06-11; RD Heanor 99-06; rtd 11; PtO *Cov* from 12. *13 Harris Drive, Rugby CV22 6DX* E: c.l.hughes@fsmail.net

HUGHES, Christopher Clarke. b 40. MRAC 61. ALCD 65. **d** 65 **p** 66. C Broadclyst *Ex* 65-68; C Chenies and Lt Chalfont *Ox* 68-70; TV Lydford w Bridestowe and Sourton *Ex* 70-72; TV Lydford, Brent Tor, Bridestowe and Sourton 72-74; V Buckland Monachorum 74-83; R Ashtead *Guildf* 83-98; R Aboyne and Ballater *Ab* 98-03; rtd 03. *Stone Farmhouse, Thorveton, Exeter EX5 5LL* T: (01884) 855250

HUGHES, Clive. b 54. Univ of Wales BA 77 MA 82. St Mich Coll Llan BD 95. **d** 95 **p** 96. C Carmarthen St Dav *St D* 95-97;

TV Aberystwyth 97-04; P-in-c Hanmer, Bronington, Bettisfield, Tallarn Green *St As* 04-09; P-in-c Hanmer and Bronington and Bettisfield 09-12; V Hanmer, Bronington, Bettisfield and Penley from 12. *The Vicarage, Hanmer, Whitchurch SY13 3DE* T: (01948) 830468 E: clive@hughes2003.fsnet.co.uk

HUGHES, Cynthia May. b 45. **d** 10 **p** 11. NSM Middlewich w Byley *Ches* from 10. *The Vicarage, 50 Norley Road, Sandiway, Northwich CW8 2JU* T: (01606) 883266 E: thiahughes@hotmail.com

HUGHES, Daniel James. b 86. Birm Univ BA 07 PGCE 10. Ridley Hall Cam 13. **d** 15. C Elmdon St Nic *Birm* from 15. *26 Hillside Croft, Solihull B92 9DL* M: 07811-180917 E: danhughes001@hotmail.com

HUGHES, David Anthony. b 25. Trin Coll Cam BA 48 MA 55. Linc Th Coll 74. **d** 76 **p** 77. C Boston *Linc* 76-78; R Graffoe 78-90; rtd 90; PtO *Linc* from 91. *27 St Clement's Road, Ruskington, Sleaford NG34 9AF* T: (01526) 832618

HUGHES, David Howard. b 55. Univ of Wales (Ban). St Mich Coll Llan. **d** 79 **p** 80. C Llanrhos *St As* 79-82; C Eckington w Handley and Ridgeway *Derby* 82-83; C Staveley and Barrow Hill 83-85; TV Whitworth St Bart *Man* 89-00. *2 Cromwell Road, Chesterfield S40 4TH* T: (01246) 277361

HUGHES, Canon David Michael. b 41. Oak Hill Th Coll BD 67. **d** 68 **p** 69. C Tunbridge Wells St Jo *Roch* 68-73; C Crookes St Thos *Sheff* 73-81; V Normanton *Wakef* 81-90; TR Didsbury St Jas and Em *Man* 90-09; AD Withington 00-04; Hon Can Man Cathl 06-09; rtd 09; PtO *Ches* from 09; *Man* from 09. *41 Cross Lane, Marple, Stockport SK6 6DG* M: 07929-114143 E: davidmichaelhughes@btinternet.com

HUGHES, Debbie Ann. *See* PEATMAN, Debbie Ann

HUGHES, Canon Elizabeth Jane. b 58. K Coll Lon BD 81 AKC 81. Ripon Coll Cuddesdon 81. **dss** 83 **d** 87 **p** 94. Chipping Barnet w Arkley *St Alb* 83-86; Dunstable 86-93; Hon Par Dn 87-93; NSM Boxmoor St Jo 93-03; Chapl Hospice of St Fran Berkhamsted 99-13; Sen Chapl Luton Airport *St Alb* from 13; Hon Can St Alb from 13. *London Luton Airport Operations Ltd, Navigation House, Airport Way, London Luton Airport, Luton LU2 9LY* T: (01582) 405100 E: liz.hughes@stfrancis.org.uk

HUGHES, Canon Evelyn. b 31. Gilmore Ho 73. **dss** 79 **d** 87 **p** 94. Fetcham *Guildf* 79-82; Dioc Adv Lay Min 82-86; Farnborough 83-87; C 87-92; Bp's Adv for Women's Min 87-94; Dn-in-c Badshot Lea CD 92-94; C-in-c 94-96; Hon Can Guildf Cathl 94-96; rtd 96; PtO *Guildf* from 96. *4 Oaklands, Haslemere GU27 3RD* T: (01428) 651576

HUGHES, Gareth Francis. b 73. St Jo Coll Dur MSc 94 Wolfs Coll Ox MSt 07 GInstP 94. St Mich Coll Llan BD 98. **d** 98 **p** 99. C Haughton le Skerne *Dur* 98-02; TV White Horse *Sarum* 02-06; PtO *Lon* 09-11; Chapl Hertf Coll Ox from 11. *Hertford College, Catte Street, Oxford OX1 3BW* T: (01865) 279411 E: gareth.hughes@hertford.ox.ac.uk

HUGHES, The Very Revd Geraint Morgan Hugh. b 34. Keble Coll Ox BA 58 MA 63. St Mich Coll Llan 58. **d** 59 **p** 60. C Gorseinon *S & B* 59-63; C Oystermouth 63-68; R Llanbadarn Fawr, Llandegley and Llanfihangel etc 68-76; R Llandrindod w Cefnllys 76-86; R Llandrindod w Cefnllys and Disserth 87-98; Can Brecon Cathl 89-98; Prec Brecon Cathl 95-98; RD Maelienydd 95-98; Dean Brecon 98-00; V Brecon St Mary and Battle w Llanddew 98-00; rtd 00. *Hafod, Cefnllys Lane, Penybont, Llandrindod Wells LD1 5SW* T: (01597) 851830

HUGHES, Canon Gerald Thomas. b 30. Lon Univ BD 63 MTh. Qu Coll Birm 72. **d** 72 **p** 73. LtO *Cov* 72-80; P-in-c Birdingbury 80-81; P-in-c Leamington Hastings 80-81; V Leamington Hastings and Birdingbury 81-82; V Dunchurch 82-89; RD Rugby 85-89; Can Res Cov Cathl 89-94; rtd 94; PtO *Cov* from 94; *Worc* from 94. *Loafers' Cottage, Lazy Lane, Fladbury, Pershore WR10 2QL* T: (01386) 860650 E: gerald@loafers.plus.net

HUGHES, Canon Gwilym Berw. b 42. St Mich Coll Llan. **d** 68 **p** 69. C Conwy w Gyffin *Ban* 68-71; V Llandinorwig 71-75; TV Llandudno 75-80; V Dwygyfylchi 80-96; RD Archllechwedd 88-96; V Bodelwyddan *St As* 96-09; Can Cursal St As Cathl 08-09; rtd 09; PtO *Ban* from 09; *St As* from 10. *Glanfa, Glanyrafon Road, Dwygyfylchi, Penmaenmawr LL34 6UD* T: (01492) 623365

HUGHES, Gwilym Lloyd. b 48. Univ of Wales (Cardiff) BD 76 MA 79 Univ of Wales (Ban) CertEd 84. St Mich Coll Llan 71. **d** 99 **p** 00. NSM Caerwys and Bodfari *St As* 99-14; Warden of Readers 99-02; PtO from 14. *Adlonfa, Bodfari, Denbigh LL16 4DA* T: (01745) 710385

HUGHES, Harold John (Hadge). b 55. St Jo Coll Nottm 83. **d** 86 **p** 87. C Man Miles Platting 86-87; C Man Apostles w Miles Platting 87-89; V Roughtown 89-93; Chapl Chich Univ 04-09; Australia 09-10; TV Horsham *Chich* 10-13; Chapl Sir Robert

Woodard Academy Lancing from 13. *Sir Robert Woodard Academy, 44 Upper Boundstone Lane, Sompting, Lancing BN15 9QZ* T: (01903) 767434

HUGHES, Canon Hazel. b 45. Cranmer Hall Dur 75. **dss** 78 **d** 87 **p** 94. Lower Mitton *Worc* 78-81; Worc St Martin w St Pet, St Mark etc 82-86; Worc SE 86-87; Par Dn 87-88; Dn-in-c Wribbenhall 88-94; V 94; P-in-c 94-10; Chapl to Mentally Handicapped 94-10; Hon Can Worc Cathl 95-10; rtd 11. *8 Hidcote Close, Worcester WR5 3SX* T: (01905) 353817 E: hazel.hughes1@btopenworld.com

HUGHES, Heather Alice. b 48. Open Univ BA 91 Kent Univ 97. **d** 99 **p** 00. NSM Pembury *Roch* from 99. *7 Henwoods Crescent, Pembury TN2 4LJ* T: (01892) 822764 E: heather.hughes@diocese-rochester.org

HUGHES, Ian Peter. b 55. Fitzw Coll Cam BA 76 MA 93. Ridley Hall Cam 05. **d** 07 **p** 08. C Wadhurst *Chich* 07-11; C Howell Hill w Burgh Heath *Guildf* from 11. *19 Ballards Green, Burgh Heath, Tadworth KT20 6DA* T: (01737) 213771 M: 07718-909695 E: ian@hughes.name *or* ianh@saintpauls.co.uk

HUGHES, Preb Ivor Gordon. b 45. Westmr Coll Ox MTh 94 Culham Coll of Educn CertEd 68. Ripon Coll Cuddesdon 75. **d** 77 **p** 78. C Newport w Longford *Lich* 77-79; Children's Work Officer CMS 79-82; V Gt and Lt Bedwyn and Savernake Forest *Sarum* 82-86; P-in-c Urchfont w Stert 86-90; TR Redhorn 90-92; Nat Children's Officer Gen Syn Bd of Educn 92-95; R Yeovil w Kingston Pitney *B & W* 95-06; Preb Wells Cathl 02-06; RD Yeovil 04-06; Chapl St Marg Hospice Yeovil 04-06; P-in-c Klamath Falls and Bonanza USA 06-08; rtd 08; PtO *B & W* from 08; *Sarum* from 13. *15 Leventon Place, Hilperton, Trowbridge BA14 7US* T: (01225) 760275

HUGHES, Canon Jacqueline Louise. b 50. Birm Poly BEd 86 ACP 81. WMMTC 89. **d** 92. NSM Edgbaston St Geo *Birm* 92-95; Tutor Qu Coll Birm 96-00; Educn Chapl Birm City Coun 00-10; Dir of Educn *Birm* 10-15; Hon Can Birm Cathl 14-15; rtd 15; PtO *Birm* from 05. *267 Stoney Lane, Yardley, Birmingham B25 8YG* T: 0121-628 4184 E: jackielhughes1950@gmail.com

HUGHES, James Thomas. b 74. St Anne's Coll Ox BA 95 Liv Hope PGCE 97. Oak Hill Th Coll BA 02. **d** 03 **p** 04. C Virginia Water *Guildf* 03-07; C Hartford *Ches* from 07. *52 Stones Manor Lane, Hartford, Northwich CW8 1NU* T: (01606) 77740 *or* 77277 E: james@christchurchgreenbank.org

HUGHES, John. *See* HUGHES, Arthur John

HUGHES, John David. b 58. Leeds Univ BA 79 Man Univ PGCE 82. Ripon Coll Cuddesdon 97. **d** 99 **p** 00. C Wythenshawe *Man* 99-06; P-in-c Old Trafford St Jo from 06; AD Stretford 10-15. *St John's Rectory, 1 Lindum Avenue, Manchester M16 9NQ* T: 0161-872 0500 E: john_dhughes@yahoo.co.uk

HUGHES, John Lloyd. b 48. **d** 08 **p** 09. NSM Abergavenny St Mary w Llanwenarth Citra *Mon* 08-09 and 11-13; NSM Abergavenny H Trin 11-13; NSM Govilon w Llanfoist w Llanelen 09-11; PtO 13-15; NSM Llantilio Pertholey w Bettws Chpl etc from 15. *Emmanuel, 7 Orchard Close, Gilwern, Abergavenny NP7 0EN* T: (01873) 832368 E: john997hughes@btinternet.com

HUGHES, John Malcolm. b 47. Man Univ BSc 68. Coll of Resurr Mirfield 68. **d** 71 **p** 72. C Newton Nottage *Llan* 71-78; V Llanwynno 78-92; R Cadoxton-juxta-Barry 92-11; AD Penarth and Barry 08-11; rtd 11; PtO *Llan* from 14; *Mon* from 14. *3 The Terrace, Rhymney, Tredegar NP22 5LY* T: (01685) 555374

HUGHES, Canon John Patrick. b 41. Oak Hill Th Coll. **d** 67 **p** 68. C Chorleywood St Andr *St Alb* 67-71; C E Twickenham St Steph *Lon* 71-76; TV High Wycombe *Ox* 77-92; Chapl Wycombe Gen Hosp 77-83; V Harborne Heath *Birm* 92-09; Hon Can Birm Cathl 99-09; rtd 09; PtO *Ox* from 10. *59 Witney Road, Ducklington, Witney OX29 7TS* T: (01993) 358781 M: 07817-465996 E: johnandanniehughes@googlemail.com

HUGHES, Canon John Tudor. b 59. Nottm Univ BSc 81 Univ of Wales (Cardiff) BD 84. St Mich Coll Llan 81. **d** 84 **p** 85. C Mold *St As* 84-88; Asst Dioc Youth Chapl 86-90; Dioc Youth Chapl 90-97; Min Can St As Cathl 88-90; Min St As and Tremeirchion 88-90; V Holt 90-96; V Buckley 96-04; RD Mold 00-03; V Gresford 04-09; V Holt and Gresford from 09; Can Cursal St As Cathl 05-13; Can Res, Preb and Sacr from 13. *The Vicarage, Church Green, Gresford, Wrexham LL12 8RG* T: (01978) 852236 E: tudorhughes53@gmail.com

HUGHES, Lindsay. *See* HUGHES, Carol Lindsay

HUGHES, Martin Conway. b 40. Ex Coll Ox BA 61 MA 67. Chich Th Coll. **d** 63 **p** 64. C Roehampton H Trin *S'wark* 63-67; C Addlestone *Guildf* 67-71; V Burpham 71-88; V Shamley Green 88-05; RD Cranleigh 90-95; rtd 05; PtO *Portsm* from 05; *Win* from 08. *22 Siskin Close, Bishops Waltham, Southampton SO32 1RQ* T: (01489) 890365 E: martin@mchughes.org.uk

HUGHES, Matthew James. b 66. K Coll Lon BD 88. Westcott Ho Cam 89. **d** 91 **p** 92. C Heston *Lon* 91-94; C Fulham All SS 94-96; TV St Laur in Thanet *Cant* 96-01; R Farnborough *Roch* from 01. *The Rectory, Farnborough Hill, Orpington BR6 7EQ* T: (01689) 856931 E: jmath@btinternet.com

HUGHES, Michael John Minto. b 50. Liv Univ MB, ChB 74 Westmr Coll Ox MTh 94. Wycliffe Hall Ox 76. **d** 79 **p** 80. C Stranton *Dur* 79-82; Chapl Intercon Ch Soc Peru 82-86; PtO *Dur* 86-87; *Carl* 87-89; TV Thetford *Nor* 89-97; P-in-c Downham *Ely* 97-05; Hon C Ely 05-13; Uganda from 13. *Georgian House, 63a Station Road, Ely CB7 4BS* T: (01353) 615682 E: mikeandsue.hughes@gmail.com

HUGHES, Canon Neville Joseph. b 52. NUU BA 79 MBIM 93. CITC 97. **d** 91 **p** 92. NSM Mullabrack w Markethill and Kilcluney *Arm* 91-98; I from 00; C Portadown St Mark 98-00; Can Arm Cathl from 14. *The Rectory, 6 Mullurg Road, Markethill BT60 1QN* T: (028) 3755 1092

HUGHES, The Ven Paul Vernon. b 53. Ripon Coll Cuddesdon 79. **d** 82 **p** 83. C Chipping Barnet w Arkley *St Alb* 82-86; TV Dunstable 86-93; P-in-c Boxmoor St Jo 93-98; V 98-03; RD Hemel Hempstead 96-03; Adn Bedford from 03. *17 Lansdowne Road, Luton LU3 1EE* T: (01582) 730722 F: 877354 E: archdbedf@stalbans.anglican.org

HUGHES, Mrs Penelope Patricia. b 47. Sheff Univ LLB. WMMTC 95. **d** 98 **p** 99. NSM Whitley *Cov* 98-01; NSM Leamington Spa H Trin and Old Milverton 01-03; P-in-c Berkswell 03-08; PtO from 08; rtd 08. *8 Albany Terrace, Leamington Spa CV32 5LP* T: (01926) 330204 E: penhughes@aol.com

HUGHES, Peter. b 79. Nottm Univ BSc 02. Westmr Th Cen 06. **d** 08 **p** 09. C Bryanston Square St Mary w St Marylebone St Mark *Lon* 08-09; Pioneer Min King's Cross from 10. *16 Bewdley Street, London N1 1HB* E: pete@stmaryslondon.com

HUGHES, Peter John. b 43. Melbourne Univ BA 67 Ch Ch Ox BPhil 77. Trin Coll Melbourne 64 ACT 69. **d** 70 **p** 70. C Warrnambool Australia 70-72; C Croydon St Jo 72-74; PtO *Ox* 75-77; Chapl Ripon Coll Cuddesdon 77-79; Chapl Lon Univ 79-84; Australia from 84; rtd 08. *c/o P J Miller & Co, PO Box 626, North Sydney NSW 2059, Australia* E: pjmillerandco@ozemail.com.au

HUGHES, Peter John. b 59. Wolv Poly BA 83 Lon Univ PGCE 85. Wycliffe Hall Ox 90. **d** 92 **p** 93. C Ecclesall *Sheff* 92-96; V Kimberworth 96-05; R Wickersley from 05. *The Rectory, 5 Church Lane, Wickersley, Rotherham S66 1ES* T: (01709) 543111 E: peter.j.hughes59@btinternet.com

HUGHES, Peter Knowles. b 61. Sarum & Wells Th Coll 87. **d** 90 **p** 91. C Whitchurch *Bris* 90-93; PtO *Worc* 93-97 and from 02; Chapl Univ Coll Worc 97-02. *Woodside Farmhouse, Blakes Lane, Guarlford, Malvern WR13 6NZ* T: (01684) 311308 E: peterknowleshughes@btinternet.com

HUGHES, Canon Philip. b 47. St Jo Coll Nottm 79. **d** 81 **p** 82. C Dolgellau w Llanfachreth and Brithdir etc *Ban* 81-83; Asst Youth Chapl 82-83; R Llaneugrad w Llanallgo and Penrhoslugwy etc 82-95; R Llanberis w Llanrug 95-03; R Llanberis, Llanrug and Llandinorwig 03; Dioc Youth Chapl 93-98; RD Arfon 00-02; R Llanfair-pwll and Llanddaniel-fab etc 03-12; AD Tindaethwy and Menai 07-10; Can Ban Cathl 10-12; rtd 12; PtO *Ban* from 12. *Address temp unknown* E: revphiliphughes@yahoo.co.uk

HUGHES, Philip Geoffrey John. b 60. Nottm Univ BCombStuds 82. Qu Coll Birm 86. **d** 89 **p** 90. C Sedgley All SS *Worc* 89-94; V Boscoppa *Truro* 94-96; Chapl Gatwick Airport and Chapl Sussex Police 96-02; P-in-c Harmondsworth *Lon* 02-07; Chapl Heathrow Airport 02-07; Chapl Metrop Police 02-07; V Seghill *Newc* from 07; AD Bedlington from 13; Chapl Northumbria Police from 07. *Seghill Vicarage, Mares Close, Seghill, Cramlington NE23 7EA* T: 0191-298 0925 E: p.hughes.1@btinternet.com

HUGHES, Philip John. b 70. Trin Coll Bris BA 07. **d** 07 **p** 08. C Ashby-de-la-Zouch and Breedon on the Hill *Leic* 07-10; V Bishops Hull *B & W* from 10; Chapl Somerset Coll of Arts and Tech from 10. *The Vicarage, Bishops Hull Hill, Bishops Hull, Taunton TA1 5EB* E: phil2overflowing@tesco.net

HUGHES, Philip Stephen. b 34. Dur Univ BA 59. Coll of Resurr Mirfield 59. **d** 62 **p** 63. C Horfield St Greg *Bris* 62-66; C Bedminster St Mich 66-69; P-in-c Chippenham St Pet 69-71; V 71-83; TR Bedminster 83-91; V Ashton Keynes, Leigh and Minety 91-00; rtd 00; PtO *Worc* from 00. *19 Fairways, Pershore WR10 1HA* T: (01386) 552375 E: p-jhughes@tiscali.co.uk

HUGHES, Poppy. *See* HUGHES, Veronica Jane

HUGHES, Richard Clifford. b 24. Pemb Coll Cam BA 57 MA 59. Ely Th Coll 48. **d** 50 **p** 51. C Wandsworth St Anne *S'wark* 50-53; S Rhodesia 53-65; S Africa 65-86; Adn Pinetown 75-80;

Australia from 86; rtd 89. *1/184 Springfield Road, Blackburn North Vic 3130, Australia* T: (0061) (3) 9894 4889
E: cherryh@smart.net.au

HUGHES, Richard Jeffrey. b 47. Trin Coll Carmarthen CertEd 68. St Mich Coll Llan 74. **d** 76 **p** 77. C Llanbeblig w Caernarfon and Betws Garmon etc *Ban* 76-78; Dioc Youth Chapl 78-82; TV Holyhead w Rhoscolyn w Llanfair-yn-Neubwll 78-83; R Llanfachraeth 83-92; R Llangefni w Tregaean and Llangristiolus etc 92-95; TV Llanbeblig w Caernarfon and Betws Garmon etc 95-12; rtd 12; PtO *Ban* from 12. *Hafodty, 30 Bryn Rhos, Rhosbodrual, Caernarfon LL55 2BT* T: (01286) 674181

HUGHES, Richard Millree. b 33. Univ of Wales BA 56 MA 79. St Mich Coll Llan 56. **d** 58 **p** 59. C Mold *St As* 58-61; V Choral St As Cathl 61-64; V Towyn 64-67; Asst Master Marlborough Sch Woodstock 77-79; R Whitchurch St Mary *Ox* 79-00; rtd 00; PtO *St As* 13-14; P-in-c Llansilin w Llangadwaladr and Llangedwyn from 14. *The Vicarage, Pentre Felin, Oswestry SY10 7PX* T: (01691) 791876 M: 07798-790369
E: rmillree@aol.com

HUGHES, Robert Elistan-Glodrydd. b 32. Trin Coll Ox BA 54 MA 58 Birm Univ MLitt 85. Westcott Ho Cam 55. **d** 57 **p** 58. C Stoke *Cov* 57-61; Ind Chapl S'wark 61-64; Chapl Birm Univ 64-69; Lodgings Warden and Student Welfare Adv 69-87; Dir Housing Study Overseas Students Trust 88-91; PtO *Ban* 88-94; V Harlech and Llanfair-juxta-Harlech etc 94-99; rtd 97. *Clogwyn Melyn, Ynys, Talsarnau LL47 6TP* T: (01766) 780257
E: shebob.clog1@virgin.net

HUGHES, Robert John. b 46. Liv Univ MB, ChB 69. St Jo Coll Nottm 05. **d** 07 **p** 08. NSM Davenham *Ches* 07-11; V Sandiway from 11. *The Vicarage, 50 Norley Road, Sandiway, Northwich CW8 2JU* T: (01606) 350132 M: 07966-470761
E: jh@doctors.org.uk

HUGHES, Robert Leslie. b 52. Qu Coll Birm 98. **d** 00 **p** 01. C The Quinton *Birm* 00-05; P-in-c Appleby Gp *Leic* 05-08; TV Woodfield 08-09; rtd 09; PtO *Chelmsf* from 11. *42 Peto Avenue, Colchester CO4 5WJ* T: (01206) 841191
E: roberthgs@mac.com

HUGHES, Rodney Thomas. b 39. Dur Univ BA 60. Wycliffe Hall Ox 60. **d** 62 **p** 63. C Edin St Thos 62-65; C Harlow New Town w Lt Parndon *Chelmsf* 65-67; R Haworth *Bradf* 67-74; R W Knighton w Broadmayne *Sarum* 74-77; R Broadmayne, W Knighton, Owermoigne etc 77-82; V Crosthwaite Keswick *Carl* 82-02; rtd 02; PtO *Carl* from 02. *2 Bewcastle Close, Carlisle CA3 0PU* T: (01228) 401680

HUGHES, Roger. *See* HUGHES, William Roger

HUGHES, Mrs Sally Lorraine. b 59. Open Univ BA 98. EAMTC 99. **d** 02 **p** 03. NSM Gretton w Rockingham and Cottingham w E Carlton *Pet* 02-05; Asst Chapl Kettering Gen Hosp NHS Trust 02-04; P-in-c Stoke Albany w Wilbarston and Ashley etc *Pet* from 05; Rural Adv Oakham Adnry from 05. *28 Rushton Road, Wilbarston, Market Harborough LE16 8QL* T/F: (01536) 770998 E: sally@hughes.uk.com

HUGHES, Mrs Sheila. b 52. NOC 92. **d** 95 **p** 96. NSM Birkenhead Priory *Ches* 95-97; C 97-99; P-in-c Northwich St Luke and H Trin 99-01; V 01-07; Bp's Adv for Women in Min 00-07; Chapl Mid Cheshire Hosps Trust 99-07; P-in-c Barrow St Jo *Carl* 07-14; rtd 14; P-in-c Lorton and Loweswater w Buttermere *Carl* from 14. *The Vicarage, Loweswater, Cockermouth CA13 0RU* T: (01900) 85237
E: vicarlolobu@hotmail.com

HUGHES, Sheila Norah. b 40. **d** 06 **p** 07. NSM Ellesmere Port *Ches* 06-10; rtd 10. *13 Bridle Way, Great Sutton, Ellesmere Port CH66 2NJ* T: 0151-339 9777
E: sheila.hughes67@ntlworld.com

HUGHES, Steven Philip. b 52. MBE 01. St Jo Coll Dur BA 80. Ridley Hall Cam 80. **d** 82 **p** 83. C Chilvers Coton w Astley *Cov* 82-86; TV Kings Norton *Birm* 86-91; PtO *Eur* 92-96; Asst Chapl Bucharest w Sofia 96-98; P-in-c 98-01; P-in-c Belgrade 98-00; P-in-c Hoole *Blackb* 02-09; Inter-Faith Development Officer Chs Together in Lancs 09-12; P-in-c Otham w Langley *Cant* from 12; AD N Downs from 14. *4 Kings Acre, Downswood, Maidstone ME15 8UP* E: steven.hughes24@btinternet.com

HUGHES, Timothy David Llewelyn. b 77. St Mellitus Coll. **d** 13 **p** 14. C Onslow Square and S Kensington St Aug *Lon* 13-15; P-in-c Birm St Luke from 15. *1B Arthur Road, Edgbaston, Birmingham B15 2UW* M: 07590-692535
E: tim@worshipcentral.org

HUGHES, Trystan Owain. b 72. Univ of Wales (Ban) BD 94 PhD 98. Wycliffe Hall Ox MTh. **d** 05 **p** 07. C Llantwit Major *Llan* 05-09; C Whitchurch 09; Chapl Cardiff Univ 09-13; P-in-c Cardiff Ch Ch Roath Park from 13; Dioc Dir of Ords from 13. *Christ Church Vicarage, 154 Lake Road East, Cardiff CF23 5NQ* T: (029) 2075 7190
E: trystanhughes@churchinwales.org.uk

HUGHES, Tudor. *See* HUGHES, John Tudor

HUGHES, Ms Valerie Elizabeth. b 53. Birm Univ BA 75 CertEd 76. Wycliffe Hall Ox 85. **d** 87 **p** 94. C Hallwood *Ches* 87-90; Par Dn Garston *Liv* 90-93; Asst Chapl Liv Univ 93; Team Dn Gateacre 93-94; TV 94-00; C St Helens St Helen 00-09; TV Newton from 09 and from 14. *Emmanuel Rectory, 333 Wargrave Road, Newton-le-Willows WA12 8RR* T: (01925) 224920

HUGHES, Veronica Jane (Poppy). b 60. Ex Univ BA 82 Birkbeck Coll Lon MSc 04. SEITE 07. **d** 10 **p** 11. C Dulwich St Clem w St Pet S'wark 10-13; P-in-c Tetbury, Beverston, Long Newnton etc *Glouc* 13-14; R from 14; R Avening w Cherington from 14. *The Vicarage, 6 The Green, Tetbury GL8 8DN* T: (01666) 502333
E: poppy_hughes@hotmail.co.uk

HUGHES, William. *See* HUGHES, Albert William

HUGHES, Canon William Piers Maximillian. b 76. Ex Univ BA 99. Ripon Coll Cuddesdon 99. **d** 01 **p** 02. C Cley Hill Warminster *Sarum* 01-05; V Blackmoor and Whitehill *Portsm* 05-11; V Petersfield from 11; R Buriton from 11; AD Petersfield from 11; Hon Can Portsm Cathl from 15. *12 Dragon Street, Petersfield GU31 4AB* T: (01730) 260464
E: revwillhughes@btinternet.com

HUGHES, The Ven William Roger. b 47. ACCA MCIPD MBIM. Trin Coll Carmarthen. **d** 91 **p** 92. NSM Llan-non *St D* 91-93; V Llangathen w Llanfihangel Cilfargen etc 93-10; Dioc Officer for Soc Resp 93-10; V Catheiniog 10-14; P-in-c Llangunnor w Cwmffrwd from 14; Hon Can St D Cathl 06-09; Can St D Cathl from 09; AD Llangadog and Llandeilo 06-12; Adn Carmarthen from 12. *The Vicarage, Llangunnor Road, Llangunnor, Carmarthen SA31 2HY* T: (01267) 236435

HUGHESDON, James Carlyle. b 82. Ex Univ BA 05. Westcott Ho Cam 10. **d** 12 **p** 13. C Old Ford St Paul and St Mark *Lon* 12-15; V from 15. *The Vicarage, St Stephen's Road, London E3 5JL* M: 07841-123869 E: jchughesdon@gmail.com

HUGHMAN, June Alison. b 58. Kingston Poly BSc 81 Southn Univ PhD 84. Trin Coll Bris 86. **d** 89 **p** 94. Par Dn Penge St Jo *Roch* 89-93; C Woking Ch Ch *Guildf* 93-98; V Croydon Ch Ch S'wark 98-00; C Uxbridge *Lon* from 00; Town Cen Min from 00. *84 Harefield Road, Uxbridge UB8 1PN* T/F: (01895) 254121 T: 258766 E: junehughman@tiscali.co.uk

HUGO, Canon Keith Alan. b 41. Nottm Univ BA 62. Chich Th Coll 62. **d** 64 **p** 65. C Pontefract St Giles *Wakef* 64-68; C Chesterfield St Mary and All SS *Derby* 68-71; V Allenton and Shelton Lock 71-77; Dioc Communications Officer *Sarum* 77-89; V Potterne 77-84; V Worton 77-84; V Potterne w Worton and Marston 84-89; R Wyke Regis 89-06; Can and Preb Sarum Cathl 84-06; RD Weymouth 94-04; rtd 06. *15 Steepdene, Poole BH14 8TE* T: (01202) 734971
E: keith.hugo@ntlworld.com

HUISH, Barnaby Thomas. b 71. St Chad's Coll Dur BA 94 MA 95. Ripon Coll Cuddesdon BA 98. **d** 99 **p** 00. C Darlington H Trin *Dur* 99-02; Prec and Min Can St Alb Abbey *St Alb* 02-06; R Dur St Marg and Neville's Cross St Jo from 06. *St Margaret's Rectory, 10 Westhouse Avenue, Durham DH1 4FH*

HUITSON, Christopher Philip. b 45. Keble Coll Ox BA 66 MA 70. Cuddesdon Coll 67. **d** 69 **p** 70. C Croydon St Sav *Cant* 69-71; Soc Service Unit St Martin-in-the-Fields Lon 71-73; C St Alb St Pet *St Alb* 73-77; V Cople 77-78; P-in-c Willington 77-78; V Cople w Willington 78-89; V Leavesden 89-96; V Totteridge 96-11; RD Barnet 99-05; rtd 11. *Abbotsleigh, 1A Gainsborough Drive, Sherborne DT9 6DS* T: (01935) 815187
E: c.huitson@btinternet.com

HULBERT, Hugh Forfar. b 22. Bris Univ BA 49. Bible Churchmen's Coll Bris 46. **d** 50 **p** 51. C Summerstown S'wark 50-53; C Felixstowe SS Pet and Paul *St E* 53-55; Min Collier Row St Jas CD *Chelmsf* 55-59; SW Area Sec CPAS 59-63; V Portsea St Luke *Portsm* 63-75; V Worthing H Trin *Chich* 75-81; C-in-c Hove H Trin CD 81-85; C Hailsham 86-87; rtd 87; PtO *Chich* from 87. *8 Ramsay Hall, 11-13 Byron Road, Worthing BN11 3HN* T: (01903) 209594

HULBERT, John Anthony Lovett. b 40. Trin Coll Cam BA 63 MA 67. Wells Th Coll 64. **d** 66 **p** 67. C Fareham H Trin *Portsm* 66-70; R Wickham 70-79; RD Bishop's Waltham 74-79; V Bedford St Andr *St Alb* 79-92; RD Bedford 87-92; V Leighton Buzzard w Eggington, Hockliffe etc 92-03; Hon Can St Alb 91-03; C Stansted *Chich* 03-04; P-in-c Lynch w Iping Marsh and Milland 04-10; rtd 10; PtO *Chich* from 10; *Portsm* from 11. *Cherry Trees, Buckshead Hill, Meonstoke, Southampton SO32 3NA* T: (01489) 878289 E: anthonic@btinternet.com

HULBERT, Canon Martin Francis Harrington. b 37. Dur Univ BSc 58 MA 62. Ripon Hall Ox 58. **d** 60 **p** 61. C Buxton *Derby* 60-63; C Eglingham *Newc* 63-67; C-in-c Loundsley Green Ascension CD *Derby* 67-71; P-in-c Frecheville 71-72; R Frecheville and Hackenthorpe *Sheff* 72-77; P-in-c Hathersage *Derby* 77-83; V 83-90; RD Bakewell and Eyam 81-90; R Brailsford w Shirley and Osmaston w Edlaston 90-93; V Tideswell 93-02; RD Buxton 96-99; Hon Can Derby Cathl

89-02; rtd 02; PtO *Derby* from 02. *22 Yokecliffe Crescent, Wirksworth, Matlock DE4 4ER* T: (01629) 825148
E: martin.hulbert1@btinternet.com

HULETT, Peter. b 31. Leeds Univ CertEd 74. Wycliffe Hall Ox 75. **d** 77 **p** 78. C Eastwood *S'well* 77-80; C Granby w Elton 80-83; V Gilling and Kirkby Ravensworth *Ripon* 83-90; P-in-c Bishop Monkton and Burton Leonard 90-96; rtd 96; PtO *Bradf* 96-11. *2 Cardan Drive, Ilkley LS29 8PH* T: (01943) 604202

HULKS, Mrs Nicola Ann. b 84. Ripon Coll Cuddesdon 12. **d** 15. C Maidenhead St Luke *Ox* from 15. *2 Belmont Vale, Maidenhead SL6 6BH* M: 07884-264131
E: nicolahulks@hotmail.co.uk

HULL, Araminta Jane. b 51. **d** 13 **p** 14. OLM Bris St Matt and St Nath from 13. *13 Somerset Street, Kingsdown, Bristol BS2 8NB* T: 0117-942 1366

HULL, Mrs Bernadette Mary. b 46. E Lon Univ BA 92 PGCE 93. NTMTC 99. **d** 02 **p** 03. NSM Becontree S *Chelmsf* 02-04; NSM Marks Gate 04-09; P-in-c Romford Ascension Collier Row from 09. *Ascension Vicarage, 68 Collier Row Road, Romford RM5 2BA* T: (01708) 741658 M: 07990-730293
E: bernadettehull@btinternet.com

HULL, David John. b 44. Linc Th Coll 88. **d** 90 **p** 91. C Mansfield Woodhouse *S'well* 90-93; P-in-c Mansfield St Lawr 93-00; V Mosbrough *Sheff* 00-03; V Elmton *Derby* 03-09; P-in-c Whitwell 05-09; rtd 10; PtO *Derby* from 10; *S'well* from 10. *5 Beeley Close, Creswell, Worksop S80 4GA* T: (01909) 724104 E: rev.dhull@tiscali.co.uk

HULL, John Hammond. b 36. Brasted Th Coll 58 Sarum Th Coll 60. **d** 61 **p** 62. C Gt Clacton *Chelmsf* 61-66; Area Chapl (E Anglia) Toc H 66-70; (Midl Region) 70-75; LtO *Chelmsf* 66-75; Chapl Toc H HQ 75-82; LtO *Ox* 75-01; rtd 01; PtO *Ox* from 01. *66 Grenville Avenue, Wendover, Aylesbury HP22 6AL* T: (01296) 624487

HULL, Stuart James. b 90. Essex Univ BA 11. Wycliffe Hall Ox BA 15. **d** 15. C Springfield H Trin *Chelmsf* from 15. *58 Navigation Road, Chelmsford CM2 6ND* M: 07941-712532
E: preatorian1990@hotmail.co.uk

HULL, The Very Revd Thomas Henry. b 55. QUB BD 79. NTMTC 94. **d** 97 **p** 98. C Kidbrooke *S'wark* 97-99; TV 99-01; I Lecale Gp *D & D* from 01; Min Can Down Cathl 03-06; Dean Down from 06. *Lecale Rectory, 9 Quoile Road, Downpatrick BT30 6SE* T: (028) 4461 3101 *or* 4461 4922 F: 4461 4456
E: henryhull@downcathedral.org

HULL, Timothy David. b 60. Lon Bible Coll 87 K Coll Lon PhD 97. St Jo Coll Nottm BTh 90. **d** 90 **p** 91. C Leyton St Mary w St Edw *Chelmsf* 90-95; Chapl Havering Coll of F&HE 94-98; C Harold Hill St Geo *Chelmsf* 95-98; TV Becontree W 98-05; Co-ord NTMTC 98-01; Registrar 01-05; Tutor St Jo Coll Nottm from 05. *2 Peache Way, Chilwell Lane, Bramcote, Nottingham NG9 3DX* T: 0115-943 6988 E: t.hull@stjohns-nottm.ac.uk

HULL, Suffragan Bishop of. *See* WHITE, The Rt Revd Alison Mary

✠**HULLAH, The Rt Revd Peter Fearnley.** b 49. K Coll Lon BD 71 AKC 71 FRSA 93. Cuddesdon Coll 73. **d** 74 **p** 75 **c** 99. Asst Chapl St Edw Sch Ox 74-77; C Summertown *Ox* 74-76; C Wolvercote w Summertown 76-77; Chapl Sevenoaks Sch 77-82; Hon C Sevenoaks St Nic *Roch* 77-82; Ho Master Internat Cen Sevenoaks Sch 82-87; Hon C Kippington *Roch* 82-87; Sen Chapl K Sch and Hon Min Can Cant Cathl 87-92; Hd Master Chetham's Sch of Music 92-99; Hon Can Man Cathl 96-99; Area Bp Ramsbury *Sarum* 99-05; Prin Northn Academy 05-11; NSM St Martin-in-the-Fields *Lon* from 11; Dir Ethos, United Learning Trust/Ch Schs Trust from 11. *62 St Margarets Road, Twickenham TW1 2LP*

HULLYER, Paul Charles. b 68. Anglia Poly Univ MA 98 Lambeth MA 04 FRSA 04. Aston Tr Scheme 92 Westcott Ho Cam 94. **d** 97 **p** 98. C Stoke Newington St Mary *Lon* 97-00; C Addlestone *Guildf* 00-03; V Hillingdon All SS *Lon* 03-08; V Pinner from 08; Dir Post-Ord Tr from 10; CF(V) from 12. *The Vicarage, 2 Church Lane, Pinner HA5 3AA* T: (020) 8866 3869
E: paulhullyer.vicar@btinternet.com

HULME, Alan John. b 60. Birm Univ BSc 81. Wycliffe Hall Ox BA 90. **d** 91 **p** 92. C Chilwell *S'well* 91-96; TV Roxeth *Lon* 96-02; V S Harrow St Paul 02-08; TR Ely 08-13; Dioc Dir Par Development and Evang *Guildf* from 13. *The Education Centre, Guildford Cathedral, Stag Hill, Guildford GU2 7UP* T: (01483) 484921 E: alan.hulme@cofeguildford.org.uk

HULME (*née* ASHLEY), Mrs Jane Isobel. b 59. Birm Univ BSc 81. **d** 05 **p** 06. NSM S Harrow St Paul *Lon* 05-08; NSM Ely 08-13. *66 Westfield Road, Woking GU22 9NG* T: (01483) 351219
E: janehulme@aol.com

HULME, Ms Juliette Mary. b 57. Whitelands Coll Lon BEd 81. Cranmer Hall Dur 94. **d** 94 **p** 95. C Crayford *Roch* 94-98; C Leatherhead *Guildf* 98-01; CF 02-05; PtO *Sarum* 05-08; Chapl Wells Cathl Sch from 06. *18 Vicars Close, Wells BA5 2UJ* T: (01749) 834207 E: j.hulme@wells-cathedral-school.com

HULME, Norman. b 31. Kelham Th Coll 50. **d** 54 **p** 55. C Blackb St Pet 54-57; C Blakenall Heath *Lich* 57-59; V Gannow *Blackb* 59-64; V Anwick *Linc* 64-74; V S Kyme 64-74; V Moulton 74-83; V Earl Shilton w Elmesthorpe *Leic* 83-88; Chapl Harperbury Hosp Radlett 88-96; rtd 96. *Moorcroft, 9 Birch Grove, Spalding PE11 2HL* T: (01775) 710127
E: norjoan@yahoo.co.uk

HULME, Susan. b 52. **d** 08 **p** 09. NSM Kinsley w Wragby *Wakef* 08-12; NSM Brotherton *Leeds* from 12; NSM Ferrybridge from 12; Chapl Mid Yorks Hosps NHS Trust from 13. *4 Balmoral Drive, Knottingley WF11 8RQ* T: (01977) 676808
E: bedeuk@talk21.com

HULSE, Mrs Ruth Carole. b 80. Ripon Coll Cuddesdon 11. **d** 13 **p** 14. C W Heref from 13. *79 Bridle Road, Hereford HR4 0PW* T: (01432) 273086 M: 07733-323290
E: revdruthhulse@gmail.com

HULSE, William John. b 42. Dur Univ BA 65. Linc Th Coll 65. **d** 67 **p** 68. C S Westoe *Dur* 67-70; LtO *Newc* 70-72; C Far Headingley St Chad *Ripon* 72-76; R Swillington 76-88; V Shadwell 88-95; V Oulton w Woodlesford 95-02; P-in-c Spennithorne w Finghall and Hauxwell 02-12; Chapl MU 03-09; rtd 12; PtO *Leeds* from 13. *5 Hargill Close, Harmby, Leyburn DL8 5QE* T: (01969) 623396
E: wjhulse@btinternet.com

HUME, Mrs Barbara Christine. b 56. NTMTC 94. **d** 97 **p** 98. NSM Romford St Edw *Chelmsf* 97-01; C 01-11; P-in-c Upper Colne from 11. *The Rectory, Church Road, Great Yeldham, Halstead CO9 4PT* T: (01787) 237138
E: revbarbara8@btinternet.com

HUME, Miss Clephane Arrol. b 46. Open Univ BA 87 Edin Univ MTh 98 DipOT 68. Edin Dioc NSM Course 88. **d** 92 **p** 94. NSM Edin St Jo from 92. *30 Findhorn Place, Edinburgh EH9 2JP* T: 0131-667 2996 F: 668 3568 E: cah@clephane.plus.com

HUME, Ernest. b 45. Linc Th Coll 77. **d** 79 **p** 80. C Ilkeston St Mary *Derby* 79-81; C Sheff Manor 81-82; TV 82-88; V Norton Woodseats St Chad 88-99; V Woodhouse St Jas 99-02; rtd 02. *Shadwell, 6 Canal Bridge, Killamarsh, Sheffield S21 1DJ* T: 0114-248 1769
E: ehume@vicarage51.freeserve.co.uk

HUME, Martin. b 54. Coll of Resurr Mirfield 89. **d** 91 **p** 92. C Brentwood St Thos *Chelmsf* 91-94; P-in-c Corringham 94-04; V E Wickham *S'wark* 04-10; rtd 10; PtO *Chich* from 11. *45 Holland Mews, Hove BN3 1JG* T: (01273) 206478 M: 07901-553522 E: martinhume@aol.com

HUME, Robert Roy. b 47. **d** 09 **p** 10. OLM Ashmanhaugh, Barton Turf etc *Nor* from 09. *Owls Dene, Ferry Cott Lane, Horning, Norwich NR12 8PP* T: (01692) 630029
E: robhume1@btinternet.com

HUMM, Andrew James. b 72. St Jo Coll Nottm 10. **d** 12 **p** 13. C Loughborough Em and St Mary in Charnwood *Leic* 12-14; C Loughborough Em from 15. *Emmanuel House, 47 Brookfield Avenue, Loughborough LE11 3LN* E: as_humm@yahoo.com

HUMMERSTONE, Jeremy David. Mert Coll Ox BA 65 MA 70. Wells Th Coll 70. **d** 72 **p** 73. C Helmsley and Pockley cum E Moors *York* 72-75; TV Swanborough *Sarum* 75-80; P-in-c Gt Torrington *Ex* 80-81; P-in-c Lt Torrington 80-81; P-in-c Frithelstock 80-81; V Gt and Lt Torrington and Frithelstock 81-10; rtd 10. *1 Undercliffe, Pickering YO18 7BB*
E: jdhummerstone@tiscali.co.uk

HUMPHREY, Alan. b 48. Open Univ BA 74. Qu Coll Birm 07. **d** 10 **p** 11. C Kirby Muxloe *Leic* 10-15; R Leicester Forest East from 15. *44 Somerfield Way, Leicester Forest East, Leicester LE3 3LX* T: 0116-239 2404 M: 07768-374200
E: alan.humphrey@me.com

HUMPHREY, Mrs Betty. b 37. St Mich Ho *Ox* 59. **d** 90 **p** 94. C Hardwicke, Quedgeley and Elmore w Longney *Glouc* 90-93; Dn-in-c Swindon w Uckington and Elmstone Hardwicke 93-94; P-in-c 94-96; R 96-98; rtd 98; PtO *Glouc* from 00. *11 Lower Orchard, Tibberton, Gloucester GL19 3AX* T: (01452) 790790

HUMPHREY, David Lane. b 57. Maine Univ BA 79. St Jo Coll Nottm 84. **d** 88 **p** 89. C Springfield All SS *Chelmsf* 88-91; C Thundersley 91-96; V Standon *St Alb* 96-04; RD Bishop's Stortford 01-04; R Portland St Matt USA from 04. *11229 NE Prescott Street, Portland OR 97220-2457, USA* T: (001) (503) 252 5720 E: humphrey@iinet.com

HUMPHREY, Derek Hollis. b 37. Chich Th Coll 69. **d** 72 **p** 73. C Havant *Portsm* 72-75; C Southsea H Spirit 75-78; V Finsbury Park St Thos *Lon* 78-88; V S Patcham *Chich* 88-03; rtd 03; C Clayton w Keymer *Chich* 03-05; C Bolney 05-07; C Lurgashall, Lodsworth and Selham 07-10; P-in-c Portslade Gd Shep 10-13; LtO from 13. *21 Gibson Road, Tangmere, Chichester PO20 2JA* T: (01243) 785089

HUMPHREY, Canon George William. b 38. Lon Bible Coll BD 61 Lon Univ CertEd 74. Oak Hill Th Coll 61. **d** 62 **p** 63. C Heigham H Trin *Nor* 62-64; P-in-c Buckenham w

Hassingham and Strumpshaw 64-67; Chapl St Andr Hosp Norwich 64-67; Asst Master Mexborough Gr Sch 67-69; Hd RE Cheadle Gr Sch 69-76; Hon C Cheadle Hulme St Andr *Ches* 70-76; P-in-c Kellington w Whitley *Wakef* 76-80; Teacher Thurnscoe Comp Sch 76-80; RE Insp Glos Co Coun and Dio *Glouc* 80-93; Dioc RE Adv 93-99; Hon Can Glouc Cathl 95-99; rtd 00; PtO *Glouc* from 00. *11 Lower Orchard, Tibberton, Gloucester GL19 3AX* T: (01452) 790790

HUMPHREY, Heather Mary. b 46. CertEd 68. WMMTC 87. **d** 90 **p** 94. NSM Overbury w Teddington, Alstone etc *Worc* 90-96; NSM Berrow w Pendock, Eldersfield, Hollybush etc 96-98; C Coseley Ch Ch 98-00; V 00-14; rtd 14; Hon C The Bourne and Tilford *Guildf* from 14. *All Saints' Vicarage, Tilford Road, Tilford, Farnham GU10 2DA*

HUMPHREY, Richard Anthony. b 44. **d** 13 **p** 14. OLM Warmley, Syston and Bitton *Bris* from 13. *103 High Street, Hanham, Bristol BS15 3QG* T: 0117-949 0502

HUMPHREY, Timothy Martin. b 62. Ex Univ BA 83. St Jo Coll Nottm 86. **d** 89 **p** 90. C Wallington *S'wark* 89-92; P-in-c 92-97; C Oakley w Wootton St Lawrence *Win* 97-02; Faith Development Field Officer 97-02; V Kensington St Barn *Lon* from 02. *St Barnabas's Vicarage, 23 Addison Road, London W14 8LH* T: (020) 7471 7019 or 7471 7000 F: 7471 7001 E: tim@stbk.org.uk

HUMPHREY, Mrs Anne-Marie (Anna). b 44. SRN 67 K Coll Lon BD 92 AKC 92 Man Univ MA 96. NOC 92. **d** 95 **p** 96. NSM Manchester Gd Shep and St Barn *Man* 95-98; NSM Burnage St Nic 98-03; Chapl Cen Man Healthcare NHS Trust 96-01; Chapl Cen Man/Man Children's Univ Hosp NHS Trust 01-06; rtd 06; PtO *Ban* from 10. *Tyn-y-Coed, Henryd Road, Conwy LL32 8YF* T: (01492) 573396

HUMPHREYS, Brian Leonard. b 29. MChS 51 SRCh. Bp Attwell Tr Inst. **d** 87 **p** 88. NSM Maugholld *S & M* 87-91; NSM S Ramsey St Paul 91-92; NSM Andreas 92-94; PtO from 94. *Thie Cassan Yack, Jack's Lane, Port E Vullen, Ramsey, Isle of Man IM7 1AW* T: (01624) 813694

HUMPHREYS, John Louis. b 51. Jes Coll Cam BA 72 MA 76 Nottm Univ BA 75. St Jo Coll Nottm 73. **d** 76 **p** 77. C W Bromwich Gd Shep w St Jo *Lich* 76-79; C Woodford Wells *Chelmsf* 79-83; V Werrington *Lich* 83-08; Chapl HM YOI Werrington Ho 83-98; PtO *Lich* from 09. *18 Omega Way, Stoke-on-Trent ST4 8TF* T/F: (01782) 658575

HUMPHREYS, Canon Kenneth Glyn. b 28. Bps' Coll Cheshunt 64. **d** 66 **p** 67. C New Windsor St Jo *Ox* 66-67; C Whitley Ch Ch 67-70; V Compton 70-74; R Compton w E Ilsley 74-75; C Wokingham All SS 75-77; Chapl Lucas Hosp Wokingham (Almshouses) 77-81; V California *Ox* 81-94; RD Sonning 86-88; Hon Can Ch Ch 91-94; rtd 95; PtO *Ox* from 96. *3 Milton Court, Milton Road, Wokingham RG40 1DQ* T: 0118-977 2096

HUMPHREYS, Mrs Lydia Ann. b 60. Sarum & Wells Th Coll 91. **d** 93 **p** 94. C Gaywood *Nor* 93-95 and 95-97; TV Cov E 97-10; P-in-c Kempston Transfiguration *St Alb* 10-14; V from 14. *The Vicarage, Cleveland Street, Kempston, Bedford MK42 8DW* T: (01234) 854886 E: lydia@humphreys.clara.co.uk

HUMPHREYS, Canon Philip Noel. b 34. Bps' Coll Cheshunt 62. **d** 64 **p** 65. C Plymouth St Andr *Ex* 64-68; Chapl Lee Abbey 68-73; V Porchester *S'well* 73-82; RD W Bingham 82-87; P-in-c W Leake w Kingston-on-Soar and Ratcliffe-on-Soar 82-87; R W Bridgford 82-00; Hon Can *S'well* Minster 93-00; rtd 00; PtO *S'well* from 00. *57 Foxhall Court, School Lane, Banbury OX16 2AU* T: (01295) 273577

HUMPHREYS, Canon Roger John. b 45. CertEd 66 Open Univ BA 76. Wycliffe Hall Ox 81. **d** 83 **p** 84. Chapl Dragon Sch Ox 83-87; C Ox St Andr 83-87; V Carterton 87-94; R Bladon w Woodstock 94-05; TR Blenheim 05-09; AD Woodstock 01-06; Chapl Cokethorpe Sch Witney 09-13; Hon Can Ch Ch *Ox* 05-14; PtO from 09; *Eur* from 15. *12 The Pieces, Bampton, Oxford OX18 2JZ* T: (01993) 850199 M: 07788-717214 E: rev.rog@zen.co.uk

HUMPHREYS, Stephen Robert Beresford. b 52. K Coll Lon BA 98. 74. **d** 76 **p** 77. C Northwood Hills St Edm *Lon* 76-79; C Manningham St Mary and Bradf St Mich 79-81; Chapl Bradf R Infirmary 82-86; C Leeds St Pet *Ripon* 87-90; PtO *B & W* 94-99; C Selworthy, Timberscombe, Wootton Courtenay etc 02-07; C Porlock and Porlock Weir w Stoke Pero etc from 07. *Stowey Farm, Timberscombe, Minehead TA24 7BW* T: (01643) 841265 M: 07973-409536

HUMPHRIES, Anthony Roy. b 49. Lon Univ BSc 73. Wycliffe Hall Ox. **d** 94 **p** 95. C Worksop St Jo *S'well* 94-96; C Retford St Sav 96-98; TV Grantham *Linc* 98-00; TV Bestwood *S'well* 00-03; V Branston w Tatenhill *Lich* 03-07; P-in-c Gisburn *Bradf* 12-14; P-in-c Blackb from 14. *St Mary's Vicarage, Main Street, Gisburn, Clitheroe BB7 4HR* T: (01200) 445118 E: revtonyhumphries@hotmail.com

HUMPHRIES, Benjamin Paul. b 56. Man Univ BA 77 FRGS 85. Qu Coll Birm 82. **d** 85 **p** 86. C Hall Green Ascension *Birm* 85-88; P-in-c Belmont *Man* 88-96; Fieldworker USPG Blackb, Bradf, Carl and Wakef 96-98; Area Co-ord Chr Aid (Cumbria, Lancs and Isle of Man) 98-07; C Shepherd's Bush St Steph w St Thos *Lon* 07-12; Chapl Mombasa Miss to Seafarers Kenya 12-15; Chapl Dunkirk Miss to Seafarers *Eur* from 15. *Mission to Seafarers, 130 rue de l'Ecole Maternelle, 59140 Dunkerque, France* E: ben.humphries@mtsmail.org *or* bphumphries1@hotmail.com

HUMPHRIES, Catherine Elizabeth. *See* NICHOLLS, Catherine Elizabeth

HUMPHRIES, Canon Christopher William. b 52. St Jo Coll Cam BA 73 MA 77 Lon Inst of Educn CertEd 74. St Jo Coll Nottm 77. **d** 79 **p** 80. C Eccleshill *Bradf* 79-82; Chapl Scargill Ho 82-86; TV Guiseley w Esholt *Bradf* 86-91; V Filey *York* 91-05; RD Scarborough 98-04; Can Res Ches Cathl 05-14; V Whitegate w Lt Budworth from 14; Hon Can Ches Cathl from 14. *The Vicarage, Cinderhill, Whitegate, Northwich CW8 2BH* T: (01606) 301563

HUMPHRIES, David. *See* HUMPHRIES, William David

HUMPHRIES, David Graham. b 48. St Mich Coll Llan 67. **d** 71 **p** 72. C Neath w Llantwit *Llan* 71-72; C Bishop's Cleeve *Glouc* 81-83; C Cirencester 83-87; V Glouc St Steph 87-96; P-in-c Mickleton 96-03; Assoc P Up Hatherley 03-06; rtd 06; Chapl Glouc Charities Trust from 06. *19 Gurney Avenue, Tuffley, Gloucester GL4 0YJ* T: (01452) 529582

HUMPHRIES, David John. b 51. BSc CertEd BD. Edin Th Coll. **d** 84 **p** 85. C Vsychale *Cov* 84-88; V Greetland and W Vale *Wakef* 88-96; V Shawbury *Lich* from 96; R Moreton Corbet from 96; V Stanton on Hine Heath from 96. *New Vicarage, Church Street, Shawbury, Shrewsbury SY4 4NH* T: (01939) 250419

HUMPHRIES, Donald. b 43. Bris Univ BA 66. Clifton Th Coll 66. **d** 68 **p** 69. C Selly Hill St Steph *Birm* 68-74; Chapl Warw Univ *Cov* 74-79; V Bedford Ch Ch *St Alb* 79-85; V Cambridge H Trin w St Andr Gt *Ely* 85-92; V Cambridge H Trin 92-94; rtd 94; PtO *Ely* from 94. *25 Park Avenue, Beverley HU17 7AT* T: (01482) 871471

HUMPHRIES, Grahame Leslie. b 44. Lon Coll of Div ALCD 70 LTh. **d** 71 **p** 72. C Wandsworth St Mich *S'wark* 71-74; C Slough *Ox* 74-77; P-in-c Arley *Cov* 77-82; R 82-84; Norfolk Churches' Radio Officer *Nor* 84-96; P-in-c Bawdeswell w Foxley 84-96; P-in-c Mayfield *Lich* 96-02; Local Min Adv (Stafford) 96-02; RD Uttoxeter 98-02; P-in-c Blockley w Aston Magna and Bourton on the Hill *Glouc* 02-12; Local Min Officer 02-12; rtd 12; PtO *Ox* from 13. *1 Lees Heights, Charlbury, Chipping Norton OX7 3EZ* T: (01608) 819270

HUMPHRIES, Mrs Janet Susan. b 46. SAOMC 02. **d** 04 **p** 05. NSM Potton w Sutton and Cockayne Hatley *St Alb* 04-07; NSM Caldecote, Northill and Old Warden from 07. *7 Shakespeare Drive, Upper Caldecote, Biggleswade SG18 9DD* T: (01767) 220365 E: janet.humphries1@ntlworld.com

HUMPHRIES, John. b 49. St Mich Coll Llan 73. **d** 76 **p** 77. C Pontnewynydd *Mon* 76-78; C Ebbw Vale 78-81; V Pet Ch Carpenter 81-86; P-in-c King's Cliffe 86-87; R King's Cliffe w Apethorpe 87-93; R King's Cliffe 93-97; V Finedon 97-09; Chapl Northants Fire and Rescue Service 03-09; TR Mynyddislwyn *Mon* 09-12; P-in-c Llanddewi Rhydderch w Llangattock-juxta-Usk etc from 12. *The Vicarage, Llanddewi Rhydderch, Abergavenny NP7 9TS* T: (01873) 840707 M: 07976-370434 E: frjohn13@btinternet.com

HUMPHRIES, Mrs Julie Ann. b 64. Birm Univ BA 02. Qu Coll Birm 06. **d** 08 **p** 09. C Redditch H Trin *Worc* 08-12; TV Salter Street and Shirley *Birm* from 12. *68 Tythe Barn Lane, Shirley, Solihull B90 1RW* T: 0121-733 6706 E: juliehumphries@yahoo.co.uk

HUMPHRIES, Richard James Robert. b 44. Anglia Ruskin Univ MA 12 FRAM 95. EAMTC 99. **d** 01 **p** 02. NSM Heybridge w Langford *Chelmsf* 01-02; NSM Maldon All SS w St Pet 02-09; Asst Chapl Mid-Essex Hosp Services NHS Trust 01-04; Chapl Colchester Hosp Univ NHS Foundn Trust 04-09; rtd 09; PtO *Chelmsf* from 09. *116 Fronks Road, Harwich CO12 4EQ* T: (01255) 502649 M: 07803-281036 E: richard.humphries1@btopenworld.com

HUMPHRIES, Robert William. b 36. Open Univ BA 87. SWMTC 96. **d** 99 **p** 00. OLM Kenwyn w St Allen *Truro* from 99. *27 Penhalls Way, Playing Place, Truro TR3 6EX* T: (01872) 862827 E: rev.bob@tiscali.co.uk

HUMPHRIES, Sidney. b 53. **d** 13 **p** 14. NSM Littleham-cum-Exmouth w Lympstone *Ex* from 13. *36 Trafalgar Road, Lympstone, Exmouth EX8 5HX*

HUMPHRIES, Mrs Susan Joy. b 45. Open Univ BSc 98. Cranmer Hall Dur 05. **d** 06 **p** 07. NSM Beverley Minster *York* 06-09; NSM N Cave w Cliffe and Hotham 09-12; P-in-c 12-14. *119 Old Station Road, Bromsgrove B60 2AS* T: (01527) 577808 M: 07930-803601 E: rev.s.humphries@btinternet.com

HUMPHRIES, Canon William David. b 57. QUB BEd LTCL. CITC. **d** 86 **p** 87. C Ballyholme *D & D* 86-90; Min Can Belf Cathl 89-12; V Choral Belf Cathl 90-93; Can Belf Cathl from 12; C Belfast St Anne *Conn* 90-93; I Stormont *D & D* from 93. *St Molua's Rectory, 3 Rosepark, Belfast BT5 7RG*   T: (028) 9048 2292 *or* 9041 9171   E: stormont@down.anglican.org

HUMPHRIS, Richard. b 44. Sarum & Wells Th Coll 69. **d** 72 **p** 73. C Cheltenham St Luke and St Jo *Glouc* 72-77; C Lydney w Aylburton 77-82; Chapl RAF 82-85; TV Kippax w Allerton Bywater *Ripon* 85-92; RSPCA 92-95; rtd 95; PtO *York* from 98. *4 Belle Vue Terrace, Bellerby, Leyburn DL8 5QL*   T: (01969) 622004

HUMPHRISS, Canon Reginald George. b 36. Kelham Th Coll 56. **d** 61 **p** 62. C Londonderry *Birm* 61-63; Asst Dir RE *Cant* 63-66; Dioc Youth Chapl 63-66; V Preston next Faversham 66-72; P-in-c Goodnestone St Bart and Graveney 71-72; V Spring Park 72-76; R Cant St Martin and St Paul 76-90; R Saltwood 90-01; RD Cant 82-88; Hon Can Cant Cathl 85-01; RD Elham 93-00; rtd 01; PtO *Cant* from 01. *Winsole, Faussett, Lower Hardres, Canterbury CT4 7AH*   T: (01227) 765264

HUMPHRY, Toby Peter. b 66. Man Univ BA 88. Ripon Coll Cuddesdon BA 90 MA 96 Qu Coll Birm 92. **d** 93 **p** 94. C Westhoughton *Man* 93-96; C Westhoughton and Wingates 97; TV Atherton 97-99; TV Atherton and Hindsford 99-02; TV Atherton and Hindsford w Howe Bridge 02-03; Chapl K Ely 03-13; Min Can Ely Cathl 03-13. *The King's School, Barton Road, Ely CB7 4DB*   T: (01353) 659653   E: chaplain@kingsely.org

HUMPHRYES, Garry James. b 62. Coll of Resurr Mirfield 92. **d** 95 **p** 96. C Lt Marsden *Blackb* 95-98; C Darwen St Cuth w Tockholes St Steph 98-00; V Nelson St Bede 00-03; V Morecambe St Barn 03-08; Dioc Race and Community Relns Officer 98-03; CF from 08. *c/o MOD Chaplains (Army)* F: 381824   T: (01264) 383430

HUMPHRYS, Kevin Luke. b 73. Surrey Univ BA 97. St Steph Ho Ox. **d** 99 **p** 00. C Moulsecoomb *Chich* 99-03. *2 Adur Court, 463 Brighton Road, Lancing BN15 8LF*   T: (01903) 609260   E: kevinhumphrys@hotmail.com

HUNDLEBY, Alan. b 41. **d** 86 **p** 87. OLM Fotherby *Linc* 86-02; NSM Barnoldby le Beck 02-14; NSM Waltham Gp from 14. *35 Cheapside, Waltham, Grimsby DN37 0HE*   T: (01472) 827159

HUNG, Frank Yu-Chi. b 45. Birm Univ BSc 68 BA 75 Liv Univ MSc 71. Wycliffe Hall Ox 76. **d** 78 **p** 79. C Walton H Trin *Ox* 78-82; C Spring Grove St Mary *Lon* 82-85; TV Wexcombe *Sarum* 85-92; V Hatcham St Jas *S'wark* 92-98; Chapl Goldsmiths' Coll Lon 95-98; Chapl Lon S Bank Univ 98-10; rtd 10; Hon C S'wark St Geo w St Alphege and St Jude from 10. *151 Graham Road, London SW19 3SL*   T: (020) 8542 1612

HUNGERFORD, Robin Nicholas. b 47. Redland Coll of Educn CertEd 74. Trin Coll Bris 86. **d** 88 **p** 89. C Swindon Dorcan *Bris* 88-92; TV Melbury *Sarum* 92-01; P-in-c Winterbourne Stickland and Turnworth etc 01-05; V Winterborne Valley and Milton Abbas 05-12; rtd 12. *Church House, 53A High Street, Heytesbury, Warminster BA12 0EA*   T: (01985) 840522   E: rhungerford157@btinternet.com

HUNNISETT, John Bernard. b 47. AKC 73. **d** 73 **p** 74. C Charlton Kings St Mary *Glouc* 73-77; C Portsea St Mary *Portsm* 77-80; V Badgeworth w Shurdington *Glouc* 80-87; R Dursley 87-99; TR Ross *Heref* 99-07; RD Ross and Archenfield 02-07; Chapl Huggens Coll Northfleet 07-12; rtd 12. *1 Fernleigh Villas, Old Bristol Road, Nailsworth, Stroud GL6 0LQ*   T: (01453) 833491   M: 07970-280274   E: john.hunnisett@tiscali.co.uk

HUNNYBUN, Martin Wilfrid. b 44. Oak Hill Th Coll 67. **d** 70 **p** 71. C Ware Ch Ch *St Alb* 70-74; C Washfield, Stoodleigh, Withleigh etc *Ex* 74-75; TV 75-80; R Braunston *Pet* 80-85; Asst Chapl HM Pris Onley 80-85; R Berry and Kangaroo Valley Sydney Australia 85-94; Sen Chapl Angl Retirement Village 94-98; TV Parkham, Alwington, Buckland Brewer etc *Ex* 98-00; Dioc Ecum Adv 98-00; R Glebe Australia 00-03; rtd 03. *204 Beacon Road, North Tambrine QLD 4272, Australia*   T: (0061) (7) 5545 4310   E: m.hunnybun@bigpond.com

HUNT, Alan. b 31. GIMechE 51 GIPE 51. St Mich Coll Llan 65. **d** 67 **p** 68. C Standish *Blackb* 66-72; V Clitheroe St Paul Low Moor 72-76; LtO 76-85; rtd 85; PtO *Blackb* from 85. *68 Coniston Drive, Walton-le-Dale, Preston PR5 4RQ*   T: (01772) 339554

HUNT, Andrew Collins. b 54. Reading Univ BA 77 Hull Univ PGCE 79. St Alb Minl Tr Scheme 82 Sarum & Wells Th Coll 89 WEMTC 99. **d** 00 **p** 01. NSM Cainscross w Selsley *Glouc* 00-02; NSM Wells St Thos w Horrington *B & W* 07-10; PtO 10-12; NSM Polden Wheel from 12. *67 Wells Road, Glastonbury BA5 9BY*   T: (01458) 830914   E: r54hunt@btinternet.com

HUNT, Ashley Stephen. b 50. St Jo Coll Nottm 81. **d** 83 **p** 84. C Southchurch H Trin *Chelmsf* 83-86; TV Droitwich *Worc* 86-87; USA 88-91; TV Melton Gt Framland *Leic* 92-93; TV Melton Mowbray 93-98; TV Grantham *Linc* 98-00; Chapl Mental Health 98-01; C Stamford All SS w St Jo *Linc* 00-01; TV Mynyddislwyn *Mon* from 02. *The Vicarage, Commercial Road, Cwmfelinfach, Ynysddu, Newport NP11 7HW*   T: (01495) 228445   E: louhunt3@aol.com

HUNT, Mrs Beverley Cecilia. b 49. **d** 08 **p** 09. NSM E Molesey *Guildf* 08-11; TV Godalming 11-15; PtO from 15. *29 Franklyn Road, Godalming GU7 2LD*   T: (01483) 424710   E: revbevppm@btinternet.com

HUNT, Mrs Christina. b 24. Qu Mary Coll Lon BSc 45. S Dios Minl Tr Scheme 78. **dss** 81 **d** 87 **p** 94. Alderbury and W Grimstead *Sarum* 81-87; Hon Par Dn 87-91; Hon Par Dn Alderbury Team 91-94; rtd 94; PtO *Sarum* 94-08. *37 Elizabeth Court, Crane Bridge Road, Salisbury SP2 7UX*   T: (01722) 336002   E: chrishunt37@btinternet.com

HUNT, Christopher Paul Colin. b 38. Ch Coll Cam BA 62 MA 62. Clifton Th Coll 63. **d** 65 **p** 66. C Widnes St Paul *Liv* 65-68; Singapore 68-70; Malaysia 70-71; Hon C Folkestone St Jo *Cant* 72-73; Iran 74-80; Overseas Service Adv CMS 81-91; P-in-c Claverdon w Preston Bagot *Cov* 91-02; rtd 02; PtO *Worc* from 04. *Birchfield House, 18 Oaklands, Malvern WR14 4JE*   T: (01684) 578803   E: pauldianamalvern@gmail.com

HUNT, David John. b 35. Kelham Th Coll 60. **d** 65 **p** 66. C Bethnal Green St Jo w St Simon *Lon* 65-69; C Mill Hill St Mich 69-73; R Staple Fitzpaine, Orchard Portman, Thurlbear etc *B & W* 73-79; P-in-c E Coker w Sutton Bingham 79-88; V E Coker w Sutton Bingham and Closworth 88-00; RD Merston 85-94; rtd 00; PtO *B & W* from 01. *Meadowside, Head Street, Tintinhull, Yeovil BA22 8QH*   T: (01935) 824554

HUNT, Derek Henry. b 38. ALCD 61. **d** 62 **p** 63. C Roxeth Ch Ch *Lon* 62-66; C Radipole *Sarum* 66-70; P-in-c Shalbourne w Ham 70-72; V Burbage 72-73; V Burbage and Savernake Ch Ch 73-78; P-in-c Hulcote w Salford *St Alb* 78-88; R Cranfield 78-88; R Cranfield and Hulcote w Salford 88-95; rtd 95; PtO *St Alb* 95-98. *26 Jowitt Avenue, Kempston, Bedford MK42 8NW*

HUNT, Ernest Gary. b 36. Univ Coll Dur BA 57. Carl Dioc Tr Inst 90. **d** 93 **p** 94. NSM Salesbury *Blackb* 93-95; NSM Blackb St Mich w St Jo and H Trin 95-98; NSM Balderstone 98-01; rtd 01; PtO *Blackb* from 01. *Dunelm, 10 Pleckgate Road, Blackburn BB1 8NN*   T: (01254) 52531   E: eg.andk.hunt@talktalk.net

HUNT, Miss Gabrielle Ann. b 59. STETS BA 10. **d** 08 **p** 09. C Salisbury St Fran and Stratford sub Castle *Sarum* 08-12; C Bourne Valley 09-12; TV Avon River from 12. *The Vicarage, High Street, Netheravon, Salisbury SP4 9QP*   T: (01980) 670326   E: galehunt@btinternet.com

HUNT, Giles Butler. b 28. Trin Hall Cam BA 51 MA 55. Cuddesdon Coll 51. **d** 53 **p** 54. C N Evington *Leic* 53-56; C Northolt St Mary *Lon* 56-58; Bp's Dom Chapl *Portsm* 58-59; Bp's Chapl *Nor* 59-62; R Holt 62-67; R Kelling w Salthouse 63-67; C Pimlico St Pet w Westmr Ch Ch *Lon* 67-72; V Barkway w Reed and Buckland *St Alb* 72-79; V Preston next Faversham, Goodnestone and Graveney *Cant* 79-92; rtd 92; PtO *Nor* from 92. *The Cottage, The Fairstead, Cley-next-the-Sea, Holt NR25 7RJ*   T: (01263) 740471

HUNT, Canon Ian Carter. b 34. Chich Th Coll 61. **d** 64 **p** 65. C Plymouth St Pet *Ex* 64-67; C Daventry *Pet* 67-70; V Northampton St Paul 70-91; Can Pet Cathl 91-99; V Wellingborough All Hallows 91-99; rtd 99; Chapl Allnutt's Hosp Goring Heath 99-12; PtO *Ox* from 12. *49 Devonshire Gardens, Tilehurst, Reading RG31 6FW*   T: 0118-942 5006

HUNT, James Allen. b 49. Linc Th Coll 92. **d** 92 **p** 93. C Huddersfield St Pet and All SS *Wakef* 92-95; V Longwood 95-10; rtd 10. *3 Moor Close, Huddersfield HD4 7BP*   T: (01484) 315498   E: jandchunt1@ntlworld.com

HUNT, James Castle. b 66. Univ of Ulster BSc 90 MRICS 92. Wycliffe Hall Ox 02. **d** 04 **p** 05. C N Farnborough *Guildf* 04-08; R Bishop's Waltham *Portsm* from 08; R Upham from 08. *The Rectory, Maypole Green, Bishops Waltham, Southampton SO32 1PW*   T: (01489) 892618   E: jameshunt1966@gmail.com

HUNT, Jeremy Mark Nicholas. b 46. Open Univ BA 73 FRGS 70. Ridley Hall Cam 83. **d** 85 **p** 86. C Leckhampton SS Phil and Jas w Cheltenham St Jas *Glouc* 85-87; Asst Chapl Vevey w Château d'Oex and Villars *Eur* 87-89; Chapl Berne w Neuchâtel 89-90; Dep Chapl HM Pris Pentonville 94-95; Chapl HM Pris Highpoint 95-05; TV Bury St Edmunds All SS w St Jo and St Geo *St E* 05-06; rtd 06; PtO *St E* from 06. *44 Queens Road, Bury St Edmunds IP33 3EP*   T: (01284) 723918

HUNT, John Barry. b 46. Lich Th Coll 70 Qu Coll Birm 72. **d** 73 **p** 74. C Auckland St Andr and St Anne *Dur* 73-77; C Consett 77-79; R Lyons 79-89; P-in-c Hebburn St Cuth 89-05; P-in-c Hebburn St Oswald 01-05; V Hebburn St Cuth and St Oswald

05-11; rtd 11; PtO *Dur* from 11. *11 Parklands, Gateshead NE10 8YP* T: 0191-438 3022

HUNT, John Edwin. b 38. ARCO Dur Univ BA 60 DipEd. EMMTC 78. **d** 81 **p** 82. NSM Newbold w Dunston *Derby* 81-92; NSM Chesterfield St Mary and All SS 92-02. *4 Ardsley Road, Ashgate, Chesterfield S40 4DG* T: (01246) 275141
E: fredwin@cwcom.net

HUNT, John Stewart. b 37. Nor Ord Course 75. **d** 78 **p** 79. NSM Hunstanton St Edm *Nor* 78-81; NSM Hunstanton St Mary w Ringstead Parva, Holme etc 81-86; NSM Sedgeford w Southmere 84-86; C Lowestoft and Kirkley 86-89; R Blundeston w Flixton and Lound 89-93; P-in-c Kessingland w Gisleham 93-99; R Kessingland, Gisleham and Rushmere 99-00; rtd 00; PtO *Nor* from 00. *10 Peddars Drive, Hunstanton PE36 6HF* T: (01485) 533424
E: chippyhunt@btinternet.com

HUNT, Canon Judith Mary. b 57. Bris Univ BVSc 80 Lon Univ PhD 85 Fitzw Coll Cam BA 90 MRCVS 80. Ridley Hall Cam 88. **d** 91 **p** 94. Par Dn Heswall *Ches* 91-94; C 94-95; P-in-c Tilston and Shocklach 95-03; Bp's Adv for Women in Min 95-00; Can Res Ches Cathl and Dioc Dir of Min 03-09; Can Emer Ches Cathl from 09; Adn Suffolk *St E* 09-12; R Whitchurch *Lich* from 12; P-in-c Edstaston, Fauls, Prees, Tilstock and Whixall from 13. *The Rectory, Church Street, Whitchurch SY13 1LB* T: (01948) 667253

HUNT, Canon Kevin. b 59. St Jo Coll Dur BA 80 Ox Univ BA 84 MA 88. St Steph Ho Ox 81. **d** 84 **p** 85. C Mansfield St Mark *S'well* 84-85; C Hendon and Sunderland *Dur* 85-88; V Sunderland St Mary and St Pet 88-95; TR Jarrow 95-02; V Walker *Newc* 02-12; Can Res Newc Cathl 12-15; Asst Dioc Dir of Ords 03-15; AD Newc E 04-12; Hon Can Newc Cathl 10-12; P-in-c Vancouver St Jas Canada from 15. *Address temp unknown* E: kevin@hunt10.plus.com

HUNT, Mark. *See* HUNT, Jeremy Mark Nicholas

HUNT, Michael David. b 64. Southn Univ BSc 86. Ox Min Course 09. **d** 12 **p** 13. NSM Wendover and Halton *Ox* from 12. *Autumn Winds, Aylesbury Road, Princes Risborough HP27 0JP* T: (01844) 344150 M: 07712-851381
E: midahunt@yahoo.co.uk

HUNT, Miss Nicola Mary. b 54. SRN 77 RSCN 77 RHV 87. Ripon Coll Cuddesdon 93. **d** 95 **p** 96. C Broughton Astley and Croft w Stoney Stanton *Leic* 95-98; C Plymouth Em, St Paul Efford and St Aug *Ex* 98-01; V Ermington and Ugborough 01-10; TV Yelverton, Meavy, Sheepstor and Walkhampton 10-12; rtd 12. *45 Clifton Street, Bideford EX39 4EU* T: (01237) 424179 E: nicolahunt361@btinternet.com

HUNT, Paul. *See* HUNT, Christopher Paul Colin

HUNT, Paul Edwin. b 47. Ripon Coll Cuddesdon 93. **d** 95 **p** 96. C Cleobury Mortimer w Hopton Wafers etc *Heref* 95-98; P-in-c Fritwell w Souldern and Ardley w Fewcott *Ox* 98-05; TR Cherwell Valley 05-12; AD Bicester and Islip 05-08; rtd 12. *32 Dalestones, Northampton NN4 9UU* T: (01604) 460539
E: paul.jehu@mac.com *or* paul.e.hunt@me.com

HUNT, Paul Michael. b 57. St Chad's Coll Dur BA 79 K Coll Lon PGCE 80 MA 96 Univ of Wales (Lamp) MTh 04. Chich Th Coll 91. **d** 92 **p** 93. Chapl Brighton Coll 92-93; NSM St Leonards SS Pet and Paul *Chich* 92-93; Chapl Mill Hill Sch Lon 93-98; Hon C Hendon St Paul Mill Hill *Lon* 95-98; P in O 96-98; V Southgate St Andr *Lon* 98-05; Warden of Readers Edmonton Area 01-05; Chapl Em Sch Wandsworth from 05. *Emanuel School, Battersea Rise, London SW11 1HS* T: (020) 8870 4171 E: pmh@emanuel.org.uk

HUNT, Canon Peter John. b 35. AKC 58. St Boniface Warminster. **d** 59 **p** 60. C Chesterfield St Mary and All SS *Derby* 59-61; C Matlock and Tansley 61-63; Chapl Matlock Hosp 61-63; Lect Matlock Teacher Tr Coll 61-63; V Tottington *Man* 63-69; CF (TA) 65-67 and from 75; V Bollington St Jo *Ches* 69-76; R Wilmslow 76-98; Hon Can Ches Cathl 94-02; P-in-c Brereton w Swettenham 98-02; rtd 02; PtO *Ches* from 02. *1 Varden Town Cottages, Birtles Lane, Over Alderley, Macclesfield SK10 4RZ* T: (01265) 829593 E: canonhari@gmail.com

HUNT, Philip Gerald. b 51. LCTP. **d** 11 **p** 12. NSM Rishton *Blackb* from 11. *11 Poplar Avenue, Great Harwood, Blackburn BB6 7RZ* T: (01254) 889808 E: j.a.hunt@sky.com

HUNT, Canon Richard William. b 46. G&C Coll Cam BA 67 MA 71. Westcott Ho Cam 68. **d** 72 **p** 73. C Bris St Agnes and St Simon w St Werburgh 72-77; Chapl Selw Coll Cam 77-84; V Birchfield *Birm* 84-01; R Chich St Paul and Westhampnett 01-11; RD Chich 06-11; Can and Preb Chich Cathl 10-11; rtd 11; PtO *Sarum* from 12. *76 Warminster Road, Bath BA2 6RU* T: (01225) 938529 M: 07504-089009
E: richard@hunts.fsnet.co.uk

HUNT, Ms Rosalind Edna Mary. b 55. Man Univ BA 76. St Steph Ho Ox 86. **d** 88 **p** 94. Chapl Jes Coll Cam 88-92; Hon Chapl to the Deaf *Ely* 92-04; C Cambridge St Jas 00; PtO *Man* from 05. *Address temp unknown* E: ros.hunt@virgin.net

HUNT, Canon Russell Barrett. b 35. NY Univ Virginia Univ Fitzw Ho Cam. Westcott Ho Cam 73. **d** 75 **p** 76. C Leic St Mary 75-78; V Leic St Gabr 78-82; Chapl Leic Gen Hosp 82-95; Hon Can Leic Cathl 88-95; rtd 95; PtO *Leic* from 15. *33 Braunstone Avenue, Leicester LE3 0JH* T: 0116-254 9101
E: c.p.k@btinternet.com

HUNT, Simon John. b 60. Pemb Coll Ox BA 81 MA 85. St Jo Coll Nottm 87. **d** 90 **p** 91. C Stalybridge St Paul *Ches* 90-93; C Heysham *Blackb* 93-99; V Higher Walton from 99. *The Vicarage, Blackburn Road, Higher Walton, Preston PR5 4EA* T: (01772) 335406 E: simon.hunt15@btinternet.com

HUNT, Stephen. b 38. Man Univ BSc 61 MSc 62 PhD 64 DSc 80. Carl Dioc Tr Inst 88. **d** 91 **p** 92. C Broughton *Blackb* 91-95; Chapl Preston Acute Hosps NHS Trust 94-95; V Preston Em *Blackb* 95-03; rtd 03; PtO *Blackb* from 05. *8 Wallace Lane, Forton, Preston PR3 0BA* T: (01524) 792563

HUNT, Stephen Christopher. b 65. **d** 13 **p** 14. NSM Bideford, Northam, Westward Ho!, Appledore etc *Ex* from 13. *63 High Street, Bideford EX39 2AN* E: viney.hill@bigfoot.com

HUNT, Timothy Collinson. b 48. ASVA 91 Univ of Wales (Cardiff) BD 95 Ox Univ MTh 98. Ripon Coll Cuddesdon 95. **d** 97 **p** 98. C Ex St Dav 97-01; Chapl Blundell's Sch Tiverton from 01. *1B Hillands, 39 Tidcombe Lane, Tiverton EX16 4EA* T: (01884) 242343 E: tc@collhunt.fsnet.co.uk

HUNT, Vera Susan Henrietta. b 33. MBE 06. S Dios Minl Tr Scheme 88. **d** 91 **p** 94. Hon Chapl RAD from 91; PtO *Lon* from 03. *54 Highway Avenue, Maidenhead SL6 5AQ* T: (01628) 623909 E: vera.hunt@yahoo.co.uk

HUNTE (*née* FRANKLIN), Ms Roxanne Fay. b 60. Gama Filho Univ Brazil BSc 93 Huron Univ MBA 94 Leeds Univ BA 08. Coll of Resurr Mirfield 07. **d** 09 **p** 10. C Newington St Mary *S'wark* 09-13; P-in-c S Norwood H Innocents from 13; P-in-c S Norwood St Mark from 15. *The Vicarage, 192A Selhurst Road, London SE25 6XX* M: 07747-896779 T: (020) 8653 2063
E: roxannefranklinhunte@btinternet.com

HUNTER, Allan Davies. b 36. Univ of Wales (Lamp) BA 57. Coll of Resurr Mirfield 57. **d** 59 **p** 60. C Cardiff St Jo *Llan* 59-68; V Llansawel 68-76; Youth Chapl 71-77; V Llansawel w Briton Ferry 76-79; V Canton St Cath 79-01; rtd 01; PtO *Llan* from 04. *9 Avonridge, Thornhill, Cardiff CF14 9AU* T: (029) 2069 3054 E: allanhunter@talk21.com

HUNTER, David Hilliard Cowan. b 48. Massey Univ (NZ) BA 92. St Jo Coll Auckland LTh 74. **d** 73 **p** 74. C Stoke New Zealand 73-75; C Christchurch Cathl 75-78; V Waimea 78-79; Chapl Tongariro Pris Farm 79-85; Chapl Waikune Pris 81-85; Chapl Rangipo Pris 81-85; Chapl Rimutuka Pris and Pris Staff Coll 86-92; P Asst Silverstream 86-92; Chapl NZ Army 88-92; P Asst Marton 92-97; P Asst Cambridge 97-01; Chapl Bruton Sch for Girls 02-06; P-in-c Stevington *St Alb* 03-06; Australia from 06. *Rockhampton Grammar School, Archer Street, Rockhampton Qld 4700, Australia* T: (0061) (7) 4936 0600

HUNTER, Edwin Wallace. b 43. NUI BA 83 FCIM. CITC 91. **d** 94 **p** 95. NSM Cork St Fin Barre's Union *C, C & R* from 94; Min Can Cork Cathl from 95; Bp's Dom Chapl from 03. *Cedar Lodge, Church Road, Carrigaline, Co Cork, Republic of Ireland* T: (00353) (21) 437 2338 E: enjhunter@eircom.net

HUNTER, Canon Frank Geoffrey. b 34. Keble Coll Ox BA 56 MA 60 Fitzw Coll Cam BA 58 MA 62. Ridley Hall Cam 57. **d** 59 **p** 60. C Bircle *Man* 59-62; C Jarrow Grange *Dur* 62-65; V Kingston upon Hull St Martin *York* 65-72; V Linthorpe 72-76; V Heslington 76-99; RD Derwent 78-98; Can and Preb York Minster 85-99; rtd 99; PtO *Leeds* from 01. *2 Flexbury Avenue, Morley, Leeds LS27 0RG* T: 0113-253 9213

HUNTER, Graham. b 78. K Coll Lon BA 02. Ridley Hall Cam 05. **d** 07 **p** 08. C Holloway St Mary Magd *Lon* 07-10; C Hoxton St Jo w Ch Ch 10-11; V from 11. *St John's Vicarage, Crondall Street, London N1 6PT* T: (020) 7739 9823
E: graham@stjohnshoxton.org.uk

HUNTER, Ian Paton. b 20. Em Coll Cam BA 46 MA 50. Tyndale Hall Bris 40. **d** 43 **p** 47. C Harrington *Pet* 43-47; C Portman Square St Paul *Lon* 47-50; V Furneux Pelham w Stocking Pelham *St Alb* 50-54; V Moulton *Pet* 54-60; V Danehill *Chich* 60-67; R Plumpton w E Chiltington 67-77; V Burwash Weald 77-83; P-in-c Stonegate 83-85; rtd 85; PtO *Chich* 86-08. *The College of St Barnabas, Blackberry Lane, Lingfield RH7 6NJ* T: (01342) 872856

HUNTER, James. b 38. Union Th Coll Belf BD 90. **d** 92 **p** 92. In Presbyterian Ch of Ireland 82-92; V Werneth *Man* 92-98; V Woking St Paul *Guildf* 98-05; Asst Chapl HM Pris Coldingley 01-05; rtd 06; PtO *Pet* from 06. *31 The Ridings, Desborough, Kettering NN14 2LP* T: (01536) 660328
E: jimo.hunter2@gmail.com

HUNTER, John Crichton. b 38. Univ of Wales (Cardiff) BA 59 DipEd 60 LTCL. St Steph Ho Ox 98. **d** 99 **p** 00. NSM Walham Green St Jo w St Jas *Lon* 99-05; NSM S Kensington

St Steph 05-08; PtO from 08. *57 Manor Court, 23 Bagleys Lane, London SW6 2BN* T: (020) 7736 7544
E: frjohnhunter@hotmail.com

HUNTER, Canon John Gaunt. b 21. St Jo Coll Dur BA 49 Leeds Univ MA 94 Lanc Univ MPhil 08. Ridley Hall Cam 49. **d** 51 **p** 52. C Bradf Cathl 51-54; C Compton Gifford *Ex* 54-56; V Bootle St Matt *Liv* 56-62; Prin Bp Tucker Coll Uganda 62-65; V Altcar *Liv* 65-78; Dioc Missr 65-71; Abp's Miss Adv *York* 71-78; Hon Can Liv Cathl 71-78; TR Buckhurst Hill *Chelmsf* 78-79 and 79-89; Dioc Adv in Evang *Bradf* 89-92; rtd 92; PtO *Leeds* from 92. *Westhouse Lodge, Lower Westhouse, Ingleton, Carnforth LA6 3NZ* T: (015242) 41305
E: canonjgh@gmail.com

HUNTER, Mrs Linda Margaret. b 47. STETS 95. **d** 98. NSM Wootton *Portsm* 98-02; NSM Chale, Gatcombe and Shorwell w Kingston 02-05; NSM Ruskington Gp *Linc* 07-13; NSM N Lafford Gp from 13. *12 Hillside Estate, Ruskington, Sleaford NG34 9TJ*

HUNTER, Lionel Lawledge Gleave. b 24. ALCD 53. **d** 53 **p** 54. C Leic H Trin 53-56; C Northampton St Giles *Pet* 56-58; C Everton St Chrys *Liv* 58-59; P-in-c Liv St Mich 59-61; Chile 61-72; R Diddlebury w Bouldon and Munslow *Heref* 72-75; P-in-c Abdon w Clee St Margaret 73-75; P-in-c Holdgate w Tugford 73-75; Canada 75-85; V N Elmham w Billingford *Nor* 85-89; R N Elmham w Billingford and Worthing 89-90; rtd 90; PtO *Heref* 93-07. *Flat 3, Manormead, Tilford Road, Hindhead GU26 6RA* T: (01428) 602500

HUNTER, Malcolm Leggatt. b 61. Middx Univ BA 97 MA 97. SAOMC 03. **d** 05 **p** 07. NSM Old St Pancras *Lon* 05-06; C 06-09; Chapl HM Pris Bronzefield 09-10; Co-ord Chapl HM YOI Aylesbury 10-14; PtO *St Alb* from 15. *Address temp unknown*

HUNTER, Matthew Gawain. b 83. LMH Ox BA 04 Man Univ MA 08 Northumbria Univ MA 11. Ripon Coll Cuddesdon 10. **d** 12 **p** 13. C Halifax *Leeds* from 12. *27 Central Park, Halifax HX1 2BT* T: (01422) 361942 E: mwg_hunter@yahoo.co.uk

HUNTER, Michael John. b 45. CCC Cam BA 67 MA 71 PhD 71 Ox Univ BA 75. Wycliffe Hall Ox 73. **d** 76 **p** 77. C Partington and Carrington *Ches* 76-79; CMS 80-90; Uganda 80-89; C Penn Fields *Lich* 90-02; RD Trysull 97-02; V Dore *Sheff* 02-12; rtd 12; PtO *Sheff* from 12. *18 Linnet Grove, Kendal LA9 7RP* E: mutagwok@aol.com

HUNTER, Canon Michael Oram. b 40. MBE 10. K Coll Lon BD 64 AKC 64. **d** 65 **p** 66. C Tividale *Lich* 65-68; C Harrogate St Wilfrid *Ripon* 68-70; V Hawksworth Wood 70-78; V Whitkirk 78-86; TR Gt Grimsby St Mary and St Jas *Linc* 86-10; Can and Preb Linc Cathl 89-10; rtd 10. *12 Osborne Road, Harrogate HG1 2EA* T: (01423) 313825
E: mo.hunter@talktalk.net

HUNTER, Paul. b 55. Huddersfield Poly BEd 82 Cliff Coll MA 05. Chich Th Coll 86. **d** 88 **p** 90. C Weymouth H Trin *Sarum* 88-92; P-in-c Hucknall Torkard *S'well* 92; TV 92-96; V Thurcroft *Sheff* 96-06; R Cleethorpes *Linc* from 06. *3 Taylors Avenue, Cleethorpes DN35 0LF* T: (01472) 291156
E: paul@paulhunter03.wanadoo.co.uk

HUNTER, Paul Andrew. b 40. Trin Coll Bris 09. **d** 11 **p** 12. OLM Brislington St Chris *Bris* from 11. *17 Friendship Road, Bristol BS4 2RW* T: 0117-971 9390
E: paulzhunter@blueyonder.co.uk

HUNTER, Paul Graham. b 64. Sheff Univ LLB 85 Solicitor 86. St Jo Coll Nottm MA 96. **d** 04 **p** 05. Prin Morogoro Bible Coll Tanzania 04-06; PtO *Blackb* from 08. *1 Ferndale Close, Leyland PR25 3BS* T: (01772) 624492 M: 07731-924289
E: pp.hunter@sky.com

HUNTER, Peter Wells. b 52. Bris Univ BSc 73. Trin Coll Bris BA 91. **d** 91 **p** 92. C New Borough and Leigh *Sarum* 91-97; P-in-c Warminster Ch Ch from 97. *The Vicarage, 13 Avon Road, Warminster BA12 9PR* T: (01985) 212219
E: peter.wh@btopenworld.com

HUNTER, Robert. b 36. Man Univ BSc 60. Clifton Th Coll. **d** 63 **p** 64. C Chadderton Ch Ch *Man* 63-65; C Balderstone 65-69; C Newburn *Newc* 69-73; TV Sutton St Jas and Wawne *York* 73-81; V Bilton St Pet 81-82; Hon C N Hull St Mich 82-91; TV Howden 91-97; P-in-c Ashton St Pet *Man* 97-99; TV Ashton 00-01; rtd 01; PtO *Leeds* from 02. *2 Adel Park Gardens, Leeds LS16 8BN* T: 0113-285 7088

HUNTER, Stephen Albert Paul. b 52. JP 96. NOC 01. **d** 04 **p** 05. NSM Ecclesall *Sheff* 04-13; Bp's Adv for SSM 10-14; Dioc Dir of Ords from 13. *Overhill, Townhead Road, Dore, Sheffield S17 3GE* T: 0114-236 9978 F: 275 9769 M: 07739-949473
E: stephenaphunter@btinternet.com

HUNTER DUNN, Jonathan. b 69. Sussex Univ BSc 91 Uppsala Univ PhD 98. Oak Hill Th Coll BA 09. **d** 10 **p** 11. C Burford w Fulbrook, Taynton, Asthall etc *Ox* 10-15; R Shepton Mallet w Doulting *B & W* from 15. *11 Naisholt Road, Shepton Mallet BA4 5GD* E: jonathanhunterdunn@btinternet.com

HUNTER SMART, Ian Douglas. b 60. St Jo Coll Dur BA 83 MA 99. Edin Th Coll 83. **d** 85 **p** 86. C Cockerton *Dur* 85-89; TV Jarrow 89-92; TV Sunderland 92-98; Chapl Sunderland Univ 92-98; Ecum Chapl Newcastle Coll 98-00; PtO *Dur* from 98; *Leeds* from 12. *Gardeners Cottage, Carlton, Richmond DL11 7AG* T: (01325) 710481 E: ihs@dunelm.org.uk

HUNTER SMART, William David. b 75. Bris Univ BSc 97. Wycliffe Hall Ox BA 01. **d** 02 **p** 03. C Watford *St Alb* 02-05; C Muswell Hill St Jas w St Matt *Lon* 05-11; TR Newbury *Ox* 11-15; R Newbury St Nic and Speen from 15. *The Rectory, 64 Northcroft Lane, Newbury RG14 1BN* T: (01635) 47018
E: rector@st-nicolas-newbury.org

HUNTINGDON AND WISBECH, Archdeacon of. See McCURDY, The Ven Hugh Kyle

HUNTINGDON, Suffragan Bishop of. See THOMSON, The Rt Revd David

HUNTLEY, David Anthony. b 32. AMInstT 56 MRTvS 78 MILT 98. Lon Bible Coll BA 60 Fuller Sch of World Miss MTh 81 Trin Coll Singapore 65. **d** 64 **p** 65. OMF Internat from 61; Singapore 61-71; Indonesia 72-73; Philippines 74-75; Hong Kong 77-81; Seychelles 82-87; Thailand 88-97; NSM S Croydon Em *Cant* 76-77 and 81-82; NSM S'wark 87-88 and 91-92 and 98-04; PtO from 05. *42 Farnborough Avenue, South Croydon CR2 8HD* T: (020) 8657 5673

HUNTLEY, David George. b 63. St Cuth Soc Dur BA 02. Coll of Resurr Mirfield 05. **d** 07 **p** 08. C Owton Manor *Dur* 07-09; C Houghton le Spring 09-11; P-in-c Horsley Hill St Lawr from 11. *St Lawrence Vicarage, 84 Centenary Avenue, South Shields NE34 6SF* T: 0191-427 6680

HUNTLEY, Denis Anthony. b 56. Saltley Tr Coll Birm CertEd 77. Qu Coll Birm 77. **d** 80 **p** 81. C Llanblethian w Cowbridge and Llandough etc *Llan* 80-83; TV Glyncorrwg w Afan Vale and Cymmer Afan 83-86; R 86-89; Chapl Asst Walsgrave Hosp Cov 89-92; Chapl Halifax Gen Hosp 92-94; Chapl Calderdale Healthcare NHS Trust 94-97; C Leeds City *Ripon* 97-02; Chapl to the Deaf 97-02; Chapl amongst Deaf People and Adv for Deaf Min 02-06; Chapl amongst Deaf and Deaf-blind People *Chelmsf* 06-14; Lead Min Deaf Community from 15; Adv on Disability Issues *Chelmsf* from 06. *17 Oakham Close, Langdon Hills, Basildon SS16 6NX* T: (01268) 490471 or 546026
E: denishuntley@gmail.com

HUNTLEY, Heidi Anne. b 71. Ripon Coll Cuddesdon 07. **d** 09 **p** 10. C Sydenham St Bart *S'wark* 09-12; V Royston *St Alb* from 12. *The Vicarage, 20 Palace Gardens, Royston SG8 5AD* T: (01763) 243145 E: hahlive@yahoo.co.uk

HUNTLEY, Stuart Michael. b 73. BEng BA. Trin Coll Bris. **d** 08 **p** 09. C Jersey St Lawr *Win* 08-09; C Jersey St Helier 09-11; R Port Washington St Steph USA 11-15; R Wulfric Benefice *B & W* from 15 and from 15. *83 Brutton Way, Chard TA20 2HB* M: 07479-532355 E: revstuarthuntley@gmail.com

HUPFIELD, Mrs Hannah Elizabeth. b 84. New Hall Cam BA 06 MA 10. Westcott Ho Cam 08. **d** 11 **p** 12. C Woodbridge St Mary *St E* 11; C Saxilby Gp *Linc* 12-15. *Flat 4, Westcott House, Jesus Lane, Cambridge CB5 8BP*
E: hannahhupfield@cantab.net

HURCOMBE, Thomas William. b 45. BD 74 AKC 76. **d** 76 **p** 77. C Hampstead All So *Lon* 76-79; C Is of Dogs Ch Ch and St Jo w St Luke 79-83; C Bromley All Hallows 83-89; C E Greenwich Ch Ch w St Andr and St Mich *S'wark* 89-96; Ind Chapl 89-97; Dioc Urban Missr 90-96; Greenwich Waterfront Chapl 96-98; C Charlton St Luke w H Trin 97-98; P-in-c S Norwood St Mark 98-14; rtd 14. *39A Warminster Road, London SE25 4DL* M: 07939-289196 E: hurcomt@aol.com

HURD, Alun John. b 52. Trin Coll Bris BA 86 New Coll Edin MTh 97. **d** 86 **p** 87. C Chertsey *Guildf* 86-90; Chapl St Pet Hosp Chertsey 86-90; V W Ewell *Guildf* 90-04; Chapl NE Surrey Coll Ewell 01-05; CF (TA) 99-05; Distr P Lower Yorke Peninsula Australia 05-07; P-in-c Gt Wakering w Foulness *Chelmsf* from 08; P-in-c Barling w Lt Wakering from 08; P-in-c Rochford and Sutton w Shopland from 14. *The Rectory, 36 Millview Meadows, Rochford SS4 1EF* T: (01702) 817991 M: 07941-417135 E: alunjhurd@gmail.com

HURD, Brenda Edith. b 44. Sittingbourne Coll DipEd 75. Cant Sch of Min 87. **d** 92 **p** 94. NSM Birling, Addington, Ryarsh and Trottiscliffe *Roch* 92-02; P-in-c Wrotham 02-12; R 12-14; RD Shoreham 06-11; Hon Can Roch Cathl 09-14; rtd 14; PtO *Roch* from 15. *South View, London Road, Ryarsh, West Malling ME19 5AW* T: (01732) 842255 E: b.hurd@virgin.net

HURD, John Patrick. b 37. CertEd 65 Open Univ BA 73 Kent Univ MA 92. S Dios Minl Tr Scheme 77. **d** 80 **p** 81. NSM Billingshurst *Chich* 80-82 and 89-94; NSM Itchingfield w Slinfold 82-89. *Groomsland Cottage, Parbrook, Billingshurst RH14 9EU* T: (01403) 782167

HURFORD, Colin Osborne. b 33. Qu Coll Ox BA 55 MA 59. Wells Th Coll 55. **d** 57 **p** 58. C Barnoldswick w Bracewell *Bradf*

57-61; C Warrington St Elphin *Liv* 61-63; Malaysia 63-70; P-in-c Annscroft *Heref* 71-79; P-in-c Longden 71-79; P-in-c Pontesbury III 71-79; R Longden and Annscroft 79-85; P-in-c Church Pulverbatch 81-85; R Longden and Annscroft w Pulverbatch 85-86; Tanzania 86-87; TR Billingham St Aid *Dur* 87-96; rtd 96; PtO *Heref* from 96; *Lich* 01-10. *14 Station Road, Pontesbury, Shrewsbury SY5 0QY* T: (01743) 792605

✠**HURFORD, The Rt Revd Richard Warwick.** b 44. OAM 99. Trin Coll Bris BA 96 Univ of Wales MTh 02 Hon FGCM 96 MACE 81. St Jo Coll Morpeth. **d** 69 **p** 70 **c** 01. Prec Grafton Cathl Australia 69-71; P-in-c Tisbury *Sarum* 71-73; R 73-75; R Tisbury and Swallowcliffe w Ansty 75-76; P-in-c Chilmark 76; P-in-c Tisbury 76-78; TR Coffs Harbour Australia 78-83; Dean Grafton 83-97; Adn The Clarence and Hastings Australia 85-87; Adn Grafton 87-92; R Sydney St Jas 97-01; Bp Bathurst from 01. *Bishopscourt, 288 William Street, PO Box 23, Bathurst NSW 2795, Australia* T: (0061) (2) 6331 3550 *or* 6331 1722 F: 6331 3660 *or* 6332 2772 E: bxbishop@ix.net.au

HURLE, Canon Anthony Rowland. b 54. Lon Univ BSc Em Coll Cam PGCE. Wycliffe Hall Ox 80. **d** 83 **p** 84. C Ipswich St Mary at Stoke w St Pet *St E* 83-87; TV Barking St Marg w St Patr *Chelmsf* 87-92; V St Alb St Paul *St Alb* from 92; RD St Alb 95-05; Hon Can St Alb from 05. *St Paul's Vicarage, 7 Brampton Road, St Albans AL1 4PN* T/F: (01727) 836810 T: 846281 E: tony@stpauls-stalbans.org *or* vicar@stpauls-stalbans.org

HURLE (*née* POWNALL), Mrs Lydia Margaret. b 53. SRN SCM. Wycliffe Hall Ox 78. **dss** 81 **d** 94 **p** 95. Ipswich St Mary at Stoke w St Pet etc *St E* 81-83; NSM St Alb St Paul *St Alb* from 93. *St Paul's Vicarage, 7 Brampton Road, St Albans AL1 4PN* T/F: (01727) 836810 E: tony.hurle@ntlworld.com

HURLEY, Daniel Timothy. b 37. St Mich Coll Llan 68. **d** 70 **p** 71. C Llanfabon *Llan* 70-73; CF 73-79; R W Walton *Ely* 79-86; V Cwmdauddwr w St Harmon and Llanwrthwl *S & B* 86-02; rtd 02. *39 Ellesmere Orchard, Emsworth PO10 8TP* T: (01243) 376923

HURLEY, Mark Tristan. b 57. Trin Coll Bris BA 89. Sarum & Wells Th Coll 89. **d** 91 **p** 92. C Gainsborough All SS *Linc* 91-94; TV Grantham 94-00; V Donington and Bicker 00-02; PtO *Ox* 08-09; Hon C Wolverton 09-12; P-in-c Swanscombe *Roch* from 12. *The Rectory, 116 Swanscombe Street, Swanscombe DA10 0JZ* T: (01322) 383160 E: markcsb@gmail.com

HURLEY, Robert. b 64. Univ of Wales (Cardiff) BD 86. Ridley Hall Cam 88. **d** 90 **p** 91. C Dagenham *Chelmsf* 90-93; C Egg Buckland *Ex* 93-96; C Devonport St Budeaux 96; P-in-c Camberwell All SS *S'wark* 96-99; V 99-02; R Oldbury *Sarum* 02-04; Chapl Grenoble *Eur* from 13. *14 rue Gérard Philipe, 38100 Grenoble, France* T: (00330 9 66 89 03 27 E: janeandbobhurley@aol.com *or* chaplain@grenoblechurch.org

HURLSTON, Mrs Jean Margaret. b 54. Crewe Coll of Educn CertEd 75 Keele Univ BEd 76. **d** 06 **p** 07. OLM High Crompton *Man* 06-10; OLM Oldham 10-11; OLM Oldham St Mary w St Pet from 11. *24 Taunton Lawns, Ashton-under-Lyne OL7 9EL* T/F: 0161-344 2854 M: 07885-406808 E: jeanhurlston@btinternet.com

HURN, Mrs June Barbara. b 32. Birm Univ CertEd 53. Cant Sch of Min 87. **d** 90 **p** 94. NSM Chislehurst St Nic *Roch* from 90. *Hawkswing, Hawkwood Lane, Chislehurst BR7 5PW* T: (020) 8467 2320 E: junehurn@yahoo.co.uk

HURREN, Timothy John. b 46. York Univ BA 74 ACIB 70. NEOC 99. **d** 02 **p** 03. C High Harrogate St Pet *Leeds* from 02. *1 South Park Road, Harrogate HG1 5QU* T: (01423) 541696 E: tim.hurren@ntlworld.com

HURRY, Lynn Susan. b 59. Middx Univ BA 05. NTMTC 02. **d** 05 **p** 06. C Southchurch H Trin *Chelmsf* 05-08; V St Mary-at-Latton from 08. *St Mary-at-Latton Vicarage, The Gowers, Harlow CM20 2JP* T: (01279) 424005 E: revlynn@btinternet.com

HURST, Alaric Desmond St John. b 24. New Coll Ox BA 50 MA 70. Wells Th Coll 48. **d** 51 **p** 53. C Huddersfield H Trin *Wakef* 51-52; C Leeds St Geo *Ripon* 52-54; Bp's Chapl for Rehabilitation *Roch* 55-56; C St Steph Walbrook and St Swithun etc *Lon* 57-59; V Pudsey St Paul *Bradf* 59-63; V Writtle *Chelmsf* 63-69; rtd 89. *Heathlands, Station Road, Pershore WR10 1NG* T: (01386) 562220

HURST, Canon Brian Charles. b 58. Nottm Univ BA Sheff Univ MA 07. Ripon Coll Cuddesdon 82. **d** 84 **p** 85. C Cullercoats St Geo *Newc* 84-87; C Prudhoe 87-88; TV Willington 88-95; V Denton 95-03; RD Newc W 97-98; TV Glendale Gp 03-09; V Bamburgh from 09; V Ellingham from 09; AD Bamburgh and Glendale from 06; Hon Can Newc Cathl from 10. *The Vicarage, 7 The Wynding, Bamburgh NE69 7DB* T: (01668) 214748 E: brian.hurst1@btopenworld.com

HURST, Colin. b 49. Linc Th Coll 88. **d** 90 **p** 91. C Wavertree H Trin *Liv* 90-93; C Croft and Stoney Stanton *Leic* 93-95; TV Broughton Astley and Croft w Stoney Stanton 95-97;

V Wigan St Andr *Liv* 97-14; AD Wigan W 03-05; AD Wigan 05-08; Hon Can Liv Cathl 03-08; rtd 14. *19 Foxfield Grove, Shevington, Wigan WN6 8AJ* E: churst6000@gmail.com

HURST, Colin. b 58. Westmr Coll Ox BA 90. St Jo Coll Nottm MA 95. **d** 95 **p** 96. C Warboys w Broughton and Bury w Wistow *Ely* 95-98; P-in-c Wisbech St Mary 98-04; P-in-c Guyhirn w Ring's End 98-04; V Wisbech St Mary and Guyhirn w Ring's End etc 05-07; P-in-c Eye *Pet* 07-14; P-in-c Newborough 07-14; P-in-c Thorney Abbey *Ely* 07-14; V Eye, Newborough and Thorney *Pet* from 14. *The Vicarage, Thorney Road, Eye, Peterborough PE6 7UN* T: (01733) 222334 E: cehurst@globalnet.co.uk

HURST, Edward. b 57. SEITE 09. **d** 11 **p** 12. NSM S Gillingham *Roch* from 11; PtO *Cant* from 14. *83A Otterham Quay Lane, Rainham, Gillingham ME8 8NE* T: (01634) 263580 M: 07791-994933 E: notfatherted@gmail.com

HURST, Canon Jeremy Richard. b 40. Trin Coll Cam BA 61 MA MPhil FCP. Linc Th Coll 62. **d** 64 **p** 65. C Woolwich St Mary w H Trin *S'wark* 64-69; PtO *Ex* 69-76; *Ox* 76-84; TV Langley Marish 84-85; TR 85-05; Hon Can Ch Ch 05; Chapl Thames Valley Univ *Lon* 92-98; rtd 05. *Hortus Lodge, 22A Bolton Avenue, Windsor SL4 3JF* T: (01753) 863693 E: jeremyhurst@lineone.net

HURST, Mrs Joanna. b 74. Cranmer Hall Dur 13. **d** 15. C Kendal H Trin *Carl* from 15. *64 Valley Drive, Kendal LA9 7AG* T: (01539) 721248 E: curate@kendalparishchurch.co.uk

HURST, John. b 31. NW Ord Course 76. **d** 79 **p** 80. C Flixton St Jo *Man* 79-82; P-in-c Hindsford 82-86; V 86-88; V Halliwell St Paul 88-93; rtd 93; PtO *Man* 99-14. *26 Cornwall Avenue, Bolton BL5 1DZ* T: (01204) 659233

HURT, Mrs Grenda Mary. b 36. LSE BSc(Econ) 63. STETS 96. **d** 99 **p** 01. NSM Freshwater and Yarmouth *Portsm* 99-10; Asst Chapl Isle of Wight Healthcare NHS Trust 03-05; Chapl Earl Mountbatten Hospice 03-05; rtd 10; PtO *Portsm* from 10. *Benhams, Victoria Road, Freshwater PO40 9PP* T: (01983) 759931 E: grenda.hurt@tiscali.co.uk

✠**HURTADO, The Rt Revd Jorge A Perera.** b 34. **d** 57 **p** 58 **c** 94. Bp Cuba from 94. *Calle 6 No 273, Vedado, Plaza de la Revolución, Havana 4, 10400, Cuba* T: (0053) (7) 35655, 38003, 321120 *or* 312436 F: 333293 E: episcopal@ip.etecsa.cu

HUSBAND, Mrs Caroline Elizabeth. b 72. STETS 11. **d** 14 **p** 15. NSM Paulton w Farrington Gurney and High Littleton *B & W* from 14. *Sunnyside, Broadway, Chilcompton, Radstock BA3 4JW* T: (01761) 233178 E: husbandcc@gmail.com

HUSS, The Ven David Ian. b 75. Jes Coll Ox MPhys 97. Wycliffe Hall Ox BA 07. **d** 07 **p** 08. C Banbury St Paul *Ox* 07-11; I Donegal w Killymard, Lough Eske and Laghey *D & R* from 11; Adn Raphoe from 13. *The Rectory, The Glebe, Donegal, Republic of Ireland* T: (00353) (74) 972 1075 E: donegal@raphoe.anglican.org

HUSTWAYTE, Samantha Jane. b 73. Lon Univ BD 96 Ches Univ MTh 13. St Jo Coll Nottm LTh 13. **d** 13 **p** 14. NSM Arnold *S'well* from 13. *3 Ashington Drive, Arnold, Nottingham NG5 8GH* M: 07801-364984 E: revsam@hustwayte.co.uk

HUSTWICK, Mrs Joanne Patricia. b 59. Trin Coll Bris 11. **d** 13 **p** 14. C Tong *Leeds* 13-15; C Tong and Laisterdyke from 15. *St Christopher's Vicarage, 207 Broadstone Way, Bradford BD4 9BT* E: jhustwick@tiscali.co.uk

HUTCHEON, Mrs Elsie. b 39. RGN 63 CertEd UEA MEd 98. EAMTC 89. **d** 92 **p** 94. NSM Heigham St Thos *Nor* 92-02; P-in-c Heigham St Barn w St Bart 02-15; RD Nor S 06-09; rtd 15. *6 St Julian's Alley, Norwich NR1 1QD* E: elsie.hutcheon@tiscali.co.uk

HUTCHERSON, Justin Francis. b 87. Jes Coll Cam BA 08 MA 11 Univ of E Lon PGCE 11 Open Univ MEd 12 Heythrop Coll Lon MA 12. St Steph Ho Ox BA 12 MA 12. **d** 14 **p** 15. C Corringham and Fobbing *Chelmsf* from 14. *The Glebe House, High Road, Fobbing, Stanford-le-Hope SS17 9JH* T: (01375) 644906 M: 07515-946575 E: justinhutcherson@cantab.net *or* frjustin@ubocaf.org.uk

HUTCHIN, David William. b 37. Man Univ MusB 58 CertEd 59 DipEd 59 LRAM ARCM LTCL. Glouc Sch of Min 85. **d** 88 **p** 89. NSM Northleach w Hampnett and Farmington *Glouc* 88-94; NSM Cold Aston w Notgrove and Turkdean 88-94; NSM Chedworth, Yanworth and Stowell, Coln Rogers etc 94-01; RD Northleach 96-99; PtO *Leic* 01-06; *Derby* 02-06; *Leeds* from 06. *Bank Side Garden, Glasshouses, Harrogate HG3 5QY* T: (01423) 712733

HUTCHINGS, Colin Michael. b 36. Clifton Th Coll 66. **d** 68 **p** 69. C Worksop St Jo *S'well* 68-71; C Hampreston *Sarum* 71-76; TV Tisbury 76-82; R Waddesdon w Over Winchendon and Fleet Marston *Ox* 82-00; rtd 00; PtO *Pet* from 01. *Nimrod, 4 The Beeches, Pattishall, Towcester NN12 8LT* T: (01327) 830563

HUTCHINGS, Ian James. b 49. Ches Coll of HE MA 03. Clifton Th Coll 69 Trin Coll Bris 72. **d** 73 **p** 74. C Parr *Liv* 73-77;

C Timperley *Ches* 77-81; V Partington and Carrington 81-96; V Huntington 96-12; Chapl Bp's Blue Coat C of E High Sch 96-08; rtd 12; PtO *Lich* from 12. *52 Hillcrest, Ellesmere SY12 0LJ* T: (01691) 622304 E: ihutchings@aol.com

HUTCHINGS, James Benjamin Balfour. b 62. Ex Univ BA 84. STETS 03. **d** 06 **p** 07. C Ex St Jas 06-09; C Cen Ex 09-11; P-in-c Littleham w Exmouth 11-13; TR Littleham-cum-Exmouth w Lympstone from 13; RD Aylesbeare from 15. *The Rectory, 1 Maer Road, Exmouth EX8 2DA* T: (01395) 225212 E: hutchingsjames@sky.com

HUTCHINGS, John Denis Arthur. b 29. Keble Coll Ox BA 53 MA 59 MSc 59. Chich Th Coll 58. **d** 60 **p** 61. C St Pancras w St Jas and Ch Ch *Lon* 60-63; Asst Chapl Denstone Coll Uttoxeter 63-67 and 79-83; C Stepney St Dunstan and All SS *Lon* 67-78; V Devonport St Boniface *Ex* 83-86; TR Devonport St Boniface and St Phil 86-93; P-in-c Lydford and Brent Tor 93-95; rtd 96; PtO *Ex* from 96. *Maisonette, 40 Brook Street, Tavistock PL19 0HE* T: (01822) 616946

HUTCHINGS, Thomas George. b 84. Qu Coll Cam BA MPhil 07 BA 13. Ridley Hall Cam 11. **d** 14 **p** 15. C Sileby, Cossington and Seagrave *Leic* from 14. *52 Main Street, Cossington, Leicester LE7 4UU* M: 07740-008757 E: tghutchings@gmail.com

HUTCHINS, Miss Katrina Mary. b 62. Ripon Coll Cuddesdon 13. **d** 15. C Kingsthorpe *Pet* from 15. *89 Park Avenue North, Northampton NN3 2HX* M: 07710-464675 E: katrinahutchins94@yahoo.co.uk

HUTCHINS, Paul. b 79. Coll of Resurr Mirfield 99 NOC 04. **d** 05 **p** 06. C Royton St Paul *Man* 05-10; TV Swinton and Pendlebury 10-13; P-in-c Southport St Luke *Liv* from 13. *33 Abington Drive, Banks, Southport PR9 8FL* M: 07818-022678 E: fr.hutchins@btinternet.com

HUTCHINSON, Alison Joyce. b 62. Leeds Univ BA 84 RMN 90. Aston Tr Scheme 92 Ripon Coll Cuddesdon 94. **d** 97 **p** 98. C Benfieldside *Dur* 97-00; C Bishopwearmouth St Nic 00-02; PtO *Carl* 02-07; C Penrith w Newton Reigny and Plumpton Wall 07-08; PtO 09; Hon C Crathorne *York* from 09; Hon C Kirklevington w Picton, and High and Low Worsall from 09; Hon C Rudby in Cleveland w Middleton from 09; Hon C Stokesley from 09. *The Rectory, Leven Close, Stokesley, Middlesbrough TS9 5AP* T: (01642) 710405 E: alison.hutchinson@btinternet.com

HUTCHINSON, Canon Andrew Charles. b 63. Univ of Wales (Ban) BA 84 MEd 96. Aston Tr Scheme 85 Chich Th Coll 87. **d** 89 **p** 90. C Burnley St Cath w St Alb and St Paul *Blackb* 89-92; C Shrewsbury St Chad w St Mary *Lich* 92-94; Chapl Heref Cathl Sch 94-97; Succ Heref Cathl 94-97; Chapl Solihull Sch from 97; Can St Jo Pro-Cathl Katakwa from 00. *2 St Alphege Close, Church Hill Road, Solihull B91 3RQ* T: 0121-704 3708

HUTCHINSON, Andrew George Pearce. b 78. Glos Univ BA 01 PGCE 02. Oak Hill Th Coll BA 08. **d** 08 **p** 09. C Normanton *Derby* 08-15; Chapl Monkton Combe Sch Bath from 15. *Monkton Combe School, Church Lane, Monkton Combe, Bath BA2 7HG* M: 07877-831506 T: (01225) 721208 E: andy_hutchinson@hotmail.com

HUTCHINSON, Andrew Paul. b 65. Trin Hall Cam BA 87 MA 91 Solicitor 90. Aston Tr Scheme 92 Ripon Coll Cuddesdon BTh 97. **d** 97 **p** 98. C Stanley *Dur* 97-99; C Sunderland 99-01; TV 01-02; Chapl Sunderland Univ 99-02; TV Penrith w Newton Reigny and Plumpton Wall *Carl* 02-09; Chapl Cumbria Campus Cen Lancs Univ 02-07; Chapl Cumbria Univ *Carl* 07-09; R Stokesley w Seamer *York* from 09. *The Rectory, Leven Close, Stokesley, Middlesbrough TS9 5AP* T: (01642) 710405 E: paul.hutchinson5@btinternet.com

HUTCHINSON, Anthony Hugh. b 47. Open Univ BSc 00 Liv Univ MA 09. **d** 10 **p** 11. OLM Stafford St Chad *Lich* from 10. *Kilsall Hall, Kilsall, Shifnal TF11 8PL* T: (01902) 373145 E: revdtony@softersolutions.co.uk

HUTCHINSON, Mrs Barbara Anne. b 55. **d** 05 **p** 06. OLM Holbeach Fen *Linc* 05-14; OLM Elloe Stone from 14; Chapl United Lincs Hosps NHS Trust from 10. *3 Sholtsgate, Whaplode, Spalding PE12 6TZ* T: (01406) 422354 E: revbarbara@uwclub.net

HUTCHINSON, Canon Cyril Peter. b 37. Dur Univ BA 61. Wm Temple Coll Rugby 61. **d** 63 **p** 64. C Birm St Paul 63-67; Prin Community Relns Officer 66-69; Dir Bradf SHARE 69-76; Hon C Manningham *Bradf* 75-76; V Clayton 76-83; RD Bowling and Horton 80-83; TR Keighley St Andr 83-94; Hon Can Bradf Cathl 84-03; rtd 94; Hon C Keighley All SS *Bradf* 94-03; PtO *Leeds* from 04. *Wellcroft, Laycock Lane, Laycock, Keighley BD22 0PN* T: (01535) 606145 E: peter_hutchinson@hotmail.co.uk

HUTCHINSON, David. *See* HUTCHINSON, William David

HUTCHINSON, Hugh Edward. b 27. CEng FICE. Bps' Coll Cheshunt. **d** 61 **p** 62. C Limehouse St Anne *Lon* 61-64; C Townstall w Dartmouth *Ex* 64-67; V Ex St Mark 67-75; P-in-c Foston on the Wolds *York* 75-77; P-in-c N Frodingham

75-77; R Beeford w Lissett 75-77; R Beeford w Frodingham and Foston 77-80; RD N Holderness 79-80; P-in-c Appleton Roebuck w Acaster Selby 80-84; P-in-c Etton w Dalton Holme 84-91; rtd 91; PtO *York* 91-11. *33 Limestone Grove, Burniston, Scarborough YO13 0DH* T: (01723) 871116

HUTCHINSON, Jeremy Olpherts. b 32. Oriel Coll Ox BA 55 MA 60. Cranmer Hall Dur. **d** 57 **p** 58. C Shoreditch St Leon *Lon* 57-60; V Hoxton St Jo w Ch Ch 60-78; Hon C Hackney 78-85; C Highbury Ch Ch w St Jo and St Sav 85-91; P-in-c Hanley Road St Sav w St Paul 91-92; TV Tollington 92-96; rtd 96; PtO *Lon* from 96. *8 Casimir Road, London E5 9NU* T: (020) 8806 6492 E: jeremy.hutch@virgin.net

HUTCHINSON, John Charles. b 44. K Coll Lon 64. **d** 69 **p** 70. C Portsea All SS *Portsm* 69-71; C Portsea All SS w St Jo Rudmore 71-73; TV Fareham H Trin 73-78; P-in-c Pangbourne *Ox* 78-86; P-in-c Tidmarsh w Sulham 84-86; R Pangbourne w Tidmarsh and Sulham 86-96; PtO from 07. *90 Fir Tree Avenue, Wallingford OX10 0PL* T: (01491) 832445 E: cavea@btinternet.com

HUTCHINSON, John Maxwell. b 48. RIBA 72. **d** 14. NSM St Jo on Bethnal Green *Lon* from 14. *Hutchinson Studios, 26 Curtain Market, London EC1R 4QE*

HUTCHINSON, Jonathan Graham. b 62. Bris Univ BA 01. Trin Coll Bris 98. **d** 01 **p** 02. C Church Stretton *Heref* 01-04; P-in-c Aspley *S'well* 04-11; V from 11. *St Margaret's Vicarage, 319 Aspley Lane, Nottingham NG8 5GA* T: 0115-929 2920 or T/F: 929 8899 E: jghutchinson@btinternet.com

HUTCHINSON, Jonathan Mark. b 45. Open Univ BA 73 E Lon Univ MSc 94. Cant Sch of Min 85. **d** 89 **p** 90. NSM Wickham Market w Pettistree and Easton *St E* 89-93; V Thorington w Wenhaston, Bramfield etc 94-97; TV Ipswich St Mary at Stoke w St Pet and St Fran 97-02; PtO *B & W* from 02. *27 Milton Lane, Wells BA5 2QS* T: (01749) 676096 E: mark.hutchinson@which.net

HUTCHINSON, Canon Julie Lorraine. b 55. WMMTC 90. **d** 93 **p** 94. C Northampton St Mary *Pet* 93-95; P-in-c Morcott w Glaston and Bisbrooke 95-97; P-in-c Lyddington w Stoke Dry and Seaton etc 97-02; V 03; Dir of Ords and Voc 03-10; Bp's Chapl 11-15; Can Pet Cathl from 04; TV Oakham, Ashwell, Braunston, Brooke, Egleton etc from 15. *The Vicarage, 67 Church Street, Oakham LE15 7JE* E: juliehutchinson@uwclub.net

HUTCHINSON, June. *See* HUTCHINSON, Margaret June

HUTCHINSON, Canon Karen Elizabeth. b 64. LMH Ox BA 85 MA 89 Kent Univ MA 06 Solicitor 89. Wycliffe Hall Ox. **d** 01 **p** 02. C Alton St Lawr *Win* 01-06; V Crondall and Ewshot *Guildf* 06-12; V The Bourne and Tilford from 12; Hon Can Guildf Cathl from 13. *The Vicarage, 2 Middle Avenue, Farnham GU9 8JL* T: (01252) 820771 E: vicar@thebourne.org.uk

HUTCHINSON, Mrs Margaret June. b 45. ERMC 03. **d** 06 **p** 07. C Midi-Pyrénées and Aude *Eur* 06-10; Asst Chapl from 10. *Le Cru, 46150 Thedirac, France* T/F: (0033) 5 65 21 68 52 E: hutchinsonlecru@compuserve.com

HUTCHINSON, Mark. *See* HUTCHINSON, Jonathan Mark

HUTCHINSON, Maxwell. *See* HUTCHINSON, John Maxwell

HUTCHINSON, Nicholas Paul. b 72. Univ Coll Lon BA 97 Lon Inst of Educn PGCE 98. Ripon Coll Cuddesdon 11. **d** 13 **p** 14. C Southampton Thornhill St Chris *Win* from 13. *22 Lydgate Green, Southampton SO19 6LP* T: (023) 8036 8512 M: 07888-732238 E: mrnickyhutch@googlemail.com

HUTCHINSON, Paul. *See* HUTCHINSON, Andrew Paul

HUTCHINSON, Paul Edward. b 33. K Coll Lon. **d** 59 **p** 60. C Bromley St Mich *Lon* 59-63; C Mill Hill St Mich 63-66; C Sandridge *St Alb* 66-73; V St Alb St Mary Marshalswick 73-80; V Tunstall *Lich* 80-91; RD Stoke N 82-91; V Lower Gornal 91-93; V *Worc* 93-98; rtd 98; PtO *Lich* from 99. *55 Mill Hayes Road, Burslem, Stoke-on-Trent ST6 4JB* T: (01782) 813361

HUTCHINSON, Miss Pauline. b 49. St Jo Coll Nottm 88. **d** 90 **p** 94. Par Dn Sherwood *S'well* 90-94; C 94-95; TV Newark 95-09; Chapl Newark Hosp NHS Trust 95-04; rtd 09. *18 Cardinal Hinsley Close, Newark NG24 4NQ* T: (01636) 681931

HUTCHINSON, Peter. *See* HUTCHINSON, Cyril Peter

HUTCHINSON, Peter Francis. b 52. Sarum & Wells Th Coll 87. **d** 89 **p** 90. C Honiton, Gittisham, Combe Raleigh, Monkton etc *Ex* 89-93; V Valley Park *Win* from 93. *35 Raglan Close, Eastleigh SO53 4NH* T: (023) 8025 5749 E: st.francis@ukgateway.net

HUTCHINSON, Canon Raymond John. b 51. Liv Univ BSc 73. Westcott Ho Cam 73. **d** 76 **p** 77. C Peckham St Jo *S'wark* 76-78; C Peckham St Jo w St Andr 78-79; C Prescot *Liv* 79-81; V Edgehill St Dunstan 81-87; P-in-c Litherland Ch Ch 87-89; P-in-c Waterloo Park 87-89; V Waterloo Ch Ch and St Mary 90-97; Chapl Wigan and Leigh Health Services NHS Trust 97-01; Chapl Wrightington Wigan and Leigh NHS Trust 01-15; P-in-c Wigan All SS *Liv* 04-08; P-in-c Wigan St Geo 05-08; R Wigan All SS and St Geo 08-15; TR Wigan All SS 15; Hon

Can Liv Cathl 13-15; rtd 15. *9 Chequers Gardens, Liverpool L19 3PD* T: 0151-291 5803 E: rayh365@gmail.com

HUTCHINSON, Canon Stephen. b 38. St Chad's Coll Dur BA 60. **d** 62 **p** 63. C Tividale *Lich* 62-68; V Walsall St Andr 68-73; R Headless Cross *Worc* 73-81; TR Redditch, The Ridge 81-91; RD Bromsgrove 85-91; V Stourbridge St Thos 91-03; Hon Can Worc Cathl 88-03; rtd 03; PtO *Worc* from 03. *251 Stourbridge Road, Kidderminster DY10 2XJ* T: (01562) 631658

E: stephen.hutchinson71@virginmedia.com

HUTCHINSON, Canon William David. b 27. Wycliffe Hall Ox 55. **d** 57 **p** 58. C Ipswich St Jo *St E* 57-60; R Combs 60-65; V Ipswich St Aug 65-76; R Ewhurst *Guildf* 76-81; V Aldeburgh w Hazlewood *St E* 81-92; RD Saxmundham 83-88; Hon Can St E Cathl 87-92; rtd 92. *Hazelwood, 1 Birch Close, Woodbridge IP12 4UA* T: (01394) 383760

HUTCHINSON CERVANTES, Canon Ian Charles. b 62. Cant Univ (NZ) BSc 84 Reading Univ MSc 86 Jes Coll Cam BA 89 MA 92. Westcott Ho Cam 86. **d** 89 **p** 90. C Iffley *Ox* 89-92; USPG 92-04; Locum P Caracas Cathl Venezuela 93; P-in-c El Cayo St Andr Belize 93-97; USPG Staff 97-04; Chapl Madrid *Eur* 04-12; World Miss Officer and P-in-c Nuthurst and Mannings Heath *Chich* 12-15; R from 15; Hon Can Madrid Cathl from 01; Hon Can Buenos Aires from 02; Hon Can Pelotas from 06; Can Gib Cathl from 10. *The Rectory, Nuthurst Street, Nuthurst, Horsham RH13 6LH* T: (01403) 891449 M: 07733-023880

✠**HUTCHISON, The Most Revd Andrew Sandford.** b 38. Montreal Dioc Th Coll Hon DD 93. Trin Coll Toronto. **d** 69 **p** 70 **c** 70. Canada from 69; Dean Montreal 84-90; Bp Montreal 90-04; Primate of Angl Ch of Canada from 04. *80 Hayden Street, Toronto ON M4Y 3G2, Canada* T: (001) (416) 924 9119 F: 924 0211 E: primate@national.anglican.ca

HUTCHISON, Geoffrey John. b 52. Trin Hall Cam MA 76 Lon Univ CertEd 76. Ridley Hall Cam 77. **d** 79 **p** 80. C Harold Wood *Chelmsf* 79-83; CF 83-89; Warden Viney Hill Chr Adventure Cen 89-96; P-in-c Viney Hill *Glouc* 89-96; V Wadsley *Sheff* 96-11; Chapl Sheff Children's NHS Foundn Trust from 11. *Children's Hospital NHS Trust, Western Bank, Sheffield S10 2TH* T: 0114-271 7000

E: rev.hutch@googlemail.com

HUTCHISON, Ross. b 61. Wadh Coll Ox BA 83 MA 86 DPhil 88. SEITE 03. **d** 06 **p** 07. NSM Newington St Mary *S'wark* 06-10; NSM Kilburn St Mary w All So and W Hampstead St Jas *Lon* from 10. *12A Cumberland Mansions, West End Lane, London NW6 1LL* T: (020) 7794 6087 E: rossnw6@gmail.com

HUTSON, Mark Arthur. b 61. OLM Barrow and Goxhill *Linc* from 13. *Lindum Lodge, Spruce Lane, Ulceby DN39 6UL* T: (01469) 566292

HUTT, Canon David Handley. b 38. Lambeth MA 05 AKC 68. **d** 69 **p** 70. C Bedford Park *Lon* 69-70; C Westmr St Matt 70-73; PV and Succ S'wark Cathl 73-78; Chapl K Coll Taunton 78-82; V Bordesley SS Alb and Patr *Birm* 82-86; V St Marylebone All SS *Lon* 86-95; Can Steward Westmr Abbey 95-05; Sub-Dean and Adn Westmr 99-05; rtd 05; PtO *Lon* 06-13; *Eur* from 06. *14A The Quadrangle, Morden College, 19 St Germans Place, London SE3 0PW*

HUTTON, Christopher. b 81. Sussex Univ BSc 04. Wycliffe Hall Ox BTh 10. **d** 10 **p** 11. C Southgate *Chich* 10-14; R Ditchingham, Hedenham, Broome, Earsham etc *Nor* from 14. *The Rectory, School Road, Earsham, Bungay NR35 2TF* T: (01986) 895423 E: chrishutton@hotmail.com

HUTTON, Elizabeth. See HUTTON, Susan Elizabeth

HUTTON, Griffith Arthur Jeremy. b 31. Trin Hall Cam BA 56 MA 59. Linc Th Coll 56. **d** 58 **p** 59. C Hexham *Newc* 58-60; C Gosforth All SS 60-65; V Whitegate *Ches* 65-71; V Whitegate w Lt Budworth 71-78; R Dowdeswell and Andoversford w the Shiptons etc *Glouc* 78-91; V Newnham w Awre and Blakeney 91-96; rtd 96; PtO *Heref* from 99. *6 Farmington Rise, Northleach, Cheltenham GL54 3HU*

HUTTON, Matthew Charles Arthur. b 53. Ch Ch Ox BA 75 MA 79. St Mellitus Coll BA 14. **d** 14 **p** 15. OLM Nor St Steph from 14. *Broom Farm, Chedgrave, Norwich NR14 6BQ* T: (01508) 520775 *or* 528388 F: 528099

E: mhutton@paston.co.uk

HUTTON, Sarah Fielding. b 63. **d** 11 **p** 12. NSM Shere, Albury and Chilworth *Guildf* from 11; Spiritual Growth Facilitator from 14. *Netley House, Shere Road, Gomshall, Guildford GU5 9QA* T: (01483) 203800 E: sarah@handr.co.uk

HUTTON, Mrs Serena Quartermaine. b 35. Nottm Univ BA 57 Lon Univ BA 73 Stranmillis Coll PGCE 68 FRSA 87. SAOMC 95. **d** 98 **p** 99. OLM Chinnor, Sydenham, Aston Rowant and Crowell *Ox* from 98. *Elma Cottage, The Green, Kingston Blount, Chinnor OX9 4SE* T: (01844) 354173

HUTTON, Susan Elizabeth. b 70. Univ of Wales (Cardiff) BD 91. Ripon Coll Cuddesdon 93. **d** 95 **p** 96. C W Parley *Sarum*

95-99; C Trowbridge H Trin 99-05; P-in-c 05-09; PtO 09-14; Lic to RD Devizes from 14. *10 Thestfield Drive, Staverton, Trowbridge BA14 8AD* T: (01225) 751275

E: rev.beth@virgin.net

HUTTON-BURY, Canon David. b 44. BA. **d** 94 **p** 95. Aux Min Geashill w Killeigh and Ballycommon *M & K* 94-97; Aux Min Clane w Donadea and Coolcarrigan 97-00; Aux Min Mullingar, Portnashangan, Moyliscar, Kilbixy etc 00-05; Aux Min Clane w Donadea and Coolcarrigan 05-10; P-in-c Geashill w Killeigh and Ballycommon from 10; Can Meath from 10. *Chorleyville Farm, Tullamore, Co Offaly, Republic of Ireland* T: (00353) (57) 932 1813 E: davidhuttonbury@yahoo.ie

HUXHAM, Hector Hubert. b 29. Bris Univ BA 55. Tyndale Hall Bris 52. **d** 56 **p** 57. C Eccleston St Luke *Liv* 56-58; C Heworth H Trin *York* 59-60; V Burley *Ripon* 61-66; Chapl St Jas and Seacroft Univ Hosp Trust Leeds 67-94; rtd 94; PtO *Bradf* 94-98; *Leeds* from 94. *3 Oakwell Oval, Leeds LS8 4AL* T: 0113-266 8851

HUXHAM, Canon Peter Richard. b 38. Worc Coll Ox BA 61 MA 74. St Steph Ho Ox 61. **d** 63 **p** 64. C Gillingham *Sarum* 63-67; C Osmondthorpe St Phil *Ripon* 67-70; V Parkstone St Osmund *Sarum* 70-75; TR Parkstone St Pet w Branksea and St Osmund 75-92; RD Poole 85-92; Can and Preb Sarum Cathl 85-92; Chapl Taunton and Somerset NHS Trust 92-03; rtd 03. *Salterns House, 34 Brownsea View Avenue, Poole BH14 8LQ* T: (01202) 707431

HUXLEY, Craig John. b 85. Cant Ch Ch Univ BA 06 MCollT 09. SEITE 11. **d** 14. NSM Hackington *Cant* 14-15; NSM Goudhurst w Kilndown from 15; Chapl Benenden Sch from 14. *Flat E Meadows, Benenden School, Cranbrook Road, Benenden, Cranbrook TN17 4AE* M: 07872-554044 T: (01580) 236691

HUXLEY, Canon Stephen Scott. b 30. Linc Th Coll 53. **d** 56 **p** 57. C Cullercoats St Geo *Newc* 56-59; C Eglingham 59-60; C N Gosforth 60-63; V Nether Witton and Hartburn and Meldon 63-65; V Tynemouth Priory 65-74; V Warkworth and Acklington 74-78; P-in-c Tynemouth St Jo 78-81; V 81-87; Hon Can Newc Cathl 82-92; V Wylam 87-92; rtd 92; PtO *Newc* 92-10. *7 Langside Drive, Comrie, Crieff PH6 2HR* T: (01764) 679877

HUXTABLE, Christopher Michael Barclay. b 61. Ex Univ BA 83 Qu Coll Cam PGCE 84. St Steph Ho Ox 93. **d** 95 **p** 96. C Chich 95-98; C Haywards Heath St Wilfrid 98-99; TV 99-01; Chapl Geelong Gr Sch (Timbertop) Australia 01-04; Chapl St Mary's Sch Wantage 04-05; C Blewbury, Hagbourne and Upton *Ox* 05-06; C S w N Moreton, Aston Tirrold and Aston Upthorpe 05-06; R Mansfield Australia 06-11; Chapl Westbourne Gr Sch 11; Chapl Stowe Sch from 12. *Stowe School, Stowe, Buckingham MK18 5EH* T: (01280) 818144

E: cmbhux@gmail.com

HUXTABLE, Peter Alexander. b 68. Southn Univ BEng 90. St Jo Coll Nottm MTh 01. **d** 01 **p** 02. C Kidderminster St Geo *Worc* 01-05; V Bestwood Em w St Mark *S'well* 05-10; P-in-c Stapleford 10-11; V from 11. *The Vicarage, 61 Church Street, Stapleford, Nottingham NG9 8GA* T: 0115-854 0196

HUYTON, Canon Susan Mary. b 57. Birm Univ BA 79. Qu Coll Birm 83. **d** 86 **p** 97. C Connah's Quay *St As* 86-89; C Wrexham 89-90; Dn-in-c 90-91; TV 91-99; V Gwersyllt 99-14; AD Alyn 05-12; R Bangor Monachorum, Worthenbury and Marchwiel from 14; AD Dee Valley from 14; Can Cursal St As Cathl from 08. *The Rectory, 8 Ludlow Road, Bangor-on-Dee, Wrexham LL13 0JG* T: (01978) 780608

E: suehuyton@aol.com

HUZZEY, Canon Peter George. b 48. Trin Coll Bris 74. **d** 76 **p** 77. C Bishopsworth *Bris* 76-79; V 86-96; C Downend 79-80; TV Kings Norton *Birm* 80-86; TR Bishopsworth and Bedminster Down *Bris* 97-00; RD Bedminster 98-99; TR Kingswood 00-15; P-in-c Hanham 12-15; Hon Can Bris Cathl 12-15; rtd 15. *134 Guest Avenue, Emersons Green, Bristol BS16 7DA* M: 07855-768856 E: peterhuzzey@tiscali.co.uk

HYATT, Robert Keith. b 34. Em Coll Cam BA 59 MA 63. Ridley Hall Cam 58. **d** 60 **p** 61. C Cheltenham St Mary *Glouc* 60-63; Asst Chapl K Edw Sch Witley 63-65; C Godalming *Guildf* 65-69; Hong Kong 69-78; V Claygate *Guildf* 78-91; TV Whitton *Sarum* 91-96 and 99; TV 96-99; rtd 00; PtO *B & W* 00-04; *Bris* from 02; May Moore Chapl Malmesbury w Westport and Brokenborough 02-05; Chapl Kennet and N Wilts Primary Care Trust 02-05. *19 Dark Lane, Malmesbury SN16 0BB* T: (01666) 829026 E: bobnhelen@dsl.pipex.com

HYDE, Ann. b 42. **d** 09 **p** 10. NSM Bramhall *Ches* 09-12; NSM Low Marple from 12. *Mellor View, 25 St Martin's Road, Marple, Stockport SK6 7BY* T: 0161-427 5767

E: ann.hyde@btinternet.com

HYDE, Mrs Denise. b 54. WEMTC 05. **d** 08 **p** 09. OLM Fairford Deanery *Glouc* 08-12; NSM S Cotswolds from 12. *14 Park Street, Fairford GL7 4JJ* T: (01285) 713285 M: 07816-500269

E: denisehyde15@googlemail.com

HYDE, Mrs Jacqueline Diane. b 66. Glos Univ BA 12. WEMTC 06. **d** 09 **p** 10. NSM Leckhampton SS Phil and Jas w Cheltenham St Jas *Glouc* 09; NSM S Cheltenham 09-15; V Churchdown St Jo and Innsworth from 15; Dioc Ecum Officer from 13. *The Vicarage, 2 St John's Avenue, Churchdown, Gloucester GL3 2DB* T: (01452) 713421 E: revdjacqui@talktalk.net

HYDE, Jeremy Richard Granville. b 52. Sch of Pharmacy Lon BPharm 75 PhD 80. SAOMC 01. **d** 04 **p** 05. NSM Furze Platt *Ox* 04-11; AD Maidenhead and Windsor 08-11; V Finham *Cov* from 11. *St Martin's Vicarage, 136 Green Lane South, Coventry CV3 6EA* T: (024) 7669 0855 E: jeremy.hyde@btinternet.com

HYDE-DUNN, Keith Frederick. b 43. Sarum Th Coll. **d** 69 **p** 70. C Selukwe St Athan Rhodesia 69-72; C Horsham *Chich* 73-77; P-in-c Fittleworth 77-86; P-in-c Graffham w Woolavington 86-00; PtO from 01; rtd 04. *The Hermitage, Church Place, Pulborough RH20 1AF* T: (01798) 873892

HYDER-SMITH, Brian John. b 45. FInstAM MCMI MBIM. EAMTC 84. **d** 87 **p** 88. NSM Huntingdon *Ely* 87-90; P-in-c Abbots Ripton w Wood Walton 90-98; P-in-c Kings Ripton 90-98; C Whittlesey, Pondersbridge and Coates 98-99; TV 99-04; rtd 04; Hon C Ironstone *Ox* 10-12; PtO *Ely* from 13. *The Cherry Trees, New Road, Woodwalton, Huntingdon PE28 5YT* T: (01295) 730951 E: revbh-s@hotmail.com

HYDON, Canon Veronica Weldon. b 52. N Lon Poly BA 73 Maria Grey Coll Lon CertEd 74. Aston Tr Scheme 87 Westcott Ho Cam 89. **d** 91 **p** 94. Par Dn Poplar *Lon* 91-94; C 94-95; P-in-c Roxwell *Chelmsf* 95-00; Lay Development Officer 95-00; V Forest Gate Em w Upton Cross 00-03; Assoc V Timperley *Ches* 03-07; V Bollington from 07; RD Macclesfield from 14; Hon Can Ches Cathl from 14. *The Vicarage, 35A Shrigley Road, Bollington, Macclesfield SK10 5RD* T: (01625) 573162 E: vhydon@hotmail.com

HYETT, Dawn Barbara. b 53. Cyncoed Coll CertEd 74 Open Univ BA 79. WEMTC 99. **d** 02 **p** 03. NSM Bromyard *Heref* 02-08; NSM Bromyard and Stoke Lacy from 09. *Roberts Hill, Norton, Bromyard HR7 4PB* T: (01885) 483747

HYGATE, Paul. b 72. Bolton Inst of HE BA 95. EMMTC 07. **d** 10 **p** 11. NSM Aston on Trent, Elvaston, Weston on Trent etc *Derby* from 10. *38 Oaklands Avenue, Littleover, Derby DE23 2QH* T: (01332) 772779 E: paulhygate@fsmail.net *or* frpaulhygate@gmail.com

HYLAND, Cecil George. b 38. TCD BA 62 MA 78. CITC Div Test . **d** 63 **p** 64. C Belfast St Nic *Conn* 63-66; C Monkstown *D & G* 66-68; Ch of Ireland Youth Officer 68-73; Chapl TCD 73-79; I Tullow *D & G* 79-90; I Howth 90-05; Dir of Ords (Dub) 91-98; Can Ch Ch Cathl Dublin 91-05; Cen Dir of Ords 98-05; rtd 05. *34 The Vale, Skerries Road, Skerries, Co Dublin, Republic of Ireland* T: (00353) (1) 810 6884 M: 86-838 5317 E: cecilhyland@hotmail.com

HYLTON, Jane Lois. *See* NURSEY, Jane Lois

HYSLOP, Mrs Catherine Graham Young. b 53. Carl Dioc Tr Inst 90. **d** 92 **p** 94. NSM St Bees *Carl* 92-95; NSM Upperby St Jo 95-98; C 98-03; C Upperby from 03. *St John's Vicarage, Manor Road, Upperby, Carlisle CA2 4LH* T: (01228) 523380 E: katie.hyslop2010@gmail.com

HYSLOP, Canon Thomas James. b 54. St Andr Univ BD 76. Edin Th Coll 76. **d** 78 **p** 79. C Whitehaven *Carl* 78-81; C Walney Is 81-83; P-in-c Gt Broughton and Broughton Moor 83-85; V 85-88; V Kells 88-95; P-in-c Upperby St Jo 95-97; V 97-03; TR S Carl 03-12; R Upperby from 12; Dioc Chapl MU from 02; Hon Can Carl Cathl from 06. *St John's Vicarage, Manor Road, Upperby, Carlisle CA2 4LH* T: (01228) 523380 E: jim.hyslop@talk21.com

HYSON, Peter Raymond. b 51. Open Univ BA 80 Bris Univ MSc 05. Oak Hill Th Coll BA 86. **d** 87 **p** 88. C Billericay and Lt Burstead *Chelmsf* 87-92; TV Whitton *Sarum* 92-99; PtO *Lon* from 07. *53 Plough Way, London SE16 2LS* T: (020) 3509 2796 M: 07951-767113 E: peter@change-perspectives.com

---

I

I'ANSON, Frederick Mark. b 43. MRAC 68. Carl Dioc Tr Inst 89. **d** 92 **p** 93. NSM Sedbergh, Cautley and Garsdale *Bradf* 92-98; P-in-c Kirkby-in-Malhamdale w Coniston Cold 98-08; rtd 08; PtO *Leeds* from 09. *The Bowers, Firbank, Sedbergh LA10 5EG* T: (015396) 21757 M: 07815-552778 E: mark@mmia.demon.co.uk

IBADAN SOUTH, Bishop of. *See* AJETUNMOBI, Jacob Ademola

IBALL, Charles Martin John. b 40. Lich Th Coll 67. **d** 69 **p** 70. C Dudley St Edm *Worc* 69-73; C W Bromwich St Jas *Lich* 73-76; V Oxley 76-80; Hon C Whittington w Weeford 86-10; Hon C Clifton Campville w Edingale and Harlaston 96-06; Hon C Hints 06-10; rtd 04. *21 Lion Court, Worcester WR1 1UT* T: (01905) 724695

IBBETSON, Stephen Andrew. b 59. Portsm Poly BSc 82. STETS 04. **d** 07 **p** 08. NSM Southbroom *Sarum* from 07; Chapl HM Pris Erlestoke from 11. *HM Prison Erlestoke, Westbury Road, Erlestoke, Devizes SN10 5TU* T: (01380) 814250 E: s.ibbetson@btinternet.com

IBBOTSON, David Paul. b 64. Man Univ BSc 85 PGCE 86. STETS 09. **d** 12 **p** 13. C Tewkesbury w Walton Cardiff and Twyning *Glouc* 12-14; Chapl Monmouth Schs from 14. *Address temp unknown* M: 07876-333390 E: dpibbotson@tesco.net

IBBOTSON, Miss Tracy Alexandra. b 63. Cranmer Hall Dur 01. **d** 03 **p** 04. C Todmorden *Wakef* 03-08; V Airedale w Fryston *Leeds* from 08; Adv on Urban Issues from 12. *Holy Cross Vicarage, The Mount, Castleford WF10 3JN* T: (01977) 553157 E: ibbotson457@btinternet.com

IBE-ENWO, Ogbonnia. b 62. Univ of Nigeria BSc 84 Univ of Northumbria at Newc MSc 04 Ex Univ MSc 11 MBCS 05. Trin Coll Umuahia 00. **d** 00 **p** 02. C Unwana St Luke Nigeria 00-01; Chapl Akanu Ibiam Federal Poly Unwana 00-10; V Unwana Em 02-03; NSM Benwell *Newc* 03-04; V Unwana St Luke Nigeria 07-10; C Kenton, Mamhead, Powderham, Cofton and Starcross *Ex* 11-13; C Exminster and Kenn 11-13. *All Saints' House, Kenton, Exeter EX6 8NG* T: (01626) 890034 M: 07760-927950 E: ibeenwo@yahoo.com

IBIAYO, David Akindayo Oluwarotimi. b 71. Lagos Univ BSc. Ridley Hall Cam. **d** 06 **p** 07. C Barking St Marg w St Patr *Chelmsf* 06-10; R Vange from 11; P-in-c Bowers Gifford w N Benfleet from 11. *Vange Rectory, 782 Clay Hill Road, Basildon SS16 4NG* T: (01268) 581404 M: 07904-846028 E: david_ibiayo@hotmail.com

IDDON, Jonathan Richard. b 82. **d** 11 **p** 12. C Glascote and Stonydelph *Lich* 11-13; V Fazeley from 13; V Canwell from 13; R Drayton Bassett from 13. *The Vicarage, 35 Moat Drive, Drayton Bassett, Tamworth B78 3UG* E: jonathan.iddon@me.com

IDDON, Roy Edward. b 40. TCert 61 Lanc Univ MA 88. NOC 83. **d** 83 **p** 84. Hd Teacher St Andr Primary Sch Blackb from 83; NSM Bolton St Matt w St Barn *Man* 83-88; Lic to AD Walmsley 88-93; NSM 93-01; NSM Turton Moorland 01-04; NSM Bolton St Phil 04-10. *28 New Briggs Fold, Egerton, Bolton BL7 9UL* T: (01204) 306589

IDLE, Christopher Martin. b 38. St Pet Coll Ox BA 62. Clifton Th Coll 62. **d** 65 **p** 66. C Barrow St Mark *Carl* 65-68; C Camberwell Ch Ch *S'wark* 68-71; P-in-c Poplar St Matthias *Lon* 71-76; R Limehouse 76-89; R N Hartismere *St E* 89-95; PtO *S'wark* 95-03; St E 01-03; rtd 03; PtO *Roch* from 04; S'wark from 13. *50 Park View House, Hurst Street, London SE24 0EH* T: (020) 3490 7828 E: christophermidle@gmail.com

IEVINS, Mrs Catherine Ruth. b 54. LMH Ox BA 77 MA 80 Solicitor 81. EAMTC 98. **d** 01 **p** 02. C Pet Ch Carpenter 01-05; PtO 05-06; P-in-c Polebrook and Lutton w Hemington and Luddington 06-07; P-in-c Barnwell w Tichmarsh, Thurning and Clapton 06-07; R Barnwell, Hemington, Luddington in the Brook etc from 07; Warden of Readers 12-14. *The Rectory, Main Street, Polebrook, Peterborough PE8 5LN* T: (01832) 270162 E: revci9@gmail.com

IEVINS, Paul Janis. b 58. Linc Sch of Th and Min 12. **d** 15. NSM Welton and Dunholme w Scothern *Linc* from 15. *Address temp unknown*

IEVINS, Peter Valdis. b 54. St Jo Coll Ox BA 75 MA 81 Solicitor 79. Westcott Ho Cam 86. **d** 88 **p** 89. C Sawston and Babraham *Ely* 88-91; NSM Pet Ch Carpenter 01-06; LtO from 06. *The Rectory, Main Street, Polebrook, Peterborough PE8 5LN* T: (01832) 270162 E: peter.ievins@judiciary.gsi.gov.uk

IGENOZA, Andrew Olu. b 50. Ife Univ Nigeria BA 75 Man Univ PhD 82. Immanuel Coll Ibadan 87. **d** 88 **p** 89. Nigeria 88-99; C Gorton St Phil *Man* 00-01. *17 Northmoor Road, Longsight, Manchester M12 4NF* T: 0161-248 8758

IJAZ, Luke Anthony. b 76. Univ Coll Lon MSci 99 Lon Inst of Educn PGCE 01. Wycliffe Hall Ox BA 06. **d** 07 **p** 08. C Wallington *S'wark* 07-11; C Redhill H Trin 11-13; C Langham Place All So *Lon* from 14. *25 Fitzroy Street, London W1T 6DR* E: luke_ijaz@hotmail.com

IKECHUKWU, Eliakim Chinonyerem. b 62. Calabar Univ Nigeria BA 01. Trin Coll Umuahia 08. **d** 07 **p** 08. Chapl Calabar Univ Nigeria 07-10; Chapl Calabar Pris 10-15; C Calabar Cathl 11-13; Chapl 13-15; PtO *Birm* from 15. *100 Bridge Street West, Birmingham B19 2YX* M: 07438-547469 T: 0121-359 2000 E: eliakimike@yahoo.com

IKIN, Gordon Mitchell. b 30. AKC 57. **d** 58 **p** 59. C Leigh St Mary *Man* 58-61; V Westleigh St Paul 61-72; V Thornham St Jas 72-95; rtd 95; PtO *Man* 95-08. *3 Lygon Lodge, Newland, Malvern WR13 5AX* T: (01684) 564948

ILECHUKWU, Gideon. b 70. Nnamdi Azikiwe Univ Nigeria MB, BS 97. Trin Coll Umuahia 04. **d** 04 **p** 06. Chapl Univ of Nigeria Teaching Hosp Nigeria 04-09; Dioc Dir of Ords & Miss & Adn Awgu/Aninri 07-09; NSM Dublin St Patr Cathl Gp 10; PtO *Man* from 11. *12 Morrell Road, Manchester M22 4WH* T: 0161-270 2656 M: 07411-239576 E: venerablegideon@yahoo.co.uk

ILES, Canon Paul Robert. b 37. Fitzw Coll Cam BA 59 MA 64 St Edm Hall Ox MA 80 FRCO 65. Sarum Th Coll 59. **d** 61 **p** 62. Chapl Bp Wordsworth Sch Salisbury 61-67; C Salisbury St Mich *Sarum* 61-64; Min Can Sarum Cathl 64-67; C Bournemouth St Pet *Win* 67-72; R Filton *Bris* 72-79; V Ox SS Phil and Jas w St Marg 79-83; Can Res and Prec Heref Cathl 83-03; rtd 03; Hon C Prestbury and All SS *Glouc* 03-08; Hon C N Cheltenham 08-12. *10 Muscroft Road, Prestbury, Cheltenham GL52 5DG* T: (01242) 321398 E: paulri@talktalk.net

ILIFFE, Mrs Alison Jane. b 63. Birm Poly BA 86. Qu Coll Birm 13. **d** 15. NSM Gilmorton, Peatling Parva, Kimcote etc *Leic* from 15. *The Rectory, 21 Dag Lane, North Kilworth, Lutterworth LE17 6HD* E: ailiffe@talktalk.net

ILIFFE, Mrs Felicity Mary. b 57. Glam Univ BA 79 Normal Coll Ban PGCE 82. SEITE 06 WEMTC 07. **d** 09 **p** 10. C Ledbury *Heref* 09-13; V Highley w Billingsley, Glazeley etc 13-14. *Address temp unknown* E: revfliss@googlemail.com

ILLING, Eric James. b 33. Kelham Th Coll 54 Chich Th Coll 55. **d** 57 **p** 58. C Leeds St Aid *Ripon* 57-60; C Leeds All SS 60-62; C E Grinstead St Swithun *Chich* 62-65; V Middleton St Mary *Ripon* 65-74; R Felpham w Middleton *Chich* 74-81; Chapl R Devon and Ex Hosp (Wonford) 81-91; TR Heavitree w Ex St Paul 81-91; R Bradninch and Clyst Hydon 91-94; rtd 94; PtO *B & W* from 94; *Eur* from 98. *2 Magdalene Court, Magdalene Street, Taunton TA1 1QY* T: (01823) 289203 M: 07709-658070 E: eric.illing@btinternet.com

ILLINGWORTH, John Patrick Paul. b 34. New Coll Ox BA 59 MA 63. Chich Th Coll 61. **d** 63 **p** 64. C Brighouse *Wakef* 63-66; C Willesden St Andr *Lon* 66-70; Chapl Gothenburg w Halmstad and Jönköping *Eur* 70-74; PtO *Chich* 74-82; V Ryhill *Wakef* 74-82; R Weston Longville w Morton and the Witchinghams *Nor* 82-04; P-in-c Alderford w Attlebridge and Swannington 94-04; RD Sparham 95-00; rtd 04; PtO *Nor* from 04. *38 Eckling Grange, Dereham NR20 3BB* T: (01362) 690407

ILORI, Emmanuel. b 57. **d** 04 **p** 05. NSM New Addington *S'wark* 04-15; PtO from 15. *Lian-May, Watson's Hill, Sittingbourne ME10 2JW* M: 07734-929501 E: e.ilori@opmaritime.com

ILSLEY (née ROGERS), Mrs Anne Frances. b 50. Heythrop Coll Lon BA 00 RGN 72. Wycliffe Hall Ox 00. **d** 02 **p** 03. NSM Harefield *Lon* 02-06; NSM Dorchester *Ox* from 06. *The Vicarage, High Street, Long Wittenham, Abingdon OX14 4QQ* T: (01865) 407605 M: 07956-374624 E: annefi36@aol.com

ILSON, John Robert. b 37. Leeds Univ BSc 59 Lon Univ BD 64 CertEd 65. ALCD 63. **d** 64 **p** 65. C Kennington St Mark *S'wark* 64-67; C Sydenham H Trin 67-70; Asst Dir RE *Sheff* 70-77; R Hooton Roberts 70-75; R Hooton Roberts w Ravenfield 75-77; P-in-c Kidderminster St Geo *Worc* 77-81; TR 81-85; P-in-c Powick 85-96; Chapl N Devon Healthcare NHS Trust 97-04; rtd 04; PtO *Roch* from 07. *14 Bromley College, London Road, Bromley BR1 1PE* T: 020-8460 3927 E: johnilson88@hotmail.com

ILTON, Mrs Jennifer Jane. b 38. S Dios Minl Tr Scheme 92. **d** 95 **p** 96. NSM Jersey St Sav *Win* 95-08; PtO from 08. *38 Maison St Louis, St Saviour, Jersey JE2 7LX* T: (01534) 722327 E: curasea@jerseymail.co.uk

ILYAS, Marilyn. b 51. Oak Hill Th Coll 92. **d** 95 **p** 96. C Roch 95-98; TV S Chatham H Trin 98-01; TR 01-12; rtd 12; PtO *Roch* from 12. *5 Pepperidge Way, Hoo, Rochester ME3 9FY* E: milyas@blueyonder.co.uk

IMPEY, Miss Joan Mary. b 35. Dalton Ho Bris 65. **dss** 74 **d** 87 **p** 94. Kennington St Mark *S'wark* 74-75; Barking St Marg w St Patr *Chelmsf* 75-81; Harwell w Chilton *Ox* 81-87; Par Dn 87-92; Par Dn Didcot All SS 92-94; C 94-97; rtd 98; PtO *Ox* from 99. *15 Loder Road, Harwell, Didcot OX11 0HR* T: (01235) 820346

IMPEY, Canon Patricia Irene. b 45. Birm Univ BA 67 Lanc Univ MPhil 01. Carl Dioc Tr Course 88. **d** 90 **p** 94. Par Dn Blackpool St Paul *Blackb* 90-94; C 94-95; Chapl Asst Victoria Hosp Blackpool 94-95; Asst Chapl Norfolk and Nor Health Care NHS Trust 95-96; Hon C Sprowston w Beeston *Nor* 96; R King's Beck 96-02; V Ecclesfield *Sheff* 02-10; Dean of Women's Min 03-06 and 06-08; Hon Can Sheff Cathl 04-10; rtd 10; PtO *Blackb* from 11. *22 Hala Grove, Lancaster LA1 4PS* T: (01524) 36617 E: patriciaimpey@btinternet.com

IMPEY, Richard. b 41. Em Coll Cam BA 63 MA 67 Harvard Univ ThM 67. Ridley Hall Cam 67. **d** 68 **p** 69. C Birm St Martin 68-72; Dir of Tr *B & W* 72-79; Dir of Ords 76-79; V Blackpool St Jo *Blackb* 79-95; RD Blackpool 84-90; Hon Can Blackb Cathl 89-95; Dioc Dir of Tr *Nor* 95-00; P-in-c Heigham St Barn w St Bart 00-02; V Wentworth *Sheff* 02-06; Bp's Adv in Par Development 04-10; rtd 06; PtO *Blackb* from 10. *22 Hala Grove, Lancaster LA1 4PS* T: (01524) 36617 E: richardimpey@btinternet.com

INALL, Mrs Elizabeth Freda. b 47. Univ of Wales (Lamp) MA 06. St Alb Minl Tr Scheme 88. **d** 92 **p** 94. NSM Tring *St Alb* 92-01; C Harpenden St Nic 01-09; P-in-c Milton Ernest, Pavenham and Thurleigh 09-13; rtd 13. *Grange House, Village Road, Christleton, Chester CH3 7AS* T: (01244) 336500 E: elizabeth@inall.co.uk

INCE, Peter Reginald. b 26. Bp's Coll Calcutta 48. **d** 51 **p** 52. C Calcutta St Jas India 51-52; V 52-53; Chapl Khargpur 53-54; Chapl Asanol 54-55; C Leek St Luke *Lich* 55-57; C Milton 57-59; C Lewisham St Jo Southend *S'wark* 59-62; R Loddington w Cransley *Pet* 62-75; V Snibston *Leic* 75-79; R Mickleham *Guildf* 79-92; rtd 92; PtO *Guildf* 92-03. *Bickerton, 8 Rockdale, Headley Road, Grayshott, Hindhead GU26 6TU* T: (01428) 604694

INCH, Vivian. b 57. **d** 13 **p** 14. OLM High Wycombe *Ox* from 13. *1 Glade View, High Wycombe HP12 4UN*

IND, Canon Dominic Mark. b 63. Lanc Univ BA 87. Ridley Hall Cam 87. **d** 90 **p** 91. C Birch w Fallowfield *Man* 90-93; SSF 93-95; PtO *Glas* 95-96; C Byker St Martin *Newc* 96-98; C Walker 96-98; P-in-c Cambuslang and Uddingston *Glas* 98-07; R Bridge of Allan *St And* from 07; Chapl Stirling Univ from 07; Can St Ninian's Cathl Perth from 10; Dioc Dir of Ords from 11. *The Rectory, 21 Fountain Road, Bridge of Allan FK9 4AT* T: (01786) 832368 E: dom.ind@btinternet.com

IND, Philip William David. b 35. K Coll Lon BD 82. Wycliffe Hall Ox 74 Cranmer Hall Dur 59. **d** 65 **p** 66. C Ipswich St Jo *St E* 65-67; C Charlton Kings St Mary *Glouc* 67-71; R Woolstone w Gotherington and Oxenton 71-74; Chapl Alleyn's Sch Dulwich 76-81; C Beckenham St Geo *Roch* 83-85; V Bromley St Jo 85-87; PtO *Ox* 88-91 and 95-12; P-in-c Hurley 91-92; P-in-c Stubbings 91-92; rtd 92; PtO *St E* from 12. *Church View, Station Road, Melton, Woodbridge IP12 1PX* T: (01394) 384392 E: mtpipind@aol.com

✠**IND, The Rt Revd William.** b 42. Leeds Univ BA 64. Coll of Resurr Mirfield 64. **d** 66 **p** 67 **c** 87. C Feltham *Lon* 66-71; C Northolt St Mary 71-73; TV Basingstoke *Win* 73-87; Vice-Prin Aston Tr Scheme 79-82; Dioc Dir of Ords *Win* 82-87; Hon Can Win Cathl 84-87; Suff Bp Grantham *Linc* 87-97; Dean Stamford 87-97; Can and Preb Linc Cathl 87-97; Bp Truro 97-08; rtd 08. *15 Dean Close, Melksham SN12 7EZ* T: (01225) 340979 E: frances.bill@blueyonder.co.uk

INDER, Patrick John. b 30. K Coll Lon BD 54 AKC 54 Huddersfield Univ MA 98. St Boniface Warminster. **d** 55 **p** 56. C St Margaret's-on-Thames *Lon* 55-57; C Golders Green 57-61; V Hanwell St Mellitus 61-77; R Rawmarsh w Parkgate *Sheff* 77-80; rtd 80; Hon C Sheff St Matt 82-88; PtO *Leeds* from 98; *Win* from 02. *14 Gracey Court, Woodland Road, Broadclyst, Exeter EX5 3GA* T: (01392) 462280 E: roucoulement@cwgsy.net

INESON, David Antony. b 36. ALCD 62. **d** 62 **p** 63. C Sandal St Helen *Wakef* 62-65; C Birm St Geo 66-71; V Horton *Bradf* 71-80; RD Bowling and Horton 78-80; V Sedbergh, Cautley and Garsdale 80-86; C Firbank, Howgill and Killington 81-86; TV Langley and Parkfield *Man* 86-88; TR Banbury *Ox* 92-98; R 98-01; rtd 01; PtO *Leeds* from 01. *11 Church Close, Redmire, Leyburn DL8 4HF* T: (01969) 624631 E: d.ineson@tiscali.co.uk

INESON, Emma Gwynneth. b 69. Birm Univ BA 92 MPhil 93 PhD 98. Trin Coll Bris BA 99. **d** 00 **p** 01. C Dore *Sheff* 00-03; Chapl Lee Abbey 03-06; Partnership P Inner Ring Partnership *Bris* 06-13; Tutor Trin Coll Bris 07-13; Bp's Chapl *Bris* 13-14; Prin Trin Coll Bris from 14; NSM Bris St Matt and St Nath 06-14. *Trinity College, Stoke Hill, Bristol BS9 1JP* T: 0117-968 2803 F: 968 7470 E: emmaineson@blueyonder.co.uk

INESON, John Michael. b 57. Leeds Univ BA 12. Yorks Min Course 09. **d** 12 **p** 13. NSM Utley *Leeds* from 12. *7 Badgergate, Wilsden, Bradford BD15 0NP* T: (01535) 273670 M: 07850-204114 E: ineson50@btinternet.com

INESON, Mathew David. b 69. Birm Univ BEng 91. Trin Coll Bris BA 99 MA 00. **d** 00 **p** 01. NSM Dore *Sheff* 00-03; Chapl

Lee Abbey 03-06; P-in-c Bris St Matt and St Nath 06-14; V 14; Min Inner Ring Partnership 06-14; AD City 10-14; P-in-c Stoke Bishop 14-15; V from 15. *St Mary's Vicarage, Mariner's Drive, Bristol BS9 1QJ* M: 07896-997604
E: matineson@blueyonder.co.uk

INESON, Matthew. b 68. Leeds Univ BA 00. Coll of Resurr Mirfield 97. **d** 00 **p** 01. C Owton Manor *Dur* 00-03; V Dalton *Sheff* 03-13. *17 Caulms Wood Road, Dewsbury WF13 1RU* M: 07780-686310 E: frmatt_@excite.com

INGALL, David Lenox. b 81. Jes Coll Cam MA 08. Wycliffe Hall Ox BA 08. **d** 09 **p** 10. C Holborn St Geo w H Trin and St Bart *Lon* 09-12; C Onslow Square and S Kensington St Aug 12-13; P-in-c St Sepulchre w Ch Ch Greyfriars etc from 13. *The Watch House, 10 Giltspur Street, London EC1A 9DE* M: 07968-119017
E: davidingall@gmail.com

INGAMELLS, Ronald Sidney. b 32. FCIPD 92. AKC 56. **d** 57 **p** 58. C Leeds Gipton Epiphany *Ripon* 57-59; C Gt Yarmouth *Nor* 59-64; Dioc Youth Officer 64-79; Hon C Nor St Pet Mancroft 64-79; P-in-c Lemsford *St Alb* 79-02; Sec Tr Development and Chr Educn Nat Coun YMCAs 79-92; Consultant to Romania Euro Alliance YMCAs 93-97; rtd 02; PtO *Ely* from 03. *2 Aragon Close, Buckden, St Neots PE19 5TY* T: (01480) 811608 E: rjingamells@btinternet.com

✠**INGE, The Rt Revd John Geoffrey.** b 55. St Chad's Coll Dur BSc 77 MA 94 PhD 02 Keble Coll Ox PGCE 79. Coll of Resurr Mirfield. **d** 84 **p** 85 **c** 03. Asst Chapl Lancing Coll 84-86; Jun Chapl Harrow Sch 86-89; Sen Chapl 89-90; V Wallsend St Luke *Newc* 90-96; Can Res Ely Cathl 96-03; Vice-Dean 99-03; Suff Bp Huntingdon *Ely* 03-07; Bp Worc from 07; Ld High Almoner from 13. *The Bishop's Office, The Old Palace, Deansway, Worcester WR1 2JE* T: (01905) 731599 F: 739382
E: bishop.worcester@cofe-worcester.org.uk

INGHAM, Anthony William. b 55. Ven English Coll Rome PhB 75 STB 78 NOC 98. **d** 78 **p** 79. In RC Ch 78-98; NSM Tottington *Man* 99-01; CF 01-15; P-in-c Beaulieu-sur-Mer *Eur* from 15. *Presbytère Anglican, 9 rue Paul-Doumer, 06310 beaulieu-sur-Mer, France* T: (0033) 4 93 01 45 61
E: chaplain@stmichaelsbeaulieusurmer.org

INGHAM, John Edmund. b 34. Reading Univ BA 56. Clifton Th Coll 58. **d** 60 **p** 61. C Rodbourne Cheney *Bris* 60-63; C Tunbridge Wells St Jo *Roch* 63-67; V Sevenoaks Weald 67-82; V Farrington Gurney *B & W* 82-92; V Paulton 82-92; RD Midsomer Norton 88-91; R Aspley Guise w Husborne Crawley and Ridgmont *St Alb* 92-99; rtd 99; PtO *B & W* from 00. *1 Garden Ground, Shepton Mallet BA4 4DJ* T: (01749) 345403
E: jsingham@talktalk.net

INGHAM, Malcolm John. b 68. Wycliffe Hall Ox BTh 99. **d** 99 **p** 00. C Moreton-in-Marsh w Batsford, Todenham etc *Glouc* 99-03; C Leckhampton SS Phil and Jas w Cheltenham St Jas 03-04; TV The Ortons, Alwalton and Chesterton *Ely* 04-10; P-in-c Elton w Stibbington and Water Newton 06-10; V Alwalton and Chesterton from 10. *St Andrew's Rectory, 4 Alwalton Hall, Alwalton, Peterborough PE7 3UN* T: (01733) 239289 M: 07974-394984
E: malcolm.ingham@yahoo.com

INGHAM, Mrs Carol Helen. *See* PHARAOH, Carol Helen

INGHAM, Mrs Pamela. b 47. MBE 96. NEOC 93. **d** 96 **p** 97. C Newc Epiphany 96-99; C Fawdon 99-00; P-in-c 00-06; Dioc Development Officer for Partners in Community Action 06-10; rtd 10; Hon C Tynemouth St Jo *Newc* from 12. *15 St George's Road, Cullercoats NE30 3JZ* E: pimbe@o2.co.uk

INGLE-GILLIS, William Clarke. b 68. Baylor Univ (USA) BA 90 MA 95 K Coll Lon PhD 04. Westcott Ho Cam 02. **d** 04 **p** 05. C Caldicot *Mon* 04-08; Dioc Soc Resp Officer 06-08; P-in-c Caerwent w Dinham and Llanvair Discoed etc 08-14; P-in-c Wentwood from 14; Tutor St Mich Coll Llan from 07. *19 Buzzard Close, Rogiet, Caldicot NP26 3UY* M: 07722-500805
E: w.c.ingle-gillis@cantab.net

INGLEBY, Canon Anthony Richard. b 48. Keele Univ BA 72. Trin Coll Bris. **d** 83 **p** 84. C Plymouth St Jude *Ex* 83-88; R Lanreath *Truro* 88-97; V Pelynt 88-97; RD W Wivelshire 96-97; P-in-c Stoke Climsland 97-05; P-in-c Linkinhorne 03-05; P-in-c Liskeard and St Keyne from 05; Chapl Cornwall and Is of Scilly Primary Care Trust 05-09; Hon Can Truro Cathl from 04; RD W Wivelshire 08-13; C Duloe, Herodsfoot, Morval and St Pinnock from 10. *The Rectory, Church Street, Liskeard PL14 3AQ* T: (01579) 342178
E: revtonyingleby@gmail.com

INGLEDEW, Peter David Gordon. b 48. AKC 77 Jo Dalton Coll Man CertEd 73 Croydon Coll DASS 92 CQSW 92 Univ Coll Chich BA 03. St Steph Ho Ox 77. **d** 78 **p** 79. C Whorlton *Newc* 78-81; C Poplar *Lon* 81-83; TV 83-85; V Tottenham H Trin 85-90; PtO *Chich* from 90. *11 St Luke's Terrace, Brighton BN2 2ZE* T: (01273) 689765 F: 389115
E: david.ingledew2@ntlworld.com

INGLES, Daniel Edward. b 78. Plymouth Univ BA 00. Ridley Hall Cam 12. **d** 14 **p** 15. C Beaminster Area *Sarum* from 14. *Orchard Cottage, Mosterton, Beaminster DT8 3HH* T: (01308) 867215 E: revdanielingles@hotmail.com

INGLESBY, Richard Eric. b 47. Birm Univ BSc 69 Bris Univ CertEd 74. Wycliffe Hall Ox 85. **d** 87 **p** 88. C Cheltenham Ch Ch *Glouc* 87-92; P-in-c Paulton *B & W* 92-94; V 94-01; P-in-c Farrington Gurney 92-94; V 94-01; P-in-c Moxley *Lich* 01-09; V 09-13; C Darlaston All SS 01-13; C Darlaston St Lawr 01-13; Ecum Adv (Wolverhampton Area) 04-08; RD Wednesbury *Lich* 05-12; Preb Lich Cathl 09-13; rtd 13. *32 Sandycroft Road, Churchdown, Gloucester GL3 1JH* T: (01452) 541509 E: r_inglesby@hotmail.com

INGLIS, Kelvin John. b 62. Ripon Coll Cuddesdon MTh 00. **d** 00 **p** 01. C Southampton Maybush St Pet *Win* 00-04; V Whitchurch w Tufton and Litchfield from 04; AD Whitchurch from 14. *The Vicarage, Church Street, Whitchurch RG28 7AS* T: (01256) 892535

INGLIS, Mark John. b 67. **d** 13 **p** 14. C Tupsley w Hampton Bishop *Heref* from 13. *23 Penn Grove Road, Hereford HR1 1BH* T: (01432) 360564

INGLIS-JONES, Valentine Walter. b 72. UEA BA 94 Univ of N Lon PGCE 95 Cam Univ BTh 07. Ridley Hall Cam 04. **d** 07 **p** 08. C Combe Down w Monkton Combe and S Stoke *B & W* 07-11; P-in-c Bramshott and Liphook *Portsm* from 11. *The Rectory, 22 Portsmouth Road, Liphook GU30 7DJ* T: (01428) 723750 M: 07917-151108 E: vwi20@cam.ac.uk

INGRAM, Canon Bernard Richard. b 40. Lon Coll of Div 66. **d** 66 **p** 67. C Bromley Common St Aug *Roch* 66-70; C Gravesend St Geo 70-74; Chapl Joyce Green Hosp Dartford 75-83; V Dartford St Edm *Roch* 75-83; V Strood St Fran 83-04; RD Strood 91-97; Hon Can Roch Cathl 00-04; rtd 04; PtO *Heref* from 05. *1 Hillview Cottage, Upper Colwall, Malvern WR13 6DH* T/F: (01684) 540475

INGRAM, Clodagh Mary. b 65. **d** 10 **p** 11. C Tuffley *Glouc* 10-13; NSM Churchdown from 13. *2 Coxmore Close, Hucclecote, Gloucester GL3 3SA* T: (01452) 618255 M: 07583-754960

INGRAM, Gary Simon. b 58. K Coll Lon BD AKC. Ripon Coll Cuddesdon. **d** 83 **p** 84. Chapl Nelson and Colne Coll 92-98; C Spalding St Mary and St Nic *Linc* 83-87; C Heaton Ch Ch *Man* 87-89; V Colne H Trin *Blackb* 89-98; RD Pendle 96-98; R Poulton-le-Sands w Morecambe St Laur 98-09; AD Lancaster 98-04; P-in-c Ferring *Chich* 09-11; V from 11. *The Vicarage, 19 Grange Park, Ferring, Worthing BN12 5LS* T: (01903) 241645
E: revgaryingram@googlemail.com

INGRAM, Canon Peter Anthony. b 53. NOC 83. **d** 86 **p** 87. C Maltby *Sheff* 86-89; TV Gt Snaith 89-92; R Adwick-le-Street w Skelbrooke 92-05; AD Adwick 01-05; V Millhouses H Trin 05-15; P-in-c Abbeydale St Jo 11-15; V Abbeydale and Millhouses from 15; AD Ecclesall 07-11; Hon Can Sheff Cathl from 05. *The Vicarage, 80 Millhouses Lane, Sheffield S7 2HB* T: 0114-236 2838
E: peter.ingram@sheffield.anglican.org

INGRAMS, Peter Douglas. b 56. Wheaton Coll Illinois BA 77 Ox Univ BA 80. Wycliffe Hall Ox 78. **d** 83 **p** 84. C Rowner *Portsm* 83-86; C Petersfield w Sheet 86-90; V Sheet 90-96; V Locks Heath 96-07; Local Min Officer *Cant* 07-15; Local Min and Growth Adv from 15. *12 Guildford Road, Canterbury CT1 3QD*

INKPIN, David Leonard. b 32. Liv Univ BSc 54 CChem MRSC 55. EMMTC 83. **d** 86 **p** 87. NSM Legsby, Linwood and Market Rasen *Linc* 86-04; PtO from 04. *Weelsby House, Legsby Road, Market Rasen LN8 3DY* T: (01673) 843360
E: inkypens@yahoo.co.uk

INKPIN, Jonathan David Francis. b 60. Mert Coll Ox MA 81 Dur Univ PhD 96. Ripon Coll Cuddesdon BA 85. **d** 86 **p** 87. C Hackney *Lon* 86-88; Tutor Ripon Coll Cuddesdon 88-90; C Cuddesdon *Ox* 88-90; TV Gateshead *Dur* 90-95; C Stanhope w Frosterley 95-01; C Eastgate w Rookhope 95-01; Dioc Rural Development Officer 95-01; Australia from 01. *78 Henry Parry Drive, PO Box 4255, Gosford East NSW 2250, Australia* T: (0061) (2) 4324 2630

INMAN, Daniel David. b 84. Wycliffe Hall Ox BA 05 Qu Coll Ox MSt 06 DPhil 09. Ripon Coll Cuddesdon 07. **d** 10 **p** 11. C Deddington w Barford, Clifton and Hempton *Ox* 10-13; Chapl Win Coll 13; Chapl Qu Coll Ox from 13. *The Queen's College, High Street, Oxford OX1 4AW* T: (01865) 279143 M: 07747-016370 E: daniel.inman@queens.ox.ac.uk

INMAN, Malcolm Gordon. b 33. Edin Th Coll 58. **d** 60 **p** 61. C Lundwood *Wakef* 60-63; C Heckmondwike 63-70; V Wrenthorpe 70-75; Chapl Cardigan Hosp 70-73; Asst Chapl Pinderfields Gen Hosp Wakef 72-73; V Cleckheaton St Jo *Wakef* 75-98; rtd 98; PtO *Wakef* 00-07; Hon C Staincliffe and Carlinghow *Leeds* from 07. *14 Briestfield Road, Thornhill Edge, Dewsbury WF12 0PW* T: (01924) 437171

INMAN, Mark Henry. b 31. Lon Univ BSc 53. EAMTC 80. d 83 p 84. Hon C Orford w Sudbourne, Chillesford, Butley and Iken *St E* 83-85; Chapl HM YOI Hollesley Bay Colony 85-91; Hon C Alderton w Ramsholt and Bawdsey *St E* 85-92; P-in-c 92-00; P-in-c Shottisham w Sutton 92-00; TV Wilford Peninsula 00-01; rtd 01; PtO *Nor* from 01. *Mill Farm House, Newton Road, Sporle, King's Lynn PE32 2DB* T: (01760) 722544

INMAN, Canon Thomas Jeremy. b 45. Rhodes Univ BA 67. St Steph Ho Ox 67. d 69 p 70. C Deptford St Paul *S'wark* 69-72; C Bellville S Africa 72-73; R Malmesbury 73-76; P-in-c Donnington *Chich* 76-80; V Hangleton 80-86; V Bosham 86-10; RD Westbourne 91-99; Can and Preb Chich Cathl 00-10; rtd 10; PtO *Bris* from 10. *3S Hunters Road, Bristol BS15 3EZ* T: 0117-960 5045 M: 07941-834914 E: tjinman45@gmail.com

INNES, Donald John. b 32. St Jo Coll Ox BA 54 MA. Westcott Ho Cam 56. d 56 p 57. C St Marylebone St Mark Hamilton Terrace *Lon* 56-58; C Walton-on-Thames *Guildf* 58-67; Chapl Moor Park Coll Farnham 67-76; P-in-c Tilford *Guildf* 76-97; rtd 97; PtO *Guildf* from 97. *Watchetts, 67A Upper Hale Road, Farnham GU9 0PA* T: (01252) 734597

INNES, Donald Keith. b 33. St Jo Coll Ox BA 56 MA 60 Lon Univ BD 58 Bris Univ MPhil 01. Clifton Th Coll 56. d 58 p 59. C Harold Hill St Paul *Chelmsf* 58-61; C Ealing Dean St Jo *Lon* 61-65; V Westacre and R Gayton Thorpe w E Walton *Nor* 65-70; V Woking St Paul *Guildf* 70-78; R Alfold and Loxwood 78-88; V Doddington w Wychling *Cant* 88-90; V Newnham 88-90; V Doddington, Newnham and Wychling 90-97; rtd 97; PtO *Chich* from 98. *6 Vicarage Close, Ringmer, Lewes BN8 5LF* T: (01273) 814995

✠**INNES, The Rt Revd Robert Neil.** b 59. K Coll Cam BA 82 MA 85 St Jo Coll Dur BA 91 Dur Univ PhD 95. Cranmer Hall Dur 89. d 95 p 96 c 14. C Dur St Cuth 95-97; C Shadforth and Sherburn w Pittington 97-99; Lect St Jo Coll Dur 95-99; P-in-c Belmont *Dur* 99-00; V 00-05; Sen Chapl and Chan Brussels Cathl 05-14; Chapl to The Queen 12-14; Bp Eur from 14. *avenue Princesse Paola 15, 1410 Waterloo, Belgium* T: (0032) (2) 213 7480 E: bishop.europe@churchofengland.org

INNES, Ms Ruth. b 56. New Coll Edin BD 00. TISEC 97. d 00 p 01. Prec St Ninian's Cathl Perth 00-02; P-in-c Linlithgow and Bathgate *Edin* 02-06; P-in-c Edin St Mark 06-10; R Falkirk from 10. *The Rectory, 55 Kerse Lane, Falkirk FK1 1RX* T: (01324) 623709 M: 07765-908829 E: ruth@ruthinnes.me.uk

INSLEY, Canon Michael George Pitron. b 47. Trin Coll Ox BA 69 MA 70 Nottm Univ MPhil 85. Wycliffe Hall Ox 69. d 72 p 73. C Beckenham Ch Ch *Roch* 72-76; P-in-c Cowden 76-79; Lect St Jo Coll Nottm 79-85; V Tidebrook and Wadhurst *Chich* 85-98; P-in-c Stonegate 95-98; Can and Preb Chich Cathl 94-98; P-in-c Horsmonden and Dioc Rural Officer *Roch* 98-03; V Bromley Common St Luke 03-12; Hon Can Th Roch Cathl 06-12; rtd 12; PtO *Roch* from 13. *22 Bridport Road, Dorchester DT1 1RS* T: (01305) 262412 E: michael.insley1@btinternet.com

INSTON, Brian John. b 47. SAOMC 95. d 98 p 99. C Bentley *Sheff* 98-01; V Balby 01-12; AD W Doncaster 07-11; rtd 12; PtO *Sheff* from 12. *62 Hindburn Close, Doncaster DN4 7RP* T: (01302) 534976 M: 07990-513120 E: bjinston@yahoo.co.uk

INVERNESS, Provost of. See STRANGE, The Rt Revd Jeremy

✠**INWOOD, The Rt Revd Richard Neil.** b 46. Univ Coll Ox BSc 70 MA 73 Nottm Univ BA 73. St Jo Coll Nottm 71. d 74 p 75 c 03. C Fulwood *Sheff* 74-78; C St Marylebone All So w SS Pet and Jo *Lon* 78-81; V Bath St Luke *B & W* 81-89; R Yeovil w Kingston Pitney 89-95; Preb Wells Cathl 90-95; Adn Halifax *Wakef* 95-03; Suff Bp Bedford *St Alb* 03-12; Cen Chapl MU 05-12; rtd 12; Hon Asst Bp Derby from 12. *43 Whitecotes Park, Chesterfield S40 3RT* T: (01246) 766288 E: richardinwood@btconnect.com

✠**IPGRAVE, The Rt Revd Michael Geoffrey.** b 58. OBE 11. Oriel Coll Ox BA 78 MA 94 St Chad's Coll Dur PhD 00 SOAS Lon MA 04. Ripon Coll Cuddesdon BA 81. d 82 p 83 c 12. C Oakham, Hambleton, Egleton, Braunston and Brooke *Pet* 82-85; Asst P Chiba Resurr Japan 85-87; TV Leic Ascension 87-90; TV Leic H Spirit 91-95; TR 95-99; P-in-c St Mary 93-94; Bp's Adv on Relns w People of Other Faiths 91-99; Bp's Dom Chapl 92-99; Hon Can Leic Cathl 94-04; Adv Inter-Faith Relns Abp's Coun 99-04; Sec Ch's Commission Inter Faith Relns 99-04; Hon C Leic Presentation 02-04; Adn S'wark 04-12; P-in-c S'wark St Geo w St Alphege and St Jude 06-07; P-in-c Peckham St Jo w St Andr 09-10; Can Missr 10-12; Area Bp Woolwich from 12; Dioc Warden of Readers from 14. *Trinity House, 4 Chapel Court, London SE1 1HW* T: (020) 7939 9407 E: bishop.michael@southwark.anglican.org

IQBAL, Javaid. b 71. Birm Univ MA 09. St Jo Coll Nottm BA 97. d 97 p 99. C Lahore St Thos Pakistan 97-99; P-in-c Lashore Ch Ch 99-00; Dir Miss and Evang Raiwind 98-99; PtO *Leic* 00-05; C Evington 05-07; P-in-c Thurmaston 07-08; TV Fosse 08-13; Hon Can Leic Cathl 11-13; TR Aldenham, Radlett and Shenley *St Alb* from 13. *The Vicarage, Church Field, Watling Street, Radlett WD7 8EE* T: (01923) 856606 M: 07782-169987 E: canoniqbal@gmail.com

IREDALE, Simon Peter. b 56. Cam Univ BA 78 MPhil 80. Wycliffe Hall Ox 83. d 86 p 87. C Thirsk *York* 86-89; Asst Chapl Norfolk and Nor Hosp 89-90; P-in-c Kexby w Wilberfoss *York* 90-93; Sub-Chapl HM Pris Full Sutton 90-93; Chapl RAF 93-06; PtO *Lich* from 14. *5 Grange Road, Albrighton, Wolverhampton WV7 3LD*

IRELAND, David Arthur. b 45. Mert Coll Ox BA 67 MA 71 MICFM 87. Cuddesdon Coll 67. d 69 p 70. C Chapel Allerton *Ripon* 69-72; C Harpenden St Nic *St Alb* 72-76; R Clifton 76-84; PtO *Guildf* 91-00; NSM Tattenham Corner and Burgh Heath 01-02; NSM Leatherhead and Mickleham 02-12; Chapl Box Hill Sch 05-12; rtd 12; PtO *Guildf* from 12. *St Michael's Lodge, Old London Road, Mickleham, Dorking RG5 6DU* E: rev.ireland43@btinternet.com

IRELAND, Leslie Sydney. b 55. York Univ BA 76. St Jo Coll Nottm 83. d 86 p 87. C Harwood *Man* 86-89; C Davyhulme St Mary 89-90; V Bardsley 90-99; R Levenshulme St Andr and St Pet 99-06; P-in-c Levenshulme St Mark 05-06; R Levenshulme 06-12; AD Heaton 04-12; R Lenzie *Glas* from 12. *58 Waverley Park, Kirkintilloch, Glasgow G66 2BP* T: 0141-776 3866 M: 07757-946184 E: rector@stcyprianslenzie.com or les949@btinternet.com

IRELAND, Mrs Lucy Annabel. b 53. Univ of Zimbabwe BSc 74. St Jo Coll Nottm. dss 85 d 87 p 95. Mansfield St Jo *S'well* 85-87; Hon Par Dn Harwood *Man* 87-89; NSM Bardsley 90-99; C Levenshulme St Andr and St Pet 99-06; C Levenshulme 06-12; NSM Glas E End from 13. *58 Waverley Park, Kirkintilloch, Glasgow G66 2BP* T: 0141-776 3866 M: 07583-884336 E: irelandla@hotmail.com

IRELAND, Mark Campbell. b 60. St Andr Univ MTheol 81 Sheff Univ MA 01. Wycliffe Hall Ox 82. d 84 p 85. C Blackb St Gabr 84-87; C Lancaster St Mary 87-89; Sub-Chapl HM Pris Lanc 87-89; V Baxenden *Blackb* 89-97; Dioc Missr *Lich* 98-07; TV Walsall 98-07; V Wellington All SS w Eyton from 07. *All Saints' Vicarage, 35 Crescent Road, Wellington, Telford TF1 3DW* T: (01952) 641251 E: vicar@allsaints-wellington.org

IRELAND, Mrs Mary Janet. b 52. EMMTC 96. d 99 p 00. NSM Kibworth and Smeeton Westerby and Saddington *Leic* 99-02; C Lutterworth w Cotesbach and Bitteswell 02-05; P-in-c Glen Magna cum Stretton Magna etc 05-13; R Gt w Lt Harrowden and Orlingbury and Isham etc *Pet* from 13. *The Vicarage, 18 King's Lane, Little Harrowden, Wellingborough NN9 5BL* E: mary_ireland@btinternet.com

IRELAND, Mrs Sharran. b 49. SEITE 95. d 98 p 99. C Appledore w Brookland, Fairfield, Brenzett etc *Cant* 98-01; TV St Laur in Thanet 01-03; TR 03-13; rtd 13; PtO *Cant* from 13. *Jamark, 13 Norman Road, Faversham ME13 8PX*

IRESON, David Christopher. b 45. Man Univ TCert 67 Birm Univ BEd 80. St Steph Ho Ox. d 93 p 94. C Minehead *B & W* 93-97; V St Decumans 97-08; rtd 08; PtO *B & W* from 11. *50 Camperdown Terrace, Exmouth EX8 1EQ* T: (01395) 263307 M: 07786-943967 E: decuman@hotmail.co.uk

IRESON, Ms Gillian Dorothy. b 39. Gilmore Ho 67. dss 72 d 87 p 94. Stepney St Dunstan and All SS *Lon* 72-99; Par Dn 87-94; C 94-99; rtd 99; PtO *Nor* from 00. *67 Glebe Road, Norwich NR2 3JH* T: (01603) 451969

IRESON, Philip. b 52. Newc Univ BSc 73. St Jo Coll Nottm. d 84 p 85. C Owlerton *Sheff* 84-87; V The Marshland 87-94; PtO *Linc* 90-93; Chapl HM YOI Hatfield 91-92; Bp's Rural Adv *Sheff* 91-00; R Firbeck w Letwell 94-01; V Woodsetts 94-01; Chapl HM Pris and YOI Doncaster 01-11; V Pitsmoor Ch Ch *Sheff* from 11; P-in-c Ellesmere St Pet from 13. *The Vicarage, 257 Pitsmoor Road, Sheffield S3 9AQ* T: 0114-272 7756 E: ireson61@gmail.com

IRESON, Richard Henry. b 46. Linc Th Coll 69. d 71 p 72. C Spilsby w Hundleby *Linc* 71-74; TV Grantham w Manthorpe 74-76; R Claypole 76-79; P-in-c Westborough w Dry Doddington and Stubton 76-77; R 77-79; R Bratoft w Irby-in-the-Marsh 79-86; V Burgh le Marsh 79-86; V Orby 79-86; R Welton-le-Marsh w Gunby 79-86; R Wyberton 86-01; RD Holland W 95-97; V Frampton 97-01; V Alford w Rigsby 01-06; R Well 01-06; R Saleby w Beesby and Maltby 01-06; V Bilsby w Farlesthorpe 01-06; R Hannah cum Hagnaby w Markby 01-06; R N Beltisloe Gp 06-11; rtd 11. *36 St Michael's Road, Louth LN11 9DA* T: (01507) 607170 E: r.ireson@uwclub.net

IRETON, Paul. b 65. Cranmer Hall Dur 99. d 01 p 02. C Southway *Ex* 01-06; P-in-c Torquay St Jo and Ellacombe

06-11; P-in-c Ellacombe Ch Ch from 11. *Silver Hill Lodge, Meadfoot Road, Torquay TQ1 2JP* T: (01803) 392813
E: revpireton@eurobell.co.uk

IRETON, Robert John. b 56. Bris Univ BEd. Oak Hill Th Coll BA. d 84 p 85. C Bromley Ch Ch *Roch* 84-87; TV Greystoke, Matterdale, Mungrisdale etc *Carl* 87-90; V Falconwood *Roch* 90-97; V Stanwix *Carl* 97-04; P-in-c Erith St Jo *Roch* 04-10; Chapl Trin Sch Belvedere 04-10; P-in-c Brinklow *Cov* 10-11; P-in-c Harborough Magna 10-11; P-in-c Monks Kirby w Pailton and Stretton-under-Fosse 10-11; P-in-c Churchover w Willey 10-11; R Revel Gp 11-13; rtd 13. *7 The Meadows, Bempton, Bridlington YO15 1LU* E: rireton@talktalk.net

IRONS, Nigel Richard. b 55. Aston Univ BSc 77. St Jo Coll Nottm MA 95. d 97 p 98. C Newchapel *Lich* 97-00; V Burton All SS w Ch Ch 00-14; TR Leek and Meerbrook from 14. *St Edward's Vicarage, 24 Ashenhurst Way, Leek ST13 5SB* E: mail@nigelirons.co.uk

IRONSIDE, John Edmund. b 31. Peterho Cam BA 55 MA 59. Qu Coll Birm 55. d 57 p 58. C Spring Park *Cant* 57-60; C Guernsey St Sampson *Win* 60-63; Thailand 63-66; V Guernsey St Jo *Win* 66-72; V Sholing 72-82; R Guernsey St Sampson 82-98; Miss to Seamen 82-98; rtd 98; PtO *Win* 98-07; P-in-c Guernsey St Andr 07-11; PtO *Chich* from 11. *1 Johnson Way, Ford, Arundel BN18 0TD* T: (01903) 722884 E: sarniaford@hotmail.co.uk

IRVINE, Mrs Andrea Mary. b 49. Sussex Univ BA 70 Ox Univ PGCE 71. NTMTC 99. d 02. NSM Cov H Trin 02-05; PtO 05-06; NSM Cov Cathl 06-12; PtO *Ely* from 13. *42 Pretoria Road, Cambridge CB4 1HE* T: (01223) 364128
E: amirvine@lineone.net

IRVINE (formerly SADLER), Ann Penrith. b 50. STETS 98. d 01 p 02. C Len Valley *Cant* 01-04; P-in-c Aylesham w Adisham 04-08; C Nonington w Wymynswold and Goodnestone etc 04-08; PtO 08-10. *Pilgrim Cottage, 16 Kilmahamogue Road, Moyarget, Ballycastle BT54 6JH* T: (028) 2076 3748
E: revann@uwclub.net

IRVINE, Barry. See IRVINE, William Barry

IRVINE, Mrs Catherine Frances. b 70. K Coll Lon BA 97. Ripon Coll Cuddesdon 99. d 01 p 02. C Romsey *Win* 01-05; TV Richmond St Mary w St Matthias and St Jo *S'wark* 05-11; Chapl R Holloway and Bedf New Coll *Guildf* from 11. *The Chaplaincy Office, Royal Holloway College, Egham Hill, Egham TW20 0EX* T: (01784) 443070 E: cate.irvine@rhul.ac.uk

IRVINE, Canon Christopher Paul. b 51. Nottm Univ BTh 75 Lanc Univ MA 76 St Martin's Coll Lanc PGCE 77. Kelham Th Coll 73. d 76 p 76. Chapl Lanc Univ *Blackb* 76-77; C Stoke Newington St Mary *Lon* 77-80; Chapl Sheff Univ 80-85; Chapl St Edm Hall Ox 85-90; Tutor St Steph Ho Ox 85-90; Vice-Prin 91-94; V Cowley St Jo *Ox* 94-98; Prin Coll of Resurr Mirfield 98-07; Can Res and Lib Cant Cathl from 07. *19 The Precincts, Canterbury CT1 2EP* T: (01227) 762862
E: irvinec@canterbury-cathedral.org

IRVINE, Clyde. See IRVINE, James Clyde

IRVINE, David John. b 50. Trin Coll Cam BA 72 MA 75. NOC 91. d 94 p 95. C Hexham *Newc* 94-99; P-in-c Blanchland w Hunstanworth and Edmundbyers etc 99-13; P-in-c Slaley 99-13; P-in-c Healey 03-13; P-in-c Whittonstall 03-13; rtd 13. *25 Charles Street, Pittenweem, Anstruther KY10 2QH* T: (01333) 311868 E: davidirvine190@btinternet.com

IRVINE, Donald Andrew. b 45. Trin Coll Bris 94. d 96 p 97. C Allington and Maidstone St Pet *Cant* 96-99; P-in-c Harrietsham w Ulcombe 99-02; P-in-c Lenham w Boughton Malherbe 00-02; R Len Valley 02-07; TV Whitstable 07-10. *Pilgrim Cottage, 16 Kilmahamogue Road, Moyarget, Ballycastle BT54 6JH* T: (028) 2076 3748 M: 07932-149495
E: don.irvine35@gmail.com

IRVINE, Gerard Philip. b 30. QUB BA 52. Edin Th Coll 56. d 56 p 57. Chapl St Andr Cathl 56-58; Prec St Andr Cathl 58-59; C Belfast Malone St Jo *Conn* 61-66; Chapl Community of St Jo Ev Dublin 67-77; C Dublin Sandymount *D & G* 77-97; rtd 97. *12A Carraig na Greine House, Coliemore Road, Dalkey, Co Dublin, Republic of Ireland* T: (00353) (1) 230 1430

IRVINE, James Clyde. b 35. QUB BA 57 NUU BPhil(Ed) 83. CITC 59. d 59 p 60. C Belfast St Luke *Conn* 59-62; C Lisburn Ch Ch Cathl 62-65; R Duneane w Ballyscullion 65-69; I Kilbride 69-74; Hd of RE Ballyclare High Sch 73-98; Bp's C Killead w Gartree 98-05; rtd 05. *1A Rathmena Avenue, Ballyclare BT39 9HX* T: (028) 9332 2933
E: irvineclyde@live.co.uk

IRVINE, The Very Revd John Dudley. b 49. Sussex Univ BA 70. Wycliffe Hall Ox BA 80. d 81 p 82. C Brompton H Trin w Onslow Square St Paul *Lon* 81-85; P-in-c Kensington St Barn 85-94; V 94-01; Dean Cov 01-12; P-in-c Cov St Fran N Radford 06-12; C Cambridge H Trin *Ely* from 12. *42 Pretoria Road, Cambridge CB4 1HE* T: (01223) 364128
E: jdirvine@lineone.net

IRVINE, Simon Timothy. b 74. CITC 00. d 03 p 04. C Dublin Ch Ch Cathl Gp 03-06; Chapl Dublin Sandymount 06-11; Chapl Rathdown Sch 06-10; C Kilkenny w Aghour and Kilmanagh *C & O* 12-14; I from 14. *The Vicar's Residence, The Close, Coach Road, Kilkenny, Republic of Ireland* T: (00353) (56) 777 1998 M: 87-944 4113 E: vicar.cathedral@ossory.anglican.org

IRVINE, Stanley. b 35. TCD. d 83 p 84. C Arm St Mark w Aghavilly 83-85; I Kilmoremoy w Castleconnor, Easkey, Kilglass etc *T, K & A* 85-93; Dom Chapl to Bp Tuam 88-94; I Stranorlar w Meenglas and Kilteevogue *D & R* 94-05; Bp's Dom Chapl 01-05; Can Raphoe Cathl 02-05; rtd 05. *3 Inisfayle Crescent, Bangor BT19 1DT* T: (028) 9146 2012

IRVINE, Suzanne. See VERNON-YORKE, Suzanne

IRVINE, William Barry. b 48. QUB BD 75. St Jo Coll Nottm 75. d 76 p 77. C Belfast St Mich *Conn* 76-80; C Mansfield SS Pet and Paul *S'well* 80-84; V Chapel-en-le-Frith *Derby* 84-90; Chapl Cheltenham Gen and Delancey Hosps 90-94; Chapl E Glos NHS Trust 94-02; Chapl Glos Hosps NHS Foundn Trust from 02. *Cheltenham General Hospital, Sandford Road, Cheltenham GL53 7AN* T: (01242) 274286 or 222222 ext 4286

IRVINE-CAPEL, Luke Thomas. b 75. Greyfriars Ox BA 97 MA 01 Leeds Univ MA 99. Coll of Resurr Mirfield 97. d 99 p 00. C Abertillery w Cwmtillery w Six Bells *Mon* 99-01; Chapl Coleg Gwent 99-01; Min Can St Woolos Cathl 01-03; Sub-Chapl HM Pris Cardiff 02-03; R Cranford *Lon* 03-08; V Pimlico St Gabr 08-13; P-in-c St Leonards Ch Ch and St Mary etc *Chich* 13-14; R from 14. *Christ Church Rectory, 3 Silchester Road, St Leonards-on-Sea TN38 0JB*
E: ltic75@hotmail.com

IRVING, Canon Andrew. b 27. St Deiniol's Hawarden 62. d 65 p 66. C Benwell St Jas *Newc* 65-69; C Langley Marish *Ox* 69-73; V Moulsford 73-81; Canada from 81; rtd 92. *3615 Lever Court, Peachland BC V0H 1X5, Canada* T: (001) (250) 767 9582

IRVING, Canon Michael John Derek. b 43. LVO 07 DL 09. BEd 80. Qu Coll Birm 80. d 81 p 82. C Coleford w Staunton *Glouc* 81-84; V Dean Forest H Trin 84-91; RD Forest S 88-91; P-in-c Hempsted and Dir of Ords 91-96; R Minchinhampton 96-08; Hon Can Glouc Cathl 94-08; rtd 08. *9 Canton Acre, Painswick, Stroud GL6 6QX* T: (01452) 814242
E: irvings@vale-view.co.uk

IRVING, Paul John. b 74. Univ of Wales (Ban) BA 96 Bris Univ PGCE 97. Trin Coll Bris BA 10. d 10 p 11. C Galmington *B & W* 10-14; TV Redditch H Trin *Worc* from 14. *St Leonard's Vicarage, Church Hill, Beoley, Redditch B98 9AR*
E: irvings@waitrose.com

IRWIN, Mrs Patricia Jane. b 49. CBDTI 02. d 05 p 06. NSM S Carl 05-10; rtd 10; PtO *Carl* from 11. *31 Blackwell Road, Carlisle CA2 4AB* T: (01228) 526885
E: patriciairwin057@btinternet.com

IRWIN, Patrick Alexander. b 55. BNC Ox BA 77 MA 81 Edin Univ BD 81. Edin Th Coll 77 Liturgisches Inst Trier 79. d 81 p 82. Hon C Cambridge St Botolph *Ely* 81-84; Chapl BNC Ox 84-92; Lect Th 86-92; CF 92-99; Sen CF 99-10; Chapl Guards Chpl Lon 05-07; Dir of Ords 05-07; Chapl Udruga Hrvata Sv Dominik Gorazde 94-95; PtO *D & G* from 87; *Arm* from 96; *Guildf* 99-02; *Leeds* from 00; Hon V Choral Arm Cathl 02-07; PtO *Eur* 08-10 and from 13; Chapl Bucharest w Sofia 10-13; Lect St Trivelius Inst Sofia Bulgaria 13-14. *Hedgebank, 8 Paganel Road, Minehead TA24 5ET* T: (01643) 703509
E: patalexirwin@yahoo.co.uk

IRWIN, Stewart. b 53. Sarum & Wells Th Coll 80. d 83 p 84. C Brighouse *Wakef* 83-87; V Stockton St Jo *Dur* 87-95; V Howden-le-Wear and Hunwick 95-13; rtd 13; PtO *Dur* from 13. *22 South View, Hunwick, Crook DL15 0JW*

IRWIN, Miss Susan Elizabeth. b 47. Cranmer Hall Dur 77. dss 79 d 87 p 94. Harborne St Faith and St Laur *Birm* 79-82; Caterham *S'wark* 82-88; Par Dn 87-88; Par Dn Kidlington w Hampton Poyle *Ox* 88-94; C 94-95; TV Gt Marlow w Marlow Bottom, Lt Marlow and Bisham 95-06; R Powick and Guarlford and Madresfield w Newland *Worc* from 06. *The Vicarage, 31 The Greenway, Powick, Worcester WR2 4RZ* T: (01905) 830270 M: 07703-350301
E: vicarage@powickparish.org.uk

IRWIN, Canon William George. b 53. QUB BSc 77. CITC 80. d 80 p 81. C Lisburn St Paul *Conn* 80-83; C Seagoe *D & D* 83-85; C Newtownards w Movilla Abbey 85-88; I Ballymacash *Conn* from 88; Preb Conn Cathl from 04; Treas Conn Cathl from 12. *St Mark's Rectory, 97 Antrim Road, Lisburn BT28 3EA* T: (028) 9266 2393 E: wgirwin@btopenworld.com

IRWIN-CLARK, Peter Elliot. b 49. Univ Coll Lon LLB 71 Barrister 72. Cranmer Hall Dur BA 80. d 81 p 82. C Kirkheaton *Wakef* 81-86; V Shirley *Win* 86-96; PtO *Chich* 96-97; *S'wark* 97; V Prestonville St Luke *Chich* 97-03; Missr Warham Trust and Faith Development Officer (Basingstoke Adnry) *Win* 03-08; TR Broadwater *Chich* from 08. *The Rectory, 8 Sompting Avenue, Worthing BN14 8HN* T: (01903) 823996 E: rector@broadwaterparish.com

ISAAC, Canon David Thomas. b 43. Univ of Wales BA 65. Cuddesdon Coll 65. **d** 67 **p** 68. C Llandaff w Capel Llanilltern *Llan* 67-71; P-in-c Swansea St Jas *S & B* 71-73; Chapl Ch in Wales Youth Coun 73-77; V Llangiwg *S & B* 77-79; Dioc Youth Officer *Ripon* 79-83; Nat Officer for Youth Work Gen Syn Bd of Educn 83-90; Can Res Portsm Cathl 90-14; Dioc Dir of Educn 90-06; Hd Miss and Discipleship 06-14; Warden of Readers 11-14; rtd 14; PtO *Portsm* from 15. *11 Wray Street, Ryde PO33 3ED* M: 07768-997220

ISAAC, Mrs Patricia Jane. b 59. Leeds Univ BA 80 Univ Coll Lon MA 82. STETS 11. **d** 14 **p** 15. C Ryde All SS *Portsm* from 14; C Swanmore St Mich from 14. *St Michael's Vicarage, 11 Wray Street, Ryde PO33 3ED* T: (01983) 616678
E: pjisaac@btinternet.com

ISAACS, James Alexander. b 84. Ex Univ BA 06. Oak Hill Th Coll BA 15. **d** 15. C Hailsham *Chich* from 15. *9 Riggers Way, Hailsham BN27 1FL* M: 07872-111354
E: jamesis84@hotmail.com

ISAACS, John Kenneth. b 36. Cam Univ MA. EAMTC. **d** 82 **p** 83. NSM Ely 82-85; Chapl K Sch Ely 85-94; LtO *Ely* 85-94; P-in-c Denver 94-02; P-in-c Ryston w Roxham 94-02; P-in-c W Dereham 94-02; R Denver and Ryston w Roxham and W Dereham etc 02-03; rtd 03; PtO *Ely* from 03. *18 Barton Road, Ely CB7 4DE* T: (01353) 666936
E: john.isaacs@ely.anglican.org

ISAACSON, Alan Timothy. b 55. York Univ BA 77 Sheff Univ PGCE 84 Leeds Univ MA 97. NOC 94. **d** 96 **p** 97. C Kimberworth *Sheff* 96-99; TV Brinsworth w Catcliffe and Treeton 99-03; TV Rivers Team 03-07; R Bradfield from 07; Dioc Discipleship Development Officer from 07; AD Ecclesfield from 14. *The Rectory, High Bradfield, Bradfield, Sheffield S6 6LG* T: 0114-285 1225
E: alan.isaacson@sheffield.anglican.org

ISAACSON, Hilda Ruth. b 57. Leeds Univ BA 10. NOC 07. **d** 09 **p** 10. C Deepcar *Sheff* 09-13; P-in-c from 13; P-in-c Bolsterstone from 14. *The Rectory, High Bradfield, Bradfield, Sheffield S6 6LG* T: 0114-285 1225 M: 07762-075687
E: hilda.isaacson@sheffield.anglican.org

ISABEL, Sister. *See* KEEGAN, Frances Ann

ISAM, Miss Margaret Myra Elizabeth (Wendy). b 35. Nottm Univ BEd 73. EMMTC 78. **dss** 81 **d** 87 **p** 94. Humberston *Linc* 81-84; Gt Grimsby St Andr and St Luke 85-93; Dn-in-c 87-93; P-in-c Gt Grimsby St Andr w St Luke and All SS 94-97; V 97-00; rtd 00; PtO *Linc* from 00. *18 Grainsby Avenue, Cleethorpes DN35 9PA* T: (01472) 699821 M: 07950-464542

ISBISTER, Charles. b 27. Chich Th Coll 58. **d** 60 **p** 61. C Tynemouth Ch Ch *Newc* 60-64; C Boyne Hill *Ox* 64-67; V Cookridge H Trin *Ripon* 67-83; rtd 83; PtO *Leeds* from 01. *2 Church Mount, Horsforth, Leeds LS18 5LE* T: 0113-239 0813 M: 07714-356059

ISHERWOOD, Mrs Claire Virginia. b 54. Liv Univ BDS 76 K Alfred's Coll Win PGCE 92. **d** 10 **p** 11. OLM Camberley St Paul *Guildf* from 10. *37 Watchetts Drive, Camberley GU15 2PQ* T: (01276) 505015 M: 07854-549154
E: claire.isherwood@ntlworld.com

ISHERWOOD, Canon David Owen. b 46. BA 68 Lon Univ MA 95 MPhil 87. Ridley Hall Cam 76. **d** 78 **p** 79. C Sanderstead All SS *S'wark* 78-82; C Horley 82-84; TV 84-88; P-in-c Streatham Immanuel and St Andr 88-89; V 89-95; TR Clapham Team 95-01; V Clapham H Trin and St Pet from 02; Hon Can S'wark Cathl from 06. *25 The Chase, London SW4 0NP* T: (020) 7498 6879 *or* 7627 0941 F: 7978 1327 *or* 7627 5065
E: rector@holytrinityclapham.org *or* david.htc@lineone.net

ISHERWOOD, Robin James. b 56. Hull Univ BA 78 Uppsala Univ MDiv 92. Ripon Coll Cuddesdon 92. **d** 94 **p** 95. C Bramhall *Ches* 94-98; V Alsager St Mary 98-14; Chapl Charterhouse from 14; Hon Chapl ATC from 99. *Charterhouse Sutton's Hospital, The Charterhouse, Charterhouse Square, London EC1M 6AN* T: (020) 7253 9503
E: robinjisherwood@googlemail.com

ISHERWOOD, Samuel Peter. b 34. Lon Coll of Div ALCD 62 LTh 74. **d** 62 **p** 63. C Bacup St Sav *Man* 62-65; C Man Albert Memorial Ch 65-67; V Livesey *Blackb* 67-79; V Handforth *Ches* 79-99; RD Cheadle 92-99; rtd 99; PtO *York* from 00. *1 Andrew Drive, Huntington, York YO32 9YF* T: (01904) 438116

ISIORHO, David John Phillip. b 58. Liv Poly BA 80 Warwick Univ MA 93 Bradf Univ PhD 98. Westcott Ho Cam 87. **d** 90 **p** 91. C Nuneaton St Mary *Cov* 90-93; P-in-c Bradf St Oswald Chapel Green 93-96; P-in-c Brereton *Lich* 96-00; P-in-c Arthingworth, Harrington w Oxendon and E Farndon *Pet* 00-05; P-in-c Maidwell w Draughton, Lamport w Faxton 01-05; V Kempston Transfiguration *St Alb* 05-09; V Handsworth St Jas *Birm* from 09. *St James's Vicarage, 21 Austin Road, Birmingham B21 8NU* T: 0121-554 4151
E: davidisiorho@catholic.org

ISIORHO (née NORTHALL), Mrs Linda Barbara. b 50. Birm Univ BA 72 Worc Coll of Educn PGCE 75. Qu Coll Birm 88. **d** 90 **p** 94. C Wood End *Cov* 90-91; PtO 91-93; *Bradf* 93-94; NSM Low Moor St Mark 94-96; PtO *Lich* 96-97; NSM Alrewas 97-00; PtO *Pet* 01-05; *Birm* from 10. *St James's Vicarage, 21 Austin Road, Birmingham B21 8NU* T: 0121-507 0370

ISITT, Norman. b 34. St Jo Coll Dur BA 56. Cranmer Hall Dur. **d** 59 **p** 60. C Loughton St Mary *Chelmsf* 59-62; C Moulsham St Jo 62-64; Billericay Co Sch 64-90; Squirrels Heath Sch Romford 64-90; Althorpe and Keadby Co Sch 66-95; rtd 95. *21 Cambridge Avenue, Bottesford, Scunthorpe DN16 3LT* T: (01724) 851489

ISKANDER, Mrs Susan Mary Mackay. b 64. Ox Univ BA 85 MBA 93. NTMTC 05. **d** 08 **p** 09. NSM Writtle w Highwood *Chelmsf* 08-12; PtO 12-13; P-in-c E Hanningfield 13-15; P-in-c Springfield All SS from 15. *The Rectory, 4 Old School Field, Springfield, Chelmsford CM1 7HU* M: 07710-646297
E: revsusaniskander@gmail.com

ISLE OF WIGHT, Archdeacon of. *See* SUTTON, The Ven Peter Allerton

ISON, Andrew Phillip. b 60. Imp Coll Lon BEng 82 Penn Univ MSE 83 Univ Coll Lon PhD 87 CEng 92 MIChemE 92. Trin Coll Bris BA 01. **d** 01 **p** 02. C Cleethorpes *Linc* 01-05; V Bestwood Park w Rise Park *S'well* 05-07; Chapl Voorschoten *Eur* 07-12; V Gt and Lt Driffield *York* from 12; V Langtoft w Foxholes, Butterwick, Cottam etc from 12. *The Vicarage, Downe Street, Driffield YO25 6DX* T: (01377) 257712 M: 07599-125700 E: rev.andrew.ison@btinternet.com

ISON, The Very Revd David John. b 54. Leic Univ BA 76 Nottm Univ BA 78 K Coll Lon PhD 85. St Jo Coll Nottm 76. **d** 79 **p** 80. C Deptford St Nic and St Luke *S'wark* 79-85; Lect CA Tr Coll Blackheath 85-88; V Potters Green *Cov* 88-93; Jt Dir SWMTC *Ex* 93-95; Dioc Officer for CME 93-05; Bp's Officer for NSMs 97-05; Can Res Ex Cathl 95-05; Chan 97-05; Dean Bradf 05-12; Dean St Paul's Lon from 12. *The Chapter House, St Paul's Churchyard, London EC4M 8AD* T: (020) 7236 2827 F: (020) 7248 3104 E: dean@stpaulscathedral.org.uk

ISON, Mrs Hilary Margaret. b 55. Leic Univ BA 76 E Lon Univ MA 02. Gilmore Course 77. **d** 87 **p** 94. NSM Deptford St Nic and St Luke *S'wark* 87-88; NSM Potters Green *Cov* 88-90; C Rugby 90-93; Chapl Ex Hospiscare 93-00; C Ex St Mark, St Sidwell and St Matt 99-02; Bp's Adv for Women in Min 02-05; Area Tutor SWMTC 03-05; PV Ex Cathl 04-05; Tutor Coll of Resurr Mirfield 05-08; Selection Sec Min Division from 08; Hon C Calverley Deanery *Bradf* 06-12. *The Deanery, 9 Amen Court, London EC4M 7BU*
E: hilary.ison@churchofengland.org

ISSBERNER, Norman Gunther Erich. b 34. Fitzw Ho Cam BA 58 MA 61. Clifton Th Coll 57. **d** 59 **p** 60. C Croydon Ch Ch Broad Green *Cant* 59-61; C Surbiton Hill Ch Ch *S'wark* 61-66; V Egham *Guildf* 66-75; V Wallington *S'wark* 75-86; UK Chmn Africa Inland Miss from 77; Adv on Miss and Evang *Chelmsf* 86-91; P-in-c Castle Hedingham 91-93; V Clacton St Paul 93-99; RD St Osyth 94-99; rtd 99; PtO *Chelmsf* from 99. *14 Darcy Close, Frinton-on-Sea CO13 0RR* T: (01255) 673548
E: nissb@zoom.co.uk

ITALY AND MALTA, Archdeacon of. *See* BOARDMAN, The Ven Jonathan

ITUMU, John Murithi. b 65. Lon Sch of Th BA 04 Heythrop Coll Lon MA 10. Lon Bible Coll 01. **d** 02 **p** 03. C Cricklewood St Gabr and St Mich *Lon* 02-07; C Herne Hill *S'wark* 07-10; P-in-c Glouc St Cath 10-12; V from 12. *5 Kenilworth Avenue, Gloucester GL2 0QJ* T: (01452) 502673 M: 07946-000364
E: vicar@stcatharine.org.uk

IVE, Jeremy George Augustus. b 57. Rhodes Univ BA 81 Ch Coll Cam PhD 86 K Coll Lon MPhil 95. Wycliffe Hall Ox 89. **d** 91 **p** 92. NSM Ivybridge w Harford *Ex* 91-95; P-in-c Abbotskerswell 95-99; P-in-c Tudeley cum Capel w Five Oak Green *Roch* from 99; Dioc Lay Min Adv 99-01. *The Vicarage, Sychem Lane, Five Oak Green, Tonbridge TN12 6TL* T/F: (01892) 836653 M: 07720-841169 E: jeremy.ive@diocese-rochester.org *or* jeremy@tudeley.org

IVE (née KNOTT), Mrs Pamela Frances. b 58. Bedf Coll of Educn BEd 79. Wycliffe Hall Ox 88. **d** 90. Par Dn Ivybridge w Harford *Ex* 90-95; Par Dn Abbotskerswell 95-99; Par Dn Tudeley cum Capel w Five Oak Green *Roch* from 99. *The Vicarage, Sychem Lane, Five Oak Green, Tonbridge TN12 6TL* T/F: (01892) 836653 T: 835548
E: pamela.ive@diocese-rochester.org *or* pamela@tudeley.org

IVELL, Robert William. b 45. Lon Univ BSc 71 Liv Univ CertEd. Ridley Hall Cam 83. **d** 85 **p** 86. C Wadsley *Sheff* 85-88; V Laughton w Throapham 88-96; V Wadworth w Loversall 96-06; rtd 06. *1 Wellbank, 20 Burrell Street, Crieff PH7 4DT* T: (01764) 652057

IVES, Mrs Susan Ethel. b 48. EAMTC 98. **d** 01 **p** 02. NSM Moulsham St Luke *Chelmsf* 01-08; Educn and Par Links Adv Chelmsf Deaneries 07-13; NSM Chelmsf St Andr 08-15; NSM Roxwell from 15; NSM Writtle w Highwood from 15. *47 Long Brandocks, Writtle, Chelmsford CM1 3JL* T: (01245) 420325 M: 07964-538485 E: revdsusanives@gmail.com

IVESON, Mrs Patricia Jill. b 35. Cam Univ CertEd 55 K Coll Lon BD 76 AKC 76. **dss** 81 **d** 87 **p** 94. Wilmington *Roch* 81-87; Hon Par Dn 87-94; Hon C from 94; Chapl Dartford and Gravesham NHS Trust 87-04. *The Birches, 15 Wallis Close, Wilmington, Dartford DA2 7BE* T: (01322) 279100 M: 07811-286219 E: pat.iveson@diocese-rochester.org

IVESON, Robert George. b 70. Oak Hill Th Coll BA 01. **d** 01 **p** 02. C Cheadle All Hallows *Ches* 01-04; C-in-c Cheadle Hulme Em CD 04-14; R Davenham from 14. *The Rectory, 44 Church Street, Davenham, Northwich CW9 8NF* E: rob.iveson@btinternet.com

IVESON, Ronald Edward. b 68. Ches Coll of HE RMN 92. Aston Tr Scheme 95 Oak Hill Th Coll BA 00. **d** 00 **p** 01. C Lache cum Saltney *Ches* 00-03; V Bidston from 03. *The Vicarage, 6 Statham Road, Prenton CH43 7XS* T: 0151-652 4852 *or* 653 4584 E: roniveson@hotmail.com

IVISON, Norman William. b 54. Hull Univ BA 75 DipEd 76 Dur Univ MA(Theol) 12. Trin Coll Bris. **d** 82 **p** 83. C Barrow St Mark *Carl* 82-85; Ecum Liaison Officer BBC Radio Furness 82-85; Chapl Barrow Sixth Form Coll 83-85; Dioc Broadcasting Officer *Lich* 85-91; Relig Progr Producer BBC Radio Stoke 85-91; Hon C Bucknall and Bagnall *Lich* 85-91; Asst Producer Relig Progr BBC TV Man 91-93; Producer Relig and Ethics BBC TV Man 93-05; Dir Tr and Events Fresh Expressions 05-08; Dir Communications and Resources from 08; PtO *Blackb* from 98. *18 Spa Garth, Clitheroe BB7 1JD* T/F: (01200) 442004 M: 07885-866317 E: norman.ivison@freshexpressions.org.uk

IVORSON, David. b 51. Mansf Coll Ox MA 73 York Univ BPhil 75 ACA 80. SEITE 05. **d** 08 **p** 09. NSM E Grinstead St Swithun *Chich* 08-11; Chapl Whittington Coll Felbridge from 11. *Woodhurst, Portland Road, East Grinstead RH19 4DZ* T: (01342) 316451 M: 07787-155154 E: david@ivorson.com

IVORY, Canon Christopher James. b 54. Reading Univ BSc 76. Qu Coll Birm. **d** 81 **p** 82. C Waltham Cross *St Alb* 81-84; C Is of Dogs Ch Ch and St Jo w St Luke *Lon* 84-88; V Streatham Ch Ch *S'wark* 88-03; Lambeth Adnry Ecum Officer 90-95; RD Streatham 00-03; R King's Lynn St Marg w St Nic *Nor* from 03; RD Lynn 08-13; Hon Can Nor Cathl from 08. *St Margaret's Vicarage, St Margaret's Place, King's Lynn PE30 5DL* T: (01553) 767090 E: vicar@stmargaretskingslynn.org.uk

IWANUSCHAK, Victor. b 51. Coll of Ripon & York St Jo MA 00. NOC 97. **d** 00 **p** 01. C Pontefract All SS *Wakef* 00-03; P-in-c *Leeds* from 03. *All Saints' Vicarage, Grenton, South Baileygate, Pontefract WF8 2JL* T: (01977) 695590 M: 07734-710254 E: iwanuschak@triom.net

IWUAGWU, Chukwuemeka Onundgbo. b 82. Imo State Univ Nigeria BSc 04 Glas Caledonian Univ MSc 07. **d** 09 **p** 12. NSM St Mary's Cathl 10-15; Chapl Glas Caledonian Univ 12-15; NSM Haslemere and Grayswood *Guildf* from 15. *Address temp unknown* M: 07878-854220 E: chukusus@yahoo.com

IZOD, Mrs Wendy Janet. b 47. Sheff Univ BSc(Econ) 68. SEITE 98. **d** 01 **p** 02. NSM Hever, Four Elms and Mark Beech *Roch* from 01; Chapl ATC from 01. *West Lodge, Stick Hill, Edenbridge TN8 5NJ* T: (01342) 850738 F: 850077 M: 07703-107496 E: izod.calligraphy@btinternet.com

IZZARD, David Antony. b 55. Trin Coll Bris 92. **d** 94 **p** 95. C E Bris 94-98; V Sea Mills from 98. *St Edyth's Vicarage, Avonleaze, Bristol BS9 2HU* T: 0117-968 1912 *or* 968 6965 E: clan.izzard@ukgateway.net

IZZARD, Ms Susannah Amanda. b 59. Hatf Poly BA 82 Birm Univ MEd 93 Wolv Univ PGCE 92. Trin Coll Bris BA 86. **dss** 86 **d** 87 **p** 01. Birm St Martin w Bordesley St Andr 86-89; Par Dn 87-89; C Handsworth St Jas 89-91; Asst Chapl Qu Eliz Hosp Birm 90-91; Lect Birm Univ 93-02; NSM Selly Oak St Mary 01-12; PtO from 12; Bp's Adv for Pastoral Care from 07. *2 Hemyock Road, Birmingham B29 4DG* M: 07702-571760 E: susannah.izzard@blueyonder.co.uk

J

JABLONSKI, Andrew Philip. b 54. St Jo Coll Cam MA 76 Nottm Univ MBA 90 Anglia Ruskin Univ MA 10 CEng 90 FIMechE 02. Ridley Hall Cam 07. **d** 09 **p** 10. NSM Grantham, Harrowby w Londonthorpe *Linc* 09-12; C Bromley SS Pet and Paul *Roch* from 12. *The Vicarage, 9 St Paul's Square, Bromley BR2 0XH* T: (020) 8460 6275 M: 07736-649401 E: andrewjab@virginmedia.com

JABLONSKI, Mrs Anne Judith. b 54. Girton Coll Cam BA 76 MA 79. Ridley Hall Cam 07. **d** 09 **p** 10. C Grantham *Linc* 09-12; V Bromley SS Pet and Paul *Roch* from 12. *The Vicarage, 9 St Paul's Square, Bromley BR2 0XH* T: (020) 8460 6275 M: 07759-661836 E: annejab1@virginmedia.com

JACK, Judith Ann. *See* JEFFERY, Judith Ann

JACK, Paul. b 65. QUB BSc 92 Univ Coll Galway MSc 94 TCD BTh 99. CITC 96. **d** 99 **p** 00. C Jordanstown *Conn* 99-01; C Seagoe *D & D* 01-07; I Belfast St Simon w St Phil *Conn* 07-12; I Belfast St Thos from 12; Bp's Dom Chapl from 08. *St Thomas's Rectory, 1A Eglantine Avenue, Belfast BT9 6DW* T: (028) 9066 8332 *or* 9066 6426 E: paul@jack11.wanadoo.co.uk

JACK, Philip Andrew. b 76. Nottm Univ BA 98. Oak Hill Th Coll BA 08. **d** 08 **p** 09. C Ox St Ebbe w H Trin and St Pet 08-12; NSM 12-13; Chapl Canford Sch from 13. *Canford School, Canford Magna, Wimborne BH21 3AD* T: (01202) 841254 M: 07972-078148 E: phil.a.jack@gmail.com

JACKLIN, John Frederick. b 30. Oak Hill Th Coll 72. **d** 72 **p** 72. Chile 72-75; C Roxeth Ch Ch *Lon* 75-78; V Selston *S'well* 78-95; rtd 95; PtO *Derby* from 97. *5 Rose Avenue, Borrowash, Derby DE72 3GA* T: (01332) 669670

JACKS, David. b 59. Nottm Univ BTh 87 Birm Univ MA 95 PhD 08. Linc Th Coll 84. **d** 87 **p** 88. C Oakham, Hambleton, Egleton, Braunston and Brooke *Pet* 87-90; V Weedon Bec w Everdon 90-96; V Weedon Bec w Everdon and Dodford 96-01; V Llandrillo-yn-Rhos *St As* from 01; AD Llanrwst and Rhos 14-15; AD Rhos from 14. *Llandrillo Vicarage, 36 Llandudno Road, Colwyn Bay LL28 4UD* T: (01492) 548878 M: 07850-597891 E: david.jacks@live.co.uk

JACKSON, Alan. b 44. Newc Univ BA 67 DipEd 68 MEd 79. NEOC 79. **d** 81 **p** 82. NSM Jesmond H Trin *Newc* 81-82; Chapl Bp Wand Sch Sunbury-on-Thames 82-89; V Hanworth St Rich *Lon* 89-10; rtd 10. *7 Uxbridge Road, Feltham TW13 5EG* T: (020) 8898 3093 E: alan11144@gmail.com

JACKSON, Alison. b 58. St Mellitus Coll. **d** 14 **p** 15. NSM Rye Park St Cuth *St Alb* from 14. *95 New Road, Ware SG12 7BY*

JACKSON, Barry. b 30. St Jo Coll Cam BA 53 DipEd 54 MA 57. Westcott Ho Cam 63. **d** 65 **p** 66. C Stockport St Geo *Ches* 65-68; C Bridgwater St Mary, Chilton Trinity and Durleigh *B & W* 68-70; P-in-c Thurloxton 70-75; Chapl Wycliffe Coll Glos 75-88; V Heathfield *Chich* 88-97; rtd 97; PtO *Chich* from 98. *11 Glenleigh Walk, Robertsbridge TN32 5DQ* T: (01580) 880667

JACKSON, Barry James. b 65. Sheff Univ BEng 87. St Jo Coll Nottm 05. **d** 07 **p** 08. C Leamington Priors St Mary *Cov* 07-10; P-in-c Kineton 10-14; P-in-c Combroke w Compton Verney 10-14; P-in-c Warmington w Shotteswell and Radway w Ratley 10-14; R Edgehill Churches from 14. *The Vicarage, Warwick Road, Kineton, Warwick CV35 0HW* T: (01926) 640248 E: revbarryjackson@btinternet.com

JACKSON, The Very Revd Brandon Donald. b 34. Liv Univ LLB 56 Bradf Univ Hon DLitt 90. Wycliffe Hall Ox. **d** 58 **p** 59. C New Malden and Coombe *S'wark* 58-61; C Leeds St Geo *Ripon* 61-65; V Shipley St Pet *Bradf* 65-77; Relig Adv Yorkshire TV 69-79; Provost Bradf 77-89; Dean Linc 89-97; rtd 97; PtO *Leeds* from 98. *1 Kingston Way, Market Harborough LE16 7XB* T: (01858) 462425 E: brandon.j@talktalk.net

JACKSON, Christopher John Wilson. b 45. St Pet Coll Ox BA 67 MA 87. Ridley Hall Cam 69. **d** 72 **p** 73. C Putney St Marg *S'wark* 72-76; C Battersea St Pet and St Paul 76-79; TV Preston St Jo *Blackb* 79-87; P-in-c Sandal St Cath *Wakef* 87-90; V Shenley Green *Birm* 90-01; AD Kings Norton 95-99; P-in-c Chesterfield H Trin and Ch Ch *Derby* 01-10; R 10; rtd 10; PtO *Blackb* from 10. *5 Beech Grove, Ashton-on-Ribble, Preston PR2 1DX* T: (01772) 721772 E: chrisaliz5@talktalk.net

JACKSON, Cuthbert. b 53. **d** 12 **p** 13. OLM Skelmersdale St Paul *Liv* from 12; Chapl Wrightington Wigan and Leigh NHS Trust from 12. *36 High Street, Skelmersdale WN8 8AP*

JACKSON, Miss Cynthia. b 42. Open Univ BA 07. S'wark Ord Course 93. **d** 96 **p** 97. NSM Wimbledon *S'wark* 96-12; PtO from 12. *39 Panmuir Road, London SW20 0PZ* T: (020) 8947 5940 E: revcynthia@timetalk.co.uk

JACKSON, David. b 48. Open Univ BA 85. St Deiniol's Hawarden 91. **d** 91 **p** 92. C Scotforth *Blackb* 91-95; Chapl Ox Radcliffe Hosps NHS Trust 95-00; C Banbury *Ox* 95-96; TV 96-98; V Banbury St Hugh 98-07; V Banbury St Fran 07-12; rtd 12. *16 rue Soeur Marie Antoinette, 50720 Barenton, France* E: vicardavyjax@tiscali.co.uk

JACKSON, Canon David. b 33. Leeds Univ BA 60. Coll of Resurr Mirfield 60. **d** 62 **p** 63. C Lewisham St Steph *S'wark* 62-65; P-in-c New Charlton H Trin 65-69; C Charlton St Luke w St Paul 69-72; Sen Tutor Coll of the Resurr Mirfield 72-75; R Clapham H Trin *S'wark* 75-78; P-in-c Clapham St Pet 76-78; TR Clapham Old Town 78-84; Hon Can S'wark Cathl 80-96; V Battersea St Mary-le-Park 84-89; V Surbiton St Andr and St Mark 89-96; rtd 96; Chapl St Mich Convent Ham 96-03. *18 Tower Lane, Bearsted, Maidstone ME14 4JJ* T: (01622) 730041

JACKSON, David Hilton. b 62. Stanford Univ BA 84 Princeton Th Sem MDiv 90 Ox Univ MSt 94. Wycliffe Hall Ox 94. **d** 95 **p** 96. C Ox St Andr 95-98; TV Thame 98-00; USA from 00; Assoc R and Chapl Upland St Mark 01-03; Sen Assoc for Par Life Pasadena All SS from 03. *614 Occidental Drive, Claremont CA 91711, USA* E: david.jackson@cgu.edu

JACKSON, David Reginald Estcourt. b 25. OBE. Qu Coll Cam BA 45 MA 49. Cranmer Hall Dur 80. **d** 81 **p** 82. Hon C Douglas *Blackb* 81-82; C 82-87; rtd 90. *64 The Common, Parbold, Wigan WN8 7EA* T: (01257) 462671

JACKSON, David Robert. b 51. Lon Univ BDS. Linc Th Coll 81. **d** 83 **p** 84. C Hatcham St Cath *S'wark* 83-87; V Sydenham St Bart 87-93; PtO *Lon* 03-05; Hon C St Martin-in-the-Fields from 05. *168 Manor Park, London SE13 5RH* T: (020) 8297 9132 E: djsaab@aol.com

JACKSON, David William. b 53. Goldsmiths' Coll Lon BA 75 PGCE 76. Cranmer Hall Dur 90. **d** 92 **p** 93. C Desborough *Pet* 92-95; C Eastham *Ches* 95-98; P-in-c Taverham w Ringland *Nor* 98-05; R Taverham 05-06; R Redenhall, Harleston, Wortwell and Needham 06-12; rtd 12; PtO *Nor* from 13. *11 Laxfield Road, Sutton, Norwich NR12 9QP* T: (01692) 218634 E: d.jackson38@yahoo.co.uk

JACKSON, Canon Derek. b 26. Ex Coll Ox BA 51 MA 55. Westcott Ho Cam 51. **d** 53 **p** 54. C Radcliffe-on-Trent *S'well* 53-56; C Frome St Jo *B & W* 56-57; V Eaton Socon *St Alb* 57-63; V Boxmoor St Jo 63-74; V Bishop's Stortford St Mich 74-85; Hon Can St Alb 82-85; Bermuda 85-89; P-in-c Cerne Abbas w Godmanstone and Minterne Magna *Sarum* 89-95; rtd 95; Chapl Menorca *Eur* 95-96; PtO *St Alb* from 96; *Chelmsf* from 12. *43B Fairfield Road, Saxmundham IP17 1BB* T: (01728) 604210

JACKSON, Canon Derek Reginald. b 49. K Coll Lon BD 72 AKC 72. **d** 73 **p** 74. C Westhoughton *Man* 73-75; C Kendal H Trin *Carl* 75-78; V Pennington w Lindal and Marton 78-83; Warden of Readers 82-92; V Kendal St Geo 83-94; Hon Can Carl Cathl 89-00; V Applethwaite 94-96; P-in-c Troutbeck 94-96; V Windermere St Mary and Troutbeck 96-00; RD Windermere 98-00; Can Res Bradf Cathl 00-03; P-in-c Bingley All SS 03-10; RD Airedale 05-10; rtd 10; PtO *Carl* from 11. *3 Ellas Orchard, Green Lane, Flookburgh, Grange-over-Sands LA11 7JT* T: (015395) 58370 E: derekjackson2901@hotmail.com

JACKSON, Doreen May. b 35. SRN. S Dios Minl Tr Scheme. **d** 88 **p** 94. NSM Fareham H Trin *Portsm* 88-05; rtd 05; PtO *Portsm* from 12. *134 Oak Road, Fareham PO15 5HR* T: (01329) 841429

JACKSON, Mrs Elizabeth Barbara. b 67. EMMTC 07. **d** 10 **p** 11. C Linc St Pet-at-Gowts and St Andr 10-13; C Linc St Botolph 10-13; C Linc St Mary-le-Wigford w St Benedict etc 10-13; P-in-c Cov St Fran N Radford from 13. *St Francis's Vicarage, 110 Treherne Road, Coventry CV6 3DY* M: 07799-724908 E: liz.jack@ntlworld.com

JACKSON, Mrs Elizabeth Mary. b 41. Man Univ BA 67 Leeds Univ MA 01. Ox Min Course 90. **d** 92 **p** 94. Chapl Reading Hosps 86-95; NSM Reading St Mary the Virgin *Ox* 92-94; Chapl R Berks and Battle Hosps NHS Trust 95-02; NSM Reading Deanery *Ox* 02-07; PtO *Carl* from 08. *The Hayloft, 2 Hall Court, Tallentire, Cockermouth CA13 0PU* T: (01900) 825799 E: mjack2bl@aol.com

JACKSON, The Ven Frances Anne (Peggy). b 51. Somerville Coll Ox BA 72 MA 76 ACA 76 FCA 81. Ripon Coll Cuddesdon 85. **d** 87 **p** 94. C Ilkeston St Mary *Derby* 87-90; TM Hemel Hempstead *St Alb* 90-94; TV 94-98; TR Mortlake w E Sheen *S'wark* 98-09; RD Richmond and Barnes 00-05; Hon Can S'wark Cathl 03-09; Dean of Women's Min 04-09; Adn Llan from 09; P-in-c Penmark w Llancarfan w Llantrithyd 09-14; P-in-c St Fagans and Michaelston-super-Ely from 14. *The Rectory, Greenwood Lane, St Fagans, Cardiff CF5 6EL* T: (029) 2056 7393 E: archdeacon.llan@churchinwales.org.uk

JACKSON, Miss Freda. b 41. Bp Otter Coll TCert 61. **d** 92 **p** 94. OLM Middleton *Man* 92-94; OLM Middleton and Thornham 94-12; rtd 12; PtO *Man* from 12. *Address temp unknown*

JACKSON, Ms Gillian Rosemary. b 52. Newc Univ BA 75 PGCE 76 Aber Univ MLitt 80 Nottm Univ MA 04 AFBPsS. EMMTC 01. **d** 04 **p** 05. NSM Bosworth and Sheepy Gp *Leic* 04-08; Dioc Dir Soc Resp 04-08; Bp's Exec Asst 08-10. *Address temp unknown*

JACKSON, Miss Hannah Louise. b 81. St Cuth Soc Dur BA 04 St Jo Coll Dur MA 06. St Mellitus Coll 10. **d** 12 **p** 13. C Pitsmoor Ch Ch *Sheff* from 12. *46 Shirecliffe Lane, Sheffield S3 9AE* M: 07702-163138 E: jacksonhan@hotmail.co.uk

JACKSON, Harry Francis. b 30. K Coll Lon BD 61 AKC 61 Ex Univ BTh 05 FBCO 80. Sarum Th Coll 61. **d** 62 **p** 62. Bermuda 62-65; C Cobham *Guildf* 65-69; R Ash 69-96; Chapl RAF Farnborough 80-96; rtd 96; P-in-c Mawnan *Truro* 96-01; PtO from 02. *Rosnython, Treliever Road, Mabe Burnthouse, Penryn TR10 9EX* T: (01326) 372532 E: harry.jackson4@btinternet.com

JACKSON, Hilary Walton. b 17. St Chad's Coll Dur BA 40 MA 48. **d** 46 **p** 47. C Selby Abbey *York* 46-49; C Middlesbrough All SS 49-51; V Thornley *Dur* 51-56; V Beamish 56-66; V Heighington 66-82; rtd 82. *54 Squires Court, Woodland Road, Darlington DL3 9XZ* T: (01325) 389495 E: hilary.jackson@durham.anglican.org

JACKSON, Ian. b 53. Jes Coll Ox BA 75. Linc Th Coll 76. **d** 78 **p** 79. C Holbeach *Linc* 78-82; V Newsome *Wakef* 82-85; V Newsome and Armitage Bridge 85-03; TR Em TM 03-04; P-in-c Corfe Castle, Church Knowle, Kimmeridge etc *Sarum* 04-14; R from 14. *The Rectory, East Street, Corfe Castle, Wareham BH20 5EE* T: (01929) 480257 E: rev.ianjackson@btinternet.com

JACKSON, Mrs Isobel Margaret. b 69. Uganda Chr Univ BD 04. **d** 04. CMS Uganda 04-05; C Lismore w Cappoquin, Kilwatermoy, Dungarvan etc *C & O* 05-10; I Templebreedy w Tracton and Nohoval *C, C & R* from 10. *Templebreedy Rectory, Church Road, Crosshaven, Co Cork, Republic of Ireland* T: (00353) (21) 483 1236 M: 86-743 5424 E: isobel@njjackson.com *or* templebreedyrector@ccrd.ie

JACKSON, Mrs Janet Lesley. b 45. CQSW 78. NEOC 93. **d** 96 **p** 97. NSM Whorlton *Newc* 96-98; Chapl St Oswald's Hospice Newc 98-07; Bereavement Services Co-ord Tynedale Hospice 10-12; Chapl from 12. *1 St Andrews Road, Hexham NE46 2EY* T: (01434) 602929

JACKSON, Mrs Joan. b 44. Bolton Coll of Educn CertEd 71 Lanc Univ MA 98. CBDTI 95. **d** 98 **p** 99. NSM Staveley, Ings and Kentmere *Carl* 98-00; Chapl Furness Hosps NHS Trust 98-00; Asst Chapl Bradf Hosps NHS Trust 00-04; NSM Bingley H Trin *Bradf* 03-07; PtO 07-10; *Carl* from 11. *3 Ellas Orchard, Green Lane, Flookburgh, Grange-over-Sands LA11 7JT* T: (015395) 58370 E: jjacksonddp@yahoo.co.uk

JACKSON, John Edward. b 29. K Coll Lon BD 57 AKC 57. St Boniface Warminster 57. **d** 58 **p** 59. C Crofton Park St Hilda w St Cypr *S'wark* 58-61; V Bremhill w Foxham *Sarum* 61-69; V Netheravon w Fittleton 69-73; V Netheravon w Fittleton and Enford 73-85; OCM 69-85; V Salisbury St Mark *Sarum* 85-92; P-in-c Bryngwyn and Newchurch and Llanbedr etc *S & B* 92-96; rtd 96. *Llwyndyrys Care Home, Llechryd, Cardigan SA43 2QP* T: (01239) 682263

JACKSON, Miss Kathryn Dianne. b 64. Leeds Univ BA 87 MA 01. St Steph Ho Ox 87. **d** 90 **p** 94. Par Dn Headingley *Ripon* 90-94; C Hawksworth Wood 94-00; P-in-c Scarborough St Columba *York* 00-14; Chapl St Cath Hospice Scarborough 00-14; R Haxby and Wigginton *York* from 14. *5 Back Lane, Wigginton, York YO32 2ZH* T: (01904) 765155 E: kathryn.columba@btinternet.com

JACKSON, Lisa Helen. *See* BARNETT, Lisa Helen

JACKSON, Malcolm. b 58. NEOC 01. **d** 04 **p** 05. C Guisborough *York* 04-08; V Kirkleatham 08-14; C Whitby w Ruswarp from 14. *23 Abbeville Avenue, Whitby YO21 1JD* T: (01947) 605686 E: maljackoagain@gmail.com

JACKSON, Mrs Margaret Elizabeth. b 47. Lon Univ BSc 68 MSc 95 Univ of Wales (Lamp) MTh 05 FCIPD 91. S'wark Ord Course 80. **dss** 83 **d** 92 **p** 94. Subiton Hill Ch Ch *S'wark* 83-84; Saffron Walden w Wendens Ambo and Littlebury *Chelmsf* 84-85; Dulwich St Barn *S'wark* 86-97; Hon C 92-97; Personal Asst to Bp S'wark 92-94; Selection Sec Min Division 96-00 and from 03; NSM Churt *Guildf* 98-00; NSM The Bourne and Tilford 00-10; NSM Churt and Hindhead 10-14; Convenor STETS 00-02; Dioc Dir of Ords S'wark 05-06; Dir of Ords Kingston Area 10-11; PtO *Guildf* from 14. *67 Parkhurst Fields, Churt, Farnham GU10 2PQ* T: (01428) 714411 F: 714426 E: revjackson@btinternet.com

JACKSON, Mrs Margaret Elizabeth. b 47. Mon Dioc Tr Scheme. **d** 87 **p** 94. C Chepstow *Mon* 87-90; C Exhall *Cov* 90-92; C Leamington Priors All SS 92-96; R Hulme Ascension *Man* 96-99; V Alstonfield, Butterton, Ilam etc *Lich* 99-08; RD Alstonfield 00-03; R Stonehaven *Bre* 08-15; R Catterline

08-15; P-in-c Muchalls 12-15; rtd 15. *St Simon's Vicarage, 134 Wenlock Road, South Shields NE34 9AL* M: 07936-366626 T: 0191-454 8834 E: maggiejackson29@gmail.com

JACKSON, Margaret Jane. b 50. RGN 72. S'wark Ord Course 89. **d** 92 **p** 94. Par Dn Hatcham St Cath *S'wark* 92-94; C 94-98; V Mottingham St Edw from 98. *St Edward's Vicarage, St Keverne Road, London SE9 4AQ* T: (020) 8857 6278 E: margaretjjackson@compuserve.com

JACKSON, Ms Marie Ann. b 45. Nottm Univ BSc 66. SAOMC 98. **d** 98 **p** 99. OLM High Wycombe *Ox* from 98. *19 New Road, Sands, High Wycombe HP12 4LH* T: (01494) 530728

JACKSON, Mark Benjamin. b 77. Dur Univ BSc 00. Wycliffe Hall Ox BTh 13. **d** 13 **p** 14. C Langham Place All So *Lon* from 13. *Flat 1, 169 Central Street, London EC1V 8BS* E: mark.jackson@allsols.org

JACKSON, Mark Harding. b 51. Open Univ BA 87. Sarum & Wells Th Coll 76. **d** 79 **p** 80. C Hobs Moat *Birm* 79-83; Chapl RN from 83. *Bush House, 12 Palmer Street, South Petherton TA13 5DB* T: (01460) 242171 M: 07960-733472 E: maundycottage@talktalk.net

JACKSON, Martin. b 56. Clare Coll Cam BA 77 MA 81 St Jo Coll Dur BA 80 MA 97. Cranmer Hall Dur. **d** 81 **p** 82. C Houghton le Spring *Dur* 81-84; C Bishopwearmouth St Mich w St Hilda 84-86; TV Winlaton 86; V High Spen and Rowlands Gill 86-94; P-in-c Benfieldside 94-97; V from 97; P-in-c Castleside from 11; AD Lanchester 00-06. *St Cuthbert's Vicarage, Church Bank, Consett DH8 0NW* T: (01207) 503019 E: martin.jackson@durham.anglican.org

JACKSON, Matthew Christopher. b 75. Univ of Wales (Abth) BD 96 MTh 98. Ripon Coll Cuddesdon. **d** 01 **p** 02. C King's Lynn St Marg w St Nic *Nor* 01-05; V Pembury *Roch* 05-10; R Attleborough w Besthorpe *Nor* from 10; RD Thetford and Rockland from 11. *The Rectory, Surrogate Street, Attleborough NR17 2AW* T: (01953) 453185 E: therectory@me.com

JACKSON, Mrs Melanie Jane Susann. b 60. UWE BA 83 Leic Univ MA 94. SWMTC 97. **d** 00 **p** 01. C Ottery St Mary, Alfington, W Hill, Tipton etc *Ex* 00-04; PtO 04-08; NSM Linc St Jo 08-15. *Address temp unknown* E: melaniejackson.amia@btinternet.com

✠**JACKSON, The Most Revd Michael Geoffrey St Aubyn.** b 56. TCD BA 79 MA 82 St Jo Coll Cam BA 81 MA 85 PhD 86 Ch Ch Ox MA 89 DPhil 89. CITC 86. **d** 86 **p** 87 **c** 02. C Dublin Zion Ch *D & G* 86-89; Chapl Ch Ch Ox 89-97; Student 93-97; Dean Cork *C, C & R* 97-02; I Cork St Fin Barre's Union 97-02; Chapl and Asst Lect Univ Coll Cork 98-02; Chapl Cork Inst of Tech 98-02; Bp Clogh 02-11; Abp Dublin *D & G* from 11. *The See House, 17 Temple Road, Dartry, Dublin 6, Republic of Ireland* T: (00353) (1) 497 7849 F: 497 6355 E: archbishop@dublin.anglican.org

JACKSON, Michael Ian. b 51. Southn Univ BA 73. STETS 00. **d** 03 **p** 04. Dir St Jo Win Charity 87-13; NSM Twyford and Owslebury and Morestead etc *Win* 03-13; V Kirkby-in-Malhamdale *Leeds* from 13. *The Vicarage, Kirkby Malham, Skipton BD23 4BS* T: (01729) 830144 E: michael.jackson@morestead.com

JACKSON, Canon Michael James. b 44. Liv Univ BEng 65 Newc Univ PhD 84 CEng 69 MICE 69. NEOC 82. **d** 84 **p** 85. C Houghton le Spring *Dur* 84-87; V Millfield St Mark 87-95; V Ponteland *Newc* 95-07; AD Newc W 03-07; Hon Can Newc Cathl 06-07; rtd 07. *1 St Andrews Road, Hexham NE46 2EY* T: (01434) 602929

JACKSON, Michael Richard. b 31. Selw Coll Cam BA 54 MA 58. Westcott Ho Cam 54. **d** 56 **p** 57. C Gosforth All SS *Newc* 56-62; R Dinnington *Sheff* 62-76; V Swinton 76-97; rtd 97; PtO *Sheff* from 97. *10 Elmhirst Drive, Rotherham S65 3ED* T: (01709) 531065

JACKSON, Nicholas David. b 54. Wadh Coll Ox MA 75 Bris Univ PGCE 76. Wycliffe Hall Ox 06. **d** 08 **p** 09. C Branksome Park All SS *Sarum* 08-12; V Southlake *Ox* from 12. *97 Reading Road, Woodley, Reading RG5 3AE* M: 07969-831963 T: 0118-969 3445 *or* 966 2568 E: rev.nickj@gmail.com

JACKSON, Norman. b 20. CEng MIMechE 53. S'wark Ord Course 74. **d** 77 **p** 78. NSM Erith Ch Ch *Roch* 77-82; NSM Bishopstoke *Win* 82-95; rtd 95; PtO *Win* 95-04. *7 Otter Close, Eastleigh SO50 8NF* T: (023) 8069 5045

JACKSON, Paul Andrew. b 65. NEOC 05. **d** 08 **p** 09. NSM Haxby and Wigginton *York* from 08. *16 Linley Avenue, Haxby, York YO32 3NE* T: (01904) 763921 E: pjacko99@aol.com

JACKSON, Peggy. *See* JACKSON, Frances Anne

JACKSON, Peter. *See* JACKSON, Thomas Peter

JACKSON, Peter Charles. b 71. Univ of Northumbria at Newc BA 95. Oak Hill Th Coll BA 01. **d** 02 **p** 03. C Lowestoft Ch Ch *Nor* 02-07; P-in-c Kendray *Sheff* 07-10; V from 10. *St Andrew's Vicarage, 84 Hunningley Lane, Barnsley S70 3DT* T: (01226) 205826 E: jacko.pete@googlemail.com

JACKSON, Peter Jonathan Edward. b 53. St Pet Coll Ox BA 74 MA 78 PGCE 78. St Steph Ho Ox 79. **d** 79 **p** 80. Lect Westmr Coll Ox 79-80; Hon C Ox St Mich w St Martin and All SS 79-80; C Malvern Link w Cowleigh *Worc* 79-82; Chapl Aldenham Sch Herts 82-89; Chapl and Hd RE Harrow Sch 89-01; Lect K Coll Lon 92-99; Dir Chr Educn and Assoc R Washington St Patr USA 01-03; V Southgate Ch Ch *Lon* 03-14; Chapl Nice w Vence *Eur* from 14. *Holy Trinity, 11 rue de la Buffa, 06000 Nice, France* T: (0033) 4 93 87 19 83 M: 7 83 28 39 53 E: peterjejackson@aol.com

JACKSON, Philip Michael. b 74. Chelt & Glouc Coll of HE BA 95 Brunel Univ PGCE 97. Trin Coll Bris BA 05. **d** 06 **p** 07. C W Kilburn St Luke w St Simon and St Jude *Lon* 06-09; C Reigate St Mary *S'wark* 09-13; P-in-c Chipstead 13-14; R from 14. *The Rectory, Starrock Lane, Chipstead, Coulsdon CR5 3QD* T: (01737) 552160 M: 07545-054022 E: phil.jackson74@googlemail.com

JACKSON (née PRICE), Mrs Rachel Anne. b 57. **d** 03 **p** 04. OLM Barnham Broom and Upper Yare *Nor* from 03. *Red Hall, Red Hall Lane, Southburgh, Thetford IP25 7TG* T: (01362) 821032 F: 820145 E: revrachel@edwardjacksonltd.com

✠**JACKSON, The Rt Revd Richard Charles.** b 61. Ch Ch Ox BA 83 Cranfield Inst of Tech MSc 85. Trin Coll Bris 92. **d** 94 **p** 95 **c** 14. C Lindfield *Chich* 94-98; V Rudgwick 98-09; RD Horsham 05-09; Dioc Adv for Miss and Renewal 09-14; Area Bp Lewes from 14. *Fir Trees, Kingston Ridge, Kingston, Lewes RH17 5QR* E: bishop.lewes@chichester.anglican.org

JACKSON, Richard Hugh. b 44. St Jo Coll York CertEd 66 UEA MA 84. **d** 98 **p** 99. OLM Stalham and E Ruston w Brunstead *Nor* 98-00; OLM Stalham, E Ruston, Brunstead, Sutton and Ingham 00-14; PtO from 14. *The Croft, Camping Field Lane, Stalham, Norwich NR12 9DT* T: (01692) 581389 E: richard.jackson@intamail.com

JACKSON, Robert. b 69. Nottm Univ BA 01. St Jo Coll Nottm 98. **d** 01 **p** 02. C Altham w Clayton le Moors *Blackb* 01-03; C Blackb St Gabr 03-05; TV Westhoughton and Wingates *Man* 05-10; TV Cartmel Peninsula *Carl* from 10; Lay Development Co-ord from 10. *The Vicarage, Boarbank Lane, Allithwaite, Grange-over-Sands LA11 7QR* T: (015395) 32437 M: 07703-824849 E: revrobjackson@live.co.uk

JACKSON, Robert Brandon. b 61. Lanchester Poly Cov BA 86 Ox Univ BA 88 MA 95. Wycliffe Hall Ox 86. **d** 89 **p** 90. C Bromley Common St Aug *Roch* 89-92; P-in-c Stowe Ox 92-97; Asst Chapl Stowe Sch 92-97; Chapl 02-11; Chapl Lord Wandsworth Coll Hook 97-02; PtO *Ox* from 11. *16 Parkland Place, Wren Way, Bicester OX26 6UH* T: (01869) 571650 E: hittiterev@msn.com

JACKSON, Robert Fielden. b 35. St D Coll Lamp BA 57. Sarum Th Coll 57. **d** 59 **p** 60. C Altham w Clayton le Moors *Blackb* 59-62; C Lytham St Cuth 62-64; V Skerton St Chad 64-69; V Preesall 69-90; RD Garstang 85-89; V Wray w Tatham and Tatham Fells 90-00; rtd 00; PtO *Blackb* from 01. *8 Squirrel's Chase, Lostock Hall, Preston PR5 5NE* T: (01772) 338756

JACKSON, The Ven Robert William. b 49. K Coll Cam MA 73 Man Univ MA. St Jo Coll Nottm 78. **d** 81 **p** 82. C Fulwood *Sheff* 81-84; V Grenoside and Chapl Grenoside Hosp 84-92; V Scarborough St Mary w Ch Ch and H Apostles *York* 92-01; Springboard Missr 01-04; Adn Walsall and Hon Can Lich Cathl 05-09; rtd 09. *4 Glebe Park, Eyam, Hope Valley S32 5RH* T: (01433) 631212 E: archbob@gmail.com

JACKSON, Roger. b 57. Chich Th Coll 85. **d** 88 **p** 89. C Hale *Guildf* 88-92; V Barton w Peel Green *Man* 92-95; P-in-c Long Crendon w Chearsley and Nether Winchendon *Ox* 95-00; V 00-08; V Clevedon St Jo *B & W* 08-14; P-in-c Fareham SS Pet and Paul *Portsm* from 14. *The Vicarage, 22 Harrison Road, Fareham PO16 7EJ* T: (01329) 281521 E: frrjackson@gmail.com

JACKSON, Canon Ronald William. b 37. Lon Univ MA 71 ALCD. **d** 69 **p** 70. C Crofton *Portsm* 69-74; V Wolverhampton St Matt *Lich* 74-85; V Bloxwich 85-89; C Tamworth 89-92; Bp's Officer for Par Miss and Development *Bradf* 92-98; Hon Can Bradf Cathl 94-98; rtd 98; PtO *Leeds* from 99; *Blackb* from 14. *24 Fosbrooke House, Clifton Drive, Lytham St Annes FY8 5RQ* T: (01253) 667024 E: rw.jackson@icloud.com

JACKSON, Ruth Ellen. b 69. Dub City Univ BBS 91. CITC BTh 02. **d** 02 **p** 03. C Portadown St Mark *Arm* 02-05; C Carrigrohane Union *C, C & R* 05-10; I Mountmellick w Coolbanagher, Rosenallis etc *M & K* 10-15; I Dublin Crumlin w Chapelizod *D & G* from 15. *St Mary's Rectory, 118 Kimmage Road West, Dublin 12, Republic of Ireland* M: (00353) 87-052 3450 E: ruthjnoble@gmail.com

JACKSON, Ruth Victoria. *See* HAKE, Ruth Victoria

JACKSON, Ms Sarah Diana. b 53. Birkbeck Coll Lon MSc 01 Dorset Ho Sch of Occupational Therapy DipCOT 74. SEITE 09. **d** 12 **p** 13. NSM Wandsworth Common St Mary *S'wark* from 12. *25 Mantilla Road, London SW17 8DY* T: (020) 8767 4667 M: 07719-876610 E: mail@sarahjackson.me

JACKSON (née STAFF), Mrs Susan. b 59. Leeds Univ BA 82. Ridley Hall Cam 88. **d** 90 **p** 94. Par Dn Mickleover All SS *Derby* 90-93; Par Dn Chatham St Wm *Roch* 93-94; C 94-97; TV Walton Milton Keynes *Ox* 97-13; PtO from 13. *11 Herdwyck Close, Oakridge Park, Milton Keynes MK14 6GR* T: (01908) 317515 E: revsusanjackson@tiscali.co.uk

JACKSON, Thomas Charles. b 70. St Mellitus Coll 13. **d** 15. NSM Onslow Square and S Kensington St Aug *Lon* from 15. *Address temp unknown*

JACKSON, Thomas Peter. b 27. Univ of Wales (Lamp) BA 50. St Mich Coll Llan 50. **d** 52 **p** 53. C Swansea St Mary and H Trin *S & B* 52-58; Area Sec (S Midl and S Wales) UMCA 58-60; V Glouc St Steph 60-73; R Upton St Leonards 73-92; RD Glouc N 82-91; rtd 92; PtO *Glouc* from 92. *44 Grebe Close, Gloucester GL4 9XL* T: (01452) 533769

JACKSON, Wendy Pamela. *See* JACKSON-HILL, Wendy Pamela

JACKSON, William Dalton. b 48. Sunderland Poly DCYW 83 Sunderland Univ CertEd 96. Linc Th Coll 86. **d** 89 **p** 90. C Heworth St Mary *Dur* 89-91; C Tudhoe Grange 91-93; Churches' Regional Commn in the NE 97-01; NSM Dipton and Leadgate 03-08; V Burnham *Ox* from 08. *The Rectory, The Precincts, Burnham, Slough SL1 7HU* T: (01628) 559992 M: 07793-750652 E: jackson.bill39@yahoo.co.uk

JACKSON, Canon William Stanley Peter. b 39. St Mich Coll Llan 63. **d** 66 **p** 67. C Llandrindod w Cefnllys *S & B* 66-69; C Gowerton w Waunarlwydd 69-73; V Crickadarn w Gwenddwr and Alltmawr 73-79; R Llanfeugan w Llanthetty etc 79-04; Dioc GFS Chapl 84-92; Can Res Brecon Cathl 90-04; Prec Brecon Cathl 98-99; Treas Brecon Cathl 99-00; Chan Brecon Cathl 00-04; Dioc Communications Officer 92-94; RD Crickhowell 98-02; rtd 04. *9 St Peter's Avenue, Fforestfach, Swansea SA5 5BX* T: (01792) 541229 E: canonjacko@aol.com

JACKSON-HILL, Mrs Wendy Pamela. b 45. Th Ext Educn Coll 99. **d** 00 **p** 02. Community P Woodlands S Africa 02-03; C Crediton, Shobrooke and Sandford etc *Ex* 03-05; P-in-c Southway 05-15; C Tamerton Foliot 06-15; rtd 15. *33 Colmanton Grove, Sholden, Deal CT14 0FF* E: wendypjackson@blueyonder.co.uk

JACKSON NOBLE, Ruth Ellen. *See* JACKSON, Ruth Ellen

JACKSON-PARR, Andrew Jason. b 81. Linc Sch of Th and Min. **d** 13 **p** 14. C Bassingham Gp *Linc* from 13. *8 Doe Close, Witham St Hughs, Lincoln LN6 9UW* E: andyjp81@gmail.com

JACKSON-STEVENS, Preb Nigel. b 42. St Steph Ho Ox. **d** 68 **p** 69. C Babbacombe *Ex* 68-73; V Swimbridge 73-75; P-in-c W Buckland 73-75; V Swimbridge and W Buckland 75-84; P-in-c Mortehoe 84-85; P-in-c Ilfracombe, Lee, W Down, Woolacombe and Bittadon 84-85; TR Ilfracombe, Lee, Woolacombe, Bittadon etc 85-08; RD Barnstaple 93-97; Preb Ex Cathl 95-08; rtd 08. *Rose Cottage, Eastacombe, Barnstaple EX31 3NT* T: (01271) 325283

JACOB, Mrs Amelia Stanley. b 52. Punjab Univ BA 73. Oak Hill Th Coll. **d** 90 **p** 94. NSM Asian Chr Congregation All SS Tufnell Park *Lon* 90-92; NSM Alperton 92-12. *39 Chester Drive, Harrow HA2 7PX* T: (020) 8902 4592 E: ameliastanley39@yahoo.com

JACOB, John Lionel Andrew. b 26. Selw Coll Cam BA 50 MA 54. Westcott Ho Cam 50. **d** 52 **p** 53. C Brightside St Thos *Sheff* 52-55; C Maltby 55-58; V Doncaster Intake 58-67; V Sheff St Aid w St Luke 67-75; TR Sheff Manor 75-82; R Waddington *Linc* 82-91; rtd 91; PtO *Linc* 91-00. *Flat 21, Manormead, Tilford Road, Hindhead GU26 6RA* T: (01428) 602559

JACOB, Canon Joseph. b 38. CITC 65. **d** 68 **p** 69. C Belfast St Aid *Conn* 68-70; Bp's Dom Chapl 70-71; I Kilscoran w Killinick and Mulrankin *C & O* 71-80; I Geashill *M & K* 80-83; Asst Warden Ch's Min of Healing 83-86; Gen Sec (Ireland) CMJ 87-91; I Ardamine, Kilnamanagh w Monamolin *C & O* 91-98; Preb Ferns Cathl 96-98; rtd 98. *Crannaulin, Clonmullen, Bunclody, Co Wexford, Republic of Ireland* T: (00353) (53) 937 7532

JACOB, Neville Peter. b 60. Kent Univ BA 82 Leeds Metrop Univ PGCE 86. Ripon Coll Cuddesdon 94. **d** 96 **p** 97. C Market Harborough *Leic* 96-97; C Market Harborough Transfiguration 96-97; C Market Harborough and The Transfiguration etc 97-99; Chapl Miss to Seafarers 99-03; P-in-c Copythorne *Win* 03-11; Chapl Ibex 03-09; PtO *Win* from 11. *3 Elmsleigh Court, Glen Eyre Road, Southampton SO16 3NT* E: raveknave@tinyworld.co.uk

JACOB, The Ven William Mungo. b 44. Hull Univ LLB 66 Linacre Coll Ox BA 69 MA 73 Ex Univ PhD. St Steph Ho Ox 70. **d** 70 **p** 71. C Wymondham *Nor* 70-73; Asst Chapl Ex Univ 73-75; Dir Past Studies Sarum & Wells Th Coll 75-80; Vice-Prin 77-80; Selection Sec and Sec Cttee for Th Educn ACCM 80-86; Warden Linc Th Coll 85-96; Can and Preb Linc Cathl 86-96; Hon C Linc Minster Gp 88-96; Adn Charing Cross *Lon* 96-14; Bp's Sen Chapl 96-00; R St Giles-in-the-Fields 00-15; P-in-c Soho St Anne w St Thos and St Pet 11-13;

rtd 15; P-in-c E Dulwich St Jo *S'wark* from 15. *4 St Mary's Walk, London SE11 4UA* T: (020) 7582 2025 E: wmjacob15@gmail.com

JACOBS, Mrs Brenda Mary. b 61. Birm Univ BA 85 Glos Univ PGCE 04. WEMTC 06. **d** 09 **p** 10. C Holmer w Huntington *Heref* 09-10; C W Heref 10-12; R Pembridge w Moor Court, Shobdon, Staunton etc from 12. *The Rectory, Manley Crescent, Pembridge, Leominster HR6 9EB* E: jacobs200@btinternet.com

JACOBS, Kevin David. b 55. SEITE 11. **d** 14 **p** 15. NSM Tunstall and Bredgar *Cant* from 14. *2 Acacia Terrace, Cryalls Lane, Sittingbourne ME10 1NU* T: (01795) 424538 M: 07572-690460 E: frkevin.0614@gmail.com

JACOBS, Prof Michael David. b 41. Ex Coll Ox BA 63 MA 67. Chich Th Coll 63. **d** 65 **p** 66. C Walthamstow St Pet *Chelmsf* 65-68; Chapl Sussex Univ *Chich* 68-72; Student Cllr Leic Univ 72-84; Lect 84-97; Sen Lect 97-00; Dir Past Care *Derby*, *Linc* and *S'well* 84-94; Visiting Prof Bournemouth Univ *Sarum* from 03. *12 Atlantic Road, Swanage BH19 2EG* T/F: (01929) 423068

JACOBS, Neville Robertson Eynesford. b 32. Lon Coll of Div ALCD 59. **d** 59 **p** 60. C Chesham St Mary *Ox* 59-62; CMS 62-67; C Keynsham *B & W* 67-71; R Croscombe and Dinder 72-80; R Pilton w Croscombe, N Wootton and Dinder 80-83; V Biddenham *St Alb* 83-89; V Chipping Sodbury and Old Sodbury *Glouc* 89-97; RD Hawkesbury 91-94; rtd 97; PtO *S'wark* from 98. *22 Comforts Farm Avenue, Hurst Green, Oxted RH8 9DH* T: (01883) 714127

JACOBS, Peter John. b 33. JP. MICFM. SEITE 96. **d** 96 **p** 97. NSM Boughton under Blean w Dunkirk and Hernhill *Cant* 96-99; NSM Murston w Bapchild and Tonge 99-02; rtd 02; PtO *Cant* from 02. *16 Temple Road, Canterbury CT2 8JD* T: (01227) 455733 E: peter@pjacobs72.freeserve.co.uk

JACOBSON, Ian Andrew. b 61. FRGS 94. STETS 02. **d** 05 **p** 06. NSM Ewell St Fran *Guildf* 05-08; NSM Headley w Box Hill 08-11; Asst Chapl Gibraltar Cathl 11-14; P-in-c Margate St Jo in Thanet *Cant* from 14; CF (TA) 07-10; OCM 11-14. *The Rectory, 2 Newington Road, Ramsgate CT11 0QT* T: (01843) 582672 M: 07711-716254 E: andrew.jacobson@waitrose.com

JACQUES, Barry John. b 52. Open Univ BSc 95. Wycliffe Hall Ox 00. **d** 02 **p** 03. NSM Attleborough *Cov* 02-03; C Weddington and Caldecote 03-07; PtO from 07. *23 Ferndale Close, Nuneaton CV11 6AQ* T: (024) 7767 7044 E: bazjac1702@gmail.com

JACQUES, Mrs Margaret Irene. b 53. St Jo Coll Nottm BA 03. **d** 03 **p** 04. C W Hallam and Mapperley w Stanley *Derby* 03-07; P-in-c Morton and Stonebroom w Shirland 07-12; R from 12. *The Rectory, 10 Main Road, Shirland, Alfreton DE55 6BB* T: (01773) 836003 E: margaret@ajacques.plus.com

JACQUES, Martin. b 62. Ch Ch Coll Cant BA 05. Coll of Resurr Mirfield 00. **d** 02 **p** 03. C Margate St Jo *Cant* 02-06; P-in-c Bucharest w Sofia *Eur* 06-09; P-in-c Gainford *Dur* from 09; P-in-c Winston from 09. *The Vicarage, Low Green, Gainford, Darlington DL2 3DS* T: (01325) 733268 M: 07706-875741 E: revmartinjacques@gmail.com

JACQUET, Linda. b 44. Hatf Poly BA 84. ERMC 06. **d** 08 **p** 09. NSM Bungay St E 08-14; rtd 15. *Roseheath, 10 Sun Road, Broome, Bungay NR35 2RW* M: 07890-216889 T: (01986) 896780 E: l.jacquet@talktalk.net

JACQUET, Trevor Graham. b 56. Man Univ BSc 77. Oak Hill Th Coll BA 88. **d** 88 **p** 89. C Deptford St Nic and St Luke *S'wark* 88-92; Chapl HM Pris Brixton 92-95; Chapl HM Pris Elmley 95-08; Chapl HM Pris Belmarsh from 08. *HM Prison Belmarsh, Western Way, London SE28 0EB* T: (020) 8331 4400 F: 8331 4401 E: trevor@jacquet2.freeserve.co.uk

JACSON, Edward Shallcross Owen. b 38. St Steph Ho Ox 61. **d** 64 **p** 65. C Yate *Glouc* 64-67; C Churchdown 67-70; P-in-c Sandhurst 70-75; V Sherborne w Windrush and the Barringtons 75-76; V Sherborne, Windrush, the Barringtons etc 76-80; TV Shaston *Sarum* 80-87; LtO 87-03; PtO from 03. *Grove Farm House, Melbury Abbas, Shaftesbury SP7 0DE* T: (01747) 853688

JAGE-BOWLER, Canon Christopher William. b 61. Nottm Univ BA 83 Ch Ch Ox PGCE 84 Down Coll Cam BA 89 MA 95. Ridley Hall Cam 87. **d** 90 **p** 91. C Downend *Bris* 90-94; Chapl Bris Univ 94-96; C Bris St Mich and St Paul 94-96; Asst Chapl Berlin *Eur* 96-97; Chapl from 97; Can Malta Cathl from 10. *Goethestrasse 31, 13158 Berlin, Germany* T/F: (0049) (30) 917 2248 E: office@stgeorges.de

JAGGER, The Ven Ian. b 55. K Coll Cam BA 77 MA 81 St Jo Coll Dur BA 80 MA 87. Cranmer Hall Dur 78. **d** 82 **p** 83. C Twickenham St Mary *Lon* 82-85; P-in-c Willen *Ox* 85-87; TV Stantonbury and Willen 87-94; TR Fareham H Trin *Portsm* 94-98; Dioc Ecum Officer 94-96; RD Fareham 96-98; Can Missr 98-01; Adn Auckland *Dur* 01-06; Dioc Rural Development Officer 01-06; Adn Dur and Can Res Dur Cathl from 06; Can Res Dur Cathl from 06. *15 The College, Durham DH1 3EQ* T: 0191-384 7534 E: archdeacon.of.durham@durham.anglican.org

JAGGER (née GREEN), Mrs Ruth Valerie. b 56. Ex Univ CertEd 77. Ox NSM Course 87. **d** 90 **p** 94. NSM Stantonbury and Willen *Ox* 90-94; NSM Fareham H Trin *Portsm* 94-98; NSM Portsm Deanery 98-01; PtO *Dur* from 01. *15 The College, Durham DH1 3EQ* T: 0191-384 7534

JAGO, Christine May. b 52. SRN 73. **d** 94 **p** 95. OLM St Buryan, St Levan and Sennen *Truro* 94-11; rtd 11. *Boscarne House, St Buryan, Penzance TR19 6HR* T: (01736) 810374 F: 810070 E: wandcmjago@btinternet.com

JAGO, David. b 48. Shoreditch Coll Lon CertEd 69 Birm Univ BPhil 77. St Steph Ho Ox 95. **d** 97 **p** 98. C S Bank *York* 97-00; V Middlesbrough St Martin w St Cuth 00-05; V Kingston upon Hull St Alb from 05. *St Alban's Vicarage, 62 Hall Road, Hull HU6 8SA* T: (01482) 443566 E: jago@jago.karoo.co.uk

JAKEMAN, Francis David. b 47. Leeds Univ BSc 69. Cuddesdon Coll 71. **d** 74 **p** 75. C Gt Grimsby St Mary and St Jas *Linc* 74-77; Ind Chapl *Lon* 77-88; V Harrow Weald All SS 88-03; V Bexleyheath Ch Ch *Roch* 03-13; AD Erith 04-09; rtd 13; PtO *Ox* from 14. *50 Eastern Avenue, Reading RG1 5SE* T: 0118-327 3326 M: 07899-922883 E: francisjakeman@tiscali.co.uk

JALLAND, Hilary Gervase Alexander. b 50. Ex Univ BA 72. Coll of Resurr Mirfield 74. **d** 76 **p** 77. C Ex St Thos 76-80; C Portsea St Mary *Portsm* 80-86; V Hempton and Pudding Norton *Nor* 86-90; TV Hawarden *St As* 90-93; R Llandysilio and Penrhos and Llandrinio etc 93-03; V Towyn and St George 03-06; rtd 06. *Flat 7, Sexeys Hospital, Bruton BA10 0AS* M: 07814-132259 E: hgaj@jalland1504.freeserve.co.uk

JAMES, Andrew Nicholas. b 54. BSc 76. Trin Coll Bris 77. **d** 80 **p** 81. C Prescot *Liv* 80-83; C Upholland 83-85; V Hindley Green 85-91; V Dean Forest H Trin *Glouc* 91-06; RD Forest S 97-03; P-in-c Hardwicke and Elmore w Longney 06-09; V from 09. *Church House, Cornfield Drive, Hardwicke, Gloucester GL2 4QJ* T: (01452) 720015 E: vicarage@inbox.com

JAMES, Andrew Peter. b 69. Glam Univ BSc 96 Univ of Wales (Cardiff) BTh 99. St Mich Coll Llan 96. **d** 99 **p** 00. C Roath *Llan* 99-01; C Radyr 01-06; TV Whitchurch 06-14; P-in-c St Andrews Major w Michaelston-le-Pit from 14. *The Rectory, Lettons Way, Dinas Powys CF64 4BY* T: (029) 2051 2555 E: frjames@totalise.co.uk

JAMES, Anne Loraine. b 45. St Jo Coll Nottm. **d** 90 **p** 94. NSM Ellon and Cruden Bay *Ab* 90-99; NSM Alford 99-02; P-in-c from 02. *St Andrew's House, 53 Main Street, Alford AB33 8PX* T: (01975) 564006 E: revanne.alford@virgin.net

JAMES, Barry Paul. b 49. BSc. Sarum & Wells Th Coll. **d** 82 **p** 83. C Bitterne Park *Win* 82-86; V Southampton St Mary Extra 86-00; R Fawley 00-14; rtd 14; PtO *Win* from 14. *7 Cleveland Drive, Dibden Purlieu, Southampton SO45 5QR* T: (023) 8087 9872 E: bpjames@email.com

JAMES, Brian. See JAMES, David Brian

JAMES, Brother. See PICKEN, James Hugh

JAMES, Brunel Hugh Grayburn. b 70. Selw Coll Cam BA 93 MA 97 Leeds Univ MA 02. Wycliffe Hall Ox BA 97. **d** 98 **p** 99. C Thornbury *Bradf* 98-02; R Barwick in Elmet *Ripon* 02-08; Abp's Dom Chapl *York* 08-10; P-in-c Cleckheaton St Luke and Whitechapel *Wakef* 10-13; P-in-c Cleckheaton St Jo 10-13; V Cleckheaton *Leeds* from 13. *The Vicarage, 33 Ashbourne Avenue, Cleckheaton BD19 5JH* T: (01274) 873471 M: 07811-195280 E: bruneljames@orange.net

JAMES, Miss Carolyn Anne. b 65. Coll of Ripon & York St Jo BA 87 Nottm Univ BTh 91 Leeds Univ MA 03. Linc Th Coll 88. **d** 91 **p** 94. Par Dn Middleton St Mary *Ripon* 91-94; C Wetherby 94-97; V Kirkstall 97-05; Chapl and Sen Warden Bp Grosseteste Coll Linc 05-12; P-in-c Manston *Leeds* from 12. *Manston Vicarage, Church Lane, Leeds LS15 8JB* T: 0113-264 2206 E: carolyn.james@bgc.ac.uk

JAMES, Christyan Elliot. b 68. Westcott Ho Cam. **d** 09 **p** 10. C Maidstone St Martin *Cant* 09-11; rtd 11; Hon C Brighton Gd Shep Preston *Chich* from 11. *14 St Mary's Square, Brighton BN2 1FZ* T: (01273) 241753 E: christyanj@yahoo.co.uk

JAMES, Colin Robert. b 39. Magd Coll Ox BA 61 MA 65 DipEd 62. SAOMC 93. **d** 96 **p** 97. NSM Wokingham All SS *Ox* 96-13; PtO from 13. *7 Sewell Avenue, Wokingham RG41 1NT* T: 0118-978 1515

JAMES, David. See JAMES, Richard David

JAMES, The Ven David Brian. b 30. FCA 52 Univ of Wales (Swansea) BA 63. St Mich Coll Llan 55. **d** 57 **p** 58. C Llandeilo Tal-y-bont *S & B* 57-59; C Swansea Ch Ch 59-63; V Bryngwyn and Newchurch and Llanbedr etc 63-70; R Llanfeugan w Llanthetty and Glyncollwng etc 70-79; V Ilston w Pennard 79-94; Hon Can Brecon Cathl 87-89; RD Gower 89-94; Can Brecon Cathl 89-94; Chan Brecon Cathl 93-94; Adn Brecon 94-99; P-in-c Llanllyr-yn-Rhos w Llanfihangel Helygen 94-99; Adn Gower 99-00; rtd 00. *1 Llys Ger-y-Llan, Pontarddulais, Swansea SA4 8HJ* T: (01792) 883023

✠**JAMES, The Rt Revd David Charles.** b 45. Ex Univ BSc 66 PhD 71. St Jo Coll Nottm BA 73. **d** 73 **p** 74 **c** 98. C Portswood Ch Ch *Win* 73-76; C Goring-by-Sea *Chich* 76-78; Chapl UEA *Nor* 78-82; V Ecclesfield *Sheff* 82-90; RD 87-90; V Portswood Ch Ch *Win* 90-98; Hon Can Win Cathl 98; Suff Bp Pontefract *Wakef* 98-02; Bp Bradf 02-10; rtd 10. *7 Long Lane, Beverley HU17 0NH* T: (01482) 871240 E: davidcharlesjames@googlemail.com

JAMES, David Clive. b 40. Bris Univ BA 61 K Coll Lon DipEd 87. Lich Th Coll 62 St Steph Ho Ox 64. **d** 65 **p** 66. C Portslade St Nic *Chich* 65-68; C Haywards Heath St Wilfrid 68-71; Chapl Brighton Poly 71-75; PtO from 75. *22 Bradford Road, Lewes BN7 1RB* T: (01273) 471851 E: davidcjames@talktalk.net

JAMES, David Henry. b 45. Univ of Wales MB, BCh 68 Univ of Wales (Swansea) MA 92 MRCPsych 75. SWMTC 95. **d** 98. NSM Truro Cathl 98-00; rtd 00; PtO *Truro* 00-03; *Sarum* 03-05; LtO *Arg* from 06. *Glencruitten House, Glencruitten, Oban PA34 4QB* T: (01631) 562431 E: david.james.855@btinternet.com

JAMES, Preb David Howard. b 47. Ex Univ BA 70 MA 73 Pemb Coll Cam CertEd 72. Linc Th Coll 81. **d** 83 **p** 84. C Tavistock and Gulworthy *Ex* 83-86; C E Teignmouth 86-88; C W Teignmouth 86-88; P-in-c Bishopsteignton 88-89; P-in-c Ideford, Luton and Ashcombe 88-89; TV Teignmouth, Ideford w Luton, Ashcombe etc 90-95; P-in-c Sidmouth, Woolbrook, Salcombe Regis, Sidbury etc 95-97; TR 97-13; Preb Ex Cathl 99-13; RD Ottery 03-13; rtd 13. *1 Farm Close, Exeter EX2 5PJ* T: (01392) 424690 E: rev.davidjames@btinternet.com

JAMES, David William. b 55. Birm Univ BA 99. Coll of Resurr Mirfield 86. **d** 88 **p** 88. C New Rossington *Sheff* 88-90; V Yardley Wood *Birm* 90-95; P-in-c Allens Cross 95-96; V 96-06; P-in-c Rubery 05-12; V Sutton in Ashfield St Mary *S'well* from 12. *St Mary's Vicarage, 11 Church Avenue, Sutton-in-Ashfield, Nottingham NG17 2EB* T: (01623) 554509 M: 07511-918806 E: david.james5@btinternet.com

JAMES, Gerwyn. See JAMES, Joshua John Gerwyn

JAMES, Gillian Mary. b 49. **d** 99. OLM Bassaleg *Mon* 99-05. *69 Hollybush Road, Cyncoed, Cardiff CF2 4SZ* T: (029) 2073 2673

JAMES, Glyn. See JAMES, Henry Glyn

JAMES, Canon Godfrey Walter. b 36. Univ of Wales (Lamp) BA 58 Univ of Wales (Cardiff) MA 60 St Pet Coll Ox DipEd 61 BA 63 MA 67. St Mich Coll Llan 63. **d** 64 **p** 65. C Canton St Jo *Llan* 64-71; V Dinas and Penygraig w Williamstown 71-85; V Kenfig Hill 85-01; Hon Can Llan Cathl 96-01; rtd 01; PtO *Llan* from 04. *23 Crossfield Avenue, Porthcawl CF36 3LA*

✠**JAMES, The Rt Revd Graham Richard.** b 51. Lanc Univ BA 72 Hon FGCM 92. Cuddesdon Coll 72. **d** 75 **p** 76 **c** 93. C Pet Ch Carpenter 75-79; C Digswell *St Alb* 79-82; TV Digswell and Panshanger 82-83; Sen Selection Sec and Sec Cand Cttee ACCM 83-87; Abp's Chapl *Cant* 87-93; Hon Can Dallas from 89; Suff Bp St Germans *Truro* 93-99; Bp Nor from 99. *The Bishop's House, Norwich NR3 1SB* T: (01603) 629001 F: 761613 E: bishop@dioceseofnorwich.org

JAMES, Helen Alison. See JONES, Helen Alison

JAMES, Henley George. b 31. Sarum & Wells Th Coll 79. **d** 81 **p** 82. C Tottenham H Trin *Lon* 81-85; C Cricklewood St Pet 85-88; P-in-c 88-89; V Bearwood *Birm* 89-97; rtd 97; PtO *Birm* from 97. *32 Antrobus Road, Birmingham B21 9NZ*

JAMES, Henry Glyn. b 26. Keble Coll Ox BA 50 MA 58 Toronto Univ MEd 74. Wycliffe Hall Ox 50. **d** 52 **p** 53. C Edgbaston St Aug *Birm* 52-54; C Surbiton St Matt *S'wark* 54-57; Housemaster Kingham Hill Sch Oxon 57-62; Chapl St Lawr Coll Ramsgate 62-68; Canada 68-73; Hon C Kidmore End *Ox* 74-77; K Jas Coll of Henley 74-87; Hon C Remenham *Ox* 77-88; Chapl The Henley Coll 87-88; Chapl Toulouse *Eur* 88-91; rtd 91; PtO *Win* from 93. *13 Harbour Road, Bournemouth BH6 4DD* T: (01202) 427697 E: glyn.james55@gmail.com

JAMES, Prof Ian Nigel. b 48. Leeds Univ BSc 69 Man Univ PhD 74. SAOMC 99. **d** 02 **p** 03. NSM Bracknell *Ox* 02-04; NSM Winkfield and Cranbourne 04-10; P-in-c Bootle, Corney, Whicham and Whitbeck *Carl* 10-15; rtd 15. *High Pasture, Crook Road, Kendal LA8 8LY* M: 07808-207422 E: dr.i.n.james@btinternet.com

JAMES, Jane Eva. b 55. Birm Univ BSc 76 W Midl Coll of Educn PGCE 77. St Mich Coll Llan 08. **d** 11 **p** 12. NSM Llansantffraid-ym-Mechain and Llanfechain *St As* 11-13; P-in-c Meifod w Llangynyw w Pont Robert w Pont Dolanog from 13. *The Vicarage, Meifod SY22 6DH* M: 07748-697112 T: (01938) 500231 E: pilotjj55@gmail.com

JAMES, Jeffrey Aneurin. b 53. Univ of Wales (Cardiff) BScEcon 80 Bris Univ MSc 85 MHSM 83. WEMTC 98. **d** 01 **p** 02. NSM Minchinhampton *Glouc* 01-07; NSM Painswick, Sheepscombe, Cranham, The Edge etc 07-13; P-in-c Mylor w

Flushing *Truro* from 13. *17 Olivey Place, Bells Hill, Mylor Bridge, Falmouth TR11 5RX* T: (01326) 374408
E: jayscott@dsl.pipex.com

JAMES, Canon Jeremy Richard. b 52. Jes Coll Cam BA 73 MA 77 York Univ CertEd 77. Cranmer Hall Dur 86. **d** 88 **p** 89. C Broxbourne w Wormley *St Alb* 88-91; C Hailsham *Chich* 91-99; V Wadhurst from 99; V Tidebrook from 99; P-in-c Stonegate from 99; RD Rotherfield 03-14; Can and Preb Chich Cathl from 12. *The Vicarage, High Street, Wadhurst TN5 6AA* T: (01892) 782083 E: jeremy@rjames.freeserve.co.uk

JAMES, Mrs Joanna Elizabeth. b 72. SAOMC. **d** 06 **p** 07. C Northwood Em *Lon* 06-10; C S Mimms Ch Ch from 10. *8 Wentworth Road, Barnet EN5 4NT* T: (020) 8441 0645

JAMES, John Charles. b 35. Keble Coll Ox BA 59. Linc Th Coll 68. **d** 70 **p** 71. C S Shields St Hilda w St Thos *Dur* 70-77; P-in-c Jarrow Docks 77-78; Adn Seychelles 78-92; V Mylor w Flushing *Truro* 92-05; rtd 06; PtO *Dur* from 11. *172 Westoe Road, South Shields NE33 3PH*

JAMES, John David. b 23. CCC Cam MA. Wells Th Coll. **d** 50 **p** 51. C Romford St Edw *Chelmsf* 50-54; C Cannock *Lich* 54-56; R Wickham Bishops *Chelmsf* 56-61; V Stansted Mountfitchet 61-71; V Clacton St Jas 71-84; R Poulshot *Sarum* 84; V Rowde 84; R Rowde and Poulshot 84-88; rtd 88; PtO *Heref* 92-14. *15 Beaconsfield Park, Ludlow SY8 4LY* T: (01584) 873754

JAMES, John Hugh Alexander. b 56. St Jo Coll Dur BA 78. St Mich Coll Llan. **d** 81 **p** 82. C Newton Nottage *Llan* 81-84; Prov Youth and Children's Officer Ch in Wales 84-92; V Llanfihangel-ar-arth 84-92; V Llanfihangel-ar-arth w Capel Dewi 97-04; RD Emlyn 01-04; V Cydweli and Llandyfaelog 04-12; AD Cydweli 05-07; R Norwich Ch Ch USA from 12. *226 Hunter's Road, Norwich CT 06360, USA* T: (001) (860) 887 4249

JAMES, John Paul. b 30. Sarum Th Coll 58. **d** 60 **p** 61. C Milton *Portsm* 60-65; C Stanmer w Falmer and Moulsecoomb *Chich* 65-69; PC Brighton H Trin 69-71; R Saguenay St Jean Canada 71; Dean Quebec 77-87; R Westmount St Matthias 87-96; rtd 96. *301-97 Huron Street, Stratford ON N5A 5S7, Canada* F: (001) (519) 273 9226 E: helenandpaul@rogers.com

JAMES, Joshua John Gerwyn. b 31. St D Coll Lamp BA 52. **d** 54 **p** 55. C Haverfordwest St Mary w St Thos *St D* 54-56; C Llanaber w Caerdeon *Ban* 56-57; CF 57-76; V Tidenham w Beachley and Lancaut *Glouc* 76-80; R Aberdovey *Ban* 80-82; V Quinton w Marston Sicca *Glouc* 82-90; R Campden 88-90; P-in-c Upper Chelsea St Simon *Lon* 90-96; rtd 96; PtO *S'wark* from 97. *25 The Watergardens, Warren Road, Kingston upon Thames KT2 7LF* T: (020) 8974 6889

JAMES, Mrs Julie Margaret. b 55. Shenstone Coll of Educn TCert 76 BEd 77. Qu Coll Birm 01. **d** 04 **p** 05. NSM Salwarpe and Hindlip w Martin Hussingtree *Worc* 04-06; NSM St Jo in Bedwardine 06-09; NSM Abberton, The Flyfords, Naunton Beauchamp etc 09-14; R Berrow w Pendock, Eldersfield, Hollybush etc from 14. *Thistledown, Pendock, Gloucester GL19 3PW* M: 07751-465241 T: (01531) 650563
E: julie.m.james@btinternet.com.uk

JAMES, Keith Edwin Arthur. b 38. Sarum & Wells Th Coll 85. **d** 87 **p** 88. C Hempnall *Nor* 87-91; R Roughton and Felbrigg, Metton, Sustead etc 91-98; V Ascension Is 98-01; rtd 02; Chapl Laslett's *Worc* from 05. *30 Woodland Rise, Tasburgh, Norwich NR15 1NF* T: (01508) 470032
E: keith.james2011@btinternet.com

JAMES, Keith Nicholas. b 66. Leeds Univ BA 91. St Jo Coll Nottm MA 93. **d** 93 **p** 94. C Crosby *Linc* 93-96; P-in-c Cherry Willingham w Greetwell 96-00; R S Lawres Gp 00-03; RD Lawres 01-03; R Ribbesford w Bewdley and Dowles *Worc* 03-11; R Ribbesford w Bewdley and Dowles and Wribbenhall 11-15; RD Kidderminster 07-13; Can Res Nor Cathl from 15; CMD Officer from 15. *The Rectory, 57 Park Lane, Bewdley DY12 2HA* T: (01299) 402275 or 404773
E: kn.james@btinternet.com

JAMES, Malcolm. b 37. CEng MICE MIStructE. NOC 80. **d** 83 **p** 84. NSM Ripponden *Wakef* 83-10; PtO *Leeds* from 10. *Lower Stones, Bar Lane, Rishworth, Sowerby Bridge HX6 4EY* T: (01274) 677439 E: malcolm@mjconsultancy.demon.co.uk

JAMES, Ms Manon Ceridwen. b 69. Poly of Wales BA 90 Selw Coll Cam BA 93 MA 97. Ridley Hall Cam. **d** 94 **p** 97. C Llandudno *Ban* 94-98; P-in-c Glanogwen w St Ann's w Llanllechid 98-99; V 99-05; V Pentir 04-05; Dir of Ords 02-05; Dioc Dir Lifelong Learning 05-08; R Llanddulas and Llysfaen from 08; Bp's Adv for Min 12-13; Dir Min from 14. *The Rectory, 2 Rhodfa Wen, Llysfaen, Colwyn Bay LL29 8LE* T: (01492) 516728
E: manoncjames@gmail.com

JAMES, Mark Nicholas. b 55. Jes Coll Ox BA 77 MA 80 PGCE 79. Ridley Hall Cam 03. **d** 05 **p** 06. C Gt Dunmow and Barnston *Chelmsf* 05-09; R Bentley Common, Kelvedon Hatch and

Navestock from 09; P-in-c Doddinghurst from 14. *The Rectory, 2 Church Road, Kelvedon Hatch, Brentwood CM14 5TJ* T: (01277) 373486 E: revmarkjames@btinternet.com

JAMES, Martin. b 40. ACII. **d** 94 **p** 95. OLM N Farnborough *Guildf* 94-08; OLM Camberley St Martin Old Dean 08-09; NSM 09-10; rtd 10; PtO *Guildf* from 10. *43 Ashley Road, Farnborough GU14 7HB* T: (01252) 544698
E: martinjean.james@ntlworld.com

JAMES, Michael Howard. b 55. Bris Univ LLB 73 Solicitor 92. WEMTC 04. **d** 06 **p** 07. NSM Clifton H Trin, St Andr and St Pet *Bris* 06-08; NSM Westbury Park LEP 08-15; Chapl Partis Coll Bath from 15. *10 Hill Drive, Failand, Bristol BS8 3UX* T: (01275) 393729 E: jamfam@jamfam4.wanadoo.co.uk *or* cranmer1662@hotmail.co.uk

JAMES, Paul Maynard. b 31. Univ of Wales (Ban) BA 52 Fitzw Ho Cam BA 54 MA 58. Ridley Hall Cam 56. **d** 57 **p** 58. C Newhaven *Chich* 57-60; Kenya 60-65; SW Area Sec CCCS 65-68; V Shrewsbury St Julian *Lich* 68-76; V Shrewsbury H Trin w St Julian 76-90; P-in-c Woore and Norton in Hales 90-98; Adn Salop's Adv on Evang 90-98; RD Hodnet *Lich* 93-97; rtd 98; PtO *Heref* from 00; *Lich* from 00. *Nettledene, Elms Lane, Little Stretton, Church Stretton SY6 6RD* T: (01694) 722559

JAMES, Canon Peter David. b 42. Keble Coll Ox BA 63 Lon Univ BD 67. Tyndale Hall Bris 64. **d** 67 **p** 68. C Haydock St Mark *Liv* 67-69; C Ashton-in-Makerfield St Thos 69-74; V Whiston 74-80; V Harlech and Llanfair-juxta-Harlech etc *Ban* 80-94; R Botwnnog w Bryncroes 94-99; V Botwnnog w Bryncroes w Llangwnnadl w Penllech 99-07; Hon Can Ban Cathl 02-07; rtd 07. *Tabor, Llithfaen, Pwllheli LL53 6NL* T: (01758) 750202 E: peterjames@botwnnog.fsnet.co.uk

JAMES, Raymond John. b 36. Linc Th Coll 85. **d** 87 **p** 88. C Cov E 87-91; V Wolvey w Burton Hastings, Copston Magna etc 91-01; rtd 01. *46 Cornmore, Pershore WR10 1HX* T: (01336) 556537

JAMES, Richard Andrew. b 44. Mert Coll Ox BA 67 MA 70. Tyndale Hall Bris. **d** 70 **p** 71. C Bebington *Ches* 70-73; C Histon *Ely* 73-77; Chapl Guildf Coll of Tech 77-80; C Guildf St Sav w Stoke-next-Guildford 77-80; Ecum Chapl Bedf Coll of HE *St Alb* 81-83; TV Ipsley *Worc* 84-89; R Mulbarton w Kenningham *Nor* 89-92; rtd 93. *5 Links Way, Harrogate HG2 7EW* T: (01423) 889410 E: hilaryqjames@hotmail.com

JAMES, Richard David. b 65. Clare Coll Cam MA 88 Lon Hosp MB, BChir 90. Ridley Hall Cam 92. **d** 95 **p** 96. C Clifton Ch Ch w Em *Bris* 95-98; C Enfield Ch Ch Trent Park *Lon* 98-00; V from 00; AD Enfield from 09. *The Vicarage, 2A Chalk Lane, Cockfosters, Barnet EN4 9JQ* T: (020) 8441 1230 *or* T/F: 8449 0556 E: richard@ccc1.fsnet.co.uk

JAMES, Richard David. b 45. Cheltenham & Glouc Coll of HE MA 97. Lon Coll of Div 66. **d** 70 **p** 71. C Boultham *Linc* 70-74; C New Waltham 74-77; TV Cleethorpes 77-87; TR E Bris 87-99; Partnership P E Bris from 99; V E Bris St Ambrose and St Leon from 99. *St Ambrose Vicarage, 487 Whitehall Road, Bristol BS5 7DA* T: 0117-951 2270 M: 07749-243407
E: rd.james@live.co.uk

JAMES, Richard Lindsay. b 39. Kelham Th Coll 61. **d** 66 **p** 67. C Seacroft *Ripon* 66-74; rtd 04. *3 Cavendish Mews, Hove BN3 1AZ* T: (01273) 324672

JAMES, Richard William. b 47. St D Coll Lamp. **d** 75 **p** 76. C Hubberston *St D* 75-78; R Pendine w Llanmiloe and Eglwys Gymyn w Marros 78-83; V Caerwent w Dinham and Llanfair Discoed etc *Mon* 83-84; Chapl Gothenburg w Halmstad, Jönköping etc *Eur* 84-89; P-in-c Shooters Hill Ch Ch *S'wark* 89-97; V Plumstead St Mark and St Marg 97-07; rtd 07. *Gärdesvägen 9H, 87162 Härnösand, Sweden* T: (0046) (611) 435557 E: eva.jame@comhem.se

JAMES, Robert William. b 79. Kent Univ BA 01 SOAS Lon MA 02 PhD 10 CCC Cam MPhil 03 St Andr Univ MLitt 13. Westcott Ho Cam 02. **d** 05 **p** 06. C St Edm Way and Bradfield St Clare, Bradfield St George etc *St E* 05-07; PtO *Glouc* 12-13; NSM Coleford, Staunton, Newland, Redbrook etc 13-14; V Newnham w Awre and Blakeney from 14. *The Vicarage, 1 Whetstones, Unlawater Lane, Newnham GL14 1BT* T: (01594) 516671 E: robdogcollar@yahoo.co.uk

JAMES, Roger Michael. b 44. K Coll Lon BD 66 AKC 66. **d** 69 **p** 70. C Frindsbury w Upnor *Roch* 69-72; LtO *St Alb* 73-78; C Digswell 78-81; R Knebworth 81-92; P-in-c Upper Team and Local Min Adv (Stafford) *Lich* 92-99; Dir Cottesloe Chr Tr Progr *Ox* 99-03; R Cusop w Blakemere, Bredwardine w Brobury etc *Heref* 03-09; RD Abbeydore 06-09; rtd 09. *Ty Siloh, Llandeilo'r Fan, Brecon LD3 8UD* T: (01874) 636126
E: tysiloh@googlemail.com

JAMES, Sandra Kay. See GARDNER, Sandra Kay

JAMES, Ms Sheridan Angharad. b 71. Univ of Wales (Abth) BA 93 PGCE 94 MPhil 00. SEITE 04. **d** 07 **p** 08. C Catford (Southend) and Downham *S'wark* 07-11; V Hatcham St Cath

from 11; Dean of Women's Min Woolwich Area from 12. *St Catherine's Vicarage, 102A Pepys Road, London SE14 5SG* T: (020) 7639 1050 M: 07703-291594
E: revsheridanjames@gmail.com

JAMES, Stephen Lynn. b 53. Oak Hill Th Coll BA 86. **d** 86 **p** 87. C Heigham H Trin *Nor* 86-89; C Vancouver St Jo Canada 89-93; R Bebington *Ches* 93-06; R Rusholme H Trin *Man* from 06. *Holy Trinity Rectory, Platt Lane, Manchester M14 5NF* T: 0161-224 1123 F: 224 1144 E: office@plattchurch.org

JAMES, Canon Stephen Nicholas. b 51. Reading Univ MA 87 Bris Univ EdD 95 ARCM 72 LTCL 72 FTCL 73 FRSA 00. SAOMC 01. **d** 04 **p** 05. NSM Hanney, Denchworth and E Challow *Ox* 04-07; P-in-c Goetre w Llanover *Mon* 07-13; Dioc Dir Educn from 11; Hon Can St Woolos Cathl from 14. *Pear Tree Cottage, Llanfair Kilgeddin, Abergavenny NP7 9DY* T: (01873) 840229 E: ddemonmouth@churchinwales.org.uk

JAMES, Mrs Susan Margaret. b 58. SRN 81 RSCN 81 St Jo Coll Dur BA 04. Cranmer Hall Dur 00. **d** 04 **p** 05. NSM Derby St Paul 04-07. *267 Victoria Avenue, Ockbrook, Derby DE72 3RL* T: (01332) 673551 E: suzejames@hotmail.com

JAMES, Susikaran. b 75. Ripon Coll Cuddesdon 10. **d** 12 **p** 13. C Tulse Hill H Trin and St Matthias *S'wark* from 12. *132 Trinity Rise, London SW2 2QT* M: 07943-306963
E: susikaranjames@gmail.com

JAMES, Thomas Martin St John. b 85. St Jo Coll Cam MA 12. Westcott Ho Cam 09. **d** 12 **p** 13. C Petersfield *Portsm* 12-15; Chapl RN from 15. *Royal Naval Chaplaincy Service, Mail Point 1.2, Leach Building, Whale Island, Portsmouth PO2 8BY* T: (023) 9262 5055 F: 9262 5134

JAMES, Veronica Norma. b 59. STETS 99. **d** 02 **p** 03. NSM Ashton Keynes, Leigh and Minety *Bris* 02-05; R Merriott w Hinton, Dinnington and Lopen *B & W* 05-10; R The Guitings, Cutsdean, Farmcote etc *Glouc* 10-14; AD N Cotswold 10-14; Hon Can Glouc Cathl 12-14; R Skipton H Trin *Leeds* from 14. *The Rectory, Rectory Lane, Skipton BD23 1ER*
E: rev.veronica@btinternet.com

JAMES, William Glynne George. b 39. Trin Coll Carmarthen 82. **d** 85 **p** 86. NSM Gorseinon *S & B* 85-09; PtO from 09. *23 Cecil Road, Gowerton, Swansea SA4 3DF* T: (01792) 872363

JAMESON, Miss Beverley Joyce. b 60. St Jo Coll Nottm 09. **d** 11 **p** 12. C en Telford *Lich* 11-15; TV Droitwich Spa *Worc* from 15; C Salwarpe and Hindlip w Martin Hussingtree from 15. *The Rectory, Salwarpe, Droitwich WR9 0AH* M: 07817-379583 T: (01905) 799002 E: bevjameson@live.co.uk

JAMESON, Canon Dermot Christopher Ledgard. b 27. TCD BA 49 MA 54. CITC 49. **d** 50 **p** 51. C Seagoe *D & D* 50-53; C Holywood 53-57; I Kilkeel 57-62; I Donaghcloney w Waringstown 62-79; Can Dromore Cathl 77-93; I Kilbroney 79-93; Treas Dromore Cathl 81-83; Prec Dromore Cathl 83-90; Chan Dromore Cathl 90-93; rtd 93. *Concord, 10B Kilbroney Road, Rostrevor, Newry BT34 3BH* T: (028) 4173 9728

JAMESON, Howard Kingsley. b 63. Warwick Univ BSc 84. Trin Coll Bris 99. **d** 02 **p** 03. C Wareham *Sarum* 02-05; P-in-c Monkton Farleigh, S Wraxall and Winsley 05-11; P-in-c Bradford-on-Avon Ch Ch 10-11; R N Bradford on Avon and Villages 11-12; P-in-c Patchway *Bris* from 12. *86 Oakleaze, Patchway, Bristol BS34 5AW* T: 0117-370 8279
E: revh.jameson@gmail.com

JAMESON, Peter. b 31. Trin Coll Cam BA 54 MA 60. Linc Th Coll. **d** 62 **p** 63. C Earl's Court St Cuth w St Matthias *Lon* 62-68; C Notting Hill St Clem 68-72; C Notting Hill St Clem and St Mark 72-74; TV Notting Hill 74-77; V Stoke Newington St Olave 77-95; rtd 95; PtO *Chich* from 95. *Colemans, Warren Lane, Cross in Hand, Heathfield TN21 0TB* T: (01435) 863414

JAMIE, Mrs Katherine Elizabeth. b 81. Cranmer Hall Dur 12. **d** 15. C Easington and Easington Colliery *Dur* from 15. *The Bungalow, Church Walk, Eastington Village, Peterlee SR8 3BW* M: 07792-159154 E: rev.katejamie@gmail.com

JAMIESON, Christopher Donald. b 50. Man Univ MEd 89 Westmr Coll Ox BEd 72. SNWTP. **d** 13 **p** 14. OLM Turton Moorland *Man* from 13. *25 Timberbottom, Bolton LB2 3DG* T: (01204) 302346 M: 07726-349195
E: roscanvel@hotmail.com

JAMIESON, Douglas. *See* JAMIESON, William Douglas

JAMIESON, Emma Victoria. *See* HIGGINS, Emma Victoria

JAMIESON, Guy Stuart. b 66. Leeds Univ BA 98. Ripon Coll Cuddesdon. **d** 00 **p** 01. C Woodhall *Bradf* 00-03; V Southowram and Claremount *Leeds* from 03. *St Anne's Vicarage, Church Lane, Southowram, Halifax HX3 9TD* T: (01422) 365229 E: guy.jamieson@virgin.net

JAMIESON, Iain Blair. b 66. Lon Univ BA 90 TCD MTh 12. **d** 11 **p** 12. C Ballymena w Ballyclug *Conn* from 11. *38 Ballee Road East, Ballymena BT42 3DH* T: (028) 2564 7049 M: 07872-966119 E: i.jamieson@hotmail.com

JAMIESON, Ian David. b 73. Leeds Univ BA 99 PGCE 00. St Jo Coll Nottm 11. **d** 13 **p** 14. C Em TM *Leeds* from 13. *12 Moor Close, Huddersfield HD4 7BP* M: 07594-552519
E: revianjamieson@gmail.com

JAMIESON, Kenneth Euan Oram. b 24. Roch Th Coll 60. **d** 62 **p** 63. C Bromley SS Pet and Paul *Roch* 62-66; R Colchester St Mary Magd *Chelmsf* 66-71; V Bexleyheath St Pet *Roch* 71-78; P-in-c Maidstone St Faith *Cant* 78-83; P-in-c Maidstone St Paul 78-83; Ind Chapl *St Alb* 83-89; rtd 89; PtO *B & W* from 89. *4 Ashley Road, Taunton TA1 5BP* T: (01823) 289367
E: ken@keoj4.plus.com

JAMIESON, Canon Marilyn. b 52. Cranmer Hall Dur IDC 80. **d** 91 **p** 94. Par Dn Bensham *Dur* 91-93; Par Dn Ryton w Hedgefield 93-94; Chapl Metro Cen Gateshead 94-02 and from 06; Bp's Sen Chapl 02-05; Hon C Ryton 05-06; Hon Can Dur Cathl from 97. *Barmoor House, 64 Main Road, Ryton NE40 3AJ* T: 0191-413 4592 *or* 493 0259

JAMIESON, Mrs Moira Elizabeth. b 50. **d** 08 **p** 09. C Lenzie *Glas* from 08. *3 Cawder Place, Cumbernauld, Glasgow G68 0BG* M: 07977-096446 T: (01236) 597633
E: jamiemoi60@sky.com

JAMIESON, Peter Grant. b 64. Liv Univ BA 87. Coll of Resurr Mirfield 90. **d** 93 **p** 94. C Charlton Kings St Mary *Glouc* 93-96. *Broncroft Castle, Broncroft, Craven Arms SY7 9HL* T: (01584) 841203 M: 07779-148898 E: ottershrew@gmail.com

JAMIESON, Miss Rosalind Heather. b 49. CertEd 71. Cranmer Hall Dur 79. **dss** 81 **d** 87 **p** 94. Queensbury All SS *Lon* 81-85; Richmond H Trin and Ch Ch *S'wark* 85-87; Par Dn 87-91; Par Dn Burmantofts St Steph and St Agnes *Ripon* 91-94; C 94-99; TV Seacroft *Leeds* 99-14; rtd 14. *The Vicarage, 134 Leeds Road, Allerton Bywater, Castleford WF10 2HB*
E: heather.jamieson1@ntlworld.com

JAMIESON, Mrs Susan Jennifer. b 49. Liv Univ SRN 71. Dioc OLM tr scheme 97. **d** 00 **p** 01. OLM Clubmoor *Liv* from 00. *15 Winsford Road, Liverpool L13 0BJ* T: 0151-475 7562 M: 07879-425277 E: susiejam@blueyonder.co.uk

JAMIESON, Thomas Lindsay. b 53. N Lon Poly BSc 74. Cranmer Hall Dur. **d** 77 **p** 78. C Gateshead Fell *Dur* 77-80; C Gateshead 80-84; TV 84-90; P-in-c Gateshead St Cuth w St Paul 90-91; TV Bensham 91-93; P-in-c Ryton w Hedgefield 93-95; R 95-05; R Ryton from 05; AD Gateshead W 94-98. *Barmoor House, 64 Main Road, Ryton NE40 3AJ* T: 0191-413 4592
E: atl.jamieson@talk21.com

JAMIESON, William Douglas. b 38. Oak Hill Th Coll 63. **d** 66 **p** 67. C Shrewsbury St Julian *Lich* 66-68; C Bucknall and Bagnall 68-70; C Otley *Bradf* 70-74; TV Keighley 74-81; V Utley 81-00; rtd 00; PtO *Ches* from 00. *11 The Quay, Frodsham, Warrington WA6 7JG* T: (01928) 731085 M: 07974-947838
E: douglasjamieson@lineone.net

JAMIESON, William Mervyn Noel. b 66. CITC 03. **d** 07 **p** 08. NSM Ballybeen *D & D* 07-10; NSM Comber from 10. *Millview House, 1 Old Ballygowan Road, Comber, Newtownards BT23 5NP* T: (028) 9187 1881 *or* 9187 3963 M: 07808-481669
E: rev.merv@btinternet.com

JANES, Austin Steven. b 75. York Univ BA 97. Ripon Coll Cuddesdon 06. **d** 08 **p** 09. C Crewe St Andr w St Jo *Ches* 08-11; Min Can St Alb Abbey *St Alb* 11-14; TV Hemel Hempstead from 14. *33 Craigavon Road, Hemel Hempstead HP2 6BA* E: austinjanes@gmail.com

JANES, David Edward. b 40. Lon Univ BSc 67. Glouc Sch of Min 86. **d** 89 **p** 90. NSM Church Stretton *Heref* 89-00; rtd 00; PtO *Heref* from 00. *Bourton Westwood Farm, 3 Bourton Westwood, Much Wenlock TF13 6QB* T: (01952) 727393

JANICKER, Laurence Norman. b 47. SS Mark & Jo Coll Chelsea DipEd 69. St Jo Coll Nottm 83. **d** 85 **p** 86. C Beverley Minster *York* 85-89; R Lockington and Lund and Scorborough w Leconfield 89-94; V Cov St Geo 94-08; rtd 08; PtO *Nor* from 09. *136 Manor Road, Newton St Faith, Norwich NR10 3LG* T: (01603) 898614 E: winnieaurens@gmail.com

JANSMA, Henry Peter. b 57. NE Bible Coll (USA) BA 79 Westmr Th Sem (USA) MA 85 St Jo Coll Dur PhD 91. Linc Th Coll 89. **d** 91 **p** 92. C Spalding St Mary and St Nic *Linc* 91-96; P-in-c Cleethorpes St Aid 96-97; V 97-01; R Haddon Heights St Mary USA from 01. *501 Green Street, Haddon Heights NJ 08035-1903, USA* T: (001) (856) 547 0565 *or* 547 3240 F: 310 0565
E: stmaryshh@juno.com

JANSSON, The Very Revd Maria Patricia. b 55. Milltown Inst Dub MReISc 93. CITC 00. **d** 01 **p** 02. C Galway w Kilcummin *T, K & A* 01-02; C Wexford w Ardcolm and Killurin *C & O* 02-04; I Cork w Killinick and Mulrankin 02-04; P-in-c 04-09; I Wexford and Kilscoran Union 10-11; Dean Waterford from 11; I Waterford w Killea, Drumcannon and Dunhill from 11; Preb Ossory Cathl from 12. *The Deanery, 41 Grange Park Road, Waterford, Republic of Ireland* T: (00353) (51) 874119 *or* 858958 M: 87-225 5793
E: miajansson@eircom.net *or* dean@waterford.anglican.org

JANVIER, Philip Harold. b 57. Trin Coll Bris BA 87. **d** 87 **p** 88. C Much Woolton *Liv* 87-90; TV Toxteth St Philemon w St Gabr and St Cleopas 90-97; TR Gateacre from 97. *St Stephen's Rectory, Belle Vale Road, Liverpool L25 2PQ* T/F: 0151-487 9338 E: philjanvier.home@virgin.net

JAONA, Ramahalefitra Hyacinthe <u>Arsène</u>. b 70. St Paul's Th Coll Ambatoharanana Madagascar 89. **d** 94 **p** 96. Madagascar 94-97 and from 98; C Caldicot *Mon* 97-98. *Mission Angelican, BP 126, 206 Antalaha, Antsiranana, Madagascar*

JAQUES, Geoffrey Sanderson. b 48. Man Univ BSc. NEOC 94. **d** 97 **p** 98. NSM Gt Ayton w Easby and Newton under Roseberry *York* from 97. *132 Roseberry Crescent, Great Ayton, Middlesbrough TS9 6EW* T: (01642) 722979 E: jaques132@btinternet.com

JAQUISS, Mrs Gabrielle <u>Clair</u>. b 56. Clare Coll Cam BA 79 MA 83 LRAM 76. NOC 06. **d** 08 **p** 09. NSM Bowdon *Ches* 08-11; NSM Hale Barns w Ringway from 11. *Ingersley, Belgrave Road, Bowdon, Altrincham WA14 2NZ* T: 0161-928 0717 M: 07843-375494 E: clairjq@aol.com

JARAM, Peter Ellis. b 45. Lon Univ BSc 70 CEng 77 MIET 77 MBIM 88. Linc Th Coll 94. **d** 94 **p** 95. C Bridlington Priory *York* 94-96; C Rufforth w Moor Monkton and Hessay 96-97; C Healaugh w Wighill, Bilbrough and Askham Richard 96-97; P-in-c 97-01; Chapl Askham Bryan Coll 97-01; V Brompton by Sawdon w Hutton Buscel, Snainton etc *York* 01-05; r-d 05; PtO *York* from 05. *74 Eastgate, Pickering YO18 7DY* T: (01751) 477831 E: pwj74@btinternet.com

JARDINE, Canon Anthony. b 38. Qu Coll Birm 64. **d** 67 **p** 68. C Baldock w Bygrave and Clothall *St Alb* 67-71; C N Stoneham *Win* 71-73; P-in-c Ecchinswell cum Sydmonton 73-79; P-in-c Burghclere w Newtown 78-79; R Burghclere w Newtown and Ecchinswell w Sydmonton 79-87; R Wonston and Stoke Charity w Hunton 87-97; P-in-c Chawton and Farringdon 97-04; Dioc Rural Officer 97-04; Hon Can Win Cathl 99-04; rtd 04; Hon C Knight's Enham and Smannell w Enham Alamein *Win* 04-08; PtO *Heref* from 09. *9 The Meads, Kington HR5 3DQ* E: rev_jardine@hotmail.com

JARDINE, Canon David John (<u>Brother David</u>). b 42. QUB BA 65. CITC 67. **d** 67 **p** 68. C Ballymacarrett St Patr *D & D* 67-70; Asst Chapl QUB 70-73; SSF from 73; Asst Chapl HM Pris Belfast 75-79; Chapl 79-85; USA 85-88; Sen Asst Warden Ch of Ireland Min of Healing 88-92; Dir Divine Healing Min 92-08; Can Belf Cathl from 07. *3 Richmond Park, Stranmillis, Belfast BT9 5EF* T: (028) 9066 6200 or 9031 1532 E-mail divinehealing@live.co.uk or davidjjardine@gmail.com

JARDINE, Canon Norman. b 47. QUB BSc 72. Trin Coll Bris 74. **d** 76 **p** 77. C Magheralin *D & D* 76-78; C Dundonald 78-80; Bp's C Ballybeen 80-88; I Willowfield 88-00; Dir Think Again 00-04; I Ballynafeigh St Jude from 04; Can Belf Cathl from 03. *10 Mornington, Belfast BT7 3JS* T: (028) 9050 4976 E: norman.jardine2@ntlworld.com

JARDINE, Thomas Parker. b 44. Oak Hill Th Coll BA 87. **d** 87 **p** 88. C Crowborough *Chich* 87-91; R Dersingham w Anmer and Shernborne *Nor* 91-00; P-in-c Southport SS Simon and Jude *Liv* 00-03; V Southport SS Simon and Jude w All So 03-09; C Southport All SS 03-09; rtd 09; PtO *Win* from 10. *16 Donnelly Road, Bournemouth BH6 5NW*

JARMAN, Christopher (<u>Kit</u>). b 38. QUB BA 63. Wells Th Coll 69. **d** 71 **p** 72. C Leckhampton SS Phil and Jas *Glouc* 71-73; Chapl RN 73-93; Chapl Rossall Sch Fleetwood 94; R Stirling *St And* 94-03; Chapl ATC 97-03; rtd 03; Warrant from 04. *Ground Floor Flat 2, 4 Branksome Park, Longsdale Road, Oban PA34 5JZ* T/F: (01631) 563535

JARMAN, John Geoffrey. b 31. IEng. S'wark Ord Course 75. **d** 78 **p** 79. NSM Chigwell *Chelmsf* 78-81; NSM Leytonstone St Marg w St Columba 81-87; C Walthamstow St Sav 87-89; V Gt Bentley and P-in-c Frating w Thorrington 89-92; C Wanstead St Mary w Ch Ch 92-95; rtd 95; PtO *Chelmsf* from 95. *c/o Mrs P J Thurston, 18 Heol Tyn-y-Fron, Penparcau, Aberystwyth SY23 3RP*

JARMAN, Michael Robert. b 48. Trin Coll Bris 07. **d** 09 **p** 10. NSM Caerleon and Llanfrechfa *Mon* 09-12; P-in-c Newport Ch Ch from 12. *The Vicarage, Christchurch, Newport NP18 1JJ* T: (01633) 420701 E: michael@ahlan48.fsnet.co.uk

JARMAN, Robert Joseph. b 59. Van Mildert Coll Dur BA 90. **d** 92 **p** 93. C Llanishen and Lisvane *Llan* 92-93; C Whitchurch 93-94. *47 Penydre, Rhiwbina, Cardiff CF14 6EJ*

JARMAN, Rosemary Susan. See GREEN, Rosemary Susan

JARRATT, David. b 70. Herts Univ BSc 92 Univ of N Lon PhD 97 UEA PGCE 97. Ox Min Course 10. **d** 12 **p** 13. C Felpham *Chich* from 12. *3 Byron Close, Bognor Regis PO22 6QU* M: 07911-132417 E: david.jarratt@btinternet.com

JARRATT, Canon Robert <u>Michael</u>. b 39. K Coll Lon BD 62 AKC 62 NY Th Sem DMin 85. **d** 63 **p** 64. C Corby St Columba *Pet* 63-67; Lay Tr Officer *Sheff* 67-71; Ind Chapl *S'wark* 72-80; P-in-c Betchworth 76-80; V Ranmoor *Sheff* 80-01; P-in-c

Worsbrough and Dir Post-Ord Tr 01-05; RD Hallam 87-94; Hon Can Sheff Cathl 95-05; rtd 05. *9 St Andrew's Plaza, 14 St Andrew's Road, Sheffield S11 9AL* T: 0114-258 2686 E: michaeljarratt42@yahoo.co.uk

JARRATT, Stephen. b 51. Edin Univ BD 76 St Kath Coll Liv CertEd 77. **d** 78 **p** 79. C Horsforth *Ripon* 78-81; C Stanningley St Thos 81-84; P-in-c Fishponds St Jo *Bris* 84-85; V 85-92; V Chapel Allerton *Ripon* 92-04; AD Allerton 97-04; TR Clifton *S'well* 04-08; AD W Bingham 07-08; P-in-c Haxby and Wigginton *York* 08-09; R 09-13; rtd 13; PtO *York* from 14. *The Lighthouse, 18 Longbridge Drive, Easingwold, York YO61 3FH* T: (01347) 823047 E: jarratt312@btinternet.com

✠**JARRETT, The Rt Revd Martyn William.** b 44. K Coll Lon BD 67 AKC 67 Hull Univ MPhil 91. **d** 68 **p** 69 **c** 94. C Bris St Geo 68-70; C Swindon New Town 70-74; C Northolt St Mary *Lon* 74-76; V Northolt St Jos 76-81; V Hillingdon St Andr 81-83; P-in-c Uxbridge Moor 82-83; V Uxbridge St Andr w St Jo 83-85; Selection Sec ACCM 85-88; Sen Selection Sec 89-91; V Chesterfield St Mary and All SS *Derby* 91-94; Suff Bp Burnley *Blackb* 94-00; Hon Can Blackb Cathl 94-00; Suff Bp Beverley (PEV) *York* 00-12; Hon Asst Bp S'well and Nottm from 01; Dur, Ripon and Sheff 00-12; Man and Wakef 01-12; Bradf 02-12; Liv 03-12; Newc 10-12; Hon Can Wakef Cathl 01-10; rtd 12. *91 Beaumont Rise, Worksop S80 1YG* T: (01909) 477847 E: martyn.jarrett@yahoo.co.uk

JARRETT, René Isaac Taiwo. b 49. Milton Margai Teachers' Coll Sierra Leone TCert 79 Lon Inst of Educn BEd 94. Sierra Leone Th Hall 80. **d** 83 **p** 85. Dn Freetown St Luke Sierra Leone 83-85; C Freetown Bp Elwin Memorial Ch 85-89; Hon C St Pancras w St Jas and Ch Ch *Lon* 89-95; C Bloomsbury St Geo w Woburn Square Ch Ch 95-11; rtd 11; PtO *Lon* from 11; S'wark from 13. *2 Woburn Mansions, Torrington Place, London WC1E 7HL* T: (020) 7580 5165 M: 07853-348143 E: jarrorene@yahoo.co.uk

JARROW, Suffragan Bishop of. See BRYANT, The Rt Revd Mark Watts

JARVIS, Ian Frederick Rodger. b 38. Bris Univ BA 60. Tyndale Hall Bris 61. **d** 63 **p** 64. C Penge Ch Ch w H Trin *Roch* 63-67; C Bilston St Leon *Lich* 67-71; V Lozells St Silas *Birm* 71-76; V Chaddesden St Mary *Derby* 76-95; V Newhall 95-02; rtd 02; PtO *Derby* from 02. *29 Springfield Road, Midway, Swadlincote DE11 0BZ* T: (01283) 551589 E: ianandirenejarvis@btinternet.com

JARVIS, Mrs Lynda Claire. b 46. Southn Univ CQSW 87. STETS 95. **d** 98 **p** 99. C Chandler's Ford *Win* 98-01; rtd 01. *Largo Santana 3, Tavira, 8800-701 Algarve, Portugal* T: (00351) (281) 323553 M: 961-166240

JARVIS, Miss Mary. b 35. Leeds Univ BA 57 Lon Univ CertEd 59. Cranmer Hall Dur 78. **dss** 80 **d** 87 **p** 94. Low Harrogate St Mary *Ripon* 80-84; Wortley-de-Leeds 84-87; C 87-88; C Upper Armley 88-94; C Holbeck 94-95; rtd 95; PtO *Leeds* from 01. *71 Burnsall Croft, Leeds LS12 3LH* T: 0113-279 7832 E: mjarvis@amserve.com

JARVIS, Nathan John. b 73. Ox Brookes Univ BA 97 Leeds Univ MA 04. St Steph Ho Ox BTh 06. **d** 06 **p** 07. C Hartlepool H Trin *Dur* 06-09; V Kingstanding St Luke *Birm* 09-12; TV Blenheim *Ox* from 12. *The Rectory, 26 Church Lane, Yarnton, Kidlington OX5 1PY* E: fr.nathan@yahoo.com

JARVIS, Mrs Pamela Ann. b 51. Sussex Univ BEd 74. SWMTC 97. **d** 00 **p** 01. C Braunton *Ex* 00-03; C Combe Martin, Berrynarbor, Lynton, Brendon etc 03-04; TV 04-10; rtd 10. *Crocnamac, Tomouth Road, Appledore, Bideford EX39 1QD* T: (01237) 420454 M: 07773-900523 E: pajarvis@virgin.net

JARVIS, Peter Timothy. b 64. St Jo Coll Nottm 02. **d** 04 **p** 05. C Thatcham *Ox* 04-06; TV 06-11; Chapl John Madejski Academy 11-13; Hon C Reading St Agnes w St Paul and St Barn *Ox* 11-13; C Loddon Reach from 13. *11 Clares Green Road, Spencers Wood, Reading RG7 1DY* T: 0118-988 3215 E: revdpj@btinternet.com

JARVIS, Rupert Charles Melbourn. b 69. St Andr Univ MA 92 Univ of Wales (Swansea) MPhil 96. Cuddesdon Coll 96. **d** 98 **p** 99. C Swansea St Mary w H Trin *S & B* 98-99; Min Can Brecon Cathl 99-01; CF 01-08; Asst Chapl Shiplake Coll Henley 08-09; Chapl Denstone Coll Uttoxeter from 09. *Denstone College, Uttoxeter ST14 5HN* T: (01889) 590484

JARVIS, Stephen John. b 55. WEMTC 04. **d** 07 **p** 08. NSM Bisley, Chalford, France Lynch, and Oakridge and Bussage w Eastcombe *Glouc* from 07. *8 Ollney Road, Minchinhampton, Stroud GL6 9BX* T: (01453) 884545 M: 07921-548467 E: stephenjarvis88@talktalk.net

JARVIS, Steven Roy. b 73. NE Wales Inst of HE BA 05. WEMTC 04. **d** 07 **p** 08. NSM Ludlow *Heref* 07-10; Dioc Youth Officer *Glouc* 10-13; TV White Horse *Sarum* from 13. *The Vicarage, The Hollow, Dilton Marsh, Westbury BA13 4BU* T: (01373) 302985 M: 07879-442751 E: steve.the.vicar@btinternet.com

JARY, Ms Helen Lesley. b 69. Lanc Univ BA 91. St Jo Coll Nottm 05. **d** 07 **p** 08. C Oulton Broad *Nor* 07-11; TV Thetford from 11. *Cloverfield Vicarage, 24 Foxglove Road, Thetford IP24 2XF* T: (01842) 755769 M: 07990-501683
E: helenjary@btinternet.com

JASON, Mark Andrew. b 73. Madras Univ BA 94 S Asia Inst for Advanced Chr Studies MA 96. Gurukul Lutheran Th Coll & Research Inst BD 00. **p** 01. India 01-03; PtO *Ab* from 03. *31 Gladstone Place, Aberdeen AB10 6UX* T: (01224) 321714
E: m.a.jason@abdn.ac.uk

JASPER, Prof David. b 51. Jes Coll Cam BA 72 MA 76 Keble Coll Ox BD 80 Dur Univ PhD 83 Ox Univ DD 02 Uppsala Univ Hon ThD 07 FRSE 06. St Steph Ho Ox BA 75 MA 79. **d** 76 **p** 77. C Buckingham *Ox* 76-77; C Dur St Oswald 80; Chapl Hatf Coll Dur 81-88; Dir Cen Study of Lit and Th Dur 88-91; Prin St Chad's Coll Dur 88-91; Reader and Dir Cen Study of Lit and Th Glas Univ from 91; Vice-Dean of Div 95-98; Dean of Div 98-02; LtO *Glas* 91-08; NSM Hamilton 08-14; P-in-c Cambuslang from 14; P-in-c Uddingston from 14. *Netherwood, 124 Old Manse Road, Wishaw ML2 0EP* T/F: (01698) 373286
E: david.jasper@glasgow.ac.uk

JASPER, David Julian McLean. b 44. Dur Univ BA 66. Linc Th Coll 66. **d** 68 **p** 69. C Redruth Truro 68-72; TV 72-75; V St Just in Penwith 75-86; P-in-c Sancreed 82-86; C Reading St Matt *Ox* 96-00; P-in-c 00-02; R S Petherton w The Seavingtons *B & W* 02-11; rtd 11; RD Trigg Major *Truro* from 12. *East Barton, North Petherwin, Launceston PL15 8LR* T: (01566) 785996 M: 07767-814533
E: davidjasper5dy@btinternet.com

JASPER, James Roland. b 32. CA Tr Coll 56 NEOC 82. **d** 84 **p** 84. C Newburn *Newc* 84-86; V Ansley *Cov* 86-97; rtd 97; PtO *Leic* from 97; *Cov* from 03. *69 Desford Road, Newbold Verdon, Leicester LE9 9LG* T: (01455) 822567

JASPER, Jonathan Ernest Farley. b 50. AKC 72. St Aug Coll Cant 73. **d** 73 **p** 74. C Cheshunt *St Alb* 73-75; C Bedford St Paul 75-77; C Bedford St Pet w St Cuth 75-77; Chapl Southn Univ *Win* 77-80; Chapl Lon Univ Medical Students 80-86; PV Chich Cathl 86-89; P-in-c Earls Colne and White Colne *Chelmsf* 89-94; P-in-c Colne Engaine 89-94; R Earls Colne w White Colne and Colne Engaine 95-02; C Christchurch *Win* 02-08; PtO 08-12; P-in-c Barkway, Reed and Buckland w Barley *St Alb* 12-13; R 13-14; rtd 14. *37 St Augustine Mews, Colchester CO1 2PF* E: jefjasper@btinternet.com

JAUNDRILL, John Warwick. b 47. MCIM 81. Qu Coll Birm 86. **d** 88 **p** 89. C Bistre *St As* 88-91; P-in-c Towyn and St George 91-92; V 92-02; C Llanrhos 06-09; C Rhos-Cystennin 09-10; TV 10-12; rtd 12; PtO *St As* from 14. *20 Avon Court, Mold CH7 1JP* T: (01352) 218350

JAY, Colin. b 62. Keble Coll Ox BA 85 St Jo Coll Dur BA 89. Cranmer Hall Dur 87. **d** 90 **p** 91. C Bishopwearmouth St Gabr *Dur* 90-94; C Newton Aycliffe 94; TV 94-96; TV Gt Aycliffe 96-03; AD Sedgefield 99-03; Chapl Co Dur & Darlington Priority Services NHS Trust 03-07; Chapl Tees, Esk and Wear Valley NHS Trust from 07. *The Chaplaincy, West Park Hospital, Edward Pease Way, Darlington DL2 2TS* T: (01325) 552045
E: colin.jay@tewv.nhs.uk

JAY, Ms Nicola Mary. b 37. SRN 58. NEOC 88. **d** 91 **p** 94. Par Dn Whitburn *Dur* 91-94; C 94-95; P-in-c Sacriston and Kimblesworth 95-00; rtd 00. *29 Church Street, Sacriston, Durham DH7 6JL* T: 0191-371 0152

JAY, Mrs Sarah Clare. b 52. **d** 12 **p** 13. NSM Stranton *Dur* from 12. *Address temp unknown* E: colsarjay@yahoo.co.uk

JAYNE, Martin Philip. b 48. Man Univ BA 71 MRTPI 73. Carl Dioc Tr Course 87. **d** 90 **p** 91. NSM Natland *Carl* from 90; Dioc Officer for NSM 04-08. *12 Longmeadow Lane, Natland, Kendal LA9 7QZ* T: (01539) 560942 E: martjay@btinternet.com

JEANES, Gordon Paul. b 55. Ox Univ BA 79 MA 82 BD 90 Univ of Wales (Lamp) PhD 99. St Steph Ho Ox 80. **d** 82 **p** 83. C S Wimbledon H Trin and St Pet *S'wark* 82-85; C Surbiton St Andr and St Mark 85-90; Chapl St Chad's Coll Dur 90-93; Sub-Warden St Mich Coll Llan 94-98; Lect Th Univ of Wales (Cardiff) 94-98; V Wandsworth St Anne *S'wark* 98-08; P-in-c Wandsworth St Faith 05-08; V Wandsworth St Anne w St Faith from 08; Dioc Voc Adv from 99. *St Anne's Vicarage, 182 St Ann's Hill, London SW18 2RS* T: (020) 8874 2809
E: gordon.jeanes@virgin.net

JEANS, The Ven Alan Paul. b 58. MIAAS 84 MIBCO 84 Southn Univ BTh 89 Univ of Wales (Lamp) MA 03. Sarum & Wells Th Coll 86. **d** 89 **p** 90. C Parkstone St Pet w Branksea and St Osmund *Sarum* 89-93; P-in-c Bishop's Cannings, All Cannings etc 93-98; Par Development Adv from 98; Can and Preb Sarum Cathl from 02; Adn Sarum from 03; RD Alderbury 05-07; Dioc Dir of Ords 07-13. *Herbert House, 118 Lower Road, Salisbury SP2 9NW* T: (01722) 336290 F: 411990
E: adsarum@salisbury.anglican.org

JEANS, David Bockley. b 48. Mert Coll Ox BA 71 MA 80 PGCE 73 Man Univ MPhil 98. Trin Coll Bris 83. **d** 85 **p** 86. C Clevedon St Andr and Ch Ch *B & W* 85-88; V Wadsley *Sheff* 88-96; Dir Studies Wilson Carlile Coll of Evang 96; Prin 97-06; Dean Coll of S Cross New Zealand 06-08; P-in-c Deepcar *Sheff* 08-13; rtd 13; PtO *Sheff* from 13. *112 Airedale Road, Sheffield S6 4AW* T: 0114-221 7829 E: jeansville@hotmail.co.uk

JEANS, Miss Eleanor Ruth. b 75. Man Univ BMus 97 GRNCM 97. Ridley Hall Cam 09. **d** 11 **p** 12. C Thurnby w Stoughton *Leic* 11-14; C Kettering Ch the King *Pet* from 14. *11 Churchill Way, Kettering NN15 5DP* M: 07795-660144
E: eleanor@thisman.co.uk

JEAPES (née PORTER), Mrs Barbara Judith. b 47. Cam Inst of Educn TCert 68. Carl Dioc Tr Inst 91. **d** 94 **p** 95. NSM Egremont and Haile *Carl* 94-14; TV 09-14; rtd 14. *15 Millfields, Beckermet CA21 2YY* T: (01946) 841489
E: barbara.jeapes@btinternet.com

JEAVONS, Mrs Margaret Anne. b 51. Liv Poly BA 72 Bris Univ BA 01 St Kath Coll Liv PGCE 74. Trin Coll Bris 99. **d** 01 **p** 02. C Totnes w Bridgetown, Berry Pomeroy etc *Ex* 01-05; V Sutton St Mich *York* from 05; AD E Hull from 13. *St Michael's Vicarage, 751 Marfleet Lane, Hull HU9 4TJ* T: (01482) 374509
E: jeavons2951@jeavons2951.karoo.co.uk

JEAVONS, Maurice. b 32. Ely Th Coll 60. **d** 62 **p** 63. C Longton St Jo *Lich* 62-68; V Wednesfield St Greg 68-81; V Lower Gornal 81-90; NSM Willenhall St Anne 92-93; C Tunstall 93-99; rtd 99; Hon C Wolverhampton St Steph *Lich* 99-09; PtO from 09. *17 Colaton Close, Wolverhampton WV10 9BB* T: (01902) 351118

JEE, Jonathan Noel. b 63. BNC Ox BA 84 MA 88. Wycliffe Hall Ox 85. **d** 88 **p** 89. C Brampton St Thos *Derby* 88-92; TV Hinckley H Trin *Leic* 92-00; V Leamington Priors St Paul *Cov* from 00. *The Vicarage, 15 Lillington Road, Leamington Spa CV32 5YS* T: (01926) 772132 *or* 427149
E: jonathan@stpl.org.uk

JEEWAN, Alexander. b 71. Univ of E Lon BA 95 PGCE 97. Westcott Ho Cam 13. **d** 15. C Witham and Villages *Chelmsf* from 15. *23 Forest Road, Witham CM8 2PF* M: 07801-946217
E: alex_jeewan@hotmail.com

JEFF, Canon Gordon Henry. b 32. St Edm Hall Ox BA 56 MA 60. Wells Th Coll 59. **d** 61 **p** 62. C Sydenham St Bart *S'wark* 61-64; C Kidbrooke St Jas 64-66; V Clapham St Paul 66-72; V Raynes Park St Sav 73-79; RD Merton 77-79; V Carshalton Beeches 79-86; P-in-c Petersham 86-90; Chapl St Mich Convent 90-96; Hon Can S'wark Cathl 93-96; rtd 96; PtO *B & W* from 07. *9 Barnetts Well, Draycott, Cheddar BS27 3TF* T: (01934) 744943
E: rumpus9bw@hotmail.com

JEFFCOAT, Rupert Edward Elessing. b 70. St Cath Coll Cam BA 92 MA 96 FRCO 91. WMMTC 02. **d** 05. NSM Brisbane Cathl Australia from 05. *GPO Box 421, Brisbane Qld 4001, Australia* T: (0061) (7) 3835 2231
E: rjeffcoat@freenetname.co.uk

JEFFERIES, Michael Lewis. b 45. St Jo Coll Nottm. **d** 87 **p** 88. C Pudsey St Lawr and St Paul *Bradf* 87-93; V Beckenham St Jo *Roch* 93-00; TV Modbury, Bigbury, Ringmore w Kingston etc *Ex* 00-10; rtd 10. *6 Sherford Down Road, Sherford, Kingsbridge TQ7 2BQ* T: (01548) 531644 E: mandejefferies@fsmail.net

JEFFERIES, Preb Phillip John. b 42. St Chad's Coll Dur BA 65 MA 91. **d** 67 **p** 68. C Tunstall *Ch* Lich 67-71; C Wolverhampton St Pet 71-74; P-in-c Oakengates 74-80; V 80-82; P-in-c Ketley 78-82; V Horninglow 82-00; RD Tutbury 97-00; TR Stafford 00-07; Bp's Adv on Hosp Chapl 82-06; Preb Lich Cathl 99-07; rtd 07; PtO *Lich* from 07. *16 Morley's Hill, Burton-on-Trent DE13 0TA* T: (01283) 544013

JEFFERS, Cliff Peter. b 69. CITC BTh 98. **d** 98 **p** 99. C Limerick City *L & K* 98-01; I Clonenagh w Offerlane, Borris-in-Ossory etc *C & O* 01-04; I Athy w Kilberry, Fontstown and Kilkea *D & G* 04-13; Chapl Dub Inst of Tech 13-14; I Fanlobbus Union *C, C & R* from 14. *The Rectory, Sackville Street, Dunmanway, Co Cork, Republic of Ireland* T: (00353) (23) 884 5151 E: cliff4b@gmail.com

JEFFERS, Mellissa Elizabeth. QUB BEd Loughb Univ MLS. **d** 11 **p** 12. NSM Finaghy *Conn* 11-14; P-in-c Fiddown w Clonegam, Guilcagh and Kilmeaden *C & O* from 14. *The Rectory, Hillcrest, Piltown, Co Kilkenny, Republic of Ireland* M: (00353) 87-101 6421

JEFFERS, Neil Gareth Thompson. b 78. St Jo Coll Ox BA 99 MA 05. Oak Hill Th Coll MTh 07. **d** 07 **p** 08. C Lowestoft Ch Ch *Nor* 07-11; Chapl Pangbourne Coll from 11. *Sunbeam, Bere Court Road, Pangbourne, Reading RG8 8JY*
M: 07769-586260 E: neiljeffers2003@yahoo.co.uk

JEFFERSON, Charles Dudley. b 55. St Pet Coll Ox BA 78 MA 81. Ridley Hall Cam 79. **d** 81 **p** 82. C Chadkirk *Ches* 81-84; C Macclesfield St Pet 84-85; C Macclesfield Team 85-89; R Elworth and Warmingham 89-99; Chapl Framlingham Coll 99-01; Chapl Rendcomb Coll Cirencester and P-in-c

Rendcomb *Glouc* 01-09; R Thrapston, Denford and Islip *Pet* 09-15; R Chenderit from 15. *The Rectory, Marston St Lawrence, Banbury OX17 2DB* T: (01295) 712418
E: revcjefferson@tiscali.co.uk

JEFFERSON, David Charles. b 33. Leeds Univ BA 57. Coll of Resurr Mirfield 57. **d** 59 **p** 60. C Kennington Cross St Anselm *S'wark* 59-62; C Richmond St Mary 62-64; Chapl Wilson's Gr Sch Camberwell 64-93; Chapl Wilson's Sch Wallington 75-99; Public Preacher *S'wark* 64-74; Hon C Carshalton Beeches 74-04; rtd 93; PtO *S'wark* 04-13. *15 Sandown Drive, Carshalton SM5 4LN* T: (020) 8669 0640 *or* 8773 2931

JEFFERSON, Michael William. b 41. K Coll Lon AKC 64. WMMTC 96. **d** 98 **p** 99. C Four Oaks *Birm* 98-02; P-in-c Longdon *Lich* 02-08; Local Min Adv (Wolverhampton) 02-08; rtd 08; PtO *Lich* from 09; *Portsm* from 09; *Birm* from 10. *9 Soma House, 380 Springfield Road, Sutton Coldfield B75 7JH* T: 0121-329 2214 E: rev_michael_uk@yahoo.co.uk

✠**JEFFERTS SCHORI, The Most Revd Katharine.** b 54. Stanford Univ BS 74 Oregon State Univ MS 77 PhD 83. Ch Div Sch of Pacific MDiv 94 Hon DD 01. **d** 94 **p** 94 **c** 01. C Corvallis Gd Samaritan USA 94-01; Chapl Benton Hospice Service 95-00; Instructor Oregon State Univ 96-99; Bp Nevada 01-06; Presiding Bp from 06. *Episcopal Church Center, 815 Second Avenue, New York NY 10017, USA* T: (001) (212) 716 6271 F: 490 3298 E: pboffice@episcopalchurch.org

JEFFERY, Graham. b 35. Qu Coll Cam BA 58. Wells Th Coll 58. **d** 60 **p** 61. C Southampton Maybush St Pet *Win* 60-63; Australia 63-66; C E Grinstead St Swithun *Chich* 66-68; C-in-c The Hydneye CD 68-74; V Wick 74-76; C Hove 76-78; P-in-c Newtimber w Pyecombe 78-82; R Poynings w Edburton, Newtimber and Pyecombe 82-92; P-in-c Sullington and Thakeham w Warminghurst 92-95; rtd 96; NSM Edburton *Chich* 97-99; PtO from 00. *6 Orchard Close, Small Dole, Henfield BN5 9YA*

JEFFERY (née CAW), Mrs Hannah Mary. b 69. Birm Univ BMus 91. St Jo Coll Nottm MA 95. **d** 95 **p** 96. C Northampton St Giles *Pet* 95-99; Hon C Hanger Hill Ascension and W Twyford St Mary *Lon* 99-04; TV Northampton Em *Pet* 04-11; CMD Officer from 11; Chapl Bp Stopford Sch from 11. *19 Rosemount Road, Kettering NN15 6EU* T: (01536) 660415 *or* (01604) 887000 E: hannah.jeffery@peterborough-diocese.org.uk

JEFFERY, Mrs Jennifer Ann. b 45. Philippa Fawcett Coll CertEd 66. STETS. **d** 02 **p** 03. NSM Wilton *B & W* 02-15; Chapl Bp Henderson Sch from 07; rtd 15; PtO *B & W* from 15. *4 Southwell, Trull, Taunton TA3 7HU* T: (01823) 286589 E: jenny@jajeffery.freeserve.co.uk

JEFFERY, Jonathan George Piers. b 63. Man Univ LLB 84. Ripon Coll Cuddesdon 95. **d** 97 **p** 98. C Lee-on-the-Solent *Portsm* 97-01; V Leigh Park from 01; V Warren Park from 01; AD Havant 09-14. *The Vicarage, Riders Lane, Havant PO9 4QT* T: (023) 9247 5276

JEFFERY (née JACK), Mrs Judith Ann. b 54. Wycliffe Hall Ox 03. **d** 05 **p** 06. C Tetbury, Beverston and Long Newnton and Shipton Moyne *Glouc* 05-10; P-in-c Baltonsborough w Butleigh, W Bradley etc *B & W* 10-15; R Crook Peak from 15. *The Vicarage, Old Hall House, Ham Street, Baltonsborough, Glastonbury BA6 8PX* T: (01458) 851681
E: judithjack@talktalk.net

JEFFERY, Kenneth Charles. b 40. Univ of Wales BA 64 Linacre Coll Ox BA 67 MA 70. St Steph Ho Ox 64. **d** 67 **p** 68. C Swindon New Town *Bris* 67-68; C Summertown *Ox* 68-71; C Brighton St Pet *Chich* 71-77; V Ditchling 77-00; rtd 05. *19A Goldstone Road, Hove BN3 3RN* T: (01273) 208833
E: kenneth@jeffery333.fslife.co.uk

JEFFERY, Michael Frank. b 48. Linc Th Coll 74. **d** 76 **p** 77. C Caterham Valley *S'wark* 76-79; C Tupsley *Heref* 79-82; P-in-c Stretton Sugwas 82-84; P-in-c Bishopstone 83-84; P-in-c Kenchester and Bridge Sollers 83-84; V Whiteshill *Glouc* 84-92; P-in-c Randwick 92; V Whiteshill and Randwick 93-02; TV Bedminster *Bris* 02-09; P-in-c 09-13; rtd 13. *Old Hall House, Ham Street, Baltonsborough, Glastonbury BA6 8PX* E: michael@not2arty.com

JEFFERY, Peter James. b 41. Leeds Univ BSc 63. Oak Hill Th Coll 64. **d** 66 **p** 67. C Streatham Park St Alb *S'wark* 66-70; C Northampton St Giles *Pet* 70-73; C Rushden St Pet 73-76; C Rushden w Newton Bromswold 77-78; V Siddal *Wakef* 78-85; V Sowerby Bridge w Norland 85-98; P-in-c Cornholme 98-00; P-in-c Walsden 98-00; V Cornholme and Walsden 00-05; rtd 05; PtO *Leeds* from 07. *12 Highcroft Road, Todmorden OL14 5LZ* T: (01706) 839781
E: jeffrey@cornden.freeserve.co.uk

JEFFERY, Peter Noel. b 37. Pemb Coll Ox BA 60 MA 64. Linc Th Coll 60. **d** 62 **p** 63. C W Smethwick *Birm* 62-64; P-in-c Bordesley St Andr 64-69; R Turvey *St Alb* 69-98; P-in-c

Stevington 79-98; rtd 98. *Franconia Cottage, The Gardens, Adstock, Buckingham MK18 2JF* T: (01296) 715770

JEFFERY, Richard William Christopher. b 43. Ex Univ BA 65. Coll of Resurr Mirfield 66. **d** 68 **p** 69. C Widley w Wymering *Portsm* 68-71; C Salisbury St Mich *Sarum* 71-74; TV Ridgeway 74-80; V Stanford in the Vale w Goosey and Hatford *Ox* 80-89; V Topsham *Ex* 89-09; RD Aylesbeare 01-07; rtd 09; P-in-c Topsham and Wear *Ex* 09-13. *5 Brownlees, Exminster, Exeter EX6 8SW* T: (01392) 823526 E: richardwcj@gmail.com

JEFFERY, The Very Revd Robert Martin Colquhoun. b 35. K Coll Lon BD 58 AKC 58 Birm Univ Hon DD 99 FRSA 91. **d** 59 **p** 60. C Grangetown *Dur* 59-61; C Barnes St Mary *S'wark* 61-63; Asst Sec Miss and Ecum Coun Ch Assembly 64-68; Sec Dept Miss and Unity BCC 68-71; V Headington *Ox* 71-78; RD Cowley 73-78; P-in-c Tong *Lich* 78-83; V 83-87; Dioc Missr 78-80; Adn Salop 80-87; Dean Worc 87-96; Can Res and Sub-Dean Ch Ch Ox 96-02; Select Preacher Ox 91, 97, 98 and 02; rtd 02. *47 The Manor House, Bennett Crescent, Cowley, Oxford OX4 2UG* T: (01865) 749706
E: rmcj@btopenworld.com

JEFFERYES, June Ann. b 37. Dur Univ BA 58. WMMTC 87. **d** 90 **p** 94. NSM Caverswall *Lich* 90-92; NSM Caverswall and Weston Coyney w Dilhorne 92-02; rtd 02; PtO *Lich* 02-14. *24 Glen Drive, Alton, Stoke-on-Trent ST10 4DJ* T: (01538) 702150 E: ann@jefferyes.co.uk

JEFFORD, Canon Margaret June. b 50. Univ of Wales RGN 81. St Mich Coll Llan 94. **d** 96 **p** 97. C Risca *Mon* 96-98; C Pontypool 98-00; TV 00-02; V Newbridge w Crumlin 02-04; V Newbridge 04-14; V Lower Islwyn from 14; Can St Woolos Cathl from 12. *St Paul's Vicarage, High Street, Newbridge, Newport NP11 4FW* T: (01495) 240794
E: rev.marg@btinternet.com

JEFFORD, Peter Ernest. b 29. AKC 53. **d** 54 **p** 55. C Berkeley *Glouc* 54-57; C Petersfield w Sheet *Portsm* 57-61; Chapl Churcher's Coll 57-61; R Rollesby w Burgh w Billockby *Nor* 62-71; V Watton 71-81; V Watton w Carbrooke and Ovington 81-82; OCM 71-82; P-in-c Brampford Speke *Ex* 82-83; P-in-c Cadbury 82-83; P-in-c Thorverton 82-83; P-in-c Upton Pyne 82-83; TR Thorverton, Cadbury, Upton Pyne etc 83-92; rtd 92; PtO *Ox* 92-96 and from 03; Hon C Ox St Mary V w St Cross and St Pet 96-99; P-in-c Whitchurch St Mary 00-03; Chapl Plater Coll 94-05. *27 Ashlong Road, Headington, Oxford OX3 0NH* T: (01865) 760593

JEFFORD, Ronald. b 46. St Mich Coll Llan. **d** 91 **p** 92. C Ebbw Vale *Mon* 91-94; TV 94-95; R Bedwas and Rudry 95-98; V Abersychan and Garndiffaith 98-03; TV Mynyddislwyn 03-05; rtd 05; PtO *Mon* from 06. *St Paul's Vicarage, High Street, Newbridge, Newport NP11 4FW* T: (01495) 240794

JEFFREE, Robin. b 29. AKC 54. **d** 55 **p** 56. C N Harrow St Alb *Lon* 55-59; C Hendon St Mary 59-62; V Manea *Ely* 62-67; V Hartford 67-83; R Denver 83-94; V Ryston w Roxham 83-94; V W Dereham 83-94; rtd 94; PtO *Nor* from 94. *3 Church Lane, Hindolveston, Dereham NR20 5BT* T: (01263) 861857

JEFFREY, Katrina. *See* METZNER, Katrina

JEFFREYS, David John. b 45. S Dios Minl Tr Scheme 89. **d** 92 **p** 93. NSM Bexhill St Barn *Chich* 92-95; Chapl Hastings and Rother NHS Trust 95-02; Chapl E Sussex Hosps NHS Trust 02-05; Chapl Team Ldr 05-09; rtd 09; PtO *Chich* from 10. *4 Osbern Close, Bexhill-on-Sea TN39 4TJ* T: (01424) 843672
E: frdavid@onetel.com

JEFFREYS (née DESHPANDE), Lakshmi Anant. b 64. Liv Univ BSc 86 St Luke's Coll Ex PGCE 87. Wycliffe Hall Ox BTh 94. **d** 94 **p** 95. C Long Eaton St Jo *Derby* 94-97; Chapl Nottm Trent Univ *S'well* 98-03; PtO *Derby* 03-04; Dioc Miss Adv 04-13; P-in-c Wootton w Quinton and Preston Deanery *Pet* from 13; Asst Dir Ords from 14. *The Rectory, Water Lane, Wootton, Northampton NN4 6HH* T: (01604) 962061
E: wootton vicar@talktalk.net

JEFFREYS, Timothy John. b 58. Man Univ BSc 79. Cranmer Hall Dur 83. **d** 86 **p** 87. C Goodmayes All SS *Chelmsf* 86-88; PtO *S'wark* 92-93; Hon C S Lambeth St Anne and All SS 93-96; C Croydon St Jo 96-06; P-in-c Brixton Road Ch Ch 06-12; V from 12. *The Vicarage, 96 Brixton Road, London SW9 6BE* T: (020) 7793 0621 E: vicar@christchurchbr.org.uk

JEFFRIES, Miss Frances Alyx. b 59. Bris Poly BA 82. Local Minl Tr Course 00. **d** 04 **p** 05. OLM Gainsborough and Morton *Linc* 04-11; C Skegness Gp 11-14; TV Bolingbroke Deanery from 14. *The Rectory, Horbling Lane, Stickney, Boston PE22 8DQ* E: fjeffries@primusbroadband.co.uk

JEFFRIES, Keith. b 48. St Steph Ho Ox 91. **d** 93 **p** 94. C St Marychurch *Ex* 93-96; TV Wood Green St Mich w Bounds Green St Gabr etc *Lon* 96-98; V The Hydneye *Chich* 98-00; Chapl Univ of Greenwich *Roch* 00-02; Chapl Kent Inst of Art and Design 00-02; Chapl Tenerife Sur *Eur* 02-03; PtO *Roch* 03-04; Bp's Adv on Chr/Muslim Relns *Birm* 04-07; Chapl Oakington Immigration Reception Cen 07-09; rtd 09.

Edificio las Tejas, Bloque 3, Vivenda 12, Lugar Pasitos 38, Pueblo de Mogan, 35140 Las Palmas, Spain
E: fatherkeithjeffries@hotmail.com

JEFFS, Mrs Stephanie Kathleen. b 58. Loughb Univ BA 79 Goldsmiths' Coll Lon PGCE 81. Trin Coll Bris 11. **d** 13 **p** 14. C Tiverton St Pet and Chevithorne w Cove *Ex* from 13. *St Andrew's Vicarage, Blackmore Road, Tiverton EX16 4AR* T: (01884) 250417   M: 07772-571282
E: steph-jeffs@hotmail.co.uk

JELF, Miss Pauline Margaret. b 55. Chich Th Coll 88. **d** 90 **p** 94. Par Dn Clayton *Lich* 90-94; C Knutton 94-98; P-in-c Silverdale and Alsagers Bank 94-98; PtO 98-02; C Clayton 02; C Betley and Madeley 02-04; C Trent Vale 03-06. *11 Stafford Avenue, Newcastle ST5 3BN* T: (01785) 639545

JELLEY, Ian. b 54. Newc Univ MA 94 Dur Univ MA 03. NEOC 89. **d** 91 **p** 92. C Jarrow *Dur* 91-95; P-in-c Leam Lane 95-96; Chapl HM Pris Holme Ho 96-01; R Grindon, Stillington and Wolviston *Dur* 01-03; rtd 03; PtO *Dur* from 03. *1 Rievaulx Avenue, Billingham TS23 2BP*

JELLEY, James Dudley. b 46. Linc Th Coll 78. **d** 80 **p** 81. C Stockwell Green St Andr *S'wark* 80-85; V Camberwell St Phil and St Mark 85-93; PtO 93-96; V Camberwell St Luke 96-13; RD Camberwell 00-06; rtd 13; PtO *S'wark* from 13. *58 Wydehurst Road, Croydon CR0 6NG* T: (020) 8405 6097

JELLEY (*née* CAPITANCHIK), Canon Sophie Rebecca. b 72. Leeds Univ BA 93. Wycliffe Hall Ox MPhil 97. **d** 97 **p** 98. C Shipley St Pet *Bradf* 97-00; CMS Uganda 00-03; C Churt and Hindhead *Guildf* 03-10; V Burgess Hill St Andr *Chich* 10-15; Can Res Dur Cathl from 15. *3 The College, Durham DH1 3EQ* E: sophie@jelley.f9.co.uk

JEMMETT, Mrs Melanie Jane. b 72. Roehampton Inst BA 93. Westcott Ho Cam 12. **d** 14. C Fawkham and Hartley *Roch* from 14. *23 Cherry Trees, Hartley, Longfield DA3 8DS* M: 07976-240888   T: (01474) 703072
E: melaniejemmett@btinternet.com

JENKIN, Charles Alexander Graham. b 54. BScEng. Westcott Ho Cam 81. **d** 84 **p** 85. C Binley *Cov* 84-88; TV Canvey Is *Chelmsf* 88-94; TR Melton Mowbray *Leic* 94-08; RD Framland 98-02; Hon Can Leic Cathl 06-08; V Ipswich St Mary-le-Tower *St E* from 08; Bp's Interfaith Adv from 09; RD Ipswich from 12. *The Vicarage, 18 Kingsfield Avenue, Ipswich IP1 3TA* T/F: (01473) 289001   E: charles@jenkin.uk.net

JENKIN, Christopher Cameron. b 36. BNC Ox BA 61 MA 64. Clifton Th Coll 61. **d** 63 **p** 64. C Walthamstow St Mary *Chelmsf* 63-68; C Surbiton Hill Ch Ch *S'wark* 68-78; V Newport St Jo *Portsm* 78-88; TR Newbarns w Hawcoat *Carl* 88-01; rtd 01; PtO *Carl* from 01. *Beckside, Orton, Penrith CA10 3RX* T: (01539) 624410   E: chriscjenkin@aol.com

JENKINS, Alan David. b 60. Bris Poly BA 83 Spurgeon's Coll MTh 02. Wycliffe Hall Ox 93. **d** 95 **p** 96. C Tunbridge Wells St Jas w St Phil *Roch* 95-01; TV S Gillingham 01-07; R Gt Bookham *Guildf* from 07. *The Rectory, 2A Fife Way, Bookham, Leatherhead KT23 3PH* T: (01372) 452405
E: alan.jenkins@stnicolasbookham.org.uk

JENKINS, Miss Anne Christina. b 47. Birm Univ BA 70 Hull Univ CertEd 71 St Jo Coll Dur BA 77. Cranmer Hall Dur 74. **dss** 78 **d** 87 **p** 94. E Coatham *York* 78-81; OHP 81-87; PtO *York* 81-87; Ghana 87-88; Par Dn Beeston *Ripon* 88-93; Par Dn Leeds Gipton Epiphany 93-94; V Leeds St Marg and All Hallows 94-99; rtd 99; PtO *York* from 00; P-in-c Costa Brava *Eur* from 12. *28 Hill Cottages, Rosedale East, Pickering YO18 8RG* T: (01751) 417130

JENKINS, Audrey Joan. b 36. TCert 61. St D Coll Lamp. **d** 01 **p** 06. Par Dn Marshfield and Peterstone Wentloog etc *Mon* 01-06; NSM Llanrumney from 06. *10 Cwrt Pencraig, 8 Caerau Crescent, Newport NP20 4HG* T: (01633) 263470
E: glyn.jenkins@homecall.co.uk

JENKINS, Catherine. b 34. SWMTC 04. **d** 05 **p** 06. NSM Silverton, Butterleigh, Bickleigh and Cadeleigh *Ex* from 05. *Butterleigh House, Butterleigh, Cullompton EX15 1PH* T: (01884) 855379

JENKINS, Clifford Thomas. b 38. Westmr Coll Ox MTh 02 IEng MIEIecIE. Sarum & Wells Th Coll 74. **d** 77 **p** 78. Chapl Yeovil Coll 77-86; Hon C Yeovil w Kingston Pitney *B & W* 77-80; P-in-c 80-86; Chs FE Liaison Officer B & W, Bris and Glouc 87-90; PtO *B & W* from 87; FE Adv Gen Syn Bd of Educn and Meth Ch 90-98; rtd 98. *Bethany, 10 Grove Avenue, Yeovil BA20 2BB* T: (01935) 475043   E: clifford.jenkins@virgin.net

JENKINS, Clive Ronald. b 57. Chich Univ BA 08. Ripon Coll Cuddesdon 81. **d** 84 **p** 85. C E Grinstead St Swithun *Chich* 84-87; C Horsham 87-88; TV 88-90; Dioc Youth Chapl 90-96; P-in-c Amberley w N Stoke and Parham, Wiggonholt etc 93-96; V Southbourne w W Thorney 96-15; RD Westbourne 11-15; P-in-c Wisborough Green from 15. *The Vicarage, Billingshurst Road, Wisborough Green, Billingshurst RH14 0DZ* T: (01403) 700339

JENKINS, David. *See* JENKINS, William David
JENKINS, David. *See* JENKINS, Richard David
✠**JENKINS, The Rt Revd David Edward.** b 25. Qu Coll Ox BA 51 MA 54 Dur Univ DD 87. Linc Th Coll 52. **d** 53 **p** 54 **c** 84. C Birm Cathl 53-54; Lect Qu Coll Birm 53-54; Chapl Qu Coll Ox 54-69; Lect Th Ox Univ 55-69; Can Th Leic Cathl 66-82; Dir WCC Humanum Studies 69-73; Dir Wm Temple Foundn Man 73-78; Jt Dir 79-94; Prof Th and RS Leeds Univ 79-84; Bp Dur 84-94; rtd 94; Hon Asst Bp Ripon and Leeds 94-14. *5 Chapel Court, Newgate, Barnard Castle DL12 8NG* T: (01833) 631012

JENKINS, The Ven David Harold. b 61. SS Coll Cam BA 84 MA 87 Ox Univ BA 88 MA 94 Univ of Wales (Lamp) PhD 08. Ripon Coll Cuddesdon 86. **d** 89 **p** 90. C Chesterton Gd Shep *Ely* 89-91; C Earley St Pet *Ox* 91-94; V Blackpool St Mich *Blackb* 94-99; V Broughton 99-04; AD Preston 04; Can Res Carl Cathl 04-10; Dir of Educn 04-10; Adn Sudbury *St E* from 10. *Sudbury Lodge, Stanningfield Road, Great Whelnetham, Bury St Edmunds IP30 0TL* T: (01284) 386942   M: 07900-990073
E: archdeacon.david@cofesuffolk.org

JENKINS, Prof David Harrison. b 52. **d** 15. NSM St Ishmael's w Llan-saint and Ferryside *St D* from 15. *17 Parc Y Ffynnon, Ferryside SA17 5TQ* T: (01267) 268230
E: davidjenkins77@outlook.com

JENKINS, David Noble. b 25. CCC Cam BA 47 MA 50. Cuddesdon Coll 48. **d** 50 **p** 51. C Northampton St Matt *Pet* 50-54; Chapl Hurstpierpoint Coll 54-59; USPG 60-65; Chapl Eastbourne Coll 66-74; V Jarvis Brook *Chich* 75-90; rtd 90; USA 90-92; PtO *Chich* from 92. *25 Ramsay Hall, 9-13 Byron Road, Worthing BN11 3HN* T: (01903) 207524
E: dnjlittleb@waitrose.com

JENKINS, David Thomas. b 43. Ox Univ MA 94 RIBA 70. S'wark Ord Course 76. **d** 79 **p** 80. NSM Merthyr Tydfil and Cyfarthfa *Llan* 79-86; NSM Brecon St David w Llanspyddid and Llanilltyd *S & B* 86-91; P-in-c Llangiwg *S & B* 92-01; V 92-01; Chapl Puerto de la Cruz Tenerife *Eur* 02-09; rtd 09. *15 Highmoor, Maritime Quarter, Swansea SA1 1YE* M: 07974-748476
E: djenkins@tinyonline.co.uk

JENKINS, David William. b 43. **d** 12 **p** 13. OLM Busbridge and Hambledon *Guildf* from 12. *Medlar House, 6 Quartermile Road, Godalming GU7 1TG* T: (01483) 416084

JENKINS, Eric Robert. b 52. Poly Cen Lon BSc 74. STETS 97. **d** 00 **p** 01. C Weybridge *Guildf* 00-04; R Cobham and Stoke D'Abernon from 04; RD Leatherhead from 08. *The Vicarage, St Andrew's Walk, Cobham KT11 3EQ* T: (01932) 862109   M: 07747-844689   E: er.jenkins@btinternet.com

JENKINS, Mrs Fiona. b 59. Dur Univ BSc 80 York St Jo Coll MA 04. St Jo Coll Nottm 04. **d** 06 **p** 07. C Settle *Bradf* 06-08; C Linton in Craven *Leeds* 08-15; C Kettlewell w Conistone, Hubberholme etc 08-15; C Burnsall w Rylstone 08-15. *The Rectory, Church Lane, Burnsall, Skipton BD23 6BP* T: (01756) 720331   E: fiona.jenkins@bradford.anglican.org

JENKINS, Garry Frederick. b 48. Southn Univ BTh 79. Chich Th Coll 75. **d** 79 **p** 80. C Kingsbury St Andr *Lon* 79-84; C Leigh St Clem *Chelmsf* 84-88; P-in-c Brentwood St Geo 88-94; V from 94; Chapl NE Lon Foundn Trust from 02. *The Vicarage, 28 Robin Hood Road, Brentwood CM15 9EN* T: (01277) 213618   E: g.jenkins197@btinternet.com

JENKINS, Canon Gary John. b 59. Warw Univ BA 80 CertEd 81. Oak Hill Th Coll BA 89. **d** 89 **p** 90. C Norwood St Luke *S'wark* 89-94; P-in-c St Helier 94-95; V 95-01; V Redhill H Trin 01-12; AD Reigate 12; V Bermondsey St Jas and St Anne from 13; Hon Can S'wark Cathl from 06. *St James's Vicarage, 4 Thurland Road, London SE16 4AA* T: (020) 7394 1482
E: garyjjenkins@outlook.com

JENKINS, Glyn Frank. b 34. Keble Coll Ox BA 55 MA 59 DipEd 58. **d** 14 **p** 14. NSM Bassaleg *Mon* from 14. *10 Cwrt Pencraig, 9 Caerau Crescent, Newport NP20 4HG* E: glynandmegjenkins@talktalk.net

JENKINS, Canon Jeanette. b 42. St Jo Coll Nottm 83. **dss** 84 **d** 86 **p** 94. NSM Kilmarnock *Glas* 84-94; NSM Irvine St Andr LEP 84-94; NSM Ardrossan 84-94; Asst Chapl Crosshouse Hosp 86-94; Chapl Ayrshire Hospice 90-02; Can St Mary's Cathl from 99. *4 Gleneagles Avenue, Kilwinning KA13 6RD* T: (01294) 553383   M: 07775-595109
E: revj.jenkins@btinternet.com

JENKINS, John. **d** 14 **p** 15. NSM Uxbridge *Lon* from 14. *Address temp unknown*

JENKINS, John Francis. b 46. Ripon Hall Ox 77 Ripon Coll Cuddesdon 75. **d** 77 **p** 78. C Filton *Bris* 77-79; C Bris St Andr Hartcliffe 79-84; P-in-c Bris H Cross Inns Court 84-85; V 85-95; R Odcombe, Brympton, Lufton and Montacute *B & W* 95-14; rtd 14. *10 Cursley Path, Wells BA5 1FF* E: johnjenkins382@btinternet.com

JENKINS, John Morgan. b 33. Open Univ BA 96. Mon Dioc Tr Scheme 82. **d** 85 **p** 86. NSM Cwmbran *Mon* 85-02; rtd 02. *5 Ridgeway Avenue, Newport NP20 5AJ* T: (01633) 662231

JENKINS, John **Rhys**. b 64. Southn Univ BM 89 MRCGP 94 DRCOG 93. St Mich Coll Llan 09. **d** 13 **p** 14. NSM Roath *Llan* from 13. *1 Thompson Avenue, Cardiff CF5 1EX* E: jrhysj@ntlworld.com

JENKINS, John **Richard**. b 68. Dundee Univ LLB 90 Leeds Univ MA 98. St Steph Ho Ox BA 94. **d** 94 **p** 95. C Brighouse and Clifton *Wakef* 94-97; C Barnsley St Mary 97-99; Dir Affirming Catholicism from 05. *St Matthew's House, 20 Great Peter Street, London SW1P 2BU* T: (020) 7233 0235 E: director@affirmingcatholicism.org.uk

JENKINS, Julian James. b 56. St Mich Coll Llan 97. **d** 99 **p** 00. C Whitchurch *Llan* 99-01; TV Aberavon 01-05; TV Cowbridge 05-11; P-in-c Llandyfodwg and Cwm Ogwr from 11. *The Vicarage, Coronation Street, Ogmore Vale, Bridgend CF32 7HE* T: (01656) 840248

JENKINS, Canon Lawrence Clifford. b 45. Open Univ BA 77 AKC 70. St Aug Coll Cant. **d** 71 **p** 72. C Osmondthorpe St Phil *Ripon* 71-74; C Monkseaton St Mary *Newc* 74-78; V Shiremoor 78-84; V Wheatley Hills *Sheff* 84-95; RD Doncaster 92-95; V Greenhill 95-10; Hon Can Sheff Cathl 08-10; rtd 10; PtO *Sheff* from 11. *10 Chiltern Crescent, Sprotbrough, Doncaster DN5 7RE* T: (01302) 856587 E: lawriejenkins@virginmedia.com

JENKINS, Canon Paul Morgan. b 44. Sussex Univ BEd 68 Fitzw Coll Cam BA 73 MA 76. Westcott Ho Cam 71. **d** 74 **p** 75. C Forest Gate St Edm *Chelmsf* 74-77; Chapl Bryanston Sch 77-85; P-in-c Stourpaine, Durweston and Bryanston *Sarum* 77-83; Asst Chapl and Housemaster Repton Sch Derby 84-89; Dean of Chpl 89-91; R Singleton *Chich* 91-97; V E Dean 91-97; V W Dean 91-97; Dir St Columba's Retreat and Conf Cen 97-07; Chapl Community of St Pet Woking 03-07; P-in-c Dunsfold and Hascombe *Guildf* 07-12; Hon Can Guildf Cathl 05-12; Master Hugh Sexey's Hosp Bruton from 12. *The Master's House, Sexey's Hospital, Bruton BA10 0AS* T: (01749) 813369 M: 07973-848941 E: pjenkins44@aol.com

JENKINS (*née* RICHARDSON), Pauline Kate. b 41. RGN 62 Nottm Univ CertEd 80 RNT 83. St Jo Coll Nottm 91. **d** 94 **p** 98. Uganda 94-96; PtO *S'well* 96-98; NSM Selston 98-01; NSM Annesley w Newstead 01-03; rtd 03; PtO *S'well* from 03; Leic from 07. *The Cottage, 5 Main Street, Stathern, Melton Mowbray LE14 4HW* T: (01949) 869474 E: revd.p.k.jenkins@gmail.com

JENKINS, Rhys. *See* JENKINS, John Rhys

JENKINS, Richard. *See* JENKINS, John Richard

JENKINS, Preb Richard **David**. b 33. Magd Coll Cam BA 58 MA. Westcott Ho Cam 59. **d** 61 **p** 62. C Staveley *Derby* 61-64; C Billingham St Aid *Dur* 64-68; V Walsall Pleck and Bescot *Lich* 68-73; R Whitchurch 73-97; RD Wem and Whitchurch 85-95; P-in-c Tilstock and Whixall 92-95; Preb Lich Cathl 93-97; rtd 97; PtO *Lich* from 99. *The Council House, Council House Court, Castle Street, Shrewsbury SY1 2AU* T: (01743) 270051

JENKINS, Richard Morvan. b 44. St Mich Coll Llan 65. **d** 69 **p** 70. C Tenby *St D* 69-73; V Llanrhian w Llanhywel and Carnhedryn etc 73-80; R Johnston w Steynton 80-93; V St Ishmael's w Llan-saint and Ferryside 93-09; rtd 09; PtO *St D* from 11. *Geirionydd, 7 Dwynant, Furnace Road, Burry Port SA16 0YQ* T: (01554) 834761

JENKINS, Robert. *See* JENKINS, Eric Robert

JENKINS, Timothy David. b 52. Pemb Coll Ox BA 73 MLitt 77 MA 82 St Edm Ho Cam BA 84 PhD 01. Ridley Hall Cam 82. **d** 85 **p** 86. C Kingswood *Bris* 85-87; Sen Chapl Nottm Univ *S'well* 88-92; Dean of Chpl Jes Coll Cam 92-10; Fell from 92; Can Th Leic Cathl 04-09. *50 Stanley Road, Cambridge CB5 8BL* T: (01223) 363185 or 339303 E: tdj22@jesus.cam.ac.uk

JENKINS, Canon William **David**. b 42. Birm Univ BA 63. St D Coll Lamp LTh 65. **d** 65 **p** 66. C Gorseinon *S & B* 65-67; C Llanelli *St D* 67-72; V Clydach *S & B* 72-82; Chapl Gwynedd Hosp NHS Trust 82-97; V Llanrhos *St As* 82-97; RD Llanrwst 84-96; Can Cursal St As Cathl 93-97; TR Tenby *St D* 97-07; rtd 07; PtO *St As* from 09. *Kildare, 96 Conway Road, Llandudno LL30 1PP* M: 07791-738018

JENKINSON, Margaret. b 40. MCSP 62. Carl Dioc Tr Inst 89. **d** 92 **p** 94. NSM Preesall *Blackb* 92-96; NSM Lanercost, Walton, Gilsland and Nether Denton *Carl* 96-04; P-in-c Lorton and Loweswater w Buttermere 04-13; rtd 13; PtO *Blackb* from 14. *10 The Conifers, Hambleton, Poulton-le-Fylde FY6 9EP* T: (01253) 702237 E: margaret.jenkinson@btinternet.com

JENKINSON, Rachel Elisabeth. *See* GIBSON, Rachel Elisabeth

JENKYNS (*formerly* EVANS), Ms Elaine. b 63. St Mich Coll Llan BTh 02. **d** 02 **p** 03. C Llantwit Major *Llan* 02-05; C Penarth All SS 05-09; P-in-c Pontypridd St Matt and Cilfynydd w Llanwynno 09-13; P-in-c Cwmafan from 13; C Baglan from 13. *66 Dinas Baglan Road, Baglan, Port Talbot SA12 8AF* T: (01639) 282216

JENKYNS, Preb Henry Derrik George. b 30. Sarum Th Coll 57. **d** 60 **p** 61. C Kettering SS Pet and Paul 60-64; V Shrewsbury St Geo *Lich* 64-71; V Wednesbury St Paul Wood Green 71-76; V Stokesay *Heref* 76-86; P-in-c Acton Scott 76-86; RD Condover 80-86; Preb Heref Cathl 83-96; R Kington w Huntington, Old Radnor, Kinnerton etc 86-96; rtd 96; PtO *Heref* from 96. *Sarum House, 9 Bromley Road, Ludlow SY8 1QY*

JENKYNS, John Thomas William **Basil**. b 30. Univ of Wales (Lamp) BA 54 St Cath Coll Ox BA 57 MA 62. Wycliffe Hall Ox 54. **d** 57 **p** 58. C Neasden cum Kingsbury St Cath *Lon* 57-60; C S Lyncombe *B & W* 60-64; V Gt Harwood St Bart *Blackb* 64-66; R Colne St Bart 66-69; V Chard St Mary *B & W* 69-87; Preb Wells Cathl 87; V Swaffham *Nor* 87-89; V Overbury w Teddington, Alstone etc *Worc* 89-95; rtd 95; PtO *St E* from 10. *9 Aldeburgh Road, Leiston IP16 4JY*

JENKYNS, Stephen. b 60. Univ of Wales (Cardiff) BTh 02. St Mich Coll Llan 99. **d** 02 **p** 03. C Penarth w Lavernock *Llan* 02-04; C Penarth and Llandough 04-06; TV Cyncoed *Mon* 06-09; P-in-c Llandaff N *Llan* 09-13; P-in-c Baglan from 13; C Cwmafan from 13. *66 Dinas Baglan Road, Baglan, Port Talbot SA12 8AF* T: (01639) 282216

JENNER, Miss Brenda Ann. b 54. Culham Coll Ox BEd 80. St Jo Coll Nottm 86. **d** 88. Par Dn Leigh St Mary *Man* 88-92; Par Dn Leic Ch Sav 92-94. *18 Chatsworth Avenue, Wigston, Leicester LE18 4LF*

JENNER, Michael Albert. b 37. Oak Hill Th Coll 75. **d** 77 **p** 78. C Mile Cross *Nor* 77-80; P-in-c Easton *Ely* 80-86; P-in-c Ellington 80-86; P-in-c Grafham 80-86; P-in-c Spaldwick w Barham and Woolley 80-86; PtO *Roch* from 01; rtd 02. *Saffron Meadow, Manaccan, Helston TR12 6EN* T: (01326) 231965 M: 07831-826954

JENNER, Peter. b 67. **d** 95 **p** 96. C Staines *Lon* from 15. *The Vicarage, Kenilworth Gardens, Staines-upon-Thames TW18 1DR* T: (01784) 469155 M: 07824-323815 E: fr.peter.jenner@gmail.com

JENNER, Canon Peter John. b 56. Chu Coll Cam BA 77 PhD 80 MA 81. St Jo Coll Nottm 82. **d** 85 **p** 86. C Upperby St Jo *Carl* 85-88; Chapl Reading Univ *Ox* 88-96; P-in-c Mellor *Derby* 96-99; V 99-06; V *Ches* 06-12; RD Chadkirk 08-11; Can Res Ches Cathl 12-15; Chapl Ches Univ from 12. *11 Abbey Street, Chester CH1 2JF* T: (01244) 401818 E: jennerfamily@btinternet.com

JENNER, William George. b 37. Nottm Univ BSc 59 K Coll Lon PGCE 60. **d** 97 **p** 98. OLM Gillingham w Geldeston, Stockton, Ellingham etc *Nor* 97-05; PtO from 05. *3 Woodland Drive, Kirby Cane, Bungay NR35 2PT* T: (01508) 518229

JENNETT, The Ven Maurice Arthur. b 34. St Jo Coll Dur BA 60. Cranmer Hall Dur 60. **d** 62 **p** 63. C Marple All SS *Ches* 62-67; V Withnell *Blackb* 67-75; V Stranton *Dur* 75-91; Crosslinks Zimbabwe 92-99; Asst P Nyanga Mary Magd 92-93; R 93-99; Can and Adn Manicaland N 97; rtd 99; PtO *Leeds* from 01. *2 Southfield Avenue, Ripon HG4 2NR* T: (01765) 607842 E: maurice@mjennett.fsnet.co.uk

JENNINGS, Anne. *See* SMITH, Anne

JENNINGS, Clive John. b 57. Trin Coll Bris. **d** 00 **p** 01. C Milton *B & W* 00-02; C Clevedon St Andr and Ch Ch from 02. *12 Princes Road, Clevedon BS21 7SZ* T: (01275) 872134 E: clive.jennings@blueyonder.co.uk

✠JENNINGS, The Rt Revd David Willfred Michael. b 44. AKC 66. **d** 67 **p** 68 **c** 00. C Walton St Mary *Liv* 67-69; C Christchurch *Win* 69-73; V Hythe 73-80; V Romford St Edw *Chelmsf* 80-92; RD Havering 85-92; Hon Can Chelmsf Cathl 87-92; Adn Southend 92-00; Suff Bp Warrington *Liv* 00-09; rtd 09; PtO *Ox* 10-13; Hon Asst Bp Ox from 13; Hon Asst Bp Glouc from 10. *The Laurels, High Street, Northleach, Cheltenham GL54 3ET* T: (01451) 860743

JENNINGS, Duncan William. b 54. UWE MA. STETS 05. **d** 08 **p** 09. C Southampton Thornhill St Chris *Win* 08-11; P-in-c from 11. *St Christopher's Vicarage, 402 Hinkler Road, Southampton SO19 6DF* T: (023) 8122 5911

JENNINGS, Canon Frederick **David**. b 48. K Coll Lon BD 73 AKC 73 Loughb Univ MPhil 98. St Aug Coll Cant 73. **d** 74 **p** 75. C Halesowen *Worc* 74-77; PtO *Birm* 78-80; *Leic* 78-80 and 85-87; P-in-c Snibston 80-85; Community Relns Officer 81-84; P-in-c Burbage w Aston Flamville 87-91; R 91-14; Hon Can Leic Cathl 03-10; Project officer for Ch and Soc 11-14; rtd 14; Can Th Leic Cathl from 10; PtO from 14. *59 Pipistrelle Drive, Market Bosworth, Nuneaton CV13 0NW* T: (01455) 698805 M: 07710-205582 E: revdavidjennings@talktalk.net

JENNINGS, Ian. b 47. Leeds Univ MA 98. NOC 95. **d** 97 **p** 97. NSM Hackenthorpe *Sheff* 97-01; Asst Chapl HM Pris and YOI Doncaster 97-98; Chapl 98-01; V Sheff St Cuth 01-06; TR Aston cum Aughton w Swallownest and Ulley 06-15; rtd 15. *24 Brincliffe Court, Nether Edge Road, Sheffield S7 1RX* T: 0114-418 9687

JENNINGS, Ian Richard. b 65. Liv Univ BA 88 Wolv Poly PGCE 91. Trin Coll Bris 07. **d** 09 **p** 10. C Pedmore *Worc* 09-13; C The Lye and Stambermill 13-14; V Low Moor and Oakenshaw *Leeds* from 14. *The Vicarage, Park House Road, Low Moor, Bradford BD12 0HR* M: 07722-019096 E: ianrichardjennings@gmail.com

JENNINGS, Janet. b 38. SCM 71 SRN 74. Oak Hill Th Coll BA 87. **d** 88 **p** 97. Par Dn Stevenage St Pet Broadwater *St Alb* 88-90; PtO *St As* 92-14. *Address temp unknown*

JENNINGS, Jonathan Peter. b 61. K Coll Lon BD 83. Westcott Ho Cam 84. **d** 86 **p** 87. C Peterlee *Dur* 86-89; C Darlington St Cuth 89-92; Dioc Communications Officer *Man* 92-95; Broadcasting Officer Gen Syn 95-01; PtO *S'wark* 95-98; Hon C Banstead *Guildf* 98-04; Abp Cant's Press Sec 01-08; PtO *Cant* 05-08; *Roch* 05-08; P-in-c Gillingham St Aug from 08; RD Gillingham 10-11. *St Augustine's Vicarage, Rock Avenue, Gillingham ME7 5PW* T: (01634) 850288 E: revjpj@aol.com

JENNINGS, Margaret. b 50. **d** 11 **p** 12. OLM Marsh Green w Newtown *Liv* 11-14; OLM Newtown from 14. *26D Mill Lane, Upholland, Skelmersdale WN8 0HJ* T: (01695) 627804

JENNINGS, Mrs Pamela. b 49. SRN 71. NEOC 05. **d** 08 **p** 09. NSM Scarborough St Mary w Ch Ch and H Apostles *York* 08-13; PtO from 14. *26 Ling Hill, Scarborough YO12 5HS* T: (01723) 365528 E: kenandpamjennings@gmail.com

JENNINGS, Peter James. b 28. Univ of Wales (Lamp) BA 56. St D Coll Lamp LTh 57. **d** 57 **p** 58. C Dudley St Jo *Worc* 57-60; C Dudley St Thos and St Luke 61-64; Chapl HM Borstal Portland 64-66; Chapl HM Pris Wakef 66-70; Chapl HM Pris Liv 70-76; RD Walton *Liv* 75-76; Chapl HM Pris Styal 76-77 and 88-92; N Regional Chapl 76-82; Asst Chapl Gen (N) 82-88; PtO *Man* 77-89 and 00-08; *Ches* from 79; rtd 93. *6 St Ann's Road South, Cheadle SK8 3DZ* T: 0161-437 8828

JENNINGS, Robert Henry. b 46. St Jo Coll Dur BA 69 MA 79. Qu Coll Birm. **d** 72 **p** 73. C Dursley *Glouc* 72-74; C Coleford w Staunton 75-78; TV Bottesford w Ashby *Linc* 78-83; TV Witney *Ox* 83-89; V Lane End w Cadmore End from 89. *The Vicarage, 7 Lammas Way, Lane End, High Wycombe HP14 3EX* T: (01494) 881913

JENNINGS, Mrs Susan Mary. b 61. MCSP 82. St Jo Coll Nottm BA 15. **d** 15. C Manningham *Leeds* from 15. *The Vicarage, Park House Road, Low Moor, Bradford BD12 0HR* T: (01274) 421077 M: 07963-279153 E: suemaryjennings@gmail.com

JENNINGS, Thomas Robert. b 24. TCD BA 47 MA 51. **d** 48 **p** 49. C Drumragh *D & R* 48-51; CF 51-67; I Killeshandra *K, E & A* 67-70; I Newcastle w Newtownmountkennedy and Calary *D & G* 70-92; Can Ch Ch Cathl Dublin 88-92; rtd 92. *66 Seacourt, Newcastle, Greystones, Co Wicklow, Republic of Ireland* T: (00353) (1) 281 0777 M: 87-763 3418 E: clojen66@gofree.indigo.ie

JENNINGS, Walter James. b 37. Birm Univ BMus 60 MA 90. Qu Coll Birm 77. **d** 80 **p** 81. Hon C Hampton in Arden *Birm* 80-84; Chapl St Alb Aided Sch Highgate Birm 84-86; C Wotton-under-Edge w Ozleworth and N Nibley *Glouc* 86-89; V Pittville All SS 89-98; rtd 98; Chapl Beauchamp Community 98-00; PtO *Worc* from 98. *Address temp unknown* E: walter.linda@virgin.net

JENSEN, Alexander Sönderup. b 68. Tübingen Univ 94 St Jo Coll Dur PhD 97 Ox Univ MTh 01. St Steph Ho Ox 97. **d** 99 **p** 00. C Norton St Mich *Dur* 99-02; Lect CITC 02-05; Lect Murdoch Univ Australia from 05. *School of Social Sciences and Humanities, Murdoch University, South Street, Murdoch, W Australia 6150* T: (0061) (8) 9360 6625 F: 9360 6480 E: a.jensen@murdoch.edu.au

JENSEN, Erik Henning. b 33. Copenhagen Univ BPhil 55 Harvard Univ STM 54 Worc Coll Ox BLitt 58 DPhil 69. Ripon Hall Ox 56. **d** 58 **p** 59. C Highwood *Chelmsf* 58-59; C Simanggang Sarawak 59-61; Borneo 61-62; Malaysia 63-02; rtd 02. *The Rock House, Maugersbury, Stow-on-the-Wold GL54 1HP* T: (01451) 830171

JENSEN, Juliet Helen. b 68. Man Univ MB, ChB 92 Univ Coll Lon MSc 97. STETS 11. **d** 13 **p** 14. C Forest Gate Em w Upton Cross *Chelmsf* from 13. *146 Godwin Road, London E7 0LP* M: 07946-869324 E: juliet.jensen@btinternet.com

✠**JENSEN, The Rt Revd Peter Frederick.** b 43. Lon Univ BD 70 Sydney Univ MA 76 Ox Univ DPhil 80. Moore Th Coll Sydney. **d** 69 **p** 70 **c** 01. C Broadway Australia 69-76; PtO *Ox* 76-79; Lect Moore Th Coll 73-76 and 80-84; Prin 85-01; Can Sydney 89-01; Abp Sydney 01-13; rtd 13. *PO Box Q190, Queen Victoria Building, Sydney NSW 1230, Australia* T: (0061) (2) 9265 1521 F: 9265 1504

JENSON, Philip Peter. b 56. Ex Coll Ox BA 78 MA 82 Down Coll Cam BA 80 MA 86 PhD 88. Ridley Hall Cam 80. **d** 87 **p** 88. C Gt Warley Ch Ch *Chelmsf* 87-89; Lect Trin Coll Bris 89-05; Lect Ridley Hall Cam from 05. *Ridley Hall, Cambridge CB3 9HG* T: (01223) 746580 F: 746581 E: ppj22@cam.ac.uk

JEPP, Malcolm Leonard. b 44. SWMTC 06. **d** 09 **p** 10. NSM Meneage *Truro* 09-14; rtd 14. *Polpidnick Cottage, Porthallow, St Keverne, Helston TR12 6PL* T/F: (01326) 281031 M: 07797-505539 E: lenjepp@jeppassociates.co.uk

JEPP (née NUGENT), Mrs Mary Patricia. b 55. Mt St Vincent Univ Canada BA 79 Univ of New Brunswick BEd 80 Open Univ MA 03. ERMC 05. **d** 08 **p** 09. C Godmanchester *Ely* 08-11; P-in-c Alconbury cum Weston 11-14; P-in-c Winwick 11-14; P-in-c Hamerton 11-14; P-in-c Gt w Lt Gidding and Steeple Gidding 11-14; P-in-c Upton and Copmanford 11-14; P-in-c Buckworth 11-14; R N Leightonstone from 14. *The Vicarage, Church Way, Alconbury, Huntingdon PE28 4DX* T: (01480) 890284 E: m.jepp@btinternet.com

JEPPS, Philip Anthony. b 34. BNC Ox BA 58 MA 68. Wycliffe Hall Ox 58. **d** 60 **p** 73. C Elton All SS *Man* 60; PtO *Pet* 70-73; R Church w Chapel Brampton 74-80; P-in-c Harlestone 79-80; V Kettering St Andr 80-94; V Conisbrough *Sheff* 94-01; rtd 01; PtO *Heref* from 01. *2 Eagle Cottages, Church Lane, Orleton, Ludlow SY8 4HT* T: (01568) 780517

JEPSON, Mrs Ann Brenda. b 46. Open Univ BA 81 Hockerill Coll Cam CertEd 68. LCTP 10. **d** 11 **p** 12. NSM Hurst Green and Mitton *Bradf* 11-13; NSM Ribchester w Stidd *Blackb* from 13. *Ribblesdale View, Greenside, Ribchester, Preston PR3 3ZJ* T: (01254) 878177 E: annjepson@btinternet.com

JEPSON, Joanna Elizabeth. b 76. Trin Coll Bris BA 99 Cam Univ MA 03. Ridley Hall Cam 01. **d** 03 **p** 04. C Plas Newton *Ches* 03-06; Chapl Lon Coll of Fashion 06-11; P-in-c Fulham St Pet 06-09; PtO *Portsm* 12-13. *4 The Liberty, Wells BA5 2SU* T: (01749) 673188 E: joeyjep@yahoo.com

JEPSON-BIDDLE, Canon Nicholas Lawrence. b 71. K Coll Lon BA 94 Leeds Univ MA 98. Coll of Resurr Mirfield 96. **d** 98 **p** 99. C Bedford St Andr *St Alb* 98-01; Bp's Dom Chapl and Research Asst *Chich* 01-04; P-in-c Brighton Gd Shep Preston 04-05; TV Putney St Mary *S'wark* 07-10; PV Westmr Abbey 08-10; Can Res Portsm Cathl 10-13; Can Res and Prec Wells Cathl from 13. *4 The Liberty, Wells BA5 2SU* T: (01749) 673188 M: 07825-322326 E: nicklb@hotmail.com

JEREMIAH, Anderson Harris Mithra. b 75. Madras Univ BA 95 MA 97 MPhil 98 Edin Univ PhD 09. United Th Coll Bangalore BD 02. **d** 03 **p** 04. C Ranipet St Mary India 03; Chapl Chr Medical Coll and Hosp Vellore 03-05; LtO *Edin* 06-13; C Edin Ch Ch 08-11; PtO *Blackb* 12-14; P-in-c Gisburn from 14. *2 Ribblesdale Court, Gisburn, Clitheroe BB7 4HB* E: a.jeremiah@lancaster.ac.uk

JERMAN, Edward David. b 40. Trin Coll Carmarthen CertEd 61. **d** 87 **p** 88. NSM Llandrygarn w Bodwrog and Heneglwys etc *Ban* 87-12; rtd 12; PtO *Ban* from 12. *Haulfre, Gwalchmai, Holyhead LL65 4SG* T: (01407) 720856

JERMY, Stuart John. b 66. Middx Univ BEd 90. Wycliffe Hall Ox 01. **d** 03 **p** 04. C New Thundersley *Chelmsf* 03-07; V St Martins and Weston Rhyn *Lich* from 07. *The Vicarage, Church Lane, St Martins, Oswestry SY11 3AP* T: (01691) 778468 M: 07801-071443 E: sjermy@toucansurf.com

JERSEY, Dean of. See KEY, The Very Revd Robert Frederick

JERVIS, Christopher. b 53. Loughb Univ BEd 75. Wycliffe Hall Ox 80. **d** 82 **p** 83. C Woodford Wells *Chelmsf* 82-85; Chapl Felsted Sch 85-87; Chapl Canford Sch 87-13; C Jersey St Helier *Win* from 13. *8 Fairways, Plat Douet Road, St Clements, Jersey JE2 6PN*

JERVIS, William Edward. b 47. MRICS 74. Linc Th Coll 74. **d** 77 **p** 78. C W Bromwich All SS *Lich* 77-80; C Horsham *Chich* 80-86; R W Tarring 86-14; rtd 14. *5 Broadmark Beach, Broadmark Lane, Rustington, Littlehampton BN16 2JF* T: (01903) 785434 E: eandj.jervis@gmail.com

JERWOOD, Eleanor Alice Jerwood. See CLACK, Eleanor Alice Jerwood

JESSETT, David Charles. b 55. K Coll Lon BD 77 AKC 77 MTh. Westcott Ho Cam 78. **d** 79 **p** 80. C Aveley *Chelmsf* 79-82; C Walthamstow St Pet 82-85; P-in-c Hunningham *Cov* 85-91; P-in-c Wappenbury w Weston under Wetherley 85-91; Progr Dir Exploring Chr Min Scheme 85-91; Dir CME 87-90; PtO *Cov* 90-97; P-in-c Barford w Wasperton and Sherbourne from 97; P-in-c Hampton Lucy w Charlecote and Loxley from 07. *The Rectory, Church Lane, Barford, Warwick CV35 8ES* T: (01926) 624238 E: david@jessetts.freeserve.co.uk

JESSIMAN, Elaine Rae. b 59. Wall Hall Coll Aldenham BEd 95. STETS 05. **d** 08 **p** 09. C Leigh Park *Portsm* 08-10; R Dorrington w Leebotwood, Longnor, Stapleton etc *Heref* 12-15; rtd 15; R Dorrington w Leebotwood, Longnor, Stapleton etc *Heref* from 12. *The Rectory, Church Road, Dorrington, Shrewsbury SY5 7JL* E: elaine.jessiman@ntlworld.com

JESSIMAN, Timothy Edward. b 58. Portsm Univ MA 06. Oak Hill Th Coll 88. **d** 91 **p** 92. C Baldock w Bygrave *St Alb* 91-95; C Bideford *Ex* 95-96; TV Bideford, Northam, Westward Ho!,

Appledore etc 96-00; Chapl Grenville Coll Bideford 95-00; Chapl N Devon Healthcare NHS Trust 98-00; P-in-c Hartplain *Portsm* 00-06; V 06-13; P-in-c Stokesay *Heref* from 13; P-in-c Halford w Sibdon Carwood from 13; P-in-c Wistanstow from 13; P-in-c Acton Scott from 13. *The Vicarage, Church Road, Dorrington, Shrewsbury SY5 7JL* T: (01743) 719578 E: tim.jessiman@ntlworld.com

JESSON, Alan Francis. b 47. TD 89. Ealing Coll of Educn 70 Loughb Univ MLS 77 Selw Coll Cam MA 87 ALA 70 FLA 91 MBIM 82. EAMTC 88. **d** 91 **p** 92. NSM Swavesey *Ely* 91-95; NSM Fen Drayton w Conington and Lolworth etc 95-00; CF (ACF) 92-96; Sen Chapl ACF from 96; R Outwell *Ely* 00-12; R Upwell St Pet 00-12; rtd 12; PtO *Ely* from 12; *Nor* from 01. *9 Lawn Lane, Sutton, Ely CB6 2RE* T: (01353) 776172 E: alan.jesson@ely.anglican.org

JESSON, George Albert Oswald (Ossie). b 54. Trin Coll Bris 90. **d** 92 **p** 93. C Thorpe Acre w Dishley *Leic* 92-01; C Chilwell *S'well* 01-08; Chapl HM Pris and YOI Doncaster from 12. *HM Prison and Young Offender Institution Doncaster, Marshgate, Doncaster DN5 8UX* T: (01302) 760870 E: revo.jesson@ntlworld.com

JESSON, Julia Margaret. b 54. St Matthias Coll Bris CertEd 75 Nottm Univ MA 04. EMMTC 01. **d** 04 **p** 05. NSM Stapleford *S'well* 04-07; C Kimberley 07-08; P-in-c E Markham w Askham, Headon w Upton and Grove 08-11; P-in-c Dunham w Darlton, Ragnall, Fledborough etc 08-11; TV Retford Area from 11. *The Rectory, Lincoln Road, East Markham, Newark NG22 0SH* T: (01777) 870965 E: julia.jesson@btinternet.com

JESSOP, Canon Gillian Mary. b 48. Hatf Poly BSc 71 Nottm Univ MEd 85 Homerton Coll Cam PGCE 80. EAMTC 91. **d** 94 **p** 95. C Gt Yarmouth *Nor* 94-97; R Gt w Lt Addington and Woodford *Pet* 97-02; R Paston 02-15; Asst Dir Tr for Readers 00-02; Dir 02-10; RD Pet 10-15; Can Pet Cathl 11-15; rtd 15; PtO *Pet* from 15. *35 Gidding Road, Sawtry, Huntingdon PE28 5TS* T: (01487) 832237 E: rev.gill@tesco.net

JESSOP, John Edward. b 46. RMCS BSc 71 CEng 78 MIET 78. S Dios Minl Tr Scheme 87 Ridley Coll Melbourne 89. **d** 90 **p** 90. C Mooroolbark Australia 90-91; P-in-c S Yarra 92-93; I Blackburn St Jo 93-98; I Kew H Trin 98-02; P-in-c Brimpsfield w Birdlip, Syde, Daglingworth etc *Glouc* 02-04; R 04-11; AD Cirencester 08-11; rtd 11. *176 Thornton Road, Taggerty VIC 3714, Australia*

JESTY, Mrs Helen Margaret. b 51. York Univ BA 72. Cranmer Hall Dur BA 81. **dss** 82 **d** 87. C Chilwell *S'well* 82-86; Norbiton 86-93; Par Dn 87-90; Hon Par Dn 91-93; Chapl Naomi Ho Hospice 05-13; rtd 13. *Fairfield, 1 Downside Road, Winchester SO22 5LT* T: (01962) 849190 E: helen.jesty@btinternet.com

JESUDASON, Leslie Peter Prakash. b 58. Wycliffe Hall Ox 05. **d** 07 **p** 08. C Throop *Win* 07-11; TV Bracknell 11-15. *54 Vulcan Drive, Bracknell RG12 9GN* T: (01344) 304973 E: ljesudason@gmail.com

JEVONS, The Ven Alan Neil. b 56. Ex Univ BA 77 Selw Coll Cam BA 80 MA 84. Ridley Hall Cam. **d** 81 **p** 82. C Halesowen *Worc* 81-84; C Heywood St Luke w All So *Man* 84-87; TV Heref St Martin w St Fran 87-93; P-in-c Much Birch w Lt Birch, Much Dewchurch etc 93-02; RD Ross and Archenfield 98-02; TR Tenbury Wells 02-07; Preb Heref Cathl 02-07; RD Ludlow 05-07; V Llyn Safaddan *S & B* 07-15; C Crickhowell from 15; Dioc Tourism Officer 07-13; Asst Dioc Soc Resp Officer 09-13; Adn Brecon from 13. *The Vicarage, Llangorse, Brecon LD3 7UG* T: (01874) 658298 E: archdeacon.brecon@churchinwales.org.uk

JEVONS, Harry Clifford. b 46. Bp Otter Coll 01. **d** 04 **p** 05. C Ifield *Chich* 04-07; C Milton *Win* 07-11; rtd 11; C Ermington and Ugborough *Ex* 11-14; C Diptford, N Huish, Harberton, Harbertonford etc 11-14; P-in-c Torquay St Luke from 14. *St Luke's Vicarage, 1 Mead Road, Torquay TQ2 6TE* T: (01803) 368047 M: 07881-527050 E: fr.harry@hotmail.co.uk

JEWELL, Alan David John. b 59. St Cath Coll Ox MA 86. Wycliffe Hall Ox 83. **d** 86 **p** 87. C Walton H Trin *Ox* 86-91; TV Sutton *Liv* 91-97; TV Halewood 97-01; TR 01-12; TR Halewood and Hunts Cross 12-14; V Stretton and Appleton Thorn *Ches* from 14. *The Vicarage, Stretton Road, Stretton, Warrington WA4 4NT* T: (01925) 730276 E: alandjjewell@btopenworld.com

JEWISS, Anthony Harrison. b 39. Virginia Th Sem MDiv 92. **d** 92 **p** 93. Chapl to Bp Los Angeles USA 92-99; Can Prec Los Angeles 99; Dep Exec Officer Episc Ch Cen New York 99-07; rtd 07; Asst Chapl Midi-Pyrénées and Aude *Eur* from 09. *3 rue Mandrière, 11580 Alet-les-Bains, France* T: (0033) 4 68 69 01 22 E: tonyjewiss@gmail.com

JEWITT, Martin Paul Noel. b 44. AKC 69. St Aug Coll Cant. **d** 70 **p** 71. C Usworth *Dur* 70-74; TV 77-78; Tutor Newton Coll Papua New Guinea 74-77; V Balham Hill Ascension *S'wark*

78-93; R N Reddish *Man* 93-99; V Thornton Heath St Paul *S'wark* 99-10; rtd 10; PtO *Cant* from 10. *12 Abbott Road, Folkestone CT20 1NG* T: (01303) 211491 M: 07981-754738 E: martin.jewitt@virginmedia.com

JEWSBURY, Jonathan Mark. b 64. St Jo Coll Dur BA 86. NEOC 04. **d** 06 **p** 07. NSM E Rainton *Dur* 06-14; NSM W Rainton 06-14. *62 Grange Road, Durham DH1 1AL* E: j.jewsbury100@durhamlea.org.uk

JEWSON, Dawn. b 56. **d** 13 **p** 14. C Southall St Geo *Lon* from 13. *17 Montague Road, London W13 8HA* T: (020) 8991 2608 M: 07930-902507 E: dawn.jewson@gmail.com

JEYES, Caroline Helen. *See* WALKER, Caroline Helen

JEYNES, Anthony James. b 44. AKC 68. St Boniface Warminster 68. **d** 69 **p** 70. C Ellesmere Port *Ches* 69-73; C Birkenhead St Pet w St Matt 73-74; R Oughtrington 75-80; C Timperley 80-85; C Eastham 85-89; V New Brighton St Jas 89-96; P-in-c New Brighton Em 94-96; R Tarleton *Blackb* 96-04; P-in-c Kyrenia St Andr and Chapl N Cyprus 04-07; Chapl Paphos 07-09; PtO from 09; Cyprus and the Gulf from 09. *PO Box 54612, 3726 Limassol, Cyprus* T: (00357) (25) 342908 M: 99-806109 E: tony_irene@cytanet.com.cy

JOACHIM, Margaret Jane. b 49. St Hugh's Coll Ox BA 70 MA 74 Birm Univ PhD 77 W Midl Coll of Educn PGCE 71 FGS 91. S Dios Minl Tr Scheme 91. **d** 94 **p** 95. NSM Ealing St Barn *Lon* 94-97; NSM Ealing St Pet Mt Park from 97. *8 Newburgh Road, London W3 6DQ* T: (020) 8723 4514 E: margaret.joachim@london.anglican.org

JOB, Canon Evan Roger Gould. b 36. Magd Coll Ox BA 60 MA 64 ARCM 55. Cuddesdon Coll 60. **d** 62 **p** 63. C Liv Our Lady and St Nic 62-65; V New Springs 65-70; Min Can and Prec Man Cathl 70-74; Prec and Sacr Westmr Abbey 74-79; Can Res, Prec and Sacr Win Cathl 79-94; Vice-Dean Win 91-94; Select Preacher Ox Univ 74 and 91; PtO *Win* from 94; rtd 01; PtO *Portsm* from 04. *Kitwood Farmhouse, Kitwood Lane, Ropley, Alresford SO24 0DB* T: (01962) 772303

JOBBER, Barry William. b 38. N Staffs Poly BA 84. Cuddesdon Coll 73. **d** 75 **p** 76. C Fenton *Lich* 76-79; V Goldenhill 79-80; PtO *Ches* 90-02 and from 12; NSM Middlewich w Byley 02-08; NSM Witton 08-12; rtd 12. *16 Angus Grove, Middlewich CW10 9GR* T: (01606) 737386 M: 07974-380234 E: barry.jobber@uwclub.net

JOBLING, Jeremy Charles. b 72. Natal Univ BSc 95. Wycliffe Hall Ox 03. **d** 05 **p** 06. C Watford *St Alb* 05-08; C Kenilworth S Africa from 08. *16 Summerley Road, Kenilworth, 7708 South Africa* T: (0027) (21) 797 6332 E: jeremy.jobling@googlemail.com

JOBLING, Miss Mary. b 77. Aachen University BPharm 99 Derby Univ MSc 03. Cranmer Hall Dur 13. **d** 15. C Cayton w Eastfield *York* from 15. *160 Dean Road, Scarborough YO12 7JH* E: maryjobling@hotmail.com

JOBSON, Clifford Hedley. b 31. St Jo Coll Dur BA 54 MA 81. **d** 56 **p** 57. C Hall Green Ascension *Birm* 56-59; C Ambleside w Rydal *Carl* 59-60; R Arthuret 60-62; CF 62-73; Dep Asst Chapl Gen 73-78; Asst Chapl Gen 78-84; QHC from 80; V Fleet *Guildf* 84-96; rtd 96; PtO *B & W* 96-06. *Vine Cottage, 25 Silver Street, South Petherton TA13 5AL* T: (01460) 241783

JOEL, Mrs Mary Tertia. b 35. **d** 99 **p** 00. OLM Blyth Valley *St E* 99-05; rtd 05; PtO *St E* from 05. *38 Saxmundham Road, Aldeburgh IP15 5JE* T: (01728) 454886 M: 07790-910554 E: maryt@joel12.freeserve.co.uk

JOHN, Alexander Dominic. b 26. Madras Univ BA 47. Episc Sem Austin Texas MDiv 63. **d** 63 **p** 64. C Millhouses H Trin *Sheff* 63-65; Switzerland 65-68; India 68-78; Australia from 78; rtd 85. *12 Bentwood Avenue, Woodlands WA 6018, Australia* T: (0061) (8) 9445 3530 E: remo@space.net.au

✠**JOHN, The Rt Revd Andrew Thomas Griffith.** b 64. Univ of Wales LLB. St Jo Coll Nottm BA. **d** 89 **p** 90 **c** 08. C Cardigan w Mwnt and Y Ferwig *St D* 89-91; P Aberystwyth 91-92; TV 92-99; V Henfynyw w Aberaeron and Llanddewi Aberarth etc 99-06; V Pencarreg and Llancrwys 06-08; Adn Cardigan 06-08; Bp Bangor from 08. *Ty'r Esgob, Upper Garth Road, Bangor LL57 2SS* T: (01248) 362895 E: bishop.bangor@churchinwales.org.uk

JOHN, Canon Arun Andrew. b 54. **d** 77 **p** 78. India 77-96; S Africa 97-04; TV Manningham *Bradf* 04-11; P-in-c Blackb St Steph 11-12; P-in-c Blackb St Jas 11-12; V Blackb St Steph and St Jas from 12. *St James's Vicarage, Cromer Place, Blackburn BB1 8EL* T: (01254) 51864

JOHN, Barbara. b 34. Gilmore Ho. **dss** 67 **d** 80 **p** 97. Merthyr Tydfil *Llan* 67-71; Loughton St Jo *Chelmsf* 71-73; Newport St Woolos *Mon* 73-78; Asst Chapl Univ Hosp of Wales Cardiff 78-85; C Radyr *Llan* 85-00; rtd 00; PtO *Llan* from 04. *14 Pace Close, Cardiff CF5 2QZ* T: (029) 2055 2989

JOHN, Canon Beverley Hayes. b 49. Qu Coll Birm 83. **d** 85 **p** 86. C Oystermouth *S & B* 85-87; C Morriston 87-88; V Cefn

Coed w Vaynor 88-14; P-in-c Penderyn Mellte 12-14; AD Brecon 99-14; Can Res Brecon Cathl 04-14; rtd 14; PtO *S & B* from 14. *63 Kingrosia Park, Clydach, Swansea SA6 5PL* T: (01792) 842911

JOHN, Brother. *See* HENNINGS, John Richard

JOHN, Caroline Victoria. b 64. Cam Univ BA 86 MA 90. St Jo Coll Nottm. **d** 90. NSM Cardigan w Mwnt and Y Ferwig *St D* 90-91; NSM Aberystwyth 91-96. *Ty'r Esgob, Upper Garth Road, Bangor LL57 2SS* T: (01248) 362895

JOHN, Canon David Michael. b 36. Univ of Wales (Lamp) BA 57. St Mich Coll Llan 57. **d** 59 **p** 60. C Pontypool *Mon* 59-61; C Roath *Llan* 61-66; Asst Chapl HM Pris Liv 66-67; Chapl HM Pris Ex 67-68; V Ystrad Rhondda *Llan* 68-76; V Ponytclun w Talygarn 76-84; R Newton Nottage 84-91; Can Llan Cathl 85-91; rtd 91; PtO *Llan* from 91; *Mon* from 91. *1 Hornbeam Close, St Mellons, Cardiff CF3 0JA* T: (029) 2079 7496

JOHN, David Wyndham. b 61. Lon Bible Coll. NTMTC. **d** 01 **p** 02. NSM Hampstead Em W End *Lon* 01-04; NSM W Hampstead St Cuth from 04; P-in-c from 06. *Flat A, 247 Fordwych Road, London NW2 3LY* M: 07719-333389 E: david.john6@btopenworld.com

JOHN, The Very Revd Jeffrey Philip Hywel. b 53. Hertf Coll Ox BA 75 Magd Coll Ox DPhil 84. St Steph Ho Ox BA 77 MA 78. **d** 78 **p** 79. C Penarth w Lavernock *Llan* 78-80; Asst Chapl Magd Coll Ox 80-82; Fell and Dean of Div 84-91; Chapl and Lect BNC Ox 82-84; V Eltham H Trin *S'wark* 91-97; Chan and Can Th S'wark Cathl 97-04; Bp's Adv for Min 97-04; Dean St Alb *St Alb* from 04. *The Deanery, Sumpter Yard, St Albans AL1 1BY* T: (01727) 890203 F: 890227 E: dean@stalbanscathedral.org

JOHN, Mrs Marie. b 48. **d** 04 **p** 05. OLM Camberwell St Geo *S'wark* from 04. *8 Caroline Gardens, Asylum Road, London SE15 2SQ* T: (020) 7635 5534

JOHN, Mark Christopher. b 61. SS Mark & Jo Univ Coll Plymouth BA 83. St Steph Ho Ox 84. **d** 87 **p** 88. C Treboeth *S & B* 87-90; V Swansea St Mark and St Jo 90-94; Chapl HM Pris Swansea 91-94; Chapl HM Pris Cardiff from 97; LtO *Mon* from 99. *HM Prison Cardiff, Knox Road, Cardiff CF24 0UG* T: (029) 2043 3100 EXT 3233 F: 2043 3318

JOHN, Meurig Hywel. b 46. St D Coll Lamp 67. **d** 71 **p** 72. C Llanelli Ch Ch *St D* 71-74; V Penrhyncoch and Elerch 74-79; V Llanfihangel Aberbythych 79-81; R Cilgerran w Bridell and Llantwyd 81-83; V Gwaun-cae-Gurwen 83-89; V Llanfihangel Genau'r-glyn and Llangorwen 89-95; V Newcastle Emlyn w Llandyfriog etc 95-01; Assoc V Lampeter and Llanddewibrefi Gp 01-03; rtd 03. *Arosfa, Llanybri, Carmarthen SA33 5HQ* T: (01267) 241096

JOHN, Michael Ioannou. b 86. City Univ BA 09. Wycliffe Hall Ox BTh 15. **d** 15. C Muswell Hill St Jas w St Matt *Lon* from 15. *8 St James Lane, London N10 3DB* M: 07540-469052 E: mikeyijohn@gmail.com

JOHN, Napoleon. b 55. Punjab Univ BA 76. Lahetysteologisen Inst Ryttyla Finland 84 Oak Hill Th Coll BA 93. **d** 93 **p** 94. C Leyton St Mary w St Edw *Chelmsf* 93-96; C Leyton St Mary w St Edw and St Luke 96-97; P-in-c Becontree St Elisabeth 97-04; V 04-07; TR Walton and Trimley *St E* 07-13; R Hayes *Roch* from 13. *The Rectory, Hayes Street, Hayes, Bromley BR2 7LH* T: (020) 8462 1373 E: napojohn@gmail.com

JOHN, Nigel. b 59. Univ of Wales (Cardiff) BA 87 Selw Coll Cam MPhil 90. Westcott Ho Cam 88. **d** 91 **p** 92. C Carmarthen St Pet *St D* 91-94; Chapl Roehampton Inst *S'wark* 94-96; V Gors-las *St D* 96-98; V Llanelli Ch Ch 98-02; Chapl Univ of Wales (Swansea) *S & B* from 02. *23 Mayals Avenue, Blackpill, Swansea SA3 5DE* T: (01792) 401703

JOHN, Robert Michael. b 46. Edin Univ BSc 67 Man Univ MSc 68 PhD 70 Otago Univ BD 78. St Jo Coll Auckland 76. **d** 78 **p** 79. C Tauranga New Zealand 78-80; C Hastings 80-83; V Hauraki *St & B* 87-88; V Otumoetai New Zealand 88-94; Chapl Auckland Hosps 94-09; Chapl Univ Hosps of Morecambe Bay NHS Trust 09-11; C N Barrow *Carl* 11-13; rtd 13. *56 Flass Lane, Barrow-in-Furness LA13 0DF* T: (01229) 821613 E: robertmichaeljohn@btinternet.com

JOHN, Stephen Michael. b 63. Univ of Wales (Lamp) BA 85. Coll of Resurr Mirfield 87. **d** 89 **p** 90. C Coity w Nolton *Llan* 89-91; C Merthyr Dyfan 91-94; V Tredegar St Geo *Mon* 94-99; Chapl HM Pris Gartree 99-04; TV Tenby *St D* 04-12; V Pentyrch w Capel Llanillterne *Llan* from 12. *The Vicarage, Church Road, Pentyrch, Cardiff CF15 9QF* T: (029) 2140 3854 E: michaeljohn@dialstart.net

JOHNES, Philip Sydney. b 45. St Mich Coll Llan 90. **d** 92 **p** 93. C Cardigan w Mwnt and Y Ferwig *St D* 92-95; V Llanegwad w Llanfynydd 95-10; rtd 10; PtO *St D* from 10. *Keeper's Cottage, Ferryside SA17 5TY* T: (01267) 267081 E: pjohnes@aol.com

JOHN-FRANCIS, Brother. *See* FRIENDSHIP, Roger Geoffrey

JOHNS, Adam Aubrey. b 34. TCD BA 57 MA 76 NUU BA 75. CITC Div Test 58. **d** 58 **p** 59. C Aghalee *D & D* 58-61; C Derriaghy *Conn* 61-63; I Billy 63-77; I Billy w Derrykeighan 77-03; Can Conn Cathl 98-03; rtd 03. *26 Chatham Road, Armoy, Ballymoney BT53 8TT* T: (028) 2075 1978 E: chathambrae@btinternet.com

JOHNS, Canon Bernard Thomas. b 36. Birm Univ BSc 58. St Mich Coll Llan 61. **d** 63 **p** 64. C Aberavon *Llan* 63-65; C St Andrews Major w Michaelston-le-Pit 65-70; V Cardiff St Andr and St Teilo 70-76; Asst Dioc Dir of Educn 72-91; V Roath 76-88; R Wenvoe and St Lythans 88-02; Dioc Dir Community Educn 91-02; Can Llan Cathl 96-02; rtd 02. *Bay Tree Cottage, 13 Badgers Meadow, Pwllmeyric, Chepstow NP16 6UE* T: (01291) 623254

JOHNS, Mrs Patricia Holly. b 33. Girton Coll Cam BA 56 MA 60 Hughes Hall Cam PGCE 57. Ox NSM Course 87. **d** 90 **p** 94. NSM Wantage *Ox* 90-94; NSM Marlborough *Sarum* 94-95; rtd 95; PtO *Sarum* 95-08. *1 Priory Lodge, 93 Brown Street, Salisbury SP1 2BX* T: (01722) 328007 E: payjohns70@hotmail.com

JOHNS, Thomas Morton. b 43. Oak Hill Th Coll 67. **d** 70 **p** 71. C N Meols *Liv* 70-73; C Farnborough *Guildf* 73-76; P-in-c Badshot Lea CD 76-83; Dep Chapl HM Pris Man 83; Chapl HM Youth Cust Cen Wellingborough 83-88; Chapl HM YOI Swinfen Hall 88-90; Chapl Tr Officer 88-95; Chapl HM Pris Service Coll 90-95; Asst Chapl Gen of Pris (HQ) 95-01; Acting Chapl Gen 00-01; P-in-c Colbury *Win* 02-08; Chapl Hants Constabulary 02-08; rtd 08; PtO *Portsm* from 02. *18 Southbrook Mews, Bishops Waltham, Southampton SO32 1RZ* T: (01489) 891585 M: 07988-314928 E: tomjohns585@btinternet.com

JOHNSEN, Edward Andrew. b 67. Birm Univ BTheol 89. Qu Coll Birm 95. **d** 97 **p** 98. C Birm St Luke 97-01; C Handsworth St Mary 01-04; PtO 05-06; TV Eden, Gelt and Irthing *Carl* from 06. *The Vicarage, Hayton, Brampton CA8 9HR* T: (01228) 670248 E: mail@johnsen3671.fsworld.co.uk

JOHNSON, Amanda Saffery. b 58. K Alfred's Coll Win BEd 83. Wycliffe Hall Ox. **d** 97 **p** 98. C Oxhey All SS w All SS 97-00; C Bricket Wood 00-02; Teacher Bp Wand Sch Sunbury-on-Thames 02-04; C Dorking St Paul *Guildf* 05-09; C Bisley and W End 09-10; V Addiscombe St Mary Magd w St Martin *S'wark* from 10. *The Vicarage, 15 Canning Road, Addiscombe CR0 6QD* T: (020) 8654 3459 *or* 8656 3457 M: 07905-893394 E: amanda@hut.co.uk

JOHNSON, Dom Andrew. b 59. **d** 08 **p** 09. OSB from 85; PtO *Win* from 09. *Abbey of Our Lady and St John, Abbey Road, Beech, Alton GU34 4AP* T: (01420) 562145 F: 561691 E: altonabbey@supanet.com

JOHNSON, Andrew Paul. b 69. **d** 14 **p** 15. C W Ealing St Jo w St Jas *Lon* from 14. *127 Coldershaw Road, London W13 9DU* M: 07958-604708 E: revandyjohnson@me.com

JOHNSON, Andrew Paul. b 56. W Surrey Coll of Art & Design BA 79 Kent Coll for Careers CertEd 82 TCD BTh 96. CITC 93. **d** 96 **p** 97. C Penarth w Lavernock *Llan* 96-99; R Walton W w Talbenny and Haroldston W *St D* 99-15; P-in-c Dale and St Brides w Marloes and Hasguard w St Ishmael's from 15. *The Vicarage, Castle Way, Dale, Haverfordwest SA62 3RN* T: (01646) 636966 E: frandrewj@btinternet.com

JOHNSON, Andrew Peter. b 67. Westf Coll Lon BA 89 St Jo Coll Nottm MA 98 LTh 99. Aston Tr Scheme 94. **d** 99 **p** 00. C Hitchin *St Alb* 99-03; V Batley All SS and Purlwell *Wakef* 03-13; R Barton-le-Cley w Higham Gobion and Hexton *St Alb* from 13. *The Rectory, 2 Manor Farm Close, Barton-le-Clay, Bedford MK45 4TB* T: (01582) 881873 E: johnsons@care4free.net

JOHNSON, Andrew Peter. **d** 12. NSM Ex Cathl from 12. *Elm Brook House, 348 Topsham Road, Exeter EX2 6HF* T: (01392) 271059 E: andrewjohnson1@btinternet.com

JOHNSON, Mrs Angela Carolyn Louise. b 52. RGN 76. STETS 00. **d** 03 **p** 04. NSM Catherington and Clanfield *Portsm* 03-07; NSM Denmead from 07. *90 Downhouse Road, Waterlooville PO8 0TY* T: (023) 9264 4595 E: angela.johnson52@ntlworld.com

JOHNSON, Anthony. *See* JOHNSON, Edward Anthony

JOHNSON, Anthony Peter. b 45. K Coll Lon BD 76 AKC 76 MTh 79. Wells Th Coll 67. **d** 70 **p** 71. C Goldington *St Alb* 70-73; C Hainault *Chelmsf* 73-76; TV Loughton St Mary 76-81; V Scunthorpe All SS *Linc* 81-85; V Alkborough 85-87; Chapl Man Univ and TV Man Whitworth 87-96; P-in-c Chorlton-cum-Hardy St Werburgh 96-00; R 00-05; P-in-c Yardley St Cypr Hay Mill *Birm* 05-08; V 08-10; rtd 10; PtO *Birm* from 10. *St Barnabas' Vicarage, 51 Over Green Drive, Kingshurst, Birmingham B37 6EY* T: 0121-770 3972 E: ajohnson940@btinternet.com

JOHNSON, Anthony Warrington. b 40. Goldsmiths' Coll Lon CertEd 60. St Jo Coll Nottm 86. **d** 88 **p** 89. C Lutterworth w Cotesbach *Leic* 88-92; V Countesthorpe w Foston 92-06; P-in-c Arnesby w Shearsby and Bruntingthorpe 94-01; rtd 06; Hon C Lutterworth w Cotesbach and Bitteswell *Leic* 06-09; PtO from 13. *9 Forest Road, Loughborough LE11 3NW* T: (01509) 210942

JOHNSON, Miss Barbara. b 45. St Jo Coll Nottm 04. **d** 07 **p** 08. NSM Royston *St Alb* 07-08; NSM Goldington 08-10; Chapl Beds and Luton Fire and Rescue Service from 07; PtO *Ely* from 10; Ox from 11. *4 Hicks Lane, Girton, Cambridge CB3 0JS* T: (01223) 276282   M: 07768-560646 E: barbara.johnson@bedsfire.com

JOHNSON, Barry Charles Richard. b 48. EAMTC 96. **d** 99 **p** 00. C Gt Burstead *Chelmsf* 99-02; C Bowers Gifford w N Benfleet 02-04; P-in-c Woodham Mortimer w Hazeleigh 04-06; R Vange 06-10; P-in-c Bowers Gifford w N Benfleet 07-10; V Folkestone St Mary, St Eanswythe and St Sav *Cant* 10-12; rtd 12; P-in-c Gt Parndon *Chelmsf* 13-14; V Staple Tye 14-15; P-in-c Mayland from 15; C Althorne and Latchingdon w N Fambridge from 15. *The Vicarage, 31 Imperial Avenue, Mayland, Chelmsford CM3 6AH* T: (01621) 742352 E: revbj@btinternet.com

JOHNSON, Beverley Charles. b 35. Bp Gray Coll Cape Town 59. **d** 61 **p** 62. C Woodstock St Mary S Africa 61-64; C Clanwilliam St Jo 64-65; C Plumstead St Mark 65-67; C Southsea St Pet *Portsm* 68-69; C Southwick St Cuth CD *Dur* 70-71; P-in-c Waterhouses 71-80; R Burnmoor 80-85; V Brandon 85-89; Australia 89-91; Asst P Sea Point St Jas S Africa 91-01; rtd 01. *43 Oxford Street, Goodwood, 7460 South Africa* T/F: (0027) (21) 592 1180   M: 82-202 5260

JOHNSON, Mrs Brenda Margaret. b 47. TISEC 93. **d** 00. NSM Edin St Salvador 00-03; NSM Wester Hailes St Luke 00-03; NSM Edin Gd Shep from 03. *58 Ratho Park Road, Ratho, Newbridge EH28 8PQ* T: 0131-333 1742   M: 07713-154744 E: brenmj@btinternet.com

JOHNSON, Brian. b 42. S'wark Ord Course 84. **d** 87 **p** 88. NSM Dulwich St Barn *S'wark* 87-92; NSM Herne Hill 92-94; PtO 94-96; Chapl HM Pris Man 96-01; P-in-c Rotterdam *Eur* 01-02; Operations Manager ICS 03; PtO *Cov* 03; *Ches* from 04; Man from 11. *11A Lynton Park Road, Cheadle Hulme, Cheadle SK8 6JA* T: 0161-485 3787   E: revbfg@talktalk.net

JOHNSON, Christopher Dudley. b 26. Worc Coll Ox BA 44 MA 51. Cuddesdon Coll 53. **d** 56 **p** 57. C Basingstoke *Win* 56-61; V Bethnal Green St Barn *Lon* 61-67; V Eton w Eton Wick and Boveney *Ox* 67-88; rtd 91; PtO *Sarum* from 96. *Lavinces Cottage, Netherbury, Bridport DT6 5LL*

JOHNSON, Christopher Frederick. b 43. MRICS 67. Ripon Hall Ox 71. **d** 74 **p** 75. C Chatham St Steph *Roch* 74-78; V Slade Green 78-85; V Wilmington 85-95; R Chevening 95-09; rtd 09; PtO *Roch* from 09. *7 Kennedy Gardens, Sevenoaks TN13 3UG* T: (01732) 456626   E: c.f.johnson@waitrose.com

JOHNSON, Christopher James. b 88. Cant Ch Ch Univ BA 11. Ripon Coll Cuddesdon MTh 13. **d** 13 **p** 14. C Weobley w Sarnesfield and Norton Canon *Heref* from 13. *St Mary's House, Staunton-on-Wye, Hereford HR4 7LT* T: (01981) 500280 M: 07969-432481   E: christopher.johnson121@gmail.com

JOHNSON, Christopher Neil. b 87. St Benet's Hall Ox BA 10 MA 14. St Steph Ho Ox MSt 10 MLitt 14. **d** 13 **p** 14. C Pickering w Lockton and Levisham *York* from 13. *Savanna, Whitby Road, Pickering YO18 7HD* T: (01751) 269061 E: fr.christopher.johnson@gmail.com

JOHNSON, Christopher Paul. b 47. Leeds Univ MA 01. St Jo Coll Nottm BTh 74. **d** 74 **p** 75. C Normanton *Wakef* 74-78; P-in-c Dewsbury St Mark 78-82; V Harden and Wilsden *Bradf* 82-88; P-in-c Holbeck *Ripon* 88-94; V 94-97; Asst Chapl Leeds Teaching Hosps NHS Trust 97-00; Chapl Bradf Hosps NHS Trust 00-13; rtd 13; PtO *Leeds* from 13. *The Old School House, 20 Street Lane, Gildersome, Morley, Leeds LS27 7HT* T: 0113-252 9313   E: christopherjohnson1947@live.co.uk

JOHNSON, Christopher Robert. b 43. Lon Coll of Div 66. **d** 70 **p** 71. C Everton St Geo *Liv* 70-71; C Childwall All SS 71-75; TV Gateacre 75-76; TV Bushbury *Lich* 76-87; R Burslem 87-10; rtd 10; PtO *Lich* from 11. *102 Chell Green Avenue, Stoke-on-Trent ST6 7LA* T: (01782) 850169 E: rob.johnson60@talk21.com

JOHNSON, Claire Elisabeth. *See* PARR, Claire Elisabeth

JOHNSON, Canon Colin Gawman. b 32. Leeds Univ BA 59. Coll of Resurr Mirfield 59. **d** 61 **p** 62. C Barrow St Matt *Carl* 61-67; V 90-96; V Addingham 67-71; V Carl H Trin 71-80; V Wigton 80-90; Hon Can Carl Cathl 85-96; rtd 96; PtO *Carl* from 97. *Hemp Garth, Ireby, Wigton CA7 1EA* T: (016973) 71578

JOHNSON, Colin Leslie. b 41. Trin Coll Cam MA 65. Cheshunt Coll Cam 62. **d** 93 **p** 94. Publications Dir Chr Educn Movement from 89; NSM Brailsford w Shirley and Osmaston

w Edlaston *Derby* 93-04; PtO from 04. *33 The Plain, Brailsford, Ashbourne DE6 3BZ* T: (01335) 360591 E: cj@acjohnson.plus.com

JOHNSON, Colin Stewart. b 46. SEITE 99. **d** 02 **p** 03. NSM Borden *Cant* 02-05; C Charlton-in-Dover 05-06; P-in-c 06-13; rtd 13; PtO *Cant* from 14. *423 Minster Road, Minster on Sea, Sheerness ME12 3NS* T: (01795) 857175   M: 07740-775277 E: frcj@dsl.pipex.com

JOHNSON, Cyril Francis. b 22. St Cath Coll Cam BA 49 MA 54. Ely Th Coll 50. **d** 52 **p** 53. C Twickenham All Hallows *Lon* 52-56; C Kingsthorpe *Pet* 56-61; R Harpole 61-87; rtd 87; PtO *Chich* from 01. *16 Blake's Way, Eastbourne BN23 6EW* T: (01323) 723491

JOHNSON, David. b 68. Cranmer Hall Dur 13. **d** 15. C Monk Fryston and S Milford *York* from 15. *32 Sand Lane, South Milford, Leeds LS25 5AU* T: (01977) 689334   M: 07515-288105 E: davidjohnsonihs@gmail.com

JOHNSON, David. *See* JOHNSON, John David

JOHNSON, David Alan. b 43. Lon Univ BSc 63 PhD 67. Trin Coll Bris 78. **d** 80 **p** 81. C Watford *St Alb* 80-85; V Idle *Bradf* 85-08; P-in-c Greengates 08; rtd 08; PtO *Dur* from 09. *15 Blackburn Close, Bearpark, Durham DH7 7TQ* T: 0191-373 7953 E: david@fss.me.uk

JOHNSON, David Bryan Alfred. b 36. Kelham Th Coll 56. **d** 61 **p** 62. C Streatham St Paul *S'wark* 61-63; Malaysia 63-71; V Worc St Mich 71-74; Warden Lee Abbey Internat Students' Club Kensington 74-77; V Plumstead St Mark and St Marg *S'wark* 77-86; Chapl W Park Hosp Epsom 86-96; Chapl Laslett's *Worc* 96-01; rtd 96. *3 St Birinus Cottages, Wessex Way, Bicester OX26 6DX* T: (01869) 320839

JOHNSON, David Francis. b 32. Univ Coll Ox BA 55 MA 59. Westcott Ho Cam 55. **d** 57 **p** 58. C Earlsdon *Cov* 57-59; C Willenhall 59-61; C Attenborough w Bramcote *S'well* 61-62; V Ravenstone w Weston Underwood *Ox* 62-66; V Crewe Ch Ch *Ches* 66-70; P-in-c Crewe St Pet 67-70; V Thornton w Allerthorpe *York* 70-79; V N Hull St Mich 79-81; V Leyburn w Bellerby *Ripon* 81-88; V Coxwold and Husthwaite *York* 88-97; rtd 97; PtO *York* 98-03; *Heref* 05-13. *Fleur de Lys, Coleford Road, Tutshill, Chepstow NP16 7BU* T: (01291) 621636

JOHNSON, David John. b 49. Lanc Univ BA 72. Linc Th Coll 78. **d** 81 **p** 82. C Stockport St Thos *Ches* 81-84; OGS from 83; C Stockton Heath *Ches* 84-88; V Tranmere St Paul w St Luke 88-99; P-in-c Antrobus 99-02; P-in-c Aston by Sutton 99-02; P-in-c Lt Leigh and Lower Whitley 99-02; V Antrobus, Aston by Sutton, Lt Leigh etc 02-07; C Coppenhall 07-10; rtd 11; PtO *Ches* from 11. *14 Manor Way, Crewe CW2 6JX* T: (01270) 250256

JOHNSON, David Richard. b 67. Birm Univ BSc 88. Ripon Coll Cuddesdon BA 92 MA 97. **d** 94 **p** 95. C Horfield H Trin *Bris* 94-97; V Two Mile Hill St Mich 97-01; Asst Chapl Haileybury Coll 01-02; Chapl Dauntsey's Sch Devizes from 02. *Dauntseys School, High Street, West Lavington, Devizes SN10 4HE* T: (01380) 814500   E: chaplain@dauntseys.org

JOHNSON, David William. b 53. Selw Coll Cam BA 76. Ripon Coll Cuddesdon 76. **d** 78 **p** 79. C Fulham St Etheldreda w St Clem *Lon* 78-82; Communications Sec Gen Syn Bd for Miss and Unity 82-87; PV Westmr Abbey 85-87; R Gilmorton w Peatling Parva and Kimcote etc *Leic* 87-91; R Cogenhoe *Pet* 91-95; R Whiston 93-95; rtd 95; PtO *Ox* from 00. *Seaview Cottage, 115 Hurst Street, Oxford OX4 1HE* T: (01865) 793393

JOHNSON, David William. b 40. Oak Hill Th Coll BD 64. **d** 65 **p** 66. C Tunbridge Wells St Jas *Roch* 65-68; C Kirby Muxloe *Leic* 68-72; V Burton Joyce w Bulcote *S'well* 72-83; V Mitford and Chapl Northgate Mental Handicap Unit Morpeth 83-87; Asst Chapl R Victoria Infirmary Newc 87-89; Chapl R Shrewsbury Hosps NHS Trust 89-04; rtd 04. *42 Hartlands, Bedlington NE22 6JG* T: (01670) 828693

JOHNSON, Preb Derek John. b 36. St Aid Birkenhead 65. **d** 68 **p** 69. C Eccleshall *Lich* 68-73; C Stafford St Mary 73-74; C Stafford St Mary and St Chad 74-75; Chapl New Cross Hosp Wolv 75-96; Preb Lich Cathl 83-96; rtd 96; PtO *St E* from 96. *6 St Paul's Close, Aldeburgh IP15 5BQ* T: (01728) 452474

JOHNSON, Canon Diana Margaret. b 46. MCSP 68 SRP 68. Cranmer Hall Dur 92. **d** 94 **p** 95. C Birtley *Dur* 94-99; TV Gateshead 99-06; AD 03-06; P-in-c Belmont 06-07; V Belmont and Pittington 07-12; Hon Can Dur Cathl 06-12; rtd 12; PtO *Dur* from 12. *3 Avenue Street, High Shincliffe, Durham DH1 2PT* E: dmjohnson462@btinternet.com

JOHNSON (née DEER), Mrs Diane Antonia. b 45. SEITE 97. **d** 00 **p** 01. C Hackington *Cant* 00-04; P-in-c Pitsea w Nevendon *Chelmsf* 04-06; R 06-09; RD Basildon 07-09; P-in-c Eastry and Northbourne w Tilmanstone etc *Cant* 09-10; AD Sandwich 09-10; rtd 10; PtO *Cant* 11-12. *The Vicarage, 31 Imperial Avenue, Mayland, Chelmsford CM3 6AH* M: 07957-758721   T: (01621) 742352 E: revdiane@btinternet.com

JOHNSON, Mrs Diane Pearl. b 47. Leeds Univ BA 68 Cam Univ PGCE 69. EAMTC 95. **d** 98 **p** 99. NSM Gt Bowden w Welham, Glooston and Cranoe *Leic* 98-01; C Evington and Leic St Phil 01-04; P-in-c 04-07; rtd 07; PtO *Pet* from 10. *16 Oaklands Park, Market Harborough LE16 8EU* T: (01858) 434118 E: gandi2007@btinternet.com

JOHNSON, Mrs Dorothy. Leic Univ BSc 89 Ox Univ MTh 95 RGN FRSH 91. Qu Coll Birm 77. **dss** 80 **d** 87 **p** 94. Coventry Caludon *Cov* 80-81; Wolston and Church Lawford 81-86; NSM Stoneleigh w Ashow 87-08; Bp's Asst Officer for Soc Resp 87-96; PtO from 11. *119 Hillside Drive, Christchurch BH23 2SZ* M: 07975-893114 E: e.djohnson@btinternet.com

JOHNSON, Douglas Leonard. b 45. St Paul's Coll Chelt CertEd 67 Lon Bible Coll MA 95 Roehampton Univ PhD 13. Tyndale Hall Bris 70. **d** 73 **p** 74. C New Malden and Coombe *S'wark* 73-76; P-in-c Upper Tulse Hill St Matthias 76-82; CPAS Staff 82-88; Lect and Tutor CA Coll 88-91; Dir Crossways Chr Educn Trust 92-08; Hon V Wimbledon Em Ridgway Prop Chpl *S'wark* 91-94; Lect Cornhill Tr Course 94-06; Crosslinks Kenya 08-10; rtd 11; PtO *B & W* from 12. *The Stables, Mudford, Yeovil BA21 5TD* T: (01935) 432304 E: douglasjohnson@btinternet.com

JOHNSON, Edward Anthony (Tony). b 32. Univ of Wales (Swansea) BSc 54. St Steph Ho Ox 79. **d** 81 **p** 82. C Wolvercote w Summertown *Ox* 81-84; P-in-c Ramsden 84-87; P-in-c Finstock and Fawler 84-87; P-in-c Wilcote 84-87; V Ramsden, Finstock and Fawler, Leafield etc 87-92; rtd 92; Hon C Kennington *Ox* 92-98; PtO from 98. *15 Cranbrook Drive, Kennington, Oxford OX1 5RR* T: (01865) 739751

JOHNSON, Mrs Elizabeth Jane. b 47. St Hilda's Coll Ox MA 69. Wycliffe Hall Ox 84. **dss** 86 **d** 87 **p** 94. NSM Ox St Aldate w St Matt 86-91; NSM Marston 91-94; NSM Ox St Clem 94-95; NSM Islip w Charlton on Otmoor, Oddington, Noke etc 95-99; OLM Officer (Dorchester) 99-00; Asst Chapl Oxon Mental Healthcare NHS Trust 00-04; NSM Bladon w Woodstock Ox 99-04; NSM Shill Valley and Broadshire 04-09 and 11-14; PtO 09-11 and from 14. *11 Oakey Close, Alvescot, Bampton OX18 2PX* T: (01993) 846169 E: liz.johnson@talktalk.net

JOHNSON, Emma Louise. See COLEY, Emma Louise

JOHNSON, Emma Louise. See PARKER, Emma Louise

JOHNSON, Eric. b 38. Nottm Univ BSc 60 Man Univ CertEd 65 Open Univ BA 92 SS Paul & Mary Coll Cheltenham MA 94 Birm Univ BA 06. Qu Coll Birm 74. **d** 77 **p** 78. Sen Lect Cov Tech Coll 66-91; NSM Earlsdon *Cov* 77-81; NSM Wolston and Church Lawford 81-86; NSM Stoneleigh w Ashow and Baginton 90-98; FE Liaison Officer *B & W, Bris* and *Glouc* 91-93; Dioc Dir of Educn *Worc* 93-98; rtd 98; PtO *Cov* from 11. *119 Hillside Drive, Christchurch BH23 2SZ* M: 07773-748967 E: e.djohnson@btinternet.com

JOHNSON, Frances Josephine. b 53. Leeds Univ CertEd 74 Open Univ BA 90. NOC 02. **d** 05 **p** 06. C Hall Green St Pet *Birm* 05-08; V Kingshurst from 08. *St Barnabas' Vicarage, 51 Overgreen Drive, Birmingham B37 6EY* T: 0121-770 3972 E: j.johnson2@tiscali.co.uk

JOHNSON, Geoffrey Stuart. b 39. ALCD 65 Wolv Poly DipEd Sussex Univ DPhil 01. **d** 65 **p** 66. C Worksop St Jo *S'well* 65-68; Taiwan 68-71; C St Andr Cathl Singapore 71-76; Aber Univ Ab 76-78; PtO *Heref* 78-82; P-in-c Hoarwithy, Sellack and Hentland 82-84; Chapl Horton Hosp Epsom 84-90; Distr Chapl Brighton HA 90-94; Managing Chapl Brighton Healthcare NHS Trust 94-99; Managing Chapl S Downs Health NHS Trust 94-99; rtd 99; Chapl S Downs Health NHS Trust 00-06; Chapl Sussex Partnership NHS Foundn Trust from 06; PtO *Chich* from 01. *5 Garden Mews, 15 Beachy Head Road, Eastbourne BN20 7QP* T: (01323) 644083

JOHNSON, Gillian Margaret. b 55. Bretton Hall Coll CertEd 76 Coll of Ripon & York St Jo MA 03. NOC 00. **d** 03 **p** 04. C Thornhill and Whitley Lower *Wakef* 03-07; V Horbury Bridge 07-10; Curriculum Development Officer Dioc Bd Educn *Leeds* from 10. *5 Wood Mount, Overton, Wakefield WF4 4SB* T: (01924) 262181 M: 07966-783644 E: gilljohnson99@hotmail.com

JOHNSON, Helen Louise. b 74. **d** 13 **p** 14. C Bedminster *Bris* from 13; C Whitchurch 13-15; C Whitchurch St Aug from 15. *78 Leighton Road, Southville, Bristol BS3 1NU*

JOHNSON, Canon Hilary Ann. b 51. RGN 72 RHV 74. S'wark Ord Course 82. **dss** 85 **d** 87 **p** 94. Hon Par Dn Salfords *S'wark* 85-90; Chapl St Geo Hosp Lon 90-94; Chapl St Geo Healthcare NHS Trust Lon 94-15; NSM Wimbledon *S'wark* 95-10; Bp's Adv for Healthcare Chapl 11-15; Hon Can S'wark Cathl 07-15; r-d 15. *203 Moor Lane, Chessington KT9 2AB* T: (020) 8397 0952 M: 07764-221116 E: hilary1j@gmail.com

JOHNSON, Ian Leslie. b 44. Wells Th Coll 68. **d** 71 **p** 72. C Benhilton *S'wark* 71-73; C Weymouth H Trin *Sarum* 73-76; R Pewsey 76-81; R Maiden Newton and Valleys 81-83; Youth Officer (Sherborne Area) 81-83; Dioc Youth Officer *Sarum* 83-88; TR Langley and Parkfield *Man* 88-95; P-in-c Haughton St Anne 95-99; Dioc Adv on Evang 95-99; TR Southampton (City Cen) *Win* 99-08; rtd 08. *Farthing Cottage, 71 St Andrew Street, Tiverton EX16 6PL* T: (01884) 251974

JOHNSON, Ian Leslie. b 51. Bede Coll Dur TCert 73. Wycliffe Hall Ox 91. **d** 93 **p** 94. C Evington *Leic* 93-96; Sub Chapl HM Pris Gartree 96-97; C Foxton w Gumley and Laughton and Lubenham *Leic* 96-97; C Foxton w Gumley and Laughton 97-00; P-in-c 00-12; Sub Chapl HM Pris Gartree 97-12; Co-ord Chapl from 12. *HM Prison Gartree, Gallows Field Road, Market Harborough LE16 7RP* T: (01858) 426600 E: ijoh270951@aol.com

JOHNSON (née SILINS), Ms Jacqueline. b 62. Coll of Ripon & York St Jo BA 85. Ripon Coll Cuddesdon 01. **d** 03 **p** 04. C Torpoint *Truro* 03-08; P-in-c Harworth *S'well* 08-12; Dioc Min Development Adv from 12. *27 Sunnyside, Worksop S81 7LN* M: 07827-291724 T: (01636) 817208 E: jackie.johnson@southwell.anglican.org or jackie@benedict.f9.co.uk

✠**JOHNSON, The Rt Revd James Nathaniel.** b 32. Wells Th Coll 63. **d** 64 **p** 65 **c** 85. C Lawrence Weston *Bris* 64-66; P-in-c St Paul's Cathl St Helena 66-69; V 69-71; Hon Can from 75; Area Sec USPG Ex and Truro 72-74; R Combe Martin *Ex* 74-80; V Thorpe Bay *Chelmsf* 80-85; Bp St Helena 85-91; R Byfield w Boddington and Aston le Walls *Pet* 91-92; Asst Bp Pet 91-92; V Hockley *Chelmsf* 92-97; Asst Bp Chelmsf 92-97; Can Chelmsf Cathl 94-97; rtd 97; Hon Asst Bp Chelmsf 97-04; PtO *Eur* 98; Hon Asst Bp Ox from 04; PtO *Cov* from 05. *St Helena, 28 Molyneux Drive, Bodicote, Banbury OX15 4AP* T: (01295) 255357 E: bpjnj@talktalk.net

JOHNSON, Canon John Anthony. b 18. Selw Coll Cam BA 48 MA 53 St Jo Coll Dur. **d** 51 **p** 52. C Battersea St Mary *S'wark* 51-54; C Merton St Mary 54-56; V Balderton *S'well* 56-60; V Mansfield Woodhouse 60-70; V Beeston 70-85; RD 81-85; Hon Can S'well Minster 82-85; rtd 86; PtO *Blackb* 90-02. *Driftwood, Ireleth Road, Askam-in-Furness LA16 7JD* T: (01229) 462291

JOHNSON, John David. b 38. Claremont Sch of Th 65 St Deiniol's Hawarden 71. **d** 71 **p** 72. C Heref St Martin 71-73; P-in-c Ewyas Harold w Dulas 73-79; P-in-c Kilpeck 73-79; P-in-c St Devereux w Wormbridge 73-79; P-in-c Kenderchurch 73-79; P-in-c Bacton 78-79; TR Ewyas Harold w Dulas, Kenderchurch etc 79-81; R Kentchurch w Llangua, Rowlestone, Llancillo etc 79-81; Chapl Napsbury Hosp St Alb 81-96; Chapl Horizon NHS Trust Herts 96-00; Chapl Barnet Healthcare NHS Trust 96-00; Chapl Barnet and Chase Farm Hosps NHS Trust 00-05; Chapl Herts Partnerships NHS Trust 02-03; rtd 03. *10 Highcroft Road, Sharpthorne, East Grinstead RH19 4NX* T: (01342) 810314

JOHNSON, Josephine. See JOHNSON, Frances Josephine

JOHNSON, Mrs Julie Margaret. b 47. **d** 98 **p** 99. OLM Welton and Dunholme w Scothern *Linc* 98-07; NSM Edgeley and Cheadle Heath *Ches* from 07. *10 Delaford Close, Stockport SK3 8XA* T: 0161-456 6463 E: johnson-julie2@sky.com

JOHNSON, Kathryn Ann. **d** 03 **p** 04. C Wrexham *St As* 03-04; C Prestatyn 04-11; V Abergele and St George from 11. *The Vicarage, 28 Lon Dirion, Abergele LL22 8PX* T: (01745) 822493 M: 07801-541380 E: pastorkate@btinternet.com

JOHNSON, Keith Henry. b 64. Keele Univ BA 91 Leeds Univ BA 97 MA 09 CQSW 91. Coll of Resurr Mirfield 95. **d** 97 **p** 98. C W Bromwich St Fran *Lich* 97-00; P-in-c Willenhall St Giles 00-05; V 05-06; PtO *Lon* 06-08; *Lich* 07-08; *Sheff* 08; P-in-c Handsworth 08-10; R from 10. *St Mary's Rectory, Handsworth Road, Handsworth, Sheffield S13 9BZ* T: 0114-269 3983 E: keithhjohnson@hotmail.com

JOHNSON, Keith Martyn. b 68. St Jo Coll Nottm 04. **d** 06 **p** 07. C Ipsley *Worc* 06-10; V Chatham St Paul w All SS *Roch* from 10. *The Vicarage, 2A Waghorn Street, Chatham ME4 5LT* M: 07772-642393 E: keiththevicar@gmail.com

JOHNSON, The Very Revd Keith Winton Thomas William. b 37. K Coll Lon BD 63 Open Univ MA 06 AKC 63. **d** 64 **p** 65. C Dartford H Trin *Roch* 64-69; Chapl Kuwait 69-73; V Erith St Jo *Roch* 73-80; V Bexley St Jo 80-91; V Royston *St Alb* 91-94; R Sandon, Wallington and Rushden w Clothall 94-97; Dean St Chris Cathl Bahrain 97-02; rtd 02; Hon C Balsham, Weston Colville, W Wickham etc *Ely* 04-10; RD Linton 07-09; PtO from 10. *17 The Rookery, Balsham, Cambridge CB21 4EU* T: (01223) 890835 E: jkeith1412@gmail.com

JOHNSON, Kenneth William George. b 53. Hull Univ BA 76 PGCE 77. EMMTC 92. **d** 95 **p** 96. NSM Ilkeston H Trin *Derby* 95-99; NSM Sandiacre from 99; Chapl Bluecoat Sch Nottm 02-11. *18 Park Avenue, Awsworth, Nottingham NG16 2RA* T: 0115-930 7830 E: kwjohnson@ntlworld.com

JOHNSON, Miss Lesley Denise. b 47. WMMTC 95. **d** 98 **p** 99. NSM Stockingford *Cov* 98-01; TV Cov E 01-10; rtd 10; PtO *Cov* from 12. *212 Sedgemoor Road, Coventry CV3 4DZ* T: (024) 7630 1241

JOHNSON, Malcolm Arthur. b 36. Univ Coll Dur BA 60 MA 64 Lon Metrop Univ Hon MA 02 Lambeth MA 06 K Coll Lon PhD 10 FSA 04. Cuddesdon Coll 60. **d** 62 **p** 63. C Portsea N End St Mark *Portsm* 62-67; Chapl Qu Mary Coll *Lon* 67-74; V St Botolph Aldgate w H Trin Minories 74-92; P-in-c St Ethelburga Bishopsgate 85-89; AD The City 85-90; Master R Foundn of St Kath in Ratcliffe 93-97; Bp's Adv for Past Care and Counselling *Lon* 97-01; rtd 02; PtO *Lon* from 07; *Guildf* from 09. *1 Foxgrove Drive, Woking GU21 4DZ* T: (01483) 720684 E: malcolm.johnson4@btinternet.com

JOHNSON, Canon Malcolm Stuart. b 35. AKC 60. **d** 61 **p** 62. C Catford St Laur *S'wark* 61-64; Hon C Hatcham St Cath 66-76; P-in-c Kingstanding St Luke *Birm* 76-77; V 77-82; P-in-c Peckham St Jo w St Andr *S'wark* 82-92; V 92-03; Hon Can Sabongidda-Ora from 98; rtd 04. *34 Sheppard's College, London Road, Bromley BR1 1PF* T: (020) 8466 5276

JOHNSON, Canon Margaret Anne Hope. b 52. Fitzw Coll Cam BA 95. Ridley Hall Cam 93. **d** 95 **p** 96. C Northampton Em *Pet* 95-97; P-in-c 97-98; TR from 98; Adv in Women's Min 03-06; Can Pet Cathl from 04. *13 Booth Lane North, Northampton NN3 6JE* T: (01604) 648974 *or* 402150 E: revmahj@gmail.com

JOHNSON, Margaret Joan (Meg). b 41. S'wark Ord Course 92. **d** 95 **p** 96. NSM Sanderstead St Mary *S'wark* 95-04; PtO from 13. *Rose Cottage, 89 Durrington Lane, Worthing BN13 2TQ* E: megjohnson@uwclub.net

JOHNSON, Mark. b 62. Leic Poly BSc 84 Loughb Univ PhD 88. Ripon Coll Cuddesdon 88. **d** 94 **p** 95. C Bishop's Cleeve *Glouc* 94-98; TV Heref S Wye 98-09; R Wormelow Hundred from 09; RD Ross and Archenfield from 13. *Becket House, Much Birch, Hereford HR2 8HT* T: (01981) 540390

JOHNSON, Michael. b 42. Birm Univ BSc 63. S'wark Ord Course 68. **d** 71 **p** 72. C Kidbrooke St Jas *S'wark* 71-74; NSM Eynsford w Farningham and Lullingstone *Roch* 74-89; NSM Selling w Throwley, Sheldwich w Badlesmere etc *Cant* 89-12; rtd 12; PtO *Cant* from 12. *1 Halke Cottages, North Street, Sheldwich, Faversham ME13 0LR* T: (01795) 536583 M: 07860-635728 E: onehalke@aol.com

JOHNSON, Canon Michael Anthony. b 51. Ex Univ BA 76. Ripon Coll Cuddesdon 76 Ch Div Sch of the Pacific (USA) 77. **d** 78 **p** 79. C Primrose Hill St Mary w Avenue Road St Paul *Lon* 78-81; C Hampstead St Jo 81-85; TV Mortlake w E Sheen *S'wark* 85-93; V Wroughton *Bris* from 93; RD 97-99; AD Swindon 99-06; Hon Can Bris Cathl from 99. *The Vicarage, Church Hill, Wroughton, Swindon SN4 9JS* T: (01793) 812301 F: 814582 E: canonmike@hotmail.com

JOHNSON, Michael Colin. b 37. S'wark Ord Course 77. **d** 80 **p** 81. NSM New Eltham All SS *S'wark* 80-84; NSM Woldingham 84-98; rtd 98; PtO *Chich* 99-07. *The College of St Barnabas, Blackberry Lane, Lingfield RH7 6NJ* T: (01342) 872832 E: tandem@collegeofstbarnabas.com

JOHNSON, Michael Douglas. b 64. St Jo Coll Nottm 11. **d** 13 **p** 14. C Woodthorpe *S'well* from 13. *12 Arno Vale Road, Woodthorpe, Nottingham NG5 4JJ* T: 0115-920 4885 E: michael.johnsons@hotmail.com

JOHNSON, Michael Gordon. b 45. Kelham Th Coll 64. **d** 68 **p** 69. C Holbrooks *Cov* 68-72; C Cannock *Lich* 72-75; V Coseley Ch Ch 75-79; P-in-c Sneyd 79-82; R Longton 82-88; Chapl Pilgrim Hosp Boston 88-96; TV Jarrow *Dur* 96-98; Chapl Monkton and Primrose Hill Hosp 96-98; R Burghwallis and Campsall *Sheff* 98-10; rtd 10; PtO *Sheff* from 10. *8 Harmby Close, Skellow, Doncaster DN6 8PA* T: (01302) 330700

JOHNSON, Michael Robert. b 68. Aston Business Sch BSc 90. Ridley Hall Cam 94. **d** 97 **p** 98. C E Greenwich *S'wark* 97-00; C Perry Hill St Geo 00-03; Chapl W Lon YMCA 03-05; C Wokingham All SS *Ox* from 05; Pioneer Min Sonning Deanery from 11. *38 Carey Road, Wokingham RG40 2NP* T: 0118-979 0098 E: michael@allsaintswokingham.org.uk

JOHNSON, Mrs Nancy May. b 46. TCert 67 Sheff Poly MA 86. NOC 00. **d** 02 **p** 03. NSM Sheff Cathl 02-04; Asst Chapl Sheff Teaching Hosps NHS Foundn Trust 04-10; rtd 10; PtO *Sheff* from 10. *121 Rustlings Road, Sheffield S11 7AB* T: 0114-266 6456 E: nancyjohnson@hotmail.co.uk

JOHNSON, Canon Nigel Victor. b 48. ARCM 68 LTCL 75 Cam Univ DipEd 69. Linc Th Coll 80. **d** 82 **p** 83. C Lindley *Wakef* 82-85; P-in-c Upperthong 85-87; PtO *Derby* 88-89; NSM Calow and Sutton cum Duckmanton 89-90; R 90-00; RD Bolsover and Staveley 98-00; V Newbold w Dunston 00-15; RD Chesterfield 02-11; Hon Can Derby Cathl 05-15; rtd 15. *Yew Tree Cottage, Wheatley Road, Two Dales, Matlock DE4 2FF* E: nvjohnson@tiscali.co.uk

JOHNSON, Paul James. b 56. Teesside Coll of Educn BEd 80 Dur Sch of Educn MA 95. NEOC 06. **d** 09 **p** 10. NSM Whorlton w Carlton and Faceby *York* 09-12; Chapl Ian Ramsey Sch Stockton from 12; NSM Norton St Mary *Dur* from 13; NSM

Norton St Mich from 13. *18 Priorwood Gardens, Ingleby Barwick, Stockton-on-Tees TS17 0XH* T: (01642) 761941 E: pauljohnson452@btinternet.com

JOHNSON, Peter Colin. b 54. SS Mark & Jo Univ Coll Plymouth BEd 89 Univ of Wales (Lamp) PhD 00 Nottm Univ MSc 10. SWMTC 97. **d** 00 **p** 01. NSM Godrevy *Truro* 00-05 and 08-13; Public Preacher 06-11; P-in-c Breage w Godolphin and Germoe 13-14; P-in-c Porthleven w Sithney 14; V W Kerrier from 14. *Seascape, Trewelloe Road, Praa Sands, Penzance TR20 9SU* T: (01736) 763407 M: 07713-624877 E: peter@seascape.ndo.co.uk

JOHNSON, Canon Peter Frederick. b 41. Melbourne Univ BA 63 Ch Ch Ox BA 68 MA 72. St Steph Ho Ox 68. **d** 69 **p** 70. C Banbury *Ox* 69-71; Tutor St Steph Ho Ox 71-74; Chapl St Chad's Coll Dur 74-80; Vice-Prin 78-80; Chapl K Sch Cant 80-90; PtO *Cant* 80-81; Hon Min Can Cant Cathl 81-90; Can Res Bris Cathl 90-08; rtd 08; PtO *Ox* from 08. *4 St John's Road, Windsor SL4 3QN* T: (01753) 865914 E: pf.johnson@btinternet.com

JOHNSON, Prof Peter Stewart. b 44. Nottm Univ BA 65 PhD 70. Cranmer Hall Dur 01. **d** 03 **p** 04. NSM Dur St Nic from 03; PtO from 14. *126 Devonshire Road, Durham DH1 2BH* T: 0191-386 6334 M: 07949-680467

JOHNSON, Philip Anthony. b 69. All Nations Chr Coll BA 97 MA 98 FIBMS 94. Ridley Hall Cam 00. **d** 02 **p** 03. C Witham *Chelmsf* 02-06; P-in-c Holland-on-Sea 06-13; V Sleaford *Linc* from 13. *1A Northfield Road, Quarrington, Sleaford NG34 8RT* E: revdphilip@aol.com

JOHNSON, Phillip Thomas. b 75. City Univ BA 03 FRSA. Ripon Coll Cuddesdon 06. **d** 08 **p** 09. C Cheam *S'wark* 08-11; V Weston *Guildf* from 11. *All Saints' Vicarage, 1 Chestnut Avenue, Esher KT10 8JL* T: (020) 8398 9685 M: 07815-018846 E: vicar@allsaintschurchweston.org.uk

JOHNSON (née DAVIES), Rhiannon Mary Morgan. b 69. St Anne's Coll Ox BA 90 MA 96 Univ of Wales (Cardiff) PhD 94 BD 96. St Mich Coll Llan 94. **d** 97 **p** 98. C Whitchurch *Llan* 97-99; NSM Walton W w Talbenny and Haroldston W *St D* 99-00; Chapl Trin Coll Carmarthen 00; NSM Walton W w Talbenny and Haroldston W *St D* 00-08; P-in-c Walwyn's Castle 08-14; P-in-c Walwyn's Castle and Robeston W from 15; Dioc Course Dir for Exploring Faith from 11. *The Vicarage, Castle Way, Dale, Haverfordwest SA62 3RN* T: (01646) 636966 E: rhiannon.johnson@tesco.net

JOHNSON, Richard Miles. b 59. Bris Univ BSc 82. St Jo Coll Nottm 87. **d** 90 **p** 91. C Bromley SS Pet and Paul *Roch* 90-94; USPG/CMS Philippines 94-97; Ind Chapl *Roch* 97-06; C Bexleyheath Ch Ch 97-06; Ind Chapl *Worc* from 06; TV Redditch H Trin from 06. *120 Carthorse Lane, Redditch B97 6SZ* T: (01527) 61936 E: dickim@globalnet.co.uk

JOHNSON, Richard William. b 76. St Cath Coll Cam BA 98 MA Glos Univ PhD 05. Westmr Th Cen. **d** 05 **p** 06. C Symonds Street St Paul New Zealand 05-09; C Worc City 09-14; V Worc St Nic and All SS w St Helen from 14. *All Saints' Church, Quay Turn, Quay Street, Worcester WR1 2JJ* T: (01905) 734625 E: rich@allsaintsworcester.org.uk

JOHNSON, Robert. See JOHNSON, Christopher Robert

JOHNSON, Canon Robert Kenneth. b 48. NOC 83. **d** 86 **p** 87. C Hattersley *Ches* 86-88; C Brinnington w Portwood 88-90; V Gospel Lane St Mich *Birm* 90-97; P-in-c Birm St Geo 97-07; R 07; Hon Can Birm Cathl 05-07; rtd 07. *9 Briants Piece, Hermitage, Thatcham RG18 9SX* T: (01635) 203419 E: robkj@btopenworld.com

JOHNSON, Ronald George. b 33. Chich Th Coll 75. **d** 76 **p** 77. NSM Shipley *Chich* 76-79; C Brighton St Matthias 79-82; Sutton w Bignor 82; R Barlavington, Burton w Coates, Sutton and Bignor 82-93; rtd 93; PtO *Chich* from 93. *1 Highdown Drive, Littlehampton BN17 6HJ* T: (01903) 732210

JOHNSON, Ruth Alice Edna. See LAMBERT, Ruth Alice Edna

JOHNSON, The Very Revd Samuel Hugh Akinsope. b 30. K Coll Lon BD 61. Lich Th Coll 52. **d** 55 **p** 56. C Whitechapel St Paul w St Mark *Lon* 55-58; C Sunbury 58-59; C Lisson Grove w St Marylebone St Matt w Em 59-60; C St Martin-in-the-Fields 60-62; Nigeria from 63; Provost Lagos Cathl 70-95; rtd 95. *1 Oba Nle Aro Crescent, Ilupeju, PO Box 10021, Marina, Lagos, Nigeria*

JOHNSON (née ROWE), Mrs Shiela. b 43. CITC 93. **d** 96 **p** 97. Aux Min Urney w Denn and Derryheen *K, E & A* 96-97; Aux Min Boyle and Elphin w Aghanagh, Kilbryan etc 97-01; Aux Min Roscommon w Donamon, Rathcline, Kilkeevin etc 97-01; P-in-c Clondevaddock w Portsalon and Leatbeg *D & R* 02-08; rtd 08. *Rainbow's End, Carrickmacafferty, Derrybeg, Co Donegal, Republic of Ireland* T: (00353) (74) 953 2843 M: 087-6350776

JOHNSON, Stanley. b 42. QUB BSc 63 TCD BTh 89. CITC 86. **d** 89 **p** 90. C Kilmore w Ballintemple, Kildallan etc *K, E & A* 89-96; Adn Elphin and Ardagh 97-01; Can Elphin Cathl

97-01; I Templemichael w Clongish, Clooncumber etc 97-01; I Clondehorkey w Cashel *D & R* 01-09; Can Raphoe Cathl 08-09; rtd 09. *Rainbow's End, Carrickmacafferty, Derrybeg, Co Donegal, Republic of Ireland* T: (00353) (74) 953 2843 M: 87-973 5775 E: sjohnsons@eircom.net

JOHNSON, Stephen. b 57. Cranmer Hall Dur. **d** 00 **p** 01. C Longton *Blackb* 00-02; C Longridge 03-04; V Preston Em 04-13; Chapl Cen Lancs Univ 08-13; P-in-c Bamber Bridge St Aid from 13; P-in-c Walton-le-Dale St Leon from 13. *St Aidan's Vicarage, Longworth Street, Bamber Bridge, Preston PR5 6GN* T: (01772) 335310 M: 07790-917504 E: stephen@johnsonstephen.orangehome.co.uk

JOHNSON, Stephen Ashley. b 79. York Univ BA 01 MA 02. Wycliffe Hall Ox BTh 06. **d** 06 **p** 07. C Sunningdale *Ox* 06-09; V Sunninghill and S Ascot from 09. *Sunninghill Vicarage, Church Lane, Ascot SL5 7DD* T: (01344) 873202 M: 07799-834250 E: vicar@ssaparish.org

JOHNSON, Stephen William. b 63. Trent Poly BEd 86 Keele Univ MA 94 Univ Coll Ches BA 05 ALCM 85. NOC 02. **d** 05 **p** 06. NSM Silverdale *Lich* 05-08; PtO *Linc* 09-10; *Lich* 10-12; Community Chapl *Linc* 13-14; P-in-c Market Rasen from 14; P-in-c Legsby from 14; P-in-c Linwood from 14; P-in-c Lissington from 14. *The Vicarage, 13 Lady Frances Drive, Market Rasen LN8 3JJ* M: 07766-411090 T: (01673) 844770

JOHNSON, Stuart. *See* JOHNSON, Geoffrey Stuart

JOHNSON, Mrs Susan Constance. b 46. EAMTC 01. **d** 03 **p** 04. NSM Heald Green St Cath *Ches* 03-07; PtO from 10. *11A Lynton Park Road, Cheadle Hulme, Cheadle SK8 6JA* T: 0161-485 3787 E: revsusan@talktalk.net

JOHNSON, Terence John. b 44. Cov Poly BA 89. ALCD 70. **d** 69 **p** 70. C Woodside *Ripon* 69-72; C Leeds St Geo 72-76; C Heworth H Trin *York* 76-81; V Budbrooke *Cov* 81-97; Chapl Wroxall Abbey Sch 83-93; V Stone Ch Ch and Oulton *Lich* 97-02; P-in-c Collingtree w Courteenhall and Milton Malsor *Pet* 02-08; rtd 08; PtO *Pet* from 09. *18 Northgate, Towcester NN12 6HT* T: (01327) 351408 E: terencejohnson194@btinternet.com

JOHNSON, Thomas Bernard. b 44. BA CertEd. Oak Hill Th Coll. **d** 84 **p** 85. C Birkenhead St Jas w St Bede *Ches* 84-88; R Ashover and Brackenfield *Derby* 88-01; P-in-c Wessington 99-01; R Ashover and Brackenfield w Wessington *Derby* 01-03; RD Chesterfield 97-02; V Swanwick and Pentrich 03-10; Hon Chapl Derbyshire St Jo Ambulance 91-09; rtd 10. *11 The Spinney, Ripley DE5 3HW* T: (01773) 570375 E: t.b.johnson2000@gmail.com

JOHNSON, Victor Edward. b 45. Linc Th Coll 83. **d** 85 **p** 86. C Garforth *Ripon* 85-90; Dioc Video Officer 90-92; V Wyther 92-00; V Shelley and Shepley *Wakef* 00-01; rtd 01; PtO *Bradf* 02-04. *Low Farm, Marsh Lane Gardens, Kellington, Goole DN14 0PG* T: (01977) 661629 E: vej@onetel.com

JOHNSON, Canon Victoria Louise. b 75. Leic Univ BSc 96 PhD 00 SS Coll Cam BA 06. Westcott Ho Cam 04 Yale Div Sch 06. **d** 07 **p** 08. C Baguley *Man* 07-10; P-in-c Flixton St Mich 10-15; Can Res Ely Cathl from 15. *The Black Hostelry, The College, Ely CB7 4DL* T: (01353) 660302 M: 07713-478609 E: v.johnson@elycathedral.org *or* vickyjohnson@cantab.net

JOHNSTON, Alexander Irvine. b 47. Keele Univ BA 70 LRAM. St Alb Minl Tr Scheme 77. **d** 80 **p** 81. NSM Hockerill *St Alb* 80-95; NSM High Wych and Gilston w Eastwick 95-96; TV Bottesford w Ashby *Linc* 96-01; P-in-c St Germans *Truro* 01-12; rtd 12; PtO *Truro* from 12. *31 Longmeadow Road, Saltash PL12 6DP* T: (01752) 842328 E: alecjohnston@btinternet.com

JOHNSTON, Allen Niall. b 61. Southn Univ BTh 92 Kent Univ MA 97 AMBIM 87 MISM 87 MInstAD 00. Sarum & Wells Th Coll 89. **d** 92 **p** 93. C Roehampton H Trin *S'wark* 92-95; Dir Past Services Richmond, Twickenham and Roehampton NHS Trust 95-98; Tutor SEITE 95-97; PtO *Eur* 01-02; Sierra Leone 02-03; Asst P St Jo Cathl Freetown 03; PtO *Ely* from 03; *D & R* from 04. *50 Vestry Court, 5 Monck Street, London SW1P 2BW* E: niall@nialljohnston.org

JOHNSTON, Austin. b 50. Huddersfield Poly CertEd 76 BEd 90. Chich Th Coll 92. **d** 94 **p** 95. C Peterlee *Dur* 94-97; C Stockton St Pet 97-00; TR Stanley and Tanfield 00-01; TR Ch the K 01-15; V Stanley and S Moor from 15. *The Rectory, Church Bank, Stanley DH9 0DU* T: (01207) 233936

JOHNSTON, Brian. *See* JOHNSTON, Wilfred Brian

JOHNSTON, Charles Walter. *See* BARR JOHNSTON, Charles Walter

JOHNSTON, David George Scott. b 66. Avery Hill Coll BA 88. SEITE 00. **d** 03 **p** 04. C Frindsbury w Upnor and Chattenden *Roch* 03-06; R Longfield 06-11; C Chislehurst Ch Ch 11-15; V from 15. *The Vicarage, 62 Lubbock Road, Chislehurst BR7 5JK* T: (020) 8467 3185 E: rev.dj@btinternet.com

JOHNSTON, Canon Donald Walter. b 28. Trin Coll Melbourne BA 51 Lon Univ PGCE 52 Em Coll Cam BA 63 MA 67. Ridley Hall Cam 64. **d** 64 **p** 65. C Cottingham *York* 64-66; Australia from 66; Min Nunawading Melbourne 67-69; Chapl Brighton Gr Sch Melbourne 70-73; Chapl Melbourne C of E Gr Sch 74-84; Angl Bd of Miss 85-90; Chapl H Name Sch Dogura 85; Hd Martyrs' Memorial Sch Popondetta 86-89; Papua New Guinea from 90; rtd 91. *22 Albert Street, PO Box 114, Point Lonsdale Vic 3225, Australia* T: (0061) (3) 5258 2139 *or* 9690 0549 F: 5258 3994 E: dncjohnston@al.com.au

JOHNSTON, Duncan Howard. b 63. Hull Univ BA 85 Nottm Univ MA 93. St Jo Coll Nottm 91. **d** 93 **p** 94. C Werrington *Pet* 93-96; V Gt Doddington and Wilby 96-01; Dioc Adv in Local Miss *Dur* 02-03; R Fremont St Jo USA from 03. *515 East Pine Street, Fremont MI 49412-1739, USA* T: (001) (231) 924 7120 E: djepisc@joimal.com

JOHNSTON, Edith Violet Nicholl. b 28. **d** 87. Par Dn Bentley *Sheff* 87-88; rtd 88; PtO *Sheff* 88-08. *30 Sharman Road, Belfast BT9 5FW* T: (028) 9066 6776

JOHNSTON, Elizabeth Margaret. b 37. QUB BA 58 DipEd 69 Serampore Univ BD 87. Dalton Ho Bris. **d** 81 **p** 94. BCMS India 62-92; C Belfast St Chris *D & D* 93-94; Bp's C 94-02; Can Down Cathl 01-03; rtd 03. *103 Ballydorn Road, Killinchy, Newtownards BT23 6QB* T: (028) 9754 2518 M: 07762-821569 E: elizabeth_johnston@amserve.com

JOHNSTON, Frank. *See* JOHNSTON, William Francis

JOHNSTON, The Ven Geoffrey Stanley. b 44. Aston Univ MBA 81 Birm Univ CertEd 78. Kelham Th Coll 64. **d** 68 **p** 69. C Blakenall Heath *Lich* 68-72 and 73-75; C St Buryan, St Levan and Sennen *Truro* 72-73; P-in-c Willenhall St Steph *Lich* 75-76; C W Bromwich All SS 76-77; Lect W Bromwich Coll of Commerce and Tech 78-82; Ind Chapl *Worc* 82-94; TV Halesowen 82-94; NSM Dudley St Fran 94-99; P-in-c 99-08; P-in-c Dudley St Edm 04-08; rtd 08; P-in-c Nerja and Almuñécar *Eur* 08-14; Adn Gib from 14. *5 Crown Terrace, Bridge Street, Belper DE56 1BD* M: 07507-391297 T: (01773) 270972 E: vengeoffrey@gmail.com

JOHNSTON, Mrs Helen Kay. b 48. SRN 70. SAOMC 95. **d** 98 **p** 99. OLM Banbury St Paul *Ox* 98-01; P-in-c Flimby *Carl* 01-03; C Netherton 01-03; PtO *Derby* 04-11; *Lich* from 11. *Merryfields, Whitehorn Avenue, Barleston, Stoke-on-Trent ST12 9EF* T: (01782) 372618 E: kaybees@supanet.com

JOHNSTON, Miss Henrietta Elizabeth Ann. b 59. St Jo Coll Dur BA 03. Cranmer Hall Dur 01. **d** 03 **p** 04. C Cov H Trin 03-07; C Dorridge *Birm* 07-11; V Lache cum Saltney *Ches* from 11. *St Mark's Vicarage, 5 Cliveden Road, Chester CH4 8DR* T: (01244) 671702 *or* 675372 M: 07796-948904 E: hennie.johnston@gmail.com

JOHNSTON, Ian. b 61. Hull Univ CertEd 82 BEd 84. LCTP 08. **d** 13 **p** 14. NSM Carl H Trin and St Barn from 13. *Watch Hill, Burgh-by-Sands, Carlisle CA5 6AQ* T: (01228) 576097

JOHNSTON, Ian Harold. b 50. Ex Univ BA 72 McMaster Univ Ontario MA 74 Sheff Univ BA 13. Yorks Min Course 10. **d** 13 **p** 14. NSM Adel *Leeds* from 13; NSM Ireland Wood from 13; Min to Business Leeds from 14. *4 Buttercup Close, Killinghall, Harrogate HG3 2WU* M: 07914-750969 E: revianjohnston@gmail.com

JOHNSTON, Kay. *See* JOHNSTON, Helen Kay

JOHNSTON, Malcolm. *See* JOHNSTON, William Malcolm

JOHNSTON, Michael David Haigh. b 44. S Dios Minl Tr Scheme 88. **d** 91 **p** 92. NSM Wootton Portsm 91-95; NSM Ryde H Trin 95-99; NSM Swanmore St Mich 95-99; P-in-c Cowes St Faith 99-03; Asst Chapl Isle of Wight NHS Primary Care Trust 03-11; Chapl HM Pris Kingston (Portsm) 03-05; P-in-c St Lawrence Portsm 11-14; rtd 14; PtO Portsm from 15. *8 Coniston Drive, Ryde PO33 3AE* T: (01983) 611291 E: rvdmikej@fastmail.fm

JOHNSTON, Canon Michael Edward. b 68. TCD BA 97 MA 04. CITC BTh 00. **d** 00 **p** 01. Bp's V and Lib Kilkenny Cathl and C Kilkenny w Aghour and Kilmanagh *C & O* 00-03; V Waterford w Killea, Drumcannon and Dunhill 03-09; I Shinrone w Aghancon etc *L & K* from 09; Can Limerick, Killaloe and Clonfert Cathls from 14. *St Mary's Rectory, Shinrone, Birr, Co Offaly, Republic of Ireland* T: (00353) (505) 47164 E: shinrone@killaloe.anglican.org

JOHNSTON, Niall. *See* JOHNSTON, Allen Niall

JOHNSTON, Patricia Anne. *See* FLEMING, Patricia Anne

JOHNSTON, Canon Robert John. b 31. Oak Hill Th Coll 64. **d** 64 **p** 65. C Bebington *Ches* 64-68; I Lack *Clogh* 68-99; Can Clogh Cathl 89-99; rtd 99. *2 Beechcroft, Semicock Road, Ballymoney BT53 6NF* T: (028) 2766 9317

JOHNSTON, Samuel Hamilton. b 44. Lurgan Ch the Redeemer *D & D* 14-15; C from 15. *15 Waverley Drive, Bangor BT20 5LD*

JOHNSTON, Thomas Cosbey. b 15. Em Coll Cam BA 40 MA 44. Ridley Hall Cam 40. **d** 42 **p** 43. C Handsworth St Mary *Birm*

42-48; New Zealand from 48. *254 Main Road, Moncks Bay, Christchurch 8081, New Zealand* T: (0064) (3) 384 1224

JOHNSTON, Trevor Samuel. b 72. Ulster Univ BMus 96 TCD BTh 01. CITC 98. **d** 01 **p** 02. C Carrickfergus *Conn* 01-04; C Jordanstown and Chapl Jordanstown and Belf Campuses Ulster Univ 04-09; Crosslinks Ireland Team Ldr 09-14; I Belfast All SS *Conn* from 14. *All Saints' Rectory, 171 Malone Road, Belfast BT9 6TA* M: 07776-178248 E: trev@tjohnston.net

JOHNSTON, Wilfred Brian. b 44. TCD BA 67 MA 70. Div Test 68. **d** 68 **p** 70. C Seagoe *D & D* 68-73; I Inniskeel *D & R* 73-82; I Castlerock w Dunboe and Fermoyle 82-02; Bp's C Gweedore, Carrickfin and Templecrone 02-08; Dioc Registrar 89-06; Can Derry Cathl 92-02; Preb 99-02; Can Raphoe Cathl 05-08; rtd 08. *2 The Apple Yard, Coleraine BT51 3PP* T: (028) 7032 6406 E: b.johnston@talk21.com

JOHNSTON, William Derek. b 40. CITC 68. **d** 68 **p** 69. V Choral Derry Cathl 68-70; I Swanlinbar w Templeport *K, E & A* 70-73; I Billis Union 73-84; Glebes Sec (Kilmore) 77-03; I Annagh w Drumaloor and Cloverhill 84-86; Preb Kilmore Cathl 85-89; I Annagh w Drumgoon, Ashfield etc 87-99; Adn Kilmore 89-03; I Lurgan w Billis, Killinkere and Munterconnaught 99-03; rtd 03. *Ballaghanea, Mullagh Road, Virginia, Co Cavan, Republic of Ireland* T: (00353) (49) 854 9960 M: 86-832 9911

JOHNSTON, William Francis (Frank). b 30. CB 83. TCD BA 55 MA 69. **d** 55 **p** 56. C Orangefield *D & D* 55-59; CF 59-77; Asst Chapl Gen 77-80; Chapl Gen 80-87; P-in-c Winslow *Ox* 87-91; RD Claydon 89-94; R Winslow w Gt Horwood and Addington 91-95; rtd 95; PtO *Ex* from 95. *Lower Axehill, Chard Road, Axminster EX13 5ED* T: (01297) 33259

JOHNSTON, Canon William John. b 35. Lon Univ BA 85 MA 90 PhD. CITC 67. **d** 70 **p** 71. C Belfast St Donard *D & D* 70-72; C Derg *D & R* 72-78; I Drumclamph w Lower and Upper Langfield 78-91; I Kilskeery w Trillick *Clogh* 91-10; Preb Clogh Cathl 04-10; Prec 09-10; rtd 10. *Ernedene, 61 Dublin Road, Enniskillen BT74 6HN* T: (028) 6632 2268

JOHNSTON, William Malcolm. b 48. SAOMC 92. **d** 95 **p** 96. NSM Banbury *Ox* 95-01; P-in-c Netherton *Carl* 01-03; C Flimby 01-03; PtO *Derby* 04-11; *Lich* from 11. *Merryfields, Whitehorn Avenue, Barleston, Stoke-on-Trent ST12 9EF* T: (01782) 372618 E: kaybees@supanet.com

JOHNSTON, William McConnell. b 33. TCD BA 57. **d** 58 **p** 59. C Ballymena w Ballyclug *Conn* 58-61; C Belfast St Thos 61-63; C Finaghy 63-66; R Kambula S Africa 66-74; Dean Eshowe 74-86; R Mtubatuba 86-99; rtd 00; PtO *Chich* from 04. *Honeysuckle Cottage, Redford, Midhurst GU29 0QG* T: (01428) 741131

JOHNSTONE, William Henry Green. b 26. **d** 92 **p** 94. Belize 92-98; Hon C Tollard Royal w Farnham, Gussage St Michael etc *Sarum* 98-01; Hon C Chase from 01; OCM 94-98 and from 01. *Church Cottage, Chettle, Blandford Forum DT11 8DB* T: (01258) 830396 E: padrewmchettle@aol.com

JOINT, Canon Michael John. b 39. Sarum & Wells Th Coll 79. **d** 79 **p** 79. CA from 61; Hon C Chandler's Ford *Win* 79-83; Youth Chapl 79-83; V Lymington 83-95; Co-ord Chapl R Bournemouth and Christchurch Hosps NHS Trust 96-03; Hon Can Win Cathl 00-03; rtd 03; PtO *Win* 03-04 and from 12. *20 Wavendon Avenue, Barton on Sea, New Milton BH25 7LS* T: (01425) 628952 E: michjoin@aol.com

JOLLEY, Canon Andrew John. b 61. Nottm Univ BSc 83 PhD 06 Warwick Univ MBA 88 CEng 88 MIMechE 88. St Jo Coll Nottm BTh 97. **d** 98 **p** 99. C Sparkhill w Greet and Sparkbrook *Birm* 98-02; V Aston SS Pet and Paul 02-08; P-in-c Aston St Jas 05-08; P-in-c Nechells 05-08; V Aston and Nechells from 08; AD Aston 05-12; Hon Can Birm Cathl from 15. *The Vicarage, Sycamore Road, Aston, Birmingham B6 5UH* T: 0121-327 5856 E: andy@astonnechellscofe.org.uk

JONAS, Alan Charles. b 56. Leeds Univ BA 79 Univ of Wales (Abth) PGCE 80. Wycliffe Hall Ox 92. **d** 94 **p** 95. C Hersham *Guildf* 94-98; P-in-c Westcott from 98; Chapl Priory Sch 01-07; RD Dorking *Guildf* from 14. *The Vicarage, Guildford Road, Westcott, Dorking RH4 3QB* T: (01306) 885309 E: alchasjonas@aol.com

JONAS, Canon Ian Robert. b 54. St Jo Coll Nottm BTh 80. **d** 80 **p** 81. C Portadown St Mark *Arm* 80-82; C Cregagh *D & D* 82-85; BCMS Sec *D & G* 85-90; V Langley Mill *Derby* 90-97; I Kilgariffe Union *C, C & R* 97-09; I Carrigrohane Union from 09; Can Cork Cathl from 11; Can Cloyne Cathl from 11. *The Rectory, Church Hill, Carrigrohane, Co Cork, Republic of Ireland* T: (00353) (21) 487 1106 E: revianjonas@yahoo.co.uk

JONES, Preb Alan John. b 47. Nottm Univ BA 71. Coll of Resurr Mirfield 71. **d** 73 **p** 74. C Sedgley St Mary *Lich* 73-76; C Cov St Jo 76-78; V W Bromwich St Fran *Lich* 78-94; V Ettingshall 94-13; AD Wolverhampton 03-11; Preb Lich Cathl 11-13; rtd 13; PtO *Lich* from 13. *65 Birches Road, Codsall, Wolverhampton WV8 2JQ* T: (01902) 900878 E: fatheralanjones@sky.com

JONES, Alan Pierce. *See* PIERCE-JONES, Alan
JONES, Alison. *See* JONES, Helen Alison
JONES, Alison. *See* WAGSTAFF, Alison
JONES, Alison Fiona Kay. b 67. St Mellitus Coll. **d** 13 **p** 14. C Burghfield *Ox* from 13. *St Peter's House, Sulhamstead Road, Ufton Nervet, Reading RG7 4DH* M: 07818-806403 E: alison@jones-tribe.com

JONES, Alun. b 52. Leeds Univ BA 96. Cuddesdon Coll 94. **d** 96 **p** 97. C Newc St Geo 96-98; C Cowgate 98-99; C Fenham St Jas and St Basil 99-04; P-in-c Carl St Herbert w St Steph 04-07; V from 07. *St Herbert's Vicarage, Blackwell Road, Carlisle CA2 4RA* T: (01228) 523375 E: alun52@sky.com

JONES, Alwyn Humphrey Griffith. b 30. Leeds Univ BSc 51. Coll of Resurr Mirfield 53. **d** 55 **p** 56. C W Hackney St Barn *Lon* 55-58; C-in-c Dacca St Thos E Pakistan 58-64; Ox Miss to Calcutta India 65-68; Chapl R Bombay Seamen's Soc 68-73; P-in-c Bedminster St Fran *Bris* 73-74; TR Bedminster 75-83; TV Langport Area *B & W* 83-85; Dep Chapl HM Pris Nor 85; Chapl HM Pris Preston 85-89; Chapl HM Pris Ashwell 89-91; C Acton Green *Lon* 91-93; rtd 93; NSM Langport Area *B & W* 93-98; PtO from 98; *Bris* from 98. *2 All Saints House, 33 Cumberland Street, Bristol BS2 8NU* T: 0117-923 2331 E: alwyn_j@btinternet.com

JONES, Alyson Elizabeth. *See* DAVIE, Alyson Elizabeth
JONES, Mrs Andrea Margaret. b 46. Qu Coll Birm 88. **d** 90 **p** 94. Par Dn Kidderminster St Geo *Worc* 90-94; TV 94-95; C Penn Fields *Lich* 95-00; C Gt Wyrley 00-06; rtd 06; PtO *Worc* from 07. *57 Woodward Road, Kidderminster DY11 6NY* T: (01562) 823555 E: aam57@blueyonder.co.uk

JONES, Ms Andrea Susan. b 55. SNWTP 08. **d** 10 **p** 11. OLM Davyhulme St Mary *Man* 10-11; C Newton Heath 11-13; C Moston St Jo 11-13; C Moston St Chad 11-13; R Manchester Gd Shep and St Barn from 13; Borough Dean Man from 12. *St Barnabas' Rectory, 1 South Street, Openshaw, Manchester M11 2EY* T: 0161-223 9182 E: andysjones@hotmail.co.uk

JONES, Andrew. *See* JONES, Ian Andrew
JONES, Andrew. b 64. York Univ BA 85. Westmr Th Sem (USA) MDiv 91 St Jo Coll Nottm 92. **d** 94 **p** 95. C Win Ch Ch 94-98; C St Helen Bishopsgate w St Andr Undershaft etc *Lon* from 98. *89 Forest Road, London E8 3BL* T: (020) 7254 5942 E: a.jones@st-helens.org.uk

JONES, The Ven Andrew. b 61. Univ of Wales (Ban) BD 82 PGCE 82 TCD BTh 85 MA 91 Univ of Wales MPhil 93. CITC 82 St Geo Coll Jerusalem 84. **d** 85 **p** 86. Min Can Ban Cathl 85-88; R Dolgellau w Llanfachreth and Brithdir etc 88-92; Warden of Readers 91-92; Dir Past Studies St Mich Coll Llan 92-96; Lect Th Univ of Wales (Cardiff) 92-96; Visiting Prof St Geo Coll Jerusalem from 94; Research Fell from 96; R Llanbedrog w Llanfihangel etc *Ban* 96-01; R Llanbedrog w Llannor and Llangian 01-12; Dioc CME and NSM Officer 96-00; AD Llyn and Eifionydd 99-10; Hon Can Ban Cathl 04-05; Can Ban Cathl from 05; Dioc Dir of Ords from 06; Adn Meirionnydd from 10; C Bro Enlli from 12. *Ty'n Llan Rectory, Llanbedrog, Pwllheli LL53 7TU* T/F: (01758) 740919 E: archdeacon.meirionnydd@churchinwales.org.uk

JONES, Preb Andrew Christopher. b 47. Southn Univ BA 69 PhD 75. Ridley Hall Cam 78. **d** 80 **p** 81. C Wareham *Sarum* 80-83; P-in-c Symondsbury 83; P-in-c Chideock 83; R Symondsbury and Chideock 84-91; V Shottermill *Guildf* 91-99; P-in-c Bishopsnympton, Rose Ash, Mariansleigh etc *Ex* 99-14; rtd 14; Preb Ex Cathl from 14. *57 Raleigh Mead, South Molton EX36 4BT* E: acjtherectory@btinternet.com

JONES, Andrew Collins. b 62. Univ Coll Dur BA 83 MA 84 MLitt 92. St Steph Ho Ox 88. **d** 90 **p** 91. C Llangefni w Tregaean and Llangristiolus etc *Ban* 90-94; C Hartlepool St Aid *Dur* 94-98; Chapl Hartlepool Gen Hosp 94-98; R Hendon *Dur* from 98; CMP from 95. *St Ignatius' Rectory, Bramwell Road, Sunderland SR2 8BY* T: 0191-567 5575

JONES, Andrew Edward. b 71. Ridley Hall Cam 10. **d** 12 **p** 13. C Sprowston w Beeston *Nor* 12-15; R Trunch Group from 15. *The Rectory, Knapton Road, Trunch, North Walsham NR28 0QE* E: revandrewjones@gmail.com

JONES, Angela Mary. *See* AUSTIN, Angela Mary
JONES, Anne. *See* FURNESS, Christine Anne
JONES, Anthony. b 43. WEMTC 99. **d** 01 **p** 02. OLM Lydney *Glouc* 01-07; NSM Woolaston w Alvington and Aylburton from 07. *The Rectory, Main Road, Alvington, Lydney GL15 5AT* T: (01594) 529387 M: 07860-331755 E: jones_rev@yahoo.co.uk

JONES, Canon Anthony Spacie. b 34. AKC 58. **d** 59 **p** 60. C Bedford St Martin *St Alb* 59-63; Br Guiana 63-66; Guyana 66-71; V Ipswich All Hallows *St E* 72-80; RD Ipswich 78-86; Bp's Dom Chapl 80-82; V Rushmere 82-91; Hon Can St E Cathl 83-99; R Brantham w Stutton 91-99; P-in-c Bentley w

Tattingstone 95-99; rtd 99; PtO *St E* from 99. *6 Fritillary Close, Pinewood, Ipswich IP8 3QT* T: (01473) 601848
E: tonyjones.pinewood@btinternet.com

JONES, April Elizabeth. b 46. WEMTC. d 12 p 13. NSM Badgeworth, Shurdington and Witcombe w Bentham *Glouc* from 12. *Charnwood, Bryerland Road, Witcombe, Gloucester GL3 4TA* T: (01452) 864469
E: aprilalan.philsroom@blueyonder.co.uk

JONES, Barbara Christine. b 48. St Hugh's Coll Ox BA 71 MA 74 Lady Spencer Chu Coll of Educn PGCE 74. CBDTI 97. d 00 p 01. NSM Bolton-le-Sands *Blackb* 00-13; Bp's Adv on Healing from 09. *11 Sandown Road, Lancaster LA1 4LN* T: (01524) 65598 E: bcjones@mypostoffice.co.uk

JONES, Barry Mervyn. b 46. St Chad's Coll Dur BA 68. d 70 p 71. C Bloxwich *Lich* 70-72; C Norwood All SS *Cant* 72-76; C New Addington 76-78; Chapl Mayday Univ Hosp Thornton Heath 78-86; Chapl Qu Hosp Croydon 78-86; Chapl St Mary's Hosp Croydon 78-86; Chapl Bromsgrove and Redditch DHA 86-94; Chapl Alexandra Healthcare NHS Trust Redditch 94-00; Chapl Worcs Acute Hosps NHS Trust 00-03; Chapl Team Ldr 03-05; PtO *Worc* from 05. *46 Barlich Way, Redditch B98 7JP* T: (01527) 520659 E: jones@jonesbarry52.orangehome.co.uk

JONES, Canon Basil Henry. b 26. Bps' Coll Cheshunt 63. d 64 p 65. C Gt Berkhamsted *St Alb* 64-67; V Leagrave 68-74; RD Luton 71-74; P-in-c Bedford St Paul 74-75; V Wigginton 75-93; Hon Can St Alb 82-93; rtd 93; PtO *St Alb* 00-15. *18 Gracey Court, Woodland Road, Broadclyst, Exeter EX5 3GA* T: (01392) 469884 E: bazilhjones@aol.com

JONES, Benjamin Jenkin Hywel. b 39. Univ of Wales BA 61. St Mich Coll Llan 61. d 64 p 65. C Carmarthen St Pet *St D* 64-70; V Cynwyl Gaeo w Llansawel and Talley 70-79; R Llanbadarn Fawr 79-82; V Llanbadarn Fawr w Capel Bangor and Goginan 82-92; V Llanychaearn w Llanddeiniol 92-05; Warden of Readers from 82; Can St D Cathl 86-90; RD Llanbadarn Fawr 89-90; Adn Cardigan 90-06; rtd 06. *Dowerdd, Waun Fawr, Aberystwyth SY23 3QF* T: (01970) 617100

JONES, Benjamin Mark. b 85. Univ Coll Lon LLB 06. Trin Coll Bris 11. d 14 p 15. C Bryanston Square St Mary w St Marylebone St Mark *Lon* from 14. *Garden Flat, 14 The Avenue, London NW6 7YD* M: 07941-838117
E: benmarkjones@gmail.com

JONES, Benjamin Mark Oscar. b 79. Kent Univ BA 00 Cant Ch Ch Univ PGCE 01. Trin Coll Bris BA 11 MPhil 12. d 12 p 13. C Folkestone St Jo *Cant* from 12. *2 Chalk Close, Folkestone CT19 5TD* M: 07779-494372
E: benmarkjones@hotmail.com

JONES, Benjamin Tecwyn. b 17. Univ of Wales BA 38. K Coll Lon 38. d 40 p 41. C Hawarden *St As* 40-45; C Pleasley *Derby* 45-46; C Ormskirk *Liv* 46-49; R Rufford *Blackb* 49-55; V S Shore St Pet 55-65; C Oldham St Mary w St Pet *Man* 65-69; Hd Master St Mary's Sch Bexhill-on-Sea 69-71; V Blackb St Luke 71-72; P-in-c Griffin 71-72; V Blackb St Luke w St Phil 72-83; rtd 83; PtO *Blackb* 83-11. *Cheshire Grange, Booths Hill Road, Lymm WA13 0EG*

JONES, Bernard Lewis. b 48. Llan Dioc Tr Scheme 89. d 93 p 94. NSM Aberaman and Abercwmboi w Cwmaman *Llan* 93-99; V Hirwaun 99-13; AD Cynon Valley 08-12; rtd 13; PtO *Llan* from 13. *21 Parc Aberaman, Aberaman, Aberdare CF44 6EY* T: (01685) 870607

JONES, Brenda. *See* CAMPBELL, Brenda

JONES, Brenda. b 50. Cranmer Hall Dur 02. d 04 p 05. C Jarrow *Dur* 04-07; C-in-c Bishop Auckland Woodhouse Close CD 07-14; rtd 14. *33 Walden Close, Ouston, Chester le Street DH2 1TF*

JONES, Canon Brian Howell. b 35. Univ of Wales MPhil 96. St Mich Coll Llan. d 61 p 62. C Llangiwg *S & B* 61-63; C Swansea St Mary and H Trin 63-70; R New Radnor w Llanfihangel Nantmelan etc 70-78; Dioc Dir of Stewardship 82-89; P-in-c Capel Coelbren 89-94; Dioc Missr 89-95; Can Res Brecon Cathl 89-00; Can Tres Brecon Cathl 98-00; Chan Brecon Cathl 99-00; RD Cwmtawe 89-93; V Killay 95-00; rtd 00. *125 Homegower House, St Helens Road, Swansea SA1 4DW*

JONES, Canon Brian Michael. b 34. Trin Coll Bris 79 Oak Hill Th Coll BA 82. d 84 p 84. CMS 82-93; Sierra Leone 84-93; Can Bo from 91; C Frimley *Guildf* 93-99; rtd 99; PtO *Newc* 00-01; Hon C N Tyne and Redesdale 01-08; PtO *Carl* from 09. *20 Campfield Road, Ulverston LA12 9PB* T: (01229) 480380
E: bmj.retired@btopenworld.com

JONES, Brian Robert. b 53. Surrey Univ BSc 76. SAOMC 02. d 05 p 06. NSM Greenham Ox from 05. *27 Three Acre Road, Newbury RG14 7AW* T: (01635) 34875

JONES, Canon Bryan Maldwyn. b 32. St Mich Coll Llan. d 62 p 63. C Swansea St Barn *S & B* 62-69; V Trallwng and Betws Penpont 69-75; V Trallwng, Bettws Penpont w Aberyskir

etc 75-00; RD Brecon 80-91 and 91-99; Hon Can Brecon Cathl 92-00; rtd 00. *Plas Newydd, 8 Camden Crescent, Brecon LD3 7BY* T: (01874) 625063

JONES, Bryan William. b 30. Selw Coll Cam BA 53 MA 57. Linc Th Coll 53. d 55 p 56. C Bedminster Down *Bris* 55-58; C Filton 58-62; P-in-c Bedminster St Mich 62-65; V 65-72; P-in-c Moorfields 72-75; TV E Bris 75-95; rtd 95; PtO *Bris* from 95. *89 Canterbury Close, Yate, Bristol BS37 5TU* T: (01454) 316795

JONES, Bryn Parry. b 49. Univ of Wales BSc 98 MCIH 98 FCIH 03. St As Minl Tr Course 04. d 06 p 10. NSM Connah's Quay *St As* 06-15; C Pontrobin from 15. *7 Fron Las, Pen y Maes, Holywell CH8 7HX* T: (01352) 714781

JONES, Bryon. b 34. Open Univ BA 84. St D Coll Lamp 61. d 64 p 65. C Port Talbot St Theodore *Llan* 64-67; C Aberdare 68-69; C Up Hatherley *Glouc* 69-71; C Oystermouth *S & B* 71-74; V Camrose *St D* 74-77; V Camrose and St Lawrence w Ford and Haycastle 77-04; rtd 04. *31 New Road, Haverfordwest SA61 1TU* T: (01437) 760596

JONES, Cameron Charles Wallace. d 14. Carrickfergus *Conn* 14-15; C from 15. *28 Summerhill Park, Belfast BT5 7HE* T: (028) 9028 2429 M: 07742-617224
E: cameron.c.jones@ntlworld.com

JONES, Mrs Carol. b 45. d 04 p 05. OLM Shirley St Geo *S'wark* 04-15; PtO from 15. *50 Belgrave Court, Sloane Walk, Croydon CR0 7NW* T: (020) 8777 6247 E: caroljonesolm@yahoo.co.uk

JONES, Carol Ann. b 58. d 13 p 14. OLM Welton and Dunholme w Scothern *Linc* from 13. *1 Rivehall Avenue, Welton, Lincoln LN2 3LH* T: (01673) 861907

JONES, Miss Celia Lynn. b 54. Univ of Wales (Lamp) MTh 09. Trin Coll Bris. d 01 p 08. C Bris St Paul's 01-08; C Barton Hill St Luke w Ch Ch and Moorfields 08-09; TV Magor *Mon* from 09. *The Vicarage, Station Road, Llanwern, Newport NP18 2DW* T: (01633) 413647 E: clynnjones@talktalk.net

JONES, Charles Derek. b 37. K Coll Lon BD 60 AKC 60. d 61 p 62. C Stockton St Chad *Dur* 61-64; C Becontree St Elisabeth *Chelmsf* 64-66; C S Beddington St Mich *S'wark* 66-73; LtO *Ex* 73-77; PtO *Liv* 77-99; rtd 02. *4 Bryn Glas, Graigfechan, Ruthin LL15 2EX* T: (01824) 705015

JONES, Christopher Howell. b 50. BA FCCA. Oak Hill Th Coll 80. d 83 p 84. C Leyton St Mary w St Edw *Chelmsf* 83-86; C Becontree St Mary 86-90; P-in-c Bootle St Matt *Liv* 90-93; V 93-99; AD Bootle 97-99; V Ormskirk from 99; Chapl W Lancashire NHS Trust 99-11. *The Vicarage, Park Road, Ormskirk L39 3AJ* T: (01695) 572143

JONES, Christopher Ian. b 63. Moorlands Coll BA 98 Southn Univ PGCE 03. Ripon Coll Cuddesdon MTh 11. d 11 p 12. C Windermere *Carl* 11-15; R Newchurch w Croft *Liv* from 15. *Newchurch Rectory, Jackson Avenue, Culcheth, Warrington WA3 4ED* M: 07745-410487 E: agalliao@hotmail.co.uk

JONES, Christopher Mark. b 56. St Jo Coll Cam BA 78 MA 82 Wycliffe Hall Ox BA 81 MA 85. d 82 p 83. C Walsall *Lich* 82-84; Chapl St Jo Coll Cam 84-89; Chapl Eton Coll from 89; Ho Master 97-10. *2 Hodgson House, Eton College, Windsor SL4 6DE* T: (01753) 671330 M: 07794-136258
E: c.m.jones@etoncollege.org.uk

JONES, Christopher Richard. b 80. Trin Coll Bris 12. d 14 p 15. C Watford St Luke *St Alb* from 14. *18 Park Road, Watford WD17 4QN* M: 07796-674435
E: chrisrichardjones@yahoo.co.uk

JONES, Christopher Yeates. b 51. STETS 97. d 00 p 01. NSM Yeovil St Mich *B & W* 00-12; rtd 12. *26 Glenthorne Avenue, Yeovil BA21 4PG* T: (01935) 420886 M: 07944-461154
E: fathercj@gmail.com

JONES, Clive. b 51. BA 82. Oak Hill Th Coll 79. d 82 p 83. C Brunswick *Man* 82-85; V Pendlebury St Jo 85-96; V Attleborough *Cov* from 96. *Attleborough Vicarage, 5 Fifield Close, Nuneaton CV11 4TS* T: (024) 7635 4114
E: clivej@hta1.freeserve.co.uk

JONES, Clive Morlais Peter. b 40. Univ of Wales (Cardiff) BA 63 CertEd 64 LTCL 71. Chich Th Coll 64. d 66 p 67. C Llanfabon *Llan* 66-70; PV Llan Cathl 70-75; R Gelligaer 75-85; Prec and Can Llan Cathl 84-85; R Tilehurst St Mich *Ox* 85-94; Chapl Costa Blanca *Eur* 94-97; V Newton St Pet *S & B* 97-06; P-in-c Haarlem *Eur* 07-10; PtO *Ox* from 10. *31 Lowbury Gardens, Compton, Newbury RG20 6NN* T: (01635) 579409
E: clive.jones857@btinternet.com

JONES, Clive Wesley. b 68. St Steph Ho Ox 95. d 98 p 99. C Swanley St Mary *Roch* 98-02; P-in-c Belvedere St Aug 02-07; V from 07; Chapl Trin Sch Belvedere 02-04. *The Vicarage, St Augustine's Road, Belvedere DA17 5HH* T: (020) 8311 6307
E: clive.jones@diocese-rochester.org *or* frclive@tiscali.co.uk

JONES, Colin Stuart. b 56. Southn Univ LLB 77. Coll of Resurr Mirfield 81. d 84 p 85. C Mountain Ash *Llan* 84-86; C Castle Bromwich SS Mary and Marg *Birm* 86-89; V Kingshurst 89-94;

V Perry Barr 94-05; P-in-c Wordsley *Worc* 05-07; TR from 07. *The Rectory, 13 Dunsley Drive, Stourbridge DY8 5RA* T: (01384) 400709

JONES, Collette Moyra Yvonne. b 50. Liv Univ BSc 71 PhD 75 ALCM 91. SNWTP 08. **d** 11 **p** 12. NSM Gt Sutton *Ches* 11-14; V Aston by Sutton, Lt Leigh and Lower Whitley from 14. *The Vicarage, Street Lane, Lower Whitley, Warrington WA4 4EN* T: (01925) 730158
E: collettemyjones@jonesc94.freeserve.co.uk

JONES, Dafydd. *See* JONES, William Dafydd

JONES, Daniel. b 78. St Andr Univ MTheol 01 PGCE 02. Qu Coll Birm 06. **d** 08 **p** 09. NSM Barbourne *Worc* 08-11; Chapl St Pet Sch York from 11. *St Peter's School, Clifton, York YO30 6AB* T: (01904) 527412 E: daniel_a_jones@btopenworld.com

JONES, David. *See* JONES, Wilfred David

JONES, David. *See* JONES, William David

JONES, David. b 55. CA Tr Coll 74 St Steph Ho Ox 83. **d** 85 **p** 86. C Fleur-de-Lis *Mon* 85-87; V Ynysddu 87-93; V Blackwood 93-08; AD Bedwellty 06-08; V Landore w Treboeth *S & B* from 08. *St Alban's Vicarage, Heol Fach, Treboeth, Swansea SA5 9DE* T: (01792) 310586

JONES, David Arthur. b 44. Liv Univ BA 66 Sussex Univ MA 68. St D Coll Lamp LTh 74. **d** 74 **p** 75. C Tenby *St D* 74-76; C Chepstow *Mon* 76-78; P-in-c Teversal *S'well* 78-81; R 81-91; Chapl Sutton Cen 78-89; V Radford All So w Ch Ch and St Mich 91-04; Adv to Urban Priority Par 96-01; Officer for Urban Life and Miss 04-09; rtd 09. *37 Devonshire Road, Nottingham NG5 2EW* T: 0115-962 2115
E: urbanrover@gmail.com

JONES, David Ceri. b 74. Univ of Wales (Abth) BA 95 PhD 01. **d** 12 **p** 13. NSM Llanfihangel Genau'r-glyn and Llangorwen *St D* 12-14; NSM Aberystwyth from 14. *2 Clos y Dderwen, Blaenplwyf, Aberystwyth SY23 4BL* T: (01970) 610286
E: dmj@aber.ac.uk

JONES, David Gornal. b 47. **d** 74 **p** 75. In RC Ch 75-80; Asst P Durban St Paul 87-88; R Durban St Aid 89-91; Justice and Reconciliation Officer Natal 92-94; Port Chapl Miss to Seafarers Walvis Bay 95-00; Vlissingen (Flushing) *Eur* 00-02; R Ayr, Girvan and Maybole *Glas* 02-06; V Sunderland St Thos and St Oswald *Dur* 06-14; rtd 14. *Address temp unknown*
E: dgjones@clara.co.uk

JONES, David Hugh. b 34. St D Coll Lamp BA 56. St Mich Coll Llan 58. **d** 58 **p** 59. C Swansea St Mary and H Trin *S & B* 58-61; Inter-Colleg Sec SCM (Liv) 61-63; Hon Chapl Liv Univ 61-63; C Swansea St Pet *S & B* 63-69; V Llanddewi Ystradenni and Abbey Cwmhir 69-75; R Port Eynon w Rhosili and Llanddewi and Knelston 75-83; V Swansea St Barn 83-92; rtd 92. *16 Lon Ger-y-Coed, Cockett, Swansea SA2 0YH*

JONES, Prof David Huw. b 49. Univ of Wales MB, BCh 72 MD 79 Chelsea Coll Lon MSc 78 FRCR 83 FRCP 96 Hon FFPM 07. EAMTC 95. **d** 98 **p** 99. NSM Trumpington *Ely* 98-02; PtO 02; Dean's V G&C Coll Cam from 06; RD Cambridge S *Ely* from 11; Hon Can Ely Cathl from 14. *17 Barrow Road, Cambridge CB2 8AP* T: (01223) 358458
E: drhuw@btopenworld.com *or* huw.jones49@gmail.com

✠**JONES, The Rt Revd David Huw.** b 34. Univ of Wales (Ban) BA 55 Univ Coll Ox BA 58 MA 62. St Mich Coll Llan 58. **d** 59 **p** 60 **c** 93. C Aberdare *Llan* 59-61; C Neath w Llantwit 61-65; V Crynant 65-69; V Cwmavon 69-74; Lect Th Univ of Wales (Cardiff) 74-78; Sub-Warden St Mich Coll Llan 74-78; V Prestatyn *St As* 78-82; Dioc Ecum Officer 78-82; Dean Brecon *S & B* 82-93; V Brecon w Battle 82-93; V Brecon St Mary and Battle w Llanddew 83-93; Asst Bp St As 93-96; Bp St D 96-01; rtd 02. *31 The Cathedral Green, Llandaff, Cardiff CF5 2EB*

JONES, David Ian Stewart. b 34. Selw Coll Cam BA 57 MA 61. Westcott Ho Cam 57. **d** 59 **p** 60. C Oldham *Man* 59-63; V Elton All SS 63-66; Chapl Eton Coll 66-70; Sen Chapl 70-74; Hd Master Bryanston Sch 74-82; P-in-c Bris Ch Ch w St Ewen and All SS 82-84; P-in-c Bris St Steph w St Nic and St Leon 82-84; Soc Resp Adv 84-85; Dir Lambeth Endowed Charities 85-94; Hon PV S'wark Cathl 85-94; rtd 94; PtO *Ox* 08-12. *33 St Lucian's Lane, Wallingford OX10 9ER* T: (01491) 836052
E: davidandsuejones@aol.com

JONES, David Mark. b 73. St Mich Coll Llan 03. **d** 06 **p** 07. C Llansamlet *S & B* 06-08; Min Can Brecon Cathl 08-13; P-in-c Rhondda Fach Uchaf *Llan* from 13. *Ty Nant, Margaret Street, Pontygwaith, Ferndale CF43 3EH* T: (01443) 732321
E: revdmj@yahoo.co.uk

JONES, David Michael. b 48. Chich Th Coll 75. **d** 78 **p** 79. C Yeovil *B & W* 78-84; C Barwick 81-84; V Cleeve w Chelvey and Brockley 84-92; V Heigham St Barn w St Bart *Nor* 92-00; V Writtle w Highwood *Chelmsf* 00-14; rtd 14; PtO *Sarum* from 15. *5 Rope Yard Court, Rope Yard, Royal Wootton Bassett, Swindon SN4 7FD* E: revmjoneswrittle@aol.com

JONES, David Ormond. b 46. Llan Dioc Tr Scheme 90. **d** 94 **p** 95. NSM Resolven w Tonna *Llan* 94-01; C Skewen 01-07;

C Neath 07-11; rtd 12; PtO *Llan* from 12. *30 Henfaes Road, Tonna, Neath SA11 3EX* T: (01639) 770930
E: ormond.jones@ntlworld.com

JONES, David Raymond. b 34. Univ of Wales (Lamp) BA 54 St Cath Coll Ox BA 57 MA 61. Wycliffe Hall Ox 58. **d** 58 **p** 59. C Ex St Dav 58-60; C Bideford 60-63; Chapl Grenville Coll Bideford 63-66; Chapl RN 66-89; QHC 84-89; Dir and Warden Divine Healing Miss Crowhurst 89-97; rtd 97; PtO *Chich* from 97. *9 Perrots Lane, Steyning BN44 3NB* T: (01903) 815236

JONES, David Robert Deverell. b 50. Sarum & Wells Th Coll 72. **d** 75 **p** 78. C Altrincham St Geo *Ches* 75-76; C Clayton *Lich* 77-80; Carriacou 80-81; P-in-c Baschurch *Lich* 81-83; R Baschurch and Weston Lullingfield w Hordley 83-96; RD Ellesmere 85-95; P-in-c Criftins 94-96; P-in-c Dudleston 94-96; P-in-c Jersey St Luke w St Jas *Win* 96-99; V 99-15; R Jersey St Mary 02-07; rtd 15. *Address temp unknown*
M: 07797-757765

JONES, David Roy. b 47. Hull Univ BA 74 CQSW 76 Man Univ DipAdEd 76 Bradf Univ MA 85. NOC 77. **d** 80 **p** 81. C New Bury *Man* 80-83; NSM Ringley w Prestolee 92-97; NSM Belmont 97-01; TV Turton Moorland 01-12; rtd 12; PtO *Man* from 12. *2 Affleck Avenue, Radcliffe, Manchester M26 1HN*

JONES, David Sebastian. b 43. St Cath Coll Cam BA 64 MA 73. Linc Th Coll 66. **d** 68 **p** 69. C Baguley *Man* 68-71; C Bray and Braywood *Ox* 71-73; V S Ascot 73-07; AD Bracknell 96-04; Chapl Heatherwood Hosp E Berks 81-94; Chapl Heatherwood and Wexham Park Hosps NHS Trust 94-07; rtd 07. *Fairhaven, 1 St Clement's Terrace, Mousehole, Penzance TR19 6SJ* T: (01736) 732938 E: sebastianjones@talk21.com

JONES, David Victor. b 37. St Jo Coll Dur BA 59. Cranmer Hall Dur Bossey Ecum Inst Geneva 61. **d** 62 **p** 63. C Farnworth *Liv* 62-65; CF 65-68; Asst Master Hutton Gr Sch Preston 68-97; rtd 02. *10 Houghton Close, Penwortham, Preston PR1 9HT* T: (01772) 745306 E: d.v.jones@btinternet.com

JONES, David William. b 42. St Mark & St Jo Coll Lon CertEd 64 Open Univ BA 79. SEITE 97. **d** 00 **p** 01. NSM Coxheath, E Farleigh, Hunton, Linton etc *Roch* from 00; PtO *Cant* from 04; *Roch* from 13. *13 Woodlands, Coxheath, Maidstone ME17 4EE* T: (01622) 741474 E: david.jones@diocese-rochester.org

JONES, Denise Gloria. b 56. Cov Univ BA 93 Leeds Univ MA 06. WMMTC 95. **d** 98 **p** 99. C Hobs Moat *Birm* 98-02; C Olton and Chapl S Birm Mental Health NHS Trust 02-06; Chapl Manager Birm Women's NHS Foundn Trust 06-08; TV Bridgnorth, Tasley, Astley Abbotts, etc *Heref* 08-10; PtO *Birm* 10-11; Chapl Co-ord Birm Women's NHS Foundn Trust from 11; Hon C Yardley Wood *Birm* from 14. *Birmingham Women's NHS Foundn Trust, Mindelsohn Way, Birmingham B15 2TG* T: 0121-472 1377 *or* 472 4208 M: 07747-385006
E: revddee@aol.com

JONES, Miss Diana. b 46. Qu Coll Birm 89. **d** 91 **p** 94. Par Dn Harnham *Sarum* 91-94; C 94-95; C Tidworth, Ludgershall and Faberstown 95-00; P-in-c Hazelbury Bryan and the Hillside Par 00-06; rtd 06. *47 Gloucester Road, Trowbridge BA14 0AB* T: (01225) 755826

JONES, Canon Dick Heath Remi. b 32. Jes Coll Cam BA 56. Linc Th Coll 56. **d** 58 **p** 59. C Ipswich St Thos *St E* 58-61; C Putney St Mary *S'wark* 61-65; P-in-c Dawley Parva *Lich* 65-75; P-in-c Lawley 65-75; RD Wrockwardine 70-72; P-in-c Malins Lee 72-75; RD Telford 72-80; P-in-c Stirchley 74-75; TR Cen Telford 75-80; Preb Lich Cathl 76-80; TR Bournemouth St Pet w St Swithun, H Trin etc *Win* 80-96; RD Bournemouth 90-95; Hon Can Win Cathl 91-96; rtd 96; PtO *Sarum* from 96. *Maltings, Church Street, Fontmell Magna, Shaftesbury SP7 0NY* T: (01747) 812071 E: dick.jones@talk21.com

JONES, Dominic Jago Francis. b 78. St Jo Coll Nottm 09. **d** 11 **p** 12. C Ludgvan, Marazion, St Hilary and Perranuthnoe *Truro* 11-15; C Feock from 15; C Devoran from 15; C St Stythians w Perranarworthal and Gwennap from 15; C Chacewater w St Day and Carharrack from 15. *The Vicarage, 2 Jago Lane, Devoran, Truro TR3 6PA* M: 07904-500882 T: (01872) 863116

JONES, Donald. b 50. BA BSc. St Jo Coll Nottm 79. **d** 82 **p** 83. C Hutton *Chelmsf* 82-86; C E Ham w Upton Park and Forest Gate 86-88; TV 88-96; V Nuneaton St Nic *Cov* 96-14; P-in-c Weddington and Caldecote 09-14; RD Nuneaton 01-06; rtd 14; C Atherstone *Cov* 14-15. *65 Charnwood Avenue, Nuneaton CV10 7NY* T: (024) 7634 8837
E: don.jones4718@gmail.com

JONES, Douglas. *See* JONES, William Douglas

JONES, Edward. b 36. Dur Univ BA 60. Ely Th Coll 60. **d** 62 **p** 63. C S Shields St Hilda w St Thos *Dur* 62-65; C Cleadon Park 65-68; V Hebburn St Cuth 68-79; R Winlaton 79-00; rtd 00; PtO *Newc* from 01. *10 Melkridge Gardens, Benton, Newcastle upon Tyne NE7 7GQ* T: 0191-266 4388

JONES, Elaine. b 62. SNWTP. **d** 10 **p** 11. C Wavertree St Mary *Liv* 10-14; V Toxteth St Bede w St Clem from 14. *29 Moel Famau View, Liverpool L17 7ET* M: 07787-550622

JONES, Miss Elaine Edith. b 58. St Jo Coll Nottm BA 99. **d** 99 **p** 00. C Gainsborough and Morton *Linc* 99-02; C Netherton *Carl* 02-04; TV Maryport, Netherton and Flimby 04-05; Lay Tr Officer 02-05; V Binley *Cov* 05-14; V Peterlee *Dur* from 14. *St Cuthbert's Vicarage, Manor Way, Peterlee SR8 5QW* T: 0191-586 2630 E: reveej@tiscali.co.uk

JONES, Canon Elaine Joan. b 50. Oak Hill Th Coll. **d** 87 **p** 94. Par Dn Tottenham H Trin *Lon* 87-92; Par Dn Clay Hill St Jo and St Luke 92-94; C St Botolph Aldgate w H Trin Minories 94-96; V Hackney Wick St Mary of Eton w St Aug 96-04; AD Hackney 99-04; Can Res Derby Cathl 04-13; rtd 13; Hon Can Derby Cathl from 13; C Derby St Jo from 13. *The Vicarage, 2 Glebe Crescent, Stanley, Ilkeston DE7 6FL* T: 0115-930 2080 M: 07749-867347 E: canonelaine.stjohns@gmail.com

JONES, Elizabeth. **d** 14. NSM Bulkington *Cov* from 14; Chapl Univ Hosps Cov and Warks NHS Trust from 14. *Address temp unknown*

JONES, Mrs Elizabeth. b 52. St Mich Coll Llan 09. **d** 12 **p** 13. NSM Tredegar *Mon* from 12. *Allesley, Ashville, Tredegar NP22 4LN* T: (01495) 726251 E: ejones8@talktalk.net

JONES, Mrs Elizabeth Jane. b 57. Derby Univ BSc 00. St Jo Coll Nottm MTh 02. **d** 02 **p** 03. C Leek and Meerbrook *Lich* 02-05; C Harlescott and Chapl Shropshire Co Primary Care Trust 05-11; R Darlaston St Lawr *Lich* 11-14; TR Darlaston and Moxley from 14. *The Rectory, 1 Victoria Road, Darlaston, Wednesbury WS10 8AA* M: 07852-856533 T: 0121-526 2240 E: rector.stlawrence@gmail.com

JONES, Mrs Elizabeth Mary. b 48. QUB BA 69. NOC 88. **d** 91 **p** 94. Par Dn Kippax w Allerton Bywater *Ripon* 91-94; C 94-95; R Swillington 95-00; TV Wordsley *Worc* 00-02; rtd 02. *33 Pill Way, Clevedon BS21 7UW* T: (01275) 876297

JONES, Mrs Elizabeth Somerset. b 49. St Jo Coll Nottm. **d** 88 **p** 94. NSM Duns *Edin* 88-99; NSM Selkirk 89-90; Dioc Dir of Ords 95-05; NSM Dalkeith from 02; NSM Lasswade from 02. *255 Carnethie Street, Rosewell EH24 9DR* T: 0131-653 6767 F: 653 3646 E: esomersetjones@btinternet.com

JONES, Ernest Edward Stephen. b 39. Lon Univ BD 76. St D Coll Lamp. **d** 66 **p** 67. C N Meols *Liv* 66-69; C Kirkby 69-71; V Farnworth All SS *Man* 71-75; P-in-c Bempton *York* 75-78; R Rufford *Blackb* 78-84; V Cropredy w Gt Bourton and Wardington *Ox* 84-90; R York St Clem w St Mary Bishophill Senior 90-98; P-in-c York All SS N Street 90-98; V Northampton St Benedict *Pet* 98-05; rtd 05; P-in-c Wootton w Glympton and Kiddington *Ox* from 05; AD Woodstock 09-12. *The Rectory, 22 Castle Road, Wootton, Woodstock OX20 1EG* T: (01993) 812543 E: three.churches@virgin.net

JONES, Evan Hopkins. b 38. St Mich Coll Llan 65. **d** 67 **p** 68. C Churston Ferrers w Goodrington *Ex* 67-70; C Tavistock and Gulworthy 70-73; R Ashprington and V Cornworthy 73-78; R S Hackney St Jo w Ch Ch *Lon* 78-92; AD Hackney 84-89; V Islington St Jas w St Pet 92-08; rtd 08; PtO *Lon* from 08. *5 St James's Close, Bishop Street, London N1 8PH* T: (020) 7226 0104 E: fr.evan@virgin.net

JONES, Evan Trefor. b 32. Univ of Wales (Ban) BA 54. Coll of Resurr Mirfield 54. **d** 56 **p** 57. C Ban St Mary 56-62; V Llandinorwig 62-71; TV Llanbeblig w Caernarfon and Betws Garmon etc 71-84; Ed dioc magazine *The Link* 79-89; R Llanfairfechan w Aber *Ban* 84-97; Can Ban Cathl 95-97; rtd 97. *19 Marlborough Place, Vaughan Street, Llandudno LL30 1AE* T: (01492) 878411

JONES, Frederick Morgan. b 19. Univ of Wales (Lamp) BA 40 BD 49. St Mich Coll Llan 42. **d** 42 **p** 43. C Llanelli St Paul *St D* 42-50; Org Sec (Wales) Ind Chr Fellowship 50-53; C-in-c Llwynhendy CD *St D* 52-56; C Llanelli 56-57; V Penrhyncoch and Elerch 57-61; R Llanbedrog and Penrhos *Ban* 61-74; R Llanbedrog w Llannor w Llanfihangel etc 74-84; C Llangefni w Tregaean and Llangristiolus etc 84-85; rtd 85; PtO Ban from 85. *15 Ponc-y-Fron, Llangefni LL77 7NY* T: (01248) 722850

JONES, Gareth. b 35. St Aid Birkenhead 58. **d** 61 **p** 62. C Doncaster Ch Ch *Sheff* 61-65; Min Can Ripon Cathl 65-68; Chapl RAF 68-85; St Jo Cathl Hong Kong 85-89; R Spofforth w Kirk Deighton *Ripon* 89-00; rtd 00; PtO *Leeds* from 00. *36 Whitcliffe Lane, Ripon HG4 2JL* T: (01765) 601745 E: garjones1549@yahoo.co.uk

JONES, Gareth Edward John Paul. b 79. Leeds Univ BA 06 Lon Univ MA 14 FRSA 15. Coll of Resurr Mirfield 03. **d** 06 **p** 07. C Brighton St Mich *Chich* 06-10; P-in-c Gt Ilford St Mary *Chelmsf* 10-14; V from 14. *St Mary's Vicarage, 26 South Park Road, Ilford IG1 1SS* T: (020) 8478 0546 E: parishpriest@stmarysilford.org.uk

JONES, Gareth Lewis. b 42. K Coll Lon BD 64 AKC 64. **d** 65 **p** 66. C Risca *Mon* 65-70; PtO *Win* 70-74; Newc 74-75; *Sarum* 75; C Pontesbury I and II *Heref* 75-77; P-in-c Presteigne w Discoed 77-79; TV Hemel Hempstead *St Alb* 79-86; R Longden and Annscroft w Pulverbatch *Heref* 86-93; TV Leominster 93-07; rtd 07; PtO *Heref* from 08. *33 Danesfield Drive, Leominster HR6 8HP* T: (01568) 620453

JONES, Prof Gareth Lloyd. b 38. Univ of Wales BA 61 Selw Coll Cam BA 63 MA 67 Yale Univ STM 69 TCD BD 70 Lon Univ PhD 75. Episc Sem Austin Texas Hon DD 90 Westcott Ho Cam 62. **d** 65 **p** 66. C Holyhead w Rhoscolyn *Ban* 65-68; USA 68-70; P-in-c Merton *Ox* 70-72; Tutor Ripon Hall Ox 72; Sen Tutor 73-75; Lect Ex Coll Ox 73-77; Tutor and Lib Ripon Coll Cuddesdon 75-77; Lect Th Univ of Wales (Ban) 77-89; Sen Lect 89-95; Reader and Hd of Sch from 95; Prof from 98; Sub-Dean Faculty of Th 80-89; Dean 89-92; Chan Ban Cathl 90-09; Select Preacher Ox Univ 89. *22 Bron-y-Felin, Llandegfan, Menai Bridge LL59 5UY* T: (01248) 712786

JONES, Glyn. b 71. **d** 12 **p** 13. NSM Ches Ch Ch from 12. *2 Hall Lane, Shotwick, Chester CH1 6JB*

JONES, Glyn Evan. b 44. Lon Coll of Div ALCD 67 LTh. **d** 67 **p** 68. C Gt Horton *Bradf* 67-70; SAMS Argentina 71-78; V Idle *Bradf* 78-84; V Hyson Green *S'well* 84-87; V Nottingham St Steph 84-87; V Hyson Green St Paul w St Steph 87-89; V Hyson Green 89-91; V Basford w Hyson Green 91-92; V Worksop St Jo 92-99; RD Worksop 93-99; V Nottingham St Sav 99-08; rtd 08. *65 Conifer Crescent, Nottingham NG11 9EP* T: 0115-846 9947 M: 07885-816697 E: chezjones@ntlworld.com

JONES, Canon Glyndwr. b 35. St Mich Coll Llan. **d** 62 **p** 63. C Clydach *S & B* 62-64; C Llangyfelach 64-67; C Sketty 67-70; V Bryngwyn and Newchurch and Llanbedr etc 70-72; Miss to Seafarers 72-00; Swansea 72-76; Port of Lon 76-81; Aux Min Sec 81-85; Asst Gen Sec 85-90; Sec Gen 90-00; V St Mich Paternoster Royal *Lon* 91-00; rtd 01; Hon Can Kobe Japan from 88; Chapl to The Queen 90-05; PtO *Chelmsf* from 91. *5 The Close, Grays RM16 2XU* T: (01375) 375053 E: glynita.tomdavey@blueyonder.co.uk

JONES, Glynn. b 56. Ches Univ MA 14. NEOC 91. **d** 94 **p** 95. NSM Glendale Gp *Newc* 94-97; Sen Chapl HM Pris Leeds 97-99; Chapl HM Pris Dur 99-00; Chapl HM YOI Wetherby 00-05; Chapl HM Pris Wymott 06-07; Co-ord Chapl HM Pris Haverigg from 07. *HM Prison, North Lane, Haverigg, Millom LA18 4NA* T: (01229) 713025 E: glynn.jones@hmps.gsi.gov.uk

JONES, Godfrey Caine. b 36. Dur Univ BA 59 Lon Univ CertEd 60 Birm Univ MEd 71. St Deiniol's Hawarden 76. **d** 78 **p** 79. Hd Humanities Denbigh High Sch 75-81; NSM Ruthin w Llanrhydd *St As* 78-81; C 83-84; Sen Lect Matlock Coll 81-85; P-in-c Llanfwrog and Clocaenog and Gyffylliog *St As* 84-85; R 85-93; V Ruabon 93-02; RD Llangollen 93-02; rtd 02; Min Pradoe *Lich* 02-08; PtO from 08; *St As* from 09. *Idoma, Penylan, Ruabon, Wrexham LL14 6HP* T: (01978) 812102 E: dorothy.e.jones@btopenworld.com

JONES, Graham Frederick. b 37. Leeds Univ BA 60 GradIPM 63. ALCD 66. **d** 66 **p** 67. C Chesterfield H Trin *Derby* 66-70; C Leeds St Geo *Ripon* 70-73; P-in-c Newcastle St Geo *Lich* 73-83; New Zealand 83-87; P-in-c Westcote w Icomb and Bledington *Glouc* 89-94; rtd 94. *7 Keynsham Bank, Cheltenham GL52 6ER* T: (01242) 238680

JONES, Griffith Trevor. b 56. BSc MPS Univ of Wales BD. **d** 87 **p** 88. C Llandrygarn w Bodwrog and Heneglwys etc *Ban* 87-89; R Llangefni w Tregaean and Llangristiolus etc 89-91; TV Bangor 91-94; Chapl Ysbyty Gwynedd 91-94; Hon C Bro Tysilio from 14. *8 Carreg-y-Gad Estate, Ffordd Penmynydd, Llanfairpwllgwyngyll LL61 5QF* T: (01248) 713094 E: gjones2747@aol.com

JONES, Canon Griffith William. b 31. St D Coll Lamp BA 53 LTh 55. **d** 55 **p** 56. C Llanycil w Bala and Frongoch *St As* 55-58; V Llandrillo 58-66; V Llandrillo and Llandderfel 66-96; RD Penllyn 83-96; Can Cursal St As Cathl from 87; rtd 96. *45 Yr Hafan, Bala LL23 7AU* T: (01678) 520217

JONES, Gwynfryn Lloyd. b 35. Univ of Wales (Lamp) BA 59. St Mich Coll Llan 59. **d** 61 **p** 62. C Rhyl w St Ann *St As* 61-64; C Prestatyn 64-67; V Whitford 67-75; V Llay 75-83; V Northop 83-98; rtd 98. *Tryfan, 41 Snowdon Avenue, Bryn-y-Baal, Mold CH7 6SZ* T: (01352) 751036

JONES, Gwynn Rees. b 32. St D Coll Lamp BA 55. **d** 57 **p** 58. C Llangystennin *St As* 57-59; C Llanrhos 59-64; R Cefn 64-68; R Llanfyllin 68-80; V Bistre 80-89; R Flint 89-97; rtd 97; PtO *St As* 09-13. *3 Lon Derw, Abergele LL22 7EA* T: (01745) 825188

JONES, Harold Philip. b 49. Leeds Univ BA 72 St Jo Coll Dur BA 84. Cranmer Hall Dur 82. **d** 85 **p** 86. C Scartho *Linc* 85-88; V Dodworth *Wakef* 88-91; C Penistone and Thurlstone 91-95; C Scunthorpe All SS *Linc* 95-96; TV Brumby 96-02; Chapl Derby Hosps NHS Foundn Trust 02-14; rtd 14. *53 Beech Avenue, Alvaston, Derby DE24 0EA*

JONES, Haydn Llewellyn. b 42. Edin Th Coll 63. **d** 65 **p** 66. C Towcester w Easton Neston *Pet* 65-68; C Northampton St Matt 68-72; CF 72-97; PtO *Roch* 97-98; *Ex* from 99; rtd 99. *11 Lady Park Road, Livermead, Torquay TQ2 6UA* T: (01803) 690483

JONES (*née* JAMES), **Ms Helen** Alison. b 59. St Andr Univ BSc 81. EMMTC 93. **d** 96 **p** 97. C Brocklesby Park *Linc* 96-98; PtO 06-08; C Bassingham Gp 08-10; R Dundee St Jo *Bre* 10-14; R Dundee St Marg 10-14; R Dundee St Martin 10-14; NSM Alexandria and Dumbarton *Glas* 14-15. *Address temp unknown* M: 07814-789817 E: halisonjones@gmail.com

JONES, Hester. See JONES, Susannah Hester Everett

JONES, Hilary Christine. b 55. Ch Ch Coll Cant CertEd 76 Lon Univ BEd 77. SEITE. **d** 99 **p** 00. C Kennington *Cant* 99-02; R Cheriton St Martin 02-11; P-in-c Cheriton All So w Newington 06-11; Bp's Adv for Women's Min 04-11; AD Elham 08-11; Asst Chapl Basle *Eur* 11-15; Chapl from 15. *Stadtweg 38, 4310 Rheinfelden, Switzerland* E: hilarycjones@lycos.co.uk

JONES, Howard. See JONES, John Howard

JONES, Hugh Vaughan. b 44. **d** 07 **p** 08. C Holyhead *Ban* 07-09; P-in-c Bodedern w Llanfaethlu 09-11; P-in-c Amlwch 11-15; rtd 15. *The Old Police Station, Machine Street, Amlwch LL68 9HA* T: (01407) 832941 M: 07795-578932 E: hughvaughan.santelbod@btinternet.com

JONES, Hugh William Fawcett. b 68. Ripon Coll Cuddesdon. **d** 10 **p** 11. C Boston *Linc* 10-14; V Linc St Nic w St Jo Newport from 14. *The Vicarage, 59 Yarborough Crescent, Lincoln LN1 3NE* E: hugh.wf.jones@talk21.com

JONES, Hughie. See JONES, Thomas Hughie

JONES, Huw. See JONES, David Huw

JONES, Ian. b 63. Trin Coll Carmarthen BEd 88. St Mich Coll Llan 95. **d** 97 **p** 98. NSM Tycoch *S & B* 97-01; NSM Swansea St Nic 01-04; Chapl Wymondham Coll from 04. *Staff House 8, Wymondham College, Golf Links Road, Wymondham NR18 9SX* T: (01953) 607120 E: ianjones99@yahoo.com

JONES, Ian Andrew. b 65. Lanc Univ BA 87. St Mich Coll Llan. **d** 90 **p** 91. C Caerphilly *Llan* 90-96; Chapl RAF from 96. *Chaplaincy Services (RAF), HQ Air Command, RAF High Wycombe HP14 4UE* T: (01494) 496800 F: 496343

JONES, Ian Robert. b 69. Sheff Univ BA 92. Trin Coll Bris 11. **d** 13 **p** 14. C Burscough Bridge *Liv* from 13. *3 Thistle Court, Burscough, Ormskirk L40 4AW* T: (01704) 897913 M: 07546-414283 E: revianjones@gmail.com

JONES, Idris. b 31. **d** 88 **p** 94. NSM Llanfihangel Ysgeifiog and Llanffinan etc *Ban* 88-97; NSM Llangefni w Tregaean and Llangristiolus etc 98-01; NSM Llanfihangel Ysgeifiog w Llangristiolus etc 01-02; PtO from 10. *8 Swn yr Engan, Gaerwen LL60 6LS* T: (01248) 421797

✠**JONES, The Rt Revd Idris.** b 43. St D Coll Lamp BA 64 NY Th Sem DMin 86. Edin Th Coll 64. **d** 67 **p** 68 **c** 98. C Stafford St Mary *Lich* 67-70; Prec St Paul's Cathl Dundee 70-73; P-in-c Gosforth All SS *Newc* 73-80; R Montrose and Inverbervie *Bre* 80-89; Can St Paul's Cathl Dundee 84-92; Chapl Angl Students Dundee Univ 89-92; P-in-c Invergowrie 89-92; TR S Ayrshire TM 92-98; Bp Glas 98-09; Primus 06-09; rtd 09; Hon Fell Univ of Wales (Trin St Dav) from 07; LtO *Glas* from 10. *27 Donald Wynd, Largs KA30 8TH* T: (01475) 674919 E: idrisjones43@hotmail.co.uk

JONES, Ivor Wyn. b 56. Trin Coll Bris 92. **d** 94 **p** 95. C Gabalfa *Llan* 94-97; TV Daventry, Ashby St Ledgers, Braunston etc *Pet* 97-01; P-in-c Dawley St Jerome *Lon* 01-08; C-in-c Harlington Ch Ch CD 03-08; V W Hayes from 08. *St Jerome's Lodge, 42 Corwell Lane, Uxbridge UB8 3DE* T: (020) 8561 7393 *or* 8573 1895 E: wynjones@blueyonder.co.uk

JONES, Jacqueline Primrose. b 47. **d** 09 **p** 10. NSM Chipping Norton *Ox* 09-12; Chapl Ox Univ Hosps NHS Trust 12-13; C Chipping Norton *Ox* from 13; Chapl Kath Ho Hospice from 13. *Old Appleyard, 18 Kingham Road, Churchill, Chipping Norton OX7 6NE* T: (01608) 658616 E: jackie.clark-jones@virgin.net

JONES, James Richard. b 65. SS Hild & Bede Coll Dur BA 87 Open Univ MBA 95. Wycliffe Hall Ox 02. **d** 04 **p** 05. C Ashtead *Guildf* 04-08; P-in-c Burscough Bridge *Liv* 08-15; V 15; R Ashtead *Guildf* from 15. *Ashdene, Dene Road, Ashtead KT21 1EE* T: (01372) 805182 E: jrj37@aol.com *or* richard.jones@ashteadparish.org

✠**JONES, The Rt Revd James Stuart.** b 48. Ex Univ BA 70 PGCE 71 Hull Univ Hon DD 99 Lincs & Humberside Univ Hon DLitt 01. Wycliffe Hall Ox 81. **d** 82 **p** 83 **c** 94. C Clifton Ch Ch w Em *Bris* 82-90; V S Croydon Em *S'wark* 90-94; Suff Bp Hull *York* 94-98; Bp Liv 98-13; Bp HM *Pris* 07-13; rtd 13; Asst Bp York from 14. *Mount Pleasant Cottage, Burythorpe, Malton YO17 9LJ* T: (01653) 658325 E: bishopjamesjones@btinternet.com

JONES, Canon Jacqueline Dorian. b 58. K Coll Lon BD 80 AKC 80 MTh 81. Westcott Ho Cam 84. **dss** 86 **d** 87 **p** 94. Epsom St Martin *Guildf* 86-91; C 87-91; Chapl Chelmsf Cathl 91-97; V Brademary *Portsm* 97-03; Can Res S'well Minster from 03. *2 Vicars Court, Southwell NG25 0HP* T: (01636) 813188 *or* 817282 E: jacquijones@southwellminster.org.uk

JONES, Jeffrey Lloyd. b 66. Univ of Wales (Abth) BD 87 PGCE 90. Wycliffe Hall Ox 95. **d** 97 **p** 98. C Lampeter Pont Steffan w Silian *St D* 97; C Carmarthen St Dav 97-00; TV Llantwit Major *Llan* 00-08; V Llanddeiniolen w Llanfair-is-gaer etc *Ban* 08-13; AD Arfon 09-12; V Uwch Gwyrfai Beuno Sant from 13. *Y Ficerdy, Clynnogfawr, Caernarfon LL54 5PE* T: (01286) 660656

JONES, Jennifer Margaret. b 49. Lon Univ CertEd. Cranmer Hall Dur 87. **d** 89 **p** 94. C Musselburgh *Edin* 89-93; Dn-in-c 93-94; P-in-c 94-95; R 95-02; C Prestonpans 89-93; Dn-in-c 93-94; P-in-c 94-95; R 95-02; LtO *Mor* from 02; NSM Rothiemurchus from 07. *Meadowbank, Main Street, Newtonmore PH20 1DD* T: (01540) 673532 E: jennifer.jones32@btinternet.com

JONES, Jennifer Margaret. b 47. **d** 13 **p** 14. OLM Sunninghill and S Ascot *Ox* from 13. *Two Chimneys, North Street, Winkfield, Windsor SL4 4TE*

JONES, Mrs Joanne. b 64. Warwick Univ BA 88. St Mellitus Coll BA 10. **d** 10 **p** 11. C Maldon All SS w St Pet *Chelmsf* 10-14; P-in-c Writtle w Highwood from 14; P-in-c Roxwell from 15. *The Vicarage, 19 Lodge Road, Writtle, Chelmsford CM1 3HY* T: (01245) 421282 E: revdjojones@gmail.com *or* jojones44@btinternet.com

JONES, John Bernard. b 49. Qu Coll Birm 86. **d** 88 **p** 89. C Mold *St As* 88-91; P-in-c Treuddyn and Nercwys and Eryrys 91-92; V Treuddyn w Nercwys 92-14; RD Mold 95-00; rtd 14. *The Vicarage, Ffordd y Llan, Treuddyn, Mold CH7 4LN* T: (01352) 770919 E: revjbj@hotmail.com

JONES, John Brian. St Mich Coll Llan. **d** 05 **p** 06. NSM Gors-las *St D* from 05. *Penpentre, 79 Carmarthen Road, Cross Hands, Lanelli SA14 6SU* T: (01269) 842236 E: brianandjanet1@hotmail.co.uk

JONES, John David Emrys. b 36. Trin Coll Carmarthen. **d** 96 **p** 97. NSM Llanfihangel Ystrad and Cilcennin w Trefilan etc *St D* 96-97; P-in-c Llangeitho and Blaenpennal w Betws Leucu etc 97-06; PtO from 06. *Dolfor, Ciliau Aeron, Lampeter SA48 8DE* T: (01570) 470569

JONES, John Hellyer. b 20. Birm Univ LDS 43. Westcott Ho Cam 65. **d** 67 **p** 68. C Haddenham *Ely* 67-70; P-in-c Lolworth 70-79 and 81-85; P-in-c Conington 75-76; P-in-c Fen Drayton w Conington 76-85; R Houghton w Wyton 79; rtd 85; PtO *Ely* 85-02. *13 High Street, Haddenham, Ely CB6 3XA* T: (01353) 740530 E: jonhadnam@ntlworld.com

JONES, John Howard. b 48. New Coll Ox BA 69 MA 73 K Coll Cam CertEd 70. Sarum & Wells Th Coll 76. **d** 77 **p** 78. C Salisbury St Mark *Sarum* 77-78; C Morriston *S & B* 78-80; Dir of Ords 80-83; V Gowerton 80-83; V Swansea St Jas 85-89; Chapl Alleyn's Sch Dulwich 89-08; Hon C Dulwich St Barn *S'wark* 90-08; rtd 08. *112 New Dock Road, Llanelli SA15 2HE*

JONES, Canon Joyce Rosemary. b 54. Newnham Coll Cam BA 76 MA 82 Coll of Ripon & York St Jo MA 97 Solicitor 79. NOC 94. **d** 97 **p** 98. C Pontefract All SS *Wakef* 97-00; NSM Cumberworth, Denby and Denby Dale 00-01; Dioc Voc Adv 00-01; Asst Chapl Kirkwood Hospice Huddersfield 00-01; P-in-c Shelley and Shepley *Leeds* from 01; AD Kirkburton *Leeds* from 11; Hon Can Wakef Cathl from 10. *Oakfield, 206 Barnsley Road, Denby Dale, Huddersfield HD8 8TS* T/F: (01484) 862350 E: joycerjones@aol.com

JONES, Julie Ann. b 59. STETS. **d** 10 **p** 11. NSM W Meon and Warnford *Portsm* 10-11; NSM Portchester 11-14; NSM Purbrook from 14. *Orchard View, Hill Pound, Swanmore, Southampton SO32 2UN* T: (01489) 891402 M: 07800-553920 E: jones59ja@btinternet.com

JONES, Mrs Julie Denise. b 63. CBDTI 03. **d** 06 **p** 07. C Darwen St Pet w Hoddlesden *Blackb* 06-09; P-in-c Wesham and Treales 09-11; V from 11. *The Vicarage, Mowbreck Lane, Wesham, Preston PR4 3HA* T: (01772) 682206 M: 07814-500855 E: jones@julie794.orangehome.co.uk

JONES, Karen Elizabeth. b 64. Univ of Ulster BA 87. Wycliffe Hall Ox 04. **d** 06 **p** 07. C Northolt Park St Barn *Lon* 06-07; NSM Longwell Green *Bris* 08-10; Chapl UWE 10-11; C Stoke Gifford from 10. *119 North Road, Stoke Gifford, Bristol BS34 8PE* T: 0117-979 1656 M: 07876-752745 E: karen@stmichaelsbristol.org

JONES, Karen Sheila Frances. See ROOMS, Karen Sheila Frances

JONES, Kathryn Mary. See BUCK, Kathryn Mary

JONES (*née* SANDELLS-REES), **Ms Kathy Louise.** b 68. Univ of Wales (Ban) BTh 96 Leeds Univ MA 13 Northumbria Univ PGCE 11. Qu Coll Birm 90. **d** 92 **p** 97. C Holyhead w Rhoscolyn w Llanfair-yn-Neubwll *Ban* 92-94; C Bangor 94-95; Chapl Gwynedd Hosp Ban 94-99; P-in-c Bangor *Ban* 95-99; V Betws-y-Coed w Capel Curig w Penmachno etc 99-06; Chapl Newcastle upon Tyne Hosps NHS Foundn Trust 06-12; Chapl Team Ldr Northumbria Healthcare NHS Foundn

Trust from 12. *North Tyneside General Hospital, Rake Lane, North Shields NE29 8NH* T: 08448-118111
E: kathy.jones@northumbria.nhs.uk

JONES, Mrs Katie Ann. b 37. **d** 99 **p** 00. NSM Sutton Courtenay w Appleford *Ox* 99-04; PtO *Cant* 04-11; *Ox* from 12. *St Edward's School, Woodstock Road, Oxford OX2 7NN*

JONES, Kay Sandra. b 61. **d** 12 **p** 13. OLM New Clee *Linc* from 12. *197 Sanctuary Way, Grimsby DN37 9RY* T: (01472) 884434

JONES, The Very Revd Keith Brynmor. b 44. Selw Coll Cam BA 65 MA 69. Cuddesdon Coll 67. **d** 69 **p** 70. C Limpsfield and Titsey *S'wark* 69-72; Dean's V St Alb Abbey *St Alb* 72-76; P-in-c Boreham Wood St Mich 76-79; TV Borehamwood 79-82; V Ipswich St Mary-le-Tower *St E* 82-96; RD Ipswich 92-96; Hon Can St E Cathl 93-96; Dean Ex 96-04; Dean York 04-12; rtd 12; PtO *St E* from 13. *7 Broughton Road, Ipswich IP1 3QR* T: (01473) 413436 E: keithbjones@gmail.com

JONES, Keith Ellison. b 47. Wycliffe Hall Ox 72. **d** 75 **p** 76. C Everton St Chrys *Liv* 75-79; C Buckhurst Hill *Chelmsf* 79-81; TV 81-88; TR Leek and Meerbrook *Lich* 88-99; V Formby H Trin *Liv* 99-11; AD Sefton 05-08; Hon Can Liv Cathl 05-08; rtd 11; PtO *Lich* from 13. *77 Woodhouse Lane, Biddulph, Stoke-on-Trent ST8 7EN*

JONES, Kingsley Charles. b 45. Birm Univ BSc 66 Open Univ BA 75. Sarum Th Coll 66. **d** 69 **p** 70. C Penwortham St Mary *Blackb* 69-72; C Broughton 72-74; P-in-c Gt Wollaston *Heref* 74-77; Chapl RAF 77-83; V Colwich w Gt Haywood *Lich* 83-94; V Winshill *Derby* 94-01; P-in-c Glouc St Aldate 01-11; rtd 11. *Orchard House, Sandhurst Road, Gloucester GL1 2SE* T: (01452) 690406 E: arkj.kcj@care4free.net

JONES, Lesley Anne. b 46. Luton Coll of HE CertEd 77. SAOMC 01. **d** 04 **p** 06. NSM Gravenhurst, Shillington and Stondon *St Alb* 04-06; NSM Leagrave from 06; NSM Officer Bedford Adnry from 14. *91 Manton Drive, Luton LU2 7DL* T: (01582) 616888 E: lesleyjones31647@aol.com

JONES, Mrs Lesley Marie. b 66. **d** 12 **p** 13. NSM N Wearside *Dur* 12-13; C Milton next Sittingbourne *Cant* from 13; C Murston w Bapchild and Tonge from 13. *The Rectory, School Lane, Bapchild, Sittingbourne ME9 9NL* M: 07881-555580 E: revlesleyjones@gmail.com

JONES, Leslie Joseph. b 23. Linc Th Coll. **d** 57 **p** 58. C Penhill *Bris* 57-60; C-in-c Lockleaze St Mary CD 60-62; V Bris Lockleaze St Mary Magd w St Fran 62-74; V Bedminster St Aldhelm 69-75; TV Bedminster 75-80; V Abbots Leigh w Leigh Woods 80-88; rtd 88; PtO *Bris* from 88. *4 Summerleaze, Bristol BS16 4ER* T: 0117-965 3597

JONES, Lloyd. *See* JONES, Jeffrey Lloyd

JONES, Lloyd. *See* JONES, Gareth Lloyd

JONES, Miss Mair. b 41. Cartrefle Coll of Educn TCert 61. St Mich Coll Llan 91. **d** 93 **p** 97. C Llangollen w Trevor and Llantysilio *St As* 93-97; V Llandrillo and Llandderfel 97-00; R Llanelian w Betws-yn-Rhos w Trofarth 00-03; R Llanelian 03-08; P-in-c Brynymaen 04-08; rtd 08; PtO *St As* from 09. *5 Ffordd Daguil, Colwyn Bay LL29 8TN* T: (01492) 517866 E: mair@jones6527.fsnet.co.uk

JONES, Malcolm. *See* JONES, Philip Malcolm

JONES, Canon Malcolm Francis. b 44. Open Univ BA 88 Hull Univ MA 96 Univ of Wales (Cardiff) LLM 05 FInstLM 10. Chich Th Coll 67. **d** 70 **p** 71. C Prestbury *Ches* 70-73; Chapl RAF 73-91; R Heaton Reddish *Man* 81-84; CF (ACF) 82-84 and from 98; CF (TA) 83-84; CF 84-93; CF (R of O) 93-99; TV Cleethorpes *Linc* 93-97; V Ryde H Trin *Portsm* 97-10; V Swanmore St Mich 97-10; rtd 10; P-in-c Win H Trin 10-11; R from 11; Hon Can Win Cathl from 14. *Holy Trinity Rectory, 60 Upper Brook Street, Winchester SO23 8DG* T: (01962) 869707 M: 07710-543155 E: frmalcolmjones@virginmedia.com

JONES, Malcolm Stuart. b 41. Sheff Univ BA 62. Linc Th Coll 64. **d** 66 **p** 67. C Monkseaton St Mary *Newc* 66-69; C Ponteland 69-72; Chapl Lake Maracaibo Venezuela 73-75; C Hexham *Newc* 75-77; P-in-c Killingworth 77-92; V Delaval 92-01; TV Ch the King 01-07; rtd 07. *13 Valeside, Newcastle upon Tyne NE15 9LA*

JONES, Ms Margaret. b 28. TCD BA 53 Man Univ PGCE 54 Lon Univ BD 66. **d** 87 **p** 94. NSM Stanstead Abbots *St Alb* 87-88; NSM Grappenhall *Ches* 88-98; rtd 98; PtO *Ches* from 98. *19 Hill Top Road, Grappenhall, Warrington WA4 2ED* T: (01925) 261992

JONES, Mrs Margaret Angela. b 53. Wolv Univ CertEd 91 Univ of Wales (Lamp) MA 04. Qu Coll Birm BA 99. **d** 99 **p** 00. C Pershore w Pinvin, Wick and Birlingham *Worc* 99-03; TV Solihull *Birm* 03-11; P-in-c Pon+esbury I and II *Heref* from 11; RD Pontesbury from 13. *The Deanery, Main Road, Pontesbury, Shrewsbury SY5 0PS* T: (01743) 792221
E: magz.stgeorges@talktalk.net

JONES, Mrs Margaret Anne. b 47. Lon Univ TCert 68 Ches Coll of HE BTh 04. NOC 01. **d** 04 **p** 05. NSM Altrincham St Geo *Ches* 04-07; C 07-12; C Altrincham St Jo 07-12; P-in-c

Whaley Bridge from 12; Chapl Trin C of E High Sch Man 05-07. *46 Buxton Road, Whaley Bridge, High Peak SK23 7JE* M: 07748-645596 E: margaret_jones@talk21.com

JONES, Margaret Mary. b 47. Oak Hill Th Coll 92. **d** 95 **p** 96. C Sydenham H Trin *S'wark* 95-98; V Anerley St Paul *Roch* 98-09; TV Anerley 09-11; rtd 11; PtO *S'wark* from 12. *10 Lower Road, Redhill RH1 6NN* T: (01737) 247998

JONES, Mark. *See* JONES, Christopher Mark

JONES, Mark. b 70. Warwick Univ BSc 92 Univ of Wales PGCE 93. Ripon Coll Cuddesdon 06. **d** 08 **p** 09. C Old Basing and Lychpit *Win* 08-12; R Bratton, Edington and Imber, Erlestoke etc *Sarum* from 12. *The Vicarage, Upper Garston Lane, Bratton, Westbury BA13 4SN* T: (01380) 830374
E: revmarkjones@sky.com

JONES, Mark Andrew. b 60. Southn Univ BSc 82 Sussex Univ PGCE 83. Oak Hill Th Coll BA 91. **d** 91 **p** 92. C Wolverhampton St Luke *Lich* 91-96; I Inishmacsaint *Clogh* 96-01; V Padiham w Hapton and Padiham Green *Blackb* from 01; AD Burnley from 10. *The Vicarage, 1 Arbory Drive, Padiham, Burnley BB12 8JS* T: (01282) 772442
E: jones.padiham@btinternet.com

JONES, Mark Vincent. b 60. St Mich Coll Llan 81. **d** 84 **p** 85. C Whitchurch *Llan* 84-89; V Pwllgwaun w Llanddewi Rhondda 89-90; CF from 90. *c/o MOD Chaplains (Army)* F: 381824 T: (01264) 383430

JONES, Martin. b 58. Leeds Univ BA 07. NOC 04. **d** 07 **p** 08. NSM Winwick *Liv* 07-13; Chapl St Helens and Knowsley Hosps NHS Trust 09-13; NSM Aisholt, Enmore, Goathurst, Nether Stowey etc *B & W* from 13. *The Rectory, Church Road, Spaxton, Bridgwater TA5 1DA* E: martinjones9558@aol.com

JONES, Martin David. b 50. Liv Univ MB, ChB 73. **d** 13 **p** 14. OLM Codnor *Derby* from 13; OLM Horsley and Denby from 13; OLM Horsley Woodhouse from 13; OLM Loscoe from 13. *Meadow Rise, Smalley Mill Road, Horsley, Derby DE21 5BL* T: (01332) 882929 M: 07788-641946
E: martinjones2812@gmail.com

JONES, Martin Patrick. b 62. K Coll Lon BDS 85. Dioc OLM tr scheme 02. **d** 05 **p** 06. NSM Kingsnorth and Shadoxhurst *Cant* 05-09; PtO 09-11; NSM Aldington w Bonnington and Bilsington etc 11-13; C Saxon Shoreline from 13. *The Rectory, Roman Road, Aldington, Ashford TN25 7EF* T: (01233) 721986
E: martin.jones62@icloud.com

JONES, Mary Catherine Theresa Bridget. b 41. Westhill Coll Birm CertEd 77 Birm Univ BA 80 MA 09. Qu Coll Birm 04. **d** 05 **p** 06. NSM Bromsgrove St Jo *Worc* 05-08; PtO from 08. *Fairways, 197A St Bernard's Road, Solihull B92 7DL* T: 0121-706 4099 E: theresa-j@sky.com

JONES, Canon Mary Nerissa Anna. b 41. MBE 02. Qu Mary Coll Lon BA 86 FRSA 91. Ripon Coll Cuddesdon 86. **d** 88 **p** 94. Par Dn St Botolph Aldgate w H Trin Minories *Lon* 88-93; P-in-c Wood End *Cov* 93-95; V 95-01; Hon Can Cov Cathl 01; rtd 01; P-in-c Askerswell, Loders and Powerstock *Sarum* 01-10; P-in-c Symondsbury 07-10. *Church Farm Cottage, West Milton, Bridport DT6 3SL* T: (01308) 485304
E: nerissa@nerissajones.plus.com

JONES, Canon Mary Valerie. b 37. Univ of Wales (Ban) BD 84. St Deiniol's Hawarden 84. **d** 85 **p** 97. C Holyhead w Rhoscolyn w Llanfair-yn-Neubwll *Ban* 85-87; C Ynyscyn-haearn w Penmorfa and Porthmadog 87-90; Dn-in-c Llansantffraid Glyn Ceirog and Llanarmon etc *St As* 90-97; V 97-98; R Overton and Erbistock and Penley 98-04; RD Bangor Isycoed 98-04; Can Cursal St As Cathl 01-04; rtd 04; PtO *St As* from 09. *Cysgod y Coed, 12 Church View, Ruabon, Wrexham LL14 6TD* T: (01978) 822206
E: valerie@hywyn.freeserve.co.uk

JONES, Matthew Brooks. b 58. St Fran Coll Brisbane BTh 94. **d** 93 **p** 95. C Caloundra Australia 94-97; P-in-c Goondiwindi 97-01; R Ipswich St Paul 01-11; Adn Cunningham 05-11; Hamburg *Eur* 11-15; R Ballina Australia from 15. *The Rectory, Burnet Street, Ballina, NSW 2478, Australia* T: (0061) (2) 6686 2094

JONES, Maurice Maxwell Hughes. b 32. Clifton Th Coll 56. **d** 60 **p** 61. C Islington St Andr w St Thos and St Matthias *Lon* 60-63; Argentina 63-71; C Whitchurch *Llan* 72-73; Area Sec (NW England) SAMS 73-77; V Haydock St Mark *Liv* 78-87; V Paddington Em Harrow Road *Lon* 87-97; rtd 98. *Glyn Orig, Cemmaes, Machynlleth SY20 9PR* T/F: (01650) 511632

JONES, Canon Melville Kenneth. b 40. Open Univ BA 82. St D Coll Lamp. **d** 66 **p** 67. C Aberdare *Llan* 66-71; C Caerau w Ely 71-72; Chapl Pontypridd Hosps 72-89; V Graig *Llan* 72-89; P-in-c Cilfynydd 86-89; V Llantwit Fardre 89-07; Chapl E Glam NHS Trust 89-99; RD Pontypridd *Llan* 99-05; Hon Can Llan Cathl 04-07; Chapl Pontypridd and Rhondda NHS Trust 99-01; rtd 07; PtO *Llan* from 10. *Nanteos, 7 Meadow Hill, Church Village, Pontypridd CF38 1RX* T: (01443) 217213
E: melville_k.jones@virgin.net

JONES, Michael. *See* JONES, David Michael

JONES, Michael. b 49. Leeds Univ BA 71 Man Univ MA 73 Padgate Coll of Educn PGCE 73. Qu Coll Birm 83. **d** 85 **p** 86. C Leigh St Mary *Man* 85-88; C-in-c Holts CD 88-93; V Hamer 93-05; rtd 09; PtO *Man* 06-12; *St As* from 09. *Ty Coch Cottage, Llangynhafal, Ruthin LL15 1RT* T: (01824) 703037 E: mike@ashborn.force9.co.uk

JONES, Michael Adrian. b 62. Reading Univ BSc 83 PGCE 84. Trin Coll Bris 07. **d** 09 **p** 10. C Bath Weston All SS w N Stoke and Langridge *B & W* 09-13; Bp's Chapl and Policy Adv *Leic* from 13; LtO from 14. *256 Milligan Road, Leicester LE2 8FD* T: 0116-283 0510 E: adrianjones.bath@yahoo.co.uk

JONES, Michael Barry. b 48. MCIEH 88 MIOSH 88. ERMC 04. **d** 07 **p** 08. NSM Whittlesey, Pondersbridge and Coates *Ely* 07-13; PtO from 13; Chapl Peterborough and Stamford Hosps NHS Foundn Trust from 13. *Chaplaincy Department, Peterborough City Hospital, Bretton Gate, Peterborough PE3 9GZ* T: (01733) 673115 E: michael.jones@pbh-tr.nhs.uk

JONES, Michael Christopher. b 67. Southn Univ BSc 88. St Jo Coll Nottm MTh 03 MA 04. **d** 04 **p** 05. C Aldridge *Lich* 04-07; V Lilleshall and Muxton 07-13; V Luton St Mary *St Alb* from 13. *32 Whitehill Avenue, Luton LU1 3SP*

JONES, Michael Denis Dyson. b 39. CCC Cam BA 62 MA 66 Lon Univ MSc 73. Wycliffe Hall Ox. **d** 76 **p** 77. C Plymouth St Andr w St Paul and St Geo *Ex* 76-81; V Devonport St Budeaux 81-00; RD Plymouth Devonport 93-95; TV Barnstaple 00-07; RD 03-07; rtd 07. *The Spinney, 40 West Drive, Harrow HA3 6TS* T: (020) 8954 1530 E: mddjamj@onetel.com

JONES, Michael Emlyn. b 47. Aber Univ MB, ChB 72 MRCP 75 FRCP 95. **d** 79 **p** 79. Asst P Moshi St Marg Tanzania 79-82; NSM Duns *Edin* 83-99; NSM Dalkeith from 02; NSM Lasswade from 02. *255 Carnethie Street, Rosewell EH24 9DR* T: 0131-440 2602 or 653 6767 F: 653 3646 M: 07710-276208 E: michaelejones@doctors.org.uk

JONES, Michael Gerald. b 46. Ban Ord Course 05. **d** 07 **p** 08. NSM Ystumaner *Ban* 07-09; NSM Dolgellau w Llanfachreth and Brithdir etc 09-14. *Bryn-Hyfryd, 1 St Mary's Terrace, Arthog LL39 1BQ* T: (01341) 250406

JONES, Michael Kevin. b 57. Llan Ord Course 94. **d** 98 **p** 99. NSM Caerau w Ely *Llan* 98-00; NSM Cen Cardiff 01; P-in-c Tremorfa St Phil CD 02-05; Area Fundraising Manager Children's Soc Llan and Mon 98-00; Ch Strategy Manager Wales 01-02; LtO *Llan* 05-09; V Mountain Ash and Miskin from 09; AD Cynon Valley from 13. *5 Lon-y-Felin, Cefn Pennar, Mountain Ash CF45 4ES* T: (01443) 473700

JONES, Morgan. See JONES, Frederick Morgan

JONES, Canon Neil Crawford. b 42. Univ of Wales BA 63 K Coll Lon BD 66 AKC 66. **d** 67 **p** 68. C Holywell *St As* 67-69; C Rhyl w St Ann 69-73; C Christchurch *Win* 73-77; V Stanmore 77-84; RD Win 82-84; V Romsey 84-07; RD 89-94; Hon Can Win Cathl 93-07; rtd 07; PtO *Nor* from 12. *23 Merton Road, Watton, Thetford IP25 6BD* T: (01953) 889846

JONES, Nerissa. See JONES, Mary Nerissa Anna

JONES, Canon Neville George. b 36. Univ of Wales (Ban) BA 59. St Mich Coll Llan 59. **d** 61 **p** 62. C Broughton *St As* 61-65; C Newcastle *Llan* 65-68; V Laleston w Tythegston 68-83; V Llanishen and Lisvane 84-93; V Llanishen 93-02; Hon Can Llan Cathl 96-02; rtd 02; PtO *Llan* from 10. *21 Cwm Gwynlais, Tongwynlais, Cardiff CF15 7HU* T: (029) 2081 1150

JONES, Nicholas Godwin. b 58. St Jo Coll Cam BA 81 MA 84 Hughes Hall Cam PGCE 90. Ridley Hall Cam 91. **d** 93 **p** 94. C Cambridge H Trin *Ely* 93-97; Chapl St Bede's Sch Cam 97-00; C Fulbourn w Gt and Lt Wilbraham 97-00; V Harston w Hauxton and Newton 00-03; V Gt Horton *Bradf* 03-10; Chapl HM Pris Man 10-11; Chapl HM Pris Hindley 10-15; Hon C Halifax *Leeds* 13-15; Hon C Siddal 13-15; R Acton St Mary *Lon* from 15. *The Rectory, 14 Cumberland Park, London W3 6SX* T: (020) 8992 8876 or 8993 0422 E: nickjones114@gmail.com

JONES, Nicholas Peter. b 55. St Mich Coll Llan. **d** 82 **p** 83. C St Andrews Major w Michaelston-le-Pit *Llan* 82-84; C Aberdare 84-88; Youth Chapl 85-89; V Abercynon 88-96; R Llanilid w Pencoed 96-10; AD Bridgend 10; Chapl Miss to Seafarers from 12. *55 William Belcher Drive, St Mellons, Cardiff CF3 0NZ* E: nicholas.jones@mtsmail.org

JONES, Nicholas Trevor. b 79. Southn Univ LLB 02. Oak Hill Th Coll BA 12. **d** 12 **p** 13. C Frogmore *St Alb* from 12. *56 Maplefield, Park Street, St Albans AL2 2BQ* T: (01727) 568946 M: 07740-718122 E: nickjones2011@gmail.com

JONES, Nigel David. b 69. Qu Coll Cam MA 95. Westcott Ho Cam 97. **d** 00 **p** 01. C Abbots Langley *St Alb* 00-03; TV Dunstable 03-08; V Caversham St Andr *Ox* from 08. *St Andrew's Vicarage, Harrogate Road, Reading RG4 7PW* T: 0118-947 2788

JONES, Nigel Ivor. b 54. Sheff Univ MMin 04. WMMTC 91. **d** 94 **p** 95. C Shirley *Birm* 94-99; TV Salter Street and Shirley 99-01; V Olton 01-08; Chapl HM Pris Rye Hill from 10; PtO *Birm* from 13. *HM Prison Rye Hill, Willoughby, Rugby CV23 8SZ* T: (01788) 523300 E: revnigel@aol.com

JONES, Norman. b 50. Oak Hill Th Coll BA 83. **d** 83 **p** 84. C Ulverston St Mary w H Trin *Carl* 83-87; Hong Kong 88-92; TR Eccles *Man* 92-01; AD 95-00; R Haslemere and Grayswood *Guildf* 01-10; RD Godalming 02-07; Chapl Wispers Sch Haslemere 01-10; rtd 11; Chapl E Cheshire Hospice from 12. *51 Freshwater Drive, Weston, Crewe CW2 5GR* T: (01270) 829141 E: revnjones@aol.com

JONES, Norman Burnet. b 52. St Andr Univ BSc 74 Man Univ PhD 78 CChem 81 CBiol 78. SEITE 08. **d** 11 **p** 12. NSM Southgate *Chich* from 11. *1 Saxon Road, Crawley RH10 7SA* T: (01293) 885209 M: 07766-367983 E: normanbjones1@virginmedia.com

JONES, Ormond. See JONES, David Ormond

JONES, Mrs Patricia Ann. b 43. **d** 97 **p** 98. OLM Bincombe w Broadwey, Upwey and Buckland Ripers *Sarum* 97-05; NSM 06-10; rtd 11; PtO *Sarum* from 11. *23 Camedown Close, Weymouth DT3 5RB* T: (01305) 813056

JONES, Mrs Patricia Anne. b 55. CSS 81. Oak Hill Th Coll 92. **d** 95. NSM Mill Hill Jo Keble Ch *Lon* 95-01; NSM Queensbury All SS 01-08; PtO 08-12; TV Thatcham *Ox* from 12. *1 Cowslip Crescent, Thatcham RG18 4DE* T: (01635) 865388 E: revpatsy55@gmail.com

JONES, Canon Patrick Geoffrey Dickson. b 28. Ch Ch Ox BA 51 MA 55 Aber Univ MLitt 98. St Deiniol's Hawarden 79. **d** 82 **p** 83. NSM Sandbach *Ches* 82-84; R Aboyne *Ab* 84-96; R Ballater 84-96; P-in-c Braemar 84-96; rtd 96; P-in-c Cen Buchan *Ab* 96-98; LtO from 06; P-in-c Cuminestown from 09; Hon Can St Andr Cathl from 01. *Byebush of Fedderate, New Deer, Turriff AB53 6UL* T: (01771) 644110 E: patrickj786@btinternet.com

JONES, Patrick George. b 42. Cant Ch Ch Univ Coll MA 99. Lich Th Coll 69. **d** 72 **p** 73. C Chesterton St Geo *Ely* 72-75; P-in-c Waterbeach 75-78; P-in-c Landbeach 76-78; R Charlton-in-Dover *Cant* 78-90; Chapl Cautley Ho Chr Cen 90-96; rtd 06. *149 London Road, Temple Ewell, Dover CT16 3DA* T: (01304) 829377 E: patrickjones303@btinternet.com

JONES, Paul Anthony. b 72. Cov Univ BSc 95. Ripon Coll Cuddesdon BTh 99. **d** 99 **p** 00. C Dolgellau w Llanfachreth and Brithdir etc *Ban* 99-02; P-in-c Ffestiniog w Blaenau Ffestiniog 02-04; PtO 04-06; Newc 06-07; Hon C Long Benton St Mary 07-10; V Newc St Fran 10-14. *164 Abbotts Way, North Shields NE29 8LY* M: 07810-686072 E: paul.ajones@yahoo.co.uk

JONES, Paul Evan. b 62. York Univ BA 84 CPFA 89. SEITE 02. **d** 05 **p** 06. C Kingstanding St Luke *Birm* 05-09; P-in-c Babbacombe *Ex* from 09. *Babbacombe Vicarage, 4 Cary Park, Torquay TQ1 3NH* T: (01803) 323002 E: liberty.hall@me.com

JONES, Paul Terence. b 35. Dur Univ BA 60. Qu Coll Birm 60. **d** 62 **p** 63. C Rainford *Liv* 62-65; C Skelmersdale St Paul 65-68; V Huyton Quarry 68-78; V Widnes St Ambrose 78-00; rtd 00; PtO *Liv* from 00. *9 Hunter Court, Prescot L34 2UH* T: 0151-430 6057

JONES, Pauline Edna. b 55. Liv Univ BA 77. **d** 10 **p** 11. OLM Langley *Man* from 10; Chapl Pennine Acute Hosps NHS Trust from 13. *9 Hopwood Avenue, Heywood OL10 2AX* T: (01706) 368829 E: pej123@hotmail.co.uk

JONES, Penelope Howson. b 58. Girton Coll Cam BA 80 MA 83 LGSM 79. Ripon Coll Cuddesdon BA 85 MA 88. **dss** 86 **d** 87 **p** 94. Hackney *Lon* 86-87; Par Dn 87-88; Tutor Ripon Coll Cuddesdon 88-90; Par Dn Cuddesdon *Ox* 88-90; PtO *Dur* 92-95; Dir Practical Th NEOC *Newc* 93-97; Hon C Eastgate w Rookhope *Dur* 93-97; Hon C Stanhope w Frosterley 93-97; PtO *York* 93-97; P-in-c Stanhope w Frosterley *Dur* 97-01; P-in-c Eastgate w Rookhope 97-01; Woman Adv in Min 97-01; Hon Can Dur Cathl 98-01; Sen Assoc P Gosford Australia from 01. *78 Henry Parry Drive, PO Box 4255, Gosford East NSW 2250, Australia* T: (0061) (2) 4324 2630 E: redimp@bigpon.com

JONES, Canon Peter Anthony Watson. b 53. AKC 75. Sarum & Wells Th Coll 76. **d** 77 **p** 78. C Hessle *York* 77-81; C Stainton-in-Cleveland 81-82; P-in-c Weston Mill *Ex* 82-84; Chapl Plymouth Poly 82-90; V Gt Ayton w Easby and Newton-in-Cleveland *York* 90-92; C Devonport St Aubyn *Ex* 92-98; P-in-c Yealmpton and Brixton 98-01; Team Chapl Portsm Hosps NHS Trust 01-05; Chapl Portsm Univ 05-09; Can Res Portsm Cathl 05-09; R Havant 09-14; Dioc Interfaith Adv 06-11; rtd 14; Hon C York All SS Pavement w St Crux and St Mich from 14; Hon C York St Olave w St Giles from 14; Hon C York St Helen w St Martin from 14; Hon C York St Denys from 14. *52 St Andrewgate, York YO1 7BZ*

JONES, Peter Brian. b 81. Ulster Univ BA 02 PGCE 03. MTh 14. **d** 13 **p** 14. Maghera w Killelagh *D & R* 13-14; C Drumglass w Moygashel *Arm* from 14. *Kinore, 84 Killyman Road, Dungannon BT71 6DQ* T: (028) 8772 4264 E: peterjones917@hotmail.com

JONES, Peter Charles. b 60. Univ of Wales BA 81 MA 82 PGCE 97. St Mich Coll Llan 80. **d** 83 **p** 84. C Pontnewynydd *Mon* 83-85; C Bassaleg 85-87; TV Cwmbran 87-94; V Blaenavon w Capel Newydd 94-01; Chapl CME 00-01; Chapl and Fell Trin Coll Carmarthen 01-05; V Llangennech and Hendy *St D* 05-11; AD Cydweli 08-11; V Keele *Lich* from 11; V Silverdale from 11. *The Vicarage, 21 Pepper Street, Silverdale, Newcastle ST5 6QJ* T: (01782) 624455
E: tadjones@btinternet.com

JONES, Peter David. b 48. S'wark Ord Course 89. **d** 92 **p** 93. NSM Coulsdon St Andr *S'wark* 92-04; PtO 04-13. *79 Beverley Road, Whyteleafe CR3 0DU* T: (020) 8668 6398
E: revpeter79@gmail.com

JONES, Peter Gordon Lewis. b 31. Llan Dioc Tr Scheme. **d** 82 **p** 83. NSM Llangynwyd w Maesteg *Llan* 82-84; Deputation Appeals Org (S & M Glam) CECS 84-87; Appeals Manager (Wales and Glouc) Children's Soc 87-97; NSM Pyle w Kenfig *Llan* 89-97; rtd 97. *18 Fulmar Road, Porthcawl CF36 3UL*
T: (01656) 785455 M: 07785-755399

JONES, Peter Henry. b 50. Qu Coll Cam MA 72 Ex Univ CertEd 73 Bradf Univ MSc 81 Nottm Univ MA 05. EMMTC 02. **d** 05 **p** 06. NSM Annesley w Newstead *S'well* 05-11; NSM Hucknall Torkard 11-12; NSM Kimberley 12-13; NSM Nuthall 12-13; rtd 13; PtO *S'well* from 13. *3 Roland Avenue, Nuthall, Nottingham NG16 1BB* T: 0115-975 1868
E: maryandpeterjones@btinternet.com

JONES, Peter Owen. b 64. Hull Univ BSc 86. Oak Hill Th Coll BA 08. **d** 08 **p** 09. C Hubberston *St D* 08-11; P-in-c Llanfihangel Genau'r Glyn and Llangorwen from 11; AD Llanbadarn Fawr from 14. *The Vicarage, Maes-y-Garn, Bow Street SY24 5DS* T: (01970) 822267
E: rev.peterjones@btinternet.com

JONES, Peter Robin. b 42. Open Univ BA 75 Bp Otter Coll Chich CertEd 68. EMMTC 79. **d** 82 **p** 83. NSM Doveridge *Derby* 82-97; NSM Doveridge, Scropton, Sudbury etc 98-10; NSM S Dales from 11; Bp's Inspector of Th Colls and Courses from 98; PtO *Lich* 93-10. *4 Cross Road, Uttoxeter ST14 7BN*
T: (01889) 565123 E: rev.jon@talktalk.net

JONES, Canon Peter Russell. b 48. St Jo Coll Cam BA 71 MA 75 Univ of Wales MTh 86. Wycliffe Hall Ox. **d** 75 **p** 76. C Northampton All SS w St Kath *Pet* 75-79; C Ban Cathl 79-81; Min Can Ban Cathl 79-81; R Pentraeth and Llanddyfnan 81-85; V Conwy w Gyffin 85-14; Lect Univ of Wales (Ban) 89-95; AD Archllechwedd *Ban* 96-09; Can and Treas Ban Cathl 99-09; Chan Ban Cathl 09-14; rtd 14; PtO *St As* from 14; *Ban* from 14. *Encilfa, 14 Victoria Park, Colwyn Bay LL29 7AX*
T: (01492) 531711

JONES, The Ven Philip Hugh. b 51. Solicitor . Chich Th Coll 92. **d** 94 **p** 95. C Horsham *Chich* 94-97; V Southwater 97-05; RD Horsham 02-04; Adn Hastings from 05. *The Archdeaconry, High Street, Maresfield, Uckfield TN22 2EH* T: (01825) 763326
E: archlandh@chichester.anglican.org

JONES, Philip Malcolm. b 43. Qu Coll Birm. **d** 04 **p** 05. NSM Birm St Paul 04-08; P-in-c Heathfield St Rich *Chich* 08-13; V 13-15; P-in-c from 15. *St Richard's Vicarage, Hailsham Road, Heathfield TN21 8AF* T: (01435) 862744
E: malcolm@peri.co.uk

JONES, Philip Thomas Henry. b 34. Qu Coll Birm 58. **d** 60 **p** 61. C Castle Bromwich SS Mary and Marg *Birm* 60-67; C Reading St Mary V *Ox* 67-72; C-in-c Reading All SS CD 72-75; V Reading All SS 75-95; PtO *Portsm* from 97; Hon Chapl Portsm Cathl from 97. *13 Oyster Street, Portsmouth PO1 2HZ*
T: (023) 9275 6676

JONES, Canon Phillip Bryan. b 34. St Mich Coll Llan. **d** 61 **p** 62. C Hope *St As* 61-64; C Llanrhos 64-67; V Kerry 67-74; R Newtown w Llanllwchaiarn w Aberhafesp 74-97; RD Cedewain 76-97; Sec Ch in Wales Prov Evang Cttee 80-83; Hon Can St As Cathl 86-93; Can St As Cathl 93-97; rtd 97. *7 Dalton Drive, Shrewsbury SY3 8DA* T: (01743) 351426

JONES, Phillip Edmund. b 56. Man Poly BA 78 Fitzw Coll Cam BA 84 MA 88 GradCIPD 79. Westcott Ho Cam 82. **d** 85 **p** 86. C Stafford St Jo and Tixall w Ingestre *Lich* 85-89; TV Redditch, The Ridge *Worc* 89-97; TV Worc SE 95-08; Ind Chapl 89-08; Team Ldr Worcs Ind Miss 01-08; Team Ldr and Chapl Faith at Work in Worcs 08-11; Miss Development Officer from 11; C Worc St Barn w Ch Ch from 08. *7 Egremont Gardens, Worcester WR4 0QH* T: (01905) 755037 M: 07586-303831
E: phillipjones@faithatwork.co.uk

JONES, Phyllis Gwendoline Charlotte. b 44. **d** 05 **p** 06. OLM Talbot Village *Sarum* 05-12; rtd 13. *Bluebell Cottage, 112 Wallisdown Road, Bournemouth BH10 4HY* T: (01202) 528956 E: revphyllisjones@fsmail.net

JONES, Ray. See JONES, David Raymond

JONES, Raymond. b 43. NOC 99. **d** 02 **p** 03. NSM Ashton-in-Makerfield St Thos *Liv* 02-03; C Widnes St Mary w St Paul 03-05; V 05-08; rtd 08; Hon C Farnworth *Liv* 10-13; Hon C E Widnes 13. *4 Norlands Park, Widnes WA8 5BH*

JONES, Raymond Alban. b 34. RGN 55 RMN 63. Chich Th Coll 64. **d** 67 **p** 68. C Ocker Hill *Lich* 67-70; C Truro St Paul 70-71; Chapl Selly Oak Hosp Birm 71-76; USPG Bahamas 76-79; Chapl Willen Hospice Milton Keynes 80-83; Chapl St Jas Hosp Balham 83-87; NSM Leamington Spa H Trin and Old Milverton *Cov* 87-92; TV Probus, Ladock and Grampound w Creed and St Erme *Truro* 92-94; In Orthodox Ch from 95; rtd 94; PtO *Sarum* from 09. *2 St Catherine's Terrace, Rodden Row, Abbotsbury, Weymouth DT3 4JL* T: (01305) 871836

JONES, Raymond Sydney. b 35. MSERT 71. Glouc Th Course 85. **d** 87 **p** 88. NSM Madley *Heref* 87-89; NSM Preston-on-Wye w Blakemere 87-89; NSM Madley w Tyberton, Preston-on-Wye and Blakemere 89; Chapl St Mich Hospice Hereford 90-00; PtO *Heref* 00-06. *The Old Cedars, Much Birch, Hereford HR2 8HR* T: (01981) 540851

JONES, Canon Raymond Trevor. b 35. Linc Th Coll. **d** 82 **p** 83. C Rushmere *St E* 82-85; Bp's Dom Chapl 85-86; CF 86-91; TV Ridgeway *Sarum* 91-97; Relig Programmes Producer BBC Wiltshire Sound 91-97; Chapl Fuengirola St Andr *Eur* 97-00; P-in-c Ypres 00-10; P-in-c Ostend 06-08; Can Gib Cathl 04-10; PtO *Portsm* from 10. *St Pierre, 3 Diana Close, Totland Bay PO39 0EE* E: raymondstg@hotmail.com

JONES (née WELCH), Mrs Rebecca Anne. b 79. Leic Univ BSc 00. Wycliffe Hall Ox BTh 10. **d** 09 **p** 10. C Cov Cathl 09-12; C Aston and Nechells *Birm* from 12. *The Vicarage, Duddeston Manor Road, Birmingham B7 4QD* T: 0121-359 6965 M: 07712-632504 E: becky@astonnechellscofe.org.uk

JONES, Miss Rhiannon Elizabeth. b 69. Univ of Wales (Cardiff) BA 91 Ox Cen for Miss Studies MA 04 Cam Univ BTh 11. Ridley Hall Cam 09. **d** 11 **p** 12. C Man Cathl from 11. *9.6A Melia House, 19 Lord Street, Manchester M4 4AX*
M: 07765-241093 E: rhinoharpy@yahoo.co.uk

JONES, Ms Rhiannon Elizabeth. b 72. Ex Univ BA 93 Brunel Univ MA 95 Anglia Poly Univ MA 05. Ridley Hall Cam 98. **d** 00 **p** 01. C Huntingdon *Ely* 00-04; R Fulbourn 04-10; V Gt Wilbraham 04-10; R Lt Wilbraham 04-10; Transforming Ch Co-ord *Birm* 10-14; Dir of Miss from 14; Dom Chapl to Bp Aston from 12. *23 Hallewell Road, Birmingham B16 0LP*
T: 0121-454 5040 M: 07595-880584
E: rhiannonejones@me.com *or*
rhiannonj@birmingham.anglican.org

JONES, Richard. See JONES, James Richard

JONES, Richard. b 23. BEM. St Deiniol's Hawarden 74. **d** 76 **p** 77. NSM Welshpool w Castle Caereinion *St As* 76-94; rtd 94. *Sherwood, Rhos Common, Llandrinio, Llanymynech SY22 6RN*
T: (01691) 830534

JONES, Canon Richard. b 28. St D Coll Lamp 54. **d** 56 **p** 57. C Llanaber w Caerdeon *Ban* 56-61; R Aberffraw w Llangwyfan 61-74; CF (TA) 61-71; V Llanfairisgaer *Ban* 74-79; Bp's Private Chapl 78-82; V Llanfair-is-gaer and Llanddeiniolen 79-89; RD Arfon 82-89; Can Ban Cathl from 86; V Llandegfan w Llandysilio 89-96; Chapl ATC from 90; rtd 96; PtO *Ban* from 96. *Bryniau, Rhostrehwfa, Llangefni LL77 7YS* T: (01248) 724609

JONES, Richard Christopher Bentley. b 53. Pemb Coll Ox BA 77 MA 79. SEITE 03. **d** 06 **p** 07. NSM Clapham H Trin and St Pet *S'wark* 06-13; PtO *Heref* from 13. *Langstone Court, Llangarron, Ross-on-Wye HR9 6NR* T: (01989) 770254
E: richard.jones@langstone-court.org.uk

JONES, Richard Keith. b 40. Jes Coll Ox BA 63. Wycliffe Hall Ox 61. **d** 63 **p** 64. C Blaenavon w Capel Newydd *Mon* 63-67; C Mynyddislwyn 67-71; C Pontypool 71; V Abercarn 71-81; V Penhow, St Brides Netherwent w Llandavenny etc 81-88. *32 Quantock Court, South Esplanade, Burnham-on-Sea TA8 1DL* T: (01278) 458123

JONES, Robert. b 45. Culham Coll Ox CertEd 67. St Steph Ho Ox. **d** 85 **p** 86. C High Wycombe *Ox* 85-89; V Beckenham St Barn *Roch* 89-90; C Swanley St Mary 90-91; C Edenbridge and Crockham Hill H Trin 91-93; rtd 13. *23 Bromley College, London Road, Bromley BR1 1PE* E: r.jones52@btinternet.com

JONES, Robert. b 40. **d** 80 **p** 81. C St Laur in Thanet *Cant* 80-83. *Erbacher Strasse 72, 64287 Darmstadt, Germany* T: (0049) (6151) 422913

JONES, Robert Cecil. b 32. Univ of Wales (Abth) BA 54 DipEd 55. Qu Coll Birm 84. **d** 86 **p** 87. C Llanbadarn Fawr w Capel Bangor and Goginan *St D* 86-88; R Llanllwchaearn and Llanina 88-91; R Newport w Cilgwyn and Dinas w Llanllawer 91-98; rtd 98; PtO *Derby* from 05. *Old Craigstead Works, High Street, Stoney Middleton, Hope Valley S32 4TL* T: (01433) 631857
E: robbie@rjones48.freeserve.co.uk

JONES, Robert David. b 73. UCD BSc 97 TCD BTh 07. CITC 04. **d** 07 **p** 08. C Dublin St Patr Cathl Gp 07-10; V Dublin Rathmines w Harold's Cross from 10. *25 Airfield Road, Rathgar, Dublin 6, Republic of Ireland* M: (00353) 86-285 4098
E: rob@htrinity.ie

JONES, The Ven Robert George. b 55. Hatf Coll Dur BA 77 Ox Univ BA 79 MA 87. Ripon Coll Cuddesdon BA 79 MA 87. **d** 80 **p** 81. C Foley Park *Worc* 80-84; V Dudley St Fran 84-92; TR Worc St Barn w Ch Ch 92-06; Dir Development 06-14; RD Worc E 99-05; Hon Can Worc Cathl 03-14; Adn Worc from 14; V Gt Malvern Ch Ch from 15. *The Archdeacon's House, Walkers Lane, Whittington, Worcester WR5 2RE* T: (01905) 773301
E: rjones@cofe-worcester.org.uk

JONES, Canon Robert George. b 42. St Mich Coll Llan 93. **d** 95 **p** 96. NSM Treboeth *S & B* 95-02; P-in-c 02-07; P-in-c Landore 03-07; Can Res Brecon Cathl 06-07; rtd 07. *106 Plunch Lane, Mumbles, Swansea SA3 4JE*

JONES, Canon Robert William. b 55. Open Univ BA 85 MA 88. Ian Ramsey Coll Brasted 75 Chich Th Coll 76 TCD Div Sch 77. **d** 79 **p** 80. C Seapatrick *D & D* 79; C Bangor Abbey 81-83; I Drumgath w Drumgooland and Clonduff 83-89; I Finaghy *Conn* 89-93; I Kilwaughter w Cairncastle and Craigy Hill 94-98; I Athlone w Benown, Kiltoom and Forgney *M & K* 98-02; Dean Clonmacnoise 02-12; I Trim and Athboy Gp 02-12; I Belfast Malone St Jo *Conn* from 12; Can Belf Cathl from 13. *St John's Rectory, 86 Maryville Park, Belfast BT9 6LQ* T: (028) 9066 6644 *or* 9066 7861
E: stjohnsmalone@btinternet.com *or* rectorstjohns@btconnect.com

JONES, Robert William Aplin. b 32. Univ of Wales (Cardiff) BSc 52 MSc 65 FRSC 71 CChem 72. St Deiniol's Hawarden 72. **d** 73 **p** 74. C Bassaleg *Mon* 73-77; V Nantyglo 77-82; PtO 82-86; R Colwinston w Llandow and Llysworney *Llan* 86-95; rtd 95; PtO *St D* from 99. *Golwg-y-Lan, Feidr Ganol, Newport SA42 0RR* T: (01239) 820297 M: 07968-173759

JONES, Robin Dominic Edwin. b 78. St Chad's Coll Dur BA 00 K Coll Lon MA 01. St Steph Ho Ox MTh 07. **d** 04 **p** 05. C Ealing Ch the Sav *Lon* 04-08; V Hammersmith St Luke 08-12; V Sevenoaks St Jo *Roch* from 12. *St John's Clergy House, 62 Quakers Hall Lane, Sevenoaks TN13 3TX* T: (01732) 451710 M: 07779-299924

JONES, Roderick. b 48. Leeds Univ BA 70 PGCE 72. Westmr Th Sem (USA) 73 Oak Hill Th Coll 74. **d** 76 **p** 77. C Beckenham Ch Ch *Roch* 76-80; C Uphill *B & W* 80-84; V Springfield All SS *Chelmsf* 84-90; Selection Sec ABM 91-96; V Horsell *Guildf* 96-13; rtd 13. *3 Pine Close, New Haw, Addlestone KT15 3BW* E: rjones2558@aol.com

JONES, Canon Roger. b 49. St Mich Coll Llan 84. **d** 86 **p** 87. C Llangynwyd w Maesteg *Llan* 86-90; V Wiston w Walton E and Clarbeston *St D* 90-01; V Pembroke Gp 01-04; TV Monkton from 04; Can St D Cathl from 09. *The Vicarage, Lower Lamphey Road, Pembroke SA71 4AF* T/F: (01646) 682710 M: 07971-528933 E: roger@royres.fsnet.co.uk

JONES, Russell Frederick. b 55. Man Univ BA 77 Edin Univ BD 84. Edin Th Coll 81. **d** 84 **p** 85. C Croxteth *Liv* 84-87; V Edgehill St Dunstan 87-98; R Glas St Bride 98-08; Hon Chapl Glas Univ 00-06; Chapl Marie Curie Hospice Glasgow from 08. *Marie Curie Cancer Care, 133 Balornock Road, Glasgow G21 3US* T: (01415) 577465
E: howisonandjones@btinternet.com

JONES, Mrs Sally. b 41. **d** 09 **p** 10. NSM Teme Valley N *Worc* from 09. *2 Old School House, Eastham, Tenbury Wells WR15 8PB* T: (01584) 781526 E: revsally@live.com

JONES, Miss Sally Jennifer. b 86. St Mich Coll Llan. **d** 11 **p** 12. C Bro Ardudwy Uchaf *Ban* 11-13; C Bro Ardudwy 13-14; St Alb Abbey from 14. *2 Dean Moore Close, St Albans AL1 1DW* T: (01707) 810802 E: sallyjjones@hotmail.co.uk

JONES, Samuel. b 44. CITC. **d** 86 **p** 87. C Agherton *Conn* 86-88; I Connor w Antrim St Patr 88-97; I Whitehead and Islandmagee 97-01; Bp's C Kilbroney *D & D* 01-10; rtd 10. *2 The Brambles, Coleraine BT52 1PN* T: (028) 7031 0076

JONES, Sarah Charlotte. b 57. SRN 79. SAOMC 01. **d** 04 **p** 05. NSM Forest Edge *Ox* from 04. *4 Tower Hill, Witney OX28 5ER* T: (01993) 200483 E: sarahtandem@hotmail.com

JONES, Ms Sarah Jane. b 61. St Hugh's Coll Ox BA 95 MA 03 Northumbria Univ MSc 02. Westcott Ho Cam 02. **d** 04 **p** 05. C Ross *Heref* 04-07; P-in-c 07-08; R Ross w Walford and Brampton Abbotts from 08. *The Rectory, Church Street, Ross-on-Wye HR9 5HN* T: (01989) 562175
E: sarah.jones@rawchurch.org.uk

JONES, Sebastian. See JONES, David Sebastian

JONES, Sharon. b 74. Liv Univ MA 00 PhD 05. Westcott Ho Cam 05. **d** 07 **p** 08. C Warwick *Cov* 07-11; P-in-c New Springs and Whelley *Liv* 11-13. *Address temp unknown*
E: rev.sharonjones@googlemail.com

JONES, Canon Sharon Ann. b 60. St Kath Coll Liv BA 82. Cranmer Hall Dur 83. **dss** 85 **d** 87 **p** 94. Rubery *Birm* 85-89; Par Dn 87-89; C-in-c Chelmsley Wood St Aug CD 89-92; PtO *Newc* 92-93; Chapl HM Pris Acklington 93-97; Chapl HM YOI Castington 97-00; Chapl HM Pris Forest Bank 00-06;

P-in-c Dearnley *Man* 06-14; P-in-c Wardle and Smallbridge 13-14; V Dearnley, Wardle and Smallbridge from 14; AD Salford 03-06; AD Rochdale 06-15; Hon Can Man Cathl from 13. *St Andrew's Vicarage, Arm Road, Littleborough OL15 8NJ* T: (01706) 378466 M: 07738-966271
E: vicar@dearnleyvicarage.plusnet.com

JONES, Mrs Shelagh Deirdre. b 46. St Mary's Coll Dur BA 68. NEOC 01. **d** 04 **p** 05. NSM Burnby *York* 04-07; NSM Londesborough 04-07; NSM Nunburnholme and Warter and Huggate 04-07; NSM Shiptonthorpe and Hayton 04-07; PtO from 07; Chapl HM YOI Wetherby 04-10; PtO *Eur* from 13. *Red Gables, Fair View, Town Street, Shiptonthorpe, York YO43 3PE* T/F: (01430) 871612 E: revd-shelagh@red-gables.org.uk

JONES, Canon Sian Eira. b 63. Univ of Wales (Lamp) BA 84 Southn Univ BTh 88. Sarum & Wells Th Coll 85. **d** 88 **p** 97. C Llan-llwch w Llangain and Llangynog *St D* 88-93; Dn-in-c Llansteffan and Llan-y-bri etc 93-97; V 97-06; AD Carmarthen 00-06; R Llanelli 06-14; P-in-c 14-15; AD Cydweli 13-15; P-in-c Catheiniog from 15; AD Llandeilo from 15; Can St D Cathl from 09. *The Vicarage, Llangathen, Carmarthen SA32 8QD* T: (01558) 668918 E: revsainjones@btinternet.com

JONES, Sian Hilary. See WIGHT, Sian Hilary

JONES, Simon. b 63. Trin Coll Bris BA 89. **d** 89 **p** 90. C Hildenborough *Roch* 89-93; C Crofton *Portsm* 93-96; C Northwood Em *Lon* 96-01; Min in charge Ignite 01-07; TR Stoke Gifford *Bris* from 07; AD Kingswood and S Glos from 11. *119 North Road, Stoke Gifford, Bristol BS34 8PE* T: 0117-979 1656 *or* 969 2486 F: 959 9264
E: simon@st-michaels-church.org.uk

JONES, Canon Simon Matthew. b 72. SS Hild & Bede Coll Dur BA 93 MA 94 Selw Coll Cam PhD 00 Ox Univ MA 02 DPhil 03. Westcott Ho Cam 95. **d** 99 **p** 00. C Tewkesbury w Walton Cardiff and Twyning *Glouc* 99-02; Chapl and Fell Mert Coll Ox from 02; Hon Can Ch Ch *Ox* from 15. *Merton College, Oxford OX1 4JD* T: (01865) 276365 *or* 281793 F: 276361
E: simon.jones@merton.ox.ac.uk

JONES, Stella Frances. TCD BTh 02. CITC. **d** 02 **p** 03. C Bandon Union *C, C & R* 02-05; I Clonenagh w Offerlane, Borris-in-Ossory etc *C & O* 05-10; I Kinneigh Union *C, C & R* from 10. *The Rectory, Ballineen, Co Cork, Republic of Ireland* T: (00353) (23) 884 7047 E: sfjones2013@gmail.com

JONES, Stephen. See JONES, Ernest Edward Stephen

JONES, Stephen Frederick. b 53. Magd Coll Ox BA 75 MA 79 Lon Univ BD 89 Leeds Univ MA 96. Linc Th Coll BCombStuds 84. **d** 84 **p** 85. C Kingswinford St Mary *Lich* 84-87; Min Can, Succ and Dean's V Windsor 87-94; C Howden *York* 94-96; Chapl St Elphin's Sch Matlock 96-01; C Worksop Priory *S'well* 01-03; R Longton *Lich* 03-13; TR Staveley and Barrow Hill *Derby* from 13. *The Rectory, Church Street, Staveley, Chesterfield S43 3TN* T: (01246) 498603
E: sfjones53@googlemail.com

JONES, Stephen John. b 56. **d** 14 **p** 15. NSM Rednal *Birm* from 14. *19 Meadowfield Road, Rubery, Rednal, Birmingham B45 9BY* T: 0121-460 1173 M: 07866-748932
E: stephen.jones@forumpm.com

JONES, Canon Stephen Leslie. b 59. Hull Univ BA 80 Lanc Univ MA 06. Sarum & Wells Th Coll 82. **d** 85 **p** 86. C Perry Barr *Birm* 85-88; C Blackpool St Steph *Blackb* 88-90; V Greenlands 90-95; V Carnforth from 95; Hon Can Blackb Cathl from 11. *The Vicarage, North Road, Carnforth LA5 9LJ* T: (01524) 732948
E: stephenjones17@hotmail.com

JONES, Stephen Richard. b 49. Heythrop Coll Lon MA 01. Oak Hill Th Coll 72. **d** 75 **p** 76. C Welling *Roch* 75-79; C Cheltenham St Mark *Glouc* 79-82; V Shiregreen St Jas and St Chris *Sheff* 82-86; P-in-c Harold Hill St Geo *Chelmsf* 86-88; V 88-97; P-in-c Harold Hill St Paul 94-95; V Kippington *Roch* 97-08; RD Sevenoaks 00-05; R Ightham 08-14; RD Shoreham 11-14; rtd 14; PtO *Roch* from 14. *The Rectory, Bates Hill, Ightham, Sevenoaks TN15 9BG* T: (01732) 886827
E: srjones49@hotmail.com
or stephen.jones@diocese-rochester.org

JONES, Stephen William. b 46. K Coll Lon BD 70 AKC 70. **d** 71 **p** 72. C Streatham St Pet *S'wark* 71-76; C Leeds St Pet *Ripon* 76-79; C Leeds Richmond Hill 79-85; R Gourock *Glas* 85-88; V Porthleven w Sithney *Truro* 88-94; Miss to Seamen 88-94; P-in-c Portsea Ascension *Portsm* 96-00; V Grimsby St Aug *Linc* 00-12; rtd 12. *20 Westbury Road, Cleethorpes DN35 0QE* T: (01472) 813304

JONES, Canon Stewart William. b 57. Heriot-Watt Univ BA 79 Bris Univ BA 88. Trin Coll Bris 86. **d** 88 **p** 89. C Stoke Bishop *Bris* 88-92; P-in-c Brislington St Luke 92-97; Abp's Chapl and Dioc Missr *Cant* 97-03; P-in-c Cant All SS 01-05; AD Cant and Hon Prov Can Cant Cathl 02-05; R Bordesley St Martin w Bordesley St Andr from 05; Hon Can Birm Cathl from 11. *St Martin's Rectory, 37 Barlows Road, Birmingham B15 2PN* T: 0121-604 0850 M: 07793-724949 E: stewart@bullring.org

JONES, Mrs Susan. b 55. Liv Hope BA 03 St Jo Coll Dur MA 05. Cranmer Hall Dur 03. **d** 05 **p** 06. C Skelmersdale St Paul *Liv* 05-09; TV Maghull and Melling from 09. *23 Green Link, Maghull L31 8DW* T: 0151-526 6626 E: rev_sue@talktalk.net

JONES, Susan Catherine. *See* ASHTON, Susan Catherine

JONES, Canon Susan Helen. b 60. Trin Coll Carmarthen BEd 92 MPhil 94 Univ of Wales (Ban) PhD. Ripon Coll Cuddesdon 93. **d** 95 **p** 97. Chapl Univ of Wales (Swansea) *S & B* 95-98; Hon C Sketty 95-98; Dir Past Studies St Mich Coll Llan 98-00; TV Bangor *Ban* 00-09; AD Ogwen 07-09; Can Missr Ban Cathl 10-11; Dean Ban 11-15; TR Bro Deiniol 14-15; Dir of Miss and Min *Derby* from 15. *Derby Church House, Full Street, Derby DE1 3DR* T: (01332) 388676

JONES, Susan Jean. b 47. Bp Grosseteste Coll CertEd 68 Heythrop Coll Lon MA 01. SAOMC 93. **d** 96 **p** 97. C S Ascot *Ox* 96-07; NSM 01-07; rtd 07. *Fairhaven, 1 St Clement's Terrace, Mousehole, Penzance TR19 6SJ* T: (01736) 732938 E: sebastian143@btinternet.com

JONES, Susannah Hester Everett. b 67. **d** 07 **p** 08. NSM Bris St Mary Redcliffe w Temple etc 07-13; P-in-c Abbots Leigh w Leigh Woods 13-14; V from 14. *The Vicarage, 51 Church Road, Abbots Leigh, Bristol BS8 3QU* E: hester.jones2@googlemail.com

JONES, Tegid Owen. b 27. Univ of Wales (Abth) LLB 47. St Deiniol's Hawarden. **d** 68 **p** 69. C Rhosddu *St As* 68-71; C Wrexham 71-75; R Marchwiel 75-83; R Marchwiel and Isycoed 83-92; RD Bangor Isycoed 86-92; rtd 92; PtO *St As* 09-13. *Teglys, 2 Bungalow, Pentre, Chirk, Wrexham LL14 5AW*

JONES, Theresa. *See* JONES, Mary Catherine Theresa Bridget

JONES, Thomas Glyndwr. b 41. Clifton Th Coll 65. **d** 65 **p** 66. C Islington St Mary *Lon* 65-69; R Fairfield Ch Ch USA 69-73; R Anniston Grace Ch 73-87; R Columbus Trin Ch 87-04; rtd 04. *1106 Placid Grove Lane, Goodlettsville TN 37072, USA* E: welshwiz@knology.net

JONES, Canon Thomas Graham. b 33. St D Coll Lamp BA 57. **d** 59 **p** 60. C Llanelli *St D* 59-64; V Ysbyty Cynfyn 64-69; V Ysbyty Cynfyn w Llantrisant 69-72; V Llanelli Ch Ch 72-94; RD Cydweli 89-93; V Carmarthen St Dav 94-00; Hon Can St D Cathl 93-99; Can St D Cathl from 99; RD Carmarthen 98-00; rtd 00. *32 Pen y Morfa, Llangunnor, Carmarthen SA31 2NP* T: (01267) 231846

JONES, The Ven Thomas Hughie. b 27. Univ of Wales BA 49 LLM 94 Lon Univ BD 53 Leic Univ MA 72 FRSA. St Deiniol's Hawarden. **d** 66 **p** 67. Hon C Evington *Leic* 66-76; Hon C Kirby Muxloe 76-81; Dioc Adult Educn Officer 81-85; R Church Langton w Thorpe Langton and Tur Langton 81-85; Hon Can Leic Cathl 83-86; R Church Langton w Tur Langton, Thorpe Langton etc 85-86; Adn Loughborough 86-92; rtd 92; PtO *Leic* 92-12; *St Alb* from 12. *2 Leigh Court, Moor Pond Piece, Ampthill, Bedford MK45 2GR* T: (01525) 405993 E: thj@connectfree.co.uk

JONES, Canon Thomas Peter. b 20. Ex Coll Ox BA 43 MA 46. St Mich Coll Llan 43. **d** 45 **p** 46. C Wrexham *St As* 45-48; C Llandrillo-yn-Rhos 48-57; R Erbistock and Overton 57-83; Can St As Cathl 78-84; Preb and Prec St As Cathl 84-86; RD Bangor Isycoed 80-86; R Overton and Erbistock and Penley 83-86; rtd 86; PtO *Cov* 86-98; *St As* from 98. *18 All Hallows Close, Retford DN22 7UP* T: (01777) 700481

JONES, Timothy Llewellyn. b 67. York Univ BA 90. Ripon Coll Cuddesdon BA 94. **d** 94 **p** 95. C Middlesbrough St Martin *York* 94-96; P-in-c Rounton w Welbury 96-02; Chapl HM YOI Northallerton 96-99; Adv for Young Adults and Voc (Cleveland) 99-02; R Corinth St Paul USA 02-07; P-in-c York St Hilda 07-14; P-in-c York St Lawr w St Nic 07-14; Dioc Dir of Ords *St E* from 14; Hon C Lark Valley from 14; Hon C Bury St Edmunds All SS w St Jo and St Geo from 14. *28 Philip Road, Bury St Edmunds IP32 6DQ* M: 07525-776406 *or* 07468-474065 T: (01284) 765018 E: tim.jones@cofesuffolk.org

JONES, Timothy Richard Nigel. b 54. Collingwood Coll Dur BSc 75 Birm Univ MSc 76 FGS. Trin Coll Bris 84. **d** 86 **p** 87. C Hailsham *Chich* 86-91; V Madley w Tyberton, Preston-on-Wye and Blakemere *Heref* 91-00; R Madley w Tyberton, Peterchurch, Vowchurch etc 00-06; V Taunton St Jas *B & W* from 06. *69 Richmond Road, Taunton TA1 1EN* T: (01823) 333194 E: timjones@tesco.net

JONES, Tracy Jane. **d** 12 **p** 13. NSM Seintiau Braint a Chefni *Ban* 12-14; R Bro Padrig from 14. *Y Ficerdy, Cemaes Bay LL67 0LB* T: (01407) 711371 E: tracy.jane1@btinternet.com

JONES, Trevor Blandon. b 43. Oak Hill Th Coll 77. **d** 80 **p** 81. NSM Homerton St Barn w St Paul *Lon* 80-83; NSM Harlow New Town w Lt Parndon *Chelmsf* 83-90; C 90-92; V Leyton Em 92-01; rtd 92; PtO *Chelmsf* from 03. *5 Wheatley Close, Sawbridgeworth CM21 0HS* T: (01279) 600248 E: rev.trev@lineone.net

JONES, Trevor Edwin. b 49. Heythrop Coll Lon MA 05 K Coll Lon DThMin 12. Ripon Coll Cuddesdon 74. **d** 76 **p** 77. C Cannock *Lich* 76-79; C Middlesbrough Ascension *York* 79-81; V Oldham St Steph and All Martyrs *Man* 81-84; V Perry Beeches *Birm* 84-90; P-in-c Saltley 90-93; P-in-c Shaw Hill 90-93; V Saltley and Shaw Hill 93-97; R Lon Docks St Pet w Wapping St Jo from 97. *St Peter's Clergy House, Wapping Lane, London E1W 2RW* T: (020) 7481 2985 E: father.jones@btinternet.com *or* frtejones@aol.com

JONES, The Ven Trevor Pryce. b 48. Southn Univ BEd 76 BTh 79 Univ of Wales (Cardiff) LLM 04 St Jo Coll Dur DThM 13. Sarum & Wells Th Coll 73. **d** 76 **p** 77. C Glouc St Geo 76-79; Warden Bp Mascall Cen *Heref* 79-84; Dioc Communications Officer 81-86; TR Heref S Wye 84-97; Preb Heref Cathl 93-97; OCM 85-97; Adn Hertford and Hon Can St Alb *St Alb* from 97. *Glebe House, St Mary's Lane, Hertingfordbury, Hertford SG14 2LE* T: (01992) 581629 F: 535349 E: archdhert@stalbans.anglican.org

JONES, Canon Tudor Howell. b 39. Univ of Wales (Cardiff) BD 91. St Mich Coll Llan. **d** 68 **p** 69. C Clydach *S & B* 68-72; C Swansea St Pet 72-75; V Ystradfellte 75-79; V Llangiwg 79-91; V Manselton 91-05; RD Penderi 98-05; Can Res Brecon Cathl 00-05; rtd 05. *15 Glasfryn Close, Cockett, Swansea SA2 0FP*

JONES, Miss Victoria Kay. b 83. St Mich Coll Llan 09. **d** 12 **p** 13. C Llangwm w Freystrop and Johnston *St D* from 12. *The Vicarage, Steynton, Milford Haven SA73 1AW* T: (01646) 690895 M: 07976-836209 E: rev.vjones@gmail.com

JONES, Preb Wilfred David. b 22. Keble Coll Ox BA 47 MA 48. St Mich Coll Llan 47. **d** 48 **p** 49. C Aberaman *Llan* 48-50; C Cardiff St Jo 50-55; Chapl Kelly Coll Tavistock 55-62; V St Decumans *B & W* 62-76; V Ilminster w Whitelackington 76-92; RD Ilminster 78-87; Preb Wells Cathl 81-05; rtd 92; PtO *B & W* 92-06. *Dragons, Lambrook Road, Shepton Beauchamp, Ilminster TA19 0NA* T: (01460) 240967

JONES, Wilfred Lovell. b 39. Lon Univ BD 71 Cam Univ CertEd. St D Coll Lamp. **d** 63 **p** 64. C Llanllyfni *Ban* 63-65; C Llanbeblig w Caernarfon 65-68; V Llanwnog w Penstrowed 68-72; V Llanwnnog and Caersws w Carno 72-75; Asst Chapl Dover Coll 77-90; Chapl Wrekin Coll Telford 91-94; V Llangollen w Trevor and Llantysilio *St As* 94-04; AD Llangollen 03-04; rtd 04; PtO *St As* from 09. *21 Ashley Drive, Blackwater, Camberley GU17 0PR*

JONES, Canon William. b 30. BTh 92. St Mich Coll Llan 54. **d** 55 **p** 56. C Denio w Abererch *Ban* 55-60; V Aberdaron and Bodferin 60-66; R Llandwrog 66-71; R Llanstumdwy, Llangybi w Llanarmon 71-74; R Dolbenmaen w Llanystymdwy w Llangybi etc 74-99; RD Eifionydd 75-99; Can Ban Cathl 84-93; Can and Treas Ban Cathl 93-99; rtd 99; PtO *Ban* from 99. *Y Fachwen, Rhoshirwaun, Pwllheli LL53 8LB* T: (01758) 760262

JONES, William Dafydd. **d** 10 **p** 11. NSM Bro Teifi Sarn Helen *St D* 10-12; C Llanddewi Brefi and Llangeitho 12-13; P-in-c from 13. *Llwynteg, Felinfach, Lampeter SA48 8BQ* T: (01570) 470691 E: dafydd.aeron1@btinternet.com

JONES, Canon William David. b 28. St D Coll Lamp BA 48 Lon Univ BD 57 Leeds Univ MA 73. St Mich Coll Llan 48. **d** 51 **p** 52. C Risca *Mon* 51-54; C Chepstow St Arvan's w Penterry 54-55; C St Geo-in-the-East w Ch Ch w St Jo *Lon* 55-59; C Farnham Royal *Ox* 59-64; Lect Div Culham Coll 65-67; Hd RS Doncaster Coll of Educn 67-74; Vice-Prin St Bede Coll Dur 74; Vice-Prin SS Hild and Bede Coll Dur 75-89; Lect Th Dur Univ 75-89; Dir of Miss Ch in Wales 89-93; Metropolitical and Hon Can St D Cathl 90-93; rtd 93; PtO *Glouc* 93-08; *Llan* from 12. *Triscombe Lodge, 55 Llantrisant Road, Cardiff CF5 2PU* T: (029) 2019 3914 E: wdavidjones@ntlworld.com

JONES, William Douglas. b 28. St Fran Coll Brisbane ThL 56. **d** 56 **p** 58. Australia 56-58; Papua New Guinea 58-72; C Manston *Ripon* 72-75; V Middleton St Mary 75-87; V Ireland Wood 87-94; rtd 94; PtO *Ripon* 94-13. *6 Willow Court, Pool in Wharfedale, Otley LS21 1RX* T: 0113-284 2028

JONES, William John. b 59. St Mich Coll Llan 91. **d** 93 **p** 94. C Pembroke Dock w Cosheston w Nash and Upton *St D* 93-96; C Tenby 96; TV 96-99; V Llanrhian w Llanhywel and Carnhedryn etc 99-00; rtd 00. *13 George Street, Milford Haven SA73 2AY* T: (01646) 697094

JONES, William Lincoln. b 19. St D Coll Lamp BA 41 St Mich Coll Llan 41. **d** 43 **p** 44. C Roath *Llan* 43-47; C Wooburn *Ox* 47-50; C Bridgwater w Chilton *B & W* 50-55; V Langford Budville w Runnington 55-60; V Winscombe 60-71; V Bishops Lydeard 71-73; V Bishops Lydeard w Cothelstone 73-80; P-in-c Bagborough 78-80; R Bishops Lydeard w Bagborough and Cothelstone 80-84; rtd 84; PtO *Ex* from 86. *Holme Lea, Well Mead, Kilmington, Axminster EX13 7SQ* T: (01297) 32744

JONES, Wyn. *See* JONES, Ivor Wyn

JONES, Mrs Wyn. b 49. **d** 01 **p** 02. OLM Linslade *Ox* 01-08; OLM Ouzel Valley *St Alb* from 08. *2 Woodside Way, Linslade, Leighton Buzzard LU7 7PN* T: (01525) 373638

JONES-BLACKETT, Enid Olive. b 40. Reading Univ BA 61. **d** 97 **p** 98. OLM Hellesdon *Nor* 97-10; rtd 10; PtO *Nor* from 10. *8 Fastolf Close, Hellesdon, Norwich NR6 5RE* T: (01603) 424769 E: enidjonesblackett@btinternet.com

JONES-CRABTREE, Stephen. *See* CRABTREE, Stephen

JONES PARRY, Mark. b 77. Oak Hill Th Coll. **d** 12 **p** 13. C Enfield Ch Ch Trent Park *Lon* from 12. *45 Osier Crescent, London N10 1QS*

JONG, Jonathan. **d** 14 **p** 15. NSM Ox St Mary Magd from 14. *64 Banbury Road, Oxford OX2 6PN* E: jonathan.jong@anthro.ox.ac.uk

JONGMAN, Canon Kären Anngel Irene. b 43. EMMTC 97. **d** 01 **p** 02. NSM Northampton St Mary *Pet* 01-03; NSM Guilsborough w Hollowell and Cold Ashby 03-04; P-in-c Walgrave w Hannington and Wold and Scaldwell from 04; Chapl Northants Fire and Rescue Service from 03; Can Pet Cathl 12-13. *The Rectory, Lower Green, Walgrave, Northampton NN6 9QF* T/F: (01604) 781974 M: 07980-881252 E: jongman@ncounterus.org.uk

JORDAN, Anne. b 42. RGN 66. **d** 02 **p** 03. OLM Crofton *Leeds* from 02. *95 Ashdene Avenue, Crofton, Wakefield WF4 1LY* T: (01924) 865527 M: 07450-475184

JORDAN, Anthony John. b 50. Birm Univ BEd 73. LNSM course. **d** 83 **p** 84. Asst Chapl Uppingham Sch 83-86; NSM Uppingham w Ayston and Wardley w Belton *Pet* 83-86; Asst Chapl Sherborne Sch 86-87; NSM Bournemouth St Fran *Win* 88-03; PtO *Leic* 04-06; NSM Leic St Aid 06-08; V Eyres Monsell 08-13; rtd 13. *St Hugh's Vicarage, 51 Pasley Road, Leicester LE2 9BU* T: 0116-278 0940 M: 07798-860106 E: fathertonyjordan@ntlworld.com

JORDAN, Avril Marilyn. *See* COURTNEY, Avril Marilyn

JORDAN, Darryl Mark. b 62. Univ of Texas at Dallas BSc 85 S Methodist Univ Dallas MDiv 05. Perkins Sch of Th (USA) 01. **d** 04 **p** 04. C Dallas Ch Ch USA 04-05; C Bishop's Stortford St Mich *St Alb* 05-09; C Christchurch *Win* 09-13. *6 Gleadowe Avenue, Christchurch BH23 1LR* T: (01202) 470722

JORDAN, Mrs Elizabeth Ann. b 58. New Hall Cam MA 82. St Jo Coll Nottm 82. **d** 87 **p** 94. Par Dn Blackpool St Jo *Blackb* 87-90; Par Dn Ewood 90-94; C 94-95; Asst Dir of Ords 90-95; Min Shelfield St Mark CD *Lich* 95-00; Local Min Adv (Wolverhampton) 95-05; OLM Course Ldr and Team Ldr Min Division 03-05; Dir Local Min Development 06-10; C Blakenall Heath 10-11; Lay Educn and Tr Adv *Chelmsf* from 11; Hon C Rawreth from 12. *Diocesan Office, 53 New Street, Chelmsford CM1 1AT* T: (01245) 294454 F: 294477 E: ejordan@chelmsford.anglican.org

JORDAN, John Charles. b 37. CQSW 81. NOC 84. **d** 87 **p** 88. C Southport Em *Liv* 87-90; V Abram and Bickershaw 90-95; V Bempton w Flamborough, Reighton w Speeton *York* 95-00; rtd 01; PtO *York* from 05. *35 Hollycroft, Barnston, Driffield YO25 8PP* T: (01262) 468925 E: barmstonbonnie@yahoo.co.uk *or* bonnie.35@btinternet.com

JORDAN, Miss Pamela Mary. b 43. Univ of Wales (Cardiff) BSc 64 Ox Univ DipEd 65. WEMTC 02. **d** 05 **p** 06. NSM Coalbrookdale, Iron-Bridge and Lt Wenlock *Heref* from 05. *2 Madeley Wood View, Madeley, Telford TF7 5TF* T: (01952) 583254

JORDAN, Patrick Glen. b 69. SEITE 01. **d** 04 **p** 05. C Charlton *S'wark* 04-07; C Catford (Southend) and Downham 07-08; TV from 08. *233 Bellingham Road, London SE6 1EH* T: (020) 8697 3220 E: revpatrickjordan@yahoo.co.uk

JORDAN, Peter Harry. b 42. Leeds Univ BA 64 Leeds Coll of Educn PGCE 65. Cranmer Hall Dur 70. **d** 73 **p** 74. C Nottingham St Ann w Em *S'well* 73-77; C Edgware *Lon* 77-82; V Everton St Chrys *Liv* 82-94; Dioc Ev and V Bootle St Mary w St Paul 94-02; Chapl Barcelona *Eur* 02-08; rtd 08; PtO *Eur* from 08; *Ches* from 10. *11 Stanford Avenue, Wallasey CH45 5AP* T: 0151-639 7860 E: peterybarbara@gmail.com

JORDAN, Richard William. b 56. Lanchester Poly Cov BSc 78 Sheff Univ MA 07. St Jo Coll Nottm 84. **d** 87 **p** 88. C Blackpool St Jo *Blackb* 87-90; V Ewood 90-95; PtO *Lich* 95-97; Co-ord Walsall Town Cen Min 97-00; Ch Links Projects Officer 00-06; Dioc Ch and Soc Officer *Derby* 06-11; P-in-c Rawreth *Chelmsf* from 11; RD Rochford from 15. *The Rectory, Church Road, Rawreth, Wickford SS11 8SH* T: (01268) 766565 E: rwjordan@gmx.com *or* richard@st.nicholas.rawreth.org.uk

JORDAN, Robert Brian. b 43. Qu Coll Birm 68. **d** 69 **p** 70. C Norton St Mich *Dur* 69-73; C Hastings St Clem and All SS *Chich* 73-74; C Carshalton *S'wark* 74-81; V Catford St Andr 81-08; rtd 08. *5 St Patrick's Road, Deal CT14 6AN* T: (01304) 368607

JORDAN, Steven Paul. b 52. **d** 11. NSM Church Lench w Rous Lench and Abbots Morton etc *Worc* from 11. *Chadbury House, Worcester Road, Chadbury, Evesham WR11 4TD* T: (01386) 45041 E: bspj@live.co.uk

JORDAN, Thomas. b 36. NW Ord Course 76. **d** 79 **p** 80. NSM Prenton *Ches* 79-84; NSM Egremont St Jo 84-91; C 91-96; Ind Chapl 91-96; TV Birkenhead Priory 96-01; rtd 01; PtO *Ches* from 02. *31 Willowbank Road, Birkenhead CH42 7JU* T: 0151-652 4212 E: thomas.t.jordan@btinternet.com

JORDAN, Trevor. b 44. Lon Hosp MB, BS 67 LRCP 68 MRCS 68 Nottm Univ MA 99. EMMTC 96. **d** 03 **p** 04. NSM Seamer *York* 03-07; PtO 07-11; NSM Long Buckby w Watford and W Haddon w Winwick *Pet* from 11. *The Vicarage, West End, West Haddon, Northampton NN6 7AY* T: (01788) 510535 M: 07887-537244 E: trevor@trevorsweb.net

JORDINSON, Vera (Sister Hilary). b 37. Liv Univ BA 60 CertEd 61. Westcott Ho Cam 88. **d** 89 **p** 94. CSF from 74; Prov Sec 90-01; Gen Sec 96-02; Sec for Miss SSF 96-99; Gift Aid Sec 01-11; LtO *Heref* 89-92; PtO *Lich* 90-92; *Birm* 92-94 and 97-06 and from 12; *B & W* 06-10; NSM Birchfield *Birm* 94-96. *St Francis House, 113 Gillott Road, Birmingham B16 0ET* E: hilarycsf@franciscans.org.uk

JØRGENSEN (née BURGESS), Mrs Laura Jane. b 74. Imp Coll Lon BSc 95 ARSM 95. Ripon Coll Cuddesdon BTh 00. **d** 00 **p** 01. C St Alb Abbey 00-01; C Boxmoor St Jo 01-04; Min Can and Sacr St Paul's Cathl 04-09; V St Botolph Aldgate w H Trin Minories from 09; PV Westmr Abbey from 10. *St Botolph's Church, Aldgate High Street, London EC3N 1AB* T: (020) 7283 2154 E: rector@stbotolphs.org.uk

JORYSZ, Ian Herbert. b 62. Van Mildert Coll Dur BSc 84 MA 95 Liv Univ PhD 87. Ripon Coll Cuddesdon BA 89 MA 95. **d** 90 **p** 91. C Houghton le Spring *Dur* 90-93; C Ferryhill 93-95; Research Officer to Bp of Bradwell 95-15; P-in-c S Weald *Chelmsf* 95-00; V 00-15; RD Brentwood 08-15; Bp's Sen Chapl *Man* from 15. *Bishopscourt, Bury New Road, Salford M7 4LE* T: 0161-792 2096 E: chaplain@bishopscourt.manchester.anglican.org *or* ian@jorysz.com *or* ianjorysz@gmail.com

JOSEPH EMMANUEL, Brother. *See* DICKSON, Colin James

JOSS, Capt Martin James Torquil. b 60. Univ of Wales (Lamp) BA 79. EAMTC 03. **d** 03 **p** 04. C Harlow Town Cen w Lt Parndon *Chelmsf* 03-07; P-in-c Coalville and Bardon Hill *Leic* 07-09; C Ravenstone and Swannington 07-09; V Coalville w Bardon Hill and Ravenstone from 09. *Christ Church Vicarage, 28 London Road, Coalville LE67 3JA* T: (01530) 838287 M: 07875-494588 E: martinjoss52@gmail.com

JOUSTRA, The Very Revd Jan Tjeerd. b 57. Univ of Tasmania BA 83 La Trobe Univ Vic MA 97. Melbourne Coll of Div BTh 91. **d** 89 **p** 91. C Melbourne E Australia 90-91; C Wangaratta Cathl 91-93; R Rutherglen w Chiltern 93-97; P-in-c St Steph Cathl Hong Kong 97-03; Sen Chapl St Jo Cathl 00-03; Chapl Monte Carlo *Eur* 04-07; Dean Hamilton New Zealand from 07. *PO Box 338, Hamilton, New Zealand*

JOWETT, Ms Hilary Anne. b 54. Hull Univ BA 75. Cranmer Hall Dur IDC 80. **dss** 82 **d** 87 **p** 94. Par Dn Brampton Bierlow 87-89; Hon Par Dn Sharrow St Andr 89-95; Chapl Nether Edge Hosp Sheff 89-95; C Sheff St Mark Broomhill 95-97; C Mosbrough 97-00; TR Gleadless 00-12; R Dinnington w Laughton and Throapham from 12. *The Rectory, 217 Nursery Road, Dinnington, Sheffield S25 2QU* T: (01909) 562335 E: hilary.jowett@sheffield.anglican.org

JOWETT, Canon Nicholas Peter Alfred. b 44. St Cath Coll Cam BA 66 MA Bris Univ CertEd 67. Qu Coll Birm 72. **d** 75 **p** 76. C Wales *Sheff* 75-78; TV Sheff Manor 78-83; V Brampton Bierlow 83-89; V Psalter Lane St Andr 89-12; Dioc Ecum Adv 01-09; Hon Can Sheff Cathl 06-12; rtd 12; PtO *Sheff* from 12. *The Rectory, 217 Nursery Road, Dinnington, Sheffield S25 2QU* T: (01909) 562335 E: mail@njowett.plus.com

JOWITT, Andrew Robert Benson. b 56. Down Coll Cam BA 78 PGCE 79 MA 81. Wycliffe Hall Ox 88. **d** 90 **p** 91. C Northampton Em *Pet* 90-94; C Barking St Marg w St Patr *Chelmsf* 94-98; TV 98-00; TV Stantonbury and Willen *Ox* from 00; Bp's Officer for Evang from 00. *Church House, 1A Atterbrook, Bradwell, Milton Keynes MK13 9EY* T: (01908) 320850 E: jowitts@btinternet.com

JOY, Bernard David. b 50. Sarum & Wells Th Coll 90. **d** 92 **p** 93. C Shortlands *Roch* 92-94; C Henbury *Bris* 94-96; V Bristol St Aid w St Geo 96-03; P-in-c Bridgwater St Fran *B & W* 03-07; V from 07. *The Vicarage, Saxon Green, Bridgwater TA6 4HZ* T: (01278) 422744 M: 07796-678478 E: rev.obejoyful@gmail.com

JOY, Canon Matthew Osmund Clifton. b 40. St Edm Hall Ox BA 62 MA 66. St Steph Ho Ox 62. **d** 64 **p** 65. C Brinksway *Ches* 64-66; C Southwick St Columba *Dur* 66-69; V Hartlepool H Trin 69-85; V Rotherham St Paul, St Mich and St Jo Ferham

Park *Sheff* 85-88; V Masbrough 88-95; RD Rotherham 88-93; P-in-c Bordesley St Benedict *Birm* 95-01; V 01-05; Bp's Adv on Chr/Muslim Relns 95-05; rtd 05; PtO *Leeds* from 05; *Sheff* from 06. *Lindisfarne, Eddyfield Road, Oxspring, Sheffield S36 8YH* T: (01226) 762276

JOYCE, Canon Alison Jane. b 59. Univ of Wales (Swansea) BA 81 Bris Univ MLitt 87 Birm Univ PhD 00 SS Coll Cam PGCE 84. Ripon Coll Cuddesdon BA 87 MA 94. **d** 88 **p** 94. Par Dn Chalgrove w Berrick Salome *Ox* 88-90; Tutor WMMTC 90-95; Tutor Qu Coll Birm 95-96; NSM Moseley St Anne *Birm* 96-04; Dean NSMs 00-03; NSM Birm Cathl 04-05; P-in-c Edgbaston St Bart 05-11; V 11-14; Chapl Birm Univ 05-14; Chapl Elmhurst Sch for Dance 05-14; Hon Can Birm Cathl 06-14; R St Bride Fleet Street w Bridewell etc *Lon* from 14. *St Bride's Rectory, St Bride's Avenue, London EC4Y 8AU* T: (020) 7427 0133
E: ajjoyce.oldedg@btinternet.com

JOYCE, Anthony Owen. b 35. Selw Coll Cam BA 60 MA 64. Wycliffe Hall Ox 60. **d** 62 **p** 63. C Birm St Martin 62-67; Rhodesia 67-70; V Birm St Luke 70-79; V Downend *Bris* 79-01; RD Stapleton 83-89; rtd 01; PtO *Bris* from 02. *116 Jellicoe Avenue, Stapleton, Bristol BS16 1WJ* T: 0117-956 2510
E: tony@joycet.freeserve.co.uk

JOYCE, Gordon Franklin. b 51. Birm Univ BA 72. St Jo Coll Nottm 86. **d** 88 **p** 89. C Didsbury St Jas and Em *Man* 88-92; V Tonge w Alkrington 92-06; C Bury St Mary from 06; P-in-c Bircle from 12; V Bury, Roch Valley from 13; AD Bury from 10. *1A Pimhole Road, Bury BL9 7EY* T: 0161-764 1157
E: gordonjoyce@gordonjoyce.eclipse.co.uk

JOYCE, Graham Leslie. b 49. Lon Univ CertEd 71. Trin Coll Bris 87. **d** 89 **p** 90. C Heald Green St Cath *Ches* 89-93; R Church Lawton 93-14; rtd 14. *11 Fields Close, Alsager, Stoke-on-Trent ST7 2ND* E: grahamljoyce@btinternet.com

JOYCE, Jennifer Claire. *See* BRIDGMAN, Jennifer Claire

JOYCE, John Barnabas Altham. b 47. St Chad's Coll Dur BA 69 Lon Univ DipEd 86. St Steph Ho Ox 72. **d** 74 **p** 75. C Reading St Giles *Ox* 74-77; C Cowley St Jo 77-80; Dioc Youth and Community Officer 80-87; V Hangleton *Chich* 87-94; Dioc Adv for Schs and Dir Educn 94-99; R Hurstpierpoint 99-13; rtd 13. *3 Wolstonbury Road, Hove BN3 6EJ* T: (01273) 773150

JOYCE, Kingsley Reginald. b 49. TD 91 MBE 00. Man Univ BSc 70. Cuddesdon Coll 70. **d** 73 **p** 74. C High Wycombe *Ox* 73-76; C Fingest 76-79; C Hambleden 76-79; C Medmenham 76-79; C Fawley (Bucks) 76-79; C Turville 76-79; P-in-c Hambleden Valley 79-80; R 80-87; R Friern Barnet St Jas *Lon* 87-91; CF 91-08; Chapl Naples w Sorrento, Capri and Bari *Eur* 08-13. *Address temp unknown*

JOYCE, Margaret. b 47. Oak Hill NSM Course 86. **d** 89 **p** 94. NSM Chadwell Heath *Chelmsf* 89-92; NSM Bath Odd Down w Combe Hay *B & W* from 92; Chapl Bath and West Community NHS Trust from 95. *69 Bloomfield Rise, Bath BA2 2BN* T: (01225) 840864
E: margaretjoyce@stphilipstjames.org

JOYCE, Martin Ernest Chancellor. b 50. K Coll Lon 69. **d** 73 **p** 74. C Leigh Park *Portsm* 73-77; C Milton 77-83; TV Cambridge Ascension *Ely* 83-85; V Blackpool St Mich *Blackb* 85-87; PtO *Glas* 94-11; *Carl* 00-11; P-in-c Gt and Lt Dunham w Gt and Lt Fransham *Nor* from 11. *The Rectory, Pound Lane, Litcham, King's Lynn PE32 2QR*

JOYCE, Paul David. b 70. Qu Coll Birm 00. **d** 02 **p** 03. C Perry Beeches *Birm* 02-05; V Eastwood St Dav *Chelmsf* from 05. *St David's Vicarage, 400 Rayleigh Road, Leigh-on-Sea SS9 5PT* T: (01702) 523126 E: joycefamily400@btinternet.com

JOYCE, Miss Penelope Anne. b 53. St Mary's Coll Chelt CertEd 74. Wycliffe Hall Ox. **d** 00 **p** 01. C Ox St Clem 00-03; C Cogges and S Leigh 03-09; Hon C Bourne Valley *Sarum* from 11; Hon C Salisbury St Fran and Stratford sub Castle from 11. *60 Endless Street, Salisbury SP1 3UH* M: 07808-181885
E: pennyoldsarum@gmail.com

JOYCE, Philip Rupert. b 38. Selw Coll Cam BA 68 MA 72. Cranmer Hall Dur 68. **d** 70 **p** 71. C Newland St Jo *York* 70-73; C Woolwich St Mary w H Trin *S'wark* 73-77; Chapl Thames Poly 77-87; Chapl S Bank Poly 77-79; rtd 03. *37 Fulcher Avenue, Cromer NR27 9SG* T: (01263) 519405
E: philipjoyce@ntlworld.com

JOYCE, Canon Terence Alan. b 57. St Jo Coll Nottm BTh 84. **d** 84 **p** 85. C Mansfield SS Pet and Paul *S'well* 84-88; V Greasley 88-00; Dioc Dir of Ords 99-11; Dir Post-Ord Support and Tr 01-11; Hon Can S'well Minster 02-11; York Adnry Tr Adv and Dioc Adv for Clergy CMD from 12; NSM Rural E York from 12. *The Rectory, Sandy Lane, Stockton-on-the-Forest, York YO32 9UR* T: (01904) 400811
E: terry.joyce@yorkdiocese.org

JOYNER, Mrs Susan Diane. b 58. Nene Coll Northn BA 79 Open Univ MA 99 Leic Univ PGCE 84. NEOC 05. **d** 08 **p** 09.

NSM Upper Coquetdale *Newc* from 08. *The Old Church, Harbottle, Morpeth NE65 7DQ* T: (01669) 650385
E: suejoyner2@aol.com

JOYNES, David. b 51. Leeds Univ BSc 74. Ripon Coll Cuddesdon 12. **d** 13 **p** 14. OLM The Cookhams *Ox* from 13. *1 Keeleys Cottages, High Street, Cookham, Maidenhead SL6 9SF* T: (01628) 528622 E: revdavidjoynes@gmail.com

JUBA, Bishop of. *See* MARONA, The Most Revd Joseph Biringi Hassan

JUCKES, Jonathan Sydney. b 61. St Andr Univ MA 83. Ridley Hall Cam BA 87. **d** 88 **p** 89. C Sevenoaks St Nic *Roch* 88-92; Proclamation Trust 92-95; C St Helen Bishopsgate w St Andr Undershaft etc *Lon* 95-98; TR Kirk Ella and Willerby *York* 98-14; R from 14. *The Rectory, 2 School Lane, Kirk Ella, Hull HU10 7NR* T: (01482) 653040
E: juckes@juckes.karoo.co.uk

JUDD, Adrian Timothy. b 67. Lanc Univ BA 88 St Jo Coll Dur BA 92. Cranmer Hall Dur 90 Trin Coll Singapore 92. **d** 93 **p** 94. C Dudley St Aug Holly Hall *Worc* 93-97; V Stockbridge Village *Liv* 97-99; V Went Valley *Leeds* from 00. *The Vicarage, Marlpit Lane, Darrington, Pontefract WF8 3AB* T: (01977) 704744 E: thevicar@darringtonchurch.com

JUDD, Colin Ivor. b 35. Dur Univ BA 61. Ridley Hall Cam 61. **d** 63 **p** 64. C Stratford St Jo w Ch Ch *Chelmsf* 63-66; C Kimberworth *Sheff* 66-68; Area Sec CMS *Bradf* and *Wakef* 68-80; V Bradf St Columba w St Andr 80-00; rtd 00; PtO *Leeds* from 00. *57 Grosvenor Road, Shipley BD18 4RB* T: (01274) 584775 E: thejudds@saltsvillage.co.uk

JUDD, Mrs Nicola Jane. b 51. Birm Coll of Educn CertEd 72. S Dios Minl Tr Scheme 87. **d** 90 **p** 94. NSM Abbotts Ann and Upper and Goodworth Clatford *Win* 90-11; Adv for NSM 01-11; rtd 11; PtO *Win* from 11. *13 Belmont Close, Andover SP10 2DE* T: (01264) 363364
E: nicola.judd@ukonline.co.uk

JUDD, The Very Revd Peter Somerset Margesson. b 49. Trin Hall Cam BA 71. Cuddesdon Coll 71. **d** 74 **p** 75. C Salford St Phil w St Steph *Man* 74-76; Chapl Clare Coll Cam 76-81; C Burnham *Ox* 81-82; TV Burnham w Dropmore, Hitcham and Taplow 82-88; V Iffley 88-97; RD Cowley 94-97; Provost Chelmsf 97-00; Dean Chelmsf 00-13; rtd 13; PtO *Ely* from 14. *18 Baycliffe Close, Cambridge CB1 8EE*

JUDD, Susan Elizabeth. b 48. Bris Univ BSc 74 Univ of Wales MA 04 ACA 80. STETS 05. **d** 08 **p** 09. NSM Portsm Cathl 08-12; PtO from 12. *16 Bepton Down, Petersfield GU31 4PR* T: (01730) 266819 E: susan.judd@ntlworld.com

JUDGE, Mrs Alison Gwendolyn. b 60. SEITE BA 10. **d** 10 **p** 11. C W Wickham St Fran and St Mary *S'wark* 10-14; PtO from 14. *7 Woodland Way, West Wickham BR4 9LL* T: (020) 8616 5794 M: 07939-495710 E: alison@judge-family.com

JUDGE, Andrew Duncan. b 50. Cape Town Univ BCom 72 Keble Coll Ox MA 81. Pietermaritzburg Th Sem 82. **d** 83 **p** 84. C Westville S Africa 84-87; R Prestbury 88-94; R Westville 94-01; TV Keynsham *B & W* from 01. *St Francis's Vicarage, Warwick Road, Keynsham, Bristol BS31 2PW* T: 0117-373 7478 E: revjudge@blueyonder.co.uk

JUDSON, Miss Christine Alison. b 64. Surrey Univ BSc 86 Birm Univ PGCE 88. Ripon Coll Cuddesdon 05. **d** 07 **p** 08. C Highbridge *B & W* 07-10; TV Portishead from 10. *77 Nightingale Rise, Portishead, Bristol BS20 8LX* T: (01275) 397232 E: c.judson@btinternet.com

JUDSON, Mrs Mary Ruth. b 47. Bretton Hall Coll DipEd 68. NEOC 89. **d** 92 **p** 94. Par Dn Chester le Street *Dur* 92-94; C 94-96; V Millfield St Mark and Pallion St Luke 96-04; V Hartlepool St Luke 04-11; rtd 11; PtO *Dur* from 12. *5 Caxton Way, Chester le Street DH3 4BW* T: 0191-388 0512 E: maryjudson7@gmail.com

JUDSON, Paul Wesley. b 46. Leic Poly ATD 71. Cranmer Hall Dur 87. **d** 89 **p** 90. C Lobley Hill *Dur* 89-92; C Chester le Street 92-96; Ed Dioc Publications and Sec Dioc Bd of Soc Resp 96-98; C Millfield St Mark and Pallion St Luke 96-04; C Hartlepool St Luke 04-11; Dioc Publications Officer 98-11; Dioc Dir of Communications 02-11; rtd 11; PtO *Dur* from 12. *5 Caxton Way, Chester le Street DH3 4BW* T: 0191-388 0512 E: pwjudson@gmail.com

JUDSON, Peter. b 39. Lon Univ BSc 61 Plymouth Univ PGCE 87. SWMTC 99. **d** 02 **p** 03. OLM Bude Haven and Marhamchurch *Truro* 02-09; rtd 09. *Meadowcroft, Bagbury Road, Bude EX23 8QJ* T/F: (01288) 356597 M: 07970-115538

JUKES, John Christopher. b 61. Ex Univ BTh 13. SWMTC 10. **d** 13 **p** 14. C Saltash *Truro* from 13. *35 Lower Port View, Saltash PL12 4BY* T: (01752) 842034 M: 07443-414436
E: johnjukes101@yahoo.co.uk

JUKES (*née* WEATHERHOGG), Mrs Susanne. b 56. Leeds Univ BA 77 Coll of Ripon & York St Jo PGCE 78. NEOC 98. **d** 01 **p** 02. C Monk Fryston and S Milford *York* 01-05; P-in-c 05-07;

Assoc Min Aldborough w Boroughbridge and Roecliffe *Ripon* 07-09; Asst Dir of Ords 07-09; Chapl HM Pris Full Sutton 09-14; V Topcliffe, Baldersby w Dishforth, Dalton etc *York* from 14. *The Vicarage, Front Street, Topcliffe, Thirsk YO7 3RU*

JUMP, Elizabeth Anne. b 63. Liv Inst of Educn BA 95. NOC 97. **d** 00 **p** 01. C Walkden and Lt Hulton *Man* 00-03; P-in-c Elton St Steph 03-05; C Ashton Ch Ch 05-06; PtO 06-07; TV Blackbourne *St E* 07-14; R Wroxham w Hoveton and Belaugh *Nor* from 14. *The Rectory, 11 Church Lane, Wroxham, Norwich NR12 8SH* T: (01359) 269265
E: revlizj@btinternet.com

JUMP, Paul Gordon. b 77. St Andr Univ BSc 99. Oak Hill Th Coll 04. **d** 07 **p** 08. C Rusholme H Trin *Man* 07-10; NSM 10-12; P-in-c Higher Openshaw from 12. *St Clement's Rectory, Ashton Old Road, Manchester M11 1HF* T: 0161-826 7587
E: paulandgilljump@gmail.com *or* paul@st-clement.org

JUNG, Mrs Jennifer Margaret. b 61. STETS 95. **d** 98 **p** 99. NSM Fareham H Trin *Portsm* 98-02. *42 Clifton Road, Winchester SO22 5BU*

JUNIPER, Sandra Elizabeth. b 42. SWMTC. **d** 11 **p** 12. NSM Bideford, Northam, Westward Ho!, Appledore etc *Ex* from 11. *6 Acacia Close, Bideford EX39 3BA* T: (01237) 425982
E: sandra.juniper@talktalk.net

✠**JUPP, The Rt Revd Roger Alan.** b 56. St Edm Hall Ox BA 78 MA 82 Surrey Univ PGCE 96. Chich Th Coll 79. **d** 80 **p** 81 **c** 03. C Newbold w Dunston *Derby* 80-83; C Cowley St Jo *Ox* 83-85; C Islington St Jas w St Phil *Lon* 85-86; V Lower Beeding *Chich* 86-90; Dom Chapl to Bp Horsham 86-91; V Burgess Hill St Jo 90-93; TR Burgess Hill St Jo w St Edw 93-94; PtO 97-98;

C Aldwick 98-00; Prin Newton Th Coll Papua New Guinea 00-03; Bp Popondota 03-05; P-in-c St Leonards Ch Ch and St Mary *Chich* 05-06; R St Leonards Ch Ch and St Mary etc 06-12; Hon Asst Bp Chich 05-12; V Long Eaton St Laur *Derby* from 12; P-in-c Ilkeston H Trin from 12. *St Laurence's Vicarage, Regent Street, Long Eaton, Nottingham NG10 1JX* T: 0115-973 5168 E: rajupp1@hotmail.com

JUPP, Vincent John. b 64. St Jo Coll Nottm BA(ThM) 06. **d** 00 **p** 01. C Evington *Leic* 00-03; TV Ascension TM 03-07; TR 07-11; AD City of Leic 09-11; V Birstall and Wanlip from 11. *The Rectory, 251 Birstall Road, Birstall, Leicester LE4 4DJ* T: 0116-267 4517 E: vince@nursery73.plus.com

JUSTICE, Keith Leonard. b 42. Wolv Univ BSc 68 CEng 83 MIMechE 83. Wycliffe Hall Ox 91. **d** 93 **p** 94. C Penwortham St Mary *Blackb* 93-96; C Dovercourt and Parkeston w Harwich *Chelmsf* 96-98; V Wentworth *Sheff* 98-01; Chapl Rotherham Gen Hosps NHS Trust 98-01; Chapl Rotherham Priority Health Services NHS Trust 98-01; R Melrose *Edin* 01-04; P-in-c Royton St Anne *Man* 04-08; P-in-c Lawton Moor 08-13; rtd 13; PtO *Man* from 13. *228A Wythenshawe Road, Manchester M23 0PH* E: keith.justice@ntlworld.com

JUSTICE, Simon Charles. b 66. Univ of Wales (Lamp) BD 88 Edin Univ MTh 90. Cranmer Hall Dur 90. **d** 92 **p** 93. C Tilehurst St Mich *Ox* 92-95; R Troy St Paul USA 95-01; R Tigard St Jas 02-04; Can All SS Cathl Albany 98-04; R Edin Ch Ch 04-06; R Corvallis Gd Samaritan USA from 06. *445 NW Elizabeth Drive, Corvallis OR 97330, USA* E: simon.justice@googlemail.com

JUTSUM, Linda Mary. *See* ELLIOTT, Linda Mary

K

KABOLEH, David Reardon. b 64. Westmr Coll Ox MTh 00. Trin Coll Nairobi 88. **d** 90 **p** 91. C-in-c Nairobi St Phil Kenya 90-92; TV Nairobi St Luke and Immanuel 93-95; NSM Hoddesdon *St Alb* 95-97; NSM Ox St Matt 97-99; NSM Blackbird Leys 99-02; NSM Ox St Aldate 03-04; NSM Akeman 04-07; P-in-c Worminghall w Ickford, Oakley and Shabbington 07-10; R from 10. *The Rectory, 32A The Avenue, Worminghall, Aylesbury HP18 9LE* T: (01844) 338839
E: kaboleh@btinternet.com

✠**KAFITY, The Rt Revd Samir.** b 33. Beirut Univ BA 57. Near E Sch of Th 57. **d** 57 **p** 58 **c** 86. Israel 57-64 and 77-98; Lebanon 64-77; Adn Jerusalem 77-82; Bp Jerusalem 84-98; Pres Bp Episc Ch Jerusalem and Middle E 86-96; rtd 98. *11964 Callado Road, San Diego CA 92128, USA*

KAGGWA, Nelson Sonny. b 58. E Lon Univ BA 91. Bp Tucker Coll Mukono 77. **d** 80 **p** 80. Kenya 80-83; USA 83; Hon C Ox SS Phil and Jas w St Marg 84-85; C W Ham *Chelmsf* 86-87; TV Walthamstow St Mary w St Steph 87-92; PtO *Sheff* 92-95; V Sheff St Paul 96-97; rtd 98. *Al-Salam, 36 Standish Gardens, Sheffield S5 8YD* T: 0114-273 1428 F: 273 1348 M: 07989-261278 E: kaggwanelsonibrahim@msn.com

KAJUMBA, The Ven Daniel Steven Kimbugwe. b 52. S'wark Ord Course. **d** 85 **p** 86. C Goldington *St Alb* 85-87; Uganda 87-99; TV Horley *S'wark* 99-01; Adn Reigate from 01. *84 Higher Drive, Purley CR8 2HJ* T: (020) 8660 9276 *or* 8681 5496 F: 8686 2074 M: 07949-594460
E: daniel.kajumba@southwark.anglican.org

KAKURU (*née* ASHBRIDGE), Mrs Clare Patricia Esther. b 80. QUB BTh 03 MTh 07. **d** 07 **p** 08. C Donaghcloney w Waringstown *D & D* 07-12; V Lurgan Ch the Redeemer from 12. *28 Bowens Meadow, Lurgan, Craigavon BT66 7UT* T: (028) 3832 9420 *or* 3832 5673 E: weedoll@gmail.com

KALENIUK, Nicholas George. b 69. WEMTC. **d** 09 **p** 10. C Claines St Jo *Worc* 09-13; P-in-c Wollaston from 13; P-in-c Stourbridge St Mich Norton from 13. *The Wollaston Vicarage, 46 Vicarage Road, Wollaston, Stourbridge DY8 4NP*

KALSI, Mrs Gina Louise. b 68. Leeds Univ BA 09. NOC 06. **d** 09 **p** 10. C Netherthorpe St Steph *Sheff* 09-13; V Malin Bridge from 13. *St Polycarp's Vicarage, 33 Wisewood Lane, Sheffield S6 4WA* T: 0114-234 3450 M: 07787-578721
E: ginalkalsi@hotmail.co.uk

KALUS, Rupert. b 61. St Jo Coll Dur BA 85 MA 93 BA 01 W Sussex Inst of HE PGCE 87. Cranmer Hall Dur 99. **d** 02 **p** 03. C Dur N 02-06; P-in-c Shildon 06-07; V 08-12; V Lanchester and Burnhope from 12. *The Vicarage, 1 Lee Hill Court, Lanchester, Durham DH7 0QE* T: (01207) 521170

KAMBLE-HANSELL, Anupama. b 76. Pune Univ India BSc 97 Serampore Univ BD 03 Birm Univ MA 06. **d** 02 **p** 04. C Birm St Martin w Bordesley St Andr 04-08; Chapl Aston Univ 05-08;

TV Coventry Caludon *Cov* 08-10; C Bure Valley *Nor* 11-13. *Address temp unknown* E: revd.akh@btinternet.com

KAMEGERI, Stephen. *See* NSHIMYE, Stephen Kamegeri

KAMINSKI, Julia Ann. *See* HOOK, Julia Ann

KAMPALA, Bishop of. *See* OROMBI, Henry Luke

KAMUYU, Elpiety Wanjiku. b 53. St Jo Coll Nottm 06. **d** 93 **p** 09. Kenya 93-01; NSM Edgware *Lon* 01-03; NSM Bilborough w Strelley *S'well* 04-06; C Lenton 08-10; C Nottingham St Ann w Em 10-12. *99 Allington Avenue, Lenton, Nottingham NG7 1JY* T: 0115-845 3922 M: 07985-424139
E: pietykamuyu@yahoo.co.uk

KANE, Peter David Colin. b 72. K Coll Lon BMus 92 Fitzw Coll Cam BA 05 MA 09 ARCO 91 ARCM 94. Wycliffe Hall Ox BA 08. **d** 09 **p** 10. C Chich St Paul and Westhampnett 09-13; V Clacton St Jas *Chelmsf* from 13. *The Vicarage, 44 Wash Lane, Clacton-on-Sea CO15 1DA* T: (01255) 429896
E: p.kane.03@cantab.net

KANERIA, Rajni. b 57. Bath Univ BPharm 82. Wycliffe Hall Ox 83. **d** 86 **p** 87. C Hyson Green *S'well* 86-87; C Hyson Green St Paul w St Steph 87-89; C Harold Hill St Geo *Chelmsf* 89-91; TV Oadby *Leic* 91-97; PtO from 15. *32 Rendall Road, Leicester LE4 6LE* T: 0116-266 6613

KAOMA, John Kafwanka. b 66. Trin Coll Melbourne BTh 97 Ridley Coll Melbourne MA 00. St Jo Sem Lusaka 90. **d** 93 **p** 94. C Chingola St Barn Zambia 93-94; PtO Melbourne Australia 94-00; Lect St Jo Coll Lusaka Zambia 00-03; Prin 01-03; Regional Manager (S Africa) CMS 03-06; Research Officer Miss Dept Angl Communion Office 06-09; Dir for Miss from 09; PtO *Lon* 06-12; Hon C Isleworth St Jo 12-14; Hon C Isleworth St Jo w St Mary from 15. *11 Silverhall Street, Isleworth TW7 6RF* T: (020) 7313 3940 F: 7313 3999 M: 07901-987239
E: john.kafwanka@anglicancommunion.org

KARAMURA, Grace Patrick. b 62. Nat Teachers' Coll Uganda DipEd 89 Rob Coll Cam MPhil 95 Leeds Univ PhD 98. Bp Tucker Coll Mukono BD 92. **d** 92 **p** 93. C All SS Cathl Kampala Uganda 92-93; C Ebbw Vale *Mon* 98-01; TV 01-03; V Pontyclun w Talygarn *Llan* 03-14. *17 Muchelney Way, Yeovil BA21 3RB* T: (01935) 700371 E: tuungi@gmail.com

KARRACH, Herbert Adolf. b 24. TCD BA 46 MB, BCh 48 BAO 48. EAMTC 85. **d** 88 **p** 89. NSM Snettisham w Ingoldisthorpe and Fring *Nor* 88-95; PtO from 95. *Narnia, 5 Docking Road, Fring, King's Lynn PE31 6SQ* T: (01485) 518346

KASHOURIS, Peter Zacharias. b 66. Peterho Cam BA 89 MA 93. St Steph Ho Ox 92. **d** 94 **p** 95. C Hampstead St Jo *Lon* 94-97; R Hartlepool St Hilda *Dur* 97-03; P-in-c Dur St Oswald 03-06; P-in-c Dur St Oswald and Shincliffe from 06; Dioc Ecum Officer 03-09. *St Oswald's Vicarage, Church Street, Durham DH1 3DG* T: 0191-374 1681 E: p.j.kashouris@durham.anglican.org

KASIBANTE, Amos Sebadduka. b 54. Trin Coll Cam BA 83 MA 87 Yale Univ STM 89. Bp Tucker Coll Mukono 76. **d** 79 **p** 80. C Lyantonde Uganda 79-80; Tutor Bp Tucker Coll Mukono 83-92; Tutor Coll of Ascension Selly Oak 92-95; Prin Simon of Cyrene Th Inst 95-97; Vice Prin St Mich Coll Llan 97-02; Chpl Leic Univ and Co-ord Reader Tr *Leic* 02-09; P-in-c Burmantofts St Steph and St Agnes *Leeds* from 10; P-in-c Leeds St Cypr Harehills from 10; Racial Justice Officer from 12. *St Agnes' Vicarage, 21 Shakespeare Close, Leeds LS9 7UQ* T: 0113-248 2648 M: 07990-938122
E: amos.kasibante@virgin.net

KASOZI, Jackson Nsamba. b 50. Bp Tucker Coll Mukono BD 91 Birm Univ MPhil 94 All Nations Chr Coll MA 00. **d** 83 **p** 84. V St Andr Cathl Mityana Uganda 84-88; Adn 86-88; Chapl to Bp W Buganda 91-92; PtO *Cov* 93-94; Adn W Buganda Uganda 95-98; Acting Dean St Paul's Cathl 98-99; NSM Limehouse *Lon* 00-02; NSM Old Ford St Paul and St Mark 02-03; C Harold Hill St Geo *Chelmsf* 04-08; rtd 08. *c/o Christian Vision Uganda, PO Box 37269, Kampala, Uganda*
E: christian.vision.uganda@live.com

KASSELL, Colin George Henry. b 42. Ripon Coll Cuddesdon 76. **d** 68 **p** 69. In RC Ch 69-75; PtO *Ox* 76-77; C Denham 77-80; V Brotherton *Wakef* 80-84; Chapl and Past Ldr St Cath Hospice Crawley 84-91; R Rogate w Terwick and Trotton w Chithurst *Chich* 91-94; C Heene 94-06; Chapl Worthing Hosp 94-07; rtd 07; P-in-c Worthing St Andr *Chich* from 06. *Park House, 3 Madeira Avenue, Worthing BN11 2AT*
T: (01903) 526571 M: 07802-259310
E: colin.kassell@ntlworld.com

KATE, Sister. See BURGESS, Kate Lamorna

KAUNHOVEN, Canon Anthony Peter. b 55. Leeds Univ BA 78 Coll of Ripon & York St Jo PGCE 79. Edin Th Coll 79. **d** 81 **p** 82. C Leeds St Aid *Ripon* 81-84; C Hawksworth Wood 84-89; V Upper Nidderdale 89-91; Hon C Rawdon *Bradf* 96-99; P-in-c Old Brampton *Derby* 99-07; P-in-c Gt Barlow 04-07; P-in-c Bakewell 07-11; C Ashford w Sheldon and Longstone 07-11; P-in-c Rowsley 07-11; V Bakewell, Ashford w Sheldon and Rowsley from 11; RD Bakewell and Eyam 12-15; Dioc Ecum Officer from 01; Hon Can Derby Cathl from 11. *The Vicarage, South Church Street, Bakewell DE45 1FD* T: (01629) 814462
E: jazzyrector@aol.com

KAUTZER, Benjamin Allen. b 85. Pt Loma Nazarene Univ (USA) BA 07 Nottm Univ MA 08 St Jo Coll Dur PhD 15. Ripon Coll Cuddesdon 13. **d** 15. C Earley St Nic *Ox* from 15. *3 Hengrave Close, Lower Earley, Reading RG6 3AR*
E: benkautzer@gmail.com

KAVANAGH, John Paul. b 63. St Fran Coll Brisbane BTh 94. **d** 94 **p** 96. C Indooroopilly Australia 94-95; C Centenary Suburbs 96-98; R Forest Lake 98; P-in-c Texas w Inglewood 99-00; Chapl Wolston Park Hosp and Asst Chapl R Brisbane Hosp 00-02; Chapl Matthew Flinders Angl Coll Australia 02-08; I Kells Gp *C & O* 08-10; Chapl Dub Inst of Tech 11; Australia from 12. *Address temp unknown* E: jpandmary@gmail.com

KAVANAGH, Canon Michael Lowther. b 58. York Univ BA 80 Newc Univ MSc 82 Leeds Univ BA 86 MBPsS 90. Coll of Resurr Mirfield 84. **d** 87 **p** 88. C Boston Spa *York* 87-91; C Clifford 89-91; Chapl Martin House Hospice for Children Boston Spa 87-91; V Beverley St Nic *York* 91-97; RD Beverley 95-97; Abp's Dom Chapl and Dioc Dir of Ords 97-05; Chapl HM Pris Full Sutton 05-08; Angl Adv HM Pris Service from 08; Can Th Liv Cathl from 09. *Chaplaincy HQ, Post Point 3.08, 3rd Floor Red Zone, Clive House, 70 Petty France, London SW1H 9HD* T: 03000-475182 F: 476822/3

KAY, Alasdair Stewart. b 61. St Jo Coll Nottm. **d** 14 **p** 15. NSM Walbrook Epiphany *Derby* from 14. *132 St Chad's Road, Derby DE23 6RN* T: (01332) 601848 M: 07885-858709
E: director@derbycitymission.org.uk

KAY, Mrs Audrey Elizabeth. b 60. NOC 04. **d** 07 **p** 08. NSM Ramsbottom and Edenfield *Man* 07-10; V Cadishead from 10; Chapl Salford City Academy from 10. *St Mary's Vicarage, Penry Avenue, Cadishead, Manchester M44 5ZE* T: 0161-775 2171 M: 07752-526140 E: kaynacg@aol.com

KAY, Clifford. b 60. Leeds Metrop Univ BA 94 Ban Univ MA 09. Ridley Hall Cam 10. **d** 12 **p** 13. C Warley *Leeds* from 12; C Halifax St Hilda from 12. *41 Gibraltar Road, Halifax HX1 4HE* E: cliffkay1@gmail.com

KAY, Dennis. b 57. St As Minl Tr Course 96. **d** 99 **p** 00. NSM Llangystennin *St As* 99-01; NSM Colwyn Bay w Brynymaen 01-03; NSM Petryal 03-07. *41 Ffordd Ffynnon, Rhuddlan, Rhyl LL18 2SP* M: 07748-312067

KAY, Ian Geoffrey. NOC. **d** 89 **p** 90. NSM Rochdale *Man* 89-91 and 95-11; NSM Heywood St Luke w All So 91-95; rtd 11. *161 Norden Road, Rochdale OL11 5PT* T: (01706) 639497

KAY, Marjory Marianne Kate. b 61. **d** 97. NSM Godshill *Portsm* 97-05; NSM Askerswell, Loders, Powerstock and Symondsbury *Sarum* 06-14. *76A East Street, Bridport DT6 3LL* T: (01308) 422453 E: kateallen76@btinternet.com

KAY, Peter Richard. b 72. St Cath Coll Cam BA 93 MA 00 PGCE 95. Trin Coll Bris 09. **d** 11 **p** 12. C Letchworth St Paul w Willian *St Alb* 11-14; P-in-c Milton Ernest, Pavenham and Thurleigh from 14. *The Vicarage, Thurleigh Road, Milton Earnest, Bedford MK44 1RF* M: 07718-201449
E: rev.peter.kay@outlook.com

KAYE, Canon Alistair Geoffrey. b 62. Reading Univ BSc 85. St Jo Coll Nottm 87. **d** 90 **p** 91. C Gt Horton *Bradf* 90-94; C Rushden w Newton Bromswold *Pet* 94-98; V Upper Armley *Ripon* 98-08; Armley Deanery Missr 08-13; AD Armley 05-08; P-in-c Beeston Hill and Hunslet Moor 13-14; Hon Can Ripon Cathl from 13. *St Luke's Vicarage, Malvern View, Leeds LS11 8SG* M: 07881-804104
E: alistair@armley.freeserve.co.uk

KAYE, Bruce Norman. b 39. Lon Univ BD 64 Sydney Univ BA 66 Basel Univ DrTheol 75. Moore Th Coll Sydney ThL 64. **d** 64 **p** 65. Australia 64-66 and from 83; PtO *Dur* 67-69; Tutor St Jo Coll Dur 68-75; Sen Tutor 75-83; Vice Prin 79-83; rtd 04. *217 Hopetown Avenue, Watsons Bay NSW 2030, Australia* T: (0061) (2) 9337 6795

KAYE, Canon Gerald Trevor. b 32. Man Univ BSc 54. Oak Hill Th Coll. **d** 56 **p** 57. C Widnes St Ambrose *Liv* 56-58; C St Helens St Mark 58-62; V Brixton Hill St Sav *S'wark* 62-65; Canada 65-85; Hon Can Keewatin 70-75; Adn Patricia 75-78; V Slough *Ox* 85-97; rtd 97; LtO *Arg* from 08. *Craiguanach, Torlundy, Fort William PH33 6SW* T: (01397) 705395
E: eleanorado@aol.com

KAYE, Peter Alan. b 47. K Coll Lon BD 71 AKC 71 Leic Univ MA 82 CQSW 82. St Aug Coll Cant 71. **d** 72 **p** 73. C Fulham All SS *Lon* 72-74; Chapl Rubery Hill, Jo Conolly and Jos Sheldon Hosps Birm 74-80; Hon C Northfield *Birm* 80-83; PtO 99-06; P-in-c Stirchley 06-12; rtd 12; PtO *Birm* from 12; *Ban* from 12. *Ty Gwyn, Factory Place, Tremadog, Porthmadog LL49 9RE* T: (01766) 513732 M: 07769-944070
E: peterakaye@gmail.com

KAYE, Mrs Sharon Vernie. b 72. Bradf Coll of Educn BEd 97. Trin Coll Bris 06. **d** 08 **p** 09. C Yeadon *Bradf* 08-12; TV Moor Allerton and Shadwell *Leeds* from 12. *St Stephen's House, Tynwald Drive, Leeds LS17 5DR* T: 0113-226 4502 M: 07871-768774 E: verniekaye@hotmail.com

KAYE, Simon Keith. b 66. Ridley Hall Cam 11. **d** 13 **p** 14. C Eye and Newborough *Pet* 13-14; C Eye, Newborough and Thorney from 14. *The Vicarage, The Green, Thorney, Peterborough PE6 0QD* T: (01733) 271184 E: simonkaye748@gmail.com

KAYE, Stephen Michael. b 72. Trin Coll Bris 06. **d** 08 **p** 09. C Calverley *Bradf* 08-12; C Washburn and Mid-Wharfe 12-13; C Abbeylands *Leeds* from 13. *St Stephen's House, Tynwald Drive, Leeds LS17 5DR* T: 0113-226 4502 M: 07756-274011
E: revkaye@gmail.com

KAYE, Timothy Henry. b 52. Linc Th Coll 77. **d** 80 **p** 81. C Warsop *S'well* 80-83; C Far Headingley St Chad *Ripon* 83-86; P-in-c Birkby *Wakef* 86; TV N Huddersfield 86-91; R Stone St Mich w Aston St Sav *Lich* 91-95; V S Kirkby *Leeds* from 95. *The Vicarage, Bull Lane, South Kirkby, Pontefract WF9 3QD* T/F: (01977) 642795 E: mail@kaye5.fsworld.co.uk

KAYE-BESLEY, Mrs Lesley Kathleen. b 47. Cam Inst of Educn CertEd 69 Kingston Univ MA 94 FRSA 85. **d** 04 **p** 05. OLM Walton-on-Thames *Guildf* 04-11; NSM Hinchley Wood 11-12; PtO 12-14; NSM E Molesey from 14. *Minggay, 1 Park Road, Esher KT10 8NP* T: (01372) 465185
E: lesley@waltonparish.org.uk

KAYLA, Ms Giyanow Sophia. b 62. St Jo Coll Nottm 13. **d** 15. NSM Aston and Nechells *Birm* from 15. *11 Tansley Road, Birmingham B44 0DN* T: 0121-384 1795 M: 07944-365778
E: giyanow@yahoo.co.uk

KAZICH, Ms Anne. b 69. Cranmer Hall Dur 12. **d** 14 **p** 15. C Tanhouse The Oaks CD *Liv* from 14. *63 Enstone, Skelmersdale WN8 6AW* E: anneatoaks@btinternet.com

KAZIRO, Godfrey Sam. b 48. BDSc Lon Univ MSc FDSRCPSGlas FFDRCSI. **d** 02 **p** 03. OLM Waterloo St Jo w St Andr *S'wark* 02-12; NSM from 12. *19 Hampshire Road, Hornchurch RM11 3EU* T: (01708) 441609

KEAL, Barry Clifford. b 57. Leeds Univ BA 06. NOC 03. **d** 06 **p** 07. NSM Halsall, Lydiate and Downholland *Liv* 06-11. *46 Eastway, Liverpool L31 6BS* T: 0151-526 4508
E: barry@keal.me.uk

KEAN, Robert John. b 64. St Mellitus Coll BA 11. **d** 11 **p** 12. C Black Notley *Chelmsf* 11-14; P-in-c Fairstead w Terling and White Notley etc 14; TV Witham and Villages from 14. *The Rectory, New Road, Terling, Chelmsford CM3 2PN* T: (01245) 206266 E: revrobkean@gmail.com

KEANE, Christian John. b 74. Rob Coll Cam BA 95 MA 99. Wycliffe Hall Ox BA 06 MA 06. **d** 06 **p** 07. C Eastrop *Win* 06-11; C Ex St Leon w H Trin from 11. *St Leonard's Church, Topsham Road, Exeter EX2 4NG* T: (01392) 286995
E: chris@stlens.org.uk

KEANE, Damien. *See* O'CATHAIN, Damien
KEARLEY-HEYWOOD, Deiniol John Owen. b 73. K Coll Lon BA 95 Peterho Cam MPhil 03. Westcott Ho Cam 02. **d** 04 **p** 05. C Paddington St Jo w St Mich *Lon* 04-08; R Prestwood and Gt Hampden Ox from 08. *The Rectory, 140 Wycombe Road, Prestwood, Great Missenden HP16 0HJ* T: (01494) 866530 E: rector@htprestwood.org.uk
KEARNEY, Mrs Sandra. b 55. Bolton Inst of HE BSc 89 Univ Coll Ches BTh 04. NOC 01. **d** 04 **p** 05. C Blackpool Ch Ch w All SS *Blackb* 04-08; P-in-c Ordsall and Salford Quays *Man* from 08. *The Rectory, Parsonage Close, Salford M5 3GS* T: 0161-872 0800 E: rev.sandra@sky.com
KEARNS, Andrew Philip. b 76. Wycliffe Hall Ox. **d** 09 **p** 10. C Maidenhead St Andr and St Mary Ox 09-15. *Chemin Neuf 2, 1028 Préverenges, Switzerland* T: (0041) (22) 990 2450 E: andrewpkearns@gmail.com
✠**KEARON, The Rt Revd Kenneth Arthur.** b 53. TCD BA 76 MA 79 MPhil 91. CITC 78. **d** 81 **p** 82 **c** 15. C Raheny w Coolock *D & G* 81-84; Lect TCD 82-90; Dean of Res TCD 84-90; I Tullow *D & G* 91-99; Can Ch Ch Cathl Dublin 95-15; Dir Irish Sch Ecum 99-05; Sec Gen Angl Communion Office 05-15; Hon Prov Can Cant Cathl 06-15; Bp L & K from 15. *Rien Roe, Adare, Co Limerick, Republic of Ireland* T: (00353) (61) 396244 E: bishop@limerick.anglican.org
KEARTON, Canon Janet Elizabeth. b 54. Univ Coll Lon BSc 78 Birkbeck Coll Lon MSc 81. NEOC 01. **d** 04 **p** 05. C Richmond w Hudswell and Downholme and Marske *Ripon* 04-08; V Hipswell 08-13; Can Res Carl Cathl from 13. *3 The Abbey, Carlisle CA3 8TZ* M: 07816-278267 T: (01228) 521857 E: canonwarden@carlislecathedral.org.uk
KEAST, William. b 43. Univ Coll Ox BA 65 DipEd 66. **d** 88 **p** 89. OLM Scotton w Northorpe *Linc* from 88. *4 Crapple Lane, Scotton, Gainsborough DN21 3QT* T: (01724) 763190 E: wkeast@hotmail.com
KEATES, Thomas Frederick. b 45. Southn Univ BSc 96. WEMTC 09. **d** 12 **p** 13. NSM Thornbury and Oldbury-on-Severn w Shepperdine *Glouc* from 12. *80 Knapp Road, Thornbury, Bristol BS35 2HJ* M: 07905-834870 T: (01454) 885058 F: 856981 E: tomkeates@blueyonder.co.uk
KEATING, Mrs Ann Barbara. b 53. Open Univ BA 85. STETS 06. **d** 09 **p** 10. NSM Fisherton Anger *Sarum* 09-11; NSM Avon River 11-13; Asst Chapl Win Univ 12-13; R N Bradford on Avon and Villages *Sarum* from 13. *The Rectory, 6 Milbourn Close, Winsley, Bradford-on-Avon BA15 2NN* T: (01225) 722230 M: 07510-588007 E: rev.ann.keating@btinternet.com
KEATING, Christopher Robin. b 39. K Coll Lon BD AKC 84. Sarum Th Coll 62. **d** 65 **p** 66. C Baildon *Bradf* 65-67; CF 67-72; V Thornton Heath St Paul *Cant* 72-79; C Harold Hill St Geo *Chelmsf* 85-89; V Goodmayes All SS 89-07; rtd 07; PtO *York* from 09. *Ghyll View, Goathland, Whitby YO22 5AP* T: (01947) 896406
KEATING, Geoffrey John. b 52. Open Univ BA 94. St Steph Ho Ox 81. **d** 84 **p** 85. C Lancaster Ch Ch w St Jo and St Anne *Blackb* 84-85; C Rotherham *Sheff* 85-87; V Bentley 87-91; V Penponds *Truro* 91-96; V Pet St Jude from 96. *St Jude's Vicarage, 49 Atherstone Avenue, Peterborough PE3 9TZ* T/F: (01733) 264169 E: geoffrey.keating@btinternet.com
KEATING, Mrs Valerie. b 54. Leeds Metrop Univ BSc 87 Huddersfield Univ MEd 92 CertEd 89 FHEA 06. Yorks Min Course 12. **d** 14 **p** 15. NSM Batley All SS and Purlwell *Leeds* from 14. *35 Moorside Green, Drighlington, Bradford BD11 1HG* T: 0113-285 4682 M: 07505-134105 E: valkeating@sky.com
KEAY, Alfred David. b 26. Aston Univ MSc 72. Qu Coll Birm 76. **d** 79 **p** 80. Hon C Penkridge w Stretton *Lich* 79-82; C Rugeley 82-85; V Cheswardine 85-95; V Hales 85-95; rtd 95; PtO *Lich* from 98. *2 The Coppice, Farcroft Gardens, Market Drayton TF9 3UA* T: (01630) 657924
KEAY, Charles Edward. b 70. Glos Univ BA 94. St Steph Ho Ox 01. **d** 03 **p** 04. C Havant *Portsm* 03-07; P-in-c Alford w Rigsby *Linc* 07-11; TV Portsea N End St Mark *Portsm* from 11. *St Nicholas House, 90A Compton Road, Portsmouth PO2 0SR*
KEDDIE, Canon Tony. b 37. Qu Coll Birm 63. **d** 66 **p** 67. C Barnoldswick w Bracewell *Bradf* 66-69; C New Bentley *Sheff* 69-71; TV Seacroft *Ripon* 71-79; V Kippax 79-84; TR Kippax w Allerton Bywater 84-92; R Fountains Gp 92-02; Hon Can Ripon Cathl 94-02; rtd 02; PtO *Ripon* 02-14; *Bradf* 03-14; *Leeds* from 14. *2 Westcroft, Station Road, Otley LS21 3HX* T: (01943) 464146 E: tbmk@metronet.co.uk
KEDDILTY, Matthew Paul. b 79. St Jo Coll Nottm 12. **d** 14 **p** 15. C Ulverston St Mary w H Trin *Carl* from 14. *21 Victoria Park, Ulverston LA12 7TT* M: 07872-620605 T: (01229) 588081 E: matthew.keddilty@hotmail.com
KEEBLE, Leslie Bruce. b 32. Spurgeon's Coll Lon BD 59. Bapt Th Sem Ruschlikon Zürich ThM 63. **d** 08 **p** 08.

NSM Harwell w Chilton Ox 08-11; PtO 11-13. *13 Limetrees, Chilton, Didcot OX11 0HW* T: (01235) 852203 E: bk@brucekeeble.org.uk
KEEBLE, Philip Wade. b 47. St Seiriol Cen 09. **d** 13. Min Can Ban Cathl 13-14. *12 Glasffordd, Marianglas, Anglesey LL73 8PB* T/F: (01248) 853802 M: 07944-671444 E: keeblephil@gmail.com
KEECH, April Irene. b 52. Penn State Univ BA 76. Trin Coll Bris BA 89. **d** 89 **p** 92. C Walthamstow St Luke *Chelmsf* 89-92; USA 92-95; V Deptford St Jo w H Trin *S'wark* 95-02; Asst Dioc Dir of Ords 96-00; Hon Can S'wark Cathl 99-02; V Hoxton St Jo w Ch Ch *Lon* 02-10; Chapl St Mary Magd Academy Lon from 10; PtO *Lon* 10-15; NSM Old Ford St Paul and St Mark from 15. *13 Regents Wharf, Wharf Place, London E2 9BD* T: (020) 7739 7621 or 7697 0123 E: april.keech@smmacademy.org
KEECH, Dominic. b 83. Keble Coll Ox BA 05 MA 14 MSt 06 DPhil 10. St Steph Ho Ox 10. **d** 12 **p** 13. C Wantage Ox 12-14; Chapl BNC Ox from 14; C Ox St Mary Magd from 14. *Brasenose College, Radcliffe Square, Oxford OX1 4AJ* T: (01865) 277833 M: 07920-761546 E: chaplain@bnc.ox.ac.uk
KEEGAN, Frances Ann (Sister Isabel). b 44. SEN 74. Franciscan Study Cen 87. **d** 99 **p** 00. NSM Sherborne w Castleton and Lillington *Sarum* 99-01; NSM Golden Cap Team 01-08; NSM Crosslacon *Carl* 08-11; P-in-c Brigham, Gt Broughton and Broughton Moor 11-12; rtd 12; PtO *Truro* 13-14; *Sarum* from 14. *The Hermitage, 67 Acreman Street, Sherborne DT9 3PH* T: (01935) 817718 E: revik@hotmail.co.uk
KEEGAN, Graham Brownell. b 40. Nottm Univ CertEd 68. NOC 81. **d** 84 **p** 85. C Highfield *Liv* 84-87; V Ince St Mary 87-95; V Newton in Makerfield St Pet 95-05; rtd 05. *5 Scott Road, Lowton, Warrington WA3 2HD* T: (01942) 713809
KEELER, Alan. b 58. City Univ BSc 84. St Jo Coll Nottm MA 01. **d** 90 **p** 91. C Paddock Wood *Roch* 90-94; V Blendon 94-06; V Plaistow St Mary from 06; AD Bromley from 15. *St Mary's Vicarage, 74 London Lane, Bromley BR1 4HE* T: (020) 8460 1827 E: alan.keeler@diocese-rochester.org or agkeeler@tiscali.co.uk
KEELEY, John Robin. b 38. G&C Coll Cam BA 62. Clifton Th Coll 62. **d** 64 **p** 65. C Onslow Square St Paul *Lon* 64-66; C Hove Bp Hannington Memorial Ch *Chich* 66-69; C Harborne Heath *Birm* 69-72; V Leic H Trin 72-74; V Leic H Trin w St Jo 74-80; PtO St Alb 81-86; NSM Carterton Ox 89-95; Tutor EAMTC *Ely* 95-99; TV Bishopsnympton, Rose Ash, Mariansleigh etc *Ex* 99-03; RD S Molton 01-03; rtd 03. *74 Pacific Parade, Mount Tamborine QLD 4272, Australia* T: (0061) (7) 5545 0966 E: robandpaulkeeley@bigpond.com
KEELEY-PANNETT, Peter George. *See* PANNETT, Peter George
KEELING, Peter Frank. b 34. Kelham Th Coll. **d** 58 **p** 59. C S Elmsall *Wakef* 58-63; C Barnsley St Mary 63-67; V Ravensthorpe 67-73; V Cudworth 73-83; R Downham Market w Bexwell *Ely* 83-00; RD Fincham 83-94; V Crimplesham w Stradsett 85-00; rtd 00; P-in-c Hempton and Pudding Norton *Nor* 00-04; PtO from 04. *23 Cleaves Drive, Walsingham NR22 6EQ* T: (01328) 820310
KEEN, David Mark. b 69. Oriel Coll Ox BA 91. St Jo Coll Nottm BTh 96 MPhil 98. **d** 98 **p** 99. C Yeovil w Kingston Pitney *B & W* 98-02; C Haughton le Skerne *Dur* 02-06; C Preston Plucknett *B & W* from 06. *3 Poplar Drive, Yeovil BA21 3UL* T: (01935) 422286 E: revdmkeen@btinternet.com
KEEN, Michael Spencer. b 41. St Pet Coll Ox BA 68 MA 72 GRSM 62 ARCM Reading Univ CertEd. Westcott Ho Cam 68. **d** 73 **p** 74. NSM W Derby St Jo *Liv* 73-74; NSM Stanley 74-76; Chs Youth and Community Officer Telford *Lich* 77-82; Dioc Unemployment Officer *Sheff* 82-89; NSM Brixton Road Ch Ch *S'wark* 89-92; Employment Development Officer 89-92; PtO 92-99; NSM Camberwell St Giles w St Matt 99-11. *40 Sheppard's College, London Road, Bromley BR1 1PF* T: (020) 8313 0490
KEEN, Ms Miriam Frances. b 65. Ex Univ BSc 87 Glos Univ MA 10 Westmr Coll of Educn PGCE 88. Wycliffe Hall Ox 04. **d** 05 **p** 06. C Cogges and S Leigh Ox 05-14; C N Leigh 13-14; TV Marlborough *Sarum* from 14. *Preshute Vicarage, 7 Golding Avenue, Marlborough SN8 1TH*
KEENAN, Leslie Herbert (Bertie). b 32. Cranmer Hall Dur. **d** 66 **p** 67. C Anston *Sheff* 66-70; C Woodsetts 66-70; Chapl HM Borstal Pollington 70-78; V Balne *Sheff* 70-78; V Poughill *Truro* 78-99; rtd 99; PtO *Chich* from 01. *Rosedene, Southdown Road, Seaford BN25 4JS* T: (01323) 899507
KEENE, Canon David Peter. b 32. Trin Hall Cam BA 56 MA 60. Westcott Ho Cam. **d** 58 **p** 59. C Radcliffe-on-Trent *S'well* 58-61; C Mansfield SS Pet and Paul 61-64; V Nottingham St Cath 64-71; R Bingham 71-81; Dioc Dir of Ords 81-90; Can Res S'well Minster 81-97; rtd 97; PtO *S'well* from 02. *Averham Cottage, Church Lane, Averham, Newark NG23 5RB* T: (01636) 708601 E: keene@averham.fsnet.co.uk

KEENE, Mrs Muriel Ada. b 35. dss 83 d 87 p 94. Dioc Lay Min Adv *S'well* 87-88; Asst Dir of Ords 88-90; Dn-in-c Oxton 90-93; Dn-in-c Epperstone 90-94; Dn-in-c Gonalston 90-94; NSM Lowdham w Caythorpe, and Gunthorpe 94-00; rtd 95; PtO *S'well* from 05. *Averham Cottage, Church Lane, Averham, Newark NG23 5RB* T: (01636) 708601
E: keene@averham.fsnet.co.uk

KEEP, Andrew James. b 55. Collingwood Coll Dur BA 77 Yale Univ STM 84 K Coll Lon MA 14. Sarum & Wells Th Coll 78. d 80 p 81. C Banstead *Guildf* 80-83; Chapl Qu Eliz Hosp Banstead 80-83; USA 83-84; Chapl Cranleigh Sch Surrey 84-98; Chapl Wells Cathl Sch 98-06; PV Wells Cathl 01-06; Chapl Mill Hill Sch Lon 07-10; PtO *Lon* 10-14; NSM St Marg Pattens from 14. *193 Foundling Court, Brunswick Centre, London WC1N 1QF* T: (020) 7837 5327 M: 07740-647813
E: andrew.keep@me.com *or* vicar@stmargaretpattens.org

KEETON, Barry. b 40. Dur Univ BA 61 MA 69 MLitt 78 K Coll Lon BD 63 AKC 63. d 64 p 65. C S Bank *York* 64-67; C Middlesbrough St Cuth 67-69; C Kingston upon Hull St Alb 70-71; V Appleton-le-Street w Amotherby 71-74; Dioc Ecum Adv 74-81; R Ampleforth w Oswaldkirk 74-78; V Howden 78-79; P-in-c Barmby on the Marsh 78-79; P-in-c Laxton w Blacktoft 78-79; P-in-c Wressell 78-79; TR Howden 80-91; Can and Preb York Minster 85-91; RD Howden 86-91; TR Yawes All SS, St Anne, St Mich and St Thos *Chich* 91-96; R Cov St Jo 96-01; RD Cov N 97-01; rtd 01; PtO *Sheff* from 01; *York* from 05. *19 Shardlow Gardens, Bessacarr, Doncaster DN4 6UB* T: (01302) 532045 E: barry.k3@ukonline.co.uk

KEFFORD, Canon Peter Charles. b 44. Nottm Univ BTh 74. Linc Th Coll 70. d 74 p 75. C W Wimbledon Ch Ch *S'wark* 74-77; C All Hallows by the Tower etc *Lon* 77-81; C-in-c Pound Hill CD *Chich* 81; TV Worth 82-93; TR 83-92; R Henfield w Shermanbury and Woodmancote 92-01; Can Res and Treas Chich Cathl 01-09; Adv for Ord Min and Dioc Dir of Ords 01-06; Dioc Adv for Min 07-09; rtd 09. *17 North Close, Mickleover, Derby DE3 9JA* T: (01332) 549534
E: peter.kefford@hotmail.com

KEGG, Mrs Georgina. b 47. Oak Hill Th Coll BA 99. EAMTC 02. d 05 p 06. NSM Mattishall and the Tudd Valley *Nor* 05-11; NSM Moulton *Ches* from 12. *The Vicarage, 66 Jack Lane, Moulton, Northwich CW9 8NR* T: (01606) 593355
E: georginakegg@waitrose.com

KEGG, Gordon Rutherford. b 45. Reading Univ BSc 66 Imp Coll Lon PhD 71 Lon Univ CertEd 74. Oak Hill Th Coll 88. d 90 p 91. C Luton Lewsey St Hugh *St Alb* 90-94; TV Hemel Hempstead 94-01; P-in-c Mattishall w Mattishall Burgh, Welborne etc *Nor* 01-08; P-in-c Hockering, Honingham, E and N Tuddenham 04-08; R Mattishall and the Tudd Valley 08-11; rtd 11; P-in-c Moulton *Ches* from 11. *The Vicarage, 66 Jack Lane, Moulton, Northwich CW9 8NR* T: (01606) 593355
E: gordon.kegg@btinternet.com

KEIGHLEY, Mrs Amanda Jane. b 56. Garnett Coll Lon CertEd 85 Leeds Univ MA 98. Cranmer Hall Dur 04. d 07 p 08. NSM Is of Dogs Ch Ch and St Jo w St Luke *Lon* 07-12; P-in-c Elm Park St Nic Hornchurch *Chelmsf* 12-13; V from 13. *The Vicarage, 17 St Nicholas Avenue, Hornchurch RM12 4PT* T: (01708) 474639 M: 07889-486354 E: akeighley@clara.co.uk

KEIGHLEY, Andrew Kenneth. b 62. Nottm Univ LLB 84 Solicitor 85. Wycliffe Hall Ox 94. d 97 p 98. C Westminster St Jas the Less *Lon* 97-00; NSM 00-04; C Brompton H Trin w Onslow Square St Paul 04-06; P-in-c W Hampstead Trin 06-09; V from 09. *10 Lisburne Road, London NW3 2NR*
M: 07747-611577

KEIGHLEY, David John. b 48. Open Univ BA 88 CertEd. Sarum & Wells Th Coll 82. d 83 p 84. C Sawbridgeworth *St Alb* 83-86; TV Saltash *Truro* 86-89; V Lanlivery w Luxulyan 89-00; P-in-c The Candover Valley *Win* 00-08; P-in-c Wield 03-08; P-in-c Hurstbourne Tarrant, Faccombe, Vernham Dean etc from 08. *The Vicarage, The Dene, Hurstbourne Tarrant, Andover SP11 0AH* T: (01264) 736222 M: 07736-799262
E: davidkeighley@hotmail.com

KEIGHLEY, Martin Philip. b 61. Edin Univ MA 83. Westcott Ho Cam 86. d 88 p 89. C Lytham St Cuth *Blackb* 88-91; C Lancaster St Mary 91-93; R Halton w Aughton 93-00; V Poulton-le-Fylde 00-04; V Poulton Carleton and Singleton from 04; AD Poulton from 08. *The Vicarage, 7 Vicarage Road, Poulton-le-Fylde FY6 7BE* T: (01253) 883086
E: martinkeighley@btconnect.com

KEIGHLEY, Thomas Christopher. b 51. Open Univ BA 85. NEOC 00. d 03 p 04. NSM Upper Nidderdale *Ripon* 03-06; NSM Dacre w Hartwith and Darley w Thornthwaite 06-07; NSM Is of Dogs Ch Ch and St Jo w St Luke *Lon* 07-12; Chapl St Joseph's Hospice Hackney 09-10; NSM Elm Park St Nic Hornchurch *Chelmsf* from 12. *The Vicarage, 17 St Nicholas Avenue, Hornchurch RM12 4PT* T: (01708) 474639 M: 07889-486354 E: nurprc@nursing.u-net.com

KEIGHTLEY, Canon Thomas. b 44. CITC 79. d 79 p 80. C Seagoe *D & D* 79-83; I Belvoir from 83; Can Down Cathl from 95; Treas Down Cathl 00-01; Prec Down Cathl from 01. *The Rectory, 86B Beechill Road, Belfast BT8 7QN* T: (028) 9064 3777 M: 07919-366660 E: tmgktly@googlemail.com

KEIGHTLEY, Trevor Charles. b 54. St Jo Coll Nottm. d 03 p 04. C Wombwell *Sheff* 03-07; V Worsbrough Common w Worsbrough St Thos from 07. *St Thomas's Vicarage, 80 Kingwell Road, Worsbrough, Barnsley S70 4HG* T: (01226) 286505 E: trevorkeightley@aol.com

KEILLER, Canon Jane Elizabeth. b 52. Westmr Coll Ox BEd 74. Cranmer Hall Dur 76. dss 80 d 87 p 94. Cambridge H Trin w St Andr Gt *Ely* 80-86; NSM Cambridge St Barn 86-88 and 90-94; NSM Cambridge H Cross 95-02; Chapl and Tutor Ridley Hall Cam from 96; Hon Can Ely Cathl from 05; Bp's Adv for Spirituality from 14. *68 Pierce Lane, Cambridge CB21 5DL* T: (01223) 575776 *or* T/F: 741076 E: jk271@cam.ac.uk

KEIR, Mrs Gillian Irene. b 44. Westf Coll Lon BA 66 Somerville Coll Ox BLitt 70 Lon Univ MA 95. SAOMC 95. d 98 p 99. NSM St Alb St Steph *St Alb* 98-08; PtO from 08; NSM Officer St Alb Adnry from 06. *17 Battlefield Road, St Albans AL1 4DA* T: (01727) 854885 E: gillikeir@gmail.com

KEIRLE, Michael Robert. b 62. Trin Coll Bris BA 89. d 89 p 90. C Orpington Ch Ch *Roch* 89-92; Zimbabwe 92-95; R Keston *Roch* 95-03; R Guernsey St Martin *Win* from 03; Vice-Dean Guernsey from 13. *St Martin's Rectory, La Grande Rue, St Martin, Guernsey GY4 6RR* T: (01481) 238303 F: 237710
E: mrkeirle@cwgsy.net

KEITH, Andrew James Buchanan. b 47. Qu Coll Cam BA 69 MA 73. Wycliffe Hall Ox 71. d 74 p 75. C Warrington St Elphin *Liv* 74-77; C Southgate *Chich* 77-80; C-in-c Broadfield CD 80-82; P-in-c Walberton w Binsted 85-85; P-in-c Aldingbourne 83-85; Chapl Oswestry Sch 85-95; Chapl HM Pris Liv 95-96; Chapl HM Pris Preston 96-01; Chapl HM Pris Garth 01-06; NSM Chipping Norton *Ox* 07-13; rtd 13. *20 Sheraton Park, Ingol, Preston PR2 7AZ* E: janda@uwclub.net

KEITH, Gary Mark Wayne. b 71. Ripon Coll Cuddesdon 01. d 03 p 04. C Botley, Curdridge and Durley *Portsm* 03-06; Chapl RNR 05-06; Chapl RN 06-08; C N Hants Downs *Win* 08-12; CF from 12. *c/o MOD Chaplains (Army)* T: (01264) 383430 F: 381824 M: 07971-448049
E: thebishmeister@btinternet.com

KEITH, John. b 25. LRAM 50 LGSM 50 AGSM 51. Cuddesdon Coll 60. d 62 p 63. C Lee-on-the-Solent *Portsm* 62-65; C Raynes Park St Sav *S'wark* 65-68; rtd 90. *7 Torr An Eas, Glenfinnan PH37 4LS* T: (01397) 722314

KELHAM, Adèle. b 46. St Andr Univ BSc 69. Cranmer Hall Dur. d 98 p 99. Asst Chapl Zürich *Eur* 98-01; P-in-c Bishop Middleham *Dur* 01-05; AD Sedgefield 03-05; P-in-c Lausanne *Eur* from 05; Dioc Adv for Women's Min from 05. *Avenue Floréal 3, 1006 Lausanne, Switzerland* T: (0041) (21) 312 6563 E: info@christchurch-lausanne.ch

KELK, Michael Anthony. b 48. Sarum & Wells Th Coll. d 83 p 84. C Ross w Brampton Abbotts, Bridstow and Peterstow *Heref* 83-86; P-in-c Burghill 86-97; P-in-c Stretton Sugwas 86-97; P-in-c Walford and St John w Bishopswood, Goodrich etc 97-02; P-in-c Llangarron w Llangrove, Whitchurch and Ganarew 02-08. *Highland Cottage, Fownhope, Hereford HR1 4NX* T: (01432) 860565

KELLAGHER, Christopher John Bannerman. b 55. Aber Univ MA 79 UMIST MSc 88. STETS MA 88. d 09 p 10. NSM Aldershot H Trin *Guildf* from 09. *8 Elsenwood Crescent, Camberley GU15 2BA* T: (01276) 508193
E: jkellagher@ntlworld.com

KELLEHER, Mrs Cheryl. b 56. Sheff Univ BA 97. NOC 98. d 01 p 02. NSM Worsbrough St Mary *Sheff* 01-03; PtO from 04. *10 Fieldsend, Oxspring, Sheffield S36 8WH* T: (01226) 763236 E: cheryl@kelnet.com

KELLEN, David. b 52. St Mich Coll Llan 70. d 75 p 76. C Mynyddislwyn *Mon* 75-77; C Risca 77-78; C Malpas 78-81; V Newport All SS 81-88; V St Mellons from 88; R Michaelston-y-Fedw 89-96. *The Vicarage, Ty'r Winch Road, St Mellons, Cardiff CF3 5UP* T: (029) 2079 6560 E: hyweldda1067@gmail.com

KELLETT, Garth. See KELLETT, Ronald Garth

KELLETT, Neil. b 41. Bps' Coll Cheshunt 64. d 66 p 67. C Ex St Thos 66-72; C Win H Trin 72-74; P-in-c Redditch St Geo *Worc* 74-77; Canada from 77. *39 Fox Avenue, St John's NL A1B 2H8, Canada* T: (001) (709) 726 2883

KELLETT, Canon Richard. b 64. Leeds Univ BSc 85 PhD 89. St Jo Coll Nottm BTh 95 MA 96. d 96 p 97. C Nottingham St Jude *S'well* 96-00; P-in-c Skegby 00-02; P-in-c Teversal 00-02; R Skegby w Teversal from 02; AD Newstead from 06; Hon Can *S'well* Minster from 10. *The Vicarage, Mansfield Road, Skegby, Sutton-in-Ashfield NG17 3ED* T/F: (01623) 558800
E: richard@kellett.com

KELLETT, Ronald Garth. b 41. NOC 04. **d** 05 **p** 06. NSM Ilkley St Marg *Bradf* 05-12; PtO *Win* 12-15. *9 Church Court, Church Road, Fleet GU51 4ND* T: (01252) 642940

KELLEY, Neil George. b 64. ARCM 85. Westcott Ho Cam 88. **d** 91 **p** 92. C E Bedfont *Lon* 91-93; C Chiswick St Nic w St Mary 93-97; C Kirkby *Liv* 97-99; V Gt Crosby St Faith and Waterloo Park St Mary 99-12; Dioc Adv on Worship and Liturgy 06-12; R Bushey *St Alb* from 12. *The Rectory, High Street, Bushey WD23 1BD* T: (020) 8950 1546 M: 07980-872203 E: frneilkelley@gmail.com

KELLEY, Peter John. b 55. Poly of the S Bank BSc 85 Kingston Univ MBA 97 Cant Ch Ch Univ BA 12. SEITE 06. **d** 09 **p** 10. NSM Hook *S'wark* from 09. *95 Lime Grove, New Malden KT3 3TR* T: (020) 8336 1639 E: peter.kelley@stpaulschurchhook.org.uk

KELLOW, Richard James. b 78. Kent Univ BA 00 Cam Univ PGCE 01. Trin Coll Bris MA 12. **d** 12 **p** 13. C Histon *Ely* from 12; C Impington from 12. *The Vicarage, 60 Impington Lane, Impington, Cambridge CB24 9NJ* T: (01223) 236887 E: revrkellow@gmail.com

KELLY, Mrs Ann Clarke Thomson. b 60. WMMTC 04. **d** 07 **p** 08. C Stafford St Jo and Tixall w Ingestre *Lich* 07-11; PtO 11-12; C Hednesford from 12. *The Vicarage, Church Hill, Hednesford, Cannock WS12 1BD* T: (01543) 426954 E: scottyann@blueyonder.co.uk

KELLY, Anthony. b 60. UCD BA 92 St Thos Aquinas Pontifical Univ Rome BDiv 95 All Hallows Coll Dublin MA 99. CITC 11. **d** 94 **p** 95. In RC Ch 94-08; Bp's C Holmpatrick w Balbriggan and Kenure *D & G* from 12. *73 Townparks, Skerries, Co Dublin, Republic of Ireland* T: (00353) (1) 849 3886 M: 87-178 7186 E: kellyanto@aim.com

KELLY, Brian Eugene. b 56. Otago Univ BA 77 Dunedin Coll PGCE 79 Bris Univ PhD 93. Trin Coll Bris BA 89. **d** 90 **p** 91. NSM Redland *Bris* 90-93; C Scarborough St Mary w Ch Ch and H Apostles *York* 93-96; Dean Chpl Cant Ch Ch Univ Coll 96-03; PtO *Cant* from 06. *Address temp unknown* E: brian@kelly1915.fsnet.co.uk

KELLY, Canon Brian Horace. b 34. St Jo Coll Dur BA 57 MA 69. **d** 58 **p** 59. C Douglas St Geo and St Barn *S & M* 58-61; V Foxdale 61-64; V Bolton All So w St Jas *Man* 64-73; V Maughold *S & M* 73-77; Dir of Ords 76-93; V German 77-06; Can and Prec St German's Cathl 80-06; RD Castletown and Peel 97-04; rtd 06; PtO *S & M* from 09. *16 Slieau Whallian Park, St Johns, Isle of Man IM4 3JH* T: (01624) 801479

KELLY, Canon Dennis Charles. b 31. Liv Univ BA 52. Lich Th Coll 54. **d** 56 **p** 57. C Tranmere St Paul *Ches* 56-59; C-in-c Grange St Andr CD 59-63; P-in-c Grange St Andr 63-65; V 65-67; R Coppenhall 67-82; V W Kirby St Andr 82-01; Hon Can Ches Cathl 86-01; rtd 01; PtO *Ches* from 01. *26 Lyndhurst Road, Hoylake, Wirral CH47 7BP* T: 0151-632 0335

KELLY, Desmond Norman. b 42. Oak Hill Th Coll BA 95. **d** 90 **p** 91. C Braintree *Chelmsf* 90-94; P-in-c Sible Hedingham 94-95; P-in-c Castle Hedingham 94-95; R Sible Hedingham w Castle Hedingham 95-08; rtd 08; PtO *St E* from 11; *Chelmsf* from 11. *Wykhams, Mill Common, Westhall, Halesworth IP19 8RQ* T: (01502) 575493 E: rev.des@btinternet.com

KELLY, Canon Edward William Moncrieff. b 28. AKC 57. **d** 57 **p** 58. C Petersfield w Sheet *Portsm* 57-60; Papua New Guinea 60-65; Dioc Sec Samarai 61; Hon Chapl Miss to Seamen 61-62; V Gosport Ch Ch *Portsm* 65-69; Hon C Eltham St Jo *S'wark* 69-87; Org Sec New Guinea Miss 69-77; Org Sec Papua New Guinea Ch Partnership 77-87; Hon Can Papua New Guinea from 78; TR Trowbridge H Trin *Sarum* 87-94; Chapl St Jo Hosp Trowbridge 87-94; Acting RD Bradford *Sarum* 91-92; rtd 94; PtO *Portsm* from 94. *133 Borough Road, Petersfield GU32 3LP* T: (01730) 260399

KELLY, John Adrian. b 49. Qu Coll Birm 70. **d** 73 **p** 74. C Formby St Pet *Liv* 73-77; Org Sec CECS Liv, Blackb and S & M 77-92; Deputation Appeals Org (Lancs and Is of Man) 88-92; PtO *Liv* 77-05; *Blackb* 77-00; *Man* 88-97. *4 Blandford Close, Southport PR8 2DB*

KELLY, Canon John Dickinson. b 42. Nottm Univ BA 63. Ripon Hall Ox 63. **d** 65 **p** 66. C Egremont *Carl* 65-67; C Upperby St Jo 67-70; V Arlecdon 70-73; V Barrow St Aid 73-79; V Milnthorpe 79-83; V Beetham and Milnthorpe 83-85; V Camerton St Pet 85-88; P-in-c Camerton H Trin W Seaton 86-88; V Camerton, Seaton and W Seaton 88-01; P-in-c Kells 01-05; Hon Can Carl Cathl from 00; Chapl N Cumbria Acute Hosps NHS Trust 03-05; rtd 05; P-in-c Kirkland, Lamplugh w Ennerdale *Carl* 05-07; Hon C Whitehaven 07-12. *The Vicarage, Oakfield Court, Hillcrest, Whitehaven CA28 6TG* T: (01946) 692630

KELLY, John Graham. b 60. Lanc Univ LLB 82 Sheff Univ PhD 95 Solicitor 84. St Jo Coll Nottm BTh 91. **d** 94 **p** 95. C Normanton *Derby* 94-97; P-in-c Ockbrook 97-01; Lect St Jo

Coll Nottm 01-07; rtd 07. *15 Stanley Road, Whitstable CT5 4NJ* T: (01227) 280209 E: jgkelly34@btinternet.com

KELLY, Malcolm Bernard. b 46. St Mich Coll Llan 72. **d** 74 **p** 75. C Tranmere St Paul w St Luke *Ches* 74-77; C Barnston 77-80; R Thurstaston 80-92; R Grappenhall 92-11; rtd 11; PtO *Ches* from 11. *22 Boswell Avenue, Warrington WA4 6DQ* T: (01925) 423871 E: malcolmkelly25@yahoo.co.uk

KELLY, Martin Herbert. b 55. Selw Coll Cam MA 90. Aston Tr Scheme 78 Ripon Coll Cuddesdon 80. **d** 83 **p** 84. C Clapham Old Town *S'wark* 83-87; Chapl and Fell Selw Coll Cam 87-92; Chapl Newnham Coll Cam 87-92; Chapl St Piers Hosp Sch Lingfield *S'wark* 95-01; C Limpsfield and Titsey 95-01; Chapl Basildon and Thurrock Gen Hosps NHS Trust 03-04; Chapl Dartford and Gravesham NHS Trust from 04; PtO *S'wark* from 14. *Darent Valley Hospital, Darenth Wood Road, Dartford DA2 8DA* T: (01322) 428100 ext 4640 E: martin.kelly@dvh.nhs.uk

KELLY, Neil Anthony. St Mich Coll Llan. **d** 10 **p** 11. C Llangollen w Trevor and Llantysilio *St As* 10-12; C Mold 12-14; P-in-c Buckley from 14. *St Matthew's Vicarage, 114 Church Road, Buckley CH7 3JN* T: (01244) 550645 E: neilanthonykelly@gmail.com

KELLY, Nigel James (Ned). b 60. N Staffs Poly BSc 83. Ripon Coll Cuddesdon 83. **d** 86 **p** 87. C Cen Telford *Lich* 86-90; TV 90-92; Chapl RN from 92. *Royal Naval Chaplaincy Service, Mail Point 1-2, Leach Building, Whale Island, Portsmouth PO2 8BY* T: (023) 9262 5055 F: 9262 5134

KELLY, Paul. b 60. Qu Coll Birm 02. **d** 04 **p** 05. C Ogley Hay *Lich* 04-07; V Stafford St Paul Forebridge 07-11; V Hednesford from 11. *The Vicarage, Church Hill, Hednesford, Cannock WS12 1BD* T: (01543) 426954 M: 07815-452616

KELLY, Canon Peter Hugh. b 46. Sarum & Wells Th Coll 81. **d** 84 **p** 85. C Fareham H Trin *Portsm* 84-87; Chapl and Prec Portsm Cathl 87-90; V Eastney 90-97; P-in-c Swanmore St Barn 97-06; V 07-11; RD Bishop's Waltham 03-09; Hon Can Portsm Cathl 07-11; rtd 11; PtO *Portsm* from 11. *16 Rosedale Close, Fareham PO14 4EL* T: (01329) 849567

KELLY, Stephen Alexander. b 61. Man Univ BSc 84. Ridley Hall Cam 03. **d** 05 **p** 06. C Meole Brace *Lich* 05-08; C Cen Telford 08-13; Fresh Expressions Adv 12-13; V Northampton St Giles *Pet* from 13. *St Giles's Vicarage, 2 Spring Gardens, Northampton NN1 1LX* T: (01604) 627680 E: revstevekelly@gmail.com

KELLY, Canon Stephen Paul. b 55. Keble Coll Ox BA 77 MA 07 Leeds Univ MA 06. Linc Th Coll 77. **d** 79 **p** 80. C Illingworth *Wakef* 79-82; C Knottingley 82-84; V Alverthorpe 84-93; Dioc Ecum Officer 88-93; TR Bingley All SS *Bradf* 93-03; P-in-c Woolley *Leeds* from 03; Dioc CME Officer from 03; AD Wakef from 14; Hon Can Wakef Cathl from 08. *The Vicarage, Church Street, Woolley, Wakefield WF4 2JU* T: (01226) 382550 E: stephen.kelly@wakefield.anglican.org

KELLY, Trevor Samuel. b 67. QUB BEd 88 Open Univ CertEd 09. CITC 06. **d** 10 **p** 11. NSM Craigs w Dunaghy and Killagan *Conn* from 10. *1 Galgorm Lodge, Ballymena BT42 1GL* T: (028) 2565 4128 M: 07793-005275 E: tkhazelwood@yahoo.co.uk

KELLY, Canon William. b 35. Dur Univ BA 58. Lambeth STh 75 Wycliffe Hall Ox 58. **d** 60 **p** 61. C Walney Is *Carl* 60-66; R Distington 66-71; V Barrow St Matt 71-81; RD Furness 77-81; Hon Can Carl Cathl 79-00; Dir of Ords 81-97; V Dalston 81-92; RD Carl 83-88; P-in-c Raughton Head w Gatesgill 86-92; P-in-c Maryport 92-97; P-in-c Flimby 93-96; P-in-c Arthuret and Nicholforest and Kirkandrews on Esk 97-00; rtd 00; PtO *Carl* from 00. *73 Upperby Road, Carlisle CA2 4JE* T: (01228) 514013

KELSEY, George Robert. b 61. Imp Coll Lon BSc 83 Newc Univ MSc 84 PhD 92. Cranmer Hall Dur 95. **d** 97 **p** 98. C Denton *Newc* 97-01; TV Glendale Gp 01-10; V Norham and Duddo from 10; P-in-c Cornhill w Carham from 10; P-in-c Branxton from 10; AD Norham from 10. *The Vicarage, Church Lane, Norham, Berwick-upon-Tweed TD15 2LF* T: (01289) 382325 E: robert.josephkelsey@live.com

KELSEY, Michael Ray. b 22. FEPA 57. Wycliffe Hall Ox 60. **d** 62 **p** 63. C Lower Broughton St Clem *Man* 62-64; V Ingleby Greenhow *York* 64-68; V Scarborough St Jas 68-71; Asst to the Gen Sec USCL 71-74; V Blackheath St Jo *S'wark* 74-87; rtd 87; PtO *St E* 88-05. *20 Sweet Briar, Marcham, Abingdon OX13 6PD* T: (01865) 391835

KELSO, Andrew John. b 47. Lon Univ BA 70 LRAM 73. St Jo Coll Nottm 83. **d** 85 **p** 86. C Gorleston St Mary *Nor* 85-87; C Hellesdon 87-90; TV Ipsley *Worc* 90-09; rtd 09. *2 The Close, Throckmorton, Pershore WR10 2JU* T: (01386) 462087 - M: 07795-431382 E: andy.kelso@sky.com

KEMBER, Ms Ann Elizabeth. b 58. ERMC 12. **d** 15. C Wolverton Ox from 15. *62 Anson Road, Wolverton, Milton Keynes MK12 5BP* M: 07855-470522 E: annkember@hotmail.com

KEMM, William St John. b 39. Birm Univ BA 62 MA 65. Ridley Hall Cam 62. **d** 64 **p** 65. C Kingswinford H Trin *Lich* 64-68;

C Hednesford 68-71; V Hanbury 71-76; R Berrow and Breane *B & W* 76-92; V Hertford All SS *St Alb* 92-06; rtd 06. *Holtye, Nether Lane, Nutley, Uckfield TN22 3LE* T: (01825) 713704 E: billkemm@waitrose.com

KEMP, Mrs Alice Mary Elizabeth. b 59. Kent Univ BA 82 Thames Poly PGCE 91. STETS 07. **d** 10 **p** 11. NSM Box w Hazlebury and Ditteridge *Bris* from 10; NSM Colerne w N Wraxall from 11. *Barn House, Barn Piece, Box, Corsham SN13 8LF* T: (01225) 742128 E: amekemp@aol.com

KEMP, Canon Allan. b 43. Bps' Coll Cheshunt 65 Oak Hill Th Coll 67. **d** 68 **p** 69. C Tunbridge Wells St Jas *Roch* 68-76; V Becontree St Mary *Chelmsf* 76-90; RD Barking and Dagenham 81-86; V Gt w Lt Chesterford 90-07; Hon Can Chelmsf Cathl 99-07; rtd 07. *6 Freemans Orchard, Newent GL18 1TX* T: (01531) 822041 E: canonkemp@waitrose.com

KEMP, Prof Anthony Eric. b 34. St Mark & St Jo Coll Lon CertEd 57 LTCL 63 FTCL 63 Lon Inst of Educn DipEd 70 Sussex Univ MA 71 DPhil 79 Hon FLCM 83 CPsychol 89 FBPsS 97 Helsinki Univ Hon MusDoc 03. SAOMC 96. **d** 98 **p** 99. NSM Wokingham All SS *Ox* 98-05; NSM Wokingham St Paul 05-09; PtO 09-13; *Portsm* from 14. *40 Sea Grove Avenue, Hayling Island PO11 9EU* T: (023) 9378 6659 E: ae.kemp@yahoo.co.uk

KEMP, Ms Audrey. b 26. MSR 49. Gilmore Ho 62. **dss** 69 **d** 87 **p** 94. Cranford *Lon* 67-70; S Ockendon Hosp 70-71; N Greenford All Hallows *Lon* 71-72; Feltham 72-80; Brentford St Faith 80-83; Hanworth All SS 83-85; Hanworth St Geo 85-87; Par Dn 87-88; rtd 88; PtO *B & W* 88-89 and 99-07; Hon Par Dn Ditcheat w E Pennard and Pylle 89-94; P-in-c 94-95; PtO *Win* 95-98. *Address temp unknown*

KEMP, Christopher Michael. b 48. K Coll Lon BD 71 AKC 71. St Aug Coll Cant 75. **d** 76 **p** 77. C Weaverham *Ches* 76-79; C Latchford St Jas 79-82; P-in-c Sandbach Heath 82-88; V Macclesfield St Paul 88-89; C Cheadle Hulme All SS 89-93; C Oxton 93-98; P-in-c Seacombe 98-02; P-in-c Brereton w Swettenham 02-05; P-in-c Brereton w Eaton and Hulme Walfield 05-10; rtd 10. *1 Orchard Rise, Droitwich WR9 8NU* T: (01905) 774372

KEMP, Ian Andrew. b 88. Trin Coll Bris BA 13 MA 14. **d** 14 **p** 15. C Penn *Lich* from 14. *204 Warstones Road, Penn, Wolverhampton WV4 4LF* T: (01902) 576809 M: 07507-367089 E: curate@stbarts.org.uk

KEMP, John Graham Edwin. b 29. Bris Univ BA 51 PGCE 52 Lon Univ BD 65. Wells Th Coll 63. **d** 65 **p** 66. C Maidenhead St Luke *Ox* 65-70; R Rotherfield Greys 70-78; V Highmore 70-78; Dep Dir Tr Scheme for NSM 78-84; P-in-c Taplow 78-82; TV Burnham w Dropmore, Hitcham and Taplow 82-84; Prin EAMTC 84-92; rtd 92; Chapl Kyrenia Cyprus 92-95; PtO *St E* from 95. *Lea Cottage, The Street, Middleton, Saxmundham IP17 3NJ* T: (01728) 648324 E: revdjgk@waitrose.com

KEMP, John Robert Deverall. b 42. City Univ BSc 65 BD 69. Oak Hill Th Coll 66. **d** 70 **p** 71. C Fulham Ch Ch *Lon* 70-73; C Widford *Chelmsf* 73-79; P-in-c New Thundersley 79-84; V 84-98; Chapl HM Pris Bullwood Hall 79-98; R S Shoebury *Chelmsf* 98-09; rtd 09; PtO *Chelmsf* from 09. *36 Macmurdo Road, Leigh-on-Sea SS9 5AQ*

KEMP, Mrs Karen Margaret. b 62. Victoria Univ Wellington MA 11 RGN 82. ACT BTh 89. **d** 13. C Glouc City and Hempsted 13. *24 Kingscroft Road, Hucclecote, Gloucester GL3 3RG* T: (01452) 614402 M: 07787-620765 E: karen.m.kemp@btinternet.com

KEMP, Mrs Pamela Ann. b 52. Coll of St Matthias Bris CertEd 73 RMN 98. Ripon Coll Cuddesdon BTh 07. **d** 02 **p** 03. C Portland All SS w St Pet *Sarum* 02-04; C Verwood 04-06; R Highnam, Lassington, Rudford, Tibberton etc *Glouc* 06-11; P-in-c Stokenham, Slapton, Charleton w Buckland etc *Ex* 11-14. *Address temp unknown* M: 07989-604543 E: pamelakemp@btinternet.com

KEMP, Ralph John. b 71. Wye Coll Lon BSc 93 Trin Hall Cam BTh 04. Ridley Hall Cam 01. **d** 04 **p** 05. C Astbury and Smallwood *Ches* 04-07; V Burton and Shotwick 07-08; NSM Plas Newton w Ches Ch Ch 09-11; NSM Ches Ch Ch from 11. *38 Ethos Court, City Road, Chester CH1 3AT* M: 07762-847211 E: ralphjkemp@googlemail.com

KEMP, Trevor George. b 62. Trin Coll Bris 98. **d** 00 **p** 01. C Old Catton *Nor* 00-03; V S Nutfield w Outwood *S'wark* 03-13; R Kemble, Poole Keynes, Somerford Keynes etc *Glouc* from 13. *The Vicarage, Coates, Cirencester GL7 6NR* T: (01285) 770550 E: rev.trev@btinternet.com

KEMP, William. b 57. St Anne's Coll Ox BA 91 Brunel Univ PGCE 92 Wolfs Coll Cam BTh 99. Ridley Hall Cam 96. **d** 99 **p** 00. C Kensington St Barn *Lon* 99-04; P-in-c Mid-Sussex Network Ch *Chich* from 04. *C Hurstpierpoint* from 04. *12 Western Road, Hurstpierpoint BN6 9TA* T: (01273) 835829

KEMPSTER, Miss Helen Edith. b 49. **d** 00 **p** 01. OLM Weybridge *Guildf* 00-06; OLM Esher 06-14; PtO 14-15; NSM Headley All

SS from 15. *Perrymead, May Close, Headley, Bordon GU35 8LR* T: (01428) 713973 E: helen.kempster@btinternet.com

KEMPTHORNE, Renatus. b 39. Wadh Coll Ox BA 60 MA 64. Wycliffe Hall Ox 60. **d** 62 **p** 63. C Stoke *Cov* 62-65; Lect St Jo Coll Auckland New Zealand 65-68; R Wytham *Ox* 68-75; Chapl Bp Grosseteste Coll Linc 75-83; V Waimea New Zealand 83-90; Th Consultant 90-96; Researcher and Educator from 97; rtd 04. *140 Nile Street, Nelson 7010, New Zealand* T: (0064) (3) 546 7447 E: kempthorne@xtra.co.nz

KENCHINGTON, Canon Jane Elizabeth Ballantyne. b 58. Hull Univ BSc 79 Trin Coll Bris MA 05 Hughes Hall Cam PGCE 83. Westcott Ho Cam 88. **d** 90 **p** 94. C Winchcombe, Gretton, Sudeley Manor etc *Glouc* 90-96; PtO 96-99; NSM Dursley 99-02; Dir Reader Tr and Tutor WEMTC 01-06; Dean of Women Clergy 06-09; R Sodbury Vale 09-15; AD Wotton 13-15; Hon Can Glouc Cathl 06-15; TR Solihull *Birm* from 15. *45 Park Avenue, Solihull B91 3EJ* E: jane@kenchington.plus.com

KENCHINGTON, Paul Henry. b 54. Worc Coll Ox MA 76. St Jo Coll Nottm BA 81. **d** 82 **p** 83. C Scarborough St Mary w Ch Ch and H Apostles *York* 82-85; C Caversham St Pet and Mapledurham etc *Ox* 85-89; V Hucclecote *Glouc* 89-00; V Kowloon St Andr Hong Kong 00-05; Chapl Versailles w Chevry *Eur* 05-11; P-in-c Combe Down w Monkton Combe and S Stoke *B & W* from 11. *Lonsdale, 81 Church Road, Combe Down, Bath BA2 5JJ* T: (01225) 835998 *or* 835835 M: 07825-482225 E: vicar@htcd.org

KENDAL, Henry David. b 59. ASVA 83. Lon Bible Coll 90 Oak Hill NSM Course 92. **d** 94 **p** 95. C Roxeth *Lon* 94-99; C Woodside Park St Barn 99-06; V from 06. *78 Woodside Avenue, London N12 8TB* T: (020) 8343 7776 *or* 8343 5775 M: 07977-521656 F: 8446 7492 *or* 8343 5771 E: henrykendal@compuserve.com *or* henrykendal@stbarnabas.co.uk

KENDALL, Edward Jonathan. b 76. Nottm Univ BA 98 Ox Univ PGCE 99. Oak Hill Th Coll BA 10. **d** 10 **p** 11. C Fulham St Pet *Lon* 10-14; C Teddington SS Pet and Paul and Fulwell from 14. *25 Rivermead Close, Teddington TW11 9NL* M: 07813-610977 E: ed@stmichaelsfulwell.co.uk

KENDALL, Edward Oliver Vaughan. b 33. Dur Univ BA 59. Ridley Hall Cam 59. **d** 61 **p** 62. C Corsham *Bris* 61-64; C Portsea St Mary *Portsm* 64-67; Asst Chapl HM Pris Pentonville 67-68; Chapl HM Borstal Portland 68-71; LtO *Bradf* 71-94; rtd 94. *10 Halsteads Cottages, Settle BD24 9QJ* T/F: (01729) 822207

KENDALL, Frank. b 40. CCC Cam BA 62 MA 68 FRSA 90. S'wark Ord Course 74. **d** 74 **p** 75. NSM Lingfield *S'wark* 74-75 and 77-82; NSM Sketty *S & B* 75-78; NSM Limpsfield and Titsey *S'wark* 82-84; LtO *Man* 84-89; *Liv* 89-96; NSM Adnry St Helens 96-00; PtO from 01; NSM Farington Moss and Lostock Hall *Blackb* 03-06; PtO from 06. *52 Kingsway, Penwortham, Preston PR1 0ED* T: (01772) 748021

KENDALL, Giles. b 57. Lon Univ BA 80 Univ Coll Lon BSc 86 Lon Univ PhD 90. STETS BTh 98. **d** 98 **p** 99. C Wareham *Sarum* 98-01; V Sawston *Ely* 01-08; P-in-c Babraham 01-08; P-in-c Kingswinford St Mary *Worc* from 08. *15 Penzer Street, Kingswinford DY6 7AA* E: revg.kingswinford@virginmedia.com

KENDALL, Gordon Sydney. b 41. **d** 72 **p** 74. NSM Old Ford St Paul w St Steph and St Mark *Lon* 72-82; NSM Homerton St Luke 86-92; Asst Chapl Hackney and Homerton Hosp Lon 87-92; Chapl S Devon Healthcare NHS Trust 92-06; rtd 06. *Shiloh, Beech Trees Lane, Ipplepen, Newton Abbot TQ12 5TW* T: (01803) 814054

KENDRA, Neil Stuart. b 46. JP 96. Leeds Univ BA 67 Bradf Univ MSc 80 PhD 84. Linc Th Coll 67. **d** 69 **p** 70. C Allerton *Liv* 69-72; Ldr Leeds City Cen Detached Youth Work Project 73-75; Dioc Youth Officer *Ripon* 75-77; Lect Ilkley Coll 77-78; Sen Lect Bradf and Ilkley Community Coll 78-88; Hd Community and Youth Studies St Martin's Coll 88-94; Hd Applied Soc Sciences 94-06; Hd Sch Soc Sciences and Business Studies 01-06; P-in-c Settle *Bradf* 06-11; P-in-c Giggleswick and Rathmell w Wigglesworth 08-11; rtd 11; PtO *Leeds* from 11. *Cravendale, Belle Hill, Giggleswick, Settle BD24 0BA* T: (01729) 825307 E: neil.kendra@totalise.co.uk

KENDREW, Geoffrey David. b 42. K Coll Lon BD 66 AKC 66. **d** 67 **p** 68. C Bourne *Guildf* 67-70; C Haslemere 70-76; V Derby St Barn 76-95; R Deal St Leon w St Rich and Sholden etc *Cant* 95-07; Chapl E Kent NHS and Soc Care Partnership Trust 00-06; Chapl Kent & Medway NHS and Soc Care Partnership Trust 06-07; rtd 07. *2 Mill Lane, Butterwick, Boston PE22 0JE* T: (01205) 760977 E: david-kendrew@supanet.com

KENDRICK, Dale Evans. b 62. Ch Ch Coll Cant BA 86 Nottm Univ MA 87 Leeds Univ MA 95 Birm Univ PhD 13. Coll of Resurr Mirfield 94. **d** 95 **p** 96. C Tividale *Lich* 95-96; C Blakenall Heath 96-97; C Stafford 97-98; Dep Chapl HM Pris

Birm 98-01; Chapl HM Pris Drake Hall 01-03; Chapl RAF 03-04; Chapl HM YOI Werrington Ho 04-08; Chapl HM Pris Lewes from 08. *HM Prison Lewes, 1 Brighton Road, Lewes BN7 1EA* T: (01273) 785100
E: dale.kendrick@hmps.gsi.gov.uk

KENDRICK, Canon Desmond Max. b 22. Leeds Univ BA 47. Wycliffe Hall Ox 50. **d** 52 **p** 53. C Glodwick St Mark *Man* 52-54; Chapl Leeds Road Hosp Bradf 54-77; V Bradf St Clem 54-77; RD Bradf 63-73; Hon Can Bradf Cathl 64-89; V Otley 77-89; Chapl Wharfdale Gen Hosp 77-90; rtd 89; PtO *Leeds* from 89. *26 Ashtofts Mount, Guiseley LS20 9DB* T: (01943) 870430

KENDRICK, Mrs Helen Grace. b 66. Bris Univ BA 88. SAOMC 96. **d** 99 **p** 00. C Icknield *Ox* 99-03; P-in-c Sutton Courtenay w Appleford from 03. *The Vicarage, 3 Tullis Close, Sutton Courtenay, Abingdon OX14 4BD* T: (01235) 848297
E: helen@kendricks.fsnet.co.uk

KENNAR, Canon Thomas Philip. b 66. Surrey Univ BA 08. STETS 02. **d** 05 **p** 06. C Warblington w Emsworth *Portsm* 05-08; Chapl Portsm Coll 06-08; TR Portsea N End St Mark *Portsm* 08-15; P-in-c Havant from 15; Hon Can Cape Coast Ghana from 13. *St Faith's Rectory, 5 Meadowlands, Havant PO9 2RP* T: (023) 9307 1946 M: 07881-025592 E: tomkennar@gmail.com

KENNARD, Mark Philip Donald. b 60. Man Univ BSc 82 Cardiff Univ MTh 08. Cranmer Hall Dur 85. **d** 88 **p** 89. C Newark w Hawton, Cotham and Shelton *S'well* 88-89; C Newark 89-91; C Cropwell Bishop w Colston Bassett, Granby etc 91-93; P-in-c Shireoaks 93-99; Chapl Bassetlaw Hosp and Community Services NHS Trust 93-96; Chapl RAF from 99. *Chaplaincy Services (RAF), HQ Air Command, RAF High Wycombe HP14 4UE* T: (01494) 496800 F: 496343

KENNAUGH, Gary. b 80. Trin Coll Bris 12. **d** 15. C Lache cum Saltney *Ches* from 15. *69 Sandy Lane, Saltney, Chester CH4 8UB* M: 07584-176632 E: garykennaugh@gmail.com

KENNEDY, Aaron John. b 82. Westcott Ho Cam 13. **d** 15. C Newc St Gabr from 15. *260 Heaton Road, Newcastle upon Tyne NE6 5QE* M: 07815-180273 E: curateofheaton@gmail.com

KENNEDY, Alan. b 52. Liv Univ BSc 95. NOC 01. **d** 03 **p** 04. C Westbrook St Phil *Liv* 03-07; TV Mossley Hill from 07. *The Vicarage, Rose Lane, Liverpool L18 8DB* T: 0151-724 1915

KENNEDY, Ms Alison Mary. b 66. K Coll Lon BMus 87 Heythrop Coll Lon MA 95 LTCL 90. NTMTC 96. **d** 99 **p** 00. C De Beauvoir Town St Pet *Lon* 99-02; TV Walthamstow *Chelmsf* 02-07; TV N Lambeth *S'wark* from 07. *60A Harleyford Road, London SE11 5AY* T: (020) 7820 9445
E: alison_m_kennedy@hotmail.com

KENNEDY, Anthony Reeves. b 32. Roch Th Coll 64. **d** 67 **p** 68. C Ross *Heref* 67-69; C Marfleet *York* 69-71; TV 72-76; V Lightwater *Guildf* 76-83; V W Ham *Chelmsf* 83-89; V Lutton w Gedney Drove End, Dawsmere *Linc* 89-94; PtO *Chich* from 94; rtd 97; PtO *Win* 01-12. *40 Haydock Close, Alton GU34 2TL* T: (01420) 549860 E: anthreev.kennedy@virgin.net

KENNEDY, Ms Caroline Jane. b 62. St Andr Univ MA 85 York Univ PGCE 86. LCTP 11. **d** 14 **p** 15. NSM Harraby *Carl* 14-15; NSM Aspatria w Hayton and Gilcrux from 15; Chapl Trin Sch Carl from 15. *4 The Courtyard, Broadwath, Heads Nook, Brampton CA8 9BL* T: (01228) 561885 M: 07506-563393

KENNEDY, Miss Carolyn Ruth. b 59. Univ of Wales (Ban) BA 81 GradCertEd(FE) 83. Ripon Coll Cuddesdon BA 90. **d** 91 **p** 94. C Frodingham *Linc* 91-95; Chapl Cov Univ 95-00; R Uffington Gp *Linc* from 00. *The Rectory, 67 Main Road, Uffington, Stamford PE9 4SN* T: (01780) 481786 E: rector@uffingtongroup.org.uk

KENNEDY, David George. b 46. Hull Univ BEd 71 MA 76. Linc Th Coll 77. **d** 79 **p** 80. C Linc St Faith and St Martin w St Pet 79-82; V Bilton St Pet *York* 82-90; V New Seaham *Dur* 90-92; Chapl Lincs and Humberside Univ *York* 92-97; P-in-c Barrow St Matt *Carl* 97-99; TR 99-03; Chapl Furness Coll 97-03; P-in-c Blackb St Aid 03-04; V Blackb St Fran and St Aid 04-06; Chapl Nord Pas de Calais *Eur* 06-08; P-in-c Bierley *Bradf* 08-12; V *Leeds* 12-15; PtO *Blackb* from 15. *53 Parklands Way, Blackburn BB2 4QS* T: (01254) 600515
E: therevdavid@yahoo.com

KENNEDY, Canon David John. b 57. St Jo Coll Dur BA 78 Nottm Univ MTh 81 Birm Univ PhD 96. St Jo Coll Nottm 79. **d** 81 **p** 82. C Tudhoe Grange *Dur* 81-87; C Merrington 84-87; Tutor Qu Coll Birm 88-96; R Haughton le Skerne *Dur* 96-01; Can Res Dur Cathl from 01; Chapl Grey Coll Dur 01-09. *7 The College, Durham DH1 3EQ* T: 0191-375 0242 F: 386 4267
E: canon.precentor@durhamcathedral.co.uk

KENNEDY, Gary. b 63. Qu Coll Birm BA 02. **d** 03 **p** 04. C New Bury *Man* 03-06; C New Bury w St Lever 06; P-in-c Bolton SS Simon and Jude 06-11; TR Broughton from 11. *St James's Rectory, Great Cheetham Street East, Salford M7 4UH* T: 0161-312 8353 E: therev@talktalk.net

KENNEDY, Ian Duncan. b 53. **d** 04 **p** 05. OLM Whitnash *Cov* 04-07; NSM Leek Wootton 07-08; P-in-c Fillongley and Corley 08-15; V from 15. *The Vicarage, Holbeche Crescent, Fillongley, Coventry CV7 8ES* T: (01676) 540320
E: reviankennedy@aol.com

KENNEDY, James Edward. b 72. Magd Coll Cam MA 97 Imp Coll Lon MB, BS 97 Wolfs Coll Ox DPhil 05. Wycliffe Hall Ox BA 09. **d** 10 **p** 11. C High Wycombe *Ox* 10-13; TR Chipping Norton from 13. *The Vicarage, Church Street, Chipping Norton OX7 5NT* T: (01608) 642688 M: 07899-751931
E: james.kennedy@stmaryscnorton.com

KENNEDY, Mrs Jane Rowston. b 47. Dudley Coll of Educn CertEd 70 Leic Univ DipEd 93. EMMTC 04. **d** 07 **p** 08. NSM Gilmorton, Peatling Parva, Kimcote etc *Leic* from 07. *17 Cromwell Close, Walcote, Lutterworth LE17 4JJ* T: (01455) 554065 E: jane@kennedyjane.wanadoo.co.uk

KENNEDY, Jason Grant. b 68. Oak Hill Th Coll BA 95. **d** 98 **p** 99. C Beccles St Mich *St E* 98-01; R Hollington St Leon *Chich* 01-05; C Tonbridge St Steph *Roch* 05-10; V Ripley *Derby* 10-14; Ch Growth Officer Derby Adnry from 14. *Derby Church House, Full Street, Derby DE1 3DR* T: (01332) 388691
E: jason.kennedy@derby.anglican.org

KENNEDY, John Frederick. b 42. Birm Univ BSc 64 PhD 67 DSc 73 BA 12. Qu Coll Birm 05. **d** 06 **p** 07. NSM Edgbaston St Geo *Birm* 06-10; PtO from 11; *Heref* from 11. *Kyrewood House, Kyrewood, Tenbury Wells WR15 8SG* M: 07801-624749

KENNEDY, Joseph. b 69. Edin Univ BSc 91 BD 94 Moray Ho Coll of Educn PGCE 97 St Hugh's Coll Ox MSt 00 Keble Coll Ox DPhil 06. St Steph Ho Ox 98. **d** 02 **p** 03. C Stratfield Mortimer and Mortimer W End etc *Ox* 02-03; C Abingdon 03-05; Dean of Chpl, Chapl and Fell Selw Coll Cam 05-08; Chapl Newnham Coll Cam 05-08; Prin Coll of Resurr Mirfield 08-11; Hon Can Wakef Cathl 10-11; V Oxton *Ches* from 11. *The Vicarage, 7 Willow Lea, Prenton CH43 2GQ* T: 0151-652 2402 E: revd.j.kennedy@gmail.com

KENNEDY, Revd Michael Charles. b 39. TCD BA 63 MA 79 BD 79 Open Univ PhD 87. TCD Div Sch 61. **d** 63 **p** 64. C Drumglass *Arm* 63-66; I Lisnadill w Kildarton 66-14; Warden Dioc Guild of Lay Readers from 74; Hon V Choral Arm Cathl 75-14; Tutor for Aux Min (Arm) 82-14; Preb Yagoe St Patr Cathl Dublin 92-14; rtd 14. *8 Vicar's Hill, Armagh BT61 7ED* T: (028) 3752 3630
E: michaelkennedy2@btinternet.com

KENNEDY, Paul Alan. b 67. ACA 92. St Steph Ho Ox BA 95. **d** 95 **p** 96. C Romford St Andr *Chelmsf* 95-98; C Cheam *S'wark* 98-01; V Steep and Froxfield w Privett *Portsm* 01-08; Bp's Adv on Healing 04-08; R E Win from 08; AD Win from 13. *The Rectory, 19 Petersfield Road, Winchester SO23 0JD* T: (01962) 853777 M: 07877-211303
E: rectoreastwinchester@googlemail.com

KENNEDY, Paul Joseph Alan. b 57. Newc Univ MA 93. Sarum & Wells Th Coll 81. **d** 84 **p** 85. C Shildon w Eldon *Dur* 84-86; C Shotton 86-88; V Waterhouses *Dur* 89-93; V Denton *Newc* 93-95; CF 95-98; P-in-c Leam Lane *Dur* 98-99; V 99-05; P-in-c S Westoe 05-15; V from 15. *St Michael's Vicarage, Westoe Road, South Shields NE33 3PD* T: 0191-422 1299

KENNEDY, Miss Penelope Ann Cheney. b 49. STETS 08. **d** 11 **p** 12. NSM Buckland Newton, Cerne Abbas, Godmanstone etc *Sarum* 11-13; NSM Charminster and Stinsford from 13. *8 Abbots Walk, Cerne Abbas, Dorchester DT2 7JN* T: (01300) 341390 E: penekennedy@tiscali.co.uk

KENNEDY, Brother Philip Bartholomew. b 47. STETS 95. **d** 98 **p** 99. SSF from 77; C Plaistow and N Canning Town *Chelmsf* from 08. *St Matthias' Vicarage, 45 Mafeking Road, London E16 4NS* T: (020) 7511 7848
E: philipbartholomewssf@googlemail.com

KENNEDY, Ross Kenneth. b 40. Edin Th Coll 83. **d** 85 **p** 86. C Hexham *Newc* 85-89; TV Glendale Gp 89-93; TR Ch the King 93-05; rtd 05; Hon C Dunfermline *St And* from 05. *12 Calaisburn Place, Dunfermline KY11 4RD* T: (01383) 625887 E: rk.kennedy@talktalk.net

KENNEDY, Samuel (Uell). b 51. Heriot-Watt Univ BSc 72. CBDTI 06. **d** 07 **p** 08. NSM Baildon *Leeds* from 07. *The Moorings, Hunsingore, Wetherby LS22 5HY* T: (01535) 650531 F: 650550 E: uell@kadugli.org.uk

KENNEDY, Wendy Patricia. b 58. STETS 00. **d** 03 **p** 04. NSM Warren Park and Leigh Park *Portsm* 03-07; Dioc Sec from 07; PtO 07-11; Public Preacher from 11. *13 Ashcroft Lane, Waterlooville PO8 0AX* T: (023) 9241 3190
E: wendy.kennedy@portsmouth.anglican.org

KENNERLEY, Katherine Virginia (Ginnie). Somerville Coll Ox BA 58 MA 65 TCD BA 86 Princeton Th Sem DMin 98. CITC 86. **d** 88 **p** 90. Lect Applied Th CITC 88-93; NSM Bray *D & G* 88-93; I Narraghmore and Timolin w Castledermot etc 93-05; Can Ch Ch Cathl Dublin 96-05; rtd 05. *4 Seafield*

Terrace, Dalkey, Co Dublin, Republic of Ireland T: (00353) (1) 275 0737 M: 87-647 5092 E: vkennerley@gmail.com

KENNETT-ORPWOOD, Jason Robert. b 55. St Mich Coll Llan. **d** 78 **p** 79. Chapl St Woolos Cathl 78-82; Chapl St Woolos Hosp Newport 79-82; Dioc Youth Chapl *Mon* 82-85; V Cwmcarn 82-85; TV Wrexham *St As* 85-89; Dioc Ecum Officer 94-99; Chapl Maelor Hosp 86-89; V Bistre *St As* 89-99. *94 Erddig Road, Wrexham LL13 7DR*

KENNEY, Canon Peter. b 50. Edin Univ BD 75 Dur Univ MA 97 Essex Univ MA 05. Edin Th Coll 73. **d** 76 **p** 77. C Cullercoats St Geo *Newc* 76-81; TV Whorlton 81-88; TR Ch the King 88-93; P-in-c Newc St Jo 93-02; P-in-c Gosforth St Hugh 02-09; P-in-c Chapel House 09-12; Dioc Adv in Past Care and Counselling 02-12; Min Development Officer from 12; Hon Can Newc Cathl from 04. *7 Spring Gardens Court, North Shields NE29 0AN* T: 0191-257 9512
E: peter.kenney5@btinternet.com

KENNING, Canon Michael Stephen. b 47. St Chad's Coll Dur BA 68. Westcott Ho Cam 69. **d** 71 **p** 72. C Hythe *Cant* 71-75; TV Bow w Bromley St Leon *Lon* 75-77; C-in-c W Leigh CD *Portsm* 77-81; V Lee-on-the-Solent 81-92; R N Waltham and Steventon, Ashe and Deane *Win* 92-10; RD Whitchurch 03-08; Hon Can Win Cathl 09-10; rtd 10; PtO *Win* from 10. *20 Teal Crescent, Basingstoke RG22 5QX* T: (01256) 817989
E: michael.kenning@telorycoed.co.uk

KENNINGTON, The Very Revd John Paul. b 61. Collingwood Coll Dur BA 85. St Steph Ho Ox BA 87 MA 92. **d** 88 **p** 89. C Headington *Ox* 88-91; C Dulwich St Clem w St Pet *S'wark* 91-94; TV Mortlake w E Sheen 94-01; V Battersea St Mary 01-10; Dean Montreal Canada from 11. *1444 Union Avenue, Montreal QC H3A 2B8, Canada* E: pkennington@clara.net

KENNY, Charles John. b 39. QUB BA 61 MEd 78 LGSM 74. CITC 69. **d** 69 **p** 70. C Belfast St Paul *Conn* 69-71; Hd of RE Grosvenor High Sch 71-94; V Choral Belf Cathl 94-00; Can Belf Cathl 95-00; Treas Belf Cathl 99-00; rtd 00; LtO *Conn* from 84. *45 Deramore Drive, Belfast BT9 5JS* T: (028) 9066 9632 *or* 9032 8332 F: 9023 8855 E: c.kenny142@btinternet.com

KENNY, Frederick William Bouvier. b 28. TCD BA 53 DipEd 54 MA 56. **d** 56 **p** 57. C Ballymacarrett St Patr *D & D* 56-58; C Blackpool St Jo *Blackb* 58-61; V Preston St Paul 61-66; Chapl Preston R Infirmary 61-66; Youth Adv CMS (Lon) 66-70; Youth Sec (Ireland) CMS 70-75; I Belfast St Clem *D & D* 75-80; V Preston St Cuth *Blackb* 80-86; TV Bushbury *Lich* 86-90; P-in-c Stambridge *Chelmsf* 90-97; Chapl Southend Community Care Services NHS Trust 90-97; rtd 97; PtO *Pet* 97-99; *Chelmsf* from 99. *89 Cavendish Gardens, Westcliff-on-Sea SS0 9XP* T: (01702) 781671 E: c-jkenny@dial.pipex.com

KENNY, Mrs Lynda Ann. b 57. **d** 14. C N Ormesby *York* from 14. *45 Lothian Road, Middlesbrough TS4 2HS*
E: lynkenny@yahoo.co.uk

KENNY, Mark Anthony. b 74. Leeds Univ BA 97 PGCE 98. NTMTC 02. **d** 04 **p** 05. NSM Covent Garden St Paul *Lon* 04-08; NSM Aldersbrook *Chelmsf* 08-10 and from 12; PtO 10-12. *110 Perth Road, Ilford IG2 6AS* T: (020) 8554 2492 M: 07974-572074 E: mark.kenny@btinternet.com

KENRICK, Kenneth David Norman. b 44. RMN. Ripon Hall Ox 70 NW Ord Course 77. **d** 77 **p** 78. C Stockport St Geo *Ches* 77-83; R Stockport St Thos 83-85; R Stockport St Thos w St Pet 86-12; Chapl St Thos Hosp 88-12; Chapl Cheadle R Hosp 88-12; rtd 12. *88 Woodlands Drive, Stockport SK2 5AP*
E: truefaith_@hotmail.com

KENSINGTON, Area Bishop of. *See* WILLIAMS, The Rt Revd Paul Gavin

KENT, Alan Gilbert. b 56. Univ of Wales (Ban) BTh 09 Univ of Wales (Trin St Dav) MTh 15. **d** 14 **p** 15. NSM Cardigan w Mwnt and Y Ferwig w Llangoedmor *St D* from 14. *44 Bro Teifi, Cardigan SA43 1DQ* T: (01239) 613907
E: albewaiting@gmail.com

KENT, Barry James. b 41. **d** 02 **p** 03. OLM Kinson *Sarum* 02-07; NSM Hordle *Win* 07-12; rtd 12; PtO *Win* from 12. *6 Orchard Leigh, 2 Herbert Road, New Milton BH25 6BX*
T: (01202) 611348 M: 07733-048534
E: barrykent@minister.com

KENT, Christopher Alfred. b 48. Birm Univ BSc 69 PhD 72 CEng 77 MIChemE 77. St Jo Coll Nottm 82. **d** 84 **p** 85. C Bucknall and Bagnall *Lich* 84-86; Hon C Halesowen *Worc* 86-96; NSM Reddal Hill St Luke 96-01; NSM The Lye and Stambermill from 01. *40 County Park Avenue, Halesowen B62 8SP* T: 0121-550 3132 E: c.a.kent@bham.ac.uk

KENT, Miss Cindy. b 45. SEITE 03. **d** 07 **p** 08. NSM Whetstone St Jo *Lon* from 07; P-in-c from 10. *St John the Apostle Vicarage, 1163 High Road, London N20 0PG* T: (020) 8445 3682 M: 07879-642100 E: cindykent58@hotmail.com

KENT, David. b 44. CEng MIMechE. NOC. **d** 83 **p** 84. NSM Huddersfield St Pet and All SS *Wakef* 83-98; NSM Newsome and Armitage Bridge 98-03; NSM Em TM *Leeds* from 03.

2 Hillside Crescent, Huddersfield HD4 6LY T: (01484) 324049 M: 07949-762186 E: david.kent3@ntlworld.com

KENT, Frank. b 44. Open Univ BA 82 ARCM 76. Ridley Hall Cam. **d** 86 **p** 87. C Faversham *Cant* 86-89; R Lyminge w Paddlesworth, Stanford w Postling etc 89-99; P-in-c Sittingbourne St Mich 99-00; V Sittingbourne St Mary and St Mich 01-04; R Eastry and Northbourne w Tilmanstone etc 04-07; rtd 07; PtO *Cant* from 14. *3 Balfour Road, Walmer, Deal CT14 7HU* T: (01304) 375080 *or* 619346
E: revkent@francikent.freeserve.co.uk

KENT, Hugh. *See* KENT, Richard Hugh

KENT, Keith Meredith. b 32. St Aid Birkenhead 55. **d** 58 **p** 59. C Fulwood Ch Ch *Blackb* 58-60; C Everton St Chrys *Liv* 60-62; C Litherland St Phil 64-68; P-in-c Everton St Polycarp 68-74; V Liv All So Springwood 74-78; V Carr Mill 78-86; V Beddgelert *Ban* 86-91; rtd 91; PtO *Blackb* from 91. *14 Crow Hills Road, Penwortham, Preston PR1 0JE* T: (01772) 746831

KENT, Mrs Mary. b 51. Birm Univ BA 72. St Steph Ho Ox 06. **d** 08 **p** 09. NSM Alveston *Cov* 08-13; PtO 13-14; P-in-c Wexham *Ox* from 14. *7 Grangewood, Wexham, Slough SL3 6LP* T: (01753) 523852 M: 07597-382594

KENT, Richard Hugh. b 38. Worc Coll Ox BA 61 MA 63. Chich Th Coll 61. **d** 63 **p** 64. C Emscote *Cov* 63-66; C Finham 66-70; V Parkend *Glouc* 70-75; V Glouc St Aldate 75-86; Chapl and Warden Harnhill Healing Cen 86-96; R N Buckingham *Ox* 96-04; AD Buckingham 00-04; rtd 04; PtO *Pet* from 05. *10 Booth Close, Pattishall, Towcester NN12 8JP*
T: (01327) 836231 E: hugh.hilary38@btinternet.com

KENT, Ms Susan Elizabeth. b 52. St Aid Coll Dur BA 74 St Mary's Coll Newc PGCE 77. Ripon Coll Cuddesdon 98. **d** 00 **p** 01. C Westgate Common *Wakef* 00-03; P-in-c Oxclose *Dur* 03-08; R Upper Weardale from 08. *12 Kirk Rise, Frosterley, Bishop Auckland DL13 2SF* T: (01388) 528722 M: 07884-024202 E: susankent@aol.com

KENTIGERN-FOX, Canon William Poyntere Kentigern. b 38. AKC 63. **d** 64 **p** 65. C S Mimms St Mary and Potters Bar *Lon* 64-67; C S Tottenham 67-70; R Barrowden and Wakerley *Pet* 70-76; P-in-c Duddington w Tixover 70-76; P-in-c Morcott w S Luffenham 75-76; R Barrowden and Wakerley w S Luffenham 77-79; R Byfield w Boddington 79-86; V Northampton St Mich w St Edm 86-95; V Raunds 95-03; Can Pet Cathl 94-03; RD Higham 97-02; rtd 03. *41 Parkfield Road, Ruskington, Sleaford NG34 9HT* T: (01526) 830944

KENT-WINSLEY, Cindy. *See* KENT, Cindy

KENWARD, Roger Nelson. b 34. Selw Coll Cam BA 58 MA 62. Ripon Hall Ox 58. **d** 60 **p** 61. C Paddington St Jas *Lon* 60-63; Chapl RAF 64-82; Asst Chapl-in-Chief RAF 82-89; P-in-c Lyneham w Bradenstoke *Sarum* 72-76; QHC 85-89; R Laughton w Ripe and Chalvington *Chich* 90-95; Chapl Laughton Lodge Hosp 90-95; rtd 95; NSM Chiddingly w E Hoathly *Chich* 96; PtO from 96. *The Coach House, School Hill, Old Heathfield, Heathfield TN21 9AE* T: (01435) 862618

KENWAY, Ian Michael. b 52. Leeds Univ BA 74 Bris Univ PhD 86. Coll of Resurr Mirfield 74. **d** 76 **p** 77. C Cov 76-79; C Southmead *Bris* 79-81; P-in-c Shaw Hill *Birm* 82-88; Asst Sec Gen Syn Bd for Soc Resp 88-93; Chapl Essex Univ *Chelmsf* 93-99; Dir Studies Cen for Study of Th 93-99; PtO *S & B* from 01. *The Beast House, Cwmdu, Crickhowell NP8 1RT* T: (01874) 730143 M: 07748-223090 F: 07092-315825
E: iankenway@phidoc.fsnet.co.uk

KENWAY, Robert Andrew. b 56. Bris Univ BA 78. Westcott Ho Cam 80. **d** 82 **p** 83. C Birchfield *Birm* 82-85; C Queensbury All SS *Lon* 87-89; R Birm St Geo 89-97; V Calne and Blackland *Sarum* 97-10; TR Marden Vale from 10. *The Vicarage, 4 Vicarage Close, Calne SN11 8DD* T: (01249) 812340
E: kenway@gotadsl.co.uk

KENWORTHY (née SWALLOW), Mrs Judith Hazel. b 46. Dioc OLM tr scheme 99. **d** 01 **p** 02. OLM Meltham *Leeds* 01-14; rtd 14; PtO *Leeds* from 14. *3 Upper Wilshaw, Meltham, Holmfirth HD9 4EA* T: (01484) 851158

KENYA, Archbishop of. *See* WABUKALA, The Most Revd Eliud

KENYON, Caroline Elizabeth. *See* HOLMES, Caroline Elizabeth

KENYON, Lee Stuart. b 78. Lanc Univ BA 01 Leeds Univ BA 04 MA 05. Coll of Resurr Mirfield 02. **d** 05 **p** 06. C Darwen St Cuth w Tockholes St Steph *Blackb* 05-09; P-in-c Calgary St Jo Canada from 09. *St John's Rectory, 1421 8th Avenue SE, Calgary AB T2G 0N1, Canada* E: leekenyon@fsmail.net

KEOGH, Anthony. b 35. St Mich Coll Llan 63. **d** 66 **p** 67. C Aberaman and Abercwmboi *Llan* 66-70; Hon C Penarth All SS 70-76; St Jersey H Trin *Win* 76-05; PtO *Win* from 08. *9 La Ville des Chenes, St John, Jersey JE3 4BG* T: (01534) 869655
E: jill.keogh@virgin.net

KEOGH, Henry James. b 39. TCD BA 61 NUI BMus 65. **d** 62 **p** 63. C Cork St Fin Barre's Cathl 62-65; C Belfast St Luke *Conn* 65-66; C Dromore Cathl 66-68; I Castlecomer *C & O* 68-83; I Castlecomer w Colliery Ch, Mothel and Bilboa 84-85;

I Kilscoran w Killinick and Mulrankin 85-02; Hon Chapl Miss to Seafarers 85-02; Preb Ferns Cathl 96-02; rtd 02. *5 Ard na Gréine, Dark Road, Midleton, Co Cork, Republic of Ireland* T: (00353) (21) 463 0841

KEOGH, Paul Anthony. b 37. Order of Friars Minor 55. **d** 62 **p** 63. In RC Ch 62-66; Hon C Eltham Park St Luke *S'wark* 00-07; PtO from 07. *78 Greenvale Road, London SE9 1PD* T: (020) 8850 9958 *or* 8303 4786 E: pak.637@btinternet.com

KEOGH, Robert Gordon. b 56. CITC. **d** 84 **p** 85. C Mossley *Conn* 84-87; I Taunagh w Kilmactranny, Ballysumaghan etc *K, E & A* 87-90; I Swanlinbar w Tomregan, Kinawley, Drumlane etc 90-02; Preb Kilmore Cathl 98-02; I Drumclamph w Lower and Upper Langfield *D & R* from 02. *Drumclamph Rectory, 70 Greenville Road, Castlederg BT81 7NU* T: (028) 8167 1433 E: rkeogh@utvinternet.com

KEOWN, Paul Gabriel. b 53. Univ of Wales (Swansea) BA 95 PGCE 97 LGSM 76. Ripon Coll Cuddesdon 00 St Steph Ho Ox BTh 06. **d** 02 **p** 03. C Llansamlet *S & B* 02-04; P-in-c Swansea St Nic 04-07; R Haddington *Edin* 07-08; V Salfords *S'wark* 08-12; P-in-c Beckenham St Mich w St Aug *Roch* 12-15; P-in-c Footscray w N Cray from 15. *The Rectory, Rectory Lane, Sidcup DA14 5BP* T: (020) 8300 70796 E: frpaulkeown@mac.com

KER, Robert Andrew. **d** 05 **p** 06. Aux Min Larne and Inver *Conn* 05-13; Dioc C from 13. *24 Ravensdale, Newtownabbey BT36 6FA* T: (028) 9083 6901 E: a.ker@btinternet.com *or* templepatrick@connor.anglican.org

KERL, Ms Elizabeth. b 72. **d** 13 **p** 14. NSM Bassaleg *Mon* from 13. *46 Laurel Road, Bassaleg, Newport NP10 8NT* T: (01633) 893739 E: e.kerl@sky.com

KERLEY, Brian Edwin. b 36. St Jo Coll Cam BA 57 MA 61. Linc Th Coll 59. **d** 61 **p** 62. C Sheerness H Trin w St Paul *Cant* 61-64; C St Laur in Thanet 64-69; C Coulsdon St Andr *S'wark* 69-76; P-in-c Fulbourn *Ely* 76-77; R 77-03; P-in-c Gt and Lt Wilbraham 86-03; RD Quy 83-93 and 97-00; rtd 03; PtO *Ely* from 03. *11 Dalton Way, Ely CB6 1DS* T: (01353) 665641 E: brian.kerley@ely.anglican.org

KERLEY, Patrick Thomas Stewart. b 42. Linc Th Coll. **d** 85 **p** 86. Hon C Thorpe St Andr *Nor* 85-90; C Wymondham 90-94; C Gt Yarmouth 94-95; TV 95-00; TV Wilford Peninsula *St E* 00-07; rtd 07; PtO *Nor* from 08. *3 St Leonard's Close, Wymondham NR18 0JF* T: (01953) 606618 M: 07940-739769 E: patrick_kerley@sky.com

KERNEY, Barbara. *See* SHERLOCK, Barbara Lee Kerney

KERNOHAN, Jason William. b 79. TCD BTh 10. CITC 07. **d** 10 **p** 11. C Drumachose *D & R* 10-15; I Eglantine *Conn* from 15. *All Saints' Rectory, 16 Eglantine Road, Lisburn BT27 5RQ* T: (028) 9266 1406 E: jasonkernohan79@gmail.com

KERR, Mrs Alison. b 76. Ripon Coll Cuddesdon 06. **d** 09 **p** 10. C Lytchett Minster *Sarum* 09-10; C The Lytchetts and Upton 10-12; P-in-c Whippingham w E Cowes *Portsm* from 12. *The Rectory, 69 Victoria Grove, East Cowes PO32 6DL* T: (01983) 299930 M: 07833-450780 E: rev.allie@hotmail.com

KERR, Andrew Harry Mayne. b 41. TCD BA 63. Melbourne Coll of Div MMin 98. **d** 65 **p** 66. C Belfast St Luke *Conn* 65-68; SCM Sec (Ireland) 68-72; C Clooney *D & R* 72-74; C Swinburne Australia 74-80; I Dallas 80-88; I Mont Albert 88-94; P-in-c W Geelong from 96. *101 Katrina Street, Blackburn North Vic 3130, Australia* T: (0061) (3) 5221 6694 *or* 9893 4946 F: 9893 4946 E: ahmkerr@hotmail.com

KERR, Mrs Anita Dawn Christina. b 63. SRN 81 SCM 86 PGCE 04. CITC 04. **d** 07 **p** 08. Aux Min Sligo w Knocknarea and Rosses Pt *K, E & A* 07-09; LtO *Clogh* 09-10; Chapl to Bp Clogh from 10; NSM Devenish w Boho 10-12; NSM Garrison w Slavin and Belleek 12-13; Dioc C Galloon w Drummully and Sallaghy 13-15; I from 15. *The Rectory, 23 Drumcru Road, Aghagay, Newtownbutler, Enniskillen BT92 8GP* T: (028) 6773 8245 E: st_kerr@btopenworld.com

KERR, Anthony. b 43. Sheff Univ BA 64 Man Univ CertEd 65. NOC. **d** 85 **p** 86. NSM Greenfield *Man* 85-87; NSM Leesfield 87-97; P-in-c Oldham St Steph and All Martyrs 97-02; NSM Lydgate w Friezland 02-03; NSM Saddleworth 03-09. *16 Netherlees, Lees, Oldham OL4 5BA* T: 0161-620 6512

KERR, Arthur Henry. LRAM 47 TCD BA 48. **d** 49 **p** 50. C Templemore *D & R* 49-50; C Dublin Harold's Cross *D & G* 50-57; ICM 57-60; Chapl Rotunda Hosp 60-75; LtO *Conn* 88-94; P-in-c Clondevaddock w Portsalon and Leatbeg *D & R* 94-01; rtd 01. *Halothane, 172 Mountsandel Road, Coleraine BT52 1JE* T: (028) 7034 4940

KERR, The Very Revd Bryan Thomas. b 70. QUB BD 91 TCD MPhil 96. CITC 94. **d** 96 **p** 97. C Enniskillen *Clogh* 96-99; I Garrison w Slavin and Belleek 99-05; I Lisbellaw 05-14; Dioc Communications Officer 00-13; Can Clogh Cathl 12-14; Dean Dromore *D & D* from 14; I Dromore Cathl from 14. *The Deanery, Church Street, Dromore BT25 1AA* T: (028) 9269 2275 *or* 9269 3968 E: brykerr@tesco.net *or* dean@dromore.anglican.org

KERR, Charles. *See* KERR, Ewan Charles

KERR, Charles Alexander Gray. b 33. Open Univ BA 75 Birm Univ MA 83 MA 88. Edin Th Coll 63. **d** 67 **p** 68. C Hawick *Edin* 67-70; C Edgbaston St Geo *Birm* 70-72; Chapl Birm Skin Hosp 70-75; P-in-c Quinton Road W St Boniface *Birm* 72-79; V 79-84; R Musselburgh *Edin* 84-86; P-in-c Prestonpans 84-86; NSM Reighton w Speeton *York* 89-91; P-in-c Burton Pidsea and Humbleton w Elsternwick 91-95; V Anlaby Common St Mark 95; rtd 96; PtO *York* 96-02. *29 Kinsbourne Avenue, Bournemouth BH10 4HE*

KERR, David James. b 36. TCD BA 58 MA 61 BD 61 HDipEd 66. TCD Div Sch Div Test 59. **d** 60 **p** 61. C Belfast Trin Coll Miss *Conn* 60-63; Dean's V St Patr Cathl Dublin 63-66; Chapl Beechwood Park Sch St Alb 66-01; Hon C Flamstead *St Alb* 74-00; PtO 00-13; rtd 01. *Trumpton Cottage, 12A Pickford Road, Markyate, St Albans AL3 8RU* T: (01582) 841191 E: kerr_david@hotmail.com

KERR, Derek Preston. b 64. TCD BTh 90. Oak Hill Th Coll 85. **d** 90 **p** 91. C Belfast St Donard *D & D* 90-93; C Carrickfergus *Conn* 93-96; I Devenish w Boho *Clogh* 96-07; I Drummaul w Duneane and Ballyscullion *Conn* from 07. *The Vicarage, 1A Glenkeen, Randalstown, Antrim BT41 3JX* T: (028) 9447 2561 E: derekpkerr@gmail.com

KERR, Miss Dora Elizabeth. b 41. QUB BA 65 Southn Univ DipEd 66. St Jo Coll Nottm 82. **dss** 84 **d** 87 **p** 94. Becontree St Mary *Chelmsf* 84-88; Par Dn 87-88; Par Dn Rushden w Newton Bromswold *Pet* 88-93; C Finham and Chapl Walsgrave Hosps NHS Trust 94-00; C Belper *Derby* 00-07; rtd 07; PtO *Cov* from 08. *23 Worcester Close, Allesley, Coventry CV5 9FZ* T: (024) 7640 2413 E: elizabeth@ekerr1.plus.com

KERR, Ewan Charles. b 74. Fitzw Coll Cam BA 96 MA 00. Ripon Coll Cuddesdon MTh 01. **d** 01 **p** 02. C Nor St Pet Mancroft w St Jo Maddermarket 01-04; Chapl Glenalmond Coll *St And* 04-07; Chapl St Edw Sch Ox from 07. *281 Woodstock Road, Oxford OX2 7NY* T: (01865) 319460 *or* 510210 E: kerrc@stedwards.oxon.sch.uk

KERR, Frank George. b 52. **d** 05 **p** 06. OLM Levenshulme *Man* from 05. *4 Limefield Terrace, Levenshulme, Manchester M19 2EP* T: 0161-225 4200 E: frankkerr@btinternet.com

KERR, Canon Jean. b 46. Man Univ MA 93 SS Hild & Bede Coll Dur CertEd 69. NOC 84. **d** 87 **p** 94. NSM Peel *Man* 87-93; Par Dn Dixon Green 88-89; Par Dn New Bury 89-93; Par Dn Gillingham St Mark *Roch* 93-94; C 94-98; Chapl Medway Secure Tr Cen 98-01; Warden of Ev *Roch* 98-05; NSM Roch St Justus 01-05; Hon Can Roch Cathl 03-05; Can Missr from 05; Tr Officer for Lay Minl Educn *Roch* 03-05; Bp's Officer for Miss and Unity from 05. *Prebendal House, 1 Kings Orchard, Rochester ME1 1TG* T/F: (01634) 844508 E: jean.kerr@rochester.anglican.org

KERR, John Maxwell. b 43. Toronto Univ BASc 66 Leeds Univ MSc 70 MSOSc 88. Linc Th Coll 75. **d** 77 **p** 78. C New Windsor *Ox* 77-80; Asst Chapl Cheltenham Coll 80-81; Chapl 81-82; NSM Win St Lawr and St Maurice w St Swithun 82-94; Chapl Win Coll 82-92; Hd RS 86-97; Visiting Lect Dept of Continuing Educn Ox Univ 92-04; rtd 02; PtO *Portsm* 03-04; USA from 05. *111 Rolfe Road, Williamsburg VA 23185-3920, USA* E: jmk@kerr.newnet.co.uk

KERR, Karleen Theresa Kamella. b 58. **d** 13 **p** 14. C Harefield *Lon* 13-14; C Wealdstone H Trin from 14. *29 Lowick Road, Harrow HA1 1UP* M: 07989-467276 E: karlenekerr@aol.com

KERR, Canon Nicholas Ian. b 46. Em Coll Cam BA 68 MA 72. Westcott Ho Cam 74. **d** 77 **p** 78. C Merton St Mary *S'wark* 77-80; C Rainham *Roch* 80-84; Chapl Joyce Green Hosp Dartford 84-90; V Dartford St Edm *Roch* 84-90; V Lamorbey H Redeemer 90-11; RD Sidcup 98-03; Hon Can Roch Cathl 02-11; rtd 11; PtO *Roch* from 11. *11 Cobdown Grove, Rainham, Gillingham ME8 7PN* T: (01634) 389960 M: 07885-619595 E: mizeki@mac.com

KERR, Canon Paul Turner. b 47. Man Univ MA 92. Cranmer Hall Dur 68. **d** 71 **p** 72. C Kingston upon Hull St Martin *York* 71-72; C Linthorpe 72-76; C Cherry Hinton St Jo *Ely* 76-78; Chapl Addenbrooke's Hosp Cam 76-78; TV Rochdale *Man* 78-84; Chapl Birch Hill Hosp 78-84; V New Bury *Man* 84-87; TR 87-93; C Gillingham St Mark *Roch* 93-98; RD Gillingham 96-98; V Roch St Justus 98-11; RD Roch 02-11; Chapl Roch Cathl from 11; Hon Can Roch Cathl from 11; rtd 12. *Prebendal House, 1 Kings Orchard, Rochester ME1 1TG* T/F: (01634) 844508 E: paul.kerr@diocese-rochester.org *or* ptkerr@hotmail.com

KERR, Canon Stephen Peter. b 46. TCD BA 68 Edin Univ BD 71 MPhil 80. **d** 71 **p** 72. C Belfast H Trin *Conn* 72-76; C Ballywillan 76-78; Lect Linc Th Coll 78-87; Dioc Officer for Adult Educn and Minl Tr *Worc* 87-99; P-in-c Ombersley w Doverdale 87-13; P-in-c Hartlebury 08-13; P-in-c Elmley Lovett w Hampton Lovett and Elmbridge etc 10-13; Bp's Th Adv 99-07; RD Droitwich 07-13; Hon Can Worc Cathl 93-13; rtd 13. *27 Witton Avenue, Droitwich WR9 8NX* T: (01905) 776423 E: stephen.kerr46@yahoo.co.uk

KERR, Terence Philip. b 54. QUB BD 97. CITC 97. **d** 99 **p** 00. C Antrim All SS *Conn* 99-01; I Drummaul w Duneane and Ballyscullion 01-07; I Belfast St Aid 07-12; rtd 13. *8 Garley Mews, Tullygarley Road, Ballymena BT42 2HF* T: (028) 9543 8841 M: 07727-877830 E: terryrevkerr@talktalk.net

KERRIDGE, Benjamin. b 82. Clare Coll Cam BA 04. Coll of Resurr Mirfield 11. **d** 14 **p** 15. C Hornsey St Mary w St Geo *Lon* from 14. *145A North View Road, London N8 7ND* T: (020) 8883 6846 E: frbenhornseyparishchurch@gmail.com

KERRIDGE, Donald George. b 32. Bede Coll Dur CertEd 72 Hull Univ BA 84. Wesley Coll Leeds 57 Bps' Coll Cheshunt 61. **d** 62 **p** 63. C Manston *Ripon* 62-66; C Hawksworth Wood 66-71; Asst Chapl Brentwood Sch 72-74; LtO *Linc* 81-89; R Tetney, Marshchapel and N Coates 89-91; P-in-c Linc St Swithin 91-95; P-in-c Linc St Swithin w All SS 95-99; Asst Chapl Linc Co Hosp 91-94; rtd 99; PtO *S'wark* from 03. *28 Caverleigh Way, Worcester Park KT4 8DG* T: (020) 8337 3886

KERRIN, Albert Eric. b 26. Aber Univ MA 51. Edin Th Coll 51. **d** 53 **p** 54. C Dumfries *Glas* 53-55; P-in-c Cambuslang w Newton Cathl Miss 55-57; R Alford *Ab* 57-69; P-in-c Portpatrick *Glas* 69-98; P-in-c Stranraer 69-98; rtd 91; PtO *Glas* from 98. *Morroch, 15 London Road, Stranraer DG9 8AF* T: (01776) 702822

KERRY, Martin John. b 55. Ox Univ MA 78. St Jo Coll Nottm BA 81 MTh 83. **d** 82 **p** 83. C Everton St Geo *Liv* 82-85; LtO *S'well* 85-04; Chapl Asst Nottm City Hosp 85-89; Chapl 89-94; Hd Chapl Nottm City Hosp NHS Trust 94-04; Lead Chapl (NE) Caring for the Spirit NHS Project 04-07; Chapl Manager Sheff Teaching Hosps NHS Foundn Trust from 07. *Chaplaincy Services, Royal Hallamshire Hospital, Glossop Road, Sheffield S10 2JF* T: 0114-271 2718 E: martin.kerry@sth.nhs.uk

KERRY, Paul Matthew. b 84. Oak Hill Th Coll BA 07. Wycliffe Hall Ox 10. **d** 12 **p** 13. C Houghton *Carl* from 12. *7 The Green, Houghton, Carlisle CA3 0LN* M: 07834-525243 T: (01228) 595761 E: paulkerry84@gmail.com

KERSHAW, Ms Diane Justine. b 70. Sheff Univ BA 92. Yorks Min Course 09. **d** 11 **p** 12. C Shiregreen *Sheff* 11-14; C Sheff St Paul 11-14; NSM Shiregreen from 14; NSM Sheff St Paul from 14; NSM from 14. *St Paul's Vicarage, Wheata Road, Sheffield S5 9FP* T: 0114-246 8494 M: 07905-475121 E: diane.kershaw@sheffield.anglican.org

KERSHAW, Johanna. b 81. Clare Coll Cam BA 12 St Andr Univ MA 04 Oriel Coll Ox MSt 05 DPhil 10. Westcott Ho Cam 10. **d** 13 **p** 14. C Todmorden w Cornholme and Walsden *Leeds* from 13. *12 Phoenix Court, Todmorden OL14 5SJ* M: 07979-042694 E: johanna.kershaw@gmail.com

KERSHAW, John Harvey. b 51. Coll of Resurr Mirfield 84. **d** 86 **p** 87. C Hollinwood *Man* 86-89; V Audenshaw St Hilda from 89; Chapl Tameside Gen Hosp 90-94; Chapl Tameside and Glossop NHS Trust 94-95. *St Hilda's Vicarage, Denton Road, Audenshaw, Manchester M34 5DR* T: 0161-336 2310

KERSHAW, Savile. b 37. Bernard Gilpin Soc Dur 60 Chich Th Coll 61. **d** 64 **p** 65. C Staincliffe *Wakef* 64-66; C Saltley *Birm* 66-68; C Birm St Aid Small Heath 68-72; PtO 88-02; rtd 02. *74 Longmore Road, Shirley, Solihull B90 3EE* T: 0121-744 3470

KERSLAKE, Mrs Mary. b 39. **d** 05 **p** 06. OLM Hethersett w Canteloff w Lt and Gt Melton *Nor* 05-09; rtd 09; PtO *Nor* from 10. *Melton Vista, Green Lane, Little Melton, Norwich NR9 3LE* T: (01603) 811228 E: hjbk@btinternet.com

KERSLEY, Stuart Casburn. b 40. CEng MIET. Trin Coll Bris. **d** 82 **p** 83. C Lancing w Coombes *Chich* 82-87; TV Littlehampton and Wick 87-90; R Kingston Buci 90-98; V Kirdford 98-06; rtd 06; Hon C Appleshaw, Kimpton, Thruxton, Fyfield etc *Win* 06-12. *7 Hormare Crescent, Storrington, Pulborough RH20 4PW*

KERSWILL, Canon Anthony John. b 39. Lambeth STh 85. Linc Th Coll 72. **d** 73 **p** 73. C Boultham *Linc* 73-76; P-in-c N Kelsey and Cadney 76-83; V Gainsborough St Geo 83-91; V Bracebridge 91-00; P-in-c Linc St Swithin 00-01; V Linc All SS 01-05; RD Christianity 96-02; Can and Preb Linc Cathl 02-05; rtd 05; Chapl Trin Hosp Retford 05-12. *Tenterflat Cottage, Tenterflat Walk, Retford DN22 7PZ* T: (01777) 862533 E: kerswill@btinternet.com

KERTON-JOHNSON, Peter. b 41. St Paul's Coll Grahamstown. **d** 81 **p** 82. S Africa 81-99; PtO *Sarum* 99-00; P-in-c Stoke sub Hamdon *B & W* 00-11; Chapl St Marg Hospice Yeovil 07-08; rtd 11. *50 Brutton Way, Chard TA20 2HB* E: peter.kertonjohnson@btinternet.com

KESLAKE, Peter Ralegh. b 33. Sarum & Wells Th Coll. **d** 83 **p** 84. C Glouc St Geo w Whaddon 83-86; P-in-c France Lynch 86-91; V Chalford and France Lynch 91-03; rtd 03; PtO *Glouc* from 04. *4 Farmcote Close, Eastcombe, Stroud GL6 7EG*

KESTER, Jonathan George Frederick. b 66. Ex Univ BA 90 FRSA 14. Coll of Resurr Mirfield 91. **d** 93 **p** 94. C Cheshunt *St Alb* 93-96; Chapl to Bp Edmonton *Lon* 96-00; Hon C

Munster Square Ch Ch and St Mary Magd 96-00; V Gt Ilford St Mary *Chelmsf* 00-08; P-in-c Hampstead Em W End *Lon* 08-13; V from 13; Asst Dir of Ords from 09; CMP 00-14. *Emmanuel Vicarage, Lyncroft Gardens, London NW6 1JU* T: (020) 7435 1911 E: frjonathan@mac.com

KESTERTON, David William. b 59. Man Univ BSc 80. Cranmer Hall Dur 85. **d** 88 **p** 89. C Cheddleton *Lich* 88-92; TV Dunstable *St Alb* 92-97; Chapl Dunstable Coll 92-97; PtO *St Alb* 12-13; C Luton All SS w St Pet 13-14; P-in-c from 14. *All Saints' Vicarage, Shaftesbury Road, Luton LU4 8AH* T: (01582) 526662 M: 07957-228102 E: dkesterton01@gmail.com

KESTEVEN, Elizabeth Anne. b 79. Newc Univ LLB 01. St Steph Ho Ox 05. **d** 08 **p** 09. C Bris St Steph w St Jas and St Jo w St Mich etc 08-12; C Bedminster 12-13; C Whitchurch 12-13; P-in-c Fishponds All SS from 13; P-in-c Fishponds St Mary from 13. *11 Vicar's Close, Bristol BS16 3TH* T: 0117-965 7740 M: 07973-917720 E: lizzie.kesteven@live.co.uk

KESTON, Marion. b 44. Glas Univ MB, ChB 68 Edin Univ MTh 95. St And Dioc Tr Course 87 Edin Th Coll 92. **d** 90 **p** 94. NSM W Fife Team Min *St And* 90-93; C Dunfermline 93-96; Priest Livingston LEP *Edin* 96-04; P-in-c Kinross *St And* 04-11; rtd 11; LtO *St And* from 11. *Hattonburn Lodge, Milnathort, Kinross KY13 0SA* T: (01577) 866834 E: marionkeston2@gmail.com

KETLEY, Christopher Glen. b 62. Aston Tr Scheme 91 Coll of Resurr Mirfield 93. **d** 95 **p** 96. C Gt Crosby St Faith *Liv* 95-98; C Swinton and Pendlebury *Man* 98-00; V Belfield 00-08; R Elgin w Lossiemouth *Mor* from 08; R Dufftown from 08; R Aberlour from 08. *Holy Trinity Rectory, 8 Gordon Street, Elgin IV30 1JQ* T: (01343) 547505 M: 07932-183069 E: cgketley@waitrose.com *or* rector@trinityelgin.org

KETLEY, Michael James. b 39. Oak Hill Th Coll 79. **d** 81 **p** 82. C Bedhampton *Portsm* 81-85; R St Ive w Quethiock *Truro* 85-86; NSM Basildon St Andr w H Cross *Chelmsf* 89-90; C Barkingside St Cedd 90-92; P-in-c 92-95; R Hadleigh St Jas 95-08; rtd 08; PtO *Chelmsf* from 08. *40 Commonhall Lane, Hadleigh, Benfleet SS7 2RN* T: (01702) 556318 E: mikeketley@aol.com

KETTLE, Alan Marshall. b 51. Leeds Univ BA 72. Wycliffe Hall Ox MA 78. **d** 78 **p** 79. C Llantwit Fardre *Llan* 78-81; Prov RE Adv Ch in Wales 81-84; Chapl Llandovery Coll 84-92; P-in-c Cil-y-Cwm and Ystrad-ffin w Rhandir-mwyn etc *St D* 85-92; Chapl W Buckland Sch Barnstaple 92-11; rtd 11; PtO *Llan* 11-12; P-in-c Colwinston, Llandow and Llyswornev from 12; PtO *St D* from 15. *Moat Farm, Llysworney, Cowbridge CF71 7NQ* T: (01446) 679186 E: kettlesatmoat@hotmail.co.uk

KETTLE, Martin Drew. b 52. New Coll Ox BA 74 Selw Coll Cam BA 76 Cam Univ MA 85. Ridley Hall Cam 74. **d** 77 **p** 78. C Enfield St Andr *Lon* 77-80; Chapl Ridley Hall Cam 80-84; V Hendon St Paul Mill Hill *Lon* 85-98; AD W Barnet 90-95; PtO *Ely* 03-04; Hon C Huntingdon 04-06; Hon C E Leightonstone 06-10; Hon C Hamerton, Winwick and Gt w Lt Gidding and Steeple Gidding 09-10; PtO *Ox* from 11. *Apple Tree House, 97 New Road, Bampton OX18 2NP* T: (01993) 852454 E: mdkettle@msn.com

KETTLE, Mrs Patricia Mary Carole. b 41. Worc Coll of Educn CertEd 61. Dalton Ho Bris 66. **d** 87 **p** 94. C Wonersh *Guildf* 87-98; C Wonersh w Blackheath 98-01; rtd 01; PtO *Guildf* 02-13; Dioc Widow/Widowers' Officer from 13. *Wakehurst Cottage, Links Road, Bramley GU5 0AL* T: (01483) 898856 E: patsykettle@talktalk.net

KETTLE, Peter. b 51. K Coll Lon BD 74 AKC 74. St Aug Coll Cant 74. **d** 75 **p** 76. C Angell Town St Jo *S'wark* 75-78; C Putney St Mary 78-80; V Raynes Park St Sav 80-85; PtO from 85; *Lon* 03-13; NSM S Kensington H Trin w All SS from 13. *46 Allenswood, Albert Drive, London SW19 6JX* T: (020) 8785 3797 E: peter@levelsix.plus.com

KEULEMANS, Andrew Francis Charles. b 68. Univ of Wales (Abth) BSc 90. St Jo Coll Nottm BTh 93. **d** 94 **p** 95. C Mold *St As* 94-97; TV Wrexham 97-02; Chapl Loretto Sch Mussel-burgh 02-10; R Musselburgh and Prestonpans *Edin* 10-15. *12 Windsor Gardens, Musselburgh EH21 7LP* T: 0131-653 4809 E: andrewkeulemans@btinternet.com

KEULEMANS, Michael Desmond. b 42. SS Mark & Jo Univ Coll Plymouth TCert 65 Univ of Wales (Ban) MPhil 06 DMin 10. St As Minl Tr Course 02. **d** 92 **p** 93. PtO *St As* 03-11; Hon C Llanfyllin, Bwlchycibau and Llanwddyn 11-13; PtO *Lich* from 13. *The Poplars, Llanyblodwell, Porth-y-Waen, Oswestry SY10 8LR* T: (01691) 830010 E: theomots931@gmail.com

KEVILL-DAVIES, Christopher Charles. b 44. AKC 69. St Aug Coll Cant 70. **d** 70 **p** 72. C Folkestone St Sav *Cant* 70-75; V Yaxley *Ely* 75-78; R Chevington w Hargrave and Whepstead w Brockley *St E* 78-86; PtO *St Alb* 86-89; NSM Stansted Mountfitchet *Chelmsf* 87-89; R Barkway, Reed and Buckland w

Barley *St Alb* 89-97; R Chelsea St Luke and Ch Ch *Lon* 97-05; rtd 06; PtO *S'wark* from 06; Hon Chapl S'wark Cathl from 06. *York House, 35 Clapham Common South Side, London SW4 9BS* T: (020) 7622 9647 E: christopherkd@hotmail.com

KEVIN, Brother. *See* GOODMAN, Kevin Charles

KEVIS, Lionel William Graham. b 55. York Univ BA. Wycliffe Hall Ox 83. **d** 86 **p** 87. C Plaistow St Mary *Roch* 86-90; R Ash 90-00; R Ridley 90-00; P-in-c Bidborough 00-02; P-in-c Leigh 00-09; V from 09; RD Tonbridge 03-10. *The Vicarage, The Green, Leigh, Tonbridge TN11 8QJ* T: (01732) 833022

KEW, Canon William Richard. b 45. Lon Univ BD 69. ALCD 68. **d** 69 **p** 70. C Finchley St Paul Long Lane *Lon* 69-72; C Stoke Bishop *Bris* 72-76; C Hamilton and Wenham USA 76-79; R Rochester All SS 79-85; Exec Dir SPCK 85-95; Co-ord Russian Min Network 95-00; Convenor US Angl Congregation 00-02; V Franklin Apostles 02-06; R Franklin Resurr 06-07; Development Dir Ridley Hall Cam from 07; PtO *Ely* from 12; Hon Can Missr Owerri from 12. *Ridley Hall, Ridley Hall Road, Cambridge CB3 9HG* T: (01223) 741069 F: 746581 E: richardkew@aol.com *or* rk383@cam.ac.uk

KEY, Christopher Halstead. b 56. St Jo Coll Dur BA 77 K Coll Lon MTh 78. Ridley Hall Cam 79. **d** 81 **p** 82. C Balderstone *Man* 81-84; C Wandsworth All SS *S'wark* 84-88; C-in-c W Dulwich Em CD 88-93; V W Dulwich Em 93-95; R Ore St Helen and St Barn *Chich* 95-13; RD Hastings 03-13; V Maidstone St Luke *Cant* from 13. *St Luke's Vicarage, 24 Park Avenue, Maidstone ME14 5HN* T: (01622) 754856 E: revchriskey@gmail.com

KEY (née LANDER), Mrs Pauline. b 50. Leeds and Carnegie Coll CertEd 71. EMMTC 07. **d** 10 **p** 11. NSM Selston *S'well* 10-13; Chapl Nottm Univ Hosp NHS Trust from 13. *8 High Edge Drive, Heage, Belper DE56 2TB* T: (01773) 853749 M: 07779-132476 E: keyholistic1@hotmail.com

KEY, The Very Revd Robert Frederick. b 52. Bris Univ BA 73. Oak Hill Th Coll 74. **d** 76 **p** 77. C Ox St Ebbe w St Pet 76-80; C Wallington *S'wark* 80-85; V Eynsham and Cassington *Ox* 85-91; V Ox St Andr 91-01; Gen Dir CPAS 01-05; Dean Jersey *Win* from 05; P-in-c Jersey St Helier 05-08; R from 08. *The Deanery, David Place, St Helier, Jersey JE2 4TE* T: (01534) 720001 E: deanofjersey@gov.je

KEY, Roderick Charles Halstead. b 57. MTh. **d** 84 **p** 85. C Up Hatherley *Glouc* 84-87; V Glouc St Paul 87-04; TR Trunch *Nor* 04-14; V Chippenham St Andr w Tytherton Lucas *Bris* from 14. *St Andrew's Vicarage, 54A St Mary Street, Chippenham SN15 3JW* T: (01249) 652788

KEY, Roger Astley. b 49. Coll of Resurr Mirfield 72. **d** 74 **p** 75. PtO *Wakef* 74-75; P-in-c Khomasdal Grace Ch Namibia 75-77; R Luдеritz 77-81; Adn The South 77-80; R Walvis Bay 81-85; Personal Asst to Bp Windhoek 85-86; Dean Windhoek 86-00; V Hopton w Corton *Nor* from 00. *The Vicarage, 51 The Street, Corton, Lowestoft NR32 5HT* T: (01502) 730977 M: 07733-028048 E: thekeybunch@aol.com *or* rogerkey30@hotmail.com

KEYES, Graham George. b 44. St Cath Coll Cam BA 65 MA 68 Lanc Univ MA 74 Nottm Univ MTh 85 MPhil 92. EMMTC 82. **d** 84 **p** 85. C Evington *Leic* 84-86; Vice-Prin NEOC 86-89; C Monkseaton St Mary *Newc* 86-89; P-in-c Newc St Hilda 89-94; TV Ch the King 94-99; rtd 99. *1 East Avenue, Newcastle upon Tyne NE12 9PH* T: 0191-259 9024 E: graham.keyes@btinternet.com

KEYMER, Philip John. b 72. Bris Univ BSc 93. Oak Hill Th Coll 96. **d** 99 **p** 00. C Partington and Carrington *Ches* 99-02; C Cheadle 02-04; PtO *Man* 05-12. *10 Central Avenue, Levenshulme, Manchester M19 2EN* T: 0161-224 2384 E: phil.keymer@ntlworld.com

KEYS, Christopher David. b 56. Southn Univ BTh 95. Trin Coll Bris. **d** 02 **p** 03. C Fressingfield, Mendham, Metfield, Weybread etc *St E* 02-04; C Ipswich St Helen, H Trin, and St Luke 04-05; P-in-c Swineshead and Brothertoft Gp *Linc* 05-07; P-in-c Weston Zoyland w Chedzoy *B & W* 07-10; V from 10; RD Sedgemoor from 11. *The Vicarage, Church Lane, Weston Zoyland, Bridgwater TA7 0EP* T: (01278) 691098 E: revcdkeys@googlemail.com

KEYT, Fitzroy John. b 34. Linc Th Coll. **d** 67 **p** 68. C Highters Heath *Birm* 67-70; Hon C Sheldon 70-73; V Miles Australia 73-76; R Rayton 76-86; R Coolangatta 86-98; P-in-c Clayfield 98-01. *58 Thompson Street, Zillmere Qld 4034, Australia* T: (0061) (7) 3314 3011 E: dskeyt@optusnet.com.au

KEYTE, Mrs Christine Evi. b 73. UNISA BA 98. Westcott Ho Cam 13. **d** 14 **p** 15. C Rustington *Chich* from 14. *23 Henry Avenue, Rustington, Littlehampton BN16 2PA* E: revcdkeys@googlemail.com

KHAKHRIA, Rohitkumar Prabhulal (Roy). b 60. Sheff Univ BSc 82 PGCE 83. Oak Hill Th Coll 94. **d** 96 **p** 97. C Muswell Hill St Jas w St Matt *Lon* 96-01; C Stoughton *Guildf* 01-04;

V Boscombe St Jo *Win* from 04. *St John's Vicarage, 17 Browning Avenue, Bournemouth BH5 1NR* T: (01202) 396667 *or* T/F: 301916 E: roy.khakhria@lycosmax.co.uk

KHAMBATTA, Neville Holbery. b 48. St Chad's Coll Dur BA 74. S'wark Ord Course 81. **d** 84 **p** 85. Asst Chapl Em Sch Wandsworth 84-87; Hon C Thornton Heath St Jude w St Aid S'wark 84-87; Asst Warden Horstead Cen 87-01; Hon C Coltishall w Gt Hautbois and Horstead *Nor* 87-01; V Ludham, Potter Heigham, Hickling and Catfield 01-11; rtd 11; PtO *Nor* from 11. *The Spinney, Butchers Common, Neatishead, Norwich NR12 8XH* T: (01692) 630231 E: khambatta@lineone.net

KHAN, Rayman Anthony. b 63. Ripon Coll Cuddesdon 09. **d** 11 **p** 12. C Tamworth *Lich* 11-15; TV Bromsgrove *Worc* from 15. *12 Kidderminster Road, Bromsgrove B61 7JW* M: 07952-170840 E: captain.rayman@gmail.com

KHARITONOVA, Natalia. *See* CRITCHLOW, Natalia

KHATUN, Hasna. b 70. Ridley Hall Cam. **d** 13. C Newbold Pacey w Moreton Morrell *Cov* 13-15. *Address temp unknown*

KHOVACS, Ivan Patricio. **d** 14 **p** 15. NSM Willesborough w Sevington *Cant* from 14. *24 Sweet Bay Crescent, Ashford TN23 3QA* T: (01233) 620672 M: 07540-418621 E: ivankhovacs@gmail.com

KHOVACS, Mrs Julie Marie. b 67. Univ of California BA 94 Leeds Univ MA 04. Westcott Ho Cam 09. **d** 11 **p** 12. C Ashford *Cant* 11-15; C Pimlico St Pet w Westmr Ch Ch *Lon* from 15. *Address temp unknown* M: 07540-418623 E: khovacs@yahoo.com

KICHENSIDE, David Alexander. b 78. St Jo Coll Nottm BA 10. **d** 10 **p** 11. C Lilleshall and Muxton *Lich* 10-14; TV S Chatham H Trin *Roch* from 14. *26 Mayford Road, Chatham ME5 8SZ* E: david.kichenside@gmail.com

KICHENSIDE, Mark Gregory. b 53. Nottm Univ BTh 83. St Jo Coll Nottm 80. **d** 83 **p** 84. C Orpington Ch Ch *Roch* 83-86; C Bexley St Jo 86-90; V Blendon 90-93; V Welling 93-00; R Flegg Coastal Benefice *Nor* 00-05; RD Gt Yarmouth 02-05; TV High Oak, Hingham and Scoulton w Wood Rising 05-10; TV Walton and Trimley *St E* from 10. *The Vicarage, 2 Blyford Way, Felixstowe IP11 2FW* T: (01394) 548929 E: markatk1che39@tiscali.co.uk

KIDD, Anthony John Eric. b 38. Solicitor. Oak Hill NSM Course. **d** 89 **p** 90. NSM Rawdon *Bradf* 89-91; C Ilkley All SS 91-93; PtO 93-95; *York* 95-96; Hon C Gt and Lt Driffield 96-98; PtO 98-04; P-in-c The Beacon 04-08; PtO from 08; *Chich* from 08; *Leeds* from 12. *23 Sitwell Grove, York YO26 5JG* T: (01904) 849488 M: 07795-109090 E: tony.kidd546@gmail.com

KIDD, Kerry. b 57. **d** 08. NSM Alverthorpe *Leeds* from 08. *49 Wrenthorpe Lane, Wrenthorpe, Wakefield WF2 0PX* T: (01924) 368811 E: kskrpe@hotmail.com

KIDD, Maurice Edward. b 26. **d** 55 **p** 56. C Wembley St Jo *Lon* 55-58; C Middleton *Man* 58-61; Chapl Pastures Hosp Derby 61-69; Chapl Guild of Health *Lon* 69-72; R Hanworth St Geo *Lon* 72-82; R Chartham *Cant* 82-91; rtd 91; PtO *Cant* 91-13; *Lon* 96-97. *4 Cornwallis Circle, Whitstable CT5 1DU* T: (01227) 282658

KIDD, Mrs Ruth. b 62. Southn Univ BSc 83 Westmr Coll of Educn PGCE 84. **d** 12 **p** 13. OLM Lightwater *Guildf* from 12. *11 Aplin Way, Lightwater GU18 5TY* T: (01276) 471193 M: 07738-263057 E: ruth.kidd@btinternet.com

KIDDLE, Canon John. b 58. Qu Coll Cam BA 80 MA 83 Heythrop Coll Lon MTh 02. Ridley Hall Cam 79. **d** 82 **p** 83. C Ormskirk *Liv* 82-86; V Huyton Quarry 86-91; V Watford St Luke *St Alb* 91-08; RD Watford 99-04; Officer for Miss and Development from 08; Hon Can St Alb 05-10; Can Res St Alb from 10; Dir Miss from 11; Adn Wandsworth *S'wark* from 15. *19 Stanbury Avenue, Watford WD17 3HW* T: (01923) 460083 *or* (01727) 851748 E: john.kiddle@stalbans.anglican.org

KIDDLE, Mark Brydges. b 34. ACP 61. Wycliffe Hall Ox. **d** 63 **p** 64. C Scarborough St Luke *York* 63-66; C Walthamstow St Sav *Chelmsf* 66-71; V Nelson St Bede *Blackb* 71-76; V Perry Common *Birm* 76-79; R Grayingham *Linc* 79-84; V Kirton in Lindsey 79-84; R Manton 79-84; Hon C St Botolph Aldgate w H Trin Minories *Lon* 85-91; Hon C St Clem Eastcheap w St Martin Orgar 91-08. *12 Tudor Rose Court, 35 Fann Street, London EC2Y 8DY* E: mk@fpsi.org

KIDDLE, Martin John. b 42. Open Univ BA 80. St Jo Coll Nottm 74. **d** 76 **p** 77. C Gt Parndon *Chelmsf* 76-80; Asst Chapl HM Pris Wakef 80-81; Asst Chapl HM Youth Cust Cen Portland 81-88; Chapl HM Pris Cardiff 88-97; Chapl HM Pris Channings Wood 97-02; rtd 02; PtO *Ex* 02-09. *2 Cricketfield Close, Chudleigh, Newton Abbot TQ13 0GA* T: (01626) 853980 E: mkiddle@talktalk.net

KIDDLE, Miss Susan Elizabeth. b 44. Birm Univ BSc 66 Nottm Univ CertEd 67. **d** 89 **p** 95. OLM Waddington *Linc* 89-97; OLM Bracebridge 98-06; PtO from 06. *Rose Cottage, 30 Finningley Road, Lincoln LN6 0UP*

KIGALI, Bishop of. *See* KOLINI, The Most Revd Emmanuel Musaba

KIGGELL, Mrs Anne. b 36. Liv Univ BA 57. SAOMC 99. **d** 02 **p** 03. OLM Basildon w Aldworth and Ashampstead *Ox* 02-09; PtO from 09. *6 Quarry Hollow, Headington, Oxford OX3 8JR* T: (01865) 766235 E: anne.kiggell@virgin.net *or* anne.kiggell@btinternet.com

KILBEY, Mrs Sarah. b 39. MBE 98. Edin Univ MA 75 Man Poly CETD 82. Bp Otter Coll TDip 59 Edin Dioc NSM Course 84. **d** 93 **p** 97. NSM Edin St Columba 93-96; NSM Edin St Martin 96-11; NSM Edin St Jo from 11. *77 Morningside Park, Edinburgh EH10 5EZ* T: 0131-447 2378

KILBOURN-MACKIE, Canon Mary Elizabeth. b 26. Toronto Univ BA 48 Harvard Univ MA 49. Trin Coll Toronto MDiv 78 Hon DD 02. **d** 77 **p** 78. C Norway St Jo Canada 78-80; Chapl Toronto Gen Hosp 78-80; Dir Chapl Toronto 80-89; Hon Can Toronto from 95; PtO *Sarum* from 01; *B & W* from 01. *Address temp unknown* E: meskm1807@hotmail.co.uk

KILCOOLEY, Christine Margaret Anne. *See* ROBINSON, Christine Margaret Anne

KILDARE, Archdeacon of. *See* STEVENSON, The Ven Leslie Thomas Clayton

KILFORD, William Roy. b 38. Bris Univ BA 60. Sarum & Wells Th Coll 82. **d** 84 **p** 85. C Herne *Cant* 84-87; Chapl Wm Harvey Hosp Ashford 87-93; R Mersham w Hinxhill *Cant* 87-93; P-in-c Sevington 87-93; V Reculver and Herne Bay St Bart 93-95; Chapl Paphos Cyprus 95-98; P-in-c Doddington, Newnham and Wychling *Cant* 98-02; P-in-c Teynham w Lynsted and Kingsdown 98-02; P-in-c Norton 98-02; AD Ospringe 01-02; rtd 02; Chapl Nord Pas de Calais *Eur* 02-04; Hon C Burton Fleming w Fordon, Grindale etc *York* 04-08; Chapl St Jo Hosp Cant 08-09; P-in-c Burpham *Chich* 09-13; P-in-c Poling 09-13; PtO *Leic* from 14; Hon C Daventry, Ashby St Ledgers, Braunston etc *Pet* from 14. *The Vicarage, 19 Church Street, Staverton, Daventry NN11 6JJ* T: (01664) 668127 E: revkilford@aol.com

KILGOUR, Christine Mary. *See* CROMPTON, Christine Mary

KILGOUR, Christopher Richard Hargrave. b 74. York Univ BSc 97 MSc 00. Oak Hill Th Coll BA 13. **d** 13. C Chalk *Roch* from 13. *7 Brooke Drive, Gravesend DA12 4XP* M: 07905-992924 E: chris@kilgour.org.uk

KILGOUR, Richard Eifl. b 57. Edin Univ BD 85. Edin Th Coll 81. **d** 85 **p** 86. C Wrexham *St As* 85-88; V Whitford 88-97; Ind Chapl 89-97; R Newtown w Llanllwchaiarn w Aberhafesp 97-03; RD Cedewain 01-03; Provost St Andr Cathl 03-15; R Aberdeen St Andr 03-15; P-in-c Aberdeen St Ninian 03-15; Gen Sec Internat Chr Maritime Assn from 15. *ICMA Secretariat, Herald House, 15 Lambs Passage, London EC1Y 8TQ* T: (020) 7256 9216 F: 7256 9217 E: secretariat@icma.as

KILLALA, Dean of. *See* GRIMASON, The Very Revd Alistair John

KILLALOE, KILFENORA AND CLONFERT, Dean of. *See* PAULSEN, The Very Revd Gary Alexander

KILLALOE, KILFENORA, CLONFERT AND KILMACDUAGH, Archdeacon of. *See* CARNEY, The Ven Richard Wayne

KILLE, Vivian Edwy. b 30. Tyndale Hall Bris 60. **d** 62 **p** 63. C Dublin Miss Ch *D & G* 62-66; I Emlaghfad *T, K & A* 66-74; I Aghadrumsee w Clogh and Drumsnatt 74-05; Can Clogh Cathl 93-05; rtd 05. *16 Greer House, 115 Castlereagh Road, Belfast BT5 5FF* T: (028) 9073 1135 E: vek@hallelujah.demon.co.uk

KILLWICK, Canon Simon David Andrew. b 56. K Coll Lon BD 80 AKC 80. St Steph Ho Ox 80. **d** 81 **p** 82. C Worsley *Man* 81-84; TV 84-97; P-in-c Moss Side Ch 97-06; R from 06; Hon Can Man Cathl from 04; AD Hulme 07-12. *Christ Church Rectory, Monton Street, Manchester M14 4LT* T/F: 0161-226 2476 E: frskillwick@btinternet.com

KILMISTER, David John. b 46. Open Univ BA 88. **d** 06 **p** 07. OLM Chippenham St Paul w Hardenhuish etc *Bris* from 06; OLM Kington St Michael from 06. *22 The Common, Langley Burrell, Chippenham SN15 4LQ* T/F: (01249) 650926 M: 07747-331971 E: dave@kilmister.eclipse.co.uk

KILMORE, Archdeacon of. *See* MACCAULEY, The Ven Craig William Leslie

KILMORE, ELPHIN AND ARDAGH, Bishop of. *See* GLENFIELD, The Rt Revd Samuel Ferran

KILNER, Canon Frederick James. b 43. Qu Coll Cam BA 65 MA 69. Ridley Hall Cam 67. **d** 70 **p** 71. C Harlow New Town w Lt Parndon *Chelmsf* 70-74; C Cambridge St Andr Less *Ely* 74-79; P-in-c Milton 79-88; R 88-94; P-in-c Ely 94-96; P-in-c Chettisham 94-96; P-in-c Prickwillow 94-96; P-in-c Stretham w Thetford 94-96; P-in-c Stuntney 95-96; TR Ely 96-08; Hon Can Ely Cathl 88-08; Hon C Somersham w Pidley and Oldhurst and Woodhurst from 08; RD St Ives from 10. *125 High Street, Somersham, Huntingdon PE28 3EN* T: (01487) 842864 E: kilner@btinternet.com

KILNER, Mrs Valerie June. b 42. Univ of Wales (Abth) BSc 64 Hughes Hall Cam PGCE 65 MICFM 91. EAMTC 98. **d** 98 **p** 99. NSM Ely 98-08; PtO from 08. *125 High Street, Somersham, Huntingdon PE28 3EN* T: (01487) 842864 E: vjkilner@btinternet.com

KILPATRICK, Alan William. b 64. Oak Hill Th Coll BA 96. **d** 96 **p** 97. C Ealing St Paul *Lon* 96-01; Assoc R Mt Pleasant USA 01-04; P-in-c Prestonville St Luke *Chich* 04-09; R Diep River S Africa 09-13; I Knocknamuckley *D & D* from 13. *The Rectory, 30 Moss Bank Road, Portadown, Craigavon BT63 5SL* T: (028) 3883 1227 E: alanwkilpatrick@gmail.com

KILPATRICK, Edmund Stuart. b 52. **d** 12 **p** 13. NSM Southowram and Claremount *Leeds* from 12. *17 Athol Green, Halifax HX3 5RN* E: readersto@gmail.com

KILSBY, Miss Joyce (Jocelyn). b 40. Univ Coll Lon BSc 62 Ox Univ DipEd 63. NOC 98. **d** 01 **p** 02. NSM Stanley *Leeds* from 01. *18 Hazelwood Court, Outwood, Wakefield WF1 3HP* T: (01924) 824396 E: hilkil.hazco@virgin.net

KIM, Ho-Kwan Crispin. b 68. Sung-Gong-Hoe Univ Korea BA 98. Trin Coll Bris MA 03. **d** 07 **p** 09. C Nam-Yang-Ju St Fran Korea 07-09; C Dae-Hak-Ro St Bede 09; C Hendon St Alphage *Lon* 09-12; Chapl Angl Korean Community 09-12. *Address temp unknown* M: 07834-831022 E: kimcrispin@hotmail.com

KIMARU, Benson Mbure. b 54. St Andr Coll Kabare 81. **d** 83 **p** 84. V Mitinguu Kenya 85; Dioc Radio Producer 86-88; Asst to Provost Nairobi 88; V Kangaru 89-90; V Kayole 91-94; V Nyari 95-98; V Maringo 99-02; V Githurai 03-05; PtO *Sheff* 06-07; NSM Brightside w Wincobank 07; NSM Penistone and Thurlstone *Wakef* 07-09; Chapl SW Yorks Partnership NHS Foundn Trust from 09; Chapl Leeds and York Partnership NHS Foundn Trust from 13. *41 Holgate Mount, Worsbrough, Barnsley S70 6SR* M: 07919-988131 T: (01226) 891185 E: benititu@gmail.com

KIMBALL, Melodie Irene. b 49. **d** 99 **p** 06. USA 99-01; Chapl Asst S Man Univ Hosps NHS Trust 01-02; Asst Chapl Qu Medical Cen Nottm Univ Hosp NHS Trust 02-03; Chapl Leeds Mental Health Teaching NHS Trust 03-12; Chapl Manager Leeds and York Partnership NHS Foundn Trust from 12; Hon C Far Headingley St Chad *Ripon* 08-11; Hon C Thirkleby w Kilburn and Bagby *York* from 12; Hon C Sowerby from 12; Hon C Sessay from 12. *The Becklin Centre, Alma Street, Leeds LS9 7BE* T: 0113-305 6639 M: 07985-803834 E: melodie.kimball@nhs.net

KIMBER, Geoffrey Francis. b 46. Univ Coll Lon BA 67 Birm Univ MPhil 01. St Jo Coll Nottm 86. **d** 88 **p** 89. C Buckhurst Hill *Chelmsf* 88-92; R Arley *Cov* 92-02; P-in-c Ansley 97-02; CMS Romania 02-07; R Birm Bp Latimer w All SS 07-12; rtd 12. *10A Belle Vue Road, Paignton TQ4 6ER* T: (01803) 556773 E: geoff.kimber@gmail.com

KIMBER, Mrs Gillian Margaret. b 48. Bedf Coll Lon BA 70. Oak Hill Th Coll 89. **d** 91. NSM Buckhurst Hill *Chelmsf* 91-92; C Arley *Cov* 92-97; C Ansley 97-02; CMS Romania 02-07; PtO *Birm* 08-11; rtd 11. *10A Belle Vue Road, Paignton TQ4 6ER* T: (01803) 556773 E: deacon_gill@yahoo.co.uk

KIMBER, Mrs Hazel Olive. b 33. Lon Univ CertEd 73. **d** 95 **p** 96. OLM W Dulwich Em *S'wark* 95-03; PtO 03-14. *18 Michaelson House, Kingswood Estate, London SE21 8PX* T: (020) 8670 5298

KIMBER, Jennifer Carole Mary. **d** 15. NSM Lampeter w Maestir and Silian and Llangybi and Betws Bledrws *St D* from 15. *Creuddyn, Bryn Steffan, Lampeter SA48 8BS* T: (01570) 422770 E: jcm.kimber@gmail.com

KIMBER, John Keith. b 45. Bris Univ BSc 66. St Mich Coll Llan. **d** 69 **p** 70. C Caerphilly *Llan* 69-72; Chapl Birm Univ 72-75; TR Bris St Agnes and St Simon w St Werburgh 75-82; P-in-c Bris St Paul w St Barn 80-82; Hon C Westbury-on-Trym H Trin 82-83; Area Sec (Wales) USPG 83-89; TR Halesowen *Worc* 89-92; Chapl Geneva *Eur* 92-01; Chapl Monte Carlo 01-02; TR Cen Cardiff *Llan* 02-06; V Cardiff City Par 07-10; rtd 10; PtO *Llan* from 10. *13 Meadow Street, Cardiff CF11 9PY* T: (029) 2023 5809 E: johnkeith.k@gmail.com

KIMBER, Canon Jonathan Richard. b 69. K Coll Cam BA 91 MA 95 St Jo Coll Dur MA 02 K Coll Lon PhD 15. Cranmer Hall Dur 99. **d** 02 **p** 03. C Weston Favell *Pet* 02-05; P-in-c Northampton St Benedict 05-10; V 10-15; Can Pet Cathl 14-15; Dioc Dir Min and Discipleship *Worc* from 15. *The Old Palace, Deansway, Worcester WR1 2JE* E: jkimber@cofe-worcester.org.uk

KIMBER, Stuart Francis. b 53. Qu Eliz Coll Lon BSc 74 Fitzw Coll Cam BA 79 MA 83. Ridley Hall Cam 77. **d** 80 **p** 81. C Edgware *Lon* 80-83; C Cheltenham St Mark *Glouc* 83-84; TV 84-92; C Hawkwell *Chelmsf* 92-01; V Westcliff St Andr 01-15; rtd 15. *210 Staple Lodge Road, Birmingham B31 3DL* M: 07758-468052 E: revskimber@blueyonder.co.uk

KIMBERLEY, Canon Carol Lylie Wodehouse, Countess of. b 51. St Hugh's Coll Ox BA 73 MA 77 CertEd 74. Ripon Coll Cuddesdon 87. **d** 89 **p** 94. NSM Hambleden Valley *Ox* 89-02;

P-in-c Hormead, Wyddial, Anstey, Brent Pelham etc *St Alb* 02-12; P-in-c Sandon, Wallington and Rushden w Clothall 10-11; RD Buntingford 06-11; Hon Can St Alb 10-12; rtd 12; PtO *Ox* from 12; *St Alb* from 12. *Fieldfares, Ferry Lane, Medmenham, Marlow SL7 2EZ* T: (01491) 413155
E: ck@womvic.demon.co.uk

KIMBERLEY, The Ven Owen Charles Lawrence. b 27. Univ of NZ BCom 53. Tyndale Hall Bris 57. **d** 59 **p** 60. C Higher Openshaw *Man* 59-62; C Nelson All SS New Zealand 62-64; V Motupiko 64-69; V Kaikoura 69-76; V Tahunanui 76-85; Can Nelson Cathl 77-78; Adn Waimea 78-92; V Richmond 85-92; Chapl Port Said Egypt 94-98; Adn Egypt 96-98. *11B Gilbert Street, Richmond, Nelson 7020, New Zealand* T: (0064) (3) 544 2115 E: okimberley@xtra.co.nz

KIMMIS, Ms Sally Elizabeth. b 59. Westcott Ho Cam 08. **d** 10 **p** 11. C King's Lynn St Marg w St Nic *Nor* 10-14; P-in-c Foulsham, Guestwick, Stibbard, Themelthorpe etc from 14. *The Rectory, Guist Road, Foulsham, Dereham NR20 5RZ* T: (01362) 680148 M: 07548-741159
E: sally.kimmis@live.co.uk

KINAHAN, Canon Timothy Charles. b 53. Jes Coll Cam BA 75. CITC 77. **d** 78 **p** 79. C Carrickfergus *Conn* 78-81; Papua New Guinea 81-84; I Belfast Whiterock *Conn* 84-90; I Gilnahirk *D & D* 90-06; I Helen's Bay from 06; Can Belf Cathl from 04; Preb Monmohenock St Patr Cathl Dublin from 12. *The Rectory, 2 Woodland Avenue, Helen's Bay, Bangor BT19 1TX* T: (028) 9185 3601

KINCH, Christopher David. b 81. K Alfred's Coll Win BTh 02. St Steph Ho Ox 03. **d** 05 **p** 06. C Long Eaton St Laur *Derby* 05-09; TV Swindon New Town *Bris* 09-11; Partnership P Bris S 11-15; P-in-c Knowle H Nativity from 12; CF (TA) from 09. *Holy Nativity Vicarage, 41 Lilymead Avenue, Bristol BS4 2BY* T: 0117-971 2496 E: frchristopherkinch@gmail.com

KINCHIN-SMITH, John Michael. b 52. Fitzw Coll Cam MA. Ridley Hall Cam 79. **d** 82 **p** 83. C Sanderstead All SS *S'wark* 82-87; TV Halesworth w Linstead, Chediston, Holton etc *St E* 87-92; R Mursley w Swanbourne and Lt Horwood *Ox* 92-02; R Newton Longville and Mursley w Swanbourne etc 03-06; R Chinnor, Sydenham, Aston Rowant and Crowell 06-13; rtd 13; PtO *Nor* from 13. *The Old Vicarage, Duke Road, Gorleston, Great Yarmouth NR31 6LL* T: (01493) 717739
E: johnks1881@aol.com

KINDER, David James. b 55. EAMTC 01. **d** 04 **p** 05. NSM Warboys w Broughton and Bury w Wistow *Ely* 04-08; Chapl HM Pris Littlehey from 08. *Chaplain, HM Prison Littlehey, Perry, Huntingdon PE28 0SR* T: (01480) 335252
E: david.kinder@hmps.gsi.gov.uk

KINDER, Mark Russell. b 66. Univ of Wales (Swansea) BA(Econ) 88. St Jo Coll Nottm 91. **d** 94 **p** 95. C Pheasey *Lich* 94-98; TV Tettenhall Regis 98-07; P-in-c Walsall St Paul 07-11; V from 11; C Walsall St Matt 07-11; V Walsall St Luke from 11; C Walsall Pleck and Bescot from 11. *St Paul's Vicarage, 57 Mellish Road, Walsall WS4 2DG* T: (01922) 624963

KINDER, Mrs Sylvia Patricia. b 61. Ridley Hall Cam 03. **d** 05 **p** 06. C Warboys w Broughton and Bury w Wistow *Ely* 05-09; C Werrington *Pet* 09-12; P-in-c Hampton *Ely* from 13. *105 Eagle Way, Hampton Vale, Peterborough PE7 8EL* T: (01733) 240196 M: 07876-204624 E: sylvia@5kinders.com or vicar@hamptonchurch.co.uk

KING, Mrs Angela Margaret. b 45. Bedf Coll Lon BA 67 Lon Inst of Educn PGCE 68. SEITE 00. **d** 03 **p** 04. NSM Bromley St Andr *Roch* 03-15; P-in-c 11-15; rtd 15. *4 Avondale Road, Bromley BR1 4EP* T/F: (020) 8402 0847
E: angelaking45@hotmail.com

KING, Mrs Barbara Anne. b 55. St Mich Coll Sarum BEd 78. SNWTP 07. **d** 13 **p** 14. NSM Plemstall w Guilden Sutton *Ches* from 13. *17 Cathcart Green, Guilden Sutton, Chester CH3 7SR* T: (01244) 300756 E: barbara.king65@yahoo.com

KING, Benjamin John. b 74. Down Coll Cam BA 96 MA 00 Harvard Univ MTh 03 Dur Univ PhD 07. Westcott Ho Cam 97. **d** 00 **p** 00. C Boston the Advent USA 00-06; Chapl Harvard Univ 06-09; Asst Prof Ch Hist Univ of the South 09-14; Assoc Prof from 14. *University of the South, 335 Tennessee Avenue, Sewanee TN 37383, USA* T: (001) (931) 598 1619 E: bjking@sewanee.edu

KING, Benjamin William. b 76. Dijon Univ BA 97 Man Univ BA 98 Univ Coll Lon MA Cam Univ BA 05. Ridley Hall Cam 03. **d** 06 **p** 07. C Stanwix *Carl* 06-10; TV Chigwell and Chigwell Row *Chelmsf* from 10. *St Winifred's Vicarage, 115 Manor Road, Chigwell IG7 5PS* T: (020) 8500 4608
M: 07752-708207 E: kingbw2001@yahoo.com

KING, Brian Henry. b 39. Chich Th Coll 63. **d** 65 **p** 66. C Castle Bromwich SS Mary and Marg *Birm* 65-67; C Southwick St Mich *Chich* 68-70; V Southwater 70-73; C Brighton St Alb Preston 73-74; TV Brighton Resurr 74-75; V Eastbourne St Elisabeth 75-96; rtd 96; PtO *Chich* 96-11. *17 Hartford House, Blount Road, Portsmouth PO1 2TN* T: (023) 9281 7051

KING, Caroline Naomi. b 62. New Coll Edin BD 94. Ripon Coll Cuddesdon 94. **d** 97 **p** 98. C Wheatley *Ox* 97-12; TV Dorchester from 12. *The Vicarage, 49 The Green North, Warborough, Wallingford OX10 7DW* T: (01865) 858525
M: 07540-051798 E: reverend.caroline@gmail.com

KING, Christopher John. b 56. Chelsea Coll Lon BSc 78 CertEd 79. St Jo Coll Nottm LTh 87. **d** 88 **p** 89. C Wandsworth All SS *S'wark* 88-92; R Geraldton w Jellicoe, Longlac etc Canada 92-97; R Toronto Lt Trin Ch from 97. *425 King Street East, Toronto ON M5A 1L3, Canada* T: (001) (416) 367 0272 F: 367 2074 E: chrisking@sympatico.ca

KING, Clare Maria. b 68. St Andr Univ BD 91 K Coll Lon MPhil 98. Westcott Ho Cam 91. **d** 94. Hon C Norbury St Phil *S'wark* 94-96; Chapl Croydon Coll 95-96; Asst Chapl Cen Sheff Univ Hosps NHS Trust 96-01; C Leic Presentation 02-08; C Leic St Chad from 08. *The Vicarage, 12 Saddington Road, Fleckney, Leicester LE8 8AW* T: 0116-240 2215

KING, Mrs Daphne Eileen. b 37. EMMTC 78. **dss** 81 **d** 87 **p** 94. Dn-in-c Theddlethorpe *Linc* 87-89; Saltfleetby 84-89; Dn-in-c 87-89; Dn-in-c Healing and Stallingborough 89-94; P-in-c 94-97; rtd 97; PtO *Linc* 99-02. *28 Charles Street, Louth LN11 0LE* T: (01507) 606062
E: daphneking@lud28.freeserve.co.uk

KING, David Charles. b 52. K Coll Lon 73 Coll of Resurr Mirfield 77. **d** 78 **p** 79. C Saltburn-by-the-Sea *York* 78-81; Youth Officer 81-85; P-in-c Crathorne 81-85; Par Deacon 85-91; Min Coulby Newham LEP *York* 91-94; P-in-c Egton w Grosmont 94-00; P-in-c Goathland and Glaisdale 99-00; V Middle Esk Moor 00-07; PtO 12-13; V Middlesbrough St Martin w St Cuth from 13; Chapl Cleveland Police from 13. *St Chad's Vicarage, 9 Emerson Avenue, Middlesbrough TS5 7QW* T: (01642) 814999 E: meaux1@hotmail.co.uk

KING, David Frederick. b 32. Sarum Th Coll 59. **d** 61 **p** 72. C Hanworth All SS *Lon* 61-62; Hon C Andover St Mich *Win* 71-83; P-in-c 83-88; V 88-90; Chapl R S Hants Hosp 90-92; Chapl Countess Mountbatten Hospice 90-92; Chapl Andover District Community Health Care NHS Trust from 92; PtO *Win* 92-97; rtd 97; P-in-c Smannell w Enham Alamein *Win* 97-04; PtO from 04. *158 Weyhill Road, Andover SP10 3BG* T: (01264) 365694

KING, David John. b 67. W Sussex Inst of HE BEd 91. St Steph Ho Ox 98. **d** 00 **p** 01. C Bexhill St Pet *Chich* 00-03; TV 03-08; V Eastbourne St Andr from 08. *St Andrew's Vicarage, 425 Seaside, Eastbourne BN22 7RT* T: (01323) 723739

KING, David Michael. b 73. St Jo Coll Dur BA 95 PGCE 96 Cam Univ BA 02. Ridley Hall Cam 00. **d** 03 **p** 04. C Claygate *Guildf* 03-07; C Redhill H Trin *S'wark* 07-10; C Wallington 10-11; V Wallington St Patr from 12. *St Patrick's House, 47 Park Hill Road, Wallington SM6 0DY* T: (020) 8647 1026 M: 07901-700958 E: david.king@stpats.org.uk

KING, Canon David Russell. b 42. Univ of Wales (Lamp) BA 67. St D Coll Lamp. **d** 68 **p** 69. C Barrow St Geo w St Luke *Carl* 68-72; P-in-c Kirkland 72-74; V Edenhall w Langwathby 72-73; P-in-c Culgaith 72-73; V Edenhall w Langwathby and Culgaith 73-74; V Flookburgh 75-79; V Barrow St Jas 79-82; P-in-c Bolton w Ireby and Uldale 82-83; R 83-90; R Burgh-by-Sands and Kirkbampton w Kirkandrews etc 90-00; P-in-c Aikton and Orton St Giles 95-00; R Barony of Burgh 00-02; P-in-c Gt Broughton and Broughton Moor 02-05; V Brigham, Gt Broughton and Broughton Moor 05-07; Hon Can Carl Cathl 01-07; rtd 07; Hon C Aspatria w Hayton and Gilcrux *Carl* from 10. *27 King Street, Aspatria, Wigton CA7 3AF* T: (016973) 23580 E: drking27@tiscali.co.uk

KING, Canon David William Anthony. b 42. Ch Ch Ox BA 63 MA 68. Westcott Ho Cam 63. **d** 65 **p** 66. C Cayton w Eastfield *York* 65-68; C Southbroom *Sarum* 68-71; V Holt St Jas 71-72; R Hinton Parva 71-72; V Holt St Jas and Hinton Parva 72-75; P-in-c Horton and Chalbury 73-75; R Holt St Jas, Hinton Parva, Horton and Chalbury 75-79; TV Melton Mowbray w Thorpe Arnold *Leic* 79-83; V Foxton w Gumley and Laughton and Lubenham 83-90; P-in-c Boreham *Chelmsf* 90-00; R Tendring and Lt Bentley w Beaumont cum Moze 00-06; rtd 06; PtO *Ely* from 06. *14 The Hythe, Reach, Cambridge CB25 0JQ* T: (01638) 742924 E: dking66@btinternet.com

KING, Dennis. b 31. ACA 53 FCA 64. EMMTC 73. **d** 76 **p** 77. NSM Chesterfield St Mary and All SS *Derby* 76-00; PtO from 00. *Hillcrest, Stubben Edge, Ashover, Chesterfield S45 0EU* T: (01246) 590279

KING, Dennis Keppel. b 33. Lich Th Coll 63. **d** 65 **p** 66. C Eccleston St Thos *Liv* 65-68; C W Derby St Mary 68-71; V Aintree St Giles 71-96; rtd 96; PtO from 96; *Liv* 00-05. *8 Whiteoak Avenue, Easingwold, York YO61 3GB* T: (01347) 822625 E: dennis.k.king@btinternet.com

KING, Mrs Elaine Rosemary. b 55. Qu Coll Birm. **d** 13 **p** 14. NSM Ward End w Bordesley Green *Birm* from 13. *283 George Road, Erdington, Birmingham B23 7SD* M: 07582-407188 E: rev.eking@hotmail.co.uk

KING, Eleanor Olwen. b 61. d 14 p 15. C Alfred Jewel *B & W* from 14. *Sunnyside, Church Road, North Newton, Bridgwater TA7 0BG* T: (01278) 662597 M: 07803-243823
E: eleanor.king@hotmail.com

KING, Ellen Francis. *See* LOUDON, Ellen Francis

KING, Canon Fergus John. b 62. St Andr Univ MA Edin Univ BD 89. Edin Th Coll 86. d 89 p 90. Chapl St Jo Cathl Oban 89-92; C Oban St Jo 89-92; Tanzania 92-98; Hon Can and Can Th Tanga from 01; PtO *S'wark* 99-03; Hon C Thamesmead 03-05; R Kotara South Gd Shep Australia from 05. *The Rectory, 10 Melissa Avenue, Adamstown Heights NSW 2289, Australia* T: (0061) (2) 4943 0103 E: revfking@bigpond.net.au

KING, George Henry. b 24. St Alb Minl Tr Scheme. d 79 p 80. Hon C Flamstead *St Alb* 79-98; Dioc Agric Chapl 90-98; PtO from 98. *Chad Lane Farm, Chad Lane, Flamstead, St Albans AL3 8HW* T: (01582) 841648

KING, Miss Helen Sarah Elizabeth. b 81. Middx Univ BSc 04. Ripon Coll Cuddesdon BA 15. d 15. C Aldenham, Radlett and Shenley *St Alb* from 15. *51 Gills Hill Lane, Radlett WD7 8DG* M: 07809-361039 E: hseking@outlook.com

KING, James Anthony. b 46. CBE 76. K Coll Lon BA 69 AKC 69 Lon Inst of Educn DipEd 77. SAOMC 99. d 01 p 02. NSM Gerrards Cross and Fulmer *Ox* 01-03; NSM S Tottenham St Ann *Lon* 03-08; NSM Chalfont St Peter *Ox* 08-15; PtO from 15. *7 Meadowcroft, Chalfont St Peter, Gerrards Cross SL9 9DH* T: (01753) 887386 E: jim@jimking.co.uk

KING, Canon Jeffrey Douglas Wallace. b 43. AKC 67. d 68 p 69. C S Harrow St Paul *Lon* 68-71; C Garforth *Ripon* 71-74; V Potternewton 74-83; TR Moor Allerton 83-99; RD Allerton 85-89; P-in-c Thorner and Dioc Ecum Officer 99-08; Hon Can Ripon Cathl 90-08; rtd 08; PtO *Leeds* from 09. *17 Barleyfields Terrace, Wetherby LS22 6PW* T: (01937) 520646

KING, Jennifer. b 48. d 08 p 09. OLM Chorlton-cum-Hardy St Clem *Man* from 08. *8 St Clements Road, Manchester M21 9HU* T: 0161-861 0898 M: 07918-702572
E: jen.king@stclement-chorlton.org.uk

KING, Jennifer Mary. b 41. Lon Univ BDS 65 MSc 75 PhD. Ripon Coll Cuddesdon 86. d 88 p 94. NSM S Hackney St Mich w Haggerston St Paul *Lon* 88-99; NSM St John-at-Hackney 99-10; Lic Preacher 10-14; Chapl St Bart's and RLSMD Qu Mary and Westf Coll 98-14; PtO *St Alb* from 11. *3 Thornton Road, Barnet EN5 4JE* T: (020) 8449 5947

KING, Jeremy Norman. *See* CLARK-KING, Jeremy Norman

KING, Mrs Joanna Claire. b 72. Chelt & Glouc Coll of HE BEd 96. Ripon Coll Cuddesdon 12. d 14 p 15. C Pagham *Chich* 14. *8 Tennyson Road, Bognor Regis PO21 2SB* E: joannaclaireking@gmail.com

KING, John. b 38. S'wark Ord Course 77. d 80 p 81. C S Gillingham *Roch* 80-85; Min Joydens Wood St Barn CD 85-90; V Borstal 90-98; Chapl HM Pris Cookham Wood 90-98; Chapl The Foord Almshouses 90-98; rtd 98; PtO *Cant* 99-15. *14 Lamberhurst Way, Cliftonville, Margate CT9 3HH* T: (01843) 229405 M: 07889-277195

KING, John. b 58. d 05 p 06. NSM Buckingham *Ox* from 05. *Wood End Farm, 2 Wood End, Nash, Milton Keynes MK17 0EL* T: (01908) 501860 E: john@kingsfold100.freeserve.co.uk

KING, John Andrew. b 50. Qu Coll Birm 72. d 75 p 76. C Halesowen *Worc* 75-77; C Belper Ch Ch and Milford *Derby* 78-81; PtO from 87. *Address temp unknown*
E: jaking49@hotmail.com

KING, John Charles. b 27. St Pet Hall Ox BA 51 MA 55. Oak Hill Th Coll 51. d 53 p 54. C Slough *Ox* 53-57; V Ware Ch Ch *St Alb* 57-60; Ed C of E Newspaper 60-68; LtO *St Alb* 60-70; Teacher St Fran Bacon Sch St Alb 68-71; Boston Gr Sch 71-88; LtO *Linc* 74-92; rtd 92. *6 Somersby Way, Boston PE21 9PQ* T: (01205) 363061

KING, John Colin. b 39. Cuddesdon Coll 69. d 71 p 72. C Cookham *Ox* 71-75; Youth Chapl *B & W* 75-80; P-in-c Merriott 76-80; P-in-c Hinton w Dinnington 79-80; R Merriott w Hinton, Dinnington and Lopen 80-04; rtd 04. *Les Chênes, Les Arquies, St Henri, 46000 Cahors, France* T: (0033) 5 65 31 14 46

KING, Joseph Stephen. b 39. St Chad's Coll Dur BA 62 MPhil 83. d 64 p 65. C Lewisham St Mary *S'wark* 64-69; Hon C Milton next Gravesend Ch Ch *Roch* 70-85; V 85-07; rtd 07. *40 Thistledown, Gravesend DA12 5EU* T: (01474) 748121
E: patandjoe48@blueyonder.co.uk

KING, Mrs Katharine Mary. b 63. St Hugh's Coll Ox BA 85 MA 89 SS Coll Cam BA 88. Ridley Hall Cam 86. d 89 p 94. C Ipswich St Aug *St E* 89-91; NSM Bures 92-02; NSM Bures w Assington and Lt Cornard 02-13; PtO *Chelmsf* 14-15; NSM Coggeshall w Markshall from 15; NSM Cressing w Stisted and Bradwell etc from 15. *The House, The Street, Bradwell, Braintree CM77 8EL* M: 07984-010485 T: (01376) 563662
E: kmking100@gmail.com *or* kking@chelmsford.anglican.org

KING, Malcolm Charles. b 37. Chich Th Coll 67. d 70 p 71. C Mill End *St Alb* 70-72; Chapl RAF 72-76; R W Lynn *Nor* 76-81; V Croxley Green All SS *St Alb* 81-90; V Grimsby St Aug *Linc* 90-99; Asst Local Min Officer 90-95; V Bury w Houghton and Coldwaltham and Hardham *Chich* 99-02; rtd 02; OGS from 90; PtO *Chich* 02-11; Warden Community of St Pet Woking 02-03. *20 The Quadrangle, Morden College, 19 St Germans Place, London SE3 0PW* T: (020) 8858 5313

KING, Malcolm Stewart. b 56. Univ of Wales (Lamp) MA 09. Sarum & Wells Th Coll 77. d 80 p 81. C Farnham *Guildf* 80-83; C Chertsey and Chapl St Pet Hosp Chertsey 83-86; V Egham Hythe *Guildf* 86-91; TR Cove St Jo 91-98; RD Aldershot 93-98; V Dorking w Ranmore 98-04; Hon Can Guildf Cathl 99-04; RD Dorking 01-04; P-in-c Portsea N End St Mark *Portsm* 04-06; TR 06-07; Warden Iona Community *Arg* 07-10; R Robina w Mermaid Beach Australia 10-12; PtO *Carl* from 12; TR Stroud Team *Glouc* from 13; AD Stroud from 13. *The Vicarage, Church Street, Stroud GL5 1JL* T: (01453) 765827
E: malcolmsking@btinternet.com

KING (née COWIE), Mrs Margaret Harriet. b 53. Glas Univ BSc 76 AMA 85 FMA 97. TISEC 95. d 98 p 99. NSM Montrose and Inverbervie *Bre* 98-05; Dioc Dir of Ord 00-05; TV N Hinckford *Chelmsf* 05-13; TR from 13. *The Vicarage, Great Henny, Sudbury CO10 7NW* T: (01787) 269385
M: 07855-558056 E: mandgking39@hotmail.com

KING, Marie. b 40. CertEd 78. d 03 p 04. OLM Addiscombe St Mildred *S'wark* 03-10; PtO from 10. *8 Annandale Road, Croydon CR0 7HP* T: (020) 8654 2651
E: marie.king@virgin.net

KING, Martin Harry. b 42. St Jo Coll Cam MA 68 MBCS 85. SAOMC 03. d 05 p 06. NSM Wheathampstead *St Alb* 05-12; Dioc Environment Officer 08-12; rtd 12; PtO *St Alb* from 13. *29 Parkfields, Welwyn Garden City AL8 6EE* T: (01707) 328905
E: martin-king-priestley.freeserve.co.uk

KING, Martin Peter James. b 73. Bris Univ BEng 95. Oak Hill Th Coll BA 05. d 05 p 06. C Leamington Priors St Paul *Cov* 05-09; V Rudgwick *Chich* from 10. *The Vicarage, Cox Green, Rudgwick, Horsham RH12 3DD* T: (01403) 822127
E: martinthevicar@googlemail.com

KING, Martin Quartermain. b 39. Reading Univ BA 61. Cuddesdon Coll 62. d 64 p 65. C S Shields St Hilda w St Thos *Dur* 64-66; C Newton Aycliffe 66-71; V Chilton Moor 71-78; R Middleton St George 78-91; R Sedgefield 91-04; RD 91-96; Chapl Co Dur & Darlington Priority Services NHS Trust 91-04; rtd 04; PtO *Dur* from 04. *3 White House Drive, Sedgefield, Stockton on Tees TS21 3BX* T: (01740) 620424
E: martin.king@durham.anglican.org

KING, Mrs Melanie Jane. b 58. Lindisfarne Regional Tr Partnership 13. d 15. NSM Brompton w Deighton *York* from 15. *The Vicarage, Moor Road, Knayton, Thirsk YO7 4AZ* T: (01845) 537227 E: penskills@tiscali.co.uk

KING, Michael Charles. b 86. Worc Coll Ox BA 56 MA 60. Coll of Resurr Mirfield. d 62 p 63. Hon C Hampstead All So *Lon* 62-65; Ed Asst SCM Press 62-65; C Thorpe St Andr *Nor* 66-69; Ed Sec BRF 69-90; Hon C Queensbury All SS *Lon* 69-79; Hon C Lt Stanmore St Lawr 80-90; R Cawston w Haveringland, Booton and Brandiston *Nor* 91-96; P-in-c Cawston w Booton and Brandiston etc 94-96; R 96-01; rtd 01; PtO *Leic* from 01. *84 Beacon Road, Loughborough LE11 2BH* T: (01509) 563103

KING, Nathan Richard. b 68. Whitelands Coll Lon BA 89 Univ of Wales (Cardiff) BTh 94 Man Univ MA 00. St Mich Coll Llan 91. d 94 p 95. C Hawarden *St As* 94-99; P-in-c 99-00; P-in-c Coreley w Doddington *Heref* 00-02; P-in-c Knowbury w Clee Hill 00-02; TV Ellesmere Port *Ches* 02-07. *Thornycroft, Aston Hill, Ewloe CH5 3AL* E: nathanking@onetel.com

KING, Nicholas Bernard Paul. b 46. Wycliffe Hall Ox 72. d 75 p 76. C Pitsmoor w Wicker *Sheff* 75-78; C Erdington St Barn *Birm* 78-80; C Sutton Coldfield H Trin 80-84; V Lynesack *Dur* 84-92; rtd 93. *16 Chatsworth Avenue, Bishop Auckland DL14 6AX* T: (01388) 605614

KING, Patrick Stewart. b 84. St Chad's Coll Dur BA 06 Jes Coll Cam MPhil 10. Westcott Ho Cam 08. d 10 p 11. C Dorchester *Sarum* 10-13; C Wokingham St Paul *Ox* from 13. *23 Sheridan Way, Wokingham RG41 3AP* T: 0118-977 3397
E: patrick.s.king@gmail.com

KING, Penelope Ann. b 86. Cant Ch Ch Univ BA 07 Sheff Univ MA 13. Coll of Resurr Mirfield 11. d 13 p 14. C Reddish *Man* from 13. *44 Luton Road, Stockport SK5 6AG* T: 0161-376 5689 M: 07747-836411 E: revdpennyking@outlook.com

KING, Peter Duncan. b 48. TD. K Coll Lon LLB 70 AKC 70 Fitzw Coll Cam BA 72 MA 77. Westcott Ho Cam 70. d 80 p 81. Hon C Notting Hill 80-84; Hon C Mortlake w E Sheen *S'wark* from 84; Dean MSE from 99. *49 Leinster Avenue, London SW14 7JW* T: (020) 8876 8997 F: 8287 9329
E: kingpd@hotmail.com

KING, Peter John Ryland. b 49. Kent Univ BA 72 Ex Univ BPhil 76 Cam Univ PhD 84. Qu Coll Birm 06. **d** 09. NSM Northampton Em *Pet* 09-12. *7 Manor Road, Pitsford, Northampton NN6 9AR* T: (01604) 880522
E: p.j.r.king@open.ac.uk

KING, Peter William Stephen. b 65. St Steph Ho Ox BTh 01. **d** 01 **p** 02. C Abertillery w Cwmtillery w Six Bells *Mon* 01-06; C Abertillery w Cwmtillery 06; CF from 06. *c/o MOD Chaplains (Army)* F: 381824 T: (01264) 383430

KING, Canon Philipa Ann. b 65. Westcott Ho Cam 91. **d** 95 **p** 96. C Cambridge Ascension *Ely* 95-00; TV 00-02; TR from 02; Hon Can Ely Cathl from 11. *2 Stretten Avenue, Cambridge CB4 3EP* T: (01223) 366665 *or* 315000 M: 07816-833363
E: pipking@btinternet.com *or* rectoratcastle@btinternet.com

KING, Richard Andrew. b 51. Linc Th Coll. **d** 84 **p** 85. C Bramhall *Ches* 84-87; V Heald Green St Cath 87-92; P-in-c Ashprington, Cornworthy and Dittisham *Ex* 92-99; RD Totnes 97-99; P-in-c Torquay St Jo and Ellacombe 99-02; P-in-c Stoneleigh and Dioc Spirituality Adv *Guildf* 02-07; P-in-c S Framland *Leic* 08-11; rtd 12. *18 Whitehall Grove, Lincoln LN1 1PG* T: (01522) 524003 E: rking11@hotmail.com

KING, Richard David. b 63. Oak Hill Th Coll 87. **d** 90 **p** 91. C Folkestone St Jo *Cant* 90-94; P-in-c Orlestone w Snave and Ruckinge w Warehorne 94-02; Dioc Ecum Officer 97-02; CA Field Officer Cant, Lon, Roch and S'wark 02-06; Dioc Missr *Cant* 06-11; C Charing w Charing Heath and Lt Chart 06-11; P-in-c Kennington from 11. *The Vicarage, 212 Faversham Road, Kennington, Ashford TN24 9AF* T: (01233) 623334
E: richarddking@hotmail.com

KING, Revd Robert Dan. b 57. Sarum & Wells Th Coll 92. **d** 94 **p** 95. C Heref H Trin 94-97; TV W Heref 97-00; V Weobley w Sarnesfield and Norton Canon 00-14; P-in-c Letton w Staunton, Byford, Mansel Gamage etc 00-04; R 04-14; Preb Heref Cathl 10-14; R Kelso *Edin* from 14. *St Andrew's Rectory, 6 Forestfield, Kelso TD5 7BX* T: (01573) 224163
E: bobking@wbsnet.co.uk

KING, The Ven Robin Lucas Colin. b 59. Dundee Univ MA 81. Ridley Hall Cam 87. **d** 89 **p** 90. C Ipswich St Aug *St E* 89-92; V Bures 92-02; C Assington w Newton Green and Lt Cornard 00-02; V Bures w Assington and Lt Cornard 02-13; RD Sudbury 06-13; Hon Can St E Cathl 08-13; Adn Stansted *Chelmsf* from 13. *The House, The Street, Bradwell, Braintree CM77 8EL* T: (01376) 563357 M: 07813-633096
E: a.stansted@chelmsford.anglican.org

KING, Mrs Rowena Niesje. b 77. WEMTC 13. **d** 15. C Dursley *Glouc* from 15. *The Vicarage, Church Street, Stroud GL5 1JL* T: (01453) 765827 E: rowenaking@gmail.com

KING, Stuart John. b 77. **d** 10 **p** 11. NSM Winnersh *Ox* 10-14; Chapl Bearwood Coll Wokingham 10-14; P-in-c Ashford St Matt *Lon* from 14. *St Matthew's Vicarage, 99 Church Road, Ashford TW15 2NY* T: (01784) 252459
E: fr_stuart@scbw.co.uk

KING, Tony Christopher. b 62. Lanc Univ BA 83. Coll of Resurr Mirfield 83. **d** 86 **p** 87. C Stansted Mountfitchet *Chelmsf* 86-89; USPG 89-92; Botswana 90-92; C Chingford SS Pet and Paul *Chelmsf* 92-93. *252 Brettenham Road, London E17 5AY*

KING, Canon Walter Raleigh. b 45. New Coll Ox BA 67 MA 74. Cuddesdon Coll 71. **d** 74 **p** 75. C Wisbech SS Pet and Paul *Ely* 74-77; C Barrow St Geo w St Luke *Carl* 77-79; P-in-c Clifford *Heref* 79-83; P-in-c Cusop 79-83; P-in-c Hardwick 79-83; P-in-c Whitney w Winforton 81-84; R Cusop w Clifford, Hardwicke, Bredwardine etc 83-86; R Heref St Nic 86-92; Dir of Ords 86-92; Preb Heref Cathl 86-92; TR Huntingdon *Ely* 92-01; RD 94-99; Hon Can Ely Cathl 99-01; Vice Dean and Can Res Chelmsf Cathl 01-10; rtd 10; PtO S'wark from 13. *8 Woodlands, Clapham Common North Side, London SW4 0RJ*
E: walterking@btinternet.com

KING, William. b 46. **d** 14 **p** 15. OLM N Beltisloe Gp *Linc* from 14. *Tanglewood, Grantham Road, Old Somerby, Grantham NG33 4AB* M: 07568-075680 E: bill.king@hotmail.co.uk

KING, Zoë Elizabeth. St Mich Coll Llan. **d** 06 **p** 07. C Neath *Llan* 06-10; P-in-c Llansawel, Briton Ferry 10-15; AD Neath 12-15; P-in-c Tongwynlais from 15; Dioc Officer for IME from 15. *33 Castell Coch View, Tongwynlais, Cardiff CF15 7LA* T: (029) 2081 0437 E: revdzoeking@gmail.com

KING-BROWN, Ian Barry. b 53. St Cuth Soc Dur BA 80 PGCE 81. Sarum & Wells Th Coll 84. **d** 86 **p** 87. C Winchmore Hill St Paul *Lon* 86-89; Hon Chapl Chase Farm Hosp Enfield 86-88; Hon Chapl Harley Street Area Hosps 88-90; Hon Chapl RAM 89; C St Marylebone w H Trin *Lon* 89-94; rtd 94; Hon Chapl Regent's Coll Lon 96-05; PtO *Lon* from 11. *Flat 4, 9 Welbeck Street, London W1G 9YB* T: (020) 3624 4433

KING-SMITH, Preb Giles Anthony Beaumont. b 53. Univ Coll Ox BA 75. Trin Coll Bris 86. **d** 88 **p** 89. C Gtr Corsham *Bris* 88-92; V Two Mile Hill St Mich 92-96; TV Ilfracombe, Lee, Woolacombe, Bittadon etc *Ex* from 96; RD Barnstaple from 14; Preb Ex Cathl from 14. *The Vicarage, Springfield Road, Woolacombe EX34 7BX* T: (01271) 870467

KING-SMITH, Philip Hugh (Brother Robert Hugh). b 28. CCC Cam BA 52 MA 56. Cuddesdon Coll 52. **d** 54 **p** 55. C Stockton St Pet *Dur* 54-59; V Bishopwearmouth Gd Shep 59-64; SSF from 64; USA from 66; rtd 98. *San Damiano, 573 Dolores Street, San Francisco CA 94110-1564, USA* T: (001) (415) 861 1372 F: 861 7952

KINGDOM, Paul Anthony. b 62. Ex Univ BA 83 FCA 86 ATII 87. STETS 07. **d** 10 **p** 11. NSM Burnham *B & W* 10-14; NSM Wedmore w Theale and Blackford from 15; NSM Chapel Allerton from 15. *1 Red House Road, East Brent, Highbridge TA9 4RX* T: (01278) 760920 M: 07803-922605
E: paul@kingdom.fsnet.co.uk

KINGDON, Mrs Chloe Elizabeth May. b 80. Lanc Univ BMus 01 Ban Univ MA 12. Ripon Coll Cuddesdon BTh 12. **d** 12 **p** 13. C Winsmoor *B & W* 12-15; R Aisholt, Enmore, Goathurst, Nether Stowey etc from 15. *The Rectory, St Mary Street, Nether Stowey, Bridgwater TA5 1LJ* T: (01935) 824378
M: 07714-790591 E: c.e.m.kingdon@gmail.com

KINGHAM, Derek Henry. b 29. Oak Hill Th Coll 56. **d** 58 **p** 59. C Deptford St Jo *S'wark* 58-60; C Normanton *Derby* 60-63; R Gaulby w Kings Norton and Stretton Parva *Leic* 63-73; V Bacup St Sav *Man* 73-95; rtd 95; PtO *Carl* from 95. *3 The Green, Blencogo, Wigton CA7 0DF* T: (016973) 61435

KINGMAN, Paul Henry Charles. b 64. Reading Univ BSc 86. Wycliffe Hall Ox BTh 95. **d** 95 **p** 96. C Whitton *Sarum* 95-99; C Harold Wood *Chelmsf* 99-03; V Stone Ch Ch and Oulton *Lich* from 03. *Christ Church Vicarage, Bromfield Court, Stone ST15 8ED* T: (01785) 812669

KINGS, Mrs Frances Bridget (Biddi). b 48. City Univ BSc 70 Birm Univ MSc 77. WEMTC 00. **d** 03 **p** 04. NSM Eckington and Defford w Besford *Worc* 03-06; NSM Powick and Guarlford and Madresfield w Newland 06-08; PtO 08-09; NSM Bowbrook S and Bowbrook N 09-12; NSM Berrow w Pendock, Eldersfield, Hollybush etc from 12. *Merebrook Farm, Hanley Swan, Worcester WR8 0DX* T: (01684) 310950 E: biddi@mostblessed.me.uk

✠**KINGS, The Rt Revd Graham Ralph.** b 53. Hertf Coll Ox BA 77 MA 80 Utrecht Univ PhD 02. Ridley Hall Cam 78. **d** 80 **p** 81 **c** 09. C Harlesden St Mark *Lon* 80-84; CMS Kenya 85-91; Dir Studies St Andr Inst Kabare 85-88; Vice Prin 89-91; Lect Miss Studies Cam Th Federation 92-00; Overseas Adv Henry Martyn Trust 92-95; Dir Henry Martyn Cen Westmr Coll Cam 95-00; Hon C Cambridge H Trin *Ely* 92-96; Hon C Chesterton St Andr 96-00; V Islington St Mary *Lon* 00-09; Area Bp Sherborne *Sarum* 09-15; Can and Preb Sarum Cathl 09-15; Hon Asst Bp S'wark from 15; Miss Th Angl Communion from 15. *Society for Promoting Christian Knowledge, 36 Causton Street, London SW1P 4ST* T: (01865) 787501 M: 07786-071677
E: graham.kings@durham.ac.uk

KINGS, Jean Alison. See THORN, Jean Alison

KINGSLEY, Miss Mary Phyllis Lillian. b 48. ERMC. **d** 09 **p** 10. NSM Croxley Green All SS *St Alb* 09-13; NSM Bushey from 13. *19 The Cloisters, Rickmansworth WD3 1HL* T: (01923) 771172

KINGSLEY-SMITH, John Sydney. b 45. ARCM. Ridley Hall Cam 78. **d** 80 **p** 81. C Nailsea H Trin *B & W* 80-84; TV Whitton *Sarum* 84-91; V Chorleywood Ch Ch *St Alb* 91-01; RD Rickmansworth 98-01; rtd 01; PtO *St Alb* from 01. *29 Lewes Way, Croxley Green, Rickmansworth WD3 3SW* T: (01923) 249949

KINGSMILL-LUNN, Brooke. See LUNN, Brooke Kingsmill

KINGSTON, Canon Albert William. b 47. Bernard Gilpin Soc Dur 68 Oak Hill Th Coll 69. **d** 72 **p** 73. C Walton Breck *Liv* 72-74; C Templemore *D & R* 74-76; I Kildallon w Newtowngore and Corrawallen *K, E & A* 76-82; Bp's C Ardagh w Tashinny, Shrule and Kilcommick from 82; Can and Preb Elphin Cathl from 95. *Oakhill Lodge, Rathmore, Ballymahon, Co Longford, Republic of Ireland* M: (00353) 87-919 5473

KINGSTON, Mrs Avril Dawson. b 34. Local Minl Tr Course 91. **d** 94 **p** 95. Aux Min Douglas Union w Frankfield *C, C & R* 94-02; rtd 02. *Ballymartin House, Glencairn, Lismore, Co Waterford, Republic of Ireland* T: (00353) (58) 56227
E: purdy@gaelic.ie

KINGSTON (née LUCAS), Mrs Barbara Margaret. b 44. Lon Univ CertEd 70. **d** 06 **p** 07. NSM Lee Gd Shep w St Pet *S'wark* 06-12; PtO from 12. *375 Westmount Road, London SE9 1NS* T: (020) 8856 6468 E: revbkingston@gmail.com

KINGSTON, Desmond. See KINGSTON, John Desmond George

KINGSTON, Eric. b 24. **d** 69 **p** 70. C Ballymacarrett St Patr *D & D* 69-72; C Knock 72-76; I Annahilt w Magherahamlet 76-93; Can and Prec Dromore Cathl 93; rtd 93. *38 Kinedale Park, Ballynahinch BT24 8YS* T: (028) 9756 5715

KINGSTON, John Desmond George. b 40. TCD BA 63 MA 66. CITC 64. **d** 64 **p** 65. C Arm St Mark w Aghavilly 64-70; Hon

V Choral Arm Cathl 69-70; Chapl Portora R Sch Enniskillen 70-01; LtO *Clogh* 70-01; Can Clogh Cathl 96-01; rtd 01. *Ambleside, 45 Old Rossory Road, Enniskillen BT74 7LF* T: (028) 6632 4493

KINGSTON, Kenneth Robert. b 42. TCD BA 65 MA 69. **d** 66 **p** 67. C Enniscorthy *C & O* 66-69; C Ballymena w Ballyclug *Conn* 70-72; C Drumragh w Mountfield *D & R* 72-78; I Badoney Lower w Greenan and Badoney Upper 78-84; I Desertmartin w Termoneeny 84-13; Can Derry Cathl 97-13; rtd 13. *3 Mountview Avenue, Moneymore, Magherafelt BT45 7GY* T: (028) 8674 7905

KINGSTON, Malcolm Trevor. b 75. QUB BSc 97 MSc 98 TCD BTh 04. CITC 01. **d** 04 **p** 05. C Portadown St Mark *Arm* 04-07; I Kilmore St Aid w St Sav 07-14; I Arm St Mark from 14. *St Mark's Rectory, 14 Portadown Road, Armagh BT61 9EE* T: (028) 3752 2970 E: malcolm.kingston@btinternet.com

KINGSTON, Canon Michael Joseph. b 51. K Coll Lon BD 73 AKC 73. St Aug Coll Cant 73. **d** 74 **p** 75. C Reading H Trin *Ox* 74-77; C New Eltham All SS *S'wark* 77-83; V Plumstead Ascension 83-94; Sub-Dean Greenwich N 92-94; V Sydenham St Bart from 94; RD W Lewisham from 04; Hon Can S'wark Cathl from 15. *St Bartholomew's Vicarage, 4 Westwood Hill, London SE26 6QR* T: (020) 8778 5290 E: thekingstons@btopenworld.com

KINGSTON, Michael Marshall. b 54. St Jo Coll Nottm MA 94. **d** 96 **p** 97. C Drayton w Felthorpe *Nor* 96-99; R Gt and Lt Plumstead w Thorpe End and Witton 99-09; RD Blofield 06-08; Chapl Norfolk Primary Care Trust 01-09; TR Hempnall *Nor* from 09; RD Depwade from 13. *The Rectory, The Street, Hempnall, Norwich NR15 2AD* T: (01508) 498157 E: hempnallgroup.office@btinternet.com

KINGSTON, Robert George. b 46. TCD BA 68 Div Test 69. **d** 69 **p** 72. C Belfast St Thos *Conn* 69-72; C Kilkenny St Canice Cathl 72-75; I Ballinasloe w Taughmaconnell *L & K* 77-79; I Maryborough w Dysart Enos and Ballyfin *C & O* 79-85; I Lurgan w Billis, Killinkere and Munterconnaught *K, E & A* 85-88; Registrar Kilmore 87-92; I Lurgan etc w Ballymachugh, Kildrumferton etc *K, E & A* 88-92; I Tallaght *D & G* 92-98; Warden of Readers 93-98; I Mallow Union *C, C & R* 98-07; I Carrickmacross w Magheracloone *Clogh* 07-13; Chapl Mageough Home *D & G* from 13. *Chaplain's Apartment, The Mageough, Cowper Road, Dublin 6, Republic of Ireland* T: (00353) (1) 555 2179 E: rgk@eircom.net

KINGSTON, Roy William Henry. b 31. Chich Th Coll 60. **d** 62 **p** 63. C Leeds St Aid *Ripon* 62-66; S Africa 66-73; V Bramley *Ripon* 74-81; TR Hemel Hempstead *St Alb* 81-85; TR Fareham H Trin *Portsm* 85-93; RD Alverstoke 89-90; RD Fareham 90-93; P-in-c Hambledon 93-97; rtd 97; PtO *Guildf* from 97; *Portsm* from 97; *Win* 97-14. *8 Pengilly Road, Farnham GU9 7XQ* T: (01252) 711371 M: 07855-457670 E: roy@roykingston.plus.com

KINGSTON-UPON-THAMES, Area Bishop of. *See* CHEETHAM, The Rt Revd Richard Ian

KINGTON, Canon David Bruce. b 45. Trin Coll Bris 72. **d** 72 **p** 73. C Wellington w Eyton *Lich* 72-77; C Boscombe St Jo *Win* 77-81; R Michelmersh, Timsbury, Farley Chamberlayne etc 81-98; R Michelmersh and Awbridge and Braishfield etc 98-10; RD Romsey 95-05; Hon Can Win Cathl 02-10; rtd 11; PtO *Win* from 11. *St Swithun's Cottage, Main Road, Littleton, Winchester SO22 6QS* T: (01962) 882698 E: dbruce.kington245@btinternet.com

KINKEAD, John Alfred Harold. b 84. TCD BA 06. CITC BTh 10. **d** 10 **p** 11. C Cregagh *D & D* 10-13; C Taney *D & G* 13-15; Chan V St Patr Cathl Dublin 13-15; P-in-c Wicklow w Killiskey *D & G* from 15. *6 Glendasan Drive, Wicklow, Co Wicklow, A67 C822, Republic of Ireland* M: (00353) 86-172 7654 E: kinkeadj@gmail.com

KINNA, Preb Michael Andrew. b 46. Chich Th Coll 84. **d** 86 **p** 87. C Leominster *Heref* 86-90; TV Wenlock 90-93; R Broseley w Benthall, Jackfield, Linley etc 94-11; P-in-c Coalbrookdale, Iron-Bridge and Lt Wenlock 07-11; RD Telford Severn Gorge 03-10; Preb Heref Cathl 07-11; rtd 11. *15 Underwood, Broseley TF12 5NZ* T: (01952) 881169 E: mak@ridewise.fsnet.co.uk

KINNAIRD, Jennifer. b 41. Hull Univ BA 62 Ex Univ PGCE 63. NEOC 94. **d** 97 **p** 98. NSM Corbridge w Halton and Newton Hall *Newc* 97-11; rtd 11. *17 Glebelands, Corbridge NE45 5DS* T: (01434) 632695 E: j.kinnaird@btopenworld.com

KINNAIRD, Keith. b 42. Chich Th Coll 72. **d** 75 **p** 76. C Didcot St Pet *Ox* 75-78; C Abingdon w Shippon 78-82; P-in-c Sunningwell 82-90; P-in-c Radley 88-90; R Radley and Sunningwell 90-95; Chapl Abingdon Hosp 79-92; V Old Shoreham *Chich* 95-00; V New Shoreham 95-00; V Caversham St Andr *Ox* 00-07; Voc Adv and Adv for Min of Healing 00-07; rtd 07; PtO *Ox* from 07. *2 Weaver Row, Garston Lane, Wantage OX12 7DZ* T/F: (01235) 760867 E: keithkinnaird@btinternet.com

KINRADE, Mrs Nicol Wendy. b 73. St Chad's Coll Dur BA 97 Newc Univ MA 98. Westcott Ho Cam 13. **d** 15. C Ditchling, Streat and Westmeston *Chich* from 15. *8 High Street, Ditchling, Hassocks BN6 8TA* M: 07981-644497 E: nicolkinrade@hotmail.co.uk

KINSELLA, Joseph Thomas. b 78. St Jo Coll Nottm BA 10. **d** 10 **p** 11. C Bromyard and Stoke Lacy *Heref* 10-13; R Buckrose Carrs *York* from 13. *The Rectory, High Street, Rillington, Malton YO17 8LA* E: thekinsellas@btinternet.com

KINSELLA, Nigel Paul. b 66. Wolv Univ LLB 95. Westcott Ho Cam 00. **d** 02 **p** 03. C Attleborough w Besthorpe *Nor* 02-03; C Quidenham Gp 03-05; R E w W Harling, Bridgham w Roudham, Larling etc 05-10; CF from 10. *c/o MOD Chaplains (Army)* F: 381824 T: (01264) 383430 E: nigelkinsella@btinternet.com

KINSEY, Bruce Richard Lawrence. b 59. K Coll Lon BD 81 AKC 81 MTh 86 MA 94. Wycliffe Hall Ox. **d** 84 **p** 85. C Gt Stanmore *Lon* 84-88; C Shepherd's Bush St Steph w St Thos 88-91; Chapl and Fell Down Coll Cam 91-01; Hd Philosophy and RS Perse Sch Cam 01-14; Fell and Chapl Ball Coll Ox from 14; PtO *Ely* from 07. *Balliol College, Broad Street, Oxford OX1 3BJ* T: (01865) 277777 E: brkinsey@perse.co.uk

KINSEY, Paul. b 56. Nottm Univ BTh 89. Linc Th Coll 86. **d** 89 **p** 90. C Connah's Quay *St As* 89-91; Min Can St As Cathl 91-94; Asst Chapl Univ Coll Lon Hosps NHS Trust 94-00; R S Lynn *Nor* 00-11; Ind Chapl 00-11. *13 Bridewell Street, Little Walsingham, Fakenham NR22 6BJ* T: (01328) 820925

KINSEY, Russell Frederick David. b 34. Sarum Th Coll 59. **d** 62 **p** 63. C Twerton *B & W* 62-66; C N Cadbury 66-75; C Yarlington 66-75; P-in-c Compton Pauncefoot w Blackford 66-75; P-in-c Maperton 66-75; P-in-c N Cheriton 66-75; TV Camelot Par 76-79; V Pill 79-82; P-in-c Easton-in-Gordano w Portbury and Clapton 80-82; V Pill w Easton in Gordano and Portbury 82-92; rtd 94. *25 Newbourne Road, Weston-super-Mare BS22 8NF*

KIPLING, Miss Susan Jane. b 49. Girton Coll Cam BA 70 MA 73. Westcott Ho Cam 04. **d** 06 **p** 08. C Old Basing and Lychpit *Win* 06-07; C N Hants Downs 07-10; R Brington w Whilton and Norton etc *Pet* from 10. *The Rectory, Main Street, Great Brington, Northampton NN7 4JB* T: (01604) 770402 E: suekipling@btinternet.com

KIPPAX, Canon Michael John. b 48. Open Univ BA 82. SWMTC 89. **d** 92 **p** 93. C Camborne *Truro* 92-95; C Woughton *Ox* 95-96; TV 96-98; R St Illogan *Truro* 98-12; Hon Can Truro Cathl 08-12; rtd 12. *33 Berkeley Crescent, Lydney GL15 5SH* T: (01594) 840497 E: mikekippax@gmail.com

KIRBY, Antony Philip. b 60. Leeds Univ BA 11. Yorks Min Course 08. **d** 11 **p** 12. C Richmond w Hudswell and Downholme and Marske *Leeds* from 11. *The Vicarage, Gilling West, Richmond DL10 5JG* T: (01748) 850349 M: 07594-615190 E: antonykirby01@btinternet.com

KIRBY, Barbara Anne June (Sister Barbara June). b 34. St Andr Univ MA 55. SAOMC 95. **d** 96 **p** 97. NSM Cowley St Jo *Ox* 96-05; rtd 06; PtO *Ox* from 06. *Convent of the Incarnation, Fairacres, Oxford OX4 1TB* T: (01865) 721301

KIRBY, Bernard William Alexander (Alex). b 39. Keble Coll Ox BA 62. Coll of Resurr Mirfield 62. **d** 65 **p** 72. C Is of Dogs Ch Ch and St Jo w St Luke *Lon* 65-66; Hon C Battersea St Phil *S'wark* 72; Hon C Battersea St Phil w St Bart 72-76; PtO 76-78 and 83-95. *28 Prince Edward Road, Lewes BN7 1BE* T: (01273) 474935 F: 486685

KIRBY, David Anthony. b 42. Dur Univ BA 64 PhD 68 Huddersfield Univ Hon DLitt 98. NOC 84. **d** 87 **p** 88. NSM Crosland Moor *Wakef* 87-00; Asst Chapl Algarve *Eur* 00-05; PtO *Leeds* from 05. *4 North Head, Bramhope, Leeds LS16 9DT* T: 0113-267 8695 E: revdakirby@hotmail.com

KIRBY, David Graham. b 58. Univ of Wales (Cardiff) BA 80. Wycliffe Hall Ox BA 85 MA 92. **d** 86 **p** 87. C Northallerton w Kirby Sigston *York* 86-89; C Southport Ch Ch *Liv* 89-92; R Bishop Burton w Walkington *York* 92-07; R Weston Favell *Pet* from 07; Warden Lay Past Min from 10. *The Rectory, Church Way, Northampton NN3 3BX* T: (01604) 413218 E: kirbydg@gmail.com

KIRBY, Mrs Elizabeth. b 56. City Univ BSc 79. ERMC 06. **d** 10 **p** 11. NSM Bury St Edmunds All SS w St Jo and St Geo *St E* 10-12; C Ipswich St Mary at Stoke w St Pet and St Fran 12-14; P-in-c Elmton *Derby* from 14; P-in-c Whitwell from 14. *The New Rectory, 31 High Street, Whitwell, Worksop S80 4RE* T: (01909) 722378 E: liz.kirby@btinternet.com

KIRBY, Mrs Joan Florence. b 32. St Hugh's Coll Ox MA 57 Lon Univ BA 66. St Alb Minl Tr Scheme 70. **d** 87 **p** 94. NSM Hemel Hempstead *St Alb* 87-90; C Blisland w St Breward *Truro* 90-94; NSM Cardynham 94-96; rtd 96; PtO *Truro* 96-04. *Penrose Barn, Bodmin PL30 4QY* T: (01208) 850252

KIRBY, Miss Kathryn Margaret. b 52. Girton Coll Cam BA 74 MA 78 Hughes Hall Cam PGCE 75 Leeds Univ MA 08 MCLIP 82. Coll of Resurr Mirfield 06. **d** 07 **p** 08. NSM Sale St Paul *Ches* 07-09; NSM Gatley 09-10; V Macclesfield St Paul 10-15; rtd 15. *Address temp unknown* M: 07745-434266
E: k.m.kirby@btinternet.com

KIRBY, Maurice William Herbert. b 31. K Coll Lon CertEd AKC. **d** 55 **p** 56. C Eltham Park St Luke *S'wark* 55-56; C Horley 56-59; C Westbury *Sarum* 59-62; R Poulshot w Worton 62-66; P-in-c Gt Cheverell 65; P-in-c Burcombe 66-68; V 68-70; V Salisbury St Mich 70-73; Chapl SS Helen and Kath Sch Abingdon 73-79; Chapl and Hd RS Wrekin Coll Telford 79-84; V Frensham *Guildf* 84-93; Dir of Reader Tr 84-93; rtd 93; PtO *Ex* 93-94; *Chich* 94-97; *York* 01-10 and from 12. *13 The Crescent, Helmsley, York YO62 5DF*

KIRBY, Meg. b 50. STETS 03. **d** 06 **p** 07. NSM Portsea St Cuth *Portsm* 06-09; NSM Calne and Blackland *Sarum* 09-10; TV Marden Vale 09-14; NSM Hermitage *Ox* from 14. *The Rectory, Yattendon, Thatcham RG18 0UR* M: 07940-419649 T: (01635) 201213 E: meg@kirby.myzen.co.uk

KIRBY, Michael Christopher. b 63. **d** 13 **p** 14. NSM Blackb Cathl from 13. *65 Church Street, Ribchester, Preston PR3 3XP* T: (01254) 820056 E: mkirby1821@aol.com

KIRBY, Paul Michael. b 51. Wycliffe Hall Ox 74 Seabury-Western Th Sem DMin 99. **d** 76 **p** 77. C Gateacre *Liv* 76-79; C Barton Seagrave w Warkton *Pet* 79-83; V Bidston *Ches* 83-93; V Ormskirk *Liv* 93-99; Team Ldr Chapl E Kent Hosps NHS Trust 99-00; Sen Team Ldr Chapl 00-14; Chapl Manager E and Coastal Kent Primary Care Trust 08-14; Bp's Adv for Hosp Chapl *Cant* 02-14; rtd 14. *74 Churchfield Way, Wye, Ashford TN25 5ET* T: (01233) 812347 M: 07834-262410

KIRBY, Richard Arthur. b 48. Lon Univ BSc 69. **d** 05 **p** 06. OLM Wellington All SS w Eyton *Lich* 05-07; NSM from 11; PtO 07-11. *4 Donnerville Gardens, Admaston, Telford TF5 0DE* T: (01952) 411358 E: richard.kirby@lichfield.anglican.org

KIRBY, Simon Thomas. b 67. Lon Bible Coll BA 92. NTMTC 00. **d** 03 **p** 04. C Woodside Park St Barn *Lon* 03-06; Lic Preacher 06-11; Chapl Wren Academy 08-12; C Friern Barnet St Jas *Lon* 11-12; V Cogges and S Leigh *Ox* from 13; V N Leigh from 13. *Cogges Priory, Church Lane, Witney OX28 3LA* T: (01993) 702155 M: 07862-254540 E: simonkirby@gmail.com

KIRBY, Stennett Roger. b 54. St Pet Coll Ox BA 75 MA 79. Sarum & Wells Th Coll 75. **d** 77 **p** 78. C Belsize Park *Lon* 77-79; NSM Plumstead St Nic *S'wark* 88; C Leic Ch Sav 90-91; TV Hanley H Ev *Lich* 91-95; P-in-c Walsall St Pet 95-01; V 01-07; V W Ham *Chelmsf* from 07. *The Vicarage, 94 Devenay Road, London E15 4AZ* T: (020) 8519 0955
E: skcse15@virgin.net

KIRK, Alastair James. b 71. St Jo Coll Dur BSc 93 PhD 98 Fitzw Coll Cam BA 06. Ridley Hall Cam 04. **d** 07 **p** 08. C Tong *Bradf* 07-10; C Laisterdyke 08-10; Chapl Warw Univ *Cov* 10-14; V Burley in Wharfedale *Bradf* from 14. *The Vicarage, 21 Southfield Lane, Burley in Wharfedale, Ilkley LS29 7PB* M: 07725-991073 T: (01943) 863216
E: alastair_kirk@yahoo.co.uk

KIRK, Andrew. *See* KIRK, John Andrew

KIRK, Clive John Charles. b 37. TD 81. FIBMS 66. Guildf Dioc Min Course 95. **d** 98 **p** 99. OLM E Molesey St Paul *Guildf* 98-04; NSM E Horsley and Ockham w Hatchford and Downside 04-10; rtd 10; PtO *Guildf* from 10. *The Rectory, Ockham Lane, Ockham, Woking GU23 6NP* T: (01483) 210167
E: candakirk@btinternet.com

KIRK, Miss Erika Cottam. b 55. Nottm Univ LLB 76 Solicitor 81. St Jo Coll Nottm MA 98. **d** 98 **p** 99. NSM Epperstone *S'well* 98-03; NSM Gonalston 98-03; NSM Oxton 98-03; NSM Calverton 98-03; NSM Woodborough 98-03; NSM Burton Joyce w Bulcote and Stoke Bardolph 03-08; NSM Edingley w Halam 08-10; NSM Gedling from 11. *24 St Helen's Crescent, Burton Joyce, Nottingham NG14 5DW* T: 0115-931 4125 E: erika.kirk@btinternet.com

KIRK, Canon Gavin John. b 61. Southn Univ BTh Heythrop Coll Lon MA. Chich Th Coll 83. **d** 86 **p** 87. C Seaford w Sutton *Chich* 86-89; Chapl and Succ Roch Cath 89-91; Min Can 89-91; Hon PV 91-98; Asst Chapl K Sch Roch 91-98; Can Res Portsm Cath 98-03; Can Res and Prec Linc Cathl from 03. *The Precentory, 16 Minster Yard, Lincoln LN2 1PX* T: (01522) 561632 E: precentor@lincolncathedral.com

KIRK, Geoffrey. b 45. Keble Coll Ox BA 67. Coll of Resurr Mirfield 71. **d** 72 **p** 73. C Leeds St Aid *Ripon* 72-74; C St Marylebone St Mark w St Luke *Lon* 74-76; C Kennington St Jo *S'wark* 77-79; C Kennington St Jo w St Jas 79-81; P-in-c Lewisham St Steph and St Mark 81-87; V 87-12; rtd 12. *60 Burnt Ash Road, London SE12 8PY* E: gkirkuk@aol.com

KIRK, Miss Geraldine Mercedes. b 49. Hull Univ MA 89. **d** 87 **p** 94. Ind Chapl *Linc* 87-99; P-in-c Bridgwater St Jo *B & W* 99-14; Chapl Somerset Primary Care Trust 99-14; rtd 14. *121 Newton Road, Bath BA2 1RU* E: revkirk52@gmail.com

KIRK, Henry Logan. b 52. Adelaide Univ BA 74 New Coll Edin BD 77 K Coll Lon MA 96. **d** 80 **p** 81. Chapl Dioc Coll Cape Prov S Africa 80-85; Asst Master Haileybury Coll 86; Asst Chapl Rugby Sch 86-93; Dep Hd Dulwich Coll Prep Sch 93-94; NSM S Dulwich St Steph *S'wark* 93-94; C Linslade *Ox* 94-96; Chapl Birkenhead Sch Merseyside 96-03; Chapl Abingdon Sch 04-11; Chapl R Russell Sch Croydon from 12. *Royal Russell School, Coombe Lane, Croydon CR0 5RN* T: (020) 8657 4433
E: hkirk@royalrussell.co.uk

KIRK, John Andrew. b 37. Lon Univ BD 61 AKC 61 MPhil 75 Fitzw Ho Cam BA 63. Ridley Hall Cam 61. **d** 63 **p** 64. C Finchley Ch Ch *Lon* 63-66; Argentina 66-79; SAMS 79-81; CMS 82-90; Dean of Miss Selly Oak Coll Birm 90-99; Dept of Th Birm Univ 99-02; PtO *Glouc* from 99; rtd 02. *The Old Stable, Market Square, Lechlade GL7 3AB* T: (01367) 253254

KIRK, Natalie Roberta. *See* GARRETT, Natalie Roberta

KIRK, Canon Steven Paul. b 59. Ex Univ LLB 80 Univ of Wales (Cardiff) BD 87 LLM 94. St Mich Coll Llan 84. **d** 87 **p** 88. C Ebbw Vale *Mon* 87-89; PV Llan Cathl 89-91; PV and Succ 91-94; V Port Talbot St Agnes w Oakwood *Llan* 94-01; TR Aberavon 01-07; AD Margam 06-07; V Ystrad Mynach w Llanbradach from 07; Can Llan Cathl from 07; AD Merthyr Tydfil and Caerphilly from 14. *The Vicarage, Cedar Way, Ystrad Mynach, Hengoed CF82 7DR* T: (01443) 813246

KIRKBRIDE, Martin Lea. b 51. Oak Hill Th Coll BA 94. **d** 97 **p** 98. C Lancaster St Thos *Blackb* 97-00; TV Hampreston *Sarum* 00-05; V Lenton *S'well* 05-11; Dioc Learning Adv *Cov* 11-14; Assoc Min Cov Cathl 12-14; P-in-c Wembury *Ex* from 14 and from 14. *The Vicarage, 63 Church Road, Wembury, Plymouth PL9 0JJ* T: (01752) 863510 M: 07983-852456
E: martinkirkbride@aol.com

KIRKBY, Canon John Victor Michael. b 39. Lon Univ BScEng 62 BD 73. Ridley Hall Cam 65. **d** 67 **p** 68. C Muswell Hill St Jas *Lon* 67-70; Chapl Hatf Poly *St Alb* 71-75; V Wootton 75-86; RD Elstow 82-86; R Byfleet *Guildf* 86-92; P-in-c Potten End w Nettleden *St Alb* 92-97; V 97-05; TV Gt Berkhamsted, Gt and Lt Gaddesden etc 05-08; Chapl Ashridge Business Sch 92-08; rtd 08; PtO *St Alb* from 08; Can Masindi Uganda from 09. *3 Hillside Gardens, Berkhamsted HP4 2LE* T: (01442) 872725
E: jvmkirkby@aol.com

KIRKE, Miss Annie Noreen. b 74. Univ of Wales (Cardiff) BA 96 Reading Univ MA 04. Westmr Th Cen 06. **d** 08 **p** 09. C Bryanston Square St Mary w St Marylebone St Mark *Lon* 08-09; Pioneer of Missional Communities 09-15; C Kenilworth Ch Ch S Africa from 15. *Christ Church Kenilworth, Summerley Road, Kenilworth, Cape Town 7745, South Africa* M: 07971-128498 E: revkirke@gmail.com

KIRKE, Clive Henry. b 51. Ridley Hall Cam. **d** 83 **p** 84. C Ainsdale *Liv* 83-86; Gen Asst Bootle Deanery 86-89; P-in-c Litherland St Andr 89-98; V Ingrow w Hainworth *Leeds* from 98. *St John's Vicarage, Oakfield Road, Keighley BD21 1BT* T: (01535) 604069 E: rachelkirke@hotmail.com

KIRKER, Richard Ennis. b 51. Sarum & Wells Th Coll 72. **d** 77. C Hitchin *St Alb* 77-78; Chief Exec LGCM 79-08. *10 Coopers Close, London E1 4BB* T: (020) 7791 1802 M: 07798-805428
E: richard@richardkirker.com

KIRKHAM, Alan. b 46. **d** 01 **p** 02. OLM Parr *Liv* from 01. *21 Avondale Road, Haydock, St Helens WA11 0HJ* T: (01744) 28046

✠**KIRKHAM, The Rt Revd John Dudley Galtrey.** b 35. Trin Coll Cam BA 59 MA 63. Westcott Ho Cam 60. **d** 62 **p** 63 **c** 76. C Ipswich St Mary le Tower *St E* 62-65; Bp's Chapl *Nor* 65-69; P-in-c Rockland St Mary w Hellington 67-69; Papua New Guinea 69-70; C St Martin-in-the-Fields *Lon* 70-72; C Westmr St Marg 70-72; Abp's Dom Chapl *Cant* 72-76; Area Bp Sherborne *Sarum* 76-81 and 81-01; Can and Preb Sarum Cathl 77-01; Abp's Adv to the Headmasters' Conf from 90; Bp HM Forces 92-01; rtd 01; Hon Asst Bp Sarum from 01; Can and Preb Sarum Cathl from 02. *Flamstone House, Flamstone Street, Bishopstone, Salisbury SP5 4BZ* T: (01722) 780221
E: jsherborne@salisbury.anglican.org

KIRKHAM, Mrs Judith Mary. b 52. **d** 13 **p** 14. OLM Stalmine w Pilling *Blackb* from 13; OLM Waterside Par from 13. *4 Stalmine Country Park, Neds Lane, Stalmine, Poulton-le-Fylde FY6 0LW* M: 07508-884528 T: (01253) 702711
E: judith.kirkham@fsmail.net

KIRKHAM, June Margaret. b 54. EMMTC 99. **d** 02 **p** 03. C Nottingham St Jude *S'well* 02-06; P-in-c Broxtowe 06-11; V from 11. *St Martha's Vicarage, 135 Frinton Road, Nottingham NG8 6GR* T: 0115-927 8837
E: june@kirkham7260.fsnet.co.uk

KIRKHAM, Stephen Gawin. b 51. MC 74. Ridley Hall Cam 96. **d** 98 **p** 99. C Histon and Impington *Ely* 98-02; P-in-c N Leigh *Ox* 02-07; rtd 07. *2 College Row, Crawley, Witney OX29 9TP* T: (01993) 706405 E: sg.kirkham@btinternet.com

KIRKLAND, Richard John. b 53. Leic Univ BA 75. Cranmer Hall Dur 76. **d** 79 **p** 80. C Knutsford St Jo and Toft *Ches* 79-82; C Bebington 82-89; V Poulton Lancelyn H Trin 89-95; V Hoole from 95. *All Saints' Vicarage, 2 Vicarage Road, Chester CH2 3HZ* T: (01244) 322056 E: j.kirkland@hender.org.uk

KIRKMAN, Richard Marsden. b 55. Cranmer Hall Dur. **d** 87 **p** 88. C Bridlington Priory *York* 87-90; TV Thirsk 90-96; R Escrick and Stillingfleet w Naburn from 96; RD Derwent 01-11; P-in-c Bubwith w Skipwith from 11. *The Rectory, York Road, Escrick, York YO19 6EY* T: (01904) 728406 E: richard@kirkman.orangehome.co.uk

KIRKMAN, Trevor Harwood. b 51. Trin Hall Cam BA 73 MA 77. EMMTC 94. **d** 96 **p** 97. NSM Hickling w Kinoulton and Broughton Sulney *S'well* 96-01; NSM Keyworth and Stanton-on-the-Wolds and Bunny etc 01-10; P-in-c Plumtree 10-11; R from 11; Dioc Registrar and Bp's Legal Adv *Leic* from 02. *The Rectory, 1 Church Hill, Plumtree, Nottingham NG12 5ND* E: trevorkirkman@btinternet.com

KIRKPATRICK, The Very Revd Jonathan Richard. b 58. CA 81 Goldsmiths' Coll Lon BA 85 Otago Univ MBA 02. Wilson Carlile Coll 78 S'wark Ord Course 83. **d** 85 **p** 85. C Lewisham St Mary *S'wark* 85-87; Chapl Lewisham Hosp 85-87; Selection Sec ACCM 88-91; Sec Aston Tr Scheme 89-91; Hon C Noel Park St Mark *Lon* 88-91; V Christchurch St Mich New Zealand 91-96; Dean Dunedin 96-01; V Gen Dunedin New Zealand 97-01; LtO Auckland from 02. *33 Haycock Avenue, Mount Roskill, Auckland 1041, New Zealand* T: (0064) (9) 627 7225 E: jonrk@xtra.co.nz

KIRKPATRICK, Nigel David Joseph. b 68. CITC BTh 96. **d** 96 **p** 97. C Portadown St Columba *Arm* 96-99; C Lecale Gp *D & D* 99-01; I Killinchy w Kilmood and Tullynakill 01-07; I Gilnahirk from 07. *St Dorothea's Rectory, 237 Lower Braniel Road, Belfast BT5 7NQ* T: (028) 9079 1748 or 9070 4123 E: crisnig@btinternet.com *or* gilnahirk@down.anglican.org

KIRKPATRICK, Reginald. b 48. **d** 07 **p** 08. OLM Ditchingham, Hedenham, Broome, Earsham etc *Nor* from 07. *18 Clark Road, Ditchingham, Bungay NR35 2QQ* T: (01986) 893645 E: regkirkpatrick@aol.com

KIRKPATRICK, Roger James (Brother Damian). b 41. FCA. **d** 86 **p** 87. SSF from 66; Guardian Belf Friary 80-88; Birm 89-93; Prov Min 91-02; NSM Belfast St Pet *Conn* 86-88; Chapl V Victoria Hosp Belf 86-88; LtO *Linc* 94-96; PtO *Lon* 97-01; *Sarum* 01-03; V Holy Is *Newc* 03-10; rtd 10. *25 Karnac Road, Leeds LS8 5BL* E: damianssf@franciscans.org.uk

KIRKPATRICK, William John Ashley. b 27. SEN SRN RMN. Sarum Th Coll 63. **d** 68 **p** 70. NSM St Mary le Bow w St Pancras Soper Lane etc *Lon* 68-70; NSM Soho St Anne w St Thos and St Pet 70-75; SSF 76-79; NSM S Kensington St Aug *Lon* 79-80; NSM Earl's Court St Cuth w St Matthias 80-98; rtd 98; PtO *Lon* 98-13. *c/o Ms V R F Tschudin, 26 Cathcart Road, London SW10 9NN*

KIRKUP, Nigel Norman. b 54. K Coll Lon BD 79 AKC 79. **d** 80 **p** 80. Hon C Catford (Southend) and Downham *S'wark* 80-83; Hon C Surbiton St Andr and St Mark 83-85; Hon C Shirley St Geo 85-93; PtO *Lon* 96-09. *10 Norfolk Buildings, Brighton BN1 2DZ* M: 07817-458076 E: nigelkirkup@hotmail.com

KIRKWOOD, Canon David Christopher. b 40. Pemb Coll Ox BA 63. Clifton Th Coll 63. **d** 65 **p** 66. C Wilmington *Roch* 65-68; C Green Street Green 68-72; Youth and Area Sec BCMS 72-73; Educn and Youth Sec 73-80; Hon C Sidcup Ch Ch *Roch* 74-80; V Rothley *Leic* 80-92; RD Goscote II 84-88; RD Goscote 88-90; P-in-c Toxteth St Philemon w St Gabr and St Cleopas *Liv* 92-95; TR 95-01; TR Harlow Town Cen w Lt Parndon *Chelmsf* 01-07; AD Toxteth and Wavertree *Liv* 96-01; AD Harlow *Chelmsf* 04-07; Hon Can Chelmsf Cathl 07; rtd 07. *7 Dunoon Close, Sinfin, Derby DE24 9NF* E: davidk@minternet.org

KIRLEW, John Richard Francis. b 52. STETS 92. **d** 05 **p** 06. NSM Castle Cary w Ansford *B & W* 05-08; P-in-c Colwyn *S & B* 08-13; V 13-15; Dioc Rural Life Adv 09-15; TV Three Valleys *Sarum* from 15. *The Rectory, Holwell, Sherborne DT9 5LF* T: (01963) 23570 E: richard.kirlew@btinternet.com

KIRTLEY, Georgina. b 44. St Jo Coll Dur BA 94. Cranmer Hall Dur. **d** 95 **p** 96. NSM Barnard Castle w Whorlton *Dur* 95-00; Chapl HM YOI Deerbolt 00-05; Bp's Asst Adv Self-Supporting Min *Dur* 00-08. *Ryelands, Stainton, Barnard Castle DL12 8RD* T: (01833) 630859

KIRTON, Canon Richard Arthur. b 43. Dur Univ BA 67 MA 73. Wycliffe Hall Ox 68. **d** 69 **p** 70. C Warsop *S'well* 69-72; C Newark St Mary 72-75; Lect Kelej Theolojo Malaysia 76-79; Dean of Studies Th Sem Kuala Lumpur 79-82; P-in-c Kuala Lumpur St Gabr 79-81; Hon Can Kuala Lumpur from 88; P-in-c Bleasby w Halloughton *S'well* 83-89; V Thurgarton w Hoveringham 83-89; V Thurgarton w Hoveringham and Bleasby etc 89-91; Bp's Adv on Overseas Relns 85-91; Tutor Wilson Carlile Coll of Evang 91-98; P-in-c Ollerton w

Boughton *S'well* 98-08; rtd 08. *Hill Top, Mosscar Close, Warsop, Mansfield NG20 0BW* T: (01623) 842915 M: 07803-627574 E: richardkirton1@btinternet.com

KISH, Paul Alexander. b 68. K Coll Lon BD 92 AKC 92 Leeds Univ MA 96. St Steph Ho Ox 96. **d** 98 **p** 99. C Prestbury *Glouc* 98-01; Chapl Sutton Valence Sch Kent 01-13; PtO *Cant* from 14. *Risebridge Farmhouse, Ranters Lane, Goudhurst, Cranbrook TN17 1HN* T: (015890) 212569 M: 07760-355434 E: pkish@btinternet.com

KISSELL, Barrington John. b 38. Lon Coll of Div 64. **d** 67 **p** 68. C Camborne *Truro* 67-71; C Chorleywood St Andr *St Alb* 71-00; C Bryanston Square St Mary w St Marylebone St Mark *Lon* from 00; Dir Faith Sharing Min from 74. *Garden Flat, 19 Lena Gardens, London W6 7PY* T: (020) 7258 5040 E: bkissell@aol.com

KISSELL, Jonathan Mark Barrington. b 66. Trin Coll Bris 99. **d** 01 **p** 02. C Stevenage St Pet Broadwater *St Alb* 01-05; C Dublin St Patr Cathl Gp 05-11; PtO *S'wark* 12-13; C Surbiton St Matt from 13. *127 Hamilton Avenue, Surbiton KT6 7QA* M: 07708-934268 E: jonkissell@me.com

KITCHEN, Ian Brian. b 60. Worc Coll Ox BA 81 Southn Univ PGCE 82. Wycliffe Hall Ox 98. **d** 00 **p** 01. C Brandesburton and Leven w Catwick *York* 00-03; P-in-c Coxwold and Husthwaite 03-11; V 11-12; P-in-c Crayke w Brandsby and Yearsley 03-11; R 11-12; R Derwent Ings from 12. *The Rectory, Church Lane, Wheldrake, York YO19 6AW* T: (01904) 448230 E: dulloldman@gmail.com

KITCHEN, Martin. b 47. N Lon Poly BA 71 K Coll Lon BD 76 AKC 77 Man Univ PhD 88. S'wark Ord Course 77. **d** 79 **p** 80. Lect CA Tr Coll Blackheath 79-83; Hon C Kidbrooke St Jas *S'wark* 79-83; Chapl Man Poly 83-88; TV Man Whitworth 83-86; TR 86-88; Adv In-Service Tr *S'wark* 88-95; Dioc Co-ord of Tr 95-97; Can Res S'wark Cathl 88-97; Can Res Dur Cathl 97-05; Sub-Dean 99-05; Dean Derby 05-07; P-in-c S Rodings *Chelmsf* 08-11; rtd 11. *4 Town Farm Close, Wall, Hexham NE46 4DH* T: (01434) 689696 E: martinx.kitchen@btinternet.com

KITCHENER, Christopher William. b 46. Open Univ BA. Sarum & Wells Th Coll 82. **d** 84 **p** 85. C Bexleyheath Ch Ch *Roch* 84-88; V Gravesend St Mary 88-97; V Biggin Hill 97-07; V St Mary Cray and St Paul's Cray 07-11; rtd 11; Bp's Officer for retired Clergy Widows and Widowers *Roch* from 11; PtO from 11. *St Lawrence Vicarage, Stone Street, Seal, Sevenoaks TN15 0LQ* T: (01732) 761766 E: chris@chriskitchener.freeserve.co.uk

KITCHENER, Mrs Evarina Carol. b 51. Stockwell Coll of Educn CertEd 70 Heythrop Coll Lon MA 00. Cant Sch of Min 89. **d** 92 **p** 94. NSM Gravesend St Mary *Roch* 92-97; NSM Biggin Hill 97-07; Asst Chapl Bromley Hosps NHS Trust 98-99; Distr Evang Miss Enabler S Prov URC 99-01; Par Development Officer *Roch* 01-07; C Chislehurst St Nic 07-11; P-in-c Seal St Lawr 11-12; V from 12; P-in-c Underriver 11-12; V from 12. *St Lawrence Vicarage, Stone Street, Seal, Sevenoaks TN15 0LQ* T: (01732) 761766 E: carol.kitchener@diocese-rochester.org

KITCHENER, Canon Michael Anthony. b 45. Trin Coll Cam BA 67 MA 70 PhD 71. Cuddesdon Coll 70. **d** 71 **p** 72. C Aldwick *Chich* 71-74; C Caversham Ox 74-77; Tutor Coll of Resurr Mirfield 77-83; Prin NEOC *Dur* 83-90; Hon Can Newc Cathl 84-90; Can Res and Chan Blackb Cathl 90-95; P-in-c Rydal *Carl* 95-99; Warden Rydal Hall 95-99; Warden Rydal Hall and Ldr Rydal Hall Community 95-99; Can Res Nor Cathl 99-05; Dioc Dir of Ords 99-04; Bp's Officer for Ord and Initial Tr 04-05; rtd 05; LtO *Edin* 06-10; *Arg* from 10. *Bullrock Cottage, Ford, Lochgilphead PA31 8RH* T: (01546) 810062 E: kitcheners@yahoo.co.uk

KITCHIN, Kenneth. b 46. Trin Coll Bris. **d** 89 **p** 90. C Barrow St Mark *Carl* 89-93; C Dalton-in-Furness 93-95; P-in-c Dearham 95-01; P-in-c Clifton 01-07; P-in-c Dean 01-07; P-in-c Mosser 01-07; R Clifton, Dean and Mosser 07-10; rtd 10; PtO *Carl* from 10. *7 Allerdale, Cockermouth CA13 0BN* E: kenneth.kitchin@sky.com

KITCHING, Daphne. b 48. Yorks Min Course. **d** 09 **p** 10. NSM Swanland *York* from 09. *21 Old Pond Place, North Ferriby HU14 3JE* T: (01482) 635159 E: daphnekitching@hotmail.com

KITCHING, Miss Elizabeth. b 49. Trent Park Coll of Educn CertEd 74. St Jo Coll Nottm. **d** 01 **p** 02. C Northallerton w Kirby Sigston *York* 01-05; V Cloughton and Burniston w Ravenscar etc 05-13; V Hackness w Harwood Dale 05-13; rtd 13. *12 Burnsall Close, Filey YO14 0DW* T: (01723) 513967 - M: 07889-425025 E: elizabethkitching@btinternet.com

KITE, Paul Anthony. b 64. SEITE BA 14. **d** 14 **p** 15. C W Sheppey *Cant* from 14. *The Vicarage, North Road, Queenborough ME11 5HA* T: (01795) 663791 M: 07414-528194 E: paulkites@btinternet.com

KITELEY, Robert John. b 51. Hull Univ BSc 73 Univ of Wales (Abth) MSc 75 Lon Univ PhD 82. Trin Coll Bris. **d** 83 **p** 84. C Bebington *Ches* 83-88; C Hoole 88-91; V Plas Newton 91-99; R Ashtead *Guildf* 99-14; rtd 14. *Address temp unknown* E: bobkiteley@gmail.com

KITLEY, Canon David Buchan. b 53. St Jo Coll Dur BA. Trin Coll Bris 78. **d** 81 **p** 82. C Tonbridge St Steph *Roch* 81-84; C-in-c Southall Em CD *Lon* 84-91; V Dartford Ch *Roch* 91-09; RD Dartford 98-07; V Kippington from 09; Bp's Adv for Overseas Links from 09; Hon Can Roch Cathl from 05; Hon Can Mpwapwa from 05. *The Vicarage, 59 Kippington Road, Sevenoaks TN13 2LL* T: (01732) 452112 E: kitley@clara.net

KITSON, Kevin. b 64. **d** 14 **p** 15. NSM Dur N from 14. *24 Village Gate, Howden le Wear, Crook DL15 8EF* T: (01388) 763775 M: 07950-341110 E: kevinkitson64@gmail.com

KIVETT, Michael Stephen. b 50. Bethany Coll W Virginia BA 72. Chr Th Sem Indiana MDiv 76 Sarum & Wells Th Coll 76. **d** 77 **p** 78. C Harnham *Sarum* 77-80; C E Dereham *Nor* 80-83; R S Walsham and V Upton 83-88; Chapl Lt Plumstead Hosp 84-88; V Chard St Mary *B & W* 88-99; TR Chard and Distr 99-04; RD Crewkerne and Ilminster 93-98; R Staplegrove w Norton Fitzwarren from 04. *The Rectory, Rectory Drive, Staplegrove, Taunton TA2 6AP* T: (01823) 270211 E: kivett@btinternet.com

KLIMAS, Miss Lynda. b 58. Jes Coll Cam BA 89 MA 93. Cranmer Hall Dur 89. **d** 90 **p** 94. Par Dn Sandy *St Alb* 90-93; Par Dn Bishop's Stortford St Mich 93-94; C 94-98; P-in-c Weston and C Baldock w Bygrave 98-03; TV Baldock w Bygrave and Weston 03-04; V Cople, Moggerhanger and Willington 04-13; R Maulden from 13; RD Ampthill and Shefford from 13. *The Rectory, Clophill Road, Maulden, Bedford MK45 2AA* E: rev.l.klimas@btinternet.com

KNAPP, Antony Blair. b 48. Imp Coll Lon BSc 68. NOC 86. **d** 89 **p** 90. C Bolton St Jas w St Chrys *Bradf* 89-92; V Kettlewell w Conistone, Hubberholme etc 92-00; TR Swindon Dorcan *Bris* 00-13; rtd 13; PtO *Llan* from 14. *5 Mountjoy Place, Penarth CF64 2TB* T: (01793) 525130 E: tonybknapp@aol.com

KNAPP, Bryan Thomas. b 61. Trin Coll Bris BA 91. **d** 91 **p** 92. C S Gillingham *Roch* 91-95; V Chatham St Paul w All SS 95-09; V Paddock Wood from 09. *The Vicarage, 169 Maidstone Road, Paddock Wood, Tonbridge TN12 6DZ* T: (01892) 833917 E: bryan.knapp@diocese-rochester.org

KNAPP, Jeremy Michael. b 67. Westhill Coll Birm BEd 91. Ripon Coll Cuddesdon BTh 99. **d** 99 **p** 00. C Hill *Birm* 99-02; TV Salter Street and Shirley 02-09; V Olton 09-15; rtd 15. *St Margaret's Vicarage, 5 Old Warwick Road, Solihull B92 7JU* T: 0121-706 2318 E: jeremy.knapp@btinternet.com

KNAPP (née STOCKER), Mrs Rachael Ann. b 64. Bris Univ BA 86. Trin Coll Bris BA 91. **d** 91 **p** 94. C Ditton *Roch* 91-95; C Chatham St Paul w All SS 95-08; Chapl Bennett Memorial Dioc Sch Tunbridge Wells from 08. *The Vicarage, 169 Maidstone Road, Paddock Wood, Tonbridge TN12 6DZ* T: (01892) 833917 or 521595 E: knapp@bennett.kent.sch.uk

KNAPPER, Peter Charles. b 39. Lon Univ BA 61. St Steph Ho Ox 61. **d** 63 **p** 64. C Carl H Trin 63-68; V Westfield St Mary 68-76; V Bridekirk 76-83; P-in-c Blackheath Ascension *S'wark* 83-96; P-in-c Holmwood *Guildf* 96-03; TV Surrey Weald 03-04; rtd 04; PtO *S'wark* 09-14. *The Cottage, 8 Moores Road, Dorking RH4 2BJ* E: peter/pat@pknapper.fsnet.co.uk

KNEE, Geoffrey. b 31. Whitelands Coll Lon CertEd 71 Anglia Poly Univ MA 05. CA Tr Coll 56 Glouc Sch of Min 91. **d** 92 **p** 93. NSM Hampton *Worc* 92-97; Chapl St Richard's Hospice Worc 95-97; NSM Badsey w Aldington and Offenham and Bretforton *Worc* 97; rtd 97; PtO *Worc* from 98. *8 Mayfair, Fairfield, Evesham WR11 1JJ* T: (01386) 443574 E: geoff@kneehome.freeserve.co.uk

KNEE, Jacob Samuel. b 66. LSE BSc(Econ) 87 MSc(Econ) 88. Ripon Coll Cuddesdon BA 92. **d** 93 **p** 94. C Ashby-de-la-Zouch St Helen w Coleorton *Leic* 93-96; C Boston *Linc* 96-00; Chapl Boston Coll of FE 96-00; V Cam w Stinchcombe *Glouc* 00-07; R Billings St Steph USA from 07. *1241 Crawford Drive, Billings MT 59102, USA* T: (001) (406) 259 5017 F: 259 1150 E: jknee@globalnet.co.uk

KNEE-ROBINSON, Keith Frederick. b 40. Thames Poly BSc 75 MICE 76. SAOMC 99. **d** 01 **p** 02. OLM Caversham St Pet and Mapledurham *Ox* 01-10; OLM Caversham Thameside and Mapledurham 10-12; rtd 12; PtO *Ox* from 12. *8 Hewett Close, Reading RG4 7ER* T: 0118-947 7868 E: kkrmill@globalnet.co.uk

KNEEBONE, Canon Patricia Jane. b 53. Man Univ BA 74 Lon Univ BD 94. SWMTC 08. **d** 10 **p** 11. NSM Newquay *Truro* from 10; Hon Can Truro Cathl from 15. *34 Henver Road, Newquay TR7 3BN* M: 07966-703924 E: janekneebone@gmail.com

KNEEN, Michael John. b 55. Univ Coll Lon BSc 76 MSc 77 St Jo Coll Dur BA 85. Cranmer Hall Dur 83. **d** 86 **p** 87. C Bishop's Castle w Mainstone *Heref* 86-90; TV Bridgnorth, Tasley, Astley Abbotts, etc 90-08; TV Leominster 08-10; TR from 10; RD from 14. *The Rectory, Church Street, Leominster HR6 8NH* T: (01568) 615709 E: mjkneen@btinternet.com

KNIBBS, Peter John. b 55. Birm Univ BDS 78 DDS 93. SWMTC 04. **d** 07 **p** 08. NSM St Illogan *Truro* 07-11; P-in-c Chacewater w St Day and Carharrack 11-14; C 14; P-in-c St Stythians w Perranarworthal and Gwennap 11-14; P-in-c Devoran 11-14; P-in-c Feock 11-14; V Monkseaton St Mary *Newc* from 14. *St Mary's Vicarage, 77 Holywell Avenue, Whitley Bay NE26 3AG* T: 0191-252 2484 E: peter.knibbs@lineone.net

KNIFTON, Gladys Elizabeth. b 52. Kingston Univ BSc 95 SRN 73 SCM 75 TCert 84. NTMTC 95. **d** 98 **p** 99. NSM Churt *Guildf* 98-01; Asst Chapl Surrey Hants Borders NHS Trust 01-05; Chapl Acorn Chr Foundn from 05; Hon C Grayshott *Guildf* from 07. *Bryanston, Boundary Road, Grayshott, Hindhead GU26 6TX* T/F: (01428) 604977 E: elizabeth@knifton.com or eknifton@acornchristian.org

KNIGHT, The Very Revd Alexander Francis (Alec). b 39. OBE 06. St Cath Coll Cam BA 61 MA 65. Wells Th Coll. **d** 63 **p** 64. C Hemel Hempstead *St Alb* 63-68; Chapl Taunton Sch 68-75; Dir Bloxham Project 75-81; Dir of Studies Aston Tr Scheme 81-83; P-in-c Easton and Martyr Worthy *Win* 83-91; Adn Basingstoke 90-98; Can Res Win Cathl 91-98; Dean Linc 98-06; rtd 06. *Shalom, Clay Street, Whiteparish, Salisbury SP5 2ST* T: (01794) 884402 E: sheelagh_knight@hotmail.com

KNIGHT, Canon Andrew James. b 50. Grey Coll Dur BA 72 Ox Univ BA 74 MA 81. Wycliffe Hall Ox 72. **d** 75 **p** 76. Min Can Brecon Cathl 75-78; C Brecon w Battle 75-78; C Morriston 78-82; V 89-00; V Llanwrtyd w Llanddulas in Tir Abad etc 82-89; RD Cwmtawe 97-00; V Sketty 00-15; Can Res Brecon Cathl 98-04; Treas Brecon Cathl 04-15. *The Vicarage, De La Beche Road, Sketty, Swansea SA2 9AR* T: (01792) 202767 E: andrewknight@phonecoop.coop

KNIGHT, Andrew Ronald. b 67. **d** 06 **p** 07. C Wolstanton *Lich* 06-09; V 09-14; Chapl Staffs and Stoke on Trent Partnership NHS Trust 09; R Shrewsbury St Giles w Sutton and Atcham *Lich* from 14. *The Rectory, 127 Abbey Foregate, Shrewsbury SY2 6LY* E: andykn@aol.com

KNIGHT, Andrew William. b 71. Hull Univ BSc 92 PhD 96. St Jo Coll Nottm 12. **d** 14 **p** 15. C Mottram in Longdendale *Ches* from 14. *59 Lower Market Street, Broadbottom, Hyde SK14 6AA* T: (01457) 763152 M: 07899-724760 E: andrewknight247@gmail.com

KNIGHT, Mrs Anne. b 54. Chorley Coll of Educn CertEd 75. Trin Coll Bris. **dss** 84 **d** 87 **p** 94. Wigan St Jas w St Thos *Liv* 84-87; Par Dn 87-90; C Costessey *Nor* 90-96; R Gt and Lt Ellingham, Rockland and Shropham etc 96-03; Chapl Norwich Primary Care Trust 96-02; P-in-c Worthen *Heref* 03-07; P-in-c Hope w Shelve 03-07; TV Ross 07-08; V Brampton 08-14; rtd 14. *6 Chatsworth Road, Rainhill, Prescot L35 8LG*

KNIGHT, Arthur Clifford Edwin. b 42. Univ of Wales BSc 64. Wells Th Coll 64. **d** 66 **p** 67. C Llangyfelach *S & B* 66-68; C Oystermouth 68-73; Chapl RAF 73-95; PtO *Heref* 95-97; P-in-c Brant Broughton and Beckingham *Linc* 97-99; P-in-c Credenhill w Brinsop and Wormsley etc *Heref* 99-10; RD Heref Rural 05-07; rtd 10. *26 Meadow Drive, Credenhill, Hereford HR4 7EE* T: (01432) 760530 E: cknight@aol.com

KNIGHT, Mrs Barbara. b 46. St Alb Minl Tr Scheme 86. **d** 90 **p** 94. NSM Weston and Ardeley *St Alb* 90-95; C Norton 95-97; R Barkway, Reed and Buckland w Barley 97-05; rtd 05. *16 Keynshambury Road, Cheltenham GL52 6HB* T: (01242) 238805

KNIGHT, Mrs Barbara Mary. b 43. SRN 64 SCM 70. EMMTC 94. **d** 97 **p** 98. NSM Market Harborough and The Transfiguration etc *Leic* 97-99; C Church Langton cum Tur Langton etc 99-02; P-in-c Billesdon and Skeffington 02; R Church Langton cum Tur Langton etc 02-07; rtd 07; PtO *Blackb* from 07. *1 Whittlewood Drive, Accrington BB5 5DJ* T: (01254) 395549 E: revbarbarak@btopenworld.com

KNIGHT, Brenda Evelyn. b 27. SAOMC 96. **d** 98 **p** 99. OLM Wheatley *Ox* 98-09; PtO from 09. *22 Middle Road, Stanton St John, Oxford OX33 1HD* T: (01865) 351227

KNIGHT, Christopher. b 61. Aston Univ BSc 84. Wycliffe Hall Ox 94. **d** 96 **p** 97. C Banbury *Ox* 96-98; C Banbury St Paul 98-01; Chapl HM Pris Lowdham Grange 01-11; V Leamington Priors St Mary *Cov* from 11. *The Vicarage, 28 St Mary's Road, Leamington Spa CV31 1JP* T: (01926) 778502 E: chrisknight07@hotmail.co.uk

KNIGHT, Christopher Colson. b 52. Ex Univ BSc 73 Man Univ PhD 77 SS Coll Cam MA 90. Sarum & Wells Th Coll BTh 83. **d** 81 **p** 82. Chapl St Mary's Cathl *Edin* 81-84; V Chesterton

Cov 84-87; R Lighthorne 84-87; V Newbold Pacey w Moreton Morrell 84-87; Chapl and Fell SS Coll Cam 87-92; Sen Research Assoc St Edm Coll Cam from 92. *Hope Cottage, Hindringham Road, Walsingham NR22 6DR* T: (01328) 820108

KNIGHT, Clifford. *See* KNIGHT, Arthur Clifford Edwin

KNIGHT, David Alan. b 59. Lanc Univ BA 81. Ripon Coll Cuddesdon 82. **d** 85 **p** 86. C Stretford All SS *Man* 85-88; C Charlestown 88-89; TV Pendleton St Thos w Charlestown 89-94; V Tysoe w Oxhill and Whatcote *Cov* 94-05; RD Shipston 04-05; Chapl Marie Curie Cen Solihull 06-08; Chapl St Richard's Hospice Worc from 06. *St Richard's Hospice, Wild Wood Drive, Worcester WR5 2QT* T: (01905) 763963 E: chaplain@strichards.org.uk

KNIGHT, Canon David Charles. b 45. Lon Univ BA 66 St Edm Hall Ox BA 68 MA 73 ATCL 63. St Steph Ho Ox 68. **d** 70 **p** 71. C Northwood H Trin *Lon* 70-73; C Stevenage All SS Pin Green *St Alb* 73-77; C Cippenham CD *Ox* 77-78; TV W Slough 78-83; Dep Min Can Windsor 81-08; R Lt Stanmore St Lawr *Lon* 83-91; Ecum Officer to Bp Willesden 83-91; Prec and Can Res Chelmsf Cathl 91-01; V Ranmoor *Sheff* 01-08; rtd 08; PtO *Ox* from 09. *12 Bankside, Headington, Oxford OX3 8LT* T: (01865) 761476 E: davidcknight45@gmail.com

KNIGHT, Canon David Lansley. b 33. Em Coll Cam BA 58 MA 61 PGCE 76. Ridley Hall Cam 57. **d** 59 **p** 60. C Chatham St Steph *Roch* 59-63; C Plymouth St Andr *Ex* 63-65; V Gravesend St Aid *Roch* 65-71; V Bexley St Mary 71-98; RD Sidcup 93-97; Hon Can Roch Cathl 97; rtd 98; PtO *Chich* from 98. *1 Newlands Avenue, Bexhill-on-Sea TN39 4HA* T: (01424) 212120

KNIGHT (née SMITH), Frances Mary. b 48. St Jo Coll York CertEd 69. EMMTC 98. **d** 03 **p** 04. NSM Braunstone *Leic* 03-07; NSM The Abbey *Leic* 07-12; rtd 12. *32 Aster Way, Burbage, Hinckley LE10 2UQ* T: (01455) 618218 E: frances@knight-t.freeserve.co.uk

KNIGHT, Gavin Rees. b 65. St Andr Univ MTheol 94. Ripon Coll Cuddesdon MTh 96. **d** 98 **p** 99. C Solihull *Birm* 98-02; P-in-c Fulham St Andr *Lon* 02-05; P-in-c Fulham St Alb w St Aug 04-05; Chapl Mon Sch 05-11; V Summertown *Ox* from 11. *The Vicarage, 33 Lonsdale Road, Oxford OX2 7ES* T: (01865) 557079 E: vicar@stmichaels-summertown.org.uk

KNIGHT, Henry Christian. b 34. Fitzw Ho Cam BA 62 MA 66. Ridley Hall Cam 62. **d** 63 **p** 64. Succ Bradf Cathl 63-64; Chapl 64-66; Chapl Tel Aviv Israel 67-79; CMJ 79-86; V Allithwaite *Carl* 86-93; rtd 93; PtO *Leic* from 93. *20 Saxon Way, Ashby-de-la-Zouch LE65 2JR* T: (01530) 460709

KNIGHT, Canon John Bernard. b 34. Fuller Th Sem California DMin 91 ACIS 60. Oak Hill Th Coll 61. **d** 65 **p** 66. C Morden *S'wark* 65-69; USA 69-71; V Summerfield *Birm* 71-07; Hon Can Birm Cathl 01-07; rtd 07; PtO *Worc* from 08. *102 High Haden Road, Cradley Heath B64 7PN* T: 0121-559 0108 E: home@jandmknight.go-plus.net

KNIGHT, Canon John Francis Alan Macdonald. b 36. Coll of Resurr Mirfield 59. **d** 61 **p** 62. C Gwelo Rhodesia 61-66; R Melfort 66-68; C Highlands amd P-in-c Chikwata 68-70; LtO Mashonaland 70-75; R Umtali Zimbabwe 76-81; Dean Mutare 81-87; TR Northampton Em *Pet* 87-97; RD Northn 88-92; P-in-c Greens Norton w Bradden and Lichborough 97-05; Bp's Adv for Min of Healing 99-05; Can Pet Cathl 01-05; rtd 05; PtO *Pet* 06-11; P-in-c Weedon Bec w Everdon and Dodford from 11. *16 Glebe Drive, Brackley NN13 7BX* T: (01280) 706258 E: theknights16@tiscali.co.uk

KNIGHT, Jonathan Morshead. b 59. Fitzw Coll Cam BA 81 MA 85 Jes Coll Cam PhD 91 Jes Coll Ox MA 87 Worc Coll Ox DPhil 02 W Lon Inst of HE PGCE 82 Sheff Univ PGCE 00. Wycliffe Hall Ox 86. **d** 88 **p** 89. C Hillingdon St Jo *Lon* 88-91; NSM Baslow *Derby* 91-92; NSM Curbar and Stoney Middleton 91-92; Lect Bibl Studies Sheff Univ 91-92; Research Fell 92-94; NSM Sheff St Paul 92-94; Bp's Research Asst *Ely* 94-98; Min Whittlesford LEP 95-96; Bp's Dom Chapl 96; Sec Doctrine Commn 96-98; P-in-c Holywell w Needingworth *Ely* 98-01; Tutor Westcott Ho Cam 98-99; OCM from 99; CF (TAVR) 00-03; Hon Lect Th Kent Univ 00-03; Chapl Worc Coll Ox 02-03; Visiting Fell York St Jo Univ from 07; Tutor Grey Coll Dur from 10. *36 Ninth Street, Peterlee SR8 4LZ* M: 07549-170031 E: jonathanknight5@hotmail.com

KNIGHT, Mrs June. b 28. Glouc Sch of Min 85. **d** 87 **p** 94. NSM Leckhampton SS Phil and Jas w Cheltenham St Jas *Glouc* 87-96; rtd 96; PtO *Glouc* from 96. *31 St Michael's Road, Woodlands, Cheltenham GL51 5RP* T: (01242) 517911

KNIGHT, Mrs June Elizabeth. b 42. St Alb Minl Tr Scheme 90. **d** 93 **p** 94. NSM Stanstead Abbots *St Alb* 93-96; NSM Gt Amwell w St Margaret's and Stanstead Abbots 96-97; NSM Lt Hadham w Albury 97-98; NSM Bishop's Stortford St Mich 98-12; PtO from 12. *The White Cottage, Albury Hall Park, Albury, Ware SG11 2HX* T: (01279) 771756 E: june.e.knight@btopenworld.com

KNIGHT, Keith Kenneth. b 36. Southn Univ BSc 58. Wycliffe Hall Ox 59. **d** 62 **p** 63. C Lower Darwen St Jas *Blackb* 62-64; C Leyland St Andr 64-68; P-in-c Blackb All SS 68-71; Dioc Youth Chapl 71-88; Hon C Burnley St Pet 71-74; Warden Scargill Ho 88-01; rtd 01; PtO *Leeds* from 01. *4 The Hawthorns, Sutton-in-Craven, Keighley BD20 8BP* T: (01535) 632920

KNIGHT, Mrs Margaret Owen. b 34. Oak Hill Th Coll 78. dss 80 **d** 87 **p** 94. Chorleywood St Andr *St Alb* 80-04; Par Dn 87-94; C 94-04; rtd 94; PtO *St Alb* from 04. *15A Blacketts Wood Drive, Chorleywood, Rickmansworth WD3 5PY* T: (01923) 283832 E: moknight@waitrose.com

KNIGHT, Canon Michael Richard. b 47. St Jo Coll Dur BA 69 MA 79 Fitzw Coll Cam BA 73 MA 78 St Cross Coll Ox MA 92. Westcott Ho Cam 71. **d** 74 **p** 75. C Bishop's Stortford St Mich *St Alb* 74-75; C Bedford St Andr 75-79; Chapl Angl Students Glas 79-86; V Riddings and Ironville *Derby* 86-91; Lib Pusey Ho 91-94; Fell St Cross Coll Ox 92-94; V Chesterfield St Mary and All SS *Derby* 94-13; P-in-c Chesterfield SS Aug 05-09; Hon Can Derby Cathl 06-13; rtd 13. *1 Leabrook Close, Nottingham NG11 8NW*

KNIGHT, Paul James Joseph. b 50. Oak Hill Th Coll. **d** 84 **p** 85. C Broadwater St Mary *Chich* 84-87; R Itchingfield w Slinfold 87-92; Chapl Highgate Sch Lon from 92. *15A Bishopswood Road, London N6 4PB* T: (020) 8348 9211 *or* 8340 1524 E: paul.knight@highgateschool.org.uk

KNIGHT, Paul Jeremy. b 53. **d** 94 **p** 95. C Moreton Say *Lich* 94-96; C Adderley, Ash, Calverhall, Ightfield etc 96-97; V Birstall *Leeds* from 97; AD from 14. *St Peter's Vicarage, King's Drive, Birstall, Batley WF17 9JJ* T/F: (01924) 473715 E: vicar@stpetersbirstall.co.uk

KNIGHT, Peter John. b 51. AKC 73 Ch Ch Coll Cant CertEd 77. Sarum & Wells Th Coll 77. **d** 80 **p** 81. C Greenford H Cross *Lon* 80-83; C Langley Marish *Ox* 83; NSM W Acton St Martin *Lon* 88-90; C E Acton St Dunstan w St Thos 90-92; V Malden St Jo *S'wark* 92-02; Co-ord Chapl HM Pris Long Lartin 02-05; TR Malvern Link w Cowleigh *Worc* 05-10; V from 10; RD Malvern from 13. *St Matthias' Rectory, 12 Lambourne Avenue, Malvern WR14 1NL* T: (01684) 566054 E: revpeterknight@hotmail.com

KNIGHT, Peter Malcolm. b 55. Cam Univ BA 76 Lon Hosp MB, BS 76 MRCGP 85. Trin Coll Bris BA 94. **d** 94 **p** 95. C Quidenham *Nor* 94-97; R Thurton 97-14; RD Loddon 99-05; NSM Tunis St Geo Tunisia from 14; PtO *Nor* from 14. *5 rue Ahmed Beyrem, 1006 Souika, Tunis, Tunisia* E: pandcknight@gmail.com

KNIGHT, Peter Michael. b 47. St Luke's Coll Ex BEd 71. Trin Coll Bris 90. **d** 92 **p** 93. C Bris Ch the Servant Stockwood 92-95; Chapl St Brendan's Sixth Form Coll 92-94; C W Swindon and the Lydiards *Bris* 95-96; TV 96-07; P-in-c The Claydons *Ox* 07-09; TV The Claydons and Swan 09-12; rtd 12; PtO *Ox* from 12. *Bramble Cottage, 17 The Green, Aston Abbotts, Aylesbury HP22 4LX* T: (01296) 680322 E: peterknight15@tiscali.co.uk

KNIGHT, Philip Stephen. b 46. Ian Ramsey Coll Brasted 74 Oak Hill Th Coll 75. **d** 77 **p** 78. C Pennycross *Ex* 77-80; C Epsom St Martin *Guildf* 80-83; V Clay Hill St Jo *Lon* 83-86; TV Washfield, Stoodleigh, Withleigh etc *Ex* 86-90; Chapl ATC from 86; Chapl S Warks Hosps 90-94; Chapl S Warks Health Care NHS Trust 94-05; PtO *Cov* from 05; *Ex* from 10; rtd 11. *Coombeside, 122 Alexandria Road, Sidmouth EX10 9HG* T: (01395) 514166 E: psk54@hotmail.co.uk

KNIGHT, Canon Roger George. b 41. Culham Coll Ox CertEd 63. Linc Th Coll 65. **d** 67 **p** 68. C Bris St Andr Hartcliffe 67-69; Hd Master Twywell Sch Kettering 69-74; V Naseby *Pet* 74-79; P-in-c Haselbech 74-79; R Clipston w Naseby and Haselbech 79-82; P-in-c Arthingworth w Kelmarsh and Harrington 79-82; TR Corby SS Pet and Andr w Gt and Lt Oakley 82-88; R Irthlingborough 88-99; RD Higham 89-94; R Burton Latimer 99-03; Can Pet Cathl 92-03; rtd 03; PtO *Pet* from 03. *9 Hollow Wood Road, Burton Latimer, Kettering NN15 5RB* T: (01536) 628480 E: rogerknight41@outlook.com

KNIGHT, Roger Ivan. b 54. K Coll Lon BD 79 AKC 79. Ripon Coll Cuddesdon 79. **d** 80 **p** 81. C Orpington All SS *Roch* 80-84; C St Laur in Thanet *Cant* 84-87; R Cuxton and Halling *Roch* from 87. *The Rectory, 6 Rochester Road, Cuxton, Rochester ME2 1AF* T: (01634) 717134 E: roger@cuxtonandhalling.org.uk

KNIGHT, Stephen. *See* KNIGHT, Philip Stephen

KNIGHT, Ms Sue Elizabeth. b 47. Southlands Coll Lon CertEd 68. SEITE 01. **d** 03 **p** 04. NSM Lee St Mildred *S'wark* 03-09; NSM Cheltenham St Mary w St Matt and St Luke *Glouc* from 12. *20 Longway Avenue, Charlton Kings, Cheltenham GL53 9JL* T: (01242) 234363

KNIGHT, Mrs Susan Jane. b 57. Open Univ BSc 99. NTMTC BA 09. **d** 09 **p** 10. C Harlow Town Cen w Lt Parndon *Chelmsf*

09-12; TV from 12. *The Vicarage, 4A The Drive, Harlow CM20 3QD* T: (01279) 420744 E: sue@kerryknight.co.uk

KNIGHT, Mrs Susan Margaret. d 02 **p** 03. C Clydach *S & B* 02-03; C Cen Swansea 04-05; TV from 05. *The Vicarage, 27 Bowen Street, Swansea SA1 2NA* T: (01792) 473047

KNIGHT, Suzanne. b 55. **d** 00 **p** 01. NSM Reading St Jo *Ox* 00-13; rtd 13; PtO *Ox* from 13. *9 Victoria Way, Reading RG1 3HD* T: 0118-967 5645 E: suz-knight@yahoo.co.uk

KNIGHT, William Lawrence. b 39. Univ Coll Lon BSc 61 PhD 65. Coll of Resurr Mirfield 75. **d** 77 **p** 78. C Bp's Hatfield *St Alb* 77-81; Asst Chapl Brussels Cathl 81-84; V Pet H Spirit Bretton 84-89; P-in-c Marholm 84-89; TR Riverside *Ox* 89-04; rtd 04. *90 Norfolk Gardens, Littlehampton BN17 5PF* T: (01903) 716750 E: knightsmvd@dial.pipex.com

KNIGHTS, Christopher Hammond. b 61. St Jo Coll Dur BA 83 PhD 88. Linc Th Coll 87. **d** 89 **p** 90. C Stockton St Pet *Dur* 89-92; C Chich St Paul and St Pet 92-94; Tutor Chich Th Coll 92-94; V Ashington *Newc* 94-00; V Monkseaton St Mary 00-04; Dioc Moderator Reader Tr 03-10; P-in-c Scotswood 04-11; R Kelso *Edin* 11-13; P-in-c Coldstream 11-13; PtO from 13; Development Worker Hawick Acorn Project 13-14; Ch and Community Development Worker Musselburgh from 14. *The Barnekin, 7 Cheviot View, Lempitlaw, Kelso TD5 8BN* T: (01573) 430741 E: revchrisknights@gmail.com

KNIGHTS, James William. b 34. AKC 66. **d** 67 **p** 68. C Kettering St Andr *Pet* 67-71; V Braunston w Brooke 71-81; V Dudley St Jo *Worc* 81-97; rtd 97; PtO *Worc* from 98. *192 Brook Farm Drive, Malvern WR14 3SL* T: (01684) 561358

KNIGHTS JOHNSON, Nigel Anthony. b 52. Ealing Tech Coll BA 74 Westmr Coll Ox MTh 99. Wycliffe Hall Ox 78. **d** 80 **p** 81. C Beckenham Ch Ch *Roch* 80-84; CF 84-07; P-in-c Ockley, Okewood and Forest Green *Guildf* from 07. *The Rectory, Stane Street, Ockley, Dorking RH5 5SY* T: (01306) 711550 E: nknightsj@hotmail.com

KNILL-JONES, Jonathan Waring (Jack). b 58. Univ Coll Lon BSc 79. St Jo Coll Nottm 88. **d** 90 **p** 91. C Northolt St Jos *Lon* 90-94; C Hayes St Nic CD 94-99; V Airedale w Fryston *Wakef* 99-07; V Teddington SS Pet and Paul and Fulwell *Lon* from 07; Chapl Richmond and Twickenham Primary Care Trust from 08. *The Vicarage, 1 Bychurch End, Teddington TW11 8PS* T: (020) 8977 0054 E: jackknill@aol.com

KNOTT, Graham Keith. b 53. Oak Hill Th Coll BA 80. **d** 80 **p** 81. C Normanton *Derby* 80-83; C Ripley 83-87; TV Newark w Hawton, Cotham and Shelton *S'well* 87-89; TV Newark 89-97; P-in-c Mansfield St Jo 97-06; AD Mansfield 03-06; P-in-c Croajingolong Australia 06-09; P-in-c Watford *St Alb* 09-11; R Maffra Australia from 11. *14 Church Street, PO Box 32, Maffra VIC 3860, Australia*

KNOTT, Preb Janet Patricia. b 50. Avery Hill Coll CertEd 71. S Dios Minl Tr Scheme MTS 91. **d** 92 **p** 94. NSM Clutton w Cameley *B & W* 92-99; Chapl R Sch Bath 94-98; Chapl R High Sch Bath 98-99; R Farmborough, Marksbury and Stanton Prior *B & W* from 99; Chapl Bath Spa Univ from 99; RD Chew Magna *B & W* 04-14; Preb Wells Cathl from 07. *The Rectory, Church Lane, Farmborough, Bath BA3 1AN* T: (01761) 479311 E: jpknott@btinternet.com

KNOTT, John Wensley. b 51. Fitzw Coll Cam MA 75 FIA 84. S Dios Minl Tr Scheme 87. **d** 90 **p** 91. NSM Canford Magna *Sarum* 90-94; NSM Northchurch and Wigginton *St Alb* 94-95; NSM Munich Ascension Germany 95-97; PtO *Eur* from 09; NSM Colne and Villages *Blackb* 12-14; R Foulridge, Laneshawbridge and Trawden from 14. *Christ Church Vicarage, Keighley Road, Colne BB8 7HF* E: judy.knott@t-online.de

KNOTT, Pamela Frances. *See* IVE, Pamela Frances

KNOTT, Miss Wendy Gillian. b 47. Adelaide Univ BA 78. Melbourne Coll of Div BD 95. **d** 94 **p** 96. NSM Sandy Bay Australia 94-98; NSM New Town St Jas 98-01; NSM Franklin w Esperance 01-05; Hon Chapl Ch Coll Tasmania 97-06; R Wick Mor from 06; P-in-c Thurso from 06. *The Parsonage, 5 Naver Place, Thurso KW14 7PZ* T: (01847) 893393 E: rev.wendy@btinternet.com

KNOWD, George Alexander. b 31. St Deiniol's Hawarden. **d** 88 **p** 89. NSM Aghalurcher w Tattykeeran, Cooneen etc *Clogh* 88-91; Dioc Communications Officer 89-90 and 92-97; NSM Ballybay w Mucknoe and Clontibret 91-92; C 92-94; I 94-97; I Clonmel w Innislounagh, Tullaghmelan etc *C & O* 97-06; Can Ossory Cathl 05-06; rtd 06. *Sunhaven, Knockelly Road, Fethard, Co Tipperary, Republic of Ireland* T/F: (00353) (52) 613 0821 M: 87-284 2350 E: gknowd@eircom.net

KNOWERS, Stephen John. b 49. K Coll Lon BD 72 AKC 72. **d** 73 **p** 74. C Bp's Hatfield *St Alb* 73-77; C Cheshunt 77-81; P-in-c Barnet Vale St Mark 81-83; V 83-85; Chapl S Bank Poly *S'wark* 85-92; Chapl S Bank Univ 92-94; V Croydon St Pet 94-06; P-in-c Croydon St Aug 04-06; V S Croydon St Pet and St Aug

06-07; V Shirley St Jo from 07; AD Croydon Addington 11-15. *The Vicarage, 49 Shirley Church Road, Croydon CR0 5EF* T: (020) 8654 1013 E: frstiiv@hotmail.com

KNOWLES, Andrew John. b 66. Wimbledon Sch of Art BA 88. St Jo Coll Nottm 05. **d** 07 **p** 08. C Long Buckby w Watford and W Haddon w Winwick and Ravensthorpe *Pet* 07-11; V Camberley St Mary *Guildf* from 11. *St Mary's Vicarage, 37 Park Road, Camberley GU15 2SP* T: (01276) 22085 or 685167 E: vicar@stmaryscamberley.org.uk

KNOWLES, Canon Andrew William Allen. b 46. St Cath Coll Cam BA 68 MA 72. St Jo Coll Nottm 69. **d** 71 **p** 72. C Leic H Trin 71-74; C Cambridge H Trin *Ely* 74-77; C Woking St Jo *Guildf* 77-81; V Goldsworth Park 81-93; V Wyke 93-98; Dioc Officer Educn and Development of Lay People 93-98; Can Res Chelmsf Cathl 98-11; rtd 11. *68 Appleby Road, Kendal LA9 6HE* T: (01539) 723478 E: andrew.knowles@btinternet.com

KNOWLES, Charles Howard. b 43. Sheff Univ BSc 65 Fitzw Coll Cam BA 69 MA 73. Westcott Ho Cam 67. **d** 69 **p** 70. C Bilborough St Jo *S'well* 69-72; V Choral S'well Minster 72-82; V Cinderhill 82-94; AD Nottingham W 91-94; V Cov St Mary 94-06; AD Cov S 96-02; C Kettlewell w Conistone, Hubberholme etc 06-08; rtd 08; PtO *Leeds* from 08. *Ivy Cottage, Linton, Skipton BD23 5HH* E: charles.knowles@sky.com

KNOWLES, Clay. *See* KNOWLES, Melvin Clay

KNOWLES, Clifford. b 35. Open Univ BA 82. NW Ord Course 74. **d** 77 **p** 78. C Urmston *Man* 77-80; V Chadderton St Luke 80-87; V Heywood St Luke w All So 87-95; AD Heywood and Middleton 92-95; PtO *Linc* 95-98; rtd 00; PtO *Linc* from 02. *12B Far Lane, Coleby, Lincoln LN5 0AH* T: (01522) 810720

KNOWLES, Canon Eric Gordon. b 44. WMMTC 79. **d** 82 **p** 83. NSM Gt Malvern St Mary *Worc* 82-83; NSM Malvern H Trin and St Jas 83-90; NSM Lt Malvern, Malvern Wells and Wyche 90-99; NSM Lt Malvern 99-00; P-in-c 00-13; V from 13; Hon Can Worc Cathl from 05. *45 Wykewane, Malvern WR14 2XD* T: (01684) 567439 E: skypilot@homecall.co.uk

KNOWLES, George. b 37. **d** 95 **p** 96. NSM Hucknall Torkard *S'well* 95-02; rtd 02; PtO *S'well* from 02. *8 North Hill Avenue, Hucknall, Nottingham NG15 7FE* T: 0115-955 9822 E: g.knowles3@ntlworld.com

✠**KNOWLES, The Rt Revd Graeme Paul. b** 51. CVO 12. AKC 73 FKC 11. St Aug Coll Cant 73. **d** 74 **p** 75 **c** 03. C St Peter-in-Thanet *Cant* 74-79; C Leeds St Pet *Ripon* 79-81; Chapl and Prec Portsm Cathl 81-87; Chapter Clerk 85-87; V Leigh Park *Portsm* 87-93; RD Havant 90-93; Adn Portsm 93-99; Dean Carl 99-03; Bp S & M 03-07; Dean St Paul's *Lon* 07-12; Hon Asst Bp St E from 12; Hon Asst Bp Ely from 12; PtO *Lon* from 12. *102A Barons Road, Bury St Edmunds IP33 2LY* T: (01284) 723823 E: graeme.knowles@clergycharities.org.uk

KNOWLES, Irene. *See* KNOWLES, Margaret Irene

KNOWLES, James Russell. b 80. Sydney Univ BA 01. Oak Hill Th Coll BTh 13. **d** 13 **p** 14. C High Ongar w Norton Mandeville *Chelmsf* from 13. *49 Kettlebury Way, Ongar CM5 9HA* M: 07791-371808 E: james.knowles@parishofhighongar.org

KNOWLES, Mrs Jane Frances. b 44. GGSM 66 Lon Inst of Educn TCert 67. Ox Min Course 90. **d** 93 **p** 94. NSM Sandhurst *Ox* 93-97; C Wargrave 97-99; P-in-c Ramsden, Finstock and Fawler, Leafield etc 99-01; V Forest Edge 01-09; rtd 09. *41 Martin's Road, Keevil, Trowbridge BA14 6NA* T: (01380) 870325 E: janeknowles@tiscali.co.uk

KNOWLES, John Geoffrey. b 48. Man Univ BSc 69 Lon Univ MSc 75 Ox Univ PGCE 70 FRSA. WMMTC 95. **d** 98 **p** 99. NSM The Lickey *Birm* 98-99; R Hutcheson's Gr Sch 99-04; P-in-c Woodford *Ches* 05-12; V 12; Dioc Warden of Readers from 05; NSM Handforth from 13; NSM Norbury 13-14. *15 Clare Avenue, Handforth, Wilmslow SK9 3EQ* T: (01625) 526531 E: john.knowles92@btinternet.com

KNOWLES, Margaret Irene. b 48. EAMTC 96. **d** 99 **p** 00. C Gt Yarmouth *Nor* 99-03; TV 03-11; RD 05-10; Chapl Norfolk & Waveney Mental Health NHS Foundn Trust 00-11; R Bunwell, Carleton Rode, Tibenham, Gt Moulton etc *Nor* 11-13; rtd 13. *21 rue de Parthenay, 79340 Ménigoute, France* T: (0033) 5 49 70 68 13 E: revmik@hotmail.co.uk

KNOWLES, Melvin Clay. b 43. Stetson Univ (USA) BA 66 Ex Univ MA 73. Ripon Coll Cuddesdon 75. **d** 77 **p** 78. C Minchinhampton *Glouc* 77-80; St Helena 80-82; TV Haywards Heath St Wilfrid *Chich* 82-88; Adult Educn Adv 88-94; TR Burgess Hill St Jo w St Edw 94-00; V Burgess Hill St Jo 00-09; rtd 09. *32 Livingstone Road, Burgess Hill RH15 8QP* T: (01444) 254429 E: cknowles@waitrose.com

KNOWLES, Philip Andrew. b 63. Leeds Univ BA 07. NOC 04. **d** 07 **p** 08. C Blackb St Mich w St Jo and H Trin 07-10; C Blackb St Thos w St Jude 07-10; P-in-c Lt Marsden w

Nelson St Mary and Nelson St Bede 10-11; V 11-15; V Sheff St Cath Richmond Road from 15. *St Catherine's Vicarage, 300 Hastilar Road South, Sheffield S13 8EJ* T: 0114-239 9598 M: 07813-966257 E: philip.knowles1@btinternet.com

KNOWLES, Philip John. b 48. MA PhD BTh LTCL ALCM LLAM. CITC 76. **d** 76 **p** 77. C Lisburn St Paul *Conn* 76-79; I Cloonclare w Killasnett and Lurganboy *K, E & A* 79-87; I Gorey w Kilnahue, Leskinfere and Ballycanew *C & O* 87-89 and I 89-95; Preb Ferns Cathl 91-95; Dean Cashel 95-13; I Cashel w Magorban, Tipperary, Clonbeg etc 95-13; Chan Waterford Cathl 95-13; Chan Lismore Cathl 95-13; Can Ossory and Leighlin Cathls 96-13; Preb Stagonil St Patr Cathl Dublin 09-13; rtd 13. *99 Kingsgrove, Athy, Co Kildare, Republic of Ireland* M: 87-264 3111 T: (00353) (59) 863 8936 E: philipknowles65@gmail.com

KNOWLES, Richard John. b 47. EAMTC 00. **d** 01 **p** 02. C Burlingham St Edmund w Lingwood, Strumpshaw etc *Nor* 01-04; TV Gt Yarmouth 04-10; rtd 11; PtO *Nor* 11-13. *21 rue de Parthenay, 79340 Ménigoute, France* T: (0033) 5 49 70 68 13 E: revrjk@hotmail.co.uk

KNOWLING, Richard Charles. b 46. K Coll Lon BSc 67 St Edm Hall Ox BA 70 MA 89. St Steph Ho Ox 69. **d** 71 **p** 72. C Hobs Moat *Birm* 71-75; C Shrewsbury St Mary w All SS and St Mich *Lich* 75-77; V Rough Hills 77-83; Dir Past Th Coll of Resurr Mirfield 83-90; V Palmers Green St Jo *Lon* 90-05; AD Enfield 96-01; V Edmonton St Alphege from 05; P-in-c Ponders End St Matt from 05. *St Alphege's Vicarage, Rossdale Drive, London N9 7LG* T: (020) 8245 3588 E: richard.knowling@london.anglican.org

KNOX, Canon Geoffrey Martin. b 44. Dur Univ BA 66 Sheff City Coll of Educn DipEd 73. St Chad's Coll Dur 63. **d** 67 **p** 68. C Newark St Mary *S'well* 67-72; PtO *Derby* 72-74; V Woodville 74-81; RD Repton 79-81; V Long Eaton St Laur 81-00; V Somercotes 00-09; RD Alfreton 04-09; Hon Can Derby Cathl 08-09; rtd 09. *9 Treveryn Parc, Budock Water, Falmouth TR11 5EH* T: (01326) 373142

KNOX, Canon Ian Stephen. b 44. Leeds Univ LLB 64 Solicitor 66 Brunel Univ MPhil 03. **d** 05 **p** 05. PtO *Cov* 05-06; Newc from 06; Exec Dir 40:33 Trust from 05. *16 East Moor, Loughoughton, Alnwick NE66 3JB* T: (01665) 572939 E: office@fortythreetrust.com

KNOX, Janet. b 57. **d** 11 **p** 12. NSM Quinton Road W St Boniface *Birm* from 11. *405 Simmons Drive, Quinton, Birmingham B32 2UH* T: 0121-426 3575 or 426 3166 E: janet_405@hotmail.com

KNOX, Matthew Stephen. b 75. Man Univ BSc 98 Newc Univ PGCE 02 St Jo Coll Dur BA 07. Cranmer Hall Dur 04. **d** 07 **p** 08. C Newburn *Newc* 07-11; P-in-c Tweedmouth from 11; P-in-c Spittal from 11; P-in-c Scremerston from 11. *The Vicarage, 124 Main Street, Tweedmouth, Berwick-upon-Tweed TD15 2AW* T: (01289) 305296 E: knoxmatthew@yahoo.com

KOCH, John Dunbar. b 77. Washington & Lee Univ BA 00 Humboldt Univ Berlin PhD 14. Trin Episc Sch for Min Penn MDiv 07. **d** 07 **p** 08. C Wiesbaden Austria 07-09; C Vienna *Eur* 09-12; R Harrods Creek St Fran USA from 12. *436 Club Lane, Louisville KY 40207, USA* T: (001) (502) 544 5711 E: jadykoch@gmail.com

KOEPPING, Elizabeth Rosalind. b 47. Edin Univ MA 71 Man Univ MA 73 Univ of Qld PhD 81 Westmr Coll Ox MTh 98. **d** 09 **p** 10. NSM Edin Ch Ch 09-14; PtO *Eur* 11-14; P-in-c Heidelberg from 14. *Erbprinzenstrasse 30, 69126 Heidelberg, Germany* E: e.koepping@ed.ac.uk

KOHNER, Canon Jeno George. b 31. K Coll Lon BD 56 AKC 56 Concordia Univ Montreal MA 82. Westcott Ho Cam 56. **d** 57 **p** 58. C Eccleston St Thos *Liv* 57-60; Canada from 60; Hon Can Montreal from 75. *H3-850 Lakeshore Drive, Dorval QC H9S 5T9, Canada* T: (001) (514) 631 0066

KOLAWOLE, Canon Peter Adeleke. b 36. Immanuel Coll Ibadan 91. **d** 85 **p** 86. C Lagos Abp Vining Memorial Nigeria 85-87; P Isolo St Paul 88-96; P Lagos Cathl 97-99; Can Res 99-03; PtO *Chelmsf* from 04. *58 Shaftesbury Point, High Street, London E13 0AB* T: (020) 8503 1620

✠**KOLINI, The Most Revd Emmanuel Musaba.** b 44. Balya Bible Coll Uganda 67 Can Werner Coll Burundi 68 Bp Tucker Coll Mukono 75. **d** 69 **c** 80. Kyangwali Uganda 69-74; Bulinda 77-79; Adn Bukavu Zaïre 80; Asst Bp Bukavu 81-85; Bp Shaba 86-97; Bp Kigali from 97; Abp Rwanda from 98. *PO Box 61, Kigali, Rwanda* T: (00250) 576340 F: 573213 or 576504 E: ek@rwanda1.com

KOLOGARAS, Mrs Linda Audrey. b 48. Humberside Univ BA 97. EMMTC 89. **d** 95 **p** 96. NSM Gt and Lt Coates w Bradley *Linc* 95-98; C Immingham 98-02; R Rosewood Australia 03-06; PtO Dio Brisbane from 06. *33 Whyandra Close, Doonan QLD 4562, Australia* T: (0061) (7) 5471 0482 M: 405-834640

KOMOR, Canon Michael. b 60. Univ of Wales BSc 83. Chich Th Coll 83. **d** 86 **p** 87. C Mountain Ash *Llan* 86-89; C Llantwit Major 89-91; TV 91-00; V Ewenny w St Brides Major 00-05; R Coity, Nolton and Brackla 05-14; R Coity, Nolton and Brackla w Coychurch from 14; AD Bridgend 04-10; Can Llan Cathl from 14. *Nolton Rectory, Merthyr Mawr Road North, Bridgend CF31 3NH* T: (01656) 652247 E: revd@komors.org.uk

KONIG, Peter Montgomery. b 44. Univ of Wales (Lamp) MA 10. Westcott Ho Cam 80. **d** 82 **p** 83. C Oundle *Pet* 82-86; Chapl Westwood Ho Sch Pet 86-92; Chapl Pet High Sch 92-95; Chapl Worksop Coll Notts 95-99; Chapl Glenalmond Coll *St And* 99-04; rtd 04; PtO *Pet* from 04. *Crossways, Main Street, Yarwell, Peterborough PE8 6PR* T: (01780) 782873 - M: 07764-586619 E: pandakonig@talktalk.net

KOPSCH, Hartmut. b 41. Sheff Univ BA 63 Univ of BC MA 66 Lon Univ PhD 70. Trin Coll Bris 78. **d** 80 **p** 81. C Cranham Park *Chelmsf* 80-85; V Springfield *Birm* 85-92; V Dover St Martin *Cant* 92-96; R Bath Walcot *B & W* 96-06; rtd 06; PtO *Glouc* 07-09. *10 St Edyths Road, Bristol BS9 2ES* T: 0117-968 8683 E: harmutandjane@gmail.com

KORN, Sam Christopher. b 89. Trin Hall Cam MA 14. Westcott Ho Cam 12. **d** 14 **p** 15. C E Barnet *St Alb* from 14. *109 Margaret Road, Barnet EN4 9RA* M: 07900-827371 E: sam.korn@cantab.net

KORNAHRENS, Wallace Douglas. b 43. The Citadel Charleston BA 66 Gen Th Sem (NY) STB 69. **d** 69 **p** 70. USA 69-72; C Potters Green *Cov* 72-75; Chapl Community of Celebration Wargrave Oxon 75-76; P-in-c Cumbrae (or Millport) *Arg* 76-78; R Grantown-on-Spey *Mor* 78-83; R Rothiemurchus 78-83; R Edin H Cross from 83. *Holy Cross Rectory, 18 Barnton Gardens, Edinburgh EH4 6AF* T: 0131-336 2311 E: info@holycrossedinburgh.org

KOSLA, Mrs Ann Louise. b 56. Middx Univ BA 04. NTMTC 01. **d** 04 **p** 05. NSM Thorley *St Alb* 04-07; NSM Chelmsf S Deanery 08-10; NSM Boreham *Chelmsf* 10-12; V Church Langley from 12. *7 Ashworth Place, Harlow CM17 9PU* T: (01279) 629950 M: 07563-548337 E: ann.kosla@sky.com

KOSLA, Charles Antoni. b 58. Ridley Hall Cam 97. **d** 99 **p** 00. C Widford *Chelmsf* 99-03; C Thorley *St Alb* 03-07; Dioc Adv for Miss and Par Development *Chelmsf* from 07; Hon C E Springfield 08-12; Hon C Church Langley from 12. *7 Ashworth Place, Harlow CM17 9PU* T: (01279) 629950 or (01245) 294419 E: ckosla@chelmsford.anglican.org

KOTHARE, Jayant Sunderrao. b 41. Bombay Univ BA Heidelberg Univ MDiv. **d** 86 **p** 87. C Handsworth St Mich *Birm* 86-89; C Southall St Geo *Lon* 89-92; TV Thamesmead *S'wark* 92-97; Dioc Community Relns Officer *Man* 97-00; P-in-c Moston St Chad 97-02; rtd 02; PtO *Man* 09-14. *27 Charlesworth Court, 18 Bingley Close, Manchester M11 3RF* E: jaysohum@yahoo.co.uk

KOUBLE (née MACKIE), Fiona Mary. b 66. Anglia Ruskin Univ BA 94 MSc 95 St Jo Coll Dur BA 09 RGN 88. Cranmer Hall Dur 07. **d** 11 **p** 12. C Hillsborough and Wadsley Bridge *Sheff* 11-13; V Ardsley from 13. *Christ Church Vicarage, Doncaster Road, Barnsley S71 5EF* M: 07817-167386 E: fionakouble@yahoo.co.uk

KOUSSEFF, Mrs Karen Patricia. b 60. Ex Univ BA 83. STETS 06. **d** 09 **p** 10. NSM Lower Dever *Win* from 09. *15 Long Barrow Close, South Wonston, Winchester SO21 3ED* T: (01962) 885114 E: kkousseff@tiscali.co.uk

KOVOOR, Canon George Iype. b 57. Delhi Univ BA 77 Serampore Univ BD 80. Union Bibl Sem Yavatmal 78. **d** 80 **p** 80. Chapl Leprosy Miss Hosp Kothara India 80-81; Assoc Presbyter Shanti Nivas Ch Faridabad 82; Presbyter Santokh Majra 83; Dean St Paul's Cathl Ambala 84-88; Chapl St Steph Hosp Delhi 88-90; C Derby St Aug 90-94; Min Derby Asian Chr Min Project 90-94; Tutor Crowther Hall CMS Tr Coll Selly Oak 94-97; Prin 97-05; Hon Can Worc Cathl 01-05; Prin Trin Coll Bris 05-13; R New Haven St Jo Connecticut USA from 13; Chapl to The Queen from 03; Can Th Niger Delta N from 10; Can Missiologist Sabah from 10; R New Haven St Jo Connecticut USA from 13. *490 Prospect Street, New Haven, CT 06511, USA* T: (001) (203) 668 3237 E: stjohnsnewhaven.rector@gmail.com

KOZAK, Robert Jozef. b 84. SS Coll Cam BTh 15. Westcott Ho Cam 12. **d** 15. C Leavesden *St Alb* from 15. *49 Ross Crescent, Watford WD25 0DA* M: 07803-086370 E: kozacco@gmail.com

KRAFT (née STEVENS), Mrs Jane. b 45. SRN 66 SCM 68. NTMTC 01. **d** 03 **p** 04. NSM Finchley St Mary *Lon* 03-07; TV Chipping Barnet 07-14; rtd 15; PtO *St Alb* from 15; *Ox* from 15. *66 Yeovil Road, Owlsmoor, Sandhurst GU47 0TE -* M: 07803-868482 T: (01276) 36402 E: revd.janekraft@btinternet.com

KRAMER, Beaman Kristopher (Kris). b 67. Mars Hill Coll (USA) BS 88 Duke Univ (USA) MTS 95. Wycliffe Hall Ox MTh 98. **d** 98 **p** 99. C Hersham *Guildf* 98-99; C Paddington St Jo w St Mich *Lon* 99-00; R Radford Grace USA 00-10; PtO *Ox* 10-12; Chapl St Edm Hall Ox 12-13; Fellows' Chapl Magd Coll Ox 12-13; USA from 13. *304 S Mill View Way, Ponte Vedra Beach FL 32082, USA* E: frkris@gmail.com

KRAMER, Mrs Caroline Anne. b 70. Wycliffe Hall Ox BTh 98. **d** 98. C Oatlands *Guildf* 98-99; USA 00-10; C Wokingham All SS *Ox* 10-13; C Ponte Vedra Beach USA from 13. *304 S Mill View Way, Ponte Vedra Beach FL 32082, USA* E: revcarolinekramer@googlemail.com

KRAMER, Maxwell James. b 85. Ball Coll Ox BA 07 MA 11 St Jo Coll Cam BA 10 MPhil 11. Westcott Ho Cam 08. **d** 13 **p** 14. NSM Cambridge St Mary Less *Ely* from 13. *St John's College, Cambridge CB2 1TP* M: 07796-673081 E: max_kramer@hotmail.com

KRAWIEC, Christopher James Michael. b 86. Cranmer Hall Dur 12. **d** 15. C Gt Harwood *Blackb* from 15. *16 Mill Gardens, Great Harwood, Blackburn BB6 7FN*

KRINKS, Philip Lewis. b 72. Magd Coll Ox BA 95 MA 99 INSEAD MBA 00 K Coll Lon PhD 11 MA 12. Westcott Ho Cam 12. **d** 14 **p** 15. C Battersea St Mary *S'wark* from 14. *35 Kerrison Road, London SW11 2QG* M: 07899-813650 E: philip@krinks.com

KROLL, Una Margaret Patricia. b 25. Girton Coll Cam MB 51 BChir 51. S'wark Ord Course 68. **d** 88 **p** 97. NSM Monmouth *Mon* 88-97; LtO 97-04. *6 Hamilton House, 57 Hanson Street, Bury BL9 6LR* T: 0161-797 7877

KRONBERGS, Paul Mark. b 55. NEOC 02. **d** 05 **p** 06. NSM Middlesbrough St Columba w St Paul *York* from 05. *39 Northumberland Grove, Stockton-on-Tees TS20 1PB* T: (01642) 365160 E: fr-paul.kronbergs@hotmail.co.uk

KRONENBERG, John Simon. b 59. Greenwich Univ BSc 85 Open Univ BA 00 MRICS 87 MBEng 94. Ripon Coll Cuddesdon BTh 06. **d** 02 **p** 03. C Chandler's Ford *Win* 02-06; V Hinchley Wood *Guildf* from 06. *The Vicarage, 98 Manor Road North, Esher KT10 0AD* T: (020) 8786 6391 M: 07500-954963 E: vicar@stchristopherschurch.org.uk

KROUKAMP, Nigel John Charles. b 53. Cen Lancs Univ BSc 93 Bolton Inst of HE CertEd 86 RNMH 75 RGN 78. LCTP 05. **d** 08 **p** 09. NSM Colne and Villages *Blackb* 08-14; rtd 14; PtO *Blackb* from 14. *56 Kelswick Drive, Nelson BB9 0SZ* T: (01282) 698261 M: 07725-858433 E: nigelkroukamp@googlemail.com

KRZEMINSKI, Stefan. b 51. Nottm Univ BTh 77. Linc Th Coll 74. **d** 77 **p** 78. C Sawley *Derby* 77-79; Asst Chapl Bluecoat Sch Nottm 79-86; Hon C W Hallam and Mapperley *Derby* 84-96; Hd of RE Nottm High Sch from 86; PtO *Derby* from 96. *12 Newbridge Close, West Hallam, Ilkeston DE7 6LY* T: 0115-930 5052

KTORIDES, Nicholas. b 59. Sheff Univ MA 97. Ridley Hall Cam. **d** 14 **p** 15. C Gorleston St Andr *Nor* from 14. *2 Elmgrove Road, Gorleston, Great Yarmouth NR31 7PP* T: (01493) 652361 M: 07812-170911

KUHRT, The Ven Gordon Wilfred. b 41. Lon Univ BD 63 Middx Univ DProf 01. Oak Hill Th Coll 65. **d** 67 **p** 68. C Illogan *Truro* 67-70; C Wallington *S'wark* 70-73; V Shenstone *Lich* 73-79; P-in-c S Croydon Em *Cant* 79-81; V S'wark 81-89; RD Croydon Cen *Cant* 81-84; RD S'wark 85-86; Hon Can S'wark Cathl 87-89; Adn Lewisham 89-96; Dir Chief Sec ABM 96-98; Min Division Abps' Coun 99-06; rtd 06; Hon C Ilmington w Stretton-on-Fosse etc *Cov* 06-12. *87 Churchway, Haddenham, Aylesbury HP17 8DT* T: (01844) 292870 E: omkuhrt@tiscali.co.uk

KUHRT, Martin Gordon. b 66. Nottm Univ LLB 88. Trin Coll Bris 93. **d** 96 **p** 97. C Morden *S'wark* 96-00; Chapl Lee Abbey 00-02; TV Melksham *Sarum* 02-08; C Atworth w Shaw and Whitley 07-08; C Broughton Gifford, Gt Chalfield and Holt 07-08; P-in-c Bedgrove *Ox* 08-09; V from 09. *The Vicarage, 252 Wendover Road, Aylesbury HP21 9PD* T: (01296) 435546 E: mgkuhrt555@btinternet.com

KUHRT, Stephen John. b 69. Man Univ BA 91 Lon Inst of Educn PGCE 93. Wycliffe Hall Ox BA 03. **d** 03 **p** 04. C New Malden and Coombe *S'wark* 03-07; P-in-c from 07. *55 Woodside Road, New Malden KT3 3AW*

KUIN LAWTON, Theresa. b 69. St Aid Coll Dur BA 91 TCD MPhil 96. Ox Min Course 05. **d** 07 **p** 08. NSM Bampton w Clanfield *Ox* 07-10; Chapl Magd Coll Sch Ox from 09. *Manor Croft, Church Close, Bampton OX18 2LW* T: (01993) 850468 *or* (01865) 242191 E: tessa.lawton@talktalk.net *or* tkuin-lawton@mcsoxford.org

KUMAR, Suresh. b 59. Madras Univ MSc 81 Leic Univ MA 91 Alagappa Univ MA 05. Serampore Th Coll BD 85. **d** 85 **p** 88. India 85-08; C Braunstone Park *Leic* 08-09; TV Emmaus Par Team 09-11; P-in-c Leic St Phil 11-14; Sec to Bp Trichy India from 14. *CSI Diocesan Office, Puthur, Trichy-620017, India* E: suresh@skumar.plus.com

KURK, Pamela Ann. b 56. Univ of Wales (Ban) BTh 06. **d** 04 **p** 05. NSM Wandsworth St Mich w St Steph *S'wark* 04-11; Chapl St Cecilia's Wandsworth C of E Sch from 07; P-in-c Battersea St Mich *S'wark* from 13. *64 Pulborough Road, London SW18 5UJ* T: (020) 8265 8985 M: 07774-437471 E: thekurks@aol.com *or* akurk@saintcecilias.wandsworth.sch.uk

KURRLE, Canon Stanley Wynton. b 22. OBE 82. Melbourne Univ BA 47 St Cath Soc Ox BA 50 MA 54. Wycliffe Hall Ox 49. **d** 52 **p** 53. C Sutton *Liv* 52-54; Australia from 54; Fell St Paul's Coll Univ of Sydney from 69; Can Sydney 81-95; Can Emer from 95. *25 Marieba Road, PO Box 53, Kenthurst NSW 2156, Australia* T: (0061) (2) 9654 1334 M: 427-277919 F: 9654 1368 E: mathourastation@bigpond.com

KURTI, Peter Walter. b 60. Qu Mary Coll Lon LLB 82 K Coll Lon MTh 89. Ch Div Sch of Pacific 82 Ripon Coll Cuddesdon 83. **d** 86 **p** 87. C Prittlewell *Chelmsf* 86-90; Chapl Derby Coll of HE 90-92; Chapl Derby Univ 92-94; Dep Hd Relig Resource and Research Cen 90-94; Prec St Geo Cathl Perth Australia 94-97; R Scarborough 97-01; R Sydney St Jas from 01. *Level 1, 169-171 Phillip Street, Sydney NSW 2000, Australia* T: (0061) (2) 9363 3335 *or* 9232 3022 M: 412-049271 F: 9232 4182 E: peter.kurti@bigpond.com

KURZ, Nathaniel William. b 84. Trin Coll Bris BA 15. **d** 15. C Esher *Guildf* from 15. *74 Cranbrook Drive, Esher KT10 8DP* M: 07912-037246 E: nate.esherparish@gmail.com

KUSTNER, Ms Jane Lesley. b 54. Lanchester Poly Cov BA 76 FCA 79. St Steph Ho Ox 03. **d** 05 **p** 06. C Waterloo St Jo w St Andr *S'wark* 05-08; P-in-c Lewisham St Swithun from 08; AD E Lewisham from 13. *St Swithun's Vicarage, 191 Hither Green Lane, London SE13 6QE* M: 00734-113741 E: jane.kustner@btinternet.com

KUTIWULU, Calixte. b 63. Qu Coll Birm 12. **d** 92 **p** 93. In RC Ch Democratic Republic of Congo 92-03; C Pet St Mary Boongate from 14. *45 Huntly Grove, Peterborough PE1 2QW* M: 07417-433229 E: ckutiwulu@yahoo.co.uk

✠**KWONG KONG KIT, The Most Revd Peter.** b 36. Kenyon Coll Ohio BD 65 DD 86 Hong Kong Univ DD 00. Bexley Hall Div Sch Ohio MTh 71 DD 98. **d** 65 **p** 66 **c** 81. P-in-c Hong Kong Crown of Thorns Hong Kong 65-66; C Hong Kong St Paul 71-72; Bp Hong Kong and Macao 81-98; Bp Hong Kong Is from 98; Abp Hong Kong Sheng Kung Hui from 98. *Bishop's House, 1 Lower Albert Road, Hong Kong, China* T: (00852) 2526 5355 F: 2525 2537 E: office1@hkskh.org

KYLE, Miss Sharon Patricia Culvinor. b 55. Open Univ BA 90 Edin Univ BD 94 MTh 96. Coates Hall Edin 91. **d** 94 **p** 95. C Edin SS Phil and Jas 94-96; C Neston *Ches* 96-99; TV Kirkby Liv 99-01. *22 Oak Tree Close, Kingsbury, Tamworth B78 2JF* T: (01827) 874445

KYRIACOU, Brian George. b 42. Lon Univ LLB 64. Oak Hill Th Coll 79. **d** 81 **p** 82. C Becontree St Mary *Chelmsf* 81-83; C Becontree St Cedd 83-85; C Becontree W 85; TV 85-87; V Shiregreen St Jas and St Chris *Sheff* 87-92; TV Schorne *Ox* 92-98; V Edmonton All SS w St Mich *Lon* 98-07; rtd 07; PtO *Chelmsf* from 07. *58 Morant Road, Colchester CO1 2JA* T: (01206) 520699 M: 07970-719094 E: brian.kyriacou@ntlworld.com

KYRIAKIDES-YELDHAM, Preb Anthony Paul Richard. b 48. Birkbeck Coll Lon BSc 82 Warwick Univ MSc 90 Univ of Wales (Lamp) MMin 10 CQSW 83 CPsychol 91. K Coll Lon BD 73 AKC 73. **d** 74 **p** 75. C Dalston H Trin w St Phil *Lon* 74-78; NSM Lon Docks St Pet w Wapping St Jo 79-81; NSM Hackney Wick St Mary of Eton w St Aug 81-85; NSM Wandsworth Common St Mary *S'wark* 85-87; Chapl Wandsworth HA Mental Health Unit 87-93; Chapl Springfield Univ Hosp Lon 87-93; PtO *Ex* 94-98; LtO 98-08; Sen Chapl Plymouth Hosps NHS Trust 98-08; P-in-c Kingsbridge and Dodbrooke *Ex* 08-11; Preb Ex Cathl 07-11; Chapl Imp Coll Healthcare NHS Trust 11-12; rtd 13; Chapl and PV Westmr Abbey from 13. *The Chapter Office, 20 Dean's Yard, London SW1P 3PA* T: (020) 7654 4957 E: tony.yeldham@talk21.com

KYTE, Eric Anthony. b 62. Leeds Univ BSc 84 PGCE 85. Trin Coll Bris BA 98. **d** 98 **p** 99. C Pudsey St Lawr and St Paul *Bradf* 98-01; P-in-c Gisburn and Hellifield 01-11; New Zealand from 11. *353 Highgate, Roslyn, Dunedin, New Zealand* E: thereverick@aol.com

KYUMU MOTUKO, Norbert. See CHUMU MUTUKU, Norbert

L

LA TOUCHE, Francis William Reginald. b 51. Linc Th Coll 73. d 76 p 77. C Yate *Bris* 76-77; C Yate New Town 77-79; Chapl Vlissingen (Flushing) Miss to Seamen *Eur* 79-83; Port Chapl Hull Miss to Seamen 83-91; V Burstwick w Thorngumbald *York* 91-02; PtO *Ches* from 11. *10A Leamington Close, Neston CH64 0SL* T: 0151-336 3238
E: frank@latouche.fsnet.co.uk

LABDON, David William. b 64. St Jo Coll Nottm 07. d 09 p 10. C Bebington *Ches* 09-13; R Winnipeg St Aid Canada from 13. *St Aidan's Anglican Church, 274 Campbell Street, Winnipeg, MB R3N 1B5, Canada* T: (001) (204) 489 3390
E: dlabdon@staidanswinnipeg.ca

LABDON, John. b 32. Oak Hill Th Coll. d 84 p 85. C Formby H Trin *Liv* 84-87; P-in-c St Helens St Mark 87-97; rtd 97; PtO *Ches* from 97. *80 Burton Road, Little Neston, Neston CH64 9RA* T: 0151-336 7039

LABOUREL, Elaine Odette. b 58. St Jo Coll Nottm 03. d 05 p 06. C Paris St Mich *Eur* 05-08; P-in-c Rouen All SS 06-08; Asst Chapl Versailles w Chevry from 08. *4 avenue de Savigny, 91700 Ste Geneviève des Bois, France* T: (0033) 1 69 04 09 91 M: 6 60 59 65 98 E: elaine.labourel@wanadoo.fr

LABRAN, Stuart. b 79. Leeds Univ BA 00 PGCE 02 Clare Coll Cam MPhil 09. Westcott Ho Cam 07. d 71 p 72. C Stratford-upon-Avon, Luddington etc *Cov* 09-12. *Flat 2, 38 Nottingham Place, London W1U 5NU* E: stuartlabran@hotmail.com

LACEY, Canon Allan John. b 48. Sheff Univ MA 02. Wycliffe Hall Ox. d 82 p 83. C Greasbrough *Sheff* 82-85; R Treeton 85-92; V Thorpe Hesley 92-00; R Rossington 00-07; CMS Uganda 07-13; Can Em Cathl Arua from 12; rtd 13; PtO *Leic* from 14. *28 Stanfell Road, Leicester LE2 3GA* T: 0116-270 2751 - M: 07887-473540 E: allanandanne@btinternet.com

LACEY, Carol Ann. b 62. Qu Coll Birm 07. d 09 p 10. NSM Leic St Anne, St Paul w St Aug 09-14; V Brampton Bierlow *Sheff* from 14. *The Vicarage, Christchurch Road, Wath-upon-Dearne, Rotherham S63 6NW* T: (01709) 873210 M: 07971-519705
E: carolannlacey@gmail.com

LACEY, Charles Richard. b 76. St Mellitus Coll BA 13. d 13 p 14. C S Tottenham St Ann *Lon* from 13. *134 Sherringham Avenue, London N17 9RR* M: 07506-648744
E: delacey76@hotmail.com

LACEY, Mrs Christina Nancy. b 83. Ox Brookes Univ BA 05. St Mellitus Coll BA 12. d 12 p 13. C Knaphill w Brookwood *Guildf* from 12. *St Andrew's Church, The Goldsworth Park Centre, Woking GU21 3LG* T: (01483) 762424 M: 07528-809065
E: chrissie@scat.org.uk

LACEY, Colin Brian. d 10 p 11. C Ballymena w Ballyclug *Conn* 10-13; I Belfast St Pet and St Jas from 13. *St Peter's Rectory, 17 Waterloo Park South, Belfast BT15 5HX* T: (028) 9077 7053 M: 07563-531082 E: brianlacey@hotmail.co.uk

LACEY, Eric. b 33. Cranmer Hall Dur 69. d 71 p 72. C Blackpool St Jo *Blackb* 71-75; V Whittle-le-Woods 75-88; R Heysham 88-98; rtd 98; PtO *Blackb* from 98. *143 Bredon Avenue, Chorley PR7 6NS* T: (01257) 273040

LACEY, Nigel Jeremy. b 59. St Jo Coll Nottm BTh 94. d 94 p 95. C Mildenhall *St E* 94-97; C Selly Park St Steph and St Wulstan *Birm* 97-01; P-in-c W Wycombe w Bledlow Ridge, Bradenham and Radnage *Ox* 01-09; R from 09. *The Rectory, Church Lane, West Wycombe, High Wycombe HP14 3AH* T: (01494) 529988 E: nigel.lacey@whsmithnet.co.uk

LACK, Miss Catherine Mary. b 59. Clare Coll Cam BA 81 Ox Univ MTh 00 ARCM 78. Qu Coll Birm 90. d 92 p 94. C Leiston *St E* 92-95; TV Ipswich St Mary at Stoke w St Pet and St Fran 95-98; Chapl Keele Univ *Lich* 98-07; Cultural and Relig Affairs Manager Yarl's Wood Immigration Removal Cen 07-08; Warden Ferrar House Lt Gidding Community 08-09; Chapl Newc Univ from 09; Master Newc St Thos Prop Chpl from 09. *9 Chester Crescent, Newcastle upon Tyne NE2 1DH* T: 0191-231 2750 M: 07913-721989
E: catherine.lack50@gmail.com

LACK, Martin Paul. b 57. St Jo Coll Ox MA 79 MSc 80. Linc Th Coll 83. d 86 p 87. C E Bowbrook and W Bowbrook *Worc* 86-89; C Bowbrook S and Bowbrook N 89-90; R Teme Valley S 90-01; rtd 01. *Colbridge Cottage, Bottom Lane, Whitbourne, Worcester WR6 5RT* T: (01886) 821978

LACKENBY, George Joseph. b 48. d 13 p 14. NSM Harlow Green and Lamesley *Dur* from 13. *68 Ashford, Gateshead NE9 6YG* T: 0191-421 9173
E: george.lackenby@hotmail.co.uk

LACKEY, Michael Geoffrey Herbert. b 42. Oak Hill Th Coll 73. d 75 p 76. C Hatcham St Jas *S'wark* 75-81; V New Barnet St Jas

St Alb 81-91; V Hollington St Jo *Chich* 91-02; Dir Crowhurst Chr Healing Cen 02-05; rtd 05; Hon C Gt Amwell w St Margaret's and Stanstead Abbots *St Alb* 05-09. *5 Vicarage Close, St Albans AL1 2PU* E: glackey@toucansurf.com

LACKEY, William Terence Charles. b 32. St Mich Coll Llan 80. d 82 p 83. C Wrexham *St As* 82-85; V Gwersyllt 85-93; R Trefnant 93-98; rtd 98. *42 Osborne Street, Neath SA11 1NN*

LACY, Melanie June. b 75. TCD BA 98 All Hallows Coll Dublin MA 00. CITC 98. d 00. C Bangor St Comgall *D & D* 00-02; N Ireland Regional Co-ord Crosslinks 02-06; C Knutsford St Jo and Toft *Ches* 06-09; Dir Youth and Children's Min Oak Hill Th Coll from 10. *Oak Hill College, Chase Side, London N14 4PS* T: (020) 8449 0467 F: 8441 5996 E: mell@oakhill.ac.uk

LACY, Sarah Frances. b 49. Sarum Th Coll 93. d 96 p 97. C Weston Zoyland w Chedzoy *B & W* 96-00; C Middlezoy and Othery and Moorlinch 00-01; R Berrow and Breane 01-15; rtd 15. *16 Peach Tree Close, Bridgwater TA6 4XF* E: sallylacy010@yahoo.co.uk

LACY-SMITH, Mrs Joanna. b 55. STETS 05. d 08 p 09. OLM Dorchester *Sarum* 08-12; NSM 12-14; NSM Dorchester and the Winterbournes from 14. *2 Ackerman Road, Dorchester DT1 1NZ* T: (01305) 266721 E: jolacysmith@copperstream.co.uk

LADD, Mrs Anne de Chair. b 56. Nottm Univ BA 78 CQSW 80. St Jo Coll Nottm. dss 86 d 87 p 94. Bucknall and Bagnall *Lich* 86-91; Par Dn 87-91; NSM Bricket Wood *St Alb* 91-01; Chapl Garden Ho Hospice Letchworth 98-06; Befriending Co-ord Mencap 07-08; Soc worker 08-11; Chapl Nottm Univ Hosp NHS Trust from 11; Hon C Chilwell *S'well* from 15. *Church House, Barn Croft, Beeston, Nottingham NG9 4HU* T: 0115-925 1114

LADD, John George Morgan. b 36. Univ of Wales (Ban) BA 58 MA 65. St Mich Coll Llan. d 90 p 91. NSM Nevern and Y Beifil w Eglwyswrw and Meline etc *St D* 90-92; NSM Llandysilio w Egremont and Llanglydwen etc 92-93; V Gwaun-cae-Gurwen 93-04; rtd 04. *Rhosdirion, Peniel, Carmarthen SA32 7HT* T: (01267) 236107

LADD, Nicholas Mark. b 57. Ex Univ BA 78 Selw Coll Cam BA 81 Anglia Ruskin Univ MA 03. Ridley Hall Cam 79. d 82 p 83. C Aston SS Pet and Paul *Birm* 82-86; TV Bucknall and Bagnall *Lich* 86-91; V Bricket Wood *St Alb* 91-01; V Cambridge St Barn *Ely* 01-09; Dean and Lect St Jo Coll Nottm from 09; Hon C Chilwell *S'well* from 15. *Church House, Barn Croft, Beeston, Nottingham NG9 4HU* T: 0115-925 1114 F: 943 6438 M: 07540-425381 E: n.ladd@stjohns-nottm.ac.uk

✠**LADDS, The Rt Revd Robert Sidney.** b 41. Lon Univ BEd 71 LRSC 72. Cant Sch of Min 79. d 80 p 81 c 99. C Hythe *Cant* 80-83; R Bretherton *Blackb* 83-91; Chapl Bp Rawstorne Sch Preston 83-87; Bp's Chapl for Min and Adv Coun for Min *Blackb* 86-91; P-in-c Preston St Jo 91-96; R Preston St Jo and St Geo 96-99; Hon Can Blackb Cathl 93-97; Adn Lancaster 97-99; Suff Bp Whitby *York* 99-08; rtd 09; Hon C Hendon St Mary and Ch Ch *Lon* from 09. *Christ Church House, 76 Brent Street, London NW4 2ES* T: (020) 8202 8123
E: episcopus@ntlworld.com

LADIPO, Canon Adeyemi Olalekan. b 37. Trin Coll Bris 63. d 66 p 76. C Bilston St Leon *Lich* 66-68; Nigeria 68-84; V Canonbury St Steph *Lon* 85-87; Sec for Internat Miss BCMS 87-90; Hon C Bromley SS Pet and Paul *Roch* 89-90; V Herne Hill *S'wark* 90-99; Hon Can Jos from 95; V S Malling *Chich* 99-02; rtd 02; PtO *Chich* from 03; *S'wark* from 07. *63 Elm Grove, London SE15 5DB* T: (020) 7639 8150 E: thelapidos@hotmail.com

LAFFERTY, Miss Kim Elvin. b 62. RGN 85 RM 89. Wycliffe Hall Ox 10. d 12 p 13. C Horwich and Rivington *Man* from 12. *St Elizabeth's Vicarage, Cedar Avenue, Horwich, Bolton BL6 6HT* T: (01204) 410582 M: 07712-698295
E: kelafferty@hotmail.co.uk

LAFFORD, Sylvia June. b 46. Middx Univ BA 04. NTMTC 01. d 04 p 05. NSM Hayes St Edm *Lon* 04-12; Asst Chapl Hillingdon Hosps NHS Foundn Trust 10-13; PtO *Lon* from 13; *Pet* from 13. *18 Blenheim Croft, Brackley NN13 7ET* T: (01280) 700122 E: sylvia.lafford@btinternet.com

LAIDLAW, Juliet. See MONTAGUE, Juliet

LAIN-PRIESTLEY, Ms Rosemary Jane. b 67. Kent Univ BA 89 K Coll Lon MA 02. Carl Dioc Tr Course 92. d 96 p 97. C Scotforth *Blackb* 96-98; C St Martin-in-the-Fields *Lon* 98-06; Dean of Women's Min Two Cities Area from 06. *13D Hyde Park Mansions, Cabbell Street, London NW1 5BD -* M: 07941-265316
E: rosemarylainpriestley@btopenworld.com

LAING, Canon Alexander Burns. b 34. RD 90. Edin Th Coll 57. **d** 60 **p** 61. C Falkirk *Edin* 60-62; C Edin Ch Ch 62-70; Chapl RNR 64-91; P-in-c Edin St Fillan 70-74; Chapl Edin R Infirmary 74-77; Dioc Supernumerary *Edin* from 77; R Helensburgh *Glas* 77-03; Can St Mary's Cathl 87-03; rtd 03; LtO *Glas* from 06. *13 Drumadoon Drive, Helensburgh G84 9SF* T: (01436) 675705

LAING, Miss Catriona Hannah. b 79. Jes Coll Cam BA 02 PhD 12 Institut d'Études Politiques Paris MA 04. Westcott Ho Cam 08. **d** 12 **p** 13. C Dulwich St Barn *S'wark* 12-15; USA from 15. *Financial Times, 1023 15th Street NW, STE 700, Washington DC 20005, USA* M: 07900-313892 E: catrionalaing@cantab.net

LAING, William Sydney. b 32. TCD BA 54 MA 62. **d** 55 **p** 56. C Dublin Crumlin *D & G* 55-59; C Dublin St Ann 59-65; I Carbury *M & K* 65-68; I Dublin Finglas *D & G* 68-80; I Tallaght 80-91; Can Ch Ch Cathl Dublin 90-94; Preb 94-97; I Dublin Crumlin w Chapelizod *D & G* 91-97; rtd 97. *42 Hazelwood Crescent, Clondalkin, Dublin 22, Republic of Ireland* T: (00353) (1) 459 3893 M: 87-760 1210

LAIRD, Alisdair Mark. b 60. Auckland Univ BA 84. Trin Coll Bris BA 92. **d** 92 **p** 93. C Linthorpe *York* 92-98; V Hull St Cuth 98-06; P-in-c Alne and Brafferton w Pilmoor, Myton-on-Swale etc 06-07; LtO 07-08; PtO from 08; Chapl Hull and E Yorks Hosps NHS Trust from 09. *Hull Royal Infirmary, Anlaby Road, Hull HU3 2JZ* T: (01482) 875875 E: alisdair@trackways.net

LAIRD, Canon John Charles. b 32. Sheff Univ BA 53 MA 54 St Cath Coll Ox BA 58 MA 62 Lon Univ DipEd 70. Ripon Hall Ox 56. **d** 58 **p** 59. C Cheshunt *St Alb* 58-62; Chapl Bps' Coll Cheshunt 62-64; Vice-Prin 64-67; Prin 67-69; V Keysoe w Bolnhurst and Lt Staughton *St Alb* 69-01; Hon Can St Alb 87-02; LtO 01-15. *The College of St Barnabas, Blackberry Lane, Lingfield RH7 6NJ*

LAIRD, Robert George (Robin). b 40. TCD Div Sch 58 Edin Th Coll 63. **d** 65 **p** 66. C Drumragh *D & R* 65-68; CF 68-93; QHC 91-93; Sen Chapl Sedbergh Sch 93-98; LtO *Bradf* 93-98; rtd 98; PtO *Sarum* from 98; Ex from 98. *Barrule, Hillside Road, Sidmouth EX10 8JD* T: (01395) 513948

LAIRD, Stephen Charles Edward. b 66. Oriel Coll Ox BA 88 MA 92 MSt 93 K Coll Lon MTh 91 Kent Univ PhD 06 FHEA 12. Wycliffe Hall Ox MPhil 96. **d** 94 **p** 95. C Ilfracombe, Lee, Woolacombe, Bittadon etc *Ex* 94-98; Chapl Kent Univ *Cant* 98-03; Dean of Chapl from 03; Hon Lect from 98; Hon C Hackington from 03; Chapl Kent Inst of Art and Design 98-02; P-in-c Blean *Cant* from 09. *24 Tyler Hill Road, Blean, Canterbury CT2 9HT* T: (01227) 763373 or 787476 M: 07970-438840 E: s.c.e.laird@kent.ac.uk

LAKE, David Michael. b 57. St Mary's Sem Oscott 76. St Jo Coll Nottm BA 01. **d** 01 **p** 02. C Lilleshall, Muxton and Sheriffhales *Lich* 01-05; P-in-c Crick and Yelvertoft w Clay Coton and Lilbourne *Pet* 05-09; R from 09. *The Rectory, Main Road, Crick, Northampton NN6 7TU* T: (01788) 822147 E: d.m.lake@btinternet.com

LAKE, Eileen Veronica. See CREMIN, Eileen Veronica

LAKE, Jeffrey Ronald. b 70. SEITE 12. **d** 15. NSM St Bride Fleet Street w Bridewell etc *Lon* from 15. *Address temp unknown*

LAKE, Kevin William. b 57. St Mich Coll Llan 97. **d** 99 **p** 00. C Penarth w Lavernock *Llan* 99-02; Chapl Marie Curie Cen Holme Tower 02-04; P-in-c Cwm Ogwr *Llan* 04-06; P-in-c Llandyfodwg and Cwm Ogwr 06-08; V Aberdare St Fagan 08-12; V Caerleon and Llanfrechfa *Mon* 12-15; P-in-c Barry All SS *Llan* from 15. *The Rectory, 3 Park Road, Barry CF62 6NU* T: (01446) 701206 E: kevin.lake1@btinternet.com

LAKE, The Very Revd Stephen David. b 63. Southn Univ BTh. Chich Th Coll 85. **d** 88 **p** 89. C Sherborne w Castleton and Lillington *Sarum* 88-92; P-in-c Branksome St Aldhelm 92-96; V 96-01; RD Poole 00-01; Can Res and Sub-Dean St Alb *St Alb* 01-11; Dean Glouc from 11. *The Deanery, 1 Miller's Green, Gloucester GL1 2BP* T: (01452) 524167 E: dean@gloucestercathedral.org.uk

LAKE, Thomas Wesley Cellan. b 77. Univ Coll Lon MEng 01. Oak Hill Th Coll BTh 08. **d** 08 **p** 09. C Enfield Ch Ch Trent Park *Lon* 08-12; V Lee St Mildred *S'wark* from 12. *The Vicarage, 1A Helder Grove, London SE12 0RB* T: (020) 8449 4042

LAKE, Vivienne Elizabeth. b 38. Westcott Ho Cam 84. **dss** 86 **d** 87 **p** 94. Chesterton Gd Shep *Ely* 86-90; C 87-90; Ecum Min K Hedges Ch Cen 87-90; NSM Bourn Deanery *Ely* 90-01; NSM Papworth Everard 94-96; PtO from 01. *15 Storey's House, Mount Pleasant, Cambridge CB3 0BZ* T: (01223) 369523 E: vel.camb@gmail.com

LAKER, Clive Sheridan. b 59. Greenwich Univ BSc 92 RGN 82. Aston Tr Scheme 93 SEITE 95. **d** 98 **p** 99. C Bridlington Quay Ch Ch *York* 98-00; C Bridlington Em 00-01; TV Bucknall *Lich* 01-04; C Surbiton St Matt *S'wark* 04-08; TV 08-13; rtd 13. *27 St Davids Road, Swanley BR8 7RJ* E: lakerfamily@ntlworld.com

LAKEY, Elizabeth Flora. b 46. DipOT 69 Open Univ BA 81. SAOMC 98. **d** 01 **p** 02. OLM Nettlebed w Bix, Highmoor, Pishill etc *Ox* 01-11; rtd 12. *Bank Farm, Pishill, Henley-on-Thames RG9 6HJ* T/F: (01491) 638601 M: 07799-752933 E: bankfarm@btinternet.com

LAKEY, Michael John. b 70. Ches Coll of HE BA 98 MTh 98 St Jo Coll Dur PhD 08. St Steph Ho Ox 13. **d** 14 **p** 15. Lect Ripon Coll Cuddesdon from 08; NSM Dorchester *Ox* from 14. *4 Church Close, Cuddesdon, Oxford OX44 9HD* T: (01865) 874406 E: michael.lakey@theology.ox.ac.uk

LALL, Mrs Julia Carole. b 56. Ch Ch Coll Cant CertEd 78 BEd 79. ERMC 07. **d** 10 **p** 11. C Bacton w Wyverstone, Cotton and Old Newton etc *St E* 10-13; P-in-c S Hartismere from 13. *The Rectory, Stanwell Green, Thorndon, Eye IP23 7JL* M: 07837-785607 E: julia.lall@hotmail.co.uk

LAMB, Alison. See EARL, Alison

LAMB, Alyson Margaret. b 55. LMH Ox BA 77 MA 80. Ridley Hall Cam 03. **d** 05 **p** 06. C York St Mich-le-Belfrey 05-09; V Eastbourne St Jo *Chich* 09-13; Can and Preb Chich Cathl 12-13; Chapl Paris St Mich *Eur* from 13. *St Michael, 5 rue d'Aguesseau, 75008 Paris, France* T: (0033) 1 47 42 70 88

LAMB, Bruce. b 47. Keble Coll Ox BA 69 MA 73. Coll of Resurr Mirfield 70. **d** 73 **p** 74. C Romford St Edw *Chelmsf* 73-76; C Canning Town St Cedd 76-79; V New Brompton St Luke *Roch* 79-83; Chapl RN 83-87; C Rugeley *Lich* 87-88; V Trent Vale 88-92; Bereavement Cllr Cruse 94-99; Hon C Chorlton-cum-Hardy St Clem *Man* 98-99; Asst Chapl N Man Health Care NHS Trust 99-02; P-in-c Barton w Peel Green *Man* 02-14; rtd 14. *Address temp unknown*

LAMB, Bryan John Harry. b 35. Leeds Univ BA 60. Coll of Resurr Mirfield 60. **d** 62 **p** 63. C Solihull *Birm* 62-65 and 88-89; Asst Master Malvern Hall Sch Solihull 65-74; Alderbrook Sch and Hd of Light Hall Adult Educn Cen 74-88; V Wragby *Linc* 89; Dioc Dir of Readers 89; PtO *Birm* 89-13; rtd 95. *27 Ladbrook Road, Solihull B91 3RN* T: 0121-705 2489

LAMB, Canon Christopher Avon. b 39. Qu Coll Ox BA 61 MA 65 Birm Univ MA 78 PhD 87. Wycliffe Hall Ox BA 63. **d** 63 **p** 64. C Enfield St Andr *Lon* 63-69; Pakistan 69-75; Tutor Crowther Hall CMS Tr Coll Selly Oak 75-78; Co-ord BCMS/CMS Other Faiths Th Project 78-87; Dioc Community Relns Officer *Cov* 87-92; Can Th Cov Cathl from 92; Sec Inter Faith Relns Bd of Miss 92-99; R Warmington w Shotteswell and Radway w Ratley *Cov* 99-06; rtd 06; PtO *Cov* from 06. *8 Brookside Avenue, Wellesbourne, Warwick CV35 9RZ* T: (01789) 842060 E: christophertinalamb@tiscali.co.uk

LAMB, David Andrew. b 60. Liv Inst of HE BA 94 Man Univ MA 01 PhD 12. NOC 90. **d** 94 **p** 95. C Formby H Trin *Liv* 94-97; C St Helens St Matt Thatto Heath 97-98; C Halewood 98-01; Lect Liv Hope 99-00; V Birkenhead St Jas w St Bede *Ches* 01-08; NSM Wallasey St Nic w All SS 08-12; V Ashton Hayes from 12. *The Vicarage, 14 Dunns Lane, Ashton, Chester CH3 8BU* T: (01829) 751440 E: david.a.lamb@btinternet.com

LAMB, Mrs Jean Evelyn. b 57. Reading Univ BA 79 Nottm Univ MA 88. St Steph Ho Ox 81. **dss** 84 **d** 88 **p** 01. Leic H Spirit 84-87; Asst Chapl Leic Poly 84-87; Par Dn Beeston *S'well* 88-91; Hon C and Artist in Res Nottingham St Mary and St Cath 92-95; Hon Par Dn Sneinton St Steph w St Alb 97-01; NSM Rolleston w Fiskerton, Morton and Upton 01-02; PtO 02-04; C Bilborough St Jo 04-11; C Bilborough w Strelley 04-11; C Colwick 11-12; C Gedling from 12. *St Alban's House, 4 Dale Street, Nottingham NG2 4JX* T: 0115-958 5892 M: 07851-792552

LAMB, Mary. b 52. **d** 10 **p** 11. OLM Framlingham w Saxtead *St E* 10-13; NSM from 13. *2 The Coach House, The Square, Dennington, Woodbridge IP13 8AB* T: (01728) 638897 E: marylamb1952@googlemail.com

LAMB, Nicholas Henry. b 52. St Jo Coll Dur BA 74. St Jo Coll Nottm 76. **d** 79 **p** 80. C Luton Lewsey St Hugh *St Alb* 79-84; Bethany Fellowship 84-86; In Bapt Min 86-94; PtO *Chich* 97-99; C E Grinstead St Swithun 99-04; V Forest Row 04-13; Asst Chapl Highgate Sch *Lon* from 13. *Highgate School, North Road, London N6 4AY* T: (020) 8340 1524 E: revnhlamb@hotmail.com

LAMB, Philip Richard James. b 42. Sarum & Wells Th Coll. **d** 83 **p** 84. C Wotton-under-Edge w Ozleworth and N Nibley *Glouc* 83-86; TV Worc SE 86-91; R Billingsley w Sidbury, Middleton Scriven etc *Heref* 91-96; R St Dominic, Landulph and St Mellion w Pillaton *Truro* 96-11; rtd 11. *3 Trelinnoe Gardens, South Petherwin, Launceston PL15 7TH*

LAMB, Phillip. b 68. NEOC 00. **d** 03 **p** 04. C Bridlington Priory *York* 03-06; V Hornsea w Atwick from 06. *The Vicarage, 9 Newbegin, Hornsea HU18 1AB* T: (01964) 532531 M: 07803-239611 E: phil_lamb2002@yahoo.co.uk

LAMB, Scott Innes. b 64. Edin Univ BSc 86 Fitzw Coll Cam BA 92. Ridley Hall Cam 90. **d** 93 **p** 94. C E Ham w Upton Park and Forest Gate *Chelmsf* 93-97; V W Holloway St Luke *Lon* 97-00; P-in-c Hammersmith H Innocents 00-03; Chapl RN

03-09; V Bexley St Jo *Roch* 09-12; TR Bexley from 12. *St John's Vicarage, 29 Parkhill Road, Bexley DA5 1HX* T: (01322) 521786 E: lambscott@sky.com

LAMB, William Robert Stuart. b 70. Ball Coll Ox BA 91 MA 95 Peterho Cam MPhil 94 Sheff Univ PhD 10. Westcott Ho Cam 92. **d** 95 **p** 96. C Halifax *Wakef* 95-98; TV Penistone and Thurlstone 98-01; Chapl Sheff Univ 01-10; Can Res Sheff Cathl 05-10; Vice-Prin Westcott Ho Cam from 10. *Westcott House, Jesus Lane, Cambridge CB5 8BP* T: (01223) 272975 *or* 741013 E: wrsl100@cam.ac.uk

LAMBERT, Antony. *See* LAMBERT, John Clement Antony

LAMBERT, David Francis. b 40. Oak Hill Th Coll 72. **d** 74 **p** 75. C Paignton St Paul Preston *Ex* 74-77; C Woking Ch Ch *Guildf* 77-84; P-in-c Willesden Green St Gabr *Lon* 84-91; P-in-c Cricklewood St Mich 85-91; V Cricklewood St Gabr and St Mich 92-93; R Chenies and Lt Chalfont, Latimer and Flaunden *Ox* 93-01; Chapl Izmir (Smyrna) w Bornova *Eur* 01-03; TV Brixham w Churston Ferrers and Kingswear *Ex* 03-05; rtd 05. *54 Brunel Road, Broadsands, Paignton TQ4 6HW* T: (01803) 842076

LAMBERT, David Hardy. b 44. AKC 66. **d** 67 **p** 68. C Marske in Cleveland *York* 67-72; V 85-09; V N Ormesby 73-85; RD Guisborough 86-91; rtd 09; PtO *York* from 10. *13 Fell Briggs Drive, Marske-by-the-Sea, Redcar TS11 6BU* T: (01642) 490235 E: david@lambert9139.freeserve.co.uk

LAMBERT, David Joseph. b 66. Coll of Resurr Mirfield 99. **d** 01 **p** 02. C Camberwell St Geo *S'wark* 01-04; C Walworth St Jo 04-06; V Stoke Newington St Faith, St Matthias and All SS *Lon* from 06. *St Matthias Vicarage, Wordsworth Road, London N16 8DD* T: (020) 7254 5063 E: frdavidlambert@aol.com

LAMBERT, David Nathaniel. b 34. Headingley Meth Coll 58 Linc Th Coll 66. **d** 66 **p** 67. In Methodist Ch 58-66; C Canwick *Linc* 66-68; C-in-c Bracebridge Heath CD 68-69; R Saltfleetby All SS w St Pet 69-73; R Saltfleetby St Clem 70-73; V Skidbrooke 70-73; V Saltfleetby 73-80; R Theddlethorpe 74-80; RD Louthesk 76-82; R N Ormsby w Wyham 80; R Fotherby 81-94; rtd 94; PtO *Linc* 94-03; *York* 03-05; *Ripon* 03-05; *Dur* from 06. *Sandcroft, Market Place, Houghton-le-Spring DH5 8AJ* T: 0191-584 1387

LAMBERT, Ian Anderson. b 43. Lon Univ BA 72 Nottm Univ MTh 87. Ridley Hall Cam 66. **d** 67 **p** 68. C Bermondsey St Mary w St Olave, St Jo etc *S'wark* 67-70; R Lluidas Vale Jamaica 71-75; Chapl RAF 75-98; rtd 98; P-in-c N and S Muskham *S'well* 01-03; P-in-c Averham w Kelham 01-03; Bp's Adv for Past Care and Counselling from 04. *34 Hayside Avenue, Balderton, Newark NG24 3GB* T: (01636) 659101 M: 07788-171958 E: revianlambert@mac.com

LAMBERT, John Clement Antony. b 28. St Cath Coll Cam BA 48 MA 52. Cuddesdon Coll 50. **d** 52 **p** 53. C Hornsea and Goxhill *York* 52-55; C Leeds St Pet *Ripon* 55-59; R Carlton in Lindrick *S'well* 59-93; rtd 93; PtO *Derby* from 93; *S'well* 93-00; *York* from 14. *4 Old Tatham, Holme-on-Spalding-Moor, York YO43 4BN* T: (01430) 860531

LAMBERT, John Connolly. b 61. Univ of Wales (Ban) BTh 04. EAMTC 01. **d** 04 **p** 05. C Paris St Mich *Eur* 04-08; C Preston-on-Tees and Longnewton *Dur* 08-10; P-in-c from 10. *The Vicarage, Quarry Road, Eaglescliffe, Stockton-on-Tees TS16 9BD* T: (01642) 789814 E: johnlambert@allsaints-church.co.uk

LAMBERT, Malcolm Eric. b 58. Leic Univ BSc 80 Fitzw Coll Cam BA 89 Nottm Univ MPhil 02 RMN 84. Ridley Hall Cam 87. **d** 90 **p** 91. C Humberstone *Leic* 90-94; R S Croxton Gp 94-99; V Birstall and Wanlip 99-05; TR Leic Resurr 05-07; RD Christianity N 05-07; Warden of Readers 97-05; Dir Angl Th Inst Belize 08-09; TR Chigwell and Chigwell Row *Chelmsf* 09-15; P-in-c Annesley w Newstead *S'well* from 15. *The Vicarage, Annesley Cutting, Annesley, Nottingham NG15 0AJ* T: (01623) 759666 E: malcolm.lambert@gmail.com

LAMBERT, Michael Roy. b 25. Univ Coll Dur BSc 49. Cuddesdon Coll 52. **d** 52 **p** 53. C Middlesbrough St Oswald *York* 52-56; C Romsey *Win* 56-59; C Cottingham *York* 59-64; Chapl Hull Univ 59-64; V Saltburn-by-the-Sea 64-72; P-in-c Shaftesbury H Trin *Sarum* 72-73; R Shaston 74-76; TR 76-78; R Corfe Mullen 78-91; rtd 91; PtO *Glouc* from 91. *6 Capel Court, The Burgage, Prestbury, Cheltenham GL52 3EL* T: (01242) 300644

LAMBERT, Neil James. b 58. Goldsmiths' Coll Lon BA 81. Ridley Hall Cam 02. **d** 04 **p** 05. C Wisley w Pyrford *Guildf* 04-08; V Ash Vale from 08. *The Vicarage, 203 Vale Road, Ash Vale, Aldershot GU12 5JE* T: (01252) 325295 M: 07812-385392 E: revneill@me.com

LAMBERT, Miss Olivia Jane. b 48. Matlock Coll of Educn BEd 70. Trin Coll Bris 84. **dss** 86 **d** 87 **p** 94. York St Luke 86-90; Par Dn 87-90; Chapl York Distr Hosp 86-90; Par Dn Huntington *York* 90-94; C 94-95; TV 95-00; TV Marfleet 00-07; C Harrogate St Mark *Ripon* 07-08; rtd 08. *7 Almsford Place, Harrogate HG2 8EH* T: (01423) 202243 E: oliviajlambert@aol.com

LAMBERT, Peter George. b 29. Coll of Resurr Mirfield 86. **d** 87 **p** 88. NSM Rothwell w Orton, Rushton w Glendon and Pipewell *Pet* 87-93; P-in-c Corby Epiphany w St Jo 93-96; rtd 96; PtO *Pet* from 96. *4 Cogan Crescent, Rothwell, Kettering NN14 6AS* T: (01536) 710692 E: pglambert@tiscali.co.uk

LAMBERT, Peter Jose. b 59. STETS. **d** 12 **p** 13. NSM Gosport Ch Ch *Portsm* from 12; NSM Gosport H Trin from 12. *57 Elmhurst Road, Gosport PO12 1PQ* T: (023) 9252 4106 M: 07926-382725 E: peterjoselambert@btinternet.com

LAMBERT, Canon Philip Charles. b 54. St Jo Coll Dur BA 75 Fitzw Coll Cam BA 77 MA 81. Ridley Hall Cam 75. **d** 78 **p** 79. C Upper Tooting H Trin *S'wark* 78-81; C Whorlton *Newc* 81-84; P-in-c Alston cum Garrigill w Nenthead and Kirkhaugh 84-87; TV Alston Team 87-89; R Curry Rivel w Fivehead and Swell *B & W* 89-01; RD Crewkerne and Ilminster 98-01; TR Dorchester *Sarum* 01-06; RD 02-06; Can Res Truro Cathl 06-14; Asst Chapl Gtr Athens *Eur* from 14. *Church House, Gavalochori, Chania 73008, Crete, Greece* T: (0030) (282) 502 3270 M: 6947-600686 E: cretechaplainphilip@yahoo.co.uk

LAMBERT (née JOHNSON), Mrs Ruth Alice Edna. b 59. Leic Univ BA 80 PGCE 93 Nottm Univ MA 01 RGN 85. EMMTC 98. **d** 01 **p** 02. C Mountsorrel Ch Ch and St Pet *Leic* 01-04; Chapl Univ Hosps Leic NHS Trust 04-07; P-in-c Belmopan St Ann Belize 08-09; Chapl Barking Havering and Redbridge Hosps NHS Trust 09-12; Sen Chapl Guy's and St Thos' NHS Foundn Trust 12-15; Chapl Sherwood Forest Hosps NHS Trust from 15. *The Vicarage, Annesley Cutting, Annesley, Nottingham NG15 0AJ* T: (01623) 759666 E: ruth.lambert@gmail.com

LAMBERT, Mrs Ruth Eleanor. b 52. ERMC. **d** 14 **p** 15. OLM Mile Cross *Nor* from 14. *22 Blomefield Road, Norwich NR3 2RA* T: (01603) 410565 E: ruthless52@hotmail.com

LAMBERT, William John. b 59. St Mich Coll Llan. **d** 13 **p** 14. C Upper Ebbw Valleys *Mon* from 13. *The New Vicarage, 19 Crosscombe Terrace, Cwm, Ebbw Vale NP23 7SP* T: (01495) 524283 E: williamlambert314@hotmail.com

LAMBETH, Mrs Dorothy Anne. b 57. Yorks Min Course 13. **d** 15. NSM Barlby and Riccall *York* from 15. *Field View, Back Lane, North Duffield, Selby YO8 5RJ* T: (01757) 288857 E: dorothy.lambeth@gmail.com

LAMBETH, Archdeacon of. *See* GATES, The Ven Simon Philip

LAMBOURN, David Malcolm. b 37. Lanc Univ BEd 76 Man Univ MEd 78 Warwick Univ PhD 01. Linc Th Coll 63. **d** 65 **p** 66. C Camberwell St Geo *S'wark* 65-67; C Mottingham St Andr w St Alban 67-70; rtd 03. *28 Frederick Road, Birmingham B15 1JN* T: 0121-242 3953 E: david.lambourn@blueyonder.co.uk

LAMBOURNE, Max. b 80. Ripon Coll Cuddesdon 12. **d** 15. C Pontesbury I and II *Heref* from 15. *Hills View, The Grove, Minsterley, Shrewsbury SY5 0AG* M: 07736-839858 E: lambourne_m@yahoo.co.uk

LAMDIN, Canon Keith Hamilton. b 47. Bris Univ BA 69. Ripon Coll Cuddesdon 86. **d** 86 **p** 87. Adult Educn Officer *Ox* 83-98; Team Ldr Par Resources Dept 88-94; Dioc Dir Tr 04-08; Prin Sarum Coll 08-15; NSM Cowley St Jo *Ox* 98-06; P-in-c Upper Kennet *Sarum* 08-10; Hon Can Ch Ch *Ox* 97-08; Hon Can Kimberley S Africa from 08; Can and Preb Sarum Cathl from 09. *2 Forge Close, West Overton, Marlborough SN8 4PG* T: (01672) 861550 E: klamdin@sarum.ac.uk *or* khlamdin@gmail.com

LAMEY, Richard John. b 77. Keble Coll Ox BA 98 MA 02 Em Coll Cam BA 01 MA 05. Westcott Ho Cam 99. **d** 02 **p** 03. C Stockport SW *Ches* 02-05; P-in-c Newton in Mottram 05-11; P-in-c Newton in Mottram w Flowery Field 11-12; V Newton w Flowery Field 12; RD Mottram 08-12; R Wokingham St Paul *Ox* from 12. *St Paul's Rectory, Holt Lane, Wokingham RG41 1ED* T: 0118-327 9116 E: richardlamey@btinternet.com

LAMMAS, Miss Diane Beverley. b 47. Trin Coll Bris 76. **dss** 79 **d** 87 **p** 94. Lenton Abbey *S'well* 79-84; Wollaton Park 79-84; E Regional Co-ord and Sec for Voc and Min CPAS 84-89; Hon C Cambridge St Paul *Ely* 87-90; Voc and Min Adv CPAS 89-92; Sen Voc and Min Adv CPAS 92-95; R Hethersett w Canteloff w Lt and Gt Melton *Nor* 95-12; RD Humbleyard 98-03; rtd 12; PtO *Nor* from 13. *3 Turnberry Close, Lowestoft NR33 9JN* T: (01502) 218599 E: di.lammas@talktalk.net

LAMMENS, Erwin Bernard Eddy. b 62. Catholic Univ Leuven BA 86 Gregorian Univ Rome MDiv 90. Grootseminarie Gent 84. **d** 87 **p** 88. In RC Ch 87-96; Asst Chapl Antwerp St Boniface *Eur* 98-05; TV Harwich Peninsula *Chelmsf* 05-10; R Wivenhoe from 10. *The Rectory, 44 Belle Vue Road, Wivenhoe, Colchester CO7 9LD* T: (01206) 822511 E: erwinlammens@btinternet.com

LAMMING, Sarah Rebecca. b 77. Middx Univ BA 02. Westcott Ho Cam 03 Yale Div Sch 05. **d** 06 **p** 07. C Handsworth St Jas *Birm* 06-09; USA from 09. *1000 Spa Road, Apt #202, Annapolis MD 21403, USA* E: fr.sarah@gmail.com

LAMOND, Stephen Paul. b 64. Trin Coll Bris BA 99. **d** 99 **p** 00. C Weston-super-Mare Ch Ch *B & W* 99-02; C Congresbury w Puxton and Hewish St Ann 02-03; Chapl RAF from 03. *Chaplaincy Services (RAF), HQ Air Command, RAF High Wycombe HP14 4UE* T: (01494) 496800 F: 496343

LAMONT, Charles John David. b 91. **d** 14 **p** 15. C Wisley w Pyrford *Guildf* from 14. *Church House, Coldharbour Road, Woking GU22 8SP*

LAMONT, Canon Euphemia Margaret (Fay). b 53. N Coll of Educn BA 98. TISEC 00. **d** 00 **p** 00. C Monifieth and Carnoustie *Bre* 00-07; P-in-c Dundee St Ninian from 07; Can St Paul's Cathl Dundee from 08. *St Ninian's Church House, Kingsway East, Dundee DD4 7RW* T: (01382) 453818 M: 07931-222092 E: fay.lamont@sky.com

LAMONT, Roger. b 37. Jes Coll Ox BA 60 MA 62 MBACP 00. St Steph Ho Ox 59. **d** 61 **p** 62. C Northampton St Alb *Pet* 61-66; V Mitcham St Olave *S'wark* 66-73; V N Sheen St Phil and All SS 73-85; P-in-c Richmond St Luke 82-85; Chapl St Lawr Hosp Caterham 85-93; Chapl Surrey Oaklands NHS Trust 94-01; rtd 01; PtO *S'wark* from 02. *36 Hillcroft Court, Chaldon Road, Caterham CR3 5XB* T: (01883) 340803 E: rmglamont@gmail.com

LAMONT, Ms Veronica Jane (Ronni). b 56. Bp Grosseteste Coll CertEd 77 Anglia Poly Univ MA 06. St Jo Coll Nottm 90. **d** 92 **p** 94. Par Dn St Alb St Pet *St Alb* 92-94; C 94-96; TV Hemel Hempstead 96-01; V Bexley St Jo *Roch* 01-08; PtO *Cant* from 08; *Roch* from 08; Dioc Faith and Nuture Adv *Cant* from 15. *86 Ufton Lane, Sittingbourne ME10 1EX* T: (01795) 553603 M: 07802-793910 E: ronni@lamonts.org.uk *or* rlamont@diocant.org

LAMPARD, Ms Ruth Margaret. b 65. St Jo Coll Dur BA 87 Jes Coll Cam BA 99 MA 04 Heythrop Coll Lon MA 04. Westcott Ho Cam 97 Berkeley Div Sch 99. **d** 00 **p** 01. C Ealing St Pet Mt Park *Lon* 00-01; C Eastcote St Lawr 01-04; Hon C Norton *St Alb* 05-06; PtO *S'wark* 06-12; Chapl to Bp Kensington *Lon* 07-08; C W Brompton St Mary w St Peter and St Jude 08-13; Chapl Chapter 1 from 13; Hon C Waterloo St Jo w St Andr *S'wark* from 13. *St Barnabas' Vicarage, 146A Lavenham Road, London SW18 5EP* T: (020) 7835 1440 *or* 7593 0470 F: 7593 0478 M: 07712-321253 E: ruthl@chapter1.org.uk

LANCASTER, Mrs Jennifer. b 48. NEOC 00. **d** 03 **p** 04. C Walker *Newc* 03-07; TV Jarrow *Dur* 07-12; rtd 12. *2 Heathdale Gardens, High Heaton, Newcastle upon Tyne NE7 7QR* E: jenny.lancaster@gmail.com

LANCASTER, John Rawson. b 47. BSc. NOC. **d** 82 **p** 83. C Bolton St Jas w St Chrys *Bradf* 82-86; V Barnoldswick w Bracewell 86-12; rtd 12; PtO *Leeds* from 13. *Harold's Laithe, High Bradley Lane, Bradley, Keighley BD20 9ES* T: (01535) 634264 E: johnlancaster@btinternet.com

LANCASTER, Ronald. b 31. MBE 93. St Jo Coll Dur BA 53 MA 56 Hon MSc 09 FRSC 83 CChem 83. Cuddesdon Coll 55. **d** 57 **p** 58. C Morley St Pet w Churwell *Wakef* 57-60; C High Harrogate St Pet *Ripon* 60-63; LtO *Ely* 63-88; Chapl Kimbolton Sch 63-88; Asst Chapl 88-91; PtO *Ely* from 88; rtd 96; PtO *St Alb* from 13. *7 High Street, Kimbolton, Huntingdon PE28 0HB* T: (01480) 860498 F: 861277

LANCASTER, Archdeacon of. See EVERITT, The Ven Michael John

LANCASTER, Suffragan Bishop of. See PEARSON, The Rt Revd Geoffrey Seagrave

LANCHANTIN, Mrs Eve Line. b 51. Sorbonne Univ Paris BA 79 MA 80 MPhil 83. Protestant Inst of Th Paris BDiv 95 MDiv 99. **d** 07 **p** 08. C Ashford *Cant* 07-10; PtO from 15. *25 Sackville Crescent, Ashford TN23 1LT* T: (01233) 632472 E: evelanchantin@gmail.com

LAND, Edward Charles. b 79. Trin Coll Bris 13. **d** 15. C Heigham St Thos *Nor* from 15. *363 Earlham Road, Norwich NR2 3RQ* T: (01603) 465758 M: 07917-285072 E: edwardland79@gmail.com *or* edward@stthomasnorwich.org

LAND, Michael Robert John. b 43. Ripon Hall Ox BA 72 MA. **d** 72 **p** 73. C Newbury St Nic *Ox* 72-73; C Newbury 73-75; TV Chigwell *Chelmsf* 75-80; V Walthamstow St Andr 80-08; rtd 08; PtO *Heref* from 08. *20 St Mary's Lane, Burghill, Hereford HR4 7QL* T: (01432) 760452 E: land117@btinternet.com

LANDALL, Allan Roy. b 55. Qu Coll Birm BA 98. **d** 98 **p** 99. C Thurnby w Stoughton *Leic* 98-02; R Walsoken *Ely* from 02. *The Rectory, Church Road, Wisbech PE13 3RA* T: (01945) 583740 E: arlandall@btinternet.com

LANDAU, Christopher David. b 80. Trin Coll Cam BA 01 MA 05 MPhil 02. Ripon Coll Cuddesdon MPhil 12. **d** 13 **p** 14. C W Kilburn St Luke and Harrow Road Em *Lon* from 13. *2 Church Flats, Fernhead Road, London W9 3EH* M: 07703-958084 E: christopher@cantab.net

LANDER, Mrs Eileen Sylvia. b 47. Cant Ch Ch Univ BA 12. **d** 09 **p** 10. NSM Maidstone St Paul *Cant* 09-14; C Eastry

and Woodnesborough from 14. *The Vicarage, The Street, Woodnesborough, Sandwich CT13 0NQ* T: (01304) 613056 E: eileenlander@yahoo.co.uk

LANDER, Mrs Elizabeth Anne. b 69. St Andr Univ BSc 93 Ox Univ PGCE 94. Wycliffe Hall Ox 00. **d** 02 **p** 03. C Glascote and Stonydelph *Lich* 02-07; C Beckenham St Jo *Roch* 08-13; V from 13. *The Vicarage, 249 Eden Park Avenue, Beckenham BR3 3JN* T: (020) 8650 6110 M: 07790-212302 E: landerliz@yahoo.co.uk

LANDER, John Stanley. b 55. **d** 04 **p** 05. OLM Uttoxeter Area *Lich* from 04. *9 Overcroft, Bramshall, Uttoxeter ST14 5NQ* T: (01889) 565228 E: john_lander@lineone.net

LANDER, Pauline. See KEY, Pauline

LANDMAN, Denis Cooper. b 21. MBE 60 OM(Ger) 80. Lon Univ BA 41 DipEd 52. St Deiniol's Hawarden 79. **d** 82 **p** 83. Hon C Tranmere St Paul w St Luke *Ches* 82-86; C Southport St Pet Australia 86-88; P-in-c Biggera Waters 88-92; rtd 92. *1/24 Stretton Drive, Helensvale Qld 4212, Australia* T: (0061) (7) 5573 4660 M: 407-758376

LANDMANN, Ulrike Helene Kathryn. b 57. **d** 06 **p** 07. NSM Balsall Heath and Edgbaston SS Mary and Ambrose *Birm* 06-10; PtO 10-13. *Address temp unknown*

LANE, Alexander John. b 71. Leeds Univ BA 02. Coll of Resurr Mirfield 99. **d** 02 **p** 03. C Eastbourne St Andr *Chich* 02-06; C Littlehampton and Wick 06-08; V Hunslet w Cross Green *Ripon* 08-12; V Twickenham All SS *Lon* from 12; CMP from 08. *All Saints' House, Church View Road, Twickenham TW2 5BX* T: (020) 8894 3580 E: fr.alex.lane@googlemail.com

LANE, Andrew Harry John. b 49. MBE 92. Lanc Univ BA 71. Cuddesdon Coll 71. **d** 73 **p** 74. C Abingdon w Shippon *Ox* 73-78; Chapl Abingdon Sch 75-78; Chapl RAF 78-94; rtd 94; PtO *Nor* 94-01; Public Preacher from 01; RD Repps 02-05. *Society of St Luke, 32B Beeston Common, Sheringham NR26 8ES* T: (01263) 825623 F: 820334 E: superior@ssluke.org.uk

LANE, Anthony James. b 29. Leeds Univ BA 53. Coll of Resurr Mirfield 53. **d** 55 **p** 56. C Tilehurst St Nich *Ox* 55-60; Min Can Win Cathl 60-63; R Handley w Pentridge *Sarum* 64-80; V Thurmaston *Leic* 80-85; TV Bournemouth St Pet w St Swithun, H Trin etc *Win* 85-93; rtd 93. *5 Richards Way, Salisbury SP2 8NT* T: (01722) 332163

LANE, Anthony Richard. b 42. St Jo Coll Nottm 07. **d** 09 **p** 10. C Gtr Athens *Eur* from 09. *Kefalas, Chania 73008, Crete, Greece* T: (0030) (282) 502 2345 M: 6944-131257 E: kritilanes@yahoo.co.uk

LANE, Canon Antony Kenneth. b 58. Ripon Coll Cuddesdon 84. **d** 87 **p** 88. C Crediton and Shobrooke *Ex* 87-90; C Amblecote *Worc* 90-94; C Sedgley All SS 94-95; TV 95-00; R Crayford *Roch* from 00; AD Erith 09-15; Hon Can Roch Cathl from 09. *The Rectory, 1 Claremont Crescent, Crayford, Dartford DA1 4RJ* T: (01322) 522078 M: 07928-769882 E: rector@stpaulinus.co.uk

LANE, Denis John Victor. b 29. Lon Univ LLB 49 BD 55. Oak Hill Th Coll 50. **d** 53 **p** 54. C Deptford St Jo *S'wark* 53-56; C Cambridge St Steph CD *Ely* 56-59; OMF S Perak Malaysia 60-66; Promotion Sec OMF Singapore 66-70; Overseas Dir 70-82; Dir Home Min 82-88; Internat Min 88-94; LtO *Chich* 91-94; rtd 94; PtO *Chich* from 94. *2 Parry Drive, Rustington, Littlehampton BN16 2QY* T/F: (01903) 785430

✠**LANE, The Rt Revd Elizabeth Jane Holden (Libby).** b 66. St Pet Coll Ox BA 89 MA 93. Cranmer Hall Dur 91. **d** 93 **p** 94 **c** 15. C Blackb St Jas 93-96; PtO *York* 96-99; Family Life Educn Officer *Ches* 00-02; TV Stockport SW 02-07; Asst Dir of Ords 05-07; V Hale and Ashley 07-15; Dean of Women in Min 10-15; Suff Bp Stockport from 15. *Bishop's Lodge, Back Lane, Dunham Town, Altrincham WA14 4SG* T: 0161-928 5611 F: 929 0692 E: bpstockport@chester.anglican.org

LANE, Gareth Ernest. b 71. Westmr Univ BSc 94 Univ of Wales MA 08. Wycliffe Hall Ox 08. **d** 10 **p** 11. C Bedgrove *Ox* 10-14; TV Aylesbury from 14. *28 Domino Way, Aylesbury HP18 0FZ* M: 07919-332859 T: (01296) 328523 E: garethlane@hotmail.com *or* gareth@churchonberryfields.org

LANE, George David Christopher. b 68. St Pet Coll Ox BA 89 MA 93. Cranmer Hall Dur 91. **d** 93 **p** 94. C Blackb St Jas 93-96; C Beverley Minster *York* 96-99; V Heald Green St Cath *Ches* 99-07; PtO from 07; *Man* 08-12; Chapl Man Airport from 12; Lic Preacher from 12. *Bishop's Lodge, Back Lane, Dunham Town, Altrincham WA14 4SG* T: 0161-489 2838 E: george.lane@manairport.co.uk

LANE, Iain Robert. b 61. CCC Ox BA 83. Ripon Coll Cuddesdon BA 86 MA 88. **d** 87 **p** 88. C Rotherhithe St Mary w All SS *S'wark* 87-91; V Bierley *Bradf* 91-00; Can Res St Alb *St Alb* 00-08; Admin St Alb Cen for Chr Studies from 08; PtO *St Alb* from 08. *Hill House, Wild Hill, Hatfield AL9 6EB* T: (01707) 660485 E: iain.lane@christianstudies.org.uk

LANE, Jennifer Mary. b 73. Leeds Univ BA 08 MA 12. NOC 05. **d** 08 **p** 09. C Crosland Moor and Linthwaite *Wakef* 08-11; P-in-c Crofton and Warmfield *Leeds* 11-14; Par Educn Adv 11-14; P-in-c E Richmond from 14. *The Rectory, 13 Kneeton Park, Middleton Tyas, Richmond DL10 6SB* E: jennilane2013@btinternet.com

LANE, John Ernest. b 39. OBE 94. MBIM 76 Cranfield Info Tech Inst MSc 80. Handsworth Coll Birm 58. **d** 80 **p** 80. In Methodist Ch 62-80; Hon C Peckham St Jo w St Andr *S'wark* 80-95; Hon C Greenwich St Alfege 98-99; Dir St Mungo Housing Assn 80-94; Dir Corporate Affairs from 94; PtO *S'wark* 95-98; *Lich* 02-14. *2 Tregony Rise, Lichfield WS14 9SN* T: (01543) 415078

LANE, Libby. *See* LANE, Elizabeth Jane Holden

LANE, Mrs Lilian June. b 37. Stockwell Coll Lon TCert 59. **d** 02 **p** 03. OLM E Knoyle, Semley and Sedgehill *Sarum* 02-08; OLM St Bartholomew 08-09; Chapl St Mary's Sch Shaftesbury from 09. *Ashmede, Watery Lane, Donhead St Mary, Shaftesbury SP7 9DP* T: (01747) 828427 E: rev.jlane@hotmail.co.uk

LANE, Mrs Linda Mary. b 41. Lon Univ BD 87 ACIB 66. Gilmore Ho 67. **dss** 82 **d** 87 **p** 94. Hadlow *Roch* 82-94; Hon Par Dn 87-94; PtO 94-96; C Dartford H Trin 96-97; V Kensworth, Studham and Whipsnade *St Alb* 97-03; rtd 03; PtO *Wakef* 05-10. *2 Half Moon Cottage, Harewood Road, Collingham, Wetherby LS22 5BL* T: (01937) 579816

LANE, Malcolm Clifford George. b 48. JP. ACIB. St D Coll Lamp. **d** 02 **p** 05. Par Dn Abergavenny St Mary w Llanwenarth Citra *Mon* 02-08; P-in-c Michaelston-y-Fedw 08-14; Asst Chapl Gwent Healthcare NHS Trust 02-14; rtd 14. *14 Coed y Brennin, Llantilio Pertholey, Abergavenny NP7 6PY* E: st8711@msn.com

LANE, Martin Guy. b 70. Oak Hill Th Coll BA 08. **d** 08 **p** 09. C Herne Bay Ch Ch *Cant* 08-12; V Hastings Em and St Mary in the Castle *Chich* from 12. *Emmanuel Vicarage, Vicarage Road, Hastings TN34 3NA* T: (01424) 272395 M: 07765-861939 E: martlane@hotmail.com *or* martin@emmanuelhastings.org.uk

LANE, Martin John. b 69. Open Univ BSc 03 Cardiff Univ LLM 08. Coll of Resurr Mirfield 92. **d** 95 **p** 96. C Liss *Portsm* 95-98; C Stamford and Leigh Park 98-00; TV Littlehampton and Wick *Chich* 00-04; P-in-c Harting w Elsted and Treyford cum Didling 04-10; RD Midhurst 06-10; V Bosham from 10; RD Westbourne from 15. *The Vicarage, Bosham Lane, Bosham, Chichester PO18 8HX* T: (01243) 573228 E: martinjlane@btinternet.com

LANE, Mrs Pamela. b 44. **d** 00 **p** 01. OLM Betley *Lich* 00-15; PtO from 15. *Brandon, Main Road, Betley, Crewe CW3 9BH* T: (01270) 820258

LANE, Richard Peter. b 60. Linc Th Coll 85. **d** 88 **p** 89. C Towcester w Easton Neston *Pet* 88-91; Asst Chapl Oslo w Bergen, Trondheim, Stavanger etc *Eur* 91-93; V Writtle w Highwood *Chelmsf* 93-99; Chapl Whitelands Coll Roehampton Inst *S'wark* 99-03; P-in-c W Wimbledon Ch Ch 03-04; V from 04; AD Merton from 12. *The Vicarage, 16 Copse Hill, London SW20 0HG* T: (020) 8946 4491

LANE, Robert David. b 66. St Steph Ho Ox 05. **d** 07 **p** 08. C Corringham *Chelmsf* 07-10; V Petts Wood *Roch* from 10. *St Francis's Vicarage, 60 Willett Way, Orpington BR5 1QE* T: (01689) 829971 M: 07807-224748 E: robert.lane2@virgin.net

LANE, Ms Rosalind Anne. b 69. Trevelyan Coll Dur BA 91 Heythrop Coll Lon MTh 93 Man Univ MA 01. Westcott Ho Cam. **d** 95 **p** 96. C Huddersfield St Pet and All SS *Wakef* 95-99; Sub Chapl HM Pris and YOI New Hall 97-99; Asst Chapl HM Pris and YOI Doncaster 99-01; Chapl 01; Chapl HM Pris Wymott 01-05; Kirkham 05-08; Whitemoor 08-11; Ashwell 11; Chapl N Essex Partnership NHS Foundn Trust 11-12; Chapl Cambs and Pet NHS Foundn Trust 12-15; Chapl Peterborough and Stamford Hosps NHS Foundn Trust 12-15; Chapl K Ely from 15. *King's, Barton Road, Ely CB7 4EW* T: (01353) 660700 E: rosalind.lane@cpft.nhs.uk

LANE, Roy Albert. b 42. Bris Sch of Min 82. **d** 85 **p** 86. NSM Bedminster *Bris* 85-97; PtO 97-02; NSM Bishopsworth and Bedminster Down from 02. *20 Ashton Drive, Bristol BS3 2PW* T: 0117-983 0747 M: 07747-808972 E: roypeg@blueyonder.co.uk

LANE, Simon. *See* DOUGLAS LANE, Charles Simon Pellew

LANE, Stuart Alexander Rhys. *See* LANE, Alexander John

LANE, Terry. b 50. STETS 94. **d** 97 **p** 98. NSM Freemantle *Win* 97-99; Chapl HM Pris Kingston (Portsm) 99-01; Chapl HM Pris Parkhurst 01-06; Co-ord Chapl HM Pris Win 06-10; r-d 10; PtO *Win* from 10. *24 Claremont Crescent, Southampton SO15 4GS*

LANE, William Henry Howard. b 63. Bris Poly BA 85. Trin Coll Bris 00. **d** 02 **p** 03. C Frome H Trin *B & W* 02-06; P-in-c Woolavington w Cossington and Bawdrip 06-08; R 09-11; RD Sedgemoor 09-11; V Bridgwater H Trin and Durleigh

from 11. *The New Vicarage, Hamp Avenue, Bridgwater TA6 6AN* T: (01278) 455022 E: reverend.lane@googlemail.com

LANG, Geoffrey Wilfrid Francis. b 33. St Jo Coll Ox BA 56 MA 61. Cuddesdon Coll 56. **d** 58 **p** 59. C Spalding St Mary and St Nic *Linc* 58-61; Asst Chapl Leeds Univ *Ripon* 61-62; C Chesterton St Luke *Ely* 62-63; C-in-c Chesterton Gd Shep CD 63-69; V Chesterton Gd Shep 69-72; V Willian *St Alb* 72-76; Dioc Dir of Educn 72-76; R N Lynn w St Marg and St Nic *Nor* 77-86; V Hammersmith St Pet *Lon* 86-00; rtd 00. *53A Ridgmount Gardens, London WC1E 7AU* T: (020) 7580 4692

LANG, Nicholas. b 45. SEITE 94. **d** 97 **p** 98. NSM Beckenham St Jo *Roch* 97-98; NSM Penge Lane H Trin 98-01; Chapl St Chris Hospice Lon 00; V Beckenham St Jo *Roch* 01-12; rtd 12; PtO *S'wark* from 13; *Roch* from 13. *23 Hayes Chase, West Wickham BR4 0HU* T: (020) 8650 6151 M: 07506-106360 E: niklang23@gmail.com

LANG, William David. b 51. K Coll Lon BD 74 MA 94 AKC 74. St Aug Coll Cant 74. **d** 75 **p** 76. C Fleet *Guildf* 75-79; C Ewell St Fran 79-82; C W Ewell 79-82; V Holmwood 82-92; R Elstead 92-10; V Thursley 92-10; P-in-c Redhorn *Sarum* 10-12; P-in-c Bishop's Cannings, All Cannings etc 11-12; TR The Cannings and Redhorn from 12. *The Rectory, High Street, Urchfont, Devizes SN10 4QP* T: (01380) 840672 E: william@lang.net

LANGAN, Mrs Eleanor Susan. b 56. Homerton Coll Cam BEd 78. Ripon Coll Cuddesdon 84. **d** 87 **p** 94. Hon Par Dn Grays Thurrock *Chelmsf* 87-89; LtO 89-94; NSM Creeksea w Althorne, Latchingdon and N Fambridge 94-95; NSM S Woodham Ferrers 95-99; NSM Overstrand, Northrepps, Sidestrand etc *Nor* 99-03; Chapl Norfolk and Nor Univ Hosp NHS Trust 00-10; Lead Chapl from 10. *Norfolk and Norwich Univ Hospital, Colney Lane, Cromer NR4 7UY* T: (01603) 287470 E: eleanor.langan@nnuh.nhs.uk

LANGAN, Michael Leslie. b 54. Cam Univ BA PGCE. Cranmer Hall Dur. **d** 84 **p** 85. C Grays Thurrock *Chelmsf* 84-89; R Creeksea w Althorne, Latchingdon and N Fambridge 89-95; RD Maldon and Dengie 92-95; P-in-c S Woodham Ferrers 95-99; R Overstrand, Northrepps, Sidestrand etc *Nor* 99-11; RD Repps 05-10; PtO 11-12; P-in-c Gt and Lt Ellingham, Rockland and Shropham etc 12-15; R from 15. *The Rectory, 2 Rectory Lane, Great Ellingham, Attleborough NR17 1LD* T: (01953) 455657 E: shellrock5555@btinternet.com

LANGDON, John Bonsall. b 21. Linc Coll Ox BA 51 MA 55. Ripon Hall Ox 52. **d** 54 **p** 55. C Erith St Jo *Roch* 54-57; C Christchurch *Win* 57-60; Min Can Ripon Cathl 60-63; R Swillington 63-75; P-in-c Wrangthorn 75-76; V Leeds All Hallows w St Simon 75-76; V Leeds All Hallows w Wrangthorn 76-87; P-in-c Woodhouse St Mark 85-87; V Woodhouse and Wrangthorn 87-92; rtd 92; PtO *Leeds* from 92; Hon Min Can Ripon Cathl from 02. *32 Magdalen's Road, Ripon HG4 1HT* T: (01765) 606814

LANGDON, Ms Susan Mary. b 48. RN 69. Ripon Coll Cuddesdon 01. **d** 03 **p** 04. C Amesbury *Sarum* 03-06; Jt Ldr Pilgrimage Community of St Wite from 06. *St Wite House, Whitchurch Canonicorum, Bridport DT6 6RQ* T: (01297) 489401 E: suelangdon@btinternet.com

LANGDON-DAVIES, Mrs Stella Mary. b 44. Bris Univ BSc 85 Nottm Univ MBA 97. St Jo Coll Nottm MTh 01. **d** 01 **p** 02. C Stamford All SS w St Jo *Linc* 01-04; V Herne *Cant* 04-06; P-in-c Saxonwell *Linc* 06-08; rtd 08; PtO *Leic* from 14. *5 Manor Paddock, Allington, Grantham NG32 2DL* T: (01400) 281395 M: 07976-380659 E: stellalangdondavies@btinternet.com

LANGDON-GRIFFITHS, Daniel Steven. b 82. St Jo Coll Dur BA 14. Cranmer Hall Dur 11. **d** 14 **p** 15. C Sutton *Liv* from 14. *80 Waterdale Crescent, St Helens WA9 3PD* T: (01744) 605362 M: 07411-795237 E: griff_200@hotmail.com

LANGDOWN, Jennifer May. b 48. STETS 95. **d** 98 **p** 99. C S Petherton w The Seavingtons *B & W* 98-02; R Curry Rivel w Fivehead and Swell 02-12; rtd 12. *61 Vereland Road, Hutton, Weston-super-Mare BS24 9TH* T: (01934) 815499 - M: 07850-245948 E: mrsvic7548@gmail.com

LANGE-SMITH, Michael Leslie. b 56. Bris Univ BSc 83 Lon Bible Coll MA 90. Trin Coll Bris 87. **d** 90 **p** 91. C Greendale Zimbabwe 90-92; R Melfort 93-98; Dir Th Educn by Ext Coll of Zimbabwe 99-02; R Chinnor, Sydenham, Aston Rowant and Crowell *Ox* 03-05; P-in-c Jersey Grouville *Win* 05-06; R from 06. *The Rectory, La Rue à Don, Grouville, Jersey JE3 9GB* T: (01534) 853073

LANGERHUIZEN, Sandra Marilyn. b 45. **d** 11 **p** 12. NSM Birkenhead St Jas w St Bede *Ches* 11-15; rtd 15; PtO *Ches* from 15. *43 Shamrock Road, Birkenhead CH41 0EG* T: 0151-652 3109 E: w.langerhuizen@btinternet.com

LANGFORD, Mrs Carol Mary. b 60. Southn Univ BTh 93 MTh 97 SS Mark & Jo Univ Coll Plymouth PGCE 06. STETS 03. **d** 06 **p** 07. C Parkstone St Pet and St Osmund w

Branksea *Sarum* 06-09; C Lilliput 09-10; P-in-c 10-14; V from 14; Chapl Talbot Heath Sch Bournemouth 09-12. *The Vicarage, 55 Lilliput Road, Poole BH14 8JX* T: (01202) 708567 E: carol.langford1@btinternet.com

LANGFORD, David Laurence. b 51. d 88 p 89. OLM Scotton w Northorpe *Linc* from 88. *1 Westgate, Scotton, Gainsborough DN21 3QX* T: (01724) 763139

LANGFORD, Prof Michael John. b 31. New Coll Ox BA 54 MA 58 Cam Univ MA 59 Lon Univ PhD 66. Westcott Ho Cam 55. d 56 p 57. C Bris St Nath w St Kath 56-59; Chapl Qu Coll Cam 59-63; C Hampstead St Jo *Lon* 63-67; Philosophy Dept Memorial Univ Newfoundland 67-96; Prof Philosophy 82-96; Prof Medical Ethics 87-96; rtd 96; PtO *Ely* from 96. *19 High Street, Dry Drayton, Cambridge CB23 8BS* T: (01954) 789593 E: ml297@hermes.cam.ac.uk

LANGFORD, Peter Francis. b 54. Sarum & Wells Th Coll 76. d 79 p 80. C N Ormesby *York* 79-82; Ind Chapl 83-91; V Middlesbrough St Chad 91-96; R Easington w Liverton 96-07; rtd 07. *17 The Cranbrooks, Wheldrake, York YO19 6AZ* T: (01904) 448944 E: peterlangford444@gmail.com

LANGFORD, Peter Julian. b 33. Selw Coll Cam BA 58. Westcott Ho Cam 59. d 60 p 61. C E Ham St Mary *Chelmsf* 60-67; Hon C 67-68; Hon C E Ham w Upton Park 68-71; Hon C Beccles St Mich *St E* 71-76; Warden Ringsfield Hall Suffolk 71-87; P-in-c Ringsfield w Redisham *St E* 76-80; TV Seacroft *Ripon* 87-98; rtd 98; PtO *St E* from 99. *22 Alexander Road, Beccles NR34 9UD* T: (01502) 710034

LANGHAM, Paul Jonathan. b 60. Ex Univ BA 81 Fitzw Coll Cam BA 86 MA 91. Ridley Hall Cam 84. d 87 p 88. C Bath Weston All SS w N Stoke *B & W* 87-91; Chapl and Fell St Cath Coll Cam 91-96; V Combe Down w Monkton Combe and S Stoke *B & W* 96-10; P-in-c Clifton Ch Ch w Em *Bris* 10-15; V from 15. *Christ Church Clifton Church Office, Linden Gate, Clifton Down Road, Bristol BS8 4AH* T: 0117-973 6524 E: paul.langham@ccweb.org.uk

LANGILLE, Canon Melvin Owen. b 58. St Mary's Univ Halifax NS BA 79. Atlantic Sch of Th MDiv 82. d 82 p 83. Dn-in-c Falkland Canada 82; R Lockeport and Barrington 83-86; R French Village 87-90; R Cole Harbour St Andr 90-96; R Yarmouth H Trin 97-03; P-in-c Brora *Mor* 03-09; P-in-c Dornoch 03-09; R Arpafeelie from 09; R Cromarty from 09; R Fortrose from 09; Syn Clerk and Can St Andr Cathl Inverness from 07; Dioc Dir of Ords from 08. *The Rectory, 1 Deans Road, Fortrose IV10 8TJ* T: (01381) 622241 M: 07780-512990 E: mel@langille.freeserve.co.uk

LANGLANDS, John. Qu Coll Birm. d 15. C Allesley Park and Whoberley *Cov* from 15. *Address temp unknown*

LANGLEY, Ms Emma Louise. b 70. Bris Univ BA 93 MA 98. STETS 01. d 03 p 04. C Horfield H Trin *Bris* 03-07; P-in-c Westbury-on-Trym St Alb from 07; Min Westbury Park LEP from 07. *St Alban's Vicarage, 21 Canowie Road, Bristol BS6 7HR* T: 0117-951 9771 M: 07974-658619 E: emmalang@aol.com

LANGLEY, Jean. See PHILLIPS, Jean

LANGLEY, Canon Myrtle Sarah. b 39. TCD BA 61 HDipEd 62 MA 67 Bris Univ PhD 76 Lon Univ BD 66 FRAI. Dalton Ho Bris 64. d 88 p 94. Dir Chr Development for Miss *Liv* 87-89; Dir Dioc Tr Inst *Carl* 90-98; Dioc Dir of Tr 90-98; Hon Can Carl Cathl 91-98; P-in-c Long Marton w Dufton and w Milburn 98-06; rtd 06; PtO *Carl* from 07. *Grania, 5 Farbrow Road, Carlisle CA1 3HW* T: (01228) 539291 E: canonmlangley@hotmail.com

LANGLEY, The Ven Robert. b 37. St Cath Soc Ox BA 61. St Steph Ho Ox. d 63 p 64. C Aston cum Aughton *Sheff* 63-68; Midl Area Sec Chr Educn Movement 68-71; HQ Sec Chr Educn Movement 71-74; Prin Ian Ramsey Coll Brasted 74-77; Can Res St Alb and Dir St Alb Minl Tr Scheme 77-85; Can Res Newc Cathl 85-01; Dioc Missr 85-98; Dioc Dir of Min and Tr 98-01; Adn Lindisfarne 01-07; Local Min Development Officer 01-07; rtd 08; PtO *York* from 09. *Brook House, Middlewood Lane, Fylingthorpe, Whitby YO22 4TT* T: (01947) 880355 E: r.langley648@btinternet.com

LANGMAN, Barry Edward. b 46. RD. Master Mariner 73. Cant Sch of Min 87. d 90 p 91. NSM St Margarets-at-Cliffe w Westcliffe etc *Cant* 90-92; C Sandgate St Paul w Folkestone St Geo 92-95; P-in-c Headcorn 95-01; V 01-08; rtd 08; PtO *Cant* 08-14. *Address temp unknown*

LANGRELL, Gordon John. b 35. Cant Univ (NZ) BA 58. Ridley Hall Cam 65. d 67 p 68. C Tonbridge SS Pet and Paul *Roch* 67-71; New Zealand from 71; rtd 05. *11A Henry Wigram Drive, Hornby, Christchurch 8042, New Zealand* T: (0064) (3) 348 9554 E: gorlang@paradise.net.nz

✠**LANGRISH, The Rt Revd Michael Laurence.** b 46. Birm Univ BSocSc 67 Fitzw Coll Cam BA 73 MA 77 Ex Univ Hon DD 07. Ridley Hall Cam 71. d 73 p 74 c 93. C Stratford-on-Avon w Bishopton *Cov* 73-76; Chapl Rugby Sch 76-81; P-in-c Offchurch *Cov* 81-87; Dioc Dir of Ords 81-87; P-in-c Rugby

87-91; Hon Can Cov Cathl 90-93; TR Rugby 91-93; Suff Bp Birkenhead *Ches* 93-00; Bp Ex 00-13; rtd 13; Hon Asst Bp Chich from 13. *39 The Meadows, Walberton, Arundel BN18 0PB* T: (01243) 551704 E: langrishm@btinternet.com

✠**LANGSTAFF, The Rt Revd James Henry.** b 56. St Cath Coll Ox BA 77 MA 81 Nottm Univ BA 80. St Jo Coll Nottm 78. d 81 p 82 c 04. C Farnborough *Guildf* 81-84 and 85-86; P-in-c 84-85; P-in-c Duddeston w Nechells *Birm* 86; V 87-96; RD Birm City 95-96; Bp's Dom Chapl 96-00; P-in-c Short Heath 98-00; R Sutton Coldfield H Trin 00-04; AD Sutton Coldfield 02-04; Suff Bp Lynn *Nor* 04-10; Bp Roch from 10; Bp HM Pris from 13. *Bishopscourt, 24 St Margaret's Street, Rochester ME1 1TS* T: (01634) 842721 F: 831136 E: bishop.rochester@rochester.anglican.org

LANGSTON, Clinton Matthew. b 62. Derby Coll of Educn BCombStuds 86. Qu Coll Birm 87. d 90 p 91. C Shirley *Birm* 90-94; CF from 94. *c/o MOD Chaplains (Army)* F: 381824 T: (01264) 383430

LANGTON, Robert. b 45. SAOMC 97. d 00 p 01. C Boyne Hill *Ox* 00-03; Chapl St Mich Hospice 03-08; TV Cwmbran *Mon* 08-15; Hon C from 15; rtd 15. *The Vicarage, 87 Bryn Eglwys, Croesyceiliog, Cwmbran NP44 2LF* T: (01633) 483945 E: robertlangton.langton@gmail.com

LANHAM, Geoffrey Peter. b 62. Cam Univ MA 84 Ox Univ MPhil 86. Wycliffe Hall Ox 86. d 89 p 90. C Southborough St Pet w Ch Ch and St Matt *Roch* 89-92; C Harborne Heath *Birm* 92-00; C Birm St Paul 00-07; Deanery Missr 00-09; C Birm Cathl 07-09; V Selly Park Ch Ch from 09. *16 Over Mill Drive, Selly Park, Birmingham B29 7JL* T: 0121-472 7074 E: geoff@b1church.net

LANHAM, Richard Paul White. b 42. Dur Univ BA 64. Wycliffe Hall Ox 65. d 67 p 68. C Gerrards Cross *Ox* 67-69; C Horwich H Trin *Man* 69-72; C Worsley 72-74; V Accrington St Andr *Blackb* 74-80; V Shillington *St Alb* 80-85; V Upper w Lower Gravenhurst 80-85; rtd 85; PtO *St Alb* from 85. *10 Alexander Close, Clifton, Shefford SG17 5RB* T: (01462) 813520

LANKESTER, Mrs Jane Elizabeth. b 53. Qu Mary Coll Lon BScEcon 74 SS Mark & Jo Univ Coll Plymouth MA 04. SWMTC 05. d 08 p 09. NSM Totnes w Bridgetown, Berry Pomeroy etc *Ex* 08-12; TV Honiton, Gittisham, Combe Raleigh, Monkton etc from 12. *The Vicarage, Awliscombe, Honiton EX14 3PJ* T: (01404) 234088 E: jane.lankester@gmail.com

LANKSHEAR, Jane Frances. See MAINWARING, Jane Frances

LANSDALE, Canon Charles Roderick. b 38. Leeds Univ BA 59. Coll of Resurr Mirfield 59. d 61 p 62. C Nunhead St Antony *S'wark* 61-65; Swaziland 65-71; V Benhilton *S'wark* 72-78; TR Catford (Southend) and Downham 78-87; TR Moulsecoomb *Chich* 87-97; V Eastbourne St Mary 97-08; Can and Preb Chich Cathl 98-08; rtd 08; PtO *Chich* from 08. *102 Channel View Road, Eastbourne BN22 7LJ* T: (01323) 646655

LANYON-HOGG, Mrs Anne Chester. b 49. St Anne's Coll Ox BA 71 MA 75 Worc Coll of Educn PGCE 92. WEMTC 01. d 04 p 05. NSM Colwall w Upper Colwall and Coddington *Heref* from 04; NSM Malvern H Trin and St Jas *Worc* from 07; Bp's Adv for SSM *Heref* from 15. *7 Lockyear Close, Colwall, Malvern WR13 6NR* T: (01684) 541979 M: 07890-995297 E: annelh@stillanne.org

LANYON JONES, Keith. b 49. Southn Univ BTh 79. Sarum & Wells Th Coll 74. d 77 p 78. C Charlton Kings St Mary *Glouc* 77-81; Sen Chapl Rugby Sch 81-99; LtO *Truro* 83-00; P-in-c St Cleer 00-15; C St Ive and Pensilva w Quethiock 02-15; Chapl Kelly Coll Tavistock from 08. *Address temp unknown* E: lanyon67@hotmail.com

LAPAGE, Michael Clement. b 23. Selw Coll Cam BA 47 MA 73. Clifton Th Coll 60. d 61 p 62. C Weithaga Kenya 61-65; V Nanyuki 65-72; Chapl Bedford Sch 73-75; Chapl Lyon w Grenoble *Eur* 76-79; V Walford w Bishopswood *Heref* 79-88; P-in-c Goodrich w Welsh Bicknor and Marstow 83-88; rtd 88; PtO *Ex* from 88. *Flat 3, 60 Plymouth Road, Tavistock PL19 8BU* T: (01822) 615949

LAPWOOD, Robin Rowland John. b 57. Selw Coll Cam MA. Ridley Hall Cam 80. d 82 p 83. C Bury St Edmunds St Mary *St E* 82-86; P-in-c Bentley w Tattingstone 86-93; P-in-c Copdock w Washbrook and Belstead 86-93; TV High Wycombe *Ox* 93-96; P-in-c Marcham w Garford 96-02; Chapl Summer Fields Sch Ox 02-12; PtO *Ox* from 12. *Address temp unknown* E: robin.lapwood@gmail.com

LARCOMBE, Paul Richard. b 57. Portsm Poly BSc 79 CEng MIET. Trin Coll Bris 94. d 96 p 97. C Werrington *Pet* 96-98; C Longthorpe 98-00; V Pet St Paul 00-07; TR Worle *B & W* from 07. *The Vicarage, 93 Church Road, Worle, Weston-super-Mare BS22 9EA* T: (01934) 510694 E: plarcombe@mac.com

LARGE, William Roy. b 40. Dur Univ BA DipEd. Edin Th Coll 82. d 84 p 85. C Leamington Priors All SS *Cov* 84-88; V Bishop's Tachbrook 88-99; Warden of Readers and Sen Tutor 88-99;

TV N Tyne and Redesdale *Newc* 99-01; TR 01-05; rtd 05. *4 Osborne Court, Osborne Avenue, Newcastle upon Tyne NE2 1LE* T: 0191-281 1894

LARK, William Donald Starling. b 35. Keble Coll Ox BA 59 MA 63. Wells Th Coll 59. **d** 61 **p** 62. C Wyken *Cov* 61-64; C Christchurch *Win* 64-66; V Yeovil St Mich *B & W* 66-75; V Earley St Pet *Ox* 75-85; V Prittlewell *Chelmsf* 85-88; V Dawlish *Ex* 88-00; rtd 00; P-in-c Lanzarote *Eur* 00-05. *Las Alondras, 6 Cummings Court, Cummings Cross, Liverton, Newton Abbot TQ12 6HJ* T: (01626) 824966
E: lanzalarks2000@yahoo.co.uk

LARKEY, Mrs Deborah Frances. b 63. Univ of Wales (Abth) BA 85 Liv Inst of Educn PGCE 90. **d** 98 **p** 99. OLM Toxteth St Cypr w Ch Ch *Liv* 98-01; OLM Edge Hill St Cypr w St Mary 01-04; C Netherton 04-07; TV Vale of Pewsey *Sarum* 07-11; TR from 11. *The Vicarage, Church Road, Woodborough, Pewsey SN9 5PH* T: (01672) 851746
E: deborahlarkey@btinternet.com

LARKIN, Andrew Brian. b 70. Warwick Univ BEng 92 PhD 95. Trin Coll Bris BA 06. **d** 06 **p** 07. C Littleover *Derby* 06-08; C Brailsford w Shirley, Osmaston w Edlaston etc 08-10; R Fenny Bentley, Thorpe, Tissington, Parwich etc from 10; RD Ashbourne from 12. *The Vicarage, Parwich, Ashbourne DE6 1QD* T: (01335) 390226 M: 07758-704452
E: andy@larkin.me.uk *or* andy@peakfive.org

LARKIN, Mrs Karen Maria. b 74. Qu Coll Birm BA 08. **d** 08 **p** 09. C Coleshill and Maxstoke *Birm* 08-12; Chapl Lon City YMCA from 12. *116 Damsonwood Road, Southall UB2 4RW* M: 07956-923653 E: karen_larkin@hotmail.co.uk

LARKIN, Lucy. b 66. Birm Univ BA 87 MPhil 91 PhD 01 Westmr Coll Ox PGCE 89. **d** 08 **p** 09. C Hawthorn Australia 08-10; C St Pet Cathl Adelaide 10-11; Tutor SWMTC from 13; PtO *Truro* 13-14; Public Preacher from 14. *3 The Cedars, Truro TR1 2FD* T: (01872) 241716 M: 07757-917473
E: lucylarkin@swmtc.org.uk

LARKIN, Canon Peter John. b 39. ALCD 62. **d** 62 **p** 63. C Liskeard w St Keyne *Truro* 62-65; C Rugby St Andr *Cov* 65-67; Sec Bp Cov Call to Miss 67-68; V Kea *Truro* 68-78; P-in-c Bromsgrove St Jo *Worc* 78-81; R Torquay St Matthias, St Mark and H Trin *Ex* 81-97; Can Sokoto Nigeria 91-98; Can Kaduna from 98; TR Plymouth Em, St Paul Efford and St Aug *Ex* 97-00; rtd 00; PtO *Ex* from 00. *Picklecombe, 57 Babbacombe Downs Road, Torquay TQ1 3LP* T: (01803) 326888
E: mollypeterlarkin@tiscali.co.uk

LARKIN, Simon George David. b 69. Birm Univ BSocSc 90 PGCE 91 Reading Univ MA 96. Trin Coll Bris BTh 09. **d** 09 **p** 10. C Kensington St Barn *Lon* 09-14; P-in-c Hastings H Trin *Chich* from 14. *31 Amhurst Road, Hastings TN34 1TT* M: 07954-600258 E: siandsair@gmail.com

LARKIN, Mrs Susan Jane. b 52. MBE 07. Qu Foundn (Course) 10. **d** 12 **p** 13. NSM Garretts Green and Tile Cross *Birm* from 12. *48 Horrell Road, Birmingham B26 2PD* T: 0121-574 3152 E: susanjlarkin@hotmail.co.uk

LARLEE, David Alexander. b 78. Univ of W Ontario MA 01. Wycliffe Hall Ox BTh 04. **d** 04 **p** 05. NSM Battersea Rise St Mark *S'wark* 04-13; USA from 13. *8815 Tudor Place, Dallas, TX 75228, USA* E: david.larlee@gmail.com

LARNER, Gordon Edward Stanley. b 30. Brasted Th Coll 54 Oak Hill Th Coll 55. **d** 59 **p** 60. C Peckham St Mary Magd *S'wark* 59-62; C Luton w E Hyde *St Alb* 62-68; V Lower Sydenham St Mich *S'wark* 68-73; Ind Chapl 73-84; Chapl HM Pris Ranby 84-92; rtd 92. *Glen Rosa, Meshaw, South Molton EX36 4NE*

LARSEN, Clive Erik. b 55. St Jo Coll Nottm 88. **d** 90 **p** 91. C Weaverham *Ches* 90-92; C Alvanley and Helsby and Dunham-on-the-Hill 92-95; P-in-c Cheadle Heath 95-02; P-in-c N Reddish *Man* from 05; P-in-c Heaton Reddish from 14. *The Rectory, 551 Gorton Road, Stockport SK5 6NX* T: 0161-223 0692 M: 07789-915263
E: clive.larsen@ntlworld.com

LASKEY, Cyril Edward. b 44. RMN 71 RGN 74. Llan Dioc Tr Scheme 85. **d** 88 **p** 89. NSM Troedrhiwgarth *Llan* 88-93; NSM Caerau St Cynfelin 94-01; P-in-c Glyncorrwg and Upper Afan Valley 01-10; rtd 10; PtO *Llan* from 11. *207 Bridgend Road, Maesteg CF34 0NL* T: (01656) 734639

LASKEY, Stephen Allan. b 56. Manitoba Univ BA 85. St Jo Coll Winnipeg MDiv 88. **d** 89 **p** 89. C Labrador W Canada 89; C Battle Harbour 89-91; V Goulds St Paul 96-99; Assoc P Foxtrap All SS 00-01; C Paddington St Jo w St Mich *Lon* 01-02; P-in-c Sydenham H Trin *S'wark* 02-07; P-in-c Forest Hill St Aug 03-07; V Sydenham H Trin and St Aug 07-09; R Dartmouth Ch Ch Canada from 09. *172 Green Village Lane, Dartmouth NS B2Y 4V4, Canada*
E: stephenlaskey@onetel.com

LASLETT, Christopher John. b 42. Leeds Univ BA 64 Lon Univ PGCE 73. Lich Th Coll 64. **d** 66 **p** 67. C Bradf St Clem 66-69; C Upper Armley *Ripon* 69-70; PtO *Dur* 71-72; Hon C Stranton

79-81; PtO *Ripon* 87-88; rtd 07. *20 Richmond Street, Bridlington YO15 3DJ* T: (01262) 671527 E: mfl@ntlworld.com

LAST, Eric Cyril. b 30. Oak Hill Th Coll 77. **d** 79 **p** 80. C Wandsworth All SS *S'wark* 79-83; V Earlsfield St Andr 83-88; V S Merstham 88-96; Asst RD Reigate 92-96; rtd 96; Hon C Upper Tean *Lich* 96-10; PtO from 10. *29 Vicarage Road, Tean, Stoke-on-Trent ST10 4LE* T/F: (01538) 723551
E: eric.last1@btopenworld.com

LAST, Mrs Estella Ruth. b 76. Brunel Univ LLB 98. SEITE 11. **d** 14 **p** 15. C Herne *Cant* from 14. *2 Bridle Way, Herne Bay CT6 7PQ* T: (01227) 503093 M: 07951-607334
E: estellalast@gmail.com

LAST, Michael Leonard Eric. b 60. St Jo Coll Nottm 92. **d** 94 **p** 95. C Tettenhall Wood *Lich* 94-98; V Pelsall 98-02; V Alton w Bradley-le-Moors and Oakamoor w Cotton 02-09; P-in-c Mayfield and Denstone w Ellastone and Stanton 06-09; I Saskatchewan Gateway Canada 09-11; R Adderley, Ash, Calverhall, Ightfield etc *Lich* from 11. *The Rectory, Moreton Say, Market Drayton TF9 3RS* T: (01630) 638054 M: 07510-179425
E: rev.last@btinternet.com *or* michael.last@amica.org.uk

LATHAM, Christine Elizabeth. b 46. S'wark Ord Course 87. **d** 90 **p** 94. Par Dn Battersea St Pet and St Paul *S'wark* 90-94; Par Dn S'wark Ch Ch 94; C 94-97; C Merstham and Gatton 97-05; Chapl E Surrey Learning Disability NHS Trust 97-05; Chapl R Marsden NHS Foundn Trust 05-10; rtd 10; PtO *S'wark* from 10. *4 Bromley College, London Road, Bromley BR1 1PE* T: (020) 3489 7213 E: christine.latham@talktalk.net

LATHAM, Henry Nicholas Lomax. b 64. Reading Univ BA 86. Wycliffe Hall Ox BTh 93. **d** 93 **p** 94. C Aberystwyth *St D* 93-99; P-in-c Stoke Poges *Ox* 99-08; V from 08. *The Vicarage, Park Road, Stoke Poges, Slough SL2 4PE* T: (01753) 642261
E: isaiah61@uwclub.net

LATHAM, John Montgomery. b 37. Univ of NZ BA Cam Univ MA Cant Univ (NZ) MEd. Westcott Ho Cam 60. **d** 62 **p** 63. C Camberwell St Geo *S'wark* 62-65; Chapl Trin Coll Cam 65-70; Chapl Wanganui Colleg Sch New Zealand 71-79; Min Enabler New Brighton 96-01; V Christchurch St Luke 98-02; rtd 02. *43 Rugby Street, Christchurch 8014, New Zealand* T: (0064) (3) 355 6654 F: 355 6658 E: latham@xtra.co.nz

LATHAM, Robert Norman. b 53. Qu Coll Birm 82. **d** 85 **p** 86. C Tamworth *Lich* 85-89; TV Wordsley *Worc* 89-96; P-in-c Hallow 96-97; R Hallow and Grimley w Holt from 97. *Hallow Vicarage, 26 Baveney Road, Worcester WR2 6DS* T: (01905) 748711 E: robert@hallowvicarage.freeserve.co.uk

LATHAM, Roger Allonby. b 69. Leic Univ BA 90 Warwick Univ MA 92 Leeds Univ PGCE 93 Nottm Univ PhD 07. St Jo Coll Nottm BTh 98. **d** 99 **p** 00. C Paston *Pet* 99-02; TV Cartmel Peninsula *Carl* 02-09; Officer for IME 4-7 from 08; Vice-Prin LCTP and C Beacon from 09. *St George's Vicarage, 3 Firbank, Kendal LA9 6EG* T: (01539) 738480
E: rogerlatham54@aol.com

LATHAM (née WEBSTER), Mrs Rosamond Mary. b 54. Coll of Ripon & York St Jo BEd 90 MA 00. Westcott Ho Cam 00. **d** 02 **p** 03. C Frodingham *Linc* 02-05; TV Dur N 05-07; TV Dorchester *Ox* 07-13; P-in-c Alford w Rigsby *Linc* from 13. *The Vicarage, 15 Bilsby Road, Alford LN13 9EW* M: 07779-784320

LATHAM, Trevor Martin. b 56. BD 84. Ripon Coll Cuddesdon 84. **d** 86 **p** 87. C Cantril Farm *Liv* 86-89; TV Croxteth Park 89-98; V 98-99; TR Walton-on-the-Hill from 99. *Walton Cornertone, 2 Liston Street, Liverpool L4 5RT* T/F: 0151-525 3130 E: trevor.latham@talktalk.net

LATHE, Canon Anthony Charles Hudson. b 36. Jes Coll Ox BA 59 MA 64. Lich Th Coll 59. **d** 61 **p** 62. C Selby Abbey *York* 61-63; V Hempnall *Nor* 63-72; R Woodton w Bedingham 63-72; R Fritton w Morningthorpe w Shelton and Hardwick 63-72; R Topcroft 63-72; R Banham 72-76; TR Quidenham 76-83; P-in-c New Buckenham 78-79; V Heigham St Thos 83-94; Hon Can Nor Cathl 87-99; RD Nor S 90-94; P-in-c Sheringham 94-99; rtd 99; PtO *Nor* 99-06. *15A Kingsdale Road, Berkhamsted HP4 3BS* T: (01442) 863115

LATIFA, Andrew Murdoch. b 73. Univ of Wales (Abth) BTh 96 Univ of Wales (Cardiff) MTh 00. St Mich Coll Llan 99. **d** 01 **p** 02. C Betws w Ammanford *St D* 01-03; C Llangynwyd w Maesteg *Llan* 03-05; CF from 05. *c/o MOD Chaplains (Army)* F: 381824 T: (01264) 383430

LATIMER, Andrew John. b 78. Qu Coll Cam MA 04 Lon Univ MB, BS 05. Oak Hill Th Coll BTh 10. **d** 10 **p** 11. C Limehouse *Lon* from 10. *169 Wheat Sheaf Close, London E14 9UZ* M: 07740-287543 E: andrew@thelatimers.net *or* a.latimer@stpetersbarge.org

LATIMER, Clifford James. b 45. City Univ BSc 68. **d** 99 **p** 00. OLM Burntwood *Lich* 99-10; rtd 10; PtO *Lich* 11-14. *24 Dove Close, Burntwood WS7 9JL* T: (01543) 671471
E: cliff.latimer@btinternet.com

LATTEY, Susan. *See* CUMMING-LATTEY, Susan Mary Ruth

LATTIMER, Nicholas William. b 84. Leeds Univ BA 08. Trin Coll Bris 12. **d** 15. C Woodside *Leeds* from 15. *12 Beech Walk, Adel, Leeds LS16 8NY* M: 07912-321377 T: 0113-281 7309
E: nicklattimer@hotmail.com

LATTIMORE, Anthony Leigh. b 35. Dur Univ BA 57. Lich Th Coll 60. **d** 62 **p** 63. C Aylestone *Leic* 62-66; C-in-c Eyres Monsell CD 66-69; V Eyres Monsell 69-73; V Somerby, Burrough on the Hill and Pickwell 73-86; RD Goscote l 80-86; R Glenfield 86-95; rtd 95; PtO *Leic* from 95; *Pet* 95-11. *28 Elizabeth Way, Uppingham, Oakham LE15 9PQ* T: (01572) 823193

LATTY, Howard James. b 54. SRCh 71. WEMTC 98. **d** 01 **p** 02. NSM Bath St Mich w St Paul *B & W* 01-08; NSM Chewton Mendip w Ston Easton, Litton etc from 08. *The Rectory, Lower Street, Chewton Mendip, Radstock BA3 4GP* T: (01761) 241189
E: howard.latty@yahoo.co.uk

LAU, Paul Chow Sing. b 49. Nat Chengchi Univ BA 74 Chinese Univ of Hong Kong MDiv 80. **d** 80 **p** 81. C Hong Kong H Trin Hong Kong 80-82; V Macao St Mark Macao 82-83; P-in-c Hong Kong Ch of Our Sav Hong Kong 83-94; V Angl Chinese Miss Ch Dio Wellington New Zealand 94-01; Chapl Chinese Congregation *Lon* from 01. *3 Strutton Court, 54 Great Peter Street, London SW1P 2HH* T: (020) 7233 4027 *or* 7766 1106
E: paul.lau@smitf.org

LAUCKNER, Averil Ann. b 55. Lanc Univ BSc 76. Ripon Coll Cuddesdon 03. **d** 04 **p** 05. C Royston *St Alb* 04-07; C Lich Ch Ch and Lich St Mich w St Mary and Wall 07-09; P-in-c Lich Ch Ch 09-11; P-in-c Hatfield Hyde *St Alb* 11-14; V from 14. *St Mary Magdalene Vicarage, Hollybush Lane, Welwyn Garden City AL7 4JS* T: (01707) 322313
E: averil.lauckner@btinternet.com

LAUENER (née MULLINER), Angela Margaret. b 54. Collingwood Coll Dur BSc 75 Sheff City Poly MSc 91 Sheff Hallam Univ PhD. Yorks Min Course 12. **d** 14 **p** 15. NSM Ranmoor *Sheff* from 14. *82 Pingle Road, Sheffield S7 2LL* T: 0114-236 2188 M: 07949-403992
E: angielauener@me.com *or*
angela.lauener@sheffield.anglican.org

LAUGHTON, Derek Basil. b 24. Worc Coll Ox BA 49 MA 52. Westcott Ho Cam 49. **d** 51 **p** 52. C Wareham w Arne *Sarum* 51-53; CF 53-56; C Hemel Hempstead St Mary *St Alb* 56-59; V Stretton cum Wetmoor *Lich* 59-64; Chapl Wellington Sch Somerset 64-73; Chapl Ardingly Coll 73-77; R Plumpton w E Chiltington *Chich* 77-88; PtO *B & W* from 88; rtd 89. *13 Pyles Thorne Road, Wellington TA21 8DX* T: (01823) 667386

LAUNDON, Timothy James. b 83. CCC Cam MA 07 SS Coll Cam BTh 11. Westcott Ho Cam 09. **d** 12 **p** 13. C Wetherby *Leeds* from 12. *10 Victoria Avenue, Knaresborough HG5 9EU*
E: revtimlaundon@gmail.com

LAURENCE, The Ven John Harvard Christopher. b 29. Trin Hall Cam BA 53 MA 57. Westcott Ho Cam 53. **d** 55 **p** 56. C Linc St Nic w St Jo Newport 55-59; V Crosby 59-74; Can and Preb Linc Cathl 74-94 and 85-94; Dioc Missr 74-79; Bp's Dir of Clergy Tr *Lon* 80-85; Adn Lindsey *Linc* 85-94; rtd 94; PtO *Linc* 94-97. *5 Haffenden Road, Lincoln LN2 1RP* T: (01522) 531444

LAURENCE, John-Daniel. b 79. Mansf Coll Ox MPhys 02. Trin Coll Bris BA 09 MA 10. **d** 10 **p** 11. C Aberystwyth *St D* from 10. *Fenton, Queen's Square, Aberystwyth SY23 2HL* T: (01970) 624537 E: jd@stmikes.net

LAURENCE, Julian Bernard Vere. b 60. Kent Univ BA 82. St Steph Ho Ox 86. **d** 88 **p** 89. C Yeovil St Mich *B & W* 88-91; Chapl Yeovil Coll 90-91; Chapl Yeovil Distr Hosp 91; P-in-c Barwick *B & W* 91-94; V Taunton H Trin from 94; Dioc Adv in Deliverance Min from 14. *15 The Square, Hillyfields, Taunton TA1 2LU* E: jlaurence@htvicarage.fsnet.co.uk

LAURIE, Canon Donovan Hugh. b 40. Man Univ MSc. Oak Hill NSM Course. **d** 82 **p** 83. NSM Cudham and Downe *Roch* 82-84; C Tunbridge Wells St Jas 84-88; P-in-c Ventnor St Cath *Portsm* 88-99; V 99-04; P-in-c Ventnor H Trin 88-99; V 99-04; P-in-c Bonchurch 00-03; R 03-04; Hon Chapl St Cath Sch Ventnor 88-04; Hon Can Portsm Cathl 01-04; rtd 04; PtO *Roch* from 05. *39 Cleveland, Tunbridge Wells TN2 3NH* T: (01892) 539951 E: don@dlaurie.fsbusiness.co.uk

LAUT, Graham Peter. b 37. Chich Th Coll 63. **d** 67 **p** 68. C Corringham *Chelmsf* 67-68; C Leytonstone St Marg w St Columba 68-71; P-in-c Leytonstone St Andr 71-75; V 75-80; V Romford Ascension Collier Row 80-06; rtd 06; PtO *Chelmsf* from 07. *11 Archers Close, Billericay CM12 9YF* T: (01277) 630395
E: grahamlaut10497@btinternet.com

LAUTENBACH, Edward Wayne. b 59. Univ Coll Ches BTh 04. St Paul's Coll Grahamstown 85. **d** 88 **p** 88. C Weltevredenpark St Mich S Africa 88-89; Asst P Florida St Gabr 89-91; Sen Asst P Bryanston St Mich 91-94; R Brakpan St Pet 94-99; P-in-c Grange St Andr *Ches* 99-04; P-in-c Runcorn H Trin 99-04;

V Prenton from 04. *The Vicarage, 1 Vicarage Close, Birkenhead CH42 8QX* T: 0151-608 1808
E: waynelautenbach@gmail.com

LAUTENBACH, Mrs Glynnis Valerie. b 59. Leeds Univ BA 08. NOC 05. **d** 08 **p** 09. C Oxton *Ches* from 08. *The Vicarage, 1 Vicarage Close, Birkenhead CH42 8QX*
E: glynn.laut@gmail.com

LAVENDER, Christopher Piers. b 61. Ridley Hall Cam 08. **d** 10 **p** 11. C Headcorn and The Suttons *Cant* 10-13; P-in-c Allington and Maidstone St Pet from 13; P-in-c Barming Heath from 13. *The Rectory, Poplar Grove, Maidstone ME16 0DE* T: (01622) 299715 M: 07910-442247
E: chris_piers@yahoo.com

LAVERTY, Walter Joseph Robert. b 49. CITC 70 Glouc Th Course 73. **d** 73 **p** 74. C Belfast St Donard *D & D* 73-77; C Ballymacarrett St Patr 77-82; I Kilwarlin Upper w Kilwarlin Lower 82-86; I Orangefield w Moneyreagh 86-14; Warden of Readers 96-14; Can Down Cathl 97-00; Preb Down Cathl 97-00; Treas Down Cathl 01-14; rtd 14. *6 Hanwood Heights, Dundonald, Belfast BT16 1XU* T: (028) 9573 8743
E: barbaralaverty58@hotmail.com

LAVERY, Edward Robinson. Lon Univ BA. St Aid Birkenhead 65. **d** 67 **p** 68. C Belfast Trin Coll Miss *Conn* 67-69; C Belfast St Mary Magd 69-71; CF (TA) 70-95; OCM from 75; I Belfast St Phil *Conn* 71-74; I Craigs w Dunaghy and Killagan 74-83; I Ballymoney w Finvoy and Rasharkin 83-05; Dioc Info Officer 83-05; Can Conn Cathl 96-05; Treas Conn Cathl 98-01; Chan Conn Cathl 01-05; rtd 05; P-in-c Ballyscullion *D & R* from 09. *11 Drummallaght Park, Ballymoney BT53 7QZ* T: (028) 2766 9147

LAVIN, Alexandra Elizabeth. b 67. **d** 12 **p** 13. NSM Sheldon *Birm* from 12. *24 Ivyfield Road, Birmingham B23 7HH* T: 0121-384 5666 M: 07963-558242
E: alexlavin@hotmail.co.uk

LAW, Andrew Philip. b 61. BNC Ox BA 83 MA 93 G&C Coll Cam PGCE 86 Leic Univ MBA 04. WEMTC 90. **d** 93 **p** 94. C Tupsley w Hampton Bishop *Heref* 93-95; Chapl Heref Sixth Form Coll 94-95; Chapl City of Lon Freemen's Sch 95-97; LtO *Guildf* 95-97; Chapl and Hd RS Heref Cathl Sch 97-02; Chapl Malvern Coll from 02; Ho Master 05-07; PtO *Heref* from 02; Fell Harris Manchester Coll Ox 13. *The Chaplain's House, College Road, Malvern WR14 3DD* T: (01684) 581540 F: 581617 E: apl@malcol.org

LAW, David Richard. b 60. Keble Coll Ox BA 82 Wolfs Coll Ox MA 89 DPhil 89. NOC 98 Predigerseminar Preetz Germany 99. **d** 01 **p** 02. NSM Ashton-upon-Mersey St Martin *Ches* 01-09; NSM Timperley 09-14; NSM Altrincham St Geo from 14. *2 Winston Close, Sale M33 6UG* T: 0161-962 0297
E: david.law@manchester.ac.uk

LAW, Mrs Elizabeth Ann. b 49. Doncaster Coll of Educn CertEd 70 Loughb Univ MA 00. EAMTC 97. **d** 01 **p** 02. C Wickham Bishops w Lt Braxted *Chelmsf* 01-05; P-in-c Rattlesden w Thorpe Morieux, Brettenham etc *St E* 05-08; R 08-11; rtd 11; PtO *St E* 11-13; Hon C Gt Finborough w Onehouse, Harleston, Buxhall etc 13-15; Hon C Combs and Lt Finborough 13-15; Hon C Bildeston w Wattisham and Lindsey, Whatfield etc from 15; Asst Dioc Dir of Ords from 08. *7 Chamberlin Close, Bildeston, Ipswich IP7 7EZ* T: (01449) 740085 E: rev.liz@btinternet.com

LAW, Jeremy Stuart Alan. b 67. RMN 93 Man Metrop Univ BSc 96. Westcott Ho Cam. **d** 00 **p** 01. C Newton Heath *Man* 00-01; C Wythenshawe 01-04; P-in-c Lawton Moor 04-07; Chapl Cen Man/Man Children's Univ Hosp NHS Trust from 07; Chapl Gtr Man W Mental Health NHS Foundn Trust from 13. *Manchester Royal Infirmary, Cobbett House, Oxford Road, Manchester M13 9WL* T: 0161-276 1234
E: jeremylaw@ntlworld.com

LAW, Jeremy Thomson. b 61. Univ of Wales (Abth) BSc 82 Southn Univ BTh 89 Ox Univ DPhil 00. Sarum & Wells Th Coll 84. **d** 87 **p** 88. C Wimborne Minster and Holt *Sarum* 87-90; C Highfield *Ox* 90-94; Chapl and Lect Ex Univ 94-03; Dean of Chpl Cant Ch Ch Univ from 03; PtO *Roch* from 13. *Canterbury Christ Church University, North Holmes Road, Canterbury CT1 1QU* T: (01227) 782747
E: jeremy.law@canterbury.ac.uk

LAW, John Francis. b 35. Bps' Coll Cheshunt 65. **d** 67 **p** 68. C Styvechale *Cov* 67-71; P-in-c Cov St Anne and All SS 71-73; TV Cov E 73-77; P-in-c Fillongley 77-82; P-in-c Corley 77-82; V Fillongley and Corley 82-00; RD Nuneaton 90-95; rtd 00; PtO *Cov* from 00. *10 Brodick Way, Nuneaton CV10 7LH* T: (024) 7632 5582 E: johnflaw@sky.com

LAW, Canon John Michael. b 43. Open Univ BA 79. Westcott Ho Cam 65. **d** 68 **p** 69. C Chapel Allerton *Ripon* 68-72; C Ryhope *Dur* 72-73; Mental Health Chapl Fulbourn Hosp Cam 74-04; Chapl Ida Darwin Hosp Cam 74-96; Hon Can Ely Cathl 04-05; rtd 04; PV Ely Cathl 06-08; PtO from 08. *2 Suffolk Close, Ely CB6 3EW* T: (01353) 659084

LAW, Nicholas Charles. b 58. Trin Coll Bris BA 89. **d** 89 **p** 90. C Goldington *St Alb* 89-92; C Teignmouth, Ideford w Luton, Ashcombe etc *Ex* 92-97; R Bere Ferrers from 97. *The Rectory, Bere Alston, Yelverton PL20 7HH* T: (01822) 840229
E: nicklaw@breathemail.net

LAW, Peter James. b 46. Ridley Hall Cam 85. **d** 87 **p** 88. C Bournemouth St Jo w St Mich *Win* 87-91; V Chineham 91-96; V Luton Lewsey St Hugh *St Alb* 96-11; rtd 11; PtO *Portsm* from 13. *7 Anmore Drive, Waterlooville PO7 6DY* T: (023) 9226 8336 E: revpjl@btinternet.com

LAW, Richard Anthony Kelway. b 57. UWIST BEng 79. St Jo Coll Nottm MA(TS) 01 99. **d** 01 **p** 02. C Brundall w Braydeston and Postwick *Nor* 01-04; V Hollingworth w Tintwistle *Ches* 04-14; TV N Wingfield, Clay Cross and Pilsley *Derby* from 14. *The Vicarage, Stretton Road, Clay Cross, Chesterfield S45 9AQ* T: (01246) 250110
E: vicar@richardaklaw.plus.com

LAW, Richard Lindsey. b 34. Univ Coll Ox BA 58 MA 63 St Pet Coll Birm DipEd 70. Cuddesdon Coll 58. **d** 60 **p** 61. C Leighton Buzzard *St Alb* 60-63; Trinidad and Tobago 63-67; V Stottesdon *Heref* 67-72; P-in-c Farlow 67-72; Chapl Framlingham Coll 72-83; V Leigh-on-Sea St Marg *Chelmsf* 83-91; Warden Framlingham Ho of Prayer and Retreat 91-94; In Orthodox Ch 94-04; rtd 96. *Room 15, Manormead, Tilford Road, Hindhead GU26 6RA*

LAW, Canon Robert Frederick. b 43. St Aid Birkenhead 67. **d** 69 **p** 70. C Bengeo *St Alb* 69-72; C Sandy 72-76; P-in-c St Ippolyts 76-81; Chapl Jersey Gp of Hosps 81-84; V Crowan w Godolphin *Truro* 84-92; RD Kerrier 90-91; R St Columb Major w St Wenn 92-02; RD Pydar 95-02; P-in-c St Minver 02-05; Hon Can Truro Cathl 98-05; rtd 05; PtO *York* from 07. *24 Parkfield, Stillington, York YO61 1JW* T: (01347) 810940 M: 07842-111525 E: robertlaw43@btinternet.com

LAW, Robert James. b 31. Lon Univ MB, BS 55. Ridley Hall Cam 62. **d** 64 **p** 65. C Barnehurst *Roch* 64-66; C Edgware *Lon* 66-72; V Halwell w Moreleigh *Ex* 72-94; P-in-c Woodleigh and Loddiswell 76-79; R 79-94; rtd 96. *38 Wheatlands Road, Paignton TQ4 5HU* T: (01803) 559450

LAW, Simon Anthony. b 55. Middx Univ BA 93 K Coll Lon MA 10. NTMTC 94. **d** 96 **p** 97. NSM Forest Gate St Mark *Chelmsf* 96-98; C Becontree W 98-99; TV 99-02; TR 02-07; V Becontree St Cedd 07-10; R Pitsea w Nevendon from 10. *The Rectory, Rectory Road, Pitsea, Basildon SS13 2AA* T: (01268) 556874 E: simon@revlaw.co.uk

LAW-JONES, Peter Deniston. b 55. Newc Univ BA 77 Nottm Univ BTh 87 Lanc Univ MA 03 Man Univ PGCE 81. Linc Th Coll 84. **d** 87 **p** 88. C Chorley St Laur *Blackb* 87-91; V Feniscliffe 91-96; V St Annes St Thos 96-13; AD Kirkham 09-13; Chapl Blackpool, Wyre and Fylde Community NHS Trust 97-04; TR Salter Street and Shirley *Birm* from 13. *The Rectory, 2 Bishopton Close, Shirley, Solihull B90 4AH* T: 0121-744 3123 E: pljz1000@gmail.com

LAWAL, Miss Basirat Adebanke Amope (Ade). b 67. Lon Bible Coll BTh 02. SAOMC 03. **d** 05 **p** 06. C Blurton *Lich* 05-09; V Wyther *Ripon* 09-13; Racial Justice Officer *Leeds* 10-15; Chapl Leeds Teaching Hosps NHS Trust 13-15; P-in-c Gillingham St Mary *Roch* from 15. *The Vicarage, 27 Gillingham Green, Gillingham ME7 1SS* T: (01634) 850529
E: baasiratlawal166@btinternet.com

LAWES, Geoffrey Hyland. b 37. St Jo Coll Dur BA 58 Hertf Coll Ox BA 60 MA 64 Newc Univ PGCE 76 MEd 79. Cranmer Hall Dur 61. **d** 63 **p** 64. C Millfield St Mark *Dur* 63-66; C Jarrow Grange 66-69; Hon C 69-86; LtO 86-90; V Collierley w Annfield Plain 90-05; rtd 05; Hon C Satley, Stanley and Tow Law *Dur* from 05; PtO from 06. *Netherwood, St Mary's Avenue, Crook DL15 9HY* T: (01388) 766585

LAWES, Stephen George. b 40. Nottm Univ PGCE 75. St Jo Coll Nottm BTh 74. **d** 82 **p** 83. NSM Hillmorton *Cov* 82-86; NSM Daventry Deanery *Pet* 87-03. *Irrisfree, Barleyfield, Kilbrittain, Co Cork, Republic of Ireland*

LAWES, Timothy Stanley. b 57. Nottm Univ BTh 88. Linc Th Coll 85. **d** 88 **p** 89. C Wymondham *Nor* 88-92; R Felmingham, Skeyton, Colby, Banningham etc 92-96; Sweden 96-12; Asst V Byske 98-09; TR Skelleftea Landsforsamling 11-12; V Swaffham and Sporle *Nor* from 12. *The Vicarage, White Cross Road, Swaffham PE37 7QY* E: timothylawes@hotmail.com

LAWLESS, Mrs Patricia Elizabeth. b 36. Bris Univ BA 58 PGCE 59. S Dios Minl Tr Scheme 91. **d** 93 **p** 94. NSM Frome Ch Ch *B & W* 93-95; NSM Mells w Buckland Dinham, Elm, Whatley etc 96; NSM Frome St Jo and St Mary 96-00; Chapl Victoria Hosp Frome 96-98; rtd 00; PtO *B & W* from 00. *22 Braithwaite Way, Frome BA11 2XG* T: (01373) 466106

LAWLEY, Peter Gerald Fitch. b 52. Chich Th Coll 77. **d** 80 **p** 81. C Pet St Jo 80-83; C Daventry 83-87; P-in-c Syresham w Whitfield 87-90; TV Cen Telford *Lich* 90-98; V Priors Lee and

St Georges' 98-12; rtd 12; PtO *Lich* from 13. *11 Kingsley Drive, Donnington, Telford TF2 8DH* T: (01952) 606160
E: peterlawley12@googlemail.com

LAWLEY, Rosemary Ann. b 47. WMMTC 00. **d** 03 **p** 04. NSM Kinver and Enville *Lich* 03-07; TV Kidderminster St Mary and All SS w Trimpley etc *Worc* 07-15; TV Kidderminster Ismere from 15; Ind Chapl from 07; Hon Can Worc Cathl from 15. *186 Birmingham Road, Kidderminster DY10 2SJ*
T: (01562) 748274 E: rosemarylawley@tiscali.co.uk

LAWLOR, Anne Louise. b 61. UEA BEd 83 Surrey Univ Roehampton BA 02 Cam Univ BTh 12. Westcott Ho Cam 10. **d** 12 **p** 13. C Everton St Pet w St Chrys *Liv* from 12. *The Vicarage, 105 Queens Road, Liverpool L6 2NF* T: 0151-260 9172
E: alawlor61@btinternet.com

LAWLOR, Colin Robert. b 63. Lanc Univ BA 89 MPhil 97 St Martin's Coll Lanc PGCE 90. Chich Th Coll 90. **d** 93 **p** 94. C Moulsecoomb *Chich* 93-97; TV 97-99; Chapl Brighton Univ from 99; P-in-c Stanmer w Falmer from 13. *St Laurence House, Park Street, Falmer, Brighton BN1 9PG* M: 07733-225263
E: c.r.lawlor@bton.ac.uk

LAWLOR, Paul. b 60. Nottm Univ BSc 82. St Jo Coll Nottm 06. **d** 08 **p** 09. C Warsop *S'well* 08-11; TV Redditch H Trin *Worc* from 11. *The Vicarage, 219 St George's Road, Redditch B98 8EE* T: (01527) 62375 M: 07807-611090 E: paul@pjlawlor.me.uk

LAWRANCE, Hugh Norcliffe. b 49. N Riding Coll of Educn BEd 79. Linc Th Coll 83. **d** 85 **p** 86. C Lindley *Wakef* 85-87; C Barkisland w W Scammonden and Ripponden 87-92; V Knottingley 92-98; C Thorp Arch w Walton, Boston Spa and Clifford *York* 98-00; P-in-c Bramham and 00-08; C Whitby w Ruswarp 08-13. *44 Ferrybridge Road, Pontefract WF8 2PD* E: frhugh@norcliffe.com

LAWRANCE, Canon Robert William. b 63. Jes Coll Ox BA 85 MA 89 Man Univ MA 93. Ripon Coll Cuddesdon BA 87. **d** 88 **p** 89. C Astley *Man* 88-91; Lect Bolton St Pet 91-94; V Bury St Jo w St Mark 94-00; Chapl Bury Healthcare NHS Trust 95-00; Dir of Ords *Dur* 00-08; Chapl Hatf Coll Dur 00-05; Chapl Collingwood Coll Dur 05-08; TR Dur N from 08; AD Dur from 10; Hon Can Dur Cathl from 10; Hon Chapl Dur and Darlington Fire and Rescue Brigade from 09. *St Cuthbert's Vicarage, 1 Aykley Court, Durham DH1 4NW* T: 0191-386 0146 E: robert.lawrance@durham.anglican.org

LAWRENCE, Charles Anthony Edwin. b 53. AKC 75. St Aug Coll Cant 75. **d** 76 **p** 77. C Mitcham St Mark *S'wark* 76-80; C Haslemere *Guildf* 80-82; P-in-c Ashton H Trin *Man* 82-84; V 84-93; AD Ashton-under-Lyne 91-93; V Saddleworth 93-97; V Effingham w Lt Bookham *Guildf* 97-05; Chapl Manor Ho Sch 97-05; R Shere, Albury and Chilworth *Guildf* 05-09; R Northfield *Birm* 09-15. *The Rectory, Rectory Road, Birmingham B31 2NA* T: 0121-477 3111 E: fathercharles@hotmail.co.uk

LAWRENCE, Christopher David. b 73. Liv Jo Moores Univ BEd 98. Ridley Hall Cam 03. **d** 05 **p** 06. C Letchworth St Paul w Willian *St Alb* 05-08; Chapl RAF from 08. *Chaplaincy Services (RAF), HQ Air Command, RAF High Wycombe HP14 4UE* T: (01494) 496800 F: 496343
E: revchrislawrence@yahoo.co.uk

LAWRENCE, Christopher David. b 55. Wycliffe Hall Ox 01. **d** 03 **p** 04. C Wadhurst *Chich* 03-07; C Tidebrook 03-07; C Stonegate 03-07; P-in-c Framfield 07-11; V from 11. *The Vicarage, Brookhouse Road, Framfield, Uckfield TN22 5NH* T: (01825) 890365 M: 07941-557537
E: cdsjlawrence@tiscali.co.uk

LAWRENCE, Canon David Ian. b 48. Univ Coll Lon BSc 74 AIMLS 71 MSB 76. Glouc Sch of Min 84 Sarum & Wells Th Coll 87. **d** 88 **p** 89. C Wotton St Mary *Glouc* 88-91; P-in-c Cheltenham St Mich 91-93; V 93-06; V Coleford, Staunton, Newland, Redbrook etc 06-11; Hon Can Glouc Cathl 06-11; rtd 12; PtO *Sarum* from 12. *14 Clappentail Park, Lyme Regis DT7 3NB* T: (01297) 442140
E: dandhlawrence@tiscali.co.uk

LAWRENCE, Miss Helen. b 30. St Mich Ho Ox 62. **dss** 74 **d** 87 **p** 94. Par Dn Braintree *Chelmsf* 87-90; rtd 90; PtO *Chelmsf* 90-08; *Ely* from 09. *28 Storeys House, Mount Pleasant, Cambridge CB3 0BZ* T: (01223) 360017
E: helen@helenlawrence1.plus.com

LAWRENCE, Isaac Sartaj. b 72. Peshawar Univ BSc 95 Philippine Chr Univ MBA 97. **d** 08 **p** 09. C Ripon H Trin 08-12; V Scotby and Cotehill w Cumwhinton *Carl* from 12. *The Vicarage, Lambley Bank, Scotby, Carlisle CA4 8BX* T: (01228) 513205 M: 07837-395770
E: revisaac.lawrence@gmail.com

LAWRENCE, James Conrad. b 62. St Jo Coll Dur BA 85. Ridley Hall Cam 85. **d** 87 **p** 88. Min Bar Hill LEP *Ely* 87-92; Min Bar Hill 92-93; Deanery Adv in Evang 90-93; CPAS Evang 93-98; PtO *Cov* from 93; Springboard Missr from 97; CPAS Dir Evang Projects from 99. *Cotton Mill Spinney, Cubbington, Leamington Spa CV32 7XH* T: (01926) 426761 *or* 334242 F: 337613
E: jlawrence@cpas.org.uk

LAWRENCE, Mrs Janet Maureen. b 43. Hockerill Teacher Tr Coll
TCert 64. Ox Min Course 89. **d** 92 **p** 94. Hon Par Dn Bletchley
Ox 92-94; NSM N Bletchley CD 94-05; rtd 05; PtO Ox 05-08;
Hon C Gayhurst w Ravenstone, Stoke Goldington etc 08-14;
PtO from 14. *10 Thornlea Croft, Olney MK46 5HZ*
T: (01234) 240568 E: jmlawrence7@btinternet.com

LAWRENCE, John Graham Clive. b 47. ACIB. Trin Coll Bris.
d 78 **p** 79. C Chatham St Phil and St Jas *Roch* 78-83; V Roch
St Justus 83-97; Asst Chapl HM Pris Roch 83-97; UK Dir CMJ
97-00; Internat Co-ord Light to the Nations UK 00-10; Chapl
Maidstone and Tunbridge Wells NHS Trust 03-04; Chapl W
Kent NHS and Soc Care Trust 05-06; Chapl Kent & Medway
NHS and Soc Care Partnership Trust 06-08; Chapl Team Ldr
Bucks Hosps NHS Trust 08-10; rtd 10. *55 Elmshurst Gardens,
Tonbridge TN10 3QT* T: (01732) 490549 M: 07984-951534
E: jgcl38@gmail.com

LAWRENCE, Mrs Judith Patricia. b 53. WEMTC 01. **d** 04
p 05. C Glastonbury w Meare *B & W* 04-09; PtO 09-11;
Chapl Somerset Community Health NHS Trust 10-11;
Chapl Somerset Partnership NHS Foundation Trust 10-11;
Asst Chapl Taunton and Somerset NHS Trust 09-11; Chapl
from 11. *12 Glanvill Road, Street BA16 0TN* T: (01458) 445451
E: j.lawrence123@btinternet.com

LAWRENCE, Canon Leonard Roy. b 31. Keble Coll Ox BA 56
MA 59. Westcott Ho Cam 56. **d** 58 **p** 59. C Stockport St Geo
Ches 58-62; V Thelwall 62-68; V Hyde St Geo 68-75; V Prenton
75-96; Hon Can Ches Cathl 86-96; rtd 96; PtO *Ches* from 96;
Acorn Chr Foundn from 97. *39 Mockbeggar Drive, Wallasey
CH45 3NN* T: 0151-346 9438

LAWRENCE, Leslie. b 44. S'wark Ord Course 86. **d** 88 **p** 89. NSM
Stanwell *Lon* 88-92; C Hounslow H Trin w St Paul 92-97; P-in-c
Norwood St Mary 97-06; R 06-09; rtd 09. *22 Chestnut Road,
Ashford TW15 1DG* T: (01784) 241773
E: leslielawrencestd@googlemail.com

LAWRENCE, Lorraine Margaret. b 58. Open Univ BA 08.
SEITE 08. **d** 11 **p** 12. NSM Gravesend St Geo *Roch* 11-15;
C Wye *Cant* from 15. *The Vicarage, Pilgrims Way, Hastingleigh,
Ashford TN25 5HP* M: 07894-034409 T: (01233) 750987
E: lorraine_lawrence@btinternet.com

LAWRENCE, Martin Kenneth. b 59. Univ Coll Dur BA 82.
St Steph Ho Ox 94. **d** 96 **p** 97. C Wanstead St Mary w Ch Ch
Chelmsf 96-00; PV Westmr Abbey 99-00; Chapl Malta and
Gozo *Eur* 00-01; C Becontree S *Chelmsf* 02; C Romford St Edw
02-05; P-in-c Cranham 05-08; rtd 08. *20 Grosvenor Court,
Varndean Road, Brighton BN1 6RR* M: 07776-267950
E: martinlawrence@dunelm.org.uk

LAWRENCE, Norman. b 45. Lon Univ BEd 75. S'wark Ord
Course 77. **d** 80 **p** 81. NSM Hounslow H Trin *Lon* from 80.
89 Bulstrode Avenue, Hounslow TW3 3AE T: (020) 8572 6292
E: nlawrence@lampton.hounslow.sch.uk

LAWRENCE, Canon Patrick Henry Andrew. b 51. TCD Div
Test 79 BA 81. **d** 81 **p** 82. C Templemore *D & R* 81-84;
C Kilkenny St Canice Cathl 84-85; I Templebreedy w Tracton
and Nohoval *C, C & R* 85-92; I Geashill w Killeigh and
Ballycommon *M & K* 92-98; Can Kildare Cathl 92-09; Adn
Kildare 93-09; Adn Meath 97-09; Warden of Readers 97-09;
I Julianstown and Colpe w Drogheda and Duleek 98-09;
I Monkstown *D & G* 09-15; Preb Monmohenock St Patr Cathl
Dublin 00-12; Chan St Patr Cathl Dublin 12-15. *Address temp
unknown* E: patricklawrence@eircom.net

LAWRENCE, Canon Peter Anthony. b 36. Lich Th Coll 67.
d 69 **p** 70. C Oadby *Leic* 69-74; P-in-c Northmarston and
Granborough *Ox* 74-81; P-in-c Hardwick St Mary 74-81; P-in-c
Quainton 76-81; P-in-c Oving w Pitchcott 76-81; TR Schorne
81-91; RD Claydon 84-88; V Ivinghoe w Pitstone and Slapton
91-97; Hon Can Ch Ch 97; rtd 97; PtO *Ox* 99-07; *Worc* from 01.
Hill House, Back Lane, Malvern WR14 2HJ T: (01684) 564075
E: peter.molly2@waitrose.com

LAWRENCE, Ralph Guy. b 55. Trin Coll Bris 87. **d** 89 **p** 90.
C Cotmanhay *Derby* 89-93; P-in-c Tansley, Dethick, Lea and
Holloway 93-04; R Ashover and Brackenfield w Wessington
from 04; C N Wingfield, Clay Cross and Pilsley from 06.
The Rectory, Narrowleys Lane, Ashover, Chesterfield S45 0AU
T: (01246) 590246 E: ralphlawrence@tiscali.co.uk

LAWRENCE, Roy. *See* LAWRENCE, Leonard Roy

LAWRENCE (née MASON), Sarah Catherine. b 79. K Coll
Lon BA 02 PGCE 03 Chu Coll Cam MPhil 06. Ridley Hall
Cam 05. **d** 08 **p** 10. NSM Carr Dyke Gp *Linc* 08-10; C Shifnal
and Sheriffhales *Lich* 10-13; C Tong 11-13. *12 Adams Close,
Rhosneigr LL64 5QG* M: 07766-348170 T: (01407) 811371
E: revsarahlawrence@btinternet.com

LAWRENCE, Simon Peter. b 60. TD . Nottm Univ BTh 88
MA 97 Indiana State Univ DMin 01. St Jo Coll Nottm 85.
d 88 **p** 89. C Holbeach *Linc* 88-90; C Alford w Rigsby 90-91;
R Rattlesden w Thorpe Morieux and Brettenham *St E* 91-93;

V Churchdown *Glouc* 93; V Maenclochog w Henry's Moat and
Mynachlogddu etc *St D* 93-94; R Overstrand, Northrepps,
Sidestrand etc *Nor* 95-98; CF (TA) 89-05; CF (ACF) 90-05;
PtO *Nor* 02-06; Public Preacher 06-07; R Stalham, E Ruston,
Brunstead, Sutton and Ingham from 07; RD St Benet from 12;
Dioc Chapl MU from 11. *The Rectory, Camping Field Lane,
Stalham, Norwich NR12 9DT* T: (01692) 580250
E: simon.stalham@btinternet.com

LAWRENCE, Victor John. b 43. ACII. Oak Hill Th Coll. **d** 83
p 84. C Paddock Wood *Roch* 83-87; R Milton next Gravesend
w Denton 87-09; RD Gravesend 05-09; rtd 09. *5 Riplingham,
41 Gaudick Road, Eastbourne BN20 7LW*
E: victorjlaw@googlemail.com

LAWRENCE-MARCH, David Lawrence. b 61. Univ of Wales
(Lamp) BA 83. Coll of Resurr Mirfield 83. **d** 85 **p** 86. C Pet
St Jude 85-89; Chapl St Aug Sch Kilburn 89-92; C Kilburn
St Aug w St Jo *Lon* 89-90; C Paddington St Mary 90-92; Chapl
Bearwood Coll Wokingham 92-96; R Holt w High Kelling *Nor*
96-98; Sen Chapl Bedford Sch 98-09; Chapl Ardingly Coll
from 09. *Ardingly College, Haywards Heath RH17 6SQ*
T: (01444) 892656 E: father.david@ardingly.com

LAWRENSON, Ronald David. b 41. CITC 68. **d** 71 **p** 72.
C Seapatrick *D & D* 71-78; Min Can Down Cathl 78-79;
V Choral Belf Cathl 79-86; Bp's C Tynan w Middletown and
Aghavilly *Arm* 86-90 and 91-93; Hon V Choral Arm Cathl
87-02; Bp's C Tynan w Middletown 92-93; I Donaghmore w
Upper Donaghmore 93-98; rtd 02. *Riverbrook Apartments,
5 Brookland Drive, Whitehead, Carrickfergus BT38 9SL*
T: (028) 9337 3625

LAWRIE (née VENTON), Ms Kathryn Magdelena. b 56. Reading
Univ BA 78. NEOC 03. **d** 06 **p** 07. C Skelton w Upleatham *York*
06-10; P-in-c Hedon w Paull 10-11; R Hedon, Paull, Sproatley
and Preston 12-13; rtd 13; PtO *York* from 15. *6 Hurn Close, Hull
HU8 0PQ* T: (01482) 706460
E: revkathy@revkathy.karoo.co.uk

LAWRIE, Peter Sinclair. b 39. Clifton Th Coll 62. **d** 65 **p** 66.
C Derby St Chad 65-68; C Toxteth Park St Philemon w St Silas
Liv 68-71; V Ramsey St Mary's w Ponds Bridge *Ely* 71-81;
V Whitwick St Jo the Bapt *Leic* 81-96; P-in-c Felixstowe
SS Pet and Paul *St E* 96-03; rtd 03. *71 Lincroft, Oakley, Bedford
MK43 7SS* T: (01234) 824055 E: p.lawrie@talk21.com

LAWRINSON, Leslie Norman. b 35. IEng MCIPD 90 MCMI 84.
d 99 **p** 00. OLM Onchan *S & M* 99-05; NSM Scarisbrick *Liv*
05-08; rtd 08; PtO *S & M* from 09. *8 Hillary Wharf Apartments,
South Quay, Douglas, Isle of Man IM1 5BL* T: (01624) 627664
M: 07749-687469 E: leslawrinson05@aol.com

LAWRY, Richard Henry. b 57. Bris Univ BA 79 Wolfs Coll Cam
PGCE 81. St Jo Coll Nottm MA 01. **d** 99 **p** 00. C Macclesfield
Team *Ches* 99-02; P-in-c Stalybridge St Paul 02-06; V 06-09;
V Norbury from 09. *Norbury Vicarage, 75 Chester Road, Hazel
Grove, Stockport SK7 5PE* T: 0161-483 8640
E: richardlawry@talk21.com

LAWS, Clive Loudon. b 54. UEA BEd 76 Leeds Univ CertEd 75.
Wycliffe Hall Ox 79. **d** 82 **p** 83. C Newcastle w Butterton
Lich 82-85; C Gabalfa *Llan* 85-88; R Pendine w Llanmiloe
and Eglwys Gymyn w Marros *St D* 89-94; CF 89-94; PtO
B & W 95-96; C Portishead 96-02; TV 02-08; P-in-c High
Laver w Magdalen Laver and Lt Laver etc *Chelmsf* 08-10;
Chapl St Clare Hospice 08-10; rtd 10. *36 Alexandra Close,
Illogan, Redruth TR16 4RS* T: (01209) 843117
E: clive_anne@yahoo.co.uk

LAWSON, Canon Alma Felicity. b 51. St Hugh's Coll Ox BA 73
MA 78. St Jo Coll Nottm. **d** 98 **p** 99. Dean of Min and Dir of
Ords *Wakef* 93-00; Hon C Wakef Cathl 98-00; V Gildersome
Leeds from 00; P-in-c Drighlington from 12; Hon Can Wakef
Cathl from 01; RD Birstall *Wakef* 10-14. *St Peter's House, 2A
Church Street, Gildersome, Morley, Leeds LS27 7AF*
T/F: 0113-253 3339 E: felicity.lawson@tiscali.co.uk

LAWSON, Anne. *See* LAWSON, Sarah Anne

LAWSON, Canon David McKenzie. b 47. Glas Univ MA 69 Edin
Univ BD 76. Edin Th Coll 73. **d** 76 **p** 77. C Glas St Mary 76-82;
V Keighley All SS *Bradf* 82-85; Chapl Asst Univ Coll Hosp Lon
85-91; Hon C St Pancras w St Jas and Ch Ch *Lon* 86-91;
R Smithfield St Bart Gt 91-93; Hon C Paddington St Jas 94-00;
TV Chambersbury *St Alb* 00-03; TR 03-09; TR Langelei from
09; RD Hemel Hempstead 08-14; Hon Can St Alb from 12. *The
Rectory, The Glebe, Kings Langley WD4 9HY* M: 07939-473717
T: (01923) 291077 E: davidmlawson@btinternet.com

LAWSON, David William. b 50. ACA. Linc Th Coll. **d** 82 **p** 83.
C Stafford *Lich* 82-85; TV Redruth w Lanner *Truro* 85-87;
C Whitley *Cov* 87-93; Chapl Whitley Hosp Cov 87-94;
Chapl Gulson Road Hosp Cov 87-94; Chapl Walsgrave
Hosps NHS Trust 87-94; V S Leamington St Jo *Cov* from 93.
St John's Vicarage, Tachbrook Street, Leamington Spa CV31 3BN
T: (01926) 422208

LAWSON, Felicity. *See* LAWSON, Alma Felicity

LAWSON, The Very Revd Frederick Quinney (Rick). b 45. Leic Univ BA. St Steph Ho Ox. **d** 83 **p** 84. Hon C Loughborough Em *Leic* 83-86; NSM Somerby, Burrough on the Hill and Pickwell 86-87; USA from 87; Hon Can Salt Lake City 87-02; Dean from 02. *4294 Adonis Drive, Salt Lake City UT 84124, USA* T: (001) (801) 595 5380 *or* (001) (801) 322-3400 F: 278 5903
E: rlawson@stmarkscathedral-ut.org

LAWSON, Gary Austin. b 53. Man Univ BA 80. Ripon Coll Cuddesdon 80. **d** 82 **p** 83. C Nunhead St Antony *S'wark* 82-86; Hon C Reddish *Man* 86-87; Hon C Longsight St Jo w St Cypr 87-88; V Wythenshawe St Rich 88-98; Chapl Bolton Inst of F&HE 98-03; C Bolton St Pet 98-03; TR Westhoughton and Wingates 03-13; C Daisy Hill 11-13; TR Daisy Hill, Westhoughton and Wingates 13-14; rtd 14. *4 Brookfold Road, Stockport SK4 5EJ* T: 0161-442 7970
E: garyaustinlawson@btinternet.com

LAWSON, James Barry. b 68. Edin Univ MA 91 New Coll Ox DPhil 96. Coll of Resurr Mirfield 98. **d** 99 **p** 00. C Poplar *Lon* 99-02; Chapl CCC Cam 02-07; Bp's Sen Chapl *Sarum* 07-08; V Stoke Newington Common St Mich *Lon* from 09. *St Michael's Vicarage, 55 Fountayne Road, London N16 7ED* T: (020) 8806 4225

LAWSON, Canon John Alexander. b 62. Sheff Univ BA 84 Nottm Univ MA 97 PhD 06. St Jo Coll Nottm 85. **d** 87 **p** 88. C Wellington All SS w Eyton *Lich* 87-92; TV Dewsbury *Wakef* 92-98; P-in-c Birchencliffe 98-05; Dioc Vocations Adv and Asst Dir of Ords 02-05; Can Res Wakef Cathl from 05; Dioc Dir Tr from 05; Warden Wakef Min Scheme from 06. *7 Belgravia Road, Wakefield WF1 3JP* T: (01924) 380182 *or* 371802
E: john.lawson@wakefield.anglican.org

LAWSON, Jonathan Halford. b 68. Westcott Ho Cam 91. **d** 93 **p** 94. C Sedgefield *Dur* 93-96; C Usworth 96-97; TV 97-00; TV Epping Distr *Chelmsf* 00-04; Chapl St Hild and St Bede Coll *Dur* 04-14; V Newc St Gabr from 14. *St Gabriel's Vicarage, 9 Holderness Road, Newcastle upon Tyne NE6 5RH* T: 0191-908 7835 E: vicarofheaton@gmail.com

LAWSON, June Margaret. b 62. Birm Univ BA 83 Didsbury Coll of Educn PGCE 84 St Jo Coll York MA 02. NOC 00. **d** 02 **p** 03. C Huddersfield H Trin *Wakef* 02-05; Dir Adult Chr Educn Mirfield Cen 05-08; Dir Mirfield Cen from 08; PV Wakef Cathl from 05; Dean of Women's Min from 09. *The Mirfield Centre, Stocks Bank Road, Mirfield WF14 0BW* T: (01924) 481911
E: jlawson@mirfield.org.uk

LAWSON, Mrs Katherine Ellen. b 53. SEITE 11. **d** 14 **p** 15. NSM Hove All SS *Chich* from 14. *Moray Cottage, 31 Oaklands Avenue, Saltdean, Brighton BN2 8LQ* T: (01273) 709330 M: 07878-959327 E: kate.tuppen.lawson@gmail.com

LAWSON, Matthew Charles Outram. b 71. Trin Coll Bris. **d** 11 **p** 12. C Bury St Edmunds St Mary *St E* 11-14; R Chadbrook from 14. *The Rectory, The Green, Long Melford, Sudbury CO10 9DT* M: 07834-507086 E: mattisfound@gmail.com

LAWSON, Matthew James. b 67. St Andr Univ MTheol 91 FRSA 02. Ripon Coll Cuddesdon MTh 94. **d** 94 **p** 95. C Bedford St Andr *St Alb* 94-97; Chapl and Hd RS St Jo Sch Leatherhead 97-07; Tutor Dioc Min Course *Guildf* 98; Chapl Hurstpierpoint Coll 07-10. *54 Hipwell Court, Olney MK46 5QB* M: 07768-515950 E: frlawson@aol.com

LAWSON, The Ven Michael Charles. b 52. Sussex Univ BA 75. Trin Coll Bris 75. **d** 78 **p** 79. C Horsham *Chich* 78-81; C St Marylebone All So w SS Pet and Jo *Lon* 81-87; V Bromley Ch Ch *Roch* 87-99; adn Hampstead *Lon* 99-10; R Guildf St Sav 10-12; rtd 12; PtO *Ely* from 13. *Arosfa, Stonely Road, Easton, Huntingdon PE28 0TT*
E: m.c.lawson@btinternet.com

LAWSON, Rick. *See* LAWSON, Frederick Quinney

LAWSON, Robert William. b 60. MSB 89. CITC 05. **d** 08 **p** 09. NSM Celbridge w Straffan and Newcastle-Lyons *D & G* 08-11; NSM Dublin Ch Ch Cathl Gp from 11. *6 Roselawn Close, Castleknock, Dublin 15, Republic of Ireland* T: (00353) (1) 820 5129 M: 86-394 3151 E: lawson.rw@gmail.com

LAWSON, Russell Thomas. b 70. Leeds Univ BA 92 Ox Univ BTh 98. St Steph Ho Ox 98. **d** 98 **p** 99. C Cheshunt *St Alb* 98-02; C Cheam *S'wark* 02-06; TV 06-07; P-in-c S Norwood St Alb 07-13; V from 13. *The Vicarage, 6 Dagmar Road, London SE25 6HZ* T: (020) 8653 6092 M: 07703-176001
E: rtl70@btopenworld.com

LAWSON, Miss Sarah Anne. b 66. Ches Coll of HE BA 87 Univ of Wales MA 12. Ridley Hall Cam. **d** 00 **p** 01. C Hollingworth w Tintwistle *Ches* 00-05; V Haslington w Crewe Green 05-14; V Acton and Worleston, Church Minshull etc from 14. *St Mary's Vicarage, Chester Road, Acton, Nantwich CW5 8LG* E: revanne@uwclub.net

LAWSON-JONES, Christopher Mark. b 68. Open Univ BA 98. St Mich Coll Llan 98. **d** 00 **p** 01. C Risca *Mon* 00-03; Chapl Cross Keys Campus Coleg Gwent 00-03; TV Cyncoed 03-06; Dioc Soc Resp Officer 04-06; P-in-c Magor 06-09; TR 09-12; TR Cyncoed from 12; AD Bassaleg from 12. *The Rectory, 256 Cyncoed Road, Cardiff CF23 6RU* T: (029) 2075 2138
E: marklawsonjones@gmail.com

LAWTON, Christopher. *See* LAWTON, Robin David Christopher

LAWTON, Donald John William. b 48. Huron Coll Ontario BMin 77. **d** 77 **p** 78. I Elsa Mayo Canada 77-80; C Ch Ch Cathl Whitehorse 80-13; C Eastling w Ospringe and Stalisfield w Otterden *Cant* 13-14; C Selling w Throwley, Sheldwich w Badlesmere etc 13-14; V High Downs from 14; Co-Warden of Readers from 14. *The Rectory, Newnham Lane, Eastling, Faversham ME13 0AS* T: (01795) 890487
E: donaldjlawton@gmail.com *or* dlawton@diocant.org

LAWTON, Robin David Christopher. b 73. St Jo Coll Dur BATM 14. Cranmer Hall Dur 12. **d** 14 **p** 15. C Leyburn w Bellerby *Leeds* from 14. *The Rectory, 68 The Springs, Middleham, Leyburn DL8 4RB* T: (01969) 625980
M: 07814-731265

LAXON, Canon Colin John. b 44. FRSA. Cant Sch of Min 86. **d** 89 **p** 90. C Folkestone St Mary and St Eanswythe *Cant* 89-94; P-in-c Barrow St Jas *Carl* 94-01; Soc Resp Officer 01-09; C Brampton and Farlam and Castle Carrock w Cumrew 01-02; TV Eden, Gelt and Irthing 02-06; C Carl St Cuth w St Mary 06-09; Hon Can Carl Cathl 06-09; rtd 09; PtO *Carl* from 09. *15 Knowefield Avenue, Carlisle CA3 9BQ* T: (01228) 544215
E: c.laxon@btinternet.com

LAY, Mrs Alison Margaret. b 57. **d** 07 **p** 09. OLM Needham Market w Badley *St E* 07-08; OLM Combs and Lt Finborough 08-12. *The Hideaway, Park Road, Needham Market, Ipswich IP6 8BH* T: (01449) 721115 E: ali@divineone.f9.co.uk

LAY, Brian Robert. b 37. Bernard Gilpin Soc Dur 59 Chich Th Coll 60. **d** 63 **p** 64. C Battyeford *Wakef* 63-66; C Belhus Park *Chelmsf* 66-73; P-in-c Sutton on Plym *Ex* 73-80; V 80-07; rtd 07; PtO *Ex* from 08. *18 Dunstone Drive, Plymouth PL9 8SQ* T: (01752) 407348

LAY, Geoffrey Arthur. b 54. Leic Poly BA 77 Man Univ MA 83 Lon Univ BD 88. Ridley Hall Cam 90. **d** 92 **p** 93. C St Neots *Ely* 92-95; P-in-c Long Stanton w St Mich 95-01; P-in-c Dry Drayton 95-97; R Chailey *Chich* 01-06; Chapl Chailey Heritage Hosp Lewes 01-06; rtd 06. *77 Firle Road, Peacehaven BN10 7QH* T: (01273) 588048
E: geofflay@btinternet.com

LAYBOURNE, Mrs Teresa Margaret. b 52. **d** 12 **p** 13. NSM Washington *Dur* from 12. *Address temp unknown*
E: twalton2207@gmail.com

LAYCOCK, Charles. b 37. Open Univ BA 88. NOC 80. **d** 83 **p** 84. C Astley Bridge *Man* 83-86; R Crumpsall 86-94; V Ashton Ch Ch 94-00; rtd 00; PtO *Man* from 00; *Ches* from 03. *23 The Mere, Ashton-under-Lyne OL6 9NH* T: 0161-330 2824

LAYNESMITH, Mark David. b 74. York Univ BA 97 MA 99. Ripon Coll Cuddesdon BA 01. **d** 02 **p** 03. C Tadcaster w Newton Kyme *York* 02-05; Chapl Reading Univ *Ox* from 05. *30 Shinfield Road, Reading RG2 7BW* T: 0118-987 1495

LAYTON, Miss Norene. b 39. Trin Coll Bris 84. **d** 86 **p** 87 **p** 94. Lindfield *Chich* 86-92; Par Dn 87-92; Par Dn Loughborough Em *Leic* 92-94; C Loughborough Em and St Mary in Charnwood 94-96; V Hengrove *Bris* 96-04; rtd 04; PtO *Leic* from 14. *104 Outwoods Drive, Loughborough LE11 3LU* T: (01509) 218127

LAYZELL, Martyn Paul. b 75. Wycliffe Hall Ox 08. **d** 10 **p** 11. C Onslow Square and S Kensington St Aug *Lon* from 10. *101 Fernside Road, London SW12 8LH* M: 07891-015221 *or* 07702-968022 E: martyn.layzell@htb.org.uk

LAZENBY, Donna Jannine. b 83. Qu Coll Cam BA 04 MPhil 05 PhD 09. Westcott Ho Cam 09. **d** 11 **p** 12. C Wallington Springfield Ch *S'wark* 11-14; Tutor St Mellitus Coll from 15. *The Vicarage, 3 Valley Road, Kenley CR8 5DJ* T: (020) 8660 6981 *or* 8660 1914 M: 07732-175107
E: donna.lazenby@btinternet.com

LE BAS, Mrs Jennifer Anne. b 60. Hull Univ BSc 81 Univ of Wales (Lamp) MA 06. S Dios Minl Tr Scheme 90. **d** 93 **p** 94. C Alverstoke *Portsm* 93-96; C Elson 97-01; P-in-c Gosport Ch Ch and Dioc FE Officer 01-04; PtO *Roch* 05-06; P-in-c Seal SS Pet and Paul 06-12; V from 12. *The Vicarage, Church Street, Seal, Sevenoaks TN15 0AR* T: (01732) 762955
E: annelebas@dsl.pipex.com

LE BILLON, Mrs Janet. b 42. STETS 99. **d** 02 **p** 03. NSM Guernsey St Jo *Win* 02-06; NSM Guernsey Ste Marie du Castel 06-09; NSM Guernsey St Matt 06-09; PtO from 09; Chapl States of Guernsey Bd of Health from 02. *Tranquillité, Clos des Quatre Vents, St Martin, Guernsey GY4 6SU* T: (01481) 234283

LE COUTEUR, Miss Tracy. b 41. STETS. **d** 09 **p** 10. NSM Jersey St Clem *Win* from 09. *2 La Cachette, La Cache du Bourg, St Clement, Jersey JE2 6FX* T: (01534) 857693
E: tracylecouteur@hotmail.com

LE DIEU, Miss Heather Muriel. b 41. Birm Univ BA 62 MA 67. Cranmer Hall Dur 77. **dss** 79 **d** 87. Birchfield *Birm* 79-82; Kings Heath 82-84; Walsall Pleck and Bescot *Lich* 84-88; Par Dn 87-88; rtd 88. *159 Swarthmore Road, Selly Oak, Birmingham B29 4NW* T: 0121-475 1236

LE GRICE, Elizabeth Margaret. b 53. Man Univ BA 75 MA(Theol) 78. N Bapt Coll 75 Westcott Ho Cam 87. **d** 88 **p** 97. In Bapt Ch 78-82; C Whitchurch *Llan* 88-95; Chapl among the Deaf SE Wales *Mon* 95-12; P-in-c Grwp Bro Ystwyth a Mynach *St D* from 12. *The Vicarage, Llanafan, Aberystwyth SY23 4AZ* T: (01974) 261185 E: emlegrice@btinternet.com

LE GRYS, Alan Arthur. b 51. K Coll Lon BD 73 AKC 73 MTh 90. St Aug Coll Cant 73. **d** 74 **p** 75. C Harpenden St Jo *St Alb* 74-77; C Hampstead St Jo *Lon* 77-81; Chapl Westf Coll and Bedf Coll 81-83; V Stoneleigh *Guildf* 84-91; Lect Ripon Coll Cuddesdon 91-96; Prin SEITE 96-05; Hon PV Roch Cathl from 96; PtO from 06. *2 Blenheim Avenue, Chatham ME4 6UU* T: (01634) 814298 M: 07958-547053
E: a.legrys@btinternet.com

LE ROSSIGNOL, Richard Lewis. b 52. Aston Univ BSc 75. Oak Hill Th Coll BA 79. **d** 79 **p** 80. C E Ham St Paul *Chelmsf* 79-81; C Willesborough w Hinxhill *Cant* 81-85; PtO 85-94; NSM Brabourne w Smeeth 94-01; NSM Mersham w Hinxhill and Sellindge 01-06; NSM Smeeth w Monks Horton and Stowting and Brabourne 06-07; P-in-c 07-14; P-in-c Mersham w Hinxhill and Sellindge 07-14; V A20 Benefice from 14. *The Rectory, Church Road, Smeeth, Ashford TN25 6SA* T: (01303) 812697 E: rlerossi@ntlworld.com

LE SÈVE, Mrs Jane Hilary. b 63. SS Hild & Bede Coll Dur BA 86. EAMTC 01. **d** 04 **p** 05. NSM Brightlingsea *Chelmsf* 04-08; TV Greenstead w Colchester St Anne 08-15; P-in-c Wickham Bishops w Lt Braxted from 15; Asst Dir of Ords from 15. *The Rectory, 1 Church Road, Wickham Bishops, Witham CM8 3LA* E: revhilary@btinternet.com

LE SUEUR, Paul John. b 38. Lon Univ BSc 59. Wycliffe Hall Ox 60. **d** 62 **p** 63. C Mortlake w E Sheen *S'wark* 62-65; C Witney *Ox* 65-69; R Sarsden w Churchill 69-74; P-in-c Clifton Hampden 74-77; P-in-c Rotherfield Greys H Trin 77-82; V 82-90; V Blacklands Hastings Ch Ch and St Andr *Chich* 90-97; V Ticehurst and Flimwell 97-00; rtd 00; PtO *Chich* from 01. *80 Barnhorn Road, Bexhill-on-Sea TN39 4QA* T: (01424) 844747 E: halomanpaul@talk21.com

LE VASSEUR, Mrs Linda Susan. b 48. Shenstone Coll of Educn CertEd 70. S Dios Minl Tr Scheme 92. **d** 95 **p** 96. NSM Guernsey Ste Marie du Castel and Guernsey St Matt *Win* 95-01; NSM Guernsey St Sav and Guernsey St Marguerite de la Foret 01-14; P-in-c Guernsey St Jo from 14; Chapl Princess Eliz Hosp Guernsey from 00. *Coin des Arquets, Les Arquets, St Pierre du Bois, Guernsey GY7 9HE* T: (01481) 264047

LE VAY, Clare Forbes Agard Bramhall Joanna. b 41. St Anne's Coll Ox BA 64 MA 66 Univ of Wales (Abth) MSc 72 PhD 86. Westcott Ho Cam 86. **d** 88 **p** 94. C Stamford Hill St Thos *Lon* 88-89; C Hackney 89-92; Asst Chapl Brook Gen Hosp Lon 92-95; Asst Chapl Greenwich Distr Hosp Lon 92-95; Chapl Greenwich Healthcare NHS Trust 95-01; PtO *S'wark* 02-06; Lon 04-06; *Glouc* from 09. *Winton, Beards Lane, Stroud GL5 4HD* T: (01453) 767020 M: 07816-468112
E: clarelevay@yahoo.com

LE-WORTHY, Michael Raymond. b 50. **d** 98 **p** 99. OLM Glascote and Stonydelph *Lich* 98-12; NSM from 12; NSM Tamworth from 12. *15 Abbey Road, Glascote, Tamworth B77 2QE* T: (01827) 55252
E: michael.leworthy1@btinternet.com

LEA, Carolyn Jane. See COOKE, Carolyn Jane

LEA, Canon Montague Brian. b 34. OBE 00. St Jo Coll Cam BA 55 Lon Univ BD 71. St Jo Coll Nottm 68. **d** 71 **p** 72. C Northwood Em *Lon* 71-74; Chapl Barcelona *Eur* 74-79; V Hove Bp Hannington Memorial Ch *Chich* 79-86; Adn N France *Eur* 86-94; Chapl Paris St Mich 86-94; Hon Can Gib Cathl from 95; R Chiddingly w E Hoathly *Chich* 94-96; Chapl The Hague *Eur* 96-00; rtd 01; PtO *Chich* from 01. *35 Summerdown Lane, East Dean, Eastbourne BN20 0LE* T: (01323) 423226 E: brian.lea@freedom255.co.uk

LEA, Norman. b 42. JP 89. Univ of Wales (Lamp) BA 67. Coll of Resurr Mirfield 66. **d** 68 **p** 69. C Newton St Pet *S & B* 68-71; C Oystermouth 71-73; C Brecon w Battle 73-74; TV Cwmbran *Mon* 74-77; V Talgarth and Llanelieu *S & B* 77-84; V Port Talbot St Theodore *Llan* 84-95; Hon Chapl Miss to Seafarers 84-08; V Cadoxton-juxta-Neath *Llan* 95-08; P-in-c Tonna 04-08; rtd 08. *67 Leonard Street, Neath SA11 3HW*

LEA, Canon Richard John Rutland. b 40. Trin Hall Cam BA 63 MA 67. Westcott Ho Cam 63. **d** 65 **p** 66. C Edenbridge *Roch* 65-68; C Hayes 68-71; V Larkfield 71-86; P-in-c Leybourne 76-86; RD Malling 79-84; V Chatham St Steph 86-88; Can Res and Prec Roch Cathl 88-98; V Iffley *Ox* 98-06; rtd 06; PtO *Roch* from 06. *The Gate House, Malling Abbey, Swan Street, West Malling ME19 6LP* T: (01732) 522887
E: richard.lea@lineone.net

LEA-WILSON, Nicholas Hugh. b 61. Man Poly BA 83 Univ Coll Ches BA 08 MLI 90. NOC 05. **d** 08 **p** 09. C Gateacre *Liv* 08-12; P-in-c Knowsley 12-14; TV 4Saints Team from 14. *The Vicarage, Tithebarn Road, Prescot L34 0JA* T: 0151-546 4266 M: 07968-290553 E: hugh.leawilson@virgin.net

LEACH, Alan Charles Graham. b 46. Univ Coll Ches BTh 04 Master Mariner 73. NOC 04. **d** 05 **p** 06. NSM Neston *Ches* 05-08; NSM Heswall from 08. *8 Hill Top Lane, Ness, Neston CH64 4EL* T: 0151-336 5046 M: 07802-622143
E: alan.leach5@btinternet.com

LEACH, Alan William Brickett. b 28. MSc CEng FIStructE FASI FICE. S'wark Ord Course. **d** 89 **p** 90. NSM Forest Row *Chich* 89-98; PtO from 98. *High Beeches, Priory Road, Forest Row RH18 5HP* T: (01342) 823778
E: alanleach@mail.adsl4less.com

LEACH, Andrew John Philip. b 54. Univ of Wales (Lamp) BA 77 Univ of Wales (Abth) PGCE 78. WEMTC 07. **d** 10 **p** 11. NSM Painswick, Sheepscombe, Cranham, The Edge etc *Glouc* from 10. *Melrose Cottage, Cheltenham Road, Painswick GL6 6SJ* T: (01452) 813609 M: 07564-448692
E: ajpleach@googlemail.com

LEACH, Miss Bethia Morag. b 62. Sheff Univ BA 84 Liv Inst of Educn PGCE 85. Ripon Coll Cuddesdon 95. **d** 97 **p** 98. C Stafford *Lich* 97-00; TV Bilston 00-07; V Pennsett *Worc* 07-10; rtd 10. *66 Lichfield Road, Walsall WS4 2DJ* T: (01922) 446956
E: bethialeach@virginmedia.com

LEACH, Clive. See LEACH, James Clive

LEACH, Gerald. b 27. Sarum & Wells Th Coll 85. **d** 73 **p** 74. NSM Cyncoed *Mon* 73-86; C 86-87; V Dingestow and Llangovan w Penyclawdd etc 87-94; rtd 94; PtO *Heref* from 95; LtO *Mon* from 98. *19 Grange Park, Whitchurch, Ross-on-Wye HR9 6EA* T: (01600) 890397

LEACH, James Clive. b 65. Homerton Coll Cam BEd 88 Open Univ MA 98. SWMTC 04. **d** 09 **p** 10. NSM Shalfleet *Portsm* 09-14; Hd Teacher Walkwood C of E Middle Sch from 15. *Walkwood C of E Middle School, Feckenham Road, Headless Cross, Redditch B97 5AQ* M: 07535-670089 T: (01527) 543361
E: rev.clive@gmail.com

LEACH, James Roger. b 66. Ball Coll Ox BA 89 MA 99. Wycliffe Hall Ox BA 98. **d** 99 **p** 00. C Knowle *Birm* 99-06; C Gerrards Cross and Fulmer *Ox* from 06. *3 The Uplands, Gerrards Cross SL9 7JQ* T: (01753) 886480 E: james.leach@saintjames.org.uk

LEACH, Jeffrey Alan. b 64. Bournemouth Univ MSc 00. Qu Coll Birm BA 11. **d** 11 **p** 12. NSM Wednesfield St Greg *Lich* from 11; Chapl Sandwell Coll from 11; Chapl R Wolv Hosps NHS Trust from 15. *36 Clewley Drive, Wolverhampton WV9 5LB* M: 07805-273277 E: fr.jeffreyleach@btinternet.com

LEACH, John. b 52. K Coll Lon BD 79 AKC 79 St Jo Coll Dur MA 83 Lambeth STh 02. **d** 81 **p** 82. C N Walsham w Antingham *Nor* 81-85; C Crookes St Thos *Sheff* 85-89; V Styvechale *Cov* 89-97; Dir Angl Renewal Min 97-02; R Jersey St Lawr *Win* 02-04; Par Development Adv *Mon* 04-09; V Folkestone St Jo *Cant* 09-13; PtO 13-14; Developing Discipleship Adv and Tr *Linc* from 14. *105 Nettleham Road, Lincoln LN2 1RU* E: john.leach@lincoln.anglican.org

LEACH, Mrs Rebecca Mary. b 65. St Aid Coll Dur BA 87 Bris Univ PGCE 90. ERMC 05. **d** 08 **p** 09. C E Barnet *St Alb* 08-11; C Harpenden St Nic from 11. *122 Hazelwood Drive, St Albans AL4 0UZ* T: (01727) 840182 E: p.r.leach@ntlworld.com

LEACH, Robert Neville. b 54. Trin Coll Bris 91. **d** 93 **p** 94. C Towcester w Easton Neston *Pet* 93-96; P-in-c Cowley *Lon* 96-01; P-in-c Brandon and Santon Downham w Elveden *St E* 01-04; P-in-c Lakenheath 02-04; R Brandon and Santon Downham w Elveden etc 04-10; P-in-c Chirbury *Heref* 10-13; P-in-c Marton 10-13; P-in-c Middleton 10-13; P-in-c Trelystan w Leighton 10-13; V Chirbury, Marton, Middleton and Trelystan etc from 13. *The Vicarage, Chirbury, Montgomery SY15 6BN* T: (01938) 561822 E: revtrebor@hotmail.com

LEACH, Samuel Mark. b 76. Westmr Coll Ox BEd 99. Ridley Hall Cam 05. **d** 08 **p** 09. C Walsall St Paul *Lich* 08-11; TV Wednesfield from 11. *The Vicarage, St Albans House, Griffiths Drive, Wolverhampton WV11 2LJ* M: 07915-668714
E: samuelmw@hotmail.co.uk

LEACH, Stephen Lance. b 42. St Steph Ho Ox 66. **d** 69 **p** 70. C Higham Ferrers w Chelveston *Pet* 69-72; TV Ilfracombe H Trin *Ex* 72; TV Ilfracombe, Lee and W Down 72-74; V Barnstaple St Mary 74-77; R Goodleigh 74-77; P-in-c Barnstaple St Pet w H Trin 76-77; P-in-c Landkey 77-79; TR Barnstaple and Goodleigh 77-79; TR Barnstaple, Goodleigh and Landkey 79-82; V Paignton St Jo 82-95; Chapl Paignton and Kings Ash Hosps 82-95; Gen Sec ACS 95-08; Public

Preacher *Birm* from 95; rtd 07; PtO *Ex* from 07. *16 Kings Avenue, Paignton TQ3 2AR* T: (01803) 552335

LEACH, Stephen Windsor. b 47. St Chad's Coll Dur BSc 70 Linacre Coll Ox BA 72 MA 76. Ripon Hall Ox 70. **d** 73 **p** 74. C Swinton St Pet *Man* 73-77; C Oldham St Chad Limeside 77-79; V Shaw 79-87; V St Just in Penwith *Truro* 87-14; V Sancreed 87-14; rtd 14. *Porthpean, 4 Bentham Avenue, Fleetwood FY7 8RH* T: (01253) 771624
E: windsorleach@aol.com

LEACH, Timothy Edmund. b 41. Dur Univ BA 63. Ridley Hall Cam 63. **d** 65 **p** 66. C Ecclesfield *Sheff* 65-68; C Stocksbridge 68-71; C-in-c W Bessacarr CD 71-80; V Goole and Hon Chapl Miss to Seamen 80-95; V Wath-upon-Dearne *Sheff* 95-08; rtd 08; PtO *Sheff* from 09. *6 Sawn Moor Avenue, Thurcroft, Rotherham S66 9DQ* T: (01709) 701263
E: komedy@btopenworld.com

LEADBEATER, Richard Paul. b 77. Birm Univ BA 04. Wycliffe Hall Ox 08. **d** 10 **p** 11. C Selly Park St Steph and St Wulstan *Birm* 10-14. *Christianity Explored, 14 Harley Street, London W1G 9PQ* M: 07799-795928
E: richardleadbeater@hotmail.com

LEADER, Miss Janette Patricia. b 46. EAMTC 94. **d** 97 **p** 98. C Desborough, Brampton Ash, Dingley and Braybrooke *Pet* 97-01; V Wellingborough St Barn 01-12; rtd 12; PtO *Pet* from 14. *15 Salisbury Road, Peterborough PE4 6NL* T: (01733) 685672
E: revjanleader@virginmedia.com

LEADER, Stephen. b 64. Ripon Coll Cuddesdon 99. **d** 01 **p** 02. C Battersea St Luke *S'wark* 01-04; V Enfield St Jas *Lon* 04-12; V Palmers Green St Jo from 12. *St John's Vicarage, 1 Bourne Hill, London N13 4DA* T: (020) 8886 1348
E: stephenthevicar@gmail.com

LEAF, Edward David Hugh. b 65. Oak Hill Th Coll BA 97. **d** 98 **p** 99. C Bath St Bart *B & W* 98-01; C Minehead 01-05; V Chadderton Em *Man* from 05. *Emmanuel Vicarage, 15 Chestnut Street, Chadderton, Oldham OL9 8HB* T: 0161-688 8655 *or* 681 1310 E: david.leaf@btopenworld.com

LEAF, William Peter Geard. b 67. Edin Univ BEng 90. Ridley Hall Cam 08. **d** 10 **p** 11. C Fulham St Dionis *Lon* 10-13; C Hammersmith St Paul from 13. *4 Margravine Road, London W6 8HJ* E: will@stdionis.org.uk

LEAH, William Albert. b 34. K Coll Lon BA 56 AKC 57 K Coll Cam MA 63. Ripon Hall Ox 60. **d** 62 **p** 63. C Falmouth K Chas *Truro* 62-63; Chapl K Coll Cam 63-67; Min Can Westmr Abbey 67-74; V Hawkhurst *Cant* 74-83; Hon Min Can Cant Cathl 78-83; V St Ives *Truro* 83-94; rtd 98. *Trerice Cottage, Sancreed Newbridge, Penzance TR20 8QR* T: (01736) 810987

LEAHY, David Adrian. b 56. Open Univ BA 90. Qu Coll Birm. **d** 85 **p** 86. C Tile Cross *Birm* 85-88; C Warley Woods 88-91; V Hobs Moat 91-07; AD Solihull 97-04; V Four Oaks from 07; AD Sutton Coldfield from 13. *The Vicarage, 26 All Saints Drive, Sutton Coldfield B74 4AG* T: 0121-308 5315
E: revaleahy@gmail.com

LEAK, Adrian Scudamore. b 38. Ch Ch Ox BA 60 MA 65 BD 89. Cuddesdon Coll 64. **d** 66 **p** 67. C Cov St Mark 66-69; C Dorchester *Ox* 69-73; V Badsey *Worc* 73-80; V Wickhamford 73-78; V Badsey w Aldington and Wickhamford 78-80; P-in-c Monkwearmouth St Pet *Dur* 80-81; V Choral and Archivist York Minster 81-86; Can Res and Prec Guildf Cathl 86-90; Hon C Guildf H Trin w St Mary 96-00; Hon C Worplesdon 00-06; P-in-c Withyham St Mich *Chich* 06-13; rtd 13; PtO *Guildf* from 14. *14 Fisher Rowe Close, Bramley, Guildford GU5 0EH* T: (01483) 894030 E: adrian.leak@btinternet.com

LEAK, Harry Duncan. b 30. St Cath Coll Cam BA 53 MA 57. Ely Th Coll 53. **d** 54 **p** 55. S Africa 54-57; Portuguese E Africa 57-61; C Eccleshall *Lich* 62-64; V Normacot 64-66; C Stoke upon Trent 66-68; V Hanley All SS 68-71; R Swynnerton 71-80; PtO 80-03; rtd 92. *15 Sutherland Road, Tittensor, Stoke-on-Trent ST12 9JQ* T: (01782) 374341

LEAK, John Michael. b 42. St Jo Coll Nottm. **d** 84 **p** 85. NSM Beeston *Ripon* 84-87; C Far Headingley St Chad 87-88; Hon C 88-90; C Headingley 90-95; TV Bramley 95-98; rtd 98. *23 Arthington Close, Tingley, Wakefield WF3 1BT* T: 0113-253 3061

✠**LEAKE, The Rt Revd David.** b 35. CBE 03. ALCD 59 LTh 74. **d** 59 **p** 60 **c** 69. C Watford *St Alb* 59-61; Lect 61-63; SAMS Argentina 63-69; Asst Bp Paraguay 69-73; Asst Bp N Argentina 69-80; Bp N Argentina 80-90; Bp Argentina 90-02; rtd 02; Hon Asst Bp Nor from 03; PtO from 03. *The Anchorage, Lower Common, East Runton, Cromer NR27 9PG* T: (01263) 513536
E: david@leake8.wanadoo.co.uk

LEAKE, Duncan Burton. b 49. Leeds Univ BA 71 Leeds and Carnegie Coll PGCE 72 Keele Univ MA 85. Oak Hill Th Coll 90. **d** 92 **p** 93. C Stanwix *Carl* 92-97; C Chasetown *Lich* 97-00; V Chase Terrace 00-14; rtd 14; PtO *Lich* from 15. *12 Outwoods Close, Weston, Stafford ST18 0JR* E: duncan.leake@ntlworld.com

LEAKEY, Ian Raymond Arundell. b 24. K Coll Cam BA 47 MA 49. Ridley Hall Cam 48. **d** 50 **p** 51. C Litherland St Jo and St Jas *Liv* 50-53; Rwanda Miss 53-73; Can Burundi 66; V Cudham *Roch* 73-76; P-in-c Downe 76; V Cudham and Downe 76-89; rtd 89; PtO *Sarum* from 89. *10 Francis Court, Spire View, Salisbury SP2 7GE* T: (01722) 329243
E: iandf.leakey@btinternet.com

LEAKEY, Peter Wippell. b 39. Lon Univ BSc 60. Trin Coll Bris 73. **d** 75 **p** 76. C Colne St Bart *Blackb* 75-79; V Copp 79-85; V Pennington *Man* 85-05; AD Leigh 93-00; Hon Can Man Cathl 02-05; rtd 05; PtO *Man* from 05. *28 Gilda Road, Worsley, Manchester M28 1BP* T: 0161-703 8076

LEAL, John. **d** 14. NSM Rock Ferry *Ches* from 14. *16 Green Mount, Wirral CH49 6NR*

LEAL, Malcolm Colin. b 33. Chich Th Coll 72. **d** 75 **p** 76. NSM Shoreham St Giles CD *Chich* 75-87; Chapl NE Surrey Coll Ewell 87-95; NSM Arundel w Tortington and S Stoke *Chich* 88-95; PtO 95-06. *8 West Park Lane, Goring-by-Sea, Worthing BN12 4EK* T: (01903) 244160

LEALMAN, Helen. b 46. NOC 03. **d** 05 **p** 06. NSM Ben Rhydding *Bradf* 05-06; NSM Bolton St Jas w St Chrys 06-10; NSM Shipley St Paul *Leeds* from 10. *8 Parkfield Road, Shipley BD18 4EA* T: (01274) 584569 E: helen.lealman@bradford.anglican.org

LEAMY, Stuart Nigel. b 46. Pemb Coll Ox BA 68 MA 73 ACA 76 FCA 81. Sarum Th Coll 68. **d** 70 **p** 71. C Upholland *Liv* 70-78; LtO *Lon* 78-83 and 94-97; NSM Pimlico St Mary Bourne Street from 97. *92 Gloucester Road, Hampton TW12 2UJ* T: (020) 8979 9068 E: leamy@blueyonder.co.uk

LEAN, The Very Revd David Jonathan Rees. b 52. Coll of Resurr Mirfield 74. **d** 75 **p** 76. C Tenby St D 75-79; C Tenby w Gumfreston 80-81; V Llanrhian w Llanhywel and Carnhedryn etc 81-88; V Haverfordwest St Martin w Lambston 88-00; RD Roose 99-00; Can St D Cathl from 00; TV Dewisland 01-09; TR from 09; Dean St D from 09. *The Deanery, St Davids, Haverfordwest SA62 6RD* T: (01437) 720202
E: dean@stdavidscathedral.org.uk

LEAR, Peter Malcolm. b 45. FCMA. SEITE 95. **d** 98 **p** 99. NSM Ham St Andr *S'wark* 98-03; NSM Wandsworth St Anne 03-04; NSM Upper Coquetdale *Newc* 04-11; rtd 11; PtO *Newc* from 11. *39 Farmanby Close, Thornton Dale, Pickering YO18 7TD*
E: peter@learpm.com

LEARMONT, Oliver James. b 62. UEA BA 83 Wolv Univ LLM 96 SS Coll Cam BTh 07. Westcott Ho Cam 05. **d** 07 **p** 08. C Hitchin *St Alb* 07-11; P-in-c E Bridgford and Kneeton *S'well* from 11; P-in-c Flintham from 11; P-in-c Car Colston w Screveton from 11. *The Rectory, Kirk Hill, East Bridgford, Nottingham NG13 8PE* M: 07966-459315
E: oliver.learmont@btinternet.com

LEARMOUTH, Michael Walter. b 50. FCA. Oak Hill Th Coll 84. **d** 84 **p** 85. C Harlow St Mary and St Hugh w St Jo the Bapt *Chelmsf* 84-89; V Hainault 89-97; TR Harlow Town Cen w Lt Parndon 97-00; TR Barnsbury *Lon* from 00; AD Islington 08-14. *The Rectory, 10 Thornhill Square, London N1 1BQ* T: (020) 7607 9039 *or* 7607 4552
E: michael@learmouth.fsworld.co.uk

LEARY, Thomas Glasbrook. b 42. AKC 66. **d** 67 **p** 68. C W Bromwich All SS *Lich* 67-70; TV Croydon St Jo *Cant* 70-75; C Limpsfield and Titsey *S'wark* 75-83; V Sutton New Town St Barn 83-92; V Merton St Mary 92-07; RD Merton 98-01; rtd 07; PtO *S & B* 12-14. *Conduit Cottage, Livesey Road, Ludlow SY8 1EZ* T: (01584) 875619 E: glassbrook@msn.com

LEATHARD, Preb Brian. b 56. Sussex Univ BA Cam Univ MA Loughb Univ PhD 91. Westcott Ho Cam 79. **d** 82 **p** 83. C Seaford w Sutton *Chich* 82-85; Chapl Loughb Univ *Leic* 85-89; V Hampton Hill *Lon* 89-06; R Chelsea St Luke and Ch Ch from 06; Dir of Ords 99-09; Preb St Paul's Cathl from 05. *The Rectory, 64A Flood Street, London SW3 5TE* T: (020) 7352 6331 *or* 7351 7365 E: brianleathard@chelseaparish.org

LEATHARD, Prof Helen Louise. b 47. Chelsea Coll Lon BSc 70 K Coll Lon PhD 74 St Martin's Coll Lanc MA 06 FBPharmacolS 06. LCTP 12. **d** 13 **p** 14. NSM Slyne w Hest and Halton w Aughton *Blackb* from 13. *29 Coronation Way, Lancaster LA1 2TQ* T: (01524) 849495
E: helenleathard@btinternet.com

LEATHERBARROW, Andrew James Howard. b 68. All SS Cen for Miss & Min 12. **d** 15. C Rainhill *Liv* from 15. *18 Chadwick Lane, Widnes WA8 9NN* M: 07557-132262

LEATHERBARROW, Mrs Laura. b 70. **d** 14 **p** 15. C E Widnes *Liv* from 14. *18 Chadwick Lane, Widnes WA8 9NN*

LEATHERBARROW, Ronald. b 35. Chester Coll TCert 59. NW Ord Course 71. **d** 75 **p** 76. C Eccleston Ch Ch *Liv* 75-80; C Eccleston St Thos 80-83; R Kirklinton w Hethersgill and Scaleby *Carl* 83-86; R Blackley St Mark White Moss *Man* 86-99; rtd 99. *1 Chapel Street, St Helens WA10 2BG* T: (01744) 614426

LEATHERS, Brian Stanley Peter. b 61. Nottm Univ BSc 83. Oak Hill Th Coll BA 89. **d** 89 **p** 90. C Watford *St Alb* 89-92; C Welwyn w Ayot St Peter 92-96; V Heacham *Nor* 96-99; P-in-c Stapenhill Immanuel *Derby* 99-00; V 00-09; V Alton w Bradley-le-Moors and Oakamoor w Cotton *Lich* 09-10; P-in-c Denstone w Ellastone and Stanton 09-10; P-in-c Mayfield 09-10; V Alton w Bradley-le-Moors and Denstone etc from 10; RD Uttoxeter from 11. *The New Vicarage, Limekiln Lane, Alton, Stoke-on-Trent ST10 4AR* T: (01538) 702469 E: briantopsey@googlemail.com

LEATHERS, Daniel Brian. b 88. Derby Univ BA 10 Trin Hall Cam BTh 15. Ridley Hall Cam 12. **d** 15. C Whitfield *Derby* from 15. *12 Rushmere, Glossop SK13 8TH* M: 07526-660791 E: dan_leathers@hotmail.co.uk

LEATHES, David Burlton de Mussenden. b 49. St Jo Coll Nottm 90. **d** 92 **p** 93. C Kirkby Stephen w Mallerstang etc *Carl* 92-00; C Brough w Stainmore, Musgrave and Warcop 94-00; PtO from 11. *Low Beck House, Rookby, Kirkby Stephen CA17 4HX* T: (017683) 71713 E: leathesrookby@btinternet.com

LEATHLEY, Susan Mary. b 57. Bath Univ BPharm 78 Trin Coll Bris MA 98 MRPharmS. Oak Hill Th Coll 92. **d** 94 **p** 98. C Weston-super-Mare Ch Ch *B & W* 94-95; C Toxteth St Philemon w St Gabr and St Cleopas *Liv* 97-01; TV Maghull 01-08; TV Mildenhall *St E* 08-14; C from 14. *The Rectory, 8 Church Walk, Mildenhall, Bury St Edmunds IP28 7ED* T: (01638) 711930 E: sueleathley@aol.com

LEATHLEY, Terence Michael. b 63. Coll of Resurr Mirfield 99. **d** 01 **p** 02. C Whitby w Aislaby and Ruswarp *York* 01-04; TV 04-07; V S Bank from 07; V Middlesbrough St Thos from 07. *The Vicarage, 259 Normanby Road, Middlesbrough TS6 6TB* T: (01642) 453679 M: 07678-986916 E: terence.leathley@ntlworld.com

LEATON, Martin John. b 46. Clifton Th Coll 68. **d** 71 **p** 72. C Kenilworth St Jo *Cov* 71-74; C Stratford-on-Avon w Bishopton 74-77; P-in-c Meriden 77-81; R Meriden and Packington 82-84; R Heanton Punchardon w Marwood *Ex* 84-87; PtO 95-97; P-in-c Rampton w Laneham, Treswell, Cottam and Stokeham *S'well* 97-06; P-in-c N and S Leverton 03-06; rtd 06; Hon C Tysoe w Oxhill and Whatcote *Cov* from 06. *The Vicarage, Peacock Lane, Tysoe, Warwick CV35 0SG* T: (01295) 680201 E: martinleaton@yahoo.co.uk

LEAVER, David Noel. b 63. Hatf Coll Dur BA 85. Wycliffe Hall Ox 89. **d** 91 **p** 92. C Blackheath Park St Mich *S'wark* 91-95; C Upton (Overchurch) *Ches* 95-98; C Wilmslow 98-99; PtO from 99. *42 Hill Top Avenue, Cheadle Hulme, Cheadle SK8 7HY* T: 0161-485 4302 E: davidleaver@btconnect.com

LEAVER, Mrs Janice Patricia. b 56. EAMTC 03. **d** 06 **p** 07. C Desborough, Brampton Ash, Dingley and Braybrooke *Pet* 06-09; TV Wilford Peninsula *St E* from 09. *The Vicarage, 11 Walnut Tree Avenue, Rendlesham, Woodbridge IP12 2GG* T: (01394) 460547 M: 07913-977218 E: rendleshamvicarage@gmail.com

LEAVER (née SMYTH), Mrs Lucinda Elizabeth Jane (Liz). b 67. New Hall Cam BA 88 MA 92. Wycliffe Hall Ox BTh 93. **d** 93 **p** 94. C Cambridge St Barn *Ely* 93-97; Chapl St Kath Hall Liv Inst of HE 97-98; TV Stockport SW *Ches* 99-01; Chapl Stockport Gr Sch from 99; Chapl Univ Hosp of S Man NHS Foundn Trust from 14. *42 Hill Top Avenue, Cheadle Hulme, Cheadle SK8 7HY* T: 0161-485 4302 E: liz.leaver@boltblue.net

LEAVER, Prof Robin Alan. b 39. Groningen Univ DTh 87. Clifton Th Coll 62. **d** 64 **p** 65. C Gipsy Hill Ch Ch *S'wark* 64-67; C Gt Baddow *Chelmsf* 67-71; P-in-c Reading St Mary Castle Street Prop Chpl *Ox* 71-77; P-in-c Cogges 77-84; Chapl Luckley-Oakfield Sch Wokingham 73-75; Lect Wycliffe Hall Ox 84-85; Prof Ch Music Westmr Choir Coll USA 84-08; Visiting Prof Liturgy Drew Univ 88-00; Visiting Prof Juilliard Sch from 04; Visiting Prof Yale Univ from 08; Visiting Prof QUB from 08. *10 Finch Lane, Dover NH 03820-4707, USA* T: (001) (603) 343 4251 E: leaver@rider.edu

LEAVES (née CRAIG), Julie Elizabeth. b 63. Southn Univ BTh 87. Sarum & Wells Th Coll 82. **dss** 86 **d** 87 **p** 92. Thatcham *Ox* 86-87; Par Dn 87-88; Hong Kong 88-92; Assoc P Fremantle Australia 92-95; Chapl St Mary's Angl Girls' Sch Karrinyup from 96. *Wollaston College, Wollaston Road, Mount Claremont WA 6010, Australia* T: (0061) (8) 9383 2774 *or* 9341 9102 F: 9341 9222 E: jleaves@stmarys.wa.edu.au

LEAVES, Nigel. b 58. Keble Coll Ox BA 80 MA 83 K Coll Lon PGCE 81 MA 86. Sarum & Wells Th Coll 84. **d** 86 **p** 87. C Boyne Hill *Ox* 86-88; Chapl Hong Kong Cathl 88-92; Australia from 92; Abp's Chapl and R W Perth 92-98; Tutor and Research Fell Murdoch Univ 98-00; Warden Wollaston Coll & Dir Cen for Belief, Spirituality and Aus Culture from 00. *Wollaston College, Wollaston Road, Mount Claremont WA 6010, Australia* T: (0061) (8) 9384 5511 *or* T/F: 9383 2774 F: 9385 3364 E: leaves@iinet.net.au

LEAWORTHY, John Owen. b 40. Univ of Wales (Swansea) BSc 62. Oak Hill Th Coll 80. **d** 82 **p** 83. C Compton Gifford *Ex* 82-85; C Plymouth Em w Efford 85-86; P-in-c Marks Tey w Aldham and Lt Tey *Chelmsf* 86-88; R 88-89; Chapl HM Pris Full Sutton 89-91; NSM Portree *Arg* 96-04; rtd 05; PtO *Chelmsf* from 05. *46 Wilkin Drive, Tiptree, Colchester CO5 0QP* T: (01621) 810905 E: jleaworthy@btinternet.com

LECK, Stuart David. b 62. Cant Ch Ch Univ BA 11 ACIB 84. SEITE 03. **d** 06 **p** 07. NSM Brockley Hill St Sav *S'wark* 06-10; NSM Nunhead St Antony w St Silas 10-12; C Catford (Southend) and Downham 12-14; TV from 14. *St Barnabas' Vicarage, 1 Churchdown, Bromley BR1 5PS* T: (020) 8698 4851 M: 07811-384420 E: stuart.leck@btinternet.com

LECKEY, Paul Robert. b 61. QUB. Ripon Coll Cuddesdon Aston Tr Scheme. **d** 96 **p** 97. C Eastleigh *Win* 96-01; P-in-c Upton St Leonards *Glouc* 01-13; V Hall Green Ascension *Birm* from 13. *592 Fox Hollies Road, Hall Green, Birmingham B28 9DX* E: rev_leckey@blueyonder.co.uk

LECLÉZIO, Ms Marie Katryn. b 62. Natal Univ BA 83 All Nations Chr Coll MA 00. WEMTC 05. **d** 08 **p** 09. C Halas *Worc* 08-12; TV from 12; Deanery Miss Enabler from 12. *34 Beecher Road, Halesowen B63 2DJ* T: (01384) 411383 E: revkat@halasteam.org.uk

LEDBETTER, Canon Shannon Carroll. b 64. Louisville Univ (USA) BA 85 Liv Univ PhD 00. Virginia Th Sem MTS 96. **d** 03 **p** 04. NSM Knowsley *Liv* 03-08; NSM W Derby St Mary and St Jas 08-11; Can Res Blackb Cathl from 11. *20 Buncer Lane, Blackburn BB2 6SE* T: (01254) 503090 M: 07720-072787 E: shannon.ledbetter@blackburncathedral.co.uk

LEDGER, Mrs Margaret Phyllis. b 47. **d** 04 **p** 05. OLM Newburn Newc from 04. *14 Woodside Avenue, Throckley, Newcastle upon Tyne NE15 9BE* T: 0191-267 2953 E: margaret.p.ledger@btinternet.com

LEDWARD, John Archibald. b 30. Lon Univ BD 58 Man Univ MA 81 FRSA 85. ALCD 57. **d** 58 **p** 59. C St Helens St Helen *Liv* 58-62; V Dearham *Carl* 62-66; V Mirehouse 66-71; V Daubhill *Man* 71-77; R Newcastle w Butterton *Lich* 77-88; R Rockland St Mary w Hellington, Bramerton etc *Nor* 88-94; P-in-c Kirby Bedon w Bixley and Whitlingham 92-94; R Rockland St Mary w Hellington, Bramerton etc 94-95; RD Loddon 92-95; rtd 95; PtO *Nor* from 95. *41 Lackford Close, Brundall, Norwich NR13 5NL* T: (01603) 714745 E: jledward@talktalk.net

LEE, Agnes Elizabeth. b 31. Open Univ BA 87 Whitelands Coll Lon TCert 51 ACP 76. NOC 97. **d** 98 **p** 99. NSM Dewsbury *Wakef* 98-02; rtd 02; PtO *Leeds* from 02. *1 Moor Park Court, Dewsbury WF12 7AU* T: (01924) 467319

LEE, Andrew. *See* LEE, Sang Youn

LEE, Mrs Anne Louise. b 65. St Jo Coll Nottm BTh 90. Wycliffe Hall Ox 94. **d** 95 **p** 96. C Wembley St Jo *Lon* 95-98; NSM S Gillingham *Roch* 98-07; Jt P-in-c Locking *B & W* 07-09; Jt P-in-c Hutton and Locking 09-13; R from 13. *The Vicarage, The Green, Locking, Weston-super-Mare BS24 8DA* T: (01934) 823556 E: revdannelee@yahoo.co.uk

LEE, Anthony Maurice. b 35. Bps' Coll Cheshunt 62. **d** 65 **p** 66. C Pinner *Lon* 65-71; Asst Youth Chapl *Glouc* 71-72; V Childswyckham 72-73; R Aston Somerville 72-73; V Childswyckham w Aston Somerville 73-91; P-in-c Stanton w Snowshill 88-91; R Childswyckham w Aston Somerville, Buckland etc 91-94; RD Winchcombe 86-94; rtd 94. *11 Holly Close, Broadclyst, Exeter EX5 3JB*

LEE, Canon Brian. b 37. Linc Th Coll 78. **d** 80 **p** 81. C Duston *Pet* 80-84; P-in-c Spratton 84-89; V 89-06; Jt P-in-c Maidwell w Draughton, Lamport w Faxton 89-01; Jt P-in-c Cottesbrooke w Gt Creaton and Thornby 89-06; RD Brixworth 94-01; Can Pet Cathl 98-06; rtd 06; PtO *Pet* from 06. *8 Clive Close, Kettering NN15 5BQ* T: (01536) 484407 E: brian.lee18@btopenworld.com

LEE, Canon Brian Ernest. b 32. ARCA 59 FCA 70. Linc Th Coll 60. **d** 62 **p** 63. C Birch St Jas *Man* 62-65; C Withington St Paul 65-66; R Abbey Hey 66-70; Hon C Gatley *Ches* 86-88; V Egremont St Jo 88-97; RD Wallasey 91-96; OGS from 92; Hon Can Ches Cathl 96-97; rtd 97; PtO *Nor* from 97. *St Fursey House, Convent of All Hallows, Ditchingham, Bungay NR35 2DZ* T: (01986) 892308 F: 894215

LEE, Brian John. b 51. K Coll Lon BD 78 AKC 78. Coll of Resurr Mirfield 78. **d** 79 **p** 80. C Ham St Rich *S'wark* 79-82; C Surbiton St Andr and St Mark 82-85; V Shirley St Geo 85-93; V St Botolph Aldgate w H Trin Minories *Lon* 93-08; rtd 08. *6 Shore Cottages, Silverdale, Carnforth LA5 0TS*

LEE, Christopher James. b 52. FIBMS 77. St Mich Coll Llan 10. **d** 13 **p** 14. NSM Caerau w Ely *Llan* from 13. *10 Coronation Road, Cardiff CF14 4QY* T: (029) 2061 8054 M: 07831-500738 E: seejayenterprises@ntlworld.com

LEE, Christopher John Bodell. b 82. Kingston Univ BA 01 Cam Univ BTh 11. Ridley Hall Cam 08. **d** 07 **p** 11. C Onslow Square and S Kensington St Aug *Lon* 11-14; P-in-c Cobbold

Road St Sav w St Mary from 15. *St Saviour's Vicarage, Cobbold Road, London W12 9LN* M: 07966-632161
E: revchris7@gmail.com

LEE, Clifford Samuel (Sam). b 53. **d** 95 **p** 96. OLM S Elmham and Ilketshall *St E* 95-10; NSM Worlingham w Barnby and N Cove 10-12; rtd 12. *Packway Lodge, Park Road, Flixton, Bungay NR35 1NR* T: (01986) 782300

LEE, Clive Warwick. b 34. St Pet Coll Ox BA 58 MA 62 Ox Univ PGCE 73. Coll of Resurr Mirfield 58. **d** 60 **p** 61. C W End *Win* 60-64; C Upper Norwood St Jo *Cant* 65-69; Chapl Vinehall Sch Robertsbridge 69-94; rtd 94; PtO *Cant* 04-12. *Old Farmhouse Rest Home, 48 Hollow Lane, Canterbury CT1 3SA*

LEE, David Alexander. b 83. Imp Coll Lon MSci 05 PhD 10. Oak Hill Th Coll BA 14. **d** 14 **p** 15. C Fulham St Pet *Lon* from 14. *St Peter's Vicarage, St Peter's Terrace, London SW6 7JS*
E: david.a.lee@gmail.com

LEE, The Ven David John. b 46. Bris Univ BSc 67 Fitzw Coll Cam BA 76 MA 79 Birm Univ PhD 96. Ridley Hall Cam 74. **d** 77 **p** 78. C Putney St Marg *S'wark* 77-80; Tutor Bp Tucker Th Coll Uganda 80-86; Tutor Crowther Hall CMS Tr Coll Selly Oak 86-91; P-in-c Wishaw and Middleton *Birm* 91-96; Can Res Birm Cathl 96-04; Dir Dioc Bd for Miss 96-04; Adn Bradf 04-15; rtd 15; Adn for Miss Resources from 15. *47 Kirkgate, Shipley BD18 3EH* T: (01274) 200698 *or* T/F: 730196 M: 07711-671351
E: david.lee@westyorkshiredales.anglican.org

LEE, The Ven David Stanley. b 30. Univ of Wales (Cardiff) BSc 51. St Mich Coll Llan 56. **d** 57 **p** 58. C Caerau w Ely *Llan* 57-60; C Port Talbot St Agnes 60-70; Ind Chapl 60-70; R Merthyr Tydfil 70-72; Chapl Merthyr Tydfil Hosp 70-91; R Merthyr Tydfil and Cyfarthfa *Llan* 72-91; RD Merthyr Tydfil 82-91; Can Llan Cathl 84-97; Adn Llan 91-97; R Llanfabon 91-97; rtd 97; PtO *Llan* from 97; *Mon* from 98. *2 Old Vicarage Close, Llanishen, Cardiff CF14 5UZ* T: (029) 2075 2431

LEE, David Wight Dunsmore. b 39. Wells Th Coll 61. **d** 63 **p** 64. C Middlesbrough St Oswald *York* 63-67; C Northallerton w Kirby Sigston 67-69; R Limbe W Thyolo and Mulanje Malawi 69-71; R S Highlands 71-75; V Newington Transfiguration *York* 76-81; P-in-c Sheriff Hutton 81-85; P-in-c Sheriff Hutton and Farlington 85-97; V Sheriff Hutton, Farlington, Stillington etc 97-04; rtd 04; PtO *York* from 04. *Kirkstone Cottage, Main Street, Oswaldkirk, York YO62 5XT* T: (01439) 788283
E: dawdle@dwdlee.plus.net *or* dwdlee@talk21.com

LEE, Derek Alfred. **d** 00. Hon Par Dn Llantilio Pertholey w Bettws Chpl etc *Mon* 00-05; Hon Par Dn Llanfihangel Crucorney w Oldcastle etc from 05. *94 Croesonen Parc, Abergavenny NP7 6PF* T: (01873) 855042

LEE, Edmund Hugh. b 53. Trin Coll Ox BA 75 MA 79 Goldsmiths' Coll Lon BMus 83 K Coll Lon MA 98. Ripon Coll Cuddesdon 93. **d** 95 **p** 96. C Malden St Jas *S'wark* 95-99; TV Mortlake w E Sheen 99-08. *67 North Worple Way, London SW14 8PP* T: (020) 8876 5270 E: edknife@aol.com

LEE, Elizabeth. *See* LEE, Agnes Elizabeth

LEE, Gilbert. b 51. Hong Kong Univ BD 80 Kent Univ MA 98. Chung Chi Coll Hong Kong 77. **d** 80 **p** 81. C Angl Ch Hong Kong 80-81; V 81-88; NSM St Martin-in-the-Fields *Lon* 88-00; Chapl Chinese Congregation 88-00; I St Jo Chinese Ch Toronto Canada 00-07; I Markham All SS from 07. *142 Dunbar Crescent, Markham ON L3R 6V8, Canada* T: (001) (905) 946 1637 F: 946 9782 E: allsts@arex.com

LEE, Hugh. *See* LEE, John Charles Hugh Mellanby

LEE, Canon Hugh Gordon Cassels. b 41. St Andr Univ BSc 64. Edin Th Coll 64. **d** 67 **p** 68. C Dumfries *Glas* 67-70; C Totteridge *St Alb* 70-73; R Glas St Jas 73-80; R Bishopbriggs 80-86; R St Fillans *St And* 86-89; R Crieff and Comrie 86-01; P-in-c Muthill 86-01; P-in-c Lochearnhead 89-01; R Dunoon *Arg* 01-06; Dioc Supernumerary from 06; Dioc Dir of Ord from 06; Can St Jo Cathl Oban from 01; Can Cumbrae from 04. *Chapel Hall, Toward, Dunoon PA23 7UA* T: (01369) 870237
E: fish4hill@yahoo.co.uk

LEE, Miss Iris Audrey Olive. b 26. Gilmore Ho. **dss** 76 **d** 87. N Weald Bassett *Chelmsf* 76-87; rtd 87; NSM Clacton St Jas *Chelmsf* 87-00; Chapl Clacton Hosp 90-95; PtO *Chelmsf* 00-04. *30 Marine Court, Marine Parade West, Clacton-on-Sea CO15 1ND* T: (01255) 423719

LEE, Janet. b 58. **d** 13 **p** 14. OLM Clifton Ch Ch w Em *Bris* from 13. *45 Alma Road, Clifton, Bristol BS8 2DE*

LEE, Mrs Jayne Christine. b 53. Dundee Univ MA 75. **d** 06 **p** 07. OLM Roberttown w Hartshead *Wakef* 06-12; OLM Heckmondwike 06-12; OLM Heckmondwike (w Norristhorpe) and Liversedge *Leeds* from 12; OLM Liversedge w Hightown *Wakef* 06-12; OLM Hartshead, Hightown, Roberttown and Scholes *Leeds* from 12. *58 Prospect View, Liversedge WF15 8BD* T: (01924) 401264 E: jayneclee@hotmail.com

LEE, Mrs Jennifer. b 42. Westf Coll Lon BA 64 CQSW 78. NOC 01. **d** 03 **p** 04. NSM Millhouses H Trin *Sheff* 03-06;

PtO 06-13; NSM Compton w Shackleford and Peper Harow *Guildf* 07-12; rtd 12; PtO *Guildf* from 12. *The Old Cottage Barn, Peper Harow Park, Peper Harow, Godalming GU8 6BQ* T: (01483) 424468 E: revjenny@btinternet.com

LEE, John. b 47. Univ of Wales (Swansea) BSc 70 MSc 73 MInstGA 87. Ripon Hall Ox 73. **d** 75 **p** 76. C Swansea St Pet *S & B* 75-78; C St Botolph Aldgate w H Trin Minories *Lon* 79-84; P-in-c Chiddingstone w Chiddingstone Causeway *Roch* 84-89; R 89-98; Clergy Appts Adv from 98; Chapl to The Queen from 10. *Church House, Great Smith Street, London SW1P 3AZ* T: (020) 7898 1898 F: 7898 1899
E: admin.caa@churchofengland.org

LEE, John Charles Hugh Mellanby. b 44. Trin Hall Cam BA 66 MA 69 Brunel Univ MTech 71. Ox NSM Course 78. **d** 81 **p** 82. NSM Amersham on the Hill *Ox* 81-88; NSM Ox St Aldate w St Matt 88-93; NSM Wheatley 93-95; Dioc Development Officer Miss in Work and Economic Life 95-02; P-in-c Ox St Mich w St Martin and All SS 02-09; LtO from 09; NSM Wheatley 13-14; NSM Beckley, Forest Hill, Horton-cum-Studley and Stanton St John from 14. *64 Observatory Street, Oxford OX2 6EP* T: (01865) 316245 M: 07879-426625
E: hugh.lee@btinternet.com

LEE, John Michael Andrew. b 62. Leeds Univ BA 84. Trin Coll Bris 88. **d** 90 **p** 91. C Norbiton *S'wark* 90-94; C Leic H Trin w St Jo 94-02; R York St Paul from 02. *St Paul's Rectory, 100 Acomb Road, York YO24 4ER* T: (01904) 792304
E: johnmalee@btinternet.com

LEE, John Samuel. b 47. Chich Th Coll 74. **d** 77 **p** 78. C Bramley *Ripon* 77-80; C Bideford *Ex* 81-84; TV Littleham w Exmouth 84-90; P-in-c Sidbury 90-91; TV Sidmouth, Woolbrook, Salcombe Regis, Sidbury etc 91-04; rtd 04. *Westward Ho!, Torpark Road, Torquay TQ2 5BQ* T: (01803) 293086
E: johnslee@glensidf.freeserve.co.uk

LEE, Joseph Patrick. b 53. St Jos Coll Upholland 72 Ushaw Coll Dur 75. **d** 78 **p** 79. In RC Ch 78-99; Hon C Charlton *S'wark* 99-09; Hon C E Greenwich from 09. *45 Chestnut Rise, London SE18 1RJ* T: (020) 8316 4674 M: 07956-294429
F: 8317 7304 E: joe_lee@lineone.net

LEE, Mrs Judith Mary. b 44. Doncaster Coll of Educn TCert 65. **d** 06 **p** 07. OLM Frenchay and Winterbourne Down *Bris* from 06. *8 Beaufort Road, Frampton Cotterell, Bristol BS36 2AD* T: (01454) 772381 E: jrplee@btinternet.com

LEE, Canon Kenneth Peter. b 45. Em Coll Cam BA 67 MA 71. Cuddesdon Coll 67. **d** 69 **p** 70. C Stoke Poges *Ox* 69-72; C Witton *Ches* 72-74; V Frankby w Greasby 74-92; R Christleton 92-10; Hon Can Ches Cathl 05-10; rtd 10; PtO *Ches* from 10. *16 Rookery Drive, Tattenhall, Chester CH3 9QS* T: (01829) 770292 E: leepf@btinternet.com

LEE, Lloyd Han. b 81. Man Univ BA 03. Wycliffe Hall Ox. **d** 12 **p** 13. C Pennington *Man* from 12. *11 Ruby Grove, Leigh WN7 4JW* T: (01942) 607695
E: lloyd@christchurchpennington.com

LEE, Luke Gun-Hong. b 37. Univ of Yon Sei BTh 62. St Jo Coll Morpeth 64. **d** 67 **p** 68. LtO Taejon Korea 67-79; C Bloxwich *Lich* 79-83; TV Dunstable *St Alb* 83-90; V Croxley Green All SS 90-07; rtd 07. *101 Larkvale, Aylesbury HP19 0YP* T: (01296) 423133 E: luke.gh.lee@gmail.com

LEE, Miss Lynley Hoe. b 52. St Jo Coll Nottm BTh 89 K Coll Lon MA 93. **d** 90 **p** 94. Par Dn Pitsea *Chelmsf* 90-95; Singapore 95-98; C Gt Ilford St Andr *Chelmsf* 99-02; TV Grays Thurrock 02-07; Chapl Salford R NHS Foundn Trust from 07. *Hope Hospital, Stott Lane, Salford M6 8HD* T: 0161-789 7373
E: lynleyhoe@aol.com

LEE, Mrs Margaret. b 48. Coll of Ripon & York St Jo BEd 71. NEOC 03. **d** 06 **p** 07. NSM Houghton le Spring *Dur* from 06. *2 Rectory View, Shadforth, Durham DH6 1LF* T: 0191-372 0595 E: margaretlee595@hotmail.com

LEE, Martin Paul. b 66. Leeds Univ BA 13. Aston Tr Scheme 91 Linc Th Coll 93 St Steph Ho Ox 94. **d** 96 **p** 97. C Wells St Thos w Horrington *B & W* 96-00; P-in-c Brent Knoll, E Brent and Lympsham 00-01; R 01-08; RD Axbridge 03-08; V Long Benton *Newc* from 08; AD Newc E from 12. *The Vicarage, 3 Station Road, Benton, Newcastle upon Tyne NE12 8AN* T: 0191-266 1921 E: martinlee903@btinternet.com

LEE, Mary Elizabeth. *See* DUNN, Mary Elizabeth

LEE, Michael. b 45. **d** 07 **p** 08. OLM Chickerell w Fleet *Sarum* 07-11; NSM from 11. *45 Lower Way, Chickerell, Weymouth DT3 4AR* T: (01305) 777031
E: michael.lynda@googlemail.com

LEE, Ms Michele Julie. b 57. St Mellitus Coll 12. **d** 15. NSM Paddington St Steph w St Luke *Lon* from 15; NSM Bayswater from 15. *Address temp unknown*

LEE, Nicholas Knyvett. b 54. Trin Coll Cam BA 76 MA 77. Cranmer Hall Dur 82. **d** 85 **p** 86. C Brompton H Trin w Onslow Square St Paul *Lon* 85-11; C Onslow Square and S Kensington St Aug from 11; Chapl R Brompton and

Harefield NHS Trust 86-90 and from 94. *St Paul's Church House, Onslow Square, London SW7 3NX* T: 08456-447533 E: nicky.lee@htb.org.uk

LEE, On Yip Franklin. b 82. York Univ BA 04 MA 06 Leeds Univ MA 07 Cam Univ BTh 12. Westcott Ho Cam 09. **d** 12 **p** 13. C Spalding St Mary and St Nic *Linc* from 12. *The Chantry, 7 Church Street, Spalding PE11 2PB* T: (01775) 711400 M: 07879-542831 E: franklinleeuk@yahoo.co.uk

LEE, Peter. *See* LEE, Kenneth Peter

LEE, Peter Alexander. b 44. Hull Univ BSc(Econ) 65. Ex & Truro NSM Scheme 80. **d** 83 **p** 84. NSM Ex St Sidwell and St Matt 83-89; NSM Ex St Dav 90-98; C Paignton St Jo 98-01; PtO 01-03; Hon C Ex St Dav from 03. *Windyridge, Beech Avenue, Exeter EX4 6HF* T: (01392) 254118

✠**LEE, The Rt Revd Peter John.** b 47. St Jo Coll Cam BA 69 MA 73 CertEd 70 Lambeth BD 06. Ridley Hall Cam 70 St Jo Coll Nottm 72. **d** 73 **p** 74 **c** 90. C Onslow Square St Paul *Lon* 73-76; S Africa from 76; V-Gen and Bp Ch the K from 90. *PO Box 1653, Rosettenville, 2130 South Africa* T: (0027) (11) 435 0097 *or* 942 1179 F: 435 2868 E: dckpeter@netactive.co.za

LEE, Peter Kenneth. b 44. Selw Coll Cam BA 66 MA 69. Cuddesdon Coll 67. **d** 69 **p** 70. C Manston *Ripon* 69-72; C Bingley All SS *Bradf* 72-77; Chapl Bingley Coll of Educn 72-77; V Cross Roads cum Lees *Bradf* 77-90; V Auckland St Pet *Dur* 90-09; Tutor NEOC 91-09; rtd 09; Tutor NEITE from 03; PtO *York* from 10. *2 Winston Court, Northallerton DL6 1PY* T: (01609) 777539

LEE, Canon Raymond John. b 30. St Edm Hall Ox BA 53 MA 57. Tyndale Hall Bris 54. **d** 56 **p** 57. C Tooting Graveney St Nic *S'wark* 56-59; C Muswell Hill St Jas *Lon* 59-62; V Woking St Mary *Guildf* 62-70; V Gt Crosby St Luke *Liv* 70-82; Dioc Adv NSM 79-95; V Allerton 82-94; P-in-c Altcar 94-98; Hon Can Liv Cathl 89-95; rtd 95; PtO *Liv* from 98. *15 Barkfield Lane, Liverpool L37 1LY* T: (01704) 872670 E: rjlee@btinternet.com

LEE, Rebecca Susan. *See* HARRIS, Rebecca Susan

LEE, Richard. *See* LEE, Thomas Richard

LEE, Robert David. b 53. QUB BD 75. CITC 77. **d** 77 **p** 78. C Comber *D & D* 77-83; I Mt Merrion 83-87; CMS 89-92; Egypt 89-97; R Peebles *Edin* 97-11; P-in-c Innerleithen 97-11; rtd 11. *Flat 6, 32 Montgomery Street, Edinburgh EH7 5JS* T: 0131-623 1850 E: robindavidlee@gmail.com

LEE, Robert William. b 31. Keele Univ BA 54 St Cath Soc Ox BA 58 MA 63. Ripon Hall Ox 56. **d** 59 **p** 60. C Dawley St Jerome *Lon* 59-62; C Bromley H Trin *Roch* 62-65; R Clayton *Man* 65-70; P-in-c Man St Paul 65-70; TV Hemel Hempstead *St Alb* 70-72; TV Corby SS Pet and Andr w Gt and Lt Oakley 72-80; V Weedon Lois w Plumpton and Moreton Pinkney etc 80-88; R Thornhams Magna and Parva, Gislingham and Mellis *St E* 88-96; rtd 96; PtO *Carl* from 96; *Leeds* from 97. *2 Guldrey Fold, Sedbergh LA10 5DY* T: (01539) 621907

LEE, Roderick James. b 50. Linc Th Coll 88. **d** 90 **p** 91. C Rushden w Newton Bromswold *Pet* 90-93; C Kingsthorpe w Northampton St Dav 93-94; TV 94-99; R Mears Ashby and Hardwick and Sywell etc 99-04; P-in-c Corby St Columba 04-12; RD Corby 07-12; rtd 12; Chapl Northants Fire and Rescue Service *Pet* 08-15. *79 Stanley Road, Northampton NN5 5EH* M: 07806-262822 E: revrjl@btinternet.com

LEE, Sai Kuen. *See* LEE, Gilbert

LEE, Sam. *See* LEE, Clifford Samuel

LEE, Sang Youn (Andrew). b 65. Pontifical Gregorian Univ BPh 95 BTh 98 MTh 00. St Steph Ho Ox 10. **d** 98 **p** 99. In RC Ch 98-06; C Goldthorpe w Hickleton *Sheff* 12-14; P-in-c Dalton from 14; P-in-c Ryecroft St Nic from 14. *The Vicarage, 2 Vicarage Close, Rotherham S65 3QL* M: 07870-885705 E: frandrewlee@yahoo.co.kr

LEE, Steven Michael. b 56. Van Mildert Coll Dur BA 78. Trin Coll Bris 80. **d** 83 **p** 84. C Beckenham St Jo *Roch* 83-86; C Leic Martyrs 86-90; V Coalville and Bardon Hill 90-95; P-in-c Kibworth and Smeeton Westerby and Saddington 95-00; P-in-c Foxton w Gumley and Laughton 96-00; R Kibworth and Smeeton Westerby and Saddington 00-06; Chapl St Lawr Coll Ramsgate 06-08; R Newcastle w Butterton *Lich* 08-14; V Holmer w Huntington *Heref* from 14. *The New Vicarage, Holmer, Hereford HR4 9RG* T: (01432) 273200 E: revslee@btinternet.com

LEE, Stuart Graham. b 73. Roehampton Inst BA 94. St Steph Ho Ox BTh 00. **d** 00 **p** 01. C Eltham H Trin *S'wark* 00-03; TV Wimbledon 03-10; TV Mortlake w E Sheen from 10. *86 East Sheen Avenue, London SW14 8AU* T: (020) 8287 0090 E: stuartlee73@blueyonder.co.uk

LEE, Stuart Michael. b 67. SEITE 06. **d** 09 **p** 10. NSM St Jo on Bethnal Green *Lon* 09-14; NSM Bethnal Green St Barn from 14. *29 Brierly Gardens, London E2 0TE* T: (020) 8980 1699 M: 07855-703766 E: stuartm.lee@virgin.net

LEE, Thomas Richard. b 52. AKC 73 FRSA 03. St Aug Coll Cant 74. **d** 75 **p** 76. C Leam Lane CD *Dur* 75-80; Chapl

RAF 80-09; Prin Armed Forces Chapl Cen Amport Ho 03-06; Hon C St Mary le Strand w St Clem Danes *Lon* 06-09; QHC 06-09; TR Egremont and Haile *Carl* from 09. *The Rectory, Grove Road, Egremont CA22 2LU* T/F: (01946) 820268 E: lee535877@aol.com

LEE, Veronica. b 47. Redland Coll of Educn TCert 68 Open Univ BA 84 Bris Poly MEd 89. STETS 02. **d** 05 **p** 06. NSM Bishopston and St Andrews *Bris* from 05. *48 Chesterfield Road, Bristol BS6 5DL* T: 0117-949 8325 E: vronlee@hotmail.com

LEE, Young. b 75. Korea Univ MA 98. St Mellitus Coll BA 12. **d** 12 **p** 13. C Walthamstow *Chelmsf* 12-15; P-in-c Barking St Erkenwald from 15. *St Erkenwald Vicarage, Levett Road, Barking IG11 9JZ* M: 07800-969706 E: gleeofgod@gmail.com

LEE-BARBER, Evelyn Mary. b 62. **d** 13 **p** 14. NSM Bath Abbey w St Jas *B & W* from 13. *6 Cranhill Road, Bath BA1 2YF* E: evelyn@evelynleebarber.plus.com

LEE-PHILPOT, Derreck Anthony John. b 56. Ripon Coll Cuddesdon 08. **d** 11 **p** 12. NSM Cholsey and Moulsford *Ox* from 11. *49 Elmhurst Road, Thatcham RG18 3DQ* T: (01635) 290973 E: derrecke21@btinternet.com

LEECE, Roderick Neil Stephen. b 59. Wadh Coll Ox BA 81 MA 85 Leeds Univ BA 84 ARCM 85. Coll of Resurr Mirfield 82. **d** 85 **p** 86. C Portsea St Mary *Portsm* 85-91; V Stamford Hill St Bart *Lon* 91-05; R Hanover Square St Geo from 05. *21A Down Street, London W1J 7AW* T: (020) 7629 0874 E: rleece@lineone.net

LEECH, Kenneth. b 39. Lon Univ BA 61 AKC 61 Trin Coll Ox BA 63 MA 71 Lambeth DD 98. St Steph Ho Ox 62. **d** 64 **p** 65. C Hoxton H Trin w St Mary *Lon* 64-67; C Soho St Anne w St Thos and St Pet 67-71; Tutor St Aug Coll Cant 71-74; R Bethnal Green St Matt *Lon* 74-79; Field Officer Community & Race Relns Unit BCC 80; Race Relns Officer Gen Syn Bd for Soc Resp 81-87; Hon C Notting Hill St Clem and St Mark *Lon* 82-85; Hon C Notting Dale St Clem w St Mark and St Jas 85-88; Dir Runnymede Trust 87-90; Hon C St Botolph Aldgate w H Trin Minories *Lon* 91-04; rtd 04; PtO *Man* from 05; *Ches* from 06. *Sandon House, Market Street, Mossley, Ashton-under-Lyne OL5 0JG* T: (01457) 838655 E: kenleech@aol.com

LEECH, Pieter-Jan Bosdin. b 73. K Alfred's Coll Win BA 96. St Jo Coll Nottm 08. **d** 10 **p** 11. C Stalham, E Ruston, Brunstead, Sutton and Ingham *Nor* 10-13; R Brundall w Braydeston and Postwick from 13. *The Rectory, 73 The Street, Brundall, Norwich NR13 5LZ* M: 07504-171311 E: peter.leech@live.co.uk

LEEDS, Archdeacon of. *See* HOOPER, The Ven Paul Denis Gregory

LEEDS, Bishop of. *See* BAINES, The Rt Revd Nicholas

LEEFIELD, Michael John. b 37. Liv Univ BA 60 K Coll Lon BD 65 AKC 65. St Boniface Warminster 62. **d** 66 **p** 67. C Gt Yarmouth *Nor* 66-70; V Trowse 70-75; V Arminghall 70-75; R Caistor w Markshall 70-75; Chapl Norfolk and Nor Hosp 70-75; V Lydney w Aylburton *Glouc* 75-84; RD Forest S 82-84; LtO from 85; rtd 01. *Brays Court, Awre, Newnham GL14 1EP* T: (01594) 510483

LEEKE, Charles Browne. b 39. Stranmillis Coll CertEd 62. CITC 80. **d** 83 **p** 84. C Ballymoney w Finvoy and Rasharkin *Conn* 83-86; I Faughanvale *D & R* 86-97; Chapl Port Londonderry Miss to Seamen 92-97; Bp's Dom Chapl *D & R* 92-96; Can Derry Cathl 96-00; I Drumragh w Mountfield 97-00; Reconciliation Development Officer *D & D* 00-06; Can Dromore Cathl 05-06; rtd 06; I Dromara w Garvaghy *D & D* 08-13. *41 Beechfield Lodge, Aghalee, Craigavon BT67 0GA* T: (028) 9265 0179 M: 07712-870799 E: charlieleeke@yahoo.co.uk

LEEKE, Canon Stephen Owen. b 50. EAMTC 82 Ridley Hall Cam 83. **d** 84 **p** 85. C Cherry Hinton St Andr *Ely* 84-87; P-in-c Warboys 87-91; P-in-c Bury 87-91; P-in-c Wistow 87-91; R Warboys w Broughton and Bury w Wistow 91-01; RD St Ives 92-01; V Cambridge St Martin 01-15; Hon Can Ely Cathl 05-15; rtd 15. *Address temp unknown* E: stephen.leeke@ely.anglican.org

LEEMAN, John Graham. b 41. NOC 78. **d** 80 **p** 81. NSM Hull St Mary Sculcoates *York* 80-96; PtO 96-99; Hon C Hull St Mary Sculcoates 99-04; P-in-c 04-14; Hon C Hull St Steph Sculcoates 99-04; Hon C Sculcoates St Paul w Ch Ch and St Silas 99-04. *1 Snuff Mill Lane, Cottingham HU16 4RY* T: (01482) 840355

LEEMAN, Miss Penelope Anne. b 51. SNWTP 10. **d** 12 **p** 13. C Kirkdale St Athanaseus with St Mary *Liv* from 12. *St Athanasius Vicarage, 54 Fonthill Road, Liverpool L4 1QQ* T: 0151-284 4703 E: pennyleeman@blueyonder.co.uk

LEEMING, Jack. b 34. Kelham Th Coll 56. **d** 61 **p** 62. C Sydenham St Phil *S'wark* 61-64; Chapl RAF 64-84; Chapl Salisbury Gen Infirmary 84-89; R Barford St Martin, Dinton, Baverstock etc *Sarum* 89-99; rtd 99; PtO *Sarum* from 01. *8 Bower Gardens, Salisbury SP1 2RL* T: (01722) 416800

LEEMING, Mrs Janice Doreen. b 45. EMMTC 97. **d** 00 **p** 01. NSM Lenton *S'well* 00-06; NSM Radford All So and St Pet 06-13; rtd 13. *5 Hollinwell Avenue, Wollaton, Nottingham NG8 1JY* T: 0115-928 2145

LEES, Allan Garside. b 38. **d** 99 **p** 00. OLM Hurst *Man* 99-09; r-d 09; PtO *Man* from 10. *1 Exeter Drive, Ashton-under-Lyne OL6 8BZ* T: 0161-339 3105

LEES, Brian James. b 52. Lon Univ BA 74 Leeds Univ BA 08 Univ of Wales (Abth) PGCE 75. NOC 05. **d** 08 **p** 09. NSM Hutton Cranswick w Skerne, Watton and Beswick *York* 08-11; P-in-c from 11; P-in-c Nafferton w Wansford from 14. *The Old Post House, 20 Main Street, Beswick, Driffield YO25 9AS* T: (01377) 270806 E: brianjlees@tiscali.co.uk

LEES, Charles Alan. b 38. RGN TCert. WMMTC 78. **d** 81 **p** 82. NSM Yardley St Cypr Hay Mill *Birm* 81-84 and 86-87; Hon C Dorridge 84-86; Chapl E Birm Hosp 85-87; Hon C Leamington Spa H Trin and Old Milverton *Cov* 89-90; PtO *Birm* 95-01. *8 Fairlawn Close, Leamington Spa CV32 6EN*

LEES, Christopher John. b 58. Fitzw Coll Cam BA 80 Birkbeck Coll Lon MA 86 FCIPD. NOC 01. **d** 04 **p** 05. NSM Wilmslow *Ches* 04-14; Asst Dir of Ords 07-14. *3 Vicarage Street, Colyton EX24 6LJ* T: (01297) 551351 E: info@johnleescareers.com

LEES, John Raymond. b 57. Selw Coll Cam BA 78 MA 82. St Steph Ho Ox 89. **d** 91 **p** 92. C Eastbourne St Mary *Chich* 91-93; Min Can and Succ St Paul's Cathl 93-98; TR Swindon New Town *Bris* 98-01; Asst to AD Swindon and C Highworth w Sevenhampton and Inglesham etc 01-02; PtO *Lon* 02-05; *Pet* 04-06; *Ely* 04-06; Can Res and Prec Wakef Cathl 06-09; r-d 09; PtO *Lich* 09-14; *Nor* from 14; Hon PV Nor Cathl from 15. *The Beeches, 58 Church Lane, Sprowston, Norwich NR7 8AZ* T: (01603) 423571 E: frjrl01@gmail.com

LEES, Mrs Kathleen Marion. b 30. Birkbeck Coll Lon BA 60. S'wark Ord Course 84. **dss** 80 **d** 87 **p** 94. Epping St Jo *Chelmsf* 80-86; Hon C Hunstanton St Mary w Ringstead Parva, Holme etc *Nor* 87-88; PtO 88-94; Chapl King's Lynn and Wisbech Hosps NHS Trust 94-00; NSM Gaywood *Nor* 94-00; rtd 00; PtO *Nor* from 00. *15 Lavender Court, King's Lynn PE30 4HL* T: (01553) 661294

LEES, Peter John. b 39. St Jo Coll Nottm 91. **d** 95 **p** 96. NSM Buckie and Turriff *Ab* 95-00; P-in-c Fraserburgh 00-01; R 01-06; rtd 06; LtO *Ab* from 06; P-in-c Turriff 08-09. *7 Whitefield Court, Buckie AB56 1EY* T: (01542) 835011 M: 07929-668027

LEES, Peter John William. b 37. **d** 02. NSM Walsall St Paul *Lich* 02-12; rtd 12; PtO *Lich* from 13. *66 Cresswell Crescent, Bloxwich, Walsall WS3 2UH* T: (01922) 497869

LEES, Stephen. b 55. St Jo Coll York CertEd 77 BEd 78 Nottm Univ MA 96. St Jo Coll Nottm 88. **d** 90 **p** 91. C Mansfield St Jo *S'well* 90-93; TV Bestwood 93-98; V Baxenden *Blackb* 98-08; P-in-c Halifax All SS *Leeds* from 08. *All Saints' Vicarage, Greenroyd Avenue, Halifax HX3 0LP* T: (01422) 251016 E: theleeslot@blueyonder.co.uk

LEES, Stephen David. b 63. Sheff City Poly BA 84 Bradf Coll of Educn PGCE 92 St Jo Coll Dur BA 09. Cranmer Hall Dur 07. **d** 09 **p** 10. C Frizinghall St Marg *Bradf* 09-13; C Wrose 13-14; C Bolton St Jas w St Chrys 13-14; V from 14. *St James's Vicarage, 1056 Bolton Road, Bradford BD2 4LH* T: (01274) 772097 E: stephen.lees@bradford.anglican.org *or* stelees51@gmail.com

LEES, Stuart Charles Roderick. b 62. Trin Coll Bris BA. **d** 89 **p** 90. C Woodford Wells *Chelmsf* 89-93; C Brompton H Trin w Onslow Square St Paul *Lon* 93-97; Chapl Stewards Trust 93-97; P-in-c Fulham Ch Ch *Lon* 97-03; V from 03. *Christ Church Vicarage, 40 Clancarty Road, London SW6 3AA* T: (020) 7736 4261 E: stuart@ccfulham.com

LEES-SMITH, Anthony James. b 77. Selw Coll Cam BA 99 MA 02 St Jo Coll Dur BA 08 MA 09 Westmr Inst of Educn PGCE 02. Cranmer Hall Dur 06. **d** 09 **p** 10. C Chesterton Gd Shep *Ely* 09-12; V Evington *Leic* from 12. *The Vicarage, Rectory Gardens, Leicester LE2 2FU* T: 0116-215 5500 M: 07967-353857 E: singers99@virginmedia.com

LEESE, Arthur Selwyn Mountford. b 09. K Coll Lon BD 31 AKC 31 St Cath Soc Ox BA 33 MA 44. Ripon Hall Ox 31. **d** 33 **p** 34. C Bexleyheath Ch Ch *Roch* 33-37; C Cockington *Ex* 37-39; C Langley Mill *Derby* 39-51; V Hawkhurst *Cant* 51-74; rtd 74; PtO from 74; *Chich* 75-08. *84 Wickham Avenue, Bexhill-on-Sea TN39 3ER* T: (01424) 213137

LEESE, Mrs Jane Elizabeth. b 50. Man Univ BA(Econ) 72 Avery Hill Coll PGCE 73. Sarum Th Coll 93. **d** 96 **p** 97. NSM Kempshott *Win* 96-01; NSM Herriard w Winslade and Long Sutton etc 01-08; NSM N Hants Downs from 08. *The Rectory, Greywell Road, Up Nately, Hook RG27 9PL* T: (01256) 765547 E: reverendjane@hotmail.co.uk

LEESE, Katherine Helen. *See* CUNLIFFE, Katherine Helen

LEESON, Bernard Alan. b 47. Bris Univ CertEd 68 Open Univ BA 75 Southn Univ MA 78 Sheff Univ PhD 97 FCollP 92 FRSA 92. EMMTC 84. **d** 87 **p** 88. Dep Hd Master Ripley Mill Hill Sch 80-91; NSM Breadsall *Derby* 87-91; Hd St Aid C of E Tech Coll Lancs 91-06; NSM Officer *Blackb* 92-96; Clergy Support and Development Officer 06-09; PtO 91-92; LtO from 92. *The Lodge, Daggers Lane, Preesall, Poulton-le-Fylde FY6 0QN* T: (01253) 811020 E: leeson@mail.org

LEESON, Mrs Sally Elizabeth. b 57. Sussex Univ BA 79. Westcott Ho Cam 83. **dss** 85 **d** 87 **p** 94. Battersea St Pet and St Paul *S'wark* 85-90; Par Dn 87-90; Par Dn Limpsfield and Titsey 90-94; PtO from 94; Chapl Bp Wand Sch Sunbury-on-Thames from 05. *32 Albany Road, New Malden KT3 3NY* T: (020) 8942 5198

LEFFLER, Christopher. b 33. Em Coll Cam BA 57 MA 61. Linc Th Coll. **d** 59 **p** 60. C Bermondsey St Mary w St Olave and St Jo *S'wark* 59-60; C Herne Hill St Paul 60-63; C-in-c Canley CD *Cov* 63-67; R Gt and Lt Glemham *St E* 67-72; R Badwell Ash w Gt Ashfield, Stowlangtoft etc 72-82; R Trimley 82-99; rtd 99; PtO *St E* from 99. *308 High Street, Felixstowe IP11 9QJ* T: (01394) 672279 M: 07765-785958 E: chrisleffler@uwclub.net

LEFFLER, Jeremy Paul (Jem). b 62. Westmr Coll Ox BEd 88. Wycliffe Hall Ox BTh 94. **d** 94 **p** 95. C Ormskirk *Liv* 94-97; C Much Woolton 97-00; P-in-c Widnes St Ambrose 00-03; V 03-12; P-in-c Birkdale St Jo from 12. *St John's Vicarage, 17 Kirkstall Road, Southport PR8 4RA* T: (01704) 568318 E: info@stambrose.fsnet.co.uk

LEFROY, John Perceval. b 40. Trin Coll Cam BA 62. Cuddesdon Coll 64. **d** 66 **p** 67. C Maidstone St Martin *Cant* 66-69; C St Peter-in-Thanet 69-74; V Barming Heath 74-82; V Upchurch w Lower Halstow 82-05; P-in-c Iwade 95-05; rtd 05. *23 Heather Avenue, Melksham SN12 6FX* T: (01225) 704012 E: jclefroy@tiscali.co.uk

LEFROY, Kathleen Christine. *See* ENGLAND, Kathleen Christine

LEFROY, Matthew William. b 62. Trin Coll Cam BA 84 Keele Univ PGCE 91. St Jo Coll Nottm MTh 02. **d** 02 **p** 03. C Portswood Ch Ch *Win* 02-06; TV Madeley *Heref* 06-13; RD Telford Severn Gorge 11-13; V Lilleshall and Muxton *Lich* from 13. *The Vicarage, 25 Church Road, Lilleshall, Newport TF10 9HE* T: (01952) 604281 E: matthew@mjlefroy.freeserve.co.uk

LEFROY-OWEN, Neal. b 62. Bradf Univ BA 99. NOC 00. **d** 03 **p** 04. C Sandal St Cath *Wakef* 03-06; Asst Chapl HM Pris Hull 06-08; Chapl HM Pris Lindholme 08-12; Chapl HM Pris Wakef 12-14; P-in-c Warley *Wakef* from 15; P-in-c Halifax St Hilda from 15. *The Vicarage, 466 Burnley Road, Halifax HX2 7LW* T: (01422) 363623 E: revneal.owen@gmail.com

LEGG, Adrian James. b 52. St Jo Coll Nottm BTh 82. **d** 82 **p** 83. C Haughton le Skerne *Dur* 82-85; C Llanishen and Lisvane *Llan* 85-89; V Llanwddyn and Llanfihangel-yng-Nghwynfa etc *St As* 89-93; V Llansadwrn w Llanwrda and Manordeilo *St D* 93-10; Chapl Wadham Sch Crewkerne from 11; C Yeovil St Mich *B & W* 12-14. *The Rectory, Cucklington, Wincanton BA9 9PY* T: (01747) 840230 E: adrianlegg@btinternet.com

LEGG, Alison Grant. *See* MILBANK, Alison Grant

LEGG, Joanna Susan Penberthy. *See* PENBERTHY, Joanna Susan

LEGG, Margaret. b 50. SEITE. **d** 07 **p** 08. NSM Paddington St Jo w St Mich *Lon* from 07. *9 Wilton Street, London SW1X 7AF* T: (020) 7235 4944

LEGG, Peter Ellis. b 51. STETS 02. **d** 05 **p** 06. NSM Radipole and Melcombe Regis *Sarum* from 05. *449 Dorchester Road, Weymouth DT3 5BW* T: (01305) 815342 M: 07779-334520 E: pleggwey@aol.com

LEGG, Richard. b 37. Selw Coll Cam BA 62 MA 66 Brunel Univ MPhil 77 NY Th Sem DMin 85. Coll of Resurr Mirfield 63. **d** 65 **p** 66. C Ealing St Pet Mt Park *Lon* 65-68; Chapl Brunel Univ 68-78; Wychcroft Ho (Dioc Retreat Cen) *S'wark* 78-81; C Chipping Barnet w Arkley *St Alb* 81-83; TV 83-85; R St Buryan, St Levan and Sennen *Truro* 85-93; Subwarden St Deiniol's Lib Hawarden 93; PtO *Ches* 93; TV Beaminster Area *Sarum* 93-97; P-in-c Veryan w Ruan Lanihorne *Truro* 97-00; rtd 00; PtO *Truro* 03-09; *B & W* from 10. *27A Bath Road, Wells BA5 3HR* T: (01749) 670468 E: richardlegg@blue-earth.co.uk

LEGG, Roger Keith. b 35. Lich Th Coll 61. **d** 63 **p** 64. C Petersfield w Sheet *Portsm* 63-66; C Portsea St Mary 66-70; Rhodesia 70-75; V Clayton *Lich* 75-00; rtd 01; PtO *Lich* from 01. *High Crest, Chapel Lane, Hookgate, Market Drayton TF9 4QP* T: (01630) 672766 E: rogjud@aol.com

LEGG, Miss Ruth Helen Margaret. b 52. Hull Univ BA 74 Homerton Coll Cam CertEd 75. Trin Coll Bris 86. **d** 88 **p** 94. C Clevedon St Andr and Ch Ch *B & W* 88-92; C Nailsea Ch Ch 92-96; C Nailsea Ch Ch w Tickenham 96-97; V Pill, Portbury and Easton-in-Gordano from 97. *The Rectory, 17 Church Road, Easton-in-Gordano, Bristol BS20 0PQ* T: (01275) 372804

LEGG, Sandra Christine. *See* FACCINI, Sandra Christine

LEGGATE, Colin Archibald Gunson. b 44. Bris Sch of Min 86. **d** 88 **p** 89. NSM Brislington St Luke *Bris* 88-97; Asst Chapl Frenchay Healthcare NHS Trust *Bris* 97-99; Asst

Chapl N Bris NHS Trust from 99. *Frenchay Hospital, Frenchay Park Road, Bristol BS16 1LE* T: 0117-970 1212 *or* 965 1434

LEGGE, Mrs Anne Christine. b 53. Ex Univ BA 73 BPhil 76 PGCE 94. Trin Coll Bris BA 10. **d** 10 **p** 11. C Newton Ferrers w Revelstoke *Ex* 10-13; P-in-c from 13; C Holbeton 11-13; P-in-c from 13. *The Rectory, 8 Court Road, Newton Ferrers, Plymouth PL8 1DL* T: (01752) 873192 M: 07929-153132
E: annelegge@live.com

LEGGE, Robert James. b 63. BSc 92. Ox Min Course. **d** 09 **p** 10. C Walton H Trin *Ox* 09-13; TV Kidderminster E *Worc* from 13. *38 Comberton Avenue, Kidderminster DY10 3EG* M: 07809-227660 E: rjlegge@live.co.uk

LEGGE, Trevor Raymond. b 42. Liv Univ BEng 63. **d** 11 **p** 12. NSM Oughtrington and Warburton *Ches* from 11. *17 Wychwood Avenue, Lymm WA13 0NE* T: (01925) 756872
E: trlegge@talktalk.net

LEGGETT, James Henry Aufrere. b 61. Oak Hill Th Coll 91. **d** 93 **p** 94. C Hensingham *Carl* 93-97; C-in-c Ryde St Jas Prop Chpl *Portsm* from 97. *84 Pellhurst Road, Ryde PO33 3BS* T: (01983) 565621 *or* 566381 E: jleggett@onetel.com

LEGGETT, Nicolas William Michael. b 62. St Steph Ho Ox 00. **d** 02 **p** 04. C Clevedon St Jo *B & W* 02-06; P-in-c Bridgwater H Trin and Durleigh 06-07; V 07-10; V Tile Hill *Cov* from 10; Hon Chapl ATC from 04. *St Oswald's Vicarage, 228 Jardine Crescent, Coventry CV4 9PL* M: 07762-156380
E: leggett1uwe@yahoo.co.uk

LEGGETT, Vanessa Gisela. *See* CATO, Vanessa Gisela

LEGH, Mrs Jane Mary. b 52. Southn Univ BSc 73. Qu Coll Birm 08. **d** 09 **p** 10. NSM S Dales *Derby* from 09; NSM Boylestone, Cubley, Church Broughton, Dalbury, etc from 09. *Cubley Lodge, Cubley, Ashbourne DE6 2FB* T: (01335) 330297
E: jane.legh@cubleylodge.com

LEGOOD, Giles Leslie. b 67. MBE 14. K Coll Lon BD 88 AKC 88 Heythrop Coll Lon MTh 98 Derby Univ DMin 04. Ripon Coll Cuddesdon 90. **d** 92 **p** 93. C N Mymms St Alb 92-95; Chapl R Veterinary Coll *Lon* 95-07; Chapl R Free and Univ Coll Medical Sch 95-07; Chapl RAuxAF 04-07; Chapl RAF from 07. *Chaplaincy Services (RAF), HQ Air Command, RAF High Wycombe HP14 4UE* T: (01494) 496800 F: 496343

LEGRAND, Nigel Stuart. b 51. STETS 96. **d** 99 **p** 00. NSM Boscombe St Jo *Win* 99-03; NSM Pokesdown All SS 03-07; NSM Holdenhurst and Iford from 07; NSM Southbourne St Chris from 03. *50 Meon Road, Bournemouth BH7 6PP* T: (01202) 428603 F: 300400 E: nlegrandfamily@aol.com

LEHANEY, Frank George. b 44. MCIT 75 MILT 99 MIAM 78. **d** 99 **p** 00. OLM Brockham Green *S'wark* 99-07; NSM 07-14; OLM Leigh 99-07; NSM 07-14; PtO from 14; Chapl Surrey and Sussex Healthcare NHS Trust from 99. *Twelve Trees, Small's Hill Road, Leigh, Reigate RH2 8PE* T: (01306) 611201

LEICESTER, Archdeacon of. *See* STRATFORD, The Ven Timothy Richard

LEICESTER, Bishop of. *See* STEVENS, The Rt Revd Timothy John

LEICESTER, Dean of. *See* MONTEITH, The Very Revd David Robert Malvern

LEIGH, Mrs Alison Margaret. b 40. CertEd 63 Goldsmiths' Coll Lon BEd 75. Sarum & Wells Th Coll 85. **d** 87 **p** 94. C Chessington *Guildf* 87-90; C Green Street Green *Roch* 90-92; Dn-in-c E Peckham and Nettlestead 92-94; P-in-c 94-95; R 95-01; rtd 01; PtO *Heref* from 02. *17 Orchard Green, Hereford HR1 3ED* T: (01432) 882032
E: alison.leigh@which.net

LEIGH, Dennis Herbert. b 34. Lon Univ BSc 56. Chich Th Coll 58. **d** 60 **p** 61. C Roehampton H Trin *S'wark* 60-62; C E Wickham 62-67; C Plumstead St Mark and St Marg 67-73; C Corby Epiphany w St Jo *Pet* 73-74; C Paston 84-86; C Aylestone St Andr w St Jas *Leic* 86-95; rtd 95; PtO *Pet* 95-10; *Leic* from 00. *14 Willowbrook Road, Corby NN17 2EB* T: (01536) 263405

LEIGH, James William. b 87. St Chad's Coll Dur BA 08 MA 09. St Steph Ho Ox BA 13. **d** 13 **p** 14. C Horden *Dur* from 13. *15 Park View, Peterlee SR8 4DE* M: 07837-977723
E: fr.james@outlook.com

LEIGH, Mary Elizabeth. b 42. K Coll Lon BA 64 Univ of Wales (Lamp) MMin 06. Westcott Ho Cam 89. **d** 91 **p** 94. NSM Chesterfield St Mary and All SS *Derby* 91-92; C Hall Green Ascension *Birm* 92-94; Asst P Yardley St Edburgha 94-97; Chapl and Tutor NOC 97-08; rtd 08; PtO *Lich* 99-11. *Downing Cottage, Jaggers Lane, Hathersage, Hope Valley S32 1AZ* T: (01433) 650567 M: 07796-980636
E: maryelizabethleigh@gmail.com

LEIGH, Michael John. b 69. Leeds Univ BA 02 LWCMD 93. Coll of Resurr Mirfield 00. **d** 02 **p** 03. C N Hull St Mich *York* 02-06; P-in-c Newby 06-14; V from 14; V Cloughton and Burniston from 14. *St Mark's Vicarage, 77 Green Lane, Scarborough YO12 6HT* T: (01723) 363205 E: mike@singingvicar.co.uk

LEIGH, Raymond. b 37. Lon Univ BEd 81. Clifton Th Coll 65. **d** 68 **p** 69. C Chadwell *Chelmsf* 68-71; Chapl RAF 71-77;

Asst Teacher Swakeleys Sch Hillingdon 81-82; Hd RE 83-88; NSM Hillingdon St Jo *Lon* 87-88; C Rowley Regis *Birm* 88-90; V Londonderry 90-95; R Westbury w Turweston, Shalstone and Biddlesden *Ox* 95-99; CF (ACF) 95-02; rtd 99; PtO *Chich* from 07. *32 Wellington Court, 34-42 Waterloo Road, Epsom KT19 8EX* T: (01372) 436114
E: rayleigh37@sky.com

LEIGH, Richenda Mary Celia. b 71. St Mary's Coll Strawberry Hill BA 93. Ripon Coll Cuddesdon BTh 98. **d** 99 **p** 00. C Dalston H Trin w St Phil and Haggerston All SS *Lon* 99-02; Asst Chapl R Free Hampstead NHS Trust 02-05; Chapl Lon Metrop Univ 05-10; Chapl Derby Univ 10-14; Chapl Derby Cathl 10-14; PtO *S'wark* from 15. *7 Sidney Square, London E1 2EY* M: 07971-659534 E: richenda@leigh.me

LEIGH, Roy Stephen. b 28. Imp Coll Lon BSc 49. S'wark Ord Course 87. **d** 90 **p** 92. NSM Green Street Green *Roch* 90-92; NSM E Peckham and Nettlestead 92-00; PtO 01; *Heref* from 02. *17 Orchard Green, Marden, Hereford HR1 3ED* T: (01432) 882032 E: roy@leighmarden.plus.com

LEIGH-HUNT, Nicolas Adrian. b 46. MIEx 70. Qu Coll Birm 85. **d** 87 **p** 88. C Tilehurst St Geo *Ox* 87-91; TV Wexcombe *Sarum* 91-99; TR 99-02; TR Savernake 02-11; RD Pewsey 97-10; rtd 11; PtO *Sarum* from 15. *Steeles Cottage, 22 Eastcourt, Burbage, Marlborough SN8 3AG* T: (01672) 810953
E: leighhunt@aol.com

LEIGHLIN, Dean of. *See* GORDON, The Very Revd Thomas William

LEIGHTON, Adrian Barry. b 44. LTh. Lon Coll of Div 65. **d** 69 **p** 70. C Erith St Paul *Roch* 69-72; C Ipswich St Marg *St E* 72-75; P-in-c Ipswich St Helen 75-82; R 82-88; P-in-c Holbrook w Freston and Woolverstone 88-97; R Holbrook, Freston, Woolverstone and Wherstead 94-97; R Holbrook, Freston, Woolverstone and Wherstead 97-98; RD Samford 90-93; P-in-c Woore and Norton in Hales *Lich* 98-09; Local Min Adv (Shrewsbury) 99-09; rtd 09; PtO *Ches* from 09. *2 Tollgate Drive, Audlem, Crewe CW3 0EA* T: (01270) 812209 E: adrianleighton@btinternet.com

LEIGHTON, Alan Granville Clyde. b 37. MInstM AMIDHE. S'wark Ord Course 73. **d** 76 **p** 77. C Silverhill St Matt *Chich* 76-79; C Eston *York* 79-82; V 82-84; TR Eston w Normanby 84-02; rtd 02; PtO *York* from 02. *Priory Lodge, 86B Church Lane, Eston, Middlesbrough TS6 9QR* T: (01642) 504798 F: 283016
E: alan.leighton@ntlworld.com

LEIGHTON, Anthony Robert. b 56. Trin Coll Bris BA 88. **d** 88 **p** 89. C Harrow Trin St Mich *Lon* 88-92; TV Ratby cum Groby *Leic* 92-94; TR Bradgate Team 94-00; P-in-c Newtown Linford 95-98; V Thorpe Acre w Dishley 00-08; NSM S Croxton Gp 08-14; Master Wyggeston's Hosp Leic from 14; NSM Leic H Apostles from 14. *The Master's House, Wyggeston's Hospital, Hinckley Road, Leicester LE3 0UX* T: 0116-254 8682
E: tony0leighton@btinternet.com

LEIGHTON, Mrs Susan. b 58. Bretton Hall Coll BEd 80. Trin Coll Bris BA 89. **d** 89 **p** 94. Par Dn Harrow Weald All SS *Lon* 89-92; NSM Ratby cum Groby *Leic* 92-96; C Bradgate Team 96-00; Asst Warden of Readers 96-00; NSM Thorpe Acre w Dishley 00-08; TV S Croxton Gp 08-10; P-in-c 10-14; P-in-c Burrough Hill Pars 10-14; NSM Leic Martyrs from 15. *The Master's House, Wyggeston's Hospital, Hinckley Road, Leicester LE3 0UX* T: 0116-254 8682 E: susan.leighton2@btinternet.com

LEIGHTON, Mrs Suzanne Elizabeth. b 59. Hertf Coll Ox BA 81. Ripon Coll Cuddesdon 11. **d** 13 **p** 14. C Charlton Kings St Mary *Glouc* from 13. *Rambler Cottage, Houndscroft, Rodborough, Stroud GL5 5DG* M: 07753-832316
E: suzanne.leighton@btinternet.com

LEIPER, Nicholas Keith. b 34. SS Coll Cam BA 55 MB 58 BChir 58 MA 65. St Jo Coll Nottm LTh 82. **d** 84 **p** 85. C Bidston *Ches* 84-87; TV Gateacre *Liv* 87-92; P-in-c Bickerstaffe 92-94; P-in-c Melling 92-94; V Bickerstaffe and Melling 94-00; rtd 00; PtO *Liv* from 00. *31 Weldale House, Chase Close, Southport PR8 2DX* T: (01704) 566393

LEITCH, Miss Carolyn Audrey. b 65. LCTP 12. **d** 15. C Poulton Carleton and Singleton *Blackb* from 15. *24 Roylen Avenue, Poulton-le-Fylde FY6 7PH*

LEITCH, Peter William. b 36. FCA 58 ATII 59. Coll of Resurr Mirfield 83. **d** 85 **p** 86. C Newsome and Armitage Bridge *Wakef* 85-88; P-in-c Upper Hopton 88-91; P-in-c Mirfield Eastthorpe St Paul 88-91; Chapl Rouen Miss to Seamen Eur 92-94; Sen Chapl Rotterdam Miss to Seamen 94-97; Chapl Felixstowe Miss to Seafarers *St E* 97-01; rtd 01; PtO *St E* from 01. *104 St Andrew's Road, Felixstowe IP11 7ED* T: (01394) 285320

LEITHEAD, Mrs Lynette. b 54. SEITE. **d** 08 **p** 09. NSM Kippington *Roch* 08-13; NSM Sundridge w Ide Hill and Toys Hill from 13. *45 Chipstead Park, Sevenoaks TN13 2SL* T: (01732) 742272 M: 07958-145959
E: lynetteleithead@hotmail.co.uk

LEMMEY, William Henry Michael. b 59. Jes Coll Cam BA 81 Jes Coll Ox PGCE 82. Westcott Ho Cam 03. **d** 05 **p** 06. C Milton *Win* 05-09; R Porlock and Porlock Weir w Stoke Pero etc *B & W* from 09. *The Rectory, Parsons Street, Porlock, Minehead TA24 8QL* T: (01643) 863135 E: billlemmey@yahoo.co.uk

LENG, Bruce Edgar. b 38. St Aid Birkenhead 68. **d** 69 **p** 70. C Sheff St Swithun 69-74; TV Speke St Aid *Liv* 74-78; TV Yate New Town *Bris* 78-82; R Handsworth *Sheff* 82-95; R Thrybergh 95-05; Warden for Past Workers 96-05; rtd 05; PtO *Sheff* from 06. *Tinsley Marina, Lock House Walk, Sheffield S9 2FN* M: 07908-448337 E: brucelenguk@gmail.com

LENNARD, Mrs Elizabeth Jemima Mary Patricia (Mary Pat). b 21. Edin Dioc NSM Course 78. **dss** 82 **d** 86 **p** 94. Falkirk *Edin* 82-86; Hon C 86-91; Asst Dioc Supernumerary 91-96; rtd 92; Hon C Grangemouth *Edin* 96-04; Hon C Bo'ness 96-04. *36 Heugh Street, Falkirk FK1 5QR* T: (01324) 623240

LENNOX, Joan Baxter. *See* LYON, Joan Baxter

LENNOX, Mark. Ulster Univ BA St Jo Coll Nottm MA. CITC. **d** 09 **p** 10. NSM Maghera w Killelagh *D & R* 09-12; NSM Camus-juxta-Mourne 12-15; C from 15. *The Rectory, 27 Newtown Street, Strabane BT82 8DW* M: 07752-152991 T: (028) 7188 2314 E: mark.lennox6@btopenworld.com

LENOX-CONYNGHAM, Canon Andrew George. b 44. Magd Coll Ox BA 65 MA 73 CCC Cam PhD 73. Westcott Ho Cam 72. **d** 74 **p** 75. C Poplar *Lon* 74-77; TV 77-80; Chapl Heidelberg *Eur* 80-82; 91-95; Chapl R Marsden Hosp 95-96; Chapl Coll Cam 82-86; Chapl and Fell St Cath Coll Cam 86-91; V Birm St Luke 96-14; AD Cen Birm 04-12; Hon Can Birm Cathl 14; rtd 14; PtO *Birm* from 14. *9 Hitches Lane, Birmingham B15 2LS* T: 0121-446 6783 E: lenox@birm.eclipse.co.uk

LENS VAN RIJN, Robert Adriaan. b 47. St Jo Coll Nottm 78. **d** 80 **p** 81. C Gt Baddow *Chelmsf* 80-83; C Edgware *Lon* 83-86; C Derby St Pet and Ch Ch w H Trin 86-90; Chapl Eindhoven *Eur* 91-00; Chapl Burrswood Chr Cen 04-08; rtd 08; PtO *York* from 09; Chapl Dove Ho Hospice Hull from 09. *15 Spinnaker Close, Hull HU9 1UL* T: (01482) 212082 E: rlvr@iae.nl

LENTHALL, Mrs Nicola Yvonne. b 73. Southn Univ BA 95. Westcott Ho Cam. **d** 99 **p** 00. C Leighton Buzzard w Eggington, Hockliffe etc *St Alb* 99-03; V Kensworth, Studham and Whipsnade from 03. *The Vicarage, Clay Hall Road, Kensworth, Dunstable LU6 3RF* T: (01582) 872223

LENTON, John Robert. b 46. Ex Coll Ox BA 69 Harvard Univ MBA 74. Oak Hill Th Coll. **d** 00. NSM Muswell Hill St Jas w St Matt *Lon* 00-09; NSM Hampstead St Jo Downshire Hill Prop Chpl 09-10; NSM Bramley *Win* 10-14; NSM Sherfield-on-Loddon and Stratfield Saye etc from 14. *Address temp unknown* M: 07714-237235 E: johnlenton@iname.com

LENTON, Patricia Margarita. *See* DICKIN, Patricia Margarita

LEON (née HOLLAND), Mrs Lesley Anne. b 52. Univ Coll Chich BA 04. STETS 04. **d** 07 **p** 08. NSM Northanger *Win* from 07; PtO *Portsm* from 11. *11A Tilmore Gardens, Petersfield GU32 2JQ* E: lesley.leon@ntlworld.com

LEONARD, Mrs Andrea Susan. b 60. SRCh 81. SEITE 13. **d** 15. C Roch St Justus from 15. *St Justus Church, The Fairway, Rochester ME1 2LT* T: (01634) 818353 M: 07752-626644 E: andreaumiak@yahoo.co.uk

LEONARD, Ms Ann Cressey. b 50. Open Univ BA 90 Lon Univ MA. S Dios Minl Tr Scheme 90. **d** 94 **p** 95. C Portsea St Cuth *Portsm* 94-96; C Farlington 96-00; Asst to RD Petersfield 00-03; Deanery Co-ord for Educn and Tr 00-03; V Hayling St Andr 03-15; V N Hayling St Pet 03-15; Dioc Ecum Officer 02-03; rtd 15. *10 Trent Way, Lee-on-the-Solent PO13 8JF* E: anncleonard@gmail.com

LEONARD, John Francis. b 48. Lich Th Coll 69. **d** 72 **p** 73. C Chorley St Geo *Blackb* 72-75; C S Shore H Trin 75-80; V Marton Moss 81-89; V Kingskerswell w Coffinswell *Ex* from 89; P-in-c Abbotskerswell from 06. *The Vicarage, Pound Lane, Kingskerswell, Newton Abbot TQ12 5DW* T: (01803) 407217 *or* 873006 E: kingskerswell.parish.church@tinyworld.co.uk

LEONARD, Canon John James. b 41. Sheffn Univ BSc 62. Sarum Th Coll 63. **d** 65 **p** 66. C Loughborough Em *Leic* 67-70; V New Humberstone 70-78; C-in-c Rushey Mead CD 78-85; V Leic St Theodore 85-05; Hon Can Leic Cathl 96-05; RD Christianity N 97-05; rtd 05; PtO *Leic* from 05. *1339 Melton Road, Syston, Leicester LE7 2EP* T: 0116-269 2691 E: j2.leonard@btinternet.com

LEONARD, Nicola Susan. *See* TERRY, Nicola Susan

LEONARD, Canon Peter Michael. b 47. Portsm Poly BSc MRTPI. Sarum & Wells Th Coll 82. **d** 84 **p** 85. C Llantwit Major *Llan* 84-88; V Cymmer and Porth 88-96; R Colwinston, Llandow and Llysworney 96-12; AD Vale of Glam 02-08 and 11-12; Can Llan Cathl 11-12; rtd 12. *9 Illtyd Avenue, Llantwit Major CF61 1TG* E: peter@theleonards.org.uk

LEONARD, Canon Peter Philip. b 70. Trin Coll Bris BA 94. **d** 97 **p** 98. C Haslemere *Guildf* 97-00; C Haslemere and

Grayswood 00-01; C Woodham 01-06; PtO 07-10; *Portsm* 12-14; Can Res Portsm Cathl from 14. *Cathedral Office, 63-68 St Thomas's Street, Portsmouth PO1 2HA* T: (023) 9282 3300 M: 07817-722219 E: peterleonard200@gmail.com

LEONARD-JOHNSON, Canon Philip Anthony. b 35. Selw Coll Cam BA 58 MA 60. Linc Th Coll 63. **d** 65 **p** 66. C Wymondham *Nor* 65-68; Zimbabwe 69-82; V Drayton in Hales *Lich* 82-92; R Adderley 82-92; P-in-c Moreton Say 88-92; S Africa 92-98; rtd 97; Hon Can Grahamstown from 97; PtO *Lich* 99-14. *Hillside, Mount Lane, Market Drayton TF9 1AG* T: (01630) 655480

LEONARDI, Preb Jeffrey. b 49. Warwick Univ BA 71. Carl Dioc Tr Course 85. **d** 88 **p** 89. C Netherton *Carl* 88-91; V Cross Canonby 91-97; V Allonby 91-97; Bp's Adv for Past Care and Counselling *Lich* 97-14; C Colton, Colwich and Gt Haywood 97-10; C Abbots Bromley, Blithfield, Colton, Colwich etc 11-14; Preb Lich Cathl 12-14; rtd 14; PtO *St D* from 14. *Llwyncelyn, Cribyn, Lampeter SA48 7NH* E: jeff.leonardi@btinternet.com

LEPINE, The Very Revd Jeremy John. b 56. BA. St Jo Coll Nottm 82. **d** 84 **p** 85. C Harrow Trin St Mich *Lon* 84-88; TV Horley *S'wark* 88-95; Evang Adv Croydon Area Miss Team 95-02; Dioc Evang Adv and Hon Chapl S'wark Cathl 97-02; R Wollaton *S'well* 02-13; AD Nottm N 08-13; Hon Can S'well Minster 09-13; Dean Bradf *Leeds* from 13. *The Deanery, 1 Cathedral Close, Bradford BD1 4EG* T: (01274) 777722 F: 777730 E: jerry.lepine@bradfordcathedral.org

LEPLEY, Mrs Kim Angela. b 60. St Mellitus Coll BA 12. **d** 12 **p** 13. C Takeley w Lt Canfield *Chelmsf* from 12. *Laywood, Canfield Drive, Takeley, Bishop's Stortford CM22 6SZ* M: 07540-065877 E: curate@tlcchurch.co.uk

LEPPARD, Miss Heather Sian. b 85. Westcott Ho Cam 12. **d** 15. C Harnham *Sarum* from 15. *Address temp unknown*

LEPPINGTON, Dian Marjorie. b 45. Leeds Univ BA 85. Cranmer Hall Dur 81. **dss** 83 **d** 87 **p** 94. Potternewton *Ripon* 83-85; Ind Chapl 85-97; Chapl Teesside Univ *York* 97-04; Can and Preb York Minster 03-04; Par Resources Adv *Man* 05-14; rtd 13; PtO *Man* from 13. *39 Derwent Mews, York YO10 3DN* T: (01904) 500253 E: dianleppington@hotmail.com

LERRY, Keith Doyle. b 49. St Mich Coll Llan 69. **d** 72 **p** 73. C Caerau w Ely *Llan* 72-75; C Roath St Martin 75-84; V Glyntaff 84-11; rtd 11. *8 Wenvoe Terrace, Barry CF62 7AS*

LERVY, Hugh Martin. b 68. Univ of Wales (Lamp) BA 89. Qu Coll Birm 89. **d** 91 **p** 92. C Brecon St Mary and Battle w Llanddew *S & B* 91-93; C Oystermouth 93-95; V Glantawe 95-00; V Morriston from 00; AD Cwmtawe from 12. *The Vicarage, Vicarage Road, Morriston, Swansea SA6 6DR* T: (01792) 771329 M: 07976-725644 E: hugh@lervy.net

LESITER, The Ven Malcolm Leslie. b 37. Selw Coll Cam BA 61 MA 65. Cuddesdon Coll 61. **d** 63 **p** 64. C Eastney *Portsm* 63-66; C Hemel Hempstead *St Alb* 66-71; TV 71-73; V Leavesden 73-88; RD Watford 81-88; V Radlett 88-93; Hon Can St Alb Abbey 90-93; Adn Bedford 93-03; rtd 03; PtO *Ely* from 03; *Chelmsf* from 04. *349 Ipswich Road, Colchester CO4 0HN* T: (01206) 841479 E: mllesiter@hotmail.com

LESLIE, Christopher James. b 42. Open Univ BA 75. Wycliffe Hall Ox 97. **d** 05 **p** 06. NSM Loddon Reach *Ox* from 05. *Church Farm House, Church Lane, Shinfield, Reading RG2 9BY* T: 0118-988 8642 E: cj.leslie@btinternet.com

LESLIE, David Rodney. b 43. Liv Univ MEd 94 Birm Univ PhD 01 AKC 67. **d** 68 **p** 69. C Belmont *Lon* 68-71; C St Giles Cripplegate w St Bart Moor Lane etc 71-75; TV Kirkby *Liv* 76-84; TR Ditton St Mich 84-98; V Ditton St Mich w St Thos 98-03; V Croxteth Park 03-08; rtd 08; PtO *Ches* from 09. *10 Eversley Close, Frodsham WA6 6AZ* T: (01928) 732463 E: davidrleslie@o2.co.uk

LESLIE, Richard Charles Alan. b 46. ACIB 71. St Alb Minl Tr Scheme 76. **d** 79 **p** 91. NSM Redbourn *St Alb* 79-88; NSM Newport Pagnell w Lathbury and Moulsoe *Ox* 88-94; Stewardship Adv St Alb Adnry *St Alb* 94-97; TV Borehamwood 97-05; TV Elstree and Borehamwood 05-15; rtd 15; PtO *St Alb* from 15. *17 George Street, Hemel Hempstead HP2 5HJ* E: rcaleslie@idreamtime.com

LESTER, David Charles. b 46. BSc. **d** 99 **p** 00. NSM Trowell *S'well* 99-02; NSM Trowell, Awsworth and Cossall 02-06; rtd 06. *25 Ruby Street, Saltburn-by-the-Sea TS12 1EF* E: d.lester@ntlworld.com

LESTER, Canon Trevor Rashleigh. b 50. CITC 83. **d** 89 **p** 90. NSM Douglas Union w Frankfield *C, C & R* 89-93; Bp's V and Lib Kilkenny Cathl and C Kilkenny w Aghour and Kilmanagh *C & O* 93-95; I Abbeystrewry Union *C, C & R* 95-03; Dean Waterford *C & O* 03-11; I Waterford w Killea, Drumcannon and Dunhill 03-11; I Kilmoe Union *C, C & R* from 11; Can Cork and Ross Cathls from 14. *Altar Rectory, Toormore, Skibbereen, Co Cork, Republic of Ireland* T: (00353) (28) 28249 M: 86-313 4617

L'ESTRANGE, Timothy John Nicholas. b 67. Surrey Univ BA 90. St Steph Ho Ox BA 92 MA 96. **d** 93 **p** 94. C Halesworth w Linstead, Chediston, Holton etc *St E* 93-96; Dom Chapl to Bp Horsham *Chich* 96-98; R Beeding and Bramber w Botolphs 98-08; R Monken Hadley *Lon* 08-11; V N Acton St Gabr from 11. *St Gabriel's Vicarage, 15 Balfour Road, London W3 0DG* T: (020) 8259 2138 M: 07845-211617
E: sacerdotal@gmail.com *or* vicar@saintgabrielacton.org

LETALL, Ronald Richard. b 29. ACII 76. Linc Th Coll 82. **d** 84 **p** 85. C Scarborough St Martin *York* 84-86; C Middlesbrough St Thos 86-88; R Kirby Misperton w Normanby, Edston and Salton 88-90; TV Louth *Linc* 90-94; rtd 94; PtO *Sheff* from 95; *Wakef* 95-97; *Chich* 97-99. *6 Windlesham Court, Grand Avenue, Worthing BN11 5AE* E: ronald@letall.fsnet.co.uk

LETCHER, Canon David John. b 34. K Coll Lon 54. Chich Th Coll 56. **d** 58 **p** 59. C St Austell *Truro* 58-62; C Southbroom *Sarum* 62-64; R Odstock w Nunton and Bodenham 64-72; RD Alderbury 68-73 and 77-82; V Downton 72-85; Can and Preb Sarum Cathl 79-99; TV Dorchester 85-97; RD 89-95; rtd 97; PtO *Sarum* from 97; CF 97-00; PtO *Ex* from 12. *1 Stonehouse, Pound Lane, Fordington, Dorchester DT1 1LP* T: (01305) 459557 E: letcher@uwclub.net

LETHBRIDGE, Christopher David. b 43. NOC 90. **d** 93 **p** 94. NSM S Elmsall *Wakef* 93-95; C Knottingley 95-97; R Badsworth 97-01; P-in-c Bilham *Sheff* 01-13; Chapl HM YOI Hatfield 01-03; Chapl HM Pris Moorland 03-12; rtd 13; PtO *Sheff* from 13. *25 Mayfield, Scawthorpe, Doncaster DN5 7UA*

LETHEREN, William Neils. b 37. St Aid Birkenhead 61. **d** 64 **p** 65. C Liv St Mich 64-67; V 71-75; C Kirkdale St Athanasius 67-69; C Walsall Wood *Lich* 69-71; V W Derby St Jas *Liv* 75-84; R Newton in Makerfield Em 84-88; V Garston 88-04; rtd 04. *24 Pitville Avenue, Liverpool L18 7JG* T: 0151-724 5543

LETSCHKA, Mrs Alison Clare. b 58. Sussex Univ BA 79 Anglia Ruskin Univ BA 08. Westcott Ho Cam 06. **d** 08 **p** 09. C Haywards Heath St Wilfrid *Chich* 08-12; TV Bexley *Roch* from 12. *St Mary's Vicarage, 29 Hill Crescent, Bexley DA5 2DA* T: (01322) 523457 M: 07950-152229
E: acletschka@yahoo.co.uk

LETSOM-CURD, Clifford John. *See* CURD, Clifford John Letsom

LETSON, Barry. b 55. Univ of Wales (Lamp) BA 77. St Deiniol's Hawarden 82. **d** 83 **p** 84. C Flint *St As* 83-86; V Llansantffraid Glyn Ceirog and Llanarmon etc 86-89; R Montgomery and Forden and Llandyssil 89-96; RD Pool 92-96; V Mountain Ash *Llan* 96-97; V Mountain Ash and Miskin 97-02; V Crickhowell w Cwmdu and Tretower *S & B* from 02; AD Crickhowell from 14. *The Rectory, Rectory Road, Crickhowell NP8 1DW* T: (01873) 810017

LETTERS, Mark Ian. b 68. Keble Coll Ox BA 89 MA 93 Magd Coll Cam PGCE 90. SAOMC 03. **d** 05 **p** 06. NSM Ox St Barn and St Paul 05-07; Asst Chapl Campsfield Ho Immigration Removal Cen 05-07; Denmark and Sweden 09-13; Chapl K Ely 13-14; Min Can Ely Cathl 13-14. *Address temp unknown* E: culeitreach@msn.com

LETTS, Canon Kenneth John. b 42. Melbourne Univ BA 65 DipEd 67. Coll of Resurr Mirfield 68. **d** 71 **p** 72. C Mt Waverley St Steph Australia 71-74; Chapl Melbourne C of E Gr Sch 74-81; P-in-c Albert Park 81-94; Sen Chapl St Mich Sch 82-94; Nice w Vence *Eur* 94-13; Can Gib Cathl 04-13; Adn France 07-12; rtd 13. *7 Dalgety Street, St Kilda, VIC 3182, Australia* T: (0061) (3) 9534 3945

LEUNG, Peter. b 36. Trin Coll Singapore BTh 60 St Andr Univ PhD 73. SE Asia Sch of Th MTh 69. **d** 60 **p** 61. Singapore 60-62 and 65-76; Br N Borneo 62-63; Malaysia 63-65; Lect Congr Coll Man 76-77; USPG 77-83; PtO *Roch* 83-89; CCBI 83-90; CTBI from 90; PtO *S'wark* 88-94; Hon C Shortlands *Roch* 90-01; Regional Sec (S and E Asia) CMS 91-99; rtd 99. *35 Tufton Gardens, West Molesey KT8 1TD* T: (020) 8650 4157

LEVASIER, James Arjen. b 67. Heriot-Watt Univ BSc 95. Wycliffe Hall Ox 07. **d** 09 **p** 10. C Ashtead *Guildf* 09-12; V Burpham from 12. *17 Loraine Gardens, Ashtead KT21 1PD* T: (01372) 813366 E: levasier@googlemail.com

LEVASIER, Joanna Mary. b 68. Jes Coll Cam BA 89 MA 90. Wycliffe Hall Ox 07. **d** 09 **p** 10. C Ashtead *Guildf* 09-12; C Burpham from 12. *17 Loraine Gardens, Ashtead KT21 1PD* T: (01372) 813366 E: j.levasier@ntlworld.com

LEVELL, Peter John. b 40. Bris Univ BA 62 CertEd 63. STETS 99. **d** 02 **p** 03. NSM Guildf St Sav 02-10; rtd 10; PtO *Guildf* from 11. *23 Mountside, Guildford GU2 4JD* T: (01483) 871656 E: plevell@ntlworld.com

LEVER, Canon Julian Lawrence Gerrard. b 36. Fitzw Coll Cam BA 60 MA 64. Sarum Th Coll 60. **d** 62 **p** 63. C Amesbury *Sarum* 62-66; R Corfe Mullen 66-78; RD Wimborne 73-75; P-in-c Wilton w Netherhampton and Fugglestone 78-82; R 82-86; R Salisbury St Martin 86-94; PtO *Win* 96-13; rtd 98; Can Ruvuma Tanzania from 14. *6 St John's Close, Wimborne BH21 1LY* T: (01202) 848249

LEVERTON, Mrs Judith. b 55. Eaton Hall Coll of Educn CertEd 76. St Jo Coll Nottm 02. **d** 04 **p** 05. C Doncaster St Jas *Sheff* 04-07; TV Rivers Team 07-15; rtd 15; Chapl to Deaf People *Sheff* 09-15. *The Rectory, Church Lane, Treeton, Rotherham S60 5PZ* M: 07960-573529 T: 0114-269 6542
E: judy.leverton@yahoo.co.uk

LEVERTON, Michael John. b 52. K Coll Lon BD 76 AKC 76 MTh 77. Cant Sch of Min 84. **d** 87 **p** 88. NSM Elham w Denton and Wootton *Cant* 87-92; C Yelverton, Meavy, Sheepstor and Walkhampton *Ex* 92-93; TV 93-98; C Tavistock and Gulworthy 98-00; P-in-c Stevenage All SS Pin Green *St Alb* 00-10; P-in-c Ardeley 10-12; P-in-c Benington w Walkern 10-12; P-in-c Cottered w Broadfield and Throcking 10-12; R Ardeley, Benington, Cottered w Throcking etc from 12. *The Rectory, Cottered, Buntingford SG9 9QA* T: (01763) 281218 E: michael.leverton@btinternet.com

LEVERTON, Peter Robert. b 25. Lich Th Coll 59. **d** 60 **p** 61. C Shepshed *Leic* 60-64; Australia 64-69; V Marshchapel *Linc* 70-73; V Grainthorpe w Conisholme 70-73; R N Coates 70-73; Miss to Seamen 73-77; P-in-c Brislington St Luke *Bris* 77-84; V Avonmouth St Andr 84-87; Ind Chapl 84-87; P-in-c Ugborough *Ex* 87-91; P-in-c Ermington 88-91; rtd 91; PtO *Ex* from 91. *4 Drakes Avenue, Sidford, Sidmouth EX10 9QY* T: (01395) 579835

LEVETT, The Ven Howard. b 44. AKC 67. **d** 68 **p** 69. C Rotherhithe St Mary w All SS *S'wark* 68-72; P-in-c Walworth St Jo 72-77; V 77-80; P-in-c Walworth Lady Marg w St Mary 78; RD S'wark and Newington 78-80; Adn Egypt 80-94; Miss to Seafarers 80-10; JMECA 80-10; V Holborn St Alb w Saffron Hill St Pet *Lon* 94-10; rtd 10; P-in-c Venice w Trieste *Eur* from 10. *Chaplain's House, 253 Dorsoduro, 30123 Venice, Italy* T: (0039) (041) 099 0019 E: stgeorgesvenice@virgilio.it

LEVETT, Julie. b 60. **d** 11. OLM Knaphill w Brookwood *Guildf* from 10. *7 Larks Way, Knaphill, Woking GU21 2LE* T: (01483) 850623 E: julie-levett@ntlworld.com *or* levtherev@knaphillchurch.co.uk

LEVY, Christopher Charles. b 51. Southn Univ BTh 82. Sarum & Wells Th Coll 79. **d** 82 **p** 83. C Rubery *Birm* 82-85; C Stratford-on-Avon w Bishopton *Cov* 85-87; TV Clifton *S'well* 87-95; V Egmanton from 95; R Kirton from 95; V Walesby from 95; P-in-c Kneesall w Laxton and Wellow from 07; Chapl Center Parcs Holiday Village from 01. *St Edmund's Vicarage, Walesby, Newark NG22 9PA* T: (01623) 860522
E: chris@walesbyvic.fsnet.co.uk

LEW, Henry. b 39. **d** 96 **p** 97. LtO *D & G* from 99; NSM Delgany from 10. *Lotts Cottage, Drummin West, The Downs, Delgany, Co Wicklow, Republic of Ireland* T: (00353) (1) 287 2957 M: 87-628 8049 E: healew@outlook.com

LEWER ALLEN, Mrs Patricia (Paddy). b 47. UNISA BA 79 HDipEd 85 Cape Town Univ BA 86 SRN 70. Th Ext Educn Coll 94. **d** 97 **p** 98. P-in-c Dunbar *Edin* 98-08; R Crieff *St And* from 08; R Comrie from 08; R Lochearnhead from 08; Dioc Dir of Ords from 10. *Strathearn Churches Office, St Columba's Church, Perth Road, Crieff PH7 3EB* T: (01764) 656222 *or* 655389 M: 07810-746121
E: stcolumbacrieff@tiscali.co.uk

LEWES AND HASTINGS, Archdeacon of. *See* JONES, The Ven Philip Hugh

LEWES, Area Bishop of. *See* JACKSON, The Rt Revd Richard Charles

LEWIS, Prof Andrew Dominic Edwards. b 49. St Jo Coll Cam LLB 71 MA 74. SWMTC 04. **d** 07 **p** 08. NSM St Endellion w Port Isaac and St Kew *Truro* 07-12; NSM St Minver 07-12; NSM N Cornwall Cluster from 12. *Moorgate, Advent, Camelford PL32 9QH* T: (01840) 211161 E: a.d.e.lewis@ucl.ac.uk

LEWIS, Miss Angela Jane. b 69. Portsm Univ BA 92. St Jo Coll Nottm 13. **d** 15. C Uxbridge *Lon* from 15. *St Peter's House, 32A The Greenway, Uxbridge UB8 2PJ* M: 07860-824314 E: angelalewisjane@gmail.com

LEWIS, Ann Theodora Rachel. b 33. Univ of Wales (Ban) BA 55. Qu Coll Birm 78. **d** 80 **p** 97. C Swansea St Mary w H Trin *S & B* 80-96; Chapl St Mary's Coll 90-96; rtd 96; Public Preacher *St D* from 96. *Fisherywish, Maes yr Eglwys, Llansaint, Kidwelly SA17 5JE* T: (01267) 267386

LEWIS, Arthur Jenkin Llewellyn. b 42. Univ of Wales (Cardiff) MPS 67 BPharm. Coll of Resurr Mirfield 71. **d** 73 **p** 74. C Cardiff St Jo *Llan* 73-78; C Christchurch *Win* 78-82; R Lightbowne *Man* 82-04; rtd 07. *25 Dene Street Gardens, Dorking RH4 2DN* T: (01306) 879743

LEWIS, Benjamin William Donald. b 78. Northumbria Univ BA 00. Ripon Coll Cuddesdon 12. **d** 14 **p** 15. C Goldington *St Alb* from 14. *1 Atholl Walk, Bedford MK41 0BG* T: (01234) 353928 M: 07977-243197 E: ben.lewis33@live.co.uk

LEWIS, Brian James. b 52. Cant Univ (NZ) BA 75. St Jo Coll Auckland 76. **d** 78 **p** 79. C Ashburton New Zealand 78-80; C Shrub End *Chelmsf* 80-82; P-in-c Colchester St Barn 82-84;

V 84-88; P-in-c Romford St Andr 88-90; R 90-99; RD Havering 93-97; R Lt Ilford St Mich from 99. *The Rectory, 124 Church Road, London E12 6HA* T: (020) 8478 2182
E: brian@littleilford.fsnet.co.uk

LEWIS, Mrs Cheryl Irene. **d** 11 **p** 12. NSM Blaina and Nantyglo *Mon* 11-13; NSM Upper Ebbw Valleys from 13. *13 Newchurch Road, Ebbw Vale NP23 5NL* T: (01495) 446054
E: revlewis@sky.com

LEWIS, The Very Revd Christopher Andrew. b 44. Bris Univ BA 69 CCC Cam PhD 74. Westcott Ho Cam 71. **d** 73 **p** 74. C Barnard Castle *Dur* 73-76; Dir Ox Inst for Ch and Soc 76-79; Tutor Ripon Coll Cuddesdon 76-79; Sen Tutor 79-81; Vice-Prin 81-82; P-in-c Aston Rowant w Crowell *Ox* 78-81; V Spalding St Mary and St Nic *Linc* 82-87; Can Res Cant Cathl 87-94; Dir of Minl Tr 89-94; Dean St Alb *St Alb* 94-03; Dean Ch Ch *Ox* 03-14; rtd 14; PtO *St E* from 15. *The Old Brewery, 16 Victoria Road, Aldeburgh IP15 5ED* T: (017228) 454263
E: christopher.lewis@chch.ox.ac.uk

LEWIS, Canon Christopher Gouldson. b 42. K Coll Cam BA 64 MA 68. Cuddesdon Coll 65. **d** 67 **p** 68. C Gosforth All SS *Newc* 67-71; Malaysia 71-74; V Luton St Chris Round Green *St Alb* 74-80; RD Reculver *Cant* 80-86 and 92-93; V Whitstable All SS w St Pet 80-84; TR Whitstable 84-93; Dir Post-Ord Tr 88-93; Hon Can Cant Cathl 91-93; Can Res Bradf Cathl 93-01; Bp's Officer for Min and Tr 93-01; P-in-c Riding Mill *Newc* 01-07; Chapl Shepherd's Dene Retreat Ho 01-07; Adv for Spirituality and Spiritual Direction 02-07; Hon Can Newc Cathl from 07; rtd 07. *The Old School, Bingfield, Hexham NE46 4HR*
T: (01434) 672729

LEWIS, David Antony. b 48. Dur Univ BA 69 Nottm Univ MTh 84. St Jo Coll Nottm 81. **d** 83 **p** 84. C Gateacre *Liv* 83-86; V Toxteth St Cypr w Ch Ch 86-01; V Edge Hill St Cypr w St Mary 01-07; AD Liv N 94-03; Urban Development Adv 07-08; rtd 08. *48 Coulsdon Road, Sidmouth EX10 9JP*
T: (01395) 516762 E: davenwend@gmail.com

LEWIS, David Hugh. b 45. Oak Hill Th Coll 88. **d** 90 **p** 91. C Oakham, Hambleton, Egleton, Braunston and Brooke *Pet* 90-94; R Ewhurst *Guildf* 94-99; V Southway *Ex* 99-03; RD Plymouth Moorside 01-03; P-in-c Anglesey Gp *Ely* 03-04; V 04-11; rtd 11. *5 Buttercup Road, Willand, Cullompton EX15 2TX* E: revdavidhlewis@btinternet.com

LEWIS, David Tudor. b 61. Jes Coll Cam BA 83. Trin Coll Bris BA 88. **d** 88 **p** 89. C Tile Cross *Birm* 88-91; C Woking St Jo *Guildf* 91-95; TV Carl H Trin and St Barn 95-97; Chapl Carl Hosps NHS Trust 95-97; Asst Chapl Oslo w Bergen, Trondheim and Stavanger *Eur* 97-04; TV E Richmond *Leeds* from 04. *The Rectory, Great Smeaton, Northallerton DL6 2EP* T: (01609) 881205 E: dtlewis@freenet.co.uk

LEWIS, David Tudor Bowes. b 63. Keele Univ BA 85 Univ of Wales (Cardiff) BTh 90. St Mich Coll Llan 87. **d** 90 **p** 91. C Llangollen w Trevor and Llantysilio *St As* 90-93; C Bistre 93-97; V Berse and Southsea 97-02; V Bwlchgwyn w Berse w Southsea 02-04; R Overton and Erbistock and Penley 04-11; AD Bangor Isycoed 09-11; TR Hawarden from 11. *The Rectory, 2 Birch Rise, Hawarden, Deeside CH5 3DD* T: (01244) 538526
E: david.lewis962@btinternet.com

LEWIS, Canon David Vaughan. b 36. Trin Coll Cam BA 60 MA 64. Ridley Hall Cam 60. **d** 62 **p** 63. C Rugby St Matt *Cov* 62-65; Asst Chapl K Edw Sch Witley 65-71; Hon C Rainham *Chelmsf* 71-76; V Stoke Hill *Guildf* 76-87; V Wallington *S'wark* 87-03; Hon Can *S'wark* Cathl 95-03; RD Sutton 97-00; rtd 03; PtO *Ely* from 03. *11 The Meadows, Haslingfield, Cambridge CB23 1JD* T: (01223) 874029
E: david@hmlewis.freeserve.co.uk

LEWIS, Canon David Watkin. b 40. Univ of Wales (Lamp) BA 61. Wycliffe Hall Ox 61. **d** 63 **p** 64. C Skewen *Llan* 63-66; Field Tr Officer Prov Youth Coun Ch in Wales 66-68; C Gabalfa *Llan* 68-71; P-in-c Marcross w Monknash and Wick 71-73; R 73-83; RD Llantwit Major and Cowbridge 81-83; V Baglan 83-10; Can Llan Cathl 00-10; Treas Llan Cathl 04-10; rtd 10; PtO *Llan* from 14. *23 St Illtyd's Close, Baglan, Port Talbot SA12 8BA* T: (01639) 821778

LEWIS, Dorothy Julie. **d** 15. NSM Clydach *S & B* from 15. *Valldemossa, 377 Birchgrove Road, Birchgrove, Swansea SA7 9NN* T: (01792) 814321 E: dottylewis@btinternet.com

LEWIS, Edward John. b 58. JP 93. Univ of Wales BEd 80 BA 82 Surrey Univ MA 07 FRSA 97 MInstD 01. Chich Th Coll 82. **d** 83 **p** 84. C Llangiwg *S & B* 83-85; C Morriston 85-87; Asst Chapl Morriston Hosp 85-87; V Tregaron w Ystrad Meurig and Strata Florida *St D* 87-89; Chapl Tregaron Hosp 87-89; Chapl Manor Hosp Walsall 89-92; Distr Co-ord Chapl Walsall Hosps 90-92; Sen Chapl Walsall Hosps NHS Trust 92-00; Chapl Walsall Community Health Trust 92-00; Chief Exec and Dir Tr Gen Syn Hosp Chapl Coun 00-10; PtO *St Alb* 02-10; P-in-c Watford St Jo 10-11; V Kenton *Lon* from 11; Visiting Lect St Mary's Univ Twickenham from 04; PV Westmr Abbey 07-12; Chapl to The Queen from 08; PtO *Lich* from 00.

St Mary's Vicarage, 3 St Leonard's Avenue, Harrow HA3 8EJ
T: (020) 8907 2914 M: 07500-557953 E: fr@fredward.org.uk

LEWIS, Ella Pauline. b 41. SWMTC 94. **d** 98. NSM Paignton Ch Ch and Preston St Paul *Ex* 98-07; NSM Torquay St Luke 07-15; rtd 15. *Roselands, 5 Great Headland Road, Paignton TQ3 2DY* T: (01803) 555171 E: paulinelewis@eclipse.co.uk

LEWIS, Eric. b 47. NEOC 04. **d** 07 **p** 08. NSM Monkseaton St Mary *Newc* 07-11; P-in-c Ovingham from 11. *The Vicarage, 2 Burnside Close, Ovingham, Prudhoe NE42 6BS* T: (01661) 836072 E: e.lewis129@gmail.com

LEWIS, Gary. b 61. Lanc Univ BA 85. Ripon Coll Cuddesdon 86. **d** 89 **p** 90. C Blackb St Mich w St Jo and H Trin 89-92; C Altham w Clayton le Moors 92-95; V Lea 95-01; V Skerton St Luke 01-14; V Cockerham w Winmarleigh and Glasson from 14. *The Vicarage, 5 Lancaster Road, Cockerham, Lancaster LA2 0EB* T: (01524) 791390

LEWIS, Graham Rhys. b 54. Loughb Univ BTech 76 Cranfield Inst of Tech MBA 89. SEITE 95. **d** 98 **p** 99. NSM S Gillingham *Roch* from 98; TV from 12. *53 Oastview, Gillingham ME8 8JG* T: (01634) 373036 *or* T/F 389224 M: 07740-915826
E: graham.lewis@diocese-rochester.org

LEWIS, Gwynne. *See* LEWIS, Hywel Gwynne

LEWIS, Ms Hannah Margaret. b 71. CCC Cam BA 93 MA 96 Birm Univ PhD 03. Qu Coll Birm 95. **d** 97 **p** 98. C Cannock *Lich* 97-00; NSM Cen Telford 00-06; Team Ldr Past Services for Deaf Community *Liv* from 06. *9 Hougoumont Avenue, Liverpool L22 0LL* T: 0151-705 2130
E: hannah.lewis@liverpool.anglican.org

LEWIS, Hubert Godfrey. b 33. Univ of Wales (Lamp) BA 59. **d** 60 **p** 61. C Merthyr Tydfil *Llan* 60-64; C Caerphilly 64-66; PtO *S'wark* 66-76; *Cant* 76-82; Hon C Shirley St Jo *S'wark* 82-93; Hon C Whitchurch *Llan* from 94. *2 Heol Wernlas, Cardiff CF14 1RY* T: (029) 2061 3079

LEWIS, Hywel Gwynne. b 37. FCA 75. St D Dioc Tr Course 94. **d** 97 **p** 98. NSM Henfynyw w Aberaeron and Llanddewi Aberarth etc *St D* 97-07; rtd 07; PtO *St D* from 07. *Danycoed, Lampeter Road, Aberaeron SA46 0ED* T: (01545) 570577

LEWIS, Ian. b 33. Lon Univ MB, BS 57. Oak Hill Th Coll 61. **d** 63 **p** 64. C Heatherlands St Jo *Sarum* 63-66; Hd CMJ Ethiopia 66-73; Hon C Bath Walcot *B & W* 75-77; LtO 78-98; Hon C Bath St Bart 80-04; rtd 98; PtO *B & W* from 04. *22C Ashley Road, Bathford, Bath BA1 7TT* T: (01225) 859818
E: i.lewis2@btinternet.com

LEWIS, Preb Ian Richard. b 54. Sheff Univ BA 76 Ox Univ BA 83 MA 87. Wycliffe Hall Ox 81. **d** 84 **p** 85. C Rusholme H Trin *Man* 84-88; C Sandal St Helen *Wakef* 88-91; V Bath St Bart *B & W* from 91; Preb Wells Cathl from 11. *St Bartholomew's Vicarage, 6A Oldfield Road, Bath BA2 3ND* T/F: (01225) 422070 E: ian.ir.lewis@btinternet.com *or* ianlewis@stbartsbath.org

LEWIS, James Edward. b 22. St D Coll Lamp BA 50. **d** 51 **p** 52. C Gorseinon *S & B* 51-52; C Defynnog w Rhydybriw and Llandeilo'r Fan 52-56; R Llangynllo w Troed-yr-aur *St D* 56-61; V Brynamman 61-72; R Llangathen w Llanfihangel Cilfargen 72-82; V Llangathen w Llanfihangel Cilfargen etc 82-90; RD Llangadog and Llandeilo 85-89; rtd 90. *4 Ger y Llan, The Parade, Carmarthen SA31 1TN* T: (01267) 221660

LEWIS, James Michael. b 51. Trin Coll Carmarthen CertEd 73 Open Univ BA 86 MA 91. St Mich Coll Llan 98. **d** 02 **p** 03. NSM Laleston w Tythegston and Merthyr Mawr *Llan* 02-09; NSM Laleston and Merthyr Mawr 09-13; NSM Laleston and Merthyr Mawr w Penyfai from 13. *19 Austin Avenue, Laleston, Bridgend CF32 0LG* T: (01656) 660648 M: 07951-300206
E: mike.lewis11@virgin.net

LEWIS, Jane. b 59. **d** 13 **p** 14. OLM Woodley *Ox* from 13. *19 Uppingham Drive, Woodley, Reading RG5 4TH* T: 0118-969 1976 E: revjrl.jl@gmail.com

LEWIS, Mrs Jayne Lisa. b 63. Hull Univ BA 84 Leic Univ PGCE 99. Qu Coll Birm 12. **d** 15. C Market Harborough and The Transfiguration etc *Leic* from 15. *69 Tymecrosse Gardens, Market Harborough LE16 7US* M: 07875-011924
E: jaynelewis28@sky.com

LEWIS, Jean Anwyl. b 34. Surrey Univ BA 03. K Coll Lon MA 05. **d** 05 **p** 06. OLM Windlesham *Guildf* 05-09; PtO from 09. *2 Hillside Cottages, Broadway Road, Windlesham GU20 6BY* T: (01276) 472681 E: jean.lewis1@btopenworld.com

LEWIS, Mrs Jennifer Jane. b 56. All SS Cen for Miss & Min 12. **d** 15. OLM Eccles *Man* from 15. *4 Welbeck Road, Eccles, Manchester M30 9EH* M: 0161-707 6230
E: jennylewis28@dsl.pipex.com

LEWIS, Jocelyn Vivien. b 49. Trevelyan Coll Dur BSc 70 Sheff Univ PhD 75. EMMTC 91. **d** 94 **p** 95. NSM Brimington *Derby* 94-99; P-in-c Whittington 99-09; Dioc Dir Reader Tr 99-09; P-in-c New Whittington 04-09; rtd 09. *13 Gower Crescent, Chesterfield S40 4LX* T: (01246) 229539
E: jocelyn@gandjlewis.plus.com

LEWIS, The Ven John Arthur. b 34. Jes Coll Ox BA 56 MA 60. Cuddesdon Coll 58. **d** 60 **p** 61. C Prestbury *Glouc* 60-63; C Wimborne Minster *Sarum* 63-66; R Eastington and Frocester *Glouc* 66-70; V Nailsworth 70-78; Chapl Memorial and Querns Hosp Cirencester 78-88; V Cirencester *Glouc* 78-88; RD 84-88; Hon Can Glouc Cathl 85-98; Adn Cheltenham 88-98; rtd 98; PtO *Glouc* from 98. *5 Vilverie Mead, Bishop's Cleeve, Cheltenham GL52 7YY* T: (01242) 678425

LEWIS, John Edward. b 31. SS Mark & Jo Coll Chelsea CertEd 53. Qu Coll Birm 83. **d** 85 **p** 86. C Leominster *Heref* 85-87; TV 87-95; rtd 95; PtO *Heref* 97-13. *The Holms, 253 Godiva Road, Leominster HR6 8TB* T: (01568) 612280

LEWIS, John Goddard. b 52. Houston Bapt Univ (USA) BA 74 JD 77 Ox Univ 98. Virginia Th Sem MDiv 97. **d** 97. USA 97-98 and from 01; Hon C Bladon w Woodstock *Ox* 98-01; Min Cen for Faith in the Workplace San Antonio from 01. *2015 NE Loop 410, San Antonio TX 78217, USA* T: (001) (210) 599 4224 E: jlewis@theworkshop-sa.org

LEWIS, John Herbert. b 42. Selw Coll Cam BA 64 MA 68. Westcott Ho Cam 64. **d** 66 **p** 67. C Wyken *Cov* 66-70; C Bedford St Andr *St Alb* 70-73; Lib Pusey Ho and Bp's Chapl for Graduates *Ox* 73-77; TV Woughton 78-82; TV Gt Chesham 82-88; P-in-c Newport Pagnell w Lathbury and Moulsoe 88-91; R 91-07; rtd 07; PtO *Ox* from 08. *54 Sparrows Way, Oxford OX4 7GE*

LEWIS, John Horatio George. b 47. Southn Univ BEd 72 MA 85. Ox NSM Course 86. **d** 89 **p** 90. NSM Newbury *Ox* 89-04; PtO *Win* 94-04; P-in-c Borden *Cant* 05-08; V from 08; AD Sittingbourne 09-15. *The Vicarage, School Lane, Borden, Sittingbourne ME9 8JS* T: (01795) 472986 M: 07973-406622 E: fr.johnlewis@tiscali.co.uk

✠**LEWIS, The Rt Revd John Hubert Richard.** b 43. AKC 66. **d** 67 **p** 68 **c** 92. C Hexham *Newc* 67-70; Ind Chapl 70-77; Communications Officer *Dur* 77-82; Chapl for Agric *Heref* 82-87; Adn Ludlow 87-92; Suff Bp Taunton *B & W* 92-97; Bp St E 97-07; rtd 07. *Kenwater House, 14A Green Lane, Leominster HR6 8QJ* T: (01568) 613982 E: lewis310@btinternet.com

LEWIS, John Malcolm. b 41. Reading Univ BEd. Trin Coll Bris. **d** 82 **p** 83. C Kingswood *Bris* 82-85; TV Weston-super-Mare Cen Par *B & W* 85-91; Dioc Children's Adv *Nor* 91-97; TV Bishopsworth and Bedminster Down *Bris* 97-06; Hon Min Can Bris Cathl 04-06; rtd 06. *35 Lodge Way, Weymouth DT4 9UU* T: (01305) 776560 E: monandjohn@btinternet.com

LEWIS, Canon John Pryce. b 65. Trin Coll Carmarthen BA 87. Wycliffe Hall Ox 92. **d** 94 **p** 95. C Carmarthen St Pet *St D* 94-97; V Nevern and Y Beifil w Eglwyswrw and Meline etc 97-07; V Henfynyw w Aberaeron and Llanddewi Aberarth etc from 07; Can St D Cathl from 14. *The Vicarage, Panteg Road, Aberaeron SA46 0EP* T: (01545) 570433 E: vicar@aberaeronparish.org.uk

LEWIS, The Very Revd John Thomas. b 47. Jes Coll Ox BA 69 MA 73 St Jo Coll Cam BA 72 MA 92. Westcott Ho Cam 71. **d** 73 **p** 74. C Whitchurch *Llan* 73-77; C Llanishen and Lisvane 77-80; Asst Chapl Univ of Wales (Cardiff) 80-85; Warden of Ords 81-85; V Brecon St David w Llanspyddid and Llanilltyd *S & B* 85-91; Sec Prov Selection Panel and Bd Ch in Wales 87-94; V Bassaley *Mon* 91-96; TR 96-00; Bp's Chapl for CME 98-00; Dean Llan 00-12; V Llandaff 00-12; rtd 12; PtO *S & B* 12-15. *8 Daniell Close, Sully, Penarth CF64 5JY* T: (029) 2053 1315

LEWIS, Joycelyn. See LEWIS-GREGORY, Joycelyn

LEWIS, Kevin James. b 76. Nottm Univ BA 98. St Jo Coll Nottm MTh 04 MA(MM) 05. **d** 05 **p** 06. C Southgate *Chich* 05-09; C St Helier *S'wark* from 09. *59 Wigmore Road, Carshalton SM5 1RG* T: (020) 8644 9203 M: 07739-139389 E: kevinjlewis@btinternet.com

LEWIS, Leslie. b 28. LRAM 56. St Aid Birkenhead 61. **d** 63 **p** 64. C Eastham *Ches* 63-66; C W Kirby St Bridget 66-72; V Rainow w Saltersford 72-73; V Rainow w Saltersford and Forest 73-02; Dioc Clergy Widows and Retirement Officer 88-93; rtd 02; PtO *Ches* from 02. *25 Appleby Close, Macclesfield SK11 8XB* T: (01625) 616395

LEWIS, Marjorie Ann. See BROOKS, Marjorie Ann

LEWIS, Mrs Mary Carola Melton. b 51. LRAM 72 S Glam Inst HE CertEd 76 Lon Univ BD 93. St Mich Coll Llan 97. **d** 98 **p** 99. NSM Aberedw w Llandeilo Graban and Llanbadarn etc *S & B* 98-03. *The Breeze, Balmartin, Isle of North Uist HS6 5DQ* T: (01876) 510789 M: 07833-767273 E: mcmlewis@aol.com

LEWIS, Maureen. b 50. Ches Coll of HE BA 92. St Jo Coll Nottm 92. **d** 94 **p** 95. C Ellesmere Port *Ches* 94-98; C Prenton 98-00; C New Brighton St Jas w Em 00-05; rtd 05; PtO *Ches* from 06. *27 Wimborne Avenue, Wirral CH61 7UL* T: 0151-648 0605

LEWIS, Michael. See LEWIS, James Michael

✠**LEWIS, The Rt Revd Michael Augustine Owen.** b 53. Mert Coll Ox BA 75 MA 79. Cuddesdon Coll 75. **d** 78 **p** 79 **c** 99. C Salfords *S'wark* 78-80; Chapl Thames Poly 80-84; V Welling 84-91; TR Worc SE 91-99; RD Worc E 93-99; Hon Can Worc Cathl 98-99; Suff Bp Middleton *Man* 99-07; Bp Cyprus and the Gulf from 07. *PO Box 22075, CY 1517-Nicosia, Cyprus* T: (00357) (22) 671220 F: 674553 E: bishop@spidernet.com.cy *or* maolewis_2000@yahoo.com

LEWIS, Canon Michael David Bennett. b 41. Portsm Univ MA 01. St Mich Coll Llan 65. **d** 68 **p** 69. C Penarth w Lavernock *Llan* 68-72; Chapl RAF 72-74; C Llanishen and Lisvane *Llan* 74-77; V Penyfai w Tondu 77-82; Chapl Ardingly Coll 82-90; R Merrow *Guildf* 90-95; RD Guildf 94-95; V Southsea H Spirit *Portsm* 95-11; RD Portsm 06-11; Hon Can Portsm Cathl 06-11; rtd 11; PtO *St D* from 11. *Stepping Stones, Reynalton, Kilgetty SA68 0PG* T: (01834) 891529 - M: 07808-609912 E: fr.lewis@btinternet.com

LEWIS, Michael John. b 37. LLAM 86. St Aid Birkenhead 64. **d** 66 **p** 67. C Whitnash *Cov* 66-69; C Nuneaton St Nic 69-73; TV Basildon St Martin w H Cross and Laindon *Chelmsf* 73-79; V W Bromwich St Jas *Lich* 79-85; TV Buxton w Burbage and King Sterndale *Derby* 85-95; P-in-c Brampton St Mark 95-02; rtd 02; PtO *Lich* from 03. *15 Langley Street, Basford, Stoke-on-Trent ST4 6DX* T: (01782) 622762

LEWIS, Norman Eric. b 34. SRN 55 Open Univ BA 77. Roch Th Coll 59 Lich Th Coll 60. **d** 63 **p** 64. C Hope St Jas *Man* 63-67; V Hindsford 67-77; V Bolton SS Simon and Jude 77-90; rtd 90; PtO *York* from 90. *Millbank Cottage, Kirby Misperton, Malton YO17 6XZ* T: (01653) 668526 E: norman@btinternet.com

LEWIS, Patrick Mansel. See MANSEL LEWIS, Patrick Charles Archibald

LEWIS, Pauline. See LEWIS, Ella Pauline

LEWIS, Peter. See LEWIS, Thomas Peter

LEWIS, Peter Andrew. b 67. Pemb Coll Ox MA PhD Univ of Wales (Abth) Bris Univ BA. Trin Coll Bris 92. **d** 96 **p** 97. C Cardigan w Mwnt and Y Ferwig *St D* 96-98; C Gabalfa *Llan* 98-01; V Aberpergwm and Blaengwrach 01-04; V Vale of Neath 04-12; AD Neath 10-12; V Pontypridd St Cath from 12. *St Catherine's Vicarage, Gelliwastad Grove, Pontypridd CF37 2BS* T: (01443) 402021 E: revpeterlewis@gmail.com

LEWIS, Peter Richard. b 40. Dur Univ BA 62. Qu Coll Birm 62. **d** 64 **p** 65. C Moseley St Mary *Birm* 64-67; C Sherborne w Castleton and Lillington *Sarum* 67-71; P-in-c Bishopstone w Stratford Tony 72-80; V Amesbury 80-02; rtd 02; PtO *Sarum* from 02; *B & W* from 05. *Rose Cottage, Silton Road, Bourton, Gillingham SP8 5DE*

LEWIS, Miss Rachel Veronica Clare. b 59. St Jo Coll Dur BA 80 Man Univ PGCE 81 Univ of Wales (Cardiff) MSc. Sarum & Wells Th Coll 86. **d** 86 **p** 94. C Caereithin *S & B* 86-88; Par Dn Bolton St Pet *Man* 88-91; Chapl Bolton Colls of H&FE 88-91; Chapl Trin Coll Carmarthen 91-94; C Yatton Keynell *Bris* 94-97; P-in-c 97-99; C Biddestone w Slaughterford 94-97; P-in-c 97-99; C Castle Combe 94-97; P-in-c 97-99; C W Kington 94-97; P-in-c 97-99; C Nettleton w Littleton Drew 94-97; P-in-c 97-99; P-in-c Grittleton and Leigh Delamere 94-99; TR By Brook 99-02; I Adare and Kilmallock w Kilpeacon, Croom etc *L & K* 02-07; P-in-c Peterston-super-Ely w St Brides-super-Ely *Llan* 07-12; P-in-c St Nicholas w Bonvilston and St George-super-Ely 07-12; P-in-c Pendoylan w Welsh St Donats 07-12; R Walbury Beacon *Ox* from 12. *3 Elizabeth Gardens, Kintbury, Hungerford RG17 9TB* T: (01488) 608400 M: 07912-646040 E: rev.lewis@btinternet.com

LEWIS, Ray Arthur. b 63. Oak Hill Th Coll 87. **d** 90 **p** 91. C Holloway St Mary Magd *Lon* 90-93; TV Forest Gate St Sav w W Ham St Matt *Chelmsf* 93-97; St Vincent 97-98; Grenada 98-99. *45 Avenue Road, London E7 0LA*

LEWIS, Raymond James. b 34. Univ of Wales (Cardiff) BA Open Univ BSc. St Mich Coll Llan. **d** 91 **p** 92. C Llanelli *St D* 91-94; rtd 99. *36 Yorath Road, Whitchurch, Cardiff CF14 1QD* T: (029) 2061 6267

LEWIS, Richard. See LEWIS, John Hubert Richard

LEWIS, The Very Revd Richard. b 35. Fitzw Ho Cam BA 78 MA 63. Ripon Hall Ox 58. **d** 60 **p** 61. C Hinckley St Mary *Leic* 60-63; C Sanderstead All SS *S'wark* 63-66; V W Merstham 67-72; V S Wimbledon H Trin 72-74; P-in-c S Wimbledon St Pet 72-74; V S Wimbledon H Trin and St Pet 74-79; V Dulwich St Barn 79-90; Chapl Alleyn's Foundn Dulwich 79-90; RD Dulwich *S'wark* 83-90; Hon Can *S'wark* Cathl 87-90; Dean Wells *B & W* 90-03; Warden of Readers 91-03; rtd 03; PtO *Worc* 03-08. *1 Monmouth Court, Union Street, Wells BA5 2PX* T: (01749) 672677 M: 07788-413525 E: dean.richard@btinternet.com

LEWIS, Canon Richard Charles. b 44. Univ of Wales (Lamp) MA 94 Sheff Univ MEd 96. ALCD 69. **d** 69 **p** 70. C Kendal H Trin *Carl* 69-72; C Chipping Barnet *St Alb* 72-76; V Watford Ch Ch 76-12; Chapl Abbot's Hill Sch Herts 81-96; Hon Can

St Alb Abbey *St Alb* 90-12; Can Emer St Alb from 12; Chapl from 12; Chapl Trin Hosp Retford from 12. *Rectory Farm, Rectory Road, Retford DN22 7AY* T: (01777) 719200
E: dick@ccwatford.u-net.com

LEWIS, Robert. b 38. St Pet Coll Ox BA 62 MA 66. Cuddesdon Coll 62. **d** 64 **p** 65. C Kirkby *Liv* 64-67 and 70-71; TV 71-75; Chapl St Boniface Coll Warminster 68-69; Tutor St Aug Coll Cant 69-70; Abp's Dom Chapl and Dir of Ords *York* 76-79; TR Thirsk 79-92; Chapl Oslo w Bergen, Trondheim, Stavanger etc *Eur* 93-96; P-in-c Danby *York* 96-98; V 98-04; RD Whitby 98-04; rtd 04; PtO *York* from 04. *19 Long Street, Thirsk YO7 1AW* T: (01845) 523256

LEWIS, Robert. **d** 14. NSM Begelly w Ludchurch and E Williamston *St D* from 14. *Valley View, Manorbier, Tenby SA70 7TE* T: (01834) 870218 E: revboblewis@gmail.com

LEWIS, Robert Charles. **d** 14. NSM Begelly w Ludchurch and E Williamston *St D* 14-15; NSM Jeffreyston w Reynoldston and Loveston etc from 15. *15 Churchill Park, Jeffreyston, Kilgetty SA68 0SD* T: (01646) 651659 E: revboblewis@gmail.com

LEWIS, Canon Robert George. b 53. Lanc Univ BEd 76. Ripon Coll Cuddesdon. **d** 78 **p** 79. C Liv Our Lady and St Nic w St Anne 78-81; Asst Dir of Educn 81-88; P-in-c Newchurch 88-89; P-in-c Glazebury 88-89; R Newchurch and Glazebury 89-94; R Winwick 94-09; R Glazebury w Hollinfare 04-09; AD Winwick 01-09; Hon Can Liv Cathl from 01; Chapl Liv Univ from 09; Chapl Liv Jo Moores Univ from 09; Bp's Adv Sector Min from 11; P-in-c Toxteth St Marg from 14. *10 Ladychapel Close, Liverpool L1 7BZ* T: 0151-707 2988
E: thelewises@hotmail.com

LEWIS, Roger Gilbert. b 49. St Jo Coll Dur BA 70. Ripon Hall Ox 70. **d** 72 **p** 73. C Boldmere *Birm* 72-76; C Birm St Pet 76-77; TV Tettenhall Regis *Lich* 77-81; V Ward End *Birm* 81-91; rtd 91; PtO *Birm* 91-06. *8 Tudor Terrace, Ravenhurst Road, Birmingham B17 9SB* T: 0121-427 4915

LEWIS, Simon Wilford. b 66. Westmr Coll Ox BTh 94 Roehampton Inst PGCE 95. STETS 03. **d** 06 **p** 07. C Ventnor St Cath, Ventnor H Trin and Bonchurch *Portsm* 06-09; P-in-c Brent Knoll, E Brent and Lympsham *B & W* from 09. *The Rectory, 3 Ash Trees, East Brent, Highbridge TA9 4DQ* T: (01278) 760496 E: rev.simonlewis@gmail.com

LEWIS, Stuart William. b 54. Newc Univ BA 79 Newc Poly PGCE 80. Edin Th Coll 84. **d** 86 **p** 87. C Ledbury w Eastnor *Heref* 86-89; Chapl Malvern Coll 89-96; Chapl and Prec Portsm Cathl 96-97; TV Ross *Heref* 97-01; P-in-c Lower Wharfedale *Ripon* 01-03; R Leeds from 03; Chapl St Aid Sch Harrogate 01-05. *Hayfield House, Strait Lane, Huby, Leeds LS17 0EA* E: stuartlewis@wyenet.co.uk

LEWIS, Thomas Peter. b 45. Selw Coll Cam BA 67 MA. Ripon Hall Ox 68. **d** 70 **p** 71. C Bp's Hatfield *St Alb* 70-74; C Boreham Wood All SS 74-78; Chapl Haileybury Coll 78-85; Chapl Abingdon Sch 86-03; R Narberth w Mounton w Robeston Wathen etc *St D* 03-14; rtd 14. *Nantyfelin, Old St Clears Road, Johnstown, Carmarthen SA31 3HN* T: (01267) 234667 E: revtplewis@btinternet.com

LEWIS, Timothy Mark Philip. b 82. Worc Coll Ox BA 05. Wycliffe Hall Ox M1 11. **d** 11 **p** 12. C Yeovil w Kingston Pitney *B & W* 11-14; Chapl Cranleigh Sch Surrey from 14. *Brannocks, Edgefield Close, Cranleigh GU6 8PX* M: 07739-026939
E: timothymplewis@hotmail.co.uk

LEWIS, Timothy Paul. b 84. Nottm Univ BA 07. Trin Coll Bris MA 11. **d** 11 **p** 12. C Cottingley *Leeds* 11-14; V Girlington from 14. *The Vicarage, 27 Baslow Grove, Bradford BD9 5JA* E: tim.paul.lewis@gmail.com *or* tim.lewis@bradford.anglican.org

LEWIS, Trevor Arnold. b 55. York St Jo Univ BA 12. NEOC 06. **d** 09 **p** 10. NSM Middlesbrough St Martin w St Cuth *York* 09-10; NSM Osmotherley w Harlsey and Ingleby Arncliffe from 10; NSM Leake w Over and Nether Silton and Kepwick from 10; NSM Felixkirk w Boltby from 10; NSM Kirkby Knowle from 10; NSM Cowesby from 10. *Orchard House, Ingleby Arncliffe, Northallerton DL6 3LN* T: (01609) 882937
E: revtrev02@gmail.com

LEWIS, Vera Elizabeth. b 45. Lon Univ BA 66 Univ of Wales (Abth) DipEd 67. St As Minl Tr Course 82. **d** 85 **p** 97. NSM Garthbeibio and Llanerfyl and Llangadfan *St As* 85-86; C 87-88; NSM Llanfair Caereinion w Llanllugan 85-86; C 87-88; Dn-in-c Llanrhaeadr-ym-Mochnant etc 88-96; Dn-in-c Llanddulas and Llysfaen 96-97; rtd 03; P-in-c Henllan and Llannefydd and Bylchau *St As* from 12. *Heulwen, Bronwylfa Square, St Asaph LL17 0BU* T: (01745) 584261

LEWIS, Canon Walter Arnold. b 45. NUI BA 68 TCD MPhil 91. TCD Div Sch 71. **d** 71 **p** 72. C Belfast Whiterock *Conn* 71-73; C Belfast St Mark 73-80; Bp's C Belfast St Andr 80-84; I Belfast St Thos 84-12; Can Belf Cathl 97-12; rtd 12. *145 Mountsandel Road, Coleraine BT52 1TA* T: (028) 7034 0929
M: 07715-358127 E: waltera.lewis@btinternet.com

LEWIS, William George Rees. b 35. Hertf Coll Ox BA 59 MA 63. Tyndale Hall Bris 61. **d** 63 **p** 64. C Tenby w Gumfreston *St D* 63-66; C Llanelli St Paul 66-69; R Letterston 69-73; R Letterston w Llanfair Nantygof, Jordanston etc 73-84; R Jordanston w Llanstinan 73-78; R Letterston w Llanfair Nant-y-Gof etc 78-84; R Hubberston w Herbrandston and Hasguard etc 84-88; R Hubberston 89-90; Prov Officer for Evang and Adult Educn 90-94; V Gabalfa *Llan* 94-00; rtd 00. *5 Westaway Drive, Hakin, Milford Haven SA73 3EG* T: (01646) 692280

LEWIS, William Rhys. b 20. St Mich Coll Llan 53. **d** 55 **p** 56. C Ystrad Mynach *Llan* 55-58; C Bassaleg *Mon* 58-59; V Cwmtillery 59-62; V Newport St Andr 62-64; TR Ebbw Vale 64-73; R Llangattock and Llangynidr *S & B* 73-78; V Swansea St Luke 78-85; rtd 85; PtO *Llan* from 85. *6 Beech Avenue, Llantwit Major CF61 1RT* T: (01446) 796741

LEWIS-ANTHONY, Justin Griffith. b 64. LSE BA 86 Kent Univ PhD 12. Ripon Coll Cuddesdon BA 91 MA 97. **d** 92 **p** 93. C Cirencester *Glouc* 92-98; Prec Ch Ch *Ox* 98-03; R Hackington *Cant* 03-13; Assoc Dean of Students Virginia Th Sem USA from 13. *Virginia Theological Seminary, 3737 Seminary Road, Alexandria VA 22304, USA* T: (001) (703) 461 1724 M: 678 3937 E: jlewis-anthony@vts.edu

LEWIS-GREGORY, Mrs Joycelyn. b 60. Qu Coll Birm. **d** 08 **p** 09. C Hall Green St Pet *Birm* 08-12; P-in-c Cotteridge 12; V from 12; Bp's Adv for Minority Ethnic Angl from 12. *118 Northfield Road, Kings Norton, Birmingham B30 1DX* T: 0121-433 5518
E: revjoycelyn@gmail.com *or* cotteridgechurch@btconnect.com

LEWIS-JENKINS, Christopher Robin. b 50. St Mich Coll Llan 94. **d** 96 **p** 97. C Barry All SS *Llan* 96-01; V Dinas and Penygraig w Williamstown 01-14; V Dinas w Penygraig from 14; AD Rhondda 06-11. *The Vicarage, 1 Llanfair Road, Tonypandy CF40 1TA* T: (01443) 423364

LEWIS LLOYD, Canon Timothy David. b 37. Clare Coll Cam BA 58 MA 62. Cuddesdon Coll 58. **d** 60 **p** 61. C Stepney St Dunstan and All SS *Lon* 60-64; C St Alb Abbey 64-67; Prec St Alb Abbey 67-69; V St Paul's Walden 69-78; V Braughing w Furneux Pelham and Stocking Pelham 78-79; P-in-c Lt Hadham 78-79; V Braughing, Lt Hadham, Albury, Furneux Pelham etc 79-82; V Cheshunt 82-95; RD 89-94; Hon Can St Alb 94-01; V Sawbridgeworth 95-01; rtd 01. *c/o M Lewis Lloyd Esq, 219C Goldhawk Road, London W12 8ER* T: (020) 8576 6122

LEWIS-MORRIS, Catherine Mary. *See* DAWKINS, Catherine Mary
LEWISHAM AND GREENWICH, Archdeacon of. *See* CUTTING, The Ven Alastair Murray

LEWORTHY, Graham Llewelyn. b 47. Reading Univ BA 69. S Dios Minl Tr Scheme 91. **d** 94 **p** 95. V Sark *Win* 94-11; rtd 11. *The Lodden, La Route des Blanches, St Martin, Guernsey GY4 6AF* T: (01481) 238125

LEWRY, Glyn. **d** 14. NSM Sampford Peverell, Uplowman, Holcombe Rogus etc *Ex* from 14. *1 Shillands, Tiverton EX16 5AA* T: (01884) 243727

LEYDEN, Michael John. b 85. St Pet Coll Ox MA 07 MSt 08. St Jo Coll Nottm 08. **d** 11 **p** 12. C Rainhill *Liv* 11-14; Tutor St Mellitus Coll 13-14; V Weston *Ches* from 14. *All Saints' Vicarage, 13 Cemetery Road, Weston, Crewe CW2 5LQ* M: 07771-923672 E: michael.leyden@spc.oxon.org

LEYLAND, Derek James. b 34. Lon Univ BSc 55. Qu Coll Birm 58. **d** 60 **p** 61. C Ashton-on-Ribble St Andr *Blackb* 60-63; V 80-87; C Salesbury 63-65; V Preston St Oswald 65-67; V Pendleton 67-74; Dioc Youth Chapl 67-69; Ind Youth Chapl 70-74; R Brindle 74-80; V Garstang St Helen Churchtown 87-94; Sec SOSc 90-94; rtd 94; PtO *Blackb* from 94. *Greystocks, Goosnargh Lane, Goosnargh, Preston PR3 2BP* T: (01772) 865682

LEYLAND, Stephen Robert. b 63. Portsm Poly BSc 84. St Seiriol Cen 07. **d** 11 **p** 12. C Llandegfan w Llandysilio w Llansadwrn *Ban* 11-14; R Bro Cyngar from 14. *The Rectory, SO Bro Ednyfed, Llangefni LL77 7WB* T: (01248) 521230
E: curate.steve@gmail.com

LEYLAND, Tyrone John. b 49. Aston Univ BSc 68. St Jo Coll Nottm 89. **d** 91 **p** 92. C Lich St Mary w St Mich 91-94; TV Willenhall H Trin 94-99; P-in-c The Ridwares and Kings Bromley 99-08; R from 08. *The Rectory, Alrewas Road, Kings Bromley, Burton-on-Trent DE13 7HP* T/F: (01543) 472932 E: ty.leyland@gmail.com

LEYSHON, Philip Alan. b 76. Glam Univ BA. Ripon Coll Cuddesdon BTh 03. **d** 03 **p** 04. C Newton Nottage *Llan* 03-07; C Caerphilly 07-09; V Tonypandy w Clydach Vale 09-14; V Tonypandy w Clydach Vale w Williamstown 14-15; P-in-c Pen Rhondda Fawr from 15. *The Vicarage, Vicarage Terrace, Treorchy CF42 6NA* T: (01443) 773303 E: pleyshon3@sky.com

LEYSHON, Simon. b 63. Trin Coll Carmarthen BA 86 Southn Univ BTh 89. Sarum & Wells Th Coll. **d** 89 **p** 90. C Tenby *St D*

89-92; TV 92-96; Chapl and Hd RS Llandovery Coll 96-02; Chapl Lord Wandsworth Coll Hook 02-13. *Address temp unknown* E: simonleyshon@hotmail.com

LIBBY, Canon John Ralph. b 55. Trin Coll Cam BA 83. Ridley Hall Cam 89. **d** 91 **p** 92. C Enfield St Andr *Lon* 91-93; C Northwood Em 93-96; V Denton Holme *Carl* 96-14; RD Carl 04-10; Hon Can Carl Cathl from 08. *Address temp unknown* E: john.libby@btinternet.com

LICHFIELD, Archdeacon of. *See* BAKER, The Ven Simon Nicholas Hartland

LICHFIELD, Bishop of. *See* GLEDHILL, The Rt Revd Jonathan Michael

LICHFIELD, Dean of. *See* DORBER, The Very Revd Adrian John

LICHTENBERGER, Miss Ruth Eileen. b 34. NY Th Sem 64 NOC 95. **d** 96 **p** 97. NSM Warrington H Trin *Liv* 96-05; rtd 05. *8 Towers Court, Warrington WA5 0AH* T: (01925) 656763

LICKESS, Canon David Frederick. b 37. St Chad's Coll Dur BA 63. **d** 65 **p** 66. C Howden *York* 65-70; V Rudby in Cleveland w Middleton 70-07; Can and Preb York Minster 90-07; RD Stokesley 93-00; rtd 07; PtO *York* from 07. *Bridge House, Snape, Bedale DL8 2SZ* T: (01677) 470077 E: davidlickess@gmail.com

LIDDELL, Mark. b 55. Birm Univ LLB BA 00. Coll of Resurr Mirfield 96. **d** 98 **p** 99. C Wednesbury St Jas and St Jo *Lich* 98-00; C Walsall St Andr 00-01; P-in-c 01-05; V 06-08; V Nuneaton St Mary *Cov* from 08. *St Mary's Abbey Vicarage, 99 Bottrill Street, Nuneaton CV11 5JB* T: (024) 7638 2936

LIDDELL, Canon Peter Gregory. b 40. St Andr Univ MA 63 Linacre Ho Ox BA 65 MA 70 Andover Newton Th Sch DMin 75. Ripon Coll Ox 63. **d** 65 **p** 66. C Bp's Hatfield *St Alb* 65-71; USA 71-76; P-in-c Kimpton w Ayot St Lawrence *St Alb* 77-83; Dir of Past Counselling 80-05; Hon Can St Alb 99-05; rtd 05. *12 Old Hall Court, Horn Hill, Whitwell, Hitchin SG4 8AS* T: (01438) 832266 E: petermary.liddell@btinternet.com

LIDDELOW, Peter William. b 33. Oak Hill NSM Course. **d** 82 **p** 83. NSM Finchley Ch Ch *Lon* 82-84; NSM S Mimms Ch Ch 84-11; PtO *St Alb* from 95; Chapl Magic Circle from 02. *23 King's Road, Barnet EN5 4EF* T: (020) 8441 2968 E: chaplain@themagiccircle.co.uk

LIDDLE, George. b 48. NEOC 88. **d** 90 **p** 91. C Auckland St Andr and St Anne *Dur* 90-92; C Crook 92-94; C Stanley 92-94; P-in-c Evenwood 94-96; V 96-03; R Blackhall, Castle Eden and Monkhesleden 03-13; rtd 13; PtO *Dur* from 13. *3 Rush Park, Bishop Auckland DL14 6NR*

LIDDLE, Harry. b 36. Wadh Coll Ox BA 57 MA 61. Wycliffe Hall Ox 62. **d** 64 **p** 65. C Withington St Paul *Man* 64-68; R Broughton St Jo 68-73; V Balby *Sheff* 73-82; R Firbeck w Letwell 82-94; V Woodsetts 82-94; TV Aston cum Aughton w Swallownest, Todwick etc 94-01; rtd 01; PtO *Sheff* from 01. *30 Meadow Grove Road, Totley, Sheffield S17 4FF* T: 0114-236 4941

LIDGATE, Mrs Jacqueline Mary. b 56. **d** 01 **p** 02. Hon C Milton Australia 01-02; C Indooroopilly 02-04; P-in-c Jimboomba 04-07; P-in-c Coolum 07-10; Chapl St Andr Angel Coll 08-10; PtO *S'well* 10-11; NSM Brampton St Thos *Derby* 11; PtO *S'well* from 13; *Sheff* from 15. *4 Granary Court, Carlton-in-Lindrick, Worksop S81 9JZ* T: (01909) 733820 E: pandjlidgate@sky.com

LIDSTONE, Vernon Henry. b 43. SWMTC 89. **d** 92 **p** 93. NSM Bovey Tracey SS Pet, Paul and Thos w Hennock *Ex* 92-94; Sub-Chapl HM Pris Channings Wood 92-96; Asst Dioc Chr Stewardship Adv *Ex* 92-93; Dioc Chr Stewardship Adv 93-96; Dioc Officer for Par Development *Glouc* 96-97; Chapl HM Pris Leyhill 97-03; rtd 03. *The Pike House, Saul, Gloucester GL2 7JD* T: (01452) 741410 E: vernon@lidstone.net

LIDWILL, Canon Mark Robert. b 57. CITC. **d** 87 **p** 88. C Annagh w Drumgoon, Ashfield etc *K, E & A* 87-90; I Urney w Denn and Derryheen from 90; Dioc Youth Adv from 92; Preb Kilmore Cathl from 98. *The Rectory, Keadue Lane, Cavan, Co Cavan, Republic of Ireland* T: (00353) (49) 436 1016

LIEBERT, Ms Sarah Jane. b 66. Pemb Coll Ox BA 88 MA 14 Imp Coll Lon MSc 89 Fitzw Coll Cam BA 13. Westcott Ho Cam 11. **d** 14 **p** 15. C Upper Tooting H Trin w St Aug *S'wark* from 14. *59 Glenburnie Road, London SW17 7NG*

LIEVESLEY, Mrs Joy Margaret. b 48. Lady Mabel Coll CertEd 69. Guildf Dioc Min Course 98. **d** 00 **p** 01. NSM Farnham *Guildf* 00-14; NSM Frimley from 15. *3 Kingfisher Close, Church Crookham, Fleet GU52 6JP* T: (01252) 690223 E: joy.lievesley@ntlworld.com

LIGHT, Mrs Madeline Margaret. b 54. Girton Coll Cam BA 77 MA 80 Lon Inst of Educn PGCE 78. EAMTC 96. **d** 99 **p** 00. C Eaton *Nor* 99-02; P-in-c Nor St Helen 02-09; Chapl GR Hosp Nor 02-09; P-in-c Nor St Steph from 09. *12 The Crescent, Chapel Field Road, Norwich NR2 1SA* T: (01603) 219927 E: madelinelight@gmail.com

LIGHT, Mrs Penelope Ann. b 46. Madeley Coll of Educn TCert 71 N Lon Poly BEd 81. WEMTC 06. **d** 09 **p** 10. NSM

Cirencester *Glouc* from 09. *Toad Cottage, 22 Bingham Close, Cirencester GL7 1HJ* T: (01285) 640125 E: jonpen22@tiscali.co.uk

LIGHTBOWN, Richard Andrew. b 66. Buckingham Univ MBA 07. Ripon Coll Cuddesdon MA 13. **d** 13 **p** 14. C Schorne Ox from 13. *Andover House, Main Street, Padbury, Buckingham MK18 2AN* T: (01280) 815042 M: 07500-015623 E: alightbown@hotmail.co.uk

LIGHTFOOT, The Very Revd Vernon Keith. b 34. St Jo Coll Dur BA 58. Ripon Hall Ox 58. **d** 60 **p** 61. C Rainhill *Liv* 60-62; C Liv Our Lady and St Nic 62-65; V Stanley 65-75; Chapl St Edm Coll Liv 66-68; Chapl Rathbone Hosp Liv 70-75; V Mt Albert St Luke New Zealand 75-85; Waikato 85-97; Dean from 98. *16C Acacia Crescent, Hamilton 3206, New Zealand* T/F: (0064) (7) 843 1381 E: keith.jennie@xtra.co.nz

LIGHTOWLER, Joseph Trevor. b 33. **d** 79 **p** 80. Hon C Leverstock Green *St Alb* 79-80; Hon C Chambersbury 80-84; C Woodmansterne *S'wark* 84-88; R Odell and Pavenham *St Alb* 88-97; rtd 97; PtO *St Alb* from 97. *18 The Dell, Sandpit Lane, St Albans AL1 4HE* T: (01727) 833422

LILBURN, Robert Irvine Terence. b 47. CITC 07. **d** 10 **p** 11. NSM Kilternan *D & G* 10-11; NSM Powerscourt w Kilbride from 11. *13 Churchfields, Dundrum Road, Milltown, Dublin 14, Republic of Ireland* T: (00353) (1) 260 0003 M: 86-886 5361 E: terrylilburn@gmail.com

LILES, Malcolm David. b 48. Nottm Univ BA 69. St Steph Ho Ox 69. **d** 71 **p** 72. C Corby Epiphany w St Jo *Pet* 71-74; C New Cleethorpes *Linc* 74-76; TV Lt Coates 76-77; TV Gt and Lt Coates w Bradley 78-82; Soc Resp Sec 82-93; Hon C Gt Grimsby St Mary and St Jas 82-93; P-in-c Grimsby All SS 88-93; TV Dronfield w Holmesfield *Derby* 93-98; TR Crawley *Chich* 98-14; rtd 14. *Address temp unknown*

LILEY, The Ven Christopher Frank. b 47. Nottm Univ BEd 70. Linc Th Coll 72. **d** 74 **p** 75. C Kingswinford H Trin *Lich* 74-79; TV Stafford 79-84; V Norton *St Alb* 84-96; RD Hitchin 89-94; V Shrewsbury St Chad w St Mary *Lich* 96-01; P-in-c Shrewsbury St Alkmund 96-01; Adn Lich 01-13; Can Res and Treas Lich Cathl 01-13; rtd 13. *15 Holloway Drive, Pershore WR10 1JL* T: (01386) 561608 E: lileyc@aol.com

LILEY, Peter James. b 60. Liv Univ BA 82 Westmr Coll Ox PGCE 83. Oak Hill Th Coll 91. **d** 93 **p** 94. C Exning St Martin w Landwade *St E* 93-96; V Acton w Gt Waldingfield 96-00; TV Bottesford w Ashby *Linc* 00-05; TR 05-12; Lic Preacher 12-14; R Mablethorpe w Trusthorpe from 14; R Sutton, Huttoft and Anderby from 14. *The Vicarage, 7A Huttoft Road, Sutton-on-Sea, Mablethorpe LN12 2QZ* T: (01507) 443948 E: rev.p.liley@btinternet.com

LILEY, Stephen John. b 65. Liv Univ BA 87 MMus 88 ARCM 93. Wycliffe Hall Ox 97. **d** 99 **p** 00. C Throop *Win* 99-03; V Clapham *St Alb* from 03; RD Elstow 08-10; RD Sharnbrook from 15. *The Vicarage, Green Lane, Clapham, Bedford MK41 6ER* T: (01234) 352814 E: the.lileys@ukgateway.net

LILLEY, Mrs Alexandra Mary. b 80. St Pet Coll Ox BA 01 MA 06. St Mellitus Coll BA 14. **d** 14 **p** 15. C Shadwell St Paul w Ratcliffe St Jas *Lon* from 14. *21 Redcastle Close, London E1W 3DQ* M: 07986-433658 E: alexandra_lilley@hotmail.com

LILLEY, Canon Christopher Howard. b 51. FCA 75 FTII 83. LNSM course 83 St Jo Coll Nottm 91. **d** 85 **p** 86. OLM Skegness and Winthorpe *Linc* 85-93; C Limber Magna w Brocklesby 93-96; PtO *S'well* 93-96; P-in-c Middle Rasen Gp *Linc* 96-97; R 97-02; V Scawby, Redbourne and Hibaldstow 02-10; P-in-c Bishop Norton, Waddingham and Snitterby 06-10; P-in-c Kirton in Lindsey w Manton 06-10; RD Yarborough 02-09; Hon C Mablethorpe w Trusthorpe from 10; Hon C Sutton, Huttoft and Anderby from 10; Can and Preb Linc Cathl from 05. *The Chrysalis, 12 Hillside Avenue, Sutton-on-Sea, Mablethorpe LN12 2JH* T: (01507) 440039 E: c.lilley@btinternet.com

LILLEY, Ivan Ray. b 32. Bps' Coll Cheshunt 58. **d** 61 **p** 62. C Kettering SS Pet and Paul 61-64; C Gt Yarmouth *Nor* 64-75; P-in-c Tottenhill w Wormegay *Ely* 76-83; P-in-c Watlington 76-83; P-in-c Holme Runcton w S Runcton and Wallington 76-83; V Tysoe w Oxhill and Whatcote *Cov* 83-86; C Langold *S'well* 87-91; P-in-c 91-98; rtd 98; PtO *Nor* from 98. *Linden Lea, 41 Cedar Drive, Attleborough NR17 2EY* T/F: (01953) 452710 E: ivanlinlea@hotmail.co.uk

LILLEY, Thomas Robert. b 84. UEA BA 05 PGCE 06 Fitzw Coll Cam BTh 11. Westcott Ho Cam 08. **d** 11 **p** 12. C Attleborough w Besthorpe *Nor* 11-14; P-in-c Southchurch H Trin *Chelmsf* from 14. *Southchurch Rectory, 8 Pilgrims Close, Southend-on-Sea SS2 4XF* M: 07984-181919 E: tom.lilley@gmail.com

LILLIAN, Mother. *See* MORRIS, Lillian Rosina

LILLICRAP, Peter Andrew. b 65. Hatf Poly BEng 87 CEng 93 MIMechE 93. Trin Coll Bris 00. **d** 02 **p** 03. C Kineton *Cov* 02-04; C Napton-on-the-Hill, Lower Shuckburgh etc 04-07;

V Acton and Worleston, Church Minshull etc *Ches* 07-13; V Layton and Staining *Blackb* from 13. *St Mark's Vicarage, 163 Kingscote Drive, Blackpool FY3 8EH* T: (01253) 392895 E: peterlillicrap@gmail.com

LILLICRAP, Canon Stephen Hunter. b 58. Newc Univ MB, BS 81 MRCGP 85. SEITE 00. **d** 03 **p** 04. C Wye w Brook and Hastingleigh etc *Cant* 03-08; C Stone Street Gp 06-08; C Mersham w Hinxhill and Sellindge 08; P-in-c Teynham w Lynsted and Kingsdown 08-14; P-in-c Norton 08-14; V Kingsdown and Creekside from 14; AD Ospringe from 11; Hon Can Cant Cathl from 14. *The Vicarage, 76 Station Road, Teynham, Sittingbourne ME9 9SN* T: (01795) 522510 M: 07971-224094 E: steve.lillicrap@btopenworld.com

LILLIE, Benjamin James. b 73. Ox Min Course 13. **d** 15. C Churchdown *Glouc* from 15. *32 Gratton Road, Cheltenham GL50 2BU* M: 07870-805642 E: benlillie@me.com

LILLIE, Judith Virginia. See THOMPSON, Judith Virginia

LILLIE, Mrs Shona Lorimer. b 49. St Jo Coll Nottm BA 03. **d** 03 **p** 04. C Bishopbriggs *Glas* 03-06; Dioc Supernumerary 06-07; Assoc P Glas St Mary 07-09; R Cambuslang 09-12; R Uddingston 09-12. *Address temp unknown* M: 07982-451745 E: shonalillie@hotmail.com

LILLINGTON (née POLLIT), Mrs Ruth Mary. b 65. SS Paul & Mary Coll Cheltenham BA 88. St Jo Coll Nottm 88. **d** 90 **p** 94. Par Dn Caverswall *Lich* 90-92; Par Dn Caverswall and Weston Coyney w Dilhorne 92-93; Par Dn Luton St Mary *St Alb* 93-94; C 94-97; Chapl Luton Univ 93-97. *20 Harcourt Road, Bracknell RG12 7JD* T: (01344) 423025

LILLISTONE, Canon Brian David. b 38. SS Coll Cam BA 61 MA 65. St Steph Ho Ox 61. **d** 63 **p** 64. C Ipswich All Hallows *St E* 63-66; C Stokesay *Heref* 66-71; P-in-c Lyonshall w Titley 71-76; R Martlesham w Brightwell *St E* 76-03; Hon Can St E Cathl 98-03; rtd 03; PtO *St E* from 03. *23 Woodland Close, Risby, Bury St Edmunds IP28 6QN* T: (01284) 811330 E: canon.b.lillistone@onetel.net

LIMA, Luiz Henrique. See Henrique, DE ANDRADE LIMA, Luiz

LIMBERT, Chrichton. b 57. Reading Univ BSc 79 St Jo Coll Cam PhD 87. St Mellitus Coll BA 12. **d** 12 **p** 13. C Ouzel Valley *St Alb* from 12. *138 Brooklands Drive, Leighton Buzzard LU7 3PG* T: (01525) 384453 M: 07711-751501 E: frch138@btinternet.com

LIMBERT, Kenneth Edward. b 25. CEng 69 MIMechE. S'wark Ord Course 72. **d** 75 **p** 76. NSM Northwood Hills St Edm *Lon* 75-90; PtO 90-13. *55 York Road, Northwood HA6 1JJ* T: (01923) 825791

LIMBRICK, Gordon. b 36. Open Univ BA 88. St Jo Coll Nottm. **d** 87 **p** 91. Hon C Troon *Glas* 87-90; Hon C Yaxley *Ely* 90-97; Hon C Yaxley and Holme w Conington 97-04; rtd 04; PtO *Pet* 98-14; *Ely* from 04. *271 Broadway, Yaxley, Peterborough PE7 3NR* T: (01733) 243170 E: revgordonlimbrick@gmail.com

LIMERICK AND ARDFERT, Dean of. See PRAGNELL, The Very Revd Sandra Ann

LIMERICK, ARDFERT AND AGHADOE, Archdeacon of. See WATTERSON, The Ven Susan Mary

LIMERICK, ARDFERT, AGHADOE, KILLALOE, KILFENORA, CLONFERT,KILMACDUAGH AND EMLY, Bishop of. See KEARON, The Rt Revd Kenneth Arthur

LINAKER, Canon David Julian John Ramage. b 65. Ripon Coll Cuddesdon BTh 95. **d** 95 **p** 96. C Colehill *Sarum* 95-99; V Mere w W Knoyle and Maiden Bradley 99-06; P-in-c Salisbury St Thos and St Edm 06-13; R from 13; Little Bower, *Campbell Road, Salisbury SP1 3BG* T: (01722) 504462 *or* 322537 E: davidlinaker65@gmail.com

LINCOLN, Archdeacon of. See BARKER, The Ven Timothy Reed

LINCOLN, Bishop of. See LOWSON, The Rt Revd Christopher

LINCOLN, Dean of. See BUCKLER, The Very Revd Philip John Warr

LIND-JACKSON, Peter Wilfrid. b 35. Leeds Univ BA 67. Linc Th Coll 67. **d** 68 **p** 69. C Heref St Martin 68-71; P-in-c Burghill 71-78; V 78-82; V Barnard Castle *Dur* 82-83; P-in-c Whorlton 82-83; V Barnard Castle w Whorlton 83-00; rtd 00; PtO *Leeds* from 03. *5 Gill Lane, Barnard Castle DL12 9AS* T: (01833) 630027 E: lindjacksons@googlemail.com

LINDARS, Frank. b 23. Wycliffe Hall Ox 54. **d** 56 **p** 57. C Beeston Hill St Luke *Ripon* 56-59; C Harrogate St Wilfrid 59-61; V Shadwell 61-80; RD Allerton 73-78; V Masham and Healey 80-88; rtd 88; PtO *Leeds* from 88. *Hope Cottage, Reeth, Richmond DL11 6SF* T: (01748) 884685

LINDECK, Peter Stephen. b 31. Oak Hill Th Coll 57. **d** 59 **p** 60. C Homerton St Luke *Lon* 59-62; C Salterhebble All SS *Wakef* 62-63; C Islington St Andr w St Thos and St Matthias *Lon* 64-67; PtO *Derby* 67-68; St Alb 67-68; V Toxteth Park St Bede *Liv* 68-74; V Kano St Geo Nigeria 74-76; C Netherton *Liv* 76-77; C Ollerton and Boughton *S'well* 77-80; V Whitgift w Adlingfleet and Eastoft *Sheff* 80-86; P-in-c Swinefleet 81-86;

V Kilnhurst 86-94; Chapl Montagu Hosp Mexborough 86-94; rtd 94; PtO *Sheff* 94-06; *Leic* from 14. *27 Stuart Court, High Street, Kibworth, Leicester LE8 0LR* T: 0116-279 6347 E: peter@lindeck.freeserve.co.uk

LINDISFARNE, Archdeacon of. See ROBINSON, The Ven Peter John Alan

LINDLEY (née FLYNN), Mrs Anna Therese. b 42. Leeds Univ BSc 63 Surrey Univ MPhil 72 Westmr Coll Ox DipEd 64. Yorks Min Course 08. **d** 09 **p** 11. NSM York St Mich-le-Belfrey 09-12; NSM Skelton w Shipton and Newton on Ouse from 12. *35 Manor Garth, Wigginton, York YO32 2WZ*

LINDLEY, Mrs Danie Maria. b 71. Lindisfarne Regional Tr Partnership 12. **d** 15. NSM Chester le Street *Dur* from 15. *23 Lime Street, Waldridge, Chester le Street DH2 3SG* T: 0191-389 0215 M: 07764-946645 E: danielindley@gmail.com

LINDLEY, Graham William. b 47. CIPFA 77. **d** 97 **p** 98. OLM E Crompton *Man* 97-02; NSM Newhey 02-08; P-in-c 08-13; P-in-c Belfield from 09. *37 Jordan Avenue, Shaw, Oldham OL2 8DQ* T: (01706) 845677 E: g.lindley7@ntlworld.com

LINDLEY, Harold Thomas. b 28. St Jo Coll Ox BA 51 MA 73. Wells Th Coll 51. **d** 53 **p** 54. C Normanton *Wakef* 53-57; C-in-c Rawthorpe CD 57-63; P-in-c Longstone *Derby* 63-67; V 68-74; P-in-c Barrow w Twyford 74-84; V Barrow-on-Trent w Twyford and Swarkestone 84-93; rtd 93. *Gorwel, 35 Nant Bychan, Moelfre LL72 8HE* T: (01248) 410484

LINDLEY, Canon Richard Adrian. b 44. Hull Univ BA 65 Man Univ MA 79 Win Univ PhD 14. Cuddesdon Coll 66. **d** 68 **p** 69. C Ingrow w Hainworth *Bradf* 68-70; PtO *Birm* 70-74; TV Ellesmere Port *Ches* 74-79; V Westborough *Guildf* 79-80; TR 80-84; Dir of Educn *Birm* 84-96; Hon Can Birm Cathl 96; Dir of Educn *Win* 96-04; Hon Can Win Cathl 03-04; rtd 04; PtO *Win* 04-13; NSM Win Cathl from 13. *28 Denham Close, Winchester SO23 7BL* T: (01962) 621851 M: 07743-758639 E: lindleyrs@ntlworld.com

LINDNER, Christoph Walter. b 67. St Mellitus Coll BA 12. **d** 12 **p** 13. NSM Gerrards Cross and Fulmer *Ox* from 12. *7 Gaviots Close, Gerrards Cross SL9 7EJ* M: 07905-530996 E: christoph.lindner@saintjames.org.uk

LINDOP, Andrew John. b 57. Cam Univ MA. Cranmer Hall Dur 80. **d** 82 **p** 83. C Brinsworth w Catcliffe *Sheff* 82-85; C S Shoebury *Chelmsf* 85-89; V Mosley Common *Man* 89-99; V Astley Bridge 99-11; AD Walmsley 02-10; TR Ramsbottom and Edenfield from 11. *St Andrew's Vicarage, 2 Henhall Hall Avenue, Ramsbottom, Bury BL0 9YH* T/F: (01706) 826482 E: andylindop95@tiscali.co.uk

LINDOP, Canon Kenneth. b 45. Linc Th Coll 71. **d** 74 **p** 75. C Leic St Phil 74-77; C Cov H Trin 77-80; P-in-c Cubbington 80-82; V 82-07; RD Warwick and Leamington 91-96; Jt P-in-c Leamington Spa H Trin and Old Milverton 03-07; Hon Can Cov Cathl 04-07; rtd 07; PtO *B & W* from 09. *2 Grove House, Blue Anchor, Minehead TA24 6JU* T: (01643) 821940 E: rev.lindop@gmail.com

LINDSAY, Canon Alexandra Jane (Sandra). b 43. CITC 90. **d** 93 **p** 94. LtO *K, E & A* 93-94; Aux Min Bailieborough w Knockbride, Shercock and Mullagh 94-05; Aux Min Roscommon w Donamon, Rathcline, Kilkeevin etc 05-12; P-in-c Drumgoon from 12; Can Kilmore Cathl from 14. *Clementstown House, Cootehill, Co Cavan, Republic of Ireland* T/F: (00353) (49) 555 2207

LINDSAY, Anne. See LINDSAY, Mary Jane Anne

LINDSAY, Anthony. b 38. Trin Coll Bris 92. **d** 89 **p** 90. CMS 76-92; Dioc Admin Bo Sierra Leone 89-92; C Rainham w Wennington *Chelmsf* 93-96; R Quendon w Rickling and Wicken Bonhunt etc 96-03; rtd 03; PtO *Derby* 03-07 and from 10; P-in-c Langtoft w Foxholes, Butterwick, Cottam etc 07-10; Rtd Clergy and Widows Officer (E Riding) from 12. *5 Bursary Court, Pickering YO18 8BF* T: (01751) 476849 E: tonyandpamlindsay@yahoo.co.uk

LINDSAY, Ashley. See LINDSAY, Robert Ashley Charles

LINDSAY, Calum Oran. b 73. Edin Univ BEng 97. Ridley Hall Cam 09. **d** 11 **p** 12. C St Margaret's-on-Thames *Lon* 11-14; USA from 14. *101 Ivy Drive, Appt 9, Charlottesville VA 22903, USA* E: revcalumlindsay@gmail.com

LINDSAY, David Macintyre. b 46. Trin Hall Cam BA 68 MA 72. Cuddesdon Coll 68. **d** 71 **p** 72. C Gosforth All SS *Newc* 71-74; C Keele *Lich* 74-78; PtO *St E* 79-80; Chapl Haberdashers' Aske's Sch Elstree 80-06; rtd 06; PtO *St Alb* 06-07; *Portsm* from 07; Co-ord Reader Tr from 10. *Kentmere, Ashling Close, Waterlooville PO7 6NQ* T: (023) 9225 7662 M: 07769-814165 E: lindsay_d46@hotmail.com

LINDSAY, Eric Graham. b 30. Witwatersrand Univ BA 51 Lon Univ MA 80 DipAdEd 78. Coll of Resurr Mirfield 55. **d** 57 **p** 59. C Stella *Dur* 57-58; C W Hartlepool St Aid 58-60; C St Geo Grenada 60-61; PtO *Win* 61-65; *Roch* 65-72; *Chelmsf* 72-84; C Stepney St Dunstan and All SS *Lon* 84-85;

P-in-c Stepney St Dunstan LEP 84-85; R Bridge of Weir *Glas* 85-98; R Kilmacolm 85-98. *1 Woodrow Court, 26-32 Port Glasgow Road, Kilmacolm PA13 4QA* T: (01505) 874668 E: priestssc@yahoo.co.uk

LINDSAY, Canon John Carruthers. b 50. Edin Univ MA 72 BD 82. Edin Th Coll 79. **d** 82 **p** 83. C Broughty Ferry *Bre* 82-84; C Edin St Hilda 84-85; TP 85-88; C Edin St Fillan 84-85; TP 85-88; R N Berwick 88-15; R Gullane 88-15; Can St Mary's Cathl 00-15; rtd 15. *2 West Meikle Pinkerton Cottages, Dunbar EH42 1RX* M: 07977-520277 E: canonjohnlindsay@gmail.com

LINDSAY, Mrs Linda. b 53. Lindisfarne Regional Tr Partnership 13. **d** 15. NSM Crook *Dur* from 15. *16 Priors Path, Ferryhill DL17 8UA* T: (01740) 655649 M: 07940-985217 E: linda.lindsay16@btinternet.com

LINDSAY (*née* CLEALL), Mrs Mary Jane Anne. b 54. Keele Univ BA 77 Herts Univ PGCE 92. SAOMC 00. **d** 03 **p** 04. C Chipping Barnet *St Alb* 03-07; Chapl Portsm Hosps NHS Trust from 07. *Kentmere, Ashling Close, Waterlooville PO7 6NQ* T: (023) 9225 7662 *or* 9228 6000 M: 07769-814166 E: anne.lindsay@porthosp.nhs.uk

LINDSAY, Richard John. b 46. Sarum & Wells Th Coll 74. **d** 78 **p** 79. C Aldwick *Chich* 78-81; C Almondbury w Farnley Tyas *Wakef* 81-84; V Mossley *Man* 84-15; rtd 15; PtO *Man* from 15. *The Vicarage, Stamford Street, Mossley, Ashton-under-Lyne OL5 0LP* T: (01457) 832219

LINDSAY, Robert Andrew Duquemin. St Mich Coll Llan. **d** 09 **p** 10. C Blaenavon w Capel Newydd *Mon* 09-13; TV Bassaleg 13-15; P-in-c Rhymney from 15; P-in-c Pontlottyn w Fochriw *Llan* from 15. *St Tyfaelog's Vicarage, Picton Street, Pontlottyn, Bargoed CF81 9PS* T: (01685) 841322 E: fatherrobthevicarage@gmail.com

LINDSAY, Robert Ashley Charles. b 43. Leeds Univ BA 66 Ex Univ BPhil 81. Coll of Resurr Mirfield 66. **d** 68 **p** 69. C Mill Hill Jo Keble Ch *Lon* 68-72; C Sherborne w Castleton and Lillington *Sarum* 73-78; Chapl Coldharbour Hosp Dorset 73-78; PtO *Leic* 87-92; rtd 08. *Breezedown Cottage, East Melbury, Shaftesbury SP7 0DS* T: (01747) 850145

LINDSAY, Sandra. See LINDSAY, Alexandra Jane

LINDSAY-SCOTT, Jonathan Mark. b 82. Bath Univ MEng 06. Ridley Hall Cam 11. **d** 14 **p** 15. C Romiley *Ches* from 14. *21 Guywood Lane, Romiley, Stockport SK6 4AN* T: 0161-430 4652 E: jon@stchadsromiley.co.uk

LINDSAY-SMITH, Kevin Roy. b 55. **d** 05 **p** 06. OLM Glascote and Stonydelph *Lich* from 05. *34 Castlehall, Tamworth B77 2EJ* T: (01827) 251557 E: lindsay-smith1@sky.com

LINDSEY, Anna Elizabeth. b 65. Cuddesdon Coll 95. **d** 97 **p** 98. C Limpsfield and Titsey *S'wark* 97-00; C Warlingham w Chelsham and Farleigh 00-03; TV 03-06; rtd 06. *2/13 Currey Crescent, Milford, Auckland 0620, New Zealand* T: (0064) (9) 410 1554 E: anna@heffs.demon.co.uk

LINDSEY, John (Sami). b 73. Ch Ch Ox BA 95 Cranfield Univ MSc 97. Trin Coll Bris 11. **d** 13 **p** 14. C Leic H Trin w St Jo from 13; C Emmaus Par Team from 14. *11 Dixon Drive, Leicester LE2 1RA* M: 07850-326991 E: samilindsey@googlemail.com

LINECAR, Rhian Wynn. **d** 15. NSM Cardiff City Par *Llan* from 15; NSM Cardiff Dewi Sant from 15. *Ty Llwyd, Drope Road, St George's-super-Ely, Cardiff CF5 6EP* T: (01446) 760007 E: rlinecar@gmail.com

LINES, Canon Andrew John. b 60. Univ Coll Dur BA 82. All Nations Chr Coll 88. **d** 97 **p** 98. Paraguay 91-99; Dir Caleb Bible Cen 91-99; SAMS 97-00; Miss Dir/Chief Exec Officer Crosslinks from 00; Hon Can Paraguay from 00; PtO *S'wark* from 01. *59 Woodside Road, New Malden KT3 3AW* T: (020) 8942 2179 *or* 8691 6111 F: 8694 8023 E: alines@crosslinks.org

LINES, Graham Martin. b 55. St Jo Coll Nottm 97. **d** 99 **p** 00. C Crosby *Linc* 99-02; C Bottesford w Ashby 02-03; TV 03-14; V Crowle Gp from 14. *The Vicarage, Church Street, Crowle, Scunthorpe DN17 4LE* E: graham@ml47.fslife.co.uk

LINES, Nicholas David John. b 64. St Jo Coll Nottm 94. **d** 96 **p** 97. C Burton All SS w Ch Ch *Lich* 96-01; P-in-c Rodbourne Cheney *Bris* 01-02; R from 02. *St Mary's Rectory, 298 Cheney Manor Road, Swindon SN2 2PF* T: (01793) 522379 E: nick.lines1@gmail.com

LINFORD, Preb John Kenneth. b 31. Liv Univ BA 52. Chich Th Coll 54. **d** 56 **p** 57. C Stoke upon Trent *Lich* 56-61; V Tunstall Ch Ch 61-70; V Sedgley All SS 70-78; Chapl Chase Hosp Cannock 78-91; TR Cannock *Lich* 78-91; V Hatherton 80-91; Preb Lich Cathl 88-98; rtd 91; PtO *Lich* 91-00. *16 School Lane, Hill Ridware, Rugeley WS15 3QN* T: (01543) 492831

LINFORD, Susan (Sue). b 51. STETS 10. **d** 13 **p** 14. OLM Bride Valley *Sarum* from 13. *North Hill Cottage, Shipton Lane, Burton Bradstock, Bridport DT6 4NQ* T: (01308) 897363 E: sue.linford@btopenworld.com

LING, Adrian Roger. b 66. Goldsmiths' Coll Lon BA 89 Leeds Univ BA 02. Coll of Resurr Mirfield 00. **d** 02 **p** 03. C Mill End

and Heronsgate w W Hyde *St Alb* 02-06; P-in-c Flegg Coastal Benefice *Nor* 06-08; R 08-12; R S Lynn from 12. *All Saints' Rectory, 33 Goodwins Road, King's Lynn PE30 5QX* T: (01553) 771779 E: adrianrling@btinternet.com

LING, Andrew Joyner. b 35. ACP 69 St Luke's Coll Ex TCert 63 Open Univ BA 80. SWMTC 83. **d** 86 **p** 87. NSM St Dominic, Landulph and St Mellion w Pillaton *Truro* 86-90; C Saltash 90-94; TV 94-97; Chapl Montreux w Gstaad *Eur* 97-03; r-d 03. *Martinets, chemin des Martinets 7, 1872 Troistorrents, Switzerland* T: (0041) (24) 477 2408

LING, Mrs Claire Louise. b 67. ERMC 12. **d** 15. C Kesgrave *St E* from 15. *The Vicarage, 18 Bell Lane, Kesgrave, Ipswich IP5 1JQ* E: claire.ling@yahoo.co.uk *or* claire@revlings.co.uk

LING, Matthew Keith. b 65. ERMC 12. **d** 15. C E Bergholt and Brantham *St E* from 15. *The Vicarage, 18 Bell Lane, Kesgrave, Ipswich IP5 1JQ* E: matthew@revlings.co.uk *or* matthew.ling@talk21.com

LING, Rebecca (Jordan). b 75. Leic Univ BSc 00. St Jo Coll Nottm 04. **d** 08 **p** 09. C Leic St Chris 08-13; P-in-c Bristol St Aid w St Geo *Bris* from 13; P-in-c Fishponds St Jo from 13; P-in-c Two Mile Hill St Mich from 13. *St John's Vicarage, Mayfield Park, Bristol BS16 3NW* E: jordanling@ntlworld.com

LING, Timothy Charles. b 61. Ex Univ BA 85 Selw Coll Cam BA 91. Ridley Hall Cam 89. **d** 92 **p** 93. C Gerrards Cross and Fulmer *Ox* 92-96; C Woking St Pet *Guildf* 96-00; V Bathford *B & W* 00-09; PtO from 10. *Slade Cottage, Church Lane, Monkton Combe, Bath BA2 7HF* T: (01225) 722622 M: 07760-785829 E: tim.ling@whsmithnet.co.uk

LINGARD, Colin. b 36. Kelham Th Coll 58. **d** 63 **p** 64. C Middlesbrough St Martin *York* 63-66; C Stainton-in-Cleveland 66-71; V Eskdaleside w Ugglebarnby 71-77; P-in-c Redcar w Kirkleatham 77; V Kirkleatham 78-86; RD Guisborough 83-86; V Linc St Botolph 86-89; Dioc Dir of Readers 86-89; R Washington *Dur* 89-93; P-in-c Middleton St George 93-97; R 97-01; Chapl Teesside Airport 97-01; rtd 01; PtO *Dur* from 01. *29 Belgrave Terrace, Hurworth Place, Darlington DL2 2DW* M: 07752-179418

LINGARD, Jennifer Mary. See ALIDINA, Jennifer Mary

LINGS, Canon George William. b 49. Nottm Univ BTh 74 Ox Univ PGCE 75 Lambeth MLitt 93 Man Univ PhD 09. St Jo Coll Nottm 70. **d** 75 **p** 76. C Harold Wood *Chelmsf* 75-78; C Reigate St Mary *S'wark* 78-85; V Deal St Geo *Cant* 85-97; First Dir CA Sheff Cen for Ch Planting and Evang from 97; NSM Norfolk Park St Leonard *CD Sheff* 97-03; NSM Arbourthorne and Norfolk Park 03-05; Hon Can Sheff Cathl from 11. *The Sheffield Centre, 50 Cavendish Street, Sheffield S3 7RZ* T: 0114-272 7451 E: g.lings@churcharmy.org.uk

LINGWOOD, Preb David Peter. b 51. Lon Univ BEd 73 Southn Univ BTh 80. Sarum & Wells Th Coll 75. **d** 78 **p** 79. C Ashford St Hilda *Lon* 78-81; TV Redditch, The Ridge *Worc* 81-86; TR Blakenall Heath *Lich* 86-96; V Rushall 96-04; RD Walsall 98-03; TR Stoke-upon-Trent from 04; RD Stoke 07-14; Preb Lich Cathl from 02. *Stoke Rectory, 172 Smithpool Road, Stoke-on-Trent ST4 4PP* T: (01782) 747737 E: dp.lingwood@btinternet.com

LINKENS, Timothy Martin. b 67. Strathclyde Univ MEng 90. Wycliffe Hall Ox BTh 99. **d** 99 **p** 00. C Blackheath St Jo *S'wark* 99-03; V Kidbrooke St Nic from 03. *66A Whetstone Road, London SE3 8PZ* T: (020) 8856 6317

LINN, Frederick Hugh. b 37. Em Coll Cam BA 61 MA 65. Ripon Hall Ox 61. **d** 63 **p** 64. C Bramhall *Ches* 63-68; V Liscard St Mary 68-71; V Liscard St Mary w St Columba 71-74; V Wybunbury 74-82; R Eccleston and Pulford 82-98; rtd 98; PtO *Ches* from 98; *St As* from 09. *4 Stonewalls, Rossett, Wrexham LL12 0LG* T: (01244) 571942 *or* (01407) 810372 E: hugh.linn@btinternet.com

LINNEGAR, George Leonard. b 33. CGA. Kelham Th Coll 63. **d** 62 **p** 63. C Wellingborough St Mary *Pet* 62-65; LtO *Lich* 65-69; PtO *B & W* 69-80; Hon C Lewes All SS, St Anne, St Mich and St Thos *Chich* 80-86; C 87-99; rtd 99; PtO *Chich* from 99. *20 Morris Road, Lewes BN7 2AT* T: (01273) 478145

LINNEY, Barry James. b 64. Spurgeon's Coll BD 97 Anglia Poly Univ MA 02 Univ of Wales (Trin St Dav) MMin 14. Westcott Ho Cam 99. **d** 01 **p** 02. C Chingford SS Pet and Paul *Chelmsf* 01-04; V Cherry Hinton St Andr *Ely* 04-15; P-in-c Chatham St Steph *Roch* from 15. *St Stephen's Vicarage, 55 Pattens Lane, Chatham ME4 6JR* T: (01634) 305786 E: barryjameslinney@gmail.com

LINNEY, The Ven Gordon Charles Scott. b 39. CITC 66. **d** 69 **p** 70. C Agherton *Conn* 69-72; Min Can Down Cathl 72-75; V Dublin St Cath w St Jas *D & G* 75-80; Preb Tipperkevin St Patr Cathl Dublin 77-80; I Glenageary *D & G* 80-04; Adn Dublin 88-04; Lect CITC 89-93; rtd 04. *208 Upper Glenageary Road, Glenageary, Co Dublin, Republic of Ireland* T: (00353) (1) 284 8503 M: 87-254 1775 E: glinney@eircom.net

LINTERN, John. b 61. Linc Th Coll BTh 93. **d** 93 **p** 94. C Preston on Tees *Dur* 93-96; Asst Dioc Youth Adv 96-99; P-in-c W Pelton 96-07; P-in-c Pelton 99-07; V Pelton and W Pelton from 07. *The Vicarage, West Pelton, Stanley DH9 6RT* T: 0191-370 2146 F: 07971-114359 E: john.lintern@durham.anglican.org

LINTERN, Robert George. b 47. **d** 10 **p** 11. OLM Codsall *Lich* from 10. *43 Castle Street, Oswestry SY11 1JZ* M: 07971-403157 E: lintern@gmail.com

LINTHICUM, James Douglas. b 58. Towson State Univ (USA) BSc 81 Leeds Univ MA 00. Wesley Th Sem Washington MDiv 86. **d** 01 **p** 02. Chapl Barnet and Chase Farm Hosps NHS Trust 01-06; NSM Monken Hadley *Lon* 01-06; Sen Chapl Gt Ormond Street Hosp NHS Foundn Trust from 06. *Great Ormond Street Hospital, Great Ormond Street, London WC1N 3JH* T: (020) 7813 8232 M: 07921-140825 E: jlinth5481@aol.com

LINTON, Mrs Angela Margaret. b 45. SAOMC 97. **d** 00 **p** 01. NSM Langtree *Ox* from 00. *10 Yew Tree Court, Goring, Reading RG8 9HF* T/F: (01491) 874236 M: 07884-346552 E: dormouse62@yahoo.co.uk

LINTON, The Ven Barry Ian. b 76. Glas Univ BSc 98 TCD BTh 04 MCIBS 01. CITC 01. **d** 04 **p** 05. C Enniskillen *Clogh* 04-08; I Drumcliffe w Lissadell and Munninane *K, E & A* 08-15; Adn Elphin and Ardagh 12-15; I Drumragh w Mountfield *D & R* from 15. *The Rectory, 8 Mullaghmenagh Avenue, Omagh BT78 5QH* M: 07931-600920

LINTOTT, William Ince. b 36. St Cath Coll Cam BA 58. Ely Th Coll 58. **d** 60 **p** 61. C Brighton St Wilfrid *Chich* 60-62; C Chingford SS Pet and Paul *Chelmsf* 62-66; Chapl Fulbourn Hosp Cam 66-73; LtO *Ely* 66-97; rtd 01. *7 Haverhill Road, Stapleford, Cambridge CB22 5BX* T: (01223) 842008

LINZEY, Prof Andrew. b 52. K Coll Lon BD 73 PhD 86 AKC 73 Lambeth DD 01. St Aug Coll Cant 75. **d** 75 **p** 76. C Charlton-in-Dover *Cant* 75-77; Chapl and Lect Th NE Surrey Coll of Tech 77-81; Chapl Essex Univ *Chelmsf* 81-92; Dir of Studies Cen for Study of Th 87-92; Sen Research Fell Mansf Coll Ox 92-00; Tutor Chr Ethics 93-00; Special Prof Th Nottm Univ 92-96; Special Prof St Xavier Univ Chicago from 96; Hon Prof Birm Univ 97-07; Sen Research Fell Blackfriars Hall Ox 00-06; Dir Ox Cen for Animal Ethics from 06; Hon Prof Win Univ from 07; Hon Res Fell St Steph Ho Ox from 08. *91 Iffley Road, Oxford OX4 1EG* T: (01865) 201565 E: andrewlinzey@aol.com *or* director@oxfordanimalethics.com

LION, Christopher Mark. b 84. St Mellitus Coll 12. **d** 15. C Gerrards Cross and Fulmer *Ox* from 15. *1 Manor House Mews, Oxford Road, Gerrards Cross SL9 7DW* M: 07796-115951 E: candclion@gmail.com

LIONEL, Brother. *See* PEIRIS, Lionel James Harold

LIPP-NATHANIEL, Julie Christiane. b 41. Melbourne Univ BA 63 MA 72. **d** 95 **p** 95. Tutor United Coll of Ascension Selly Oak 96-99; LtO *Birm* 96-99; Regional Desk Officer S Asia & Middle East USPG 99-05; PtO *S'wark* 00-05; rtd 05. *Frankentobel Strasse 4, 73079 Suessen, Germany* T: (0049) (71) 625846 E: julinath@aol.com

LIPPIATT, Michael Charles. b 39. Oak Hill Th Coll BD 71. **d** 71 **p** 72. C Ardsley *Sheff* 71-74; C Lenton *S'well* 74-78; V Jesmond H Trin *Newc* 78-96; rtd 96. *69 Lansdowne Crescent, Stanwix, Carlisle CA3 9ES* T: (01228) 537080

LIPPIETT, Canon Peter Vernon. b 47. Lon Univ MB, BS 73 MRCGP 80 Univ of Wales (Lamp) MA 08. Ripon Coll Cuddesdon 86. **d** 88 **p** 89. C Pinner *Lon* 88-91; V Twyford and Owslebury and Morestead *Win* 91-99; P-in-c Rydal *Carl* 99-03; Warden Rydal Hall and Ldr Rydal Hall Community 99-03; Dioc Spirituality Adv *Portsm* 03-10; Hon Can Portsm Cathl 10; rtd 11; PtO *Win* from 11. *Pax Lodge, Cox's Hill, Twyford, Winchester SO21 1PQ.* T: (01962) 717438 E: peterlippiett@gmail.com

LIPSCOMB, Ian Craig. b 30. Wells Th Coll 61. **d** 63 **p** 64. C Feltham *Lon* 63-65; Australia from 65; rtd 94. *South Hill, Garroorigang Road, PO Box 118, Goulburn NSW 2580, Australia* T/F: (0061) (2) 4821 9591

LIPSCOMB, Canon Timothy William. b 52. Chich Th Coll 82. **d** 85 **p** 86. C Sevenoaks St Jo *Roch* 85-89; C Stanningley St Thos *Ripon* 89-92; V Armley w New Wortley 92-05; AD Armley 98-05; R Preston St Jo and St Geo *Blackb* from 05; AD Preston 08-14; Hon Can Blackb Cathl from 10. *The Rectory, 13 Ribblesdale Place, Preston PR1 3NA* T: (01772) 252528 M: 07855-396452 E: lavish@ermine2.fsnet.co.uk

LIPSCOMBE, Brian. b 37. Bris Univ BA 62. Tyndale Hall Bris 62. **d** 64 **p** 65. C Eccleston Ch Ch *Liv* 64-66; C Halliwell St Pet *Man* 66-69; C Frogmore *St Alb* 69-72; V Richmond Ch Ch *S'wark* 72-75; TV Mortlake w E Sheen 76-80; P-in-c Streatham Vale H Redeemer 80-85; V 85-91; R Norris Bank *Man* 91-96; V Droylsden St Martin 96-02; rtd 02; PtO *Leeds* from 02 and from 13. *15 St Anne's Drive, Leeds LS4 2SA* T: 0113-275 1893 M: 07743-168641 E: yvonne@ylipscombe.freeserve.co.uk

LISK, Canon Stewart. b 62. Regent's Park Coll Ox BA 84 MA 88. St Mich Coll Llan 86. **d** 88 **p** 89. C Glan Ely *Llan* 88-92; Chapl Cardiff Inst of HE 92-96; Chapl Welsh Coll of Music and Drama 92-96; Asst Chapl Univ of Wales (Cardiff) 92-96; V Glan Ely 96-06; AD Llan 04-06; V Roath from 06; Can Llan Cathl from 14. *Roath Vicarage, Waterloo Road, Cardiff CF23 5AD* T: (029) 2048 4808

LISMORE, Dean of. *See* DRAPER, The Very Revd Paul Richard

LISTER, Mrs Jennifer Grace. b 44. Totley Hall Coll CertEd 65. NOC 87. **d** 92 **p** 94. C Cowgate *Newc* 92-95; C Wall and Lich St Mary w St Mich 95-96; P-in-c Yoxall and Asst P The Ridwares and Kings Bromley 96-07; rtd 07; PtO *Cov* from 09. *81 Kingsley Road, Bishops Tachbrook, Leamington Spa CV33 9RZ* T: (01926) 427922 E: jenny.lister@waitrose.com

LISTER (née AISBITT), Mrs Joanne. b 69. St Jo Coll Dur BA 91. St Steph Ho Ox 91. **d** 93. NSM Mill End and Heronsgate w W Hyde *St Alb* 93-96. *St Mark, via Maggio 18, 50125 Florence, Italy* T/F: (0039) (055) 294764 E: listerwilliam@hotmail.com

LISTER, Joseph Hugh. b 38. Tyndale Hall Bris 61. **d** 64 **p** 65. C Pemberton St Mark Newtown *Liv* 64-68; Hon C Braintree *Chelmsf* 68-71; C Darfield *Sheff* 71-73; P-in-c Sheff St Swithun 73-75; TV Sheff Manor 76-80; TR Winfarthing w Shelfanger *Nor* 80-81; P-in-c Burston 80-81; P-in-c Gissing 80-81; P-in-c Tivetshall 80-81; R Winfarthing w Shelfanger w Burston w Gissing etc 81-88; P-in-c Sandon, Wallington and Rushden w Clothall *St Alb* 88-89; R 89-93; R Nether and Over Seale *Derby* 93-96; V Lullington 93-96; R Seale and Lullington 96-98; Dean Ndola Repton 96-98; Zambia 99-02; rtd 02; Hon C Hartington, Biggin and Earl Sterndale *Derby* 02-04; C Stoke Canon, Poltimore w Huxham and Rewe etc *Ex* 05-06; PtO *Carl* from 10. *11 Sir Josephs Lane, Darley Dale, Matlock DE4 2GY* E: joe@ndolarola.co.uk

LISTER, Miss Mary Phyllis. b 28. St Andr Ho Portsm 52. **dss** 80 **d** 87. Inkberrow w Cookhill and Kington w Dormston *Worc* 80-82; Ancaster *Linc* 82-87; C 87-88; rtd 88; PtO *Worc* 88-00. *6 Stuart Court, High Street, Kibworth, Leicester LE8 0LR* T: 0116-279 3763

LISTER, Peter. b 42. Leeds Univ BA 64 Newc Univ PGCE 75. Coll of Resurr Mirfield 63. **d** 65 **p** 66. C Monkseaton St Pet *Newc* 65-68; C Cramlington 68-70; Hon C 71-78; C Morpeth 79-83; V Shilbottle 83-88; Asst Dioc Dir of Educn 83-88; Dir of Educn 88-95; Hon Can Newc Cathl 88-95; Dioc Dir of Educn *Lich* 95-06; rtd 07; PtO *Lich* 07-09; *Cov* from 09. *81 Kingsley Road, Bishops Tachbrook, Leamington Spa CV33 9RZ* T: (01926) 427922 E: peterlister@globalnet.co.uk

LISTER, Peter William Ryley. b 56. **d** 10 **p** 11. OLM Bourne *Linc* from 10. *4 Linden Rise, Bourne PE10 9TD* T: (01778) 423730 E: pwr.lister@btinternet.com

LISTER, William Bernard. b 67. Keble Coll Ox BA 88 MA 92. St Steph Ho Ox BA 91. **d** 92 **p** 93. C Mill End and Heronsgate w W Hyde *St Alb* 92-96; CF 96-06; Sen CF 06-12; Chapl Florence w Siena *Eur* from 12. *St Mark, via Maggio 18, 50125 Florence, Italy* T/F: (0039) (055) 294764 E: listerwilliam@hotmail.com

LITHERLAND, Norman Richard. b 30. Lon Univ BA 51 BA 52 Man Univ MEd 72. NOC 78. **d** 81 **p** 82. NSM Flixton St Mich *Man* 81-94; rtd 94; PtO *Man* from 94. *1 Overdale Crescent, Urmston, Manchester M41 5GR* T: 0161-748 4243

LITHERLAND, Terence. b 46. **d** 93 **p** 94. OLM Horwich and Rivington *Man* from 93; OLM Blackrod from 11. *61 Tomlinson Street, Horwich, Bolton BL6 5QR* T: (01204) 692201

LITJENS, Shan Elizabeth. b 55. **d** 95. C Fareham SS Pet and Paul *Portsm* 95-96; C Fareham H Trin 96-99; NSM Hedge End St Jo *Win* from 00. *11 Abraham Close, Botley, Southampton SO30 2RQ* T: (01489) 796321 E: shanlitjens@aol.com

LITTLE, Andrew. b 27. Open Univ BA 83 UEA BA 03. AKC 51. **d** 52 **p** 53. C Fulham All SS *Lon* 52-54; C Epsom St Barn *Guildf* 54-61; V Northwood *Lich* 61-72; V Stowe 72-85; P-in-c Hixon 72-85; V Hixon w Stowe-by-Chartley 86-89; rtd 89; PtO *Nor* 89-09; Hon PV Nor Cathl 93-09. *4 Capel Court, The Burgage, Prestbury, Cheltenham GL52 3EL* T: (01242) 285800

LITTLE, Ms Christine. b 60. Lanc Univ BA 83. St Jo Coll Nottm 88. **d** 91 **p** 94. Par Dn Meltham *Wakef* 91-94; C Hatcham St Jas *S'wark* 94-99; P-in-c 99-04; C Nottingham St Pet and All SS *S'well* 04-07; C Nottingham All SS, St Mary and St Pet 07-14; C Bestwood Em w St Mark from 14. *5 Hatton Close, Arnold, Nottingham NG5 9QG*

LITTLE, David John. b 65. Oak Hill Th Coll BA 94. **d** 94 **p** 95. C Chislehurst Ch Ch *Roch* 94-98; TV Bath Twerton-on-Avon *B & W* 98; Dep Chapl HM Pris Bris 98-99; Chapl HM Pris Reading 99-14; PtO *Ox* from 14. *Address withheld by request* T: 0118-437 4861 E: revdjlittle@gmail.com

LITTLE, Derek Peter. b 50. St Jo Coll Dur BA 72. Trin Coll Bris. **d** 75 **p** 76. C Bradley *Wakef* 75-78; C Kidderminster St Geo *Worc* 78-82; V Lepton *Wakef* 82-85; E Regional Sec CPAS 85-88; V Canonbury St Steph *Lon* 88-96; R Bedhampton *Portsm*

96-99; rtd 09. *Sunnyside House, 14 Culimore Road, West Wittering, Chichester PO20 8HB* T: (01243) 671114 E: deepy@blueyonder.co.uk

LITTLE, George Nelson. b 39. CITC 70. **d** 72 **p** 73. C Portadown St Mark *Arm* 72-76; I Newtownhamilton w Ballymoyer and Belleek 76-80; I Aghaderg w Donaghmore *D & D* 80-82; I Aghaderg w Donaghmore and Scarva 82-05; Can Dromore Cathl 93-05; Treas Dromore Cathl 93-05; Chan Dromore Cathl 03-05; rtd 05. *22 Willow Dean, Markethill, Armagh BT60 1QG* T: (028) 3755 2848

LITTLE, Herbert Edwin Samuel. b 21. Lon Univ BA 54 BD 68. NEOC 79. **d** 80 **p** 81. NSM Dur St Cuth 80-88; rtd 88. *Address temp unknown*

LITTLE, Ian Dawtry Torrance. b 49. Keele Univ BEd 72. SWMTC 81. **d** 85 **p** 86. NSM St Stythians w Perranarworthal and Gwennap *Truro* 85-97; NSM Chacewater w St Day and Carharrack 97-06; PtO from 06. *Kernyk, Crellow Fields, Stithians, Truro TR3 7RE*

LITTLE, James Harry. b 57. York Univ BA 79. Qu Coll Birm 84. **d** 87 **p** 88. C Wollaton *S'well* 87-90; C N Wheatley, W Burton, Bole, Saundby, Sturton etc 90-93; R E Markham w Askham, Headon w Upton and Grove 93-06; P-in-c Dunham w Darlton, Ragnall, Fledborough etc 04-06; TR Howden *York* from 06; RD 10-15. *The Minster Rectory, Market Place, Howden, Goole DN14 7BL* T: (01430) 432056 E: revjlittle@aol.com

LITTLE, Nigel James. b 73. Middx Univ BA 93. Oak Hill Th Coll 98. **d** 01 **p** 02. C Highgate St Mich *Lon* 01-07; TV Kirk Ella and Willerby *York* 07-12; Chapl Felsted Sch from 12. *Stavells, Braintree Road, Felsted, Dunmow CM6 3DR* T: (01371) 822600 E: nigel_little@yahoo.com

LITTLE, Rebekah Mary. b 70. Oak Hill Th Coll. **d** 97 **p** 03. NSM Chislehurst Ch Ch *Roch* 97-98; NSM Bath Twerton-on-Avon *B & W* 98; PtO *Ox* 00-04; NSM Reading St Mary the Virgin 04-05. *Address withheld by request*

LITTLE, Canon Stephen Clifford. b 47. Man Univ MEd 81. AKC 72. **d** 72 **p** 73. C Grange St Andr *Ches* 72-73; C E Runcorn w Halton 73-75; P-in-c Newbold *Man* 75-77; P-in-c Broughton and Milton Keynes *Ox* 77-82; Sector Min Milton Keynes Chr Coun 77-84; TR Warwick *Cov* 84-93; R Harvington and Norton and Lenchwick *Worc* 93-96; R Harvington 96-98; Exec Officer Dioc Bd for Ch and Soc *Man* 98-05; Exec Officer Dioc Bd for Min and Soc 01-05; Hon Can Man Cathl 00-05; PtO from 05. *12 Redwood, Westhoughton, Bolton BL5 2RU* T: 0161-832 5253

LITTLEFAIR, David. b 38. ACCA 71 FCCA 85 Lon Univ BD 79. Trin Coll Bris 76. **d** 79 **p** 80. C Bursledon *Win* 79-82; V Charles w Plymouth St Matthias *Ex* 82-89; Warden Lee Abbey Internat Students' Club Kensington 89-94; V Malmesbury w Westport and Brokenborough *Bris* 94-03; rtd 03. *6 Matford Mews, Matford, Exeter EX2 8XP* T: (01392) 218784

LITTLEFORD, Peter John. b 40. St Mark & St Jo Coll Lon CertEd 63 ACP 65 Birkbeck Coll Lon BSc 70 Lon Inst of Educn DipEd 73 MA 76. SAOMC 96. **d** 99 **p** 00. Chapl De Montfort Univ *Leic* 99-01; NSM Bedf St Mark *St Alb* 99-01; NSM Bedford St Mich 01-04; NSM Elstow 04-10; rtd 10; PtO *St Alb* from 10. *1 Bindon Abbey, Bedford MK41 0AZ* T: (01234) 356645 E: peterlittleford@btinternet.com

LITTLEJOHN, Keith Douglas. b 59. Ripon Coll Cuddesdon BTh 03. **d** 03 **p** 04. C Horsham *Chich* 03-07; P-in-c Bolney from 07; P-in-c Cowfold from 07. *The Vicarage, Horsham Road, Cowfold, Horsham RH13 8AH* T: (01403) 865945 M: 07905-544366 E: keithdlj@aol.com

LITTLER, Alison Susan. **d** 12 **p** 13. NSM Caldicot *Mon* 12-14; NSM Magor from 14. *The Vicarage, 6 Old Barn Court, Undy, Caldicot NP26 3TE* T: (01633) 882719 E: alisonlittler1@btinternet.com

LITTLER, Eric Raymond. b 36. AMIC 93. Roch Th Coll 65. **d** 68 **p** 69. C Hatfield Hyde *St Alb* 68-73; Chapl Welwyn Garden City Hosp 70-73; TV Pemberton St Jo *Liv* 73-78; Chapl Billinge Hosp Wigan 76-81; V Pemberton St Fran Kitt Green *Liv* 78-81; V White Notley, Faulkbourne and Cressing *Chelmsf* 81-88; V Westcliff St Andr 88-96; Chapl Westcliff Hosp 88-96; Chapl Southend HA 89-96; R E and W Tilbury and Linford *Chelmsf* 96-98; Chapl Orsett Hosp 96-98; RD Thurrock *Chelmsf* 96-98; R Gt Oakley w Wix and Wrabness 98-02; Chapl Essex Rivers Healthcare NHS Trust 98-02; rtd 02; PtO *Sarum* from 98; *Chelmsf* from 02; *B & W* from 02; Chapl St Jo Hosp Heytesbury 03-08. *Minster Hall, 1 Pound Row, Warminster BA12 8NQ* T: (01985) 218818 E: ericandsuzette@uwclub.net

LITTLEWOOD, Alan James. b 51. Man Poly BEd 77. **d** 95 **p** 96. OLM Gosberton *Linc* 95-97; OLM Gosberton, Gosberton Clough and Quadring 97-01; C Bourne 01-03; P-in-c Leasingham and Cranwell 03-08; P-in-c Ancaster Wilsford Gp 08-14; P-in-c Barkston and Hough Gp 11-14; rtd 15. *26 Alexander Road, Lincoln LN2 4FA* E: alan@littlewood35.freeserve.co.uk

LITTLEWOOD, Alistair David. b 68. St Cath Coll Ox BA 89. Qu Coll Birm 93. **d** 96 **p** 97. C Keyworth and Stanton-on-the-Wolds *S'well* 96-00; Chapl Birm Univ 00-05; P-in-c Edwinstowe *S'well* 05-10; P-in-c Perlethorpe 05-10; Hon C Mansfield Deanery from 10. *St Lawrence Vicarage, 3 Shaw Street, Mansfield NG18 2NP*

LITTLEWOOD, Miss Jacqueline Patricia. b 52. Linc Th Coll 77. **dss** 80 **d** 87 **p** 94. Crayford *Roch* 80-84; Gravesend H Family w Ifield 84-87; Par Dn 87-93; rtd 93; NSM Gravesend St Aid *Roch* from 93. *25 Beltana Drive, Gravesend DA12 4BT* T: (01474) 560106

LITTLEWOOD, Mrs Penelope Anne. b 47. WEMTC 05. **d** 08 **p** 09. NSM Burghill *Heref* 08-12; P-in-c from 12; NSM Pipe-cum-Lyde and Moreton-on-Lugg 08-12; P-in-c from 12; NSM Stretton Sugwas 08-12; P-in-c from 12. *Cobwebs, Burghill, Hereford HR4 7RL* T: (01432) 760835 M: 07734-347327 E: penny.cobwebs@virgin.net

LITTON, Alan. b 42. Ridley Hall Cam 66. **d** 69 **p** 70. C Bolton St Bede *Man* 69-71; C Ashton St Mich 71-73; V Haslingden St Jo Stonefold *Blackb* 73-77; Ind Chapl *York* 77-81; V Crewe All SS and St Paul *Ches* 81-84; Ind Chapl *Liv* 84-89; V Spotland *Man* 89-94; R Newchurch *Liv* 94-02; P-in-c Croft w Southworth 99-02; R Newchurch w Croft 02; rtd 02; PtO *Liv* 03-08; Hon C Burtonwood from 08. *3 Rosemary Close, Great Sankey, Warrington WA5 1TL* T: (01925) 222944

LITZELL, Sven Anders. b 80. Wheaton Coll Illinois BA 03 Stockholm Univ MSc 04. Ridley Hall Cam 10. **d** 12 **p** 13. C Holborn St Geo w H Trin and St Bart *Lon* 12-15; Community of St Anselm Cant from 15; PtO *S'wark* from 15. *Lambeth Palace, London SE1 7JU* T: (020) 7898 1200 E: anders.litzell@lambethpalace.org.uk

LIVERPOOL, Archdeacon of. *See* PANTER, The Ven Richard James Graham

LIVERPOOL, Bishop of. *See* BAYES, The Rt Revd Paul

LIVERPOOL, Dean of. *See* WILCOX, The Very Revd Peter Jonathan

LIVERSIDGE, Mrs Linda Sheila. b 48. Oak Hill Th Coll BA 98. **d** 98 **p** 99. C Kensal Rise St Mark and St Martin *Lon* 98-01; TV N Wingfield, Clay Cross and Pilsley *Derby* 01-11; P-in-c Willingham *Ely* from 11. *The Rectory, 23 Rampton End, Willingham, Cambridge CB24 5JB* T: (01954) 263187 M: 07941-667616 E: revlin@me.com

LIVERSUCH, Ian Martin. b 56. St Jo Coll Dur BA 79. Wycliffe Hall Ox 79. **d** 83 **p** 84. C Newport St Mark *Mon* 83-85; C Risca 85-88; P-in-c Newport All SS 88-91; R Hemmingford w Clarenceville Canada 92-98; R La Salle St Lawr from 98. *350 12th Avenue, La Salle QC H8P 3P7, Canada* T: (001) (514) 364 5718 E: islwyn@total.net

LIVESEY, Rachel Elizabeth. *See* DALE, Rachel Elizabeth

LIVESLEY, John. b 80. Magd Coll Ox BA 02 MSt 03 MA 07 Leeds Univ MA 07. Coll of Resurr Mirfield 04. **d** 07 **p** 08. C Swinton and Pendlebury *Man* 07-10; P-in-c Tudhoe Grange *Dur* from 10; P-in-c Cassop cum Quarrington from 10. *St Andrew's Vicarage, St Andrew's Road, Spennymoor DL16 6NE* T: (01388) 814817 M: 07796-117568 E: johnlivesley1980@yahoo.co.uk

LIVINGSTON, Andrew Stuart. b 56. Sheff Univ BSc 79 Man Univ PGCE 85. SNWTP 07. **d** 10 **p** 11. C Poynton *Ches* from 10. *5 Eveside Close, Cheadle Hulme, Cheadle SK8 5RW* T: 0161-291 0650 M: 07925-589841 E: andy.livo@ntlworld.com

LIVINGSTON, Bertram. TCD BA 56. **d** 57 **p** 58. C Enniscorthy *C & O* 57-59; I Carrickmacross *Clogh* 59-61; I Carrickmacross w Magheracloone 61-63; C-in-c Derryvolgie *Conn* 63-78; I 78-79; I Monaghan w Tydavnet and Kilmore *Clogh* 79-86; I Desertlyn w Ballyeglish *Arm* 86-94; rtd 94. *6 The Green, Portadown, Craigavon BT63 5LH* T: (028) 3835 1859

LIVINGSTON, Richard. b 46. Qu Coll Birm. **d** 83 **p** 84. C Hobs Moat *Birm* 83-87; V Droylsden St Martin *Man* 87-95; P-in-c Wolverton w Norton Lindsey and Langley *Cov* 95-14; Chapl to the Deaf 95-03; P-in-c Snitterfield w Bearley 03-14; R Arden Valley from 14; P-in-c Aston Cantlow and Wilmcote w Billesley from 08. *The Rectory, Wolverton, Stratford-upon-Avon CV37 0HF* T: (01789) 731278 E: richard@livingstonr.freeserve.co.uk

LIVINGSTONE, Canon John Morris. b 28. Peterho Cam BA 53 MA 56. Cuddesdon Coll 53. **d** 55 **p** 56. C Hunslet St Mary and Stourton *Ripon* 55-60; Chapl Liddon Ho Lon 60-63; V Notting Hill St Jo *Lon* 63-74; P-in-c Notting Hill St Mark 66-73; P-in-c Notting Hill All SS w St Columb 67-74; P-in-c Notting Hill St Clem 68-74; TR Notting Hill 74-75; Chapl Paris St Geo *Eur* 75-84; Adn N France 79-84; Adn Riviera 84-93; Chapl Nice w Vence 84-93; Chapl Biarritz 93-05; rtd 93. *47 Côte des Basques, 64200 Biarritz, France* T/F: (0033) 5 59 24 71 18 E: j.livingstone@infonie.fr

LIVINGSTONE, John Philip. b 51. Univ of Wales (Abth) BA PGCE. St D Dioc Tr Course. **d** 96 **p** 97. NSM Maenclochog and New Moat etc *St D* 96-02; V Elerch w Penrhyncoch w Capel Bangor and Goginan 02-12; AD Llanbadarn Fawr 10-12;

rtd 12; PtO *St D* from 12. *Clyd Fan, Llysyfran, Clarbeston Road SA63 4RR*

LIYANAGE, Sylvester. b 78. Kingston Univ BEng 01 Surrey Univ MSc 03 Cam Univ BTh 08. Ridley Hall Cam 05. **d** 08 **p** 09. C Kingston Hill St Paul *S'wark* 08-12; TV Gt Chesham *Ox* from 12. *The Vicarage, 95 Latimer Road, Chesham HP5 1QQ* T: (01494) 773318 E: s.liyanage@btinternet.com

LLANDAFF, Archdeacon of. *See* JACKSON, The Ven Frances Anne

LLANDAFF, Bishop of. *See* MORGAN, The Most Revd Barry Cennydd

LLANDAFF, Dean of. *See* CAPON, The Very Revd Gerwyn Huw

✠**LLEWELLIN, The Rt Revd John <u>Richard</u> Allan.** b 38. Fitzw Ho Cam BA 64 MA 78. Westcott Ho Cam 61. **d** 64 **p** 65 **c** 85. C Radlett *St Alb* 64-68; C Johannesburg Cathl S Africa 68-71; V Waltham Cross *St Alb* 71-79; R Harpenden St Nic 79-85; Hon Can Truro Cathl 85-92; Suff Bp St Germans 85-92; Suff Bp Dover *Cant* 92-99; Bp at Lambeth (Hd of Staff) 99-03; rtd 03; PtO *Truro* 03-07; Hon Asst Bp Cant from 08. *15A The Precincts, Canterbury CT1 2EL* T: (01227) 764645 M: 07850-185869 E: rllewellin@clara.co.uk

LLEWELLYN, Brian Michael. b 47. Univ of Wales (Cardiff) LLM 99 MRICS 73. Sarum & Wells Th Coll 78. **d** 80 **p** 81. C Farncombe *Guildf* 80-83; Chapl RAF 83-87; R Hethersett w Canteloff w Lt and Gt Melton *Nor* 87-95; RD Humbleyard 94-95; P-in-c Smallburgh w Dilham w Honing and Crostwight 95-98; R 98-00; P-in-c Folkestone St Sav *Cant* 00-07; rtd 07; P-in-c Ypres *Eur* from 10. *Haiglaan 12, 8900 Ieper, Belgium* T: (0032) (57) 215685 F: 215927 E: bllewy@gmail.com

LLEWELLYN, Canon Christine Ann. b 46. Univ of Wales (Ban) BA 69 DipEd 70. **d** 89 **p** 97. NSM Arthog w Fairbourne w Llangelynnin w Rhoslefain *Ban* 90-93; NSM Holyhead w Rhoscolyn w Llanfair-yn-Neubwll 93-94; C 94-95; C Holyhead 95-97; TV 97-04; TR 04-11; Hon Can Ban Cathl 03-07; Can Cursal Ban Cathl 07-11; rtd 12; PtO *Ban* from 12; AD Llifon and Talybolion from 13. *The Old School, Rhoscolyn, Holyhead LL65 2RQ* T: (01407) 741593 E: holyislland2@sky.com

LLEWELLYN, Neil Alexander. b 55. LWCMD 78. Westcott Ho Cam 79 Sarum & Wells Th Coll 83. **d** 84 **p** 85. C Heref St Martin 84-86; Chapl Rotterdam Miss to Seamen *Eur* 86-89; R Docking w The Birchams and Stanhoe w Barwick *Nor* 89-92; Chapl Ypres *Eur* 92-95; Toc H 92-95; P-in-c Newport w Cilgwyn and Dinas w Llanllawer *St D* 06-07; V Newport w Cilgwyn and Nevern and Y Beifil etc 07-11; V Newport w Cilgwyn and Dinas w Llanllawer etc from 11. *The Rectory, Long Street, Newport SA42 0TJ* T: (01239) 820380

LLEWELLYN, Richard <u>Morgan</u>. b 37. MBE 76 OBE 79 CB 91. FCMI 81. Sarum & Wells Th Coll 91. **d** 93 **p** 94. C Brecon St Mary and Battle w Llanddew *S & B* 93-95; Min Can Brecon Cathl 93-95; Chapl Ch Coll Brecon from 95. *Field House, Llangattock, Crickhowell NP8 1HL* T: (01873) 810116

LLEWELLYN-MACDUFF, Ms Lindsay. b 75. Kent Univ BA 97. St Mich Coll Llan 97. **d** 99 **p** 00. C Milton next Sittingbourne *Cant* 99-01; C Barham w Bishopsbourne and Kingston 01-03; C Margate All SS and Westgate St Sav 03-05; P-in-c Gt Finborough w Onehouse, Harleston, Buxhall etc *St E* 05-09; Chapl HM Pris Littlehey 10-14; Bp's Dom Chapl *Roch* from 14. *Bishopscourt, 24 St Margaret's Street, Rochester ME1 1TS* T: (01634) 814439
E: bishops.chaplain@rochester.anglican.org

LLEWLYN, Miss Gabrielle Jane. b 48. Trin Coll Bris 08. **d** 09 **p** 10. NSM Fair Oak *Win* 09-12; Chapl HM Pris Northd 12-15; PtO *Newc* from 12. *4 Albion Close, Warkworth, Morpeth NE65 0UE* M: 07817-731036 T: (01665) 713451
E: gabbyllewelyn@hotmail.com

LLEWELYN, Canon Robert John. b 32. Keble Coll Ox BA 54 MA 58 Cheltenham & Glouc Coll of HE PhD 01. Cuddesdon Coll 65. **d** 66 **p** 67. C Bedford St Andr *St Alb* 66-69; C Cheltenham St Luke and St Jo *Glouc* 69-75; V S Cerney w Cerney Wick 75-80; V Glouc St Cath 80-99; P-in-c Glouc St Mark 87-89; Hon Can Glouc Cathl 94-99; rtd 99; PtO *Glouc* from 99. *2 The Limes, South Cerney, Cirencester GL7 5RF* T: (01285) 861529 E: robert@llewe4.freeserve.co.uk

LLEWELYN-EVANS, Catherine Ruth. b 55. St Mary's Coll Dur BA 76 Southlands Coll Lon PGCE 78. STETS 99. **d** 02 **p** 03. NSM Yatton Moor *B & W* 02-13; NSM E w W Harptree and Hinton Blewett from 13. *The Old Vicarage, 1 St Cuthbert's Street, Wells BA5 2AW* T: (01749) 674061 E: cthlle@btinternet.com

LLOYD, Ann. b 47. **d** 13 **p** 14. OLM Almondsbury and Olveston *Bris* from 13; OLM Compton Greenfield from 13. *13 Manor Park, Tockington, Bristol BS32 4NS* T: (01454) 613302

LLOYD, Canon Bernard James. b 29. AKC 56. **d** 57 **p** 58. C Laindon w Basildon *Chelmsf* 57-65; V E Ham St Geo 65-82; RD Newham 76-82; Hon Can Chelmsf Cathl 82-94; R Danbury 82-94; P-in-c Woodham Ferrers 87-90; rtd 94; PtO *Chelmsf* from 94. *Chanterelle, 47 Seaview Avenue, West Mersea, Colchester CO5 8HE* T: (01206) 383892

LLOYD, Bertram John. b 26. St Mich Coll Llan 81. **d** 83 **p** 84. C Malpas *Mon* 83-85; V Blaenavon w Capel Newydd 85-93; rtd 93; LtO *Mon* 93-96; St Vincent 96-02. *91 Hillside Avenue, Blaenavon, Pontypool NP4 9JL* T: (01495) 792616
E: llwydunion@cardiff.surf.com

LLOYD, The Ven Bertram <u>Trevor</u>. b 38. Hertf Coll Ox BA 60 MA 64. Clifton Th Coll 62. **d** 64 **p** 65. C S Mimms Ch Ch *Lon* 64-70; V Wealdstone H Trin 70-84; RD Harrow 77-82; P-in-c Harrow Weald St Mich 80-84; V Harrow Trin St Mich 84-89; Adn Barnstaple *Ex* 89-02; Preb Ex Cathl 91-02; rtd 02. *8 Pebbleridge Road, Westward Ho!, Bideford EX39 1HN* T: (01237) 424701 E: trevor@stagex.fsnet.co.uk

LLOYD, Mrs Carole Barbara. b 53. Sheff Univ BA 74 Coll of Ripon & York St Jo MA 03 Leeds Metrop Univ PGCE 93. NOC 00. **d** 03 **p** 04. C Bolton St Jas w St Chrys *Bradf* 03-06; C Gt Aycliffe and Chilton *Dur* 06-07; TV Gt Aycliffe 07-09; P-in-c Chilton 09-11; P-in-c Kelloe and Coxhoe 08-11; P-in-c Swanwick and Pentrich *Derby* 11-12; V 12-15; rtd 15; PtO *Derby* from 15. *Address temp unknown* E: carole.lloyd@amnos.co.uk

LLOYD, David Edgar Charles. b 59. St Mich Coll Llan 97. **d** 99 **p** 00. C Newton Nottage *Llan* 99-03; V Newcastle from 03. *The Vicarage, 1 Walters Road, Bridgend CF31 4HE* T: (01656) 655999 E: revd.lloyd@virgin.net

LLOYD, David Hanbury. b 28. Univ of Wales (Abth) BSc 49 Reading Univ PhD 70. LNSM course 97. **d** 97 **p** 98. NSM Swanage and Studland *Sarum* 97-98; PtO 98-06. *Scar Bank House, Russell Avenue, Swanage BH19 2ED* T: (01929) 426015

LLOYD, David John. b 52. Lon Univ BD 82. Burgess Hall Lamp 73. **d** 76 **p** 77. C Pembroke St Mary w St Mich *St D* 76-77; C Llanelli 77-80; V Cil-y-Cwm and Ystrad-ffin w Rhandir-mwyn etc 80-82; Oman 82-84; R Llanllwchaearn and Llanina *St D* 84-88; V Llangennech and Hendy 88-90; PtO *St Alb* 91-95; V Bampton w Clanfield *Ox* from 96; AD Witney 02-03. *5 Deanery Court, Broad Street, Bampton OX18 2LY* T: (01993) 851222 E: revdjlloyd@hotmail.co.uk

LLOYD, David Matthew. b 76. SS Hild & Bede Coll Dur BA 98. Oak Hill Th Coll 06. **d** 09 **p** 10. C St Helen Bishopsgate w St Andr Undershaft etc *Lon* 09-13; C Bromley Ch Ch *Roch* from 15. *Flat 1, 14 Highland Road, Bromley BR1 4AD* M: 07721-745165 E: dmattlloyd@yahoo.co.uk *or* matt.lloyd@christchurchbromley.org

LLOYD, David Peter. b 58. Kingston Poly BA 81 DipArch 84. Sarum & Wells Th Coll 88. **d** 90 **p** 91. C N Dulwich St Faith *S'wark* 90-94; TV Bedminster *Bris* 94-00; V Henbury from 00; Tutor STETS from 11. *87 Sea Mills Lane, Bristol BS9 1DX* T/F: 0117-950 0536 M: 07939-264261 E: dlloyd@stets.ac.uk

LLOYD, David Zachary. b 80. Wycliffe Hall Ox BA 01 Anglia Ruskin Univ MA 10 Solicitor 05. Ridley Hall Cam 08. **d** 10 **p** 11. C Hampton St Mary *Lon* 10-13; C Heigham St Thos *Nor* from 13. *St Alban's Vicarage, Eleanor Road, Norwich NR1 2RE* M: 07916-295154 E: davidzacharylloyd@gmail.com

LLOYD, Dennis John. b 46. BSc 70 MSc 74 PhD 81. S Dios Minl Tr Scheme. **d** 90 **p** 91. C Hamworthy *Sarum* 90-92; Chapl UEA *Nor* 92-97; P-in-c Malvern St Andr *Worc* 97-99; V 99-01; Chapl Defence Evaluation Research Agency 97-01; RD Malvern *Worc* 98-01; P-in-c Rowlands Castle *Portsm* 01-11; Warden of Readers 01-11; rtd 11; PtO *Portsm* from 11. *24 Forest Hills, Newport PO30 5NQ* E: revdrdjlloyd@aol.com

LLOYD, Derek James. b 78. Birm Univ BA 00 Leeds Univ BA 03. Coll of Resurr Mirfield 02. **d** 04 **p** 05. C Burnley St Andr w St Marg and St Jas *Blackb* 04-07; C W Burnley All SS 07-09; V Cross Heath *Lich* from 09; V Newcastle St Paul from 09; CMP from 05. *St Michael's Presbytery, Linden Grove, Newcastle ST5 9LJ* T: (01782) 662839

LLOYD, Dyfrig Cennydd. b 80. K Coll Lon BA 01. Ripon Coll Cuddesdon 01. **d** 04 **p** 05. C Llandysul w Bangor Teifi and Llanfairollwyn etc *St D* 04-06; C Bro Teifi Sarn Helen 06-07; TV 07-11; V Cardiff Dewi Sant *Llan* from 11. *6 Rachel Close, Cardiff CF5 2SH* T: (029) 2056 6001
E: dyfriglloyd@hotmail.com

LLOYD, Edward <u>Gareth</u>. b 60. K Coll Cam BA 81 MA 85 Dur Univ PhD 98. Ridley Hall Cam 85. **d** 88 **p** 89. C Jarrow *Dur* 88-91; C Monkwearmouth St Pet 91-92; P-in-c 92-96; TV Monkwearmouth 97-99; V Birtley from 99. *6 Ruskin Road, Birtley, Chester le Street DH3 1AD* T: 0191-410 2115
E: gareth@dunelm.org.uk

LLOYD, Eileen. *See* TAVERNOR, Eileen

LLOYD, Canon Elizabeth <u>Jane</u>. b 52. GRIC 74 CChem MRIC 77. Linc Th Coll 77. **dss** 80 **d** 87 **p** 94. Linc St Nic w St Jo Newport 80-81; LtO *Sarum* 81-87; Hon Par Dn Lytchett Matravers 87-92; Chapl Poole Gen Hosp 85-94; Chapl Poole Hosp NHS Trust from 94; Pres Coll of Health Care Chapl 02-04; Can and Preb Sarum Cathl from 03. *St John's Vicarage, Macaulay Road, Broadstone BH18 8AR* T: (01202) 694109
E: jane.lloyd@poole.nhs.uk *or* janelloyd52@googlemail.com.

LLOYD, Gareth. *See* LLOYD, Edward Gareth

LLOYD, Geoffrey. *See* LLOYD, William Geoffrey

LLOYD, Graham. b 36. Brasted Th Coll 62 St Aid Birkenhead 64 Glouc Sch of Min 86. **d** 89 **p** 90. NSM Churchstoke w Hyssington and Sarn *Heref* 89-97; NSM Lydbury N w Hopesay and Edgton 97-01; rtd 01; PtO *Heref* from 01. *The Pullets Cottage, Church Stoke, Montgomery SY15 6TL*
T: (01588) 620285

LLOYD, Gwilym Wyn. b 50. Leic Univ BA 72 Birm Univ MSc 73 Lon Univ LLB 78. Trin Coll Bris 83. **d** 87 **p** 88. C Bexleyheath Ch Ch *Roch* 87-91; R Darlaston St Lawr *Lich* 91-98. *24 Grosvenor Avenue, Streetly, Sutton Coldfield B74 3PB*

LLOYD, Harry James. b 22. Univ of Wales (Lamp) BA 50. **d** 51 **p** 52. C Hay *S & B* 51-55; C Llanigon 51-55; C Hillingdon St Jo *Lon* 55-56; C Marlborough *Sarum* 56-60; V Kingston and Worth Matravers 60-83; C Milton Abbas, Hilton w Cheselbourne etc 83-87; rtd 87; PtO *Sarum* 87-00. *Riverside Cottage, 35 Rockbridge Park, Presteigne LD8 2NF* T: (01547) 560115

LLOYD, Jane. *See* LLOYD, Elizabeth Jane

LLOYD, Canon Jonathan Wilford. b 56. Surrey Univ & City of Lon Poly BSc 80 N Lon Poly MA 86 CQSW 82 DASS 82. S'wark Ord Course 87. **d** 90 **p** 91. NSM Sydenham St Bart *S'wark* 90-93; P-in-c 93-94; Dir of Soc Resp 91-95; Bp's Officer for Ch in Soc 95-97; Hon PV S'wark Cathl 91-97; Chapl Team Ldr Bath Univ *B & W* 97-04; P-in-c Charlcombe w Bath St Steph 04-09; Chapl Denmark *Eur* 09-14; Adn Germany and N Eur 10-14; Can Brussels Cathl 10-14; PtO from 14; P-in-c Bridge *Cant* from 14; P-in-c Littlebourne and Ickham w Wickhambreaux etc from 14; Asst Dir of Ords from 15. *The Vicarage, 23 High Street, Bridge, Canterbury CT4 5JZ*
T: (01227) 830250 E: canonjonathanlloyd@gmail.com

LLOYD, Marc Andrew. b 78. LMH Ox BA 99 Middx Univ MA 02. Oak Hill Th Coll 04. **d** 07 **p** 08. C Eastbourne H Trin *Chich* 07-11; P-in-c Warbleton and Bodle Street Green 11-12; R Warbleton, Bodle Street Green and Dallington from 12; RD Dallington from 14. *Warbleton Rectory, Rookery Lane, Rushlake Green, Heathfield TN21 9QJ* T: (01435) 830421
M: 07812-054820 E: marc_lloyd@hotmail.com

LLOYD, Matthew. *See* LLOYD, David Matthew

LLOYD, Michael Francis. b 57. Down Coll Cam BA 79 MA 82 St Jo Coll Dur BA 83 Worc Coll Ox DPhil 97. Cranmer Hall Dur 81. **d** 84 **p** 85. C Locks Heath *Portsm* 84-87; Asst Chapl Worc Coll Ox 89-90; Chapl Ch Coll Cam 90-94; Chapl Fitzw Coll Cam 95-96; Hon C Westminster St Jas the Less *Lon* 96-03; Tutor St Steph Ho Ox 03-05; Tutor St Paul's Th Cen *Lon* 06-13; C St Andr Holborn 06-10; Chapl Qu Coll Ox 10-13; Prin Wycliffe Hall Ox from 13. *Wycliffe Hall, 54 Banbury Road, Oxford OX2 6PW* T: (01865) 274200 F: 274215

LLOYD, Canon Nigel James Clifford. b 51. Nottm Univ BTh 81 Lambeth STh 90 Win Univ MA 10. Linc Th Coll 77. **d** 81 **p** 82. C Sherborne w Castleton and Lillington *Sarum* 81-84; R Lytchett Matravers 84-92; TR Parkstone St Pet w Branksea and St Osmund 92-02; R Parkstone St Pet and St Osmund w Branksea 02-12; Ecum Officer (Sherborne Area) 92-00; Dioc Ecum Officer 00-01; RD Poole 01-09; V Broadstone from 12; Can and Preb Sarum Cathl from 02. *St John's Vicarage, Macaulay Road, Broadstone BH18 8AR* T: (01202) 694109
M: 07940-348776 E: canon.nigel@gmail.com

LLOYD, Mrs Pamela Valpy. b 25. Gilmore Ho 48 St Aug Coll Cant 76. **dss** 76 **d** 87 **p** 94. Chartham *Cant* 76-78; Cant All SS 78-85; rtd 85; Chapl Asst Kent and Cant Hosp 87; Chapl Chaucer Hosp Cant 87-90; NSM Elham w Denton and Wootton *Cant* 87-93; Sub-Chapl HM Pris Cant 88-96; Hon C Cant St Martin and St Paul 93-95; PtO 96-15. *Cavendish House, 9 North Holmes Road, Canterbury CT1 1QJ* T: (01227) 457782

LLOYD (née WALMSLEY), Patricia Jane. b 62. Bris Univ BSc 83 PhD 87 Trin Coll Cam BTh 01. Ridley Hall Cam 99. **d** 01 **p** 02. C Bowdon *Ches* 01-05; V Over Peover w Lower Peover from 05. *The Vicarage, The Cobbles, Lower Peover, Knutsford WA16 9PZ* T: (01565) 722304
E: jane@janelloyd6.wanadoo.co.uk

LLOYD, Peter Vernon James. b 36. St Jo Coll Cam BA 61 MA. Ridley Hall Cam 60. **d** 62 **p** 63. C Keynsham w Queen Charlton *B & W* 62-65; PtO *Sarum* from 65; NSM Bournemouth St Jo w St Mich *Win* 87-90; NSM Bournemouth St Pet w St Swithun, H Trin etc 90-93; PtO 93-95 and from 13. *18 Cornelia Crescent, Branksome, Poole BH12 1LU* T/F: (01202) 741422

LLOYD, Rebecca Joanne. b 78. Univ of Wales (Ban) BA 00 K Coll Lon MMus 01 PhD 06 Cam Univ BA 13. Westcott Ho Cam 11. **d** 14 **p** 15. C S Dulwich St Steph *S'wark* from 14. *18 Talisman Square, London SE26 6XY* E: rebecca.j.lloyd5@gmail.com

LLOYD, Richard Gary. b 75. Ex Coll Ox BA 98 St Jo Coll Dur MA 00. Cranmer Hall Dur 98. **d** 00 **p** 01. C Dibden *Win* 00-03; Asst Chapl Charterhouse Sch Godalming 04-11; C Claygate *Guildf* 11-13; C E Molesey from 13. *The Vicarage, St Mary's Road, East Molesey KT8 0ST* T: (020) 8941 5901
M: 07753-835744 E: church.office@smem.org.uk

LLOYD, Robert Graham. b 42. St Jo Coll Nottm 82. **d** 84 **p** 85. C Tonyrefail *Llan* 84; C Tonyrefail w Gilfach Goch 85-87; V Martletwy w Lawrenny and Minwear and Yerbeston *St D* 87-91; V Monkton 91-96; V Cymmer and Porth *Llan* 96-07; AD Rhondda 04-06; rtd 07; PtO *St D* from 06. *7 Greenhill Park Drive, Haverfordwest SA61 1LS* T: (01437) 783682

LLOYD, Roger Bernard. b 58. K Coll Lon BA. Cranmer Hall Dur. **d** 84 **p** 85. C Hornchurch St Andr *Chelmsf* 84-87; C Gt Parndon 87-94; V Elm Park St Nic Hornchurch 94-99. *494 Heathway, Dagenham RM10 7SH* T: (020) 8984 9887
M: 07703-383176

LLOYD, Ronald. b 37. St Mich Coll Llan. **d** 83 **p** 84. C Penarth All SS *Llan* 83-85; V Cwmbach 85-91; PtO from 91. *23 Teilo Street, Cardiff CF11 9JN*

LLOYD, Canon Ronald Henry. b 32. Univ of Wales (Lamp) BA 52 LTh 54. **d** 54 **p** 56. C Manselton *S & B* 54-56; C Sketty 56-59; C Swansea St Mary and H Trin 59-63; CF (TA) 59-65; V Elmley Castle w Netherton and Bricklehampton *Worc* 63-69; Chapl Dragon Sch Ox 69-82; Chapl St Hugh's Coll Ox 75-80; P-in-c Ox St Marg 75-76; Chapl Magd Coll Ox 75-82; Prec and Chapl Ch Ch *Ox* 82-87; R Alvescot w Black Bourton, Shilton, Holwell etc 87-95; R Shill Valley and Broadshire 95-01; rtd 01; PtO *Glouc* from 02; *Ox* from 02. *2 The Farriers, Southrop, Lechlade GL7 3RL* T: (01367) 850071

LLOYD, Mrs Sandra Edith. b 48. Sarum & Wells Th Coll 83. **dss** 86 **d** 87 **p** 94. Freshwater *Portsm* 86-87; C 87-89; C Whitwell 89-95; V 95-14; C Niton 89-95; P-in-c 95-96; R 96-14; R St Lawrence 96-04; rtd 14; PtO *Portsm* from 14. *St Kenelm, Guyers Road, Freshwater PO40 9QA* T: (01983) 756865
E: rhadegunde@aol.com

LLOYD, Ms Sarah Jane. b 67. MBE 12. Leic Univ BA 88. Ripon Coll Cuddesdon MA 15 MA 15. **d** 15. NSM Old Basing and Lychpit *Win* from 15. *6 St Mary's Close, Old Basing, Basingstoke RG24 7DQ* E: slloydcloud@icloud.com

LLOYD, Stephen Russell. b 47. Worc Coll Ox BA 69 MA 77 CertEd. Oak Hill Th Coll 76. **d** 77 **p** 78. C Canonbury St Steph *Lon* 77-80; C Braintree *Chelmsf* 80-92; V Braintree St Paul 92-01; V Ipswich St Andr *St E* 01-14; rtd 14; PtO *St E* from 14. *26 Endsleigh Court, Colchester CO3 3QN* T: (01206) 560172
E: stephenrlloyd@btinternet.com

LLOYD, Canon Stuart George Errington. b 49. TCD BA 72. **d** 75 **p** 76. C Cloughfern *Conn* 75-79; C Cregagh *D & D* 79-82; I Eglantine *Conn* 82-89; I Ballymena w Ballyclug from 89; Can Conn Cathl from 97; Preb 97-01; Prec from 01. *St Patrick's Rectory, 102 Galgorm Road, Ballymena BT42 1AE* T/F: (028) 2565 2253 T: 2563 0741 E: ballymena@connor.anglican.org

LLOYD, Timothy David Lewis. *See* LEWIS LLOYD, Timothy David

LLOYD, Trevor. *See* LLOYD, Bertram Trevor

LLOYD, William Geoffrey. b 48. Man Univ BA 70. Oak Hill Th Coll 92. **d** 95 **p** 96. C Plaistow St Mary *Roch* 95-99; TV Ottery St Mary, Alfington, W Hill, Tipton etc *Ex* 99-04; P-in-c Sampford Spiney w Horrabridge 04-11; RD Tavistock 07-11; rtd 11. *24 Mills Bakery, 4 Royal William Yard, Plymouth PL1 3GD* T: (01752) 227680 E: geofflloyd@ukgateway.net

LLOYD HUGHES, Gwilym. *See* HUGHES, Gwilym Lloyd

LLOYD-JAMES, Duncan Geraint. b 66. St Steph Ho Ox BTh 94. **d** 94 **p** 96. C St Leonards Ch Ch and St Mary *Chich* 94-96; C Rottingdean 96-99; R Brede w Udimore 99-07; rtd 07; PtO *Guildf* 08-10. *62 Richmond Street, Brighton BN2 9PE* T: (01273) 606550 M: 07511-772256
E: duncanlj@btinternet.com

LLOYD JONES, Ieuan. b 31. St Cath Coll Cam BA 51 MA 54 FBIM. Sarum & Wells Th Coll 80. **d** 83 **p** 84. NSM Claygate *Guildf* 83-89; PtO *Ox* 89-06; *Guildf* from 07. *20 Aldersey Road, Guildford GU1 2ES* T: (01483) 449605 E: lloyd.jones4@ntlworld.com

LLOYD MORGAN, Richard Edward. b 48. Trin Coll Cam MA 70 Ox Univ DipEd 71. SEITE 95. **d** 98 **p** 99. NSM Clapham St Paul *S'wark* 98-03; Chapl K Coll Cam from 03. *King's College, Cambridge CB2 1ST* T: (01223) 331100 or 331418
E: chaplain@kings.cam.ac.uk

LLOYD-RICHARDS, David Robert. b 48. Open Univ BA 84 Hull Univ MA 87. St D Coll Lamp. **d** 71 **p** 72. C Skewen *Llan* 71-73; C Neath w Llantwit 73-76; Miss to Seamen 76-77; V Pontlottyn w Fochriw *Llan* 77-84; R Merthyr Dyfan 84-90; Chapl Barry Neale-Kent Hosp 84-90; Tutor Open Univ 85-10; Sen Chapl Univ Hosp of Wales NHS Trust 90-95; Sen Chapl Univ Hosp of Wales and Llandough NHS Trust 95-00; Sen Chapl Manager Cardiff and Vale NHS Trust 00-08; rtd 08. *Jeantique, La Butte, La Trinité des Laitiers, Gace, 61230 Orne, France* T: (0033) (2) 33 36 11 15
E: robertlloydrichards@googlemail.com

LLOYD ROBERTS, Mrs Kathleen Ada May. b 49. Bordesley Coll of Educn CertEd 71. Qu Coll Birm 03. **d** 06 **p** 07. NSM Temple Balsall *Birm* 06-09; V from 09. *The Master's House, Temple Balsall, Knowle, Solihull B93 0AL* T: (01564) 772415
E: klloydroberts@leveson.org.uk

LLOYD WILLIAMS, The Ven Martin Clifford. b 65. Westmr Coll Lon BEd 87. Trin Coll Bris BA 93. **d** 93 **p** 94. C Bath Walcot *B & W* 93-97; R Bath St Mich w St Paul 97-14; R Bath St Mich Without 14-15; RD Bath 10-15; Adn Brighton and Lewes *Chich* from 15. *12 Walsingham Road, Hove BN3 4FF* M: 07732-676273

LO, Peter Kwan Ho. b 54. Chinese Univ of Hong Kong BD 84 Stirling Univ MBA 92 K Coll Lon LLB 99. **d** 84 **p** 85. Hong Kong 84-91; PtO *Chich* 02-03; C Uckfield 03-06; R Monterey Park USA from 07. *133 East Graves Avenue, Monterey Park CA 91755-3915, USA* T: (001) (626) 571 2714
E: peterkwanholo@hotmail.com

lo POLITO, Nicola. b 59. Catholic Th Union Chicago MDiv 85 MA(Theol) 87. Comboni Miss. **d** 85 **p** 86. In RC Ch 85-94; Egypt 86-88; Sudan 88-91; Italy 91-94; Asst Chapl Malta and Gozo *Eur* 94-98; C Castle Bromwich SS Mary and Marg *Birm* 98-01; TV Salter Street and Shirley 01-05; Chapl Birm Univ 05-13; P-in-c Highgate from 13; Chapl St Alb Academy from 13. *258 Mary Vale Road, Birmingham B30 1PJ* T: 0121-458 7432 M: 07813-937756 E: nlopolito@hotmail.com

LOACH, Michael Graham. b 72. Bris Univ BA 94 Chelt & Glouc Coll of HE PGCE 95 Heythrop Coll Lon MA 03 St Jo Coll Dur MA 12. Cranmer Hall Dur 10. **d** 12 **p** 13. C W Kirby St Bridget *Ches* 12-15; V Higher Bebington from 15. *The Vicarage, King's Road, Bebington, Wirral CH63 8LX* M: 07878-338546 E: mgloach@gmail.com

LOADER, Michael John. b 43. Hull Univ BSc 64 Chelsea Coll Lon MSc 72. **d** 05 **p** 14. Asst Chapl Nicosia Cyprus Cyprus 05-12; NSM Tavistock and Gulworthy *Ex* 13-15; NSM Tavistock, Gulworthy and Brent Tor from 15. *20 Edgcumbe Drive, Tavistock PL19 0ET* T: (01822) 613231 M: 07799-766755 E: michaelloader@supanet.com

LOAT, Andrew Graham. b 61. Aber Univ BD 83 Univ of Wales (Ban) MTh 00. St Jo Coll Nottm. **d** 87 **p** 88. C Llangynwyd w Maesteg *Llan* 87-90; C Llansamlet *S & B* 90-91; R Whitton and Pilleth and Cascob etc 91-98; R Llandrindod w Cefnllys and Disserth 98-09; R Lower Ithon Valley 09-14; V Upper Ithon Valley 09-14; Warden of Readers 02-08; AD Maelienydd 06-14; Can Res Brecon Cathl 03-14; P-in-c Llanbadarn Fawr and Elerch and Penrhyncoch etc *St D* from 14. *The Vicarage, Llanbadarn Fawr, Aberystwyth SY23 3TT* T: (01970) 624638 E: vicarage.llanbadarn@gmail.com

LOBB, Edward Eric. b 51. Magd Coll Ox BA 74 MA 76. Wycliffe Hall Ox 73. **d** 76 **p** 77. C Haughton St Mary *Man* 76-80; C Rusholme H Trin 80-84; P-in-c Whitfield *Derby* 84-90; V 90-92; V Stapenhill w Cauldwell 92-03; rtd 03; PtO *Derby* 03-05. *Middleton House, Beith KA15 1HX* T: (01505) 500232

LOBB, Miss Josephine Mary. b 57. SRN 83. **d** 96 **p** 97. OLM St Germans *Truro* 96-06; NSM Saltash 06-12; TV from 12. *19 Lowertown Close, Landrake, Saltash PL12 5DG* T: (01752) 851488 E: jolobb@btinternet.com

LOBSINGER, Eric John. b 78. Washington Univ AB 00 JD 03 Kyushu Univ Japan LLM 04 LLD 07. **d** 10. USA 10-13; Jun Chapl Mert Coll Ox 13-14; Jun Dean St Steph Ho Ox 13-14; C Hornsey H Innocents *Lon* from 15. *St Paul's Church House, Wightman Road, London N4 1RW* T: (020) 8341 3306 E: fr.eric.lobsinger@gmail.com

LOCK, Mrs Beverley. b 59. Loughb Univ BA 81 York St Jo Univ MA 12 Bris Univ PGCE 82. CBDTI 01. **d** 04 **p** 05. C Kendal St Geo *Carl* 04-07; C Beacon 07-08; P-in-c Orton and Tebay w Ravenstonedale etc from 08; P-in-c Shap w Swindale and Bampton w Mardale from 08. *The Vicarage, Orton, Penrith CA10 3RQ* T: (015396) 24045 E: rev.bev@btinternet.com

LOCK, Mrs Jacqueline. b 43. **d** 08 **p** 09. OLM High Wycombe *Ox* from 08. *15 Kingsley Crescent, High Wycombe HP11 2UN* T: (01494) 532216 E: jackie@thelocks.org.uk

LOCK, Paul Alan. b 65. St Chad's Coll Dur BA 86. Coll of Resurr Mirfield 87. **d** 89 **p** 90. C Upholland *Liv* 89-92; C Teddington SS Pet and Paul and Fulwell *Lon* 92-95; V 95-99; V Wigan St Anne *Liv* 99-04; Dioc Dir of Educn *Blackb* 13-14. *Lindsay Cottage, Crawford Road, Crawford Village, Skelmersdale WN8 9QP* M: 07813-019863 T: (01744) 883732 E: paul.a_lock@btinternet.com

LOCK, The Ven Peter Harcourt D'Arcy. b 44. AKC 67. **d** 68 **p** 69. C Meopham *Roch* 68-72; C Wigmore w Hempstead 72; C S Gillingham 72-77; R Hartley 77-83; R Fawkham and Hartley 83-84; V Dartford H Trin 84-93; Hon Can Roch Cathl 90-01; V Bromley SS Pet and Paul 93-01; RD Bromley 96-01; Adn Roch and Can Res Roch Cathl 01-09; PtO *Cant* from 11; *Roch* from 11. *53 Preston Park, Faversham ME13 8LH* T: (01795) 529161 E: peter.lock123@btinternet.com

LOCK, Thomas. **d** 05 **p** 06. OLM N Poole Ecum Team *Sarum* 05-11; rtd 11. *103 Copeland Drive, Poole BH14 8NP* T: (01202) 880702 E: thomas@thomaslock.orangehome.co.uk

LOCKE, Mrs Jennifer Margaret. b 52. Edin Univ BEd 74. Ox Min Course 06. **d** 08 **p** 09. NSM Wexham *Ox* 08-11; TV Risborough from 11. *The Rectory, Church End, Bledlow, Princes Risborough HP27 9PD* T: (01844) 344762 E: revjmlocke@gmail.com

LOCKE, Nigel Richard. *See* HESFORD-LOCKE, Richard Nigel

LOCKE, Robert Andrew. b 62. St Steph Ho Ox 89. **d** 92 **p** 93. C Colchester St Jas, All SS, St Nic and St Runwald *Chelmsf* 92-95; CF 95-00; V Burnham *Chelmsf* 00-04. *331 Broomfield Road, Chelmsford CM1 4DU* T: (01245) 440745 M: 07949-862867 E: robert@robertlocke.wanadoo.co.uk

LOCKE, Stephen John. b 60. St Chad's Coll Dur BA 82. Sarum & Wells Th Coll 84. **d** 86 **p** 87. C Blackb St Mich w St Jo and H Trin 86-89; C Oswaldtwistle Immanuel and All SS 89-92; V Blackb St Mich w St Jo and H Trin 92-98; Chapl to the Deaf 98-04; V Owton Manor *Dur* from 04. *The Vicarage, 18 Rossmere Way, Hartlepool TS25 5EF* T: (01429) 290278

LOCKETT, Preb Paul. b 48. Sarum & Wells Th Coll 73. **d** 76 **p** 77. C Horninglow *Lich* 76-78; C Tewkesbury w Walton Cardiff *Glouc* 78-81; P-in-c W Bromwich St Pet *Lich* 81-90; R Norton Canes 90-95; V Longton St Mary and St Chad 95-12; Dean's V Lich Cathl 91-12; Preb Lich Cathl 04-12; rtd 12; P-in-c Hempton and Pudding Norton *Nor* from 12; Chantry P Shrine of Our Lady of Walsingham from 12; Chapl to The Queen from 12. *20 Cleaves Drive, Walsingham NR22 6EQ* T: (01328) 820030

LOCKETT, Simon David. b 66. Stirling Univ BA 96. Wycliffe Hall Ox 00. **d** 02 **p** 03. C Ray Valley *Ox* 02-06; R Madley w Tyberton, Peterchurch, Vowchurch etc *Heref* from 06. *The Vicarage, Madley, Hereford HR2 9LP* T: (01981) 250245 E: simonlizlockett@hotmail.com

LOCKEY, Malcolm. b 45. Sunderland Poly BA 67 Newc Univ DipEd 68 FRSA 75. NEOC 87. **d** 90 **p** 91. NSM Yarm *York* 90-97; C 97-98; TV Whitby w Aislaby and Ruswarp 98-03; Hon Chapl Miss to Seafarers 98-03; Chapl RNLI 00-03; P-in-c Coldstream *Edin* 04-09; R Kelso 05-09; Offg Chapl RAF and Chapl ATC 02-03; rtd 09; PtO *Newc* 10-13; Hon C Bilbrook and Coven *Lich* 13-14; V Coven from 14. *The Vicarage, Church Lane, Wolverhampton WV9 5DE* M: 07710-467785 T: (01902) 791923 E: macbrac@hotmail.com

LOCKHART, Clare Patricia Anne (Sister Clare). b 44. Bris Univ BA 74 Newc Univ MLitt 96. Cranmer Hall Dur 84. **d** 87 **p** 94. Sisters of Charity from 63; Chapl Asst Sunderland Distr Gen Hosp 84-89; Chapl 89-94; Chapl City Hosps Sunderland NHS Trust 94-95; NSM N Hylton St Marg Castletown *Dur* 87-95; P-in-c 95-99; NSM Eorropaidh *Arg* from 99; PtO *Dur* from 02; Dioc Supernumerary *Arg* from 09; P-in-c Stornoway 11-12. *The Sisters of Charity, Carmel, 7A Gress, Isle of Lewis HS2 0NB* T: (01851) 820484 *or* 820734 E: srlockhart@btinternet.com

LOCKHART, David. b 68. QUB BSc 90 TCD BTh 93. CITC 90. **d** 93 **p** 94. C Belfast St Mary w H Redeemer *Conn* 93-96; I Belfast St Steph w St Luke 96-03; I Cloughfern from 03. *Cloughfern Rectory, 126 Doagh Road, Newtownabbey BT37 9QR* T: (028) 9086 2437 E: dandblockhart@btinternet.com

LOCKHART, Eileen Ann. b 52. Open Univ BA 93 ACII 74. EAMTC 95. **d** 98 **p** 99. NSM Shenfield *Chelmsf* from 98. *6 Granary Meadow, Wyatts Green, Brentwood CM15 0QD* T/F: (01277) 822537 E: eileenlockhart@gmail.com

LOCKHART, Raymond William. b 37. Qu Coll Cam BA 58 MA 61 LLB 60. St Jo Coll Nottm 72. **d** 74 **p** 75. C Aspley *S'well* 74-76; V 81-88; R Knebworth *St Alb* 76-81; Warden Stella Carmel Haifa (CMJ) Israel 88-91; R Jerusalem Ch Ch 91-99; Dir CMJ 99-02; rtd 02; PtO *B & W* from 03. *1 The Old Playground, Alexandra Place, Bath BA2 5EU* T: (01225) 840432 M: 07817-330831 E: raylockhart1@gmail.com

LOCKLEY, Miss Pauline Margaret. b 41. **d** 02. OLM Stoke-upon-Trent *Lich* 02-13; PtO from 13. *Highfields, 89 Tolkien Way, Stoke-on-Trent ST4 7SJ* T: (01782) 849806 E: plock@cix.co.uk

LOCKWOOD, Richard John. b 46. **d** 01 **p** 02. OLM Glascote and Stonydelph *Lich* from 01. *26 Mossdale, Wilnecote, Tamworth B77 4PJ* T: (01827) 738105 *or* 330306

LOCKWOOD, Mrs Thelma. b 42. WEMTC 01. **d** 03 **p** 04. OLM Bourton-on-the-Water w Clapton etc *Glouc* 03-07; NSM Wimborne Minster *Sarum* 07-11. *82 Merley Ways, Wimborne BH21 1QR* T: (01202) 882488

LOCKYER, David Ralph George. b 41. Wells Th Coll 65. **d** 67 **p** 68. C Bottesford *Linc* 67-69; C Eling *Win* 69-72; C Eling, Testwood and Marchwood 72-73; TV 73-77; TR Speke St Aid *Liv* 77-84; V Halifax St Jude *Wakef* 84-96; Chapl Halifax R Infirmary 84-96; V Banwell *B & W* 96-06; rtd 06. *The Old Quarry, Stour Provost, Gillingham SP8 5SB* T: (01747) 839970 E: david.r.g.lockyer@btinternet.com

LOCKYER, Peter Weston. b 60. Linc Coll Ox BA 80 MA 83 PGCE 98. St Jo Coll Nottm 84. **d** 87 **p** 88. C Rowner *Portsm* 87-90; C Beaconsfield *Ox* 90-91; TV 91-95; Dep Chapl HM YOI Glen Parva 95; Chapl Wellingborough Sch 96-00; R Ewhurst

Guildf 00-03; Hd Schs & Youth Chr Aid from 03. *3 King George Avenue, Petersfield GU32 3EU* T: (01730) 269661
E: peterlockyer@btinternet.com

LOCOCK (née MILES), Mrs Jillian Maud. b 33. Lon Univ BSc 55. NOC 81. **dss** 84 **d** 87 **p** 95. Didsbury Ch Ch *Man* 84-86; Chapl Asst Man R Infirmary 85-87; Chapl Asst Withington Hosp Man 86-88; Chapl Asst RN 88-93; NSM Dumbarton *Glas* 93-96; PtO *Ex* from 02. *Glebe Cottage, Dousland, Yelverton PL20 6LU* T: (01822) 854098 E: rjbirtles@aol.com

LODER, Sister Helen. b 43. S'wark Ord Course 91. **d** 94 **p** 95. Soc of St Marg from 70; Hon C S Hackney St Mich w Haggerston St Paul *Lon* 94-01; Hon C Bethnal Green St Matt w St Jas the Gt 02-10. *St Saviour's Priory, 18 Queensbridge Road, London E2 8NS* T: (020) 7613 1464 E: helenloder@aol.com

LODGE, Canon Michael John. b 53. Wycliffe Hall Ox 87. **d** 89 **p** 90. C Highworth w Sevenhampton and Inglesham etc *Bris* 89-93; P-in-c Cheltenham St Luke and St Jo *Glouc* 93-05; TR Rayleigh *Chelmsf* from 05; RD Rochford 08-15; Hon Can Chelmsf Cathl from 12. *The Rectory, 3 Hockley Road, Rayleigh SS6 8BA* T: (01268) 742151 E: mike.lodge@btinternet.com

LODGE, Mrs Patricia Evelyn. b 46. City of Birm Coll CertEd 68. **d** 08 **p** 09. OLM Ashton *Man* 08-14; rtd 14; PtO *Man* from 14. *250 Yew Tree Lane, Dukinfield SK16 5DE* T: 0161-338 5303 E: patterry@lodge250.freeserve.co.uk

LODGE, Robin Paul. b 60. Bris Univ BA 82 Ch Ch Coll Cant PGCE 83. Chich Th Coll 88. **d** 90 **p** 91. C Calne and Blackland *Sarum* 90-94; Asst Chapl St Mary's Sch Calne 90-94; TV Wellington and Distr *B & W* 94-03; V Highbridge 03-09; V Taunton St Andr from 09. *The Vicarage, 118 Kingston Road, Taunton TA2 7SR* T: (01823) 365730 M: 07707-439808 E: robin.lodge1@btinternet.com

LODGE, Roy Frederick. b 38. MBE 97. BTh DPhil 93. Tyndale Hall Bris 63. **d** 66 **p** 67. C Tardebigge *Worc* 66-67; Chapl and Warden Probation Hostel Redditch 67-69; Chapl RAF 69-75; C Kinson *Sarum* 76; LtO *Pet* 76-77; Asst Chapl HM Pris Stafford 77-78; Chapl HM Pris Ranby 78-84; Chapl HM Pris Long Lartin 84-93; Chapl HM Pris Service Coll 87-93; Chapl HM Pris Hewell Grange 93-98; Chapl HM Pris Brockhill 93-98; rtd 98; PtO *Cov* from 98; *Glouc* from 99. *44 Eton Road, Stratford-upon-Avon CV37 7ER* E: lodgeconstantia1@btinternet.com

LODGE, Mrs Sally Nicole. b 61. Keele Univ BA 83 St Jo Coll Dur BA 09. Cranmer Hall Dur 07. **d** 09 **p** 10. C Halstead Area *Chelmsf* 09-12; P-in-c Witham 12-14; TR Witham and Villages from 14. *The Rectory, 7 Chipping Dell, Witham CM8 2JX* M: 07747-612817 E: sally.lodge@btinternet.com

LODWICK, Brian Martin. b 40. Leeds Univ BA 61 MPhil 76 Linacre Coll Ox BA 63 MA 67 Univ of Wales PhD 87. St Steph Ho Ox 61. **d** 64 **p** 65. C Aberaman *Llan* 64-66; C Newton Nottage 66-73; R Llansannor and Llanfrynach w Penllyn etc 73-94; R Llandough w Leckwith 94-04; RD Llantwit Major and Cowbridge 83-94; Warden of Readers 92-03; Chan Llan Cathl 92-02; Treas Llan Cathl 02-04; Chapl Llandough Hosp 94-99; Chapl Univ Hosp of Wales and Llandough NHS Trust 99-00; Chapl Cardiff and Vale NHS Trust 00-01; rtd 04; PtO *Llan* from 04. *26 New Road, Neath Abbey, Neath SA10 7NH*

LODWICK, Stephen Huw. b 64. Plymouth Poly BSc 85. St Mich Coll Llan. **d** 94 **p** 95. C Clydach *S & B* 94-95; Chapl St Woolos Cathl 95-98; R Grosmont and Skenfrith and Llangattock etc 98-01; CF from 01. *c/o MOD Chaplains (Army)* F: 381824 T: (01264) 383430

LOEWE, The Very Revd Jost Andreas. b 73. St Pet Coll Ox BA 95 MA 99 MPhil 97 Selw Coll Cam PhD 01 FRHistS 11. Westcott Ho Cam 97. **d** 01 **p** 02. C Upton cum Chalvey *Ox* 01-04; C Cambridge Gt St Mary w St Mich *Ely* 04-09; Chapl Trin Coll Melbourne Australia 09-12; Lect Th Trin Coll Th Sch 10-12; Dean Melbourne from 12. *St Paul's Cathedral, 209 Flinders Lane, Melbourne VIC 3000, Australia* T: (0061) (3) 9653 4333 F: 9653 4307 E: dean@stpaulscathedral.org.au

LOEWENDAHL, David Jacob (Jake). b 50. SS Coll Cam BA 74 MA 77. Ripon Coll Cuddesdon 75. **d** 77 **p** 78. C Walworth *S'wark* 77-80; Chapl St Alb Abbey *St Alb* 80-83; Chapl St Alb Sch 80-83; Team Ldr Community Service Volunteers 84-90; PtO *Lon* 83-90; R E and W Tilbury and Linford *Chelmsf* 90-95; V Menheniot *Truro* 95-98; RD W Wivelshire 97-98; rtd 98; PtO *Truro* from 98. *Ashpark House, Ash Park Terrace, Liskeard PL14 4DN* T: (01579) 348205

LOFT, Edmund Martin Boswell. b 25. St Jo Coll Cam BA 49 MA 55. Ely Th Coll 49. **d** 51 **p** 52. C Carl H Trin 51-54; C Barrow St Geo 54-56; V Allonby w W Newton 56-62; V Fillongley *Cov* 62-77; V Earlsdon 77-90; rtd 90; PtO *Sheff* from 90. *10 Quarry Road, Sheffield S17 4DA* T: 0114-236 0759

LOFTHOUSE, Canon Brenda. b 33. RGN 60 RM 62 RNT 69. NOC 84. **d** 87 **p** 94. Hon Par Dn Greengates *Bradf* 87-89; Par Dn Farsley 89-94; V Bolton St Jas w St Chrys 94-00; Hon Can Bradf Cathl 98-00; rtd 00; PtO *Leeds* from 00. *33 Myrtle Court, Bingley BD16 2LP* T: (01274) 771476 E: brenloft@blueyonder.co.uk

LOFTHOUSE, Mrs Diane Lesley. b 66. Yorks Min Course 08. **d** 11 **p** 12. NSM Moor Allerton and Shadwell *Leeds* from 11; Chapl St Gemma's Hospice from 15. *33 Jackson Avenue, Leeds LS8 1NP* T: 0113-266 6495
E: dianelofthouse@virginmedia.com

LOFTS, Sally Anne. *See* BAYLIS, Sally Anne

LOFTUS, Francis. b 52. Newc Univ BA 73 St Andr Univ BPhil 76 York St Jo Coll PGCE 76 FRSA 94. NEOC 93. **d** 96 **p** 97. Hd Master Barlby High Sch 90-10; rtd 10; NSM Barlby and Riccall *York* 96-10; P-in-c 10-13; NSM Hemingbrough 06-10; P-in-c 10-13; V Riccall, Barlby and Hemingbrough from 13. *19 Green Lane, North Duffield, Selby YO8 5RR* T: (01757) 288030 *or* 706161 M: 07850-839419
E: francisloftus@btinternet.com

LOFTUS, John Michael. b 52. Sheff Univ BSc 74 Solicitor 77. **d** 00 **p** 01. OLM Hundred River *St E* 00-13; NSM Hundred River and Wainford from 13. *Keld House, Hulver Street, Henstead, Beccles NR34 7UE* T: (01502) 476257 F: 533001 E: jloftus@nortonpeskett.co.uk

LOGAN, Ms Alexandra Jane. b 73. Trin Coll Carmarthen BA 94. Ridley Hall Cam 99. **d** 02 **p** 03. C Penwortham St Mary *Blackb* 02-07; V Bethnal Green St Jas Less *Lon* 07-13; Chapl Co-ord Cumbria Univ *Blackb* from 14. *University of Cumbria, Bowerham Road, Lancaster LA1 3JD*
E: alexandra.logan@btopenworld.com

LOGAN, Elisabeth Jane. b 59. **d** 10 **p** 11. NSM Copthorne *Chich* from 10. *Fermandy House, Fermandy Lane, Crawley Down, Crawley RH10 4UB* T: (01342) 713338

LOGAN, Ms Joanne. b 64. Ch Coll Cam BA 87 St Jo Coll Dur BA 04 MA 05. Cranmer Hall Dur 02. **d** 05 **p** 06. C Harrogate St Mark *Ripon* 05-09; PtO *Lich* 11-12; *St Alb* from 12. *22 Molewood Road, Hertford SG14 3AQ*
E: jo_logan@btopenworld.com

LOGAN, Kevin. b 43. Oak Hill Th Coll 73. **d** 75 **p** 76. C Blackb Sav 75-78; C Leyland St Andr 78-82; V Gt Harwood St Jo 82-91; V Accrington Ch Ch 91-08; rtd 08; PtO *Blackb* from 08. *119 Kingsway, Church, Accrington BB5 5EL* T: (01254) 396139 M: 07776-007694 E: kevin-logan@sky.com

LOGAN, Samuel Desmond. b 39. TEng. CITC. **d** 78 **p** 79. NSM Belvoir *D & D* 78-85; NSM Knock 85-87; NSM Belfast St Brendan 87-91; LtO 91-95; C Bangor Abbey 95-97; I Belfast St Clem 97-11; rtd 11. *8 Casaeldona Crescent, Belfast BT6 9RE* T: (028) 9079 5473

LOGUE, Mrs Rosemary Christine. TCD BTh 93. CITC 90. **d** 93 **p** 94. C Clooney w Strathfoyle *D & R* 93-96; I Londonderry St Aug 96-03; I Tullyaughnish w Kilmacrenan and Killygarvan 03-05; I Sixmilecross w Termonmaguirke *Arm* 05-08; P-in-c Cambuslang and Uddingston *Glas* 08; I Kilskeery w Trillick *Clogh* from 11. *The Rectory, 130 Kilskeery Road, Trillick, Omagh BT78 3RJ* T: (028) 8956 1457
E: r.logue@btinternet.com

LOH, Tom. b 79. UEA BSc 01. Wycliffe Hall Ox BTh 11. **d** 11 **p** 12. C Billericay and Lt Burstead *Chelmsf* 11-14; P-in-c Westcliff St Mich from 14. *St Michael's Vicarage, 5 Mount Avenue, Westcliff-on-Sea SS0 8PS* M: 07905-743419 T: (01702) 716782 E: tomloh79@yahoo.co.uk

LOMAS, Anthony David. b 59. Cranfield Inst of Tech BSc 81. WEMTC 04. **d** 07 **p** 08. C Sevenhampton w Charlton Abbots, Hawling etc *Glouc* 07-11; R Redmarley D'Abitot, Bromesberrow, Pauntley etc from 11. *The Rectory, Redmarley, Gloucester GL19 3HS* M: 07793-564877 T: (01531) 650991
E: adlomas@aol.com

LOMAS, Mrs Catherine Mary. b 72. St Jo Coll Cam MA 93. STETS 07. **d** 10 **p** 11. C Wellingborough All SS *Pet* 10-11; C Cogenhoe and Gt and Lt Houghton w Brafield 11-14; LtO from 15. *12 Bush Close, Wellingborough NN8 3GL* T: (01933) 385430 E: revdcatherine@virginmedia.com

LOMAS, David Xavier. b 39. St Jo Coll Dur BA 78. Cranmer Hall Dur 75. **d** 78 **p** 79. C Chester le Street *Dur* 78-81; C-in-c Newton Hall LEP 81-84; C-in-c Newton Hall 84-85; Chapl Scunthorpe Distr HA 85-93; Sen Chapl Linc and Louth NHS Trust 93-01; Sen Chapl Chapl Manager United Lincs Hosps NHS Trust 01-04; rtd 04. *9 Hazel Grove, Welton, Lincoln LN2 3JZ* T: (01673) 861409 E: xavlomas@aol.com

LOMAS, The Ven John Derrick Percy. b 58. St Mich Coll Llan 94. **d** 94 **p** 95. C Rhyl w St Ann *St As* 94-00; Chapl RN 00-01; V Holywell *St As* 01-11; AD 08-11; C Corwen w Llangar w Glyndyfrdwy etc 11-13; C Bangor Monachorum, Worthenbury and Marchwiel 13-14; Adn St As from 14; R Caerwys and Bodfari from 15; Can Cursal St As Cathl from 08. *14 Lon yr Ysgol, Caerwyd, Mold CH7 5PZ* T: (01352) 720092 E: archdeacon.stasaph@churchinwales.org.uk

LOMAX, Canon Barry Walter John. b 39. Lambeth STh Lon Coll of Div 63. **d** 66 **p** 67. C Sevenoaks St Nic *Roch* 66-71; C Southport Ch Ch *Liv* 71-73; V Bootle St Matt 73-78; P-in-c Litherland St Andr 76-78; V New Borough and Leigh

Sarum 78-94; Can and Preb Sarum Cathl 91-02; R Blandford Forum and Langton Long 94-02; rtd 02; PtO *Sarum* from 03. *Shiloh, 2 Colborne Avenue, Wimborne BH21 2PZ* T: (01202) 856104 E: barry.lomax@talktalk.net

LOMAX, Eric John. b 64. St Jo Coll Dur BA 96 Leeds Univ PGCE 04. Cranmer Hall Dur 93. **d** 96 **p** 97. C Goodshaw and Crawshawbooth *Man* 96-00; V Copmanthorpe *York* 00-01; P-in-c Colsterworth Gp *Linc* from 10. *The Rectory, 13A Back Lane, Colsterworth, Grantham NG33 5NJ* T: (01476) 861959 E: ericjohnlomax64@aol.com

LOMAX, Mrs Kate Jane. b 73. RGN 96. St Jo Coll Nottm BA 02. **d** 02 **p** 03. C Luton St Mary *St Alb* 02-04; Asst Chapl Cam Univ Hosps NHS Foundn Trust 04-05; Chapl 05-07; NSM Penn Fields *Lich* 08-10; NSM Bayston Hill from 10. *The Vicarage, 42 Eric Lock Road West, Bayston Hill, Shrewsbury SY3 0QA* T: (01743) 872472 E: kate.lomax@btinternet.com

LOMAX, Timothy Michael. b 73. Derby Univ BEd 95 Nottm Univ MA 11. Ridley Hall Cam 05. **d** 07 **p** 08. C Penn Fields *Lich* 07-10; V Bayston Hill from 10. *The Vicarage, 42 Eric Lock Road West, Bayston Hill, Shrewsbury SY3 0QA* T: (01743) 872472 E: tim.lomax@btinternet.com

LONDON (St Paul's), Dean of. *See* ISON, The Very Revd David John

LONDON, Archdeacon of. *See* MERCER, The Ven Nicholas Stanley

LONDON, Bishop of. *See* CHARTRES, The Rt Revd and Rt Hon Richard John Carew

LONEY, Mark William James. b 72. Cen Lancs Univ BSc 94 MA 97 TCD BTh 03. CITC 00. **d** 03 **p** 04. C Larne and Inver *Conn* 03-06; I Ahoghill w Portglenone 06-11; TV Digswell and Panshanger *St Alb* 12-15; I Dungiven w Bovevagh *D & R* from 15. *The Rectory, 14 Main Street, Dungiven, Londonderry BT47 4LB* E: rev.loney@btopenworld.com

LONG, Canon Anne Christine. b 33. Leic Univ BA 56 Ox Univ DipEd 57 Lon Univ BD 65 ALBC. **dss** 80 **d** 87 **p** 94. Lect St Jo Coll Nottm 73-84; Acorn Chr Healing Trust 85-98; Stanstead Abbots *St Alb* 85-92; Hon Par Dn 87-92; Hon Par Dn Camberley St Paul *Guildf* 92-94; Hon C 94-03; Hon Can Guildf Cathl 96-03. *3 Chiselbury Grove, Salisbury SP2 8EP* T: (01722) 341488 E: annelong33@talktalk.net

LONG, Anthony Auguste. b 45. Linc Th Coll 79. **d** 81 **p** 82. C Kingswinford St Mary *Lich* 81-84; TV Ellesmere Port *Ches* 84-87; V Witton 87-97; P-in-c Wybunbury w Doddington 97-02; V 02-10; rtd 10. *23 Osborne Grove, Shavington, Crewe CW2 5BY* T: (01270) 561113 E: tojolong@hotmail.co.uk

LONG, Anthony Robert. b 48. SS Mark & Jo Coll Chelsea CertEd 70 Southn Univ BTh 93 UEA MA 96 Lambeth MA 04. Chich Th Coll 74. **d** 77 **p** 78. C Chiswick St Nic w St Mary *Lon* 77-80; C Earley St Pet *Ox* 80-85; P-in-c Worstead w Westwick and Sloley *Nor* 85-92; R Worstead, Westwick, Sloley, Swanton Abbot etc from 92; P-in-c Tunstead w Sco' Ruston from 85; Chapl Nor Cathl from 85. *The Vicarage, Withergate Road, Worstead, North Walsham NR28 9SE* T: (01692) 536800

LONG, Bill. *See* LONG, Edward Percy Eades

LONG, Bradley. b 65. St Jo Coll Dur BA 08 Lon Inst of Educn PGCE 94. Cranmer Hall Dur 06. **d** 08. C The Hague *Eur* 08-11. *Address temp unknown* M: 68-236 6789 E: bradley_long@hotmail.com

LONG, The Ven Christopher William. b 47. MBE 94. Nottm Univ BTh 78 Open Univ BA 80. Linc Th Coll 75. **d** 78 **p** 79. C Shiregreen St Jas and St Chris *Sheff* 78-81; V 81-82; Chapl RAF 82-05; I Enniscorthy w Clone, Clonmore, Monart etc *C & O* 05-15; Adn Ferns 08-15; Adn Cashel, Waterford and Lismore 14-15. *The Rectory, St John's, Enniscorthy, Co Wexford, Republic of Ireland* T: (00353) (53) 923 9009 E: chriswlong1@eircom.net

LONG, David William. b 47. St Aug Coll Cant 70. **d** 72 **p** 73. C Stanley *Liv* 72-73; C W Derby St Luke 73-76; C Cantril Farm 76-79; V Warrington St Barn 79-81; V Westbrook St Jas 82-96; V Ince St Mary 96-12; AD Wigan E and Hon Can Liv Cathl 03-05; rtd 12; PtO *Blackb* from 14. *25 Almond Brook Road, Standish, Wigan WN6 0TB* T: (01257) 400720 E: david@scars.org.uk

LONG, Edward Percy Eades (Bill). b 14. Liv Univ BA 36 MA 38. Linc Th Coll 73. **d** 73 **p** 74. C Sedbergh, Cautley and Garsdale *Bradf* 73-84; rtd 85; PtO *Bradf* 85-11. *4 Derry Cottages, Sedbergh LA10 5SN* T: (015396) 20577

LONG, Mrs Frances Mary. b 58. SEITE 98. **d** 01 **p** 02. NSM Caterham *S'wark* 01-05; Chapl Surrey and Sussex Healthcare NHS Trust 01-03; C Riddlesdown *S'wark* 05-08; P-in-c Purley St Mark 08-12; P-in-c Purley St Swithun 08-12; PtO 12-14; NSM Caterham from 14. *Address temp unknown* E: franyb8@hotmail.com

LONG, Frederick Hugh. b 43. EMMTC 90. **d** 90 **p** 91. NSM Grantham *Linc* 90-00; C 00-01; TV 01-02; V Grantham St Anne New Somerby and Spitalgate 02-08; rtd 08; Hon

C Drybrook, Lydbrook and Ruardean *Glouc* 08-13. *The Rectory, High Street, Ruardean GL17 9US* T: (01594) 541070

LONG, Geoffrey Lawrence. b 47. La Sainte Union Coll BTh 93 PGCE 94. Portsm Dioc Tr Course 88. **d** 89 **p** 98. NSM Whippingham w E Cowes *Portsm* 89-01; Chapl HM Pris Maidstone 01-12; rtd 12; PtO *Ely* from 13. *2 Fallowfield, Littleport, Ely CB6 1GY* T: (01353) 360702 E: geoffreylong@outlook.com

LONG, Hermione Jane. *See* MORRIS, Hermione Jane

LONG, John. b 48. ACIB 72. Yorks Min Course 09. **d** 10 **p** 11. NSM Utley *Leeds* from 10. *Rosslyn House, Cold Street, Haworth BD22 8AY* T: (01535) 646592 E: haworthlongs@tiscali.co.uk

LONG, Canon John Sydney. b 25. Lon Univ BSc 49. Wycliffe Hall Ox 50. **d** 51 **p** 52. C Plaistow St Andr *Chelmsf* 51-54; C Keighley *Bradf* 54-57; C-in-c Horton Bank Top CD 57-59; V Buttershaw St Aid 59-64; V Barnoldswick w Bracewell 64-85; Hon Can Bradf Cathl 77-91; RD Skipton 83-90; R Broughton, Marton and Thornton 85-91; rtd 91. *1 Church Villa, Carleton, Skipton BD23 3DQ* T: (01756) 799095

LONG, Kingsley Edward. b 41. CITC 90. **d** 93 **p** 94. NSM Swords w Donabate and Kilsallaghan *D & G* 93-94 and 96-99; NSM Howth 94-96; NSM Holmpatrick w Balbriggan and Kenure 99-01; NSM Dublin Clontarf 02-03; NSM Swords w Donabate and Kilsallaghan from 03. *Crimond, 125 Seapark, Malahide, Co Dublin, Republic of Ireland* T: (00353) (1) 845 3179

LONG, Canon Michael David Barnby. b 32. AKC 55. **d** 56 **p** 57. C Whitby *York* 56-59; C Cottingham 59-61; V Elloughton 61-66; P-in-c Brantingham 61-66; V Sheff St Cecilia Parson Cross 66-68; V Flamborough *York* 68-73; R Litcham w Kempston w E and W Lexham *Nor* 73-75; P-in-c York St Luke 75-77; V 77-80; V Hatton w Haseley and Rowington w Lowsonford *Cov* 80-82; V Derringham Bank *York* 82-85; R Castleacre w Newton, Rougham and Southacre *Nor* 85-86; TV Grantham *Linc* 86-89; V Cayton w Eastfield *York* 89-98; RD Scarborough 94-98; Can and Preb York Minster 97-03; rtd 98; P-in-c York St Clem w St Mary Bishophill Senior 98-03; P-in-c Trowse *Nor* 03-12; PtO from 13. *17 Albany Court, Cromer NR27 9AZ* T: (01263) 514059 E: michaeldbl17@gmail.com

LONG, Peter Ronald. b 48. Cuddesdon Coll 71. **d** 73 **p** 74. Chapl RAFVR 74-99; C Bodmin *Truro* 73-75; C Newquay 75-76; Asst Youth Chapl 75-76; Dioc Youth Chapl 76-79; PtO *Eur* 76 and 78-85 and 87-98; Public Preacher Truro 77; P-in-c Mawgan w St Martin-in-Meneage *Truro* 79-82; Chapl Helston-Meneage Community and Geriatric Hosp 80-95; Miss to Seamen 80-98; P-in-c Cury w Gunwalloe *Truro* 80-82; R Cury and Gunwalloe w Mawgan 83-98; PtO *Ex* 82-93; Ecum Th in UK Rail Ind from 97; rtd 08. *26 Jubilee Street, Newquay TR7 1LA* M: 07780-976113 F: (01637) 877060 E: ipsn2009@yahoo.co.uk

LONG, Richard John William. b 59. Hull Univ BA 80 PGCE 81. Cranmer Hall Dur 03. **d** 05 **p** 06. C Beverley St Nic *York* 05-09; TV Marfleet from 09. *St Philip's House, 107 Amethyst Road, Hull HU9 4JG* T: (01482) 376208 E: richlong@fsmail.net

LONG, Roger Eric. b 36. Univ Coll Dur BSc 59 PhD 62. NEOC 90. **d** 93 **p** 94. C Street *York* 93-97; P-in-c Coxwold and Husthwaite 97-02; rtd 02. *Ivy House, Coxwold, York YO61 4AD* T: (01347) 868301

LONG, Samuel Allen. b 48. EAMTC 03. **d** 05 **p** 06. NSM Barrow *St E* 05-08; NSM Pakenham w Norton and Tostock 08-10; P-in-c Badwell and Walsham 10-15; C Hepworth, Hinderclay, Wattisfield and Thelnetham 15; rtd 15. *16 Drury Close, Rougham, Bury St Edmunds IP30 9JE* M: 07732-971925 E: samlong167@aol.com

LONG, Canon Samuel Ernest. b 18. JP 68. ALCD 50 LTh MTh ThD. **d** 49 **p** 50. C Belfast St Clem *D & D* 49-52; C Willowfield 52-56; I Dromara w Garvaghy 56-85; Can Dromore Cathl 81-85; Treas Dromore Cathl 82-85; rtd 85. *9 Cairnshill Court, Saintfield Road, Belfast BT8 4TX* T: (028) 9079 3401

LONG, Simon Richard. b 40. Bernard Gilpin Soc Dur 61 Ely Th Coll 62 Coll of Resurr Mirfield 64. **d** 65 **p** 66. C Bournemouth St Fran *Win* 65-68; C Brussels *Eur* 68; V Portales and Fort Sumner USA 69-79; V Lincoln St Mark 79-81; V Martin St Kath 81-83; R Louisville Em 83-86; V Elizabethtown Ch Ch 86-88; P-in-c Medbourne cum Holt w Stockerston and Blaston *Leic* 88-89; P-in-c Bringhurst w Gt Easton 88-89; R Six Saints circa Holt 90-99; RD Gartree I 93-97; rtd 99. *17C Craft Village, Balnakeil, Durness, Lairg IV27 4PT* T: (01971) 511757

LONG, Timothy Martin Stuart. b 44. Witwatersrand Univ BA 69 Natal Univ MA 89 PhD 95. **d** 84 **p** 84. C Waterkloof S Africa 84-85; R Lynnwood 86-95; R Atteridgeville 95-02; R Weltevreden Park 02-10; PtO *Guildf* from 11. *11 White Lodge, 90 Leatherhead Road, Ashtead KT21 2SU* T: (01372) 273441 M: 07586-296062 E: timmslong@gmail.com

LONG, William Thomas. b 53. Dur Univ MA 88 QUB PhD 99. **d** 81 **p** 82. C Orangefield *D & D* 81-84; C Portadown St Mark

Arm 84-86; I Dromara w Garvaghy *D & D* 86-91; I Aghalurcher w Tattykeeran, Cooneen etc *Clogh* 91-96; I Annalong *D & D* 96-03; I Belfast St Simon w St Phil *Conn* 03-06; I Carnteel and Crilly *Arm* 06-13; I Convoy w Monellan and Donaghmore *D & R* from 13. *The Rectory, Convoy, Lifford, Co Donegal, Republic of Ireland* T: (00353) (74) 910 1817 M: 89-418 2436 E: wl21011@outlook.com

LONGBOTTOM, Canon Frank. b 41. Ripon Hall Ox 65. **d** 68 **p** 69. C Epsom St Martin *Guildf* 68-72; Chapl St Ebba's Hosp Epsom 68-72; Chapl Qu Mary's Hosp Carshalton 68-72; Chapl Henderson Hosp Sutton 68-72; Chapl Highcroft Hosp Birm 72-94; Chapl Northcroft Hosp Birm 74-94; Dioc Adv for Past Care of Clergy & Families *Birm* 89-94; Bp's Adv 94-06; Bp's Adv on Health and Soc Care *Birm* 01-06; P-in-c Middleton 99-00; Hon Can Birm Cathl 91-06; rtd 07; PtO *Birm* from 09. *46 Sunnybank Road, Sutton Coldfield B73 5RE* T/F: 0121-350 5823

LONGBOTTOM, Canon Paul Edward. b 44. Kent Univ MA 02 AKC 67. **d** 68 **p** 69. C Rainham *Roch* 68-71; C Riverhead 71-75; C Dunton Green 71-75; V Penge Lane H Trin 75-84; V Chatham St Wm 84-94; V Shorne and Dioc Dir of Ords 94-09; Hon Can Roch Cathl 96-09; rtd 09; PtO *Roch* from 09; *Cant* from 10. *30 Doubleday Drive, Bapchild, Sittingbourne ME9 9PJ* T: (01795) 428300 E: paul.longbottom@ymail.com

LONGDEN, Lee Paul. b 70. Peterho Cam BA 91 MA 95 Ches Coll of HE MTh 03 Birm Univ ThD 12 Huddersfield Univ MSc 13 FRCO 91 LLCM 93 ARCM 93 LRSM 96 FHEA 12 FInstLM 13. Qu Coll Birm 03. **d** 05 **p** 06. C Langley and Parkfield *Man* 05-08; V Ashton St Ch Ch 08-15; Hon Assoc Dir of Ords 09-15; Vice Prin All SS Cen for Miss & Min from 15; PtO *Man* from 15; Extraordinary Sen Lect NW Univ S Africa from 13. *All Saints Centre, 113 Aiken Hall, Crab Lane, Fearnhead, Warrington WA2 0DB* T: (01925) 534373 E: viceprincipal@allsaintscentre.org

LONGDON, Anthony Robert James. b 44. STETS 00. **d** 03 **p** 04. OLM N Bradley, Southwick and Heywood *Sarum* 03-08; OLM N Bradley, Southwick, Heywood and Steeple Ashton 08-14; PtO from 14. *1A Holbrook Lane, Trowbridge BA14 0PP* T/F: (01225) 754771 E: tony.longdon@homecall.co.uk

LONGE, David John Hastings. b 75. New Coll Edin BD 99. Ripon Coll Cuddesdon 07. **d** 09 **p** 10. C N Lambeth *S'wark* from 09. *12 Moat Place, London SW9 0TA* T: (020) 7735 3403

LONGE, James Robert. b 46. EAMTC 02. **d** 04 **p** 05. NSM Pakenham w Norton and Tostock *St E* 04-07; NSM St Edm Way 07-14; rtd 14; PtO *St E* from 14. *Bush House, Bradfield St Clare, Bury St Edmunds IP30 0EQ*

LONGFELLOW, Erica Denise. b 74. Duke Univ (USA) BA 97 Linc Coll Ox MSt 98 DPhil 01. SEITE 02. **d** 05 **p** 06. NSM Kew St Phil and All SS w St Luke *S'wark* 05-09; NSM Surbiton St Andr and St Mark 09-11; Chapl and Dean of Div New Coll Ox from 11. *New College, Holywell Street, Oxford OX1 3BN* T: (01865) 279555 E: chaplain@new.ox.ac.uk

LONGFOOT, Canon Richard. b 46. Oak Hill Th Coll 76. **d** 78 **p** 79. C Chaddesden St Mary *Derby* 78-81; C Cambridge St Martin *Ely* 81-83; R Folksworth w Morborne 83-89; R Stilton w Denton and Caldecote 83-89; R Stilton w Denton and Caldecote etc 90-11; RD Yaxley 02-07; Hon Can Ely Cathl 04-11; rtd 11; PtO *Ely* from 11; *Pet* from 12. *5 Westfield Close, Yaxley, Peterborough PE7 3NW* T: (01733) 247700 E: richard.lfoot@lineone.net

LONGMAN, Edward. b 37. Hatf Coll Dur BSc 62 Fitzw Coll Cam BA 66 MA 70. Clifton Th Coll 62. **d** 66 **p** 67. C Lower Homerton St Paul *Lon* 66-72; C Parr *Liv* 72-73; TV 74-85; PtO 87-02; *Ches* from 96. *21 Canadian Avenue, Hoole, Chester CH2 3HG* T: (01244) 317544 M: 07779-650791 F: 400450 E: elongman@onetel.com

LONGMAN, Edward George. b 35. St Pet Hall Ox BA 58 MA 62. Westcott Ho Cam 59. **d** 60 **p** 61. C Sheff St Mark Broomhall 61-65; V Brightside St Thos 65-74; V Yardley St Edburgha *Birm* 74-84; RD Yardley 77-84; Hon Can Birm Cathl 81-96; R Sutton Coldfield H Trin 84-96; RD Sutton Coldfield 94-96; Chapl Gd Hope Distr Gen Hosp Sutton Coldfield 84-96; P-in-c Cerne Abbas w Godmanstone and Minterne Magna *Sarum* 96-02; RD Dorchester 00-02; rtd 02; PtO *B & W* from 04. *5 Old Wells Road, Shepton Mallet BA4 5XN* T: (01749) 343699 E: ted@roseted.co.uk

LONGUET-HIGGINS, John. b 62. Leeds Univ BA 85. St Jo Coll Nottm 88. **d** 91 **p** 92. C Kidlington w Hampton Poyle *Ox* 91-95; TV N Huddersfield *Wakef* 95-01; V Painswick, Sheepscombe, Cranham, The Edge etc *Glouc* 02-12; R Ashleworth, Corse, Hartpury, Hasfield etc from 12. *The Rectory, Over Old Road, Hartpury, Gloucester GL19 3BJ* T: (01452) 700965 E: vicar.westof7@gmail.com

LONSDALE, Mrs Gillian. b 36. Qu Mary Coll Lon BA 57 MA 59 Ex Univ MPhil 81 AIMSW 61. SWMTC 96. **d** 99 **p** 00. NSM Duloe, Herodsfoot, Morval and St Pinnock *Truro* 99-06;

NSM Lansallos and Talland 01-03; RD W Wivelshire 03-06; rtd 06. *2 Garden Terrace, Whittingham, Alnwick NE66 4RD* T: (01665) 574907 E: gill@glonsdale.freeserve.co.uk

LONSDALE, Ms Linda. b 49. SWMTC 08. **d** 10 **p** 11. NSM Alderley Edge *Ches* 10-13; P-in-c Beetham *Carl* from 13. *The Parsonage, Stanley Street, Beetham, Milnthorpe LA7 7AS* T: (015395) 62412 E: rev.beetham@gmail.com *or* rev@jandll.plus.com

LOOKER, Clare Margaret. *See* FLEMING, Clare Margaret

LOOMES, Gaenor Mary. *See* HOCKEY, Gaenor Mary

LORAINE, Kenneth. b 34. Cranmer Hall Dur 63. **d** 66 **p** 67. C Hartlepool All SS Stranton *Dur* 66-69; C Darlington St Cuth 69-72; V Preston on Tees 72-79; V Staindrop 79-87; P-in-c Haynes *St Alb* 87-96; Dioc Stewardship Adv 87-96; rtd 96; PtO *York* from 96. *116 Turker Lane, Northallerton DL6 1QD* T: (01609) 771277

LORD, Andrew Michael. b 66. Warwick Univ BSc 87 Birm Univ MA 99 PhD 10 Fitzw Coll Cam BA 02. Ridley Hall Cam 00. **d** 03 **p** 04. C Long Buckby w Watford *Pet* 03-06; C W Haddon w Winwick and Ravensthorpe 03-06; R Trowell, Awsworth and Cossall *S'well* from 06. *The Rectory, 47 Nottingham Road, Trowell, Nottingham NG9 3PF* T: 0115-849 5195 E: revandylord@gmail.com

LORD, Clive Gavin. b 69. St Martin's Coll Lanc BA. St Steph Ho Ox BTh. **d** 96 **p** 97. C Penwortham St Leon *Blackb* 96-98; C Blackpool St Mary 98-01; P-in-c 01-04; V 04-06; Chapl Blackpool, Fylde and Wyre Hosps NHS Trust from 06. *Chaplaincy Office, Victoria Hospital, Whinney Heys Road, Blackpool FY3 8NR* T: (01253) 306875 E: livecg@aol.com *or* clive.lord@bfwhospitals.nhs.uk

LORD, Mrs Deborah Alice. b 69. Reading Univ BSc 90 Univ of Wales (Swansea) PGCE 93. St Jo Coll Nottm 10. **d** 13 **p** 14. C Toton *S'well* from 13. *47 Nottingham Road, Trowell, Nottingham NG9 3PF* T: 0115-849 5195 E: debbie.lord@gmail.com

LORD, Mrs Sharon Ruth. b 68. Staffs Univ BSc 03 RGN 89 RM 92. Cranmer Hall Dur 13. **d** 15. C Burton All SS w Ch Ch *Lich* from 15. *242 Blackpool Road, Burton-on-Trent DE14 3AU* M: 07711-030203 E: rev@lord-family.co.uk *or* curate@disciples.com

LORD, Stuart James. b 59. K Coll Lon BD 81 AKC 81. Sarum & Wells Th Coll 83. **d** 85 **p** 86. C Darwen St Pet w Hoddlesden *Blackb* 85-88; C Otley *Bradf* 88-93; P-in-c Low Moor St Mark 93-02; TV Brighouse and Clifton *Wakef* 02-09; R Norton in the Moors *Lich* from 10. *The New Rectory, Norton Lane, Stoke-on-Trent ST6 8BY* T: (01484) 534622

LORD, Mrs Tanya Marie. b 66. Trin Coll Bris. **d** 09 **p** 10. C Bris St Matt and St Nath 09-13; P-in-c Southmead from 13. *St Stephen's Vicarage, Wigton Crescent, Bristol BS10 6DR* M: 07852-928881 E: tanyalord@aol.com

LORD-LEAR, Mark. b 40. Ex Univ DipEd 70 Sussex Univ MA 74. SWMTC 10. **d** 11 **p** 12. NSM Torquay St Matthias, St Mark and H Trin Ex 11-14; C Kenton, Mamhead, Powderham, Cofton and Starcross 14-15; C Exminster, Kenn, Kenton w Mamhead, and Powderham from 15. *All Saints' House, Kenton, Exeter EX6 8NG* T: (01626) 891795 E: markll@talktalk.net

LORDING, Miss Claire Ann. b 75. Roehampton Inst BA 96. Ripon Coll Cuddesdon BTh 96. **d** 99 **p** 00. C Ledbury *Heref* 99-02; TV Tenbury Wells 02-08; TR 08-10; P-in-c Clee Hill 09-10; TR Tenbury 10-15; RD Ludlow 10-15; P-in-c Pershore w Pinvin, Wick and Birlingham *Worc* from 15. *58 Three Springs Road, Pershore WR10 1HS* T: (01386) 300053 E: claire.lording@virgin.net

LORIMER, Eileen Jean. b 35. CertEd 56. Dalton Ho Bris 62. **dss** 84 **d** 89 **p** 94. Chiddingstone w Chiddingstone Causeway *Roch* 84-04; NSM 89-04; PtO from 04. *3 Causeway Cottages, Chiddingstone Causeway, Tonbridge TN11 8JR* T: (01892) 871393

LORT-PHILLIPS, Mrs Elizabeth Priscilla. b 47. STETS 02. **d** 05 **p** 06. NSM Redhorn *Sarum* 05-12; NSM The Cannings and Redhorn from 12. *The Cottage on the Green, 1 Manor Farm Lane, Patney, Devizes SN10 3RB* T: (01380) 840071 E: e.lortphillips@btinternet.com

LOSACK, Marcus Charles. b 53. Ch Coll Cam BA 76 MA 78 MPhil. Sarum & Wells Th Coll 78. **d** 80 **p** 81. C Hattersley *Ches* 80-82; C Dublin Zion Ch *D & G* 83-86; Libya 86-89; CMS Jerusalem 89-92; I Newcastle w Newtownmountkennedy and Calary *D & G* 93-95; Exec Dir Céile Dé 95-13 and from 14; P-in-c Palermo w Taormina *Eur* 13-14. *Céile Dé Castlekevin, Annamoe, Bray, Co Wicklow, Republic of Ireland* T/F: (00353) (404) 45595

LOTHIAN, Iain Nigel Cunningham. b 59. Aber Univ MA 84 Bath Univ PGCE 86 Leeds Univ MA 05. NOC 02. **d** 05 **p** 06. C Sheff St Pet Abbeydale 05-09; C Sheff St Pet and St Oswald 09; PtO from 09. *33 Gatefield Road, Sheffield S7 1RD* T: 0114-250 9736 E: i.lothian@btopenworld.com

LOTT, Eric John. b 34. Lon Univ BA 65 Lanc Univ MLitt 70 PhD 77. Richmond Th Coll BD 59. **d** 60 **p** 61. India 60-88; Prof United Th Coll Bangalore 77-88; Wesley Hall Ch and Community Project Leics 88-94; rtd 94; PtO *Leic* from 94. *16 Main Road, Old Dalby, Melton Mowbray LE14 3LR* T: (01664) 822405 E: eric.lott@breathemail.net

LOUDEN, Canon Terence Edmund. b 48. Ch Coll Cam BA 70 MA 74. Sarum & Wells Th Coll 72. **d** 75 **p** 76. C Portsea N End St Mark *Portsm* 75-78; C-in-c Leigh Park St Clare CD 78-81; R Chale 81-88; R Niton 81-88; P-in-c Whitwell 82-84; V Cosham 88-96; V E Meon 96-13; V Langrish 96-13; CME Officer 96-03; Hon Can Portsm Cathl 92-13; rtd 13; Hon Can Cape Coast Ghana from 12; PtO *Portsm* from 13. *34 Claire Gardens, Waterlooville PO8 0JH* T: (023) 9259 6525 M: 07711-319752 E: terrylouden@btinternet.com

LOUDON (née KING), Canon Ellen Francis. b 67. Liv Poly BA 90 Liv Univ MA 96 PhD 11. Trin Coll Bris 06. **d** 08 **p** 09. C Everton St Pet w St Chrys *Liv* 08-12; P-in-c Walton St Luke from 12; P-in-c Walton St Jo from 14; AD Walton from 13; Hon Can Liv Cathl from 13. *25 Stuart Road, Walton, Liverpool L4 5QS* T: 0151-521 1344 M: 07718-806891 E: ellen@ellenloudon.com

LOUGHBOROUGH, Archdeacon of. *See* NEWMAN, The Ven David Maurice Frederick

LOUGHEED, Brian Frederick Britain. b 38. TCD BA 60. CITC 61. **d** 61 **p** 62. C Dublin St Pet w St Audoen *D & G* 61-63; C Glenageary 63-66; I Rathmolyon Union *M & K* 66-79; I Killarney w Aghadoe and Muckross *L & K* 79-04; Can Limerick and Killaloe Cathls 87-95; Preb Taney St Patr Cathl Dublin 89-04; Dioc Info Officer (Limerick) *L & K* 90-91; Radio Officer 91-04; rtd 04. *2 Arlington Heights, Park Road, Killarney, Co Kerry, Republic of Ireland* T: (00353) (64) 21642 E: brianlougheed1@eircom.net

LOUGHLIN, George Alfred Graham. b 43. Clifton Th Coll 65. **d** 69 **p** 70. C Plumstead All SS *S'wark* 69-73; C Bromley Ch Ch *Roch* 73-76; P-in-c Bothenhampton w Walditch *Sarum* 76-79; TV Bridport 79-83; V Heatherlands St Jo 83-08; rtd 08. *239 rue de Florieye, 83460 Taradeau, France* E: vicar@gagl.co.uk

LOUGHTON, Michael. b 34. K Coll Lon BD 58 AKC 58. **d** 59 **p** 60. C Chingford SS Pet and Paul *Chelmsf* 59-62; C Eastbourne St Elisabeth *Chich* 62-65; R Lewes St Jo sub Castro 65-74; PtO from 87; rtd 99. *Green Woodpecker, 1 Kammond Avenue, Seaford BN25 3JL* T: (01323) 893506

LOUIS, Ms Emma Christine. b 69. Coll of Ripon & York St Jo BA 92 St Jo Coll Dur BA 96. Cranmer Hall Dur 94. **d** 97 **p** 98. C Birm St Martin w Bordesley St Andr 97-00; Arts Development Officer 97-00; Asst Chapl Harrogate Health Care NHS Trust 00-02; Chapl Co-ord St Mich Hospice Harrogate 01-02; Asst Chapl Birm Heartlands and Solihull NHS Trust 02-04; Lead Chapl Sandwell Mental Health NHS and Social Care Trust from 04; PtO *Birm* from 05. *Sandwell Mental Health Trust, Delta House, Greets Green Road, West Bromwich B70 9PL* T: 0121-612 8067 M: 07813-015325 E: emma.louis@bcpft.nhs.uk

LOUIS, Canon Peter Anthony. b 41. St Cath Coll Ox BA 63 MA 77 Man Univ MPhil 85 Jes Coll Cam CertEd 64. Wells Th Coll 66. **d** 68 **p** 70. C E Grinstead St Mary *Chich* 68-75; C Radcliffe-on-Trent *S'well* 75-80; Hd Master Blue Coat Comp Sch Cov 80-85; V Welwyn Garden City *St Alb* 85-08; Chapl Oaklands Coll 93-95; Hon Can St Alb St Alb 04-08; rtd 08; PtO *St Alb* 10-14. *27 Aylesbury Road, Wendover, Aylesbury HP22 6JG* T: (01296) 582683 E: plouis@ntlworld.com

LOVATT, Bernard James. b 31. Lich Th Coll 64. **d** 65 **p** 66. C Burford III w 1t Heref 65-67; C Cleobury Mortimer w Hopton Wafers 67-68; C Bradford-on-Avon H Trin *Sarum* 68-69; C Wootton Bassett 69-72; C Broad Town 69-72; R Bishopstrow and Boreham 72-79; P-in-c Brighton St Geo *Chich* 79-83; V Brighton St Anne 79-83; V Brighton St Geo and St Anne 83-86; P-in-c Kemp Town St Mark and St Matt 85-86; V Brighton St Geo w St Anne and St Mark 86-95; rtd 95; PtO *Ex* from 95. *7 Cambridge Terrace, Salcombe Road, Sidmouth EX10 8PL* T: (01395) 514154

LOVATT, James Arthur Roy. b 36. **d** 08 **p** 09. OLM Horton, Lonsdon and Rushton Spencer *Lich* 08-14; OLM Cheddleton, Horton, Longsdon and Rushton Spencer from 14. *25 Kent Drive, Endon, Stoke-on-Trent ST9 9EH* T: (01782) 504723 E: jarl25kd@tiscali.co.uk

LOVATT, Mrs Pamela. b 50. **d** 98 **p** 99. OLM Warrington St Ann *Liv* 98-14; OLM Warrington H Trin and St Ann from 14; Chapl Warrington Community Health Care NHS Trust from 99. *59 Amelia Street, Warrington WA2 7QD* T: (01925) 650849 *or* 655221 E: pam.lovatt@ntlworld.com

LOVATT, William Robert. b 54. SS Coll Cam MA 75 K Coll Lon PGCE 77 MA 78. Oak Hill Th Coll 85. **d** 87 **p** 88. C Devonport St Budeaux *Ex* 87-90; Asst Chapl Paris St Mich *Eur* 90-94; P-in-c Lenton *S'well* 94-00; V 00-04; V Eastbourne All SS

Chich from 04; RD Eastbourne 06-09. *All Saints' Vicarage, 1A Jevington Gardens, Eastbourne BN21 4HR* T: (01323) 410033 M: 07815-138202 E: robertlovatt@tiscali.co.uk

LOVE, Mrs Alison Jane. b 63. Lanc Univ BA 84 Westmr Coll Ox PGCE 85 Win Univ BA 11. STETS 08. **d** 11 **p** 12. NSM Chippenham St Pet *Bris* 11-14; P-in-c Draycot from 14. *Draycot Rectory, Seagry Road, Sutton Benger, Chippenham SN15 4RY* T: (01249) 720619 E: palove@tiscali.co.uk

LOVE, Ms Anette. b 53. Matlock Coll of Educn CertEd 74 Nottm Univ BEd 75. Cranmer Hall Dur 88. **d** 90 **p** 94. Par Dn Gresley *Derby* 90-92; C Heanor 92-94; C Loscoe 94-02; V Heath 02-15; rtd 15; PtO *Derby* from 15. *Address temp unknown-* M: 07713-955249 E: anette.love@btinternet.com

LOVE, Joel Andrew. b 77. Birm Univ BA 99 MPhil 04 PhD 08 Cam Univ BA 11. Westcott Ho Cam 09. **d** 11 **p** 12. C Lancaster St Mary w St John and St Anne *Blackb* 11-15; V Roch from 15. *The Vicarage, 138 Delce Road, Rochester ME1 2EH* M: 07519-620889 E: joel.loves.trees@gmail.com

LOVE, Pamela Elizabeth. **d** 14 **p** 15. NSM Llangybi and Coedypaen w Llanbadoc *Mon* 14-15; NSM Usk Min Area from 15. *15 Ty Cybi Drive, Llangybi, Usk NP15 1TU* T: (01633)450347 E: pljl13@aol.com

LOVE, Richard Angus. b 45. AKC 67. **d** 68 **p** 69. C Balham Hill Ascension *S'wark* 68-71; C Amersham *Ox* 71-73; R Scotter w E Ferry *Linc* 73-79; P-in-c Petham w Waltham and Lower Hardres w Nackington *Cant* 79-85; R Petham and Waltham w Lower Hardres etc 85-90; V Sittingbourne H Trin w Bobbing 90-02; P-in-c Aldington w Bonnington and Bilsington etc 02-10; rtd 10; PtO *Cant* from 10. *45 Greystones Road, Bearsted, Maidstone ME15 8PD* E: revralove@msn.com

LOVE, Robert. b 45. Bradf Univ BSc 68 PhD 74 NE Lon Poly PGCE 89. Trin Coll Bris. **d** 75 **p** 76. C Bowling St Jo *Bradf* 75-79; TV Forest Gate St Sav w W Ham St Matt *Chelmsf* 79-85; P-in-c Becontree St Elisabeth 85-96; V S Hornchurch St Jo and St Matt 96-10; AD Havering 08-10; rtd 10. *7 Chelmer Drive, South Ockendon RM15 6EE* T: (01708) 530915 M: 07767-279598 E: priestwalking11@gmail.com *or* robert-love2@sky.com

LOVEDAY, Mrs Jean Susan. b 47. Ex Univ BTh 10. SWMTC 09. **d** 11. NSM Braunton *Ex* from 11. *Cowley, Parracombe, Barnstaple EX31 4PQ* T: (01598) 763373 E: jean@castlemaker.com

LOVEDAY, Joseph Michael. b 54. AKC 75. St Aug Coll Cant 75. **d** 78 **p** 79. C Kettering SS Pet and Paul 78-81; C Upper Teddington SS Pet and Paul *Lon* 81-84; CF 84-09; rtd 09; PtO *Ox* from 13. *6 Mansell Close, Towcester NN12 7AY*

LOVEDAY, Susan Mary. b 49. Sussex Univ BA 70 Surrey Univ MSc 81. STETS 94. **d** 97 **p** 98. NSM New Haw *Guildf* 97-03; NSM Egham Hythe from 03; Ecum Co-ord Churches Together in Surrey from 00. *10 Abbey Gardens, Chertsey KT16 8RQ* T: (01932) 566920 E: sue.loveday.ctsurrey@lineone.net

LOVEGROVE, Anne Maureen. b 44. Oak Hill Th Coll 88. **d** 90 **p** 94. Par Dn Thorley *St Alb* 90-94; C 94-95; V Croxley Green St Oswald 95-02; V Letchworth St Paul w Willian 02-09; rtd 09. *24 Chenies Avenue, Amersham HP6 6PP* T: (01494) 763151 E: anne.lovegrove1@btinternet.com

LOVEGROVE, Michael John Bennett. b 42. FCII FCIPD ACIArb. SEITE. **d** 00 **p** 01. NSM Saffron Walden w Wendens Ambo, Littlebury etc *Chelmsf* 00-08; TV 05-08; rtd 08; PtO *Chelmsf* from 09. *Craigside, 8 Beck Road, Saffron Walden CB11 4EH* T: (01799) 528232 M: 07980-103541 E: lovegrove8_@btinternet.com

LOVELESS, Martin Frank. b 46. N Bucks Coll of Educn CertEd 68. Wycliffe Hall Ox 72. **d** 75 **p** 76. C Caversham *Ox* 75-81; V Carterton 81-86; Chapl RAF 86-02; Chapl K Coll Taunton 02-04; PtO *Heref* 04-05 and from 07; P-in-c Glossop *Derby* 05-07. *Ridge Cottage, Staunton-on-Wye, Hereford HR4 7LP* T: (01981) 500311 M: 07810-002079 E: martinloveless@hotmail.com

LOVELESS, Mrs Natalie Louise. b 78. Southn Univ BA 01. SEITE 08. **d** 11 **p** 12. NSM Horsham *Chich* 11-14; TV from 14. *The Vicarage, Church Street, Warnham, Horsham RH12 3QW* T: (01403) 243254 E: revnloveless@gmail.com

LOVELESS, Robert Alfred. b 43. Birm Univ BA 66. Westcott Ho Cam 66. **d** 68 **p** 69. C Kenilworth St Nic *Cov* 68-72; C Costessey *Nor* 73-75; R Colney 75-80; R Lt w Gt Melton, Marlingford and Bawburgh 75-80; V Lt and Gt Melton w Bawburgh 80-82; P-in-c Westwood *Sarum* 82-83; P-in-c Wingfield w Rowley 82-83; R Westwood and Wingfield 83-87; Chapl Stonar Sch Melksham 82-87; R Paston *Pet* 87-93; V Nassington w Yarwell and Woodnewton 93-07; rtd 07. *93 The Pollards, Bourne PE10 0FR* T: (01778) 393561

LOVELL, Ben Robert. b 82. UMIST BEng 03 Ox Brookes Univ BA 09. St Mellitus Coll MA 14. **d** 14 **p** 15. C S Harrow St Paul *Lon* from 14. *39 Eastcote Lane, Harrow HA2 8DE* M: 07734-775102 E: benlovell@me.com

LOVELL, Charles Nelson. b 34. Oriel Coll Ox BA 57 MA 61. Wycliffe Hall Ox. **d** 59 **p** 60. C Walsall St Matt *Lich* 59-63; C St Giles-in-the-Fields *Lon* 63; Argentina 64-67; C Cambridge H Trin *Ely* 64; V Esh *Dur* 67-75; V Hamsteels 67-75; Chapl Winterton Hosp Sedgefield 75-83; R Stanhope *Dur* 83-86; Chapl Horn Hall Hosp Weardale 83-97; R Stanhope w Frosterley *Dur* 86-97; V Eastgate w Rookhope 86-97; RD Stanhope 87-97; rtd 97; PtO *Dur* from 97. *10 Riverside, Wolsingham, Bishop Auckland DL13 3BP* T: (01388) 527038 E: charles@thefreeinternet.co.uk

LOVELL, David John. b 38. JP 89. Univ of Tasmania BEcon 86. Qu Coll Birm 60. **d** 59 **p** 60. C Glouc St Steph 60-64; C Lower Tuffley St Geo CD 64-67; V Lydbrook 67-73; R Oatlands Australia 73-75; PtO *Tas* 76-81; rtd 98. *26 Lynden Road, Bonnet Hill Tas 7053, Australia* T: (0061) (3) 6229 2838

LOVELL, Mrs Gillian Jayne. b 58. Univ of Wales (Ban) BA 79 PGCE 80. Qu Coll Birm MA 04. **d** 04 **p** 05. C Burnham *Ox* 04-08; P-in-c Burghfield 08-10; R from 10; R Sulhamstead Abbots and Bannister w Ufton Nervet 10-14. *The Rectory, Hollybush Lane, Burghfield Common, Reading RG7 3JL* T: 0118-983 4433 E: keith@mary.freewire.co.uk
E: gill.lovell@stmarysburghfield.org

LOVELL, Helen Sarah. *See* HOUSTON, Helen Sarah

LOVELL, Keith Michael Beard. b 43. K Coll Lon 67. **d** 68 **p** 69. C Romford St Edw *Chelmsf* 68-73; P-in-c Elmstead 73-79; V Tollesbury w Salcot Virley 79-09; rtd 09; PtO *Chelmsf* from 09. *14 Brierley Avenue, West Mersea, Colchester CO5 8HG* T: (01206) 386626 E: keith@mary.freewire.co.uk

LOVELL, Laurence John. b 31. St D Coll Lamp BA 54 Tyndale Hall Bris 54. **d** 56 **p** 57. C Penge Ch Ch w H Trin *Roch* 56-61; C Illogan *Truro* 61-63; V St Keverne 63-68; C-in-c Oatley Australia 68-72; R 72-95; rtd 95. *Donald Robinson Village, 105/81 Flora Street, Kirrawee NSW 2223 Australia* E: ljl01@bigpond.com

LOVELUCK, Canon Allan (Illtyd). b 30. Univ of Qld BSW 74 MSocWork 79. St D Coll Lamp BA 52 St Mich Coll Llan 52. **d** 55 **p** 56. C Dowlais *Llan* 55-58; SSF 58-79; LtO *Chelmsf* 62-64; Australia from 64; Hon Can Brisbane 92-00; rtd 95. *5/48 Dunmore Terrace, Auchenflower Qld 4066, Australia* T: (0061) (7) 3719 5342 *or* 3870 2566 M: 414-500837

LOVELUCK, Canon Graham David. b 34. Univ of Wales (Abth) BSc 55 PhD 58 CChem FRSC. St Deiniol's Hawarden 77. **d** 78 **p** 79. NSM Llanfair Mathafarn Eithaf w Llanbedrgoch *Ban* 78-87; NSM Llaneugrad w Llanallgo and Penrhosllugwy etc 87-96; P-in-c 96-03; R 03-04; Dioc Dir of Educn 92-03; Can Cursal Ban Cathl 00-04; rtd 04; PtO *Ban* from 11. *Gwenallt, Marianglas LL73 8PE* T: (01248) 853741

LOVEMAN, Mrs Ruth. b 45. STETS 01. **d** 04 **p** 05. NSM Portsea N End St Mark *Portsm* 04-09; NSM Cowplain 09-12; NSM Blendworth w Chalton w Idsworth from 12. *3 Cotwell Avenue, Waterlooville PO8 9AP* T: (023) 9259 1933 E: ruthlvm@googlemail.com

LOVERIDGE, Douglas Henry. b 52. Sarum & Wells Th Coll. **d** 84 **p** 85. C Earley St Pet *Ox* 84-88; V Hurst 88-03; Asst Chapl R Berks NHS Foundn Trust 03-07; Chapl Mid-Essex Hosp Services NHS Trust 07-09; Chapl W Herts Hosps NHS Trust from 09. *All Saints' Vicarage, Churchfields, Hertford SG13 8AE* T: (01992) 584899 *or* (01923) 217994 E: dhloveridge@hotmail.com *or* douglas.loveridge@whht.nhs.uk

LOVERIDGE, Emma Warren. b 65. St Jo Coll Cam BA 87 MA 90 PhD 01. **d** 99 **p** 00. NSM Highbury Ch Ch w St Jo and St Sav *Lon* 99-02; NSM Islington St Mary 03-05; Prin Adv to Abp York 06-07. *6 Prior Bolton Street, London N1 2NX* M: 07000-777977 E: eloveridge@windsandstars.co.uk

LOVERIDGE (née RODEN), Canon Joan Margaretha Holland (Jo). b 57. K Coll Lon BD 78 AKC 78 Regent's Park Coll Ox MTh 98. SAOMC 95. **d** 97 **p** 98. NSM Caversham St Jo *Ox* 97-98; C Earley St Pet 98-03; P-in-c Burghfield 03-07; AD Bradfield 04-07; P-in-c Hertford All SS *St Alb* 07-08; TR Hertford from 08; Hon Can St Alb from 14; RD Hertford and Ware from 15. *All Saints' Vicarage, Churchfields, Hertford SG13 8AE* T: (01992) 584899 E: jonloveridge@hotmail.com

LOVERING, Mrs Jennifer Mary. b 39. Eastbourne Tr Coll CertEd 59. Wycliffe Hall Ox 81. **dss** 84 **d** 87 **p** 94. Abingdon w Shippon *Ox* 84-87; Par Dn Abingdon 87-94; C 94-97; r-d 98. *5 Monksmead, Brightwell-cum-Sotwell, Wallingford OX10 0RL* T: (01491) 825329

LOVERN, Mrs Sandra Elaine. b 48. Trin Coll Bris BA 07. **d** 07 **p** 08. NSM Chew Magna w Dundry, Norton Malreward etc *B & W* from 07. *Willow Lodge, Breach Hill Lane, Chew Stoke, Bristol BS40 8YA* T: (01275) 332657 E: sandra.lovern@yahoo.com

LOVESEY, Katharine Patience Beresford. b 62. Trin Coll Bris 00. **d** 03 **p** 04. C Nor Lakenham St Jo and All SS and Tuckswood 03-08; C Stoke H Cross w Dunston, Arminghall

etc 08-10; P-in-c Aldborough Hatch *Chelmsf* from 12. *Aldborough Hatch Vicarage, 89 St Peter's Close, Ilford IG2 7QN* T: (020) 8599 5413 E: katelovesey@btinternet.com

LOVETT, Frances Mary Anderson. b 46. Plymouth Univ BA 92. NOC 00. **d** 03 **p** 04. NSM Newton in Makerfield St Pet *Liv* 03-05; Hon Chapl Liv Cathl 05-10; rtd 10; PtO *Liv* from 10. *The Rectory, Fore Street, Northam, Bideford EX39 1AW* T: (01237) 470183 M: 07989-099483 E: fran.lovett@googlemail.com

LOVETT, Francis Roland. b 25. Glouc Th Course. **d** 85 **p** 86. NSM Ludlow *Heref* 85-91; rtd 92; PtO *Heref* 96-05. *7 Poyner Road, Ludlow SY8 1QT* T: (01584) 872470

LOVETT, Ian Arthur. b 43. NE Lon Poly BSc 74. Linc Th Coll 85. **d** 87 **p** 88. C Uppingham w Ayston and Wardley w Belton *Pet* 87-91; R Polebrook and Lutton w Hemington and Luddington 91-04; Asst to RD Corby 05-08; rtd 08; PtO *Pet* from 09. *38 Northbrook, Corby NN18 9AX* T: (01536) 747644 E: ian.lovett@tiscali.co.uk

LOVETT, Canon Ian James. b 49. JP 99. CertEd 72 BTh 89 MA 92. S'wark Ord Course 73. **d** 76 **p** 77. NSM Gravesend St Geo *Roch* 76-77; NSM Willesborough w Hinxhill *Cant* 77-83; NSM Landcross, Littleham, Monkleigh etc *Ex* 83-85; C Compton Gifford 85-86; TV Plymouth Em w Efford 86-92; TV Plymouth Em, St Paul Efford and St Aug 93-97; Chapl Aintree Hosps NHS Trust Liv 97-10; Bp's Adv for Hosp Chapl *Liv* 03-10; Hon Can Liv Cathl 08-10; TV Bideford, Northam, Westward Ho!, Appledore etc *Ex* from 11. *The Rectory, Fore Street, Northam, Bideford EX39 1AW* T: (01237) 470183

LOVITT, Gerald Elliott. b 25. St Mich Coll Llan 59. **d** 61 **p** 62. C Aberdare *Llan* 61-66; C Whitchurch 66-71; V Grangetown 71-76; V Rockfield and Llangattock w St Maughan's *Mon* 76-83; V Rockfield and St Maughen's w Llangattock etc 83-93; rtd 93; PtO *Llan* from 93; LtO *Mon* from 93. *104A Albany Road, Cardiff CF24 3RT* T: (029) 2041 1697

LOW, Prof Adrian Andrew. b 56. UEA BSc 77 Hull Univ MSc 78 Nottm Univ MA 10 CertEd 82 FBCS FIMA CEng CITP. EMMTC 08. **d** 10 **p** 11. NSM Alrewas *Lich* 10-14; NSM Wychnor 10-14; C Abbots Bromley, Blithfield, Colton, Colwich etc 14-15; P-in-c Costa del Sol W *Eur* from 15. *Calle Juan de Fuca 27, Beverly Hills, 29680, Estepona, Malaga, Spain* T: (0034) 952 808 605 E: a.a.low@staffs.ac.uk

LOW, Alastair Graham. b 43. Brunel Univ BSc 68 Reading Univ PhD 74. Ripon Coll Cuddesdon 90. **d** 92 **p** 93. C Brighton Gd Shep Preston *Chich* 92-96; TV Ifield 96-99; TV Horsham 99-08; Chapl Surrey and Sussex Healthcare NHS Trust 02-08; rtd 08; PtO *Ox* from 08. *3 Sheepway Court, Iffley, Oxford OX4 4JL* T: (01865) 777257 E: graham@glowpigs.freeserve.co.uk

LOW, Mrs Christine Mabel. b 48. Southlands Coll Lon CertEd 69 SS Mark & Jo Univ Coll Plymouth BEd 87. SWMTC. **d** 99 **p** 00. NSM Bideford, Northam, Westward Ho!, Appledore etc *Ex* 99-03; P-in-c Thornton in Lonsdale w Burton in Lonsdale *Bradf* 03-08; NSM Bingley All SS and Bingley H Trin 08-12; PtO *Sheff* from 12. *37 The Brideway, Rawmarsh, Rotherham S62 5PY* T: (01709) 208794 M: 07870-766634 E: chris.low@talktalk.net

LOW, Canon David Anthony. b 42. AKC 66. **d** 67 **p** 68. C Gillingham St Barn *Roch* 67-70; V 82-88; C Wallingford *Ox* 70-73; V Spencer's Wood 73-82; P-in-c Grazeley and Beech Hill 77-82; Chapl Medway Hosp Gillingham 86-88; V Hoo St Werburgh *Roch* 88-02; RD Strood 97-02; Hon Can Roch Cathl 01-02; rtd 02. *12 Stonecrop Close, St Mary's Island, Chatham ME4 3HA*

LOW, Canon David Michael. b 39. Cape Town Univ BA 60. Cuddesdon Coll 61. **d** 63 **p** 64. C Portsea St Cuth *Portsm* 63-65; S Africa 65-69; C Havant *Portsm* 69-72; V St Helens 72-88; V Sea View 81-88; V Sandown Ch Ch 88-95; V Lower Sandown St Jo 88-95; R Brading w Yaverland 95-01; Hon Can Portsm Cathl 00-01; rtd 01. *Copeland, Lane End Close, Bembridge PO35 5UF* T: (01983) 874306

LOW, Mrs Jennifer Anne. b 49. St Anne's Coll Ox MA 70 Nottm Univ PGCE 71. Trin Coll Bris 01. **d** 03 **p** 04. C Bris St Andr Hartcliffe 03-07; P-in-c Lawrence Weston and Avonmouth 07-14; Deanery Growth Officer Bris W 07-14; rtd 14. *Address temp unknown* E: revjennylow@gmail.com

LOW, Peter James. b 52. Nottm Univ BTh 89. Linc Th Coll 86. **d** 89 **p** 90. C Dartford H Trin *Roch* 89-92; C Plympton St Mary *Ex* 92-94; TR Devonport St Boniface and St Phil 94-08; V Heybridge w Langford *Chelmsf* from 08. *The Vicarage, 1A Crescent Road, Heybridge, Maldon CM9 4SJ* T: (01621) 841274 E: peter@lowuk.wanadoo.co.uk

LOW, Robbie. *See* LOW, William Roberson

LOW, Stafford. b 42. N Lon Poly BSc 65. Trin Coll Bris 82. **d** 85 **p** 86. C Yeovil *B & W* 85-88; C Glastonbury w Meare, W Pennard and Godney 88-92; R Berrow and Breane 92-00; R Wincanton 00-07; R Pen Selwood 00-07; Chapl Voc and Min 97-07; RD Bruton and Cary 03-06; rtd 07; P-in-c Le Gard

Eur from 13. *Les Acacias, route d'Uzès Prolongée, Le Moulinet, 30500 Saint-Ambroix, France* E: lowandco@aol.com

LOW, Terence John Gordon. b 37. Oak Hill Th Coll 75. **d** 77 **p** 78. C Kensal Rise St Martin *Lon* 77-79; C Longfleet *Sarum* 79-83; P-in-c Maiden Newton and Valleys 83-84; TV Melbury 84-88; TV Buckhurst Hill *Chelmsf* 88-92; R Gt Hallingbury and Lt Hallingbury 92-01; rtd 01; PtO *Sarum* from 02. *37 Vicarage Lane, Charminster, Dorchester DT2 9QF* T: (01305) 260180 E: terrylow@talktalk.net

LOW, William Roberson (Robbie). b 50. Pemb Coll Cam BA 73 MA 77. Westcott Ho Cam 76. **d** 79 **p** 80. C Poplar *Lon* 79-83; Chapl St Alb Abbey *St Alb* 83-88; V Bushey Heath 88-03; rtd 10. *3 Trewince Lane, Bodmin Hill, Lostwithiel PL22 0AJ* T: (01208) 871517 E: robbielow2@hotmail.com

LOWATER, Canon Jennifer Blanche. b 34. Eastbourne Tr Coll TCert 54. Sarum & Wells Th Coll 82. **dss** 85 **d** 87 **p** 94. Locks Heath *Portsm* 85-88; Hon C 87-88; NSM Southsea St Pet 88-94; NSM Hook w Warsash 94-01; Asst Dir of Ords 91-99; Hon Can Portsm Cathl 95-97; rtd 97. *Lower Gubbles, Hook Lane, Warsash, Southampton SO31 9HH* T: (01489) 572156 F: 572252 E: jenny.lowater@care4free.net

LOWDON, Christopher Ian. b 63. Plymouth Univ LLB 93 Barrister 94. Aston Tr Scheme 86 St Mich Coll Llan 04. **d** 06 **p** 07. C Chaddesden St Phil *Derby* 06-09; TV Buxton w Burbage and King Sterndale 09-13; P-in-c Maughold and S Ramsey *S & M* 13; V from 13. *Address temp unknown* M: 07871-087294

LOWE, Anthony Richard. b 45. York Univ BA 66. Qu Coll Birm 66. **d** 69 **p** 70. C Greasbrough *Sheff* 69-71; C Thrybergh 71-75; P-in-c Sheff St Mary w St Thomas w St Matthias 75; P-in-c Sheff St Barn and St Mary 75-78; V Shiregreen St Hilda 78-85; V Hoxne w Denham St Jo and Syleham *St E* 85-89; P-in-c Fressingfield w Weybread and Wingfield 86-89; R Hoxne w Denham, Syleham and Wingfield 90-05; rtd 06. *9 Alfred Road, Dover CT16 2AB* T: (01304) 214047

LOWE, Mrs Brenda June. b 53. Cranmer Hall Dur 75. **d** 88 **p** 94. Chapl to Families Trin Coll and Mortimer Ho Bris 86-91; NSM Clifton Ch Ch w Em *Bris* 88-91; Asst Chapl Southmead Health Services NHS Trust 86-91; NSM Marple All SS *Ches* from 91; PtO *Man* 91-97; Asst Chapl Wythenshawe Hosp Man 94-96; Chapl Stockport Acute Services NHS Trust 96-98; Sen Chapl Stockport NHS Trust from 98. *4 Greenway Road, Heald Green, Cheadle SK8 3NR* T: 0161-282 3850 *or* 419 5889 E: malowe@mail.com

LOWE, Christopher Alan. b 75. Imp Coll Lon MEng 97. Oak Hill Th Coll MTh 08. **d** 08 **p** 09. C Cambridge St Andr Less *Ely* 08-13; C Chesterton Gd Shep from 13. *3 Iceni Way, Cambridge CB4 2NZ* T: (01223) 354207 M: 07962-060786 E: chris.lowe@christchurchcambridge.org.uk

LOWE, Canon David Charles. b 43. Kelham Th Coll 62. **d** 67 **p** 68. C Wingerworth *Derby* 67-70; C Greenhill St Pet 70-73; TV Eckington 73-74; TV Eckington w Handley and Ridgeway 74-78; V Bury St Edmunds St Geo *St E* 78-86; V Leiston 86-98; RD Saxmundham 88-96; P-in-c Felixstowe St Jo 98-08; Hon Can St E Cathl 98-08; rtd 08; PtO *St E* from 08. *21 Firebrass Lane, Sutton Heath, Woodbridge IP12 3TS* T: (01394) 421722 E: david_lowechurch@lineone.net

LOWE, David Reginald. b 42. K Coll Lon BD 65 AKC 65. St Boniface Warminster 65. **d** 66 **p** 67. C Tupsley *Heref* 66-69; C Lewes St Anne *Chich* 69-73; C Heref H Trin 73-77; P-in-c Lyonshall w Titley 77-88; V Lyonshall w Titley, Almeley and Kinnersley 88-96; PtO 97-00; rtd 00. *28 Rodney Close, Longlevens, Gloucester GL2 9DG*

LOWE, Donald. b 33. Lich Th Coll 57. **d** 60 **p** 61. C Horwich H Trin *Man* 60; C Wythenshawe St Martin CD 60-62; C Bury St Paul 62-65; S Africa 65-69; V Gannow *Blackb* 70-73; R Virginia St Alb S Africa 73-81; V Colne H Trin *Blackb* 81-89; TV Melbury *Sarum* 89-94; RD Beaminster 93-94; rtd 94; PtO *Leeds* from 13. *28 High Bank, Threshfield, Skipton BD23 5BU* T: (01756) 752344

LOWE, Mrs Elaine Mary. b 55. **d** 98 **p** 99. OLM Bardsley *Man* from 98. *5 Danisher Lane, Bardsley, Oldham OL8 3HU* T: 0161-633 4535

LOWE, The Ven Frank McLean Rhodes. b 26. ACT 59. **d** 61 **p** 63. Australia 61-86 and from 87; Hon Can Gippsland 73-81; Adn Latrobe Valley 81-86; Adn Gippsland 81-86; P-in-c Kirkby in Ashfield St Thos *S'well* 86-87; C Mansfield Woodhouse 87; rtd 91. *Unit 2, 3 Berg Street, Morwell Vic 3840, Australia* T: (0061) (3) 5134 1338

LOWE, Mrs Janet Eleanor. b 56. Univ Coll Lon BSc 77. NTMTC 98. **d** 01 **p** 02. C Hendon St Paul Mill Hill *Lon* from 01. *12 Frobisher Road, London N8 0QS* T: (020) 8340 8764 E: janlowe@btinternet.com

LOWE, John Forrester. b 39. Nottm Univ BA 61. Lich Th Coll 61. **d** 64 **p** 65. C N Woolwich *Chelmsf* 64-70; V Marks Gate 70-74; V Moulsham St Jo 74-79; V N Woolwich w

Silvertown 79-82; V Birm St Pet 82-86; Gen Sec SOMA UK 86-91; V Heckmondwike *Wakef* 92-98; rtd 98; PtO *Heref* from 99. *37 Jubilee Close, Ledbury HR8 2XA* T: (01531) 631890

LOWE, Jonathan David. b 66. ACII 04. Trin Coll Bris 08. **d** 10 **p** 11. C Icknield Way Villages *Chelmsf* 10-13; P-in-c Steeple Bumpstead and Helions Bumpstead 13-15; V from 15; R Two Rivers from 15; AD Hinckford from 15. *The Vicarage, Church Street, Steeple Bumpstead, Haverhill CB9 7DG* T: (01440) 731687 M: 07771-850705 E: jonathan.lowe@worship.org.uk

LOWE, Keith Gregory. b 50. Sarum & Wells Th Coll 91. **d** 93 **p** 94. C Wallasey St Hilary *Ches* 93-94; C W Kirby St Bridget 94-98; V Sandbach Heath w Wheelock 98-01; V High Lane 01-04; Chapl Stockport NHS Trust 01-04; Asst Chapl Sheff Teaching Hosps NHS Trust 04-06; Chapl Sheff Teaching Hosps NHS Foundn Trust from 06. *169 Mortomley Lane, High Green, Sheffield S35 3HT* T: 0114-284 4076 E: keithglowe@mail.com

LOWE, Canon Michael Arthur. b 46. Lon Univ BD 67 Hull Univ MA 85. Cranmer Hall Dur. **d** 76 **p** 77. C Thorpe Edge *Bradf* 76-79; C N Ferriby *York* 79-84; TV 84-86; Dir Past Studies Trin Coll Bris 86-91; V Marple All SS *Ches* 91-00; RD Chadkirk 95-00; Dir of Miss and Unity 00-05; C Delamere 00-02; C Wilmslow 05-08; Hon Can Ches Cathl 00-08; rtd 08; Dioc Ecum Officer *Ches* from 09; Hon C Cheadle from 10. *4 Greenway Road, Heald Green, Cheadle SK8 3NR* T: 0161-282 3850 *or* 419 5889 E: malowe@mail.com

LOWE, Samuel. b 35. St D Coll Lamp. **d** 65 **p** 66. C Tenby w Gumfreston *St D* 65-67; C Lower Mitton *Worc* 67-69; C Halesowen 69-72; R Droitwich St Nic w St Pet 72; TR Droitwich 72-73; TV 73-77; P-in-c Claines St Geo 77-78; P-in-c Worc St Mary the Tything 77-78; P-in-c Worc St Geo w St Mary Magd 78-84; V 84-00; rtd 00. *57 Camp Hill Road, Worcester WR5 2HG* T: (01905) 357807

LOWE, Preb Stephen Arthur. b 49. Nottm Univ BSc 71. Cuddesdon Coll 71. **d** 74 **p** 75. C Mansfield St Mark *S'well* 74-77; Chapl Martyrs' Sch Papua New Guinea 77-78; P-in-c Nambaiyufa 79; V Kirkby Woodhouse *S'well* 80-86; V Beeston 86-99; TR Wenlock *Heref* 99-14; RD Condover 06-11; Preb Heref Cathl 10-14; rtd 14. *Faith Cottage, West Lambrook, South Petherton TA13 5HA* T: (01460) 249447

✠LOWE, The Rt Revd Stephen Richard. b 44. Lon Univ BSc 66. Ripon Hall Ox 68. **d** 68 **p** 69 **c** 99. C Gospel Lane St Mich *Birm* 68-72; C-in-c Woodgate Valley CD 72-75; V E Ham w Upton Park *Chelmsf* 75-76; TR E Ham w Upton Park and Forest Gate 76-88; Hon Can Chelmsf Cathl 85-88; Adn Sheff 88-99; Can Res Sheff Cathl 88-99; Suff Bp Hulme *Man* 99-09; rtd 09; PtO *St As* 09-11 and from 12; P-in-c Towyn 11-12; Hon Asst Bp Liv from 15. *2 Pen y Glyn, Bryn-y-Maen, Colwyn Bay LL28 5EW* T: (01492) 533510 M: 07801-505277 E: lowehulme@btinternet.com

LOWE, Mrs Valerie Anne. b 51. CBDTI. **d** 07 **p** 08. NSM Skipton Ch Ch w Carleton *Leeds* from 07. *126A Keighley Road, Skipton BD23 2QT* T: (01756) 790132

LOWELL, Ian Russell. b 53. AKC 75. St Aug Coll Cant 75. **d** 76 **p** 77. C Llwynderw *S & B* 76-79; C Swansea St Mary w H Trin and St Mark 79-81; Chapl Ox Hosps 81-83; TV Gt and Lt Coates w Bradley *Linc* 83-88; V Wellingborough St Mark *Pet* 88-02; V Northampton St Alb 02-13; Chapl Northants Ambulance Service 92-03; Officer for Major Emergencies 03-13; rtd 13. *24 Gwel Lewern, Eastern Green, Penzance TR18 3AX* T: (01736) 361924 E: ianlowell@btinternet.com

LOWEN, Mrs Anne Lois. b 60. DipCOT 82. ERMC 03. **d** 06 **p** 07. NSM Basle *Eur* from 06; Asst Chapl from 11. *Im Wygaertli 15, 4114 Hofstetten, Switzerland* T: (0041) (61) 731 1485 E: anne.lowen@bluewin.ch

LOWEN, David John. b 42. Sussex Univ BSc 74 Univ of Wales (Lamp) MA 84. Llan Dioc Tr Scheme 86. **d** 88 **p** 89. C Carmarthen St Pet *St D* 89-90; P-in-c Walwyn's Castle w Robeston W 90-92; R 92-08; rtd 08. *The Vicarage, Rock Lane, Llawhaden, Narberth SA67 8HL*

LOWEN, John Michael. b 47. Nottm Univ BTh 77. Linc Th Coll 73. **d** 77 **p** 78. C Beeston *S'well* 77-80; C Stratford-on-Avon w Bishopton *Cov* 80-82; V Monkseaton St Mary *Newc* 82-90; V Ponteland 90-95; Chapl HM Pris Leeds 95; P-in-c Sutton St Mary *Linc* 95-00; R Dunvegan Canada 00-05; rtd 07. *9 Alden Hubley Drive, RR1, Annapolis Royal NS B0S 1A0, Canada* T: (001) (902) 532 1981

LOWER, David John. b 77. Huddersfield Univ BA 99. Wycliffe Hall Ox 08. **d** 10 **p** 11. C Sileby, Cossington and Seagrave *Leic* 10-14; P-in-c Clacton St Paul *Chelmsf* from 14; C Holland-on-Sea from 14. *St Paul's Vicarage, 7 St Albans Road, Clacton-on-Sea CO15 6BA* T: (01255) 475900 M: 07709-451681 E: davidandnaomi@o2.co.uk

LOWLES, Martin John. b 48. Thames Poly BSc 72. Cranmer Hall Dur. **d** 78 **p** 79. C Leyton St Mary w St Edw *Chelmsf* 78-81; C Waltham Abbey 81-85; V E Ham St Paul 85-95;

TR N Huddersfield *Wakef* 95-06; V Birkenshaw w Hunsworth 06-13; rtd 13. *Shaw Fields Farm, Slaithwaite, Huddersfield HD7 5XA* E: martin.lowles@btinternet.com

LOWMAN, The Ven David Walter. b 48. K Coll Lon BD 73 AKC 73. St Aug Coll Cant 73. **d** 75 **p** 76. C Notting Hill *Lon* 75-78; C Kilburn St Aug w St Jo 78-81; Selection Sec and Voc Adv ACCM 81-86; TR Wickford and Runwell *Chelmsf* 86-93; Dioc Dir of Ords 93-01; C Chelmsf All SS 93-01; C Chelmsf Ascension 93-01; Hon Can Chelmsf Cathl 93-01; Adn Southend 01-13; Adn Chelmsf from 13. *The Archdeacon's Lodge, 136 Broomfield Road, Chelmsford CM1 1RN* T: (01245) 258257 F: 250845 E: a.chelmsford@chelmsford.anglican.org

LOWNDES, Harold John (Nobby). b 31. SAOMC 96. **d** 99 **p** 00. OLM Lamp *Ox* from 99. *98 Wolverton Road, Haversham, Milton Keynes MK19 7AB* T: (01908) 319939 E: hlowndes@vivao.net

LOWNDES, Canon Richard Owen Lewis. b 63. Univ of Wales (Ban) BD 86. Coll of Resurr Mirfield 87. **d** 89 **p** 90. C Milford Haven *St D* 89-91; C Roath St German *Llan* 91-94; Chapl Cardiff Royal Infirmary 91-94; V Tylorstown w Ynyshir *Llan* 94-96; Asst Chapl St Helier NHS Trust 96-98; Chapl Team Ldr W Middx Univ Hosp NHS Trust 98-03; Chapl Team Ldr Ealing Hosp NHS Trust 01-03; Chapl Team Ldr Univ Hosp Southn NHS Foundn Trust 03-11; Hon Can Win Cathl 11; Coaching and Lay Tr Officer *Llan* from 11. *28 Thornhill Road, Cardiff CF14 6PF*

LOWRIE, David Andrew. b 81. **d** 14 **p** 15. C Gt Crosby St Luke *Liv* from 14. *17 Moor Coppice, Liverpool L23 2XJ* E: lowzie@yahoo.co.uk

LOWRIE, Ronald Malcolm. b 48. Bath Spa Univ MA 07. Ripon Hall *Ox* 70. **d** 72 **p** 73. C Knowle *Birm* 72-75; C Bourton-on-the-Water w Clapton *Glouc* 75-79; R Broadwell, Evenlode, Oddington and Adlestrop 79-81; TV Trowbridge H Trin *Sarum* 81-88; P-in-c Westwood and Wingfield 88-90; R 90-13; P-in-c Bradford-on-Avon Ch Ch 03-10; Chapl Wilts and Swindon Healthcare NHS Trust 88-05; rtd 13. *9 Thestfield Drive, Staverton, Trowbridge BA14 8TT* T: (01225) 768310 E: rmlowrie@btinternet.com

LOWRY, Canon Stephen Patrick. b 58. QUB BSc 79 CertEd 80. CITC 82. **d** 85 **p** 86. C Coleraine *Conn* 85-88; I Greenisland 88-98; I Dromore Cathl 98-13; Dean Dromore 02-13; I Killaney w Carryduff from 13; Can Belf Cathl from 13. *The Rectory, 700 Saintfield Road, Carryduff, Belfast BT8 8BU* T: (028) 9081 2342 *or* 9081 3489 M: 07834-584932 E: stephenlowry@me.com

✠**LOWSON, The Rt Revd Christopher.** b 53. AKC 75 Heythrop Coll Lon MTh 96 Univ of Wales (Cardiff) LLM 03. St Aug Coll Cant 76 Pacific Sch of Relig Berkeley STM 78. **d** 77 **p** 78 **c** 11. C Richmond St Mary *S'wark* 77-79; C Richmond St Mary w St Matthias and St Jo 79-82; P-in-c Eltham H Trin 82-83; V 83-91; R Buriton *Portsm* 91-99; V Petersfield 91-99; RD 95-99; Adn Portsdown 99-06; Bp's Liaison Officer for Pris 00-03; Bp's Adv to Hosp Chapl 03-06; Dir Min Division Abps' Coun 06-11; PV Westmr Abbey 06-11; Bp Linc from 11. *The Old Palace, Lincoln LN2 1PU* T: (01522) 504090 E: bishop.lincoln@lincoln.anglican.org

LOWSON, Canon Geoffrey Addison. b 47. Bede Coll Dur BEd 70 PGCE 70. NEOC 95. **d** 98 **p** 99. NSM Sherburn in Elmet w Saxton *York* 98-04; Fieldworker (NE England) USPG 98-06; P-in-c Tynemouth Priory *Newc* 06-14; Hon Can Newc Cathl 11-14; rtd 14. *85 Keble Park South, Bishopthorpe, York YO23 2SU* E: geoffl@freenet.co.uk

LOWTHER, Ms Kareen Anne. b 59. Loughb Univ BSc 81. WMMTC 98. **d** 01 **p** 02. C Lich St Mich w St Mary and Wall 01-04; TV Bloxwich 04-13; TV Penkridge 13-15. *17 Leyfields, Lichfield WS13 7NJ* M: 07940-936033 E: kareenlowther@hotmail.com

LOWTHER, Peter Mark. b 56. GTCL 77. NTMTC BA 08. **d** 08 **p** 09. C Pimlico St Pet w Westmr Ch Ch *Lon* 08-15; P-in-c Aldeburgh w Hazlewood *St E* from 15; P-in-c Whinlands from 15. *The Vicarage, Church Walk, Aldeburgh IP15 5DU* M: 07801-258503 T: (01728) 452807 E: mark@thelowthers.com

LOWTON, Nicholas Gerard. b 53. St Jo Coll Ox BA 76 FRSA 94. Glouc Sch of Min 86. **d** 89 **p** 90. NSM Prestbury *Glouc* 89-94; V Clodock and Longtown w Craswall, Llanveynoe etc *Heref* from 10; RD Abbeydore from 14. *Forest Mill, Craswall, Hereford HR2 0PW* T: (01981) 510675

LOXHAM, Edward. b 49. BEd. **d** 04 **p** 05. OLM Birkdale St Pet *Liv* from 04. *34 Alma Road, Southport PR8 4AN* T: (01704) 568141

LOXHAM, Geoffrey Richard. b 40. Hull Univ BA 62. Cranmer Hall Dur. **d** 65 **p** 66. C Darwen St Barn *Blackb* 65-68; C Leyland St Andr 68-72; V Preston St Mark 72-79; V Edgeside *Man* 79-91; P-in-c Heapey and Withnell *Blackb* 91-92; V 92-99; V Grimsargh 99-10; rtd 10; PtO *Blackb* from 10. *63 Preston Road, Preston PR3 3AY* T: (01772) 780511

LOXLEY, Harold. b 43. NOC 79. **d** 82 **p** 83. NSM Sheff St Cecilia Parson Cross 82-87; C Gleadless 87-90; V Sheff St Cath Richmond Road 90-14; rtd 14. *508 Richmond Road, Sheffield S13 8NB* E: father.loxley@sky.com

LOXTON, John Sherwood. b 29. Bris Univ BSc 50 Birm Univ BA 53. Handsworth Coll Birm 50 Chich Th Coll 80. **d** 80 **p** 81. In Meth Ch 50-80; C Haywards Heath St Wilfrid *Chich* 80-82; TV 82-89; V Turners Hill 89-96; rtd 96; PtO *Chich* 96-10; *Win* from 13. *2 Blackbird Court, Andover SP10 5PA* T: (01264) 358179

LOXTON, Mrs Susan Ann. b 57. EAMTC 02. **d** 05 **p** 06. NSM Colchester, New Town and The Hythe *Chelmsf* 05-08; P-in-c Fressingfield, Mendham, Metfield, Weybread etc *St E* 08-13; C Hoxne w Denham, Syleham and Wingfield 08-13; R Sancroft from 13; RD Hoxne from 13; RD Hartismere from 14. *The Rectory, Doctors Lane, Stradbroke, Eye IP21 5HU* T: (01379) 388493 E: revloxton@gmail.com

LOZADA-UZURIAGA, Ernesto. b 61. Wycliffe Hall Ox. **d** 02 **p** 03. C Henley w Remenham *Ox* 02-06; P-in-c Milton Keynes 06-11; V from 11. *1 Cottage Common, Loughton, Milton Keynes MK5 8AE* T: (01908) 231260 E: leon-judah@hotmail.com

LUBBOCK, David John. b 34. S'wark Ord Course. **d** 87 **p** 88. NSM Tulse Hill H Trin and St Matthias *S'wark* 87-04; rtd 04; PtO *S'wark* from 04. *The Old Vicarage, 107 Upper Tulse Hill, London SW2 2RD* T: (020) 8674 6146 E: lubodj@dircon.co.uk

LUBKOWSKI, Richard Jan. b 51. Westmr Coll Ox BEd 75 Warw Univ MA 79. Cranmer Hall Dur 86. **d** 88 **p** 89. C Duston *Pet* 88-90; C Hellesdon *Nor* 90-91; PtO *Sheff* 91-94; In RC Ch 94-00; Chapl HM Pris Ashwell 00-10; P-in-c Cottesmore and Barrow w Ashwell and Burley *Pet* 10; V Cottesmore and Burley, Clipsham, Exton etc 11; rtd 11. *11 Bracken Way, Malvern WR14 1JH* M: 07502-487683 T: (01684) 562177 E: richardmain812@btinternet.com

LUCAS, Anthony Stanley. b 41. Man Univ BA 62 K Coll Lon MA 99. Qu Coll Birm 63. **d** 65 **p** 66. C N Hammersmith St Kath *Lon* 65-69; C W Wimbledon Ch Ch *S'wark* 69-74; C Caterham 74-78; P-in-c Stockwell St Mich 78-86; V 86-91; R S'wark St Geo the Martyr w St Jude 91-94; P-in-c S'wark St Alphege 92-94; R S'wark St Geo w St Alphege and St Jude 95-06; rtd 06; PtO *S'wark* from 10. *23 Clements Road, London SE16 4DW* T: (020) 7064 9088 E: tonyslucas@btinternet.com

LUCAS, Barbara Margaret. *See* KINGSTON, Barbara Margaret

LUCAS, The Ven Brian Humphrey. b 40. CB 93. FRSA 93 Univ of Wales (Lamp) BA 62. St Steph Ho Ox 62. **d** 64 **p** 65. C Llandaff w Capel Llanilltern *Llan* 64-67; C Neath w Llantwit 67-70; Chapl RAF 70-87; Asst Chapl-in-Chief RAF 87-91; Chapl-in-Chief RAF 91-95; QHC from 88; PtO *Llan* from 88; Can and Preb Linc Cathl 91-95; P-in-c Caythorpe 96-00; R 00-03. *Pen-y-Coed, 6 Arnhem Drive, Caythorpe, Grantham NG32 3DQ* T: (01400) 272085 E: brian@pen-y-coed.co.uk

LUCAS, Mrs Carolyn. b 61. Surrey Univ MSc 06. SEITE 06. **d** 09 **p** 10. NSM New Malden and Coombe *S'wark* from 09. *10 Presburg Road, New Malden KT3 5AH* E: clucas@blueyonder.co.uk

LUCAS, Glyn Andrew. b 63. Oak Hill Th Coll. **d** 09 **p** 10. C Cheadle *Ches* 09-12; R Stanton-by-Dale w Dale Abbey and Risley *Derby* from 12. *The Rectory, Stanhope Street, Stanton-by-Dale, Ilkeston DE7 4QA* T: 0115-932 4584 E: glynlucas@googlemail.com

LUCAS, Mrs Jane Eleanor. b 49. SWMTC 00. **d** 03 **p** 04. NSM N Creedy *Ex* 03-07; NSM Burrington, Chawleigh, Cheldon, Chulmleigh etc 07-08; P-in-c Ashwater, Halwill, Beaworthy, Clawton etc 08-15; R from 15. *The Rectory, Ashwater, Beaworthy EX21 5EZ* T/F: (01409) 211205 E: jane.e.lucas@btinternet.com

LUCAS, John Kenneth. b 32. LNSM course 92. **d** 95 **p** 96. NSM Deptford St Nic and St Luke *S'wark* 95-97; PtO 97-00 and from 03. *4 The Colonnade, Grove Street, London SE8 3AY* T: (020) 8691 3161 E: johnl1932@tiscali.co.uk

LUCAS, Julia Mary. *See* MYLES, Julia Mary

LUCAS, Lorna Yvonne. b 48. Bp Lonsdale Coll TCert 69. EMMTC 95. **d** 98 **p** 99. NSM Haxey and Owston *Linc* 98-00; NSM Scawby, Redbourne and Hibaldstow 00-04; NSM Lea Gp from 05. *4 Willingham Road, Lea, Gainsborough DN21 5EH* T: (01427) 811463 E: lorna.lucas@virgin.net

LUCAS, Mark Wesley. b 62. Man Univ BSc 83. Oak Hill Th Coll BA 94. **d** 94 **p** 95. C Harold Wood *Chelmsf* 94-98; Dir Oast Ho Retreat Cen *Chich* 98-00; Co-ord for Adult Educn (E Sussex Area) 98-00; V Polegate 00-10; R Barton Seagrave w Warkton *Pet* from 10. *The Rectory, St Botolph's Road, Kettering NN15 6SR* T: (01536) 628501 M: 07788-100757 E: rector@stbots.org.uk

LUCAS, Ms Pamela Turnbull. b 68. Westmr Coll Ox BA 91 Glas Univ MSW 98 Edin Univ MTh 99 UNISA MTh 05. TISEC 98. **d** 00 **p** 01. C Easington, Easington Colliery and S Hetton *Dur* 00-04; CSC 04-06; Asst Chapl Basingstoke and N Hants NHS Foundn Trust 06-09; Chapl St Mich Hosp Toronto Canada

from 09; Hon C Toronto St Monica 09-10; Hon C Toronto St Pet 11-14; Hon C Toronto St Leon from 14. *St Michael's Hospital, Spiritual Care, Room 3-018a, 30 Bond Street, Toronto ON M5B 1W8, Canada* T: (001) (647) 238 1499
E: lucas52727@gmail.com

LUCAS, Paul de Neufville. b 33. Ch Ch Ox BA 59 MA 59 Cam Univ MA 63. Cuddesdon Coll 57. **d** 59 **p** 60. C Westmr St Steph w St Jo *Lon* 59-63; Chapl Trin Hall Cam 63-69; V Greenside *Dur* 69-73; Chapl Shrewsbury Sch 73-77; V Batheaston w St Cath *B & W* 78-88; Preb Wells Cathl 87-88; Can Res and Prec Wells Cathl 88-99; rtd 99; PtO *Sarum* from 01. *11 Fisherton Island, Salisbury SP2 7TG* T/F: (01722) 325266 E: plucas@givemail.co.uk

LUCAS, Pauline. b 60. SEITE 10. **d** 13 **p** 14. C Seaford w Sutton *Chich* from 13. *2 Benenden Close, Seaford BN25 3PG* T: (01323) 891831

LUCAS, Peter Stanley. b 21. Sarum Th Coll 48. **d** 50 **p** 51. C Gillingham *Sarum* 50-53; Min Heald Green St Cath CD *Ches* 53-58; V Heald Green St Cath 58-62; V Egremont St Jo 62-65; Canada from 66. *404-1241 Fairfield Road, Victoria BC V8V 3B3, Canada* E: pmlucas@smartt.com

LUCAS, Preb Richard Charles. b 25. Trin Coll Cam BA 49 MA 57. Ridley Hall Cam. **d** 51 **p** 52. C Sevenoaks St Nic *Roch* 51-55; Cand Sec CPAS 55-61; Asst Sec 61-67; R St Helen Bishopsgate w St Martin Outwich *Lon* 61-80; P-in-c St Andr Undershaft w St Mary Axe 77-80; R St Helen Bishopsgate w St Andr Undershaft etc 80-98; Preb St Paul's Cathl 85-98; rtd 98. *16 Merrick Square, London SE1 4JB* T: (020) 7407 4164

LUCAS, Ronald James. b 38. St Aid Birkenhead 64. **d** 67 **p** 68. C Swindon Ch Ch *Bris* 67-71; C Knowle St Martin 71-74; V Swindon St Jo 74-77; TR Swindon St Jo and St Andr 77-81; V Wroughton 81-83; TV Liskeard w St Keyne, St Pinnock and Morval *Truro* 83-87; R St Ive w Quethiock 87-91; R St Ive and Pensilva w Quethiock 91-01; rtd 01; PtO *Truro* from 01. *Ough's Folly, Castle Lane, Liskeard PL14 3AH* T: (01579) 345611 E: mlcs2658@gmail.com

LUCAS, Ms Susan Catherine. b 59. City of Lon Poly BSc 90. STETS 97. **d** 00 **p** 01. C Streetly *Lich* 00-02; C Pheasey 02-04; Chapl HM Pris Albany 04-09; Chapl HM Pris Wandsworth 09-11; Chapl HM Pris High Down 11-15; Chapl HM YOI Aylesbury from 15. *HM YOI Aylesbury, Bierton Road, Aylesbury HP20 1EH* T: (01296) 444000 E: sue.lucas@hmps.gsi.gov.uk

LUCAS, Susan Joyce. b 61. Bedf Coll Lon BA 83 Univ of Wales (Swansea) PGCE 90 Birkbeck Coll Lon MPhil 95 PhD 07 Leeds Univ MA 08. **d** 08 **p** 09. NSM Anfield St Marg *Liv* 08-12; C Walton-on-the-Hill 12-14; P-in-c Gt Crosby St Faith and Waterloo Park St Mary from 14. *The Vicarage, 2 Milton Road, Waterloo, Liverpool L22 4RE* M: 07976-901389
E: sue.lucas@dsl.pipex.com

LUCAS, Mrs Vivienne Kathleen. b 44. Sarum & Wells Th Coll 84. **d** 87 **p** 94. Chapl Asst W Middx Univ Hosp Isleworth 87-92; Par Dn Whitton St Aug *Lon* 87-94; C Isleworth St Jo 94-97; P-in-c Isleworth St Mary 97-01; P-in-c Pirbright *Guildf* 01-06; rtd 06; PtO *York* from 07. *36 Harthill Avenue, Leconfield, Beverley HU17 7LN* T/F: (01964) 551519
E: v.lucas224@btinternet.com

LUCAS, William Wallace. b 29. Sarum Th Coll 56. **d** 59 **p** 60. C Stockton St Jo *Dur* 59-63; V Norton St Mich 63-81; R Broseley w Benthall *Heref* 81-93; P-in-c Jackfield and Linley w Willey and Barrow 81-93; rtd 93; PtO *Dur* 93-02. *1 Beckwith Mews, Seaham Street, Sunderland SR3 1HN*

LUCK, Benjamin Paul. b 53. BD. St Mich Coll Llan 80. **d** 83 **p** 84. C Blakenall Heath *Lich* 83-87; C Torpoint *Truro* 87-89; V Tuckingmill 89-96; C Knowle St Barn and H Cross Inns Court *Bris* 96-02; V Inns Court H Cross 02-05; C Washfield, Stoodleigh, Withleigh etc *Ex* 05-07; Chapl N Devon Hospice from 07. *North Devon Hospice, Deer Park, Rumsam Road, Barnstaple EX32 0HU* T: (01271) 344248

LUCKETT, Nicholas Frank. b 43. Ch Ch Ox BA 65 DipEd 66 MA 69. OLM course 95. **d** 98 **p** 99. Hd Master St Edw C of E Middle Sch Leek 94-00; OLM Ipstones w Berkhamsytch and Onecote w Bradnop *Lich* 98-02; NSM Siddington w Preston *Glouc* 02-07; NSM S Cerney w Cerney Wick, Siddington and Preston 07-08; rtd 08; PtO *Nor* from 09. *Shillingstone, Church Road, Beetley, Dereham NR20 4AB* T: (01362) 860738
E: nandeluckett@hotmail.com

LUCKETT, Virginia. b 67. **d** 11 **p** 12. NSM Isleworth All SS *Lon* from 11. *156 Windmill Road, Brentford TW8 9NQ* M: 07812-056564 E: virgina.luckett@allsaints-isleworth.org

LUCKING, Mrs Linda Pauline. b 61. St Jo Coll Nottm BA 10. **d** 10 **p** 11. C Caverswall and Weston Coyney w Dilhorne *Lich* from 10; Chapl N Staffs Combined Healthcare NHS Trust from 13. *5 Welsh Close, Lightwood Grange, Stoke-on-Trent ST3 4TQ* T: (01782) 321246 M: 07778-896584
E: linda.lucking.me@googlemail.com

LUCKMAN, David Thomas William. b 71. Oak Hill Th Coll BA 95 K Coll Lon PGCE 96. CITC 98. **d** 00 **p** 01. C Portadown St Mark *Arm* 00-02; C Enniskillen *Clogh* 02-03; I Galloon w Drummully and Sallaghy 03-04; N Ireland Field Worker ICM 05-08; C Ardmore w Craigavon *D & D* 10-11; C Donaghcloney w Waringstown 12-13; Crosslinks Ireland Team Ldr from 15. *53 Taughrane Lodge, Dollingstown, Craigavon BT66 7UH* T: (028) 3832 4936 M: 07742-513845
E: daveluckman@hotmail.com or dluckman@crosslinks.org

LUCKRAFT, Christopher John. b 50. K Coll Lon BD 80 AKC 80. Ripon Coll Cuddesdon 80. **d** 81 **p** 82. C Sherborne w Castleton and Lillington *Sarum* 81-84; Bermuda 84-87; Chapl RN 87-07; R Merrow *Guildf* from 07. *St John's Rectory, 232 Epsom Road, Guildford GU4 7AA* T: (01483) 452390
E: chrisluckraft@sky.com

LUCKRAFT, Ian Charles. b 47. Qu Coll Ox BA 70 BSc 81. Ripon Hall Ox 70. **d** 73 **p** 74. C Totteridge *St Alb* 73-77; C Broxbourne w Wormley 77-78; Lect Harrow Tech Coll 78-81; PtO *Ox* from 06. *4 Willes Close, Faringdon SN7 7DU* T: (01367) 240135

LUCY CLARE, Sister. *See* WALKER, Margaret

LUDKIN, Miss Linda Elaine. b 50. NEOC 02. **d** 05 **p** 06. NSM Dunnington *York* 05-10; NSM Ireland Wood *Leeds* from 10. *St Paul's Vicarage, Raynel Drive, Leeds LS16 6BS* T: 0113-230 1564 E: l.e.ludkin@btinternet.com

LUDLOW, Brian Peter. b 55. Lon Univ MB, BS 78 Birm Univ MMedSc 90 LRCP 90 MRCS 90 MRAeS 87 AFOM 90 MFOM 92 FFOM 01. WEMTC 01. **d** 04 **p** 05. NSM Winchcombe *Glouc* 04-06; NSM Cainscross w Selsley 06-09; NSM Rodborough from 09; NSM The Stanleys 12-13; NSM The Stanleys w Selsley from 13. *The Rectory, Walkley Hill, Stroud GL5 3TX* T: (01453) 752659 M: 07836-667530
E: revbrian@btopenworld.com

LUDLOW, Mrs Lesley Elizabeth. b 43. SEITE 97 OLM course 04. **d** 06 **p** 07. NSM Allington and Maidstone St Pet *Cant* 06-10; NSM Bearsted w Thurnham 11-13; rtd 13; PtO *Cant* from 13. *37 Tudor Avenue, Maidstone ME14 5HJ* T: (01622) 673536 - M: 07778-027031 E: lesley.ludlow@blueyonder.co.uk

LUDLOW, Lady Margaret Maude. b 56. WEMTC 98. **d** 01 **p** 02. C Winchcombe *Glouc* 01-05; P-in-c Rodborough from 05; P-in-c The Stanleys 12-13; V The Stanleys w Selsley from 13. *The Rectory, Walkley Hill, Stroud GL5 3TX* T: (01453) 752659
E: revpeggy@btopenworld.com

LUDLOW, Archdeacon of. *See* MAGOWAN, The Rt Revd Alistair James

LUDLOW, Suffragan Bishop of. *See* MAGOWAN, The Rt Revd Alistair James

LUFF, Canon Alan Harold Frank. b 28. Univ Coll Ox MA 54 ARCM 77 Hon FGCM 93. Westcott Ho Cam 54. **d** 56 **p** 57. C Stretford St Matt *Man* 56-59; C Swinton St Pet 59-61; Prec Man Cathl 61-68; V Dwygyfylchi *Ban* 68-79; Prec and Sacr Westmr Abbey 79-86; Prec 86-92; Can Res Birm Cathl 92-96; rtd 96; PtO *Llan* from 96. *12 Heol Ty'n-y-Cae, Cardiff CF14 6DJ* T/F: (029) 2061 6023

LUFF, Mrs Caroline Margaret Synia. b 44. St Hild Coll Dur BA 65 Bris Univ CertEd 66. SWMTC 87. **d** 90 **p** 94. NSM Teignmouth, Ideford w Luton, Ashcombe etc *Ex* 90-07; Chapl Trin Sch Teignmouth 97-11; C Diptford, N Huish, Harberton, Harbertonford etc *Ex* from 07; C Ermington and Ugborough from 11. *The Vicarage, Harberton, Totnes TQ9 7SA* T: (01803) 868445 E: pgandcmsl@btinternet.com

LUFF, John Edward Deweer. b 46. STETS 04. **d** 07 **p** 08. NSM Guernsey St Peter Port *Win* 07-14; Chapl States of Guernsey Bd of Health from 07; Chapl HM Pris Guernsey from 12; PtO *Win* from 15. *Le Courtil La Chapelle, Rohais de Haut, St Andrews, Guernsey GY6 8YX* T: (01481) 257694
E: johnluff@cwgsy.net

LUFF, Matthew John. b 70. Brighton Univ BA 95. Wycliffe Hall Ox 07. **d** 09 **p** 10. C Broadwater *Chich* 09-13; P-in-c Worthing H Trin w Ch Ch from 13. *5 Christchurch Road, Worthing BN11 1JH* T: (01903) 209222 M: 07875-190203
E: matthewluff39@gmail.com

LUFF, Preb Philip Garth. b 42. St Chad's Coll Dur BA 63. **d** 65 **p** 66. C Sidmouth St Nic *Ex* 65-69; C Plymstock 69-71; Asst Chapl Worksop Coll Notts 71-74; V Gainsborough St Jo *Linc* 74-80; V E Teignmouth *Ex* 80-89; P-in-c W Teignmouth 85-89; TR Teignmouth, Ideford w Luton, Ashcombe etc 90-07; RD Kenn 01-05; Preb Ex Cathl 02-07; Chapl S Devon Healthcare NHS Trust 85-07; Chapl Trin Sch Teignmouth 88-97; rtd 07; PtO *Ex* from 07. *The Vicarage, Harberton, Totnes TQ9 7SA* T: (01803) 868445 E: pgandcmsl@btinternet.com

LUGG, Donald Arthur. b 31. St Aid Birkenhead 56. **d** 59 **p** 60. C Folkestone H Trin w Ch Ch *Cant* 59-62; V Seasalter 62-66; Iran 67-73; V Cliftonville *Cant* 74-94; rtd 94; PtO *Cant* from 94. *Redcroft, Vulcan Close, Whitstable CT5 4LZ* T: (01227) 770434

LUKE, Anthony. b 58. Down Coll Cam BA 81 MA 85. Ridley Hall Cam 82. **d** 84 **p** 85. C Allestree *Derby* 84-87; C Oakham, Hambleton, Egleton, Braunston and Brooke *Pet* 87-88; V Allenton and Shelton Lock *Derby* 88-02; Dir Reader Tr 95-97; Warden of Readers *Derby* 97-00; R Aston on Trent, Elvaston, Weston on Trent etc from 02; RD Melbourne from 07. *The Rectory, Rectory Gardens, Aston-on-Trent, Derby DE72 2AZ* T: (01332) 792658 E: theramsrev@gmail.com

LUMB, David Leslie. b 28. Jes Coll Cam BA 52 MA 56. Oak Hill Th Coll 52. **d** 54 **p** 55. C Walcot *B & W* 54-58; C Lenton *S'well* 58-60; V Handforth *Ches* 60-71; V Plymouth St Jude *Ex* 71-87; V Southminster *Chelmsf* 87-93; rtd 93; PtO *Worc* from 93. *11 Gracey Court, Woodland Road, Broadclyst, Exeter EX5 3GA*

LUMBY, Jonathan Bertram. b 39. Em Coll Cam BA 62 MA 66 Lon Univ PGCE 66. Ripon Hall Ox 62. **d** 64 **p** 65. C Moseley St Mary *Birm* 64-65; Asst Master Enfield Gr Sch 66-67; C Hall Green Ascension *Birm* 67-70; V Melling *Liv* 70-81; P-in-c Milverton w Halse and Fitzhead *B & W* 81-82; R 82-86; P-in-c Gisburn and Dioc Rural Adv *Bradf* 90-93; P-in-c Easton w Colton and Marlingford *Nor* 95-98; Dioc Missr 95-98; R Eccleston and Pulford *Ches* 98-05; rtd 05; Hon C Redmarley D'Abitot, Bromesberrow, Pauntley etc *Glouc* 05-08. *Valentines Cottage, Hollybush, Ledbury HR8 1ET* T: (01531) 650641

LUMBY, Simon. b 70. Coll of Resurr Mirfield 99. **d** 02 **p** 03. C Worksop Priory *S'well* 02-06; P-in-c Leic St Aid 06-09; V from 09. *St Aidan's Vicarage, St Oswald's Road, Leicester LE3 6RJ* T: 0116-287 2342 M: 07983-609290 E: fathersimonlumby@gmail.com

LUMBY, Simon John. b 56. Hull Univ BSc 80 Open Univ MTh 01. St Jo Coll Nottm 99. **d** 01 **p** 04. C Wirksworth *Derby* 01-06; R Clifton Campville w Edingale and Harlaston *Lich* 06-10; P-in-c Thorpe Constantine 06-10; P-in-c Elford 06-10; Chapl OHP 10-13; P-in-c Killarney w Aghadoe and Muckross *L & K* from 14. *The Rectory, Rookery Road, Ballycasheen, Killarney, Co Kerry, Republic of Ireland* T: (00353) (64) 663 1832 E: wl21011@outlook.com

LUMGAIR, Michael Hugh Crawford. b 43. Lon Univ BD 71. Oak Hill Th Coll 66. **d** 71 **p** 72. C Chorleywood Ch Ch *St Alb* 71-74; C Prestonville St Luke *Chich* 74-75; C Attenborough *S'well* 75-80; R Tollerton 80-91; V Bexleyheath St Pet *Roch* 91-06; rtd 06; PtO *Roch* from 06. *11 Bromley College, London Road, Bromley BR1 1PE* T: (020) 8290 2011 E: michael@lumgair.plus.com

LUMLEY (née HATFIELD), Rebecca Alison. b 76. St Andr Univ MTheol 99. Cranmer Hall Dur 02. **d** 04 **p** 05. C Haughton le Skerne *Dur* 04-09; V Windy Nook St Alb 09-11; V Beverley St Mary *York* from 11; Chapl Bp Burton Coll York 11-13. *St Mary's Vicarage, 15 Molescroft Road, Beverley HU17 7DX* T: (01482) 881437 M: 07930-631936 E: becky@lumleyfamily.karoo.co.uk

LUMMIS, Elizabeth Howieson. See McNAB, Elizabeth Howieson

LUMSDON, Keith. b 45. Linc Th Coll 68. **d** 71 **p** 72. C S Westoe *Dur* 71-74; C Jarrow St Paul 74-77; TV Jarrow 77-88; V Ferryhill 88-07; P-in-c Cornforth 03-07; V Cornforth and Ferryhill 07-15; AD Sedgefield 05-15; rtd 15. *32 Witton Road, Ferryhill DL17 8QE*

LUND, David Peter. b 46. NOC 88. **d** 91 **p** 92. C Maghull *Liv* 91-94; V Hindley All SS 94-01; V Teddington St Mark and Hampton Wick *Lon* 01-14; rtd 14. *Address temp unknown* M: 07813-493761

LUND, John Edward. b 48. Cranmer Hall Dur 78. **d** 80 **p** 81. C Peterlee *Dur* 80-83; C Bishopton w Gt Stainton 83-85; C Redmarshall 83-85; C Grindon and Stillington 83-85; V Hart w Elwick Hall 85-09; Hon Chapl Miss to Seamen 85-99; Chapl Hartlepool and E Durham NHS Trust 94-99; Chapl N Tees and Hartlepool NHS Trust 99-04; rtd 09. *16 Chelker Close, Hartlepool TS26 0QW* E: lund@telco4u.net

LUND (née BEST), Karen Belinda. b 62. Qu Coll Birm 92. **d** 94 **p** 95. C Southall Green St Jo *Lon* 94-97; C Northolt Park St Barn 97-00; V Gillingham St Barn *Roch* 00-08; P-in-c Roxwell *Chelmsf* 08-14; Lay Discipleship Adv (Bradwell Area) 08-14; TV Turton Moorland *Man* from 14. *2 Higher Dunscar, Egerton, Bolton BL7 9TE* T: (01204) 304283 E: revkbest@aol.com

✠**LUNGA, The Rt Revd Cleophus.** b 66. UNISA BTh 00. Bp Gaul Th Coll Harare 91. **d** 93 **p** 94 **c** 09. Zimbabwe 94-03 and from 09; TV Coventry Caludon *Cov* 03-09; Bp Matabeleland from 09. *PO Box 2422, Bulawayo, Zimbabwe* T: (00263) (9) 61370 F: 68353

LUNN, Preb Brooke Kingsmill. b 32. TCD BA 62 MA 66. Chich Th Coll 62. **d** 64 **p** 65. C Northolt Park St Barn *Lon* 64-66; C N St Pancras All Hallows 66-68; P-in-c Hornsey St Luke 68-79; V Stroud Green H Trin 79-02; AD W Haringey 90-95; Preb St Paul's Cathl 96-02; rtd 02; PtO *Lon* from 02. *The Charterhouse, Charterhouse Square, London EC1M 6AN* T: (020) 7251 5143

LUNN, David. b 47. Bris Univ BSc 69 St Jo Coll Dur BA 73. Cranmer Hall Dur. **d** 74 **p** 75. C Aigburth *Liv* 74-77; C Slough *Ox* 77-81; P-in-c Haversham w Lt Linford 81-84; R Haversham w Lt Linford, Tyringham w Filgrave 84-93; RD Newport 86-92; R Walton Milton Keynes 93-12; Dioc Ecum Officer 00-10; rtd 12; Hon C Billing *Pet* from 13. *38 Riverwell, Northampton NN3 5EG* T: (01604) 784241 E: david@thelunns.vispa.com

✠**LUNN, The Rt Revd David Ramsay.** b 30. K Coll Cam BA 53 MA 57. Cuddesdon Coll 53. **d** 55 **p** 56 **c** 80. C Sugley *Newc* 55-59; C N Gosforth 59-63; Chapl Linc Th Coll 63-66; Sub-Warden 66-70; V Cullercoats St Geo *Newc* 71-72; TR 72-80; RD Tynemouth 75-80; Bp Sheff 80-97; rtd 97; PtO *York* 97-99; Hon Asst Bp York 99-14. *Rivendell, 28 Southfield Road, Wetwang, Driffield YO25 9XX* T: (01377) 236657

LUNN, Edward James. b 85. St Jo Coll Dur BA 12. Cranmer Hall Dur 09. **d** 12 **p** 13. C Acomb St Steph and St Aid *York* from 12. *36 Fellbrook Avenue, York YO26 5PT* M: 07834-532768 E: ned_lunn@msn.com or nedlunn@gmail.com

LUNN, Graham Edward. b 86. Wycliffe Hall Ox BA 08. St Steph Ho Ox 09. **d** 11 **p** 12. C Reading St Mark and All SS *Ox* 11-15; Shrine of Our Lady of Walsingham from 15. *The Shrine of Our Lady of Walsingham, The College, Knight Street, Walsingham NR22 6EF* T: (01328) 820909 M: 07708-887898 E: shrine.pr@olw-shrine.org.uk or frgrahamlunn@gmail.com

LUNN, Leonard Arthur. b 42. Culham Coll of Educn CertEd 64. Trin Coll Bris 69. **d** 72 **p** 73. C Walthamstow St Mary w St Steph *Chelmsf* 72-75; V Collier Row St Jas 75-85; V Collier Row St Jas and Havering-atte-Bower 86-87; Sen Chapl St Chris Hospice Sydenham *S'wark* 87-04; Hon C Redlynch and Morgan's Vale *Sarum* 04-06; Hon C Forest and Avon 06-09. *Summerhayes, Whiteshoot, Redlynch, Salisbury SP5 2PR* T: (01725) 510322 E: len.lunn@btopenworld.com

LUNN, Mrs Lucy Ann (Lucie). b 71. Lanc Univ BA 93. Cranmer Hall Dur 11. **d** 13 **p** 14. C Binsey *Carl* from 13. *The Vicarage, Ireby, Wigton CA7 1EX* T: (016973) 71265 M: 07739-180241 E: lucielunn299@btinternet.com or assistantcurate@binsey.org.uk

LUNN, Maureen Susan. b 48. Middx Univ BSc 00. NTMTC BA 07. **d** 07. NSM Enfield St Jas *Lon* 07-10; NSM Enfield Chase St Mary from 10. *62 First Avenue, Enfield EN1 1BN* T: (020) 8366 0592 E: deacon@saintmarymagdalene.org.uk

LUNN, Mrs Rosemary Christine. b 51. Bris Univ BA 72. Trin Coll Bris 98. **d** 00 **p** 01. NSM Stoke Bishop *Bris* 00-01; C Chippenham St Pet 01-04; Hon Min Can Bris Cathl 02-04; P-in-c Wraxall *B & W* 04-09; R 09-12; P-in-c Evercreech w Chesterblade and Milton Clevedon from 12; C Bruton and Distr from 12. *The Vicarage, Church Lane, Evercreech, Shepton Mallet BA4 6HU* T: (01749) 830322 M: 07786-118762 E: rosemarylunn@btinternet.com

LUNN, Sarah Anne. b 63. Lanc Univ BMus 84 Man Metrop Univ MA 93. Cranmer Hall Dur 00. **d** 02 **p** 03. C Kirkby Lonsdale *Carl* 02-07; P-in-c Long Marton w Dufton and w Milburn 07-08; TV Heart of Eden 08-10; TR from 10; P-in-c Kirkby Thore w Temple Sowerby and Newbiggin from 11; Dioc Rural Officer from 09. *The Rectory, Long Marton, Appleby-in-Westmorland CA16 6BN* T: (017683) 61269 E: sarahlunn@care4free.net

LUNNON, Canon Robert Reginald. b 31. K Coll Lon BD 55 AKC 55 Kent Univ MA 99. St Boniface Warminster 55. **d** 56 **p** 57. C Maidstone St Mich *Cant* 56-58; C Deal St Leon 58-62; V Sturry 63-68; V Norbury St Steph 68-77; V Orpington All SS *Roch* 77-96; RD Orpington 79-95; Hon Can Roch Cathl 96; rtd 96; PtO *Cant* from 96. *10 King Edward Road, Deal CT14 6QL* T: (01304) 364898

LUNT, Colin Peter. b 54. York Univ BA 75 Bris Univ MA 02. Trin Coll Bris 95. **d** 97 **p** 98. C Westbury-on-Trym H Trin *Bris* 97-00; V Coalpit Heath from 00. *The Vicarage, Beesmoor Road, Coalpit Heath, Bristol BS36 2RP* T/F: (01454) 775129 E: colin@lunt.co.uk

LUNT, Margaret Joan. b 44. Leeds Univ MB, ChB 68. Cranmer Hall Dur 91. **d** 94 **p** 95. C Stanford-le-Hope w Mucking *Chelmsf* 94-97; C Rayleigh 97-00; TV 00-03; TV Rivers Team *Sheff* 03-10; rtd 10; Hon C Todwick *Sheff* 10-12. *1 Rodwell Close, Treeton, Rotherham S60 5UF* T: 0114-269 4479 E: margaretlunt@yahoo.co.uk

LURIE, Miss Gillian Ruth. b 42. LRAM 62 GNSM 63. Gilmore Ho 68. **dss** 74 **d** 87 **p** 94. Camberwell St Phil and St Mark *S'wark* 74-76; Haddenham *Ely* 76-79; Dioc Lay Min Adv *Pet* 79-86; Longthorpe 79-81; Pet H Spirit Bretton 81-86; Bramley *Ripon* 86-93; C 87-88; Team Dn 88-93; P-in-c Methley w Mickletown 93-98; R 98-01; rtd 02; PtO *Cant* from 02. *42A Cuthbert Road, Westgate-on-Sea CT8 8NR* T/F: (01843) 831698 E: gillandjean@hotmail.com

LURY, Anthony Patrick. b 49. K Coll Lon BD 71 AKC 71. St Aug Coll Cant 71. **d** 72 **p** 73. C Richmond St Mary *S'wark* 72-76;

P-in-c Streatham Hill St Marg 76-81; V Salfords 81-90; V Emscote *Cov* 90-01; P-in-c Ascot Heath *Ox* 01-06; NSM The Churn 06-10; PtO *St E* from 11. *8 St Anthonys Crescent, Ipswich IP4 4SY* T: (01473) 273395 E: anthonylury@gmail.com

LUSCOMBE, John Nickels. b 45. Birm Univ BA 99. AKC 68. **d** 69 **p** 70. C Stoke Newington St Faith, St Matthias and All SS *Lon* 69-74; V Tottenham St Phil 74-81; Zimbabwe 82-86; V Queensbury All SS *Lon* 86-99; V Estover *Ex* 99-01; Dioc Ecum Officer 99-01; V Norton *St Alb* 01-10; RD Hitchin 02-07; rtd 10. *8 Manor Way, Totnes TQ9 5HP* T: (01803) 864514 E: jnluscombe@btinternet.com

✠**LUSCOMBE, The Rt Revd Lawrence Edward (Ted).** b 24. Dundee Univ LLD 87 MPhil 91 PhD 93 ACA 52 FSA 80 FRSA 87. K Coll Lon 63. **d** 63 **p** 64 **c** 75. C Glas St Marg 63-66; R Paisley St Barn 66-71; Provost St Paul's Cathl Dundee 71-75; R Dundee St Paul 71-75; Bp Bre 75-90; Primus 90; rtd 90; PtO *Bre* 90-08; LtO *St And* from 05; *Bre* from 08; *Glas* from 08. *Woodville, Kirkton of Tealing, Dundee DD4 0RD* T: (01382) 380331

LUSITANIAN CHURCH, Bishop of the. See SOARES, The Rt Revd Fernando da Luz

LUSTY, Tom Peter. b 71. Glas Univ BD 94 Leeds Univ MA 06. Coll of Resurr Mirfield 97. **d** 99 **p** 00. C Billingshurst *Chich* 99-02; Asst Chapl Leeds Teaching Hosps NHS Trust 02-06; Chapl Wheatfields Hospice 06-11; P-in-c Far Headingley St Chad *Ripon* 11-14. *St Chad's Vicarage, Otley Road, Leeds LS16 5JT* T: 0113-275 2224

LUTHER, Canon Richard Grenville Litton. b 42. Lon Univ BD 64. Tyndale Hall Bris 66. **d** 68 **p** 69. C Preston St Mary *Blackb* 68-70; C Bishopsworth *Bris* 70-71; C Radipole *Sarum* 72-76; TV Radipole and Melcombe Regis 77-90; TR Hampreston 90-07; Can and Preb Sarum Cathl 00-07; rtd 07. *49 North Street, Charminster, Dorchester DT2 9RN* T: (01305) 251547 E: dickluther@talktalk.net

LYALL, Canon Graham. b 37. Univ of Wales (Lamp) BA 61. Qu Coll Birm 61. **d** 63 **p** 64. C Middlesbrough Ascension *York* 63-67; C Kidderminster St Mary *Worc* 67-72; V Dudley St Aug Holly Hall 72-79; P-in-c Barbourne 79-81; V 81-93; RD Worc E 83-89; TR Malvern Link w Cowleigh 93-04; Hon Can Worc Cathl 85-04; rtd 04; PtO *Worc* from 04. *44 Victoria Street, Worcester WR3 7BD* T: (01905) 20511 E: lambourne43@hotmail.co.uk

LYDDON, David Andrew. b 47. Lon Univ BDS 70 LDS 70. SWMTC 90. **d** 93 **p** 94. NSM Tiverton St Pet *Ex* 93-95; NSM Tiverton St Pet w Chevithorne 95-96; NSM W Exe 96-01; NSM Tiverton St Geo and St Paul from 01. *Hightrees, 19 Patches Road, Tiverton EX16 5AH* T: (01884) 257250 E: dlyddon597@aol.uk

LYDON, Mrs Barbara. b 34. Gilmore Ho 64. **dss** 72 **d** 87 **p** 94. Rastrick St Matt *Wakef* 72-85; Upper Hopton 85-87; Par Dn 87; Dn-in-c Kellington w Whitley 87-94; P-in-c 94-95; rtd 95; PtO *Leeds* from 95. *17 Garlick Street, Brighouse HD6 3PW* T: (01484) 722704

LYES-WILSDON, Canon Patricia Mary. b 45. Open Univ BA 87 ALA 65. Glouc Sch of Min 84 Qu Coll Birm 86. **d** 87 **p** 94. C Thornbury *Glouc* 87-94; P-in-c Cromhall w Tortworth and Tytherington 94-03; Asst Dioc Dir of Ords 90-98; Dioc Voc Officer 94-01; RD Hawkesbury 98-04; R Cromhall, Tortworth, Tytherington, Falfield etc 02-09; Dioc Adv for Women's Min 01-09; Hon Can Glouc Cathl 02-09; rtd 09. *24 Maple Avenue, Thornbury, Bristol BS35 2JW* E: revd.pat@virgin.net

LYMBERY, Peter. b 32. JP 73. SAOMC 95. **d** 98 **p** 99. OLM Stewkley w Soulbury and Drayton Parslow *Ox* 98-05; Hon C 05-09; Hon C Stewkley w Soulbury 09-12; Hon C Cottesloe from 12; Dep Chapl Guild of Servants of the Sanctuary from 00; P Assoc Shrine of Our Lady of Walsingham from 00. *19 White House Court, Hockliffe Street, Leighton Buzzard LU7 1FD* T: (01525) 371235

LYNAS, Mrs Angela. b 56. ERMC. **d** 14 **p** 15. NSM Cheshunt *St Alb* from 14. *8 Parkwood Close, Broxbourne EN10 7PF*

LYNAS, Preb Stephen Brian. b 52. MBE 00. St Jo Coll Nottm BTh 77. **d** 78 **p** 79. C Penn *Lich* 78-81; Relig Progr Org BBC Radio Stoke-on-Trent 81-84; C Hanley H Ev *Lich* 81-82; C Edensor 82-84; Relig Progr Producer BBC Bris 85-88; Relig Progr Sen Producer BBC S & W England 88-91; Hd Relig Progr TV South 91-92; Community (and Relig) Affairs Ed Westcountry TV 92-96; Abps' Officer for Millennium 96-01; Dioc Resources Adv *B & W* 01-07; Sen Chapl and Adv to Bps B & W and Taunton from 07; Preb Wells Cathl from 07. *Old Honeygar Cottage, Honeygar Lane, Westhay, Glastonbury BA6 9TS* T: (01749) 672341 E: chaplain@bathwells.anglican.org

LYNCH, Canon Eithne Elizabeth Mary. b 45. TCD BTh. CITC 94. **d** 97 **p** 98. C Douglas Union w Frankfield *C, C & R* 97-01; I Kilmoe Union 01-10; I Mallow Union from 10;

Min Can Cork Cathl 98-07; Bp's Dom Chapl from 99; Can Cork and Ross Cathls from 09. *The Rectory, Lower Bearforest, Mallow, Co Cork, Republic of Ireland* T: (00353) (22) 21473 M: 86-253 5002 E: eithnel@eircom.net *or* mallowunion@eircom.net

LYNCH, James. b 44. EAMTC 93. **d** 96 **p** 97. NSM High Oak *Nor* 96-97; NSM High Oak, Hingham and Scoulton w Wood Rising 97-99; Asst Chapl Norfolk Mental Health Care NHS Trust 99-03; P-in-c Nor St Steph 99-03; NSM Blanchland w Hunstanworth and Edmundbyers etc *Newc* 03-13; NSM Slaley 03-13; NSM Healey 03-13; NSM Whittonstall 03-13; rtd 13. *Beechenlea, 61 Church Lane, Wicklewood, Wymondham NR18 9QH* T: (01953) 798417 E: justjimlynch@hotmail.com

LYNCH, Ms Sally Margaret. b 60. St Jo Coll Dur BA 81 UEA MA 94 FRSA 96. Westcott Ho Cam 04. **d** 08 **p** 09. C Romford St Edw *Chelmsf* 08-11; V Maidenhead St Luke *Ox* from 11. *St Luke's Vicarage, 26 Norfolk Road, Maidenhead SL6 7AX* T: (01628) 783033 E: sally514@btinternet.com

LYNCH, Sheila. b 56. **d** 09 **p** 10. OLM Rossendale Middle Valley *Man* 09-14. *70 Fairfield Avenue, Rossendale BB4 9TH* T: (01706) 217438 M: 07711-992004 E: sheila.lynch@btinternet.com

LYNCH-WATSON, Graham Leslie. b 30. AKC 55. **d** 56 **p** 57. C New Eltham All SS *S'wark* 56-60; C W Brompton St Mary *Lon* 60-62; V Camberwell St Bart *S'wark* 62-66; V Purley St Barn 67-77; C Caversham *Ox* 77-81; C Caversham St Pet and Mapledurham etc 81-85; P-in-c Warwick St Paul *Cov* 85-86; V 86-92; rtd 92; PtO *Ox* 96-00. *11 Crouch Street, Banbury OX16 9PP* T: (01295) 263172

LYNES, Ann Louise. b 79. Moray Ho Edin BSc 01. Ripon Coll Cuddesdon BA 12. **d** 13 **p** 14. C Barnes *S'wark* from 13. *52 Boileau Road, London SW13 9BL* E: annlynes@gmail.com

LYNESS, Nicholas Jonathan. b 55. Oak Hill Th Coll BA 97. **d** 97. C Reading Greyfriars *Ox* 97-98; PtO *St Alb* from 13. *2 Flint Cottages, Mill End, Sandon, Buntingford SG9 0RN* T: (01763) 288172 M: 07802-730485

LYNETT, Canon Anthony Martin. b 54. K Coll Lon BD 75 AKC 75 Darw Coll Cam PGCE 76. Sarum & Wells Th Coll 77. **d** 78 **p** 79. C Swindon Ch Ch *Bris* 78-81; C Leckhampton SS Phil and Jas w Cheltenham St Jas *Glouc* 81-83; Asst Chapl HM Pris Glouc 83-88; Chapl 91-98; V Coney Hill *Glouc* 83-88; Chapl HM YOI Deerbolt 88-91; P-in-c Glouc St Mark 91-99; P-in-c Glouc St Mary de Crypt w St Jo, Ch Ch etc 98-99; Chapl HM Pris Wellingborough 99-01; V Wellingborough All SS *Pet* from 01; P-in-c Wellingborough All Hallows from 10; RD Wellingborough 07-15; Can Pet Cathl from 12. *The Vicarage, 154 Midland Road, Wellingborough NN8 1NF* T: (01933) 227101 E: tartleknock@btinternet.com

LYNN, Anthony Hilton. b 44. Golds Coll Lon TCert 66 Open Univ BA 80. SAOMC 95. **d** 98 **p** 99. NSM Stanford in the Vale w Goosey and Hatford *Ox* 98-00; NSM Cherbury w Gainfield 00-03; TV Hermitage 03-13; rtd 13; PtO *Ox* from 13. *36 High Street, Stanford in the Vale, Faringdon SN7 8NQ* E: revtonylynn@btinternet.com

LYNN, Mrs Antonia Jane. b 59. Girton Coll Cam BA 80 MA 84. St Steph Ho Ox 82. **dss** 84 **d** 87. Portsm Cathl 84-87; Dn-in-c Camberwell St Mich w All So w Em *S'wark* 87-91; Par Dn Newington St Mary 87-91; PtO 91-94; Chapl Horton Hosp Epsom 91-94; Gen Sec Guild of Health from 94; Hon Par Dn Ewell *Guildf* 94-99. *7 Kingsmead Close, West Ewell, Epsom KT19 9RD* T: (020) 8786 8983

LYNN, Frank Trevor. b 36. Keble Coll Ox BA 61 MA 63. St Steph Ho Ox 61. **d** 63 **p** 64. C W Derby St Mary *Liv* 63-65; C Chorley *Ches* 65-68; V Altrincham St Jo 68-72; Chapl RN 72-88; Hon C Walworth St Jo *S'wark* 88-90; C Cheam 90-96; rtd 99. *7 Kingsmead Close, West Ewell, Epsom KT19 9RD* T: (020) 8786 8983

LYNN, Jeffrey. b 39. Moore Th Coll Sydney 67 EMMTC 76. **d** 79 **p** 80. C Littleover *Derby* 79-80; Hon C Allestree 80-85; Chapl HM Pris Man 85-86; Kirkham 86-93; Wakef 93-95; Sudbury and Foston Hall 95-96; rtd 96; PtO *Blackb* 98-11. *48 South Park, Lytham St Annes FY8 4QQ* T: (01253) 730490

LYNN, Peter Anthony. b 38. Keele Univ BA 62 St Jo Coll Cam BA 64 MA 68 PhD 72. Westcott Ho Cam 67. **d** 68 **p** 69. C Soham *Ely* 68-72; Min Can St Paul's Cathl 72-78; PtO *St Alb* 78-86; Min Can and Sacr St Paul's Cathl 86-88; C Westmr St Matt 89-91; V Glynde, W Firle and Beddingham *Chich* 91-03; rtd 03. *119 Stanford Avenue, Brighton BN1 6FA* T: (01273) 553361

LYNN, Trevor. See LYNN, Frank Trevor

LYNN, Archdeacon of. See ASHE, The Ven Francis John

LYNN, Suffragan Bishop of. See MEYRICK, The Rt Revd Cyril Jonathan

LYON, Adrian David. b 55. Coll of Resurr Mirfield 84. **d** 87 **p** 88. C Crewe St Andr *Ches* 87-90; C Altrincham St Geo 90-91; TV Accrington *Blackb* 91-00; TR Accrington Ch the King 00-10;

P-in-c St Annes St Anne 10-11; V from 11. *St Anne's Vicarage, 4 Oxford Road, Lytham St Annes FY8 2EA* T: (01253) 722725 E: david.lyon1955@googlemail.com

LYON, Christopher David. b 55. Strathclyde Univ LLB 75 Edin Univ BD 81. Edin Th Coll 78. **d** 81 **p** 82. C Dumfries *Glas* 81-84; P-in-c Alexandria 84-88; R Greenock 88-00; R Ayr, Girvan and Maybole 00-02; Chapl Luxembourg *Eur* from 02. *89 rue de Mühlenbach, L-2168 Luxembourg* T/F: (00352) 439593 E: chris.lyon@escc.lu

LYON, Dennis. b 36. Wycliffe Hall Ox 64. **d** 67 **p** 68. C Woodthorpe *S'well* 67-70; Warden Walton Cen 70-72; V W Derby Gd Shep *Liv* 72-81; V Billinge 81-00; AD Wigan W 89-00; rtd 00; PtO *Liv* from 01. *10 Arniam Road, Rainford, St Helens WA11 8BU* T: (01744) 885623

LYON, Miss Jane Madeline. b 50. Derby Univ MA 05. Ripon Coll Cuddesdon 07. **d** 09 **p** 10. NSM Derby St Andr w St Osmund 09-12; Asst Chapl Derby Hosps NHS Foundn Trust 12-14; C Marlpool *Derby* from 14. *31 Lady Well Views, Springwood Gardens, Belper DE56 1RT* M: 07974-806636 E: janelyon0910@tiscali.co.uk

LYON, Joan Baxter. b 50. Strathclyde Univ BA 70. TISEC 94. **d** 96 **p** 00. NSM Glas E End 96-00; Asst Chapl Luxembourg *Eur* 05-11; TV Sole Bay *St E* 11-15; P-in-c Aberdeen St Ninian *Ab* from 15. *15 Corse Wynd, Kingswells, Aberdeen AB15 8TP* M: 07513-421700 E: joanblyon@gmail.com

LYON, John Forrester. b 39. Edin Th Coll CertEd 95. **d** 95 **p** 96. C Greenock *Glas* 95-98; C Gourock 95-98; Chapl Ardgowan Hospice 95-98; Chapl HM Pris Greenock 97-04; P-in-c Glas Gd Shep and Ascension 98-07; Chapl Rosshall Academy from 02; rtd 07; PtO *Bre* from 09. *28 Demondale Road, Arbroath DD11 1TR* T: (01241) 433601 E: revjohnlyon@btinternet.com *or* lyon68@btinternet.com

LYON, John Harry. b 51. S Dios Minl Tr Scheme 86. **d** 89 **p** 90. NSM S Patcham *Chich* 89-91; C Chich St Paul and St Pet 91-94; R Earnley and E Wittering 94-04; V E Preston w Kingston from 04. *The Vicarage, 33 Vicarage Lane, East Preston, Littlehampton BN16 2SP* T: (01903) 783318 E: revdjohnlyon@tiscali.co.uk

LYON, Mark John. b 82. St Steph Ho Ox 08. **d** 11 **p** 12. C Brighton St Mich and St Paul *Chich* 11-15; C W Tarring from 15. *West Tarring Rectory, Glebe Road, Worthing BN14 7PF* E: frmarklyon@gmail.com

LYONS, Bruce Twyford. b 37. K Alfred's Coll Win CertEd 61. Tyndale Hall Bris. **d** 70 **p** 71. C Virginia Water *Guildf* 70-73; Chapl Ostend w Knokke and Bruges *Eur* 73-78; V E Ham St Paul *Chelmsf* 78-85; V St Alb Ch Ch 85-91; Chapl Wellingborough Sch 92-95; P-in-c Stogumber w Nettlecombe and Monksilver *B & W* 96-98; P-in-c Ostend w Knokke and Bruges *Eur* 98-00; NSM Newbury Deanery *Ox* 01; Chapl

Milton Abbey Sch Dorset 01-02; rtd 02; PtO *Sarum* 01-11. *34 Merryfield Close, Bransgore, Christchurch BH23 8BS* T: (01425) 672105 E: bruce.lyons1@virgin.net

LYONS, Canon Edward Charles. b 44. Nottm Univ BTh 75 LTh. St Jo Coll Nottm 71. **d** 75 **p** 76. C Cambridge St Martin *Ely* 75-78; P-in-c Bestwood Park *S'well* 78-85; R W Hallam and Mapperley *Derby* 85-98; P-in-c Brownsover CD *Cov* 98-02; V Brownsover 02-06; V Clifton w Newton and Brownsover 07-09; RD Rugby 99-06; Dioc Ecum Officer 03-06; Hon Can Cov Cathl 07-09; rtd 09; PtO *Cov* from 10. *68 Juliet Drive, Rugby CV22 6LY* T: (01788) 333277 E: ted.lyons@virginmedia.com

LYONS, Graham Selby. b 29. MBE 84. Open Univ BA 79. **d** 97 **p** 98. OLM New Eltham All SS *S'wark* 97-04. *56 Cadwallon Road, London SE9 3PY* T: (020) 8850 6576 E: holyons2@aol.com

LYONS, Margaret Rose Marie. b 47. **d** 89. OLM Gainsborough All SS *Linc* 89-91; Hon C Low Moor *Bradf* 04-05; Hon C Oakenshaw, Wyke and Low Moor 06-12; Hon C Wyke *Leeds* from 12. *1A Common Road, Low Moor, Bradford BD12 0PN* M: 07940-558062

LYONS, Paul. b 67. Ulster Univ BA 91. TCD Div Sch BTh 98. **d** 98 **p** 99. C Seapatrick *D & D* 98-03; I Greenisland *Conn* from 03. *4 Tinamara, Upper Station Road, Greenisland, Carrickfergus BT38 8FE* T: (028) 9086 3421 *or* 9085 9676 M: 07791-472225 E: revpaul.lyons@btinternet.com

LYONS, Paul Benson. b 44. Qu Coll Birm 68. **d** 69 **p** 70. C Rugby St Andr *Cov* 69-70; C Moston St Jo *Man* 70-72; PV Llan Cathl 73-74; C Brookfield St Anne, Highgate Rise *Lon* 74-75; PtO 76-82; C Westmr St Sav and St Jas Less 82-86; V Gt Cambridge Road St Jo and St Jas 86-12; rtd 12. *22 Standard Road, Enfield EN3 6DR*

LYSSEJKO, Mrs Janet Lesley. b 64. **d** 10 **p** 11. OLM Walmersley Road, Bury *Man* from 10. *31 Burrs Lea Close, Bury BL9 5HT* T: 0161-764 6882 E: janetlyssejko@sky.com

LYTHALL, Andrew Simon. b 86. Keele Univ BSc 07 St Jo Coll Dur BA 09 MA 11. Cranmer Hall Dur 07. **d** 10 **p** 11. C Stockport St Geo *Ches* 10-13; V Offerton St Alb and Stockport St Thos from 13. *The Vicarage, Salcombe Road, Stockport SK2 5AG* M: 07706-036425 E: alythall@btinternet.com

LYTHALL, Jennifer Elizabeth. See MAYO-LYTHALL, Jennifer Elizabeth

LYTTLE, Norma Irene. b 47. CITC. **d** 01 **p** 02. Aux Min Drumachose *D & R* 01-04; Aux Min Dungiven w Bovevagh 04-07; Bp's C Leckpatrick w Dunnalong 07-09; I from 09. *The Rectory, 1 Lowertown Road, Ballymagorry, Strabane BT82 0LE* T/F: (028) 7188 3545 M: 07742-836688 E: leckpatrick@derry.anglican.org

M

MABBS, Miss Margaret Joyce. b 24. St Hilda's Coll Ox BA 45 MA 47 DipEd 46. S'wark Ord Course 79. **dss** 82 **d** 87 **p** 94. Eltham Park St Luke *S'wark* 82-05; NSM 87-05; PtO from 05. *70 Westmount Road, London SE9 1JE* T: (020) 8850 4621

MABIRE, Gillian Mary. b 69. STETS. **d** 12. NSM Guernsey St Peter Port *Win* from 12. *L'Hyvreuse Avenue, St Peter Port, Guernsey GY1 1UZ* T: (01481) 722542

McADAM, Gordon Paul. b 66. QUB BSc 88 TCD BTh 93. CITC 90. **d** 93 **p** 94. C Drumglass w Moygashel *Arm* 93-96; I Dungiven w Bovevagh *D & R* 96-02; I Loughgall w Grange *Arm* from 02. *The Rectory, 2 Main Street, Loughgall, Armagh BT61 8HZ* T: (028) 3889 1587 E: loughgall@armagh.anglican.org

McADAM, Canon Michael Anthony. b 30. K Coll Cam BA 52 MA 56. Westcott Ho Cam 54. **d** 56 **p** 57. C Towcester w Easton Neston *Pet* 56-59; Chapl Hurstpierpoint Coll 60-68; Bp's Chapl *Lon* 69-73; R Much Hadham *St Alb* 73-95; Hon Can St Alb 89-95; rtd 95; RD Oundle *Pet* 96-97; PtO from 98; *St Alb* from 03. *28 West Street, Oundle, Peterborough PE8 4EF* T: (01832) 273451

McALISTER, Canon David. b 39. St Jo Coll Nottm 83. **d** 87 **p** 88. NSM Arpafeelie *Mor* 87-93; NSM Cromarty 87-93; NSM Fortrose 87-93; C Broughty Ferry *Bre* 93-95; P-in-c Nairn *Mor* 95-09; P-in-c Kishorn 08-09; P-in-c Lochalsh 08-09; P-in-c Poolewe 08-09; Chapl Inverness Airport 98-09; Can St Andr Cathl Inverness 01-09; Hon Can St Andr Cathl Inverness from 09; OCM from 03; rtd 09; LtO *Mor* from 10. *36 Feddon Hill, Fortrose IV10 8SP* T: (01381) 622530 E: david.mcalister@btinternet.com

McALISTER, Kenneth Bloomer. b 25. TCD BA 51. **d** 51 **p** 53. C Cregagh *D & D* 51-54; C Monaghan *Clogh* 54-57; C Portadown St Mark *Arm* 57-62; R Ripley *Ripon* 62-91; rtd 91; PtO *Leeds* from 91. *31 Wetherby Road, Knaresborough HG5 8LH* T: (01423) 860705

McALISTER, Margaret Elizabeth Anne (Sister Margaret Anne). b 55. St Mary's Coll Dur BA 78 Ex Univ PGCE 79. Wycliffe Hall Ox 83 SAOMC 99. **d** 01 **p** 02. ASSP from 91; NSM Cowley St Jas *Ox* 01-04; NSM Cowley St Jo 04-09; NSM Ox St Mary Magd 09-11; PtO 11-14; Asst Chapl St Jo Home 11-14; PtO *S'wark* from 15. *25 Orchard Road, Richmond TW9 4AQ* T: (020) 8876 5079 E: margaretanne@socallss.co.uk

McALLEN, James. b 38. Lon Univ BD 71. Oak Hill Th Coll 63. **d** 66 **p** 67. C Blackheath St Jo *S'wark* 66-69; C Edin St Thos 69-73; V Selby St Jas *York* 73-80; V Wistow 75-80; V Houghton *Carl* 80-91; Gen Sec Lon City Miss 92-03; Hon C Blackheath St Jo *S'wark* 94-04; rtd 04; PtO *Carl* from 04. *205 Brampton Road, Carlisle CA3 9AX* T: (01228) 540505

McALLEN, Julian William. b 71. Lon Guildhall Univ BA 94 Avery Hill Coll PGCE 95. Wycliffe Hall Ox 11. **d** 13 **p** 14. C Epsom Common Ch Ch *Guildf* from 13. *278 The Greenway, Epsom KT18 7JF* M: 07817-745378 E: curate@christchurchepsom.org.uk

McALLEN, Robert Roy. b 41. Bps' Coll Cheshunt 62. **d** 65 **p** 66. C Seagoe *D & D* 65-67; C Knockbreda 67-70; CF 70-96; Chapl R Memorial Chpl Sandhurst 87-92; Chapl Guards Chpl Lon 92-96; Hon CF 96; R Ockley, Okewood and Forest Green 98-06; rtd 06. *Maranatha, Church Street, Rudgwick, Horsham RH12 3EG* T: (01403) 823172 E: roy-gill@mcallenr.freeserve.co.uk

MACAN, Peter John Erdley. b 36. Bp Gray Coll Cape Town 58. **d** 60 **p** 61. C Matroosfontein S Africa 60-64; C Maitland Gd Shep 64-67; C S Lambeth St Ann *S'wark* 68-71; V Nunhead St Silas 72-81; P-in-c Clapham H Spirit 81-87; TV Clapham Team 87-90; V Dulwich St Clem w St Pet 90-02; rtd 02; PtO *S'wark* from 04; Retirement Officer Croydon Area from 08. *19 The Windings, South Croydon CR2 0HW* T: (020) 8657 1398 E: peter.macan@virgin.net

McARTHUR, Duncan Walker. b 50. Strathclyde Univ BSc 73 Moore Th Coll Sydney ThL 80 Melbourne Univ BD 82 Newc Univ MA 94. **d** 82 **p** 82. C Hornsby Australia 82-85; Asst Chapl Barker Coll Hornsby 86-88; Asst Min 88-89; P-in-c Harraby *Carl* 90-93; R Hurstville Australia 93-95; Hon Asst P Wauchope St Matt from 99; Chapl St Columba Sch Port Macquarie from 02. *43 Narran River Road, Wauchope NSW 2446, Australia* T: (0061) (2) 6585 1147 *or* 6583 6999 F: 6583 6982 M: 412-828341 E: dmcarthe@bigpond.net.au

MACARTHUR, Helen Anne. b 45. Ulster Univ BEd 90 QUB MSc 96. CITC 05. **d** 08 **p** 09. NSM Derriaghy w Colin *Conn* 08-11; P-in-c Ardclinis and Tickmacrevan w Layde and Cushendun from 11. *76 Largy Road, Carnlough, Ballymena BT44 0JJ* M: 07818-027040 T: (028) 2888 5932 E: helenmacar@btinternet.com

McARTHUR-EDWARDS, Mrs Judith Sarah. b 71. Westmr Coll Ox BTh 94. Cranmer Hall Dur 97. **d** 99 **p** 00. C Cradley *Worc* 99-02; C Quarry Bank 02-03; Asst Chapl Frimley Park Hosp NHS Trust 04-05; Asst Chapl R Surrey Co Hosp NHS Trust from 05. *The Vicarage, 1 Garrison Lane, Chessington KT9 2LB* T: (020) 8397 3016 E: scott-edwards@btopenworld.com *or* judyedwards@nhs.net

MACARTNEY, Gerald Willam. b 52. TCD BTh 03. CITC. **d** 03 **p** 04. C Drumglass w Moygashel *Arm* 03-05; I Milltown 05-14; Dioc Communications Officer 09-10 and 11-14; I Drumgath w Drumgooland and Clonduff *D & D* from 14. *The Rectory, 29 Cross Road, Hilltown, Newry BT34 5TF* M: 07850-040027 T: (028) 4063 1829 E: drumgath@dromore.anglican.org

McATEER (née ROBINSON), Katharine Mary. b 51. NUU BA 73. CITC 03. **d** 06 **p** 07. NSM Conwal Union w Gartan *D & R* 06-08; NSM Londonderry Ch Ch, Culmore, Muff and Belmont from 08. *27 Northland Road, Londonderry BT48 7NF* T: (028) 7137 4544 F: 7127 1991 M: 07813-885145 E: kmcateer51@gmail.com

MACAULAY (née BRAYBROOKS), Mrs Bridget Ann. b 63. Trin Coll Bris BA 92 DipCOT 84. TISEC 96. **d** 98 **p** 99. C Edin Old St Paul 98-01; C Edin St Pet 01-06; Dir Coracle Trust 01-09; Warden Epiphany Ho *Truro* 09-12; Public Preacher from 09. *Lismore, Perranuthnoe, Penzance TR20 9NF* T: (01736) 711343 E: bridgetbraybrooks@googlemail.com

MACAULAY, Jide. *See* MACAULAY, Rowland Ayoola Babajide

MACAULAY, John Roland. b 39. Man Univ BSc 61 Liv Inst of Educn PGCE 80. Wells Th Coll 61. **d** 63 **p** 64. C Padgate Ch Ch *Liv* 63-66; C Upholland 66-73; TV 73-75; V Hindley St Pet 75-81; Chapl Liv Coll 81-96; Sub-Chapl HM Pris Risley 85-96; R Lowton St Luke *Liv* 96-05; rtd 05. *83 Severn Road, Culcheth, Warrington WA3 5ED* T: (01925) 502639

MACAULAY, Kenneth Lionel. b 55. Edin Univ BD 78. Edin Th Coll 74. **d** 78 **p** 79. C Glas St Ninian 78-80; Dioc Youth Chapl 80-87; P-in-c Glas St Matt 80-87; R Glenrothes *St And* 87-89; Chapl St Mary's Cathl 89-92; Min Glas St Mary 89-92; Min Glas St Serf 92-94; PtO 94-96; NSM Glas St Oswald 96-98; P-in-c 98-01; Chapl HM Pris Glas (Barlinnie) 99-00; P-in-c Dumbarton *Glas* 01-06; R from 06; R Alexandria from 14. *St Mungo's Rectory, Queen Street, Alexandria G83 0AS* T: (01389) 734514 *or* 513365 M: 07734-187250 E: frkenny@sky.com *or* frkenny@icloud.com

MACAULAY, Kenneth Russell. b 63. Strathclyde Univ BSc 85. TISEC 95. **d** 98 **p** 99. C Edin Old St Paul 98-01; C Edin St Pet 01-06; Dir Coracle Trust 01-09; Warden Epiphany Ho *Truro* 09-12; Public Preacher from 09. *Lismore, Perranuthnoe, Truro TR20 9NF* T: (01736) 711343 E: kennymacaulay@gmail.com

McAULAY, Mark John Simon. b 71. Lanc Univ LLB 92 Leeds Univ BA 04 Heythrop Coll Lon MA 11 Barrister-at-Law (Inner Temple) 93. Coll of Resurr Mirfield 02. **d** 04 **p** 05. C Ruislip St Martin *Lon* 04-07; V New Southgate St Paul from 07. *The Vicarage, 11 Woodland Road, London N11 1PN* T: (020) 8361 1946 E: frmarkmcaulay@hotmail.com

MACAULAY, Rowland Ayoola Babajide. b 65. Thames Valley Univ LLB 96. Westcott Ho Cam 11. **d** 13. C E Ham w Upton Park and Forest Gate *Chelmsf* 13-14. *Address temp unknown* M: 07521-130179 E: ramacaulay@gmail.com

MACAULEY, Marionette Austina Constance. **d** 14. OLM Forest Gate All SS *Chelmsf* from 14. *98 Courtland Avenue, Ilford IG1 3UP* E: marionmacauley@yahoo.co.uk

McAUSLAND, Canon William James. b 36. Edin Th Coll 56. **d** 59 **p** 60. C Dundee St Mary Magd *Bre* 59-64; R 71-79; R Glas

H Cross 64-71; Chapl St Marg Old People's Home 79-85; R Dundee St Marg *Bre* 79-01; Chapl St Mary's Sisterhood 82-87; Chapl Ninewells Hosp Dundee 85-01; Can St Paul's Cathl Dundee 93-01; rtd 01; Hon Can from 01; NSM Monifieth *Bre* from 03. *18 Broadford Terrace, Broughty Ferry, Dundee DD5 3EF* T: (01382) 737721 E: billmcausland@talktalk.net

McAVOY, George Brian. b 41. MBE 78. TCD BA 67 MA 72. Div Test 63. **d** 63 **p** 65. C Cork St Luke w St Ann *C, C & R* 63-66; I Timoleague w Abbeymahon 66-68; Chapl RAF 68-88; Asst Chapl-in-Chief RAF 88-95; QHC 91-95; Chapl Fosse Health NHS Trust 95-98; Chapl Oakham Sch 98-03; rtd 03; PtO *Pet* 03-11; *Leic* from 05; Past Care and Counselling Adv *Pet* 04-10. *1 The Leas, Cottesmore, Oakham LE15 7DG* T: (01572) 812404 - M: 07967-967803 E: gbm825@outlook.com

McAVOY, Philip George. b 63. Imp Coll Lon BSc 85 SS Coll Cam BA 90. Westcott Ho Cam 88. **d** 91 **p** 92. C W End *Win* 91-95; TV Swanage and Studland *Sarum* 95-00; P-in-c Littleton *Lon* 00-06; V Weston *Guildf* 06-10; PtO from 10. *Four Acorns, Molesey Road, Walton-on-Thames KT12 3PP* T: (01932) 225098 E: pandk.mac@btinternet.com

MACBAIN, Patrick. b 77. G&C Coll Cam BA 99. Oak Hill Th Coll BTh 06. **d** 09 **p** 10. C Worksop St Anne *S'well* 09-13; V Danehill Chich from 13. *The Vicarage, Lewes Road, Danehill, Haywards Heath RH17 7ER* T: (01825) 790269 E: pmacbain@hotmail.com

McBETH, David Ronald. **d** 06 **p** 07. C Glendermott *D & R* 06-09; Australia 09-11; I Dungiven w Bovevagh *D & R* 11-15; I Clooney w Strathfoyle from 15. *All Saints' Rectory, 20 Limavady Road, Londonderry BT47 6JD* T: (028) 7134 4306

McBRIDE, Ms Catherine Sarah. b 64. Trent Poly BSc 87. Ridley Hall Cam 06. **d** 08 **p** 09. C Meole Brace *Lich* 08-12; C Busbridge and Hambledon *Guildf* from 12. *Mervil Bottom, Malthouse Lane, Hambledon, Godalming GU8 4HG* E: cathmcb@yahoo.co.uk

McBRIDE, Murray. b 61. Trin Coll Bris BA 00. **d** 00 **p** 01. C S Lawres Gp *Linc* 00-04; V Aspatria w Hayton and Gilcrux *Carl* 04-06; CF 06-09; V Shrewsbury St Geo w Greenfields *Lich* from 09. *The Vicarage, St George's Street, Shrewsbury SY3 8QA* T: (01743) 235461

McBRIDE, Peter William Frederick. b 66. Trin Coll Ox BA 88 MA 03 Solicitor 91. SEITE 03. **d** 06 **p** 07. C Guildf H Trin w St Mary 06-09; TV Poplar *Lon* 09-11; PtO *S'wark* from 11. *G10 The School House, Pages Walk, London SE1 4HG* T: (020) 7252 2328 M: 07887-551077

McBRIDE, The Ven Stephen Richard. b 61. QUB BSc 84 TCD BTh 89 MA 92 QUB PhD 96. CITC 84. **d** 87 **p** 88. C Antrim All SS *Conn* 87-90; I Belfast St Pet 90-95; Bp's Dom Chapl 94-02; I Antrim All SS from 95; Adn Conn from 02; Prec Belf Cathl from 02. *The Vicarage, 10 Vicarage Gardens, Antrim BT41 4JP* T/F: (028) 9446 2186 M: 07718-588191 E: archdeacon@connor.anglican.org

McCABE, Alan. b 37. Lon Univ BScEng 61. Ridley Hall Cam 61. **d** 63 **p** 64. C Bromley SS Pet and Paul *Roch* 63-67; PV Roch Cathl 67-70; V Bromley H Trin 70-77; V Westerham 77-88; V Eastbourne St Jo *Chich* 88-99; rtd 00; PtO *Chich* 00-14. *Dairy Cottage, Dunorlan Farm, Halls Hole Road, Tunbridge Wells TN2 4RE* T: (01892) 458620 E: romy@talktalk.net

McCABE, Carol. b 49. **d** 03 **p** 04. OLM Blackrod *Man* 03-14; OLM Horwich and Rivington 11-14; PtO from 14. *27 Lymbridge Drive, Blackrod, Bolton BL6 5TH* T: (01204) 669775

McCABE, Revd Dr John Hamilton. b 59. St Edm Hall Ox MA 82 PGCE 84. Trin Coll Bris MA 01. **d** 01 **p** 02. C Burpham *Guildf* 01-05; LtO 05-06; R Byfleet from 06. *The Rectory, 81 Rectory Lane, Byfleet, West Byfleet KT14 7LX* T: (01932) 342374 M: 07710-094357 E: john.h.mccabe@btinternet.com

McCABE, The Ven John Trevor. b 33. RD 78. Nottm Univ BA 55. Wycliffe Hall Ox 57. **d** 59 **p** 60. C Compton Gifford *Ex* 59-63; P-in-c Ex St Martin, St Steph, St Laur etc 63-66; Chapl RNR 63-03; Chapl Ex Sch 64-66; V Capel *Guildf* 66-71; V Scilly Is *Truro* 71-74; TR Is of Scilly 74-81; Can Res Bris Cathl 81-83; V Manaccan w St Anthony-in-Meneage and St Martin *Truro* 83-96; RD Kerrier 87-90 and 94-96; Chmn Cornwall NHS Trust for Mental Handicap 91-00; Hon Can Truro Cathl from 93; Adn Cornwall 96-99; rtd 00; Non Exec Dir Cornwall Healthcare NHS Trust from 99; PtO *Truro* from 99. *1 Sunhill, School Lane, Budock Water, Falmouth TR11 5DG* T: (01326) 378095

McCABE, Terence John. b 46. Sarum Th Coll 71. **d** 74 **p** 75. C Radford *Cov* 74-77; P-in-c Bris St Paul w St Barn 77-80; TV E Bris 80-84; USA 84-90; R Eynesbury *Ely* 90-11; rtd 11. *21 Hardy Drive, Eastbourne BN23 6ED* E: terry.mccabe@ntlworld.com

McCAFFERTY, Andrew. *See* McCAFFERTY, William Andrew

McCAFFERTY, Canon Christine Ann. b 43. FCA 76. Gilmore Course 76. **dss** 79 **d** 87 **p** 94. Writtle w Highwood *Chelmsf*

79-94; C 87-94; Chapl to Bp Bradwell 87-92; Dioc NSM Officer 87-94; TR Wickford and Runwell 94-00; Hon C Lt Baddow 00-09; Hon Can Chelmsf Cathl 91-09; rtd 09; PtO *Chelmsf* from 09. *68 Galleywood Road, Great Baddow, Chelmsford CM2 8DN* T: (01245) 690043 E: jcmccafferty@hotmail.co.uk

McCAFFERTY (née BACK), Mrs Esther Elaine. b 52. Saffron Walden Coll CertEd 74. Trin Coll Bris 79 Oak Hill Th Coll BA 81. **dss** 81 **d** 87 **p** 94. Collyhurst *Man* 81-84; Upton (Overchurch) *Ches* 84-88; Par Dn 87-88; Par Dn Upper Holloway St Pet w St Jo *Lon* 88-90; Min in charge 90-97; P-in-c Pitsea w Nevendon *Chelmsf* 97-02; R Basildon St Martin from 02; RD Basildon 99-04. *The Rectory, St Martin's Square, Basildon SS14 1DX* T/F: (01268) 522455 E: emccafferty@talk21.com

McCAFFERTY, Keith Alexander. *See* DUCKETT, Keith Alexander

McCAFFERTY, William Andrew. b 49. Open Univ BA 93. SWMTC 94. **d** 97 **p** 98. NSM Lapford, Nymet Rowland and Coldridge *Ex* 97-00; CF 00-04; TR Crosslacon *Carl* 04-08; R Forfar *St And* 08-14; R Lunan Head 08-14; CF (TA) 09-14; rtd 14. *Address temp unknown* M: 07891-119684 E: normandy08@btinternet.com

McCAGHREY, Mark Allan. b 66. Warwick Univ BSc 87. St Jo Coll Nottm BTh 93. **d** 94 **p** 95. C Byfleet *Guildf* 94-97; V Lowestoft St Andr *Nor* 97-12; R Mattishall and the Tudd Valley from 12. *The Vicarage, Back Lane, Mattishall, Dereham NR20 3PU* E: mmccaghrey@gmail.com

McCALL, Adrienne. b 49. **d** 08 **p** 09. OLM Hawkhurst *Cant* 08-11; rtd 11; PtO *Roch* from 12; *Cant* from 12. *5 Noah's Place, Noah's Ark, Kemsing, Sevenoaks TN15 6QQ* T: (01732) 669268 E: adiemcall@gmail.com

McCALLA, Robert Ian. b 31. AKC 55. St Boniface Warminster 56. **d** 56 **p** 57. C Barrow St Jo *Carl* 56-58; C Penrith St Andr 58-61; R Greenheys St Clem *Man* 61-64; V Glodwick 64-71; R Distington *Carl* 71-73; V Howe Bridge *Man* 73-87; Chapl Atherleigh Hosp 75-98; R Heaton Mersey *Man* 87-92; V Tyldesley w Shakerley 92-98; rtd 98; PtO *Carl* from 98. *17 Brunswick Square, Penrith CA11 7LW* T: (01768) 895212

McCALLA, Sandra Sheron. b 63. Westcott Ho Cam. **d** 12 **p** 13. C Poplar *Lon* from 12. *The Manse, 1 Rigden Street, London E14 6DJ* E: sandramccalla@lawyer.com

McCALLIG, Darren Martin. **d** 05 **p** 06. C Monkstown *D & G* 05-07; Dean of Res and Chapl TCD 07-15; Denmark *Eur* from 15. *St Alban's House, Tuborgvej 82, 2900 Hellerup, Copenhagen, Denmark* T: (0045) 3311 8518 E: darrenmccallig@hotmail.com *or* chaplain@st-albans.dk

MacCALLUM, The Very Revd Norman Donald. b 47. Edin Univ LTh 70. Edin Th Coll 67. **d** 71 **p** 72. TV Livingston LEP *Edin* 71-82; P-in-c Bo'ness and R Grangemouth 82-00; Syn Clerk 96-00; Can St Mary's Cathl 96-00; Provost St Jo Cathl Oban 00-12; R Oban St Jo 00-12; R Ardchattan 00-12; R Ardbrecknish 00-12; Dean Arg 05-12; rtd 12. *Kinnoul, 57 Nant Drive, Oban PA34 4NL* T: (01631) 569846 - M: 07776-496487 E: normanmaccallum@gmail.com

McCAMLEY, Gregor Alexander. b 42. TCD BA 64 MA 67. CITC 65. **d** 65 **p** 66. C Holywood *D & D* 65-68; C Bangor St Comgall 68-72; I Carnalea 72-80; I Knock 80-07; Stewardship Adv 89-07; Can Down Cathl 90-07; Dioc Registrar 90-95; Adn Down and Chan Belf Cathl 95-07; rtd 07. *1 Rocky Lane, Seaforde, Downpatrick BT30 8PW* T: (028) 4481 1111

McCAMMON, John Taylor. b 42. QUB BSc 65 Lon Univ BD 70. Clifton Th Coll 67. **d** 71 **p** 72. C Lurgan Ch the Redeemer *D & D* 71-75; I Kilkeel 75-82; I Lisburn Ch Ch Cathl 82-98; Treas Lisburn Ch Ch Cathl 94-96; Prec Lisburn Ch Ch Cathl 96; Chan Lisburn Ch Ch Cathl 96-98; Can Conn Cathl 85-98; CMS Kenya 99-05; CMS Ireland 05-09; rtd 09. *9 Beechfield Park, Coleraine BT52 2HZ* T: (028) 7032 6046 E: jmmccammon@hotmail.com

McCANDLESS, John Hamilton Moore. b 24. QUB BA Ulster Poly BEd. **d** 63 **p** 64. C Belfast St Matt *Conn* 63-66; I Termonmaguirke *Arm* 66-69; C Jordanstown *Conn* 69-70; I Ballinderry, Tamlaght and Arboe *Arm* 70-74; I Kilbarron w Rossnowlagh and Drumholm *D & R* 84-87; rtd 87. *4 Greenhill Drive, Ballymoney BT53 6DE* T: (028) 2766 2078 E: jack@theloughan.fsnet.co.uk

McCANN, Alan. *See* McCANN, Thomas Alan George

McCANN, Hilda. b 36. NOC. **d** 03. OLM Parr *Liv* from 03. *25 Newton Road, St Helens WA9 2HZ* T: (01744) 758759

McCANN, Michael Joseph. b 61. Man Univ BSc 82 TCD BTh 91 FCA. **d** 91 **p** 92. C Derryloran *Arm* 91-94; I Dunmurry *Conn* 94-99; I Kilroot and Templecorran from 99. *Kilroot Rectory, 29 Downshire Gardens, Carrickfergus BT38 7LW* T: (028) 9336 2387

McCANN, Roland Neil. b 39. Serampore Coll BD 73. Bp's Coll Calcutta. **d** 70 **p** 73. C Calcutta St Jas India 70-73; V Calcutta St Thos 73-74; C Earley St Bart *Ox* 74-77; C-in-c Harlington Ch

Ch CD *Lon* 77-99; rtd 99; PtO *Lon* 02-13. *195 Park Road, Uxbridge UB8 1NP* T: (01895) 259265

McCANN, Stephen Thomas. b 60. Benedictine Coll Kansas BA 83 Boston Coll (USA) MA 89 Creighton Univ Nebraska MA 94. Pontifical Gregorian Univ 96. **d** 97 **p** 98. In RC Ch 97-01; Rydal Hall *Carl* 02-05; C Kendal H Trin 05-10; I Ballydehob w Aghadown *C, C & R* from 10; Chapl Lay Min from 14. *The Rectory, Church Road, Ballydehob, Co Cork, Republic of Ireland* T: (00353) (28) 37117 E: ballydehobrector@gmail.com

McCANN, Thomas Alan George. b 66. Ulster Univ BA 90 TCD BTh 93 QUB MPhil 99. CITC 90. **d** 93 **p** 94. C Carrickfergus *Conn* 93-00; I Woodburn H Trin from 00. *20 Meadow Hill Close, Carrickfergus BT38 9RQ* T: (028) 9336 2126 E: alan@thehobbit.fsnet.co.uk

McCARTAN, Mrs Audrey Doris. b 50. Keele Univ CertEd 71 BEd 72 Lanc Univ MA 75 Northumbria Univ MSc 99. NEOC 01. **d** 04 **p** 05. NSM Gosforth St Hugh *Newc* 04-07; P-in-c Heddon-on-the-Wall from 07. *St Andrew's Vicarage, The Towne Gate, Heddon-on-the-Wall, Newcastle upon Tyne NE15 0DT* T: (01661) 853142

McCARTER, Mrs Suzanne. b 63. Hull Univ BA 85 PGCE 86. CBDTI 04. **d** 07 **p** 08. C Standish *Blackb* 07-10; C Cullingworth *Bradf* 10-13; TV Harden and Wilsden, Cullingworth and Denholme *Leeds* from 13; Area Missr S Craven Deanery from 10. *The Vicarage, Halifax Road, Cullingworth, Bradford BD13 5DE* T: (01535) 270687 E: suzanne_mccarter@msn.com

McCARTHY, Christopher James. b 61. NEOC 04. **d** 06 **p** 07. C Bessingby *York* 06-08; C Bridlington Quay Ch Ch 06-08; V Bridlington Em 08-15; P-in-c Skipsea and Barmston w Fraisthorpe 08-12; V 12-15; P-in-c Doncaster St Jas *Sheff* from 15. *15 Grange View, Doncaster DN4 0XL* E: chrismbrid@aol.com

McCARTHY, Daniel Michael. b 76. Wolv Univ LLB 98. Trin Coll Bris 08. **d** 10 **p** 11. C Long Benton *Newc* 10-13; TV Aldenham, Radlett and Shenley *St Alb* from 13. *The Rectory, 63 London Road, Shenley, Radlett WD7 9BW* T: (01923) 855383 M: 07855-941184 E: danielmccarthy7x77@yahoo.com

McCARTHY, David William. b 63. Edin Th Coll BD 88. **d** 88 **p** 89. C Edin St Paul and St Geo 88-91; P-in-c S Queensferry 91-95; R Glas St Silas 95-14; I Edin St Thos from 14. *St Thomas's Church, 75-79 Glasgow Road, Edinburgh EH12 8LJ* M: 07411-236433 T: 0131-316 4292

MacCARTHY, Denis Francis Anthony. b 60. St Patr Coll Maynooth BD 85 CITC 05. **d** 85 **p** 86. In RC Ch 85-05; C Bandon Union *C, C & R* 06-08; I from 10; I Mallow Union 08-10. *The Rectory, Castle Road, Bandon, Co Cork, Republic of Ireland* T: (00353) (23) 884 1259 E: noden1@eircom.net

McCARTHY, Lorraine Valmay. *See* REED, Lorraine Valmay

MacCARTHY, The Very Revd Robert Brian. b 40. TCD BA 63 MA 66 PhD 83 NUI MA 65 Ox Univ MA 82. Cuddesdon Coll 77. **d** 79 **p** 80. C Carlow w Urglin and Staplestown *C & O* 79-81; LtO Cashel, Waterford and Lismore 81-86; Lib Pusey Ho and Fell St Cross Coll Ox 81-82; C Bracknell *Ox* 82-83; TV 83-86; Bp's V and Lib Kilkenny Cathl and C Kilkenny w Aghour and Kilmanagh *C & O* 86-88; Chapl Kilkenny Coll 86-88; Bp's Dom Chapl 86-89; I Castlecomer w Colliery Ch, Mothel and Bilboa 88-95; Dioc Info Officer (Ossory and Leighlin) 88-90; Glebes Sec (Ossory and Leighlin) 92-94; Preb Monmohenock St Patr Cathl Dublin 94-99; Provost Tuam *T, K & A* 95-99; I Galway w Kilcummin 95-99; Chapl Univ Coll Galway 95-99; Dean St Patr Cathl Dublin 99-12; rtd 12. *Suirmount, Clonmel, Co Tipperary, Republic of Ireland* T: (00353) (52) 36395

McCARTHY, Sandra Ellen. *See* MANLEY, Sandra Ellen

MacCARTHY, Stephen Samuel. b 49. ACII 81 Univ Coll Chich BA 02. **d** 01. NSM Burgess Hill St Edw *Chich* from 01. *St Edward's House, 9 Coopers Close, Burgess Hill RH15 8AN* T: (01444) 248520 M: 07802-734903 E: ssmaccarthy@aol.com

McCARTHY, Terence Arthur. b 46. Open Univ BA 90. Kelham Th Coll 66. **d** 70 **p** 71. C Gt Burstead *Chelmsf* 70-74; C Wickford 74-76; TV E Runcorn w Halton *Ches* 76-80; V Runcorn H Trin 80-84; Chapl HM Pris Liv 84; Chapl HM Pris Acklington 84-92; Chapl HM Pris Holme Ho 92-11; rtd 11; PtO *Dur* from 12. *33 Leicester Way, Eaglescliffe, Stockton-on-Tees TS16 0LP* T: (01642) 651179 E: artyter@yahoo.co.uk

McCARTNEY, Adrian Alexander. b 57. Stranmillis Coll BEd 79 TCD BTh 88. CITC 86. **d** 88 **p** 89. C Jordanstown w Monkstown *Conn* 88-91; Bp's C Monkstown 91-94; I 94-96; C Belvoir *D & D* from 02. *94 Comber Road, Dundonald, Belfast BT16 2AG* T: (028) 9067 3379 M: 07970-626384 E: adrian@boringwells.org

✠**McCARTNEY, The Rt Revd Darren James.** **d** 03 **p** 04 **c** 12. P-in-c Pangnirtung Canada 03-06; C Carrickfergus *Conn*

06-09; I Knocknamuckley *D & D* 09-12; Suff Bp Arctic from 12. *PO Box 190, Yellowknife NT X1A 2N2, Canada* T: (001) (867) 873 5432 F: 837 8478 E: diocese@arcticnet.org

McCARTNEY, Ellis. b 47. Univ Coll Lon BSc 73 Lon Inst of Educn MA 82. NTMTC 94. **d** 97 **p** 98. NSM Tollington *Lon* 97-05. *6 Elfort Road, London N5 1AZ* T: (020) 7226 1533 E: macfour@btinternet.com

McCARTNEY, Robert Charles. CITC. **d** 85 **p** 85. C Portadown St Mark *Arm* 85-88; I Errigle Keerogue w Ballygawley and Killeshil 88-89; CF 89-04; I Belfast St Donard *D & D* 04-08; I Aghalee from 08. *The Rectory, 39 Soldierstown Road, Aghalee, Craigavon BT67 0ES* T: (028) 9265 0407 M: 07846-610977 E: dunroamin.mccartney@btopenworld.com

McCARTY, Colin Terence. b 46. Loughb Univ BTech 68 PhD 71 Lon Univ PGCE 73 FRSA 89. EAMTC 91. **d** 94 **p** 95. NSM Exning St Martin w Landwade *St E* from 94; Bp's Officer for Self-Supporting Min from 09; PtO *Ely* from 96. *1 Seymour Close, Newmarket CB8 8EL* T: (01638) 669400 *or* (01223) 552716 F: 553537 M: 07970-563166 E: test_and_eval@btinternet.com

MacCARTY, Paul Andrew. b 34. Sarum & Wells Th Coll 73. **d** 75 **p** 76. Ind Chapl *Win* 75-80; C Bournemouth St Andr 75-84; Hon C Christchurch 80-91; C 91-99; rtd 99; PtO *Win* from 01. *3 Douglas Avenue, Christchurch BH23 1JT* T: (01202) 483807 E: paulmaccarty@aol.com

McCASKILL, James Calvin. b 73. Wheaton Coll Illinois BA 95 Leeds Univ MA 02. Coll of Resurr Mirfield 00. **d** 02 **p** 03. C Mt Lebanon St Paul USA 02-04; P-in-c Lundwood *Wakef* 04-09; R Bailey's Crossroads USA from 09. *The Rectory, 5850 Glen Forest Drive, Falls Church VA 22041-2527, USA* T: (001) (828) 335 1382 E: james@mccaskill.info

McCATHIE, Neil. b 62. N Staffs Poly BA 84 De Montfort Univ MA 00 Huddersfield Univ PGCE 93 MAAT 96. St Jo Coll Nottm 03. **d** 05 **p** 06. C Shipley St Pet *Bradf* 05-09; TV Parr *Liv* 09-14; TR from 14. *St Peter's Vicarage, Broad Oak Road, St Helens WA9 2DZ*

McCAULAY, Stephen Thomas John. b 61. Leeds Univ BA 98 Cardiff Univ MTh 14. Coll of Resurr Mirfield 96. **d** 98 **p** 99. C Chaddesden St Phil *Derby* 98-02; V Mackworth St Fran 02-04; CF from 04. *c/o MOD Chaplains (Army)* F: 381824 T: (01264) 383430 E: mccaulay@armymail.mod.uk

McCAULEY, The Ven Craig William Leslie. b 72. Glam Univ BA 95 TCD BTh 99. CITC 96. **d** 99 **p** 00. C Seapatrick *D & D* 99-02; C Kill *D & G* 02-04; I Lurgan w Billis, Killinkere and Munterconnaught *K, E & A* from 04; Adn Kilmore from 10. *The Rectory, Virginia, Co Cavan, Republic of Ireland* T: (00353) (49) 854 8465 E: virginia@kilmore.anglican.org

McCAUSLAND, Norman. b 58. TCD BTh 89. CITC 89. **d** 89 **p** 90. C Portadown St Columba *Arm* 89-91; P-in-c Clonmel Union *C, C & R* 91-94; Miss to Seamen 91-94; CMS 94-95; Bp's V and Lib Ossory Cathl 96; Chapl and Tutor CITC 96-00; PV Ch Ch Cathl Dublin 96-00; CMS 00-01; LtO *D & G* 01-13; I Raheny w Coolock from 13. *The Rectory, 403 Howth Road, Raheny, Dublin 5, Republic of Ireland* T: (00353) (1) 831 3929 M: 86-837 0450 E: raheny@dublin.anglican.org

M'CAW, Stephen Aragorn. b 61. Magd Coll Cam BA 83 Lon Univ MB, BS 86 FRCS 90 MRCGP 92. Cranmer Hall Dur 97. **d** 99 **p** 00. C Thetford *Nor* 99-02; R Steeple Aston w N Aston and Tackley *Ox* 02-10; AD Woodstock 06-09; TR Keynsham *B & W* from 10. *68 Park Road, Keynsham, Bristol BS31 1DE* T: 0117-986 4437 E: samcaw@talk21.com

McCLAY, The Ven David Alexander. b 59. TCD MA 87. **d** 87 **p** 88. C Magheralin w Dollingstown *D & D* 87-90; I Kilkeel 90-01; I Willowfield from 01; P-in-c Mt Merrion from 07; Can Belf Cathl from 05; Adn Down *D & D* from 13. *Willowfield Rectory, 149 My Lady's Road, Belfast BT6 8FE* T/F: (028) 9046 0105 T: 9045 7654 M: 07854-395797 E: mcclayd@googlemail.com

McCLEAN, Derek Alistair. b 69. Poly of Wales BA 92 QUB PGCE 94. Ridley Hall Cam 08. **d** 10 **p** 11. C Drayton *Nor* 10-13; R Hethersett w Canteloff w Lt and Gt Melton from 13. *The Rectory, 27 Norwich Road, Hethersett, Norwich NR9 3AR* M: 07889-284921 E: revdmac@googlemail.com

McCLEAN, Dominic Joseph James Albert Francis. b 59. Trin & All SS Coll Leeds BEd 82 De Montfort Univ MSc 07. Allen Hall Qu Coll Birm. **d** 89 **p** 11. NSM Leic St Aid 10-11; NSM Burbage w Aston Flamville 11-13; P-in-c Bosworth and Sheepy Gp 13-15; P-in-c Nailstone and Carlton w Shackerstone 13-15. *Address temp unknown* E: dominic.mcclean@gmail.com

McCLEAN, Lydia Margaret Sheelagh. See COOK, Lydia Margaret Sheelagh

McCLEAN, Robert Mervyn. b 38. Greenwich Univ BTh 91. Edgehill Th Coll Belf 57. **d** 85 **p** 88. NSM Seapatrick *D & D* 85-99. *2 Kiloanin Crescent, Banbridge BT32 4NU* T: (028) 4062 7419 E: r.m.mcclean@btinternet.com

McCLEAVE, George. d 12 **p** 13. NSM Stokesley w Seamer *York* from 12. *52 The Stripe, Middlesbrough TS9 5PU* T: (01642) 714254 E: gmccleave@btinternet.com

McCLELLAN, Andrew David. b 71. St Jo Coll Cam BA 93 MA 96. Oak Hill Th Coll BA 05. **d** 05. C Sevenoaks St Nic *Roch* 05-09; P-in-c Bromley St Jo 09-12; V from 12; Chapl St Olave's Gr Sch Orpington from 09. *St John's Vicarage, 9 Orchard Road, Bromley BR1 2PR* T: (020) 8460 1844 M: 07931-731062 E: aj_mcc@btinternet.com

McCLELLAND (née FARLEY), Mrs Claire Louise. b 69. Man Univ BA 91 Heythrop Coll Lon MTh 99. Westcott Ho Cam 96. **d** 99 **p** 00. C Sherborne w Castleton and Lillington *Sarum* 99-00; C Weymouth H Trin 00-02; Chapl Barts and The Lon NHS Trust 02-03; Chapl Ealing Hosp NHS Trust 03-06; Chapl W Middx Univ Hosp NHS Trust 03-06; Hon C Pimlico St Pet w Westmr Ch Ch *Lon* 08-14; Hon C Charminster and Stinsford *Sarum* from 14. *33 Marie Road, Dorchester DT1 2LF* T: (01305) 250158 M: 07813-894621 E: clairemcclelland@icloud.com

McCLENAGHAN, John Mark. b 61. TCD BTh 05. CITC 02. **d** 05 **p** 06. C Portadown St Columba *Arm* 05-08; I Keady w Armaghbreague and Derrynoose 08-13; Hon V Choral Arm Cathl 07-13; I Aghalurcher w Tattykeeran, Cooneen etc *Clogh* from 13. *Colebrook Rectory, 8 Owenskerry Lane, Fivemiletown BT75 0SP* T: (028) 8953 1822 E: aghalurcher@clogher.anglican.org

MACCLESFIELD, Archdeacon of. See BISHOP, The Ven Ian Gregory

McCLINTOCK, Darren John. b 77. Hull Univ BA 98 Open Univ MA(TS) 00. St Jo Coll Nottm 98. **d** 01 **p** 02. C Drypool *York* 01-04; C Bilton *Ripon* 04-06; TV *Leeds* 06-15; Dioc Ecum Adv *Ripon* 08-09; Chapl Wakefield Hospice from 15. *Wakefield Hospice, Aberford Road, Wakefield WF1 4TS* T: (01924) 213900 E: darren@djmcclintock.freeserve.co.uk

McCLOSKEY, Robert Johnson. b 42. Stetson Univ (USA) AB 63. Gen Th Sem NY STB 67. **d** 67 **p** 68. C Gt Medford USA 67-69; R Somerville w St Jas and Chapl Tufts Univ 69-72; Dioc Adv for Liturgy and Music Mass 71-76; R Westford St Mark 72-76; R Blowing Rock St Mary 76-82; Liturg and Musical Adv and Ecum Officer Dio W N Carolina 76-81; Dio SE Florida USA 90-93; Ecum Officer Dio Long Is 81-89; R Bay Shore St Pet and St Pet Sch 82-89; R Miami St Steph and St Steph Sch 89-01; Staff Officer Lambeth Conf 98; rtd 01. *PO Box 1691, West Jefferson NC 28694-1691, USA*

McCLURE, Mrs Catherine Abigail. b 63. Birm Univ BA 84 SS Hild & Bede Coll Dur PGCE 85. Ripon Coll Cuddesdon BTh 07. **d** 03 **p** 04. C Cirencester *Glouc* 03-07; Chapl Glos Hosps NHS Foundn Trust 07-13; Chapl Cheltenham Ladies' Coll from 13. *Cheltenham Ladies' College, Bayshill Road, Cheltenham GL50 3EP* T: (01242) 520691 M: 07824-476505

McCLURE, Jennifer Lynne. See MOBERLY, Jennifer Lynne

McCLURE, John. d 07 **p** 08. NSM Skerry w Rathcavan and Newtowncrommelin *Conn* 07-09; NSM Belfast St Mich 09-14; C Ballymena w Ballyclug from 14; Bp's Dom Chapl from 11. *69 Parkgate Road, Kells, Ballymena BT42 3PF* T: (028) 2589 2324 *or* 9024 1640 M: 07841-866414 E: mcclurejohn@hotmail.com *or* belfast@icm-online.ie

McCLURE, The Ven Timothy Elston. b 46. St Jo Coll Dur BA 68. Ridley Hall Cam 68. **d** 70 **p** 71. C Kirkheaton *Wakef* 70-73; C Chorlton upon Medlock *Man* 74-79; Chapl Man Poly 74-82; TR Man Whitworth 79-82; Gen Sec SCM 82-92; Bp's Soc and Ind Adv and Dir Chs' Coun for Ind and Soc Resp LEP *Bris* 92-99; Hon Can Bris Cathl 92-12; Hon C Cotham St Sav w St Mary 96; Chapl Lord Mayor's Chpl 96-99; Adn Bris 99-12; rtd 12. *Park House, Denton, Gilsland, Brampton CA8 7AG*

McCLUSKEY, Coralie Christine. b 52. Univ of Wales (Cardiff) BEd 74. SAOMC 98. **d** 01 **p** 02. C Welwyn w Ayot St Peter *St Alb* 01-04; P-in-c Datchworth 04-05; TV Welwyn 05-11; P-in-c Eaton Bray w Edlesborough 11-12; V from 12; Agric Chapl for Herts 09-13; Agric Chapl for Beds from 13. *The Vicarage, High Street, Eaton Bray, Dunstable LU6 2DN* T: (01525) 220261 E: coralie_mccluskey@yahoo.co.uk

McCLUSKEY, James Terence. b 65. Coll of Resurr Mirfield 01. **d** 03 **p** 04. C Swanley St Mary *Roch* 03-06; V Prittlewell St Luke *Chelmsf* from 06. *The Vicarage, St Luke's Road, Southend-on-Sea SS2 4AB* T/F: (01702) 467620 M: 07761-632734 E: mccluskey@katy-james.freeserve.co.uk

McCLUSKEY, Miss Lesley. b 45. Hull Univ LLB 72 Bolton Coll of Educn PGCE 77. NOC 89. **d** 92 **p** 94. C Bootle St Mary w St Paul *Liv* 92-94; C Wigan St Anne 94-98; P-in-c Newton in Makerfield Em 98-07; TV Newton 08; Chapl St Helens and Knowsley Hosps NHS Trust 98-08; rtd 09. *9 Mulberry Court, Stockton Heath, Warrington WA4 2DB* T: (01925) 602286 E: lesley-mccluskey@yahoo.co.uk

McCOACH, Jennifer Sara. See CROFT, Jennifer Sara

McCOLL, Iain Gordon. b 75. Cardiff Univ BA 97 Lon Univ MA 98 Bris Univ MA 00. Westcott Ho Cam 12. **d** 14 **p** 15. C Henleaze *Bris* from 14. *9 Dorset Road, Westbury-on-Trym, Bristol BS9 4BJ* M: 07746-951187 E: mccoll.iain@gmail.com

McCOLLUM, Alastair Colston. b 69. Whitelands Coll Lon BA 91. Westcott Ho Cam 95. **d** 96 **p** 97. C Hampton All SS *Lon* 96-98; C S Kensington St Aug 98-00; Chapl Imp Coll 98-00; TV Papworth *Ely* 00-08; V Kilmington, Stockland, Dalwood, Yarcombe etc *Ex* 08-13; R Victoria St Jo Canada from 13. *395 St Charles Street, Victoria BC V8S 3N5, Canada* E: revdalmac@gmail.com

McCOLLUM, Canon Charles James. b 41. TCD BTh 89. CITC 85. **d** 89 **p** 90. C Larne and Inver *Conn* 89-91; Bp's C Belfast Whiterock 91-96; I Belfast St Pet and St Jas 96-08; I Dunleckney w Nurney, Lorum and Kiltennel *C & O* 08-12; Can Ossory Cathl 12; rtd 12. *Curragho, Cavan, Republic of Ireland* M: 87-288 5019 E: charlesjmccollum@gmail.com

McCOMB, Samuel. b 33. CITC 70. **d** 71 **p** 72. C Belfast St Mich *Conn* 71-74; C Lisburn Ch Ch 74-79; I Ballinderry *Arm* 79-83; I Lisburn Ch Ch *Conn* 83-04; Can Conn Cathl 98-04; Treas Conn Cathl 01-04; rtd 04. *209 Hillsborough Old Road, Lisburn BT27 5QE* T: (028) 9260 5812

McCONACHIE, Robert Noel. b 40. Goldsmiths' Coll Lon BA 86. Oak Hill Th Coll 86. **d** 88 **p** 89. C Larkfield *Roch* 88-93; R Mereworth w W Peckham 93-10; rtd 11; PtO *Cant* from 15. *25 Sturmer Court, Kings Hill, West Malling ME19 4ST* T: (01732) 874195 E: robertmcconachie@ymail.com

McCONAGHIE, Colin Andrew. b 75. CITC MTh 12. **d** 11 **p** 12. C Drumglass w Moygashel *Arm* 11-14; C Dunboyne and Rathmolyon *M & K* from 14. *Rathflesk, Mill Road, Rathmolyon, Enfield, Co Meath, Republic of Ireland* T: (00353) (46) 954 2939 M: 87-346 6190 E: colinmcconaghie@hotmail.com

McCONKEY, Brian Robert. b 62. Carl Dioc Tr Inst 92. **d** 95 **p** 96. C Blackb St Gabr 95-98; Dioc Youth Officer 99-04; V Fulwood Ch Ch from 04; Dioc Voc Team Co-ord from 06; AD Preston from 15; Chapl Preston Coll 05-09. *Christ Church Vicarage, 19 Vicarage Close, Fulwood, Preston PR2 8EG* T: (01772) 719210 E: christchurchfulwood@btinternet.com

McCONKEY, David Benton. b 53. Kansas Wesleyan Univ (USA) BA 75 Yale Univ MusM 77. Yale Div Sch MDiv 79. **d** 83 **p** 84. Dn Ch Cathl Salina USA 83-84; C S Lake Anchorage 84-85; P-in-c Louisville St Luke 85-86; R Warrensburgh H Cross 86-94; Can Capitular All SS Cath Albany 88-93; R Belvedere St Eliz Zimbabwe 94-03; P-in-c Norton St Fran and St Jas 94-99; Lect Bp Gaul Coll 94-01; TR Swindon New Town *Bris* 03-12; P-in-c Northampton All SS w St Kath and St Pet from 12. *All Saints' Rectory, 6 Albion Place, Northampton NN1 1UD* T: (01604) 621854 *or* 632194 E: frdbmcconkey@yahoo.co.uk

McCONNAUGHIE, Adrian William. b 66. Jes Coll Ox BA 89 MA 06 Lon Univ PhD 93 Cam Univ PGCE 96. Trin Coll Bris BA 08. **d** 08 **p** 09. C Bath Abbey w St Jas *B & W* 08-11; Chapl Mon Sch 11-13; Chapl Brentwood Sch from 13; C Warley Ch Ch and St Warley St Mary *Chelmsf* from 15. *Mitre House, 6 Shenfield Road, Brentwood CM15 8AA* T: (01277) 203280 E: awm@brentwood.essex.sch.uk

McCONNELL, Canon Brian Roy. b 46. St Paul's Coll Grahamstown. **d** 71 **p** 72. C Plumstead S Africa 71-74; C St Geo Cathl Cape Town 74-77; C Prestwich St Marg *Man* 77-79; R Sea Point S Africa 79-85; V Liscard St Mary w St Columba *Ches* 85-90; V Altrincham St Geo 90-06; RD Bowdon 95-03; Hon Can Ches Cathl 97-06; Can Res Carl Cathl 06-13; rtd 13. *30 Countisbury Gardens, Milborne Port, Sherborne DT9 5FF* T: (01963) 251511

McCONNELL, Peter Stuart. b 54. Linc Th Coll 89. **d** 91 **p** 92. C N Shields *Newc* 91-95; V Balkwell 95-03; C Killingworth 03-07; P-in-c Longhorsley and Hebron 08-10; P-in-c Longhorsley from 11; Sen Chapl Northumbria Police from 98; PtO *Dur* from 01. *The Vicarage, Longhorsley, Morpeth NE65 8UU* T: (01670) 788218 E: mcconnell@balkwell.freeserve.co.uk

McCONNELL, Robert Mark. b 60. Oak Hill Th Coll BA 88. **d** 89 **p** 90. C Bedford Ch Ch *St Alb* 89-92; C Bangor St Comgall *D & D* 92-94; I Killyleagh 94-99; I Ballynure and Ballyeaston *Conn* from 99. *The Rectory, 11 Church Road, Ballyclare BT39 9UF* T: (028) 9332 2350 *or* 9335 4814 M: 07801-235330 E: david@theunitedparish.org.uk

McCORMACK, Alan William. b 68. Jes Coll Ox BA 90 MA 94 DPhil 94. CITC 93. **d** 96 **p** 97. C Knock *D & D* 96-98; Dean of Res and Chapl TCD 98-07; Succ St Patr Cathl Dublin 98-06; Abp's Dom Chapl *D & G* 03-07; P-in-c St Botolph without Bishopgate *Lon* from 07; P-in-c St Vedast w St Mich-le-Querne etc from 07. *St Vedast's Rectory, 4 Foster Lane, London EC2V 6HH* T: (020) 7588 3388 E: rector@botolph.org.uk

McCORMACK, Colin. b 47. QUB BSc 70 DipEd 71. St Jo Coll Nottm BA 75. **d** 78 **p** 79. C Carl St Jo 78-81; C Ballynafeigh St Jude *D & D* 81-84; V Harraby *Carl* 84-89; NSM Carl H Trin and St Barn 95-99; Asst Chapl Costa Blanca *Eur* 00-04;

Chapl Torrevieja 04-08; I Clonallon and Warrenpoint w Kilbroney *D & D* from 11. *Clonallon Rectory, 8 Donaghaguy Road, Warrenpoint, Newry BT34 3RZ* T: (028) 4175 3497 E: colinmccormack6@btinternet.com

McCORMACK, Canon David Eugene. b 34. Wells Th Coll 66. **d** 68 **p** 69. C Lillington *Cov* 68-71; C The Lickey *Birm* 71-75; V Highters Heath 75-82; V Four Oaks 82-00; Hon Can Birm Cathl 95-00; PtO *Linc* from 00; Pet from 00; *Birm* from 05. *27 Rockingham Close, Market Deeping, Peterborough PE6 8BY* T: (01778) 347569

McCORMACK, George Brash. b 32. ACIS 65 FCIS 75. S'wark Ord Course 82. **d** 85 **p** 86. Hon C Crofton St Paul *Roch* 85-89; C Crayford 89-91; R Fawkham and Hartley 91-97; rtd 97; PtO *Roch* from 98. *11 Turnpike Drive, Pratts Bottom, Orpington BR6 7SJ* E: geomacc@uwclub.net

McCORMACK, Ian Douglas. b 80. St Anne's Coll Ox BA 02 MA 06 MSt 03 Leeds Univ MA 10. Coll of Resurr Mirfield 07. **d** 10 **p** 11. C Horbury w Horbury Bridge *Wakef* 10-13; V Grimethorpe w Brierley *Leeds* from 13. *The Vicarage, 7 St Luke's Road, Grimethorpe, Barnsley S72 7FN* E: fatherianmccormack@hotmail.co.uk

McCORMACK, John Heddon. b 58. Chich Th Coll 85. **d** 88 **p** 89. C Cleobury Mortimer w Hopton Wafers *Heref* 88-90; C Lymington *Win* 90-92; C Portsea N End St Mark *Portsm* 92-95; Chapl St Barn Hospice Worthing 95-06. *10 Columbia Walk, Worthing BN13 2ST* T: (01903) 263700 M: 07974-603518 E: humanrites1@sky.com

McCORMACK, Canon Kevan Sean. b 50. Chich Th Coll 77. **d** 80 **p** 81. C Ross *Heref* 80-81; C Ross w Brampton Abbotts, Bridstow and Peterstow 81-83; C Leominster 83; TV 84-87; Chapl R Hosp Sch Holbrook 87-00; R Woodbridge St Mary *St E* from 00; Hon Can St E Cathl from 09; Chapl to The Queane from 14. *St Mary's Rectory, Church Street, Woodbridge IP12 1DS* T/F: (01394) 610424 E: rector@stmaryswoodbridge.org

McCORMACK, Canon Lesley Sharman. b 50. EAMTC. **d** 88 **p** 94. Hon Par Dn Chevington w Hargrave and Whepstead w Brockley *St E* 88-95; Asst Chapl W Suffolk Hosp Bury St Edm 88-95; Chapl Kettering Gen Hosp NHS Trust 95-09; Chapl Cransley Hospice from 09; NSM Kettering SS Pet and Paul from 09; Bp's Hosp Chapl Adv from 00; Can Pet Cathl from 03. *Barnbrook, Water Lane, Chelveston, Wellingborough NN9 6AP* T: (01933) 626636 E: lesleybarnbrook@hotmail.co.uk

MacCORMACK, Michael Ian. b 54. Kent Univ BA 77 Ch Ch Coll Cant MA 87 Bris Univ PGCE 78. STETS 02. **d** 05 **p** 06. NSM Martock w Kingsbury Episcopi and Ash *B & W* from 05. *12A Middle Street, Montacute TA15 6UZ* T: (01935) 827823 M: 07717-847736 E: michael.maccormack@nationaltrust.org.uk

McCORMACK, Mrs Susan. b 60. NEOC 00. **d** 03 **p** 04. C Newburn *Newc* 03-07; P-in-c Fawdon 07-13; TR Willington from 13. *St Mary's Vicarage, 67 Churchill Street, Wallsend NE28 7TE* T: 0191-262 8208 E: suemc@mccormacks4.fsnet.co.uk

McCORMICK, Mrs Anne Irene. b 67. Sheff Univ BA 89 Hull Univ PGCE 90. Ripon Coll Cuddesdon 90. **d** 92 **p** 94. C Spalding St Mary and St Nic *Linc* 92-96; C Gt Grimsby St Mary and St Jas 96-01; C Gt and Lt Coates w Bradley from 98; Chapl Rotherham, Doncaster and S Humber NHS Trust 07-12; Chapl N Lincs and Goole Hosps NHS Trust from 12. *Glebe House, 11 Church Lane, Limber, Grimsby DN37 8JN* E: anneoflimber@btinternet.com

McCORMICK, David Mark. b 68. Univ of Wales (Ban) BD 89. Ripon Coll Cuddesdon 90. **d** 92 **p** 93. C Holbeach *Linc* 92-96; TV Gt Grimsby St Mary and St Jas 96-01; Prin Linc Min Tr Course 01-09; CME Officer 09-12; TV Gt and Lt Coates w Bradley from 12; Chapl St Andr Hospice Grimsby from 12. *St Nicholas' Vicarage, Great Coates Road, Great Coates, Grimsby DN37 9NS* T: (01472) 882495 E: david.mccormick@lincoln.anglican.org

McCOSH, Andrew James. **d** 14 **p** 15. NSM Shelfield and High Heath *Lich* from 14. *4 Larch Close, Lichfield WS14 9UR* T: (01543) 256075 E: ajmccosh@tiscali.co.uk

McCOSH, Canon Duncan Ian. b 50. Edin Dioc NSM Course 82. **d** 91 **p** 92. C Dalkeith *Edin* 91-96; C Lasswade 91-96; P-in-c Falkirk 96-97; R 97-03; R Galashiels from 03; Hon Can Cape Coast from 06. *The Rectory, 6 Parsonage Road, Galashiels TD1 3HS* T: (01896) 753118 E: stpeters.gala@btopenworld.com

McCOUBREY, William Arthur. b 36. CEng MIMechE. Sarum & Wells Th Coll 86. **d** 89 **p** 90. C Bedhampton *Portsm* 89-92; V Stokenham w Sherford *Ex* 92-96; R Stokenham w Sherford and Beesands, and Slapton 96-02; rtd 02; PtO *Portsm* from 02; *Chich* from 02. *19 Warblington Road, Emsworth PO10 7HE* T: (01243) 374011

McCOULOUGH, David. b 61. Man Univ BA 84 St Jo Coll Dur BA 88 Leeds Univ MA 01. Cranmer Hall Dur 86. **d** 89 **p** 90.

C Man Apostles w Miles Platting 89-92; C Elton All SS 92-94; V Halliwell St Marg 94-98; Min Can Ripon Cathl 98-01; Chapl Univ Coll of Ripon and York St Jo 98-01; Ind Chapl S'well 01-07; Chapl Boots PLC 01-07; C Nottingham St Pet and St Jas 01-02; C Nottingham St Pet and All SS 02-07; Assoc Dir Partnerships 07-09; Dir from 09; P-in-c Edingley w Halam 07-14. *15 Adams Row, Southwell NG25 0FF* T: (01636) 812029 E: davidmcc@southwell.anglican.org

McCOULOUGH, Thomas Alexander. b 32. AKC 59. **d** 60 **p** 61. C Norton St Mich *Dur* 60-63; USPG India 63-67; P-in-c Derby St Jas 67-72; Ind Chapl *York* 72-82; P-in-c Sutton on the Forest 82-96; Dioc Sec for Local Min 82-89; Lay Tr Officer 89-96; rtd 96; PtO *Newc* from 96. *1 Horsley Gardens, Holywell, Whitley Bay NE25 0TU* T: 0191-298 0332

McCRACKEN, William. **d** 08 **p** 09. C Camlough w Mullaglass *Arm* from 08. *1 Aughlish Road, Tandragee, Craigavon BT62 2EE* T: (028) 3884 0655

McCREA, Christina Elizabeth. b 53. **d** 08 **p** 09. NSM Glanogwen and Llanllechid w St Ann's and Pentir *Ban* 08-14; NSM Bro Ogwen from 14. *2 Bron-y-Waun, Rhiwlas, Bangor LL57 4EX* T: (01248) 372249 E: christinaemcc@aol.com

McCREA, Canon Francis. b 53. BTh. **d** 91 **p** 92. C Dundonald *D & D* 91-94; I Belfast St Brendan 94-15; Can Down Cathl 14-15; rtd 15. *1 Pine Lodge, 3A Cherryvalley, Belfast BT5 6PH*

McCREADIE, Mrs Lesley Anne. b 51. Bp Otter Coll CertEd 73 Open Univ BA 93. STETS BA 10. **d** 10 **p** 11. NSM Sherborne w Castleton, Lillington and Longburton *Sarum* from 10. *5 Kings Close, Longburton, Sherborne DT9 5PW* T: (01963) 210548 E: revdlesley@aol.com

McCREADY, Kennedy Lemar. b 26. Birkbeck Coll Lon BSc 59 Sussex Univ MA 94 Garnett Coll Lon TCert 54 CEng 50 FIEE 56. Chich Th Coll 91. **d** 92 **p** 99. NSM Mayfield *Chich* 92-97; PtO 97-00; NSM New Groombridge 99-01; PtO from 01. *Quarry House, Groombridge Road, Groombridge, Tunbridge Wells TN3 9PS* T: (01892) 864297

McCRORY, Canon Peter. b 34. Chich Th Coll 63. **d** 67 **p** 68. C St Marychurch *Ex* 67-72; R Kenn w Mamhead 72-74; R Kenn 75-78; Bp's Dom Chapl *S'wark* 78-81; V Kew 81-00; RD Richmond and Barnes 84-89; Hon Can S'wark Cathl 90-00; rtd 00; PtO *Nor* from 00; RD Burnham and Walsingham 11-14. *Dane House, The Street, Kettlestone, Fakenham NR21 0AU* T: (01328) 878455 E: canonpeter.mcc@gmail.com

McCROSKERY, Andrew. b 74. Glas Univ BD 97 TCD MPhil 99. CITC 98. **d** 99 **p** 00. C Newtownards *D & D* 99-02; Dean's V Cork Cathl 02-04; I Youghal Union 04-08; Chapl Univ Coll Cork 04-08; Bp's Dom Chapl 03-08; Min Can Cork Cathl 04-08; I Dublin St Bart w Leeson Park *D & G* from 08. *The Rectory, 12 Merlyn Road, Ballsbridge, Dublin 4, Republic of Ireland* T: (00353) (1) 269 4813 E: wolfram100@hotmail.com

McCRUM, Michael Scott. b 35. Glas Univ BSc 57 UNISA BTh 85. **d** 85 **p** 85. Asst P Lynnwood S Africa 86-87; P-in-c Mamelodi 87; P-in-c Villieria 87-88; Kerygma Internat Chr Min 89-92; PtO *Nor* 93-94; NSM Chesham Bois *Ox* 94-95; PtO *St Alb* 95-98 and from 05; Hon C Chorleywood St Andr 98-05. *Cranbrook, 31 South Road, Chorleywood, Rickmansworth WD3 5AS* T/F: (01923) 336897 M: 07792-621587 E: michael.s.mccrum@gmail.com

McCULLAGH, Elspeth Jane Alexandra. See SAVILLE, Elspeth Jane Alexandra

McCULLAGH, Canon John Eric. b 46. TCD BA 68 BTh 88 QUB DipEd 70. **d** 88 **p** 89. C Stillorgan w Blackrock *D & G* 88-91; Chapl and Hd of RE Newpark Sch Dub 90-99; I Clondalkin w Rathcoole *D & G* 91-99; Sec Gen Syn Bd of Educn 99-08; I Rathdrum w Glenealy, Derralossary and Laragh *D & G* 08-14; Can Ch Ch Cathl Dublin 99-14; Treas Ch Ch Cathl Dublin 09-14; rtd 14. *Harcourt Villa, Kimberley Road, Greystones, Co Wicklow, Republic of Ireland* T: (00353) (1) 287 1408 M: 86-837 0384 E: jemccullagh@gmail.com

McCULLOCH, Alistair John. b 59. Univ of Wales (Lamp) BA 81 Leeds Univ BA 86 Lon Univ MA 07. Coll of Resurr Mirfield 84. **d** 87 **p** 88. C Portsm Cathl 87-90; C Portsea St Mary 90-94; V Reading St Matt *Ox* 94-95; PtO *S'wark* 99; Chapl King's Coll Hosp NHS Trust 00-04; Chapl R Marsden NHS Foundn Trust from 04. *The Royal Marsden Hospital, Fulham Road, London SW3 6JJ* T: (020) 7808 2818 E: alistair.mcculloch@rmh.nhs.uk

McCULLOCH, Mrs Celia Hume. b 53. Leeds Univ BA 08. NOC 05. **d** 08 **p** 09. C Cheetham *Man* 08-10; rtd 10; PtO *Man* 11-13. *Stonelea, 1 Heads Drive, Grange-over-Sands LA11 7DY* - M: 07943-366331 E: celiamcculloch@yahoo.co.uk

MacCULLOCH, Prof Diarmaid Ninian John. b 51. Kt 12. Chu Coll Cam BA 72 MA 76 PhD 77 FSA 78 FRHistS 81. Ripon Coll Cuddesdon 86. **d** 87. NSM Clifton All SS w St Jo *Bris* 87-88. *St Cross College, St Giles, Oxford OX1 3LZ* T: (01865) 270794 F: 270795 E: diarmaid.macculloch@theology.ox.ac.uk

✠**McCULLOCH, The Rt Revd Nigel Simeon.** b 42. KCVO 13. Selw Coll Cam BA 64 MA 69. Cuddesdon Coll 64. **d** 66 **p** 67

c 86. C Ellesmere Port *Ches* 66-70; Dir Th Studies Ch Coll Cam 70-75; Chapl 70-73; Dioc Missr *Nor* 73-78; P-in-c Salisbury St Thos and St Edm *Sarum* 78-81; R 81-86; Adn Sarum 79-86; Can and Preb Sarum Cathl 79-86; Suff Bp Taunton *B & W* 86-92; Preb Wells Cathl 86-92; Bp Wakef 92-02; Bp Man 02-13; Ld High Almoner 97-13; rtd 13. *Stonelea, 1 Heads Drive, Grange-over-Sands LA11 7DY*

McCULLOCK, Mrs Patricia Ann. b 46. EMMTC 87. **d** 90 **p** 94. C Bottesford w Ashby *Linc* 90-95; P-in-c Wragby 95-98; Chapl N Lincs Coll of FE 95-98; Ind Chapl 98-01; rtd 01; PtO *Linc* 01-11; NSM Marden w Preston Grange and Billy Mill *Newc* 12-13. *1 Orchard Close, Morpeth NE61 1XE* T: (01670) 519800 E: patricia.mccullock@virgin.net

McCULLOUGH, Mrs Aphrodite Maria. b 47. Derby Univ MSc 95. EMMTC 97. **d** 00 **p** 01. NSM Kirby Muxloe *Leic* 00-04; TV 04-08; rtd 08; PtO *Leic* from 08. *33 Alton Road, Leicester LE2 8QB* T: 0116-283 7887 E: aphro.mccullough@btinternet.com

McCULLOUGH, Canon Roy. b 46. MBE 13. Brasted Th Coll 69 Linc Th Coll 70. **d** 73 **p** 74. Chapl Highfield Priory Sch Lancs 73-77; C Ashton-on-Ribble St Andr *Blackb* 73-77; V Rishton 77-86; V Burnley St Matt w H Trin 86-97; RD Burnley 91-97; Chapl Victoria Hosp Burnley 86-91; V Walton-le-Dale St Leon w Samlesbury St Leon *Blackb* 97-11; Hon Can Blackb Cathl 97-11; rtd 11; PtO *Blackb* from 11; *Carl* from 11. *Wescoe, Kirkby Thore, Penrith CA10 1XE* T: (01768) 361656 E: randjmcc@googlemail.com

McCURDY, The Ven Hugh Kyle. b 58. Portsm Poly BA Univ of Wales (Cardiff) PGCE. Trin Coll Bris. **d** 85 **p** 86. C Egham *Guildf* 85-88; C Woking St Jo 88-91; V Histon *Ely* 91-95; P-in-c Impington 98-05; RD N Stowe 94-05; Hon Can Ely Cathl 04-05; Adn Huntingdon and Wisbech from 05. *Whitgift House, The College, Ely CB7 4DL* T: (01353) 658404 or 652709 F: 652745 E: archdeacon.handw@ely.anglican.org

McDERMOTT, Christopher Francis Patrick. b 54. Southeastern Coll USA BA 84 Wheaton Coll Illinois MA 87. EAMTC. **d** 95 **p** 96. C Gt Ilford St Clem and St Marg *Chelmsf* 95-99; PtO from 06; Chapl Sussex Univ *Chich* from 14. *The Chaplaincy, University of Sussex, Southern Ring Road, Falmer, Brighton BN1 9RH* T: (01273) 877123 E: chrismcd54@aol.com or c.mcdermott@sussex.ac.uk

McDERMOTT, Fraser Graeme. b 65. NTMTC 97. **d** 98 **p** 00. NSM Oak Tree Angl Fellowship *Lon* 98-02; V N Wembley St Cuth 02-14; V Hillsborough New Zealand from 14. *102 Hillsborough Road, Hillsborough 1042, New Zealand* E: frasermcdermot@me.com

MacDONALD, Preb Alan Hendry. b 49. St Steph Ho Ox 86. **d** 88 **p** 89. C Heavitree w Ex St Paul 88-91; C Withycombe Raleigh 91-92; TV 92-95; R Silverton, Butterleigh, Bickleigh and Cadeleigh from 95; RD Tiverton 00-02 and 08-12; RD Cullompton 08-12; Preb Ex Cathl from 10. *The Rectory, 21A King Street, Silverton, Exeter EX5 4JG* T: (01392) 860350 E: almac1@talktalk.net

MacDONALD, Alastair Douglas. b 48. Cranmer Hall Dur 71. **d** 74 **p** 75. C Mottingham St Andr w St Alban *S'wark* 74-78; C Woolwich St Mary w St Mich 78-81; V S Wimbledon St Andr 81-89; V Brighton St Matthias *Chich* 89-94; Chapl Southn Community Services NHS Trust 94-01; Mental Health Chapl Hants Partnerships NHS Trust 01-04. *Episkopi, Fontwell Avenue, Eastergate, Chichester PO20 3RU* T: (01243) 542771

MacDONALD, Alastair Robert. b 72. Edin Univ MA 94 MTh 03. TISEC. **d** 02 **p** 03. C Edin St Thos 02-06; Asst Chapl Amsterdam w Den Helder and Heiloo *Eur* 06-13. *17 South Road, Insch AB52 6XG* M: 07513-400081 E: macinsch@gmail.com

McDONALD, Barbara Joy. b 58. **d** 12 **p** 13. OLM Gt Bookham *Guildf* from 12. *3 Fiona Close, Great Bookham KT23 3JU* T: (01372) 454187 E: barbarajoymcdonald@gmail.com

MACDONALD, Cameron. b 51. Open Univ BA 89. Wilson Carlile Coll 76 NEOC 89. **d** 90 **p** 91. CA from 76; C Nairn *Mor* 90-92; P-in-c 92-95; CF 95-05; Chapl HM YOI Thorn Cross 05-07; Port Chapl Aqaba Jordan from 07. *Church of St Peter and St Paul, PO Box 568, Aqaba 77100, Jordan* T: (00962) (3) 201 8630 E: mtsaqaba@go.com.jo

McDONALD, Carollyn Elisabeth. b 54. Edin Univ BSc 76. EMMTC 07. **d** 09 **p** 10. C Sawley *Derby* 09-13; C Ashbourne St Oswald w Mapleton from 13; C Ashbourne St Jo from 13; C Clifton from 13. *12 Meynell Rise, Ashbourne DE6 1RU* T: (01335) 664132 E: carollyn4ashbourne@sky.com

MacDONALD, Christina Mary. b 72. SWMTC. **d** 12 **p** 13. NSM Minehead *B & W* from 12. *14 Glenmore Road, Minehead TA24 5BH* T: (01643) 709322 E: teena.macdonald@btinternet.com

MACDONALD, Christopher Kenneth. b 57. Ex Univ BA 79 PGCE 80. Trin Coll Bris 91. **d** 93 **p** 94. C Eastbourne All SS *Chich* 93-96; C Polegate 96-99; Chapl Eastbourne Coll from 99. *14A Grange Road, Eastbourne BN21 4HJ* T: (01323) 452317 E: ckm@eastbourne-college.co.uk

MACDONALD, Colin. b 47. St Jo Coll Nottm 87. **d** 89 **p** 90. C Limber Magna w Brocklesby *Linc* 89-92; P-in-c Barrow and Goxhill 92-97; V 97-99; R Hemingby 99-02; V Fulletby 99-02; R Belchford 99-02; TV Wilford Peninsula *St E* 02-09; rtd 09; P-in-c Siddal *Wakef* 09-12. *2 Southdale Gardens, Ossett WF5 8BB* T: (01924) 276965 E: cmacdonald@aol.com

MACDONALD, Canon Donald Courtenay. b 45. Nottm Univ BTh 74 St Martin's Coll Lanc CertEd 75. Kelham Th Coll 70. **d** 75 **p** 76. C Clifton All SS w Tyndalls Park *Bris* 75-78; C Clifton All SS w St Jo 78-79; Chapl Derby Lonsdale Coll 79-82; Chapl Derby Coll of HE 83-84; V Derby St Andr w St Osmund 84-10; RD Derby S 89-99; Dioc Communications Officer 89-93; Hon Can Derby Cathl 95-10; rtd 10. *13 Langford Road, Mickleover, Derby DE3 0PD* E: donald.c.macdonald@btinternet.com

MACDONALD, Helen Maria. See BARTON, Helen Maria

McDONALD, Ian Henry. b 40. TD. St Aid Birkenhead 65. **d** 68 **p** 69. C Kingston upon Hull H Trin *York* 68-70; C Drumglass *Arm* 70-73; I Eglish w Killylea 73-80; I Maghera w Killelagh *D & R* 80-91; I Killowen 91-98; I Errigal w Garvagh 98-05; Can Derry Cathl 94-00; Preb 00-05; CF (TAVR) 91-05; rtd 05. *4 Ballylagan Lane, Aghadowey, Coleraine BT51 4DD* T: (028) 7086 9150 M: 07740-708402 E: ihmcd@hotmail.co.uk

McDONALD, James Alexander. b 88. Leeds Univ BSc 10. Ripon Coll Cuddesdon BA 14. **d** 14 **p** 15. C Brackley St Pet w St Jas from 14. *36 Price's Way, Brackley NN13 6NR* M: 07981-429338 E: james.a.mcdonald@live.co.uk

McDONALD, Canon James Damian (Jack). b 66. Pemb Coll Cam BA 87 MA 91 K Coll Lon MA 96 SS Hild & Bede Coll Dur PGCE 88 Strasbourg Univ Dr Théol 07. Qu Coll Birm 90. **d** 92 **p** 93. C Camberwell St Geo *S'wark* 92-95; Chapl G&C Coll Cam 95-99; Fell and Dean 99-06; Sen Proctor Cam Univ 02-03; Headmaster Sancton Wood Sch 06-09; PtO *Eur* 09-12; P-in-c Leuven from 12; Can Th Brussels Cathl from 12. *Leeuwerikenstraat 57/0608, 3001 Heverlee, Belgium* T: (0032) (49) 737 9365 E: jackmcdonald@hotmail.be *or* chaplain@anglicanchurchleuven.be

MACDONALD, Mrs Janice Margaret. b 57. SCRTP 13. **d** 15. C Aldermaston and Woolhampton *Ox* from 15. *Address temp unknown*

McDONALD, Lawrence Ronald. b 32. St Alb Minl Tr Scheme 84. **d** 87 **p** 88. NSM Sharnbrook and Knotting w Souldrop *St Alb* 87-90; C Bromham w Oakley and Stagsden 90-93; P-in-c Renhold 93-98; rtd 99; P-in-c Stevington *St Alb* 99-02; PtO from 02. *16 Townsend Road, Sharnbrook, Bedford MK44 1HY* T: (01234) 782849 E: fathermac@ukgateway.net

MACDONALD, Malcolm Crawford. b 75. St Andr Univ MA 97 MLitt 98. Wycliffe Hall Ox BTh 05. **d** 05 **p** 06. C Kensington St Barn *Lon* 05-09; V Loughton St Mary *Chelmsf* from 09. *The Vicarage, 4 St Mary's Close, Loughton IG10 1BA* T: (020) 8508 7892 M: 07821-011435 E: malcolmandcaroline@talktalk.net

MACDONALD, Martin Stanley Harrison. b 51. Dur Univ BSc 72 ACA 75 FCA 82. SAOMC 98. **d** 01 **p** 02. NSM Tring *St Alb* 01-08; PtO *Leeds* from 09. *Broad Head End, Cragg Vale, Hebden Bridge HX7 5RT* T: (01422) 881543 M: 07883-091787 E: mshmacdonald@gmail.com

MACDONALD, Canon Murray Somerled. b 23. Pemb Coll Cam BA 46 MA 49. Ely Th Coll 47. **d** 48 **p** 49. C Hendon St Mary *Lon* 48-51; C Hanover Square St Geo 51-53; P-in-c Upton and Copmanford *Ely* 53-54; R Sawtry 53-54; R Sawtry, Upton and Copmanford 54-57; V Upwood w Gt and Lt Raveley 57-62; R Wood Walton 57-62; V Fenstanton 62-70; V Hilton 62-70; RD Huntingdon 69-76; R Huntingdon All SS w St Jo 70-82; R Huntingdon St Mary w St Benedict 71-82; Hon Can Ely Cathl 72-82; Can Res Ely Cathl 82-88; rtd 89; PtO *Linc* 89-01; *Ely* 89-97. *4 Hacconby Lane, Morton, Bourne PE10 0NT* T: (01778) 570711

McDONALD, Robert William. b 72. Otago Univ BA 94 MA 96 Fitzw Coll Cam BA 06 MA 10 MPhil 07 PhD 12 LTCL 95. Ridley Hall Cam 04. **d** 10 **p** 11. C Shrewsbury St Geo w Greenfields *Lich* 10-13; Tutor Ridley Hall Cam from 13. *Ridley Hall, Ridley Hall Road, Cambridge CB3 9HG* T: (01223) 746580 F: 746581 E: rwm40@cam.ac.uk

MACDONALD (formerly WIFFIN), The Very Revd Susan Elizabeth. b 51. Edin Th Coll 93. **d** 96 **p** 97. NSM Jedburgh *Edin* 96-98; C Galashiels 98-01; P-in-c Fochabers and Dioc Miss Co-ord *Mor* 01-04; Can St Andr Cathl Inverness 03-04; Miss and Min Officer *Ab* 05-07; R Edin Ch Ch from 07; Dean Edin from 12. *4 Morningside Road, Edinburgh EH10 4DD* M: 07753-684923 T: 0131-229 6556 *or* 229 0090 E: susan@6a.org.uk *or* dean@dioceseofedinburgh.org

MACDONALD, Warren. Monash Univ Aus BEng Leeds Univ MPhil Gothenburg Univ PhD 00 CEng CPEng MIEAust. Trin Coll Bris 93. **d** 95 **p** 96. NSM Iford *Win* 95-98; PtO 98-12;

Sarum from 11. *5 St James's Square, Bournemouth BH5 2BX* T: (01202) 422131 M: 07774-497872 F: 422101 E: warren@warrenmacdonald.com

MACDONALD-MILNE, Canon Brian James. b 35. CCC Cam BA 58 MA 62 St Pet Coll Ox MA 81. Cuddesdon Coll 58. **d** 60 **p** 61. C Fleetwood St Pet *Blackb* 60-63; Solomon Is 64-78; Vanuatu 78-80; Acting Chapl Trin Coll Ox 81; Acting Chapl St Pet Coll Ox 81-82; Relief Chapl HM Pris Grendon and Spring Hill 81-82; Research Fell Qu Coll Birm 82-83; Hon Asst P Bordesley SS Alb and Patr *Birm* 82-83; R Landbeach *Ely* 83-88; V Waterbeach 83-88; OCM 83-88; R Radwinter w Hempstead *Chelmsf* 88-97; RD Saffron Walden 91-97; P-in-c The Sampfords 95-97; rtd 97; PtO *Ely* from 97; *Chelmsf* from 02; Dioc Rep Melanesian Miss and Papua New Guinea Ch Partnership from 99; Chapl Ely Chapter Guild of Servants of the Sanctuary from 00; Adv Melanesian Brotherhood 05-13; PtO Melanesia from 07; Can Honiara from 07. *39 Way Lane, Waterbeach, Cambridge CB25 9NQ* T: (01223) 861631 E: bj.macdonaldmilne@homecall.co.uk

MacDONNELL, David. b 80. TCD BEd 02 BTh 09 MA 09. CITC. **d** 09 **p** 10. C Dublin Ch Ch Cathl Gp 09-14; Treas V St Patr Cathl Dublin 11-14; I Dunfanaghy, Raymunterdoney and Tullaghbegley *D & R* from 14. *The Rectory, Horn Head Road, Dunfanaghy, Co Donegal, Republic of Ireland* T: (00353) (74) 913 6187 E: htdunfanaghy@gmail.com

McDONNELL, Mrs Mavis Marian. b 42. **d** 98 **p** 99. OLM Warrington St Ann *Liv* 98-12; rtd 12. *32 Shaws Avenue, Warrington WA2 8AX* T: (01925) 634408 E: mmavis@aol.com

McDONOUGH, David Sean. b 55. **d** 89 **p** 90. C Moseley St Mary *Birm* 89-92; TV Glascote and Stonydelph *Lich* 92-11; R Anstey and Thurcaston w Cropston *Leic* from 11. *The Rectory, 1 Hurd's Close, Anstey, Leicester LE7 7GH* T: 0116-236 2176 E: david@dmcdonough.freeserve.co.uk

McDONOUGH, Terence. b 57. St Jo Coll Nottm LTh 86. **d** 89 **p** 90. C Linthorpe *York* 89-94; TV Heworth H Trin 94-98; V Heworth Ch Ch 98-11; P-in-c York St Thos w St Maurice 06-09; V Fulford from 11; RD City of York from 12. *The Vicarage, 1 Fulford Park, Fulford, York YO10 4QE* T: (01904) 633261 E: tmcd@st-oswalds-fulford.org.uk

McDOUGAL, John Anthony Phelps Standen. See STANDEN McDOUGAL, John Anthony Phelps

McDOUGALL, David Robin. b 61. Avery Hill Coll CertEd BEd 84. Ridley Hall Cam 85. **d** 87 **p** 88. C Bletchley *Ox* 87-91; C High Wycombe 91-93; C E Twickenham St Steph *Lon* 93-02; P-in-c Upper Sunbury St Sav 02-14; AD Spelthorne 10-14; R Bletchley *Ox* from 14. *The Rectory, 101 Whalley Drive, Bletchley, Milton Keynes MK3 6HX* T: (01908) 630305 E: davidrobinmcdougall@gmail.com

McDOUGALL, Mrs Denise Alma. b 48. Ban Coll TCert 69. NOC 00. **d** 03 **p** 04. NSM Waterloo Ch Ch and St Jo *Liv* 03-09; Chapl St Fran of Assisi City Academy Liv 05-09; NSM Gt Crosby St Faith and Waterloo Park St Mary *Liv* 09-13; rtd 13. *27 Mayfair Avenue, Crosby, Liverpool L23 2TL* T: 0151-924 8870 E: denisemcdougall@yahoo.com

MacDOUGALL, Canon Iain William. b 20. TCD BA 43 MA 59. CITC 43. **d** 43 **p** 44. C Belfast St Steph *Conn* 43-45; C Enniskillen and Trory *Clogh* 45-48; I Drumlane *K, E & A* 48-50; I Ballinaclash *D & G* 51-54; I Moate *M & K* 54-58; I Ballyloughloe 54-58; I Ferbane 54-58; I Mullingar, Portnashangan, Moyliscar, Kilbixy etc 58-85; Can Meath 81-85; rtd 85. *18 Denville Court, Killiney, Co Dublin, Republic of Ireland* T: (00353) (1) 285 4751

McDOUGALL, Sally-Anne. b 64. Glas Univ BMus 86 Edin Univ BD 04. TISEC 01. **d** 04 **p** 11. C Glas St Marg 04-06; C Studley *Sarum* 10-12; Bp's Dom Chapl *Linc* from 12; PV Linc Cathl from 13. *The Old Palace, Lincoln LN2 1PU* T: (01522) 504094 E: bishops.chaplain@lincoln.anglican.org

McDOUGALL, Stuart Ronald. b 28. Leeds Univ DipAdEd MEd 84. Roch Th Coll 64. **d** 66 **p** 67. C Gravesend St Aid *Roch* 66-69; C Wells St Thos w Horrington *B & W* 69-70; TV Tong *Bradf* 70-73; V Cononley w Bradley 73-82; C Thornthwaite w Thruscross and Darley *Ripon* 82-83; P-in-c Dacre w Hartwith 83-86; rtd 86; PtO *Sarum* 90-08. *13 Bromley College, London Road, Bromley BR1 1PE* T: (020) 8313 1342

MacDOUGALL, William Duncan. b 47. Anglia Ruskin Univ MA 04. St Jo Coll Nottm BTh 74 LTh 74. **d** 74 **p** 75. C Highbury New Park St Aug *Lon* 74-77; C Tunbridge Wells St Jo *Roch* 77-78; SAMS Argentina 78-82; V Rashcliffe and Lockwood *Wakef* 83-87; V Tonbridge St Steph *Roch* 87-03; RD Tonbridge 01-03; Dir Past and Evang Studies Trin Coll Bris 03-12; rtd 12; P-in-c Bradley Stoke N CD *Bris* 12-15. *Address temp unknown* M: 07710-067239 E: bill.macdougall@btinternet.com

McDOWALL, Julian Thomas. b 39. CCC Cam BA 62 MA 67 Barrister 61. Linc Th Coll 62. **d** 64 **p** 65. C Rugby St Andr *Cov* 64-70; C-in-c Stoke Hill CD *Guildf* 70-72; V Stoke Hill 72-76;

R Elstead 76-91; V Thursley 82-91; TV Wellington and Distr *B & W* 91-93; C Lymington *Win* 93-04; rtd 04; PtO *Win* from 04. *Juniper Cottage, 20 Solent Avenue, Lymington SO41 3SD* T: (01590) 676750

McDOWALL, Robert Angus (Robin). b 39. AKC 66. **d** 67 **p** 68. C Bishopwearmouth St Mich w St Hilda *Dur* 67-69; CF 69-05; Sen CF 80-91; Asst Chapl Gen 91-94; QHC 93-05; rtd 04; PtO *York* from 05. *c/o Crockford, Church House, Great Smith Street, London SW1P 3AZ* T: (01482) 862504

McDOWALL, Roger Ian. b 40. AKC 64. **d** 65 **p** 66. C Peterlee *Dur* 65-68; C Weaste *Man* 68-70; C Tonge Moor 70-73; V Whitworth St Bart 73-80; TV Torre *Ex* 80-88; V Torre All SS 88-00; Chapl S Devon Tech Coll Torbay 80-00; rtd 04. *1 Dunanellerich, Dunvegan, Isle of Skye IV55 8ZH* T: (01470) 521271 E: rogers@sagart.co.uk

✠**McDOWELL, The Rt Revd Francis John.** b 56. QUB BA 78. CITC BTh 93. **d** 96 **p** 97 **c** 11. C Antrim *Conn* 96-99; I Ballyrashane w Kildollagh 99-02; I Dundela St Mark *D & D* 02-11; Bp Clogh from 11. *The See House, Ballagh Road, Fivemiletown BT75 0QP* T: (028) 8952 2461 E: bishop@clogher.anglican.org

McDOWELL, Ian. b 67. Ch Coll Cam MA 88 BA 92. Westcott Ho Cam 90. **d** 93 **p** 94. C Hackney *Lon* 93-96; Asst Chapl Homerton Hosp NHS Trust Lon 96-98; Chapl Newham Healthcare NHS Trust Lon 98-03. *37 Hemsworth Street, London N1 5LF* T: (020) 7363 8053 E: mcdow@dircon.co.uk

McDOWELL, Ian James. b 37. St Jo Coll Morpeth ACT ThL 60 St Aug Coll Cant. **d** 61 **p** 62. C Naracoorte Australia 61-66; P-in-c Elliston Miss 63-66; C S Harrow St Paul *Lon* 66; C Southgate Ch Ch 67; V Ganton *York* 67-71; P-in-c Foxholes and Butterwick 67-68; R 68-71; R Angaston Australia 71-76; R Colonel Light Gardens 76-94; R Gawler 94-98; R Merriwa 98-02; rtd 02. *1516 New England Highway, Harpers Hill NSW 2321, Australia* T: (0061) (2) 4930 9051

McDOWELL, John. *See* McDOWELL, Francis John

McDOWELL, Canon Peter Kerr. b 69. QUB BA 91. CITC BTh 94. **d** 94 **p** 95. C Lisburn St Paul *Conn* 94-98; C Arm St Mark 98-99; I Belfast Upper Malone (Epiphany) *Conn* 99-05; I Ballywillan from 05; Can St Patr Cathl Dublin from 11. *The Rectory, 10 Coleraine Road, Portrush BT56 8EA* T: (028) 7082 4298 M: 07724-072944 E: revpetermcdowell@hotmail.co.uk

McDOWELL, Sheilah Rosamond Girgis. b 72. **d** 05. NSM Hammersmith H Innocents and St Jo *Lon* 05-13; PtO from 13. *36 Avenue Gardens, Teddington TW11 0BH* T: (020) 8943 9259 E: rosamond.mcdowell@collyerbristow.com

McDOWELL, William. b 61. Ox Min Course 12. **d** 15. C E Downland *Ox* from 15. *Address temp unknown*

MACE, Alan Herbert. b 28. Lon Univ BA 49 Ex Inst of Educn TCert 50. Wycliffe Hall Ox 59. **d** 60 **p** 61. C Disley *Ches* 60-63; C Folkestone H Trin w Ch Ch *Cant* 63-67; LtO *Win* 67-93; rtd 93; Public Preacher *Win* from 93. *15 Bassett Heath Avenue, Southampton SO16 7GP* T: (023) 8076 8161

MACE, David Sinclair. b 37. Cam Univ BA 61. **d** 95 **p** 96. OLM Godalming *Guildf* 95-07; rtd 07; PtO *Guildf* from 07. *Torridon, Grosvenor Road, Godalming GU7 1NZ* T: (01483) 414646 E: dsmace@btinternet.com

McELHINNEY, Canon Mary Elizabeth Ellen. b 45. TCD BSSc 67 BA 67. CITC BTh 94. **d** 97 **p** 98. C Magheralin w Dollingstown *D & D* 97-01; I Calry *K, E & A* 01-07; Preb Elphin Cathl 04-07; rtd 07; P-in-c Roscommon w Donamon, Rathcline, Kilkeevin etc *K, E & A* 13-15. *10 Taughrane Heights, Dollingstown, Craigavon BT66 7RS* E: lizmcelhinney@hotmail.com

McELHINNEY, Robert Stephen. b 70. Aston Univ BSc 91. CITC BTh 05. **d** 05 **p** 06. C Kill *D & G* 05-08; C Drumglass w Moygashel *Arm* 08-11; P-in-c Derryvolgie *Conn* 11-15; I from 15. *The Rectory, 35 Kirkwoods Park, Lisburn BT28 3RR* E: scrap5@eircom.net

McELVEE, Rachel. b 49. **d** 10 **p** 11. NSM Clapham St Paul *S'wark* 10-13; USA from 13. *Address temp unknown*

McENDOO, Canon Neil Gilbert. b 50. TCD BA 72. CITC 75. **d** 75 **p** 76. C Cregagh *D & D* 75-79; C Dublin St Ann *D & G* 79-82; I Dublin Rathmines w Harold's Cross from 82; Can Ch Ch Cathl Dublin 92-02; Preb from 02; Chan from 05. *The Rectory, Purser Gardens, Church Avenue, Rathmines, Dublin 6, Republic of Ireland* T: (00353) (1) 497 1797 E: neil.mcendoo@oceanfree.net

McEUNE, Patrick John. b 55. Sarum Coll MA 12. **d** 04 **p** 05. NSM White Horse *Sarum* 04-12; TV 07-12; Liturg Chapl Bp Ramsbury 08-12; PtO *Nor* from 08; R Bradwell on Sea and St Lawrence *Chelmsf* 12-14; P-in-c Fingringhoe w E Donyland and Abberton etc from 14. *The Rectory, Rectory Road, Rowhedge, Colchester CO5 7HR* M: 07411-761883 E: mceune@gmail.com

McEVITT, Canon Peter Benedict. b 58. Coll of Resurr Mirfield 91. **d** 93 **p** 94. C Swinton and Pendlebury *Man* 93-96; TV 96-97; V Darwen St Cuth w Tockholes St Steph *Blackb*

97-02; P-in-c Failsworth H Family *Man* 02-04; R 04-08; AD Oldham 02-08; Dioc Stewardship Officer 08-11; V Royton St Paul and Shaw from 11; Hon Can Man Cathl from 07. *The Vicarage, 13 Church Road, Shaw, Oldham OL2 7AT* T: (01706) 843485 E: frpetermcevitt@googlemail.com

MACEY, Preb Anthony Keith Frank. b 46. St Steph Ho Ox 69. **d** 71 **p** 72. C Ex St Thos 71-76; V Wembury 76-88; RD Ivybridge 83-91; V Cockington 88-12; RD Torbay 98-03; Preb Ex Cathl 05-12; rtd 12. *28 All Saints Road, Torquay TQ1 3RD* T: (01803) 329540 E: p.macey1953@btinternet.com

MACEY, Michael David. b 81. Ex Univ BA 03 St Jo Coll Dur MATM 08. Cranmer Hall Dur 03. **d** 05 **p** 06. C Dartmouth and Dittisham *Ex* 05-08; Min Can and Prec Westmr Abbey 08-14; V Boxmoor St Jo *St Alb* from 14; PV Westmr Abbey from 15. *Boxmoor Vicarage, 10 Charles Street, Hemel Hempstead HP1 1JH* T: (01442) 243258 M: 07972-266881 E: vicar@stjohnsboxmoor.org.uk

McFADDEN, Canon Ronald Bayle. b 30. TCD BA 53 MA 55. **d** 54 **p** 55. C Drumglass *Arm* 54-58; S Africa 58-62; Bp's Dom Chapl *D & D* 62-64; C Dundela St Mark 62-64; V Pateley Bridge and Greenhow Hill *Ripon* 64-73; V Knaresborough St Jo 73-79; P-in-c Knaresborough H Trin 78-79; Can Res Ripon Cathl 79-90; rtd 90; Chapl Qu Mary's Sch Baldersby Park 90-00; PtO *Leeds* from 90; *York* from 97. *12 Ure Bank Terrace, Ripon HG4 1JG* T: (01765) 604043

McFADDEN, Terrance. b 61. NTMTC 05. **d** 08 **p** 09. C Greenstead w Colchester St Anne *Chelmsf* 08-12; TV Eccleston *Liv* 12-15; Chapl HM Pris Littlehey from 15. *HM Prison Littlehey, Perry, Huntingdon PE28 0SR* M: 07856-981104 T: (01480) 335000 E: terry1117@hotmail.co.uk

McFADYEN, Donald Colin Ross. b 63. Wolfs Coll Cam BTh 00 Peterho Cam MPhil 02 SS Coll Cam PhD 06. Ridley Hall Cam 97. **d** 01 **p** 02. NSM Haslingfield w Harlton and Gt and Lt Eversden *Ely* 01-05; P-in-c Bassingbourn 05-12; P-in-c Whaddon 05-12; Course Dir Ridley Hall Cam 05-08; V Orton Longueville w Bottlebridge *Ely* 12-14; P-in-c Orton Waterville 14; V The Ortons from 14; RD Yaxley from 14. *The New Rectory, 2A The Village, Orton Longueville, Peterborough PE2 7DN* T: (01733) 371071 M: 07595-539507 E: donald.mcfadyen@me.com

McFADYEN (formerly TALBOT), Canon Mair Josephine. b 59. Univ Coll Lon BA 84. Ridley Hall Cam 85. **d** 88 **p** 94. C Gt Yarmouth *Nor* 88-94; Sen Asst P Raveningham Gp 94-99; Chapl Norfolk Mental Health Care NHS Trust 94-02; Bp's Adv for Women's Min *Nor* 01-04; P-in-c Watton w Carbrooke and Ovington 02-06; Project Manager Magd Gp 06-10; Chapl Norfolk Primary Care Trust from 10; NSM Nor St Geo Colegate from 14; Hon Can Nor Cathl from 02. *The Chaplaincy, Priscilla Bacon Lodge, Unthank Road, Norwich NR2 2PJ* T: (01603) 225728 E: mair.mcfadyen@nchc.nhs.uk

McFADYEN, Canon Phillip. b 44. K Coll Lon BD 69 AKC 69 MTh 70 ATD. St Aug Coll Cant 69. **d** 71 **p** 72. C Sheff St Mark Broomhall 71-74; Chapl Keswick Hall Coll of Educn 74-79; V Swardeston *Nor* 79-81; P-in-c E Carleton 79-81; P-in-c Intwood w Keswick 79-81; R Swardeston w E Carleton, Intwood, Keswick etc 81-90; R Ranworth w Panxworth, Woodbastwick etc 90-05; Dioc Clergy Tr Officer 90-98; P-in-c Nor St Geo Colegate from 05; Hon Can Nor Cathl from 97; Bp's Officer for Visual Arts from 01; Relig Adv Anglia TV from 01. *54 The Close, Norwich NR1 4EG* T: (01603) 621570 E: phillipmcfadyen@aol.com

McFARLAND, Alan Malcolm. b 24. Lon Univ BA 53. Bris Sch of Min 82. **d** 85 **p** 86. NSM Westbury-on-Trym H Trin *Bris* 85-88; Asst Lect Bris Sch of Min 85-88; PtO *Glouc* 88-89; NSM Lechlade 89-93; PtO *Sarum* 93-08. *11 The Seahorse, Higher Sea Lane, Charmouth, Bridport DT6 6BB* T: (01297) 560414

McFARLAND, Darren William. b 71. QUB BA 93. CITC BTh 96. **d** 96 **p** 97. C Greystones *D & G* 96-98; PV Ch Ch Cathl Dublin 97-99; P-in-c Clydebank *Glas* 99-02; Asst Dioc Miss 21 Co-ord 99-02; R Paisley St Barn and Paisley H Trin 02-11; V Headington *Ox* from 11. *The Vicarage, 33 St Andrew's Road, Oxford OX3 9DL* T: (01865) 761094 M: 07773-772610 E: vicar.headington@gmail.com

MACFARLANE, Elizabeth Clare. b 71. St Hugh's Coll Ox BA 92 MA 03 St Cross Coll Ox DPhil 12. Ripon Coll Cuddesdon BA 02. **d** 03 **p** 04. C Watford St Mich *St Alb* 03-06; TV Gt Marlow w Marlow Bottom, Lt Marlow and Bisham *Ox* 06-11; Chapl and Fell St Jo Coll Ox from 11. *St John's College, Oxford OX1 3JP* T: (01865) 277660 F: 277435 E: elizabeth.macfarlane@sjc.ox.ac.uk

MACFARLANE, Iain Philip. b 64. Essex Univ BSc 85 W Sussex Inst of HE PGCE 88. Trin Coll Bris BA 99. **d** 99 **p** 00. C Fishponds St Jo *Bris* 99-03; TV Yate from 03. *The Vicarage, 57 Brockworth, Bristol BS37 8SJ* T: (01454) 322921 E: imacfarlane@ukonline.co.uk

McFARLANE, Iain Scott. b 70. St Jo Coll Nottm 02. **d** 04 **p** 05. C Malvern St Andr and Malvern Wells and Wyche *Worc* 04-07; V Taunton Lyngford *B & W* 07-14; P-in-c Boyatt Wood *Win* from 14. *St Peter's Church House, 53 Sovereign Way, Eastleigh SO50 4SA* T: (023) 8184 5032 M: 07834-191507 E: revmcfarlane@gmail.com

McFARLANE, The Ven Janet Elizabeth. b 64. Sheff Univ BMedSci 87 St Jo Coll Dur BA 92. Cranmer Hall Dur 93. **d** 93 **p** 94. Par Dn Stafford *Lich* 93-94; C 94-96; Chapl and Min Can Ely Cathl 96-99; Dioc Communications Officer *Nor* from 99; Hon PV Nor Cathl 00-09; Bp's Chapl 01-09; Adn Nor from 09. *31 Bracondale, Norwich NR1 2AT* T: (01603) 620007 E: archdeacon.norwich@dioceseofnorwich.org

MACFARLANE, Katy Antonia. b 69. STETS. **d** 09. NSM Crofton *Portsm* 09-15; Dn-in-c Hartplain from 15. *The Vicarage, 61 Hart Plain Avenue, Waterlooville PO8 8RG*

McGAFFIN, Judith Hilary. CITC. **d** 09 **p** 10. NSM Donagheady *D & R* 09-14; NSM Fahan Lower and Upper from 14. *32 Berryhill Road, Artigarvan, Strabane BT82 0EL* M: 07738-505464 E: judi.mcgaffin@hscni.net *or* judimcgaffin@aol.com

McGANITY, Canon Steven. b 61. Nottm Univ BTh 93. St Jo Coll Nottm 90. **d** 93 **p** 94. C Gateacre *Liv* 93-97; V Clubmoor from 97; AD W Derby from 08; Hon Can Liv Cathl from 08. *St Andrew's Vicarage, 176 Queen's Drive, West Derby, Liverpool L13 0AL* T: 0151-226 1977 E: smcganity@bigfoot.com

McGARAHAN, Kevin Francis. b 51. Oak Hill Th Coll BA 84 MA 90. **d** 84 **p** 85. C Balderstone *Man* 84-87; C Stoughton *Guildf* 87-89; Par Lect Ashton St Mich *Man* 89-92; TV Madeley *Heref* 92-96; CF 96-99; TV Woughton *Ox* 99-06; rtd 07; Hon C Hanger Hill Ascension and W Twyford St Mary *Lon* 07-10. *7 Wesley Terrace, Pensilva, Liskeard PL14 5PD* T: (01579) 363336 E: revkev_mcgarahan@hotmail.co.uk

McGARRIGLE, John James Samuel (Don). b 51. QUB BSc 77 CEng 85 MIET 85. ERMC 12. **d** 14 **p** 15. C Ketton, Collyweston, Easton-on-the-Hill etc *Pet* from 14. *48 Main Street, Greetham, Oakham LE15 7NL* T: (01572) 812804 M: 07802-401798 E: escapeenergy@btconnect.com

McGARVEY, Mrs Muriel Dorothy. b 51. SEITE 12. **d** 14. NSM Eynsford w Farningham and Lullingstone *Roch* from 14. *17 Tilmans Mead, Farningham, Dartford DA4 0BY* - M: 07969-175768 E: eflcurate@gmail.com

McGEARY, Peter. b 59. K Coll Lon BD AKC. Chich Th Coll 84. **d** 86 **p** 87. C Brighton St Pet and St Nic w Chpl Royal *Chich* 86-90; C St Marylebone All SS *Lon* 90-95; P-in-c Hayes St Anselm 95-97; V 97-98; V St Geo-in-the-East St Mary from 98; PV Westmr Abbey from 00. *The Clergy House, All Saints Court, 68 Johnson Street, London E1 0BQ* T/F: (020) 7790 0973 E: mcgeary@pmcg.demon.co.uk

MacGEOCH, David John Lamont. b 64. Bath Univ BSc 90 CQSW 90. Westcott Ho Cam 97. **d** 99 **p** 00. C Midsomer Norton w Clandown *B & W* 99-03; V Puriton and Pawlett 03-08; P-in-c Glastonbury w Meare 08-11; V from 11; RD Glastonbury from 11. *The Vicarage, 24 Wells Road, Glastonbury BA6 9DJ* T: (01458) 834281 E: all@macgeoch.fsnet.co.uk *or* vicarabbeyparish@btinternet.com

McGHIE, Clinton Adolphus. b 41. Univ of W Indies. **d** 78 **p** 79. Jamaica 78-96; PtO *Chelmsf* 96-97; P-in-c Highams Park All SS 97-02; V 02-11; rtd 11. *10 Sussex Way, Billericay CM12 0FA* T: (01277) 634389 E: rev.mcghie@btinternet.com

McGILL, Francis Leonard. b 31. **d** 93 **p** 94. NSM Howell Hill *Guildf* 93-01; PtO from 02. *12 Hampton Grove, Ewell, Epsom KT17 1LA* T: (020) 8393 2226

MacGILLIVRAY, Jonathan Martin. b 53. Aber Univ MA 75. Coll of Resurr Mirfield. **d** 80 **p** 81. C Hulme Ascension *Man* 80-84; P-in-c Birch St Agnes 84-85; R 85-91; V Hurst 91-96; Chapl Tameside Gen Hosp 92-96; Dir of Ords and OLM Officer *Man* 96-02; V Carrington *S'well* 02-13; P-in-c Cawthorne *Leeds* from 13; P-in-c Darton from 13. *The Vicarage, 6 Jacobs Hall Court, Darton, Barnsley S75 5LY* T: (01226) 384596 E: j.macg@virgin.net

McGINLEY, Canon Jack Francis. b 36. ALCD 65. **d** 65 **p** 66. C Erith St Paul *Roch* 65-70; C Morden *S'wark* 70-74; V New Catton Ch Ch *Nor* 74-94; RD Nor N 84-89; Hon Can Nor Cathl 90-94; R Carlton-in-the-Willows *S'well* 94-02; R Colwick 96-02; rtd 02; PtO *Nor* from 03. *14 Clovelly Drive, Norwich NR6 5EY* T: (01603) 788848 E: jack.mcginley14@btinternet.com

McGINLEY, John Charles. b 69. Birm Univ BSocSc 90. Trin Coll Bris BA 96. **d** 96 **p** 97. C Hounslow H Trin w St Paul *Lon* 96-00; TV Hinckley H Trin *Leic* 00-04; TR 04-09; V Leic H Trin w St Jo from 09; P-in-c Emmaus Par Team from 14. *5 Ratcliffe Road, Leicester LE2 3JE* E: john.mcginley1@ntlworld.com

McGINTY, Ms Nicola Jane. b 61. Bath Univ BSc 83 Warwick Univ MBA 06. Qu Coll Birm MA 09. **d** 09 **p** 10. NSM Barrow upon Soar w Walton le Wolds *Leic* 09-12; NSM Wymeswold and Prestwold w Hoton 09-12; PtO from 12. *5 Station Road, Rearsby, Leicester LE7 4YX* T: (01664) 424869 E: nicky@njmcginty.co.uk

McGIRR, Canon William Eric. b 43. CITC 68. **d** 71 **p** 72. C Carrickfergus *Conn* 71-74; C Mt Merrion *D & D* 74-77; I Donacavey w Barr *Clogh* 77-88; I Ballybeen *D & D* 88-94; I Magheraculmoney *Clogh* 94-10; Can Clogh Cathl 95-10; Chan Clogh Cathl 06-10; rtd 10. *11 Castle Manor, Kesh, Enniskillen BT93 1RT* T: (028) 6863 2221

McGIVERN, Mrs Ann Margaret. b 49. Newc Poly BSc 79 MPhil 92 Newc Univ PGCE 80. Lindisfarne Regional Tr Partnership 10. **d** 11. NSM Long Benton *Newc* 11-15; NSM Balkwell from 15. *9 Albany Avenue, Newcastle upon Tyne NE12 8AS* T: 0191-266 5442 M: 07940-211004 E: annpope@hotmail.com

McGLADDERY, David John. b 62. Homerton Coll Cam BEd 85 Univ of Wales (Cardiff) MA 93. St Mich Coll Llan 02. **d** 05 **p** 06. NSM Monmouth w Overmonnow etc *Mon* 05-09; V from 09; AD Monmouth from 13; Asst Chapl Mon Sch from 05. *The Vicarage, The Parade, Monmouth NP25 3PA* T: (01600) 715941 E: mcgladdery5@btinternet.com

McGLINCHEY, Patrick Gerard. b 59. NUU BA 82 Nottm Univ BTh 95 MA 06 QUB PhD 13. St Jo Coll Nottm 93. **d** 95 **p** 96. C Kettering Ch the King *Pet* 95-97; C Gorleston St Andr *Nor* 97-02; Assoc Min Cliff Park Community Ch 99-02; Chapl and Dean of Res QUB 03-09; TCD from 09; Lect Ch of Ireland Th Inst from 09. *40 Thorncliffe Park, Churchtown, Dublin 14, Republic of Ireland* T: (00353) (1) 405 5202 *or* 499 7279 M: (00353) 89-475 3105 *or* 07500-464542 E: patrickmcglinchey@theologicalinstitute.ie

McGLYNN, Mrs Lesley Anne. b 59. St Mellitus Coll 12. **d** 15. OLM Canvey Is *Chelmsf* from 15. *3 Thorney Bay Road, Canvey Island SS8 0HG*

McGONIGLE, Martin Leo Thomas. b 64. Univ of Greenwich BA 94 Anglia Poly Univ MA 99. EAMTC 96. **d** 98 **p** 99. C Forest Gate All SS *Chelmsf* 98-01; PtO *Lon* 01-02; Chapl Asst Cen Man/Man Children's Univ Hosp NHS Trust 02-03; Lead Chapl 03-07; Spiritual Care Co-ord 07-11; Chapl Springhill Hospice 06-11; V Southgate St Andr *Lon* 11-13; Chapl Cen Lon Community Healthcare NHS Trust from 13. *Central London Community Healthcare, 7th Floor, 64 Victoria Street, London SW1E 6QP* T: (020) 7798 1300

McGOVERN, Mrs Leisa Caroline. b 69. Plymouth Univ BSc 92. SWMTC. **d** 14. C Ottery St Mary, Alfington, W Hill, Tipton etc *Ex* from 14. *The Vicarage, Bendarroch Road, West Hill, Ottery St Mary EX11 1UW* T: (01404) 234498 M: 07766-702076 E: lcmcgv@sky.com

McGOWAN, Anthony Charles. b 57. Jes Coll Cam BA 79 MA 83. Coll of Resurr Mirfield 80. **d** 82 **p** 83. C Milford Haven *St D* 82-85; C Penistone and Thurlstone *Wakef* 85-88; Asst Chapl Radcliffe Infirmary Ox 91-94; Chapl Radcliffe Infirmary NHS Trust 94-99; Chapl Ox Radcliffe Hosps NHS Trust 99-04; V Northampton H Trin and St Paul *Pet* from 05. *The Vicarage, 24 Edinburgh Road, Northampton NN2 6PH* T: (01604) 711468 E: anthony.mcgowan@tiscali.co.uk

McGOWAN, Daniel Richard Hugh. b 71. Oak Hill Th Coll. **d** 03 **p** 04. C Peterlee *Dur* 03-07; TV Morden *S'wark* from 07. *49 Camborne Road, Morden SM4 4JL* T: (020) 8542 2966

McGOWAN, James. b 83. York St Jo Coll BA 04 St Hild Coll Dur PGCE 05 St Jo Coll Dur BA 11. Cranmer Hall Dur 08. **d** 11 **p** 12. C St German's Cathl 11-14; C W Coast 12-14; V Malew and Santan from 14. *Malew Vicarage, Crossag Road, Ballasalla, Isle of Man IM9 3EF* T: (01624) 822469 M: 07624-488008 E: revdjamesmcgowan@outlook.com

McGOWAN, Timothy Julien. b 68. Wycliffe Hall Ox 05. **d** 07 **p** 09. C N Wembley St Cuth *Lon* 07-08; C Fulham St Matt 08-11; C Umhlali All So S Africa from 14. *Address temp unknown* E: tmcgowan@tmls.co.uk

McGRATH, Prof Alister Edgar. b 53. Wadh Coll Ox BA 75 Mert Coll Ox MA 78 DPhil 78 BD 83 DD 01 DLitt 13 FRSA 05. Westcott Ho Cam 78. **d** 80 **p** 81. C Wollaton *S'well* 80-83; Chapl St Hilda's Coll Ox 83-87; Tutor Wycliffe Hall Ox 83-06; Prin 95-04; Prof Systematic Th Regent Coll Vancouver 93-97; Research Lect in Th Ox Univ 93-99; Prof Hist Th 99-08; Dir Ox Cen for Evang and Apologetics 04-08; President from 06; Sen Research Fell Harris Manchester Coll Ox 06-13; Fell from 14; Prof Th, Min and Educn K Coll Lon 08-14; Andreas Idreos Prof of Science and Relig Ox Univ from 14; NSM Shill Valley and Broadshire *Ox* from 09. *Harris Manchester College, Mansfield Road, Oxford OX1 3TD*

McGRATH, Gavin John. b 53. Marietta Coll (USA) BA 76 Trin Episc Sch for Min MDiv 81 Dur Univ PhD 90. **d** 81 **p** 82. USA 81-87 and 99-05; C Fulwood *Sheff* 87-95; Assoc Th Prof Trin Episc Sch for Min Ambridge 99-05; PtO *S'wark* 07-12; C Sevenoaks St Nic *Roch* from 12. *4 Braeside Close, Sevenoaks TN13 2JL* E: mcgrath.gavin@gmail.com

McGRATH, Ian Denver. b 47. Leeds Univ CertEd 72. **d** 87 **p** 88. OLM Ancaster Wilsford Gp *Linc* 87-92; C Spilsby w Hundleby

92-95; P-in-c Asterby Gp 95-99; R 99-09; rtd 09. *14 Park Crescent, Metheringham, Lincoln LN4 3HH* T: (01526) 321918
E: ian@idmcgrath.fsnet.co.uk

McGRATH, Joanna Ruth. *See* COLLICUTT McGRATH, Joanna Ruth

McGRATH, John. b 49. Salford Univ BSc 78 Univ of Wales (Lamp) MA 10 Man Poly CertEd 79. NOC 82. **d** 85 **p** 86. C Horwich *Man* 85-88; P-in-c Hillock 88-89; V 89-94; V York St Luke 94-97; V Hollinwood *Man* 97-02; P-in-c Oldham St Chad Limeside 97-02; V Hollinwood and Limeside 02-03; TV Turton Moorland 03-07; P-in-c Littleborough, Calderbrook and Shore 07-13; V Littleborough 13-14; rtd 14; PtO *Blackb* from 15. *15 Hall Park Avenue, Burnley BB10 4JJ* T: (01282) 760256 E: johnbede@live.co.uk

McGRATH, Kenneth David. b 59. Surrey Univ BSc 82 QUB PGCE 83 TCD BTh 03. CITC 00. **d** 03 **p** 04. C Lisburn Ch Ch *Cath* 03-05; V 05-09; I Kilkeel *D & D* from 09. *The Rectory, 44 Manse Road, Kilkeel, Newry BT34 4BN* T: (028) 4176 2300 or 4176 5994 E: revken.mcgrath@btopenworld.com

McGRATH, Patrick Desmond. b 64. Liv Univ LLB 86. Wycliffe Hall Ox 92. **d** 96 **p** 97. C Netherton *Liv* 96-98; C Ravenhead 98-02; P-in-c Ightham *Roch* 02-07; PtO *Cant* from 08. *c/o Crockford, Church House, Great Smith Street, London SW1P 3AZ*

MacGREGOR, Alan John. b 31. Jes Coll Ox MA 57. S Tr Scheme 94. **d** 97 **p** 98. NSM Worting *Win* 97-00; PtO *Lon* 01; NSM Poole *Sarum* 03-11; PtO *Derby* 11-12; NSM Ockbrook from 12. *12 Chevin Avenue, Borrowash, Derby DE72 3HR* T: (01332) 678183

McGREGOR, Alexander Scott. b 72. Ch Ch Ox BA 95 MA 00 Barrister 96. SAOMC 03. **d** 06 **p** 07. NSM Harrow St Mary *Lon* 06-09; NSM Pimlico St Barn from 09; NSM Pimlico St Mary Bourne Street 09-14; Legal Adv Legal Office Nat Ch Inst 06-08; Dep Legal Adv Gen Syn and Abps' Coun from 09; Dep Chan *Ox* 07-13; Chan from 13. *Church House, Great Smith Street, London SW1P 3AZ* T: (020) 7898 1748
E: asmcg@hotmail.com

MacGREGOR, Colin Highmoor. b 19. Lon Univ BSc 45 Magd Coll Cam BA 47 MA 50. Wells Th Coll 54. **d** 56 **p** 57. C Camberwell St Giles *S'wark* 56-60; V Clapham St Pet 60-73; V Riddlesdown 73-87; rtd 87; PtO *S'wark* from 03. *3 Longacre Court, 21 Mayfield Road, South Croydon CR2 0BG* T: (020) 8651 2615

MacGREGOR, Donald Alexander Thomson. b 52. Loughb Univ BSc 75 Nottm Univ MA 97 Leic Univ CertEd 78. St Jo Coll Nottm 91. **d** 93 **p** 94. C Walmley *Birm* 93-96; C Braunstone *Leic* 96-97; TV 97-99; Chapl Loughb Univ 99-04; V Fishguard w Llanychar and Pontfaen w Morfil etc *St D* 04-13; P-in-c Llanrhian and Mathry w Grandstone etc from 13; AD Dewisland and Fishguard 13-14. *The Vicarage, Llanrhian, Haverfordwest SA62 5BG* T: (01348) 837750
E: donmacg@live.co.uk

McGREGOR, Mrs Eileen. b 50. Ex Univ BA 71. STETS 07. **d** 10 **p** 11. NSM Fulham All SS *Lon* from 10. *44 Abinger Road, London W4 1EX* T: (020) 8994 2088 M: 07899-928785
E: mcgeileen@aol.com

McGREGOR, Mrs Lorraine Louise. b 59. Sarum Th Coll 02. **d** 05 **p** 06. OLM Colehill *Sarum* from 05. *Tapiola, Marianne Road, Wimborne BH21 2SQ* T: (01202) 886519
E: lorraine@hayeswood.dorset.sch.uk

McGREGOR, Mrs Lynn. b 61. Ches Coll of HE BTh 00. NOC 97. **d** 00 **p** 01. C Colne and Villages *Blackb* 00-03; C Gt Harwood 03-06; P-in-c Wigan St Mich *Liv* 06-07; V 07-10; P-in-c Platt Bridge from 10. *240A Warrington Road, Ince, Wigan WN3 4NH* E: macnmac@sky.com

MacGREGOR, Preb Neil. b 35. Keble Coll Ox BA 60 MA 80. Wells Th Coll. **d** 65 **p** 66. C Bath Bathwick St Mary w Woolley *B & W* 65-70; R Oare w Culbone 70-74; C Lynton, Brendon, Countisbury and Lynmouth *Ex* 70-74; P-in-c Kenn w Kingston Seymour *B & W* 74-76; R 76-80; R Wem and V Lee Brockhurst *Lich* 80-01; P-in-c Loppington w Newtown 95-01; RD Wem and Whitchurch 95-01; Preb Lich Cathl 97-01; rtd 01; PtO *Heref* from 01. *19 Castle View Terrace, Ludlow SY8 2NG* T: (01584) 872671 E: hatchment@talktalk.net

McGREGOR, Nigel Selwyn. b 47. FCA 69. Sarum & Wells Th Coll 87. **d** 89 **p** 90. C Charlton Kings St Mary *Glouc* 89-92; P-in-c Seale *Guildf* 92-95; P-in-c Puttenham and Wanborough 92-95; R Seale, Puttenham and Wanborough 95-04; R Barming *Roch* 04-12; rtd 12; PtO *York* from 12. *14 Chestnut Croft, Hemingbrough, Selby YO8 6UD* E: nigelmcgregor@ymail.com

McGREGOR, Stephen Paul. b 55. **d** 03 **p** 04. OLM Tonge Fold *Man* 03-10; OLM Leverhulme from 10. *32 Rawcliffe Avenue, Bolton BL2 6JX* T: (01204) 391205
E: steve.mcgregor2@ntlworld.com

McGUFFIE, Duncan Stuart. b 45. Man Univ MA 70 Regent's Park Coll Ox DPhil 80. S Dios Minl Tr Scheme 84. **d** 85 **p** 85.

C Sholing *Win* 85-89; V Clavering and Langley w Arkesden etc *Chelmsf* 89-10; rtd 10; PtO *Sheff* from 11. *April Cottage, 15 High Street, Snaith, Goole DN14 9HF*

McGUINNESS, Canon Gordon Baxter. b 57. St Andr Univ BSc 79 BNC Ox MSc 80. Oak Hill NSM Course 86. **d** 89 **p** 90. NSM Loudwater *Ox* 89-92; C Chilwell *S'well* 92-01; TR Ellesmere Port *Ches* 01-09; R from 09; Hon Can Ches Cathl from 14. *The Rectory, Vale Road, Whitby, Ellesmere Port CH65 9AY* T: 0151-356 8351 or 355 2516
E: revgordon@supanet.com

McGUIRE, John. b 31. Oak Hill Th Coll 59. **d** 62 **p** 65. C Tooting Graveney St Nic *S'wark* 62-64; C Normanton *Derby* 64-67; N Area Sec ICM 67-71; Chapl RNR 67-81; R Biddulph Moor *Lich* 71-00; rtd 00; PtO *Blackb* 00-11. *25 Victoria Road, Fulwood, Preston PR2 8NE* T: (01772) 719549
E: jmcguire@argonet.co.uk

McGURK, Michael Joseph Patrick. b 68. St Jo Coll Nottm 05. **d** 07 **p** 08. C Haughton St Mary *Man* 07-09; C Harpurhey 09-10; R from 10; AD N Man from 12. *The Rectory, 95 Church Lane, Manchester M9 5BG* T/F: 0161-205 4020 M: 07811-360432 E: rev.mikemcgurk@hotmail.co.uk

MACHA, David. b 65. Keele Univ BA 88 CertEd 88 St Jo Coll Dur BA 97 Nottm Univ MA 03. Cranmer Hall Dur 94. **d** 97 **p** 98. C Loughborough Em and St Mary in Charnwood *Leic* 97-01; CMS Tanzania 02-09; R Linton in Craven *Leeds* from 09; P-in-c Burnsall w Rylstone from 09. *The Rectory, Hebden Road, Grassington, Skipton BD23 5LA* T: (01756) 752575
E: mchdmacha@gmail.com

McHAFFIE, Alistair. b 57. Oak Hill Th Coll 92. **d** 94 **p** 95. C Braintree *Chelmsf* 94-98; R Falkland Is 98-03; V Leyland St Jo *Blackb* from 03; AD Leyland from 11. *St John's Vicarage, Leyland Lane, Leyland PR25 1XB* T: (01772) 621646
E: alistair@mchaffie.com

McHALE, John Michael. b 61. Ch Ch Coll Cant BA 84 Kingston Univ PGCE 89 Univ of Wales (Cardiff) BTh 08. St Mich Coll Llan 03. **d** 08 **p** 09. NSM Llandingat w Myddfai and Chapl Llandovery Coll 08-10; Chapl Lich Cathl Sch and Prec's V Lich Cathl 10-12; Chapl Wycliffe Coll Glos from 12. *Wycliffe College, Bath Road, Stonehouse GL10 2JQ* T: (01453) 822432 M: 07912-143374 E: john.mchale8@btinternet.com

MACHAM, Miss Anna Jane Mary. b 77. Trin Coll Ox BA 98 Cam Univ BA 02 MPhil 04. Ridley Hall Cam 00. **d** 04 **p** 05. C Cheshunt *St Alb* 04-07; Succ S'wark Cathl 07-13; Chapl K Coll Lon 07-13; P-in-c Camberwell St Phil and St Mark *S'wark* from 13. *St Philip's Vicarage, Avondale Square, London SE1 5PD* T: (020) 7237 3239 M: 07796-590024
E: anna.macham@southwark.anglican.org

McHARDIE, Douglas John Low. b 64. Dundee Univ MA 85. St Jo Coll Nottm 08. **d** 10 **p** 11. C Horley *S'wark* 10-14; R Woodmansterne from 14. *The Rectory, Woodmansterne Street, Banstead SM7 3NL* M: 07958-675530
E: revdougmch@btinternet.com

McHARDY, David William. b 61. Edin Univ BD 88 BD 90 PhD 97 Aber Coll of Educn DCE 82. Edin Th Coll 85. **d** 88 **p** 03. C Dumfries *Glas* 88-89; Lect in World Religions Open Univ 97-08; Hon C Oldmeldrum *Ab* 99-08; P-in-c 08; Chapl Blue Coat Sch Reading 08-10; V Meir Heath and Normacot *Lich* from 10. *St Francis's Vicarage, Sandon Road, Stoke-on-Trent ST3 7LH* T: (01782) 398585 M: 07855-581714
E: david.mchardy@hotmail.com

McHENRY, Brian Edward. b 50. CBE 08. New Coll Ox BA 73 MA 77 Cant Ch Ch Univ BA 12 Barrister 76. SEITE 05. **d** 08 **p** 09. NSM Deptford St Paul *S'wark* 08-11; V Orpington All SS *Roch* from 11. *The Vicarage, 1A Keswick Road, Orpington BR6 0EU* T: (01689) 824624 M: 07887-802641
E: brian@mchenry.co.uk

MACHIN, Mrs Jacqueline June. b 62. STETS. **d** 10 **p** 11. C Romsey *Win* 10-14; R The Downs from 14. *c/o Crockford, Church House, Great Smith Street, London SW1P 3AZ*
E: jax.machin@btinternet.com

MACHIN, Roy Anthony. b 38. BA 79. Oak Hill Th Coll 76. **d** 79 **p** 80. C Halliwell St Pet *Man* 79-83; V Eccleston St Luke *Liv* 83-91; V Kendal St Thos and Crook *Carl* 91-99; V Wigan St Barn Marsh Green *Liv* 99-03; rtd 03; PtO *Man* from 03. *56 Ferndown Road, Harwood, Bolton BL2 3NN*
T/F: (01204) 362220 E: roy.machin@btinternet.com

MACHIRIDZA, Douglas Tafara. b 71. Univ of Zimbabwe BSW 99 Birm Univ BPhil 07 St Edm Coll Cam BTh 10. Westcott Ho Cam 08. **d** 10 **p** 11. C Perry Barr and Perry Beeches *Birm* 10-14; V Handsworth St Andr from 14. *The Vicarage, 55 Laurel Road, Handsworth, Birmingham B21 9PB* T: 0121-551 2097 M: 07887-741029
E: dtmachiridza@yahoo.co.uk

McHUGH, Brian Robert. b 50. York Univ BA 72 Keele Univ CertEd 73 IEng 92 MIMA 98 CMath 98. S Dios Minl Tr Scheme 79. **d** 82 **p** 83. NSM Sarisbury *Portsm* 82-86; NSM

Shedfield 86-06; NSM Shedfield and Wickham from 07; PtO Cyprus and the Gulf from 10. *28 Siskin Close, Bishops Waltham, Southampton SO32 1RQ* T: (01489) 896658 E: brian.mchugh@bcs.org.uk

McHUGH, Michael. b 57. **d** 87 **p** 88. In RC Ch 87-05; NSM Cley Hill Warminster *Sarum* 05-07; C Salisbury St Thos and St Edm 07-10; TV Vale of Pewsey 10-12; TR Savernake from 12. *The Rectory, Church Street, Great Bedwyn, Marlborough SN8 3PF* E: mtmch@hotmail.com

McILROY (née NEWBY), Mrs Claire. b 77. UWE BSc 00 Ox Brookes Univ MA 09. Trin Coll Bris 12. **d** 14 **p** 15. C Torpoint *Truro* 14-15; C Antony w Sheviock from 14; C Antony w Sheviock and Torpoint from 14. *25 Maker Road, Torpoint PL11 2HY* M: 07766-556321 E: revclairemcilroy@gmail.com

McILROY, Sister Honor Margaret. b 24. LRAM 44 GRSM 45. **d** 98 **p** 99. CSMV from 55. *St Mary's Convent, Challow Road, Wantage OX12 9DJ* T: (01235) 763141 E: sisterscsmv@btinternet.com

McINDOE, Darren Lee. b 76. Univ of Wales (Lamp) BA 97. Trin Coll Bris BA 05. **d** 06 **p** 07. C Stratford St Jo w Ch Ch and St Jas *Chelmsf* 06-09; C Forest Gate Em w Upton Cross 09-10; R Burslem *Lich* from 10. *The Rectory, 16 Heyburn Crescent, Burslem, Stoke-on-Trent ST6 4DL* T: (01782) 838932 M: 07886-502307 E: rev.darren.mcindoe@gmail.com

MACINNES, Canon David Rennie. b 32. Jes Coll Cam BA 55 MA 59. Ridley Hall Cam 55. **d** 57 **p** 58. C Gillingham St Mark *Roch* 57-61; C St Helen Bishopsgate w St Martin Outwich *Lon* 61-67; Prec Birm Cathl 67-78; Angl Adv Cen TV 67-82 and 82-93; Dioc Missr *Birm* 79-87; Hon Can Birm Cathl 81-87; R Ox St Aldate w St Matt 87-94; R Ox St Aldate 95-02; Hon Can Ch Ch 98-02; rtd 02. *Pear Tree Cottage, Milcombe, Banbury OX15 4RS* T: (01295) 721119

MacINNES, Harry Campbell. b 67. Nottm Poly BA 89. Wycliffe Hall Ox BTh 94. **d** 97 **p** 98. C E Twickenham St Steph *Lon* 97-00; P-in-c St Margaret's-on-Thames 00-04; R Shill Valley and Broadshire *Ox* from 04. *The Rectory, Church Lane, Shilton, Burford OX18 4AE* T: (01993) 845954 E: harry@hcmacinnes.wanadoo.co.uk

MACINNES (née HITCHEN), Mrs Lisa Jan. b 73. Linc Univ NZ BPR&TM 95 Graduate Sch of Educn Dip Teaching 01. Trin Coll Bris BA 09. **d** 09 **p** 10. C Brinnington w Portwood *Ches* 09-12; V Hallwood Ecum Par from 12. *The Vicarage, 6 Kirkstone Crescent, Beechwood, Runcorn WA7 3JQ* T: (01928) 713101 M: 07769-800915 E: lisahitchen.angel@gmail.com

MACINTOSH, Andrew Alexander. b 36. St Jo Coll Cam BA 59 MA 63 BD 80 DD 97. Ridley Hall Cam 60. **d** 62 **p** 63. C S Ormsby Gp *Linc* 62-64; Lect St D Coll Lamp 64-67; LtO *Ely* 67-04; Chapl St Jo Coll Cam 67-69; Asst Dean 69-79; Dean 79-02; Lect Th from 70; Pres 95-99; PtO *Ely* from 14. *St John's College, Cambridge CB2 1TP* T: (01223) 338709 E: aam1003@cus.cam.ac.uk

MacINTOSH, Canon George Grant. b 41. St Jo Coll Dur BA 75. Cranmer Hall Dur. **d** 76 **p** 77. C Ecclesall *Sheff* 76-79; Hon C Sheff St Oswald 79-81; Research Fell Sheff Univ 79-81; Dioc Adult Educn Officer 81-88; V Crookes St Tim 81-88; V Abbeydale St Jo 88-97; RD Ecclesall 89-94; P-in-c Cuminestown and Turriff *Ab* 97-06; Dioc Dir Ords 01-03; Can St Andr Cathl 01-06; rtd 06. *9 Millar Street, Carnoustie, Angus DD7 7AS* T: (01241) 854678 E: ggrantmacintosh@gmail.com

McINTOSH, Canon Ian MacDonald. b 64. Jes Coll Cam BA 86. Trin Coll Bris BA 90. **d** 90 **p** 91. C Belmont *Lon* 90-92; C Pinner 92-95; Chapl Leic Univ 96-02; TV Leic H Spirit 96-02; Co-ord Reader Tr 00-02; Dir Cen for Ecum Studies Westcott Ho Cam 02-04; C Milton Ernest, Pavenham and Thurleigh *St Alb* 02-06; Hon C 06-08; RD Sharnbrook 04-06; Lect and Dir Studies ERMC *Ely* 06-07; Prin from 07; Hon Can St E Cathl from 12. *22 Devon Road, Bedford MK40 3DJ* T: (01234) 302362 *or* (01223) 741740 E: mcintosh@ermc.cam.ac.uk

McINTOSH, Mrs Nicola Ann. b 60. Trin Coll Bris 87. **d** 90 **p** 94. Par Dn Queensbury All SS *Lon* 90-93; Par Dn Ruislip Manor St Paul 93-94; C 94-95; NSM Clarendon Park St Jo w Knighton St Mich *Leic* 96-02; Asst Dioc Dir of Ords 00-02; V Milton Ernest, Pavenham and Thurleigh *St Alb* 02-08; PtO 08-12; Lead Chapl Bedford Hosp NHS Trust from 12. *31 Paddock Close, Clapham, Bedford MK41 6BD* T: (01234) 302362 *or* 355122 ext 5901 E: nicola.mcintosh@bedfordhospital.nhs.uk

McINTYRE, Ms Iris Evelyn. b 60. Worc Coll Ox BA 82 MA 90. St Steph Ho Ox 82. **dss** 84 **d** 87 **p** 97. Southbroom *Sarum* 84-86; Oakdale 86-88; Par Dn 87-88; Par Dn Ireland Wood *Ripon* 88-89; Area Co-ord (NW) Chr Aid 92-94; Hon C W Derby St Mary *Liv* 94-98; R Bangor Monachorum and Worthenbury *St As* 98-03; Chapl HM Pris Brockhill 03-06; V Stourport and Wilden *Worc* from 06. *The Vicarage, 20 Church Avenue, Stourport-on-Severn DY13 9DD* T: (01299) 822041 E: evacymru@btinternet.com

McINTYRE, Preb Robert Mark. b 69. Nottm Univ BA 91. Coll of Resurr Mirfield 92. **d** 94 **p** 95. C Wednesbury St Jas and St Jo *Lich* 94-97; TV Wolstanton 97-05; P-in-c Rickerscote 05-10; V 10-11; C Stafford 05-11; V Walsall St Gabr Fulbrook from 11; Preb Lich Cathl from 15; CMP from 97. *St Gabriel's Vicarage, Walstead Road, Walsall WS5 4LZ* T: (01922) 622583 E: stgabriels.frmark@gmail.com

MACIVER, Donald. b 46. Heriot-Watt Univ BSc 69 Nazarene Th Coll Man ThB 82 Lon Univ BD 82. **d** 08 **p** 09. OLM Heatons *Man* 08-14; NSM Cloughton and Burniston *York* from 14; NSM Newby from 14; NSM Hackness w Harwood Dale from 14; NSM Ravenscar and Staintondale from 14; NSM Scarborough St Luke from 14; NSM Scalby from 14. *Address temp unknown* T: E: dmaciver@eclipse.co.uk

McIVER, Lyn Cavell. b 56. SNWTP. **d** 10 **p** 11. C Toxteth Park Ch Ch and St Mich w St Andr *Liv* 10-13; TV E Widnes from 13. *St John's House, 134 Greenway Road, Widnes WA8 6HA* M: 07791-650911

MACK, Mrs Gillian Frances. b 50. SCM 72. Cant Sch of Min 84. **d** 87 **p** 94. NSM Deal St Geo *Cant* 87-88; NSM Deal St Leon and St Rich and Sholden 88-92; Par Dn 93-94; C 94-97; rtd 97; PtO *Cant* 97-06; Hon Chapl Cautley Ho Chr Cen 98-06; Hon C Hurst Green and Mitton *Bradf* 06-07; P-in-c 07-13; V 13-14; Hon C Waddington 06-14; Pioneer Min Craven Adnry 08-11; V Hurst Green and Mitton *Blackb* from 14; Hon C Waddington from 14. *The Vicarage, Shire Lane, Hurst Green, Clitheroe BB7 9QR* T: (01254) 826686 E: gfmack@talktalk.net

McKAE, William John. b 42. Liv Univ BSc 63 St Mark & St Jo Coll Lon PGCE 64. Wells Th Coll 68. **d** 71 **p** 72. C Tranmere St Paul w St Luke *Ches* 71-74; C Midsomer Norton *B & W* 74-75; TV Birkenhead Priory *Ches* 75-80; R Oughtrington 80-91; Chapl Asst Hope, Salford R and Ladywell Hosps Man 91-92; Lic Preacher *Man* 91-92; R Heaton Reddish 92-06; rtd 06; PtO *Ches* from 06. *3 Grantham Close, Wirral CH61 8SU* T: 0151-648 0858 E: john.g4ila@tiscali.co.uk

MACKARILL, Ian David. b 54. York St Jo Univ BA 09. NEOC 01. **d** 04 **p** 05. NSM Waggoners *York* 04-12; NSM Woldsburn 11-12; V Lesbury w Alnmouth *Newc* from 12; V Longhoughton w Howick from 12. *The Vicarage, Lesbury, Alnwick NE66 3AU* T/F: (01665) 830281 M: 07933-161419 E: rev@mackarill.co.uk

McKAVANAGH, Dermot James. b 51. TCD BA 75 MA 78 K Coll Lon BD 78 AKC 78. **d** 78 **p** 79. C Croydon H Sav *Cant* 78-82; Asst Chapl Wellington Coll Berks 82-87; Chapl RAF 87-00; rtd 02. *42 Freshfields, Lea, Preston PR2 1TJ*

McKAY, Alastair James Mark. b 63. York Univ BA 85 Leeds Univ PGCE 87 E Mennonite Univ (USA) MA 99 Univ of Wales (Trin St Dav) DMin 14. St Mellitus Coll 12. **d** 15. C St Martin-in-the-Fields Lon from 15. *26 Midhurst Avenue, London N10 3EN* T: (020) 8883 1336 M: 07999-492511 E: ajmmckay@gmail.com

MACKAY, Alison. See PHILLIPSON, Alison

MACKAY, Canon Douglas Brysson. b 27. Edin Th Coll 56. **d** 58 **p** 59. Prec St Andr Cathl Inverness 58-61; P-in-c Fochabers 61-70; R 70-72; P-in-c Aberlour 64-72; Syn Clerk 65-72; Can St Andr Cathl Inverness 65-72; Hon Can St Andr Cathl Inverness 72; R Carnoustie *Bre* 72-98; Can St Paul's Cathl Dundee 81-97; Hon Can St Paul's Cathl Dundee from 98; Syn Clerk 81-97; rtd 97; PtO *Bre* 98-06; LtO from 06; Tutor Dundee Univ from 97; Chapl St Paul's Cathl Dundee from 99; Vice-Provost St Paul's Cathl Dundee 06-12. *24 Philip Street, Carnoustie DD7 6ED* T: (01241) 852362 E: db.mackay@btinternet.com

MACKAY, Hedley Neill. b 27. St Aid Birkenhead 53. **d** 56 **p** 57. C Beverley St Mary *York* 56-59; C Scarborough St Mary 59-60; Nigeria 61-70; C Wawne *York* 70-71; TV Sutton St Jas and Wawne 72-76; V Huntington 76-82; TR 82-93; rtd 93; PtO *York* from 93; Rtd Clergy and Widows Officer (York Adnry) 94-98. *2 Elmfield Terrace, Heworth, York YO31 1EH* T: (01904) 412971

MACKAY, James Hugh. b 57. Ridley Hall Cam. **d** 09 **p** 10. C Walesby *Linc* 09-13; R Stixwould w Denton and Caldecote etc *Ely* 13-15; P-in-c Elton 13-15. *5 Hayford Place, Derby DE22 3SL* M: 07946-895858 E: mackay1957@btinternet.com

MACKAY, Margaret. b 59. St Martin's Coll Lanc BEd 82. Lindisfarne Regional Tr Partnership 12. **d** 14 **p** 15. NSM High Spen and Rowlands Gill *Dur* from 14. *48 Cedarway, Gateshead NE10 8LD* T: 0191-438 3808 M: 07910-697308 E: margaretmackay1@talktalk.net

McKAY, Margaret McLeish. See HALE, Margaret McLeish,

MACKAY, Neill. See MACKAY, Hedley Neill

MACKAY, Paul Douglas. b 60. Trin Coll Bris. **d** 00 **p** 01. C Becontree St Mary *Chelmsf* 00-03; V Mile Cross *Nor* from 03; RD Nor N from 10. *St Catherine's Vicarage, Aylsham Road, Norwich NR3 2RJ* T: (01603) 426767 E: vicar@stcatherinesmilecross.org.uk

MACKAY, Phyllis Marion. *See* BAINBRIDGE, Phyllis Marion
MACKAY, Rupert. b 61. Oak Hill Th Coll BA 00. **d** 00 **p** 01. C Knutsford St Jo and Toft *Ches* 00-04; Min Hadley Wood St Paul Prop Chpl *Lon* from 04. *28 Beech Hill, Barnet EN4 0JP* T/F: (020) 8449 2572 E: rupmac@mac.com
McKEACHIE, The Very Revd William Noble. b 43. Univ of the South (USA) BA 66. Trin Coll Toronto STB 70. **d** 70 **p** 70. Asst Chapl St Jo Coll Ox 70-72; Dioc Th Toronto Canada 73-78; Dir Ch Relns and Tutor Univ of the South USA 78-80; R Baltimore St Paul 81-95; Dean S Carolina and R Charleston Cathl from 95. *126 Coming Street, Charleston SC 29403-6151, USA* T: (001) (843) 722 7345　F: 722 2105 E: cathchlp@dycon.com
McKEARNEY, Andrew Richard. b 57. Selw Coll Cam MA. Edin Th Coll 81. **d** 82 **p** 83. Prec St Ninian's Cathl Perth 82-84; Chapl St Mary's Cathl 84-88; R Hardwick and Toft w Caldecote and Childerley *Ely* 88-94; RD Bourn 92-94; V Chesterton Gd Shep 94-06; V Iffley Ox from 06. *The Rectory, Mill Lane, Iffley, Oxford OX4 4EJ* T: (01865) 773516 E: mckearney@windmillweb.net
McKEE, Douglas John Dunstan. b 34. Univ of W Aus BA 65. St Mich Th Coll Crafers 54. **d** 57 **p** 58. Australia 57-72 and from 85; SSM from 58; LtO *S'well* 73-85. *12 Kensington Mews, 69 Maesbury Street, Kensington, SA 5068 Australia* T: (0061) (8) 8331 3853 *or* 8416 8445　F: 8416 8450 E: dunstan.mckee@flinders.edu.au
McKEE, Joanna Elizabeth. b 77. RNCM BMus 99. St Jo Coll Nottm 09. **d** 13 **p** 14. C Harwood *Man* from 13. *Flat 2, 17-19 Recreation Street, Bradshaw, Bolton BL2 3HT* T: (01204) 304119 M: 07870-605533 E: jo.mckee@live.co.uk
McKEE, Nicholas John. b 71. Nottm Univ MEng 94. Ridley Hall Cam 05. **d** 08 **p** 09. C Didsbury St Jas and Em *Man* 08-11; V Astley Bridge from 11. *St Paul's Vicarage, Sweetloves Lane, Bolton BL1 7ET* T: (01204) 304119 E: rev.nick@live.co.uk
McKEE, Patrick Joseph. b 49. Ripon Coll Cuddesdon 92. **d** 94 **p** 95. C Oakham, Hambleton, Egleton, Braunston and Brooke *Pet* 94-97; V Ryhall w Essendine and Carlby from 97. *The Vicarage, Church Street, Ryhall, Stamford PE9 4HR* T: (01780) 762398 E: revpaddymckee@aol.com
McKEE HANNA, Patricia Elizabeth. TCD BA HDipEd QUB BD NUU MA. **d** 99 **p** 00. Aux Min Nenagh *L & K* from 99; Aux Min Drumcliffe w Kilnasoolagh from 00. *Seafield Cottage, Quilty, Co Clare, Republic of Ireland* M: (00353) 87-660 6003 E: hannape@tcd.ie
McKEEMAN, David Christopher. b 36. AKC 58 DipEd 76. **d** 60 **p** 61. C Catford St Andr *S'wark* 60-64; P-in-c W Dulwich Em 64-66; P-in-c W Dulwich All SS and Em 66-69; LtO *Win* 70-82; R Silchester 82-01; rtd 01; PtO *Heref* from 01. *The Maltings, Woodend Lane, Stoke Lacy, Bromyard HR7 4HQ* T: (01885) 490705 E: david.mckeeman@ntlworld.com
McKEGNEY, Canon John Wade. b 47. TCD BA 70 MA 81. CITC 70. **d** 72 **p** 73. C Ballynafeigh St Jude *D & D* 72-75; C Bangor St Comgall 75-80; I Drumgath w Drumgooland and Clonduff 80-83; I Gilnahirk 83-90; I Arm St Mark 90-13; Can Arm Cathl 01-13; rtd 13. *Tany Bwlch, 2 Magheramenagh Gardens, Portrush BT56 8SU* T: (028) 7082 5019 M: 07801-866555 E: john.mckegney@virgin.net
MacKEITH (*née* GODFREY), Mrs Ann Veronica. b 35. Bris Univ BSc 57 CertEd. Gilmore Course 78. **dss** 79 **d** 87 **p** 94. Bishopwearmouth Ch Ch *Dur* 79-83; Bishopwearmouth St Gabr 83-86; Ryhope 86-88; Par Dn 87-88; Par Dn Darlington H Trin 88-94; C 94-95; Family Life Officer 95-97; rtd 98. *26 Withdean Court, London Road, Brighton BN1 6RN* T: (01273) 552376 E: annmackeith@talktalk.net
McKELLEN, Pamela Joyce. b 47. Homerton Coll Cam TCert 69 BEd 70. Cranmer Hall Dur 01. **d** 02 **p** 03. C Ox St Matt 02-04; P-in-c Radley and Sunningwell 04-15; P-in-c Kennington 09-15; R Radley, Sunningwell and Kennington from 15; AD Abingdon 07-12. *The Vicarage, Kennington Road, Radley, Abingdon OX14 2JN* T: (01235) 554739 E: p.mckellen@btinternet.com
McKELVEY, Mrs Jane Lilian. b 48. Liv Inst of Educn BA 94. N Bapt Coll 94. **d** 97 **p** 98. C Aughton St Mich *Liv* 97-01; TV Gateacre from 01. *St Mark's Vicarage, Cranwell Road, Liverpool L25 1NZ* T: 0151-487 9634 E: revjanemc1@yahoo.co.uk
McKELVEY, The Very Revd Robert Samuel James Houston. b 42. TD QVRM 00 OBE 10. QUB BA 65 MA(Ed) 88 Garrett-Evang Th Sem DMin 93. CITC 67. **d** 67 **p** 68. C Dunmurry *Conn* 67-70; CF (TAVR) 70-99; P-in-c Kilmakee *Conn* 70-77; I 77-81; Sec Gen Syn Bd of Educn (N Ireland) 81-01; Preb Newcastle St Patr Cathl Dublin 89-01; Dean Belf 01-11; rtd 11. *9 College Park, Coleraine BT51 3HE* T: (028) 7035 3621 - M: 07802-207825 E: houston.mckelvey@btinternet.com
McKEMEY, Mrs Norma Edith. b 47. St Mary's Coll Chelt CertEd 71. STETS BA 10. **d** 10 **p** 11. NSM Swindon Ch Ch *Bris* from 10. *Bethany, Greens Lane, Wroughton, Swindon SN4 0RJ* T: (01793) 845917 M: 07760-457739 E: mckemeyn@talktalk.net

McKENDREY, Susan Margaret. b 55. **d** 02 **p** 03. NSM Allonby, Cross Canonby and Dearham *Carl* 02-08; TV Maryport, Netherton and Flimby from 08; C Broughton Moor from 14. *The Vicarage, Church Street, Maryport CA15 6HE* T: (01900) 813077 E: s.mckendrey@btinternet.com
MACKENNA, Christopher. *See* MACKENNA, Robert Christopher Douglass
McKENNA, Edward Patrick. b 48. Liv Univ BTh 02. NOC 05. **d** 06 **p** 07. NSM Stretton and Appleton Thorn *Ches* 06-09; Asst Chapl HM Pris Risley 08-09; P-in-c Low Marple *Ches* 09-14; V from 14. *15 Brabyns Brow, Marple Bridge, Stockport SK6 5DT* T: 0161-427 2736 M: 07979-624271 E: ed1mckenna@aol.com
McKENNA (*née* ALLEN), Mrs Jacqueline Lesley. b 54. EMMTC 99. **d** 02 **p** 03. NSM Huthwaite *S'well* 02-05; P-in-c Shireoaks 05-12; Asst Chapl Notts Healthcare NHS Trust 07-12; Chapl Doncaster and Bassetlaw Hosps NHS Foundn Trust from 12. *Bassetlaw District General Hospital, Kilton Hill, Worksop S81 0BD* T: (01909) 500990 E: jackie@serv77.netscapeonline.com
McKENNA, Lindsay Taylor. b 62. Glas Univ MA 83 Aber Univ BD 86. Edin Th Coll 87. **d** 87 **p** 88. C Broughty Ferry *Bre* 87-90; C Wantage Ox 90-93; V Illingworth *Wakef* 93-99; Dir CARA 99-02; V Hanworth All SS *Lon* 02-08; Provost St Paul's Cathl Dundee 08-09; R Dundee St Paul 08-09; PtO *Win* 09-10; P-in-c Catford St Andr *S'wark* 10-11; V from 11; Dir Ords Woolwich Area from 13. *St Andrew's Parsonage, 119 Torridon Road, London SE6 1RG* T: (020) 8697 2600 E: lindsay.m@virgin.net
MACKENNA, Richard William. b 49. Pemb Coll Cam BA 71 MA 75. Ripon Coll Cuddesdon BA 77 MA 81. **d** 78 **p** 79. C Fulham St Dionis *Lon* 78-81; C Paddington St Jas 81-85; Tutor Westcott Ho Cam 85-89; V Kingston All SS w St Jo *S'wark* 90-91; PtO 94-01; *Nor* 99-04. *Flat 5, 11 Grassington Road, Eastbourne BN20 7BJ* T: (01323) 730477
MACKENNA, Robert Christopher Douglass. b 44. Oriel Coll Ox BA 72 MA 75 MBAP 85. Cuddesdon Coll 71. **d** 73 **p** 74. C Farncombe *Guildf* 73-77; C Tattenham Corner and Burgh Heath 77-80; P-in-c Hascombe 80-90; R 90-00; RD Godalming 91-96; Hon Can Guildf Cathl 99-00; Dir St Marylebone Healing and Counselling Cen from 00; NSM St Marylebone w H Trin *Lon* from 00; rtd 09. *17 Victory Road, London E11 1UL* T: (020) 7935 5066 E: chrismackenna@aol.com *or* cmackenna@stmarylebone.org
MACKENZIE, Andrew John Kett. b 46. Southn Univ BA 68. Guildf Dioc Min Course 98. **d** 91 **p** 92. Fullbrook Sch New Haw 76-99; OLM Woodham *Guildf* 91-99; C Aldershot St Mich 99-05; V Effingham w Lt Bookham 05-15; rtd 15; Hon C Bradford Peverell, Stratton, Frampton etc *Sarum* from 15; Hon C Charminster and Stinsford from 15. *The Rectory, 4 Meadow Bottom, Stratton, Dorchester DT2 9WH* M: 07511-756407 E: revandy1@btinternet.com
MACKENZIE, Miss Ann. b 54. CertEd 76. Trin Coll Bris 82. **dss** 85 **d** 87 **p** 94. Normanton *Wakef* 85-90; Par Dn 87-90; Par Dn Bletchley Ox 90-94; C 94-98; TV W Swindon and the Lydiards *Bris* 98-04; P-in-c E Springfield *Chelmsf* from 04. *The Vicarage, Ashton Place, Chelmsford CM2 6ST* T: (01245) 460205 E: ann.mackenzie@btinternet.com
MACKENZIE, Mrs Ann Elizabeth. b 45. Leic Univ BA 67 PGCE 68. STETS 95. **d** 98 **p** 99. NSM Appleshaw, Kimpton, Thruxton, Fyfield etc *Win* 98-15; rtd 15. *The Post House, Thruxton, Andover SP11 8LZ* T: (01264) 772788 M: 07733-112975 E: ann.mackenzie@waitrose.com
McKENZIE, Cilla. *See* McKENZIE, Priscilla Ann
MACKENZIE, David Stuart. b 45. Open Univ BA 95 FRSA 00. Linc Th Coll 66. **d** 69 **p** 70. C Bishopwearmouth St Mary V w St Pet CD *Dur* 69-72; C Pontefract St Giles *Wakef* 72-74; Chapl RAF 74-02; Chapl OHP 02-08; RD Whitby *York* 04-08; QHC from 00; PtO *Ely* from 09. *57 London Road, Godmanchester, Huntingdon PE29 2HZ* T: (01480) 413120 E: ds@mack60.wanadoo.co.uk
McKENZIE, Ian Colin. b 31. CA 56. EMMTC 89. **d** 93. NSM Edin St Mark and Edin St Andr and St Aid 93-94; PtO *S'well* from 01. *21 Crafts Way, Southwell NG25 0BL* T: (01636) 815755
MACKENZIE, Ian William. b 46. Trin Coll Bris 93. **d** 95 **p** 96. C Bideford *Ex* 95-96; C Bideford, Northam, Westward Ho!, Appledore etc 96-99; TV Littleham w Exmouth 99-11; rtd 11; PtO *Heref* from 13. *Ballavayre, New Street, Ledbury HR8 2EL* T: (01531) 579009 E: billandmaggiemackenzie@gmail.com
McKENZIE, Jack Llewellyn. b 29. FRSH AMIEHO MAMIT. S'wark Ord Course. **d** 79 **p** 80. Hon C Stonebridge St Mich *Lon* 79-88; Hon C Willesden St Mary 88-91; PtO *St Alb* 00-08. *2 Beckets Square, Berkhamsted HP4 1BZ* T: (01442) 874265
MACKENZIE, Miss Janet. b 62. Westmr Coll Ox BEd 86 Anglia Ruskin Univ BA 08. Westcott Ho Cam 04. **d** 06 **p** 07. C Sandy

St Alb 06-10; P-in-c Luton St Aug Limbury 10-14; V from 14; AD Luton from 12. *The Vicarage, 215 Icknield Way, Luton LU3 2JR* T: (01582) 572415
E: revjanetmackenzie@tiscali.co.uk

McKENZIE (née DOORES), Mrs Jennifer Mary. b 78. Hull Univ BA 99 St Jo Coll Dur BA 03. Cranmer Hall Dur 01. **d** 04 **p** 05. C Old Swinford Stourbridge *Worc* 04-08; V Cam w Stinchcombe *Glouc* from 08. *The Vicarage, Church Road, Cam, Dursley GL11 5PQ* T: (01453) 542084
E: mckenzie.jennifer@btinternet.com

MacKENZIE, John Christopher Newman. b 67. Trin Coll Bris 02. **d** 04 **p** 05. C Staplehurst *Cant* 04-07; P-in-c Willesborough 07-13; P-in-c Sevington 07-13; R Willesborough w Sevington from 13. *The Rectory, 66 Church Road, Willesborough, Ashford TN24 0JG* T: (01233) 624064 E: john@jjsmack.me.uk

MACKENZIE, Peter Sterling. b 65. Univ Coll Lon BSc 88. Oak Hill Th Coll BA 95. **d** 95 **p** 96. C Roxeth *Lon* 95-99; Assoc V 99-00; TV 00-08; V W Ealing St Jo w St Jas from 08. *23 Culmington Road, London W13 9NJ* T: (020) 8566 3462
E: petersmackenzie@btinternet.com

MACKENZIE, Canon Peter Thomas. b 44. Lon Univ LLB 67 Westmr Coll Ox MTh 97 Univ of E Lon MA 01. Cuddesdon Coll 68. **d** 70 **p** 71. C Leigh Park *Portsm* 70-75; P-in-c Sittingbourne St Mary *Cant* 75-82; V Folkestone St Sav 82-90; RD Elham 89-90; R Cant St Martin and St Paul 90-99; RD Cant 95-99; V Goudhurst w Kilndown 99-07; Hon Can Cant Cathl 97-07; AD Cranbrook 01-06; rtd 07; PtO Cant 09-11; P-in-c Turvey *St Alb* 11-14; P-in-c Stevington 11-14; PtO *Leic* from 15. *5 Madeline Close, Great Bowden, Market Harborough LE16 7HX* T: (01858) 440049 E: canonmack@talk21.com

MACKENZIE, Mrs Priscilla Ann. b 47. St Jo Coll Nottm 87. **d** 93 **p** 94. NSM Ellon *Ab* 93-96; NSM Cruden Bay 93-96; PtO *Roch* 96-99 and from 04; Chapl Medway NHS Trust 99-04. *Iona, Linton Hill, Linton, Maidstone ME17 4AW* T: (01622) 741318
E: johncilla.mackenzie@talktalk.net

MACKENZIE, Richard Graham. b 49. St Aug Coll Cant 72. **d** 73 **p** 74. C Deal St Leon *Cant* 73-75; C Deal St Leon w Sholden 75-78; C Herne 78-81; I Pakenham Canada 81-88; I Richmond 88-90; I Petawawa 90-12; rtd 12. *1022 Pembroke Street E, Pembroke ON K8A 8A7, Canada*

MACKENZIE, Robin Peter. b 61. Sheff Univ BEng 82 Birm Univ MSc(Eng) 87 Dur Univ BA 02 Warwick Univ EngD 02 CEng MIET. Cranmer Hall Dur 00. **d** 03 **p** 04. C Shrewsbury St Chad w St Mary *Lich* 03-07; P-in-c Hilton *Ely* 07-11; P-in-c Fenstanton from 07. *The Vicarage, 16 Church Street, Fenstanton, Huntingdon PE28 9JL* T: (01480) 466162
E: mckenzie_robin@hotmail.com

MACKENZIE, Simon Peter Munro. b 52. Univ Coll Ox BA 74. Coll of Resurr Mirfield 82. **d** 85 **p** 86. C Tipton St Jo *Lich* 85-91; V Perry Beeches *Birm* 91-13; P-in-c Lochgilphead *Arg* from 13; P-in-c Inveraray from 13; P-in-c Kilmartin from 13; P-in-c Is of Arran from 13. *Bishopton House, Bishopton Road, Lochgilphead PA31 8PY* E: dr.lachlan@zen.co.uk

McKENZIE, Stephen George. b 58. Leeds Univ BSc 80 Imp Coll Lon PhD 85. Oak Hill Th Coll 03. **d** 05 **p** 06. C Barton Seagrave w Warkton *Pet* 05-08; P-in-c Swynnerton and Tittensor *Lich* 08-09; C Broughton w Croxton and Cotes Heath w Standon 08-09; R Cotes Heath and Standon and Swynnerton etc from 09. *3 Rectory Gardens, Swynnerton, Stone ST15 0RT* T: (01782) 796564 M: 07986-558861
E: stephen_gill.swyn@btinternet.com

MACKENZIE, William. See MACKENZIE, Ian William

MACKENZIE MILLS, David Graham. b 75. Bris Univ BA 96 St Jo Coll Dur BA 01. Cranmer Hall Dur. **d** 01 **p** 02. C Glas St Marg 01-04; Chapl Trin Coll Cam 04-09; Min Can and Prec Cant Cathl 09-12; R Kinross *St And* from 13. *36 Manse Road, Milnathort, Kinross KY13 9YQ* T: (01577) 863795
E: frdavidkinross@gmail.com

McKEON, Linda. b 60. **d** 09 **p** 10. OLM Gentleshaw *Lich* 09-13; NSM from 13. *17 Bradwell Lane, Rugeley WS15 4RW* T: (01543) 670739

McKEOWN, Trevor James. b 53. Glos Univ BA 12. CITC 01. **d** 04 **p** 05. Aux Min Dromore Cathl from 04. *39 Cedar Park, Portadown, Craigavon BT63 5LL* T: (028) 3832 1217
E: trevor.mckeown3@hotmail.com

McKERAN, The Very Revd James Orville. b 71. Kent Univ BA 94 K Coll Lon MA 06 Leeds Univ MA 08 Solicitor 98 ACIArb 08 FRGS 11 MCMI 13. Coll of Resurr Mirfield 06. **d** 08 **p** 09. C Altrincham St Geo and Altrincham St Jo *Ches* 08-11; Chapl Trafford Coll 08-11; Tutor SSM Lesotho 11-12; Asst P Maseru St Jo and Maseru E 11-12; V Gen Botswana from 12; Dean Gaborone from 12. *Cathedral of the Holy Cross, PO Box 1315, Gaborone, Botswana* E: james.mckeran@yahoo.com

MACKEY, John. b 34. Lich Th Coll. **d** 64 **p** 65. C Kells *Carl* 64-67; C Barrow St Matt 67-70; R Clayton *Man* 70-75; V Low Marple *Ches* 75-83; R Coppenhall 83-00; rtd 00; PtO *Ches* from 00. *361 Hungerford Road, Crewe CW1 5EZ* T: (01270) 254951

MacKICHAN, Gillian Margaret. b 34. Cam Univ CertEd 56 CQSW 80. S Dios Minl Tr Scheme 90. **d** 93 **p** 94. NSM Upper Kennet *Sarum* 93-04; TV 95-04; RD Marlborough *Sarum* 02-04; rtd 04; PtO *Sarum* 04-08. *West Bailey, Lockeridge, Marlborough SN8 4ED* T: (01672) 861629 E: g.mackichan@btinternet.com

MACKIE, Andrew. b 53. Glas Univ BSc 74 CEng MIET. SAOMC 00. **d** 00 **p** 01. OLM Purley *Ox* from 00. *12 Church Mews, Purley-on-Thames, Pangbourne, Reading RG8 8AG* T: 0118-941 7170 E: mackie.family@btinternet.com

MACKIE, Fiona Mary. See KOUBLE, Fiona Mary

MACKIE, Ian William. b 31. Lon Univ BSc 53 Ex Univ PGCE 54. Linc Th Coll 81. **d** 83 **p** 84. C Market Rasen *Linc* 83-87; V Bracebridge Heath 87-96; RD Christianity 92-96; rtd 96; PtO *Sheff* 96-02. *57 Bridle Crescent, Chapeltown, Sheffield S35 2QX* T: 0114-284 4073

McKIE, The Very Revd Kenyon Vincent. b 60. Aus Nat Univ BA 83 ACT BTh 88 K Coll Lon MTh 92 Canberra Coll DipEd 84. **d** 86 **p** 87. Dn Queanbeyan Australia 86; C 87; Lucas-Tooth Scholar K Coll Lon 89-91; Hon C Coulsdon St Andr *S'wark* 89-91; R Monaro S Australia 91-94; R Bega 94-99; Adn S Coast and Monaro 96-99; Dean Goulburn from 99. *PO Box 205, Goulburn NSW 2580, Australia* T: (0061) (2) 4821 9192 or 4821 2206 F: 4822 2639
E: mesacgbn@tpgi.com.au *or* deanery@tpgi.com.au

McKILLOP, Mrs Caroline Annis. b 47. Glas Univ MB, ChB 72 PhD 77. TISEC 95. **d** 98 **p** 99. NSM Glas St Matt 98-01; Chapl Stobhill NHS Trust 99-00; NSM Glas St Mary from 02. *Flat 1, 6 Kirklee Gate, Glasgow G12 0SZ* T: 0141-339 7000
E: caroline.mckillop@yahoo.co.uk

McKILLOP, Iain Malcolm. b 54. Man Univ BA 75 Man Poly PGCE 76 Kingston Univ MA 95. Guildf Dioc Min Course 07. **d** 10 **p** 11. NSM Effingham w Lt Bookham *Guildf* from 10. *10 Hopfield Avenue, Byfleet, West Byfleet KT14 7PE* T: (01932) 341687 E: imckillopi@aol.com

McKINLEY, Canon Arthur Horace Nelson. b 46. TCD BA 69 MA 79. CITC 70. **d** 70 **p** 71. C Taney Ch Ch *D & G* 71-76; I Dublin Whitechurch from 76; Preb Dunlavin St Patr Cathl Dublin from 91. *The Vicarage, Whitechurch Road, Rathfarnham, Dublin 16, Republic of Ireland* T: (00353) (1) 493 3953 or 493 4972 E: whitechurchparish@eircom.net

McKINLEY, George Henry. b 23. TCD BA 44 MA 51. **d** 46 **p** 47. C Waterford Ch Ch *C & O* 46-49; I Fiddown 49-51; I Fiddown w Kilmacow 51-54; C S Harrow St Paul *Lon* 54-58; V Stonebridge St Mich 58-65; R Hackney St Jo 65-72; TR Hackney 72-77; V Painswick w Sheepscombe *Glouc* 77-83; Bp's Chapl 83-87; C Sandhurst 83-85; C Twigworth, Down Hatherley, Norton, The Leigh etc 85-87; rtd 88; PtO *Heref* from 96; *Worc* from 96. *Middlemarch, 2 Old Barn Court, Bircher, Leominster HR6 0AU* T: (01568) 780795

✠**McKINNEL, The Rt Revd Nicholas Howard Paul.** b 54. Qu Coll Cam BA 75 MA 79. Wycliffe Hall Ox BA 79 MA 86. **d** 80 **p** 81 **c** 12. C Fulham St Mary N End *Lon* 80-83; Chapl Liv Univ 83-87; P-in-c Hatherleigh *Ex* 87-88; R Hatherleigh, Meeth, Exbourne and Jacobstowe 88-94; P-in-c Plymouth St Andr w St Paul and St Geo *S'wark* 94-95; TR Plymouth St Andr and Stonehouse 95-12; RD Plymouth Sutton 01-06; Preb Ex Cathl 02-12; Suff Bp Crediton 12-15; Suff Bp Plymouth from 15. *108 Molesworth Road, Stoke, Plymouth PL3 4AQ*
E: bishop.of.plymouth@exeter.anglican.org

McKINNEY, James Alexander. b 52. Ex Univ BA 74 Hull Univ MA 87. Ripon Coll Cuddesdon 75. **d** 78 **p** 79. C Wath-upon-Dearne w Adwick-upon-Dearne *Sheff* 78-82; V Doncaster Intake 82-87; Ind Chapl 84-87; Chapl Bramshill Police Coll *Win* 87-92; V Cleator Moor w Cleator *Carl* 92-96; Chapl Cumbria Constabulary 93-96; P-in-c Frizington and Arlecdon *Carl* 94-96; V Roehampton H Trin *S'wark* from 96. *The Vicarage, 7 Ponsonby Road, London SW15 4LA* T: (020) 8788 9460 E: mckinneyja@hotmail.com

McKINNEY, Canon Mervyn Roy. b 48. St Jo Coll Nottm. **d** 81 **p** 82. C Tile Cross *Birm* 81-84; C Bickenhill w Elmdon 84-89; V Addiscombe St Mary *S'wark* 89-93; V Addiscombe St Mary Magd w St Martin 93-99; P-in-c W Wickham St Fran 99-02; V W Wickham St Fran and St Mary 02-14; AD Croydon Addington 04-11; Hon Can S'wark Cathl 05-14; rtd 14; PtO *Chelmsf* from 15. *12 Dedham Mill, Mill Lane, Dedham, Colchester CO7 6DJ* T: (01206) 323565
E: mervmckinney@btinternet.com

MacKINNON, Canon Karen Audrey. b 64. Ex Univ BA 85. Linc Th Coll 92. **d** 92 **p** 94. Par Dn Filton *Bris* 92-93; Par Dn Bris Lockleaze St Mary Magd w St Fran 93-94; C 94-96; P-in-c 96-98; V 98-00; Asst Chapl Southn Univ Hosps NHS Trust 00-03; Chapl 03-04; Dep Team Ldr 04-11; Spiritual Care Manager Univ Hosp Southn NHS Foundn Trust from 11; Hon Can Win Cathl from 14. *Chaplaincy Department, MP 201, Univ Hospital Southampton NHS Trust, Tremona Road, Southampton SO16 6YD* T: (023) 8120 8517
E: karen.mackinnon@uhs.nhs.uk

McKINNON, Neil Alexander. b 46. Wycliffe Hall Ox 71. **d** 74 **p** 75. C Deptford St Nic w Ch Ch *S'wark* 74-76; C St Helier 76-79; Min W Dulwich All SS and Em 79-81; TV Thamesmead 87-95; R S'wark H Trin w St Matt from 95. *The Rectory, Meadow Row, London SE1 6RG* T: (020) 7407 1707 *or* 7357 8532
E: neilatelephant@yahoo.com

MACKINTOSH, Canon Robin Geoffrey James. b 46. Rhodes Univ BCom 71 Cranfield Inst of Tech MBA 78. Ripon Coll Cuddesdon BA 85 MA 91. **d** 86 **p** 87. C Cuddesdon *Ox* 86; C Cannock *Lich* 86-89; R Girton *Ely* 89-01; Exec Dir The Leadership Inst 01-06; PtO *Cant* from 03; Dir Min and Tr 06-14; rtd 14; Hon Can Cant Cathl from 09; PtO from 14. *4 Loop Court Mews, Sandwich CT13 9HF*
E: robmackintosh@btinternet.com

McKINTY, Norman Alexander (Fionn). b 63. St D Coll Lamp BA 86. Westcott Ho Cam 97. **d** 99 **p** 00. C Yeovil St Mich *B & W* 99-03; C Gillingham and Milton-on-Stour *Sarum* 03-05; P-in-c Portland All SS w St Andr 05-09; TV Portland 10-13. *Address temp unknown* E: fionn@mckinty.fsworld.co.uk

McKITTRICK, The Ven Douglas Henry. b 53. St Steph Ho Ox 74. **d** 77 **p** 78. C Deptford St Paul *S'wark* 77-80; C W Derby St Jo *Liv* 80-81; TV St Luke in the City 81-89; V Toxteth Park St Agnes and St Pancras 89-97; V Brighton St Pet w Chpl Royal *Chich* 97-02; RD Brighton 98-02; Can and Preb Chich Cathl 98-02; Adn Chich from 02. *2 Yorklands, Dyke Road Avenue, Hove BN3 6RW* T: (01273) 505330 *or* 421021
E: archchichester@chichester.anglican.org

MACKLEY, Robert Michael. b 78. Ch Coll Cam BA 99 MA 03. Westcott Ho Cam 00. **d** 03 **p** 04. C Clerkenwell H Redeemer *Lon* 03-06; C Clerkenwell St Mark 03-06; C Liv Our Lady and St Nic 06-09; Asst Chapl Em Coll Cam 09-12; V Cambridge St Mary Less *Ely* from 12. *The Vicarage, 1B Summerfield, Cambridge CB3 9HE* T: (01223) 356641 *or* 366202
M: 07866-445877 E: rmm28@cam.ac.uk *or* vicar@lsm.org.uk

MACKLIN, Reginald John. b 29. Bris Univ BA 52. Ely Th Coll 54. **d** 55 **p** 56. C W Hackney St Barn *Lon* 55-58; C E Ham St Mary *Chelmsf* 58-61; C Northolt St Mary *Lon* 61-64; Jordan 64-68; Palma de Mallorca and Balearic Is *Eur* 68-69; P-in-c Hammersmith St Matt *Lon* 69-70; V Stanwell 70-82; V Kimbolton *Ely* 82-88; V Stow Longa 82-88; RD Leightonstone 82-88; P-in-c Keyston and Bythorn 85-88; P-in-c Catworth Magna 85-88; P-in-c Tilbrook 85-88; P-in-c Covington 85-88; R Coveney 88-96; R Downham 88-96; RD Ely 89-96; rtd 96; PtO *Ely* from 96. *11 Castelhythe, Ely CB7 4BU* T/F: (01353) 662205
E: macklinrj@aol.com

MACKNESS, Canon Paul Robert. b 73. Univ of Wales (Lamp) BA 96 Univ of Wales (Cardiff) BA 01. St Mich Coll Llan 98. **d** 01 **p** 02. C Llanelli *St D* 01-04; P-in-c Maenordeifi and Capel Colman w Llanfihangel etc 04-05; R 05-07; R Maenordeifi Gp 07-10; AD Cemais and Sub-Aeron 08-10; V Haverfordwest 10-14; Bp's Chapl from 14; Can St D Cathl from 14; Asst Dioc Warden Ords from 15. *The Vicarage, Wellfield Road, Abergwili, Carmarthen SA31 2JQ* T: (01267) 236597
E: paulmackness@churchinwales.org.uk

McKNIGHT, Elizabeth Ann. **d** 15. NSM Cil-y-Cwm and Ystradffin w Rhandir-mwyn etc *St D* from 15. *The Vicarage, Cilycwm, Llandovery SA20 0SP* T: (01550) 721109
E: ann.mcknight@btinternet.com

MACKNIGHT, Glen. b 62. Lindisfarne Regional Tr Partnership 10. **d** 13 **p** 14. C Herrington, Penshaw and Shiney Row *Dur* from 13. *The Rectory, Bournmoor, Houghton le Spring DH4 6EX* T: 0191-435 8356 M: 07983-572472
E: glenmacknight@mac.com

McKNIGHT, Thomas Raymond. b 48. QUB BEd 71. CITC 74. **d** 77 **p** 78. C Lisburn Ch Ch Cathl 77-80; C Carrickfergus 80-82; I Kilcronaghan w Draperstown and Sixtowns *D & R* 82-86; I Magheragall *Conn* 86-91; CF 91-07; I Urney w Sion Mills *D & R* 07-11; rtd 11. *5 Pembury Mews, Brompton on Swale, Richmond DL10 7SG* T: (01748) 810348

MACKRELL, Catherine Anita. *See* SPENCE, Catherine Anita

MACKRIELL, Peter John. b 64. Mansf Coll Ox BA 85 MA 93 Man Univ PGCE 87. St Jo Coll Nottm BTh 93 MA 94. **d** 94 **p** 95. C Hale and Ashley *Ches* 94-96; C Marple All SS 96-98; V Brandwood *Birm* 98-01; V Pontblyddyn *St As* 01-05; Chapl to Deaf People 01-11; Dioc Communications Officer 06-11; V Kelsall *Ches* from 11. *St Philip's Vicarage, Chester Road, Kelsall, Tarporley CW6 0SA* T: (01829) 752639
E: vicar@kelsallparishchurch.org.uk

MACKRILL, Mrs Deirdre Anne. b 49. ACIS 95. SAOMC 01. **d** 05 **p** 06. NSM Hemel Hempstead *St Alb* 05-09; NSM St Keverne *Truro* from 11; NSM St Ruan w St Grade and Landewednack from 11. *Rosenithon House, Rosenithon, St Keverne, Helston TR12 6QR* T: (01326) 281178
E: deirdre.mackrill@btinternet.com

MACKRILL, Robert John. b 51. Univ Coll Lon BSc 73 RIBA 79. EMMTC 92. **d** 93 **p** 94. NSM Stamford All SS w St Jo *Linc* 93-97; P-in-c Stamford Ch Ch 97-10; RD Aveland and Ness w Stamford 09-10; C Oakham, Hambleton, Egleton, Braunston and Brooke *Pet* 10; TV Oakham, Ashwell, Braunston, Brooke, Egleton etc 11; rtd 11; PtO *Pet* from 12. *8 St Lawrence Way, Tallington, Stamford PE9 4RH* T: (01780) 749283
E: bobmackrill@btinternet.com

MacLACHLAN (née GRIFFITHS), Mrs Margaret. b 44. Birm Poly CertEd 81 Open Univ BA 82 SRN 67. WMMTC 92. **d** 95 **p** 96. NSM Tile Cross *Birm* 95-08; NSM Garretts Green 07-08; NSM Garretts Green and Tile Cross 08-13; PtO from 13; Chapl Heart of England NHS Foundn Trust from 08. *Wayside, 17 Chester Road, Birmingham B36 9DA* T: 0121-747 2340
E: revmac@talktalk.net

MacLACHLAN, Michael Ronald Frederic. b 39. Wycliffe Hall Ox 75. **d** 75 **p** 76. C Mansfield SS Pet and Paul *S'well* 75-78; P-in-c Newark Ch Ch 78-80; TV Newark w Hawton, Cotham and Shelton 80-86; P-in-c Sparkhill St Jo *Birm* 86-90; P-in-c Sparkbrook Em 86-90; V Sparkhill w Greet and Sparkbrook 90-92; RD Bordesley 90-92; P-in-c Kugluktuk Canada 92-97; R Stoke-next-Guildf 97-05; rtd 05; Hon C Drayton Bassett *Lich* 05-12; Hon C Canwell 09-12; PtO *Birm* from 13; *Cov* from 13. *36A Grendon Road, Polesworth, Tamworth B78 1NU* T: (01827) 893109 E: michaelmaclachlan@btinternet.com

McLACHLAN, Canon Sheila Elizabeth. b 52. SRN 73 Kent Univ MA 89. Wycliffe Hall Ox 80. **dss** 83 **d** 87 **p** 94. Chapl Kent Univ *Cant* 83-94; Dep Master Rutherford Coll 87-94; Dn-in-c Kingsnorth w Shadoxhurst *Cant* 94; P-in-c Kingsnorth and Shadoxhurst 94-15; AD Ashford 03-09; Hon Can Cant Cathl 08-15; rtd 15. *33 Josephs Way, New Romney TN28 8AQ* - M: 07771-691164 E: sheila.mclachlan@tesco.net

MacLAREN, Ms Clare. b 67. Edin Univ LLB 88 Leeds Univ MA 14. Linc Th Coll BTh 95. **d** 95 **p** 96. C Benchill *Man* 95-98; C Bilton *Ripon* 98-03; TV Seacroft 03-10; P-in-c Heaton St Martin *Leeds* 10-15; P-in-c Heaton St Barn 10-15; Can Res Newc Cathl from 15. *The Vicarage, 130 Haworth Road, Bradford BD9 6LL* T: (01274) 409313 M: 07952-760168
E: claremaclaren@gmail.com

MacLAREN, Duncan Arthur Spencer. b 69. Oriel Coll Ox BA 90 MA 96 K Coll Lon MA 97 PhD 03. Oak Hill Th Coll 92. **d** 94 **p** 95. C Ox St Clem 94-97; Chapl St Edm Hall Ox 97-04; Assoc R Edin St Paul and St Geo 04-09; R Edin St Jas 09-13. *8 Keith Terrace, Edinburgh EH4 3NJ* T: (01314) 678481
E: duncan@mclaren.org

MacLAREN (née ALEXANDER), Mrs Jane Louise. b 69. LMH Ox BA 90 MA 96. Oak Hill Th Coll BA 95. **d** 95 **p** 96. C Ox St Clem 95-98; Chapl St Aug Sch 98-02; Chapl Ox Brookes Univ 02-04; Assoc R Edin St Paul and St Geo 04-09; NSM Edin St Jas from 09. *8 Keith Terrace, Edinburgh EH4 3NJ* M: 07709-905528 T: (01314) 678481
E: janelmaclaren@hotmail.com

MacLAREN, Mrs Jeanette Moira. b 59. **d** 95 **p** 96. C Dulwich St Clem w St Pet *S'wark* 95-99; P-in-c Brixton St Paul 99-05; P-in-c Brixton St Paul w St Sav 05-08; V Biggin Hill *Roch* 08-15; C W Sheppey *Cant* from 15. *Holy Trinity Vicarage, 241 High Street, Sheerness ME12 1UR* E: jmmclaren@tiscali.co.uk

MacLAREN, Richard Francis. b 46. S'wark Ord Course 72. **d** 75 **p** 76. C Charlton St Luke w H Trin *S'wark* 75-78; C Kensington St Mary Abbots w St Geo *Lon* 78-81; Hon C St Marylebone w H Trin 82-96; P-in-c 96-97; Development Officer CUF 97; Chmn Art and Christianity Enquiry Trust 97-11; Hon C Regent's Park St Mark *Lon* 97-11; rtd 11. *The Chapter House, 2 East Wing, Stoneleigh Abbey, Kenilworth CV8 2LF* T: (01926) 851977 E: richardmclaren8@hotmail.com

McLAREN, Canon Robert Ian. b 62. Bris Univ BSc 84 St Jo Coll Dur BA 87. Cranmer Hall Dur 85. **d** 88 **p** 89. C Birkenhead Ch Ch *Ches* 88-90; C Bebington 90-95; V Cheadle All Hallows 95-05; V Poynton from 05; RD Cheadle from 09; Hon Can Ches Cathl from 14. *The Vicarage, 41 London Road North, Poynton, Stockport SK12 1AF* T: (01625) 850524 *or* 879277
E: poyntonvicar@talktalk.net

McLAREN-COOK, Paul Raymond. b 43. **d** 66 **p** 67. C Mt Lawley Australia 66-67; C Perth Cathl 67-69; R Carnarvon 69-72; V Seremban Malaysia 72-75; Warden Coll of Th 75-76; R Kensington 76-79; R Narrogin 79-84; P-in-c Wellington Australia 84-85; R Eugowra 85-86; P-in-c Berrigan 86-87; P-in-c Hay 87-88; P-in-c Yass 88; R Moruya 88-90; R Heywood 90-92; R Warracknabeal 92-95; Chapl Ballarat Base and St Jo of God Hosps 95-00; R Kansas City St Mary USA 00-03; R Stanway *Chelmsf* 03-13; rtd 13. *Ascot Priory, Priory Road, Ascot SL5 8RT* T: (01344) 882067 E: mclarencook@btinternet.com

McLARNON, Mrs Sylvia Caroline Millicent. b 45. S Dios Minl Tr Scheme 92. **d** 95 **p** 96. NSM Burgess Hill St Andr *Chich* 95-99; C 99-09; rtd 09; Asst Chapl St Pet and St Jas Hospice N Chailey from 05. *23 The Warren, Burgess Hill RH15 0DU* T: (01444) 233902

McLAUGHLIN, Adrian Robert. QUB BTh MTh PhD PGCE. **d** 07 **p** 08. C Bangor Abbey *D & D* 07-13; LtO 13-14; I Dunmurry *Conn* from 14. *The Rectory, 27 Church Avenue, Dunmurry, Belfast BT17 9RS* T: (028) 9061 0984 E: revadrian@btinternet.com

McLAUGHLIN, Hubert James Kenneth. b 45. CITC 85. **d** 88 **p** 89. NSM Donagheady *D & R* 88-89; NSM Glendermott 89-98; P-in-c Inver w Mountcharles, Killaghtee and Killybegs 98-02; I 02-10; rtd 10. *9 Cadogen Park, Londonderry BT47 5QW* T: (028) 7134 8916 E: kenandmart@yahoo.com

McLAUGHLIN, Capt Michael Anthony. b 48. **d** 97 **p** 98. C Gt Chart *Cant* 97-01; C-in-c Parkwood CD 01-11; rtd 11; PtO *Roch* from 12. *12 Medway Road, Gillingham ME7 1NH* M: 07977-051681 E: macl@blueyonder.co.uk

McLAUGHLIN, Mrs Teresa Marguerite Irene Mary. b 54. Linc Sch of Th and Min 11. **d** 13 **p** 14. NSM S Ormsby Gp *Linc* from 13. *Woodside, Aswardby Road, Harrington, Spilsby PE23 4NL* T: (01790) 753158 E: tmcmclaughlin@tiscali.co.uk

MACLAURIN, Ms Anne Fiona. b 62. St Andr Univ MA 84. Ridley Hall Cam. **d** 99 **p** 00. C Crookes St Thos *Sheff* 99-04; TV 04-05; Miss P Philadelphia St Thos 05-10; V Cambridge St Barn *Ely* from 10. *The Vicarage, 57 St Barnabas Road, Cambridge CB1 2BX*

MACLAY, Christopher Willis. b 64. Stirling Univ BA 88 Reading Univ MA 92. Trin Coll Bris BA 01. **d** 01 **p** 02. C Bedhampton *Portsm* 01-05; P-in-c Ashington, Washington and Wiston w Buncton *Chich* 05-11; R 11-12; Chapl Versailles w Chevry *Eur* 12-15; V Bream *Glouc* from 15. *St James's Vicarage, Coleford Road, Bream, Lydney GL15 6ES* E: chris.maclay@gmail.com

McLAY, Robert James. b 49. Cant Univ (NZ) BA 71. St Jo Coll Auckland. **d** 73 **p** 74. C Fendalton New Zealand 73-75; Hon C Yardley St Edburgha *Birm* 75-77; V Banks Peninsular New Zealand 77-80; V Marchwiel 80-83; V Huntly 83-89; Lect St Jo Coll 86-88; V Stokes Valley 89-93; V Pauatahanui 93-04; V Brooklyn from 04; Can Wellington Cathl 96-00. *13 Garfield Street, Brooklyn, Wellington 6021, New Zealand* T: (0064) (4) 389 8003 *or* 389 3470 E: stmattes@actrix.gen.nz

MACLEAN, Canon Allan Murray. b 50. Edin Univ MA 72. Cuddesdon Coll 72. **d** 76 **p** 77. Chapl St Mary's Cathl 76-81; Tutor Edin Univ 77-80; R Dunoon *Arg* 81-86; R Tighnabruaich 84-86; Provost St Jo Cathl Oban 86-99; R Oban St Jo 86-99; R Ardbrecknish 86-99; R Ardchattan 89-99; Hon Can St Jo Cathl Oban from 99; LtO *Edin* from 00; PtO *Mor* from 00; P-in-c Edin St Vin from 15. *5 North Charlotte Street, Edinburgh EH2 4HR* T: 0131-225 8609 E: editoredge@aol.com

McLEAN, Bradley Halstead. b 57. McMaster Univ Ontario BSc Toronto Univ MDiv MTh PhD. **d** 83 **p** 84. C Dur St Giles 83-84; Canada from 84. *38 Tweedsmuir Road, Winnipeg MB R3P 1Z2, Canada*

MacLEAN, Christopher Gavin. b 57. Kent Univ BA 85. SEITE 10. **d** 13 **p** 14. C Walmer *Cant* from 13. *24 Thistledown, Walmer, Deal CT14 7XE* T: (01304) 761630 E: busyonasunday@gmail.com

McLEAN, Dominic. **d** 89 **p** 11. NSM Leic St Aid 10-11; NSM Burbage w Aston Flamville from 11; PtO *Pet* from 12. *50 Stokes Drive, Leicester LE3 9BS*

McLEAN, Donald Stewart. b 48. TCD BA 70. CITC 70. **d** 72 **p** 73. C Glendermott *D & R* 72-75; I Castledawson 75-87 and I 03-12; I Londonderry Ch 87-03; Dioc Dir of Ords 79-96; Adn Derry 96-12; Can Derry Cathl 91-12; rtd 12. *99 Oldtown Road, Castledawson, Magherafelt BT45 8BZ* T: (028) 7946 8656 M: 07710-387436 E: donaldmclean@btinternet.com

McLEAN, Mrs Eileen Mary. b 44. City Univ BSc 67. NOC 85. **d** 88 **p** 94. Par Dn Burley in Wharfedale *Bradf* 88-92; Par Dn Nottingham St Pet and St Jas *S'well* 92-94; C 94-02; AD Nottingham Cen 98-02; V Bamburgh *Newc* 02-08; V Ellingham 02-08; rtd 08; PtO *Ripon* 08-13; *Sarum* from 15. *8 Fordington Dairy, Athelstan Road, Dorchester DT1 1FD* T: (01305) 260126 E: eileen.mclean6@btinternet.com

MACLEAN, Kenneth John Forbes. b 31. St Deiniol's Hawarden 80. **d** 81 **p** 82. C Sedgley All SS *Lich* 81-85; V Shareshill 85-90; R Bicton, Montford w Shrawardine and Fitz 90-96; rtd 96; PtO *Lich* from 99. *7 The Armoury, Wenlock Road, Shrewsbury SY2 6PA* T: (01743) 243308

MacLEAN, Lawrence Alexander Charles. b 61. K Coll Lon BD 84 AKC 84. Chich Th Coll 86. **d** 88 **p** 89. C Cirencester *Glouc* 88-91; C Prestbury 91-96; PtO 01-02; Chapl Florence w Siena *Eur* 02-11; V Gt and Lt Torrington and Frithelstock *Ex* 11-14; RD Torrington 12-14; V Hove St Barn and St Agnes *Chich* from 14; P-in-c Hove St Andr from 14; Dioc Development Officer from 14. *30 Bigwood Avenue, Hove BN3 6FQ* E: lm61@live.co.uk

McLEAN, Canon Margaret Anne. b 62. Birm Univ BA 91 Heythrop Coll Lon MA 99. Qu Coll Birm 88. **d** 91 **p** 94. Par Dn Bedford All SS *St Alb* 91-94; C 94; Chapl St Alb High Sch for Girls 94-98; Asst Soc Resp Officer *Derby* 98-99; Chapl Huddersfield Univ *Wakef* 99-02; P-in-c Scholes 02-09; P-in-c Cleckheaton St Luke and Whitechapel 02-09; P-in-c Battyeford 09-14; V from 14; Dioc Tr Officer (Reader Formation) from 09; Hon Can Wakef Cathl from 11. *Battyeford Vicarage, 107A Stocksbank Road, Mirfield WF14 9QT* T: (01924) 493277 M: 07777-673172 E: m.a.mclean@btinternet.com

McLEAN, Canon Michael Stuart. b 32. Dur Univ BA 57. Cuddesdon Coll 57. **d** 59 **p** 60. C Camberwell St Giles *S'wark* 59-61; LtO *Nor* 61-68; R Marsham 68-74; R Burgh 68-74; RD Ingworth 70-74; P-in-c Nor St Pet Parmentergate w St Jo 74-75; TV 75-78; TR 78-86; Hon Can Nor Cathl 82-86; Can Res Nor Cathl 86-94; P-in-c Nor St Mary in the Marsh 87-94; PtO from 94; rtd 97. *8 Blickling Court, Recorder Road, Norwich NR1 1NW* T: (01603) 630398 E: canonm@talktalk.net

McLEAN, Peter. b 50. **d** 94 **p** 95. NSM Mold *St As* 94-02; PtO 02-03; P-in-c Bodedern w Llanfaethlu *Ban* 03-05; R Llangefni w Tregaean 05-11; AD Malltraeth 06-11; PtO from 11. *Trelawney, Bryn Coch Lane, Mold CH7 1PS* T: (01352) 700387

McLEAN, Canon Robert Hedley. b 47. St Jo Coll Dur BA 69. Ripon Hall Ox 69. **d** 71 **p** 72. C Redhill St Jo *S'wark* 71-74; C S Beddington St Mich 74-77; C-in-c Raynes Park H Cross CD 77; P-in-c Motspur Park 77-80; V 80-84; V Tadworth 84-00; Asst RD Reigate 92-93; RD Reigate 93-00; R Morpeth *Newc* 00-12; AD 04-08; Chapl Northd Mental Health NHS Trust 00-09; Chapl Northumbria Healthcare NHS Foundn Trust 00-09; rtd 12; P-in-c Wylam *Newc* from 12; Hon Can Newc Cathl from 11. *The Vicarage, Church Road, Wylam NE41 8AT* T: (01661) 853254 E: rhm47@hotmail.co.uk

MacLEAY, Angus Murdo. b 59. Univ Coll Ox BA 81 MA 86 Man Univ MPhil 92 Solicitor 83. Wycliffe Hall Ox 85. **d** 88 **p** 89. C Rusholme H Trin *Man* 88-92; V Houghton *Carl* 92-01; R Sevenoaks St Nic *Roch* from 01. *The Rectory, Rectory Lane, Sevenoaks TN13 1JA* T: (01732) 740340 F: 742810 E: angus.macleay@diocese-rochester.org

MacLEOD, Alan Roderick Hugh (Roddie). b 33. St Edm Hall Ox BA 56 MA 61 Ox Univ DipEd 62. Wycliffe Hall Ox 56. **d** 58 **p** 59. C Bognor St Jo *Chich* 58-61; Chapl Wadh Coll Ox 62; Hd of RE Picardy Boys' Sch Erith 62-68; C Erith St Jo *Roch* 63-69; Dean Lonsdale Coll Lanc Univ 70-72; Hd of RE K Edw VI Sch Totnes 72-73; Dir of Resources St Helier Boys' Sch Jersey 73-84; V Shipton Bellinger *Win* 84-02; rtd 02; PtO *Win* from 02. *Pippins Toft, Lashmar's Corner, East Preston, Littlehampton BN16 1EZ* T: (01903) 783523

McLEOD, David Leo Roderick. b 71. Westmr Coll Ox BA 92 DipCOT 96. **d** 05 **p** 06. OLM Coddenham w Gosbeck and Hemingstone w Henley *St E* 05-10; OLM Crowfield w Stonham Aspal and Mickfield 05-10; Chapl Team Co-ord Univ Campus Suffolk 07-10; Chapl Team Co-ord Suffolk New Coll 07-10; C Wokingham St Sebastian *Ox* 10-15; V Greenham from 15. *St Mary's Vicarage, New Road, Greenham, Thatcham RG19 8RZ* M: 07706-429805 T: (01635) 41075 E: davidmcleod01@btinternet.com

McLEOD, Everton William. b 57. Oak Hill Th Coll 89. **d** 91 **p** 92. C New Ferry *Ches* 91-93; C Moreton 93-98; Chapl R Liv Univ Hosp NHS Trust 98-01; R Weston-super-Mare St Nic w St Barn *B & W* 01-11; V Trentham *Lich* from 11; V Hanford from 11. *The Vicarage, Trentham Park, Stoke-on-Trent ST4 8AE* T: (01782) 658194 E: vicar@trenthamchurch.org.uk

MACLEOD, John Bain Maclennan. b 50. Aber Univ LLB 86 Solicitor 03. TISEC 03. **d** 06 **p** 08. NSM Hamilton *Glas* 06-12; NSM Annan from 12; NSM Eastriggs from 12; NSM Gretna from 12; NSM Lockerbie from 12; NSM Moffat from 12. *All Saints' Rectory, Ashgrove Terrace, Lockerbie DG11 2BP* T: (01576) 204163 M: 07826-163415 E: macleod.greenrig@btinternet.com

MacLEOD, John Malcolm (Jay). b 61. Harvard Univ AB 84 Pemb Coll Ox BA 87 MA 91. Linc Th Coll MDiv 93. **d** 93 **p** 94. C Chesterfield SS Aug *Derby* 93-96; C Stalybridge St Paul *Ches* 96-98; P-in-c Micklehurst 98-03; P-in-c Bedford All SS *St Alb* 03-13; Dioc Interfaith Adv 03-13; R New London USA from 13. *184 Shindagan Road, Wilmot Flat NH 03287, USA* E: jaymacleod@mac.com

McLEOD, Neil Raymond. b 61. Trin Coll Bris 06. **d** 08 **p** 09. C N w S Wootton *Nor* 08-12; P-in-c Newport and Widdington *Chelmsf* 12-13; V Newport w Widdington, Quendon and Rickling from 13. *The Vicarage, 5 Meadowford, Newport, Saffron Walden CB11 3QL* T: (01799) 540339 E: mcleod444@btinternet.com

McLEOD, Paul Douglas. b 66. Cuddesdon Coll BTh 95. **d** 98 **p** 99. C Morpeth *Newc* 98-02; V Newbiggin Hall 02-10; R Silverstone and Abthorpe w Slapton etc *Pet* from 10; RD Towcester from 11. *The Vicarage, 24A High Street, Silverstone, Towcester NN12 8US* T: (01327) 858101 M: 07780-834099 E: revpaulmcleod@btinternet.com

MacLEOD, Roderick. *See* MacLEOD, Alan Roderick Hugh

MacLEOD, Talisker Isobel. *See* TRACEY-MacLEOD, Talisker Isobel

MacLEOD-MILLER, The Ven Peter Norman. b 66. **d** 91 **p** 91. C Cardiff Australia 91-92; C Hillston 92-94; C Fitzroy 95-97; PtO Melbourne 97-01; P-in-c Risby w Gt and Lt Saxham *St E* 02-04; V Barrow 05-10; Min Can St E Cathl 05-10; R Albury and Adn Hume Australia from 10. *St Matthew's Rectory, PO Box 682, Albury NSW 2640, Australia* T: (0061) (2) 6021 3022 *or* 6041 1916

McLOUGHLIN, Ian Livingstone. b 38. CEng MICE 64. Carl Dioc Tr Course 78. **d** 83 **p** 84. NSM Stanwix *Carl* 83-88; C Barrow St Geo w St Luke 88-90; R Kirkby Thore w Temple Sowerby and Newbiggin 90-01; rtd 01; PtO *Carl* from 01; *Bradf* 01-10. *29 Wordsworth Drive, Kendal LA9 7JW* T: (01539) 728209
E: nohastle@googlemail.com

McLOUGHLIN, John Robert. b 70. QUB BEng 92 Open Univ MSc 02. CITC BTh 09. **d** 09 **p** 10. C Arm St Mark 09-11; I Clonfeacle w Derrygortreavy from 11. *The Rectory, 4 Clonfeacle Road, Dungannon BT71 7LQ* T: (028) 3754 8289 M: 07515-353023 E: johnnymcloughlin@gmail.com

McLOUGHLIN, Ms Tracey. b 65. Liv Hope Univ Coll BA 05. SNWTP 09. **d** 12 **p** 13. C Skelmersdale St Paul *Liv* from 12. *6 Wilcove, Skelmersdale WN8 8NF* T: (01695) 51596
M: 07990-545489 E: tracey_lamia_1@yahoo.co.uk

McLUCKIE, John Mark. b 67. St Andr Univ BD 89. Edin Th Coll MTh 91. **d** 91 **p** 92. C Perth St Ninian *St And* 91-94; Chapl K Coll Cam 94-96; TV Glas E End 96-00; Assoc R Edin St Jo 00-03; PtO from 08; Chapl Asst R Marsden NHS Foundn Trust 10-12; Vice Provost St Mary's Cathl from 12. *33/1 Manor Place, Edinburgh EH3 7EB* M: 07967-711884
E: john.mcluckie@hotmail.co.uk

MACLURE, David Samuel. b 80. York Univ BA 02 MA 06. Oak Hill Th Coll BA 14. **d** 14 **p** 15. C Isleworth St Jo w St Mary *Lon* from 14. *11 Paget Lane, Isleworth TW7 6ED*
E: davidmaclure@gmail.com

MACLUSKIE, Mrs Linda. b 55. Lanc Univ MA 99. CBDTI 95. **d** 98 **p** 99. NSM Halton w Aughton *Blackb* 98-02; NSM Bolton-le-Sands 02-10; P-in-c Sandylands 10-11; V from 11. *St John's Vicarage, 2 St John's Avenue, Morecambe LA3 1EU* T: (01524) 411039 M: 07827-923222 E: linda.macluskie@virgin.net

McMAHON, Stephen. b 66. Newc Univ BSc 87 MSc 89 Leeds Univ BA 03 CEng 97 MBES 97. Coll of Resurr Mirfield 01. **d** 03 **p** 04. C Lancaster St Mary w St John and St Anne *Blackb* 03-07; P-in-c Lowther and Askham and Clifton and Brougham *Carl* 07-10; P-in-c Kirkby Thore w Temple Sowerby and Newbiggin 07-10; Chapl Rossall Sch Fleetwood 10; NSM Lancaster St Mary w St John and St Anne *Blackb* 10-11; V Blyth St Cuth Newc from 11. *The Vicarage, 29 Ridley Avenue, Blyth NE24 3BA* T: (01670) 354218 E: steve1345.mcmahon@virgin.net

McMAIN, Sheena Stuart. b 56. Edin Univ BSc 77 MB, ChB 80 Leeds Univ MMedSc 00 FRCGP 03. Ripon Coll Cuddesdon 11. **d** 13 **p** 14. C Rothwell *Leeds* 13-15; C Rothwell, Lofthouse, Methley etc from 15. *The Vicarage, 46 Holmsley Lane, Woodlesford, Leeds LS26 8RY* T: 0113-282 6239 M: 07545-240004
E: revsheenamcmain@gmail.com

McMANN, Duncan. b 34. Jes Coll Ox BA 55 MA 60. Clifton Th Coll 55. **d** 58 **p** 59. C Newburn *Newc* 58-60; C Bishopwearmouth St Gabr *Dur* 60-62; N Area Sec BCMS 62-66; Midl and E Anglia Area Sec 66-92; Support Co-ord 84-92; LtO *Man* 62-66; *Cov* 66-92; P-in-c Awsworth w Cossall *S'well* 92-99; Chapl Notts Constabulary 93-99; rtd 99; PtO *Nor* from 00. *7 Evans Drive, Lowestoft NR32 2RX* T: (01502) 531337

McMANN, Canon Judith. b 46. Hull Univ BTh 96. EMMTC MA 98. **d** 98 **p** 99. NSM Gt Grimsby St Mary and St Jas *Linc* 98-08; NSM Caistor Gp from 08; Can and Preb Linc Cathl from 05. *23 Grasby Crescent, Grimsby DN37 9HE*
T: (01472) 887523 E: jmcmann@btopenworld.com

McMANNERS, John Roland. b 46. Liv Univ LLB 68. Cranmer Hall Dur 99. **d** 01 **p** 02. C Monkwearmouth *Dur* 01-05; P-in-c Bishopwearmouth St Gabr 05-15; rtd 15. *40 Bek Road, Durham DH1 5LD* T: 0191-567 5200

McMANUS, James Robert. b 33. Wycliffe Hall Ox 56. **d** 58 **p** 59. C Leic H Trin 58-60; C Aylestone 60-63; India 66-79; V Oldham St Barn *Man* 79-83; Asst Regional Sec CMS 83-85; V Wolverhampton St Matt *Lich* 85-93; V Lapley w Wheaton Aston 93-99; P-in-c Blymhill w Weston-under-Lizard 93-99; rtd 99; PtO *Lich* from 99. *Delamere, McBean Road, Wolverhampton WV6 0JQ* T: (01902) 833436 F: 834170
E: jimvicar@aol.com

McMANUS-THOMPSON, Elizabeth Gray. *See* THOMPSON, Elizabeth Gray McManus

McMASTER, James Alexander. b 43. **d** 69 **p** 70. C Dundonald *D & D* 69-73; C Antrim All SS *Conn* 73-78; I Tempo and Clabby *Clogh* 78-83; I Knocknamuckley *D & D* 83-95; I Carrickfergus *Conn* 95-08; rtd 08. *78 Murray Wood, Waringstown, Craigavon BT66 7SX* T: (028) 3882 0741

MacMASTER, Mrs Norma. QUB BA DipEd McGill Univ Montreal MEd. **d** 04 **p** 05. NSM Dublin St Geo and St Thos *D & G* 04-07; rtd 07. *1 The Orchard, Tennis Court Lane, Skerries, Co Dublin, Republic of Ireland* T: (00353) (1) 849 1387
E: nmacmaster@eircom.net

McMASTER, William Keith. b 57. TCD. **d** 82 **p** 84. C Portadown St Columba *Arm* 82-84; C Erdington St Barn *Birm* 84-87; TV Shirley 87-00; TV Salter Street and Shirley 00-02; rtd 02. *1 Hockley Terrace, Banbridge BT32 3QB* T: (028) 4062 2582

MACMATH, Terence Handley. *See* HANDLEY MACMATH, Terence

McMICHAEL, Andrew Hamilton. b 48. Univ of Wales (Ban) BA 77. Chich Th Coll 87. **d** 89 **p** 90. C Chorley St Geo *Blackb* 89-92; C Burnley St Andr w St Marg 92-94; Chapl Burnley Health Care NHS Trust 92-94; R Eccleston *Blackb* 94-99; V Lt Marsden w Nelson St Mary 99-04; P-in-c Tain, Lochinver and Invergordon St Ninian *Mor* 04-07; P-in-c Harrington *Carl* 07-09; R Port Glas 09-13; rtd 13. *11 Howard Court, 77 Albert Road, Southport PR9 9LN*
E: andrew.mcmichael@tesco.net

MacMILLAN, Douglas Middleton. b 41. RCM DMus 13 St Thos Hosp Lon MB, BS 66 FRCS 70 FTCL 82 AMusLCM 80 FLCM 83. Guildf Dioc Min Course 96. **d** 00. NSM Guildf Cathl 00-02; PtO 02-04; NSM E and W Clandon 04-11; rtd 12; PtO *Guildf* from 12. *Rivendell, 50 Speedwell Close, Guildford GU4 7HE* T: (01483) 533019
E: douglas.oriana@btinternet.com

✤**McMULLAN, The Rt Revd Gordon.** b 34. ACIS 57 QUB BSc 61 PhD 71 TCD MPhil 90 Univ of the South (USA) DMin 95. Ridley Hall Cam 61. **d** 62 **p** 63 **c** 80. C Ballymacarrett St Patr *D & D* 62-67; Cen Adv on Chr Stewardship to Ch of Ireland 67-70; C Knock *D & D* 70-71; I 76-80; I Belfast St Brendan 71-76; OCM 71-78; Bp's Dom Chapl *D & D* 72-78; Adn Down 79-80; Bp Clogh 80-86; Bp D & D 86-97; rtd 97. *Abbeyfield House, 2A Ward Avenue, Bangor BT20 5JW* T: (028) 9146 0821

McMULLEN, Philip Kenneth. b 55. RMN 80. St Mich Coll Llan 93. **d** 95 **p** 96. C Coity w Nolton *Llan* 95-98; V Fleur-de-Lis *Mon* 98-04. *29 Clos Coed Bach, Blackwood NP12 1GT*
T: (01495) 220210

McMULLEN, Ronald Norman. b 36. TCD BA 61 MA 66 California Inst of Integral Studies MA 92. Ridley Hall Cam 61. **d** 63 **p** 64. C Fulham St Mary N End *Lon* 63-67; C Cambridge St Sepulchre *Ely* 67-70; C Everton St Ambrose w St Tim *Liv* 70-73; Community Work Course & Research Asst York Univ 73-75; P-in-c Heanor *Derby* 75-79; V 79-88; RD 76-83; USA 88-93; rtd 98. *Apple Tree Cottage, 38A Main Street, Lowick, Berwick-upon-Tweed TD15 2UA* T/F: (01289) 388301

McMULLON, Andrew Brian. b 56. Sheff Univ BSc. St Jo Coll Nottm. **d** 83 **p** 84. C Stainforth *Sheff* 83-86; V Blackb Redeemer 86-90; Chapl RAF 90-13; V Sedbergh, Cautley and Garsdale *Carl* from 13; P-in-c Firbank, Howgill and Killington from 15. *20 Winfield Road, Sedbergh LA10 5AZ* T: (015396) 20018

McMUNN, Lee James. b 78. LSE BSc 99. Wycliffe Hall Ox BA 04. **d** 05 **p** 06. C Hull St Jo Newland *York* from 05. *32 Riversdale Road, Hull HU6 7HA* T: (01482) 802611 M: 07957-898884
E: lee@stjohnnewland.org.uk

McMURRAY, Gary. b 81. QUB BA 02. CITC BTh 08. **d** 08 **p** 09. C Dundonald *D & D* 08-11; I Aghavea *Clogh* from 11. *The Rectory, 256 Belfast Road, Lurgan, Brookeborough, Enniskillen BT94 4DS* T: (028) 8953 1210 E: garymcmurray@gmail.com

McMURRAY, Matthew Paul. b 79. Trin Hall Cam BTh 11. Westcott Ho Cam 08. **d** 11 **p** 12. C Hawes Side and Marton Moss *Blackb* 11-14; C Fleetwood St Pet and St Dav from 14. *96 Promenade Road, Fleetwood FY7 6RF* T: (01253) 878310
E: frmatthew@cantab.net

McMURTARY, Simon Alexander. b 79. Wycliffe Hall Ox BA 00 MA 05. Ripon Coll Cuddesdon 10. **d** 12 **p** 13. C Four Marks *Win* 12-15; Chapl Dur Sch from 15. *Durham School, Durham DH1 4SZ* T: 0191-386 4783 E: simon.mcmurtary@oba.co.uk

McNAB (née LUMMIS), Mrs Elizabeth Howieson. b 44. Lon Univ BDS 68 LDS 68. St Jo Coll Nottm 85. **d** 88 **p** 95. NSM Lerwick *Ab* from 88; NSM Burravoe from 88. *Waters Edge, Bridge of Walls, Shetland ZE2 9NP* T: (01595) 809441
E: j.mcnab840@btinternet.com

McNAIR SCOTT, Benjamin Guthrie. b 76. K Coll Lon BA 98 MA 05. Ridley Hall Cam 05. **d** 07 **p** 08. NSM Guildf Ch Ch w St Martha-on-the-Hill from 07; Chapl St Cath Sch Bramley from 12. *21 Lancaster Avenue, Guildford GU1 3JR* T: (01483) 455645 M: 07968-617084 E: benjaming@lycos.co.uk *or* benji@christchurchguildford.com

McNALLY-CROSS, Samuel John. b 85. **d** 14 **p** 15. C Reading St Giles *Ox* from 14. *St Saviour's House, 31 Holybrook Road, Reading RG1 6DG* M: 07841-973045
E: frsamuelcross@gmail.com

McNAMARA, Barbara. *See* SMITH, Barbara Mary

McNAMARA, Michael Ian. b 59. Van Mildert Coll Dur BA 81. Ridley Hall Cam 83. **d** 85 **p** 86. C Bedford Ch Ch *St Alb* 85-89; BCMS Tanzania 89-92; TV Bolton St Paul w Em *Man* 93-97; C Galleywood Common *Chelmsf* 97-03; R Elmswell *St E* 03-12; RD Lavenham 11-12; C Blackburn N Australia from 12. *5 Wilton Street, Blackburn North, Melbourne VIC 3130, Australia* E: mwanza@lineone.net

McNAUGHTAN-OWEN, James Thomas. b 48. Liv Univ MA 00. Linc Th Coll 77. **d** 80 **p** 81. C Palmers Green St Jo *Lon* 80-84; C Timperley *Ches* 84-87; C Bramhall 87-92; V Latchford St Jas 92-14; RD Gt Budworth 96-03; rtd 14. *9 Melton Road, Runcorn WA7 4AH*

MACNAUGHTON, Mrs Diana. b 54. St Hugh's Coll Ox BA 76 MA 90 Northumbria Univ MA 11 Dur Univ PGCE 78. NEOC 95. **d** 98 **p** 99. NSM Gosforth All SS *Newc* 98-01; C Willington 01-04; Chapl Team Ldr Northumbria Healthcare NHS Foundn Trust 04-11; P-in-c Byker St Silas *Newc* from 11. *40 Heaton Grove, Newcastle upon Tyne NE6 5NP* T: 0191-276 5005 M: 07950-627799 E: dmacnaughton@btinternet.com

MACNAUGHTON, Canon James Alastair. b 54. St Jo Coll Ox BA 78 MA 82 Fitzw Coll Cam BA 80. Ridley Hall Cam 78. **d** 81 **p** 82. C Rounds Green *Birm* 81-85; TV Bestwood Park *S'well* 85-86; TV Bestwood 86-90; V Amble *Newc* 90-97; TR Cramlington 97-07; Jt Newc/Dur Development Officer for Educn for Discipleship 07-13; Hon Can Newc Cathl 13; rtd 13; PtO *Dur* from 13. *40 Heaton Grove, Newcastle upon Tyne NE6 5NP* T: 0191-276 5005 E: macnaughton@btinternet.com

McNAUGHTON, John. b 29. St Chad's Coll Dur. **d** 54 **p** 55. C Thorney Close CD *Dur* 54-58; C-in-c E Herrington St Chad CD 58-62; PC E Herrington 62-66; CF 66-94; V Hutton Cranswick w Skerne, Watton and Beswick *York* 94-99; rtd 99; PtO *York* from 99. *47 Southgate, Cranswick, Driffield YO25 9QX* T: (01377) 270869

MACNAUGHTON, Mrs Pamela Jean. b 63. Ox Min Course. **d** 08 **p** 09. NSM Bishopthorpe *York* from 08; NSM Acaster Malbis from 08; NSM Appleton Roebuck w Acaster Selby from 08; Dioc Adv for Pioneer Min 12-14; CPAS from 13. *64 Copmanthorpe Lane, Bishopthorpe, York YO23 2RS* T: (01904) 700141 E: workspacepjm@aol.com

MACNAUGHTON, William Malcolm. b 57. Qu Coll Cam BA 80. Ridley Hall Cam 79. **d** 81 **p** 82. C Haughton le Skerne *Dur* 81-85; P-in-c Newton Hall 85-90; TV Shoreditch St Leon and Hoxton St Jo *Lon* 90-00; AD Hackney 94-99; V Hoxton St Jo w Ch Ch 00-02; R Hambleden Valley *Ox* 02-07; AD Wycombe 05-07; Chief of Staff to Abp York from 07. *The Palace, Bishopthorpe, York YO23 2GE* T: (01904) 772362 E: malcolm.macnaughton@archbishopofyork.org

MacNEANEY, Jonathan Niall Agnew. b 88. Oriel Coll Ox BA 09. Ripon Coll Cuddesdon MTh 13. **d** 13 **p** 14. C Hadleigh St Jas and Hadleigh St Barn *Chelmsf* 13-14; C Epping Distr from 14. *12 Kendal Avenue, Epping CM16 4PP* E: macneaneyj@gmail.com

McNEE, Canon William Creighton. Ulster Univ MA NUU MA FCIPD. **d** 82 **p** 83. C Larne and Inver *Conn* 82-84; I Donagheady *D & R* 84-91; I Kilwaughter w Cairncastle and Craigy Hill *Conn* 91-93; I Ardstraw w Baronscourt, Badoney Lower etc *D & R* 93-04; P-in-c Londonderry Ch Ch 04-05; I 05-08; I Londonderry Ch Ch, Culmore, Muff and Belmont 08-09; Bp's Dom Chapl 96-07; Can Derry Cathl 00-09; rtd 09. *14 Tartnakilly Road, Limavady BT49 9NA* T: (028) 7727 8873 M: 07770-767737 E: billmcnee@usa.net

MACNEICE, Alan Donor. b 34. TCD Div Sch 62. **d** 64 **p** 65. C Ballymoney w Finvoy and Rasharkin *Conn* 64-67; R Christiana Jamaica 67-70; C Winchmore Hill H Trin *Lon* 71-76; C Harringay St Paul 76-77; C Kensington St Barn 77-78; P-in-c 78-79; USA 83-06; rtd 99. *29Eo, Street 178, Commond Choychom, nas Distrib Daun Penh, Phnom Penh, Cambodia* T: (00855) (23) 986064 E: donor@online.com.kh

McNEICE, Kathleen Mary. b 42. SEITE. **d** 07 **p** 08. NSM Folkestone Trin *Cant* from 07. *19 Beachborough Road, Folkestone CT19 4AA* T: (01303) 278791

McNEIL, Mrs Ann. b 41. **d** 89 **p** 94. NSM Henfield w Shermanbury and Woodmancote *Chich* 89-99; PtO from 00. *6 The Daisy Croft, Henfield BN5 9LH* T: (01273) 492606 E: annmcneil@onetel.com

McNEIL, Kyle Gillies. b 86. Univ Coll Dur BA 09. St Steph Ho Ox BA 14. **d** 14 **p** 15. C Cockerton *Dur* from 14. *19 Holmlands Road, Darlington DL3 9JE* T: (01325) 483187 E: kyle.g.mcneil@gmail.com

MACNEILL, Nicholas Terence. b 62. St Steph Ho Ox BTh 93. **d** 93 **p** 94. C Ex St Thos and Em 93-97; TV 97-98; V Cople, Moggerhanger and Willington *St Alb* 98-03; R Toddington and Chalgrave 03-06; rtd 07. *20 Black Path, Polegate BN26 5AP* T: (01323) 485399 E: nick.macneill@ntlworld.com

McNELLY, The Very Revd Nicola. b 62. Cranmer Hall Dur 07. **d** 09 **p** 10. Chapl St Mary's Cathl 09-10; C 10-12; Provost St Jo Cathl Oban from 12; R Ardchattan from 12; R Ardbrecknish from 12. *The Rectory, Ardconnel Terrace, Oban PA34 5DJ* M: 07825-440580 T: (01631) 562323 E: nicki.mcnelly@googlemail.com

McNICOL, Andrew Keith. b 45. Westmr Coll of Educn CertEd 69 Open Univ BA 79 Westmr Coll Ox MA 90. Westcott Ho Cam 92. **d** 92 **p** 93. C Whitstable *Cant* 92-95; V Ferring *Chich* 95-00; P-in-c Willesborough *Cant* 00-06; P-in-c Tunstall w Rodmersham 06-11; R Tunstall and Bredgar 11-14; rtd 14; PtO *Cant* from 15. *63 Shearwater Avenue, Whitstable CT5 4DY* T: (01227) 264592 E: keiththerector@gmail.com

McNIVEN, Mrs Betty. b 47. Lanc Univ BA 68. NOC 83. **dss** 86 **d** 87 **p** 94. Baguley *Man* 86-87; Hon Par Dn 87-88; Par Dn Newton Heath All SS 88-91; Par Dn E Farnworth and Kearsley 91-94; TV 94-95; P-in-c Spotland 95-02; Hon Can Man Cathl 00-02; TV Cwm Gwendraeth *St D* 02-06; rtd 07; P-in-c Llansteffan and Llan-y-bri etc *St D* 07-08. *105 Homegower House, St Helens Road, Swansea SA1 4DN* T: (01792) 469995 E: betty.mcniven@talk21.com

McPHATE, The Very Revd Gordon Ferguson. b 50. Aber Univ MB, ChB 74 Fitzw Coll Cam BA 77 MA 81 MD 88 Surrey Univ MSc 86 Edin Univ MTh 94 FRCPEd 98. Westcott Ho Cam 75. **d** 78 **p** 79. NSM Sanderstead All SS *S'wark* 78-81; Hon PV S'wark Cathl 81-86; Lect Lon Univ 81-86; Chapl St Andr Univ *St And* 86-02; Lect 86-93; Sen Lect 93-02; Dean Ches from 02. *The Deanery, 7 Abbey Street, Chester CH1 2JF* T: (01244) 500956 *or* 500971 F: 341110 E: dean@chestercathedral.com

McPHEE, Mrs Margaret Theresa Maria. b 65. Nottm Univ BA 88 Anglia Ruskin Univ PGCE 97 FCIPD 04. ERMC 09. **d** 12 **p** 13. C Mile Cross *Nor* 12-13; C Stalham, E Ruston, Brunstead, Sutton and Ingham from 13. *1 Bullemer Close, Stalham, Norwich NR12 9AY* M: 07759-913802 E: revmargaretmcphee@gmail.com

MACPHERSON, Aian Jonathan. b 84. BSc 07 St Jo Coll Dur BA 13. Cranmer Hall Dur 10. **d** 13 **p** 14. C Drypool *York* from 13. *St Andrew's House, 2 Harcourt Drive, Hull HU9 2AR* T: (01482) 225130 M: 07929-733555 E: aian.macpherson2012@gmail.com

McPHERSON, Andrew Lindsay. b 58. St Jo Coll Dur BA 79 MCIPD 84. **d** 88 **p** 89. C Bitterne *Win* 88-92; V Weston 92-99; V Holdenhurst and Iford from 99; P-in-c Southbourne St Chris from 07; P-in-c Bournemouth H Epiphany 12-14; AD Bournemouth from 08. *The Vicarage, 53A Holdenhurst Avenue, Bournemouth BH7 6RB* T: (01202) 425978 E: parish.office@stsaviours.f2s.com

MACPHERSON, Canon Anthony Stuart. b 56. Qu Coll Birm 77. **d** 80 **p** 81. C Morley St Pet w Churwell *Wakef* 80-84; C Penistone 84-85; P-in-c Thurlstone 85-86; TV Penistone and Thurlstone 86-88; V Grimethorpe 88-95; P-in-c Westgate Common 95-96; V 96-07; P-in-c Horbury Junction 02-07; RD Wakef 99-07; Hon Can Wakef Cathl 06-07; Can Missr *Leeds* from 07; Sub Dean *Wakef* from 15. *3 Cathedral Close, Wakefield WF1 2DP* M: 07780-990354 E: canontonymac@gmail.com

MACPHERSON, Archibald McQuarrie. b 27. Edin Th Coll 50. **d** 52 **p** 53. Asst Chapl St Andr Cathl 52-55; Prec 55-56; P-in-c Airdrie *Glas* 56-63; R Dumbarton 63-92; rtd 92. *29 Bramblehedge Path, Alexandria G83 8PH* T: (01389) 753981

MACPHERSON, Miss Catherine Annunciata. b 86. Univ of Wales (Lamp) BA 07 Em Coll Cam MPhil 10. Westcott Ho Cam 08. **d** 10 **p** 11. C Mirfield *Wakef* 10-14; P-in-c Fawdon *Newc* from 14. *St Mary's Vicarage, 7 Fawdon Lane, Newcastle upon Tyne NE3 2RR* T: 0191-285 6153 M: 07961-699486 E: catherine.a.macpherson@gmail.com

MacPHERSON, David Alan John. b 42. Lon Univ BD 75 Open Univ BA 83 Hatf Poly MSc 89. Clifton Th Coll 69 Trin Coll Bris 72. **d** 72 **p** 73. C Drypool St Columba w St Andr and St Pet *York* 72-76; Asst Chapl HM Pris Hull 72-76; P-in-c Bessingby and Carnaby *York* 76-78; Chapl RAF 78-83; P-in-c Chedgrave w Hardley and Langley *Nor* 83-87; R 87-97; Chapl Langley Sch *Nor* 83-97; P-in-c Brington w Whilton and Norton *Pet* 97-98; R Brington w Whilton and Norton etc 98-02; rtd 02; PtO *Pet* 02-14; Chapl to Retired Clergy and Clergy Widows' Officer 10-14. *24 Coldstream Close, Daventry NN11 9HL* T: (01327) 704500 E: dmacp@compuserve.com

MACPHERSON, Ewan Alexander. b 43. Toronto Univ BA 74. Wycliffe Coll Toronto MDiv 78. **d** 78 **p** 79. C Toronto St Cuth Canada 78-81; C Toronto Apostles 81-86; V Priddy and Westbury sub Mendip w Easton *B & W* 86-06; rtd 06. *20 Tuddington Gardens, Wells BA5 2EJ* T: (01749) 675876

MACPHERSON, Peter Sinclair. b 44. Lich Th Coll 68. **d** 71 **p** 72. C Honiton, Gittisham and Combe Raleigh *Ex* 71-72; C Bideford 72-74; C Devonport St Mark Ford 74-75; V Thorncombe *Sarum* 75-79; TV Dorchester 79-85; Chapl Jersey Gp of Hosps 85-90; Chapl Derriford Hosp Plymouth

90-98; rtd 98; PtO *Ex* 04-09. *Pump Cottage, 1 Rosemary Lane, Musbury, Axminster EX13 6AT* T: (01297) 552524

McQUAID, Mrs Jennifer Claire. b 79. Univ of Wales (Abth) BA 01. St Mellitus Coll BA 13 MA 14. **d** 14 **p** 15. NSM Hitchin *St Alb* 14-15; C from 15. *60 Old Park Road, Hitchin SG5 2JX* E: jennifercmcquaid@gmail.com

McQUILLEN, Brian Anthony. b 45. Ripon Hall Ox 73. **d** 75 **p** 76. C Northfield *Birm* 75-78; C Sutton Coldfield H Trin 78-80; V Bearwood *Birm* 80-86; V Glouc St Geo w Whaddon 89-96; R St Martin w Looe *Truro* 96-11; RD W Wivelshire 98-03 and 06-08; rtd 11. *7 Bonython Drive, Grampound, Truro TR2 4RL* T: (01726) 883184 E: revmcq.looe@btinternet.com

McQUILLEN-WRIGHT, Christopher Charles. b 71. Kent Univ BA 92. Westcott Ho Cam 92. **d** 95 **p** 96. C Hayle, St Erth and Phillack w Gwithian and Gwinear *Truro* 95-96; C Godrevy 96-99; TV Bodmin w Lanhydrock and Lanivet 99-02; P-in-c St Columb Minor and St Colan from 02. *19 Eliot Gardens, Newquay TR7 2QE* T: (01637) 873496 *or* 877165 E: newquaychurches@icloud.com

MacRAE, Mrs Rosalind Phyllis. b 41. Sarum & Wells Th Coll 81. **dss** 84 **d** 87 **p** 94. Feltham *Lon* 84-87; Asst Chapl R Cornwall Hosps Trust 87-88; Chapl Mt Edgcumbe Hospice 88-92; Chapl St Austell Hosp 88-92; Chapl Penrice Hosp St Austell 88-92; NSM St Austell *Truro* 88-92; Chapl R Cornwall Hosps Trust 92-95; rtd 95. *16 Rosparc, Probus, Truro TR2 4TJ*

McREYNOLDS, Canon Kenneth Anthony. b 48. **d** 83 **p** 84. C Ballymena w Ballyclug *Conn* 83-86; I Rathcoole 86-90; I Lambeg from 90; Can Conn Cathl from 08. *Lambeg Rectory, 58 Belfast Road, Lisburn BT27 4AT* T/F: (028) 9266 3872 E: rector@lambegparish.co.uk

MacROBERT, Iain. b 49. Wolv Univ BA 80 PGCE 81 Birm Univ MA 85 PhD 89. **d** 00 **p** 00. NSM S Queensferry *Edin* from 00. *21 Long Crook, South Queensferry EH30 9XR* T/F 0131-319 1558 T: (01506) 600292 E: iain0macrobert@aol.com

McROBERTS, Ms Tracey. b 68. QUB BTh 99 PGCE 00 Dub City Univ MA 09. CITC 08. **d** 09 **p** 10. C Belfast St Thos *Conn* 09-12; I Belfast St Matt from 12; Bp's Dom Chapl from 11. *Shankill Rectory, 51 Ballygomartin Road, Belfast BT13 3LA* T: (028) 9071 4325 M: 07718-490040 E: tracey.mcroberts@btinternet.com

McROSTIE, Ms Lyn. b 50. Canberra Univ BA 77 Portsm Univ MA 03 MIInfSc 81. STETS 95. **d** 98 **p** 99. C Portsea St Cuth *Portsm* 98-02; P-in-c Shadwell St Paul w Ratcliffe St Jas *Lon* 02-04; Course Ldr NTMTC 04-06; P-in-c Northwood *Portsm* 06-07; R 07-11; P-in-c Gurnard 06-07; V 07-11; P-in-c Cowes St Faith 06-07; V 07-11; P-in-c Elizabeth Australia from 11. *13 Ashley Street, Elizabeth North SA 5113, Australia* T: (0061) (8) 8287 6722 E: lyn.mcrostie@mcrostie.info

MACROW-WOOD, The Ven Antony Charles. b 60. York Univ BA 82 Jes Coll Cam BA 91 ACA 86. Westcott Ho Cam 89. **d** 92 **p** 93. C Swindon St Jo and St Andr *Bris* 92-96; TV Preston w Sutton Poyntz, Littlemoor etc *Sarum* 96-04; P-in-c N Poole Ecum Team 04-06; TR 06-15; Adn Dorset from 15; Can and Preb Sarum Cathl from 12. *28 Merriefield Drive, Broadstone BH18 8PB* E: amacrowwood@mac.com *or* addorset@salisbury.anglican.org

MacSWAIN, Robert Carroll. b 69. Liberty Univ USA BA 92 Princeton Th Sem MDiv 95 Edin Univ MTh 96 St Andr Univ PhD 10. Virginia Th Sem 99. **d** 01 **p** 02. C Kinston St Mary USA 01-04; Chapl and Fell St Chad's Coll Dur 05-08; Instructor Univ of the South USA 09-10; Asst Prof from 10. *The School of Theology, University of the South, Sewanee TN 37383-0001, USA* E: robert.macswain@sewanee.edu

McTEER, Canon Robert Ian. b 56. Chich Th Coll 90. **d** 92 **p** 93. C S Shields All SS *Dur* 92-95; P-in-c Auckland St Helen 95-97; V from 97; Chapl Bishop Auckland Hospitals NHS Trust 95-98; Chapl S Durham Healthcare NHS Trust 98-02; Hon Can Koforidua from 07. *The Vicarage, 8 Manor Road, St Helen Auckland, Bishop Auckland DL14 9EN* T: (01388) 604152 E: fr.r.mcteer@btinternet.com

McTERNAN, Ms Margaret Siobhan. b 70. Edin Univ LLB 92 Dundee Univ MSc 95 DipSW 95. **d** 11 **p** 12. C Glas St Marg from 11. *Flat 0/1, 9 Kennoway Drive, Glasgow G11 7UA* T: 0141-337 2604 M: 07738-054461 E: maggsmct@gmail.com

McTIGHE, Ann-Margaret. b 67. Brunel Univ BSc 97 PGCE 98. Trin Coll Bris BA 10. **d** 10 **p** 11. C Woodford St Mary w St Phil and St Jas *Chelmsf* 10-12; C Woodford Wells 12-14; Pioneer Min Olympic Park from 14; C Stratford St Paul and St Jas *Chelmsf* from 14; C Stratford St Jo w Ch Ch from 15. *33 Carina House, 25 Cheering Lane, London E20 1BA* T: (020) 3579 3195 M: 07940-892391 E: revanniemct@gmail.com

MacVANE, Ms Sara Ann Andrew. b 44. Wellesley Coll (USA) BA 66 Univ of Wales (Ban) BA 05. EAMTC 03. **d** 05 **p** 06. C Rome *Eur* 05-09; Asst Dir Angl Cen Rome 05-09; P-in-c Nord Pas de Calais *Eur* 09-11; Asst Chapl Zürich from 11. *St Andrew,*

Promenadengasse 9, 8001 Zürich, Switzerland T/F: (0041) (44) 252 6024 E: macvanesara@gmail.com *or* zurich@anglican.ch

McVEAGH, Paul Stuart. b 56. Southn Univ BA 78. Oak Hill Th Coll BA 88. **d** 88 **p** 89. C Bebington *Ches* 88-92; Crosslinks Portugal 92-95; R High Halstow w All Hallows and Hoo St Mary *Roch* 95-02; V Westerham 02-15; P-in-c Ashburnham w Penhurst *Chich* from 15. *The Granary, Agmerhurst Farm, Kitchenham Road, Ashburnham, Battle TN33 9NB* T: (01424) 532443 E: pmcveagh@aol.com

MACVEAN, Mrs Amanda Sharon. b 58. K Alfred's Coll Win BEd 80. STETS 09. **d** 12 **p** 13. C Banstead *Guildf* from 12. *14 Glenfield Road, Banstead SM7 2DG* M: 07969-135657 E: mandy.m@mypostoffice.co.uk

McVEETY, Canon Ian. b 46. NOC 82. **d** 85 **p** 86. C Langley and Parkfield *Man* 85-89; V Castleton Moor 89-99; AD Heywood and Middleton 95-99; V Baguley 99-12; AD Withington 06-12; Hon Can Man Cathl 07-12; rtd 12; PtO *Man* from 12. *873 Walmersley Road, Bury BL9 5LE* T: 0161-797 3575

McVEIGH, Miss Dorothy Sarah. b 67. QUB BA 89 TCD BTh 93. CITC 90. **d** 93 **p** 94. C Belfast St Matt *Conn* 93-96; C Carrickfergus 96-99; C Lurgan Ch the Redeemer *D & D* 99-04; I Annaghmore *Arm* from 04. *54 Moss Road, Portadown, Craigavon BT62 1NB* T: (028) 3885 2751 M: 07786-454346

McVEIGH, Canon Samuel. b 49. DL 14. CITC 77. **d** 79 **p** 80. C Drumragh w Mountfield *D & R* 79-82; I Dromore *Clogh* 82-90; I Drumachose *D & R* from 90; Can Derry Cathl from 01. *49 Killane Road, Limavady BT49 0DJ* T: (028) 7776 2680

McVEIGH, Sandra. See BARTON, Sandra

MACVICAR, Miss Mary. b 23. Edin Univ MA 44 Ox Univ DipEd 45. Ripon Coll Cuddesdon 85. **dss** 86 **d** 87 **p** 94. Bishop's Waltham *Portsm* 86-89; Hon C 87-89; PtO 89-94; Hon C Portsm Cathl 94-95; Hon Chapl from 94; rtd 95; PtO *Portsm* 95-09. *8/17 Victoria Grove, Southsea PO5 1NF* T: (023) 9275 1207

McWATT, Glenn Ellsworth. b 48. S'wark Ord Course 89. **d** 92 **p** 93. NSM Tulse Hill H Trin and St Matthias *S'wark* 92-99; C New Malden and Coombe 99-03; C Reigate St Mary 03-08; C Gillingham St Mark *Roch* 08-12; P-in-c Grain w Stoke 12-14; rtd 14. *10 Marigolds Lodge, Holmes Lane, Rustington, Littlehampton BN16 2PT* T: (01903) 774750 E: glennmcwatt@btinternet.com

McWHIRTER, James Angus. b 58. Portsm Poly BA 91 Trin Coll Carmarthen PGCE 93 Warwick Univ PGCE 07. St Steph Ho Ox 00. **d** 02 **p** 03. C Shifnal *Lich* 02-06; CF from 07. *c/o MOD Chaplains (Army)* F: 381824 T: (01264) 383430 E: revdjames.mcwh@btopenworld.com

McWHIRTER (née BELL), Jennifer Kathryn. b 77. Harper Adams Univ Coll BSc 99. CITC BTh 04. **d** 04 **p** 05. Asst Chapl R Gp of Hosps Health and Soc Services Trust 04-06; Asst Chapl Belfast City Hosp Health and Soc Services Trust 04-06; Chapl Belfast Health and Soc Care Trust 06-13; C Belfast St Anne *Conn* 04-06; C Belfast St Nic 06-08; I Templepatrick w Donegore 08-13; Bp's Dom Chapl 08-13; Dir CME Ch of Ireland Th Inst from 13; Chapl Ch of Ireland Min to Deaf People from 13. *St Michael's Rectory, Church Road, Ballina, Co Mayo, Republic of Ireland* T: (028) 9753 2330 *or* (00353) (1) 499 7271 E: revjkmcwhirter@yahoo.co.uk

McWHIRTER, Stephen Joseph. b 64. Open Univ BA 02. St Jo Coll Nottm MTh 11. **d** 13. C Lisburn St Paul *Conn* 13-15. *St Michael's Rectory, Church Road, Ballina, Co Mayo, Republic of Ireland* T: revsjmcwhirter@eircom.net

McWILLIAMS, Amelia. CITC. **d** 09 **p** 10. NSM Brackaville w Donaghendry and Ballyclog *Arm* 09-12; NSM Portadown St Mark from 12. *47 Alexander Avenue, Armagh BT61 7JD* T: (028) 3752 7456 E: amcwilliams861@btinternet.com

McWILLIAMS, Mrs Laura Jane. b 67. Cranmer Hall Dur 01. **d** 03 **p** 04. C Kingston upon Hull St Aid Southcoates *York* 03-07; V Seamer w East Ayton 07-14; TR Billingham *Dur* from 14. *1 Clifton Avenue, Billingham TS22 5DE* M: 07500-345058 E: revlaurajane@yahoo.co.uk

MACY, Jonathan Edward Gordon. b 68. Oak Hill Th Coll BA 96 Heythrop Coll Lon MTh 98 K Coll Lon PhD 04. Wycliffe Hall Ox MTh 09. **d** 10 **p** 11. C Plumstead St Jo w St Jas and St Paul *S'wark* 10-14; TV Thamesmead from 14. *62-64 Battery Road, London SE28 0JT* M: 07910-988014 T: (020) 8836 9069 E: jegmacy@googlemail.com

MADDEN, Kenneth Usher. b 48. St Jo Coll Dur BA 70 Lon Inst of Educn PGCE 73. WEMTC 06. **d** 09 **p** 10. NSM Newent and Gorsley w Cliffords Mesne *Glouc* 09-13. *Plantation Cottage, Ganders Green, May Hill, Longhope GL17 0NJ* T: (01452) 831401 M: 07894-208501 E: kenandlibby@virginmedia.com

MADDERN, James Thomas. b 76. New Coll Edin BD 99. Wycliffe Hall Ox MTh 03. **d** 02 **p** 03. C Stratford St Jo w Ch Ch and St Jas *Chelmsf* 02-06; PtO Ox 07-09; TV Brize Norton and Carterton from 09. *The Vicarage, 8 Trefoil Way, Carterton OX18 1JQ* T: (01993) 844175 E: vicbrizecarterton@btinternet.com

MADDISON, Simon Christopher. b 63. St Steph Ho Ox 10. **d** 12 **p** 13. C Hendon St Alphage Lon 12-15; V Edmonton St Aldhelm from 15. St Aldhelm's Vicarage, 2 Windmill Road, London N18 1PA M: 07906-156932 T: (020) 8807 5336 E: simon.c.maddison@talktalk.net

MADDOCK, Claire Louise. See McCLELLAND, Claire Louise

MADDOCK, David John Newcomb. b 36. Qu Coll Cam BA 60 MA 64. Oak Hill Th Coll 60. **d** 62 **p** 63. C Bispham Blackb 62-65; R 82-93; RD Blackpool 90-93; Miss Payne Bay Canada 65-69; R Frobisher Bay 70; R Walsoken Ely 70-77; V Ore Ch Ch Chich 77-82; V Fowey Truro 93-02; Chapl Cornwall Healthcare NHS Trust 94-02; rtd 02; PtO Truro from 02. 3 The Moorings, 25 St John's Road, Eastbourne BN20 7NL T: (01323) 749172

MADDOCK, Nicholas Rokeby. b 47. ABSM 72 Birm Coll of Educn CertEd 73. Linc Th Coll 82. **d** 82 **p** 83. C Romford St Edw Chelmsf 82-87; V Sway Win 87-94; V Taunton St Mary B & W 94-04; R Wrington w Butcombe and Burrington from 04. The Rectory, 3 Alburys, Wrington, Bristol BS40 5NZ T: (01934) 862201 E: n.maddock@rectory.org.uk

MADDOCK, Philip Arthur Louis. b 47. Open Univ BA 82 Lanc Univ MPhil 02. Oak Hill Th Coll 75. **d** 78 **p** 79. C New Ferry Ches 78-81; C Barnston 81-82; V Over St Jo 82-85; V Norley and Chapl to the Deaf 85-88; P-in-c Treales and Blackb 88-96; Lich 96-02; C Yoxall and The Ridwares and Kings Bromley 98-02; Adv for Deaf and Disabled People Min Div 03-12; rtd 13; NSM Alrewas and Wychnor Lich 03-13; PtO Blackb from 14. 28 Kendal Road, Lytham St Annes FY8 2LQ T: (01253) 279833 E: pcmaddock@gmail.com

MADDOCK, Canon Philip Lawrence. b 20. Bris Univ BA 42. Cuddesdon Coll 42. **d** 43 **p** 44. C Kilburn St Aug Lon 43-48; C Weston-super-Mare All SS B & W 48-57; Chapl Community of the Epiphany Truro 57-60; Sub-Warden 60-63; Chapl HM Pris Wandsworth 63-64; HM Pris Birm 64-67; Ex 67-69; Chapl St Lawr Hosp Bodmin 69-76; Can Res and Treas Truro Cathl 76-88; rtd 88; PtO Truro from 88. 32A Coinagehall Street, Helston TR13 8EQ

MADDOCKS, Alison Julie. b 63. Birm Univ BSc 84 Loughb Univ MBA 92. St Jo Coll Nottm MTh 03. **d** 03 **p** 04. C Wollaton S'well 03-06; Retail Chapl Birm City Cen 06-08; Ind Chapl S'well 08-11; C Nottingham All SS, St Mary and St Pet 08-11; P-in-c Breadsall Derby from 11. The Rectory, 57 Rectory Lane, Breadsall, Derby DE21 5LL T: (01332) 835468 E: revmaddocks@aol.com or alison.maddocks@derby.anglican.org

MADDOX, David John. b 34. AIMLS 58. Sarum & Wells Th Coll 92. **d** 81 **p** 93. In RC Ch 81-91; NSM Wimborne Minster and Holt Sarum 93-95; NSM Broadstone 95-01; PtO 00-08; Win 00-12. 298 Wimborne Road, Poole BH15 3EG T: (01202) 672597 E: david.maddox123@btinternet.com

MADDOX, Derek Adrian James. b 64. Kingston Poly BA 88. Trin Coll Bris 02. **d** 04 **p** 05. C Mitcham St Mark S'wark 04-07; P-in-c S Yardley St Mich Birm 07-08; V 08-13; P-in-c Withywood Bris from 13; P-in-c Bris St Andr Hartcliffe from 13. St Oswald's Vicarage, Cheddar Grove, Bristol BS13 7EN E: derekmaddox8@gmail.com

MADDOX, Hugh Inglis Monteath. b 37. CCC Cam BA 60. Westcott Ho Cam 61. **d** 63 **p** 64. C Attercliffe Sheff 63-66; C Maidstone All SS w St Phil Cant 66-67; C Folkestone St Mary and St Eanswythe 67-69; C St Martin-in-the-Fields Lon 69-73; R Sandwich Cant 73-81; V St Peter-in-Thanet 81-84; V Red Post Sarum 84-03; rtd 03; PtO Sarum from 03. 36 Corfe Road, Stoborough, Wareham BH20 5AD T: (01929) 550872

MADDY, Kevin. b 58. Selw Coll Cam BA 83 MA 87 GRNCM 79 FRSA 96. Westcott Ho Cam 81. **d** 85 **p** 86. C St Peter-in-Thanet Cant 85-88; Chapl RAF 88-02; CF 02-07; Chapl Miss to Seafarers and R Yokohama Ch Ch 07-11; V Monk Bretton Leeds 11-14; P-in-c Lundwood 11-14; P-in-c Hackington Cant from 14; Chapl Abp's Sch Cant from 14. The Rectory, St Stephen's Green, Canterbury CT2 7JU M: 07720-499403 T: (01227) 477171 E: revkmaddy@gmail.com

MADELEY, Mark Keith. b 68. AVCM 96. Oak Hill Th Coll BA 93. **d** 93 **p** 94. C Mickleover All SS Derby 93-96; C Charlesworth and Dinting Vale 96-99; Chapl Chr Tours (UK) Ltd 99-00; NSM Moldgreen and Rawthorpe Wakef 99-00; V Coley 00-11; R Weston-super-Mare St Nic w St Barn B & W from 12. Uphill Rectory, 3 Old Church Road, Uphill, Weston-super-Mare BS23 4UH T/F: (01934) 620156 M: 07947-159795 E: mark@mibtravel.co.uk

MADGWICK, Mrs Philippa Jane. b 60. Magd Coll Ox BA 83 DPhil 86. SAOMC 04 ERMC 05. **d** 07 **p** 08. NSM St Alb St Steph St Alb from 07; NSM Officer St Alb Adnry from 14. 22 Blenheim Road, St Albans AL1 4NR T: (01727) 842449 E: pippa.madgwick1@btinternet.com

MADZIMURE, Dominic Makusha. b 52. Middx Univ MA 03. **d** 77 **p** 78. Zimbabwe 77-99; PtO Cant 01-03; P-in-c Wood-

church 03-06; P-in-c Byker St Ant Newc 06-12. St Anthony's Vicarage, Enslin Gardens, Newcastle upon Tyne NE6 3ST T: 0191-265 1683 E: dominic@madzimure.fsnet.co.uk

MAGEE, Canon Frederick Hugh. b 33. Yale Univ BA 56. Westcott Ho Cam 58. **d** 59 **p** 60. C Bury St Mark Man 59-62; USA 63-64 and 87-05; Chapl St Paul's Cathl Dundee 74-79; P-in-c Invergowrie 76-79; R St Andrews St Andr St And 79-83; R Forfar 83-87; rtd 05; PtO Bre from 07; Hon Can St Paul's Cathl Dundee from 08. 17 North Street, St Andrews KY16 9PW T: (01334) 470446 M: 07726-106236 E: hugh@twomagees.plus.com

MAGEE, Keith Robert. b 60. Bris Univ BA 95 PGCE 96. Trin Coll Bris 92 Westcott Ho Cam 99. **d** 01 **p** 02. C S Woodham Ferrers Chelmsf 01-05; V Moulsham St Jo 05-12; V Knighton St Mary Magd Leic from 12. The Vicarage, Church Lane, Leicester LE2 3WG T: 0116-212 3176 E: keith.magee@btinternet.com

MAGILL, Robert James Henderson. b 59. Paisley Coll of Tech BSc 81. Sarum & Wells Th Coll 92. **d** 94 **p** 95. C W Moors Sarum 94-98; P-in-c Hilperton w Whaddon and Staverton etc 98-05; Community Affairs Chapl 02-05. The Vicarage, 1A The Weir, Edington, Westbury BA13 4PX

MAGINN, Ms Penny. b 73. Humberside Univ BA 94 Liv Univ MA 05. St Jo Coll Nottm 06. **d** 08 **p** 09. C Much Woolton Liv 08-12; P-in-c Carl St Luke Morton from 12. St Luke's Vicarage, Brownrigg Drive, Carlisle CA2 6PA M: 07522-472272 T: (01228) 513460 E: revpenny@gmail.com

MAGNESS, Anthony William John. b 37. New Coll Ox BA 62 MA 65 Ch Coll Liv PGCE 76. Coll of Resurr Mirfield 78. **d** 80 **p** 81. C Gt Crosby St Faith Liv 80-83; C Newc St Jo 83-85; P-in-c Newc St Luke 85-88; P-in-c Newc St Andr 88; V Newc St Andr and St Luke 89-99; Chapl Hunter's Moor Hosp 89-95; P-in-c Cambois Newc 99-00; P-in-c Sleekburn 99-00; V Cambois and Sleekburn 00-03; rtd 03; PtO Newc from 03. 59 Firtree Crescent, Newcastle upon Tyne NE12 7JU T/F: 0191-268 4596

MAGNUSSON, Lisbet Maria. b 50. Mid-Sweden Univ BSc 85 Uppsala Univ MDiv 93 ML 98. Past Inst Uppsala 93. **p** 94. In Ch of Sweden 94-98; C Crosby Linc 98-99; TV Gainsborough and Morton 99-04; P-in-c Swallow and Chapl Doncaster and S Humber Healthcare NHS Trust 04-06; Sweden from 06. Haggkullevagen 26, 184 37 Akersberga, Stockholm, Sweden T: (0046) (8) 1205 9082 or (278) 41023 M: 72-231 5990 E: dalhemrectory@hotmail.com

MAGOR, Robert Jolyon. b 47. Sarum & Wells Th Coll 91. **d** 93 **p** 94. C Plaistow Chelmsf 93-96; TV Plaistow and N Canning Town 96-99; V Leigh-on-Sea St Aid 99-01; C Thorpe Bay 01-06; R E and W Tilbury and Linford 06-09; rtd 09; PtO Chelmsf from 12. 31 Selwyn Road, Southend-on-Sea SS2 4DR T: (01702) 467269 E: robert.magor@googlemail.com

MAGORRIAN, Brian Geoffrey. b 64. St Aid Coll Dur BSc 85 York Univ DPhil 89. St Jo Coll Nottm. **d** 01 **p** 02. C Bishop-wearmouth St Gabr Dur 01-04; P-in-c Brough w Stainmore, Musgrave and Warcop Carl 04-10; C Whitfield Derby 10-14; V Walton St Jo from 14. 6 Medlock Road, Chesterfield S40 3NH T: (01246) 731366 E: brianmagorrian@tiscali.co.uk

✠**MAGOWAN, The Rt Revd Alistair James.** b 55. Leeds Univ BSc 77 Ox Univ MTh 02. Trin Coll Bris 78. **d** 81 **p** 82 **c** 09. C Owlerton Sheff 81-84; C Dur St Nic 84-89; Chapl St Aid Coll 85-89; V Egham Guildf 89-00; RD Runnymede 93-98; Adn Dorset Sarum 00-09; Can and Preb Sarum Cathl 00-09; Suff Bp Ludlow Heref from 09; Adn Ludlow from 09. Bishop's House, Corvedale Road, Halford, Craven Arms SY7 9BT T: (01588) 673571 F: 673585 E: office@bishopofludlow.co.uk

MAGOWAN, Harold Victor. b 34. QUB BA 55 Dip(Econ) 66 DipEd 69 ACII 69 FCII 73. TCD Div Sch Div Test 57. **d** 57 **p** 58. C Antrim All SS w Muckamore Conn 57-59. 6 Fold Mews, 22 Ballyholme Road, Bangor BT20 5JS T: (028) 9146 5091

MAGOWAN, Ian Walter. b 51. St Paul's Coll Chelt CertEd 73 Ulster Poly BEd 82 TCD BTh 07. CITC 04. **d** 07 **p** 08. C Killowen D & R 07-10; I Connor w Antrim St Patr Conn from 10. Connor Rectory, 50 Church Road, Kells, Ballymena BT42 3JU T: (028) 2589 1254 M: 07810-636167 E: iwmagowan@hotmail.com

MAGOWAN, Margaret Louise. b 57. SRN 77 SCM 80. WEMTC 11. **d** 14. NSM Church Stretton Heref from 14. Bishop's House, Corvedale Road, Halford, Craven Arms SY7 9BT T: (01588) 673810 E: mlmagowan@fsmail.net

MAGUIRE, Alan. b 45. CBDTI 03. **d** 06 **p** 07. NSM Croglin and Holme Eden and Wetheral w Warwick Carl 06-09; NSM Carl H Trin and St Barn 09-12; P-in-c Lowther and Askham and Clifton and Brougham from 12. The Rectory, Clifton, Penrith CA10 2EA T: (01768) 892807 E: alan.maguire24@btinternet.com

MAGUIRE, Canon Brian William. b 33. Hull Univ BTh 84 MA 88. Coll of Resurr Mirfield 70. **d** 72 **p** 73. C Guisborough

York 72-76; TV Haxby w Wigginton 76-77; TR 78-89; V Huddersfield St Pet and All SS *Wakef* 89-00; Hon Can Wakef Cathl 94-00; rtd 00; PtO *Leeds* from 00; Bp's Dom Chapl *Wakef* 03-04; PtO *Lich* from 12. *33 Chapel Lane, Lichfield WS14 9BA* T: (01543) 305936

MAGUIRE, Luke Karl. b 87. Warwick Univ BA 09 Leeds Univ BA 11. Coll of Resurr Mirfield 09. **d** 12 **p** 13. C Rochdale *Man* 12-13; C Salford All SS from 13. *89 Clement Royds Street, Rochdale OL12 6PL* T: (01706) 632809 M: 07919-018681 E: lukekarlmaguire@googlemail.com

MAGUIRE, Michael Timothy Gale (Tim). b 34. Ox Univ Inst of Educn DipEd 61. Wycliffe Hall Ox 58. **d** 61 **p** 62. C Southampton St Mary Extra *Win* 61-63; Bp's Youth Chapl 63-66; PtO from 97; rtd 99; PtO *Truro* from 02. *6 Bercote Close, Littleton, Winchester SO22 6PX* T: (01962) 889172

MAGUIRE (formerly GRATTON), Canon Patricia Margaret. b 46. Leeds Univ BTh 94 MA 96 SRN 67 TCert 84 CertEd 88. EMMTC 89 NOC 96. **d** 97 **p** 98. NSM Shipley St Pet *Bradf* 97-99; C Brighouse and Clifton *Wakef* 99-00; Chapl Wakef Cathl Sch 00-05; P-in-c Lupset *Wakef* 05-11; P-in-c Thornes 00-11; RD Wakef 08-11; Hon Can Wakef Cathl 08-11; rtd 11; PtO *Lich* from 12. *33 Chapel Lane, Lichfield WS14 9BA* T: (01543) 305936 E: revmaguire@virginmedia.com

MAGUIRE, Sarah Alison. *See* EDMONDS, Sarah Alison

MAHER, David James. b 70. St Jo Coll Dur BA 01. Cranmer Hall Dur 98. **d** 01 **p** 02. C Hounslow H Trin w St Paul and St Mary *Lon* 01-04; C Staines 04-07; Chapl to Bp Kensington 04-07; V Chesterton Gd Shep *Ely* from 07; RD Cambridge N from 14. *The Good Shepherd Vicarage, 51 Highworth Avenue, Cambridge CB4 2BQ* T: (01223) 351844 *or* 312933 E: vicar@churchofthegoodshepherd.co.uk

MAHER, Capt Ian. b 58. Open Univ BA 97 MEd 01. CA Tr Coll 88 Yorks Min Course 11. **d** 12 **p** 13. Multifaith Chapl Co-ord Sheff Hallam Univ from 06; Hon C Sheff Cathl 12-14; Min Can from 14. *3 Parsonage Street, Walkley, Sheffield S6 5BL* T: 0114-232 2330 *or* 225 4577 M: 07791-639820 E: i.maher@shu.ac.uk *or* ian.maher@sheffield.anglican.org

MAHILUM, Bello. b 60. **d** 10 **p** 11. NSM Notting Hill St Jo *Lon* 10-14; NSM Wood Green St Mich w Bounds Green St Gabr etc from 14. *5 Faith Court, Cooper's Road, London SE1 5HD* M: 07738-330861 E: belkiewtz@aol.com

MAHON, Stephanie Mary. *See* SOKOLOWSKI, Stephanie Mary

MAHONEY, William Denis. b 35. Sem of the Immaculate Conception (NY) 77. **d** 79 **p** 95. In RC Ch USA 79-87; NSM Egremont and Haile *Carl* 92-93; NSM Kells 93-96; R Cohoes USA 96-98; P-in-c Beckermet St Jo and St Bridget w Ponsonby *Carl* 98-05; rtd 05. *2 Bowden Drive, Huntington Station NY 11746-4218, USA* E: vlwd17@aol.com

MAHONY, Conal Martin. b 38. Pontificio Ateneo Antoniano Rome Lic in Sacred Th 64 Lateran Univ Rome ThD 66. Franciscan Ho of Studies 57. **d** 62 **p** 63. In RC Ch 62-89; Dir Folkestone Family Care Cen 90-92; C Hempnall *Nor* 92-94; TV 94-97; TR 97-08; rtd 08; PtO *Nor* from 08. *6 Rigby Close, Framingham Earl, Norwich NR14 7TL* T: (01508) 491646

MAIDEN, Charles Alistair Kingsley. b 60. Trent Poly BSc 84. St Jo Coll Nottm LTh 88. **d** 89 **p** 90. C Porchester *S'well* 89-93; C Selston 93-96; P-in-c Huthwaite 96-11; V from 11. *The Vicarage, Blackwell Road, Huthwaite, Sutton-in-Ashfield NG17 2QT* T: (01623) 555053 E: charliemaiden@hotmail.com

MAIDMENT, Thomas John Louis. b 43. Lon Univ BSc 65. St Steph Ho Ox. **d** 67 **p** 68. C Westmr St Steph w St Jo *Lon* 67-73; P-in-c Twickenham Common H Trin 73-77; V 77-80; V Heston 80-98; V Bolton-le-Sands *Blackb* 98-08; P-in-c Tunstall w Melling and Leck 02-03; AD Tunstall 99-05; rtd 08; PtO *Blackb* from 08. *69 Aintree Road, Thornton-Cleveleys FY5 5HW* T: (01253) 829399 E: t.j.l.m@btinternet.com

MAIDSTONE, Archdeacon of. *See* TAYLOR, The Ven Stephen Ronald

MAIN, Mrs Brigid Mary Harvey. b 49. EAMTC 96. **d** 99 **p** 00. NSM Tillingham *Chelmsf* 99-03; NSM Pleshey 03-11; PtO 11-13; NSM Bradwell on Sea and St Lawrence from 13. *White Lyons Cottage, High Street, Bradwell on Sea, Southminster CM0 7QL* T: (01621) 776438 E: brigid@lauriebrigid.co.uk *or* bmain@chelmsford.anglican.org

MAIN, Clive Timothy. b 53. St Andr Univ MA 75 Cam Univ PGCE 76. Oak Hill Th Coll BA 94. **d** 96 **p** 97. C Alperton *Lon* 96-00; V Highbury New Park St Aug 00-12; TR Hackney Marsh from 12. *St Barnabas' Rectory, 111 Homerton High Street, London E9 6DL* T: (020) 8533 1156 E: clivemain@blueyonder.co.uk

MAIN, Canon David Murray. b 28. Univ Coll Ox BA 52 MA 56. St Deiniol's Hawarden 73. **d** 73 **p** 74. C Glas St Marg 73-75; R Challoch w Newton Stewart 75-79; R Kilmarnock 79-93;

Can St Mary's Cathl 85-93; rtd 93; Hon Can St Mary's Cathl from 93. *Sunnybrae, 50 Abercromby Road, Castle Douglas DG7 1BA* T: (01556) 504669

MAINA, Simon Mwangi. b 52. Nairobi Univ 85. **d** 80 **p** 81. Kenya 80-95; C Acton St Mary *Lon* 95-97; Worthing Churches Homeless Project from 98; rtd 08. *49 Cambourne Court, Shelley Road, Worthing BN11 4BQ* T: (01903) 205042

MAINE, Michael John. b 57. FGMS 95. Coll of Resurr Mirfield 09. **d** 11 **p** 12. C Willingdon *Chich* 11-15; V Cuckfield from 15. *The Vicarage, 5 Barrowfield, Cuckfield, Haywards Heath RH17 5ER* M: 07895-415143 E: michaeljmaine@btinternet.com

MAINES, Canon Trevor. b 40. Leeds Univ BSc 63. Ripon Hall Ox 63. **d** 65 **p** 66. C Speke All SS *Liv* 65-70; C Stevenage St Geo *St Alb* 70-73; V Dorridge *Birm* 73-78; Org Sec CECS *Ex* 79-80; Hon C Tiverton St Pet *Ex* 79-80; Org Sec (Wales) CECS 80-87; Hon C Newton Nottage *Llan* 81-83; PtO *Mon* 83-87; V Arlesey w Astwick *St Alb* 87-95; RD Shefford 91-95; V Goldington 95-05; RD Bedford 98-05; Hon Can St Alb 04-05; rtd 05; Hon C Beedon and Peasemore w W Ilsley and Farnborough *Ox* 05-07; Hon C Brightwalton w Catmore, Leckhampstead etc 05-07; PtO from 12. *1 Adlam Villas, Greenham Road, Newbury RG14 7HX* T: (01635) 551352 E: trevor.maines@tesco.net

MAINEY, Ian George. b 51. CertEd 73. Oak Hill Th Coll BA 87. **d** 87 **p** 88. C Denton Holme *Carl* 87-91; V Hensingham 91-02; RD Calder 01-02; TR Deane *Man* 02-09; P-in-c Birkdale St Jas *Liv* from 09; P-in-c Birkdale St Peter from 09. *The Vicarage, 26 Lulworth Road, Southport PR8 2BQ* T: (01704) 566255 E: ian.mainey@lineone.net

MAINWARING, Islwyn Paul. b 52. Univ of Wales (Swansea) BD 75. St Mich Coll Llan 77. **d** 79 **p** 80. C Llanilid w Pencoed *Llan* 79-82; C Llanishen and Lisvane 82-85; TV Cwmbran *Mon* 85-88; V Troedyrhiw w Merthyr Vale *Llan* 88-91. *Pennant, 109 Penygroes Road, Blaenau, Ammanford SA18 3BZ* T: (01269) 850350

MAINWARING (née LANKSHEAR), Jane Frances. b 70. Leeds Univ BA 92 Trin Coll Carmarthen MPhil 97 PhD 99. EAMTC 98. **d** 00 **p** 01. C Sudbury and Chilton *St E* 00-03; TV Hitchin *St Alb* from 03. *St Mark's Vicarage, St Mark's Close, Hitchin SG5 1UR* T: (01462) 422862 *or* 434686 E: jane@stmarks-hitchin.org.uk

MAIRS, Canon Adrian Samuel. b 43. Oak Hill Th Coll 76. **d** 78 **p** 79. C Rugby St Matt *Cov* 78-82; P-in-c Mancetter 82-84; V 84-08; P-in-c Hartshill 97-01; Hon Can Cov Cathl 03-08; rtd 08; PtO *Blackb* from 14. *15 Salter Fell Road, Lancaster LA1 2PX* T: (01524) 382206 E: adrian.mairs@tesco.net

MAIS, Jeremy Hugh. b 47. **d** 00 **p** 01. NSM Bibury w Winson and Barnsley *Glouc* 00-02; P-in-c 04-08; NSM Stratton, N Cerney, Baunton and Bagendon 02-04; NSM Fairford Deanery 09; NSM Hambleden Valley *Ox* from 09. *The Vicarage, Turville, Henley-on-Thames RG9 6QU* T: (01491) 638539 E: jeremy.mais@tiscali.co.uk

MAITIN, Ito. b 36. Open Univ BA. Kelham Th Coll 63. **d** 68 **p** 69. C Longton St Jo *Lich* 68-69; C Leek St Edw 69-71; C Lich St Chad 71-74; C Tamworth 74-81; V Penkhull 81-06; rtd 06; PtO *Lich* 06-08 and from 12; C Hanley H Ev 08-09; C Stoke-upon-Trent 10-12; PtO from 12. *18 Crescent Grove, Stoke-on-Trent ST4 6EN* T: (01782) 878788

MAITLAND, The Hon Sydney Milivoje Patrick. b 51. Edin Univ BSc MRTPI. St Jo Coll Nottm. **d** 86 **p** 87. Hon C Glas St Geo 86-01; C Glas St Bride 03-11; R Glas All SS from 11. *14 Kersland Street, Glasgow G12 8BL* T: 0141-339 4573 E: sydneymaitland@btinternet.com

MAJOR, Richard James Edward. b 54. Trin Coll Bris 78. **d** 81 **p** 82. C Parr *Liv* 81-84; V Burton Fleming w Fordon *York* 84-85; V Grindale and Ergham 84-85; P-in-c Wold Newton 84-85; V Burton Fleming w Fordon, Grindale etc 85-91; V Bilton St Pet 91-15; R Woodhall Spa Gp *Linc* from 15. *The Vicarage, Alveston Avenue, Woodhall Spa LN10 6SN* E: revrichardmajor@gmail.com

MAJOR, Richard John Charles. b 63. Massey Univ (NZ) BA 85 Ex Coll Ox BA 91 MA 93 Magd Coll Ox DPhil 91. St Steph Ho Ox 92. **d** 94 **p** 95. C Truro Cathl 94-97; C Putney St Mary *S'wark* 97-98; Chapl Florence w Siena *Eur* 98-01; USA from 01. *Nansough Manor, Ladock, Truro TR2 4PB* T: (01726) 883315 *or* (001) (718) 442 1589 F: 442 4555 E: email@richardmajor.com

MAK, Marcus Andreas. b 81. Ox Brookes Univ BA 10 St Jo Coll Dur BA 15. Cranmer Hall Dur 13. **d** 15. C N Poole Ecum Team *Sarum* from 15. *43 Sandpiper Close, Poole BH17 7YE* M: 07978-588524 E: revmmak@gmail.com

MAKEL, Arthur. b 39. AKC 63. **d** 64 **p** 65. C Beamish *Dur* 64-68; Ind Chapl *York* 68-72; Ind Chapl and P-in-c Scotton w Northorpe *Linc* 72-81; R Epworth 81-89; P-in-c Wroot 81-89; R Epworth and Wroot 89-92; R Sigglesthorne and Rise w Nunkeeling and Bewholme *York* 92-04; P-in-c Aldbrough,

Mappleton w Goxhill and Withernwick 98-04; rtd 04; PtO *York* 04-11. *43 Lowfield Road, Beverley HU17 9RF* T: (01482) 865798

MAKEPEACE, David Norman Harry. b 51. Magd Coll Ox BA 74. Trin Coll Bris 83. **d** 85 **p** 86. C Romford Gd Shep *Chelmsf* 85-88; Tanzania 88-89; C York St Paul 89-91; TV Radipole and Melcombe Regis *Sarum* 91-98; V Sandgate St Paul w Folkestone St Geo *Cant* 98-00; PtO from 01. *Flat 1, 33 Augusta Gardens, Folkestone CT20 2RT* T: (01303) 259342
E: dmakepeace51@gmail.com

MAKEPEACE, Preb James Dugard. b 40. Keble Coll Ox BA 63 MA 67. Cuddesdon Coll 63. **d** 65 **p** 66. C Cullercoats St Geo *Newc* 65-68; Lib Pusey Ho and Chapl Wadh Coll Ox 68-72; V Romford St Edw *Chelmsf* 72-79; V Tettenhall Regis *Lich* 79-80; TR 80-89; RD Trysull 87-97; Preb Lich Cathl 96-99; rtd 00; PtO *Lich* from 00. *3 Shaw Lane, Albrighton, Wolverhampton WV7 3DS* T: (01902) 375472

✠**MAKHULU, The Most Revd Walter Paul Khotso.** b 35. CMG 00. Kent Univ Hon DD 88 Gen Th Sem NY Hon DD 99. St Pet Rosettenville Selly Oak Coll. **d** 57 **p** 58 **c** 79. S Africa 57-61; Bechuanaland 61-63; C Poplar All SS w St Frideswide *Lon* 64-66; C Pentonville St Silas w Barnsbury St Clem 66-68; V Battersea St Phil *S'wark* 68-72; V Battersea St Phil w St Bart 72-75; Bp Botswana 79-00; Abp Cen Africa 80-00; rtd 00. *16 Downside, 8-10 St John's Avenue, London SW15 2AE* E: makhulu@btinternet.com

MAKIN, Miss Pauline. b 45. Cranmer Hall Dur 75. **dss** 78 **d** 87 **p** 94. Ashton-in-Makerfield St Thos *Liv* 78-89; Par Dn 87-89; Par Dn Rainford 89-94; C 94-95; C Farnworth 95-10; Asst Dioc Chapl to the Deaf 89-10; rtd 10. *50 Farm Meadow Road, Orrell, Wigan WN5 8TE* T: (01695) 624995
E: paulinemakin@aol.com

MAKIN, Susan. b 65. **d** 13 **p** 14. NSM Hoxton St Anne w St Columba *Lon* 13-14; C St John-at-Hackney from 14. *21B Blurton Road, London E5 0NL* M: 07749-532978
E: stepneyd@london.anglican.org

MAKIN, Valerie Diana. b 33. S'wark Ord Course 86. **d** 88 **p** 94. Hon Par Dn Bryanston Square St Mary w St Marylebone St Mark *Lon* 88-94; Chapl St Marylebone Healing and Counselling Cen 88-94; NSM Godalming *Guildf* 94-95; PtO *Lon* 95-97; *Guildf* 95-05. *41 Broad Street, Alresford SO24 9AS*

MÄKIPÄÄ, Tuomas. b 78. Helsinki Univ 97. **d** 05 **p** 10. C Helsinki *Eur* 05-12; Chapl from 12. *Brysselinkatu 6 D 70, 00550 Helsinki, Finland* T: (00358) (50) 309 9132
E: tuomas.makipaa@anglican.fi

MAKOWER, Canon Malory. b 38. TCD BA 61 MA 68 St Jo Coll Ox MA 64 DPhil 64. Ridley Hall Cam 64. **d** 66 **p** 67. C Onslow Square St Paul *Lon* 66-69; Tutor Ridley Hall Cam 69-71; Sen Tutor 71-76; P-in-c Lode and Longmeadow *Ely* 76-84; Warden EAMTC 77-79; Prin 79-84; Dir of Post-Ord Tr for NSM *Nor* 84-90; C Gt Yarmouth 84-89; TV 89-95; Dioc NSM Officer 88-95; Hon Can Nor Cathl 94-97; Prin LNSM Tr Scheme 94-97; rtd 97; PtO *Nor* from 98. *114 Yarmouth Road, Lowestoft NR32 4AQ* T: (01502) 574769

MALAM, Susan Mary. St Mellitus Coll BA 14. **d** 14 **p** 15. NSM Witham and Villages *Chelmsf* from 14. *2 John Ray Street, Braintree CM7 9DZ* T: (01376) 329958
E: sue.malam18@gmail.com

MALAN, Victor Christian de Roubaix. b 39. Cape Town Univ BA 60 Linacre Coll Ox BA 63 MA 68. Wycliffe Hall Ox 61. **d** 63 **p** 64. C Springfield *Birm* 63-66; P-in-c 66-67; C New Windsor Ox 67-69; Chapl St Jo Coll Cam 69-74; V Northampton All SS w St Kath *Pet* 74-86; V Stockport St Geo *Ches* 86-89; R N Mundham w Hunston and Merston *Chich* 89-06; rtd 06; PtO *Cant* 07-15. *2 The Hermitage, North Mundham, Chichester PO20 1LE* T: (01243) 781054

MALBON, Canon John Allin. b 36. Oak Hill Th Coll 62. **d** 65 **p** 66. C Wolverhampton St Jude *Lich* 65-68; C Hoole *Ches* 68-71; P-in-c Crewe Ch Ch 71-75; V 75-79; V Plemstall w Guilden Sutton 79-01; Hon Can Ches Cathl 96-01; rtd 01; PtO *Ches* from 02. *22 Hawksey Drive, Nantwich CW5 7GF* T: (01270) 611584

MALCOLM, Andrew Alexander. b 55. Open Univ BA 99 Leic Univ MSc 99 Leeds Univ BA 08 Man Metrop Univ MRes 11. NOC 05. **d** 08 **p** 09. NSM Salesbury *Blackb* from 08; V Langho Billington from 12. *Middle Bulls Head Farm, Red Lees Road, Burnley BB10 4TD* M: 07957-846428

MALCOLM, Brother. See FOUNTAIN, David Roy

MALCOLM, Miss Mercia Alana. b 54. St Andr Univ MA 77. S'wark Ord Course 84. **d** 87 **p** 94. C Dartford Ch Ch *Roch* 87-91; Par Dn Stockport St Geo *Ches* 91-94; C Jordanstown *Conn* 95-99; Chapl Ulster Univ 95-03; I Carnmoney *Conn* from 03. *Coole Glebe, 20 Glebe Road, Newtownabbey BT36 6UW* T: (028) 9083 6337 E: carnmoney@connor.anglican.org

MALE, Canon David Edward. b 62. Southn Univ BA 83 St Jo Coll Dur BA 90. Cranmer Hall Dur 88. **d** 91 **p** 92. C Leic

St Chris 91-94; C Kirkheaton *Wakef* 94-98; P Missr Huddersfield 99-06; Dioc Fresh Expressions Adv *Ely* from 06; Tutor Ridley Hall Cam from 06; Hon Can Ely Cathl from 14. *130 Hulatt Road, Cambridge CB1 8TH* T: (01223) 410581 or 741102 E: dm432@cam.ac.uk

✠**MALECDAN, The Most Revd Edward Pacyaya.** Episc Th Sem of the SW MA 93 Hon DD. St Andr Th Sem Manila BTh 77 MDiv 85. **d** 79 **p** 80 **c** 97. Philippines from 79; Dean St Andr Th Sem 94-97; Bp N Philippines 97-09; Prime Bp from 09. *Provincial Office, PO Box 10321, Broadway Centrum, 1112 Quezon City, Philippines* T: (0063) (2) 722 8478 or 722 8481 F: 721 1923 E: ednpvic@hotmail.com

MALEK, Mark Mayool. b 44. Khartoum Univ BSc 69 Salford Univ BSc 76 Bradf Coll of Educn PGCE 93. **d** 03 **p** 04. NSM Horton *Bradf* 03-04; NSM Bradf St Oswald Chapel Green 03-04; NSM Lt Horton *Leeds* from 04. *26 Martlett Drive, Bradford BD5 8QG* T: (01274) 732712

MALES, Jeanne Margaret. b 49. Reading Univ BA 71 Lon Univ MPhil 73 Surrey Univ PhD 86 AFBPsS 75 CPsychol 88. S'wark Ord Course 93. **d** 96 **p** 97. NSM Caterham *S'wark* 96-00; C Addington 00-03; V 03-15; rtd 15; PtO *S'wark* from 15. *Collingwood House, 53 High Street, Sandwich CT13 9EG* T: (01304) 612050 E: rev.jeanne@tiscali.co.uk

MALIK, The Rt Revd Alexander John.. Moderator Ch of Pakistan from 03. *Bishopsbourne, Cathedral Close, The Mall, Lahore 54000, Pakistan* T: (0092) (42) 723 3560 F: 722 1270

MALINS, Mrs Judith. b 47. Bris Univ BA 69. STETS 97. **d** 00 **p** 01. NSM Wilton w Netherhampton and Fugglestone *Sarum* 00-04; P-in-c Kingston, Langton Matravers and Worth Matravers 04-10; P-in-c Wrington w Butcombe and Burrington *B & W* 10-12; rtd 12; PtO *B & W* from 12. *87 Knightcott Road, Banwell BS29 6HR* T: (01934) 824162 E: judith.malins@btinternet.com

MALINS, Matthew John. b 80. St Jo Coll Nottm MTh 12. **d** 12 **p** 13. C Glascote and Stonydelph *Lich* from 12. *9 Friars Walk, Tamworth B77 2FH* T: (01827) 59334 M: 07932-721131 E: mattmalins@hotmail.co.uk

MALKIN, Thomas Ross. b 64. Hertf Coll Ox BA 86. Trin Coll Bris BA 98 MPhil 00. **d** 99 **p** 00. C Old Trafford St Bride *Man* 99-03; P-in-c Firswood and Gorse Hill 03-10; R from 10. *The Rectory, 24 Canute Road, Stretford, Manchester M32 0RJ* T: 0161-865 1802 M: 07973-240023 E: rev.trm@ntlworld.com

MALKINSON, Canon Christopher Mark. b 47. Chich Th Coll 84. **d** 86 **p** 87. C Stroud and Uplands w Slad *Glouc* 86-89; V Cam w Stinchcombe 89-00; P-in-c Tywardreath w Tregaminion *Truro* 00-02; P-in-c St Sampson 00-02; V Padstow from 02; RD Pydar 03-13; Hon Can Truro Cathl from 07; Chapl Miss to Seafarers from 00. *The Vicarage, 46 Treverbyn Road, Padstow PL28 8DN* T: (01841) 533776
E: chrismalk@hotmail.com

MALKINSON, Michael Stephen. b 43. St Steph Ho Ox 65. **d** 68 **p** 69. C New Addington *Cant* 68-71; C Blackpool St Steph *Blackb* 71-74; V Wainfleet St Mary *Linc* 74-81; R Wainfleet All SS w St Thos 74-81; P-in-c Croft 80-81; V Lund *Blackb* 81-93; V Heyhouses on Sea 93-00; R Balcombe *Chich* 00-09; P-in-c Staplefield Common 00-03; rtd 09. *8 Haines Avenue, Wyre Piddle, Pershore WR10 2RQ* T: (01386) 556102
E: malkinson@msn.com

MALLAS, Mrs Wendy Norris. b 42. Reading Univ MA 91 Cov Coll of Educn CertEd 63. STETS 00. **d** 03 **p** 04. NSM Liss *Portsm* 03-07; NSM Blackmoor and Whitehill 07-12; PtO from 12; NSM Bordon *Guildf* from 07. *Mayfield, 45 Hogmoor Road, Whitehill, Bordon GU35 9ET* T: (01420) 478883
E: wendy.mallas@gmail.com or
wendy.mallas@mayfieldjays.co.uk

MALLETT, John Christopher. b 44. EAMTC. **d** 82 **p** 83. NSM Hethersett w Canteloff *Nor* 82-85; NSM Hethersett w Canteloff w Lt and Gt Melton 85-90; Chapl Wayland Hosp Norfolk 88-94; Chapl Norwich Community Health Partnership NHS Trust 94-00; PtO *Nor* 00-03; NSM Hethersett w Canteloff w Lt and Gt Melton 03-10; rtd 10; PtO *Nor* from 10. *2 Bailey Close, Hethersett, Norwich NR9 3EU* T: (01603) 811010
E: christophersheila@tiscali.co.uk

MALLETT, Canon Marlene Rosemarie. b 59. Sussex Univ BA 81 Warwick Univ PhD 94. SEITE 01. **d** 04 **p** 05. C Brixton Road Ch Ch *S'wark* 04-07; P-in-c Angell Town St Jo 07-13; V from 13; Dir Ords Kingston Area from 13; Hon Can S'wark Cathl from 13. *St John's Vicarage, 49 Wiltshire Road, London SW9 7NE* T: (020) 7733 0585 E: rosemarie.mallett@gmail.com

MALLINSON, Peter Albert. b 57. St Jo Coll Nottm 06 BA(ThM) 12. **d** 08 **p** 09. NSM Allestree St Edm and Darley Abbey *Derby* 08-12; TV Canvey Is *Chelmsf* from 12. *St Anne's House, 51 St Anne's Road, Canvey Island SS8 7LS* T: (01268) 698620 E: peter6hq@btinternet.com

MALLINSON, Canon Ralph Edward. b 40. Oriel Coll Ox BA 63 MA 66. St Steph Ho Ox 63. **d** 66 **p** 67. C Bolton St Pet

Man 66-68; C Elton All SS 68-72; V Bury St Thos 72-76; V Bury Ch King 76-81; P-in-c Goodshaw 81-82; V 82-84; V Goodshaw and Crawshawbooth 84-93; AD Rossendale 83-93; V Unsworth 93-06; Hon Can Man Cathl 92-06; Vice Prin Dioc OLM Scheme 98-06; rtd 06; PtO Man from 06. *18 Woodgate Avenue, Bury BL9 7RU* T: 0161-797 2006
E: ralphandhelen@rmallinson.fsnet.co.uk

MALLON, Allister. b 61. Sheff Univ BA 83 TCD BTh 89 MA. CITC. **d** 87 **p** 88. C Ballymoney w Finvoy and Rasharkin *Conn* 87-90; C Belfast St Mary w H Redeemer 90-92; Bp's C Belfast St Mary Magd 92-00; Bp's C Stoneyford 00-11; Chapl R Gp of Hosps Health and Soc Services Trust from 00. *9 The Rose Garden, Dunmurry, Belfast BT17 9GZ* T: (028) 9030 1272 M: 07719-833034 E: bigal@talk21.com

MALLORY, George Henry. b 14. JP. Lon Univ BSc 63. St Deiniol's Hawarden. **d** 80 **p** 81. NSM Oaks in Charnwood and Copt Oak *Leic* 80-88; rtd 88; PtO *Leic* 88-91; *Worc* from 91. *Claudina, Bewdley Road North, Stourport-on-Severn DY13 8PX* T: (01299) 827969

MALMESBURY, Archdeacon of. *See* FROUDE, The Ven Christine Ann

MALONE, Richard Patrick. b 66. Wycliffe Hall Ox BTh 03. **d** 03 **p** 04. C Fulham Ch Ch *Lon* 03-06; C Battersea St Pet and St Paul *S'wark* 06-12; P-in-c from 12. *22 Rochelle Close, London SW11 2RX* T: (020) 7738 9943 M: 07973-104941
E: patrick@stpetersbattersea.org.uk

MALONEY, Ms Fiona Elizabeth. b 60. Bradf Univ BSc 82 St Jo Coll Dur BA 91. NOC 91. **d** 92 **p** 94. Par Dn Castleton Moor *Man* 92-94; C 94-96; C Pendlebury St Jo 96-99; C Fatfield *Dur* 99-03; NSM Harrow Trin St Mich *Lon* 03-05; NSM Wealdstone H Trin from 05. *The Vicarage, 39 Rusland Park Road, Harrow HA1 1UN* T: (020) 8863 5844 *or* 8863 6131
E: fiona@cofe.org.uk

MALONEY, Terence Mark. b 63. York Univ BSc 84. Cranmer Hall Dur 88. **d** 91 **p** 92. C Blackley St Andr *Man* 91-96; P-in-c Pendlebury St Jo 96-99; C-in-c Fatfield *Dur* 99-03; P-in-c Harrow Trin St Mich *Lon* 03-05; V Wealdstone H Trin from 05. *The Vicarage, 39 Rusland Park Road, Harrow HA1 1UN* T: (020) 8863 5844 *or* 8863 6131 E: mark@cofe.org.uk

MALTBY, Canon Geoffrey. b 38. Leeds Univ BA 62. Wells Th Coll 68. **d** 70 **p** 71. C Mansfield St Mark *S'well* 70-73; V Skegby 73-78; V Carrington 78-87; C Rainworth 87-90; Chapl for People w Learning Disability (Mental Handicap) 90-03; Hon Can S'well Minster 99-03; rtd 03; PtO *S'well* from 03. *18 Beverley Close, Rainworth, Mansfield NG21 0LW* T: (01623) 474452

MALTBY, Canon Judith Diane. b 57. Univ of Illinois BA 79 Newnham Coll Cam PhD 92 FRHistS 99. S Dios Minl Tr Scheme 89. **d** 92 **p** 94. Tutor Sarum & Wells Th Coll 87-93; Hon Par Dn Wilton w Netherhampton and Fugglestone *Sarum* 92-93; Chapl and Fell CCC Ox from 93; Reader Ch Hist Ox Univ from 04; Can Th Leic Cathl from 04; Hon Can Ch Ch Ox from 06; Can Th Win Cathl from 11. *Corpus Christi College, Oxford OX1 4JF* T: (01865) 276722
E: judith.maltby@ccc.ox.ac.uk

MALTIN, Basil St Clair Aston. b 24. Qu Coll Cam BA 49 MA 54. Westcott Ho Cam 50. **d** 51 **p** 52. C Dursley *Glouc* 51-53; C Bathwick w Woolley *B & W* 53-57; V Frome Ch Ch 57-63; P-in-c Marston Bigot 57-59; V Bishops Lydeard 63-71; R Pulborough *Chich* 71-90; RD Storrington 84-89; rtd 90; PtO *Chich* from 90. *13 Somerstown, Chichester PO19 6AG* T: (01243) 786740

MALTON, William Peter Antony. b 33. K Coll Lon AKC 56. **d** 57 **p** 58. C N Hammersmith St Kath *Lon* 57-60; C-in-c Blackbird Leys CD *Ox* 60-65; R Pitsford *Pet* 65-66; Canada from 66; rtd 93. *97 Queen Street, PO Box 1433, Digby NS B0V 1A0, Canada*

MAN, Archdeacon of the Isle of. *See* BROWN, The Ven Andrew

MANCHESTER, Canon John Charles. b 45. Lon Univ BD 69. ALCD 68. **d** 69 **p** 70. C Scarborough St Martin *York* 69-73; C Selby Abbey 73-76; P-in-c Old Malton 76-79; V 79-10; RD Bulmer and Malton 85-91; Can and Preb York Minster 05-10; rtd 10; PtO *York* from 10. *18 Castle Howard Road, Malton YO17 7AY* T: (01653) 690671

MANCHESTER, Archdeacon of. *See* ASHCROFT, The Ven Mark David

MANCHESTER, Bishop of. *See* WALKER, The Rt Revd David Stuart

MANCHESTER, Dean of. *See* GOVENDER, The Very Revd Rogers Morgan

MANCO, Gwenda Diane. b 54. NOC 97. **d** 99 **p** 00. NSM Rochdale *Man* 99-02; NSM Dearnley 02-04; Asst Chapl HM Pris Buckley Hall 99-03; Chapl HM Pris Styal 03; NSM Spotland *Man* 04-06; NSM Dearnley 06-13; NSM Littleborough 13-14. *5 Stansfield Hall, Littleborough OL15 9RH* T: (01706) 370264 M: 07966-217252
E: gwenda.manco@tesco.net

MANCOR, Neil McKay. Univ of BC MA Reading Univ PhD. Wycliffe Hall Ox. **d** 99 **p** 00. C Llandeilo Fawr and Taliaris *St D* 99-02; Canada from 02. *1490 Nanton Avenue, Vancouver BC V6H 2E2, Canada* E: neilmancor@hotmail.com

MANDER, Patricia. b 51. **d** 13 **p** 14. OLM Haddenham w Cuddington, Kingsey etc *Ox* from 13. *7 Stockwell Furlong, Haddenham, Aylesbury HP17 8HD* T: (01844) 290985

MANDER, Peter John. b 52. Liv Univ BEd 75 Anglia Ruskin Univ MA 09. Sarum & Wells Th Coll 85. **d** 87 **p** 88. C Hale and Ashley *Ches* 87-90; TV Grantham *Linc* 90-00; P-in-c Quarrington w Old Sleaford 00-08; P-in-c Silk Willoughby 00-08; RD Lafford 03-07; Can and Preb Linc Cathl 05-08; R Ellon *Ab* 08-15; R Cruden Bay 08-15; TV N Tyne and Redesdale *Newc* from 15. *The Vicarage, Otterburn, Newcastle upon Tyne NE19 1NP* M: 07929-140425 T: (01830) 520212
E: peter.mander@gmail.com

MANDER, Canon Thomas Leonard Frederick. b 33. Roch Th Coll 59 Ely Th Coll 60. **d** 62 **p** 63. C Cov St Mary 62-66; V Bishop's Tachbrook 66-70; V Earlsdon 70-76; V Chesterton 76-83; R Lighthorne 76-83; V Newbold Pacey w Moreton Morrell 76-83; Hon Can Cov Cathl 80-92; P-in-c S Leamington St Jo 83-84; V 84-92; rtd 92; PtO *Cov* from 92. *59 Murcott Road East, Whitnash, Leamington Spa CV31 2JJ* T: (01926) 339950

MANDERSON, Robert Dunlop (Leslie). b 35. LDS 59 FDS 65. Ox Min Course 92. **d** 94 **p** 95. NSM Maidenhead St Andr and St Mary *Ox* 94-00; PtO 00-02; NSM Chipping Norton 02-03; rtd 03; PtO Ox 03-04; *Ely* from 04. *67 Park Street, Dry Drayton, Cambridge CB23 8DA* T: (01954) 782388
E: lesmanderson@tiscali.co.uk

MANGA, Amos Morris Yorobama. **d** 06 **p** 07. C Helsinki *Eur* from 06. *Thölberginkatu 5 B 15, 65380 Vaasa, Finland* T: (00358) (9) 680 1515 F: 698 6302

MANHOOD, Phyllis. *See* DELVES, Phyllis

✠**MANKTELOW, The Rt Revd Michael Richard John.** b 27. Ch Coll Cam BA 48 MA 52. Chich Th Coll 51. **d** 53 **p** 54 **c** 77. C Boston *Linc* 53-56; Chapl Ch Coll Cam 57-61; Chapl Linc Th Coll 61-63; Sub-Warden 64-66; V Knaresborough St Jo *Ripon* 66-73; RD Harrogate 72-77; V Harrogate St Wilfrid 73-77; P-in-c Harrogate St Luke 75-77; Hon Can Ripon Cathl 75-77; Suff Bp Basingstoke *Win* 77-93; Can Res Win Cathl 77-91; Hon Can Win Cathl 91-93; Vice-Dean Win 87-93; rtd 93; Hon Asst Bp Chich from 94; Hon Asst Bp Eur from 94; Wiccamical Preb Chich Cathl 97-02. *14 Little London, Chichester PO19 1NZ* T: (01243) 531096

MANLEY, Mrs Gillian. b 59. St Martin's Coll Lanc BEd 80. St Jo Coll Nottm MA 00. **d** 00 **p** 01. C Eckington and Ridgeway *Derby* 00-04; TV Wirksworth 04-09; V Blackwell w Tibshelf from 09; C Pinxton from 14. *The Vicarage, 67 High Street, Tibshelf, Alfreton DE55 5NU* T: (01773) 873305
E: gill-manley@sky.com

MANLEY, Canon Gordon Russell Delpratt. b 33. Ch Coll Cam BA 56 MA 60. Linc Th Coll 57. **d** 59 **p** 60. C Westbury-on-Trym St Alb *Bris* 59-61; Chapl Ch Coll Cam 61-66; V Radlett *St Alb* 66-75; V Faversham *Cant* 75-99; RD Ospringe 84-90; Hon Can Cant Cathl 90-99; rtd 99; PtO *Cant* from 99; Retirement Officer (Cant Adnry) 01-10. *170 Old Dover Road, Canterbury CT1 3EX* T: (01227) 784016

MANLEY, Mrs Jane Elizabeth. b 58. Ox Min Course 05. **d** 08 **p** 09. C Bracknell *Ox* 08-11; C Crowthorne 11-12; V Ruislip Manor St Paul *Lon* from 12; Dean of Women's Min Willesden Area from 13. *St Paul's Vicarage, Thurlstone Road, Ruislip HA4 0BP* T: (01895) 633499 M: 07711-613057
E: jane.e.manley@btinternet.com

MANLEY, Canon Michael Alan. b 60. SS Hild & Bede Coll Dur BA 82. Trin Coll Bris. **d** 86 **p** 87. C Accrington St Jo w Huncoat *Blackb* 86-90; V Preston St Luke and St Oswald 90-96; V Blackpool St Jo 96-07; Can Res Carl Cathl from 07; RD Carl from 10. *1 The Abbey, Carlisle CA3 8TZ* T: (01228) 542790
E: canonmissioner@carlislecathedral.org.uk

MANLEY (née McCARTHY), Mrs Sandra Ellen. b 56. Man Univ MusB 77 Goldsmiths' Coll Lon PGCE 79 ARCM 75 FRCO 77 GRNCM 78. S'wark Ord Course 92. **d** 95 **p** 96. C Beckenham St Geo *Roch* 95-99; V Heybridge w Langford *Chelmsf* 99-06; R Creeksea w Althorne, Latchingdon and N Fambridge 06-09; P-in-c Purleigh, Cold Norton and Stow Maries 08-09; V Althorne and Latchingdon w N Fambridge from 09; V Cold Norton w Stow Maries from 09; RD Maldon and Dengie from 11. *The Vicarage, Fambridge Road, Althorne, Chelmsford CM3 6BZ* T: (01621) 742947 M: 07777-673096
E: sandra.manley@btinternet.com

MANLEY-COOPER, Simon James. b 46. S Dios Minl Tr Scheme 91. **d** 94 **p** 95. NSM Soho St Anne w St Thos and St Pet *Lon* 94-96; Ind Chapl 94-96; P-in-c Bedford St Mich *St Alb* 96-01; Ind Chapl 96-01; R Bramfield, Stapleford, Waterford etc 01-02; Chapl E and N Herts NHS Trust 03-11; rtd 11; PtO *St Alb* from 11. *19 Barnfield Road, Harpenden AL5 5TH* T: (01582) 460797 E: manley-c@hotmail.co.uk

MANN, Alexandrina Elizabeth. b 67. Westmr Coll Ox BA 92 PGCE 93 Birm Univ MA 95 FGA 90. Trin Coll Bris 01. **d** 03 **p** 04. C Austrey and Warton *Birm* 03-06; V Hanbury, Newborough, Rangemore and Tutbury *Lich* 06-13; C Branston 13; C Cannock and Huntington from 13. *18 Queen Street, Cannock WS11 1AE* T: (01543) 577846 M: 07761-263849 E: alexandrina.shalom@virgin.net

MANN, Ms Angela. b 58. Bath Univ BA 80 Bris Univ PGCE 83. Trin Coll Bris 92. **d** 94 **p** 95. C Marlborough *Sarum* 94-97; PtO 97-98; *Ox* 98-09; NSM The Claydons and Swan from 09. *The Rectory, Grendon Underwood, Aylesbury HP18 0SY* T: (01296) 770240 M: 07982-770161 E: angela.mann@o2.co.uk

MANN, Canon Charmion Anne Montgomery. b 36. Liv Univ BA 57 CertEd 62 AdDipEd 79 Univ of Wales (Lamp) MA 06. Trin Coll Bris 80. **dss** 82 **d** 87 **p** 94. Bris St Nath w St Kath 82-84; Bris St Matt and St Nath 84-85; Asst Chapl Bris City Hosp 85-88; Chapl Bris Maternity Hosp 88-94; Chapl Bris R Hosp for Sick Children 88-94; Chapl Bris R Infirmary 88-94; Hon Can Bris Cathl 93-00; P-in-c Lacock w Bowden Hill 94-00; C Gtr Corsham 97-00; rtd 00; PtO *Bris* 00-06; *Sarum* 01-06; *Ex* from 07. *21 Oak Gardens, Ivybridge PL21 0NB* T: (01752) 896636 E: charmion.mann@danmat.co.uk

MANN, Christopher John. b 57. Glas Univ BSc 79. Westcott Ho Cam 83. **d** 86 **p** 87. C Worc SE 86-89; Min Can and Sacr St Paul's Cathl 89-96; R Upminster *Chelmsf* 96-06; Chapl to Bp Bradwell 06-10; C Corringham 07-10; P-in-c Christchurch *Win* 10-14. *3 Park View, Wells BA5 1UW* T: (01749) 686996 M: 07931-116897 E: fatherchris@domus.org.uk

MANN, David. b 57. St Jo Coll Dur BA 78. Ridley Hall Cam. **d** 82 **p** 83. C Monkwearmouth St Andr *Dur* 82-86; Chapl Sheff Cathl 86-87; C Leeds St Geo *Ripon* 87-94; V Ripon H Trin 94-06; Asst Dir of Ords 02-06; Nat Adv for Pre-Th Educn and Selection Sec Min Division 06-09; Dioc Voc Adv *York* from 09. *64 Strensall Road, Huntington, York YO32 9SH* T: (01904) 768668 E: david.mann@yorkdiocese.org

MANN, Donald Leonard. b 22. Westcott Ho Cam. **d** 47 **p** 48. C S'well Minster 47-49; C Edwinstowe 49-51; C St Alb St Paul *St Alb* 51-54; C Baldock w Bygrave and Clothall 54-56; V Guilden Morden *Ely* 56-59; V Rocester *Lich* 59-63; V Gnosall w Knightley 63-67; V Gnosall and Moreton 68-69; V Sheen 69-76; P-in-c Calton 72-76; P-in-c Ellastone 76; rtd 76; PtO *Ches* from 93. *Bungalow 24, Lyme Green Settlement, Macclesfield SK11 0LD* T: (01260) 252209

MANN (*née* WELLS), Ms Gillian Mary. b 46. Bedf Coll Lon BA 67 Goldsmiths' Coll Lon TCert 68 MCIPD 89. EMMTC 99. **d** 01 **p** 02. NSM Wirksworth *Derby* 01-05; P-in-c The Sampfords and Radwinter w Hempstead *Chelmsf* 05-13; rtd 13. *56 Well Creek Road, Outwell, Wisbech PE14 8SA* T: (01945) 773078 M: 07719-470363 E: gillianmarymann@yahoo.co.uk

MANN, Ivan John. b 52. Brunel Univ BTech 74 Southn Univ BTh 80. Sarum & Wells Th Coll 75. **d** 78 **p** 79. C Hadleigh w Layham and Shelley *St E* 78-81; C Whitton and Thurleston w Akenham 81-83; V Leiston 83-86; PtO 86-89; R Aldringham w Thorpe, Knodishall w Buxlow etc 89-93; V Ipswich St Jo 93-96; Chapl St Mary's Convent Wantage 96-00; Asst Chapl R Berks and Battle Hosps NHS Trust 00; TV Gt Yarmouth *Nor* 00-03; Team Member Loyola Hall Jesuit Spirituality Cen Prescot 03-04; Prec and Hon Can Cumbrae *Arg* 04-06; Can St Jo Cathl Oban 04-06; rtd 06. *140 Somerleyton Gardens, Norwich NR2 2BS* T: (01603) 929591 E: ivan@ivanmann.f2s.com

MANN, Mrs Joan. b 41. **d** 98. NSM Eastbourne St Mary *Chich* 98-02; NSM The Hydneye 02-10; NSM Hampden Park and The Hydnye from 10. *39 Cherry Garden Road, Eastbourne BN20 8HF* T: (01323) 728259

MANN, John. b 35. ISO 91. Oak Hill NSM Course 89. **d** 92 **p** 93. NSM Springfield All SS *Chelmsf* 92-05; RD Chelmsf N 99-04; rtd 05; PtO *Chelmsf* from 05. *18 Humber Road, Chelmsford CM1 7PE* T: (01245) 259596

MANN, The Very Revd John Owen. b 55. QUB BD 77 MTh 86 MPhil 98. CITC 79. **d** 79 **p** 81. C Cloughfern *Conn* 79-82; C Knock *D & D* 82-85; I Ballyrashane w Kildollagh *Conn* 85-89; R Bentworth and Shalden and Lasham *Win* 89-93; RD Alton 92-93; I Cloughfern *Conn* 93-02; I Belfast Malone St Jo 02-11; Dean Belf from 11; I Belfast St Anne *Conn* from 11; Preb Clonmethan St Patr Cathl Dublin from 99. *St Anne's Cathedral, Donegall Street, Belfast BT1 2HB* T: (028) 9032 8332 *or* 9066 0980 E: dean@belfastcathedral.org

MANN, Julia Corinne. b 52. Open Univ BA 92 Anglia Poly Univ BA 03 RGN 91. **d** 08 **p** 09. OLM Bury St Edmunds All SS w St Jo and St Geo *St E* 08-13; NSM from 13; NSM Lark Valley from 14. *Orchard House, 13 Orchard Street, Bury St Edmunds IP33 1EH* T: (01284) 753984 E: jc.mann@btinternet.com

MANN, Julian Farrer Edgar. b 64. Peterho Cam MA 90. Oak Hill Th Coll BA 93. **d** 96 **p** 97. C Hoole *Ches* 96-00; V Oughtibridge

Sheff from 00. *The Vicarage, Church Street, Oughtibridge, Sheffield S35 0FU* T: 0114-286 2317 E: julianlisa@oughtimann.freeserve.co.uk

MANN, Mrs Nicola Antoinette. b 70. Man Univ BA 92. SEITE 12. **d** 14 **p** 15. C Stamford All SS w St Jo *Linc* from 14. *26 Hazel Grove, Stamford PE9 2HJ* M: 07738-266057 T: (01780) 759053 E: nikkimann40@hotmail.co.uk

MANN, Mrs Patricia Ann. b 62. STETS 08. **d** 11 **p** 12. C Havant *Portsm* 11-15; Chapl RN Coll Greenwich from 15. *39 Burney Street, Greenwich, London SE10 8EX* M: 07890-304670 T: (020) 8269 4750 E: patmann17@yahoo.co.uk

MANN, Paul William. b 63. Leeds Univ BSc 84 CEng MIET. EAMTC 01. **d** 04 **p** 05. NSM Lawford *Chelmsf* from 04. *8 Cherrywoods, Great Bentley, Colchester CO7 8QF* T: (01206) 252420 E: lima3papa-lawford@yahoo.co.uk

MANN, Peter Eric. b 51. St Jo Coll Dur BA 73. Westcott Ho Cam 73. **d** 75 **p** 76. C Barrow St Jo *Carl* 75-78; C Egremont 78-80; V Carl St Luke Morton 80-86; TR Egremont and Haile 86-93; P-in-c Barrow St Geo w St Luke 93-99; TR S Barrow 99-06; P-in-c Barrow St Jo 95-96; RD Furness 94-01; RD Barrow 01-06; Hon Can Carl Cathl 95-06; TR Harwich Peninsula *Chelmsf* from 06; RD Harwich 09-14. *The Rectory, 51 Highfield Avenue, Harwich CO12 4DR* T: (01255) 502033 E: cookbird@gmail.com

MANN, Philip David. b 78. **d** 08 **p** 09. NSM Guildf St Sav 08-10; C Gerrards Cross and Fulmer *Ox* from 10. *Willowbrook, 54 The Uplands, Gerrards Cross SL9 7JG* E: philip.mann@saintjames.org.uk

MANN, Ms Rachel. b 70. Lanc Univ BA 91 MA 93. Qu Coll Birm 03. **d** 05 **p** 06. C Stretford St Matt *Man* 05-08; P-in-c Burnage St Nic from 08. *The Rectory, 408 Kingsway, Burnage, Manchester M19 1PL* T: 0161-432 7009 M: 07834-403195 E: rachelmann994@gmail.com

MANN, Robin. b 45. Fitzw Coll Cam BA 76 MA 80 MRTPI 73. Ridley Hall Cam 73. **d** 77 **p** 78. C Wetherby *Ripon* 77-80; V Hipswell 80-86; V Mamble w Bayton, Rock w Heightington etc *Worc* 86-96; V Avon Valley *Sarum* 96-02; R Selworthy, Timberscombe, Wootton Courtenay etc *B & W* 02-07; rtd 07. *Hoarthorns Cottage, Malvern Way, Edge End, Coleford GL16 7DZ* T: (01594) 833576 E: hoarthorns@tiscali.co.uk

MANN, Stephen Paul. b 52. Staffs Univ BA 76 Keele Univ PGCE 78. Cranmer Hall Dur 96. **d** 98 **p** 99. C Spennymoor, Whitworth and Merrington *Dur* 98-03; Chapl Dur Constabulary 99-03; Chapl Butterwick Hospice Bishop Auckland 00-03; TV Madeley *Heref* 03-04; rtd 05. *42 The Crescent, Montford Bridge, Shrewsbury SY4 1EA* E: steve.mann99@telco4u.net

MANN, Mrs Susan Mary. b 66. Coll of Ripon & York St Jo BA 89 Loughb Univ PGCE 90. St Mellitus Coll BA 12. **d** 12 **p** 13. C Wickford and Runwell *Chelmsf* from 12. *8 Honington Close, Wickford SS11 8XB* T: (01268) 730972 E: suemann@tiscali.co.uk

MANN, Terence John. b 47. Miami Univ MA 80 Lon Univ PGCE 69 GGSM 68 LRSM 79 FTCL 79. Ox Min Course 91. **d** 94 **p** 95. NSM Kingham w Churchill, Daylesford and Sarsden *Ox* 94-00; Chapl HM Pris Camp Hill 00-12; rtd 12. *Address temp unknown*

MANN, Mrs Tessa Gillian. b 62. Nottm Univ BA 84. STETS 05. **d** 08 **p** 09. C Bourne Valley *Sarum* 08-11; C Salisbury St Fran and Stratford sub Castle from 11. *Barton Mead, Tanners Lane, Winterbourne Earls, Salisbury SP4 6HD* T: (01980) 611942 M: 07588-533283 E: tessamann@fsmail.net

MANNALL, Michael John Frederick. b 37. St Mich Coll Llan 61. **d** 63 **p** 64. C Clapham H Spirit *S'wark* 63-66; C Brighton St Bart *Chich* 66-68; C Willesden St Matt *Lon* 68-69; C-in-c Cricklewood St Pet CD 69-73; R Broughton *Pet* 73-75; Hon C Kingston St Luke *S'wark* 76-94; rtd 84; PtO *Nor* from 95. *The Blessings, 55 Sculthorpe Road, Fakenham NR21 9ET* T: (01328) 863496 E: michael.mannall@btinternet.com

MANNERS, Jennifer Helen Edith. b 50. K Coll Lon MB, BS 73 AKC 73. **d** 06 **p** 07. OLM Bearsted w Thurnham *Cant* 06-13; PtO 13-14. *Address temp unknown* E: jhemanners@hotmail.com

MANNERS, Kenneth. b 29. NOC. **d** 84 **p** 85. NSM Brayton *York* 84-00; rtd 00; PtO *York* 00-11. *16 Wistow Road, Selby YO8 3LY* T: (01757) 702129

MANNING, Adrian Peter. b 63. St Cath Coll Cam BA 84 MA 88 K Coll Lon PGCE 88. Ridley Hall Cam 92. **d** 95 **p** 96. C Oxhey All SS *St Alb* 95-97; Asst Chapl Bedford Sch 97-02; Chapl St Geo Sch Harpenden 02-15; V Ivinghoe w Pitstone and Slapton and Marsworth *Ox* from 15. *The Vicarage, Station Road, Ivinghoe, Leighton Buzzard LU7 9EB* T: (01296) 660127 E: revadrianmanning@gmail.com

MANNING, Mrs Ann. b 42. Liv Univ CertEd 75. St Jo Coll Nottm 93 NOC 94. **d** 95 **p** 96. NSM Grasmere *Carl* 95-96; NSM Delamere *Ches* 96-99; C Middlewich w Byley 99-02;

Chapl Mid Cheshire Hosps Trust 99-02; P-in-c Dunton w Wrestlingworth and Eyeworth *St Alb* 02-05; R 05-08; rtd 08; PtO *Ches* from 10. *27 Barley Croft, Great Boughton, Chester CH3 5SP* T: (01244) 316781 E: revmanning@hotmail.co.uk

MANNING, David Godfrey. b 47. Trin Coll Bris 73. **d** 76 **p** 77. C Richmond H Trin and Ch Ch *S'wark* 76-79; C Anston *Sheff* 79-83; V Blackpool St Mark *Blackb* 83-91; V Creech St Michael *B & W* 91-08; PtO 10-12. *The Priest Hole, 11 Bittern Avenue, Portishead BS20 7NT* T: (01275) 848016

MANNING, Mrs Jean Margaret. b 46. Oak Hill NSM Course 07. **d** 08 **p** 09. NSM Herstmonceux and Wartling *Chich* 08-13; PtO from 13. *Little Bathurst Farm, Cowbeech Road, Rushlake Green, Heathfield TN21 9QA* T/F: (01435) 831105 M: 07711-052131 E: jmm60@btinternet.com

MANNING, Neville Alexander. b 41. Lon Univ BD 68. ALCD 68. **d** 68 **p** 69. C Belvedere All SS *Roch* 68-71; C Hollington St Leon *Chich* 71-73; C Hersham *Guildf* 73-77; V Dawley St Jerome *Lon* 77-94; R Denton w S Heighton and Tarring Neville *Chich* 94-06; rtd 06. *7 Salvador Close, Eastbourne BN23 5TB* T: (01323) 479359

MANNING, Virginia Ann. b 47. Univ of Wales (Ban) BTh 07. **d** 07 **p** 08. OLM N Hartismere *St E* 07-13; NSM from 13. *Fernleigh, Mill Road, Winfarthing, Diss IP22 2DZ* T: (01379) 644229 E: colgin.manning@tesco.net

MANNINGS, Andrew James. b 52. Trent Park Coll of Educn CertEd 73. St Jo Coll Nottm 90. **d** 92 **p** 94. C Over St Chad *Ches* 92-93; C Sale St Anne 93-96; C Timperley 96-98; P-in-c Egremont St Jo 98-04; P-in-c Liscard St Mary w St Columba 03-04; V Liscard Resurr from 04; RD Wallasey 02-07. *The Vicarage, 107 Manor Road, Wallasey CH45 7LU* T: 0151-638 4360 M: 07814-878175 F: 513 0172 E: frandrew2004@yahoo.co.uk

MANNS, Edwin Ernest. b 30. Portsm Dioc Tr Course 84. **d** 85. C Paulsgrove *Portsm* 85-95; Chapl St Mary's Hosp Portsm 90-91; Team Chapl Portsm Hosps NHS Trust 91-95; rtd 95. *17 Kelvin Grove, Portchester, Fareham PO16 8LQ* T: (023) 9232 4818

MANOUCH, Miss Sarah Jane. b 65. SEITE 12. **d** 15. NSM W Wittering and Birdham w Itchenor *Chich* from 15. *9 Kent Road, Chichester PO19 7NH* T: (01243) 774841 M: 07833-914545 E: sarah035@btinternet.com

MANSEL LEWIS, Patrick Charles Archibald. b 53. Solicitor 79. St Mich Coll Llan 01. **d** 04 **p** 05. NSM Llandeilo Fawr and Taliaris *St D* 04-12; NSM Llanelli from 12. *Stradey Castle, Pwll, Llanelli SA15 4PL* T: (01554) 774626 E: patmanlew@btconnect.com

MANSELL, Carol. b 52. Lon Bible Coll BA 75 Nottm Univ MA 86 CQSW 86 Leic Univ MBA 05 Anglia Ruskin Univ MA 11. ERMC 08. **d** 10 **p** 11. NSM Rattlesden w Thorpe Morieux, Brettenham etc *St E* 10-13; P-in-c Monks Eleigh w Chelsworth and Brent Eleigh etc from 13. *The Rectory, The Street, Monks Eleigh, Ipswich IP7 7AU* T: (01449) 744484 M: 07788-157147 E: carol.mansell@btinternet.com

MANSELL, Mrs Caroline Andrea. **d** 14 **p** 15. C Pembroke Dock *St D* from 14. *22 Glenview Avenue, Pembroke Dock SA72 6EJ* T: (01646) 279818 E: mansellc@btinternet.com

MANSELL, The Ven Clive Neville Ross. b 53. Leic Univ LLB 74 Solicitor 77. **d** 82 **p** 83. C Gt Malvern St Mary *Worc* 82-85; Min Can Ripon Cathl 85-89; R Kirklington w Burneston and Wath and Pickhill 89-02; AD Wensley 98-02; Adn Tonbridge *Roch* from 02. *3 The Ridings, Blackhurst Lane, Tunbridge Wells TN2 4RU* T/F: (01892) 520660 E: archdeacon.tonbridge@rochester.anglican.org

MANSELL, Paul John. b 67. Staffs Univ MSc 05. Ripon Coll Cuddesdon 05. **d** 07 **p** 08. C Schorne *Ox* 07-10; V Forest Edge from 10. *The Vicarage, Mount Skippett, Ramsden, Chipping Norton OX7 3AP* T: (01993) 868687 M: 07983-707560 E: paul@deepblueocean.co.uk

MANSFIELD, Alastair John Fraser. b 60. Ex Univ BA 82 Ch Coll Cam PGCE 84 City Univ MSc 92. SEITE. **d** 99 **p** 00. C Palmers Green St Jo *Lon* 99-02; P-in-c Enfield St Mich 02-07; Chapl RN from 08. *Royal Naval Chaplaincy Service, Mail Point 1-2, Leach Building, Whale Island, Portsmouth PO2 8BY* T: (023) 9262 5055 F: 9262 5134

MANSFIELD, Ms Coralie Patricia. b 58. Nene Coll Northn BA 95. Ripon Coll Cuddesdon. **d** 13 **p** 14. NSM Olney *Ox* from 13. *8 Slated Row, Old Wolverton Road, Old Wolverton, Milton Keynes MK12 5NJ* T: (01908) 317038 E: cortims@aol.com

MANSFIELD, Glen Robert. b 76. St Jo Coll Ox BA 97. Oak Hill Th Coll BA 11. **d** 11 **p** 12. C Aldershot H Trin *Guildf* 11-15; C Rhyl w St Ann *St As* from 15. *122 Rhuddlan Road, Rhyl LL18 2RD* T: (01745) 798864 E: tellspartans@yahoo.co.uk *or* glen@parishofrhyl.co.uk

MANSFIELD, Gordon Reginald. b 35. Lon Univ BA CertEd. Clifton Th Coll 58. **d** 63 **p** 64. C Carl St Jo 63-65;

C Westcombe Park St Geo *S'wark* 65-68; C Rashcliffe *Wakef* 68-70; V Woodlands *Sheff* 70-80; V Steeple Bumpstead and Helions Bumpstead *Chelmsf* 80-02; PtO *Ely* 03-04 and from 13; *Heref* 04-13; *S & B* 04-13. *25 Rampton End, Willingham, Cambridge CB24 5JB* T: (01954) 261540

MANSFIELD, Julian Nicolas (Nick). b 59. K Coll Lon BD AKC. Edin Th Coll 83. **d** 85 **p** 86. C Kirkby *Liv* 85-89; TV Ditton St Mich 89-96; P-in-c Preston St Oswald *Blackb* 96-01; V Penwortham St Leon from 01. *St Leonard's Vicarage, Marshall's Brow, Penwortham, Preston PR1 9HY* T: (01772) 742367 E: nickthevic1@googlemail.com

MANSFIELD, Robert William. b 45. **d** 88 **p** 89. OLM Louth *Linc* from 88. *The Old Railway House, Stewton, Louth LN11 8SD* T: (01507) 327533 E: mansfieldstewton@hotmail.com

MANSFIELD, Simon David. b 55. Brunel Univ BSc 81 Lon Univ MA 94 Univ of Wales (Ban) MPhil 06. Ripon Coll Cuddesdon 88. **d** 90 **p** 91. C N Harrow St Alb *Lon* 90-93; C Birchington w Acol and Minnis Bay *Cant* 93-97; TV Accrington *Blackb* 97-00; TV Accrington Ch the King 00-05; P-in-c Wednesfield St Greg *Lich* 05-15; V Hockerill *St Alb* from 15. *Hockerill Vicarage, 4A All Saints Close, Bishop's Stortford CM23 2EA* T: (01279) 506542 E: smansfeeld@toucansurf.com

MANSFIELD, Stephen McLaren. b 59. FGA. Cranmer Hall Dur 86. **d** 89 **p** 90. C Poynton *Ches* 89-92; C Bromborough 92-94; V Bidston 94-02; C Heswall 02-09; V Birkenhead St Jas w St Bede from 09. *St James's Vicarage, 56 Tollemache Road, Prenton CH43 8SZ* T: 0151-652 1016 E: steve.mansfield@mac.com

MANSHIP, Charmian Margaret. b 45. RCM BMus 68 ARCM 65 GRSM 67 FRCO 68. SAOMC 95. **d** 98 **p** 99. NSM Abingdon *Ox* 98-04; Succ and Min Can Worc Cathl from 04. *22 Stanmore Road, Worcester WR2 4PW* T: (01905) 421147 M: 07986-657110 E: charmian@manships.co.uk

MANSHIP, Canon David. b 27. ARCO Keble Coll Ox BA 52 MA 58. Qu Coll Birm 52. **d** 54 **p** 55. C Hackney St Jo *Lon* 54-58; C Preston Ascension 58-61; C St Andr Holborn 61-65; Members' Tr Officer C of E Youth Coun 65-68; Clergy Tr Officer 68-70; Dir of Educn *Win* 70-79; Hon Can Win Cathl 74-79; R Old Alresford 76-79; V Abingdon w Shippon *Ox* 79-89; TR Abingdon 89-93; V Shippon 89; RD Abingdon 87-90; rtd 93; PtO *Ox* 93-03; *Worc* from 04. *22 Stanmore Road, Worcester WR2 4PW* T: (01905) 421147 E: david@manships.co.uk

MANSLEY, Caroline Anne Bimson. b 58. Bris Univ BA 80. TCD Div Sch MTh 12. **d** 11 **p** 12. Par Dn Willowfield *D & D* 11-12; C Magheraculmoney *Clogh* from 12. *3 Castle Manor, Kesh, Enniskillen BT93 1RT* T: (028) 6863 2751 M: 07850-836997 E: caroline@mansley.net

MANSLEY, Colin Edward. b 56. Edin Univ MA 80 BA 85. Ripon Coll Cuddesdon 83. **d** 86 **p** 87. C Worle *B & W* 86-89; C Baguley *Man* 89-91; C Radcliffe St Mary 91; TV Radcliffe 91-96; V Bartley Green *Birm* 96-08; R Trefnant w Tremeirchion w Cefn *St As* from 08; AD Denbigh from 14. *The Rectory, Trefnant, Denbigh LL16 5UG* T: (01745) 730584 E: colin@archangel.clara.co.uk

MANSON-BRAILSFORD, Andrew Henry. b 64. NUU BA 86 Liv Univ MPhil 98 Sussex Univ DPhil 09. Ripon Coll Cuddesdon 87. **d** 90 **p** 91. C Warrington St Elphin *Liv* 90-93; C Torrisholme *Blackb* 93-96; V Brighton St Geo w St Anne and St Mark *Chich* from 96; RD Brighton 10-15; Chapl St Mary's Hall Brighton from 97. *St George's House, 6 Sussex Mews, Brighton BN2 1GZ* T: (01273) 625538 E: revmanson-brailsford@hotmail.co.uk

MANTON, Paul Arthur. b 45. Oak Hill Th Coll BD 77. **d** 77 **p** 78. C Wolverhampton *Lich* 77-80; Ind Chapl *Lon* 80-87; Hon C St Marylebone All So w SS Pet and Jo 80-87; PtO from 03. *75 Homefield Gardens, London N2 0XL* T: (020) 3224 3001 M: 07847-425946 E: paulikann@me.com

MANUEL, Paul. b 55. Univ of Wales (Ban) BA 76 Lon Sch of Th MA 09 ACIS 79 FCIS 88. SAOMC 97. **d** 00 **p** 01. NSM Luton St Paul *St Alb* 00-03; C Chorleywood Ch Ch 03-07; P-in-c New Milverton *Cov* 07-10; V from 10; AD Warwick and Leamington 10-14. *St Mark's Vicarage, 2 St Mark's Road, Leamington Spa CV32 6DL* T: (01926) 421004 E: paul.manuel4@ntlworld.com

MAPES, David. Brunel Univ BSc 71 CEng 75 MIET 74 MIMechE 78 EurIng 89 FInstD 77 MBACP 99. NTMTC BA 07. **d** 07 **p** 08. NSM Feltham *Lon* 07-10; P-in-c Southampton St Mark *Win* 10-15; Hon C The Downs from 15. *The Rectory, Chilbolton, Stockbridge SO20 6BA* M: 07885-635378 E: davemapes@aol.com

MAPLE, David Charles. b 34. Sarum Th Coll 64. **d** 66 **p** 66. C Buckland in Dover *Cant* 66-67; C St Laur in Thanet 67-71; Chapl RAF 71-75; P-in-c Ivychurch w Old Romney and Midley *Cant* 75-76; P-in-c Newchurch 75-78; P-in-c Burmarsh 75-78;

P-in-c St Mary in the Marsh 75-76; R Dymchurch 76-78; R Dymchurch w Burmarsh and Newchurch 78-81; Hon Min Can Cant Cathl from 79; Abp's Dioc Chapl 81-91; Chapl St Jo Hosp Cant 91-95; rtd 95; PtO *Cant* from 98. *1 Mount Pleasant, Blean, Canterbury CT2 9EU* T: (01227) 459044

MAPLE, John Philip. b 50. Chich Th Coll 71. **d** 74 **p** 79. C Notting Hill St Mich and Ch Ch *Lon* 74-75; LtO 78-79; C Barnsbury St Dav w St Clem 79-80; C Cotham St Sav w St Mary *Bris* 80-83; TV St Marylebone Ch Ch *Lon* 83-91; R St Marylebone St Paul 91-99; P-in-c Fulham St Alb w St Aug 99-04; P-in-c Fulham St Pet 99-02; Community Min Adv 04-15; rtd 15. *Address temp unknown*

MAPLEY, Mrs Barbara Jean. b 46. Guy's Hosp Medical Sch MCSP 69. Oak Hill NSM Course 86. **d** 89 **p** 94. NSM Kelvedon *Chelmsf* 89-93; C Witham 93-94; TV 94-01; R Belbroughton w Fairfield and Clent *Worc* 01-11; rtd 12. *2 Leamington Gate, Coxwell Road, Faringdon SN7 7FP* T: (01367) 615009
E: barbaramapley@waitrose.com

MAPPLEBECKPALMER, Richard Warwick. b 32. CCC Cam BA 56 MA 60. Cuddesdon Coll 56. **d** 58 **p** 59. C Redcar *York* 58-60; C Drypool St Jo 61-63; V Pendleton St Ambrose *Man* 63-77; P-in-c Piddington *Ox* 77; P-in-c Ambrosden w Arncot and Blackthorn 77; P-in-c Merton 77; V Ambrosden w Merton and Piddington 77-88; USA from 88; rtd 97. *472 Dale Road, Martinez CA 94553-4829, USA* T: (001) (510) 228 5252

MAPSON, Preb John Victor. b 31. Lon Univ BA 60. Oak Hill Th Coll 55. **d** 60 **p** 61. C Littleover *Derby* 60-62; C Wandsworth St Mich *S'wark* 62-65; R Willand *Ex* 65-71; P-in-c Axmouth 71-72; V 72-75; V Axmouth w Musbury 75-77; RD Honiton 76-77; V Cullompton 77-89; R Kentisbeare w Blackborough 77-89; RD Cullompton 81-89; P-in-c Sidmouth All SS 89-96; Preb Ex Cathl 91-01; RD Ottery 94-96; rtd 96; Ed Exeter Diocesan Directory *Ex* 00-10. *47 Head Weir Road, Cullompton EX15 1NN* T: (01884) 38037 E: jmapson@care4free.net

MAPSTONE, Canon Trevor Anthony. b 63. Lanc Univ BSc 84 MA 96. St Jo Coll Nottm 86. **d** 89 **p** 90. C Hoole *Ches* 89-92; C Lancaster St Thos *Blackb* 92-96; V Harrow Trin St Mich *Lon* 96-03; Dir of Ords Willesden Area 98-03; V S Croydon Em *S'wark* from 03; AD Croydon Cen from 09; Hon Can S'wark Cathl from 14. *33 Hurst Way, South Croydon CR2 7AP* T: (020) 8688 6676 E: tmapstone@emmanuelcroydon.org.uk

MARAIS, Rudolph James. b 41. St Bede's Coll Umtata BTh. **d** 81 **p** 82. S Africa 81-85 and from 87; C Belmont *S'wark* 85-87. *PO Box 101, Jefferys Bay, 6300 South Africa* T: (0027) (42) 291 1659 M: 82-578 7522

MARBUS, Alida Janny. *See* WHITTOCK, Alida Janny

MARCER, Graham John. b 52. Ripon Coll Cuddesdon 75. **d** 78 **p** 79. C Sherborne w Castleton and Lillington *Sarum* 78-81; C Christchurch *Win* 81-84; V Southampton St Jude 84-90; P-in-c Moordown 90-91; C Sheff St Cecilia Parson Cross 91-93; V Balby 93-00; RD W Doncaster 97-00; V Radford *Cov* 00-11; AD Cov N 01-04; rtd 11. *1 Bosworth Close, Ashby de la Zouch LE65 1LB* T: (01530) 563767
E: graham.marcer@btinternet.com

MARCETTI, Alvin Julian. b 41. San Jose State Univ BA 66 Santa Clara Univ MA 76. Cranmer Hall Dur 85. **d** 87 **p** 88. C Stepney St Dunstan and All SS *Lon* 87-91; Chapl Lon Guildhall Univ 91-92 and 92-96; Chapl Homerton Univ Hosp NHS Trust Lon 96-03; Chapl City and Hackney Community Services NHS Trust 96-03; rtd 03. *5 Burrs Lane, Providence RI 02904, USA* E: almarcetti@yahoo.co.uk

MARCH, Alan Mervyn. b 48. Open Univ BA 91 CPFA 73. EAMTC 00. **d** 03 **p** 04. NSM Northampton St Alb *Pet* 03-06; NSM Northampton Ch Ch from 06; NSM Northampton H Sepulchre w St Andr and St Lawr from 06; NSM Northampton St Mich w St Edm from 06; NSM Northampton H Trin and St Paul from 06. *236 Beech Avenue, Northampton NN3 2LE* T: (01604) 405722 E: march100@o2.co.uk

MARCH, Andrew. b 81. UEA BA 03. St Jo Coll Nottm MA 09. **d** 09 **p** 10. C Werrington and Wetley Rocks *Lich* 09-12; V Allesley Park and Whoberley *Cov* from 12. *St Christopher's Vicarage, 99 Buckingham Rise, Coventry CV5 9HF* M: 07816-998642 E: revandymarch@googlemail.com

MARCH, Charles Anthony Maclea (Tony). b 32. CCC Cam BA 55 MA 70. Oak Hill Th Coll 55. **d** 57 **p** 58. C S Croydon Em *Cant* 57-60; C Eastbourne H Trin *Chich* 60-63; V Whitehall Park St Andr Hornsey Lane *Lon* 63-67; V Tunbridge Wells H Trin w Ch Ch *Roch* 67-82; V Prestonville St Luke *Chich* 82-97; rtd 97; PtO *Roch* from 99. *The Barn, 2 Town Farm Dairy, Brenchley Road, Brenchley, Tonbridge TN12 7PA* T: (01892) 722802

MARCH, Gerald. b 44. Nottm Univ BA 75. Oak Hill Th Coll 92. **d** 95 **p** 96. C Sandgate St Paul w Folkestone St Geo *Cant* 95-99; P-in-c Southampton St Mark *Win* 99-03; V 03-09; rtd 09; PtO *Ox* from 10; *Cov* 13-15. *Dovetrees, 2B Curbridge Road, Witney OX28 5JR* E: rev.gerald@gmail.com

MARCH, Jonathan. b 79. Wycliffe Hall Ox. **d** 05 **p** 06. C Brompton H Trin w Onslow Square St Paul *Lon* 05-11; V Oseney Crescent St Luke from 11. *1 Bartholomew Road, London NW5 2AH*

MARCH, Peter John. b 75. Cov Univ BA 97 Univ Coll Worc PGCE 98. SWMTC 10. **d** 13 **p** 14. C Heavitree and St Mary Steps *Ex* from 13. *10 Sherwood Close, Exeter EX2 5DX*

MARCHAND, Canon Rex Anthony Victor (Toby). b 47. K Coll Lon BD 69 AKC 69. St Aug Coll Cant 69. **d** 70 **p** 71. C Leigh Park *Portsm* 70-73; C Bp's Hatfield *St Alb* 73-80; R Deal St Leon and St Rich and Sholden *Cant* 80-85; RD Sandwich 91-94; Hon Can Cant Cathl 94-95; V Bishop's Stortford St Mich *St Alb* 95-12; RD Bishop's Stortford 03-06; Hon Can St Alb 08-12; rtd 12; PtO *Cant* from 13. *12 Langton Close, Deal CT14 6UL* T: (01304) 371419
E: tandmmarchand@ntlworld.com

MARCHANT, Canon Iain William. b 26. Wells Th Coll 59. **d** 60 **p** 61. C Dalston *Carl* 60-63; V Hawkesbury *Glouc* 63-76; R Newent 76-85; Hon Can Glouc Cathl 84-92; R Newent and Gorsley w Cliffords Mesne 85-92; rtd 92; PtO *Glouc* from 92. *34 Parklands, Wotton-under-Edge GL12 7LT* T: (01453) 844779

MARCHANT, John Bennet. b 46. St Jo Coll Nottm. **d** 06 **p** 07. Aux Min Powerscourt w Kilbride *D & G* 06-12; P-in-c Dublin Clontarf 12-13; P-in-c Dublin Irishtown w Donnybrook 13-14; Bp's C from 14; Chapl Dublin City Univ from 07. *The Rectory, 4 Ailesbury Grove, Donnybrook, Dublin 4, Republic of Ireland* T: (00353) (1) 494 2408 M: 87-239 3682
E: revjmarchant@yahoo.ie *or* john.marchant@dcu.ie

MARCHANT, Neil. b 62. Sheff Poly BA 84. St Jo Coll Nottm 12. **d** 15. C Penistone and Thurlstone *Sheff* from 15. *87 High Street, Penistone, Sheffield S36 6BR* M: 07808-081344
E: neilmarchant2@googlemail.com

MARCHANT (née ROWLAND), Sally Margaret. b 58. SEITE. **d** 10 **p** 11. C Melton Mowbray *Leic* 10-13; TV Totton *Win* from 13. *The Vicarage, Cooks Lane, Calmore, Southampton SO40 2RU*
E: revsallymarchant@gmail.com

MARCHMENT, Mrs Ethel Diane. b 53. Ridley Hall Cam. **d** 11 **p** 12. NSM Douglas St Ninian *S & M* 11-14; NSM W Coast from 14. *Thie Peddyr, Glen Vine Road, Glen Vine, Isle of Man IM4 4HG* T: (01624) 851754
E: dianemarchment@hotmail.com

MARCUS, Mrs Candice Ann. b 52. FInstLEx 80. Trin Coll Bris 05. **d** 07 **p** 08. C Timsbury and Priston *B & W* 07-10; C Timsbury w Priston, Camerton and Dunkerton 10-11; TV Whitton *Sarum* from 11. *Willow Tree Cottage, Throop Road, Templecombe BA8 0HR* T: (01963) 370603 M: 07788-437063
E: revcandicemarcus@gmail.com

MARCUS, Sarah Caroline. *See* ROWLAND JONES, Sarah Caroline

MARCUSSEN, Mrs Yolande Roberta. b 47. SEITE 98. **d** 01 **p** 02. NSM Bromley Common St Aug *Roch* 01-03; NSM Orpington All SS 03; Asst Chapl HM Pris Roch 03-06; Chapl 03-06; rtd 06; PtO *Roch* from 09. *24 Lucerne Road, Orpington BR6 0EP* T: (01689) 833599 E: yolande.marcussen@ntlworld.com

MARFLITT, Belinda-Jane. b 59. STETS 10. **d** 13 **p** 14. C Wimborne Minster *Sarum* from 13; C Witchampton, Stanbridge and Long Crichel etc from 15; C Horton, Chalbury, Hinton Martel and Holt St Jas from 15. *29 Venator Place, Wimborne BH21 1DQ* T: (01202) 736931 E: supermum2@hotmail.co.uk

MARGAM, Archdeacon of. *See* MORRIS, The Ven Philip Gregory

MARGARET ANNE, Sister. *See* McALISTER, Margaret Elizabeth Anne

MARGARET JOY, Sister. *See* HARRIS, Margaret Claire

MARIES, Phillip John.. C Normanton *Leeds* from 15. *54 Dalefield Road, Normanton WF6 1HD* T: (01924) 891578
E: phil@pmaries.freeserve.co.uk

MARINER, Aris. b 43. Alexandria Univ BSc 65. St Alb Minl Tr Scheme 84. **d** 87. NSM Stevenage H Trin *St Alb* 87-14. *13 Church Lane, Stevenage SG1 3QS* T: (01438) 365596

MARION EVA, Sister. *See* RECORD, Marion Eva

MARK, Timothy John. b 34. Bris Univ BA 57 PGCE 58 MLitt 68 MEd 71 Leeds Univ PhD 79. Didsbury Methodist Coll 54. **d** 59 **p** 61. India 59-69; PtO *Sheff* 73-08. *Spindrift, 61 Craig-yr-Eos Road, Ogmore-by-Sea, Bridgend CF32 0PH* T: (01665) 880908
E: tjm@timothymark.plus.com

MARKBY, Ms Jane Elizabeth. b 67. Em Coll Cam BA 88 Homerton Coll Cam PGCE 89. Ridley Hall Cam 00. **d** 02 **p** 03. NSM Edmonton All SS w St Mich *Lon* 02-06; Chapl Haberdashers' Aske's Sch Elstree 06-10; Chapl Berkhamsted Sch Herts from 10. *Adelbert House, Mill Street, Berkamsted HP4 2BA* T: (01442) 358095
E: jmarkby@berkhamstedschool.org

MARKBY, Peter John Jenner. b 38. Em Coll Cam BA 60. Clifton Th Coll 62. **d** 64 **p** 65. C Tufnell Park St Geo *Lon* 64-68; C Crowborough *Chich* 68-73; C Polegate 73-77; R Southover 77-02; rtd 02; PtO *Chich* from 02. *66 Leylands Road, Burgess Hill RH15 8AJ* T: (01444) 870831
E: petermarkby@gmail.com

MARKEY, Andrew John. b 73. Univ of Wales (Swansea) BSc 96. Westcott Ho Cam BTh 02. **d** 02 **p** 03. C Wotton-under-Edge w Ozleworth, N Nibley etc *Glouc* 02-06; Chapl Ox Brookes Univ 09-12; Chapl Luxembourg *Eur* from 12. *Address temp unknown*

MARKHAM, Deryck O'Leary. b 28. Oak Hill Th Coll 66. **d** 68 **p** 69. C Purley Ch Ch *S'wark* 68-72; V E Budleigh and Bicton *Ex* 72-93; RD Aylesbeare 89-93; rtd 93; PtO *Ex* 93-03; *Win* from 03. *8 Milford House, Milford on Sea, Lymington SO41 0QJ* T: (01590) 643515 E: dolm@onetel.com

MARKS, Allan Willi. b 56. Cranmer Hall Dur 92. **d** 94 **p** 95. C Barnoldswick w Bracewell *Bradf* 94-96; C Willington *Newc* 96-98; TV 98-02; V Newc H Cross 02-09; P-in-c Newc Ch Ch w St Ann from 09; AD Newc Cen from 13. *St Ann's Vicarage, 11 Gibson Street, Newcastle upon Tyne NE1 6PY* T: 0191-232 0516 E: fatherallan@blueyonder.co.uk

MARKS, Anthony Alfred. b 28. AKC 53. **d** 54 **p** 55. C Fleetwood St Pet *Blackb* 54-58; V Burnley St Cuth 58-63; Chapl RN 63-83; P-in-c Bradninch *Ex* 83-88; R Bradninch and Clyst Hydon 88-90; rtd 90; PtO *B & W* from 90; QHC from 81. *45 Mondyes Court, Milton Lane, Wells BA5 2QX* T: (01749) 671609

MARKS, Dennis Ray. b 37. Lon Univ BSc 58 PhD 67 PGCE 59 Univ of Wales (Ban) BTh 04 CChem 85 MRSC 85. **d** 06 **p** 07. OLM Willesden St Mary *Guildf* 06-12; PtO from 12. *Green Tiles, Shaftesbury Road, Woking GU22 7DU* T: (01483) 762030 E: ray.marks@mypostoffice.co.uk

MARKS, Mrs June Margaret. b 49. LCTP. **d** 08. NSM Oakworth *Bradf* 08-09. *49 Larkfield Terrace, Oakworth, Keighley BD22 7HJ* T: (01535) 648328 E: emrysandjune@talktalk.net

MARKS, Robert Wesley. b 58. Guelph Univ (Canada) BSc 81. Cranmer Hall Dur 03. **d** 05 **p** 06. C Baxenden *Blackb* 05-06; C Anchorsholme 06-09; P-in-c Ribby cum Wrea and Weeton 09-11; V from 11. *The Vicarage, 1 Vicarage Close, Wrea Green, Preston PR4 2PQ* T: (01772) 687644 E: wesmarks@btinternet.com

MARKS, Timothy John. b 45. Man Univ BA 76 Anglia Poly Univ MA 96. **d** 88 **p** 89. NSM Burton and Sopley *Win* 88-91; R Croxton and Eltisley *Ely* 91-96; R Graveley w Papworth St Agnes w Yelling etc 91-96; Dir Network Counselling and Tr 96-05; Nat Adv for Personal/Spiritual Development YMCA 05-07. *102 Woodfarm Road, Malvern WR14 4PP* T: (01684) 564925 M: 07817-465213 E: tim@timmarksconsulting.com

MARL, David John. b 42. ARCA 67. **d** 01 **p** 02. OLM Okeford *Sarum* 01-12; PtO from 12. *Bow Cottage, Shute Lane, Iwerne Minster, Blandford Forum DT11 8LZ* T: (01747) 812048 E: burgoyne.marl@tiscali.co.uk

MARLEY, The Very Revd Alan Gordon. b 59. Birm Univ BA 89. Qu Coll Birm 87. **d** 89 **p** 90. C Blandford Forum and Langton Long *Sarum* 89-93; Chapl HM YOI Aylesbury 93-97; I Fermoy Union *C, C & R* 97-03; Bp's Dom Chapl 99-03; Dean Cloyne from 03; I Cloyne Union from 03; Dioc Dir of Ords from 05. *The Deanery, Deanery Road, Midleton, Co Cork, Republic of Ireland* T: (00353) (21) 463 1449 E: dean@cloyne.anglican.org

MARLOW, Jonathan James. b 76. SS Hild & Bede Coll Dur MEng 99. Wycliffe Hall Ox BTh 06. **d** 06 **p** 07. C Elburton *Ex* 06-10; P-in-c Pennycross from 10. *St Pancras' Vicarage, 66 Glentor Road, Plymouth PL3 5TR* T: (01752) 395300 E: jon.marlow@stps.org.uk

MARLOW, Mrs Kathryn Elizabeth. b 67. STETS 12. **d** 15. NSM Portsea St Cuth *Portsm* from 15. *276 Powerscourt Road, Portsmouth PO2 7JR* T: (023) 9236 2259 M: 07772-061118 E: stanandkate@ntlworld.com

MARLOW (née SIBBALD), Mrs Olwyn Eileen. b 57. Aston Tr Scheme 85 Linc Th Coll 87. **d** 89 **p** 94. Par Dn Wythenshawe St Martin *Man* 89-93; Par Dn Baguley 93-94; C 94-95; Asst Chapl Cen Man Healthcare NHS Trust 95-00; NSM Newall Green St Fran *Man* 97-98; rtd 01; NSM Wythenshawe *Man* 01-05; PtO from 05; *Ches* from 05. *28 Arcadia Avenue, Sale M33 3SA* T: 0161-962 9292

MARLOW, Ms Tracy Margaret. b 64. St Mellitus Coll 12. **d** 15. C Rayleigh *Chelmsf* from 15. *15 The Limes, Rayleigh SS6 8TH* M: 07886-442264 T: (01268) 770752 E: t-marlow@hotmail.co.uk *or* tracy.marlo@parishofrayleigh.org.uk

MARNHAM, Preb Charles Christopher. b 51. Jes Coll Cam BA 73 MA 77. Cranmer Hall Dur. **d** 77 **p** 78. C Brompton H Trin *Lon* 77-78; C Brompton H Trin w Onslow Square St Paul 78-80; C Linthorpe *York* 80-84; R Haughton le Skerne *Dur* 84-95; V Ches Square St Mich w St Phil *Lon* from 95; Preb St Paul's Cathl from 10. *St Michael's Vicarage, 4 Chester Square, London SW1W 9HH* T: (020) 7730 8889 F: 7730 0043 E: charles@stmichaelschurch.org.uk

MARNS, Nigel Geoffrey. b 63. Univ of Wales (Abth) BSc(Econ) 85 Birm Univ BD 92 MA 10. Qu Coll Birm 90. **d** 93 **p** 94. C Addington *S'wark* 93-96; P-in-c W Bromwich Gd Shep

w St Jo *Lich* 96-01; V Bromsgrove St Jo *Worc* 01-09; R Ludgvan, Marazion, St Hilary and Perranuthnoe *Truro* from 09. *The Rectory, Ludgvan, Penzance TR20 8EZ* T: (01736) 740784 E: nigelmarns@yahoo.co.uk

✠**MARONA, The Most Revd Joseph Biringi Hassan.** b 41. Bp Gwynne Th Coll 78. **d** 81 **p** 82 **c** 84. Chapl Rumbek State Secondary Sch Sudan 81-82; Chapl Maridi Teachers' Tr Coll 82-83; Area Bp Maridi 85-89; Bp Maridi 89-00; Dean of Prov Sudan from 98; Abp Sudan and Bp Juba from 00. *ECS Liaison Office, PO Box 604, Khartoum, Sudan* T: (00249) (811) 20040 *or* (11) 485720 F: (811) 20065 (11) 485717 E: ecsprovince@hotmail.com

MARQUEZ, Edilberto. b 57. Bible Sem Alliance Peru BA 80 Westmr Coll Ox MTh 93. St Steph Ho Ox 92. **d** 94 **p** 95. C Reading St Jo *Ox* 94-98; C New Malden and Coombe *S'wark* 98-01; P-in-c Bucklebury w Marlston *Ox* 01-08; P-in-c Bradfield and Stanford Dingley 04-08; P-in-c Woodley 08-09; V from 09. *6 Denmark Avenue, Woodley, Reading RG5 4RS* T: 0118-969 6540 E: emarquez@tiscali.co.uk

MARR (née PARKER), Mrs Anne Elizabeth. b 46. Hull Univ BSc 67 CertEd 68. NEOC 91. **d** 96 **p** 12. NSM Whorlton *Newc* 96-97; NSM Chapel House 97-14; Chapl Newc City Health NHS Trust 96-01; Chapl Newc Mental Health Unit 01-14; rtd 14. *26 The Chesters, Newcastle upon Tyne NE5 1AF* T: 0191-267 4808

MARR, Derek Paul. b 33. Dur Univ TCert 69. **d** 00 **p** 01. OLM Chapel House *Newc* from 00. *26 The Chesters, Newcastle upon Tyne NE5 1AF* T: 0191-267 4808

MARR, Canon Donald Radley. b 37. K Coll Lon 57. St Aid Birkenhead 61. **d** 64 **p** 65. C Macclesfield St Mich *Ches* 64-66; C Sale St Anne 66-67; V Marthall 67-72; C W Kirby St Bridget 72-76; R Waverton 76-83; R Nantwich 83-87; RD 86-87; RD Malpas 87-91; V Bunbury 87-91; rtd 91; Dioc Rural Officer *Ches* 91-07; Hon Can Ches Cathl 91-92; PtO *Truro* from 94; *Ches* from 07. *St Boniface, 5 Hockenhull Crescent, Tarvin, Chester CH3 8LJ* T: (01829) 741302 E: revsdonaldandmargaret@btinternet.com

MARR, Mrs Margaret Rose. b 36. JP 81. St Mary's Coll Ban TCert 56 Open Univ BA 00. Ripon Coll Cuddesdon 02. **d** 02 **p** 03. NSM Tarvin *Ches* 02-11; PtO *Truro* from 02; *Ches* from 11. *St Boniface, 5 Hockenhull Crescent, Tarvin, Chester CH3 8LJ* T: (01829) 741302 E: revsdonaldandmargaret@btinternet.com

MARR, Peter. b 36. Reading Univ PhD 78. Ox NSM Course 84. **d** 87 **p** 88. NSM Reading St Giles *Ox* 87-89; C Beverley Minster *York* 90-92; P-in-c Beckenham St Barn *Roch* 92-96; V 96-03; rtd 03; PtO *Ex* from 04. *31 Kingsley Road, Plymouth PL4 6QP* T: (01752) 228426 E: pbmarr@dircon.co.uk

MARRIAGE, Sophia Briony. b 71. Rob Coll Cam BA 93 Edin Univ PhD 98 Glas Univ MTh 05. TISEC 03. **d** 05 **p** 06. C Edin St Martin 05-11; R Edin St Mark from 11. *15 Viewforth Terrace, Edinburgh EH10 4LJ* T: 0131-229 8939 *or* 629 1219 E: sophia.marriage@stmarksportobello.org

MARRIOTT (née REID), Mrs Amanda Joy. b 63. Nottm Univ BTh 92. Linc Th Coll 89. **d** 92 **p** 96. Par Dn Rothwell *Ripon* 92-94; C 94-95; C Manston 95-97; C Wetherby 97-01; P-in-c Water Eaton *Ox* 01-06; AD Milton Keynes 05-06; P-in-c Sherington w Chicheley, N Crawley, Astwood etc 06-09; R 09-15; TR Duston *Pet* from 15. *The Rectory, 3 Main Road, Duston, Northampton NN5 6JB* T: (01908) 610521 E: aj.marriott123@gmail.com

MARRIOTT, Frank Lewis. b 29. Lich Th Coll 57. **d** 60 **p** 61. C Earlsdon *Cov* 60-64; R Tysoe w Compton Winyates and Oxhill 64-70; P-in-c Cov St Marg 70-77; R Ufton 77-83; V Long Itchington 77-83; RD Southam 82-89; V Long Itchington and Marton 83-95; rtd 95; PtO *Heref* 95-13. *12 Traherne Close, Ledbury HR8 2JF* T: (01531) 634576

MARRIOTT, Stanley Richard. b 36. AKC 60 Warwick Univ MA 92. **d** 61 **p** 62. C Coleshill *Birm* 61-64; C Maxstoke 61-64; V Ansley *Cov* 64-78; Org Sec (E Midl) CECS 79-83; P-in-c Baxterley w Hurley and Wood End and Merevale etc *Birm* 83-84; R 84-87; R Newton Regis w Seckington and Shuttington 87-97; rtd 97; PtO *B & W* from 97. *Dunkery Pleck, Wootton Courtenay, Minehead TA24 8RH* T: (01643) 841058 E: joanmarriott@btinternet.com

MARRISON, Geoffrey Edward. b 23. Lon Univ BA 48 PhD 67. Bps' Coll Cheshunt 49 Kirchliche Hochschule Berlin 50. **d** 51 **p** 52. C Wormley *St Alb* 51-52; SPG Miss Selangor Malaya 52-55; C St Andr Cathl Singapore 55-56; C Radlett *St Alb* 56-57; C St Botolph Aldgate w H Trin Minories *Lon* 57-58; V Crookes St Tim *Sheff* 58-61; SPG India 62-64; PtO *Cant* 64-69; LtO 69-82; PtO *Carl* 83-07; Tutor Carl Dioc Tr Course 83-07. *c/o The Parish Office, 20 Church Walk, Ulverston LA12 7EN* T: (01229) 588081

MARROW, David Edward Armfield. b 42. Nottm Univ BA 65 MA. Tyndale Hall Bris 65. **d** 67 **p** 68. C Clifton Ch Ch w Em

Bris 67-70; BCMS Ethiopia 70-75; N Area Sec BCMS 75-77; C-in-c Ryde St Jas Prop Chpl *Portsm* 77-84; V Worthing St Geo *Chich* 84-07; rtd 07. *West View, 65 St Michael's Road, St Helens, Ryde PO33 1YJ* T: (01983) 872729

MARRY, Sarah Louise. d 11 **p** 12. C Douglas Union w Frankfield *C, C & R* 11-15; P-in-c Cork St Ann's Union from 15. *The Rectory, 49 Ard na Laoi, Montenotte, Cork, Republic of Ireland* M: 86-171 3936   T: (00353) (21) 229 1371 *or* 455 2605
E: sarah_marry@hotmail.com *or* sarah.marry@stlukeshome.ie

MARSBURG, John Edward. b 53. Oak Hill Th Coll BA 96. Coll of Resurr Mirfield 98. **d** 99 **p** 00. NSM Selby Abbey *York* 99-02; R Lenzie *Glas* 02-06; I Donacavey w Barr *Clogh* 06-15; rtd 15. *Address temp unknown*

MARSDEN, Canon Andrew Philip. b 63. Keble Coll Ox BA 85 MA 90 Birm Univ MA 86. Wycliffe Hall Ox BA 90. **d** 91 **p** 92. C Newport *St Jo Portsm* 91-94; C Cowplain 94-97; V Wokingham St Sebastian *Ox* from 97; Hon Can Ch Ch from 15. *St Sebastian's Vicarage, Nine Mile Ride, Wokingham RG40 3AT*   T: (01344) 761050   E: revamarsden@tiscali.co.uk

MARSDEN, Andrew Robert. b 49. AKC 71. St Aug Coll Cant 68. **d** 72 **p** 73. C New Addington *Cant* 72-75; C Prudhoe *Newc* 75-77; Asst Chapl HM Pris Wakef 77; Chapl HM Borstal Portland 77-82; Chapl HM YOI Onley 82-89; V Ulceby Gp *Linc* 89-98; Chapl Calderdale Healthcare NHS Trust 98-01; Chapl St Andr Hospice Grimsby 01-05; Community Chapl *Linc* 01-05; Chapl Hull and E Yorks Hosps NHS Trust 05-13; rtd 13. *Address temp unknown*

MARSDEN, Canon Carole. b 44. Avery Hill Coll TCert 65 Sheff Poly DipEd 87. NOC 88. **d** 91 **p** 94. NSM Saddleworth *Man* 91-92; Par Dn 92-94; C 94-95; P-in-c Oldham St Paul 95-02; C Werneth 98-02; P-in-c Shap w Swindale and Bampton w Mardale *Carl* 02-08; P-in-c Orton and Tebay w Ravenstonedale etc 07-08; rtd 08; PtO *Carl* from 09; RD Appleby 09-13; Hon Can Carl Cathl from 11; PtO *Blackb* from 13. *Fairfield, Faraday Road, Kirby Stephen CA17 4QL*   T: (017683) 71279
M: 07866-006849   E: carole.sam@hotmail.com

MARSDEN, Mrs Diana Marion (Dodie). b 53. Deakin Univ Australia BEd 88. STETS 00. **d** 03 **p** 04. NSM Hurstbourne Priors, Longparish etc *Win* from 03. *Little Brook House, Church Street, St Mary Bourne, Andover SP11 6BG*
T: (01264) 738211   E: dodie.marsden@ukgateway.net

MARSDEN, The Very Revd John Joseph. b 53. York Univ BA 74 Nottm Univ MTh 81 Kent Univ PhD 88. St Jo Coll Nottm 77. **d** 80 **p** 81. C Leigh St Mary *Man* 80-83; Hon C Chatham St Steph *Roch* 83-91; Ind Chapl 83-91; Lect Systematic Th CITC and TCD from 91; I Newbridge w Carnalway and Kilcullen *M & K* 97-14; I Kildare w Kilmeague and Curragh 06-14; Dean Kildare 06-14; rtd 14. *Firgrove House, Military Road, Killiney, Co Dublin, Republic of Ireland*
E: johnmarsden@eircom.net

MARSDEN, Canon Joyce. b 47. Eliz Gaskell Coll Man TCert 68. Trin Coll Bris 78. **dss** 83 **d** 87 **p** 94. Wavertree H Trin *Liv* 83-85; Much Woolton 85-97; Par Dn 87-94; C 94-97; TV Parr 97-05; C 05-07; Hon Can Liv Cathl 03-07; rtd 07. *4 Mackets Close, Liverpool L25 9NU*   T: 0151-428 2798
E: joyceamarsden@hotmail.co.uk

MARSDEN, Michael John. b 59. St Mich Coll Llan 78. **d** 82 **p** 83. C Neath w Llantwit *Llan* 82-85; Asst Chapl Univ Hosp of Wales Cardiff 85-89; V Graig *Llan* 89-93; P-in-c Cilfynydd 89-93; R Merthyr Tydfil St Dav 93-01; Chapl Gwent Healthcare NHS Trust from 01. *Nevill Hall Hospital, Brecon Road, Abergavenny NP7 7EG*   T: (01873) 732112
E: michael.marsden@gwent.wales.nhs.uk

MARSDEN, Robert. b 59. Ch Ch Ox BA 81 PGCE 82. Oak Hill Th Coll BA 92. **d** 92 **p** 93. C Sevenoaks St Nic *Roch* 92-95; Chapl Fettes Coll Edin 95-99; C-in-c Buxton Trin Prop Chpl *Derby* from 99. *37 Temple Road, Buxton SK17 9BA*
T: (01298) 73656   E: bobinbuxton@sky.com

MARSDEN, Robert James. b 56. Ch Ch Coll Cant BEd 79. Oak Hill Th Coll 90. **d** 94 **p** 95. C Margate H Trin *Cant* 94-98; P-in-c Brinton, Briningham, Hunworth, Stody etc *Nor* 98-08; P-in-c Gressenhall w Longham w Wendling etc from 08; RD Dereham in Mitford 13-15. *The Rectory, Bittering Street, Gressenhall, Dereham NR20 4EB*   T: (01362) 860102
E: robert@camelhome.co.uk

MARSDEN, Robert William. b 24. TCD BA 49 MA 52. CITC 50. **d** 50 **p** 51. C Dublin St Jas *D & G* 50-54; Asst Chapl Miss to Seamen 54-58; I Currin w Drum *Clogh* 58-66; I Clones w Killeevan 66-94; Prec Clogh Cathl 86-94; rtd 94. *30 Claremont Park, Sandymount, Dublin 4, Republic of Ireland*
T: (00353) (1) 668 0210

MARSDEN, Samuel Edward. b 44. Keble Coll Ox BA 66 MA 85. Linc Th Coll 66. **d** 68 **p** 69. C Liskeard w St Keyne *Truro* 68-72; R Gerrans w St Anthony in Roseland 72-77; V Kowloon Ch Ch Hong Kong 77-81; P-in-c Ingrave *Chelmsf* 81-82; P-in-c Gt Warley w Childerditch 81-82; R Gt Warley w Childerditch

and Ingrave 82-89; R Gilgandra Australia 89-93; R Kelso 94-00; Adn Wylde 00-01; R Parkes 01-07; Adn Bathurst 05-07; R Coffs Harbour 07-10; rtd 10; PtO *Ely* 10-12. *7 Penmare Court, Hayle TR27 4RD*   T: (01736) 756669
E: samuelmarsden@hotmail.com

MARSDEN-JONES, Watkin David. b 22. St D Coll Lamp BA 48. **d** 49 **p** 50. C Flint *St As* 49-54; C Forest Row *Chich* 54-56; V Copthorne 56-70; RD E Grinstead 66-70; V Bosham 70-86; rtd 86; PtO *Chich* from 86. *10 Fairfield Road, Bosham, Chichester PO18 8JH*   T: (01243) 575053   E: dmj@wdmarjon.go-plus.net

MARSH, Anderson Jason. b 74. STETS 06. **d** 09. NSM Sheet *Portsm* from 09. *12 Rother Close, Petersfield GU31 4DN*
T: (01730) 268156   E: amarsh@rotherbank.co.uk

MARSH, Anthony David. b 29. Roch Th Coll 64. **d** 66 **p** 67. C Liskeard w St Keyne *Truro* 66-69; R Wrentham w Benacre and Covehithe *St E* 69-75; R Wrentham w Benacre, Covehithe, Frostenden etc 75-80; P-in-c Beyton and Hessett 80-86; C Felixstowe St Jo 86-88; rtd 88; PtO *St E* 88-03 and from 07; B & W 01-03. *24 Winston Close, Felixstowe IP11 2FA*

MARSH, Carol Ann. *See* HATHORNE, Carol Ann

MARSH, Colin Arthur. b 54. Edin Univ PhD 02. St Jo Coll Nottm 79. **d** 82 **p** 83. C Kirkby *Liv* 82-86; TV St Luke in the City 86-91; P-in-c Chingola St Barn Zambia 91-95; PtO *Edin* 95-03; Tutor United Coll of Ascension Selly Oak 03-06; Ecum Development Officer Chs Together *Birm* from 06. *St George's Community Hub, Great Hampton Row, Birmingham B19 3JG*
T: 0121-236 3966   E: office@birminghamchurches.org.uk

MARSH, David. b 32. St Jo Coll Dur BA 54. Cranmer Hall Dur. **d** 57 **p** 58. C Bilston St Leon *Lich* 57-62; LtO Dio Maseno Kenya 63-66; Chapl Scargill Ho 67-69; Adn S Maseno 70-72; V Meole Brace *Lich* 72-77; V Westlands St Andr 77-86; V Trentham 86-96; P-in-c Alstonfield, Butterton, Warslow w Elkstone etc 96-99; rtd 99; PtO *Ches* from 99; Chapl Mid Cheshire Hosps Trust from 02. *31 Spring Gardens, Nantwich CW5 5SH*   T: (01270) 610079   E: dlmarsh@btinternet.com

MARSH, Mrs Deborah Lindsay. b 59. Westcott Ho Cam 13. **d** 15. C Hardingstone and Piddington w Horton *Pet* from 15. *1 Willoughby Way, Piddington, Northampton NN7 2EH*
M: 07919-385314   E: debmarsh37@yahoo.com

MARSH, Donald. b 35. WMMTC. **d** 90 **p** 91. NSM Wednesbury St Bart *Lich* 90-03; NSM Wednesbury Deanery 03-13; PtO from 13. *Holly Rise, 19 Trouse Lane, Wednesbury WS10 7HR*
T/F: 0121-556 0095

MARSH, Mrs Elaine Daphne. b 42. **d** 07 **p** 08. OLM Askerswell, Loders, Powerstock and Symondsbury *Sarum* 07-12; NSM from 12. *Powerstock Mill Farm, West Milton, Bridport DT6 3SL*
T: (01308) 485213   F: 485160

MARSH, Francis John. b 47. York Univ BA 69 DPhil 76 ATCL 65 ARCM 66 ARCO 71. Oak Hill Th Coll 72 Selw Coll Cam 73. **d** 75 **p** 76. C Cambridge St Matt *Ely* 75-78; C Pitsmoor w Wicker *Sheff* 79; C Pitsmoor w Ellesmere 79-81; C Crookes St Thos 81-85; V S Ossett *Wakef* 85-96; RD Dewsbury 93-96; Adn Blackb 96-01; Bp's Adn on Hosp Chapls 96-01; P-in-c Emley *Leeds* from 11; P-in-c Flockton cum Denby Grange from 11. *14 Grange Drive, Emley, Huddersfield HD8 9SF*   T: (01924) 849161   E: john.marsh747@sky.com

MARSH, John. b 60. **d** 10 **p** 11. OLM Ockley, Okewood and Forest Green *Guildf* from 10. *2 Chatsworth Row, Caburn Heights, Crawley RH11 8RT*   T: (01293) 401639
E: home@john-marsh.co.uk

MARSH, Lawrence Allan. b 36. Sarum Th Coll 66. **d** 67 **p** 68. C Waterlooville *Portsm* 67-70; V Shedfield 70-76; R Fen Ditton *Ely* 76-01; P-in-c Horningsea 83-01; rtd 01; PtO *Ely* from 01. *The Old Bakery, 22 High Street, Bottisham, Cambridge CB25 9DA*
T: (01223) 811314   E: landjmarsh@aol.com *or* l.marsh142@btinternet.com

MARSH, Leonard Stuart Alexander. b 55. Hull Univ BA 77 SOAS Lon MA 00. Linc Th Coll 77. **d** 79 **p** 80. C Eltham St Barn *S'wark* 79-81; C Camberwell St Giles 81-83; Hon C Clifton St Paul *Bris* 83-86; Asst Chapl Bris Univ 83-86; Area Sec (Dio S'wark) USPG 86-91; Chapl Guildhall Sch of Music and Drama *Lon* 91-97; Chapl City Univ 91-98; NSM Clerkenwell H Redeemer and St Mark 94-95; P-in-c Finsbury St Clem w St Barn and St Matt 95-01; P-in-c Upper Norwood All SS *S'wark* 01-08; V from 08; AD Croydon N from 12. *The Vicarage, 49 Chevening Road, London SE19 3TD*   T: (020) 8653 2820

MARSH, Mrs Margaret Ann. b 37. Nottm Univ BSc 59 Ox Univ DipEd 60 Lambeth STh 87 Newc Univ MA 93 Man Univ MPhil 95. Carl Dioc Tr Course 86. **d** 87. Asst Chapl Garlands Cumberland and Westmoreland Hosps 87-92; Dn Carl Cathl 87-93; NSM Carl St Luke Morton 93-94; Hon Chapl Carl Hosps NHS Trust 94-00; rtd 00; PtO *Carl* 00-02; *St Alb* 02-10. *1 The Maltings, Leighton Buzzard LU7 4BS*   T: (01525) 384655

MARSH, Canon Margaret Evaline. b 47. STETS 96. **d** 99 **p** 00. NSM Tattenham Corner and Burgh Heath *Guildf* 99-03; NSM Epsom St Martin 03-04; P-in-c Walton-on-the-Hill 04-15;

Hon Can Guildf Cathl from 10; PtO from 15. *The Rectory, Breech Lane, Tadworth KT20 7SD* T: (01737) 812105 F: 814333 E: maggiemarsh17@gmail.com

MARSH, Michael John. b 47. Reading Univ BA 69 DipEd 70 York Univ MA 91 Leeds Univ BA 07. Coll of Resurr Mirfield 05. **d** 07 **p** 08. NSM Castleford *Wakef* 07-11; NSM Knottingley and Kellington w Whitley *Leeds* from 11. *The Vicarage, 1 Manor Farm Close, Kellington, Goole DN14 0PF* T: (01977) 663553 M: 07802-734900 E: frmike.marsh@hotmail.com

MARSH, Peter Charles Ernest. b 57. Southn Univ CertEd 03 IEng 87. WEMTC 04. **d** 06 **p** 07. NSM Tyndale *Glouc* from 06. *1 Pitt Court Villas, Pitt Court, North Nibley, Dursley GL11 6EB* T: (01453) 547521 E: pete.marsh@cityofbristol.ac.uk

MARSH, Phillip Edward. b 73. Univ of Wales (Abth) BSc 94 Ch Ch Coll Cant PGCE 96. Wycliffe Hall Ox BTh 02. **d** 02 **p** 03. C Hubberston *St D* 02-05; C Werrington *Pet* 05-09; P-in-c Wilford *S'well* 09-11; R from 11. *St Wilfrid's New Rectory, Main Road, Wilford, Nottingham NG11 7AJ* T: 0115-981 7328 M: 07766-314957 E: revdphilmarsh@aol.com

MARSH, Ralph. b 42. Ches Coll of HE CertEd 63 Birm Univ BPhil 77 Liv Univ MA 00 ACP 65. St Deiniol's Hawarden 86. **d** 88 **p** 89. NSM Tranmere St Paul w St Luke *Ches* 88-90; C Guiseley w Esholt *Bradf* 90-92; V Broughton *St As* 92-94; Hon C W Derby St Jo *Liv* 94; C Ribbleton *Blackb* 94-97; NSM Man Victoria Park 98-00; NSM Croxteth *Liv* 00-07; rtd 07. *47 Rolleston Drive, Wallasey CH45 6XE*

MARSH, Richard St John Jeremy. b 60. Keble Coll Ox BA 82 MA 86 Dur Univ PhD 91. Coll of Resurr Mirfield 83. **d** 85 **p** 86. C Grange St Andr *Ches* 85-87; Solway Fell and Chapl Univ Coll Dur 87-92; Abp's Asst Sec for Ecum Affairs *Cant* 92-95; Abp's Sec for Ecum Affairs 95-01; Hon C Westmr St Steph w St Jo *Lon* 94-96; Assoc P Westmr St Matt 96-01; Can Gib Cathl 95-01; Hon Prov Can Cant Cathl 98-01; Can Res Cant Cathl 01-06; Dir of Educn 01-05; Dir ImpACT Coalition from 07. *Institute of Fundraising, 2 Park Place, 10-12 Lawn Lane, London SW8 1UD* T: (020) 7840 1038 E: richardm@institute-of-fundraising.org.uk

MARSH, Robert Charles. b 58. Linc Univ BA 13. Linc Sch of Th and Min 09. **d** 13 **p** 14. NSM Whitwick, Thringstone and Swannington *Leic* 13-15; NSM Kirby Muxloe 15; NSM Desford and Kirby Muxloe from 15. *43 Chevin Avenue, Leicester LE3 6PX* M: 07557-536926 E: rob.ministry@btinternet.com

MARSH, Robert Christopher. b 53. Ex Univ BEd 76. St Steph Ho Ox 86. **d** 88 **p** 89. C St Leonards Ch Ch and St Mary *Chich* 88-91; TV Crawley 91-00; V Maybridge 00-02. *67 Hythe Crescent, Seaford BN25 3TZ* E: rmarsh6204@aol.com

MARSH, Roger Philip. b 44. K Coll Lon BD 72 AKC 72 Sussex Univ MA 95 K Alfred's Coll Win CertEd 66 FRSA 13. St Aug Coll Cant 73. **d** 73 **p** 74. C Leagrave *St Alb* 73-76; Asst Youth Officer 76-77; Resources Officer 77-80; Chapl Marlborough Coll 80-86; Master Ardingly Coll Jun Sch Haywards Heath 86-95; Hd Master St Geo Sch Windsor 95-99; Chapl Lancing Coll 99-09; rtd 09; PtO *Cant* from 09; Chapl St Edm Sch Cant 10-11; Chapl Heathfield Sch Ascot 11-12; PtO *Chich* from 14. *107 College Road, Deal CT14 6BU* T: (01304) 362851 E: frrogermarsh@hotmail.com

MARSH, Mrs Shelley Ann. b 54. SRN 75 SCM 76. St Jo Coll Nottm 84. **d** 89 **p** 94. Hon C Glas Gd Shep and Ascension 89-96; P-in-c Johnstone and Renfrew 96-06; R Bishopbriggs from 06; Chapl Paisley Univ 98-00. *St James's Rectory, 9 Meadowburn, Bishopbriggs, Glasgow G64 3HA* T: 0141-563 5154 E: revshelleymarsh@ntlworld.com

MARSH, Simon Robert. b 59. Sarum & Wells Th Coll 79. **d** 82 **p** 83. C Mottram in Longdendale w Woodhead *Ches* 82-85; Bp's Dom Chapl *Bradf* 85-87; V Ashton Hayes *Ches* 87-90; V Macclesfield St Paul 90-96; V Ringway 96-01; V Bollington St Jo 01-06; V Bramhall from 06. *The Vicarage, 66 St Michael's Avenue, Bramhall, Stockport SK7 2PG* T: 0161-439 6532 E: frsimon@btinternet.com

MARSH, Steven Philip. b 73. Lon Inst BA 96 Cov Univ MA 98 Lon Sch of Th BA 05. Ripon Coll Cuddesdon MA 13. **d** 13 **p** 14. C Crofton *Portsm* from 13. *3 Martlet Close, Lee-on-the-Solent PO13 8FP* T: (023) 9255 0042 M: 07817-872163 E: s.p.marsh@hotmail.com

MARSH, Susan Edith. b 42. Southn Univ BA 63 CertEd 64. SAOMC 01. **d** 01 **p** 02. NSM Bp's Hatfield *St Alb* 01-05; NSM Bp's Hatfield, Lemsford and N Mymms 05-15; rtd 15; PtO *St Alb* from 15. *141 Handside Lane, Welwyn Garden City AL8 6TA* T: (01707) 329744 E: susanianmarsh@ntlworld.com

MARSHALL, Alexander John. b 53. Leeds Univ BSc. **d** 95 **p** 96. OLM Holbrook, Stutton, Freston, Woolverstone etc *St E* 95-05; PtO 05-06 and from 09. *Well Cottage, 1 The Street, Freston, Ipswich IP9 1AF* T: (01473) 780738

MARSHALL, Alexander Robert. b 43. Glouc Sch of Min 84. **d** 87 **p** 88. NSM Newtown w Llanllwchaiarn w Aberhafesp *St As*

87-00; P-in-c Mochdre 00-06. *31 Bromley College, London Road, Bromley BR1 1PE* T: (020) 8464 9727 E: marshall@rhayapow.kc3ltd.co.uk

MARSHALL, Mrs Alison Mary. b 54. Middx Hosp MB, BS 79 MRCGP 84. SAOMC 98. **d** 01 **p** 02. NSM Reading St Jo *Ox* 01-14; PtO from 14; Progr Co-ordinator Iona Community *Arg* 14-15. *The Iona Community, The Macleod Centre, Isle of Iona PA76 6SN* T: (01681) 700404 M: 07740-944102 E: ali.m@rshall.org.uk

MARSHALL, Ms Alison Rose Marie. b 60. Leic Univ BA 83 Birkbeck Coll Lon MA 86 UEA PGCE 87. Ridley Hall Cam. **d** 95 **p** 96. C Whittlesey, Pondersbridge and Coates *Ely* 95-98; Dep Chapl HM Pris Nor 98-99; Chapl HM Pris Northallerton 99-03; TV Sunderland and Chapl Sunderland Univ *Dur* 03-04; rtd 04. *9 Glamis Avenue, Sunderland SR4 8PB* T: 0191-520 2580 M: 07905-173171

MARSHALL, Andrew Stephen. b 74. UNISA BTh 00. Coll of Resurr Mirfield 02. **d** 99 **p** 00. C Port Elizabeth St Hugh S Africa 00-02; C Port Elizabeth St Jo 02; C Easthampstead *Ox* 03-06; Sen Chapl South Solent Univ *Win* 06-09; Chapl Portsm Univ from 09; Dioc Interfaith Adv from 11. *15 Grays Court, Portsmouth PO1 2PN* T: (023) 9284 3030 E: andyroo74@btinternet.com

MARSHALL, Mrs Angela. b 48. Trin Coll Bris 74. **d** 88 **p** 96. Hon Par Dn Newcastle St Geo *Lich* 88-92; LtO *Eur* 92-94; Dn Versailles 94-96; Asst Chapl 96-04; PtO *St E* 04-07; Hon C Collier Row St Jas and Havering-atte-Bower *Chelmsf* 07-15; rtd 15. *Sous le Figuier, Hameau de Manieu, 32100 Condom, France* E: revdave@dsl.pipex.com

MARSHALL, Basil Eustace Edwin. b 21. OBE 69. Westcott Ho Cam 71. **d** 73 **p** 74. C Edenbridge *Roch* 73-78; P-in-c Matfield 78-85; P-in-c Lamberhurst 78-85; C Farnborough 85-86; rtd 86; PtO *Roch* from 86; *Chich* from 01. *3 Church Close, Brenchley, Tonbridge TN12 7AA* T: (01892) 724403

MARSHALL, Canon Bryan John. b 40. Chich Th Coll 63. **d** 65 **p** 66. C Poulton-le-Fylde *Blackb* 65-68; C S Shore H Trin 68-70; V Wesham 70-74; PV Chich Cathl 74-82; V Boxgrove 82-91; P-in-c Tangmere 82-84; R 84-91; R Westbourne 91-95; V E Preston w Kingston 95-03; Can and Preb Chich Cathl 94-10; rtd 03. *11 Priory Close, Boxgrove, Chichester PO18 0EA* T: (01243) 536337

MARSHALL, Christine. See MARSHALL, Melinda Christine

MARSHALL, Mrs Christine Anne. b 40. Leeds Univ BSc 64. **d** 95 **p** 96. OLM Holbrook, Stutton, Freston, Woolverstone etc *St E* 95-05; PtO 05-06 and from 09. *Well Cottage, 1 The Street, Freston, Ipswich IP9 1AF* T: (01473) 780738 E: marshall@freston40.freeserve.co.uk

MARSHALL, Christopher John. b 56. Edge Hill Coll of HE BEd 79. St Alb Minl Tr Scheme 83. **d** 86 **p** 87. C Biggleswade *St Alb* 86-89; Chapl Asst S Beds Area HA 89-91; Chapl St Helier Hosp Carshalton 91-93; Sen Chapl St Helier NHS Trust 93-98; Gen Office and Bereavement Manager Newham Healthcare NHS Trust from 98; Gen Services Manager from 99. *Newham General Hospital, Glen Road, London E13 8SL* T: (020) 7363 8462

MARSHALL, Preb Christopher John Bickford. b 32. TD 78. AKC 56. **d** 57 **p** 58. C Leatherhead *Guildf* 57-60; C Crewkerne *B & W* 60-63; V Long Sutton 63-72; V Long Sutton w Long Load 72-76; V Wiveliscombe 76-93; RD Tone 78-87; Preb Wells Cathl 88-96; P-in-c Chipstable w Huish Champflower and Clatworthy 93; R Wiveliscombe w Chipstable, Huish Champflower etc 93-96; rtd 96; PtO *B & W* from 96. *Tap Cottage, High Street, Milverton, Taunton TA4 1LL* T: (01823) 400419

MARSHALL, Craig Laurence. b 64. Southn Univ BEd 87 Open Univ MA 93. St Jo Coll Nottm MTh 01. **d** 01 **p** 02. C Staplegrove w Norton Fitzwarren *B & W* 01-04; Chapl K Coll Taunton 04-06; R Aisholt, Enmore, Goathurst, Nether Stowey etc *B & W* 06-14; RD Quantock 12-14; V Hurstbourne Priors, Longparish etc *Win* from 14; Dioc Rural Officer from 14. *The Vicarage, St Mary Bourne, Andover SP11 6AY* T: (01264) 738308 E: craig785@btinternet.com

MARSHALL, David. b 66. Liv Univ BA 88. Ripon Coll Cuddesdon 89. **d** 92 **p** 93. C Dovecot *Liv* 92-96; P-in-c Westbrook St Jas 96-98; Dioc Communications Officer 95-98; *Ches* 98-03; *Man* from 06; LtO *Ches* 98-06. *Diocesan Church House, 90 Deansgate, Manchester M3 2GJ* T: 0161-828 1421 E: dmarshall@manchester.anglican.org

MARSHALL, David Charles. b 52. St Chad's Coll Dur BA 73. Trin Coll Bris 74. **d** 76 **p** 77. C Meole Brace *Lich* 76-78; C W Teignmouth *Ex* 78-80; C Broadwater St Mary *Chich* 80-84; V Newcastle St Geo *Lich* 84-92; Chapl Versailles w Chevry *Eur* 92-04; Min Southgate LEP *St E* 04-07; P-in-c Collier Row St Jas and Havering-atte-Bower *Chelmsf* 07-15; V 15; AD Havering 10-14; rtd 15. *Sous le Figuier, Hameau de Manieu, 32100 Condom, France* E: vicar@jamesandjohn.org.uk

MARSHALL, Canon David Evelyn. b 63. New Coll Ox BA 85 Birm Univ MA 88 PhD 96. Ridley Hall Cam 88. **d** 90 **p** 91. C Roundhay St Edm *Ripon* 90-92; Chapl Ex Coll Ox 95-98; Lect St Paul's United Th Coll Limuru Kenya 98-99; P-in-c Buckden and Hail Weston *Ely* 99-00; Abp's Dom Chapl *Cant* 00-05; Hon Can All SS Cathl Cairo from 02; PtO *S'wark* 05-09; *Carl* from 09; Assoc Prof Duke Div Sch USA from 13. *2A Eskin Street, Keswick CA12 4DH* T: (017687) 72467
E: revdem63@yahoo.co.uk

MARSHALL, Derek Stanley. b 53. All SS Cen for Miss & Min 11. **d** 14 **p** 15. NSM Tranmere St Cath *Ches* from 14; Chapl YMCA Birkenhead from 14. *5 Bowfell Close, Wirral CH62 9EX*
T: 0151-328 0655   M: 07746-943178
E: derek.m777@yahoo.co.uk

MARSHALL, The Very Revd Geoffrey Osborne. b 48. St Jo Coll Dur BA 71. Coll of Resurr Mirfield 71. **d** 73 **p** 74. C Waltham Cross *St Alb* 73-76; C Digswell 76-78; P-in-c Belper Ch Ch and Milford *Derby* 78-86; V Spondon 86-93; Chapl Derby High Sch 87-01; RD Derby N 90-95; Can Res Derby Cathl 93-02; Dioc Dir of Ords 95-00; TR Wrexham *St As* 02-08; AD 02-08; Dean Brecon *S & B* 08-14; Warden of Readers 08-14; V Brecon St Mary w Llanddew 08-11; P-in-c Llanddew 11-14; rtd 14. *36 Saundersfoot Way, Oakwood, Derby DE21 2RH*
T: (01332) 280452

MARSHALL, Mrs Gillian Kathryn. b 54. Glouc Sch of Min 84. **d** 87 **p** 97. NSM Newtown w Llanllwchaiarn w Aberhafesp *St As* 87-98; P-in-c Betws Cedewain and Tregynon and Llanwyddelan 98-02; V 02-06. *31 Bromley College, London Road, Bromley BR1 1PE* T: (020) 8464 9727

MARSHALL, Graham George. b 38. Dur Univ BA 60 St Chad's Coll Dur. **d** 65 **p** 66. C Ashton-on-Ribble St Mich *Blackb* 65-67; C Lancaster St Mary 67-71; R Church Eaton *Lich* 71-75; Prec Man Cathl 75-78; R Reddish 78-85; V Chadderton St Luke 87-02; rtd 02; PtO *Man* from 02. *7 The Woods, Rochdale OL11 3NT* T: (01706) 642139 E: ggm@manutd.com

MARSHALL (née CHADWICK), Mrs Helen Jane. b 63. UEA BA 84. St Jo Coll Nottm MTh 91. **d** 91 **p** 94. Par Dn Easton H Trin w St Gabr and St Lawr and St Jude *Bris* 91-94; C 94-95; PtO *Ox* 95-98; Lect St Paul's Th Coll Limuru Kenya 98-99; PtO *Ely* 99-00; Chapl K Coll Lon 01-05; P-in-c Addiscombe St Mildred *S'wark* 05-06; V 06-09; PtO *Carl* 09-13; NSM Keswick St Jo from 13. *2A Eskin Street, Keswick CA12 4DH* T: (017687) 72467 E: helenmarshall2592@yahoo.co.uk

MARSHALL, Canon Hugh Phillips. b 34. SS Coll Cam BA 57 MA 61. Linc Th Coll 57. **d** 59 **p** 60. C Westmr St Steph w St Jo *Lon* 59-65; V Tupsley *Heref* 65-74; V Wimbledon *S'wark* 74-78; TR 78-87; RD Merton 79-86; V Mitcham SS Pet and Paul 87-90; Hon Can S'wark Cathl 89-90; PtO 90-96; Chief Sec ABM 90-96; V Wendover *Ox* 96-01; P-in-c Halton 96-01; rtd 01; Hon Can Bulawayo from 96; PtO *Ox* from 01. *7 The Daedings, Deddington, Banbury OX15 0RT* T: (01869) 337761 E: hughm34@btinternet.com

MARSHALL, James Hudson. b 48. Sheff Univ CertEd 70 Open Univ BA 74 Cumbria Univ BA 08. LCTP 05. **d** 08 **p** 09. NSM Lamplugh w Ennerdale *Carl* 08-13; P-in-c 11-13; rtd 14. *28 Arlecdon Road, Arlecdon, Frizington CA26 3UX* E: revjimmarshall@gmail.com

MARSHALL, Mrs Jean. b 36. SWMTC 84. **d** 87 **p** 94. NSM Stratton *Truro* 87-89; NSM Bodmin w Lanhydrock and Lanivet 89-94; P-in-c Lezant w Lawhitton and S Petherwin w Trewen 94-98; rtd 98; Hon C Bodmin w Lanhydrock and Lanivet *Truro* 00-06; PtO from 06. *10 Springwell View, Love Lane, Bodmin PL31 2QP* T: (01208) 79891

MARSHALL, John. b 50. St Luke's Coll Ex CertEd 74 W Lon Inst of HE DEHC 79. S'wark Ord Course 88. **d** 91 **p** 92. Hon C Brixton Hill St Sav *S'wark* 91-95; Hon C Clapham St Jas from 95. *57A Kingscourt Road, London SW16 1JA* T: (020) 8769 3665

MARSHALL, John. b 37. Kelham Th Coll 53. **d** 62 **p** 63. C Winshill *Derby* 62-64; C Chaddesden St Phil 64-65; Chapl HM YOI Morton Hall 65-75; V Swinderby *Linc* 66-77; R Church Aston *Lich* 77-84; V Auckland St Andr and St Anne *Dur* 84-02; P-in-c Hunwick 88-90; Chapl Bishop Auckland Gen Hosp 84-94; Chapl Bishop Auckland Hospitals NHS Trust 94-98; Chapl S Durham Healthcare NHS Trust 98-02; rtd 02; PtO *Derby* 02-06; Hon C S Darley, Elton and Winster 06-12; Hon C Darley, S Darley and Winster from 12. *Croft House, West Bank, Winster, Matlock DE4 2DQ* T: (01629) 650310

MARSHALL, John Linton. b 42. Worc Coll Ox BA 64 MA 68 Bris Univ MLitt 75. Wells Th Coll 66. **d** 68 **p** 69. C Bris St Mary Redcliffe w Temple etc 68-71; Tutor Sarum & Wells Th Coll 71-73; PtO *Pet* 74-77; LtO *S'well* 77-81; V Choral S'well Minster 79-81; R Ordsall 81-88; P-in-c Grove 84-88; RD Retford 84-88; V Northowram *Wakef* 88-99; P-in-c Glouc St Mark and St Mary de Crypt w St Jo etc 99-00; R Glouc St Mary de Lode and St Mary de Crypt etc 00-09; rtd 09. *166 Calton Road, Gloucester GL1 5ER* E: cyprianus@btopenworld.com

MARSHALL, Mrs Julie. b 62. **d** 08 **p** 09. OLM Bucknall *Lich* from 08. *27 Meadow Avenue, Wetley Rocks, Stoke-on-Trent ST9 0BD* T: (01782) 550993 E: julie.marshall@stokecoll.ac.uk

MARSHALL, Ms Karen Lesley. b 59. Coll of Ripon & York St Jo BA 82 Leeds Metrop Univ BSc 96 Huddersfield Univ MA 05. NEOC 04. **d** 07 **p** 08. C Horsforth *Ripon* 07-11; P-in-c Leeds All SS w Osmondthorpe 11-14; P-in-c Urmston *Man* from 14; P-in-c Davyhulme Ch Ch from 14. *Address temp unknown* E: karenlmarshall@btinternet.com

MARSHALL, Keith William. **d** 11 **p** 12. C Portadown St Mark *Arm* from 11. *4 Killycomain Drive, Portadown, Craigavon BT63 5JJ* E: keithmarshall777@yahoo.com

MARSHALL, Kirstin Heather. *See* FREEMAN, Kirstin Heather

MARSHALL, Canon Lionel Alan. b 41. TEng. St Deiniol's Hawarden 84 Qu Coll Birm 86. **d** 87 **p** 88. C Llandudno *Ban* 87-90; V Rhayader and Nantmel *S & B* 90-01; P-in-c Llanbister w Llanbadarn Fynydd w Llananno etc 01-06; AD Maelienydd 98-06; Hon Can Brecon Cathl 00-04; Can Res Brecon Cathl 04-06; rtd 06. *46 Gordon Road, Blackwood NP12 1DW* T: (01495) 223371

MARSHALL, Mrs Margaret Elizabeth. b 60. New Hall Cam BA 81 MA 84. EAMTC 01. **d** 04 **p** 05. C St Neots *Ely* 04-09; P-in-c Riversmeet *St Alb* 09-13; R from 13. *The Vicarage, 57 High Street, Great Barford, Bedford MK44 3JJ* T: (01234) 870363 E: riversmeetvicar@ntlworld.com

MARSHALL, Melanie Kirsten. b 80. Ch Ch Ox BA 02 MSt 06 Toronto Univ MA 07 BNC Ox DPhil 11 Em Coll Cam MA 12. Westcott Ho Cam 10. **d** 13 **p** 14. C Bedford Park *Lon* from 13. *33 Quick Road, London W4 2BU* M: 07967-762558 E: mthrmelanie@gmail.com

MARSHALL, Melinda Christine. b 54. Cov Coll of Educn CertEd 76. Ridley Hall Cam. **d** 01 **p** 02. C Exning St Martin w Landwade *St E* 01-05; TV Heatons *Man* 05-10. *52 Osborne Road, Tweedmouth TD15 2HS*

MARSHALL, Michael David. b 51. BSc. Trin Coll Bris. **d** 84 **p** 85. C Kennington St Mark *S'wark* 84-88; V Streatham Park St Alb 88-96; RD Tooting 93-96; V Blackheath St Jo 96-06; RD Charlton 01-06; Chapl Bishop's Stortford Coll 06-11; V St Austell *Truro* from 11. *12 North Hill Park, St Austell PL25 4BJ* T: (01726) 64990 *or* 61930 E: mikemarshall51@hotmail.com

✠**MARSHALL, The Rt Revd Michael Eric.** b 36. Ch Coll Cam BA 58 MA 60. Cuddesdon Coll 58. **d** 60 **p** 61 **c** 75. C Birm St Pet 60-62; Tutor Ely Th Coll 62-64; Min Can Ely Cathl 62-64; Chapl Lon Univ 64-69; V St Marylebone All SS 69-75; Suff Bp Woolwich *S'wark* 75-84; Episc Dir Angl Inst Missouri 84-92; Abps' Adv Springboard for Decade of Evang 92-97; Hon Asst Bp Lon 84-07; Hon Asst Bp Chich from 92; Can and Preb Chich Cathl 90-99; Bp in Res Upper Chelsea H Trin *Lon* 97-02; R 02-07; rtd 07. *53 Oakley Gardens, London SW3 5QQ* T: (020) 7351 0928   M: 07710-215131

MARSHALL, Mrs Michèle Jane. b 60. SEN 82. NTMTC 05. **d** 08 **p** 09. C Orsett and Bulphan and Horndon on the Hill *Chelmsf* 08-11; C Pitsea w Nevendon 11-13; C Woodham Ferrers and Bicknacre from 13; C S Woodham Ferrers from 13; Lead Chapl (Essex) St Andr Healthcare from 13. *Church House, Main Road, Bicknacre, Chelmsford CM3 4HA* E: mjmarshall@fastmail.co.uk

MARSHALL, Pauline Nikola. b 49. WMMTC 84. **d** 87 **p** 94. C Walsgrave on Sowe *Cov* 87-91; Team Dn Grantham *Linc* 91-94; TV 94-96; Ind Chapl 91-96; PtO 01-02; C Boston 02-05; TV 05-06; Mental Health Chapl Lincs Partnership NHS Trust 05-06; Lead Chapl Mental Health Beds and Luton Mental Health and Soc Care NHS Trust 06-11; rtd 12; PtO *Linc* from 12. *18 Dudley Road, Grantham NG31 9AA* T: (01476) 405371 M: 07792-981768 E: nikola.marshall@ntlworld.com

MARSHALL, Canon Peter Arthur. b 31. AKC 58. **d** 59 **p** 60. C Hutton *Chelmsf* 59-61; C Rickmansworth *St Alb* 61-66; Chapl Orchard View and Kingsmead Court Hosps 66-94; R Lexden *Chelmsf* 66-94; RD Colchester 88-93; Hon Can Chelmsf Cathl 90-94; rtd 94; PtO *Win* 94-14. *21 Manor Close, Wickham, Fareham PO17 5BZ* T: (01329) 832988

MARSHALL, Peter James. b 48. Qu Coll Birm 78. **d** 80 **p** 81. C Ormskirk *Liv* 80-83; V Dallam 83-14; rtd 14. *Address temp unknown* E: pjorm.marshall@btinternet.com

MARSHALL, The Very Revd Peter Jerome. b 40. Westcott Ho Cam 61. **d** 63 **p** 64. C E Ham St Mary *Chelmsf* 63-66; C Woodford St Mary 66-71; C-in-c S Woodford 66-71; V Walthamstow St Pet 71-81; Can Res Chelmsf Cathl 81-85; Dep Dir of Tr 81-84; Can Res Ripon Cathl and Dioc Dir of Tr *Ripon* 85-97; Dean Worc 97-06; rtd 06. *433 Gordon Avenue, Peterborough ON K9J 6G6, Canada* T: (001) (705) 876 3381 E: petermarshall@bell.net

MARSHALL, Peter John Charles. b 35. Bris Univ BA 60. Ridley Hall Cam 60. **d** 62 **p** 63. C Lindfield *Chich* 62-65; Travelling Sec Scripture Union 65-83; Hon C Nottingham St Nic *S'well* 65-67; Hon C Cheadle Hulme St Andr *Ches* 67-83; V Ilkley All

SS *Bradf* 83-98; RD Otley 92-97; rtd 98; PtO *Ches* 00-03; *St As* from 03; *Ban* from 11. *Creuddyn Barn, Glanwydden, Llandudno Junction LL31 9JL* T: (01492) 547352
E: revmarsh35@gmail.com

MARSHALL, Richard Arthur Howard. b 66. Regent's Park Coll Ox BA 88 MA 92 SS Coll Cam PGCE 89. Wycliffe Hall Ox BTh 99. **d** 98 **p** 99. C Broughton *Man* 98-02; Asst Chapl Sedbergh Sch 02-03; Sub Chapl HM Pris Man 02-04; V Blackb Redeemer from 04. *2 Kendall Close, Blackburn BB2 4FB* T: (01254) 51206 E: vicar@the-redeemer.org.uk

MARSHALL, Robert David. b 52. TCD BA 75 MA 00 Solicitor 77. CITC 99. **d** 02 **p** 03. NSM Stillorgan w Blackrock *D & G* from 02. *The Tontine, 84 The Rise, Mount Merrion, Co Dublin, Republic of Ireland* T: (00353) (1) 288 6170 *or* 649 2137 F: 649 2649 M: 86-815 3089
E: curate@stillorgan.dublin.anglican.org

MARSHALL, Robert Paul. b 60. Sheff Univ BA 81 PhD 14 St Jo Coll Dur MA 85. Cranmer Hall Dur 81. **d** 83 **p** 84. C Kirkstall *Ripon* 83-85; C Otley *Bradf* 85-87; Dioc Communications Officer 87-91; P-in-c Embsay w Eastby 87-91; Dioc Communications Officer *Lon* 91-95; P-in-c S Kensington St Aug 95-00; Media Adv to Abp *York* 95-05; Communications Adv *Sheff* 04-13; Public Relns Adv Fresh Expressions from 05; Hd of Marketing St Mary's Univ Coll Twickenham *Lon* 05-07; Hon C Kensington St Mary Abbots w Ch Ch and St Phil 07-13; PtO *Ely* 08-13; *Derby* 08-13; *Sarum* 08-13; P-in-c E Ham w Upton Park and Forest Gate *Chelmsf* 13; TR 13-15; C Digswell and Panshanger *St Alb* from 15. *The Rectory, 354 Knightsfield, Welwyn Garden City AL8 7NG* M: 07766-952113
E: robmarshalluk@gmail.com

MARSHALL, Canon Rodney Henry. b 46. Bernard Gilpin Soc Dur 71 St Steph Ho Ox 72. **d** 75 **p** 76. C Gorton Our Lady and St Thos *Man* 75-78; C Bedford Leigh 78-82; V Goldthorpe w Hickleton *Sheff* 82-90; Dioc Dir of In-Service Tr 88-90; NSM Hemsworth *Wakef* 96-97; P-in-c Athersley 97-98; V 98-12; P-in-c Monk Bretton 04-07; P-in-c Carlton 10-12; V Athersley and Carlton *Leeds* from 12; Hon Can Wakef Cathl from 07. *St Helen's Vicarage, 27 Laithes Lane, Barnsley S71 3AF* T: (01226) 245361

MARSHALL, Simon. b 54. Kingston Poly BSc 77 Leeds Univ PGCE 78 MA(Ed) 79. Qu Coll Birm 91. **d** 93 **p** 94. C Gt Clacton *Chelmsf* 93-97; TV Chigwell and Chigwell Row 97-02; C Woodford Wells from 02. *3 Inmans Row, Woodford Green IG8 0NH* T: (020) 3302 1856
E: simon.marshall17@ntlworld.com

MARSHALL, Simon Hardy. b 69. Bp Grosseteste Coll BA 92. St Jo Coll Nottm 00. **d** 02 **p** 03. C Bartley Green *Birm* 02-05; TV Solihull from 05. *Oak Cottage, Bryanston Road, Solihull B91 1BS* T: 0121-704 4730

MARSHALL, Mrs Sonia Margaret Cecilia. b 49. Westf Coll Lon BA 71 Nottm Univ MA 03. EMMTC 01. **d** 03 **p** 04. NSM Deeping St James *Linc* from 03. *135C Eastgate, Deeping St James, Peterborough PE6 8RB* T: (01778) 346420
E: curate@dsj.org.uk

MARSHALL, Sonya Tolley. b 62. Hull Univ BA 84 Lon Inst of Educn PGCE 85. NOC 04. **d** 06 **p** 07. NSM Southport Ch Ch *Liv* 06-13; C N Meols from 13. *112 Linaker Street, Southport PR8 5DG* M: 07834-170070

MARSHALL, Susan. *See* PANTER MARSHALL, Susan Lesley

MARSHALL, Trevor. b 60. SEITE 08. **d** 11 **p** 12. C Bognor *Chich* 11-15. *2 Shelley Road, Bognor Regis PO21 2SL* T: (01243) 920681 M: 07900-158982 E: curate@wilfrid.com

MARSHALL, William John. b 35. TCD BA 57 BD 61 PhD 75. TCD Div Sch 59. **d** 59 **p** 60. C Ballyholme *D & D* 59-61; India 62-72; Asst Dean of Residence TCD 73-76; I Rathmichael *D & G* 76-92; Can Ch Ch Cathl Dublin 90-02; Chan Ch Ch Cathl Dublin 91-02; Vice-Prin CITC 92-02; rtd 02. *115 The Elms, Abberley, Killiney, Co Dublin, Republic of Ireland* T: (00353) (1) 239 0832

MARSHALL, William Michael. b 30. Pemb Coll Ox BA 53 MA 57 DipEd 65 Bris Univ MLitt 72 PhD 79. Wells Th Coll 63 Sarum & Wells Th Coll 79. **d** 80 **p** 81. Asst Chapl Millfield Sch Somerset 80-96; Hon C Glastonbury St Jo w Godney *B & W* 80-84; Hon C Glastonbury w Meare, W Pennard and Godney 84-96; rtd 96; PtO *Portsm* 96-01; *Win* 96-01; *Ely* 01-08. *7 The Paddock, Ely CB6 1TP* T/F: (01353) 612287
E: william.m247@gmail.com

MARSHALL, William Roger. b 82. New Coll Ox MPhys 05. Wycliffe Hall Ox BTh 13. **d** 13 **p** 14. C Handforth *Ches* from 13. *71 Blackden Walk, Wilmslow SK9 2EL* M: 07790-821366

MARSHMAN, Mrs Elizabeth Maryan. b 53. York St Jo Coll CertEd 74 Leeds Univ BEd 75. NEOC 03. **d** 06 **p** 07. C Clifton *York* 06-10; P-in-c Lockington and Lund and Scorborough w Leconfield 10-14; R from 14. *Rectory House, Church Lane, Lockington, Driffield YO25 9SU* T: (01430) 810604
E: emmarshman@yahoo.co.uk

MARSTON, David Howarth. b 48. St Jo Coll Dur BA 69. Edin Th Coll 69. **d** 71 **p** 72. C Kendal H Trin *Carl* 71-75; PtO *Glas* 75-78; NSM Barrow St Matt *Carl* 79-86; PtO *York* 86-91; *Liv* 91-93 and 99-00; NSM Southport All SS and All So 93-99; NSM Southport St Luke 99-00; PtO from 11. *33 Sandringham Road, Ainsdale, Southport PR8 2NY* T: (01704) 578303

MARSTON, Neville Charles. b 37. Univ of Wales (Cardiff) BA 65 Waterloo Univ (Canada) MA 67. Ox Cen for Miss Studies 95. **d** 97 **p** 99. Dioc Dir Tr Seychelles 92-00; C Coven *Lich* 00-02; rtd 02; PtO *York* 05-11. *8 Appleton Gardens, South Cave, Brough HU15 2EN* T: (01430) 471093 M: 07866-935844
E: nevillemarston@aol.com

MARSTON, William Thornton. b 59. Worc Coll Ox BA 81 MA 85 Cam Univ CertEd 83. St Steph Ho Ox BA 87. **d** 88 **p** 89. C Beckenham St Geo *Roch* 88-92; TV Ifield *Chich* 92-97; C-in-c Middleton-on-Sea CD 97-99; V Middleton from 99. *The Vicarage, 106 Elmer Road, Middleton-on-Sea, Bognor Regis PO22 6LJ* T: (01243) 586348 E: w.marston@btinternet.com

MARSZALEK, Mrs Rachel Emma. b 74. St Jo Coll Nottm 08. **d** 11 **p** 12. C Belper *Derby* 11-14; V Ealing All SS *Lon* from 14. *All Saints' Vicarage, Elm Grove Road, London W5 3JH* M: 07906-632972 E: revrachelemma@gmail.com

MART, Terence Eugene. b 47. CertEd 76 BA 82. St Jo Coll Nottm LTh 87. **d** 87 **p** 88. C Prestatyn *St As* 87-91; Chapl Theatr Clwyd Mold 87-91; R Llangystennin *St As* 91-01; RD Llanrwst 96-00; V Llanfair DC, Derwen, Llanelidan and Efenechtyd 01-07. *31 Pengarth, Conwy LL32 8RW*

MARTIN, Mrs Adele Joan. b 51. BSc 74. Cranmer Hall Dur 05. **d** 07 **p** 08. C Seacroft *Ripon* 07-11; P-in-c Dinsdale w Sockburn *Dur* from 11; P-in-c Hurworth from 11; Chapl HM YOI Deerbolt 11-15. *Address temp unknown*

MARTIN, Alexander Lewendon. b 26. Em Coll Cam BA 47 MA 51. Ridley Hall Cam 56. **d** 57 **p** 58. C Ashtead *Guildf* 57-59; Asst Chapl Tonbridge Sch 59-64; Chapl Felsted Sch 64-74; Chapl Sedbergh Sch 74-84; R Askerswell, Loders and Powerstock *Sarum* 84-89; RD Lyme Bay 86-89; rtd 89; PtO *Ex* from 89. *Thirtover, 7 Alexandra Way, Crediton EX17 2EA* T: (01363) 776206 E: alexmartin777@hotmail.com

MARTIN, Andrew Philip. b 78. **d** 14 **p** 15. C Selly Park St Steph and St Wulstan *Birm* from 14. *103 Bournbrook Road, Selly Park, Birmingham B29 7BY* M: 07799-990179 T: 0121-247 6763
E: andy.martin@sssw.org.uk

MARTIN, Angela Frances. b 66. SEITE 05. **d** 08 **p** 09. C Henfield w Shermanbury and Woodmancote *Chich* 08-12; C Worth, Pound Hill and Maidenbower 12-14; V Forest Row from 14. *The Vicarage, Ashdown Road, Forest Row RH18 5BW* T: (01342) 458263 E: revd.angelamartin@gmail.com

MARTIN, Angela Lee. b 61. EMMTC 00. **d** 03 **p** 04. NSM Derby St Barn 03-08; P-in-c Hatton from 08. *The Joiners' Arms, 60 Church Road, Quarndon, Derby DE22 5JA* T: (01332) 552876 M: 07967-180531 E: hattonlee1968@yahoo.co.uk

MARTIN, Bryan Robert. b 71. TCD BTh 01. CITC 98. **d** 01 **p** 02. C Magheralin w Dollingstown *D & D* 01-04; C Knockbreda 04-07; I Dromore *Clogh* 07-10; I Donaghcloney w Waringstown *D & D* from 10. *The Rectory, 54 Banbridge Road, Waringstown, Craigavon BT66 7QD* T: (028) 3888 1218
E: brymrtn@aol.com *or* bryan.martin@btinternet.com

MARTIN, Canon Cameron Anthony Brian. b 56. Cape Town Univ BA 93 Cant Univ (NZ) MBA 02 MA 05. St Bede's Coll Umtata 82. **d** 84 **p** 85. C Nigel Ch the K S Africa 84-86; R Ennerdale St Nic 87-89; R Eldorado Park Transfiguration 89-90; P-in-c Kenwyn 90-95; R Woodlands 95-02; Adn Mitchell's Plain 98-02; Dioc Admin Kimberley and Kuruman 02-05; Can from 03; P-in-c Brumby *Linc* 05-07; TR from 07. *St Hugh's Rectory, 114 Ashby Road, Scunthorpe DN16 2AG* E: cameron.martin@ntlworld.com

MARTIN (*née* GILES), Mrs Caroline Evelyn. b 76. York Univ BA 98 Homerton Coll Cam PGCE 99. St Mellitus Coll BA 15. **d** 15. C Berechurch St Marg w St Mich *Chelmsf* from 15. *3 Helen Ewing Place, Colchester CO2 8WS* M: 07889-259398
E: carolinemartin002@gmail.com

MARTIN, Christopher Edward. b 70. Bris Poly BA 92 ACA 97. Trin Coll Bris 07. **d** 09 **p** 10. C Newton Flotman, Swainsthorpe, Tasburgh, etc *Nor* 09-12; C Whimple, Talaton and Clyst St Lawr *Ex* 12-13; P-in-c from 13; C Bradninch and Clyst Hydon from 13. *The Rectory, Grove Road, Whimple, Exeter EX5 2TP* T: (01404) 822427 E: cemartin70@googlemail.com

MARTIN, Christopher John. b 45. Ball Coll Ox BA 67 MA 87 Aber Univ MTh 09. Wycliffe Hall Ox 86. **d** 88 **p** 89. C Edin St Thos 88-90; R Duns 90-00; Chapl Lyon *Eur* 00-13; rtd 13. *10 Kirkhill Terrace, Edinburgh EH16 5DQ*
E: revchris.martin@free.fr

MARTIN, David. **d** 14. Howth *D & G* 14-15; C Hillsborough *D & D* from 15. *Address temp unknown*

MARTIN, Prof David Alfred. b 29. LSE BSc PhD. Westcott Ho Cam. **d** 83 **p** 84. Hon C Guildf Cathl 83-99; PtO from 99. *174 St John's Road, Woking GU21 7PQ* T: (01483) 762134

MARTIN, David Howard. b 47. Worc Coll Ox BEd 79. AKC 70 St Aug Coll Cant 70. **d** 71 **p** 72. C Sedgley All SS *Lich* 71-75; Dioc Youth Chapl *Worc* 75-81; P-in-c Worc St Andr and All SS w St Helen 75-81; R Newland, Guarlford and Madresfield 81-91; R Alvechurch 91-13; rtd 13. *4 Denison Close, Malvern WR14 2EU* T: (01684) 577425 E: davidmartin@lynkserve.net

MARTIN, Dennis. b 50. St Mellitus Coll. **d** 13 **p** 14. OLM Woodford Wells *Chelmsf* from 13. *7 Knighton Drive, Woodford Green IG8 0NY* E: dennis.martin9@btinternet.com

MARTIN, Donald Philip (Ralph). b 30. Trin Coll Toronto MA 55 STB 55. **d** 54 **p** 55. C Toronto St Simon Canada 54-57; Tutor Kelham Th Coll 57-73; SSM from 60; P-in-c Willen *Ox* 73-81; Japan 81-82; Ghana 83-89; Dir Cleveland Lay Tr Course 89-91; C Middlesbrough All SS York 89-91; Kuwait 92-93; Italy 93-94; Canada 94-95; Tutor SAOMC *Ox* 95-96; Chapl OHP 96; Lesotho 97-00; rtd 98. *The Well, Newport Road, Willen, Milton Keynes MK15 9AA* T: (01908) 242190 E: ralphssm@yahoo.co.uk

MARTIN, Edward Eldred William. b 37. Cranfield Inst of Tech MSc 84 Herts Univ MA 88. S'wark Ord Course 65. **d** 68 **p** 69. C Greenwich St Alfege w St Pet *S'wark* 68-71; C Kidbrooke St Jas 71-75; V Peckham St Jo 75-78; P-in-c Peckham St Andr w All SS 76-78; V Peckham St Jo w St Andr 78-81; Hon Chapl S'wark Cathl 81-02; Chapl Guy's Hosp Lon 81-88; rtd 02; PtO *S'wark* 02-03 and from 07; Hon C Lee St Marg 03-07. *17 Honor Oak Rise, London SE23 3QY* T: (020) 8699 2303 M: 07956-204869 E: emartin1722@yahoo.co.uk

MARTIN, Edward James Russell. b 76. Hull Univ BA 98 Leeds Univ BA 02 MA 06. Coll of Resurr Mirfield 00. **d** 03 **p** 04. C Carrington *S'well* 03-06; P-in-c Chapel St Leonards w Hogsthorpe *Linc* 06-09; R Scartho 09-14; V Grimsby St Aug from 14; V Gt Grimsby St Andr w St Luke and All SS from 14. *St Augustine's Vicarage, 145 Legsby Avenue, Grimsby DN32 0LA* M: 07736-711360 E: fatheredward@ntlworld.com

MARTIN, Mrs Eileen. b 43. City of Portsm Coll of Educn TCert 65. **d** 03 **p** 15. OLM Queen Thorne *Sarum* 03-08; C Is of Scilly *Truro* from 15. *Mellyns, Church Road, St Mary's, Isles of Scilly TR21 0NA* T: (01720) 423660 E: rev_eileenm@yahoo.co.uk

MARTIN, Miss Eileen Susan Kirkland. b 45. LCST 66. Cranmer Hall Dur 77. **dss** 83 **d** 86. Kilmarnock *Glas* 84-86; Par Dn Heanor *Derby* 87-92; PtO 92-95. *1 Malin Court, Hardings Close, Hemel Hempstead HP3 9AQ* T: (01442) 216768

MARTIN, Elizabeth Anne. *See* DADY, Elizabeth Anne

MARTIN, Glenn. b 52. Qu Coll Birm 84. **d** 86 **p** 87. C Chatham St Wm *Roch* 86-89; Chapl Pastures Hosp Derby 89-94; Chapl Kingsway Hosp Derby 89-94; Sen Chapl S Derbys Mental Health NHS Trust 94-97; Sen Chapl Community Health Sheff NHS Trust 97-01; Professional Development Officer for Chapl and Spiritual Healthcare 01-07; NSM Gilmorton, Peatling Parva, Kimcote etc *Leic* 04-07; NSM Guilsborough w Hollowell and Cold Ashby *Pet* 07-08; NSM Cottesbrooke w Gt Creaton and Thornby 07-08; NSM Spratton 07-08; NSM W Haddon w Winwick and Ravensthorpe 07-08; R Sutton Bonington w Normanton-on-Soar *S'well* 08-11; P-in-c Derby St Andr w St Osmund 11-13; P-in-c Allenton and Shelton Lock 11-13; rtd 13; PtO *Derby* from 13; *Leic* from 14. *27 Shields Crescent, Castle Donington, Derby DE74 2JS* T: (01332) 818858 E: glenn.martinrev@btinternet.com

MARTIN, Graham Michael. b 39. Liv Univ CertEd 58 Lon Univ BD 70 Bris Univ BEd 73 FRSA LCP. Wells Th Coll 71. **d** 71 **p** 72. Hon C Glouc St Cath 71-76; P-in-c Brookthorpe w Whaddon 76-78; PtO 78-80; Hon C Hucclecote 80-82; Hon C Tuffley 82-88; NSM Hardwicke, Quedgeley and Elmore w Longney 88-89; V Kemble, Poole Keynes, Somerford Keynes etc 89-96; P-in-c Bibury w Winson and Barnsley 96-04; Dioc Ecum Officer 96-04; rtd 04; PtO *Glouc* from 04. *Wharf Cottage, Wharf Lane, Lechlade GL7 3AU* T: (01367) 252825

MARTIN, Henry Rowland Felix. b 67. Leeds Univ BA 89 SS Coll Cam BA 95. Ridley Hall Cam 93. **d** 96 **p** 97. C Becontree St Mary *Chelmsf* 96-00; C Broughton *Man* 00-02; TR 02-10; Chapl HM Pris Man from 10. *HM Prison Manchester, 1 Southall Street, Manchester M60 9AH* T: 0161-817 5600 E: h3nrymartin@googlemail.com

MARTIN, James Alwyn. b 47. St Paul's Coll Grahamstown 76. **d** 78 **p** 79. C Highlands St Mary Rhodesia 78-80; P-in-c Lowveld Zimbabwe 80-84; Adn Victoria 82-87; R Masvingo St Mich 84-87; R Borrowdale Ch Ch 87-98; Adn Harare S 96-98; Dean Bulawayo 98-04; V Aldershot St Mich *Guildf* from 05. *St Michael's Vicarage, 120 Church Lane East, Aldershot GU11 3SS* T: (01252) 320108 M: 07749-770035 E: jamesmartin858@btinternet.com

MARTIN, James Smiley. b 32. MBE 98. TCD 65. **d** 67 **p** 68. C Glenavy *Conn* 67-70; C Belfast St Mary 70-73; I Carnmoney 73-74; I Mallusk 74-94; rtd 94. *7 Dundesert Road, Nutts Corner, Crumlin BT29 4SL* T: (028) 9082 5636

MARTIN, Mrs Jane Juliet. b 56. Warwick Univ BA 77 Solicitor 81. ERMC 03. **d** 06 **p** 07. NSM Huntingdon w the Stukeleys *Ely* 06-09. *Address temp unknown* E: jjmandsm@aol.com

MARTIN, Canon Jessica Heloise. b 63. Trin Hall Cam BA 86 PhD 93. EAMTC 00. **d** 03 **p** 04. NSM Trin Coll Cam 03-09; NSM Fen Ditton *Ely* 08-09; NSM Horningsea 08-09; NSM Teversham 08-09; P-in-c Duxford from 10; P-in-c Hinxton from 10; P-in-c Ickleton from 10; Bp's Adv for Women's Min from 14; Hon Can Ely Cathl from 14. *The Rectory, 13 St John's Street, Duxford, Cambridge CB22 4RA* T: (01223) 832137 M: 07780-704006 E: jessicamartin@virginmedia.com

MARTIN, John Eric Terence. b 75. SS Coll Cam MA 99 MEng 99. Wycliffe Hall Ox BTh 10. **d** 10 **p** 11. C Wolverhampton St Luke *Lich* 10-13. *18 Galileo Gardens, Cheltenham GL51 0GA* M: 07941-978856 E: john@gracechurchcheltenham.org

MARTIN, John Henry. b 42. St Jo Coll Cam BA 63 MA 67. St Jo Coll Nottm BA 73. **d** 73 **p** 74. C Ecclesall *Sheff* 73-77; C Hednesford *Lich* 77-82; V Walsall Pleck and Bescot 82-92; V Whittington w Weeford 92-08; V Hints 05-08; rtd 08. *2 Churn Close, South Cerney, Cirencester GL7 6HX* T: (01285) 869585

MARTIN, John Hunter. b 42. AKC 64. **d** 65 **p** 66. C Mortlake w E Sheen *S'wark* 65-69; C-in-c Bermondsey St Hugh CD 69-72; V Bermondsey St Anne 72-78; P-in-c Lt Ouse *Ely* 78; V Littleport 78-89; V Attercliffe *Sheff* 89-90; P-in-c Darnall 89-90; TR Darnall-cum-Attercliffe 90-96; TR Attercliffe, Darnall and Tinsley 96; R Kirk Sandall and Edenthorpe 96-07; rtd 07; PtO *Glas* from 09. *Salara Haven, Sandgreen, Gatehouse of Fleet, Castle Douglas DG7 2DU* T: (01557) 815068 E: vanessaandjohnmartin@gmail.com

MARTIN, Canon Jonathan Patrick McLeod. b 55. Leic Univ BA 81. Sarum & Wells Th Coll 84. **d** 86 **p** 87. C Southampton Thornhill St Chris *Win* 86-89; PtO 89-92; C Heatherlands St Jo *Sarum* 92-97; Dioc Link Officer for ACUPA 95-97; Chief Exec Dame Agnes Weston's R Sailors' Rests from 97; PtO *Sarum* 98-01 and from 12; NSM Parkstone St Pet and St Osmund w Branksea 01-12; Can and Preb Sarum Cathl from 06. *32 Gladstone Road, Poole BH12 2LY* T: (01202) 748566 E: jonathanmartin@mchap.co.uk

MARTIN, Joseph Edward. b 35. Bps' Coll Cheshunt 58. **d** 60 **p** 61. C Short Heath *Birm* 60-62; C Caterham Valley *S'wark* 63-66; R W Hallam and Mapperley *Derby* 66-70; P-in-c Mapperley 66-67; V Wykeham and Hutton Buscel *York* 71-78; Chapl HM Pris Askham Grange 78-82; V Askham Bryan w Askham Richard *York* 78-82; R Amotherby w Appleton and Barton-le-Street 82-84; C Banbury *Ox* 85-88; C Warsop *S'well* 88-90; V Tuxford w Weston and Markham Clinton 90-00; rtd 00; PtO *Carl* from 03. *Windsmead, Allithwaite Road, Cartmel, Grange-over-Sands LA11 7SB* T: (015395) 32693

MARTIN, Lee. *See* MARTIN, Angela Lee

MARTIN (née BULLEN), Mrs Marilyn Patricia. b 46. Liv Hope Univ Coll BA(Theol) 00 MA 05. NOC 06. **d** 06 **p** 07. NSM Stretton and Appleton Thorn *Ches* 06-09; Asst Chapl HM YOI Thorn Cross from 06. *HM Young Offender Institution, Thorn Cross, Arley Road, Appleton, Warrington WA4 4RL* T: (01925) 805100 E: malmartin@btinternet.com

MARTIN, Miss Marion. b 47. Oak Hill Th Coll 83. **dss** 86 **d** 87. Ditton *Roch* 86-88; C 87-88; PtO *Glouc* 89-01; rtd 01. *16 Garborough Close, Crosby, Maryport CA15 6RZ* T: (01900) 810776

MARTIN, Michelle Karen. b 81. Ripon Coll Cuddesdon 11. **d** 14 **p** 15. C Bristol St Aid w St Geo *Bris* from 14; C Fishponds St Jo from 14; C Two Mile Hill St Mich from 14. *St Aidan's Vicarage, 2 Jockey Lane, Bristol BS5 8NZ* M: 07883-072847 E: michellemartin72@googlemail.com

MARTIN, Preb Nicholas Roger. b 53. St Jo Coll Dur BA 74. Ripon Coll Cuddesdon 75. **d** 77 **p** 78. C Wolvercote w Summertown *Ox* 77-82; C Kidlington 80-82; TV 82-84; V Happisburgh w Walcot *Nor* 84-85; P-in-c Hempstead w Lessingham and Eccles 84-85; R Happisburgh w Walcot, Hempstead, Lessingham etc 85-89; R Blakeney w Cley, Wiveton, Glandford etc 89-97; TR Totnes w Bridgetown, Berry Pomeroy etc *Ex* 97-05; RD Totnes 99-03; Co-ord Chapl HM Pris Channings Wood from 05; Preb Ex Cathl from 14. *HM Prison, Channings Wood, Denbury, Newton Abbot TQ12 6DW* T: (01803) 814647 E: nick.martin@hmps.gsi.gov.uk

MARTIN, Paul Dexter. b 50. Wabash Coll (USA) BA 72 Univ of the South (USA) MDiv 75. **d** 75 **p** 76. Educn Tutor Cov Cathl 75-76; C Norbury St Phil *Cant* 76-80; USA from 80. *275 Southfield Road, Shreveport LA 71105, USA* T: (001) (318) 865 8469 E: pdmartin@iamerica.net

MARTIN, Canon Penelope Elizabeth. b 44. Cranmer Hall Dur 83. **dss** 86 **d** 87 **p** 94. Seaham w Seaham Harbour *Dur*

86-89; Par Dn 87-89; Par Dn Cassop cum Quarrington 89-93; Par Dn Sherburn w Pittington 93-94; C 94-95; V 95-02; R Shadforth 95-02; R Pittington, Shadforth and Sherburn 02-03; Hon Can Dur Cathl 01-03; rtd 03; PtO *Dur* from 03. *34A Rosemount, Durham DH1 5GA* T: 0191-386 1742
E: penny.martin@charis.co.uk

MARTIN, Preb Peter. b 50. MCIH 75. Linc Th Coll 82. **d** 84 **p** 85. C Taunton H Trin *B & W* 84-86; C Bath Bathwick 86-88; R Cannington, Otterhampton, Combwich and Stockland 88-15; RD Sedgemoor 00-06; Warden of Readers Taunton Adnry 06-14; Chapl Cannington Coll 89-15; Preb Wells Cathl 09-15; rtd 15. *55 Irnham Road, Minehead TA24 5DW*
T: (01643) 706552 E: revd.petermartin@tiscali.co.uk

MARTIN, Philip James. b 58. Cam Univ BA. Coll of Resurr Mirfield. **d** 84 **p** 85. C Pontefract St Giles *Wakef* 84-88; C Wantage *Ox* 88-90; C Didcot All SS 90; V Alderholt *Sarum* from 90. *The Vicarage, Daggons Road, Alderholt, Fordingbridge SP6 3DN* T: (01425) 653179 E: vicar@stjamesalderholt.org.uk

MARTIN, Ralph. *See* MARTIN, Donald Philip

MARTIN, Raymond William. b 32. Lon Univ BSc 66 MBIM. Glouc Th Course 73. **d** 76 **p** 76. NSM Glouc St Mary de Lode and St Nic 76-77; NSM Redmarley D'Abitot, Bromesberrow w Pauntley etc 77-84; R 84-91; P-in-c Falfield w Rockhampton 91-98; P-in-c Oldbury-on-Severn 91-98; Chapl HM YOI Eastwood Park 91-92; rtd 98; PtO *Glouc* 98-00 and from 02; Clergy Widows' Officer (Glouc Adnry) from 99; P-in-c Shipton Moyne w Westonbirt and Lasborough 00-02; PtO *Heref* 03-15; *Worc* from 03 and from 03. *Tree Tops, 35 Thirlstane Road, Malvern WR14 3PL* T: (01684) 562714

MARTIN, Richard. b 34. Rhodes Univ BA 54 Em Coll Cam BA 57 MA 58. Wells Th Coll 57. **d** 59 **p** 60. C Portsea St Mary *Portsm* 59-60; C Bloemfontein Cathl S Africa 60-62; R Wepener 62-64; R Odendaalsrus 64-67; R Newton Park St Hugh 67-76; Chapl St Bede's Coll Umtata 77-79; R Hillcrest 79-87; C Aldershot St Mich *Guildf* 87-94; R Wick *Mor* 94-99; P-in-c Thurso 94-99; rtd 99; Hon C Diptford, N Huish, Harberton, Harbertonford etc *Ex* 99-01; PtO 01-03; LtO *Mor* from 03. *59 Cradlehall Park, Westhill, Inverness IV2 5DA* T: (01463) 791759
E: martin@chilledthames.com

MARTIN, Richard Arthur. b 59. Leeds Univ BA 91 MA 97 Cant Ch Ch Univ Coll PGCE 03. SEITE 07. **d** 09 **p** 10. C Gravesend St Aid *Roch* 09-12; P-in-c Gravesend H Family w Ifield from 12; Bp's Adv for Inter-Faith Concerns from 15. *18 Brenchley Avenue, Gravesend DA11 7RQ* T: (01474) 249792
M: 07593-092758 E: ramartin@talktalk.net

MARTIN, Richard Charles de Villeval. b 41. St Jo Coll Ox BA 63 MA 67. Ox Ord Course. **d** 84 **p** 85. NSM Ox St Thos w St Frideswide and Binsey 84-04; Asst Chapl Highgate Sch Lon 86-92; Asst Master Magd Coll Sch Ox 92-02; Chapl 94-02; rtd 04; LtO *Ox* 05-12; PtO from 12. *11 Benson Place, Oxford OX2 6QH* T: (01865) 510694 E: richardcmartin@tiscali.co.uk

MARTIN, Richard Hugh. b 55. Van Mildert Coll Dur BA 78 St Jo Coll Nottm BA 81 Leeds Univ MA 01. Cranmer Hall Dur 79. **d** 82 **p** 83. C Gateshead *Dur* 82-85; C Redmarshall 85-88; V Scarborough St Jas w H Trin *York* 88-96; Chapl R Wolv Hosps NHS Trust 96-02; V Bris St Andr Hartcliffe 02-12; rtd 12. *197 Preston Road, Weymouth DT3 6BG* M: 07709-429631
E: richardtherev55@gmail.com

✠**MARTIN, The Rt Revd Robert David Markland.** b 49. Trin Coll Cam BA 71 MA 74 FCA 80. Trin Coll Bris BA 91. **d** 91 **p** 92 **c** 08. C Kingswood *Bris* 91-95; V Frome H Trin *B & W* 95-08; RD Frome 03-08; Suff Bp Marsabit Kenya 08-11; Bp from 11. *ACK Marsabit Mission Area, c/o MAF Kenya, PO Box 21123/00505, Nairobi, Kenya*

MARTIN, Robert Paul Peter. b 58. Chich Th Coll. **d** 83 **p** 84. C Anfield St Columba *Liv* 83-86; C Orford St Marg 86-87; R Blackley H Trin *Man* 87-90; C Oseney Crescent St Luke *Lon* 90-93; C Kentish Town 93-96; V Harringay St Paul 96-09; P-in-c W Green Ch Ch w St Pet 04-08; Chapl St Paul's Coll Hong Kong from 09; CMP from 01. *St Paul's College, 69 Bonham Road, Hong Kong, China* T: (00852) 2546 2241
E: fr.robert@btinternet.com

MARTIN, Robin. *See* MARTIN, Thomas Robin

MARTIN, Robin Hugh. b 35. Rhodes Univ BA 56. **d** 58 **p** 59. C Darnall *Sheff* 58-62; C-in-c Kimberworth Park 62-65; LtO 65-66; *Newc* 67-71; PtO *Sheff* 65-66; *Newc* 67-71; *Man* 79-93; Lich 97-99 and from 11; *Heref* from 97; P-in-c Maesbury Lich 99-11. *Offa House, Treflach, Oswestry SY10 9HQ* T: (01691) 657090

MARTIN, Roger Allen. b 38. Westmr Coll Lon CertEd 59 Birkbeck Coll Lon BA 64 FRMetS 79. SAOMC 97. **d** 99 **p** 00. NSM Bramfield, Stapleford, Waterford etc *St Alb* 99-06; NSM Broxbourne w Wormley 06-10; rtd 10; PtO *St Alb* from 10. *41 The Avenue, Bengeo, Hertford SG14 3DS* T: (01992) 422414
E: roger.martin@ntlworld.com

MARTIN, Canon Roger Ivor. b 42. MCMI. Cant Sch of Min. **d** 85 **p** 86. NSM Saltwood *Cant* 85-90; P-in-c Crundale w Godmersham 90-01; Dioc Exec Officer for Adult Educn and Lay Tr 90-96; CME Officer 94-96; Chapl to Bp Maidstone *Cant* 96-01; R Saltwood 01-09; Hon Can Cant Cathl 09; rtd 09; PtO *Cant* 09-11 and from 12; Hon C Aldington w Bonnington and Bilsington etc 11-12. *Kwetu, 23 Tanners Hill Gardens, Hythe CT21 5HY* T: (01303) 237204
E: rogmartin@btinternet.com

MARTIN, Ronald Charles John Richard. b 61. Bris Univ BA 92. Wesley Coll Bris 88. **d** 15 **p** 15. Lead Chapl Dorset Co Hosp NHS Foundn Trust from 15; C Sherborne w Castleton, Lillington and Longburton *Sarum* from 15. *The Old Coach House, South Street, Sherborne DT9 3LZ* M: 07701-091627

MARTIN, Rosanna Stuart. *See* STUART-MARTIN, Rosanna

MARTIN, Rupert Gresley. b 57. Worc Coll Ox BA 78 Ox Univ MA 95. Trin Coll Bris 89. **d** 91 **p** 92. C Yateley *Win* 91-95; V Sandal St Helen *Leeds* from 95. *The Vicarage, 333 Barnsley Road, Wakefield WF2 6EJ* T: (01924) 255441
E: office@sandalmagna.fsnet.co.uk

MARTIN, Russell Derek. b 47. Cranmer Hall Dur 71. **d** 74 **p** 75. C Hartlepool H Trin *Dur* 74-78; C Swindon St Jo and St Andr *Bris* 78-79; V Penhill 79-91; V Haselbury Plucknett, Misterton and N Perrott *B & W* 91-99. *59 North Street, Martock TA12 6EH* T: (01935) 829266 M: 07770-783893

MARTIN, Scott. b 73. Herts Univ BA 99 Leeds Univ BA 04 MA 05. Coll of Resurr Mirfield 02. **d** 05 **p** 06. C Leagrave St Alb 05-09; P-in-c Bishop's Stortford 09-13. *Address temp unknown* M: 07766-295678 E: scottmar73@hotmail.com

MARTIN, Sean Cal Hugh. b 69. Wycliffe Coll Toronto MDiv 04. **d** 04 **p** 05. C Rio Grande St Andr USA 05-06; Asst P ICM 06-08; Canada from 08. *587 Laurel Crescent, Campbell River BC V9W 6K8, Canada*

MARTIN, Steven. b 50. Qu Coll Birm BA 08. **d** 08 **p** 09. C Malvern St Andr and Malvern Wells and Wyche *Worc* 08-12; TV Brierley Hill 12-15; rtd 15. *Address temp unknown* E: smartin1006@sky.com

MARTIN, Steven Edward. b 81. Ex Univ BA 03 MA 04 Bris Univ PhD 10 LRSM 03. St Steph Ho Ox 13. **d** 15. Tavistock, Gulworthy and Brent Tor *Ex* from 15. *1 St Andrews Road, Tavistock PL19 9BY* M: 07866-582519
E: stevenemartin@gmail.com

MARTIN, Miss Susan. b 56. Nottm Univ BA 77. Edin Th Coll 86. **d** 88 **p** 94. C Leigh Park *Portsm* 88-91; C Sandown Ch Ch 91-94; C Portsea St Cuth 94-95; rtd 95; PtO *Portsm* 95-01 and from 04; NSM Portsea St Geo 01-04. *2 Charminster, 46 Craneswater Park, Southsea PO4 0NU* T: (023) 9307 9389

MARTIN, Mrs Susan Jane. b 69. SEITE BA 10. **d** 10 **p** 11. C Minster-in-Sheppey *Cant* 10-12; C W Sheppey 12-14; P-in-c Reculver and Herne Bay St Bart and Hoath from 14. *The Vicarage, 25 Dence Park, Herne Bay CT6 6BQ* T: (01227) 360948 E: revsuemartin@btinternet.com

MARTIN, Mrs Susan Mary. b 49. UEA BEd 94. ERMC 04. **d** 09 **p** 10. NSM Gayton, Gayton Thorpe, E Walton, E Winch etc *Nor* 09-13; Chapl Norfolk Hospice from 13. *The Limes, Lynn Road, Gayton, King's Lynn PE32 1QJ* T/F: (01553) 636570 M: 07801-701677 E: suemartin2gayton@hotmail.com

MARTIN, Sylvia. b 24. dss 75 **d** 87 **p** 94. NSM Selsdon St Jo w St Fran *S'wark* 87-99; PtO 99-07. *17 Frobisher Court, Sydenham Rise, London SE23 3XH* T: (020) 8699 6247

MARTIN, Sylvia. b 43. Sarum Th Coll 94. **d** 97 **p** 98. NSM Locks Heath *Portsm* 97-02; PtO 02-04; NSM Fareham H Trin 04-07; Chapl Fareham Coll of F&HE 04-07; rtd 07; PtO *Portsm* from 07. *9 Harvester Drive, Fareham PO15 5NR* T: (01329) 312269
E: sylvia.martin43@yahoo.com

MARTIN, Thomas Robin. b 40. Bps' Coll Cheshunt 64. **d** 67 **p** 68. C Ripley *Derby* 67-70; C Ilkeston St Mary 70-74; V Chinley w Buxworth 74-83; V Knighton St Mich *Leic* 83-85; V Thurmaston 85-05; rtd 05; C Leic Resurr 08; C Braunstone Park 09; C Birstall and Wanlip 10-11; PtO from 14. *22 Sycamore Road, Birstall, Leicester LE4 4LT* T: 0116-267 1651
E: tr.martin@btinternet.com

MARTIN, Warrick David. b 71. Stirling Univ BA 94. Oak Hill Th Coll BA 09. **d** 09 **p** 10. C Lt Heath *St Alb* 09-13; C Terrington St Clement *Ely* from 13. *8 Sutton Road, Terrington St Clement, King's Lynn PE34 4PQ* T: (01553) 390308 M: 07738-127587
E: tscassociate@gmail.com

MARTIN, William Harrison. b 38. Sarum & Wells Th Coll 91. **d** 87 **p** 88. NSM Rushen *S & M* 87-92; C German 92-97; V Lonan and Laxey 97-08; rtd 08; PtO *S & M* from 09. *Crossag Villa, Crossag Road, Ballasalla, Isle of Man IM9 3EF* T: (01624) 825982 E: billmartin@manx.net

MARTIN-DOYLE, Mrs Audrey Brenda. b 35. Cranmer Hall Dur 80. dss 82 **d** 87 **p** 95. The Lye and Stambermill *Worc* 82-86; Chapl Lee Abbey 86-88; Ldr Aston Cottage Community

88-93; C Cheltenham St Mary, St Matt, St Paul and H Trin *Glouc* 94-97; rtd 97; PtO *Glouc* from 97. *39 Moorend Street, Cheltenham GL53 0EH* T: (01242) 510352
E: audrey@martin-doyle.freeserve.co.uk

MARTIN-SMITH, Paul. b 38. TCD BA 64 Lon Univ MSc 67 FIPEM 88. WMMTC 94. **d** 97 **p** 98. NSM Tile Hill *Cov* 97-99; PtO *Ex* 00-09. *12 Emmasfield, Exmouth EX8 2LS* T: (01395) 269505

MARTINEAU, Canon David Richards Durani. b 36. AKC 59. **d** 60 **p** 61. C Ches St Jo 60-64; C St Mark's Cathl George S Africa 64; C Riversdale 64-66; R Beaufort W and Victoria W 66-69; C Jarrow St Paul *Dur* 69-72; TV 72-75; TR Jarrow 76-85; V Gildersome *Wakef* 85-00; Hon Can Wakef Cathl 94-00; rtd 00; PtO *Linc* from 00; Hon Asst Chapl Voorschoten *Eur* 02-03. *Harlough, St Chad, Barrow-upon-Humber DN19 7AU* T: (01469) 531475
E: david-martineau@harlough.freeserve.co.uk

MARTINEAU, Canon Jeremy Fletcher. b 40. OBE 03. K Coll Lon BD 65 AKC 65. **d** 66 **p** 67. C Jarrow St Paul *Dur* 66-73; Bp's Ind Adv 69-73; P-in-c Raughton Head w Gatesgill *Carl* 73-80; Chapl to Agric 73-80; Ind Chapl *Bris* 80-90; Nat Rural Officer Gen Syn Bd of Miss 88-90 and 90-03; Hon Can Cov Cathl 01-03; rtd 04; LtO *St D* from 05. *11 New Hill Villas, Goodwick SA64 0DT* T: (01348) 874886 E: jeremy.m@talktalk.net

MARTINSON, Matthew Allan. b 74. Mattersey Hall BA 03. St Jo Coll Nottm. **d** 09 **p** 10. C Beverley St Nic *York* 09-12; V Bransholme from 12. *St John's Vicarage, Wawne Road, Sutton-on-Hull, Hull HU7 4YR* T: (01482) 828169
E: matt@martinson.org.uk

MARTLEW, Andrew Charles. b 50. Nottm Univ BTh 76 Lanc Univ MA 80. Linc Th Coll 72. **d** 76 **p** 77. C Poulton-le-Fylde *Blackb* 76-79; Hon C Lancaster Ch Ch 79-80; Malaysia 81-83; V Golcar *Wakef* 83-89; Dioc Schs Officer 89-95; V Warmfield 89-95; Dioc Dir of Educn *York* 95-02; CF (TA) 87-02; CF 02-10; Chapl HM Pris Ranby 10-11; rtd 11; PtO *Wakef* 10-13; V Womersley *Leeds* from 13; PtO *York* from 11. *Balne Moor Farm, Balne Moor Road, Balne, Goole DN14 0EN* T: (01405) 862484
E: 762martl@armymail.mod.uk

MARTLEW, Mrs Catherine Linda. b 54. Bolton Inst of Educn BSc 84 Lon Inst of Educn MSc 85. LCTP 09. **d** 12 **p** 15. NSM Chorley St Geo *Blackb* from 12. *148 Appley Lane North, Appley Bridge, Wigan WN6 9DX* T: (01257) 253345
M: 07969-878655 E: smartlew@sky.com

MARVELL, John. b 32. Lon Univ BD 63 Leic Univ MEd 73 PhD 85. Oak Hill Th Coll 79. **d** 80 **p** 81. NSM Colchester Ch Ch w St Mary V *Chelmsf* 80-85; PtO 85-87; P-in-c Stisted w Bradwell and Pattiswick 87-98; rtd 98. *3 impasse de Genets, 35800 Dinard, France* T: (0033) 2 99 16 56 74
E: jmarvell@nordnet.fr

MARVIN, David Arthur. b 51. St Jo Coll Nottm 96. **d** 97 **p** 98. C Mansfield St Jo *S'well* 97-01; P-in-c Greasley 01-11; V from 11. *The Vicarage, 36 Moorgreen, Newthorpe, Nottingham NG16 2FB* T: (01773) 712509
E: dave.marvin1@ntlworld.com

MARWOOD, Canon Timothy John Edmonds. b 51. Whitelands Coll Lon CertEd 72 Open Univ BA 89 Lon Inst of Educn MA 91. S'wark Ord Course 92. **d** 95 **p** 96. NSM Putney St Mary *S'wark* 95-00; PtO *Ex* 00-07; P-in-c Petersham *S'wark* 07-11; V from 11; P-in-c Earlsfield St Jo from 15; Chapl K Coll Sch Wimbledon 08-10; AD Richmond and Barnes *S'wark* 10-15; Hon Can S'wark Cathl from 08. *The Vicarage, Bute Avenue, Richmond TW10 7AX* T: (020) 8940 8435 -
M: 07973-518742 E: timmarwood@yahoo.co.uk

MARY CLARE, Sister. *See* FOGG, Cynthia Mary

MARY STEPHEN, Sister. *See* BRITT, Mary Stephen

MASCALL, Mrs Margaret Ann. b 43. LRAM 64 Bris Univ CertEd 65 St Jo Coll Dur BA 71 MA 79. Cranmer Hall Dur 69. **dss** 76 **d** 87 **p** 94. Hertford St Andr *St Alb* 75-79; Herne Bay Ch Ch *Cant* 79-82; Seasalter 82-84; Whitstable 84-90; Par Dn 87-90; PtO 91-94; Hon C Hackington 94-95; V Newington w Hartlip and Stockbury 95-03; rtd 03; PtO *Cant* from 03. *48 Holmside Avenue, Minster on Sea, Sheerness ME12 3EY* T: (01795) 663095 E: margaret.mascall@btopenworld.com

MASCARENHAS, Felix Pedro Antonio. b 55. Bombay Univ BA 80 Pontifical Univ Rome JCD 88. Pilar Major Th Sem Goa BTh 81. **d** 82 **p** 82. In RC Ch 82-02; C Chich St Paul and Westhampnett 02-06; P-in-c Brighton Gd Shep Preston from 06. *The Vicarage, 272 Dyke Road, Brighton BN1 5AE* T: (01273) 882987 M: 07814-739312 E: felixmas@hotmail.com

MASDING, John William. b 39. Magd Coll Ox BA 61 DipEd 63 MA 65 Univ of Wales (Cardiff) LLM 94 FRSA 96. Ridley Hall Cam 63. **d** 65 **p** 66. C Boldmere *Birm* 65-71; V Hamstead St Paul 71-97; rtd 97; PtO *B & W* from 00; *Bris* from 00. *The Old School House, Norton Hawkfield, Pensford, Bristol BS39 4HB* T/F: (01275) 830017 E: john.masding@magd.oxon.org

MASH, William Edward John. b 54. Imp Coll Lon BSc 75 Open Univ MA 00 ARCS. St Jo Coll Nottm 87. **d** 89 **p** 90. C Beverley Minster *York* 89-93; V Elloughton and Brough w Brantingham 93-01; P-in-c Newcastle St Geo *Lich* 01-08; V 08-10; P-in-c Knutton 06-08; V 08-10; Chapl Town Cen and Newcastle Coll 01-10; Team Ldr Black Country Urban Ind Miss *Lich* from 10; Dioc Officer for Miss in the Economy from 10. *20 Mahogany Drive, Stafford ST16 2TS* T: (01785) 509231 M: 07714-103007
E: william.e.j.mash@gmail.com

MASHEDER, Canon Peter Timothy Charles. b 49. AKC 71. St Aug Coll Cant 71. **d** 72 **p** 73. C Barkingside St Fran *Chelmsf* 72-75; C Chingford SS Pet and Paul 75-91; P-in-c High Laver w Magdalen Laver and Lt Laver etc 91-98; R 98-07; RD Ongar 98-04; R Ray Valley *Ox* 07-14; AD Bicester and Islip 08-13; Hon Can Ch Ch 13-14; rtd 14; Hon C Honiton, Gittisham, Combe Raleigh, Monkton etc *Ex* 14-15; Hon C Bere Regis and Affpuddle w Turnerspuddle *Sarum* from 15. *Address temp unknown* E: chasmash@ic24.net

MASHITER, Mrs Marion. b 48. CBDTI 01. **d** 04 **p** 05. NSM Burneside *Carl* 04-07; NSM Beacon 07-10; NSM Natland from 10; NSM Old Hutton and New Hutton from 10. *The Maples, 5 Esthwaite Avenue, Kendal LA9 7NN* T: (01539) 731957 M: 07748-771836 E: revquackers@tiscali.co.uk

MASIH, Wilson. b 49. **d** 12. NSM Hanwell St Mellitus w St Mark *Lon* 11-15; NSM Southall Ch Redeemer from 15. *37 Western Avenue, Southall UB1 2AP* E: masih37@aol.com

MASKELL, John Michael. *See* MILLER-MASKELL, John Michael

MASKELL, Miss Rosemary Helen. b 58. Ripon Coll Cuddesdon. **d** 00 **p** 01. C Goodrington *Ex* 00-04; V Littleport *Ely* 04-13; R Huntingdon St Barn and the Riptons from 13. *St Barnabas' Vicarage, Coneygear Road, Huntingdon PE29 1RQ* T: (01480) 434637 M: 07794-938501 E: rhmaskell@gmail.com

MASKREY, Mrs Susan Elizabeth. b 43. Cranmer Hall Dur IDC 70. **dss** 76 **d** 92 **p** 94. C Billingham St Aid *Dur* 92-95; Asst Chapl HM Pris Holme Ho 94-95; Asst Chapl HM Pris Preston 95-01; Chapl HM Pris Kirkham 01-05; rtd 05; PtO *Blackb* from 05. *c/o the Bishop of Blackburn, Bishop's House, Ribchester Road, Blackburn BB1 9EF*

MASLEN, Mrs Linda Jane. b 62. Yorks Min Course 12. **d** 15. C Halifax St Aug and Mount Pellon *Leeds* from 15. *12 Warren Lodge Gardens, Halifax HX3 0RB* M: 07595-949153
E: linda-maslen@hotmail.com

MASLEN (formerly CHILD), Mrs Margaret Mary. b 44. ALA 76 Open Univ BA 79. S Dios Minl Tr Scheme 89. **d** 92 **p** 94. C Portishead *B & W* 92-93; C Ilminster w Whitelackington 93-94; C Ilminster and Distr 94-96; C Tatworth 96-99; C Chaffcombe, Cricket Malherbie etc 99-00; TV Chard and Distr 00-05; Chapl Taunton and Somerset NHS Trust 97-05; rtd 05; Hon C Sherston Magna, Easton Grey, Luckington etc *Bris* from 06; Hon C Hullavington, Norton and Stanton St Quintin from 06. *2 Woods Close, Sherston, Malmesbury SN16 0LF* T: (01666) 840387 E: maslens@tiscali.co.uk

MASLEN, Richard Ernest. b 34. S Dios Minl Tr Scheme 89. **d** 92 **p** 93. NSM Sherston Magna, Easton Grey, Luckington etc *Bris* 92-93; NSM Ilminster w Whitelackington *B & W* 93-94; NSM Ilminster and Distr 94-96; P-in-c Tatworth 96-99; TV Chard and Distr 99-00; rtd 00; PtO *B & W* 00-05. *2 Woods Close, Sherston, Malmesbury SN16 0LF* T: (01666) 840387

MASLEN, Canon Stephen Henry. b 37. CCC Ox BA 62 MA 65. Ridley Hall Cam 62. **d** 64 **p** 65. C Keynsham w Queen Charlton *B & W* 64-67; C Cheltenham St Mary *Glouc* 67-71; P-in-c St Mary-at-Lambeth *S'wark* 72-73; TV N Lambeth 74-79; V Horley 79-84; TR 84-94; RD Reigate 86-91; R Coulsdon St Jo 94-02; Hon Can S'wark Cathl 95-02; rtd 02; PtO *Worc* from 02. *The Red House, Back Lane, Bredon, Tewkesbury GL20 7LH* T: (01684) 772575 E: stephen.maslen@hotmail.co.uk

MASON, Adrian Stanley. b 54. Hatf Poly BSc 77. Ripon Coll Cuddesdon 77. **d** 80 **p** 81. C Mill End and Heronsgate w W Hyde *St Alb* 80-83; TV Axminster, Chardstock, Combe Pyne and Rousdon *Ex* 83-87; TV Halesworth w Linstead, Chediston, Holton etc *St E* 87-88; R Brandon and Santon Downham 88-91; R Glemsford, Hartest w Boxted, Somerton etc 91-95; Min Can St E Cathl 95-97; R S Hartismere 06-11; P-in-c Stoke by Nayland w Leavenheath and Polstead 11-15; R Mid Elloe Gp *Linc* from 15. *The Rectory, Wood Lane, Fleet, Holbeach, Spalding PE12 8NN* T: (01406) 821755
E: fr.adrian.mason@gmail.com

MASON, Ambrose. *See* MASON, Thomas Henry Ambrose

MASON, Andrew. b 73. **d** 10 **p** 11. NSM Chelsea St Jo w St Andr *Lon* from 10. *Flat 2, 465 Kings Road, London SW10 0LU* T: (020) 7351 1447 E: andymason73@yahoo.com *or* andy@stjohnchelsea.org

MASON, Andrew John. b 77. St Jo Coll Nottm BA 06. **d** 06 **p** 07. C Bemerton *Sarum* 06-09; TV Kingswood *Bris* from 09. *60 Lavers Close, Bristol BS15 9ZG* T: 0117-960 3195
E: revandymason06@hotmail.co.uk

MASON, Miss Beverley Anne. Trin Coll Bris BA 00. **d** 01 **p** 03. C Rusthall *Roch* 01-02; C Rainham 02-05; V Upper Norwood St Jo *S'wark* 05-12; AD Croydon N 10-12; P-in-c Bingley All SS *Bradf* 12-13; V *Leeds* from 13. *Woodlands, 26 Falcon Road, Bingley BD16 4DW* T: (01274) 563113
E: revdbeverley@yahoo.co.uk

MASON, Miss Chantal Marie. b 73. Ex Univ BA 96 St Luke's Coll Ex PGCE 98. Trin Coll Bris MA 08. **d** 08 **p** 09. C Alphington, Shillingford St George and Ide *Ex* 08-12; Bp's Chapl *Chelmsf* 12-14; Chapl Ex Univ from 15. *The Chaplaincy, University of Exeter, St Luke's Campus, Heavitree Road, Exeter EX1 2LU* E: revchantalmason@yahoo.co.uk

MASON, Charles Oliver. b 51. Jes Coll Cam BA 73 MA 99 St Jo Coll Dur BA 79. **d** 80 **p** 81. C Cheltenham St Mary, St Matt, St Paul and H Trin *Glouc* 80-84; C Enfield Ch Ch Trent Park *Lon* 84-88; P-in-c W Hampstead St Cuth 88-93; V 93-01; AD N Camden 98-01; V Braintree *Chelmsf* from 01. *St Michael's Vicarage, 10A Marshalls Road, Braintree CM7 2LL* T: (01376) 322840 E: revdcom@btinternet.com

MASON, Christina Mary. b 42. Univ of Wales BMus 63 MA 67 BSc(Econ) 70 Dundee Univ PhD 84 Middx Univ MSc 02. St Jo Coll Nottm 81. **d** 83 **p** 10. LtO *Bre* 83-92; PtO *Nor* 09-10; NSM Gt and Lt Ellingham, Rockland and Shropham etc from 10. *44 Long Street, Great Ellingham, Attleborough NR17 1LN* T: (01953) 451354 E: cmason@patsltd.co.uk

MASON, Mrs Christine Mary. b 43. Sarum & Wells Th Coll 91. **d** 93 **p** 94. Par Dn Blakenall Heath *Lich* 93-94; C 94-97; TV Rugeley 97-06; TV Brereton and Rugeley 06-08; rtd 08; PtO *Lich* from 09. *The Old School, Sutton Maddock, Shifnal TF11 9NQ* T: (01952) 730442

MASON, Christopher David. b 51. Lanc Univ BA 72 Leic Univ MEd 82. EAMTC 91. **d** 94 **p** 95. NSM Pet St Mary Boongate 94-00 and 03-05; P-in-c Newborough 00-02; Chapl Pet High Sch 05-10; rtd 10; PtO *Pet* 10-12; Hon C Charfield and Kingswood w Wickwar etc *Glouc* from 12. *The Rectory, 36 Wotton Road, Charfield, Wotton-under-Edge GL12 8TG* T: (01454) 261971
E: christopher.mason2012@btinternet.com

MASON, Damien David Robert. b 85. Edin Univ BD 11. St Steph Ho Ox MTh 15. **d** 15. C Hendon St Mary and Ch Ch *Lon* from 15. *St Mary's Cottage, 48 Church End, London NW4 4JT* M: 07505-723596 E: damienmason@btinternet.com

MASON, David Gray. b 37. Birm Univ LDS 61 K Coll Lon MPhil 94. St Alb Minl Tr Scheme 83. **d** 95 **p** 95. NSM Biddenham *St Alb* 95-98; P-in-c Felmersham 98-05; NSM Sharnbrook, Felmersham and Knotting w Souldrop 05-12; RD Sharnbrook 06-12; PtO from 12. *2A Devon Road, Bedford MK40 3DF* T/F: (01234) 309737
E: david.mason93@ntlworld.com

MASON, Dawn Lavinia. b 53. Ripon Coll Cuddesdon 95. **d** 97 **p** 98. C Wisbech St Aug *Ely* 97-00; V Emneth and Marshland St James 00-09; P-in-c Elm and Friday Bridge w Coldham 04-09; V Fen Orchards from 09. *The Vicarage, 72 Church Road, Emneth, Wisbech PE14 8AF* T: (01945) 583089
E: dmason889@btinternet.com

MASON, Dennis Wardell. b 28. Ox NSM Course 83. **d** 86 **p** 87. NSM Ox St Barn and St Paul 86-08. *26 John Lopes Road, Eynsham, Witney OX29 4JR* T: (01865) 880440

MASON, Edward. *See* MASON, Thomas Edward

MASON, Mrs Elizabeth Ann. b 42. Homerton Coll Cam TCert 64 Open Univ BA 90. Ox Min Course 91. **d** 94 **p** 95. NSM Worminghall w Ickford, Oakley and Shabbington *Ox* 94-95; NSM Swan 95-98; TV 98-05; rtd 05. *35 Common Road, North Leigh, Witney OX29 6RD* T: (01993) 883966

MASON, Francis Robert Anthony. b 56. Trin Coll Bris BA 90. **d** 90 **p** 91. C Denham *Ox* 90-94; P-in-c Jersey Grouville *Win* 94-98; R 98-04; R Tendring and Lt Bentley w Beaumont cum Moze *Chelmsf* 07-15; C Gt Oakley w Wix and Wrabness 13-15; R Fakenham w Alethorpe *Nor* from 15; P-in-c Fulmodeston w Croxton from 15. *The Rectory, 21 Gladstone Road, Fakenham NR21 9BZ* T: (01328) 862268 E: revmason@btinternet.com

✠**MASON, The Rt Revd James Philip.** b 54. Solomon Is Coll of HE TCert 73 St Jo Coll Auckland STh 86. Bp Patteson Th Coll (Solomon Is) 78. **d** 81 **p** 82 **c** 91. C St Barn Cathl Honiara Solomon Is 81-82; Sec to Abp Melanesia 83-86; Lect Bp Patteson Th Coll 87; Dean Honiara 88-91; Bp Hanuato'o 91-04; P-in-c Plympton St Maurice *Ex* 05-14; Hon Asst Bp Ex 07-14; rtd 14. *The Anglican Church of Melanesia, PO Box 19, Honiara, Solomon Islands* T: (00677) 769 8586
E: ellisonmason77@gmail.com

MASON, John Evans. b 32. RD . Linc Th Coll 57. **d** 59 **p** 60. C Putney St Mary *S'wark* 59-62; C Berry Pomeroy *Ex* 62-64; Chapl RN 64-68; V Hopton *Nor* 68-72; Chapl RNR 69-82; P-in-c Roydon St Remigius *Nor* 72-76; R Diss 72-80; Dir YMCA Cam 80-85; Prin YMCA Dunford Coll 85-88; PtO *Glouc* 88-97;

Ox 89-99; rtd 96; PtO *Nor* 98-02; *Sarum* 02-04; *B & W* from 05. *8 Nursteed Meadows, Nursteed, Devizes SN10 3HL* T: (01380) 728674

MASON, John Martin. b 41. UMIST BSc 63. Glouc Sch of Min 80 Qu Coll Birm 82. **d** 84 **p** 85. C Tuffley *Glouc* 84-87; P-in-c Willersey, Saintbury, Weston-sub-Edge etc 87-92; R 92-96; P-in-c Selling w Throwley, Sheldwich w Badlesmere etc *Cant* 96-06; Dioc Rural Officer 96-06; rtd 06; PtO *Cant* from 06. *26 High Snoad Wood, Challock, Ashford TN25 4DQ* M: 07951-024355 E: ruraljoe@btinternet.com

MASON, Jonathan Patrick. b 55. Edin Th Coll 90. **d** 92 **p** 93. C Edin Ch Ch 92-94; C Edin Old St Paul 94-96; R St Andrews All SS *St And* 96-14; Chapl St Andr Univ 97-14; Dioc Dir of Ords 02-11; Can St Ninian's Cathl Perth 07-14. *36 High Street, Belford NE70 7NJ* E: northmasons@gmail.com

MASON, Ms Josephine Margaret. b 41. Edin Univ BMus 64. WMMTC 88. **d** 93 **p** 94. Chapl Asst S Birm Mental Health NHS Trust 91-06; C Birm St Jo Ladywood 93-01; C Ladywood St Jo and St Pet 01-06; rtd 06; PtO *Birm* from 06. *340 Selly Oak Road, Birmingham B30 1HP* T: 0121-451 1412
E: jo.mason@freeuk.com

MASON, Julia Ann. b 43. St Jo Coll Nottm 89. **d** 91 **p** 95. NSM Troon *Glas* 91-93; NSM Ayr, Maybole and Girvan 93-05; LtO *Edin* from 08; PtO *Glas* from 08. *13/2 Rocheid Park, Edinburgh EH4 1RU* T: 0131-343 1165
E: revdjuliamason@btinternet.com

MASON, Canon Kenneth Staveley. b 31. ARCS 53 Lon Univ BSc 53 BD 64. Wells Th Coll 56. **d** 58 **p** 59. C Kingston upon Hull St Martin *York* 58-61; C Pocklington w Yapham-cum-Meltonby, Owsthorpe etc 61-63; C Millington w Gt Givendale 61-63; V Thornton w Allerthorpe 63-69; Sub-Warden St Aug Coll Cant 69-76; Abp's Adv in Past Min 76-77; Dir Cant Sch of Min 77-81; Prin 81-89; Sec to Dioc Bd of Min *Cant* 77-87; Six Preacher Cant Cathl 79-84; Hon Can Cant Cathl 84-89; Prin Edin Th Coll 89-94; Prin TISEC 95; Can St Mary's Cathl 89-96; rtd 95; PtO *Leeds* from 96. *2 Williamson Close, Ripon HG4 1AZ* T: (01765) 607041

MASON, Lesley Jane. b 55. Newnham Coll Cam BA 76 FInstD. St Jo Coll Nottm 04. **d** 07 **p** 08. NSM Busbridge and Hambledon *Guildf* 07-10; Chapl HM Pris Send from 10. *HM Prison Send, Ripley Road, Woking GU23 7LJ* T: (01483) 471000 E: ljmason@btinternet.com

MASON, Nigel Frederick. b 60. Wycliffe Hall Ox 93. **d** 95 **p** 96. C Highbury Ch Ch w St Jo and St Sav *Lon* 95-98; C Seaford w Sutton *Chich* 98-01; R Rotherfield w Mark Cross from 01. *The Rectory, Mayfield Road, Rotherfield, Crowborough TN6 3LU* T: (01892) 852536

MASON, Nigel James. b 56. Culham Coll of Educn BEd 78. St Steph Ho Ox 95. **d** 97 **p** 98. C Hove *Chich* 97-00; V Kemp Town St Mary 00-07; Chapl St Mary's Hall Brighton 03-07; V Smethwick *Birm* 07-13; P-in-c Smethwick St Matt w St Chad 10-13; Chapl Ex Hospiscare from 13. *4 Velwell Road, Exeter EX4 4LE* T: (01392) 688000 E: n.mason@talktalk.net

MASON, Paul. b 51. Cranmer Hall Dur 93. **d** 93 **p** 94. C Handforth *Ches* 93-97; V Partington and Carrington 97-04; V Church Hulme from 04. *The Vicarage, 74 London Road, Holmes Chapel, Crewe CW4 7BD* T/F: (01477) 533124 E: paulandsuemason@tiscali.co.uk

MASON, Mrs Pauline. b 49. LCTP. **d** 08 **p** 09. NSM Chorley St Geo *Blackb* 08-12; V Wrightington from 12. *The Vicarage, Church Lane, Wrightington, Wigan WN6 9SL* T: (01257) 452133 E: pollymason@qualitas.f9.co.uk

MASON, Peter Charles. b 45. K Coll Lon BD 72 AKC 72 Birm Univ PGCE 89. St Aug Coll Cant 72. **d** 73 **p** 74. C Ilkeston St Mary *Derby* 73-76; C Bridgnorth St Mary *Heref* 76-78; TV Bridgnorth, Tasley, Astley Abbotts, etc 78-88; RE Teacher from 89; rtd 10; PtO *Heref* 89-04; *St D* from 04. *63 Nun Street, St Davids, Haverfordwest SA62 6NU* T: (01437) 721715

MASON, Canon Peter Joseph. b 34. Lon Univ BA 58. Coll of Resurr Mirfield 58. **d** 60 **p** 61. C Belhus Park CD *Chelmsf* 60-63; LtO *Eur* 63-64; Asst Chapl Lon Univ 64-70; Chapl City Univ 66-70; R Stoke Newington St Mary 70-78; V Writtle *Chelmsf* 78-81; P-in-c Highwood 78-81; V Writtle w Highwood 81-86; R Shenfield 86-93; Hon Can Chelmsf Cathl 89-00; P-in-c Maldon All SS w St Pet 93-95; V 95-00; RD Maldon and Dengie 95-00; rtd 00; PtO *Chelmsf* from 00. *8 Canuden Road, Chelmsford CM1 2SX* T: (01245) 351465
E: petermason32@waitrose.com

MASON, Robert Herbert George. b 48. ACII. Oak Hill Th Coll 82. **d** 84 **p** 85. C Ware Ch Ch *St Alb* 84-88; V Eastbourne All So *Chich* 88-98; P-in-c Poole *Sarum* 98-01; R 01-11; rtd 11; PtO *Portsm* from 11; Chapl Miss to Seafarers 98-11. *63 Tredegar Road, Southsea PO4 9BJ* T: (023) 928 24712
E: revbobmelmason@hotmail.com

MASON, Mrs Sally Lynne. b 52. EMMTC 05. **d** 08 **p** 09. NSM Alfreton *Derby* 08-12; NSM Blackwell w Tibshelf 12-13;

Spiritual Dir Derby Angl Cursillo from 13. *27 Stretton Road, Morton, Alfreton DE55 6GW* T: (01773) 873508
E: sallymason@live.co.uk

MASON, Mrs Sally-Anne. b 55. Open Univ BA 86 C F Mott Coll of Educn CertEd 77. SNWTP 07. **d** 10 **p** 11. NSM Childwall St Dav *Liv* from 10; NSM Stoneycroft All SS from 10. *2 Reedale Road, Liverpool L18 5HL* T: 0151-724 1142 M: 07889-584885
E: sallyanne.mason@o2.co.uk

MASON, Sarah Catherine. *See* LAWRENCE, Sarah Catherine

MASON (formerly FOALE), Sheila Rosemary. b 40. Saffron Walden Coll CertEd 61 ARCM 62. SWMTC 98. **d** 01 **p** 02. NSM Shebbear, Buckland Filleigh, Sheepwash etc *Ex* 01-04; C Cobham and Stoke D'Abernon *Guildf* 04-08; rtd 08; PtO *Bre* 09-10; *Guildf* from 14. *1 Heron Place, Broughty Ferry, Dundee DD5 3PR* T: (01382) 350568 M: 07783-965119
E: rosemarymason16@mypostoffice.co.uk

MASON, Simon Ion Vincent. b 60. Birm Univ BA 82. Trin Coll Bris BA 00. **d** 00 **p** 01. C Nottingham St Nic *S'well* 00-05; P-in-c Newent and Gorsley w Cliffords Mesne *Glouc* from 05. *The Rectory, 43 Court Road, Newent GL18 1SY* T: (01531) 820248 E: mason.simon@ntlworld.com *or* stmarys.church@talk21.com

MASON, Stephen David. b 65. Univ of Wales (Lamp) BA 87. Ripon Coll Cuddesdon 89. **d** 92 **p** 93. C Gt Grimsby St Mary and St Jas *Linc* 92-97; V Southborough St Thos *Roch* 97-02; V Paddington St Jo w St Mich *Lon* from 02. *18 Somers Crescent, London W2 2PN* T: (020) 7262 1732 F: 7706 4475
E: parishadmin@stjohns-hydepark.com

MASON, Terry Mathew. b 56. Trin Coll Bris 94. **d** 96 **p** 97. C Bexleyheath Ch Ch *Roch* 96-99; P-in-c Stone 99-03; V Broadway w Wickhamford *Worc* 03-11; RD Evesham 05-10; P-in-c Wootton Wawen *Cov* 11-14; P-in-c Claverdon w Preston Bagot 11-14; AD Alcester 11-14; Deanery Missr 11-14; R Ditton Priors w Neenton, Burwarton etc *Heref* from 14. *The Vicarage, Ditton Priors, Bridgnorth WV16 6SQ* T: (01746) 712426
E: terrymason56@gmail.com

MASON, Preb Thomas Edward. b 52. Bris Univ MEd 80. Trin Coll Bris BA 91. **d** 91 **p** 92. C Glouc St Jas and All SS 91-94; V Churchdown 94-04; RD Glouc N 99-04; R Bath Abbey w St Jas *B & W* from 04; Preb Wells Cathl from 05. *The Rectory, 12 Cleveland Walk, Bath BA2 6JX* T: (01225) 318267 *or* 422462
E: rector@bathabbey.org

MASON, The Ven Thomas Henry Ambrose. b 51. Solicitor 75. Oak Hill Th Coll BA 86. **d** 86 **p** 87. C W Drayton *Lon* 86-89; Field Officer Oak Hill Ext Coll 89-94; Eur Sec ICS 94-95; Dir of Tr *Eur* 95-03; Dir Min and Dir of Ords 01-03; Can Brussels Cathl 00-03; Hon Can Brussels Cathl 03-07; R Grosmont and Skenfrith and Llangattock etc *Mon* 03-08; Dir Min from 06; Adn Mon from 13. *The Rectory, Gwernesney, Usk NP15 1HP* T: (01291) 672152
E: archdeacon.monmouth@churchinwales.org.uk

MASON, William Frederick. b 48. Linc Th Coll 75. **d** 78 **p** 79. C Ipswich St Aug *St E* 78-81; TV Dronfield *Derby* 81-88; V Ellesmere St Pet *Sheff* 88-91; V Bedgrove *Ox* 91-00; C Hazlemere 00-07; V Penn Street 07-13; rtd 14. *The Vicarage, Penn Street, Amersham HP7 0PX* T: (01494) 715195
E: willfmason@aol.com

MASSEY, Alison June. b 63. **d** 13 **p** 14. C Stourdene Gp *Cov* from 13. *27 Pebworth Drive, Hatton, Warwick CV35 7UD* T: (01926) 401781

MASSEY, Brenda Margaret. b 60. OLM Frimley *Guildf* from 14. *69 Old Pasture Road, Frimley, Camberley GU16 8RT* T: (01276) 684907
E: margaret@masseyonline.co.uk

MASSEY, Mrs Elizabeth Ann. b 53. N Staffs Poly BSc 75. STETS 04. **d** 07 **p** 08. C Whitton *Sarum* 07-10; TV Marden Vale from 10. *The Vicarage, Church Road, Derry Hill, Calne SN11 9NN* T: (01249) 817926 M: 07777-800084
E: ea.massey@btinternet.com

MASSEY, George Douglas. b 44. St Jo Coll Nottm 91. **d** 93 **p** 94. C Higher Bebington *Ches* 93-98; V Messingham *Linc* 98-14; rtd 14. *Address temp unknown*

MASSEY, Mrs Kate Ishbel. b 77. Aber Univ MB, ChB 99. Qu Coll Birm 08. **d** 11 **p** 12. C Kenilworth St Nic *Cov* 11-13; C Meriden 13-15; V Stockingford from 15. *Stockingford Vicarage, 90 Church Road, Nuneaton CV10 8LG*
E: katemassey@virginmedia.com

MASSEY, Keith John. b 46. Oak Hill Th Coll 69. **d** 72 **p** 73. C Bermondsey St Jas w Ch Ch *S'wark* 72-76; C Benchill *Man* 76-82; V Clifton Green 82-97; V Flixton St Jo 97-11; rtd 11; PtO *Man* from 11. *42 Curzon Road, Stockport SK2 5DH* E: keithjmassey@yahoo.co.uk

MASSEY, Margaret. *See* MASSEY, Brenda Margaret

MASSEY, Michelle Elaine. *See* WARD, Michelle Elaine

MASSEY, Nigel John. b 60. Birm Univ BA 81 MA 82. Wycliffe Hall Ox. **d** 87 **p** 88. C Bearwood *Birm* 87-90; C Warley Woods

90; C Tottenham St Paul *Lon* 91-94; USA from 94. *French Church du St Spirit, 111 East 60th Street #4, New York NY 10022, USA* T: (001) (212) 838 5680 E: stesprit@msn.com

MASSEY, Paul Daniel Shaw. b 70. Nottm Univ BA 93. Westcott Ho Cam 94. **d** 96 **p** 97. C Ashby-de-la-Zouch St Helen w Coleorton *Leic* 96-01; R Cotgrave *S'well* from 01; P-in-c Owthorpe from 01; P-in-c Hickling w Kinoulton and Broughton Sulney from 14. *The Rectory, 2 Thurman Drive, Cotgrave, Nottingham NG12 3LG* T/F: 0115-989 2223
E: pdsmassey@tiscali.co.uk

MASSEY, Peter. *See* MASSEY, William Peter

MASSEY, Peter William. b 45. St Mark & St Jo Coll Lon TCert 66 Open Univ BA 75. WMMTC 96. **d** 99 **p** 00. Lay Tr Officer *Heref* 97-09; NSM Holmer w Huntington 99-03; NSM Heref St Pet w St Owen and St Jas 03-15; PtO from 15. *15 Thoresby Drive, Hereford HR2 7RF* T/F: (01432) 270248 M: 07803-826728
E: p.massey@hereford.anglican.org

MASSEY, Shellie. *See* WARD, Michelle Elaine

MASSEY, Stephen William. b 56. Hatf Poly BSc 79 PhD 86 MIMA 04. ERMC 06. **d** 09 **p** 10. NSM Watford St Luke *St Alb* 09-12; PtO 12-14. *19 South Riding, Bricket Wood, St Albans AL2 3NG* T: (01923) 662368 E: swmportraits@xalt.co.uk

MASSEY, Wayne Philip. b 74. Brunel Univ BSc 97. Wycliffe Hall Ox BA 05. **d** 06 **p** 07. C Clifton Ch Ch w Em *Bris* 06-12; TV Bishopston and St Andrews from 12. *8 Windsor Road, Bristol BS6 5BP*

MASSEY, Preb William Cyril. b 32. Lich Th Coll 58. **d** 61 **p** 62. C Heref St Martin 61-66; V Kimbolton w Middleton-on-the-Hill 66-75; V Alveley 75-83; P-in-c Quatt 81-83; R Alveley and Quatt 84-85; R Llangarron w Llangrove, Whitchurch and Ganarew 85-97; Preb Heref Cathl 92-97; rtd 97; PtO *Heref* from 97. *16 Siward James Close, Bodenham, Hereford HR1 3LS* T: (01568) 797520

MASSEY, William Peter. b 50. CITC 96. **d** 99 **p** 00. C Fermoy Union *C, C & R* 99-00; C Carrigrohane Union and Kinsale Union 00-03; PtO *Eur* 04-13; P-in-c Lorgues w Fayence from 13. *1801 chemin des Pailles, 83510 Lorgues, France* T: (0033) 4 94 73 93 37 *or* 4 94 99 40 74 E: peter@themasseys.fr

MASSHEDAR, Richard Eric. b 57. Nottm Univ BTh 86. Linc Th Coll 83. **d** 86 **p** 87. C Cassop cum Quarrington *Dur* 86-89; C Ferryhill 89-91; V Leam Lane 91-94; P-in-c Hartlepool St Paul 94-96; V from 96. *St Paul's Vicarage, 6 Hutton Avenue, Hartlepool TS26 9PN* T: (01429) 272934
E: r.masshedar@ntlworld.com

MASSINGBERD-MUNDY, Roger William Burrell. b 36. TD. Univ of Wales (Lamp) BA 59. Ridley Hall Cam 59. **d** 61 **p** 62. C Benwell St Jas *Newc* 61-64; C Whorlton 64-72; TV 73; P-in-c Healey 73-85; Dioc Stewardship Adv 73-85; Hon Can Newc Cathl 82-85; CF (TA) 63-68; CF (TAVR) 71-83; R S Ormsby w Ketsby, Calceby and Driby *Linc* 85-86; P-in-c Harrington w Brinkhill 85-86; P-in-c Haugh 85-86; P-in-c Oxcombe 85-86; P-in-c Ruckland w Farforth and Maidenwell 85-86; P-in-c Somersby w Bag Enderby 85-86; P-in-c Tetford and Salmonby 85-86; R S Ormsby Gp 86-96; RD Bolingbroke 88-96; rtd 96; Chapl Taverham Hall Sch from 03. *The Old Post Office, West Raynham, Fakenham NR21 7AD* T: (01328) 838611 F: 838698
E: rogermundy@markeaton.co.uk

MASSON, Canon Philip Roy. b 52. Hertf Coll Ox BA 75 Leeds Univ BA 77. Coll of Resurr Mirfield 75. **d** 78 **p** 79. C Port Talbot St Theodore *Llan* 78-82; V Penyfai w Tondu 82-92; Dioc Dir Post-Ord Tr 85-88; Warden of Ords 88-01; R Newton Nottage from 92; AD Margam 01-06 and from 12; Can Llan Cathl from 02. *The Rectory, 64 Victoria Avenue, Porthcawl CF36 3HE* T: (01656) 782042 *or* 786899
E: porthcawl.church@tiscali.co.uk *or* philipmasson@hotmail.com

MASTERMAN, Malcolm. b 49. City Univ MSc 00. K Coll Lon 73 Chich Th Coll 76. **d** 77 **p** 78. C Peterlee *Dur* 77-80; Chapl Basingstoke Distr Hosp 80-85; Chapl Freeman Hosp Newc 85-95; Tr and Development Officer Hosp Chapl Coun 96-00; Sen Chapl N Dur Healthcare NHS Trust 00-02; Sen Chapl Co Durham and Darlington Acute Hosps NHS Trust 02-06; Lead Chapl S Tees Hosps NHS Trust 06-14; rtd 14; Bp's Adv on Hosp Chapl (Whitby Area) *York* from 06. *8 Fulthorpe Grove, Wynyard, Billingham TS22 5QZ*

MASTERMAN, Miss Patricia Hope. b 28. St Mich Ho Ox 59. dss 79 **d** 87. Asst CF 79-90; rtd 90; PtO *Chich* from 90. *33 Sea Lane Gardens, Ferring, Worthing BN12 5EQ* T: (01903) 245231

MASTERS, Mrs Carol. b 61. SNWTP 11. **d** 13 **p** 14. OLM Denton Ch Ch *Man* from 13. *55 Hulme Road, Denton, Manchester M34 2WX* T: 0161-320 5485 M: 07759-130100
E: carol1masters@aol.com

MASTERS, Kenneth Leslie. b 44. Leeds Univ BA 68. Cuddesdon Coll 68. **d** 70 **p** 71. C Wednesbury St Paul Wood Green *Lich* 70-71; C Tettenhall Regis 71-75; TV Chelmsley Wood *Birm* 75-79; R Harting *Chich* 79-87; V Rustington 87-00; TR

Beaminster Area *Sarum* 00-09; rtd 09; PtO *B & W* from 10. *9 Carrington Way, Wincanton BA9 9NX* T: (01963) 824209 E: k2masters4@btinternet.com

MASTERS, Rupert Paul Falla. b 52. Hull Univ BA 74 Ex Univ PGCE 75 Lon Inst of Educn MA 88. **d** 10 **p** 11. OLM Stoughton *Guildf* from 10. *32 Sheepfold Road, Guildford GU2 9TT* T: (01483) 573785 E: rupert.masters@talk21.com

MASTERS, Stephen Michael. b 52. St Chad's Coll Dur BA 75. Coll of Resurr Mirfield 85. **d** 87 **p** 88. C Primrose Hill St Mary w Avenue Road St Paul *Lon* 87-90; C Hornsey St Mary w St Geo 90-91; Bp's Dom Chapl *Chich* 91-96; V Brighton St Mich 96-99; C Eastbourne St Andr 00-01; Chapl to Bp Lewes 00-01; P-in-c Alderney *Win* 01-03; V from 03. *The New Vicarage, La Vallee, Alderney, Guernsey GY9 3XA* T: (01481) 824866

MASTERS, Ms Vivien. b 63. Yorks Min Course. **d** 14 **p** 15. C Kippax w Allerton Bywater *Leeds* from 14. *The Vicarage, 134 Leeds Road, Allerton Bywater, Castleford WF10 2HB* E: masters.vivien77@gmail.com

MASTIN, Brian Arthur. b 38. Peterho Cam BA 60 MA 63 BD 80 Mert Coll Ox MA 63. Ripon Hall Ox 62. **d** 63 **p** 64. Asst Lect Hebrew Univ Coll of N Wales (Ban) 63-65; Lect Hebrew 65-82; Sen Lect 82-98; Chapl Ban Cathl 63-65; LtO 65-98; rtd 98; PtO *Ely* from 98. *2A Gurney Way, Cambridge CB4 2ED* T: (01223) 355078

MATABELELAND, Bishop of. *See* LUNGA, The Rt Revd Cleophus

MATANA, Bishop of. *See* NTAHOTURI, The Rt Revd Bernard

MATCHETT, Christopher Jonathan. b 65. QUB BSSc TCD BTh 98. **d** 98 **p** 99. C Ballynafeigh St Jude *D & D* 98-01; C Holywood 01-04; I Magheraconmse *Clogh* 04-11; I Newtownards *D & D* from 11. *The Rectory, 36 Belfast Road, Newtownards BT23 4TT* T: (028) 9181 2527 *or* 9181 3193 M: 07875-179060 E: chris.matchett@btinternet.com

MATCHETT, Miss Diane Margaret. b 71. Open Univ BA 98. TCD Div Sch BTh 05. **d** 05 **p** 06. C Lisburn Ch Ch *Conn* 05-08; I Castlerock w Dunboe and Fermoyle *D & R* from 08. *The Rectory, 52 Main Street, Castlerock, Coleraine BT51 4RA* T: (028) 7084 8127 M: 07853-186509 E: revdiane@hotmail.co.uk

MATHER, David Jonathan. b 65. New Coll Ox BA 88 MA 95. St Steph Ho Ox BTh 95. **d** 95 **p** 96. C Pickering w Lockton and Levisham *York* 95-98; P-in-c Bridlington H Trin and Sewerby w Marton 98-99; V from 99. *Sewerby Vicarage, Cloverley Road, Bridlington YO16 5TX* T: (01262) 675725

MATHER, Mrs Elizabeth Ann. b 45. CertEd 66. Dalton Ho Bris IDC 70 St Jo Coll Nottm 92. **d** 94 **p** 95. NSM Littleover *Derby* 94-02; LtO *St Alb* 02-05; rtd 05; PtO *York* 05-10. *Angel Court, 2 Rose Street, Fortrose IV10 8TN* T: (01381) 621745 E: revlib@libbymather.freeserve.co.uk

MATHER, James William. b 63. Sheff Univ BA 86. St Steph Ho Ox 88. **d** 91 **p** 92. C Doncaster St Leon and St Jude *Sheff* 91-94; C Cantley 94-95; V Lakenheath *St E* 95-01; P-in-c Downham Market w Bexwell *Ely* 01-02; P-in-c Crimplesham w Stradsett 01-02; R Downham Market and Crimplesham w Stradsett from 02; RD Fincham and Feltwell 06-09. *The Rectory, King's Walk, Downham Market PE38 9LF* T: (01366) 382187 E: james.mather@ely.anglican.org

MATHER, William Bernard George. b 45. St Jo Coll Nottm 77. **d** 79 **p** 80. C St Leonards St Leon *Chich* 79-82; TR Netherthorpe *Sheff* 82-90; V Littleover *Derby* 90-02; Assoc Dir SOMA UK 02-05; TR Drypool *York* 05-10; rtd 10. *Angel Court, 2 Rose Street, Fortrose IV10 8TN* T: (01381) 621745 E: williammather@aol.com

MATHERS, Alan Edward. b 36. Lon Univ BA FPhS. Oak Hill Th Coll 61. **d** 64 **p** 65. C Ox St Matt 64-66; C Bootle St Leon *Liv* 66-68; C Hampreston *Sarum* 68-70; P-in-c Damerham 70-71; V Queniborough *Leic* 71-76; USA 76-77; V Tipton St Matt *Lich* 77-86; P-in-c Tipton St Paul 77-84; V 85-86; V Sutton Ch Ch *S'wark* 86-95; Chapl Cannes *Eur* 95-98; rtd 98; PtO *Chich* from 98; *S'wark* from 98. *52 The Meadow, Copthorne, Crawley RH10 3RQ* T: (01342) 713325 E: alanandmuriel@talktalk.net

MATHERS, David Michael Brownlow. b 43. Em Coll Cam BA 65 MA 69. Clifton Th Coll 65. **d** 67 **p** 68. C Branksome St Clem *Sarum* 67-70; C Bromley Ch Ch *Roch* 70-73; V Bures *St E* 73-80; Brazil 80-82; P-in-c Old Newton w Stowupland *St E* 82-86; V 87-90; V Thurston 90-11; RD Ixworth 94-03; rtd 11; P-in-c Laughton w Ripe and Chalvington *Chich* from 11. *The Rectory, Church Lane, Laughton, Lewes BN8 6AH* T: (01323) 811177 *or* 811624

MATHERS, Derek. b 48. NOC 82. **d** 85 **p** 86. C Huddersfield St Jo *Wakef* 85-86; C N Huddersfield 86-88; TV Almondbury w Farnley Tyas 88-92; V Marsden 92-02; R Badsworth 02-12; rtd 12. *17 Union Street, Slaithwaite, Huddersfield HD7 5ED* E: father.derek@badsworth.com

MATHERS, Kenneth Ernest William. b 56. Trin Coll Bris 93. **d** 95 **p** 96. C Bournemouth St Jo w St Mich *Win* 95-99; NSM Darenth *Roch* 99-04; Chapl Dartford and Gravesham

NHS Trust 01-04; Chapl N Devon Healthcare NHS Trust from 05. *The Rectory, Newton Tracey, Barnstaple EX31 3PL* T: (01271) 858292 E: revkmathers@btinternet.com

MATHERS (née STEWART), Mrs Kim Deborah. b 61. Southn Univ LLB 82. Trin Coll Bris 86. **d** 89 **p** 94. Par Dn Bitterne *Win* 89-93; NSM Stoke Bishop *Bris* 93-95; NSM Bournemouth St Jo w St Mich *Win* 95-99; P-in-c Darenth *Roch* 99-04; TR Newton Tracey, Horwood, Alverdiscott etc *Ex* from 04; RD Torrington 09-12. *The Rectory, Newton Tracey, Barnstaple EX31 3PL* T: (01271) 858292 E: revkimmathers@btinternet.com

MATHESON, Alexander John. b 59. Lon Bible Coll BA 84 S Tr Scheme 94. **d** 97 **p** 98. NSM Cowplain *Portsm* 97-01; C Portchester 01-04; V Sarisbury from 04; P-in-c Whiteley CD from 12. *The Vicarage, 149 Bridge Road, Sarisbury Green, Southampton SO31 7EN* T: (01489) 572207 E: sandy@mathesonuk.com

MATHEW, Mrs Alison Kate. b 65. Glas Coll of Tech BA 86 Glas Univ MPH 95 Kingston Univ BA 08. Ripon Coll Cuddesdon 10. **d** 12 **p** 13. C Spring Grove St Mary *Lon* from 12. *22 Kenley Road, Twickenham TW1 1JU* T: (020) 8892 9509 M: 07980-262912 E: alisonmathew@gmail.com

MATHEW, Laurence Allen Stanfield. b 47. Sarum Th Coll 99. **d** 02 **p** 03. OLM Warminster Ch Ch *Sarum* 02-12; NSM Ross w Walford and Brampton Abbotts *Heref* from 12. *The Vicarage, Walford, Ross-on-Wye HR9 5QP* M: 07768-006245 E: laurence01@blueyonder.co.uk

MATHEW (née HOLLIS), Rebecca Catherine. b 78. St Martin's Coll Lanc BA 99. Ripon Coll Cuddesdon BTh 03. **d** 03 **p** 04. C Broughton *Blackb* 03-07; C Mirihana Ch Ch Sri Lanka 07-08; Chapl St Thos Coll Mt Lavina 08-11; TV Bicester w Bucknell, Caversfield and Launton Ox from 11. *The Vicarage, The Spinney, Launton, Bicester OX25 6EP* E: revdrebh@hotmail.com

MATHEW, Shemil. b 82. Glos Univ MA 14 Ox Univ MTh 14. **d** 14 **p** 15. C Aynho and Croughton w Evenley etc *Pet* from 14. *The Vicarage, The Spinney, Launton, Bicester OX25 6EP* M: 07401-587151 E: mathew.shemil@gmail.com

MATHEWS, Richard Twitchell. b 27. Bps' Coll Cheshunt 57. **d** 59 **p** 60. C Leic St Phil 59-62; Chapl Beirut 62-63; Qatar 63-67; V Riddlesden *Bradf* 67-74; Australia 74-78; P-in-c Medbourne cum Holt w Stockerston and Blaston *Leic* 78-82; Chapl Alassio *Eur* 82-83; Chapl San Remo 82-83; Chapl Palma and Balearic Is w Ibiza etc 83-87; P-in-c Witchford w Wentworth *Ely* 87-91; rtd 91; PtO *Cant* from 96-09. *1/1 Richmond Village Centre, Stroud Road, Painswick, Stroud GL6 6UL* T: (01452) 812857

MATHEWS, Trevor John. b 50. Goldsmiths' Coll Lon MSc 98. St Steph Ho Ox 87. **d** 89 **p** 90. C Cheltenham St Steph *Glouc* 89-91; C Up Hatherley 89-91; PtO *Chelmsf* from 08; CF from 09. *c/o MOD Chaplains (Army)* T: (01264) 381140 F: 381824 E: mathews@conflict.co.uk

MATHIAS, Ms Lesley. b 49. Portsm Poly BA 72 Nottm Univ MTh 90. EMMTC 93. **d** 96 **p** 97. C Oadby *Leic* 96-98; Asst Chapl United Bris Healthcare NHS Trust 98-99; C Pet St Mary Boongate 99-01; V Kings Heath 01-06; Bp's Interfaith Adv 01-05; PtO *B & W* 99-01; *Pet* from 06; *Ely* from 08; *Leic* from 13. *8 Big Green, Warmington, Peterborough PE8 6TU* E: lesley@mathias.me.uk

MATHIAS-JONES, Edward Lloyd. b 71. Univ of Wales (Lamp) BA 93. St Mich Coll Llan BD 96. **d** 97 **p** 98. C Llanelli *St D* 97-00; C Milford Haven 00-04; V Newport St Steph and H Trin *Mon* from 04. *St Stephen's Vicarage, Adeline Street, Newport NP20 2HA* T: (01633) 265192 E: frmathias-jones@aol.com

MATHIE, Patricia Jean (Sister Donella). b 22. Worc Coll of Educn CertEd 49. dss 79 **d** 87. CSA from 74; Asst Superior 82-94; Mother Superior 94-00; Notting Hill St Jo *Lon* 79-80; Abbey Ho Malmesbury 81-82; Notting Hill St Clem and St Mark *Lon* 82-84; Kensal Town St Thos w St Andr and St Phil 85-87; Hon C 87-96; PtO 00-13. *St Mary's Convent and Nursing Home, Burlington Lane, London W4 2QE* M: 07583-546278 T: (020) 8747 3172

MATHOLE, Paul Mark. b 76. St Anne's Coll Ox BA 98 R Holloway Coll Lon MA 00 PhD 04. Oak Hill Th Coll 07. **d** 10 **p** 11. C Rusholme H Trin *Man* from 10. *3A Eileen Grove West, Manchester M14 5NW* T: 0161-224 1123 M: 07733-185670 E: paulmathole@gmail.com

MATLOOB, Canon Nazir Ahmad Barnabas. b 48. Punjab Univ BA 79. Gujranwala Th Sem BTh 77 BD 81 MDiv 85. **d** 78 **p** 78. Pakistan 78-93; PtO *Chelmsf* 94-97; C Forest Gate All SS 98-06; C Lt Ilford St Barn 06; Inter-Faith Worker Newham Deanery from 07; Hon Can Chelmsf Cathl from 12. *64 Henderson Road, London E7 8EF* T: (020) 8552 4280

MATON, Oswald. b 24. St Aug Coll Cant 75. **d** 77 **p** 78. NSM Chatham St Steph *Roch* 77-94; PtO 94-04. *304 Maidstone Road, Chatham ME4 6JJ* T: (01634) 843568

MATSON de LAURIER, Mrs Sarah Kennerley. b 46. EMMTC 00. **d** 02 **p** 03. NSM Hilton w Marston-on-Dove *Derby* 02-14;

PtO from 14. *1 Park Way, Etwall, Derby DE65 6HU* T: (01283) 732859 E: pskmdl@aol.com *or* peteandrev@gmail.com

MATTACKS, Mrs Lesley Anne. b 58. Birm Univ BA 79 K Coll Lon MA 86 Leeds Univ BA 07 W Lon Inst of HE PGCE 80. NOC 04. d 07 p 08. C Birkenshaw w Hunsworth *Wakef* 07-10; P-in-c Middlestown *Leeds* 10-15; Dioc Tr Officer (Reader Formation) 10-15; V Brownhill from 15. *St Saviour's Vicarage, 24 Intake Lane, Batley WF17 0BT* M: 07952-375176 T: (01924) 471999 E: revles.mattacks@hotmail.co.uk

MATTAPALLY, Sebastian Thomas. b 57. N Bengal Univ BA 77 Pontifical Salesian Univ BTh 84 Pontifical Gregorian Univ LTh 98 DTh 05. d 83 p 83. In RC Ch 83-00; PtO *Eur* 01-04; C Patcham *Chich* 05-07; P-in-c Kirdford 07-10; V Eastbourne St Mich from 10. *St Michael's Vicarage, 15 Long Acre Close, Eastbourne BN21 1UF* T: (01323) 646569 E: smattapally@btinternet.com

MATTHEW, Peter. b 73. d 11 p 13. Kenya 11-12; C Woking St Jo *Guildf* from 12. *13 Ashley Road, Woking GU21 8SR* T: (01483) 351294 E: pete@stjohnswoking.org.uk

MATTHEWS, Adrian James. b 51. Edge Hill Coll of HE CertEd 73. NOC. d 87 p 88. C Blackley St Andr *Man* 87-90; NSM Tonge w Alkrington 96-01; R Failsworth St Jo 01-12; rtd 12. *Address withheld by request*

MATTHEWS, The Rt Revd Alan Montague (Dom Basil). b 37. Ex Univ BA 86. d 02 p 02. OSB from 65; Abbot Elmore Abbey from 88. *Elmore Abbey, Church Lane, Speen, Newbury RG14 1SA* T: (01635) 33080 F: 580729

MATTHEWS, Anita Kathryn. b 70. Dur Univ BTh 91. Ripon Coll Cuddesdon 93. d 97 p 98. C E Barnet *St Alb* 97-01; Chapl Derby High Sch 01-05; Nat Adv for Children's Work CMS 05-12; C Derby St Pet and Ch Ch w H Trin from 12. *5 Bamford Avenue, Derby DE23 8DT* T: (01332) 270917 E: anita@stpetersderby.org.uk

MATTHEWS, Mrs Anna Ruth. b 78. Rob Coll Cam BA 99 MA 03 MPhil 03. Westcott Ho Cam 01. d 03 p 04. C Abbots Langley *St Alb* 03-06; Min Can St Alb Abbey 06-12; V Cambridge St Benedict *Ely* from 12; Dioc Dir of Ords from 12. *1 Hedgerley Close, Cambridge CB3 0EW* T: (01223) 321312 E: anna.matthews@ely.anglican.org

MATTHEWS, Barry Alan. b 46. AKC 68. St Boniface Warminster 68 St Paul's Coll Grahamstown 69. d 69 p 70. C De Aar S Africa 69-72; C Kimberley St Aug 72-74; P-in-c Kimberley St Matt 74-75; C Leeds St Aid *Ripon* 75-77; R Vryburg St Steph S Africa 77-81; Dioc Missr 81-82; R Kimberley St Aug 82-83; C Shotton *St As* 83-84; R Hwange St Jas Zimbabwe 84-89; R Bulawayo N St Marg 89-95; R Nkulumane H Family S Africa 95-97; Adn N Matabeleland 89-97; Sen P St Mary's Cathl Harare 97-00; rtd 01. *21 Lord Roberts Road, PO Box 1083, Hermanus 7200, Republic of South Africa*

MATTHEWS, Basil. *See* MATTHEWS, Alan Montague

MATTHEWS, Canon Campbell Thurlow. b 33. Lon Univ BA 56 Dur Univ DipEd 57. St Jo Coll Nottm 70. d 71 p 72. C Ryton *Dur* 71-74; Chapl R Victoria Infirmary Newc 74-82; V Greenside *Dur* 74-82; R Wetheral w Warwick *Carl* 82-93; RD Brampton 83-91; P-in-c Farlam and Nether Denton 87-93; P-in-c Gilsland 87-93; Hon Can Carl Cathl 87-00; P-in-c Thornthwaite cum Braithwaite and Newlands 93-00; P-in-c Borrowdale 97-00; rtd 00; PtO *Carl* from 00; *Newc* from 01. *The Hayes, Newcastle Road, Corbridge NE45 5LP* T: (01434) 632010

MATTHEWS, Celia Inger. b 30. St Chris Coll Blackheath 50. d 86 p 94. Dioc Missr *St And* from 86; rtd 95. *24 Barossa Place, Perth PH1 5HH* T: (01738) 623578 E: cmatthews@toucansurf.com

MATTHEWS, Cilla. *See* MATTHEWS, Francilla Lacey

MATTHEWS, Canon Colin John. b 44. Jes Coll Ox BA 67 MA 71 Fitzw Coll Cam BA 70 MA 74. Ridley Hall Cam 68. d 71 p 72. C Onslow Square St Paul *Lon* 71-74; C Leic H Apostles 74-78; Bible Use Sec Scripture Union 78-89; Dir Ch Cen Guildf St Sav 89-95; V Burpham 95-12; RD Guildf 01-06; Hon Can Guildf Cathl 02-12; rtd 12; PtO *Guildf* from 12. *Bargate, Little Tangley, Wonersh Common, Wonersh, Guildford GU5 0PW* T: (01483) 575334 M: 07787-575923 E: colinjmatthews@gmail.com

MATTHEWS, David Charles. b 61. TCD BA 84 HDipEd 86 MA 87 BTh 95 Lille Univ LèsL 85. CITC 95. d 95 p 96. C Arm St Mark 95-97; Hon V Choral Arm Cathl 96-97; Min Can and Chapl St Woolos Cathl 97-01; V Marshfield and Peterstone Wentloog etc 01-12; P-in-c Newport St Julian from 12. *The Vicarage, 41 St Julian's Avenue, Newport NP19 7JT* T: (01633) 258046 E: david@hebron97.freeserve.co.uk

MATTHEWS, David William. b 49. St Paul's Coll Grahamstown 88. d 90 p 91. C Port Eliz St Sav S Africa 90-91; C Port Eliz St Paul 91-94; R Zwartkops River Valley Par 94-00; Chapl Miss to Seafarers 00-03; R Boxford, Edwardstone, Groton etc

St E 03-09; P-in-c Southampton St Anne Bermuda from 09. *St Anne's Rectory, 74 Middle Road, Southampton SB 04, Bermuda* T: (001) (441) 238 0370 E: stannesrectory@logic.bm

MATTHEWS, David William Grover. b 73. Acadia Univ (NS) BA 93 Toronto Univ MDiv 98. Trin Coll Toronto 95. d 98 p 99. C Newport St Teilo *Mon* 98-00; NSM Cobbold Road St Sav w St Mary *Lon* 00-03; P-in-c Hammersmith H Innocents 03-05; P-in-c Hammersmith H Innocents and St Jo from 05. *35 Paddenswick Road, London W6 0UA* T: (020) 8741 1006 E: holyinnocentsw6@yahoo.com

MATTHEWS, Mrs Deborah Lynne. b 57. Southn Univ BTh 98 MCIPD 92. Ripon Coll Cuddesdon MTh 01. d 00 p 01. C Southampton (City Cen) *Win* 00-04; V Clapham St Paul *S'wark* from 04; P-in-c Clapham H Spirit 12-13; Dir IME Kingston Area from 13; AD Lambeth N from 13. *St Paul's Vicarage, Rectory Grove, London SW4 0DX* T: (020) 7622 2128 E: revdebmatthews@waitrose.com

MATTHEWS, Mrs Diana Elizabeth Charlotte. b 43. MCSP 65. d 93 p 96. OLM Merrow *Guildf* 93-11; rtd 11; PtO *Guildf* from 11. *Avila, 13 Wells Road, Guildford GU4 7XQ* T: (01483) 839738 E: diana.matthews@ntlworld.com

MATTHEWS, Elis Alun. b 82. York Univ BA 04 Cam Univ BTh 15. Ridley Hall Cam 12. d 15. C E Ham St Paul *Chelmsf* from 15. *281 Central Park Road, London E6 3AF* M: 07739-020288 E: elismatthews@yahoo.co.uk

MATTHEWS, Mrs Francilla Lacey. b 37. S'wark Ord Course 83. dss 86 d 87 p 94. Bromley St Mark *Roch* 86-90; Hon Par Dn 87-90; Par Dn Hayes 90-94; C 94-02; rtd 02; PtO *Roch* from 02. *71 Hayes Road, Bromley BR2 9AE* T: (020) 8464 4083 E: cillajohn@waitrose.com

MATTHEWS, Frederick Peter. b 45. Grey Coll Dur BA 66 MA 68 K Coll Lon PGCE 68 Lon Univ BSc(Econ) 75. Sarum & Wells Th Coll 70. d 72 p 73. C W Wickham St Jo *Cant* 72-74; C Sholing *Win* 74-77; LtO 78-79; V Woolston 79-03; P-in-c Over Wallop w Nether Wallop 03-07; Dioc Ecum Officer 03-07; rtd 07; PtO *Sarum* from 07; *Win* 07-14. *19 Berkshire Road, Salisbury SP2 8NY* T: (01722) 340508 E: fpetermatthews@hotmail.co.uk

MATTHEWS, George Charles Wallace. b 27. Sarum Th Coll 58. d 60 p 61. C Coppenhall St Paul *Ches* 60-63; C Lewes St Anne *Chich* 63-67; V Wheelock *Ches* 67-76; V Mossley 76-93; rtd 93; PtO *Ches* from 93. *145 Primrose Avenue, Haslington, Crewe CW1 5QB* T: (01270) 587463

MATTHEWS, Gerald Lancelot. b 31. Bris Univ LLB 50. Ripon Hall Ox 55. d 57 p 58. C The Quinton *Birm* 57-60; C Olton 60-63; V Brent Tor *Ex* 63-72; P-in-c Lydford w Bridestowe and Sourton 70-72; TR Lydford, Brent Tor, Bridestowe and Sourton 72-78; P-in-c Black Torrington, Bradford w Cookbury etc 78-90; PtO from 90; rtd 94. *The Larches, Black Torrington, Beaworthy EX21 5PU* T: (01409) 231228

MATTHEWS, Harold James. b 46. Leeds Univ BSc 68 Fitzw Coll Cam BA 70 MA 74 Goldsmiths' Coll Lon PGCE 71. Westcott Ho Cam 68. d 71 p 72. C Mossley Hill St Matt and St Jas *Liv* 71-74; C Stanley 74-76; TV Hackney Lon 76-78; Chapl Forest Sch Snaresbrook 78-83; Hd Master Vernon Holme Sch Cant 83-88; Hd Master Heath Mt Sch Hertf 88-06; Chapl Roedean Sch Brighton 06-08; Chapl Kent Coll Pembury from 10. *18 Oak Hall Road, London E11 2JT* T: (020) 8257 2925 M: 07515-857110 E: hjmatth46@hotmail.com

MATTHEWS, Hayley Deborah Yeshua. b 68. Ridley Hall Cam 05. d 07 p 08. C Lancaster St Mary w St John and St Anne *Blackb* 07-10; Chapl MediaCityUK *Man* 10-13; R Birch w Fallowfield from 13. *197 Old Hall Lane, Manchester M14 6HJ* T: 0161-224 1310 M: 07928-786915 E: rector@holyinnocentsff.org

MATTHEWS, Mrs Heather Ann. b 49. Bris Univ BA 71 Lon Univ CertEd 72. Trin Coll Bris 87. d 89 p 94. C Blagdon w Compton Martin and Ubley *B & W* 89-93; Dn-in-c 93-94; R 94-01; R Hodnet *Lich* 01-03; C Skipton Ch Ch *Bradf* 03-04; rtd 04. *9 Hayslan Green, Malvern WR14 2RG*

MATTHEWS, Canon Joan Muriel. b 53. NOC 89. d 92 p 94. C Aughton St Mich *Liv* 92-97; R Wavertree St Mary 97-06; AD Toxteth and Wavertree 04-06; Hon Can Liv Cathl 04-06 and from 07; P-in-c Newton in Makerfield St Pet 06-07; P-in-c Earlestown 06-07; TR Newton from 08; AD Winwick from 09; TR Newton from 14. *130 Belvedere Road, Newton-le-Willows WA12 0LG* T: (01925) 299668 E: revjoan@hotmail.com

MATTHEWS, John Goodman. b 77. Univ of Wales BTh 99. St Mich Coll Llan 99. d 02 p 03. C Lampeter and Llanddewibrefi Gp *St D* 02-05; P-in-c Aberporth w Tremain w Blaenporth and Betws Ifan 05-07; V 07-09; V Aberporth w Blaenporth w Betws Ifan 09; P-in-c Tregarth and Llandygai and Maes y Groes *Ban* 09-14; V Bro Ogwen from 14. *Pentir Vicarage, Pentir, Bangor LL57 4YB* T: (01248) 364991

MATTHEWS, Lewis William (Bill). b 29. St Jo Coll Dur BA 53 MSc 76. d 55 p 56. C Eston *York* 55-57; Ind Chapl *Sheff* 57-61;

V Copt Oak *Leic* 61-64; R Braunstone 64-70; V Thornaby on Tees St Paul *York* 70-72; TR Thornaby on Tees 72-78; Dir Dioc Bd for Soc Resp *Lon* 79-84; PtO 84-94; Warden Durning Hall Chr Community Cen Forest Gate 84-94; rtd 94; Hon C Jersey Gouray St Martin *Win* 94-06; PtO from 06. *2 Malvern, La Ruelle es Ruaux, St Brelade, Jersey JE3 8BB* T: (01534) 498368 M: 07797-731143 E: billmatthews@jerseymail.co.uk

MATTHEWS, Liam. *See* MATTHEWS, William Temple Atkinson

MATTHEWS, Canon Melvyn William. b 40. St Edm Hall Ox BA 63 MA 68. K Coll Lon BD 66 AKC 67. **d** 67 **p** 68. C Enfield St Andr *Lon* 67-70; Asst Chapl Southn Univ *Win* 70-72; Lect Univ of Nairobi Kenya 72-76; V Highgate All SS *Lon* 76-79; P-in-c Clifton St Paul *Bris* 79-87; Sen Chapl Bris Univ 79-87; Dir Ammerdown Cen for Study and Renewal 87-93; V Chew Magna w Dundry *B & W* 93-97; Can and Chan Wells Cathl 97-05; rtd 05; PtO *B & W* from 05. *Yew Tree House, 22 Beaufort Avenue, Midsomer Norton, Radstock BA3 2TG* T: (01761) 413630 E: mwmatthews@onetel.com

MATTHEWS, Michael Raymond. b 55. JP 96. Huddersfield Univ MBA 96 Leeds Univ BA 04 CQSW 82. Coll of Resurr Mirfield 02. **d** 04 **p** 05. C Featherstone and Purston cum S Featherstone *Wakef* 04-07; P-in-c Haslingfield w Harlton and Gt and Lt Eversden *Ely* 07-10; TV Lordsbridge 10-13; RD Bourn 10-13; P-in-c Nassington w Yarwell and Woodnewton w Apethorpe *Pet* 13-15; V Nassington, Apethorpe, Thornhaugh etc from 15. *The Vicarage, 34 Station Road, Nassington, Peterborough PE8 6QB* T: (01780) 470368 E: frmichaelmatthews@btinternet.com

MATTHEWS, Paul. b 47. Brunel Univ BTech 70. S Dios Minl Tr Scheme 89. **d** 92 **p** 93. NSM Goring-by-Sea *Chich* 92-12; P-in-c Chidham 12-14; V from 14. *The Vicarage, Cot Lane, Chidham, Chichester PO18 8TA* T: (01243) 575067 E: frpaulm@virginmedia.com

MATTHEWS, Peter. *See* MATTHEWS, Frederick Peter

MATTHEWS, Peter John. b 69. Leic Poly BEng 92. Wycliffe Hall Ox 07. **d** 09 **p** 10. C Catterick *Ripon* 09-13; Chapl St Fran Xavier Sch Richmond 09-13; P-in-c Old Trafford St Bride *Man* from 13; Young Adults Missr Man Adnry from 13. *St Bride's Rectory, 29 Shrewsbury Street, Manchester M16 9BB* M: 07590-698333 E: revpetermatthews@gmail.com

MATTHEWS, Canon Rodney Charles. b 36. Sarum Th Coll 62. **d** 64 **p** 65. C Gt Clacton *Chelmsf* 64-68; C Loughton St Mary 68-74; TV 74-76; V Goodmayes All SS 76-87; V Woodford Bridge 87-02; Hon Chapl Sail Tr Assn from 89; P-in-c Barkingside St Cedd *Chelmsf* 90-92; Hon Can Chelmsf Cathl 99-02; rtd 02; PtO *Chelmsf* from 03. *93 King's Head Hill, London E4 7JG* T: (020) 8529 4372 E: canonrodney@ntlworld.com

MATTHEWS, Canon Roger Charles. b 54. Man Univ BSc 75 Nottm Univ MA 02 Fuller Th Sem California DMin 10 MBCS 82 CEng 90. Trin Coll Bris 87. **d** 89 **p** 90. C Gt Baddow *Chelmsf* 89-93; P-in-c Chigwell Row 93-94; TV Chigwell and Chigwell Row 94-96; Dioc Miss Officer 96-00; Millennium Ecum Officer 98-00; Dean of Miss and Min 01-12 and from 12; Hon C Gt Baddow from 01; Hon Can Chelmsf Cathl from 00. *42 Riffhams Drive, Great Baddow, Chelmsford CM2 7DD* T: (01245) 478959 *or* 294455 F: 294477 E: rmatthews@chelmsford.anglican.org

MATTHEWS, Canon Roy Ian John. b 27. TD 71. St Cath Soc Ox BA 52 MA 56. St Steph Ho Ox 52. **d** 54 **p** 55. C Barnsley St Mary *Wakef* 54-58; V Staincliffe 58-65; CF (TA) 58-92; V Penistone w Midhope *Wakef* 65-72; V Brighouse 72-84; Hon Can Wakef Cathl 76-92; V Darrington 84-92; Dioc Schs Officer 84-89; Dep Dir of Educn 85-89; rtd 92; PtO *Leeds* from 92; *York* from 92; P-in-c Selby Abbey 96-97. *14 Spring Walk, Brayton, Selby YO8 9DS* T: (01757) 707259

MATTHEWS, Canon Royston Peter. b 39. Univ of Wales (Lamp) BA 61. St Mich Coll Llan 61. **d** 64 **p** 65. C Fairwater CD *Llan* 64-67; C Cadoxton-juxta-Barry 67-71; V Bettws *Mon* 71-84; V Abergavenny H Trin 84-05; Hon Can St Woolos Cathl 05; rtd 05; PtO *Win* from 08. *1 Hoburne Gardens, Christchurch BH23 4PP* T: (01425) 271216 E: roymatt1@aol.com

MATTHEWS, Simon David. b 64. Qu Coll Birm 12. **d** 15. C Wistow *Leic* from 15. *Address temp unknown*

MATTHEWS, Canon Stuart James. b 37. St Jo Coll Dur BA 60. Bps' Coll Cheshunt 60. **d** 62 **p** 63. C Horsham *Chich* 62-65; C Rednal *Birm* 65-67; Min Bradwood St Bede CD 67-68; C Northfield 68-73; V Thurcroft *Sheff* 73-82; RD Laughton 79-82; R Sprotbrough 82-00; RD Adwick 84-89; Hon Can Sheff Cathl 92-00; rtd 00; PtO *Sheff* from 00. *43 Dinnington Road, Woodsetts, Worksop S81 8RL* T: (01909) 560160

MATTHEWS, Terence Leslie. b 35. Handsworth Coll Birm 55. **d** 61 **p** 62. C W Acklam *York* 61-64; V Horden *Dur* 64-72; R Wroton Gilbert 72-77; P-in-c Grangetown 77-85; V Cleadon 85-86; V Hebburn St Cuth 86-88; rtd 88; PtO *Lich* from 08. *22 Bankfield Grove, Scot Hay, Newcastle ST5 6AR*

MATTHEWS, Thomas Bartholomew Hall. *See* HALL, Thomas Bartholomew Berners

MATTHEWS, Timothy John. b 73. Univ of Wales (Cardiff) BScEcon 97 PhD 00 ACA 03. Wycliffe Hall Ox 06. **d** 08 **p** 09. C Brompton H Trin w Onslow Square St Paul *Lon* 08-11; C Onslow Square and S Kensington St Aug 11-14; C Bournemouth Town Cen *Win* from 14. *11 Beechey Road, Bournemouth BH8 8LL* E: tim@stswithuns.me

MATTHEWS, William. *See* MATTHEWS, Lewis William

MATTHEWS, William John Joseph. b 48. **d** 08 **p** 08. NSM Lee-on-the-Solent *Portsm* 08-10; TV St Helens Town Cen *Liv* 11-15; TV Wigan All SS from 15. *St Stephen's Vicarage, Whelley, Wigan WN2 1BL* E: revbillmatthews@outlook.com

MATTHEWS, William Temple Atkinson (Liam). b 47. EMMTC 86. **d** 83 **p** 83. SSF 83-86; C Brinsley w Underwood *S'well* 86-89; TV Hitchin *St Alb* 89-97; R Toddington and Chalgrave 97-03; R N Albury Australia from 03; RD Murray Valley from 05. *St Mark's Rectory, 328 Gulpha Street, North Albury NSW 2640, Australia* T: (0061) (2) 5794 2443 E: liammatthews@bigpond.com

MATTHEWS-LOYDALL, Mrs Elaine. b 63. Bp Otter Coll BA 85. St Jo Coll Nottm 87. **d** 90 **p** 94. Par Dn Nottingham All SS *S'well* 90-94; C 94-95; Asst Chapl to the Deaf 91-93; Chapl to the Deaf 93-99; Chapl for Deaf People *Leic* 99-10; TV Leic H Spirit 99-10. *Pumpkin Cottage, 54 Wilne Road, Long Eaton, Nottingham NG10 3AN* T: 0115-972 8943

MATTHIAE, Canon David. b 40. Fitzw Ho Cam BA 63 MA 69. Linc Th Coll 63. **d** 65 **p** 66. C New Addington *Cant* 65-70; C Charlton-by-Dover SS Pet and Paul 70-72; C Charlton-in-Dover 72-75; V Cant All SS 75-84; P-in-c Tunstall 84-87; R Tunstall w Rodmersham 87-05; RD Sittingbourne 88-94; Hon Can Cant Cathl 99-05; rtd 05; PtO *Ely* from 06. *7 Bustlers Rise, Duxford, Cambridge CB22 4QU* T: (01223) 835471 - M: 07719-716240 E: david@matthiae.demon.co.uk

MATTHIAS, George Ronald. b 30. CertEd 51. St Deiniol's Hawarden 76. **d** 78 **p** 79. NSM Broughton *St As* 78-83; NSM Wrexham 83-85; C 85-87; V Brymbo 87-95; rtd 95; PtO *St As* 09-13. *Bryn Adref, Pisgah Hill, Pentre Hill, Wrexham LL11 5DB* T: (01978) 750757

MATTHIAS, Canon John Rex. b 61. St Mich Coll Llan. **d** 94 **p** 95. C Llandrillo-yn-Rhos *St As* 94-98; R Llanfair Talhaearn and Llansannan etc 98-03; V Petryal 03-10; P-in-c Betws-yn-Rhos 03-10; Warden of Readers 09-10; P-in-c Newport St Julian *Mon* 10-12; V Mold *St As* 12-15; Can Prec St As Cathl from 15. *Cefn Coed, Upper Denbigh Road, St Asaph LL17 0RR* E: rexmatthias61@gmail.com

MATTHIAS, Paul. b 47. Philippa Fawcett Coll CertEd 75 Kent Univ DipEd 84. Cant Sch of Min 92. **d** 94 **p** 95. Head RE Hever Sch Maidstone 80-94; Chapl Ch Ch High Sch Ashford 94-07; NSM Gillingham St Aug *Roch* 94-10; P-in-c New Brompton St Luke from 10. *33 Malvern Road, Gillingham ME7 4BA* T: (01634) 576197 E: paul.matthias@diocese-rochester.org

MATTOCK, Colin Graham. b 38. Chich Th Coll. **d** 84 **p** 85. C Hove All SS *Chich* 84-87; C Bexhill St Pet 87-90; V Henlow *St Alb* 90-96; V Linslade *Ox* 96-00; P-in-c Pebworth w Dorsington and Honeybourne *Glouc* 00-02; R Pebworth, Dorsington, Honeybourne etc 02-10; AD Campden 06-10; rtd 10. *14 Mullings Court, Cirencester GL7 2AW* T: (01285) 653828 E: colin.mattock@btinternet.com

MATTOCKS, Mrs Margaret. b 61. **d** 06 **p** 07. C Tettenhall Regis *Lich* 06-09; V Burntwood from 09; P-in-c Hammerwich from 13; RD Lich from 14. *The Vicarage, Church Road, Burntwood, Walsall WS7 9EA* T: (01543) 675014

MAUCHAN, Andrew. b 44. Hertf Coll Ox BA 65 MA 69 Man Univ CertEd 66. Oak Hill Th Coll 88. **d** 90 **p** 91. C Bridlington Priory *York* 90-94; V Alverthorpe *Wakef* 94-01; R Wombwell *Sheff* 01-07; rtd 07. *Hollins Barn, Top o' the Hill, Slaithwaite, Huddersfield HD7 5UA* T: (01484) 846371 E: andrew.mauchan@yahoo.co.uk

MAUDE, Alexander. b 53. Bingley Coll of Educn TCert 74. NOC. **d** 02 **p** 03. NSM Erringden *Leeds* from 02; Chapl Ravenscliffe High Sch from 02. *47 Vicar Park Drive, Norton Tower, Halifax HX2 0NN* T: (01422) 355856 M: 07816-597074 E: sandiemaude@hotmail.com

MAUDE, Gillian Hamer. b 53. St Anne's Coll Ox BA 75 MA 79 Edin Univ MSc 77. St Steph Ho Ox 99. **d** 01 **p** 02. C Hackney Wick St Mary of Eton w St Aug *Lon* 01-05; P-in-c Goodrington *Ex* 05-06; V 06-14; V Goodrington and Collaton St Mary 14-15; RD Torbay 09-15; P-in-c Jarrow *Dur* from 15. *St Peter's House, York Avenue, Jarrow NE32 5LP* M: 07932-056071 T: 0191-483 3371 E: revgilly.jarrow@gmail.com

MAUDLIN, David. b 39. EAMTC 92. **d** 95 **p** 96. NSM Bury St Edmunds St Jo *St E* 95-97; NSM Haverhill w Withersfield 97-98; P-in-c The Sampfords and Radwinter w Hempstead *Chelmsf* 98-04; RD Saffron Walden 00-04; rtd 04; PtO *Leic*

04-13; P-in-c Leic St Mary from 13; PtO *Pet* from 04; *Eur* from 04. *3 Goldfinch Road, Uppingham LE15 9UJ* T: (01572) 820181

MAUDSLEY, Canon George Lambert. b 27. St Jo Coll Nottm 74. **d** 75 **p** 76. C Binley *Cov* 75-77; Chapl Barn Fellowship Winterborne Whitechurch 77-83; V Salford Priors *Cov* 83-94; RD Alcester 87-92; Hon Can Cov Cathl 91-94; rtd 94; PtO *Cov* from 94; *Worc* from 94. *12 Moorlands Lodge, Moorlands Avenue, Kenilworth CV8 1RT* T: (01926) 512206 E: lambert.maudsley@yahoo.co.uk

MAUDSLEY, Keith. b 51. York Univ BA 72. Ripon Hall Ox 72. **d** 75 **p** 76. C Rugby St Andr *Cov* 75-79; C Cambridge Gt St Mary w St Mich *Ely* 79-82; Chapl Girton Coll 79-82; P-in-c Binley *Cov* 82-89; RD Cov E 87-89; P-in-c Leek Wootton 89-91; Dioc Policy Development Adv 89-91; Dioc Adv on UPA *Liv* 91-97; Soc Resp Officer 91-97; R Lymm *Ches* from 97. *The Rectory, 46 Rectory Lane, Lymm WA13 0AL* T: (01925) 752164 E: keith@maudsley5234.wanadoo.co.uk

MAUDSLEY, Canon Michael Peter. b 38. St Andr Univ BSc 61. Oak Hill Th Coll 65. **d** 67 **p** 68. C Blackpool St Mark *Blackb* 67-70; C Hartford *Ches* 70-72; R Balerno *Edin* 72-82; V Stapenhill w Cauldwell *Derby* 82-91; Assoc R Edin St Paul and St Geo 91-95; C 00-03; R 95-00; rtd 03. *44 Buckstone Loan, Edinburgh EH10 6UG*

MAUDSLEY, Philip. b 73. St Martin's Coll Lanc BA(QTS) 96. St Jo Coll Nottm 13. **d** 15. C Fulwood Ch Ch *Blackb* from 15. *58 Garstone Croft, Fulwood, Preston PR2 3WY* E: philmaudsley7@gmail.com

MAUDSLEY, Richard Leonard. b 55. Trent Park Coll of Educn BEd 76. NTMTC 04. **d** 07 **p** 08. NSM Clay Hill St Jo and St Luke *Lon* 07-09; NSM Silverton, Butterleigh, Bickleigh and Cadeleigh *Ex* from 09. *The Old Coach House, 5B Fore Street, Silverton, Exeter EX5 4HP* T: (01392) 860883 E: richard.maudsley@exeter.anglican.org

MAUGHAN, Angela. b 54. Newc Univ BA 93. NEOC 94. **d** 97 **p** 98. C Willington *Newc* 97-01; V Weetslade from 01. *Weetslade Vicarage, 59 Kirklands, Burradon, Cramlington NE23 7LE* T: 0191-268 9366

MAUGHAN, Canon Geoffrey Nigel. b 48. CCC Cam BA 69 MA 73 Wycliffe Hall Ox MA 98. Oak Hill Th Coll 75. **d** 77 **p** 78. C New Malden and Coombe *S'wark* 77-81; C Abingdon w Shippon *Ox* 81-89; TV Abingdon 89-98; Dir of Min and Chapl Wycliffe Hall Ox 98-07; V Cumnor *Ox* from 07; Hon Can Ch Ch from 15. *The Vicarage, 1 Abingdon Road, Cumnor, Oxford OX2 9QN* T: (01865) 865402 E: geoff.maughan@btinternet.com

MAUND, Mrs Margaret Jennifer. b 42. RGN 64 RM 65. Llan Dioc Tr Scheme 89. **d** 94 **p** 97. NSM Cymmer and Porth *Llan* 94-97; NSM Pwllgwaun w Llanddewi Rhondda 97-04. *27 Mill Street, Tonyrefail, Porth CF39 8AB* T: (01443) 670085

MAUNDER, Alan John. b 52. UWIST BSc 74. Oak Hill Th Coll 88. **d** 90 **p** 91. C Birkenhead Ch Ch *Ches* 90-95; P-in-c Poulton 95-05; V Cwmaman *St D* from 05. *The Vicarage, 118 Heol Cae Gurwen, Gwaun Cae Gurwen, Ammanford SA18 1PD* T: (01269) 822426 E: aljomau@tiscali.co.uk

MAUNDER, Miss Vicky Alexandra. b 73. Leeds Univ BA 95. Ripon Coll Cuddesdon BA 01. **d** 02 **p** 03. C Swaythling *Win* 02-05; C Pimlico St Pet w Westmr Ch Ch *Lon* 05-07; TV Kingston All SS w St Jo *S'wark* 07-12; TV Kingston from 12. *30 Bloomfield Road, Kingston upon Thames KT1 2SE* T: (020) 8546 9882

MAURICE, David Pierce. b 50. Pemb Coll Cam BA 72 MA 76 BChir 76. Dioc OLM tr scheme. **d** 01 **p** 02. OLM Marlborough *Sarum* from 01. *Isbury House, Kingsbury Street, Marlborough SN8 1JA* T: (01672) 514119 E: david_maurice2000@yahoo.com

✠**MAURICE, The Rt Revd Peter David.** b 51. St Chad's Coll Dur BA 72. Coll of Resurr Mirfield. **d** 75 **p** 76 **c** 06. C Wandsworth St Paul *S'wark* 75-79; TV Mortlake w E Sheen 79-85; V Rotherhithe H Trin 85-96; RD Bermondsey 91-96; V Tooting All SS 96-03; Adn Wells, Can Res and Preb Wells Cathl 03-06; Suff Bp Taunton 06-15; rtd 15. *14 Saltwood Road, Maidstone ME15 6UY*

MAURITZ, Willem Jacobus. b 72. Fontys Univ Netherlands BA 98 Stoas Univ BSc 00 Surrey Univ MSc 04. St Mellitus Coll BA 14. **d** 14. C Tunbridge Wells St Jas *Roch* from 14. *3 Andrew Close, Tunbridge Wells TN2 3PA* T: (01892) 514860 M: 07799-076690 E: wim.mauritz@gmail.com

MAW, Mrs Jacqueline. b 59. Wycliffe Hall Ox 04. **d** 06 **p** 07. C Iwerne Valley *Sarum* 06-10; TV Wareham from 10. *St Martin's Vicarage, 9 Keysworth Road, Wareham BH20 7BD* T: (01929) 556796 M: 07747-561375 E: jackiemaw@yahoo.co.uk

MAWBEY, Diane. See COUTURE, Diane

MAWDITT, Stephen Donald Harvey. b 56. **d** 96 **p** 97. OLM Ashill w Saham Toney *Nor* 96-05; OLM Watton w Carbrooke

and Ovington 00-05; Min Fountain of Life from 05. *43 Cressingham Road, Ashill, Thetford IP25 7DG* T: (01760) 440363 E: themawditts@tiscali.co.uk

MAWER, Canon David Ronald. b 32. Keble Coll Ox BA 55 MA 58 Dur Univ BA 57 McGill Univ Montreal PhD 77. Wells Th Coll 58. **d** 59 **p** 60. C Cullercoats St Geo *Newc* 59-61; Canada 61-92; Co-ord Angl Studies St Paul Univ Ottawa 81-92; Can Ottawa from 85; rtd 92; PtO *Newc* from 93. *Moorside, Church Lane, Thropton, Morpeth NE65 7JA* T: (01669) 620597

MAWSON, Canon Arthur Cyril. b 35. St Pet Coll Ox BA 56 MA 61. Wycliffe Hall Ox 61. **d** 62 **p** 63. C Walsall *Lich* 62-66; V Millhouses H Trin *Sheff* 66-73; Selection Sec ACCM 73-79; Can Res and Treas Ex Cathl 79-98; Dioc Dir of Ords 81-87; rtd 99. *4 Woodlands Close, Headington, Oxford OX3 7RY* T: (01865) 764099

MAXFIELD, Roberta. b 60. WMMTC. **d** 09 **p** 10. NSM Oxley *Lich* 09-13; NSM Penn 13-15; Chapl R Wolv Sch from 15. *53 Swan Bank, Wolverhampton WV4 5PZ* T: (01902) 834023

MAXFIELD-COOTE, Ms Olivia Constance. b 86. Kent Univ BA 09 Univ Coll Lon MA 10 Jes Coll Cam BTh 14. Westcott Ho Cam 12. **d** 15. C Black Notley *Chelmsf* from 15. *The Rectory, Shalford Road, Rayne, Braintree CM77 6BT* M: 07939-297048 T: (01376) 795199 E: olivia.maxfield-coote@cantab.net

MAXIM, Claire Margaret Astrid. b 68. Birm Univ BEng 90 Reading Univ MBA 03 MIET 95. Qu Coll Birm 07. **d** 10 **p** 11. C Ampfield, Chilworth and N Baddesley *Win* 10-14; V Ludgershall and Faberstown *Sarum* from 14. *The Rectory, 10 St James Street, Ludgershall, Andover SP11 9QF* T: (01264) 393026 E: rector@themaxims.co.uk

MAXTED, Neil Andrew. b 58. Aston Tr Scheme 88 Sarum & Wells Th Coll 90. **d** 92 **p** 93. C Folkestone St Sav *Cant* 92-96; CF 96-05; P-in-c Frome Ch Ch *B & W* from 05; V Frome St Mary from 11. *The Vicarage, 73 Weymouth Road, Frome BA11 1HJ* T: (01373) 473249 E: vicarchchfrome@aol.com

MAXWELL, Alan. b 75. Strathclyde Univ BSc 96 Aber Univ MSc 97 Selw Coll Cam BTh 08. Ridley Hall Cam 05. **d** 08 **p** 09. C Gosforth All SS *Newc* 08-12; V Hebburn St Cuth and St Oswald *Dur* from 12. *St Cuthbert's Vicarage, Argyle Street, Hebburn NE31 1RD* T: 0191-420 2792 M: 07790-913581 E: alan.maxwell@hotmail.co.uk

MAXWELL, Christopher John Moore (Bill). b 31. Qu Coll Cam MA 75 MRCS 59 LRCP 59. Trin Coll Bris 74. **d** 75 **p** 76. SAMS Chile 75-81; Hon C Homerton St Luke *Lon* 81-94; Chapl Ibiza *Eur* 94-99; rtd 99; PtO *Chich* 99-08; *Win* from 08. *Willowbank, Sycamore Close, Milford on Sea, Lymington SO41 0RY* T: (01590) 643110 E: abmaxwell@btinternet.com

MAXWELL, Marcus Howard. b 54. Liv Univ BSc 76 Man Univ MPhil 89. St Jo Coll Nottm BA 79. **d** 80 **p** 81. C Chadderton St Matt *Man* 80-84; V Bircle 84-93; P-in-c Heaton Mersey 93-02; TR Heatons from 02; AD Heaton 98-04 and from 13. *St John's Rectory, 15 Priestnall Road, Stockport SK4 3HR* T: 0161-442 1932 E: marcus.maxwell@ntlworld.com

MAY, Charles Henry. b 29. LTh 58. **d** 58 **p** 59. C Bethnal Green St Jas Less *Lon* 58-61; C Woking St Pet *Guildf* 61-64; Area Sec (W Midl) CPAS 64-67; V Homerton St Luke *Lon* 67-80; Home Sec SAMS 80-84; V Fulham Ch Ch *Lon* 84-94; rtd 94; PtO *Ely* from 94; *Pet* from 94; *Linc* 95-15. *16 Kilverstone, Werrington, Peterborough PE4 5DX* T: (01733) 328108 E: clergy.c.may@gmail.com

MAY, Mrs Deborah Kim. b 60. Trin Coll Bris. **d** 01 **p** 02. C Haughley w Wetherden and Stowupland *St E* 01-04; R Ashwater, Halwill, Beaworthy, Clawton etc *Ex* 04-08; R Melville Australia from 08. *6 Donavon Rise, Murdoch, Perth WA 6150, Australia* T: (0061) (8) 9310 7767 M: 41-817 8688 E: revd.debbie@gmail.com

MAY, Donald Charles Leonard. b 25. Chich Th Coll 72. **d** 73 **p** 74. C Barkingside H Trin *Chelmsf* 73-77; V Aldersbrook 77-91; rtd 92; PtO *Chelmsf* from 92. *236 Prospect Road, Woodford Green IG8 7NQ* T: (020) 8504 6119 E: donald.may1@ntlworld.com

MAY, George Louis. b 27. Selw Coll Cam BA 52 MA 55 Cam Univ PGCE 67 AdDipEd 78. Ridley Hall Cam 52. **d** 54 **p** 55. C St Mary Cray and St Paul's Cray *Roch* 54-56; C St Barnabas's Cray St Barn CD 56-57; C-in-c Elburton CD *Ex* 57-66; Asst Master Guthlaxton Sch Wigston 67-70; Ixworth Sch 70-72; Thurston Upper Sch 73-74; Perias Sch New Alresford 75-85; Hon C Ropley w W Tisted *Win* 78-79; PtO 79-96; rtd 92; PtO *Derby* 07-13. *Oven House, Water Lane, Eyam, Hope Valley S32 5RG* T: (01433) 630599

MAY, Janet Isabel. b 51. Lon Univ CertEd 72. **d** 00 **p** 01. OLM Gt and Lt Ellingham, Rockland and Shropham etc *Nor* 00-05; PtO from 05. *The Mill House, Church Street, Great Ellingham, Attleborough NR17 1LE* T: (01953) 452198 E: rev.may@btopenworld.com

MAY, Preb John Alexander Cyril. b 52. K Coll Lon BD 77 PhD 98 Ch Ch Ox PGCE 78. Linc Th Coll 79. **d** 80 **p** 81. C Tynemouth Ch Ch *Newc* 80-82; C Tynemouth Ch Ch w H Trin 82-85; C Tynemouth St Aug 82-85; TV Glendale Gp 85-90; V Wotton-under-Edge w Ozleworth, N Nibley etc *Glouc* 90-07; P-in-c St Endellion w Port Isaac and St Kew *Truro* 07-12; P-in-c St Minver 07-12; R N Cornwall Cluster 12-14; Preb St Endellion 07-14; rtd 14. *The Lawns, 31 St Peter Street, Tiverton EX16 6NW* T: (01208) 881041
E: johnmay187@hotmail.com

MAY, Peter Richard. b 43. St Jo Coll Cam BA 64 MA 68 MICE 70. Trin Coll Bris 77. **d** 79 **p** 80. C Lancaster St Thos *Blackb* 79-85; V Darwen St Barn 85-91; Chapl Lyon w Grenoble *Eur* 91-92; Chapl Lyon 92-94; PtO *S'wark* 94-95; TR Horley 95-02; rtd 03; PtO *Chich* 04-11. *North Lodge, Exminster, Exeter EX6 8AT* T: (01392) 823047
E: openhearts.2@btinternet.com

MAY, Roger Austin. b 45. SWMTC 07. **d** 10 **p** 11. NSM Bodmin w Lanhydrock and Lanivet *Truro* 10-15; rtd 15. *12 Hanson Road, Liskeard PL14 3NT* T: (01579) 342924 -
M: 07779-349257 E: rogermay@clara.co.uk

MAY, Preb Simon George. b 47. Ex Univ BA 69 Univ of Wales (Ban) CertEd 72 FCA 77. Sarum & Wells Th Coll 86. **d** 88 **p** 89. C Tamworth *Lich* 88-92; V Whitchurch *Ex* 92-07; Warden of Readers (Plymouth Adnry) 00-07; RD Tavistock 02-07; C Barnstaple from 07; Preb Ex Cathl from 09. *Holy Trinity Vicarage, Victoria Road, Barnstaple EX32 9HP* T: (01271) 344321 E: vicar@trinitybarnstaple.eclipse.co.uk

MAY, Stephen Charles Arthur. b 52. Mert Coll Ox BA 73 Edin Univ BD 78 Aber Univ PhD 86. Ridley Hall Cam 84. **d** 86 **p** 87. C Sawley *Derby* 86-88; V Norden w Ashworth *Man* 01-11; rtd 11. *11 Wood Leason Avenue, Lyppard Hanford, Worcester WR4 0EU* T: (01905) 312509 E: smaysfiction@hotmail.com

MAY, Toby Sebastian. b 67. Bris Univ BEng 89. St Jo Coll Nottm MTh 02. **d** 02 **p** 03. C Kendal St Thos *Carl* 02-06; V Alsager Ch Ch *Ches* from 06. *Christ Church Vicarage, 43 Church Road, Alsager, Stoke-on-Trent ST7 2HS* T: (01270) 873727
E: toby@mays-in-grace.co.uk

MAYBEE, Christine. *See* DALE, Christine

MAYBURY, David Kaines. b 32. G&C Coll Cam BA 55 MA 59. Ridley Hall Cam 55. **d** 57 **p** 58. C Sydenham H Trin *S'wark* 57-60; C Rainham *Chelmsf* 60-63; R Edin St Jas 63-75; R Jedburgh 75-84; NSM Duns 84-91; Warden Whitchester Conf Cen 84-91; NSM Hawick *Edin* 91-97; Warden Whitchester Chr Guest Ho and Retreat Cen 91-97; Admin from 97; rtd 97. *DaDo Heights, Borthaugh, Hawick TD9 7LN* T: (01450) 370809 *or* 377477 M: 07570-597835 F: 371080
E: dado@maybud.fsnet.co.uk *or* enquiries@whitchester.org.uk

MAYBURY, Doreen Lorna. b 33. RGN 54 SCM 56. Edin Th Coll 76. **dss** 81 **d** 95 **p** 95. Jedburgh *Edin* 81-84; Warden Whitchester Conf Cen 84-91; Duns *Edin* 84-91; Hawick 91-97; NSM 95-97; rtd 97; Chapl Borders Gen Hosp NHS Trust 98-04. *DaDo Heights, Borthaugh, Hawick TD9 7LN* T: (01450) 370809 -
M: 07801-354134 E: dado1@homecall.co.uk

MAYBURY, Canon John Montague. b 30. G&C Coll Cam BA 53 MA 57. Ridley Hall Cam 53. **d** 55 **p** 56. C Allerton *Liv* 55-59; C Rowner *Portsm* 59-62; V Wroxall 62-67; V Southsea St Simon 67-78; V Crofton 78-91; Hon Can Portsm Cathl 81-95; C Locks Heath 91-95; rtd 95; PtO *Portsm* from 95. *19 Netley Road, Titchfield Common, Fareham PO14 4PE* T: (01489) 584168

MAYBURY, Canon Paul Dorian. b 58. Trin Coll Bris 93. **d** 95 **p** 96. C Spondon *Derby* 95-99; V Gawthorpe and Chickenley Heath *Wakef* 99-02; P-in-c Ossett cum Gawthorpe 01-02; V Ossett and Gawthorpe 02-13; RD Dewsbury 08-13; Hon Can Wakef Cathl 13; Spirituality Co-ord and Bp's Missr SE Cyprus from 13. *PO Box 36034, Deryneia 5385, Cyprus*
E: paul.maybury@cypgulf.org

MAYCOCK, Ms Jane Ellen. b 66. Somerville Coll Ox BA 90 MA 95 Glas Univ MPhil 98. Cranmer Hall Dur 90. **d** 92 **p** 94. Par Dn Harrow Trin St Mich *Lon* 92-94; C 94-95; C Kendal H Trin *Carl* 95-99; Dir of Ords 01-07. *The Rectory, Longlands Road, Bowness-on-Windermere, Windermere LA23 3AS* T: (015394) 43063 E: j.e.maycock@btinternet.com

MAYELL, Howard John. b 50. Bris Sch of Min 81. **d** 84 **p** 88. NSM Patchway *Bris* 84-86; NSM Weston-super-Mare Cen Par *B & W* 87-88; C N Stoneham *Win* 88-91; P-in-c Black Torrington, Bradford w Cookbury etc *Ex* 91-97; C Ledbury w Eastnor *Heref* 97-98; TV Ledbury from 98. *27 Hazle Close, Ledbury HR8 2XX* T: (01531) 631530

MAYER, Alan John. b 46. AKC 70. St Aug Coll Cant 70. **d** 71 **p** 72. C Stanningley St Thos *Ripon* 71-74; C St Helier *S'wark* 74-79; TV Wimbledon 79-85; V Reigate St Luke S Park 85-00; R Oxted and Tandridge 00-11; rtd 11; PtO *S'wark* 11-14. *17 Saxon Crescent, Horsham RH12 2HX*
E: aandkmayer@gmail.com

MAYER, Graham Keith. b 46. St Cath Coll Ox BA 68 Nottm Univ PGCE 69 Ex Univ MA 93. Linc Th Coll 78. **d** 80 **p** 81. C Paignton St Jo *Ex* 80-93; PtO 93-96; P-in-c Christow, Ashton and Bridford 96-10; P-in-c Dunchideock 97-10; V Christow, Ashton, Bridford, Dunchideock etc from 10; RD Kenn from 05. *The Rectory, Dry Lane, Christow, Exeter EX6 7PE* T: (01647) 252845 E: rivertide@btinternet.com

MAYER, Mrs Paula Denise. b 45. St Hilda's Coll Ox BA 68 Nottm Univ CertEd 69. SWMTC 84. **d** 88 **p** 07. Hon Par Dn Paignton St Jo *Ex* 88-90; Par Dn 90-93; PtO from 93. *The Haven, 1 Parkside Road, Paignton TQ4 6AE* T: (01803) 558727
E: paula.haven@aniserve.com

MAYER-JONES, Miss Fiona Ruth. b 70. Westcott Ho Cam 08. **d** 10 **p** 11. C Beverley Minster *York* 10-14; V Northallerton w Kirby Sigston from 14. *27 Mowbray Road, Northallerton DL6 1QT* E: fionaruth@gmail.com

MAYES, Miss Alexier Olwen. St Mich Coll Llan 08. **d** 11 **p** 12. C Bistre *St As* 11-14; V Kerry, Llanmerewig, Dolfor and Mochdre from 14. *The Vicarage, 47 Willan's Drive, Kerry, Newtown SY16 4DB* T: (01686) 670482
E: rev.alex@btinternet.com

MAYES, Canon Andrew Dennis. b 56. K Coll Lon BD 79 AKC 79 Man Univ MA 97. Armenian Orthodox Sem Jerusalem 79 St Steph Ho Ox 80. **d** 81 **p** 82. C Hendon St Alphage *Lon* 81-84; C Hockley *Chelmsf* 84-87; V Kingstanding St Mark *Birm* 87-92; V Saltdean *Chich* 92-01; P-in-c Ovingdean 01-09; CME Officer 01-09; Course Dir St Geo Coll and C St Geo Cathl Jerusalem 09-11; R E Blatchington and Bishopstone *Chich* from 11; Hon Can Niger Delta from 96. *The Rectory, 86 Belgrave Road, Seaford BN25 2HE* T: (01323) 892964
E: andrew.mayes@gmail.com

MAYES, Aonghus William Alun. **d** 05 **p** 06. C Cregagh *D & D* 05-10; I Moy w Charlemont *Arm* from 10; Dioc Communications Officer 10-11. *The Rectory, 37 The Square, Moy, Dungannon BT71 7SG* T: (028) 8778 4312
M: 07748-710148 E: aonghusmayes@yahoo.ie

MAYES, John Charles Dougan. b 44. Bps' Coll Cheshunt 63. **d** 67 **p** 68. C Portadown St Mark *Arm* 67-74; I Aghadowey w Kilrea *D & R* 74-86; USPG Area Sec 77-94; I Clooney w Strathfoyle *D & R* 86-07; Can Derry Cathl 92-96; Preb 96-07; rtd 07. *10 Ebrington Park, Londonderry BT47 6JE*
T: (028) 7131 2973

✠**MAYES, The Rt Revd Michael Hugh Gunton.** b 41. TCD BA 62 Lon Univ BD 85. TCD Div Sch Div Test 64. **d** 64 **p** 65 **c** 93. C Portadown St Columba *Arm* 64-68; USPG Kobe Japan 68-69; Tokyo 69-70; Yokkaichi 70-74; Area Sec USPG C & O, C, C & R, L & K and T, K & A 75-93; I Cork St Mich Union C, C & R 75-86; Adn Cork, Cloyne and Ross 86-93; I Moviddy Union 86-88; I Rathcooney Union 88-93; Bp L & K 93-00; Bp L & K 00-08; rtd 08. *4 Langford Place, Langford Row, Cork, Republic of Ireland*
T: (00353) (21) 496 7688

MAYES, Canon Stephen Thomas. b 47. St Jo Coll Nottm 67. **d** 71 **p** 72. C Cullompton *Ex* 71-75; C Cheltenham St Mark *Glouc* 76-84; P-in-c Water Orton *Birm* 84-91; V 91-12; AD Coleshill 95-05; Hon Can Birm Cathl 05-12; rtd 12; P-in-c Barston *Birm* 12-14; PtO from 14. *47 Yew Tree Lane, Solihull B91 2NX* T: 0121-704 1356 E: stmayes@yahoo.co.uk

MAYES, Suzanne Janette. b 55. NTMTC 95. **d** 98 **p** 99. NSM E Ham w Upton Park and Forest Gate *Chelmsf* 98-02; Chapl HM Pris Wellingborough 02-04; Sessional Chapl HM Pris Chelmsf 05-07; HM Pris Wormwood Scrubs 07-08; HM Pris Hollesley Bay 07-10; HM Pris and YOI Warren Hill 07-10; Chapl HM Pris Bullwood Hall 11-13; PtO *Chelmsf* 04-11; Hon C Romford St Andr 11-12; Hon C Romford Ascension Collier Row from 12. *37 Netherpark Drive, Romford RM2 5RJ* T: (01708) 728095
E: suzannemayes@btinternet.com

✠**MAYFIELD, The Rt Revd Christopher John.** b 35. G&C Coll Cam BA 57 MA 61 Cranfield Inst of Tech MSc 83. Wycliffe Hall Ox 61. **d** 63 **p** 64 **c** 85. C Birm St Martin 63-67; Lect 67-71; V Luton St Mary *St Alb* 71-80; RD Luton 74-80; Adn Bedford 80-85; Suff Bp Wolverhampton *Lich* 85-92; Area Bp Wolverhampton 92-93; Bp Man 93-02; rtd 02; Hon Asst Bp Worc from 02. *Harewood House, 54 Primrose Crescent, Worcester WR5 3HT* T: (01905) 764822

MAYFIELD, Timothy James Edward. b 60. LMH Ox BA 82. Trin Coll Bris BA 88. **d** 88 **p** 89. C Ovenden *Wakef* 88-92; V Mount Pellon 92-03; V Cheltenham Ch Ch *Glouc* from 03. *Christ Church Vicarage, Malvern Road, Cheltenham GL50 2NU* T: (01242) 515983

MAYFIELD, Timothy John Joseph. b 59. BA MA. **d** 99 **p** 00. C Battersea Rise St Mark *S'wark* 99-10; C Fairfax *Truro* Ch USA from 10. *10520 Main Street, Fairfax VA 22030-3380, USA* T: (001) (703) 273 1300

MAYHEW, David Francis. b 51. Ch Ch Ox BA 72 MA 76 Wycliffe Hall Ox BA 75. NEOC 89. **d** 91 **p** 92. NSM High Elswick St Paul *Newc* 91-94; Toc H 91-94; V Mitford *Newc*

94-09; C Longhorsley and Hebron 07-09; Chapl Northgate and Prudhoe NHS Trust 94-09; V Cov H Trin from 09. *Holy Trinity Vicarage, 4 Bishop's Walk, Coventry CV5 6RE* T: (024) 7671 2114 E: dfmayhew@me.com

MAYHEW (née GURNEY), Jean Elizabeth. b 39. OBE 97. New Hall Cam BA 61 MA 85 K Coll Lon BD 84 AKC 84 PGCE 85 Ulster Univ Hon DUniv 98 FKC 00. SEITE 02. **d** 05 **p** 06. NSM Maidstone St Paul *Cant* 05-10; PtO from 11. *Twysden, Riseden Lane, Kilndown, Cranbrook TN17 2SG* T: (01580) 211820 F: 212232 M: 07773-404554 E: jean@jmayhew.free-online.co.uk

MAYLAND, Mrs Jean Mary. b 36. JP 77. LMH Ox BA 58 MA 61 TCert 60. St Deiniol's Hawarden 91. **d** 91 **p** 94. NSM York Minster 91-93; Lect and Tutor NOC 91-93; Lect NEOC 93-96; Dioc Ecum Officer *Dur* 93-96; Local Unity Officer Dur Ecum Relns Gp 93-96; Assoc Sec CCBI 96-99; Co-ord Sec for Ch Life CTBI 99-03; Asst Gen Sec 99-03; PtO *Lon* 97-03; *S'wark* 97-00; *Chelmsf* 00-03; rtd 03; PtO *York* 03-09; *Newc* from 04. *5 Hackwood Glade, Hexham NE46 1AL* T: (01434) 600339 E: jeanmayland@btinternet.com

MAYLAND, Canon Ralph. b 27. VRD 63. Ripon Hall Ox 57. **d** 59 **p** 60. C Lambeth St Andr w St Thos *S'wark* 59-62; Chapl RNR 61-94; C-in-c Worksop St Paul CD *S'well* 62-68; V Brightside St Marg *Sheff* 68-72; Ind Chapl 68-81; V Ecclesfield 72-81; Can Res and Treas York Minster 82-94; rtd 94; Hon C Brancepeth *Dur* 94-96; PtO *York* from 96; *Chelmsf* 01-03. *5 Hackwood Glade, Hexham NE46 1AL* T: (01434) 600339

MAYLES, Miss Helena Rosemary Laura. b 84. Nottm Univ BA 06. Westcott Ho Cam 12. **d** 14 **p** 15. C Over St Chad *Ches* from 14. *31 Vauxhall Way, Winsford CW7 1NQ* E: h.mayles@gmail.com

MAYLOR, David Charles. b 59. Lanc Univ BSc 80 Edge Hill Coll of HE PGCE 81. St Jo Coll Nottm 89. **d** 91 **p** 92. C Hindley All SS *Liv* 91-94; P-in-c Spalding St Paul *Linc* 94-07; Chapl United Lincs Hosps NHS Trust 99-07; Lic Gen Preacher *Linc* 07-12; Music Dir Stamford St Geo w St Paul 07-12; P-in-c Barnack w Ufford and Bainton *Pet* from 12. *The Rectory, Millstone Lane, Barnack, Stamford PE9 3ET* T: (01780) 740234 E: dmaylor@btinternet.com

MAYLOR, Miles Edward. b 55. St Andr Univ BD 85 Glam Univ PhD 00 PGCE 02. St Mich Coll Llan 03. **d** 05 **p** 06. NSM Mountain Ash and Miskin *Llan* 05; NSM Wheatley *Ox* 06-09; NSM Ox St Barn and St Paul 09-11; C Carew *St D* 11-13. *St David's Cathedral Clergy House, 38 Charles Street, Cardiff CF10 2SF* E: miles.maylor@btinternet.com

MAYNARD, Adam Richard. b 86. Cranmer Hall Dur 12. **d** 15. C Liv Ch Ch Norris Green from 15. *9 Kingsland Crescent, Liverpool L11 7AN*

MAYNARD, John William. b 37. Lon Univ BSc 58. Ripon Hall Ox 60. **d** 62 **p** 63. C St Laur in Thanet *Cant* 62-67; C S Ashford Ch Ch 67-70; V Pagham *Chich* 70-00; rtd 00. *2 West Checkstone, 2 Douglas Avenue, Exmouth EX8 2AU* T: (01395) 222675

MAYNARD, Jonathan Mark (Josh). b 80. Ex Univ BA 02. Trin Coll Bris BA 09. **d** 10 **p** 11. C Woodchester and Brimscombe *Glouc* 10-15; V Styvechale *Cov* from 15. *Styvechale Vicarage, 16 Armorial Road, Coventry CV3 6GJ* M: 07825-795257 T: (024) 7641 6074 E: jmaynard1044@googlemail.com

MAYNARD, Joshua Phillip. b 88. St Mich Coll Llan BTh 14. **d** 14 **p** 15. C Hubberston and Herbrandston *St D* from 14. *95 Waterloo Road, Hakin, Milford Haven SA73 3PE* T: (01646) 279884 M: 07849-991706 E: revjoshmaynard@gmail.com

MAYNARD, Canon Richard Edward Buller. b 42. AKC 66. **d** 67 **p** 68. C St Ives *Truro* 67-71; C Falmouth K Chas 71-74; V St Germans 74-85; RD E Wivelshire 81-85; TR Saltash 85-08; Hon Can Truro Cathl 82-08; Chapl St Barn Hosp Saltash 90-93; Chapl Cornwall Healthcare NHS Trust 93-02; Chapl N and E Cornwall Primary Care Trust 02-06; Chapl Cornwall and Is of Scilly Primary Care Trust 06-08; rtd 08; C Altarnon w Bolventor, Laneast and St Clether *Truro* 11-12. *Harewood, Dunheved Road, Launceston PL15 9JJ* T: (01752) 843142 E: canonrichardmaynard@btinternet.com

MAYNE, Canon Brian John. b 52. Univ of Wales (Cardiff) BA 73 LTCL 75 MRICS 81. NEOC 82 Coll of Resurr Mirfield 84. **d** 85 **p** 86. C Stainton-in-Cleveland *York* 85-89; P-in-c Rounton w Welbury 89-96; Chapl HM YOI Northallerton 89-96; Chapl HM YOI Lanc Farms 96-10; Chapl HM Pris Kirkham from 10; Hon Can Blackb Cathl from 09. *HM Prison Kirkham, Freckleton Road, Kirkham, Preston PR4 2RN* T: (01772) 675625 E: brianmayne@tiscali.co.uk

MAYO, Christopher Paul. b 68. Heythrop Coll Lon BD 91 Birm Univ PGCE 96. Qu Coll Birm 91. **d** 93 **p** 94. C Wednesfield *Lich* 93-94; C Bilston 94-95; Miss P E Sutherland *Mor* from 10; P-in-c Tain from 12. *9 Academy Street, Brora KW9 6QP* T: (01408) 600818 M: 07860-333892 E: frchrismayo@gmail.com *or* chris.mayo@mac.com

MAYO, Deborah Ann. *See* MURPHY, Deborah Ann

MAYO, Inglis John. b 46. FCA. Ripon Hall Ox 74. **d** 77 **p** 78. C Bitterne Park *Win* 77-81; C Christchurch 81-86; P-in-c Sturminster Marshall *Sarum* 86-89; P-in-c Kingston Lacy and Shapwick 86-89; V Sturminster Marshall, Kingston Lacy and Shapwick 89-00; P-in-c Lilliput 00-06; V 06-08; rtd 08; PtO *Sarum* from 08; *Win* from 08. *49B St Catherine's Road, Bournemouth BH6 4AQ* T: (01202) 424971 E: inglis.mayo@btinternet.com

MAYO, Robert William. b 61. Keble Coll Ox BA 83 Trin Coll Carmarthen PhD 00. Cranmer Hall Dur 85. **d** 87 **p** 88. C Luton Lewsey St Hugh *St Alb* 87-90; Hd Cam Univ Miss and NSM Bermondsey St Jas w Ch Ch *S'wark* 90-95; Chapl S Bank Univ 95-98; Dir Youth Work Tr Ridley Hall Cam 98-05; V Shepherd's Bush St Steph w St Thos *Lon* from 05. *St Stephen's Vicarage, 1 Coverdale Road, London W12 8JJ* T: (020) 8743 3166 M: 07977-003227 E: bobmayo43@gmail.com

MAYO, Mrs Susan. b 53. Didsbury Coll Man BEd 78. St Jo Coll Nottm 08. **d** 10 **p** 11. NSM Edgeley and Cheadle Heath *Ches* 10-15; NSM Cheadle All Hallows from 15; Chapl Stockport Academy 11-15. *38 Brookhead Drive, Cheadle SK8 2JA* T: 0161-428 5375 E: mayos32@waitrose.com *or* sue@edgeleyandcheadleheath.org.uk

MAYO-LYTHALL, Ms Jennifer Elizabeth. b 83. St Jo Coll Dur BA 10. Cranmer Hall Dur 07. **d** 10 **p** 11. C Norbury *Ches* 10-14; Transforming Lives Together Development Officer from 14; NSM Offerton St Alb and Stockport St Thos from 14. *The Vicarage, Salcombe Road, Stockport SK2 5AG* M: 07749-949830 E: jmayo-lythall@hotmail.com

MAYO-SMITH, Peter. b 49. Open Univ BA 80. Ridley Hall Cam 05. **d** 06 **p** 07. C Greengates *Bradf* 06-09; C Idle 06-09; C Cottingley 08-09; P-in-c Haworth *Leeds* 09-15; P-in-c Cross Roads cum Lees 09-15; P-in-c Oxenhope *Bradf* 10-13; R Haworth and Cross Roads cum Lees *Leeds* from 15. *78 Prince Street, Haworth, Keighley BD22 8JD* T: (01535) 648464 M: 07880-866222 E: peter@mayo-smith.net *or* rector@haworthchurch.co.uk

MAYOR, Henry William. b 39. Oriel Coll Ox BA 62. Westcott Ho Cam 62. **d** 64 **p** 65. C The Quinton *Birm* 64-66; C Dudley St Thos and St Luke *Worc* 67-71; R Birch St Agnes *Man* 71-83; Community Chapl Aylesbury *Ox* 83-89; Community Chapl Aylesbury w Bierton and Hulcott 89; R Cheetham St Luke and Lower Crumpsall St Thos *Man* 89-96; R Cheetham and Lower Crumpsall 97-01; rtd 01; PtO *Man* from 01. *57 Hill Street, Manchester M20 3FY* T: 0161-434 2955 M: 07960-767155 E: henrywmayor@hotmail.com

MAYOR, Janet Hilary. *See* TAYLOR, Janet Hilary

MAYOSS, Anthony (Aidan). b 31. Leeds Univ BA 55. Coll of Resurr Mirfield 55. **d** 57 **p** 58. C Meir *Lich* 57-62; LtO *Wakef* 62-72; *Leeds* from 78; CR from 64; S Africa 73-75; Asst Chapl Lon Univ 76-78; Bursar CR 84-90; rtd 98; PtO *Lon* 98-07. *House of the Resurrection, Stocks Bank Road, Mirfield WF14 0BN* T: (01924) 483330 E: amayoss@mirfield.org.uk

MAYOSS-HURD, Canon Susan Patricia. b 59. Lanc Univ BA 81. Cranmer Hall Dur 82. **dss** 84 **d** 87 **p** 94. Ribbesford w Bewdley and Dowles *Worc* 84-88; Par Dn 87-88; Chapl W Heath Hosp 88-96; C W Heath *Birm* 88-96; V 96-03; V Peachland St Marg Canada from 03. *6146 Turner Avenue, Peachland BC V0H 1X4, Canada* T: (001) (250) 767 9682 E: revsuemh@shaw.ca

MAZUR, Mrs Ann Carol. b 47. St Mich Coll Sarum CertEd 69. TISEC 01. **d** 04 **p** 05. NSM St Ninian's Cathl Perth 04-07; Prec 07-12; Chapl Craigclowan Sch Perth 04-07; rtd 12. *Fairmead, Langton-by-Wragby, Market Rasen LN8 5PX* T: (01673) 857720 E: ann@mazur.org.uk

MBALI, Escourt Zolile. b 40. Fort Hare Univ BA 68 Ox Univ BA 71. St Bede's Coll Umtata 62. **d** 71 **p** 72. S Africa 71-74 and from 93; Botswana 74-81; V Preston on Tees *Dur* 81-83; C Knighton St Mary Magd *Leic* 84-88; P-in-c Church Langton w Tur Langton, Thorpe Langton etc 88-92; Community Relns Officer 88-93; Hon Can Leic Cathl 92-93; rtd 02. *1 Halford Road, Berea, Durban, 4001 South Africa* T: (0027) (31) 201 6195

MDUMULLA, Jonas Habel. b 50. Nairobi Univ Hull Univ BTh 87 MA 89. St Phil Coll Kongwa. **d** 74 **p** 75. Tanzania 74-82; C Sutton St Jas and Wawne *York* 82-96; P-in-c Carlton and Drax 96-15; Ind Chapl 96-15; rtd 15. *Address temp unknown*

MEACHAM, John David. b 24. AKC 51 Lambeth STh 77 Open Univ MPhil 90. **d** 52 **p** 53. C Maidenhead St Luke *Ox* 52-55; Asst Master Linton Ho Maidenhead 52-55; C Croydon St Jo *Cant* 55-58; V Sittingbourne St Mich 58-74; Teacher St Jo Boys' High Sch 64-74; V Brenchley *Roch* 74-83; Teacher Tunbridge Wells Girls' Gr Sch 78-83; P-in-c Gt Wishford and S Newton *Sarum* 83-88; Bp's Chapl and Research Asst 83-86; Sec C of E Doctrine Commn 84-89; rtd 88; PtO *Sarum* 88-98. *Trewinnard, Grams Road, Walmer, Deal CT14 7NT* T: (01304) 239613

MEAD, Arthur Hugh. b 39. K Coll Cam BA 60 MA 64 New Coll Ox BLitt 66. St Steph Ho Ox 61. **d** 80 **p** 80. NSM Hammersmith St Jo *Lon* 80-05; NSM Hammersmith H Innocents and St Jo from 05; Chapl St Paul's Sch Barnes 82-97; rtd 97; Dep P in o 85-90 and 95-09; P in O 90-95; Reader of The Temple from 95. *11 Dungarvan Avenue, London SW15 5QU* T: (020) 8876 5833

MEAD, Canon John Harold. b 37. Wells Th Coll 69. **d** 71 **p** 72. C Charlton Kings St Mary *Glouc* 71-75; R Stratton w Baunton 75-82; R Bishop's Cleeve 82-00; RD Tewkesbury 88-97; Hon Can Glouc Cathl 90-00; rtd 00; PtO *Glouc* from 00. *13 Cleevemount Close, Cheltenham GL52 3HW* T: (01242) 241050

MEAD, Mrs Lynda Roberta. b 44. Open Univ BA 91. STETS. **d** 99 **p** 00. NSM Hythe *Win* 99-04. *22 Furzedale Park, Hythe, Southampton SO45 3HW* T: (023) 8084 8901

MEAD, Nicholas Charles. b 50. Newc Univ BEd 73 Reading Univ MA 76. Ridley Hall Cam 83. **d** 85 **p** 86. C Bilton *Cov* 85-88; C Whittlesey *Ely* 88-89; Hd RS Neale-Wade Community Coll March 89-97; Fell Farmington Inst for Chr Studies Ox from 96; Sen Lect RE Westmr Coll Ox 97-00; Sen Lect RE Ox Brookes Univ 00-13. *9 Yarnells Road, Oxford OX2 0JY* T: (01865) 240865 E: nmead@brookes.ac.uk

MEAD, Peter Tony. b 63. St Jo Coll Dur BA 08. Cranmer Hall Dur 06. **d** 08 **p** 09. C Yeovil H Trin w Barwick *B & W* 08-12; R St Leonards St Ethelburga and St Leon *Chich* from 12. *The Rectory, 81A Filsham Road, St Leonards-on-Sea TN38 0PE* T: (01424) 433705 M: 07791-642598 E: pete.mead@sky.com

MEADEN, Philip George William. b 40. Open Univ BA 75. Lich Th Coll 63. **d** 66 **p** 67. C Aston SS Pet and Paul *Birm* 66-70; V Lozells St Paul 70-76; Asst Chapl HM Pris Brixton 76-77; Chapl HM Pris Lewes 77-84; Chapl HM Pris Aylesbury 84-88; Chapl HM Pris Wandsworth 88-01; rtd 01; PtO *St E* 01-05. *2 Waterloo Lane, Fairford GL7 4BP* T: (01285) 713917

MEADER, Jennifer Lindsay. b 68. UEA BA 89. Westcott Ho Cam. **d** 01 **p** 02. C Teversham and Cherry Hinton St Andr *Ely* 01-05; C Westmr St Jas *Lon* from 05. *St James's Church, 197 Piccadilly, London W1J 9LL* T: (020) 7734 4511
E: revlindsaym@gmail.com

MEADER, Philip John. b 44. Oak Hill Th Coll 73. **d** 75 **p** 76. C E Ham St Paul *Chelmsf* 75-77; CMJ 77-90; TV Lowestoft and Kirkley *Nor* 90-94; V Lowestoft St Andr 94-96; R Panfield and Rayne *Chelmsf* 96-09; RD Braintree 06-09; rtd 09. *39 Langdale Avenue, Chichester PO19 8JQ* T: (01243) 528783 E: philip@revdmeader.fsnet.co.uk

MEADOWS, Mrs Freda Angela. b 46. CertEd 68. Oak Hill Th Coll 93. **d** 96 **p** 97. NSM N Wembley St Cuth *Lon* 96-01; NSM Roxeth 01-07; rtd 07; PtO *Lon* 07-12; *B & W* from 12. *38 Maple Rise, Radstock BA3 3LH* T: (01761) 435320
E: fred@famead.net

MEADOWS, Philip Michael. b 71. Univ of Wales (Lamp) BA 95. St Steph Ho Ox BTh 01. **d** 01 **p** 03. C W Bromwich St Fran *Lich* 01; C Leeds Belle Is St Jo and St Barn *Ripon* 02-06; PtO *Ches* from 06; CMP from 04. *13 Naburn Close, Stockport SK5 8JQ* T: 0161-494 8073 M: 07971-035513
E: frmeadows@hotmail.co.uk

MEADS, William Ivan. b 35. Qu Mary Coll Lon BA 56 ACIS 67 ACMA 75. Linc Th Coll 75. **d** 77 **p** 78. C Cheltenham St Luke and St Jo *Glouc* 77-81; Chapl HM Pris Pentonville 81-82; Preston 82-85; Wakef 85-88; P-in-c Wroxton w Balscote and Shenington w Alkerton *Ox* 88-90; R Broughton w N Newington and Shutford etc 90-95; P-in-c Week St Mary w Poundstock and Whitstone *Truro* 95-97; rtd 97; PtO *B & W* 97-00; *St E* from 08. *The Meads, Briswell Green, Thorndon, Eye IP23 7JF* T: (01379) 678670 E: nanmeads@whsmithnet.co.uk

MEADWAY, Prof Jeanette Valerie. b 47. Edin Univ MB, ChB 69 FRCP 87 FRCPEd 87. Oak Hill NSM Course 89. **d** 93 **p** 94. NSM Stratford St Jo w Ch Ch and St Jas *Chelmsf* 93-14; NSM Forest Gate St Sav and St Jas from 14; PtO *Lon* 99-03; Hon Prof Gulu Univ Uganda from 09; Can Mbale Cathl from 09. *4 Glebe Avenue, Woodford Green IG8 9HB* T: (020) 8504 1958 E: drjeanettemeadway@btinternet.com

MEAKIN, Canon Anthony John. b 28. TD 76. Down Coll Cam BA 52 MA 56. Westcott Ho Cam 52. **d** 54 **p** 55. C Gosforth All SS *Newc* 54-60; V Alnwick St Paul 60-71; V Edlingham 62-71; CF (TA) 63-83; R Whickham *Dur* 71-88; RD Gateshead W 78-88; Hon Can Dur Cathl 83-93; Bp's Sen Chapl and Exec Officer for Dioc Affairs 88-93; rtd 93; PtO *Dur* from 94. *73 Oakfields, Burnopfield, Newcastle upon Tyne NE16 6PQ* T: (01207) 270429 E: a.meakin2@homecall.co.uk

MEAKIN, Catherine Mary. b 77. LMH Ox BA 99 Selw Coll Cam BA 02. Ridley Hall Cam 02. **d** 04 **p** 05. NSM Cambridge H Trin *Ely* from 04. *Holy Trinity Church, Market Street, Cambridge CB2 3NZ* T: (01223) 355397
E: cat.meakin@htcambridge.org.uk

MEAKIN, David John. b 61. Hull Univ BA 82 Dur Univ MA 96 Hughes Hall Cam PGCE 83 Lambeth STh 88. Westcott Ho Cam 86. **d** 88 **p** 89. C Upminster *Chelmsf* 88-92; Prec and Sacr Dur Cathl 92-97; V Ryhope 97-04; P-in-c Schorne *Ox* 04-11; TR from 11; AD Claydon from 11. *The Rectory, 1 Green Acres Close, Whitchurch, Aylesbury HP22 4JP* T: (01296) 641606
E: d.meakin@btinternet.com

MEARA, The Ven David Gwynne. b 47. Oriel Coll Ox BA 70 MA 73. Lambeth STh 76 Cuddesdon Coll 71. **d** 73 **p** 74. C Whitley Ch Ch *Ox* 73-77; Chapl Reading Univ 77-82; V Basildon 82-87; P-in-c Aldworth and Ashampstead 85-87; V Basildon w Aldworth and Ashampstead 87-94; RD Bradfield 90-94; V Buckingham w Radclive cum Chackmore 94-97; P-in-c Nash w Thornton, Beachampton and Thornborough 96-97; R Buckingham 97-00; RD 95-00; Hon Can Ch Ch 98-00; R St Bride Fleet Street w Bridewell etc *Lon* 00-14; Adn Lon 09-14; P-in-c St Mary Aldermary 10-12; rtd 14. *Stonewalls Barn, 10 The Closes, Kidlington OX5 2DP*

MEARDON, Canon Brian Henry. b 44. Reading Univ BSc 66 PhD 71. Oak Hill Th Coll MPhil 84. **d** 79 **p** 80. C Reading St Jo *Ox* 79-82; V Warfield 82-09; Hon Can Ch Ch 03-09; rtd 09; Hon C Bemerton *Sarum* 10-12; PtO from 12. *382 Devizes Road, Salisbury SP2 9LY* T: (01722) 501300
E: brian.meardon@googlemail.com

MEARDON, Mark James. b 73. Southn Univ BSc 94. Trin Th Coll Singapore MTS 07 St Jo Coll Nottm MA 09. **d** 09 **p** 10. C Hazlemere *Ox* from 09. *17 Southcote Way, Penn, High Wycombe HP10 8JG* T: (01494) 812748 M: 07905-887125
E: mark.meardon@gmail.com

MEARS, Mrs Hannah Marie. b 80. St Cuth Soc Dur BA 02 St Mary's Ho Dur MA 03. Trin Coll Bris 06. **d** 08 **p** 09. NSM Henbury *Bris* 08-09; C St Austell *Truro* 09-13; V Rugby W *Cov* from 13. *St Matthew's Vicarage, 7 Vicarage Road, Rugby CV22 7AJ*

MEARS, Oliver Harry John. b 80. Ball Coll Ox BA 02. Trin Coll Bris BA 08. **d** 09 **p** 10. C St Austell *Truro* 09-13; NSM Rugby W *Cov* 13-14; V from 14. *The Vicarage, 7 Vicarage Road, Rugby CV22 7AJ* E: ollymears@yahoo.co.uk

MEARS, Phillip David. b 40. Dur Univ BA 62. **d** 65 **p** 66. C Sandylands *Blackb* 65-68; C Chorley St Geo 68-71; V Leyland St Ambrose 71-81; Chapl Warrington Distr Gen Hosp 81-00; PtO *Ches* 81-06; Hon C Schorne *Ox* from 06. *The Rectory, Church Street, Quainton, Aylesbury HP22 4AP* T: (01296) 655237

MEATH AND KILDARE, Bishop of. *See* STOREY, The Most Revd Patricia Louise

MEATH, Archdeacon of. *See* STEVENSON, The Ven Leslie Thomas Clayton

MEATHREL, Timothy James. b 78. Ox Brookes Univ BSc 99. Wycliffe Hall Ox BTh 07. **d** 08 **p** 09. C Harborne Heath *Birm* 08-13; C Clifton Ch Ch w Em *Bris* from 13. *60 Clifton Park Road, Bristol BS8 3HN* T: 0117-325 1226 M: 07818-401372
E: tim.meathrel@ccweb.org.uk

MEATS, Canon Alan John. b 41. Univ of Wales (Cardiff) BA 62 DipEd 63 Lon Univ BD 70 Trin Coll Carmarthen MTh 00. St Mich Coll Llan 68. **d** 70 **p** 71. C Pontypridd St Cath *Llan* 70-73; TV Ystradyfodwg 73-75; Dioc Inspector of Schs 73-75 and 83-89; V Llandeilo Tal-y-bont *S & B* 75-83; RD Llwchwr 81-83; V Aberdare St Fagan *Llan* 83-89; V Felin-foel *St D* 89-01; Asst Dioc Dir of Educn 89-92; Dioc Dir of Educn 92-97; V Pen-bre 01-07; Can St D Cathl 94-07; rtd 07; PtO *S & B* from 12. *45A Capel Road, Llanelli SA14 8SL* T: (01554) 229427

MEATYARD, Mrs Christina. b 51. SRN 74. STETS 96. **d** 99 **p** 01. NSM S Hayling *Portsm* 99-05; NSM N Hayling St Pet and Hayling Is St Andr 05-06. *38 Staunton Avenue, Hayling Island PO11 0EW* T: (023) 9234 8886 *or* 9263 7649 M: 07979-096779

MECHANIC, Mrs Bridget Elisheva. b 54. Cape Town Univ TDip 74 Nazarene Th Coll Man BA 08 Anglia Ruskin Univ MA 10. Ridley Hall Cam 08. **d** 10 **p** 11. C Ipswich St Jo *St E* 10-13; rtd 13; Academic Supervisor Africa Sch of Miss S Africa 13-14; P-in-c Escomb *Dur* from 14; P-in-c Etherley from 14; P-in-c Witton Park from 14; P-in-c Hamsterley and Witton-le-Wear from 14. *1 Vicarage Court, Howden le Wear, Crook DL15 8RB* T: (01388) 768898
E: elishevamechanic@gmail.com

MECHANIC, Rodney Ian (Roni). b 48. Man Univ MA(Theol) 00. **d** 78 **p** 78. S Africa 78-98; P-in-c Shebbear, Buckland Filleigh, Sheepwash etc *Ex* 98-01; Australia 01-02; TV Heatons *Man* 02-08; TV Mildenhall *St E* 08-13; rtd 13; Tr Dir Africa Sch of Miss S Africa 13-14; Hon C Escomb *Dur* from 14; Hon C Etherley from 14; Hon C Witton Park from 14; Hon C Hamsterley and Witton-le-Wear from 14. *1 Vicarage Court, Howden le Wear, Crook DL15 8RB* T: (01388) 768898
E: ronimechanic@gmail.com

MECREDY, Ruth. b 60. STETS 09. **d** 12 **p** 13. NSM Broughton Gifford, Gt Chalfield and Holt *Sarum* from 12. *9 Little Parks, Holt, Trowbridge BA14 6QR* T: (01225) 783197
E: rmecredy@gmail.com

MEDCALF, James Gordon. b 31. CB . Solicitor 63. S'wark Ord Course 87. **d** 90 **p** 91. NSM Shortlands *Roch* 90-00. *15 Losecoat Close, Stamford PE9 1DU* T: (01780) 482583

MEDFORTH, Allan Hargreaves. b 27. Qu Coll Cam BA 48 MA 52. Westcott Ho Cam 50. **d** 51 **p** 52. C Hexham *Newc* 51-55; PV S'well Minster 55-59; V Farnsfield 59-72; RD S'well 66-72; V St Alb St Pet *St Alb* 72-95; RD St Alb 74-84; rtd 95; PtO *St Alb* from 95. *62 Cuckmans Drive, St Albans AL2 3AF* T: (01727) 836437

MEDHURST, Mrs June. b 44. St Hild Coll Dur TCert 66. NOC 99. **d** 02 **p** 03. C Silsden *Bradf* 02-06; P-in-c Oxenhope 06-10; PtO *Leeds* from 10. *100 Langley Lane, Baildon, Shipley BD17 6TD* T: (01274) 599177 E: medjune@tiscali.co.uk

MEDHURST, Prof Kenneth Noel. b 38. Edin Univ MA 61 Man Univ PhD 69. **d** 91 **p** 93. NSM Baildon *Bradf* 91-06; NSM Oxenhope 06-09; PtO *Leeds* from 10; Can Th Bradf Cathl from 00. *100 Langley Lane, Baildon, Shipley BD17 6TD* T: (01274) 599177 E: kenmed@btinternet.com

MEDHURST, Leslie John. b 56. TCD BTh 90 MA 93 Open Univ BA 91. **d** 85 **p** 86. C Seapatrick *D & D* 85-90; I Belfast St Mark *Conn* 90-97; I Helen's Bay *D & D* 97-05. *25 Ballyhalbert Gardens, Bangor BT19 1SE* T: (028) 9107 0820

MEDLEY, Philip James Anthony. b 81. St Jo Coll Dur BA 03 PGCE 04. Trin Coll Bris 08. **d** 10 **p** 11. C Walker *Newc* 10-13; P-in-c Byker St Mich w St Lawr from 13. *63 Rosebery Crescent, Newcastle upon Tyne NE2 1EX* T: 0191-281 5639 M: 07735-990077 E: phil_medley@hotmail.com

MEDLEY, Canon Philip Roger. b 46. Birm Univ CertEd 73 Sheff Univ MA 00 FCollP 96. SWMTC. **d** 85 **p** 86. NSM Ottery St Mary, Alfington and W Hill *Ex* 85-86; C S Hill w Callington *Truro* 86-89; C Linkinhorne 86-89; V 89-03; Dioc Officer for Evang 93-99; Warden Cornwall Preachers' Coll 93-99; Hon Can Truro Cathl 01-03; Dioc Missr *B & W* from 03. *The Old Deanery, Wells BA5 2UG* T: (01749) 670777
E: roger.medley@bathwells.anglican.org

MEDLEY, Stephen. b 70. **d** 15. C Chilvers Coton w Astley *Cov* from 15. *35 Carnation Way, Nuneaton CV10 7SR* M: 07751-384297 T: (024) 7667 2268
E: steve.medley42@gmail.com

MEDWAY, Mrs Christine Jean. b 57. Qu Coll Birm 93. **d** 95 **p** 98. C Milton *Win* 95-97; C Southampton St Mary Extra 97-01; P-in-c Haselbury Plucknett, Misterton and N Perrott *B & W* 01-03; rtd 03; PtO *Win* 04-13. *40 Lime Avenue, Southampton SO19 8NZ* T: (023) 8044 5105

MEDWAY, Daron. b 72. Univ of N Lon BA 98. Wycliffe Hall Ox BTh 04. **d** 04 **p** 05. C Crofton *Portsm* 04-08; V Penge St Jo *Roch* 08-13; P-in-c Weston *Win* from 13. *Weston Vicarage, Weston Lane, Southampton SO19 9HG* T: (023) 8044 8421 M: 07900-574691 E: d.medway@mac.com

MEE, Colin Henry. b 36. Reading Univ BSc 58. Bris Sch of Min 83. **d** 85 **p** 86. NSM Stanton St Quintin, Hullavington, Grittleton etc *Bris* 85-87; C Swindon Ch Ch 88-90; TV Washfield, Stoodleigh, Withleigh etc *Ex* 90-95; TR 95-99; Chapl Marie Curie Foundn (Tidcombe Hall) 95-99; rtd 99; PtO *B & W* from 02. *Rickstones, Burgundy Road, Minehead TA24 5QJ* T: (01643) 706048

MEEHAN, Cyril Frederick. b 52. St Jo Coll Nottm BTh 80. **d** 80 **p** 81. C Keresley and Coundon *Cov* 80-83; P-in-c Linton and Castle Gresley *Derby* 83-90; P-in-c Alvaston 90-00; V 00; Chapl Asst Freeman Gp of Hosps NHS Trust 00-03; Chapl Northumbria Healthcare NHS Trust 03-04. *9 Vanburgh Gardens, Morpeth NE61 2YF*

MEEK, Anthony William. b 45. ACIB. Ox NSM Course 80. **d** 83 **p** 84. NSM Gt Chesham *Ox* 83-01; PtO *Ex* from 01; Clergy Widow(er)s Officer 02-12. *The Willows, Orley Road, Ipplepen, Newton Abbot TQ12 5SA* T: (01803) 814370
E: frtonymeek@aol.com

MEERE, Mrs Alison Elizabeth. b 44. SRN 65. Ripon Coll Cuddesdon 85. **d** 87 **p** 94. Par Dn Hengrove *Bris* 87-88; Par Dn Winterbourne 88-91; Par Dn Southmead 91-93; Par Dn Hackney *Lon* 93-94; TV 94-95; Asst Chapl R Berks Hosp Reading 95-96; Asst Chapl Battle Hosp Reading 95-96; Indonesia 02-03; rtd 03. *19 St Elmos Road, London SE16 1SA* T: (020) 7231 2601 M: 07754-808579

MEERING, Dominic William Edward. b 78. Bris Univ BSc 00 PGCE 02. Trin Coll Bris 12. **d** 14 **p** 15. C Hazlemere *Ox* from 14. *Church House, 70 George's Hill, Widmer End, High Wycombe HP15 6BH* T: 07811-814528
E: dominicmeering@hotmail.com

MEERING, Laurence Piers Ralph. b 48. Man Univ BSc 70. Trin Coll Bris 79. **d** 81 **p** 82. C Downend *Bris* 81-84; C Crofton

Portsm 84-87; V Witheridge, Thelbridge, Creacombe, Meshaw etc *Ex* 87-94; TV Southgate *Chich* 94-02; TV Walton H Trin *Ox* 02-07; P-in-c Bedgrove 02-07; P-in-c Newton Longville and Mursley w Swanbourne etc 07-08; R 08-09; V Newton Longville, Mursley, Swanbourne etc 09-14; AD Mursley 11-14; rtd 14. *21 St Michael's Gardens, South Petherton TA13 5BD* E: laurencemeering@yahoo.co.uk

MEESE, Dudley Noel. b 63. Leic Univ BA 86 Nottm Univ PGCE 87. Ridley Hall Cam 99. **d** 01 **p** 02. C Sheff St Jo 01-05; Chapl Lee Abbey 05-13. *1 Borrowdale Close, Nottingham NG2 6PD*

MEESON, Andrew Scott. b 86. Man Univ MB, ChB 09. Oak Hill Th Coll MTheol 15. **d** 15. C Whittle-le-Woods *Blackb* from 15. *16 Carr Meadow, Bamber Bridge, Preston PR5 8HS* M: 07532-271740 E: andyandamymeeson@aol.co.uk

MEGARRELL, Miss Joanne Myrtle. b 70. QUB BA 93 PGCE 94. CITC BTh 03. **d** 03 **p** 04. C Moira *D & D* 03-12; I from 12. *The Rectory, Main Street, Moira, Craigavon BT67 0LE* T: (028) 9261 1268 E: jmegarrell@talk21.com *or* joanne@moiraparish.org.uk

✠**MEHAFFEY, The Rt Revd James.** b 31. TCD BA 52 MA 56 BD 56 QUB PhD 75 Ulster Univ Hon DLitt 99. **d** 54 **p** 55 **c** 80. C Ballymacarrett St Patr *D & D* 54-56; C Deptford St Jo *S'wark* 56-58; C Down Cathl 58-60; C-in-c Ballymacarrett St Chris 60-62; I Kilkeel 62-66; I Cregagh 66-80; Bp's Private Chapl 72-76; Dean Derry 76-80; Dioc Missr 76-80; Bp D & R 80-02; rtd 02. *10 Clearwater, Londonderry BT47 6BE* T: (028) 7134 2624 E: james.mehaffey@btinternet.com

MEHEN, Donald Wilfrid. b 44. Birkbeck Coll Lon BSc 72 CertEd 66. **d** 00 **p** 01. OLM Sproughton w Burstall, Copdock w Washbrook etc *St E* 00-13; NSM 13-14; rtd 14; PtO *St E* from 14; RD Samford 13-15. *19 The Link, Bentley, Ipswich IP9 2DJ* T: (01473) 310383 E: donmehen@gmail.com

MEIER, Paul. b 64. St Jo Coll Nottm BA 98. **d** 98 **p** 99. C Highley w Billingsley, Glazeley etc *Heref* 98-01; C Hildenborough *Roch* 01-07; Storrington Deanery Youth Missr *Chich* 07-10; P-in-c Horsmonden *Roch* 10-13. *Address temp unknown* E: paulmeier@bleev.co.uk

MEIGHEN, Alan Hugh. b 54. **d** 15. NSM Killingworth *Newc* from 15. *4 Hazelwood, Killingworth, Newcastle upon Tyne NE12 6FF*

MEIN, The Very Revd James Adlington. b 38. Nottm Univ BA 60. Westcott Ho Cam 61. **d** 63 **p** 64. C Edin St Columba 63-67; Bp's Dom Chapl 65-67; Malawi 67-72; R Grangemouth *Edin* 72-82; P-in-c Bo'ness 76-82; TV Livingston LEP 82-90; R Edin Ch Ch 90-04; Can St Mary's Cathl 90-01; Syn Clerk 00-01; Dean Edin 01-04; rtd 04. *Cardhu, Bridgend, Linlithgow EH49 6NH* T: (01506) 834317 E: jim@meins.plus.com

MEIRION-JONES, Dafydd Padrig ap Geraint. b 70. Magd Coll Cam BA 91 PGCE 92. Oak Hill Th Coll BA 01. **d** 01 **p** 02. C Ex St Leon w H Trin 01-05; V Preston All SS *Blackb* from 05. *All Saints' Vicarage, 94 Watling Street Road, Fulwood, Preston PR2 8BP* T: (01772) 700672 M: 07989-390028
E: dafandboo@hotmail.com *or* daf@allsaintspreston.org.uk

MEIRIONNYDD, Archdeacon of. See JONES, The Ven Andrew

MELANESIA, Archbishop of. See VUNAGI, The Most Revd David

MELANIPHY, Miss Angela Ellen. b 55. SRN 79. Cranmer Hall Dur 87. **d** 90 **p** 94. Par Dn Leytonstone St Jo *Chelmsf* 90-94; C 94-95; TV Harlow Town Cen w Lt Parndon 95-06; TV Hackney Marsh *Lon* 06-15; R Fowlmere, Foxton, Shepreth and Thriplow *Ely* from 15. *The Rectory, High Street, Fowlmere, Royston SG8 7SU* E: angels25@virginmedia.com

MELBOURNE, Brian Kenneth. b 45. Trin Coll Toronto 79. **d** 82 **p** 82. R Fogo Is Canada 82-84; R Welland 84-87; C Pembroke Bermuda 88-94; P-in-c Biddenden and Smarden *Cant* 94-97; Hon C Isfield *Chich* 04-06; R Ponoka Canada 06-10. *Casita La Montana, Puerto de Sedella, 29715 Sedella (Málaga), Spain* E: melbournebk@gmail.com

MELDRUM, Andrew John Bruce. b 66. Univ of Wales (Abth) LLB 89 Lon Univ MA 98. Westcott Ho Cam 91. **d** 94 **p** 95. C Paddington St Jas *Lon* 94-99; P-in-c Brookfield St Anne, Highgate Rise 99-02; V from 02; Communications Adv to Bp Edmonton from 00; AD S Camden from 08. *St Anne's Vicarage, 106 Highgate West Hill, London N6 6AP* T/F: (020) 8340 5190 E: javintner@aol.com

MELDRUM, David Peter John. b 73. St Andr Univ MA 95. Oak Hill Th Coll BA 01. **d** 01 **p** 02. C Leyton St Mary w St Edw and St Luke *Chelmsf* 01-03; C Cranham Park 03-05; C Wandsworth St Steph *S'wark* 05-06; C Wandsworth St Mich w St Steph 06-10; R Mowbray St Pet S Africa from 10. *St Peter's Church, Church Street, Mowbray 7700, South Africa* T: (0027) (21) 689 1903 M: 72-165 4438 E: meldrum@gmail.com

MELINSKY, Canon Michael Arthur Hugh. b 24. Ch Coll Cam BA 47 MA 49. Ripon Hall Ox 57. **d** 57 **p** 59. C Wimborne Minster *Sarum* 57-59; C Wareham w Arne 59-61; V Nor St Steph 61-68; Chapl Norfolk and Nor Hosp 61-68; Hon Can Nor Cathl and Can Missr 68-73; Chief Sec ACCM 73-78;

Prin NOC 78-88; rtd 88; PtO *Nor* from 88. *15 Parson's Mead, Norwich NR4 6PG* T: (01603) 455042

MELLERUP, Miss Eiler Mary. b 37. Saffron Walden Coll CertEd 58. **d** 96 **p** 97. OLM Happisburgh, Walcott, Hempstead w Eccles etc *Nor* 96-08; PtO from 08. *Channings, The Crescent, Walcott, Norwich NR12 0NH* T: (01692) 651393

MELLISH, John. b 26. Cranmer Hall Dur 67. **d** 69 **p** 70. C Ulverston St Mary w H Trin *Carl* 69-72; V Bromfield 72-73; V Bromfield w Waverton 73-79; P-in-c Allonby w W Newton 77-79; V Shap w Swindale 79-86; RD Appleby 82-86; V Bassenthwaite, Isel and Setmurthy 86-90; rtd 90; PtO *Carl* from 90. *Wyndham, 3 Old Road, Longtown, Carlisle CA6 5TH* T: (01228) 791441

MELLOR, The Very Revd Kenneth Paul. b 49. Southn Univ BA 71 Leeds Univ MA 72. Cuddesdon Coll 72. **d** 73 **p** 74. C Cottingham *York* 73-76; C Ascot Heath *Ox* 76-80; V Tilehurst St Mary 80-85; V Menheniot *Truro* 85-94; Hon Can Truro Cathl 90-94; Can Res and Treas Truro Cathl 94-03; RD W Wivelshire 88-96; R Guernsey St Peter Port *Win* 03-14; P-in-c Sark 03-14; Dean Guernsey 03-14; Hon Can Win Cathl 03-14; rtd 14; PtO *Win* from 14. *10 Magdalene Court, Gigant Street, Salisbury SP1 2DL* T: (01722) 320184 - M: 07720-506863 E: kpaulmellor@cwgsy.net

MELLOR, Roy. b 52. Lanc Univ BA 92. Cuddesdon Coll 94. **d** 96 **p** 97. C Oakdale *Sarum* 96-00; TV Kingsthorpe w Northampton St Dav *Pet* 00-03; R Blisworth and Stoke Bruerne w Grafton Regis etc 03-10; P-in-c Collingtree w Courteenhall and Milton Malsor 09-10; rtd 10; PtO *Dur* 11-15. *7 Honeysuckle Way, Ambrosden, Bicester OX25 2AN* M: 07914-767191 E: roy_mellor2002@yahoo.co.uk

MELLOR-SMITH, Sarah Victoria. b 80. St Hilda's Coll Ox BA 02 Liv Hope Univ Coll PGCE 03 Man Univ MA 05. Wycliffe Hall Ox 07. **d** 09 **p** 10. C Dur St Nic 09-13; C Ray Valley *Ox* from 15. *St Mary's House, High Street, Charlton on Otmoor, Kidlington OX5 2UG* E: victorialis@googlemail.com

MELLORS, Derek George. b 38. Bris Univ CertEd 60 Lon Univ BSc 71 Nottm Univ DipEd 74 Liv Univ MEd 83. NOC 81. **d** 84 **p** 85. NSM Eccleston Ch Ch *Liv* 84-92; C Lowton St Mary 92-93; V Ashton-in-Makerfield St Thos 93-99; rtd 99; PtO *Liv* from 00. *20 Millbrook Lane, Eccleston, St Helens WA10 4QU* T: (01744) 28424

MELLORS, James. b 32. Kelham Th Coll 52. **d** 56 **p** 57. C Horbury *Wakef* 56-61; V Scholes 61-72; V Mirfield 72-88; Hon Can Wakef Cathl 83-88; V Leyburn w Bellerby *Ripon* 88-93; rtd 93; PtO *Ripon* 93-13. *Broomhill, 22 The Shawl, Leyburn DL8 5DG* T: (01969) 622452 E: jj.ww@virgin.net

MELLOWS, Canon Alan Frank. b 23. Qu Coll Cam BA 45 MA 49. Tyndale Hall Bris 47. **d** 49 **p** 50. C Morden *S'wark* 49-54; V Brimscombe *Glouc* 54-62; R Mileham *Nor* 62-74; P-in-c Beeston next Mileham 62-66; R 66-74; P-in-c Stanfield 62-74; P-in-c Gt w Lt Dunham 70-73; R Ashill 74-79; P-in-c Saham Toney 78-79; R Ashill w Saham Toney 79-88; Hon Can Nor Cathl 82-88; rtd 88; PtO *Nor* from 88. *c/o S Mellows Esq, 29 Cavell Close, Swardeston, Norwich NR14 8DH*

MELLOWSHIP, Robert John. b 52. St Mich Coll Llan BD 92. **d** 92 **p** 93. C Brecon St Mary and Battle w Llanddew *S & B* 92-94; Min Can Brecon Cathl 92-94; C Pontypool *Mon* 94-95; TV 95-97; P-in-c Bressingham w N and S Lopham and Fersfield *Nor* 97-07; P-in-c Roydon St Remigius 04-07; R Upper Waveney 07-12; rtd 12. *51 Sharman Avenue, Watton, Thetford IP25 6EG* T: (01953) 889917 E: robmellowship@msn.com

MELLUISH, Preb Mark Peter. b 59. Oak Hill Th Coll. **d** 89 **p** 90. C Ashtead *Guildf* 89-93; V Ealing St Paul *Lon* from 93; P-in-c Hanwell St Mellitus w St Mark from 14; Preb St Paul's Cathl from 13. *St Paul's Vicarage, 102 Elers Road, London W13 9QE* T/F: (020) 8567 4628 T: 8799 3779 E: mark@stpaulsealing.com

MELLUISH, Stephen. b 60. Trin Coll Bris 91. **d** 93 **p** 94. C Gipsy Hill Ch Ch *S'wark* 93-96; V Wandsworth St Steph 96-06; P-in-c Wandsworth St Mich 01-06; V Wandsworth St Mich w St Steph from 06. *St Michael's Vicarage, 73 Wimbledon Park Road, London SW18 5TT* T: (020) 8874 5610 or 8877 3003 E: smelluish@aol.com

MELLY, Aleck Emerson. b 24. Oak Hill Th Coll 50. **d** 53 **p** 54. C Chadderton Ch Ch *Man* 53-56; C Cheltenham St Mark *Glouc* 56-59; V Tipton St Paul *Lich* 59-68; R Kemberton w Sutton Maddock 68-80; P-in-c Stockton 74-80; R Kemberton, Sutton Maddock and Stockton 81-89; rtd 89; PtO *Lich* 89-03; *Heref* from 90. *Bethany, 47 Greenfields Road, Bridgnorth WV16 4JG* T: (01746) 762711

MELTON, Mrs Anne. b 44. N Riding Coll of Educn CertEd 65. Cranmer Hall Dur 80. **dss** 83 **d** 87 **p** 94. Newton Aycliffe *Dur* 83-88; Par Dn 87-88; Par Dn Shildon w Eldon 88-94; Asst Dir of Ords 88-94; P-in-c Usworth 94-96; TR 96-06; rtd 06; PtO *Dur* from 07. *4 Lindisfarne, High Shincliffe, Durham DH1 2PH* T: 0191-416 3533

MELVILLE, Carl Nicholas. b 87. Trin Coll Bris BA 13. **d** 13 **p** 14. C St E Cathl Distr from 13. *2 Fen Way, Bury St Edmunds IP33 3ZA* T: (01284) 748720 M: 07554-014695 E: carlmelville@hotmail.com

MELVILLE, Dominic. b 63. Sussex Univ BA 84 Southn Univ BTh 90. Sarum & Wells Th Coll 87. **d** 90 **p** 91. C Willenhall H Trin *Lich* 90-94; V Wednesfield St Greg 94-99; V Worc St Wulstan 99-11; TV Halas from 11; RD Dudley from 13. *506 Bromsgrove Road, Hunnington, Halesowen B62 0JJ* T: 0121-550 7426

MELVIN, Gordon Thomas. b 55. BA 86. Sarum & Wells Th Coll 86. **d** 88 **p** 89. C Linc St Faith and St Martin w St Pet 88-91; TV Horsham *Chich* 91-94; Chapl Horsham Gen Hosp 91-94; Chapl Ipswich Hosp NHS Trust 94-00; Sen Chapl 00-06; Chapl Local Health Partnerships NHS Trust 94-00; Sen Chapl from 00; PtO *St E* from 04. *50 Constable Road, Ipswich IP4 2UZ* T: (01473) 233517

MENDEL, Canon Thomas Oliver. b 57. Down Coll Cam BA 79 MA 82. Cranmer Hall Dur 79. **d** 81 **p** 82. Chapl Down Coll Cam 81-86; Fell 84-86; Hon C Cambridge St Mary Less *Ely* 81-86; V Minsterley *Heref* 86-92; R Habberley 86-92; Chapl Shrewsbury Sch 93-95; Chapl Milan w Genoa and Varese *Eur* 95-96; Chapl Copenhagen w Aarhus 96-04; Sen Chapl Malta and Gozo 04-08; Can and Chan Malta Cathl 04-08; V Eastbourne St Mary *Chich* from 08. *St Mary's Vicarage, 2 Glebe Close, Eastbourne BN20 8AW* T: (01323) 720420

✠**MENIN, The Rt Revd Malcolm James.** b 32. Univ Coll Ox BA 55 MA 59. Cuddesdon Coll 55. **d** 57 **p** 58 **c** 86. C Southsea H Spirit *Portsm* 57-59; C Fareham SS Pet and Paul 59-62; V Nor St Jas w Pockthorpe 62-72; P-in-c Nor St Martin 62-74; P-in-c Nor St Mary Magd 68-72; V Nor St Mary Magd w St Jas 72-86; RD Nor E 81-86; Hon Can Nor Cathl 82-86; Suff Bp Knaresborough *Ripon* 86-97; rtd 97; PtO *Nor* 97-04; Hon Asst Bp Nor from 00. *32C Bracondale, Norwich NR1 2AN* T: (01603) 627987

MENNISS, Canon Andrew Philip. b 49. Univ of Wales (Swansea) BSc 73. Sarum & Wells Th Coll 83. **d** 85 **p** 86. C Horsell *Guildf* 85-89; V Bembridge *Portsm* 89-14; RD E Wight 95-00; Hon Can Portsm Cathl 09-14; PtO *Birm* from 14. *102 Sunnybank Road, Sutton Coldfield B73 5RL* - M: 07762-228629 E: andrewpm49@gmail.com

MENON, Nicholas Anthony Thotekat. b 39. Mert Coll Ox BA 61 MA 65. St Steph Ho Ox 61. **d** 63 **p** 64. C Paddington Ch Ch *Lon* 63-66; Hon C 66-70; V Thorpe *Guildf* 70-76; V Ox SS Phil and Jas w St Marg 76-79; Chapl Surrey Univ *Guildf* 79-82; Chapl and Ho Master Cranleigh Sch Surrey 82-00; Asst Chapl Malvern Coll 00-06; rtd 04; PtO *Worc* from 05; *Heref* from 06. *Pilgrim Cottage, 187 West Malvern Road, Malvern WR14 4BB* T: (01684) 577189 E: nicholasmenon159@btinternet.com

MENSINGH, Gregg Richard. b 69. Portsm Univ BSc 94. Westcott Ho Cam 95. **d** 97 **p** 98. C Birchfield *Birm* 97-01; V Gravelly Hill 01-12; V Botley *Portsm* from 12; V Curdridge from 12; R Durley from 12; AD Bishop's Waltham from 14. *The Rectory, 46 High Street, Botley, Southampton SO30 2EA* T: (01489) 796703 or 780994 E: gregg.mensingh@gmail.com

MENTZEL, Kevin David. b 60. Reading Univ BSc 82 Down Coll Cam BA 87 MA 91 QUB MTh 04 Heythrop Coll Lon MA 09. Ridley Hall Cam 85. **d** 88 **p** 89. C Ditton *Roch* 88-91; Asst Chapl Eton Coll 91-93; Asst Chapl R Hosp Sch Holbrook 93-94; Sen C Fulham St Dionis *Lon* 94-97; CF from 97. *c/o MOD Chaplains (Army)* F: 381824 T: (01264) 383430 E: kdmentzel@gmail.com

MENZIES, James Kingsley. b 86. St Jo Coll Dur BA 08. Cranmer Hall Dur 08. **d** 10 **p** 11. C Hetton-Lyons w Eppleton *Dur* 10-14; TV Portland *Sarum* from 14. *All Saints' Vicarage, Straits, Portland DT5 1HG* T: (01305) 458593 E: jameskmenzies@yahoo.com

MENZIES, Stanley Hay. b 33. Edin Univ MA 55 BD 58. New Coll Edin 55. **d** 02 **p** 03. NSM Boston Spa *York* 02-10; rtd 10; PtO *York* from 10. *Cairn Croft, 2 Crag Gardens, Bramham, Wetherby LS23 6RP* T/F: (01937) 541047 E: stanley.menzies@virgin.net

MEON, Archdeacon of the. *See* COLLINS, The Ven Gavin Andrew

MEPHAM, Alistair. b 75. Trin Coll Bris BA 07. **d** 07 **p** 08. C Warminster Ch Ch *Sarum* 07-10; TV The Lytchetts and Upton from 10. *The Rectory, Jenny's Lane, Lytchett Matravers, Poole BH16 6BP* T: (01929) 459200 M: 07540-745210 E: ali@smlm.co.uk

MEPHAM, Stephen Richard. b 64. K Coll Lon BD 85 AKC 85. Linc Th Coll 87. **d** 89 **p** 90. C Newark *S'well* 89-92; C Cheshunt *St Alb* 92-95; C-in-c Turnford St Clem CD 95-98; V Rickmansworth 98-06. *46 Thellusson Way, Rickmansworth WD3 8RQ* E: sr.mepham@ntlworld.com

MERCER, James John. b 56. Bp Otter Coll Chich BEd 79 Lon Inst of Educn MA 85. Ridley Hall Cam 00. **d** 02 **p** 03. C Heref St Pet w St Owen and St Jas 02-07; V Harrow Weald

All SS *Lon* from 07; Lic Lay Min Tr Officer Willesden Area 08-14. *All Saints' Vicarage, 175 Uxbridge Road, Harrow HA3 6TP* T: (020) 8954 0247 M: 07940-506188
E: james_ashw@mac.com

MERCER, Jarred Austin. b 86. SE Coll (USA) BA 09 St Andr Univ MLitt 10 Qu Coll Ox DPhil 15. St Steph Ho Ox 13. **d** 15. C Ox St Mary Magd from 15; Jun Chapl Mert Coll Ox from 15. *67 Iffley Road, Oxford OX4 1EF* M: 07583-503796
E: jarred.mercer@gmail.com

MERCER, Lt Col Nicholas Justin. b 62. St Andr Univ BD 85 Cardiff Univ LLM 99 Solicitor 91. Ripon Coll Cuddesdon 08. **d** 11 **p** 12. C Gillingham and Milton-on-Stour *Sarum* 11-14; Asst Chapl Sherborne Sch from 14. *Sherborne School, Abbey Road, Sherborne DT9 3AP* T: (01935) 812249
M: 07912-619533 E: mercer-family@hotmail.com

MERCER, The Ven Nicholas Stanley. b 49. Selw Coll Cam BA 72 MA 76 PGCE 73 Spurgeon's Coll BA 78 Lon Bible Coll MPhil 86. Cranmer Hall Dur 95. **d** 95 **p** 95. C Northwood Hills St Edm *Lon* 95-98; C Pimlico St Mary Bourne Street 98-03; Dir of Min 03-07; V Gen Lon Coll of Bps from 07; Dir of Ords from 03; Hon C Wilton Place St Paul from 04; Preb St Paul's Cathl from 08; Adn Lon from 15. *The Old Deanery, Dean's Court, London EC4V 5AA* T: (020) 7489 4274
M: 07782-250377 E: nick.mercer@london.anglican.org

MERCER, Timothy James. b 54. Fitzw Coll Cam BA 76 MA 80. Westcott Ho Cam 78. **d** 81 **p** 82. C Bromley SS Pet and Paul *Roch* 81-85; R Swanscombe 85-96; Chapl Bromley Hosps NHS Trust 96-09; Chapl S Lon Healthcare NHS Trust 09-14; Hon Can Roch Cathl 10-14; Dep Hd of Chapl King's Coll Hosp NHS Foundn Trust from 14. *King's College Hospital, Denmark Hill, London SE5 9RS* T: (020) 3299 9000
E: mercer180@btinternet.com

MERCERON, Daniel John. b 58. Lon Univ BA 81. Westcott Ho Cam 88. **d** 90 **p** 91. C Clevedon St Jo *B & W* 90-94; CF 94-14; P-in-c Alfriston w Lullington, Litlington and W Dean *Chich* 14-15; R Alfriston w Lullington, Litlington, W Dean and Folkington from 15. *The Vicarage, Sloe Lane, Alfriston, Polegate BN26 5UP* T: (01323) 870376
E: rectory@alfriston-churches.co.uk

MERCHANT, Robert Ian. b 73. Keele Univ BA 98. Wycliffe Hall Ox BA 00 MA 05. **d** 01 **p** 02. C Harborne Heath *Birm* 01-04; Prin Lect Spirituality and Health Staffs Univ *Lich* 05-09; Dep Dir Cen for Ageing and Mental Health 05-09; NSM Cheltenham St Mark *Glouc* 05-06; C Cheltenham St Mich and Cheltenham St Luke and St Jo 06-10; R Ashleworth, Corse, Hartpury, Hasfield etc 10-12; Dir Dispersed Learning St Mellitus Coll from 12; PtO *Lon* 12-13; NSM Hornsey Rise from 13. *3 Highcroft Road, London N19 3AQ* T: (020) 7281 1459 E: revrobmerchant@googlemail.com

MERCHANT, Mrs Tamsin Laetitia Rachel. b 70. Wycliffe Hall Ox BTh 01. **d** 01 **p** 02. C Harborne Heath *Birm* 01-04; Sen Chapl Glos Univ 04-12; V Hornsey Rise *Lon* from 12. *3 Highcroft Road, London N19 3AQ* T: (020) 7281 1459
E: revtamsinmerchant@gmail.com

MERCURIO, Frank James Charles. b 46. Webster Univ (USA) BA 73 MA 75. St Alb Minl Tr Scheme 87. **d** 89 **p** 90. C Cheshunt *St Alb* 89-93; TV Hitchin 93-00; RD 94-00; TR Tring 00-07; P-in-c Alfreton *Derby* from 07; P-in-c Riddings and Ironville from 08. *The Vicarage, 13 Church Street, Alfreton DE55 7AH* T: (01773) 833280 E: frankmercurio@dialstart.net

MEREDITH, Andrew James MacPherson. b 59. St Jo Coll Nottm 91. **d** 93 **p** 94. C Killay S *B & W* 93-97; V Waunarllwydd 97-00; V Swansea St Thos and Kilvey 00-13; AD Swansea 13; P-in-c Cadoxton-juxta-Neath and Tonna *Llan* from 13. *St Catwg's Vicarage, Glebeland Street, Cadoxton, Neath SA10 8AY* T: (01639) 646055

MEREDITH, Ian. b 53. Univ of Wales BA 85 K Coll Lon MTh 89 Edin Univ MTh 96 Dur Univ PhD 07. K Coll Lon 86. **d** 02 **p** 03. Assoc Min Dumfries *Glas* 02-06; NSM Annan 06-07; NSM Eastriggs 06-07; NSM Gretna 06-07; NSM Lockerbie 06-07; NSM Moffat 06-07; R Ayr 07-13; R Girvan 07-13; R Maybole 07-13; P-in-c Portchester *Portsm* from 13. *The Vicarage, 164 Castle Street, Portchester, Fareham PO16 9QH* T: (023) 9237 5422 E: irev@ymail.com

MEREDITH, Canon Roland Evan. b 32. Trin Coll Cam BA 55 MA 59. Cuddesdon Coll 55. **d** 57 **p** 58. C Bishopwearmouth St Mich *Dur* 57-59; Dioc Chapl *Birm* 59-60; C Kirkby *Liv* 60-63; V Hitchin St Mary *St Alb* 63-72; TR Preston St Jo *Blackb* 72-76 and 76-79; RD Preston 72-79; Hon Can Blackb Cathl 77-79; TR Witney *Ox* 79-94; P-in-c Hailey w Crawley 79-82; RD Witney 89-97; Hon Can Ch Ch 92-97; rtd 94; PtO *Ox* from 97; *Eur* from 98. *37 Otters Court, Priory Mill Lane, Witney OX28 1GJ* T: (01993) 703698 M: 07971-370647
E: roland@canonmeredith.free-online.co.uk

MERIVALE, Charles Christian Robert. b 44. Cranmer Hall Dur 76. **d** 78 **p** 79. C Highbury Ch Ch w St Jo *Lon* 78-81; P-in-c Hawes *Ripon* 81-82; P-in-c Hardrow and St Jo w Lunds 81-82; V Hawes and Hardraw 82-84; Chapl R Cornwall Hosps Trust 85-92; PtO *B & W* 92-00; *Ex* 00-02; TV Shebbear, Buckland Filleigh, Sheepwash etc 02-08; rtd 08; PtO *B & W* from 10. *The Cider House, Coxs Close, North Cadbury, Yeovil BA22 7DY* T: (01963) 440917 E: christianandjane@hotmail.co.uk

MERRICK, Harry. b 50. Yorks Min Course 08. **d** 10. OLM Pontefract All SS *Leeds* from 10. *18 Eastbourne Terrace, Pontefract WF8 2HF* T: (01977) 780831 M: 07785-981159
E: harry.merrick1@btinternet.com

MERRICK, Dr James. b 81. Taylor Univ (USA) BA 03 MA 06 Aber Univ PhD 13 Trin Evang Div Sch (USA) MTh 07. 04. **d** 06 **p** 07. NSM Aberdeen St Jo *Ab* 08-10; Instructor Loretto Sr Fran Univ USA 11-13; Instructor Ambridge Trin Epis Sch 11-14; Asst Prof Grand Canyon Univ 13-15; Th in Res Phoenix All SS 14-15; R Aberdeen St Mary *Ab* from 15. *28 Stanley Street, Aberdeen AB10 6UR* T: (01224) 561383
E: jmerrick@stmaryscardenplace.org.uk

MERRICK, Canon John. b 51. New Univ of Ulster BA 72 DipAdEd 75 TCD HDipEd 73. CITC 89. **d** 92 **p** 93. Hd Master Sligo Gr Sch from 86; LtO *K, E & A* from 92; Preb Elphin Cathl from 01. *Pier Lodge, Dunfanaghy PO, Letterkenny, Co Donegal, Republic of Ireland* T/F: (00353) (74) 913 6971 M: 87-227 4978

MERRICK, Richard Christopher. b 57. Qu Coll Birm 08. **d** 11 **p** 12. C Bushbury *Lich* 11-14; V Heath Town from 14. *Holy Trinity Vicarage, Bushbury Road, Wolverhampton WV10 0LY* T: (01902) 772840 E: revrichht@gmail.com

MERRIMAN, Stephen Richard. b 74. Leeds Univ BA 02. Coll of Resurr Mirfield 99. **d** 02 **p** 03. C Littlehampton and Wick *Chich* 02-06; TV from 08; C Brighton St Matthias 06-08. *St James's Vicarage, 12 Cornwall Road, Littlehampton BN17 6EE* T: (01903) 724311

MERRINGTON, Bill. b 55. Sheff Hallam Univ BSc 78 Birm Univ MPhil 95 Warwick Univ PhD 03. Cranmer Hall Dur 80. **d** 83 **p** 84. C Harborne Heath *Birm* 83-88; V Leamington Priors St Paul *Cov* 88-99; RD Warwick and Leamington 97-99; R Ilmington w Stretton-on-Fosse etc 99-07; R Tredington and Darlingscott 05-07; RD Shipston 99-03; Hon Can Cov Cathl 01-07; Sen Chapl Bournemouth Univ *Sarum* from 07; PtO *Win* from 09. *Chaplaincy, Bournemouth University, Fern Barrow, Poole BH12 5BB* T: (01202) 965383
E: bmerrington@bournemouth.ac.uk

MERRINGTON, Mrs Hilary. b 47. **d** 14 **p** 15. NSM Norley, Crowton and Kingsley *Ches* from 14. *Cartref, Ball Lane, Kingsley, Frodsham WA6 8HP* T: (01928) 788087
E: hilary.merrington@btinternet.com

MERRIOTT, Mrs Pamela Ann. b 51. SNTS. **d** 12 **p** 13. OLM Abbots Bromley, Blithfield, Colton, Colwich etc *Lich* from 12. *The Oaklands, 1 Billington Avenue, Little Haywood, Stafford ST18 0UZ* T: (01889) 881030 M: 07967-717181
E: davidmerriott@btinternet.com

MERRY, David Thomas. b 48. St Chad's Coll Dur BA 70. AKC 73. **d** 74 **p** 75. C Cirencester *Glouc* 74-78; TV Bridgnorth, Tasley, Astley Abbotts and Oldbury *Heref* 78-83; P-in-c Quatford 81-83; P-in-c Stroud H Trin *Glouc* 83-87; V 87-01; Chapl Severn NHS Trust 83-93 and 93-01; Chapl Cheltenham Ladies' Coll 01-13; Hon Min Can Glouc Cathl 04-13; rtd 13. *3 Rose Hill, Far Wells Road, Bisley, Stroud GL6 7AQ* T: (01452) 770517

MERRY, Ivor John. b 28. WMMTC 84. **d** 87 **p** 88. NSM Redditch, The Ridge *Worc* 87-94; NSM Astwood Bank 94-98; PtO from 98. *186 Moorcroft Gardens, Redditch B97 5WQ*

MERRY, Philip John. b 58. ERMC 11. **d** 14 **p** 15. NSM Gt and Lt Bealings w Playford and Culpho *St E* from 14. *Abbey School, Church Street, Woodbridge IP12 1DS* T: (01394) 610972 M: 07900-058418 E: philipmerry@hotmail.co.uk

MERRY, Rex Edwin. b 38. AKC 67. **d** 68 **p** 69. C Spalding St Jo *Linc* 68-73; C Boxmoor St Jo *St Alb* 73-83; TV Hemel Hempstead 83-95; V Farley Hill St Jo 95-06; rtd 06; PtO *St Alb* from 06. *4 Wellcroft, Hemel Hempstead HP1 3EG* T: (01442) 401122

MERRY, Thomas. See MERRY, David Thomas

MERRY, Tommy Philip. b 85. UEA BA 08 Sheff Univ BA 13. Coll of Resurr Mirfield 10. **d** 13 **p** 14. C Hanley H Ev *Lich* from 13. *18 Cromer Road, Northwood, Stoke-on-Trent ST1 6QN* T: (01782) 267828 M: 07585-954122 E: frtommymerry@gmail.com

MERRYWEATHER, Mrs Rosalynd. b 50. Hull Coll of Educn CertEd 72. NEOC. **d** 00 **p** 01. NSM Beverley St Nic *York* 00-12; PtO from 12. *10 West Close, Beverley HU17 7JJ* T: (01482) 867958 E: rmerryweather@rmerryweather.karoo.co.uk

MESLEY, Mark Terence. b 59. Plymouth Poly BSc 88. St Steph Ho Ox 98. **d** 00 **p** 01. C Bickleigh and Shaugh Prior *Ex* 00-03; P-in-c Llanhilleth *Mon* 03-06; P-in-c Llanhilleth w Six Bells

06-08; P-in-c Penwerris *Truro* from 08; Chapl Miss to Seafarers 08-13. *The Vicarage, Pellew Road, Falmouth TR11 2NS* T: (01326) 218947 E: revmarkmesley@btinternet.com

MESLEY-SPONG, Terence John. b 32. Roch Th Coll 63. **d** 66 **p** 67. C Forton *Portsm* 66-68; Rhodesia 68-80; Zimbabwe 80-84; R Christow, Ashton, Trusham and Bridford *Ex* 84-86; Chapl Puerto de la Cruz Tenerife *Eur* 86-93; Miss to Seamen 86-93; rtd 93; PtO *Win* 93-13; Chapl R Bournemouth and Christchurch Hosps NHS Trust 97-98. *14B Stuart Road, Highcliffe, Christchurch BH23 5JS* T: (01425) 277833

MESSAM, Paul James. b 65. Lon Coll of Printing BA 87. Cranmer Hall Dur 01. **d** 03 **p** 04. C Market Harborough and The Transfiguration etc *Leic* 03-07; P-in-c Bulkington *Cov* from 07; Lead Chapl Cov Blue Coat C of E Sch from 07. *St James's Vicarage, School Road, Bulkington, Nuneaton CV12 9JB* T: (024) 7631 8241 M: 07711-098209 E: paul.messam@virgin.net

MESSENGER, Paul. b 38. Univ of Wales (Lamp) BA 63. Coll of Resurr Mirfield 63. **d** 65 **p** 66. C Battersea St Luke *S'wark* 65-69; C Ainsdale *Liv* 69-71; V Wigan St Steph 71-74; Asst Chapl St Marg Convent E Grinstead 74-76; Chapl Kingsley St Mich Sch W Sussex 74-76; P-in-c Southwater *Chich* 76-81; V 81-97; R Sullington and Thakeham w Warminghurst 97-07; rtd 07. *122 Ninfield Road, Bexhill-on-Sea TN39 5BB* T: (01424) 220044

MESSER, David Harry. b 61. MCIH 93. EAMTC 01. **d** 04 **p** 05. C Stanton, Hopton, Market Weston, Barningham etc *St E* 04-07; R from 07; C Hepworth, Hinderclay, Wattisfield and Thelnetham from 15; RD Ixworth from 14. *The Rectory, 1 Old Rectory Gardens, Stanton, Bury St Edmunds IP31 2JH* T: (01359) 250239 E: david@dmesser.freeserve.co.uk

MESSERVY, Mrs Cassandra. b 75. Ox Brookes Univ BA 99 PGCE 02. Ripon Coll Cuddesdon BTh 11. **d** 11 **p** 12. C Beaconsfield *Ox* 11-14; NSM Seer Green and Jordans 14-15; NSM Chalfont St Giles, Seer Green and Jordans from 15. *Holy Trinity Vicarage, 43 Long Grove, Seer Green, Beaconsfield HP9 2YN* M: 07886-331714 E: cassamesservy@gmail.com

MESSHAM, Canon Barbara Lynn. b 52. Bretton Hall Coll CertEd 75. STETS 96. **d** 99 **p** 00. C The Bourne and Tilford *Guildf* 99-03; V Guildf All SS 03-13; RD Guildf 06-11; Hon Can Guildf Cathl 10-13; P-in-c Deerhurst and Apperley w Forthampton etc *Glouc* from 13; C Tewkesbury w Walton Cardiff and Twyning from 13. *The Vicarage, 1 The Green, Apperley, Gloucester GL19 4DQ* M: 07932-615132 T: (01452) 780880 E: barbara@messhams.co.uk *or* barbaramessham@gmail.com

METCALF, Preb Michael Ralph. b 37. Clare Coll Cam BA 61 MA 65 Birm Univ MA 80. Ridley Hall Cam 63. **d** 64 **p** 65. C Downend *Bris* 64-67; PtO *Birm* 68-78; *Lich* 72-81; Lect W Midl Coll of Educn 72-77; Sen Lect 77-81; Dioc Dir of Educn *Lich* 83-94; V Stafford St Paul Forebridge 94-05; Preb Lich Cathl 91-05; RD Stafford 00-05; rtd 05; PtO *Heref* from 87; *Lich* from 05. *196 Stone Road, Stafford ST16 1NT* T/F: (01785) 600260 E: prebmetcalf@hotmail.com *or* berylm@ntlworld.com

METCALFE, Bernard. *See* METCALFE, William Bernard

METCALFE, Reginald Herbert. b 38. **d** 79. Hon C Aspley Guise *St Alb* 79; Hon C Aspley Guise w Husborne Crawley and Ridgmont 80-84; Hon C Bovingdon 84-03. *30 Manorville Road, Hemel Hempstead HP3 0AP* T: (01442) 242952 F: 213137

METCALFE, Canon Ronald. b 41. BA. Edin Th Coll 67. **d** 69 **p** 70. C Saltburn-by-the-Sea *York* 69-72; P-in-c Crathorne 73-77; Youth Officer 73-77; Dioc Adult Tr Officer 78-88; Can Res York Minster 88-00; Sec for Miss and Min 88-00; V Kendal H Trin *Carl* 00-07; rtd 07; PtO *Dur* from 08. *50 Carlton Moor Crescent, Darlington DL1 4RF* T: (01325) 367219

METCALFE, Canon William Bernard. b 47. St Jo Coll Cam BA 69 MA 73 Ball Coll Ox BA 71. Ripon Hall Ox 70. **d** 72 **p** 73. C Caversham *Ox* 72-75; C Aylesbury 75-79; Ind Chapl 75-79; TV Thamesmead *S'wark* 79-84; TR Totton *Win* 84-94; R Gt Bentley and Frating w Thorrington *Chelmsf* 94-10; V Gt Bentley 10-12; RD St Osyth 99-07; Hon Can Chelmsf Cathl 06-12; rtd 12; PtO *Ox* from 13. *60 Elmhurst Road, Reading RG1 5HY* T: 0118-975 6586 E: bernard.metcalfe@btinternet.com

METHUEN, Canon Charlotte Mary. b 64. Girton Coll Cam BA 85 MA 89 New Coll Edin BD 91 PhD 95. Edin Th Coll 87. **d** 98 **p** 99. C E Netherlands *Eur* 98-01; C Bonn w Cologne 01-03; Hon Asst Chapl 03-05; Dioc Dir of Tr 03-05; Hon C Offenbach (Old Catholic Ch) 05-07; Hon C Bottrop (Old Catholic Ch) from 08; Lect Ecclesiastical Hist Ox Univ 05-11; Dioc Can Th Glouc 07-13; Lect Ripon Coll Cuddesdon 09-11; Lect Ch History Glas Univ from 11. *2/1, 34 Keir Street, Glasgow G41 2NW* T: 0141-429 4716 E: charlotte.methuen@glasgow.ac.uk

METHVEN, Alexander George. b 26. Lon Univ BD 52 Em Coll Cam BA 54 MA 58. ACT ThL 47 Lon Coll of Div 50. **d** 52 **p** 53. C Cambridge St Andr Less *Ely* 52-54; Chapl RAF 55-60; V Lower Sydenham St Mich *S'wark* 60-67; Australia from 68; rtd 91. *PO Box 494, Belgrave Vic 3160, Australia* T: (0061) (3) 9754 8056 E: agmethven@hotmail.com

METIVIER, Canon Robert John. b 31. Lon Univ BA 68. Lambeth STh 61 Ch Div Sch of the Pacific (USA) BD 66 MDiv 69 Codrington Coll Barbados 56. **d** 60 **p** 61. Trinidad and Tobago 61-64 and 68-78; USPG 66-67; C Gt Berkhamsted *St Alb* 78-82; V Goff's Oak St Jas 82-90; V Tokyngton St Mich *Lon* 90-01; Hon Can Trinidad from 98; rtd 01; PtO *Lon* from 02. *17 Willowcourt Avenue, Kenton, Harrow HA3 8ET* T: (020) 8909 1371 E: ej.metivier@googlemail.com

METRY, Sameh Farid. b 63. Assiut Univ Egypt BA 87. **d** 09 **p** 10. C W Ealing St Jo w St Jas *Lon* 09-14; C Northolt St Jos from 14. *St Hugh's House, 22 Gosling Close, Greenford UB6 9UE* M: 07971-257287 E: smetry@msn.com

METTERS, Anthony John Francis. b 43. AKC 65. **d** 68 **p** 69. C Heavitree *Ex* 68-74; V Plymouth Crownhill Ascension 74-79; RD Plymouth 77-79; Chapl RN 79-99; rtd 99. *Knightshayes, 1 De Port Heights, Corhampton, Southampton SO32 3DA*

METTERS, Mrs Henrietta Louise. b 83. Dur Univ BA 05. NTMTC 08. **d** 10 **p** 11. C Onslow Square and S Kensington St Aug *Lon* 10-14. *86 Colehill Lane, London SW6 5EH* M: 07862-258706 E: henriettametters@yahoo.co.uk

METZ, Susanna. b 50. Immaculata Univ (USA) BA 72 W Chester State Coll (USA) MA 82 Univ of the S (USA) MDiv 96 DMin 03. **d** 96 **p** 97. C Battle Creek St Jo USA 96-07; R 07-11; TV Shebbear, Buckland Filleigh, Sheepwash etc *Ex* from 11. *The Rectory, Petrockstow, Okehampton EX20 3HQ* T: (01837) 810621

METZNER (née JEFFREY), Mrs Katrina. b 73. St Jo Coll Ox BA 96 MA 01. St Steph Ho Ox 97. **d** 99 **p** 00. C Glouc St Geo w Whaddon 99-00; C Parkstone St Pet and St Osmund w Branksea *Sarum* 00-04; PtO *S'wark* from 05. *All Saints' Vicarage, 84 Franciscan Road, London SW17 8DQ* T: (020) 8672 3706 E: katemetzner@sky.com

METZNER, Simon David. b 64. Magd Coll Ox BA 85 K Coll Lon MA 95 St Luke's Coll Ex PGCE 93. St Steph Ho Ox 88. **d** 00 **p** 01. C Branksome St Aldhelm *Sarum* 00-04; V Tooting All SS *S'wark* from 04. *All Saints' Vicarage, 84 Franciscan Road, London SW17 8DQ* T: (020) 8672 3706 E: simon.metzner@ntlworld.com

MEWIS, Canon David William. b 47. Leeds Inst of Educn CertEd 68 Leeds Poly BEd 83. NOC 87. **d** 90 **p** 91. C Skipton Ch Ch *Bradf* 90-92; R Bolton by Bowland w Grindleton 92-12; C Waddington, Hurst Green and Mitton 05-12; RD Bowland 99-08; Hon Can Bradf Cathl 00-12; rtd 12; PtO *Leeds* from 13; *Blackb* from 14. *23 Darkwood Crescent, Chatburn, Clitheroe BB7 4AL* T: (01200) 440335 E: dwm.dmewis@uwclub.net *or* david.mewis@bradford.anglican.org

MEWS, Stuart Paul. b 44. Leeds Univ BA 64 MA 67 Trin Hall Cam PhD 74 FRHistS 75. Westcott Ho Cam 86. **d** 87 **p** 88. Lect Lanc Univ 68-92; NSM Caton w Littledale *Blackb* 87-90; Hon C Lancaster St Mary 88-92; Reader RS Cheltenham and Glouc Coll of HE 92-00; Acting P-in-c Croxton and Eltisley *Ely* 97-98; P-in-c Tilbrook 00-07; P-in-c Keyston and Bythorn 00-07; P-in-c Catworth Magna 00-07; P-in-c Covington 00-07; P-in-c Grantchester 07-14. *The Vicarage, 44 High Street, Grantchester, Cambridge CB3 9NF* T: (01223) 845664

MEYER, Jonathan Peter. b 55. Keble Coll Ox BA 76 MA. SAOMC 03. **d** 05 **p** 06. NSM Kintbury w Avington *Ox* 05-08; NSM W Woodhay w Enborne, Hampstead Marshall etc 05-09; P-in-c Ewelme, Brightwell Baldwin, Cuxham w Easington from 09. *The Rectory, Ewelme, Wallingford OX10 6HP* T: (01491) 837823 E: revdjonathan@btinternet.com

MEYER, William John. b 46. ACIB. Cranmer Hall Dur 83. **d** 85 **p** 86. C Merrow *Guildf* 85-89; V Grayshott 89-98; R Binfield *Ox* 98-11; rtd 11. *27A Oxford Drive, Bognor Regis PO21 5QU* E: bill.meyer@hotmail.com

MEYNELL, Canon Andrew Francis. b 43. Westcott Ho Cam 70. **d** 73 **p** 74. C Cowley St Jas *Ox* 73-79; TV 79-81; P-in-c Halton 81-95; V Wendover 81-95; P-in-c Monks Risborough 95-98; TV Risborough 98-08; Dir Ords Bucks Adnry 95-08; Hon Can Ch Ch 01-08; rtd 08; PtO *Ox* from 09. *Pettits House, The Green, Great Milton, Oxford OX44 7NT* T: (01844) 277912 E: andrew.meynell@oxford.anglican.org

MEYNELL, Mrs Honor Mary. b 37. EMMTC 84. **d** 87 **p** 94. NSM Kirk Langley *Derby* 87-03; NSM Mackworth All SS 87-03; NSM Mugginton and Kedleston 87-03; rtd 04; PtO *Derby* from 04. *The Coachman's Cottage, Meynell Langley, Kirk Langley, Ashbourne DE6 4NT* T: (01332) 824207

MEYNELL, Mark John Henrik. b 70. New Coll Ox MA 93. Ridley Hall Cam MA 97. **d** 97 **p** 98. C Fulwood *Sheff* 97-01; Dean Kampala Evang Sch of Th Uganda 01-05; C Langham Place All So *Lon* 05-14; Hon C from 14. *36 Honeyman Close, London NW6 7AZ*

✠**MEYRICK, The Rt Revd Cyril Jonathan.** b 52. St Jo Coll Ox BA 73 MA 77. Sarum & Wells Th Coll 74. **d** 76 **p** 77 **c** 11. C Bicester *Ox* 76-78; Bp's Dom Chapl 78-81; Tutor Codrington Coll Barbados 81-84; TV Burnham w Dropmore, Hitcham and Taplow *Ox* 84-90; TR Tisbury *Sarum* 90-98; Link Officer Black Angl Concerns 90-98; RD Chalke 97-98; Can Res Roch Cathl 98-05; Dean Ex 05-11; P-in-c Cen Ex 06-11; Suff Bp Lynn *Nor* from 11. *The Old Vicarage, Priory Road, Castle Acre, King's Lynn PE32 2AA* T: (01760) 755553 F: 755085
E: bishoplynn@norwich.anglican.org

MEYRICK, Thomas Henry Corfe. b 67. Magd Coll Ox BA 88 MA 92 Leeds Univ PhD 05. St Steph Ho Ox BA 94. **d** 95 **p** 96. C Bierley *Bradf* 95-99; Chapl Oriel Coll Ox 99-04; P-in-c Ox St Thos w St Frideswide and Binsey 04-05; P-in-c Newbold de Verdun and Kirkby Mallory *Leic* 05-10; P-in-c Barlestone 09-10; R Newbold de Verdun, Barlestone and Kirkby Mallory from 10; AD Sparkenhoe W 08-15. *The Rectory, 6 The Paddock, Newbold Verdon, Leicester LE9 9NW* T: (01455) 824986
E: tom_meyrick@ekit.com

MIALL, Mrs Hazel Henrietta. b 49. Open Univ BSc 97 DipCOT 70. St Mellitus Coll BA 12. **d** 12. NSM Southgate Ch *Lon* from 12. *85 Conway Road, London N14 7BD*
T: (020) 8882 6738 M: 07890-740587
E: hazelhmiall@btinternet.com

MIALL, Peter Brian. b 30. Scawsby Coll of Educn TCert 69. **d** 89 **p** 89. Hon C Bolsterstone *Sheff* 89-98; PtO from 98. *Address temp unknown*

MICHAEL, Canon Ian MacRae. b 40. Aber Univ MA 62 Hertf Coll Ox DPhil 66. Westcott Ho Cam 77. **d** 79 **p** 80. C Kings Heath *Birm* 79-82; Vice-Provost St Paul's Cathl Dundee 82-88; V Harborne St Faith and St Laur *Birm* 88-03; RD Edgbaston 91-98; Hon Can Birm Cathl 00-03; rtd 03; PtO *Birm* from 03; LtO *St And* from 04; NSM St Andrews All SS from 05. *46 Argyle Court, St Andrews KY16 9BW* T: (01334) 473901

MICHAELS, David Albert Emmanuel. b 49. Bede Coll Dur BA 72 Barrister-at-Law (Inner Temple) 73. Westcott Ho Cam 86. **d** 88 **p** 89. C Hampstead St Jo *Lon* 88-91; TV Wolvercote w Summertown *Ox* 91-04; P-in-c Launceston *Truro* 04-13; rtd 13; PtO *Ox* from 15. *5 Northmoor Place, Northmoor Road, Oxford OX2 6XB* T: (01865) 558035
E: david.michaels@dunelm.org.uk

MICHAUX, Mrs Teresa Mary. b 56. STETS 09. **d** 12 **p** 13. NSM Swindon St Jo and St Andr *Bris* from 12. *3 Campden Road, Swindon SN3 1DB* M: 07963-399645
E: tmx256@hotmail.co.uk

MICHELL, Canon Francis Richard Noel. b 42. St Cath Coll Cam BA 64 MA 68. Tyndale Hall Bris 64. **d** 66 **p** 67. C Northampton St Giles *Pet* 66-69; C Gateacre *Liv* 69-72; V Litherland St Paul Hatton Hill 72-79; V Rainhill 79-88; V Rainford 88-07; Hon Can Liv Cathl 06-07; rtd 07; Hon C Ludgvan, Marazion, St Hilary and Perranuthnoe *Truro* 07-13. *2 Chycelin, Alverton Terrace, Penzance TR18 4JH*
E: noel.michell@sky.com

MICHELL, Philip Leonard. b 69. Trin Coll Bris 08. **d** 10 **p** 11. C Brailsford w Shirley, Osmaston w Edlaston etc *Derby* 10-13; R Hulland, Atlow, Kniveton, Bradley and Hognaston from 13. *The Rectory, 16 Eaton Close, Hulland Ward, Ashbourne DE6 3EX* M: 07815-940409 E: phil.michell@live.co.uk

MICKLEFIELD, Andrew Mark. b 71. K Alfred's Coll Win BEd 93. Ridley Hall Cam 04. **d** 06 **p** 07. C Alton *Win* 06-10; R Itchen Valley 10-14; V Alton from 14. *St Lawrence Vicarage, Church Street, Alton GU34 2BW* T: (01420) 88794 M: 07749-483707
E: andrewmicklefield@gmail.com

MICKLETHWAITE, Andrew Quentin. b 67. Univ Coll Dur BA 89. Trin Coll Bris BA 94. **d** 94 **p** 95. C Abington *Pet* 94-97; TV Duston 97-04; V Castle Donington and Lockington cum Hemington *Leic* from 04. *The Vicarage, 6 Delven Lane, Castle Donington, Derby DE74 2LJ* T: (01332) 810364
E: revandrew@talk21.com

MICKLETHWAITE, Mrs Dorothy Eileen. b 41. SAOMC 98. **d** 01 **p** 02. NSM Astwell Gp *Pet* 01-12; Asst Chapl Ox Radcliffe Hosps NHS Trust 02-09; rtd 12; PtO *Pet* from 12. *54 Stuart Road, Brackley NN13 6HZ* T: (01280) 703697
E: dorothy.mick@talktalk.net

MICKLETHWAITE, Jane Catherine. b 56. Lanc Univ BSc 78. Trin Coll Bris 92. **d** 95 **p** 96. C Kings Heath *Pet* 95-98; Chapl Nene Coll of HE Northn 97-98; PtO *Pet* 98-01; NSM Kings Heath 01-04; PtO *Leic* 04-13; Chapl E Midl Airport and NSM Loughborough All SS w H Trin from 13. *The Vicarage, 6 Delven Lane, Castle Donington, Derby DE74 2LJ* T: (01332) 810364
E: j.micklethwaite@talk21.com

MICKLETHWAITE, Peter William. b 62. Peterho Cam BA 84 MA 88. St Jo Coll Nottm 87. **d** 90 **p** 91. C Leatherhead *Guildf* 90-93; C Wisley w Pyrford 93-97; R Windlesham 97-09; PtO *Portsm* 09-13; NSM Sheet from 13. *Cloncaird, Durford Wood, Petersfield GU31 5AS* T: (01730) 893303

MIDDLEBROOK, Canon David John. b 61. Newc Univ BSc 83 Cranfield Inst of Tech MSc 85. Trin Coll Bris BA 98. **d** 98 **p** 99. C Chorleywood Ch Ch *St Alb* 98-02; TV Hemel Hempstead 02-08; P-in-c Watford St Luke 08-12; V from 12; RD Watford from 09; Hon Can St Alb from 13. *St Luke's Vicarage, Devereux Drive, Watford WD17 3DD* T: (01923) 231205
E: dmiddlebrook@btinternet.com

MIDDLEDITCH, Terry Gordon. b 30. Univ of Wales (Lamp) BA 62 St Martin's Coll Lanc PGCE 68. St D Coll Lamp 59. **d** 63 **p** 64. C Poulton-le-Fylde *Blackb* 63-65; C-in-c Heysham 65-67; Sch Master 68-88; Hon C Cheltenham St Pet *Glouc* 75-87; Hon C Badgeworth w Shurdington 75-87; Hon C Up Hatherley 75-87; C Poulton-le-Sands w Morecambe St Laur *Blackb* 88-91; V Stalmine 91-00; rtd 00; PtO *Blackb* from 00. *93 Thornton Road, Morecambe LA4 5PG* T: (01524) 413378 -
M: 07879-426173

MIDDLEMISS, Fritha Leonora. b 47. Man Univ BA 68 CertEd 69. Glouc Sch of Min 86. **d** 89 **p** 94. NSM Bengeworth *Worc* 89-94; NSM Stoulton w Drake's Broughton and Pirton etc 94-96; Chapl Malvern Girls' Coll 96-03; Asst Chapl HM Pris Long Lartin 03-08. *1 Ravensdowne, Berwick-upon-Tweed TD15 1HX* T: (01289) 308553

MIDDLEMISS, Mrs Justine. b 68. Aston Univ BSc 90. Ripon Coll Cuddesdon 00. **d** 02 **p** 03. C Lee St Marg *S'wark* 02-06; P-in-c Beddington 06; R 06-13; TR Sutton from 13. *The Rectory, 34 Robin Hood Lane, Sutton SM1 2RG* T: (020) 8642 3499

MIDDLESEX, Archdeacon of. *See* WELCH, The Ven Stephan John

MIDDLETON, Alan Derek. b 46. St Jo Coll Dur BA 68 MA 85 Bris Univ PGCE 70 Sheff Univ MMin 00. Qu Coll Birm. **d** 72 **p** 73. C Cannock *Lich* 72-76; Warden St Helen's Youth & Community Cen Bp Auckd 76-79; V Darlington St Jo *Dur* 79-89; TR E Darlington 89-90; V Upper Norwood All SS *S'wark* 90-99; TR Warlingham w Chelsham and Farleigh 99-11; Bp's Ecum Adv 96-11; AD Caterham 05-11; rtd 11; PtO *Dur* from 11. *21 Boste Crescent, Durham DH1 5US*
T: 0191-386 4467 E: alan.middleton21@btinternet.com

MIDDLETON, Arthur. *See* MIDDLETON, Thomas Arthur

MIDDLETON, Barry Glen. b 41. Lich Th Coll 68. **d** 70 **p** 71. C Westhoughton *Man* 70-73; C Prestwich St Marg 73-74; TV Buxton w Burbage and King Sterndale *Derby* 74-77; Chapl Worc R Infirmary 77-83; Chapl Fairfield Hosp Hitchin 83-85; P-in-c Erpingham w Calthorpe *Nor* 85-86; R Erpingham w Calthorpe, Ingworth, Aldborough etc 86-92; R Badingham w Bruisyard, Cransford and Dennington *St E* 92-96; V Sidcup St Jo *Roch* 96-98; V Gt and Lt Bardfield w Gt and Lt Saling *Chelmsf* 98-00; rtd 00; PtO *St E* from 00. *20 Lynwood Avenue, Felixstowe IP11 9HS* T: (01394) 286506
E: bgm.jfm@btinternet.com

MIDDLETON, David Jeremy. b 68. Ex Univ BSc 90. Wycliffe Hall Ox 01. **d** 03 **p** 04. C Ipswich St Jo *St E* 03-06; Hon C Wimbledon Park St Luke *S'wark* 06-09; C Fulwood *Sheff* 09-11; C Heeley and Gleadless Valley 11-12; V Gleadless Valley from 12. *The Vicarage, 5 Blackstock Close, Sheffield S14 1AE* T: 0114-239 3808 E: djm.middleton@googlemail.com

MIDDLETON, Hugh Charles. b 50. Nottm Univ BTh 77. Linc Th Coll 73. **d** 77 **p** 78. C New Sleaford *Linc* 77-81; C Grantham 81; TV 81-83; R Caythorpe 83-95; P-in-c Bracebridge Heath 97-00; V 00-15; P-in-c Bracebridge 07-15; rtd 15. *Address temp unknown*

MIDDLETON, Miss Jennifer Ann. b 82. St Jo Coll Dur BA 03. St Jo Coll Nottm 06. **d** 08 **p** 09. C Fatfield *Dur* 08-12; NE Regional Dir Urban Saints from 12; PtO *Dur* from 14. *Urban Saints, Kestin House, 45 Crescent Road, Luton LU2 0AH*
T: (01582) 589850 E: jmiddleton@urbansaints.org

MIDDLETON, Kent. **d** 15. NSM Cardiff Ch Ch Roath Park *Llan* from 15. *Address temp unknown*

MIDDLETON, Canon Michael John. b 40. Dur Univ BSc 62 Fitzw Ho Cam BA 66 MA 70. Westcott Ho Cam 63. **d** 66 **p** 67. C Newc St Geo 66-69; V 77-85; Chapl St Geo Gr Sch Cape Town S Africa 69-72; Chapl K Sch Tynemouth 72-77; R Hexham *Newc* 85-92; Hon Can Newc Cathl 90-92; Adn Swindon *Bris* 92-97; Can and Treas Westmr Abbey 97-04; rtd 04; PtO *Carl* from 05. *37 High Fellside, Kendal LA9 4JG* T: (01539) 729320

MIDDLETON, Canon Rodney. b 54. St Andr Univ BD 80. St Steph Ho Ox 80. **d** 82 **p** 83. C Walton St Mary *Liv* 82-87; C-in-c Kew St Fran CD 87-94; V Kew 94-95; Chapl Southport and Formby Distr Gen Hosp 87-95; V Haydock St Jas *Liv* from 95; Hon Can Wiawso Ghana from 13. *The Vicarage, 169 Church Road, Haydock, St Helens WA11 0NJ* T: (01942) 727956
E: rodmid169@yahoo.co.uk

MIDDLETON, Canon Thomas Arthur. b 36. Dur Univ MLitt 95 FRHistS 04. K Coll Lon AKC 61 St Boniface Warminster 61. **d** 62 **p** 63. C Sunderland *Dur* 62-63; C Auckland St Helen 63-67; C Winlaton 67-70; C-in-c Pennywell St Thos and Grindon St Oswald CD 70-79; Chapl Grindon Hall Hosp 73-79; R Boldon *Dur* 79-03; Adv in Stewardship Dur Adnry 87-92; Acting Prin St Chad's Coll Dur 97; Hon Fell from 07; Hon Can Dur Cathl 98-03; rtd 03; PtO *Dur* from 03. *1 St Mary's Drive, Sherburn Village, Durham DH6 1RL* T: 0191-372 3436
E: thomas@thomas.middleton.wanadoo.co.uk

MIDDLETON, Suffragan Bishop of. See DAVIES, The Rt Revd Mark

MIDDLETON-DANSKY, Serge Wladimir. b 45. Cuddesdon Coll 74. **d** 77 **p** 78. C Wisbech SS Pet and Paul *Ely* 77-79; LtO Adnry Riviera *Eur* from 80; C Ox St Giles and SS Phil and Jas w St Marg 83-86; PtO 86-88; *Truro* 88-90; P-in-c Zennor and Towednack 90-96; PtO 97-99; LtO from 99. *The Old Vicarage, Zennor, St Ives TR26 3BY* T: (01736) 796955

MIDDLEWICK, Robert James. b 44. Lon Univ BD 76 K Alfred's Coll Win CertEd 67. Ripon Coll Cuddesdon 75. **d** 77 **p** 78. C Bromley SS Pet and Paul *Roch* 77-81; C Belvedere All SS 81-84; P-in-c Lamberhurst 85-88; P-in-c Matfield 85-88; V Lamberhurst and Matfield 88-99; rtd 09. *12 Mill Stream Place, Tonbridge TN9 1QJ* T: (01732) 352480
E: middlewick@btinternet.com

MIDGLEY, George William. b 38. NOC. **d** 83 **p** 84. C Penistone and Thurlstone *Wakef* 88-89; TV 89-94; TR 94-04; rtd 04; PtO *Leeds* from 06. *20 Smithies Moor Lane, Batley WF17 9AR* T: (01924) 472289

MIDGLEY, Stephen Nicholas. b 60. Jes Coll Cam BA 83 MA 86 Lon Hosp MB, BS 86. Wycliffe Hall Ox. **d** 97 **p** 98. C Hove Bp Hannington Memorial Ch *Chich* 97-01; C Cambridge H Sepulchre *Ely* 01-04; P-in-c Cambridge St Andr Less 04-09; V from 09. *St Andrew the Less Vicarage, 21 Parsonage Street, Cambridge CB5 8DN* T: (01223) 353794 *or* 750450
E: steve.midgley@christchurchcambridge.org.uk

MIDLANE, Colin John. b 50. Qu Mary Coll Lon BA 72. Westcott Ho Cam 73 Sarum & Wells Th Coll 77. **d** 78 **p** 79. C Bethnal Green St Pet w St Thos *Lon* 78-82; P-in-c Haggerston All SS 82-88; Chapl Hengrave Hall Ecum Cen 88-89; P Cllr St Botolph Aldgate *Lon* 89-94; C St Botolph Aldgate w H Trin Minories 93-94; TV Haywards Heath St Wilfrid *Chich* 94-97; C Brighton St Geo w St Anne and St Mark 97-01; Chapl Brighton and Sussex Univ Hosps NHS Trust 01-03; rtd 03; PtO *Lon* from 04. *30 Damien Court, Damien Street, London E1 2HL* T: (020) 7791 0001

MIDWINTER, Sister Josie Isabel. b 46. Open Univ BA 84 Univ of Wales (Lamp) MA 98. CA Tr Coll IDC 71. **d** 87 **p** 99. C Didcot All SS *Ox* 98-05; P-in-c Drayton St Pet (Abingdon) 05-10; rtd 06; PtO *Ox* from 10. *32 Barnes Close, Didcot OX11 8JN* T: (01235) 759398 E: josie.midwinter@lineone.net

MIDWOOD, Canon Peter Stanley. b 47. CertEd 69. Linc Th Coll 80. **d** 82 **p** 83. C Garforth *Ripon* 82-85; C-in-c Grinton w Arkengarthdale, Downholme and Marske 85-86; C-in-c Melbecks and Muker 85-86; V Swaledale 86-97; R Romaldkirk w Laithkirk 97-08; AD Richmond 97-08; R Walkingham Hill 08-13; Hon Can Ripon Cathl 05-13; rtd 13; PtO *Nor* from 14. *4 Larch Crescent, Holt NR25 6TU*
E: ps.midwood@googlemail.com

MIELL (née OOSTRA), Catharina Henriët. b 60. Uppsala Univ MDiv 92. **p** 92. C Linköping Cathl Sweden 92-93; V Simrishamn 93-96; V Lund Cathl 96-99; V Stora Köpinge 99-01; V Brösarp - Tranås 01-04; C Upton cum Chalvey *Ox* 04-05; PtO *Win* from 11. *The Vicarage, 65 Southampton Road, Ringwood BH24 1HE* T: (01425) 476462
E: henrietmiell@gmail.com

MIELL, David Keith. b 57. Lanc Univ BSc 78 PhD 81 Trin Coll Cam BA 85. Westcott Ho Cam 83. **d** 86 **p** 87. C Blackbird Leys CD *Ox* 86-88; C Blackbird Leys 88-89; C Walton Milton Keynes 89-90; TV 90-96; RD Milton Keynes 93-95; TR Upton cum Chalvey 96-05; AD Burnham and Slough 02-05; PtO 05-08; *Sarum* 10-11; P-in-c Ringwood *Win* from 11. *Devizes Marina, Horton Avenue, Devizes SN10 2RH* T: (01425) 476462
E: vicar@ringwoodparish.org.uk

MIER, Ms Catherine Elizabeth. b 60. Bris Univ BSc 81 Chelsea Coll Lon MSc 84 Dur Univ BA 95. Cranmer Hall Dur 93. **d** 96 **p** 97. C Royston *St Alb* 96-00; C Bilton *Cov* 00-04; P-in-c Wellesbourne 04-14; V from 14; P-in-c Walton d'Eiville 04-14; R from 14; AD Fosse from 11. *The Vicarage, Church Street, Wellesbourne, Warwick CV35 9LS* T: (01789) 840262
E: kate.mier@virgin.net

MIGHALL, Robert. b 33. St Pet Coll Ox BA 57 MA 61. Wycliffe Hall Ox 57. **d** 58 **p** 59. C Stoke *Cov* 58-62; C Rugby

St Andr 62-64; V Newbold on Avon 64-76; V Combroke w Compton Verney 76-96; V Kineton 76-96; rtd 96; PtO *Glouc* from 97. *40 Rempstone Road, Wimborne BH21 1RP* T: (01202) 883522 E: randm@qvalley.tesco.net

MIHILL, Dennis George. b 31. St Alb Minl Tr Scheme 78. **d** 81 **p** 82. NSM Harpenden St Nic *St Alb* 81-86; C Sawbridgeworth 86-89; V Motspur Park *S'wark* 89-96; rtd 96; PtO *St Alb* 96-98 and 01-08; Hon C Biddenham 98-01; PtO *Roch* from 06. *7 Bourchier Close, Sevenoaks TN13 1PD* T: (01732) 459760 E: d.mihill@sky.com

MIKHAIL, Stella Frances. See JONES, Stella Frances

MILBANK (née LEGG), Alison Grant. b 54. Girton Coll Cam BA 78 MA 81 PGCE 79 Lanc Univ PhD 88. EMMTC 05. **d** 06 **p** 07. NSM Lambley *S'well* 06-09; PV S'well Minster from 09. *Burgage Hill Cottage, Burgage, Southwell NG25 0EP* T: (01636) 819224 E: alison.milbank@nottingham.ac.uk

MILBURN, John Frederick. b 56. Westmr Coll Ox BA 84. Sarum & Wells Th Coll 84. **d** 86 **p** 87. C Leavesden *St Alb* 86-89; C Broxbourne w Wormley 89-93; CF (TA) 90-93; R Inglewood w Texas Australia 93-98; P-in-c Holland Park 98-04; R Bulimba from 04. *171 Oxford Street, PO Box 271, Bulimba QLD 4171, Australia* T: (0061) (7) 3397 1508 F: 3397 3253 M: 415-838239 E: johnmilburn@hotmail.com *or* anglicanbulimba@ozemail.com.au

MILES, Mrs Beverley Anne. b 54. **d** 09 **p** 15. NSM Findon Valley *Chich* from 09; Dn-in-c from 15. *6 Cissbury Gardens, Worthing BN14 0DX* T: (01903) 873732

MILES, Damian Stewart. b 76. Fitzw Coll Cam BTh 02. Westcott Ho Cam 99. **d** 02 **p** 03. C Willingdon *Chich* 02-06; P-in-c Nork *Guildf* 06-11; P-in-c Thorpe 11-15; V from 15. *The Vicarage, Church Approach, Egham TW20 8TQ* T: (01932) 565986 M: 07815-848735 E: damomiles@btinternet.com

MILES, Gerald Christopher Morgan. b 36. Peterho Cam BA 57 MA 72 Cranfield Inst of Tech MSc 72 CEng MIET. Wycliffe Hall Ox 74. **d** 76 **p** 77. C Tunbridge Wells St Jas *Roch* 76-80; V Leigh 80-90; R Addington w Trottiscliffe 90-91; P-in-c Ryarsh w Birling 90-91; R Birling, Addington, Ryarsh and Trottiscliffe 91-00; Chapl ATC 80-11; rtd 00; PtO *Roch* from 00. *2 Spa Close, Hadlow, Tonbridge TN11 0JX* T/F: (01732) 852323 E: gcmmiles@btinternet.com

MILES (née HOARE), Ms Janet Francis Mary. b 48. St Aid Coll Dur BA 70 Bris Univ MEd 84. Sarum & Wells Th Coll 91. **d** 93 **p** 94. C Bruton and Distr *B & W* 93-98; P-in-c Llangarron w Llangrove, Whitchurch and Ganarew *Heref* 98-04; P-in-c Dixton 02-04; P-in-c Chewton Mendip w Ston Easton, Litton etc *B & W* 04-08; Dir Studies WEMTC 04-07; rtd 11; PtO *B & W* from 11; *Ex* from 12. *The Sanctuary, Bridford, Exeter EX6 7HS* T: (01647) 252750 E: jfm@btinternet.com

MILES, Jillian Maud. See LOCOCK, Jillian Maud

MILES, Marion Clare. b 41. S Dios Minl Tr Scheme 86. **d** 88 **p** 94. NSM Blandford Forum and Langton Long *Sarum* 88-01; NSM Winterborne Valley and Milton Abbas 01-14; Chapl Blandford Community Hosp 88-11; PtO *Sarum* from 14. *153 Salisbury Road, Blandford Forum DT11 7SW* T: (01258) 452010 E: marionclare07@yahoo.co.uk

MILES, Ms Patricia Ellen. b 56. RGN 79. STETS 00. **d** 03 **p** 04. NSM Verwood *Sarum* from 03. *4 Firs Glen Road, Verwood BH31 6JB* T: (01202) 824211 E: pe.miles@btinternet.com

MILES, Robert Anthony. b 71. Nottm Univ BSc 92 PGCE 94 All Nations Chr Coll BA 01. Wycliffe Hall Ox MTh 08. **d** 08 **p** 09. C Moulton *Pet* 08-11; C Houghton-on-the-Hill, Keyham and Hungarton *Leic* 11-13; TV Cornerstone Team from 13. *The Rectory, 16 Main Street, Houghton-on-the-Hill, Leicester LE7 9GD* T: 0116-241 4783 E: robmiles100@btinternet.com

MILES, Miss Sharon Elizabeth Ann. b 66. Westcott Ho Cam 00. **d** 02 **p** 03. C Shrub End *Chelmsf* 02-05; P-in-c Rivenhall 05-10; P-in-c St Osyth 10-15; V St Osyth and Great Bentley from 15; Adv for Ordained Women's Min (Colchester Area) from 07. *The Vicarage, The Bury, St Osyth, Clacton-on-Sea CO16 8NX* T: (01255) 822055 E: revdsmiles@hotmail.com

MILES, Stephen John. b 44. Monash Univ Aus BA 66 Worc Coll Ox DipEd 68 Univ Coll Lon MA 75 California Univ PhD 80. Melbourne Coll of Div BTheol 86. **d** 87 **p** 88. C Malvern St Jo Australia 87; C Clifton Hill St Andr 87-89; Chapl Co-ord and Angl Chapl Monash Med Cen 89-97; Asst Chapl Bonn w Cologne *Eur* 97-00; Chapl 00-03; PtO Melbourne Australia from 03. *24 Dorothea Crescent, Dromana VIC 3936, Australia* E: stephenmiles@iprimus.com.au

MILFORD, Canon Catherine Helena. b 39. LMH Ox BA 61 MA 65 FRSA 92. Gilmore Course 81. **dss** 82 **d** 87 **p** 94. Heaton St Barn *Bradf* 82-88; Par Dn 87-88; Adult Educn Adv *Win* 88-96; TR Barnham Broom *Nor* 96-00; P-in-c Reymerston w Cranworth, Letton, Southburgh etc 96-00; TR Barnham Broom and Upper Yare 00-04; Hon Can Nor Cathl 00-04; rtd 04; PtO *Leeds* from 05. *6 Leylands Grove, Bradford BD9 5QP*

MILFORD, Graham Alan. b 57. Trin Coll Bris 00. **d** 02 **p** 03. C Wolborough and Ogwell *Ex* 02-08; P-in-c Newburgh w Westhead *Liv* 08-10; V from 10. *The Vicarage, 12 New Acres, Newburgh, Wigan WN8 7TU* T: (01257) 463267
E: grahammilford@btinternet.com

MILFORD, Mrs Nicola Claire. b 75. Univ Coll Ches BTh 03. Trin Coll Bris 00 NOC 02. **d** 04 **p** 05. C Alphington, Shillingford St George and Ide *Ex* 04-08; Dioc Adv NSM *Liv* from 11; C Sefton from 13. *The Vicarage, 12 New Acres, Newburgh, Wigan WN8 7TU* T: (01257) 463267 E: milford.nicola@virgin.net

MILLAR, Alan William. b 46. Nottm Univ MDiv. **d** 00 **p** 01. C Drumglass w Moygashel *Arm* 00-02; I Dromara w Garvaghy *D & D* 02-06; I Rathcoole *Conn* 06-11; rtd 11. *6 Primrose Court, 1 Doagh Road, Newtownabbey BT37 9PA* T: (028) 9085 4215 E: alan.millar3@btinternet.com

MILLAR, Alexander. *See* MILLAR, John Alexander Kirkpatrick

MILLAR, Andrew Charles. b 48. Hull Univ BSc 69. Cuddesdon Coll 71. **d** 73 **p** 74. C Rushmere *St E* 73-76; C Ipswich All Hallows 76-79; Dioc Youth Chapl *Sheff* 79-83; Youth Chapl *Win* 83-92; V Colden 92-08; V Twyford and Owslebury and Morestead etc 08-10; rtd 10; PtO *St As* from 13. *22 Fford Bryn Estyn, Mold CH7 1TJ* T: (01352) 754745
E: acmillar@btinternet.com

MILLAR, Christine. *See* WHEELER, Christine

MILLAR, David Glassell. b 43. Dur Univ BSc 64 St Cath Coll Cam BA 66 MA 71 Birkbeck Coll Lon BSc 78 Leeds Univ MSc 80. Cuddesdon Coll 66. **d** 68 **p** 69. C Pershore w Wick *Worc* 68-72; C Malden St Jas *S'wark* 72-73; V W Dean *Chich* 73-75; rtd 08. *5 Beacon Hill, London N7 9LY*
T/F: (020) 7607 3809

MILLAR, Gary. b 67. St Mich Coll Llan 88. **d** 91 **p** 92. C Tonyrefail w Gilfach Goch *Llan* 91-93; C Barry All SS 93-95; TV Cowbridge 95-97; I Dromara w Garvaghy *D & D* 97-01; I Kilkeel 01-08; I Belfast St Paul w St Barn *Conn* 08-12; I Ahoghill w Portglenone from 12. *The Rectory, 42 Church Street, Ahoghill, Ballymena BT42 2PA* T: (028) 2587 1240 M: 07817-968357 E: revgarymillar@gmail.com

✠**MILLAR, The Rt Revd John Alexander Kirkpatrick (Sandy).** b 39. Trin Coll Cam BA 62 MA 66. Cranmer Hall Dur 74. **d** 76 **p** 77 **c** 05. C Brompton H Trin w Onslow Square St Paul *Lon* 76-85; V 85-05; Hon C 05-11; Hon C Onslow Square and S Kensington St Aug from 11; P-in-c Tollington 03-10; AD Chelsea 89-94; Preb St Paul's Cathl from 97; Asst Bp Uganda from 05; Hon Asst Bp St E from 12. *Fairlawn, 37 Alde Lane, Aldeburgh IP15 3DZ* T: (01728) 452926

MILLAR, Mrs Julie Ann. b 65. Bris Poly BA 87 Ex Univ BTh 08 FCA 09. SWMTC 02. **d** 05 **p** 06. NSM Penzance St Mary w St Paul and St Jo *Truro* 05-08; Asst Chapl R Cornwall Hosps Trust 08-13; NSM St Agnes and Mount Hawke w Mithian *Truro* 10-13. *6 Brunel Court, Truro TR1 3AE*
E: julie.millar@truro.anglican.org

MILLAR, Canon Sandra Doreen. b 57. Univ of Wales (Cardiff) BA 79 Warwick Univ MA 94 PhD 99. Ripon Coll Cuddesdon 98. **d** 00 **p** 01. C Chipping Barnet w Arkley *St Alb* 00-03; TV Dorchester *Ox* 03-07; Dioc Children's Officer *Glouc* 07-13; Hd of Projects and Development Abps' Coun from 13; Public Preacher *Glouc* from 13; Hon Can Glouc Cathl from 14. *Church House, Great Smith Street, London SW1P 3AZ* T: (020) 7898 1458 M: 07976-823986
E: sandra.millar@churchofengland.org *or* revdocsand@gmail.com

MILLARD, Canon Jane Mary. b 43. Open Univ BA 80. Edin Dioc NSM Course 81. **d** 90 **p** 94. Chapl HIV/AIDS 90-94; NSM Edin St Mary 90-94; C 94-98; Can St Mary's Cathl 95-09; Vice Provost 98-09; rtd 09; LtO *Edin* from 09; Hon Can St Mary's Cathl from 10. *22/1 Kinellan Road, Edinburgh EH12 6ES* T: 0131-346 2469 M: 07712-898805
E: jmmillard@btinternet.com

MILLARD, Jonathan Neil. b 62. Aston Univ BSc 83 Barrister-at-Law (Gray's Inn) 84. Wycliffe Hall Ox 89. **d** 92 **p** 93. C Haddenham w Cuddington, Kingsey etc *Ox* 92-94; R Washington Trin USA 94-00; R Church Stretton *Heref* 00-03; R Pittsburgh Ascension USA from 04. *4729 Ellsworth Avenue, Pittsburgh PA 15213-2888, USA* T: (001) (412) 621 5378 F: 621 5746 E: jonathan.millard@comcast.net

MILLARD, Malcolm Edoric. b 38. Lon Univ BA 60 AKC 60 Lon Inst of Educn PGCE 61. St Jo Coll Nottm 80. **d** 77 **p** 81. Dn Banjul Cathl The Gambia 77-79; Dn Lamin St Andr 79-81; P-in-c 81-82; P-in-c Fajara St Paul 82-88; V Gen 86-88; 89-95; C S Shoebury *Chelmsf* 95-97; C Rainham w Wennington 97-02; P-in-c N Ockendon 02-08; PtO *Sarum* from 08. *29 Moorcombe Drive, Preston, Weymouth DT3 6NP* T: (01305) 834060 E: weeksmary@gmail.com

MILLARD, Richard Stuart Marsh. b 33. St Pet Coll Ox BA 57 MA. Oak Hill NSM Course 90. **d** 93 **p** 94. NSM Laleham

Lon 93-94; NSM Neatishead, Barton Turf and Irstead *Nor* 94-95; NSM Ashmanhaugh, Barton Turf etc 95-99; rtd 99; PtO *Nor* from 99. *Semaphore Lodge, 30 Weybourne Road, Sheringham NR25 8HF*

MILLER, Adrian David. b 74. Open Univ BSc 02. St Jo Coll Nottm MTh 06. **d** 06 **p** 07. C Newton Flotman, Swainsthorpe, Tasburgh, etc *Nor* 06-09; TV 09-14; R Mulbarton w Bracon Ash, Hethel and Flordon from 14. *The Rectory, The Common, Mulbarton, Norwich NR14 8JS* M: 07871-085013
E: aidymiller@i12.com

MILLER, Mrs Alison. b 75. Liv Univ BSc 97 St Jo Coll Dur BATM 15. Cranmer Hall Dur 13. **d** 15. C Lanchester and Burnhope *Dur* from 15. *The Vicarage, Bryans Leap, Burnopfield, Newcastle upon Tyne NE16 6HQ* M: 07557-148689
E: alison.miller@durham.anglican.org

MILLER, Andrew. *See* MILLER, Ronald Andrew John

MILLER, Andrew Philip. b 72. Liv Univ BSc 94 PhD 98. Cranmer Hall Dur 09. **d** 11 **p** 12. C Barnard Castle w Whorlton *Dur* 11-15; V Tanfield w Burnopfield and Dipton from 15. *The Vicarage, Bryans Leap, Burnopfield, Newcastle upon Tyne NE16 6HQ* M: 07747-191989 E: a235miller@btinternet.com *or* amcurate@btinternet.com

MILLER, Mrs Annette. b 53. W Midl Coll of Educn BEd 83. LCTP 07 Cranmer Hall Dur 12. **d** 13 **p** 14. NSM Levens *Carl* from 13. *Airton, Eden Park Road, Grange-over-Sands LA11 6BW* T: (015395) 33840 E: miller3637@btinternet.com

MILLER, Anthony. *See* MILLER, Ronald Anthony

MILLER, Barry. b 42. Bede Coll Dur TCert 63 Open Univ BA 79 Leic Univ MEd 86. Linc Th Coll 63. **d** 65 **p** 66. C Greenside *Dur* 65-68; C Auckland St Andr and St Anne 68-71; Adv in Educn *Leic* 71-77; C Leic St Nic 77-80; Asst Chapl Leic Univ 77-80; Lect RS Leic Poly 77-80; Children's Officer Gen Syn Bd of Educn 80-84; Hd RS W Midl Coll of HE 84-89; Hd Initial Teacher Educn Wolv Univ *Lich* 89-93; Hd Teacher Educn Bradf Coll 94-10; PtO *Leeds* from 06; Co-ord Yorks Regional Tr Partnership from 10. *32 Nab Lane, Shipley BD18 4HH* T: (01274) 590630 E: revbarrymiller@gmail.com

MILLER, Charles. *See* MILLER, Ernest Charles

MILLER, Charles Irvine. b 35. Nottm Univ BEd 76. Bps' Coll Cheshunt 61. **d** 63 **p** 64. C Anlaby Common St Mark *York* 63-66; C Whitby 66-68; R Ingoldmells w Addlethorpe *Linc* 68-72; P-in-c Bishop Norton 72-76; V Scunthorpe St Jo 76-83; Chapl Manor Hosp Walsall 83-89; rtd 89; PtO *Ely* 89-98 and from 99; P-in-c Isleham 98-99. *The Old Studio, 6 Chapel Street, Duxford, Cambridge CB22 4RJ*

MILLER, Darren Noel. b 67. Birm Univ BSocSc 89. Chich Th Coll BTh 95 Coll of Resurr Mirfield 94. **d** 95 **p** 96. C Weoley Castle *Birm* 95-98; C Shard End 98-00; V Castle Vale St Cuth 00-06; AD Sutton Coldfield 04-06; TR Cheam *S'wark* from 06; AD Sutton from 13. *The Rectory, 33 Mickleham Gardens, Cheam, Sutton SM3 8QJ* T: (020) 8641 4664 M: 07747-858697 E: dnmiller@dandsmiller.me.uk

MILLER, Canon David George. b 54. Oriel Coll Ox BA 76 MA 80. Ripon Coll Cuddesdon 78. **d** 81 **p** 82. C Henfield w Shermanbury and Woodmancote *Chich* 81-84; C Monk Bretton *Wakef* 84-87; V Rastrick St Jo 87-93; TR Helston and Wendron *Truro* from 93; Chapl R Cornwall Hosps Trust 95-01; Chapl W of Cornwall Primary Care Trust 01-06; Hon Can Truro Cathl from 06. *St Michael's Rectory, Church Lane, Helston TR13 8PF* T: (01326) 572516
E: millerourrectory@googlemail.com

MILLER, David James Tringham. b 45. AKC 70. Sarum & Wells Th Coll 76. **d** 77 **p** 78. C Abington *Pet* 77-80; TV Corby SS Pet and Andr w Gt and Lt Oakley 80-83; V Kettering All SS 83-94; RD Kettering 87-94; V Pet All SS 94-09; rtd 09; C Penrith w Newton Reigny and Plumpton Wall *Carl* 10-11; PtO from 11. *27 Drovers Terrace, Penrith CA11 9EN* T: (01768) 840406
E: djtmiller@o2.co.uk

MILLER, David John. b 37. Louvain Univ Belgium Lic en Sciences Catéchétiques 68. Chich Th Coll 60. **d** 62 **p** 63. C Southsea H Spirit *Portsm* 62-65; C Roehampton H Trin *S'wark* 67-68; Chapl Luxembourg *Eur* 68-72; Chapl Lausanne 72-91; P-in-c Gstaad Switzerland 82-88; Chapl Le Rossey Sch 72-02; Asst Chapl Lausanne *Eur* 91-93; rtd 02; PtO *Eur* from 94. *63 avenue de Savoie, 74500 Publier, France*
T: (0033) 4 50 26 89 41

MILLER, David Robert. b 47. Middx Univ BA 98. ERMC 94. **d** 08 **p** 09. C Eaton Socon *St Alb* 08-12; rtd 12. *32 Cornwall Court, Eaton Socon, St Neots PE19 8PR* T: (01480) 471132 E: davidmiller@care4free.net

MILLER, Ernest Charles. b 56. Franklin & Marshall Coll (USA) BA 78 Univ of Michigan MA 79 Keble Coll Ox DPhil 90. Nashotah Ho MDiv 82. **d** 82 **p** 83. C Dallas St Andr USA 82-84; Warden Ho of SS Greg and Macrina 84-90; Asst Chapl Keble Coll Ox 84-88; P-in-c New Marston *Ox* 91-96; Ramsey

Prof Th Nashotah Ho Wisconsin USA 96-00; R New York Transfiguration USA 00-04; Adjunct Prof Ch Hist Gen Th Sem 02-04; TR Abingdon *Ox* from 06. *The Rectory, St Helen's Court, Abingdon OX14 5BS* T: (01235) 532722 M: 07726-743924 E: rector@sthelens-abingdon.org.uk

MILLER, Francis Rogers. b 54. Ex Univ BA 86. St Steph Ho Ox 86. **d** 88 **p** 89. C Wednesfield *Lich* 88-93; P-in-c Caldmore 93-99; V 99-02; C Walsall St Mary and All SS Palfrey 93-97; P-in-c 97-02; V Caldmore w Palfrey 02-11; rtd 11. *12 Brooke Road, Braunston, Oakham LE15 8QR* E: rogermiller@live.co.uk

MILLER, Gareth. *See* MILLER, John Gareth

MILLER, Gary Russell. b 58. **d** 07 **p** 08. OLM Wythenshawe *Man* from 07. *77 Mayfair Road, Manchester M22 9ZE* T: 0161-436 8151 E: gary-miller@hotmail.co.uk

MILLER, The Ven Geoffrey Vincent. b 56. Dur Univ BEd 78 Newc Univ MA 94. St Jo Coll Nottm 81. **d** 83 **p** 84. C Jarrow *Dur* 83-86; TV Billingham St Aid 86-92; Dioc Urban Development Officer 91-97; Community Chapl Stockton-on-Tees 92-94; P-in-c Darlington St Cuth 94-96; V 96-99; Soc Resp Officer 97-99; Can Res Newc Cathl 99-05; Dioc Urban Officer 99-05; Adn Northd and Can Res Newc Cathl from 05. *80 Moorside North, Newcastle upon Tyne NE4 9DU* T: 0191-273 8245 F: 226 0286 E: g.miller@newcastle.anglican.org

MILLER, Graham William. b 71. St Andr Univ BD 94 Dur Univ MA 98. Westcott Ho Cam 99. **d** 01 **p** 02. C Ex St Dav 01-03; C Sunderland St Mary and St Pet and Sunderland Pennywell St Thos *Dur* 03-07; C Paddington St Jas *Lon* 07-14; R Greenford H Cross from 14. *The Rectory, 75 Oldfield Lane South, Greenford UB6 9JT* T: (020) 8575 5402 M: 07851-013457 E: graham.miller@london.anglican.org

✠**MILLER, The Rt Revd Harold Creeth.** b 50. TCD BA 73 MA 78. St Jo Coll Nottm BA 75. **d** 76 **p** 77 **c** 97. C Carrickfergus *Conn* 76-79; Dir Ext Studies St Jo Coll Nottm 79-84; Chapl QUB 84-89; I Carrigrohane Union *C, C & R* 89-97; Bp's Dom Chapl 91-97; Can Cork and Cloyne Cathls 94-96; Treas Cork Cathl 96-97; Can Cork Cathl 96-97; Preb Tymothan St Patr Cathl Dublin 96-97; Bp D & D from 97. *The See House, 32 Knockdene Park South, Belfast BT5 7AB* T: (028) 9047 1973 *or* 9023 7602 F: 9023 1902 E: bishop@down.anglican.org

MILLER (née BLUNDEN), Mrs Jacqueline Ann. b 63. Leic Univ BA 86 SS Coll Cam BA 90. Ridley Hall Cam 88. **d** 91. Par Dn Bedford St Paul *St Alb* 91-94; C 94-95; PtO *Lon* 05-13. *39 Bounds Green Road, London N22 8HE* T: (020) 8829 0450 E: jacqui.miller7@btinternet.com

MILLER, John David. b 76. Ch Ch Ox BA 98 MA 07. Oak Hill Th Coll BA 10. **d** 10 **p** 11. C Bath St Bart *B & W* 10-13. *37 Osler Road, Headington, Oxford OX3 9BH* M: 07821-180901 E: johnmiller.jdm@gmail.com

MILLER, Canon John David. b 50. Nottm Univ BTh 73 Lanc Univ CertEd 74 Newc Univ MA 93. Kelham Th Coll 68. **d** 74 **p** 75. C Horden *Dur* 74-79; C Billingham St Aid 79-80; TV 80-84; TR S Shields All SS 84-10; Hon Can Dur Cathl 04-10; rtd 10; PtO *Dur* from 10. *6 Tynedale Road, South Shields NE34 6EX* T: 0191-455 6911

MILLER, John Gareth. b 57. St Jo Coll Dur BA 78. Ridley Hall Cam 79 Ven English Coll Rome 80. **d** 81 **p** 82. C Addiscombe St Mary *Cant* 81-84; TV Melbury *Sarum* 84-88; TR 88-91; V Leamington Priors All SS *Cov* 91-94; PtO *Ox* from 15. *6 Woodfield Drive, Charlbury, Chipping Norton OX7 3SE* E: garethmiller@tiscali.co.uk

MILLER (née BAILEY), Judith Elizabeth Anne. b 61. RGN RSCN 84. **d** 99 **p** 00. OLM Blyth Valley *St E* 99-07; OLM Bungay H Trin w St Mary 11-13; OLM Wainford 11-13; NSM Bungay from 13. *Moonrakers, Back Road, Wenhaston, Halesworth IP19 9DY* T: (01502) 478882 E: judym61@btinternet.com

MILLER, Dr Kathryn Rebecca. b 63. Ex Univ BSc 84 Abth Univ MSc 05 UEA PhD 10. Ridley Hall Cam 13. **d** 15. C Speke St Aid *Liv* from 15. *1 Gatley Walk, Liverpool L24 2UY* M: 07914-529310 E: katie.miller.063@gmail.com

MILLER, Kenneth Leslie. b 50. Lanc Univ BEd 74 Liv Univ BPhil 94 FRSA. NOC 78. **d** 80 **p** 81. NSM Formby St Pet *Liv* 80-87; NSM Anfield St Columba from 87; Chapl St Marg C of E High Sch Aigburth Liv from 86. *9 Hampton Road, Liverpool L37 6EJ* T: (01704) 831256 E: jenke_2@hotmail.co.uk

MILLER, Kim Hurst. b 49. Ex Univ Hon PhD 89. Canberra Coll of Min BTh 82. **d** 82 **p** 83. C Goulburn Cathl Australia 83-84; P-in-c Koorawatha 84-85; PtO *Ex* 85-89; R Wagga Wagga St Alb Australia 89-98; Chapl Bathurst Gaol from 98. *3 Oates Place, Eglinton NSW 2795, Australia* T: (0061) (2) 6337 1841 *or* 6338 3282 E: kkmiller@globalfreeway.com.au

MILLER, The Ven Luke Jonathan. b 66. SS Coll Cam BA 87 MA 91. St Steph Ho Ox BA 90. **d** 91 **p** 92. C Oxhey St Matt *St Alb* 91-94; C Tottenham St Mary *Lon* 94-95; V 95-10; AD E Haringey 05-10; Adn Hampstead from 10; P-in-c Winchmore

Hill H Trin 11-12. *39 Bounds Green Road, London N22 8HE* T: (020) 8829 0450 E: archdeacon.hampstead@london.anglican.org

MILLER, Mark George. b 69. Cranmer Hall Dur 10. **d** 12 **p** 13. C Stockton *Dur* from 12. *12 Pennypot Lane, Eaglescliffe, Stockton-on-Tees TS16 0BN* E: hello@markmiller.co.uk

MILLER, Martin Michael. b 55. St Jo Coll Dur BSc 78. Trin Coll Bris 94. **d** 96 **p** 97. C Leamington Priors St Paul *Cov* 96-99; C Bermondsey St Anne and St Aug *S'wark* 99-05; R Newhaven *Chich* from 05. *The Rectory, 36 Second Avenue, Newhaven BN9 9HN* T: (01273) 515251 E: martinmrev@aol.com

MILLER, Michael Andrew. b 58. Ripon Coll Cuddesdon 03. **d** 05 **p** 06. C Hockerill *St Alb* 05-08; P-in-c Kensal Town St Thos w St Andr and St Phil *Lon* 08-12; V from 12. *St Thomas's Vicarage, 231 Kensal Road, London W10 5DB* T: (020) 8960 3703 M: 07778-617482 E: mmiller363@tiscali.co.uk

MILLER, Michael Daukes. b 46. Qu Coll Cam MA 71 Lon Univ BCh 70 MB 71 MRCGP 74. Glouc Th Course 82. **d** 85 **p** 94. NSM Lydney w Aylburton *Glouc* 85-95; NSM Lydney 95-06; Asst Chapl HM Pris Ex from 07; PtO *Ex* from 07. *HM Prison, 30 New North Road, Exeter EX4 4EX* T: (01392) 415650 E: mmiller@btinternet.com

MILLER, Patrick Figgis. b 33. Ch Coll Cam BA 56 MA 60 Surrey Univ PhD 95. Cuddesdon Coll 56. **d** 58 **p** 59. C Portsea St Cuth *Portsm* 58-61; C Cambridge Gt St Mary w St Mich *Ely* 61-63; Chapl SCM 61-63; Hd RS Man Gr Sch 63-69; Can Res and Lib S'wark Cathl 69-72; Dir of Soc Studies Qu Mary's Coll Basingstoke 72-79; Prin Sunbury Coll 79-80; Prin Esher Coll 81-98; Project Dir Learning for Living 00-05; Chapl London Flotilla from 00; PtO *Guildf* from 01. *9 Fairfax Avenue, Epsom KT17 2QN* T: (020) 8394 0970 M: 07740-909414 E: patrickmiller@ntlworld.com

MILLER, Canon Paul. b 49. Oak Hill Th Coll 71. **d** 74 **p** 75. C Upton *Ex* 74-77; C Farnborough *Guildf* 77-78; P-in-c Torquay St Luke *Ex* 78-81; V 81-86; V Green Street Green *Roch* 86-94; V Green Street Green and Pratts Bottom 94-01; RD Orpington 96-01; V Shortlands 01-12; Hon Can Roch Cathl 00-12; AD Beckenham 09-12; Chapl Is of Scilly *Truro* 12-15; Chapl to The Queen from 05. *Address temp unknown* M: 07940-582010 E: canonpmiller@aol.com

MILLER, Paul Richard. b 37. K Coll Lon BSc 60 AKC 60. Linc Th Coll 60. **d** 62 **p** 63. C Sheff St Geo 62-65; C Bottesford *Linc* 65-67; Bp's Youth Chapl 67-69; C Corringham 67-69; Dioc Youth Officer *Ripon* 69-74; Sec Nat Coun for Voluntary Youth Services 74-79; Hd Youth Nat Coun of Soc Services 74-79; P-in-c Battlesden and Pottesgrove *St Alb* 79-80; P-in-c Eversholt w Milton Bryan 79-80; P-in-c Woburn 79-80; V Woburn w Eversholt, Milton Bryan, Battlesden etc 80-98; rtd 98; PtO *Heref* 98-12; *Lich* from 03. *6 Elms Paddock, Little Stretton, Church Stretton SY6 6RD* T: (01694) 724596 E: paulmiller@macunlimited.net

MILLER, Canon Philip Harry. b 58. Leeds Univ BA 79. Chich Th Coll 80. **d** 82 **p** 83. C Reddish *Man* 82-86; R Lower Broughton Ascension 86-94; P-in-c Cheetwood St Alb 91-94; P-in-c Langley and Parkfield 95-00; TR 00-10; V Langley from 10; AD Heywood and Middleton 10-15; Hon Can Man Cathl from 07. *The Rectory, Wood Street, Middleton, Manchester M24 5GL* T: 0161-643 5013

MILLER, Philip Howard. b 40. Tyndale Hall Bris 67. **d** 72 **p** 73. Argentina 72-73; C Rusholme H Trin *Man* 73-74; SAMS Paraguay 74-77; C Toxteth St Cypr w Ch Ch *Liv* 78-80; V Burscough Bridge 80-85; V Woodbridge St Jo *St E* 85-91; P-in-c Combs 91-92 and 93-96; Chapl Burrswood Chr Cen 92-93; V Yoxford and Peasenhall w Sibton *St E* 96-01; rtd 01; PtO *St E* from 07. *Salta, 54 Orchard Close, Melton, Woodbridge IP12 1LD* T: (01394) 388615 E: phm914@lineone.net

MILLER, Philip Hugh Owen. b 62. **d** 13 **p** 14. NSM Beccles St Mich and St Luke *St E* from 13. *Ty Bach, 19 Rigbourne Hill, Beccles NR34 9JG* T: (01502) 714786 E: windy.miller.321@btinternet.com

MILLER, Richard Bracebridge. b 45. Wycliffe Hall Ox 68. **d** 70 **p** 71. C Lee Gd Shep w St Pet *S'wark* 70-74; C Roehampton H Trin 74-77; C Earley St Pet *Ox* 77-80; V Aldermaston w Wasing and Brimpton 80-96; C Newbury 96-01; PtO from 03. *14 Burcot Park, Burcot, Abingdon OX14 3DH* T: (01865) 407521 E: rbmoxford@breathe.com

MILLER, The Ven Robert Stephen. b 71. QUB BSc 92. CITC BTh 95. **d** 95 **p** 96. C Lurgan Ch the Redeemer *D & D* 95-99; I Tullylish 99-03; I Maghera w Killelagh *D & R* 03-10; I Londonderry Ch Ch, Culmore, Muff and Belmont from 10; Adn Derry from 12. *The Rectory, 1B Heathfield, Londonderry BT48 8JD* T: (028) 7135 2396 *or* 7135 8925 M: 07711-748406 E: rector@cccmsp.org *or* archdeacon@derry.anglican.org

MILLER, Ronald Andrew John. b 46. **d** 96 **p** 97. OLM Heywood *Man* 96-09. *16 Bryn Morfa, Bodelwyddan, Rhyl LL18 5TP* T: (01745) 530055 E: andrew.miller1@virgin.net

MILLER, Ronald Anthony. b 41. CEng CPA MRAeS City Univ BSc 63. S'wark Ord Course 69. **d** 72 **p** 80. NSM Crookham *Guildf* 72-73 and 80-85; NSM New Haw 85-95; NSM Effingham w Lt Bookham 95-04; PtO 05-09; NSM Nork 09-11; rtd 11. *190 Gossops Drive, Crawley RH11 8LD* M: 07710-294786 E: ramiller@sky.com

MILLER, Rosamund Joy. *See* SEAL, Rosamund Joy

MILLER, Roy. b 29. **d** 88 **p** 93. NSM Leic Cathl 88-91; NSM Leic H Apostles 91-97; PtO 97-99. *Address temp unknown*

MILLER, Miss Sarah Lydia. b 65. St Andr Univ BD 90 Hughes Hall Cam PGCE 91. EAMTC 98. **d** 01 **p** 02. NSM Nor St Pet Mancroft w St Jo Maddermarket 01-03; C Wythenshawe *Man* 03-07; C Tewkesbury w Walton Cardiff and Twyning *Glouc* 07-11; V Newbiggin Hall *Newc* from 11. *St Wilfrid's Vicarage, Trevelyan Drive, Newcastle upon Tyne NE5 4DA* T: 0191-214 0833 E: revsarah1@tiscali.co.uk

MILLER, Canon Stephen Michael. b 63. NE Lon Poly BSc 86 Nottm Univ BTh 91. Linc Th Coll 88. **d** 91 **p** 92. C Dudley St Fran *Worc* 91-94; V Sedgley St Mary 94-99; Miss to Seafarers from 99; Chapl Rotterdam w Schiedam Miss to Seafarers *Eur* 99-02; Chapl Dubai and UAE 02-11; Sen Chapl Hong Kong from 11; Hon Can Manila Philippines from 15. *The Mission to Seafarers, 11 Middle Road, Kowloon, Hong Kong, China* T: (00852) 2368 8261 F: 2366 0928 E: seamenhk@biznetvigator.com

MILLER, Stuart William. b 71. Univ of Wales (Cardiff) BA 92. Trin Coll Bris BA 97. **d** 97 **p** 98. C Fordingbridge *Win* 97-98; C Bursledon 98-02; V W Moors *Sarum* 02-05; Chapl Bournemouth and Poole Coll of FE *Win* 05-10; C Bournemouth Town Cen 05-10; V Moordown from 10. *1 Gervus Road, Bournemouth BH1 3ED*

MILLER, Timothy Ian. b 85. Ustinov Coll Dur MA 09 St Jo Coll Dur MATM 14. Cranmer Hall Dur 12. **d** 14 **p** 15. C Primrose Hill St Mary w Avenue Road St Paul *Lon* from 14. *Flat 2, St John's Hall, St John's Wood High Street, London NW8 7NE* M: 07588-644217 E: believethesescars@gmail.com

MILLER, William David. b 45. Man Univ BA 66. Linc Th Coll 69. **d** 71 **p** 72. C Newc St Geo 71-74; C Corbridge w Halton 74-77; C N Gosforth 77-81; TV Whorlton 81-90; Chapl K Sch Tynemouth 90-09; rtd 09. *7 Strawberry Terrace, Hazlerigg, Newcastle upon Tyne NE13 7AR* T: 0191-236 5024

MILLER-MASKELL, John Michael. b 45. Sarum & Wells Th Coll 86. **d** 88 **p** 89. C Swanborough *Sarum* 88-91; Chapl RAF 91-95; P-in-c Ollerton w Boughton *S'well* 95-97; P-in-c Capel *Guildf* 97-02; TV Walton H Trin *Ox* 02-03; Healing Co-ord Acorn Chr Foundn 03-04; rtd 04; PtO *Chich* 04-10; P-in-c Chailey from 10. *The Rectory, Chailey Green, Lewes BN8 4DA* T: (01825) 722286 M: 07852-741515 E: johnm1@madasafish.com

MILLEST, Daniel John. b 86. St Mellitus Coll. **d** 13 **p** 14. C Onslow Square and S Kensington St Aug *Lon* 13-14; Malaysia from 14. *C-20-6, The Capers, Jalan Enam, 51000, Kuala Lumpur, Malaysia* E: dan.millest@htbb.org

MILLETT, Maxwell Roy. b 45. Clare Coll Cam BA 67. S Dios Minl Tr Scheme 92. **d** 95 **p** 96. NSM Southsea St Pet *Portsm* 95-03; PtO from 03. *70 Waverley Road, Southsea PO5 2PR* T: (023) 9281 7216 E: max.millett@ntlworld.com

MILLGATE, Victor Frederick. b 44. St Mich Coll Llan 81. **d** 83 **p** 84. C Pembroke St Mary w St Mich *St D* 83-85; V Manorbier and St Florence w Redberth 85-04; TR Carew 04-09; AD Castlemartin 03-09; rtd 09. *3 Grove Drive, Pembroke SA71 5QB* T: (01646) 621683 E: esmillgate@yahoo.co.uk

MILLICHAMP, Mrs Penelope Mary. b 39. CertEd 60. WMMTC 82. **dss** 85 **d** 87 **p** 94. Wednesfield *Lich* 85-94; Par Dn 87-90; Team Dn 90-94; PtO 94-95; NSM Wrockwardine Deanery 95-99; rtd 99; PtO *Lich* 99-00 and from 06. *18 Nursery Walk, Tettenhall, Wolverhampton WV6 8QY* T: (01902) 741996 M: 07971-421562 E: penny@millichamp.com

MILLIER, Gordon. b 28. OBE 95. Em Coll Cam BA 49. Cuddesdon Coll 53. **d** 55 **p** 56. C Portsea N End St Mark *Portsm* 55-62; V New Eltham All SS *S'wark* 62-71; V Roehampton H Trin 71-79; Can Res St Alb 79-86; Chapl Strasbourg *Eur* 86-95; Angl Rep Eur Insts 90-95; rtd 95; PtO *S'wark* 95-00; *Sarum* from 98. *3 East Street, Beaminster DT8 3DS* T: (01308) 862806 E: milligan@uwclub.net

MILLIGAN, Peter John. b 52. **d** 01 **p** 02. NSM Putney St Marg *S'wark* 01-06; NSM Angell Town St Jo from 06. *39 Stapleton Road, London SW17 8BA* T: (020) 8767 3497

MILLIGAN, Canon William John (Barney). b 28. OBE 95. Em Coll Cam BA 49. Cuddesdon Coll 53. **d** 55 **p** 56. C Portsea N End St Mark *Portsm* 55-62; V New Eltham All SS *S'wark* 62-71; V Roehampton H Trin 71-79; Can Res St Alb 79-86; Chapl Strasbourg *Eur* 86-95; Angl Rep Eur Insts 90-95; rtd 95; PtO *S'wark* 95-00; *Sarum* from 98. *3 East Street, Beaminster DT8 3DS* T: (01308) 862806 E: milligan@uwclub.net

MILLIKEN, Matthew Henry Thomas. **d** 11 **p** 12. C Lisburn Ch Ch *Conn* 11-15; I Milltown *Arm* from 15. *10 Derrylileagh Road, Portadown, Craigavon BT62 1TQ* M: 07886-413543 E: matthew28181920@hotmail.com

MILLINCHIP (née DAVENPORT), Susan Jane. b 56. Somerville Coll Ox MA 79. All SS Cen for Miss & Min 10. **d** 14 **p** 15. NSM Witton *Ches* from 14. *2 Manor Grove, Northwich CW8 1JE* T: (01606) 784042 M: 07591-942297 E: revjanemillinchip@outlook.com

MILLING, David Horace. b 29. Oriel Coll Ox BA 51 MA 54 Cam Univ PhD 73. Cuddesdon Coll 54. **d** 56 **p** 57. C Bris St Mary Redcliffe w Temple 56-59; C Fishponds St Jo 59-62; India 62-69; Lect St D Coll Lamp 73-75; C Caversham *Ox* 77-81; C Mapledurham 77-81; C Caversham St Andr 81-86; TV Upper Kennet *Sarum* 86-88; rtd 88; PtO *Glouc* 90-99; *Ex* 00-09. *16 Loram Way, Exeter EX2 8GG* T: (01392) 436261

MILLINGTON, Stuart. b 45. Lich Th Coll 67. **d** 70 **p** 71. C Boulton *Derby* 70-73; C Moseley St Mary *Birm* 73-76; TV Staveley and Barrow Hill *Derby* 76-82; R Wingerworth 82-99; RD Chesterfield 91-97; P-in-c Elton All SS *Man* 99-09; P-in-c Woolfold 07-09; V Kirklees Valley 09-10; AD Bury 05-10; rtd 10; PtO *Man* 10-12. *33 Westways, Wrenthorpe, Wakefield WF2 0TE* T: (01924) 375996 E: stuart@revmillington.wanadoo.co.uk

MILLS, Alan Francis. b 29. Ch Coll Cam BA 52 MA 91. Linc Th Coll 52. **d** 54 **p** 55. C Hucknall Torkard *S'well* 54-58; C Bath Bathwick St Jo *B & W* 58-70; V Drayton 70-76; V Muchelney 70-76; V Alcombe 76-99; rtd 99; PtO *B & W* from 00. *194 Locking Road, Weston-super-Mare BS23 3LU* T: (01934) 622679

MILLS, Alexandra. b 56. Univ of Wales (Abth) BMus 78 CertEd 79. Ripon Coll Cuddesdon 88. **d** 90 **p** 94. Par Dn Earlsfield St Andr *S'wark* 90-94; C Kingston All SS w St Jo 94-99; C Brixton Road Ch Ch 99-00; PtO from 05. *121A Transmere Road, London SW18 3QP* T: (020) 8944 1641 M: 07900-543068 E: aggix1@gmail.com

MILLS, Anne. *See* MILLS, Leslie Anne

MILLS, Anthony James. b 55. Nottm Univ BA. Linc Th Coll. **d** 84 **p** 85. C Mexborough *Sheff* 84-86; C Howden *York* 86-89; V Fylingdales and Hawsker cum Stainsacre 89-95; V Scarborough St Sav w All SS 95-09; P-in-c Scarborough St Martin 02-05; V 05-09; R Failsworth H Family *Man* from 09. *The Rectory, 190 Lord Lane, Failsworth, Manchester M35 0QS* T/F: 0161-681 3644 E: tony.mills@talktalk.net

MILLS, David Francis. b 51. Oak Hill Th Coll 76. **d** 79 **p** 80. C Rodbourne Cheney *Bris* 79-82; C Wolverhampton St Matt *Lich* 82-85; CF 85-88; TV Braunstone *Leic* 88-95; Past Asst to Adn Leic 95-97; C Barkestone w Plungar, Redmile and Stathern 97-99; C Bottesford and Muston 97-99; C Harby, Long Clawson and Hose 97-99; C Vale of Belvoir 00-02; R Winfarthing w Shelfanger w Burston w Gissing etc *Nor* from 02. *The Rectory, Church Lane, Winfarthing, Diss IP22 2EA* T: (01379) 643646 E: revdfmills1812@gmail.com

MILLS, David Graham Mackenzie. *See* MACKENZIE MILLS, David Graham

MILLS (née SHAW), Mrs Elaine Rosemary. b 42. SRN 63. **d** 07 **p** 08. OLM Bris Lockleaze St Mary Magd w St Fran from 07. *15 Blake Road, Bristol BS7 9UJ* E: elaine.mills@lycos.co.uk

MILLS, Canon Geoffrey Charles Malcolm. b 33. Wycliffe Hall Ox 59. **d** 61 **p** 62. C Buckhurst Hill *Chelmsf* 61-65; C Ecclesall *Sheff* 65-69; V Endcliffe 69-78; R Whiston 78-99; Hon Can Sheff Cathl 96-99; rtd 99; PtO *Sheff* from 99. *8 Hall Road, Rotherham S60 2BP* T: (01709) 373863

MILLS, Miss Glenys Christine. b 38. Open Univ BA 81. Dalton Ho Bris 64. **d** 87 **p** 94. Par Dn Clifton Ch Ch w Em *Bris* 87-94; C 94-95; P-in-c Gt w Lt Abington *Ely* 95-00; Chapl Arthur Rank Hospice Cam 95-00; rtd 00; PtO *Bris* from 00. *3 St Monica Court, Cote Lane, Bristol BS9 3TL* T: 0117-949 4703

MILLS, Gordon Derek. b 35. Lich Th Coll 60. **d** 63 **p** 64. C W Derby St Mary *Liv* 63-65; C Clifton w Glapton *S'well* 65-67; V N Wilford St Faith 67-72; V Farnsfield 72-82; P-in-c Kirklington w Hockerton 77-82; P-in-c Brindle and Asst Dir of Educn *Blackb* 82-86; V Gt Budworth *Ches* 86-88; P-in-c Antrobus 87-88; V Gt Budworth and Antrobus 88-92; V Gt Budworth 92-00; rtd 00; PtO *Blackb* 01-04; *York* from 04; *Bradf* 04-07; *Dur* from 04. *Holmelands House, Raby Lane, East Cowton, Northallerton DL7 0BW* T: (01325) 378798

MILLS, Canon Hubert Cecil. b 44. TCD BA 66 MA 71 HDipEd 73. CITC 67. **d** 67 **p** 68. C Dublin Rathfarnham *D & G* 67-72; C Dublin St Steph and St Ann 72-77; I Holmpatrick w Balbriggan and Kenure 77-86; I Killiney H Trin 86-11; Min Can St Patr Cathl Dublin 69-92; Succ St Patr Cathl Dublin 77-92; Preb Rathmichael St Patr Cathl Dublin 92-01; Treas St Patr Cathl Dublin 01-11; rtd 11. *2 Verona, Queens Park, Monkstown, Co Dublin, Republic of Ireland* T: (00353) (1) 214 3689 M: 87-286 8743 E: cecil.mills@alterum.com

MILLS, Jack Herbert. b 14. Selw Coll Cam BA 38 MA 42. Cuddesdon Coll 39. **d** 40 **p** 41. C Camberwell St Geo *S'wark* 40-42; C Southfields St Barn 42-46; USPG 46-47; Chapl Hurstpierpoint Coll 47-52; Chapl K Coll Auckland New Zealand 52-56; Asst Chapl St Pet Colleg Sch Adelaide Australia 57-59; Chapl St Paul's Colleg Sch Hamilton New Zealand 59-61; Chapl Guildford Gr Sch Perth Australia 62-66; Hd Master Carpentaria Coll Darwin 66-73; Hd Master St Wilfrid's Sch Ex 74-79; Chapl Community of St Wilfrid 74-79; Hon C Ewhurst *Chich* 79-81; Hon C Bodiam 79-81; PtO Ex 81-85; Chich 85-87; rtd 87; New Zealand from 87. *14/28 Maranui Avenue, Point Chevalier 1002, Auckland, New Zealand* T: (0064) (9) 849 2243

MILLS, Jennifer Clare. *See* TOMLINSON, Jennifer Clare

MILLS, Mrs Leslie Anne. b 44. K Alfred's Coll Win CertEd 65. SWMTC 99. **d** 02 **p** 03. NSM Kilmington, Stockland, Dalwood, Yarcombe etc Ex from 02. *Gorse Bungalow, Cotleigh, Honiton EX14 9JB* T: (01404) 861430 E: revannemills@googlemail.com

MILLS, Martin. b 58. **d** 14 **p** 15. NSM Bolney *Chich* from 14; NSM Cowfold from 14. *19 Honeywood Road, Horsham RH13 6AE* T: (01403) 267284

MILLS, Melina. *See* BEDEAU, Melina

MILLS, Michael Henry. b 51. AKC 73. St Aug Coll Cant. **d** 74 **p** 75. C Newton Aycliffe *Dur* 74-78; C Padgate *Liv* 78-79; TV 79-95; V Frodsham *Ches* from 95. *The Vicarage, Vicarage Lane, Frodsham, Warrington WA6 7DU* T: (01928) 733378 E: mikehmills@mac.com

MILLS, Michael John. b 52. St Andr Univ BSc 75 Cam Univ PGCE 76. Cranmer Hall Dur 97. **d** 99 **p** 00. C Brockmoor *Worc* 99-03; P-in-c St Leonards St Ethelburga *Chich* 04-09; P-in-c St Leonards St Leon 04-09; R St Leonards St Ethelburga and St Leon 09-11; TV Glascote and Stonydelph *Lich* from 11. *The Vicarage, 90 Briar, Tamworth B77 4DZ* M: 07789-913013 E: michael_mills@talktalk.net

MILLS, Pamela Ann. b 44. Southn Univ DAES 82. S Tr Scheme 94. **d** 97 **p** 98. NSM Hurstbourne Tarrant, Faccombe, Vernham Dean etc *Win* 97-11; rtd 11. *Address temp unknown*

MILLS, Peter James. b 32. Univ Coll Lon LLB 58. **d** 99 **p** 00. NSM Woodchurch *Ches* 99-03; rtd 03; PtO *Ches* from 03. *6 West Heath Court, Gerard Road, West Kirby, Wirral CH48 4ES* T: 0151-625 3314　M: 07989-374499　E: pjmills@uwclub.net

MILLS, Peter John. b 52. Sarum & Wells Th Coll 87. **d** 89 **p** 90. C Chatham St Wm *Roch* 89-92; V Perry Street 92-95; V E Malling 95-00; CF from 00. *c/o MOD Chaplains (Army)* F: 381824　T: (01264) 383430

MILLS, Mrs Philippa Jane. b 63. Rob Coll Cam MA 86 Open Univ PGCE 96. STETS 06. **d** 09 **p** 10. NSM Hook w Warsash *Portsm* 09-12; C Whiteley CD 12-13; C-in-c from 13. *Lower Lapstone, Botley Road, Fair Oak, Eastleigh SO50 7AN* T: (023) 8069 6097　M: 07760-771667　E: revpjmills@hotmail.co.uk

MILLS, Roger Conrad. b 58. Selw Coll Cam BA 79 MA 83. St Jo Coll Nottm 83. **d** 85 **p** 86. C Jesmond H Trin *Newc* 85-88; C Alnwick 88-91; Chapl Newc Univ 91-00; P-in-c Newc St Barn and St Jude 95-97; V Kingston Park from 00. *12 Shannon Court, Newcastle upon Tyne NE3 2XF* T/F: 0191-286 4050　E: rogermills123@yahoo.co.uk

MILLS, Timothy John. b 57. Wye Coll Lon BSc 79. Trin Coll Bris 01. **d** 03 **p** 04. C Chislehurst Ch Ch *Roch* 03-07; V Ticehurst and Flimwell *Chich* from 07. *The Vicarage, Church Street, Ticehurst, Wadhurst TN5 7AB* T: (01580) 200316 M: 07786-540819　E: tim.mills60@ntlworld.com

MILLS-POWELL, Mark Oliver McLay. b 55. Edinburg Th Sem Virginia. **d** 83 **p** 84. C Huyton St Mich *Liv* 83-86; USA 86-95; P-in-c Basildon w Aldworth and Ashampstead *Ox* 95-02; TR Linton *Ely* 02-08; Warden Guild of St Jo and St Mary Magd 08-12; P-in-c Desborough, Brampton Ash, Dingley and Braybrooke *Pet* 12-13; R 13-15. *Address temp unknown* E: mmillspowell1@gmail.com

MILLSON, Brian Douglas. b 53. Univ of W Ontario BA 76 Huron Coll MDiv 84 Open Univ BSc 10. Westcott Ho Cam 82. **d** 83 **p** 84. C Walton-on-Thames *Guildf* 83-86; R Par of the Six Nations Canada 86-89; Canadian Forces Chapl 89-98; CF 98-12; Miss to Seafarers from 12. *Hoevenesbaan 253, 2950 Kapellen, Belgium* T: (0032) (3) 294 5922　M: 46-815 5522　E: brianmillson@gmail.com

MILLSON, Mrs Margaret Lily. b 41. CertEd 61. EMMTC 83. **dss** 86 **d** 87 **p** 94. NSM Bottesford w Ashby *Linc* 86-01; P-in-c St Tudy w St Mabyn and Michaelstow *Truro* 01-10; rtd 10. *Winterbourne, 2 Gwelmeneth Park, St Cleer, Liskeard PL14 5HU* T: (01579) 346338　E: mlmillson@aol.com

MILLWOOD, Stephen Grant. b 44. Sheff City Coll of Educn CertEd 77 Open Univ BA 92. St Jo Coll Nottm 92. **d** 94 **p** 95. C Anston *Sheff* 94-98; V Kimberworth Park 98-09; Bp's Urban Adv 05-09; rtd 09. *6 Quarryfield Drive, Sheffield S9 5AG* T: 0114-243 4948　E: steveandjanetm@mac.com

✠**MILMINE, The Rt Revd Douglas.** b 21. CBE 83. St Pet Hall Ox BA 46 MA 46. Clifton Th Coll 47. **d** 47 **p** 48 **c** 73. C Ilfracombe SS Phil and Jas *Ex* 47-50; C Slough *Ox* 50-53; Chile 54-69; Adn N Chile, Bolivia and Peru 63-69; Hon Can Chile from 69; Area Sec SAMS 69-72; Bp Paraguay 73-85; rtd 86. *1C Clive Court, 24 Grand Parade, Eastbourne BN21 3DD* T: (01323) 734159

MILMINE, Canon Neil Edward Douglas. b 46. Kent Univ BSc 70. Wycliffe Hall Ox 80. **d** 82 **p** 83. C Hailsham *Chich* 82-86; C Horsham 86; TV 86-93; V Patcham 93-11; Can and Preb Chich Cathl 00-11; RD Brighton 02-09; rtd 11; PtO *Chich* from 12; S'wark 12-14. *8 The Willows, Barcombe, Lewes BN8 5FJ* T/F: (01273) 401521　E: n.milmine@yahoo.co.uk

MILNE, Alan. b 54. RMN SRN TCert. Cranmer Hall Dur 89. **d** 91 **p** 92. C Hartlepool St Luke *Dur* 91-94; P-in-c Dalton le Dale 94-00; V 00-05; P-in-c Hawthorn 94-00; R 00-05; R Hawthorn and Murton from 05; AD Easington 03-14. *The Vicarage, Church Lane, Murton, Seaham SR7 9RD* T: 0191-526 2410

MILNE, Miss Christine Helen. b 48. LTCL 71. S'wark Ord Course 83. **dss** 86 **d** 87 **p** 90. Par Dn S Lambeth St Steph *S'wark* 87-89; New Zealand from 89. *NGA Tawa School, Private Bag 1101, Marton 4741, New Zealand* T: (0064) (6) 355 4566 F: 327 7954　E: hmilne@xtra.co.nz

MILNE, Canon James Harley. b 73. Univ of Wales (Lamp) BD 94 New Coll Edin MTh 96. TISEC 95. **d** 98 **p** 99. C Dundee St Mary Magd *Bre* 98-01; Chapl St Marg Res Home Dundee 98-01; R Dundee St Marg *Bre* 01-09; Chapl Ninewells Hosp Dundee 01-09; R Glas St Bride 09-15; Can St Paul's Cathl Dundee 08-09; Hon Can St Paul's Cathl Dundee 09-15; Min Can and Sacr St Paul's Cathl from 15. *8A Amen Court, London EC4M 7BU* T: (020) 7246 8331 E: sacrist@stpaulscathedral.org.uk

MILNE, Norma Campbell. b 45. TISEC 01. **d** 02 **p** 06. OLM Huntly *Mor* 02-03; NSM Elgin w Lossiemouth, Aberlour and Dufftown 05-10; NSM Huntly from 10; NSM Aberchirder from 10; Chapl Grampian Univ Hosp NHS Trust from 07. *26 Green Road, Huntly AB54 8BE* T/F: (01466) 793841 M: 07900-113933　E: normamilne@talktalk.net

MILNE, Sulin. b 54. St Mich Coll Llan BTh 13. **d** 13 **p** 14. C Catheiniog *St D* from 13. *16 Gelli Newydd, Golden Grove, Carmarthen SA32 8LP* T: (01558) 668268 E: sulinmilne@yahoo.co.uk

MILNE SMITH, Christopher. *See* SMITH, Christopher Milne

MILNER, Catherine Mary. b 56. **d** 99 **p** 00. OLM Uttoxeter Area *Lich* 99-03; Sub Chapl HM Pris Foston Hall 99-03; Sub Chapl HM YOI Werrington Ho 99-03; Chapl Blue Coat Comp Sch Walsall 03-05; Hon Chapl Lich Cathl 99-05; rtd 05. *Address temp unknown* M: 07754-444770

MILNER, Darryl Vickers. b 43. Natal Univ BA 63. St Chad's Coll Dur 64. **d** 66 **p** 67. C Oswestry H Trin *Lich* 66-69; S Africa 69-76; New Zealand from 76. *The Vicarage, 47 Church Street, Northcote, North Shore 0627, New Zealand* T: (0064) (9) 480 7568　F: 419 7459　E: dvmilner@clear.net.nz

MILNER, David. *See* MILNER, William David

MILNER, David. b 38. St Aid Birkenhead 63. **d** 66 **p** 67. C Ulverston H Trin *Carl* 66; C Ulverston St Mary w H Trin 66-68; C Mickleover All SS *Derby* 68-71; C Mickleover St Jo 68-71; V 71-82; P-in-c Sandiacre 82-86; P-in-c Doveridge 86-97; P-in-c Sudbury and Somersal Herbert 92-97; R Doveridge, Scropton, Sudbury etc 98-03; RD Longford 86-96 and 01-03; rtd 03; PtO *Lich* 04-08. *21 Greenwood Park, Hednesford WS12 4DQ* T: (01543) 428972

✠**MILNER, The Rt Revd Ronald James.** b 27. Pemb Coll Cam BA 49 MA 52. Wycliffe Hall Ox 51. **d** 53 **p** 54 **c** 88. Succ Sheff Cathl 53-58; V Westwood *Cov* 58-64; V Fletchamstead 64-70; R Southampton St Mary w H Trin *Win* 70-72; P-in-c Southampton St Matt 70-72; LtO 72-73; TR Southampton (City Cen) 73-83; Hon Can Win Cathl 75-83; Adn Linc 83-88; Can and Preb Linc Cathl 83-88; Suff Bp Burnley *Blackb* 88-93; rtd 93; Hon Asst Bp S'well and Nottm from 94. *7 Crafts Way, Southwell NG25 0BL* T: (01636) 816256

MILNER, William David. b 52. St Jo Coll Nottm. **d** 93 **p** 94. C Wollaton *S'well* 93-97; P-in-c Daybrook 97; C W Bridgford 98-99; TV Clifton 99-04; P-in-c Collingham w S Scarle and Besthorpe and Girton 04-10; P-in-c E Trent 10-11; P-in-c Farndon w Thorpe, Hawton and Cotham from 11; AD Newark and S'well from 12. *The Rectory, 3 Marsh Lane, Farndon, Newark NG24 3SS* T: (01636) 650063

MILNES, David Ian. b 45. Chich Th Coll 74. **d** 76 **p** 77. C Walthamstow St Sav *Chelmsf* 76-80; C Chingford SS Pet and Paul 80-83; P-in-c Gt Ilford St Alb 83-87; V 87-09; rtd 09. *Walsingham House, Main Road, Hadlow Down, Uckfield TN22 4ES* T: (01825) 830076　E: frmilnes@aol.com

MILNES, James Clark. b 79. St Chad's Coll Dur BA 00 MA 01. Westcott Ho Cam 03. **d** 05 **p** 06. C Newbold w Dunston *Derby*

05-08; R Alderley w Birtles *Ches* from 08. *St Mary's Rectory, Congleton Road, Nether Alderley, Macclesfield SK10 4TW* T: (01625) 585440 E: jamesclarkmilnes@yahoo.co.uk

MILSON, Julian James. b 70. De Montfort Univ BEd 96. Oak Hill Th Coll BA 04. **d** 04 **p** 05. C Bramcote *S'well* 04-07; C Hove Bp Hannington Memorial Ch *Chich* from 07. *43 Hogarth Road, Hove BN3 5RH* T: (01273) 777020 E: jmilson@bigfoot.com

MILTON, Andrew John. b 54. BD. St Steph Ho Ox. **d** 83 **p** 84. C Highfield *Ox* 83-87; TV Banbury 87-95; P-in-c Thorney Abbey *Ely* 95-02; TR Huntingdon 02-07; P-in-c Gt w Lt Stukeley 04-07; TR Huntingdon w the Stukeleys 07-13; V Huntingdon All SS w St Jo St Mary etc from 13. *The Rectory, 1 The Walks East, Huntingdon PE29 3AP* T: (01480) 412674 E: miltons@walkseast.fsnet.co.uk

MILTON, Miss Angela Daphne. b 50. FInstLEx 79. Oak Hill Th Coll 84. **d** 87 **p** 94. NSM Watford *St Alb* 87-95; NSM St Alb St Mary Marshalswick 95-97; C Stevenage St Mary Shephall w Aston 97-02; P-in-c E Molesey St Paul *Guildf* 02-05; V E Molesey 05-10; rtd 10. *75 Furtherfield, Abbots Langley WD5 0PN* T: (01923) 519453 E: angelamilton@msn.com

MILTON, Claudius James Barton. b 29. K Coll Lon BD 52 AKC 53. **d** 53 **p** 54. C Sudbury St Andr *Lon* 53-56; Asst Chapl and Asst Master Bedford Sch 57-65; Chapl, Asst Master and Ho Master Cranbrook Sch Kent 65-74; Chapl and Asst Master Clayesmore Sch Blandford 74-89; rtd 89. *28 Oakwood Drive, Iwerne Minster, Blandford Forum DT11 8QT* T: (01747) 811792

MILTON, Robert. b 48. **d** 07 **p** 08. NSM Southport Ch Ch *Liv* from 11. *28 Dover Road, Southport PR8 4TB* M: 07721-414724 E: rob.milton@openwork.uk.com

MILTON-THOMPSON, Jonathan Patrick. b 51. Nottm Univ BA 76. Oak Hill Th Coll 86. **d** 88 **p** 89. C Bispham *Blackb* 88-92; C Darfield *Sheff* 92; C-in-c Gt Houghton CD 92-03; P-in-c Livesey *Blackb* 03-11; V from 11; P-in-c Blackb St Barn 10-14; V from 14. *St Andrew's Vicarage, 112 Full View, Blackburn BB2 4QB* T: (01254) 59422 E: jarpmt51hotmail.co.uk

MILVERTON, The Revd and Rt Hon Lord (Fraser Arthur Richard Richards). b 30. Bps' Coll Cheshunt. **d** 57 **p** 58. C Beckenham St Geo *Roch* 57-59; C Sevenoaks St Jo 59-60; C Gt Bookham *Guildf* 60-63; V Okewood 63-67; R Christian Malford w Sutton Benger etc *Bris* 67-93; Public Preacher 93-95; rtd 95; PtO *Sarum* from 96. *7 Betjeman Road, Marlborough SN8 1TL* T: (01672) 514068

MILVERTON, Mrs Ruth Erica. b 32. Open Univ BA 78 Southn Univ MA 82. Sarum Th Coll 83. **dss** 86 **d** 87 **p** 95. Weymouth H Trin *Sarum* 86-87; Hon Par Dn 87-95; NSM 95-02; Dioc NSM Officer 89-97; rtd 02; PtO *Sarum* 02-07. *4 Compass South, Rodwell Road, Weymouth DT4 8QT* T: (01305) 788930 E: rev.milv.compass@care4free.net

MILWARD, Terence George. b 23. Ripon Hall Ox 66. **d** 68 **p** 69. C Selly Oak St Mary *Birm* 68-70; C Edgbaston St Bart 70-75; TV Bournemouth St Pet w St Swithun, H Trin etc *Win* 75-81; R Smannell w Enham Alamein 81-88; rtd 88; PtO *Guildf* 88-10. *Church House Flat, Church Lane, Witley, Godalming GU8 5PN* T: (01428) 685308

MINALL, Peter. b 26. Lon Univ BSc 47. Bps' Coll Cheshunt 51. **d** 53 **p** 54. C Bishop's Stortford St Mich *St Alb* 53-57; C Luton w E Hyde 57-63; C Tuffley *Glouc* 63-65; Asst Youth Chapl 65-69; V Stroud 69-84; RD Bisley 78-84; P-in-c Barnwood 84-91; rtd 91; Chapl Coney Hill Hosp Glouc 86-95; Chapl Severn NHS Trust 95-05; Chapl Glos Primary Care Trust 05-06; PtO *Glouc* from 06. *29 Queen Anne Court, Quedgeley, Gloucester GL2 4JY* T: (01452) 886811 E: peter.minall@btinternet.com

MINAY, Francis Arthur Rodney. b 44. Westcott Ho Cam 66. **d** 68 **p** 69. C Edenbridge *Roch* 68-73; C Bromley St Mark 73-75; V Tudeley w Capel 75-79; TV Littleham w Exmouth *Ex* 79-82; P-in-c Bolton Percy and Asst Chapl to Arts and Recreation in the NE *York* 82-06; rtd 06; LtO *Mor* 07-14; PtO from 14. *Rosedyke, Achintee, Strathcarron IV54 8YX* T: (01520) 722144 E: francisandjaney@btinternet.com

MINCHIN, Anthony John. b 35. St Cath Coll Cam BA 59 MA. Wells Th Coll 59. **d** 61 **p** 62. C Cheltenham St Pet *Glouc* 61-64; C Bushey *St Alb* 64-67; V Cheltenham St Mich *Glouc* 67-74; V Lower Cam 74-82; V Tuffley 82-92; R Huntley and Longhope 92-00; rtd 00; PtO *Glouc* from 00. *2 Melbourne Drive, Stonehouse GL10 2PJ* T: (01453) 828899

MINCHIN, Charles Scott. b 51. Trin Coll Cam BA 72 MA 75. Linc Th Coll 73. **d** 75 **p** 76. C Gt Wyrley *Lich* 75-78; TV Wilnecote 78-82; C Tamworth 82-84; C-in-c Glascote CD 84-88; R Brierley Hill 88-93; R *Worc* 93-03; P-in-c Stonehouse *Glouc* from 03. *The Vicarage, Elms Road, Stonehouse GL10 2NP* T: (01453) 822332 E: cminchin@talktalk.net

MINETT STEVENS, Mrs Christina Noelle. b 68. Hull Univ BSc 92 Sheff Univ BA 14. Coll of Resurr Mirfield 12. **d** 14 **p** 15.

C Scarborough St Mary w Ch Ch and H Apostles *York* from 14. *13 Woodall Avenue, Scarborough YO12 7TH* T: (01723) 378736 E: tina@minettstevens.co.uk

MINION, Canon Arthur. b 65. TCD BTh 92. CITC 89. **d** 92 **p** 93. C Bandon Union *C, C & R* 92-95; I Taunagh w Kilmactranny, Ballysumaghan etc *K, E & A* 95-99; I Shinrone w Aghancon etc *L & K* 99-08; I Crosspatrick Gp *C & O* 08-12; I Wexford and Kilscoran Union from 12; Can Ferns Cathl from 14. *The Rectory, Park, Co Wexford, Republic of Ireland* T: (00353) (53) 914 0652 M: 86-825 1065 E: minionart@gmail.com

MINION, Hazel Elizabeth Alice. b 47. TCD BA 68 HDipEd 69. CITC 00. **d** 03 **p** 04. Aux Min Templebreedy w Tracton and Nohoval *C, C & R* 03-04; Aux Min Carrigaline Union from 04; Chapl Ashton Sch Cork 03-07. *22 Inchvale Drive, Shamrock Lawn, Douglas, Cork, Republic of Ireland* T: (00353) (21) 436 1924 E: hminion22@hotmail.com

MINKKINEN, Mrs Janet Mary. b 63. Ox Brookes Univ BA 12. **d** 10 **p** 12. NSM Cippenham *Ox* 10-14; V from 14. *St Andrew's House, Washington Drive, Slough SL1 5RE* T: (01628) 661994 M: 07856-047960 E: janetminkkinen@hotmail.co.uk

MINNS, David Andrew. b 59. St Jo Coll Nottm 95. **d** 97 **p** 98. C Burpham *Guildf* 97-00; C Knaphill w Brookwood 00-04; R Ewhurst from 04. *The Rectory, The Street, Ewhurst, Cranleigh GU6 7PX* T: (01483) 277584 E: dlkminns@btinternet.com *or* dlkminns@talktalk.net

MINNS, John Alfred. b 38. Oak Hill Th Coll 63. **d** 68 **p** 69. C Cheadle Hulme St Andr *Ches* 68-72; C Hartford 72-74; V Wharton 74-85; V Halliwell St Paul *Man* 85-87; C Halliwell St Pet 87-91; rtd 91; PtO *Glouc* 91-97. *39 Hambidge Lane, Lechlade GL7 3BJ* T: (01367) 253549

MINNS, Canon John Charles. b 42. EAMTC. **d** 85 **p** 86. NSM Heigham St Barn w St Bart *Nor* 85-91; P-in-c Nor St Geo Tombland from 91; Asst Chapl Norfolk and Nor Health Care NHS Trust 92-95; Chapl Nor Sch of Art and Design 99-03; Hon Can Nor Cathl from 05. *18 Thunder Lane, Norwich NR7 0PX* T: (01603) 437000 M: 07951-434485 E: j.minns@ntlworld.com

MINORS, Canon Graham Glyndwr Cavil. b 44. Glouc Sch of Min. **d** 79 **p** 79. Hon C Lower Cam *Glouc* 79-83; C Leckhampton SS Phil and Jas w Cheltenham St Jas 83-89; V Cainscross w Selsley 89-99; RD Stonehouse 97-99; TR Bodmin w Lanhydrock and Lanivet *Truro* 99-13; P-in-c from 13; Chapl N and E Cornwall Primary Care Trust 02-06; Hon Can Truro Cathl from 07. *The Rectory, Priory Road, Bodmin PL31 2AB* T: (01208) 73867 E: revgminors@hotmail.com

MINSON, Roger Graham. b 41. Leeds Univ BA 64. Coll of Resurr Mirfield 64. **d** 66 **p** 67. C Horfield St Greg *Bris* 66-70; C Southmead 70-73; V Lawrence Weston 74-81; TV Knowle 81-93; V Knowle St Martin 93-95; V Fishponds St Mary 95-06; rtd 06; PtO *Heref* 08-13. *2 Box Tree Cottage, Turners Tump, Ruardean GL17 9XG* T: (01594) 546821

MINTON, Bernard John. b 68. St Chad's Coll Dur BA 89 Sheff Univ PhD 14 MRICS 00. Coll of Resurr Mirfield 00. **d** 04 **p** 05. C Lancing w Coombes *Chich* 04-08; TV Ouzel Valley *St Alb* from 08; RD Dunstable from 14. *St Barnabas' Vicarage, Vicarage Road, Leighton Buzzard LU7 2LP* T: (01525) 372149 E: bernardminton@aol.com

MINTY, Selwyn Francis. b 34. St D Coll Lamp 58. **d** 61 **p** 62. C Tonyrefail *Llan* 61-66; C Pontypridd St Cath 66-69; V Cilfynydd 69-84; V Crynant 84-00; rtd 00; PtO *Llan* from 00. *24 Derwen Fawr, Cilfrew, Neath SA10 8NX*

MIR, Amene Rahman. b 58. Man Univ BA 81 PhD 93. Coll of Resurr Mirfield 81. **d** 83 **p** 84. C Walton St Mary *Liv* 83-87; Chapl Walton Hosp Liv 83-87; PtO *Man* 87-90; Asst Chapl Salford Mental Health Unit 90-94; Chapl Salford Mental Health Services NHS Trust 94-96; Chapl R Marsden NHS Trust 96-04; LtO *Lon* 96-04; PtO *S'wark* 96-04. *9 Mylne Close, Upper Mall, London W6 9TE* T: (020) 8741 7961 E: amenemir@ymail.com

MIRZANIA, Ms Bassirat Bibi (Bassi). b 43. Tehran Univ MS 74 Thames Valley Coll of HE BSc 83. **d** 04 **p** 05. Chapl Persian Community UK and NSM Guildf Ch Ch w St Martha-on-the-Hill 04-13; rtd 13. *Shiraz, 11 Nelson Gardens, Guildford GU1 2NZ* T: (01483) 569316 E: bassi.mirzania@btinternet.com

MISTLIN, Mrs Donna Jane. b 68. RGN 89. STETS 03. **d** 08 **p** 09. NSM Crookham *Guildf* 08-11; R Headley All SS 11-13; PtO from 14. *37 Foxhurst Road, Ash Vale, Aldershot GU12 5DY* E: djmistl@aol.com

MITCHAM, Andrew Mark. b 66. Kent Univ BA 87 Leeds Univ BA 90. Coll of Resurr Mirfield 88. **d** 91 **p** 92. C Downham Market w Bexwell *Ely* 91-94; P Shrine of Our Lady of Walsingham 94-96; V W Worthing St Jo *Chich* 96-04; R Eye *St E* 04-13; RD Hartismere 10-13; V Walsingham, Houghton and Barsham *Nor* from 13. *New Vicarage, Church Street, Walsingham NR22 6BL* E: andrew@redmail.co.uk

MITCHELL, Alec Silas. b 52. Man Univ BA 75 MPhil 95. N Bapt Coll 77 Coll of Resurr Mirfield 98. **d** 99 **p** 99. C Ashton *Man* 99-05; TV 05-07; P-in-c Haughton St Anne from 07; Dioc Officer for Racial Justice from 02; Borough Dean Tameside from 10; C Denton Ch Ch from 13; C Denton St Lawr from 13; C Audenshaw St Steph from 13. *St Anne's Rectory, St Anne's Drive, Denton, Manchester M34 3EB*   T: 0161-336 2374 *or* 828 1400   M: 07746-873164   E: fathermit@hotmail.com

MITCHELL, Allan. b 52. Kelham Th Coll 74 Linc Th Coll 78. **d** 78 **p** 79. C Kells *Carl* 78-81; C Upperby St Jo 81-83; V Pennington w Lindal and Marton 83-88; V Westfield St Mary 88-98; P-in-c Dalton-in-Furness 98-02; V Dalton-in-Furness and Ireleth-with-Askam from 02. *The Vicarage, Market Place, Dalton-in-Furness LA15 8AZ*   T: (01229) 462526

MITCHELL, Andrew Patrick (Paddy). b 37. English Coll Valladolid 59 Ripon Coll Cuddesdon 84. **d** 64 **p** 65. In RC Ch 64-85; C Woolwich St Mary w St Mich *S'wark* 85-87; V E Wickham 87-94; P-in-c Walsall St Andr *Lich* 94-00; TV Sedgley All SS *Worc* 00-03; rtd 03; PtO *Birm* 03-04 and from 05. *74 Pershore Road, Selly Oak, Birmingham B29 7NR*   T: 0121-415 5828

MITCHELL, Anne-Marie. b 57. **d** 13 **p** 14. NSM Camberley St Mich Yorktown *Guildf* from 13. *13 Verran Road, Camberley GU15 2ND*

MITCHELL, Anthony. b 54. St Jo Coll Nottm 05. **d** 07 **p** 08. C Plas Newton w Ches Ch Ch 07-10; P-in-c Halton from 10. *27 Halton Brow, Halton, Runcorn WA7 2EH*   T: (01928) 563636   E: vicar@haltonparish.org.uk

MITCHELL, Ashley. *See* MITCHELL, Christopher Ashley

MITCHELL, Mrs Brenda Margaret. b 53. Leeds Univ BA 06. NOC 03. **d** 06 **p** 07. C Golcar *Wakef* 06-10; P-in-c Oldham Moorside *Man* from 10. *The Vicarage, 1 Glebe Lane, Oldham OL1 4SJ*   T: 0161-652 6452   M: 07976-305011   E: brenda_m_mitchell@hotmail.com

MITCHELL, Miss Catherine Amy. b 62. Cov Poly BEng St Jo Coll Dur BA 13. Cranmer Hall Dur 11. **d** 13 **p** 14. C Croxdale and Tudhoe *Dur* from 13. *4 Watson Park, Spennymoor DL16 6NB*   T: (01388) 819792

MITCHELL, Christian Strang. b 72. Ripon Coll Cuddesdon 12. **d** 14 **p** 15. C Uckfield *Chich* from 14. *7 Park View Road, Uckfield TN22 1JP*   T: (01825) 763475   E: revdmitch@gmail.com

MITCHELL, Christopher Allan. b 51. Newc Univ BA 72. Oak Hill Th Coll 82. **d** 84 **p** 85. C Guisborough *York* 84-87; C Thornaby on Tees 87-88; TV 88-92; V Dent w Cowgill *Bradf* 92-98; R Barney, Fulmodeston w Croxton, Hindringham etc *Nor* 98-03; R Hulland, Atlow, Kniveton, Bradley and Hognaston *Derby* 03-11; RD Ashbourne 09-11; rtd 11; PtO *York* from 12. *42 Melton Avenue, York YO30 5QG*   T: (01904) 623872   E: pennychris51@btinternet.com

MITCHELL, Christopher Ashley. b 69. Leeds Univ BA(Econ) 91. Ridley Hall Cam 92. **d** 95 **p** 96. Min Can St As Cathl 95-98; CF 98-02; Chapl RAF from 02. *Chaplaincy Services (RAF), HQ Air Command, RAF High Wycombe HP14 4UE*   T: (01494) 496800   F: 496343   E: mrm-chaplaincyseniorpadre@mod.uk

MITCHELL, Christopher Derek. b 61. Univ of Wales (Lamp) BA 85 Leic Univ MA 86 Qu Coll Cam BA 88 MA 92 Auckland Univ of Tech MHSc 04. Westcott Ho Cam 87. **d** 89 **p** 90. C Streetly *Lich* 89-92; C Brookfield St Mary *Lon* 92-96; Hon C Hornsey St Mary w St Geo 99-02; LtO Dio Auckland New Zealand 03-07; PtO *Lon* 07; C Hendon St Mary and Ch Ch 07-08; V Edmonton St Pet w St Martin from 08. *St Peter's Vicarage, St Peter's Road, London N9 8JP*   T: (020) 8807 7431   E: fatherchris@btinternet.com

MITCHELL, Clare Elizabeth. *See* GRIFFITHS, Clare Elizabeth

MITCHELL, Canon David George. b 35. QUB BA 56. Sarum Th Coll 59. **d** 61 **p** 62. C Westbury-on-Trym H Trin *Bris* 61-64; C Cricklade w Latton 64-68; V Fishponds St Jo 68-77; RD Stapleton 76-77; TR E Bris 77-87; R Syston 87-94; V Warmley 87-94; P-in-c Bitton 87-94; R Warmley, Syston and Bitton 94-01; RD Bitton 87-93; Hon Can Bris Cathl 87-01; rtd 01; P-in-c Chedworth, Yanworth and Stowell, Coln Rogers etc *Glouc* 01-09; AD Northleach 04-09; PtO *Bris* from 01. *32 Flower Way, Longlevens, Gloucester GL2 9JD*   T: (01452) 500119   E: canongeorgemitchell@btinternet.com

MITCHELL, Preb David Norman. b 35. Tyndale Hall Bris 64. **d** 67 **p** 68. C Marple All SS *Ches* 67-70; C St Helens St Helen *Liv* 70-72; V S Lambeth St Steph *S'wark* 72-78; P-in-c Brixton Road Ch Ch 73-75; SE Area Sec CPAS 78-81; R Uphill *B & W* 81-92; TR 92-01; Chapl Weston Area Health NHS Trust 86-01; Preb Wells Cathl 90-10; rtd 01; PtO *B & W* from 02. *3 Pizey Close, Clevedon BS21 7TP*   T: (01275) 349176   E: davidnmitchell@talktalk.net

MITCHELL, Canon Edwin. b 48. St Jo Coll Nottm BTh 74. **d** 74 **p** 75. C Worksop St Jo *S'well* 74-77; C Waltham Abbey *Chelmsf* 77-80; V Whiston *Liv* 80-91; R Wombwell *Sheff* 91-99; V Mortomley St Sav High Green 99-11; P-in-c Stocksbridge 06-07; AD Ecclesfield 01-07; Hon Can Sheff Cathl 07-11; rtd 11; PtO *Leeds* from 12. *3 North View, Lothersdale, Keighley BD20 8EX*   T: (01535) 631837   E: edwin.mitchell1@btopenworld.com

MITCHELL, Elizabeth Edgar. d 14. C S Cheltenham *Glouc* from 14. *Address temp unknown*

MITCHELL, Eric Sidney. b 24. S Dios MinI Tr Scheme 77. **d** 80 **p** 81. NSM Portland All SS w St Pet *Sarum* 80-83; C 88-92; Bermuda 83-88; Chapl HM Pris The Verne 91-92; rtd 92; PtO *Sarum* from 92. *10 Underhedge Gardens, Portland DT5 2DX*   T: (01305) 821059   E: ericandmay@talktalk.net

MITCHELL, Geoffrey. b 36. SS Coll Cam BA 60 MA 64 Nottm Univ BA 97 CEng 66 FIMechE 76 FCIT 92. EMMTC 88. **d** 91 **p** 92. NSM Oaks in Charnwood and Copt Oak *Leic* 91-94; NSM Loughborough All SS w H Trin 94-00; P-in-c Oaks in Charnwood and Copt Oak 00-03; NSM Shepshed and Oaks in Charnwood 03-04; Dioc NSM Officer 98-02; rtd 04; PtO *Leic* from 04. *36 Brick Kiln Lane, Shepshed, Loughborough LE12 9EL*   T: (01509) 502280   E: mitchell.household@talk21.com

MITCHELL, Geoffrey Peter. b 30. Liv Univ BEng 57 Man Univ MSc 68. Wells Th Coll 57. **d** 59 **p** 60. C Bradford cum Beswick *Man* 59-61; R Man St Pet Oldham Road w St Jas 61-64; LtO 64-68; Hon C Unsworth 68-86; V Woolfold 86-95; rtd 95; PtO *Man* from 95. *14 Redfearn Wood, Rochdale OL12 7GA*   T: (01706) 638180

MITCHELL, George. *See* MITCHELL, David George

MITCHELL, George Alfred. b 23. TCD BA 45 MA 56. **d** 46 **p** 47. C Belfast St Matt *Conn* 46-48; C Ballymoney w Finvoy and Rasharkin 48-51; C Cathl Miss Belfast St Anne 51-52; I Broomhedge 52-58; I Carrickfergus 59-70; I Bangor St Comgall *D & D* 70-88; Can Belf Cathl 78-88; rtd 88. *2 Glendun Park, Bangor BT20 4UX*   T: (028) 9146 0882

MITCHELL, Geraint Owain. b 71. Lincs & Humberside Univ BA 96 Leeds Univ BA. Coll of Resurr Mirfield 99. **d** 02 **p** 03. C Bridlington Em *York* 02-05; V Brigg, Wrawby and Cadney cum Howsham *Linc* from 05; V Bonby from 10; V Worlaby from 10. *The Vicarage, 10 Glanford Road, Brigg DN20 8DJ*   T: (01652) 653989   E: owain.mitchell@btopenworld.com

MITCHELL, Gordon Frank Henry. b 26. FIFireE. Sarum & Wells Th Coll 74. **d** 77 **p** 78. NSM Alderbury and W Grimstead *Sarum* 77-91; NSM Alderbury Team 91-96; PtO 96-07. *Seefeld, Southampton Road, Whaddon, Salisbury SP5 3EB*   T: (01722) 710516

MITCHELL, Graham Bell. b 40. Otago Univ BA 64 MA 65 Worc Coll Ox BA 73 MA 76. St Chad's Coll Dur 66. **d** 68 **p** 69. C Bris St Agnes w St Simon 68-71; C Bedminster St Mich 73-76; V Auckland St Pet *Dur* 76-78; Vice-Prin Chich Th Coll 78-83; C Brighton St Pet w Chpl Royal and St Jo *Chich* 83-86; P-in-c Scaynes Hill 86-96; V 96-04; rtd 04. *18B Ballin Street, Ellersie, Auckland 1051, New Zealand*   T: (0064) (9) 579 6988

MITCHELL, Mrs Helen Miranda. b 55. **d** 10 **p** 11. NSM Sudbury and Chilton *St E* from 10. *The Old Vicarage, Church Street, Stoke by Nayland, Colchester CO6 4QL*   T: (01206) 262612   E: helenoldvic@hotmail.com

MITCHELL, Ian. *See* MITCHELL, Stuart Ian

MITCHELL, Jolyon Peter. b 64. Selw Coll Cam BA 88 MA 90 St Jo Coll Dur MA 93 Edin Univ PhD 97. Cranmer Hall Dur. **d** 93 **p** 94. NSM St Mary's Cathl 93-97; NSM Edin Ch Ch 97-01; NSM Edin St Jas from 01; Lect Edin Univ 93-01; Sen Lect from 01; Visiting Fell Clare Hall Cam 02. *11 Eildon Street, Edinburgh EH3 5JU*   T: 0131-226 1092 *or* 650 8900   E: jolyon.mitchell@ed.ac.uk

MITCHELL, Karen Irene. b 68. Westcott Ho Cam 07. **d** 09 **p** 10. C Cheshunt *St Alb* 09-13; P-in-c Bridgemary *Portsm* from 13; P-in-c Elson from 13. *St Matthew's Vicarage, 7 Duncton Way, Gosport PO13 0FD*   T: (01329) 829883   M: 07834-322943   E: karen.mitchell@talk.talk.net

MITCHELL, Kevin. b 49. Newc Univ BSc 71 Ox Univ BA 83. Ripon Coll Cuddesdon 81. **d** 83 **p** 84. C Cantril Farm *Liv* 83-86; Chapl N Middx Hosp 86-90; C Gt Cambridge Road St Jo and St Jas *Lon* 86-90; P-in-c Cricklewood St Pet 90-96; V Whetstone St Jo 96-10; rtd 10. *32 Guildford Street, Brighton BN1 3LS*   T: (01273) 203429   E: kevin.mitchell.49@googlemail.com

MITCHELL, Owain. *See* MITCHELL, Geraint Owain

MITCHELL, Paddy. *See* MITCHELL, Andrew Patrick

MITCHELL, The Very Revd Patrick Reynolds. b 30. FSA 81 Mert Coll Ox BA 52 MA 56. Wells Th Coll 52. **d** 54 **p** 55. C Mansfield St Mark *S'well* 54-57; Chapl Wells Th Coll and PV Wells Cathl 57-61; V Milton *Portsm* 61-67; V Frome St Jo and P-in-c Woodlands *B & W* 67-73; Dir of Ords 70-74; Dean Wells 73-89; Dean Windsor and Dom Chapl to The Queen 89-98; rtd 98; PtO *Ex* from 98; *Sarum* from 00. *Wolford Lodge, Dunkeswell, Honiton EX14 4SQ*   T: (01404) 841244

MITCHELL, Canon Richard John Anthony. b 64. St Martin's Coll Lanc BA 85 PGCE 86. Sarum & Wells Th Coll 88. **d** 91

p 92. C Kendal H Trin *Carl* 91-95; TV Kirkby Lonsdale 95-04; P-in-c Badgeworth, Shurdington and Witcombe w Bentham *Glouc* 04-09; R from 09; AD Glouc N 04-09; AD Severn Vale from 09; Hon Can Glouc Cathl from 10. *The Vicarage, School Lane, Shurdington, Cheltenham GL51 4TF* T: (01242) 702911 E: richard.mitchell@talk21.com

MITCHELL, Robert Hugh. b 53. Ripon Coll Cuddesdon. **d** 82 **p** 83. C E Dulwich St Jo *S'wark* 82-86; C Cambridge Gt St Mary w St Mich *Ely* 86-90; Chapl Girton Coll Cam 86-90; Asst Chapl Win Coll 90-91; Chapl Addenbrooke's NHS Trust 91-93; Chapl Portsm Hosps NHS Trust 93-95; Chapl Mental Health Chapl Portsm Health Care NHS Trust 93-95; Chapl R Free London NHS Foundn Trust from 95. *The Chaplains' Office, The Royal Free Hospital, Pond Street, London NW3 2QG* T: (020) 7830 2742 *or* 7794 0500 ext 3096 E: robert.mitchell@royalfree.nhs.uk

MITCHELL, Robert McFarlane. b 50. Man Univ BA 72 Lambeth STh 92. Wycliffe Hall Ox 73. **d** 75 **p** 76. C Tonbridge SS Pet and Paul *Roch* 75-80; CF 80-08; P-in-c Tillington *Chich* from 08; P-in-c Duncton from 08; P-in-c Upwaltham from 08. *The Rectory, Tillington, Petworth GU28 9AH* T: (01798) 342827 M: 07530-852896 E: robert@revbobm.plus.com

MITCHELL, Miss Sandra Helen. b 47. ERMC 03. **d** 06 **p** 07. NSM Wroxham w Hoveton and Belaugh *Nor* 06-07; NSM Martham and Repps w Bastwick, Thurne etc from 07. *White House Farm, Tower Road, Repps with Bastwick, Great Yarmouth NR29 5JW* T: (01692) 670473 E: shmitch@tiscali.co.uk

MITCHELL, Sarah Rachel. *See* TAN, Sarah Rachel

MITCHELL, Sheila Rosemary. b 53. Univ Coll Ches CertEd 74 AdDipEd 80. NOC 93. **d** 96 **p** 97. NSM Plemstall w Guilden Sutton *Ches* 96-98; C New Brighton St Jas w Em 98-00; C New Brighton All SS 98-00; P-in-c Weston 00-02; V 02-07; PtO from 07. *Casa Robila 21, Calle Jilguero, Mondron, 29710 Periana (Málaga), Spain* E: revsmitchell@aol.com

MITCHELL, Stephen Andrew John. b 56. Ch Ch Coll Cant CertEd 78 K Coll Lon AKC 77 BD 80 MA 02 Lambeth STh 90 Heythrop Coll Lon MTh 05 PhD 10. Coll of Resurr Mirfield 80. **d** 82 **p** 83. C Chatham St Steph *Roch* 82-87; C Edenbridge 87-91; V from 91; P-in-c Crockham Hill H Trin 91-14; Chapl Invicta Community Care NHS Trust from 91. *The Vicarage, Mill Hill, Edenbridge TN8 5DA* T: (01732) 862258 F: 864335 E: sspvicarage@hotmail.com

MITCHELL, Canon Stephen John. b 51. Ex Univ BA 73 Fitzw Coll Cam BA 78 MA. Ridley Hall Cam 76. **d** 79 **p** 80. C Gt Malvern St Mary *Worc* 79-81; Prec Leic Cathl 82-85; R Barrow upon Soar w Walton le Wolds 85-02; P-in-c Gazeley w Dalham, Moulton and Kentford *St E* 02-04; V Dalham, Gazeley, Higham, Kentford and Moulton from 05; P-in-c Mildenhall from 14; RD from 08; Min Can St E Cathl 05-10; Hon Can St E Cathl from 10. *All Saints' Vicarage, The Street, Gazeley, Newmarket CB8 8RB* T: (01638) 552630 E: smitch4517@aol.com

MITCHELL, Steven. b 58. St Jo Coll Nottm BTh 83. **d** 83 **p** 84. C Ovenden *Wakef* 83-87; V Gawthorpe and Chickenley Heath 87-98; V Birkenshaw w Hunsworth 98-05; R Newport w Longford, Chetwynd and Forton *Lich* 05-11; V Newport w Longford, and Chetwynd from 11. *18A Underwood Road, Newcastle ST5 6QF* E: smitchellnewport@btinternet.com

MITCHELL, Stuart. b 53. Cranmer Hall Dur 01. **d** 03 **p** 04. C Pocklington and Owsthorpe and Kilnwick Percy etc *York* 03-06; P-in-c Edith Weston w N Luffenham and Lyndon w Manton *Pet* 06-10; P-in-c Preston and Ridlington w Wing and Pilton 06-10; C Empingham and Exton w Horn w Whitwell 06-10; R Empingham, Edith Weston, Lyndon, Manton etc 11; R Stour Valley *St E* from 11. *The Vicarage, 14 High Street, Clare, Sudbury CO10 8NY* T: (01787) 278482

MITCHELL, Stuart Ian. b 50. Wadh Coll Ox BA 71 DPhil 74. S'wark Ord Course 81. **d** 85 **p** 87. NSM Charlton St Luke w H Trin *S'wark* 85-86; NSM Kidbrooke St Jas 86-88; NSM Newbold w Dunston *Derby* 88-94; C 94-96; C Newbold and Gt Barlow 96-97; P-in-c Matlock Bank 97-03; RD Wirksworth 98-03; P-in-c Mackworth All SS 03-10; P-in-c Mugginton and Kedleston 03-10; P-in-c Kirk Langley 03-10; rtd 10. *22 Old Hall Close, Pilsley, Chesterfield S45 8JD* E: ianandmarym@tiscali.co.uk

MITCHELL, Tim. b 63. Trin Coll Bris 95. **d** 97 **p** 98. C Cromer *Nor* 97-01; P-in-c Selston *S'well* 01-05; P-in-c Sutton in Ashfield St Mich 05-13. *48 Eden Street, Alvaston, Derby DE24 8RB* T: (01332) 405131 E: timmitchell.t@googlemail.com

MITCHELL, Wendy Mary. b 47. Glas Univ MA 70 Callendar Park Coll of Educn Falkirk PGCE 71. Trin Coll Bris 99. **d** 01 **p** 02. C Yatton Moor *B & W* 01-07; TV Parkham, Alwington, Buckland Brewer etc *Ex* from 07. *The Rectory, Old Market Drive, Woolsery, Bideford EX39 5QF* T: (01237) 431160 E: revwendym@aol.com

MITCHELL-INNES, Canon Charles William. b 47. Pemb Coll Cam BA 69 MA 73. Sarum Th Coll 83. **d** 86 **p** 87. Asst Chapl Sherborne Sch 86-89; Chapl Milton Abbey Sch Dorset 90-96; Conduct Eton Coll 96-07; rtd 07; V of Close Sarum Cathl 07-14; Can and Preb Sarum Cathl from 13. *South Bank, South Street, Sherborne DT9 3LZ* T: (01935) 812656 E: charlesm-i@hotmail.com

MITCHELL-INNES, James Alexander. b 39. Ch Ch Ox BA 64 MA 66. Lon Coll of Div 65. **d** 67 **p** 68. C Cullompton *Ex* 67-71; Nigeria 71-75; P-in-c Puddletown w Athelhampton and Burleston *Sarum* 75-78; R Puddletown and Tolpuddle 78-82; V Win Ch Ch 82-92; V Titchfield *Portsm* 92-98; rtd 98; PtO *Win* from 99. *115 Battery Hill, Winchester SO22 4BH* T: (01962) 859039 E: jmitchellinnes@gmail.com

MITCHINSON, Frank. b 37. AKC 60. **d** 61 **p** 62. C Cross Heath *Lich* 61-64; C Forrabury w Minster and Trevalga *Truro* 64-68; C Harpenden St Nic *St Alb* 68-70; R Southwick St Mich *Chich* 70-83; V Billingshurst 83-88; V Preston 88-02; rtd 02; P-in-c Bolney *Chich* 02-05. *7 St Cyr, 26 Douglas Avenue, Exmouth EX8 2HA* T: (01395) 268438

MITCHINSON, Canon Ronald. b 35. Westmr Coll Ox MA 91. Linc Th Coll 66. **d** 68 **p** 69. C Heworth St Mary *Dur* 68-72; C Banbury *Ox* 72-73; TV 73-76; New Zealand 76-82; TR Banbury *Ox* 82-86; RD Deddington 84-86; Ind Chapl 86-92; Hon Can Ch Ch 90-92; TV Brayton *York* 92-96; Sen Chapl Selby Coalfield Ind Chapl 92-96; rtd 96; PtO *York* 04-11. *2 The Cottages, The Green, Stillington, York YO61 1JY* T: (01347) 810064 E: ronmitchinson@mac.com

MITFORD, Bertram William Jeremy (Bill). b 27. Wells Th Coll 62. **d** 64 **p** 65. C Hollinwood *Man* 64-67; C Atherton 67-68; C Frome St Jo *B & W* 68-71; V Cleeve 72-74; V Cleeve w Chelvey and Brockley 74-79; Chapl HM Pris Shepton Mallet 79-92; C Shepton Mallet *B & W* 79-84; C Shepton Mallet w Doulting 84-92; rtd 92. *21 Monkton Road, Honiton EX14 1PZ* T: (01404) 42632

MITRA, Avijit (Munna). b 53. Keble Coll Ox BA 76. Ox NSM Course 84. **d** 88 **p** 89. NSM Abingdon *Ox* 88-96; Asst Chapl Abingdon Sch 88-96; Sen Chapl Ch Hosp Horsham 96-09; Hd Classics K Sch Roch from 09. *The Old Archdeaconry Flat, The Precinct, Rochester ME1 1SX* T: (01634) 400576 M: 07713-727708 E: avijit@mitra1953.plus.com *or* amm@ksr.org.uk

MITRA, Mrs Nicola Jane. b 54. St Hugh's Coll Ox BA 76 MA 81 PGCE 77. Ox Min Course 92. **d** 94 **p** 95. NSM Abingdon *Ox* 94-96; Asst Chapl Ch Hosp Horsham 96-08; Asst Chapl Maidstone and Tunbridge Wells NHS Trust from 08; PtO *Roch* from 10. *The Old Archdeaconry Flat, The Precinct, Rochester ME1 1SX* T: (01634) 400576 *or* (01622) 224569 M: 07976-966105 E: nicola@mitra1953.plus.com *or* nicolamitra@nhs.net

MITSON, Mrs Carol Mae. b 46. SRN SCM. Oak Hill NSM Course 89. **d** 93 **p** 94. NSM Lawford *Chelmsf* 93-96; NSM Elmstead 96-98; NSM Harwich 96-98; NSM Dedham 98-00; PtO from 01. *Drift Cottage, The Drift, Dedham, Colchester CO7 6AH* T/F: (01206) 323116 E: mitson@onetel.net.uk

MITSON, John Dane. b 29. Solicitor 56 SS Coll Cam MA 53 LLM 54. Oak Hill Th Coll 91 EAMTC 93. **d** 94 **p** 95. Dioc Registrar and Legal Sec to Bp *St E Chelmsf* 75-97; NSM Greenstead 94-96; NSM Elmstead 96-98; NSM Dedham 98-00; PtO from 00. *Drift Cottage, The Drift, Dedham, Colchester CO7 6AH* T/F: (01206) 323116 E: mitson@onetel.net.uk

MITSON, Miss Joyce. b 37. Man Univ CertEd 64. Trin Coll Bris 77. **dss** 79 **d** 87 **p** 94. Wellington w Eyton *Lich* 79-85; Farnworth *Liv* 85-91; Par Dn 87-91; Team Dn Bilston *Lich* 91-94; TV 94; Lich Local Min Adv 91-94; C W Bromwich St Jas 94-97; C W Bromwich St Jas w St Paul 97-98; rtd 98; PtO *Man* 00-12. *13 Birkenhills Drive, Bolton BL3 4TX* T: (01204) 655081

MITSON, Miss Judith Anne. b 74. Man Metrop Univ BA 97. St Jo Coll Nottm 13. **d** 15. C Harpurhey *Man* from 15. *Address temp unknown* E: sonofmit1@gmail.com

MITTON, Christopher Michael James. b 84. Leeds Univ BA 08. Trin Coll Bris MA 13. **d** 13 **p** 14. C Holbeck *Leeds* from 13. *139 Dewsbury Road, Leeds LS11 5NW* M: 07759-558602 E: cmjmitton@hotmail.co.uk

MITTON, Canon Michael Simon. b 53. Ex Univ BA 75. St Jo Coll Nottm 76. **d** 78 **p** 79. C High Wycombe *Ox* 78-82; TV Kidderminster St Geo *Worc* 82-89; Dir Angl Renewal Min 89-97; Dep Dir Acorn Chr Foundn 97-03; Renewing Min Project Officer *Derby* 03-06; Miss and Min Development Adv 06-09; Dioc Fresh Expressions Adv 09-13; Fresh Expressions Officer from 13; P-in-c Derby St Paul from 09; Hon Can Derby Cathl from 11. *264 Broadway, Derby DE22 1BN* T: (01332) 552448 E: michaelmitton@btinternet.com

MLEMETA, Kedmon Hezron. b 60. CertEd 78. CA Tr Coll Nairobi 86. **d** 89 **p** 90. Tanzania 89-96 and from 99; P-in-c

Loughb Gd Shep *Leic* 96-99. *The Diocese of Mount Kilimanjaro, PO Box 1057, Arusha, Tanzania*

MOAT, Terry. b 61. Nottm Univ BTh 92. Aston Tr Scheme 86 Linc Th Coll 88. **d** 92 **p** 93. C Caterham *S'wark* 92-96; Hon C Tynemouth Priory *Newc* 04-06; C Morpeth 06-09; V Choppington from 09. *The Vicarage, Scotland Gate, Choppington NE62 5SX* T: (01670) 822216

MOATE, Gerard Grigglestone. b 54. BA FRSA 01. Oak Hill Th Coll 79. **d** 82 **p** 83. C Mildmay Grove St Jude and St Paul *Lon* 82-85; C Hampstead St Jo 85-88; P-in-c Pinxton *Derby* 88; V Charlesworth and Dinting Vale 88-95; V Dedham *Chelmsf* 95-15; RD Dedham and Tey 98-03; Chapl Bloxham Sch from 15; PtO *Ox* from 15. *Bloxham School, Banbury Road, Bloxham, Banbury OX15 4PE* T: (01295) 724301
E: ggm@bloxhamschool.com *or* gerard@moate.org

MOATE, Phillip. b 47. RGN 70 RNT 75. NOC 87. **d** 90 **p** 91. NSM Upper Holme Valley *Wakef* 90-92; NSM Almondbury Deanery 92-94; NSM Honley *Wakef* 94-95; P-in-c Roos and Garton w Tunstall, Grimston and Hilston *York* 95-02; R Lockington and Lund and Scorborough w Leconfield 02-09; rtd 09; PtO *York* from 09. *58 Pilmar Lane, Roos, Hull HU12 0HN* T: (01964) 671321 E: phillipmoate@btinternet.com

MOATT, Canon Richard Albert. b 54. K Coll Lon BD 76 AKC 76. Linc Th Coll 80. **d** 81 **p** 82. C Egremont and Haile *Carl* 81-85; V Addingham, Edenhall, Langwathby and Culgaith 85-04; P-in-c Skirwith, Ousby and Melmerby w Kirkland 98-04; V Cross Fell Gp 04-13; RD Penrith 09-13; Hon Can Carl Cathl 10-13; R Lewes St Anne and St Mich and St Thos etc *Chich* from 13. *St Anne's Rectory, 57 St Anne's Crescent, Lewes BN7 1SD* T: (01273) 472545
E: moatt@btinternet.com

MOBBERLEY, Keith John. b 56. BA. Westcott Ho Cam. **d** 84 **p** 85. C Coventry Caludon *Cov* 84-87; C Kenilworth St Nic 87-92; V Keresley and Coundon 92-98; P-in-c Hatton w Haseley, Rowington w Lowsonford etc 98-00; R from 00. *North Ferncumbe Rectory, Hatton Green, Hatton, Warwick CV35 7LA* T: (01926) 484332

MOBBERLEY, Mrs Susan. b 57. Kent Univ BA 79. Westcott Ho Cam 81. **dss** 84 **d** 90 **p** 94. Coventry Caludon *Cov* 84-87; LtO 87-92; NSM Keresley and Coundon 92-98; NSM Hatton w Haseley, Rowington w Lowsonford etc from 98. *North Ferncumbe Rectory, Hatton Green, Hatton, Warwick CV35 7LA* T: (01926) 484332

MOBBS, Bernard Frederick. b 26. Open Univ BA. S'wark Ord Course 71. **d** 72 **p** 73. C Purley St Barn *S'wark* 72-74; Vice-Prin S'wark Ord Course 74-80; P-in-c Sydenham St Bart *S'wark* 80-87; V Dormansland 87-92; rtd 92; PtO *Chich* from 92. *19 Ramsay Hall, 11-13 Byron Road, Worthing BN11 3HN* T: (01903) 237663

MOBERLY (née McCLURE), Mrs Jennifer Lynne. b 62. Ball State Univ (USA) BSc 84. Cranmer Hall Dur 98. **d** 01 **p** 02. C Belmont *Dur* 01-07; C Belmont and Pittington 07-08; Chapl St Mary's Coll Dur from 09. *St Mary's College, Elvet Hill Road, Durham DH1 3LR* E: j.l.moberly@durham.ac.uk

MOBERLY, Richard Hamilton. b 30. Trin Hall Cam BA 53 MA 57. Cuddesdon Coll 53. **d** 55 **p** 56. C Walton St Mary *Liv* 55-59; C Kensington St Mary Abbots w St Geo *Lon* 59-63; R Chingola Zambia 63-66; V Kennington Cross St Anselm *S'wark* 67-73; TV N Lambeth 74-80; Ind Chapl 80-95; rtd 95; PtO *S'wark* from 95. *Flat 2, 1 Chester Way, London SE11 4UT* T: (020) 7735 2233 E: richard@richardmoberly.org.uk

MOBERLY, Robert Walter Lambert. b 52. New Coll Ox MA 77 Selw Coll Cam MA 80 Trin Coll Cam PhD 81. Ridley Hall Cam 74. **d** 81 **p** 82. C Knowle *Birm* 81-85; Lect Dur Univ from 85; PtO *Dur* from 85. *Department of Theology, Abbey House, Palace Green, Durham DH1 3RS* T: 0191-334 3953
E: r.w.l.moberly@durham.ac.uk

MOBEY, Jonathan Lee. b 73. Pemb Coll Cam MA 95 St Edm Hall Ox BM, BCh 98 MRCGP 02. Wycliffe Hall Ox BA 07. **d** 08 **p** 09. NSM Ox St Andr 08-11; R Harwell w Chilton from 11. *The Rectory, Church Lane, Harwell, Didcot OX11 0EZ* T: (01235) 799376 E: rectora@harwellandchiltonchurches.org.uk

MOBSBY, Ian Jonathan. b 68. Leeds Univ BHSc 93 SROT 93 Anglia Ruskin Univ MA 06. EAMTC 00. **d** 04 **p** 05. C Westmr St Matt *Lon* 04-11; C St Mary Aldermary 11-12; P-in-c from 12. *Moot Community, St Mary Aldermary, Watling Street, London EC4M 9BW* T: (020) 7248 9902 E: ian.mobsby@moot.uk.net

MOCK, David Lawrence. b 64. Whitman Coll Washington BA 86 Heythrop Coll Lon MTh 01. Trin Coll Bris BA 98. **d** 98 **p** 99. C Tadworth *S'wark* 98-01; P-in-c Sutton St Geo *Ches* 01-02; C Macclesfield Team 01-02; TV from 02. *2 The Mallards, Chester Road, Macclesfield SK11 8PT*
E: revdavem@googlemail.com

MOCKFORD (née WATKINS), Mrs Betty Anne. b 45. Leeds Univ BA 66 Nottm Univ CertEd 67. EAMTC 94. **d** 97 **p** 98. C Ipswich St Aug *St E* 97-00; P-in-c Charsfield w Debach,

Monewden, Hoo etc 01-06; rtd 06; PtO *St E* from 06. *Mirembe, 10 Castle Brooks, Framlingham, Woodbridge IP13 9SF* T: (01728) 724193 M: 07890-110741

MOCKFORD, Preb Peter John. b 57. Nottm Univ BSc 79 St Jo Coll Dur BA 88. Cranmer Hall Dur 86. **d** 89 **p** 90. C Tamworth *Lich* 89-94; V Blurton 94-11; P-in-c Dresden 04-11; V Blurton and Dresden from 11; P-in-c Longton Hall 08-13; Preb Lich Cathl from 15. *The Vicarage, School Lane, Stoke-on-Trent ST3 3DU* T: (01782) 312163 E: p.mockford@ukgateway.net

MODY, Rohintan Keki. b 63. New Coll Ox BA 85 MA 88 Fitzw Coll Cam MPhil 05 Aber Univ PhD 08. Oak Hill Th Coll BA 00. **d** 00 **p** 01. C Wolverhampton St Luke *Lich* 00-03; C Virginia Water *Guildf* 08-11; P-in-c Throop *Win* from 11. *St Paul's Vicarage, 1 Chesildene Avenue, Bournemouth BH8 0AZ* T: (01202) 531064 E: romody@hotmail.com

MOESEL, Joseph Sams. b 65. Villanova Univ USA BA 90 Harris Man Coll Ox BTh 93 Regent's Park Coll Ox MTh 03. Ripon Coll Cuddesdon 93. **d** 95 **p** 96. C Twigworth, Down Hatherley, Norton, The Leigh etc *Glouc* 95-98; CF 98-06; Sen CF from 06. *c/o MOD Chaplains (Army)* T: (01264) 383430 F: 381824

MOFFAT, Canon George. b 46. Edin Univ BD 77 Open Univ BA 87 Bradf Univ MA 04. Edin Th Coll 67. **d** 72 **p** 73. C Falkirk *Edin* 73-76; C Edin St Pet 76-81; Chapl Edin Univ 77-81; C Heston *Lon* 81-84; V S Elmsall *Wakef* 84-93; TR Manningham *Bradf* 93-07; R Bolton Abbey 07-12; Hon Can Bradf Cathl 02-12; rtd 12; Chapl to The Queen from 00. *Fir Cottage, The Stenders, Mitcheldean GL17 0JE* T: (01594) 543668 E: rev.g.moffat@gmail.com

MOFFATT, Joseph Barnaby. b 72. Fitzw Coll Cam BA 96 MA 99. Ripon Coll Cuddesdon MTh 99. **d** 99 **p** 00. C Cen Wolverhampton *Lich* 99-03; C Chelsea St Luke and Ch Ch *Lon* 03-09; V Teddington St Mary w St Alb from 09; AD Hampton from 14. *The Vicarage, 11 Twickenham Road, Teddington TW11 8AQ* T: (020) 8977 2767

MOFFATT, Ms Lorraine Susan. b 56. LCTP 12. **d** 15. C Sandylands *Blackb* from 15. *67 Oxley Road, Heysham, Morecambe LA3 1LY*

MOFFATT, Canon Neil Thomas. b 46. Fitzw Coll Cam BA 68 MA 72. Qu Coll Birm 69. **d** 71 **p** 72. C Charlton St Luke w St Paul *S'wark* 71-74; C Walworth St Pet 74-75; C Walworth 75-77; V Dormansland 77-86; TR Padgate *Liv* 86-96; V 96-98; TR Thatcham *Ox* 98-10; AD Newbury 02-10; S Africa 10-11; Hon Can Ch Ch *Ox* 10-11; rtd 11; PtO *Ox* from 11; *Cov* from 11. *7 Jeffs Close, Upper Tysoe, Warwick CV35 0TQ* T: (01295) 688030 E: revd.tom.moffatt@googlemail.com

MOFFETT, Mrs Marie-Louise. b 25. St Andr Univ MA 46. **d** 87 **p** 94. St Andr Univ Angl Chapl Team 87-91; C St Andrews All SS *St And* from 91. *10 Queen's Gardens, St Andrews KY16 9TA* T: (01334) 473678

MOFFETT-LEVY, Joanna. b 45. **d** 11 **p** 12. NSM Ox St Mich w St Martin and All SS 11-15; NSM Osney from 15. *15 Third Acre Rise, Oxford OX2 9DA* T: (01865) 862715 M: 07765-175164 E: jo.moffett-levy@virginmedia.com

MOFFITT, Mrs Vivien Louisa. b 37. LSE BSc 59. Sarum & Wells Th Coll 90. **d** 91 **p** 94. NSM Chandler's Ford *Win* 91-99; NSM Twyford and Owslebury and Morestead 99-01; rtd 01. *Address temp unknown*

MOGER, Canon Peter John. b 64. Mert Coll Ox BA 85 BMus 86 MA 89 St Jo Coll Dur BA 93 ARSCM 08 Hon FGCM 10. Cranmer Hall Dur 89. **d** 93 **p** 94. C Whitby *York* 93-95; Prec, Sacr and Min Can Ely Cathl 95-01; V Godmanchester 01-05; Nat Worship Development Officer Abps' Coun 05-10; PtO *Ely* 05-10; Sec Liturg Commn 09-10; Can Res and Prec York Minster from 10. *2 Minster Court, York YO1 7JJ* T: (01904) 557205 *or* 557265 M: 07970-694021 E: precentor@yorkminster.org

MOGHAL, Dominic Jacob. *See* MUGHAL, Dominic Jacob

MOGRIDGE, Christopher James. b 31. Culham Coll of Educn CertEd 62 LCP 70 FCollP 86. St Steph Ho Ox 93. **d** 94 **p** 95. NSM Wellingborough St Andr *Pet* 94-98; NSM Ecton 98-02; rtd 02; PtO *Pet* from 02. *April Cottage, Little Harrowden, Wellingborough NN9 5BB* T: (01933) 678412

MOIR, Canon David William. b 38. St Aid Birkenhead 64. **d** 67 **p** 68. C Danbury *Chelmsf* 67-70; C Bollington St Jo *Ches* 70-72; V Sutton St Jas 72-81; V Prestbury 81-95; RD Macclesfield 88-98; P-in-c Bosley and N Rode w Wincle and Wildboarclough 95-98; V 98-03; Hon Can Ches Cathl 96-03; Chapl E Cheshire NHS Trust 96-03; rtd 04; PtO *Heref* from 04. *Dove Top, Bentlawnt, Minsterley, Shrewsbury SY5 0HE* T: (01743) 891209 E: moirdl@compuserve.com

MOIR, Canon Nicholas Ian. b 61. G&C Coll Cam BA 82 MA 86 Ox Univ BA 86 MA 91 Lon Univ MTh 92. Wycliffe Hall Ox 84. **d** 87 **p** 88. C Enfield St Andr *Lon* 87-91; Bp's Dom Chapl *St Alb* 91-94; Chapl St Jo Coll Cam 94-98; V Waterbeach and R Landbeach *Ely* 98-07; RD N Stowe 05-07; V Chesterton

St Andr from 07; P-in-c Cambridge St Clem from 14; RD Cambridge N 11-14; Hon Can Ely Cathl from 12. *The Vicarage, 10 Lynfield Lane, Cambridge CB4 1DR* T: (01223) 303469 E: nicholas.moir@ntlworld.com *or* vicar@standrews-chesterton.org

✠**MOKIWA, The Most Revd Valentino.** b 66. c 02. Bp Dar-es-Salaam from 02; Abp Tanzania from 08. *PO Box 25016, Ilala, Dar-es-Salaam, Tanzania* T: (00255) (22) 286 4426 M: 755-099754 E: mokiwa_valentine@hotmail.com

MOLD, Peter John. b 33. **d** 63 **p** 64. C Boston *Linc* 63-66; C Scarborough St Mary w Ch Ch, St Paul and St Thos *York* 67-68; Australia from 68; rtd 91. *Stone Grange, 29 Newcastle Street, PO Box 355, York WA 6302, Australia* T: (0061) (8) 9641 1965

MOLE, David Eric Harton. b 33. Em Coll Cam BA 54 MA 58 PhD 62. Ridley Hall Cam 55. **d** 59 **p** 59. C Selly Hill St Steph *Birm* 59-62; Tutor St Aid Birkenhead 62-63; Chapl Peterho Cam 63-69; Ghana 69-72; Lect Qu Coll Birm 72-76; Tutor USPG Coll of the Ascension Selly Oak 76-87; C Burton *Lich* 87-93; Chapl Burton Gen Hosp 90-93; Chapl Ostend w Knokke and Bruges *Eur* 93-98; rtd 98; PtO *Birm* from 99. *48 Green Meadow Road, Selly Oak, Birmingham B29 4DE* T: 0121-475 1589 E: susananddavidmole@yahoo.co.uk

MOLE, Canon Jennifer Vera. b 49. CertEd 70. Qu Coll Birm 82. **d** 84 **p** 97. C Pontypool *Mon* 84-87; C Cyncoed 87-88; TV 88-96; C Caerleon 96-99; V Maesglas and Duffryn 99-07; R Panteg w Llanfihangel Pontymoile 07-12; AD Pontypool 08-12; Can St Woolos Cathl 07-12; rtd 12; Can Res St Woolos Cathl from 12; PtO *Llan* from 13. *28 Joyce Close, Newport NP20 3JD* T: (01633) 258556 E: revcanjen63@btinternet.com

MOLL, Christopher David Edward. b 67. St Cath Coll Cam BA 89 MA 93. Ridley Hall Cam 94. **d** 98 **p** 99. C Byker St Mark and Walkergate St Oswald *Newc* 98-02; C Eastrop *Win* 02-06; V Wembdon *B & W* from 07. *The Vicarage, 12 Greenacre, Wembdon, Bridgwater TA6 7RD* T: (01278) 423647 E: ed@sgw.org.uk

MOLL, Nicola. b 47. Bedf Coll Lon BA 69. TISEC 99. **d** 03 **p** 04. C Edin Gd Shep from 03; C Edin St Salvador 03-06; TV 06-08; P-in-c from 08. *9/3 Forth Street, Edinburgh EH1 3JX* T: 0131-558 3729 *or* 557 0718 E: nicolamjmoll3@gmail.com

MOLL, Randell Tabrum. b 41. Lon Univ BD 65. Wycliffe Hall Ox 62. **d** 66 **p** 67. C Drypool St Columba w St Andr and St Pet *York* 66-70; Asst Chapl HM Pris Hull 66-70; Asst Master Hull Gr Sch 66-70; C Netherton *Liv* 70-74; C Sefton 70-72; Ind Chapl 70-74 and 92-99; Belgium 75-76; P-in-c Brockmoor *Lich* 76-81; Team Ldr Black Country Urban Ind Miss 76-81; Dir Chilworth Home Services 81-84; Asst Master Bp Reindorp Sch Guildf 84-90; France and Iraq 91; Chapl Sedbergh Sch 92; Sen Chapl Miss in the Economy (Merseyside) 92-99; Hon Can Liv Cathl 97-99; Chapl Campsfield Ho Immigration and Detention Cen 00-02; Sen Chapl Immigration Detention Services 01-02; Team Ldr Workplace Min *St Alb* 03-07; rtd 08. *Penn Cottage, Green End, Granborough, Buckingham MK18 3NT* T/F: (01296) 670970 E: randellmoll@yahoo.co.uk

MOLLAN, Patricia Ann Fairbanks. b 44. QUB BSc 67 PhD 70 BD 97. **d** 97 **p** 98. Aux Min *D & D* from 97; Aux Min Lecale Gp 02-04; Dep Dir Ch's Min of Healing from 04. *Echo Sound, 69 Killyleagh Road, Downpatrick BT30 9BN* T: (028) 4482 1620 F: 9073 8665 E: pat@mollan.net *or* cmhbel@btconnect.com

MOLLAN, Prof Raymond Alexander Boyce. b 43. QUB MB, BCh 69 BAO 69 MD 84 FRCS. CITC 97. **d** 97 **p** 98. Aux Min *D & D* from 97; NSM Comber 02-10; NSM Orangefield w Moneyreagh from 10. *Echo Sound, 69 Killyleagh Road, Downpatrick BT30 9BN* T: (028) 4482 1620 E: rab@mollan.net

MOLLER, George Brian. b 35. TCD BA 60 MA 64 Div Test 61 Lon Univ BD 84. **d** 61 **p** 62. C Belfast St Pet *Conn* 61-64; C Larne and Inver 64-68; P-in-c Rathcoole 68-69; I 69-86; Dioc Dir Ords 82-92; I Belfast St Bart 86-01; Chapl Stranmillis Univ Coll Belf 88-01; Preb Conn Cathl 90-96; Treas Conn Cathl 96; Prec Conn Cathl 96-98; Dean Conn 98-01; rtd 01. *Deneholme, 7 Sunningdale Park, Bangor BT20 4UU* T: (028) 9145 5903 E: gb@moller2.plus.com

MOLLOY, Mrs Heather. b 54. Bradf Univ BTech 76. **d** 95 **p** 96. OLM Harwood *Man* from 95; AD Walmsley from 15. *7 Fellside, Bolton BL2 4HB* T: (01204) 520395

MOLONEY, Charles Michael Stephen. b 81. Leeds Univ BA 03. Ridley Hall Cam 07. **d** 09 **p** 10. C Retford Area *S'well* 09-12; Asst Chapl Tonbridge Sch 12-15; Chapl St Jo Sch Leatherhead from 15. *St John's School, Epsom Road, Leatherhead KT22 8SP* T: (01372) 373000 E: revcharlie@gmx.co.uk

MOLONY, Canon Nicholas John. b 43. St Jo Coll Dur BA 67 Birm Univ MA 78 Fuller Th Sem California DMin 06. Qu Coll Birm 67. **d** 70 **p** 71. C Beaconsfield *Ox* 70-75; P-in-c Chesham Ch Ch 75-80; TV Gt Chesham 80-81; P-in-c Weston Turville 81-90; P-in-c Stoke Mandeville 87-89; P-in-c Gt Marlow 90-93; P-in-c Bisham 90-93; TR Gt Marlow w Marlow Bottom, Lt Marlow and Bisham 93-10; rtd 10; Hon Can Kimberley and

Kuruman from 08; PtO *Ox* from 11. *9 Culverton Hill, Princes Risborough HP27 0DZ* T: (01844) 273895 E: nick.molony@btopenworld.com

MOLUDY, Omid. b 81. All SS Cen for Miss & Min. **d** 14 **p** 14. NSM Heatons *Man* from 14; Miss Support P for Cultural Diversity from 15. *10 Dixon Drive, Chelford, Macclesfield SK11 9BU* T: (01625) 860619 M: 07590-363221 E: omidmoludy@gmail.com

MOLYNEUX, Ms Tina Mercedes. b 68. Ox Min Course 07. **d** 10 **p** 11. NSM Burchetts Green *Ox* from 10. *1 Littlewick Place, Coronation Road, Littlewick Green, Maidenhead SL6 3RA* T: (01628) 822813 E: tina.molyneux@btconnect.com

MONAGHAN, Mrs Hilary Alice. b 78. Edin Univ MA 01 Cam Univ BA 04. Ridley Hall Cam 02. **d** 06 **p** 07. C Gerrards Cross and Fulmer *Ox* 06-10; NSM Clifton Ch Ch w Em *Bris* 12-13; NSM Malmesbury w Westport and Brokenborough from 13; NSM St Somerford, Lt Somerford, Seagry, Corston etc from 13; Chapl Westonbirt Sch from 13. *1 Park Close, Malmesbury SN16 0EB* E: alicemon7@gmail.com

MONAGHAN, John Emanuel. b 80. Carlow Coll BSc 02 UEA MSc 06. Trin Coll Bris 10. **d** 13 **p** 14. C Malmesbury w Westport and Brokenborough *Bris* from 13; C Gt Somerford, Lt Somerford, Seagry, Corston etc from 13. *1 Park Close, Malmesbury SN16 0EB* M: 07791-684160 E: johnmon7@gmail.com

MONAGHAN, Teresa. b 61. **d** 14. C S Kirkby *Wakef* from 14. *52 Park Estate, South Kirkby, Pontefract WF9 3PA* T: (01977) 649251

MONBERG, Canon Ulla Stefan. b 52. Copenhagen Univ BA 79. Westcott Ho Cam 88. **d** 90 **p** 94. C Westmr St Jas *Lon* 90-94; Dean Women's Min and Area Dir of Ords Cen Lon 94-99; Dean Women's Min Kensington 94-99; C Paddington St Jo w St Mich *Lon* 96-98; P-in-c S Kensington H Trin w All SS 98-02; Dir of Ords Two Cities Area 99-02; Denmark from 02; Dioc Adv for Women's Min *Eur* 04-05; Dioc Dir of Tr from 05; Can Brussels Cathl from 10. *Borgmester Jensens Alle 2, 2th, DK-2100 Copenhagen 0, Denmark* T: (0045) 3526 0660 E: ulla.monberg@churchofengland.org

✠**MONDAL, The Rt Revd Barnabas Dwijen.** b 37. Dhaka Univ BA 61 Serampore Univ BD 64. Bp's Coll Calcutta 61. **d** 64 **p** 65 **c** 75. Barisal Bangladesh 64-67; Khulna 67-69; Rhode Is USA 69-70; Bolloropur 70-71; Thakurpukur 71-72; Prin Coll of Chr Th 72-74; Dhaka St Thos 74-75; Asst Bp Dhaka 75; Bp Dhaka and Moderator Ch of Bangladesh 75-03; rtd 03. *Merlin Apartment, 59/A-1 Barobagh, Dhaka 1216, Bangladesh* T: (00880) (2) 805 1656 M: 172-031350

MONDON, Simon Charles. b 57. WEMTC. **d** 02 **p** 03. OLM Worfield *Heref* 02-09; V Goodrich, Marstow, Welsh Bicknor, Llangarron etc from 09. *The Vicarage, Llangrove, Ross-on-Wye HR9 6EZ* T: (01989) 770341 E: revsimon@btinternet.com

MONDS, Anthony John Beatty. b 53. Solicitor 78. **d** 97 **p** 00. OLM Queen Thorne *Sarum* 97-04; C Sherborne w Castleton, Lillington and Longburton 04-06; V Piddle Valley, Hilton, Cheselbourne etc 06-15; Bp's Dom Chapl from 15. *6 Lime Kiln Way, Salisbury SP2 8RN* T: (01722) 334031 E: tony.monds@btinternet.com

MONEME, Dozie Chukwubulkem. b 79. W Africa Th Sem Lagos BA 10. **d** 08 **p** 10. Nigeria 08-11; PtO *S'wark* 11-13; C Orpington Ch Ch *Roch* from 14. *49 Star Lane, Orpington BR5 3LJ* T: (01689) 639384 M: 07915-530670 E: chuu200@yahoo.com

MONEY, John Charles. b 69. Wycliffe Hall Ox 01. **d** 03 **p** 04. C Porchester *S'well* 03-06; TV Plymouth St Andr and Stonehouse *Ex* 06-13; Chapl RN from 13. *Royal Naval Chaplaincy Service, Mail Point 1.2, Leach Building, Whale Island, Portsmouth PO2 8BY* T: (023) 9262 5055 F: 9262 5134 M: 07711-285217

MONEY, Mrs Lynn Astrid. b 59. St Martin's Coll Lanc BEd 80. WEMTC 03. **d** 06 **p** 07. C Letton w Staunton, Byford, Mansel Gamage etc *Heref* 06-09; R Bredenbury 09-14; TV Dunstable *St Alb* from 14. *St Fremund's Vicarage, 20 Friars Walk, Dunstable LU6 3JA* M: 07791-349406 E: revlynnmoney@gmail.com

MONGER, Paul James. b 54. Reading Univ BEd 77 Greenwich Univ MSc 99. NTMTC 07. **d** 10 **p** 11. NSM Chingford St Edm *Chelmsf* from 10. *25 Stanmore Road, London E11 3BU* M: 07739-905363 E: james.monger@yahoo.com

MONK, Carol Lorna. b 57. STETS 08. **d** 11 **p** 12. NSM Ash *Guildf* 11-15; PtO from 15. *The Hawthorns, 2 Rowhill Avenue, Aldershot GU11 3LU* T: (01252) 313239 E: clmonk@virginmedia.com

MONK, Mrs Mary. b 38. CertEd 58. S'wark Ord Course 85. **d** 88 **p** 94. NSM Lee Gd Shep w St Pet *S'wark* 88-99; NSM Harpenden St Jo *St Alb* 99-07; PtO from 07. *3 Hawthorn Close, Harpenden AL5 1HN* T: (01582) 462057

MONK, Nicholas John. b 32. Westcott Ho Cam 61. **d** 63 **p** 64. C Bris H Cross Inns Court 63-67; C Stoke Bishop 67-69; V Swindon All SS 69-75; V Ashton Keynes w Leigh 75-87;

P-in-c Minety w Oaksey 82-87; RD Malmesbury 85-88; V Ashton Keynes, Leigh and Minety 87-91; TR Swindon St Jo and St Andr 91-97; rtd 97; PtO Heref 97-13. 6 Bowerhill Road, Salisbury SP1 3DN T: (01722) 238214
E: n.monk@hotmail.co.uk

MONK, Paul Malcolm Spenser. b 65. Ex Univ BSc 86 PhD 90 Leeds Univ MA 07 CChem MRSC. NOC 05. **d** 07 **p** 08. C Oldham Man 07-09; TV Medlock Head from 09. St Barnabas Vicarage, 1 Arundel Street, Oldham OL4 1NL T: 0161-624 7708 M: 07854-776410 E: paul_and_jo_monk@yahoo.co.uk

MONK, Stephen David. b 74. Leuven Univ Belgium STB 03. Qu Coll Birm 05. **d** 00 **p** 01. C Knighton St Mary Magd Leic 06-08; C Wigston Magna 08-11; P-in-c Darley Derby 11-12; C S Darley, Elton and Winster 11-12; R Darley, S Darley and Winster from 12. 10 Normanhurst Park, Darley Dale, Matlock DE4 3BQ T: (01629) 734257
E: rev.stephenmonk@btinternet.com

MONKHOUSE, Henry Alistair. b 34. **d** 99 **p** 00. OLM Quidenham Gp Nor 99-05; PtO from 05. Wildwood, Mill Road, Old Buckenham, Attleborough NR17 1SG T: (01953) 860845

MONKHOUSE, William Stanley. b 50. Qu Coll Cam BA 72 MA 76 MB, BChir 75 Nottm Univ PhD 85 MA 06. EMMTC 04. **d** 06 **p** 07. C Wirksworth Derby 06-08; P-in-c Old Brampton 08-09; P-in-c Gt Barlow 08-09; P-in-c Old Brampton and Great Barlow 09-11; R 11; P-in-c Loundsley Green 09-11; Asst Dir of Ords 09-11; I Maryborough w Dysart Enos and Ballyfin C & O 11-14; Chapl Midlands and Portlaoise Pris 11-14; Chapl Midland Regional Hosp Portlaoise 11-14; V Burton St Aid and St Paul Lich from 14; V Burton St Modwen from 14. The Vicarage, Rangemore Street, Burton-on-Trent DE14 2ED T: (01283) 565570 E: wsmonkhouse@gmail.com

MONKS, Ian Kay. b 36. K Coll Lon BA 60 Lon Inst of Educn PGCE 61. Oak Hill NSM Course 90. **d** 93 **p** 94. NSM Woodford Bridge Chelmsf 93-06; PtO from 06. 46 Summit Drive, Woodford Green IG8 8QP T: (020) 8550 2390

MONMOUTH, Archdeacon of. See MASON, The Ven Thomas Henry Ambrose

MONMOUTH, Bishop of. See PAIN, The Rt Revd Richard Edward

MONMOUTH, Dean of. See TONGE, The Very Revd Lister

MONRO, Alexander James. b 55. Oriel Coll Ox BA 77 Lon Hosp MB, BS 80 MRCP 86 MRCGP 88. STETS 09. **d** 12 **p** 13. NSM Hunstanton St Mary w Ringstead Parva etc Nor from 12. Manor Cottage, Church Place, Docking, King's Lynn PE31 8LW T: (01485) 518342 E: alexander.monro@btinternet.com

MONTAGUE (née LAIDLAW), Mrs Juliet. b 52. Nottm Univ BTh 82. Linc Th Coll 78. **dss** 82 **d** 87 **p** 94. Gainsborough All SS Linc 82-86; Chapl Linc Cathl and Linc Colls of FE 86-92; Dn-in-c Gedney Hill and Whaplode Drove Linc 92-94; P-in-c 94-99; P-in-c Crawley and Littleton and Sparsholt w Lainston Win 99-03; R 03-08; R The Downs 08-13; Hon C Shedfield and Wickham Portsm from 13. The Vicarage, 52 Brooklynn Close, Waltham Chase, Southampton SO32 2RZ T: (01489) 895012

MONTAGUE-YOUENS, Canon Hubert Edward. b 30. Ripon Hall Ox 55. **d** 58 **p** 59. C Redditch St Steph Worc 58-59; C Halesowen 59-62; V Kempsey 62-69; V Kidderminster St Geo 69-72; R Ribbesford w Bewdley and Dowles 72-81; RD Kidderminster 74-81; Hon Can Worc Cathl 78-81; TR Bridport Sarum 81-86; RD Lyme Bay 82-86; V Easebourne Chich 86-89; Chapl K Edw VII Hosp Midhurst 86-89; rtd 89; PtO Worc from 89; Glouc 89-95 and from 98; P-in-c Twyning 96-98. 6 Harbour View, Bredon Road, Tewkesbury GL20 5AZ T: (01684) 292363

MONTEITH, The Very Revd David Robert Malvern. b 68. St Jo Coll Dur BSc 89 Nottm Univ BTh 92 MA 93. St Jo Coll Nottm 90. **d** 93 **p** 94. C Kings Heath Birm 93-97; C St Martin-in-the-Fields Lon 97-02; P-in-c S Wimbledon H Trin and St Pet S'wark 02-09; TR Merton Priory 09; AD Merton 04-09; Can Res and Chan Leic Cathl 09-13; Dean Leic from 13. The Deanery, 23 St Martins, Leicester LE1 5DE M: 07952-238291 T: 0116-261 5356 E: david.monteith@leccofe.org

MONTGOMERIE, Alexander (Sandy). b 47. St Jo Coll Nottm 89. **d** 94 **p** 96. NSM Irvine St Andr LEP Glas from 94; NSM Ardrossan from 94; Dioc Ecum Relns Co-ord from 05. 105 Sharphill Road, Saltcoats KA21 5QU T/F: (01294) 465193 E: sandy.montgomerie@btinternet.com

MONTGOMERIE, Andrew Simon. b 60. Keble Coll Ox BA 82. Ridley Hall Cam 83. **d** 85 **p** 86. C Childwall All SS Liv 85-87; C Yardley St Edburgha Birm 87-90; TV Solihull 90-96; V Balsall Common 96-05; P-in-c Eyam Derby 05-11; C Baslow w Curbar and Stoney Middleton 06-11; R Baslow and Eyam 11-12; RD Bakewell and Eyam 07-12; R Iver Heath Ox from 12. The Rectory, 2 Pinewood Close, Iver SL0 0QS T: (01753) 654470 M: 07545-385629 E: asmontgomerie@hotmail.co.uk

MONTGOMERY, Canon Anthony Alan. b 33. Trin Hall Cam BA 56. Edin Th Coll 56. **d** 58 **p** 59. C Dumfries Glas 58-63;

P-in-c Airdrie 63-66; R 66-68; Asst Chapl Gordonstoun Sch 68-93; Can St Andr Cathl Inverness from 81; rtd 93. Easter Hillside, Mosstowie, Elgin IV30 8XE T/F: (01343) 850282

MONTGOMERY, Canon Ian David. b 44. St Andr Univ LLB 66 Univ of the South (USA) DMin 02 FCA 69. Wycliffe Hall Ox 71. **d** 75 **p** 76. C Fulham St Dionis Lon 75-78; Chapl Amherst Coll USA 78-83; R New Orleans St Phil 83-93; R Nashville St Bart 92-97; R Menasha St Thos 97-09; rtd 09; SAMS Peru from 09; Can from 10. Iglesia Anglicana del Perú, Calle Doña Maria 141, Surco, Lima 13, Peru T: (001) (802) 428 4762 or 463 2175 E: frianm@aol.com

MONTGOMERY (née YOUATT), Canon Jennifer Alison. b 49. St Aid Coll Dur BSc 70 Homerton Coll Cam PGCE 71. NOC 89. **d** 92 **p** 94. NSM Ripon H Trin Leeds from 92; Warden of Readers from 99; Dioc Adv on Women's Min from 10; Hon Can Ripon Cathl from 10. Washington House, Littlethorpe, Ripon HG4 3LJ T: (01765) 605276 or T/F: 690930
E: montgomery@littlethorpe97.freeserve.co.uk

MONTGOMERY, Jennifer Susan. b 54. QUB MB, BCh 77 Leeds Univ MA 05. NOC 02. **d** 05 **p** 06. NSM Ackworth Wakef 05-10; P-in-c Goodshaw and Crawshawbooth Man from 10. Goodshaw Vicarage, Goodshawfold Road, Rossendale BB4 8QN T: (01706) 601262 M: 07780-764233
E: jsm1954@hotmail.com

MONTGOMERY, Laura Alice. b 77. Lon Bible Coll BTh 99. St Jo Coll Nottm MTh 09. **d** 09. C Newton Liv 09-12; P-in-c Woolston and Birchwood 12-13; TV Warrington E from 13. The Vicarage, Admirals Road, Birchwood, Warrington WA3 6QG T: (01925) 813712 M: 07511-030948
E: la.monty@yahoo.co.uk

MONTGOMERY, Mark. b 77. **d** 10 **p** 11. NSM Upton (Overchurch) Ches 10-14; Dioc Youth Officer from 14. 18 Kingfisher Way, Wirral CH49 4PR T: 0151-678 7599

MONTGOMERY, Pembroke John Charles. b 24. Codrington Coll Barbados. **d** 53 **p** 55. C St Geo Cathl St Vincent 55; R Biabou 56-65; R Calliaqua 65-73; Can Kingstown Cathl 63-73; P-in-c Derby St Jas 73-74; V 74-90; rtd 90. 39 Church Street, Tutbury, Burton-on-Trent DE13 9JE T: (01283) 814887

MONTGOMERY, Rachel. See TREWEEK, Rachel

MONTGOMERY, Canon Thomas Charles Osborne. b 59. Edin Univ BD 81. Edin Th Coll 77. **d** 82 **p** 83. C Glas St Mary 82-85; C Dumfries 85-88; R Hamilton 88-96; R Glas St Marg 96-10; R Troon from 10; Can St Mary's Cathl from 94. St Ninian's Rectory, 70 Bentinck Drive, Troon KA10 6HZ T: (01292) 313731 E: tmontgomery1@hotmail.co.uk

MONTGOMERY, Timothy Robert. b 59. Hull Univ BA 82 Cam Univ PGCE 83. EAMTC 90. **d** 93 **p** 94. Dir Romsey Mill Community Cen Ely 93-94; NSM Cambridge St Phil 93-96; Warden Kepplewray Cen Broughton-in-Furness 96-00; NSM Kendal St Thos Carl 96-00; V 00-13; Bp's Leadership and Strategy Adv 11-15; Hon Can Carl Cathl 06-15; Dir Miss Wigan Liv from 15. Address temp unknown M: 07985-290493 E: tim.montgomery@liverpool.anglican.org

MONTGOMERY, Archdeacon of. See PIKE, The Ven Peter John

MONTROSE, Michelle Ann. b 57. NOC 05. **d** 08 **p** 09. NSM W Derby St Mary and St Jas Liv 08-12; NSM Liv Our Lady and St Nic from 12. 1 Highfield View, Liverpool L13 3BP T: 0151-220 1746 M: 07528-331316
E: michelleamontrose@yahoo.co.uk

MOODY, Christopher John Everard. b 51. New Coll Ox BA 72 Lon Univ MSc 90. Cuddesdon Coll BA 74. **d** 75 **p** 76. C Fulham All SS Lon 75-79; C Surbiton St Andr and St Mark S'wark 79-82; Chapl K Coll Lon 82-87; V S Lambeth St Anne and All SS S'wark 87-95; RD Lambeth 90-95; P-in-c Market Harborough Leic 95-97; P-in-c Market Harborough Transfiguration 95-97; V Market Harborough and The Transfiguration etc 97-05; Hon Can Leic Cathl 04-05; V Greenwich St Alfege S'wark from 05. The Vicarage, Park Vista, London SE10 9LZ T: (020) 8858 6828
E: chrisjemoody@btinternet.com

MOODY, Colin John. b 36. Chich Th Coll 61. **d** 63 **p** 64. C Hove All SS Chich 63-69; C Dulwich St Barn S'wark 69-70; PtO Bris 70-71; Chich 72-78 and from 90; LtO Ely 78-89; rtd 01. 11 Hewitts, Henfield BN5 9DT T: (01273) 495062

MOODY, Ms Elizabeth Jane. b 61. Hull Univ BA 82 Westmr Coll Ox PGCE 84. Ridley Hall Cam 00. **d** 02 **p** 03. C Uxbridge Lon 02-05; C Hanwell St Mary w St Chris from 05. 26 Tentelow Lane, Southall UB2 4LE M: 07796-988302
E: lizmoody@blueyonder.co.uk

MOODY, George. b 65. Clare Coll Cam MA 88 Ox Brookes Univ MA 14. Ripon Coll Cuddesdon 11. **d** 14 **p** 15. NSM Vale Ox from 14. 11 Clifton Drive, Abingdon OX14 1ET
E: curate@valebenefice.org.uk

MOODY, Preb George Henry. b 27. ACIS 56 ARCA 68. Cranmer Hall Dur 69. **d** 71 **p** 72. C Marske in Cleveland York 71-74; Chapl to the Deaf Lich 74-89; Preb Lich Cathl 83-89; rtd 89;

PtO *York* from 90. *21 Priestcrofts, Marske-by-the-Sea, Redcar TS11 7HW* T: (01642) 489660

MOODY, Canon Ivor Robert. b 57. K Coll Lon BD 80 AKC Anglia Ruskin Univ MA 03. Coll of Resurr Mirfield. **d** 82 **p** 83. C Leytonstone St Marg w St Columba *Chelmsf* 82-85; C Leigh-on-Sea St Marg 85-88; V Tilbury Docks 88-96; Chapl Anglia Ruskin Univ 96-10; Hon Can Chelmsf Cathl 09-10; Vice-Dean and Can Res Chelmsf Cathl from 10. *83 Ridgewell Avenue, Chelmsford CM1 2GF* T: (01245) 267773 *or* 294493 E: vicedean@chelmsfordcathedral.org.uk

MOODY, John Kelvin. b 30. St Fran Coll Brisbane ThL 55. **d** 56 **p** 57. C Warwick Australia 56-57; C Southport 57-58; C Dalby 58-61; C Earl's Court St Cuth w St Matthias *Lon* 61-64; Chapl Ankara *Eur* 64-69; Chapl Istanbul 64-66; Chapl Palma 69-75; Chapl Tangier 75-79; Can Gib Cathl 74-79; Hon Can Gib Cathl from 79; Australia from 79; rtd 01. *1 Short Street, Watsons Bay NSW 2030, Australia* T: (0061) (2) 9337 2871 E: jm986672@bigpond.net.au

MOOKERJI, Michael Manoje. b 45. Baring Union Coll Punjab BSc 69. Ridley Hall Cam 83. **d** 85 **p** 86. C Heanor *Derby* 85-92; V Codnor and Loscoe 92-93; V Codnor 93-02; V Winshill 02-15; C Hartshorne and Bretby 13-15; rtd 15; PtO *Derby* from 15. *1 Plymouth Walk, Church Gresley, Swadlincote DE11 9GU* E: michael.mookerji@live.co.uk

MOON, Arthur Thomas. b 22. ACP 53 LCP 56. Sarum Th Coll 65. **d** 66 **p** 67. C Fulwood Ch Ch *Blackb* 66-71; Hon C Bispham 71-80; C 80-87; rtd 87; PtO *Blackb* 87-11. *15 Kirkstone Drive, Thornton-Cleveleys FY5 1QQ* T: (01253) 853521

MOON, Sister Catherine Joy. b 48. LRAM 68 ARCM 69. Gen Th Sem NY 84. **d** 84 **p** 85. USA 84-02; CSF from 87; Chapl Mersey Care NHS Trust from 04. *42 Boxtree Close, Liverpool L12 0PN* M: 07906-365962

MOON, John Charles. b 23. Sarum Th Coll 49. **d** 51 **p** 52. C Bottesford *Linc* 51-54; C Habrough 54-55; V Immingham 55-61; V Weaste *Man* 61-67; V Spalding St Jo *Linc* 67-82; V Spalding St Jo w Deeping St Nicholas 82-86; rtd 86; PtO *Linc* 87-02. *14 Harrox Road, Moulton, Spalding PE12 6PR* T: (01406) 370111

MOON, Revd Dr Nicola Jane. b 71. Ox Min Course 13. **d** 15. C Harbury and Ladbroke *Cov* from 15. *Address temp unknown*

MOON, Philip. b 59. CCC Ox BA 80 Warwick Univ PhD 92. Wycliffe Hall Ox BTh 01. **d** 01 **p** 02. C Otley *Bradf* 01-05; V Lt Aston *Lich* from 05. *The Vicarage, 3 Walsall Road, Little Aston, Sutton Coldfield B74 3BD* T: 0121-353 0798 E: familyofmoon@aol.com

MOON, Philip Russell. b 56. Em Coll Cam BA 78 MA 81 Reading Univ PGCE 79. Wycliffe Hall Ox BA 82. **d** 85 **p** 86. C Crowborough *Chich* 85-87; Hd of CYFA (CPAS) 87-94; V Lowestoft Ch Ch *Nor* 94-04; P-in-c Hove Bp Hannington Memorial Ch *Chich* 04-06; V from 06; RD Hove 05-08. *82 Holmes Avenue, Hove BN3 7LD* T: (01273) 732821

MOONEY, Mrs Julie. b 66. Cranmer Hall Dur 11. **d** 13 **p** 14. C Newc H Cross from 13. *2A Lanercost Drive, Newcastle upon Tyne NE5 2DE* M: 07443-410781 E: m-jmooney@supanet.com

MOONEY, The Very Revd Paul Gerard. b 58. St Patr Coll Maynooth BD 84 Asian Cen for Th Studies and Miss Seoul ThM 92 Protestant Th Faculty Brussels DrTheol 02. **d** 84 **p** 85. In RC Ch 84-90; Chapl Miss to Seamen Korea 90-94; Hon Can Pusan from 94; Chapl Antwerp Miss to Seamen 94-97; Asst Chapl Antwerp St Boniface *Eur* 94-97; C Galway w Kilcummin T, K & A 97-98; I New w Old Ross, Whitechurch, Fethard etc C & O 98-07; Hon Chapl New Ross and Waterford Miss to Seamen 98-07; Prec Ferns Cathl 07-11; Adn Ferns 02-07; Chapl Seoul Cathl Korea 07-11; Dean Ferns C & O from 11; I Ferns w Kilbride, Toombe, Kilcormack etc from 11; Prec Ossory Cathl from 14; Prec Leighlin Cathl from 14. *The Deanery, Ferns, Enniscorthy, Co Wexford, Republic of Ireland* T: (00353) (53) 936 6124 E: pgmoon@hotmail.com

MOOR, Canon Simon Alan. b 65. Nottm Univ BTh 93. Linc Th Coll 90. **d** 93 **p** 94. C Skegness and Winthorpe *Linc* 93-96; C Airedale w Fryston *Wakef* 96-98; V Hoylandswaine and Silkstone w Stainborough 98-11; V Huddersfield St Pet *Leeds* from 11; Bp's Adv for Ecum Affairs from 08; Hon Can Wakef Cathl from 11. *59 Lightridge Road, Fixby, Huddersfield HD2 2HF* T: (01484) 767708 E: samoor@talktalk.net

MOORCROFT, Steven James. b 73. Wye Coll Lon BSc 95. Cranmer Hall Dur 05. **d** 07 **p** 08. C Kendal St Thos *Carl* 07-09; NSM Probus, Ladock and Grampound w Creed and St Erme *Truro* 13-14. *Little Pendene, Fore Street, Grampound, Truro TR2 4RS* T: (01726) 882242 E: svae@btinternet.com

MOORE, Albert William. b 47. WMMTC 91. **d** 94 **p** 95. C Hobs Moat *Birm* 94-98; V Dosthill 98-06; V Hill 06-13; rtd 13; PtO *Birm* from 13. *40 Main Street, Walton-on-Trent, Swadlincote DE12 8LZ* E: bill@fammoore.plus.com

MOORE, Andrew Jonathan. b 57. York Univ BA 82 Wycliffe Hall Ox BA 84 MA 89 Worc Coll Ox DPhil 99. **d** 86 **p** 86. C Camberwell St Jo Australia 86-87; Assoc P S Yarra Ch Ch 87-90; Asst/Acting Chapl Worc Coll Ox 91-94; Chapl Jes Coll Ox 94-99; Voc Adv Ox 98-04; Dir of Ords 04-10; Hon Chapl Cen for Mediaeval and Renaissance Studies Ox 99-04; Research Fell Regent's Park Coll Ox 01-04; Chapl St Pet Coll Ox 04-07. *Theology Faculty, 41 St Giles, Oxford OX1 3LW* T: (01865) 270731 E: andrew.moore@spc.ox.ac.uk

MOORE, Anthony Harry. b 34. Westcott Ho Cam 88. **d** 90 **p** 91. C Eyke w Bromeswell, Rendlesham, Tunstall etc *St E* 90-93; V Aldeburgh w Hazlewood 93-02; rtd 02; PtO *St E* from 02; *Chelmsf* from 02. *5 Kings Meadow, Great Cornard, Sudbury CO10 0HP* T: (01787) 377967

MOORE, Canon Anthony Michael. b 71. Ex Univ BA 94 Leeds Univ BA 98 MA 99 PhD 10 Cam Univ MA 10. Coll of Resurr Mirfield 96. **d** 99 **p** 00. C Carnforth *Blackb* 99-03; Fell and Past Tutor Coll of Resurr Mirfield 03-04; C Wilton Place St Paul *Lon* 04-07; Chapl R Academy of Music 04-07; Chapl and Fell St Cath Coll Cam 07-12; Dean of Chpl 12; Can Res Lich Cathl from 13; Vice-Dean from 14. *24 The Close, Lichfield WS13 7LD* E: anthony.moore@lichfield-cathedral.org

MOORE, Anthony Richmond. b 36. Clare Coll Cam BA 59 MA 63. Linc Th Coll 59. **d** 61 **p** 62. C Roehampton H Trin *S'wark* 61-66; C New Eltham All SS 66-70; P Missr Blackbird Leys CD Ox 70-81; Dioc Ecum Officer 80-98; TV Dorchester 81-93; R Enstone and Heythrop 93-01; rtd 01; PtO Ox from 01. *13 Cobden Crescent, Oxford OX1 4LJ* T: (01865) 244673 E: moore.t@which.net

MOORE, Arlene. b 64. Dundee Univ BSc 87 N Coll of Educn PGCE 90 TCD BTh 95. CITC 92. **d** 95 **p** 96. C Portadown St Mark *Arm* 95-99; PtO *Sheff* 99-02 and 03-09; C Crookes St Thos 02-03; Chapl Belfast Health and Soc Care Trust 09-10; P-in-c Monkstown *Conn* from 09. *Monkstown Rectory, 27 Twinburn Gardens, Newtownabbey BT37 0EW* T: (028) 9086 4902 M: 07921-864024 E: sendmyemails2me@yahoo.com

MOORE, Canon Bernard Geoffrey. b 27. New Coll Ox BA 47 MA 52. Ely Th Coll 49. **d** 51 **p** 52. C Chorley St Pet *Blackb* 51-54; Bp's Dom Chapl 54-55; C-in-c Blackpool St Mich CD 55-67; Chapl Victoria Hosp Blackpool 58-67; V Morecambe St Barn *Blackb* 67-81; R Standish 81-88; Hon Can Blackb Cathl 86-92; RD Chorley 86-92; V Charnock Richard 88-92; rtd 92; PtO *Ex* from 92; *Carl* from 01; *Win* 00-12. *29 Wiltshire Close, Exeter EX4 1LU* T: (01392) 258686

MOORE, Bernard George. b 32. Qu Coll Birm 57. **d** 60 **p** 62. C Middlesbrough St Columba *York* 60-62; C Kimberley Cathl S Africa 62-64; R Kimberley St Matt 64-69; Chapl RN 70-74; C Milton *Portsm* 74-76; V Glenfield New Zealand 76-80; V Kaitala 80-84; V Gisborne 84-86; rtd 97. *45 Feasegate Street, Manurewa 2102, New Zealand* T: (0064) (9) 267 6924 E: freesaxon2000@yahoo.com

✠**MOORE, The Rt Revd Bruce Macgregor.** b 31. Univ of NZ BA 55. Coll of Resurr Mirfield. **d** 57 **p** 58 **c** 92. C Blackpool St Steph *Blackb* 57-61; New Zealand from 61; Hon Can Auckland 78-96; Adn Manukau 81-90; Asst Bp Auckland 92-97. *5 Pokaka Crescent, Taupo 3330, New Zealand* T: (0064) (7) 378 4849 E: brucemoore@xtra.co.nz

MOORE, Caroline Judith. *See* FALKINGHAM, Caroline Judith

MOORE, Miss Catherine Joy. b 63. Bretton Hall Coll BEd 85 Anglia Poly Univ MEd 94. St Mellitus Coll BA 10. **d** 10 **p** 11. NSM Springfield All SS *Chelmsf* 10-13; NSM Chelmsf Cathl from 13. *33 Church Street, Witham CM8 2JP* T: (01376) 501128 M: 07860-459465 E: katejmoore@aol.com

MOORE, Charles David. b 59. Dundee Univ BSc 82 BArch 85 Open Univ MA 96 RIBA 86. St Jo Coll Nottm 91. **d** 93 **p** 94. C Deane *Man* 93-97; Crosslinks 98-02; R and Sub Dean Mutare Zimbabwe 98-02; R Bermondsey St Mary w St Olave, St Jo etc *S'wark* from 02. *The Rectory, 193 Bermondsey Street, London SE1 3UW* T: (020) 7357 0984

MOORE, Christopher Baden. b 58. **d** 12 **p** 13. NSM Stretton and Appleton Thorn *Ches* 12-14; C Stockport St Geo from 14. *40 Beechfield Road, Stockport SK3 8SF* E: chrismoore58@aol.com

MOORE, Christopher John. b 73. Stirling Univ BA 95 K Coll Lon MA 98 PGCE 99 Anglia Ruskin Univ MA 13. Westcott Ho Cam 11. **d** 13 **p** 14. C Croydon St Jo *S'wark* from 13. *8 The Ridgeway, Croydon CR0 4AB* M: 07793-144841 E: christophermoore100@hotmail.com

MOORE, Christopher Kevin William. b 69. Ox Brookes Univ BSc 92 Bris Univ BA 01 Trin Coll Bris PhD 10 MRICS 95. Bris Bapt Coll 98. **d** 09 **p** 10. C Tenbury *Heref* 09-11; P-in-c Fownhope w Mordiford, Brockhampton etc 11-13; R from 13. *The Rectory, Fownhope, Hereford HR1 4PS* T: (01432) 860365 E: chris@cm5j.com

MOORE, Preb Clive Granville. b 31. St Pet Hall Ox BA 54 MA 58. Wycliffe Hall Ox 54. **d** 55 **p** 56. C Newbarns w

Hawcoat *Carl* 55-57; CF 57-61; Chapl Joyce Green Hosp Dartford 61-69; R Stone *Roch* 61-69; R Radstock *B & W* 69-71; P-in-c Writhlington 69-71; R Radstock w Writhlington 71-83; RD Midsomer Norton 81-83; R S Petherton w The Seavingtons 83-95; RD Crewkerne 83-95; RD Crewkerne and Ilminster 93; Preb Wells Cathl 90-95; rtd 95; PtO *B & W* from 95. *Mowries Stable, West Street, Somerton TA11 6NA* T: (01458) 274649

MOORE, Canon Colin Frederick. b 49. CITC 69. **d** 72 **p** 73. C Drumglass w Moygashel *Arm* 72-80; I Newtownhamilton w Ballymoyer and Belleek 80-15; Hon V Choral Arm Cathl 85-96; Can and Preb Arm Cathl 97-15; rtd 15; Asst Dioc and Prov Registrar *Arm* 96-09; Dioc and Prov Registrar from 09. *8 Willow Dean, Markethill, Armagh BT60 1QG* E: cf.moore@btinternet.com

MOORE, Darren Lee. b 73. Kingston Univ BEng 95. Oak Hill Th Coll BA 01. **d** 01 **p** 02. C Camberwell All SS *S'wark* 01-04; P-in-c Tranmere St Cath *Ches* 04-07; V 07-12. *104 St Fabian's Drive, Chelmsford CM1 2PR*

MOORE, Darren Richard. b 70. Univ of Wales (Abth) BD 91 Hull Univ PGCE 97 St Jo Coll York MA(Ed) 03 Leeds Univ MA 04. Coll of Resurr Mirfield 02. **d** 04 **p** 05. C Scarborough St Martin *York* 04-07; R Brayton 07-09; Chapl Ranby Ho Sch Retford 09-11; P-in-c Leeds Halton St Wilfrid 11-15; Asst Dir of Ords *Ripon* 12-14; Assoc Dioc Dir of Ords *Leeds* 14-15; Chapl Barnard Castle Sch from 15. *Littlemoor, Mount Eff Lane, Barnard Castle DL8 8UR* M: 07745-296406 T: (01833) 696043 E: drm@barneyschool.org.uk

MOORE, David James Paton. b 60. Sheff Univ BEng 82. Cranmer Hall Dur 88. **d** 91 **p** 92. C Pemberton St Mark Newtown *Liv* 91-94; C St Helens St Helen 94-97; V Canonbury St Steph *Lon* 97-07; NSM Easton H Trin w St Gabr and St Lawr and St Jude *Bris* from 08. *St Michael's Vicarage, St Michael's Court, Kingswood, Bristol BS15 1BE* T: 0117-967 9446

MOORE, David Leonard. b 51. **d** 80 **p** 82. Hon C Brixton St Matt *S'wark* 80-82; C 82-84; TV Bris St Agnes and St Simon w St Werburgh 84-86; PtO 86-88; *Blackb* from 88. *154 Victoria Road, Fulwood, Preston PR2 8NQ*

MOORE, David Metcalfe. b 41. Hull Univ BA 64 PhD 69. Trin Coll Bris 76. **d** 78 **p** 79. C Marple All SS *Ches* 78-82; V Loudwater *Ox* 82-90; V Chilwell *S'well* 90-93; rtd 93; PtO *Ely* from 95. *12 Rhugarve Gardens, Linton, Cambridge CB21 4LX* T: (01223) 894315 E: davidmmoore@mypostoffice.co.uk

MOORE, David Roy. b 39. Clare Coll Cam BA 61. Ripon Hall Ox 61. **d** 63 **p** 64. C Melton Mowbray w Thorpe Arnold *Leic* 63-66; C St Steph Walbrook and St Swithun etc *Lon* 66-72; Dep Dir The Samaritans 66-72; Public Preacher *S'well* 72-77; C Daybrook 77-80; V 80-87; V Ham St Andr *S'wark* 87-99; P-in-c Rothbury *Newc* 99-04; rtd 04; P-in-c Kneesall w Laxton and Wellow *S'well* 04-07. *Lily Cottage, Far Back Lane, Farnsfield, Newark NG22 8JX*

MOORE, Donald John. b 31. Chich Th Coll 86. **d** 87 **p** 88. C Uckfield *Chich* 87-88; C Southwick St Mich 88-90; Asst P St Geo Bermuda 90-97; P-in-c St Dav 90-97; Chapl St Brendan's Psychiatric Hosp 92-97; rtd 97. *PO Box HM122, Hamilton HM AX, Bermuda* T: (001) (441) 296 8962

MOORE, Douglas Gregory. b 49. Bris Univ BA 71 CertEd 72. Coll of Resurr Mirfield 87. **d** 89 **p** 90. C Hessle *York* 89-93; P-in-c Micklefield w Aberford 93-95; V Aberford w Micklefield 95-04; P-in-c Darwen St Cuth w Tockholes St Steph *Blackb* 04-14; rtd 14; PtO *York* from 15. *53 Saxon Road, Whitby YO21 3NU* T: (01947) 602329 E: douglasgmoore@yahoo.co.uk

MOORE, Edward James. b 32. TD 85. TCD BA 56 MA 59. **d** 56 **p** 57. C Belfast St Luke *Conn* 56-59; CF 59-62; C Dunmurry *Conn* 62-64; P-in-c Kilmakee 64-70; I Belfast H Trin 70-80; I Jordanstown w Monkstown 80-91; I Jordanstown 91-97; Chapl Ulster Univ 80-84 and 84-88; CF (ACF) 66-70 and 88-97; CF (TAVR) 70-88; Can Belf Cathl 89-97; rtd 97. *16 Langford Close, Carrickfergus BT38 8HG* T: (028) 9336 7209 E: ejm@ejmoore.plus.com

MOORE, Geoffrey David. b 51. Poly Cen Lon BA 73. ERMC 04. **d** 07 **p** 08. NSM Brackley St Pet w St Jas 07-11; NSM Aston-le-Walls, Byfield, Boddington, Eydon etc from 11. *The New Vicarage, Parsons Street, Woodford Halse, Daventry NN11 3RE* T: (01327) 264927 E: geoff@ccvp.co.uk

MOORE, Geoffrey Robert. b 46. WEMTC 03. **d** 06 **p** 07. NSM Upton-on-Severn, Ripple, Earls Croome etc *Worc* from 06. *12 Hill View Gardens, Upton-upon-Severn WR8 0QJ* T: (01684) 594531 M: 07876-162402

MOORE, Mrs Gillian Mary. b 70. NTMTC. **d** 09 **p** 10. NSM Harwich Peninsula *Chelmsf* 09-13; Chapl St Helena Hospice Colchester from 13. *15 Lushington Road, Manningtree CO11 1EE* T: (01206) 397493 or 845566 E: lushingtree@btinternet.com *or* gmoore@sthelenahospice.org.uk

MOORE, Henry James William. b 33. TCD BA 55 MA 70. **d** 56 **p** 57. C Mullabrack *Arm* 56-61; C Drumglass 61-63; I Clogherny 63-81; I Ballinderry, Tamlaght and Arboe 81-08; Can Arm Cathl 90-08; Chan 98-01; Prec 01-08; rtd 08. *20 Laragh Road, Beragh, Omagh BT79 0TH* T: (028) 8075 7384

✠**MOORE, The Rt Revd Henry Wylie.** b 23. Liv Univ BCom 50 Leeds Univ MA 72. Wycliffe Hall Ox 50. **d** 52 **p** 53 **c** 83. C Farnworth *Liv* 52-54; C Middleton *Man* 54-56; CMS 56-60; Iran 57-60; R Burnage St Marg *Man* 60-63; R Middleton 60-74; Home Sec CMS 74-80; Exec Sec CMS 80-83; Bp Cyprus and the Gulf 83-86; Gen Sec CMS 86-90; rtd 90; Asst Bp Dur 90-94; PtO *Heref* from 94. *Fern Hill Cottage, Hopesay, Craven Arms SY7 8HD* T: (01588) 660248

MOORE, Miss Hilary Jane. b 62. St Jo Coll Nottm 12. **d** 15. NSM Chesterfield SS Aug *Derby* from 15. *61 Peach Street, Derby DE22 3EQ* M: 07708-8864445 E: hilary90@hotmail.co.uk

MOORE, Preb Hugh Desmond. b 37. St Cath Soc Ox BA 58 MA 64. St Steph Ho Ox 58. **d** 61 **p** 62. C Kingston St Luke *S'wark* 61-68; Asst Chapl Lon Univ 68-70; Chapl Edgware Community Hosp 70-92; Chapl Barnet and Chase Farm Hosps NHS Trust 92-99; V Hendon St Alphage *Lon* from 70; AD W Barnet 85-90; Preb St Paul's Cathl from 95. *The Vicarage, Montrose Avenue, Edgware HA8 0DN* T: (020) 8952 4611 E: hugh.moore@tesco.net

MOORE, Ivan. MA BTh. **d** 90 **p** 91. C Knock *D & D* 90-93; I Taney *D & G* 97-99; Chapl Bancroft's Sch Woodford Green from 99. *41 Wynndale Road, London E18 1DY* T: (020) 8559 2791 *or* 8505 4821 F: 8559 0032

MOORE, James. *See* MOORE, Edward James

MOORE, Canon James Kenneth. b 37. AKC 62. St Boniface Warminster 62. **d** 63 **p** 64. C W Hartlepool St Oswald *Dur* 63-66; C-in-c Manor Park CD *Sheff* 66-76; TV Sheff Manor 76-78; R Frecheville and Hackenthorpe 78-87; V Bilham 87-91; V Sheff St Oswald 91-02; Hon Can Sheff Cathl 93-02; rtd 02; PtO *Sheff* from 02. *115 Greenhill Main Road, Sheffield S8 7RG* T: 0114-283 9634

MOORE (formerly BEVAN), Ms Janet Mary. b 46. Bris Poly CertEd 86. WMMTC. **d** 98 **p** 99. C Bishop's Cleeve *Glouc* 98-02; V Overbury w Teddington, Alstone etc *Worc* 02-08; Faith Co-ord Surrey Police *Guildf* 08-11; rtd 11. *8 St John's Close, Cirencester GL7 2JA* T: (01285) 640077 E: therevjan@btinternet.com

MOORE, Janis. b 43. **d** 05 **p** 06. OLM Bridport *Sarum* from 05. *61 North Allington, Bridport DT6 5DZ* T: (01305) 425644 E: janis@moore61.fsnet.co.uk

MOORE, John. b 26. Univ of Wales (Lamp) BA 51. Oak Hill Th Coll 51. **d** 53 **p** 54. C Illogan *Truro* 53-57; C Margate H Trin *Cant* 57-58; C Abingdon w Shippon *Ox* 58-67; V Retford St Sav *S'well* 67-73; R Aspenden and Layston w Buntingford *St Alb* 73-86; V Stanstead Abbots 86-91; rtd 91; PtO *Ox* from 95. *20 Radley Road, Abingdon OX14 3PQ* T: (01235) 532518

MOORE, John Arthur. b 33. Cuddesdon Coll 70. **d** 71 **p** 72. Hon C Gt Burstead *Chelmsf* 71-74; Chapl Barnard Castle Sch 74-97; rtd 97; PtO *Dur* from 96; *Leeds* from 02. *39 Woodside, Barnard Castle DL12 8DY* T: (01833) 690947

MOORE, John Bishop. b 53. Haverford Coll (USA) BA 75 Columbia Univ MBA 78. ERMC. **d** 08 **p** 09. C Paris St Mich *Eur* 08-12; Asst Chapl 12-15; P-in-c Guernsey St Steph *Win* from 15. *St Stephen's Vicarage, Les Gravées, St Peter Port, Guernsey GY1 1RN* T: (01481) 720268 E: frjohnbishopmoore@gmail.com

MOORE, John Cecil. b 37. TCD BA 61 MA 67 BD 69. CITC 62. **d** 62 **p** 63. C Belfast St Matt *Conn* 62-65; C Holywood *D & D* 65-70; I Ballyphilip w Ardquin 70-77; I Mt Merrion 77-79; I Donaghcloney w Waringstown 79-02; Treas Dromore Cathl 90-93; Chan Dromore Cathl 93-02; rtd 02. *22 Kensington Court, Dollingstown, Craigavon BT66 7HU* T: (028) 3832 1606 E: canonjohnmoore@gmail.com

MOORE, John David. b 30. St Chad's Coll Dur BA 54 DipEd 56. **d** 56 **p** 57. C Wallsend St Pet *Newc* 56-60; C Leamington Priors All SS *Cov* 60-62; V Longford 62-75; P-in-c Nuneaton St Mary 75-77; V 77-83; V St Ives *Ely* 83-00; rtd 00; PtO *Chelmsf* from 01. *25 Felmongers, Harlow CM20 3DU* T: (01279) 436496 M: 07890-976056 E: frjdavid@aol.com

MOORE, John Henry. b 35. Nottm Univ BMus 56 CertEd 57 MA 61. EMMTC 87. **d** 90 **p** 91. NSM Gotham *S'well* 90-95; NSM Kingston and Ratcliffe-on-Soar 90-95; NSM Bunny w Bradmore 95-00; P-in-c 97-00; rtd 00. *19 Hall Drive, Gotham, Nottingham NG11 0JT* T: 0115-983 0670 E: john@moorerev.freeserve.co.uk

MOORE, John Keith. b 26. Sarum & Wells Th Coll 78. **d** 81 **p** 82. NSM Guildf All SS 81-86; NSM Guildf H Trin w St Mary 86-94; Dean of Chapter 90-94; PtO *Chich* 94-06; *Guildf* from 94. *4 Grover's Manor, Wood Road, Hindhead GU26 6JP* T: (01428) 605871

MOORE, John Michael. b 48. Em Coll Cam BA 70 MA 73. Cuddesdon Coll 72. **d** 74 **p** 75. C Almondbury *Wakef* 74-78; TV Basingstoke *Win* 78-88; P-in-c Southampton St Alb 88-91; V Swaythling 91-99; rtd 99; Chapl St Jo Win Charity 99-11. *13 Priors Way, Winchester SO22 4HQ* T: (01962) 862341 *or* 854226 F: 840602 E: office@stjohnswinchester.co.uk

MOORE, Canon John Richard. b 45. Linc Th Coll 80. **d** 82 **p** 83. C Gt Grimsby St Mary and St Jas *Linc* 82-86; V Skirbeck Quarter 86-95; P-in-c Coningsby w Tattershall 95-99; R 99-06; R Bain Valley Gp 06-10; Can and Preb Linc Cathl 09-10; rtd 11. *23 Church Lane, Hutton, Alford LN13 9RD* T: (01507) 490246

MOORE, Canon John Richard. b 35. Lambeth MA 01. St Jo Coll Nottm 56. **d** 59 **p** 60. C Northwood Em *Lon* 59-63; V Burton Dassett *Cov* 63-66; Dioc Youth Chapl 63-71; Dir Lindley Lodge Educn Trust Nuneaton 71-82; TR Kinson *Sarum* 82-88; Gen Dir CPAS 88-96; Hon Can Cov Cathl 95-01; Internat Dir ICS 96-01; rtd 01; PtO *Cov* from 01. *26 Jourdain Park, Heathcote, Warwick CV34 6FJ* T: (01926) 429299 E: moore.fam@tiscali.co.uk

MOORE, Mrs Joyce. b 48. TCD BA 70 HDipEd 71 ARIAM 68. CITC 98. **d** 01 **p** 02. NSM Camlough w Mullaglass *Arm* 01-07; NSM Drogheda w Ardee, Collon and Termonfeckin from 07; Hon V Choral Arm Cathl from 07. *Dundalk Road, Dunleer, Co Louth, Republic of Ireland* T: (00353) (41) 685 1327 E: am.drogheda@armagh.anglican.org

MOORE, Margaret Louise. b 62. DipOT 85. SAOMC 04. **d** 06 **p** 07. C Bp's Hatfield, Lemsford and N Mymms *St Alb* 06-10; C Letchworth St Paul w Willian from 10; Chapl Garden Ho Hospice Letchworth from 09. *St Paul's Vicarage, 177 Pixmore Way, Letchworth SG6 1QT* T: (01462) 483934 M: 07729-385830 E: louisemoore85@btinternet.com

MOORE, Matthew Edward George. b 38. Oak Hill Th Coll 77. **d** 77 **p** 78. C Larne and Inver *Conn* 77-80; I Desertmartin w Termoneeny *D & R* 80-84; I Milltown *Arm* 84-96; I Culmore w Muff and Belmont *D & R* 96-06; Dioc Warden for Min of Healing 97-06; Can Derry Cathl 04-06; rtd 06. *9 Glen House Mews, Main Street, Eglinton, Londonderry BT47 3AA* T: (028) 7181 1238 M: 07720-036211 E: matt-audreymoore@hotmail.co.uk

MOORE, Canon Michael Mervlyn Hamond. b 35. LVO 99. Pemb Coll Ox BA 60 MA 63. Wells Th Coll 60. **d** 62 **p** 63. C Bethnal Green St Matt *Lon* 62-66; Chapl Bucharest w Sofia and Belgrade *Eur* 66-67; Asst Gen Sec C of E Coun on Foreign Relns 67-70; Gen Sec 70-72; Abp's Chapl on Foreign Relns *Cant* 72-82; Hon C Walworth St Pet *S'wark* 67-75; Hon C Walworth 75-80; Hon Can Cant Cathl 74-90; Chapl Chpl Royal Hampton Court Palace 82-99; Dep P in O 92-99; rtd 99. *The College of St Barnabas, Blackberry Lane, Lingfield RH7 6NJ* T: (01342) 872859

MOORE, Michael Peter John. b 60. Qu Coll Birm 05. **d** 08 **p** 09. C Pet St Mary Boongate 08-11; V from 11. *St Mary's Vicarage, 214 Eastfield Road, Peterborough PE1 4BD* T: (01733) 554815 E: revmichael@tiscali.co.uk

MOORE, Nicholas James. b 84. Magd Coll Ox BA 07 MSt 08 Keble Coll Ox DPhil 15. Wycliffe Hall Ox 09. **d** 14 **p** 15. C Stranton *Dur* from 14. *40 Browning Avenue, Hartlepool TS25 5PS* T: (01429) 597284 M: 07969-393031 E: nicholas.moore@magd.oxon.org

MOORE, The Ven Paul Henry. b 59. Ball Coll Ox BA 82 DPhil 86. Wycliffe Hall Ox 87. **d** 89 **p** 90. C Ox St Andr 89-93; V Kildwick *Bradf* 93-01; V Cowplain *Portsm* 01-14; RD Havant 04-09; Hon Can Portsm Cathl 13-14; Adn for Miss Development *Win* from 14; Hon Can Win Cathl from 14. *2 Maldon Close, Eastleigh SO50 6BD* T: (023) 8065 0824 *or* (01962) 710964 E: paul.moore@winchester.anglican.org

MOORE, Philip. b 49. York Univ MA 71 Leeds Univ MA 05 PGCE 72. NOC 02. **d** 05 **p** 06. NSM Heworth Ch Ch *York* 05-09; P-in-c York St Thos w St Maurice 09-14; PtO from 14. *14 Whitby Avenue, York YO31 1ET* T: (01904) 425250

MOORE, Raymond. b 47. QUB BSc 70. **d** 87 **p** 88. Aux Min Belfast All SS *Conn* 87-95; NSM 95-96; Aux Min Kilmakee 96-04; P-in-c Drung w Castleterra, Larah and Lavey etc *K, E & A* 04-09; NSM Albert Park Australia 09-12; P-in-c Belfast St Simon w St Phil *Conn* from 13. *21 Kilwarlin Avenue, Hillsborough BT26 6LQ* T/F: (028) 9268 2789 M: 07746-583471 E: rev.raymond.moore@gmail.com

MOORE, Richard Noel. b 34. TCD BA 56 MA 60. **d** 57 **p** 58. C Derry Cathl 57-60; I Clondehorkey 60-66; I Stranorlar w Meenglas and Kilteevogue 66-76; I Glendermott 76-00; Can Derry Cathl 89-00; rtd 00. *Evergreen House, 37 Mullanahoe Road, Dungannon BT71 5AT* T: (028) 8673 7112

MOORE, Richard Norman Theobald. b 39. St Andr Univ BSc 62 Lon Univ BD 66. Clifton Th Coll. **d** 66 **p** 67. C Stowmarket *St E* 66-69; C New Humberstone *Leic* 69-72; P-in-c Leic Martyrs 73; V 73-84; Chapl Manor Hosp Epsom 84-94; Chapl Surrey

Oaklands NHS Trust 94-00; rtd 00; PtO *Guildf* 02-07; *St E* from 07. *9 Cramner Cliff Gardens, Felixstowe IP11 7NH* T: (01394) 273889

MOORE, Richard William Robert. b 39. UCD BA 70 TCD HDipEd 71. CITC 98. **d** 01 **p** 02. Aux Min Drogheda w Ardee, Collon and Termonfeckin *Arm* 01-05; Aux Min Dundalk w Heynestown from 05; Aux Min Ballymascanlan w Creggan and Rathcor from 05. *Dundalk Road, Dunleer, Co Louth, Republic of Ireland* T: (00353) (41) 685 1327 E: richwmoore@yahoo.ie

MOORE, Robert Allen. b 32. Univ of the Pacific BA 54 Boston Univ STB 58 STM 59. **d** 63 **p** 63. USA 63-80; V Farington *Blackb* 80-83; TV Preston St Jo 83-85; P-in-c Fleetwood St Pet 85-87; V Leyland St Jas 87-97; rtd 97; PtO *Blackb* from 97. *19 Lea Road, Whittle-le-Woods, Chorley PR6 7PF* T: (01257) 265701 E: rmoore1980@aol.com

MOORE, Mrs Roberta. b 46. CITC 03. **d** 06 **p** 07. Aux Min Drung w Castleterra, Larah and Lavey etc *K, E & A* 06-09; NSM Albert Park Australia 09-12; P-in-c Belfast St Aid *Conn* from 13. *21 Kilwarlin Avenue, Hillsborough BT26 6LQ* T/F: (028) 9268 2789 M: 07746-583470 E: bobbiemoore1@gmail.com

MOORE, Robin Hugh. b 52. CertEd BEd QUB BD. **d** 84 **p** 85. C Derryloran *Arm* 84-86; C Knock *D & R* 86-89; Bp's C Belfast St Steph w St Luke *Conn* 89-94; I 94-96; I Whitehouse 96-03; Bp's C Belfast St Mary Magd 03-07; I Belfast St Mark from 07; P-in-c Belfast St Mary w H Redeemer from 12. *9 Sycamore Park, Newtownabbey BT37 0NR* T: (028) 9086 9569 E: moorerobin@sky.com

MOORE, Shaun Christopher. b 52. Open Univ BA 92 NE Lon Poly CertEd 75 K Coll Lon MA 10. NTMTC BA 08. **d** 08 **p** 09. NSM Leyton St Mary w St Edw and St Luke *Chelmsf* 08-11; TV Walthamstow 11-12; PtO 12-14; V Harold Hill St Geo from 14. *St George's Vicarage, Chippenham Road, Romford RM3 8HX* E: shaunmoore@freeola.com

MOORE, Simon Quentin. b 61. Sheff Univ BA 83 PGCE 84. St Jo Coll Nottm MA 99. **d** 00 **p** 01. C St Alb St Paul *St Alb* 00-03; TV Digswell and Panshanger 03-10; P-in-c Letchworth St Paul w Willian 10-13; V from 13. *St Paul's Vicarage, 177 Pixmore Way, Letchworth SG6 1QT* T: (01462) 483934 E: sqmoore@btinternet.com

MOORE, Thomas Sydney. b 50. St Paul's Coll Grahamstown 77. **d** 79 **p** 80. C Rondebosch St Thos 79-82 and S Africa 83-84; C Bredasdorp 82-83; R Green Pt 84-88; C Bushey *St Alb* 97-08; C Aldershot St Mich *Guildf* from 08. *Ascension House, Ayling Hill, Aldershot GU11 3LL* T: (01252) 330224 E: ts.moore@virgin.net

MOORE, Mrs Wendy. b 44. Westcott Ho Cam 92. **d** 94 **p** 95. C Rotherham *Sheff* 94-97; V Laughton w Throapham 97-01; V Bromsgrove All SS *Worc* 01-09; rtd 09; TV Saffron Walden and Villages *Chelmsf* 09-14. *Ashdown Vicarage, Radwinter Road, Ashdown, Saffron Walden CB10 2ET* T: (01799) 584171 E: wendywmoor@aol.com

MOORE, William. *See* MOORE, Albert William

MOORE, William Morris. b 33. QUB BSc 55 TCD. **d** 61 **p** 62. C Belfast St Mich *Conn* 61-64; I 70-80; C Belfast All SS 64-70; I Ballynafeigh St Jude *D & D* 80-83; Can Bell Cathl 95-03; rtd 03. *10 Hollygate Park, Carryduff, Belfast BT8 8DZ* T: (028) 9081 4896

MOORE-BICK, Miss Elizabeth Mary. b 77. Qu Coll Cam BA 99 MA 03 Anglia Poly Univ BA 04. Westcott Ho Cam 02. **d** 05 **p** 06. C Hillingdon St Jo *Lon* 05-09; TV Clarendon *Sarum* 09-15; Chapl Salisbury Cathl Sch 15. *Little Bines, Witherenden Hill, Burwash, Etchingham TN19 7JE* M: 07803-044217 E: lizmoore_bick@yahoo.co.uk

MOORE BROOKS, Dorothy Anne. b 66. York Univ BA 87 Hughes Hall Cam PGCE 88. Ridley Hall Cam 96. **d** 98 **p** 99. C S Kensington St Jude *Lon* 98-01; PtO 02-08; Chapl Gt Ormond Street Hosp for Children NHS Trust 02-08; NSM Hoddesdon *St Alb* 01-10; Chapl Isabel Hospice 08-10; Chapl Gt Ormond Street Hosp NHS Foundn Trust from 10; LtO Amersham Deanery from 10. *Great Ormond Street Hospital, Great Ormond Street, London WC1N 3JH* T: (020) 7813 8232 *or* (01494) 730876 E: moorebrooks@sky.com *or* dorothy.moorebrooks@gosh.nhs.uk

MOORES, Jonathan Ian. b 75. Glos Univ BA 10. Trin Coll Bris MA 12. **d** 12 **p** 13. C Denton Holme *Carl* from 12. *118 Dalston Road, Carlisle CA2 5PJ* M: 07753-427329 E: youthmissioner@googlemail.com

MOORES, Samantha Jane. *See* DUDDLES, Samantha Jane

MOORHEAD, Preb Michael David. b 52. BSc BA. St Steph Ho Ox. **d** 83 **p** 84. C Kilburn St Aug w St Jo *Lon* 83-87; C Kenton 87-89; Chapl Cen Middx Hosp NHS Trust from 89; V Harlesden All So *Lon* from 89; P-in-c Willesden St Matt 92-02; Preb St Paul's Cathl from 13. *All Souls' Vicarage, 3 Station Road, London NW10 4UJ* T/F: (020) 8965 4988 E: michael@allsoulschurch.fsnet.co.uk

MOORHOUSE, Humphrey John. b 18. Oak Hill Th Coll 37. **d** 41 **p** 42. C Dalston St Mark w St Bart *Lon* 41-42; C Chadwell Heath *Chelmsf* 42-45; R Vange 45-83; rtd 83; PtO *Chelmsf* from 83. *12 Waverley Road, Benfleet SS7 4AZ* T: (01268) 754952

MOORHOUSE, Peter. b 42. Liv Univ BSc 64 Hull Univ CertEd. Linc Th Coll 79. **d** 81 **p** 82. C Horsforth *Ripon* 81-85; R Ackworth *Wakef* 85-96; Dep Chapl HM Pris Leeds 96-97; Chapl HM Pris Stocken 97-98; Chapl HM Pris Everthorpe 98-07; rtd 07; PtO *York* from 07. *65 Eastfield Lane, Dunnington, York YO19 5ND* T: (01904) 481055

MOORSE, Michael William. b 36. Culham Coll of Educn TCert 63. Guildf Dioc Min Course 96. **d** 98 **p** 99. OLM Woking St Pet *Guildf* 98-06; PtO from 06. *4 Bonners Close, Woking GU22 9RA* T: (01483) 767460

MOORSOM, Canon Christopher Arthur Robert. b 55. Ox Univ BA. Sarum & Wells Th Coll 79. **d** 82 **p** 83. C Bradford-on-Avon H Trin *Sarum* 82-85; R Broad Town, Clyffe Pypard and Tockenham 85-89; V Banwell *B & W* 89-96; R Upper Stour *Sarum* 96-14; Prec and Can Res Derby Cathl from 14. *Derby Cathedral Office, 18-19 Iron Gate, Derby DE1 3GP* T: (01332) 341201 E: precentor@derbycathedral.org *or* chris@moorsom.co.uk

MORAN, Adrian Peter. CITC. **d** 09 **p** 10. NSM Cork St Ann's Union *C, C & R* 09-10; NSM Fermoy Union 10-13; NSM Bandon Union 13-14; P-in-c Cobh and Glanmire from 14. *22 Rosehill East, Ballinacurra, Midleton, Co Cork, Republic of Ireland* T: (00353) (21) 463 1611 M: 87-228 2931 E: adrianpmoran@yahoo.ie

MORAN, Patricia Margaret. b 54. Dur Univ BA 77 PGCE 81 Loyola Univ MA 99 Newc Univ PhD 10. Lindisfarne Regional Tr Partnership 12. **d** 14 **p** 15. NSM Monkseaton St Mary *Newc* from 14. *1 Woodburn Square, Whitley Bay NE26 3JE* T: 0191-251 8200 E: pmmoran@blueyonder.co.uk

MORAY, ROSS AND CAITHNESS, Bishop of. *See* STRANGE, The Rt Revd Mark Jeremy

MORAY, ROSS AND CAITHNESS, Dean of. *See* SIMPSON, The Very Revd Alison Jane

MORBY, Helen Mary. b 62. Wolv Univ BA 99. Ripon Coll Cuddesdon 99. **d** 01 **p** 02. C Lich St Chad 01-04; V Farnworth *Liv* 04-12; AD Widnes 05-07; Hon Can Liv Cathl 05-12; P-in-c Kinnerley w Melverley and Knockin w Maesbrook *Lich* from 12; P-in-c Maesbury from 12. *The Rectory, Vicarage Lane, Kinnerley, Oswestry SY10 8DE* T: (01691) 682351 E: rectory.kinnerley@btinternet.com

MORDECAI, Mrs Betty. b 27. Birm Univ BA 48 Cam Univ CertEd 49. Wycliffe Hall Ox 85. **dss** 86 **d** 87 **p** 94. Leamington Priors All SS *Cov* 86-89; Hon Par Dn 87-89; C Worc City St Paul and Old St Martin etc 89-94; rtd 94; PtO *Cov* from 00. *8 Swain Crofts, Leamington Spa CV31 1YW* T: (01926) 882001 E: bettyhoward@btinternet.com

MORDECAI, Thomas Huw. b 59. Bris Univ BA 81 St Jo Coll Dur BA 85 MA 92. Cranmer Hall Dur 83. **d** 87 **p** 88. C Gillingham St Mary *Roch* 87-90; Chapl Warw Sch 90-96; Chapl Giggleswick Sch 96-98; Chapl Westmr Sch and PV Westmr Abbey 98-01; Chapl Geelong Gr Sch Australia 02-04; Chapl Malvern Coll 05-07; Chapl K Wm's Coll Is of Man 07-12; PtO *Ox* from 13. *3 Popel's Cottages, Church Road, Winkfield, Windsor SL4 4SG* T: (01344) 893973

MORE, Ajay. b 68. **d** 14 **p** 15. C Alperton *Lon* from 14. *56 Devon Close, Perivale, Greenford UB6 7DR* M: 07868-662703 E: ajay-kavita@hotmail.com

MORE, Canon Richard David Antrobus. b 48. St Jo Coll Dur BA 70. Cranmer Hall Dur 70. **d** 72 **p** 73. C Macclesfield St Mich *Ches* 72-77; Chapl Lee Abbey 77-82; V Porchester S'well 82-96; RD Gedling 90-96; Bp's Dom Chapl *Chelmsf* 96-01; Dioc Dir of Ords 01-13; Dioc NSM Officer 01-13; Hon Can Chelmsf Cathl 96-13; rtd 13. *16 Russell Street, Chichester PO19 7EL*

MORELAND, Andrew John. b 64. St Jo Coll Nottm 09. **d** 11 **p** 12. C Bridlington Priory *York* 11-14; V Seamer w East Ayton from 14. *The Vicarage, 3 Stockshill, Seamer, Scarborough YO12 4QG* M: 07784-020848 T: (01723) 866284 E: andrew.moreland@btinternet.com

MORETON, Ann Louise. b 32. **d** 02 **p** 03. OLM Whitstable *Cant* 02-10; PtO from 11. *Church House, 24 Freemans Close, Seasalter, Whitstable CT5 4BB* T: (01227) 277140 E: annmoreton@hotmail.com

MORETON, Bernard. *See* MORETON, Michael Bernard

MORETON, Harley. *See* MORETON, Philip Norman Harley

MORETON, Preb Mark. b 39. Jes Coll Cam BA 64 MA 68. Westcott Ho Cam 63. **d** 65 **p** 66. C Portsea All SS *Portsm* 65-70; C St Martin-in-the-Fields *Lon* 70-72; Chapl Jes Coll Cam 72-77; R Stafford St Mary and St Chad *Lich* 77-79; P-in-c Stafford Ch Ch 77-79; TR Stafford 79-91; P-in-c Marston w Whitgreave 77-79; V W Bromwich All SS 91-04; Preb Lich

Cathl 99-04; rtd 04; PtO *Worc* from 05. *Rosemont, Dry Mill Lane, Bewdley DY12 2BL* T: (01299) 401965 E: moreton@fatbeehive.com

MORETON, Michael Bernard. b 44. St Jo Coll Cam BA 66 MA 70 Ch Ch Ox BA 66 MA 69 DPhil 69. St Steph Ho Ox 66. **d** 68 **p** 69. C Banstead *Guildf* 68-74; R Alburgh *Nor* 74-75; R Denton 74-75; R Middleton Cheney w Chacombe *Pet* 75-87; PtO *Cant* 00-15. *Address temp unknown*

MORETON, Philip Norman Harley. b 28. Linc Th Coll. **d** 57 **p** 58. C Howden *York* 57-60; C Bottesford *Linc* 60-65; V Linc St Giles 65-70; V Bracebridge Heath 71-77; V Seasalter *Cant* 77-84; TV Whitstable 84-88; rtd 88; PtO *York* 96-06. *112 Grantham Road, Bracebridge Heath, Lincoln LN4 2QF* T: (01522) 534672 M: 07851-717891

MORETON, Rupert Robert James. b 66. TCD BA 89. CITC BTh 92. **d** 92 **p** 93. C Dublin Ch Ch Cathl Gp 92-96; Asst Chapl Costa Blanca *Eur* 96-98; Chapl Helsinki 98-11; Dean's V Cork Cathl 11-13; Finland from 13. *Address temp unknown*

MORFILL, Mrs Mary Joanna. b 46. Seaford Coll of Educn TCert 67. STETS 01. **d** 04 **p** 08. NSM Swanmore St Barn *Portsm* 04-14; PtO from 14; Chapl MU from 12. *Whistlers, New Road, Swanmore, Southampton SO32 2PF* T: (01489) 878227 M: 07906-755145 E: mary@swanmore.net

MORGAN, Adrian. b 85. Univ of Wales (Abth) BA 06 MPhil 08 PhD 12 Peterho Cam BA 13. Ridley Hall Cam 11. **d** 14 **p** 15. C Gorseinon *S & B* from 14; Chapl Gower Coll Swansea from 14. *28 Bryneithin Road, Gorseinon, Swansea SA4 4XA* T: (01792) 897004 E: adrian@stcath.org.uk

MORGAN, Alison Jean. b 59. Girton Coll Cam BA 82 MA 85 Darw Coll Cam PhD 86. EMMTC 93. **d** 96 **p** 97. NSM Oadby *Leic* 96; NSM Leic H Trin w St Jo 98-08; Thinker and writer ReSource from 04. *10 Dairy Close, Wells BA5 2ND* T: (01749) 600341 E: alisonmorgan@resource-arm.net

MORGAN, Andrew Paul. b 80. **d** 14 **p** 15. C Trentham *Lich* from 14. *Trent Vale Vicarage, Crosby Road, Stoke-on-Trent ST4 6JY* M: 07880-730295

MORGAN, Anthony Hogarth. b 42. St Josef Missiehuis Holland 60 St Jos RC Coll Lon 62. **d** 65 **p** 66. In RC Ch 66-93; NSM Handsworth Woodhouse *Sheff* 93-94; C Sheff St Leon Norwood 94-97; P-in-c Shiregreen St Hilda 97-05; C Shiregreen St Jas and St Chris 05-07; rtd 07; PtO *York* from 09. *30 Dulverton Hall, Esplanade, Scarborough YO11 2AR*

MORGAN, Anthony Paul George. b 57. Sarum & Wells Th Coll 89. **d** 91 **p** 92. C Plymstock *Ex* 91-95; P-in-c Wolborough w Newton Abbot 95-00; V York St Hilda 01-06; rtd 06; PtO *Derby* 07-10. *54 Macaulay Road, Luton LU4 0LP* E: tony@thefms.fsnet.co.uk

✠**MORGAN, The Most Revd Barry Cennydd.** b 47. Lon Univ BA 69 Selw Coll Cam BA 72 MA 74 Univ of Wales PhD 86. Westcott Ho Cam 70. **d** 72 **p** 73 **c** 93. Chapl Bryn-y-Don Community Sch 72-75; C St Andrews Major w Michaelston-le-Pit *Llan* 72-75; Ed *Welsh Churchman* 75-82; Lect Th Univ of Wales (Cardiff) 75-77; Chapl and Lect St Mich Coll Llan 75-77; Warden Ch Hostel Ban 77-84; Chapl and Lect Th Univ of Wales (Ban) 77-84; In-Service Tr Adv Ban 78-84; Dir of Ords 82-84; Can Ban Cathl 83-84; TR Wrexham *St As* 84-86; Adn Meirionnydd Ban 86-93; R Criccieth w Treflys 86-93; Bp Ban 93-99; Bp Llan from 99; Abp Wales from 03. *Llys Esgob, The Cathedral Green, Llandaff, Cardiff CF5 2YE* T: (029) 2056 2400 F: 2057 7129 E: archbishop@churchinwales.org.uk

MORGAN, Carol Jacqueline Ann. b 62. Ox Min Course. **d** 13 **p** 14. C Reading St Matt *Ox* from 13. *29 Somerton Gardens, Earley, Reading RG6 5XG* T: 0118-986 0983 E: carolmorgan@the-network.info

MORGAN, Charles Nicholas Brendan. b 55. MBE 91. Open Univ BSc 94 Leeds Univ BA 08. NOC 05. **d** 08 **p** 09. C Derwent Ings *York* 08-12; R Howardian Gp from 12. *The Rectory, Terrington, York YO60 6PU* T: (01653) 648226 M: 07902-033174 E: dadintheditch@hotmail.com

✠**MORGAN, The Rt Revd Christopher Heudebourck.** b 47. Lanc Univ BA 73 Heythrop Coll Lon MTh 91. Kelham Th Coll 66. **d** 73 **p** 74 **c** 01. C Birstall *Leic* 73-76; Asst Chapl Brussels *Eur* 76-80; P-in-c Redditch St Geo *Worc* 80-81; TV Redditch, The Ridge 81-85; V Sonning *Ox* 85-96; Prin Berks Chr Tr Scheme 85-89; Dir Past Studies Ox Min Course 92-96; Dioc Can Res Glouc Cathl and Officer for Min 96-01; Area Bp Colchester *Chelmsf* 01-13; rtd 13; Hon Asst Bp Chich from 14. *6 Wellington Court, Grand Avenue, Worthing BN11 5AB* T: (01903) 264184

MORGAN, Christopher John. b 46. Brasted Th Coll 68 Linc Th Coll 70. **d** 72 **p** 73. C Earley St Pet *Ox* 72-76; C Epsom St Martin *Guildf* 76-79; V Stoneleigh 79-83; Ind Chapl *York* 83-92; NACRO 87-91; V York St Hilda 92-96; TV E Greenwich S'wark 96-03; P-in-c Norbury St Oswald 03-05; V 05-14; rtd 14. *5 Gilkes Walk, Middlesbrough TS4 3RT*

MORGAN, Christopher Laurence John. b 66. **d** 12 **p** 13. NSM Stepney St Dunstan and All SS *Lon* from 12. *13 Ursula Court, 146 Brownfield Street, London E14 6NF* M: 07894-099039 E: c.morgan903@btinternet.com

MORGAN, Clive. b 41. **d** 02. NSM Blaina and Nantyglo *Mon* 02-13; NSM Upper Ebbw Valleys from 13. *26 Victoria Street, Blaina, Abertillery NP13 3BG* T: (01495) 291637

MORGAN, David Farnon Charles. b 43. Leeds Univ BA 68. Coll of Resurr Mirfield 68. **d** 70 **p** 71. C Swinton St Pet *Man* 70-73; C Langley All SS and Martyrs 73-75; R Salford St Clem w St Cypr Ordsall 75-76; R Salford Ordsall St Clem 76-86; V Adlington *Blackb* 86-11; AD Chorley 98-04; rtd 11. *1 Holly Close, Farishes Lane, South Ferriby, Barton-upon-Humber DN18 6HG* T: (01652) 408500 E: morgyvic@talktalk.net

MORGAN, David Joseph. b 47. Bp Burgess Hall Lamp 66 St Deiniol's Hawarden 74. **d** 74 **p** 75. C Pembroke Dock *St D* 74-77; C Burry Port and Pwll 77-80; Miss to Seafarers 80-12; Sen Chapl and Sec Welsh Coun 85-12; rtd 12. *19 Clos Bevan, Gowerton, Swansea SA4 3GY* T: (01792) 923368

MORGAN, Deiniol Tudur. **d** 02 **p** 03. Min Can Ban Cathl 02-04; P-in-c Llanberis, Llanrug and Llandinorwig 04-05; Min Can and Prec Westmr Abbey 05-08; CF from 08. *c/o MOD Chaplains (Army)* F: 381824 T: (01264) 383430

MORGAN, Sister Enid May. b 37. St Luke's Coll Ex CertEd 69 Ex Univ DipEd 76 Univ of Wales (Lamp) BA 04. **d** 07 **p** 07. NSM Llanfrechfa and Llanddewi Fach w Llandegfeth *Mon* 07-08. *Llety'r Pererin, Whitchurch, Solva, Haverfordwest SA62 6UD* E: enidmorgan@onetel.com

MORGAN, Canon Enid Morris Roberts. b 40. St Anne's Coll Ox BA 61 Univ of Wales (Ban) MA 73. United Th Coll Abth BD 81. **d** 84 **p** 97. C Llanfihangel w Llanafan and Llanwnnws etc *St D* 84-86; Dn-in-c 86-93; Dir Bd of Miss Ch in Wales 93-00; V Llangynwyd w Maesteg *Llan* 00-05; Hon Can Llan Cathl 02-05; rtd 05. *Rhiwlas, Cliff Terrace, Aberystwyth SY23 2DN* T: (01970) 624648

MORGAN, Gareth Morison Kilby. b 33. Bris Univ BA 56. Cuddesdon Coll 57 Bangalore Th Coll. **d** 61 **p** 62. C St Helier *S'wark* 61-65; Chapl Scargill Ho 65-70; Dir RE *Linc* 71-74; Dioc Dir of Educn *St E* 74-81; TR Hanley H Ev *Lich* 81-89; TR Cen Telford 89-92; Warden Glenfall Ho *Glouc* 92-98; rtd 98; Chapl Hants Partnership NHS Trust 08-11; PtO *Win* 00-11; *Ely* from 12. *102 Lambs Lane, Cottenham, Cambridge CB24 8TA* T: (01954) 201696 E: morgan3341@virginmedia.com

MORGAN, Gary. b 61. Westmr Inst of Educn BA 03. St Steph Ho Ox 04. **d** 06 **p** 07. C Spilsby Gp *Linc* 06-10; P-in-c Kirton in Holland 10-13; P-in-c Algarkirk and Fosdyke 10-13; V Kirton in Holland w Algarkirk and Fosdyke 13-15; R The Wainfleet Gp from 15. *The Rectory, Vicarage Lane, Wainfleet St Mary, Skegness PE24 4JJ* M: 07879-068196 E: fathergaz@yahoo.co.uk

MORGAN, Geoffrey. *See* MORGAN, James Geoffrey Selwyn

MORGAN, Gerwyn. *See* MORGAN, William Charles Gerwyn

MORGAN, Glyn. b 21. Oak Hill Th Coll 73. **d** 76 **p** 77. NSM Barton Seagrave w Warkton *Pet* 76-00; PtO 00-11. *Address temp unknown*

MORGAN, Glyn. b 33. Univ of Wales (Ban) BA 55 MA 69. Coll of Resurr Mirfield 55. **d** 57 **p** 58. C Dolgellau *Ban* 57-60; C Conway 60-63; V Corris 63-68; Hd of RE Friars' Sch Ban 69-70; LtO *Ban* 70-71; Hd of RE Oswestry Boys' Modern Sch 70-74; Hd of RE Oswestry High Sch for Girls 74-79; Hon C Oswestry H Trin *Lich* 71-79; Hd of RE Oswestry Sch Oswestry 79-88; V Meifod and Llangynyw *St As* 88-01; RD Caereinion 89-01; rtd 01. *Crib y Gwynt Annexe, Trefnanney, Meifod SY22 6XX* T: (01938) 500066

MORGAN, Graham. b 47. Kt 00. S'wark Ord Course. **d** 83 **p** 84. NSM S Kensington St Steph *Lon* 83-90; NSM Hammersmith H Innocents 90-02; NSM Bedford Park from 02. *24 Charleville Court, Charleville Road, London W14 9JG* T: (020) 7381 3211 E: grahammorgan1@btinternet.com

MORGAN, Henry. b 45. Hertf Coll Ox BA 68. Westcott Ho Cam 68. **d** 70 **p** 71. C Lee St Marg *S'wark* 70-73; C Newington St Paul 73-76; V Camberwell St Mich w All So w Em 76-84; V Kingswood 84-93; PtO 93-03; *Sheff* 03-11. *2 Brook Cottage, Eckington Road, Birlingham, Pershore WR10 3DA* M: 07714-569375 E: henry.morgan10@btinternet.com

MORGAN, Mrs Hilary Jane. b 55. WEMTC 06. **d** 09 **p** 10. C Tenbury *Heref* 09-12; C Heref St Pet w St Owen and St Jas 12-14; R Cagebrook from 14. *The Rectory, Kingstone, Hereford HR2 9EY* E: revhilary2011@btinternet.com

MORGAN, The Ven Ian David John. b 57. Hull Univ BA 78 LTCL 75. Ripon Coll Cuddesdon 80. **d** 83 **p** 84. C Heref H Trin 83-86; C New Shoreham *Chich* 86-88; Researcher, Producer & Presenter BBC Local Radio 88-92; V Ipswich All Hallows, *St E* 92-95; TR Ipswich St Mary at Stoke w St Pet 95-97; TR Ipswich St Mary at Stoke w St Pet and St Fran 97-12;

RD Ipswich 08-12; Adn Suffolk from 12; CUF Link Officer from 06; Hon Can St E Cathl from 09. *Glebe House, The Street, Ashfield, Stowmarket IP14 6LX* T: (01449) 685497 E: archdeacon.ian@cofesuffolk.org

MORGAN, Ian Stephen. b 50. Open Univ BA 88. Sarum & Wells Th Coll 86. **d** 88 **p** 89. C Baldock w Bygrave *St Alb* 88-91; C S Elmham and Ilketshall *St E* 91-95; V Bungay H Trin w St Mary 95-05; R Lt Barningham, Blickling, Edgefield etc *Nor* 05-10; rtd 10. *Plessey Cottage, Oulton, Norwich NR11 6NX* T: (01263) 587535 M: 07808-451350 E: smorganciho@yahoo.co.uk

MORGAN, James Geoffrey Selwyn. b 59. Ex Univ BA 81 PGCE 82 Open Univ MPhil 97 K Coll Lon PhD 14. Cranmer Hall Dur 88. **d** 91 **p** 92. C Reading St Agnes w St Paul *Ox* 91-93; C Bromham w Oakley and Stagsden *St Alb* 94-95; PtO *Pet* 95-98; C Epsom St Martin *Guildf* 98-01; Tutor Ox Cen for Miss Studies 01-05; Lic Preacher *Ox* 01-05; PtO *Guildf* from 01; Chapl Imp Coll Healthcare NHS Trust 11-13; Lead Chapl from 13. *Lead Chaplain, Charing Cross Hospital, Fulham Palace Road, London W6 8RF* F: 3312 1843 M: 07796-315334 T: (020) 3311 1041 *or* 3311 1234 E: geoff.morgan@imperial.nhs.net *or* jgs_morgan@talktalk.net

MORGAN, Mrs Jane Elizabeth. b 60. MBE 13. Keele Univ MA 96. SNWTP 11. **d** 14 **p** 15. NSM Southport H Trin *Liv* from 14. *19 Massams Lane, Formby, Liverpool L37 7BD*

MORGAN, John. *See* MORGAN, William John

MORGAN, John Laurence. b 41. Melbourne Univ BA 62 Oriel Coll Ox BA 69 MA 73 DPhil 76. **d** 68 **p** 69. Acting Chapl Oriel Coll Ox 69; and Chapl 70-76; USA 77-78; Australia from 78. *St John's College, College Road, St Lucia Qld 4067, Australia* T: (0062) (7) 3371 3741 *or* 3842 6600 F: 3870 5124 E: john.morgan@mailbox.uq.edu.au

MORGAN, John William. **d** 15. NSM Tenby *St D* from 15. *Avalon, 80 Upper Hill Park, Tenby SA70 8JG* T: (01834) 843625 E: jmorg410@aol.com

MORGAN, John William Miller. b 34. Lon Univ BSc 56. Wycliffe Hall Ox 61. **d** 63 **p** 64. C St Alb Ch Ch 63-68; V Luton St Matt High Town 68-79; V Mangotsfield *Bris* 79-90; P-in-c Stanton St Quintin, Hullavington, Grittleton etc 90-95; R Hullavington, Norton and Stanton St Quintin 95-99; rtd 99; PtO *Bris* from 00. *3 Bouverie Park, Stanton St Quintin, Chippenham SN14 6EE* T: (01666) 837670 E: johnwmmorgan@compuserve.com

MORGAN, Joseph. *See* MORGAN, David Joseph

MORGAN, Mrs Judith. b 62. CBDTI 96. **d** 99 **p** 00. C Brigham and Gt Broughton and Broughton Moor *Carl* 99-04; P-in-c Doxford St Wilfrid *Dur* 04-12; rtd 13. *30 Queens Avenue, Seaton, Workington CA14 1DL* E: morgjud@aol.com

MORGAN, Katharine. b 41. **d** 97. NSM Loughor *S & B* 91-11; PtO from 11. *68 Borough Road, Loughor, Swansea SA4 6RT* T: (01792) 524901

MORGAN, Kathleen Irene. b 52. St Martin's Coll Lanc CertEd 74. WEMTC 93. **d** 96 **p** 97. NSM Barnwood *Glouc* 96-99; C Coney Hill 99-02; V Churchdown St Jo and Innsworth 02-14; rtd 14. *Address temp unknown* E: revkaty@aol.com

MORGAN, Linda Marianne. b 48. Bris Univ BSc 69 Surrey Univ MSc 72 Lon Univ PhD 77 FRCPath 01. STETS 99. **d** 02 **p** 03. NSM Claygate *Guildf* from 02. *8 Melbury Close, Claygate KT10 0EX* T: (01372) 462911 E: lindamorgan@holytrinityclaygate.org.uk

MORGAN, Mrs Marian Kathleen Eleanor. b 38. Birm Univ MA 94 FCMI 82. WEMTC. **d** 00 **p** 01. NSM Cusop w Blakemere, Bredwardine w Brobury etc *Heref* 00-03; P-in-c New Radnor and Llanfihangel Nantmelan etc *S & B* 03-07; rtd 08; Hon C Aberedw w Llandeilo Graban and Llanbadarn etc *S & B* 10-13; Hon C Bryngwyn and Newchurch and Llanbedr etc 10-13; PtO from 13. *Carob Tree House, 4 Koukkoulas Street, Nata, 8525 Paphos, Cyprus* E: mkemorgan@btinternet.com

MORGAN, Mark Anthony. b 58. LLB. Chich Th Coll. **d** 84 **p** 85. C Thorpe St Andr *Nor* 84-87; C Eaton 87-90; V Southtown 90-92; PtO from 92. *Nethergate End, The Street, Saxlingham Nethergate, Norwich NR15 1AJ* T: (01508) 498003

MORGAN, Mark Steven Glyn. b 60. Essex Univ BSc 83 RGN 86. Ridley Hall Cam 95. **d** 97 **p** 99. C Herne Bay Ch Ch *Cant* 97-02; TV Ipswich St Mary at Stoke w St Pet and St Fran *St E* from 02. *St Peter's Church House, Stoke Park Drive, Ipswich IP2 9TH* T: (01473) 601438 E: hama.morgan@tinyworld.co.uk

MORGAN, Martin Paul. b 46. St Steph Ho Ox 71. **d** 73 **p** 74. C Kettering St Mary *Pet* 73-76; C Fareham SS Pet and Paul *Portsm* 76-80; V Portsea Ascension 80-94; V Rottingdean *Chich* from 94. *The Vicarage, Steyning Road, Rottingdean, Brighton BN2 7GA* T: (01273) 309216 E: martin.morgan43@ntlworld.com

MORGAN, Mrs Melanie Jane. b 54. RMN. Qu Coll Birm 98. **d** 02 **p** 03. NSM Derby St Andr w St Osmund 02-05. *16 Brading Close, Alvaston, Derby DE24 0UW* T: (01332) 754419
E: clifden@btinternet.com

MORGAN, Michael John. b 45. Nottm Univ BA 66 MEd 71. Linc Th Coll 80. **d** 82 **p** 83. C Bulkington *Cov* 82-83; C Bulkington w Shilton and Ansty 83-85; V Longford 85-89; R Norton *Sheff* 89-99; R Lapworth *Birm* 99-09; R Baddesley Clinton 99-09; rtd 09; PtO *Birm* from 09. *47 Grasmere Crescent, Nuneaton CV11 6ED* T: (01564) 784127

MORGAN, Canon Nicholas John. b 50. K Coll Lon BD 71 AKC 71 CertEd. St Aug Coll Cant 72. **d** 73 **p** 74. C Wythenshawe Wm Temple Ch *Man* 73-76; C Southam w Stockton *Cov* 76-79; V Brailes from 79; R Sutton under Brailes from 79; P-in-c Tysoe w Oxhill and Whatcote from 06; RD Shipston 90-98; Hon Can Cov Cathl from 03. *The Vicarage, Brailes, Banbury OX15 5HT* T: (01608) 685230

MORGAN, Nicholas John. b 69. Surrey Univ MBus 91 Sheff Univ BA 15. Yorks Min Course 13. **d** 15. C Masham and Healey *Leeds* from 15. *Green View, 43A Watermill Lane, North Stainley, Ripon HG4 3LA* M: 07939-052689 T: (01765) 635039
E: revnjmorgan@gmail.com

MORGAN, Nicola. b 64. Nottm Univ MA 86. Linc Th Coll BTh 95. **d** 95 **p** 96. C Lillington *Cov* 95-98; C Gospel Lane St Mich *Birm* 98-01; P-in-c Gt Paxton *Ely* 01-05; P-in-c Lt Paxton 01-05; P-in-c Diddington 01-05; V The Paxtons w Diddington 05; PtO *Pet* 06-08; P-in-c Hallaton and Allexton, w Horninghold, Tugby etc *Leic* 08-12; R Quantock Coast *B & W* from 12. *The Rectory, High Street, Stogursey, Bridgwater TA5 1PL* T: (01278) 732873 E: nickymorgan25@btinternet.com

MORGAN, Philip. b 51. Lon Univ BSc 75 Univ of Wales (Cardiff) BD 78. St Mich Coll Llan 75. **d** 78 **p** 79. C Swansea St Nic *S & B* 78-81; C Morriston 81-83; C Swansea St Mary w H Trin 83-84; USA from 84. *17476 Hawthorne Avenue, Culpeper VA 22701-8003, USA* E: padre4u@hotmail.com

MORGAN, Canon Philip Brendan. b 35. G&C Coll Cam BA 59 MA 63. Wells Th Coll 59. **d** 61 **p** 62. C Paddington Ch Ch *Lon* 61-66; C Trunch w Swafield *Nor* 66-68; P-in-c Nor St Steph 68-72; Sacr Nor Cathl 72-74; Can Res and Sub-Dean St Alb *St Alb* 74-81; Hon Can St Alb 81-94; R Bushey 81-94; RD Aldenham 91-94; Can Res and Treas Win Cathl 94-01; rtd 01; PtO *Win* from 01. *9 Clifton Hill, Winchester SO22 5BL* T: (01962) 867549

MORGAN, Canon Philip Reginald Strange. b 27. St D Coll Lamp BA 51 Keble Coll Ox BA 53 MA 57. Wells Th Coll 57. **d** 57 **p** 58. C Fleur-de-Lis *Mon* 57-59; C Bassaleg 59-62; CF (TA) 62-74; V Dingestow and Wanastow *Mon* 62-64; V Dingestow and Penrhos 65-66; R Machen and Rudry 66-75; R Machen 75-76; V Caerleon 76-95; Can St Woolos Cathl 84-95; rtd 95; LtO *Mon* from 95. *4 Anthony Drive, Caerleon, Newport NP18 3DS* T: (01633) 422238

MORGAN, Philip Richard Llewelyn. b 27. Wadh Coll Ox BA 50 MA 52. St Steph Ho Ox 53. **d** 55 **p** 56. C Warlingham w Chelsham and Farleigh *S'wark* 55-58; Chapl Haileybury Coll 58-73; Hd Master Haileybury Jun Sch Berks 73-87; R The Deverills *Sarum* 87-94; rtd 94; PtO *Guildf* from 95; *Win* 95-12. *6 Phillips Close, Headley, Bordon GU35 8LY* T/F: (01428) 712194 E: philipmorgan@msn.com

MORGAN, Canon Reginald Graham. b 25. St D Coll Lamp BA 46 LTh 48. **d** 48 **p** 49. C Chirk *St As* 48-50; C Llangollen and Trevor 50-55; R Llanwyddelan w Manafon 55-66; V Rhuddlan 66-94; RD St As 78-94; Hon Can St As Cathl 83-89; Can St As Cathl from 89; rtd 94; PtO *St As* 10-13. *Manafon, 49 Ffordd Ffynnon, Rhuddlan, Rhyl LL18 2SP* T: (01745) 591036

MORGAN, Rhys Bryn. b 65. E Lon Univ BA 94. St Mich Coll Llan 00. **d** 02 **p** 03. C Carmarthen St Pet *St D* 02-05; P-in-c Cil-y-Cwm and Ystrad-ffin w Rhandir-mwyn etc 05-09. *Rhiwlas, Cliff Terrace, Aberystwyth SY23 2DN* T: (01970) 624648
M: 07973-254062 E: rhys.morgan1@btinternet.com

MORGAN, Canon Richard Mervyn. b 50. Wadh Coll Ox BA 73 MA 75 K Alfred's Coll Win PGCE 74. **d** 92 **p** 93. CMS 85-94; Kenya 88-94; PtO *S'wark* 95-96; R Therfield w Kelshall *St Alb* from 96; RD Buntingford from 11; Tutor ERMC 99-11; Hon Can St Alb *St Alb* from 14. *The Rectory, Church Lane, Therfield, Royston SG8 9QD* T: (01763) 287364
E: rm@therfieldrectory.freeserve.co.uk

MORGAN, Richard Thomas. b 70. Peterho Cam BA 91 MA 95. Wycliffe Hall Ox 94. **d** 96 **p** 97. C Bath Twerton-on-Avon *B & W* 96-99; Chapl Lee Abbey 99-01; R Marks Tey and Aldham *Chelmsf* 01-08; C Fisherton Anger *Sarum* 08-12; R Paoli USA from 12. *212 West Lancaster Avenue, Paoli PA 19301, USA* T: (001) (610) 644 4040
E: revrichardmorgan@googlemail.com

MORGAN, Robert Chowen. b 40. St Cath Coll Cam BA 63 MA 67. St Chad's Coll Dur 64. **d** 66 **p** 67. C Lancaster St Mary

Blackb 66-76; Lect Th Lanc Univ 67-76; Fell Linacre Coll Ox from 76; Lect Th Ox Univ 76-97; Reader from 97; P-in-c Sandford-on-Thames *Ox* from 87. *Lower Farm, Sandford-on-Thames, Oxford OX4 4YR* T: (01865) 748848
E: robert.morgan@theology.oxford.ac.uk

MORGAN, Canon Roger William. b 40. Mert Coll Ox BA 62 Cam Univ MA 67. Ridley Hall Cam 80. **d** 81 **p** 82. NSM Cambridge St Paul *Ely* 81-84; V Corby St Columba *Pet* 84-90; V Leic H Trin w St Jo 90-08; C-in-c Leic St Leon CD 01-08; Hon Can Leic Cathl 06-08. *10 Dairy Close, Wells BA5 2ND* T: (01749) 679865 M: 07799-403346
E: rogermorgan@resource-arm.net

MORGAN, Simon John. b 58. Univ of Wales (Swansea) BA 81 Univ of Wales (Cardiff) BD 86 MA 94 Sussex Univ PGCE 03 FRGS 03 FRSA 07. St Mich Coll Llan 83. **d** 86 **p** 87. C Penarth All SS *Llan* 86-87; C Port Talbot St Theodore 87-89; C Gelligaer 89-91; R Dowlais 91-96; Asst P Peacehaven and Telscombe w Piddinghoe and Southease *Chich* 96; P-in-c E Dean w Friston and Jevington 96-99; NSM Hellingly and Upper Dicker 99-05; NSM Fairwarp 05-08; Chapl St Bede's Sch Upper Dicker 99-08; Asst Master Abbey Sch Reading 08-10; SS Helen and Kath Sch Abingdon from 10. *19 Lister Close, Exeter EX2 4SD*

MORGAN, Stephen. See MORGAN, John Stephen

MORGAN, Stephen John. b 67. UEA BA 89 SS Coll Cam BA 02. Westcott Ho Cam 99. **d** 02 **p** 03. C Pitlochry and Kilmaveonaig *St And* 02-04; P-in-c E Knoyle, Semley and Sedgehill *Sarum* 05-08; P-in-c St Bartholomew 08-09; R 09-15; RD Chalke 12-15; Chapl RN from 15. *Royal Naval Chaplaincy Service, Mail Point 1.2, Leach Building, Whale Island, Portsmouth PO2 8BY* T: (023) 9262 5055 F: 9262 5134
E: stevethevicar@gmail.com

MORGAN, Canon Steve Shelley. b 48. St Mich Coll Llan 67. **d** 71 **p** 72. C Llanharan w Peterston-super-Montem *Llan* 71; C Llandaff w Capel Llanilltern 71-74; C Neath w Llantwit 74-77; TV Merthyr Tydfil and Cyfarthfa 77-91; V Merthyr Tydfil Ch Ch 91-13; RD Merthyr Tydfil 93-04; Can Llan Cathl 98-13; rtd 13; PtO *Llan* from 14. *33 Parc Cwm Pant Bach, Merthyr Tydfil CF48 1TQ* T: (01685) 268571
E: smorgan842@yahoo.com

MORGAN, Mrs Susan Dianne. b 53. Univ of Wales (Lamp) BA 74 Westmr Coll Ox PGCE 75. NOC 03. **d** 05 **p** 06. C Droylsden St Martin *Man* 05-07; P-in-c Kirkholt 08-13; rtd 13; PtO *Man* 13-14; Hon C Langley from 14. *Address withheld by request* M: 07837-706037 E: sue_morgan14@hotmail.com

MORGAN, Teresa Jean. b 68. Clare Coll Cam BA 90 MA 94 PhD 95 Oriel Coll Ox MA 98 BA 01 LRAM 91. SAOMC 00. **d** 02 **p** 03. NSM Littlemore *Ox* from 02. *Oriel College, Oxford OX1 4EW* T: (01865) 728807
E: teresa.morgan@oriel.ox.ac.uk

MORGAN, Trevor. b 45. **d** 01 **p** 05. C Fleur-de-Lis *Mon* 01-06; P-in-c 06-14; P-in-c Blackwood 13-14; P-in-c Blackwood w Fleur-de-Lis 14-15; AD Bedwellty 08-15; rtd 15; Hon C Blackwood w Fleur-de-Lis *Mon* from 15. *The Tidings, Woodfieldside, Blackwood NP12 0PJ* T: (01495) 222198
E: tmo1036014@aol.com

MORGAN, Verna Ireta. b 42. NEOC. **d** 89 **p** 94. NSM Potternewton *Ripon* 89-92; Par Dn Longsight St Luke *Man* 92-94; C 94-95; P-in-c Gorton St Phil 95-02; rtd 02. *Butler's Village, St James's Parish, Nevis, St Kitts and Nevis*

MORGAN, William Charles Gerwyn. b 30. Univ of Wales (Lamp) BA 52. St Mich Coll Llan 52. **d** 56 **p** 57. C Hubberston *St D* 56-62; V Ambleston w St Dogwells 62-68; Miss to Seamen 68-93; V Fishguard w Llanychar *St D* 68-84; V Fishguard w Llanychar and Pontfaen w Morfil etc 85-93; Can St D Cathl 85-93; Chan St D Cathl 91-93; rtd 93; PtO *St D* from 12. *Wrth y Llan, Pontycleifion, Cardigan SA43 1DW* T: (01239) 613943

MORGAN, William John. b 38. Selw Coll Cam BA 62 MA 66. Cuddesdon Coll 62. **d** 65 **p** 66. C Cardiff St Jo *Llan* 65-68; Asst Chapl Univ of Wales (Cardiff) 68-70; PtO *Lon* 70-73; C Albany Street Ch Ch 73-78; P-in-c E Acton St Dunstan 78-80; V E Acton St Dunstan w St Thos 80-95; V Isleworth All SS 95-04; P-in-c St Margaret's-on-Thames 95-00; rtd 04. *Marvol, 24310 Bourdeilles, France* T: (0033) 5 53 54 18 90
E: marvol24@orange.fr

MORGAN, William Stanley Timothy. b 41. Univ of Wales (Lamp) BA 63. Wycliffe Hall Ox 63. **d** 66 **p** 67. C Aberystwyth St Mich *St D* 66-67; C Aberystwyth 67-69; V Ambleston w St Dogwells 69-70; V Ambleston, St Dogwells, Walton E and Llysyfran 70-74; V Llan-non 74-80; V Lampeter 80-86; V Lampeter Pont Steffan w Silian 87-01; V Llanbadarn Fawr 01-08; rtd 08. *16 Eddystone Close, Cardiff CF11 8EB* T: (029) 2115 6388

MORGAN-GUY, John Richard. b 44. St D Coll Lamp BA 65 Univ of Wales PhD 85 ARHistS 80 FRHistS 05 FRSocMed 81. St Steph Ho Ox 65. **d** 67 **p** 68. C Canton St Cath *Llan* 67-68;

C Roath St Sav 68-70; Chapl Llandough Hosp 70-71; C Machen and Rudry *Mon* 71-74; R Wolvesnewton w Kilgwrrwg and Devauden 74-80; PtO *B & W* 80-93; V Betws Cedewain and Tregynon and Llanwyddelan *St As* 93-97; RD Cedewain 97; Lect Univ of Wales (Lamp) 98-03; Research Fell Lect Univ of Wales (Trin St Dav) from 04; Research Fell Cen for Adv Welsh & Celtic Studies 99-04; Tutor Welsh Nat Cen for Ecum Studies Carmarthen from 00. *Tyngors, Silian, Lampeter SA48 8AS* T: (01570) 422710

MORGAN-JONES, Canon Christopher John. b 43. Bris Univ BA 66 Chicago Univ MBA 68 McMaster Univ Ontario MA 69. Cuddesdon Coll 70. **d** 73 **p** 74. C Folkestone St Sav *Cant* 73-76; P-in-c Swalecliffe 76-82; V Addington 82-84; V S'wark 85-92; RD Croydon Addington 85-90; V Maidstone All SS and St Phil w Tovil *Cant* 92-14; Hon Can Cant Cathl 99-14; rtd 14; PtO *Cant* from 14. *35 Shearwater Avenue, Whitstable CT5 4DX* T: (01227) 271172
E: cmorganjones1@gmail.com

MORGANNWG, Archdeacon of. *See* SMITH, The Ven Christopher Blake Walters

MORIARTY, Mrs Susan Margaret. b 43. Cartrefle Coll of Educn TCert 65. St As Minl Tr Course. **d** 02 **p** 09. Par Dn Gorsedd w Brynford, Ysgeifiog and Whitford *St As* from 02. *7 St Michael's Drive, Caerwys, Mold CH7 5BS* T: (01352) 722074

MORING, Sally Margaret. b 61. St Martin's Coll Lanc BEd 84 Middx Univ BA 06. NTMTC 03. **d** 06 **p** 07. NSM Northolt St Mary *Lon* 06-09; V Hayes St Edm from 09. *St Edmund's Vicarage, 1 Edmund's Close, Hayes UB4 0HA* T: (020) 8573 9965 E: vicar@stedmundschurch.com

MORISON, John Donald. b 34. ALCD 60. **d** 61 **p** 62. C Rayleigh *Chelmsf* 61-64; C St Austell *Truro* 64-67; V Meltham Mills *Wakef* 67-71; Youth Chapl *Cov* 71-76; S Africa 76-82; Can Port Elizabeth 80-82; Bardsley Missr 82-86; LtO *S'wark* 82-86; Dioc Missr *Derby* 86-99; V Quarndon 86-99; rtd 99; PtO *Sarum* from 01. *Flat 1, Canford Place, 59 Cliff Drive, Canford Cliffs, Poole BH13 7JX* T: (01202) 709377
E: kayandjohn@waitrose.com

MORLEY, Alison Ruth. b 67. Sarum Coll MA 13. STETS 05 Ripon Coll Cuddesdon 13. **d** 13 **p** 14. C Devizes St Jo w St Mary *Sarum* from 13. *52 Queens Road, Devizes SN10 5HW* T: (01380) 829931 M: 07500-007437 E: alliemorley@aol.com

MORLEY, Georgina Laura (George). b 63. Dur Univ BA 84 Nottm Univ MTh 95 PhD 99. Cranmer Hall Dur. **d** 03 **p** 03. NSM Osmotherley w Harlsey and Ingleby Arncliffe *York* 03-08; Lect Cranmer Hall Dur 07-10. *Beacon Hill, High Street, Low Pittington, Durham DH6 1BE* T: 0191-372 0385

MORLEY, Miss Gillian Dorothy. b 21. Greyladies Coll 49. **dss** 70 **d** 87. Lewisham St Swithun *S'wark* 70-82; Sturry w Fordwich and Westbere w Hersden *Cant* 82-87; PtO 87-10. *28 Glen Iris Avenue, Canterbury CT2 8HP* T: (01227) 459992

MORLEY, John. b 43. AKC 67. St Deiniol's Hawarden 67. **d** 68 **p** 69. C Newbold on Avon *Cov* 69-73; C Solihull *Birm* 73-77; C-in-c Elmdon Heath CD 76-77; Chapl RAF 77-93; TR Wallingford *Ox* 93-99; RD 95-99; Dean St Paul's Cathl and Chapl Nicosia 99-02; V Henlow and Langford *St Alb* 02-08; RD Shefford 06-08; rtd 08; PtO *Leic* 08-11 and from 13; *Pet* from 08; *Lich* 09-11; P-in-c Gaulby *Leic* 11-12; Spiritual Dir Leic Angl Cursillo from 13. *31 Walcot Road, Market Harborough LE16 9DL* T: (01858) 419714 M: 07900-892566
E: revjmorley@talktalk.net

MORLEY, Keith. b 45. St Chad's Coll Dur BA 66 Open Univ BSc 93. **d** 67 **p** 68. C S Yardley St Mich *Birm* 67-70; C Solihull 70-73; V Shaw Hill 73-77; P-in-c Burton Coggles *Linc* 77-79; P-in-c Boothby Pagnell 77-79; V Lenton w Ingoldsby 77-79; P-in-c Bassingthorpe w Bitchfield 77-79; R Ingoldsby 79-87; RD Beltisloe 84-87; P-in-c Old Dalby and Nether Broughton *Leic* 87-94; RD Framland 88-90; rtd 94; PtO *Linc* 03-13. *10 Gracey Court, Woodland Road, Broadclyst, Exeter EX5 3GA*

MORLEY, Canon Leslie James. b 45. K Coll Lon BD 67 AKC 67 MTh 68. St Boniface Warminster 68. **d** 69 **p** 70. C Birm St Pet 69-72; C W Brompton St Mary *Lon* 72; C W Brompton St Mary w St Pet 73-74; Chapl Nottm Univ *S'well* 74-80; Dir Post-Ord Tr 80-85; Can Res and Vice-Provost S'well Minster 80-85; Hon Can S'well Minster 85-99; Chapl Bluecoat Sch Nottm 85-90; R Nottingham St Pet and St Jas *S'well* 85-99; AD Nottingham Cen 90-93; Dioc Rural Officer *Ripon* 99-10; Hon Chapl Yorks Agric Soc *York* from 09; rtd 10. *Beacon Hill, High Street, Low Pittington, Durham DH6 1BE* T: 0191-372 0385 M: 07879-470752 E: leslie.morley@virgin.net

MORLEY, Stephen Raymond. b 55. Birm Univ LLB 76. STETS 07. **d** 10 **p** 11. C Aisholt, Enmore, Goathurst, Nether Stowey etc *B & W* 10-14; V Bures w Assington and Lt Cornard *St E* from 14. *The Vicarage, Church Square, Bures, Sudbury CO8 5AA* M: 07723-786688 E: steve.morley@btinternet.com

MORLEY, Terence Martin Simon. b 49. SS Hild & Bede Coll Dur CertEd 78. St Steph Ho Ox 71. **d** 74 **p** 75. C Kingston upon Hull St Alb *York* 74-76; C Middlesbrough All SS 76-77; PtO *Dur* 77-78; Hon C Worthing St Andr *Chich* 78-80; C Brighton Ch Ch 80-82; C Hove St Patr 80-82; C Ayr *Glas* 83-86; C Mayble 83-84; P-in-c Coatbridge 86-88; R 88-92; P-in-c 92; V Plymouth St Jas Ham *Ex* 93-09; Chapl Plymouth Community Services NHS Trust 96-98; rtd 09. *37 Great College Street, Brighton BN2 1HJ*

MORLEY, Trevor. b 39. Man Univ BSc 62 MPS 62 MRSPH 84. Ripon Hall Ox 65. **d** 67 **p** 68. C Compton Gifford *Ex* 67-70; Chapl Hammersmith Hosp Lon 70-83; Hon C N Hammersmith St Kath *Lon* 70-83; Chapl Univ Coll Hosp Lon 83-94; Chapl Univ Coll Lon Hosps NHS Trust 94-99; Chapl St Luke's Hosp for the Clergy 89-99; V Linthwaite *Wakef* 99-06; rtd 06; PtO *Sheff* from 06. *19 Queenswood Road, Sheffield S6 1RR* T: 0114-232 5232 E: tmqwr@tiscali.co.uk

MORLEY-BUNKER, John Arthur. b 27. Wells Th Coll 67. **d** 68 **p** 69. C Horfield H Trin *Bris* 68-71; P-in-c Easton All Hallows 71-75; V 75-82; RD Bris City 74-79; V Horfield St Greg 82-93; rtd 93; PtO *Bris* from 93. *1 Knoll Court, Knoll Hill, Bristol BS9 1QX* T: 0117-968 5837

MORLEY-JONES, Anthony Roger. St Mich Coll Llan. **d** 04 **p** 05. NSM Cydweli and Llandyfaelog *St D* 04-12; P-in-c 12-15; rtd 15. *11 Westhill Crescent, Cydweli SA17 4US* T: (01554) 890458 E: revroger@btinternet.com

MORLING, David Arthur. b 45. Saltley Tr Coll Birm CertEd 66 Open Univ BA 78. S Dios Minl Tr Scheme 83 Linc Th Coll. **d** 85 **p** 86. NSM Chich 85-97; P-in-c Doncaster Intake *Sheff* 97-02; P-in-c Doncaster H Trin 97-02; rtd 02; PtO *Bradf* 02-13. *York Villa, New Road, Beer, Seaton EX12 3HS* T: (01297) 625045 E: david@morling.co.uk

MORONEY, Kevin John. b 61. Valley Forge Chr Coll Pennsylvania BS 86. Gen Th Sem NY MDiv 92. **d** 92 **p** 93. Asst Pastor Metuchen St Luke USA 92-94; R Metuchen All SS 94-98; Chapl St James Sch St James Maryland 98-00; Chapl and Tutor CITC 00-05; P-in-c Dublin Sandymount *D & G* 01-05; USA from 05. *St James School, 17641 College Road, St James MD 21781, USA* T: (001) (301) 733 9330 E: kjmcoi@yahoo.com

MORPHY, George David. b 49. Birm Univ BEd 71 Lon Univ BA 75 Warwick Univ MA 90. WMMTC. **d** 89 **p** 90. NSM Ribbesford w Bewdley and Dowles *Worc* 89-06; NSM Barbourne from 06; Dioc Dir of Educn 99-11. *41 Hallow Road, Worcester WR2 6BX* T: (01905) 422007 M: 07867-525779 E: morphy611@btinternet.com

MORPHY, Canon Michael John. b 43. Newc Univ BSc 65 Dur Univ MSc 66 QUB PhD 73. Ripon Coll Cuddesdon 82. **d** 84 **p** 85. C Halifax *Wakef* 84-86; V Luddenden w Luddenden Foot 86-97; V Corbridge w Halton and Newton Hall *Newc* 97-08; Hon Can Newc Cathl 07-08; rtd 08. *7 Mallard Drive, Montrose DD10 9NB* T: (01674) 675277 E: mj.morphy@tiscali.co.uk

MORRALL, Heather Lynne. *See* COOKE, Heather Lynne

MORRELL, Mrs Jennifer Mary. b 49. NOC 84. **d** 87 **p** 94. Par Dn Crewe All SS and St Paul *Ches* 87-90; Par Dn Padgate Liv 90-94; C 94-95; TV Kirkby 95-00; V Croxteth Park 00-02. *The MacLeod Centre, Isle of Iona PA76 6SN* T: (01681) 700405 M: 07880-757607 E: shazandjen@gmail.com

MORRELL, Canon Nigel Paul. b 38. S'wark Ord Course 73. **d** 76 **p** 77. C Letchworth St Paul w Willian *St Alb* 76-85; V Farley Hill St Jo 85-95; RD Luton 90-94; V Cardington 95-03; Hon Can St Alb 01-03; RD Elstow 03-08; rtd 03. *22 Sunderland Place, Shortstown, Bedford MK42 0FD* T/F: (01234) 743202 E: nigel.morrell@btopenworld.com

MORRELL, Paul Rodney. b 49. SRN 70. SWMTC 91. **d** 93 **p** 94. C Heavitree w Ex St Paul 93-02; C Heavitree and St Mary Steps 02-05; TV from 05. *1A St Loyes Road, Exeter EX2 5HA* T: (01392) 273430

MORRELL, His Honour Peter Richard. b 44. Univ Coll Ox MA 71 Solicitor 70 Barrister-at-Law (Gray's Inn) 74. ERMC 06. **d** 08 **p** 09. NSM Uppingham w Ayston and Wardley w Belton *Pet* 08-10; NSM Nassington w Yarwell and Woodnewton w Apethorpe 10-12; PtO from 12. *New Sulehay Lodge, Nassington, Peterborough PE8 6QT* T/F: (01780) 782281 M: 07860-573597 E: pmorrell@btinternet.com

MORRELL, Mrs Susan Marjorie. b 46. Open Univ BA 94. SEITE 93. **d** 96 **p** 97. NSM E Peckham and Nettlestead *Roch* from 96; Chapl Kent Coll Pembury 99-00. *7 Pippin Road, East Peckham, Tonbridge TN12 5BT* T: (01622) 871150

MORRIS, Miss Alison Mary. b 58. W Midl Coll of Educn BEd 81 Wolv Univ PGCE 00 MA 02. Qu Coll Birm 06. **d** 09 **p** 10. NSM Pelsall *Lich* from 09. *32 Chestnut Road, Leamore, Walsall WS3 1BD* T: (01922) 477734 M: 07837-649756 E: a.morris125@btinternet.com

MORRIS, Andy. *See* MORRIS, Edward Andrew

MORRIS, Mrs Ann. b 52. N Co Coll Newc CertEd 73. WEMTC 00. **d** 03 **p** 04. C Churchdown St Jo and Innsworth *Glouc* 03-07; P-in-c Barnwood from 07. *The Vicarage, 27A Barnwood Avenue, Gloucester GL4 3AB* T: (01452) 619531

MORRIS, Mrs Ann Veronica Marsham. b 46. Open Univ BA 83. WEMTC 99. **d** 01 **p** 02. NSM Amberley *Glouc* 01-09; NSM Minchinhampton w Box and Amberley 09-13; rtd 13. *Cotswold, Amberley, Stroud GL5 5AB* T: (01453) 872371 E: ann.morris@amberley.org

MORRIS, Anne. *See* MORRIS, Margaret Anne

MORRIS (née SHAW), Mrs Anne. b 47. LMH Ox BA 69 MA 72 Lon Univ BD 82. NOC 01. **d** 03 **p** 04. NSM Leamington Priors All SS *Cov* from 03; NSM Leamington Spa H Trin from 03. *20 Hayle Avenue, Warwick CV34 5TW* T: (01926) 403512 E: am.gm@hotmail.co.uk

MORRIS, Anthony David. b 61. Aston Univ BSc 83. Qu Coll Birm 06. **d** 09. NSM Droitwich Spa *Worc* 09-13; NSM Stoke Prior, Wychbold and Upton Warren 13-14; P-in-c Bowbrook N from 14; P-in-c Bowbrook S from 14; NSM Stoke Prior, Wychbold and Upton Warren from 14. *The Parsonage, Church Lane, Tibberton, Droitwich WR9 7NW* T: (01905) 345169 E: revdm777@gmail.com

MORRIS, Bernard Lyn. b 28. St Aid Birkenhead 55. **d** 58 **p** 59. C-in-c Hartcliffe St Andr CD *Bris* 58-61; C Bishopston 61-63; R Ardwick St Thos *Man* 63-69; R Aylton w Pixley, Munsley and Putley *Heref* 69-79; P-in-c Tarrington w Stoke Edith 72-77; R 77-79; P-in-c Queen Camel, Marston Magna, W Camel, Rimpton etc *B & W* 79-80; R 80-87; R Queen Camel w W Camel, Corton Denham etc 87-95; rtd 95; PtO *B & W* from 95; *Ex* from 01. *Canterbury Bells, Ansford Hill, Castle Cary BA7 7JL* T: (01963) 351154 E: revblmorris@supanet.com

MORRIS, Beti Elin. b 36. CertEd 57. Sarum & Wells Th Coll 87. **d** 89 **p** 97. C Llangeitho and Blaenpennal w Betws Leucu etc *St D* 89-92; C-in-c Pencarreg and Llanycrwys 92-97; V 97-05; rtd 05. *Bro Mihangel, Maes y Tren, Felinfach, Lampeter SA48 8AH*

MORRIS, Brian. *See* MORRIS, Reginald Brian

MORRIS, Brian Michael Charles. b 32. S Dios Minl Tr Scheme 82. **d** 85 **p** 86. NSM Denmead *Portsm* 85-89; C S w N Hayling 89-96; P-in-c Shalfleet 96-97; rtd 97; PtO *Portsm* from 97. *Ashleigh, 5 Ashwood Close, Hayling Island PO11 9AX* T: (023) 9246 7292 E: bmc_morris@btinternet.com

MORRIS, Ms Catharine Mary. b 75. Regent's Park Coll Ox BA 96 MA 00. Ridley Hall Cam 99. **d** 01 **p** 02. C Malpas *Mon* 01-06; C Reading Greyfriars *Ox* 06-12; Par Development Adv (Berks) from 12. *90 Tippings Lane, Woodley, Reading RG5 4RY* T: (01865) 208296 M: 07785-990208 E: catharine.morris@oxford.anglican.org

MORRIS, Canon Christopher John. b 45. K Coll Lon AKC 67 BD 68. **d** 68 **p** 69. C W Bromwich All SS *Lich* 68-72; C Porthill 72-74; Min Can Carl Cathl 74-77; Ecum Liaison Officer BBC Radio Carl 74-77; Dioc Communications Officer *Carl* 77-83; V Thursby 77-83; Angl Adv Border TV from 82; V Upperby St Jo *Carl* 83-91; P-in-c Lanercost w Kirkcambeck and Walton 91-99; P-in-c Gilsland w Nether Denton 96-99; R Lanercost, Walton, Gilsland and Nether Denton 99-10; RD Brampton 98-05; Hon Can Carl Cathl 98-10; rtd 10; PtO *Carl* from 10. *15 Nook Lane, Dalston, Carlisle CA5 7JA* T: (01228) 711872 E: chrisandmarjorie.morris@btinternet.com

MORRIS, Prof Colin. b 28. Qu Coll Ox BA 48 BA 51 MA 53 FRHistS 71. Linc Th Coll 51. **d** 53 **p** 54. Fell and Chapl Pemb Coll Ox 53-69; Prof Medieval Hist Southn Univ 69-92; rtd 92; Public Preacher *Win* from 69. *12 Bassett Crescent East, Southampton SO16 7PB* T: (023) 8076 8176

MORRIS, David. *See* MORRIS, Anthony David

MORRIS, Preb David Meeson. b 35. Trin Coll Ox BA 56 MA 60. Chich Th Coll 57. **d** 60 **p** 61. C Westmr St Steph w St Jo *Lon* 60-65; Lib Pusey Ho 65-68; Chapl Wadh Coll Ox 67-68; C Sheff St Leon Norwood 68-69; Ind Chapl 68-72; C Brightside St Marg 69-72; R Adderley *Lich* 72-82; V Drayton in Hales 72-82; RD Tutbury 82-95; Chapl Burton Gen Hosp 82-90; P-in-c Burton St Modwen *Lich* 82; V Burton 82-99; Preb Lich Cathl 93-99; P-in-c Shobnall 94-99; rtd 99; PtO *Lich* from 99; *Heref* from 99. *Watling House, All Stretton, Church Stretton SY6 6HH* T: (01694) 722243

MORRIS, David Michael. b 59. Ox Univ MA 84 Cam Univ PGCE 91. Sarum & Wells Th Coll 82. **d** 84 **p** 85. C Angell Town St Jo *S'wark* 84-87; C Mitcham SS Pet and Paul 87-90; V Llandygwydd and Cenarth w Cilrhedyn etc *St D* 90-98; Lect Th St D Coll Lamp from 90; Hd RE Lampeter Comp Sch from 98; PtO *Leic* from 15. *Bronant, Rhydargaeau, Carmarthen SA32 7DR* E: michael.morris@leccofe.org

MORRIS, Canon David Pryce. b 39. St Mich Coll Llan 62. **d** 63 **p** 64. C Colwyn Bay *St As* 63-70; St George 70-76; Dioc Children's Adv 75-87; V Bodelwyddan and St George 76-79; V Connah's Quay 79-95; St As Dioc Adult Lay Tr Team 88-06;

Ed *St Asaph Diocesan News* from 89; Dioc Communications Officer *St As* 90-06; V Shotton 95-06; Hon Can St As Cathl 96-00; Can Cursal St As Cathl 00-06; rtd 07; PtO *St As* from 09. *7 Rhuddlan Road, Buckley CH7 3QA* T: (01244) 540779 M: 07711-519752 E: david@dandpmorris.net

MORRIS, David Thomas. St Mich Coll Llan. **d** 09 **p** 10. C Merthyr Tydfil St Dav and Abercanaid *Llan* 09-12; C Cardiff St Mary w St Dyfrig and St Samson from 12; Voc Adv from 13. *St Paul's Vicarage, Llanmaes Street, Cardiff CF11 7LR* T: (029) 2221 2177 E: dtmorris@sky.com

MORRIS, Dennis Gordon. b 41. ALCM 58. St D Coll Lamp. **d** 67 **p** 68. C Neath w Llantwit *Llan* 67-92; V Troedrhiwgarth 92-10; rtd 10. *12 Cwrt yr Hen Ysgol, Tondu, Bridgend CF32 9GE*

MORRIS, Edward Andrew (Andy). b 57. St Jo Coll Nottm BTh 93. **d** 96 **p** 97. C Conisbrough *Sheff* 96-01; PtO *S'well* 01-04; V Bestwood St Matt w St Phil from 04. *St Matthew's Vicarage, Padstow Road, Nottingham NG5 5GH* T: 0115-927 7229 M: 07775-925297 E: andy-morris@ntlworld.com

MORRIS, Mrs Elizabeth Anne. b 59. BA 05. **d** 00 **p** 01. OLM Darsham and Westleton w Dunwich *St E* 00-04; C Hadleigh, Layham and Shelley 04-06; C Yoxmere 08-09; C Aquitaine *Eur* from 10. *Maison Neuve, Plaisance, 24560 Issigeac, France* T: (0033) 5 53 58 71 90 E: cookingcurate@tiscali.co.uk

MORRIS, Geoffrey. *See* MORRIS, Martin Geoffrey Roger

MORRIS, Geoffrey David. b 43. Fitzw Coll Cam BA 65 MA 69 Westmr Coll Ox DipEd 67. NOC. **d** 82 **p** 83. C Man Clayton St Cross w St Paul 82-85; V Lower Kersal 85-03; P-in-c Priors Hardwick, Priors Marston and Wormleighton *Cov* 03-08; Asst Chapl HM Pris Rye Hill 03-07; rtd 08; PtO *Cov* from 08. *20 Hayle Avenue, Warwick CV34 5TW* T: (01926) 403512 E: am.gm@hotmail.co.uk

MORRIS, Canon Graham Edwin. b 60. Sarum & Wells Th Coll 83. **d** 86 **p** 87. C Coalbrookdale, Iron-Bridge and Lt Wenlock *Heref* 86-90; TV Bilston *Lich* 90-99; R Northwood *Portsm* 99-05; V Gurnard 99-05; P-in-c Ventnor H Trin 05-06; V 06-12; P-in-c Ventnor St Cath 05-06; V 06-12; P-in-c Bonchurch 05-06; R 06-12; RD E Wight 05-12; P-in-c Ryde All SS from 12; P-in-c Swanmore St Mich from 12; Hon Can Portsm Cathl from 11. *The Vicarage, 14 Argyll Street, Ryde PO33 3BZ* T: (01983) 716435 E: graham.morris@btinternet.com

MORRIS, Preb Henry James. b 47. Lon Univ BSc 69. Wycliffe Hall Ox MA. **d** 79 **p** 80. C Woodford Wells *Chelmsf* 79-82; C Gt Baddow 82-87; R Siddington w Preston *Glouc* 87-01; RD Cirencester 97-01; TR Madeley *Heref* 01-12; Preb Heref Cathl 09-12; rtd 12; PtO *Lich* from 12. *2 Waveney Avenue, Perton, Wolverhampton WV6 7RA* T: (01902) 757797 E: henrym@dircon.co.uk

MORRIS (née LONG), Hermione Jane. b 66. Univ of Wales (Swansea) BSc 97 RGN 88. St Mich Coll Llan 05. **d** 07 **p** 08. C Bassaleg *Mon* 07-11; R Llanfyllin, Bwlchycibau and Llanwddyn *St As* from 11. *The Rectory, Coed Llan Lane, LLanfyllin SY22 5BW* T: (01691) 648306

MORRIS, Miss Jane Elizabeth. b 50. York Univ BA 71 CertEd 72 MSc 80. NEOC 92. **d** 92 **p** 94. NSM York St Mich-le-Belfrey 92-95; C Leeds St Geo *Ripon* 95-05; V Cricklewood St Gabr and St Mich *Lon* from 05. *St Gabriel's Vicarage, 156 Anson Road, London NW2 6BH* T: (020) 8452 6305 E: jane.morris10@virgin.net

MORRIS, Jeremy Nigel. b 60. Ball Coll Ox MA 81 DPhil 86 Clare Coll Cam BA 92. Westcott Ho Cam 90. **d** 93 **p** 94. C Battersea St Mary *S'wark* 93-96; Dir Studies Westcott Ho Cam 96-01; Vice-Prin 97-01; Dean and Chapl Trin Hall Cam 01-10; Dean K Coll Cam 10-14; Trin Hall Cam from 14. *Trinity Hall, Cambridge CB2 1TJ* T: (01223) 332500 E: jnm20@cam.ac.uk

MORRIS, Mrs Joanna Elizabeth. b 60. N Riding Coll of Educn CertEd 81. Qu Coll Birm 07. **d** 09 **p** 10. C Riddings and Ironville *Derby* 09-13; R Whittington from 13. *The Rectory, 84 Church Street North, Old Whittington, Chesterfield S41 9QP* E: jomorris17@gmail.com

MORRIS, Canon John. b 25. Westcott Ho Cam. **d** 65 **p** 66. C St Alb St Mich *St Alb* 65-68; V Leverstock Green 68-80; TR Chambersbury 80-82; V N Mymms 82-90; RD Hatfield 83-88; Hon Can St Alb 89-90; rtd 90; PtO *St Alb* 90-02; *Nor* 92-94; *Pet* 11-14; P-in-c Barney, Fulmodeston w Croxton, Hindringham etc *Nor* 94-95. *Highfield, 20 Teigh Road, Market Overton, Oakham LE15 7PW* T: (01572) 767212 E: morrisfulmod@aol.com

MORRIS, John Douglas. b 37. Cam Univ BA 58 Lon Inst of Educn PGCE 60 Univ of E Africa MEd 67 Ex Univ PhD 87. S Dios Minl Tr Scheme 94. **d** 95 **p** 96. NSM Twyford and Owslebury and Morestead *Win* 95-01; PtO from 01; Chapl Twyford Sch Win 95-05. *9 Parkside Gardens, Winchester SO22 5NA* T: (01962) 852033 E: johnmarymorris@btopenworld.com

MORRIS, John Dudley. b 33. Ball Coll Ox BA 57 MA 61. Wycliffe Hall Ox 58. **d** 60 **p** 61. C Tonbridge SS Pet and Paul *Roch* 60-65; C Enfield Ch Ch Trent Park *Lon* 65-69; Chapl Elstree Sch Woolhampton 70-74; Hd Master Handcross Park Sch W Sussex 74-89; V Rudgwick *Chich* 89-98; RD Horsham 93-98; rtd 98; PtO *Chich* from 98. *13 Hoadlands, Handcross, Haywards Heath RH17 6HB* T: (01444) 400184

MORRIS, John Edgar. b 20. Keble Coll Ox BA 42 MA 50. Wycliffe Hall Ox 42. **d** 44 **p** 45. C Eccleston St Thos *Liv* 44-48; C Warrington H Trin 48-50; V Newton-le-Willows 50-57; R Wavertree H Trin 57-66; V Ainsdale 66-82; R Broadwell, Evenlode, Oddington and Adlestrop *Glouc* 82-88; rtd 89; PtO *Glouc* 89-97 and 01-07. *Pen y Dref, Rhosneigr, Anglesey LL64 5JH* T: (01407) 810202

MORRIS, John Owen. b 56. Nottm Univ BCom 82. Linc Th Coll 79. **d** 82 **p** 83. C Morriston *S & B* 82-84; C Kingstone w Clehonger and Eaton Bishop *Heref* 84-87; P-in-c Lugwardine w Bartestree and Weston Beggard 87-92; Chapl RN 92-13; Chapl Lord Wandsworth Coll Hook 13-15. *Address temp unknown*

MORRIS, Jonathan Richard. b 57. Lanc Univ BA 78 Trin Coll Ox MSc 84. WEMTC 99. **d** 02 **p** 03. C Taunton St Andr *B & W* 02-06; C Wulfric Benefice from 06; RD Crewkerne from 12. *The Rectory, New Street, North Perrott, Crewkerne TA18 7ST* T: (01460) 72356 E: jonbea@supanet.com

MORRIS, Kevin John. b 63. Univ of Wales (Ban) BMus 84 Lon Univ MA 12. Westcott Ho Cam 85. **d** 88 **p** 89. C Roath Llan 88-91; C Holborn St Alb w Saffron Hill St Pet *Lon* 91-96; V Bedford Park from 96; P-in-c Acton Green from 15; Dir Post-Ord Tr from 09. *The Vicarage, Priory Gardens, London W4 1TT* T: (020) 8994 0139 *or* 8994 1380 E: frkjmorris@aol.com

MORRIS, Kirsteen Helen Grace. b 44. STETS 99. **d** 02 **p** 03. NSM Cowes H Trin and St Mary *Portsm* 02-12; rtd 12; PtO *Portsm* from 12. *Meda, Medham Farm Lane, Cowes PO31 8PH* T: (01983) 289585 F: 292919 E: morris.scawfell@onwight.net

MORRIS, Lillian Rosina (Mother Lillian). b 29. **dss** 70 **d** 87. CSA 68-97; Mother Superior 82-94 and from 00; Sherston Magna w Easton Grey *Bris* 71-73; Notting Hill All SS w St Columb *Lon* 74-82. *St Mary's Convent and Nursing Home, Burlington Lane, London W4 2QE* T: (020) 8747 0001

MORRIS, Lyn. *See* MORRIS, Bernard Lyn

MORRIS, Mrs Lynne. b 48. STETS 07. **d** 10 **p** 11. Wimborne Minster *Sarum* 10; NSM Horton, Chalbury, Hinton Martel and Holt St Jas 10-14; NSM Witchampton, Stanbridge and Long Crichel etc 11-14; PtO from 14. *2 Garth Close, St Leonards, Ringwood BH24 2RG* E: lynnemorrislp@btinternet.com

MORRIS, Mrs Lynne Margaret. b 53. SEN. WMMTC 95. **d** 98 **p** 99. NSM Wrockwardine Wood *Lich* 98-01; Chapl Birm Specialist Community Health NHS Trust from 01. *5 Kingston Road, Trench, Telford TF2 7HT* T: (01952) 618158 *or* 0121-442 4321 E: lynne.morris@southbirminghampct.nhs.uk

MORRIS, Ms Margaret Anne. b 61. Man Univ BA 82 MA 91. NOC 94. **d** 96 **p** 97. C Bury St Pet 96-98; C Accrington St Jo w Huncoat *Blackb* 98-01; V Knuzden from 01. *St Oswald's Vicarage, 68 Bank Lane, Blackburn BB1 2AP* T: (01254) 698321 E: rev_anne_morris@gn.apc.org

MORRIS, Canon Margaret Jane. Ox Univ MTh 96 Leic Univ Hon LLM 96. EMMTC 86. **d** 89 **p** 94. NSM Quorndon *Leic* 89-96; Chapl for People affected by HIV 94-05; NSM Loughborough All SS w H Trin 96-98; Chapl Asst Leic R Infirmary NHS Trust 98-00; Chapl Asst Univ Hosps Leic NHS Trust 00-10; Hon Can Leic Cathl 97-10; rtd 10; PtO *Leic* 10-13. *2 Chatsworth Close, Sandiacre, Nottingham NG10 5PF* T: 0115-949 7997 E: morris@rog15.freeserve.co.uk

MORRIS, Canon Martin Geoffrey Roger. b 41. Trin Coll Cam BA 63 MA 67. St D Coll Lamp 63. **d** 66 **p** 67. C Newport St Paul *Mon* 66-72; R Lampeter Velfrey *St D* 72-74; R Lampeter Velfrey and Llanddewi Velfrey 74-08; RD St Clears 83-98; Can St D Cathl 92-08; Chan St D Cathl 03-08; rtd 08. *Greenfield Cottage, Gilfach Hill, Lampeter Velfrey, Narberth SA67 8UL*

MORRIS, Ms Mary. b 27. Birm Univ BA 49 CertEd 50 MA 56. **dss** 68 **d** 87 **p** 94. Kinver *Lich* 83-87; Kinver and Enville 87; Hon Par Dn 87-94; Hon C 94-11; PtO from 11. *12 Pavilion End, Prestwood, Stourbridge DY7 5PF* T: (01384) 877245 E: marymorris12@tiscali.co.uk

MORRIS, Michael. *See* MORRIS, David Michael

MORRIS, Michael Alan. b 46. Jes Coll Cam BA 70 MA 74. Coll of Resurr Mirfield 79. **d** 81 **p** 82. C Leamington Priors All SS *Cov* 81-83; C Milton *Portsm* 83-88; R Petworth *Chich* 88-90; R Egdean 88-90; Chapl St Pet Hosp Chertsey 90-95; Hon C Thorpe *Guildf* 90-95; P-in-c Harbledown *Cant* 95-97; R from 97; Chapl St Nic Hosp Cant 95-00. *The Rectory, Summer Hill, Harbledown, Canterbury CT2 8NW* T: (01227) 464117 E: michael@themorrises.co.uk

MORRIS, Michael James. b 70. Univ of Wales (Abth) BScEcon 92. Qu Coll Birm BA. **d** 00 **p** 01. C Tupsley w Hampton Bishop *Heref* 00-04; TV Watling Valley *Ox* 04-12; TR from 12. *21 Edzell Crescent, Westcroft, Milton Keynes MK4 4EU* T: (01908) 507123 E: mike.morris@wvep.org

MORRIS (née ROBERTS), Nia Wyn. b 64. Univ of Wales (Ban) BA 86 PGCE 87 CQSW 90 Anglia Poly Univ MA 00. Westcott Ho Cam 98. **d** 00 **p** 01. C Rhyl w St Ann *St As* 00-03; R Bala 03-14; AD Penllyn and Edeirnion 12-13; R Llanllwchaiarn and Newtown w Aberhafesp from 14; AD Cedewain from 14. *The Rectory, 3 Old Barn Lane, Newtown SY16 2PT* T: (01678) 951395 M: 07833-302312 E: niawyn1000@yahoo.com

MORRIS, Preb Norman Foster Maxwell. b 46. Ex Univ BA 68 MA 71 Leic Univ PGCE 69 K Coll Lon MTh 85 Univ of Wales (Cardiff) MA 91 Cheltenham & Glouc Coll of HE MA 98. S'wark Ord Course 75. **d** 78 **p** 79. C Hackbridge and N Beddington *S'wark* 78-81; Chapl Tonbridge Sch 81-85; Chapl Mon Sch 85-00; Asst Warden Jones Almshouses Mon 89-00; R Wentnor w Ratlinghope, Myndtown, Norbury etc *Heref* from 00; P-in-c Churchstoke w Hyssington from 04; RD Clun Forest from 11; Preb Heref Cathl from 12; CF (ACF) from 02. *The Rectory, Wentnor, Bishops Castle SY9 5EE* T: (01588) 650244 M: 07974-771069 E: revnorm@btinternet.com

MORRIS, Canon Paul David. b 56. St Jo Coll Nottm BTh 79. **d** 80 **p** 81. C Billericay and Lt Burstead *Chelmsf* 80-84; C Luton Lewsey St Hugh *St Alb* 84-89; Dioc Adv on Evang *S'well* 89-00; Dioc Millennium Officer 97-01; Min Tommy's (ch for the unchurched) 96-01; C Barton in Fabis 01-02; C Gotham 01-02; C Thrumpton 01-02; C Kingston and Ratcliffe-on-Soar 01-02; C Sutton Bonington w Normanton-on-Soar 01-02; Dir Evang Chr Associates Internat 02-04; Assoc Eur Dir 04-06; Eur Dir 06-08; Brussels Team 08-09; P-in-c Derby St Pet and Ch Ch w H Trin from 09; Co-ord Chapl Derby City Cen from 12; Prin Chapl Workplace Chapl in Derbyshire from 12; Hon Can Derby Cathl from 12. *St Peter's Vicarage, 16 Farley Road, Derby DE23 6BX* T: (01332) 204686 E: paul@stpetersderby.org.uk

MORRIS, Peter. b 45. Leeds Univ CertEd 66. Tyndale Hall Bris 68. **d** 71 **p** 72. C Southport SS Simon and Jude *Liv* 71-74; Min-in-c Ch Ch Netherley LEP 74-76; V Bryn *Liv* 76-91; R Redenhall, Harleston, Wortwell and Needham *Nor* 91-05; rtd 05. *9 Bromley College, London Road, Bromley BR1 1PE* T: (020) 8460 3455 E: petermorris203@btinternet.com

MORRIS, The Ven Philip Gregory. b 50. Leeds Univ BA 71 MPhil 74. Coll of Resurr Mirfield 71. **d** 73 **p** 74. C Aberdare *Llan* 74-77; C Neath w Llantwit 77-80; V Cymmer and Porth 80-88; TV Llantwit Major 88-01; Dioc Missr 88-99; Can Res Llan Cathl 00-01; Adn Margam from 02; TV Aberavon 02; P-in-c Kenfig Hill 02-05; P-in-c Ewenny w St Brides Major from 05. *The Vicarage, Southerndown Road, St Brides Major, Bridgend CF32 0SD* T: (01656) 880108 E: pmorri@globalnet.co.uk

MORRIS, Philip John. b 50. FCIPD 96. St Mich Coll Llan 97. **d** 99 **p** 00. NSM Builth and Llanddewi'r Cwm w Llangynog etc *S & B* 99-04; NSM Aberedw w Llandeilo Graban and Llanbadarn etc 04-13; LtO from 14. *Lochaber, 22 North Road, Builth Wells LD2 3BU* T: (01982) 552390

MORRIS, Canon Raymond. b 48. Open Univ BA 88. NOC 80. **d** 83 **p** 84. C Tonge w Alkrington *Man* 83-86; R Blackley St Paul 86-91; V Heyside 91-14; AD Tandle 02-09; C Royton St Anne 12-14; Hon Can Man Cathl 07-14; rtd 14; PtO *Man* from 14. *46 Penthorpe Drive, Royton, Oldham OL2 6JL* T: (01706) 842192

MORRIS, Raymond Arthur. b 42. Trin Coll Ox BA 64 MA 66 Lon Univ LLB 71 CQSW 72. Clifton Th Coll 66. **d** 67 **p** 91. C Greenstead *Chelmsf* 67-68; PtO *York* 69-91; NSM Linthorpe 91-12; PtO from 12. *3 Medina Gardens, Middlesbrough TS5 8BN* T: (01642) 593726 E: morris101@btinternet.com

MORRIS, Reginald Brian. b 31. St Mich Coll Llan 56. **d** 59 **p** 60. C St Jo in Bedwardine *Worc* 59-61; P-in-c Tolladine 61-62; CF 62-78; V Cheswardine *Lich* 78-84; V Hales 78-84; PtO 84-86; C Cen Telford 86-89; rtd 89; PtO *Heref* 90-07; *Lich* from 07. *Woodside Cottage, School Lane, Prees, Whitchurch SY13 2BU* T: (01948) 840090

MORRIS, Canon Robert John. b 45. Leeds Univ BA 67. Coll of Resurr Mirfield 74. **d** 76 **p** 77. C Beeston Hill St Luke *Ripon* 76; C Holbeck 76-78; C Moseley St Mary *Birm* 78-83; P-in-c Handsworth St Jas 83-88; V 88-99; P-in-c Handsworth St Mich 86-87; AD Handsworth 92-99; TR Kings Norton 99-15; Hon Can Birm Cathl 97-15; rtd 15; PtO *Birm* from 15. *61 Oxford Street, Stirchley, Birmingham B30 2LH* M: 07973-389427 F: 0121-486 2825 E: morrisrob4@aol.com

MORRIS, Robert Lee. b 47. W Virginia Univ BA 69. Gen Th Sem (NY) MDiv 73. **d** 73 **p** 74. USA 73-74 and from 84; Community of Celebration 74-94; P-in-c Cumbrae (or Millport) *Arg* 75-76 and 79-84. *St Dunstan's Episcopal Church, 14301 Stuebner Airline Road, Houston TX 77069 USA* T: (001) (281) 440 1600

MORRIS, Robin Graham. d 14 **p** 15. NSM Grwp Bro Ystwyth a Mynach *St D* from 14. *Tynddol, Cwmystwyth, Aberystwyth SY23 4AG* T: (01974) 282618
E: robin_catherine@btinternet.com

✠**MORRIS, The Rt Revd Roger Anthony Brett. b** 68. Imp Coll Lon BSc 89 Trin Coll Cam BA 92 MA 08 ARCS 89. Ridley Hall Cam 90. **d** 93 **p** 94 **c** 14. C Northleach w Hampnett and Farmington etc *Glouc* 93-96; P-in-c Sevenhampton w Charlton Abbotts and Hawling etc 96-00; P-in-c Dowdeswell and Andoversford w the Shiptons etc 96-00; R Sevenhampton w Charlton Abbots, Hawling etc 00-03; Dioc Dir Par Development and Evang *Cov* 03-14; Adn Worc 08-14; Area Bp Colchester *Chelmsf* from 14. *1 Fitzwalter Road, Colchester CO3 3SS* T: (01206) 576648 M: 07590-696212
E: b.colchester@chelmsford.anglican.org

MORRIS, Mrs Sally Jane. b 69. Imp Coll Lon BSc 91. Qu Coll Birm 07. **d** 10 **p** 11. NSM Bowbrook S *Worc* 10-13; NSM Chipping Campden w Ebrington *Glouc* 13-14; NSM Vale and Cotswold Edge 14-15. *1 Fitzwalter Road, Colchester CO3 3SS* E: sjmorris@mypostoffice.co.uk

MORRIS (née GILES), Mrs Sarah Jayne. b 76. Aston Univ BSc 98. St Jo Coll Nottm MTh 07. **d** 06 **p** 07. C Cen Telford *Lich* 06-10; Chapl HM YOI Stoke Heath from 10; PtO *Lich* from 10. *HM Young Offender Institution, Stoke Heath, Market Drayton TF9 2JL* T: (01630) 636116 E: sarah.morris@hmps.gsi.gov.uk

MORRIS, Shaun Anthony. b 64. Keele Univ BSocSc 85. Oak Hill Th Coll 04. **d** 06 **p** 07. C Westlands St Andr *Lich* 06-10; C Hanford from 10; C Trentham from 10. *Hanford Vicarage, 76 Church Lane, Stoke-on-Trent ST4 4QD* T: (01782) 657848
E: morris.shaun@btinternet.com

MORRIS, Simon John. b 83. St Jo Coll Dur BA 05. St Steph Ho Ox BA 07. **d** 08 **p** 09. C Tottenham St Mary *Lon* 08-11; V from 11. *St Mary's Vicarage, Lansdowne Road, London N17 9XE* E: fr.morris@hotmail.com

MORRIS, Stanley James. b 35. Keble Coll Ox BA 58 MA 63. Chich Th Coll 59. **d** 61 **p** 62. C Tunstall Ch Ch *Lich* 61-64; C W Bromwich All SS 64-67; V Wilnecote 67-88; V Alrewas and Wychnor 88-00; rtd 01; PtO *Derby* from 01. *44 Pinfold Close, Repton, Derby DE65 6FR* T: (01283) 703453

MORRIS, Stephen Bryan. b 54. Linc Th Coll 88. **d** 90 **p** 91. C Glouc St Geo w Whaddon 90-94; C Glouc St Mark and St Mary de Crypt w St Jo etc 94-02; C Barnwood 02-03; Chapl for the Deaf 94-13; Dioc Chapl among Deaf and Adv on Disability from 13. *The Vicarage, 27A Barnwood Avenue, Gloucester GL4 3AB* T: (01452) 610450
E: spadework@fsmail.net

MORRIS, Stephen Francis. b 52. St Jo Coll Nottm BTh 79. **d** 79 **p** 80. C N Hinksey *Ox* 79-82; C Leic H Apostles 82-85; TV Shenley and Loughton *Ox* 85-88; TV Watling Valley 88-95; V Chatham St Wm *Roch* 95-98; TR S Chatham H Trin 98-00; Lect Nottingham St Mary and St Cath *S'well* 00-07; Lect Nottingham All SS, St Mary and St Pet 07-14; AD Nottingham Cen 02-08; Dioc Ecum Officer 10-14; P-in-c Newark w Coddington from 14. *The Rectory, 6 Bede House Lane, Newark NG24 1PY* T: (01636) 704513

MORRIS, Steven Ralph. b 62. UEA BA 84 MA 85. Wycliffe Hall Ox 08. **d** 10 **p** 11. C Ealing St Steph Castle Hill *Lon* 10-13; C Neasden St Cath w St Paul 13-15; V N Wembley St Cuth from 15. *St Cuthbert's Vicarage, 214 Carlton Avenue West, Wembley HA0 3QY* T: (020) 8904 1457
E: steve_stcuthberts@hotmail.com

MORRIS, Canon Stuart Collard. b 43. AKC 66. St Boniface Warminster 66. **d** 67 **p** 68. C Hanham *Bris* 67-71; C Whitchurch 71-74; P-in-c Westerleigh and Wapley w Codrington and Dodington 74-77; P-in-c Holdgate w Tugford *Heref* 77-82; P-in-c Abdon w Clee St Margaret 77-82; R Diddlebury w Bouldon and Munslow 77-82; P-in-c Sotterley, Willingham, Shadingfield, Ellough etc *St E* 82-87; RD Beccles and S Elmham 83-94; P-in-c Westhall w Brampton and Stoven 86-88; P-in-c Flixton w Homersfield and S Elmham 86-92; Hon Can St E Cathl 87-99; V Bungay H Trin w St Mary 87-94; P-in-c Hadleigh w Layham and Shelley 94-96; R Hadleigh 96-99; Dean Bocking 94-99; RD Hadleigh 94-98; rtd 99; Hon C Tottenhill w Wormegay *Ely* from 14; PtO 07-14; Hon C Watlington from 14; Hon C Holme Runcton w S Runcton and Wallington from 14. *Blackbank Farm, Black Bank, Southery, Downham Market PE38 0NL* T: (01366) 377567
E: stuart@bartimaeuscommunity.org.uk

MORRIS, Canon Timothy David. b 48. Lon Univ BSc 69. Trin Coll Bris. **d** 75 **p** 76. C Edin St Thos 75-77; R Edin St Jas 77-83; R Troon *Glas* 83-85; R Galashiels *Edin* 85-02; R Edin Gd Shep 02-08; Dean Edin 92-01; Hon Can St Mary's Cathl from 01; rtd 08; Canada 08-10; LtO *Edin* from 10. *2 The Firs, Foulden Newton, Berwick-upon-Tweed TD15 1UL* T: (01289) 386615 M: 07548-227963
E: tim@foulden.org.uk

MORRIS, Mrs Trudie Elizabeth. b 53. UEA BA 91 PGCE 92 Leic Univ MBA 04 Cam Univ BTh 12. Westcott Ho Cam 10. **d** 12 **p** 13. C Fowlmere, Foxton, Shepreth and Thriplow *Ely* 12-15; P-in-c Derby St Andr w St Osmund from 15; P-in-c Allenton and Shelton Lock from 15. *St Edmund's Vicarage, Sinfin Avenue, Derby DE24 9JA* M: 07710-494871 E: revtrudie@gmail.com

MORRIS, Mrs Valerie Ruth. b 46. St Hugh's Coll Ox BA 68 MA 72. Gilmore Course 76. **dss** 78 **d** 87 **p** 05. Par Dn Burton *Lich* 87-91; Dioc Children's Officer 88-89; PtO *Heref* 04-05; Hon C Church Stretton from 05. *Watling House, All Stretton, Church Stretton SY6 6HH* T: (01694) 722243
E: valerieanddavid@caradoc-as.fsnet.co.uk

MORRIS, Victor Bernard. d 14 **p** 15. OLM Wigginton *Lich* from 14. *5 Southam Drive, Sutton Coldfield B73 5PD* T: 0121-354 4333 E: vicbmorris@yahoo.co.uk

MORRIS, William Hazlitt. b 62. Trin Coll Cam BA 84 MA 88 Virginia Univ LLM 89 Solicitor 88. NTMTC BA 09. **d** 09 **p** 10. NSM St Martin-in-the-Fields *Lon* from 09. *St Martin-in-the-Fields, 6 St Martin's Place, London WC2N 4JH* T: (020) 7766 1100 E: william.morris@smitf.org

MORRIS, William James. b 23. St Deiniol's Hawarden 72. **d** 73 **p** 74. NSM Brecon Adnry *S & B* 73-78; NSM Crickhowell w Cwmdu and Tretower 78-98; rtd 98. *The School House, Cwmdu, Crickhowell NP8 1RU* T: (01874) 730355

MORRIS, William Richard Price. b 23. FCollP 82. Glouc Sch of Min 86. **d** 88 **p** 89. Hon C Bussage *Glouc* 88-90; PtO 90-91; Hon C France Lynch 91; Hon C Chalford and France Lynch 91-93; rtd 93; PtO *Glouc* from 93. *Langendun House, Manor Close, Michinhampton, Stroud GL6 9DG* T: (01453) 886382

MORRISON, Ailsa. See SPACKMAN, Ailsa

MORRISON, Alistair James. b 61. TCD MTh 12. CITC 09. **d** 11 **p** 12. Dn Dunmurry *Conn* 11-12; C Ballyholme *D & D* from 12. *34 Beverley Gardens, Bangor BT20 4NQ* T: (028) 9127 1922 M: 07917-218558 E: alistair@ballyholmeparish.co.uk

MORRISON, Barbara Anne. b 29. St Andr Univ BSc 50. **d** 95 **p** 96. NSM Eorropaidh *Arg* 95-11; P-in-c 00-04; rtd 04. *46 Upper Coll, Back, Isle of Lewis HS2 0LT* T/F: (01851) 820559 E: barbara.stmoluag@care4free.net

MORRISON, Barry John. b 44. Pemb Coll Cam BA 66 MA 70. ALCD 69. **d** 69 **p** 70. C Stoke Bishop *Bris* 69-72; C Edgware *Lon* 72-76; Chapl Poly Cen Lon 76-83; Hon C Langham Place All So 76-83; P-in-c W Hampstead St Luke 83-88; V 88-98; Chapl Westf Coll 84-92; R Rushden St Mary w Newton Bromswold *Pet* 98-08; rtd 08; PtO *Pet* from 09. *11 Lytham Park, Oundle, Peterborough PE8 4FB* T: (01832) 274242 E: gandbmorrison@btinternet.com

MORRISON, Bryony Clare. b 47. Lon Univ CertEd 77 Brentwood Coll of Educn BEd 86. NTMTC 96. **d** 99 **p** 00. C Epping Distr *Chelmsf* 99-05; TV from 05; Chapl Epping Forest Primary Care Trust 03-05. *Theydon Garnon Vicarage, Fiddlers Hamlet, Epping CM16 7PQ* T: (01992) 573672 M: 07850-876304 E: revbry@dibleyhouse.com

MORRISON, Mrs Caroline Frances. b 63. SEITE. **d** 09 **p** 10. C Bexleyheath Ch Ch *Roch* 09-13; R Keston from 13. *The Rectory, 24 Commonside, Keston BR2 6BP* T: (01689) 853186 M: 07765-244724 E: cfmorrison@sky.com

MORRISON, Diana Mary (Sister Diana). b 43. St Kath Coll Liv CertEd 64. EAMTC 02. **d** 05 **p** 06. NSM Breadsall *Derby* 05-13; PtO from 13; Man from 14. *St John's Rectory, St John's Road, Longsight, Manchester M13 0WU* E: dianachm@tiscali.co.uk

MORRISON, Edward John Scott. b 89. St Steph Ho Ox 12. **d** 15. C Cantley *Sheff* from 15. *4 Alston Road, Doncaster DN4 7HB* M: 07864-960007 E: esmorrison@hotmail.com

MORRISON, Iain Edward. b 36. St Steph Ho Ox 76. **d** 78 **p** 79. C Brighton St Aug and St Sav *Chich* 78-81; C Felpham w Middleton 81-83; P-in-c Barnham and Eastergate 83-85; R Aldingbourne, Barnham and Eastergate 85-91; V Jarvis Brook 91-98; R Hastings St Clem and All SS 98-03; rtd 03; P-in-c Arlington, Folkington and Wilmington *Chich* 03-10. *2 Priory Close, Hastings TN34 1UJ* T: (01424) 420499 E: revmorrison@btinternet.com

MORRISON, Preb James Wilson Rennie. b 42. Aber Univ MA 65. Linc Th Coll 76. **d** 78 **p** 79. C Whitley Ch Ch *Ox* 78-81; R Burghfield 81-87; CF 87-97; P-in-c Burghill *Heref* 97-03; V 03-11; P-in-c Stretton Sugwas 97-03; R 03-11; P-in-c Pipe-cum-Lyde 97-03; P-in-c Pipe-cum-Lyde and Moreton-on-Lugg *Heref* 03-11; Preb Heref Cathl 08-11; rtd 11; PtO *Heref* from 13. *Brambles, 8 Dernside Close, Wellington, Hereford HR4 8BP* T: (01432) 830911 E: jimmym@btinternet.com

MORRISON, The Ven John Anthony. b 38. Jes Coll Cam BA 60 MA 64 Linc Coll Ox MA 68. Chich Th Coll 61. **d** 64 **p** 65. C Birm St Pet 64-68; C Ox St Mich 68-71; Chapl Linc Coll Ox 68-74; C Ox St Mich w St Martin and All SS 71-74; V Basildon 74-82; RD Bradfield 78-82; V Aylesbury 82-89; RD 85-89; TR

89-90; Adn Buckingham 90-98; P-in-c Princes Risborough w Ilmer 96-97; Adn Ox and Can Res Ch Ch 98-05; rtd 05; PtO *Ox* from 05. *39 Crown Road, Wheatley, Oxford OX33 1UJ* T: (01865) 876625 E: morrison039@btinternet.com

MORRISON, Keith Charles. b 63. Wycliffe Hall Ox. **d** 01 **p** 02. C Ipswich St Aug *St E* 01-04; Asst Chapl Cam Univ Hosps NHS Foundn Trust 04-13; Chapl Arthur Rank Ho Brookfields Hosp Cam from 13. *Brookfield's Hospital, 351 Mill Road, Cambridge CB1 3DF* T: (01223) 723110 *or* 723151 M: 07798-965651 E: keith.morrison@ccs.nhs.uk

MORRISON, Raymond. *See* MORRISON, Walter John Raymond

MORRISON, Richard James. b 55. Sarum & Wells Th Coll 87. **d** 89 **p** 90. C Boston *Linc* 89-93; P-in-c Digby 93-99; V Whaplode Drove from 99; V Gedney Hill from 99; P-in-c Whaplode 10-14; P-in-c Holbeach Fen 10-14. *The Vicarage, 1 Broadgate, Whaplode Drove, Spalding PE12 0TN* T: (01406) 330392

MORRISON, Canon Robin Victor Adair. b 45. Nottm Univ BA 67. Bucharest Th Inst 67 Ripon Hall Ox 68. **d** 70 **p** 71. C Hackney St Jo *Lon* 70-73; Chapl Newc Univ 73-76; P-in-c Teversal *S'well* 76-78; Chapl Sutton Cen 76-78; Asst Hd Deans Community Sch Livingston *Edin* 78-80; R Edin St Columba 80-81; Chapl Birm Univ 81-88; Prin Soc Resp Officer *Derby* 88-96; TV Southampton (City Cen) *Win* 96-01; Ind Chapl 96-01; Non Exec Dir Southampton and SW Hants HA 00-01; Officer for Ch and Soc Ch in Wales Prov Coun 01-11; Hon Can Llan Cathl 09-11. *1 Dannog y Coed, Barry CF63 1HF* T: (01446) 741900 E: robinmore@tiscali.co.uk

MORRISON, Walter John Raymond (Ray). b 30. Jes Coll Cam BA 55 MA 58. Westcott Ho Cam 55. **d** 57 **p** 58. C Dalston St Mark w St Bart *Lon* 57-60; C Totteridge *St Alb* 60-63; V Letchworth St Paul 63-71; RD Hitchin 70-71; R Ludlow *Heref* 72-83; RD 78-83; Preb Heref Cathl 78-83; P-in-c Ludlow, Ludford, Ashford Carbonell etc 80-83; Chapl St Thos Hosp Lon 83-86; Chapl Eastbourne Distr Gen Hosp 86-95; rtd 95; PtO *Worc* 95-10. *24 West Grange Court, Lovedays Mead, Stroud GL5 1XB* E: ray_morrison@tiscali.co.uk

MORROW, Daniel Ross. b 77. Oklahoma Bapt Univ BA 01. Claremont Sch of Th MDiv 06. **d** 07 **p** 08. C San Clemente USA 07-08; Asst Chapl Zürich *Eur* 08-11; P-in-c Oregon City St Paul USA from 11. *202 Avenida Aragon, San Clemente CA 92672-5015, USA* T: (001) (503) 656 9842 E: revdanmorrow@gmail.com

MORROW, David. b 63. NUU BSc 86 TCD BTh 89. CITC 86. **d** 89 **p** 90. C Portadown St Mark *Arm* 89-91; C Ballymena w Ballyclug *Conn* 91-94; I Tempo and Clabby *Clogh* 94-01; I Kilcronaghan w Draperstown and Sixtowns *D & R* 01-11; Bp's Dom Chapl 07-11. *22 Carsonville Drive, Upperlands, Maghera BT46 5SQ* M: 07540-134601 E: davidmorrow763@btinternet.com

MORROW, Canon Henry Hugh. b 26. TCD BA 49 MA 67 Flinders Univ Aus BSocAdmin 76. TCD Div Sch Div Test 49. **d** 49 **p** 50. C Dublin St Thos *D & G* 49-53; I Rathmolyon *M & K* 53-58; I Killoughter *K, E & A* 58-63; C Portadown St Columba *Arm* 63-65; I Ballinderry w Tamlaght 65-70; Australia from 70; Hon Can Adelaide from 84. *5 Allendale Grove, Stonyfell SA 5066, Australia* T: (61) (8) 8332 5890

MORROW, Canon Joseph John. b 54. JP 87. Edin Univ BD 79 Dundee Univ LLB 92 NY Th Sem DMin 87. Edin Th Coll 76. **d** 79 **p** 80. Chapl St Paul's Cathl Dundee 79-82; P-in-c Dundee St Martin 82-85; R 85-90; P-in-c Dundee St 85-08; P-in-c Dundee St Ninian 02-07; Can St Paul's Cathl Dundee 00-08; Dioc Chan from 08; PtO from 09. *Milton Haugh, Tealing, Dundee DD4 0QZ* T: (01382) 380501 E: j.jmorrow@btinternet.com

MORROW, Nigel Patrick. b 68. Dur Univ BA 94 TCD MPhil 02 Anglia Ruskin Univ MA 05. Westcott Ho Cam 03. **d** 05 **p** 06. C Linc St Botolph and Linc St Pet-at-Gowts and St Andr 05-08; C Camberwell St Giles w St Matt *S'wark* 08-10; Chapl K Coll Lon 08-10; Chapl and Inter Faith Adv Brunel Univ 11-12; PtO 12-13; *S'wark* 13-14; C Lt Ilford St Mich *Chelmsf* from 14; Chapl Camden and Islington NHS Foundn Trust from 14. *3 Toronto Avenue, London E12 5JF* M: 07515-770440 T: (020) 8514 6703 E: patrickmorrow@live.co.uk

MORSE, Mrs Elisabeth Ann. b 51. New Hall Cam MA 73 Qu Eliz Coll Lon MSc 74 Heythrop Coll Lon MA 97. S'wark Ord Course 91. **d** 94 **p** 95. C Wimbledon *S'wark* 94-99; C Fulham All SS *Lon* 99-08; V Battersea St Luke *S'wark* from 08. *52 Thurleigh Road, London SW12 8UD* T: (020) 8673 6506 E: morseelisabeth@yahoo.co.uk

MORSHEAD, Ivo Francis Trelawny. b 27. ACA 52 FCA 63. Cuddesdon Coll 61. **d** 63 **p** 64. C Bris St Mary Redcliffe w Temple etc 63-68; C Wimbledon *S'wark* 68-73; V Elham *Cant* 73-78; V Whitchurch *Ex* 78-91; rtd 91; PtO *Lon* from 91. *28 Edge Street, London W8 7PN* T: (020) 7727 5975

MORSON, Mrs Eleanor. b 42. CA Tr Coll 63 TISEC 95. **d** 96 **p** 96. NSM Kirkwall *Ab* 96-01; R Edin St Mark 01-05. *4 Broadshaw Mews, Leazes Parkway, Newcastle upon Tyne NE15 9QL* T: 0191-264 6885

MORSON, John. b 41. CA Tr Coll 62. **d** 88 **p** 92. NSM Duns *Edin* 88-89; CF 89-92; R Kirkwall *Ab* 92-01; R Stromness 92-01; NSM Edin St Mark 01-05; rtd 06. *4 Broadshaw Mews, Leazes Parkway, Newcastle upon Tyne NE15 9QL* T: 0191-264 6885

MORT, Alister. b 52. BSc BA. Oak Hill Th Coll. **d** 82 **p** 83. C Cheadle Hulme St Andr *Ches* 82-85; C Rodbourne Cheney *Bris* 86-87; TV 87-90; V New Milverton *Cov* 90-05; PtO 05-09; TR Bilton *Ripon* 09-14; rtd 14; Tutor Johannesburg Bible Coll S Africa from 14. *c/o J Mort Esq, 168 Tachbrook Road, Leamington Spa CV31 3EF* E: alistermort@mac.com

MORT, Ivan Laurence (Laurie). b 61. Nottm Univ BTh 87. Linc Th Coll 84. **d** 87 **p** 88. C Aston cum Aughton and Ulley *Sheff* 87-90; C Greenstead *Chelmsf* 90-94; Chapl Toulouse *Eur* 94-05. *19 rue Bel Soulhel, 31700 Cornebarrieu, France* E: laurie.mort@tiscali.fr

MORTER, Canon Charles. b 54. AKC 77. Coll of Resurr Mirfield 77. **d** 78 **p** 79. C Colchester St Jas, All SS, St Nic and St Runwald *Chelmsf* 78-82; C Brixham w Churston Ferrers *Ex* 82-83; TV 84-86; TV Sidmouth, Woolbrook, Salcombe Regis, Sidbury etc 86-95; P-in-c Exminster and Kenn 95-00; TR Littleham w Exmouth 00-10; RD Aylesbeare 07-10; Preb Ex Cathl 08-10; Can Res Ex Cathl from 10. *9 Cathedral Close, Exeter EX1 1EZ* T: (01392) 285983 E: pastor@exeter-cathedral.org.uk

MORTIBOYS, John William. b 45. K Coll Lon BD 69 AKC 69. Sarum Th Coll 71. **d** 71 **p** 72. C Reading All SS *Ox* 71-95; PtO *Portsm* from 97. *13 Oyster Street, Portsmouth PO1 2HZ* T: (023) 9275 6676 F: 9266 2626

MORTIMER, Aileen Jane. b 46. Edin Univ MA 67 CQSW 69. ERMC 05. **d** 08 **p** 09. NSM E Bergholt and Brantham *St E* 08-13; rtd 13. *20 Leggatt Drive, Bramford, Ipswich IP8 4ET* T: (01473) 747419 E: ajmortimer@hotmail.co.uk

MORTIMER, Anthony John. b 42. Sarum & Wells Th Coll 68. **d** 71 **p** 72. C Heref St Martin 71-79; V Kingstone 79-85; P-in-c Clehonger and Eaton Bishop 80-85; TR Pinhoe and Broadclyst *Ex* 85-05; rtd 05. *97 Egremont Road, Exmouth EX8 1SA* T: (01395) 271390 E: themortimers@totalise.co.uk

MORTIMER, Mrs Elizabeth Anne. b 69. RGN 92. Ripon Coll Cuddesdon 05. **d** 07 **p** 08. C Minehead *B & W* 07-10; P-in-c Castle Cary w Ansford from 10. *The Vicarage, Church Street, Castle Cary BA7 7EJ* T: (01963) 351615 E: fr.liz@talktalk.net

MORTIMER, Helen Teän. *See* GREENHAM, Helen Teän

MORTIMER, Jonathan Michael. b 60. Bris Univ BA 83. Oak Hill Th Coll BA 92. **d** 92 **p** 93. C Rugby St Matt *Cov* 92-96; C Southgate *Chich* 96-98; TR 98-07; Through Faith Miss Ev 07-11; V Peckham All SS *S'wark* from 11. *78 Talford Road, London SE15 5NZ* T: (020) 7252 7549 E: mortimerj@btinternet.com

MORTIMER, Canon Lawrence George. b 45. St Edm Hall Ox BA 67 MA 71. St Chad's Coll Dur. **d** 70 **p** 71. C Rugby St Andr *Cov* 70-75; V Styvechale 75-89; Dioc Broadcasting Officer 80-89; Dioc Communications Officer 89-03; P-in-c Wootton Wawen 97-03; P-in-c Claverdon w Preston Bagot 03-10; Hon Can Cov Cathl 98-10; rtd 10; PtO *Lich* from 11. *3 Top Street, Whittington, Oswestry SY11 4DR* T: (01691) 657986 E: l.mortimer@btinternet.com

MORTIMER, Peter Aled. **d** 10 **p** 11. NSM Whitchurch *Llan* 10-12; C 13-14; TV from 14. *3 Lon Ganol, Rhiwbina, Cardiff CF14 6EB* T: (029) 2031 2326

MORTIMER, Canon Peter Jackson. b 41. TD 73 MBE 95. St Jo Coll York CertEd 63 Essex Univ MA 71 Univ Campus Suffolk DUniv 09 FRSA 97 Hon GCM 07. EAMTC 97. **d** 99 **p** 99. NSM Needham Market w Badley *St E* 98-02; NSM Ringshall w Battisford, Barking w Darmsden etc 98-02; Bp's Coun Adv from 02; Chapl to Suffolk Fire Service from 03; Hon Can St E Cathl 06-11; Hon Fell UEA *Nor* from 07; PtO *St E* from 11. *20 Leggatt Drive, Bramford, Ipswich IP8 4ET* T: (01473) 747419

MORTIMER, Richard James. b 63. Ex Univ BSc 85 Lon Bible Coll BA 97. Oak Hill Th Coll. **d** 01 **p** 02. C Ore St Helen and St Barn *Chich* 01-05; Chapl Hastings Univ and C Hastings H Trin 05-10; V Dartford Ch Ch *Roch* from 10. *The Vicarage, 67 Shepherds Lane, Dartford DA1 2NS* T: (01322) 220036 E: richardrmortimer123@btinternet.com

MORTIMORE, David Jack. b 42. Master Mariner 69. St Mich Coll Llan 90. **d** 91 **p** 92. C Pembroke St Mary w St Mich *St D* 91-92; C Bargoed and Deri w Brithdir *Llan* 92-97; PtO 98-02; P-in-c Llangeinor 02-04; P-in-c Llangeinor and the Garw Valley 04-10; rtd 12. *33 Gaddarn Reach, Neyland, Milford Haven SA73 1PW* T: (01646) 602555 E: davidmortimore139@btinternet.com

MORTIMORE, Robert Edward. b 39. Kelham Th Coll 61 Wells Th Coll 66. **d** 69 **p** 70. C Byfleet *Guildf* 69-72; C Fitzroy New Zealand 72-75; C Remuera 76-78; Min Bell Block 77-79; V Te Kuiti 79-85; Offic Min Auckland 86-89; Sen Asst P Whangarei 89-92; V Avondale 92-98; V Milford 98-04; Offic Min from 04. *69 Crawford Crescent, Kamo, Whangarei 0112, New Zealand* T/F: (0064) (9) 435 1285
E: b.jmortimore@xtra.co.nz

MORTIMORE, Robin Malcolm. b 46. **d** 11 **p** 12. NSM Yardley St Edburgha *Birm* 11-15; PtO from 15. *33 Stonebow Avenue, Solihull B91 3UP* T: 0121-705 9116 M: 07812-728526
E: robinmortimore@hotmail.com

MORTIS, Lorna Anne. b 54. Moray Ho Coll of Educn DipEd 76 Open Univ BA 88. TISEC 95. **d** 98 **p** 99. NSM Gullane and N Berwick *Edin* 98-02; P-in-c Edin St Marg 02-08; NSM Prestonpans and Musselburgh 08-10; R Airdrie *Glas* 10-14; Bp's Dom Chapl 11-14; rtd 14. *Rosebank, 2 School Cottages, Athelstaneford, North Berwick EH39 5BE* M: 07779-553807 T: (01620) 880505 E: l.mortis@btconnect.com

MORTON, Adrian Ian. b 65. Brighton Poly BSc 87 Brunel Univ MSc 93. Ridley Hall Cam 98. **d** 00 **p** 01. C Kettering Ch the King *Pet* 00-04; P-in-c Bozeat w Easton Maudit 04-06; P-in-c Wollaston and Strixton 04-06; V Wollaston w Strixton and Bozeat etc from 06. *The Vicarage, 81 Irchester Road, Wollaston, Wellingborough NN29 7RW* T: (01933) 664256
E: adrianmorton762@btinternet.com

MORTON, Albert George. b 34. Saskatchewan Univ BA 61 McGill Univ Montreal MA 73. Em Coll Saskatoon 56. **d** 61 **p** 61. Canada 61-65; C Stanford-le-Hope *Chelmsf* 66-69; V Linc St Geo Swallowbeck 69-82; R Lt Munden w Sacombe *St Alb* 82-89; R The Mundens w Sacombe 89-96; rtd 96; PtO *Sarum* from 00. *10 Church Green, Bishop's Caundle, Sherborne DT9 5NN* T: (01963) 23383 E: amorton1@waitrose.com

MORTON, Andrew Edward. b 51. Lon Univ BA 72 BD 74 AKC 74 Univ of Wales (Cardiff) MPhil 93. St Aug Coll Cant 75. **d** 76 **p** 77. C Feltham *Lon* 76-79; C Pontllottyn w Fochriw *Llan* 79-81; V Ferndale w Maerdy 81-88; V Tylorstown w Ynyshir 88-93; Dir of Studies Llan Ord Course 91-93; R Llangybi and Coedypaen w Llanbadoc *Mon* 93-13; Chapl Coleg Gwent 93-13; Dioc FE Officer 93-13; Prov HE Officer 01-13; Dioc Dir NSM Studies 00-13; rtd 13. *4 Parc Close, Llangybi, Usk NP15 1PN* M: 07894-901744
E: mortonae@hotmail.com

MORTON, Christine Marjorie. b 60. **d** 13 **p** 14. NSM Marton *Blackb* from 13. *7 Trinity Gardens, Thornton-Cleveleys FY5 2UA* T: (01253) 824657

MORTON, Mrs Christine Mary. b 39. Linc Th Coll 78. **dss** 80 **d** 87 **p** 94. Ore St Helen and St Barn *Chich* 80-84; Southwick St Mich 84-85; Winchmore Hill St Paul *Lon* 85-87; Par Dn 87-94; C 94-99; Hon C 00-02; rtd 00; PtO *Lon* from 02. *122 Bourne Hill, London N13 4BD* T: (020) 8886 3157

MORTON, Clive Frederick. b 47. Lon Univ BA 70 Birm Univ MA 98. Cranmer Hall Dur 78. **d** 80 **p** 81. C Countesthorpe w Foston *Leic* 80-83; C Glen Parva and S Wigston 83-86; Asst Chapl HM Youth Cust Cen Glen Parva 83-86; V Birm St Pet 86-98; Miss Partner CMS 99-02; Chapl St Petersburg *Eur* 99-02; Lect St Petersburg Th Academy and Sem 99-02; V Kingsbury H Innocents *Lon* 02-12; rtd 13. *14 Westfields, Catshill, Bromsgrove B61 9HJ* T: (01527) 273574 M: 07947-883559 E: cfmpam@gmail.com

MORTON, Howard Knyvett. b 30. St Jo Coll Cam BA 51 MA 67. Linc Th Coll 55. **d** 57 **p** 58. C Hatfield Hyde *St Alb* 57-60; Hd RE Heaton Gr Sch Newc 60-66; 72-75; CMS 66-72; Regional Org Oxfam 88-91; Grainger Gr Sch Newc 91-94; LtO *Newc* 73-93; Dioc World Development Officer 94-95; rtd 95; PtO *Dur* 95-98; *Newc* from 96. *Daisy Cottage, Hawthorn Lane, Rothbury, Morpeth NE65 7TL* T: (01669) 621296

MORTON, Mrs Jacqueline Mavis. b 46. UEA BSc 67 York Univ BSc 82. EMMTC 97. **d** 00 **p** 01. NSM Sibsey w Frithville *Linc* from 00. *8 Lucan Close, Sibsey, Boston PE22 0SH* T: (01205) 751378 E: jacqui.morton@care4free.net

MORTON, Jennifer. b 50. Bedf Coll Lon BA 72 Leic Univ PGCE 73. EMMTC 87. **d** 90 **p** 94. C New Mills *Derby* 90-94; Chapl Asst Nottm City Hosp NHS Trust 94-98; Chapl Basford Hosp Nottm 94-98; Chapl S Derbyshire Acute Hosps NHS Trust 98-02; Vice Prin EMMTC *S'well* 02-10; rtd 10. *56 Marshall Drive, Beeston, Nottingham NG9 3LD* T: 0115-939 5784
E: home@jennifer3.plus.com

MORTON, Jennifer. b 49. **d** 15. C Dorchester *Ox* from 15. *Address temp unknown*

MORTON, Mrs Judith. b 58. St Jo Coll Nottm 04. **d** 06 **p** 07. C Shaftesbury *Sarum* 06-10; V St Leonards and St Ives *Win* from 10. *The Vicarage, 30 Pine Drive, St Ives, Ringwood BH24 2LN* T: (01425) 483283 M: 07932-630232
E: revjude@btinternet.com

MORTON, Judith Ann. **d** 14 **p** 15. NSM Llanllwchaearn and Llanina *St D* from 14. *Cynefin, 5 Cae'r Henwas, Caerwedros, Llandysul SA44 6BE* T: (01545) 560506
E: revjudemorton@btinternet.com

MORTON, Mark Paul. b 58. Univ of Wales (Swansea) BA 79 Univ of Wales (Lamp) MA 99 Cardiff Univ MTh 08. Ridley Hall Cam 90. **d** 92 **p** 93. C Daventry, Ashby St Ledgers, Braunston etc *Pet* 92-95; Chapl Danetre Hosp 93-94; CF (TA) 93-95; CF 95-03; Sen CF 03-11; R Harting w Elsted and Treyford cum Didling *Chich* from 11. *The Rectory, The Street, South Harting, Petersfield GU31 5QB* T: (01730) 825428
E: revmpmorton@hotmail.com

MORTON, Michelle. b 67. Ripon Coll Cuddesdon 00. **d** 02 **p** 03. C Buckingham *Ox* 02-05; P-in-c Stewkley w Soulbury and Drayton Parslow 05-09. *Address temp unknown*
E: squarenalo@hotmail.com

MORTON, Philip. b 79. Birm City Univ BA 05 St Jo Coll Dur BA 11. Cranmer Hall Dur 09 St Jo Coll Dur BATM 11. **d** 12 **p** 13. C Maney *Birm* from 12. *1 Trinity Hill, Sutton Coldfield B72 1TA* M: 07739-903225
E: revphilipmorton@gmail.com

MORTON, Rex Gerald. b 61. St Jo Coll Nottm 96. **d** 98 **p** 99. C Bury St Edmunds All SS *St E* 98-01; C Woodside Park St Barn *Lon* 01-07; V Golders Green from 07. *The Vicarage, 3 St Alban's Close, London NW11 7RA* T: (020) 8455 4525 M: 07968-088714 E: sj@morton4.swinternet.co.uk

MORTON, Sister Rita. b 34. Wilson Carlile Coll. **dss** 85 **d** 94. Par Dn Harlow New Town w Lt Parndon *Chelmsf* 87-89; C Harold Hill St Geo 89-94; rtd 94; NSM Elm Park St Nic Hornchurch *Chelmsf* from 94. *14 Cheviot Road, Hornchurch RM11 1LP* T: (01708) 709842

MORTON, Robert Hart. b 28. Moray Ord Course 91. **d** 94. Hon C St Andr Cathl Inverness from 94. *75 Fairfield Road, Inverness IV3 5LJ* T: (01463) 223525

MORTON, Miss Rosemary Grania. b 65. Qu Coll Birm BA 05. **d** 05 **p** 06. C Kings Heath *Birm* 05-07; C Handsworth St Mary 07-09; Asst Chapl Northn Gen Hosp NHS Trust 09-12; Chapl Newcastle upon Tyne Hosps NHS Foundn Trust 12-13; PtO *Birm* 13-14. *8 Carolsteen Drive, Helens Bay, Bangor BT19 1HJ* T: (028) 9185 3729 M: 07753-116753
E: rosie_morton@yahoo.co.uk

MORTON, Ms Rosemary Jane. b 79. LRAM 02 Lon Univ BMus 03. Westcott Ho Cam 07. **d** 10 **p** 11. C Coggeshall w Markshall *Chelmsf* 10-14; Min Can and Succ St Paul's Cathl from 14. *7A Amen Court, London EC4M 7BU* T: (020) 7246 8338 E: rmorton@stpaulscathedral.org.uk

MORTON, Mrs Sheila. b 44. Leeds Univ. Sarum & Wells Th Coll 79. **dss** 84 **d** 87 **p** 94. HM Forces Düsseldorf 84-86; Cov St Mary 86-89; Par Dn 87-89; Par Dn Boston Spa *York* 89-92; C Flitwick *St Alb* 93-00; R Wilden w Colmworth and Ravensden 00-14; rtd 14. *11 Roundhouse Drive, Perry, Huntingdon PE28 0DJ* T: (01480) 810363
E: revsheila@btinternet.com

MORTON, Mrs Susan. b 58. Ex Univ BA 80 Warwick Univ PGCE 84. Ripon Coll Cuddesdon 10. **d** 12 **p** 13. NSM Hambleden Valley *Ox* from 12. *18 Claymore Park, Marlow SL7 3DL* T: (01494) 449197 M: 07808-517347
E: suemorton131@gmail.com

MORTON, The Very Revd William Wright. b 56. ALAM TCD BTh 88 MA 95 QUB PhD 96. CITC. **d** 88 **p** 89. C Drumachose *D & R* 88-91; I Conwal Union w Gartan 91-97; Bp's Dom Chapl 92-97; Can Raphoe Cathl 94-97; Dean Derry from 97; I Templemore from 97; Can St Patr Cathl Dublin from 13. *The Deanery, 30 Bishop Street, Londonderry BT48 6PP* T: (028) 7126 2746 E: dean@derry.anglican.org

MOSEDALE, Jonathan Ralph. b 69. Imp Coll Lon BSc 90 York Univ MSc 91 Trin Coll Ox DPhil 95. Protestant Th Inst Montpellier Lic 99 Ripon Coll Cuddesdon 07. **d** 09 **p** 10. C St Endellion w Port Isaac and St Kew *Truro* 09-12; C St Minver 09-12; C N Cornwall Cluster 12-13. *Address temp unknown* M: 07760-275087 E: mosedale@metanoa.com

MOSELEY, David John Reading. b 30. Univ Coll Ox BA 54 MA 58. Wells Th Coll 54. **d** 56 **p** 57. C Farnworth and Kearsley *Man* 56-59; Trinidad and Tobago 59-63; V Bedminster St Paul *Bris* 63-74; TV Bedminster 75-78; V Kilmington w Shute *Ex* 78-95; P-in-c Stockland w Dalwood 90; rtd 95; PtO *Ex* 95-09. *11 Alexandra Court, Gardens Road, Clevedon BS21 7PZ* T: (01275) 875922

MOSELEY, Canon Hugh Martin. b 47. St Jo Coll Dur BA 70. Westcott Ho Cam 71. **d** 73 **p** 74. C Hythe *Cant* 73-77; P-in-c Eythorne w Waldershare 77-83; V Ringmer *Chich* 83-99; RD Lewes and Seaford 93-97; P-in-c E Dean w Friston and Jevington 99-00; R 00-03; TR Rye 03-09; RD 03-09; Can and Preb Chich Cathl 07-09; rtd 09; PtO *Cant* from 11; Hon C Winchelsea and Icklesham *Chich* from 11.

Pilgrim's End, Manor Close, Icklesham, Winchelsea TN36 4BT
T: (01424) 813588 E: hugh@rabbitwarren13.freeserve.co.uk

MOSELEY, Michael. b 45. Oak Hill Th Coll 02. **d** 04 **p** 05. NSM
Forty Hill Jes Ch *Lon* 04-07; P-in-c Murston w Bapchild and
Tonge *Cant* 07-12; rtd 12; PtO *Cant* from 12. *56 Park Drive,
Sittingbourne ME10 1RD* T: (01795) 556258
E: michaelmoseley07@googlemail.com

MOSELEY, Roger Henry. b 38. Edin Th Coll 60. **d** 63 **p** 64.
C Friern Barnet All SS *Lon* 63-66; C Grantham St Wulfram
Linc 66-69; P-in-c Swaton w Spanby 69-73; P-in-c Horbling
69-73; V Soberton w Newtown *Portsm* 73-80; V Sarisbury
80-03; rtd 03; PtO *Portsm* from 03. *53B St Michael's Road,
St Helens, Ryde PO33 1YJ* T: (01983) 875203
E: roger.moseley@tesco.net

MOSELING, Canon Peter. b 48. WMMTC 92. **d** 95 **p** 96.
C Daventry, Ashby St Ledgers, Braunston etc *Pet* 95-97; P-in-c
Northampton H Trin 97-99; P-in-c Northampton St Paul
98-99; V Northampton H Trin and St Paul 99-05; Chapl Univ
Coll Northn 99-05; P-in-c Bletchingley *S'wark* 05-06;
R Bletchingley and Nutfield from 06; AD Godstone from 12;
Hon Can S'wark Cathl from 14. *The Rectory, Outwood Lane,
Bletchingley, Redhill RH1 4LR* T: (01883) 743252
E: p.moseling@tiscali.co.uk

MOSES, The Very Revd John Henry. b 38. KCVO 06. Nottm
Univ BA 59 PhD 65. Linc Th Coll 62. **d** 64 **p** 65. C Bedford
St Andr *St Alb* 64-70; P-in-c Cov St Pet 70; P-in-c Cov St Mark
71-73; TR Cov E 73-77; RD 73-77; Adn Southend *Chelmsf*
77-82; Provost Chelmsf 82-96; Chmn Coun of Cen for Th
Study Essex Univ 87-96; Dean St Paul's *Lon* 96-06; rtd 06.
Chestnut House, Burgate, Southwell NG25 0EP
T: (01636) 814880

MOSES, Preb Leslie Alan. b 49. Hull Univ BA 71 Edin Univ
BD 76. Edin Th Coll 73. **d** 76 **p** 77. C Edin Old St Paul
76-79; R Leven *St And* 79-85; R Edin Old St Paul 85-95; P-in-c
Edin St Marg 86-92; V St Marylebone All SS *Lon* from 95;
AD Westmr St Marylebone from 01; Preb St Paul's Cathl from
10. *All Saints' Vicarage, 7 Margaret Street, London W1W 8JG*
T: (020) 7636 1788 *or* 7636 9961 F: 7436 4470
E: alan@moses.org.uk

MOSFORD, Denzil Huw Erasmus. b 56. Florida State Univ
MTh 04 AKC 78. Sarum & Wells Th Coll 77. **d** 79 **p** 80.
C Clydach *S & B* 79-82; V 87-97; Jamaica 82-85; V Ystalyfera
S & B 85-87; Dioc World Miss Officer 91-10; RD Cwmtawe
93-97; V Gorseinon 97-10; AD Llwchwr 00-10; Hon Can
Brecon Cathl 01-04; Can Res Brecon Cathl 04-10; Dir of Min
Miss to Seafarers 10-14; P-in-c Dafen and Felinfoel *St D* from
14; Dioc Ecum Officer from 14. *The Vicarage, Bryngwyn Road,
Dafen, Llanelli SA14 8LW* T: (01554) 754848
E: huw.mosford@gmail.com

MOSLEY, Edward Peter. b 38. Clifton Th Coll 62. **d** 67 **p** 68.
C Mirehouse *Carl* 67-69; C Newbarns w Hawcoat 69-72;
R Aikton and Orton St Giles 72-77; V Silloth 77-78; CF 78-94;
Hon C Rothiemurchus and Grantown-on-Spey *Mor* 94-95;
rtd 98; P-in-c Strathnairn St Paul *Mor* 03-09. *52 Castle Heather
Crescent, Inverness IV2 4BF* T: (01463) 232552
E: epmos@onetel.com

MOSLEY, Robin Howarth. b 46. Birm Univ LLB 67 Leeds Univ
BA 09 Solicitor 71. NOC 06. **d** 09 **p** 10. NSM Ches St Mary
09-11; V Brereton from 11. *The Rectory, Brereton Park, Brereton,
Sandbach CW11 1RY* T: (01477) 533263 M: 07818-568017
E: robinm243@btinternet.com

MOSS, Canon Barbara Penelope. b 46. St Anne's Coll Ox
BA 66 MA 70 Lon Univ BD 97 Middx Univ MA 00.
EAMTC 95. **d** 97 **p** 98. NSM Leytonstone H Trin and St Aug
Harrow Green *Chelmsf* 97-00; C Cambridge Gt St Mary w
St Mich *Ely* 00-05; P-in-c Gothenburg w Halmstad, Jönköping
etc *Eur* from 05; Chapl Gothenburg Univ and Chalmers Univ
of Tech from 05; Hon Can *Eur* from 12. *St Andrew's Church Flat,
Norra Liden 15, S411-18 Gothenburg, Sweden* T/F: (0046) (31)
711 1915 E: bar@barmoss.demon.co.uk *or*
st.andrews.got@telia.com

MOSS, Bernard Roger. b 44. **d** 15. NSM Odd Rode *Ches* from
15. *34 Leicester Avenue, Alsager, Stoke-on-Trent ST7 2BS*
T: (01270) 882238 M: 07917-543356 E: b.r.moss@staffs.ac.uk

MOSS, Catherine. b 53. ERMC. **d** 09 **p** 10. NSM Guilsborough
and Hollowell and Cold Ashby etc *Pet* from 09. *Saxon Spires
Practice, West Haddon Road, Guilsborough, Northampton
NN6 8QE* T: (01604) 740210 F: 740869 M: 07779-000897
E: cattimoss@aol.com

MOSS (née BELL), Mrs Catherine Ann. b 63. Trin Coll Bris
BA 88. **d** 89 **p** 94. Par Dn Southsea St Jude *Portsm* 89-94; C
94-97; C Luton St Mary *St Alb* from 97; Chapl Luton Univ
97-02. *2 Saxtead Close, Luton LU2 9SQ* T: (01582) 391125

MOSS, Christopher Ashley. b 52. Ex Univ BA 73 Southn
Univ DASS 78 CQSW 78. Wycliffe Hall Ox 89. **d** 91 **p** 92.

C Malvern H Trin and St Jas *Worc* 91-96; V Longdon,
Castlemorton, Bushley, Queenhill etc from 96; RD Upton
from 11. *The Vicarage, Longdon, Tewkesbury GL20 6AT*
T/F: (01684) 833256 E: cmoss@holyplace.feeserve.co.uk

MOSS, David. b 60. WEMTC 12. **d** 15. NSM Gt Hanwood and
Longden and Annscroft etc *Heref* from 15. *Address temp
unknown*

MOSS, Preb David Glyn. b 62. St Anne's Coll Ox BA 83 Em Coll
Cam BA 89. Westcott Ho Cam 87. **d** 90 **p** 91. C Halesowen
Worc 90-93; Tutor St Steph Ho Ox 93-03; Vice-Prin 00-03; Dioc
Tr Officer *Ex* 03-04; Prin SWMTC 04-13; Preb Ex Cathl 10-13;
rtd 13. *6 St Davids Close, Sidbury, Sidmouth EX10 0QS*

MOSS, David Sefton. b 59. Sunderland Poly BSc 80 Anglia Poly
Univ MA 05 MRPharmS 81. Ridley Hall Cam 91. **d** 93 **p** 94.
C Highworth w Sevenhampton and Inglesham etc *Bris*
93-97; V Bedminster St Mich from 97. *St Michael's Vicarage,
153 St John's Lane, Bedminster, Bristol BS3 5AE* T: 0117-977
6132 M: 07890-262334 E: vicar@stmichaelandallangels.info

MOSS, James Wilfred. b 15. Oak Hill Th Coll 75. **d** 76 **p** 77.
Hon C Frogmore *St Alb* 76-78 and 81-93; Hon C Watford
St Luke 78-81; PtO 93-08. *8A The Rise, Park Street, St Albans
AL2 2NT* T: (01727) 872467

MOSS, Preb Kenneth Charles. b 37. Imp Coll Lon BSc 59
PhD 62 ARCS 59. **d** 66 **p** 67. Canada 66-73; Chapl Ex Univ
73-83; V St Marychurch 83-02; RD Ipplepen 87-93; Preb
Ex Cathl from 92; rtd 02. *3 Mondeville Way, Northam, Bideford
EX39 1DQ* T: (01237) 422251

MOSS, The Ven Leonard Godfrey. b 32. K Coll Lon BD 59
AKC 59. **d** 60 **p** 61. C Putney St Marg *S'wark* 60-63; C Cheam
63-67; R Much Dewchurch w Llanwarne and Llandinabo
Heref 67-72; Dioc Ecum Officer 69-83; V Marden w Amberley
72-78; V Marden w Amberley and Wisteston 78-84;
P-in-c 92-94; Preb Heref Cathl 79-97; Can Heref Cathl
84-91; Dioc Soc Resp Officer 84-91; Adn Heref 91-97;
rtd 97; PtO *Heref* from 97. *10 Saxon Way, Ledbury HR8 2QY*
T: (01531) 631195

MOSS, Leslie. b 52. **d** 02 **p** 03. OLM Ditton St Mich w
St Thos *Liv* from 02. *105 Heath Road, Widnes WA8 7NU*
T: 0151-423 1100

MOSS, Miss Lindsey. b 70. St Jo Coll Nottm 07. **d** 09 **p** 10.
C Standon and The Mundens w Sacombe *St Alb* 09-12;
NSM Ware Ch Ch from 12. *Christ Church, New Road, Ware
SG12 7BS* M: 07974-823727
E: lindseymoss822@yahoo.co.uk

MOSS, Miss Lucy Margaret. b 85. Cant Ch Ch Univ BA 07. St Jo
Coll Nottm MTh 15. **d** 15. C Spennymoor and Whitworth
Dur from 15. *34 Bluebell Drive, Spennymoor DL16 7YF*
M: 07891-491386 E: lucymoss1@hotmail.com

MOSS, Mrs Nelva Elizabeth. b 44. Bp Grosseteste Coll TCert 66
Sussex Univ BEd 73. S Dios Minl Tr Scheme 90. **d** 93 **p** 94.
NSM Bincombe w Broadwey, Upwey and Buckland Ripers
Sarum 93-96; NSM Langtree *Ox* 96-98; TV 98-09; rtd 09.
5 Wynnes Rise, Sherborne DT9 6DH T: (01935) 814329
E: nelvamoss@hotmail.com

MOSS, Peter Hextall. b 34. Clare Coll Cam BA 59 MA 62.
Linc Th Coll 59. **d** 61 **p** 62. C Easington Colliery *Dur* 61-63;
C Whickham 63-65; C-in-c Town End Farm CD 65-72; TV
Mattishall *Nor* 72-75; P-in-c Welborne 75-84; P-in-c Mattishall
w Mattishall Burgh 75-84; P-in-c Yaxham 80-84; TR Hempnall
84-89. *High House Cottage, Gunn Street, Foulsham, Dereham
NR20 5RN* T: (01362) 683823

MOSS, Peter John. b 41. K Coll Cam BA 64 MA 67. Westcott Ho
Cam 63. **d** 84 **p** 85. NSM Leighton Buzzard w Eggington,
Hockliffe etc *St Alb* 84-93; NSM Luton St Sav 93-98; NSM
Houghton Regis 03-05; P-in-c Devizes St Pet *Sarum* 05-13;
rtd 13; PtO *Sarum* from 13. *42 Bouverie Avenue, Salisbury
SP2 8DT* T: (01722) 326008 E: peter.moss87@virgin.net

MOSSE, Mrs Barbara Ann. b 51. CertEd 73 Open Univ BA 77
Univ of Wales (Lamp) MA 99 Lambeth STh 83. CA Tr Coll
IDC 81. **d** 90 **p** 95. CA 81-91; NSM Southbourne w
W Thorney *Chich* 90-93; Community Mental Health Chapl
Fareham/Gosport 94-97; NSM Purbrook *Portsm* 95-03; Team
Chapl Portsm Hosps NHS Trust 01-09; Asst Dioc Spirituality
Adv *Portsm* 05-09. *Drogo, 1 Grenfield Court, Emsworth PO10 7SA*
T: (01243) 376155 E: barbaramosse@btinternet.com

MOSSLEY, Iain Stephen. b 72. Univ of Wales (Ban) BTh 94.
St Steph Ho Ox 95. **d** 98 **p** 99. C Ribbleton *Blackb* 98-01;
C Marton Moss 01-03; V Burnley St Matt w H Trin 03-08;
P-in-c Leyland St Jas 08-12; V 12-13; P-in-c Ashton-upon-
Mersey St Martin *Ches* 13. *Address temp unknown*
E: fatheriain@blueyonder.co.uk

MOSSMAN, Mrs Margaret. b 46. NOC 97. **d** 00 **p** 01. NSM
Beighton *Sheff* 00-02; C 02-04; V Owston 04-12; rtd 12.
32 Tennyson Road, Rothwell, Kettering NN14 6JH
T: (01536) 660928 E: mmossman@hotmail.co.uk

MOSSOP, Patrick John. b 48. Solicitor St Jo Coll Cam MA LLB. Linc Th Coll BTh 93. **d** 93 **p** 94. C Halstead St Andr w H Trin and Greenstead Green *Chelmsf* 93-97; Assoc Chapl Essex Univ 97-99; Chapl 99-04; V Forest Gate Em w Upton Cross 04-09; TR Plaistow and N Canning Town 09-14; rtd 14; PtO *Chelmsf* from 15. *18 Aileen Walk, London E15 4BB* E: pat.mos@btinternet.com

MOSTON, William Howard. b 47. **d** 10 **p** 11. OLM E Crompton *Man* from 10. *36 Clough Road, Shaw, Oldham OL2 8QD* T: (01706) 847940 M: 07824-507354 E: whmoston@hotmail.com

MOTE, Gregory Justin. b 60. Oak Hill Th Coll BA 83. **d** 86 **p** 87. C W Ealing St Jo w St Jas *Lon* 86-90; C St Helen Bishopsgate w St Andr Undershaft etc 90-95; V Poulton Lancelyn H Trin *Ches* 96-04; PtO *Blackb* from 04. *22 Evergreen Avenue, Leyland PR25 3AW* E: gjmote@aol.com

MOTH, Miss Susan. b 44. Leic Univ BA 65 K Coll Lon CertEd 66. Linc Th Coll 83. **dss** 85 **d** 87 **p** 94. Churchdown St Jo *Glouc* 85-93; C 87-93; Dn-in-c The Rissingtons 93-94; P-in-c 94-05; rtd 05. *19 Cunliffe Close, Oxford OX2 7BJ*

MOTHERSOLE, Hugh Robert. b 43. Essex Univ BA 70 MSc 73. **d** 11 **p** 12. OLM Halstead Area *Chelmsf* 11-15; NSM from 15. *10 Park Lane, Earls Colne, Colchester CO6 2RJ* T: (01787) 222211 M: 07803-699268 E: hrmsteam@btinternet.com

MOTHERSOLE, John Robert. b 25. Lon Univ MA 99. Chich Th Coll. **d** 84 **p** 85. NSM Hayes St Anselm *Lon* 84-93; NSM Hayes St Edm 93-98; P-in-c St Mary Aldermary 98-10; rtd 10. *116 Nestles Avenue, Hayes UB3 4QD* T: (020) 8848 0626 E: jm014t1045@blueyonder.co.uk

MOTT, Julian Ward. b 52. Loughb Univ BSc 77. Ripon Coll Cuddesdon 78. **d** 81 **p** 82. C Aylestone *Leic* 81-84; C Gt Ilford St Mary *Chelmsf* 84-88; R Chevington w Hargrave and Whepstead w Brockley *St E* 88-99; V Lower Gornal *Worc* from 99. *The Vicarage, Church Street, Lower Gornal, Dudley DY3 2PF* T: (01902) 882023

MOTT, Marjorie. b 45. NSM Greenhill St Jo *Lon* from 15. *51 Brook Drive, Harrow HA1 4RT* T: (020) 8930 9119 M: 07976-609287 E: marjorie.mott@gmail.com

MOTT, Peter John. b 49. Ch Coll Cam BA 70 MA 75 Dundee Univ PhD 73. St Jo Coll Nottm BA 79. **d** 80 **p** 81. C Hull St Jo Newland *York* 80-83; C Selly Park St Steph and St Wulstan *Birm* 83-87; C Mosbrough *Sheff* 87-92; R Colne St Bart *Blackb* 92-98; TV Colne and Villages 98-01; P-in-c Keighley St Andr *Leeds* 01-14; Dioc Ecum Officer 04-14; rtd 14; PtO *York* from 14. *Cornerways, 13 Hall Park, Heslington, York YO10 5DT* T: (01904) 206958 E: petermott57@gmail.com

✠**MOTTAHEDEH, The Rt Revd Iraj Kalimi.** b 32. United Th Coll Bangalore 56. **d** 59 **p** 60 **c** 86. C Isfahan St Luke Iran 59-62; V Shiraz St Simon 62-66; V Tehran St Paul 67-75; V Isfahan St Luke 75-83; Adn Iran 83-86; Asst Bp Iran 86-90; Bp Iran 90-02; Pres Bp Episc Ch Jerusalem and Middle E 00-02; rtd 02; Interim Bp Iran 02-04; Hon Asst Bp Birm and Lich from 05. *2 Highland Road, Newport TF10 7QE* T: (01952) 813615 E: bishraj@btinternet.com

MOTTERSHEAD, Derek. b 39. Open Univ BA 74 BEd. Chich Th Coll 65. **d** 69 **p** 70. C Walthamstow St Barn and St Jas Gt *Chelmsf* 69-72; C Chelmsf All SS 72-77; P-in-c Cold Norton w Stow Maries 77-80; V Leytonstone St Andr 80-92; V Eastbourne St Sav and St Pet *Chich* 92-04; Miss to Seafarers 92-04; rtd 04; PtO *Cant* 05-06 and from 11; Hon C Preston next Faversham, Goodnestone and Graveney 06-10. *Sherwood, 25B The Paddock, Spring Lane, Canterbury CT1 1SX* T: (01227) 453118 E: dmottershead11@btinternet.com

MOTTERSHEAD, Nicholas John Leigh. b 66. SEITE 12. **d** 15. NSM St Olave Hart Street w All Hallows Staining etc *Lon* from 15. *Address temp unknown*

MOTTRAM, Andrew Peter. b 53. AKC 77. Ripon Coll Cuddesdon 77. **d** 78 **p** 79. C E Bedfont *Lon* 78-81; C Bp's Hatfield *St Alb* 81-84; V Milton Ernest 84-91; V Thurleigh 84-91; P-in-c Heref All SS 91-06; RD Heref City 02-03; PtO from 06. *Ecclesiastical Property Solutions, Mulberry Dock, Pencombe, Bromyard HR7 4SH* T: (01885) 400311 M: 07960-726717 E: andrew@abetterview.co.uk

MOTYER, John Alexander. b 24. TCD BA 46 MA 51 BD 51 Lambeth DD 97. Wycliffe Hall Ox 47. **d** 47 **p** 48. C Penn Fields *Lich* 47-50; C Bris H Trin and Tutor Clifton Th Coll 51-54; Vice-Prin 54-65; Tutor Tyndale Hall Bris 52-54; V W Hampstead St Luke *Lon* 65-70; Dep Prin Tyndale Hall Bris 70-71; Prin and Dean Trin Coll Bris 71-81; Min Westbourne Ch Ch Prop Chpl *Win* 81-89; rtd 89; PtO *Ex* from 99. *27 Georges Road West, Poynton, Stockport SK12 1JY*

MOTYER, Stephen. b 50. Pemb Coll Cam BA 73 MA 77 Bris Univ MLitt 79 K Coll Lon PhD 93. Trin Coll Bris 73. **d** 76 **p** 77. Lect Oak Hill Th Coll 76-83; C Braughing, Lt Hadham, Albury, Furneux Pelham etc *St Alb* 83-87; Lect Lon Sch of Th from 87;

PtO *Lon* 87-13; *St Alb* from 87. *7 Hangar Ruding, Watford WD19 5BH* T: (020) 8386 6829 *or* (01923) 826061 E: s.motyer@londonbiblecollege.ac.uk

MOUGHTIN, Ross. b 48. St Cath Coll Cam BA 70 St Jo Coll Dur BA 75. **d** 76 **p** 77. C Litherland St Paul Hatton Hill *Liv* 76-79; C Heswall *Ches* 79-84; Chapl Edw Unit Rochdale Infirmary 83-92; V Thornham w Gravel Hole *Man* 84-92; V Aughton Ch Ch *Liv* from 92; Chapl W Lancashire NHS Trust 94-11. *Christ Church Vicarage, 22 Long Lane, Aughton, Ormskirk L39 5AT* T: (01695) 422175 E: ross.moughtin@gmail.com

MOUGHTIN-MUMBY, Andrew Denis Paul. b 78. Birm Univ BA 00 SS Coll Cam BA 05 MA 09. Westcott Ho Cam 03. **d** 06 **p** 07. C Walworth St Chris *S'wark* 06-10; R Walworth St Pet from 10; AD S'wark and Newington from 14; PV Westmr Abbey from 14. *St Peter's Rectory, 12 Villa Street, London SE17 2EJ* T: (020) 7703 3139 E: rector@stpeterswalworth.org

MOUGHTIN-MUMBY, Sharon. b 76. St Jo Coll Dur BA 97 MA 98 Worc Coll Ox DPhil 04. Westcott Ho Cam 05. **d** 06 **p** 07. C Walworth St Pet *S'wark* 06-10; Dioc Miss Th Angl Communion 10-11; Hon C S'wark St Geo w St Alphege and St Jude 10-15; Hon C Walworth St Pet from 15. *St Peter's Rectory, 12 Villa Street, London SE17 2EJ* M: 07980-611347 E: sharon.mm@btinternet.com

MOUK, Mae Elizabeth. b 83. **d** 14 **p** 15. C Walworth St Chris *S'wark* from 14. *78 Tatum Street, London SE17 1QR* M: 07500-309540 E: mae.mouk@icloud.com

MOUL, Russell Derek. b 56. Reading Univ BA 83. Oak Hill Th Coll 97. **d** 99 **p** 00. C Harold Wood *Chelmsf* 99-02; C Harold Hill St Paul 02-03; V from 03. *St Paul's Vicarage, Redcar Road, Romford RM3 9PT* T: (01708) 341225 E: russell@themouls.fslife.co.uk

MOULAND, Norman Francis. b 38. OLM course 98. **d** 99 **p** 00. OLM Verwood *Sarum* from 99. *13 Park Drive, Verwood BH31 7PE* T: (01202) 825320

MOULD, Mrs Jacqueline. b 66. QUB BD 88. CITC BTh 91. **d** 91 **p** 92. C Belfast St Aid *Conn* 91-94; C Drumragh w Mountfield *D & R* 94-96; NSM Kinson *Sarum* 97-00; C Belvoir *D & D* from 03. *10A Ballyclough Road, Lisburn BT28 3UY* T: (028) 9264 7912 *or* 9049 1436 E: jacmould@gmail.com

MOULD, James Michael. b 46. SEITE 95. **d** 98 **p** 99. NSM Wallington *S'wark* 98-03; NSM W Wittering and Birdham w Itchenor *Chich* from 03. *Quinneys, Itchenor Road, Itchenor, Chichester PO20 7DD* T: (01243) 513600 E: revd.jim@btinternet.com

MOULD, Jeremy James. b 63. Nottm Univ BA 85 TCD BTh 91. CITC 88. **d** 91 **p** 92. C Mossley *Conn* 91-94; C Drumragh w Mountfield *D & R* 94-96; C Kinson *Sarum* 97-00. *10A Ballyclough Road, Lisburn BT28 3UY* T: (028) 9264 7912 E: jermould@gmail.com

MOULDEN, David Ivor. b 52. Cant Ch Ch Univ BA 02. SEITE 05. **d** 08 **p** 09. C Madeley *Heref* 08-12; V Canonry *Cant* from 12. *The Vicarage, Queen's Road, Ash, Canterbury CT3 2BG* E: davidmoulden@hotmail.com

MOULDER, John William Michael Cornock. b 39. City of Lon Poly ACIB 67. Glouc Sch of Min 82. **d** 86 **p** 86. C Broken Hill Australia 86-88; P-in-c Berrigan 88-94; P-in-c Edenhope y 94-98; C Tividale *Lich* 98-01; P-in-c W Bromwich St Pet 01-04; rtd 04; Hon Asst P Cobram Australia from 04. *Goldwick, 130 Jerilderie Street, Berrigan NSW 2712, Australia* T/F: (0061) (3) 5885 2913 E: fatherm@dragnet.com.au

MOULDER, Kenneth. b 53. Lon Univ BEd 75. Ridley Hall Cam 78. **d** 81 **p** 82. C Harold Wood *Chelmsf* 81-84; C Darfield *Sheff* 84-88; V Walkergate *Newc* 88-92; P-in-c Byker St Mark 90-92; V Byker St Mark and Walkergate St Oswald from 92. *St Oswald's Parsonage, Woodhead Road, Newcastle upon Tyne NE6 4RX* T: 0191-263 6249

MOULT, Jane Elizabeth Kate. b 61. Trin Coll Bris 91. **d** 94 **p** 95. C St Jo in Bedwardine *Worc* 94-97; NSM Bilton *Cov* 97-99; Chapl Staunton Harold Hosp 00-01; Sen Chapl Leics Partnership NHS Trust 01-07; PtO *Leic* 07-14. *17 The Leascroft, Ravenstone, Coalville LE67 2BL* T: (01530) 833160 E: jane.moult@btinternet.com

MOULT, Simon Paul. b 66. Trin Coll Bris BA 94. **d** 94 **p** 95. C St Jo in Bedwardine *Worc* 94-97; C Bilton *Cov* 97-99; P-in-c Thringstone St Andr *Leic* 99-05; RD Akeley S 03-05; Chapl N Warks NHS Trust from 05; Chapl Geo Eliot Hosp NHS Trust Nuneaton from 05. *The Chaplaincy, George Eliot Hospital, College Street, Nuneaton CV10 7DJ* T: (024) 7686 5046 *or* 7635 1351

MOULTON, Canon Paul Oliver. b 43. NOC 77. **d** 80 **p** 81. C Wilmslow *Ches* 80-85; V Knutsford St Cross 85-92; Chapl Mary Dendy Hosp Knutsford 86-92; V Gatley *Ches* 92-01; Chapl Cen Man Healthcare NHS Trust 92-01; P-in-c Capesthorne w Siddington and Marton *Ches* 01-11; Hon Can

Ches Cathl 07-11; rtd 11; PtO *Ches* from 11. *52 Longdown Road, Congleton CW12 4QP* T: (01260) 272627
E: paulo.moulton@btinternet.com

MOUNCER, David Peter. b 65. Univ of Wales (Abth) BA 86. Oak Hill Th Coll BA 94. d 94 p 95. C Folkestone St Jo *Cant* 94-98; Min Grove Green LEP 98-03; R Brampton St Thos *Derby* 03-07; C Walton St Jo from 07. *5 Foxbrook Drive, Chesterfield S40 3JR* T: (01246) 555113 E: therevdp@tiscali.co.uk

MOUNSEY, William Lawrence Fraser. b 51. St Andr Univ BD 75. Edin Th Coll 76. d 78 p 79. C Edin St Mark 78-81; Chapl RAF 81-90 and 96-06; R Dalmahoy and Chapl Heriot-Watt Univ *Edin* 90-96; PtO *Eur* from 06; C Roslin (Rosslyn Chpl) *Edin* 06-11; C Edin St Vin from 11. *9 Upper Coltbridge Terrace, Edinburgh EH12 6AD* M: 07967-322651
E: wlfm@hotmail.co.uk

MOUNSTEPHEN, Canon Philip Ian. b 59. Southn Univ BA 80 Magd Coll Ox MA 87 PGCE. Wycliffe Hall Ox 85. d 88 p 89. C Gerrards Cross and Fulmer *Ox* 88-92; V W Streatham St Jas *S'wark* 92-98; Hd Pathfinders CPAS 98-02; Dir CY Network 01-02; Hd Min 02-07; Dep Gen Dir 04-07; Chapl Paris St Mich *Eur* 07-12; Exec Ldr CMS from 12; Hon Can *Eur* from 12. *CMS, Watlington Road, Oxford OX4 6BZ* T: (01865) 787400 F: 776375

MOUNT, Canon Judith Mary. b 35. Bedf Coll Lon BA 56 Lon Univ CertEd 57. Ripon Coll Cuddesdon 81. dss 83 d 87 p 94. Carterton *Ox* 83-85; Charlton on Otmoor and Oddington 85-87; Dioc Lay Min Adv and Asst Dir of Ords 86-89; Par Dn Islip w Charlton on Otmoor, Oddington, Noke etc 87-94; C 94-95; Assoc Dioc Dir Ords and Adv for Women in Ord Min 89-95; Hon Can Ch Ch 92-95; rtd 95; PtO *Ox* 95-10; *Glouc* from 99. *The Owl House, Bell Lane, Poulton, Cirencester GL7 5JF* T: (01285) 850242 E: jmount315@btinternet.com

MOUNTAIN, John Raymond. b 46. LCTP 11. d 12 p 13. NSM Appley Bridge and Parbold *Blackb* from 12. *50 The Common, Parbold, Wigan WN8 7EA* T: (01257) 463919 M: 07542-000996 E: john_mountain@talktalk.net

MOUNTFORD, Canon Brian Wakling. b 45. Newc Univ BA 66 Cam Univ MA 73 Ox Univ MA 90. Westcott Ho Cam 66. d 68 p 69. C Westmr St Steph w St Jo *Lon* 68-69; C Paddington Ch Ch 69-73; Chapl SS Coll Cam 73-78; V Southgate Ch Ch *Lon* 78-86; V Ox St Mary V w St Cross and St Pet from 86; Chapl St Hilda's Coll Ox from 89; Hon Can Ch Ch Ox from 98. *9A Norham Gardens, Oxford OX2 6PS* T: (01865) 515778 *or* 279111 E: brian.mountford@oriel.ox.ac.uk

MOUNTFORD, Ian David. b 65. St Jo Coll Nottm BTh 93. d 96 p 97. C Chilwell *S'well* 96-00; TV Thame *Ox* 00-14; C Derby St Alkmund and St Werburgh from 14. *Park Hurst, 25 Highfield Road, Derby DE22 1GX* E: mounty@psaconnect.com

MOURANT, Julia Caroline. b 58. Sheff Univ BA 79. St Jo Coll Nottm 82. dss 84 d 92 p 94. Cropwell Bishop w Colston Bassett, Granby etc *S'well* 84-86; Marple All SS *Ches* 86-89; Harlow St Mary and St Hugh w St Jo the Bapt *Chelmsf* 89-92; NSM 92-04; Asst Dir of Min 98-04; CME Officer 00-02; PtO *Win* 04-05; Lay Tr Officer 05-07; Voc, Recruitment and Selection Officer from 07. *The Rectory, Church Lane, Ellisfield, Basingstoke RG25 2QR* T: (01256) 381217

MOURANT, Sidney Eric. b 39. Lon Univ BD 73. Oak Hill Th Coll. d 89 p 90. C Oxton *Ches* 89-92; V Douglas All SS and St Thos *S & M* 92-96; I Rathkeale w Askeaton, Kilcornan and Kilnaughtin *L & K* 96-00; I Nenagh 00-04; rtd 04. *12 Breezemount, Hamiltonsbawn, Armagh BT61 9SB* T: (00353) (48) 3887 2203 M: 87-239 9785
E: sid296ney@btinternet.com

MOURANT, Stephen Philip Edward. b 54. St Jo Coll Nottm BTh 83. d 83 p 84. C Cropwell Bishop w Colston Bassett, Granby etc *S'well* 83-86; C Marple All SS *Ches* 86-89; P-in-c Harlow St Mary and St Hugh w St Jo the Bapt *Chelmsf* 89-90; V 90-04; P-in-c Bitterne *Win* 04-08; C Fair Oak 08-11; C Farleigh, Candover and Wield from 11. *The Rectory, Church Lane, Ellisfield, Basingstoke RG25 2QR* T: (01256) 381217
E: stephen.mourant@btinternet.com

MOUSIR-HARRISON, Stuart Nicholas. b 68. SW Poly Plymouth BSc 89 Nottm Univ MSc 92 St Martin's Coll Lanc PhD 99 St Jo Coll Dur BA 99. Cranmer Hall Dur. d 00 p 01. C Oadby *Leic* 00-03; C W Malling w Offham *Roch* 03-07; C Mereworth w W Peckham 03-07; P-in-c Dallington *Pet* 07-12; Chapl Northn Univ from 07. *Charles Bradlaugh Hall, Flat C2, Boughton Green Road, Northampton NN2 7AL* T: (01604) 892488
E: stuart.mousir-harrison@northampton.ac.uk

MOVERLEY, Canon Ruth Elaine. b 55. K Alfred's Coll Win CertEd 76. St Mich Coll Llan. d 90 p 97. C Llangynwyd w Maesteg *Llan* 90-95; C Glan Ely 95-97; V Llanharan w Peterston-super-Montem 97-05; V Tonyrefail w Gilfach Goch from 05; Can Llan Cathl from 14. *The Vicarage, High Street, Tonyrefail, Porth CF39 8PL* T: (01443) 670330

MOWBRAY, David. b 38. Fitzw Ho Cam BA 60 MA 64 Lon Univ BD 62. Clifton Th Coll. d 63 p 64. C Northampton St Giles *Pet* 63-66; Lect Watford St Mary *St Alb* 66-70; V Broxbourne 70-77; R Broxbourne w Wormley 77-84; V Hertford All SS 84-91; V Darley Abbey *Derby* 91-03; Asst Chapl Derby R Infirmary 91-94; Chapl Derbyshire Mental Health Services NHS Trust 99-03; rtd 03. *4 Marigold Close, Lincoln LN2 4SZ* T: (01522) 546753
E: davidanddiana@hotmail.co.uk

MOWBRAY, James Edward. b 78. Univ of Wales (Abth) BTh 00 Leeds Univ BA 03. Coll of Resurr Mirfield 01. d 03 p 04. C Perry Street *Roch* 03-07; V Swanley St Mary 07-14; P-in-c Kettering St Mary *Pet* from 14. *St Mary's Vicarage, 175 Avondale Road, Kettering NN16 8PN*

MOWBRAY, Ms Jill Valerie. b 54. Sussex Univ BEd 76 Lon Inst of Educn MA 86 Anglia Poly Univ MA 01. Ridley Hall Cam 99. d 01 p 02. C Tufnell Park St Geo and All SS *Lon* 01-04; V Whitton SS Phil and Jas 04-09; CME Adv *Chelmsf* from 09; C Walthamstow from 10. *41 Fraser Road, London E17 9DD* T: (020) 8520 9740 E: revjillmowbray@googlemail.com

MOWER, Miss Marguerite Mary. b 36. Bris Univ BA 57. Cant Sch of Min 90. d 93 p 94. NSM Eythorne and Elvington w Waldershare etc *Cant* 93-03; NSM Denholme and Harden and Wilsden *Bradf* 04-07; PtO *Cant* from 07. *Meadow Bank, Eythorne Road, Shepherswell, Dover CT15 7PN*

MOWLL, John William Rutley. b 42. Sarum Th Coll 63. d 66 p 67. C Oughtibridge *Sheff* 66-69; C Hill Birm 69-73; Ind Chapl and V Upper Arley *Worc* 73-78; P-in-c Upton Snodsbury and Broughton Hackett etc 78-81; R 81-83; V Boughton under Blean w Dunkirk *Cant* 83-89; V Boughton under Blean w Dunkirk and Hernhill 89-07; RD Ospringe 95-01; Hon Min Can Cant Cathl 96-07; rtd 07; Chapl to The Queen 00-12; PtO *Cant* from 07. *Holly Cottage, Water Lane, Ospringe, Faversham ME13 8TS* T: (01795) 597597

MOXLEY, Mrs Elizabeth Jane. b 52. St Jo Coll Nottm. d 05 p 06. C Aston Clinton w Buckland and Drayton Beauchamp *Ox* 05-08; R from 08. *The Rectory, 23 New Road, Aston Clinton, Aylesbury HP22 5JD* T: (01296) 632488
E: elizabethmoxley@hotmail.com

✠**MOXON, The Most Revd Sir David John.** b 51. KNZM 14. Cant Univ (NZ) BA 74 Massey Univ (NZ) MA 76 St Pet Coll Ox BA 78 MA 82. d 78 p 79 c 93. C Havelock North New Zealand 78-81; V Gate Pa 81-87; Dir Th Educn by Ext 87-93; Bp Waikato 93-13; Abp New Zealand 06-13; Abp Cant's Rep H See and Dir Angl Cen Rome from 13. *Palazzo Doria Pamphilj, Piazzo del Collegio Romano 2, 00186 Rome, Italy* T: (0039) 066 780 302 F: 066 780 674 E: director@anglicancentre.it

MOXON, John. d 02 p 03. NSM Birm St Luke 02-04. *41 Mariner Avenue, Birmingham B16 9DF* T: 0121-456 1628 *or* 472 0726 M: 07887-573122
E: john.moxon@birminghamchristiancollege.ac.uk

MOXON, Michael Anthony. b 42. LVO 98. Lon Univ BD 78 Heythrop Coll Lon MA 96. Sarum Th Coll 67. d 70 p 71. C Kirkley *Nor* 70-73; Min Can St Paul's Cathl 74-81; Sacr 77-81; Warden Coll of Min Canons 79-81; V Tewkesbury w Walton Cardiff *Glouc* 81-90; Chapl to The Queen 86-98; Can Windsor and Chapl in Windsor Gt Park 90-98; Dean Truro and R Truro St Mary 98-04; Chapl Cornwall Fire Brigade HQ 98-04; rtd 05. *St Neots, 79 Moresk Avenue, Truro TR1 1BT* T: (01872) 274666

MOY, Miss Elizabeth. b 55. Leeds and Carnegie Coll CertEd 76. LCTP 07. d 10 p 13. NSM Harden and Wilsden, Cullingworth and Denholme *Leeds* from 10. *3 Parkside Court, Cross Roads, Keighley BD22 9DS* T: (01535) 645991 *or* 650552 F: 650550
E: liz@kadugli.org.uk

MOY (née PLUMB), Mrs Nicola Louise. b 80. Birm Univ BA 01 Bris Univ MA 03 PGCE 04. St Jo Coll Nottm 06. d 08 p 09. C Wolverhampton St Jude *Lich* 08-12; C Turnham Green Ch Ch *Lon* from 13. *The Vicarage, 2 Wellesley Road, London W4 4BL* M: 07815-077917 E: nicolalouisemoy@gmail.com

MOY, Richard John. b 78. St Cath Coll Cam BA 99. Trin Coll Bris MA 03. d 04 p 05. C Wolverhampton St Jude *Lich* 04-07; Pioneer Min Wolv City Cen 07-10; Fresh Expressions Adv 10-12; V Turnham Green Ch Ch *Lon* from 12. *The Vicarage, 2 Wellesley Road, London W4 4BL* T: (020) 8996 0366
E: notintheratrace@yahoo.co.uk

MOYES (née WATSON), Mrs Stephanie Abigail. b 61. Heriot-Watt Univ BA 84. Cranmer Hall Dur 86. d 90 p 94. C Bishop's Castle w Mainstone *Heref* 90-93; Dep Chapl HM Pris Dur 93-95; Chapl HM Rem Cen Low Newton 95-98; V Chilton and Cornforth *Dur* 98-02; Chapl Wrekin Coll Telford 02-04; PtO *Worc* from 04. *7 Birchanger Green, Worcester WR4 0DW* T: (01905) 619181

MOYNAGH, David Kenneth. b 46. LRCP 70 MRCS 70 MRCGP 76 Lon Univ MB, BS 70. S Dios Minl Tr Scheme 88.

d 91 **p** 92. NSM Ore St Helen and St Barn *Chich* 91-99; PtO *Win* from 01. *White Cottage, Jordan's Lane, Sway, Lymington SO41 6AR* T: (01590) 682475

MOYNAGH, Michael Digby. b 50. Southn Univ BA 73 Lon Univ MA 74 Aus Nat Univ PhD 78 Bris Univ MA 85. Trin Coll Bris. **d** 85 **p** 86. C Northwood Em *Lon* 85-89; P-in-c Wilton *B & W* 89-90; TR 90-96; Dir Cen for Futures Studies St Jo Coll Nottm 96-04; Co-Dir Tomorrow Project 04-14; Fresh Expressions Team *Ox* from 05. *14 Dale Close, Oxford OX1 1TU* T: (01865) 722551

MOYNAN, Canon David George. b 53. **d** 86 **p** 87. C Seagoe *D & D* 86-88; C Taney *D & G* 88-89; I Arklow w Inch and Kilbride 89-94; Dioc Stewardship Adv 92-15; Dioc Ch of Ireland Bps' Appeal Rep 92-15; I Kilternan 94-15; Dioc Dir Decade of Evang 96-15; Can Ch Ch Cathl Dublin 97-15; New Zealand from 15. *45 Thorpe-Orinoco Road, Orinoco RD1, Motueka 7196, New Zealand* M: (0064) 21-0826 6278 E: moynandg.nz@gmail.com

MOYSE, Mrs Pauline Patricia. b 42. Ex Univ CertEd 62. S Dios Minl Tr Scheme 88. **d** 91 **p** 94. NSM Fleet *Guildf* 91-92; C 93-97; Chapl Farnborough Coll of Tech 96-97; P-in-c Stoneleigh *Guildf* 97-02; Warden of Readers 97-07; Dioc Adv Lay Min 01-07; rtd 07; Tr Officer for Past Assts *Guildf* 07-09; PtO from 09. *Beechend, 2 Hillcrest, Fleet GU51 4PZ* T: (01252) 671382 E: pauline.moyse1@ntlworld.com

✠**MPALANYI-NKOYOYO, The Rt Revd Livingstone.** b 37. **d** 69 **p** 70. **c** 80. Kasubi Uganda 69-75; Nsangi 75-77; Adn Namirembe 77-79; Suff Bp 80-81; Suff Bp Mukono 81-94; Abp Uganda and Bp Kampala 94-03; rtd 03. *PO Box 14123, Kampala, Uganda* E: couab@uol.co.ug

MPUNZI, Nduna Ananias. b 46. Federal Th Coll S Africa 69. **d** 71 **p** 72. C Galeshewe St Jas S Africa 71-74; C Taung 74-75; C Vaal Hartz 75-77; R Vryberg St Phil 77-78; LtO *Glas* 82-84; C Bilston *Lich* 84-86; TV 86-90; P-in-c Walsall St Mary and All SS Palfrey 90-97; P-in-c Caldmore 90-93; P-in-c Shobnall 02-04; TV Worc St Barn w Ch Ch 04-08. *4 Forest Close, Worcester WR2 6BW*

✠**MTETEMELA, The Rt Revd Donald Leo.** b 47. St Phil Th Coll Kongwa Wycliffe Hall Ox 75. **d** 71 **p** 72. Asst Bp Cen Tanganyika 82-90; Bp Ruaha from 90; Abp Tanzania 98-08. *Box 1028, Iringa, Tanzania* T: (00255) (262) 270 1211 F: 270 2479 E: ruaha@anglican.or.tz

MUBARAK, Riaz. b 70. **d** 01. Pakistan 01-14; P-in-c W Winch w Setchey, N Runcton and Middleton *Nor* 14-15; R Middlewinch from 15. *The New Rectory, Rectory Lane, West Winch, King's Lynn PE33 0NR* T: (01553) 841519 E: rev.riaz.mubarak@gmail.com

MUDD, Mrs Linda Anne. b 59. WMMTC 00. **d** 03 **p** 04. C Exhall *Cov* 03-07; Chapl Geo Eliot Hosp NHS Trust Nuneaton 07-11; TV Coventry Caludon *Cov* from 11. *The Vicarage, 56 Wyken Croft, Coventry CV2 3AD* T: (024) 7661 8329 E: linda.mudd@btinternet.com

MUDDIMAN, John Bernard. b 47. Keble Coll Ox BA 67 MA 72 DPhil 76 Selw Coll Cam BA 71 MA 75. Westcott Ho Cam 69. **d** 72 **p** 73. Hon C Ox St Giles 72-83; Chapl New Coll Ox 72-76; Tutor St Steph Ho Ox 76-83; Vice-Prin 80-83; Lect Th Nottm Univ 83-90; Fell Mansf Coll Ox 90-12; Chapl 97-12; LtO *Ox* 90-02; NSM Littlemore 97-12; rtd 12. *16 Long Acre, Bingham, Nottingham NG13 8BG* E: john.muddiman@mansfield.ox.ac.uk

MUDGE, Frederick Alfred George. b 31. Leeds Univ BSc 58 Univ of Wales BD 67. St Mich Coll Llan 58. **d** 61 **p** 62. C Cwmavon *Llan* 61-64; PV Llan Cathl 64-70; R Llandough w Leckwith 70-88; V Penarth All SS 88-96; rtd 96; PtO *Llan* from 07. *Pathways, 6 Fairwater Road, Llandaff, Cardiff CF5 2LD*

MUDIE, Martin Bruce. b 54. Goldsmiths' Coll Lon BA 76. Sarum & Wells Th Coll 92. **d** 92 **p** 93. C Bromley St Mark *Roch* 92-95; rtd 95; PtO *B & W* 02-03; Hon C Glastonbury w Meare 03-10. *20 Oriel Road, Street BA16 0JL* T: (01458) 448034 E: mmudie5@gmail.com

MUFFETT, Mrs Sarah Susan. b 53. STETS 02. **d** 05 **p** 06. NSM Okeford *Sarum* 05-13; rtd 13; PtO *Sarum* from 13. *Prides Cottage, High Street, Child Okeford, Blandford Forum DT11 8EH* T: (01258) 860010 E: sarahmuffett@btopenworld.com

MUGAN, Miriam Ruth. b 56. RNMH 77. Oak Hill Th Coll 93. **d** 96 **p** 97. NSM St Alb St Sav *St Alb* 96-07; P-in-c Croxley Green All SS 07-12; V from 12. *All Saints' Vicarage, The Green, Croxley Green, Rickmansworth WD3 3HJ* T: (01923) 772109 E: miriam.mugan@btopenworld.com

MUGGE, Martijn. b 69. Oak Hill Th Coll BA 12. **d** 12 **p** 13. C Wombwell *Sheff* 12-15; P-in-c Conisbrough from 15. *The Vicarage, 8 Castle Avenue, Conisbrough, Doncaster DN12 3BT* M: (07732)-492998 E: mugge@onetel.com *or* martijn.mugge@sheffield.anglican.org

MUGGERIDGE, Ms Sara Ann. b 49. Westf Coll Lon BA 73 Reading Univ MBA 92 Cant Ch Ch Univ BA 13. **d** 15. C St Steph Walbrook and St Swithun etc *Lon* from 15. *8 Hayfield House, 11-15 Hayfield Passage, London E1 3LQ* M: 07770-381911 T: (020) 7790 0511 E: sally@sallymuggeridge.com

MUGGLETON, James. b 55. Bris Univ BA 80. Chich Th Coll 81 EAMTC 99. **d** 01 **p** 02. NSM E Leightonstone *Ely* 01-03; C 03-04; C Buckworth and Alconbury cum Weston 04; R Barney, Fulmodeston w Croxton, Hindringham etc *Nor* 04-15; R Barney, Hindringham, Thursford, Great Snoring, Little Snoring and Kettlestone and Pensthorpe from 15. *The Rectory, The Street, Hindringham, Fakenham NR21 0AA* T: (01328) 878159 E: jamie@muggs.myzen.co.uk

MUGGLETON, Major George. b 25. Chich Th Coll 55. **d** 57 **p** 58. C Oldham St Mary *Man* 57-59; C Ashton St Mich 59-61; V Croydon H Trin *Cant* 61-68; R Stisted *Chelmsf* 68-69; P-in-c Pattiswick 68-69; P-in-c Bradwell 68-69; R Stisted w Bradwell and Pattiswick 69-87; rtd 87. *Curvalion House, Creech St Michael, Taunton TA3 5QF* T: (01823) 443842

MUGHAL, Dominic Jacob. b 59. Asian Soc Inst Manila MSc 88 Edin Univ MTh 93 Leeds Univ MPhil 05. St Jo Coll Nottm 05. **d** 07 **p** 08. C Fairweather Green *Bradf* 07-09; Community Outreach P 09-13; C Thornbury 09-13; C Woodhall 09-13; C Bradf St Aug Undercliffe 09-13; C Bradf St Clem 09-13. *Address temp unknown* M: 07821-246891 E: dominic_moghal@hotmail.com

MUGRIDGE, Mrs Gloria Janet. b 45. R Holloway Coll Lon BA 66. S Dios Minl Tr Scheme 92. **d** 95 **p** 96. NSM Dorchester *Sarum* 95-97; Asst Chapl Weymouth Coll 95-97; Chapl 97-04; NSM Melbury *Sarum* 97-02; NSM Stour Vale 04-06. *27 St John's Priory, 1 Shaftesbury Road, Wilton, Salisbury SP2 0JN* T: (01722) 742386 E: janetmug@aol.com

MUIR, David Murray. b 49. Glas Univ MA 70. St Jo Coll Nottm BA 72. **d** 76 **p** 77. C Fulham St Mary N End *Lon* 76-80; C Aspley *S'well* 80; India 81-85; Dir Ext Studies St Jo Coll Nottm 85-02; C Upton (Overchurch) *Ches* 02-04; Adult Educn and Par Development Adv *Ex* 04-08; Pioneer Min Okehampton Deanery 08-14; rtd 14. *265 Milton Road, Weston-super-Mare BS22 8JA* T: (01934) 622036 M: 07854-845067 E: davidandjunemuir@gmail.com

MUIR, David Trevor. b 49. TCD MA MLitt 93. CITC 75. **d** 78 **p** 79. C Dublin Clontarf *D & G* 78-80; C Monkstown St Mary 80-83; I Kilternan 83-94; I Delgany 94-97; Can Ch Ch Cathl Dublin 95-97; Chapl to Ch of Ireland Assn of Deaf People from 97. *Luogh North, Doolin, Co Clare, Republic of Ireland* T: (00353) (65) 707 4778 F: 707 4871 E: muirdt@gmail.com

MUIR, John William. b 38. Dur Univ BA 59 Mansf Coll Ox MA 65. Chich Th Coll 78. **d** 78 **p** 79. In Congr Ch 62-70; United Ch of Zambia 70-78; C Brighouse *Wakef* 78-80; V Northowram 80-87; V Sowerby 87-01; rtd 01; PtO *Leeds* from 02. *8 Whitley Drive, Holmfield, Halifax HX2 9SJ* T: (01422) 244163 M: 07733-152089 E: jmuir@msn.com

MUIR, Peter Robert James. b 49. Ex Univ BSc 71. **d** 09 **p** 10. OLM Thursley *Guildf* 09-13; NSM from 13; OLM Elstead 09-13; NSM from 13. *Yew Cottage, Thursley, Godalming GU8 6QA* T: (01252) 702360 *or* 703857 M: 07747-793253 E: peter@cellarworld.co.uk *or* vicar@thursleychurch.org.uk

MUKHERJEE, Supriyo. b 42. Calcutta Univ BA 70 Serampore Th Coll BD 76 Derby Univ MA 97. Bp's Coll Calcutta 70. **d** 75 **p** 76. India 75-91; C Crook *Dur* 91-92; V Nelson in Lt Marsden *Blackb* 92-95; Dioc Community Relns Officer *Cov* 95-02; TV Cov E 95-02; rtd 02; PtO *Cov* from 02. *30 Ulverscroft Road, Coventry CV3 5EZ* T: (024) 7650 1559 E: samukh@lineone.net

MUKHOLI, Eshuchi Patrick. b 60. Nairobi Univ BSc 86 Aber Univ MTh 09. Nairobi Evang Graduate Sch of Th MDiv 98. **d** 98 **p** 99. Dioc Youth Adv Mombasa Kenya 98-02; Dioc Miss and Communications Officer 99-02; Chapl St Aug Prep Sch 99-02; NSM Blackbird Leys *Ox* 02-08; Youth Worker 03-09; NSM Penhill *Bris* from 13; NSM Upper Stratton from 13. *St Peter's Vicarage, Bremhill Close, Swindon SN2 5DS* M: 07448-794154 E: pmukholi@yahoo.com

MUKUNGA, James. b 74. Univ of Zimbabwe BA 00. Bp Gaul Th Coll Harare 95. **d** 97 **p** 99. Zimbabwe 97-04; R Kadoma All SS 01-02; R Mabelreign St Pet and Lect Bp Gaul Coll 02-04; PtO *Ox* 04-06; C High Wycombe 06-07; C Peckham St Sav *S'wark* 07-10; PtO from 11. *7 Neville Close, London SE15 5UE* M: 07886-235698 E: jamesmukunga@yahoo.com

MULCAHY, Richard Patrick. b 67. SW Poly Plymouth BSc 90. St Mich Coll Llan 02. **d** 05 **p** 06. NSM Bassaleg *Mon* from 05. *9 High Cross Drive, Rogerstone, Newport NP10 9AB* T: (01633) 894641 E: richard-mulcahy@ntlworld.com

MULFORD, Robert. b 57. Middx Poly CertEd 79 Open Univ BA 87 MA 93. Oak Hill Th Coll BA 03 ERMC 05. **d** 07 **p** 08. C Billing *Pet* 07-11; PtO 11-12; V Westfield and Guestling

Chich from 12. *The Vicarage, Vicarage Lane, Westfield, Hastings TN35 4SD* T: (01424) 751029 M: 07768-960896
E: vicar@westfieldguestlingchurches.org.uk

MULHALL, James Gerard. b 60. NUI DipSW 92 CQSW 92. Carlow Coll BA 95. d 86 p 87. C Clonmel w Innislounagh, Tullaghmelan etc *C & O* 09-10; C Lismore w Cappoquin, Kilwatermoy, Dungarvan etc from 10. *St James's Rectory, Church Lane, Stradbally, Co Waterford, Republic of Ireland* T: (00353) (51) 293129 M: 87-240 1913
E: jamesgmulhall@gmail.com

MULHOLLAND, Canon Nicholas Christopher John. b 44. Chich Th Coll 77. d 79 p 80. C Thornbury *Glouc* 79-83; R Boxwell, Leighterton, Didmarton, Oldbury etc 83-11; RD Tetbury 00-03; Hon Can Glouc Cathl 06-11; rtd 11. *Little Badminton Farmhouse, Little Badminton, Badminton GL9 1AB* T: (01454) 218427 E: revmulholland@btinternet.com

MULKERN, Richard Neville. b 39. S'wark Ord Course 88. d 91 p 92. NSM Leytonstone St Andr *Chelmsf* 91-93; Min Sec and Welfare Officer Miss to Seamen 91-93; Welfare Sec 93-94; Dir N Region 94-00; PtO *Wakef* 93-06; NSM Oulton w Woodlesford *Ripon* 96-99; rtd 00. *120 Norwood Road, Birkby, Huddersfield HD2 2XX* T: (01484) 480864

✠**MULLALLY, The Rt Revd Dame Sarah Elisabeth.** b 62. DBE 05. S Bank Univ BSc 84 MSc 92 Bournemouth Univ Hon DSc 01 Wolv Univ Hon DSc 04 Herts Univ Hon DSc 05 RGN 84. SEITE 98. d 01 p 02 c 15. C Battersea Fields *S'wark* 01-06; TR Sutton 06-12; Can Res and Treas Sarum Cathl 12-15; Suff Bp Crediton *Ex* from 15. *32 The Avenue, Tiverton EX16 4HW* M: 07909-595752 T: (01884) 250002
E: sarah.mullally@btinternet.com *or* bishop.of.crediton@exeter.anglican.org

MULLANEY, Mrs Jane Megan. b 48. Kingston Poly BA 72. d 04 p 05. OLM Kenilworth St Jo *Cov* 04-15; rtd 15. *5 Knightlow Close, Kenilworth CV8 2PX* T: (01926) 850723
E: jane_m_mullaney@tiscali.co.uk

MULLEN, Canon Charles William. b 64. CITC BTh 92. d 92 p 93. C Lecale Gp *D & D* 92-95; I Gorey w Kilnahue, Leskinfere and Ballycanew *C & O* 95-00; Dean's V St Patr Cathl Dublin from 00; Preb Rathmichael St Patr Cathl Dublin from 08. *35A Kevin Street Upper, Dublin 8, Republic of Ireland* T: (00353) (1) 453 9472 M: 87-261 8878
E: deans.vicar@stpatrickscathedral.ie

MULLEN, Lee Ross. b 73. Cranmer Hall Dur 05. d 07 p 08. C Chelmsf St Andr 07-11; V Southend St Sav Westcliff from 11. *St Saviour's Vicarage, 33 King's Road, Westcliff-on-Sea SS0 8LL* M: 07976-311906 E: tdyp@msn.com

MULLEN, Peter John. b 42. Liv Univ BA 70 Middx Univ PhD 00. St Aid Birkenhead 66. d 70 p 71. C Manston *Ripon* 70-72; C Stretford All SS *Man* 72-73; C Oldham St Mary w St Pet 73-74; LtO 74-77; V Tockwith and Bilton w Bickerton *York* 77-89; PtO 98-98; P-in-c St Mich Cornhill w St Pet le Poer etc *Lon* 98-03; R 03-12; P-in-c St Sepulchre w Ch Ch Greyfriars etc 98-12; Chapl City Inst Stock Exchange 98-12; rtd 12. *3 Naomi Close, Eastbourne BN20 7UU*

MULLENGER, William. b 44. Linc Th Coll 68. d 69 p 70. C Clapham St Jo *S'wark* 69-73; C Hook 73-81; P-in-c Camberwell St Phil and St Mark 81-85; V Hackbridge and N Beddington 85-93; rtd 93; PtO *Roch* from 93. *30 Constance Crescent, Bromley BR2 7QJ*

MULLER, Vernon. b 40. Natal Univ BA 62 Birm Univ MPhil 93. St Chad's Coll Dur 62. d 64 p 65. C Durban St Martin S Africa 64-68; R Queensburgh 68-76; C Hendon St Mary *Lon* 76-77; Chapl Friern Hosp Lon 77-91; Chapl R Berks Hosp and Battle Hosp Reading 91-95; Dep Dir Bodey Ho Counselling Cen 95-05; rtd 05; PtO *Chelmsf* from 95. *8 Ruskin Road, Chelmsford CM2 6HN* T: (01245) 345865
E: vernonmuller@aol.com

MÜLLER, Anton Michael. b 61. d 99 p 00. C Sandgate St Paul w Folkestone St Geo *Cant* 99-03; TV Penrith w Newton Reigny and Plumpton Wall *Carl* 03-04; P-in-c Dacre 03-04; Chapl N Cumbria Mental Health NHS Trust 03-04; Chapl Eden Valley Hospice Carl 06-08; PtO *Carl* from 08; Tutor LCTP from 09; PtO Blackb 14-15; V Scorton and Barnacre and Calder Vale from 15. *St Peter's Vicarage, Snow Hill Lane, Scorton, Preston PR3 1AY* E: ecumenical@ctlancashire.org.uk

MULLETT, John St Hilary. b 25. St Cath Coll Cam BA 47 MA 49. Linc Th Coll. d 50 p 51. C Tottenham All Hallows *Lon* 50-52; R Que Que S Rhodesia 52-61; V Bollington St Jo *Ches* 61-69; V Oxton 69-77; R Ashwell *St Alb* 77-90; RD Buntingford 82-86; rtd 90; Fell St Cath Coll Cam from 90; PtO *Ely* from 90. *Queen's Head Cottage, 20 Main Street, Wardy Hill, Ely CB6 2DF* T: (01353) 778711

MULLEY, Mrs Margery Ann Oclanis. b 38. d 07 p 08. OLM Iwerne Valley *Sarum* 07-12; NSM 12; PtO *Cov* from 13. *17 South Parade, Harbury, Leamington Spa CV33 9HZ*

MULLIGAN, Colin Arthur. b 42. Llan Ord Course 96. d 96 p 97. NSM Neath w Llantwit Llan 96-01; NSM Neath 01-07; rtd 07; PtO *Llan* from 07. *12 Chestnut Road, Cimla, Neath SA11 3PB* T: (01639) 630409

MULLIGAN, Ronald Leslie. b 53. LCTP. d 08 p 09. NSM Haslingden w Grane and Stonefold *Blackb* 08-11; NSM Blackb St Thos w St Jude 11-13; NSM Blackb St Mich w St Jo and H Trin 11-13; NSM N and E Blackb 13-14; Chapl Airedale NHS Foundn Trust from 14. *3 Chatburn Close, Rossendale BB4 8UT* T: (01706) 220749 E: ronmulligan@talktalk.net

MULLIN, Horace Boies (Dan). b 44. d 00 p 01. OLM Mildenhall *St E* 00-13; rtd 13; PtO *St E* from 13. *47 Oak Drive, Beck Row, Bury St Edmunds IP28 8UA* T: (01638) 718200
E: dan.marthan@btinternet.com

MULLINER, Angela Margaret. *See* LAUENER, Angela Margaret

MULLINER, Canon Denis Ratliffe. b 40. LVO 15. BNC Ox BA 62 MA 66. Linc Th Coll 70. d 72 p 73. C Sandhurst *Ox* 72-76; Chapl Bradfield Coll Berks 76-00; Chapl Chpl Royal Hampton Court Palace from 00; Can from 10; Dep P in O from 00. *Chapel Royal, Hampton Court Palace, East Molesey KT8 9AU* T: (020) 3166 6515 E: chapelroyal@hrp.org.uk

MULLINER, Miss Eliska Fiona Jo. b 71. Bp Otter Coll BA 94 W Sussex Inst of HE PGCE 98. Ridley Hall Cam 12. d 14 p 15. C Lymington *Win* from 14. *48 Courtenay Place, Lymington SO41 3NQ* T: (01590) 719528 E: jo@lymingtonchurch.org

MULLINGS, Paulette Patricia Yvonne. b 53. d 07 p 08. NSM Cobbold Road St Sav w St Mary *Lon* from 07. *53A Melina Road, London W12 9HY* T: (020) 7386 1262 M: 07751-374857
E: pmullings@aol.com *or* paulette.mullings@london.anglican.org

MULLINS, Caroline Anne. b 56. Ex Univ BA 78 St Anne's Coll Ox CertEd 79. SEITE 04. d 07 p 08. NSM Wandsworth St Paul *S'wark* 07-11; NSM Hinchley Wood *Guildf* from 11. *1 Chesterfield Drive, Esher KT10 0AH* T: (020) 8224 3334
E: rev.carolinemullins@gmail.com

MULLINS, Joe. b 20. MC 45. Trin Coll Ox BA 49 MA 59. Ridley Hall Cam 48. d 50 p 51. C Portman Square St Paul *Lon* 50-52; India 52-74; Australia from 74; rtd 86. *33/31 Cockcroft Avenue, Monash ACT 2904, Australia* T: (0061) (2) 6291 0345
E: emullins@autarmetro.com.au

MULLINS, Mrs Margaret. b 49. Southn Univ CertEd 70. Sarum & Wells Th Coll 94. d 94 p 95. C Bishopstoke *Win* 94-98; TV Bicester w Bucknell, Caversfield and Launton *Ox* 98-10; rtd 10. *5 Hardings Lane, Fair Oak, Eastleigh SO50 8GL* E: mgt.mullins@tiscali.co.uk

MULLINS, Canon Peter Matthew. b 60. Ch Ch Ox BA 82 MA 86 Irish Sch of Ecum MPhil 90. Qu Coll Birm 82. d 84 p 85. C Caversham St Pet and Mapledurham etc *Ox* 84-88; PtO *D & G* 88-89; TV Old Brumby *Linc* 89-94; Clergy Tr Adv 94-99; TR Gt and Lt Coates w Bradley from 99; Can and Preb Linc Cathl from 02; RD Grimsby and Cleethorpes 05-10. *The Rectory, 23 Littlecoates Road, Grimsby DN34 4NG* T: (01472) 346986 E: p.m.mullins@virgin.net

MULLINS, Philip James. b 82. SS Coll Cam BA 04. Oak Hill Th Coll BA 13. d 13 p 14. C Castle Church *Lich* from 13. *32 Rowley Avenue, Stafford ST17 9AA* M: 07533-905236
E: phil.mullins@cantab.net

MULLINS, Timothy Dougal. b 59. St Jo Coll Dur BA 81. Wycliffe Hall Ox 83. d 85 p 86. C Reading Greyfriars *Ox* 85-89; C Haughton le Skerne *Dur* 89-95; Chapl Eton Coll 95-05; Chapl Radley Coll 05-12; C Ches Square St Mich w St Phil *Lon* from 12. *40 Ebury Bridge Road, London SW1W 8PZ* T: (020) 7730 1673 E: tim@stmichaelschurch.org.uk

MULLIS, Robert Owen. b 49. Open Univ BA 77 Glam Univ MSc 00 St Paul's Coll Chelt CertEd 71. St Mich Coll Llan 90. d 93 p 94. NSM Llangenni and Llanbedr Ystrad Yw w Patricio *S & B* 93-03; NSM Llantilio Pertholey w Bettws Chpl etc *Mon* 03-06; PtO *Heref* from 06. *Church Gate, Almeley, Hereford HR3 6LB* T: (01544) 327801 E: bob.mullis@hotmail.co.uk

MULRAINE, Miss Margaret Haskell. b 24. Birm Univ BA 45 DipEd 46. Sarum Th Coll 83. dss 86 d 87 p 94. Wareham *Sarum* 86-93; Hon Par Dn 87-93; PtO 93-08. *9 Turnworth Close, Broadstone BH18 8LS* T: (01202) 640292

MULRYNE, Thomas Mark. b 70. St Cath Coll Cam BA 91 MA 95 Lon Inst of Educn PGCE 93. Oak Hill Th Coll BA 02. d 02 p 03. C W Streatham St Jas *S'wark* 02-06; C Gt Clacton *Chelmsf* from 06. *112 Woodlands Close, Clacton-on-Sea CO15 4RU* T: (01255) 425159
E: mark_and_caroline_mulryne@hotmail.com

MUMBY, Andrew. *See* MOUGHTIN-MUMBY, Andrew Denis Paul

MUMFORD, David. *See* MUMFORD, Michael David

MUMFORD, Prof David Bardwell. b 49. St Cath Coll Cam BA 71 MA 75 Bris Univ MB, ChB 81 MD 92 Edin Univ MPhil 89 MRCPsych 86. Bp's Coll Calcutta 71 Cuddesdon Coll 73. d 75. C Bris St Mary Redcliffe w Temple etc 75-76; NSM 76-82; NSM Edin St Columba 82-86; NSM Calverley

Bradf 86-92; PtO *B & W* 92-06 and from 11. *14 Clifton Vale, Clifton, Bristol BS8 4PT* T: 0117-927 2221 M: 07501-134525 E: david.mumford@bristol.ac.uk

MUMFORD, David Christopher. b 47. Mert Coll Ox BA 68 MA 74 York Univ MSW CQSW 81. Linc Th Coll 84. **d** 86 **p** 87. C Shiremoor *Newc* 86-89; C N Shields 89-91; V Byker St Ant 91-97; RD Newc E 96-97; V Cowgate 97-02; Internat Co-ord Internat Fellowship of Reconciliation 02-07; R Brechin *Bre* from 07; R Tarfside from 07; Dean Bre 08-12. *St Andrew's Rectory, 9 Castle Street, Brechin DD9 6JW* T: (01356) 622708 E: dmumford@phonecoop.coop

MUMFORD, Geoffrey Robert. b 70. York Univ BSc 92 St Jo Coll Nottm MA 00. **d** 00 **p** 01. C Rowley Regis *Birm* 00-03; TV Darwen St Pet w Hoddlesden *Blackb* 03-08; P-in-c Copmanthorpe *York* 08-09; V from 09; P-in-c Askham Bryan 08-09; V from 09; P-in-c Bolton Percy 08-09; R from 09. *The Vicarage, 17 Sutor Close, Copmanthorpe, York YO23 3TX* T: (01904) 707716 M: 07980-569450 E: gmumford@btinternet.com

MUMFORD, Grenville Alan. b 34. Richmond Th Coll. **d** 78 **p** 78. C Witham *Chelmsf* 78-81; C-in-c Gt Ilford St Marg CD 81-85; V Gt Ilford St Marg 85-87; P-in-c Everton and Mattersey w Clayworth *S'well* 87-89; R 89-96; RD Bawtry 93-96; rtd 96; PtO *Ches* from 96. *146 Audlem Road, Nantwich CW5 7EB* T: (01270) 610221 E: mumford7eb@btinternet.com

MUMFORD, Canon Hugh Raymond. b 24. Oak Hill Th Coll 50. **d** 53 **p** 54. C Bethnal Green St Jas Less *Lon* 53-57; C Watford St Mary *St Alb* 57-59; R Thetford St Pet w St Nic *Nor* 59-69; RD Thetford 68-69; V Nether Cerne *Sarum* 69-71; R Godmanstone 69-71; R Cerne Abbas w Upcerne 69-71; R Minterne Magna 69-71; V Cerne Abbas w Godmanstone and Minterne Magna 71-89; RD Dorchester 75-79; Can and Preb Sarum Cathl 77-89; rtd 89; PtO *Sarum* from 89. *10 South Walks Road, Dorchester DT1 1ED* T: (01305) 264971

MUMFORD, Lesley Anne. *See* CHEETHAM, Lesley Anne

MUMFORD, Michael David. b 29. **d** 79 **p** 80. Chapl Lister Hosp Stevenage 79-83; C Royston *St Alb* 83-87; P-in-c Kelshall and Therfield 83-88; C Barkway, Reed and Buckland w Barley 87-88; V Bodiam and R Ewhurst *Chich* 88-94; RD Rye 90-91; rtd 94; PtO *Chich* 94-09. *9 Colonel Stevens Court, 10A Granville Court, Eastbourne BN20 7HD* T: 07803-004492

MUNBY, Canon David Philip James. b 52. Pemb Coll Ox BA 75 MA 80. St Jo Coll Nottm 76. **d** 78 **p** 79. C Gipsy Hill Ch Ch *S'wark* 78-82; C-in-c W Dulwich Em CD 82-88; V Barnsley St Geo *Leeds* from 88; Asst Dioc Ecum Officer *Wakef* 99-01; Can Bungoma from 04. *St George's Vicarage, 100 Dodworth Road, Barnsley S70 6HL* T: (01226) 203870 E: davidmunby@bigfoot.com

MUNCEY, William. b 49. Oak Hill Th Coll BA 80. **d** 80 **p** 81. C Wandsworth St Mich *S'wark* 80-84; C Morden 84-88; TV 88-01; RD Merton 00-01; P-in-c Croydon Ch Ch 01-04; V 04-12; NSM Shelswell *Ox* from 12. *10C St Michael's Close, Fringford, Bicester OX27 8DW* T: (01869) 277986

MUNCH, Philip Douglas. b 55. Witwatersrand Univ BMus. Cranmer Hall Dur. **d** 88 **p** 89. C Wlvis Bay Namibia 88-89; P-in-c 89-92; Warden Ho of Prayer Luderitz 92-99; Prec Port Elizabeth S Africa 99-02; Warden Emmaus Ho of Prayer Northampton from 02; NSM Northampton St Mich w St Edm *Pet* from 02. *Emmaus House of Prayer, St Michael's Church, Perry Street, Northampton NN1 4HL* T: (01604) 627669 F: 230316 E: emmaushouse@btconnect.com

MUNCHIN, David Leighfield. b 67. Imp Coll Lon BSc 88 K Coll Lon MA 00 Heythrop Coll Lon PhD 09. Ripon Coll Cuddesdon 89. **d** 92 **p** 93. C Golders Green *Lon* 92-96; Prec and Min Can St Alb Abbey *St Alb* 96-02; P-in-c Hatfield Hyde 02-10; TR Welwyn from 10. *The Rectory, 2 Ottway Walk, Welwyn AL6 9AS* T: (01438) 714150 M: 07787-567747 E: davidmunchin@talktalk.net *or* rector@welwyn.org.uk

MUNCHIN, Ysmena Rachael. *See* PENTELOW, Ysmena Rachael

MUNDAY, Elaine Jeanette. b 56. SWMTC. **d** 10 **p** 11. NSM Bodmin w Lanhydrock and Lanivet *Truro* from 10. *70 St Mary's Crescent, Bodmin PL31 1NP* T: (01208) 77945 E: themunday.family@virgin.net

MUNDAY, Nicholas John. b 54. Jes Coll Cam BA 76 PGCE 77 MA 97. Ripon Coll Cuddesdon 09. **d** 11 **p** 12. C Monmouth w Overmonnow etc *Mon* 11-14; R S Lafford *Linc* from 14. *The Rectory, 16 West Street, Folkingham, Sleaford NG34 0SW* T: (01529) 497519 E: n.j.munday@btinternet.com

MUNDAY, Mrs Sandra Anne. b 61. St Jo Sem Wonersh BTh 89 Ripon Coll Cuddesdon 97. **d** 99 **p** 00. C Esher *Guildf* 99-02; Team Chapl R United Hosp Bath NHS Trust 02-03; PtO *B & W* from 03. *18 Chestnut Walk, Saltford, Bristol BS31 3BG* T: (01225) 342740 E: smunday150@hotmail.co.uk

MUNDELL, Mrs Christine Elizabeth. b 49. WEMTC 01. **d** 04 **p** 05. C Ledbury *Heref* 04-08; TV Leominster 08-15; rtd 15. *Address temp unknown*

MUNDEN, Alan Frederick. b 43. Nottm Univ BTh 74 Birm Univ MLitt 80 Dur Univ PhD 87. St Jo Coll Nottm. **d** 74 **p** 75. C Cheltenham St Mary *Glouc* 74-76; C Cheltenham St Mary, St Matt, St Paul and H Trin 76; Hon C Jesmond Clayton Memorial *Newc* 76-80; C 80-83; V Cheylesmore *Cov* 83-01; R Weddington and Caldecote 01-03; rtd 03; Hon C Jesmond Clayton Memorial *Newc* from 03; PtO *Dur* from 11. *11 The Crescent, Benton, Newcastle upon Tyne NE7 7ST* T: 0191-266 1227

MUNDY, David Hugh. b 59. Sheff Univ BA. Yorks Min Course 12. **d** 15. NSM Chapel-en-le-Frith *Derby* from 15. *103 Station Road, Hadfield, Glossop SK13 1AR* T: (01457) 856554 E: dhmundy@btinternet.com

MUNDY, Kay. **d** 14 **p** 15. C Deerhurst and Apperley w Forthampton etc *Glouc* from 14. *Address temp unknown*

MUNDY, Paul Kevin. b 68. Westcott Ho Cam 11. **d** 13 **p** 14. C Barcombe *Chich* from 13. *The Locks, Knowle Lane, Halland, Lewes BN8 6PR* T: (01825) 840869 M: 07717-000281 E: p.mundy@me.com

MUNGAVIN, David Stewart. b 60. Stirling Univ BA 80. Edin Th Coll 87. **d** 90 **p** 91. C Glas St Marg 90-92; P-in-c Airdrie, Coatbridge and Gartcosh 92-96; R 96-99; R Troon 99-09; I Greystones *D & G* from 09. *The Rectory, Church Road, Greystones, Co Wicklow, Republic of Ireland* T: (00353) (1) 287 4077 E: davidsmungavin@gmail.com

MUNGAVIN, Canon Gerald Clarence. b 27. Edin Th Coll 51. **d** 54 **p** 55. C Dunfermline *St And* 54-55; C Glas Gd Shep 55-57; CF 57-60; C Stanwix *Carl* 60-62; Chapl RAF 62-75; R Turriff *Ab* 75-81; R Cuminestown 75-81; R Banff 75-81; R Banchory 81-92; R Kincardine O'Neil 81-92; Can St Andr Cathl 89-92; Hon Can St Andr Cathl from 92; rtd 92. *5 Lade Court, Lochwinnoch PA12 4BT* T: (01505) 843972 E: mungavin@hotmail.com

MUNN, Canon Carole Christine. b 45. EMMTC 83. **d** 90 **p** 94. NSM Long Bennington w Foston *Linc* 90-95; NSM Saxonwell 95-98; NSM Claypole 98-08; Asst Chapl HM Pris Linc 94-01; Chapl HM Pris Morton Hall from 01; Gen Preacher *Linc* from 01; Can and Preb Linc Cathl from 05. *Address temp unknown*

MUNN, George. b 44. Master Mariner 72. Linc Th Coll 85. **d** 87 **p** 88. C Boston *Linc* 87-90; R Claypole 90-08; rtd 08. *15 The Meadow, Caistor, Market Rasen LN7 6XD* T: (01472) 852203 E: g.munn@tiscali.co.uk

MUNN, Richard Probyn. b 45. Selw Coll Cam BA 67 MA 69. Cuddesdon Coll 67. **d** 69 **p** 70. C Cirencester *Glouc* 69-71; Chapl St Mark's Sch Mapanze Zambia 71-74; R Livingstone 75-79; Adn S Zambia 79; P-in-c Kings Stanley *Glouc* 80-83; R Lezant w Lawhitton and S Petherwin w Trewen *Truro* 84-92; Lesotho from 93; rtd 01. *Reavenall, PO Box 249, Leribe 300, Lesotho* T: (00266) 877 8553

MUNNS, Ms Alice Wiliemhina (Mina). b 78. York Univ BA 99 Derby Univ PGCE 00. Cranmer Hall Dur BA 15. **d** 15. C Selston *S'well* from 15. *7 Pippin Close, Selston, Nottingham NG16 6JE* M: 07960-250497 E: mina_munns@yahoo.co.uk

MUNNS, John Millington. b 76. Univ Coll Dur BA 99 MA 00 Bris Univ MPhil 07 Em Coll Cam PhD 10 FRSA 04. Westcott Ho Cam 01. **d** 03 **p** 04. C Bridgwater St Mary and Chilton Trinity *B & W* 03-06; Asst Chapl Em Coll Cam 06-10; Lect Bris Univ 10-12; Chapl Fitzw Coll Cam from 11; Fell from 12; Lect Cam Univ from 12. *Fitzwilliam College, Storey's Way, Cambridge CB3 0DG* T: (01223) 332013 E: jmm89@cam.ac.uk

MUNNS, Stuart Millington. b 36. OBE 77. St Cath Coll Cam BA 58 MA 62 MCIPD 91. Cuddesdon Coll 58. **d** 60 **p** 61. C Allenton and Shelton Lock *Derby* 60-63; C Brampton St Thos 63-65; C-in-c Loundsley Green Ascension CD 65-66; Bp's Youth Chapl 66-72; Nat Dir of Community Industry 72-77; Hon C Hornsey Ch Ch *Lon* 72-77; Dioc Missr *Lich* 77-82; V Knowsley 77-82; P-in-c Stramshall *Lich* 82-88; V Uttoxeter w Bramshall 82-88; RD Uttoxeter 82-87; P-in-c Kingstone w Gratwich 84-88; P-in-c Marchington w Marchington Woodlands 84-88; P-in-c Checkley 86-88; PtO *B & W* 88-90; NSM Wells St Thos w Horrington 90-94; P-in-c Fosse Trinity 94-02; rtd 02; Dioc Pre-Th Educn Co-ord *B & W* 02-06; PtO from 03. *Applewood House, Ham Street, Baltonsborough, Glastonbury BA6 8PX* T: (01458) 851443 M: 07791-111904 E: munns@cantab.net

MUNOZ-TRIVINO, Daniel. b 75. Hatf Coll Dur BA 99. Wycliffe Hall Ox MTh 01. **d** 01 **p** 02. C Hazlemere *Ox* 01-04; TV Gt Marlow w Marlow Bottom, Lt Marlow and Bisham 04-09; Chapl Los Olivos Retreat Cen Spain from 09; PtO *Ox* from 13. *Hacienda los Olivos, Haza Llana, Sierra de Mondujar, 18656 Lecrin, Spain* T: (01865) 600698 E: daniel.munoz@haciendalosolivos.org

MUNRO, Duncan John Studd. b 50. Magd Coll Ox BA 72 MA 76 Warwick Univ MBA 96 CDir 05. Wycliffe Hall Ox 73.

d 76 **p** 77. C Ecclesall *Sheff* 76-77; C Sheff St Barn and St Mary 78-80; LtO 80-86; PtO 97-05; LtO *Edin* from 06; PtO *Glouc* from 13. *Hosanna House, 43 Cudnall Street, Charlton Kings, Cheltenham GL53 8HL* T: (01242) 321712 M: 07802-871156 E: duncan.munro@munrostrategic.co.uk

MUNRO, Ingrid Phyllis. b 51. Herts Univ BEd 80. St Jo Coll Nottm MA 96 St Alb Minl Tr Scheme 83. **d** 98 **p** 99. NSM Walbrook Epiphany *Derby* 98-01 and 05-09; NSM Alvaston from 09. *40 Brisbane Road, Mickleover, Derby DE3 9JZ*

MUNRO, Robert. b 40. Leeds Univ BA 62 Bris Univ PGCE 63. SWMTC 95. **d** 98 **p** 99. NSM Saltash *Truro* 98-03; NSM Calstock 03-11. *15 Valley Road, Saltash PL12 4BT* T: (01752) 844731 E: bobmu@valley151.fsnet.co.uk

MUNRO, Robert Speight. b 63. Bris Univ BSc 84 Man Univ PGCE 87. Oak Hill Th Coll BA 93. **d** 93 **p** 94. C Hartford *Ches* 93-97; R Davenham 97-03; R Cheadle from 03. *The Rectory, 1 Depleach Road, Cheadle SK8 1DZ* T: 0161-428 3440 *or* 428 8050 E: rob@munro.uk.net

MUNRO, Canon Terence George. b 34. Jes Coll Cam BA 56 MA 60. Linc Th Coll 59. **d** 61 **p** 62. C Far Headingley St Chad *Ripon* 61-64; Jamaica 64-70; R Methley w Mickletown *Ripon* 70-79; V Hunslet Moor St Pet and St Cuth 79-85; R Barwick in Elmet 85-93; V Woodhouse and Wrangthorn 93-99; Dioc Ecum Officer 99; Hon Can Ripon Cathl 94-99; rtd 99; PtO *York* from 00. *45 Laburnum Drive, Beverley HU17 9UQ* T: (01482) 861237

MUNRO, Teresa Frances. b 51. Leeds Poly CertEd 73 Leeds Univ BEd 74. SEITE 03. **d** 06 **p** 07. NSM Coulsdon St Andr *S'wark* 06-11; TV Rye *Chich* from 11. *21 Fair Meadow, Rye TN31 7NL* E: teresamunro@hotmail.com

MUNRO-SMITH, Alison Jean. *See* WATERS, Alison Jean

MUNT, Cyril. b 27. AKC 52. **d** 53 **p** 54. C Ashford *Cant* 53-56; C Dorking w Ranmore *Guildf* 56-60; R Cheriton w Newington *Cant* 60-68; R Harbledown 68-83; R Porlock w Stoke Pero *B & W* 83-92; rtd 92; PtO *B & W* from 92. *Applegarth, 26 Hood Close, Glastonbury BA6 8ES* T: (01458) 831842

MUNT, Mrs Linda Christine. b 55. NEOC 92. **d** 95 **p** 96. C Beverley St Nic *York* 95-98; Chapl E Yorkshire Hosps NHS Trust 97-99; V Bridlington Em *York* 99-03; P-in-c Skipsea w Ulrome and Barmston w Fraisthorpe 02-03; Chapl Martin House Hospice for Children Boston Spa 03-05; Hon C Boston Spa, Thorp Arch w Walton etc 03-05; V Market Weighton *York* 05-10; V Sancton 05-10; R Goodmanham 05-10; PtO 10-12; V Attercliffe and Darnall *Sheff* 12-15. *Flat 1, Stamford House, 14-15 Westwood, Scarborough YO11 2JD* M: 07791-748082 E: l.munt@btinternet.com

MUNYANGAJU, Canon Jerome Cassian. b 53. Serampore Univ BD 85 Open Univ MA 97. St Phil Coll Kongwa 73. **d** 75 **p** 76. Tanzania 75-80 and 85-95; India 80-85; Hon Can Kagera from 91; Overseas Resource Person *D & D* 95-97; C Bangor Abbey *D & D* 98-00; I Killyleagh 00-15; Can Belf Cathl from 12. *Address temp unknown* E: jmunyangaju@yahoo.co.uk

MURCH, Canon Robin Norman. b 37. Wells Th Coll. **d** 67 **p** 68. C Wisbech St Aug *Ely* 67-70; C Basingstoke *Win* 70-73; C Whitstable All SS *Cant* 73-75; C Whitstable All SS w St Pet 75-76; V Queenborough 76-99; Hon Can Cant Cathl 96-99; rtd 99; PtO *Ex* from 00. *3 Narenta, 22 Barton Crescent, Dawlish EX7 9QL* T: (01626) 863532 M: 07836-514528

MURDOCH, Alexander Edward Duncan. b 37. Oak Hill Th Coll 68. **d** 71 **p** 72. C Kensington St Helen w H Trin *Lon* 71-72; C Kensington St Barn 73-74; CF 74-78; C W Kirby St Bridget *Ches* 78-84; V N Shoebury *Chelmsf* 84-87; V W Poldens *B & W* 87-96; R Gayhurst w Ravenstone, Stoke Goldington etc *Ox* 96-07; rtd 07. *Hopp House, Back Lane, Old Bolingbroke, Spilsby PE23 4EU* T: (01790) 763603

MURDOCH, David John. b 58. Birm Univ BSocSc 81 Leeds Univ MA 03. Ripon Coll Cuddesdon 81. **d** 84 **p** 85. C Penwortham St Leon *Blackb* 84-87; C Wirksworth w Alderwasley, Carsington etc *Derby* 87-89; R Shirland 89-97; Dioc World Development Officer 96-00; P-in-c New Mills 97-01; V 01-05; RD Glossop 04-05; TR Wilford Peninsula *St E* from 05. *The Rectory, 109A Front Street, Orford, Woodbridge IP12 2LN* T: (01394) 450336 E: revdave@timicomail.co.uk

MURDOCH, Canon Lucy Eleanor. b 41. STETS BTh 99. **d** 99 **p** 00. NSM Warbleton and Bodle Street Green *Chich* 99-02; NSM Rye 02-12; TV 03-12; RD 10-11; P-in-c Fletching from 12; Can and Preb Chich Cathl from 10. *The Vicarage, Mill Lane, Fletching, Uckfield TN22 3SR* T: (01825) 723880 M: 07508-931198 E: dog.home@uwclub.net

MURFET, Edward David. b 36. Qu Coll Cam BA 59 MA 63. Chich Th Coll 59. **d** 61 **p** 62. C Croydon St Mich *Cant* 61-64; C Hunslet St Mary and Stourton *Ripon* 64-65; C Hackney Wick St Mary of Eton w St Aug *Lon* 65-69; Chapl Berne *Eur* 69-71; Chapl Naples 71-74; Chapl Rome 74-77; LtO *Bris* 78-81;

Gen Sec CEMS 81-86; C Leeds St Pet *Ripon* 87-89; P-in-c 89-90; C Leeds City 91-93; Min Can Ripon Cathl 93-03; rtd 03; PtO *Leeds* from 03. *3 Old Deanery Close, St Marygate, Ripon HG4 1LZ* T: (01765) 608422

MURFET, Gwyn. b 44. Linc Th Coll 71. **d** 74 **p** 75. C Scalby w Ravenscar and Staintondale *York* 74-77; P-in-c S Milford 77-83; R 83-84; V Kirkby Ireleth *Carl* 84-05; rtd 05; PtO *Carl* from 11. *75 Portsmouth Street, Walney, Barrow-in-Furness LA14 3AJ* T: (01229) 471157

MURFITT, Mrs Ruth Margaret. b 48. **d** 09 **p** 10. NSM St Goran w Caerhays *Truro* 09-12; P-in-c Roche from 12. *The Rectory, Roche, St Austell PL26 8EP* T: (01726) 890301 E: ruthmurfitt@hotmail.com

MURLEY, Anthony James Raymond. b 82. MBE 11. Univ Coll Lon BA 04. St Steph Ho Ox 12. **d** 14 **p** 15. C Small Heath *Birm* from 14. *17 Avoca Court, 146 Cheapside, Deritend, Birmingham B12 0PR* E: anthony.murley@ssho.ox.ac.uk *or* curate@allsaintsonline.co.uk

MURNANE, Terence Francis. b 62. Ex Univ BSc 83 Sheff Univ BA 13. Coll of Resurr Mirfield 11. **d** 13 **p** 14. C Accrington St Andr, St Mary and St Pet *Blackb* from 13. *St Peter's Vicarage, 151 Willows Lane, Accrington BB5 0LR* M: 07828-133030 E: terrymurnane@gmail.com

MURPHIE, Andrew Graham. b 65. Reading Univ BA 86. St Jo Coll Nottm BTh 91 MA 92. **d** 92 **p** 93. C Boulton *Derby* 92-96; C Marston on Dove w Scropton 96-97; V Hilton w Marston-on-Dove from 98; RD Longford from 04. *The Vicarage, 28 Back Lane, Hilton, Derby DE65 5GJ* T: (01283) 733433 E: andymurphie@btinternet.com

MURPHY, Alexander Charles. b 28. St Edm Coll Ware 50. **d** 55 **p** 56. NSM Edin St Jas 88-90; TV Edin St Mark 90-93; TV Edin St Andr and St Aid 90-93; TV Edin St Marg 93-96; rtd 96. *Ardleven, 48 Victoria Street, Dumbarton G82 1HP* T: (01389) 733755 E: almagda328@hotmail.com

MURPHY, Anthony. **d** 11 **p** 12. NSM Moviddy Union *C, C & R* 11-12; NSM Carrigaline Union from 12. *9 Riverside, Church Road, Carrigaline, Co Cork, Republic of Ireland* M: (00353) 87-832 7347 E: tmurphy@tmahr.com

MURPHY, Christopher Campbell. b 84. Hatf Coll Dur BA 06. Wycliffe Hall Ox 09. **d** 12. C Bovey Tracey SS Pet, Paul and Thos w Hennock *Ex* from 12. *Dunley Lodge, Bovey Tracey, Newton Abbot TQ13 9PW* T: (01626) 833487 M: 07595-742970 E: christopher.c.murphy@gmail.com

MURPHY, Mrs Deborah Ann. b 67. Newc Univ BA 89. Qu Coll Birm BD 92. **d** 93 **p** 94. C Bloxwich *Lich* 93-97; TV Gt Grimsby St Mary and St Jas *Linc* 97-00; Chapl N Lincs and Goole Hosps NHS Trust 99-00; PtO *St Alb* 01-05; Asst Chapl Walsall Hosps NHS Trust 05-08; TV Blakenall Heath *Lich* 08-10; Chapl Gd Hope Hosp NHS Trust Sutton Coldfield 10-12; Chapl Walsall Healthcare NHS Trust 12-14; C Pheasey *Lich* 12-13; PtO from 14. *84 Gainsborough Crescent, Birmingham B43 7LB* T: 0121-360 2122 E: deborah.murphy@heartofengland.nhs.uk

MURPHY, Ms Hilary Elizabeth. b 57. St Martin's Coll Lanc BSc 00. St Jo Coll Nottm MTh 05. **d** 05 **p** 06. C S Shore H Trin *Blackb* 05-08; C Bloemfontein Cathl S Africa from 08. *St Andrew's Cathedral, PO Box 1523, Bloemfontein, 9300 South Africa* T: (0027) (51) 448 3010

MURPHY, Jack. b 27. NOC 83. **d** 86 **p** 87. C Armley w New Wortley *Ripon* 86-90; C Hawksworth Wood 90-94; rtd 94; PtO *York* from 96. *70 Avocet Way, Bridlington YO15 3NT* T: (01262) 609477

MURPHY, James Royse. b 54. Bris Univ MB, ChB 77 MRCGP 81. Glouc Sch of Min 89. **d** 92 **p** 94. NSM Glouc St Cath 92-98; NSM Glouc St Paul 98-09; NSM Glouc St Paul and St Steph from 09. *52 Lansdown Road, Gloucester GL1 3JD* T: (01452) 505080 E: jrmurphy@supanet.com

MURPHY, Ms Julia Mary. b 58. Essex Univ BA 81 Lon Bible Coll BTh 00. Wycliffe Hall Ox MTh 07. **d** 07 **p** 08. C Thetford *Nor* 07-11; TV Forest Gate St Sav w H Ham St Matt *Chelmsf* 11-12; Chapl Essex Univ from 12. *Mariners, Rectory Hill, Wivenhoe, Colchester CO7 9LB* T: (01206) 683676 M: 07779-266034 E: revjuliamurphy@gmail.com

MURPHY, Keith Anthony. b 72. St Jo Coll Nottm 10. **d** 12 **p** 13. C Ware Ch Ch *St Alb* from 12. *10 Cromwell Road, Ware SG12 7JZ* M: 07980-745437 E: keithmurphymusic@gmail.com

MURPHY, Owen. b 52. Open Univ BA 85 Liv Univ MA 04. Chich Th Coll 92. **d** 94 **p** 95. C Oxhey St Matt *St Alb* 94-96; C Watford St Mich 96-98; P-in-c Shinfield *Ox* 98-05; V Barnehurst *Roch* 05-07; Dir St Columba's Retreat and Conf Cen 07-12; PtO *Guildf* 12-13; P-in-c Yealmpton and Brixton *Ex* from 13. *The Vicarage, Bowden Hill, Yealmpton, Plymouth PL8 2JX* T: (01752) 880040 E: owen.murphy52@btconnect.com

MURPHY, Peter Frederick. b 40. AKC 65. **d** 67 **p** 68. C Paddington St Jo w St Mich *Lon* 67-72; P-in-c Basingstoke *Win* 72-76; TV 76-81; V Hythe 81-92; V Lyndhurst and Emery Down 92-99; P-in-c Copythorne and Minstead 95-99; V Lyndhurst and Emery Down and Minstead 99-05; rtd 05; Hon C Fordingbridge and Breamore and Hale etc *Win* 05-10; PtO from 10. *11 Watton Road, Holbury, Southampton SO45 2LW* T: (02380) 893243 M: 07815-050096
E: petermurf@gmail.com

MURPHY, Philip John Warwick. b 65. Kent Univ BA 87 Southn Univ BTh 93. Chich Th Coll 88. **d** 91 **p** 92. C Broadstone *Sarum* 91-94; C Teddington SS Pet and Paul and Fulwell *Lon* 94-96; V Leytonstone St Marg w St Columba *Chelmsf* 96-01; P-in-c Leytonstone St Andr 96-97; R Benalla Australia 01-04; V Fitzroy 04-10; CEO Catchment Youth Services 10-13; Chapl St Paul's Coll Hong Kong from 13. *PO Box 207, Fitzroy VIC 3065, Australia* E: pjwm65@hotmail.com

MURPHY, Ronald Frederick. b 38. **d** 84 **p** 85. NSM Swindon Dorcan *Bris* 84-87; P-in-c N Cerney w Bagendon *Glouc* 87-90. *Anemone Cottage, The Village, Ashreigney, Chulmleigh EX18 7LU*

MURPHY, Rosalyn Frances Thomas. b 55. Marquette Univ (USA) BA 85 Ustinov Coll Dur MTh 00 Union Th Sem Virginia MDiv 99 St Jo Coll Dur PhD 05. Cranmer Hall Dur 04. **d** 05 **p** 06. C Dur St Nic 05-08; P-in-c Blackpool St Thos *Blackb* 08-12; V from 12. *St Thomas's Vicarage, 80 Devonshire Road, Blackpool FY3 8AE* T: (01253) 392544
E: stthomasvicar@btinternet.com

MURPHY, Royse. *See* MURPHY, James Royse

MURPHY, Wendy Susan. b 54. **d** 13 **p** 14. NSM Carlton-in-the-Willows *S'well* from 13. *22 Brooksby Lane, Clifton, Nottingham NG11 8HL*

MURPHY, Canon William Albert. b 43. MBE 98. Lon Univ BD 73 QUB MTh 78. **d** 73 **p** 74. C Lisburn Ch Ch *Conn* 73-79; Supt and Chapl Ulster Inst for the Deaf 79-98; Chapl HM Pris Maze from 82; Dioc Dir Ords *Conn* from 92; Chapl Ch of Ireland Min to Deaf People 98-13; Can Belf Cathl from 04. *2 Maghaberry Manor, Moira, Craigavon BT67 0JZ* T: (028) 9261 9140 E: murphy43@btinternet.com

MURPHY, Mrs Yvonne Letita. b 52. Brunel Univ BA 90 PGCE 91. SEITE 95. **d** 98 **p** 99. NSM Hampton St Mary *Lon* 98-01; NSM Staines St Mary and St Pet 01-04; Chapl Bp Wand Sch 98-04; P-in-c Kennington *Cant* 04-09; TV High Wycombe *Ox* 09-12; rtd 12. *41 Jersey Close, Chertsey KT16 9PA*
E: ylm.bwm@virgin.net

MURRAY, Alan. b 61. St Jo Coll Nottm BTh 92. **d** 92 **p** 93. C Wombwell *Sheff* 92-95; C Mortomley St Sav High Green 95-99; P-in-c Doncaster St Jas 99-01; V 01-13; V Normanton *Leeds* from 13. *All Saints' Vicarage, High Street, Normanton WF6 1NR* E: vicarofallsaints@gmail.com

MURRAY, Andrew James. b 72. Loughb Univ BEng 95 PhD 01. Trin Coll Bris 10. **d** 12 **p** 13. C Clifton Ch Ch w Em *Bris* 12-15; P-in-c Lawrence Weston and Avonmouth from 15. *The Vicarage, 335 Long Cross, Lawrence Weston, Bristol BS11 0NN* T: 0117-325 1227 E: rev.andymurray@icloud.com

MURRAY, Mrs Anne. b 53. MCSP 75. NOC 03. **d** 06 **p** 07. NSM Fairfield *Liv* 06-10; NSM Liv All SS from 11. *75 Priorsfield Road, Liverpool L25 8TL* T: 0151-428 2254 E: annel25@yahoo.co.uk

MURRAY, Christine Jean. *See* MEDWAY, Christine Jean

MURRAY, Christopher James. b 49. Open Univ BA 78. St Jo Coll Nottm 79. **d** 81 **p** 82. C Heatherlands St Jo *Sarum* 81-84; C Hamworthy 84-90; R Passenham *Pet* from 90. *The Rectory, Wicken Road, Deanshanger, Milton Keynes MK19 6JP* T: (01908) 262371 E: chris@murrayfamily.co.uk

MURRAY, David McIlveen. b 36. ALCD 61. **d** 61 **p** 62. C Mortlake w E Sheen *S'wark* 61-64; C Lyncombe *B & W* 64-67; C Horsham *Chich* 67-73; V Devonport St Bart *Ex* 73-79; R Chalfont St Peter *Ox* 79-95; RD Amersham 86-89; R Lower Windrush 95-03; rtd 03; PtO *Glouc* from 03. *Collum End Farm, 88 Church Road, Leckhampton, Cheltenham GL53 0PD* T: (01242) 528008

MURRAY, Elaine Mary Edel. b 58. TCD BTh 05 MICS 97. CITC 02. **d** 05 **p** 06. Bp's V and Lib Kilkenny Cathl 05-11; C Kilkenny w Aghour and Kilmanagh 05-08; V 08-11; I Carrigaline Union *C, C & R* from 11. *The Rectory, Church Road, Carrigaline, Co Cork, Republic of Ireland* T: (00353) (21) 437 2224 M: 87-236 3100 E: emit@eircom.net

MURRAY, Elizabeth. b 57. **d** 10 **p** 11. NSM Eastwood and Brinsley w Underwood *S'well* 10-13; P-in-c Elston w Elston Chapelry from 13; P-in-c E Stoke w Syerston from 13; P-in-c Kilvington from 13; P-in-c Shelton from 13; P-in-c Sibthorpe from 13; P-in-c Staunton w Flawborough from 13. *The Rectory, Top Street, Elston, Newark NG23 5NP* T: (01636) 525383 E: reveimurray24@gmail.com

MURRAY, Elizabeth Ruth. **d** 03 **p** 04. C Antrim All SS *Conn* 03-06; I Woodschapel w Gracefield *Arm* from 06. *The Rectory, 140 Ballyronan Road, Magherafelt BT45 6HU* T: (028) 7941 8311 E: ruth@mdroll.fsnet.co.uk

MURRAY, Gordon John. b 33. St Cath Coll Cam BA 57 MA 61. Clifton Th Coll 57. **d** 59 **p** 60. C Heref St Jas 59-61; C Uphill *B & W* 62-65; C-in-c Reading St Mary Castle Street Prop Chpl *Ox* 65-68; Ed *English Churchman* 65-71; Prin Kensit Coll Finchley 68-75; Hd of RE Sandown High Sch 76-78; rtd 98. *18 Longcroft, Felixstowe IP11 9QH* T: (01394) 273372

MURRAY, Gordon Stewart. b 33. Birkbeck Coll Lon BSc 72. Ripon Coll Cuddesdon 76. **d** 78 **p** 79. C Kenilworth St Nic *Cov* 78-81; V Potterspury w Furtho and Yardley Gobion *Pet* 81-83; V Potterspury, Furtho, Yardley Gobion and Cosgrove 84; TV Wolvercote w Summertown *Ox* 84-90; P-in-c Walworth *S'wark* 90-95; R Walworth St Pet 95-98; rtd 98; P-in-c Tillington, Duncton and Up Waltham *Chich* 98-01; PtO *York* 05-13. *90 Cedar Drive, Chichester PO19 3EN* T: (01243) 926182
E: gordon.murray11@ntlworld.com

MURRAY, Heather. b 62. RGN 82. NEOC 04. **d** 07 **p** 08. NSM Burnopfield *Dur* 07-12; P-in-c Collierley w Annfield Plain from 12; AD Lanchester from 14. *Moorfield Collierley Vicarage, Bourne Terrace, Stanley DH9 8QS* T: (01207) 284760
E: revheather@btinternet.com

MURRAY, Preb Ian Hargraves. b 48. Man Univ BSc 71. St Jo Coll Nottm 79. **d** 81 **p** 82. C Erith St Paul *Roch* 81-84; C Willenhall H Trin *Lich* 84-87; TV 87-92; P-in-c Moxley 92-00; C Darlaston St Lawr 99-00; TR Glascote and Stonydelph 00-14; RD Tamworth 04-09; Preb Lich Cathl 11-14; rtd 14. *9 Wenlock Drive, Hucknall, Nottingham NG15 8HX*
E: rockin.rev@ntlworld.com

MURRAY, James Beattie. b 67. Goldsmiths' Coll Lon BMus 87 Southlands Coll Lon PGCE 89. Oak Hill Th Coll 01. **d** 03 **p** 04. C Upper Holloway *Lon* 03-07; C Chesham Bois *Ox* 07-15; Australia from 15. *Address temp unknown*
E: jamiebmurray@hotmail.com

MURRAY, John Grainger. b 45. CITC 67. **d** 70 **p** 71. C Carlow w Urglin and Staplestown *C & O* 70-72; C Limerick City *L & K* 72-77; I Rathdowney w Castlefleming, Donaghmore etc *C & O* 77-14; Can Leighlin Cathl 83-88; Preb Ossory Cathl 83-88; Treas Ossory and Leighlin Cathls 88-89; Chan Ossory and Leighlin Cathls 89-90; Prec Ossory and Leighlin Cathls 90-92; Adn Ossory and Leighlin 92-14; Adn Cashel, Waterford and Lismore 94-14; rtd 14. *Vicarstown, Stradbally, Co Laois, Republic of Ireland* T: (00353) (57) 864 1682 M: 87-248 8241
E: venjgm@gmail.com

MURRAY, John Louis. b 47. Keble Coll Ox BA 67 MA 69. **d** 82 **p** 83. Asst Chapl Strasbourg *Eur* 82-05; P-in-c 05-09. *Aumônerie Anglicane, 2 Quai Mathiss, 67000 Strasbourg, France* T/F: (0033) 3 88 36 93 90 E: john.murray@coe.int

MURRAY, Mrs Kim Margaret. b 58. **d** 07 **p** 09. OLM Camberley St Mich Yorktown *Guildf* from 07. *9 Dorchester Court, 283 London Road, Camberley GU15 3JJ* T: (01276) 23354
E: k.murray208@btinternet.com

MURRAY, Mrs Margaret Janice. b 46. Carl Dioc Tr Course. **dss** 86 **d** 87 **p** 94. Walney Is *Carl* 86-87; Hon Par Dn 87-89; Par Dn Carl H Trin and St Barn 89-94; Chapl Cumberland Infirmary 90-94; C Harraby *Carl* 94-97; P-in-c W 00-02; Chapl to the Deaf and Hard of Hearing 94-02; rtd 02; PtO *Carl* from 02. *6 Follyskye Cottages, Tindale Fell, Brampton CA8 2QB* T: (016977) 46400

MURRAY, Paul Ridsdale. b 55. BEd. St Steph Ho Ox 80. **d** 83 **p** 84. C Hartlepool St Oswald *Dur* 83-86; C S Shields All SS 86-88; V Sacriston and Kimblesworth 88-94; P-in-c Waterhouses 94-98; P-in-c Chopwell from 98; PtO *Newc* from 99. *St John's Vicarage, Derwent View, Chopwell, Newcastle upon Tyne NE17 7AN* T: (01207) 561248 F: 563850 M: 07803-906727
E: p.r.murray@durham.anglican.org

MURRAY, Roy John. b 47. Open Univ BA 92 Wolv Poly CertEd 89 RGN 75 RMN 77. WMMTC 01. **d** 04 **p** 05. NSM Solihull *Birm* 04-08; C Torquay St Jo and Ellacombe *Ex* 08-11; P-in-c Torquay St Jo 11-13; rtd 13; NSM Solihull *Birm* from 13. *3 St Alphege Close, Church Hill Road, Solihull B91 3RQ* T: 0121-709 5689 M: 07768-436363
E: roymurray99@gmail.com

MURRAY, Ruth. *See* MURRAY, Elizabeth Ruth

MURRAY, Mrs Ruth Elizabeth. b 55. Dur Univ BA 77 Man Coll of Educn CertEd 78. BA. **d** 94 **p** 95. NSM Alloa *St And* 94-98; Chapl Stirling Univ 94-99. *2 Wallace Street, Alloa FK10 3RZ* T: (01259) 217432 E: ruthemurray@lineone.net

MURRAY, Sarah Elisabeth. Aber Univ BTh 12. TISEC 10. **d** 13 **p** 14. Dioc C *Mor* from 13. *Holy Trinity Rectory, Seafield Avenue, Keith AB55 5BS* T: (01542) 882782 M: 07794-532052
E: revsarahmurray@gmail.com

MURRAY, Mrs Sheila Elizabeth. b 53. Ripon Coll Cuddesdon 10. **d** 11 **p** 12. NSM Taunton St Mary *B & W* 11-14; NSM Taunton St Mary and St Jo from 14. *Courtlands, Staplehay, Trull, Taunton TA3 7HT* T: (01823) 326876
E: revsmurray@btinternet.com

MURRAY, Stephen. b 74. Windsor Univ Ontario BA 97. Trin Coll Toronto MDiv 03. **d** 03 **p** 04. C Dundas St Jas Canada 03-06; R Hamilton Resurr 06-11; P-in-c Ghent *Eur* from 11; P-in-c Knokke from 11. *Begijnhoflaan 29, B-9000 Ghent, Belgium* T: (0032) (9) 336 4722 M: (4) 9745 1809
E: stephenmurray92@gmail.com

MURRAY (née GOULD), Mrs Susan Judith. b 61. Poly of Wales BSc 83 Open Univ MA 95. St Jo Coll Nottm 90. **d** 91 **p** 94. Par Dn Stokesley *York* 91-94; CMS 94-95; Argentina 95-03; P-in-c Haddlesey w Hambleton and Birkin *York* 03-09; TV Crawley *Chich* from 09. *St Richard's Vicarage, 1 Crossways, Crawley RH10 1QF* T: (01293) 533727

MURRAY, THE. *See* FORD, John Frank

MURRAY, Canon William Robert Craufurd. b 44. St Chad's Coll Dur BA 66. **d** 68 **p** 69. C Workington St Mich *Carl* 68-71; C Harrogate St Wilfrid *Ripon* 71-74; P-in-c Sawley 74; V Winksley cum Grantley and Aldfield w Studley 74; R Fountains 75-81; V Hutt New Zealand 81-87; V Fendalton and Chapl Medbury Sch 87-00; V Merivale 00-09; Can Christchurch Cathl 91-09; rtd 09. *Oriel Cottage, 28 High Street, Waddington 7500, New Zealand* T: (0064) (3) 318 3068
E: craufurd@xtra.co.nz

MURRAY-LESLIE, Adrian John Gervase. b 46. Lich Th Coll 67. **d** 69 **p** 70. C Sheff St Cuth 69-73; C Mosbrough 73-75; C-in-c Mosborough CD 75-80; P-in-c Edale and Warden The Peak Cen 80-11; rtd 11. *Woodside House, New Road, Barlborough, Chesterfield S43 4HY* T: (01246) 819021
E: adrian@murray-leslie.org.uk

MURRAY-PETERS, Mrs Nancy Susan. b 48. WEMTC 09. **d** 11 **p** 12. NSM Worc St Barn w Ch Ch 11-14; NSM Peopleton and White Ladies Aston w Churchill etc from 14. *Wee Wee Cottage, Worcester Road, Wyre Piddle, Pershore WR10 2HR* T: (01386) 553286 E: nmp.murraypeters@btinternet.com

MURRELL, Canon John Edmund. b 28. Westcott Ho Cam. **d** 66 **p** 67. C Ivychurch w Old Romney and Midley *Cant* 66-70; R Bardwell *St E* 70-75; PtO *Ely* 75-77; V Wenhaston w Thorington and Bramfield w Walpole *St E* 77-86; V Thorington w Wenhaston and Bramfield 86-92; P-in-c Walberswick w Blythburgh 86-92; V Thorington w Wenhaston, Bramfield etc 92-93; RD Halesworth 85-90; Hon Can St E Cathl 89-93; rtd 93; PtO *St E* from 93. *Strickland Cottage, 12 Lorne Road, Southwold IP18 6EP* T: (01502) 722074

MURRIE, Clive Robert. b 44. Ripon Coll Cuddesdon 77. **d** 79 **p** 80. C Kenton Ascension *Newc* 79-80; C Prudhoe 80-83; V Burnopfield *Dur* 83-87; R Stella 87-91; V Coalpit Heath *Bris* 91-95; P-in-c Sittingbourne St Mich *Cant* 95-98; Chapl HM Pris Stocken 98-03; Chapl HM YOI Castington 03-04; rtd 04; PtO *Pet* 04-08; P-in-c Publow w Pensford, Compton Dando and Chelwood *B & W* 08-09. *1 Kingsway Cottages, Corston, Malmesbury SN16 0HW* T: (01666) 838887
E: c.murrie@btinternet.com

MURRILLS, Mrs Rosemary Jill. b 62. Cam Coll of Art & Tech BSc 84 Brunel Univ MSc 93. ERMC 09. **d** 12 **p** 13. NSM Hartford and Houghton w Wyton *Ely* 12-15; NSM Upper St Leonards St Jo *Chich* from 15. *4 Hobart Court, 5 Ellenslea Road, St Leonards-on-Sea TN37 6HX* M: 07525-186205
E: rosemary.murrills@btinternet.com

MURRIN, Robert Staddon. b 42. Reading Univ BA 68 Open Univ MA 96. WMMTC 90. **d** 93 **p** 95. NSM Peterchurch w Vowchurch, Turnastone and Dorstone *Heref* 93-95; NSM Tupsley w Hampton Bishop 95-97; Chapl Kemp Hospice Kidderminster 97-05; PtO *Heref* from 06. *Albion Cottage, Peterchurch, Hereford HR2 0RP* T: (01981) 550656 *or* 550467
F: 550432

✠**MURSELL, The Rt Revd Alfred Gordon.** b 49. BNC Ox BA 70 MA 73 BD 87 Birm Univ Hon DD 05 ARCM 74. Cuddesdon Coll 71. **d** 73 **p** 74 **c** 05. C Walton St Mary *Liv* 73-77; V E Dulwich St Jo *S'wark* 77-86; Tutor Sarum & Wells Th Coll 87-91; TR Stafford *Lich* 91-99; Dean Birm 99-02 and 02-05; Area Bp Stafford *Lich* 05-10; rtd 10; Can Th Leic Cathl from 10; LtO *Glas* from 10. *The Old Manse, Borgue, Kirkcudbright DG6 4SH* T: (01557) 870307
E: gordon.mursell@btinternet.com

MURTHEN, Mark Anthony. b 77. UEA BA 99 MA 00. Oak Hill Th Coll BA 14. **d** 14 **p** 15. C Deane *Man* from 14. *7 Bowyer Gardens, Bolton BL3 4SN* E: markmurthen@gmail.com

MUSINDI, Mrs Beatrice Nambuya Balibali. b 64. Birm Univ MA 94. Bp Tucker Coll Mukono BD 90. **d** 03 **p** 04. C Caerleon w Llanhennock *Mon* 03-07; C Malpas 07-08; PtO *Cant* 09-14; Chapl Dover Immigration Removal Cen 14; Chapl HM YOI Roch from 14. *HM Young Offender Institution, 1 Fort Road, Rochester ME1 3QS* M: 07989-469938 T: (01634) 803100
E: beatrice.musindi@hotmail.com

MUSINDI, Philip. b 63. Bp Tucker Coll Mukono BD 91 Univ of Wales (Cardiff) MA 94. **d** 87 **p** 90. C and Sch Chapl Naigana

Uganda 87-89; C Builth and Llanddewi'r Cwm w Llangynog etc *S & B* 92-94; C Newport St Teilo *Mon* 94-97; P-in-c Newport St Matt 97-04; V Newport St Andr 04-09; Min Thanet St Andr CD *Cant* 09-11; V Reading Street from 11. *St Andrew's House, 29 Reading Street, Broadstairs CT10 3AZ* T: (01843) 579945

✠**MUSK, The Rt Revd Bill Andrew.** b 49. Ox Univ BA 70 MA 75 Fuller Th Sem California ThM 80 UNISA D Litt et Phil 84. Trin Coll Bris. **d** 81 **p** 82 **c** 08. Egypt 81-86; CMS 88-89; TV Maghull *Liv* 89-97; V Tulse Hill H Trin and St Matthias *S'wark* 97-08; Hon Can S'wark Cathl 07-08; Area Bp N Africa and R Tunis St Geo from 08. *5 rue Ahmed Beylem, 1006 Tunis Bab Souika, Tunisia* T: (00216) 7133 5493 E: billamusk@gmail.com

MUSKER, Mrs Hilary. b 56. St Mellitus Coll 15. **d** 15. OLM Barkingside St Laur *Chelmsf* from 15. *13 Deacon Way, Woodford Bridge IG8 8DF*

MUSSER, Ms Christine. b 55. Ex Univ 96. **d** 00 **p** 01. C Torpoint *Truro* 00-03; P-in-c Boscastle w Davidstow 03-07; P-in-c Pirbright *Guildf* from 07. *The Vicarage, The Green, Pirbright, Woking GU24 0JE* T: (01483) 473332
E: revdchrismusser@aol.com

MUSSON, David John. b 46. Open Univ BA 86 Univ of Wales (Lamp) MPhil 96 Univ of Wales (Ban) PhD 00. Linc Th Coll 70. **d** 73 **p** 74. C New Sleaford *Linc* 73-76; C Morton 76-80; P-in-c Thurlby 80-86; R Quarrington w Old Sleaford 86-99; P-in-c Silk Willoughby 86-87; R 87-99; PtO *Chich* from 01. *Flat 9, Regency Court 4-5, South Cliff, Eastbourne BN20 7AE* T: (01323) 723345 E: davidmusson@tiscali.co.uk

MUSSON, Mrs Joanne Chatterley. b 60. Qu Coll Birm 07. **d** 09 **p** 10. C Redditch Ch the K *Worc* 09-13; P-in-c Claines St Jo from 13; V Worc City 13-14; P-in-c Worc St Geo w St Mary Magd from 14. *The Vicarage, Claines Lane, Worcester WR3 7RN* M: 07590-514115

MUSSON, John Keith. b 39. Nottm Univ BSc 61 PhD 66 CEng MIMechE. St As Minl Tr Course 85. **d** 88 **p** 89. Assoc Prin NE Wales Inst of HE 80-93; NSM Holywell *St As* 88-93; C 93-95; R Caerwys and Bodfari 95-02; rtd 02; PtO *Lich* from 02; *St As* from 09. *4 Hayes View, Oswestry SY11 1TP* T: (01691) 656212

MUSSON, William John. b 58. UMIST BSc 80 Open Univ MA 02. St Jo Coll Nottm 88. **d** 91 **p** 92. C Nantwich *Ches* 91-94; C Finchley Ch Ch *Lon* 94-97; V Lynchmere and Camelsdale *Chich* 97-10; V Cudham and Downe *Roch* from 10. *The Boundary, Hangrove Hill, Downe, Orpington BR6 7LQ* T: (01959) 540012 E: stpandp@googlemail.com

MUST, Albert Henry. b 27. Clifton Th Coll 61. **d** 63 **p** 64. C Becontree St Mary *Chelmsf* 63-68; V Highbury Vale St Jo *Lon* 68-78; V Highbury New Park St Aug 78-84; V Walthamstow St Jo *Chelmsf* 84-93; rtd 93; PtO *Cant* from 93. *24 Nightingale Avenue, Whitstable CT5 4TR* T/F: (01227) 772160

MUST, Mrs Shirley Ann. b 35. St Mich Ho Ox 61. **dss** 82 **d** 87 **p** 94. Highbury New Park St Aug *Lon* 82-84; Walthamstow St Jo *Chelmsf* 84-93; Hon Par Dn 87-93; PtO *Cant* 93-94; Hon C Herne Bay Ch Ch 94-05; PtO 05-12. *24 Nightingale Avenue, Whitstable CT5 4TR* T/F: (01227) 772160

MUSTARD, James Edmond Alexander. b 74. Ex Univ BA 95 Clare Coll Cam BA 04 MA 08 K Coll Lon MA 13. Westcott Ho Cam 02 Berkeley Div Sch 04. **d** 05 **p** 06. C Nor St Pet Mancroft w St Jo Maddermarket 05-08; C Pimlico St Pet w Westmr Ch Ch *Lon* 08-12; R E Barnet *St Alb* from 12. *The Rectory, 136 Church Hill Road, Barnet EN4 8XD* M: 07763-973647
E: rector.eastbarnet@gmail.com

MUSTOE, Alan Andrew. b 52. Man Univ BA 74. Qu Coll Birm. **d** 78 **p** 79. C Chatham St Wm *Roch* 78-82; R Burham and Wouldham 82-88; Dioc Info Officer 83-88; V Strood St Nic w St Mary 88-99; V Orpington All SS 99-10; AD Orpington 05-10; R Chislehurst St Nic from 10. *The Rectory, 2 Cardinal Close, Chislehurst BR7 6SA* T: (020) 8467 4405
M: 07725-909733 E: alan.mustoe@akmustoe.co.uk

MUSTON, James Arthur. b 48. Open Univ BA 92 Derby Univ MA. EMMTC 89. **d** 91 **p** 92. NSM Chaddesden St Mary *Derby* 91-95; Community Min E Marsh Grimsby *Linc* 95-99; V Gresley *Derby* 99-04; rtd 04; PtO *Derby* from 04. *20 Whitmore Road, Chaddesden, Derby DE21 6HR* T: (01332) 678073
M: 07946-575563

MUTCH, Canon Sylvia Edna. b 36. St Mich Ho Ox 57. **dss** 79 **d** 87 **p** 94. Clifton *York* 79-95; Par Dn 87-94; C 94-95; Chapl Clifton Hosp *York* 81-94; R Elvington w Sutton on Derwent and E Cottingwith *York* 95-01; Can and Preb York Minster 98-01; rtd 01; PtO *York* from 01. *18 Waite Close, Pocklington, York YO42 2YU* T: (01759) 307894

MUTETE, Lameck. b 61. Bp Gaul Th Coll Harare 94. **d** 96 **p** 97. C Harare St Luke Zimbabwe 96-97; Asst P Harare Cathl 97-01; P-in-c 01; Adn Harare E 01; Can Harare 01-04; PtO *Bradf* 04; P-in-c Tattenhall and Handley *Ches* 04-10; R 10-11; R Tattenhall w Burwardsley and Handley from 11; PtO *Birm* from 14. *The Rectory, Chester Road, Gatesheath, Tattenhall, Chester CH3 9AH* M: 07940-512748 T: (01829) 770245 E: lameckmutete@yahoo.co.uk

MUTHALALY, Varghese Malayil Lukose (Saju). b 79. S Asia Bible Coll Bangalore BTh 01. Wycliffe Hall Ox BTh 08. **d** 08 **p** 09. C Lancaster St Thos *Blackb* 08-11; C Kendal St Thos and Crook *Carl* 11-15; V Gillingham St Mark *Roch* from 15. *St Mark's Vicarage, 173 Canterbury Street, Gillingham ME7 5TU* T: (01634) 852910 E: sajudoj@yahoo.com *or* saju@stkmail.org.uk

MUTIKANI, Mrs Martha Tsungayi Zivito. b 66. SEITE 12. **d** 15. NSM Reigate St Luke *S'wark* from 15. *Address temp unknown*

MUTTER, Richard Douglas. b 73. **d** 14. C Cleobury Mortimer w Hopton Wafers etc *Heref* from 14. *Glebe House, 5 New Road Gardens, Cleobury Mortimer, Kidderminster DY14 8AW* M: 07791-491239 E: richard_mutter@hotmail.com

MUXLOW, Judy Ann. b 47. Univ of Wales (Cardiff) BSc 69 St Luke's Coll Ex CertEd 73. SEITE. **d** 00 **p** 01. Chapl Ch Ch High Sch Ashford 00-03; Bp's Officer for NSM *Cant* 03-07; NSM Biddenden and Smarden 00-06; NSM Appledore w Brookland, Fairfield, Brenzett etc 06-08; NSM Wittersham w Stone and Ebony 06-08; NSM Woodchurch 06-08; PtO *Roch* from 00; *Cant* from 09. *29 The Meadows, Biddenden, Ashford TN27 8AW* T: (01580) 291016 E: judy@mucat.eclipse.co.uk

MWANGI, Capt Joel Waweru. b 59. CA Tr Coll Nairobi 81. **d** 93 **p** 94. Kenya 93-96 and from 00; C Sheff St Mary Bramall Lane 96-99. *PO Box 57227, Nairobi, Kenya*

MYANMAR, Archbishop of. *See* SAN SI HTAY, The Most Revd Samuel

MYATT, Francis Eric. b 60. St Jo Coll Nottm 89. **d** 92 **p** 93. C W Derby St Luke *Liv* 92-95; TV Sutton 95-98; V Liv St Chris Norris Green 98-01; CF 01-13; C Walton St Jo *Liv* from 13. *66 Roseworth Avenue, Liverpool L9 8HF*

MYATT, Philip Bryan. b 29. Wycliffe Hall Ox 54. **d** 57 **p** 58. C Fareham St Jo *Portsm* 57-61; C Westgate St Jas *Cant* 61-64; R Woodchester *Glouc* 64-70; R Bath Walcot *B & W* 70-91; R The Edge, Pitchcombe, Harescombe and Brookthorpe *Glouc* 91-94; rtd 94; PtO *Glouc* from 94. *West Cottage, Littleworth, Amberley, Stroud GL5 5AL*

MYERS, Mrs Alison Margaret. b 66. Bris Univ BSc 88. SEITE 04. **d** 07 **p** 08. NSM Cambourne *Ely* 07-10; TV Lordsbridge from 10. *The Rectory, 50 Main Street, Hardwick, Cambridge CB23 7QS* T: (01954) 212815 M: 07884-370933 E: alisonmyers@lordsbridge.org

MYERS, Andrew Thomas Christopher. b 57. Leeds Univ BA 81 Ches Coll of HE MTh 05. NOC 02. **d** 04 **p** 05. C Leeds St Aid *Ripon* 04-08; P-in-c Middleton St Cross 08-13; P-in-c Middleton St Mary 08-13; V Middleton *Leeds* from 13. *St Cross Vicarage, Middleton Park Avenue, Leeds LS10 4HT* T: 0113-271 6398 M: 07876-431183 E: andymyers@elmet4.freeserve.co.uk

MYERS, Duncan Frank. b 57. Warwick Univ BSc. St Jo Coll Nottm 81. **d** 84 **p** 85. C Upton cum Chalvey *Ox* 84-86; C Farnborough *Guildf* 86-90; Chapl Nottm Poly *S'well* 90-92; Chapl Nottm Trent Univ 92-95; Sen Past Adv 95-02; Hon Min Can Dur Cathl 04-08; Chapl Hatf Coll Dur 06-08; Chapl Salford Univ *Man* 08-12; Chapl Lon S Bank Univ *S'wark* 12-14; Nat Adv for HE Abps' Coun from 14; Hon Min Can S'wark Cathl from 13. *Church House, Great Smith Street, London SW1P 3AZ* T: (020) 7898 1513 E: duncan.myers@churchof england.org

MYERS, Canon Gillian Mary. b 57. Warwick Univ BSc 78 Nottm Univ MA 96. St Jo Coll Nottm 83. **d** 95 **p** 97. NSM

Nottingham St Jude *S'well* 95-97; NSM Gedling 97-00; P-in-c Nottingham All SS 00-02; Succ, Sacr and Min Can Dur Cathl 02-08; Can Res Man Cathl 08-12; Can Res and Prec S'wark Cathl from 12. *7 Temple West Mews, West Square, London SE11 4TJ* T: (020) 7582 4442 E: gilly@myers.uk.net

MYERS, Paul Henry. b 49. ALA 72. Qu Coll Birm 74. **d** 77 **p** 78. C Baildon *Bradf* 77-80; C W Bromwich All SS *Lich* 80-83; Chapl RAF 83-86; V Milton *Lich* 87-92; C Baswich 96-99; C Hixon w Stowe-by-Chartley 99-02; TV Mid Trent 02-05; TR Blakenall Heath 05-14; rtd 14. *110 Buxton Road, Leek ST13 6EJ* E: rev.paulmyers@btinternet.com

MYERS, Peter Daniel. b 83. Man Univ BA 04. Oak Hill Th Coll MTh 13. **d** 13 **p** 14. NSM Cambridge St Andr Less *Ely* from 13. *2 Tyndale Court, Grange Road, Cambridge CB3 9AS* T: (01223) 566611 M: 07930-222217 E: peterdanielmyers@gmail.com

MYERS, Peter John. b 60. St Jo Coll Dur BA 81. Linc Th Coll 84. **d** 84 **p** 85. C Bulwell St Mary *S'well* 84-88; C Shrewsbury H Cross *Lich* 88-92; rtd 92. *21-22 Eastcliff, Dover CT16 1LU* T: (01304) 332179

MYERS, Robert William John. b 57. Aus Nat Univ BSc 80 Newc Univ Aus DipEd 82. Trin Coll Bris 93. **d** 95 **p** 96. C Addiscombe St Mary Magd w St Martin *S'wark* 95-98; C Surbiton St Matt 98-03; P-in-c Blayney Australia 04-10; I Bellarine from 10. *PO Box 365, Drysdale VIC 3222, Australia* T: (0061) (3) 5251 2571 M: 48-857 4855 E: rwj127@hotmail.com

MYERS, Sally Ann. b 65. Leic Univ BA 86 Nottm Univ MA 06. EMMTC 02. **d** 06 **p** 07. C Grantham *Linc* 06-08; Vice-Prin Dioc Min Tr Course 08-09; Dir of Studies Dioc Min Tr Course from 09. *15 Wain Well Mews, Lincoln LN2 4BF* T: (01522) 567804 *or* 504050 E: sally.myers@lincoln.anglican.org

MYERSCOUGH, Robin Nigel. b 44. K Coll Lon BD 69 Nottm Univ PGCE 70. Coll of Resurr Mirfield 66. **d** 81 **p** 82. Hon C Diss *Nor* 81-84; Chapl Nor Sch 81-84; Hd RS Sedbergh Sch 84-85; Chapl and Hd RS Dur Sch 85-92; Chapl Gresham's Sch Holt 92-01; Asst Chapl 01-04; rtd 04; PtO *Nor* from 04. *Hamer, The Street, Bodham, Holt NR25 6NW* T: (01263) 588859 E: rmyerscough@hotmail.com

MYLES (née LUCAS), Mrs Julia Mary. b 63. Westhill Coll Birm BEd 85 Birm Univ MA 92. Lindisfarne Regional Tr Partnership 10. **d** 13 **p** 14. C Alnwick *Newc* from 13. *10 Allerburn Lea, Alnwick NE66 2NJ* M: 07716-771164 E: juliamyles@btinternet.com

MYLNE, Mrs Christine. b 44. Open Univ BA 76 Univ of Wales (Lamp) MA 03. St Alb Minl Tr Scheme 89 NEOC 04. **d** 04 **p** 05. NSM Norham and Duddo *Newc* 04-06; NSM Cornhill w Carham 04-06; NSM Branxton 04-06; P-in-c Challoch *Glas* 06-11; rtd 11; P-in-c Glenurquhart *Mor* from 11. *St Ninian's Cottage, 32 Milton, Drumnadrochit, Inverness IV63 6UA* T: (01456) 450715 E: christinemylne@gmail.com *or* christine.mylne@btinternet.com

MYNORS, Canon James Baskerville. b 49. Peterho Cam BA 70 MA 74. Ridley Hall Cam 70 St Jo Coll Nottm 77. **d** 78 **p** 80. Hon C Leic H Apostles 78-79; C Virginia Water *Guildf* 79-83; C Patcham *Chich* 83-88; P-in-c Fowlmere and Thriplow *Ely* 88-01; Sen Tutor EAMTC 88-90; Vice-Prin 90-97; P-in-c Gt w Lt Abington 01-07; P-in-c Hildersham 01-07; Dioc Rural Miss Officer 04-07; R Aldwincle, Clopton, Pilton, Stoke Doyle etc *Pet* from 07; Can Pet Cathl from 13. *The Rectory, Main Street, Aldwincle, Kettering NN14 3EP* T: (01832) 720613 E: jim@mynors.me.uk

N

NADARAJAH (née GOODDEN), Mrs Stephanie Anne. b 81. Fitzw Coll Cam MA 04. Ripon Coll Cuddesdon MTh 10. **d** 10 **p** 11. C Caterham *S'wark* from 10. *1 Torwood Lane, Caterham CR3 0HD* T: (020) 8660 5077 E: stephnadarajah@gmail.com

NADEN, Anthony Joshua. b 38. Jes Coll Ox BA 62 MA 64 SOAS Lon PhD 73. Wycliffe Hall Ox 60. **d** 62 **p** 63. C Rowner *Portsm* 62-66; C Fisherton Anger *Sarum* 69-72; Ghana 72-10; PtO *Ox* from 10. *Lost Marbles, 31 Reading Road, Pangbourne, Reading RG8 7HY* T: 0118-984 2368 E: lostmarbles31@gmail.com

NADIN, Dennis Lloyd. b 37. St D Coll Lamp BA 60 Man Univ MEd 81. Ridley Hall Cam 60. **d** 64 **p** 65. C Childwall All SS *Liv* 64-67; P-in-c Seacroft *Ripon* 67-69; Project Officer Grubb Inst 69-70; Lect CA Tr Coll Blackheath 70-72; Community Educn Essex Co Coun 73-80; Public Preacher *Chelmsf* from 73; PtO *St Alb* 01-03. *The Hermitage, 201 Willowfield, Harlow CM18 6RZ* T: (01279) 325904

NAGEL, Canon Lawson Chase Joseph. b 49. Univ of Michigan BA 71 K Coll Lon PhD 82 ARHistS 75. Sarum & Wells Th Coll 81. **d** 83 **p** 84. C Chiswick St Nic w St Mary *Lon* 83-86; C Horsham *Chich* 86; TV 86-91; V Aldwick from 91; Sec Gen Confraternity of the Blessed Sacrament 85-10; Hon Can Popondota from 05. *The Vicarage, 25 Gossamer Lane, Aldwick, Bognor Regis PO21 3AT* T: (01243) 262049 E: lawson@nagel.me.uk

NAGEL, Miss Lucy Mary. b 86. Bris Univ BA 07 PGCE 08 Anglia Ruskin Univ MA 15. Ridley Hall Cam 13. **d** 15. C Redland *Bris* from 15. *41 Birchall Road, Bristol BS6 7TT* M: 07813-405361 E: lucynagel@hotmail.com

NAHABEDIAN, Canon Harold Joseph. b 39. Toronto Univ BA 63 MA 66. Trin Coll Toronto STB 70 Armenian Orthodox Sem Jerusalem 70. **d** 73 **p** 74. C Vancouver St Jas Canada 73-76; Chapl Trin Coll Toronto 76-81; V Toronto St Thos

81-83; P-in-c Toronto St Mary Magd 83-88; R 88-09; Hon Can Toronto from 93; rtd 09; P-in-c Strasbourg *Eur* 10-13. *Aumônerie Anglicane, 2 Quai Mathiss, 67000 Strasbourg, France* T/F: (0033) 3 88 36 93 90 E: hj.nahabedian@gmail.com

NAIDU, Michael Sriram. b 28. Univ of the South (USA) 81. Ridley Hall Cam 86. **d** 80 **p** 85. Acting Chapl Stuttgart *Eur* 85-91; Chapl 91-00; rtd 00. *Kloster Kinchberg, 72172 Sulz am Neckar, Stuttgart, Germany* T: (0049) (7454) 883136 *or* 87418 F: 883250

NAIRN, Frederick William. b 43. TCD 64. Luther NW Th Sem DMin 88. **d** 67 **p** 68. C Larne and Inver *Conn* 67-70; Chapl RAF 70-74; P-in-c Harmston *Linc* 75-77; V 77-84; V Coleby 78-84; USA from 84; rtd 04. *5895 Stoneybrook Drive, Minnetonka MN 55345-6434, USA*

NAIRN, Canon Stuart Robert. b 51. K Coll Lon BD 75 AKC 75 Univ of Wales (Lamp) MTh 04 FRSA 01. St Aug Coll Cant 75. **d** 76 **p** 77. C E Dereham *Nor* 76-80; TV Hempnall 80-88; V Narborough w Narford 88-99; R Pentney St Mary Magd w W Bilney 88-99; R Narborough w Narford and Pentney 99-10; P-in-c Castleacre, Newton, Westacre and Southacre 97-10; R Nar Valley from 11; RD Lynn 91-99; RD Breckland from 06; Hon Can Nor Cathl from 03. *The Rectory, Main Road, Narborough, King's Lynn PE32 1TE* T: (01760) 338552 *or* 338562 E: nairn.nvgrectory@btinternet.com

NAIRN-BRIGGS, The Very Revd George Peter. b 45. AKC 69. St Aug Coll Cant 69. **d** 70 **p** 71. C Catford St Laur *S'wark* 70-73; C Raynes Park St Sav 73-75; V Salfords 75-81; V St Helier 81-87; Dioc Soc Resp Adv *Wakef* 87-97; Can Res Wakef Cathl 92-97; Provost Wakef 97-00; Dean Wakef 00-07; rtd 07; PtO *Leeds* from 09. *Abbey House, 2 St James Court, Park Avenue, Wakefield WF2 8DN* T: (01924) 291029 M: 07770-636840 E: nairnbriggs@btinternet.com

NAISH, Miss Annie Claire. b 65. St Jo Coll Dur BA 04 MA 08. Cranmer Hall Dur. **d** 05 **p** 06. C Gorleston St Andr *Nor* 05-09; Dioc Ecum Miss Enabler *B & W* 09-11; Missr Lee Abbey Movement from 11. *Lee Abbey, Lynton EX35 6JJ* T: (01598) 752621 E: annie@leeabbey.org.uk

NAISH, Mrs Hilary Marilyn. b 43. Edin Univ MA 04. TISEC 04. **d** 05 **p** 07. NSM Edin Gd Shep and Edin St Salvador 05-09; LtO from 09. *26(Pf) Learmonth Grove, Edinburgh EH4 1BW* E: hmnaish@talk21.com

NAISH, Mrs Joanna Mary. b 60. Bris Univ BA 81 Southn Univ MA 92 Sheff Univ PGCE 82. STETS 06. **d** 09 **p** 10. NSM Woodford Valley w Archers Gate *Sarum* from 09; NSM Amesbury from 13. *44 Balmoral Road, Salisbury SP1 3PX* T: (01722) 504934 M: 07810-810231 E: joanna.naish44@gmail.com

NAISH, Timothy James Neville. b 57. St Jo Coll Ox BA 80 MA 88 Bris Univ PhD 05. WMMTC 86. **d** 87 **p** 88. CMS 81-00; C Cov H Trin 87; Dir Th Formation (Shaba) Zaïre 88-91; Research Fell, Tutor, and Lect Qu Coll Birm 92-93; Tutor and Lect Bp Tucker Th Coll Uganda 93-00; R Hanborough and Freeland *Ox* 00-06; Dir Studies Ox Min Course 06-09; Dean from 09; Lect Ripon Coll Cuddesdon from 06; Asst Chapl Campsfield Ho Immigration Removal Cen 07-15. *307 London Road, Headington, Oxford OX3 9EJ* T: (01865) 766627 *or* 877407 E: tim.naish@rcc.ac.uk

NAISMITH, Mrs Carol. b 37. St Andr Univ MA 59 Edin Univ MTh 98. Edin Dioc NSM Course 85. **d** 90 **p** 94. NSM Edin Old St Paul from 90; Hon C Edin St Salvador 00-03. *38 Castle Avenue, Edinburgh EH12 7LB* T: 0131-334 4486 E: carol.naismith@tiscali.co.uk

✠**NALEDI, The Rt Revd Theophilus Tswere.** b 36. UNISA BTh 82 K Coll Lon MTh 84. St Bede's Coll Umtata LTh 59. **d** 59 **p** 60 **c** 87. S Africa 59-70; R Kimberley St Jas 67-70; R Gaborone Botswana 71-73; Adn and R Lobatse 74-83; C Wimbledon *S'wark* 83-85; Prov Sec Ch of the Prov of Cen Africa 86-87; Bp Matabeleland 87-01; Bp Botswana 01-04; rtd 04. *PO Box 237, Gaborone, Botswana*

NALL, Sheila Ann. b 48. Univ of Wales (Ban) BA 69. WMMTC 00. **d** 03 **p** 04. NSM Worc St Wulstan 03-07; Chapl HM Pris Hewell 07-09. *108 Ombersley Road, Worcester WR3 7EZ* T: (01905) 26284 E: nall.mail@tiscali.co.uk

NANCARROW, Mrs Caroline Elisabeth. b 47. Trin Coll Melbourne BTheol 87. **d** 93 **p** 97. Chapl St Anne's and Gippsland Gr Sch Australia 88-96; NSM Bairnsdale 96-99; P-in-c Omeo 00-02; P-in-c Paynesville 02-07; R Stratford 07-09; R Avon 09-11; PtO *Pet* from 11; Chapl Malcolm Arnold Academy Northampton from 13; Can Gippsland from 07. *Malcolm Arnold Academy, Trinity Avenue, Northampton NN2 6JW* T: (01604) 778018 E: c.nancarrow@malcolmarnoldacademy.co.uk

NANCARROW, Mrs Rachel Mary. b 38. Cam Inst of Educn TCert 59. EAMTC 87. **d** 90 **p** 94. NSM Girton *Ely* 90-95; P-in-c Foxton 95-01; P-in-c Shepreth 98-01; C Fulbourn and Gt and Lt Wilbraham 01-03; rtd 03; PtO *Pet* from 04. *Thimble Cottage, 11 Geeston, Ketton, Stamford PE9 3RH* T: (01780) 729382 E: r.m.nancarrow@skogen.co.uk

NANKIVELL, Christopher Robert Trevelyan. b 33. Jes Coll Ox BA 55 MA 63 Birm Univ MSocSc 79. Linc Th Coll 56. **d** 58 **p** 59. C Bloxwich *Lich* 58-60; C Stafford St Mary 60-64; P-in-c Malins Lee 64-72; Soc Welfare Sector Min to Milton Keynes Chr Coun 73-76; Tutor Qu Coll Birm 76-81; rtd 96. *77 Pereira Road, Birmingham B17 9JA* T: 0121-427 1197

NAPIER, Graeme Stewart Patrick Columbanus. b 66. Magd Coll Ox BA MA MPhil LRSM. St Steph Ho Ox. **d** 95 **p** 96. C Inverness St Andr *Mor* 95-98; Asst P St Laurence Ch Ch Australia 98-02; Min Can and Succ Westmr Abbey 02-10; Prec St Geo Cathl Perth Australia from 10. *18 St George's Terrace, Perth WA 6000, Australia* T: (0061) (8) 9325 5766 E: graeme.napier@perthcathedral.org

NAPIER, Jennifer Beryl. *See* BLACK, Jennifer Beryl

NASCIMENTO COOK, Mrs Anesia. b 62. Mogidas Cruces Univ BA 86. Porto Allegre Th Sem BTh 91. **d** 91 **p** 93. Brazil 91-94; LtO *St Alb* 96-97; C Dinnington *Sheff* 97-99; P-in-c Shiregreen St Jas and St Chris 99-07; P-in-c Shiregreen St Hilda 05-07; V Shiregreen 07-08; C Rotherham 08-15; V Sheff St Pet and St Oswald from 15. *St Peter's Vicarage, 17 Ashland Road, Sheffield S7 1RH* E: anjesus@postmaster.co.uk *or* anesia.cook@sheffield.anglican.org

NASH, Alan Frederick. b 46. Sarum & Wells Th Coll 72. **d** 75 **p** 76. C Foley Park *Worc* 75-79; P-in-c Mildenhall *Sarum* 79-82; Wilts Adnry Youth Officer 79-82; TV N Wingfield, Pilsley and Tupton *Derby* 82-85. *17 Chapel Road, Astwood Bank, Redditch B96 6AL* T: (01527) 894294 E: alan.nash@bigfoot.com

NASH, David. b 25. K Coll Lon BD 51 AKC 51. **d** 52 **p** 53. C Buckhurst Hill *Chelmsf* 52-58; Min St Cedd CD Westcliff 58-66; R Rivenhall *Chelmsf* 66-83; P-in-c Boscastle w Davidstow *Truro* 83-85; TR 85-90; rtd 90; PtO *Truro* from 90. *9 Boscundle Avenue, Falmouth TR11 5BU*

NASH, Preb David John. b 41. Pemb Coll Ox BA 64 MA 70. Wells Th Coll 65. **d** 67 **p** 68. C Preston Ascension *Lon* 67-70; TV Hackney 70-75; TV Clifton *S'well* 76-82; V Winchmore Hill St Paul *Lon* 82-98; AD Enfield 87-91; R Monken Hadley 98-08; AD Cen Barnet 00-04; Preb St Paul's Cathl 96-08; rtd 08; PtO *Lon* from 08. *36 Birkbeck Road, Enfield EN2 0DX* T: (020) 8367 6873 E: prebdjnash@yahoo.co.uk

NASH, Mrs Ingrid. b 36. SRN 57 RNT 80 BEd 78. S'wark Ord Course 91. **d** 94 **p** 95. NSM Eltham Park St Luke *S'wark* 94-06; PtO *Roch* from 97; S'wark from 06. *13 Crookston Road, London SE9 1YH* T: (020) 8850 0750 E: ingrid.nash@btopenworld.com

NASH, Canon James Alexander. b 56. St Jo Coll Nottm BA 94. **d** 97 **p** 98. C Trunch *Nor* 97-01; R Stratton St Mary w Stratton St Michael etc 01-10; R N w S Wootton from 10; RD Lynn from 13; Hon Can Nor Cathl from 15. *The Rectory, 47 Castle Rising Road, South Wootton, King's Lynn PE30 3JA* E: james.nash@btopenworld.com

NASH, James David Gifford. b 76. New Coll Ox MEng 98. Wycliffe Hall Ox BTh 03. **d** 03 **p** 04. C Plymouth St Andr and Stonehouse *Ex* 03-07; Hon C Preston All SS *Blackb* 07-11; C W Preston from 11. *The Vicarage, 240 Tulketh Road, Ashton-on-Ribble, Preston PR2 1ES* T: (01772) 726848 M: 07889-424907 E: jdgnash@gmail.com

NASH, Mrs Jane. b 58. ERMC 05. **d** 08 **p** 09. C Kempston All SS and Biddenham *St Alb* 08-11; V Chadsmoor *Lich* from 11. *The Vicarage, Albert Street, Cannock WS11 5JD* T: (01543) 500015 E: janenash@hotmail.co.uk

NASH, Paul. *See* NASH, William Paul

NASH, Paul. b 59. WMMTC 94. **d** 97 **p** 98. C Aston SS Pet and Paul *Birm* 97-02; Asst Chapl Birm Children's Hosp NHS Trust from 02; Tutor St Jo Coll Nottm from 02. *13 Jaffray Road, Birmingham B24 8AZ* T: 0121-384 6034 *or* 333 8526 F: 333 8527 E: paulandsal@msn.com *or* p.nash@bch.nhs.uk

NASH, Penelope Jane. b 71. Trin Coll Bris 04. **d** 06 **p** 07. C Downend *Bris* 06-09; TV Gt Berkhamsted, Gt and Lt Gaddesden etc *St Alb* from 09. *The Vicarage, Church Road, Potten End, Berkhamsted HP4 2QY* T: (01442) 865217 E: penny@jeznash.co.uk

NASH, Robin Louis. b 51. Open Univ BA 87. Aston Tr Scheme 80 Chich Th Coll 82. **d** 84 **p** 85. C Lymington *Win* 84-86; C Andover w Foxcott 86-90; R Kegworth *Leic* 90-01; P-in-c Bournemouth St Alb *Win* 01-10; V 10-14; V Bournemouth St Luke 10-14; rtd 14; PtO *Win* from 14; *Eur* from 14. *6 Shreen Way, Gillingham SP8 4EL* T: (01747) 823183 E: my_quarters@yahoo.co.uk

NASH, Sally Ann. b 57. Sussex Univ BA 78 Sheff Univ DMinTh 03 Ox Brookes Univ MA 10 PGCE 79. Qu Coll Birm 10. **d** 12 **p** 13. NSM Hodge Hill *Birm* from 12. *Wellman, 13 Jaffray Road, Erdington, Birmingham B24 8AZ* T: 0121-384 6034 M: 07824-542104 E: revsally12@gmail.com

NASH, Thomas James. b 82. SS Hild & Bede Coll Dur BA 03 MA 04. Wycliffe Hall Ox 07. **d** 09 **p** 10. C St Helen Bishopsgate w St Andr Undershaft etc *Lon* 09-14; C Sevenoaks St Nic *Roch* from 14. *26 Woodside Road, Sevenoaks TN13 3HE* E: thomas.nash@stnicholas-sevenoaks.org

NASH, The Ven Trevor Gifford. b 30. Clare Coll Cam BA 53 MA 57. Cuddesdon Coll 53. **d** 55 **p** 56. C Cheshunt *St Alb* 55-57; CF (TA) 56-61; C Kingston All SS *S'wark* 57-61; C Stevenage *St Alb* 61-63; V Leagrave 63-67; Dir Luton Samaritans 66-67; Chapl St Geo Hosp Lon 67-73; R Win St Lawr and St Maurice w St Swithun 73-82; Bp's Adv Min of Healing 73-98; P-in-c Win H Trin 77-82; RD Win 75-82; Hon Can Win Cathl 80-90; Adn Basingstoke 82-90; Exec Co-ord Acorn Chr Healing Trust 90-97; Pres Guild of Health 92-97; Warden Guild of St Raphael 95-98; PtO *Win* from 95; rtd 97; Hon Chapl Win Cathl from 98. *Cottage D, Headbourne Worthy House, Bedfield Lane, Headbourne Worthy, Winchester SO23 7JG* T: (01962) 881184

NASH, William Paul. b 48. St Mich Coll Llan 86. **d** 87 **p** 88. C Pembroke Dock *St D* 87-89; P-in-c Llawhaden w Bletherston and Llanycefn 89-90; V 90-92; P-in-c E Brixton St Jude *S'wark* 92-96; V 96-99; V Cwmaman *St D* 99-04; R Pendine w Llanmiloe and Eglwys Gymyn w Marros 04-11; TR Monkton from 11. *The Vicarage, Church Terrace, Monkton, Pembroke SA71 4LW* T: (01646) 682723

NASH-WILLIAMS, Mrs Barbara Ruth. b 66. St Martin's Coll Lanc BA 88 Anglia Poly Univ MA 03. EAMTC 96. **d** 99 **p** 00. C Tettenhall Wood and Perton *Lich* 99-02; NSM Cheswardine, Childs Ercall, Hales, Hinstock etc 04-06; Dioc Development Officer for Youth Work *Newc* 06-14. *Parsonage House, Brampton Road, Alston CA9 3AA* T: (01434) 382558 E: bar@nash-williams.name

NASH-WILLIAMS, Mark Christian Victor. b 64. Trin Hall Cam BA 86 MA 90 PGCE 87. Qu Coll Birm BD 01. **d** 02 **p** 03. C Edgmond w Kynnersley and Preston Wealdmoors *Lich* 02-06; P-in-c Stamfordham w Matfen *Newc* 06-14; R Alston Moor from 14. *Parsonage House, Brampton Road, Alston CA9 3AA* T: (01434) 382558 E: vicar@alstonmoorcofe.org.uk

NASH-WILLIAMS, Canon Piers le Sor Victor. b 35. Trin Hall Cam BA 57 MA 61. Cuddesdon Coll 59. **d** 61 **p** 62. C Milton *Win* 61-64; Asst Chapl Eton Coll 64-66; PtO *Chich* 66-68; C Furze Platt *Ox* 69-72; V Newbury St Geo Wash Common 72-73; TV Newbury 73-91; R Ascot Heath 91-01; Hon Can Ch Ch 01; rtd 01; PtO *Ox* from 02. *18 Chiltern Close, Newbury RG14 6SZ* T: (01635) 31762 E: pnashwilliams@tesco.net

NASHASHIBI, Pauline. b 48. **d** 11 **p** 12. NSM Finsbury Park St Thos Lon 11-15; NSM Hornsey St Mary w St Geo from 15. *36A Woodstock Road, London N4 3EX* T: (020) 7263 8268 E: pauline.nashashibi@btinternet.com

NASON, Canon Thomas David. b 44. Open Univ BA 92 ACA 68 FCA 78. Ripon Coll Cuddesdon 84. **d** 86 **p** 87. C Banstead *Guildf* 86-89; Chapl Prebendal Sch Chich 89-14; PV Chich Cathl 89-14; Can and Preb Chich Cathl 06-14. *The Gables, Hambrook Hill South, Hambrook, Chichester PO18 8UJ* T: (01243) 573716 M: 07732-114279 E: d.nason@tesco.net

NASSAR, Nadim. b 64. Near E Sch of Th BTh 88. **d** 03 **p** 04. Prin Trin Foundn for Christianity and Culture 03-05; Dir Awareness Foundn from 05; Hon C Upper Chelsea H Trin *Lon* 03-11; Hon C Upper Chelsea H Trin and St Sav from 11; PtO *S'wark* from 13. *Awareness Foundation, Lodge House, 69 Beaufort Street, London SW3 5AH* T: (020) 7730 8830 M: 07961-968193 E: director@awareness-foundation.com

NATHANAEL, Martin Moses. b 43. Lon Univ BEd 73 K Coll Lon MTh 77. Ripon Coll Cuddesdon 77. **d** 79 **p** 80. C Hampton All SS *Lon* 79-82; P-in-c Kensal Town St Thos w St Andr and St Phil 82-83; Hd Div Bp Stopford Sch Lon 83-91; TV Tring *St Alb* 91-00; rtd 00. *43 Morehall Close, York YO30 4WA* T: (01904) 691201 E: martinascend@aol.com

NATHANIEL, Canon Garth Edwin Peter. b 61. Brunel Univ BTh 99. Lon Bible Coll 96. **d** 98 **p** 99. NSM Hanwell St Mary w St Chris *Lon* 98-99; C Lt Stanmore St Lawr 99-01; P-in-c Brockmoor *Worc* 02-07; TV Brierley Hill 07-10; TR Ipsley from 10; RD Bromsgrove from 15; Hon Can Worc Cathl from 15. *The Rectory, Icknield Street, Ipsley, Redditch B98 0AN* T: (01527) 522847 M: 07949-490265 E: gn004d6359@blueyonder.co.uk

NATHANIEL, Ivan Wasim. Punjab Univ MA 65. Bp's Coll Calcutta 59. **d** 62 **p** 64. India 62-68; C Newland St Aug *York* 68-70; Hon C Crawley *Chich* 70-98; Chapl H Trin Sch Crawley 76-97; Hd RS 76-97; PtO *Chich* from 97. *13 Haywards, Crawley RH10 3TR* T: (01293) 882932 E: i.nathaniel@btopenworld.com

NATHANIEL, Canon Leslie Satianathan. b 54. Bangalore Univ BA 74 Jawaharlal Nehru Univ Delhi BA 79 Birm Univ PhD 08. **d** 01 **p** 02. Interchange Adv CMS 99-04; Germany from 04;

Abp's Dep Sec Ecum Affairs and Eur Sec Coun for Chr Unity from 09; Hon Can *Eur* from 12. *Frankentobelstrasse 4, 73079 Suessen, Germany* T: (020) 7898 1474 E: leslie.nathaniel@churchofengland.org

NATNAEL, Daniel. b 66. Wycliffe Hall Ox 10. **d** 12 **p** 13. C Goldsworth Park *Guildf* from 12. *6 Waldens Park Road, Woking GU21 4RN* T: (01483) 765752 E: dnatnael@yahoo.co.uk

NATTRASS, Elizabeth Jane. b 59. CBDTI 97. **d** 00 **p** 01. C Dalston w Cumdivock, Raughton Head and Wreay *Carl* 00-03; TV S Barrow 03-08; P-in-c 08; TR 08-10; P-in-c York St Olave w St Giles from 10; P-in-c York St Helen w St Martin from 10; P-in-c York All SS Pavement w St Crux and St Mich from 10; P-in-c York St Denys from 10; P-in-c York H Trin Micklegate from 13; P-in-c York St Lawr w St Nic from 15. *St Olave's Vicarage, 52 Bootham, York YO30 7BZ* T: (01904) 623559 E: nattrassjane@aol.com

NATTRASS, Michael Stuart. b 41. CBE 98. Man Univ BA 62. Cuddesdon Coll 62. **d** 64 **p** 65. C Easington Colliery *Dur* 64-65; C Silksworth 65-68; PtO *S'well* 68-72; LtO *Dur* 72-76; PtO *Lon* 76-78 and from 05; Hon C Pinner 78-05; rtd 05. *36 Waxwell Lane, Pinner HA5 3EN* T: (020) 8866 0217 F: 8930 0622 E: msnattrass@btinternet.com

NAUDÉ, John Donald. b 62. Ridley Hall Cam 95. **d** 97 **p** 98. C Kettering Ch the King *Pet* 97-00; C Wellingborough All Hallows 00-06; Dioc Disability Adv 05-06; V Crookhorn *Portsm* 06-12. *Address temp unknown* E: john@naudeuk.com

NAUMANN, Canon David Sydney. b 26. Ripon Hall Ox 54. **d** 55 **p** 56. C Herne Bay Ch Ch *Cant* 55-58; Asst Chapl United Sheff Hosps 58-60; V Reculver *Cant* 60-64; Dioc Youth Chapl 63-70; R Eastwell w Boughton Aluph 65-67; V Westwell 65-67; Warden St Gabr Retreat Ho Westgate 68-70; V Littlebourne *Cant* 70-82; RD E Bridge 78-82; Hon Can Cant Cathl 81-00; R Sandwich 82-91; RD 85-90; rtd 91; PtO *Cant* from 91. *2 The Forrens, The Precincts, Canterbury CT1 2ER* T: (01227) 458939

NAUNTON, Hugh Raymond. b 38. Whitelands Coll Lon CertEd 69 Open Univ BA 75. Bernard Gilpin Soc Dur 59 Chich Th Coll 60. **d** 63 **p** 64. C Stanground *Ely* 63-66; NSM Woolwich St Mary w H Trin *S'wark* 66-67; NSM Wandsworth St Anne 67-69 and 71-73; NSM Paddington St Sav *Lon* 69-71; NSM Cuddington *Guildf* 73-78; Hd RE Raynes Park High Sch 69-76; Hd RE Paddington Sch 76-78; Sen Teacher and Hd RE Ch Sch Richmond 79-93; Hon C Cheam Common St Phil *S'wark* 79-95; C Cheam 95-02; PtO *Guildf* 97-02 and from 04; TV Selsdon St Jo w St Fran *S'wark* 02-03; rtd 03; PtO *S'wark* from 04. *35 Farm Way, Worcester Park KT4 8RZ* T: (020) 8395 1748 M: 07899-255852 E: hugh.naunton@blueyonder.co.uk

NAWROCKYI, Nicholas Daniel. b 85. Dur Univ BA 06 MA 07 Leeds Univ BA 10. Coll of Resurr Mirfield 09. **d** 12 **p** 13. C Gt Grimsby St Mary and St Jas *Linc* from 12. *St Mark's Vicarage, Winchester Avenue, Grimsby DN33 1EW* M: 07912-681092 E: n.d.nawrockyi@dunelm.org.uk

NAY, Ms Imogen Joyce. b 79. York Univ BA 00 Warwick Univ MA 02 Cam Univ BA 08. Westcott Ho Cam 06. **d** 09 **p** 10. C Surbiton St Andr and St Mark *S'wark* 09-13; R Rugby St Andr w St Pet and St John *Cov* from 13. *St Andrew's Rectory, Church Street, Rugby CV21 3PH* M: 07828-064710 E: imogen.nay1@btinternet.com

NAYLOR, Alison Louise. *See* CHESWORTH, Alison Louise

NAYLOR, Barry. *See* NAYLOR, James Barry

NAYLOR, Fiona. b 68. CQSW 93. St Jo Coll Nottm 02. **d** 05 **p** 08. C Len Valley *Cant* 05-06; Hon C Lower Darwen St Jas *Blackb* 07-10; P-in-c Lea 10-12; PtO from 12. *82 Pear Tree Avenue, Coppull, Chorley PR7 4NL* T: (01257) 793283 E: revfionanaylor@btinternet.com

NAYLOR, Canon Frank. b 36. Lon Univ BA 58 Liv Univ MA 63. NW Ord Course 75. **d** 75 **p** 76. NSM Eccleston Ch Ch *Liv* 75-92; Asst Dioc Chapl to the Deaf 92-94; Sen Chapl from 94; Hon Can Liv Cathl from 01. *27 Daresbury Road, Eccleston, St Helens WA10 5DR* T: (01744) 757034

NAYLOR, Ms Gloria. b 60. N Lon Poly BEd 87 Lon Inst of Educn MA 97. Westcott Ho Cam 11. **d** 13 **p** 14. C Islington St Mary *Lon* from 13. *Vicarage Apartment, St Mary's Church, Upper Street, London N1 2TX* M: 07964-951364 E: gloria.naylor@stmaryislington.org

NAYLOR, Grant Lambert. b 87. Univ of Wales (Lamp) BA 09. St Steph Ho Ox 09. **d** 11 **p** 12. C Auckland St Helen *Dur* 11-15; P-in-c Sheff St Matt from 15. *St Matthew's Vicarage, 9 Ashdell Road, Sheffield S10 3DA* E: father.naylor@gmail.com

NAYLOR, The Ven Ian Frederick. b 47. Open Univ BA 92 Heythrop Coll Lon MA 00 AKC 70. St Aug Coll Cant 70. **d** 71 **p** 72. C Camberwell St Giles *S'wark* 71-74; OSB 74-86; Chapl RN 86-04; rtd 04; P-in-c Pau *Eur* 08-15; Adn France from 13; Can Gib Cathl from 13. *Appt 23, 3 bis rue Pasteur, 64000 Pau, France* T: (0033) 5 59 30 91 84 M: 7 88 55 09 80 E: if.naylor@orange.fr

NAYLOR, Ian Stuart. b 63. Wycliffe Hall Ox. **d** 01 **p** 02. C Ipswich St Marg *St E* 01-04; P-in-c Martlesham w Brightwell 04-11; P-in-c Coalbrookdale, Iron-Bridge and Lt Wenlock *Heref* from 11; RD Telford Severn Gorge from 13. *The Rector's House, Paradise, Coalbrookdale, Telford TF8 7NR* T: (01952) 433248 M: 07712-309848 E: iandjnaylor@hotmail.co.uk

NAYLOR, Canon James Barry. b 50. Lon Univ BSc 71 St Benet's Hall Ox BA 75. Wycliffe Hall Ox 72. **d** 76 **p** 76. C Catford (Southend) and Downham *S'wark* 76-79; TV 79-82; P-in-c Lewisham St Swithun 82-87; V E Dulwich St Jo 87-97; RD Dulwich 90-97; P-in-c Blythburgh w Reydon *St E* 97-99; P-in-c Wrentham w Benacre, Covehithe, Frostenden etc 97-99; P-in-c Southwold 97-99; TR Sole Bay 99-02; Chapl Supervisor St Felix Sch Southwold 99-02; Can Res Leic Cathl 02-15; C The Abbey Leic 02-08; P-in-c 08-15; C Leic H Spirit 02-08; P-in-c 08-15; rtd 15; Chapl Trin Hosp Leic from 09. *St Andrew's House, 53B Jarrom Street, Leicester LE2 7DH*

NAYLOR, Miss Jean. b 29. Linc Th Coll 77. **dss** 79 **d** 87. Charlton St Luke w H Trin *S'wark* 79-84; Crofton Park St Hilda w St Cypr 84-89; Par Dn 87-89; rtd 89; PtO *Leeds* from 89. *12 Winter Terrace, Barnsley S75 2ES* T: (01226) 204767

NAYLOR, Martin. b 72. Leeds Univ BA 10 Darw Coll Cam PhD 98 Hertf Coll Ox BA 94 ALCM 90. Coll of Resurr Mirfield 08. **d** 10 **p** 11. C Bedford All SS *St Alb* 10-14; P-in-c Batley All SS and Purlwell *Leeds* from 14; P-in-c Hanging Heaton from 14. *The Vicarage, Churchfield Street, Batley WF17 5DL* T: (01924) 473049 E: martin.mna@gmail.com

NAYLOR, Canon Peter Aubrey. b 33. Kelham Th Coll 54 Ely Th Coll 57. **d** 58 **p** 59. C Shepherd's Bush St Steph *Lon* 58-62; C Portsea N End St Mark *Portsm* 62-66; Chapl HM Borstal Portsm 64-66; V Foley Park *Worc* 66-74; V Maidstone All SS w St Phil and H Trin *Cant* 74-81; P-in-c Tovil 79-81; V Maidstone All SS and St Phil w Tovil 81-91; Hon Can Cant Cathl 79-93; RD Sutton 80-86; R Biddenden and Smarden 91-93; P-in-c Leic St Marg and All SS 93-96; P-in-c Leic St Aug 93-96; TR The Abbey Leic 96; rtd 98; PtO *Chich* 98-02; P-in-c Crowborough St Jo 02-09. *11 Park View, Buxted, Uckfield TN22 4LS* T: (01825) 731840

NAYLOR, Peter Edward. b 30. Linc Th Coll 58. **d** 61 **p** 62. C S Beddington St Mich *S'wark* 61-64; V S Lambeth St Ann 64-77; V Nork *Guildf* 77-90; R Ecton *Pet* 90-97; Warden Ecton Ho 90-97; rtd 97; PtO *Ely* 97-01; *Eur* from 03. *48 chemin Mirassou, 64140 Lons, France* T: (0033) 5 59 62 41 68 E: naylor64@orange.fr

NAYLOR, Peter Henry. b 41. MIMechE. Chich Th Coll 64. **d** 67 **p** 68. C Filton *Bris* 67-70; C Brixham *Ex* 70-72; C Leckhampton St Pet *Glouc* 72-76; V Brockworth 76-94; P-in-c Gt Witcombe 91-94; RD Glouc N 91-94; P-in-c The Ampneys w Driffield and Poulton 94-95; R 95-99; P-in-c Cheltenham Em w St Steph 99-07; rtd 07. *20 Glebe Farm Court, Up Hatherley, Cheltenham GL51 3EB*

NAYLOR, Robert James. b 42. CQSW 66. NOC 74. **d** 77 **p** 78. C Aigburth *Liv* 77-80; Soc Resp Officer *Glouc* 80-85; Leonard Cheshire Foundn (Lon) 85-91; Dir The Stable Family Home Trust (Hants) 91-07; NSM The Lulworths, Winfrith Newburgh and Chaldon *Sarum* 98-00; P-in-c 00-07; RD Purbeck 02-07; R Jersey St Mary *Win* 07-13; PtO *Sarum* from 13; *Win* from 13. *Hybridge House, The Launches, West Lulworth, Wareham BH20 5SF* T: (01929) 400539 E: rjn-rectory@tiscali.co.uk

NAYLOR, Russell Stephen. b 45. Leeds Univ BA 70. St Chad's Coll Dur 70. **d** 72 **p** 73. C Chapel Allerton *Ripon* 72-75; Ind Chapl *Liv* 75-81; P-in-c Burtonwood 81-83; V 83-05; rtd 05; PtO *Ches* from 05. *6 Hillside Avenue, Runcorn WA7 4BW* T: (01928) 835139 E: russnaylor@ntlworld.com

NAYLOR, Mrs Shelagh. b 47. I M Marsh Coll of Physical Educn Liv CertEd 68 MBACP. Ban Ord Course 06. **d** 07 **p** 08. NSM Ardudwy *Ban* 07-12; PtO from 12. *Tanyffridd, Heol y Bryn, Harlech LL46 2TU* T: (01766) 780922 M: 07855-057037

NAYLOR, Vivien Frances Damaris. *See* BRADLEY, Vivien Frances Damaris

✠**NAZIR-ALI, The Rt Revd Michael James.** b 49. Karachi Univ BA 70 St Edm Hall Ox BLitt 74 MLitt 81 Fitzw Coll Cam MLitt 77 ACT ThD 85 Bath Univ Hon DLitt 03 Greenwich Univ Hon DLitt 03 Kent Univ Hon DD 04 Westmr Coll Penn (USA) DHumLit 04 Lambeth DD 05. Ridley Hall Cam 70. **d** 74 **p** 76 **c** 84. C Cambridge H Sepulchre w All SS *Ely* 74-76; Tutorial Supervisor Th Cam Univ 74-76; Sen Tutor Karachi Th Coll Pakistan 76-81; Provost Lahore 81-84; Bp Raiwind 84-86; Asst to Abp Cant 86-89; Co-ord of Studies and Ed Lambeth Conf 86-89; Hon C Ox St Giles and SS Phil and Jas w St Marg 86-89; Gen Sec CMS 89-94; Asst Bp S'wark 89-94; Hon C Limpsfield and Titsey 89-94; Can Th Leic Cathl 92-94; Bp Roch 94-09; Visiting Prof Th and RS Univ of Greenwich from 96; Hon Fell St Edm Hall Ox from 99. *c/o 70 Wimpole Street, London W1G 8AX* T: (020) 3327 1130 E: oxtrad@gmail.com

NDALISO, Silumko Vuyani Edwin. b 52. **d** 12. NSM Bishopwearmouth St Nic *Dur* from 12. *107 Cleveland Road, Sunderland SR4 7JP* E: endaliso@hotmail.co.uk

NDEGWA, Timothy. b 81. **d** 04 **p** 05. Kenya 04-11; PtO *S'wark* 11-14. *77 Coldharbour Lane, London SE5 9NS* M: 07504-829190 E: timobet@gmail.com

✠**NDUNGANE, The Most Revd Winston Hugh Njongonkulu.** b 41. K Coll Lon BD 78 AKC 78 MTh 79 FKC 97 Rhodes Univ Hon DD 97 Protestant Th Sem Virginia Hon DD 00 Worc State Coll USA Hon DHL 00 Natal Univ Hon DSocSc 01. St Pet Coll Alice 71. **d** 73 **p** 74 **c** 91. C Atholone S Africa 73-75; C Mitcham St Mark *S'wark* 75-76; C Hammersmith St Pet *Lon* 76-77; C Primrose Hill St Mary w Avenue Road St Paul 77-79; Asst Chapl Paris St Geo *Eur* 79; R Elsies River S Africa 80-81; Prov Liaison Officer 81-84; Prin St Bede's Th Coll Umtata 85-86; Prov Exec Officer 87-91; Bp Kimberley and Kuruman 91-96; Abp Cape Town 96-08. *African Monitor, PO Box 44986, Claremont, Cape Town, 7735 South Africa*

NEAL, Alan. b 27. Trin Coll Bris 82. **d** 84 **p** 85. Hon C Broughty Ferry *Bre* 84-85; P-in-c Dundee St Ninian 85-86; R Lockerbie and Annan *Glas* 86-94; rtd 94. *c/o Mr and Mrs Graham Rew, 3 Vallance Drive, Lockerbie DG11 2DU*

NEAL, Canon Anthony Terrence. b 42. Open Univ BA 84 Leeds Univ CertEd 73 Univ of Wales MPhil 12. Chich Th Coll 65. **d** 68 **p** 69. C Cross Green St Sav and St Hilda *Ripon* 68-73; NSM Hawksworth Wood 73-78; Asst Chapl and Hd RE Abbey Grange High Sch 73-81; NSM Farnley *Ripon* 78-81; Dioc Adv in RE *Truro* 81-85; Children's Officer 85-87; Stewardship Adv *Truro* 87-88; P-in-c St Erth 81-84; V 84-96; P-in-c Phillack w Gwithian and Gwinear 94-96; P-in-c Hayle 94-96; TR Godrevy 96-06; Hon Can Truro Cathl 94-06; C Chacewater w St Day and Carharrack 10-13; C St Stythians w Perranarworthal and Gwennap 10-13; C Devoran 10-13; C Feock 10-13. *11 Adelaide Street, Camborne TR14 8HH* T: (01209) 712733 E: steamerneal@talktalk.net

NEAL, Canon Christopher Charles. b 47. St Pet Coll Ox BA 69. Ridley Hall Cam 69. **d** 72 **p** 73. C Addiscombe St Mary *Cant* 72-76; C Camberley St Paul *Guildf* 76-83; TV 83-86; V Thame w Towersey *Ox* 86-98; TR Thame 98-03; Hon Can Ch Ch 98-03; Dir Miss and Community CMS 03-12; rtd 12. *2 Spinney Court, Brimscombe, Stroud GL5 2PY*

NEAL, Miss Frances Mary. b 37. BEd 76. S'wark Ord Course 94. **d** 96 **p** 97. NSM Catford (Southend) and Downham *S'wark* 96-07; PtO 07-08. *29 Ballamore Road, Downham, Bromley BR1 5LN* T: (020) 8698 6616

NEAL, Gary Roy. b 57. St Jo Coll Nottm 03. **d** 05 **p** 06. C Kinson *Sarum* 05-09; TV Broadwater *Chich* from 09. *St Stephen's Vicarage, 37 Angola Road, Worthing BN14 8DU* T: (01903) 235054 E: gary@cofekinson.org.uk

NEAL, Canon Geoffrey Martin. b 40. AKC 63. **d** 64 **p** 65. C Wandsworth St Paul *S'wark* 64-66; USA 66-68; C Reigate St Mark *S'wark* 68-70; P-in-c Wandsworth St Faith 70-72; V 72-75; V Houghton Regis *St Alb* 75-95; Hon Can St Alb 93-95; rtd 00; PtO *St Alb* from 00; *Pet* from 10. *63 The Moor, Carlton, Bedford MK43 7JS* T: (01234) 720938

NEAL, James Frederick Charles. b 87. Nottm Univ BA 08. Trin Coll Bris 12. **d** 14 **p** 15. C Ashton-upon-Mersey St Mary Magd *Ches* from 14. *109 Ascot Avenue, Sale M33 4GT* M: 07734-360421 E: jamesfcneal@gmail.com

NEAL, John Edward. b 44. Nottm Univ BTh 74 Heythrop Coll Lon MA 04. Linc Th Coll 70. **d** 74 **p** 75. C Lee St Marg *S'wark* 74-77; C Clapham St Jo 77; C Clapham Ch Ch and St Jo 77-81; P-in-c Eltham St Barn 81-83; V 83-98; Sub-Dean Eltham 89-90; Sub-Dean Greenwich S 91-96; RD Greenwich S 97-01; V Eltham St Jo 98-09; rtd 09; PtO *Eur* from 10. *4 Square Mantegna, 37000 Tours, France* T: (0033) 2 47 64 07 92 E: johnlesneal@orange.fr

NEAL, Mrs Maxine Elner. b 56. Univ of Wales (Abth) BA 78 Wolv Univ PGCE 94. WEMTC 09. **d** 11 **p** 12. OLM Ford, Gt Wollaston and Alberbury w Cardeston *Heref* from 11. *Bank House, Coedway, Shrewsbury SY5 9AR* T: (01743) 884095 E: nealmaxine@hotmail.com

NEAL, Stephen Charles. b 44. K Coll Lon BSc 66 MCMI 76. NOC 90. **d** 93 **p** 94. C Walmsley *Man* 93-96; P-in-c Bolton St Matt w St Barn 96-98; TV Halliwell 98-02; Chapl Bolton Hospice 02-05; PtO *Man* 05-08; *Derby* from 08; *Eur* from 08; rtd 09; Asst Chapl Derby Hosps NHS Foundn Trust from 09. *21 Utah Close, Hilton, Derby DE65 5JA* T: (01283) 480450 - M: 07775-794890 E: stephencneal@yahoo.co.uk

NEALE, Alan James Robert. b 52. LSE BSc(Econ) 73. Wycliffe Hall Ox BA 76 MA 81. **d** 77 **p** 78. C Plymouth St Andr w St Paul and St Geo *Ex* 77-80; C Portswood Ch Ch *Win* 80-82; V Stanstead Abbots *St Alb* 82-85; Asst Master Chelmsf Hall Sch Eastbourne *Chich* 85-88; R Brookings St Paul USA 88-90; R Middletown St Columba 91-04; R Philadelphia

St Columba from 04. *316 S 16th Street, Philadelphia PA 19102, USA* T: (001) (215) 567 1267 F: 567 3766

NEALE, Andrew Jackson. b 58. Oak Hill Th Coll 97. **d** 99 **p** 00. C Harold Hill St Geo *Chelmsf* 99-02; C Bentley Common, Kelvedon Hatch and Navestock 02-03; TV Chigwell and Chigwell Row 03-10; PtO from 10. *Pilgrims' Hall, Ongar Road, Brentwood CM15 9SA* T: (01277) 372206
E: andy.neale2pray@btopenworld.com

NEALE, Canon David. b 50. Lanchester Poly Cov BSc 72. St Mich Coll Llan BD 83. **d** 83 **p** 84. Min Can St Woolos Cathl 83-87; Chapl St Woolos Hosp Newport 85-87; R Blaina and Nantyglo *Mon* 87-91; Video and Tech Officer Bd of Miss 91-01; TV Cyncoed *Mon* 99-01; Creative Resources Officer 01-03; V Maindee Newport *Mon* from 03; AD Newport from 09; Can St Woolos Cathl from 12. *St John's Vicarage, 25 St John's Road, Newport NP19 8GR* T: (01633) 674155
E: dneale@ntlworld.com

NEALE, Edward. *See* NEALE, James Edward McKenzie

NEALE, Geoffrey Arthur. b 41. Brasted Th Coll 61 St Aid Birkenhead 63. **d** 65 **p** 66. C Stoke *Cov* 65-68; C Fareham H Trin *Portsm* 68-71; TV 71-72; R Binstead 72-77; TR Bottesford w Ashby *Linc* 77-80; V Horncastle w Low Toynton 80-90; V Brigg 90-95; V Blockley w Aston Magna and Bourton on the Hill *Glouc* 95-01; Local Min Officer 95-01; V Heath and Reach *St Alb* 01-05; TV Billington, Egginton, Hockliffe etc 06; RD Dunstable 02-04; rtd 06; PtO *Cant* from 06. *46 Cavendish Road, Herne Bay CT6 5BB* T: (01227) 360717 -
M: 07703-174761 E: revd.geoffn@gmail.com

NEALE, Hannah. b 40. SEITE. **d** 99 **p** 00. NSM Mitcham St Mark *S'wark* 99-00; NSM Merton St Jo 00-09; NSM Merton Priory 09; PtO from 09. *42 Palestine Grove, London SW19 2QN* T: (020) 8648 5405

NEALE, Canon James Edward McKenzie (Eddie). b 38. MBE 04. Selw Coll Cam BA 61 Nottm Trent Univ Hon DLitt 00 Nottm Univ Hon DD 03. Clifton Th Coll 61. **d** 63 **p** 64. C Everton St Ambrose w St Tim *Liv* 63-72; Relig Adv BBC Radio Merseyside 72-76; V Bestwood St Matt *S'well* 76-86; Dioc Urban Officer 86-91; V Nottingham St Mary and St Cath 91-03; Hon Can *S'well* Minster 91-03; rtd 03; PtO *S'well* from 03. *Church Cottage, Church Lane, Maplebeck, Nottingham NG22 0BS* T: (01636) 636559
E: eddie@neale007.freeserve.co.uk

NEALE, Mrs Jan Celia. b 42. EMMTC 92. **d** 92 **p** 94. C Gt and Lt Coates w Bradley *Linc* 92-96; TV 96-01; TV Chambersbury *St Alb* 01-07; rtd 07. *1 Dickens Close, St Albans AL3 5PP* T: (01727) 853936

✣**NEALE, The Rt Revd John Robert Geoffrey.** b 26. AKC 54 St Boniface Warminster 54. **d** 55 **p** 56 **c** 74. C St Helier *S'wark* 55-58; Chapl Ardingly Coll 58-62; Recruitment Sec CACTM 63-66; ACCM 66-68; R Hascombe *Guildf* 68-74; Can Missr and Dir Post-Ord Tr 68-74; Hon Can Guildf Cathl 68-74; Adn Wilts *Sarum* 74-80; Area Bp Ramsbury 74-81 and 81-88; Can and Preb Sarum Cathl 74-88; Sec Partnership for World Miss 89-91; Hon Asst Bp Lon and *S'wark* 89-91; rtd 91; Hon Asst Bp B & W 91-08; Bris 92-15; Glouc from 94. *Flat 2, 40 High Street, Corsham SN13 0HB*

NEALE, Martyn William. b 57. G&C Coll Cam BA 78 MA 82. Ripon Coll Cuddesdon 78. **d** 81 **p** 82. C Perry Hill St Geo *S'wark* 81-83; C Purley St Mark 83-85; V Abbey Wood 85-97; V Hawley H Trin *Guildf* from 97; V Minley from 97. *The Vicarage, Hawley, Blackwater, Camberley GU17 9BN* T: (01276) 35287 E: frmartyn@aol.com

NEALE, Paul Edward. b 46. Portsm Coll of Tech BSc 68. **d** 07 **p** 08. OLM Cromer *Nor* from 07. *30 Fulcher Avenue, Cromer NR27 9SG* T: (01263) 513563
E: paulneale127@btinternet.com

NEALE, Mrs Sandra Anne. b 50. Yorks Min Course 12. **d** 13 **p** 14. NSM Lt Horton *Leeds* from 13. *4 Foxcroft Close, Queensbury, Bradford BD13 2DG* T: (01274) 816168
M: 07729-338618 E: sandineale@hotmail.co.uk

NEARY (née TAYLOR), Mrs Joanna Beatrice. b 74. Warwick Univ BA 96 Homerton Coll Cam PGCE 97. St Jo Coll Nottm 04. **d** 06 **p** 07. C Northolt St Jos *Lon* 06-09; NSM Charminster and Stinsford *Sarum* 10-12; TV Beaminster Area from 12. *The Vicarage, Orchard Mead, Broadwindsor, Beaminster DT8 3RA* T: (01308) 867816 M: 07939-062409
E: revneary@gmail.com

NEAUM, Canon Andrew David Irwin. b 45. Lon Univ BA 67 PGCE 68. St Paul's Coll Grahamstown 72. **d** 74 **p** 75. C Salisbury Rhodesia 74-77; R Gatooma Zimbabwe 77-82; V St Helena 82-85; Adn 84-85; R Skipton Australia 85-89; R Ararat 89-95; Can Ballarat 93-95; R Wodonga 95-03; R Shepparton 03-13; Can Wangaratta 02-13; Hon C Boldre w S Baddesley *Win* from 13. *The Vicarage, Pilley Hill, Pilley, Lymington SO41 5QF* T: (01590) 717439
E: andrew.neaum@gmail.com

NEAUM, David Andrew. b 79. Trin Coll Melbourne BA 01 SS Coll Cam BA 06 Em Coll Cam MPhil 08. Westcott Ho Cam 04 Yale Div Sch 06. **d** 07 **p** 08. NSM Cambridge St Mary Less Ely 07-08; C Marnhull *Sarum* 08-11; C Ox St Mary V w St Cross and St Pet 11-13; Asst Chapl Keble Coll Ox 11-12; Chapl and Fell St Cath Coll Cam from 13. *St Catharine's College, Cambridge CB2 1RL* T: (01223) 338346
M: 07411-675157 E: david.neaum@gmail.com *or* chaplain@caths.cam.ac.uk

NEAVE, Garry Reginald. b 51. Leic Univ BA 72 MA 73 PGCE 74 MCMI. S'wark Ord Course. **d** 82 **p** 83. NSM Harlow St Mary Magd *Chelmsf* 82-87 and from 92; NSM St Mary-at-Latton 87-92; Chapl and Asst Prin Harlow Tertiary Coll 84-99; Dir Student Services and Admin W Herts Coll 99-04; Educn Dir Girls' Day Sch Trust from 04. *35 Perry Spring, Harlow CM17 9DQ* T: (01279) 411775

NEED, Canon Philip Alan. b 54. AKC 75. Chich Th Coll 76. **d** 77 **p** 78. C Clapham Ch Ch and St Jo *S'wark* 77-79; C Luton All SS w St Pet *St Alb* 80-83; V Harlow St Mary Magd *Chelmsf* 83-89; P-in-c Chaddesden St Phil *Derby* 89-91; Bp's Dom Chapl *Chelmsf* 91-96; R Bocking St Mary 96-13; Dean Bocking 96-13; RD Braintree 00-06 and 09-13; Dioc Dir of Ords from 13; Hon Can Chelmsf Cathl from 07. *25 The Lintons, Sandon, Chelmsford CM2 7UA* T: (01245) 472212 *or* 294421
E: ddo@chelmsford.anglican.org

NEED, Stephen William. b 57. K Coll Lon BD 79 MTh 83 PhD 93 AKC 79 FRSA 95. **d** 08 **p** 08. Dean St Geo Coll Jerusalem 05-11; C St Geo Cathl 08-11; P-in-c Stock Harvard *Chelmsf* from 11; P-in-c W Hanningfield from 11. *The Rectory, 61 High Street, Stock, Ingatestone CM4 9BN* T: (01277) 840442

NEEDHAM, Mrs Marian Ruth. b 52. Birm Univ BMus 74 City Univ MA 96. NOC 06. **d** 08 **p** 09. NSM Ches H Trin 08-12; NSM Dodleston 12-15; NSM Chase *Ox* from 15. *The Vicarage, Church Enstone, Chipping Norton OX7 4NL* T: (01244) 610339 F: 571857 E: marianrnmailbox-rev@yahoo.co.uk

NEEDHAM, Brother Peter Douglas. b 56. Chich Th Coll 86. **d** 88 **p** 88. SSF from 80; C S Moor *Dur* 88-90; Chapl RN 91-93; LtO *Newc* 91-96; *Lon* 97-99; C Ealing Ch the Sav 99-02; P-in-c Grimethorpe *Wakef* 02-05; V Grimethorpe w Brierley 05-12; Chapl Barnsley Hosp NHS Foundn Trust from 12. *The Vicarage, Manchester Road, Thurlstone, Sheffield S36 9QS*
E: needham278@oal.com

NEEDLE, Mrs Jill Mary. b 56. Matlock Coll of Educn TCert 77 BEd 78. St Jo Coll Nottm 03. **d** 05 **p** 06. NSM Allestree St Nic *Derby* from 05; NSM Quarndon from 05. *117 Hazelwood Road, Duffield, Belper DE56 4AA* T: (01332) 840746
E: jill.needle@btinternet.com

NEEDLE, Paul Robert. b 45. Oak Hill Th Coll 67. **d** 70 **p** 71. C Gt Horton *Bradf* 70-74; C Pudsey St Lawr 74-77; Hon C Horton and Chapl St Luke's Hosp Bradf 78-80; NSM Irthlingborough *Pet* 87-90; NSM Gt w Lt Addington 90-94; NSM Gt w Lt Addington and Woodford 94-98; Bp's Media Adv 94-02; NSM Higham Ferrers w Chelveston 02-06; Bp's Communications Officer *Eur* from 05; P-in-c Costa Azahar 07-12; PtO *Pet* 07-13; Hon C Higham Ferrers w Chelveston from 13. *3 Bishops Court, Chichele Street, Higham Ferrers, Rushden NN10 8HT* T: (01933) 316339 M: 07833-372439 E: paulneedle@aol.com

NEEDLE, Richard John. b 57. Bath Univ BPharm 78 PhD 83 MRPharmS 79. ERMC 04. **d** 07 **p** 08. NSM Sproughton w Burstall, Copdock w Washbrook etc *St E* 07-11; NSM E Bergholt and Brantham from 11. *Meadowside, Gandish Road, East Bergholt, Colchester CO7 6UR* T: (01206) 298859
E: richard.needle@btinternet.com

NEEDS, Michael John. b 42. Open Univ BA 82 Univ of Wales (Swansea) MSc 84 PhD 87. Wycliffe Hall Ox 91. **d** 93 **p** 94. C Aberystwyth *St D* 93-96; R Llanllwchaearn and Llanina 96-06; rtd 07; P-in-c Martletwy w Lawrenny and Minwear etc *St D* 07-09. *Inglemere, Pentwyn Road, Nelson, Treharris CF46 6HE* T: (01443) 453137 E: michaeljohnneeds@aol.com

NEIL, Prof Peter Sydney. b 62. Edin Univ MA 83 MEd 86 QUB PhD 95 MDiv 03 Cardiff Univ MPhil 10 FHEA FRSA. **d** 08 **p** 09. NSM Elerch w Penrhyncoch w Capel Bangor and Goginan *St D* 08-09; NSM Ayr *Glas* 09-13; Vice Chan Bp Grosseteste Univ from 13; Gen Preacher *Linc* from 13; Can and Preb Linc Cathl from 14. *Vice Chancellor's House, Bishop Grosseteste University, Longdales Road, Lincoln LN1 3DY* T: (01522) 523166 M: 07801-458694
E: vicechancellor@bishopg.ac.uk

NEILAND, Paul Andrew. b 62. CITC 00. **d** 01 **p** 02. Aux Min Enniscorthy w Clone, Clonmore, Monart etc *C & O* 01-05; Aux Min Wexford w Ardcolm and Killurin 05-09; Aux Min Wexford and Kilscoran Union from 10. *6 Plásán, Bridgetown, Co Wexford, Republic of Ireland* M: 87-242 2842 T: (00353) (53) 917 5606

NEILL, Barbara June. b 39. St Jo Coll Nottm. **d** 00 **p** 01. NSM Bestwood Park w Rise Park *S'well* 99-09; rtd 09. *17 Harvest Close, Nottingham NG5 9BW* T: 0115-975 3378
E: barbjn@btopenworld.com

✠**NEILL, The Rt Revd John Robert Winder.** b 45. TCD BA 66 MA 69 Jes Coll Cam BA 68 MA 72 NUI Hon LLD 03. Ridley Hall Cam 67. **d** 69 **p** 70 **c** 86. C Glenageary *D & G* 69-71; Lect CITC 70-71 and 82-84; Dioc Registrar (Ossory, Ferns and Leighlin) *C & O* 71-74; Bp's V, Lib and Registrar Kilkenny Cathl 71-74; I Abbeystrewry C, *C & R* 74-78; I Dublin St Bart w Leeson Park *D & G* 78-84; Chapl Community of St Jo the Ev 78-84; Dean Waterford *C & O* 84-86; Prec Lismore Cathl 84-86; Adn Waterford 84-86; I Waterford w Killea, Drumcannon and Dunhill 84-86; Bp T, K & A 86-97; Bp *C & O* 97-02; Abp Dublin *D & G* 02-11; Preb Cualaun St Patr Cathl Dublin 02-11; rtd 11. *Knockglass, Annamult Road, Bennettsbridge, Co Kilkenny, Republic of Ireland* T: (00353) (56) 772 7707
E: jrwneill@eircom.net

NEILL, Richard Walter. b 67. Wadh Coll Ox BA 89 Em Coll Cam BA 92. Westcott Ho Cam 90. **d** 93 **p** 94. C Abbots Langley *St Alb* 93-97; C Wisley w Pyrford *Guildf* 97-00; V Winkfield and Cranbourne *Ox* 00-08; V Wedmore w Theale and Blackford *B & W* from 08; P-in-c Chapel Allerton from 14. *The Vicarage, Manor Lane, Wedmore BS28 4EL* T: (01934) 713566 E: neill.hall@care4free.net

NEILL, Canon Robert Chapman. b 51. Lon Univ BD 82. CITC 77. **d** 77 **p** 78. C Lurgan Ch the Redeemer *D & D* 77-82; I Tullylish 82-88; I Mt Merrion 88-98; I Drumbo from 98; Can Down Cathl from 07. *Drumbo Rectory, 5 Pinehill Road, Ballylesson, Belfast BT8 8LA* T: (028) 9082 6225
E: rc.neill@talktalk.net

NEILL, Stephen Herman. b 69. TCD BA 91. CITC 91. **d** 93 **p** 94. C Monkstown *D & G* 93-95; Dom Chapl to Bp of Killaloe and Clonfert *L & K* 95-15; C Limerick City 95-98; I Cloughjordan w Borrisokane etc 98-15; Can Limerick Cathl 04-15; I Celbridge w Straffan and Newcastle-Lyons *D & G* from 15. *The Rectory, Maynooth Road, Celbridge, Co Kildare, Republic of Ireland* M: (00353) 87-232 8172 E: paddyanglican@eircom.net

NEILL, The Ven William Barnet. b 30. TCD BA 61. **d** 63 **p** 64. C Belfast St Clem *D & D* 63-66; C Dundonald 66-72; I Drumgath 72-80; I Drumgooland 76-80; I Mt Merrion 80-83; I Dromore Cathl 83-97; Adn Dromore 85-97; rtd 97. *10 Cairnshill Court, Saintfield Road, Belfast BT8 4TX* T: (028) 9079 2969

NEILL, William Benjamin Alan. b 46. Open Univ BA 76. CITC 68. **d** 71 **p** 72. C Dunmurry *Conn* 71-74; C Coleraine 75-77; C Dublin St Ann w St Steph *D & G* 77-78; I Convoy w Monellan and Donaghmore *D & R* 78-81; I Faughanvale 81-86; I Waterford w Killea, Drumcannon and Dunhill *C & O* 86-97; Dean Waterford 86-97; Prec Lismore Cathl 86-97; Prec Cashel Cathl 87-97; Can Ossory and Leighlin Cathls 96-97; I Dalkey St Patr *D & G* 97-12; Can Ch Ch Cathl Dublin 04-12; rtd 12. *Cleevaun, 77 Ballinclea Heights, Killiney, Co Dublin, Republic of Ireland* T: (00353) (1) 202 4849
E: neillben77@gmail.com

NELLIST, Canon Valerie Ann. b 48. SRN 69 SCM 71. St And Dioc Tr Course 87. **d** 90 **p** 94. NSM W Fife Team Min *St And* 90-99; R Aberdour 99-13; R Burntisland 99-13; R Inverkeithing 99-13; Hon Can St Ninian's Cathl Perth 97-13; rtd 13. *28 Glamis Gardens, Dalgety Bay, Dunfermline KY11 9TD* T: (01383) 824066 F: 824668
E: valnellist@btinternet.com

NELMES, Mrs Christine. b 41. St Mary's Coll Chelt Dip Teaching 63 UWE BA 97. S Dios Minl Tr Scheme 92. **d** 95 **p** 96. NSM Winscombe *B & W* 95-99; PtO 00-03; P-in-c Mark w Allerton 03-08; rtd 08; PtO *B & W* from 09. *Yarrow Farm, Yarrow Road, Mark, Highbridge TA9 4LW* T: (01278) 641650
E: revcnelmes@googlemail.com

NELSON, Christopher James. b 57. Lanc Univ MA 91. Aston Tr Scheme 83 St Jo Coll Nottm BTh 88. **d** 88 **p** 89. C Blackpool St Thos *Blackb* 88-90; C Altham w Clayton le Moors 90-92; V Knuzden 92-01; V Penwortham St Mary from 01; AD Leyland 04-11. *St Mary's Vicarage, 14 Cop Lane, Penwortham, Preston PR1 0SR* T: (01772) 743143 M: 07858-772421
E: kitnel@btinternet.com

NELSON, Gibson. *See* NELSON, Robert Gibson

NELSON, Graham William. b 61. St Jo Coll Nottm BA 91. **d** 91 **p** 92. C Pype Hayes *Birm* 91-93; C Lancaster St Mary *Blackb* 94-97; Chapl HM Pris Lanc Castle 94-97; P-in-c Preston St Jude w St Paul *Blackb* 97-06; P-in-c Preston St Oswald 01-06; P-in-c Preston St Oswald w St Jude from 06. *Deepdale Vicarage, 97 Garstang Road, Preston PR1 1LD* T: (01772) 252987
E: gw.nelson@btinternet.com

NELSON, Hugh Edmund. b 72. Worc Coll Ox BA 94. Ripon Coll Cuddesdon 07. **d** 09 **p** 10. C Newington w Hartlip and Stockbury *Cant* 09-12; C Iwade 09-12; C Upchurch w Lower Halstow 09-12; V Goudhurst w Kilndown from 12. *The Vicarage, Back Lane, Goudhurst, Cranbrook TN17 1AN* T: (01580) 211739 E: hugh.nelson@ymail.com

NELSON, Jane. b 42. **d** 94 **p** 99. Par Dn Muchalls *Bre* 94-99; C 99-04; Asst Chapl Grampian Healthcare NHS Trust 93-97; NSM Brechin *Bre* 04-14; NSM Tarfside from 05. *4 St Michael's Road, Newtonhill, Stonehaven AB39 3RW* T: (01569) 730967 E: nelson.jane1@btinternet.com

NELSON, Mrs Julie. b 52. St Aid Coll Dur BA 73 Ex Univ MA 95. SWMTC 92. **d** 95 **p** 96. NSM Tavistock and Gulworthy *Ex* 95-01; Germany 01-04; P-in-c Kirklington w Burneston and Wath and Pickhill *Ripon* 04-10; AD Wensley 08-10; Dioc Adv on Women's Min 08-10; R Panfield and Rayne *Chelmsf* 10-15; Dioc Rural Officer 10-15; rtd 15. *41 Blencathra Street, Keswick CA12 4HX* E: rev.julienelson@googlemail.com

NELSON, Marcus John Reginald. b 81. QUB LLB 03. Wycliffe Hall Ox BA 11. **d** 11 **p** 12. C Plymouth St Andr and Stonehouse *Ex* 11-15; V Bris St Matt and St Nath from 15. *St Matthew's Vicarage, 11 Glentworth Road, Bristol BS6 7EG* M: 07731-424874 T: 0117-942 4186
E: marcusjrnelson@gmail.com

NELSON, Michael. b 44. Newc Univ Aus BSc 68 BA 72 St Jo Coll Cam BA 74 Cam Univ MA 78. Westcott Ho Cam 74. **d** 75 **p** 76. PtO *Newc* 75; Australia from 77. *185 Burbong Street, Chapel Hill Qld 4069, Australia* T: (0061) (7) 3720 1283 F: 3720 1620 E: mnelson@hradvantage.com.au

NELSON, Sister Norma Margaret. b 34. Liv Univ DASS 77 CQSW 77. CA Tr Coll IDC 60. **d** 93 **p** 94. Team Dn Kirkby *Liv* 93-94; TV 94-95; rtd 95; PtO *Liv* from 95. *15 Pateley Close, Kirkby, Liverpool L32 4UT* T: 0151-292 0255

NELSON, Canon Paul John. b 52. Nottm Univ BCombStuds 84. Linc Th Coll 81. **d** 84 **p** 85. C Waltham Cross *St Alb* 84-87; C Sandridge 87-90; V 90-98; R Hundred River *St E* 98-13; C Wainford 06-13; R Hundred River and Wainford 13-15; RD Beccles and S Elmham 03-11; Hon Can St E Cathl 08-15; rtd 15. *The Rectory, Moll's Lane, Brampton, Beccles NR34 8DB* T: (01502) 575859

NELSON, Peter Joseph. b 46. Nottm Poly BSc 73. N Bapt Coll 82 NEOC 99. **d** 99 **p** 99. In Bapt Min 85-99; Chapl R Hull Hosps NHS Trust 94-99; Chapl Hull and E Yorks Hosps NHS Trust 99-02; Sen Chapl 02-11; NSM Sutton St Mich *York* 99-06; rtd 11; PtO *York* from 11. *Cobblestones, 1 Low Street, Sancton, York YO43 4QZ* T: (01430) 828779

NELSON, Ralph Archbold. b 27. St Cuth Soc Dur BA 50. Bps' Coll Cheshunt 50. **d** 52 **p** 53. C Penwortham St Mary *Blackb* 52-57; C Eglingham *Newc* 57-58; V Featherstone *Wakef* 58-80; V Kirkham *Blackb* 80-92; RD 88-91; rtd 92; PtO *Blackb* from 92. *6 Blundell Lane, Penwortham, Preston PR1 0EA* T: (01772) 742573

NELSON, Robert Gibson. b 34. ALCD 61. **d** 61 **p** 62. C Isleworth St Mary *Lon* 61-64; C-in-c Reading St Barn CD *Ox* 64-69; R Margaret River Australia 69-72; V Guernsey St Jo *Win* 72-78; R Guernsey Ste Marie du Castel 78-86; V Guernsey St Matt 84-86; rtd 86; PtO *Win* from 86. *Le Petit Feugre, Clos des Mielles, Castel, Guernsey GY5 7XB* T: (01481) 52726

NELSON, Robert Towers. b 43. MSOSc Liv Coll of Tech BSc 65. NW Ord Course 76. **d** 79 **p** 80. NSM Liv Our Lady and St Nic w St Anne 79-83; NSM Liscard St Thos *Ches* 83-87; P-in-c 87-12; V from 12; Ind Missr from 87; Asst Sec SOSc from 89; PtO *Liv* 89-98; Chapl Wirral and W Cheshire Community NHS Trust 98-03. *5 Sedbergh Road, Wallasey CH44 2BR* T: 0151-630 2830
E: rtnelson43@googlemail.com

NELSON, Roger Charles. b 44. ATII 74 Newc Univ LLB 66 Solicitor 69. Cant Sch of Min 88. **d** 91 **p** 92. NSM Deal St Leon and St Rich and Sholden *Cant* 91-96; NSM Northbourne and Gt Mongeham w Ripple and Sutton by Dover 96-97; PtO 97-00; Leeds from 01. *26 Meal Hill Road, Holme, Holmfirth HD9 2QQ* T: (01484) 680309
E: nelsontrap@aol.com

NELSON, Warren David. b 38. TCD BA 67. **d** 68 **p** 69. C Belfast St Mich *Conn* 68-70; I Kilcooley w Littleton, Crohane, Killenaule etc *C & O* 70-76; Chapl Coalbrook Fellowship Hosp Ho Thurles 76-94; PtO (Cashel, Waterford and Lismore) *C & O* 93-94; I Lurgan w Billis, Killinkere and Munterconnaught *K, E & A* 94-98; rtd 98. *6 Mucklagh, Tullamore, Co Offaly, Republic of Ireland* T: (00353) (57) 932 4218 E: wnelson@eircom.net

NELSON, William. b 38. Oak Hill Th Coll 74. **d** 76 **p** 77. C Hensingham *Carl* 76-80; I Widnes St Paul *Liv* 81-89; R Higher Openshaw *Man* 89-03; AD Ardwick 96-00; rtd 03; PtO *S'well* from 03. *215 Stapleford Road, Trowell, Nottingham NG9 3QE* T: 0115-932 2910

NENER, Canon Thomas Paul Edgar. b 42. Liv Univ MB, ChB FRCSEd 71 FRCS 71. Coll of Resurr Mirfield 78. **d** 80 **p** 81. C Warrington St Elphin *Liv* 80-83; V Haydock St Jas 83-95; V W Derby St Jo 95-10; Hon Can Liv Cathl 95-10; rtd 10. *16 Princes Park Mansions, Croxteth Road, Liverpool L8 3SA* T: 0151-726 7003

NENO, David Edward. b 62. SS Mark & Jo Univ Coll Plymouth BA 85. Ripon Coll Cuddesdon 85. **d** 88 **p** 89. C Chapel Allerton *Ripon* 88-91; C Acton St Mary *Lon* 91-94; V Kingsbury H Innocents 94-02; R Brondesbury Ch Ch and St Laur 02-12; V Ealing St Pet Mt Park from 12. *St Peter's Vicarage, 56 Mount Park Road, London W5 2RU* T: (020) 8997 1620 M: 07976-905294 E: david.neno@virginmedia.com

NESBITT, Heather Hastings. b 48. S'wark Ord Course 88. **d** 90 **p** 94. C Addiscombe St Mary Magd w St Martin 94-01; TV Sutton St Jas and Wawne *York* 01-10; rtd 10. *21 Glengarry Way, Greylees, Sleaford NG34 8XU* T: (01529) 419298 E: h.nesbitt@yahoo.co.uk

NESBITT, Mrs Patricia Ann. **d** 14 **p** 15. OLM Bloxwich *Lich* from 14. *39 Glastonbury Crescent, Walsall WS3 2RF* T: (01922) 446928 E: jumpforjoy1957@hotmail.com

NESBITT, Patrick Joseph. b 72. St Martin's Coll Lanc BA 96. St Jo Coll Nottm 00. **d** 03 **p** 04. C Blackpool St Thos *Blackb* 03-07; TV Kinson and W Howe *Sarum* 07-13. *16 Croft Road, Ringwood BH24 1TA* M: 07879-660100 E: patricknesbitt72@hotmail.com

NESBITT, Canon Ronald. b 58. Sheff Univ LLB. CITC 82. **d** 85 **p** 86. C Ballymena w Ballyclug *Conn* 85-88; C Holywood *D & D* 88-90; I Helen's Bay 90-96; I Bangor Abbey from 96; Can Belf Cathl from 04. *The Abbey Rectory, 5 Downshire Road, Bangor BT20 3TW* T: (028) 9146 0173 *or* 9145 1087 E: ronnienesbitt@aol.com *or* bangorabbeyparish@gmail.com

NESBITT, Miss Wilhelmina. b 65. Qu Coll Birm 98. **d** 00 **p** 01. C Bridgnorth, Tasley, Astley Abbotts, etc *Heref* 00-04; TV Saddleworth *Man* 04-08; I Fanlobbus Union *C, C & R* 08-13. *157 Fairview Road, Newtownabbey BT36 6QN*

NESTOR, Cordelia Frances. **d** 12. NSM Plumstead Common *S'wark* 12-15; NSM Catford (Southend) and Downham from 15. *19 Aislibie Road, London SE12 8QH* T: (020) 8852 8152

NETHERWAY, Diana Margaret. b 47. Bp Otter Coll 94. **d** 96. NSM Northwood *Portsm* from 96; NSM Gurnard 96-14; Asst Chapl Isle of Wight NHS Primary Care Trust from 09; NSM Gurnard w Cowes St Faith *Portsm* from 14. *138 Bellevue Road, Cowes PO31 7LD* T: (01983) 298505 E: revdiana@onwight.net

NETHERWOOD, Mrs Anne Christine. b 43. Liv Univ BArch 66 Lon Univ BD 92 ARIBA 68. St Deiniol's Hawarden 88. **d** 91 **p** 94. NSM Ellesmere and Welsh Frankton *Lich* 91-94; C Dudleston 94-97; C Criftins 94-97; C Criftins w Dudleston and Welsh Frankton 97; P-in-c 97-10; rtd 10; PtO *Lich* 10-12; Hon C Pradoe from 12. *11 Cottage Fields, St Martins, Oswestry SY11 3EJ* T: (01691) 778495 E: anne_netherwood@talk21.com

NEUDEGG, Mrs Joan Mary. b 36. Cant Sch of Min 81. **dss** 84 **d** 87 **p** 94. Chalk *Roch* 84-86; Hon C Dean Forest H Trin *Glouc* 87-90; Hon C Woolaston w Alvington 90-95; Hon C Woolaston w Alvington and Aylburton 95-96; rtd 96; PtO *Ex* from 96. *48 Marker Way, Honiton EX14 2EN* T: (01404) 43957

NEUPERT, Douglas Alan. b 46. Chris Newport Univ (USA) BA 78. **d** 99 **p** 00. OLM Blackbourne *St E* 99-13; NSM 13-14; rtd 15. *Hall Farm, Troston, Bury St Edmunds IP31 1EZ* T: (01359) 269614 M: 07944-214417 E: doug.neupert@talktalk.net

NEVILL, James Michael. b 50. Cranmer Hall Dur 84. **d** 86 **p** 87. C Sowerby Bridge w Norland *Wakef* 86-91; CF 91-94; TV Broadwater *Chich* 94-99; Chapl St Mich Hospice Hereford 99-05; Spiritual Care Co-ord St Cath Hospice Crawley 05-15; rtd 15. *Teviotdale, Ivy Close, Ashington, Pulborough RH20 3LW* E: mikenevill1509@sky.com

NEVILL, Mavis Hetty. b 45. Bradf Univ BEd 95. NOC 92. **d** 95 **p** 96. NSM Mount Pellon *Wakef* 95-99; P-in-c Mixenden 99-04; Hon C Harden and Wilsden *Bradf* 06-07; P-in-c Steeton 07-11; rtd 11; PtO *Leeds* from 11. *1 Willow Bank Close, Allerton, Bradford BD15 7YL* T: (01274) 813584 E: mh.nevill@btinternet.com

NEVILLE, Alfred John. b 21. K Coll Lon BA 40. Sarum & Wells Th Coll 80. **d** 83 **p** 84. NSM Weston-super-Mare St Paul *B & W* 83-93; PtO from 93. *10 Clarence House, 17 Clarence Road North, Weston-super-Mare BS23 4AS* T: (01934) 631176 E: john.neville@lockdeanhsl.co.uk

NEVILLE, David Bruce. b 61. Ravensbourne Coll of Art & Design BA 83. St Jo Coll Nottm 87. **d** 91 **p** 92. C Broxtowe *S'well* 91-94; C Attenborough 94-95; PtO 95-97; C Carrington 97-99; C Bulwell St Mary 99-02; PtO from 02. *3 Inham Road, Beeston, Nottingham NG9 4FL* T: 0115-854 5648 E: rev.dnev@virgin.net

NEVILLE, Michael Robert John. b 56. Hatf Coll Dur BA 80 Hughes Hall Cam PGCE 81. Wycliffe Hall Ox 82. **d** 85 **p** 86. C E Twickenham St Steph *Lon* 85-88; Asst Dir Proclamation Trust 88-93; R Fordham *Chelmsf* 93-11; P-in-c Upper Chelsea St Sav and St Simon *Lon* 11; V Upper Chelsea St Simon from

11. *St Simon Zelotes Vicarage, 34 Milner Street, London SW3 2QF* T: (020) 7589 8999 E: mike.neville@btinternet.com

NEVILLE, Paul Stewart David. b 61. Wycliffe Hall Ox 98. **d** 00 **p** 01. C Chester le Street *Dur* 00-03; R Middleton St George and Sadberge 03-13; P-in-c Stockton H Trin w St Mark from 13. *The Vicarage, 76 Fairfield Road, Stockton-on-Tees TS19 7BP* T: (01642) 640863 E: prevnev@gmail.com

NEVIN, Alan Joseph. b 51. Univ Coll Galway BA 72 MCIPD 80. CITC 87. **d** 92 **p** 93. Aux Min Youghal Union *C, C & R* 92-94; Aux Min Waterford w Killea, Drumcannon and Dunhill *C & O* 94-95; C 95-98; I Buncloudy w Kildavin, Clonegal and Kilrush 98-04; I Clonfert Gp *L & K* 04-15; rtd 15. *109 Castlelawn Heights, Galway, Republic of Ireland* M: (00353) 85-860 7597

NEVIN, Graham Harold. b 45. QUB BSc 68 MSc 72 Ulster Poly CertEd 74 FGS 75. St Jo Coll Nottm 06. **d** 09 **p** 10. NSM Billy w Derrykeighan *Conn* 09-14; NSM Armoy w Loughguile and Drumtullagh from 14. *11 Carthall Crescent, Coleraine BT51 3LT* T: (028) 7035 3713 E: graham@carthall.fsnet.co.uk

NEW, Brian Philip. b 59. **d** 13 **p** 14. NSM Nuthurst and Mannings Heath *Chich* from 13. *6 Lapwing Close, Horsham RH13 5PB* T: (01403) 251068 M: 07787-144669

NEW, David John. b 37. Lon Univ BScEng 58. Chich Th Coll 65. **d** 67 **p** 68. C Folkestone St Mary and St Eanswythe *Cant* 67-72; C Kings Heath *Birm* 72-74; V S Yardley St Mich 74-83; V Moseley St Agnes 83-00; rtd 00; PtO *Worc* from 00. *6 Falmouth, Worcester WR4 0TE* T: (01905) 458084 E: davidnew@talktalk.net

NEW, Derek. b 30. **d** 86 **p** 87. NSM Brondesbury St Anne w Kilburn H Trin *Lon* 86-98; NSM Willesden St Matt 99-02; PtO from 02. *20 Lynton Road, London NW6 6BL* T: (020) 7912 0640

NEW, Canon Thomas Stephen. b 30. K Coll Cam BA 52 MA 56. Cuddesdon Coll 52. **d** 54 **p** 55. C Greenford H Cross *Lon* 54-55; C Old St Pancras w Bedford New Town St Matt 55-58; C Woodham *Guildf* 58-64; V Guildf All SS 64-72; V Banstead 72-93; RD Epsom 76-80; Hon Can Guildf Cathl 79-93; Sub-Chapl HM Pris Downview 88-93; rtd 93; PtO *Ex* from 94. *St Katharine's, North Street, Denbury, Newton Abbot TQ12 6DJ* T: (01803) 813775

NEW ZEALAND, Archbishop of. *See* TUREI, The Most Revd William Brown

NEWALL, Arthur William. b 24. Univ of Wales (Lamp) BA 49. Chich Th Coll 49. **d** 51 **p** 52. C Hulme St Phil *Man* 51-53; C Fallowfield 53-55; V Oldham St Barn 55-60; V Aspull *Liv* 60-68; R Foots Cray *Roch* 68-78; V Henlow St Alb 78-89; rtd 89; PtO *Liv* from 89. *38 Fairhaven Road, Southport PR9 9UH* T: (01704) 26045

NEWALL, Richard Lucas. b 43. K Coll Lon AKC 66. **d** 66 **p** 67. C Roby *Liv* 66-69; C Douglas St Geo and St Barn *S & M* 69-71; LtO *Man* 72-75; C Ban St Mary 75-77; R Newborough w Llangeinwen w Llangaffo etc 77-97; R Newborough w Llanidan and Llangeinwen etc 98-07; AD Tindaethwy and Menai 03-07; V Llanilar w Rhostie and Llangwyryfon etc *St D* 07-09; rtd 09. *Himmelbjerg, 18 Maesydderwen, Cardigan SA43 1PE* T: (01239) 623816

NEWARK, Archdeacon of. *See* PICKEN, The Ven David Anthony

NEWBOLD, Mrs Caroline Sarah. b 62. K Alfred's Coll Win BA 83 Homerton Coll Cam PGCE 85. St Mellitus Coll BA 10. **d** 10 **p** 11. C Yiewsley 10-13; Chapl Lady Margaret Sch from 13; Hon C Ealing St Steph Castle Hill *Lon* from 13. *St Stephen's Vicarage, Sherborne Gardens, London W13 8AQ* T: (020) 7736 7138 M: 07958-073583 E: chaplain@ladymargaret.lbhf.sch.uk

NEWBOLD, Stephen Mark. b 60. Trin Coll Bris 01. **d** 03 **p** 04. C Roxeth *Lon* 03-09; V Ealing St Steph Castle Hill from 09. *St Stephen's Vicarage, Sherborne Gardens, London W13 8AQ* T: (020) 8810 4929

NEWBON, Kenneth. b 29. Wells Th Coll 67. **d** 69 **p** 70. C Church Stretton *Heref* 69-72; P-in-c Cressage w Sheinton 72-75; R Braunstone *Leic* 75-81; TR 81-84; P-in-c Eardisley w Bollingham and Willersley *Heref* 84-88; P-in-c Brilley w Michaelchurch on Arrow 84-88; P-in-c Whitney w Winforton 84-88; RD Kington and Weobley 87-95; R Eardisley w Bollingham, Willersley, Brilley etc 88-96; rtd 96; PtO *Heref* 96-14. *Grace Dieu House, Staunton-on-Wye, Hereford HR4 7LT* T: (01981) 500188

NEWBON, Michael Charles. b 59. Oak Hill Th Coll 92. **d** 94 **p** 95. C Bedford St Jo and St Leon *St Alb* 94-99; V Luton St Fran 99-11; P-in-c Georgeham *Ex* 11-15; R from 15. *The Rectory, Newberry Road, Georgeham, Braunton EX33 1JS* T: (01271) 890616 E: mikenewbon@aol.com

NEWBORN, Carol Margaret. b 45. **d** 05 **p** 06. OLM Styvechale *Cov* from 05. *76 The Park Paling, Coventry CV3 5LL* T: (024) 7650 3707 E: rev.carol@newborn.org.uk

NEWBY, Canon Ailsa Ballantyne. b 56. Collingwood Coll Dur BA 78. St Steph Ho Ox 98. **d** 98 **p** 99. C Streatham Ch Ch

S'wark 98-01; V S Lambeth St Anne and All SS 01-10; TR Putney St Mary from 10; Dir IME Kingston Area from 10; Hon Can S'wark Cathl from 15. *3 Wharf Terrace, Deodar Road, London SW15 2JZ* T: (020) 8785 6019
E: rev.newby@btinternet.com

NEWBY, Claire. *See* McILROY, Claire

NEWBY, Mrs Susan. b 48. Lady Spencer Chu Coll of Educn CertEd 70 BEd 71. **d** 04 **p** 05. OLM Adderbury w Milton Ox 04-10; NSM Banbury 10-13. *9 De Quincey Close, Brackley NN13 6LG* T: (01280) 840635 M: 07824-470877
E: revnewby@hotmail.co.uk

NEWCASTLE, Bishop of. *See* WHARTON, The Rt Revd John Martin

NEWCASTLE, Dean of. *See* DALLISTON, The Very Revd Christopher Charles

NEWCOMBE, Andrew Charles. b 70. Melbourne Univ BA 92 BMus 93 Ox Univ BTh 09 Monash Univ Aus DipEd 96 LTCL 93. St Steph Ho Ox 03. **d** 05 **p** 06. C Tottenham St Mary *Lon* 05-08; C Edmonton St Alphege and Ponders End St Matt 08-11; V Hoxton H Trin w St Mary from 11. *Holy Trinity Vicarage, 3 Bletchley Street, London N1 7QG* T: (020) 7253 4796 M: 07931-700675 E: andrewnewcombe@yahoo.co.uk

NEWCOMBE, John Adrian. b 61. Univ of Wales (Lamp) BA 83 SS Paul & Mary Coll Cheltenham PGCE 85. Ripon Coll Cuddesdon 90. **d** 92 **p** 93. C Stroud and Uplands w Slad *Glouc* 92-96; C Nailsworth 96-01; P-in-c Childswyckham w Aston Somerville, Buckland etc 01-05; TV Winchcombe from 05. *New Vicarage, Buckland Road, Childswickham, Broadway WR12 7HH* T: (01386) 853824

NEWCOMBE, John <u>Charles</u> Dymoke. BSc. Ridley Hall Cam. **d** 07 **p** 08. NSM Wimbledon Em Ridgway Prop Chpl *S'wark* 07-10; Asst Chapl Tervuren *Eur* 10-14; C Cambridge H Sepulchre *Ely* from 14. *St Andrew the Great, St Andrew's Street, Cambridge CB2 3AX* T: (01223) 518218
E: charlienewc@clara.co.uk

NEWCOMBE, Canon Timothy James Grahame. b 47. AKC 75. St Aug Coll Cant 75. **d** 76 **p** 77. C Heref St Martin 76-79; C Hitchin *St Alb* 79-85; R Croft and Stoney Stanton *Leic* 85-91; P-in-c Launceston *Truro* 91-92; V 92-97; TR 97-03; Hon Can Truro Cathl 01-03; Chapl Cornwall Healthcare NHS Trust 96-03; V Wotton St Mary *Glouc* 03-12; rtd 12. *18 Kempley Road, Okehampton EX20 1DS* T: (01837) 52901
E: tnewco@btinternet.com

✠**NEWCOME, The Rt Revd James William Scobie.** b 53. Trin Coll Ox BA 74 MA 78 Selw Coll Cam BA 77 MA 81. Ridley Hall Cam 75. **d** 78 **p** 79 **c** 02. C Leavesden *St Alb* 78-82; P-in-c Bar Hill LEP *Ely* 82-92; V Bar Hill 92-94; Tutor Ridley Hall Cam 83-88; P-in-c Dry Drayton *Ely* 89-94; RD N Stowe 93-94; Can Res Ches Cathl and Dioc Dir of Ords 94-02; Dir of Educn and Tr 96-02; Suff Bp Penrith *Carl* 02-09; Bp Carl from 09; Clerk of the Closet from 15. *Bishop's House, Ambleside Road, Keswick CA12 4DD* T: (01768) 773430
E: bishop.carlisle@carlislediocese.org.uk

NEWELL, Christopher David. b 53. Ex Univ MA 03 Win Univ PhD 15. S'wark Ord Course 84. **d** 87 **p** 88. C Stockwell St Mich *S'wark* 87-90; Asst Chapl R Lon Hosp (Whitechapel) 90-92; Asst Chapl R Lon Hosp (Mile End) 90-92; R Birch St Agnes *Man* 92-96; P-in-c Longsight St Jo w St Cypr 94-96; R Birch St Agnes w Longsight St Jo w St Cypr 97; R Lansallos and V Talland *Truro* 97-98; Asst P Liskeard and St Keyne 00-02; C Duloe, Herodsfoot, Morval and St Pinnock 02-03; P-in-c 03-05; C Lansallos and Talland 02-03; Chapl Cornwall Partnership NHS Trust from 02; P-in-c St Goran w Caerhays *Truro* from 14. *The Vicarage, Gorran, St Austell PL26 6HN* T: (01726) 844195
E: christopher.newell@nhs.net

NEWELL, David Walter. b 37. Nottm Univ BSc 57. WEMTC 01. **d** 03 **p** 04. OLM Painswick, Sheepscombe, Cranham, The Edge etc *Glouc* from 03. *Woodside, Kingsmill Lane, Painswick, Stroud GL6 6SA* T: (01452) 812083 E: d.newell083@btinternet.com

NEWELL, Canon Edmund John. b 61. Univ Coll Lon BSc 83 Nuff Coll Ox DPhil 88 MA 89 FRHistS 98 FRSA 08. Ox Min Course 89 Ripon Coll Cuddesdon 92. **d** 94 **p** 95. C Deddington w Barford, Clifton and Hempton *Ox* 94-98; Bp's Dom Chapl 98-01; Chapl Headington Sch 98-01; Can Res St Paul's Cathl 01-08; Chan St Paul's Cathl 03-08; Can Res and Sub-Dean Ch Ch *Ox* 08-13; Prin Cumberland Lodge Windsor from 13; PtO *Ox* from 13; Hon Can Ch Ch from 14. *Cumberland Lodge, The Great Park, Windsor SL4 2HP* T: (01784) 497786 F: 497799 E: enewell@cumberlandlodge.ac.uk

NEWELL, Jack Ernest. b 26. CEng FIChemE ARCS BSc. Glouc Th Course 80. **d** 83 **p** 84. NSM Hempsted *Glouc* 83-96; PtO from 96. *Hempsted House, Rectory Lane, Hempsted, Gloucester GL2 5LW* T: (01452) 523320

NEWELL, Kenneth Ernest. b 22. S Dios Minl Tr Scheme 77. **d** 79 **p** 80. NSM Lynton, Brendon, Countisbury, Lynmouth

etc *Ex* 79-85; TR 85-89; RD Shirwell 84-89; rtd 89; PtO *Ex* 89-09. *Mole End, Lydiate Lane, Lynton EX35 6HE*

NEWELL, Peter James. b 56. SEITE 12. **d** 15. NSM Kennington *Cant* from 15. *16 Silver Birch Grove, Kingsnorth, Ashford TN23 3LX* T: (01233) 502340 M: 07799-023598
E: peternewell06@gmail.com

NEWELL, Samuel James. b 28. TCD BA 53 MA 63. TCD Div Sch Div Test 54. **d** 54 **p** 55. C Belfast St Mary *Conn* 54-57; C Derriaghy 57-60; C Reading St Mary V *Ox* 60-63; V Chesham Ch Ch 63-74; P-in-c Wraysbury 74-78; TV Riverside 78-94; rtd 94; PtO *Ox* 97-10. *41 Redford Road, Windsor SL4 5ST* T: (01753) 862300

NEWELL OF STAFFA, Gerald Frederick Watson. b 34. Sarum Th Coll 56. **d** 59 **p** 61. C Southampton SS Pet and Paul w All SS *Win* 59-61; C Overton w Laverstoke and Freefolk 61-63; CF (TA) 61-63; CF 63-66; R Spennithorne *Ripon* 66-68; R Finghall 66-68; R Hauxwell 66-68; Hon C Steyning *Chich* 74-78; PtO *Ex* 93-95 and 99-00; P-in-c Breamore *Win* 95-98; rtd 99; P-in-c Palermo w Taormina *Eur* 99-00; R Glencarse *Bre* 00-03; PtO *Ox* 04-06 and from 10. *Church Cottage, Compton Beauchamp, Swindon SN6 8NN* T: (01738) 710334

NEWELL PRICE, John Charles. b 29. SS Coll Cam BA 50 MA MB, BChir MRCGP. **d** 91 **p** 94. OLM Frensham *Guildf* 91-99; rtd 99; PtO *Guildf* 99-05. *The Linney, Clamoak, Bere Alston, Yelverton PL20 7BU* T: (01822) 841126

NEWEY, Canon Edmund James. b 71. Linc Coll Ox BA 95 MA 97 Em Coll Cam BA 99 Man Univ PhD 08. Westcott Ho Cam 97. **d** 00 **p** 01. C Birch w Fallowfield *Man* 00-03; R Newmarket St Mary w Exning St Agnes *St E* 03-07; V Handsworth St Andr *Birm* 07-13; AD Handsworth 11-13; Can Res and Sub-Dean Ch Ch *Ox* from 13. *Christ Church, St Aldates, Oxford OX1 1DP* T: (01865) 276278 M: 07986-530511 E: subdean@chch.ox.ac.uk *or* ejnewey@phonecoop.coop

NEWHAM, Simon Frank Eric. b 65. Sheff Univ BSc 87 MSc 89. Trin Coll Bris BA 00. **d** 00 **p** 01. C Horsham *Chich* 00-04; P-in-c Wisborough Green 04-09; V 09-10; RD Petworth 06-09; TR Ifield from 10. *Ifield Rectory, Rusper Road, Ifield, Crawley RH11 0LR* T: (01293) 543126
E: rector@ifieldparish.org

✠**NEWING, The Rt Revd Dom Kenneth Albert.** b 23. Selw Coll Cam BA 53 MA 57. Coll of Resurr Mirfield 53. **d** 55 **p** 56 **c** 82. C Plymstock *Ex* 55-63; R Plympton St Maurice 63-82; RD Plympton 71-76; Preb Ex Cathl 75-82; Adn Plymouth 78-82; Suff Bp Plymouth 82-88; LtO *Ox* 88-93; OSB from 89; rtd 93. *St Benedict's Priory, 19A The Close, Salisbury SP1 2EB*

NEWING, Peter. b 33. Birm Univ CertEd 55 Dur Univ BA 63 Bris Univ BEd 76 State Univ NY BSc 85 EdD 88 Worc Univ BA 12 FRSA 60 FSAScot 59 ACP 67 MCollP 86 FCollT 95 APhS 63 FVCM 01. Cranmer Hall Dur 63. **d** 65 **p** 66. C Blockley w Aston Magna *Glouc* 65-69; P-in-c Taynton 69-75; P-in-c Tibberton 69-75; R Brimpsfield w Elkstone and Syde 75-83; R Brimpsfield, Cranham, Elkstone and Syde 83-97; P-in-c Daglingworth w the Duntisbournes and Winstone 95-97; R Brimpsfield w Birdlip, Syde, Daglingworth etc 97-01; C Redmarley D'Abitot, Bromesberrow, Pauntley etc 01-02; NSM 02-10; rtd 02; PtO *Heref* from 02; *Worc* from 04; *Glouc* from 10. *1 Hambutts Mead, Painswick, Stroud GL6 6RP* T: (01452) 814360

NEWITT, Mark Julian. b 76. Bradf Univ BSc 97 St Jo Coll Dur BA 02. Cranmer Hall Dur 00. **d** 03 **p** 04. C Billing *Pet* 03-06; Asst Chapl Sheff Teaching Hosps NHS Foundn Trust from 06. *Chaplaincy Services, Royal Hallamshire Hospital, Glossop Road, Sheffield S10 2JF* T: 0114-271 1900

NEWLAND, Mrs Patricia Frances. b 35. Edin Univ MA 56. EAMTC 96. **d** 97 **p** 98. NSM Duxford *Ely* 97-02; NSM Hinxton 97-02; NSM Ickleton 97-02; rtd 02; PtO *Ely* from 02. *Ickelton Lodge, 14 Frogge Street, Ickleton, Saffron Walden CB10 1SH* T: (01799) 530268 F: 531146
E: patricia.newland@googlemail.com

NEWLANDS, Christopher William. b 57. Bris Univ BA 79. Westcott Ho Cam 81. **d** 84 **p** 85. C Bishop's Waltham *Portsm* 84-87; Hon C Upham 85-87; Prec, Sacr and Min Can Dur Cathl 87-92; Chapl Bucharest w Sofia *Eur* 92-95; V Shrub End *Chelmsf* 96-04; Bp's Chapl 04-10; P-in-c Lancaster St Mary w St John and St Anne *Blackb* 10-11; V from 11. *The Vicarage, Priory Close, Lancaster LA1 1YZ* T: (01524) 63200
E: cnewlands@gmail.com

NEWLANDS, Prof George McLeod. b 41. Edin Univ MA 63 DLitt 05 Heidelberg Univ BD 66 PhD 70 Ch Coll Cam MA 73 FRSE 08. **d** 82 **p** 82. Lect Cam Univ 73-86; Fell and Dean Trin Hall Cam 82-86; Prof Div Glas Univ 86-08; PtO *Glas* from 86; Hon Fell New Coll Edin Univ from 10. *12 Jamaica Street Lane, Edinburgh EH3 6HQ, or 49 Highsett, Cambridge CB2 1NZ* T: 0131-225 2545 *or* (01223) 569984 M: 07979-691966
E: newlands71@hotmail.com

NEWLING, Scott John. b 77. **d** 08. C Berowra Australia 08-10; PtO *Ely* from 12. *Address temp unknown*
E: scottnewling@gmail.com

NEWLYN, Canon Edwin. b 39. AKC 64. **d** 65 **p** 66. C Belgrave St Mich *Leic* 65-68; Miss to Seamen 68-81; Chapl Santos Brazil 68-69; Asst Chapl Glas and C Glas St Gabr 69-73; Chapl E Lon S Africa 73-76; R W Bank St Pet 75-76; V Fylingdales *York* 81; P-in-c Fylingdales and Hawsker cum Stainsacre 81; V 81-88; RD Whitby 85-92; Sec Dioc Adv Cttee for Care of Chs 87-01; P-in-c Goathland 88-99; Can and Preb York Minster 90-08; rtd 01; PtO *York* from 01. *The Garden Flat, 12 Royal Crescent, Whitby YO21 3EJ* T: (01947) 604533 *or* 606578 F: 602798
E: edwin.newlyn@talktalk.net

✠**NEWMAN, The Rt Revd Adrian.** b 58. Bris Univ BSc 80 MPhil 89. Trin Coll Bris 82. **d** 85 **p** 86 **c** 11. C Forest Gate St Mark *Chelmsf* 85-89; V Hillsborough and Wadsley Bridge *Sheff* 89-96; RD Hallam 94-96; R Birm St Martin w Bordesley St Andr 96-05; Hon Can Birm Cathl 01-05; Dean Roch 05-11; Area Bp Stepney *Lon* from 11. *63 Coborn Road, London E3 2DB* T: (020) 8981 2323 F: 8981 8015
E: bishop.stepney@london.anglican.org

NEWMAN, Mrs Alison Myra. b 55. K Coll Lon BD 77. SEITE 99. **d** 02 **p** 03. C Bromley SS Pet and Paul *Roch* 02-06; C Shortlands 06-08; C Farnborough from 08. *Church House, Leamington Avenue, Orpington BR6 9QB* T: (01689) 854451
E: alison@st-nicks.org.uk

NEWMAN, Christopher David. *See* NEWMAN-DAY, Christopher David

NEWMAN, Daniel. b 85. BNC Ox BA 06 MA 12 BM, BCh 09 Fitzw Coll Cam BA 12. Ridley Hall Cam 10. **d** 13 **p** 14. C Radipole and Melcombe Regis *Sarum* from 13. *16 Lynmoor Road, Weymouth DT4 7TW* E: daniel.r.newman@gmail.com

NEWMAN, David. *See* NEWMAN, Richard David

NEWMAN, David Malcolm. b 54. FSAScot 81 Aber Univ BTh. St Steph Ho Ox 89. **d** 91 **p** 92. C St Mary-at-Latton *Chelmsf* 91-94; R Weeley and Lt Clacton from 94. *The Vicarage, 2 Holland Road, Little Clacton, Clacton-on-Sea CO16 9RS* T: (01255) 860241 E: revdnewman@btinternet.com

NEWMAN, The Ven David Maurice Frederick. b 54. Hertf Coll Ox BA 75 MA 79. St Jo Coll Nottm. **d** 79 **p** 80. C Orpington Ch Ch *Roch* 79-83; C Bushbury *Lich* 83-86; V Ockbrook *Derby* 86-97; TR Loughborough Em and St Mary in Charnwood *Leic* 97-09; RD Akeley E 99-06; Hon Can Leic Cathl 06-09; Adn Loughborough from 09. *The Archdeaconry, 21 Church Road, Glenfield, Leicester LE3 8DP* T: 0116-231 1632

NEWMAN, Mrs Diana Joan. b 43. Sarum Th Coll 81. **dss** 84 **d** 87 **p** 94. Parkstone St Pet and St Osmund w Branksea *Sarum* from 84; NSM from 87; TV 96-02. *62 Vale Road, Poole BH14 9AU* T/F: (01202) 745136 E: diana.n@sky.com

NEWMAN, Ms Elizabeth Ann. b 57. K Coll Lon BD 79 Hull Univ CQSW 81. **d** 05 **p** 06. OLM Charlton *S'wark* from 05; Chapl Blackheath Bluecoat C of E Sch from 11; Chapl Lewisham and Greenwich NHS Trust from 14. *66 Annandale Road, London SE10 0DB* T: (020) 8305 0642
E: newman66@btopenworld.com

NEWMAN, Elizabeth Margot. b 50. Reading Univ BA 92. Ox Min Course 09. **d** 12 **p** 13. NSM Earley St Nic *Ox* from 12. *37 Sevenoakes Road, Earley, Reading RG6 7NT* T: 0118-926 5557 E: libbynewman3000@gmail.com

NEWMAN, Mrs Helen Margaret. b 58. York Univ BA 80 Nottm Univ MA 02. EMMTC 99. **d** 02 **p** 03. NSM Thorpe Acre w Dishley *Leic* 02-05; NSM Loughborough Em and St Mary in Charnwood 05-09; Chapl LOROS Hospice from 09. *The Archdeaconry, 21 Church Road, Glenfield, Leicester LE3 8DP* T: 0116-231 1632 E: helen@astad.org

NEWMAN, James Edwin Michael. b 59. Nottm Univ BA 80 Ox Univ BA 90. Wycliffe Hall Ox 88. **d** 91 **p** 92. C Bidston *Ches* 91-95; C Cheadle from 95. *4 Cuthbert Road, Cheadle SK8 2DT* T: 0161-428 3983 E: mike@stcuthberts.org

NEWMAN, Mrs Lynda Elizabeth. b 61. Univ of Wales (Swansea) DipEd 81 BEd 83 MEd 93. St Mich Coll Llan 07. **d** 10 **p** 11. NSM Neath *Llan* 10-13; TV from 13; Asst Dioc Children's Officer from 12. *95 Ridgewood Gardens, Cimla, Neath SA11 3QX* E: lenewman@hotmail.co.uk

NEWMAN, Mark Stephen. b 72. Wycliffe Hall Ox 10. **d** 12 **p** 13. C Eaton Socon *St Alb* from 12. *53 Shakespeare Road, Eaton Socon, St Neots PE19 8HG* M: 07766-466072 E: newmans72@gmail.com

NEWMAN, Michael Alan. b 40. Chich Th Coll 67. **d** 70 **p** 71. C Kilburn St Aug *Lon* 70-73; C St Geo-in-the-East St Mary 75-78; rtd 78. *April Cottage, Georges Lane, Storrington, Pulborough RH20 3JH* T: (01903) 744354
E: tcepriest@tiscali.co.uk

NEWMAN, Michael John. b 50. Leic Univ BA 72 MA 75. Cuddesdon Coll 73. **d** 75 **p** 76. C Tettenhall Regis *Lich* 75-79;

C Uttoxeter w Bramshall 79-82; R Norton Canes 82-89; TR Rugeley 89-06; TR Brereton and Rugeley 06-15; RD Rugeley 07-15; Preb Lich Cathl 02-15; rtd 15. *2 Firs Close, Weeping Cross, Stafford ST17 0DW*

NEWMAN, Paul. b 65. St Martin's Coll Lanc BA 90. Oak Hill Th Coll. **d** 00 **p** 01. C Poynton *Ches* 00-04; V Barnton from 04. *The Vicarage, Church Road, Barnton, Northwich CW8 4JH* T: (01606) 74358 E: scallyvic@yahoo.com

NEWMAN, Paul Anthony. b 48. Lon Univ BSc 70. Coll of Resurr Mirfield 73. **d** 76 **p** 77. C Catford St Laur *S'wark* 76-81; TV Grays All SS and Lt Thurrock St Mary *Chelmsf* 81-83; Youth Chapl W Ham Adnry 83-87; P-in-c Forest Gate All SS 83-89; V 89-91; Dep Chapl HM Pris Wormwood Scrubs 91-92; Chapl HM Pris Downview and Asst Chapl HM Pris High Down 92-02; Chapl HM Pris Win 02-07; Chapl HM Pris Kingston (Portsm) 07-13; rtd 13; PtO *Win* 07-13. *5 Cranworth House, Cranworth Road, Winchester SO22 6EJ*
E: paul309@btinternet.com

NEWMAN, Richard David. b 38. BNC Ox BA 60 MA 63. Lich Th Coll 60. **d** 62 **p** 63. C E Grinstead St Swithun *Chich* 62-66; C Gt Grimsby St Jas *Linc* 66-69; C Gt Grimsby St Mary and St Jas 69-73; TV 73-74; V St Nicholas at Wade w Sarre *Cant* 74-75; P-in-c Chislet w Hoath 74-75; V St Nicholas at Wade w Sarre and Chislet w Hoath 75-81; V S Norwood H Innocents 81-84; V *S'wark* 85-04; rtd 04; PtO *B & W* from 04. *10 Hardy Court, Lang Road, Crewkerne TA18 8JE* T: (01460) 271496 E: david.newman123@btinternet.com

NEWMAN, William Nigel Edward. b 61. St Jo Coll Dur BA 83 Bris Univ PGCE 86. Westcott Ho Cam 99. **d** 01 **p** 02. C Halstead Area *Chelmsf* 01-04; Chapl St Jo Cathl Hong Kong from 04; P-in-c Stanley St Steph from 04. *Bungalow 5, St Stephen's College, 22 Tung Tau Wan Road, Stanley, Hong Kong, China* E: willanddot@netvigator.org

NEWMAN-DAY, Christopher David. b 81. Bath Univ BSc 02 Anglia Ruskin Univ BA 10. Ridley Hall Cam 07. **d** 11 **p** 12. C Canonbury St Steph *Lon* 11-14; V Bethnal Green St Jas Less from 14. *St James the Less Vicarage, St James's Avenue, London E2 9JD* M: 07921-505744 E: revnewmanday@gmail.com

NEWNES, Steven William. **d** 14 **p** 15. C Brockworth *Glouc* from 14. *Address temp unknown*

NEWNHAM, Carol Ann. St Mellitus Coll. **d** 15. OLM Becontree St Thos *Chelmsf* from 15. *9 Tendring Way, Romford RM6 5DX*

NEWNHAM, Eric Robert. b 43. FCA. Sarum & Wells Th Coll 70. **d** 75 **p** 76. NSM Blackheath Ascension *S'wark* 75-06; NSM Deptford St Jo w H Trin and Ascension 06-13; PtO from 13. *27 Morden Hill, London SE13 7NN* T: (020) 8692 6507 *or* 8691 6559 E: e.n@btopenworld.com

NEWPORT, Derek James. b 39. Acadia Univ (NS) BA 82 MEd 84. Sarum & Wells Th Coll 74. **d** 76 **p** 77. C Tavistock and Gulworthy *Ex* 76-78; Canada 78-86; V Malborough w S Huish, W Alvington and Churchstow *Ex* 86-95; TR Widecombe-in-the-Moor, Leusdon, Princetown etc 95-04; rtd 04. *Woodland Cottage, Southdown Woods, Yarnscombe, Barnstaple EX31 3LZ* T: (01271) 858685 E: dereknewport@dnewport.fsnet.co.uk

NEWPORT, Prof Kenneth George Charles. b 57. Columbia Union Coll (USA) BA 83 Andrews Univ (USA) MA 84 Linacre Coll Ox MSt 85 St Hugh's Coll Ox DPhil 88. NOC 98. **d** 00 **p** 01. Reader Chr Thought Liv Hope 99-01; Prof Th and RS Liv Hope Univ from 01; Asst Vice Chan from 05; Hon Research Fell Man Univ from 98; NSM Bolton St Pet 00-11; NSM Bolton St Pet w St Phil from 11; PtO *Liv* from 00. *Theology and Religious Studies, Liverpool Hope, Hope Park, Taggart Avenue, Liverpool L16 9JD* T: 0151-291 3510 F: 291 3772
E: knewport@hope.ac.uk

NEWPORT, Archdeacon of. *See* WILLIAMS, The Ven Jonathan Simon

NEWSOME, Preb David Ellis. b 55. St Jo Coll Dur BA 77. Westcott Ho Cam 80. **d** 82 **p** 83. C Finchley St Mary *Lon* 82-85; C Fulham All SS 85-87; Bp's Dom Chapl *Birm* 87-91; V Gravelly Hill 91-00; P-in-c Stockland Green 93-96; AD Aston 95-00; TR Tettenhall Regis *Lich* 00-08; Dioc Dir of Ords from 08; Preb Lich Cathl from 15. *10 The Brambles, Lichfield WS14 9SE* T: (01543) 306220

NEWSOME, Canon John Keith. b 49. Mert Coll Ox BA 73 MA 76. Ripon Coll Cuddesdon 73. **d** 76 **p** 77. C Bywell *Newc* 76-78; C Berwick H Trin 78-82; Chapl Bonn w Cologne *Eur* 86-93; Chapl Hamburg 93-00; Chapl Zürich 00-14; Can Brussels Cathl 98-14; rtd 14. *St Marien, Steinweg 25, 63500 Seligenstadt, Germany*

NEWSOME, Monica Jane. b 55. WMMTC 96. **d** 99 **p** 00. NSM Kingshurst *Birm* 99-00; Asst Chapl HM YOI Stoke Heath 00-10; Chapl HM Pris Swinfen Hall from 10. *HM Young Offender Institution, Swinfen Hall, Swinfen, Lichfield WS14 9QS* T: (01543) 484000

NEWSON, Julie. b 60. Southn Univ BA 97. Bp Otter Coll 00. **d** 03. NSM Brighton St Pet w Chpl Royal *Chich* 03-09;

NSM Brighton Chpl Royal 09-10; C Brighton St Luke Queen's Park from 10. *St Luke's Vicarage, Queen's Park Terrace, Brighton BN2 9YA* T: (01273) 570978 M: 07803-750147
E: julie.newson@btinternet.com

NEWSTEAD, Dominic Gerald Bruno. b 65. Wycliffe Hall Ox BTh 95. **d** 95 **p** 96. C Windlesham *Guildf* 95-00; Asst Chapl Fontainebleau *Eur* 00-05; V Southwater *Chich* 05-09; C Bebington *Ches* from 09. *22 Woodhey Road, Wirral CH63 9PD* T: 0151-601 7793
E: dominic.newstead@standrewsbebington.org.uk

NEWSUM, Alfred Turner Paul. b 28. Coll of Resurr Mirfield 52. **d** 53 **p** 54. C Roath St German *Llan* 53-59; C Westmr St Matt *Lon* 59-60; C Washwood Heath *Birm* 60-68; P-in-c Small Heath St Greg 68-78; V Birm St Aid Small Heath 72-80; V Stockland Green 80-93; rtd 93; PtO *Llan* from 93; *Mon* from 93. *Ty'r Offeiriad, 18 Almond Drive, Cardiff CF23 8HD*

NEWTH, Barry Wilfred. b 33. Bris Univ BA 56. ALCD 58. **d** 58 **p** 59. C Upton (Overchurch) *Ches* 58-62; C Kimberworth *Sheff* 62-63; V Clifton *Man* 63-72; V Radcliffe St Thos 72-74; V Radcliffe St Thos and St Jo 74-81; R Heaton Mersey 81-86; V Kirkby Malham *Bradf* 86-87; P-in-c Coniston Cold 86-87; V Kirkby-in-Malhamdale w Coniston Cold 87-97; r-d 97; PtO *Man* 00-08. *1 Higher Ridings, Bromley Cross, Bolton BL7 9HP* T: (01204) 451927

NEWTON, Angela Margaret. b 48. RGN 70. Ripon Coll Cuddesdon 06. **d** 07 **p** 08. NSM Luton St Aug Limbury *St Alb* 07-12; PtO from 12; NSM Christchurch *Win* from 12; Chapl R Bournemouth and Christchurch Hosps NHS Trust from 14. *23 Regency Crescent, Christchurch BH23 2YF* T: (01202) 950010 M: 07940-824206 E: angela.m.newton@talktalk.net

NEWTON, Miss Ann. b 46. Trin Coll Bris 75. **d** 87 **p** 94. Par Dn Rothley *Leic* 87-91; Par Dn Becontree St Mary *Chelmsf* 91-94; C 94-01; V Canley *Cov* 01-08; rtd 08. *35 Mossford Street, London E3 4TH* T: (020) 8981 5764 E: revanew@aol.com

NEWTON, Barrie Arthur. b 38. Dur Univ BA 61. Wells Th Coll 61. **d** 63 **p** 64. C Walton St Mary *Liv* 63-67; C N Lynn w St Marg and St Nic *Nor* 67-69; Chapl Asst The Lon Hosp (Whitechapel) 69-71; Chapl K Coll Hosp Lon 72-77; P-in-c Bishops Sutton w Stowey *B & W* 77-81; P-in-c Compton Martin w Ubley 79-81; P-in-c Bridgwater St Jo w Chedzoy 81-83; Chapl St Mary's Hosp Praed Street Lon 83-94; Chapl St Mary's NHS Trust Paddington 94-99; rtd 00; PtO *Lon* from 04. *10 Brondesbury Park Mansions, 132 Salusbury Road, London NW6 6PD* T/F: (020) 7328 0397
E: newrie@btinternet.com

NEWTON, Brian Karl. b 30. Keble Coll Ox BA 55 MA 59. Wells Th Coll 56. **d** 58 **p** 59. C Barrow St Geo *Carl* 58-61; Trinidad and Tobago 61-69 and 71-77; Gen Ed USPG 69-71; P-in-c Gt Coates *Linc* 77; TV Gt and Lt Coates w Bradley 78-88; V Burgh le Marsh 88-94; R Bratoft w Irby-in-the-Marsh 88-94; V Orby 88-94; R Welton-le-Marsh w Gunby 88-94; rtd 94; PtO *Linc* 94-97. *27 Somersby Way, Boston PE21 9PQ* T: (01205) 362433

NEWTON, Canon Christopher Wynne. b 25. Trin Hall Cam BA 46. Westcott Ho Cam 48. **d** 50 **p** 51. C Gateshead Ch Ch *Dur* 50-52; Canada 52-55; C Harrow Weald All SS *Lon* 55-58; V Radlett *St Alb* 58-66; RD St Alb 63-66; TR Hemel Hempstead 66-72; RD Milton Keynes *Ox* 72-77; TV Swan 78-84; RD Claydon 78-84; Dioc Ecum Officer 79-84; Hon Can Ch Ch 80-83; P-in-c Lt Gaddesden *St Alb* 84-86; rtd 86; PtO *St Alb* from 86. *24 Slade Court, Watling Street, Radlett WD7 7BT* T: (01923) 859131

NEWTON, David. *See* NEWTON, Michael David

NEWTON, David Ernest. b 42. Sarum & Wells Th Coll 72. **d** 74 **p** 75. C Wigan All SS *Liv* 74-80; V Choral York Minster 80-85; R Ampleforth w Oswaldkirk 85-86; P-in-c E Gilling 85-86; R Ampleforth and Oswaldkirk and Gilling E 86-97; V Ampleforth w Oswaldkirk, Gilling E etc 98-01; RD Helmsley 94-99; P-in-c Overton *Blackb* 01-10. *4 Lunesdale Court, Derwent Road, Lancaster LA1 3ET* T: (01524) 599101
E: davidnoot@aol.com

NEWTON, Derek. b 50. NEOC 89. **d** 92 **p** 93. NSM Houghton le Spring *Dur* 92-96; C 06-09; NSM Deanery of Houghton 97-06; P-in-c Chilton Moor from 09. *1 Fields View, East Rainton, Houghton le Spring DH5 9GA*

NEWTON, Canon Fiona Olive. b 46. GTCL 67. WMMTC 96. **d** 99 **p** 00. C Southam and Ufton *Cov* 99-03; P-in-c Laxfield, Cratfield, Wilby and Brundish *St E* 03-04; R 04-13; C Hoxne w Denham, Syleham and Wingfield 06-13; R Worlingworth, Southolt, Tannington, Bedfield etc 12-13; R Bedfield, Brundish, Cratfield, Laxfield etc 13; RD Hoxne 07-13; RD Hartismere 08-10; Hon Can St E Cathl 11-13; rtd 13; PtO *Nor* from 14. *Manor Farm Cottage, 67 Langham Road, Field Dalling, Holt NR25 7LG* T: (01328) 830947
E: fionanewton46@gmail.com

NEWTON, George Peter Howgill. b 62. Pemb Coll Cam BA 84 MA 88. Oak Hill Th Coll BA 93. **d** 93 **p** 94. C Blackpool

St Thos *Blackb* 93-99; P-in-c Aldershot H Trin *Guildf* 99-03; V from 03; RD Aldershot from 11; Chapl Farnborough Coll of Tech from 00. *2 Cranmore Lane, Aldershot GU11 3AS* T: (01252) 320618 E: g@gjsk.prestel.co.uk

NEWTON, Gordon. b 81. Cant Ch Ch Univ Coll BA 03. Coll of Resurr Mirfield 07. **d** 09 **p** 10. C Armley w New Wortley *Ripon* 09-12; C Harrogate St Wilfrid 12-14; TV from 14. *St Wilfrid's House, 23 Azerley Grove, Harrogate HG3 2SY* T: (01423) 525545 E: fr.gordon.newton@hotmail.co.uk

NEWTON, Canon Graham Hayden. b 47. AKC 69. St Aug Coll Cant 70. **d** 70 **p** 71. C St Mary-at-Lambeth *S'wark* 70-73; TV Catford (Southend) and Downham 73-78; P-in-c Porthill *Lich* 78-79; TV Wolstanton 79-86; V Stevenage H Trin *St Alb* 86-96; TR Dunstable 96-04; RD 96-02; R Barton-le-Cley w Higham Gobion and Hexton 04-12; Hon Can St Alb 04-12; rtd 12; PtO *St Alb* 12-15; *Win* from 12. *23 Regency Crescent, Christchurch BH23 2UF* T: (01202) 950010 E: revghnewton@talktalk.net

NEWTON, Ian. b 66. Westmr Coll Ox BEd 89 Leeds Univ BA 03. Coll of Resurr Mirfield 01. **d** 03 **p** 04. C Horninglow *Lich* 03-06; V W Bromwich St Pet 06-10; Chapl Quainton Hall Sch Harrow 10-11; V Paulsgrove *Portsm* from 11. *St Michael's Vicarage, Hempsted Road, Portsmouth PO6 4AS* T: (023) 9237 8194 E: fatheriannewton@yahoo.co.uk

NEWTON, John. b 39. AKC 65. **d** 66 **p** 67. C Whipton *Ex* 66-68; C Plympton St Mary 68-74; V Broadwoodwidger 74-81; R Kelly w Bradstone 74-81; R Lifton 74-81; Chapl All Hallows Sch Rousdon 81-94; LtO *Ex* 81-94; rtd 99. *Flat 2, 5 Eyewell Green, Seaton EX12 2BN* T: (01297) 625887

NEWTON, Michael David. b 89. Trin Hall Cam BA 11 MA 15 PGCE 12. Cranmer Hall Dur 13. **d** 15. C Ely from 15. *8 Hertford Close, Ely CB6 3QS* E: mdavidn16@gmail.com

NEWTON, Miles Julius Albert. b 69. K Alfred's Coll Win BA 91. Qu Coll Birm BTh 96. **d** 97 **p** 98. C Sholing *Win* 97-01; C Bitterne Park 01-03; V Woolston from 03; P-in-c Southampton St Mary Extra from 11. *St Mark's Vicarage, 117 Swift Road, Southampton SO19 9ER* T: (023) 8044 1124 E: milesnewton117@btinternet.com

NEWTON, Canon Nigel Ernest Hartley. b 38. St Jo Coll Nottm 87. **d** 89 **p** 90. C Largs *Glas* 89-92; Angl Chapl Ashbourne Home Largs 89-92; P-in-c Eyemouth *Edin* 92-95; Chapl Miss to Seamen 92-95; P-in-c Challoch *Glas* 95-04; R 04-06; Can St Mary's Cathl 04-06; Hon Can St Mary's Cathl from 06; rtd 06; P-in-c Stranraer *Glas* from 10. *Glenairlie, 7 Wigtown Road, Newton Stewart DG8 6JZ* T: (01671) 401228 M: 07885-436892 E: glenairlie@btinternet.com

NEWTON, Miss Pauline Dorothy. b 48. Southn Univ BA 70 PGCE 71 MPhil 79. Sarum Th Coll 79. **dss** 82 **d** 87 **p** 94. Bemerton *Sarum* 86; Hon C 87-06; Dep Hd Malvern Girls' Coll 86-06; rtd 06; PtO *Heref* from 07. *16 Weston Park, Weston under Penyard, Ross-on-Wye HR9 7FR* T: (01989) 564414 E: pnewton48@hotmail.com

NEWTON, Peter. b 39. St Jo Coll Nottm 73. **d** 75 **p** 76. C Porchester *S'well* 75-79; R Wilford 79-99; rtd 99; Warden Advent Ho Healing Min Birmingham USA 99-12; PtO *Leic* from 00. *20 Main Street, Eaton, Grantham NG32 1SE* T: (01476) 870024 E: newtonji@hotmail.com

NEWTON, Richard. b 47. Trin Coll Bris 72. **d** 73 **p** 74. C Fareham St Jo *Portsm* 73-76; C Cheltenham St Mark *Glouc* 76-83; P-in-c Malvern St Andr *Worc* 83-95; TR Kingswood *Bris* 95-99; Master St Jo Hosp Bath 00-07; rtd 07; PtO *Worc* from 08. *61 Columbia Drive, Worcester WR2 4DB* T: (01905) 426702 E: 2antiques41@talktalk.net

NEWTON, Richard John Christopher. b 60. Bris Univ BSc 81. Qu Coll Birm 85. **d** 88 **p** 89. C Bris Ch the Servant Stockwood 88-92; C Dorking w Ranmore *Guildf* 92-96; P-in-c Hagley *Worc* 96-00; R from 00. *The Rectory, 6 Middlefield Lane, Hagley, Stourbridge DY9 0PX* T: (01562) 882442 or 886363 F: 887833 E: richard.kathy@yescomputers.co.uk *or* hagley.pcc@freeuk.com

NEWTON, Ruth Katherine. b 58. **d** 10 **p** 11. NSM Rowley w Skidby *York* from 10. *6 Manor Barns, Little Weighton, Cottingham HU20 3UA* T: (01482) 841875 E: newtonrk@newtonrk.karoo.co.uk

NGOY, Lusa. *See* NSENGA-NGOY, Lusa

NGUGI, Peter Mbugua. b 65. E Africa Sch of Th BA 91 Nairobi Internat Sch of Th MDiv 94 Stellenbosch Univ MTheol 98. Trin Coll Bris. **d** 10 **p** 11. C Stratford St Jo w Ch Ch *Chelmsf* 10-15; C Walthamstow from 14. *29 Maryland Park, London E15 1HB* E: ngugip@ymail.com

NGURURI, Miss Naomi. b 73. St Jo Coll Nottm 07. **d** 09 **p** 10. C Hackney Marsh *Lon* 09-11; C Stoke Newington St Mary 11-13; TV Horley *S'wark* from 13. *St Wilfrid's Vicarage, Horley Row, Horley RH6 8DF* T: (01293) 774123 E: nguruuri.vicar@yahoo.com

NIASSA, Bishop of. *See* VAN KOEVERING, The Rt Revd Mark Allan

NIBLOCK, Mark. b 78. Fitzw Coll Cam MA 03 Milltown Inst Dub MA 08. CITC 06. **d** 08 **p** 09. C Agherton *Conn* 08-12; P-in-c Rathcoole from 12. *7 Oaklands Meadow, Newtownabbey BT37 0XN* T: (028) 9086 7714 E: mark-niblock@hotmail.com

NICE, Canon John Edmund. b 51. Univ of Wales (Ban) BA 73. Coll of Resurr Mirfield 74. **d** 76 **p** 77. C Oxton *Ches* 76-79; C Liscard St Mary w St Columba 79-82; V Latchford St Jas 82-92; TR Holyhead w Rhoscolyn w Llanfair-yn-Neubwll *Ban* 92-95; TR Holyhead 95-04; RD Llifon and Talybolion 97-01; AD 01-04; R Llandudno from 04; Can Cursal Ban Cathl 02-04; Can and Preb Ban Cathl from 04; AD Archllechwedd from 10; PtO *St As* from 14. *The Rectory, Church Walks, Llandudno LL30 2HL* T: (01492) 876624
E: john.nice2@btopenworld.com

NICHOL, William David. b 58. Hull Univ BA 84. Ridley Hall Cam 84. **d** 87 **p** 88. C Hull St Jo Newland *York* 87-90; C Kirk Ella 90-92; TV 92-98; P-in-c Powick *Worc* 98-99; R Powick and Guarlford and Madresfield w Newland 99-05; V Malvern H Trin and St Jas from 05; RD Malvern 07-13. *Holy Trinity Vicarage, 2 North Malvern Road, Malvern WR14 4LR* T: (01684) 561126 E: david@trinityandthewest.wanadoo.co.uk

NICHOLAS, Ernest Milton. b 25. ACP 50 Newc Univ DipAdEd 69 Lanc Univ MA 78. NEOC 85. **d** 86 **p** 87. NSM Hexham *Newc* 86-96; PtO from 96. *Hillside, Eilansgate, Hexham NE46 3EW* T: (01434) 603609

NICHOLAS, Jonathan. b 78. Cranmer Hall Dur 08. **d** 10 **p** 11. C Lt Horton *Bradf* 10-14; C Oldbury, Langley and Londonderry *Birm* 14-15; V Sutton Coldfield St Chad from 15. *41 Hollyfield Road, Sutton Coldfield B75 7SN*
E: rev.nicholas@chris-kent.co.uk

NICHOLAS, Malcolm Keith. b 46. Open Univ BA 79 FIBMS 71. S Dios Minl Tr Scheme 81. **d** 84 **p** 85. NSM Gatcombe *Portsm* 84-92; NSM Shorwell w Kingston 88-92; C Hartley Wintney, Elvetham, Winchfield etc *Win* 92-96; TV Grantham *Linc* 96-02; V Grantham, Harrowby w Londonthorpe 02-03; V Carr Dyke Gp 03-11; rtd 11; PtO *Nor* from 12. *20 Marrams Avenue, Cromer NR27 9BB* T: (01263) 514036
E: malnic1@yahoo.co.uk

NICHOLAS, Milton. *See* NICHOLAS, Ernest Milton

NICHOLAS, Patrick. b 37. Selw Coll Cam BA 60 MA 65. Wells Th Coll 60. **d** 62 **p** 63. C Camberwell St Giles *S'wark* 62-63; C Warlingham w Chelsham and Farleigh 63-65; C Oxted 65-68; Hong Kong 68-74; C Portsea St Mary *Portsm* 75; Hd of Ho St Chris Fellowship Chiswick 76-79; Dept of Soc Services Glos Co Coun 79-92; Probation Officer Glouc Probation Service 92-97; rtd 97; Chapl St Jo Coll Hong Kong 97-00; PtO *Glouc* from 02. *35 Norwich Drive, Cheltenham GL51 3HD* T: (01242) 510007 E: patnic@btinternet.com

NICHOLAS, Paul James. b 51. Univ of Wales (Lamp) BA. Coll of Resurr Mirfield 73. **d** 74 **p** 75. C Llanelli *St D* 74-78; C Roath Llan 78-84; P-in-c Leic St Pet 84-87; V Shard End *Birm* 87-96; rtd 96; PtO *Birm* from 96. *50 Delrene Road, Shirley, Solihull B90 2HJ* T: 0121-745 7339 E: frpaul@oikos.screaming.net

NICHOLAS, Peter. b 78. **d** 12 **p** 13. C Langham Place All So *Lon* from 12. *All Souls' Church, 2 All Souls' Place, London W1B 3DA*

NICHOLAS ALAN, Brother. *See* WORSSAM, Nicholas Alan

NICHOLL, Mrs Karen. b 65. Bradf Univ BA 99 Leeds Univ BA 07. Coll of Resurr Mirfield 05. **d** 07 **p** 08. C Lindley *Wakef* 07-10; P-in-c Gomersal *Leeds* from 10. *St Mary's Vicarage, 404 Spen Lane, Gomersal, Cleckheaton BD19 4LS*
E: nicholl.karen@googlemail.com

NICHOLLS, Brian Albert. b 39. LBIPP LMPA. WMMTC 90. **d** 93 **p** 94. NSM Oakham, Hambleton, Egleton, Braunston and Brooke *Pet* 93-96; R Edith Weston w N Luffenham and Lyndon w Manton 96-05; P-in-c Empingham and Exton w Horn w Whitwell 02-05; rtd 05; PtO *Pet* from 05; *Leic* from 05. *28 Heron Road, Oakham LE15 6BN* T: (01572) 759657
E: lizbriannicholls@tiscali.co.uk

NICHOLLS (née HUMPHRIES), Mrs Catherine Elizabeth. b 53. Anglia Poly Univ MA 97. Trin Coll Bris BA 87. **d** 87 **p** 94. C Bath Twerton-on-Avon *B & W* 87-90; Personnel Manager and Tr Officer TEAR Fund 90-95; Hon C Norbiton *S'wark* 91-95; PtO *Ely* 95-97; Dir Past Studies EAMTC 97-03; Vice Prin 01-03; Hon Min Can Pet Cathl 97-03; PtO *Nor* 03-05; Dioc Dir CME 05-10. *North Cottage, King John's Thorn, Hethel, Norwich NR14 8HE* T: (01508) 570557

NICHOLLS, Christopher Alan. b 60. Leic Univ BSc 81 Reading Univ MSc 82 FGS 91. ERMC 07. **d** 10 **p** 11. C Utrecht w Zwolle *Eur* from 10. *Baronielaan 37, 2242 RB Wassenaar, The Netherlands* T: (0031) (70) 517 5291 M: 61-097 3164
E: cajwnicholls@hetnet.nl

NICHOLLS (née TOVAR), Mrs Gillian Elaine. b 48. Sussex Univ CertEd 69. Trin Coll Bris BA 86. **dss** 86 **d** 87 **p** 94. Nuneaton SS Pet and Paul *Roch* 86-00; Par Dn 87-94; C 94-00; V Gillingham H Trin 00-10; rtd 10. *29 The Gables, Haddenham, Aylesbury HP17 8AD* T: (01844) 291993 E: gilltovar2008@gmail.com

NICHOLLS, Irene. b 60. **d** 09 **p** 10. OLM Penkridge *Lich* 09-14; PtO from 14. *79 Croydon Drive, Penkridge, Stafford ST19 5DW* T: (01785) 714686

NICHOLLS, Mrs Janet Elizabeth. b 64. Southlands Coll Lon BEd 86. ERMC 09. **d** 12 **p** 13. NSM Panfield and Rayne *Chelmsf* from 12; NSM Finchingfield and Cornish Hall End etc from 12. *Park House, Braintree Road, Shalford, Braintree CM7 5HQ* T: (01371) 851317
E: janetnicholls64@hotmail.co.uk

NICHOLLS, Mrs Joan. b 55. All SS Cen for Miss & Min 12. **d** 15. OLM New Bury w Gt Lever *Man* from 15. *144 Bradford Road, Bolton BL3 2HR* T: (01204) 531357
E: joan.nicholls187@gmail.com

✠NICHOLLS, The Rt Revd John. b 43. AKC 66. **d** 67 **p** 68 **c** 90. C Salford St Clem Ordsall *Man* 67-69; C Langley All SS and Martyrs 69-72; V 72-78; Dir Past Th Coll of Resurr Mirfield 78-83; Can Res Man Cathl 83-90; Suff Bp Lancaster *Blackb* 90-97; Bp Sheff 97-08; rtd 08; Hon Asst Bp Derby from 09; Hon Asst Bp Man from 12. *75 Rowton Grange Road, Chapel-en-le-Frith, High Peak SK23 0LD* T: (01298) 938249
E: jnseraphim@gmx.com

NICHOLLS, Keith Barclay. b 57. Nottm Univ BA 78. Wycliffe Hall Ox 03. **d** 05 **p** 06. C Bisley and W End *Guildf* 05-09; V Burchetts Green *Ox* from 09. *The Vicarage, Burchetts Green Road, Burchetts Green, Maidenhead SL6 6QS* T: (01628) 828822
E: kbnicholls@hotmail.com

NICHOLLS, Canon Mark Richard. b 60. LSE BSc(Econ) 82 Leeds Univ BA 88. Coll of Resurr Mirfield 86. **d** 89 **p** 90. C Warrington St Elphin *Liv* 89-92; V Wigan St Andr 92-96; R North End St Marg Zimbabwe 96-00; Shrine P Shrine of Our Lady of Walsingham 00-02; V Mill End and Heronsgate w W Hyde *St Alb* 02-07; P-in-c Rotherhithe St Mary w All SS *S'wark* 07-10; R from 10; P-in-c Bermondsey St Kath w St Bart from 14; AD Bermondsey from 13; Hon Can Manicaland Zimbabwe from 14. *St Mary's Rectory, 72A St Marychurch Street, London SE16 2JE* M: 07909-546659
E: mmarini2001@aol.com

NICHOLLS, Mark Simon. b 57. Down Coll Cam MA 79. Ripon Coll Cuddesdon 92. **d** 94 **p** 95. C Farnham *Guildf* 94-98; P-in-c Crookham 98-03; V 03-14; PtO from 14. *2 Ryebeck Road, Church Crookham, Fleet GU52 6HP*

NICHOLLS, Neil David Raymond. b 65. Univ Coll Lon BA 86. Wycliffe Hall Ox BA 90. **d** 91 **p** 92. C Westmr St Steph w St Jo *Lon* 91-94; C Islington St Mary 94-96; Chapl LSE 96-00; C St Bride Fleet Street w Bridewell etc 99-00; V Ealing St Barn 00-05; V Hatcham St Jas *S'wark* from 05; AD Deptford 07-12. *St James's Vicarage, St James's, London SE14 6AD* T: (020) 8691 2167 E: rev.neil@tiscali.co.uk

NICHOLLS, Rachel. b 62. BA MPhil. **d** 00 **p** 01. NSM Chesterton St Geo *Ely* 00-04; PtO 04-07; NSM Cambridge St Benedict from 07. *5 Eachard Road, Cambridge CB3 0HZ* T: (01223) 359167 E: rachel.nicholls2@btinternet.com

NICHOLLS, Robert Graham. b 56. Sheff Univ BEng 77 CEng MIET 07. STETS 05. **d** 08 **p** 09. NSM Fair Oak *Win* from 08. *20 The Spinney, Eastleigh SO50 8PF* T: (023) 8069 3716 M: 07837-804366 E: bob.nicholls@dsl.pipex.com

NICHOLLS, Roger Frank. b 43. Ox Univ MA Cam Univ DipEd. **d** 01 **p** 02. OLM Kenwyn w St Allen *Truro* 01-04; NSM Truro St Paul and St Clem 04-08; NSM Truro St Geo and St Jo 04-08; P-in-c Mylor w Flushing 08-13; rtd 13. *8 Truro Vean Terrace, Truro TR1 1HA* T: (01872) 275753
E: rognicholls@tesco.net

NICHOLLS, Simon James. b 53. Anglia Ruskin Univ MA 08 Trent Park Coll of Educn CertEd 76. Ridley Hall Cam. **d** 00 **p** 01. C Nuneaton St Nic *Cov* 00-04; R Markfield, Thornton, Bagworth and Stanton etc *Leic* from 04. *The Rectory, 3A The Nook, Markfield LE67 9WE* T: (01530) 242844
E: markfield.rector@virgin.net

NICHOLS, Barry Edward. b 40. ACA 63 FCA 73. S'wark Ord Course 66. **d** 69 **p** 70. NSM Surbiton St Andr and St Mark *S'wark* 69-92; Dean for MSE Kingston Area 90-92; Hon Can S'wark Cathl 90-92; PtO 99-01; NSM Upper Tooting H Trin 01-04; NSM Upper Tooting H Trin w St Aug 04-12; rtd 12; PtO *S'wark* from 12. *19 Arterberry Road, London SW20 8AF* T/F: (020) 8879 0154 M: 07740-152309
E: barrynichols@btinternet.com

NICHOLS, Mrs Elizabeth Margaret. b 45. WEMTC 00. **d** 02 **p** 03. NSM Ledbury *Heref* 02-05; NSM Boxwell, Leighterton, Didmarton, Oldbury etc *Glouc* from 05. *The Rectory, The Meads, Leighterton, Tetbury GL8 8UW* T: (01666) 890635 E: reverend.elizabeth@cotswoldwireless.co.uk

NICHOLS, Frank Bernard. b 43. Kelham Th Coll 64. **d** 68 **p** 69. C Luton St Andr *St Alb* 68-72; C Cheshunt 72-76; C-in-c Marsh Farm CD 76-81; PtO Brisbane Australia 08-10; PtO *Nor* from 10. *55 Pirnhow Street, Ditchingham, Bungay NR35 2SA* M: 07503-932804 T: (01986) 896171
E: lyngateman@hotmail.co.uk

NICHOLS, Howard Keith. b 41. CCC Ox BA 64 MA 68 CEng 86 FIEE 92 EurIng 94. WEMTC 98. **d** 01 **p** 02. NSM Ledbury *Heref* 01-04; NSM Boxwell, Leighterton, Didmarton, Oldbury etc *Glouc* from 04. *The Rectory, The Meads, Leighterton, Tetbury GL8 8UW* T: (01666) 890635
E: reverend.howard@cotswoldwireless.co.uk

NICHOLS, Mark Steven. b 68. Lon Bible Coll BA 94 Ridley Hall Cam 95. **d** 97 **p** 98. C Balham Hill Ascension *S'wark* 97-99. *16 Beckside Close, Rossendale BB4 9DE* M: 07875-636737
E: markn1968uk@yahoo.co.uk

NICHOLS, Robert Warren. b 54. Biola Univ (USA) BA 77 Fuller Th Sem California MA 81. SAOMC 93. **d** 96 **p** 97. C Headington Quarry *Ox* 96-00; Sen Asst P Wymondham *Nor* 00-05; Lect 01-05; R Caston, Griston, Merton, Thompson etc *Nor* from 05. *The Rectory, 4 Hunters Ride, Caston, Attleborough NR17 1DE* T: (01953) 483222 E: revbobnichols@gmail.com

NICHOLS, Stephen Robert Chamberlain. b 73. Ch Coll Cam BA 96 MA 00 SOAS Lon MA 98 Bris Univ PhD 11. Wycliffe Hall Ox BA 06. **d** 09 **p** 10. C Plymouth St Andr and Stonehouse *Ex* 09-14; C Langham Place All So *Lon* from 14. *All Souls' Church, 2 All Souls' Place, London W1B 3DA* T: (020) 7580 3522 M: 07960-063174 E: stephen.nichols@virgin.net

NICHOLSON, Andrew John. b 69. Leeds Univ BA 93 MA 00. St Jo Coll Nottm MTh 04. **d** 05 **p** 06. C E Richmond *Ripon* 05-09; P-in-c Barwick in Elmet *Leeds* from 09; P-in-c Thorner from 09. *The Vicarage, Church View, Thorner, Leeds LS14 3ED* T: 0113-289 2437 M: 07723-345917
E: andydebbie80@hotmail.com

NICHOLSON, Mrs Barbara Ruth. b 39. Nor City Coll TCert 59. **d** 02 **p** 03. OLM Reculver and Herne Bay St Bart *Cant* 02-11; PtO from 11. *34 Cliff Avenue, Herne Bay CT6 6LZ* T: (01227) 364606 F: 365384

NICHOLSON, Brian Warburton. b 44. ALCD 73 LTh 74. St Jo Coll Nottm 70. **d** 73 **p** 74. C Canford Magna *Sarum* 73-77; C E Twickenham St Steph *Lon* 77-80; V Colchester St Jo *Chelmsf* 80-96; R Oakley w Wootton St Lawrence *Win* 96-09; rtd 09; PtO *Win* from 09. *Nuthatches, 16 St Vigor Way, Colden Common, Winchester SO21 1UU* T: (01962) 713433
E: brian.nic@talktalk.net

NICHOLSON, Christina Olive. b 59. **d** 08 **p** 09. OLM Mossley Hill *Liv* 08-12; C Ince Ch Ch w Wigan St Cath 12-15; C Hindley Green from 15. *St Peter's Vicarage, 122 Wigan Road, Wigan WN2 3DF* E: tina2nic@sky.com

NICHOLSON, Miss Clare. b 46. Keele Univ BA 70 CertEd 70 RMN 80. St Jo Coll Nottm 83. **dss** 85 **d** 87 **p** 94. Bletchley *Ox* 85-89; Par Dn 87-89; Par Dn Milton Keynes 89-90; Par Dn Prestwood and St Hampden 90-94; C 94-99; P-in-c E Springfield *Chelmsf* 99-03; V Aldborough Hatch 03-11; r-d 11; PtO *Cant* from 12. *32 Craddock Road, Canterbury CT1 1YP* T: (01227) 472188 E: cnicholson@btinternet.com

NICHOLSON, David. b 57. Sarum & Wells Th Coll 80. **d** 83 **p** 84. C Trevethin *Mon* 83-85; C Ebbw Vale 85-87; V Newport St Steph and H Trin 87-95; V Abertillery w Cwmtillery w Six Bells 95-97; Hon Chapl Miss to Seamen 87-97; P-in-c Cudworth *Wakef* 97-98; V Leeds from 98; P-in-c Lundwood *Wakef* 01-04; Dioc Urban Officer *Leeds* from 08; Chapl to The Queen from 14. *The Vicarage, St John's Road, Cudworth, Barnsley S72 8DE* T: (01226) 710279 E: frnicholson@aol.com

NICHOLSON, Mrs Diane Maureen. b 45. Birm Coll of Educn CertEd 68. **d** 97 **p** 98. OLM Ludham, Potter Heigham, Hickling and Catfield *Nor* 97-14; rtd 14. *25 Latchmoor Park, Ludham, Great Yarmouth NR29 5RA* T: (01692) 678683

NICHOLSON, Dorothy Ann. b 40. Surrey Univ Roehampton MSc 04. S'wark Ord Course 81. **dss** 84 **d** 87 **p** 94. Carshalton Beeches *S'wark* 84-88; Par Dn 87-88; Par Dn Brixton Road Ch Ch 88-89; C Malden St Jo 89-95; V Balham St Mary and St Jo 95-05; rtd 05. *13 Tebbs Close, Countesthorpe, Leicester LE8 5XG* T: 0116-277 5737
E: nicholsonda@btopenworld.com

NICHOLSON, Eric. b 33. **d** 01 **p** 02. OLM W Wycombe w Bledlow Ridge, Bradenham and Radnage *Ox* 01-07; LtO *Mor* from 07. *Carlingford, Spey Road, Spey Bay, Fochabers IV32 7PY* T: (01343) 823879 E: eric.nicholson@virgin.net

NICHOLSON, Prof Ernest Wilson. b 38. Comdr OM (Italy) 90. TCD BA 60 MA 64 Glas Univ PhD 64 Cam Univ MA 67 BD 71 DD 78 Ox Univ DD 79 FBA 87. Westcott Ho Cam 69. **d** 69 **p** 70. Lect Div Cam Univ 67-79; Fell, Chapl and Dir of Th Studies Pemb Coll Cam 69-79; Dean 73-79; Prof of Interpr of H Scripture Oriel Coll Ox 79-90; Provost 90-03; Pro-Vice-Chan Ox Univ 93-03; rtd 03; LtO Ox 84-10; PtO from 10. *39A Blenheim Drive, Oxford OX2 8DJ*
E: ernest.nicholson@oriel.ox.ac.uk

NICHOLSON, Gary. b 62. Open Univ BA 89. Cranmer Hall Dur 91 NEOC 92. **d** 95 **p** 96. NSM Whitworth w Spennymoor *Dur* 95-97; NSM Spennymoor, Whitworth and Merrington 97-00; C Coundon and Eldon 00-02; P-in-c from 02. *St James's Vicarage, 2A Collingwood Street, Coundon, Bishop Auckland DL14 8LG* E: frgary@hotmail.com

NICHOLSON, Harold Sydney Leonard. b 35. Garnett Coll Lon PGCE 67 Open Univ BA 77. Oak Hill NSM Course 92. **d** 94 **p** 95. NSM Stanwell *Lon* 94-00; NSM Sunbury 98-00; NSM Shepperton 00-05; PtO from 05. *7 Academy Court, Fordbridge Road, Sunbury-on-Thames TW16 6AN* T: (01932) 787690
E: hslnicholson@onetel.com

NICHOLSON, James Benjamin. b 51. NEOC. **d** 08 **p** 09. NSM Helmsley and Upper Ryedale *York* 08-11. *5 Bells Court, Helmsley, York YO62 5BA* T: (01439) 772150
E: bnicuk@aol.com

NICHOLSON, John Paul. b 57. Sarum Th Coll. **d** 82 **p** 83. C Kirkby *Liv* 82-85; TV Speke St Aid 85-95; Ind Chapl *Ox* 95-04; Chapl Cambs and Pet NHS Foundn Trust from 04. *Chaplaincy Office, Kent House, Fulbourn Hospital, Cambridge CB21 5EF* T: (01223) 218598 M: 07771-787249
E: john.nicholson@cpft.nhs.uk

NICHOLSON, Kevin Smith. b 47. CQSW 76. Edin Th Coll 89. **d** 91 **p** 92. C W Fife Team Min *St And* 91-94; P-in-c 94-95; R Kinross 95-03; rtd 03. *Oldshoremore, 3A West Huntingtower, Perth PH1 3NU* T: (01738) 583555
E: keithnicholson7747@gmail.com

NICHOLSON, Canon Nigel Patrick. b 46. DL 07. Sarum & Wells Th Coll 72. **d** 75 **p** 76. C Farnham *Guildf* 75-78; C Worplesdon 78-81; CF (ACF) from 80; P-in-c Compton *Guildf* 81-85; R Compton w Shackleford and Peper Harow 85-89; R Cranleigh 89-12; RD 95-00; Hon Can Guildf Cathl 01-12; rtd 12; PtO *Chich* from 12; *Guildf* from 12; *Portsm* from 12. *Banford House, 25 Portsmouth Road, Liphook GU30 7DJ* T: (01428) 724979 E: nicholson.banford@outlook.com

NICHOLSON, Miss Pamela Elizabeth. b 47. Ripon Coll Cuddesdon. **d** 92 **p** 94. C Balsall Heath St Paul *Birm* 92-95; V Smethwick St Matt w St Chad 95-09; PtO 09-12; *Blackb* from 12. *1 Acresfield, Colne BB8 0PT* T: (01282) 862717
E: pamela.nicholson1@btinternet.com

NICHOLSON, Paul Shannon. b 52. York Univ BA 74 Middx Univ BA 02 Heythrop Coll Lon MA 07 ARCO 74 ARCM 75. NTMTC 99. **d** 02 **p** 03. C Primrose Hill St Mary w Avenue Road St Paul *Lon* 02-06; P-in-c S Hampstead St Sav from 06; P-in-c Belsize Park from 06. *St Saviour's Vicarage, 30 Eton Villas, London NW3 4SQ* T: (020) 7586 6522 M: 07971-223764
E: paul.nicholson@london.anglican.org

NICHOLSON, Canon Peter Charles. b 25. OBE 92. Lambeth MA 89. Chich Th Coll 57. **d** 59 **p** 60. C Sawbridgeworth *St Alb* 59-62; Min Can, Prec and Sacr Pet Cathl 62-67; V Wroxham w Hoveton *Nor* 67-74; V Lyme Regis *Sarum* 74-80; Gen Sec St Luke's Hosp for the Clergy 80-93; NSM Harlington *Lon* 80-87; Hon Chapl S'wark Cathl from 87; Can and Preb Chich Cathl 89-93; rtd 93. *St Luke's Cottage, 13 Brearley Close, Uxbridge UB8 1JJ* T: (01895) 233522

NICHOLSON, Peter Charles. b 44. Oak Hill Th Coll 74. **d** 76 **p** 77. C Croydon Ch Ch Broad Green *Cant* 76-80; C Gt Baddow *Chelmsf* 80-88; TV 88-96; V Westcliff St Mich 96-13; rtd 13. *Kiononia, 25 Eastwood Park Drive, Leigh-on-Sea SS9 5RP* T: (01702) 527444 E: pedinic@talk21.com

NICHOLSON, Canon Rodney. b 45. Mert Coll Ox BA 68 MA 71. Ridley Hall Cam 69. **d** 72 **p** 73. C Colne St Bart *Blackb* 72-75; C Blackpool St Jo 75-78; V Ewood 78-90; V Clitheroe St Paul Low Moor 90-14; P-in-c Chatburn and Downham 03-14; Hon Can Blackb Cathl 06-14; rtd 14; PtO *York* from 15. *96 Shipman Road, Market Weighton, York YO43 3RB* T: (01430) 650271 E: rodnic03@gmail.com

NICHOLSON, Roland. b 40. Sarum & Wells Th Coll 72. **d** 74 **p** 75. C Morecambe St Barn *Blackb* 74-78; V Feniscliffe 78-90; V Sabden and Pendleton 90-02; C Poulton-le-Fylde 02-04; C Poulton Carleton and Singleton 04-07; rtd 08; PtO *Blackb* from 08. *13 Laurel Bank Terrace, Feniscowles, Blackburn BB2 5JA*

NICHOLSON, Mrs Samantha. b 69. St Jo Coll York BA 92. St Jo Coll Nottm MA 95 LTh 93. **d** 96 **p** 97. C Toxteth St Cypr w Ch Ch *Liv* 96-01; P-in-c W Derby St Luke 01-08; P-in-c Ince Ch Ch 08-09; P-in-c Wigan St Cath 08-09; V Ince Ch Ch w Wigan St Cath 09-15; TV Wigan All SS from 15. *The Vicarage, 70 Belle Green Lane, Ince, Wigan WN2 2EP* T: (01942) 495831

NICHOLSON, Stephen James. b 83. Qu Coll Cam MEng 05. Oak Hill Th Coll BA 15. **d** 15. C Oswestry H Trin *Lich* from 15. *Address withheld by request*

NICHOLSON, Trevor Parry. b 35. St Edm Hall Ox BA 58 MA. Wycliffe Hall Ox 58. **d** 60 **p** 61. C Eastbourne Ch Ch *Chich* 60-63; C Ifield 63-67; Asst Youth Chapl *Win* 67-73; Chapl Shoreham Gr Sch 73-78; P-in-c Capel *Guildf* 78-85; V 85-90; Chapl Qu Anne's Sch Caversham 90-00; rtd 00; P-in-c N Chapel w Ebernoe *Chich* 00-05. *Lexham, Dodsley Lane, Easebourne, Midhurst GU29 9BB* T: (01730) 810452

NICHOLSON, Miss Velda Christine. b 44. Charlotte Mason Coll of Educn TCert 65. Cranmer Hall Dur 81. **dss** 82 **d** 87 **p** 94.

Gt and Lt Driffield *York* 82-86; Newby 86-88; Par Dn 87-88; Team Dn Cramlington *Newc* 88-94; TV 94-96; PtO from 96; rtd 04. *24 Glendale, Amble, Morpeth NE65 0RG* T: (01665) 713796

NICHOLSON, Veronica Mary. *See* WILSON, Veronica Mary

NICKLAS-CARTER, Derath May. *See* DURKIN, Derath May

NICKLESS, Christopher John. b 58. Univ of Wales BA 79. Coll of Resurr Mirfield 79. **d** 81 **p** 82. C Bassaleg *Mon* 81-85; TV Ebbw Vale 85-93; V Newport St Teilo 93-99. *c/o Bishopstow, Stow Hill, Newport NP9 4EA* T: (01633) 263510

NICKOLS, James Alexander. b 75. Regent's Park Coll Ox BA 96. Ridley Hall Cam 98. **d** 00 **p** 01. C Plymouth St Jude *Ex* 00-04; C Camberwell All SS *S'wark* 04-08; Hon C Camberwell Ch Ch from 09; PtO *Ox* from 13. *Christ Church, 676-680 Old Kent Road, London SE15 1JF* M: 07968-062339 E: jamesnkls@aol.com

NICKOLS-RAWLE, Peter John. b 44. St Luke's Coll Ex CertEd 73. Sarum & Wells Th Coll 76. **d** 78 **p** 79. C Ex St Thos 78-80; Old and New Shoreham *Chich* 80-86; P-in-c Donnington 86-90; Chapl RAF 90-92; TV Ottery St Mary, Alfington, W Hill, Tipton etc *Ex* 92-97; V Breage w Germoe and Godolphin *Truro* 98-01; rtd 01; PtO *Truro* 01-05. *14 The Copse, Exmouth EX8 4EY* T: (01395) 270068

NICKSON, Canon Ann Louise. b 58. New Hall Cam BA 80 Fitzw Coll Cam BA 95 Solicitor 81. Ridley Hall Cam PhD 98. **d** 98 **p** 99. C Sanderstead All SS *S'wark* 98-01; P-in-c Norbury St Steph and Thornton Heath 01-05; V 05-10; AD Croydon N 06-10; TR Mortlake w E Sheen from 10; Hon Can S'wark Cathl from 10. *The Rectory, 170 Sheen Lane, London SW14 8LZ* T: (020) 8876 4816 E: annnickson@aol.com

NICOL, David Christopher. b 56. Westmr Coll Ox BEd 84 Ox Univ Inst of Educn 91. SAOMC 95. **d** 98 **p** 99. NSM Deddington w Barford, Clifton and Hempton *Ox* 98-01; V Longnor, Quarnford and Sheen *Lich* 01-08; P-in-c Woore and Norton in Hales 09-12; Local Par Development Adv Shrewsbury Area 10-12; R Empingham, Edith Weston, Lyndon, Manton etc *Pet* from 12. *The Rectory, 5A Audit Hall Road, Empingham, Oakham LE15 8PH* T: (01780) 460216 E: fr.david@tinyworld.co.uk

NICOL, Harvie Thomas. b 61. Aston Tr Scheme 95 St Jo Coll Nottm 97. **d** 99 **p** 00. C Balderstone *Man* 99; C S Rochdale 00-03; TV Ashton 03-08; P-in-c Ashton St Pet 03-08; V Formby St Luke *Liv* from 08. *St Luke's Vicarage, St Luke's Church Road, Liverpool L37 2DF* T: (01704) 877655

NICOL, Stephen Trevor. b 52. Oak Hill Th Coll BA 82. **d** 82 **p** 83. C Harold Hill St Geo *Chelmsf* 82-85; C Greenstead 85-88. *7 rue des Forgerons, 87330 Nouic, France* E: stephen.nicol@nvoy.co.uk

NICOLE, Bruce. b 54. K Coll Lon MA 96 ACIB. Wycliffe Hall Ox 89. **d** 91 **p** 92. C Headley All SS *Guildf* 91-95; V Camberley St Mich Yorktown from 95; RD Surrey Heath 02-06. *The Vicarage, 286 London Road, Camberley GU15 3JP* T: (01276) 23602 E: revbrucenicole@googlemail.com

NICOLL, Alexander Charles Fiennes Jack. b 34. Lon Coll of Div 66. **d** 68 **p** 69. C Trentham *Lich* 68-71; C Hednesford 72-74; P-in-c Quarnford 74-84; V Longnor 74-84; P-in-c Sheen 80-84; V Longnor, Quarnford and Sheen 85-00; RD Alstonfield 96-00; rtd 00; PtO *Lich* 00-11. *110 Stone Road, Uttoxeter ST14 7QW* T: (01889) 569361

NICOLL, Miss Angela Olive Woods. b 50. Linc Th Coll 77. **dss** 79 **d** 87 **p** 94. Catford St Laur *S'wark* 79-83; Peckham St Jo w St Andr 83-88; Par Dn 87-88; Par Dn New Addington 88-94; C 94-02; S Africa 02-06; PtO *Ely* from 14. *15 Manor Park, Watton, Thetford IP25 6HH* T: (01953) 889074

NICOLLS, Andrew John. b 67. Regents Th Coll BA 03. Trin Coll Bris MA 05. **d** 05 **p** 06. C Higher Bebington Ches 05-08; P-in-c Bulwell St Mary *S'well* 08-11; R 11-15. *St John's Parsonage, 1 Nottingham Road, Hucknall, Nottingham NG15 7QN* M: 07594-436605 E: ajn50sm7@gmail.com

NICOLLS, Mrs Louise Victoria. b 71. Ch Ch Coll Cant BA 93. St Jo Coll Nottm 07. **d** 10 **p** 11. C Arnold *S'well* 10-14; TV Hucknall Torkard from 14; Chapl Nat C of E Academy Hucknall from 14. *St John's Parsonage, 1 Nottingham Road, Hucknall, Nottingham NG15 7QN* M: 07969-572731 E: louisestmarys@aol.com

NICOLSON, Paul Roderick. b 32. Cuddesdon Coll 65. **d** 67 **p** 68. C Farnham Royal *Ox* 67-68; LtO *St Alb* 69-82; C Hambleden Valley *Ox* 82-99; rtd 99. *93 Campbell Road, London N17 0AX* T: (020) 8376 5455 F: 8376 5319 - M: 07961-177889 E: paul@nicolson.com

NIECHCIAL, Stephen Alexander. b 53. St Chad's Coll Dur BA 74 CQSW 85. St Steph Ho Ox 12. **d** 14. NSM Sidcup St Jo *Roch* from 14. *14 Aldersmead Road, Beckenham BR3 1NA* T: (020) 8778 6427 M: 07976-011494 E: sjniechcial@hotmail.com

NIEMIEC, Paul Kevin. b 56. EAMTC 03. **d** 05 **p** 06. NSM Thrapston, Denford and Islip *Pet* 05-08; TV Barnstaple *Ex* 08-11; TV Ouzel Valley *St Alb* from 11. *4 Warneford Way, Leighton Buzzard LU7 4PX* T: (01525) 750099 E: pkniemiec@gmail.com

NIGHTINGALE, Catherine. b 72. **d** 01 **p** 02. C Birchencliffe *Wakef* 01-04; C to Dioc Chapl among Deaf People 01-04; TV E Farnworth and Kearsley *Man* 04-08; P-in-c Roughtown from 08; Chapl among Deaf People from 04. *The Vicarage, Carrhill Road, Mossley, Ashton-under-Lyne OL5 0BL* T: (01457) 832250 E: cathy.nightingale@clearclergy.org.uk

NIGHTINGALE, Mrs Jennifer. b 66. Wolv Univ BA 99. Qu Coll Birm. **d** 04 **p** 05. C Walsall St Paul *Lich* 04-07; C Holdenhurst and Iford *Win* from 07; Chapl Bp Win Comp Sch from 07. *13 Brackendale Road, Bournemouth BH8 9HY* T: (01202) 533356 M: 07703-558668

NIGHTINGALE, Canon John Brodie. b 42. Pemb Coll Ox BA 64 Qu Coll Cam BA 67. Westcott Ho Cam 65. **d** 67 **p** 68. C Wythenshawe St Martin *Man* 67-70; Nigeria 70-76; P-in-c Amberley w N Stoke *Chich* 76-79; Adult Educn Adv 76-79; Asst Home Sec Gen Syn Bd for Miss and Unity 80-84; Miss Sec 84-87; P-in-c Wolverton w Norton Lindsey and Langley *Cov* 87-95; Dioc Miss Adv 87-95; V Rowley Regis *Birm* 95-07; Hon Can Birm Cathl 01-07; Warden of Readers 03-07; rtd 07; PtO *Birm* from 07; *Lich* from 15. *19 Berberry Close, Birmingham B30 1TB* T: 0121-458 6182 M: 07811-128831 E: johnnightingale@btinternet.com

NIGHTINGALE, Susan Kay. b 44. Keele Univ BA 66 Seabury-Western Th Sem DMin 99. S'wark Ord Course 90. **d** 93 **p** 94. NSM St Giles Cripplegate w St Bart Moor Lane etc *Lon* 93-99; PtO *York* 93-99; Asst Chapl H Trin Geneva *Eur* 99-02; P-in-c Sutton on the Forest *York* 03-06; NSM Forest of Galtres 06-12; rtd 12; PtO *York* from 12. *Westfield Farm, Sheriff Hutton, York YO60 6QQ* T: (01347) 878423 E: suenightingale@barbicannet.demon.co.uk

NIMMO, The Very Revd Alexander Emsley. b 53. Aber Univ BD 76 PhD 97 Edin Univ MPhil 83 FSAScot 93. Edin Th Coll 76. **d** 78 **p** 79. Prec St Andr Cathl Inverness 78-81; P-in-c Stornoway *Arg* 81-83; R 84; R Edin St Mich and All SS 84-90; Chapl HM Pris Saughton 87-90; R Aberdeen St Marg *Ab* from 90; Can St Andr Cathl from 96; Syn Clerk 01-08; Dean Ab from 08. *St Margaret's Clergy House, Gallowgate, Aberdeen AB25 1EA* T: (01224) 644969 F: 630767 E: alexander306@btinternet.com

NIND, Robert William Hampden. b 31. Ball Coll Ox BA 54 MA 60. Cuddesdon Coll 54. **d** 56 **p** 57. C Spalding St Mary and St Nic *Linc* 56-60; Jamaica 60-67; P-in-c Battersea St Bart *S'wark* 67-70; V Brixton St Matt 70-82; LtO 82-84; Ind Chapl 84-89; *Ox* 89-95; rtd 95; PtO *Ox* from 15. *19 Binswood Avenue, Headington, Oxford OX3 8NY* T: (01865) 66604 E: b467@btinternet.com

NINEHAM, Prof Dennis Eric. b 21. Qu Coll Ox BA 43 MA 46 Cam Univ BD 64 Birm Univ Hon DD 72. Linc Th Coll 44. **d** 44 **p** 45. Asst Chapl Qu Coll Ox 44-46; Chapl 46-54; Prof Bibl and Hist Th K Coll Lon 54-58; Prof Div Lon Univ 58-64; Regius Prof Div Cam Univ 64-69; Warden Keble Coll Ox 69-79; Hon Can Bris Cathl 80-86; Prof Th Bris Univ 80-86; rtd 86; PtO *Ox* from 87. *9 Fitzherbert Close, Iffley, Oxford OX4 4EN* T: (01865) 715941

NISBECK, Peter. b 51. SOAS Lon BA 73 Aston Univ MSc 94. NOC 03. **d** 06 **p** 07. NSM Newcastle w Butterton *Lich* from 06. *The Village Farmhouse, Clayton Road, Newcastle ST5 4AB* T: (01782) 662379 E: peternisbeck@hotmail.com

NISBET, Gillian Ruth. b 65. NOC 00. **d** 03 **p** 04. NSM Childwall St Dav *Liv* 03-06; NSM Abu Dhabi St Andr UAE from 06. *PO Box 60534, Al Bateen PO, Abu Dhabi, UAE* T: (00971) 508-173234 E: gilliannisbet@hotmail.co.uk

NISBETT, Canon Thomas Norman. b 25. OBE 91. Codrington Coll Barbados. **d** 62 **p** 63. Barbados 62-64; Bermuda from 65; Hon Can Bermuda Cathl from 81; rtd 97. *2 Shelton Road, Pembroke HM 20, Bermuda* T/F: (001441) 236 0537

NIXON, David John. b 59. St Chad's Coll Dur BA 81 Ex Univ PhD 02. St Steph Ho Ox 88. **d** 91 **p** 92. C Plymouth St Pet *Ex* 91-94; Chapl Ex Univ 94-03; P-in-c Stoke Damerel 03-09; P-in-c Devonport St Aubyn 03-09; R Stoke Damerel and Devonport St Aubyn 09-13; RD Plymouth Devonport 11-13; Dean of Studies SWMTC from 13; Public Preacher *Ex* from 14. *SWMTC, St Luke's Campus, University of Exeter, Heavitree Road, Exeter EX1 2LU* T: (01392) 264404 E: rev.dave@virgin.net *or* deanofstudies@swmtc.org.uk

NIXON, Frances (Isobel). b 34. TCD BA 62. **d** 94 **p** 95. NSM Rossorry *Clogh* from 94. *59 Granshagh Road, Enniskillen BT92 2BL* T: (028) 6634 8723 M: 07710-307263 E: agfin@btinternet.com

NIXON, John David. b 38. Leeds Univ BSc 60 CEng 70 MICE. Linc Th Coll 76. **d** 78 **p** 79. C Rugby *Cov* 78-83; TV 83-86; TV Bicester w Bucknell, Caversfield and Launton *Ox* 86-98; USA from 98; rtd 03. *1209 W 21st Street, Lawrence KS 66046-2833, USA* E: frjdn@hotmail.com *or* allsaintskcrector@juno.com

NIXON, Ms Naomi Jane. b 75. Keele Univ BA 97. St Jo Coll Nottm MA 00. **d** 01 **p** 02. C Ludlow, Ludford, Ashford Carbonell etc *Heref* 01-04; Chapl N Warks and Hinckley Coll of FE 04-12; Dioc Learning Adv for Minl Development *Cov* from 12; NSM Lillington and Old Milverton from 10. *Cathedral and Diocesan Offices, 1 Hill Top, Coventry CV1 5AB* T: (024) 7652 1304 E: naomi.nixon@covcofe.org

NIXON, Pauline Margaret. b 49. **d** 05 **p** 06. NSM Perranzabuloe *Truro* 05-10; NSM Crantock w Cubert 09-10; NSM Perranzabuloe and Crantock w Cubert 10-12; Chapl Mt Edgcumbe Hospice 12; PtO *Blackb* from 13. *Address temp unknown* E: revpolly@btinternet.com

NIXON, Canon Phillip Edward. b 48. Ch Ch Ox MA 73 DPhil 73 Trin Coll Cam BA 80 K Coll Lon MA 00. Westcott Ho Cam 78. **d** 81 **p** 82. C Leeds Halton St Wilfrid *Ripon* 81-84; V Goring *Ox* 84; V Goring w S Stoke 84-03; RD Henley 94-02; Hon Can Ch Ch 00-03; P-in-c Northampton St Jas *Pet* 03-13; Warden of Readers 05-12; rtd 13; PtO *Ox* from 13. *32 Cedar Road, Oxford OX2 9EB* T: (01865) 241385 E: phillipn@btinternet.com

NIXON, Miss Rosemary Ann. b 45. Bp Grosseteste Coll CertEd 66 Dur Univ MA 83 Edin Univ MTh 95. Dalton Ho Bris BD 73. **d** 87 **p** 94. Tutor St Jo Coll w Cranmer Hall Dur 75-89; Dir St Jo Coll Ext Progr 82-89; NSM Chester le Street *Dur* 87-89; Team Dn Gateshead 89-92; Dir Cranmer Hall Urban Studies Unit 89-92; Staff Member Edin Th Coll 92-95; Prin TISEC 95-99; Can St Mary's Cathl 96-99; V Cleadon *Dur* 99-07; rtd 07; PtO *Dur* from 08. *6 Wearside Drive, Durham DH1 1LE* T: 0191-384 6558

NIXON, Mrs Tonya. b 69. Plymouth Univ BSc 93 St Mark & St Jo Coll Lon PGCE 94. Qu Coll Birm 06. **d** 09 **p** 10. C Farmborough, Marksbury and Stanton Prior *B & W* 09-13; P-in-c Huntspill from 13; P-in-c Mark w Allerton from 13; C Highbridge from 13. *Huntspill Rectory, Church Road, West Huntspill, Highbridge TA9 3RN* E: tonya39n@btinternet.com

NIXON, William Samuel. Reading Univ BSc 94 TCD BTh 00. **d** 00 **p** 01. C Lisburn St Paul *Conn* 00-02; C Hillsborough *D & D* 02-06; P-in-c Edin Clermiston Em 06-08; I Killaney w Carryduff *D & D* 08-12; I Drumbeg from 12; Warden of Readers from 11. *The Rectory, 64 Drumbeg Road, Dunmurry, Belfast BT17 9LE* T: (028) 9061 0255 M: 07764-277771 E: cazza_willie@hotmail.com

NIXSON, Peter. b 27. Ball Coll Ox BA 51 MA 59 Ex Univ PGCE 67 DipEd 72. Coll of Resurr Mirfield 51. **d** 53 **p** 54. C Babbacombe *Ex* 53-56; C Swindon New Town *Bris* 56-57; C Boyne Hill *Ox* 57-60; C-in-c Bayswater St Mary CD 60-66; PtO *Ex* 66-67 and 70-85; *Lich* 67-69; Hd RE Oswestry Boys' High Sch 67-69; Hon C Oswestry H Trin *Lich* 69-70; Sch Coun Tiverton 70-75; Newton Abbot 75-85; V Winkleigh *Ex* 85-92; R Ashreigney 85-92; R Broadwoodkelly 85-92; V Brushford 85-92; RD Chulmleigh 87-93; rtd 93; PtO *Ex* from 93. *40 Lidford Tor Avenue, Paignton TQ4 7ED* T: (01803) 522698

NIXSON, Rosemary Clare. *See* WARD, Rosemary Clare

NJENGA, Kennedy Samuel. b 60. Oak Hill Th Coll Qu Coll Birm. **d** 01 **p** 02. C Old Trafford St Jo *Man* 01-04; P-in-c Pheasey *Lich* 04-10; V W Bromwich Gd Shep w St Jo from 10; Chapl Sandwell Coll from 10. *The Vicarage, 4 Bromford Lane, West Bromwich B70 7HP* T: 0121-525 5530 E: njambinjenga@aol.com

NJENGA, Lukas. b 68. Natal Univ BTh 97 MTh 98. Trin Coll Nairobi. **d** 92 **p** 93. V Kitengela Kenya 92-96; R Sobantu S Africa 96-01; Lect Carlile Coll Nairobi 01-02; R Glas St Geo 02-05; Chapl Glas Caledonian Univ 05-11; Chapl York St Jo Univ from 11. *The Vicarage, York Road, Barlby, Selby YO8 5JP* T: (01904) 876606 M: 07534-719450 E: l.njenga@yorksj.ac.uk

✠**NJOJO, The Rt Revd Patrice Byankya.** b 38. BA 76. Montreal Dioc Th Coll 79. **d** 70 **p** 80 **c** 80. Bp Boga from 80; Abp Congo 92-02. *PO Box 25586, Kampala, Uganda* T: (00256) 77-647495 E: eac-mags@infocom.co.uk

NJOKA, Stanley. b 80. Middx Univ BA 09. St Andr Coll Kabare 01. **d** 04 **p** 05. Kenya 04-06; PtO *Lon* 06-07; *S'wark* 08-10; NSM Peckham St Jo w St Andr 10-11; NSM Camberwell St Giles w St Matt from 11; Chapl King's Coll Hosp NHS Foundn Trust from 10. *The Chaplaincy, King's College Hospital, Denmark Hill, London SE5 9RS* T: (020) 3299 3522 M: 07846-759133 E: stanley.njoka@nhs.net

NJOKU, Chinenye Ngozi. b 63. Trin Coll Bris. **d** 09 **p** 10. C Goldington *St Alb* 09-13; I Garrison w Slavin and Belleek

Clogh from 13. *Garrison Rectory, 39 Brollagh Road, Kockarevan, Garrison, Enniskillen BT93 4AE* T: (028) 6865 8699 M: 07515-171579 E: gozy78@hotmail.com *or* garrison@clogher.anglican.org

NJOROGE, John Kibe Mwangi. b 47. **d** 79 **p** 79. C Llantwit Major *Llan* 07-10; Chapl HM Pris Elmley from 11. *HM Prison Elmley, Church Road, Eastchurch, Sheerness ME12 4DZ* T: (01795) 882130 E: john.njoroge@hmps.gsi.gov.uk *or* john.njoroge@btinternet.com

NJUGUNA, Daniel Cahira. b 73. St Jo Coll Nottm BA 04. **d** 00 **p** 01. Kenya 00-03; C Balderton and Barnby-in-the-Willows *S'well* 04-06; TV Hucknall Torkard 06-11; V Wednesbury St Paul Wood Green *Lich* from 11. *St Paul's Vicarage, 68 Wood Green Road, Wednesbury WS10 9QT* M: 07817-577436 E: daniel.njuguna@btinternet.com

NJUGUNA, Timothy. b 49. St Paul's Coll Limuru BD 84 Presbyterian Th Coll Seoul ThM 89 San Francisco Th Sem DMin 03. **d** 83 **p** 84. V Nairobi St Mary Kenya 84-86; V Karura 86-87; V Kirangari 89-90; Dioc Sec Mt Kenya S 91-93; P-in-c San Bruno USA 99-03; PtO *S'wark* 05-07; Hon C Falkirk *Edin* from 07; Chapl Forth Valley NHS Trust from 07. *55 Maxwell Tower, Seaton Place, Falkirk FK1 1TF* T: (01324) 871921 M: 07805-690363 M: 07824-460903 E: tegssa@yahoo.com

NOAH, Michael John. b 44. WEMTC 00. **d** 02 **p** 03. NSM Hucclecote *Glouc* 02-05; NSM Malmesbury w Westport and Brokenborough *Bris* 05-11; NSM Frampton on Severn, Arlingham, Saul etc *Glouc* from 11. *1 Athelstan Court, Malmesbury SN16 0FD* T: (01666) 826564 E: mikenoah@supanet.com

NOAKES, Mrs Dorothy. b 35. Derby Coll of Educn CertEd 55 Ex Univ BEd 85 BPhil(Ed) 92. **d** 96 **p** 97. OLM Helston and Wendron *Truro* from 96. *6 Tenderah Road, Helston TR13 8NT* T: (01326) 573239 E: dorothy@dorothy1.wanadoo.co.uk

NOBBS, Canon Charles Henry ffrench. b 67. Hatf Coll Dur BSc 89 St Jo Coll Dur BA 99 CEng 96. Cranmer Hall Dur 97. **d** 99 **p** 00. C Northampton St Giles *Pet* 99-02; C Collingtree w Courteenhall and Milton Malsor 02-11; Min Grange Park LEP from 11; Police Chapl Co-ord from 03; Pioneer and Ch Planting Enabler from 13; Can Pet Cathl from 15. *10 Foxglove Close, Grange Park, Northampton NN4 5DD* T: (01604) 875188 M: 07742-013599 E: charlie@dunelm.org.uk

NOBBS, John Ernest. b 35. Tyndale Hall Bris 60. **d** 63 **p** 64. C Walthamstow St Mary *Chelmsf* 63-66; C Braintree 66-69; C Wakef St Andr and St Mary 69-71; C Tooting Graveney St Nic *S'wark* 71-74; C Woking St Pet *Guildf* 74-78; C Worthing St Geo *Chich* 78-88; C Rayleigh *Chelmsf* 88-94; rtd 94; PtO *Chelmsf* from 00. *89 Panfield Lane, Braintree CM7 5RP* T: (01376) 322901

NOBEL, Johannes. b 81. Evang Th Faculty Leuven BA 03 Utrecht Univ MA 05 St Jo Coll Dur MA 08. Cranmer Hall Dur 06. **d** 08 **p** 09. C Norton St Mary *Dur* 08-12; C Stockton St Chad 08-12; V Heslington *York* from 12. *The Vicarage, School Lane, Heslington, York YO10 5EE* T: (01904) 870814 or 412300 E: johannes.nobel@gmail.com *or* jan.nobel@gmail.com

NOBES, Mrs Gillian Mary. b 65. Lon Univ BA 90. Ripon Coll Cuddesdon MA 12. **d** 12 **p** 13. C Broughton, Bossington, Houghton and Mottisfont *Win* from 12. *1 Church Lane, Mottisfont, Romsey SO51 0LL* T: (01794) 341010 E: nobes@guernsey.net

NOBLE, Alexander Frederick Innes (Sandy). b 30. Selw Coll Cam BA 53 MA 58. Lon Coll of Div ALCD 55. **d** 55 **p** 56. C Stratton St Margaret *Bris* 55-57; C Brislington St Luke 57-59; Chapl Pierrepont Sch Frensham 59-61; Asst Chapl Repton Sch Derby 61-63; Chapl 63-66; Chapl Blundell's Sch Tiverton 66-72; St Jo C of E Sch Cowley 73-77; Chapl Cranbrook Sch Kent 77-81; Chapl St Geo Sch Harpenden 81-90; Hon C Herriard w Winslade and Long Sutton etc *Win* 90-94; rtd 95; P-in-c Oare w Culbone *B & W* 95-99; PtO from 00. *Upway, Church Street, Minehead TA24 5JU* T: (01643) 708976

NOBLE, Ann Carol. *See* PHILP, Ann Carol

NOBLE, Anne Valerie. b 60. Univ Coll Ox BA 82 Toronto Univ MSc 84 PhD 91. St Jo Coll Nottm 04. **d** 07 **p** 08. C Wollaton *S'well* 07-11; TV Clifton from 11. *St Mary's House, 58 Village Road, Clifton, Nottingham NG11 8NE* T: 0115-921 1188 E: nobles1@btinternet.com

NOBLE, Christopher John Lancelot. b 58. Oak Hill Th Coll 88. **d** 90 **p** 91. C Tonbridge SS Pet and Paul *Roch* 90-95; P-in-c Stansted w Fairseat and Vigo 95-98; R from 98. *The Rectory, 9 The Coach Drive, Meopham, Gravesend DA13 0SZ* T: (01732) 822494

NOBLE, David. b 37. S Dios Minl Tr Scheme 84. **d** 87 **p** 88. C Alverstoke *Portsm* 87-89; R Jerramungup Australia 90-93; R Bridgetown 93-97; R Willetton 97-02; rtd 02. *Quill Studio, 9 Chaparral Crescent, Willetton WA 6155, Australia* T/F: (0033) (8) 9259 0323 M: 41-717 2542 E: thenobles@surak.com.au

NOBLE, Canon Eileen Joan. b 45. NEOC 90. **d** 93 **p** 94. C Gosforth All SS *Newc* 93-96; C Cramlington 96-97; TV 97-01; V Ashington 01-06; rtd 06; Hon C Monkseaton St Mary *Newc* 07-15; Hon Can Newc Cathl from 12. *34 Gorsedene Road, Whitley Bay NE26 4AH* E: revnoble2000@yahoo.com

NOBLE, Canon Graham Edward. b 49. Open Univ BA 74 SS Paul & Mary Coll Cheltenham CertEd 71. EAMTC 85. **d** 88 **p** 89. C Kesgrave *St E* 88-90; P-in-c Gt and Lt Blakenham w Baylham and Nettlestead 90-95; P-in-c Debenham w Aspall and Kenton 95-04; P-in-c Helmingham w Framsden and Pettaugh w Winston 99-04; R Debenham and Helmingham 04-05; RD Loes 99-05; Hon Can St E Cathl 03-05; rtd 05; PtO *St E* from 05. *36 Gracechurch Street, Debenham, Stowmarket IP14 6RE* T: (01728) 861008
E: graham@noblefamily.fsnet.co.uk

NOBLE, Jack Michael. b 89. Bris Univ BA 12 Sheff Univ BA 14 MA 15. Coll of Resurr Mirfield 12. **d** 15. C Ruislip St Martin *Lon* from 15. *5 Wyteleaf Close, Ruislip HA4 7SP* M: 07765-771547 E: frjacknoble@gmail.com

NOBLE, Paul Vincent. b 54. Leeds Univ BA 75 PGCE 76 Ox Univ BA 81 MA 85. St Steph Ho Ox 79. **d** 82 **p** 83. C Prestbury *Glouc* 82-85; P-in-c Avening w Cherington 85-90; V The Suttons w Tydd *Linc* 90-98; R Skirbeck St Nic from 98. *The Rectory, Fishtoft Road, Skirbeck, Boston PE21 0DJ* T: (01205) 362734 E: frpnoble@skirbeckrectory.freeserve.co.uk

NOBLE, Canon Philip David. b 46. Glas Univ BSc 67 Edin Univ BD 70. Edin Th Coll 67. **d** 70 **p** 71. C Edin Ch Ch 70-72; C Port Moresby Papua New Guinea 72-73; P-in-c Sakarina 73-75; R Cambuslang *Glas* 76-83; R Uddingston 76-83; Ev Prestwick 83-85; R 85-11; Can St Mary's Cathl 99-11; rtd 11; PtO *Mor* from 12. *28 Duncraig Street, Inverness IV3 5DJ* T: (01463) 233612 E: philipdnoble@btopenworld.com

NOBLE, Robert. b 43. TCD BA 66 BD 73. **d** 68 **p** 69. C Holywood *D & D* 68-71; Chapl RAF 71-98; Chapl Holmewood Ho Sch Tunbridge Wells 98-04; PtO *Chich* 01-08; *Heref* from 08. *Temperance Cottage, Weston under Penyard, Ross-on-Wye HR9 7NX* T: (01989) 566748 E: rjnobles@tiscali.co.uk

NOBLES, Mrs Mary Joy. b 37. WEMTC 04. **d** 05 **p** 06. NSM Malvern Link w Cowleigh *Worc* from 05. *4 Hamilton Close, Powick, Worcester WR2 4NH* T: (01905) 831925
E: m.nobles@btopenworld.com

NOBLET, David. b 62. Cranmer Hall Dur 97. **d** 99 **p** 00. C Standish *Blackb* 99-03; P-in-c Langho Billington 03-11; LtO from 11; Chapl HM Pris Kirkham from 08; Chapl HM YOI Lanc Farms from 12. *HM Prison Kirkham, Freckleton Road, Kirkham, Preston PR4 2RN* T: (01772) 675625
E: davidnoblet@aol.com

NOBLETT, The Ven William Alexander. b 53. CBE 12. Southn Univ BTh 78 Westmr Coll Ox MTh 99. Sarum & Wells Th Coll 74. **d** 78 **p** 79. C Sholing *Win* 78-80; I Ardamine w Kiltennel, Glascarrig etc *C & O* 80-82; Chapl RAF 82-84; V Middlesbrough St Thos *York* 84-87; Dep Chapl HM Pris Wakef 87-89; Chapl 89-92; Chapl HM Pris Nor 92-97; Chapl HM Pris Full Sutton 97-01; Chapl Gen of Pris and Adn to HM Pris 01-12; Can and Preb York Minster 01-12; Hon Can Liv Cathl 09-12; rtd 12; PtO *York* from 12; *Eur* from 12; Chapl to The Queen from 05. *Address withheld by request*
E: williamnoblett@gmail.com

NOCK, Roland George William. b 62. St Andr Univ BSc 84 BD 89. Edin Th Coll 91. **d** 91 **p** 92. C Dunfermline *St And* 91-93; C W Fife Team Min 91-93; R Cupar 93-96; CF 96-99. *46 Heol y Parc, Cefneithin, Llanelli SA14 7DL* T: (01269) 845847 E: roland@nock.screaming.net

NOCKELS, John Martin. b 46. Lich Th Coll Qu Coll Birm 73. **d** 73 **p** 74. C Eccleshill *Bradf* 73-76; C Fawley *Win* 76-78; V Southampton St Jude 78-84; R Tadley St Pet 84-98; P-in-c Gt and Lt Massingham and Harpley *Nor* 98-99; P-in-c S Raynham, E w W Raynham, Helhoughton, etc 98-99; R Gt w Lt Massingham, Harpley, Rougham etc 99-06; rtd 06; PtO *Nor* from 06. *96 Church Lane, Beeston Regis, Sheringham NR26 8EY* T: (01263) 825404

NODDER, Marcus Charles Colmore. b 67. Pemb Coll Cam BA 89 PGCE 90. Oak Hill Th Coll BA 01. **d** 01 **p** 02. C Denton Holme *Carl* 01-04; C Limehouse *Lon* from 04. *13 Storers Quay, London E14 3BZ* T: (020) 7515 7947 M: 07727-713744
E: mnodder@hotmail.com *or* marcus@nodder.fsbusiness.co.uk

NODDINGS, John Henry. b 39. Chich Th Coll 80. **d** 81 **p** 82. C Southborough St Pet w Ch Ch and St Matt *Roch* 81-83; C Prittlewell *Chelmsf* 83-86; V Clay Hill St Jo *Lon* 86-88; V Clay Hill St Jo and St Luke 88-02; Chapl Chase Farm Hosp Enfield 88-94; Chapl Chase Farm Hosps NHS Trust 94-95; P-in-c Gt Coxwell w Buscot, Coleshill etc *Ox* 03-10; rtd 03; PtO *Sarum* from 10. *9 Fisherton Island, Salisbury SP2 7TG* T: (01722) 320177 E: johnnoddings@btinternet.com

NOEL, Rachel Naomi. b 75. BSc MBA MBA. STETS. **d** 14 **p** 15. C Fordingbridge and Breamore and Hale etc *Win* from 14.

19 Falconwood Close, Fordingbridge SP6 1TB M: 07773-717813 T: (01425) 655127 E: rachel@noels.org.uk

NOKE, Christopher. b 48. Ex Coll Ox BA 69 MA 79 LSE MSc 78 ACA 72 FCA 79. SEITE 03. **d** 06 **p** 07. NSM Raynes Park St Sav and S Wimbledon All SS *S'wark* from 06. *Cedar Lodge, Church Road, Ham, Richmond TW10 5HG* T: (020) 8948 7986

NOKES, Michael David Patrick. b 44. York St Jo Coll MA 05. **d** 02 **p** 03. CA from 88; NSM Heworth Ch Ch *York* 02-08; PtO *Bradf* 02-11; *Leeds* from 03; *York* from 08; rtd 10. *5 Fox Covert, York YO31 9EN* T: (01904) 674879 M: 07776-252440
E: michaelanddi@talktalk.net

NOKES, Canon Peter Warwick. b 48. Leic Univ BA 71. Westcott Ho Cam 79. **d** 81 **p** 82. C Northfield *Birm* 81-84; C Ludlow *Heref* 84-87; P-in-c Writtle w Highwood *Chelmsf* 87-91; V 91-92; P-in-c Epping St Jo 92-95; P-in-c Coopersale 93-95; TR Epping Distr 95-99; R Nor St Pet Mancroft w St Jo Maddermarket 99-15; Hon Can Nor Cathl 10-15; rtd 15; Chapl Beauchamp Community from 15. *The Chaplain's House, Newland, Malvern WR13 5AX* M: 07711-384009
T: (01684) 562100 E: pwnokes@gmail.com

NOKES, Robert Harvey. b 39. Keble Coll Ox BA 61 MA 65. Qu Coll Birm 61. **d** 63 **p** 64. C Totteridge *St Alb* 63-67; C Dunstable 67-73; V Langford 73-90; R Braughing w Furneux Pelham and Stocking Pelham 90-04; PtO *Ox* from 04. *92 Western Drive, Hanslope, Milton Keynes MK19 7LE* T: (01908) 337939 E: nokes@easykey.com

NOLAN, James Charles William. b 44. Chich Th Coll 75. **d** 77 **p** 78. C Crewe St Andr *Ches* 77-79; C Sale St Anne 79-83; R Holme Runcton w S Runcton and Wallington *Ely* 83-14; V Tottenhill w Wormegay 83-14; R Watlington 83-14; rtd 14; PtO *Nor* from 14. *26 Holt Road, Langham, Holt NR25 7BX*

NOLAN, Marcus. b 54. Bris Univ BEd. Ridley Hall Cam. **d** 83 **p** 84. C Dagenham *Chelmsf* 83-86; C Finchley St Paul and St Luke *Lon* 86-90; V W Hampstead Trin 90-98; rtd 99; PtO *Derby* 00-06. *55 Blanch Croft, Melbourne, Derby DE73 8GG*

NOLAN, Richard Thomas. b 68. Ex Univ LLB 89 Sheff Univ BA 14 Solicitor 90. Yorks Min Course 11. **d** 14 **p** 15. NSM High Harrogate St Pet *Leeds* from 14. *11 Thirlmere Drive, Wetherby LS22 6FE* T: (01937) 520258 M: 07528-574523
E: rpa.nolan@btinternet.com

NOLAN, Stephen Carl. b 74. Lanc Univ BSc 02 Sheff Univ BA 13 Bolton Univ PGCE 05. Coll of Resurr Mirfield 11. **d** 13 **p** 14. C Medlock Head *Man* from 13. *The Vicarage, 34 Church Street East, Oldham OL4 2JQ* T: 0161-284 8975

NOLES, Mrs Gillian. b 64. BEd 86. St Paul's Th Cen Lon. **d** 10 **p** 11. NSM Colchester St Jo *Chelmsf* 10-12; NSM Colchester St Luke from 12. *St Luke's Vicarage, 6 Baronia Croft, Colchester CO4 9EE* T: (01206) 532252 E: gillnoles@ntlworld.com *or* gill@stlukescolchester.org.uk

NOLES, Jeremy Andrew. b 67. St Jo Coll Nottm 02. **d** 04 **p** 05. C Southchurch Ch Ch *Chelmsf* 04-07; C Colchester St Jo 07-12; V Colchester St Luke from 12. *St Luke's Vicarage, 6 Baronia Croft, Colchester CO4 9EE* T: (01206) 532252 M: 07719-652333 E: jeremynoles@ntlworld.com

NOLLAND, John Leslie. b 47. New England Univ (NSW) BSc 67 Clare Coll Cam PhD 78. Moore Th Coll Sydney ThL 70 BD 71. **d** 71 **p** 72. Res Min Cabramatta Australia 71-74; Asst Prof NT Studies Regent Coll Vancouver Canada 78-86; Tutor Trin Coll Bris from 86; Vice Prin 91-97 and 06-07. *6 Phoenix Grove, Bristol BS6 7XY* T: 0117-924 4896
E: john.nolland@cantab.net

NOONAN, Deborah Anne. b 79. Virginia Univ BA 01. Yale Div Sch MDiv 10. **d** 09 **p** 10. C Trin Cathl Phoenix USA 10-12; C Eynesbury *Ely* from 12; C St Neots from 12. *14 Chestnut Grove, Eynesbury, St Neots PE19 2DW* T: (01480) 390509
E: rev.noonan@gmail.com

NOORDANUS, Francis Peter. b 61. Cant Univ (NZ) BA 82 ACT BTh 90. **d** 92 **p** 93. C Ashburton New Zealand 92-94; V Masterton St Matt 94-02; Chapl Eindhoven *Eur* from 02. *Paradijslaan 76, 5611 KR Eindhoven, The Netherlands* T: (0031) (40) 245 0601 E: f.p.noordanus@planet.nl

NOPPEN, Miss Chantal Mary. b 83. Newc Univ BMus 06 Clare Coll Cam BTh 12. Westcott Ho Cam 10. **d** 13 **p** 14. C Byker St Martin *Newc* from 13; C Byker St Mich w St Lawr from 13. *26 Crompton Road, Newcastle upon Tyne NE6 5QL* E: c.noppen@googlemail.com

NORBURN, Christopher Richard. b 62. Cov Poly BSc 85. Aston Tr Scheme 92 Ridley Hall Cam 94. **d** 96 **p** 97. C Exning St Martin w Landwade *St E* 96-99; P-in-c Redgrave cum Botesdale w Rickinghall 99-01; R from 01. *The Rectory, Bury Road, Rickinghall, Diss IP22 1HA* T: (01379) 898685

NORBURN, Canon Richard Henry. b 32. MBE 97. St Edm Hall Ox BA 57. Wycliffe Hall Ox 57. **d** 59 **p** 59. C Sudbury St Greg and St Pet *St E* 59-65; Dioc Youth Officer 65-74; P-in-c Gt Livermere 74-81; R Ampton w Lt Livermere and Ingham

74-81; RD Thingoe 78-88; Hon Can St E Cathl 81-97; R Ingham w Ampton and Gt and Lt Livermere 81-92; TV Blackbourne 92-97; rtd 97; PtO *St E* from 97. *69 Churchgate Street, Bury St Edmunds IP33 1RL* T: (01284) 702644
E: richardhnorburn@btopenworld.com

NORBURY, Robert John. b 60. Southn Univ BA 83 Univ of Wales (Ban) BTh 07. S'wark Ord Course 01. d 04 p 05. NSM Eltham Park St Luke *S'wark* 04-07; PtO *Chich* 07-08; NSM Crowborough St Jo 08-12; P-in-c 09-13; V from 13; Chapl Wandsworth Primary Care Trust 09-10; Dir of Ords Croydon Area *S'wark* 10-12. *St John's Vicarage, St John's Road, Crowborough TN6 1RZ* T: (01892) 668188 M: 07715-595828
E: frrobnorbury@aol.com

NORBY, Dean Luverne. d 11 p 12. C Edin St Paul and St Geo 11-14; P-in-c Burntisland *St And* from 14. *Address temp unknown* M: 07821-712500

NORFIELD, David Jonathan. b 67. Humberside Univ BA 89. Linc Th Coll MA 94 Westcott Ho Cam 95. d 97 p 98. C Halstead St Andr w H Trin and Greenstead Green *Chelmsf* 97-01; V Moulsham St Jo 01-04; Chapl RAF from 04. *Chaplaincy Services (RAF), HQ Air Command, RAF High Wycombe HP14 4UE* T: (01494) 496800 F: 496343
E: davidnorfield@hotmail.com

NORFOLK, The Ven Edward Matheson. b 21. Leeds Univ BA 44. Coll of Resurr Mirfield 41. d 46 p 47. C Greenford H Cross *Lon* 46-47; C S Mymms K Chas 47-50; C Bushey *St Alb* 50-53; PC Waltham Cross 53-59; V Welwyn Garden City *St Alb* 59-69; R Gt Berkhamsted 69-81; Hon Can St Alb 72-82; V Kings Langley 81-82; Adn St Alb 82-87; r-d 87; PtO *Ex* 87-09. *5 Fairlawn Court, Sidmouth EX10 8UR* T: (01395) 514222

NORFOLK, Archdeacon of. See BETTS, The Ven Steven James

NORGATE, Norman George. b 32. Qu Coll Cam BA 55 MA 58. Ridley Hall Cam. d 57 p 58. C Erith St Paul *Roch* 57-60; C E Twickenham St Steph *Lon* 60-63; V Bexleyheath St Pet *Roch* 63-71; V Woking St Mary *Guildf* 71-83; V Tunbridge Wells St Jas *Roch* 83-92; TR Tunbridge Wells St Jas w St Phil 92-97; rtd 97; PtO St E from 97. *Crathie, 58 Sexton Meadows, Bury St Edmunds IP33 2SB* T: (01284) 767363

NORKETT, Alan. b 45. Sarum & Wells Th Coll 85. d 87 p 88. C Shrewsbury St Giles w Sutton and Atcham *Lich* 87-90; V Mow Cop 90-94; NSM Astbury and Smallwood *Ches* 96-97; NSM Sandbach Heath w Wheelock 97-98; C Castleford All SS and Whitwood *Wakef* 98-01; C Glass Houghton 98-01; R Shrawley, Witley, Astley and Abberley *Worc* 01-10; r-d 10. *15 New Road, Far Forest, Kidderminster DY14 9TQ* T: (01299) 269355 E: vicaralan@btinternet.com

NORMAN, Andrew Bryan. b 90. Selwyn Coll Cam BA 11 MA 15. Ripon Coll Cuddesdon BA 14. d 15. C Cartmel Peninsula *Carl* from 15. *The Vicarage, Station Road, Flookburgh, Grange-over-Sands LA11 7JY* E: revdabn@gmail.com

NORMAN, Canon Andrew Herbert. b 54. K Coll Lon BD 77 AKC 77 Lon Univ PhD 88. St Steph Ho Ox 77. d 78 p 79. C Deal St Leon w Sholden *Cant* 78-81; C Maidstone All SS and St Phil w Tovil 81-84; V Tenterden St Mich 84-93; Chapl Benenden Hosp 86-91; Dir Post-Ord Tr *Cant* 91-93; R Guildf St Nic from 93; Hon Can Guildf Cathl from 05. *The Rectory, 3 Flower Walk, Guildford GU2 4EP* T: (01483) 504895
E: andrew@andrewnorman.orangehome.co.uk

NORMAN, Canon Andrew Robert. b 63. Univ Coll Ox BA 84 MA 99 Selw Coll Cam BA 94 MA 99 Birm Univ MPhil 08 AIL 89. Ridley Hall Cam 92. d 95 p 96. Asst Chapl Paris St Mich *Eur* 95-00; C Clifton Ch Ch w Em *Bris* 00-02; Abp's Asst Sec for Ecum and Angl Affairs *Cant* 02-05; Abp's Prin Sec for Internat, Ecum and Angl Communion Affairs 05-08; Prin Ridley Hall Cam from 08; Hon Prov Can Cant Cathl from 06; Hon Can Ely Cathl from 12. *Ridley Hall, Cambridge CB3 9HG* T: (01223) 746580 *or* 741060 F: 746581
E: arn1000@cam.ac.uk

NORMAN, Ann. See NORMAN, Margaret Ann

NORMAN, Catherine. b 53. Nottm Univ BSc 73 N Counties Coll Newc CertEd 74. Linc Th Coll 95. d 95 p 96. C Scartho *Linc* 95-99; V Ulceby Gp 99-02; TV Guiseley w Esholt *Bradf* 02-08; P-in-c Rawdon 08-13; V 13-14; RD Otley 09-14; rtd 14. *3 Borrowdale Croft, Yeadon, Leeds LS19 7FN*
E: caytenorman@aol.com

NORMAN, Canon Edward Robert. b 38. Selw Coll Cam BA 61 PhD 64 MA 65 BD 67 DD 78 FRHistS 72 FRSA 88. Linc Th Coll 65. d 65 p 71. Fell Jes Coll Cam 64-71; Lect Cam Univ 65-88; Dean Peterho Cam 71-88; Dean of Chpl Ch Ch Coll of HE Cant 88-95; Six Preacher Cant Cathl 84-90; Can Res York Minster 95-04; Can Res and Treas York Minster 95-99; Can Res and Chan York Minster 99-04; Hon Prof York Univ from 96; Hon C St Andr-by-the-Wardrobe w St Ann, Blackfriars *Lon* from 05; Hon C St Jas Garlickhythe w St Mich Queenhithe etc from 05. *Peterhouse, Cambridge CB2 1RD*

NORMAN, Mrs Elizabeth Ann. b 43. SAOMC 95. d 98 p 99. OLM Amersham *Ox* 98-04; PtO *Ex* from 11. *Lamorna, Main Road, Bickington, Barnstaple EX31 2NA* T: (01271) 859314
E: liz.norman4@btinternet.com

NORMAN, The Ven Garth. b 38. St Chad's Coll Dur BA 62 MA 68 UEA MEd 84 Cam Inst of Educn PGCE 68. d 63 p 64. C Wandsworth St Anne *S'wark* 63-66; C Trunch w Swafield *Nor* 66-71; R Gimingham 71-77; TR Trunch 77-83; RD Repps 75-83; Prin Chiltern Chr Tr Course *Ox* 83-87; C W Wycombe w Bledlow Ridge, Bradenham and Radnage 83-87; Dir of Tr *Roch* 88-94; Adn Bromley and Bexley 94-03; Hon Can Roch Cathl 91-03; rtd 03; PtO *S'well* from 03; Chapl to Retired Clergy 04-09; PtO *Ely* from 10. *12 Scotsdowne Road, Trumpington, Cambridge CB2 9HU* T: (01223) 844303
E: garthnorman@btinternet.com

NORMAN, Gary. b 64. Newc Univ BA 87. Ripon Coll Cuddesdon 02. d 04 p 05. C Spennymoor and Whitworth *Dur* 04-09; P-in-c Croxdale and Tudhoe from 08; P-in-c Merrington from 09. *The Vicarage, 21 York Villas, Spennymoor DL16 6LP* T: (01388) 811108

NORMAN, Jillianne Elizabeth. b 59. Ridley Hall Cam 85. d 88 p 94. Par Dn Fishponds St Jo *Bris* 88-92; PtO 92-94; Hon C Warmley, Syston and Bitton from 94; Chapl Univ Hosps Bris NHS Foundn Trust from 02. *74 Blackhorse Road, Mangotsfield, Bristol BS16 9AY* T: 0117-956 1551 F: 904 6894
E: jilliannenorman@blueyonder.co.uk

NORMAN, Linda Mary. b 48. Man Univ BSc 69 CertEd 70 St Jo Coll Dur BA 82. dss 83 d 87. York St Mich-le-Belfrey 83-88; Par Dn 87-88; rtd 88. *23 Ainsty Avenue, Dringhouses, York YO24 1HH* T: (01904) 706152

NORMAN, Lynette Dianne. b 52. Sussex Univ CertEd 73 Univ of Wales (Ban) BEd 89. Ripon Coll Cuddesdon 00. d 02 p 03. C Welshpool w Castle Caereinion *St As* 02-04; R LLanrwst 04-11; C Llanrhaeadr ym Mochnant etc from 11. *Maes-y-Llan, Pennant Melangell, Llangynog, Oswestry SY10 0HQ* M: 07889-184517

NORMAN, Margaret Ann. b 48. N Lon Poly CertEd 76 ALA 73. SEITE 09. d 11. NSM Erith St Paul *Roch* 11-13; NSM Erith Ch Ch from 13. *27 Kempton Close, Erith DA8 3SR* T: (01322) 340902 E: ann.norman@hotmail.com

NORMAN, Michael John. b 59. Southn Univ LLB 82. Wycliffe Hall Ox 82. d 85 p 86. C Woodley St Jo the Ev *Ox* 85-89; C Uphill *B & W* 89-92; TV 92-98; R Bath St Sav w Swainswick and Woolley from 98. *St Saviour's Rectory, Claremont Road, Bath BA1 6LX* T: (01225) 311637 E: michael@stsaviours.org.uk

NORMAN, Michael John. b 61. St Jo Coll Ox BSc 83 Univ Coll Lon MSc 84. Aston Tr Scheme 89 St Jo Coll Nottm 91. d 93 p 94. C Haughton le Skerne *Dur* 93-97; R Sapcote and Sharnford w Wigston Parva *Leic* from 97; RD Sparkenhoe W 02-07. *The Rectory, 4 Sharnford Road, Sapcote, Leicester LE9 4JN* T: (01455) 272215 E: micknorman@msn.com

NORMAN, Peter John. b 59. Chich Th Coll 84. d 87 p 88. C Farncombe *Guildf* 87-91; C Cockington *Ex* 91-94; V Winkleigh from 94; R Ashreigney from 94; R Broadwoodkelly from 94; V Brushford from 94. *The Vicarage, Torrington Road, Winkleigh EX19 8HR* T: (01837) 83719

NORMAN, Peter John. b 42. Culham Coll of Educn TCert 66 Lon Inst of Educn DipEd 83 MA 86. STETS 95. d 98 p 99. NSM Bath Weston All SS w N Stoke and Langridge *B & W* 98-13. *5 Rockliffe Avenue, Bathwick, Bath BA2 6QP* T: (01225) 465354 E: peterjnorman@sky.com

NORMAN, Canon Richard Hudson. b 58. Louisiana State Univ BS 84 MA 88. Gen Th Sem NY MDiv 93 STM 93. d 92 p 93. C Southgate St Andr *Lon* 92 and 97-98; Assoc New York City St Matt and St Tim USA 92-93; R Abbeville St Paul 93-95; Assoc R Chevy Chase All SS 95-97; V Mill Hill St Mich *Lon* 98-02; R Greenville Redeemer USA 02-05; Sen Can St Mark's Cathl Minneapolis from 05. *3734 Pleasant Avenue, Minneapolis MN 55409, USA* T: (001) (612) 870 7800 F: 870 7802
E: richardn@ourcathedral.org

NORMAN, Richard Jonathan. b 88. Ch Ch Ox BA 10 Leeds Univ MA 11. Coll of Resurr Mirfield 09. d 11 p 12. C Rotherhithe St Mary w All SS *S'wark* 11-15; V Bickley Roch from 15. *St George's Vicarage, Bickley Park Road, Bromley BR1 2BE* M: 07752-732324 T: (020) 8467 3809 *or* 8295 6411
E: rjnorman@hotmail.co.uk

NORMAN, Timothy. b 68. Jes Coll Cam BA 91 Univ Coll Lon PhD 95. Spurgeon's Coll 95 Wycliffe Hall Ox BA 00. d 01 p 02. C Chipping Norton *Ox* 01-04; Asst Chapl Paris St Mich *Eur* 04-06; PtO 06-08; C Rugby W *Cov* 09-14. *58 Park Road, Rugby CV21 2QH* T: (01788) 537468
E: tim.norman@bigfoot.com

NORMAN, Canon William Beadon. b 26. Trin Coll Cam BA 49 MA 55. Ridley Hall Cam 52. d 52 p 53. C Beckenham St Jo *Roch* 52-54; CMS Miss and Tutor Buwalasi Th Coll Uganda

55-65; Hon Can Mbale 63-65; V Alne *York* 65-74; RD Warley *Birm* 74-79; V Blackheath 74-79; Hon Can Birm Cathl 78-91; TR Kings Norton 79-91; RD 82-87; Warden Dioc Readers Bd 84-91; rtd 91; PtO *S'wark* from 91; Preacher Lincoln's Inn 94-06. *37 Cloudesdale Road, London SW17 8ET* T: (020) 8673 9134 F: 8675 6890 E: bbnorman@hotmail.com

NORMAN-WALKER, Canon Anna Elizabeth. b 67. RGN 89. St Jo Coll Nottm BA 03. **d** 03 **p** 04. C Cullompton, Willand, Uffculme, Kentisbeare etc *Ex* 03-06; TV 06-10; Chapl Stover Sch Newton Abbot 06-08; RD Cullompton *Ex* 09-10; Can Res Ex Cathl from 10; Dioc Missr 10-14; Chan from 14. *6 Cathedral Close, Exeter EX1 1EZ* M: 07557-053567 T: (01392) 255573 E: missioner@exeter.anglican.org

NORMAND, Stephen Joseph William. b 48. N Texas State Univ BSEd 80. Sarum & Wells Th Coll 90. **d** 92 **p** 93. C Norton *St Alb* 92-94; C St Alb St Pet 95-97; Chapl Oaklands Coll 95-97; TV Horsham *Chich* 97-01; R Wimbotsham w Stow Bardolph and Stow Bridge etc *Ely* 01-04; rtd 04; PtO *Ely* 05-09; *S'wark* from 13. *97 Mitre Road, London SE1 8PT* T: (020) 7633 0012 E: normasteph@aol.com

NORRINGTON, Paul Richard. b 57. Brighton Poly BSc 80. Trin Coll Bris 96. **d** 98 **p** 99. C Prittlewell St Pet w Westcliff St Cedd *Chelmsf* 98-02; R Colchester Ch Ch w St Mary V from 02; AD Colchester from 14. *The Rectory, 21 Cambridge Road, Colchester CO3 3NS* T: (01206) 563478 E: paul.nozzer@btinternet.com

NORRIS, Preb Alison. b 55. St Andr Univ MTheol 77 Dur Univ PGCE 78. Cant Sch of Min 80. **dss** 82 **d** 87 **p** 94. Warlingham w Chelsham and Farleigh *S'wark* 82-85; Willingham *Ely* 85-90; Hon Par Dn 87-90; Hon Par Dn Worle *B & W* 90-94; NSM Milverton w Halse and Fitzhead 94-02; P-in-c Deane Vale 02-10; R from 10; Preb Wells Cathl from 14. *6 Cole Close, Cotford St Luke, Taunton TA4 1NZ* T: (01823) 431567 E: revalison@revsnorris.co.uk

NORRIS, Allan Edward. b 43. St Jo Coll Dur BA 72. Cranmer Hall Dur 69. **d** 73 **p** 74. C Plumstead St Jo w St Jas and St Paul *S'wark* 73-78; C Battersea Park St Sav 78-82; C Battersea St Geo w St Andr 78-82; V Grain w Stoke *Roch* 82-92; R Sissinghurst w Frittenden *Cant* 92-12; rtd 12; PtO *Cant* from 13. *17 Abbots Road, Faversham ME13 8DD* T: (01795) 227927 E: allannorris@talktalk.net

NORRIS, Andrew David. b 54. St Andr Univ BSc 78 Lon Univ MPhil 80 CPsychol. EAMTC 87. **d** 90 **p** 91. C Worle *B & W* 90-94; R Milverton w Halse and Fitzhead 94-08; RD Tone 01-07; Nat Chapl Adv Methodist Homes for the Aged 08-14; St Monica Trust Westbury Fields from 14. *St Monica Trust, Cote Lane, Bristol BS9 3UN* M: 07812-061761 T: 0117-949 4000 E: revandrew@revsnorris.co.uk

NORRIS, Andrew Peter. b 62. Aston Univ BSc 83. St Jo Coll Nottm BA 86. **d** 87 **p** 88. C Mountsorrel Ch Ch and St Pet *Leic* 87-90; C Harborne Heath *Birm* 90-91; P-in-c Edgbaston St Germain 91-92; V 92-99; P-in-c Hook w Warsash *Portsm* 99-00; V 00-13; P-in-c Alverstoke from 13. *Alverstoke Rectory, Little Anglesey Road, Gosport PO12 2JA*

NORRIS, Barry John. b 46. Nottm Univ MTh 86 Open Univ BA 80 K Coll Lon PhD 95 CQSW 75. St Jo Sem Wonersh. **d** 70 **p** 71. In RC Ch 70-72; C Wisbech SS Pet and Paul *Ely* 76-78; TV E Ham w Upton Park and Forest Gate *Chelmsf* 78-81; Chapl RAF 81-87; V N Tadley St Mary *Win* 87-11; rtd 11. *42 Greenway, Crediton EX17 3LP* E: baz.norris@talktalk.net

NORRIS, Daniel Ross. d 15. NSM Gt Stanmore *Lon* from 15. *11 The Chantries, 18 Uxbridge Road, Stanmore HA7 3LG* M: 07779-094794 E: dnorris3@hgfl.org.uk

NORRIS, Eric Richard. b 43. Bernard Gilpin Soc Dur 65 Ripon Hall Ox 66. **d** 69 **p** 70. C Huyton St Mich *Liv* 69-72; C Mexborough *Sheff* 72-74; V Dalton 74-78; Org Sec CECS Carl 78-89; Area Appeals Manager N Co 89-93; TR Thirsk *York* 93-02; RD Mowbray 00-02; V Boosbeck w Moorsholm 02-06; Abp's Adv in Tourism 02-06; rtd 06; PtO *York* from 06. *39 Upleatham Street, Saltburn-by-the-Sea TS12 1JX* T: (01287) 280940 E: dtoyork@gmail.com

NORRIS, Mrs Helen. b 53. Univ of Wales (Abth) LLB 74 Univ Coll Lon LLM 76 Solicitor 78. **d** 04 **p** 05. OLM Coddenham w Gosbeck and Hemingstone w Henley *St E* 04-13; NSM from 13; OLM Crowfield w Stonham Aspal and Mickfield 04-13; NSM from 13. *The Villa, The Street, Stonham Aspal, Stowmarket IP14 6AQ* T: (01449) 711395 E: helen.norris@btinternet.com

NORRIS, Julie Mary. b 63. Westmr Coll Ox BA 84 Fitzw Coll Cam MPhil 88 Birm Univ PhD 03. Wesley Ho Cam 86. **d** 06 **p** 06. C Orwell Gp *Ely* 06-09; P-in-c Gt w Lt Abington from 09; P-in-c Hildersham from 09; TV Linton from 09; P-in-c Balsham, Weston Colville, W Wickham etc from 10; RD Granta from 11. *The Vicarage, 35 Church Lane, Little Abington, Cambridge CB21 6BQ* T: (01223) 891350 E: revjulienorris@gmail.com

NORRIS, Keith David. b 47. E Lon Univ BA 89 MIAM 76 MBIM 80. NTMTC 95. **d** 98 **p** 02. NSM Cranham Park *Chelmsf*

98-99; NSM S Hornchurch St Jo and St Matt 01-06; NSM Rainham w Wennington 06-14; rtd 15. *Still Waters, 8 Hesselyn Drive, Rainham RM13 7EJ* T: (01708) 780767 M: 07908-557047 E: keithdnorris@hotmail.co.uk

NORRIS, Mark. b 68. Brunel Univ BEng 90. Oak Hill Th Coll BA 93. **d** 93 **p** 94. C Roby *Liv* 93-97; C St Helens St Helen 97-00; TV Gateacre 00-09; Asst Dioc Dir of Ords 05-09; Leadership Development Adv (Voc) CPAS 09-12; V Keresley and Coundon *Cov* from 12. *Keresley Vicarage, 34 Tamworth Road, Coventry CV6 2EL* T: (024) 7633 2717 E: vicar@keresleychurches.org.uk

NORRIS, Michael Charles Latham. b 69. Reading Univ LLB. Wycliffe Hall Ox 99. **d** 01 **p** 02. C Bryanston Square St Mary w St Marylebone St Mark *Lon* 01-03; V Symonds Street St Paul New Zealand 04-13; R Guildf St Sav from 13. *St Saviour's Rectory, Wharf Road, Guildford GU1 4RP* T: (01483) 577811 E: mikenorris1@hotmail.com

NORRIS, Paul. b 48. **d** 10 **p** 11. OLM Woughton *Ox* from 10. *20 Thirsk Gardens, Bletchley, Milton Keynes MK3 5LH* T: (01908) 371824 M: 07840-296676 E: paul88547@aol.com

NORTH, Christopher David. b 69. Trin Coll Bris BA 01. **d** 01 **p** 02. C Bathampton w Claverton *B & W* 01-05; P-in-c Chilcompton w Downside and Stratton on the Fosse from 05; RD Midsomer Norton from 12. *The Rectory, The Street, Chilcompton, Radstock BA3 4HN* T: (01761) 232219 E: c.north123@btinternet.com

NORTH, Preb David Roland. b 45. Lich Th Coll 70 Qu Coll Birm 72. **d** 73 **p** 74. C Salesbury *Blackb* 73-76; C Marton 76-79; V Penwortham St Leon 79-87; R Whittington St Jo *Lich* 87-10; P-in-c W Felton 96-10; RD Oswestry 02-09; Chapl Robert Jones/Agnes Hunt Orthopaedic NHS Trust 00-01; Preb Lich Cathl 07-10; rtd 11; PtO *Lich* from 11; *St As* from 11. *Honeycroft, Daisy Lane, Whittington, Oswestry SY11 4EA* T: (01691) 676130

NORTH, Lyndon Percival. b 55. Lon Bible Coll BA 77. NTMTC. **d** 00 **p** 01. NSM Sudbury St Andr *Lon* 00-04 and 05-12; C Roxbourne St Andr 04-05; V from 12. *St Andrew's Vicarage, Malvern Avenue, Harrow HA2 9ER* T: (020) 8422 3633 M: 07747-638783 E: lyndonnorth@hotmail.com *or* revlnorth@aol.com

NORTH, Mark Richard. b 71. St Steph Ho Ox 03. **d** 05 **p** 06. C Sevenoaks St Jo *Roch* 05-09; V Burnham *Chelmsf* from 09. *The Vicarage, 2A Church Road, Burnham-on-Crouch CM0 8DA* T: (01621) 782071 M: 07776-231681 E: frmarknorth@btinternet.com

NORTH, Michael. b 50. **d** 13. NSM Stokenham, Slapton, Charleton w Buckland etc *Ex* from 13. *Figtree, Vicarage Road, Blackawton, Totnes TQ9 7AY*

✠**NORTH, The Rt Revd Philip John.** b 66. York Univ BA 88. St Steph Ho Ox BA 91 MA 01. **d** 92 **p** 93 **c** 15. C Sunderland St Mary and St Pet *Dur* 92-96; V Hartlepool H Trin 96-02; AD Hartlepool 00-02; P-in-c Hempton and Pudding Norton *Nor* 04-07; TR Old St Pancras *Lon* 08-15; Suff Bp Burnley *Blackb* from 15; CMP from 97. *Dean House, 449 Padiham Road, Burnley BB12 6TE* M: 07919-180788 T: (01282) 479300 E: bishop.burnley@blackburn.anglican.org

NORTH, Preb Robert. b 54. Lon Univ BSc 77. Ripon Coll Cuddesdon 78. **d** 81 **p** 82. C Leominster *Heref* 81-86; TV Heref St Martin w St Fran, Dewsall etc 86-92; P-in-c Heref St Nic 92-97; TR W Heref from 97; Dir of Ords 92-00; Preb Heref Cathl from 94; Dioc Chapl MU from 05. *St Nicholas's Rectory, 76 Breinton Road, Hereford HR4 0JY* T: (01432) 273810

NORTH, Canon Vernon Leslie. b 26. Bps' Coll Cheshunt 61. **d** 63 **p** 64. C N Holmwood *Guildf* 63-65; C Dunstable *St Alb* 65-68; V Stotfold 68-91; V Stotfold and Radwell 91-92; RD Shefford 79-91; Hon Can St Alb 89-92; rtd 92; PtO *Ely* from 96; *St Alb* 00-13. *Hunters Moon, 10 High Street, Little Paxton, St Neots PE19 6HA* T: (01480) 471146

NORTH, William Walter. b 77. Ox Brookes Univ BA 03. St Jo Coll Nottm 07. **d** 09 **p** 10. C N Farnborough *Guildf* 09-13; R Barming *Roch* from 13. *The Rectory, Church Lane, Barming, Maidstone ME16 9HA* T: (01622) 726263 M: 07766-560793 E: revwilnorth@hotmail.co.uk

NORTHALL, Linda Barbara. *See* ISIORHO, Linda Barbara

NORTHALL, Malcolm Walter. b 26. Cheshunt Coll Cam 59 Ely Th Coll 63. **d** 64 **p** 65. C Bromsgrove St Jo *Worc* 64-67; V Blockley w Aston Magna *Glouc* 67-82; P-in-c Churchdown 82; V 82-92; rtd 92; PtO *Ban* from 92. *5 Maethlon Close, Tywyn LL36 0BN* T: (01654) 710123

NORTHALL, Ms Sarah Elizabeth. b 69. Ex Univ BA 91 PGCE 92. Ox Min Course 09. **d** 12 **p** 13. C Iffley *Ox* from 12. *Church House, The Oval, Rose Hill, Oxford OX4 4SE* T: (01865) 579695 E: revsarahnorthall@gmail.com

NORTHAM, Cavell Herbert James Cavell. *See* CAVELL-NORTHAM, Cavell Herbert James

NORTHAM, Mrs Susan Jillian. b 36. Oak Hill Th Coll 87. **d** 89. NSM Enfield Ch Ch Trent Park *Lon* 89-91; Par Dn 91-94; C 94-97; rtd 97; PtO *Lon* from 02. *5 Beech Hill Avenue, Barnet EN4 0LW* T/F: (020) 8440 2723
E: jillandjohn.northam@btinternet.com

NORTHAMPTON, Archdeacon of. *See* ORMSTON, The Ven Richard Jeremy

NORTHCOTT, Canon Michael Stafford. b 55. St Chad's Coll Dur BA 76 MA 77 Sunderland Univ PhD 81. Cranmer Hall Dur 80. **d** 81 **p** 82. C Chorlton-cum-Hardy St Clem *Man* 81-84; USPG 84-89; Malaysia 84-89; Sen Lect Chr Ethics New Coll Edin Univ 89-91; NSM Edin Old St Paul 89-91; NSM Edin St Jas from 91; TV Edin St Marg 93-96; Can Th Liv Cathl from 05; LtO *Glas* from 12. *New College, Mound Place, Edinburgh EH1 2LX* T: 0131-554 1651 E: m.northcott@ed.ac.uk

NORTHCOTT, William Mark. b 36. Clifton Th Coll 61. **d** 64 **p** 65. C Walthamstow St Luke *Chelmsf* 64-68; C Idle *Bradf* 68-70; N Sec *CMJ* 70-79; V Withnell *Blackb* 79-90; P-in-c Glenrothes *St And* 90-91; Asst Dioc Supernumerary 90-91; PtO *Blackb* from 91; *Liv* from 91. *34 Welsby Road, Leyland PR25 1JB* T: (01772) 493932

NORTHERN, Elaine Joy. *See* TIPP, Elaine Joy

NORTHEY, Edward Alexander Anson. b 81. Trin Coll Bris BA 08. Wycliffe Hall Ox 09. **d** 11 **p** 12. C Barrow St Mark *Carl* 11-14; Chapl Univ Hosps of Morecambe Bay NHS Trust from 14. *Furness General Hospital, Dalton Lane, Barrow-in-Furness LA14 4LF* T: (01229) 870870 M: 07952-938797
E: edwardnorthey@gmail.com

NORTHEY (née GANT), Mrs Joanna Elizabeth. b 75. Dur Univ BSc 96 Ox Univ PGCE 97. Trin Coll Bris BA 09. **d** 09 **p** 10. C Swindon Ch Ch *Bris* 09-11; C Barrow St Mark *Carl* 11-14; TV S Barrow from 14. *31 Middle Hill, Barrow-in-Furness LA13 9HD* T: (01229) 826487 M: 07807-188912
E: revjonorthey@gmail.com

NORTHFIELD, Stephen Richmond. b 55. Lon Univ BSc 77 Southn Univ BTh 84. Sarum & Wells Th Coll 79. **d** 82 **p** 83. C Colchester St Jas, All SS, St Nic and St Runwald *Chelmsf* 82-85; C Chelmsf All SS 85-89; V Ramsey w Lt Oakley and Wrabness 89-95; V Hatfield Peverel w Ulting from 95. *The Vicarage, Church Road, Hatfield Peverel, Chelmsford CM3 2LE* T: (01245) 380958 E: srnorthfield@aol.com

NORTHING, Ross. b 58. St Steph Ho Ox 92. **d** 94 **p** 95. C Up Hatherley *Glouc* 94-98; C Cheltenham St Steph 94-95; C Cheltenham Em w St Steph 95-98; V Stony Stratford *Ox* 98-11; R Calverton 98-11; R Stony Stratford w Calverton from 12. *St Mary and St Giles Vicarage, 14 Willow Lane, Stony Stratford, Milton Keynes MK11 1FG* T: (01908) 562148 F: 565132 E: r.northing@btinternet.com

NORTHOLT, Archdeacon of. *See* GREEN, The Ven Duncan Jamie

NORTHOVER, Kevin Charles. b 57. Coll of Resurr Mirfield 89. **d** 91 **p** 92. C Kingston upon Hull St Alb *York* 91-94; V Moorends *Sheff* 94-00; R Guernsey St Michel du Valle *Win* from 00; Vice-Dean Guernsey 07-13; Sen Vice-Dean from 13; Chapl HM Pris Guernsey from 00; CMP from 99. *The Rectory, L'Abbaye, Vale, Guernsey GY3 5SF* T: (01481) 244088
E: frkevin@cwgsy.net

NORTHRIDGE, Herbert Aubrey Hamilton. b 16. TCD BA 40 MA 43. **d** 41 **p** 42. C Londonderry Ch Ch *D & R* 41-45; P-in-c Convoy 45-47; I 47-50; I Derg 50-70; I Derg w Termonamongan 70-81; Can Derry Cathl 72-81; rtd 81. *Goblusk, Ballinamallard BT94 2LW* T: (028) 6638 8676

NORTHUMBERLAND, Archdeacon of. *See* MILLER, The Ven Geoffrey Vincent

NORTON, Anthony Bernard. b 40. Man Univ BA 62. Linc Th Coll 63. **d** 65 **p** 66. C Westbury-on-Trym H Trin *Bris* 65-68; C Bris St Agnes w St Simon 68-70; P-in-c Bris St Werburgh 70-72; TV Bris St Agnes and St Simon w St Werburgh 72-77; V Lakenham St Alb *Nor* 77-85; TV Trunch 85-93; TV Halesworth w Linstead, Chediston, Holton etc *St E* 93-99; TV Blyth Valley 99-05; RD Halesworth 98-01; rtd 05; PtO *St E* 06-08; P-in-c Heveningham from 12. *6 Bramblewood Way, Halesworth IP19 8JT* T: (01986) 875374
E: anthonynorton@btinternet.com

NORTON, Benjamin James. b 80. Hull Univ BTh 05. St Jo Coll Nottm 06. **d** 07 **p** 08. C Bridlington Em *York* 07-12; C Marton-in-Cleveland from 12. *31 Grange Wood, Coulby Newham, Middlesbrough TS8 0RT* T: (01642) 593961 M: 07780-606314 E: thepartycanstart@yahoo.com

NORTON, Howard John. b 41. Fitzw Coll Cam BA 64 MA 68. S'wark Ord Course 78 St Jo Coll Nottm 79. **d** 80 **p** 81. C Sutton Ch Ch *S'wark* 80-82; C Morden 82-84; V Motspur Park 84-88; PtO *Chich* from 03. *Gladstone House, 8 Coburg Place, Hastings TN34 3HY*

NORTON, Michael Clive Harcourt. b 34. Selw Coll Cam BA 58 MA 60 Union Th Sem (NY) STM 69 Univ of NSW MCom 81

MACE 84. Wells Th Coll 56 Bossey Ecum Inst Geneva 57. **d** 58 **p** 59. C Gt Ilford St Jo *Chelmsf* 58-62; NSW Sec Aus Coun Chs Australia 62-68; C Manhattan St Steph USA 68-69; C-in-c Mortdale Australia 69-77; R Mortdale 77-79; Assoc Chapl and Hd RS Cranbrook Sch Sydney 79-85; R Hunter's Hill 85-00; rtd 00. *7 Dulwich Road, Chatswood NSW 2067, Australia* T: (0061) (2) 9411 8606 F: 9410 2069 M: 417-041779
E: chnorton@bigpond.com

NORTON, Michael James Murfin. b 42. Lich Th Coll 66. **d** 67 **p** 68. C W Bromwich St Fran *Lich* 67-70; C Wellington Ch Ch 70-72; C Norwood All SS *Cant* 72-76; V Elstow *St Alb* 76-82; Asst Chapl HM Pris Wakef 82-83; Chapl HM Pris Camp Hill 83-86; Parkhurst 86-88; Win 88-93; V Somborne w Ashley *Win* 93-03; rtd 03. *Bryneirian, Penparc, Cardigan SA43 1RG* T: (01239) 623512 E: revmnorton@aol.com

NORTON, Paul James. b 55. Oak Hill Th Coll BA 86. **d** 86 **p** 87. C Luton St Fran *St Alb* 86-89; C Bedworth *Cov* 89-95; TV Hitchin *St Alb* 95-02; V Portsdown *Portsm* 03-07; rtd 07; PtO *Portsm* from 11. *23 Oxford Road, Southsea PO5 1NP*

NORTON, Canon Peter Eric Pepler. b 38. TCD BA 61 G&C Coll Cam PhD 64. Cranmer Hall Dur 78. **d** 80 **p** 81. C Ulverston St Mary w H Trin *Carl* 80-83; P-in-c Warcop, Musgrave, Soulby and Crosby Garrett 83-84; R 84-90; OCM 83-90; V Appleby and R Ormside *Carl* 90-04; P-in-c Kirkby Thore w Temple Sowerby and Newbiggin 01-04; RD Appleby and Hon Can Carl Cathl 00-04; rtd 04; PtO *Nor* 05-08. *Ard na Cree, Church Hill, Wicklow, Co Wicklow, Republic of Ireland* T: (00353) (404) 62648 M: 07802-334575 E: pepnorton@gmail.com

NORTON, Sam Charles. b 70. Trin Coll Ox BA 92 MA 99 Heythrop Coll Lon MA 00. Westcott Ho Cam 97. **d** 99 **p** 00. C Stepney St Dunstan and All SS *Lon* 99-02; R W w E Mersea *Chelmsf* 03-10; P-in-c Peldon w Gt and Lt Wigborough 03-10; R W w E Mersea, Peldon, Gt and Lt Wigborough from 10. *93 Kingsland Road, West Mersea, Colchester CO5 8AG* T: (01206) 385635 E: elizaphanian@hotmail.com

NORTON (née FISHER), Mrs Susan Alexandra. b 54. Man Univ BA 75 Hughes Hall Cam PGCE 76. NEOC 01. **d** 04 **p** 05. NSM York St Olave w St Giles and York St Helen w St Martin 04-09. *21 Wentworth Road, York YO24 1DG* T: (01904) 634911 E: e.norton@tinyworld.co.uk

NORTON, William Fullerton. b 23. Selw Coll Cam BA 46 MA 52. Wycliffe Hall Ox 46. **d** 48 **p** 49. C Leic H Apostles 48-52; C Singapore St Matt 52-54; Miss Selangor Malaya 54-56; Miss Kampong Tawas 56-60; V Ipoh St Pet 60-63; R Manila St Steph Philippines 63-66; C Homerton St Luke *Lon* 67; C Tooting Graveney St Nic *S'wark* 68-71; V Hanley Road St Sav w St Paul *Lon* 71-89; rtd 89. *Charlesworth Nursing Home, 37 Beaconsfield Villas, Brighton BN1 6HB* T: (01273) 565561

NORWICH, Archdeacon of. *See* MACFARLANE, The Ven Janet Elizabeth

NORWICH, Bishop of. *See* JAMES, The Rt Revd Graham Richard

NORWICH, Dean of. *See* HEDGES, The Very Revd Jane Barbara

NORWOOD, Andrew David. b 65. Lon Bible Coll BA 91. Cranmer Hall Dur 92. **d** 94 **p** 95. C Headingley *Ripon* 94-97; C Handsworth St Mary *Birm* 97-00; PtO *Lon* 01-02; Chapl Chelsea Coll 02-12; PtO *S'wark* 06-13. *73A Crabtree Lane, London SW6 6LR* E: adn272@yahoo.co.uk

NORWOOD, David John. b 40. SS Paul & Mary Coll Cheltenham BEd 82. Linc Th Coll 65. **d** 68 **p** 69. C Hitchin St Mary *St Alb* 68-71; P-in-c Luanshya *Zambia* 72-76; C Littlehampton St Jas *Chich* 76-77; P-in-c Chacewater *Truro* 77-79; Chapl R Cornwall Hosp Treliske 77-79; Hd RE Red Maids Sch Bris 82-85; Appeals Organiser Children's Soc 86-94; P-in-c Clarkston *Glas* 94-96; R 96-99; R Dalbeattie 99-05; rtd 05; PtO *St D* 13. *Dove Cottage, Wellfield Terrace, Ferryside SA17 5SD* T: (01267) 267125
E: norwoods@talktalk.net

NORWOOD, Paul James. b 71. **d** 08 **p** 09. OLM S Lynn *Nor* from 08. *46 Tennyson Avenue, King's Lynn PE30 2QJ* T: (01553) 777455 M: 07720-806318 E: pjnorwood@hotmail.co.uk

NORWOOD, Canon Philip Geoffrey Frank. b 39. Em Coll Cam BA 62 MA 66. Cuddesdon Coll 63. **d** 65 **p** 66. C New Addington *Cant* 65-69; Abp's Dom Chapl 69-72; V Hollingbourne 72-78; P-in-c Wormshill and Huckinge 74-78; V St Laur in Thanet *Cant* 78-88; RD Thanet 86-88; V Spalding St Mary and St Nic *Linc* 88-98; RD Elloe W 96-98; R Blakeney w Cley, Wiveton, Glandford etc *Nor* 98-05; RD Holt 02-05; Hon Can Nor Cathl 03-05; rtd 05; PtO *Leic* from 14. *30 Home Close Road, Houghton-on-the-Hill, Leicester LE7 9GT* T: 0116-241 0255 E: pandanorwood@hotmail.com

NORWOOD, Robert William. b 38. Keble Coll Ox BA 71 MA 71 Lon Univ TCert 64 Lambeth STh 83. **d** 01 **p** 03. NSM St Pancras H Cross w St Jude and St Pet *Lon* 01-10; PtO *Chelmsf* from 08; *Eur* from 08; *Lon* from 10. *Carlton Court, 11A Hermon Hill, London E11 2AR* T: (020) 8530 2493 M: 07907-383926 E: robert.norwood@hotmail.co.uk

NORWOOD, Timothy. b 70. Aber Univ BD 94. Westcott Ho Cam 95. **d** 97 **p** 98. C Upton cum Chalvey *Ox* 97-00; TV Watling Valley 00-10; AD Milton Keynes from 06; C from 11. *3 Daubeney Gate, Shenley Church End, Milton Keynes MK5 6EH* T: (01908) 505812 E: tim@thenorwoods.fsnet.co.uk

NOTT, Canon George Thomas Michael. b 34. Ex Coll Ox BA 58 MA 62 Birm Univ MEd 88 Cov Univ PhD 95. Coll of Resurr Mirfield. **d** 60 **p** 61. C Solihull *Birm* 60-69; Chapl K Sch Worc and Min Can Worc Cathl 69-77; P-in-c Worc St Nic and Children's Officer 77-87; P-in-c Worc St Andr and All SS w St Helen 82-84; Droitwich Spa 87-89; V Broadheath, Crown East and Rushwick 89-04; Chapl Worc Coll of HE 89-96; RD Martley and Worc W 95-03; Hon Can Worc Cathl 99-04; P-in-c Worc St Mich 00-01; rtd 04; PtO *Worc* from 06. *17 Wirlpiece Avenue, Worcester WR4 0NF* T: (01905) 729494 E: mnott17@btinternet.com

✠**NOTT, The Rt Revd Peter John.** b 33. Fitzw Ho Cam BA 61 MA 65. Westcott Ho Cam 58. **d** 61 **p** 62 **c** 77. C Harpenden St Nic *St Alb* 61-64; Chapl Fitzw Coll Cam 64-69; Fell 66-69; Chapl New Hall Cam 66-69; R Beaconsfield *Ox* 69-76; TR 76-77; Preb Wells Cathl 77-85; Suff Bp Taunton 77-85; Bp Nor 85-99; rtd 99; Hon Asst Bp Ox from 99. *Westcot House, Westcot, Wantage OX12 9QA* T: (01235) 751233 E: peternott@btinternet.com

NOTT, Philip James. b 69. Nottm Trent Univ BA 92. Ridley Hall Cam 95. **d** 98 **p** 99. C Kersal Moor *Man* 98-01; C Ealing St Mary *Lon* 01-04; Chapl Thames Valley Univ 01-04; P-in-c Broxtowe *S'well* 04-06; P-in-c Easton H Trin w St Gabr and St Lawr and St Jude *Bris* from 06; Min Inner City Partnership from 06. *St Anne's Vicarage, 75 Greenbank Road, Greenbank, Bristol BS5 6HD* T: 0117-955 4255 E: rev@ecfc.org.uk

NOTTAGE, Preb Terence John. b 36. Oak Hill Th Coll 62. **d** 65 **p** 66. C Finchley St Paul Long Lane *Lon* 65-68; C Edgware 68-72; V Harlesden St Mark 72-86; V Kensal Rise St Mark and St Martin 86; TR Plymouth Em w Efford *Ex* 86-92; P-in-c Laira 88-92; TR Plymouth Em, St Paul Efford and St Aug 93-96; Preb Ex Cathl from 96; Adv for Voc and Dioc Dir of Ords 96-01; rtd 01. *4 Keyberry Close, Newton Abbot TQ12 1DA* T: (01626) 332277 E: terry.nottage@tesco.net

NOTTINGHAM, Archdeacon of. *See* CLARK, The Ven Sarah Elizabeth

NOVELL, Jill. b 49. Bris Univ BA 72 Open Univ MA 89 St Martin's Coll Lanc PGCE 77. CBDTI 01. **d** 04 **p** 05. NSM Silverdale *Blackb* 04-11; PtO 11-12; NSM Lancaster St Mary w St John and St Anne from 12. *29 Hall Park, Lancaster LA1 4SH* E: riverlunelancaster@yahoo.co.uk

NOVIS, Timothy Wellington George. b 70. Trin Coll Toronto BA 93 MDiv 96. **d** 96 **p** 96. C Guelph St Geo Canada 96-98; R Hornby St Steph 98-05; Chapl Ridley Coll 05-08; Chapl Wellington Coll Berks from 08. *Chapel Hill, Wellington College, Crowthorne RG45 7PT* T: (01344) 444104 E: twgn@wellingtoncollege.org.uk

NOWAK, Jurek Anthony (George). b 47. NTMTC 04. **d** 07. NSM Edmonton St Mary w St Jo *Lon* from 07. *138 Dysons Road, London N18 2DJ* T: (020) 8884 0903 M: 07944-854617 E: jurek-n@dysons.demon.co.uk

NOWELL, Canon John David. b 44. AKC 67. **d** 68 **p** 69. C Lindley *Wakef* 68-70; C Lightcliffe 70-72; V Wyke *Bradf* 72-80; V Silsden 80-92; V Baildon *Leeds* 92-14; Hon Can Bradf Cathl 00-14; rtd 14. *Fairview, Carlisle Road, Pudsey LS28 8LW* E: john@jdnowell.plus.com

NOWÉN, Lars Fredrik. b 71. Summit Pacific Coll BC BTh 93 Regent Coll Vancouver MCS 98. **d** 98 **p** 99. Dn Halifax St Geo Canada 98-99; P-in-c Meadow Lake and Loon Lake 99-04; C Pelton and W Pelton *Dur* 04-07; P-in-c St Bees *Carl* 07-10; Chapl St Bees Sch Cumbria 07-10; Chapl Chelsea Academy 11-12; Sen Chapl Algarve *Eur* 13-15; P-in-c Edmonton Ch the K Canada from 15. *Address temp unknown* T: (001) (780) 800 5515 E: revlfnowen@gmail.com

NOY, Frederick William Vernon. b 47. Sarum Th Coll 67. **d** 71 **p** 72. C Swindon St Jo *Bris* 71-75; Chapl to the Deaf *Sarum* 75-80; P-in-c Stinsford, Winterborne Came w Whitcombe etc 76-80; PtO 80-08. *54 Casterbridge Road, Dorchester DT1 2AG* T: (01305) 264269

NOY, Rufus William. b 63. St Mich Coll Llan 11. **d** 13 **p** 14. C Blaenavon w Capel Newydd *Mon* from 13. *The Vicarage, Vicarage Lane, Abersychan, Pontypool NP4 8PX* T: (01495) 524599 E: reverend.noy@gmail.com

NOYCE, Colin Martley. b 45. Brasted Th Coll 73 Ridley Hall Cam 74. **d** 76 **p** 77. C Cambridge St Jas *Ely* 76-78; Chapl RN 78-82; R Mistley w Manningtree *Chelmsf* 82-86; Miss to Seamen Kenya 86-89; Trinidad and Tobago 89-90; V Four Marks *Win* 90-99; Chapl Pilgrims Hospices E Kent 99-01; Chapl and Dir Ch Ch and Ras Morbat Clinics Yemen 01-03; Chapl Limassol St Barn and Miss to Seafarers 03-05; rtd 05; PtO *Chelmsf* 06-09; *Portsm* from 08. *64 Whitwell Road, Southsea PO4 0QS* T: (023) 9275 3517 E: candinoyce@sky.com

NOYCE, Graham Peter. b 62. Bedf Coll Lon BSc 84. Trin Coll Bris BA 92. **d** 92 **p** 93. C Sketty *S & B* 92-94; C Swansea St Jas 94-96; C Kensal Rise St Mark and St Martin *Lon* 96-04; TV 04-11; V Kensal Rise St Martin from 11; AD Brent from 13. *26 Ashburnham Road, London NW10 5SD* T: (020) 8960 6211 M: 07515-702862 E: graham@noycefamily.co.uk

NOYES, Gary Robert. b 50. Ripon Coll Cuddesdon. **d** 14. C Ipsley *Worc* from 14. *29 Sheldon Road, Redditch B98 7QS* T: (01527) 501092

NOYES, Roger. b 39. Linc Th Coll 65. **d** 67 **p** 68. C Adel *Ripon* 67-70; Chapl Aldenham Sch Herts 70-74; V Aldborough w Boroughbridge and Roecliffe *Ripon* 74-89; Rural Min Adv 89-90; PtO *Leeds* from 91. *Rose Cottage, Moor End, Nun Monkton, York YO26 8EN* T: (01423) 330846 E: r.noyes1@btinternet.com

NSENGA-NGOY, Lusa. b 77. Cranmer Hall Dur. **d** 08 **p** 09. C Staplehurst *Cant* 08-12; V Gravesend St Aid *Roch* from 12. *The Vicarage, St Gregory's Crescent, Gravesend DA12 4JL* T: (01474) 561554 E: lusansenga@gmail.com

NSHIMYE, Stephen Kamegeri. b 60. Bp Lutaya Th Coll Uganda 88. **d** 90 **p** 91. C Kamusemene Uganda 90-91; C Kigalama 92-93; C Nyagatovu Rwanda 94-99; PtO *S'wark* 02-05; NSM Greenwich St Alfege from 12. *58 Hickin Close, London SE7 8SH* T: (020) 8853 2580 M: 07950-553440

✠**NTAHOTURI, The Most Revd Bernard.** b 48. St Jo Coll Cam MA. Bp Tucker Coll Mukono 68. **d** 73 **c** 97. Burundi from 73; Bp Matana from 97; Abp Burundi from 05. *BP 447, Bujumbura, Burundi* T: (00257) (2) 70361 F: 29129 E: ntahober@cbinf.com

NTEGE, Nathan Kasolo. b 59. **d** 87 **p** 89. C St Paul's Cathl Namirembe Uganda 87-91; Bp Tucker Coll Mukono 91-94; V Luzira and Kabowa 94-96; PtO *S'wark* 97-02; P-in-c Thornton Heath St Jude w St Aid 02-07; V from 07. *St Jude's Vicarage, 11 Dunheved Road North, Thornton Heath CR7 6AH* T: (020) 8665 5564 M: 07904-197329

NTOYIMONDO, Samuel. b 54. All Nations Chr Coll BA 02 Wolv Univ BA 05 Qu Foundn for Ecum Th Educn MA 11. Butare Th Sch Rwanda 80. **d** 84 **p** 87. Pastor Mutunda Rwanda 84-87; Pastor Butare 87-92; Dioc Sec Kigeme 92-94; Germany 96-99; PtO *Birm* 08-11 and from 14; Chapl HM Pris Wellingborough 11-12; Chapl HM Pris Nottm from 13; Chapl HM Pris Stocken from 13. *HM Prison, Stocken Hall Road, Stretton, Oakham LE15 7RD* T: (01780) 795100 E: samuel.ntoyimondo@hmps.gsi.gov.uk

NUGENT, Canon Alan Hubert. b 42. Dur Univ BA 65 MA 78. Wycliffe Hall Ox 65 United Th Coll Bangalore 66. **d** 67 **p** 68. C Mossley Hill St Matt and St Jas *Liv* 67-71; C Bridgnorth St Mary *Heref* 71-72; Chapl Dur Univ 72-78; P-in-c Bishopwearmouth Ch Ch 78-85; P-in-c Brancepeth 85-94; Dioc Dir of Educn 85-97; Hon Can Dur Cathl 86-97; Dir of Miss and Tr Development Forum *Linc* 97-03; Can and Preb Linc Cathl 98-03; Can Res and Subdean Linc Cathl 03-11; rtd 11. *2 The Link, Wellingore, Lincoln LN5 0BJ*

NUGENT, David Richard. b 54. MInstPS 84 Liv Poly BA 87. Oak Hill Th Coll BA 95. **d** 95 **p** 96. C Birkenhead St Jas w St Bede *Ches* 95-99; V Blundellsands St Mich *Liv* 99-02; Asst Chapl Wirral and W Cheshire Community NHS Trust 02-03; Asst Chapl Cheshire and Wirral Partnerships NHS Trust from 03; P-in-c Gt Saughall *Ches* from 13. *Belmont Cottage, Church Road, Saughall, Chester CH1 6EP* E: dave.nugent@whnt.nhs.uk

NUGENT, Eric William. b 26. Bps' Coll Cheshunt 56. **d** 58 **p** 59. C Rochford *Chelmsf* 58-61; C Eastwood 61-62; C-in-c Eastwood St Dav 62-66; V Eastwood St Dav 66-79; P-in-c Weeley 79-81; V Lt Clacton 80-81; R Weeley and Lt Clacton 81-93; rtd 93; PtO *Chelmsf* from 93. *1 King's Court, King's Road, Dovercourt, Harwich CO12 4DS* T: (01255) 552640

NUGENT, Mary Patricia. *See* JEPP, Mary Patricia

NUNN, Ms Alice Candida. b 52. Ripon Coll Cuddesdon 95. **d** 97 **p** 98. C Margate St Jo *Cant* 97-01; V Winterton Gp *Linc* from 01. *The Vicarage, High Street, Winterton, Scunthorpe DN15 9PU* T: (01724) 732262

NUNN, The Very Revd Andrew Peter. b 57. Leic Poly BA 79 Leeds Univ BA 82. Coll of Resurr Mirfield 80. **d** 83 **p** 84. C Manston *Ripon* 83-87; C Leeds Richmond Hill 87-91; Chapl Agnes Stewart C of E High Sch Leeds 87-95; V Leeds Richmond Hill *Ripon* 91-95; Personal Asst to Bp *S'wark* 95-99; Hon PV S'wark Cathl 95-99; Sub-Dean, Prec and Can Res S'wark Cathl 99-12; Dean S'wark from 12; Dioc Warden of Readers from 01. *51 Bankside, London SE1 9JE* T: (020) 7928 3336 M: 07961-332051 E: andrew.nunn@southwark.anglican.org

NUNN, Mrs Christine Jane. b 47. **d** 05 **p** 06. OLM Kesgrave *St E* 05-13; NSM from 13. *37 Bracken Avenue, Kesgrave, Ipswich IP5 2PP* T: (01473) 622363

NUNN, Canon Peter Michael. b 38. MBE 98. Sarum Th Coll 64. **d** 66 **p** 67. C Hornsey St Geo *Lon* 66-71; C Cleator Moor w Cleator *Carl* 71-72; V Carl St Luke Morton 72-79; V Wotton St Mary *Glouc* 79-02; OCM 80-97; RD Glouc City 88-94; Hon

Can Glouc Cathl 90-02; rtd 02; PtO *Chich* from 02. *87 South Street, Tarring, Worthing BN14 7ND* T: (01903) 233748

NUNN, Peter Rawling. b 51. St Cath Coll Ox BA 73 Sheff Univ MSc 74. Oak Hill Th Coll BA 85. **d** 85 **p** 86. C Bispham *Blackb* 85-87; C-in-c Anchorsholme 87-89; V 89-08; P-in-c Preston Risen Lord from 08. *St Matthew's Vicarage, 20 Fishwick View, Preston PR1 4YA* T: (01772) 794312
E: peter@therisenlordpreston.org.uk

NUNNERLEY, William John Arthur. b 27. Univ of Wales (Lamp) BA 54. St Chad's Coll Dur. **d** 56 **p** 57. C Tredegar St Geo *Mon* 56-60; Chapl RN 60-81; QHC from 79; R Barnoldby le Beck *Linc* 81-92; R Waltham 81-92; rtd 92; PtO *B & W* from 00. *Juniper Cottage, 82B Lower Street, Merriott TA16 5NW* T: (01460) 76049

NUNNEY, Sheila Frances. b 49. SRN 74 RSCN 74 SCM 75. Oak Hill Th Coll BA 92. **d** 92 **p** 94. C Swaffham *Nor* 92-96; Chapl Asst Norfolk and Nor Health Care NHS Trust 96-00; Chapl 00-01; Chapl Norfolk Primary Care Trust 01-09; Chapl Norfolk & Waveney Mental Health NHS Foundn Trust 03-09; rtd 09; PtO *Nor* from 09. *43A Chestnut Hill, Eaton, Norwich NR4 6NL* T: (01603) 507110
E: sfn60@btinternet.com

NURSER, Canon John Shelley. b 29. Peterho Cam BA 50 MA 54 PhD 58. Wells Th Coll 58. **d** 58 **p** 59. C Tankersley *Sheff* 58-61; Dean Trin Hall Cam 61-68; Australia 68-74; R Freckenham w Worlington *St E* 74-76; Can Res and Chan Linc Cathl 76-92; Can and Preb Linc Cathl 92-94; P-in-c Shudy Camps *Ely* 92-94; rtd 94; PtO *St E* from 94; *Ely* 00-10. *68 Friars Street, Sudbury CO10 2AG* T: (01787) 378595 E: jsnurser@btinternet.com

NURSEY (née HYLTON), Mrs Jane Lois. b 56. Leeds Univ BA 78. **d** 07 **p** 08. OLM Dereham and Distr *Nor* from 07; Chapl Norfolk and Nor Univ Hosp NHS Trust from 11. *Chaplaincy Department, Norfolk and Norwich University Hospital, Colney Lane, Norwich NR4 7UY* T: (01603) 287470
E: jane.nursey@nnuh.nhs.uk *or* nursey1@btinternet.com

NURTON, Robert. b 44. Univ of Wales (Lamp) BA 67. Ridley Hall Cam 67. **d** 69 **p** 70. C Bris St Andr Hartcliffe 69-73; C Ipswich St Mary at Stoke w St Pet etc *St E* 73-77; Chapl RN 77-99; Chapl Morden Coll Blackheath 99-09; rtd 09; PtO *St E* from 11. *The Thatched Cottage, High Road, Great Finborough, Stowmarket IP14 3AQ* T: (01449) 674396

NUTH, Stephen William. b 55. St Jo Coll Nottm 93. **d** 95 **p** 96. C Wadhurst and Stonegate *Chich* 95-99; R Marks Tey and Aldham *Chelmsf* 99-01; P-in-c 01-04; P-in-c Woburn w Eversholt, Milton Bryan, Battlesden etc *St Alb* 04-08; V from 08. *The Vicarage, Park Street, Woburn, Milton Keynes MK17 9PG* T: (01525) 290225 E: stephen.nuth@googlemail.com

NUTT, Angela Karen. b 66. Homerton Coll Cam BEd 89. STETS 08. **d** 11 **p** 12. C Totton and Copythorne *Win* 11-15; P-in-c Freemantle from 15. *The Vicarage, 129 Paynes Road, Southampton SO15 3BW* M: 07740-424143
E: revdangi@gmail.com

NUTT, Susan Mary. b 45. BEM 15. OLM Blackbourne *St E* 99-13; NSM 13-15; rtd 15; PtO *St E* from 15; Hon Chapl St Nic Hospice Bury St Edmunds from 08. *Portelet, Blacksmith Lane, Barnham, Thetford IP24 2NE* T: (01842) 890409 E: suenutt@hotmail.co.uk

NUTTALL, Michael John Berkeley. b 36. K Coll Lon AKC 60. St Boniface Warminster 61. **d** 61 **p** 62. C Chapel Allerton

Ripon 61-64; C Stanningley St Thos 64-68; V Leeds Gipton Epiphany 68-76; P-in-c Stainby w Gunby *Linc* 76-83; R N Witham 76-83; R S Witham 76-83; TV Bottesford w Ashby 83-88; I Adare w Kilpeacon and Croom *L & K* 88-94; I Adare and Kilmallock w Kilpeacon, Croom etc 94-01; Chapl Limerick Univ 88-95; Adn Limerick 92-01; rtd 01; PtO *York* from 12. *29 Dulverton Hall, Esplanade, Scarborough YO11 2AR* T: (01723) 340129 E: adnmichaelnuttall@yahoo.com

NUTTER, Ms Tracy Jane. b 58. NTMTC. **d** 10 **p** 11. NSM Prittlewell St Steph *Chelmsf* 10-14; NSM Rayleigh from 14. *8 Ailsa Road, Westcliff-on-Sea SS0 8BL* T: (01702) 342470
E: t.nutter@virgin.net

NUZUM, Daniel Robert. b 73. TCD BTh 99 RGN 94. **d** 99 **p** 00. C Bandon Union *C, C & R* 99-01; I Templebreedy w Tracton and Nohoval 02-09; Chapl Cork Univ Hosp from 09; Can Cork Cathl from 14; Can Cloyne Cathl from 14. *Cork University Hospital, Wilton, Cork, Republic of Ireland* T: (00353) (21) 454 6400

NWAEKWE, Augustine Ugochukwu. b 75. Leuven Univ Belgium MA 07. St Paul's Univ Coll Awka Nigeria 95. **d** 98 **p** 00. LtO Dio Mbaise Nigeria 98-04; Asst Chapl Brussels *Eur* 06-13; Chapl Ostend from 13. *Address temp unknown* M: (0032) 48-499 5790

NWOGU, Okwunna Nketa. b 66. Uyo Univ Nigeria LLB 02 BL 02 Sunderland Univ LLM 12. Trin Coll Umuahia Nigeria 91. **d** 94 **p** 95. Can Aba Cathl Nigeria 02-08; Adn from 08; Chapl Law Sch Enugu 05-06; PtO *Dur* 12-13; NSM The Boldons from 13. *Greenriggs, Dipe Lane, East Boldon NE36 0PH* T: 0191-908 8801 M: 07407-030091
E: revdokwunnanwogu@yahoo.com

NYAONGO, Jairo Omondi. b 73. **d** 14 **p** 15. C Mill End and Heronsgate w W Hyde *St Alb* from 14. *St Thomas House, 46 Chalfont Road, Maple Cross, Rickmansworth WD3 9TB* M: 07763-104640 E: jnyaongo@hotmail.com

NYATSANZA, Petros Hamutendi. b 69. Redcliffe Coll Glouc BA 04. Bp Gaul Th Coll Harare 95. **d** 95 **p** 96. R Greendale St Luke Zimbabwe 95-96; C Highfields St Paul 96-97; R Mufakose St Luke 97-01; PtO *Glouc* 02-04; P-in-c Rounds Green *Birm* 04-08; V Goodmayes All SS *Chelmsf* from 08. *All Saints' Vicarage, 38 Broomshill Road, Ilford IG3 9SJ* T: (020) 8590 1476 M: 07877-841643
E: petrosnyatsanza@yahoo.co.uk

NYE, Canon David Charles. b 39. K Coll Lon BD 65 Glos Univ MA 01. **d** 63 **p** 64. C Charlton Kings St Mary *Glouc* 63-67; C Yeovil St Jo w Preston Plucknett *B & W* 67-70; V Lower Cam *Glouc* 70-74; Min Can Glouc Cathl 74-79; Dir of Ords 74-79; Prin Glouc Th Course 74-79; V Glouc St Mary de Lode and St Nic 74-76; V Maisemore 76-79; Chapl Grenville Coll Bideford 79-81; V Leckhampton SS Phil and Jas w Cheltenham St Jas *Glouc* 81-95; Hon Can Glouc Cathl 88-04; RD Cheltenham 89-95; P-in-c Northleach w Hampnett and Farmington 95-00; P-in-c Cold Aston w Notgrove and Turkdean 95-00; R Northleach w Hampnett and Farmington etc 00-04; RD Northleach 99-04; rtd 04. *3 Blackberry Field, Prestbury, Cheltenham GL52 5LT* T: (01242) 268964
E: tisnyes@tiscali.co.uk

NYIRONGO, David. b 79. Wycliffe Hall Ox. **d** 11 **p** 12. C Penketh *Liv* 11-14; C Warrington W 14-15. *Address temp unknown* E: davyngo@hotmail.com

O

OADES, Debbie Gaynor. b 63. Middx Univ BA 06. NTMTC 03. **d** 06 **p** 07. C Hounslow W Gd Shep *Lon* 06-08; NSM Hampton Hill 08-11; C Maybush and Southampton St Jude *Win* from 11. *St Peter's Church House, Lockerley Crescent, Southampton SO16 4BP* E: debbieoades@hotmail.com

OADES, Michael Anthony John. b 45. Brasted Th Coll 69 Sarum & Wells Th Coll 71. **d** 73 **p** 74. C Eltham Park St Luke *S'wark* 73-78; C Coulsdon St Andr 78-81; P-in-c Merton St Jas 81-86; V 86-87; V Benhilton 87-10; rtd 10. *Cranleigh, Penbothidno, Constantine, Falmouth TR11 5AU* T: (01326) 341304 E: michaelandsylvia@btinternet.com

OAKDEN, David Ian. b 60. **d** 10 **p** 11. OLM Shere, Albury and Chilworth *Guildf* from 10. *102 New Road, Chilworth, Guildford GU4 8LU* T: (01483) 578230
E: david.oakden@yahoo.co.uk

OAKE, Canon Barry Richard. b 47. MRICS 71. Ripon Coll Cuddesdon 83. **d** 85 **p** 86. C Wantage *Ox* 85-88; C Warlingham w Chelsham and Farleigh *S'wark* 88-91; R N w S Wootton *Nor* 91-05; R Thorpe St Andr 05-15; rtd 15; V Nor St Helen

from 15; Chapl Gt Hosp Nor from 15; Asst Chapl among Deaf and Hearing-Impaired People *Nor* from 01; Hon Can Nor Cathl from 07. *Calthorpe Lodge, The Great Hospital, Norwich NR1 4EL* T: E: barryoake@gmail.com

OAKES, Graham. b 42. Chich Th Coll 68. **d** 70 **p** 71. C Hulme Ascension *Man* 70-74; C Clifton All SS w Tyndalls Park *Bris* 74-76; P-in-c Chadderton St Mark *Man* 76-78; V 78-82; V King Cross *Wakef* 82-95; R Bath H Trin *B & W* 95-07; Chapl R United Hosp Bath NHS Trust 99-07; rtd 07. *St Christophers, Newland, Malvern WR13 5AX* T: (01684) 576654 E: oakes551@btinternet.com

OAKES, Miss Jennifer May. b 43. Trin Coll Bris 78. **dss** 82 **d** 87 **p** 94. Par Dn Bentley *Lich* 87-89; Par Dn Hixon w Stowe-by-Chartley 89-94; C 94-98; Par Dn Fradswell, Gayton, Milwich and Weston 93-94; C 94-98; P-in-c Standon and Cotes Heath 98-00; rtd 00; Hon C Alfrick, Lulsley, Suckley, Leigh and Bransford *Worc* 03-04; PtO *Lich* from 05. *Willow Rise, Ashbourne Road, Whiston, Stoke-on-Trent ST10 2JE* T: (01538) 260013 E: oaklud@supanet.com

OAKES, Canon Jeremy Charles. b 51. ACA 75 FCA 81. Westcott Ho Cam 75. **d** 78 **p** 79. C Evington *Leic* 78-81; C Ringwood *Win* 81-84; P-in-c Thurnby Lodge *Leic* 84-89; TV Oakdale *Sarum* 89-95; P-in-c Canford Cliffs and Sandbanks 95-03; V 03-14; rtd 14; Can and Preb Sarum Cathl from 03. *5 Townsend Road, Corfe Castle, Wareham BH20 5ET* T: (01929) 480181 E: oakesjeremyc@gmail.com

OAKES, John Cyril. b 49. AKC 71. St Aug Coll Cant 71. **d** 72 **p** 73. C Broseley w Benthall *Heref* 72-76; C Cannock *Lich* 76-79; TV 79-83; V Rough Hills 83-09; P-in-c Wolverhampton St Steph 94-09; rtd 09; PtO *Lich* from 09. *Glendower, Bull Street, Gornal Wood, Dudley DY3 2NQ* T: (01384) 232097 M: 07821-199122 E: classfortyseven@hotmail.co.uk

OAKES, Canon Leslie John. b 28. AKC 53. **d** 54 **p** 55. C Bedford Leigh *Man* 54-58; C Walsall St Matt *Lich* 58-60; Chapl Selly Oak Hosp Birm 60-64; V Longbridge *Birm* 64-93; Hon Can Birm Cathl 84-93; rtd 93; PtO *Birm* from 93. *108 Hole Lane, Birmingham B31 2DF* T: 0121-476 8514

OAKES, Melvin. b 36. Linc Th Coll 77. **d** 79 **p** 80. C Lt Ilford St Mich *Chelmsf* 79-82; V Highams Park All SS 82-96; rtd 96; PtO *Chelmsf* from 99. *115 Richmond Avenue, London E4 9RR* T: (020) 8527 0457

OAKES, Robert. b 47. Chan Sch Truro 79. **d** 82 **p** 83. NSM Probus, Ladock and Grampound w Creed and St Erme *Truro* 82-84; TV Bodmin w Lanhydrock and Lanivet 85-88; R S Hill w Callington 88-03; RD E Wivelshire 95-00; Bp's Adv on Healing Min 98-03; Hon Can Truro Cathl 01-03; C Calstock 06-14; C St Dominic, Landulph and St Mellion w Pillaton 12-14; Chapl Cornwall and Is of Scilly Primary Care Trust 09-13; rtd 14. *Kernick House, 11 Trelawney Rise, Callington PL17 7PT* T: (01579) 389109 M: 07890-099248 E: oakesrobert@hotmail.co.uk

OAKES, Simon Paul. b 77. SS Coll Cam BA 00 MA 03 PhD 06. Coll of Resurr Mirfield 11. **d** 13 **p** 14. C Walsall St Gabr Fulbrook *Lich* from 13. *20 Poplar Avenue, Walsall WS5 4EX* E: frsimonoakes@outlook.com

OAKEY-JONES, Ms Angela Jean. b 71. Keele Univ BA 93. NTMTC BA 08. **d** 08 **p** 09. C Rushmere *St E* 08-11; P-in-c Ipswich All Hallows from 11. *All Hallows' Vicarage, Reynolds Road, Ipswich IP3 0JH* T: (01473) 717084 E: angela.oj@btinternet.com

OAKHAM, Archdeacon of. *See* STEELE, The Ven Gordon John

OAKLAND, Mrs Sarah Marie. b 54. UEA BEd 85. EAMTC 99. **d** 02 **p** 03. C Diss *Nor* 02-06; V Chessington *Guildf* 06-11; R E w W Harling, Bridgham w Roudham, Larling etc *Nor* 11-15; rtd 15. *Sea Holly, Fearns Close, Cromer NR27 0DZ* E: sarahoakland@hotmail.com

OAKLEY, Barry Wyndham. b 32. TD 72. SS Coll Cam BA 53 MA 57. Ridley Hall Cam 56. **d** 58 **p** 59. C Alverstoke *Portsm* 58-61; C Bermondsey St Mary w St Olave and St Jo *S'wark* 61-63; V Crofton *Portsm* 63-78; V Edmonton All SS *Lon* 78-82; P-in-c Edmonton St Mich 80-82; V Edmonton All SS w St Mich 82-97; rtd 97; PtO *Lon* from 98. *25 Queen's Road, Enfield EN1 1NF* T: (020) 8363 3199

OAKLEY, Mrs Dawn. b 55. STETS. **d** 12 **p** 13. NSM Shanklin St Blasius *Portsm* 12-14. *1 Allandale Park Avenue, Ventnor PO38 1LE* T: (01983) 854584 E: dawn@goakley.co.uk

OAKLEY, Hilary Robert Mark. b 53. Univ of Wales (Ban) BSc 75 Ox Univ BA 78 MA 81 MCIPD 91. Ripon Coll Cuddesdon 76. **d** 79 **p** 80. C Birm St Pet 79-82; C Cambridge Gt St Mary w St Mich *Ely* 82-86; Chapl Girton Coll Cam 82-86; Chapl Zürich w St Gallen and Winterthur *Eur* 86-88; NSM Lon 88-92; PtO *St Alb* from 92. *55 Southdown Road, Harpenden AL5 1PQ* T: (01582) 761514 E: hilary.oakley@talk21.com

OAKLEY, James Robert. b 75. St Edm Hall Ox BA 96. Oak Hill Th Coll BA 05. **d** 05 **p** 06. C Audley Clk 05-09; P-in-c Kemsing w Woodlands *Roch* from 09. *The Vicarage, High Street, Kemsing, Sevenoaks TN15 6NA* T: (01732) 762556 M: 07827-299342 E: vicar@kemsing.org

OAKLEY, Jeremy Steven. b 52. Birm Univ BA 99. Trin Coll Bris 95. **d** 97 **p** 98. C Walsall *Lich* 97-02; V Penn Fields from 02. *St Philip's Vicarage, Church Road, Bradmore, Wolverhampton WV3 7EJ* T: (01902) 332749 E: jeremy@pennfieldsparish.co.uk

OAKLEY, Canon Mark David. b 68. K Coll Lon BD 90 AKC 90. St Steph Ho Ox 90. **d** 93 **p** 94. C St John's Wood *Lon* 93-96; Bp's Chapl 96-00; P-in-c Covent Garden St Paul 00-03; R 03-05; AD Westmr St Marg 04-05; Chapl RADA 03-05; Chapl Copenhagen and Jutland w Aarhus *Eur* 05-08; P-in-c Grosvenor Chpl *Lon* 08-10; Can Res St Paul's Cathl from 10; Dep P in O from 96. *6 Amen Court, London EC4M 7BU* T: (020) 7248 8572 E: mark.chaplain@gmail.com *or* canonspa@stpaulscathedral.org.uk

OAKLEY, Richard John. b 46. AKC 69 St Aug Coll Cant 69. **d** 70 **p** 71. C Wythenshawe Wm Temple Ch *Man* 70-75; V Ashton

H Trin 75-80; CR 80-93; LtO *Lon* 88-93; V Cantley *Sheff* 93-99; V Carl St Aid and Ch Ch 99-11; rtd 11; PtO *Blackb* from 12. *17 Ulpha Close, Burnley BB12 8XB* T: (01282) 787621 E: rjoakley@talktalk.net

OAKLEY, Robert Paul. b 51. Sheff Univ BScTech 72 PGCE 74 Open Univ MA(Theol) 97. St Jo Coll Nottm 87. **d** 89 **p** 90. C Heatherlands St Jo *Sarum* 89-92; V Burton All SS w Ch Ch *Lich* 92-99; V Gt Wyrley 99-07; Tutor Wilson Carlile Coll of Evang 07-12; V Totley *Sheff* from 12. *All Saints' Vicarage, 37 Sunnyvale Road, Sheffield S17 4FA* T: 0114-236 2322 M: 07971-325222

OAKLEY, Robin Ian. b 37. Ripon Hall Ox 68. **d** 70 **p** 71. C Leighton Buzzard *St Alb* 70-73; C Watford St Mich 73-76; R Ickleford 76-80; R Ickleford w Holwell 80-02; rtd 02; PtO *St Alb* from 02; *Win* from 03. *13 Anders Road, South Wonston, Winchester SO21 3EL* T: (01962) 880613

OAKLEY, Stephen Alfred. b 66. **d** 13 **p** 14. NSM Lundwood *Leeds* from 13. *9 Parkland View, Barnsley S71 5LG* T: (01226) 781797 E: stephenoakley66@googlemail.com

OAKLEY, Susan Mary. *See* HENWOOD, Susan Mary

OAKLEY, Timothy Crispin. b 45. Qu Coll Cam BA 66 MA 70 Bris Univ PGCE 69. St Jo Coll Nottm 73. **d** 76 **p** 77. C Bromley Common St Aug *Roch* 76-79; C Fairfield *Liv* 79-81; CMS Kenya 82-90; P-in-c Beaford, Roborough and St Giles in the Wood *Ex* 91-96; Chapl St Andr Sch Turi Kenya 96-98; V Woodford Halse w Eydon *Pet* 99-10; RD Brackley 03-05; rtd 10. *Sunny Bank, Clive Avenue, Church Stretton SY6 7BL* T: (01694) 724225 E: tim@revoakley.freeserve.co.uk

OATES, Alan. b 32. S'wark Ord Course 79. **d** 80 **p** 81. NSM Rayleigh *Chelmsf* 80-87; TV Jarrow *Dur* 87-92; P-in-c Stella 92-95; R 95-97; rtd 97; PtO *Dur* 98-14; Newc from 00. *1 The Haven, North Shields NE29 6YH* T: 0191-258 6984

OATES, Alexander John. b 38. Clifton Th Coll 63. **d** 67 **p** 68. C Brixton Hill St Sav *S'wark* 67-68; C Westcombe Park St Geo 68-71; C Stechford *Birm* 71-74; R Greenhithe St Mary *Roch* 74-77; Soc worker 77-02; rtd 03. *1 Fairlight Villas, North Road, Havering-atte-Bower, Romford RM4 1PP* T: (01708) 760252

OATES, Douglas. b 39. Bolton Coll of Educn CertEd 74 Ches Coll of HE BTh 97. NOC 94. **d** 97 **p** 98. NSM Balderstone *Man* 97-01; NSM Oldham St Barn 01-06; P-in-c 03-06; P-in-c Waterhead 05-06; TV Medlock Head 06-09; rtd 09; PtO *Man* from 09. *43 Devonport Crescent, Royton, Oldham OL2 6JX* T: (01706) 849929 E: doug@oates400.freeserve.co.uk

OATES, Jeanette Linda. b 50. SEN 70. NEOC 05. **d** 08 **p** 09. NSM Bridlington Priory *York* 08-13; rtd 13; PtO *York* from 13. *77 St Alban Road, Bridlington YO16 7SY* T: (01262) 678534 E: jeanetteoates@tiscali.co.uk

OATES, Canon John. b 30. Kelham Th Coll 53. **d** 57 **p** 58. C Hackney Wick St Mary of Eton w St Aug *Lon* 57-60; Development Officer C of E Youth Coun 60-64; Sec C of E Coun Commonwealth Settlement 64-65; Gen Sec 65-72; Sec C of E Cttee on Migration & Internat Affairs 68-72; Hon Can Bunbury from 69; V Richmond St Mary *S'wark* 70-79; P-in-c Richmond St Jo 76-79; V Richmond St Mary w St Matthias and St Jo 79-84; RD Richmond and Barnes 79-84; R St Bride Fleet Street w Bridewell etc *Lon* 84-00; AD The City 97-00; Preb St Paul's Cathl 97-00; rtd 00; PtO *S'wark* from 03; *Lon* from 01. *27 York Court, Albany Park Road, Kingston upon Thames KT2 5ST* T: (020) 8974 8821 E: john.oates@blueyonder.co.uk

OATES, Michael Graham. b 62. Leic Poly BSc 84. Aston Tr Scheme 87 Cranmer Hall Dur 89. **d** 92 **p** 93. C Enfield St Andr *Lon* 92-96; TV N Poole Ecum Team *Sarum* 96-07; PtO 07-08; Chapl Dorset HealthCare University NHS Foundn Trust from 14. *51 Ringwood Road, Poole BH14 0RE* E: oates@madasafish.com

OATES (née ADAMS), Canon Ruth. b 47. Bris Univ BSc 69. SEITE 97. **d** 00 **p** 01. C Rainham *Roch* 00-03; V Gravesend St Mary 03-13; RD Gravesend 09-13; P-in-c Ash from 13; P-in-c Ridley from 13; Hon Can Roch Cathl from 11. *11 Lambardes, New Ash Green, Longfield DA3 8HX* T: (01474) 872209 E: ruth.oates@diocese-rochester.org

OATRIDGE, Andrew Philip. b 77. Sheff Univ MMath 00. Oak Hill Th Coll MTh 10. **d** 10 **p** 11. C Chapeltown *Sheff* 10-13; Crosslinks Hungary from 13. *Zsigmond király utca 17, 2051 Biatorbágy, Hungary* E: andyzsofi@gmail.com

OBAN, Provost of. *See* MACNELLY, The Very Revd Nicola

OBEDOZA, William. b 58. NTMTC 05. **d** 08 **p** 09. C Walthamstow St Sav *Chelmsf* 08-12; V Woodford St Barn from 12. *St Barnabas' Vicarage, 127 Snakes Lane East, Woodford Green IG8 7HX* T: (020) 3659 4023 M: 07916-281227 E: fatherobedoza@gmail.com

O'BENEY, Robin Mervyn. b 35. Ely Th Coll 61. **d** 64 **p** 65. C Liss *Portsm* 64-65; C Portsea St Cuth 65-68; Hon C Wymondham *Nor* 74-76; R Swainsthorpe w Newton Flotman 76-80; NSM

Sparkenhoe Deanery *Leic* 87-90; V Billesdon and Skeffington 90-91; rtd 95. *19 Bridge Street, Kington HR5 3DL* T: (01544) 230416

OBIN, Raymond Clive. b 63. Girton Coll Cam BA 85 MA 89. Wycliffe Hall Ox BTh 07. **d** 04 **p** 05. NSM Bucklebury w Marlston *Ox* 04-12; NSM Bradfield and Stanford Dingley 04-12; Asst Dir of Ords (Berks) from 12; PtO *Win* from 13; LtO *Ox* from 15. *Solfonn, Enborne Row, Wash Water, Newbury RG20 0LY* T: (01635) 38212 E: raymond@obin.org.uk

OBIORA, Arthur Cuenyem. b 42. JP 91. **d** 95 **p** 95. NSM Hatcham St Cath *S'wark* 95-12; PtO from 12. *126 Perry Hill, London SE4 4EY* T: (020) 8699 3845

OBLESBY, Judith Mary. *See* COOK, Judith Mary

OBORNE, Mrs Martine Amelia. b 57. St Hilda's Coll Ox MA 80. SEITE BA 09. **d** 09 **p** 10. C Islington St Mary *Lon* 09-12; P-in-c Chiswick St Mich 12-15; V from 15. *St Michael's Vicarage, 60 Elmwood Road, London W4 3DZ* T: (020) 8994 3173 M: 07842-199556 E: maoborne@hotmail.com *or* vicar@stmichael-suttoncourt.org.uk

O'BOYLE, Liam Patrick Butler. b 66. Nottm Univ BA 90 MA 98. EMMTC 98. **d** 01 **p** 02. C Cinderhill *S'well* 01-06; TV Clifton 06-10; Dioc Partnerships Officer from 10; C Chilwell from 11; C Lenton Abbey from 11. *23 Fellows Road, Beeston, Nottingham NG9 1AQ* T: 0115-943 1032 E: liam.oboyle@ntlworld.com

O'BRIEN, Andrew David. b 61. Nottm Univ BTh 88. Linc Th Coll 85. **d** 88 **p** 89. C Clare w Poslingford *St E* 88-89; C Clare w Poslingford, Cavendish etc 89-91; V Belton *Linc* 91-97; P-in-c Melbourn *Ely* 97-99; V 99-15; P-in-c Meldreth 97-99; V 99-15; RD Shingay 13-15; V Canford Cliffs and Sandbanks *Sarum* from 15. *The Vicarage, 14 Flaghead Road, Poole BH13 7JW* E: revbrien@ntlworld.com

O'BRIEN, Andrew Peter. b 81. Jes Coll Cam BA 03. Wycliffe Hall Ox BTh 14. **d** 14 **p** 15. C Wimbledon Park St Luke *S'wark* from 14. *37 Lucien Road, London SW19 8EL*

O'BRIEN, David. b 62. Moorlands Th Coll BA 99. CBDTI 01. **d** 04 **p** 05. C Bispham *Blackb* 04-08; C S Shore H Trin 08-10; P-in-c Shelton and Oxon *Lich* from 10; Uplands Nursing Home from 15. *The Vicarage, 10A Shelton Gardens, Bicton Heath, Shrewsbury SY3 5AG* T: (01743) 232774

O'BRIEN, Mrs Elaine. b 55. CITC 94. **d** 97 **p** 98. Aux Min Killyman *Arm* 97-00; Aux Min Gilnahirk *D & D* 00-06; Bp's C Clogherny w Seskinore and Drumnakilly *Arm* 06-08; R 08-11; I Whitehouse *Conn* from 11. *The Rectory, 283 Shore Road, Newtownabbey BT37 9SR* T: (028) 9036 9955 M: 07703-618119 E: elaineobrien1@btinternet.com

O'BRIEN, George Edward. b 32. Clifton Th Coll 61. **d** 64 **p** 65. C Denton Holme *Carl* 64-68; V Castle Town *Lich* 68-88; Chapl St Geo Hosp Stafford 88-94; Chapl Kingsmead Hosp Stafford 88-94; Chapl Foundation NHS Trust Stafford 94-99; rtd 99; PtO *Lich* from 99. *Abily, 185 Tixall Road, Stafford ST16 3XJ* T: (01785) 244261

O'BRIEN, Kevin Michael. b 60. Herts Univ BA 82. St Steph Ho Ox BTh 05. **d** 01 **p** 02. C Uppingham w Ayston and Wardley w Belton *Pet* 01-04; Asst Chapl Wellington Coll Berks 04-06; Bp's Chapl and Office Manager *Eur* 06-10; V Burgess Hill St Jo *Chich* from 10; RD Hurst from 11. *St John's Rectory, 68 Park Road, Burgess Hill RH15 8HG* T: (01444) 232582

O'BRIEN, Mary. *See* GUBBINS, Mary

O'BRIEN, Shelagh Ann. *See* STACEY, Shelagh Ann

O'CATHAIN, Damien. **d** 08 **p** 09. C Bandon Union *C, C & R* 08-11; I Castlepollard and Oldcastle w Loughcrew etc *M & K* from 11. *St Michael's Rectory, Castlepollard, Co Westmeath, Republic of Ireland* T: (00353) (44) 966 1123 E: churchinfo21@gmail.com

OCHOLA, George Otieno. b 58. Lon Sch of Th BTh 02. St Jo Sch of Miss Kokise. **d** 88 **p** 89. Kenya 88-99; PtO *Lon* 00-08; NSM Watford St Mich *St Alb* 08-10; Chapl W Herts Hosps NHS Trust from 10. *Foundation Trust Office, Watford General Hospital, 60 Vicarage Road, Watford WD18 0HB* T: (01923) 436280 M: 07866-359120 E: georgeochola@hotmail.com

OCKFORD, Paul Philip. b 46. St Chad's Coll Dur BA 67. St Steph Ho Ox 68. **d** 70 **p** 71. C Streatham St Pet *S'wark* 70-74; C Cheam 74-77; P-in-c Eastrington *York* 77-79; TV Howden 80-83; R Sherburn and W and E Heslerton w Yedingham 83-92; V Bampton, Morebath, Clayhanger and Petton *Ex* 92-98; R Goodmanham *York* 98-04; V Market Weighton 98-04; V Sancton 98-04; rtd 04. *78 Wold Road, Pocklington, York YO42 2QG*

O'CONNELL, Miss Mary Joy. b 49. York Univ BA 71 Leeds Univ CertEd 74. Chich Th Coll 84. **dss** 86 **d** 87 **p** 94. Cinderhill *S'well* 86-98; Par Dn 87-94; C 94; P-in-c 94-98; V Linc St Giles 98-14; rtd 14. *Address temp unknown* E: mjoconnell@lineone.net

O'CONNELL, Peter David. b 69. St Edm Hall Ox BA 91 MA 97 Cant Ch Ch Univ BA 12. SEITE 09. **d** 12 **p** 13. C Henfield w

Shermanbury and Woodmancote *Chich* from 12. *Glebe House, 41 Furners Mead, Henfield BN5 9JA* T: (01273) 492792 E: curate@henfield.org

O'CONNELL, William Anthony. b 61. STETS. **d** 10 **p** 11. C Milton *Win* 10-13; P-in-c Lyddington and Wanborough and Bishopstone etc *Bris* from 13. *The Vicarage, 19 Church Road, Wanborough, Swindon SN4 0BZ* T: (01793) 791359 E: villagevicar@hotmail.co.uk

O'CONNOR, Canon Brian Michael McDougal. b 42. St Cath Coll Cam BA 67 MA 69. Cuddesdon Coll 67. **d** 69 **p** 70. C Headington *Ox* 69-71; Sec Dioc Past and Redundant Chs Uses Cttees 72-79; P-in-c Merton 72-76; V Rainham *Roch* 79-97; RD Gillingham 81-88; Hon Can Roch Cathl 89-97; Dean Auckland New Zealand 97-00; Hon Can from 00; PtO *Ox* 00-02 and from 04; P-in-c Lt Missenden 02-04; rtd 04. *1 Steadys Lane, Stanton Harcourt, Witney OX29 5RL* T: (01865) 882776 M: 07740-702161 E: canonmichaeloc@aol.com

O'CONNOR, Canon Daniel. b 33. Univ Coll Dur BA 54 MA 67 St Andr Univ PhD 81. Cuddesdon Coll 56. **d** 58 **p** 59. C Stockton St Pet *Dur* 58-62; C W Hartlepool St Aid 62-63; Cam Miss to Delhi 63-70; USPG India 70-72; Chapl St Andr Univ *St And* 72-77; R Edin Gd Shep 77-82; Prin Coll of Ascension Selly Oak 82-90; Dir Scottish Chs Ho (Chs Together in Scotland) 90-93; Can Res Wakef Cathl 93-96; Bp's Adv on Inter-Faith Issues 93-96; rtd 96; Hon C Cupar *St And* from 12. *15 School Road, Balmullo, St Andrews KY16 0BA* T: (01334) 871326 E: danoconnor@btinternet.com

O'CONNOR, John Goodrich. b 34. Keble Coll Ox BA 58 MA 60. Lich Th Coll. **d** 61 **p** 62. C Blackpool St Steph *Blackb* 61-66; C Holbeck *Ripon* 66-68; C Hendon St Mary *Lon* 68-73; TV Thornaby on Tees *York* 73-79; TR 79-89; V Blyth St Cuth *Newc* 89-96; Chapl Wellesley Nautical Sch 89-96; V Feniscliffe *Blackb* 96-04; rtd 04; Hon C Lightbowne *Man* 04-14; PtO from 14. *28 Boar Green Close, Manchester M40 3AW* T: 0161-376 3346

O'CONNOR, Michael. *See* O'CONNOR, Brian Michael McDougal

ODA-BURNS, John Macdonald. b 31. AKC 56. **d** 57 **p** 58. C St Marychurch *Ex* 57-59; S Africa 59-64; Bahamas 64-67; USA from 67; rtd 96. *611 La Mesa Drive, Portola Valley CA 94028-7416, USA* T/F: (001) (650) 854 2831 E: bussels@batnet.com

ODDY, Canon Frederick Brian. b 29. Univ of Wales (Lamp) BA 50. Linc Th Coll 50. **d** 52 **p** 53. C Preston Em *Blackb* 52-55; C St Annes St Thos 55-57; V Chorley St Jas 57-64; V Warton St Oswald 64-76; P-in-c Yealand Conyers 74-76; V Warton St Oswald w Yealand Conyers 76-98; RD Tunstall 84-90; Hon Can Blackb Cathl 89-98; rtd 98; PtO *Blackb* from 98. *9 Main Road, Nether Kellet, Carnforth LA6 1HG*

ODDY, Joan Winifred. b 34. **d** 97 **p** 98. OLM Kessingland w Gisleham *Nor* 97-99; OLM Kessingland, Gisleham and Rushmere 99-04; rtd 04; PtO *Nor* from 04. *Rose Cottage, Wash Lane, Kessingland, Lowestoft NR33 7QY* T: (01502) 742001 E: bracken@joanshome.freeserve.co.uk

ODDY-BATES, Mrs Julie Louise. b 61. SRN 82 SCM 85. Ridley Hall Cam 04. **d** 06 **p** 07. C Watton w Carbrooke and Ovington *Nor* 06-07; C Ashill, Carbrooke, Ovington and Saham Toney 07-09; P-in-c Gillingham w Geldeston, Stockton, Ellingham etc from 09; C Loddon, Sisland, Chedgrave, Hardley and Langley from 09. *The Rectory, 60 The Street, Geldeston, Beccles NR34 0LN* T: (01502) 715898 E: jlo32@tiscali.co.uk

O'DELL, Colin John. b 61. WEMTC 03. **d** 06 **p** 07. C Bishop's Cleeve *Glouc* 06-09; Chapl RAF from 09. *Chaplaincy Services (RAF), HQ Air Command, RAF High Wycombe HP14 4UE* T: (01494) 496800 F: 496343 M: 07779-126050 E: revdcolin@hotmail.co.uk

ODLING-SMEE, George William. b 35. K Coll Dur MB, BS 59 FRCS 68 FRCSI 86. **d** 77 **p** 78. NSM Belfast St Thos *Conn* 77-90; NSM Belfast St Geo 90-02. *The Boathouse, 24 Rossglass Road South, Killough, Downpatrick BT30 7RA* T: (028) 4484 1868 F: 4484 1143 E: wodlingsmee@aol.com

O'DONNELL, Mrs Mollie. b 39. Portsm Poly BA 91. STETS 97. **d** 00 **p** 03. NSM Calbourne w Newtown and Shalfleet *Portsm* 00-09; rtd 09; PtO *Portsm* from 09. *36 Medina Court, Old Westminster Lane, Newport PO30 5PW*

O'DONNELL, Paula Ella. *See* CHALLEN, Paula Ella

O'DONOGHUE, Mark Ronald. b 69. St Aid Coll Dur BA 91 Solicitor 93. Oak Hill Th Coll BA 04. **d** 04 **p** 05. C St Helen Bishopsgate w St Andr Undershaft etc *Lon* 04-11; C Kensington St Mary Abbots w Ch Ch and St Phil from 11. *20 South End Row, London W8 5BZ* T: (020) 7795 6330 E: odonoghue_mark@hotmail.com

O'DONOGHUE, Mrs Sarah Helen. b 75. Ches Coll of HE BA 96 Liv Hope PGCE 97. St Mellitus Coll 13. **d** 15. C Aughton Ch Ch *Liv* from 15. *13 Grasmere Road, Maghull, Liverpool L31 6BX* T: 0151-526 0220 M: 07847-931323 E: revsarahodonoghue@gmail.com

O'DONOVAN, Prof Oliver Michael Timothy. b 45. Ball Coll Ox BA 68 MA 71 DPhil 75. Wycliffe Hall Ox 68. **d** 72 **p** 73. Tutor Wycliffe Hall Ox 72-77; Prof Systematic Th Wycliffe Coll Toronto 77-82; Regius Prof Moral and Past Th Ox Univ 82-06; Can Res Ch Ch *Ox* 82-06; Prof Chr Ethics Edin Univ from 06. *New College, Mound Place, Edinburgh EH1 2LX*
T: (01383) 740797 E: oliver.odonovan@ed.ac.uk

O'DOWD-SMYTH, Christine. CITC. **d** 09 **p** 10. NSM Lismore w Cappoquin, Kilwatermoy, Dungarvan etc *C & O* 09-14; P-in-c Fiddown w Clonegam, Guilcagh and Kilmeaden 14; Dioc Spokesperson for Healing Min from 14. *Eldon, 16 John's Hill, Waterford, Republic of Ireland* T: (00353) (51) 304423 M: 87-293 3461 E: codowdsmyth@wit.ie

OEHRING, Anthony Charles. b 56. Sheff City Poly BA 79 CQSW 79 Kent Univ MA 02. Ridley Hall Cam 86. **d** 88 **p** 89. C Gillingham *Sarum* 88-91; TV S Gillingham *Roch* 91-00; P-in-c Faversham *Cant* 00-12; C Preston next Faversham, Goodnestone and Graveney 02-12; P-in-c The Brents and Davington w Oare and Luddenham 03-06; AD Ospringe 02-11; Co-ord Chapl HM Pris E Sutton Park 12-13; Co-ord Chapl HM Pris Blantyre Ho 12-13; Hon Can Cant Cathl 06-13; Managing Chapl HM Pris Ford from 13. *HM Prison Ford, Ford Road, Ford, Arundel BN18 0BX* T: (01903) 663085
E: anthony.oehring@hmps.gsi.gov.uk

OEPPEN, Canon John Gerard David. b 44. St D Coll Lamp. **d** 67 **p** 68. C-in-c Cwmmer w Abercregan CD *Llan* 67-70; TV Glyncorrwg w Afan Vale and Cymmer Afan 70-71; C Whitchurch 71-74; V Aberavon H Trin 74-78; V Bargoed and Deri w Brithdir 78-86; R Barry All SS 86-08; Can Llan Cathl 04-08; rtd 08; PtO *Llan* from 08. *6 Heol Fioled, Barry CF63 1HB* T: (01446) 421099

OESTREICHER, Canon Paul. b 31. OM(Ger) 95. Univ of NZ BA 53 MA 56 Cov Poly Hon DLitt 91 Sussex Univ Hon LLD 05 Lambeth DD 08 Otago Univ Hon DD 09. Linc Th Coll 56. **d** 59 **p** 60. C Dalston H Trin w St Phil *Lon* 59-61; C S Mymms K Chas 61-68; Asst in Relig Broadcasting BBC 61-64; Assoc Sec Internat Affairs Dept BCC 64-69; V Blackheath Ascension *S'wark* 68-81; Dir of Tr 69-72; Hon Can S'wark Cathl 78-81; Asst Gen Sec BCC 81-86; Can Res Cov Cathl 86-97; Dir of Internat Min 86-97; Humboldt Fell Inst of Th Free Univ of Berlin 92-93; rtd 98; PtO *Cov* 98-10; *Chich* from 03; Hon Chapl Sussex Univ 04-09. *97 Furze Croft, Furze Hill, Hove BN3 1PE* T: (01273) 728033
E: paul.oestreicher.nz@gmail.com

O'FARRELL, Anne Marie. d 08 **p** 09. NSM Dublin Sandford w Milltown *D & G* from 08. *138 Meadow Grove, Dundrum, Dublin 14, Republic of Ireland* T: (00353) (1) 296 6222

O'FERRALL, Patrick Charles Kenneth. b 34. OBE 89. New Coll Ox BA 58 MA 60. **d** 00 **p** 01. OLM Godalming *Guildf* 00-04; PtO from 04. *Pear Tree House, 66 Firgrove Hill, Farnham GU9 8LW* T: (01252) 724498 E: patrickoferrall@gmail.com

OFFER, The Ven Clifford Jocelyn. b 43. Ex Univ BA 67 FRSA 97. Westcott Ho Cam 67. **d** 69 **p** 70. C Bromley SS Pet and Paul *Roch* 69-74; TV Southampton (City Cen) *Win* 74-83; TR Hitchin *St Alb* 83-94; Adn Nor and Can Res Nor Cathl 94-08; rtd 08. *Chase House, Peterstow, Ross-on-Wye HR9 6JX* T: (01989) 567874

OFFER, Mrs Jill Patricia. b 44. CertEd 65. **d** 03 **p** 04. OLM Salisbury St Mark *Sarum* 03-13; OLM Salisbury St Mark and Laverstock from 13. *11 Netheravon Road, Salisbury SP1 3BJ* T: (01722) 334455 E: jill.offer418@btinternet.com

O'FLAHERTY, Mrs Sheila Mary. b 53. Huddersfield Univ MA 08 Man Univ CertEd 00. SNWTP 11. **d** 13 **p** 14. NSM Heatons *Man* 13-15; NSM Coldhurst and Oldham St Steph from 15. *7 Windsor Grove, Ashton under Lyne OL6 8UU* T: 0161-330 9641 M: 07803-084422 E: sheila@oflaherty.co.uk

OGADA, John Ochieng. b 56. Nairobi Univ LLB 83 Univ of Wales (Cardiff) LLM 89. **d** 01. PtO *York* 01-02; NSM Hull St Martin w Transfiguration 02-03. *44 Kingston Road, Willerby, Hull HU10 6BH* T: (01482) 653592

O'GARRO, Henry Roland Furlonge. b 30. Leeward Is TCert 52. St Steph Ho Ox 00. **d** 00. NSM Kilburn St Aug w St Jo *Lon* 00-05; NSM Willesden St Mary 05-12; PtO from 12. *32 Cedar Road, London NW2 6SR* T: (020) 8452 4530

OGBEDE, Ms Olufunke Oladunni. b 48. Lon Inst of Educn MA 81. **d** 05 **p** 06. OLM S Lambeth St Anne and All SS *S'wark* 05-13; NSM Stockwell St Andr and St Mich from 13. *98 Plummer Road, London SW4 8HJ* T: (020) 8678 7387 M: 07944-424931 E: fundunni@aol.com

OGILVIE, The Ven Gordon. b 42. Glas Univ MA 64 Lon Univ BD 67. ALCD 66. **d** 67 **p** 68. C Ashtead *Guildf* 67-72; V New Barnet St Jas *St Alb* 72-80; Dir Past Studies Wycliffe Hall Ox 80-87; P-in-c Harlow New Town w Lt Parndon *Chelmsf* 87-89; R 89-94; TR Harlow Town Cen w Lt Parndon 94-96; Hon Can Chelmsf Cathl 94-96; Chapl Princess Alexandra Hosp Harlow 88-96; Adn Nottingham *S'well* 96-06; rtd 07;

LtO *St And* from 07. *49 Argyle Street, St Andrews KY16 9BX* T: (01334) 470185 E: gordon.ogilvie@virgin.net

OGILVIE, Ian Douglas. b 37. Em Coll Cam BA 59 MA 63. Linc Th Coll 59. **d** 61 **p** 62. C Clapham H Trin *S'wark* 61-63; C Cambridge Gt St Mary w St Mich *Ely* 63-66; Chapl Sevenoaks Sch 66-77; Hon C Sevenoaks St Nic *Roch* 67-77; Chapl Malvern Coll 77-84; Hd Master St Geo Sch Harpenden 84-87; LtO *St Alb* 84-87; Bp's Dom Chapl 87-89; P-in-c Aldenham 87-91; Appeals Dir Mind 89-91; Fund Raising Dir Br Deaf Assn 91-94; NSM Tring *St Alb* 92-94; PtO from 94; Fund Raising Dir R Nat Miss to Deep Sea Fishermen from 94. *The White House, 19 Lower Icknield Way, Marsworth, Tring HP23 4LN* T: (01296) 661479

OGILVIE, Pamela. b 56. Brunel Univ MA 89 CQSW 82. Qu Coll Birm 01. **d** 03 **p** 04. C Hill *Birm* 03-07; V Billesley Common from 07. *Holy Cross Vicarage, 29 Beauchamp Road, Birmingham B13 0NS* T: 0121-444 1737
E: church@holycrossbillesley.co.uk

OGLE, The Very Revd Catherine. b 61. Leeds Univ BA 82 MPhil 85 MA 91 Fitzw Coll Cam BA 87. Westcott Ho Cam 85. **d** 88 **p** 94. C Middleton St Mary *Ripon* 88-91; Relig Progr Ed BBC Radio Leeds 91-95; NSM Leeds St Marg and All Hallows 91-95; P-in-c Woolley *Wakef* 95-01; P-in-c Huddersfield St Pet and All SS 01-03; V Huddersfield St Pet 03-10; RD Huddersfield 09-10; Chapl Huddersfield Univ 03-06; Hon Can Wakef Cathl 08-10; Dean Birm from 10. *38 Goodby Road, Birmingham B13 8NJ* T: 0121-262 1840 F: 262 1860
E: cogleathome@aol.com *or* dean@birminghamcathedral.com

OGLESBY, Ms Elizabeth Jane. b 73. Roehampton Inst BA 95 Man Univ BPhil 98. Westcott Ho Cam 00. **d** 03 **p** 04. C S Dulwich St Steph *S'wark* 03-06; P-in-c Camberwell St Mich w All So w Em 06-07; V 07-14; AD S'wark and Newington 13-14; V Eltham Park St Luke from 14. *St Luke's Vicarage, 107 Westmount Road, London SE9 1XX* M: 07790-219725 T: (020) 8850 3030

OGLESBY, Canon Leslie Ellis. b 46. Univ Coll Ox BA 69 MA 73 City Univ MPhil 73 Fitzw Coll Cam BA 73 MA 77 Lambeth PhD 12. Ripon Coll Cuddesdon 77. **d** 78 **p** 79. C Stevenage St Mary Shephall *St Alb* 78-80; Dir St Alb Minl Tr Scheme 80-87; V Markyate Street *St Alb* 80-87; Dir CME 87-94; Hon Can St Alb 93-01; TR Hitchin 94-01; Adult Educn and Tr Officer *Ely* 01-04; Dioc Dir Minl and Adult Learning 04-12; Dir Min 12; Hon Can Ely Cathl 04-12; rtd 12; PtO *Ely* from 12. *55 Swansholme Gardens, Sandy SG19 1HN* E: oglesbyles75@yahoo.co.uk

OGNJANOVIC, Joanne. b 65. **d** 12. NSM Wellesbourne and Walton d'Eiville *Cov* 12. *17 Ash Grove, Southam CV47 1EJ*

O'GRADY, Anthony Donald. b 87. RNMH 11. Coll of Resurr Mirfield 12. **d** 15. C Newc Ch Ch w St Ann from 15. *6 Three Indian Kings House, 31 Quayside, Newcastle upon Tyne NE1 3DE* M: 07519-683355 E: ant.ogrady@hotmail.co.uk

OGRAM, Mrs Ann. b 44. WEMTC 04. **d** 06 **p** 07. NSM Clun w Bettws-y-Crwyn and Newcastle *Heref* 06-14; NSM Clun Valley from 14. *Highbeech House, Mount Pleasant, Llwyn Road, Clun, Craven Arms SY7 8JJ* T: (01588) 640830 M: 07970-072836
E: ann@ogram.com

OGUGUO, Barnabas Ahuna. b 47. Rome Univ BA 70 BD 74 Glas Univ MTh 84 PhD 90 Strathclyde Univ PGCE 93. **d** 73 **p** 74. Nigeria 73-93; RE Teacher Lenzie Academy *Glas* 93-96; Bearsden Academy from 96; Hon C Lenzie 95-05; P-in-c Glas St Matt 05-07; P-in-c Cumbernauld 07-09; R from 09. *32 Carron Crescent, Lenzie, Glasgow G66 5PJ* T: 0141-578 9802 M: 07757-502054 E: bahunog01@yahoo.co.uk

OGUNSANYA, Olumuyiwa Adegboyega. b 67. Lagos Angl Dioc Sem 01. **d** 03 **p** 04. C Alapere Ch Ch Nigeria 04-05; PtO *S'wark* 07-10. *222 Seabrook Rise, Grays RM17 6BL* T: (01375) 369415 M: 07946-488595 E: revoolord2005@yahoo.com

OGUNYEMI, Dele Johnson. b 56. Obafemi Awolowo Univ BA 90. SEITE 04. **d** 07 **p** 08. NSM Plumstead All SS *S'wark* 07-11; C Nunhead St Antony w St Silas 11-14; P-in-c from 14. *St Antony with St Silas Vicarage, Athenlay Road, London SE15 3EP* T: (020) 7639 4261 M: 07958-396118
E: djogunyemi@tiscali.co.uk

OGUNYINKA, Olasupo. b 59. Yorks Min Course 13. **d** 15. NSM Beeston *Ripon* from 15. *36 Holmwood Avenue, Leeds LS6 4NJ* T: 0113-275 7574 E: olasupo.ognunyinka@ntlworld.com

OH, Abraham (Taemin). b 75. St Steph Ho Ox 08. **d** 11 **p** 12. C Colchester St Jas and St Paul w All SS etc *Chelmsf* 11-14; P-in-c Enfield St Geo *Lon* from 14. *St George's Vicarage, 706 Hertford Road, Enfield EN3 6NR* M: 07737-161317
E: taemin.oh@gmail.com

O'HARE, Phelim Sean. b 71. QUB BA 94 Gregorian Univ Rome STB 97 St Thos Aquinas Pontifical Univ Rome MA 98 St Mary's Coll Twickenham PGCE 02. **d** 97 **p** 98. In RC Ch 97-12; Chapl Llan Cathl Sch from 12; NSM Canton Cardiff

Llan 12-14; TV from 14. *Canton Vicarage, 3A Romilly Road, Cardiff CF5 1FH* T: (029) 2021 0732
E: phelimohare@gmail.com

OHEN, John. b 42. **d** 06 **p** 07. NSM Clapham St Jas *S'wark* 06-12; PtO from 12. *47 Kirkstall Gardens, London SW2 4HR* T: (020) 8671 0028 M: 07947-616869 E: john.ohen@btinternet.com

OHS, Lt Comdr Douglas Fredrick. b 49. Saskatchewan Univ BA 74. Em Coll Saskatoon LTh 75. **d** 74 **p** 75. C Bridgwater St Mary w Chilton Trinity *B & W* 75-77; R MacDowall Canada 77-83; R Regina St Mary 83-87; CF from 87. *14-3505 Willowdale Crescent, Brandon MB R7B 3C5, Canada*

OJI, Erasmus Oluchukwu. b 43. Lon Univ BSc 66 LRCP 70 MRCS 70 FRCS 76. Oak Hill Th Coll 75. **d** 78 **p** 79. C Ealing Dean St Jo *Lon* 78-80; Nigeria 80-90; Asst Chapl Rotherham Distr Gen Hosp 90-91; PtO *Sheff* from 92. *369 Fulwood Road, Sheffield S10 3BS* T/F: 07092-147747
E: erasmus@doctors.org.uk

OKE, Mrs Elizabeth Mary. b 43. SAOMC 96. **d** 99 **p** 00. NSM Woolhampton w Midgham and Beenham Valance *Ox* 99-08; NSM Aldermaston w Wasing and Brimpton 05-08; NSM Aldermaston and Woolhampton 08-11; PtO from 11. *Gladstone Cottage, 18 Windmill Road, Mortimer, Reading RG7 3RN* T: 0118-933 2829 E: em.oke@btinternet.com

OKE, Michael John. b 42. Ox Min Course 89. **d** 92 **p** 93. NSM Stratfield Mortimer *Ox* 92-99; NSM Stratfield Mortimer and Mortimer W End etc 99-03; NSM Tilehurst St Geo 03-12; NSM Tilehurst St Mary 03-12; rtd 12; PtO *Ox* from 12. *Gladstone Cottage, 18 Windmill Road, Mortimer, Reading RG7 3RN* T: 0118-933 2829 E: em.oke@btinternet.com

OKECHI, Patrick Otosio. b 62. Chas Univ Prague MTh 94. **d** 95 **p** 98. PtO *Eur* 95-02; Asst P Angl Episc Congregation Czech Republic 02; V W Bromwich Gd Shep w St Jo *Lich* 02-08. *8 Drake Road, Birmingham B66 1TF* M: 07951-814518
E: pokechi1@btinternet.com

OKEKE, Christian. b 71. Strathclyde Univ MSc 09. United Th Coll Harare BTheol 04. **d** 05 **p** 06. C Avondale Zimbabwe 05; C Glas St Silas 05-08; P-in-c Glas Gd Shep and Ascension 08-15; Chapl Strathclyde Univ 08-15; Chapl Princess Alexandra Hosp NHS Trust from 15. *75 Old Road, Harlow CM17 0HF* M: 07748-590407 T: (01279) 423301
E: bishopc7@yahoo.com

✠**OKEKE, The Rt Revd Ken Sandy Edozie.** b 41. Nigeria Univ BSc 67 Man Univ MA 94. Igbaja Sem Nigeria. **d** 76 **p** 76 **c** 00. Nigeria 76-80 and 87-89; Chapl to Nigerians in UK and Irish Republic 80-87; Hon Can Kwara from 85; Hon Adn from 98; C Man Whitworth 89-95; Chapl Inst of Higher Learning Man 89-95; CMS 95-01; PtO *S'wark* 96-02; Bp on the Niger 00-11. *50 Essex Road, Longfield DA3 7QL* T: (01474) 709627
E: kengozi8@yahoo.com

OKELLO, Modicum. b 53. Trin Coll Bris BA 90. St Paul's Coll Limuru 76 Wycliffe Hall Ox 86. **d** 78 **p** 79. Kenya 78-80; Uganda 80-86; NSM Goodmayes All SS *Chelmsf* 91-92; C Barking St Marg w St Patr 92-96; C Stratford St Jo and Ch Ch w Forest Gate St Jas 96-99; TV Forest Gate St Sav w W Ham St Matt 99-10; P-in-c Hall Green St Mich *Birm* 10-14. *237 Lakey Lane, Birmingham B28 8QT* T: 0121-777 8443
E: modicum.okello@btconnect.com

O'KELLY, Martin. **d** 11. C Clonsast w Rathangan, Thomastown etc *M & K* from 11. *Address temp unknown*

O'KELLY, Ruth Julia. **d** 14. Mullingar, Portnashangan, Moyliscar, Kilbixy etc *M & K* 14-15; C Dublin Rathfarnham *D & G* from 15. *Address temp unknown*

OLADUJI, Christopher Temitayo. b 57. Awosika Th Coll Nigeria 84. **d** 87 **p** 88. C Ilutitun Ebenezer Nigeria 87; Asst P Ondo Cathl 88; NSM W Ham *Chelmsf* 89-93; NSM Peckham St Jo w St Andr *S'wark* 97-98; NSM E Ham St Geo *Chelmsf* 99-01; NSM Hackney Wick St Mary of Eton w St Aug *Lon* 02-04; NSM Smithfield St Bart Gt 04-13; NSM Plaistow and N Canning Town *Chelmsf* from 13. *103 Browning Road, London E12 6RB* T: (020) 8472 4143 M: 07985-465401
E: coladuji@yahoo.com

OLANCZUK, Jonathan Paul Tadeusz. b 49. EAMTC 94. **d** 96 **p** 97. C Haverhill w Withersfield *St E* 96-00; P-in-c Badingham w Bruisyard, Cransford and Dennington 00-04; P-in-c Rendham w Sweffling 00-04; R Upper Alde from 04. *The Rectory, 5 Orchard Rise, Badingham, Woodbridge IP13 8LN* T/F: (01728) 638823 M: 07766-953558 M: 07944-186526 E: olanczuk@suffolkonline.net *or* olanczuk@me.com

OLD, Arthur Anthony George (Tony). b 36. Clifton Th Coll 69. **d** 71 **p** 72. C Clitheroe St Jas *Blackb* 71-73; C Bispham 73-77; V Haslingden St Jo Stonefold 77-81; TV Lowestoft and Kirkley *Nor* 81-83; Chapl to the Deaf *Cant* 83-01; P-in-c Hernhill 83-85; C Preston next Faversham, Goodnestone and Graveney 85-01; rtd 01; PtO *Cant* from 01. *62 Knaves Acre, Headcorn, Ashford TN27 9TJ* T: (01622) 891498

OLDFIELD, Jonathan Thomas. b 54. Bede Coll Dur TCert 76. NEOC 04. **d** 07 **p** 08. NSM Patrick Brompton and Hunton *Leeds* from 07; NSM Crakehall from 07; NSM Hornby from 07; NSM Spennithorne w Finghall and Hauxwell from 12. *12 St Mary's Mount, Leyburn DL8 5JB* T: (01969) 622958
E: jonathan@jonathanoldfield.wanadoo.co.uk

OLDFIELD, Canon Roger Fielden. b 45. Qu Coll Cam BA 67 MA 71 Lon Univ BD 75. Trin Coll Bris 75. **d** 75 **p** 76. C Halliwell St Pet *Man* 75-80 and 03-10; V 80-03; AD Bolton 93-02; Hon Can Man Cathl 00-10; rtd 10; PtO *Man* from 11. *70 Eastgrove Avenue, Bolton BL1 7HA* T: (01204) 305228
E: rogerandruth@googlemail.com

OLDHAM, Dale Raymond. b 40. NZ Coll of Pharmacy MPS 63 Cant Univ (NZ) MA 87. Ridley Hall Cam 64. **d** 67 **p** 68. C Woking St Mary *Guildf* 67-70; C Papanui New Zealand 71-73; CMS Miss Dodoma Tanzania 74-81; Sec Home CMS New Zealand 81-85; C Burnside 85-88; V Shirley St Steph 89-06; rtd 06. *58 Pitcairn Crescent, Papanui, Christchurch 8053, New Zealand* E: d.oldham@xtra.co.nz

OLDHAM, David Christian. *See* COLES, David Christian

OLDHAM, Susan Yvonne. b 60. SWMTC 07. **d** 10 **p** 11. NSM Georgeham *Ex* 10-14; P-in-c Dolton from 14; P-in-c Monkokehampton from 14; P-in-c Iddesleigh w Dowland from 14. *The Rectory, Cleave Hill, Dolton, Winkleigh EX19 8QT* E: susan.oldham7@btinternet.com

OLDNALL, Frederick Herbert. b 16. Ripon Hall Ox 56. **d** 57 **p** 58. C Radford *Cov* 57-59; C Stratford-on-Avon 59-62; V Rosliston w Coton in the Elms *Derby* 62-83; rtd 83; PtO *Cov* from 93. *4 Margetts Close, Kenilworth CV8 1EN* T: (01926) 852417

OLDROYD, David Christopher Leslie. b 42. FRICS. S Dios Minl Tr Scheme. **d** 85 **p** 86. NSM Four Marks *Win* 85-90; PtO *Portsm* from 06; *Guildf* from 08; Chich from 12. *18 Rozeldene, Grayshott, Hindhead GU26 6TW* T: (01428) 606620

OLDROYD, Mrs Sheila Margaret. b 40. Liv Univ BSc 63. St Steph Ho Ox 98. **d** 99 **p** 00. NSM Cotgrave *S'well* 99-03; NSM Keyworth and Stanton-on-the-Wolds and Bunny etc 03-08; rtd 08; PtO *S'well* from 08. *27 Lowlands Drive, Keyworth, Nottingham NG12 5HG* T: 0115-937 6344
E: margaretoldroyd@btinternet.com

OLDROYD, Trevor. b 33. Hatf Coll Dur BA 55 Lon Univ BD 60. Wycliffe Hall Ox 60. **d** 61 **p** 62. C Barnes St Mary *S'wark* 61-65; C Wimbledon 65-68; Chapl K Sch Gütersloh W Germany 68-73; Chapl Dudley Sch 73-80; Asst Chapl Wellington Coll Berks 80-82; P-in-c Rendcomb *Glouc* 82-86; Chapl Rendcomb Coll 82-86; Chapl Wrekin Coll Telford 86-90; V Deptford St Jo w H Trin *S'wark* 91-94; rtd 94; PtO *Sarum* 94-00; *Guildf* from 02. *4 The Larches, Woking GU21 4RE* T: (01483) 720398

OLEY, Mrs Carolyn Joan Macdonald. b 44. Ox Min Course 05. **d** 08 **p** 09. NSM Lambfold *Pet* 08-12; R from 12. *The Lambfold Rectory, Collswell Lane, Blakesley, Towcester NN12 8RB* T: (01327) 860507 M: 07531-768070
E: carolyn.oley@btinternet.com

OLHAUSEN, William Paul. b 67. Wycliffe Hall Ox BA 97. **d** 98 **p** 99. C Reading Greyfriars *Ox* 98-01; Sub Chapl HM YOI Reading 98-01; C Cambridge H Trin *Ely* 01-04; I Carrigrohane Union *C, C & R* 04-08; Chapl Monkton Combe Sch Bath 08-11; I Killiney Ballybrack *D & G* from 11. *The Rectory, Killiney Avenue, Killiney, Co Dublin, Republic of Ireland* T: (00353) (1) 285 2228 M: 87-166 0356 E: wolhausen@googlemail.com

OLIVE, Dan. b 29. ARIBA 54. Sarum & Wells Th Coll 79. **d** 82 **p** 83. NSM Wells St Cuth w Wookey Hole *B & W* 82-85; C Yatton Moor 86-88; R Mells w Buckland Dinham, Elm, Whatley etc 88-97; RD Frome 93-97; rtd 97; PtO *B & W* from 97. *Roseleigh, Woodcombe, Minehead TA24 8SA* T: (01643) 702218

OLIVER, Bernard John. b 31. CEng 65 MIMechE. S'wark Ord Course 75. **d** 78 **p** 79. NSM Chipping Ongar *Chelmsf* 78-81; C Waltham Abbey 81-85; C High Ongar w Norton Mandeville 85-87; C Somerton w Compton Dundon, the Charltons etc *B & W* 87-88; rtd 96; PtO *Sarum* from 01. *1 Orchard Way, Mosterton, Beaminster DT8 3LT* T: (01308) 868037

OLIVER, David Leath. b 41. **d** 96. Old Catholic Ch Germany 96-01; PtO *Eur* 10-11; Asst Chapl Helsinki from 11. *Ajurinkatu 5 A 1, 65100 Vaasa, Finland* M: (00358) 407-325250
E: tuulandavid@yahoo.com

OLIVER, Canon David Ryland. b 34. Univ of Wales (Lamp) BA 56 St Cath Coll Ox BA 58 MA 62. Wycliffe Hall Ox 56. **d** 58 **p** 59. C Carmarthen St Pet *St D* 58-61; C Llangyfelach *S & B* 61-63; R Aberedw w Llandeilo Graban etc 63-66; R Llanbadarn Fawr, Llandegley and Llanfihangel etc 66-67; LtO *Llan* 68-70; *Ban* 70-73; V Nefyn w Pistyll w Tudweiliog w Llandudwen etc 73-74; V Abercraf and Callwen *S & B* 74-77; V Llangyfelach 77-79; R Llanllwchaearn and Llanina *St D* 79-83; V Cwmaman 83-94; Can *St D* Cathl from 90; RD Dyffryn Aman 93-94; V Cynwyl Gaeo w Llansawel and Talley

94-99; rtd 99. *Maes y Gelynen, 40 Heol Bryngwili, Cross Hands, Llanelli SA14 6LR* T: (01269) 840146

OLIVER, Diane Margaret. b 49. **d** 14 **p** 15. OLM Cheddleton, Horton, Longsdon and Rushton Spencer *Lich* from 14. *17 Cauldon Close, Leek ST13 5SH* T: (01538) 373800 E: dmoliver@btinternet.com

OLIVER, Gordon. *See* OLIVER, Thomas Gordon

OLIVER, Graham Frank. b 42. St Barn Coll Adelaide. **d** 68 **p** 69. Australia 68-86; C Ealing Ch the Sav *Lon* 86-93; PtO 94-97 and 00-08; Asst Chapl Ypres *Eur* 97-99; P-in-c 99-00; rtd 07. *2 Aldridge Court, 176A High Street, London W3 9NN* T: (020) 8992 0332

✠**OLIVER, The Rt Revd John Keith.** b 35. G&C Coll Cam BA 59 MA 63 MLitt 65. Westcott Ho Cam 59. **d** 64 **p** 65 **c** 90. C Hilborough w Bodney *Nor* 64-68; Chapl Eton Coll 68-72; R S Molton w Nymet St George *Ex* 73-75; P-in-c Filleigh w E Buckland 73-75; P-in-c Warkleigh w Satterleigh and Chittlehamholt 73-75; P-in-c High Bray w Charles 73-75; TR S Molton, Nymet St George, High Bray etc 75-82; P-in-c N Molton w Twitchen 77-79; RD S Molton 74-80; TR Cen Ex 82-85; Adn Sherborne *Sarum* 85-90; P-in-c W Stafford w Frome Billet 85-90; Can Res Sarum Cathl 85-90; Bp Heref 90-03; rtd 03; Hon Asst Bp S & B from 04; PtO *Heref* from 05. *The Old Vicarage, Glascwm, Llandrindod Wells LD1 5SE* T/F: (01982) 570771

OLIVER, John Kenneth. b 47. Brunel Univ MA 92 ALBC 70. EAMTC 98. **d** 00 **p** 01. C E Ham St Paul *Chelmsf* 00-03; V Stratford New Town St Paul 03-05; TV Totton *Win* 05-12; rtd 12; PtO *Win* from 12. *91B Wentworth Avenue, Bournemouth BH5 2EH* T: (01202) 417666 E: revjohnoliver@btinternet.com

OLIVER, The Ven John Michael. b 39. Univ of Wales (Lamp) BA 62. Ripon Hall Ox 62. **d** 64 **p** 65. C High Harrogate St Pet *Ripon* 64-67; C Bramley 67-72; V Low Harrogate St Mary 72-78; V Beeston 78-92; RD Armley 86-92; Adn Leeds 92-05; Hon Can Ripon Cathl 87-05; rtd 05; PtO *Leeds* from 05. *42A Chapel Lane, Barwick in Elmet, Leeds LS15 4EJ* T: 0113-393 5019

OLIVER, The Ven John Rodney. b 31. Melbourne Univ BA 53 Lon Univ MTh 73. Bps' Coll Cheshunt 54. **d** 56 **p** 57. C Much Hadham *St Alb* 56-57; Chapl Ballarat Gr Sch Australia 58-69; C Thorley and Bishop's Stortford H Trin *St Alb* 70-73; V Aberfeldie Australia 74-77; Chapl Trin Coll Melbourne 77-81; I Dandenong 81-91; Adn Box Hill 87-00; I E Kew St Paul 91-00; rtd 00. *27 Asquith Street, Box Hill South Vic 3128, Australia* T: (0061) (3) 9888 7517 F: 9888 7598 E: rodley@smartchat.net.au

OLIVER, Jonathan Andrew. b 79. Cam Univ MPhil 11. Ridley Hall Cam 08. **d** 11 **p** 12. C Sholing *Win* from 11. *Peartree Vicarage, 65 Peartree Avenue, Southampton SO19 7JN* T: (023) 8178 2238 E: jon@sholingchurch.com

OLIVER, Mrs Josephine May. b 48. Cranmer Hall Dur. **d** 01 **p** 02. C Buckrose Carrs *York* 01-04; P-in-c Bubwith w Skipwith 04-10; rtd 10. *23 Skirbeck Road, Hull HU8 0HR* T: (01482) 784744 M: 07885-448331 E: jovicar@jovicar.plus.com

OLIVER (née TROMANS), Judith Anne. b 54. Liv Univ BSc 76 Lanc Univ PGCE 77 Birm Univ MA 07. WMMTC. **d** 96 **p** 97. C Old Swinford Stourbridge *Worc* 96-99; C Pensnett 99-01; Asst to Suff Bp Dudley 99-01; P-in-c Dudley Wood 01-08; V 08-10; TV Dudley 10-15; Hon Can Worc Cathl 11-15; rtd 15. *37 Haden Park Road, Cradley Heath B64 7HF* M: 07903-104862 T: (01384) 832095 E: juditholiver@blueyonder.co.uk

OLIVER, Mark. **d** 14 **p** 15. OLM New Haw *Guildf* from 14. *39 Kingston Rise, New Haw, Addlestone KT15 3EX* T: (01932) 910355 E: markthechurch@gmail.com

OLIVER, Canon Paul Robert. b 41. Tyndale Hall Bris 63. **d** 66 **p** 67. C Virginia Water *Guildf* 66-70; Scripture Union (E Region) 70-74; TV Thetford *Nor* 75-83; V Earlham St Anne 83-98; RD Nor S 94-98; Hon Can Nor Cathl 96-98; rtd 98; PtO *Nor* from 98. *The Sanctuary, 35A Blofield Road, Brundall, Norwich NR13 5NU* T: (01603) 712124 E: paulandliz.oliver@uwclub.net

OLIVER, Canon Philip Maule. b 38. Birm Univ LLB 59. Wells Th Coll 62. **d** 64 **p** 65. C Chesterton *Lich* 64-67; C Tettenhall Wood 67-71; V Milton 71-78; V Ixworth and Bardwell *St E* 78-92; P-in-c Honington w Sapiston and Troston 81-92; TR Blackbourne 92-08; RD Ixworth 85-94; Hon Can St E Cathl 00-08; rtd 08; PtO *St E* from 08. *25 Millfield Road, Barningham, Bury St Edmunds IP31 1DX*

OLIVER, Rodney. *See* OLIVER, John Rodney

OLIVER, Ryland. *See* OLIVER, David Ryland

OLIVER, Prof Simon Andrew. b 71. Mansf Coll Ox BA 93 MA 98 Peterho Cam BA 97 MA 00 PhD 03. Westcott Ho Cam 95. **d** 98 **p** 99. NSM Teversham *Ely* 98-01; NSM Cherry Hinton St Andr 98-01; Chapl Hertf Coll Ox 01-05; Lect Univ of Wales (Lamp)

St D 05; Sen Lect 06-09; Assoc Prof Nottm Univ *S'well* 09-15; Can Th S'well Minster 11-15; Van Mildert Prof Div Dur Univ from 15. *University of Durham, Department of Theology, Abbey House, Palace Green, Durham DH1 3RS* T: 0191-334 3293 E: simon.oliver@durham.ac.uk

✠**OLIVER, The Rt Revd Stephen John.** b 48. AKC 69. St Aug Coll Cant 70. **d** 71 **p** 72 **c** 03. C Clifton *S'well* 71-75; P-in-c Newark Ch Ch 75-79; R Plumtree 79-85; Sen Producer BBC Relig Broadcasting Dept Lon 85-87; Chief Producer 87-91; TR Leeds City *Ripon* 91-97; Can Res and Prec St Paul's Cathl 97-03; Area Bp Stepney 03-10; rtd 10. *Garden Cottage, Church Lane, Averham, Newark NG23 5RB* T: (01636) 673861 E: stephen@btinternet.com

OLIVER, Mrs Susan Jacqueline. b 54. Univ Coll Lon LLB 78 CQSW 86. Qu Coll Birm 03. **d** 05 **p** 06. C Fladbury w Wyre Piddle and Moor etc *Worc* 05-09; TV Louth *Linc* 09-12; P-in-c Pennsett *Worc* from 12. *St Mark's Vicarage, Vicarage Lane, Brierley Hill DY5 4JH* T: (01384) 261558 M: 07843-750451 E: suejoliver@tiscali.co.uk

OLIVER, Suzanne Marie. *See* PATTLE, Suzanne Marie

OLIVER, Canon Thomas Gordon. b 48. Nottm Univ BTh 72 DipAdEd 80 ALCD 72. St Jo Coll Nottm 68. **d** 72 **p** 73. C Thorpe Edge *Bradf* 72-76; C Woodthorpe *S'well* 76-80; V Huthwaite 80-85; Dir Past Studies St Jo Coll Nottm 85-94; Dir of Min and Tr *Roch* 94-09; R Meopham w Nurstead 09-13; Hon Can Roch Cathl 95-13; rtd 13; PtO *Roch* from 13. *112 Bush Road, Cuxton, Rochester ME2 1HA* E: canongordon.oliver@gmail.com

OLIVER, Mrs Trudi. b 65. Brighton Univ BA 09. Trin Coll Bris BA 11. **d** 11 **p** 12. C Southampton Lord's Hill and Lord's Wood *Win* 11-14; P-in-c Gravesend St Mary *Roch* from 14; Chapl St Geo Sch Gravesend from 14. *The Vicarage, 57 New House Lane, Gravesend DA11 7HJ* M: 07432-131079 T: (01474) 353612 E: revtrudi@gmail.com

OLIVER, Canon Wendy Louise. b 54. Aston Tr Scheme 93 Oak Hill Th Coll 94. **d** 96 **p** 97. C Walmsley *Man* 96-99; P-in-c Goodshaw and Crawshawbooth 99-08; AD Rossendale 04-08; V Harwood from 08; AD Walmsley 10-14; Hon Can Man Cathl from 11. *The Vicarage, Stitch mi Lane, Bolton BL2 4HU* T: (01204) 525196 E: wendyloliver@googlemail.com

OLIVEIRA, Bertrand Maurice Daniel. b 82. Ecole des Cadres Paris BA 84. S'wark Ord Course 93. **d** 96 **p** 97. C Walworth St Jo *S'wark* 96-00; V Southfields St Barn 00-05; RD Wandsworth 03-05; V All Hallows by the Tower etc *Lon* from 05. *The Residence, 43 Trinity Square, London EC3N 4DJ* T: (020) 7488 4772 or 7481 2928 M: 07983-720264 E: bertrand@ahbtt.org.uk

OLLIER, Mrs Jane Sarah. b 60. Leeds Univ BA 81 Ex Univ MA 05. SWMTC 02. **d** 05 **p** 06. NSM Seaton and Beer *Ex* 05-07; C Ottery St Mary, Alfington, W Hill, Tipton etc 07-10; P-in-c Ex St Mark, St Sidwell and St Matt from 10. *St Mark's Rectory, 8 Lamacraft Drive, Exeter EX4 8QS* T: (01392) 438448

OLLIER, Canon Timothy John Douglas. b 44. Trin Hall Cam BA 66 MA 69. Cuddesdon Coll 66. **d** 68 **p** 69. C Silksworth *Dur* 68-71; C St Marylebone w H Trin *Lon* 71-74; C Winlaton *Dur* 74-77; R Redmarshall and V Bishopton w Gt Stainton 77-88; P-in-c Grindon and Stillington 83-88; V Gainford and R Winston 88-00; AD Barnard Castle 88-00; P-in-c Egglescliffe 00-03; R 03-13; AD Stockton 01-07; Hon Can Dur Cathl 94-13; rtd 13; PtO *Dur* from 14. *14 Low Coniscliffe, Darlington DL2 2JY* T: (01325) 495458 E: timdollie3@gmail.com

OLLIFF, Roland. b 61. Leeds Univ BTh 95 Ex Coll Ox MA 00. Coll of Resurr Mirfield 93. **d** 95 **p** 96. C Bickleigh and Shaugh Prior *Ex* 95-98; CF 98-07; Sen CF 07-10; V Crookham *Guildf* from 15 and from 15. *The Vicarage, 14 Gally Hill Road, Church Crookham, Fleet GU52 6LH* M: 07956-028128 E: roland.olliff@gmail.com

OLLIVE, Mrs Patricia Ann. b 55. St Luke's Coll Ex BA 91. Ripon Coll Cuddesdon BTh 05. **d** 05 **p** 06. C Backwell w Chelvey and Brockley *B & W* 05-09; P-in-c Shapwick w Ashcott and Burtle 09-11; P-in-c W Poldens 09-11; V Polden Wheel 11-15; V Bridgwater St Mary and Chilton Trinity from 15. *11 Vickery Close, Bridgwater TA6 7JU* M: 07840-387121 T: (01278) 323302 E: trishollive@hotmail.com

OLLMAN, Mrs Elaine Margaret. b 45. SNWTP 07. **d** 10 **p** 11. NSM Frankby w Greasby *Ches* 10-12; P-in-c Delamere 12-14; R from 14. *The Rectory, Chester Road, Delamere, Northwich CW8 2HS* T: (01606) 882184 M: 07599-511887 E: revemollman@btinternet.com

OLNEY, Dorian Frederick. b 50. Kingston Poly BA 71 Anglia Poly Univ MA 03 MIL 88 MCIPD 88. Ridley Hall Cam 96. **d** 98 **p** 99. C Glenfield *Leic* 98-02; Chapl ATC 99-01; TV Newark *S'well* 02-07; P-in-c Shenstone *Lich* 07-09; P-in-c Stonnall 07-09; V Shenstone and Stonnall 09-13; R Sissinghurst w Frittenden *Cant* from 13. *The Rectory, Frittenden, Cranbrook TN17 2DD* T: (01580) 852275 E: fred.olney@webleicester.co.uk

OLOKOSE, Folorunso Oladosu. b 70. Lyon Univ MA 08. Trin Coll Bris 11. **d** 13 **p** 14. C Cobham and Stoke D'Abernon *Guildf* from 13. *Elm Farm House, Tilt Road, Cobham KT11 3HJ* T: (01932) 660345 E: folo.olokose@gmail.com

O'LOUGHLIN, Mrs Kathryn. b 60. Man Univ BSc 81 Win Univ MA 08. STETS 96. **d** 99 **p** 00. NSM Basing *Win* 99-03; PtO 03-08; C N Hants Downs from 08; Tutor STETS 08-11. *The Parsonage, Gaston Lane, South Warnborough, Hook RG29 1RH* E: kathy.oloughlin@gmail.com

OLSEN, Arthur Barry. b 37. Univ of NZ BA 61 Melbourne Coll of Div BD 73. ACT ThL 64. **d** 64 **p** 64. C Nelson All SS New Zealand 64-67; V Ahuara 67-69; V Motupiko 69-70; V Amuri 70-73; Maori Miss and C Dunedin St Matt 73-76; V Brooklyn 77-81; C Hersham *Guildf* 81-84; P-in-c Botleys and Lyne 84-95; V 95-03; P-in-c Long Cross 84-95; V 95-03; Chapl NW Surrey Mental Health Partnership NHS Trust 85-03; rtd 03; Hon C Rotherfield Peppard and Kidmore End etc *Ox* 03-12; PtO from 13; *St Alb* from 13. *29 Sandhill Way, Aylesbury HP19 8GU* E: barry.o22@virgin.net

OLSWORTH-PETER, Edward James. b 77. UWE BA 99. Wycliffe Hall Ox BTh 04. **d** 04 **p** 05. C Guildf Ch Ch w St Martha-on-the-Hill 04-07; C Upper Chelsea St Sav and St Simon *Lon* 07-10; V Sydenham H Trin and St Aug *S'wark* 10-15; Dioc Fresh Expressions Adv *Ely* from 15. *Ely Diocesan Office, Bishop Woodford House, Barton Road, Ely CB7 4DX* E: revedop@gmail.com

OLUKANMI, Miss Stella Grace Oluwafunmilayo Olanrewaju. b 57. St Jo Coll Nottm BTh 95 LTh 92. **d** 96 **p** 97. C Gt Ilford St Jo *Chelmsf* 96-01; V Barkingside St Cedd 01-15; P-in-c Walthamstow St Andr from 15. *St Andrew's Vicarage, 37 Sutton Road, London E17 5QA* T: (020) 8527 3969 E: revdsolukanmi@btinternet.com

OLUMIDE, The Ven Oluseye Abiola Abisogun Okikiade ('Seye). b 42. Bradf Univ BA 89 MSc 92. Clifton Th Coll 68. **d** 71 **p** 72. C Halliwell St Pet *Man* 71-72; C Salford St Phil w St Steph 72; P-in-c Wood Green St Mich *Lon* 73; C Stanmer w Falmer and Moulsecoomb *Chich* 73-75; C Hulme Ascension *Man* 76-77; Chapl Asst N Man Gen Hosp 77-80; Chapl St Bernard's and Ealing Hosps 80-86; Chapl Bradf R Infirmary 86-91; Chapl Lynfield Mt Hosp Bradf 86-91; Chapl St Luke's Hosp Bradf 86-91; Chapl Bradf Hosps NHS Trust 91-96; Chapl Co-ord Parkside Community NHS Trust Lon 96-01; rtd 01; Can Lagos Cathl from 98; Adn in Egba Nigeria from 00. *98 Brecon Road, Ystradgynlais, Swansea SA9 1HJ* M: 07427-548537

O'MALLEY, Canon Brian Denis Brendan. b 40. Univ of Wales (Lamp) MA 97 MHCIMA 60. Oscott Coll (RC) 74 Coll of Resurr Mirfield 82. **d** 77 **p** 83. In RC Ch 77-81; Warden St Greg Retreat Rhandirmwyn *St D* 80-83; Chapl and Min Can St D Cathl 83-85; V Wiston w Ambleston, St Dogwells, Walton E etc 85-88; V Wiston w Clarbeston and Walton E 89; R Walton W w Talbenny and Haroldston W 89-98; Chapl Pembrokeshire Coll of FE 93-98; Chapl St D Coll Lamp 98-07; Can St D Cathl 01-07; rtd 07. *Millbank, North Road, Lampeter SA48 7HZ* T: (01570) 422148

O'MAOIL MHEANA, Patrick John. b 66. Coll of Resurr Mirfield 12. **d** 14 **p** 15. C Paulsgrove *Portsm* from 14. *35 Newbolt Road, Portsmouth PO6 4JE* E: paji65@hotmail.com

OMOBUDE, Boyle Osaro. b 69. Ushaw Coll Dur 07. **d** 11 **p** 15. In RC Ch 11-14; NSM Fenham St Jas and St Basil *Newc* from 15. *St Margaret's Vicarage, 14 Heighley Street, Newcastle upon Tyne NE15 6AR* E: omobude@btinternet.com

OMOLE, Oluremi Richard. b 63. **d** 05 **p** 07. NSM Dur N 05-14; Chapl City Hosps Sunderland NHS Foundn Trust from 14. *7 Frensham Way, Meadowfield, Durham DH7 8UR* T: 0191-378 9756 E: romole@sky.com

OMOYAJOWO, Justus Akinwale. b 65. Obafemi Awolowo Univ BA 87 Ibadan Univ Nigeria MA 90 Bayreuth Univ PhD 99. Vining Coll Th 90. **d** 92 **p** 93. C Akure St Andr Nigeria 92; Chapl Ondo-State Pris 93; Chapl Ondo-State Univ 94; Asst Lect Bayreuth Univ Germany 95-97; PtO *S'wark* 98-99 and 00-01; C Hatcham St Jas 99-00; Chapl Goldsmiths' Coll Lon 99-00; P-in-c Sutton New Town St Barn 01-03; P-in-c Yardley St Edburgha *Birm* 03-09; V Mildmay Grove St Jude and St Paul *Lon* from 09. *The Vicarage, 71 Marquess Road, London N1 2PT* T: (020) 7226 5924 E: drjustus@icloud.com

OMUKU, Precious Sotonye. b 47. Ibadan Univ Nigeria BSc 73. Lagos Angl Dioc Sem 00. **d** 02 **p** 03. V Ikoyi Nativity Nigeria 02-06; LtO Lon 07-08; PtO *S'wark* 07-08; Hon C Morden from 08. *4 Litchfield Avenue, Morden SM4 5QS* T: (020) 8640 7311 M: 07790-593392 E: precious.omuku@yahoo.com

O'NEILL, Amanda. b 64. **d** 12 **p** 13. NSM Trumpington *Ely* 12-14; NSM Hartford and Houghton w Wyton from 14. *43 Station Road, Whittlesford, Cambridge CB22 4NL* T: (01223) 833918 E: amandacurate@trumpingtonchurch.org.uk

O'NEILL, Mrs Caroline Lois. b 55. CQSW. Trin Coll Bris BA 00. **d** 00 **p** 01. C Bath St Sav w Swainswick and Woolley *B & W* 00-03; C Charlcombe w Bath St Steph 03-08; from 13; Chapl K Edw Sch Bath from 09; Chapl Partis Coll Bath 09-10; Chapl Westonbirt Sch 11-12; PtO *B & W* from 09. *King Edward's Senior School, North Road, Bath BA2 6HU* T: (01225) 464313 E: revcaroline_oneill@yahoo.co.uk

O'NEILL, Christopher John. b 53. Worc Coll Ox BA 75 MA 80 Surrey Univ PhD 03 CertEd 91 ALAM LGSM. Ripon Coll Cuddesdon 77. **d** 78 **p** 79. Asst Chapl Rugby Sch 78-80; Chapl Charterhouse Sch Godalming 81-98; Hd of Counselling from 98. *14 Chapelfields, Charterhouse Road, Godalming GU7 2BF* T: (01483) 414437 E: cbenedictoneill@hotmail.com *or* cjon@charterhouse.org.uk

O'NEILL, Edward Daniel. b 42. Man Univ BA 62 Bradf Univ MSc 76. NOC 89. **d** 92 **p** 93. NSM Prenton *Ches* 92-94; NSM Newton 94-95; PtO *Liv* 97-98; NSM W Derby Gd Shep 98-99; C 99-02; V Stockbridge Village 02-12; rtd 12. *1 The Cross, Stanley Road, Huyton, Liverpool L36 9XL* T: 0151-449 3800 E: eddieoneill@blueyonder.co.uk

O'NEILL, Gary. b 57. K Coll Lon BD 79 AKC 79 Liv Univ MA 06. Westcott Ho Cam 80. **d** 81 **p** 82. C Oldham *Man* 81-84; C Birch w Fallowfield 84-87; R Moston St Chad 87-97; Can Res Birm Cathl 97-07; Dir Studies for Ords *Ches* from 07; Bp's Adv for Minl Development Review from 15. *10 Neston Close, Helsby, Frodsham WA6 0FH* T: (01928) 723327 M: 07976-729449 E: gary.oneill@chester.anglican.org

O'NEILL, Mrs Gillian. b 73. Westmr Coll Ox BTh 95. Ripon Coll Cuddesdon MTh 12. **d** 12 **p** 13. C W Dulwich All SS *S'wark* from 12. *All Saints' Church, Lovelace Road, London SE21 8JY* T: (020) 8676 4768 E: gill_oneilluk@hotmail.com

O'NEILL, Irene. *See* CARTER, Irene

O'NEILL, Robert Patrick. b 66. Herts Univ BA 96. Ridley Hall Cam 06. **d** 08 **p** 09. NSM Lt Berkhamsted and Bayford, Essendon etc *St Alb* 08-09; C Luton St Mary 09-12; P-in-c Caddington from 12; P-in-c Farley Hill St Jo from 12. *The Vicarage, Collings Wells Close, Caddington, Luton LU1 4BG* T: (01582) 483702 E: rob.oneill@gmail.com

O'NEILL, Miss Victoria Elaine. b 82. Lanc Univ BA 05. St Jo Coll Nottm 12. **d** 15. C Kempston Transfiguration *St Alb* from 15. *16 Rosedale Way, Kempston, Bedford MK42 8JE* T: (01234) 856640 E: rev.victoria@btinternet.com*

ONGYERTH, Michael George. b 50. **d** 13 **p** 14. OLM Crowland *Linc* from 13. *22 North Street, Crowland, Peterborough PE6 0EF*

ONIONS, Mrs Angela Ann. b 33. STETS 01. **d** 02. NSM Bradford-on-Avon H Trin *Sarum* 02-08. *27 Berryfield Road, Bradford-on-Avon BA15 1SX* T: (01225) 309001 M: 07719-726461 E: r.a.onions@btinternet.co.uk

ONUNWA, The Ven Udobata Rufus. b 47. Univ of Nigeria BA 78 MA 82 PhD 85. Trin Coll Umuahia 72. **d** 74 **p** 75. Chapl Owerri Cathl Nigeria 74-75; Chapl Univ of Nigeria 75-78 and 82-84; Chapl to Abp Nigeria 78-79; P-in-c Okebola St Paul 78-79; Lect Trin Th Coll Umuahia 79-81; Hon Can Okigwe-Orlu 84-89; Can Res Calabar 90-91; V St Jude 92-96; Adn 94-96; Tutor Crowther Hall CMS Tr Coll Selly Oak 97-02; NW Regional Dir Crosslinks 03-05; P-in-c Grange St Andr *Ches* 05-09; rtd 09. *76 Firedrake Croft, Coventry CV1 2DR* M: 07766-724510 E: uonunwa@yahoo.co.uk

ONYEKWELU, Mrs Ada. b 54. Ibadan Univ Nigeria BSc 83 SEN 98. **d** 07 **p** 08. NSM Selsdon St Fran CD *S'wark* from 07. *80 Tedder Road, South Croydon CR2 8AQ* T: (020) 8657 4018 E: a_onye@yahoo.co.uk

OOSTERHOF, Ms Liesbeth. b 61. Ripon Coll Cuddesdon 02. **d** 04 **p** 05. C E Bergholt and Brantham *St E* 04-07; R Shoreline from 07; Dioc Adv for Women's Min from 11; RD Samford from 15. *The Rectory, Rectory Field, Chelmondiston, Ipswich IP9 1HY* T: (01473) 781902 E: l.oosterhof@btinternet.com

OOSTRA, Catharina Henriët. *See* MIELL, Catharina Henriët

OPENSHAW, Steven Paul. b 62. Open Univ BA 91 Birm Univ MSc 01. SNWTP 09. **d** 12 **p** 13. C Ramsbottom and Edenfield *Man* from 12. *12 Carrwood Hey, Ramsbottom, Bury BL0 9QT* M: 07963-100345 E: steve_openshaw@hotmail.com

OPPERMAN, Graham William. b 40. Th Ext Educn Coll 98. **d** 00 **p** 03. C Linden St Thos S Africa 00-04; NSM Aberdour *St And* 04; NSM Burntisland 04; NSM Inverkeithing 04; TV Jarrow *Dur* 05-10; rtd 10; Hon C Cwmbran *Mon* 10-15; Hon C Usk Min Area from 15. *The Rectory, Parc Road, Llangybi, Usk NP15 1NL* M: 07792-451622 E: graham.opperman@uwclub.net

OPPERMAN, Mrs Jennifer Catharine. b 57. ERMC 09. **d** 12 **p** 13. NSM Pet Cathl from 12. *Littleworth Mission, Main Road, Deeping St Nicholas, Spalding PE11 3EN* T: (01775) 630497 M: 07912-380464 E: jenny@littleworthmission.com

ORAM, Anthony. b 63. York St Jo Univ BA 08 Hull Univ PGCE 09. St Jo Coll Nottm 12. **d** 15. C Kingston upon Hull St Aid Southcoates *York* from 15. *9 Lorenzos Way, Hull HU9 3HS* M: 07740-257173 E: anthony@staidans.org.uk

ORAM, John Ernest Donald. b 34. Open Univ BA 74. Tyndale Hall Bris. **d** 61 **p** 62. C Cheetham Hill *Man* 61-64; C Gt Baddow *Chelmsf* 64-67; V Blackb St Barn 67-72; Bp's Chapl for Soc Resp *Sheff* 72-86; Chapl Psychotherapist 79-86; PtO from 86; rtd 99. *12 Montgomery Road, Sheffield S7 1LQ* T: 0114-221 4982

ORAM, Roland Martin David. b 45. Trin Coll Cam BA 68 ARCM 70. Cranmer Hall Dur. **d** 78 **p** 79. C Aspley *S'well* 78-81; Chapl Alleyn's Sch Dulwich 81-88; Chapl Versailles w Grandchamp and Chevry *Eur* 88-92; Chapl Denstone Coll Uttoxeter 92-01; C Hanford and Trentham *Lich* 02-10; rtd 10; PtO *Lich* from 10; *Ches* from 10. *12 Ash Grove, Rode Heath, Stoke-on-Trent ST7 3TD* T: (01270) 747271 E: orammb@tiscali.co.uk

ORAM, Stephen John. b 58. **d** 84 **p** 85. C Kidderminster St Jo *Worc* 84-88; Chapl RAF 88-92; P-in-c Brislington St Anne *Bris* 92-97; V Cricklade w Latton 97-04; Co-ord Chapl N Bris NHS Trust from 04. *North Bristol NHS Trust, Frenchay Park Road, Bristol BS16 1LE* T: 0117-970 1212 E: stephen.oram@ntlworld.com

ORAM, Canon Vincent Charles. b 55. Rhodes Univ BA 78 Fort Hare Univ BTh 84. St Paul's Coll Grahamstown. **d** 81 **p** 82. C King Williams Town H Trin S Africa 81-85; R Barkly East St Steph 85-90; Can Grahamstown Cathl 96; Adn East London South 97-99; P-in-c Shenley *St Alb* 00-05; TV Aldenham, Radlett and Shenley 05-13; RD Aldenham 03-08; P-in-c Stevenage H Trin 13-14; V from 14; Hon Can St Alb from 15. *The Vicarage, 18 Letchmore Road, Stevenage SG1 3JD* E: vincent.oram@ntlworld.com

ORAMS, Ronald Thomas. b 49. ACMA 80. **d** 08 **p** 09. NSM Laxfield, Cratfield, Wilby and Brundish *St E* 08-13; NSM Four Rivers from 13. *Crane Lodge, Bickers Hill, Laxfield, Woodbridge IP12 8DP* T: (01986) 798901 M: 07721-682183 E: ron.orams@care4free.net

O'RAW, Canon Neal John. **d** 02 **p** 03. C Killala w Dunfeeny, Crossmolina, Kilmoremoy etc *T, K & A* 02-05; Bp's C from 05; Can Tuam Cathl from 09; Can Killala Cathl from 13; Can Raphoe Cathl from 13. *The Rectory, The Boreen, Crossmolina, Co Mayo, Republic of Ireland* T: (00353) (96) 31384 E: revdoraw@hotmail.com

ORCHARD, Canon George Richard. b 41. Ex Coll Ox BA 62 BA 64 MA 66. Ripon Hall Ox 62. **d** 65 **p** 66. C Greenhill St Pet *Derby* 65-70; Member Ecum Team Min Sinfin Moor 70-78; V Sinfin Moor *Derby* 76-78; TR Dronfield 78-86; Can Res Derby Cathl 86-92; Hon Can Derby Cathl 92-06; P-in-c Baslow 92-93; P-in-c Curbar and Stoney Middleton 92-93; V Baslow w Curbar and Stoney Middleton 93-06; rtd 06; PtO *Cant* from 07; *Chich* from 07. *7 Love Lane, Rye TN31 7NE* T: (01797) 225916 E: richardorchard41@yahoo.co.uk

ORCHARD, Helen Claire. b 65. Sheff Univ BA 87 PhD 96 Em Coll Cam MPhil 02 Ox Univ MA 06. Westcott Ho Cam 01. **d** 03 **p** 04. C Merrow *Guildf* 03-06; Chapl and Fell Ex Coll Ox 06-11; TV Wimbledon *S'wark* from 11. *St Matthew's House, 10 Coombe Gardens, London SW20 0QU* T: (020) 8286 4584 E: orchard.helen@gmail.com

ORCHARD, Nigel John. b 56. CertEd 78. St Steph Ho Ox 82. **d** 85 **p** 86. C Tottenham St Paul *Lon* 85-89; C Is of Dogs Ch Ch and St Jo w St Luke 89-90; TV 90-92; P-in-c Southall Ch Redeemer 92-99; V from 99. *Christ the Redeemer Vicarage, 299 Allenby Road, Southall UB1 2HE* T: (020) 8578 2711 E: nigel.orchard1@btinternet.com

ORCHARD, Richard. *See* ORCHARD, George Richard

ORCHARD, Mrs Tryphena Jane. b 35. Westf Coll Lon BA 57. S'wark Ord Course 87. **d** 92 **p** 94. NSM Shaston *Sarum* 92-01; rtd 01; PtO *Sarum* 01-08. *Dunscar Fold, Hawkesdene Lane, Shaftesbury SP7 8NU* T: (01747) 855228

O'REILLY, Brian. **d** 07 **p** 08. C Seagoe *D & D* 07-10; I Cobh and Glanmire *C, C & R* 10-14; I Rathdrum w Glenealy, Derralossary and Laragh *D & G* from 14. *The Rectory, Rathdrum, Co Wicklow, Republic of Ireland* T: (00353) (404) 43814 M: 86-223 0271 E: brianor@eircom.net

O'REILLY, Clare Maria. *See* KING, Clare Maria

O'REILLY, Canon Philip Jonathon. b 66. Portsm Poly BSc 87 Kent Univ MA 97 MRICS. Westcott Ho Cam 93. **d** 93 **p** 94. C Selsdon St Jo w St Fran *S'wark* 93-96; TV Staveley and Barrow Hill *Derby* 96-01; V Wistow *Leic* from 01; Hon Can Leic Cathl from 10. *The Vicarage, 12 Saddington Road, Fleckney, Leicester LE8 8AW* T: 0116-240 2215 E: philiporeilly@leicester.anglican.org

O'REILLY, William Anthony. b 62. St Mellitus Coll 12. **d** 15. NSM Bow w Bromley St Leon *Lon* from 15. *Address temp unknown*

ORFORD, Barry Antony. b 49. Univ of Wales (Ban) BA 71 MTh 97 PhD 01. St Steph Ho Ox 71. **d** 73 **p** 74. C Monmouth *Mon* 73-77; V Choral St As Cathl 77-81; CR 83-96; PtO

St As from 97; Hon Asst Chapl Univ of Wales (Ban) 99-01; Lib Pusey Ho from 01. *Pusey House, St Giles, Oxford OX1 3LZ* T: (01865) 278415

ORFORD, Canon Keith John. b 40. FCIT. EMMTC 76. **d** 79 **p** 80. NSM Matlock Bank *Derby* 79-99; NSM Wirksworth from 99; Hon Can Derby Cathl 00-10. *27 Lums Hill Rise, Matlock DE4 3FX* T/F: (01629) 55349 E: keith.orford@btinternet.com

ORGAN, Mrs Alma. b 45. Bordesley Coll of Educn CertEd 66. WEMTC 08. **d** 09 **p** 10. NSM Worc St Barn w Ch Ch 09-12; NSM Pershore w Pinvin, Wick and Birlingham from 12. *14 Ongrils Close, Pershore WR10 1QE* T: (01386) 554248 M: 07531-461810 E: piglet1723@btinternet.com

ORGAN, Peter. b 73. K Coll Lon BA 97 Birm Univ MA 01. Qu Coll Birm 99. **d** 01 **p** 02. C E Wickham *S'wark* 01-05; TV Thamesmead 05-11; V E Wickham from 11. *St Michael's Vicarage, Upper Wickham Lane, Welling DA16 3AP* T: (020) 8304 1214 E: revpeterorgan@yahoo.co.uk

ORME, Christopher Malcolm. b 60. City Univ BSc 83. Wycliffe Hall Ox 03. **d** 05 **p** 06. C Shrewsbury H Cross *Lich* 05-08; P-in-c Meanwood *Ripon* 08-12; V 12-15; R Thorley *St Alb* from 15. *The Rectory, Vicerons Place, Bishop's Stortford CM23 4EL* E: rector@stjamesthorley.org

ORME, Mrs Delia. b 57. STETS 01. **d** 08 **p** 09. NSM Haslemere and Grayswood *Guildf* 08-12; NSM Seale, Puttenham and Wanborough from 12. *Tarn House, 17 Critchmere Hill, Haslemere GU27 1LS* T: (01428) 644853 E: dj.orme@btinternet.com

ORME, Edward John Gilbert. b 42. Man Univ BSc 64. Ox Min Course 04. **d** 07 **p** 08. NSM Reading St Agnes w St Paul and St Barn *Ox* 07-12; rtd 12; PtO *Ox* 12-15. *The Barn, 1 Carr Lane, Dronfield Woodhouse, Dronfield S18 8XF* M: 07901-528971 E: eddie.orme@yahoo.co.uk

ORME, John. b 29. Sarum Th Coll 58. **d** 60 **p** 61. C Heald Green St Cath *Ches* 60-64; C Ellesmere Port 64-67; Chapl Harperbury Hosp Radlett 67-73; P-in-c Luton All SS w St Pet *St Alb* 73-79; V 79-87; V Oxhey St Matt 87-96; rtd 97; PtO *St Alb* from 97. *1 Alzey Gardens, Harpenden AL5 5SZ* T: (01582) 761931 E: john@orme117.freeserve.co.uk

ORME, Sydney. b 27. Oak Hill Th Coll 54. **d** 58 **p** 59. C Halliwell St Pet *Man* 58-61; V Friarmere 61-73; V Knypersley *Lich* 73-92; rtd 92; PtO *Ches* from 92. *10 Elworth Road, Sandbach CW11 9HQ* T: (01270) 759233

ORMEROD, Henry Lawrence. b 35. Pemb Coll Cam BA 58 MA 63. Qu Coll Birm. **d** 60 **p** 61. C Chigwell *Chelmsf* 60-64; C Thundersley 64-68; C Canvey Is 68-72; V Stanground *Ely* 72-77; TR Stanground and Farcet 77-81; TR Swindon St Jo and St Andr *Bris* 81-90; TR N Wingfield, Clay Cross and Pilsley *Derby* 90-97; rtd 97; Hon C Ironstone *Ox* 98-03; PtO from 03. *5 Waterloo Drive, Banbury OX16 3QN* T: (01295) 278483 E: henryormerod@aol.com

ORMESHER, David Rodney. b 39. **d** 05 **p** 06. OLM Delaval *Newc* from 05. *14 The Crest, Seaton Sluice, Whitley Bay NE26 4BG* T: 0191-237 1104 E: david@ormesher.fslife.co.uk

ORMROD, Jonathan Robert. b 63. Open Univ BSc 04. Wycliffe Hall Ox 06 Ripon Coll Cuddesdon 09. **d** 11 **p** 12. C Llantrisant *Llan* 11-14; P-in-c Sully from 14; P-in-c Wenvoe and St Lythans from 14; C St Andrews Major w Michaelston-le-Pit from 14. *The Rectory, Port Road, Wenvoe, Cardiff CF5 6DF* T: (029) 2059 5347 E: jonormrod@yahoo.co.uk

ORMROD, Paul William. b 57. Liv Univ BA 80 MTh 08. Westcott Ho Cam 80. **d** 83 **p** 84. C Prescot *Liv* 83-86; TV Padgate 86-95; V Formby St Pet 95-13; Chapl Madrid *Eur* from 13. *St George, Nuñez de Balboa 43, 28001 Madrid, Spain* T/F: (0034) 915 765 109 E: chaplain@stgeorgesmadrid.com

ORMSTON, Derek. b 43. St D Coll Lamp. **d** 67 **p** 68. C Ogley Hay *Lich* 67-70; C Tettenhall Regis 70-74; P-in-c Leek All SS 74-79; TV Leek and Meerbrook 79-83; Youth Chapl *Bris* 83-87; R Brinkworth w Dauntsey 87-12; Chapl New Coll Swindon 87-12; rtd 12; Hon C Garsdon, Lea and Cleverton and Charlton *Bris* from 12; Hon C Gt Somerford, Lt Somerford, Seagry, Corston etc from 12. *49 Lime Kiln, Royal Wootton Bassett, Swindon SN4 7HF* T: (01793) 852779 E: derek.ormston43@btinternet.com

ORMSTON, The Ven Richard Jeremy. b 61. Southlands Coll Lon BA 83 Brunel Univ MTh 98. Oak Hill Th Coll BA 87. **d** 87 **p** 88. C Rodbourne Cheney *Bris* 87-91; R Collingtree w Courteenhall and Milton Malsor *Pet* 91-01; RD Wootton 96-01; R Oundle w Ashton and Benefield w Glapthorn 01-14; RD Oundle 03-13; Can Pet Cathl from 03; Adn Northn from 14. *Westbrook, 11 The Drive, Northampton NN1 4RZ* T: (01604) 714015 E: archdeacon.northampton@peterborough-diocese.org.uk

✤**OROMBI, The Most Revd Henry Luke.** b 49. Bp Tucker Coll Mukono 75 St Jo Coll Nottm BTh 83. **d** 79 **p** 79 **c** 93. Dioc Youth Officer Madi/W Nile Uganda 79-86; Adn Goli 87-93;

Bp Nebbi 93-03; Abp Uganda and Bp Kampala from 03. *PO Box 14123, Kampala, Uganda* T: (00256) (41) 270218, 270219 *or* 271138 M: 77-476476 F: (41) 251925 *or* 245597 E: orombih@yahoo.com *or* couab@uol.co.ug

O'ROURKE, Brian Joseph Gerard. b 58. TCD BA 82 HDipEd 83. CITC 89. **d** 92 **p** 93. Chapl E Glendalough Sch 90-96; C Newcastle w Newtownmountkennedy and Calary *D & G* 92-96; Bp's C 96-98; I 98-00; I Cork St Ann's Union C, *C & R* 00-15; I Maryborough w Dysart Enos and Ballyfin *C & O* from 15; Hon Chapl Miss to Seafarers from 00. *The Rectory, Coote Street, Portlaoise, Co Laois, Republic of Ireland* T: (00353) (57) 862 1154 M: 86-807 9452 E: bjgorourke@gmail.com

O'ROURKE, Shaun. b 58. NOC 02. **d** 05 **p** 06. C Gorton and Abbey Hey *Man* 05-08; P-in-c Heaton Reddish 08-12; Borough Dean Stockport 10-12; P-in-c Swimbridge w W Buckland and Landkey *Ex* from 12. *The Rectory, Barnstaple Hill, Swimbridge, Barnstaple EX32 0PH* T: (01271) 830950 M: 07914-361905 E: sorourke@freezone.co.uk

ORPIN, Mrs Gillian. b 32. SRN 53. Oak Hill Th Coll 82. **d** 87 **p** 95. Par Dn Passenham *Pet* 87-92; rtd 92; NSM Oban St Jo *Arg* 92-95; Dioc Chapl 95-98; PtO *St Alb* from 98. *11 Berwick Way, Sandy SG19 1TR* T: (01767) 680629

ORR, The Ven Andrew Dermot Harman. b 66. Sheff Univ BSc 89. CITC BTh 92. **d** 92 **p** 93. C Ballymacash *Conn* 92-95; I Castlecomer w Colliery Ch, Mothel and Bilboa *C & O* 95-00; I Castleknock and Mulhuddart w Clonsilla *D & G* 00-09; I Tullow w Shillelagh, Aghold and Mullinacuff *C & O* from 09; Dioc Registrar 95-00 and from 12; Adn Ossory and Leighlin from 14. *The Rectory, Tullow, Co Carlow, Republic of Ireland* T/F: (00353) (59) 915 1481 M: 87-419 6051 E: andrewlorr1234@gmail.com

ORR, David Cecil. b 33. TCD BA 56 MA 68. **d** 57 **p** 58. C Drumragh *D & R* 57-60; I Convoy 60-70; I Maghera w Killelagh 70-80; I Drumragh w Mountfield 80-84; Dean Derry 84-97; I Templemore 84-97; Miss to Seamen 84-97; rtd 97. *Kilrory, 11 Broomhill Court, Londonderry BT47 6WP* T: (028) 7134 8183 E: dcecilorr@btopenworld.com

ORR, Donald Macrae. b 50. Humberside Poly BA 73 Glas Univ BD 02 MTh 04 PhD 08. TISEC 02. **d** 04 **p** 05. C Greenock *Glas* 04-07; P-in-c Johnstone from 07; P-in-c Renfrew from 07. *16 Neilston Road, Barrhead, Glasgow G78 1TY* T: 0141-881 1372 E: don.orrald@gmail.com

ORR, Mrs Helen McGowan. b 71. Ridley Hall Cam. **d** 14 **p** 15. C Chesterton St Andr *Ely* from 14. *36 Northampton Street, Cambridge CB3 0AD* M: 07751-490884 E: helenorr24@gmail.com

ORR, Mark. b 61. St Jo Coll Nottm BA 14. **d** 14 **p** 15. C Clifton *S'well* from 14. *1 Osprey Close, Nottingham NG11 8SX* T: 0115-922 6705 M: 07568-585638 E: odman001@yahoo.co.uk

ORR, Robert Vernon. b 50. Westmr Univ 80 MIQA 89. Wycliffe Hall Ox 96. **d** 98 **p** 99. C Cowley St Jo *Ox* 98-01; P-in-c Reading St Agnes w St Paul 01-02; R Reading St Agnes w St Paul and St Barn from 02. *The Vicarage, 290 Northumberland Avenue, Reading RG2 8DD* T: 0118-987 4448 E: vernon.orr@lineone.net

ORR, William James Craig. b 33. TCD BTh 01. CITC 98. **d** 01 **p** 02. C Lurgan Ch the Redeemer *D & D* 01-07; I Muckamore *Conn* from 07; I Killead w Gartree from 07. *43 Oldstone Road, Muckamore, Antrim BT41 4SE* M: 07850-156942 *or* 07806-882783 T: (028) 9446 6756 E: william-orr@sky.com

ORR-EWING, Francis Ian Lance (Frog). b 75. Regent's Park Coll Ox BA 97. Wycliffe Hall Ox MTh 00. **d** 00 **p** 01. C Ox St Aldate 00-03; V Camberwell All SS *S'wark* 03-10; PtO *Ox* 10-13; NSM Amersham Deanery from 13. *Applebarn, Bull Lane, Chalfont St Peter, Gerrards Cross SL9 8RH* T: (01753) 886540 M: 07979-594762 E: rector@latimerminster.org

ORRIDGE, Harriet Grace. b 72. St Jo Coll Nottm. **d** 09 **p** 10. C Ironstone Villages *Leic* 09-13; P-in-c Saxonwell *Linc* from 13. *Saxonwell Vicarage, Church Street, Long Bennington, Newark NG23 5ES* T: (01400) 281281

ORTON, Peter Joseph. b 57. **d** 03 **p** 04. OLM Burton St Chad *Lich* 03-10; NSM Burton St Aid and St Paul from 10; NSM Burton from 15. *237 Wetmore Road, Burton-on-Trent DE14 1RB* T: (01283) 537574 E: lightcommunity@yahoo.co.uk

ORTON, Canon Richard. b 33. Keble Coll Ox BA 56 MA 60 Leeds Univ. Lich Th Coll 60. **d** 61 **p** 64. C Penistone w Midhope *Wakef* 61-62; Hon C Meltham 62-69; Hon C Horsforth *Ripon* 69-72; C Far Headingley St Chad 72-75; V Hellifield *Bradf* 75-80; RD Bowland 78-80; R Hutton *Chelmsf* 80-87; R Walsey St Hilary *Ches* 87-90; Dioc Ecum Officer 92-99; RD Wallasey 96-99; Hon Can Ches Cathl 97-00; rtd 00; C Gt Sutton *Ches* 01-05; PtO from 05. *137 Brimstage Road, Barnston, Wirral CH60 1XF* T: 0151-348 4911

O'RYAN, Mrs Elizabeth Ann. b 63. Birm Univ BA 84 Glas Univ MTh 11 Roehampton Inst PGCE 85. TISEC 09. **d** 11 **p** 12. NSM Greenock *Glas* from 11. *23 Paddockdyke, Skelmorlie PA17 5DA* T: (01475) 529835 M: 07949-667135 E: lizoryan@tiscali.co.uk

OSAKA, Bishop of. *See* UNO, The Rt Revd James Toru

OSBORN, Andrew Talbot. b 62. **d** 94 **p** 95. Australia 94-13; PtO *Blackb* 13-14; R Heysham from 14. *The Rectory, Main Street, Heysham, Morecambe LA3 2RN* T: (01524) 851422 E: andrewinlancaster@gmail.com

OSBORN, Miss Anne. b 40. Reading Univ BA 62 MA 64 Lon Univ PGCE 67. Oak Hill NSM Course 87. **d** 92. Chapl Lon Univ 92-94; Chapl Lon Guildhall Univ 94-96; Chapl Univ of Westmr 94-95; Assoc Tutor NTMTC 97-03; Adv on Women's Min Edmonton Area from 03. *8 Beaufort House, Talbot Road, London N15 4DR* T: (020) 8801 0115

OSBORN, Canon David Ronald. b 42. Bris Univ BA 66 Leeds Univ CertEd 77 Bath Univ MEd 80. Clifton Th Coll 62. **d** 66 **p** 67. C Farndon *S'well* 66-69; P-in-c W Bridgford 69-72; Asst Dioc Dir Educn *Carl* 72-77; P-in-c Kirkandrews-on-Eden w Beaumont and Grinsdale 72-77; Hd RE and Chapl Dauntsey's Sch Devizes 77-83; V Southbroom *Sarum* 83-86; Hd RE Bexhill High Sch 86-93; TV Langtree *Ox* 93-95; TR 95-97; TR Bracknell 97-06; rtd 06; P-in-c Llantilio Crossenny w Penrhos, Llanvetherine etc *Mon* 06-14; AD Abergavenny 11-14; Can St Woolos Cathl from 12; PtO from 14. *51 Cornpoppy Avenue, Monmouth NP25 5SD* M: 07803-618464 E: davidosborn@ntlworld.com

OSBORN, David Thomas. b 58. K Coll Lon BD 79 AKC 79 PGCE 80. Linc Th Coll 82. **d** 83 **p** 84. C Bearsted w Thurnham *Cant* 83-86; Chapl RAF 86-90; R Bassingham *Linc* 90-91; V Aubourn w Haddington 90-91; V Carlton-le-Moorland w Stapleford 90-91; R Thurlby w Norton Disney 90-91; Chapl RAF from 91. *Chaplaincy Services (RAF), HQ Air Command, RAF High Wycombe HP14 4UE* T: (01494) 496800 F: 496343

OSBORN, Mrs Diana Marian. b 52. R Holloway Coll Lon BSc 74 Birm Univ PGCE 75. NEOC 81. **dss** 84 **d** 87 **p** 94. Malden St Jo *S'wark* 84-89; Par Dn 87-89; Par Dn Brampton *Ely* 89-92; Par Dn Richmond H Trin and Ch Ch *S'wark* 92-93; Chapl Ridley Hall Cam 94-96; Chapl Milton Children's Hospice 96-98; Chapl E Anglia's Children's Hospices 98-01; PtO *Ely* 01-07; *Guildf* 08-11. *Address temp unknown*

OSBORN, Preb John Geoffrey Rowland. b 33. Jes Coll Cam BA 55 MA 59. Wells Th Coll 63. **d** 65 **p** 66. C Easthampstead *Ox* 65-68; LtO *Blackb* 68-70; Brunei 70-75; Asst Dir RE *Blackb* 75-77; V Tockholes 75-77; Dir RE *B & W* 77-83; Dir and Sec Lon Dioc Bd for Schs 83-95; Preb St Paul's Cathl 86-95; rtd 96. *4 Musson Close, Abingdon OX14 5RE* T: (01235) 528701

OSBORNE, Anthony Russell. b 47. Sarum & Wells Th Coll 77. **d** 79 **p** 80. C Heref St Martin 79-81; TV 82-86; TV Hanley H Ev *Lich* 86-92; Can Heref Cathl and Dioc Soc Resp Officer *Heref* 92-97; TR Cannock and V Hatherton *Lich* 97-06; V Penkhull 06-07; P-in-c Hartshill 06-07; P-in-c Trent Vale 06-07; TR Hartshill, Penkhull and Trent Vale 07-11; rtd 11. *97 Victoria Street, Stoke-on-Trent ST4 6EH* E: osborne06@btinternet.com

OSBORNE, Canon Brian Charles. b 38. St Andr Univ MA 61. Clifton Th Coll 61. **d** 63 **p** 64. C Skirbeck H Trin *Linc* 63-68; V 80-03; P-in-c New Clee 68-71; V 71-75; V Derby St Aug 75-80; Chapl Pilgrim Hosp Boston 84-88; RD Holland E *Linc* 85-95; Can and Preb Linc Cathl 92-03; rtd 03; Chapl to The Queen 97-08. *3 Newlands Road, Haconby, Bourne PE10 0UT* T: (01778) 570818 E: revbrianosborne@ukonline.co.uk

OSBORNE, Christopher Hazell. b 60. Aston Tr Scheme 89 Sarum & Wells Th Coll 91. **d** 93 **p** 94. C Paignton St Jo *Ex* 93-96; C Hooe 96-97; TV Plymstock and Hooe 97-01; V Ivybridge w Harford from 01. *The Vicarage, Blachford Road, Ivybridge PL21 0AD* T: (01752) 690193 E: chrisosbornework@aol.com

OSBORNE, Preb David Robert. b 50. Birm Univ BSc 71 MEd 86 Bris Univ PGCE 73. Cranmer Hall Dur 78. **d** 80 **p** 81. C Penkridge w Stretton *Lich* 80-85; R Longdon-upon-Tern, Rodington, Uppington etc 85-94; R Pilton w Croscombe, N Wootton and Dinder *B & W* 94-13; RD Shepton Mallet 01-07; Sub-Dean Wells 11-13; rtd 13; Preb Wells Cathl from 11. *10 Millbrook Gardens, Castle Cary BA7 7EF* T: (01963) 351275 M: 07719-391485 E: drosborne@btinternet.com

OSBORNE, David Victor. b 36. Dur Univ BA 59 Univ of Wales MA 99. Cranmer Hall Dur. **d** 62 **p** 63. C Kennington Cross St Anselm *S'wark* 62-66; C Sandal St Helen *Wakef* 66-67; R Ancoats *Man* 67-73; V Claremont H Angels 73-80; R Breedon cum Isley Walton and Worthington *Leic* 80-87; V Beaumont Leys 87-92; V Billesdon and Skeffington 92-01; rtd 01; PtO *Leic* from 02; *Pet* from 02. *Rose Cottage, 12 Barlows Lane, Wilbarston, Market Harborough LE16 8QB* T: (01536) 770400

OSBORNE, Canon Derek James. b 32. Tyndale Hall Bris 53. **d** 57 **p** 58. C Weymouth St Mary *Sarum* 57-60; C Southgate *Chich* 60-63; V Croydon Ch Ch Broad Green *Cant* 63-71; V Cromer *Nor* 71-83; P-in-c Gresham w Bessingham 71-83; Hon Can Nor Cathl 77-83; V Northwood Em *Lon* 83-94; Chapl Lee Abbey 94-97; rtd 97; PtO *Nor* from 97. *50 Clifton Park, Cromer NR27 9BG* T: (01263) 511272

OSBORNE, Canon Gerald Edward Richard. b 63. Ch Ch Ox MA 85 Wye Coll Lon MSc 86. **d** 99 **p** 00. OLM Pewsey and Swanborough *Sarum* 99-10; OLM Vale of Pewsey from 10; RD Pewsey from 12; Can and Preb Sarum Cathl from 14. *Lawn Farm, Milton Lilbourne, Pewsey SN9 5LQ* T: (01672) 563459 F: 564271 M: 07798-942118 E: gerald.osborne@lawnfarm.co.uk

OSBORNE, Gillian Margaret. b 54. Open Univ BA 90 UEA PGCE 93. **d** 07 **p** 08. OLM Stratton St Mary w Stratton St Michael etc *Nor* from 07. *5 Welford Court, The Street, Long Stratton, Norwich NR15 2XL* E: d-gosborne@btinternet.com

OSBORNE, Graham Daking. b 51. Univ of Wales MPhil 13 City Univ ACII 74 FCII 77. Ripon Coll Cuddesdon 94. **d** 96 **p** 97. C Cirencester *Glouc* 96-00; V Glouc St Cath 00-09; AD Glouc City 03-08; R Leatherhead and Mickleham *Guildf* from 09. *The Rectory, 3 St Mary's Road, Leatherhead KT22 8EZ* T: (01372) 372313 E: revgdo@gmail.com

OSBORNE, The Ven Hayward John. b 48. New Coll Ox BA 70 MA 73. Westcott Ho Cam 71. **d** 73 **p** 74. C Bromley SS Pet and Paul *Roch* 73-77; C Halesowen *Worc* 77-80; TV 80-83; TR Worc St Barn w Ch Ch 83-88; V Moseley St Mary *Birm* 88-01; AD Moseley 94-01; Hon Can Birm Cathl 00-01; Adn Birm from 01; P-in-c Allens Cross 08-09. *23 Carisbrooke Road, Birmingham B17 8NN* T: 0121-420 3299 *or* 426 0441 F: 428 1114 E: archdeaconofbham@birmingham.anglican.org

OSBORNE, Preb Jonathan Lloyd. b 62. Ripon Coll Cuddesdon 95. **d** 97 **p** 98. C Mill End and Heronsgate w W Hyde *St Alb* 97-00; Asst Chapl Ealing Hosp NHS Trust 00-03; Chapl Team Ldr 03-10; Asst Chapl W Middx Univ Hosp NHS Trust 00-03; Chapl Team Ldr 03-10; Chapl Team Ldr Meadow House Hospice 03-10; Chapl W Lon Mental Health NHS Trust 03-10; Sen Chapl Metrop Police *Lon* from 10; Hon Chapl S'wark Cathl from 03; PtO *Roch* from 10; PV Westmr Abbey from 12; Preb St Paul's Cathl from 13. *2 St Alphege House, Pocock Street, London SE1 0BJ* T: (020) 7928 9203

OSBORNE, The Very Revd June. b 53. Man Univ BA 74. Wycliffe Hall Ox 78. **dss** 80 **d** 87 **p** 94. Birm St Martin 80-84; Old Ford St Paul and St Mark *Lon* 84-95; Par Dn Old Ford St Paul w St Steph and St Mark 87-94; P-in-c Old Ford St Paul and St Mark 94-95; Can Res and Treas Sarum Cathl 95-04; Bp's Dom Chapl 95-97; Dean Sarum from 04. *The Deanery, 7 The Close, Salisbury SP1 2EF* T: 555177 T: (01722) 343200 E: thedean@salcath.co.uk *or* j.osborne@salcath.co.uk

OSBORNE, Malcolm Eric (Max). b 64. EN(G) 87 RMN 92. St Jo Coll Nottm 94. **d** 96 **p** 97. C Walton *St E* 96-99; C Ipswich St Matt 99-02; Soc Resp Adv 99-02; V Newmarket All SS from 02. *All Saints' Vicarage, 32 Warrington Street, Newmarket CB8 8BA* T: (01638) 662514 E: max.osborne@stedmundsbury.anglican.org

OSBORNE, Mrs Marianne Lily-May. St Mich Coll Llan. **d** 09 **p** 10. C Tenby *St D* 09-11; P-in-c Burton and Rosemarket 11-14; P-in-c St Issell's and Amroth w Crunwere and Marros from 14; Children and Youth Development Chapl from 11. *The Vicarage, Saundersfoot SA69 9BD* T: (01834) 812375

OSBORNE, Mark William. b 67. Univ of Wales BA 89 Lon Univ MTh 06. Coll of Resurr Mirfield 94. **d** 94 **p** 95. C Goldthorpe w Hickleton *Sheff* 94-97; C-in-c Southey Green St Bernard CD 97-01; P-in-c Walham Green St Jo w St Jas *Lon* 01-12; V from 12. *The Vicarage, 40 Racton Road, London SW6 1LP* T: (020) 7385 3676 *or* 7385 7634 E: mark.osborne5@btinternet.com

OSBORNE, Norma. b 36. **d** 97 **p** 03. NSM Upper Tooting H Trin S'wark 02-03; NSM Tooting St Aug 02-03; NSM Wandsworth St Mich 03-06; NSM Wandsworth St Mich w St Steph 06-07; PtO 07-14. *Address temp unknown*

OSBORNE, Ralph. b 38. Bernard Gilpin Soc Dur 62 Clifton Th Coll 63.· **d** 66 **p** 67. C Harpurhey Ch Ch *Man* 66-68; C Chorlton on Medlock St Sav 68-71; C Wilmington *Roch* 71-74; V St Mary Cray and St Paul's Cray 74-85; P-in-c Bath St Steph *B & W* 85-88; P-in-c Charlcombe 86-88; R Charlcombe w Bath St Steph 88-03; rtd 03; PtO *B & W* from 09. *406 Bath Road, Saltford, Bristol BS31 3DH* T: (01225) 872536 E: ralph.osborne@ic24.net

OSBORNE, Canon Robin Orbell. b 29. Leeds Univ BA 54. Coll of Resurr Mirfield 52. **d** 54 **p** 55. C Wellingborough All Hallows Pet 54-58; C Oxhey St Matt *St Alb* 60-61; V Woburn and Battlesden and Pottesgrove 61-65; V Cheshunt 65-82; RD 70-81; Hon Can St Alb 76-82; V Penzance St Mary w St Paul *Truro* 82-88; Can Res and Treas Truro Cathl 88-94; rtd 94;

PtO *B & W* 94-08; S'wark 05-14. *The College of St Barnabas, Blackberry Lane, Lingfield RH7 6NJ* T: (01342) 872833 M: 07776-081564 E: orbellosborne@gmail.com

OSBORNE, Mrs Sandra Anne. b 53. SRN 74 SCM 76. STETS 09. **d** 11 **p** 12. NSM Denmead *Portsm* from 11; PtO *Win* from 14. *45 Wallisdean Avenue, Portsmouth PO3 6HA* T: (023) 9236 2591 M: 07891-432667 E: sandie.osborne@btinternet.com

OSBOURNE, Canon David John. b 56. Linc Th Coll 78. **d** 79 **p** 80. C Houghton le Spring *Dur* 79-82; C Spalding St Jo *Linc* 82-83; C Spalding St Jo w Deeping St Nicholas 83-84; V Swineshead 84-94; RD Holland W 86-92; P-in-c Boultham 94-01; R from 01; RD Christianity from 08; Can and Preb Linc Cathl from 12. *The Rectory, 2A St Helen's Avenue, Lincoln LN6 7RA* T/F: (01522) 682026 E: david.osbourne@hotmail.co.uk

OSBOURNE, Steven John. b 59. St Jo Coll Nottm 92. **d** 94 **p** 95. C Bushbury *Lich* 94-98; C Tamworth 98-03; V Caverswall and Weston Coyney w Dilhorne from 03; RD Cheadle 07-14. *8 Vicarage Crescent, Caverswall, Stoke-on-Trent ST11 9EW* T: (01782) 388037 or 312570 E: steve.osbourne@btopenworld.com

OSEI, Robert Emmanuel. b 56. **d** 76 **p** 77. Ghana 76-83; C Hangleton *Chich* 83-84; PtO *S'wark* 00-02. *8 Plummer Court, London SE13 6RA*

OSGERBY, John Martin. b 34. Sheff Univ BSc 56 PhD 59. Linc Th Coll 75. **d** 77 **p** 78. C Rotherham *Sheff* 77-80; C-in-c W Bessacarr CD 80-84; V W Bessacarr 84-87; Warden of Readers 86-99; R Fishlake w Sykehouse and Kirk Bramwith etc 87-99; RD Snaith and Hatfield 93-99; rtd 99; PtO *Sheff* from 99; *Linc* 00-02. *4 Marlborough Avenue, Haxey, Doncaster DN9 2HL* T: (01427) 754815 E: jmosgerby.hax@virgin.net

OSGOOD, Graham Dean. b 39. Lon Univ BSc 62 ALCD 71. St Jo Coll Nottm 71. **d** 71 **p** 72. C Bebington *Ches* 71-76; V Gee Cross 76-05; rtd 05. *4 Lower Close, Bodicote, Banbury OX15 4DZ* T: (01295) 266848 E: graham.htgx@btinternet.com

OSGOOD, Sylvia Joy. b 47. QUB BSc 68 Lon Univ BD 78 Man Univ PhD 92. St Jo Coll Nottm MA 98. **d** 97 **p** 98. NSM Bredbury St Mark *Ches* 97-01; Tutor and Chapl Spurgeon's Coll from 01. *4 Lower Close, Bodicote, Banbury OX15 4DZ* T: (01295) 266848 E: j.osgood@spurgeons.ac.uk

O'SHAUGHNESSY, Mrs Janice Florence. b 51. STETS 95. **d** 98 **p** 99. NSM Bembridge *Portsm* 98-02; Asst Chapl Isle of Wight Healthcare NHS Trust 99-02; C Catherington and Clanfield *Portsm* 02-07; P-in-c Arreton 07-09; V from 09; P-in-c Newchurch 07-09; V from 09; P-in-c Gatcombe 07-09. *The Vicarage, High Street, Newchurch, Sandown PO36 0NN* T: (01983) 865504

O'SHEA, Mrs Helen Mary. b 55. Univ of Wales (Abth) BA 77 SRN 79. Llan Ord Course 94. **d** 98 **p** 99. NSM Skewen *Llan* 98-01; C Llangynwyd w Maesteg 01-02; P-in-c Cwmafan 02-12; R Cilybebyll from 12. *The Rectory, 7 Cwmnantllyd Road, Gellinudd, Pontardawe, Swansea SA8 3DT* T: (01792) 862118

OSLER, Philip. b 55. SEITE 99. **d** 02 **p** 03. NSM Staplehurst *Cant* 02-07; C Thurlestone, S Milton, W Alvington etc *Ex* 07-09; P-in-c 09-13; PtO from 13. *45 Onslow Road, Plymouth PL2 3QG* T: (01752) 300186 E: philip.osler@btinternet.com

OSMAN, David Thomas. b 49. Bradf Univ BTech 72 Newc Univ MA 93. Trin Coll Bris 75. **d** 78 **p** 79. C Stranton *Dur* 78-81; C Denton Holme *Carl* 81-84; V Preston on Tees *Dur* 84-97; P-in-c Hebburn St Jo from 97; P-in-c Jarrow Grange from 00. *St John's Vicarage, 23 St John's Avenue, Hebburn NE31 2TZ* T: 0191-422 7505

OSMAN, Stephen William. b 53. Matlock Coll of Educn CertEd 74 Teesside Poly CQSW 80. Cranmer Hall Dur 88. **d** 90 **p** 91. C Newbarns w Hawcoat *Carl* 90-93; TV Marfleet *York* 93-00; P-in-c Gotham *S'well* 00-10; P-in-c Barton in Fabis 02-10; P-in-c Thrumpton 02-10; P-in-c Kingston and Ratcliffe-on-Soar 02-10; P-in-c Herrington, Penshaw and Shiney Row *Dur* 10-14; R from 14. *23 Barnwell View, Herrington Burn, Houghton le Spring DH4 7FB* T: 0191-584 5657 E: steveosman500@aol.com

OSMASTON, Canon Amiel Mary Ellinor. b 51. Ex Univ BA 73 St Jo Coll Dur BA 84. Cranmer Hall Dur 82. **dss** 84 **d** 87 **p** 94. Chester le Street *Dur* 84-88; Par Dn 87-88; Dir Miss and Past Studies Ridley Hall Cam 89-96; Min Development Officer *Ches* 96-03; C Lache cum Saltney 00-03; Min Development Officer *Carl* from 03; C Penrith w Newton Reigny and Plumpton Wall from 03; Hon Can Carl Cathl from 05. *The New Vicarage, Plumpton, Penrith CA11 9PA* T: (01768) 885756 *or* (01228) 522573 F: (01768) 885773 E: ministry.dev@carlislediocese.org.uk

✠**OSMERS, The Rt Revd John Robert.** b 35. Cant Univ (NZ) MA 58. Coll of Resurr Mirfield 59. **d** 61 **p** 62 **c** 95. C Rawmarsh w Parkgate *Sheff* 61-65; Par P Quthing Lesotho 65-73; R Masite

Miss 73-81; Asst P H Cross Cathl Botswana 82-87; R Molepolole 82-88; Chapl ANC Zambia 88-91; Dioc Tr Chapl Lusaka 90-95; Bp E 95-03; Asst Bp Lusaka 03-07; R St Jo Angl Sem Kitwe Zambia 07-10. *Holy Cross Cathedral, PO Box 30477, Lusaka, Zambia* T: (00260) 977-841215
E: josmers@zamnet.zm

OSMOND, Andrew Mark. b 62. Leeds Univ LLB 85. Wycliffe Hall Ox 02. **d** 02 **p** 09. C Cheltenham St Mary, St Matt, St Paul and H Trin *Glouc* 02-03; NSM Cheltenham St Mark 09-11; Chapl Glouc Docks Mariners' Ch from 12. *11 Sandhurst Road, Gloucester GL1 2SE* T: (01452) 699552 M: 07906-314463
E: andy@marinersgloucester.org.uk

OSMOND, David Methuen. b 38. Qu Coll Birm 75. **d** 77 **p** 78. C Yardley St Edburgha *Birm* 77-80; V Withall 80-89; R W Coker w Hardington Mandeville, E Chinnock etc *B & W* 89-95; PtO 96-98; rtd 98; Hon C Castle Town *Lich* 01-03; PtO *Blackb* 05-10; *Heref* from 14. *56 Essex Road, Church Stretton SY6 6AY* T: (01694) 328329 E: dandhosmond@hotmail.co.uk

OSMOND, Mrs Heather Christine. b 44. ABSM 64 ARCM 65 Birm Poly CertEd 65. Qu Coll Birm 83. **dss** 84 **d** 87 **p** 97. Brandwood *Birm* 84-85; Withall 85-89; Par Dn 87-89; PtO *B & W* 89-01; P-in-c Castle Town *Lich* 01-03; rtd 04; PtO *Blackb* 05-09; *Heref* from 14. *56 Essex Road, Church Stretton SY6 6AY* T: (01694) 328329 E: dandhosmond@hotmail.co.uk

OSMOND, Oliver Robert. b 44. Ch Coll Cam BA 66 MA 70. Cuddesdon Coll 66 Trin Coll Toronto STB 69. **d** 69 **p** 70. C Toronto St Jo York Mills Canada 69-71; R N Essa 71-74; R Westmoreland 74-77; P-in-c Lower Scakville 77-81; V Mill Hill Jo Keble Ch *Lon* 81-09; rtd 09. *PO Box 211, Lunenburg NS B0J 2C0, Canada* T: (001) (902) 766 4318

OSMOND, Tobias Charles. b 74. Plymouth Univ BSc 96. Ripon Coll Cuddesdon BTh 99. **d** 99 **p** 00. C Wilton *B & W* 99-02; C Bath Abbey w St Jas 02-05; I Craighurst, Midhurst and Minesing Canada 05-11; P-in-c Wells St Thos w Horrington *B & W* from 11; P-in-c Chewton Mendip w Ston Easton, Litton etc from 11. *The Vicarage, 94 St Thomas Street, Wells BA5 2UZ* T: (01749) 672193 E: tobieosmond@gmail.com

OSSORY AND LEIGHLIN, Archdeacon of. *See* ORR, The Ven Andrew Dermot Harman

OSSORY, Dean of. *See* POULTON, The Very Revd Katharine Margaret

OSTLER, Mrs Christine Anne. b 46. Bp Otter Coll CertEd 68. Westcott Ho Cam 07. **d** 09 **p** 10. NSM Gt w Lt Harrowden and Orlingbury and Isham etc *Pet* 09-12; P-in-c Wellingborough St Barn from 12. *19B Castle Street, Wellingborough NN8 1LW* T: (01933) 226730 E: c.ostler@btinternet.com

OSTLI-EAST (formerly EAST), Peter Alan. b 61. Southn Univ LLB 82. Cranmer Hall Dur 90. **d** 93 **p** 94. C Combe Down w Monkton Combe and S Stoke *B & W* 93-97; PtO *Bris* 06-09; TV Bourne Valley *Sarum* 09-15; P-in-c from 15. *The Vicarage, Winterbourne Earls, Salisbury SP4 6HA* T: (01980) 611350 M: 07805-581269 E: ostlieast@gmail.com

O'SULLIVAN, Ms Barbara Jane. b 62. McGill Univ Montreal BA 84 York Univ MA 87 MPhil 89. STETS 11. **d** 14 **p** 15. NSM Portsea St Mary *Portsm* from 14. *St Mary's Church, Fratton Road, Portsmouth PO1 5PA*
E: barbara.o'sullivan@portseaparish.co.uk

O'SULLIVAN, Mrs Hazel. b 50. S Dios Minl Tr Scheme 91. **d** 94 **p** 95. C Cove St Jo *Guildf* 94-98; TV Headley All SS 98-02; V Bordon 02-04; Chapl Whiteley Village 04-11; rtd 11; PtO *Win* 12-15; *Portsm* from 15. *3 The Avenue, Gosport PO12 2JS* T: (023) 9252 6664 E: hosull@hotmail.co.uk

O'SULLIVAN, Mrs Hazel May. b 64. Surrey Univ BSc 86 ACA 90. SEITE 09. **d** 12 **p** 13. C Reigate St Mary *S'wark* from 12. *3 St Clair Close, Reigate RH2 0QB* M: 07810-698906
E: osullivan_hazel@yahoo.co.uk

O'SULLIVAN, Helen Louise. b 68. Westmr Coll Ox BTh 96. St Steph Ho Ox 06. **d** 08 **p** 09. C Chinnor, Sydenham, Aston Rowant and Crowell *Ox* 08-11; P-in-c Brighstone and Brooke w Mottistone *Portsm* from 11; P-in-c Shorwell w Kingston from 11; P-in-c Chale 11-15. *The Rectory, Rectory Lane, Brighstone, Newport PO30 4QH* T: (01983) 740267
E: bbmcsosullivan@gmail.com

O'SULLIVAN, Richard Norton. b 59. Glas Coll of Tech BSc 80. Gregorian Univ Rome PhB 85 STB 88 STL 90. **d** 89 **p** 90. In RC Ch 89-96; NSM Clarkston *Glas* 00-02; P-in-c Glas St Oswald 02-06; P-in-c Peterhead *Ab* 06-09; R from 09. *The Rectory, 19 York Street, Peterhead AB42 1SN* T: (01779) 472217
E: richard.osullivan@virgin.net

OSWALD, John Edward Guy. b 39. Qu Coll Cam BA 63 MA 67. Ridley Hall Cam. **d** 68 **p** 69. C Chippenham St Paul w Langley Burrell *Bris* 68-72; C Hengrove 72-75; P-in-c Hardenhuish 75-79; P-in-c Kington St Michael 75-79; TV Chippenham St Paul w Hardenhuish etc 79-82; P-in-c Gt w Lt Somerford and Seagry 82-86; P-in-c Corston w Rodbourne 84-86;

R Gt Somerford, Lt Somerford, Seagry, Corston etc 86-09; rtd 09; PtO *Bris* from 09. *Chauffeur Cottage, 26 Draycot Cerne, Chippenham SN15 5LG* T: (01249) 720182

OSWIN, Frank Anthony (Tony). b 43. Chich Th Coll 69. **d** 71 **p** 72. C Radford *Cov* 71-74; C Shrub End *Chelmsf* 74-76; V Layer de la Haye 76-80; V Eastwood St Dav 80-93; TR Withycombe Raleigh *Ex* 93-10; rtd 10. *39 West Cliff Park Drive, Dawlish EX7 9ER* T: (01626) 888897

OTTER, Anthony Frank. b 32. Kelham Th Coll 54. **d** 59 **p** 60. C Bethnal Green St Jo w St Simon *Lon* 59-63; C Aylesbury *Ox* 63-68; V Hanslope w Castlethorpe 68-77; P-in-c N w S Moreton 77-79; P-in-c Aston Tirrold w Aston Upthorpe 77-79; R S w N Moreton, Aston Tirrold and Aston Upthorpe 79-97; rtd 97; PtO *Ox* 97-09. *4 Emden House, Barton Lane, Headington, Oxford OX3 9JU* T: (01865) 765447

OTTER, Martin John. b 65. Liv Poly BSc 87 Leeds Univ BA 11. Yorks Min Course 08. **d** 11 **p** 12. C Sherburn in Elmet w Saxton *York* from 11; C Aberford w Micklefield from 15. *The Old Post Office, Main Street, Barkston Ash, Tadcaster LS24 9PR* T: (01937) 557254 M: 07842-106044
E: martin@theottersholt.plus.com

OTTEY, Canon John Leonard. b 34. AKC 60 Nottm Univ BA 70. **d** 61 **p** 62. C Grantham St Wulfram *Linc* 61-64; R Keyworth *S'well* 70-85; P-in-c Stanton-on-the-Wolds 71-85; P-in-c E Retford 85-87; V 87-99; P-in-c W Retford 85-87; R 87-99; Hon Can *S'well* Minster 93-99; rtd 99; PtO *Linc* from 00; *S'well* from 04. *1 The Orchards, Grantham NG31 9GW* T: (01476) 578762

OTTLEY, David Ronald. b 57. Lanc Univ BA 78. Sarum & Wells Th Coll 79. **d** 81 **p** 82. C Urmston *Man* 81-85; Lect Bolton St Pet 85-87; P-in-c Halliwell St Thos 87-88; V Bolton St Thos 88-98; TR Halliwell 98-03; P-in-c Goostrey *Ches* 03-05; V Goostrey w Swettenham 05-09; rtd 09; PtO *Man* from 10. *77 Ravenscroft, Holmes Chapel, Crewe CW4 7HJ*

OTTO, Andrew James. b 63. St Pet Coll Ox BA 86 MA 90 Bris Univ BA 01. Trin Coll Bris 99. **d** 01 **p** 02. C Trowbridge H Trin *Sarum* 01-05. *2 Swallow Drive, Trowbridge BA14 9TW* T: (01225) 776325

OTTO, Francis James Reeve. b 42. New Coll Ox BA 64 BA 68. St Steph Ho Ox 66 Wells Th Coll 68. **d** 69 **p** 70. C St Stephen by Saltash *Truro* 69-72; C Newquay 72-73; V Lanteglos by Fowey 73-79; V St Goran w Caerhays 79-82; Chapl St Mary's Hall Brighton 82-88; Chapl Reading Sch 88-90; Chapl Lic Victuallers' Sch Ascot 91-93; LtO *Ox* 89-95; C Boyne Hill 95; P-in-c Cocking, Bepton and W Lavington *Chich* 95-99; Chapl Heathfield Sch Ascot 99-05; PtO *Ox* 05-06; C Parkham, Alwington, Buckland Brewer etc *Ex* 06-15; rtd 15. *Address temp unknown* T: (01237) 477227
E: corporaljones42@hotmail.com

OUGH, John Christopher. b 51. Lon Univ CertEd 74 Open Univ BA 82. SWMTC 91. **d** 94 **p** 95. C Plymouth Em, St Paul Efford and St Aug *Ex* 94-97; P-in-c Diptford, N Huish, Harberton and Harbertonford 97-01; P-in-c Halwell w Moreleigh 97-01; R Diptford, N Huish, Harberton, Harbertonford etc 01-14; C Ermington and Ugborough 10-14; rtd 14. *Carndu, Rosenithon, St Keverne, Helston TR12 6QR*
E: john@diptfordough.freeserve.co.uk

OULD, Julian Charles. b 52. MHCIMA 77. Coll of Resurr Mirfield 80. **d** 83 **p** 84. C Hebburn St Cuth *Dur* 83-86; C Pet H Spirit Bretton 86-90; R Peakirk w Glinton 90-95; R Peakirk w Glinton and Northborough 95-96; TR Is of Scilly *Truro* 96-98; R 98-06; TR Totnes w Bridgetown, Berry Pomeroy etc *Ex* from 06. *The Rectory, Northgate, Totnes TQ9 5NX* T: (01803) 865615 E: ypj69@dial.pipex.com

OULD, Peter. b 74. Man Univ BA 96. Wycliffe Hall Ox BTh 05. **d** 05 **p** 06. C Ware Ch Ch *St Alb* 05-11; PtO *Cant* from 12. *3 Goudhurst Close, Canterbury CT2 7TZ* T: (01227) 456209
E: mail@peter-ould.net

OULESS, John Michael. b 22. AKC 49. Ridley Hall Cam 49. **d** 50 **p** 51. C Dallington *Pet* 50-55; C Evesham *Worc* 55-56; R Halewood *Liv* 56-62; V Southwick w Glapthorn *Pet* 62-71; Chapl Glapthorn Road Hosp Oundle 63-71; R Cogenhoe *Pet* 71-89; R Whiston 71-89; rtd 89; PtO *Win* 92-06; *Pet* from 07. *15 St Peters Way, Cogenhoe, Northampton NN7 1NU* T: (01604) 891104

OUTEN (née BAILEY), Mrs Joyce Mary Josephine. b 33. St Gabr Coll Lon CertEd 69. S'wark Ord Course 80. **dss** 83 **d** 87 **p** 94. Par Dn Woolwich St Mary w St Mich *S'wark* 87-89; Par Dn Rusthall *Roch* 89-94; C 94-97; rtd 97; Asst Chapl Kent and Cant Hosps NHS Trust 97-99; Asst Chapl E Kent Hosps NHS Trust 99-00; TV Whitstable *Cant* 00-07; PtO from 07. *10 Foxgrove Road, Whitstable CT5 1PB* T: (01227) 273643
E: joyceouten@tiscali.co.uk

OUTRAM, Canon David Michael. b 42. Univ of Wales (Ban) BA 77 BD 79. Coll of Resurr Mirfield 79. **d** 80 **p** 81.

C Llandegfan and Beaumaris w Llanfaes w Penmon etc *Ban* 80-82; Chapl Prebendal Sch Chich 82-86; PV Chich Cathl 82-86; Asst Chapl Wellington Coll Berks 86-89; Chapl 89-03; Hd Div 87-03; V Dwygyfylchi *Ban* 03-11; Hon Succ Ban Cathl 08-11; Can Ban Cathl from 11; LtO 12-13; rtd 13; PtO *Ban* 13-14. *Holly Cottage, LLangoed, Beaumaris LL58 8NP* T: (01248) 490016

OVENDEN, Canon John Anthony. b 45. LVO 07. Open Univ BA 80 BA 93 K Coll Lon MA 96. Sarum & Wells Th Coll 71. **d** 74 **p** 75. C Handsworth *Sheff* 74-77; C Isfield *Chich* 77-80; C Uckfield 77-80; P-in-c Stuntney *Ely* 80-85; Min Can, Prec and Sacr Ely Cathl 80-85; V Primrose Hill St Mary w Avenue Road St Paul *Lon* 85-98; Can Windsor and Chapl in Windsor Gt Park 98-12; rtd 12; Dean of Chpl and Fell Harris Manchester Coll Ox from 12; Dir English Hymnal Co 93-00; Chapl to The Queen 02-15. *Little Croft, Great Rissington, Cheltenham GL54 2LN* E: johnovenden@btinternet.com

OVEREND, Alan. b 53. Sheff Univ BA 75. Oak Hill Th Coll 84. **d** 86 **p** 87. C Aughton St Mich *Liv* 86-89; P-in-c Eccleston Park 89-92; V 92-99; V Ainsdale 99-07; V Billinge from 07. *5 Lostock Close, Billinge, Wigan WN5 7TQ* T: (01744) 892210

OVEREND, Barry Malcolm. b 49. K Coll Lon BD 71 AKC 71. St Aug Coll Cant 71. **d** 72 **p** 73. C Nailsworth *Glouc* 72-74; C High Harrogate Ch Ch *Ripon* 75-78; V Collingham w Harewood 78-87; V Far Headingley St Chad 87-10; rtd 10; PtO *Leeds* from 10. *4 Cherington Court, Burley in Wharfedale, Ilkley LS29 7BP* T: (01943) 968248 E: barry.sue.overend@gmail.com

OVEREND, Paul. b 66. Coll of Ripon & York St Jo BA 88 Hull Univ MA 96 Univ of Wales (Cardiff) PhD 04. Coll of Resurr Mirfield 88. **d** 93 **p** 94. C Clayton w Eastfield *York* 93-96; Asst Chapl Univ of Wales (Cardiff) *Llan* 96; Sen Chapl 97-03; Tutor 03-04; Tutor St Mich Coll Llan 03-04; Teaching Fell Liv Hope Univ 04-05; Dir Initial Minl Formation *Sarum* 05-06; Vice Prin Sarum OLM Scheme 05-06; Prin OLM 06-08; Tutor STETS and Co-ord for Locally Deployable Ord Min 08-09; Tutor STETS 11-12; C Wymondham *Nor* 12-13; Lay Development Officer from 14; Asst Dir of Ords from 15. *2 Chapel Lane, Foulsham, Dereham NR20 5RA* T: (01603) 882336 E: paul.overend@gmail.com *or* paul.overend@dioceseofnorwich.org

OVERINGTON, Canon David Vernon. b 34. ALCD 60. **d** 60 **p** 61. C Penge Ch Ch w H Trin *Roch* 60-62; C Lenton *S'well* 62-65; PC Brackenfield w Wessington *Derby* 65-71; P-in-c Cubley w Marston Montgomery 71-76; R Bridgetown Australia 76-79; Par P Denmark 79-85; Can Bunbury 84-85; R E Fremantle w Palmyra Australia 85-90; Field Officer Angl Dept of Educn 90-93; R Wembley 93-99; Hon Can Perth from 96; rtd 99. P-in-c Longside *Ab* 99-03; P-in-c New Pitsligo 99-03; P-in-c Old Deer 99-03; P-in-c Strichen 99-03; PtO *Roch* from 04. *223 Ralph Perring Court, Stone Park Avenue, Beckenham BR3 3LX* T: (020) 8650 5291 E: overington@talktalk.net

OVERTHROW, Royston John. b 45. Southn Univ BTh 94. Portsm Dioc Tr Course 84. **d** 85. NSM Portsm Cathl 85-91; PtO 91-94; Bp's Dom Chapl *Sarum* 94-02; NSM Marlborough 02-04; rtd 04. *19 Bratton Avenue, Devizes SN10 5BA* T: (01380) 722404 E: liznroyuk@supanet.com

OVERTON, Andrew. b 70. **d** 13 **p** 14. NSM Sutton-on-Plym, Plymouth St Simon and St Mary *Ex* from 13; NSM Plymouth St Gabr from 13. *30 Caroline Place, Plymouth PL1 3PS*

OVERTON, Charles Henry. b 51. CCC Ox BA 74 MA 77 Fitzw Coll Cam PGCE 75 BA 79 MA 85. Ridley Hall Cam 77. **d** 80 **p** 81. C Tonbridge SS Pet and Paul *Roch* 80-84; Asst Chapl St Lawr Coll Ramsgate 84-87; P-in-c Aythorpe w High and Leaden Roding *Chelmsf* 88-95; P-in-c Hughenden *Ox* 95-01; P-in-c Chalfont St Peter 05-08; R from 08. *The Vicarage, 4 Austenway, Chalfont St Peter, Gerrards Cross SL9 8NW* T: (01753) 882389 E: vicar@csp-parish.org.uk

OVERTON, David Malcolm. b 52. Surrey Univ BA 97. Chich Th Coll. **d** 84 **p** 85. C Ches H Trin 84-86; C Woodchurch 86-88; C Coppenhall 88-91; C Croydon St Jo *S'wark* 91-94; PtO *Lon* 97-00; C Selsey *Chich* 98-02; Miss P Ribbleton *Blackb* 02-07; Hon C Preston St Jo and St Geo 07-09. *42 Altcar Road, Formby, Liverpool L37 8DT*

OVERTON, John Michael. b 48. CCC Ox BA 71 MA 74 CPA 77 MRSC 01. Ripon Coll Cuddesdon 11. **d** 12 **p** 13. NSM New Mills *Derby* from 12. *6 Brown Edge Close, Buxton SK17 7AS* T: (01298) 24845 E: jm.overton@btinternet.com

OVERTON, Keith Charles. b 28. EAMTC 78. **d** 81 **p** 82. NSM Duxford *Ely* 81-84; NSM Whittlesford 84-88; P-in-c 88-94; P-in-c Pampisford 88-90; PtO *Bris* from 94. *86 Pittsfield, Cricklade, Swindon SN6 6AW* T: (01793) 750321 E: keith@overton.org.uk

OVERTON-BENGE, Canon Angela Margaret. b 46. UEA BA 99 Anglia Poly Univ MA 04. EAMTC 94. **d** 97 **p** 98. NSM Moulsham St Jo *Chelmsf* 97-01; Ind Chapl 01-04; C Aveley and Purfleet 01-04; Bp's Soc and Ind Adv *Bris* from 04; C Swindon All SS w St Barn from 06; C Swindon St Aug from 06; Hon Can Bris Cathl from 12. *St Augustine's Vicarage, Morris Street, Swindon SN2 2HT* T: (01793) 618986

OVEY, Michael John. b 58. Ball Coll Ox BA 81 BCL 82 ACT MTh 00 Lon Univ PhD 04. Ridley Hall Cam 88. **d** 91 **p** 92. C Crowborough *Chich* 91-95; Australia 95-98; Kingham Hill Fell Oak Hill Th Coll 98-07; Prin from 07. *Oak Hill Theological College, Chase Side, London N14 4PS* T: (020) 8449 0467 ext 248 E: mikeo@oakhill.ac.uk

OWEN, Bryan Philip. b 47. Keswick Hall Coll CertEd 70. Cant Sch of Min 83. **d** 86 **p** 87. NSM Deal St Geo *Cant* 86-87; C Herne 87-89; R Clarkston *Glas* 89-93; Warden Scottish Chs Ho (Chs Together in Scotland) 93-96; V Cuddington *Guildf* 96-01; rtd 01; PtO *Glas* from 01. *Columcille, 10 Waverley Park, Kirkintilloch, Glasgow G66 2BP* T: 0141-776 0407 M: 07796-155560 E: bryan.owen@talktalk.net

OWEN, Mrs Carole Janice. b 55. **d** 01 **p** 02. NSM Cley Hill Warminster *Sarum* 01-07; NSM Warminster St Denys and Upton Scudamore from 07. *11 Stuart Green, Warminster BA12 9NU* T: (01985) 214849 E: richardowen50@hotmail.com

OWEN, Caroline Ann. b 59. Univ of Wales (Abth) BA 80 PGCE 81. St Mich Coll Llan 03. **d** 05 **p** 06. NSM Bangor *Ban* 05-09; V Cadoxton-juxta-Neath and Tonna *Llan* 09-12; V Dan yr Eppynt *S & B* from 12. *The Gardens, Cradoc, Brecon LD3 9LR* T: (01874) 409291 E: calowen18@gmail.com

OWEN, Christine Rose. b 62. Univ of Wales (Ban) BA 83 PGCE 84. Qu Coll Birm 86. **d** 88 **p** 94. C Ynyscynhaearn w Penmorfa and Porthmadog *Ban* 88-90; Chapl Lon Univ 90-96; Hon C St Marylebone w H Trin 94-96; Min Can and Prec Worc Cathl 96-00; R Llansantffraid Glan Conwy and Eglwysbach *St As* 00-12; AD Llanrwst 09-12; V Colwyn Bay w Brynymaen from 12. *The Vicarage, 27 Walshaw Avenue, Colwyn Bay LL29 7UY* T: (01492) 539522 E: revdchristine@btinternet.com

OWEN, Christopher David. b 73. Trin Coll Bris 10. **d** 12 **p** 13. C Walton-on-Thames *Guildf* from 12. *1 Egmont Road, Walton-on-Thames KT12 2NW* M: 07890-422357 E: cdowen1973@gmail.com

OWEN, Clifford. *See* OWEN, Phillip Clifford

OWEN, Canon Dafydd Gwyn. b 62. St Steph Ho Ox 95. **d** 97 **p** 98. C Whitchurch *Bris* 97-01; V Bris Ch the Servant Stockwood from 01; AD Bris S from 06; Hon Min Can Bris Cathl 04-11; Hon Can Bris Cathl from 11. *The Vicarage, Goslet Road, Stockwood, Bristol BS14 8SP* T: (01275) 831138 E: christtheservant@blueyonder.co.uk

OWEN, Daniel James. b 71. Anglia Poly Univ BSc 94 TCD BTh 00. CITC 97. **d** 00 **p** 01. C Belfast St Donard *D & D* 00-03; I Rathcooney Union *C, C & R* 03-09; I Kilgariffe Union from 09. *The Rectory, Gullanes, Clonakilty, Co Cork, Republic of Ireland* T: (00353) (23) 883 3357 E: danielsonja@eircom.net

OWEN, David Cadwaladr. b 56. Grey Coll Dur BSc 77 Univ Coll Worc PGCE 99. WEMTC 00. **d** 03 **p** 04. NSM Pershore w Pinvin, Wick and Birlingham *Worc* 03-07; TV Droitwich Spa 07-14; P-in-c Salwarpe and Hindlip w Martin Hussing-tree 10-14; V Loddon, Sisland, Chedgrave, Hardley and Langley *Nor* from 14. *The Vicarage, 4 Market Place, Loddon, Norwich NR14 6EY* M: 07837-800009 E: david.droitwich@gmail.com

OWEN, Canon David William. b 31. Down Coll Cam BA 55 MA 58. Linc Th Coll 55. **d** 57 **p** 58. C Salford St Phil w St Steph *Man* 57-61; C Grantham St Wulfram *Linc* 61-65; V Messingham 65-70; V Spilsby w Hundleby 70-77; R Aswardby w Sausthorpe 71-77; R Langton w Sutterby 71-77; R Halton Holgate 73-77; P-in-c Firsby w Gt Steeping 75-77; P-in-c Lt Steeping 75-77; TR Louth 77-92; Chapl Louth Co Hosp 77-92; RD Louthesk *Linc* 82-89; Can and Preb Linc Cathl 85-92; TR Swan *Ox* 92-97; RD Claydon 94-96; rtd 97. *19 Stephen Road, Headington, Oxford OX3 9AY* T: (01865) 766585

OWEN, Miss Denise. b 65. Warwick Univ BA 87 Westmr Coll of Educn PGCE 92. Coll of Resurr Mirfield 12. **d** 14 **p** 15. C Spotland and Oakenrod *Man* from 14. *10 Little Flatt, Rochdale OL12 7AU* T: (01706) 346846 E: owendenise4@gmail.com

OWEN, Edgar. b 26. WMMTC. **d** 82 **p** 83. NSM Garretts Green *Birm* 82-88; NSM Stechford 88-94; rtd 94; PtO *Birm* from 94. *36 Colbourne Court, 116 Frederick Road, Stechford, Birmingham B33 8AE* T: 0121-783 5603

OWEN, Emyr. b 69. Lancs Poly BSc 91. Westcott Ho Cam BA 94. **d** 95 **p** 96. C Llanbeblig w Caernarfon and Betws Garmon etc *Ban* 95-96; C Llanberis w Llanrug 96-98; TV Bangor 98-02; P-in-c Llandygai and Maes y Groes 98-02; V Nefyn w Tudweiliog w Llandudwen w Edern 02-07; PtO *St As* 08-10; TV Wrexham 10-13. *Llety Heulog, Tyn-y-Coed Road, Dolgellau LL40 2YT* T: (01341) 422495 E: emyr_owen@hotmail.com

OWEN, Eric Cyril Hammersley. b 46. Liv Univ LLB 68 Barrister 69. St As Minl Tr Course 95. **d** 97 **p** 98. NSM Gresford w Holt *St As* 97-03; NSM Rhosymedre w Penycae 03-04; PtO from 12. *Thistle Patch, 28 Wynnstay Lane, Marford, Wrexham LL12 8LG* T: (01978) 856495 E: eowen@lineone.net

OWEN, Gary John. b 72. City Univ BSc 93 Fitzw Coll Cam BA 97 MA 01. Ridley Hall Cam 95. **d** 98 **p** 99. C Welshpool w Castle Caereinion *St As* 98-01; TV Wrexham 01-10; R Eynsford w Farningham and Lullingstone *Roch* from 10. *The Rectory, Pollyhaugh, Eynsford, Dartford DA4 0HE* T: (01322) 863050 M: 07947-358050 E: eflrector@googlemail.com

OWEN, Geoffrey Neill. b 55. Chich Th Coll. **d** 85 **p** 86. C Streatham St Pet *S'wark* 85-89; C Battersea Ch Ch and St Steph 89-91; TV Surbiton St Andr and St Mark 91-97; V Merton St Jas 97-08; V Battersea Ch Ch and St Steph from 08; RD Battersea from 10. *Christ Church Vicarage, Candahar Road, London SW11 2PU* T: (020) 7228 1225

OWEN, Glyn John. b 56. Open Univ BA 91 Nottm Univ MSc 93 St Jo Coll Dur BA 05. Cranmer Hall Dur 01. **d** 03 **p** 04. C Whiston *Sheff* 03-07; V Rudston w Boynton, Carnaby and Kilham *York* from 07; P-in-c Burton Fleming w Fordon, Grindale etc from 07; RD Bridlington from 12. *The Vicarage, Rudston, Driffield YO25 4XA* T: (01262) 420313 E: revglynowen@btinternet.com

OWEN, Graham Anthony. b 54. Birm Univ BA 77. Trin Coll Bris 92. **d** 94 **p** 95. C Wiveliscombe w Chipstable, Huish Champflower etc *B & W* 94-98; R 98-09; V Frome H Trin from 09. *Holy Trinity Vicarage, Orchard Street, Frome BA11 3BX* T: (01373) 462586 E: graham-owen@hotmail.co.uk

OWEN, Canon Graham Wynne. b 46. Lon Inst of Educn MA 81 GTCL FTCL 70. Cant Sch of Min 90. **d** 93 **p** 94. C Eltham H Trin *S'wark* 93-97; P-in-c Shooters Hill Ch Ch 97-00; V 00-01; TV Sole Bay *St E* 01-04; P-in-c Framlingham w Saxtead 04-13; RD Loes 05-13; Hon Can St E Cathl 11-13; rtd 13; PtO *St E* from 14. *Clarendon House, 3 St Peter's Court, High Street, Clare, Sudbury CO10 8NY* T: (01787) 279172 E: gowen.mowen@talktalk.net

OWEN, Gwyn. *See* OWEN, Dafydd Gwyn

OWEN, Miss Hannah Mair. b 72. **d** 13 **p** 14. NSM Carmarthen St Pet and Abergwili etc *St D* from 13. *5 Ger y Llan, The Parade, Carmarthen SA31 1LY* T: (01267) 469085 E: revmair@gmail.com

OWEN, Harry Dennis. b 47. Oak Hill Th Coll 73. **d** 76 **p** 77. C Fulham Ch Ch *Lon* 76-81; V Byker St Mark *Newc* 81-89; V Plumstead All SS *S'wark* 89-14; RD Plumstead 03-14; rtd 14. *All Saints' Vicarage, 106 Herbert Road, London SE18 3PU* T: (020) 8854 2995 E: h.d.owen@talk21.com

OWEN, James Thomas. *See* McNAUGHTAN-OWEN, James Thomas

OWEN, John Edward. b 52. Middx Poly BA 75. Sarum & Wells Th Coll BTh 81. **d** 81 **p** 82. C S Ashford Ch Ch *Cant* 81-85; TV Bemerton *Sarum* 85-91; V St Leonards and St Ives *Win* 91-95; R N Stoneham 95-09; V Steep and Froxfield w Privett *Portsm* from 09. *The Vicarage, 77 Church Road, Steep, Petersfield GU32 2DF* T: (01730) 264282 *or* 260169 E: revjohnowen@gmail.com

OWEN, Karen. *See* HOPWOOD OWEN, Karen

OWEN, Keith Robert. b 57. Warwick Univ BA Ox Univ BA MA 85 Hull Univ MA(Ed) 89. St Steph Ho Ox 79. **d** 82 **p** 83. C Headingley *Ripon* 82-85; Chapl Grimsby Colls of H&FE 85-90; Ecum Chapl for F&HE Grimsby *Linc* 85-90; P-in-c Linc St Botolph 90-95; Chapl to Caring Agencies Linc City Cen 90-95; V Steeton *Bradf* 95-01; Chapl Airedale NHS Trust 95-01; P-in-c Penzance St Mary w St Paul *Truro* 01-02; P-in-c Penzance St Jo 01-02; TR Penzance St Mary w St Paul and St Jo 02-12; C from 12; P-in-c Newlyn St Pet from 12; C Paul from 12. *24 Chapel Street, Penzance TR18 4AP* T: (01736) 365079 E: stpetersnewlyn@hotmail.co.uk

OWEN, Kenneth Phillip. b 56. Liv Univ BA 77 PGCE 78. NOC 92. **d** 95 **p** 96. C Heswall *Ches* 95-01; V Frankby w Greasby from 01. *The Vicarage, 14 Arrowe Road, Greasby, Wirral CH49 1RA* T: 0151-678 6155 E: greasby@office.fsworld.co.uk

OWEN, Mair. *See* OWEN, Hannah Mair

OWEN, Mark. b 63. RMN. St Mich Coll Llan 03. **d** 05 **p** 06. C Tredegar *Mon* 05-08; V Rhymney 08-14; P-in-c Mynyddislwyn from 14; AD Bedwellty from 15. *The Vicarage, Commercial Street, Pengam, Blackwood NP12 3TX* T: (01443) 836805 E: fathermarkowen12@gmail.com

OWEN, Myles Ronald. b 85. Sheff Univ BA 07. Ripon Coll Cuddesdon 09. **d** 12 **p** 13. C Bowdon *Ches* from 12. *45 Priory Street, Bowdon, Altrincham WA14 3BQ*

OWEN, Paul Jonathan. b 59. S Bank Poly BSc 81 Anglia Poly Univ MA 03. Ridley Hall Cam 00. **d** 02 **p** 03. C Seaford w Sutton *Chich* 02-06; R Denton w S Heighton and Tarring Neville 06-11; V Seaford w Sutton from 11. *The Vicarage, 46 Sutton Road, Seaford BN25 1SH* T: (01323) 893508 E: revpowen@gmail.com

OWEN, Peter Russell. b 35. St Mich Coll Llan. **d** 63 **p** 64. C Wrexham *St As* 63-64; C Connah's Quay 64-65; Asst Chapl Miss to Seamen 66-69; P-in-c Upper Norwood All SS w St Marg *Cant* 69-72; C Hawarden *St As* 72-75; V Cilcain and Nannerch 75-79; R Cilcain and Nannerch and Rhydymwyn 79-83; V Brymbo and Bwlchgwyn 83-87; R Llangynhafal and Llanbedr Dyffryn Clwyd 87-99; P-in-c Llanynys w Llanychan 87-99; rtd 00. *Telpyn Forge, Rhewl, Ruthin LL15 1TP* T: (01824) 704051

OWEN, Phillip Clifford. b 42. G&C Coll Cam BA 65 MA 69 Birm Univ PhD 07. Ridley Hall Cam 71. **d** 73 **p** 74. C Stowmarket *St E* 73-76; C Headley All SS *Guildf* 76-81; TV 81-89; P-in-c Clifton-on-Teme, Lower Sapey and the Shelsleys *Worc* 89-97; R 97-02; Dioc Ecum Officer 89-02; P-in-c Corfu *Eur* 03-08; P-in-c Ostend 08-12; rtd 12; PtO *Ely* from 13. *147 Sapley Road, Hartford, Huntingdon PE29 1YH* T: (01480) 435488 M: 07887-745632 E: clavis@hotmail.com

OWEN, Mrs Phyllis Elizabeth. b 48. NTMTC. **d** 05 **p** 06. NSM Southend *Chelmsf* from 05. *42 Harcourt Avenue, Southend-on-Sea SS2 6HU* T: (01702) 313312 E: thephiz@blueyonder.co.uk

OWEN, Raymond Philip. b 37. Man Univ BScTech 60 AMCST 60. Chich Th Coll 65. **d** 67 **p** 68. C Elland *Wakef* 67-70; C Lindley 70-73; V Bradshaw 73-80; Ind Chapl *Dur* 80-91; TR Hanley H Ev *Lich* 91-99; Bp Stafford's Past Aux 03-04; rtd 04; PtO *Lich* 04-07; C Alton w Bradley-le-Moors and Denstone etc from 07. *The Vicarage, Church Lane, Mayfield, Ashbourne DE6 2JR* M: 07747-601379 E: revrayowen@hotmail.com

OWEN, Canon Richard Llewelyn. b 27. Univ of Wales (Lamp) BA 51. St Mich Coll Llan 51. **d** 53 **p** 54. C Holyhead w Rhoscolyn w Llanfair-yn-Neubwll *Ban* 53-57; C Porthmadog 57-59; R Llanfechell w Bodewryd, Rhosbeirio etc 59-67; Youth Chapl 66-67; V Penrhyndeudraeth and Llanfrothen 67-77; R Llangefni w Tregaean and Llangristiolus etc 77-89; Can Ban Cathl 82-93; Hon Can Ban Cathl from 93; Treas Ban Cathl 86-93; Can Missr and V Ban Cathl 89-93; RD Arfon 92-93; rtd 93; PtO *Ban* from 93. *Bodowen, Great Orme's Road, Llandudno LL30 2BF* T: (01492) 872765

OWEN, Richard Matthew. b 49. Sheff Univ BA 70 Leeds Univ CertEd 73. NOC 84. **d** 87 **p** 88. NSM Chorlton-cum-Hardy St Werburgh *Man* 87-89; C N Reddish 89-91; PtO *York* 91-96 and 97-03; NSM York St Olave w St Giles 96-97; PtO *Cant* from 12. *17 Mill Lane, St Radigunds, Canterbury CT1 2AW* T: (01227) 784430 M: 07789-923516 E: richardowen100@gmail.com

OWEN, Robert Glynne. b 33. St Mich Coll Llan 56. **d** 58 **p** 59. C Machynlleth and Llanwrin *Ban* 58-62; C Llanbeblig w Caernarfon 62-65; V Carno and Trefeglwys 65-69; Hon C Dorking w Ranmore *Guildf* 69-75; PtO *St As* 75-94; V Broughton 94-99; rtd 99. *Briarcroft, Minera Road, Cefn y Bedd, Wrexham LL12 9TR* T: (01978) 750134

OWEN, Robert Lee. b 56. Univ of Wales (Cardiff) BD 79. Qu Coll Birm 79. **d** 81 **p** 82. C Holywell *St As* 81-84; PtO *Birm* 85-87; Chapl Blue Coat Sch Birm 85-87; Chapl St Elphin's Sch Matlock 87-94; Chapl Qu Marg Sch York from 94. *Queen Margaret's School, Escrick Park, Escrick, York YO19 6EU* T: (01904) 728261

OWEN, Ronald Alfred. b 44. Wilson Carlile Coll 73 Sarum & Wells Th Coll 80. **d** 81 **p** 82. C Wotton St Mary *Glouc* 81-83; CF 83-97; P-in-c Salcombe *Ex* 97-02; V Salcombe and Malborough w S Huish 02-06; RD Woodleigh 00-03; rtd 07; PtO *B & W* from 07. *9 Reedmoor Gardens, Bridgwater TA6 3SL* T: (01278) 433801 M: 07540-805060 E: owenrarev@gmail.com

OWEN, Sally Ann. *See* ROBERTSON, Sally Ann

OWEN, Stuart James. b 68. Sunderland Poly BA 91. Ripon Coll Cuddesdon BTh 00. **d** 00 **p** 01. C Hendon St Mary *Lon* 00-01; C Hendon St Mary and Ch Ch 01-04; P Missr Edmonton St Mary w St Jo 04-08; V Edmonton All SS w St Mich from 08. *All Saints' Vicarage, 43 All Saints' Close, London N9 9AT* T: (020) 8803 9199 E: fr.stuart@gmail.com

OWEN, Susan Elizabeth. *See* WYATT, Susan Elizabeth

OWEN, Mrs Susan Margaret. b 38. St Andr Univ MA 61 Univ of Wales (Swansea) MPhil 91 Univ of Wales (Ban) BD 93. Qu Coll Birm 94. **d** 95 **p** 96. NSM Shrewsbury St Geo *Lich* 95-98; P-in-c Penrhyndeudraeth w Llanfrothen w Beddgelert *Ban* 98-99; V 99-06; V Penrhyndeudraeth and Llanfrothen w Maentwrog etc 06-07; rtd 08; PtO *Ban* from 09. *Coed Helyg, Lower Moranedd, Criccieth LL52 0LA*

OWEN-JONES, Mrs Ingrid. b 41. **d** 11 **p** 12. OLM W Hallam and Mapperley w Stanley *Derby* from 11. *Bridge Cottage, 63 Derby Road, Stanley, Ilkeston DE7 6EX* T: 0115-932 0764 M: 07977-808041 E: ingridoj@talktalk.net

OWEN-JONES, Peter Charles. b 57. Ridley Hall Cam 92. **d** 94 **p** 95. C Leverington and Wisbech St Mary *Ely* 94-97; R Haslingfield w Harlton and Gt and Lt Eversden 97-05; P-in-c Glynde, W Firle and Beddingham *Chich* from 05. *The Vicarage, The Street, Firle, Lewes BN8 6NP* T: (01273) 858005 M: 07973-265953 E: poj@lineone.net

OWEN-JONES, Peter John. b 47. RMCS BScEng 68 CEng 84 MIMechE 84 MBIM 87 FPWI 89. EMMTC 85. **d** 88 **p** 89. NSM Holbrook and Lt Eaton *Derby* 88-00; NSM W Hallam and Mapperley w Stanley 01-13; RD Erewash 12-13; MSE Officer 11-13; rtd 13; PtO *Derby* from 13. *Bridge Cottage, 63 Derby Road, Stanley, Ilkeston DE7 6EX* T: 0115-932 0764 M: 07771-828018 E: peter@ipoj.co.uk

OWENS, Canon Ann Lindsay. b 47. St Hild Coll Dur CertEd 68 Man Univ BA 94. NOC 92. **d** 95 **p** 96. Chapl St Jas Sch Farnworth 94-97; NSM New Bury *Man* 95-97; C Heywood St Luke w All So 97-98; C Heywood 98-99; P-in-c Chadderton St Matt 99-04; P-in-c Chadderton St Luke 03-04; V Chadderton St Matt w St Luke 04-05; V Hurst 05-12; Hon Can Man Cathl 10-12; rtd 12; PtO *Man* from 12. *10A Victoria Drive, Wirral CH48 0QT* T: 0151-625 9494 E: ann-lindsay.owens@virgin.net

OWENS, Christopher Lee. b 42. SS Mark & Jo Coll Chelsea 61 Lon Inst of Educn TCert. Linc Th Coll 66. **d** 69 **p** 70. C Dalston H Trin w St Phil *Lon* 69-72; C Portsea N End St Mark *Portsm* 72-81; TV E Ham w Upton Park and Forest Gate *Chelmsf* 81-92; C Is of Dogs Ch Ch and St Jo w St Luke *Lon* 92-98; P-in-c Chingford St Edm *Chelmsf* 98-02; V 02-07; rtd 07; PtO *Chelmsf* from 08. *67 Disraeli Road, London E7 9JU* T: (020) 8555 6337 E: owenseaster@gmail.com

OWENS, Mrs Janet. b 49. Ches Coll of HE MEd 99. NOC 90. **d** 13 **p** 14. NSM Stockport St Sav *Ches* 13-14; NSM Offerton St Alb and Stockport St Thos from 14. *94 Queens Road, Cheadle Hulme, Cheadle SK8 5HS* T: 0161-485 6677 M: 07990-570778 E: revandrog@gmail.com

OWENS, John David. b 83. Spurgeon's Coll BD 10. Coll of Resurr Mirfield 10. **d** 13. C Church Langton cum Tur Langton etc *Leic* 13. *Address temp unknown* M: 07930-669904 E: 39articles@gmail.com

OWENS, Mrs Margaret Jean. b 49. Man Univ BSc 70 Birm Univ MSc 72. St Jo Coll Nottm 99. **d** 01 **p** 02. NSM Hurdsfield *Ches* 01-07; V Disley from 07. *Disley Vicarage, Red Lane, Disley, Stockport SK12 2NP* T: (01663) 762068 M: 07775-801613 E: mowens44@btinternet.com

OWENS, Canon Patricia Margaret. d 07 **p** 08. NSM Buckley *St As* 07-10; NSM Ruabon and Rhosymedre from 10; Can St As Cathl from 14. *The Clappers, Pont-y-Capel Lane, Gresford, Wrexham LL12 8RS* T: (01978) 854855 E: p.owens@liv.ac.uk

OWENS, Philip Roger. b 47. Wells Th Coll 71. **d** 71 **p** 72. C Colwyn Bay *St As* 71-74; C Wrexham 74-77; TV 77-80; P-in-c Yoxford *St E* 80-85; Asst Stewardship and Resources Adv 80-85; R Bangor Monachorum and Worthenbury *St As* 85-98; Sec Dioc Stewardship Cttee 89-98; RD Bangor Isycoed *St As* 92-98; R Flint 98-03; AD Holywell 02-03; rtd 06; PtO *Ches* from 11. *101 Woolton Road, Wirral CH61 3UD* T: 0151-648 3940 M: 07808-167147 E: philipowens653@btinternet.com

OWENS, Stephen Graham Frank. b 49. Ch Coll Cam BA 71 MA 75 CertEd 72. Qu Coll Birm 73. **d** 75 **p** 76. C Stourbridge St Mich Norton *Worc* 75-80; Tanzania 80-88; V Dudley Wood *Worc* 88-99; P-in-c Mamble w Bayton, Rock w Heightington etc 99-02; V 02-14; rtd 14. *Address temp unknown*

OWERS, Ian Humphrey. b 46. Em Coll Cam BA 68 MA 72. Westcott Ho Cam 71. **d** 73 **p** 74. C Champion Hill St Sav *S'wark* 73-77; V Peckham St Sav 77-82; P-in-c E Greenwich Ch Ch w St Andr and St Mich 82-83; V 83-94; P-in-c Westcombe Park St Geo 85-94; RD Greenwich 92-94; PtO *St E* 01-07; *Bradf* 03-10; *Sheff* from 10. *St Aidan's Vicarage, 4 Manor Lane, Sheffield S2 1UF* T: 0114-272 4676 M: 07808-613252 E: ianowers@ianowers.co.uk

OXBORROW, Alison Louise. b 68. Nottm Univ BA 90 Lon Sch of Th BA 04 Solicitor 92. St Jo Coll Nottm 08. **d** 11 **p** 12. C Didsbury St Jas and Em *Man* 11-14; PtO 14-15; Chapl Springhill Hospice from 15. *St Thomas's Vicarage, Cavendish Road, Rochdale OL11 2QX* M: 07870-917710 E: alioxborrow@hotmail.com

OXBROW, Canon Mark. b 51. Reading Univ BSc 72 Fitzw Ho Cam BA 75 MA 79. Ridley Hall Cam 73. **d** 76 **p** 77. C Luton Ch Ch *Roch* 76-80; TV Newc Epiphany 80-88; Chapl Newc Mental Health Unit 80-88; Regional Sec Eur CMS 88-01; Communication Resources Sec 94-97; Internat Miss Dir 01-03; Asst Gen Sec 03-08; Internat Co-ord Faith2Share Network from 08; Hon Can Brussels Cathl from 98. *Faith2Share Network, Watlington Road, Oxford OX4 6BZ* T: (01865) 787440 E: mark.oxbrow@faith2share.net

OXENFORTH, Colin Bryan. b 45. St Chad's Coll Dur BA 67. **d** 69 **p** 70. C Bromley St Andr *Roch* 69-72; C Nunhead St Antony *S'wark* 72-76; V Toxteth St Marg *Liv* 76-89; V Brixton St Matt *S'wark* 89-00; V Pemberton St Jo *Liv* 00-10; rtd 10; PtO *Liv* from 10. *Flat 3, 5 Walmer Road, Liverpool L22 5NL* T: 0151-721 2018 E: colinoxenforth@sky.com

OXFORD (Christ Church), Dean of. *See* PERCY, The Very Revd Prof Martyn William

OXFORD, Archdeacon of. *See* GORICK, The Ven Martin Charles William

OXFORD, Bishop of. *Vacant*

OXLEY, Canon Christopher Robert. b 51. Sheff Univ BA 73 PGCE 74. Wycliffe Hall Ox BA 78 MA 83. **d** 79 **p** 80. C Greasbrough *Sheff* 79-82; C Doncaster St Leon and St Jude 82-84; Asst Chapl Brussels *Eur* 84-87; V Humberstone *Leic* 87-93; V Beaumont Leys 93-05; RD Christianity S 98-01; P-in-c Leic St Anne 05-09; P-in-c Leic St Paul and St Aug 05-09; V Leic St Anne, St Paul w St Aug 09-11; P-in-c Gilmorton, Peatling Parva, Kimcote etc from 11; Dir Post-Ord Tr 04-09; Hon Can Leic Cathl from 10. *The Rectory, Kilworth Road, Swinford, Lutterworth LE17 6BQ* T: (01788) 860445 E: oxley@leicester.anglican.org *or* oxleycr@btopenworld.com

OXLEY, David William. b 63. TCD BA 85 BTh 89. CITC 85. **d** 89 **p** 90. C Dublin Ch Ch Cathl Gp 89-92; Clerical V Ch Ch Cathl Dublin 90-92; I Templebreedy w Tracton and Nohoval *C, C & R* 92-96; Min Can Cork Cathl 95-96; I Tullow w Shillelagh, Aghold and Mullinacuff *C & O* 96-02; I Dublin Santry w Glasnevin and Finglas *D & G* from 02; Succ St Patr Cathl Dublin from 07. *The Rectory, Church Street, Finglass, Dublin 11, Republic of Ireland* T: (00353) (1) 834 1015 M: 86-881 6486 E: revdwo@hotmail.com

OXLEY, Ms Helen Mary. b 64. TCD BA 88 HDipEd 89 Univ of Wales (Trin St Dav) MMin 11. **d** 11 **p** 12. NSM Dunleckney w Nurney, Lorum and Kiltennel *C & O* from 11. *11 Ashbrook, Tullow Hill, Tullow, Co Carlow, Republic of Ireland* T: (00353) (59) 918 0975 M: 86-378 6980 E: revheleno@gmail.com

OXLEY, Martin Neil. b 65. Birm Univ BA 86 Edin Univ BD 95. Edin Th Coll 92. **d** 95 **p** 96. C Glas St Mary 95-97; C Glas St Matt 95-97; C Clydebank 95-97; P-in-c Glas St Matt 97-00; Dir Studies TISEC 97-00; R Lerwick *Ab* 00-05; P-in-c Burravoe 00-05. *1 Church Avenue, Beckenham BR3 1DT* T: (020) 8658 1846 M: 07970-266578 E: frmartin@globalnet.co.uk

OXLEY, Paul. b 80. Chelt & Glouc Coll of HE BSc 01 Glos Univ PGCE 02. Trin Coll Bris BTh 09. **d** 09 **p** 10. C Upper Sunbury St Sav *Lon* 09-12; PtO *Ox* 12-13; NSM Milton Keynes from 13. *1 East Moor Drive, Wolverton Mill, Milton Keynes MK12 5GX* T: (01908) 310987 M: 07985-937117 E: pauloxo@gmail.com

OXLEY, Mrs Paula Jane. b 51. Sheff Univ BA 74 Nottm Univ MA 00 PGCE 75. EMMTC 93. **d** 93 **p** 94. NSM Birstall and Wanlip *Leic* 93-95; C Beaumont Leys 95-05; NSM Leic St Anne, St Paul w St Aug 05-14; PtO *Cov* from 13; *Leic* from 14. *The Rectory, Kilworth Road, Swinford, Lutterworth LE17 6BQ* T: (01788) 860445 E: oxleycr@btopenworld.com

OXLEY, Mrs Velma. b 52. Trin Coll Bris. **d** 12 **p** 13. NSM By Brook *Bris* 12-15; NSM Colerne w N Wraxall 12-15. *The Gate, Brinkworth, Chippenham SN15 5BY* T: (01666) 510484 E: velmaoxley@btinternet.com

OXTOBY, David Antony. b 72. Huddersfield Univ BSc 98. Ridley Hall Cam 08. **d** 10 **p** 11. C Stamford St Geo w St Paul *Linc* 10-13; P-in-c Sutton Bridge 13-14; C The Suttons w Tydd 13-14; V Sutton Bridge and Tydd St Mary from 14. *The Vicarage, 79 Bridge Street, Sutton Bridge, Spalding PE12 9SD* M: 07595-387652 E: fynesys@gmail.com

P

PACEY, Graham John. b 52. Open Univ BA 81 Leeds Univ CertEd 74 Teesside Poly AdDipEd 85. NEOC 90. d 93 p 94. C Kirkleatham *York* 93-96; V Middlesbrough St Agnes 96-00; R Skelton w Upleatham 00-09; V Boosbeck and Lingdale 07-09; R Guisborough 09-13; RD 11-13; rtd 13. *16 Exeter Street, Saltburn-by-the-Sea TS12 1BN* E: graham.pacey@ntlworld.com

PACEY, James Stewart. b 84. Nottm Trent Univ BA 07 Cam Univ BTh 15. Westcott Ho Cam 12. d 15. C Hucknall Torkard *S'well* from 15. *149 Beardall Street, Hucknall, Nottingham NG15 7HA* M: 07595-035342 E: revjamespacey@gmail.com

PACKER, Catherine Ruth. *See* PICKFORD, Catherine Ruth

PACKER, Prof James Innell. b 26. CCC Ox BA 48 MA 52 DPhil 55. Wycliffe Hall Ox 49. d 52 p 53. C Harborne Heath *Birm* 52-54; Lect Tyndale Hall Bris 55-61; Lib Latimer Ho Ox 61-62; Warden 62-69; Prin Tyndale Hall Bris 70-72; Assoc Prin Trin Coll Bris 72-79; Prof Hist Th Regent Coll Vancouver 79-89; Prof Th from 89; rtd 91. *6017 Holland Street, Vancouver BC V6N 2B2, Canada* T: (001) (604) 266 6722

✤PACKER, The Rt Revd John Richard. b 46. Keble Coll Ox BA 67 MA. Ripon Hall Ox 67. d 70 p 71 c 96. C St Helier *S'wark* 70-73; Chapl Abingdon St Nic *Ox* 73-77; Tutor Ripon Hall Ox 73-75; Tutor Ripon Coll Cuddesdon 75-77; V Wath-upon-Dearne w Adwick-upon-Dearne *Sheff* 77-86; RD Wath 83-86; TR Sheff Manor 86-91; RD Attercliffe 90-91; Adn W Cumberland *Carl* 91-96; P-in-c Bridekirk 95-96; Suff Bp Warrington *Liv* 96-00; Bp Ripon and Leeds 00-14; rtd 14; Hon Asst Bp Newc from 14. *Devonshire House, Alma Place, Whitley Bay NE26 2EQ* T: 0191-253 4321

PACKER, Peter Aelred. b 48. St Jo Coll Dur BA 70 St Chad's Coll Dur PhD 79 Strathclyde Univ MBA 00. Ven English Coll Rome 95. d 96 p 97. SSM 91-98; Hon C S Lambeth St Anne and All SS *S'wark* 96-98; OSB and LtO *Ox* 98-99; Bp's Adv in Miss and Resources *Glas* 99-00; PtO *S'wark* 08-09; Hon C Deptford St Paul 09-10; P-in-c Peckham St Jo w St Andr from 10. *St John's Vicarage, 10A Meeting House Lane, London SE15 2UN* T: (020) 7635 4214 M: 07932-648034 E: packerpunch@gmail.com

PACKER, Preb Roger Ernest John. b 37. ARCO 59 Pemb Coll Cam BA 60 MA 64. Cuddesdon Coll 60. d 62 p 63. C Chippenham St Andr w Tytherton Lucas *Bris* 62-65; C Caversham *Ox* 65-70; R Sandhurst 70-91; V Bridgwater St Mary, Chilton Trinity and Durleigh *B & W* 91-00; RD Bridgwater 94-00; Preb Wells Cathl 96-00; rtd 00; PtO *Chelmsf* from 00. *3 Kreswell Grove, Harwich CO12 3SZ* T: (01255) 502239

PACKHAM, Ms Elizabeth Daisy. b 33. Goldsmiths' Coll Lon BSc 54 CertEd 55. NOC. dss 83 d 87 p 94. Fairfield *Derby* 83-84; Buxton w Burbage and King Sterndale 84-95; Par Dn 87-94; C 94-95; P-in-c Chinley w Buxworth 95-98; PtO from 98; rtd 98. *100 Manchester Road, Chapel-en-le-Frith, High Peak SK23 9TP* T: (01298) 812921 E: elizabeth.packham@btinternet.com

PACKMAN, James Morley. b 76. St Hild & Bede Coll Dur MSci 99. Oak Hill Th Coll BA 04. d 04 p 05. C Eastbourne All SS *Chich* 04-08; R Frant w Eridge from 08; RD Rotherfield from 15. *The Rectory, Church Lane, Frant, Tunbridge Wells TN3 9DX* T: (01892) 750638

PADDICK, Graham. b 47. S'wark Ord Course. d 89 p 90. C St Helier *S'wark* 89-93; P-in-c Thornton Heath St Paul 93-96; V 96-98; V Dormansland 98-14; Chapl MU 03-08; AD Godstone *S'wark* 08-12; Dir Ords Croydon Area 96-14; rtd 14; PtO *S'wark* from 14. *14 Went Hill Gardens, Eastbourne BN21 0QP* M: 07866-820547 T: (01323) 502970 E: graham.paddick@gmail.com

PADDISON, Mrs Jennifer Sheila. b 70. Cranmer Hall Dur. d 07 p 08. C Newc H Cross 07-11; Chapl Nottm Trent Univ *S'well* from 12. *The Rectory, 27 Cotes Road, Barrow upon Soar, Loughborough LE12 8JP* T: (01509) 412014 E: jenny.paddison@ntu.ac.uk

PADDISON, Canon Michael David William. b 41. Oak Hill Th Coll 75. d 77 p 78. C Gt Warley Ch Ch *Chelmsf* 77-80; C Rayleigh 80-83; R Scole, Brockdish, Billingford, Thorpe Abbots etc *Nor* 83-95; RD Redenhall 89-94; R Reepham, Hackford w Whitwell, Kerdiston etc 95-06; RD Sparham 00-05; Hon Can Nor Cathl 02-06; rtd 06; PtO *Nor* from 06. *4 North Street, Castle Acre, King's Lynn PE32 2BA* T: (01760) 755648 E: paddison@toucansurf.com

PADDISON, Robert Michael. b 70. Cranmer Hall Dur. d 07 p 08. C Whorlton *Newc* 07-11; P-in-c Barrow upon Soar w Walton le Wolds *Leic* from 11. *The Rectory, 27 Cotes Road,*

Barrow upon Soar, Loughborough LE12 8JP T: (01509) 412014 E: rob@paddisons.plus.com

PADDOCK, The Very Revd John Allan Barnes. b 51. Liv Univ BA 74 MA 91 Ox Univ BA 77 MA 81 Glas Univ PhD 05 Cardiff Univ LLM 08 Man Univ PGCE 75 FRSA 94. St Steph Ho Ox 75. d 80 p 81. C Matson *Glouc* 80-82; Asst Chapl Madrid *Eur* 82-83; Chapl R Gr Sch Lanc 83-86; Hon C Blackb Ch Ch w St Matt 83-86; Chapl RAF 86-91; OCM 92-94; Chapl St Olave's Gr Sch Orpington 91-94; PtO *Blackb* 94-97; Chapl R Russell Sch Croydon 97-00; Hon C Bickley *Roch* 97-00; V Folkestone St Pet *Cant* 00-03; Hon Min Can Cant Cathl 01-03; V Glouc St Geo w Whaddon 03-08; Dean Gib *Eur* from 08. *The Deanery, 41 Jumpers Building, Rosia Road, Gibraltar* T: (00350) 200 78377 F: 78463 E: deangib@gibraltar.gi

PADDOCK, Susan. b 54. NTMTC 03. d 06 p 07. NSM Upper Holloway *Lon* 06-11; NSM Upper Clapton St Matt from 13. *53 Morland Mews, London N1 1HN* T: (020) 7609 1299 E: susie.paddock@lcbroadband.co.uk

PADFIELD, Jude. b 75. St Mellitus Coll. d 12 p 13. C St Jas in the City *Liv* from 12. *6 Lady Chapel Close, Liverpool L1 7BZ*

PADFIELD, Stephen James. b 68. Exn Univ BA 90 Univ Coll Dur PGCE 92. Trin Coll Bris BA 00 MA 01. d 01 p 02. C Luton Ch Ch *Roch* 01-05; Chapl R Russell Sch Croydon 05-12; Chapl Dulwich Coll from 12; Hon C Dulwich St Barn *S'wark* from 12. *Dulwich College, Dulwich Common, London SE21 7LD* T: (020) 8693 3601 M: 07747-775385 E: stevepadfield@tiscali.co.uk

PADLEY, Miss Karen. b 68. RGN 89. St Jo Coll Nottm MA 00. d 00 p 01. C Broxtowe *S'well* 00-04; V Marlpool *Derby* from 04; RD Heanor from 13. *All Saints' Vicarage, 85 Ilkeston Road, Heanor DE75 7BP* T: (01773) 712097 E: karen@hpadley.fsnet.co.uk *or* revpadley@fsmail.net

PADLEY, Kenneth Peter Joseph. b 78. Ex Coll Ox BA 00 MA 04. Ripon Coll Cuddesdon BA 03 MSt 04. d 04 p 05. C Cen Swansea *S & B* 04-07; Warden of Ch Hostel and Chapl Ban Univ 07-12; Dir of Ords 11-12; V St Alb St Mich from 12. *St Michael's Vicarage, St Michael's Street, St Albans AL3 4SL* T: (01727) 835037 E: kennethpadley@gmail.com

PADMORE, Lynn Beverley. b 51. EMMTC. d 06 p 07. NSM Beaumont Leys *Leic* 06-09; TV Ascension TM 09-14; rtd 14; PtO *Nor* from 14. *Brightmore, 13 Clifton Way, Overstrand, Cromer NR27 0NG* T: (01263) 576720 E: lynn.padmore@hotmail.co.uk

PAGAN, Canon Keith Vivian. b 37. St Jo Coll Dur BA 60 MA 66. Chich Th Coll 60. d 62 p 63. C Clacton St Jas *Chelmsf* 62-64; C Wymondham *Nor* 64-70; P-in-c Guestwick 70-80; P-in-c Kettlestone 70-79; V Hindolveston 70-80; R Islay *Arg* 80-98; R Campbeltown 80-98; Miss to Seamen 80-98; Can St Jo Cathl Oban 85-98; Can Cumbrae 85-98; Hon Can Cumbrae from 99; rtd 98; LtO *Arg* from 04. *Mariefield, Southend, Campbeltown PA28 6RW* T: (01586) 830310

PAGE, Alan Richard Benjamin. b 38. Univ of Wales (Lamp) BA 60 BSc. St Mich Coll Llan 60. d 62 p 63. C Cardiff St Andr and St Teilo *Llan* 62-64; C Newport St Julian *Mon* 64-67; C Hoxton H Trin w St Mary *Lon* 67-69; C Winchmore Hill H Trin 69-71; V Camden Town St Mich w All SS and St Thos 71-98; Public Preacher 98-02; rtd 02. *7 Four Ash Street, Usk NP15 1BW*

PAGE, David. b 48. Bris Univ BA 70 Leic Univ MA 74 Southn Univ PGCE 74. St Jo Coll Nottm 81. d 83 p 84. C Morden *S'wark* 83-86; V Wimbledon St Luke 86-91; P-in-c Clapham Common St Barn 91-92; V 92-08; rtd 08. *Rye View, The Strand, Winchelsea TN36 4JY* T: (01797) 226524 E: david@ryeview.net

PAGE, David James. b 62. Liv Univ BSc 83 Qu Coll Ox DPhil 87. Trin Coll Bris BA 93 MA 95. d 96 p 97. C Knutsford St Jo and Toft *Ches* 96-99; R Elworth and Warmingham 99-11; V Elworth from 11; RD Congleton from 13. *The Rectory, 2 Taxmere Close, Sandbach CW11 1WT* T: (01270) 762415 E: vicar@stpeters-elworth.org.uk

PAGE, Mrs Dorothy Jean. b 29. Portsm Poly CertEd 50. Ox NSM Course 84. d 87 p 94. NSM Wantage Downs *Ox* from 87. *11 North Street, Marcham, Abingdon OX13 6NG* T: (01865) 391462

PAGE, The Ven Gilbert Alfred Derek. b 35. d 93 p 94. C Launceston St Jo Australia 94-95; P-in-c George Town 95-98; Chapl Bell Bay Miss to Seamen 95-98; Adn Burnie Australia 97-00; R Devonport 98-01; Miss Support Officer 01; rtd 01. *Unit 32/4 Brereton Street, Nowra NSW 2541, Australia* T: (0061) (02) 4422 3403 M: 41-924 1950 E: gandrpage@shoal.net.au

PAGE, Mrs Gill Lydia. b 53. Bp Grosseteste Coll PGCE 91 Derby Lonsdale Coll BCombStuds 85 Sheff Univ BA 12. Yorks Min Course 10. **d** 12 **p** 13. NSM Todmorden w Cornholme and Walsden *Leeds* from 12. *The Vicarage, 7 Fern Valley Chase, Todmorden OL14 7HB* T: (01706) 813180 M: 07974-704374 E: gillpagetod@yahoo.co.uk

PAGE, Gillian Fiona. b 55. Hull Coll of Educn CertEd 76. Cranmer Hall Dur 08. **d** 10 **p** 11. C W Bolton *Man* 10-13; TV Walkden and Lt Hulton from 13. *St Paul's Vicarage, 10 Old Vicarage Gardens, Worsley, Manchester M28 3JR* M: 07866-936323 E: gill91@btopenworld.com

PAGE, Mrs Heather. b 54. **d** 13 **p** 14. NSM Hadley and Wellington Ch Ch *Lich* from 13. *46 Appledore Gardens, Wellington, Telford TF1 1RR* T: (01952) 249165 E: h.page@blueyonder.co.uk

PAGE, Mrs Irene May. b 38. Birm Univ BA 58. NEOC 85. **d** 87 **p** 94. Par Dn Cockfield *Dur* 87-90; Par Dn Waterloo St Jo w St Andr *S'wark* 90-94; C 94-95; R Old Charlton St Thos 95-02; C Charlton 02-03; rtd 03; PtO *Birm* from 14. *40 Wolverton Road, Rednal, Birmingham B45 8RN* T: 0121-460 1745

PAGE, Jacqueline Anne. b 57. SAOMC 96. **d** 99 **p** 00. NSM Stevenage H Trin *St Alb* 99-03; NSM Benington w Walkern 03-06; P-in-c Ardeley and Cottered w Broadfield and Throcking 06-08; PtO 08-13; NSM Stevenage St Andr and St Geo from 13. *5 Sinfield Close, Stevenage SG1 1LQ* T: (01438) 368502

PAGE, Jean. *See* PAGE, Dorothy Jean

PAGE, John Jeremy. b 56. Keble Coll Ox BA 79 MA 82 New Coll Edin BD 86. Edin Th Coll 83. **d** 86 **p** 87. C Wetherby *Ripon* 86-89; TV Wrexham *St As* 89-92; Chapl Hymers Coll Hull 92-98; Chapl Charterhouse Sch Godalming 98-03; TR Hale w Badshot Lea *Guildf* 03-10; R Elstead from 10; V Thursley from 10. *The Rectory, Thursley Road, Elstead, Godalming GU8 6DG* T: (01252) 702640 E: rev.john@elsteadandthursley.org.uk

PAGE, Jonathan Michael. b 58. Ripon Coll Cuddesdon 97. **d** 99 **p** 00. C Littlemore *Ox* 99-02; V Chaddesden St Phil *Derby* 02-09; P-in-c Derby St Mark 07-09; V Chaddesden St Phil w Derby St Mark 09-10; RD Derby N 06-10; P-in-c Belper Ch Ch w Turnditch 10-13; V from 13; C Ambergate and Heage 10-12; RD Duffield from 10. *Christ Church Vicarage, Bridge Street, Belper DE56 1BA* T: (01773) 824974 E: frjonathan@philipandmark.org.uk

PAGE, Judy. b 42. Keele Univ DipEd 63 BA 63 Westmr Coll Ox BTh 02. TISEC 03. **d** 05 **p** 06. C Paisley H Trin and Paisley St Barn *Glas* 05-13; PtO *Win* from 14. *109B Priory Road, Southampton SO17 2JS* T: (023) 8032 1241 E: revjudypage@live.co.uk

PAGE, Lynda Christina. b 55. STETS 04. **d** 07 **p** 08. NSM Blackmoor and Whitehill *Portsm* 07-14; P-in-c Lyng, Sparham, Elsing, Bylaugh, Bawdeswell etc *Nor* from 14. *The Rectory, Rectory Road, Lyng, Norwich NR9 5RA* M: 07790-494296 E: lyn.page@willow-bank.co.uk

PAGE, Mathew James. b 77. WEMTC. **d** 09 **p** 10. NSM Cainscross w Selsley *Glouc* 09-13; NSM Stroud Team from 13. *Fair View, 7 Ebley Road, Stonehouse GL10 2LW* T: (01453) 821202 E: regencypages@googlemail.com

PAGE, Canon Michael John. b 42. K Coll Lon BD 66 AKC 66. **d** 67 **p** 68. C Rawmarsh w Parkgate *Sheff* 67-72; C-in-c Gleadless Valley 72-74; TR Gleadless Valley 74-77; V Lechlade *Glouc* 77-86; RD Fairford 81-86; V Winchcombe, Gretton, Sudeley Manor etc 86-02; Hon Can Glouc Cathl 91-02; RD Winchcombe 94-99; Chapl E Glos NHS Trust 94-02; rtd 02; PtO *Sheff* from 03. *18 Brocco Bank, Sheffield S11 8RR* T: 0114-266 3798 E: pages.brocco18@btinternet.com

PAGE, Owen Richard. b 53. FIBMS 83. Linc Th Coll 89. **d** 91 **p** 92. C Gt Bookham *Guildf* 91-94; V Kings Heath *Pet* 94-99; TR Daventry, Ashby St Ledgers, Braunston etc 99-07; RD Daventry 00-07; ACUPA Link Officer 00-07; CUF Project Officer 00-05; Can Pet Cathl 07; V Todmorden *Wakef* 07-13; P-in-c Cornholme and Walsden 12-13; V Todmorden w Cornholme and Walsden *Leeds* from 13; Asst Dioc Dir of Ords from 09; RD Calder Valley from 13. *The Vicarage, 7 Fern Valley Chase, Todmorden OL14 7HB* T: (01706) 813180 E: owen@todvic55.orangehome.co.uk

PAGE, Teehan Dawson. b 61. Ch Ch Ox BA 83 MA 87 K Coll Lon MA 96. St Steph Ho Ox 91. **d** 93 **p** 94. C Surbiton St Andr and St Mark *S'wark* 93-96; Chapl Reed's Sch Cobham 96-99; Asst Chapl Tonbridge Sch 99-00; Sen Chapl 00-04; Asst Master Westmr Sch from 07. *19 Dean's Yard, London SW1P 3PA*

PAGE, Thomas William. b 57. Sarum & Wells Th Coll 84. **d** 87 **p** 88. C Caterham *S'wark* 87-91; C Cheam 91-95; P-in-c Cranham *Chelmsf* 95-04; R Chingford SS Pet and Paul 04-12; V Chelmsf Ascension 12-14; P-in-c Chelmsf All SS 14; V Chelmsf Ascension w All SS from 14; AD Chelmsf N from 15; Dioc NSM Officer from 99. *Ascension Vicarage, 57 Maltese Road, Chelmsford CM1 2PB* T: (01245) 269906 E: frtom1@priest.com

PAGE, Canon Trevor Melvyn. b 41. Dur Univ BA 63 Fitzw Coll Cam BA 67 MA 72. Westcott Ho Cam 64. **d** 67 **p** 68. C Millhouses H Trin *Sheff* 67-69; Chapl Sheff Univ 69-74; V Doncaster Intake 74-82; Can Res Sheff Cathl 82-00; Dioc Dir of In-Service Tr 82-95; Dioc Dir of Ords and Post-Ord Tr 82-00; R Bradfield 00-06; Hon Can Sheff Cathl 01-06; rtd 06. *39 Benty Lane, Sheffield S10 5NF* T: 0114-268 3879

PAGE, William George. b 42. Linc Th Coll 83. **d** 85 **p** 86. C Boston *Linc* 85-89; V Sibsey w Frithville 89-07; RD Holland E 95-97; rtd 07; PtO *York* from 08. *20 Marshall Drive, Pickering YO18 7JT* T: (01751) 476915

PAGE-CHESTNEY, Michael William. b 47. Linc Th Coll 80. **d** 82 **p** 83. C Barton upon Humber *Linc* 82-85; TV Gt Grimsby St Mary and St Jas 85-91; V E Stockwith 91-96; V Blyton w Pilham and Laughton w Wildsworth 91-93; V Corringham and Blyton Gp 93-03; P-in-c Immingham 03-13; P-in-c Habrough Gp 03-13; P-in-c Keelby Gp 08-13; rtd 13. *4 Ponds Way, Barton-upon-Humber DN18 5AQ* E: mike@page-chestney.co.uk

PAGE-CHESTNEY, Mrs Susan Valerie. b 49. EMMTC. **dss** 86 **d** 87 **p** 94. NSM Gt Grimsby St Mary and St Jas *Linc* 86-91; NSM Blyton w Pilham and Laughton w Wildsworth 91-93; NSM Corringham and Blyton Gp 93-03; Chapl W Lindsey NHS Trust 94-99; Chapl Linc and Louth NHS Trust 99-01; Chapl United Lincs Hosps NHS Trust 01-03; NSM Immingham *Linc* 03-13; NSM Habrough Gp 03-13. *4 Ponds Way, Barton-upon-Humber DN18 5AQ* E: sue@heavenlyhugs.com

PAGE-CLARK, Howard David. b 53. Fitzw Coll Cam MA 77. **d** 97 **p** 98. OLM Lytchett Minster *Sarum* 97-10; OLM The Lytchetts and Upton from 10. *37 Gorse Lane, Poole BH16 5RR* T: (01202) 620239 E: hdpc@talktalk.net

PAGE DAVIES, David John. b 36. St Cath Soc Ox BA 58 MA 62. St D Coll Lamp 58. **d** 60 **p** 61. C Rhosddu *St As* 60-68; Chr Aid Area Sec (Glos, Herefords and Worcs) 68-85; Midl Regional Co-ord 78-85; Area Co-ord (Devon and Cornwall) 86-01; LtO *Truro* 86-01; PtO from 01; rtd 01. *3 Chyenhal Cottages, Buryas Bridge, Penzance TR19 6AN* T: (01736) 732466 E: johnp-d@tiscali.co.uk

PAGE-TURNER, Canon Edward Gregory Ambrose Wilford. b 31. Qu Coll Birm 57. **d** 60 **p** 61. C Helmsley *York* 60-64; C Kensington St Phil Earl's Court Lon 64-67; C Walton-on-Thames *Guildf* 67-70; V Seend *Sarum* 70-71; V Seend and Bulkington 71-79; R Bladon w Woodstock *Ox* 79-87; P-in-c Begbroke 80-86; P-in-c Shipton-on-Cherwell 80-86; P-in-c Hampton Gay 80-85; RD Woodstock 84-87; P-in-c Wootton by Woodstock 85-87; R Patterdale *Carl* 87-89; R Askerswell, Loders and Powerstock *Sarum* 89-01; RD Lyme Bay 92-98; RD Beaminster 94-97; Can and Preb Sarum Cathl 99-01; rtd 01; PtO *Sarum* from 01; B & W 02-05; Eur 02-06. *The Old School House, 9 School House Close, Beaminster DT8 3AH* T: (01308) 861410

PAGET, Alfred Ivor. b 24. St Aid Birkenhead 56. **d** 59 **p** 60. C Hoylake *Ches* 59-62; Chapl Miss to Seamen Hong Kong 62-63; Melbourne Australia 63-64; C Hyde St Geo *Ches* 64-66; R Gt and Lt Henny w Middleton *Chelmsf* 66-74; C Gt Holland 74-79; V Holland-on-Sea 79-92; rtd 92; PtO *S'wark* 92-98; Lon 96-02; *Chelmsf* 99-05. *6 Bary Close, Cheriton Fitzpaine, Crediton EX17 4JY* T: (01363) 860069

PAGET, Richard Campbell. b 54. Collingwood Coll Dur BA 76 Rob Coll Cam BA 87. Ridley Hall Cam 85. **d** 88 **p** 89. C Gipsy Hill Ch Ch *S'wark* 88-92; R Chatham St Mary w St Jo *Roch* 92-98; P-in-c Brenchley 99-00; V from 00; RD Paddock Wood 06-10. *The Vicarage, 8 Broadoak, Brenchley, Tonbridge TN12 7NN* T: (01892) 722140

PAGET, Robert James Innes. b 35. AKC 59. **d** 60 **p** 61. C Attenborough w Bramcote *S'well* 60-63; C Cheltenham St Mark *Glouc* 63-72; P-in-c Pilsley *Derby* 72-73; TV N Wingfield, Pilsley and Tupton 73-89; R Pinxton 89-97; P-in-c Ambergate and Heage 97-05; rtd 06; PtO *Derby* from 06. *1A Jeffries Lane, Crich, Matlock DE4 5DT* T: (01773) 852072

PAGET-WILKES, The Ven Michael Jocelyn James. b 41. ALCD 69. **d** 69 **p** 70. C Wandsworth All SS *S'wark* 69-74; V Hatcham St Jas 74-82; V Rugby St Matt *Cov* 82-90; Adn Warwick 90-09; rtd 09. *64 Tarlton, Cirencester GL7 6PA* T: (01285) 770553 E: michael.pw@btinternet.com

PAGETT, Andrew Stephen. b 45. Bris & Glouc Tr Course. **d** 82 **p** 83. NSM Swindon New Town *Bris* 82-01; C Paignton St Jo *Ex* 01-04; V Lifton, Broadwoodwidger, Stowford etc 04-10; rtd 10. *Merrowlea, Gas Lane, Torrington EX38 7BE* T: (01805) 624313 E: a.pagett@tiscali.co.uk

PAICE, Richard James Rowland. b 72. Ch Ch Ox BA 94 MA 99. Oak Hill Th Coll BA 00. **d** 00 **p** 01. C Eastbourne All So *Chich* 00-03; Chapl Bp Bell Sch 00-03; P-in-c Warbleton and Bodle Street Green *Chich* 03-08; V Wimbledon Park St Luke *S'wark* from 08. *St Luke's Vicarage, 28 Farquhar Road, London SW19 8DA* E: sw19church@gmail.com

PAILING, Crispin Alexander. b 75. Qu Coll Ox BA 98 MA 01 Birm Univ PhD 08. Ripon Coll Cuddesdon BA 02. **d** 03 **p** 04. C Four Oaks *Birm* 03-06; P-in-c Perry Barr 06-10; V 10-14; AD Handsworth 13-14; R Liv Our Lady and St Nic from 14. *St Nicholas' House, 71 Woodlands Road, Aigburth, Liverpool L17 0AL* T: 0151-727 4872
E: crispin.pailing@queens.oxon.org *or* rector@livpc.co.uk

PAILING, Rowena Fay. b 77. Qu Coll Ox BA 99 MA 02 Birm Univ PhD 08. Ripon Coll Cuddesdon BA 02. **d** 03 **p** 04. C Four Oaks *Birm* 03-04; C Gravelly Hill 04-07; P-in-c Handsworth St Mich 07-12; Dir Past Studies Coll of Resurr Mirfield from 12; PtO *Birm* 12-14; *Liv* from 14. *College of the Resurrection, Stocks Bank Road, Mirfield WF14 0BW* T: (01924) 481908 *or* 0151-727 4872 E: rpailing@mirfield.org.uk

PAIN, Canon David Clinton. b 36. K Coll Lon 56. **d** 64 **p** 64. Chapl Ossiomo Leper Settlement and Ika Gr Sch Nigeria 64-67; P-in-c Obuasi St Paul and Kumasi St Paul Ghana 67-70; P-in-c Teshie St Bart 70-86; Chapl Ridge Ch Accra 80-86; Hon Can Accra from 80; V Kemp Town St Mary *Chich* 86-93; Chapl St Mary's Hall Brighton 88-93; V Billingshurst *Chich* 93-05; RD Horsham 98-02; rtd 05; P-in-c Chidham *Chich* 05-11; PtO *Portsm* from 12. *6 Cremorne Place, King George Avenue, Petersfield GU32 3EP* T: (01730) 269510

PAIN, Michael Broughton George. b 37. Dur Univ BA 61. Wycliffe Hall Ox 61. **d** 63 **p** 64. C Downend *Bris* 63-67; C Swindon Ch Ch 67-70; V Alveston 70-78; V Guildf Ch Ch 78-90; TR Melksham *Sarum* 90-98; Chapl Melksham Hosp 90-91; Chapl Wilts Healthcare NHS Trust 92-98; TR Redhorn *Sarum* 98-03; rtd 03; PtO *Sarum* from 03. *Framfield, 10 Marie Road, Dorchester DT1 2LE* T: (01305) 213469

✠**PAIN, The Rt Revd Richard Edward.** b 56. Bris Univ BA 79 Univ of Wales (Cardiff) BD 84. St Mich Coll Llan 81. **d** 84 **p** 85 **c** 13. C Caldicot *Mon* 84-86; P-in-c Cwmtillery 86-88; V 88-91; V Six Bells 88-91; V Risca 91-98; V Overmonnow w Wonastow and Michel Troy 98-03; V Monmouth w Overmonnow etc 03-08; Adn Mon 08-13; P-in-c Mamhilad w Monkswood and Glascoed Chapel 08-13; Warden of Ords 01-06; Can St Woolos Cathl 03-13; Bp Mon from 13. *Bishopstow, Stow Hill, Newport NP20 4EA* T: (01633) 263510
E: bishop.monmouth@churchinwales.org.uk

PAINE, Alasdair David MacConnell. b 60. Trin Coll Cam BA 82 MA 86 MSc 84. Wycliffe Hall Ox 94. **d** 96 **p** 97. C Ex St Leon w H Trin 96-01; V Westbourne Ch Ch Chpl *Win* 02-11; V Cambridge H Sepulchre *Ely* from 11. *The Round Church Vicarage, Manor Street, Cambridge CB1 1LQ* T: (01223) 518218 E: alasdair@claranet.co.uk *or* alasdair.paine@stag.org

PAINE, Peter Stanley. b 46. K Coll Lon BD 69 AKC 69. Cuddesdon Coll 69. **d** 71 **p** 72. C Leeds St Aid *Ripon* 71-74; C Harrogate St Wilfrid 74-78; V Beeston Hill H Spirit 78-82; TV Seacroft 82-90; V Martham w Repps w Bastwick *Nor* 90-94; V Martham and Repps w Bastwick, Thurne etc 94-04; P-in-c Foremark and Repton w Newton Solney *Derby* 04-08; V 08-11; rtd 11. *Beachway House, 27 Stratford Close, Southport PR8 2RT* E: peterspaine@gmail.com

PAINE, William Barry. b 58. CITC. **d** 84 **p** 85. C Glendermott *D & R* 84-86; C Lurgan St Jo *D & D* 86-88; I Kilbarron w Rossnowlagh and Drumholm *D & R* 88-91; CF 91-00; I Tynan w Middletown and Aghavilly *Arm* 00-09; I Ballinderry, Tamlaght and Arboe from 09. *The Rectory, 10 Brookmount Road, Cookstown BT80 0BB* T: (028) 7941 8500
E: bpaine.888@hotmail.co.uk

PAINTER, Christopher Mark. b 65. Cranmer Hall Dur. **d** 00 **p** 01. C Melksham *Sarum* 00-03; Chapl Wilts and Swindon Healthcare NHS Trust 02-03; TV Eccles *Man* 03-07; PtO *Ches* 13-14; NSM Hale Barns w Ringway 14-15; P-in-c Calstock *Truro* from 15; P-in-c St Dominic, Landulph and St Mellion w Pillaton from 15. *Oaklands House, Albaston, Gunnislake PL18 9EZ* E: revchrispainter@gmail.com

PAINTER, The Ven David Scott. b 44. Worc Coll Ox BA 68 MA 72 LTCL 65. Cuddesdon Coll 68. **d** 70 **p** 71. C Plymouth St Andr w St Paul and St Geo *Ex* 70-73; Chapl Plymouth Poly 71-73; C St Marylebone All SS *Lon* 73-76; Abp's Dom Chapl and Dir of Ords *Cant* 76-80; V Roehampton H Trin *S'wark* 80-91; RD Wandsworth 85-90; PV Westmr Abbey 81-91; Can Res and Treas S'wark Cathl 91-00; Dioc Dir of Ords 91-00; Adn Oakham and Can Res Pet Cathl 00-11; rtd 11; Hon C Towcester Deanery from 11. *3 Meeting Lane, Towcester NN12 6JX* T: (01327) 438392

PAINTER, John. b 25. Selw Coll Cam BA 48 MA 53. Ripon Hall Ox 48. **d** 50 **p** 51. C Stoke Newington St Mary *Lon* 50-55; C Woodside Park St Barn 55-56; C Llangiwg *S & B* 56-59; C-in-c Swansea St Mark and St Jo 59-60; R Chipstable w Raddington *B & W* 61-64; V Audenshaw St Steph *Man* 64-66; V Sandown Ch Ch *Portsm* 66-72; R Keinton Mandeville *B & W* 72-77; P-in-c Lydford-on-Fosse 76-77; R Keinton Mandeville w Lydford on Fosse 77-90; RD Cary 81-90; RD Bruton 82-85; rtd 90; PtO *B & W* 90-05; *Sarum* from 96. *2 Juniper Gardens, Gillingham SP8 4RF* T: (01747) 823818

PAINTING, Stephen Nigel. b 60. Trin Coll Bris 01. **d** 03 **p** 04. C Heanton Punchardon w Marwood *Ex* 03-08; TV Beaconsfield *Ox* 08-11; Chapl Lee Abbey 11-14; TV Wellington and Distr *B & W* from 14. *The Vicarage, 62 Rockwell Green, Wellington TA21 9BX* T: (01823) 662742
E: s.painting@btinternet.com

PAIRMAN, David Drummond. b 47. GGSM CertEd. Chich Th Coll 82. **d** 84 **p** 85. C Cowes St Mary *Portsm* 84-87; C Marshwood Vale *Sarum* 87-88; C Hawkchurch 87-88; C Marshwood Vale 88-95; rtd 95. *Chestnut Cottage, Old Pinn Lane, Exeter EX1 3RF* T: (01392) 464488

PAISEY, Gerald Herbert John. b 31. Wm Booth Memorial Coll 51 Leic Univ CertEd 62 Nottm Univ DipAdEd 70 MPhil 77 Lanc Univ MA 78 K Coll Lon PhD 91. St Alb Minl Tr Scheme 80. **d** 88 **p** 90. NSM Montrose *Bre* 88-90; NSM Inverbervie 88-90; Lect Robert Gordon Univ *Ab* 89-97; P-in-c Stonehaven and Catterline *Bre* 90-01; rtd 01; Tutor Open Univ 90-05; PtO *Bre* 03-07; LtO *Edin* from 08. *40 South Middleton, Uphall, Broxburn EH52 5GB* T: (01506) 865937

PAISEY, Canon Jeremy Mark. b 58. Aber Univ LLB 81 Solicitor 83. Coates Hall Edin 92. **d** 94 **p** 95. C Turriff *Ab* 94-97; C Buckie 94-97; C Banff 94-97; C Cuminestown 94-97; C Portsoy 94-97; P-in-c Buckie from 97; P-in-c Portsoy from 97; P-in-c Banff from 98; Can St Andr Cathl from 08. *All Saints' Rectory, 14 Cluny Square, Buckie AB56 1HA* T: (01542) 832312 M: 07817-261435 E: jpaisey@aol.com

PAISLEY, Canon Samuel Robinson (Robin). b 51. Man Univ BSc 72. Edin Th Coll BD 91. **d** 91 **p** 92. C St Mary's Cathl 91-95; P-in-c Bishopbriggs 95-06; Teaching Consultant Glas Univ 95-99; Chapl Stobhill NHS Trust 95-99; Bp's Adv in Min *Glas* 99-07; R Dumfries from 06; Chapl NHS Dumfries and Galloway from 06; Can St Mary's Cathl from 06. *8 Newall Terrace, Dumfries DG1 1LW* T: (01387) 254126
E: rector@stjohnsdumfries.org

PAJUNEN, Mika Kari Tapani. b 76. Helsinki Univ MTh 00. **p** 01. C Helsinki *Eur* 02-04; Asst Chapl 05-12. *Kivikarintie 3, 21570 Sauvo, Finland* T: mika.pajunen@helsinki.fi

PAKENHAM, Charles Wilfrid. b 18. Trin Coll Ox BA 40 MA 52. Wycliffe Hall Ox 40. **d** 41 **p** 42. C Sutton *Liv* 41-44; CMS 44-49; Nigeria 44-49; C Cheltenham St Mary *Glouc* 49-52; V Litherland Ch Ch *Liv* 52-84; rtd 84; PtO *Sarum* from 90; P-in-c W Woodhay w Enborne, Hampstead Marshall etc *Ox* 91-92; PtO 92-00. *15 Cook Road, Marlborough SN8 2EG* T: (01672) 540531 E: cepak@btinternet.com

PAKISTAN, Moderator of the Church of. *See* MALIK, The Rt Revd Alexander John

PALIN, Elizabeth. b 62. Hull Univ BA 85 Birm Univ MA 11. WEMTC 08. **d** 11 **p** 12. Dir Glenfall Ho *Glouc* 08-13; NSM N Cheltenham 11-13; C from 13. *The Rectory, Rectory Lane, Swindon Village, Cheltenham GL51 9RD* T: (01242) 575547 E: liz.palin@northchelt.org.uk

PALIN, Roy. b 34. Man Univ BA 56. Ripon Hall Ox 65. **d** 67 **p** 68. C Ilkeston St Mary *Derby* 67-70; C Wollaton *S'well* 70-71; V Harby w Swinethorpe 71-79; V Thorney w Wigsley and Broadholme 71-79; P-in-c N Clifton 75-79; R Harby w Thorney and N and S Clifton 79-80; V Tuxford 80-81; P-in-c Laxton 80-81; P-in-c Markham Clinton 80-81; P-in-c Weston 80-81; V Tuxford w Weston and Markham Clinton 81-90; R Nuthall 90-99; rtd 99; PtO *Nor* from 00. *31 Pine Walk, Weybourne, Holt NR25 7HJ* T: (01263) 588146

PALK, Deirdre Elizabeth Pauline. b 41. Reading Univ BA 63 Lon Univ MA 94 Leic Univ PhD 02 AIL 77 FIOSH 96 FRHistS 06. S'wark Ord Course 81. **dss** 84 **d** 87. Wanstead H Trin Hermon Hill *Chelmsf* 84-88; Hon Par Dn 87-88; Hon Par Dn Walthamstow St Pet 88-93; Hon Chapl UPA Projects 93-97; Tutor NTMTC 97-01; rtd 01. *3 Ashdon Close, Woodford Green IG8 0EF* T: (020) 8498 0649

PALLANT, Canon Roger Frank. b 35. Trin Coll Cam BA 57 MA 61. Wells Th Coll 57. **d** 59 **p** 60. C Stafford St Mary *Lich* 59-62; C Ipswich St Mary le Tower *St E* 62-65; Dioc Youth Chapl 62-65; Development Officer C of E Youth Coun 65-70; Hon C Putney St Mary *S'wark* 66-71; Org Sec New Syn Gp 70-71; R Hintlesham w Chattisham *St E* 71-80; V Ipswich All Hallows 80-88; Hon Can St E Cathl 85-00; P-in-c Sproughton w Burstall 88-00; Dioc Officer for OLM 88-00; RD Samford 93-99; rtd 00; PtO *St E* from 00. *163 Fircroft Road, Ipswich IP1 6PT* T: (01473) 461148

PALLENT, Ian. b 70. Newc Poly BA 91. Ridley Hall Cam 05. **d** 07 **p** 08. C Bayston Hill *Lich* 07-10; R Jersey St Ouen w St Geo *Win* from 10. *The Rectory, La Route du Marais, St Ouen, Jersey JE3 2GG* T: (01534) 481800 *or* 485686 M: 07870-630433 E: ianpallent@hotmail.com

PALLETT, Ian Nigel. b 59. Leeds Univ BA 80. Linc Th Coll 81. **d** 84 **p** 85. C Halesowen *Worc* 84-88; C Mansfield Woodhouse *S'well* 88-91; R Morton and Stonebroom *Derby* 91-98; P-in-c Heanor 98-01; V 01-03; P-in-c Dingwall *Mor* from 03; P-in-c Strathpeffer from 03. *The Parsonage, 4 Castle Street, Dingwall IV15 9HU* T: (01349) 862204
E: pallett3000@btinternet.com

PALLIS, Mrs Maria. b 60. NOC 96. **d** 99 **p** 00. C Chapel Allerton *Ripon* 99-03; P-in-c Collingham w Harewood 03-11; P-in-c Spofforth w Kirk Deighton 07-11; V Banstead *Guildf* from 11; RD Epsom 14. *The Vicarage, 21 Court Road, Banstead SM7 2NQ* T: (01737) 351134 E: mariapallis@hotmail.com

PALMER, Alister Gordon. b 46. Univ of Tasmania BA 73 DipEd 74. Trin Coll Bris 76 Ridley Hall Cam 78. **d** 80 **p** 81. C Patchway *Bris* 80-83; C Bushbury *Lich* 83-86; V Wednesfield Heath 86-93; NSM Independent Ch Community Work 93-98; Dioc Officer for Min Tas Australia 98-02; Dir Angl Miss 99-02; C Smestow Vale *Lich* 02-03; V Knowle St Barn *Bris* 03-07; P-in-c Inns Court H Cross 05-07; V Filwood Park 07-13; rtd 13. *4 Rowberrow, Bristol BS14 0AD* T: (01275) 832208
E: agpal46@btopenworld.com

PALMER, Andrew. b 84. St Chad's Coll Dur BA 06. Oak Hill Th Coll MA 14. **d** 14 **p** 15. C Hampstead St Jo Downshire Hill Prop Chpl *Lon* from 14. *19 Parliament Court, Parliament Hill, London NW3 2TS* M: 07866-584293
E: andy.palmer@live.com

PALMER, Angus Douglas. b 40. St Chad's Coll Dur BA 62. **d** 63 **p** 64. C Wallsend St Pet *Newc* 63-66; C Newc H Cross 66-69; C Bottesford *Linc* 69-70; R Penicuik *Edin* 70-84; R W Linton 77-84. *6 Hackworth Gardens, Wylam NE41 8EJ* T: (01661) 853786

PALMER, Carol Lesley. St Mellitus Coll 13. **d** 14 **p** 15. OLM Southend St Sav Westcliff *Chelmsf* from 14. *11 Crowstone Avenue, Westcliff-on-Sea SS0 8HT* T: (01702) 330188
E: carol@mandarin-enterprises.co.uk

PALMER, Christopher John Ingamells. b 71. **d** 98 **p** 99. C Emscote *Cov* 98-02; TV Mortlake w E Sheen *S'wark* 02-10; AD Richmond and Barnes 05-10; TR Merton Priory from 10. *The Vicarage, 1 Trinity Road, London SW19 8QT* T: (020) 8542 2313 E: christopherpalmer@blueyonder.co.uk

PALMER, David Edward. *See* HAGAN-PALMER, David Edward

PALMER, David Michael. b 53. QUB BA 95 MSc. CITC 95. **d** 97 **p** 98. C Glenageary *D & G* 97-99; C Agherton *Conn* 99-00; I Ramoan w Ballycastle and Culfeightrin 00-10; I Magherally w Annaclone *D & D* from 10. *Magherally Rectory, 46 Kilmacrew Road, Banbridge BT32 4EP* T: (028) 4062 5625 M: 07591-382599 E: david.palmer@cantab.net

PALMER, Canon David Philip. b 50. Sarum & Wells Th Coll. **d** 84 **p** 85. C St Ives *Ely* 84-86; C Luton All SS w St Pet *St Alb* 86-88; V Stocksbridge *Sheff* 88-97; P-in-c Seaton Hirst *Newc* 97-98; TR 98-08; R from 08; Chapl Northd Coll from 99; Hon Can Newc Cathl from 15. *The Vicarage, Newbiggin Road, Ashington NE63 0TQ* T: (01670) 813218

PALMER, Derek James. b 54. Man Univ BA 77. Qu Coll Birm 77. **d** 79 **p** 80. C Leek *Lich* 79-83; CF 83-92; R Riviera Beach St Geo USA 92-95; C S Ockendon and Belhus Park *Chelmsf* 95-98; V Walthamstow St Mich 98-00; Chapl Salford Univ *Man* 00-06; AD Salford 02-03; P-in-c Droylsden St Andr 06-09; TR Oldham 09-11; V Oldham St Mary w St Pet from 11; Bp's Adv on New Relig Movements from 02. *The Rectory, Prince Charlie Street, Oldham OL1 4HJ* T: 0161-633 4847 M: 07504-953670 E: derek_palmer@hotmail.co.uk

PALMER, Elizabeth. *See* BLATCHLEY, Elizabeth

PALMER, Graham. b 31. Em Coll Cam BA 53 MA 57. Qu Coll Birm 56. **d** 58 **p** 59. C Camberwell St Giles *S'wark* 58-61; C Kilburn St Aug *Lon* 61-67; P-in-c Fulham St Alb 67-73; V 73-92; V Fulham St Alb w St Aug 92-97; rtd 97; PtO *Lon* 97-13. *7 Wellington Court, 116 Knightsbridge, London SW1X 7PL* T: (020) 7584 4036

PALMER, Hugh. b 50. Pemb Coll Cam BA 72 MA 76. Ridley Hall Cam 73. **d** 76 **p** 77. C Heigham H Trin *Nor* 76-80; Bp's Chapl for Tr and Miss 80-84; C St Helen Bishopsgate w St Andr Undershaft etc *Lon* 85-95; C Fulwood *Sheff* 95-97; V 97-05; Hon Can Sheff Cathl 01-05; R Langham Place All So *Lon* from 05; Chapl to The Queen from 12. *12 Weymouth Street, London W1W 5BY* T: (020) 7580 3522
E: ramona.ramsahadeo@allsouls.org

PALMER, The Ven Ian Stanley. b 50. K Coll Lon BD 71. Cranmer Hall Dur 73. **d** 75 **p** 76. C Huyton St Mich *Liv* 75-78; Chapl Dur Univ 78-83; V Collierley w Annfield Plain 83-90; Dir Evang Newc Australia 90-92; R Belmont N and Redhead 93-00; Adn Upper Hunter and R Muswellbrook 00-05; R Queanbeyan from 05; Adn Chapl from 09; Adn S Canberra and Queanbeyan from 09. *39 Rutledge Street, PO Box 103,* *Queanbeyan NSW 2620, Australia* T: (0061) (2) 6299 3920 *or* 6299 3917 F: 6299 1360 M: 41-124 2596
E: palmeris50@fastmail.fm

PALMER, John Richard Henry. b 29. AKC 52. **d** 53 **p** 54. C Englefield Green *Guildf* 53-57; P-in-c Brewarrina Australia 57-62; C Wareham w Arne *Sarum* 62-63; PC Derby St Jo 63-66; Chapl Holloway Sanatorium Virginia Water 66-70; Chapl Brookwood Hosp Woking 70-94; rtd 94; PtO *Truro* from 94. *Lightning Ridge, Pentreath Road, The Lizard, Helston TR12 7NY* T: (01326) 290654
E: vsp@oldlizardhead.freeserve.co.uk

PALMER, Judith Angela. b 47. Bris Univ MB, ChB 71. NOC 02. **d** 05 **p** 06. NSM Strensall *York* 05-14; PtO from 14. *6 Portisham Place, Strensall, York YO32 5AZ* T: (01904) 613356
E: j.palmer@phonecoop.coop

PALMER, Mrs June Ann. b 42. **d** 11 **p** 12. OLM Elmton and Whitwell *Derby* 11-14; OLM E Scarsdale from 14. *22 Field Drive, Shirebrook, Mansfield NG20 8BN* T: (01623) 744835

PALMER, Kevin Anthony. b 59. St Steph Ho Ox. **d** 01 **p** 02. C Tunstall *Lich* 01-04; R Wednesbury St Jas and St Jo 04-13; V Longton St Mary and St Chad from 13; CMP from 02. *St Mary and St Chad's Presbytery, 269 Anchor Road, Stoke-on-Trent ST3 5DN* T: (01782) 313142
E: frkevinpalmer@live.co.uk

PALMER, Malcolm Leonard. b 46. Sarum & Wells Th Coll 80. **d** 82 **p** 83. C Cannock *Lich* 82-85; Chapl RAF 85-89; Asst Chapl HM Pris Dur 89-90; Chapl HM YOI Hewell Grange 90-93; Chapl HM Rem Cen Brockhill 90-93; Chapl HM Pris Blakenhurst 93-01; Miss P Kugluktuk Canada 01-04; R Meadows from 04. *Box 3631, RR 2, Corner Brook NL A2H 6B9, Canada* T: (001) (709) 783 2194 F: 783 3093
E: atanck@excite.com

PALMER, Marc Richard. b 72. St Jo Coll Dur BA 96. Cranmer Hall Dur 93. **d** 98 **p** 99. C Chester le Street *Dur* 98-03; TV Bensham 03-08; V Bensham and Teams 08-10; V Nor St Mary Magd w St Jas from 10. *St Mary Magdalene Vicarage, 10 Crome Road, Norwich NR3 4RQ* T: (01603) 661381
E: emnk@talktalk.net

PALMER, Marion Denise. b 42. Open Univ BA 82 SRN 64 SCM 66. Linc Th Coll 84. **dss** 86 **d** 87 **p** 94. Poplar *Lon* 86-90; Par Dn 87-90; Par Dn Gillingham St Mary *Roch* 90-94; C 94-96; C Farnborough 96-02; rtd 02; PtO *St E* from 04. *14 Prestwick Avenue, Felixstowe IP11 9LF* T: (01394) 671588

PALMER, Canon Maureen Florence. b 38. Qu Eliz Coll Lon BSc 60 PhD 64. Ripon Coll Cuddesdon. **dss** 85 **d** 87 **p** 94. Tupsley *Heref* 85-88; C 87-88; Par Dn Talbot Village *Sarum* 88-91; Chapl Birm Cathl 91-96; Can Pastor and Can Res Guildf Cathl 96-06; Sub-Dean 99-06; rtd 06; PtO *Heref* from 06. *28A Green Street, Hereford HR1 2QG* T: (01432) 353771
E: drmaureenpalmer@btinternet.com

PALMER, Michael Christopher. b 43. MBE 00. AKC 67 CQSW 76. **d** 68 **p** 69. C Easthampstead *Ox* 68-71; Miss to Seamen 71-73; Hong Kong 73; LtO *Ox* 76-79; *Truro* 79-83; Dioc Soc Resp Adv 83-98; Bp's Dom Chapl 85-87; V Devoran 87-98; rtd 98; PtO *Truro* 98-08; *Ox* 08-10. *5 Little Drove, Singleton, Chichester PO18 0HD* T: (01243) 811540

PALMER, Mrs Patricia. b 41. STETS. **d** 09 **p** 10. NSM Basingstoke *Win* from 09. *97 Packenham Road, Basingstoke RG21 8YA* T: (01256) 412986 E: pat.palmer@ntlworld.com

PALMER, Canon Peter Malcolm. b 31. Chich Th Coll 56. **d** 59 **p** 60. C Leighton Buzzard *St Alb* 59-63; C Apsley End 63-65; C Hitchin H Sav 65-69; R Ickleford 69-76; V Oxhey St Matt 76-86; V Kensworth, Studham and Whipsnade 86-96; Hon Can *St Alb* 94-96; rtd 97; PtO *St Alb* from 97; Bp's Retirement Officer 97-10. *4 Sefton Close, St Albans AL1 4PF* T: (01727) 763196

PALMER, Peter Parsons. b 27. **d** 59 **p** 61. SSJE from 59; Miss at Bracebridge Canada 59-79; PtO *Leic* 80-86; *Lon* 86-94; LtO 94-02. *College of St Barnabas, Blackberry Lane, Lingfield RH7 6NJ*

PALMER, Philip Edward Hitchen. b 35. St Jo Coll Cam MA 61 DipAdEd 74. Ridley Hall Cam 61 EAMTC 87. **d** 90 **p** 91. NSM Gt Oakley w Wix *Chelmsf* 90-96; NSM Gt Oakley w Wix and Wrabness 96-00; PtO from 00. *Glebe House, Wix Road, Great Oakley, Harwich CO12 5BJ* T: (01255) 880737

PALMER, Robert William. b 28. Wells Th Coll 63. **d** 65 **p** 66. C Earlsdon *Cov* 65-69; P-in-c Cov St Mark 69-71; Chapl Cov and Warks Hosp 69-71; Hon C Binley *Cov* 72-76; V Sheff St Paul 76-84; V Deepcar 84-93; rtd 93; PtO *Sheff* 93-12. *Moorlands, 26 Coal Pit Lane, Stocksbridge, Sheffield S36 1AW*

PALMER, Steven Roy. b 51. Birm Univ BSc 71. WMMTC 91. **d** 94 **p** 95. C Sheldon *Birm* 94-97; P-in-c Duddeston w Nechells 97-99; V Nechells 99-03; R Billing *Pet* from 03; RD Northn 06-07. *The Rectory, 25 Church Walk, Great Billing, Northampton NN3 4ED* T: (01604) 788508 F: 401641
E: stevenrpalmer@hotmail.com

PALMER, Canon Terence Henry James. b 34. Univ of Wales (Lamp) BA 55 LTh 57 St Edm Hall Ox BA 65 MA 69 FRSA 08. **d** 57 **p** 58. C Griffithstown *Mon* 57-60; Min Can and C St D Cathl 60-63; PtO *Ox* 63-65; *B & W* 63-65; C Monmouth *Mon* 65-69; C-in-c St Hilary Greenway CD 69-72; R Portskewett and Rogiet w Llanfihangel Rogiet 72-00; RD Netherwent 89-00; Dir NSM Studies 91-99; Can St Woolos Cathl 96-00; rtd 00; PtO *Eur* from 99; LtO *Mon* from 00; P-in-c Newport St Teilo from 03. *Terleen, 12 Windsor Park, Magor, Caldicot NP26 3NJ* T: (01633) 881927 E: kathypalmer.1@virgin.net

PAMMENT, Gordon Charles. b 31. TCD BA 54. Linc Th Coll 56. **d** 58 **p** 60. C Hemel Hempstead *St Alb* 58-63; C Gedney Drove End *Linc* 63-65; I Macroom Union *C, C & R* 65-72; I Rathcormac Union 72-77; I Fermoy Union 78-91; Can Ross Cathl 89-91; Can Cork Cathl 89-91; rtd 91. *Magoola, Dripsey, Co Cork, Republic of Ireland* T: (00353) (21) 451 6532

PAMPHILON-GREEN, Sister Phaedra Kay. b 64. Anglia Ruskin Univ MA 12. St Mellitus Coll 12. **d** 14 **p** 15. C Gainsborough and Morton *Linc* from 14. *St George's Vicarage, Heapham Road, Gainsborough DN21 2JE* M: 07775-954144 E: pamphilon@googlemail.com

PAMPLIN, Canon Richard Lawrence. b 46. Lon Univ BScEng 68 Dur Univ BA 75 NY Th Sem DMin 85. Wycliffe Hall Ox 75. **d** 77 **p** 78. C Greenside *Dur* 77-80; C Sheff St Barn and St Mary 80-84; R Wombwell 84-90; P-in-c Madeley *Heref* 90-91; TR 91-01; Chapl Berne w Neuchâtel *Eur* 01-07; Can Gib Cathl 04-07; Chapl Viña del Mar w Valparaiso Chile 07-12; rtd 12; PtO *Cant* from 12. *126 Downs Road, Folkestone CT19 5PX* T: (01303) 779126 E: richard.l.pamplin@gmail.com

PAMPLIN, Samantha Jane. *See* FERGUSON, Samantha Jane

PANG, Mrs Heather Marian. b 46. St Jo Coll Nottm BA 08. SNWTP 09. **d** 11 **p** 12. NSM Gt Saughall *Ches* from 11. *20 Oakland Drive, Wirral CH49 6JL* T: 0151-677 2690 E: wingonheather@gmail.com

PANG, Wing-On. b 43. Manitoba Univ BA 67 SOAS Lon MA 70. Oak Hill Th Coll 85. **d** 87 **p** 88. C Pennycross *Ex* 87-91; TV Mildenhall *St E* 91-96; Assoc P Kowloon St Andr Hong Kong 96-08; rtd 08; PtO *Ches* from 09. *20 Oakland Drive, Wirral CH49 6JL* T: 0151-677 2690 E: wingonheather@gmail.com

PANGBOURNE, John Godfrey. b 36. Ridley Hall Cam 82. **d** 84 **p** 85. C Ashtead *Guildf* 84-88; V Ore Ch Ch *Chich* 88-03; rtd 03; PtO *Ex* 04-06; Hon C Ottery St Mary, Alfington, W Hill, Tipton etc from 06. *Meon Croft, Toadpit Lane, West Hill, Ottery St Mary EX11 1TR* T: (01404) 812393

PANKHURST, Donald Araunah. b 28. Qu Coll Birm. **d** 64 **p** 65. C Pemberton St Jo *Liv* 64-68; V Aspull 68-76; R Newchurch 76-88; R Winwick 88-94; rtd 94; PtO *Carl* from 94. *Hunters Hill, Spooner Vale, Windermere LA23 1AU* T: (015394) 46390

PANKHURST, Ian Charles. b 50. Trin Cath Cam BA 72 Lon Inst of Educn PGCE 88. SAOMC 01. **d** 04 **p** 05. C Watford St Luke *St Alb* 04-10; P-in-c Watford St Andr 10-13; V from 13. *2 Albert Road North, Watford WD17 1QE* T: (01923) 249139 E: ian_pankhurst@btinternet.com

PANNETT, Peter George. b 44. **d** 11. NSM Brighton St Geo w St Anne and St Mark *Chich* 11-13; NSM Portslade St Nic and St Andr and Mile Oak from 13. *Flat 4, 20 Bristol Road, Brighton BN2 1AP* T: (01273) 694023 E: peter.pannett712@gmail.com

PANTER, The Ven Richard James Graham. b 48. Oak Hill Th Coll 73. **d** 76 **p** 77. C Rusholme H Trin *Man* 76-80; C Toxteth St Cypr w Ch Ch *Liv* 80-85; V Clubmoor 85-96; P-in-c Litherland St Jo and St Jas 96-02; AD Bootle 99-02; V Orrell Hey St Jo and St Jas 02-11; Adn Liv from 02. *115 Papillon Drive, Liverpool L9 9HL* T: 0151-705 2154 E: ricky.panter@liverpool.anglican.org

PANTER MARSHALL, Canon Susan Lesley. b 49. Portsm Poly BSc 72. S Dios Minl Tr Scheme 88. **d** 91 **p** 94. NSM Southover *Chich* 91-95; C Iford w Kingston and Rodmell 95-98; C Hollington St Jo 98-02; P-in-c Herstmonceux and Wartling 02-07; R 07-10; Can and Preb Chich Cathl 07-10; rtd 10. *Glebe Farm, Woolfardisworthy, Crediton EX17 4RX* T: (01363) 866853 E: suandnigel@gmail.com

PANTING, Nigel Roger. b 47. St Pet Coll Ox BA 69 PGCE 70. Local Minl Tr Course 06. **d** 11. NSM Ruskington Gp *Linc* 11-13; NSM N Lafford Gp from 13. *The Cottage, Roxholm, Sleaford NG34 8NE* T: (01526) 832020 M: 07866-808737 E: nigelpanting@yahoo.co.uk

PANTLING, Rosemary Caroline. b 60. Ex Coll Ox BA 83 MA 89 Anglia Poly Univ MA 03 Birm Univ PGCE 84. EAMTC 98. **d** 01 **p** 02. NSM Bishop's Tachbrook *Cov* 01-08; P-in-c Cubbington 08-10; PtO from 10. *22 Touchstone Road, Heathcote, Warwick CV34 6EE* M: 07846-220974 E: kevinandrosemary@pantling.demon.co.uk

PANTON, Alan Edward. b 45. K Coll Lon BD 67 AKC 67. **d** 68 **p** 69. C Eltham St Jo *S'wark* 68-73; C Horley 73-78; V Dallington *Pet* 78-07; rtd 07; PtO *Pet* from 09. *28 Riverstone*

Way, Northampton NN4 9QH T: (01604) 755421 E: rev.panton@virgin.net

PANTRY, John Richard. b 46. Oak Hill NSM Course 90. **d** 93 **p** 94. NSM Alresford *Chelmsf* 93-04; NSM W w E Mersea 04-10; NSM W w E Mersea, Peldon, Gt and Lt Wigborough from 10. *48 Empress Avenue, West Mersea, Colchester CO5 8EX* T/F: (01206) 386910 E: johnpantry@fsmail.net

PAPADOPULOS, Canon Nicholas Charles. b 66. G&C Coll Cam BA 88 MA 92 Barrister-at-Law (Middle Temple) 90. Ripon Coll Cuddesdon. **d** 99 **p** 00. C Portsea N End St Mark *Portsm* 99-02; Bp's Dom Chapl *Sarum* 02-07; Hon Chapl 07-10; V Pimlico St Pet w Westmr Ch Ch *Lon* 07-13; Can Res Cant Cathl from 13; Dir IME 4-7 from 13. *15 The Precincts, Canterbury CT1 2EL* M: 07903-620018

PAPANTONIOU, Ms Frances Caroline. b 52. S Dios Minl Tr Scheme 89. **d** 92 **p** 94. Par Dn Harrow Weald All SS *Lon* 92-94; C 94-95; C Preston Ascension 95-98; Assoc V Wembley Park 98-99; TV 99-04; V Horton Kirby and Sutton-at-Hone *Roch* 04-12; rtd 12. *Sampsons Hall, Norman Road, Eastchurch, Sheerness ME12 4EU* T: (01795) 880297 E: fpapantoniou@aol.com

PAPE, David. b 54. **d** 98 **p** 99. OLM S'wark St Geo w St Alphege and St Jude from 98; OLM Waterloo St Jo w St Andr from 98. *10 Stopher House, Webber Street, London SE1 0RE* T: (020) 7928 3503

PAPE, Timothy Vernon Francis. b 39. OBE . Lon Univ BSc 63. Wells Th Coll 63. **d** 65 **p** 66. C Pershore w Wick *Worc* 65-69; PtO *Bris* 69-73; NSM Southbroom *Sarum* 75-08; Hd Master Chirton Primary Sch Wilts from 81; Dir Gen Shaw Trust from 90. *Mallards, Chirton, Devizes SN10 3QX* T: (01380) 840593

PAPWORTH, Daniel John. b 69. Plymouth Poly BSc 90. Trin Coll Bris BA 98 MA 00. **d** 99 **p** 00. C Gabalfa *Llan* 99-02; PtO *B & W* 03-04; Asst Chapl Dudley Gp of Hosps NHS Trust 04-07; Chapl R Devon and Ex NHS Foundn Trust 07-08; TV N Cheltenham *Glouc* 08-13; PtO from 13. *7 Campden Road, Cheltenham GL51 6AA* T: (01242) 575649 E: papworth@gmail.com

PAPWORTH, John. b 21. Lon Univ BSc(Econ). **d** 75 **p** 76. Zambia 76-81; Hon C Paddington St Sav *Lon* 81-83; Hon C St Marylebone St Mark Hamilton Terrace 85-97; PtO *Bris* from 01. *The Fourth World, The Close, 26 High Street, Purton, Swindon SN5 4AE* T: (01793) 772214 F: 772521

PAPWORTH, Miss Shirley Marjorie. b 33. CA Tr Coll. **d** 88 **p** 94. Par Dn Hornchurch H Cross *Chelmsf* 88-93; rtd 93; Chapl Havering Primary Care Trust 93-08; NSM Hornchurch St Andr *Chelmsf* 93-08; PtO from 08. *39 Heron Flight Avenue, Hornchurch RM12 5LN* T: (01708) 524348 E: sm.papworth@btinternet.com

PARAGUAY, Bishop of. *See* BARTLETT, The Rt Revd Peter

PARBURY, Mrs Heather Christina Winifred. b 56. **d** 01 **p** 02. C Long Compton, Whichford and Barton-on-the-Heath *Cov* 01-05; C Barcheston 01-05; C Cherington w Stourton 01-05; C Wolford w Burmington 01-05; TV Cherwell Valley *Ox* 05-08; P-in-c Pangbourne w Tidmarsh and Sulham 08-10; R from 10; Chapl MU from 10. *The Rectory, St James's Close, Pangbourne, Reading RG8 7AP* T: 0118-984 2928 E: parbury@btinternet.com

PARE, Stephen Charles. b 53. Sussex Univ BEd 75. St Mich Coll Llan 78. **d** 80 **p** 81. C Cardiff St Jo *Llan* 80-83; P-in-c Marcross w Monknash and Wick 83; TV Llantwit Major 83-91; V Penmark w Porthkerry 91-06; P-in-c Llansantffraid, Bettws and Aberkenfig from 06; Chapl Cardiff Wales Airport from 93. *The Paddock, Derllwyn Road, Tondu, Bridgend CF32 9HD* T: (01656) 716828 E: scpare@googlemail.com

PARES, John. b 57. Bedf Coll Lon BA 79. Westcott Ho Cam 08. **d** 10 **p** 11. C Diss *Nor* 10-14; P-in-c Pokesdown St Jas *Win* from 14. *St James's Vicarage, 12 Harewood Avenue, Bournemouth BH7 6NQ* M: 07972-075459 E: j.pares@virginmedia.com

PARFFETT, Allan John. b 51. Open Univ BA 97 CQSW 76. Qu Coll Birm MA 00. **d** 98 **p** 99. C Hall Green Ascension *Birm* 98-00; Soc Worker 00-09; rtd 09. *20 Kiln Close, Corfe Mullen, Wimborne BH21 3UR* T: (01202) 690164

PARFITT, Anthony Colin. b 44. Ox Univ Inst of Educn CertEd 66 Open Univ BA 71 Plymouth Poly MPhil 84. SWMTC 93. **d** 96 **p** 97. NSM Langport Area *B & W* 96-00; NSM Bruton and Distr 01-06; PtO from 07. *Tile Hill Cottage, North Brewham, Bruton BA10 0JT* T: (01749) 850177 M: 07930-144522 E: tonyparfitt@btinternet.com

PARFITT, Brian John. b 49. Ex Coll Ox BA 71 MA 76. Wycliffe Hall Ox 71. **d** 74 **p** 75. C Newport St Mark *Mon* 74-78; R Blaina 78-83; R Blaina and Nantyglo 83-86; Chapl Blaina and Distr Hosp Gwent 83-86; Regional Consultant (W Midlands and Wales) CPAS 86-95; V Magor w Redwick and Undy *Mon* 95-98; TR Magor 98-06; Local Min Officer *Glouc* 06-14; P-in-c Highnam, Lassington, Rudford, Tibberton etc 14-15; rtd 15. *9 Red Admiral Drive, Abbeymead, Gloucester GL4 5EA*   M: 07847-359062   T: (01452) 621979   E: brianparfitt@btinternet.com

PARFITT, David George. b 65. De Montfort Univ Leic BA 87. Wycliffe Hall Ox BTh 92. **d** 95 **p** 96. C Malpas *Mon* 95-98; C Bassaleg 98-00; TV 00-01; V Malpas from 01. *The Vicarage, Malpas Road, Newport NP20 6GQ*   T: (01633) 852047

PARFITT, George Rudolf William. b 54. WMMTC 96. **d** 99 **p** 00. OLM Highnam, Lassington, Rudford, Tibberton etc *Glouc* 99-08; NSM Hardwicke and Elmore w Longney from 08. *66 Holbeach Drive, Kingsway, Quedgeley, Gloucester GL2 2BF*   T: (01452) 728180   E: george.parfitt@btinternet.com

PARFITT, Preb John Hubert. b 29. Southn Univ MA 72 BPhil. Qu Coll Birm 78. **d** 80 **p** 81. C Fladbury, Wyre Piddle and Moor *Worc* 80-82; C Malvern Link w Cowleigh 82; V Hanley Castle, Hanley Swan and Welland 82-83; Dir RE *B & W* 84-93; Preb Wells Cathl 85-05; rtd 93; PtO *B & W* from 93; Master Hugh Sexey's Hosp Bruton 95-05. *3 Willow Farm Cottages, Brister End, Yetminster, Sherborne DT9 6NH*   T: (01935) 873260   E: passitatwillow@btinternet.com

PARFITT, Susan Mary. b 42. Bris Univ BA 63 CertEd 68. Bris Minl Tr Scheme 82. **dss** 84 **d** 87 **p** 94. Assoc Dir of Ords *Bris* 84-86; CME Officer 87-91; Dir Past Care and Counselling *S'wark* 91-01; rtd 01; PtO *Bris* from 02. *Brook End, Rectory Gardens, Bristol BS10 7AQ*   T: 0117-959 0293

PARGETER, Canon Muriel Elizabeth. b 28. St Mich Ho Ox 53. **dss** 82 **d** 87 **p** 95. Dioc Dir of Ords *Roch* 87-90; Hon Can Roch Cathl 87-90; rtd 90; Hon C Worthing Ch the King *Chich* 95-03; PtO from 03. *63 Pavilion Road, Worthing BN45 7EE*   T: (01903) 214476

PARISH, Mrs Mary Eileen. b 48. Nottm Univ BA 70. STETS BTh 98. **d** 98 **p** 99. NSM Worthing Ch the King *Chich* 98-08; NSM Worthing St Matt from 08. *The Heritage, 10 Winchester Road, Worthing BN11 4DJ*   T: (01903) 236909   E: frmary@theheritage.freeserve.co.uk

PARISH, Revd Nicholas Anthony. b 58. Oak Hill Th Coll BA 84 Kingston Univ MA 97. Ridley Hall Cam 84. **d** 86 **p** 87. C Eltham H Trin *S'wark* 86-89; C Barnes St Mary 89-91; V Streatham St Paul 91-96; Ind Chapl *Ox* 96-07; P-in-c Bracknell 07-14; AD 04-12; Hon Can Ch Ch 08-14; P-in-c Epsom St Martin *Guildf* from 14. *35 Burgh Heath Road, Epsom KT17 4LP*   E: nick.parish@ntlworld.com

PARISH, Canon Stephen Richard. b 49. Liv Univ MTh 05. Oak Hill Th Coll 74. **d** 77 **p** 78. C Chadderton Ch Ch *Man* 77-81; C Chell *Lich* 81-82; TV 82-88; V Warrington St Ann *Liv* 88-14; P-in-c Warrington H Trin 06-14; V Warrington H Trin and St Ann 14-15; Hon Can Liv Cathl 14-15; rtd 15. *26 Leamington Close, Warrington WA5 3PY*   M: (07909) 001399   E: bloovee@outlook.com

PARK, Christopher John. b 62. Sheff Poly BA 83. Cranmer Hall Dur 00. **d** 02 **p** 03. C Didsbury St Jas and Em *Man* 02-08; P-in-c Alne *York* from 08; P-in-c Brafferton w Pilmoor, Myton-on-Swale etc from 08. *Monk Green House, Main Street, Alne, York YO61 1TB*   T: (01347) 838122   E: pastaparko@tiscali.co.uk

PARK, John Charles. b 55. St Pet Coll Ox BA 77 St Mary's Coll Newc PGCE 81. Cranmer Hall Dur 00. **d** 02 **p** 03. C Morpeth *Newc* 02-06; R Bothal and Pegswood w Longhirst from 06; AD Morpeth from 13. *Bothal Rectory, Longhirst Road, Pegswood, Morpeth NE61 6XF*   T: (01670) 510793   E: john.park53@yahoo.co.uk

PARK, Tarjei Erling Alan. b 64. W Lon Inst of HE BA 88 Lanc Univ MA 89 Pemb Coll Ox DPhil 96. Ripon Coll Cuddesdon 92. **d** 94 **p** 95. C Lancaster St Mary w St John and St Anne *Blackb* 94-98; V Enfield St Mich *Lon* 98-01; Asst Dir Post-Ord Tr 98-03; V Golders Green 01-06; C St Pancras w St Jas and Ch Ch 06-08; rtd 09; PtO *Lon* from 12. *22 Colman Court, Christchurch Avenue, London N12 0DT*   T: (020) 8445 7985   M: 07929-465991   E: tarjei.park@pmb.oxon.org

PARK, Trevor. b 38. MBE 05. Lon Univ BA 64 Open Univ PhD 90 Lambeth STh 81. Linc Th Coll 64. **d** 66 **p** 67. C Crosthwaite Kendal *Carl* 66-68; Asst Chapl Solihull Sch 69-71; Chapl St Bees Sch and V St Bees *Carl* 71-77; V Dalton-in-Furness 77-84; V Natland 84-97; Hon Can Carl Cathl 86-97; RD Kendal 89-94; Chapl Oslo w Bergen, Trondheim and Stavanger *Eur* 97-05; rtd 05; P-in-c St Petersburg *Eur* 06-07; PtO *Carl* from 09. *20 Seacroft Drive, St Bees CA27 0AF*

PARKER, Angus Michael Macdonald. b 53. Bris Univ BSc 74. St Jo Coll Nottm 80. **d** 83 **p** 84. C Northampton St Giles *Pet* 83-86; C Attenborough *S'well* 86-96; V Pennycross *Ex* 96-09; P-in-c Bitterne *Win* from 09. *The Vicarage, 2 Bursledon Road, Southampton SO19 7LW*   T: (023) 8044 0493   E: angus@mmparker.wanadoo.co.uk

PARKER, Mrs Ann Jacqueline. b 41. Dur Inst of Educn TCert 63 Sunderland Poly TCert 65 Open Univ BA 82. WEMTC 91. **d** 95 **p** 96. NSM Pilning w Compton Greenfield *Bris* 95-98; NSM Almondsbury and Olveston 98-03; Asst Chapl N Bris

NHS Trust from 98. *Wyngarth, Easter Compton, Bristol BS35 5RA*   T: (01454) 632329   E: annatdibley@aol.com

PARKER, Anne Elizabeth. *See* MARR, Anne Elizabeth

PARKER, Anne Margaret. *See* HINDLE, Anne Margaret

PARKER, Mrs Brenda. b 36. **d** 00 **p** 01. OLM Eccleston Ch Ch *Liv* 00-06; rtd 06. *22 Selkirk Drive, Eccleston, St Helens WA10 5PE*   T: (01744) 757495

PARKER, Brian William. b 39. Ulster Univ BA 88. CITC 99. **d** 01 **p** 02. NSM Knock *D & D* 01-02; NSM Glencraig from 02. *7 Cairnsville Park, Bangor BT19 6EW*   T: (028) 9145 4549   F: 9147 1804   E: bwparker@ukgateway.net

PARKER, David Anthony. b 38. St Chad's Coll Dur BA 62. **d** 64 **p** 65. C Palmers Green St Jo *Lon* 64-65; C Kenton 65-71; C W Hyde St Thos *St Alb* 71-75; P-in-c Brinksway *Ches* 76-80; V 80-83; V Weston 83-92; NSM Cheadle Hulme All SS 97-98; C Offerton 98-00; TV Crosslacon *Carl* 00-02; rtd 02; C Cheadle Hulme All SS *Ches* from 02. *77 Station Road, Cheadle Hulme, Cheadle SK8 7BG*   T: 0161-485 4451

PARKER, David Charles. b 53. St Andr Univ MTheol 75 Univ of Leiden DTh 90. Ridley Hall Cam 75. **d** 77 **p** 78. C Hendon St Paul Mill Hill *Lon* 77-80; C Bladon w Woodstock *Ox* 80-85; C-in-c Shipton-on-Cherwell 80-85; C-in-c Begbroke 80-85; C-in-c Hampton Gay 80-85; Lect Qu Coll Birm 85-93; Sen Angl Tutor 89-93; Lect Birm Univ 93-96; Sen Lect 96-98; Reader in NT Textual Criticism and Palaeography from 98. *Dumbleton Cottage, 24 Church Street, Bromyard HR7 4DP*   T: 0121-415 2415   E: d.c.parker@bham.ac.uk

PARKER, Canon David John. b 33. St Chad's Coll Dur BA 55 Hull Univ MA 85. Linc Th Coll 57. **d** 59 **p** 60. C Tynemouth Ch Ch *Newc* 59-60; C Ponteland 60-63; C Byker St Mich 63-64; C-in-c Byker St Martin CD 64-69; V Whorlton 69-73; TR 73-80; Ind Chapl *Linc* 80-84; Master Newc St Thos Prop Chpl 84-89; Exec Officer Dioc Bd for Ch and Soc *Man* 90-98; Lic Preacher 90-98; Hon Can Man Cathl 97-98; rtd 98; PtO *Newc* from 98. *4 The Kylins, Morpeth NE61 2DJ*   T: (01670) 516218   E: davidparker12@sky.com

PARKER, David John. b 57. Qu Coll Birm 12. **d** 15. NSM Selly Oak St Mary *Birm* from 15. *1 Spirehouse Lane, Blackwell, Bromsgrove B60 1QE*   T: 0121-445 1901   E: davidparker124@btinternet.com

PARKER, Canon David Louis. b 47. Lon Univ LLB 70. Wycliffe Hall Ox BA 79 MA 82. **d** 80 **p** 81. C Broadwater St Mary *Chich* 80-84; TR Ifield 84-97; R Lavant 97-12; RD Chich 01-06; Can and Preb Chich Cathl 03-12; rtd 12. *6 Queens Gate, 1 Osborne Road, Southsea PO5 3LX*

PARKER, David William. b 21. SEN CQSW MBASW. Glouc Th Course 77 Sarum & Wells Th Coll 81. **d** 81 **p** 81. Chapl HM Pris Leyhill 81-84; NSM Cromhall w Tortworth *Glouc* 81-83; NSM Wickwar w Rangeworthy 83-87; PtO 88-01. *22 Durham Road, Charfield, Wotton-under-Edge GL12 8TH*   T: (01454) 260253

PARKER (née JOHNSON), Mrs Emma Louise. b 82. St Mary's Coll Dur BA 05 MA 06. Ridley Hall Cam 07. **d** 09 **p** 10. C Cockfield *Dur* 09-12; C Lynesack 09-12; C Evenwood 09-12; C Easington and Easington Colliery 12-14; P-in-c from 14. *3 The Grange, South Side, Peterlee SR8 3AX*   E: emma.parker@durham.anglican.org

PARKER, George William. b 29. Univ of K Coll Halifax NS BS 53 BD 57 Lon Univ PGCE 67. **d** 53 **p** 54. C Calgary Cathl Canada 53-55; I Cardston 55-59; C W Hackney St Barn *Lon* 59-61; V Haggerston St Mary w St Chad 61-68; Teacher St Adele Canada 68-71; C Portsea N End St Mark *Portsm* 72-75; V Darlington St Jo *Dur* 75-78; R Des Monts Canada 78-81; R Digby 81-87; R Rawdon 87-91; rtd 91. *c/o T Parker Esq, 7 McNeil Street, Dartmouth NS B2Y 2H2, Canada*

PARKER, Hugh James. b 30. ACP 55 TCD MA 57 Ulster Univ DASE 74. **d** 63 **p** 64. LtO *Conn* 63-70 and 96-01; Dioc C 70-96; Hd Master Larne High Sch 71-92; rtd 96. *25 Ballykillaire Terrace, Bangor BT19 1GS*   T: (028) 9185 7142

PARKER, Janet Elizabeth. b 54. Cranmer Hall Dur 05. **d** 07 **p** 08. C Sale St Anne *Ches* 07-10; V High Lane from 10; RD Chadkirk from 11. *35 Martlet Avenue, Disley, Stockport SK12 2JH*   T: (01663) 764519   E: janetparker1@homecall.co.uk

PARKER, Mrs Joanna Caroline. b 63. UEA BA 95 Leeds Univ MA 07 RGN 85 RM 92. NOC 04. **d** 07 **p** 08. C Pocklington Wold York 07-11; V Hyde St Geo *Ches* from 11. *The Vicarage, 85 Edna Street, Hyde SK14 1DR*   T: 0161-478 2608   E: joanna.parker@tinyworld.co.uk

PARKER, John. *See* PARKER, Linsey John Owen

PARKER, John Bristo. b 26. Edin Th Coll 61. **d** 64 **p** 65. C Barrow St Jo *Carl* 64-68; V Sledmere *York* 68-74; V Sledmere and Wetwang w Cowlan 74-79; R Cowlam 68-74; P-in-c Wetwang 69-74; V Kirkby Ireleth *Carl* 79-83; V Rillington w Scampston, Wintringham etc *York* 83-87; R Bishop Wilton w Full Sutton, Kirby Underdale etc 87-91; rtd 91; PtO *York* 91-11. *10 Easterfield Court, Driffield YO25 5PP*   T: (01377) 256582

PARKER, John David. b 61. Ridley Hall Cam 00. **d** 02 **p** 03. C Aston cum Aughton w Swallownest and Ulley *Sheff* 02-06; TV Rugby *Cov* 06-12; V Newbold Pacey w Moreton Morrell from 12; R Lighthorne from 12; V Chesterton from 12. *The Rectory, Lighthorne, Warwick CV35 0AR* E: parkersuk@aol.com

PARKER, Julian Roderick. b 57. Essex Univ BA 80. Sarum & Wells Th Coll 91. **d** 93 **p** 94. C Gillingham *Sarum* 93-97; V N Bradley, Southwick and Heywood 97-08; V N Bradley, Southwick, Heywood and Steeple Ashton from 08. *The Vicarage, 62 Church Lane, North Bradley, Trowbridge BA14 0TA* T: (01225) 752635 E: julianparker22@hotmail.com

PARKER, Justin Trevelyan. b 71. Reading Univ LLB 92. WEMTC 11. **d** 12 **p** 13. NSM Cleobury Mortimer w Hopton Wafers etc *Heref* from 12. *6 Orchard End, Cleobury Mortimer, Kidderminster DY14 8BA* T: (01299) 270603 M: 07932-606420 E: justin.parker@mfgsolicitors.com

PARKER, Linsey John Owen. b 70. Oriel Coll Ox BA 91 Lon Univ PGCE 94. Oak Hill Th Coll 02. **d** 05 **p** 06. C Arborfield w Barkham *Ox* 05-12; P-in-c Fordham *Chelmsf* from 12. *Fordham Hall, Church Road, Fordham, Colchester CO6 3NL* T: (01206) 243261 M: 07976-433107 E: johnandmim@bigfoot.com *or* john.parker@fordhamchurch.org.uk

PARKER, Canon Lynn. b 54. SS Mark & Jo Univ Coll Plymouth BEd 94. SWMTC 04. **d** 07 **p** 08. NSM S Hill w Callington *Truro* 07-10; P-in-c Antony w Sheviock 10-15; P-in-c Torpoint 10-15; R Antony w Sheviock from 12; C Maker w Rame and St John w Millbrook 12-15; V Antony w Sheviock and Torpoint from 15; Hon Can Truro Cathl from 15. *The Vicarage, 3 Grove Park, Torpoint PL11 2PP* T: (01752) 815412 E: parker3@hotmail.com

PARKER, Miss Margaret. b 27. Lightfoot Ho Dur 54. **dss** 60 **d** 87 **p** 94. Ryhope *Dur* 56-61; Monkwearmouth St Andr 61-79; Adv for Accredited Lay Min 74-87; *Newc* 79-87; Newc St Geo 79-87; C 87; rtd 87; PtO *Dur* 87-12; *Newc* 87-12; Tutor Cranmer Hall Dur 87-92; Hon C Dur Cathl 87-94; Min Can Dur Cathl 94-97; Chapl St Mary's Coll Dur 95-98. *c/o P Davies Esq, 16 The College, Durham DH1 3EQ*

PARKER, Margaret Grace. *See* TORDOFF, Margaret Grace

PARKER, The Ven Matthew John. b 63. Man Univ BA 85 SS Coll Cam BA 88. Ridley Hall Cam 85. **d** 88 **p** 89. C Twickenham St Mary *Lon* 88-91; Chapl Stockport Gr Sch 91-94; C Stockport St Geo *Ches* 91-93; P-in-c Stockport St Mark 93-94; TV Stockport SW 94-00; TR Leek and Meerbrook *Lich* 00-13; RD Leek 07-13; Adn Stoke from 13. *39 The Brackens, Newcastle ST5 4JL* T: (01782) 663066 E: matpark01@aol.com

PARKER, Michael. b 54. **d** 07. C Ebbw Vale *Mon* 07-09; Hon C Llanhilleth w Six Bells 09-10; Hon C Abertillery w Cwmtillery w Llanhilleth etc from 10. *43 Drysiog Street, Ebbw Vale NP23 6DE* T: (01495) 304193 E: mikeparker54@googlemail.com

PARKER, Michael Alan. b 70. St Jo Coll Dur BA 91. CITC BTh 93. **d** 96 **p** 97. C Dundela St Mark *D & D* 96-00; I Carnalea from 00. *St Gall's Rectory, 171 Crawfordsburn Road, Bangor BT19 1BT* T: (028) 9185 3366 *or* 9185 3810 E: carnalea@down.anglican.org *or* stgalloffice@btconnect.com

PARKER, Canon Michael John. b 57. BSc Nottm Univ MA 04. Wycliffe Hall Ox 80. **d** 83 **p** 84. C Heigham H Trin *Nor* 83-86; C Muswell Hill St Jas w St Matt *Lon* 86-90; R Bedford St Jo and St Leon *St Alb* 90-98; V Knowle *Birm* from 98; AD Solihull 04-09; Hon Can Birm Cathl from 05. *The Vicarage, 1811 Warwick Road, Knowle, Solihull B93 0DS* T/F: (01564) 773666 T: 778802 F: 779123 E: vicar@knowleparishchurch.org.uk

PARKER, Michael John. b 54. Cam Coll of Art and Tech BA 76 Lon Univ BD 85. Trin Coll Bris 82. **d** 85 **p** 86. C Leic H Trin w St Jo 85-88; P-in-c Edin Clermiston Em 88-90; I Edin St Thos 90-03; Can St Mary's Cathl 94-03; NSM Edin St Paul and St Geo 03-06; Gen Sec Evang Alliance Scotland 03-06; Middle E Dir Middle E Chr Outreach 06-09; Sen Min All SS Cathl Cairo from 09; PtO *Edin* from 06. *4 Liberton Place, Edinburgh EH16 6NA* E: revmikecairo@gmail.com *or* mikeparker@f2s.com

PARKER, Nicolas. *See* PARKER, Robert Nicolas

PARKER, Nigel Howard. b 69. St Jo Coll Dur BSc 90. CITC BTh 97. **d** 97 **p** 98. C Holywood *D & D* 97-00; Outreach Development Officer Think Again 00-04; I Bangor St Comgall from 04. *The Rectory, 2 Raglan Road, Bangor BT20 3TL* T: (028) 9145 7203 E: nigel@parkers123.plus.com

PARKER, Philip Vernon. b 60. Birm Univ BSc 82 PGCE 83 Heythrop Coll Lon MA 09. Wycliffe Hall Ox 89. **d** 90 **p** 91. C Walkergate *Newc* 90-93; Chapl Shiplake Coll Henley 93-96; C Lindfield *Chich* 97-99; Team Ldr Titus Trust 99-04; Chapl Cranleigh Sch Surrey 04-12; CF (TA) 97-05; P-in-c Frimley Green and Mytchett *Guildf* from 13. *The Vicarage, Sturt Road, Frimley Green, Camberley GU16 6HY* T: (01252) 835179 E: minister@st-andrewschurch.org.uk

PARKER, Canon Richard Bryan. b 64. Sheff Poly BA 87. Coll of Resurr Mirfield 92. **d** 95 **p** 96. C Norton *Sheff* 95-98; C Hoyland 98-00; V Moorends 00-08; V Hoyland from 08; Dioc Warden of Readers 10-13; Hon Can Sheff Cathl from 10. *The Vicarage, 104 Hawshaw Lane, Hoyland, Barnsley S74 0HH* T: (01226) 749231 E: r.b.parker@btinternet.com

PARKER, Richard Frederick. b 36. Oak Hill Th Coll 72. **d** 74 **p** 75. C Wootton *St Alb* 74-76; C Hove Bp Hannington Memorial Ch *Chich* 76-81; R Northwood *Portsm* 81-88; V W Cowes H Trin 81-88; V Aldershot H Trin *Guildf* 88-98; R Spaxton w Charlynch, Goathurst, Enmore etc *B & W* 98-03; rtd 03. *47 Banneson Road, Nether Stowey, Bridgwater TA5 1NS* T: (01278) 733883

PARKER, Robert. b 43. Lon Univ BSc 65. Cuddesdon Coll. **d** 67 **p** 68. C Sheff St Cuth 67-70; Asst Chapl Cheltenham Coll 70-74; R Yate *Glouc* 74-76; R Bris 76-77; TR Yate New Town 77-80; C of E Development Officer 80-83; NSM Pool Quay *St As* 99-07; P-in-c 99-04; PtO *Lich* 08-10; *St As* from 14. *Tedsmore Hall, Tedsmore, West Felton, Oswestry SY11 4HD* T: (01691) 610628 E: rgparker@tedsmorehall.co.uk

PARKER, Robert Lawrence. b 34. ALCD 59. **d** 59 **p** 60. C Chippenham St Paul *Bris* 59-61; C Swindon Ch Ch 61-63; New Zealand 63-71; P-in-c Over Stowey w Aisholt *B & W* 71-73; V Nether Stowey 71-73; V Nether Stowey w Over Stowey 73-93; RD Quantock 87-93; V Pitminster w Corfe 93-99; rtd 99; PtO *B & W* from 00. *Oratia, 9 Brookfield Way, Street BA16 0UE* T: (01458) 442906 E: bvparker@uwclub.net

PARKER, Robert Nicolas. b 71. Nottm Univ BA 93 PGCE 95. Ridley Hall Cam 95. **d** 98 **p** 99. C Yardley St Edburgha *Birm* 98-02; Asst P Eugene St Mary USA 02-05; P-in-c Coleshill *Birm* 05-08; V from 08; P-in-c Maxstoke 05-08; V from 11; Bp's Ecum Adv from 12. *The Vicarage, High Street, Coleshill, Birmingham B46 3BP* T: (01675) 462188 E: nickthevicparker@btinternet.com

PARKER, Roger Thomas Donaldson. b 55. Simon Fraser Univ BC BA 80 Univ of Wales (Cardiff) LLB 84 Univ Coll Lon LLM 85. Coll of Resurr Mirfield 95. **d** 95 **p** 96. C Swinton and Pendlebury *Man* 95-02; V Burnley St Cath w St Alb and St Paul *Blackb* from 02. *St Catherine's Parsonage, 156 Todmorden Road, Burnley BB11 3ER* T: (01282) 424587 F: 458579 M: 07977-291166 E: frrogerparker@aol.com

PARKER, Roland John Graham. b 48. AKC 72 Hull Univ BA(Ed) 83. St Aug Coll Cant 71. **d** 74 **p** 75. C Linc St Faith and St Martin w St Pet 74-78; V Appleby 78-84; Ind Chapl 78-84; V N Kelsey 84-92; V Cadney 84-92; P-in-c Waddington 92-97; R 97-11; rtd 11. *29 Castle Street, Kirkcudbright DG6 4JD* T: (01557) 330317 E: rolapark2@btinternet.com

PARKER, Russell Edward. b 48. Man Univ BA 80. St Jo Coll Nottm MTh 82. **d** 81 **p** 82. C Walmsley *Man* 81-85; V Coalville and Bardon Hill *Leic* 85-90; Dir Acorn Chr Foundn 90-14; Internat Ambassador from 14. *Acorn Christian Foundation, Whitehill Chase, Bordon GU35 0AP* T: (01420) 478121 E: rparker@acornchristian.org

PARKER, Stephen. b 88. Ches Univ BA 09. St Steph Ho Ox BA 12. **d** 13 **p** 14. C Worksop Priory *S'well* from 13. *6 Conrad Close, Worksop S80 2EN* T: (01909) 282283 E: stephen.parker88@gmail.com

PARKER, Stephen George. b 65. Birm Univ BEd 89 MA 97 PhD 03. Qu Coll Birm 96. **d** 98. Teaching Asst Westhill Coll of HE Birm 98-01; Sen Lect Th Univ Coll Ches 01-04; Hd RS Cadbury Sixth Form Coll 04-08; Hd Postgraduate Studies in Educn Worc Univ 08-12. *Address temp unknown*

PARKER, Stephen John. b 47. **d** 10 **p** 11. OLM Werrington and Wetley Rocks *Lich* from 10. *11 Tollbar Road, Werrington, Stoke-on-Trent ST9 0JG* T: (01782) 851933 E: stephen.parker690@ntlworld.com

PARKER, Thomas Henry Louis. b 16. Em Coll Cam BA 38 MA 42 BD 50 DD 61. Lon Coll of Div 38. **d** 39 **p** 40. C Chesham St Mary *Ox* 39-42; C Cambridge St Phil *Ely* 42-43; C Cambridge St Andr Less 43-45; C Luddesdowne *Roch* 45-47; V Brothertoft *Linc* 48-55; R Lt Ponton w Stroxton 55-59; R Lt Ponton 59-61; R Gt Ponton 58-61; V Oakington *Ely* 61-71; Lect Dur Univ 71-81; rtd 81; PtO *Ely* 97-00. *Ceriogh, Flaggoners Green, Bromyard HR7 4QR* T: (01885) 489307

PARKER, Canon Thomas Richard. b 52. Imp Coll Lon BScEng 73 Keele Univ MEd 83. Cranmer Hall Dur. **d** 94 **p** 95. C Chadkirk *Ches* 94-08; RD 04-08; P-in-c Stalybridge H Trin and Ch Ch 08-11; V from 11; Hon Can Ches Cathl from 13. *277 Mottram Road, Stalybridge SK15 2RT* T: 0161-303 1984 E: tomparker121@gmail.com

PARKER, Timothy James. b 82. Ch Ch Ox MPhys 05. Wycliffe Hall Ox BA 09. **d** 10 **p** 11. C Gamston and Bridgford *S'well* 10-13; P-in-c E and W Leake, Stanford-on-Soar, Rempstone etc from 13. *The Rectory, 3 Bateman Road, East Leake, Loughborough LE12 6LN* T: (01509) 852228 M: 07963-550964 E: vicar@ourbenefice.org

PARKER, Timothy Percy. b 58. Man Univ BA. St Jo Coll Nottm. **d** 85 **p** 86. C Pitsmoor Ch Ch *Sheff* 85-87; C Kimberworth 87-89; C Brightside w Wincobank 89-91; C Upper Armley *Ripon* 91-95; TV Billingham St Aid *Dur* 95-97; V Billingham St Luke 97-12; Chapl Harrogate and Distr NHS Foundn Trust from 12. *Harrogate District Hospital, Lancaster Park Road, Harrogate HG2 7SX* T: (01423) 885959
E: timparker17@googlemail.com

PARKER-McGEE, Robert Thomas. b 78. Leeds Univ BA 10. Coll of Resurr Mirfield 07. **d** 10 **p** 11. C Gornal and Sedgley *Worc* 10-14; P-in-c Geddington w Weekley *Pet* from 14. *The Vicarage, 25 West Street, Geddington, Kettering NN14 1BD* M: 07588-801593 E: rparkermcgee@gmail.com

PARKERSON, Trevor Richard. b 46. Qu Coll Birm 06. **d** 08 **p** 09. NSM Ashby-de-la-Zouch and Breedon on the Hill *Leic* from 08; PtO *Lich* from 14. *36 Ashby Road, Woodville, Swadlincote DE11 7BY* T: (01283) 225408 E: trp@gofast.co.uk

PARKES, Arthur Burnham. b 42. Univ of Wales MSc 72 PhD 76 FIBiol 94 LTCL 82. St Mich Coll Llan 11. **d** 12 **p** 13. NSM Cyncoed *Mon* from 12. *17 Bramshill Drive, Pontprennau, Cardiff CF23 8NX* T: (029) 2048 1970 M: 07950-454926
E: arthur.b.parkes@virginmedia.com

PARKES, Mrs Celia Anne. b 50. STETS 06. **d** 09 **p** 10. NSM Burslackdon *Win* 09-11; NSM Southampton (City Cen) 11-15; NSM Margaretting w Mountnessing and Buttsbury *Chelmsf* from 15; NSM Ingatestone w Fryerning from 15. *The Vicarage, Penny's Lane, Margaretting, Ingatestone CM4 0AH*
E: m.parkes345@btinternet.com

PARKES, Edward Patrick. b 58. Crewe & Alsager Coll BEd 80 Ban Univ MTh 11. SWMTC 10. **d** 11 **p** 12. Dioc Miss Resources Adv *Ex* from 11; NSM Dawlish 11-12; NSM Ex Cathl 12-14; C Yelverton, Meavy, Sheepstor and Walkhampton from 14; C Sampford Spiney w Horrabridge from 14; Tutor SWMTC from 14. *The Rectory, St Paul's Church, Yelverton PL20 6AB* T: (01822) 859092 *or* (01392) 294960 M: 07960-102001
E: patrick.parkes@exeter.anglican.org

PARKES, Jack Christopher. b 53. **d** 15. NSM Cleckheaton *Leeds* from 15. *29 Huntington Crescent, Leeds LS16 5RT* T: 0113-443 7383 E: jackparkes29@gmail.com

PARKES, Kevin. b 62. Trent Poly BA 84. Sarum & Wells Th Coll BTh 90. **d** 88 **p** 89. C Wandsworth St Anne *S'wark* 88-92; USPG 92-95; Trinidad and Tobago 93-95; Kingston Area Miss Team *S'wark* 95-01; V Wandsworth Common St Mary 01-09; AD Tooting 07-09; Chapl Univ Coll Lon Hosps NHS Foundn Trust 09-13; Chapl Hillingdon Hosps NHS Foundn Trust 13-14; Chapl King's Coll Hosp NHS Foundn Trust from 14. *King's College Hospital, Denmark Hill, London SE5 9RS* T: (020) 3299 9000 E: bloomsbury1@hotmail.com

PARKES, Patrick. *See* PARKES, Edward Patrick

PARKHILL, Alan John. b 43. TCD BA 66. CITC 68. **d** 67 **p** 68. C Knockbreda *D & D* 67-70; Asst Warden Elswick Lodge Newc 71-72; C Bangor St Comgall *D & D* 73-78; Bp's C Kilmore 78-81; I Kilmore and Inch 82-86; I Clonfeacle w Derrygortreavy *Arm* 86-09; rtd 09. *1 Rodney Park, Bangor BT19 6FN* T/F: (028) 9147 3916
E: aparkhill1@btinternet.com

PARKIN, Christopher. *See* PARKIN, Melvyn Christopher

PARKIN, George David. b 37. Cranmer Hall Dur BA 60. **d** 62 **p** 63. C Balderstone *Man* 62-65; C Tunstead 65-67; C Gateshead Fell *Dur* 69-73; CMS Nigeria 74-76; V Walton Breck *Liv* 80-92; V Rawtenstall St Mary *Man* 92-07; P-in-c Constable Lee 02-07; rtd 07; PtO *Man* 08. *174 Bury Road, Rawtenstall, Rossendale BB4 6DJ*
E: pamandco@googlemail.com

PARKIN, Gillian Elizabeth. b 48. Heref Coll of Educn CertEd 69. Trin Coll Bris. **d** 13 **p** 14. OLM By Brook *Bris* from 13; OLM Colerne w N Wraxall from 13. *4 Kents Bottom, Yatton Keynell, Chippenham SN14 7BW*
E: gillianparkin4@gmail.com

PARKIN, Mrs Jennifer Anne. b 47. Nene Coll Northn BEd 85. WMMTC 95. **d** 98 **p** 99. C Northampton St Alb *Pet* 98-02; P-in-c Ecton 02-07; P-in-c Wootton w Quinton and Preston Deanery 07-12; Chapl Cynthia Spencer Hospice 02-07; Warden of Past Assts *Pet* 06-10; rtd 12; Lay Voc Officer *Pet* 12-13. *40 Pinewood Road, Northampton NN3 2RB*
E: parkinjen@btinternet.com *or* jenny.johnparkin@gmail.com

PARKIN, Canon John Edmund. b 44. Open Univ BA 73. St Jo Coll Nottm 83. **d** 85 **p** 86. C Aberavon *Llan* 85-90; R Eglwysilan 90-01; P Missr Merthyr Tydfil Ch Ch 01-09; Hon Can Llan Cathl 09; rtd 09; PtO *Llan* from 12. *2 Mount Pleasant, Penderyn Road, Hirwaun, Aberdare CF44 9RT*

PARKIN, John Francis. b 40. Linc Th Coll 65. **d** 68 **p** 69. C Cullercoats St Geo *Newc* 68-72; C Stony Stratford *Ox* 72-73; TV Lt Coates *Linc* 73-76; PtO 88-93; NSM Horncastle w Low

Toynton 93-06; NSM High Toynton 93-06; NSM Horncastle Gp from 06. *The Firs, 68 Louth Road, Horncastle LN9 5LJ* T: (01507) 523208

PARKIN, Jonathan Samuel. b 73. La Sainte Union Coll BTh 95 Birm Univ MA 97. Qu Coll Birm 98. **d** 98 **p** 99. C Skegness and Winthorpe *Linc* 98-01; Chapl Leic Coll of FE 01-03; Chapl De Montfort Univ 04-07; Chapl Leic Cathl 01-07; TV Market Harborough and The Transfiguration etc 01-11; P-in-c Welham, Glooston and Cranoe and Stonton Wyville 07-11; C Branston w Nocton and Potterhanworth *Linc* from 11; C Metheringham w Blankney and Dunston from 11. *The Rectory, 19 Abel Smith Gardens, Branston, Lincoln LN4 1NN* T: (01522) 794275 E: parkin@tiscali.co.uk

PARKIN, Melvyn Christopher. b 57. NEOC 99. **d** 02 **p** 03. NSM Boston Spa *York* 02-03; C Elvington w Sutton on Derwent and E Cottingwith 03-06; R Howardian Gp 06-11; V Gt and Lt Ouseburn w Marton cum Grafton etc *Leeds* from 11. *The Vicarage, Main Street, Great Ouseburn, York YO26 9RQ* T: (01423) 330928

PARKIN, Canon Trevor Kinross. b 37. MCMI. Cranmer Hall Dur 63. **d** 66 **p** 67. C Kingston upon Hull St Martin *York* 66-69; C Reading St Jo *Ox* 69-73; Ind Chapl *Lon* 73-80; Hon C Langham Place All So 73-80; Ind Chapl *Ely* 80-82; V Maidenhead St Andr and St Mary *Ox* 82-02; Hon Can Butare from 00; rtd 02; PtO *Guildf* 03-07. *2 Yew Tree Court, 2A Trinity Trees, Eastbourne BN21 3LD* E: trevorparkin@fsmail.net

PARKINSON, Alan. *See* PARKINSON, Thomas Alan

PARKINSON, Andrew. b 74. St Steph Ho Ox. **d** 01 **p** 02. C Lancaster Ch Ch *Blackb* 01-04; P-in-c Yarnton w Begbroke and Shipton on Cherwell *Ox* 04-05; TV Blenheim 05-12; P-in-c Kirkby Stephen w Mallerstang etc *Carl* from 12. *The Vicarage, Vicarage Lane, Kirkby Stephen CA17 4QX* T: (017683) 71204
E: revparkinson@tiscali.co.uk

PARKINSON, Andrew. b 56. Keble Coll Ox BA 77 MA 80. Westcott Ho Cam 78. **d** 80 **p** 81. C S Shore H Trin *Blackb* 80-85; V Lea 85-94; V Longton from 94. *Longton Vicarage, Birchwood Avenue, Hutton, Preston PR4 5EE* T: (01772) 612179 E: andrew.parkinson@talktalk.net

PARKINSON, Miss Brenda. b 40. Lancs Poly CQSW. Dalton Ho Bris 65. **dss** 74 **d** 87 **p** 94. Ribbleton *Blackb* 75-80; Ingol 82-88; Par Dn 87-88; Par Dn Ashton-on-Ribble St Mich 88-91; Par Dn Ashton-on-Ribble St Mich w Preston St Mark 91-92; Par Dn Gt Marsden 92-94; C 94-98; C Gt Marsden w Nelson St Phil 99-00; rtd 00; PtO *Blackb* from 01. *18 Thorn Hill Close, Blackburn BB1 1YE* T: (01254) 678367

PARKINSON, David Thomas. b 42. Linc Th Coll 77. **d** 79 **p** 80. C Yate New Town *Bris* 79-82; TV Keynsham *B & W* 82-88; R Bleadon 88-07; rtd 07; PtO *B & W* from 08. *Sherwell Court, 48 Old Church Road, Uphill, Weston-super-Mare BS23 4UP* T: (01934) 708125 M: 07951-239778
E: dtparkinson@talktalk.net

PARKINSON, Francis Wilson. b 37. Open Univ BA 80 MBACP. St Aid Birkenhead 59. **d** 62 **p** 63. C Monkwearmouth St Andr *Dur* 62-64; C Speke All SS *Liv* 64-67; CF 67-92; PtO *Ox* from 92. *9 Priory Mead, Longcot, Faringdon SN7 7TJ* T: (01793) 784406

PARKINSON, Canon Ian Richard. b 58. Dur Univ BA 79 Lon Univ BD 84. Wycliffe Hall Ox 80. **d** 83 **p** 84. C Hull St Jo Newland *York* 83-86; C Linthorpe 86-92; V Saltburn-by-the-Sea 92-01; V Marple All SS *Ches* from 01; Hon Can Ches Cathl from 12. *The Vicarage, 155 Church Lane, Marple, Stockport SK6 7LD* T/F: 0161-449 0950 T: 427 2378
E: ian.parkinson7@ntlworld.com

PARKINSON, John Reginald. b 32. Qu Coll Birm 79. **d** 81 **p** 82. NSM Catshill and Dodford *Worc* 81-85; C Knightwick w Doddenham, Broadwas and Cotheridge 85-88; C Martley and Wichenford 85-88; P-in-c Berrow w Pendock and Eldersfield 88-89; R Berrow w Pendock, Eldersfield, Hollybush etc 89-97; RD Upton 95-97; rtd 97; PtO *Glouc* from 97; *Worc* from 97. *8 Glebe Close, Stow on the Wold, Cheltenham GL54 1DJ* T: (01451) 830822

PARKINSON, Nicholas John. b 46. FCCA 75 Cranfield Inst of Tech MBA 85. St Alb Minl Tr Scheme 92. **d** 95 **p** 96. NSM Woburn Sands *St Alb* 95-98; NSM Westoning w Tingrith 98-01; NSM Woburn Sands from 01. *Thornbank House, 7 Church Road, Woburn Sands, Milton Keynes MK17 8TE* T: (01908) 583397

PARKINSON, Richard Duncan. b 48. ERMC. **d** 07 **p** 08. NSM Leverington, Newton and Tydd St Giles *Ely* 07-11; NSM Wisbech St Mary and Guyhirn w Ring's End etc from 11. *166 Leverington Common, Leverington, Wisbech PE13 5BP* T: (01945) 465818 E: rykp@bigfoot.com.bt
ryk.parkinson@ely.anglican.org

PARKINSON, Richard Francis. b 76. Cranmer Hall Dur. **d** 10 **p** 11. C Ilkley All SS *Bradf* 10-13; R Cherry Burton *York* from 13; C Etton w Dalton Holme from 13; Chapl Bp Burton Coll York from 13. *The Rectory, Main Street, Cherry Burton, Beverley HU17 7RF* E: richard@poiema.co.uk

PARKINSON, Mrs Sarah Kathryn Rachel. b 80. Trin Coll Ox MMath 02. Ripon Coll Cuddesdon BA 06. **d** 07 **p** 08. NSM Steeple Aston w N Aston and Tackley Ox 07-10; Chapl HM Pris Bullingdon 05-08; Manager Relig Affairs Campsfield Ho Immigration Removal Cen 08-12; PtO *Leeds* from 13. *The Vicarage, Vicarage Lane, Kirkby Stephen CA17 4QX* T: (017683) 71204

PARKINSON, Simon George Denis. b 39. Univ of Wales (Lamp) BA 66. Westcott Ho Cam 65. **d** 67 **p** 68. C Rothwell *Ripon* 67-70; Chapl RAF 70-73; C Leeds St Pet *Ripon* 74-75; V Horbury Junction *Wakef* 76-83; V Hanging Heaton 83-92; P-in-c Upper Hopton 92; V Eastthorpe and Upper Hopton 92-02; rtd 02. *126 Edge Lane, Dewsbury WF12 0HB* T: (01924) 508885

PARKINSON, Thomas Alan. b 40. St Jo Coll York CertEd 61. NW Ord Course 75. **d** 78 **p** 79. NSM Sheff St Cecilia Parson Cross 78-82; NSM Goldthorpe w Hickleton 82-90; C Cantley 90-01; Dioc RE and Worship Adv 93-04; V Ryecroft St Nic 02-10; rtd 10; PtO *Sheff* from 10; CMP from 00. *40 South Street, Rawmarsh, Rotherham S62 5RG* T: (01709) 525654

PARKINSON, Vivian Leslie. b 54. St Luke's Coll Ex CertEd 76 Brighton Poly BEd 87. St Jo Coll Nottm. **d** 94 **p** 95. C Cowbridge *Llan* 94-97; V Llantrisant from 97; AD Pontypridd 06-10. *The Vicarage, Coed yr Esgob, Llantrisant, Pontyclun CF72 8EL* T: (01443) 223356 *or* 237983 F: 230631 E: vivparkinson@parishofllantrisant.org.uk

PARKMAN, Mrs Michelle Joy. b 77. SS Mark & Jo Univ Coll Plymouth BA 00. Trin Coll Bris BA 08. **d** 08 **p** 09. C Nailsea H Trin *B & W* 08-13. *45 Dellohay Park, Saltash PL12 6AQ* M: 07740-366597 E: mparkman@hotmail.co.uk

PARKS, Paul. b 59. K Coll Lon BA 96. St Jo Coll Nottm MA 97. **d** 98 **p** 99. C S Molton w Nymet St George, High Bray etc *Ex* 98-04; P-in-c Hurst *Ox* 04-05; C Wokingham St Sebastian 05-07; TV Wednesfield *Lich* 07-11; V Hoddesdon *St Alb* 11-15; P-in-c Ore St Helen and St Barn *Chich* from 15. *St Helen's Rectory, 23 Ore Place, Hastings TN34 2LR* M: 07872-535495 E: revpaulparks@gmail.com

PARMENTER, Canon Deirdre Joy. b 45. EAMTC 91. **d** 94 **p** 95. C Ipswich St Aug *St E* 94-97; P-in-c Haughley w Wetherden 97-00; V Haughley w Wetherden and Stowupland 00-07; RD Stowmarket 99-05; Bp's Chapl 07-10; Dioc Adv for Women's Min 08-10; Hon Can St E Cathl 03-10; rtd 10; PtO *St E* from 10; Dioc Warden of Readers 10-13; RD Loes 14-15. *Avalon, Marlesford Road, Campsea Ashe, Woodbridge IP13 0QG* T: (01728) 748145 E: deirdre@stedmundsbury.anglican.org

PARMENTIER, Martinus Franciscus Georgius. b 47. Utrecht Univ DTh 71 Pemb Coll Ox DPhil 74. Old Cath Sem Amersfoort 65. **d** 71 **p** 71. Old Catholic Ch of The Netherlands 71-73; C Wolvercote *Ox* 74-76; Chapl Amsterdam w Haarlem and Den Helder *Eur* 78-80; Lect Old Catholic Sem Utrecht 80-12; rtd 12. *Burgemeester Lambooylaan 19, 1217 LB Hilversum, The Netherlands*

PARNELL, Bryan Donald. b 38. JP . DipEd 88. Chich Th Coll 66. **d** 69 **p** 70. C Lewisham St Jo Southend *S'wark* 69-72; Asst Chapl Cooleg Sch of St Pet Australia 72-76; R Angaston 76-78; Chapl RAN 78-88; R Edwardstown 89-02; rtd 02. *PO Box 2131, Unit 19, Manson Towers, 13 Moseley Street, Glenelg SA 2035, Australia* M: 414-692340 E: trinitas@senet.com.au

PARR, Mrs Anne Patricia. b 38. Nottm Univ CertEd 59. **d** 07 **p** 08. OLM Penistone and Thurlstone *Wakef* 07-14; OLM *Sheff* from 14. *7 Rydal Close, Penistone, Sheffield S36 8HN* T: (01226) 764490 M: 07971-513301 E: mail@anneparr.co.uk

PARR (née JOHNSON), Mrs Claire Elisabeth. b 83. Wheaton Coll Illinois BA 05. Ridley Hall Cam 08. **d** 10 **p** 11. C Melksham and Broughton Gifford, Gt Chalfield and Holt 10-12; C Hampreston 12-14; C Hemingford Grey *Ely* from 14. *19 St Ives Road, Hemingford Grey, Huntingdon PE28 9DU* E: claire.e.johnson@gmail.com

PARR, Clive William. b 41. FCIS. WEMTC 02. **d** 03 **p** 04. NSM Evesham w Norton and Lenchwick *Worc* 03-07; NSM Hampton w Sedgeberrow and Hinton-on-the-Green 07-14; PtO from 14; Bp's Health Service Adv from 08. *Grace Cottage, Mill Lane, Elmley Castle, Pershore WR10 3HP* T: (01386) 710700 F: 761214 M: 07801-820006 E: cw.parr@btinternet.com

PARR, David Jonathan. b 77. Chelt & Glouc Coll of HE BA 98. Trin Coll Bris BA 04. **d** 04 **p** 05. C Whitchurch *Ex* 04-08; C Shepton Mallet w Doulting *B & W* 08-10; TV Melksham *Sarum* 10-12; PtO 13-14; C Hemingford Grey *Ely* from 14. *19 St Ives Road, Hemingford Grey, Huntingdon PE28 9DU* E: davejparr@yahoo.co.uk

PARR, Frank. b 35. Nottm Univ BCombStuds 82 Lanc Univ MA 86. Linc Th Coll 79. **d** 82 **p** 83. C Padiham *Blackb* 82-85; P-in-c Accrington St Andr 85-88; V Oswaldtwistle Immanuel and All SS 88-96; V Tunstall w Melling and Leck

96-01; rtd 01; PtO *Blackb* from 01; *Leeds* from 02. *1 Bank View, Burton Road, Lower Bentham, Lancaster LA2 7DZ* T: (015242) 61159 E: frank_parr@lineone.net

PARR, Jeffrey John. b 48. FCA 73. EMMTC 03. **d** 06 **p** 07. NSM Bassingham Gp *Linc* 06-09; NSM Claypole 09-10; LtO from 10. *3 Manor Paddocks, Bassingham, Lincoln LN5 9GW* T: (01522) 789869 M: 07785-281215 E: jparr@chesapeake.co.uk

PARR, John. b 53. St Edm Hall Ox BA 74 MA 87 Lon Univ BD 79 Sheff Univ PhD 90. Trin Coll Bris 75. **d** 79 **p** 80. C Gt Crosby St Luke *Liv* 79-82; C Walton St Mary 82-84; V Ince St Mary 84-87; Tutor and Lect Ridley Hall Cam 87-95; Chapl 87-93; Dir Studies 93-95; CME Officer *Ely* 95-99; P-in-c Harston w Hauxton 95-99; P-in-c Newton 97-99; Can Res and CME Officer *St E* 99-00; PtO 06-09; TR Bury St Edmunds All SS w St Jo and St Geo 09-12; Dir Min Educn and Tr from 12. *Diocesan Office, St Nicholas Centre, 4 Cutler Street, Ipswich IP1 1UQ* T: (01473) 298500 F: 298501 E: parr28@btinternet.com

PARR, Mabel Ann. b 37. CBDTI 07. **d** 07 **p** 08. NSM Bentham *Bradf* 07-10; PtO *Blackb* from 10; *Leeds* from 12. *1 Bank View, Burton Road, Lower Bentham, Lancaster LA2 7DZ* T: (015242) 61159 E: f.parr207@btinternet.com

PARR, Vanessa Caroline. *See* CONANT, Vanessa Caroline

PARRATT, Dennis James. b 53. Glos Coll of Art & Design BA 74. St Steph Ho Ox 82. **d** 84 **p** 85. C Cainscross w Selsley *Glouc* 84-88; C Old Shoreham and New Shoreham *Chich* 88-91; PtO *Glouc* 01-08. *11 Millbrook Gardens, Cheltenham GL50 3RQ* T: (01242) 525730 E: djparratt@hotmail.co.uk

PARRETT, Mrs Mary Margaret. b 42. Shenstone Coll of Educn DipEd 63. St Alb Minl Tr Scheme 86. **d** 98 **p** 99. NSM Barton-le-Cley w Higham Gobion and Hexton *St Alb* 98-06; PtO from 06; NSM Officer Bedford Adnry 10-14. *49 Manor Road, Barton-le-Clay, Bedford MK45 4NP* T: (01582) 883089 E: mary.parrett@btinternet.com

PARRETT, Mrs Rosalind Virginia. b 43. Ox Brookes Univ MTh 02. Cant Sch of Min 84. **d** 87 **p** 94. NSM Selling w Throwley, Sheldwich w Badlesmere etc *Cant* 87-91; Asst Chapl Cant Hosp 87-91; Par Dn Stantonbury and Willen *Ox* 91-94; TV 94-96; P-in-c Owlsmoor 96-98; V 98-03; rtd 03; PtO *Cant* 03-04; Hon C Faversham 04-11; Hon C Preston next Faversham, Goodnestone and Graveney 04-10; PtO from 11. *16 Hilton Close, Faversham ME13 8NN* T: (01795) 530380 M: 07881-788155 E: revros@talktalk.net

PARRETT, Simon Christopher. b 60. Sarum & Wells Th Coll. **d** 87 **p** 88. C Ifield *Chich* 87-91; Chapl to the Deaf *Sarum* 91-94; NSM Bournemouth H Epiphany *Win* 94-96; Asst Chapl Poole Hosp NHS Trust 96-03; Chapl Dorothy House Hospice Winsley 01-04. *252 The Common, Holt, Trowbridge BA14 6QN* T: (01225) 783163

PARRETT, Stephen. b 65. Cant Ch Ch Univ Coll BA 96. **d** 07 **p** 08. OLM Herne Bay Ch Ch *Cant* 07-14; NSM from 14. *1 Birkdale Gardens, Herne Bay CT6 7TS* T: (01227) 360139 M: 07742-439563 E: stephenparrett@lycos.co.uk

PARRI, Emyr. b 51. Univ of Wales BA 96 FRAS. Ban & St As Minl Tr Course 98. **d** 98 **p** 99. NSM Tregarth *Ban* 98-04; Bp's Chapl 04-07. *Bryn Awel, Sling, Tregarth, Bangor LL57 4RH* T: (01248) 602176

PARRIS, Mrs Alison Louise. **d** 14 **p** 15. NSM Camelot Par *B & W* from 14. *76 Combe Park, Yeovil BA21 3BE* T: (01935) 476412 E: parwych@googlemail.com

PARRISH, Ian Robert. b 62. SEITE 05. **d** 09 **p** 10. C Kingsnorth and Shadoxhurst *Cant* 09-10; C Maidstone St Paul 11-14; P-in-c Maidstone All SS and St Phil w Tovil from 14. *The Vicarage, Priory Road, Maidstone ME15 6NL* T: (01622) 756002 E: vicar@maidstoneallsaints.wanadoo.co.uk

PARRISH, Robert Carey. b 57. St Steph Ho Ox 89. **d** 91 **p** 92. C Abington *Pet* 91-94; C Leckhampton SS Phil and Jas w Cheltenham St Jas *Glouc* 94-97; PV Llan Cathl 97-02; R Merthyr Dyfan from 02. *Merthyr Dyfan Rectory, 10 Buttrills Road, Barry CF62 8EF* T: (01446) 735943

PARROTT, David Wesley. b 58. Univ of Wales (Cardiff) LLM 01. Oak Hill Th Coll BA. **d** 84 **p** 85. C Thundersley *Chelmsf* 84-87; C Rainham 87-89; P-in-c Heydon w Gt and Lt Chishill 89-90; P-in-c Chrishall 89-90; P-in-c Elmdon w Wendon Lofts and Strethall 89-90; R Heydon, Gt and Lt Chishill, Chrishall etc 91-96; R Rayleigh 96-00; TR 00-04; RD Rochford 02-04; Barking Area CME Adv 04-09; C Hornchurch St Andr 05-09; Hon Can Chelmsf Cathl 07-09; V St Lawr Jewry *Lon* from 09. *St Lawrence Jewry Vicarage, Church Passage, London EC2V 5AA* T: (020) 7600 9478 E: dwparrott01@aol.com

PARROTT, George. b 37. Leeds Univ BA 61. Bps' Coll Cheshunt 61. **d** 63 **p** 64. C Lower Mitton *Worc* 63-65; C-in-c Fairfield St Rich CD 65-68; Zambia 68-70; C Cleethorpes *Linc* 70-75; R Withern 75-80; P-in-c Gayton le Marsh 76-80; P-in-c Strubby 76-80; P-in-c Authorpe 76-80; P-in-c Belleau w Aby and Claythorpe 76-80; P-in-c N and S Reston 76-80; P-in-c

Swaby w S Thoresby 76-80; R Withern 80-90; V Reston 80-90; V Messingham 90-93; P-in-c Fincham *Ely* 95-02; P-in-c Marham 95-02; P-in-c Shouldham 95-02; P-in-c Shouldham Thorpe 95-02; rtd 02; PtO *Linc* from 03. *8 Anson Close, Skellingthorpe, Lincoln LN6 5TH* T: (01522) 694417

PARROTT, Canon Gerald Arthur. b 32. St Cath Coll Cam BA 56 MA 60. Chich Th Coll. **d** 58 **p** 59. C Ashington *Newc* 58-61; C Brighton St Pet *Chich* 61-63; V Leeds St Wilfrid *Ripon* 63-68; R Lewisham St Jo Southend *S'wark* 69-73; TR Catford (Southend) and Downham 73-77; RD E Lewisham 75-77; Can Res and Prec S'wark Cathl 77-88; TR Wimbledon 88-95; rtd 95; PtO *Chich* from 95. *10 Palings Way, Fernhurst, Haslemere GU27 3HJ* T: (01428) 641533

PARROTT, Martin William. b 57. Keele Univ BA 79 K Coll Lon MA 93 W Lon Inst of HE PGCE 80. Ripon Coll Cuddesdon 82. **d** 85 **p** 86. C Birchfield *Birm* 85-88; Chapl Univ Coll Medical Sch *Lon* 88-93; Chapl SOAS 88-93; P-in-c Univ Ch Ch the K 90-93; V Hebden Bridge *Wakef* 93-01; Asst Chapl Pinderfields and Pontefract Hosps NHS Trust 01-02; Chapl Calderdale and Huddersfield NHS Trust 02-11; V Crosland Moor and Linthwaite *Wakef* 11-12; rtd 12. *125 Chessetts Wood Road, Lapworth, Solihull B94 6EL* T: (01564) 777137 M: 07905-444872 E: martinwilliamparrott@gmail.com

PARRY, Canon Alfred Charles Ascough. b 37. Natal Univ BA 58. Westcott Ho Cam 59. **d** 61 **p** 62. C E Ham w Upton Park *Chelmsf* 61-63; C Durban N St Martin S Africa 63-64; R Newcastle H Trin 64-70; Dir Chr Educn Kloof 70-76; Sub Dean Pietermaritzburg 76-81; R Estcourt S Africa 81; Adn N Natal 81-85; R Kloof S Africa 86-93; R Berea 93-98; Hon Can Pietermaritzburg from 86; Sen Asst Min Hornchurch St Andr *Chelmsf* 99-04; C Furze Platt *Ox* 04-05; Hon C 05-07; rtd 05. *45 Windmill Drive, Croxley Green, Rickmansworth WD3 3FF* T: (01923) 771037

PARRY, Andrew Martyn. b 61. Witwatersrand Univ BA 81 MBA 91 Open Univ BSc 04. Ox Min Course 06. **d** 09 **p** 10. NSM Horton and Wraysbury *Ox* 09-12; NSM Stoke Poges from 12. *2 Pennylets Green, Stoke Poges, Slough SL2 4BT* T: (01753) 644239 E: andrew@vamparry.eclipse.co.uk

PARRY, Benjamin. *See* PARRY, Owen Benjamin

PARRY, Canon Bryan Horace. b 33. St Mich Coll Llan 65. **d** 67 **p** 68. C Holyhead w Rhoscolyn w Llanfair-yn-Neubwll *Ban* 67-71; TV 71-73; P-in-c Small Heath St Greg *Birm* 73-78; V 78-80; V Perry Barr 80-94; RD Handsworth 83-91; P-in-c Kingstanding St Luke 86-92; Hon Can Birm Cathl 87-94; rtd 94; PtO *Nor* from 94. *St Seiriol, Old Crown Yard, Walsingham NR22 6BU* T: (01328) 820019

PARRY, Charles. *See* PARRY, Alfred Charles Ascough

PARRY, Canon David Allan. b 62. Bris Univ BSc 83 Univ of Wales (Cardiff) CQSW 88. Trin Coll Bris. **d** 94 **p** 95. C Withywood *Bris* 94-98; P-in-c Litherland St Phil *Liv* 98-02; V 02-06; Hon Chapl to the Deaf 00-05; AD Bootle 02-05; Dioc Dir of Ords from 05; V Toxteth Park Ch Ch and St Mich w St Andr from 06; Hon Can Liv Cathl 03-05 and from 12. *St Michael's Vicarage, St Michael's Church Road, Liverpool L17 7BD* T: 0151-286 2411

PARRY, David Thomas Newton. b 45. Selw Coll Cam BA 67 MA 71. Lambeth STh 76 Cuddesdon Coll 67. **d** 69 **p** 70. C Oldham St Mary w St Pet *Man* 69-73; C Baguley 73-74; Tutor Sarum & Wells Th Coll 74-78; V Westleigh St Pet *Man* 78-88; TR E Farnworth and Kearsley 88-97; TR Chambersbury *St Alb* 97-03; V Blackbird Leys *Ox* 03-11; rtd 11; PtO *Llan* from 11. *32 Barry Road, Pontypridd CF37 1HY* E: davidparry912@btinternet.com

PARRY, Denis. b 34. Sarum & Wells Th Coll 83. **d** 85 **p** 86. C Hubberston w Herbrandston and Hasguard etc *St D* 85-88; C Herbrandston and Hasguard w St Ishmael's 89; P-in-c 89-90; R 90-99; Dioc RE Adv 89-99; rtd 99; PtO *Heref* from 99; *St D* from 10. *Mayfield, 33 Mill Street, Kington HR5 3AL* T: (01544) 230550

PARRY, Canon Dennis John. b 38. Univ of Wales (Lamp) BA 60. St Mich Coll Llan 60. **d** 62 **p** 63. C Caerphilly *Llan* 62-64; C Aberdare St Fagan 64-67; Miss at Povungnituk Canada 67-69; R Gelligaer *Llan* 69-75; V Llanwnnog and Caersws w Carno *Ban* 75-89; V Llanidloes w Llangurig 89-01; RD Arwystli 89-01; Hon Can Ban Cathl 90-01; Can Cursal Ban Cathl 97-01; rtd 02; PtO *Ban* from 02. *Lock Cottage, Groesfford, Brecon LD3 7UY* T: (01874) 665400 E: dj519@btinternet.com

PARRY, Derek Nugent Goulding. b 32. Ely Th Coll 60. **d** 63 **p** 64. C Fareham SS Pet and Paul *Portsm* 63-67; C Portsea N End St Mark 67-74; P-in-c Piddletrenthide w Plush, Alton Pancras etc *Sarum* 74-92; rtd 92; PtO *Sarum* from 92. *Farthing Cottage, 12 Fordington Green, Dorchester DT1 1LU* T: (01305) 269794

PARRY, Gordon Martyn Winn. b 47. Down Coll Cam BA 68 MA 70 Univ Coll Chich MA 02. **d** 04 **p** 05. NSM Turners Hill

Chich 04-07; NSM E Grinstead St Swithun from 07. *31A Mount Close, Crawley RH10 7EF* M: 07802-432398 E: gordonmwparry@btinternet.com

PARRY, Jane. *See* PARRY, Patricia Jane

PARRY, John Gareth. b 61. Univ of Wales (Abth) BA 83 Univ of Wales (Ban) PGCE 84. Westcott Ho Cam 94. **d** 96 **p** 97. C Holyhead *Ban* 96-99; C-in-c Llandinorwig w Penisa'r-waen 99-00; Asst Master Bodedern Secondary Sch 00-01; Hd RE Pensby High Sch for Boys Wirral 02; Chapl and Hd RE Tettenhall Coll Wolv 03-09; Chapl Prestfelde Sch Shrewsbury 09-11; Chapl Oswestry Sch 11-14; PtO *Ban* 00-12. *34 Merton Park, Penmaenmawr LL34 6DH* T: (01492) 622671 E: penmaen86@hotmail.com

PARRY, Keith Melville. b 31. MRICS 65. S'wark Ord Course 80. **d** 83 **p** 84. NSM Bexley St Jo *Roch* 83-88; C Orpington All SS 88-96; rtd 96; PtO *Roch* from 96. *5 Greenside, Bexley DA5 3PA* T: (01322) 555425 E: keithparry2@btinternet.com

PARRY, Canon Kenneth Charles. b 34. Ripon Hall Ox 56. **d** 58 **p** 59. C Stoke *Cov* 58-61; Chapl RN 61-65; V Cradley *Worc* 65-70; V Gt Malvern H Trin 70-83; RD Malvern 74-83; Hon Can Worc Cathl 80-83; V Budleigh Salterton *Ex* 83-91; Can Res and Prec Ex Cathl 91-00; rtd 00. *Brook Cottage, Pye Corner, Kennford, Exeter EX6 7TB* T: (01392) 832767 E: kcparry@ic24.net

PARRY, Manon Ceridwen. *See* JAMES, Manon Ceridwen

PARRY, Canon Marilyn Marie. b 46. W Coll Ohio BA 68 Man Univ MA 77 PhD 00. Epis Th Sch Cam Mass 68 Gilmore Ho 76. **dss** 79 **d** 87 **p** 94. Chapl Asst N Man Gen Hosp 85-90; Tutor NOC 90-97; Dir Studies 91-97; Lic Preacher *Man* 90-94; Hon C E Farnworth and Kearsley 94-97; Nat Adv for Pre-Th Educn and Selection Sec Min Division Abps' Coun 97-01; Public Preacher *St Alb* 98-01; Can Res Ch Ch *Ox* 01-11; Dioc Dir of Ords 01-10; IME Officer 10-11; rtd 11; PtO *Llan* from 11. *32 Barry Road, Pontypridd CF37 1HY* M: 07952-309667 E: marilyn@parsonage.org.uk

PARRY, Nicholas John Sinclair. b 56. Sarum & Wells Th Coll 82. **d** 85 **p** 86. C Hendon St Mary *Lon* 85-87; C Verwood *Sarum* 87-90; TV Witney *Ox* 90-96; V Costessey *Nor* from 96. *The Vicarage, Folgate Lane, Costessey, Norwich NR8 5DP* T: (01603) 742818 E: nicholas.parry@btinternet.com

PARRY, Mrs Olwen Margaret. b 45. Cardiff Coll of Educn CertEd 67. Llan Dioc Tr Scheme 88. **d** 92 **p** 97. NSM Newcastle *Llan* 92-04; NSM Llansantffraid, Bettws and Aberkenfig 04-15; rtd 15. *17 Wernlys Road, Bridgend CF31 4NS* T: (01656) 721860

PARRY, Owen Benjamin. b 42. St As Minl Tr Course 99. **d** 01 **p** 02. C Llangollen w Trevor and Llantysilio *St As* 01-07; rtd 07; C-in-c Pradoe *Lich* 09-11; PtO *St As* from 09; *Lich* from 14. *Fairways, Halton, Chirk, Wrexham LL14 5BD* T: (01691) 778484

PARRY, Mrs Patricia Jane. b 54. Liv Univ BTh 99. NOC 97. **d** 99 **p** 00. C Wilmslow *Ches* 99-03; V Baddiley and Wrenbury w Burleydam 03-08; V Alderley Edge from 08; RD Knutsford from 13. *The Vicarage, Church Lane, Alderley Edge SK9 7UZ* T: (01625) 583249 *or* 581477 E: vicarontheedge@hotmail.co.uk

PARRY, Peter John. b 42. Westmr Coll Ox BTh 99 Sarum Coll MA 14. EAMTC 99. **d** 01 **p** 02. NSM Montreux w Gstaad *Eur* 01-06; PtO *Pet* from 05. *Forge House, Church Road, Hargrave, Wellingborough NN9 6BQ* E: phwparry@btinternet.com

PARRY, Miss Violet Margaret. b 30. Selly Oak Coll 53. **dss** 82 **d** 87. W Kilburn St Luke w St Simon and St Jude *Lon* 82-83; St Marylebone St Mary 83-86; Stamford All SS w St Jo *Linc* 86-90; C 87-90; rtd 90; PtO *Linc* 90-01; *Leic* from 03. *2 Stuart Court, High Street, Kibworth, Leicester LE8 0LR* T: 0116-279 6858

PARRY-JENNINGS, Christopher William. b 34. Lon Coll of Div 57. **d** 60 **p** 62. C Claughton cum Grange *Ches* 60-63; C Folkestone H Trin w Ch Ch *Cant* 63-67; V Lincoln New Zealand 67-72; Chapl Cant Univ 68-72; V Riccarton St Jas 72-88; V Heathcote Mt Pleasant 88-96; First Gen Sec SPCK (NZ) 89-90; P Asst Upper Riccarton St Pet New Zealand from 96. *22 Ambleside Drive, Burnside, Christchurch 8053, New Zealand* T/F: (0064) (3) 358 9304 E: chpj@globe.net.nz

PARRY JONES, Leonard. b 29. Univ of Wales (Ban) BA 52. St Mich Coll Llan 52. **d** 54 **p** 55. C Newtown w Llanllwchaiarn w Aberhafesp *St As* 54-58; C Abergele 58-60; V Pennant, Hirnant and Llangynog 60-65; V Llanynys w Llanychan 65-71; V Brynymaen w Trofarth 71-94; RD Rhos 77-94; rtd 94; PtO *Lich* from 15. *29 Pengwern Court, Longden Road, Shrewsbury SY3 7JE*

PARSELL, Howard Vivian. b 60. Univ of Wales (Lamp) BA 87 Univ of Wales (Swansea) PGCE 88. St Mich Coll Llan 93. **d** 94 **p** 95. C Builth and Llanddewi'r Cwm w Llangynog etc *S & B* 94-96; C Swansea St Thos and Kilvey 96-98; P-in-c Swansea

St Jude 98-09; V Swansea St Jude w St Nic 09-15; AD Swansea 04-12; Chapl to the Deaf from 98. *5 Lon Einon, Penllergaer, Swansea SA4 9BP*

PARSELLE, Stephen Paul. b 53. Univ of Wales (Cardiff) MTh 06. St Jo Coll Nottm. d 82 p 83. C Boscombe St Jo *Win* 82-86; CF 86-05; Dir of Ords 02-05; Chapl RN 05-08; PtO *Win* from 09. *11 Southbourne Overcliff Drive, Bournemouth BH6 3TE* T: (01202) 433858 M: 07711-017282 E: parselle@aol.com

PARSONAGE, Robert Hugh. b 55. Nottm Trent Univ BSc 78. Trin Coll Bris BA 97. d 97 p 98. C Chell *Lich* 97-01; R Poringland *Nor* from 01; RD Loddon from 10. *The Rectory, Rectory Lane, Poringland, Norwich NR14 7SL* T: (01508) 492215 E: rector@poringland-benefice.org.uk

PARSONS, Andrew David. b 53. UEA BA 74 Fitzw Coll Cam BA 77 MA 81. Westcott Ho Cam 75. d 78 p 79. C Hellesdon *Nor* 78-82; C Eaton 82-85; P-in-c Burnham Thorpe w Burnham Overy 85-87; R Burnham Sutton w Burnham Ulph etc 85-87; R Burnham Gp of Par 87-93; P-in-c Wroxham w Hoveton and Belaugh 93; R 93-07; RD St Benet 99-07; V Old Catton from 07. *St Margaret's Vicarage, 1 Parkside Drive, Norwich NR6 7DP* T: (01603) 425615 E: 2andrew@andrewparsons.fsnet.co.uk

PARSONS, Christopher Paul. b 58. EAMTC 01. d 04 p 05. C Pakefield *Nor* 04-08; P-in-c Kenwyn w St Allen *Truro* from 08. *The Vicarage, Kenwyn Church Road, Truro TR1 3DR* T: (01872) 263015 E: chris@cpp1.freeserve.co.uk

PARSONS, David Norman. b 39. FCIB 83. Trin Coll Bris 92. d 94 p 95. NSM Swindon Dorcan *Bris* 94-03; PtO *Glouc* from 03. *31 Couzens Close, Chipping Sodbury, Bristol BS37 6BT* T: (01454) 323070 E: david.parsons1@virgin.net

PARSONS, Mrs Deborah Anne. b 66. Surrey Univ BA 87. STETS 04. d 07. C Goodrington *Ex* 07-11; TV Totnes w Bridgetown, Berry Pomeroy etc from 11. *St John's Vicarage, Crosspark, Totnes TQ9 5BQ* T: (01803) 840113 E: d.a.parsons@btinternet.com

PARSONS, Geoffrey Fairbanks. b 35. Trin Coll Cam BA 58 MA 68. Ridley Hall Cam 59. d 61 p 62. C Over St Chad *Ches* 61-64; C Heswall 64-69; V Congleton St Steph 69-75; V Weaverham 75-94; P-in-c Backford and Capenhurst 94-00; R 00-01; rtd 01; PtO *Ches* from 02. *28 Springcroft, Parkgate, South Wirral CH64 6SE* T: 0151-336 3354

PARSONS, George Edward. b 35. St D Coll Lamp BA 60 Ripon Hall Ox 60. d 62 p 63. C Leominster *Heref* 62-66; NSM Bromfield 67-72; NSM Culmington w Onibury 67-72; NSM Stanton Lacy 67-72; NSM Ludlow 72-77; P-in-c Caynham 77-79; NSM Bishop's Cleeve *Glouc* 79-91; Sub-Chapl HM Pris Glouc 88-91; P-in-c Hasfield w Tirley and Ashleworth *Glouc* 91-00; P-in-c Maisemore 91-00; rtd 00; PtO *Glouc* 00-02; *Blackb* from 02. *Ballalona, 2 The Meadows, Hollins Lane, Forton, Preston PR3 0AF* T: (01524) 792656

PARSONS, George Horace Norman. b 19. S'wark Ord Course 65. d 68 p 69. C Hatcham St Cath *S'wark* 68-72; C Horley 72-76; P-in-c S Wimbledon All SS 76-78; P-in-c Caterham 78-81; C Caterham and Chapl St Lawr Hosp Caterham 82-84; rtd 85; PtO *S'wark* from 85. *15 Whitgift House, 76 Brighton Road, Croydon CR2 6AB* T: (020) 8680 0028

PARSONS, Canon Jennifer Anne. b 53. Univ of Wales (Lamp) BA 76 MA 78 Jes Coll Cam PhD 90. Westcott Ho Cam 92. d 94 p 95. C Halesowen *Worc* 94-97; TV Worc St Barn w Ch Ch 97-04; R Matson *Glouc* 04-12; Hon Can Glouc Cathl 07-12; Asst Dean of Women Clergy 09-11; rtd 12; PtO *St D* from 12; Dioc Officer for Soc Resp from 15. *Lan Fach, Cefnypant, Whitland SA34 0TS* T: (01994) 419808 E: jeni@hencity.fsnet.co.uk

PARSONS, Jeremy Douglas Adam. b 64. Ox Univ MA. Ridley Hall Cam. d 09 p 11. NSM Cambridge St Martin *Ely* 09-13; PtO *S'well* 13-14; TV Saffron Walden and Villages *Chelmsf* from 14. *The Vicarage, Church Street, Great Chesterford, Saffron Walden CB10 1NP* M: 07980-016974 T: (01799) 667344 E: jeremy.parsons@gmail.com *or* teamvicar@outlook.com

PARSONS, Canon John Banham. b 43. Selw Coll Cam BA 65 MA 68. Ridley Hall Cam 65. d 67 p 68. C Downend *Bris* 67-71; Public Preacher Withywood LEP 71-77; P-in-c Hengrove 77-78; V 78-85; V Letchworth St Paul w Willian *St Alb* 85-94; P-in-c Barking St Marg w St Patr *Chelmsf* 94-98; TR 98-04; RD Barking and Dagenham 00-04; P-in-c Hornchurch H Cross 04-09; RD Havering 04-08; Hon Can Chelmsf Cathl 01-09; rtd 09. *8 Pound Close, Upper Caldecote, Biggleswade SG18 9AU* T: (01767) 315285 E: j.parsons986@btinternet.com

PARSONS, Canon Marlene Beatrice. b 43. Wilson Carlile Coll. **dss** 76 d 87 p 94. Coulsdon St Jo *S'wark* 76-79; Hill *Birm* 79-86; Dioc Lay Min Adv 80-90; Vice Prin WMMTC 86-90; Dioc Dir of Ords *Birm* 90-04; Dean of Women's Min 90-04; Hon Can Birm Cathl 89-04; rtd 04; PtO *Birm* from 04. *20 Copperbeech Close, Birmingham B32 2HT* T: 0121-427 2632

PARSONS, Michael. b 46. Open Univ BA 84. SWMTC 05. d 08

p 09. NSM Boscastle w Davidstow *Truro* 08-15; NSM Boscastle and Tintagel Gp from 15. *2 Penally Terrace, Boscastle PL35 0HA* T: (01840) 250625 E: mike@2penally.co.uk

PARSONS, Canon Michael William Semper. b 47. St Cath Coll Ox BA 69 MA 74 DPhil 74 Selw Coll Cam BA 77 MA 81. Ridley Hall Cam 75. d 78 p 79. C Edmonton All SS *Lon* 78-81; SPCK Research Fell Dur Univ 81-84; Hon Lect Th 84-85; SPCK Fell N of England Inst for Chr Educn 84-85; P-in-c Derby St Aug 85-95; TR Walbrook Epiphany 95-96; Dioc Voc Adv 86-96; P-in-c Hempsted *Glouc* 96-00; Dir of Ords 96-04; Dir Curates' Tr 00-04; Prin WEMTC *Glouc* 04-11; Prin Lect Glos Univ 09-11; P-in-c Coney Hill 11-15; rtd 15; Hon Can Glouc Cathl from 03. *6 Spa Villas, Montpellier, Gloucester GL1 1LB* E: mwsp@btinternet.com

PARSONS, Canon Robert Martin. b 43. Qu Coll Cam BA 65 MA 69. ALCD 68. d 68 p 69. C Chapeltown *Sheff* 68-71; C Sheff St Jo 71-75; V Swadlincote *Derby* 75-91; RD Repton 81-91; P-in-c Gresley 82-86; R Etwall w Egginton 91-93; Can Res Derby Cathl 93-98; Hon Can Derby Cathl 98-09; P-in-c Belper 98-03; V 03-09; Jt P-in-c Ambergate and Heage 06-09; rtd 09; Hon C Bicton, Montford w Shrawardine and Fitz *Lich* from 09; Hon C Leaton and Albrighton w Battlefield from 09. *The Vicarage, Baschurch Road, Bomere Heath, Shrewsbury SY4 3PN* T: (01939) 291494 E: canonparsons@tiscali.co.uk

PARSONS, Roger John. b 37. Sarum Th Coll 62. d 65 p 66. C Bitterne Park *Win* 65-69; C Clerkenwell H Redeemer w St Phil *Lon* 69-72; C Willesden St Andr 72-76; C St Laur in Thanet *Cant* 76-81; Chapl Luton and Dunstable Hosp 81-86; Chapl St Mary's Hosp Luton 81-86; C Luton All SS w St Pet *St Alb* 81-86; TV E Dereham *Nor* 86-88; TV E Dereham and Scarning 89; PtO 89-93. *Address temp unknown*

PARSONS, Stephen Christopher. b 45. Keble Coll Ox BA 67 MA 72 BLitt 78. Cuddesdon Coll 68. d 70 p 71. C Whitstable All SS *Cant* 70-71; C Croydon St Sav 71-74; PtO *Ox* 74-76; C St Laur in Thanet *Cant* 76-79; V Lugwardine w Bartestree and Weston Beggard *Heref* 79-87; V Lechlade *Glouc* 87-03; R Edin St Cuth 03-10; rtd 10. *12 The Green, Dalston, Carlisle CA5 7QB* T: (01228) 712780 E: stephen@parsons262.orangehome.co.uk

PARSONS, Stephen Drury. b 54. Qu Mary Coll Lon BSc 76 CCC Cam MSc 79. Westcott Ho Cam 79. d 82 p 83. C Stretford All SS *Man* 82-85; C Newton Heath All SS 85-86; V Ashton St Jas 86-90; PtO 97-13; TR Turton Moorland from 13. *St Anne's Vicarage, High Street, Turton, Bolton BL7 0EH* T: (01204) 777167 E: rectorturton@outlook.com

PARSONS, Mrs Susan Catherine. b 60. SWMTC 06 ERMC 08. d 09 p 10. NSM Oakham, Ashwell, Braunston, Brooke, Egleton etc *Pet* 09-11; NSM Polden Wheel *B & W* from 12. *Greystones, Broadway, Chilton Polden, Bridgwater TA7 9DJ* E: susie.parsons@hotmail.co.uk

PARSONS, Thomas James. b 74. K Coll Lon BMus 97 LRAM 96. Oak Hill Th Coll BA 06. d 06 p 07. C Hensingham *Carl* 06-10; V Sidcup Ch Ch *Roch* from 10. *The Vicarage, 16 Christchurch Road, Sidcup DA15 7HE* T: (020) 8308 0835 M: 07960-944287 E: tjparsons@tiscali.co.uk

PARTINGTON, The Ven Brian Harold. b 36. OBE 02. St Aid Birkenhead 60. d 63 p 64. C Barlow Moor *Man* 63-66; C Deane 66-68; V Patrick *S & M* 68-96; Bp's Youth Chapl 68-77; RD Peel 76-96; P-in-c German St Jo 77-78; V 78-96; P-in-c Foxdale 77-78; V 78-96; Can St German's Cathl 85-96; Adn of Man 96-05; V Douglas St Geo 96-04; rtd 04. *Brambles, Patrick Village, Peel, Isle of Man IM5 3AH* T: (01624) 844173 E: bpartington@mcb.net

PARTINGTON, John. See PARTINGTON, Peter John

PARTINGTON, Kenneth. b 41. Lanc Univ MA 86. Ripon Hall Ox. d 70 p 71. C Atherton *Man* 70-72; C Kippax *Ripon* 72-75; V Cartmel Fell *Carl* 75-95; V Crosthwaite Kendal 75-95; V Witherslack 75-95; V Winster 78-95; rtd 01; PtO *Carl* from 01; *Blackb* from 03. *Kilvert Heights, 9 Castle Park, Kendal LA9 7AX* T: (01539) 723963

PARTINGTON, Canon Kevin. b 51. Huddersfield Poly BA 73. St Jo Coll Nottm 91. d 93 p 94. C Salterhebble All SS *Wakef* 93-96; V Pontefract All SS 96-03; TR Dewsbury Leeds from 03; AD from 13; Hon Can Wakef Cathl from 07; *The Rectory, 16A Oxford Road, Dewsbury WF13 4JT* T: (01924) 465491 *or* 457057 E: kevin.partington@btinternet.com

PARTINGTON, Peter John. b 57. Peterho Cam MA. St Jo Coll Nottm 79. d 81 p 82. C Cov H Trin 81-85; C Woking St Jo *Guildf* 85-87 and 94-99; R Busbridge 87-94; Dir of Ords 94-03; P-in-c Winchcombe, Gretton, Sudeley Manor etc *Glouc* 03-05; TR Winchcombe 05-15; TV S Cotswolds from 15. *The Vicarage, Church Lane, Coln St Aldwyns, Cirencester GL7 5AG*

PARTON, John Michael. b 44. Bradf & Ilkley Community Coll MA 93. d 04 p 05. NSM Horbury w Horbury Bridge *Wakef* 04-10; NSM Dewsbury Deanery from 10. *106 Lennox Drive, Wakefield WF2 8LF* T/F: (01924) 360395 E: johnmparton@btinternet.com

PARTON, Mrs Michelle Elizabeth. b 82. Qu Coll Birm 12. **d** 15. C Wythall *Birm* from 15. *247 Alcester Road, Hollywood, Birmingham B47 5HG* T: 0121-430 2775
E: michelleparton@hotmail.co.uk

PARTRIDGE, Alan Christopher. b 55. Thames Poly BA 77 Ex Univ PGCE 78. St Jo Coll Nottm MA 00. **d** 00 **p** 01. C Woking St Jo *Guildf* 00-03; C Ely 03-08; TV 08-09; P-in-c Sawston from 09; P-in-c Babraham from 09. *The Vicarage, Church Lane, Sawston, Cambridge CB22 3JR* T: (01223) 832248
E: a.partridge7@ntlworld.com

PARTRIDGE, Anthony John. b 38. Univ of Wales (Lamp) BA 61 Linacre Ho Ox BA 63 K Coll Lon PhD 77. St Steph Ho Ox 61. **d** 64 **p** 65. C Sydenham All SS *S'wark* 64-67; Hon C 68-74; LtO 74-08; PtO from 08; Lect Woolwich Poly 67-70; Thames Poly 70-74; Prin Lect 75-92; Greenwich Univ *S'wark* 92-03; rtd 03. *40 Upwood Road, London SE12 8AN* T: (020) 8318 9901
E: tony-partridge1@o2.co.uk

PARTRIDGE, Mrs Bryony Gail. b 51. St Anne's Coll Ox BA 72 MA 76 Ox Univ PGCE 73 Leeds Univ BA 11. Yorks Min Course 09. **d** 11 **p** 12. NSM Oakworth *Leeds* from 11. *New House Farm, Oakworth, Keighley BD22 7JW* T: (01535) 643206
E: geraldandbryony@hotmail.com

PARTRIDGE, Canon David John Fabian. b 36. Ball Coll Ox BA 60 MA. Westcott Ho Cam 60. **d** 62 **p** 63. C Halliwell St Thos *Man* 62-65; C St Martin-in-the-Fields *Lon* 65-69; R Warblington w Emsworth *Portsm* 69-01; Hon Can Portsm Cathl 84-01; rtd 01. *3 Frarydene, Prinsted, Emsworth PO10 8HU*

PARTRIDGE, Ian Starr. b 36. Linc Th Coll 87. **d** 89 **p** 90. C Barton upon Humber *Linc* 89-92; P-in-c Barkwith Gp 92-97; R 97-02; rtd 02; PtO *Linc* from 02; RD Calcewaithe and Candleshoe 03-05. *Altair, 4 Thames Street, Louth LN11 7AD* T: (01507) 600398 E: ian@altair.org.uk

PARTRIDGE, Martin David Waud. b 38. Ox NSM Course 86. **d** 89 **p** 90. NSM Wargrave *Ox* 89-97; NSM Schorne 97-05; rtd 05; PtO *Ox* from 05. *Barnes House, St James Street, Eastbury, Hungerford RG17 7JL* T: (01488) 670281

PARTRIDGE, Preb Michael John. b 61. St Edm Hall Ox BA 83 MA 89 St Jo Coll Dur BA 86. Cranmer Hall Dur 84. **d** 87 **p** 88. C Amington *Birm* 87-90; C Sutton Coldfield H Trin 90-93; P-in-c W Exe *Ex* 93-01; RD Tiverton 96-00; V Tiverton St Geo and St Paul 01-06; P-in-c Pinhoe and Broadclyst 06-13; P-in-c Aylesbeare, Rockbeare, Farringdon etc 06-13; TR Broadclyst, Clyst Honiton, Pinhoe, Rockbeare etc from 13; Preb Ex Cathl from 12. *The Rectory, 9 Church Hill, Pinhoe, Exeter EX4 9ER* T: (01392) 466257 E: m.partridge@talktalk.net

PARTRIDGE, Richard Bruce. b 69. STETS. **d** 12 **p** 13. NSM Christchurch *Win* from 12. *The Paddocks, Holly Lane, Walkford, Christchurch BH23 5QQ* T: (01425) 279043 M: 07903-252230
E: richardpartridge310@btinternet.com

PARTRIDGE, Ronald Malcolm. b 49. Bris Bapt Coll LTh 74 Cuddesdon Coll 74. **d** 75 **p** 76. C Bris St Andr Hartcliffe 75-78; C E Bris 78-82; V Easton All Hallows 82-85; TV Brighton St Pet w Chpl Royal and St Jo *Chich* 85-86; TV Brighton St Pet and St Nic w Chpl Royal 86-88; C-in-c Bermondsey St Hugh CD *S'wark* 88-90; Asst Chapl Gt Ormond Street Hosp for Children NHS Trust 91-97. *29 All Saints Street, Hastings TN34 3BJ* T: (01424) 715219

PARTRIDGE, Ronald William. b 42. Shimer Coll Illinois BA 64. Cant Sch of Min 93. **d** 96 **p** 97. NSM Upchurch w Lower Halstow *Cant* 96-12; PtO *Roch* from 10; *Cant* from 12. *4 The Green, Lower Halstow, Sittingbourne ME9 7DT* T: (01795) 842007 M: 07779-789039 E: revdron.partridge@virgin.net

PARTRIDGE, Mrs Sarah Mercy. b 59. SEITE 04. **d** 07 **p** 08. NSM Tunbridge Wells K Chas *Roch* from 07. *Long Hedges, Station Road, Rotherfield, Crowborough TN6 3HP* T: (01892) 853451
E: spartridge@partridges59.fsnet.co.uk

PARTRIDGE, Stephen Hugh. b 70. Bath Univ BSc 91 Univ of Wales (Swansea) PGCE 92. St Jo Coll Nottm MTh 13. **d** 13 **p** 14. C Canford Magna *Sarum* from 13. *174 Lynwood Drive, Wimborne BH21 1UU* T: (01202) 880702
E: revspartridge@gmail.com

PARTRIDGE, Canon Timothy Reeve. b 39. Lon Univ BSc 60 AKC 60. Wells Th Coll 60. **d** 62 **p** 63. C Glouc St Cath 62-65; C Sutton St Nicholas *Linc* 65-74; R Bugbrooke *Pet* 74-95; R Bugbrooke w Rothersthorpe 95-04; RD Daventry 81-88; Can Pet Cathl 83-04; Warden of Par Ev 96-02; rtd 04. *54 Thorney Leys, Witney OX28 5LS* T: (01993) 864926
E: tim.partridge39@tiscali.co.uk

PASCHAL, Brother. *See* WORTON, David Reginald Paschal

PASCOE, Mrs Caroline Elizabeth Alice. b 57. **d** 08 **p** 09. NSM Ewenny w St Brides Major *Llan* 08-10; Lay Development Officer *Heref* from 10. *Diocesan Office, The Palace, Hereford HR4 9BL* T: (01432) 373300 F: 352952

PASCOE, Lorraine Eve. *See* SUMMERS, Lorraine Eve

PASCOE, Michael Lewis. b 43. **d** 99 **p** 00. OLM Crowan and Treslothan *Truro* 99-02; C 02-13; OLM Penponds

01-02; C 02-13; P-in-c 13-14; rtd 14. *Genesis, Bosparva Lane, Leedstown, Hayle TR27 6DN* T: (01736) 850425
E: revdmike@supanet.com

PASHLEY, Howard Thomas. b 47. Kent Univ MSc 85 Keele Univ PGCE 71 ARIC 70. **d** 06 **p** 07. OLM Sandwich *Cant* 06-12; OLM Sandwich and Worth from 12. *56 New Street, Sandwich CT13 9BB* T: (01304) 612018
E: howardpashley@yahoo.co.uk

PASK, Howard. b 54. St Jo Coll Nottm. **d** 99 **p** 00. C Todmorden *Wakef* 99-02; P-in-c Hebden Bridge 02-03; P-in-c Heptonstall 02-03; V Hebden Bridge and Heptonstall *Leeds* from 03. *The Vicarage, 12 Becketts Close, Heptonstall, Hebden Bridge HX7 7LJ* T: (01422) 842138 M: 07779-243176
E: howardpask@btinternet.com

PASKETT, Ms Margaret Anne. b 45. Northd Coll of Educn CertEd 67 York Univ BSc 81 Leeds Univ MEd 83. NEOC 84. **d** 87 **p** 94. Par Dn Marske in Cleveland *York* 87-91; C 92-96; Dioc Adv for Diaconal Mins 92-96; P-in-c Hemingbrough and Tr Officer (York Adnry) 96-05; rtd 06. *15 Hubert Street, York YO23 1EF* T: (01904) 626521
E: annepaskett62@btinternet.com

PASKINS, David James. b 52. Univ of Wales (Lamp) BA 73 Trin Hall Cam BA 76 MA 81. Westcott Ho Cam 74. **d** 77 **p** 78. C St Peter-in-Thanet *Cant* 77-80; C Swanage *Sarum* 80-82; R Waldron *Chich* 82-92; R Bere Ferrers *Ex* 92-96; V Lockerley and E Dean w E and W Tytherley *Win* 96-03; R Cranborne w Boveridge, Edmondsham etc *Sarum* from 03. *The Rectory, Grugs Lane, Cranborne, Wimborne BH21 5PX* T: (01725) 517232
E: david@paskins.eclipse.co.uk

PASSANT, Keith. b 39. St Jo Coll Dur BA 62 CertEd 70. St Alb Minl Tr Scheme 77. **d** 87 **p** 88. C Hatfield Hyde *St Alb* 87-93; rtd 93; PtO *St Alb* from 93. *26 Monk's Rise, Welwyn Garden City AL8 7NF* T: (01707) 332869

PASSEY, Miss Rhona Margaret. b 52. St Jo Coll Nottm BTh 96. EMMTC 06. **d** 09 **p** 10. NSM Hugglescote w Donington, Ellistown and Snibston *Leic* 09-13; NSM Broom Leys from 13. *14 Atherstone Road, Measham, Swadlincote DE12 7EG* T: (01530) 270823 M: 07787-573731
E: rhona.passey@btinternet.com

PASTERFIELD, Laura. b 85. Univ of the Arts Lon BA 07 Rob Coll Cam BTh 13. Ridley Hall Cam 11. **d** 13 **p** 14. C Liv All SS from 13. *12 Whitcroft Road, Liverpool L6 8NJ* M: 07557-501582
E: lpasterfield@gmail.com

PATCH, Simon John. b 63. Aus Nat Univ BA 88 Southn Univ BTh 95 Univ of S Qld MEd 15. Chich Th Coll 92 92 Westcott Ho Cam 94. **d** 95 **p** 96. C Ifield *Chich* 95-99; TV 99-03; C Stepney St Dunstan and All SS *Lon* 03-06; Hong Kong from 07. *Flat D/20F, Tower 2, Dragon View, Chung Hau Street, Ho Man Tin, Kowloon, Hong Kong, China*
E: simon_patch@yahoo.com.au

PATCHELL, Miss Gwendoline Rosa. b 49. Goldsmiths' Coll Lon BA 69 TCert 70. Trin Coll Bris 90. **d** 92 **p** 94. C Ashton-upon-Mersey St Mary Magd *Ches* 92-98; TV Hemel Hempstead *St Alb* 98-06; P-in-c Kirkby in Ashfield *S'well* 06-11; R 11-14; rtd 14. *21 Leivers Close, East Leake, Loughborough LE12 6PQ*

PATCHING, Colin John. b 47. Linc Th Coll 84. **d** 86 **p** 87. C Farnley *Ripon* 86-89; C Didcot St Pet *Ox* 89-92; P-in-c Steventon w Milton 92-97; R from 98. *The Vicarage, 73 Field Gardens, Steventon, Abingdon OX13 6TF* T: (01235) 831243
E: cpatching@toucansurf.com

PATCHING, Julian Francis. b 65. Colchester Inst BA 87 Liv Inst of HE PGCE 88. Ushaw Coll Dur 88. **d** 93 **p** 94. In RC Ch 93-09; C Langdon Hills *Chelmsf* from 13. *19 Glenwood Gardens, Langdon Hills, Basildon SS16 6TU* T: (01268) 541004
M: 07535-674594 E: jfp65@hotmail.co.uk

PATE, Barry Emile Charles. b 50. NE Lon Poly BA 80 CQSW 80. S'wark Ord Course 85. **d** 88 **p** 89. NSM E Dulwich St Jo *S'wark* 88-92; C Farnborough *Roch* 92-94; C Broxbourne w Wormley *St Alb* 94-00; V Wilbury from 00. *Church House, 103 Bedford Road, Letchworth Garden City SG6 4DU* T/F: (01462) 623119
E: b.pate@ntlworld.com

PATEL, Jitesh Krisnakavi. b 82. Jes Coll Ox MPhys 04 Kellogg Coll Ox PGCE 06. Wycliffe Hall Ox BA 09 MA 09. **d** 10 **p** 11. C Abingdon *Ox* 10-13; C N Abingdon from 13. *33 Mattock Way, Abingdon OX14 2PQ* T: (01235) 524159
E: bioneural@hotmail.com

PATEMAN, Edward Brian. b 29. Leeds Univ BA 51. Qu Coll Birm 51. **d** 53 **p** 54. C Stockton St Pet 53-57; Lect Bolton St Pet 57-58; V Coxhoe *Dur* 58-65; V Dalton le Dale 65-93; RD Houghton 72-75; R Hawthorn 88-93; rtd 93; PtO *Dur* from 93. *27 Atherton Drive, Houghton le Spring DH4 6TA* T: 0191-385 3168

PATERNOSTER, Canon Michael Cosgrove. b 35. Pemb Coll Cam BA 59 MA 63. Cuddesdon Coll 59. **d** 61 **p** 62. C Surbiton St Andr *S'wark* 61-63; Chapl Qu Coll Dundee 63-68; Dioc Supernumerary *Bre* 63-68; Chapl Dundee Univ 67-68; Sec Fellowship of SS Alb and Sergius 68-71; R Dollar *St And* 71-75;

R Stonehaven *Bre* 75-90; Hon Can St Paul's Cathl Dundee from 81; R Aberdeen St Jas *Ab* 90-00; rtd 00; PtO *B & W* from 00. *12 Priest Row, Wells BA5 2PY*

PATERSON, Alan Michael. b 64. **d** 06 **p** 07. NSM Bartley Green *Birm* 06-10; V Cowgate *Newc* from 10. *St Peter's Vicarage, Druridge Drive, Newcastle upon Tyne NE5 3LP* T: 0191-286 9913

PATERSON (*née* SOAR), Mrs Angela Margaret. b 59. Aston Univ MSc 81 MCIPD 82. SAOMC 97. **d** 00 **p** 01. NSM Icknield *Ox* from 00. *86 Hill Road, Watlington OX49 5AF* T: (01491) 614033 E: angie.paterson@btinternet.com

PATERSON, David. b 33. Ch Ch *Ox* BA 55 MA 58. Linc Th Coll 56. **d** 58 **p** 59. C Kidderminster St Mary *Worc* 58-60; C Wolverhampton St Geo *Lich* 60-64; V Loughborough St Pet *Leic* 64-04; rtd 04; PtO *Ox* from 05. *Address temp unknown* E: davidpaterson129@hotmail.com

PATERSON, Douglas Monro. b 30. Em Coll Cam BA 54 MA 57. Tyndale Hall Bris 55. **d** 57 **p** 58. C Walcot *B & W* 57-60; C Portman Square St Paul *Lon* 60-62; Lect Oak Hill Th Coll 60-62; Min Hampstead St Jo Downshire Hill Prop Chpl *Lon* 62-65; Lect All Nations Chr Coll Ware 62-65; Rwanda 67-73; C Edin St Thos 73-75; Lect Northumbria Bible Coll 73-94; PtO *Edin* 75-94; LtO *Newc* 76-94; rtd 94; PtO *Ox* 94-10; *York* from 10. *8 Dulverton Hall, Esplanade, Scarborough YO11 2AR* T: (01723) 340108

PATERSON, Geoffrey Gordon. b 45. Cant Univ (NZ) LTh 69. **d** 69 **p** 70. C Linwood New Zealand 69-71; C Belfast-Redwood 71-76; V Mayfield Mt Somers 76-78; P-in-c Astwood Bank w Crabbs Cross *Worc* 78-80; V Halswell-Prebbleton New Zealand 80-87; Chapl Sunnyside Hosp 87-95. *19 Ridder Place, Christchurch 8025, New Zealand* T: (0064) (3) 322 7787 or 365 3211 E: geoffpat@xtra.co.nz

PATERSON, James Beresford. b 21. DSC 42. St Andr Univ MPhil 85 FRSA 93. Westcott Ho Cam 59. **d** 61 **p** 62. C Woodbridge St Mary *St E* 61-64; R Broughty Ferry *Bre* 64-72; Dioc Supernumerary 72-75; Sec Scottish Ch Action for World Development 72-79; P-in-c Glencarse *Bre* 76-84; Dioc Sec 79-84; Hon Can St Paul's Cathl Dundee 79-89; rtd 84; PtO *Bre* from 84; *St E* from 84. *67 Ipswich Road, Woodbridge IP12 4BT* T: (01394) 383512

PATERSON, Mrs Jennifer Ann. b 49. Brooklands Tech Coll 69. S Dios Minl Tr Scheme 85. **d** 88 **p** 95. C Hale *Guildf* 88-92; PtO 94-95; NSM Seale, Puttenham and Wanborough 95-01; rtd 01; PtO *Guildf* from 01. *4 St George's Close, Badshot Lea, Farnham GU9 9LZ* T: (01252) 316775 E: ja.paterson@btinternet.com

✠**PATERSON, The Rt Revd John Campbell.** b 45. Auckland Univ BA 66. St Jo Coll Auckland. **d** 69 **p** 70 **c** 95. C Whangarei New Zealand 69-71; V Waimate Maori N Pastorate 71-76; Co-Missr Auckland Maori Miss 76; Chapl Qu Victoria Sch 76-82; CF 76-92; Sec Bishopric of Aotearoa New Zealand 78-87; Prov Sec 86-92; Gen Sec Angl Ch in Aotearoa NZ and Polynesia 92-95; Bp Auckland 95-10; rtd 10; PtO Auckland New Zealand from 10. *PO Box 87255, Meadowbank, Auckland 1742, New Zealand* T: (0064) (9) 524 8910 E: johnandmarionn@orcon.net.nz

PATERSON, Michael Séan. b 61. Heythrop Coll Lon BD 89 MA 95 Univ of Wales (Lamp) MMin 04. **d** 04 **p** 05. C Stonehaven *Bre* 04-05; C Arbroath 05-06; C Edin Ch Ch 06-08; Chapl St Andr Hospice Airdrie 08-09; Chapl St Columba's Hospice from 09. *St Columba's Hospice, Boswall Road, Edinburgh EH5 3RW* T: 0131-551 77706 E: mpaterson@stcolumbashospice.org.uk

PATERSON, Mrs Moira Whillans. b 53. Edin Univ BA 74 Lon Univ BA 91. TISEC 07. **d** 10 **p** 11. C St Andr Cathl from 10. *40 North Street, Inverurie AB51 4RS* T: (01467) 620428 M: 07528-774046 E: moira.paterson1@virgin.net

PATERSON, Nigel John Merrick. b 53. Lanc Univ BEd 75 Open Univ MA 89. **d** 01 **p** 02. OLM N Walsham and Edingthorpe *Nor* from 01. *Marshgate Cottage, Marshgate, North Walsham NR28 9LG* T: (01692) 406259 M: 07786-381361 E: nigel-paterson@tiscali.co.uk

PATERSON, Rex Douglas Trevor. b 27. AKC 54. **d** 55 **p** 56. C Maidenhead St Luke *Ox* 55-58; C Littlehampton St Mary *Chich* 58-62; V Woodingdean 62-73; V Ferring 73-94; rtd 94; PtO *Chich* from 94. *14 Hurst Avenue, Worthing BN11 5NY* T: (01903) 504252

✠**PATERSON, The Rt Revd Robert Mar Erskine.** b 49. St Jo Coll Dur BA 71 MA 82. Cranmer Hall Dur. **d** 72 **p** 73 **c** 08. C Harpurhey St Steph and Harpurhey Ch Ch *Man* 72-73; C Sketty *S & B* 73-78; R Llangattock and Llangynidr 78-83; V Gabalfa *Llan* 83-94; TR Cowbridge 94-00; Prin Officer Ch in Wales Coun for Miss and Min 00-06; Metrop Can 04-08; Abp's Chapl and Researcher *York* 06-08; Bp S & M from 08. *Thie yn Aspick, 4 The Falls, Tromode Road, Cronkbourne, Douglas, Isle of Man IM4 4PZ* T: (01624) 622108 E: bishop@sodorandman.im

PATERSON, Robin Fergus (Robert). b 32. Moore Th Coll Sydney 83. **d** 87 **p** 89. Singapore 87-88; NSM Crieff *St And* 88-92; NSM Comrie 88-92; R Dunkeld 93-98; R Strathtay 93-98; rtd 98; LtO *St And* from 98; *Eur* from 98. *1 Corsiehill House, Corsiehill, Perth PH2 7BN* T: (01738) 446621 E: robinatcorsie@talktalk.net

PATERSON, Robin Lennox Andrew. b 43. NOC 84. **d** 87 **p** 88. C Manston *Ripon* 87-91; P-in-c Leeds All So 91-95; V 95-98; V Middleton St Mary 98-08; rtd 08. *22 Manston Way, Leeds LS18 5BR* M: 07778-860178 E: rlap@ntlworld.com

PATERSON, Rodney John. b 62. Keele Univ BA 84. St Jo Coll Nottm MA 98. **d** 98 **p** 99. C Huddersfield H Trin *Wakef* 98-01; P-in-c Charlton Kings H Apostles *Glouc* 01-14; V from 14; P-in-c Cheltenham St Mich from 14. *The Vicarage, 1A Langton Grove Road, Charlton Kings, Cheltenham GL52 6JA* T: (01242) 512254 E: rod.paterson@holyapostles.org.uk

PATERSON, Mrs Shirley Anne. b 56. Reading Univ BA 78 Ex Univ PGCE 79. SWMTC 11. **d** 14. NSM Barnstaple *Ex* from 14. *Elm Cottage, Ladywell, Barnstaple EX31 1QS* T: (01271) 346095 M: 07971-251707 E: shirley.p@live.co.uk

PATERSON, Stuart Maxwell. b 37. Kelham Th Coll 57 Lich Th Coll 58. **d** 60 **p** 61. C Ilkeston St Mary *Derby* 60-64; V Somercotes 64-70; R Wingerworth 70-73; P-in-c Hawick *Edin* 92-95; R 95-00; rtd 00; LtO *Ab* 05-13; P-in-c Aberdeen St Jas 07-12; P-in-c Whiterashes 09-12; PtO from 13. *40 North Street, Inverurie AB51 4RS* T: (01467) 620428 E: patersonstuart1@gmail.com

PATERSON, Mrs Susan Ann. b 57. St Hilda's Coll Ox MA 84. EMMTC 92. **d** 95 **p** 96. NSM Evington *Leic* 95-98; C Humberstone 98-03; TV Melton Mowbray 03-09; P-in-c Ab Kettleby and Holwell w Asfordby 09-15; V Deeping St James *Linc* from 15. *The Vicarage, 50 Spalding Road, Deeping St James, Peterborough PE6 8UJ* E: revpaterson@gmail.com

PATO, Luke Luscombe Lungile. b 49. Fort Hare Univ BA 76 Manitoba Univ MA 80. St Bede's Coll Umtata. **d** 74 **p** 75. S Africa 73-81 and from 92; Canada 81-90; Tutor Coll of Ascension Selly Oak 90-92. *PO Box 62098, Marshalltown, 2107 South Africa* T: (0027) (11) 763 2510 or 492 1380 M: 83-367 3961 E: luke@cpsa.org.za

PATON, David. See PATON, John David Marshall

PATON, Canon Ian James. b 57. Jes Coll Cam MA 78 PGCE 79 Edin Univ MTh 07. Westcott Ho Cam MA 81. **d** 82 **p** 83. C Whitley Ch Ch *Ox* 82-84; Bp's Dom Chapl 84-86; Chapl Wadh Coll Ox 86-90; C Ox St Mary V w St Cross and St Pet 86-90; Can and Vice Provost St Mary's Cathl Edin 90-94; R Edin St Mary 90-94; R Haddington and Dunbar 94-97; R Edin Old St Paul from 97; Can St Mary's Cathl from 04; Hon Chapl Edin Univ from 11. *Lauder House, 39 Jeffrey Street, Edinburgh EH1 1DH* T: 0131-556 3332 M: 07751-510594 E: rector@osp.org.uk

PATON, Preb John David Marshall. b 47. Barrister-at-Law (Middle Temple) 71. St Steph Ho Ox 81. **d** 83 **p** 84. C Bethnal Green St Matt w St Jas the Gt *Lon* 83-86; P-in-c St Geo-in-the-East St Mary 86-89; V 89-92; P-in-c Bethnal Green St Barn 92-96; AD Tower Hamlets 92-96; Dir Post-Ord Tr 92-99; P-in-c St Vedast w St Mich-le-Querne etc 97-06; P-in-c St Botolph without Bishopgate 97-06; AD The City 00-06; Master R Foundn of St Kath in Ratcliffe 06-12; Preb St Paul's Cathl 04-12; rtd 12. *Address temp unknown*

PATON, John William Scholar. b 52. Mert Coll Ox BA 74 MA 95. St Steph Ho Ox 93. **d** 95 **p** 96. C Sherborne w Castleton and Lillington *Sarum* 95-98; Succ S'wark Cathl 98-01; Chapl Medical and Dental Students K Coll Lon 98-01; P-in-c Purley St Mark S'wark 01-07; P-in-c Purley St Swithun 05-07; Prec Ch Ch Ox from 07. *Christ Church, Oxford OX1 1DP* T: (01865) 276150 E: john_w_s_paton@msn.com

PATON, The Ven Michael John Macdonald. b 22. Magd Coll Ox BA 49 MA 54. Linc Th Coll 52. **d** 54 **p** 55. C Gosforth All SS *Newc* 54-57; V Norton Woodseats St Chad *Sheff* 57-67; Sen Chapl Sheff United Hosps 67-70; Chapl Weston Park Hosp Sheff 70-78; V Sheff St Mark Broomhall 70-78; Adn Sheff 78-87; Can Res Sheff Cathl 78-87; rtd 88; PtO *Sheff* 88-10. *Room 16, Manormead, Tilford Road, Hindhead GU26 6RA*

PATON-WILLIAMS, Canon David Graham. b 58. Warwick Univ BA 81 Selw Coll Cam BA 86 MA 90 Newc Univ MA 92. Ridley Hall Cam 84. **d** 87 **p** 88. C S Westoe *Dur* 87-90; C Newton Aycliffe 90-91; TV 91-93; Chapl Univ Coll of Ripon and York St Jo 93-98; Min Can Ripon Cathl 93-98; R Bedale 98-02; P-in-c Leeming 98-02; R Bedale and Leeming 03-08; P-in-c Thornton Watlass 07-08; R Bedale and Leeming and Thornton Watlass 08; AD Wensley 05-08; V Roundhay St Edm *Leeds* from 08; Hon Can Ripon Cathl from 11. *St Edmund's Vicarage, 5A North Park Avenue, Leeds LS8 1DN* T: 0113-266 4532 E: davidpw@onetel.net

PATRICIA, Sister. See PERKINS, Patricia Doris

PATRICIA ANN, Sister. See GORDON, Patricia Ann

PATRICK, Andrew. b 83. Hull Univ BA 06. St Jo Coll Nottm 09. **d** 12 **p** 13. C Harrogate St Mark *Leeds* from 12. *10 Merryfield, Harrogate HG2 9DH* M: 07966-360437 E: mrandrewpatrick@gmail.com

PATRICK, Charles. *See* PATRICK, Peter Charles

PATRICK, Hugh Joseph. b 37. TCD BA 62 MA 66. **d** 63 **p** 64. C Dromore Cathl 63-66; C Lurgan Ch the Redeemer 66-70; C Rothwell *Ripon* 70-73; V Thurnscoe St Hilda *Sheff* 73-78; V Wales 78-02; P-in-c Thorpe Salvin 78-82; RD Laughton 93-98; rtd 02; PtO *Sheff* from 02. *5 Fairfax Avenue, Worksop S81 7RH* T: (01909) 477622 E: hughpatrick@sky.com

PATRICK, James Harry Johnson. b 67. Birm Poly LLB 88 Barrister 89. STETS 96 St Steph Ho Ox 99. **d** 99 **p** 00. Hon C Clifton All SS w St Jo *Bris* 99-10. *4 Clifton Park Road, Bristol BS8 3HL* T: 0117-908 0460 F: 930 3813 M: 07768-340344 E: jp@guildhallchambers.co.uk

PATRICK, Canon John Andrew. b 62. St Jo Coll Dur BA 84. Ripon Coll Cuddesdon 87. **d** 89 **p** 90. C Frankby w Greasby *Ches* 89-92; Lect Boston *Linc* 92-95; P-in-c Graffoe Gp 95-97; R 97-02; P-in-c New Sleaford 02-12; P-in-c Kirkby Laythorpe 10-12; RD Lafford 08-12; Can and Preb Linc Cathl 07-12; Can Res and Subdean Linc Cathl from 12. *The Subdeanery, 18 Minster Yard, Lincoln LN2 1PX* T: (01522) 561600 E: japatrick1@btinternet.com *or* subdean@lincolncathedral.com

PATRICK, Peter Charles. b 64. Leeds Univ BA 86 Fitzw Coll Cam BA 91 MA 95. Ridley Hall Cam 89. **d** 92 **p** 93. C Barton upon Humber *Linc* 92-96; TV Gt Grimsby St Mary and St Jas 96-03; RD Grimsby and Cleethorpes 99-03; R Middle Rasen Gp 03-15; P-in-c Barkwith Gp 07-15; R Horncastle Gp from 15. *9 Langton Drive, Horncastle LN9 5AJ* E: charles.patrick@talk21.com

PATTEN (née STARNS), Mrs Helen Edna. b 43. St Hilda's Coll Ox BA 65 Maria Grey Coll Lon CertEd 70. Trin Coll Bris 73 Oak Hill Th Coll 81. **dss** 82 **d** 87 **p** 94. Tunbridge Wells St Jo *Roch* 82-86; Patcham *Chich* 86-91; Par Dn 87-91; Par Dn Eckington w Handley and Ridgeway *Derby* 91-94; C 94-95; TV 95-98; Chapl St Mich Hospice 98-03; rtd 03; Hon C Fairlight and Pett *Chich* from 04. *Holyoak, Workhouse Lane, Westfield, Hastings TN35 4QJ* T: (01424) 752052

PATTEN, Miss Ruth Janet. b 72. Roehampton Inst BA 94 Goldsmiths' Coll Lon MMus 98. Westcott Ho Cam 08. **d** 10 **p** 11. C Witham *Chelmsf* 10-14; P-in-c Gt Dunmow and Barnston from 14. *The Vicarage, Charters, Dunmow CM6 2SJ* E: ruthjpatten@googlemail.com

PATTENDEN, Mrs Alison Margaret. b 53. Eastbourne Tr Coll CertEd 75 Sussex Univ BEd 76. St Steph Ho Ox 04. **d** 06 **p** 07. C Goring-by-Sea *Chich* 06-10; P-in-c Amberley w N Stoke and Parham, Wiggonholt etc 10-14; V from 14. *The New Vicarage, School Road, Amberley, Arundel BN18 9NA* T: (01798) 831500 E: revapattenden@btinternet.com

PATTERSON, Alfred Percy. d 85 **p** 87. NSM Aghalee *D & D* 85-91; C Gilford 91-93; Bp's C 95-00; rtd 00. *Brookdale, 723 Upper Newtownards Road, Belfast BT4 3NU* T: (028) 9029 4741 E: revap.patterson@ntlworld.com

PATTERSON, Andrew John. b 56. Master Mariner 85. Qu Coll Birm 85. **d** 88 **p** 89. C Newc St Phil and St Aug 88-92; Chapl Hunter's Moor Hosp 91-92; Asst Chapl R Victoria Infirmary Newc 92-96; V Whitley *Newc* from 96; Chapl Hexham Gen Hosp from 96. *The Vicarage, Whitley, Hexham NE46 2LA* T: (01434) 673379 E: revdocpatt@doctors.org.uk

PATTERSON, Anthony. b 43. Moore Th Coll Sydney BTh 82. **d** 83 **p** 83. Australia 83-91; C Darfield *Sheff* 91-94; TR Marfleet *York* 94-99; TV Heeley and Gleadless Valley *Sheff* 99-04; TR 04-10; AD Attercliffe 04-10; rtd 11; PtO *York* 11-13; P-in-c Bempton w Flamborough, Reighton w Speeton from 13. *The Vicarage, Church Street, Flamborough, Bridlington YO15 1PE* E: tonypatterson1@gmail.com

PATTERSON, Colin Hugh. b 52. St Pet Coll Ox MA 77 Univ of Wales (Cardiff) MPhil 90 CertEd 75. Trin Coll Bris. **d** 87 **p** 88. C Blackb Sav 87-90; C Haughton le Skerne *Dur* 90-93; Adult Educn Adv 93-05; Asst Dir Bridge Builders from 05; NSM Dur St Nic from 05. *24 Monks Crescent, Durham DH1 1HD* T: 0191-386 1691 E: colinpatterson@menno.org.uk

PATTERSON, Colin Peter Matthew. b 62. Newc Poly BA 84. St Steph Ho Ox 92. **d** 94 **p** 95. C Cullercoats St Geo *Newc* 94-97; Shrine P Shrine of Our Lady of Walsingham 97-99; P-in-c Harlow St Mary Magd *Chelmsf* 99-00; V 00-09; V Willesden Green St Andr and St Fran *Lon* from 09; CMP from 97. *The Clergy House, 4 St Andrew's Road, London NW10 2QS* T: (020) 8459 2670 E: cpmp1@btinternet.com

PATTERSON, Mrs Diane Rosemary. b 46. WMMTC 88. **d** 91 **p** 94. C Hill *Birm* 91-95; PtO 95-96; C Shottery St Andr *Cov* 96-01; C Hunningham 01-13; C Wappenbury w Weston under Wetherley 01-13; C Long Itchington and Marton 01-13;

C Offchurch 01-13; RD Southam 02-08; rtd 13; PtO *Cov* from 13. *169A Clopton Road, Stratford-upon-Avon CV37 6TF*

PATTERSON, Hugh John. b 38. Southn Univ MPhil 76. AKC 63. **d** 64 **p** 65. C Epsom St Martin *Guildf* 64-65; Chapl Ewell Coll 65-68; Asst Chapl and Lect Bp Otter Coll Chich 68-71; Lect Dudley Coll of Educn 71-77; Lect Wolv Poly 77-92; Wolv Univ 92-00; Chapl 89-00; rtd 01; Hon C Morville w Aston Eyre *Heref* from 82; Hon C Upton Cressett w Monk Hopton from 82; Hon C Acton Round from 82. *6 Victoria Road, Bridgnorth WV16 4LA* T: (01746) 765298

PATTERSON, John. *See* PATTERSON, Norman John

PATTERSON, John. b 27. MBIM 76. Bps' Coll Cheshunt 60. **d** 61 **p** 62. C Maidenhead St Luke *Ox* 61-65; Chapl RAF 65-72; V Ashton St Jas *Man* 72-78; USA 78-90; R Somercotes and Grainthorpe w Conisholme *Linc* 90-92; rtd 92; PtO *Linc* from 92. *9 Simpson Close, Barrow-upon-Humber DN19 7BL* T: (01469) 30867

PATTERSON, John Norton. b 39. TCD BA 64 MA 68. **d** 65 **p** 66. C Belfast St Paul *Conn* 65-68; C Larne and Inver 68-72; I Ballintoy w Rathlin and Dunseverick 72-05; Miss to Seafarers 72-05; Can Belf Cathl 97-05; Adn Dalriada *Conn* 01-05; rtd 05. *31 Moycraig Road, Dunseverick, Bushmills BT57 8TB* T: (028) 2073 0654

PATTERSON, Marjorie Jean. *See* BROWN, Marjorie Jean

PATTERSON, Neil Sydney. b 79. BNC Ox BA 00 MA 04. Ripon Coll Cuddesdon BA 03. **d** 04 **p** 05. C Cleobury Mortimer w Hopton Wafers etc *Heref* 04-08; TV Ross 08; R Ariconium from 08. *The Rectory, Weston under Penyard, Ross-on-Wye HR9 7QA* T: (01989) 567229 E: pattersonneil@hotmail.com

PATTERSON, Norman John. b 47. Peterho Cam BA 69 ALCD. St Jo Coll Nottm 70. **d** 73 **p** 74. C Everton St Ambrose w St Tim *Liv* 73-74; C Everton St Pet 74-78; TV 79-84; C Aigburth and Dioc Adv for Past Care and Counselling 84-92; V Gt Crosby All SS 92-04; Crosslinks Uganda 05-09; rtd 12. *6 Brookside, Great Boughton, Chester CH3 5TL* T: (01244) 314613 E: johnpatterson6098@yahoo.com

PATTERSON, Patric Douglas MacRae. b 51. Wycliffe Hall Ox 73. **d** 76 **p** 77. C Bebington *Ches* 76-79; Canada from 79. *The Rectory, PO Box 10, Milford ON K0K 2P0, Canada*

PATTERSON, Scott Robert. b 71. GTCL 92. Oak Hill Th Coll 07. **d** 09 **p** 10. C Newton Tracey, Horwood, Alverdiscott etc *Ex* 09-13; P-in-c Curry Rivel w Fivehead and Swell *B & W* from 13. *The Rectory, Church Street, Curry Rivel, Langport TA10 0HQ* M: 07973-139092 E: scottr.patterson@btinternet.com

PATTERSON, Susan Margaret. b 48. Otago Univ BA 71 BD 89 PhD 92. Knox Coll Dunedin 84. **d** 88 **p** 89. C Dunedin St Martin New Zealand 88-91; Tutor Otago Univ and Knox Coll 89-91; USA 91-92; Assoc P Hawke's Bay New Zealand 92-96; Lect Trin Coll Bris 97-00; I Kildallon w Newtowngore and Corrawallen *K, E & A* 00-04; I Killala w Dunfeeny, Crossmolina, Kilmoremoy etc *T, K & A* 04-10; Dean Killala 05-10; Sen Lect and Registrar Bishopdale Th Coll New Zealand from 10. *Bishop Eaton House, 30 Vanguard Street, PO Box 100, Nelson 7040, New Zealand* T: (0064) (3) 548 8785

PATTERSON, Trevor Harold. b 60. QUB BA 82 Stranmillis Coll PGCE 83. Trin Coll Bris 91. **d** 93 **p** 94. C Ashtead *Guildf* 93-98; V Richmond H Trin and Ch Ch *S'wark* from 98; AD Richmond and Barnes from 15. *Holy Trinity Vicarage, Sheen Park, Richmond TW9 1UP* T: (020) 8241 0042 *or* 8404 1113 E: trevor.patterson@htrichmond.org.uk

PATTIMORE, Daniel James. b 64. Nottm Univ MEng 88 Lon Bible Coll BA 94. Wycliffe Hall Ox 97. **d** 99 **p** 00. C Charlesworth and Dinting Vale *Derby* 99-03; NSM Norley, Crowton and Kingsley *Ches* 03-06; P-in-c Heanor *Derby* 04-14; P-in-c Langley Mill and Aldercar 07-14; NSM Kirkby Thore w Temple Sowerby and Newbiggin *Carl* from 14; NSM Heart of Eden from 14. *The Rectory, Kirkby Thore, Penrith CA10 1UR* M: 07973-406022 T: (017683) 62655 E: danpattimore@gmail.com

PATTIMORE (née GORDON), Mrs Kristy. b 72. Leeds Univ BA 94 Newc Univ PGCE 95. Wycliffe Hall Ox 98. **d** 01 **p** 02. C Hallwood *Ches* 01-04; NSM Heanor *Derby* 04-14; NSM Kirkby Thore w Temple Sowerby and Newbiggin *Carl* from 14; NSM Heart of Eden from 14. *The Rectory, Kirkby Thore, Penrith CA10 1UR* T: (017683) 62655 E: kristy@pattimore.com

PATTINSON, Christine Brodie. b 43. Darlington Tr Coll CertEd 64. **d** 06 **p** 07. OLM Chertsey, Lyne and Longcross *Guildf* 06-13. *28 Moorfields Close, Staines TW18 3LU* T: (01784) 457260 E: cbpattinson@btinternet.com

PATTINSON, Rhobert James. St Mich Coll Llan. **d** 04 **p** 05. C Llanelli *St D* 04-07; TV Dewisland 07-10; V Llanegwad w Llanfihangel Uwch Gwili from 10; Min Can St D Cathl from 07. *Y Ficerdy, Clos y Myrtwydd, Nantgaredig, Carmarthen SA32 7LT* T: (01267) 290142

PATTINSON, Richard Clive. b 46. Keble Coll Ox BA 68 MA 84. CBDTI 98. **d** 00 **p** 01. C Hesket-in-the-Forest and Armathwaite *Carl* 00-04; C Inglewood Gp 04-05; P-in-c

Dacre 05-12; TV Penrith w Newton Reigny and Plumpton Wall 05-12; TV Gd Shep TM 10-12; rtd 12. *High Buildings, Shap, Penrith CA10 3NB* T: (01931) 716886
E: clivepattinson@btinternet.com

PATTISON, Prof George Linsley. b 50. Edin Univ MA 72 BD 77 Dur Univ PhD 83 DD 04. Edin Th Coll 74. **d** 77 **p** 78. C Benwell St Jas *Newc* 77-80; P-in-c Kimblesworth *Dur* 80-83; R Badwell Ash w Gt Ashfield, Stowlangtoft etc *St E* 83-91; Dean of Chpl K Coll Cam 91-01; Lect Aarhus Univ Denmark 01-04; Lady Marg Prof Div Ox Univ 04-13; Can Res Ch Ch *Ox* 04-13; Prof Div Glas Univ from 13. *School of Divinity, University of Glasgow, University Avenue, Glasgow G12 8QQ*

PATTISON, Stephen Bewley. b 53. Selw Coll Cam BA 76. Edin Th Coll 76. **d** 78 **p** 80. C Gosforth All SS *Newc* 78-79; NSM St Nic Hosp Newc 78-82; Hon C Newc St Thos Prop Chpl 80-82; Chapl Edin Th Coll 82-83; Lect Past Studies Birm Univ 83-88; PtO *Birm* 83-86 and 87-00; Hon C Moseley St Mary 86-87. *11A Salisbury Road, Moseley, Birmingham B13 8JS* T: 0121-449 3023

PATTLE (née OLIVER), Mrs Suzanne Marie. b 66. LMH Ox BA 88 SSEES Lon MA 91. Trin Coll Bris BTS 03. **d** 03 **p** 04. C Rainham *Roch* 03-07; P-in-c Gillingham St Mary 07-14; V Colehill *Sarum* from 14. *The Vicarage, Smugglers Lane, Colehill, Wimborne BH21 2RY* M: 07971-073093 T: (01202) 883721 E: suzanne.pattle@btinternet.com

PATTMAN, Andrew. b 53. Didsbury Coll Man BEd 75. Westcott Ho Cam. **d** 95 **p** 96. C Washington *Dur* 95-98; Children's Work Adv *St Alb* 98-02; PtO 04-05. *110 Marshalswick Lane, St Albans AL1 4XE* T: (01727) 841201

PATTON (née GRAVELING), Mrs Hannah. b 79. Univ Coll Lon BSc 03 MSc 10 Murray Edwards Coll Cam BTh 14. Ridley Hall Cam 12. **d** 14 **p** 15. C Colchester St Jo *Chelmsf* from 14. *10 Goldcrest Close, Colchester CO4 3FN* M: 07796-157724 E: hannah.patton@stjohnscolchester.org.uk *or* hannahgraveling@gmail.com

PAUL, Ian Benjamin. b 62. St Jo Coll Ox BA 84 MA 88 Southn Univ MSc 85 Nottm Univ BTh 91 PhD 98. St Jo Coll Nottm 89. **d** 96 **p** 97. C Longfleet *Sarum* 96-00; NSM 00-04; Visiting Lect Trin Coll Bris 00-01; Th Adv Dioc Bd of Min *Sarum* 00-04; Tutor Sarum OLM Scheme 00-04; Visiting Lect STETS 00-04; Dir Partnership Development St Jo Coll Nottm 04-05; Dean of Studies 05-13; NSM Nottingham St Nic *S'well* from 13. *102 Cator Lane, Beeston, Nottingham NG9 4BB* T: 0115-752 5422 E: editor@grovebooks.co.uk

PAUL, John Matthew. b 61. K Coll Lon BA 82 Fitzw Coll Cam BA 88 MA 92 FRSA 06. Westcott Ho Cam 86. **d** 89 **p** 90. C Writtle w Highwood *Chelmsf* 89-94; Min Can and Chapl St Paul's Cathl 94-96; Min Can and Sacr St Paul's Cathl 96-99; V Winchmore Hill St Paul 99-09; AD Enfield 04-09; PtO from 09. *4 Woodcroft Mews, Station Road, Petersfield GU32 3FE* M: 07800-606555 E: jm.paul@virgin.net

PAUL, Naunihal Chand (Nihal). b 40. Allahabad Univ MA. Bangalore Th Coll BD. **d** 69 **p** 70. C Simla Ch Ch India 69-70; V Kangra w Dharamsala 70-74; C Urmston *Man* 75-77; P-in-c Farnworth St Pet 77-80; TV E Farnworth and Kearsley 80-83; TV Laindon St Martin and St Nic w Nevendon *Chelmsf* 83-90; R Laindon w Dunton 90-05; rtd 05; PtO *Chelmsf* from 06. *3 Wellstye Green, Basildon SS14 2SR* T: (01268) 293965 E: rupriwas@aol.com

PAUL, Roger Philip. b 53. Clare Coll Cam BA 74 MA 88 CertEd 76 Open Univ PhD 98. Westcott Ho Cam 78. **d** 81 **p** 82. C Coventry Caludon *Cov* 81-85; R Warmington w Shotteswell and Radway w Ratley 85-98; R Kirkby Stephen w Mallerstang etc *Carl* 98-08; Nat Adv (Unity in Miss) Coun for Chr Unity from 08. *Council for Christian Unity, Church House, Great Smith Street, London SW1P 3AZ* T: (020) 7898 1473 E: roger.paul@churchofengland.org

PAUL, Rosalind Miranda. b 53. Man Univ BA 74 Bris Univ PGCE 77 Paris Univ LèsL 86 Open Univ MBA 95. Ripon Coll Cuddesdon 05. **d** 07 **p** 08. C Budock and Mawnan *Truro* 07-09; R Higham, Holton St Mary, Raydon and Stratford *St E* from 09; PtO *Chelmsf* from 13. *The Rectory, Raydon, Ipswich IP7 5LH* T: (01473) 310677 E: rosalind.paul@yahoo.co.uk

PAUL, Simon Nicholas. b 56. Hull Univ BA 81 PGCE 82. Trin Coll Bris BA 95. **d** 95 **p** 96. C Cranleigh *Guildf* 95-99; P-in-c Broughton and Duddon *Carl* 99-04; Chapl Ranby Ho Sch Retford 04-09; Chapl Chigwell Sch Essex from 09. *Chigwell School, High Road, Chigwell IG7 6QF* T: (020) 8501 5700

PAULSEN, The Very Revd Gary Alexander. UNISA BTh. Coll of Transfiguration Grahamstown. **d** 03 **p** 04. C Matroosfontein S Africa 03-05; R Clanwilliam 05-07; R Paarl H Trin 07-11; I Adare and Kilmallock w Kilpeacon, Croom etc *L & K* 11-13; Dean Killaloe and Clonfert from 13; I Killaloe w Stradbally from 13. *The Deanery, Abbey Road, Killaloe, Co Clare, Republic of Ireland* M: 85-764 0533 T: (00353) (61) 374779 E: dean@killaloe.anglican.org *or* abbeydean2@gmail.com

PAULUS, Garrett Keith. b 76. Marymount Coll California BA 98 Yale Univ MA 00 Regent Coll Vancouver MA 08. **d** 05 **p** 06. C Albuquerque St Mark on the Mesa USA 05-09; NSM N Ferriby *York* 09-11; USA from 11. *Address temp unknown* E: gadosii@aol.com

PAVEY, Canon Angela Mary. b 55. Hull Univ BA 77 Nottm Univ BCombStuds 84 Univ of Wales (Lamp) MA 06. Linc Th Coll 81. **dss** 84 **d** 87 **p** 94. Linc St Faith and St Martin w St Pet 84-86; Chapl Boston Coll of FE 87-95; Asst Min Officer *Linc* 89-95; C Birchwood 95-97; Dioc Dir of Ords 97-07; P-in-c Linc St Faith and St Martin w St Pet 07-13; Chapl Lincs Partnership NHS Foundn Trust from 07; Can and Preb Linc Cathl from 00. *The Vicarage, 165C Carholme Road, Lincoln LN1 1RU* T: (01522) 829385 E: a.pavey1@ntlworld.com

PAVEY, John Bertram. b 51. Keele Univ BA 73 Hull Univ PGCE 74 MEd 95. Linc Th Coll 81. **d** 83 **p** 84. C Boultham *Linc* 83-86; R Fishtoft 86-90; P-in-c Birchwood 95-01; V 01-12. *35 The Moorings, Burton Waters, Lincoln LN1 2WQ* E: j.pavey@ntlworld.com

PAVEY, Mark Andrew. b 79. Trin Coll Bris 13. **d** 15. C Maidstone St Paul *Cant* from 15. *St Faith's Vicarage, Moncktons Lane, Maidstone ME14 2PY* M: 07970-569423

PAVLOU, Michael. b 55. St Jo Coll Nottm BA. **d** 06 **p** 07. C Woodside Park St Barn *Lon* 06-10 and from 12; C Wandsworth St Mich w St Steph *S'wark* 10-12. *53 Gallants Farm Road, East Barnet, Barnet EN4 8ER* M: 07956-573217 E: mike.pavi@talktalk.net

PAVYER, Jennifer Elizabeth. *See* FENNELL, Jennifer Elizabeth

PAWLEY, Adam Richard. St Mich Coll Llan. **d** 10 **p** 11. C Llanllwchaiarn and Newtown w Aberhafesp *St As* 10-13; R Hope from 13. *The Rectory, Kiln Lane, Hope, Wrexham LL12 9PH* T: (01978) 760439 E: rectorofhope@live.co.uk

PAWSON (née ROYLE), Mrs Gillian Mary. b 57. Kingston Univ BA 79 Roehampton Inst PGCE 82. SEITE 99. **d** 02 **p** 03. C Wimbledon *S'wark* 02-06; P-in-c Merton St Jo 06-09; P-in-c Colliers Wood Ch Ch 06-09; TV Merton Priory 09; PtO 10-12; C Putney St Mary 12-14. *10 Bennets Courtyard, Watermill Way, London SW19 2RW* E: gillypawson@googlemail.com

PAWSON, John. b 66. Moorlands Th Coll BA 00. Wycliffe Hall Ox. **d** 02 **p** 03. C Bursledon *Win* 02-06; P-in-c Sway 06-12; V from 12. *The Vicarage, Station Road, Sway, Lymington SO41 6BA* T: (01590) 682358 M: 07762-246947 E: johnpawson1@btinternet.com

PAWSON, Preb John Walker. b 38. Kelham Th Coll 58. **d** 63 **p** 64. C N Hull St Mich *York* 63-67; C Lower Gornal *Lich* 67-70; V Tipton St Jo 70-78; V Meir Heath 78-03; RD Stoke 88-98; Preb Lich Cathl 93-03; rtd 03; PtO *Nor* from 03. *39 Runton Road, Cromer NR27 9AT* T: (01263) 511715 E: pawson.meirton@btinternet.com

PAXON, Robin Michael Cuninghame. b 46. St Jo Coll Dur BA 69. Westcott Ho Cam 69. **d** 71 **p** 72. C Croydon St Pet S End *Cant* 71-77; C Saffron Walden w Wendens Ambo and Littlebury *Chelmsf* 77-80; P-in-c Plaistow St Mary 80-83; TV Plaistow 83-89; TV Dovercourt and Parkeston 90-95; rtd 95. *20 Park Road, Harwich CO12 3BJ* T: (01255) 551139

PAXTON, Elizabeth Glynis. b 53. Salford Univ BSc 74. St Mellitus Coll BA 12. **d** 13 **p** 14. NSM Sible Hedingham w Castle Hedingham *Chelmsf* from 13. *The Old Stables, The Street, Stoke by Clare, Sudbury CO10 8HP* T: (01787) 277270 M: 07932-160594 E: liz@paxtonconsulting.co.uk

PAXTON, John Ernest. b 49. Ex Univ BA 71. Westcott Ho Cam 74. **d** 74 **p** 75. C Redditch St Steph *Worc* 74-77; UAE 77-81; C Bolton St Pet *Man* 81-91; Ind Missr 81-91; TV Southampton (City Cen) *Win* 91-96; R S'wark Ch Ch 96-03; Sen Chapl S Lon Ind Miss 96-03; Adv to Bd of Soc Resp *Worc* 03-11; Miss Development Officer 11-13; rtd 13. *57 Drovers Way, Worcester WR3 8QD* T: (01905) 456793 *or* 732819 E: jpaxton@cofe-worcester.org.uk

PAXTON, William Neil. b 60. Brunel Univ BSc 88 MA 90. Ripon Coll Cuddesdon 02. **d** 04 **p** 05. C Camberwell St Geo *S'wark* 04-08; TV Southend *Chelmsf* from 08. *All Saints' Vicarage, 1 Sutton Road, Southend-on-Sea SS2 5PA* E: neil.paxton@blueyonder.co.uk

PAY, Norman John. b 50. St Jo Coll Dur BA 72. Cranmer Hall Dur. **d** 74 **p** 75. C S Moor *Dur* 74-78; C Rawmarsh w Parkgate *Sheff* 78-80; C-in-c New Cantley CD 80-82; V New Cantley 82-89; V Doncaster St Leon and St Jude from 89; P-in-c Moorends from 11; Asst Clergy In-Service Tr Officer 90-93. *St Leonard's Vicarage, Barnsley Road, Doncaster DN5 8QE* T: (01302) 784858 E: njpay@btinternet.com

PAYN, Peter Richard. b 33. Moore Th Coll Sydney LTh 59. **d** 60 **p** 60. C Pittwater Australia 60-61; C Kensington St Matt 61-63; C Melbourne St Jas w St Jo 63-65; V E Geelong St Matt 65-79; C Blackb Ch Ch w St Matt 79-81; V Lowestoft Ch Ch *Nor* 81-92; P-in-c Tunbridge Wells St Pet *Roch* 92-96; V 96-03; rtd 03. *Vincent, 24190 Neuvic, France* T: (0033) 5 53 81 13 56 E: prpayn@hotmail.com

PAYNE, Alan. *See* PAYNE, Kenneth Alan

PAYNE, Mrs Anne. b 52. Bris Univ BA 73 Southn Univ PGCE 74. STETS 11. **d** 14 **p** 15. NSM Worplesdon *Guildf* from 14. *27 Wilderness Road, Guildford GU2 7QX* T: (01483) 565064 M: 07796-420382 E: annempayne@sky.com

PAYNE, Arthur Edwin. b 37. K Alfred's Coll Win TCert 59. St Mich Coll Llan 86. **d** 87 **p** 88. C Swansea St Gabr *S & B* 87-90; Chapl Univ of Wales (Swansea) 87-90; V Brynmawr 90-91; TV Wickford and Runwell *Chelmsf* 91-94; Chapl Runwell Hosp Wickford 91-94; P-in-c Wraxall *B & W* 94-95; PtO 95-97; V Rhymney *Mon* 97-98; rtd 98; PtO *B & W* from 99. *4 Villa Rosa, Shrubbery Road, Weston-super-Mare BS23 2JB* T: (01934) 615522 E: aepayne630@btinternet.com

PAYNE, David Charles. b 62. Univ of Wales (Abth) BLib 84. St Jo Coll Nottm MA 95. **d** 95 **p** 96. C Horncastle w Low Toynton *Linc* 95-99; V Metheringham w Blankney and Dunston 99-04; Chapl Sherwood Forest Hosps NHS Trust 04-06; R Standon and The Mundens w Sacombe *St Alb* 06-14; C Vale *Ox* 14-15; TV Vale of Belvoir *Leic* from 15. *4 Rutland Lane, Bottesford, Nottingham NG13 0DG* M: 07985-922553 E: revdpayne24@gmail.com

PAYNE, David Ronald. b 49. Open Univ BA 87. St Mich Coll Llan 88. **d** 90 **p** 91. C Oystermouth *S & B* 90-93; V Penllergaer 93-02; TV Llanelli *St D* 02-10; V Gwendraeth Fawr 10-14; rtd 14; PtO *S & B* from 14; *St D* from 15. *51 Clos y Gelli, Llanelli SA14 9BA*

PAYNE, Frederick Gates (Eric). b 19. Jes Coll Cam BA 40 MA 43. Lon Coll of Div 40. **d** 42 **p** 43. C Walcot *B & W* 42-45; CF (EC) 45-48; Hd CMJ Miss Ethiopia 48-67; SW Org Sec CMJ 68-85; rtd 84; PtO *B & W* from 85; *Truro* from 91. *Cranhill Nursing Home, Weston Road, Bath BA1 2YA* T: (01225) 422321

PAYNE, Mrs Glenys. **d** 14 **p** 15. NSM Llanelli *St D* from 14. *51 Clos y Gelli, Llanelli SA14 9BA*

PAYNE, Jeffery Mark. b 68. Lon Sch of Th BTh 99. Wycliffe Hall Ox 06. **d** 08 **p** 09. C Southall St Geo *Lon* 08-11; R Norwood St Mary from 11. *Aconbury, Tentelow Lane, Southall UB2 4LE* T: (020) 8574 1362 M: 07827-965798 E: jeff.payne5@btinternet.com

PAYNE, Mrs Joanna Nicola. b 72. Liv Univ BA 93 Homerton Coll Cam PGCE 95. Trin Coll Bris BA 00 MA 01. **d** 01 **p** 02. C Chislehurst St Nic *Roch* 01-06. *15 Nursery Lane, Costessey, Norwich NR8 5BU* T: (01603) 745792 M: 07958-598145 E: joanna.payne@hotmail.com

PAYNE, John. *See* PAYNE, Victor John

PAYNE, John Rogan. b 44. Episc Th Coll São Paulo. **d** 78 **p** 79. Brazil 78-86; C Ilkley All SS *Bradf* 86-88; R Elvington w Sutton on Derwent and E Cottingwith *York* 88-94. *Manor Farm House, East Flotmanby Road, Muston, Filey YO14 0HX* T: (01723) 513969

PAYNE, Julia Kathleen. *See* PEATY, Julia Kathleen

PAYNE, Canon Kenneth Alan. b 45. Pemb Coll Ox BA 68 MA 71. Qu Coll Birm 71. **d** 74 **p** 74. Hon C Perry Barr *Birm* 74-78; Hon C Ruislip Manor St Paul *Lon* 78-79; C Hawksworth Wood *Ripon* 79-84; R Stanningley St Thos 84-94; TR Kippax w Allerton Bywater 94-00; AD Whitkirk 95-00; P-in-c Lambley and Dioc Min Development Adv *S'well* 00-09; Dioc Dir of Min 02-09; Hon Can S'well Minster 06-09; rtd 10; PtO *York* from 10. *Fern Cottage, 2 Gladstone Terrace, Thornton Dale, Pickering YO18 7SS* T: (01751) 476243 E: alanlambley@mac.com

PAYNE, Leonard John. b 49. St Jo Coll Nottm 93. **d** 95 **p** 96. C Trimley *St E* 95-98; TV Sole Bay 98-09; P-in-c Wrentham, Covehithe w Benacre etc 09-15; V from 15. *The Vicarage, 59 Southwold Road, Wrentham, Beccles NR34 7JE* T: (01502) 675208 M: 07879-457902 E: rev.leonard.payne@gmail.com

PAYNE, Canon Mark James Townsend. b 69. Van Mildert Coll Dur BA 90. Ridley Hall Cam 92. **d** 94 **p** 95. C Angmering *Chich* 94-98; Dioc Ev and C Prestonville St Luke 98-04; P-in-c Scaynes Hill 04-10; R Chich St Pancras and St Jo from 10; Can and Preb Chich Cathl from 08. *1 Lower Walls Walk, Chichester PO19 7BH* T: (01243) 699718

PAYNE, Matthew Charles. b 62. Ex Univ LLB 85 All Nations Chr Coll BA 95 Solicitor 89. Oak Hill Th Coll 99. **d** 01 **p** 02. C Angmering *Chich* 01-05; V Lowestoft Ch Ch *Nor* from 05. *The Vicarage, 16 Corton Road, Lowestoft NR32 4PL* T: (01502) 572444 E: matthew@christ-church.info

PAYNE, Michael Frederick. b 49. St Jo Coll Nottm 81. **d** 83 **p** 84. C Hyson Green *S'well* 83-86; P-in-c Peckham St Mary Magd *S'wark* 86-90; V 90-05; Hon C Chenies and Lt Chalfont, Latimer and Flaunden *Ox* 05-09; P-in-c Tollerton *S'well* 09-11; R 11-14; rtd 14. *100 Denison Street, Beeston, Nottingham NG9 1DQ* M: 07961-515840 T: 0115-808 6506 E: mikefpayne@hotmail.com

PAYNE, Michael Jeffrey. b 75. Hull Univ MA 00 Cant Ch Ch Univ MA 08 Open Univ PGCE 09. St Steph Ho Ox 13. **d** 15.

C Northfleet and Rosherville *Roch* from 15; C Perry Street from 15. *St Mark's Vicarage, 123 London Road, Northfleet, Gravesend DA11 9NH* T: (01474) 535814 E: frmichael.anglican@gmail.com

PAYNE, Mrs Norma. b 48. Bris Univ BA 70 Homerton Coll Cam PGCE 71. STETS 98. **d** 01 **p** 02. NSM Cley Hill Warminster *Sarum* 01-04; TV 04-07; R Cley Hill Villages 07-13; rtd 13. *2 The Mews, Newport, Warminster BA12 8BX* E: revnpayne@btinternet.com

PAYNE, Mrs Penelope Kenward. b 42. LGSM 64. Bp Otter Coll 64. **d** 94 **p** 98. NSM Portsea N End St Mark *Portsm* 94-05; NSM S Hayling 05-12; rtd 12; PtO *Portsm* from 12. *35 Saltmarsh Lane, Hayling Island PO11 0JT* T/F: (023) 9246 5259 T: 9266 5753 E: pennie@ppayne.f9.co.uk

PAYNE, Philip John. b 56. Warwick Univ BA 77 UMIST MSc 94. Westcott Ho Cam 09. **d** 11 **p** 12. C Bury St Edmunds All SS w St Jo and St Geo *St E* 11-14; P-in-c Coddenham w Gosbeck and Hemingstone w Henley from 14; P-in-c Crowfield w Stonham Aspal and Mickfield from 14; P-in-c The Creetings and Earl Stonham w Stonham Parva from 14. *The Rectory, The Street, Stonham Aspal, Stowmarket IP14 6AQ* M: 07871-090557 E: revphilippayne@btinternet.com

PAYNE, Mrs Priscilla Mary. b 40. **d** 04 **p** 05. NSM Ditton *Roch* 04-15; PtO *Ripon* from 15; *Roch* from 15. *4 Station Road, Ditton, Aylesford ME20 6AX* T: (01732) 841257 E: priscillapayne@outlook.com

PAYNE, Preb Robert Christian. b 42. MBE 12. St Mich Coll Llan. **d** 65 **p** 66. C Charlton Kings St Mary *Glouc* 65-69; C Waltham Cross *St Alb* 69-71; V Falfield *Glouc* 71-72; P-in-c Rockhampton 71-72; V Falfield w Rockhampton 72-76; Chapl HM Det Cen Eastwood Park 71-76; Chapl HM Borstal Everthorpe 76-79; Chapl HM YOI Glen Parva 79-85; Pris Service Chapl Tr Officer 85-88; Chapl HM Pris Swinfen Hall 85-88; Asst Chapl Gen of Pris 88-02; rtd 02; Sessional Chapl HM YOI Stoke Heath 02-06; Sessional Chapl HM Pris Swinfen Hall from 05; Sessional Chapl HM Pris Foston Hall 06-08; Preb Lich Cathl 05-12; PtO from 13. *HM Prison Swinfen Hall, Swinfen, Lichfield WS14 9QS* T: (01543) 484125 E: bob.payne@ukgateway.net *or* bob.payne@hmps.gsi.gov.uk

PAYNE, Robert Harold Vincent. b 44. St Jo Coll York CertEd 69. St Jo Coll Nottm 77. **d** 79 **p** 80. C Didsbury St Jas *Man* 79-80; C Didsbury St Jas and Em 80-83; V Southchurch Ch Ch *Chelmsf* 83-90; P-in-c Charles w Plymouth St Matthias *Ex* 90-94; Warden Lee Abbey 94-02; R Thorley *St Alb* 02-14; rtd 14. *131 Stour View Gardens, Corfe Mullen, Wimborne BH21 3TN*

PAYNE, Robert Sandon. b 48. Reading Univ BSc 69 MRICS 72. Ripon Coll Cuddesdon 77. **d** 80 **p** 81. C Bridgnorth, Tasley, Astley Abbotts and Oldbury *Heref* 80-83; P-in-c Wistanstow 83-92; P-in-c Acton Scott 86-92; P-in-c Dorrington 92-94; P-in-c Leebotwood w Longnor 92-94; P-in-c Smethcott w Woolstaston 92-94; P-in-c Stapleton 92-94; R Dorrington w Leebotwood, Longnor, Stapleton etc 94-11; rtd 11. *6 Clun Road, Aston-on-Clun, Craven Arms SY7 8EW* T: (01588) 661008 E: robert.payne49@btinternet.com

PAYNE, Rosemary Ann. b 46. LSE LLB 68. SAOMC 97. **d** 00 **p** 01. NSM Woburn *Ox* 00-05; NSM Hedsor and Bourne End 05-14; Bp's NSM Officer (Bucks) 05-09; rtd 14. *30 Goddington Road, Bourne End SL8 5TZ* T: (01628) 521677

PAYNE, Stephen Michael. b 55. **d** 03 **p** 04. C Plymouth Em, St Paul Efford and St Aug *Ex* 03-10; TV Plymstock and Hooe 11-13; P-in-c from 13. *The Vicarage, 9 St John's Drive, Plymouth PL9 9SD* T: (01752) 213358 E: spayne55@live.co.uk

PAYNE, Mrs Trudy. b 48. K Coll Lon BA 66 Lon Inst of Educn PGCE 73. **d** 04 **p** 05. OLM Clapham Park St Steph *S'wark* 04-06; Hon C Telford Park 06-09; Hon C Mitcham St Barn from 09. *6 Clarence Road, Croydon CR0 2EN* T: (020) 8689 5857 E: paynetrudy@hotmail.com

PAYNE, Victor John. b 45. Open Univ BA 81. St Mich Coll Llan. **d** 70 **p** 71. C Ystrad Mynach *Llan* 70-72; V Whitchurch 72-75; CF (TA) 74-75; CF 75-93; V Talgarth and Llanelieu *S & B* 85-87; Chapl Mid-Wales Hosp 85-87; C Bassaleg *Mon* 93-96; TV 96-01; V Tongwynlais *Llan* 01-11; AD Llan 08-10; rtd 11. *11 Hawkhurst Court, Porthcawl CF36 3NU* E: jaypay1960@yahoo.co.uk

PAYNE COOK, Canon John Andrew Somerset. b 43. St Pet Coll Ox BA 65 MA 65. Coll of Resurr Mirfield 65. **d** 68 **p** 69. C St Mary-at-Latton *Chelmsf* 68-71; C Gt Berkhamsted *St Alb* 71-76; C-in-c N Brickhill CD 76-82; V N Brickhill and Putnoe 83-85; TR Tring 85-99; RD Berkhamsted 92-97; Hon Can St Alb 98-99; USPG 99-03; P-in-c Sandy Pt St Anne St Kitts-Nevis 00-03; P-in-c Ickleford w Holwell *St Alb* 03-05; P-in-c Pirton 03-05; R Holwell, Ickleford and Pirton 05-10; Hon Can St Alb 03-10; rtd 10. *4 Lancotbury Close, Totternhoe, Dunstable LU6 1RQ* T: (01582) 699485

PAYNTER, Stephen Denis. b 59. Bath Univ BSc 82 CertEd 82. Trin Coll Bris BA 89. **d** 89 **p** 90. C Nailsea Ch Ch *B & W* 89-92; C Farnborough *Guildf* 92-97; TV N Farnborough 97-98; V Ealing St Mary *Lon* from 98. *11 Church Place, London W5 4HN* T: (020) 8567 0414 *or* 8579 7134 F: 8840 4534 E: steve.paynter@stmarysealing.org.uk

PAYNTON, Paul Alexander. b 42. Linc Th Coll 72. **d** 74 **p** 75. C Uppingham w Ayston *Pet* 74-77; R Teigh w Whissendine 77-79; P-in-c Market Overton w Thistleton 77-79; R Teigh w Whissendine and Market Overton 79-95; V Irchester 95-00; rtd 04. *33 Sewell Road, Lincoln LN2 5QT* T: (01522) 560428

PAYTON, Paul John. b 59. Middx Poly MA 90 LRAM 79 GRSM 80. Ripon Coll Cuddesdon. **d** 05 **p** 06. C Lancaster St Mary w St John and St Anne *Blackb* 05-08; P-in-c Leeds Gipton Epiphany *Ripon* 08-13; TR Leeds All So and St Aid 13-15; rtd 15. *Address withheld by request.*

PEABODY, Anthony John. b 43. St Cuth Soc Dur BSc 64 MSc 67 Surrey Univ PhD 82 MSB 82 CBiol 82. Cuddesdon Coll 08. **d** 08. NSM Sulhamstead Abbots and Bannister w Ufton Nervet *Ox* 08-14; PtO from 14; *Eur* from 14. *Blackberries, 29 Woodlands Avenue, Burghfield Common, Reading RG7 3HU* T: 0118-983 2491 E: pisumcorporum@btinternet.com

PEACE, Brian. b 38. St Jo Coll Nottm 90. **d** 92 **p** 93. C Huddersfield H Trin *Wakef* 92-95; R Cheswardine, Childs Ercall, Hales, Hinstock etc *Lich* 95-00; TR 00-03; RD Hodnet 00-03; rtd 03; PtO *Ches* from 03. *2 Mouldsworth Close, Northwich CW9 8FT* T: (01606) 333013 E: brian@peaceb.freeserve.co.uk

PEACE, Stuart Vaughan. b 47. **d** 04 **p** 05. OLM Dorking w Ranmore *Guildf* 04-14; rtd 14; PtO *Guildf* from 14. *95 Ashcombe Road, Dorking RH4 1LW* T: (01306) 883002 E: stuart@peaces.freeserve.co.uk

PEACH, Malcolm Thompson. b 31. St Chad's Coll Dur BA 56. Sarum Th Coll 56. **d** 58 **p** 59. C Beamish *Dur* 58-61; Chapl Dur Univ 61-65; NE England Sec SCM 61-65; C-in-c Stockton St Mark CD *Dur* 65-72; P-in-c Bishopwearmouth St Nic 72-81; V 81-85; V S Shields St Hilda w St Thos 85-95; Hon Chapl Miss to Seamen 85-95; P-in-c S Shields St Aid w St Steph *Dur* 92-95; rtd 95; PtO *Dur* from 95. *116 Mount Road, Sunderland SR4 7QD* T: 0191-522 6216

PEACHELL, David John. b 45. Oak Hill Th Coll 85. **d** 86 **p** 87. C Prescot *Liv* 86-89; CF 89-98; P-in-c Hockering, Honingham, E and N Tuddenham *Nor* 98-02; rtd 02. *21 Brentwood, Eaton, Norwich NR4 6PN* T: (01603) 880121

PEACOCK, Canon David. b 39. Liv Univ BA 61 Lanc Univ MA 71 Univ of the South (USA) Hon DD 00 FRSA 95. Westcott Ho Cam 84. **d** 84 **p** 85. Prin Lect St Martin's Coll Lanc 81-85; Hon C Lancaster St Mary *Blackb* 84-85; Prin Whitelands Coll S'wark 85-00; Pro Rector Surrey Univ *Guildf* 93-00; Hon C Roehampton H Trin *S'wark* 85-92; Hon C Putney St Mary 92-00; Hon Can S'wark Cathl 97-00; PtO *Blackb* from 00. *The Old Dairy, Keerside, Arkholme, Carnforth LA6 1AP* T: (01524) 221706 E: keersidecowshed@aol.com

PEACOCK, John. b 34. ALCD 60. **d** 60 **p** 61. C Addiscombe St Mary *Cant* 60-62; C Felixstowe St Jo *St E* 62-65; Chapl RAF 65-70; C Panania Australia 71-74; R Strathfield 74-80; Chapl Gladesville Hosp Sydney 81-94; Chapl Angl Retirement Villages Sydney 94-99; rtd 99. *511/6 Tarragal Glen Avenue, Erina NSW 2250, Australia* T: (0061) (2) 4367 0936

PEACOCK, Mrs Kate Rebecca. b 78. Hatf Coll Dur BA 00. Westcott Ho Cam 01. **d** 03 **p** 04. C Cambridge Ascension *Ely* 03-07; C Three Rivers Gp 07-12; P-in-c Hormead, Wyddial, Anstey, Brent Pelham etc *St Alb* 12-13; V from 13. *The Vicarage, Great Hormead, Buntingford SG9 0NT* T: (01763) 289258 E: kate.peacock@btopenworld.com

PEACOCK, Nicholas James. b 76. CCC Cam BA 99 MA 02. Ripon Coll Cuddesdon BA 06. **d** 07 **p** 08. C Clapham Ch Ch and St Jo *S'wark* 07-10; V Wandsworth Common St Mary from 10. *The Vicarage, 291 Burntwood Lane, London SW17 0AP* T: (020) 8874 4804 M: 07837-425792 E: revd.nick@btinternet.com

PEAKE, Ms Sue. b 42. K Coll Dur BA 63. SEITE 99. **d** 02 **p** 03. NSM Clapham Ch Ch and St Jo *S'wark* 02-13; PtO from 13. *20 Gauden Road, London SW4 6LT* T: (020) 7627 4060 M: 07867-532911 E: admin@springfieldcommunityflat.com

PEAL, Jacqueline. b 46. MCSP 70. Cant Sch of Min 88. **d** 91 **p** 94. NSM Bexley St Jo *Roch* 91-97; NSM Crayford 91-94; C 94-97 and 00-01; C Dartford H Trin 97-00; Hon C Ash 01-11; Asst Chapl Thames Gateway NHS Foundn Trust 01-11; Chapl Wisdom Hospice 04-11; rtd 11. *9 Crescent Rise, Thakeham, Pulborough RH20 3NB* T: (01903) 743083 E: peal@btinternet.com

PEAL, John Arthur. b 46. K Coll Lon BD 70 AKC. **d** 71 **p** 72. C Portsea All SS w St Jo Rudmore *Portsm* 71-74; C Westbury *Sarum* 74-77; V Borstal *Roch* 77-82; Chapl HM Pris Cookham

Wood 78-82; V Erith Ch Ch *Roch* 82-91; P-in-c Erith St Jo 86-91; V Bexley St Jo 91-00; Chapl Erith and Distr Hosp 82-90; R Ash *Roch* 00-11; R Ridley 00-11; rtd 11. *9 Crescent Rise, Thakeham, Pulborough RH20 3NB* T: (01903) 743083 M: 07919-410438 E: peal@btinternet.com

PEAL, William John. b 26. K Coll Lon BSc 47 AKC PhD 52. St Jo Coll Nottm 79. **d** 80 **p** 81. C Coalville and Bardon Hill *Leic* 80-83; TV Melton Mowbray w Thorpe Arnold 83-86; TV Melton Gt Framland 86-90; rtd 90; PtO *Lich* 91-09 and 12-14; *Ches* 91-99. *20 Conway Road, Knypersley, Stoke-on-Trent ST8 7AL* T: (01782) 513580

PEALL, Mrs Linda Grace. b 66. Westmr Coll Ox BEd 88. EAMTC 99. **d** 02 **p** 03. NSM Blackwell All SS and Salutation *Dur* 02-04; C Darlington H Trin 04-07; Chapl Co Durham and Darlington NHS Foundn Trust 05-10; Chapl Basildon & Thurrock Univ Hosps NHS Foundn Trust from 10. *Basildon University Hospital, Nethermayne, Basildon SS16 5NL* T: (01268) 524900 *or* (01268) 08451-553111 E: linda.peall@btopenworld.com

PEARCE, Adrian Francis. b 55. Westmr Coll Ox BTh 05. S Dios Minl Tr Scheme 92. **d** 95 **p** 96. NSM Jersey St Luke w St Jas *Win* 95-13; NSM Jersey St Mary 01-13; P-in-c Bournemouth St Ambrose from 13; NSM Bournemouth St Fran from 13. *72A West Cliff Road, Bournemouth BH4 8BE* T: (01202) 911569 E: afpear2@gmail.com

PEARCE, Andrew John. b 66. Ex Univ BA 89 Homerton Coll Cam PGCE 93. St Mich Coll Llan 94. **d** 96 **p** 97. C Llansamlet *S & B* 96-99; C Clydach 99-00; P-in-c E Radnor 00-02; V 02-06; V Bishopston w Penmaen and Nicholaston 06-11; V Bishopston from 11. *The Rectory, 4 Portway, Bishopston, Swansea SA3 3JR* T: (01792) 232140

PEARCE, Mrs Angela Elizabeth. b 36. K Coll Lon BSc 58 CertEd 59 BD 79 AKC 79. **dss** 79 **d** 87. Chapl Raines Foundn Sch Tower Hamlets *Lon* 79-97; Homerton St Barn w St Paul *Lon* 79-85; Upper Chelsea St Simon 85-89; Hon Par Dn 87-89; Hon Par Dn Limehouse 89-97; PtO *St E* from 97. *50 Crown Street, Bury St Edmunds IP33 1QX* T: (01284) 760016

PEARCE, Canon Brian Edward. b 39. Kelham Th Coll 59. **d** 64 **p** 65. C Smethwick St Matt *Birm* 64-68; C Kings Norton 68-72; TV 73-80; TR Swindon Dorcan *Bris* 80-91; Min Withywood CD 91-94; V Withywood 94-98; V Fishponds All SS 98-05; RD Bedminster 92-98; Hon Can Bris Cathl 97-05; rtd 05; PtO *Mon* from 15. *32 Brook Estate, Monmouth NP25 5AW* T: (01600) 716057 E: rev.pearce@tesco.net

PEARCE, Preb Clive. b 40. Univ of Wales (Lamp) BA 63 Heythrop Coll Lon MA 01. St Steph Ho Ox 63. **d** 65 **p** 66. C Acton Green St Pet *Lon* 65-67; C Eastcote St Lawr 67-73; V Hatch End St Anselm from 73; Preb St Paul's Cathl from 08. *Hatch End Vicarage, 50 Cedar Drive, Pinner HA5 4DE* T/F: (020) 8428 4111 M: 07710-900545 E: ecclesianevis@aol.com

PEARCE, Colin James. b 51. Trin Coll Bris 94. **d** 96 **p** 97. C Kingswood *Bris* 96-00; TV Bedminster 00-07; Canada from 07. *189 Lafferty Avenue, Lasalle, Windsor ON N9J 1K1, Canada* T: (001) (519) 734 1476 E: colinjpearce@hotmail.com

PEARCE, Daniel. *See* PEARCE, William Philip Daniel

PEARCE, Desmond. b 30. Univ of Wales (Abth) BA 52. EMMTC 85. **d** 88 **p** 89. NSM Chellaston *Derby* 88-90; NSM Walsall St Gabr Fulbrook *Lich* 90; C Stoke Lacy, Moreton Jeffries w Much Cowarne etc *Heref* 91-97; PtO *Mon* 98-00; P-in-c New Tredegar 00-03. *56 Bedwellty Road, Cefn Forest, Blackwood NP12 3HB* T: (01443) 833015

PEARCE, Elizabeth. *See* PEARCE, Janet Elizabeth

PEARCE, Mrs Iris Rose. b 27. **d** 00 **p** 03. OLM Parkstone St Pet and St Osmund w Branksea *Sarum* 00-03; Chapl Asst Poole Hosp NHS Trust 00-03; Hon Asst Chapl from 03. *Flat 1 Pelham, 34 Lindsay Road, Poole BH13 6AY* T: (01202) 769301 E: williamraymond.pearce@yahoo.co.uk

PEARCE, Mrs Janet Elizabeth. b 49. Somerville Coll Ox BA 72 MA 76 CertEd 74. NOC 85. **d** 88 **p** 94. Par Dn Helsby and Dunham-on-the-Hill *Ches* 88-94; C 94-96; C Norley, Crowton and Kingsley 96-06; Dioc Adv in Spirituality 02-06; R Llanfair Mathafarn Eithaf w Llanbedrgoch *Ban* 06-11; TR Bangor 11-13; rtd 13; PtO *Ban* from 13. *2 Egdean Walk, Sevenoaks TN13 3UQ* T: (01732) 464598

PEARCE, Preb John Frederick Dilke. b 32. Ex Coll Ox BA 55 MA 59. Westcott Ho Cam. **d** 57 **p** 58. C Dalston St Mark w St Bart *Lon* 57-60; C Chelsea Ch Ch 60-63; R Lower Homerton St Paul 63-81; P-in-c Clapton Park All So 72-77; V 77-84; RD Hackney 74-79; R Homerton St Barn w St Paul 81-85; TR Hackney Marsh 85; P-in-c Upper Chelsea St Simon 85-89; AD Chelsea 88-89; E Limehouse 89-91; Preb St Paul's Cathl 70-97; rtd 97; PtO *St E* from 97. *50 Crown Street, Bury St Edmunds IP33 1QX* T: (01284) 760016 F: 756306 E: john@jfdp.freeserve.co.uk

PEARCE, Jonathan. b 55. St Jo Coll Nottm BTh 85. **d** 85 **p** 86. C Gt Chesham Ox 85-89; C Newport Pagnell w Lathbury and Moulsoe 89-93; TV Waltham H Cross *Chelmsf* 93-07; R Gt Totham and Lt Totham w Goldhanger from 07. *The Vicarage, 1 Hall Road, Great Totham, Maldon CM9 8NN* T/F: (01621) 893150 E: revdjpearce@aol.com

PEARCE, Kenneth Jack. b 25. CIPFA. Linc Th Coll 62. **d** 63 **p** 64. C Wootton Bassett *Sarum* 63-66; C Broad Town 63-66; P-in-c Derby St Andr 66-68; V Derby St Mark 68-87; rtd 87; PtO *St Alb* 91-15. *117 Oaks Cross, Stevenage SG2 8LT* T: (01438) 317385

PEARCE, Michael Hawkins. b 29. Sarum Th Coll 61. **d** 62 **p** 63. C Bedminster St Aldhelm *Bris* 62-65; C Bishopston 65-68; R Jacobstow w Warbstow *Truro* 68-74; V Treneglos 68-74; V St Teath 74-94; rtd 94; PtO *Truro* from 94. *32 Trenant Road, Tywardreath, Par PL24 2QJ* T: (01726) 813658

PEARCE, Neville John Lewis. b 33. CBIM 88 Leeds Univ LLB 53 LLM 54. Trin Coll Bris 90. **d** 91 **p** 92. NSM Bath Walcot *B & W* 91-93; P-in-c Bath St Sav w Swainswick and Woolley 93-98; PtO from 98. *Penshurst, Weston Lane, Bath BA1 4AB* T: (01225) 426925 E: nevillepearce@tiscali.co.uk

PEARCE, Robert John. b 47. GLCM LLCM 72 Birm Univ PGCE 73. Ripon Coll Cuddesdon 79. **d** 82 **p** 83. C Broseley w Benthall *Heref* 82-83; C Kington w Huntington, Old Radnor, Kinnerton etc 83-85; R Westbury 85-94; R Yockleton 85-94; V Gt Wollaston 85-94; V Gwersyllt *St As* 94-99; V Northop 99-03; P-in-c Cerrigydrudion w Llanfihangel Glyn Myfyr etc 08-15; Hon C Henllan and Llannefydd and Bylchau from 15. *Trigfan, Ochr y Bryn, Henllan LL16 5AT* T: (01745) 817551

PEARCE, Sacha John Tremain. b 64. Reading Univ BA 92 RGN 86. RGN 86 Ripon Coll Cuddesdon. **d** 00 **p** 01. C Tisbury *Sarum* 00-01; C Nadder Valley 01-04; V Seend, Bulkington and Poulshot 04-09; Chapl Plymouth Hosps NHS Trust from 09. *Derriford Hospital, Derriford Road, Plymouth PL6 8DH* T: (01752) 792022 E: sacha.pearce@nhs.net

PEARCE, Mrs Susan Elizabeth. b 44. NEOC 03. **d** 06 **p** 07. NSM Pannal w Beckwithshaw *Ripon* 06-11; NSM High Harrogate St Pet *Leeds* from 11. *56 Beckwith Crescent, Harrogate HG2 0BH* T: (01423) 565954 E: sue.pearce56@btopenworld.com

PEARCE, Trevor John. b 27. FSR 57. Roch Th Coll 65. **d** 67 **p** 68. C Cheriton Street *Cant* 67-69; C Willesborough w Hinxhill 69-73; V Devonport St Barn *Ex* 73-79; Chapl N Devon Healthcare NHS Trust 79-83; V Derby St Andr w St Osmund 83-84; Chapl Derbyshire R Infirmary 83-92; LtO *Derby* 84-92; rtd 92; PtO *Derby* 92-13. *4 Morrell Wood Drive, Belper DE56 0JD* T: (01773) 828450

PEARCE, Valerie Olive. b 46. Whitelands Coll Lon CertEd 67. SEITE 96. **d** 97 **p** 98. CSC 77-04; LtO *S'wark* 97-04; PtO from 09. *10 Bromley College, London Road, Bromley BR1 1PE* T: (020) 8290 6662 E: revdval@gmail.com

PEARCE, William Philip Daniel. b 26. Stanford Univ BA 48 Leeds Univ CertEd 64 MA 75. Cuddesdon Coll 54. **d** 56 **p** 57. USA 56-60; CR 60-84; C St Geo-in-the-East w St Paul *Lon* 84-86; USA from 86; rtd 02. *1037 Olympic Lane, Seaside CA 93955-6226, USA* T: (001) (831) 393 2176 E: danielp@mbay.net

PEARKES, Nicholas Robin Clement. b 49. Ex Univ BA. Linc Th Coll. **d** 82 **p** 83. C Plymstock *Ex* 82-85; P-in-c Weston Mill 85-86; TV Devonport St Boniface and St Phil 86-99; R Broadhempston, Woodland, Staverton etc 99-14; rtd 14. *The Old Post Office, 128-130 Fore Street, Barton, Torquay TQ2 8DP* E: nicholaspearkes1@yahoo.com

PEARMAIN, Andrew Neil. b 55. K Coll Lon BD 79 AKC 79. Ridley Hall Cam 79. **d** 81 **p** 82. C Cranleigh *Guildf* 81-84; P-in-c Frimley 85-86; C 86-87. *4 Laurel Close, Farnborough GU14 0PT*

PEARMAIN, Brian Albert John. b 34. Lon Univ BD 68. Roch Th Coll 63. **d** 66 **p** 67. C Shirley St Jo *Cant* 66-69; C Selsdon St Jo w St Fran 69-73; P-in-c Louth H Trin *Linc* 73-75; TV Louth 75-79; R Scartho 79-97; RD Grimsby and Cleethorpes 89-94; Can and Preb Linc Cathl 94-97; rtd 97; PtO *Linc* 00-07; *Leeds* from 07. *32 Capel Court, The Burgag, Prestbury, Cheltenham GL52 3EL* M: 07944-675321

PEARMAN, Mrs Barbara Elizabeth Anne. b 48. RGN 69 RHV 72. ERMC 07. **d** 09 **p** 10. NSM E Marshland *Ely* from 09. *Rambles, 8 School Road, Tilney All Saints, King's Lynn PE34 4RS* T: (01553) 828808 M: 07946-348744 E: barbarapearman@hotmail.com

PEARS, Anthony John. b 58. Ripon Coll Cuddesdon 00. **d** 02 **p** 03. C Watton w Carbrooke and Ovington *Nor* 02-05; R Northanger *Win* from 05. *The Rectory, Gaston Lane, Upper Farringdon, Alton GU34 3EE* T: (01420) 588398 E: tony.pears@virgin.net

PEARSE, Andrew George. b 46. Wycliffe Hall Ox 71. **d** 74 **p** 75. C Homerton St Luke *Lon* 74-77; C Chadderton Em *Man* 77-81; R Collyhurst 81-89; Area Sec (NE, E Midl and Scotland) SAMS

89-03; rtd 03; Chapl Co-ord St Leon Hospice York 03-11; PtO *York* from 11; Hon C Knaresborough *Leeds* from 14. *39 Birkdale Avenue, Knaresborough HG5 0LS* T: (01423) 797033 E: tarvethecurkey@yahoo.co.uk

PEARSE, Ronald Thomas Hennessy. b 26. AKC 52. **d** 53 **p** 54. C Leic St Pet 53-55; C Hanwell St Thos *Lon* 55-58; R Asfordby *Leic* 58-84; P-in-c Scalford w Wycombe and Chadwell 75-76; R Thurcaston 84-89; rtd 89; PtO *Leic* 89-90. *15 Burton Street, Loughborough LE11 2DT* T: (01509) 215478

PEARSON, Canon Andrew George Campbell. b 41. Qu Coll Ox BA 63 BA 66. Wycliffe Hall Ox 63. **d** 71 **p** 72. C Gillingham St Mark *Roch* 71-72; C Billingshurst *Chich* 72-77; C Ches Square St Mich w St Phil *Lon* 77-82; Co-ord Busoga Trust 82-02; Dir from 02; Hon Can Busoga from 98; P-in-c St Marg Pattens *Lon* 90-06; Hon C Kensington St Mary Abbots w St Geo 96-06; rtd 06. *Denecroft, Little East Street, Billingshurst RH14 9PN* T: (01403) 782080 E: busogatrust@hotmail.com

PEARSON, Andrew John. b 59. Westcott Ho Cam 86. **d** 89 **p** 90. C Knaresborough *Ripon* 89-92; C Wetherby 92-94; P-in-c Hunslet Moor St Pet and St Cuth 94-96; V 96-01; V Hawksworth Wood 01-06; Dioc Environment Officer 97-06; P-in-c Oulton w Woodlesford and Methley w Mickletown 06-13; P-in-c Wyther *Leeds* from 13. *Beeston Vicarage, 16 Town Street, Beeston, Leeds LS11 8PN* T: 0113-272 3337 E: revajp@btinternet.com

PEARSON, Andrew Michael. b 54. Univ of Wales (Ban) BTh 10 Solicitor 77. **d** 07 **p** 08. OLM Shere, Albury and Chilworth *Guildf* 07-12; C from 12. *Owl House, Shophouse Lane, Albury, Guildford GU5 9ET* T: (01483) 203220 M: 07815-049950 E: rev.a.m.pearson@btinternet.com

PEARSON, Mrs Béatrice Levasseur. b 53. Sorbonne Univ Paris LèsL 74 MèsL 75 Lon Inst of Educn PGCE 76. Ripon Coll Cuddesdon 01. **d** 03 **p** 04. C Easthampstead *Ox* 03-06; TV Loddon Reach 06-13; rtd 13. *1 Northanger Court, Grove Street, Bath BA2 6PE* T: (01225) 571344 M: 07981-462145 E: bea.acumen@zetnet.co.uk

PEARSON, Ms Brenda Elizabeth Frances (Brandy). b 51. SEITE 00. **d** 03 **p** 04. NSM Finsbury Park St Thos *Lon* 03-07; C Acton Green 07-15. *St Martin's Cottage, Hale Gardens, London W3 9SQ* T: (020) 8993 3237 E: brandy@brandypearson.wanadoo.co.uk *or* therevvedbee@hotmail.com

PEARSON, Canon Brian Robert. b 35. Leeds Univ BA 59. Coll of Resurr Mirfield 59. **d** 61 **p** 62. C Chesterfield St Mary and All SS *Derby* 61-66; P-in-c Derby St Jo 66-72; P-in-c Derby St Anne 66-72; R Thorpe St Andr *Nor* 72-90; Hon Can Nor Cathl 85-90; RD Nor E 86-90; V Harrogate St Wilfrid *Ripon* 90-00; rtd 00; PtO *York* from 00; *Bradf* 04-07. *Green Garth, 13 Cedar Glade, Dunnington, York YO19 5QZ* T: (01904) 481232

PEARSON, Canon Brian William. b 49. Brighton Poly BSc 71 City Univ MSc 80 Westmr Coll Ox MTh 94 FHSM. S'wark Ord Course & Clapham Ord Scheme 76. **d** 79 **p** 80. Hon C Plumstead All SS *S'wark* 79-81; PtO *Chich* 81-83; Hon C Broadwater St Mary 83-88; Bp's Research and Dioc Communications Officer *B & W* 88-90; Dioc Missr 91; Abp's Officer for Miss and Evang and Tait Missr *Cant* 91-97; Abp's Dioc Chapl 91-97; Hon Prov Can Cant Cathl 92-97; Gen Dir CPAS 97-00; P-in-c Leek Wootton and Dioc Officer for OLM *Cov* 00-06; Assoc Dir of Voc *B & W* from 11. *Woodspring, Northfield, Somerton TA11 6SL* T: (01458) 274360 E: brian@vividclouds.com

PEARSON, Christian David John (Brother Christian). b 42. Open Univ BA 76 CCC Cam BA 79 MA 83. AKC 65. **d** 66 **p** 67. C Pallion *Dur* 66-68; C Peterlee 68-71; SSF from 71; LtO *Sarum* 71-73; Tanzania 74-75; LtO *Ely* 75-90; Asst Chapl Keble Coll Ox 82-83; Chapl St Cath Coll Cam 83-86; Chapl Down Coll Cam 86-90; LtO *Lon* from 90; Dep Warden and Chapl Lon Goodenough Trust 90-95; PtO *S'wark* from 15. *St Matthias, 45 Mafeking Road, London E16 4NS* T: (020) 7511 7848

PEARSON, Christopher John. b 49. GRSM LRAM ARCM. Oak Hill NSM Course 81. **d** 84 **p** 85. NSM Barton Seagrave w Warkton *Pet* 84-86; C Kettering St Andr 86-88; V Nassington w Yarwell and Woodnewton 88-91; V Pet St Mark 91-03; P-in-c Gt Doddington and Wilby 03-12; P-in-c Ecton 07-12; R Gt Doddington and Wilby and Ecton 12-15; rtd 15. *10 Ashley Way, Weston, Northampton NN3 3DZ* T: (01604) 947861 E: c.pearson1@homecall.co.uk

PEARSON, Christopher William. b 56. Univ Coll Ox MA. St Jo Coll Nottm 07. **d** 09 **p** 10. C Norton St Mary and Stockton St Chad *Dur* 09-11; P-in-c Easington and Easington Colliery 11-14; TR Gt Aycliffe from 14. *St Clare's Rectory, St Cuthbert's Way, Newton Aycliffe DL5 5NT* T: (01325) 789439 E: cwpearson@fastmail.co.uk

PEARSON, Colin Graham. b 58. St Jo Coll Nottm 01. **d** 04 **p** 05. C Mickleover All SS *Derby* 04-09; C Breadsall 09-10; P-in-c Alvaston 10-14; V 14-15; P-in-c Chapel-en-le-Frith from 15;

AD Bakewell and Eyam from 15; AD Buxton from 15; AD Glossop from 15. *The Vicarage, 71 Manchester Road, Chapel-en-le-Frith, High Peak SK23 9TH* T: (01298) 812134 M: 07530-776406 E: colin2pearson@gmail.com

PEARSON, David. *See* PEARSON, James David

PEARSON, David. b 57. Man Poly BA 78. Trin Coll Bris 85. **d** 88 **p** 89. C Shawbury *Lich* 88-91; C Morton 88-91; C Stanton on Hine Heath 88-91; R Mattishall w Mattishall Burgh, Welborne etc *Nor* 91-00; RD Dereham in Mitford 98-00; Asst P Tawa Linden New Zealand 00-04; V Levin from 04. *120 Cambridge Street, Levin 5500, New Zealand* T: (0064) (6) 368 5955 E: vicar.levinanglicans@xtra.co.nz

PEARSON, Fergus Tom. b 58. Middx Poly BA 81 Moore Th Coll Sydney MA 98. Oak Hill Th Coll BA 95. **d** 92 **p** 93. C Mildmay Grove St Jude and St Paul *Lon* 92-95; Australia 96-98; C Heatherlands St Jo *Sarum* 98-03; V Hensingham *Carl* from 03. *St John's Vicarage, Egremont Road, Hensingham, Whitehaven CA28 8QW* T: (01946) 692822 E: fpe@rson.justbrowsing.com

PEARSON, Geoffrey Charles. b 49. Imp Coll Lon BSc 70 ARCS. Oak Hill Th Coll 80. **d** 82 **p** 83. C Folkestone St Jo *Cant* 82-86; V Ramsgate St Luke 86-93; Chapl to People at Work in Cam *Ely* 93-01; Co-ord Chapl HM Pris Chelmsf 01-07; rtd 07; PtO *Cant* from 08. *99 Cherry Drive, Canterbury CT2 8ER* T/F: (01227) 379451 M: 07890-808739 E: pearsongeoff@mail.co.uk

✠**PEARSON, The Rt Revd Geoffrey Seagrave.** b 51. St Jo Coll Dur BA 72. Cranmer Hall Dur 72. **d** 74 **p** 75 **c** 06. C Kirkheaton *Wakef* 74-77; C-in-c Blackb Redeemer 77-82; V 82-85; Asst Home Sec Gen Syn Bd for Miss and Unity 85-89; Hon C Forty Hill Jes Ch *Lon* 85-89; Exec Sec BCC Evang Cttee 86-89; V Roby *Liv* 89-06; AD Huyton 02-06; Hon Can Liv Cathl 03-06; Suff Bp Lancaster *Blackb* from 06; C Ellel w Shireshead from 08. *Shireshead Vicarage, Whinney Brow, Forton, Preston PR3 0AE* T: (01524) 799900 F: 799901 E: bishoplancaster@gmail.com

PEARSON, George Michael. b 31. FCA FBCS MIMC. Qu Coll Birm 86 Coll of Resurr Mirfield 89. **d** 88 **p** 90. NSM Solihull *Birm* 88-95; PtO from 95. *The Parsonage, 67A Hampton Lane, Solihull B91 2QD* T: 0121-705 0288 E: parsonpearson@pearwood.org.uk

PEARSON, Canon Henry Gervis. b 47. Mansf Coll Ox BA 72 MA 76. St Jo Coll Nottm 72. **d** 74 **p** 75. C Southgate *Chich* 74-76; TV 76-82; V Debenham w Aspall and Kenton *St E* 82-91; Chapl to Suffolk Fire Service 88-91; RD Loes 89-91; TR Marlborough *Sarum* 91-02; RD 94-02; R Queen Thorne 02-12; Pv-in-c Gifle Valley 10-12; RD Sherborne 04-11; Chapl Savernake Hosp Marlborough 91-94; Chapl E Wilts Health Care NHS Trust 94-99; Can and Preb Sarum Cathl 99-12; rtd 12; PtO *Sarum* from 12. *1 Morris Road, Marlborough SN8 1TJ* T: (01672) 511788 E: canonhenry@btinternet.com *or* henryandjudith@btinternet.com

PEARSON, Ian. b 49. Liv Univ BA 71. S'wark Ord Course 79. **d** 82 **p** 83. Archivist USPG 82-85; Archivist Nat Soc 85-91; NSM Lavender Hill Ascension *S'wark* 82-84; LtO Lon 84-86 and 88-90; NSM Westmr St Matt 86-88; PtO *S'wark* 85-90; *St Alb* 90-91; C Chesterfield St Mary and All SS *Derby* 91-95; R Bengeo *St Alb* 95-04; P-in-c Worc City St Paul and Old St Martin etc 04-06; R Worc City 06-10; rtd 10; PtO *B & W* from 10. *7 Rosedale Walk, Frome BA11 2JH* T: (01373) 469739 E: ianandlizpearson@waitrose.com

PEARSON, James David. b 51. Cape Town Univ BSocSc 74. St Paul's Coll Grahamstown 76. **d** 78 **p** 79. C St Geo Cathl Cape Town S Africa 78-80; R Caledon H Trin 80-84; R Tristan da Cunha St Mary 84-86; R Camps Bay St Pet 86-89; R Kuruman St Mary-le-Bourne w Wrenchville 89-91; R Amalinda Ch 92-96; Asst P Cambridge St Mark 96-98; Asst P-in-c Kidds Beach St Mary & St Andr 99; C Prittlewell St Steph *Chelmsf* 00-04; TV Barking St Marg w St Patr 04-09; P-in-c Hornchurch H Cross from 09. *Holy Cross Vicarage, 260 Hornchurch Road, Hornchurch RM11 1PX* T: (01708) 464544 E: david_pearson@dsl.pipex.com

PEARSON, Joanna Ruth. *See* SEABOURNE, Joanna Ruth

PEARSON, Mrs Katherine Elizabeth. b 77. Birm Univ LLB 99 MSc 08. Qu Coll Birm. **d** 12 **p** 13. C Brandwood *Birm* 12-15; C Weoley Castle 12-15; Chapl Warw Univ *Cov* from 15. *92 De Montfort Way, Coventry CV4 7DT* M: 07890-648008 T: (024) 7641 9666 E: kate.e.pearson@me.com

✠**PEARSON, The Rt Revd Kevin.** b 54. Leeds Univ BA 75 Edin Univ BD 79. Edin Th Coll 76. **d** 79 **p** 80 **c** 11. C Horden *Dur* 79-81; Chapl Leeds Univ *Ripon* 81-87; R Edin St Salvador 87-93; Chapl Edin Napier Univ 88-92 and 92-94; Dioc Dir of Ords 90-95; Prov Dir of Ords from 91; Assoc R Edin Old St Paul 93-94; P-in-c Linlithgow *Edin* 94-95; R Edin St Mich and All SS 95-11; Can St Mary's Cathl 03-11; Dean Edin 04-10; Bp Arg

from 11. *St Moluag's Diocesan Centre, Croft Avenue, Oban PA34 5JJ* T: (01631) 570870 *or* 562617 E: bishop@argyll.anglican.org

PEARSON, Mrs Lindsey Carole. b 61. Cov Poly BA 86 CQSW 86. Westcott Ho Cam 86. **d** 89 **p** 94. Par Dn High Harrogate St Pet *Ripon* 89-93; C Moor Allerton 93-96; Chapl St Gemma's Hospice 94-96; TV Seacroft *Ripon* 96-04; World Development Officer 97-04; Area Co-ord (N and W Yorks) Chr Aid 04-07; PtO *Ripon* 04-07; P-in-c Swillington 07-13; NSM Kippax w Allerton Bywater 12-13; P-in-c Beeston *Leeds* from 13. *Beeston Vicarage, 16 Town Street, Beeston, Leeds LS11 8PN* T: 0113-272 3337 M: 07961-016052 E: revlcp@btinternet.com

PEARSON, Michael Carden. b 38. Guy's Hosp Medical Sch MB 63 BChir 63 Down Coll Cam MA 64 Lon Univ MSc 94 FRCR 75 FRCP 94. St Steph Ho Ox 96. **d** 98 **p** 99. NSM Horsted Keynes *Chich* 98-99; NSM Worth 99-00; Chapl Gtr Athens *Eur* 00-01; PtO *Chich* 04-05; P-in-c Staplefield Common 05-08; rtd 08. *Bleak House, Station Road, Horsted Keynes, Haywards Heath RH17 7ED* T: (01825) 790617 E: michaelpearson@coxlesspair.demon.co.uk

PEARSON, Michael John. b 53. Southn Univ BTh 78. Sarum Th Coll 74. **d** 78 **p** 79. C Paignton St Jo *Ex* 78-82; TV Ilfracombe, Lee, Woolacombe, Bittadon etc 82-86; TV Barnstaple 86-88; Chapl N Devon Healthcare NHS Trust 86-96; RD Barnstaple *Ex* 97-01; C Shaldon, Stokeinteignhead, Combeinteignhead etc 08-09; rtd 09. *5 Kala Fair, Westward Ho, Bideford EX39 1TX* E: fathermichaelpearson@googlemail.com

PEARSON, Nigel Hetley Allan. b 45. Fitzw Coll Cam BA 67 MA 87. EMMTC 04. **d** 06 **p** 07. NSM Papworth *Ely* from 06. *Manor Farm House, 53 Ermine Street, Caxton, Cambridge CB23 3PQ* T: (01954) 719750 *or* 719637 F: 718566 M: 07713-639928 E: njfarm@gmail.com

PEARSON, Pauline Hilary. b 54. BA 77 PhD 88 RN 77 RHV 79. NEOC 02. **d** 05 **p** 06. NSM Denton *Newc* 05-10; NSM Newc St Geo and St Hilda from 10. *3 Belle Grove Place, Newcastle upon Tyne NE2 4LH* T: 0191-232 5980 M: 07753-744349 E: pauline.pearson@northumbria.ac.uk

PEARSON, Mrs Priscilla Dawn. b 45. Oak Hill Th Coll BA 90. **d** 90 **p** 94. Par Dn Stanford-le-Hope w Mucking *Chelmsf* 90-94; C 94; C Colchester St Jo 94-96; Hon C Woking St Jo *Guildf* 03-05; rtd 10. *Talywain Cottage, Shop Road, Cwmavon, Pontypool NP4 7RU* T: (01495) 774132 E: priscillapearson@btinternet.com

PEARSON, Raymond Joseph. b 44. AKC 71. St Aug Coll Cant 71. **d** 72 **p** 73. C Wetherby *Ripon* 72-75; C Goring-by-Sea *Chich* 75-77; C Bramley *Ripon* 77-82; V Patrick Brompton and Hunton 82-94; V Crakehall 82-94; V Hornby 82-94; World Miss Officer 88-94; RD Wensley 92-94; V Bardsey 94-09; rtd 09; PtO *York* from 09. *7 St George's Croft, Bridlington YO16 7RW* T: (01262) 424332

PEARSON, Robert James Stephen. b 52. Cov Poly BA 74. St Steph Ho Ox 85. **d** 87 **p** 88. C Stoke Newington St Mary *Lon* 87-90; C Haggerston All SS 90-97; C Dalston H Trin w St Phil and Haggerston All SS 97-98; Chapl HM Pris Wandsworth 98-02; Chapl HM Pris Pentonville 02-07; PtO *Lon* from 07. *276 Osborne Road, London W3 8SR* T: (020) 8993 3237 E: ahjay@hotmail.co.uk

PEARSON, Robert Lyon. b 57. St Jo Coll Nottm 90. **d** 92 **p** 93. C Netherton *Liv* 92-96; V Woolston 96-02; V Highfield from 02. *St Matthew's Vicarage, Billinge Road, Wigan WN3 6BL* T: (01942) 222121 F: 211332 E: vicar@stmatthewhighfield.org.uk

PEARSON, Preb Roy Barthram. b 35. K Coll Lon 56. **d** 60 **p** 61. C Brookfield St Mary *Lon* 60-64; C St Marylebone St Cypr 64-70; V Tottenham All Hallows from 70; AD E Haringey 95-00; Preb St Paul's Cathl from 96. *The Priory, Church Lane, London N17 7AA* T: (020) 8808 2470

PEARSON-GEE, William Oliver Clinton. b 61. Wycliffe Hall Ox 04. **d** 06 **p** 07. C Ox St Andr 06-10; R Buckingham from 10. *The Rectory, 8 Aris Way, Buckingham MK18 1FX* T: (01280) 830221 E: rector@buckinghambenefice.org.uk

PEARSON-MILES, David. b 37. St Jo Coll Nottm 74. **d** 76 **p** 77. C Hazlemere *Ox* 76-79; R Waddesdon w Over Winchendon and Fleet Marston 79-82; CF 82-92; P-in-c Barcombe *Chich* 92-94; V 94-00; rtd 00. *The Coach House, Holme Place, Oakford, Tiverton EX16 9DH* T: (01398) 351495

PEART, John Graham. b 36. Bps' Coll Cheshunt 65. **d** 68 **p** 69. C Cheshunt *St Alb* 68-70; C St Alb St Pet 70-73; R Hunsdon 73-76; R Widford 73-76; Ind Chapl 76-82; Chapl St Geo Hosp Stafford 82-87; Chapl Stafford Distr Gen Hosp 82-87; Chapl Qu Eliz Hosp Gateshead 87-89; Chapl Bensham Hosp Gateshead 87-89; Chapl Garlands Hosp 89-94; P-in-c Cotehill and Cumwhinton *Carl* 89-94; V Irthington, Crosby-on-Eden and Scaleby 94-98; rtd 98; Chapl Douglas MacMillan Hospice

Stoke-on-Trent 98-01; P-in-c Salt and Sandon w Burston *Lich* 01-02; TV Mid Trent 02-03; PtO 04-07; *Eur* 07-13; *Lich* from 15. *29 Little Tixall Lane, Great Haywood, Stafford ST18 0SE* T: (01889) 883340 E: johnpeart@hotmail.co.uk

PEART, Patricia Isidora. b 55. Westcott Ho Cam 97. **d** 99. C Holland-on-Sea *Chelmsf* 99-00; C Shrub End 00-01. *6 Whitsand Road, Manchester M22 4ZA*

PEASE, Alexander Michael. b 56. Mansf Coll Ox MA. St Mellitus Coll BA 12. **d** 12 **p** 13. NSM Itchen Valley *Win* from 12. *Manor Farm House, Kilmeston Road, Kilmeston, Alresford SO24 0NW* T: (01962) 793063 M: 07931-380321 E: alex@manorfarmkelmeston.com

PEAT, Mrs Ann Kathleen. b 40. TCert 60. **d** 98 **p** 99. OLM Brumby *Linc* from 98. *36 Glover Road, Scunthorpe DN17 1AS* T: (01724) 852609

PEAT, David James. b 62. Leeds Univ BA 84 Dur Univ MA 91. Cranmer Hall Dur 86. **d** 89 **p** 90. C Wetherby *Ripon* 89-92; C Beeston 92-95; Chapl St Lawr Coll Ramsgate 95-06; Hd Relig Educn Eastbourne Coll from 06. *Eastbourne College, Old Wish Road, Eastbourne BN21 4JY* T: (01323) 452244 E: djpeat@eastbourne-college.co.uk

PEAT, David William. b 37. Clare Coll Cam MA 59 PhD 62 FRAS 63. Westcott Ho Cam 72. **d** 75 **p** 76. C Chesterton St Andr *Ely* 75-77; Chapl Univ Coll of Ripon and York St Jo 77-83; V E Ardsley *Wakef* 83-87; Prin Willesden Min Tr Scheme 87-94; NSM Headingley *Leeds* from 94; P-in-c *Ripon* 06-12; Research Lect Leeds Univ from 94. *12 North Grange Mews, Headingley, Leeds LS6 2EW* T: 0113-275 3179 E: phy6dwp@phys-irc.leeds.ac.uk

PEAT, The Ven Lawrence Joseph. b 28. Linc Th Coll 55. **d** 58 **p** 59. C Bramley *Ripon* 58-61; V 65-73; R Heaton Norris All SS *Man* 61-65; P-in-c Southend St Erkenwald *Chelmsf* 73-74; TR Southend St Jo w St Mark, All SS w St Fran etc 74-79; V Skelsmergh w Selside and Longsleddale *Carl* 79-86; RD Kendal 84-89; TV Kirkby Lonsdale 86-89; Hon Can Carl Cathl 88-95; Adn Westmorland and Furness 89-95; rtd 95; PtO *Carl* from 95. *2 Primrose Court, Primley Park View, Leeds LS17 7UY* E: lawrie.peat@fsmail.net

PEAT, Matthew. b 71. Bradf and Ilkley Coll BA 97. Ripon Coll Cuddesdon BTh 03. **d** 03 **p** 04. C Walney Is *Carl* 03-06; C Barrow St Matt 06-08; TR 08-10; TR N Barrow 10-13; RD Barrow 11-12; P-in-c Whitkirk *Leeds* from 13. *Whitkirk Vicarage, 386 Selby Road, Leeds LS15 0AA* M: 07772-560014 E: matthewpeat@talktalk.net

PEATMAN (née HUGHES), Mrs Debbie Ann. b 62. SS Hild & Bede Coll Dur BA 83 St Jo Coll Dur BA 89. Cranmer Hall Dur 87. **d** 90 **p** 94. C Edin Old St Paul 90-91; NSM Greasley *S'well* 92-94; NSM Whitley *Cov* 94-02; C Lancaster St Thos *Blackb* 02-09; Co Ecum Development Officer for Churches Together in Lancs 09-13; LtO 09-15. *The Rectory, Church Walk, Morecambe LA4 5PR* M: 07806-643097 E: debbiepeat@talktalk.net

PEATMAN, Michael Robert. b 61. Keble Coll Ox BA 85 MA 89 St Jo Coll Dur BA 89 Lanc Univ MA 06. Cranmer Hall Dur 87. **d** 90 **p** 91. C Greasley *S'well* 90-94; C Whitley *Cov* 94-02; Dio Stewardship Adv 94-02; Sen Chapl St Martin's Coll *Blackb* 02-07; Sen Chapl Cumbria Univ 07-09; P-in-c Poulton-le-Sands w Morecambe St Laur 09-11; R from 11; AD Lancaster and Morecambe from 10. *The Rectory, Church Walk, Morecambe LA4 5PR* T/F: (01524) 410941 E: mikepeat@sky.com

PEATTIE, The Ven Colin Hulme Reid. b 39. Natal Univ BSc 59. Ripon Hall Ox 61. **d** 63 **p** 64. C Belmont *Lon* 63-65; R Durban St Columba S Africa 65-69; R Dundee St Jas 69-72; Chapl St Andr Sch Bloemfontein 72-76; R Pietermaritzburg St Alphege 76-83; V S Ossett *Wakef* 83-85; R York-cum-Ravensworth S Africa 85-93; R Stranger All SS 93-96; R Umhlali All So from 96; Adn N Coast from 01. *PO Box 222, Salt Rock, 4391 South Africa* T/F: (0027) (32) 947 2001 M: 82-413 8650 E: cpeattie@absamail.co.za

PEATY, Canon Julia Kathleen. b 53. Salford Univ BSc 75 Glos Univ BA 07. STETS 96. **d** 99 **p** 00. NSM E Grinstead St Swithun *Chich* 99-13; RD E Grinstead 10-13; Dean of Women's Min from 13; Can and Preb Chich Cathl from 10. *15 Overton Shaw, East Grinstead RH19 2HN* T: (01342) 322386 E: julia@peaty.net

PEBERDY (née GARNETT), Mrs Alyson Susan. b 48. Trevelyan Coll Dur BA 69 Reading Univ MA 75. Ox Min Course 95. **d** 96 **p** 97. C New Windsor *Ox* 96-99; V Brockley Hill St Sav *S'wark* from 99; P-in-c Perry Hill St Geo 00-01; P-in-c Forest Hill St Aug 00-02; Adv Women's Area Woolwich Area from 10; Dean of Women's Min from 12. *St Saviour's Vicarage, 5 Lowther Hill, London SE23 1PZ* T: (020) 8690 2499 E: alysonpeberdy@aol.com

PECK, Christopher Wallace. b 49. UEA BA 72 Lon Bible Coll BA 75 Ches Coll of HE MTh 96. Ripon Coll Cuddesdon 10.

d 11 **p** 12. C Abington *Pet* 11-15; R Guilsborough and Hollowell and Cold Ashby etc from 15. *The Vicarage, 15 Church Mount, Guilsborough, Northampton NN6 8QA* M: 07505-253096 E: revchrispeck@hotmail.co.uk

PECK, David Warner. b 66. American Univ (Washington) BA 88 Selw Coll Cam BA 94 MA 99. Westcott Ho Cam 92. **d** 95 **p** 96. C Weybridge *Guildf* 95-99; Bp's Chapl 99-05; Abp's Sec for Internat Development *Cant* 05-08; R Lancaster St Jas USA from 08. *The Rectory, 115 North Duke Street, Lancaster PA 17602, USA* T/F: (001) (717) 397 4858

PECK, Kay Margaret. b 51. Milton Keynes Coll of Ed BEd 76. Ox Min Course 04. **d** 07 **p** 08. NSM Swan *Ox* 07-09; NSM The Claydons and Swan 09-10; NSM Lenborough from 11. *21 Beamish Way, Winslow, Buckingham MK18 3EU* E: kmpeck@btinternet.com

PECK, Robert John. b 49. Bath Univ BSc 72. STETS 00. **d** 03 **p** 04. NSM Stoke-next-Guildf 03-08; V Camberley St Martin Old Dean from 08; RD Surrey Heath from 11. *St Martin's Vicarage, 2A Hampshire Road, Camberley GU15 4DW* T: (01276) 23958 E: vicar@stmartinolddean.com *or* rpeck@btinternet.com

PECKHAM, Richard Graham. b 51. Sarum & Wells Th Coll 84. **d** 86 **p** 87. C Bishop's Cleeve *Glouc* 86-89; TV Ilfracombe, Lee, Woolacombe, Bittadon etc *Ex* 89-96; TV Sidmouth, Woolbrook, Salcombe Regis, Sidbury etc 96-12; RD Ottery 98-02; P-in-c Dunkeswell, Luppitt, Sheldon and Upottery from 12; C Broadhembury, Payhembury and Plymtree from 12; Hon Chapl ATC from 98. *The Rectory, Dunkeswell, Honiton EX14 4RE* T: (01404) 891243 E: rikpeckham@btinternet.com

PEDDER, Brian. b 38. Carl Dioc Tr Inst 88. **d** 91 **p** 92. NSM Wigton *Carl* 91-93; C Cleator Moor w Cleator 93-96; P-in-c Grayrigg, Old Hutton and New Hutton 96-04; rtd 04; PtO *Carl* from 05. *5 Scholars Green, Wigton CA7 9QW* T: (016973) 45346

PEDLAR, Canon John Glanville. b 43. Ex Univ BA 68 De Montfort Univ Hon MA 06. St Steph Ho Ox 68. **d** 70 **p** 71. C Tavistock and Gulworthy *Ex* 70-73; Prec Portsm Cathl 74-77; Prec St Alb Abbey *St Alb* 77-81; V Redbourn 81-98; V Bedford St Paul 98-13; PV Westmr Abbey 87-04; Hon Can St Alb *St Alb* 06-13; rtd 13. *1 Priory Dene, Bristol BS9 3EG* E: johnpedlar@btinternet.com

PEDLEY, Canon Betty. b 49. Ripon Coll of Educn CertEd 70 Leeds Univ BEd 71 ALCM 78. NOC 85. **d** 88 **p** 03. Par Dn Sowerby *Wakef* 88-92; Par Educn Adv and Youth Chapl 92-03; P-in-c Luddenden w Luddenden Foot 03-08; P-in-c Norland 06-08; Hon Can Wakef Cathl 00-08; rtd 08; PtO *Leeds* from 08. *7 Ogden View Close, Halifax HX2 9LY* T: (01422) 882127

✠PEDLEY, The Rt Revd Geoffrey Stephen. b 40. Qu Coll Cam BA 64 MA 67. Cuddesdon Coll 64. **d** 66 **p** 67 **c** 98. C Liv Our Lady and St Nic 66-69; C Cov H Trin 69-71; P-in-c Kitwe Zambia 71-77; P-in-c Stockton H Trin *Dur* 77-83; V Stockton St Pet 77-88; Chapl to The Queen 84-98; R Whickham *Dur* 88-93; Can Res Dur Cathl 93-98; Suff Bp Lancaster *Blackb* 98-05; Hon Can Blackb Cathl 98-05; rtd 05. *The Blue House, Newbrough, Hexham NE47 5AN* T: (01434) 674238

PEDLEY, Nicholas Charles. b 48. CQSW 75. Qu Coll Birm 88. **d** 90 **p** 91. C Stafford St Jo and Tixall w Ingestre *Lich* 90-93; C Kingswinford St Mary *Worc* 93-96; TV 96-97; C Cheswardine, Childs Ercall, Hales, Hinstock etc *Lich* 97-99; Chapl HM YOI Stoke Heath 97-99; rtd 99; PtO *Worc* from 00. *33 Comber Grove, Kinver, Stourbridge DY7 6EN* T: (01384) 877219 E: nick@npedley48.freeserve.co.uk

PEDLEY, Simon David. b 76. Lon Univ BSc 98 ARCS 98. Oak Hill Th Coll BA 10. **d** 10 **p** 11. C St Helen Bishopsgate w St Andr Undershaft etc *Lon* 10-14. *30 Kirkstall Gardens, London SW2 4HS* M: 07713-897991

PEDLOW, Henry Noel. b 37. QUB BA 59. **d** 61 **p** 62. C Belfast St Phil *Conn* 61-66; C Belfast St Nic 66-70; I Eglantine 70-82; I Kilkeel *D & D* 82-89; I Belfast St Donard 89-03; rtd 03. *8 Old Mill Dale, Dundonalad, Belfast BT16 1WG* T: (028) 9048 5416

PEEBLES, David Thomas. b 64. Bris Univ BA 85 St Chad's Coll Dur PGCE 86 Man Univ MA 94. Coll of Resurr Mirfield 90. **d** 90 **p** 91. C Crewe St Andr *Ches* 90-93; Lect and Asst Dir Studies Mirfield 93-95; Chapl Qu Mary and Westf Coll *Lon* 95-00; P-in-c Bethnal Green St Matt w St Jas the Gt 97-99; Chapl LSE 00-10; R Bloomsbury St Geo w Woburn Square Ch Ch from 10; Bp's Adv on New Relig Movements from 01. *The Rectory, 6 Gower Street, London WC1E 6DP* T: (020) 7580 4010 M: 07838-388074 E: rector@stgb.org.uk

PEEK, Alan Nicholas. b 65. Ridley Hall Cam 02. **d** 04 **p** 05. C Much Woolton *Liv* 04-08; I Derg w Termonamongan *D & R* 08-14; I Movilla *D & D* from 14. *The Rectory, 34 Hollymount Road, Newtownards BT23 7DL* T: (028) 9181 0787 *or* 9181 9794 E: rev.al@sky.com

PEEK, John Richard. b 51. Bris Univ BSc 72 Nottm Univ BA 75. St Jo Coll Nottm. **d** 76 **p** 77. C Hebburn St Jo *Dur* 76-78; C Dunston 78-81; R Armthorpe *Sheff* 81-86; RE Teacher K Edw VI Sch Southn 87-88; Chapl and Hd RE Casterton Sch Lancs 89; Teacher Furze Platt Comp Sch Berks 89-90; Chapl Bearwood Coll Wokingham 96-97; Teacher K Manor Sch Guildf 97-98; Teacher Stowford Coll Sutton 98-08; Teacher Ryde Sch w Upper Chine 08-09; PtO *Portsm* 08-11. *41 North Road, Shanklin PO37 6DE* T: (01983) 719631

PEEL, Mrs Christine Mary. b 44. Whitelands Coll Lon CertEd 66. Portsm Dioc Tr Course. **d** 90. NSM Sheet *Portsm* 90-03; PtO *York* from 03. *11 Whiteoak Avenue, Easingwold, York YO61 3GB* T: (01347) 823548 E: iw.peel@homecall.co.uk *or* peel3gb@btinternet.com

PEEL, Canon David Charles. b 41. AKC 75. St Aug Coll Cant 75. **d** 76 **p** 77. C Tynemouth Cullercoats St Paul *Newc* 76-79; C Tynemouth St Jo 79-84; Ldr Cedarwood Project 84-88 and 91-11; Warden Communicare Ho 89-91; Min Killingworth 89-91; Hon Can Newc Cathl 08-11; rtd 11. *116 Grey Street, North Shields NE30 2EG* T: 0191-272 8743

PEEL, Derrick. b 50. Open Univ BA 82. Linc Th Coll 75. **d** 78 **p** 79. C Otley *Bradf* 78-82; V Shelf 82-94; P-in-c Buttershaw St Aid 89-94; TR Shelf w Buttershaw St Aid 94-95; V E Crompton *Man* 95-05; V Ware St Mary *St Alb* from 05. *St Mary's Vicarage, 31 Thunder Court, Ware SG12 0PT* T: (01920) 464817

PEELING, Mrs Pamela Mary Alberta. b 44. Oak Hill Th Coll 83. **dss** 86 **d** 87 **p** 94. NSM Moulsham St Luke *Chelmsf* 86-88; NSM N Springfield 88-95; C Basildon St Martin 95-97; TV Grays Thurrock 97-05; rtd 05; PtO *St E* from 05. *4 Heron Road, Saxmundham IP17 1WR* T: (01728) 604584 E: ppeeling@freebie.net

PEER, Charles Scott. b 69. Bris Univ BSc 91 PGCE 94 Ex Univ MA 05. Trin Coll Bris BA 02. **d** 02 **p** 03. C Dawlish *Ex* 02-05; P-in-c Kea *Truro* 05-12; Miss Development Officer *Portsm* from 12. *40 Romsey Road, Winchester SO22 5DL*

✠**PEERS, The Most Revd Michael Geoffrey.** b 34. Univ of BC BA 56. Trin Coll Toronto LTh 59 Hon DD 78. **d** 59 **p** 60 **c** 77. C Ottowa St Thos Canada 59-61; C Ottowa Trin 61-65; Chapl Carleton Univ 61-66; R Winnipeg St Bede 66-72; R Winnipeg St Martin w Middlechurch 72-74; Adn Winnipeg 69-74; R St Paul's Cathl Regina Dean Qu'Appelle 74-77; Bp Qu'Appelle 77-82; Abp Qu'Appelle and Metrop Rupert's Land 82-86; Primate Angl Ch of Canada 86-04; rtd 04. *195 Westminster Avenue, Toronto ON M6R 1N9, Canada*

PEERS, Michael John. b 65. SS Paul & Mary Coll Cheltenham BA 86. Ripon Coll Cuddesdon 88. **d** 91 **p** 92. C Birstall and Wanlip *Leic* 91-94; C Leic St Marg and All SS 94-96; TV The Abbey Leic 96-00; P-in-c Langley Park *Dur* 00-01; V from 01; P-in-c Esh 00-01; V 01-11; P-in-c Hamsteels 00-01; V 01-11; V Esh and Hamsteels from 11; P-in-c Waterhouses 00-01; V from 01. *The Vicarage, Church Street, Langley Park, Durham DH7 9TZ* T: 0191-373 3110 E: mjpeers@aol.com

PEERS, Richard Charles. b 65. K Alfred's Coll Win BEd 88 Lon Inst of Educn MA 05. Chich Th Coll BTh 93. **d** 93 **p** 94. C Grangetown *York* 93-95; C Portsea St Mary *Portsm* 95-97; Dep Hd Emsworth Primary Sch 97-01; Hon Chapl Portsm Cathl 01-03; Chapl St Luke's Sch Southsea 01-03; Dep Hd Ch Sch Richmond 03-06; Headmaster Trin Sch Lewisham from 08; Hon C Earlsfield St Andr *S'wark* 06-11; Hon C Blackheath All SS 11-13; Hon C Lewisham St Mary from 13. *Trinity Church of England School, Taunton Road, London SE12 8PD* T: (020) 8852 3191 E: richard.peers1@btopenworld.com

PEET, John Christopher. b 56. Oriel Coll Ox BA 80 MA 83 Clare Coll Cam BA 82 MA 87. Ridley Hall Cam 80. **d** 83 **p** 84. C Menston w Woodhead *Bradf* 83-86; C Prenton *Ches* 86-89; V Harden and Wilsden *Bradf* 89-97; V Cononley w Bradley *Leeds* from 97. *The Vicarage, 3 Meadow Close, Cononley, Keighley BD20 8LZ* T: (01535) 634369 E: john.peet@bradford.anglican.org

PEET, Mrs Ruth Marie. b 59. **d** 15. C Plaistow St Mary *Roch* from 15. *The Vicarage, 1 Lake Avenue, Bromley BR1 4EN* T: (020) 8460 9397 E: ruthmpeet@gmail.com

PEGG, Brian Peter Richard (Bill). b 30. Ox NSM Course 77 Sarum & Wells Th Coll 82. **d** 83 **p** 84. C Furze Platt *Ox* 83-85; V Ashbury, Compton Beauchamp and Longcot w Fernham 85-94; Chapl Málaga *Eur* 94-97; rtd 97; Hon C Shere, Albury and Chilworth *Guildf* 98-02; PtO *Eur* from 98; *Linc* from 03. *31 King Street, Winterton, Scunthorpe DN15 9TP* T: (01724) 734860

PEGG, Josephine Anne. See ROBERTSON, Josephine Anne

PEGLER, Mrs Eve Charlotte. b 73. Cheltenham & Glouc Coll of HE BSc 95. Ridley Hall Cam 05. **d** 07 **p** 08. C Hullavington, Norton and Stanton St Quintin *Bris* 07-10; C Sherston Magna, Easton Grey, Luckington etc 07-10; TV Shaftesbury *Sarum* 10-14; Chapl Port Regis Sch 10-14; C Gillingham and Milton-on-Stour *Sarum* from 14. *The Vicarage, 49 Fern Brook Lane, Gillingham SP8 4FL* T: (01747) 851442 E: evepegler@gmail.com

PEGLER, Frederic Arthur. b 19. Selw Coll Cam BA 46 MA 48. Qu Coll Birm 46. **d** 47 **p** 48. C Crawley *Chich* 47-49; C Rickmansworth *St Alb* 49-50; V Sark *Win* 50-52; PV S'well Minster 52-55; Canada 55-84 and from 86; rtd 84; PtO *St Alb* 84-85. *302 Goodwin Manor, 1148 Goodwin Street, Victoria BC V8S 5H2, Canada* T: (001) (250) 370 9300

PEILOW, Canon Lynda Elizabeth Anne. b 74. CITC BTh 97. **d** 97 **p** 98. C Castleknock and Mulhuddart w Clonsilla *D & G* 97-00; C Dublin St Ann and St Steph 00-01; Min Can St Patr Cathl Dublin 00-01; I Clonsast w Rathangan, Thomastown etc *M & K* from 01; Can Meath from 14; Can Kildare Cathl from 14. *The Rectory, Monasteroris, Edenderry, Co Offaly, Republic of Ireland* T: (00353) (46) 973 1585 E: lyndapeilow@gmail.com *or* edenderry@kildare.anglican.org

PEIRCE, John. b 35. Worc Coll Ox BA 59 MA 64 Kent Univ MA 96. Wycliffe Hall Ox 59. **d** 61 **p** 62. C Brompton H Trin *Lon* 61-64; C Wareham w Arne *Sarum* 64-68; V Sturminster Newton and Hinton St Mary 68-74; V Kingswood *Bris* 74-79; Dir Coun Chr Care *Ex* 79-89; Public Preacher 89-92; NSM Hackney *Lon* 90-94; NSM St Botolph Aldgate w H Trin Minories from 94; Co-ord Ch Action on Disability 90-98; PtO *Ex* 92-98. *3 Mile End Place, London E1 4BH* T: (020) 7790 9418

PEIRCE, Canon John Martin. b 36. Jes Coll Cam BA 59 MA 65. Westcott Ho Cam 65. **d** 66 **p** 67. C Croydon St Jo *Cant* 66-70; C Fareham H Trin *Portsm* 70-71; TV 71-76; TR Langley Marish Ox 76-85; RD Burnham 78-82; Dir of Ords and Post-Ord Tr 85-01; Can Res Ch Ch *Ox* 87-01; rtd 01. *8 Burwell Meadow, Witney, Oxford OX28 5JQ*

PEIRIS, Lionel James Harold (Brother Lionel). b 45. Serampore Coll BD 71. Bp's Coll Calcutta 67. **d** 70 **p** 71. P Lect Colombo Coll Sri Lanka 71-76 and 78-95; C Shirley *Birm* 76-78; P Brother SSF Auckland New Zealand 96-97; Asst Chapl and Past Asst Annerley Hosp Australia 97-98; Hon C Annerley St Phil 97-98; P-in-C from 99. *115 Cornwall Street, Annerley Qld 4103, Australia* T: (0061) (7) 3391 3915 F: 3391 3916

PELHAM, John. b 36. New Coll Ox BA 61 MA 65. **d** 79 **p** 80. NSM Balerno *Edin* 79-91; NSM W Linton and Penicuik 91-94; Dioc Supernumerary from 94; NSM Lanark *Glas* 03-07; I.tO *Edin* from 08. *2 Horsburgh Bank, Balerno EH14 7DA* T: 0131-449 3934 E: johnpelham21@btinternet.com

PELL, Charles Andrew. b 54. Leeds Univ CertEd 77. Aston Tr Scheme 87 St Jo Coll Nottm 87. **d** 89 **p** 90. C Mottram in Longdendale w Woodhead *Ches* 89-90; C Handforth 90-93; P-in-c Walton Breck *Liv* 93-94; V 94-96; P-in-c Glyndyfrdwy and Llansantffraid Glyn Dyfrdwy *St As* 96-01; V Rhodes *Man* 01-07; CF (ACF) 93-07; rtd 07; PtO *Man* 09-10; P-in-c Forcett and Aldbrough and Melsonby *Leeds* from 13. *The Vicarage, 1 Appleby Close, Aldbrough St John, Richmond DL11 7TT* T: (01325) 374634 E: padre@milnet.uk.net

PELLEY, John Lawless. b 34. Oak Hill Th Coll 67. **d** 69 **p** 70. C Fareham St Jo *Portsm* 69-72; C Frogmore *St Alb* 72-76; V Standon 76-96; RD Bishop's Stortford 91-95; rtd 96; PtO *Ely* from 96. *7 Home Close, Histon, Cambridge CB24 9JL* T: (01223) 234636

PELLING, Nicholas Philip. b 48. EMMTC 05. **d** 07 **p** 08. C S Cluster S'well Deanery 07-10; V Oldbury, Langley and Londonderry *Birm* from 10. *The Vicarage, 2 St John's Road, Oldbury B68 9RP* T: 0121-552 5005 M: 07804-326416 E: nick@nickandju.plus.com

PELLY, Mrs Elizabeth Wigram (Lulu). b 52. Bris Univ BA 73. ERMC 05. **d** 08 **p** 09. C Towcester w Caldecote and Easton Neston etc *Pet* from 08. *Home Farm, Wakefield Lodge, Potterspury, Towcester NN12 7QX* T: (01327) 811218 M: 07723-604316 E: lulu.pelly@farming.co.uk

PELLY, Raymond Blake. b 38. Worc Coll Ox BA 61 MA 63 Geneva Univ DTh 71. Linc Th Coll 61 Bossey Ecum Inst Geneva 62. **d** 63 **p** 64. C Gosforth All SS *Newc* 63-65; C N Lynn w St Marg and St Nic *Nor* 69-70; Vice-Prin Westcott Ho Cam 71-76; Warden St Jo Coll Auckland New Zealand 77-85; Visiting Lect Univ of Mass Boston USA 86-88 and 96; Chapl Victoria Univ of Wellington New Zealand 90-94; Asst P Wellington St Pet 92-94 and from 96; rtd 03. *12 Kio Crescent, Hataitai, Wellington 6021, New Zealand* T: (0064) (4) 386 3972 M: 21-486200 F: (4) 386 3729 E: raymond.pelly@xtra.co.nz

PEMBERTON, Anthony Thomas Christie (Chris). b 57. BA. Cranmer Hall Dur 82. **d** 84 **p** 85. C Maidstone St Luke *Cant* 84-88; Chapl Ox Pastorate 88-98; V Cant St Mary Bredin 98-09; Tr Dir New Wine from 09; PtO *Chelmsf* from 13. *Newhouse Farm, Walden Road, Radwinter, Saffron Walden CB10 2SP* T: 03000-406205 E: chrisp@nwtp.org.uk

PEMBERTON, Crispin Mark Rugman. b 59. St Andr Univ MTheol 83. St Steph Ho Ox 84. **d** 86 **p** 87. C Acton Green *Lon* 86-90; C Leckhampton SS Phil and Jas w Cheltenham St Jas *Glouc* 90-93; V Tuffley 93-97; RE Teacher Cheltenham Coll Jun Sch 97-00; PtO *Heref* from 13. *Jenny Penny Whites, Little Dewchurch, Hereford HR2 6PR* T: (01432) 840817
M: 07824-444655 E: crispinpemberton@yahoo.co.uk

PEMBERTON, Elizabeth Joan. b 70. Univ of W Aus BA 90. ACT. **d** 98. Field Officer Bible Soc Australia 98-09; PtO *Lich* from 09. *17 The Spinney, Finchfield, Wolverhampton WV3 9HE*

PEMBERTON, Canon Jeremy Charles Baring. b 56. Mert Coll Ox MA 77 Fitzw Ho Cam BA 80 Leeds Univ MA 92. Ridley Hall Cam 78. **d** 81 **p** 82. C Stranton *Dur* 81-84; C Leeds St Geo *Ripon* 84-87; CMS Miss Partner and Dir Angl Th Inst Zaïre 87-91; V Irchester *Pet* 92-94; R Bourn and Kingston w Caxton and Longstowe *Ely* 94-00; P-in-c Elsworth w Knapwell 99-00; P-in-c Boxworth 99-00; TR Papworth 00-07; RD Bourn 98-03; Hon Can Ely Cathl 05-07; Community Chapl Notts Co Teaching Primary Care Trust 08-11; Dep Sen Chapl United Lincs Hosps NHS Trust from 11; Hon Can Boga from 05. *Department of Pastoral Care, Lincoln County Hospital, Greetwell Road, Lincoln LN2 5QY* T: (01522) 597717 M: 07920-274719
E: jeremy.pemberton@ulh.nhs.uk *or* canonjpemberton@gmail.com

PEMBERTON FORD, Carrie Mary. b 55. St Hilda's Coll Ox BA 78 Cam Univ PGCE 82 Leeds Univ MA 92 Newnham Coll Cam PhD 98. Cranmer Hall Dur 83 NEOC 84. **dss** 86 **d** 87 **p** 94. NSM Leeds St Geo *Ripon* 86-87; Miss Partner CMS and Dir Women's Studies Angl Th Inst Zaïre 91-94; PtO *Pet* 92-94; NSM Bourn and Kingston w Caxton and Longstowe *Ely* 94-99; TV Elsworth w Knapwell 99; Min Cambourne LEP 00-01; PtO 01-07; Cen Chapl Yarlswood Immigration and Detention Cen 01-03; Chief Exec CHASTE 04-08; Development Officer Cam Cen for Applied Research in Human Trafficking from 08. *Address temp unknown* E: carrie@ccarht.org

PENBERTHY, Canon Joanna Susan. b 60. Newnham Coll Cam BA 81 MA 85 St Jo Coll Nottm MTh 84. Cranmer Hall Dur 83. **dss** 84 **d** 87 **p** 97. Haughton le Skerne *Dur* 84-85; Llanishen and Lisvane *Llan* 85-89; NSM 87-89; NSM Llanwddyn and Llanfihangel-yng-Nghwynfa etc *St As* 89-93; NSM Llansadwrn w Llanwrda and Manordeilo *St D* 93-95; Prov Officer Div for Par Development Ch in Wales 94-99; P-in-c Cynwyl Gaeo w Llansawel and Talley *St D* 99-01; V 01-10; Dioc Adult Educn Officer 01-02; Warden of Readers 02-10; Can St D Cathl 07-10; P-in-c Charlton Musgrove, Cucklington and Stoke Trister *B & W* 10-11; R from 11. *The Rectory, Cucklington, Wincanton BA9 9PY* T: (01747) 840230
E: cmstbcrectory@btinternet.com

PENCAVEL, Mrs Ursula Frances. b 53. Qu Coll Birm 13. **d** 15. C Bayston Hill *Lich* from 15. *Address temp unknown*

PENDLEBURY, Stephen Thomas. b 50. ACA 78 Southn Univ BSc 73. Ridley Hall Cam 86. **d** 88 **p** 89. C Birkenhead St Jas w St Bede *Ches* 88-91; V 91-00; V Ches St Paul from 00; P-in-c Huntington from 12. *St Paul's Vicarage, 10 Sandy Lane, Chester CH3 5UL* T: (01244) 351377 E: stpendleby@aol.com

PENDORF, Canon James Gordon. b 45. Drew Univ New Jersey BA 67. Episc Th Sch Cam Mass STB 71. **d** 71 **p** 71. V Newark St Greg USA 71-76; V Colne H Trin *Blackb* 76-80; Sen Dioc Stewardship Adv *Chelmsf* 80-83; Dioc Sec *Birm* 83-95; P-in-c Highgate 95-97; V 97-04; Dioc Stewardship Adv 95-04; AD Birm City Cen 96-02; Hon Can Birm Cathl 90-04; Par Resources Adv and Chapl St Nic Ch Cen *St E* 04-13; NSM Holbrook, Stutton, Freston, Woolverstone etc 05-13; P-in-c Capel St Mary w Lt and Gt Wenham from 13. *The Rectory, Days Road, Capel St Mary, Ipswich IP9 2LE* M: 07973-265037
E: canonpendorf@aol.com

PENDUCK, Joshua Paul James. b 87. Birm City Univ BMus 09 St Jo Coll Dur BA 13. Cranmer Hall Dur 11. **d** 14 **p** 15. C Lich St Chad from 14. *15 Little Barrow Walk, Lichfield WS13 7EP*

PENFOLD, Brian Robert. b 54. Lon Univ BSc 75 Bris Univ PGCE 77. Oak Hill Th Coll BA 84. **d** 84 **p** 85. C Norwood St Luke *S'wark* 84-88; C Rayleigh *Chelmsf* 88-92; V New Barnet St Jas *St Alb* 92-08; V Worthing St Geo *Chich* from 08. *14 Pendine Avenue, Worthing BN11 2NB* T: (01903) 203309 M: 07753-680839 E: brian@brpenfold.freeserve.co.uk

PENFOLD, Colin Richard. b 52. St Pet Coll Ox BA 74 MA 78. Ridley Hall Cam 81. **d** 84 **p** 85. C Buckhurst Hill *Chelmsf* 84-87; C Greenside *Dur* 87-90; V Cononley w Bradley *Bradf* 90-97; P-in-c Shipley St Paul and Frizinghall 97; V Shipley St Paul 98-08; P-in-c Gt Harwood *Blackb* 08-12; V from 12. *St Bartholomew's Vicarage, Church Lane, Great Harwood, Blackburn BB6 7PU* T: (01254) 884039
E: colin@thepenfolds.org.uk

PENFOLD, Julian Oliver Kevin. All SS Cen for Miss & Min. **d** 15. NSM Riddings and Ironville *Derby* from 15. *Shirland Park Farm, Park Lane, Shirland, Alfreton DE55 6AX* T: (01773) 833242 E: jokpenfold@aol.com

PENFOLD, Marion Jean. b 49. NEOC 96. **d** 99 **p** 00. NSM Lesbury w Alnmouth *Newc* 99-02; C 02-03; NSM Longhoughton w Howick 99-02; C 02-03; TV N Tyne and Redesdale 03-11; TV Glendale Gp from 11. *Eglingham Vicarage, The Village, Eglingham, Alnwick NE66 2TX* T: (01665) 578250 E: marion.penfold@btinternet.com

PENFOLD, Canon Susan Irene. b 52. York Univ BA 73 Bris Univ PhD 77 Selw Coll Cam BA 83 MA 87. Ridley Hall Cam 81. **dss** 84 **d** 87 **p** 94. Buckhurst Hill *Chelmsf* 84-87; Hon C Greenside *Dur* 87-90; Hon C Cononley w Bradley *Bradf* 90-97; Assoc Dioc Dir of Ords 96-01; Hon C Shipley St Paul 97-00; PtO 00-08; Dir of Ords and CME Officer *Wakef* 01-03; Dir of Ords and Dean of Min 03-08; Hon Can Wakef Cathl 04-08; Can Res Blackb Cathl 08-15; Dir of Min from 08. *The Vicarage, Church Lane, Great Harwood, Blackburn BB6 7PU* M: 07753-987977 E: sue.penfold@blackburn.anglican.org

PENGELLY, Canon Geoffrey. b 50. Oak Hill Th Coll 86. **d** 88 **p** 89. C Redruth w Lanner and Treleigh *Truro* 88-91; TV Bolventor 91-92; V Egloskerry, N Petherwin, Tremaine, Tresmere etc from 92; RD Trigg Major 04-10; Hon Can Truro Cathl from 03. *The Vicarage, Egloskerry, Launceston PL15 8RX* T: (01566) 785365

PENISTAN, Richard Luke. *See* PENNYSTAN, Richard Luke

PENMAN, John Bain. b 67. Aber Univ BD 89 New Coll Edin MTh 93. Edin Th Coll 91. **d** 93 **p** 94. C Glas St Ninian 93-96; C Ealing Ch the Sav *Lon* 96-98; P-in-c Kirkcaldy and Kinghorn *St And* 98-04; R Falkirk *Edin* 04-09; C Edin St Mich and All SS from 10. *89 Atheling Grove, South Queensferry EH30 9PG* M: 07713-254660 E: john_penman02@yahoo.co.uk

PENMAN, Robert George. b 42. St Jo Coll Auckland LTh 66. **d** 65 **p** 66. C Mt Roskill New Zealand 65-68; C Henderson 69-70; V Glen Innes 71-72; C Alverstoke *Portsm* 73-74; CF 74-77; C Bridgwater St Mary w Chilton Trinity *B & W* 77-80; P-in-c Haselbury Plucknett w N Perrott 80-81; P-in-c Misterton 80-81; V Haselbury Plucknett, Misterton and N Perrott 81-89; P-in-c Appleton *Ox* 89-07; P-in-c Besselsleigh w Dry Sandford 89-00; P-in-c Besselsleigh 00-07; rtd 07; PtO *Ox* from 07. *31 High Street, Sherington, Newport Pagnell MK16 9NU* T: (01908) 611838 E: penman29@btinternet.com

PENN, Barry Edwin. b 46. Univ of Wales (Swansea) BA 72 Trin Coll Bris MA 04. St Jo Coll Nottm 77. **d** 79 **p** 80. C New Barnet St Jas *St Alb* 79-83; TV Preston St Jo *Blackb* 83-92; V Patchway *Bris* 92-01; PtO from 01. *50 Eastfield Road, Westbury-on-Trym, Bristol BS9 4AG* T: 0117-962 2862 E: barrypenn@aol.com

PENN, Christopher Francis. b 34. ACII 63. Wells Th Coll 68. **d** 70 **p** 71. C Andover w Foxcott *Win* 70-72; C Odiham w S Warnborough 72-75; C Keynsham *B & W* 75-76; TV 76-82; R Chilcompton w Downside and Stratton on the Fosse 82-87; RD Midsomer Norton 84-86; V Bathford 87-90; V Avonmouth St Andr *Bris* 90-96; Ind Chapl 90-96; rtd 96; PtO *B & W* from 96; *Bris* from 96. *53 Caernarvon Road, Keynsham, Bristol BS31 2PF* T: 0117-986 2367 E: c.s.penn@talktalk.net

PENN, Christopher Wilson. b 60. Cranmer Hall Dur 98. **d** 00 **p** 01. C Wrockwardine Deanery *Lich* 00-03; P-in-c Llanyblodwel and Trefonen 03-07; P-in-c Llanymynech 03-07; P-in-c Morton 03-07; R Llanyblodwel, Llanymynech, Morton and Trefonen 07-13; Rural Officer (Salop Adnry) 08-13; P-in-c Holsworthy w Hollacombe and Milton Damerel *Ex* from 13; RD Holsworthy from 15. *The Rectory, Bodmin Street, Holsworthy EX22 6BH* T: (01409) 259282 E: crispy50@hotmail.co.uk

PENN, Jane Rachel. b 45. ERMC. **d** 10 **p** 11. NSM Orton Longueville w Bottlebridge *Ely* 10-13; NSM Tadley w Pamber Heath and Silchester *Win* from 13. *Address temp unknown* E: janepenn@hotmail.com

PENN, Mrs Jennifer Anne. b 61. Imp Coll Lon BEng 84 Leeds Univ BA 07. NOC 04. **d** 07 **p** 08. C Halliwell St Pet *Man* 07-10; TV New Bury w Gt Lever 10-14; P-in-c Reigate St Phil *S'wark* from 14; Chapl St Bede's Ecum Sch Reigate from 14. *The Parsonage, 102A Nutley Lane, Reigate RH2 9HA* T: (01737) 244542 E: jenpenn@virginmedia.com

PENN, Mrs Sarah Jane. b 56. City Univ BSc 83 Chelsea Coll Lon PGCE 84. Lindisfarne Regional Tr Partnership 10. **d** 14 **p** 15. OLM St John Lee *Newc* from 14; OLM Warden w Newbrough from 14. *3 Red Houses, Newbrough, Hexham NE47 5AA* T: (01434) 674518 M: 07747-865747
E: janepenn11@gmail.com

PENN-ALLISON, Mrs Nicola. b 69. Man Univ BSc 99 Open Univ MBA 11 St Jo Coll Dur BA 14 Ox Brookes Univ PGCE 04. Cranmer Hall Dur. **d** 14 **p** 15. C Redcar *York* from 14. *34 Ings Road, Redcar TS10 2DL* M: 07918-941656
E: nicky.allison@outlook.com

PENNAL, David Bernard. b 37. Ripon Hall Ox 64. **d** 67 **p** 68. C Moseley St Mary *Birm* 67-71; C Bridgwater St Mary w Chilton Trinity *B & W* 71-73; P-in-c Hilton w Cheselbourne and Melcombe Horsey *Sarum* 73-76; R Milton Abbas, Hilton w Cheselbourne etc 76-78; P-in-c Spetisbury w Charlton

Marshall 78-88; R Spetisbury w Charlton Marshall etc 89-00; rtd 00. *11 High Street, Wicken, Ely CB7 5XR*

PENNANT, David Falconer. b 51. Trin Coll Cam MA 73. Trin Coll Bris BD 84 PhD 88. **d** 86 **p** 87. C Bramcote *S'well* 86-88; C Woking St Jo *Guildf* 88-93. *30 Oriental Road, Woking GU22 7AW* T: (01483) 768055
E: david.pennant@ntlworld.com

PENNANT, Rachel Elizabeth Burrows. b 74. Ex Univ BA 95 Sheff Univ PhD 01. Trin Coll Bris MA 12. **d** 12 **p** 13. C Biggleswade *St Alb* from 12. *46 Wilsheres Road, Biggleswade SG18 0DN* T: (01767) 315032 M: 07811-774192
E: rpennant@btinternet.com

PENNELL, Ms Pamela. b 45. EAMTC 94. **d** 97 **p** 98. NSM Moulsham St Luke *Chelmsf* 97-98; NSM Writtle w Highwood 98-00; PtO 01-04; NSM Gt Waltham w Ford End 04-06; PtO 06-08; P-in-c Sandon 08-10; P-in-c E Hanningfield 08-13; rtd 13; PtO *Chelmsf* from 14. *33 Birch Lane, Stock, Ingatestone CM4 9NA* T: (01277) 841270 E: pencof.pam@btinternet.com

PENNELLS, David Malcolm Benedict. b 56. Leeds Univ BA 11 CQSW 80. Coll of Resurr Mirfield 09. **d** 11 **p** 12. C Kennington St Jo w St Jas *S'wark* 11-15; V Mitcham SS Pet and Paul from 15. *The Vicarage, 11 Vicarage Gardens, Mitcham CR4 3BE* M: 07776-242352 E: fatherdavid@btinternet.com

PENNEY, David Richard John. b 39. St Jo Coll Dur BA 63. Cranmer Hall Dur 63. **d** 67 **p** 68. C Chilvers Coton w Astley *Cov* 67-70; C Styvechale 70-72; P-in-c Shilton w Ansty 72-77; P-in-c Withybrook w Copston Magna 74-77; R Easington w Liverton *York* 77-85; Dir Soc Resp *Sarum* 85-93; PtO *Blackb* 93-02; rtd 01. *Noyna House, 2 Noyna Street, Colne BB8 0PE* T: (01282) 870076 M: 07966-157697

PENNEY, William Affleck. b 41. MBIM 75 FRSA 91. K Coll Lon BD 63 AKC 63 St Boniface Warminster 65. **d** 66 **p** 67. C Chatham St Steph *Roch* 66-70; Ind Chapl 70-77; P-in-c Bredhurst 70-72; Hon C S Gillingham 72-74; Hon C Eynsford w Farningham and Lullingstone 74-77; Bp's Dom Chapl 74-88; Hon Ind Chapl 77-88; Hon C Balham St Mary and St Jo *S'wark* 89-91; PtO *St Alb* 91-94; Hon C Bushey 94-05; rtd 05. *2 Harbord Road, Oxford OX2 8LQ* T: (01865) 557198 E: wpenney@btconnect.com

PENNIE, Mrs Fiona Clare. b 64. All SS Cen for Miss & Min 12. **d** 15. NSM Grassendale *Liv* from 15. *23 Hillside Drive, Liverpool L25 5NR* T: 0151-421 1526 M: 07941-652488
E: fionapennie@blueyonder.co.uk

PENNICEARD, Clifford Ashley. b 42. Monash Univ Aus BA 65 DipEd 71 Linacre Coll Ox BA 67 Ox Univ MA 70. St Steph Ho Ox 65. **d** 68 **p** 69. C S Leamington St Jo *Cov* 68-70; P-in-c Wantirna Australia 74; Assoc P N Brighton 76-80; P-in-c Euroa 84-91; P-in-c Nagumbie 93-95; P-in-c Cudal 96-98; R Manly St Paul 98-04; P-in-c Cen Goulburn from 04. *1700 Euroa-Strathbogie Road, Kithbrook VIC 3666, Australia* M: 41-617 7732 E: cliffpenn@dodo.com.au

PENNIECOOKE, Dorothy Victoria. b 45. Dioc OLM tr scheme 97. **d** 00 **p** 01. NSM Balham Hill Ascension *S'wark* 00-15; PtO from 15. *56 Lysias Road, London SW12 8BP* T: (020) 8673 0037

PENNINGTON, Catherine Prudence. *See* RELF-PENNINGTON, Catherine Prudence

PENNINGTON, Edward Francis Quentin. b 76. G&C Coll Cam BA 97 MA 01 Birm Univ MSc 98. Oak Hill Th Coll BTh 04. **d** 04 **p** 05. C Moulton *Pet* 04-07; C Fulwood *Sheff* from 07. *237 Bannerdale Road, Sheffield S11 9FD* T: 0114-221 9393 M: 07743-942931 E: efqpennington@hotmail.com *or* ed@endcliffechurch.co.uk

PENNINGTON, Emma Louise. b 71. Ex Univ BA 92 Kent Univ MA 96 Ox Univ DPhil 14. Ripon Coll Cuddesdon BA 00. **d** 00 **p** 01. C Shepperton *Lon* 00-03; Chapl Worc Coll Ox 03-08; TV Wheatley *Ox* 08-14; V Garsington, Cuddesdon and Horspath from 14. *Garsington Rectory, 17 Southend, Garsington, Oxford OX44 9DH* T: (01865) 361381
E: emmapennington153@gmail.com

PENNINGTON, James Edward. b 78. Essex Univ BA 00. St Jo Coll Nottm 12. **d** 14 **p** 15. C Nailsea H Trin *B & W* from 14. *26 St Mary's Grove, Nailsea, Bristol BS48 4NQ* M: 07736-299889 E: jepennington@hotmail.com

PENNINGTON, Ms Nicola Gail. b 67. Nottm Univ BA 88 Leic Univ MA 93 CQSW 93. LCTP 10. **d** 13 **p** 14. C Maryport, Netherton and Flimby *Carl* from 13. *Limetree House, Broughton Cross, Cockermouth CA13 0TY* T: (01900) 825876 M: 07824-631570 E: nickipennington@rocketmail.com

PENNOCK, Mrs Christine. b 48. Bp Grosseteste Coll BEd 71 Leeds Univ PGCE 94 Teesside Univ PGDE 05. NEOC 98. **d** 01 **p** 02. C Crowland *Linc* 01-05; P-in-c Ruskington Gp 05-13; P-in-c Leasingham 09-13; P-in-c Cranwell 11-13; R N Lafford Gp from 13; RD Lafford from 12. *The Rectory, All Saints' Close, Ruskington, Sleaford NG34 9FP* T: (01526) 832463 M: 07813-954043 E: chris@cpennock.fsnet.co.uk

PENNY, Alexander Stuart Egerton. b 52. Wolv Art Coll BA 75. Ridley Hall Cam MA 00. **d** 00 **p** 01. C Uttoxeter Area *Lich* 00-03; V Crosthwaite Keswick *Carl* from 03. *Crosthwaite Vicarage, Vicarage Hill, Keswick CA12 5QB* T: (01768) 772509 E: vicar@crosthwaitechurchkeswick.co.uk

PENNY, David Roy. b 67. Wilson Carlile Coll 89 NOC 00. **d** 03 **p** 04. C Hey and Waterhead *Man* 03-05; V Chadderton St Matt w St Luke from 05; AD Oldham W from 09. *St Matthew's Vicarage, Mill Brow, Chadderton, Oldham OL1 2RT* T: 0161-624 8600 E: revdpenny@btinternet.com

PENNY, Diana Eleanor. b 51. Open Univ BA 87 MSc 13 Birm Univ DipEd 96. Nor Ord Course 87. **d** 89 **p** 94. NSM Gillingham w Geldeston, Stockton, Ellingham etc *Nor* 89-93; NSM Upton St Leonards *Glouc* 93-97; NSM Stiffkey and Cockthorpe w Morston, Langham etc *Nor* 97-03; NSM Stiffkey and Bale 03-04; C Lowestoft St Marg 04-06; V E Marshland *Ely* 06-10; rtd 10; PtO *Ely* from 10. *Hibiscus, 33 Church Drive, Outwell, Wisbech PE14 8RH* T: (01945) 771978
E: dep451@btinternet.com

PENNY, Edwin John. b 43. Leeds Univ BA 64. Coll of Resurr Mirfield 64. **d** 66 **p** 67. C Acocks Green *Birm* 66-69; C Wombourne *Lich* 69-71; C Wednesbury St Paul Wood Green 71-74; V Kingshurst *Birm* 74-79; Chapl All Hallows Convent Norfolk 79-82; Hon Chapl Overgate Hospice Yorkshire 82-84; Hon C Raveningham *Nor* 84-90; All Hallows Hosp Nor Past Team 90-93; P-in-c Upton St Leonards *Glouc* 93-97; Dioc Communications Officer 93-97; P-in-c Stiffkey and Cockthorpe w Morston, Langham etc *Nor* 97-03; P-in-c Gunthorpe w Bale w Field Dalling, Saxlingham etc 99-03; R Stiffkey and Bale 03-04; rtd 04; PtO *Nor* from 04; *Ely* from 08; RD Wisbech Lynn Marshland 09-11. *Hibiscus, 33 Church Drive, Outwell, Wisbech PE14 8RH* T: (01945) 771978 E: noakhillpupil@dialstart.net

PENNY, Michael John. b 36. Linc Th Coll 78. **d** 80 **p** 81. C Knighton St Mary Magd *Leic* 80-83; TV Leic Resurr 83-85; V Blackfordby 85-95; V Blackfordby and Woodville 95-00; RD Akeley W 88-93; rtd 00; PtO *Nor* from 00. *15 Sarah's Road, Hunstanton PE36 5PA* T: (01485) 534957

PENNY, Stuart. *See* PENNY, Alexander Stuart Egerton

PENNYSTAN, Richard Luke. b 74. Newc Univ BA 97 St Jo Coll Cam BA 02. Ridley Hall Cam 00. **d** 03 **p** 04. C E Twickenham St Steph *Lon* 03-06; C Fulham Ch Ch 06-11; V Romiley *Ches* from 11. *18 Chadkirk Road, Romiley, Stockport SK6 3JY* T: 0161-285 7748 M: 07971-663129
E: vicar@stchadsromiley.co.uk

PENRITH, Suffragan Bishop of. *See* FREEMAN, The Rt Revd Robert John

PENTELOW, Mrs Ysmena Rachael. b 73. St Andr Univ BD 96 MLitt 99. EAMTC 01. **d** 03 **p** 04. C Stevenage H Trin *St Alb* 03-06; P-in-c Langleybury St Paul 06-13; V from 13; Dioc CME Officer from 06. *The Vicarage, 1 Langleybury Lane, Kings Langley WD4 8QQ* T: (01923) 270634 M: 07798-654194
E: pentelow@waitrose.com

PENTLAND, The Ven Raymond Jackson. b 57. CB 13. Wm Booth Memorial Coll CertEd 79 Open Univ BA 90 Westmr Coll Ox MTh 02. St Jo Coll Nottm 86. **d** 88 **p** 89. C Nottingham St Jude *S'well* 88-90; Chapl RAF 90-05; Command Chapl RAF 05-06; Adn RAF 06-14; Chapl-in-Chief RAF 09-14; QHC 06-14; Can and Preb Linc Cathl 06-14; rtd 14. *Address temp unknown*

PEOPLES, James Scott. b 59. TCD BA HDipEd 90. **d** 85 **p** 86. C Carlow w Urglin and Staplestown *C & O* 85-90; Chapl Kilkenny Coll 90-91; I Portarlington w Cloneyhurke and Lea *M & K* 91-99; Dioc Youth Officer (Kildare) 92-99; I Lucan w Leixlip *D & G* from 99. *5 Uppercross, Ballyowen Lane, Ballydowd, Lucan, Co Dublin, Republic of Ireland* T: (00353) (1) 624 9147

PEOPLES, Mervyn Thomas Edwards. b 53. Open Univ BA 88. CITC 03. **d** 06 **p** 07. NSM Raphoe w Raymochy and Clonleigh *D & R* 06-09; NSM Clooney w Strathfoyle from 09. *29 Dunnalong Road, Magheramason, Londonderry BT47 2RU* T: (028) 7184 1416 E: mervynpeoples@hotmail.com

PEPPER, David Reginald. b 50. Lon Bible Coll. St Alb Minl Tr Scheme 89. **d** 92 **p** 93. NSM Cheshunt *St Alb* 92-95; NSM Bengeo 06-08; NSM Hertford from 08. *36 Salisbury Road, Hoddesdon EN11 0HX* T: (01992) 427385
E: davidpepper2@yahoo.co.uk

PEPPER, Leonard Edwin. b 44. Ex Univ BA 71. Ripon Hall Ox 71. **d** 73 **p** 74. C Cottingham *York* 73-76; C Kingshurst *Birm* 76-79; Dir Past Studies St Steph Ho Ox 80-89; TV Aylesbury *Ox* 89-91; TV High Wycombe 91-96; rtd 96. *19 Gardiner Street, Oxford OX3 7AW* T: (01865) 66191

PEPPER, Mrs Nicola Mary. b 54. Yorks Min Course 13. **d** 15. NSM New Mills *Derby* from 15. *5 Wheston Bank, Tideswell, Buxton SK17 8LJ* T: (01298) 8711182
E: nicolapepper@hotmail.co.uk

PEPPIATT, Martin Guy. b 33. Trin Coll Ox BA 57 MA 60. Wycliffe Hall Ox 57. **d** 59 **p** 60. C St Marylebone All So w SS Pet and Jo *Lon* 59-63; Kenya 65-69; V E Twickenham St Steph *Lon* 69-96; rtd 96. *Pipers Cottage, East End, North Leigh, Witney OX29 8ND* T: (01993) 883001

PEPPIATT, Quintin Brian Duncombe. b 63. Ex Univ BSc 85 St Luke's Coll Ex PGCE 86. Ripon Coll Cuddesdon 89 Ch Div Sch of the Pacific (USA) 90. **d** 92 **p** 93. C Gt Ilford St Clem and St Marg *Chelmsf* 92-95; TV E Ham w Upton Park and Forest Gate from 95. *1 Norman Road, London E6 6HN* T: (020) 8471 8751 E: quintinpeppiatt@aol.com

PEPPIATT, Miss Sarah Frances. b 84. Ox Univ BA 05. Yorks Min Course 09. **d** 12 **p** 13. C Moston St Mary *Man* from 12. *2 Kilmaine Avenue, Manchester M9 7FN* M: 07816-592377 E: sarah.peppiatt@ntlworld.com

PERCIVAL, Brian Sydney. b 37. Univ of Wales (Ban) BA 61. NOC 81. **d** 84 **p** 85. NSM Norbury *Ches* 84-88; P-in-c Werneth 88-04; RD Chadkirk 00-04; rtd 04; PtO *Ches* from 04. *21 Holly Road, High Lane, Stockport SK6 8HW* T: (01663) 810217

PERCIVAL, Darren James. b 70. Yorks Min Course 09. **d** 12 **p** 13. NSM Dodworth *Leeds* from 12. *8 High Keep Fold, Hall Green, Wakefield WF4 3QL* T: (01924) 253045 M: 07960-555609 E: percivalfamily1@gmail.com

PERCIVAL, James Edward Charles. b 50. NOC 92. **d** 95 **p** 96. C Broughton *Blackb* 95-99; P-in-c Blackb St Steph 99-03; Chapl Blackb, Hyndburn and Ribble Valley NHS Trust 99-03; P-in-c Freckleton *Blackb* 03-11; V from 11. *Holy Trinity Vicarage, 3 Sunnyside Close, Freckleton, Preston PR4 1YJ* T: (01772) 632209 E: jamesperc2005@aol.com

PERCIVAL, James Frederick. b 74. New Coll Ox BA 96 MA 01 Barrister-at-Law (Middle Temple) 99. Ripon Coll Cuddesdon MA 02. **d** 03 **p** 04. C Redhill St Matt *S'wark* 03-06; TV Sanderstead 06-13; TR Limpsfield and Tatsfield from 13. *The Rectory, High Street, Limpsfield, Oxted RH8 0DG* T: (01883) 722351 E: james.percival7@gmail.com

PERCIVAL, Joanna Vera. b 52. Univ of San Francisco BA 87. Ch Div Sch of Pacific MDiv 94. **d** 94 **p** 94. Asst R Almaden USA 94-95; NSM Ockham w Hatchford *Guildf* 95-96; C Cobham 96-00; Dioc Spirituality Adv 00-02; V Weston 02-06; PtO *Lon* 06-07; *S'wark* 06-07; *S & B* 07-08; Chapl Univ Hosp Southn NHS Foundn Trust from 08. *Southampton General Hospital, Tremona Road, Shirley, Southampton SO16 6YD* T: (023) 8079 6745 E: joanna.percival@btinternet.com

PERCIVAL, John Harry. b 83. Pemb Coll Cam MA 08. Wycliffe Hall Ox BA 10 Oak Hill Th Coll MA 12. **d** 12 **p** 13. C Eastbourne All So *Chich* from 12. *Wellesley House, Longstone Road, Eastbourne BN21 3SL* M: 07818-028494 E: john.percival@cantab.net

PERCIVAL, Mrs Kathryn Janet. b 74. St Hilda's Coll Ox BA 95 MA 01 ARCM 89 Barrister-at-Law (Lincoln's Inn) 98. Ripon Coll Cuddesdon 08. **d** 10 **p** 11. C Purley St Mark and Purley St Swithun *S'wark* 10-13; P-in-c Lingfield and Crowhurst 13-15; C Dormansland 13-15; V Lingfield and Dormansland from 15. *The Rectory, High Street, Limpsfield, Oxted RH8 0DG* T: (01883) 722351 M: 07985-272437 E: kathryn.percival@blueyonder.co.uk

PERCIVAL, Martin Eric. b 45. Lon Univ BSc 66 Linacre Coll Ox BA 70 MA 74. Wycliffe Hall Ox 67. **d** 70 **p** 71. C Anfield St Marg *Liv* 70-73; C Witney *Ox* 73-74; TV Bottesford w Ashby *Linc* 74-76; TV Grantham 76-80; R Coningsby w Tattershall 80-82; P-in-c Coleford w Holcombe *B & W* 82-83; V 83-84; Chapl Rossall Sch Fleetwood 84-88; Chapl Woodbridge Sch 88-02; R Downham w S Hanningfield *Chelmsf* 02-05; P-in-c Ramsden Crays w Ramsden Bellhouse 02-05; P-in-c Leiston *St E* 05-13; rtd 13; PtO *St E* from 13. *18 Culcott Close, Yoxford, Saxmundham IP17 3GZ* T: (01728) 668537 E: moreteevicar@mail.com

PERCIVAL, Patricia Anne. b 52. SEITE 03. **d** 06 **p** 07. NSM Footscray w N Cray *Roch* 06-10; NSM Blendon from 10. *31 Collindale Avenue, Sidcup DA15 9DN* T: (020) 8302 9754 E: pat@thepercies.freeserve.co.uk

PERCIVAL, Richard Thomas. b 33. MRICS 59 MRTPI 67 FRICS 71. Edin Dioc NSM Course 79. **d** 91 **p** 98. S Africa 91-94; RD Adnry of Kokstad 93-94; NSM Edin St Ninian 94-01; rtd 01; LtO *Edin* from 01. *2/1 Fettes Rise, Edinburgh EH4 1QH* T: 0131-552 5271 E: rpercival@btinternet.com

PERCIVAL, Robert Standring. b 27. Sheff Univ BA 55. Qu Coll Birm 57. **d** 59 **p** 60. C Lightbowne *Man* 59-62; C Prestwich St Marg 62-63; V Pendlebury St Aug 63-68; Lect Glos Coll of Arts and Tech 68-93; NSM Glouc St Mary de Crypt w St Jo and Ch Ch 68-82; PtO 82-97 and from 01; rtd 92. *5 Firwood Drive, Gloucester GL4 0AB* T: (01452) 522739

PERCY, Brian. b 34. **d** 93 **p** 94. OLM Walton *St E* 93-00; OLM Walton and Trimley 00-04; rtd 04; PtO *St E* from 04. *16 Lynwood Avenue, Felixstowe IP11 9HS* T: (01394) 286782

PERCY, Christopher. *See* HEBER PERCY, Christopher John

PERCY, Emma Margaret. b 63. Jes Coll Cam BA 85 MA 89 St Jo Coll Dur BA 89 Nottm Univ PhD 12. Cranmer Hall Dur 87. **d** 90 **p** 94. C Bedford St Andr *St Alb* 90-94; Chapl Anglia Poly Univ *Ely* 94-97; P-in-c Millhouses H Trin *Sheff* 97-03; V 03-04; Chapl Trin Coll Ox from 05. *The Deanery, Christ Church, St Aldates, Oxford OX1 1DP* T: (01865) 276162 E: emma.percy@trinity.ox.ac.uk

PERCY, Gordon Reid. b 46. St Jo Coll Dur BA 68. Cranmer Hall Dur 69. **d** 71 **p** 72. C Flixton St Jo *Man* 71-76; C Charlesworth *Derby* 76-77; P-in-c 77-87; P-in-c Dinting Vale 80-87; V Long Eaton St Jo 87-98; RD Ilkeston 92-98; R Torquay St Matthias, St Mark and H Trin *Ex* 98-12; rtd 12. *13 Wembury Drive, Torquay TQ2 8DT* E: gordonpercy@minister.com

PERCY, The Very Revd Prof Martyn William. b 62. Bris Univ BA 84 K Coll Lon PhD 92 Sheff Univ MEd. Cranmer Hall Dur 88. **d** 90 **p** 91. C Bedford St Andr *St Alb* 90-94; Chapl and Dir Th and RS Ch Coll Cam 94-97; Dir Th and RS SS Coll Cam 95-97; Dir Linc Th Inst Man Univ 97-04; Hon C Millhouses H Trin *Sheff* 97-04; Hon Can Sheff Cathl 97-04; Can Th Sheff Cathl 04-10; Sen Lect Relig and Soc Sheff Univ 97-00; Reader 00-02; Reader Man Univ 02-04; Prof Th and Min Hartford Sem Connecticut USA 02-07; Prin Ripon Coll Cuddesdon 04-14; Prin Ox Min Course 06-14; Dean Ch Ch *Ox* from 14; Prof Th Educn K Coll Lon from 04; Can and Preb Sarum Cathl 09-14. *The Deanery, Christ Church, St Aldates, Oxford OX1 1DP* M: 07941-072542

PERCY, Mrs Pauline. b 62. Sheff City Poly BSc 84 Sheff Univ BA 14. Yorks Min Course 11. **d** 14 **p** 15. NSM Crathorne *York* from 14; NSM Kirklevington w Picton, and High and Low Worsall from 14; NSM Rudby in Cleveland w Middleton from 14. *The Vicarage, 49 Ash Grove, Kirklevington, Yarm TS15 9NQ* T: (01642) 790327 E: revd.pauline.percy@gmail.com

PERDUE, Ernon Cope Todd. b 30. TCD BA 52 MA BD 56 MEd 73 UCD MPsychSc 80. TCD Div Sch 53. **d** 54 **p** 55. C Dublin Drumcondra w N Strand *D & G* 54-58; C Dublin Booterstown w Carysfort 58-60; Dean of Res TCD 60-68; C-in-c Dublin St Mark *D & G* 66-68; C-in-c Dublin St Steph 68-69; I Rathmichael 69-76; Careers Counsellor Wicklow Voc Sch 76-82; I Limerick *L & K* 82-87; Can Limerick Cathl 82-87; Dean Killaloe, Kilfenora and Clonfert 87-95; I Killaloe w Stradbally 87-95; rtd 95. *18 The Mageough, Cowper Road, Rathmines, Dublin 6, Republic of Ireland* T/F: (00353) (1) 491 4867 M: 86-278 0354 E: ernonandheather@hotmail.com

PEREIRA, Alwyn Antonio Basilio. b 63. Trin Coll Bris. **d** 11 **p** 12. C Sea Mills *Bris* 11-15. *2 Applegate, Bristol BS10 6QJ* T: 0117-307 0120 M: 07767-702094 E: alwynper@googlemail.com

PEREIRA, Melvyn Christopher. b 52. Oak Hill Th Coll BA 04. **d** 04 **p** 05. C Kettering Ch the King *Pet* 04-07; Min Gleneagles CD 07-13; V Gleneagles from 13; Warden of Par Ev from 10. *20 Ribble Close, Wellingborough NN8 5XJ* T: (01933) 673437 M: 07810-816744 E: melvyn.pereira@gleneagleschurch.co.uk

PERERA, Ms Chandrika Kumudhini. b 61. Qu Coll Birm. **d** 03 **p** 04. C Luton All SS w St Pet *St Alb* 03-07; TV Hemel Hempstead 07-14; V Stevenage St Hugh and St Jo from 14. *St Hugh's House, 4 Mobbsbury Way, Stevenage SG2 0HL* T: (01438) 727577 E: chandy.perera@btinternet.com

PERERA, George Anthony. b 51. Edin Univ BD 74. Linc Th Coll 74. **d** 76 **p** 77. Chapl Mabel Fletcher Tech Coll Liv 76-79; C Wavertree H Trin *Liv* 76-79; TV Maghull 79-94; V Hunts Cross 94-04; Chapl Park Lane Hosp Maghull 79-89; Asst Chapl Ashworth Hosp Maghull 89-04; Chapl R Liverpool and Broadgreen Univ Hosps NHS Trust from 05. *Broadgreen Hospital, Thomas Drive, Liverpool L14 3LB* T: 0151-282 6000 F: 254 2070

✠**PERHAM, The Rt Revd Michael Francis.** b 47. Keble Coll Ox BA 74 MA 78. Cuddesdon Coll 74. **d** 76 **p** 77 **c** 04. C Addington *Cant* 76-81; Bp's Dom Chapl *Win* 81-84; Sec C of E Doctrine Commn 79-84; TR Oakdale *Sarum* 84-92; Prec and Can Res Nor Cathl 92-98; Provost Derby 98-00; Dean Derby 00-04; Bp Glouc 04-14; rtd 14. *The Old Mill, Bleadney, Wells BA5 1PF* T: (01749) 670239 E: michaelperham47@gmail.com

PERKES, Brian Robert Keith. b 46. St Andr Univ BSc 68. NOC 91. **d** 94 **p** 95. NSM Witton *Ches* 94-98; Bp's Chapl 98-00; P-in-c Ashton Hayes 98-11; P-in-c Delamere 00-11; rtd 11. *Roselea, 123 Marbury Road, Anderton, Northwich CW9 6AP* T: (01606) 784211 E: brkperkes@btinternet.com

PERKIN, Jonathan Guy. b 52. Westmr Coll Ox BEd 76. Trin Coll Bris 89. **d** 91 **p** 92. C Cullompton *Ex* 91-96; C Ashtead *Guildf* 96-01; V Egham 01-05; V Churchdown *Glouc* from 05. *The Vicarage, 5 Vicarage Close, Churchdown, Gloucester GL3 2NE* T: (01452) 713203 E: jjperkin@btconnect.com

PERKIN, Paul John Stanley. b 50. Ch Ch Ox BA 71 MA 75 CertEd. Wycliffe Hall Ox 78. **d** 80 **p** 81. C Gillingham St Mark *Roch* 80-84; C Brompton H Trin w Onslow Square St Paul *Lon*

84-87; P-in-c Battersea Rise St Mark *S'wark* 87-92; V from 92; P-in-c Battersea St Pet and St Paul 00-12. *St Mark's Vicarage, 7 Elsynge Road, London SW18 2HW*   T: (020) 8874 6023 *or* 7223 6188   E: mark.mail@ukonline.co.uk

PERKINS, Barnaby Charles Rudolf. b 80. Peterho Cam BA 08 MPhil 10. Ridley Hall Cam 06. **d** 10 **p** 11. C Guildf St Nic 10-13; R E and W Clandon from 13. *The Rectory, The Street, West Clandon, Guildford GU4 7RG*   T: (01483) 222573 E: barnaby.perkins@cantab.net

PERKINS, Colin Blackmore. b 35. FCII 65. Lon Coll of Div 68. **d** 70 **p** 71. C Hyson Green *S'well* 70-73; V Clarborough w Hayton 73-79; P-in-c Cropwell Bishop 79-84; P-in-c Colston Bassett 79-84; P-in-c Granby w Elton 79-84; P-in-c Langar 79-84; V Tithby w Cropwell Butler 79-84; R Cropwell Bishop w Colston Bassett, Granby etc 84-94; P-in-c Sutton Bonington w Normanton-on-Soar 94-01; rtd 01; PtO *Newc* from 01. *6 Ravensmede, Alnwick NE66 2PX*   T: (01665) 510445 E: cperk68836@aol.com

PERKINS, Canon David. b 51. Sarum & Wells Th Coll. **d** 87 **p** 88. C New Mills *Derby* 87-90; V Marlpool 90-95; P-in-c Turnditch 95-02; Min in charge Belper Ch Ch and Milford 95-02; V Belper Ch Ch w Turnditch 02-09; Jt P-in-c Ambergate and Heage 06-09; RD Duffield 97-09; Chapl Derbyshire Mental Health Services NHS Trust 95-09; Can Res Derby Cathl 09-13; rtd 13; P-in-c Beeley and Edensor *Derby* 13-15; V from 15. *The Vicarage, Edensor, Bakewell DE45 1PH*   T: (01246) 386385 E: revdaveperkins@aol.com

PERKINS, David John Elmslie. b 45. Dur Univ BA 66 ATII 75. Cranmer Hall Dur 66. **d** 69 **p** 70. C Wadsley *Sheff* 69-71; C Shortlands *Roch* 71-73; PtO *Lon* 76-78; B & W 78-80 and from 02; LtO 80-02; rtd 02. *Rainbow's End, Montacute Road, Stoke-sub-Hamdon TA14 6UQ*   T: (01935) 823314

PERKINS, John Everard. b 47. SEITE 04. **d** 06 **p** 07. NSM Speldhurst w Groombridge and Ashurst *Roch* 06-10; NSM Tonbridge St Steph from 10. *25 Northfields, Speldhurst, Tunbridge Wells TN3 0PN*   T: (01892) 863239

PERKINS, Miss Julia Margaret. b 49. Linc Th Coll 85. **d** 87 **p** 94. Par Dn Owton Manor *Dur* 87-89; Par Dn Leam Lane 89-94; C 94; P-in-c Stockton St Chad 94-96; V 96-00; C Eppleton and Hetton le Hole 00-06; C Heworth St Mary 06-11; rtd 11; PtO *Pet* from 14. *12 Portman Close, Peterborough PE3 9RJ* T: (01733) 262240

PERKINS, Julian John. b 67. Southn Univ BSc 90 MSc 92. Trin Coll Bris 80 60 MPhil 03. **d** 01 **p** 02. C Thornbury *Glouc* 01-02; C Thornbury and Oldbury-on-Severn w Shepperdine 02-04; C Tewkesbury w Walton Cardiff and Twyning 04-07; P-in-c Crosland Moor *Wakef* 07-08; P-in-c Linthwaite 07-08; V Crosland Moor and Linthwaite 08-10; Chapl Sheff Teaching Hosps NHS Foundn Trust from 11. *Chaplaincy Department, Northern General Hospital, Herries Road, Sheffield S5 7AU* T: 0114-271 5578   E: julian.perkins@sth.nhs.uk

PERKINS, Patricia Doris (Sister Patricia). b 29. Gilmore Ho 60. dss 73 **d** 87. CSA from 71; Sherston Magna w Easton Grey *Bris* 73-75; Cant St Martin and St Paul 76-78; Kilburn St Aug w St Jo *Lon* 80-84; Abbey Ho Malmesbury 84-87; Hon Par Dn Bayswater *Lon* 87-94; Chapl St Mary's Hosp Praed Street Lon 88-89; Chapl St Chas Hosp Ladbroke Grove 88-89; Dean of Women's Min *Lon* from 89; Dioc Dir of Ords 90-94; Hon Par Dn St Olave Hart Street w All Hallows Staining etc 94-01. *St Mary's Convent and Nursing Home, Burlington Lane, London W4 2QF*

PERKINS, Sheila Barbara. b 50. SEITE BA 07. **d** 07 **p** 08. NSM Tonbridge St Steph *Roch* from 07. *25 Northfields, Speldhurst, Tunbridge Wells TN3 0PN*   T: (01892) 863239 M: 07952-354478   E: perkins25@btinternet.com

PERKINSON, Neil Donald. b 46. Wycliffe Hall Ox 84. **d** 85 **p** 86. C Workington St Jo *Carl* 85-88; TV Cockermouth w Embleton and Wythop 88-93; TV St Laur in Thanet *Cant* 93-01; P-in-c Darlaston All SS and Ind Chapl Black Country Urban Ind Miss *Lich* 01-08; rtd 08; V Whangamata New Zealand from 08. *103 Durrant Drive, Whangamata, Waikato 3620, New Zealand* E: neil@perkinson.org.uk

PERKINTON, Keith Glyn. b 61. Humberside Poly BA 83 Leeds Univ BA 92. Coll of Resurr Mirfield 93. **d** 93 **p** 94. C Knowle H Nativity *Bris* 93-97; TV Brighton Resurr *Chich* 97-05; P-in-c Hangleton 05-07; V from 07; RD Hove 10. *The Vicarage, 127 Hangleton Way, Hove BN3 8ER*   T: (01273) 413044

PERKS, David Leonard Irving. b 38. Avery Hill Coll TCert 61 Sussex Univ MA 76. S Dios Minl Tr Scheme 84. **d** 87 **p** 88. NSM Lewes All SS, St Anne, St Mich and St Thos *Chich* 87-91; Chapl HM Pris Lewes 91-94; NSM Deanery of Lewes and Seaford *Chich* 94-96; C Peacehaven and Telscombe Cliffs 96-00; rtd 00; Hon C Lewes and Seaford *Chich* from 00; Asst to RD S Downs Health NHS Trust from 01. *45 Fitzjohns Road, Lewes BN7 1PR*   T: (01273) 478719 E: danddperks@btopenworld.com

PERKS, Edgar Harold Martin. b 31. Open Univ BA 87. Glouc Sch of Min 85. **d** 88 **p** 89. NSM Bromfield *Heref* 88-89; NSM Culmington w Onibury 88-89; NSM Stanton Lacy 88-89; NSM Culmington w Onibury, Bromfield etc 90-98; PtO from 98. *The Oaklands, Bromfield Road, Ludlow SY8 1DW* T: (01584) 875525

PERRETT, David Thomas. b 48. Cranmer Hall Dur 80. **d** 82 **p** 83. C Stapleford *S'well* 82-86; V Ollerton 86-87; P-in-c Boughton 86-87; V Ollerton w Boughton 87-93; V Winklebury *Win* 93-05; P-in-c Gresley *Derby* 05-10; V 10-13; RD Repton 11-13; rtd 13; PtO *Pet* from 14. *14 Dunbar Court, Kettering NN15 5DN*   T: (01536) 659065   E: davdotp2405@sky.com

PERRETT, Mrs Jill. b 59. Trent Poly BA 80 CQSW 82. STETS 99. **d** 02 **p** 03. C Mere w W Knoyle and Maiden Bradley *Sarum* 02-07; P-in-c Atworth w Shaw and Whitley 07-11; V 11-13; C Melksham 07-13; C Broughton Gifford, Gt Chalfield and Holt 07-13; Chapl Melksham Oak Community Sch 11-13; R Addingham *Leeds* from 13; IME Officer 4-7 from 13. *The Rectory, Low Mill Lane, Addingham, Ilkley LS29 0QP* E: revjperrett@hotmail.co.uk

PERRETT (formerly ROWE), Vanda Sheila. b 63. STETS 95. **d** 98 **p** 99. C Marlborough *Sarum* 98-01; TV Pewsey and Swanborough 01-06; TR Bourne Valley 06-14; C Salisbury St Fran and Stratford sub Castle 09-14; RD Alderbury 06-14; Can and Preb Sarum Cathl 12-14; P-in-c St Buryan, St Levan and Sennen *Truro* from 14. *The Rectory, Rectory Road, St Buryan, Penzance TR19 6BB*   T: (01736) 810216 E: rev.vandaperrett@googlemail.com

PERRICONE, Vincent James. b 50. Connecticut Univ BA 74 Pontifical Univ Rome STB 88 STL 90 Glas Univ PhD 98. **d** 90 **p** 90. In RC Ch 89-94; C Glas St Mary 94-95; P-in-c Glas All SS and Glas H Cross 95-03; USA 03-04; PtO *Eur* 04-08; Asst Chapl Florence w Siena 08-09; LtO *Ab* from 10; C Kincardine O'Neil 10-12; Chapl Grampian Univ Hosp NHS Trust 10-12; P-in-c Devizes St Pet *Sarum* 14-15; V from 15. *St Peter's Vicarage, Bath Road, Devizes SN10 2AP*   M: 07733-740372 T: (01380) 501481   E: vjperricone@googlemail.com *or* vicar@stpeters-devizes.org.uk

PERRIN, Andrew. **d** 12 **p** 13. C Morriston *S & B* 12-14; C Upper Ithon Valley from 14; C Lower Ithon Valley from 14. *The Rectory, Crossgates, Llandrindod Wells LD1 6RU*   T: (01597) 851204   E: revperrin@btinternet.com

PERRIN, Bruce Alexander. b 72. Birm Univ BSc 94 MSc 96. St Jo Coll Nottm 08. **d** 09 **p** 10. C Marple All SS *Ches* 09-12; V Hollingworth w Tintwistle from 15. *6 Taylor Street, Hollingworth, Hyde SK14 8PB*   M: 07914-211376 E: rev.bruce.perrin@gmail.com

PERRIN, Michael Leonard. b 47. Shenstone Coll of Educn CertEd 66 Lanc Univ BEd 71. Dioc OLM tr scheme 97. **d** 01 **p** 02. OLM Aspull St Eliz *Liv* 01-06; OLM Haigh and Aspull 06-15; OLM Wigan All SS from 15. *21 Firs Park Crescent, Aspull, Wigan WN2 2SJ*   T: (01942) 257418 E: mikeperrin99@hotmail.com

PERRINS, Christopher Neville. b 68. St Steph Ho Ox 01. **d** 03 **p** 04. C Warrington St Elphin *Liv* 03-08; TV Walton-on-the-Hill 08-12; C Rainhill 12-15. *1 Wesley Place, Liverpool L15 8JB* T: 0151-733 7930   E: revdcnperrins@aol.com

PERRINS, Mrs Lesley. b 53. St Hugh's Coll Ox BA 74. S Dios Minl Tr Scheme 90. **d** 93 **p** 95. NSM Stoneleigh *Guildf* 93-94; NSM Haxby w Wigginton *York* 94-00; Asst Chapl York Health Services NHS Trust 99-00. *Address temp unknown*

PERRIS, Preb Anthony. b 48. Univ of Wales (Abth) BSc 69 Selw Coll Cam BA 76 MA 79. Ridley Hall Cam 74. **d** 77 **p** 78. C Sandal St Helen *Wakef* 77-80; C Plymouth St Andr w St Paul and St Geo *Ex* 80-87; TV Yeovil *B & W* 87-88; V Preston Plucknett from 88; RD Yeovil from 06; Preb Wells Cathl from 11. *St James's Vicarage, 1 Old School Close, Yeovil BA21 3UB* T: (01935) 429398   E: antonyperris@yahoo.com

PERRIS, Mrs Jocelyn Clare. b 69. Surrey Univ BSc 91. ERMC 08. **d** 11 **p** 12. C St Alb St Pet *St Alb* from 11. *White Hart House, Sergehill Lane, Bedmond, Abbots Langley WD5 0RT*   T: (01923) 268673   M: 07979-590480   E: josperris@aol.com

PERRIS, John Martin. b 44. Liv Univ BSc 66. Trin Coll Bris 69. **d** 72 **p** 73. C Sevenoaks St Nic *Roch* 72-76; C Bebington *Ches* 76-79; V Redland *Bris* 79-97; RD Horfield 91-97; R Barton Seagrave w Warkton *Pet* 97-09; rtd 09; PtO *Carl* from 11. *3 Old Myse, Storth, Milnthorpe LA7 7HQ*   T: (01539) 564446 E: martin.perris@hotmail.co.uk

PERRY, Alan David. b 64. Avery Hill Coll BA 86 Lon Inst of Educn PGCE 87 Greenwich Univ MA 99. NTMTC 01. **d** 03 **p** 04. NSM Romford St Edw *Chelmsf* 03-08; Hd Teacher St Edw C of E Sch Havering from 08; Public Preacher *Chelmsf* from 08. *1A Lyndhurst Drive, Hornchurch RM11 1JL* T: (01708) 437852   M: 07946-730291 E: alan.perry80@ntlworld.com

PERRY, Andrew John. b 65. St Steph Ho Ox BTh 00. **d** 00 **p** 01. C Southwick St Mich *Chich* 00-03; P-in-c Upper St Leonards St Jo 03; R 03-13; P-in-c Portslade St Nic and St Andr and Mile Oak from 13. *The Vicarage, South Street, Portslade, Brighton BN41 2LE* T: (01273) 418090 M: 07900-981345
E: revajperry@btinternet.com

PERRY, Canon Andrew Nicholas. b 62. Westmr Coll Ox BA 86. Trin Coll Bris MA 91. **d** 91 **p** 92. C Bath Weston All SS w N Stoke *B & W* 91-93; C Bath Weston All SS w N Stoke and Langridge 93-95; P-in-c Longfleet *Sarum* 95-00; V from 00; Can and Preb Sarum Cathl from 12. *The Vicarage, 2 Twemlow Avenue, Poole BH14 8AN* T/F (01202) 253527 T: 338720
E: andrew.perry@smlpoole.org.uk

PERRY, Andrew William. b 44. MRAC 65. WMMTC 91. **d** 94 **p** 95. NSM Redmarley D'Abitot, Bromesberrow, Pauntley etc *Glouc* 94-14; PtO *Heref* 05-12; rtd 14. *Rye Cottage, Broomsgreen, Dymock GL18 2DP* T: (01531) 890489
E: aw@perry.net

PERRY, Anthony Henry. b 54. Leic Univ BA 76. Aston Tr Scheme 89 Linc Th Coll 93. **d** 93 **p** 94. C Bartley Green *Birm* 93-97; V Bearwood from 97; AD Warley 06-13. *St Mary's Vicarage, 27 Poplar Avenue, Birmingham B17 8EG* T: 0121-429 2165 E: trinity20@hotmail.co.uk

PERRY, David William. b 42. St Chad's Coll Dur BA 64. **d** 66 **p** 67. C Middleton St Mary *Ripon* 66-69; C Bedale 69-71; C Marton-in-Cleveland *York* 71-75; V Skirlaugh w Long Riston 75-05; V Skirlaugh w Long Riston, Rise and Swine 05-07; N Humberside Ecum Officer 84-07; RD N Holderness *York* 06-07; rtd 07. *11 Middle Garth Drive, South Cave, Brough HU15 2AY* T: (01430) 421412 E: perrydr@dsl.pipex.com

PERRY, Edward John. b 35. AKC 62. **d** 63 **p** 64. C Honicknowle *Ex* 63-65; C Ashburton w Buckland-in-the-Moor 65-70; V Cornwood 70-92; Asst Dir of Educn 71-92; Chapl Moorhaven Hosp 91-93; V Ermington and Ugborough *Ex* 92-00; rtd 00; PtO *Ex* from 01. *32 Finches Close, Elburton, Plymouth PL9 8DP* T: (01752) 405364

PERRY, Mrs Elizabeth Ann. b 59. WEMTC 04. **d** 07 **p** 08. NSM Soundwell *Bris* from 07; Chapl HM Pris Ashfield from 11. *HM Prison Ashfield, Shortwood Road, Pucklechurch, Bristol BS16 9QJ* T: 0117-303 8000

PERRY, James Marcus. b 71. Ridley Hall Cam 02. **d** 04 **p** 05. C Cen Wolverhampton *Lich* 04-07; TV Tettenhall Regis from 07. *St Paul's Vicarage, 1 Talaton Road, Wolverhampton WV9 5LS* E: revjimperry@gmail.com

PERRY, Mrs Joanna Teresa. b 60. K Coll Lon BD 82. Trin Coll Bris. **d** 96 **p** 00. C Thornbury *Glouc* 96-97; C Winchcombe, Gretton, Sudeley Manor etc 97-99; Sub Chapl HM Pris and YOI New Hall 99-06; Chapl HM Pris and YOI Warren Hill from 06; Chapl HM Pris Hollesley Bay from 06. *HM Prison Hollesley Bay, Hollesley, Woodbridge IP12 3JW* T: (01394) 412400

✠**PERRY, The Rt Revd John Freeman.** b 35. Lon Coll of Div MPhil 86 ALCD 59. **d** 59 **p** 60 **c** 89. C Woking Ch Ch *Guildf* 59-62; C Chorleywood Ch Ch *St Alb* 62; Min Chorleywood St Andr 63-66; V 66-77; RD Rickmansworth 72-77; Warden Lee Abbey 77-89; RD Shirwell *Ex* 80-84; Hon Can Win Cathl 89-96; Suff Bp Southampton 89-96; Bp Chelmsf 96-03; rtd 03; Hon Asst Bp B & W from 11. *8 The Firs, Bath BA2 5ED* T: (01225) 833987

PERRY, John Neville. b 20. Leeds Univ BA 41. Coll of Resurr Mirfield 41. **d** 43 **p** 44. C Poplar All SS w St Frideswide *Lon* 43-50; V De Beauvoir Town St Pet 50-63; V Feltham 63-75; RD Hounslow 67-75; Adn Middx 75-82; R Orlestone w Snave and Ruckinge w Warehorne *Cant* 82-86; rtd 86; PtO *Chich* from 90. *73 Elizabeth Crescent, East Grinstead RH19 3JG* T: (01342) 315446

PERRY, John Walton Beauchamp. b 43. Ex Coll Ox BA 64 Sussex Univ MA 67. EAMTC 82 Westcott Ho Cam 84. **d** 85 **p** 86. C Shrewsbury St Chad w St Mary *Lich* 85-89; V Batheaston w St Cath *B & W* 89-99; V Milborne Port w Goathill 99-07; P-in-c Charlton Horethorne w Stowell 06-07; V Milborne Port w Goathill etc 07-09; rtd 09; PtO *Heref* from 10. *67 Steventon New Road, Ludlow SY8 1JY* T: (01584) 873755
E: jwbperry@hotmail.com

PERRY, Jonathan Robert. b 55. Cranmer Hall Dur. **d** 82 **p** 83. C Filey *York* 82-84; C Rayleigh *Chelmsf* 84-88; Asst Chapl St Geo Hosp Linc 88-90; Chapl Gateshead Hosps NHS Trust 90-98; Chapl Gateshead Health NHS Trust from 98. *Queen Elizabeth Hospital, Sheriff Hill, Gateshead NE9 6SX* T: 0191-403 2072 *or* 482 0000 ext 2072

PERRY, Lesley Anne. b 52. K Coll Lon BA 73 MIPR 99. SEITE 96. **d** 99 **p** 00. NSM Fulham All SS *Lon* 99-07; NSM Kensington St Mary Abbots w Ch Ch and St Phil from 07. *Flat 3, 76 Philbeach Gardens, London SW5 9EY* T: (020) 7373 3085 *or* 7419 5404 E: lesley.perry@universitiesuk.ac.uk

PERRY, Canon Lynne Janice. b 48. **d** 90 **p** 97. NSM Llanfair Mathafarn Eithaf w Llanbedrgoch *Ban* 90-97; C Bangor 97-99;

TV 99-05; V Tregarth 04-05; V Tregarth and Llandygai and Maes y Groes 05-09; AD Ogwen 02-07; C Ogwen Deanery 09-10; Hon Chapl Ban Cathl 10-12; Hon Can 11-12; rtd 12. *Cwm Collen, 39 Tal y Cae, Tregarth, Bangor LL57 4AE* T: (01248) 600997 M: 07817-518337
E: lynne.pcc@btinternet.com

PERRY, Mark. b 71. K Alfred's Coll Win BA 97 Homerton Coll Cam PGCE FRSA 14 FCollT 15. Regent's Park Coll Ox 02 Ripon Coll Cuddesdon 09. **d** 10 **p** 11. C Bourne Valley *Sarum* 10-11; C Iwerne Valley 11-13; Asst Chapl Shaftesbury Sch 11-13; Res Chapl Port Regis Sch 13-15; P Assoc Shrine of Our Lady of Walsingham from 11; CF(V) 12-15; Chapl Sarum Cathl 13-15; Ecum Officer (Dorset) 13-15; Chapl RAF from 15. *Chaplaincy Services (RAF), HQ Air Command, RAF High Wycombe HP14 4UE* T: (01494) 496800 F: 496343

PERRY, Martin Herbert. b 43. Cranmer Hall Dur 66. **d** 70 **p** 71. C Millfield St Mark *Dur* 70-74; C Haughton le Skerne 74-77; V Darlington St Matt and St Luke 77-84; TR Oldland *Bris* 84-91; V 91-01; rtd 01; C Wellington and Distr *B & W* from 12. *51 Rockwell Green, Wellington TA21 9BZ* T: (01823) 665803 M: 07814-501261 E: bask4faith@yahoo.co.uk

PERRY, Martyn. b 57. Coll of Resurr Mirfield 89. **d** 90 **p** 91. In Bapt Ch 85-89; C Hornsey St Mary w St Geo *Lon* 90-93; V Pontllotyn w Fochriw *Llan* 93-97; R Cilybebyll 97-12; TV Cowbridge 12-13; P-in-c Merthyr Tydfil Ch from 13. *Mandian House, Brondeg, Heolgerrig, Merthyr Tydfil CF48 1TW* T: (01685) 375542 E: father_martyn@tiscali.co.uk

PERRY, Michael James Matthew. b 66. Bris Univ BSc 87 MSc 89 PhD 93. Trin Coll Bris BA 99. **d** 99 **p** 00. C Keynsham *B & W* 99-03; R Cam Vale 03-13; V Woodford Valley w Archers Gate *Sarum* from 13. *The Vicarage, Middle Woodford, Salisbury SP4 6NR* T: (01722) 782310
E: mikepqc-crockfords@yahoo.co.uk

PERRY, Nicholas Charles. **d** 07 **p** 08. NSM Ebbw Vale *Mon* 07-10; R Blaina and Nantyglo 10-13; TR Upper Ebbw Valleys from 13. *The Rectory, Station Road, Blaina NP13 3BW* T: (01495) 290130
E: nick.perry1@btinternet.com

PERRY, Russell Lee. b 38. Worc Coll Ox BA 60 MA 64. CBDTI 98. **d** 98 **p** 99. NSM Grasmere *Carl* 98-01; rtd 01; PtO *S'well* from 01. *Dumble Howe, 3 Byron Gardens, Southwell NG25 0DW* T: (01636) 815813

PERRY, Timothy Richard. b 64. Trin Coll Bris BA 93. **d** 93 **p** 95. C Abingdon *Ox* 93-97; New Life Outreach/Fit Lives 97-01; Mountaintop Life Coaching Canada 01-09; Chapl Cothill Ho Sch from 10; Chapl Cothill Trust from 11; Hon C Wootton and Dry Sandford *Ox* from 11. *6 Oakthorpe Road, Oxford OX2 7BE* T: (01865) 318922 E: perry.tim@sky.com

PERRY, Valerie Evelyn. b 39. Southn Univ CertEd 59. S'wark Ord Course 82. **dss** 85 **d** 87 **p** 94. NSM Romford St Edw *Chelmsf* 85-89; Par Dn 89-91; Asst Chapl Middx Hosp Lon 92-93; Asst Chapl Univ Coll Lon Hosps NHS Trust 94; Chapl S Kent Hosps NHS Trust 94-98; Hon C Aylesham w Adisham *Cant* 98-00; Hon C Nonington w Wymynswold and Goodnestone etc 98-00; rtd 99; PtO *Truro* from 01. *115 Century Close, St Austell PL25 3UZ* T: (01726) 68075

PERRY, Canon William Francis Pitfield. b 61. Keble Coll Ox BA 84 MA 87. Ripon Coll Cuddesdon 94. **d** 96 **p** 97. C Brockworth *Glouc* 96-01; P-in-c Millbrook *Win* from 01; Can Ruvuma Tanzania from 14. *58 Shirley Avenue, Shirley, Southampton SO15 5NJ* T: (023) 8070 1896 E: fr.will@icxc.org

PERRY-GORE, Canon Walter Keith. b 34. Univ of Wales (Lamp) BA 59. Westcott Ho Cam 60. **d** 61 **p** 62. C St Austell *Truro* 61-64; R H Innocents Barbados 64-71; R New Carlisle Canada 71-74; R N Hatley 74-96; rtd 96. *1115 Rue Massawippi, North Hatley QC J0B 2C0, Canada* T: (001) (819) 842 4665 F: 842 2176

PERRYMAN, Preb David Francis. b 42. Brunel Univ BSc 64. Oak Hill Th Coll 74. **d** 76 **p** 77. C Margate H Trin *Cant* 76-80; R Ardingly *Chich* 80-90; V Bath St Luke *B & W* 90-07; RD Bath 96-03; Preb Wells Cathl 01-07; rtd 07; PtO *Win* from 08. *Treetops, Upper Froyle, Alton GU34 4JH* T: (01420) 520647
E: david@perrypeople.co.uk

PERRYMAN, Graham Frederick. b 56. Southn Univ BA 78 Reading Univ PGCE 80. Aston Tr Scheme 90 Trin Coll Bris 92. **d** 94 **p** 95. C Hamworthy *Sarum* 94-98; P-in-c Moreton and Woodsford w Tincleton 98-02; R 02-04; TV Melbury 04-06; TR 06-15; RD Sherborne 12-14; P-in-c Upper Stour from 15. *The Rectory, Portnells Lane, Zeals, Warminster BA12 6PG* E: revgfp@btopenworld.com

PERRYMAN, James Edward. b 56. Lon Bible Coll BA 85. Oak Hill Th Coll 86. **d** 88 **p** 89. C Gidea Park *Chelmsf* 88-91; C Becontree St Mary 91-94; Chapl Lynn *Eur* 94-00; R Allington and Maidstone St Pet *Cant* 00-08; Dioc Ecum Officer 02-08; P-in-c Leek Wootton *Cov* from 08; P-in-c Stoneleigh w Ashow 08-13. *The Vicarage, 4 Hill Wootton Road, Leek Wootton,*

Warwick CV35 7QL T/F: (01926) 850610 E: jim@me16.com *or* vicar@a-lw-s.org.uk

PERRYMAN, Canon John Frederick Charles. b 49. Mert Coll Ox BA 71 MA 74 MInstGA 98. Ridley Hall Cam 72. **d** 74 **p** 75. C Shortlands *Roch* 74-78; Asst Chapl St Geo Hosp Lon 78-82; Chapl Withington Hosp Man 83-94; Chapl Univ Hosp of S Man NHS Foundn Trust 94-09; Hon Can Man Cathl 00-09; rtd 09; PtO *Man* from 09. *24 Alan Road, Manchester M20 4WG* T: 0161-445 4769

PERSSON, The Very Revd Caspar Bernhard Michael. b 59. Uppsala Univ BA 85. **p** 85. In Swedish Lutheran Ch from 85; Dean and R Swedish Ch in London from 07; LtO *Lon* from 09. *The Swedish Church in London, 6 Harcourt Street, London W1H 4AG* T: (020) 7723 5681 M: 07785-308067 E: rector@swedishchurch.com

PERSSON, Matthew Stephen. b 60. Dundee Univ BSc 82 Bris Univ MA 98. Wycliffe Hall Ox 88. **d** 91 **p** 92. C Bath Twerton-on-Avon *B & W* 91-94; Chapl HM Pris Shepton Mallet 94-97; PtO *B & W* 97-98; C Shepton Mallet w Doulting 98-00. *Grange Farm, Fair Place, West Lydford, Somerton TA11 7DN* T: (01963) 240024

✤**PERSSON, The Rt Revd William Michael Dermot.** b 27. Oriel Coll Ox BA 51 MA 55. Wycliffe Hall Ox 51. **d** 53 **p** 54 **c** 82. C S Croydon Em *Cant* 53-55; C Tunbridge Wells St Jo *Roch* 55-58; V S Mimms Ch Ch *Lon* 58-67; R Bebington *Ches* 67-79; V Knutsford St Jo and Toft 79-82; Suff Bp Doncaster *Sheff* 82-92; rtd 93; Hon Asst Bp B & W from 93. *Ryalls Cottage, Burton Street, Marnhull, Sturminster Newton DT10 1PS* T: (01258) 820452

PERTH, Provost of. *See* FARQUHARSON, The Very Revd Hunter Buchanan

PERUMBALATH, The Ven John. b 66. Calicut Univ BA 86 Union Bibl Sem Pune BD 90 Osmania Univ Hyderabad MA 93 NW Univ S Africa PhD 07. Serampore Th Coll MTh 93. **d** 94 **p** 95. C Calcutta St Jo India 94-95; V Calcutta St Jas 95-00; V Calcutta St Thos 00-01; C Beckenham St Geo *Roch* 02-05; TV Northfleet and Rosherville 05-08; V Perry Street 08-13; Dioc CUF Link Officer 08-13; Adn Barking *Chelmsf* from 13. *11 Bridgefields Close, Hornchurch RM11 1GQ* T: (01708) 474951 E: a.barking@chelmsford.anglican.org

PESCE, Fabrizio. b 73. Universidad del Salvador Buenos Aires BA MA 03 MD 09. St Steph Ho Ox 14. **d** 02 **p** 03. In RC Ch 02-09; C Bedford Park *Lon* from 15; C Acton Green St Pet from 15. *26 St Albans Avenue, London W4 5JU* M: 07713-444382 E: pesce.fabrizio@gmail.com

PESCOD, John Gordon. b 44. Leeds Univ BSc 70. Qu Coll Birm. **d** 72 **p** 73. C Camberwell St Geo *S'wark* 72-75; Chapl R Philanthropic Soc Sch Redhill 75-80; P-in-c Nunney w Wanstrow and Cloford *B & W* 80-84; R Nunney and Witham Friary, Marston Bigot etc 84-87; R Milverton w Halse and Fitzhead 87-93; V Frome St Jo and St Mary 93-00; V Frome St Jo 01; V Woodlands 93-01; RD Frome 97-01; R Castle Cary w Ansford 01-09; rtd 09. *32 Churchfield Drive, Castle Cary BA7 7LA* E: jjpescod@tiscali.co.uk

PESKETT, Richard Howard. b 42. Selw Coll Cam BA 64 MA 67. Ridley Hall Cam 64. **d** 68 **p** 69. C Jesmond H Trin *Newc* 68-71; Lect Discipleship Tr Cen Singapore 71-76; Dean 76-86; Lect Coll of SS Paul and Mary Cheltenham 86-87; Research Dir OMF 88-91; Tutor Trin Coll Bris 91-06; Vice-Prin 98-06; rtd 07; PtO *Truro* 06-08; Hon C Penzance St Mary w St Paul and St Jo 08-13; RD Penwith 08-13. *7 North Parade, Penzance TR18 4SH* T: (01736) 362913 E: howard.peskett@btinternet.com

PESKETT, Timothy Lewis. b 64. St Kath Coll Liv BA 86. Chich Th Coll BTh 90. **d** 90 **p** 91. C Verwood *Sarum* 90-91; C Southsea H Spirit *Portsm* 91-95; TV Burgess Hill St Jo w St Edw *Chich* 95-00; V Burgess Hill St Edw 00-05; R Felpham 05-14; R Whyke w Rumboldswhyke and Portfield from 14. *The Rectory, 199 Whyke Road, Chichester PO19 7AQ* T: (01243) 782535 E: rector@whyke.info

PESTELL, Robert Carlyle. b 54. Aston Tr Scheme 89 Linc Th Coll 91. **d** 93 **p** 94. C Matson *Glouc* 93-97; P-in-c Charfield 97-01; R Charfield and Kingswood 02-06; P-in-c Cheltenham St Mich 06-13; P-in-c Cheltenham St Luke and St Jo 06-12; Chapl Leckhampton Court Hospice from 13. *Leckhampton Court, Church Road, Leckhampton, Cheltenham GL53 0QJ* T: (01242) 230199

PETCH, Canon Douglas Rodger. b 57. Nottm Univ BSc 79. St Jo Coll Nottm MA 96. **d** 94 **p** 94. C Vom Nigeria 94-95; C Pendleton *Man* 96-98; P-in-c Werneth and C Oldham St Paul 98-03; CMS Nigeria 03-07; Hon Can Jos from 05; TV Halliwell *Man* 07-11; TV W Bolton from 11; AD Bolton 10-15. *101 Cloister Street, Bolton BL1 3HA* T: (01204) 842627 M: 07837-423501 E: rodgerpetch@yahoo.co.uk

PETER, Christopher Javed. b 51. Peshawar Univ BA 75. Qu Coll Birm 94. **d** 96 **p** 97. C Darwen St Pet w Hoddlesden *Blackb*

96-98; C Accrington 98-99; C Burnley St Andr w St Marg and St Jas 99-05; Chapl R Liverpool and Broadgreen Univ Hosps NHS Trust from 05. *Royal Liverpool University Hospital, Prescot Street, Liverpool L7 8XP* T: 0151-706 2826 E: christopher.peter@rlbuht.nhs.uk

PETER DOUGLAS, Brother. *See* NEEDHAM, Peter Douglas

PETERBOROUGH, Bishop of. *See* ALLISTER, The Rt Revd Donald Spargo

PETERBOROUGH, Dean of. *See* TAYLOR, The Very Revd Charles William

PETERKEN, Canon Peter Donald. b 28. K Coll Lon BD 51 AKC 51 Open Univ BA 09. **d** 52 **p** 53. C Swanley St Mary *Roch* 52-55 and 62-65; C Is of Dogs Ch Ch and St Jo w St Luke *Lon* 55-57; R S Perrott w Mosterton and Chedington *Sarum* 57-59; Br Guiana 59-62; R Killamarsh *Derby* 65-70; V Derby St Luke 70-90; RD Derby N 79-90; Hon Can Derby Cathl 85-95; R Matlock 90-95; rtd 95; PtO *Derby* from 95. *64 Brayfield Road, Littleover, Derby DE23 6GT* T: (01332) 766285 E: peter.peterken@ntlworld.com

PETERS, Ann Margaret. *See* PETERS-WOTHERSPOON, Ann Margaret

PETERS, Carl Richard. b 62. Ripon Coll Cuddesdon 95. **d** 97 **p** 98. C Coventry Caludon *Cov* 97-01; V Gt Grimsby St Andr w St Luke and All SS *Linc* 01-02; TV Leek and Meerbrook *Lich* 02-14; P-in-c Brandon and Ushaw Moor *Dur* from 14. *The Clergy House, Sawmills Lane, Brandon, Durham DH7 8NS* T: 0191-378 0845 E: carl@revpeters.wanadoo.co.uk

PETERS, Miss Carole Jean. b 61. Ripon Coll Cuddesdon 07. **d** 09 **p** 10. C Ivinghoe w Pitstone and Slapton and Marsworth *Ox* 09-11; C Aston Clinton w Buckland and Drayton Beauchamp 12-13; R Astwell Gp *Pet* from 13. *The Vicarage, The Green, Lois Weedon, Towcester NN12 8PN* T: (01933) 673437 M: 07710-128859 E: carolepeters@aol.com

PETERS, The Very Revd Christopher Lind. b 56. Oak Hill Th Coll. **d** 82 **p** 83. C Knockbreda *D & D* 82-84; C Lisburn Ch Ch Cathl 84-87; I Kilmocomogue *C, C & R* 89-91; I Kilmocomogue *C, C & R* Beara 92; I Killiney Ballybrack *D & G* 93-98; Dean Ross *C, C & R* from 98; Chan Cork Cathl from 98; I Ross Union from 98. *The Deanery, Rosscarbery, Co Cork, Republic of Ireland* T: (00353) (23) 48166 E: candjpeters@eircom.net

PETERS, David. b 62. Reading Univ BSc 83. Wycliffe Hall Ox 11. **d** 14 **p** 15. NSM Wonersh w Blackheath *Guildf* from 14. *Rushtons, 15 Longdown Road, Guildford GU4 8PP* T: (01483) 575906 E: dk.peters@btinternet.com

PETERS, David Alexander. b 72. K Coll Lon BA 94. St Steph Ho Ox BA 98 MA 08. **d** 99 **p** 00. C Paddington St Jas *Lon* 99-03; PV Westmr Abbey 01-13; V Reading H Trin and Reading St Mark *Ox* 03-08; Asst Chapl Tonbridge Sch 08-11; Sen Chapl from 11. *Tonbridge School, High Street, Tonbridge TN9 1JP* T: (01732) 365555 E: dap@tonbridge-school.org

PETERS, David Lewis. b 38. Ch Ch Ox BA 62 MA 66. Westcott Ho Cam 63. **d** 65 **p** 66. C Oldham St Mary w St Pet *Man* 65-69; C Stand 70-74; P-in-c Hillock 70-74; V 74-82; V Haslingden w Haslingden Grane *Blackb* 82-88; rtd 88; PtO *Man* 88-09; *Blackb* 88-09. *37 Cyprus Road, Faversham ME13 8HB* T: (01795) 537917

PETERS, Geoffrey John. b 51. BCom BSc MDiv MInstC(Glas). Oak Hill Th Coll 85. **d** 87 **p** 88. C Forest Gate St Saw w W Ham St Matt *Chelmsf* 87-90; C Wembley St Jo *Lon* 90-92; Chapl Wembley Hosp 90-92; TV Manningham *Bradf* 92-97; Res Scheme Manager Anchor Trust 02-04; NSM York St Clem w St Mary Bishophill from 07. *15 Cameron Walker Court, Bishopthorpe Road, York YO23 1LD* T: (01904) 638632 M: 07990-644779 E: geoffpeters04@aol.com

PETERS, Mrs Helen Elizabeth. b 67. Qu Marg Coll Edin BSc 88. Ox Min Course 08. **d** 11 **p** 12. NSM Hughenden *Ox* from 11. *Boundary House, Missenden Road, Great Kingshill, High Wycombe HP15 6EB* T: (01494) 716772 E: helen.peters@peters-research.com

PETERS, Mrs Jane Elisabeth. b 48. Kent Univ BA 08. **d** 08 **p** 09. NSM Shortlands *Roch* from 08. *27 The Gardens, Beckenham BR3 5PH* T: (020) 8650 5986 E: revjane@virginmedia.com

PETERS, John Peter Thomas. b 63. Keble Coll Ox BL 85. Wycliffe Hall Ox BA 91. **d** 95 **p** 96. C Brompton H Trin w Onslow Square St Paul *Lon* 95-99; P-in-c Bryanston Square St Mary w St Marylebone St Mark 00-04; R from 04. *13 Chomeley Crescent, London N6 5EZ* T: (020) 7258 5042

PETERS, John Thomas. b 58. Connecticut Univ BA 80. St Jo Coll Nottm 84. **d** 87 **p** 88. C Virginia Water *Guildf* 87-93; R Grand Rapids Ch CH USA 93-00; R Eden Prairie St Alb from 00. *14434 Fairway Drive, Eden Prairie MN 557344-1904, USA* E: johnpeters@isd.net

PETERS, Canon Kenneth. b 54. Newport Univ Tokyo MBA 88 Greenwich Univ MA 02 MIW 96. St Mich Coll Llan 74. **d** 77 **p** 78. C Mountain Ash *Llan* 77-80; Asst Chapl Mersey Miss to

Seamen 80-82; Chapl Miss to Seamen Japan 82-89; Hon Can Kobe from 85; Chapl Supt Mersey Miss to Seamen 89-93; Justice and Welfare Sec 94-09; Dir Justice and Welfare from 09; Hon C St Mich Paternoster Royal *Lon* from 94. *The Mission to Seafarers, St Michael Paternoster Royal, College Hill, London EC4R 2RL* T: (020) 7248 5202 F: 7248 4761
E: justice@missiontoseafarers.org

PETERS, Malcolm John. b 71. Leic Univ BA 92. Oak Hill Th Coll BA 03. **d** 03 **p** 04. C Braintree *Chelmsf* 03-06; C Hull St Jo Newland *York* 06-09; P-in-c High Ongar w Norton Mandeville *Chelmsf* from 09. *The Rectory, The Street, High Ongar, Ongar CM5 9NQ* T: (01277) 362593
E: malcolm.peters892@btinternet.com

PETERS, Preb Marilyn Ann. b 49. Open Univ BA 90. Qu Coll Birm 96. **d** 98 **p** 99. C Blakenall Heath *Lich* 98-01; TV Cen Telford 01-05; TR 05-13; Preb Lich Cathl 09-13; rtd 13; PtO *Lich* from 15. *66 Harrington Walk, Lichfield WS13 7UY* M: 07541-245618 E: marilynpeters@waitrose.com

PETERS, Canon Michael. b 41. Chich Th Coll 75. **d** 77 **p** 78. C Redruth *Truro* 77-79; TV 79-80; TV Redruth w Lanner 80-82; R St Mawgan w St Ervan and St Eval 82-86; Chapl HM Pris Liv 86-87; Chapl HM Pris Bris 87-01; Hon Can Bris Cathl 96-01; P-in-c Middlezoy and Othery and Moorlinch *B & W* 01-08; rtd 08; PtO *B & W* from 08. *Archway House, North Lane, Othery, Bridgwater TA7 0QG* T: (01823) 690208
E: archwaymike@googlemail.com

PETERS, Rebecca Ann. b 76. St Hilda's Coll Ox MPhys 98 St Cross Coll Ox PGCE 99. Wycliffe Hall Ox 06. **d** 08 **p** 09. C Roxeth *Lon* 08-11; P-in-c Drayton St Pet (Abingdon) *Ox* from 11. *The Vicarage, 8 Gravel Lane, Drayton, Abingdon OX14 4HY* T: (01235) 531374 M: 07967-598115
E: rebecca.a.peters@gmail.com

PETERS, Robert David. b 54. BA 76. Oak Hill Th Coll 78. **d** 79 **p** 80. C Hyde St Geo *Ches* 79-83; C Hartford 83-86; V Lindow 86-96; V Throop *Win* 96-10; P-in-c Bournemouth H Epiphany 08-10; AD Bournemouth 03-08; Hon Can Win Cathl 08-10; V Plas Newton w Ches Ch Ch 10-11; V Plas Newton from 11. *St Michael's Vicarage, 22 Plas Newton Lane, Chester CH2 1PA* T: (01244) 319677 *or* 315129 E: rob.peters@tiscali.co.uk

PETERS, Stephen Eric. b 45. Westcott Ho Cam 74. **d** 77 **p** 78. C Wanstead St Mary *Chelmsf* 77-79; C Leigh-on-Sea St Marg 79-81; P-in-c Purleigh 81-82; P-in-c Cold Norton w Stow Maries 81-82; R Purleigh, Cold Norton and Stow Maries 83-84; V Bedford Park *Lon* 84-87; PtO *Ex* 87-88 and 93-08; TR Totnes and Berry Pomeroy 88-90; Chapl Ex Sch and St Marg Sch 91-93. *10 rue Ronzier, 34140 Meze, France*
E: stephen.e.peters@gmail.com

PETERS-WOTHERSPOON, Ann Margaret. b 48. Lon Univ BD 84 Open Univ MA 95 UEA EdD 05 Anglia Ruskin Univ MA 09. ERMC 05. **d** 07 **p** 08. NSM Somersham w Pidley and Oldhurst and Woodhurst *Ely* 07-11; NSM Tweedmouth *Newc* from 11; NSM Spittal from 11; NSM Scremerston from 11. *St John's Vicarage, 129 Main Street, Spittal, Berwick-upon-Tweed TD15 1RD* E: ann_m_peters@hotmail.com

PETERSEN, Miss Jennifer Elizabeth. b 55. Aus Nat Univ BA 78. Moore Th Coll Sydney BTh 82 Wycliffe Hall Ox 92. **d** 94 **p** 95. C Elloughton and Brough w Brantingham *York* 94-96; C Ealing St Mary *Lon* 96-00; Chapl Thames Valley Univ 96-00; Chapl Qu Mary and Westf Coll from 00. *24 Sidney Square, London E1 2EY* T: (020) 7791 1973 *or* 7882 3179
E: j.e.petersen@qmul.ac.uk

PETERSON, David Gilbert. b 44. Sydney Univ BA 65 MA 74 Lon Univ BD 68 Man Univ PhD 78. Moore Th Coll Sydney ThL 68. **d** 68 **p** 69. C Manly St Matt Australia 68-70; Lect Moore Th Coll 71-75; C Cheadle *Ches* 75-78; Sen Can and R Wollongong Cathl Australia 80-84; Lect Moore Th Coll 84-96; Prin Oak Hill Th Coll 96-07; PtO *Lon* 96-07; *St Alb* 96-07; Research Fell Moore Th Coll Australia from 07; rtd 09. *1 Vista Street, Belrose NSW 2085, Australia*
E: davidandlesleypeterson@gmail.com

PETERSON, Dennis. b 25. Oak Hill Th Coll 51. **d** 54 **p** 55. C Leyton All SS *Chelmsf* 54-56; C Leeds St Geo *Ripon* 56-58; V E Brixton St Jude *S'wark* 58-91; rtd 91; PtO *Chelmsf* 91-12. *79 Cavendish Gardens, Westcliff-on-Sea SS0 9XP* T: (01702) 334400 E: peterson@flashbyte.co.uk

PETERSON, Canon John Louis. b 42. Concordia Coll (USA) BA 65 Harvard Div Sch STB 68 Chicago Th Sem ThD 76 Virginia Th Sem Hon DD 93. **d** 76 **p** 77. V Plainwell St Steph USA 76-82; Dean St Geo Coll Jerusalem 82-94; Can Res 82-94; Hon Can from 95; Hon Can Kalamazoo from 82; Hon Prov Can Cant Cathl from 95; Sec Gen Angl Communion Office 95-04; Hon Can Kaduna from 99; Hon Can St Paul's Cathl 00-05. *Episcopal Church House, Mount St Alban, Washington DC 20016, USA*

PETERSON, Paul John. b 67. Trin Coll Bris 94. **d** 97 **p** 98. C Burney Lane *Birm* 97-01; C-in-c Bradley Stoke N CD *Bris*

01-10; C Downend from 10. *15 Glendale, Bristol BS16 6EQ* T: 0117-330 7673 E: paul@petersonp.freeserve.co.uk

PETFIELD, Bruce le Gay. b 34. FHA. NEOC 76. **d** 79 **p** 80. NSM Morpeth *Newc* 79-86; C Knaresborough *Ripon* 86-87; V Flamborough *York* 87-94; V Bempton 87-94; rtd 94; PtO *York* from 94. *36 Maple Road, Bridlington YO16 6TE* T: (01262) 676028 E: bruce.petfield@talktalk.net

PETHERAM, Louise Anne Miranda. b 62. Nottm Univ BSc 84 PGCE 85. Qu Coll Birm 09. **d** 12 **p** 13. NSM Upper Soar *Leic* 12-15. *Address temp unknown* T: 0116-319 8703
E: louise.petheram@googlemail.com

PETHERICK, Mrs Karen Elizabeth. **d** 14 **p** 15. OLM Hanley H Ev *Lich* from 14. *80 Birches Head Road, Stoke-on-Trent ST1 6LQ* T: (01782) 865240 E: karenpetherick@ntlworld.com

PETIT, Andrew Michael. b 53. Em Coll Cam MA 78. Trin Coll Bris. **d** 83 **p** 84. C Stoughton *Guildf* 83-87; C Shirley *Win* 87-92; V Cholsey *Ox* 92-04; C Streatley w Moulsford 03-04; V Cholsey and Moulsford from 04; Chapl W Berks Priority Care Services NHS Trust 92-03. *The Vicarage, Church Road, Cholsey, Wallingford OX10 9PP* T: (01491) 651216 M: 07986-005618 E: apetit@lineone.net

PETITT, Mark Peter. b 81. Trin Coll Bris BA 12. **d** 12 **p** 13. C Langdon Hills *Chelmsf* from 12. *149 Great Berry Lane, Langdon Hills, Basildon SS16 6BP* M: 07900-466373
E: mark.petitt@yahoo.co.uk

PETITT, Michael David. b 53. BCombStuds. Linc Th Coll 79. **d** 82 **p** 83. C Arnold *S'well* 82-86; Asst Chapl HM Youth Cust Cen Glen Parva 86-87; V Blaby *Leic* 87-94; V Leagrave *St Alb* 94-98; R Badby w Newham and Charwelton w Fawsley etc *Pet* 98-08; Dioc Voc Adv 00-08; Dir Tr for Past Assts 01-03; P-in-c Guilsborough w Hollowell and Cold Ashby 08-10; P-in-c Cottesbrooke w Gt Creaton and Thornby 08-10; C W Haddon w Winwick and Ravensthorpe 08-10; P-in-c Spratton 08-10; V Ilkeston St Mary *Derby* from 10. *St Mary's Vicarage, 63B Manners Road, Ilkeston DE7 5HB* T: 0115-932 4725 *or* 932 8540 E: michael.petitt@virginmedia.com

PETRIE, Alistair Philip. b 50. Fuller Th Sem California DMin 99. Oak Hill Th Coll 76. **d** 76 **p** 77. C Eston *York* 76-79; P-in-c Prestwick *Glas* 79-81; R 81-82; Canada from 82. *PO Box 25103, Kelowna BC V1W 3Y7, Canada* T: (001) (250) 764 8590 F: 656 3298 E: alistair@partnershipministries.org

PETRIE, Ian Robert (Eric). b 53. Avery Hill Coll PGCE 84 Oak Hill Th Coll BA 83. Qu Coll Birm 93. **d** 95 **p** 96. C Sedgley All SS *Worc* 95-98; P-in-c Salwarpe and Hindlip w Martin Hussingtree 98-08; Co-ord Chapl W Mercia Police 98-08; rtd 08; PtO *B & W* from 12. *100 Highbridge Road, Burnham-on-Sea TA8 1LW* T: (01278) 787402
E: eric@petrierev.freeserve.co.uk

PETRINE, Andrei Anatolievich. b 73. St Jo Coll Dur BA 05. Cranmer Hall Dur 02. **d** 05 **p** 06. C Hounslow H Trin w St Paul and St Mary *Lon* 05-08; PtO 08-09; P-in-c Greensted-juxta-Ongar w Stanford Rivers etc *Chelmsf* 09-15; Chapl Russian Community *Lon* 09-14; P-in-c Laindon w Dunton *Chelmsf* from 15. *38 Claremont Road, Basildon SS15 5PZ* M: 07723-026925 E: pater@me.com

PETTENGELL, Ernest Terence. b 43. Ex Univ MA 98. K Coll Lon 65. **d** 69 **p** 70. C Chesham St Mary *Ox* 69-72; C Farnborough *Guildf* 72-75; Asst Master K Alfred Sch Burnham-on-Sea 75-78; C Bishop's Cleeve *Glouc* 78-80; Chapl Westonbirt Sch 80-85; P-in-c Shipton Moyne w Westonbirt and Lasborough *Glouc* 80-85; V Berkeley w Wick, Breadstone and Newport 85-92; TV Weston-super-Mare Cen Par *B & W* 92-95; P-in-c Weston super Mare Em 96-99; Chapl Staffs Univ *Lich* 99-03; V Douglas All SS and St Thos *S & M* 03-07; rtd 07; PtO *Ox* from 09. *3 Rushall Road, Thame OX9 3TR* T: (01844) 216298

PETTER, Oliver Robert Hugh. b 80. St Edm Hall Ox BA 05. St Steph Ho Ox 11. **d** 14 **p** 15. C Old St Pancras *Lon* from 14. *33B Crowndale Road, London NW1 1TN* T: (020) 7388 4990
E: oliver.petter@gmail.com

PETTERSEN, Canon Alvyn Lorang. b 51. TCD BA 73 Dur Univ BA 75 PhD 81. Sarum & Wells Th Coll 78. **d** 81 **p** 82. Chapl Clare Coll Cam 81-85; Fell and Chapl Ex Coll Ox 85-92; Research Fell Linc Coll Ox 92-93; V Frensham *Guildf* 93-02; Can Res Worc Cathl from 02. *2 College Green, Worcester WR1 2LH* T: (01905) 732900
E: alvynpettersen@worcestercathedral.org.uk

PETTET, Christopher Farley. b 54. Ox Univ BEd 78. St Jo Coll Nottm 87. **d** 90 **p** 91. C Luton St Mary *St Alb* 90-93; C Fawley *Win* 93-97; P-in-c Amport, Grateley, Monxton and Quarley 97-09; TV Portway and Danebury 09-12; V E w W Wellow and Sherfield English from 12. *Wellow Vicarage, 1 The Beeches, West Wellow, Romsey SO51 6RN* T: (01794) 323562
E: cpettet@btinternet.com

PETTIFER, Bryan George Ernest. b 32. Qu Coll Cam BA 55 MA 59 Bris Univ MEd 74. Wm Temple Coll Rugby 56 Ridley

Hall Cam 57. **d** 59 **p** 60. C Attercliffe w Carbrook *Sheff* 59-61; C Ecclesall 61-65; Chapl City of Bath Tech Coll 65-74; Adult Educn Officer *Bris* 75-80; Dir Past Th Sarum & Wells Th Coll 80-85; Can Res St Alb *St Alb* 85-92; Prin St Alb Minl Tr Scheme 85-92; Prin Ox Area Chr Tr Scheme 92-94; PtO 94-98; Min and Deployment Officer/Selection Sec ABM 94-97; rtd 97; PtO *Bris* from 98; *Glouc* 98-00; *Sarum* from 98; *B & W* 02-05; Rtd Clergy Officer Malmesbury Adnry *Bris* from 04. *23 Curlew Drive, Chippenham SN14 6YG* T: (01249) 659823

PETTIFER, John Barrie. b 38. Linc Th Coll 63. **d** 65 **p** 66. C Stretford St Matt *Man* 65-67; C Stand 67-71; V Littleborough 71-00; rtd 00. *Littleborough Christian Centre, 43 Todmorden Road, Littleborough OL15 9EL* T: (01706) 374074

PETTIFOR, Mrs Anne Elizabeth. b 64. Man Univ BSc 85 FIA 99. LCTP 10. **d** 14 **p** 15. NSM Kirkby Lonsdale *Carl* from 14. *Cross House, Whittington, Carnforth LA6 2NX* T: (015242) 71904 F: 08701-602766 M: 07973-869475
E: anne.pettifor@btinternet.com

PETTIFOR, Canon David Thomas. b 42. Ripon Coll Cuddesdon 78. **d** 81 **p** 82. C Binley *Cov* 81-84; P-in-c Wood End 84-88; V 88-92; V Finham 92-98; TV Coventry Caludon 98-07; Hon Can Cov Cathl 04-07; rtd 07; PtO *Cov* from 08. *8 Austin Edwards Drive, Warwick CV34 5GW* T: (01926) 498736 E: davidtpettifor@hayoo.co.uk

PETTIGREW, Stanley. b 27. TCD BA 49 MA 62. Div Test . **d** 50 **p** 51. C Newcastle *D & D* 50-53; C Dublin Clontarf *D & G* 53-57; I Derralossary 57-62; Miss to Seamen 62-92; I Wicklow w Killiskey *D & G* 62-92; Can Ch Ch Cathl Dublin 87-92; rtd 92. *Corr Riasc, Bollarney South, Wicklow, Republic of Ireland* T: (00353) (404) 69755

PETTINGELL, Hubert. b 32. ACA 54 FCA 65 AKC 58. **d** 59 **p** 60. C Mansfield SS Pet and Paul *S'well* 59-61; CMS Iran 61-66; C Wellington w W Buckland and Nynehead *B & W* 67-68; Warden Student Movement Ho Lon 68-69; R Holywell w Needingworth *Ely* 69-71; Dir Finance WCC 80-96; PtO *Eur* from 94; rtd 97. *chemin du Pommier 22, CH-1218 Le Grand Saconnex, Geneva, Switzerland* T: (0041) (22) 798 8586
E: hpettingell@hotmail.com

PETTIT, Mrs Alice Hazel Lester. b 78. St Mellitus Coll. **d** 11 **p** 12. C Teynham w Lynsted and Kingsdown *Cant* 11-13; C Sittingbourne w Bobbing from 13. *32 Valenciennes Road, Sittingbourne ME10 1EN* T: (01795) 479568
E: alicepettit1@gmail.com

PETTIT, Anthony David. b 72. Univ of Cen England in Birm BA 94 MA 95 St Jo Coll Dur BA 01. Cranmer Hall Dur 98. **d** 01 **p** 02. C Gt Malvern St Mary *Worc* 01-04; P-in-c Cradley 04-05; TV Halas 05-10; P-in-c Paget St Paul Bermuda from 11. *PO Box PG290, Paget PG BX, Bermuda* T: (001) (441) 236 5880 F: 236 8224 E: stpaulsoffice@logic.bm

PETTIT, James Lee. b 78. Lon Bible Coll BA 01 MA 03. Ox Min Course 07. **d** 09 **p** 10. C Faversham *Cant* 09-13; TV Sittingbourne w Bobbing from 13. *32 Valenciennes Road, Sittingbourne ME10 1EN* T: (01795) 479568
E: jamesthemonk@gmail.com

PETTITT, Canon Robin Adrian. b 50. MRTPI 79 Newc Univ BA 77. St Steph Ho Ox 81. **d** 83 **p** 84. C Warrington St Elphin *Liv* 83-87; C Torrisholme *Blackb* 87-93; P-in-c Charnock Richard 93-00; Dioc Par Development Officer 93-98; Sec Dioc Adv Cttee for the Care of Chs 98-99; C Broughton 00-01; rtd 01; PtO *Liv* 03-13; Hon Can Wiawso Ghana from 13. *The Vicarage, 169 Church Road, Haydock, St Helens WA11 0NJ* T: (01942) 727956

PETTMAN, Mrs Hilary Susan. b 45. STETS 99. **d** 02 **p** 03. NSM Shottermill *Guildf* 02-08; PtO from 08. *Stacey's Farm Cottage, Thursley Road, Elstead, Godalming GU8 6DG* T: (01252) 703217
E: hilarypettman@tiscali.co.uk

PETTS, Mrs Anna Carolyn. b 44. St Mich Coll Sarum CertEd 65. STETS 00. **d** 03 **p** 04. NSM Hordle *Win* 03-11; NSM NW Hants 11-15. *The Clergy House, 2 Flexford Close, Highclere, Newbury RG20 9PE* T: (01635) 255143 E: carolynpetts@tiscali.co.uk

PETTY, Alicia Christina Margaret. *See* DRING, Alicia Christina Margaret

PETTY, Brian. b 34. Man Univ BA 90. St Aid Birkenhead 59. **d** 62 **p** 63. C Meole Brace *Lich* 62-65; Chapl RAF 65-69; Australia 70-75; P-in-c Kimbolton w Middleton-on-the-Hill *Heref* 76-79; P-in-c Pudleston-cum-Whyle w Hatfield, Docklow etc 76-79; P-in-c Haddenham *Ely* 79-80; V 80-84; V Fairfield *Derby* 84-90; Chapl St Geo Sch Ascot 90-93; TR Sampford Peverell, Uplowman, Holcombe Rogus etc *Ex* 93-99; RD Cullompton 95-99; rtd 99; PtO *Ex* 99-02; Hon C Diptford, N Huish, Harberton, Harbertonford etc 02-13. *23 Gracey Court, Woodland Road, Broadclyst, Exeter EX5 3GA*

PETTY, Duncan. *See* PETTY, William Duncan

PETTY, The Very Revd John Fitzmaurice. b 35. Trin Hall Cam BA 59 MA 65. Cuddesdon Coll 64. **d** 66 **p** 67. C Sheff St Cuth 66-69; C St Helier *S'wark* 69-75; V Hurst *Man* 75-88; AD

Ashton-under-Lyne 83-87; Hon Can Man Cathl 86-88; Dean Cov 88-00 and 00; rtd 00; PtO *Lich* 01-14. *4 Granville Street, Copthorne, Shrewsbury SY3 8NE* T: (01743) 231513

PETTY, Neil. b 40. Coll of Resurr Mirfield 04. **d** 04 **p** 05. NSM N Thornaby *York* from 04. *28 Bader Avenue, Thornaby, Stockton-on-Tees TS17 0HQ* T: (01642) 761588 M: 07985-760490
E: neilpetty@hotmail.com

PETTY, Capt Stuart. b 56. Chich Th Coll 91. **d** 93 **p** 94. CA from 88; C W Bromwich St Andr w Ch Ch *Lich* 93-96; Asst Chapl Walsall Hosps NHS Trust 96-00; Sen Chapl 00-03; Chapl Team Ldr R Wolv Hosps NHS Trust 03-08; Sen Chapl York Hosps NHS Foundn Trust 08-14; Asst Chapl R Wolv Hosps NHS Trust from 14. *New Cross Hospital, Wolverhampton Road, Heath Town, Wolverhampton WV10 0QP* T: (01902) 307999

PETTY, William Duncan. b 55. Ex Univ BSc 76 Leic Univ PGCE 77. Oak Hill Th Coll 97. **d** 99 **p** 00. C Burscough Bridge *Liv* 99-04; Min Tanhouse The Oaks CD from 04. *181 Ennerdale, Skelmersdale WN8 6AH* T: (01704) 892444
E: duncan@thepettys.freeserve.co.uk

PETZER, Garth Stephen. MBE 99. Rhodes Univ BTh 95. St Paul's Coll Grahamstown. **d** 88 **p** 91. C Queenstown St Mich S Africa 88-89; C E London St Sav 90-93; R E London St Martin 93-95; Chapl RN 96-03 and 04-07; CF 03-04; rtd 07; PtO *Nor* 04-07. *46 Crystal Way, Waterlooville PO7 8NB* M: 07801-637205 E: petzeggs@hotmail.com

PETZSCH, Hugo Max David. b 57. Edin Univ MA 79 BD 83 PhD 95 FSAScot 91. Edin Th Coll 80. **d** 83 **p** 84. C Dollar *St And* 83-86; New Zealand 86-90; P-in-c Alyth, Blairgowrie and Coupar Angus *St And* 90-91; Chapl Glenalmond Coll 91-98; Dep Headmaster Benenden Sch 99-12; rtd 12. *45 Portland Street, Leamington Spa CV32 5EY*

PEVERELL, Canon Paul Harrison. b 57. Hull Univ BA 80. Ripon Coll Cuddesdon. **d** 82 **p** 83. C Cottingham *York* 82-85; V Middlesbrough St Martin 85-93; V Gt Ayton w Easby and Newton under Roseberry from 93; Hon Can Ho Ghana from 04. *The Vicarage, Low Green, Great Ayton, Middlesbrough TS9 6NN* T: (01642) 722333 E: revpev@btinternet.com

✠**PEYTON, The Rt Revd Nigel.** b 51. JP 87. Edin Univ MA 73 BD 76 Lanc Univ PhD 09. Union Th Sem (NY) STM 77 Edin Th Coll 73. **d** 76 **p** 77 **c** 11. Chapl St Paul's Cathl Dundee 76-82; Dioc Youth Chapl 76-85; Chapl Invergowrie 79-82; P-in-c 82-85; Chapl Univ Hosp Dundee 82-85; V Nottingham All SS *S'well* 85-91; P-in-c Lambley 91-99; Chapl Bluecoat Sch Nottm 90-92; Dioc Min Development Adv *S'well* 91-99; Adn Newark 99-11; Bp Bre from 11; Hon Teaching Fell Lanc Univ *Blackb* from 10. *Brechin Diocese Office, Unit 14, Prospect III, Technology Park, Dundee DD2 1TY* T: (01382) 641586 *or* 562244 E: bishop@brechin.anglican.org

PEYTON JONES, Mrs Dorothy Helen. b 58. LMH Ox BA 79 MPhil 80 DipSW 02. Trin Coll Bris 84. **dss** 86 **d** 87 **p** 94. W Holloway St Luke *Lon* 86-89; Par Dn 87-89; C Glas St Oswald 89-92; NSM Drumchapel 92-98; PtO *Ely* 98-03; NSM Chesterton St Andr from 03; Ind Chapl 09-12. *71 Humberstone Road, Cambridge CB4 1JD* T: (01223) 523485 *or* 311727 M: 07503-746520 E: dorothypj@ntlworld.com *or* dorothy@peytonjones.org

PHAIR, Neal David Stewart. b 70. Limerick Univ BA 98 UCD HDipEd 99 TCD MPhil 02. CITC 99. **d** 02 **p** 03. C Ballymena w Ballyclug *Conn* 02-05; I Ballintoy w Rathlin and Dunseverick 05-07; Chapl Dub Inst of Tech 07-10; R Cherbury w Gainfield *Ox* 10-14; I Ballybay w Mucknoe and Clontibret *Clogh* from 14. *The Rectory, Drumcrwe, Castleblayney, Co Monaghan, Republic of Ireland* T: (00353) (42) 974 0483
E: nealphair@hotmail.com

PHARAOH, Carol Helen. b 63. Preston Poly BTech 84. Cranmer Hall *Dur* 96. **d** 98 **p** 99. C Heaton Ch Ch *Man* 98-02; TV Walkden and Lt Hulton 02-09; P-in-c E Farnworth and Kearsley 09-10; TR Farnworth, Kearsley and Stoneclough from 10. *The Rectory, 55 Church Street, Farnworth, Bolton BL4 8AQ* T: (01204) 572819 E: pharaohingham@o2.co.uk

PHEELY, William Rattray. b 35. EN(M) 88. Edin Th Coll 57. **d** 60 **p** 61. C Glas St Mary 60-63; C Salisbury St Martin *Sarum* 63-66; Guyana 66-82; V Bordesley St Oswald *Birm* 82-86; PtO 86-00; *Ex* 00-03; rtd 00. *Flat 2, 16 Westcliffe Road, Birkdale, Southport PR8 2BN* T: (01704) 563346

PHELAN, Thomas Sylvester Patrick. b 36. CQSW 79. Chich Th Coll 72. **d** 94 **p** 95. C Somers Town *Lon* 94-96; C Old St Pancras w Bedford New Town St Matt 96-97; Chapl Camden and Islington Community Health NHS Trust 96-97; OSB 97-09; Lic Preacher *Lon* 97-02; Hon C Nor St Jo w St Julian 02-06; PtO from 06. *7 Chaplain's House, The Great Hospital, Bishopgate, Norwich NR1 4EL* T: (01603) 305522

PHELPS, Canon Arthur Charles. b 26. St Cath Coll Cam BA 50 MA 55. Ridley Hall Cam 51. **d** 53 **p** 54. C Kirkdale St Lawr *Liv* 53-56; C Rainham *Chelmsf* 56-60; Min Collier Row St Jas CD 60-65; V Collier Row St Jas 65-75; R Thorpe Morieux w

Preston and Brettenham *St E* 75-84; R Rattlesden w Thorpe Morieux and Brettenham 84-90; Hon Can St E Cathl 89-90; rtd 90; PtO *Truro* 90-00; *St E* from 01. *8 Northfield Court, Aldeburgh IP15 5LU* T: (01728) 454772

PHELPS, Ian Ronald. b 28. Lon Univ BSc 53 PhD 57 FLS 58. Chich Th Coll 57. **d** 59 **p** 60. C Brighton Gd Shep Preston *Chich* 59-61; C Sullington 62-64; C Storrington 62-64; R Newtimber w Pyecombe 64-68; V Brighton St Luke 68-74; TV Brighton Resurr 74-76; V Peacehaven 76-94; rtd 94; PtO *Chich* from 94. *2 Kingston Green, Seaford BN25 4NB* T: (01323) 899511

PHENNA, Timothy Peter. b 69. Ridley Hall Cam BTh 01. **d** 01 **p** 02. C Woodseats St Chad *Sheff* 01-04; USA from 04. *965 Colorow Road, Golden CO 80401, USA* E: timphenna@yahoo.co.uk

PHILBRICK, Canon Gary James. b 57. Southn Univ BA 78 K Alfred's Coll Win CertEd 79 MA(Theol) 00 Edin Univ BD 86. Edin Th Coll 83. **d** 86 **p** 87. C Southampton Maybush St Pet *Win* 86-90; R Fawley 90-00; P-in-c Swaythling 00-04; V 04-13; AD Southampton 07-13; P-in-c Fordingbridge and Breamore and Hale etc from 13; AD Christchurch from 13; Hon Can Win Cathl from 09. *The Rectory, 71 Church Street, Fordingbridge SP6 1BB* T: (01425) 839622 E: gary.philbrick@dsl.pipex.com

PHILBRICK, Miss Leah Karen. b 79. Gordon Coll Mass BA 01. Ridley Hall Cam 09. **d** 11 **p** 12. C Sutton *S'wark* 11-14; C Bedwellty and New Tredegar *Mon* from 14. *107 Derlwyn Street, Phillipstown, New Tredegar NP24 6BA* M: 07952-640885 T: (01443) 820778 E: l.philbrick@icloud.com

PHILIP, Mathew. b 54. Leeds Univ BSc 77 MSc 78 PhD 83 Surrey Univ 04. STETS 02. **d** 05 **p** 06. NSM Patcham *Chich* from 05. *Hillside Lodge, 76 Redhill Drive, Brighton BN1 5FL* T: (01273) 883726 M: 07760-158043 E: paluvalil@aol.com

PHILIP, Peter Wells. b 35. Ridley Hall Cam 64. **d** 67 **p** 68. C Tollington Park St Mark w St Anne *Lon* 67-70; C Battersea St Pet *S'wark* 70-72; Hon C Kennington St Mark 72-73; V Titirangi New Zealand 74-80; Hon C Blockhouse Bay 80-92; Past Dir Chr Advance Min 80-84; Dir Evang Fellowship of NZ 87-90; C Finchley Ch Ch *Lon* 92-93; V Frankton New Zealand 94-00; rtd 00. *608 Rolleston Street, Thames 3500, New Zealand* T: (0064) (7) 868 5028 E: peterp@xnet.co.nz

PHILIP BARTHOLOMEW, Brother. *See* KENNEDY, Philip Bartholomew

PHILIPPINES, Prime Bishop of the Episcopal Church in the. *See* MALECDAN, The Most Revd Edward Pacyaya

PHILLIP, Isaiah Ezekiel. b 59. Univ of W Indies BA 88. Codrington Coll Barbados 85. **d** 88 **p** 89. C St Jo Cathl Antigua 88-91; R St Geo Dominica 91-96; R All SS Antigua 96-01; P-in-c Handsworth St Mich *Birm* 02-05; V Basseterre St Kitts-Nevis from 05. *St Peter's Rectory, PO Box 702, Basseterre, St Kitts, West Indies* T: (001869) (465) 2774 E: phillipisaiah@hotmail.com

PHILLIPS, Mrs Adele. b 59. Newc Univ LLB 84. NEOC 04. **d** 07 **p** 08. NSM Gateshead *Dur* from 07. *47 Blackstone Court, Blaydon NE21 4HH* T: 0191-414 0955 M: 07752-325736 E: jophillips06@aol.com

PHILLIPS, Andrew Graham. b 58. Ex Univ BSc 79. Chich Th Coll 84. **d** 87 **p** 88. C Frankby w Greasby *Ches* 87-89; C Liv St Chris Norris Green 89-92; CF 92-97; Chapl RN 00-12; rtd 12. *Address temp unknown*

PHILLIPS, Canon Anthony Charles Julian. b 36. Lon Univ BD 63 AKC 63 G&C Coll Cam PhD 67 St Jo Coll Ox MA 75 DPhil 80. Coll of Resurr Mirfield 66. **d** 66 **p** 67. C-in-c Chesterton Gd Shep CD *Ely* 66-69; Dean, Chapl and Fell Trin Hall Cam 69-74; Hon Bp's Chapl *Nor* 70-71; Chapl and Fell St Jo Coll Ox 75-86; Lect Th Jes Coll Ox 75-86; Lect Th Hertf Coll Ox 84-86; Hd Master K Sch Cant 86-96; Hon Can Cant Cathl 87-96; Can Th Truro Cathl 86-02; PtO from 02; rtd 01. *10 St Peter's Road, Flushing, Falmouth TR11 5TP* T: (01326) 377217

PHILLIPS, Mrs Audrey Katherine. b 32. Lorain Coll Ohio BS 73. Ox Min Course 88. **d** 91 **p** 94. NSM Princes Risborough w Ilmer *Ox* 91-94; P Assoc Marco Is St Mark USA 94-98; NSM Akeman *Ox* 98-00; PtO from 08. *1 The Chestnuts, Kirtlington, Kidlington OX5 3UB* T: (01869) 350194

PHILLIPS, Benjamin Guy. b 75. Wycliffe Hall Ox. **d** 02 **p** 03. C Cockermouth w Embleton and Wythop *Carl* 02-05; V Stanwix 05-12; Chapl Rio de Janeiro Ch Ch Brazil from 12. *The Vicarage, rua Real Graneza 99, Botafo GO, Rio de Janeiro, Brazil* E: benphillips@uk2k.com

PHILLIPS, Benjamin Lambert Meyrick. b 64. K Coll Cam BA 86 MA 90. Ridley Hall Cam 87. **d** 90 **p** 91. C Wareham *Sarum* 90-94; C Chipping Barnet w Arkley *St Alb* 94-96; V Bodicote *Ox* 96-12; AD Deddington 05-10; V Towcester w Caldecote and Easton Neston etc *Pet* from 12. *The Vicarage, Chantry Lane, Towcester NN12 6YY* T: (01327) 350459 E: revbenphillips@tiscali.co.uk *or* rector@tovebenefice.co.uk

PHILLIPS, Beryl. *See* PHILLIPS, Elizabeth Beryl

PHILLIPS, Bill. *See* PHILLIPS, Edward Leigh Bill

PHILLIPS, Mrs Brenda. b 41. St Hugh's Coll Ox BA 63 MA 68. **d** 04 **p** 05. OLM Sherborne w Castleton, Lillington and Longburton *Sarum* 04-11; rtd 11; PtO *Sarum* from 11. *Address temp unknown* E: brendaphillips@courthousedairyfarm.freeserve.co.uk

PHILLIPS, Brian Edward Dorian William. b 36. Bris Univ BA 58. Ripon Hall Ox 58. **d** 60 **p** 61. C Ross *Heref* 60-64; Chapl RAF 64-68; Hon C Fringford w Hethe and Newton Purcell *Ox* 68-73; Chapl Howell's Sch Denbigh 73-76; C Cleobury Mortimer w Hopton Wafers *Heref* 76-80; V Dixton 80-02; r-d 02; PtO *Heref* from 02. *37 Duxmere Drive, Ross-on-Wye HR9 5UW* T: (01989) 562993 M: 07712-071558 E: brianphillips@u-genie.co.uk

PHILLIPS, Canon Brian Robert. b 31. Clare Coll Cam BA 53 MA 57. Linc Th Coll 54. **d** 56 **p** 57. C Tuffley *Glouc* 56-59; C Southgate Ch Ch *Lon* 59-62; R Luckington w Alderton *Bris* 62-69; V Highworth w Sevenhampton and Inglesham etc 69-84; Hon Can Bris Cathl 84-90; P-in-c Long Newnton 84-87; P-in-c Crudwell w Ashley 84-87; R Ashley, Crudwell, Hankerton, Long Newnton etc 87-90; rtd 90; PtO *Portsm* from 90; *Win* 90-09. *Hannington, Hospital Road, Shirrell Heath, Southampton SO32 2JR* T: (01329) 834547

PHILLIPS, Mrs Caroline Jill. b 80. Nottm Univ BA 02 Man Univ MA 04. Qu Coll Birm 07. **d** 10 **p** 11. C Ollerton w Boughton *S'well* 10-13; P-in-c Mansfield St Aug 13-15; P-in-c Pleasley Hill 13-15; V Mansfield St Aug and Pleasley Hill from 15. *St Augustine's Vicarage, 46 Abbott Road, Mansfield NG19 6DD* E: revcarolinephillips@gmail.com

PHILLIPS, Christopher Peter. b 82. St Jo Coll Dur BA 00. Ripon Coll Cuddesdon BA 12. **d** 13 **p** 14. C Ilkley St Marg *Leeds* from 13. *9 Hollingwood Park, Ilkley LS29 9NZ* M: 07917-798285 E: frchrisphillips@gmail.com

PHILLIPS, David Arthur. b 36. S Dios Minl Tr Scheme 90. **d** 94 **p** 95. NSM Canford Magna *Sarum* 94-06; rtd 06. *32 Lynwood Drive, Wimborne BH21 1UG* T: (01202) 880262 E: d.phillips581@btinternet.com

PHILLIPS, David Gordon. b 60. Toronto Univ BASc 82. Wycliffe Coll Toronto MDiv 95. **d** 94 **p** 95. R Kawawachikamach Canada 94-99; Exec Adn Prince Albert 99-03; R Petite Riviere and New Dublin 04-09; P-in-c Palermo w Taormina *Eur* 10-13; Chapl Utrecht w Zwolle from 13. *Van Hogendorpstraat 26, 3581 KE Utrecht, The Netherlands* T: (0031) (30) 251 3424 E: revdgphillips@hotmail.com *or* chaplain@holytrinityutrecht.nl

PHILLIPS, David Keith. b 61. New Coll Ox MA 90 St Jo Coll Dur BA 90. Cranmer Hall Dur 88. **d** 91 **p** 92. C Denton Holme *Carl* 91-94; C Chadderton Ch Ch *Man* 94-98; Gen Sec Sec Ch Soc 98-11; Public Preacher *St Alb* 98-11; V Chorley St Jas *Blackb* from 11. *St James's Vicarage, St James's Place, Chorley PR6 0NA* T: (01257) 233714 E: vicar@stjameschorley.org

PHILLIPS, David Thomas. b 47. NEOC 03. **d** 05 **p** 06. NSM Gt and Lt Driffield *York* 05-06; C Elloughton and Brough w Brantingham 06-10; rtd 11; P-in-c Vernet-les-Bains *Eur* from 11. *Lot 22, Cams de Baille, 66360 Olette, France* E: dphill9590@yahoo.co.uk

PHILLIPS, Edward Leigh Bill. b 12. St Edm Hall Ox BA 34 MA 47. Wycliffe Hall Ox 33. **d** 35 **p** 36. Asst Chapl Dean Close Sch Cheltenham 35-37; C Highfield *Ox* 37-38; C-in-c Patcham Chr the K CD *Chich* 39-41; CF (EC) 41-46; R Ide Hill *Roch* 46-49; V Moulsecoomb *Chich* 49-52; V Kingston w Iford 52-75; V Iford w Kingston and Rodmell 75-78; RD Lewes 65-77; rtd 78; PtO *Glouc* from 78. *35 Woodland Green, Upton St Leonards, Gloucester GL4 8BD* T: (01452) 619894

PHILLIPS, Edwin George. b 35. N Wales Baptist Coll 64. **d** 03 **p** 03. NSM Morriston *S & B* 03-08; rtd 09. *146 Lingfield Avenue, Port Talbot SA12 6QA* T: (01639) 886784 M: 07815-969913

PHILLIPS, Mrs Elizabeth Beryl. b 34. **d** 94 **p** 95. C N Farnborough *Guildf* 94-99; rtd 99; PtO *Sarum* from 00. *8 Byron Road, Wimborne BH21 1NX* T: (01202) 883328 E: eberylp@talktalk.net

PHILLIPS, Mrs Emma Catharine. b 62. St Anne's Coll Ox BA 84. Trin Coll Bris BA 99. **d** 99 **p** 00. C Shawbury *Lich* 99-01; C Moreton Corbet 99-01; C Stanton on Hine Heath 99-01; C Cen Telford 01-02; TV 03-07; PtO 07-09; NSM Cen Telford 09-13; Chapl Severn Hospice from 09; PtO *Lich* from 14. *11 Stocking Park Road, Lightmoor, Telford TF4 3QZ* T: (01952) 502878

PHILLIPS, Geoffrey Clarke. b 50. SWMTC 94. **d** 96 **p** 97. NSM Georgeham *Ex* 96-98; Chapl HM YOI Huntercombe and Finnamore 99-00; Chapl HM Pris Shepton Mallet 01-03; Chapl Children's Hospice SW from 07. *Children's Hospice South West, Little Bridge House, Redlands Road, Fremington, Barnstaple EX31 2PZ* T: (01271) 325270

PHILLIPS, Ms Gillian. b 44. EMMTC 07. **d** 10 **p** 12. NSM Old Brampton and Great Barlow and Loundsley Green *Derby* 10-11; NSM Wrockwardine Deanery *Lich* from 12. *78 Lawley Gate, Telford TF4 2NZ* T: (01952) 506038

PHILLIPS, Graham Donald. b 57. Magd Coll Cam BA 79 MA 83 Goldsmiths' Coll Lon PGCE 90. Qu Coll Birm 08. **d** 12 **p** 13. C Madeley *Heref* from 12. *11 Stocking Park Road, Lightmoor, Telford TF4 3QZ* T: (01952) 502878

PHILLIPS, Ivor Lyn. b 44. Leeds Univ BA 70. Cuddesdon Coll 69. **d** 71 **p** 72. C Bedlinog *Llan* 71-73; C Roath 73-77; TV Wolverhampton All SS *Lich* 77-78; TV Wolverhampton 78-81; Chapl Charing Cross Hosp Lon 81-91; Chapl Milan w Genoa and Lugano *Eur* 91-94; C Hampstead St Jo *Lon* 95-00; V Whitton St Aug 00-09; rtd 09; PtO *S'wark* from 10. *10 Northumberland Avenue, Berwick-upon-Tweed TD15 1JZ* T: (01289) 305075 E: i.lyn@virgin.net

PHILLIPS, Mrs Janet Elizabeth. b 37. Bp Grosseteste Coll CertEd 57. EMMTC 81. **dss** 84 **d** 87 **p** 94. Wisbech St Aug *Ely* 84-86; Cambridge St Jas 86-91; Par Dn 87-91; Par Dn Wisbech SS Pet and Paul 91-94; C 94-02; rtd 02; Hon C Elm and Friday Bridge w Coldham *Ely* 03-07; Hon C Leverington, Newton and Tydd St Giles 07-10; PtO from 10. *41 Mountbatten Drive, Leverington, Wisbech PE13 5AF* T: (01945) 589034

PHILLIPS, Jason Paul. b 73. Man Metrop Univ BA 95 CertEd 95 PhD 05 Ox Brookes Univ MA 09 FCollT 09. Ripon Coll Cuddesdon 07. **d** 09 **p** 10. C Mid Trent *Lich* 09-14; C Stafford St Mary and Marston 14-15; C Blakenall Heath from 15; Dioc Voc Adv from 15. *St Basil's House, 20 Sandalwood Drive, Stafford ST16 3FX* E: revdjason@fastmail.co.uk

PHILLIPS (née LANGLEY), Mrs Jean. b 52. St Mary's Coll Chelt CertEd 73. WEMTC 03. **d** 06 **p** 07. NSM Bishop's Cleeve *Glouc* 06-08; NSM Bishop's Cleeve and Woolstone w Gotherington etc 08-13; rtd 13. *3 St Nicholas Drive, Cheltenham GL50 4RY* T: (01242) 673612

PHILLIPS, Jeffery Llewellyn. b 32. Sarum & Wells Th Coll. **d** 87 **p** 88. C Ringwood *Win* 87-90; V Somborne w Ashley 90-93; rtd 93; PtO *Win* 93-12. *Queen's Acre, 3 Solent Avenue, Lymington SO41 3AH* T: (01590) 673955

PHILLIPS, Mrs Jennifer Jean. b 36. Guildf Dioc Min Course 98. **d** 01 **p** 02. OLM New Haw *Guildf* 01-07; PtO from 07. *20 Lindsay Road, New Haw, Addlestone KT15 3BD* T: (01932) 429689 E: jennifer.phillips73@ntlworld.com

PHILLIPS, John. b 50. ACIB 74. NOC 01. **d** 04. NSM Wavertree H Trin *Liv* from 04. *12 Montclair Drive, Liverpool L18 0HA* T: 0151-722 2542 E: jpipps@hotmail.com

PHILLIPS, John David. b 29. G&C Coll Cam BA 50 MA 54 CertEd 69. SWMTC 85. **d** 87 **p** 88. NSM St Martin w E and W Looe *Truro* 87-88; NSM St Merryn 88-94; rtd 94; PtO *Truro* from 94. *Restings, Plaidy, Looe PL13 1LF* T: (01503) 262121

PHILLIPS, John Eldon. b 50. Univ of Wales (Cardiff) BEd 85 MEd 92. St Mich Coll Llan. **d** 90 **p** 91. NSM Merthyr Cynog and Dyffryn Honddu etc *S & B* 90-94; LtO *St D* 94-99; NSM Ystradgynlais *S & B* 95-99; Chapl Trin Coll Carmarthen 95-99; P-in-c Llanrhidian w Llanmadoc and Cheriton *S & B* 99-05; Dioc Press Officer from 02; NSM Burry Port and Pwll *St D* 07-15. *2 Gerddi Glasfryn, Llanelli SA15 3LL* T: (01554) 744770 E: reveldon@btinternet.com

PHILLIPS, Jonathan Richard. b 79. Liv Univ BA 01 Cam Univ BTh 13. Ridley Hall Cam 10. **d** 13 **p** 14. C Lache cum Saltney *Ches* from 13. *84 Ermine Road, Chester CH2 3PW* M: 07813-709035 E: jonathanrichardphillips@gmail.com

PHILLIPS, Judith Mary. b 46. Reading Univ BA 67 Cardiff Coll of Educn PGCE 86. St Mich Coll Llan 93. **d** 95 **p** 97. Lect Neath Coll 84-00; NSM Clydach *S & B* 95-00; Dep Chapl HM Pris Bris 00-01; Chapl HM Pris Eastwood Park 01-12; rtd 12. *Gwalia, Felindre, Swansea SA5 7PQ* T: (01792) 772523

PHILLIPS, Canon Kenneth John. b 37. Coll of Resurr Mirfield 67. **d** 67 **p** 68. C Blackb St Jas 67-69; C-in-c Lea CD 70-80; V Lea 80-84; P-in-c Priors Hardwick, Priors Marston and Wormleighton *Cov* 85-02; Sec Dioc Adv Cttee 85-99; RD Southam *Cov* 89-95; Hon Can Cov Cathl 94-02; Dioc Rural Chs Officer 00-02; rtd 02; Hon C Gisburn *Bradf* 02-07; Hon C Hellifield 02-07; PtO *Leeds* from 07. *7 Temperance Square, Hellifield, Skipton BD23 4LG* T: (01729) 850340 E: kcanonic@aol.com

PHILLIPS, Lamont Wellington Sanderson. b 33. S'wark Ord Course 73. **d** 76 **p** 78. NSM Tottenham St Paul *Lon* 76-83; P-in-c Upper Clapton St Matt 83-88; V 88-97; rtd 98. *24 Berkshire Gardens, London N18 2LF* T: (020) 8807 7025

PHILLIPS, Mrs Lena. b 61. STETS 12. **d** 15. NSM Shirley *Win* from 15. *11 Clifton Road, Southampton SO15 4GU* T: (023) 8077 4307 E: lena@shirleyparishchurch.org

PHILLIPS, Lynn. *See* PHILLIPS, Ivor Lyn

PHILLIPS, Mark. b 66. STETS 10. **d** 13 **p** 14. C Portland *Sarum* from 13. *12 Fancys Close, Portland DT5 2AJ* T: (01305) 824130 E: thephillips6466@btinternet.com

PHILLIPS, Canon Martin Nicholas. b 32. Em Coll Cam BA 57 MA 61. Linc Th Coll 57. **d** 59 **p** 60. C Stocking Farm CD *Leic* 59-63; V Sheff Gillcar St Silas 63-71; V Birstall *Leic* 72-82; R Wanlip 72-82; V Birstall and Wanlip 82-88; TR Loughborough Em and St Mary in Charnwood 88-96; Hon Can Leic Cathl 90-96; rtd 96; PtO *Leic* from 96. *Foxhollow, 40A Lodge Close, Barrow upon Soar, Loughborough LE12 8ZL* T: (01509) 416361

PHILLIPS, Mary Alice. b 53. Ripon Coll Cuddesdon 97. **d** 99 **p** 00. C Addiscombe St Mildred *S'wark* 99-02; TV Basingstoke *Win* 02-12; rtd 13. *215 Paddock Road, Basingstoke RG22 6QP* E: map13@tinyworld.co.uk

PHILLIPS, Michael John. b 54. JP . Trent Poly BA 77. Sarum & Wells Th Coll 78. **d** 81 **p** 82. C Killay *S & B* 81-83; C Treboeth 83-85; Hong Kong 85-88; Japan 88-91; TR Is of Scilly *Truro* 91-95; TR Cwmbran *Mon* from 95; AD Pontypool from 12. *The Rectory, Clomendy Road, Cwmbran NP44 3LS* T: (01633) 489718 E: mj-phillips1@hotmail.com

PHILLIPS, Michael John Anselm. b 77. Leeds Univ BA 02. Coll of Resurr Mirfield 99. **d** 02 **p** 03. C Cudworth and Lundwood *Wakef* 02-03; C Castleford 03-06; In RC Ch 06-09; C Hanging Heaton and Batley St Thos *Leeds* 10-14. *Address temp unknown* M: 07970-821438 E: carpentermja@hotmail.com

PHILLIPS, Michael Thomas. b 46. CQSW 81. Linc Th Coll 89. **d** 90 **p** 91. C Hyson Green *S'well* 90-91; C Basford w Hyson Green 91-93; Chapl HM Pris Gartree 93-99; Chapl HM Pris Nottm 99-08; rtd 08; Hon C Radford All So and St Pet *S'well* from 08. *12 Edgbaston Gardens, Aspley, Nottingham NG8 5AY* T: 0115-929 7029 E: bigviola@hotmail.com

PHILLIPS, Mrs Patricia. b 45. Glouc Sch of Min 83. **dss** 86 **d** 87 **p** 94. Newent and Gorsley w Cliffords Mesne *Glouc* 86-95; C 87-95; P-in-c Childswyckham w Aston Somerville, Buckland etc 95-97; R 97-00; R Redmarley D'Abitot, Bromesberrow, Pauntley etc 00-10; rtd 10. *5 Freemans Orchard, Newent GL18 1TX* T: (01531) 828444 E: revpp@tesco.net

PHILLIPS, Miss Pauline. b 54. **d** 96 **p** 97. OLM Mossley *Man* from 96. *32 Mountain Street, Mossley, Ashton-under-Lyne OL5 0EZ* T: (01457) 832363

PHILLIPS, Peter. b 26. Oak Hill Th Coll 63. **d** 65 **p** 66. C Eastbourne All SS *Chich* 65-69; C St Alb St Paul *St Alb* 69-73; V Riseley w Bletsoe 73-84; R Arley *Cov* 84-91; rtd 91; PtO *B & W* 91-04; Clergy Retirement and Widows' Officer 99-04; PtO *Guildf* from 09. *1 Manormead, Tilford Road, Hindhead GU26 6RA* T: (01428) 601501

PHILLIPS, Peter Miles Lucas. b 44. Reading Univ BA 66 QUB DipEd 69 Univ of Wales (Cardiff) MEd 88 Bris Univ MA 07 Cardiff Univ PhD 14. St Mich Coll Llan 90. **d** 92 **p** 93. Dep Hd Teacher Dynevor Sch 82-96; NSM Llangyfelach *S & B* 92-96; Dep Chapl HM Pris Liv 96-97; Chapl HM Pris Usk and Prescoed 97-01; Chapl HM Pris Bris 01-04; rtd 04; PtO *Bris* from 04; Chapl Wesley Coll Bris 08-11. *Gwalia, Felindre, Swansea SA5 7PQ* T: (01792) 772523 E: revdpeterphillips@yahoo.co.uk

PHILLIPS, Ms Rachel Susan. b 64. Newnham Coll Cam BA 86 MA 90 Nottm Univ MPhil 11 Solicitor 89. St Jo Coll Nottm 04. **d** 07 **p** 08. C Eastcote St Lawr *Lon* 07-10; P-in-c Northaw and Cuffley *St Alb* 10-13; V from 13; RD Cheshunt from 12. *Northaw Vicarage, 58 Hill Rise, Cuffley, Potters Bar EN6 4RG* T: (01707) 874126 E: revrachelphillips@gmail.com

PHILLIPS, Rebecca Jane. *See* ROGERS, Rebecca Jane

PHILLIPS, Richard Matthew. b 76. St Cath Coll Cam BA 98 MA 02. Ripon Coll Cuddesdon 11. **d** 13 **p** 14. C Walton H Trin *Ox* from 13. *1A Limes Avenue, Aylesbury HP21 7HA* M: 07541-197220 E: richard.m.phillips@hotmail.co.uk

PHILLIPS, Richard Paul. b 76. Man Univ BA 08. Trin Coll Bris 09. **d** 11 **p** 12. C Kingston upon Hull St Aid Southcoates *York* 11-14; V from 14. *St Aidan's Vicarage, 139 Southcoates Avenue, Hull HU9 3HF* M: 07944-541968 E: rich.phillips76@gmail.com

PHILLIPS, Robin Michael. b 33. AKC 58. **d** 59 **p** 60. C Hanwell St Mellitus *Lon* 59-61; C St Margaret's-on-Thames 61-64; C Hangleton *Chich* 64-68; V Mellor *Derby* 68-95; RD Glossop 89-93; rtd 95; Hon C Bridekirk *Carl* 95-96. *27 Calgarth Park, Troutbeck Bridge, Windermere LA23 1LF* T: (015394) 88841 E: robinphillips88@hotmail.com

PHILLIPS, Mrs Sandra Georgina. b 49. STETS 01. **d** 04 **p** 05. NSM Portsdown *Portsm* from 04. *14 Forest End, Waterlooville PO7 7AB* T: (023) 9226 7740 M: 07778-921624

PHILLIPS, Thomas Wynford. b 15. Univ of Wales BA 37 BD 40. St Mich Coll Llan. **d** 43 **p** 44. C Shotton *St As* 43-46; C Rhyl 46-50; C Hall Green Ascension *Birm* 50-52; R Shustoke 52-55; P-in-c Maxstoke 52-55; V Clay Cross *Derby* 55-68; R Upton Magna *Lich* 68-73; V Withington 68-73; R Roche *Truro* 73-80;

R Withiel 73-80; RD St Austell 76-80; rtd 80; PtO *Truro* from 80. *Brynawelon, Wheal Quoit Avenue, St Agnes TR5 0SJ* T: (01872) 552862

PHILLIPS, Timothy Leo. b 72. Bris Univ BSc 95 PhD 99. Trin Coll Bris BA 01 MA 02. **d** 02 **p** 03. C Leic H Trin w St Jo 02-05; TV Ashby-de-la-Zouch and Breedon on the Hill from 05. *Holy Trinity Vicarage, 1 Trinity Close, Ashby-de-la-Zouch LE65 2GQ* T: (01530) 412339

PHILLIPS, Wayne. b 45. **d** 10 **p** 11. NSM Pontefract All SS *Leeds* from 10. *16 Maple Walk, Knottingley WF11 0PU* T: (01977) 678024 E: wayne.phillips16@btinternet.com

PHILLIPS-LAST, Martin. b 68. **d** 10 **p** 11. C Beccles St Mich and St Luke *St E* 10-14; P-in-c Leiston from 14. *The Vicarage, Church Road, Leiston IP16 4HG* M: 07746-278390 E: rev.phillips-last@sky.com

PHILLIPS-SMITH, Edward Charles. b 50. AKC 71. **d** 73 **p** 74. C Wolverhampton *Lich* 73-76; Chapl St Pet Colleg Sch Wolv 77-87; Hon C Wolverhampton *Lich* 78-87; V Stevenage St Pet Broadwater *St Alb* 87-89; Chapl Millfield Jun Sch Somerset 89-95; Chapl Papplewick Sch 95-08; rtd 08. *5 Hampton Drive, Kings Sutton, Banbury OX17 3QR* T: (01295) 811220 E: email@ecp-s.eclipse.co.uk

PHILLIPSON (née MACKAY), Alison. b 62. Teesside Univ BA 00. NEOC 01. **d** 04 **p** 05. C Stokesley w Seamer *York* 04-08; P-in-c Cosby *Leic* 08-09; P-in-c Whetstone 08-09; V Coatham and Dormanstown *York* 09-14; R Guisborough from 14. *The Rectory, Church Street, Guisborough TS14 6BS* E: alisonphillipson@aol.com

PHILLIPSON-MASTERS, Miss Susan Patricia. b 52. Sussex Univ CertEd 73 K Alfred's Coll Win BEd 81 Leeds Univ MA 04 Glos Univ MA 09 FIST 76 ACP 80. Trin Coll Bris 86. **d** 89 **p** 95. C Saltford w Corston and Newton St Loe *B & W* 89-94; C Uphill 94-97; C Nailsea Ch Ch w Tickenham 97-98; P-in-c Tredington and Darlingscott w Newbold on Stour *Cov* 98-00; P-in-c The Stanleys *Glouc* 00-11; Chapl Wycliffe Prep Sch 07-11; rtd 11. *Recsretreat, 1 Oakleaze Road, Thornbury, Bristol BS35 2LG* E: sue.pm112@btinternet.com

PHILLPOT, Donald John. b 27. St Jo Coll Dur BA 53. **d** 55 **p** 56. C Southmead *Bris* 55-60; C Brislington St Luke 60-63; R Stapleton *Heref* 63-68; V Dorrington 63-68; P-in-c Astley Abbotts 68-78; R Bridgnorth w Tasley 68-78; V Lillington *Cov* 78-92; rtd 92; PtO *Glouc* from 92. *22 Williams Orchard, Highnam, Gloucester GL2 8EL* T: (01452) 386844

PHILP (née NOBLE), Canon Ann Carol. b 42. Sarum Dioc Tr Coll CertEd 63 Southn Univ MA(Ed) 89 MCIPD. S Dios Minl Tr Scheme 93. **d** 95 **p** 96. Dir Sarum Chr Cen 93-98; Chapl Sarum Cathl 95-02; Dioc NSM Officer 98-02; P-in-c Woodford Valley w Archers Gate 02-12; Dioc Dir of Ords 02-07; Bp's Dom Chapl 07-12; Can and Preb Sarum Cathl 05-12; rtd 12. *55 The Close, Salisbury SP1 2EL* T: (01722) 555178 E: acphilp55@virginmedia.com

PHILPOTT, Canon John David. b 43. Leic Univ BA 64. Trin Coll Bris 68. **d** 72 **p** 73. C Knutsford St Jo and Toft *Ches* 72-75; C Bickenhill w Elmdon *Birm* 75-79; V Birm St Luke 79-91; RD Birm City 83-88; Hon Can Birm Cathl 89-91; V Chilvers Coton w Astley *Cov* 91-00; RD Nuneaton 95-00; Hon Can Cov Cathl 96-00; Prague *Eur* 00-08; P-in-c from 08. *2 Portland Court, 1 Portland Avenue, Exmouth EX8 2DJ* T: (01395) 225044 E: jamphilpott@yahoo.com

PHILPOTT, John Wilfred. b 44. K Coll Lon BD 67 AKC 67. **d** 68 **p** 69. C Norbury St Steph *Cant* 68-71; C Addiscombe St Mildred 71-75; V Whitfield w Guston 75-01; rtd 02; PtO *Cant* from 02. *9 Mannering Close, River, Dover CT17 0UD* T: (01304) 825875

PHILPOTT, Jonathan Mark. b 76. Chelt & Glouc Coll of HE BA 98. Trin Coll Bris BA 06 MA 10. **d** 07 **p** 08. C Lydney *Glouc* 07-10; P-in-c By Brook *Bris* from 10; P-in-c Colerne w N Wraxall 10-11; C from 11. *By Brook Rectory, 3 Church Farm, Yatton Keynell, Chippenham SN14 7FD* T: (01249) 782663 E: philpott.jonathan@gmail.com *or* bybrook.rectory@gmail.com

PHILPOTT, Ronald. b 38. IPFA 69. Cranmer Hall Dur 88. **d** 89 **p** 90. NSM S Ossett *Wakef* 89-93; R Clitheroe St Jas *Blackb* 93-03; rtd 03; PtO *York* from 03. *8 Headland Close, Haxby, York YO32 3HW* T: (01904) 758697

PHILPOTT, Preb Samuel. b 41. MBE 12. Kelham Th Coll 60. **d** 65 **p** 66. C Swindon New Town *Bris* 65-70; C Torquay St Martin Barton *Ex* 70-73; TV Withycombe Raleigh 73-76; V Shaldon 76-78; P-in-c Plymouth St Pet 78-80; V 80-09; RD Plymouth Devonport 86-93 and 95-01; Preb Ex Cathl 91-09; rtd 09; P-in-c Plymouth St Pet and H Apostles *Ex* 09-13. *21 Plaistow Crescent, Plymouth PL5 2EA* T: (01752) 298502 E: frphilpott@aol.com

PHILPOTT-HOWARD, John Nigel. b 54. Univ of Wales Coll of Medicine MB, BCh 77 FRCPath 83. SEITE 99. **d** 02 **p** 03. NSM Shooters Hill Ch Ch *S'wark* 02-11; PtO 11-15; NSM E

Greenwich from 15. *80 Charlton Road, London SE7 7EY* T: (020) 8858 4692 E: john.philpotth@kcl.ac.uk

PHILPS, Mark Seymour. b 51. Worc Coll Ox BA 73 MA 78 Lon Univ MA 75 Nottm Univ BA 79. St Jo Coll Nottm 77. **d** 80 **p** 81. C Chadwell Heath *Chelmsf* 80-83; C Woodford Wells 83-87; V Tipton St Matt *Lich* 87-02; TV Roxeth *Lon* 02-03; TR 03-11; V 11-15; rtd 15. *1 White Horse Road, Marlborough SN8 2FE* E: mark.philps@roxethteam.org

PHILSON, James Alexander Summers (Hamish). b 20. Edin Th Coll 48. **d** 51 **p** 52. C Falkirk *Edin* 51-53; R Dunblane *St And* 53-62; R Beverley Australia 62-64; R Victoria Park 64-75; R Cottesloe 75-85; rtd 85. *38 Allenswood Road, Greenwood WA 6024, Australia* T: (0061) (8) 9447 9523 M: 0416-001620 E: jasp@smartchat.net.au

PHIPPS, David John. b 46. Bris Univ BSc 68 Ex Univ PhD 94 Nottm Univ PGCE 69. Trin Coll Bris 75. **d** 78 **p** 79. C Madron w Morvah *Truro* 78-80; C Heanstown w St Jo *Cov* 80-83; TV Barnstaple *Ex* 83-95; I Abercraf w Callwen w Capel Coelbren *S & B* 95-02; P-in-c Gulval and Madron *Truro* 02-05; rtd 05. *11 Walton Way, Barnstaple EX32 8AE* T: (01271) 349746 E: phippsdv@dialstart.net

PHIPPS, Mathew Jamie David. b 76. ERMC 13. **d** 15. C Madrid *Eur* from 15. *Address temp unknown*

PHIZACKERLEY, The Ven Gerald Robert. b 29. Univ Coll Ox BA 52 MA 56. Wells Th Coll 52. **d** 54 **p** 55. C Carl St Barn 54-57; Chapl Abingdon Sch 57-64; R Gaywood, Bawsey and Mintlyn *Nor* 64-78; RD Lynn 68-78; Hon Can Nor Cathl 75-78; Adn Chesterfield 78-96; rtd 96; PtO *Derby* from 96; *Cov* from 96. *Archway Cottage, Hall Road, Leamington Spa CV32 5RA* T: (01926) 332740 E: phizleam@yahoo.co.uk

PHOEBE, Sister. *See* HANMER, Phoebe Margaret

PHYPERS, David John. b 39. Leic Univ BA 60 CertEd 61 Lon Univ BD 65. Linc Th Coll 76. **d** 78 **p** 79. NSM Normanton *Derby* 78-80; NSM Sinfin 80-87; LtO 87-88; P-in-c Denby and Horsley Woodhouse 88-00; P-in-c Wormhill, Peak Forest w Peak Dale and Dove Holes 00-07; Adv for Chr Giving 00-07; rtd 07; PtO *Derby* from 07. *15 Albert Road, Chaddesden, Derby DE21 6SL* T: (01332) 239134 E: david@phypers.co.uk

PICK, David. b 44. Linc Th Coll 85. **d** 87 **p** 88. C Howden *York* 87-90; P-in-c Sledmere and Cowlam w Fridaythorpe, Fimer etc 90-91; V 91-96; rtd 96; PtO *York* from 96. *Westwood Close, 16 North Street, Nafferton, Driffield YO25 4JW* T: (01377) 240360

PICKARD, Canon Frank Eustace. b 31. Lon Univ BScEcon 52 St Cath Soc Ox BA 56 MA 63. St Steph Ho Ox. **d** 57 **p** 58. C Haydock St Jas *Liv* 57-59; C Davenham *Ches* 59-60; Asst Master St Dunstan's Sch Lon 60-63; Min Can Pet Cathl 63-72; P-in-c Newborough 67-68; V 68-72; R Isham w Pytchley 72-76; R Abington 76-96; Can Pet Cathl 86-02; rtd 96; P-in-c Wappenham w Weedon Lois w Plumpton and Moreton Pinkney etc *Pet* 96-02; PtO from 02. *19 Watersmeet, Northampton NN1 5SQ* T: (01604) 239667 E: margaret.pickard1@btinternet.com

PICKARD, Mrs Patricia Anne. b 44. **d** 04 **p** 05. NSM Ovenden *Leeds* from 04. *Address temp unknown* E: patricia-anne.pickard@sky.com

✠**PICKARD, The Rt Revd Stephen Kim.** b 52. Newc Univ Aus BCom 74 Van Mildert Coll Dur PhD 90. Melbourne Coll of Div BD 79 St Jo Coll Morpeth 77. **d** 80 **p** 80 **c** 07. C Singleton Australia 80-82; C Dur St Cuth 82-84; Chapl Van Mildert Coll Dur 84-90; Chapl Trev Coll Dur 84-90; Lect United Th Coll Sydney Australia 91-97; Dir St Mark's Nat Th Cen 98-06; Assoc Prof and Hd Th Chas Sturt Univ 99-06; Asst Bp Adelaide 07-10; Adn The Port Australia 07-09; Visiting Fell Ripon Coll Cuddesdon 10-11; Dir Ox Cen for Ecclesiology and Practical Th 10-11; Six Preacher Cant Cathl 11-12; Chief Exec Anglicare NSW Australia from 12. *Anglicare, PO Box 427, Parramatta NSW 2124, Australia* T: (0061) (2) 9895 8000 F: 9633 4620 E: s.k.pickard@gmail.com

PICKEN, The Ven David Anthony. b 63. Lon Univ BA 84 Kent Univ PGCE 85 Nottm Univ MA 96. Linc Th Coll 87. **d** 90 **p** 91. C Worth *Chich* 90-93; TV Wordsley *Worc* 93-97; TR 97-04; RD Kingswinford 01-04; TR High Wycombe *Ox* 04-12; AD Wycombe 07-11; Hon Can Ch 11-12; Adn Newark *S'well* from 12. *22 Rufford Road, Edwinstowe, Mansfield NG21 9HY* T: (01623) 238957 E: archdeacon-newark@southwell.anglican.org

PICKEN, James Hugh. b 51. Victoria Univ (BC) BMus 75 ARCT 73. Ripon Coll Cuddesdon BA 79 MA 94. **d** 80 **p** 81. C Jarrow *Dur* 80-83; SSF 83-93; PtO *Sarum* 86-92; Guardian Alnmouth Friary 92-94; LtO *Newc* 92-94; Canada from 94. *929 4th Street NW, Calgary AB T2N 1P4, Canada* T: (001) (403) 270 9661

PICKERING, David Arthur Ashley. b 67. G&C Coll Cam BA 89. Wycliffe Hall Ox BTh 06. **d** 06 **p** 07. C Hornchurch H Cross

Chelmsf 06-09; P-in-c Fyfield w Tubney and Kingston Bagpuize *Ox* from 09. *1 Oxford Road, Kingston Bagpuize, Abingdon OX13 5FZ* T: (01865) 820451 E: vicar.kbsft@gmail.com

PICKERING, Canon David Colville. b 41. Kelham Th Coll 61. **d** 66 **p** 67. C Chaddesden St Phil *Derby* 66-70; C New Mills 70-72; C Buxton 72-74; V Chesterfield SS Aug 74-90; R Whittington 90-99; P-in-c Hathersage 99; P-in-c Bamford 99; R Hathersage w Bamford and Derwent 00-06; Hon Can Derby Cathl 05-06; rtd 06; PtO *Derby* from 06. *Les Chênes Verts, Chemin de St Laurent, Le Rang, 84750 Viens, France* T: (0033) 4 90 74 68 55 M: 6 33 84 95 86
E: pickport@gmail.com

PICKERING, Geoffrey Craig. b 40. Leic Univ CertEd 62. S Dios Minl Tr Scheme 90. **d** 93 **p** 94. C Horsham *Chich* 93-97; V Heathfield 97-08; rtd 08. *3 Bedlam Green, West End, Hertsmonceux, Hailsham BN27 4NW* T: (01323) 833325
E: pickeringgeoff@aol.com

PICKERING, John Alexander. b 41. TCD BA 63 MA 66. CITC 65. **d** 65 **p** 66. C Magheralin *D & D* 65-67; C-in-c Outeragh *K, E & A* 67-68; I 68-71; Deputation Sec Hibernian Bible Soc 71-74; C-in-c Drumgoon w Dernakesh, Ashfield etc *K, E & A* 74-80; I Keady w Armaghbreague and Derrynoose *Arm* 80-83; I Drumcree 83-07; rtd 07. *25 Twinem Court, Portadown, Craigavon BT63 5FH* M: 07752-339558

PICKERING, John David. b 38. **d** 86 **p** 86. NSM Ellon *Ab* 86-88; NSM Cruden Bay 86-88; Ind Chapl *Dur* 88-97; TV Jarrow 91-97; P-in-c Newton Hall 97-02; TV Dur N 02-03; rtd 03. *14 Denholm Avenue, Cramlington NE23 3FT* T: (01670) 716619

PICKERING, John Michael Staunton. b 34. Sarum & Wells Th Coll 71. **d** 72 **p** 73. C Gaywood, Bawsey and Mintlyn *Nor* 72-77; P-in-c Foulsham 77-81; R Foulsham w Hindolveston and Guestwick 81-88; P-in-c Bacton w Edingthorpe w Witton and Ridlington 88-98; rtd 98; PtO *Nor* from 04. *The Brambles, School Lane, Neatishead, Norwich NR12 8XH* T: (01692) 630818

PICKERING, Malcolm. b 37. Sarum Th Coll 65. **d** 68 **p** 69. C Milton *Portsm* 68-70; C Stanmer w Falmer and Moulsecoomb *Chich* 70-75; Chapl Brighton Coll of Educn 71-75; V Hooe and R Ninfield *Chich* 75-80; V Ventnor H Trin and Ventnor St Cath *Portsm* 80-88; Chapl St Cath Sch Ventnor 87-88; V Marton *Blackb* 88-97; P-in-c Badingham w Bruisyard, Cransford and Dennington *St E* 97-99; V Leiston 99-04; rtd 04; PtO *B & W* 04-07; Hon C Drybrook, Lydbrook and Ruardean *Glouc* 07-08. *51 Lydd Road, Camber, Rye TN31 7RJ* T: (01797) 458516 E: malpic@talktalk.net

PICKERING, Mark Penrhyn. b 36. Liv Univ BA 59 St Cath Coll *Ox* BA 62 MA 67. Wycliffe Hall Ox 60. **d** 63 **p** 64. C Claughton cum Grange *Ches* 63-67; C Newland St Jo *York* 67-72; TV Marfleet 72-76; V Kingston upon Hull St Nic 76-85; V Elloughton and Brough w Brantingham 85-88; Chapl R Hull Hosps NHS Trust 88-99; Chapl Hull and E Yorks Hosps NHS Trust 99-01; PtO *York* from 01. *43 Lowerdale, Elloughton, Brough HU15 1SD* T: (01482) 662102

PICKERING, Mrs Maureen Anne. b 46. Man Univ CertEd 67 Open Univ BA 88 MA 93 Leeds Univ MA 07. NOC 04. **d** 07 **p** 08. NSM Ches St Mary 07-15; PtO from 15. *Curzon Cottage, 2A Curzon Park South, Chester CH4 8AB* T: (01244) 677352 M: 07966-409404 E: mapickering@btinternet.com

PICKERING, Michael. *See* PICKERING, John Michael Staunton

PICKERING, William Stuart Frederick. b 22. K Coll Lon BD 49 AKC 49 PhD 58 Manitoba Univ Hon DCL 81. **d** 50 **p** 51. C Frodingham *Linc* 50-53; LtO *Guildf* 55-56; *Linc* 55-56; Tutor K Coll Lon 53-56; Canada 58-66; LtO *Newc* 66-87; rtd 87; PtO *Ely* 87-97 and from 03. *1 Brookfield Road, Coton, Cambridge CB23 7PT* T: (01954) 210525 E: cepickering@gmail.com

PICKERSGILL, James Richard. b 74. Brunel Univ BA 96. Trin Coll Bris 11. **d** 13 **p** 14. C Winchcombe *Glouc* from 13. *22 Delavale Road, Winchcombe, Cheltenham GL54 5HN* T: (01242) 604847 E: james@winchcombeparish.org.uk

PICKETT, Brian Laurence. b 48. Reading Univ BA 70 Qu Coll Birm BA 73 MA 77. Ripon Coll Cuddesdon. **d** 88 **p** 88. C Highcliffe w Hinton Admiral *Win* 88-91; P-in-c Colbury 91-01; P-in-c W End 01-04; V 04-12; rtd 12; PtO *Win* from 12. *6 Woodlands Gardens, Romsey SO51 7TE* T: (01794) 523463

PICKETT, David. b 65. MBE 99. Leeds Univ BA 11. Coll of Resurr Mirfield 09. **d** 11 **p** 12. C Edenham w Witham on the Hill and Swinstead *Linc* 11-14; R Guiseley w Esholt *Leeds* from 14. *The Rectory, The Green, Guiseley, Leeds LS20 9BB* T: (01943) 874321 M: 07916-825465 E: daipickett@hotmail.co.uk

PICKETT, Ms Joanna Elizabeth. b 53. Leic Univ BA 74 MA 80 Lon Univ MTh 95. Wycliffe Hall Ox 87. **d** 89 **p** 94. Chapl Southn Univ *Win* 89-94; C N Stoneham 94-95; NSM Colbury 97-01; NSM W End 01-12; PtO from 12. *6 Woodlands Gardens, Romsey SO51 7TE* T: (01794) 523463

PICKETT, Mark William Leslie. b 60. Westhill Coll Birm BEd 84. Trin Coll Bris 93. **d** 95 **p** 96. C Hellesdon *Nor* 95-98; TV

Thetford 98-03; R Clitheroe St Jas *Blackb* from 03; P-in-c Clitheroe St Paul Low Moor from 15. *The Rectory, Woone Lane, Clitheroe BB7 1BJ* T: (01200) 423608
E: rector@stjamesclitheroe.co.uk

PICKETT, Peter Leslie. b 28. Guy's Hosp Medical Sch LDS 52. S Dios Minl Tr Scheme 83. **d** 86 **p** 87. NSM Eastbourne H Trin *Chich* 86-88; P-in-c Danehill 88-93; rtd 93; PtO *Chich* from 93. *Springfield, 76 Meads Road, Eastbourne BN20 7QJ* T: (01323) 731709 M: 07733-090957
E: pjpickett@btinternet.com

PICKFORD (née PACKER), Mrs Catherine Ruth. b 76. Nottm Univ BA 97 Anglia Poly Univ MA 00. Westcott Ho Cam MA 00. **d** 00 **p** 01. C Gosforth All SS *Newc* 00-04; TV Benwell 04-09; TR 09-15; TR Benwell and Scotswood 15; P-in-c Stannington from 15; Dioc CMD Officer from 15. *The Vicarage, Stannington, Morpeth NE61 6HL* T: (01670) 789025 E: catherine_pickford@yahoo.co.uk

PICKLES, Christopher James. b 85. Huddersfield Univ BA 07. Ripon Coll Cuddesdon BTh 12. **d** 12 **p** 13. C Cant St Pet w St Alphege and St Marg etc 12-15; C Cant St Dunstan w H Cross 12-15. *Address temp unknown*

PICKLES (née BALDWIN), Mrs Julia Clare. b 81. St Chad's Coll Dur BA 02 Darw Coll Cam PGCE 05. Ripon Coll Cuddesdon BA 09. **d** 10 **p** 11. C Bridge *Cant* 10-13; Chapl to Bp Dover from 13; Abp's Chapl from 13. *The Bishop of Dover's Office, The Old Palace, The Precincts, Canterbury CT1 2EE* T: (01227) 459382 E: julia.pickles@bishcant.org

PICKLES, Mark Andrew. b 62. Edin Univ BA 83. Cranmer Hall Dur 85. **d** 88 **p** 89. C Rock Ferry *Ches* 88-91; C Hartford 91-93; V Wharton 93-00; P-in-c Duffield *Derby* 00-05; V Duffield and Lt Eaton 05-14; Dir Angl Tr Oak Hill Th Coll from 14; Hon C Oakwood St Thos *Lon* from 15. *Oak Hill College, Chase Side, London N14 4PS* T: (020) 8449 0467
E: pickles465@btinternet.com

PICKSTONE, Canon Charles Faulkner. b 55. BNC Ox BA 77 MA 81 Leeds Univ BA 80. Coll of Resurr Mirfield 78. **d** 81 **p** 82. C Birkenhead Priory *Ches* 81-84; Chapl Paris St Geo *Eur* 84; C Camberwell St Giles w St Matt *S'wark* 84-89; V Catford St Laur from 89; Asst RD E Lewisham 92-99; Hon Can S'wark Cathl from 13. *St Laurence's Vicarage, 31 Bromley Road, London SE6 2TS* T: (020) 8698 2871 or 8698 9706
E: st.laurence@btconnect.com

PICKUP, Harold. b 17. St Pet Hall Ox BA 39 MA 46. Ridley Hall Cam 46. **d** 47 **p** 48. C Middleton *Man* 47-50; V Gravesend St Mary *Roch* 51-57; Australia from 57; rtd 82. *7 Farview Avenue, Riverside Tas 7250, Australia* T: (0061) (3) 6327 4891

PICOT, Katherine Frances. b 73. Ox Brookes Univ BA. Ridley Hall Cam. **d** 09. C Houston St Martin USA 09-14; Dir Harnhill Cen of Chr Healing from 14. *Harnhill Centre of Christian Healing, Harnhill Manor, Harnhill, Cirencester GL7 5PX* T: (01285) 850283 E: picotk@googlemail.com

PIDGEON, Warner Mark. b 68. Trin Coll Bris 00. **d** 02 **p** 03. C Fair Oak *Win* 02-06; TV Billericay and Lt Burstead *Chelmsf* 06-14; V Carshalton Beeches *S'wark* from 14. *The Vicarage, 38 Beeches Avenue, Carshalton SM5 3LW* T: (020) 8647 6056 M: 07927-348741 E: revwmp@aol.co.uk

PIDOUX, Ian George. b 32. Univ Coll Ox BA 55 MA 60. Coll of Resurr Mirfield 54. **d** 57 **p** 58. C Middlesbrough All SS *York* 57-60; C Haggerston St Aug w St Steph *Lon* 60-62; C Aylesford *Roch* 80-81; TV Rye *Chich* 81-84; P-in-c Bridgwater St Jo *B & W* 84-86; V 86-98; Chapl Bridgwater Hosp 91-98; rtd 98; PtO *B & W* from 98. *18 Alexandra Road, Bridgwater TA6 3HE* T: (01278) 452882 M: 07746-615854
E: igsepidoux@btinternet.com

PIDSLEY, Preb Christopher Thomas. b 36. ALCD 61. **d** 61 **p** 62. C Enfield Ch Ch Trent Park *Lon* 61-66; C Rainham *Chelmsf* 66-70; V Chudleigh *Ex* 70-98; RD Moreton 86-91; Preb Ex Cathl 92-98; rtd 98. *Bellever, Shillingford Abbot, Exeter EX2 9QF* T: (01392) 833588

PIENAAR, Joseph. b 77. Birm Chr Coll MA 09. **d** 09 **p** 10. C Romiley *Ches* 09-12; V Luton Lewsey St Hugh *St Alb* from 12. *St Hugh's Vicarage, 367 Leagrave High Street, Luton LU4 0ND* T: (01582) 664433 M: 07758-015782
E: joepienaar@yahoo.com

PIERARD, Canon Beaumont Harold. b 21. JP 68 MBE 72. St Jo Coll Auckland. **d** 46 **p** 51. New Zealand 46-53; Chapl Hurstpierpoint Coll 53-54; Chapl Worksop Coll Notts 54-57; New Zealand from 57; Hon Can St Peter's Cathl Waikato 64-82. *287 Peachgrove Road, Hamilton 3214, New Zealand* T: (0064) (7) 855 7000

PIERCE, Alan. b 46. St Mark & St Jo Coll Lon TCert 68 Southlands Coll Lon BEd 75 K Coll Lon MA 85. NOC 89. **d** 92 **p** 93. NSM Bolton St Thos *Man* 92-98; NSM Halliwell 98-00; NSM Bolton Breightmet St Jas 00-06; NSM Leverhulme 06-15; rtd 15; PtO *Man* from 15. *3 Astley Road, Bolton BL2 4BR* T: (01204) 300071 F: 401556

✠**PIERCE, The Rt Revd Anthony Edward.** b 41. Univ of Wales (Swansea) BA 63 Linacre Coll Ox BA 65 MA 71. Ripon Hall Ox 63. **d** 65 **p** 66 **c** 99. C Swansea St Pet *S & B* 65-67; C Swansea St Mary and H Trin 67-74; Chapl Univ of Wales (Swansea) 71-74; V Llwynderw 74-92; P-in-c Swansea St Barn 92-96; Dioc Dir of Educn 93-96; Can Brecon Cathl 93-99; Adn Gower 95-99; V Swansea St Mary w H Trin 96-99; Bp S & B 99-08; rtd 08. *2 Coed Ceirios, Swansea Vale, Swansea SA7 0NU* T: (01792) 790258

PIERCE, Brian William. b 42. St Steph Ho Ox 86. **d** 88 **p** 89. C Cudworth *Wakef* 88-93; TV Manningham *Bradf* 93-98; V Tipton St Jo *Lich* 98-07; rtd 07; PtO *Blackb* from 08. *53 St Patricks Road North, Lytham St Annes FY8 2HB* T: (01253) 711247 E: loggos@btinternet.com

PIERCE, Bruce Andrew. b 58. TCD BBS 80 BTh 89 Dub City Univ MA 99 MA 02. CITC 86. **d** 89 **p** 90. C Raheny w Coolock *D & G* 89-92; C Taney 92-93; I Lucan w Leixlip 93-98; Chapl Adelaide and Meath Hosp Dublin 98-02; C Haarlem *Eur* 02-03; Chapl Toronto Gen Hosp Canada 03-04; Chapl Princess Marg Hosp Toronto 04-05; Supervisor (Assoc) Kerry Gen Hosp 06-08; Dir Educn St Luke's Home Mahon *C, C & R* from 08. *Aquila, Church Road, Blackrock, Cork, Republic of Ireland* F: 435 9450 T: (00353) (21) 435 8914 *or* 435 9444 ext 507 E: bruapierce@hotmail.com *or* bruce.pierce@stlukeshome.ie

PIERCE, Christopher Douglas. b 61. Middle Tennessee State Univ BSc 95 Covenant Th Sem St Louis MA 96. Asbury Th Sem Kentucky 92. **d** 08 **p** 09. C St Jo Cathl Antigua 08-10; I Clondehorkey w Cashel *D & R* from 10. *Ballymore Rectory, Port-na-Blagh, Letterkenny, Co Donegal, Republic of Ireland* T: (00353) (74) 913 6185 E: revcdp@gmail.com

PIERCE, David. *See* PIERCE, Thomas David Benjamin

PIERCE, David Richard. **d** 15. OLM Prittlewell St Pet w Westcliff St Cedd *Chelmsf* from 15. *7 Holmsdale Close, Westcliff-on-Sea SS0 0QW*

PIERCE, Jeffrey Hyam. b 29. Chelsea Coll Lon BSc 51 FBIM 80. Ox NSM Course 86. **d** 88 **p** 89. NSM Gt Missenden w Ballinger and Lt Hampden *Ox* 88-93; NSM Penn 93-97; rtd 97; PtO *Ox* 97-15. *Glebe Cottage, Manor Road, Penn, High Wycombe HP10 8HY* T: (01494) 817179

PIERCE, Canon Jonathan Douglas Marshall. b 70. UCD BA 91. CITC BTh 96. **d** 96 **p** 97. C Knockbreda *D & D* 96-99; L'Arche Community Dublin 99-00; C Taney *D & G* 00-03; I Kilmore and Inch *D & D* 03-09; I Cregagh from 09; Preb Down Cathl from 12. *St Finnian's Rectory, 3 Upper Knockbreda Road, Belfast BT6 9QH* T: (028) 9079 3822 E: jonopierce@btinternet.com

PIERCE, Roderick Martin. b 52. ACIB 74. **d** 06 **p** 07. OLM Guildf H Trin w St Mary from 06. *Appledore, 18 Blackwell Avenue, Guildford GU2 8LU* T: (01483) 505816 E: ann.rodpierce@ntlworld.com

PIERCE, Stephen Barry. b 60. Birm Univ BA 81 MA 82. Cranmer Hall Dur. **d** 85 **p** 86. C Huyton St Mich *Liv* 85-89; V Walton Breck Ch Ch 89-00; P-in-c Walton Breck 98-00; Resources Officer 00-08; PtO from 01. *39 Duke Street, Formby, Liverpool L37 4AP* T: (01704) 833725

PIERCE, Thomas David Benjamin. b 67. Ulster Univ BA 88. Oak Hill Th Coll BA 94. **d** 94 **p** 95. C Cromer *Nor* 94-97; C Belfast St Donard *D & D* 97-99; C Holywood 99-00; I Kilwarlin Upper w Kilwarlin Lower from 00. *Kilwarlin Rectory, 9 St John's Road, Hillsborough BT26 6ED* T: (028) 9268 3299

PIERCE, William Johnston. b 32. NOC. **d** 89 **p** 90. NSM Gt Crosby St Luke *Liv* 89-96; PtO from 96. *1 Forton Lodge, Blundellsands Road East, Liverpool L23 8SA* T: 0151-924 2400

PIERCE-JONES, Alan. b 74. Coll of Ripon & York St Jo BA 98. St Mich Coll Llan 98. **d** 00 **p** 01. C Port Talbot St Theodore Llan 00-02; TV Neath 02-05; V Lt Marsden w Nelson St Mary and Nelson St Bede *Blackb* 05-10; C W Burnley All SS 10; C Burnley St Mark 10; Chapl HM YOI Lanc Farms and HM Pris Lanc Castle 10-11; Chapl HM Pris Kennet from 11; PtO *Man* from 14. *HM Prison Kennet, Parkbourn, Liverpool L31 1HX* T: 0151-213 3000 E: alan.pierce-jones@hmps.gsi.gov.uk

PIERCY, Elizabeth Claire. *See* FRANCE, Elizabeth Claire

PIERPOINT, The Ven David Alfred. b 56. **d** 86 **p** 88. NSM Athboy w Ballivor and Killallon *M & K* 86-88; NSM Killiney Ballybrack *D & G* 88-89; NSM Narraghmore and Timolin w Castledermot etc 89-91; Chan V St Patr Cathl Dublin 90-96; C Dublin St Patr Cathl Gp 92-95; V Dublin Ch Ch Cathl Gp from 95; Can Ch Ch Cathl Dublin from 95; Adn Dublin from 04. *The Vicarage, 30 Phibsborough Road, Dublin 7, Republic of Ireland* T: (00353) (1) 830 4601 M: 87-263 0402 E: pierpoint.david@gmail.com

PIERSSENE, Frances Jane. *See* GRIEVE, Frances Jane

PIGGOTT, The Ven Andrew John. b 51. Qu Mary Coll Lon BSc(Econ) 72. St Jo Coll Nottm 83. **d** 86 **p** 87. C Dorridge *Birm* 86-89; TV Kidderminster St Geo *Worc* 89-94; V Biddulph *Lich* 94-99; Min and Voc Adv CPAS 99-01; Patr Sec 01-05; Adn Bath and Preb Wells Cathl from 05. *56 Grange Road, Saltford, Bristol BS31 3AG* T: (01225) 873609 F: 874110 E: adbath@bathwells.anglican.org

PIGGOTT, Clive. b 47. St Luke's Coll Ex CertEd 69. **d** 96 **p** 97. OLM Malden St Jas *S'wark* from 96. *84 Manor Drive North, New Malden KT3 5PA* T: (020) 8337 0801

PIGGOTT, Graham John. b 44. Lon Bible Coll BD 73 Nottm Univ MPhil 84 MEd 94 Lon Inst of Educn PGCE 74. St Jo Coll Nottm 79. **d** 81 **p** 82. C Beeston *S'well* 81-84; P-in-c W Bridgford 84-88; V Wilford Hill 88-09; AD W Bingham 97-04; Hon Can S'well Minster 04-09; rtd 09; PtO *Derby* from 09. *Tanner's House, 5A Goatscliff Cottages, Grindleford, Hope Valley S32 2HG* T: (01433) 639641 E: graham.pigott@btinternet.com

PIGGOTT, Nicholas John Capel. b 48. Qu Coll Birm 75. **d** 78 **p** 79. C Belmont *Dur* 78-79; C Folkestone St Sav *Cant* 79-82; C Birm St Geo 82-85; V Stevenage St Hugh and St Jo *St Alb* 85-91; TV Totnes w Bridgetown, Berry Pomeroy etc *Ex* 91-02; Asst P 02-04; rtd 04. *27 Croft Road, Ipplepen, Newton Abbot TQ12 5SS* T: (01803) 813664 E: njsa@pigott.freeserve.co.uk

PIGREM, Terence John (Tim). b 39. Middx Univ BA 97 MA 01. Oak Hill Th Coll 66. **d** 69 **p** 70. C Islington St Andr w St Thos and St Matthias *Lon* 69-73; C Barking St Marg w St Patr *Chelmsf* 73-75; TV 75-76; C W Holloway St Luke *Lon* 76-79; V 79-95; P-in-c Abbess Roding, Beauchamp Roding and White Roding *Chelmsf* 95-96; R S Rodings 96-07; RD Dunmow 97-02; rtd 07; PtO *Chelmsf* from 08. *96 Vicarage Lane, Great Baddow, Chelmsford CM2 8JB* T: (01245) 471878 E: pigrem@btinternet.com

PIIR, The Very Revd Gustav Peeter. b 61. St Olaf Coll Minnesota BA 83 Saskatchewan Univ MDiv 86. **p** 88. Asst Toronto St Pet Canada 88-92; Asst Chas Ch Tallinn Estonia 92-95; R Tallinn H Spirit from 95; Dean Tallinn from 99; P-in-c Tallinn SS Tim and Titus *Eur* from 00. *Pühavaimu 2, Tallinn 10123, Estonia* T: (00372) 646 4430 M: 51-76159 F: 644 1487 E: praost@hot.ee

PIKE, Mrs Amanda Shirley Gail. b 69. Cranmer Hall Dur 99. **d** 01 **p** 02. C Boston Spa *York* 01-03; C Elloughton and Brough w Brantingham 03-05; P-in-c Eggleston and Middleton-in-Teesdale w Forest and Frith *Dur* 05-08; TV Bosworth and Sheepy Gp *Leic* 08-11; C Nailstone and Carlton w Shackerstone 08-11; P-in-c Elmton and Whitwell *Derby* 11-13; P-in-c Cheddleton *Lich* 13-14; P-in-c Horton, Lonsdon and Rushton Spencer 13-14; V Cheddleton, Horton, Longsdon and Rushton Spencer from 14. *The Vicarage, Hollow Lane, Cheddleton, Leek ST13 7HP* T: (01538) 360226 M: 07968-543569 E: amanda@ichthos.me.uk

PIKE, David Frank. b 35. BA Lon Univ TCert CEng MIMechE. S Dios Minl Tr Scheme 82. **d** 85 **p** 86. NSM Lancing w Coombes *Chich* 85-88; R Albourne w Sayers Common and Twineham 88-94; V Wisborough Green 94-04; rtd 04. *42 Greenoaks, Lancing BN15 0HE* T: (01903) 766209

PIKE, George Richard. b 38. Birm Univ BSc 57. WMMTC 79. **d** 82 **p** 83. NSM Edgbaston St Bart *Birm* 82-89; NSM S Yardley St Mich 89-06; PtO from 06. *138 Charlbury Crescent, Birmingham B26 2LW* T/F: 0121-783 2818 E: kepi@geopi.fsnet.co.uk

PIKE, James. b 22. TCD 66. **d** 68 **p** 69. C Clooney *D & R* 68-72; I Ardstraw 72-76; I Ardstraw w Baronscourt, Badoney Lower etc 76-92; Can Derry Cathl 90-92; rtd 92. *19 Knockgreenan Avenue, Omagh BT79 0EB* T: (028) 8224 9007

PIKE, Nicholas Keith. b 52. Warwick Univ BA 74 Brunel Univ MA 80 CQSW 80. Ox NSM Course 10. **d** 12 **p** 13. NSM Cogges and S Leigh *Ox* from 12; NSM N Leigh from 12. *The Old Nursery, 29 Bridge Street, Witney OX28 1DA* T: (01993) 200843 M: 07962-623310 E: nick.pike@coggesparish.com

PIKE, Paul Alfred. b 38. Bognor Regis Coll of Educn CertEd 58 MIL 88. Wycliffe Hall Ox 83. **d** 84 **p** 85. C Penn Fields *Lich* 84-89; OMF Internat Japan 89-03; rtd 03; PtO *Bris* from 03; *B & W* from 09. *18 Silverlow Road, Nailsea, Bristol BS48 2AD* T: (01275) 856270 E: papike@btinternet.com

PIKE, The Ven Peter John. b 53. Southn Univ BTh 86 Lanc Univ PhD 00. Sarum & Wells Th Coll 81. **d** 84 **p** 85. C Broughton *Blackb* 84-88; V Woodplumpton 88-93; Asst Dir of Ords and Voc Adv 89-93; P-in-c Barnacre w Calder Vale 93-98; Tutor CBDTI 93-98; V Briercliffe *Blackb* 98-04; AD Burnley 01-04; V Bempton w Flamborough, Reighton w Speeton *York* 04-12; RD Bridlington 08-12; Adn Montgomery *St As* from 12; V Berriew from 12. *The Vicarage, Berriew, Welshpool SY21 8PL* T: (01686) 640223 E: archdeacon.montgomery@churchinwales.org.uk

PIKE, Robert James. b 47. Kelham Th Coll 66. **d** 70 **p** 71. C Cov E 70-74; C Bilton 74-76; P-in-c Southall St Geo *Lon* 76-81; V S Harrow St Paul 81-86; C Hillingdon St Jo 86-88; Chapl Hillingdon Hosp Uxbridge 88-90; Chapl Mt Vernon Hosp Uxbridge 88-90; PtO *Lon* 91-96. *6 Salt Hill Close, Uxbridge UB8 1PZ* T: (01895) 235212

PIKE, Timothy David. b 68. Collingwood Coll Dur BA 90 Leeds Univ BA 94. Coll of Resurr Mirfield 92. **d** 95 **p** 96. C Owton Manor *Dur* 95-98; C Old St Pancras w Bedford New Town St Matt *Lon* 98-03; CMP from 98; Warden from 05; CR 03-04; P-in-c Hornsey H Innocents *Lon* 04-07; V from 07; C Stroud Green H Trin from 04; P-in-c Harringay St Paul from 10; AD W Haringey 06-11. *99 Hillfield Avenue, London N8 7DG* T: (020) 8340 1300 E: fathertimpike@hotmail.com

PILAVACHI, Michael. b 58. St Mellitus Coll. **d** 12 **p** 13. Soul Survivor Watford St Pet from 12. *37 Maytree Crescent, Watford WD24 5NJ*

PILCHER, Mrs Jennifer. b 42. **d** 04 **p** 05. OLM Eastry and Northbourne w Tilmanstone etc *Cant* 04-12; PtO from 12. *1 Long Drive, Church Street, Eastry, Sandwich CT13 0HN* T: (01304) 611472 E: jennifer.p@torview1.freeserve.co.uk

PILGRIM, Canon Colin Mark. b 56. BA 77. Westcott Ho Cam 81. **d** 84 **p** 85. C Chorlton-cum-Hardy St Clem *Man* 84-87; C Whitchurch *Bris* 87-89; V Bedminster Down 89-95; Dioc Youth Officer 95-01; Hon C Stoke Bishop 96-01; V Henleaze from 01; AD Bris W from 06; Hon Can Bris Cathl from 09. *St Peter's Vicarage, 17 The Drive, Henleaze, Bristol BS9 4LD* T: 0117-962 0636 *or* 962 3196 E: markpilgrimis@aol.com

PILGRIM, Donald Eric. b 55. Cant Univ (NZ) BA 80 LTh 87. St Jo Coll Auckland 81. **d** 81 **p** 82. New Zealand 81-85 and from 86; C Southampton Maybush St Pet W 85-86. *212 Hoon Hay Road, Hoon Hay, Christchurch 8025, New Zealand* T/F: (0064) (3) 338 4277 E: pilgrimspalace@paradise.net.nz

PILGRIM, Ms Judith Mary. b 44. Westcott Ho Cam 88. **d** 90 **p** 94. C Probus, Ladock and Grampound w Creed and St Erme *Truro* 90-94; C Nottingham All SS *S'well* 94-97; Asst Chapl to the Deaf 94-97; PtO 97-00; C *ny* 00-01; P-in-c Zennor and Towednack *Truro* 02-06; rtd 06. *356 Bennett Street, Long Eaton, Nottingham NG10 4JD*

PILGRIM, Kenneth George. b 49. Lon Univ BEd 77 Kent Univ MA 94. **d** 01 **p** 02. OLM Alkham w Capel le Ferne and Hougham *Cant* 01-03; PtO *Nor* 04-05; NSM E Dereham and Scarning 05-06; NSM Swanton Morley w Beetley w E Bilney and Hoe 05-06; NSM Dereham and Distr from 06; Bp's Officer for Wholeness and Healing from 10. *Sunny Oak, 27 Fakenham Road, Beetley, Dereham NR20 4BT* T: (01362) 861265 E: kenpilgrim@btinternet.com

PILGRIM, Mark. *See* PILGRIM, Colin Mark

PILKINGTON, Miss Anne. b 57. Aston Tr Scheme 88 NOC 90. **d** 93 **p** 94. C Wythenshawe Wm Temple Ch *Man* 93-96; P-in-c 96-99; TV Wythenshawe 99-06; P-in-c Didsbury Ch Ch 06; P-in-c Withington St Chris 06; R W Didsbury and Withington St Chris from 06. *Christ Church Rectory, 35 Darley Avenue, Manchester M20 2ZD* T: 0161-445 4152 E: anne@christchurchdidsbury.org.uk

PILKINGTON, Charles George Willink. b 21. Trin Coll Cam BA 42 MA 64. Westcott Ho Cam. **d** 63 **p** 64. C Pendleton St Thos *Man* 63-65; C Brindle Heath 63-65; C Chorlton-cum-Hardy St Clem 65-68; R Withington St Chris 68-88; rtd 88; PtO *Man* 88-14. *32 Rathen Road, Withington, Manchester M20 9GH* T: 0161-434 5365

PILKINGTON, Edward Russell. b 39. ALCD 65. **d** 65 **p** 66. C Eccleshill *Bradf* 65-68; C Billericay St Mary *Chelmsf* 68-72; V New Thundersley 72-78; R Theydon Garnon 78-82; V Gidea Park 82-04; rtd 04. *19 Tryon Close, Swindon SN3 6HG* T: (01793) 433495

PILKINGTON, John Rowan. b 32. Magd Coll Cam BA 55 MA 59. Ridley Hall Cam 57. **d** 59 **p** 60. C Ashtead *Guildf* 59-61; C Wimbledon *S'wark* 62-65; R Newhaven *Chich* 65-75; R Farlington *Portsm* 75-89; V Darlington St Mark w St Paul *Dur* 89-97; rtd 97; PtO *Portsm* from 98. *38 Main Road, Emsworth PO10 8AU* T: (01243) 375830

PILKINGTON, Canon Timothy William. b 54. Nottm Univ BA 85 Univ of Wales (Lamp) MA 09. Linc Th Coll 82. **d** 85 **p** 86. C Newquay *Truro* 85-88; C Cockington *Ex* 88-91; R St John w Millbrook *Truro* 91-97; V Northampton St Matt *Pet* 97-02; TR Solihull *Birm* 02-14; AD 09-13; Hon Can Birm Cathl 06-14; TV St Berkhamsted, Gt and Lt Gaddesden etc *St Alb* from 14. *The Rectory, Rectory Lane, Berkhamsted HP4 2DH* T: (01442) 879739 E: rector@greatberkhamsted.org.uk

PIMENTEL, Barnabas. b 86. Lon Sch of Th BA 10. Trin Coll Bris MA 12. **d** 13 **p** 14. C Woking St Mary *Guildf* from 13. *46 Hawthorn Road, Woking GU22 0BA* M: 07882-885736 E: bushka22@hotmail.com

PIMENTEL, Peter Eric. b 55. Lon Bible Coll BA 79 MA 94. Ridley Hall Cam. **d** 82 **p** 83. C Gt Ilford St Andr *Chelmsf* 82-85; Chapl Basingstoke Distr Hosp 85-88; TV Grays Thurrock *Chelmsf* 88-96; P-in-c Barton *Portsm* 96-99; V 99-14; Dioc Ecum Officer 96-02; P-in-c Ibiza *Eur* from 14. *Address temp unknown* E: peterepimentel@gmail.com

PIMENTEL, Mrs Zoe Louise. b 84. Ox Brookes Univ BA 08. Trin Coll Bris MA 13. **d** 13 **p** 14. C Woking St Mary *Guildf* from 13. *46 Hawthorn Road, Woking GU22 0BA*

PIMM, Robert John. b 57. Bris Univ BA 78 ACIB 82. Trin Coll Bris 92. **d** 94 **p** 95. C Long Benton *Newc* 94-98; TV Bath Twerton-on-Avon *B & W* from 98. *Ascension Vicarage, 35A Claude Avenue, Bath BA2 1AG* T: (01225) 405354 E: robertjpimm@gmail.com

PINCHBECK, Canon Caroline Rosamund. b 70. Hatf Coll Dur BA 93. Wesley Ho Cam MA 00. **d** 02 **p** 03. C Mawnan *Truro* 02-06; C Budock 03-06; P-in-c Eastling w Ospringe and Stalisfield w Otterden *Cant* 06-11; Communities and Partnership Exec Officer from 11; Rural Life Adv *Cant* and *Roch* from 06; C Blean *Cant* from 12; Hon Can Cant Cathl from 11. *124 Blean Common, Blean, Canterbury CT2 9JJ* T: (01227) 463163 E: caroline.pinchbeck575@btinternet.com

PINCHES, Donald Antony. b 32. Pemb Coll Cam BA 55 MA 60 Linacre Coll Ox BA 67. Wycliffe Hall Ox 64. **d** 67 **p** 68. C Aylesbury *Ox* 67-71; C Compton Gifford *Ex* 71-74; TV Lydford, Brent Tor, Bridestowe and Sourton 74-77; V Shiphay Collaton 77-97; rtd 97; PtO *Ex* from 98. *3 Malderek Avenue, Preston, Paignton TQ3 2RP* T: (01803) 698003

PINDER, Canon John Ridout. b 43. Peterho Cam BA 65 MA 69. Cuddesdon Coll 65. **d** 73 **p** 74. C Leavesden *St Alb* 73-76; Gen Sec Melanesian Miss 77-89; P-in-c Harpsden *Ox* 82-89; R Farlington *Portsm* 89-02; R Liss 02-09; RD Petersfield 96-01; Hon Can Portsm Cathl 01-09; rtd 09; P-in-c Stapleford *Ely* 09-15; PtO from 15. *The Vicarage, 43 Mingle Lane, Stapleford, Cambridge CB22 5SY* T: (01223) 840256 E: johnpinder@waitrose.com

PINDER-PACKARD, John. b 47. Lon Univ BSc. NOC 81. **d** 84 **p** 85. NSM Mosbrough *Sheff* 84-85; C Norton 85-88; V New Whittington *Derby* 88-04; P-in-c Newbold and Gt Barlow 99-00; Chapl Whittington Hall Hosp 88-04; R Barlborough and Renishaw *Derby* 04-09; P-in-c Clowne 05-09; rtd 09. *1 Great Common Close, Barlborough, Chesterfield S43 4SY* E: packards@tiscali.co.uk

PINE, David Michael. b 41. Lich Th Coll 68. **d** 71 **p** 72. C Northam *Ex* 71-74; R Toft w Caldecote and Childerley *Ely* 74-80; R Hardwick 74-80; V Ipswich St Andr *St E* 80-84; P-in-c Hazelbury Bryan w Stoke Wake etc *Sarum* 84-91; R Hazelbury Bryan and the Hillside Par 91-93; V Steep and Froxfield w Privett *Portsm* 93-00; rtd 00; PtO *Portsm* 07-11. *3 Nansen Close, Bembridge PO35 5QD* T: (01983) 872939

PINES, Christopher Derek. b 65. Lon Univ MB, BS 89. Oak Hill Th Coll BA 93 MA 01. **d** 93 **p** 94. C Heref St Pet w St Owen and St Jas 93-97; Min Can and Chapl St Alb Abbey *St Alb* 97-03; Chapl St Alb Sch from 03. *1 Fishpool Street, St Albans AL3 4RS* T: (01727) 846508 E: cdpines@st-albans.herts.sch.uk

PINFIELD, Leslie Arthur. b 37. Birm Univ BMus 79. St Steph Ho Ox 92. **d** 94 **p** 95. C Bath Bathwick *B & W* 94-98; TV Swindon New Town *Bris* 98-07; P-in-c Huddersfield All SS and St Thos *Leeds* 07-15; Bp's Adv on Inter-Faith Issues from 07; V Huddersfield All SS and St Thos from 15. *The Vicarage, 17 Cross Church Street, Paddock, Huddersfield HD1 4SN* T: (01484) 425823 E: frleslie@btopenworld.com

PINKERTON, Ms Patricia Edith. b 38. California Univ BA 72 MA 75 BTh 80. Ch Div Sch of the Pacific (USA). **d** 81 **p** 82. USA 81-88; C Coleford w Staunton *Glouc* 88-92; Dn-in-c St Briavels w Hewelsfield 92-94; P-in-c 94-97; rtd 97; PtO *Glouc* 97-09. *97 Kingsgate Road, Apt H-21, Lake Oswego OR 97035-2371, USA*

PINNEGAR, Alan Edward. b 58. SEITE 09. **d** 12 **p** 13. C Bearsted w Thurnham *Cant* from 12. *66 Peverel Drive, Bearsted, Maidstone ME14 4PS* E: apinnegar@hotmail.com

PINNELL (formerly ALLEN), Ms Beverley Carole. b 52. Ch Ch Coll Cant CertEd 74 Open Univ BA 91. Sarum Th Coll 93. **d** 96 **p** 97. NSM Ruislip Manor St Paul *Lon* 96-12; PtO from 12; *Ox* from 14. *127 Cobden Close, Uxbridge UB8 2YH* T: (01895) 257037 E: revbev@tiscali.co.uk

PINNELL, George. b 39. NTMTC 96. **d** 99 **p** 00. NSM Hillingdon St Jo *Lon* from 99; Chapl Heathrow Airport from 08. *127 Cobden Close, Uxbridge UB8 2YH* M: 07951-124976 E: pinneg@tiscali.co.uk

PINNER, Mrs Cheri Lee. b 36. Marietta Coll (USA) BA 59. **d** 07 **p** 08. C Greytown New Zealand 07-10; P-in-c Whaley Bridge *Ches* 10-12; rtd 12. *The Maple, Westend, Wickwar, Wotton-under-Edge GL12 8LB* M: 07889-796020 E: cheri.pinner@mac.com

PINNER, John Philip. b 37. K Coll Lon BA 59 AKC 59 Lon Inst of Educn PGCE 60. Westcott Ho Cam 70. **d** 71 **p** 72. C Dover St Mary *Cant* 71-74; Chapl Felsted Sch 74-81; Chapl Rathkeale Coll New Zealand 81-02; P-in-c Greytown St Luke 04-08; rtd 10; Hon C Whaley Bridge *Ches* 10-12. *The Maple, Westend, Wickwar, Wotton-under-Edge GL12 8LB*

PINNER, Canon Terence Malcolm William. b 35. Southn Univ MA 89. AKC 59. **d** 60 **p** 61. C Eltham St Barn *S'wark* 60-64;

C Grahamstown Cathl S Africa 64-67; USPG 67-69; R King William's Town S Africa 69-72; R Beacon Bay 72-74; Sec for Home Affairs Conf of Br Miss Socs 74-76; P-in-c Hinstock *Lich* 76-79; Adult Educn Officer 76-79; Adult RE Officer 79-83; Chapl Southn Univ *Win* 83-88; Dioc Dir of Ords 88-98; Tutor S Dios Minl Tr Scheme 88-92; P-in-c Old Alresford and Bighton *Win* 93-00; Dir Old Alresford Place 93-00; Hon Can Win Cathl 92-00; rtd 00; PtO *Win* from 00. *47 Buriton Road, Winchester SO22 6JF* T: (01962) 884215   M: 07889-177203

PINNINGTON, Mrs Gillian. b 59. St Kath Coll Liv BEd 81 Ches Coll of HE BTh 02. NOC 99. **d** 02 **p** 03. C Roby *Liv* 02-06; TV Speke St Aid from 06. *62 East Millwood Road, Liverpool L24 6SQ* T: 0151-425 3388   E: pinny@supanet.com

PINNINGTON, Suzanne Jane. b 66. MBE 10. Trevelyan Coll Dur BA 89. St Steph Ho Ox 95. **d** 97 **p** 98. C Oakham, Hambleton, Egleton, Braunston and Brooke *Pet* 97-00; V Cottingley *Bradf* 00-08; Hon Can Bradf Cathl 04-08; R Houghton le Spring *Dur* from 08. *The Rectory, 5 Lingfield, Houghton le Spring DH5 8QA* T: 0191-584 3487   E: rectorpinnington@gmail.com

PINNOCK, Martyn Elliott. b 47. Linc Th Coll 93. **d** 93 **p** 94. C Fordingbridge *Win* 93-97; V St Minver *Truro* 97-01; P-in-c Luray Ch Ch USA 01-02; V Steeton *Bradf* 02-05; P-in-c Scottsville USA 05-08; rtd 09; P-in-c Tregony w St Cuby and Cornelly *Truro* 13-14; PtO from 14. *Neyth Golvan, 149 Treffry Road, Truro TR1 1WE* T: (01872) 264578 E: martynpinnock@aol.com

PINSENT, Ewen Macpherson. b 30. Edin Th Coll 67. **d** 69 **p** 70. C Holt *Nor* 69-72; R Kelso *Edin* 72-82; R Blendworth w Chalton w Idsworth etc *Portsm* 82-90; R Blendworth w Chalton w Idsworth 90-92; rtd 92; PtO *Sarum* from 94. *The Cross House, The Cross, Child Okeford, Blandford Forum DT11 8ED* T: (01258) 860803

PIPER, Canon Andrew. b 58. Magd Coll Ox BA 79 MA 83. Chich Th Coll 80. **d** 83 **p** 84. C Eastbourne St Mary *Chich* 83-88; TV Lewes All SS, St Anne, St Mich and St Thos 88-93; TR Worth 93-03; Can Res and Prec Heref Cathl from 03. *1 The Close, Hereford HR1 2NG* T: (01432) 266193   F: 374220 E: precentor@herefordcathedral.org

PIPER, Calum Lewis. b 91. Ches Univ BTh 12. St Jo Coll Nottm 12. **d** 14 **p** 15. C Wallasey St Hilary *Ches* from 14. *40 Station Road, Wallasey CH44 3AN* M: 07890-977064 E: calum.piper@btinternet.com

PIPER, Clifford John. b 53. Moray Ord Course 91. **d** 93 **p** 94. C Invergordon St Ninian *Mor* 93-96; P-in-c 00-03; NSM Tain 96-98; P-in-c 98-03; P-in-c Forres from 03; Can St Andr Cathl Inverness 00-09; Dean Mor 09-14. *St John's Rectory, Victoria Road, Forres IV36 3BN* T: (01309) 672856   F: 08712-422221 M: 07895-105104   E: stjohnsforres@btinternet.com

PIPER, Gary Quentin David. b 42. Nottm Coll of Educn TCert 65 Maria Grey Coll Lon DipEd 71. Oak Hill Th Coll 75. **d** 78 **p** 79. NSM Fulham St Matt *Lon* 78-85; V 85-13; AD Hammersmith 86-92; AD Hammersmith and Fulham 06-12; rtd 13. *The Flat, St Saviour's Church, Walton Street, London SW3 1SA* T: (020) 7730 7270   E: revgarypiper@hotmail.com

PIPER, Graham. b 58. Southn Univ BTh 91. Chich Th Coll 88. **d** 91 **p** 92. C Horsham *Chich* 91-94; TV Haywards Heath St Wilfrid 94-99; Dioc Voc Adv 96-99; V Bamber Bridge St Aid *Blackb* 99-04; V Hawes Side and Marton Moss from 04. *The Vicarage, Hawes Side Lane, Blackpool FY4 5AH* T: (01253) 697937   M: 07816-525843   E: fathergraham@fsmail.net

PIPPEN, Canon Brian Roy. b 50. St D Coll Lamp. **d** 73 **p** 74. C Maindee Newport *Mon* 73-77; TV Cwmbran 77-84; V Newport Ch Ch 84-90; R Pontypool from 90; AD 98-08; Can St Woolos Cathl from 01. *The Vicarage, Trevethin, Pontypool NP4 8JF* T: (01495) 762228 E: brian.pippen@btconnect.com

PIRET, Michael John. b 57. State Univ NY BA 79 Univ of Michigan MA 80 PhD 91 Mert Coll Ox MLitt 89. Edin Th Coll 90. **d** 92 **p** 93. C St Andr Cathl Inverness 92-94; Dean of Div and Chapl Magd Coll Ox from 94. *Magdalen College, Oxford OX1 4AU* T: (01865) 276027

PIRRIE, Stephen Robin. b 56. Kent Univ BA 79 Cam Univ MA 83 Barrister 80. EAMTC 94. **d** 97 **p** 98. C King's Lynn St Marg w St Nic *Nor* 97-99; C Bideford, Northam, Westward Ho!, Appledore etc *Ex* 99-00; TV 00-03. *Address withheld by request*

PITCHER, Canon David John. b 33. Ely Th Coll 55. **d** 58 **p** 59. C Kingswinford St Mary *Lich* 58-61; C Kirkby *Liv* 61-66; R Ingham w Sutton *Nor* 66-72; V Lakenham St Jo 72-76; R Framlingham w Saxtead *St E* 76-91; RD Loes 82-89; Hon Can St E Cathl 85-99; R Woodbridge St Mary 91-99; rtd 99; PtO *St E* from 00. *25 Coucy Close, Framlingham, Woodbridge IP13 9AX* T: (01728) 621580

PITCHER, George Martell. b 55. Birm Univ BA 77 Middx Univ BA 05. NTMTC 02. **d** 05 **p** 06. NSM St Bride Fleet Street w

Bridewell etc *Lon* 05-13; P-in-c Waldron *Chich* from 13. *Culverwood, Little London Road, Cross in Hand, Heathfield TN21 0AX* T: (01435) 865376   M: 07778-917182 E: george@pitcher.com

PITCHER, Robert Philip. b 47. Westhill Coll Birm DipEd 70. Trin Coll Bris 90. **d** 92 **p** 93. C Llansamlet *S & B* 92-96; V Caereithin 96-02; V Llanidloes w Llangurig *Ban* 02-10; AD Arwystli 04-10; rtd 10; PtO *Ban* 11-14. *22 Dysart Terrace, Canal Road, Newtown SY16 2JL* T: (01686) 627696 E: bob.pitcher@openworld.com

PITCHER, Ronald Charles Frederick. b 21. AKC 50. **d** 51 **p** 52. C Burnage St Marg *Man* 51-53; C Heywood St Jas 53-55; C Newall Green CD 55-61; V Newall Green St Fran 61-73; Chapl Wythenshawe Hosp Man 64-73; C-in-c Danesholme CD *Pet* 73-81; V Estover *Ex* 81-91; rtd 91; PtO *Sarum* 92-10. *50 Townhill Drive, Broughton, Brigg DN20 0HG* T: (01652) 653561

PITCHER, Simon John. b 63. Reading Univ BA 85. Ridley Hall Cam 00. **d** 02 **p** 03. C Lightcliffe *Wakef* 02-05; P-in-c Heckmondwike 05-10; C Liversedge w Hightown 05-10; C Roberttown w Hartshead 05-10; RD Birstall 08-10; TR Sole Bay *St E* from 10; RD Waveney and Blyth from 11. *The Vicarage, Gardner Road, Southwold IP18 6HJ* E: revsimon@talktalk.net

PITE, Sheila Reinhardt. *See* SWARBRICK, Sheila Reinhardt

PITHERS, Canon Brian Hoyle. b 34. Chich Th Coll 63. **d** 66 **p** 67. C Wisbech SS Pet and Paul *Ely* 66-70; V Fenstanton 70-75; V Hilton 70-75; V Habergham Eaves St Matt *Blackb* 75-85; P-in-c Habergham Eaves H Trin 78-85; V Burnley St Matt w H Trin 85-86; TR Ribbleton 86-92; V Torrisholme 92-00; Hon Can Blackb Cathl 97-00; rtd 01; PtO *Blackb* from 01. *37 Dallam Avenue, Morecambe LA4 5BB* T: (01524) 424786   E: brianpithers@talktalk.net

PITKETHLY (née CHEVILL), Elizabeth Jane. b 65. Colchester Inst of Educn BA 86 K Coll Lon MMus 87 PhD 93 Warwick Univ BPhil 08 AKC 89 Lon Inst of Educn PGCE 91. Wycliffe Hall Ox MSt 04 MLitt 08. **d** 08 **p** 09. C Blackheath St Jo *S'wark* 08-11; PtO *Ox* 11-12; NSM Ox St Andr from 12; Chapl St Pet Coll Ox from 14. *24 Thorncliffe Road, Oxford OX2 7BB* M: 07952-024571   E: ejpitkethly@btinternet.com

PITKIN, James Mark. b 62. Man Univ BSc 83 Glos Univ BA(Theol) 03 MRAeS 90 CEng 90. STETS. **d** 99 **p** 00. C Chilworth w N Baddesley *Win* 99-03; V Lockerley and E Dean w E and W Tytherley from 03; Corps Chapl ATC from 15. *The Vicarage, The Street, Lockerley, Romsey SO51 0JF* T: (01794) 340635   F: 08701-674691   M: 07931-736166 E: jamespitkin@priest.com

PITKIN, Mrs Susan Margaret. b 60. Man Univ BA 84 Surrey Univ BA 03. STETS 00. **d** 03 **p** 04. C Southampton Maybush St Pet *Win* 03-06; C Maybush and Southampton St Jude 06-09; Asst Chapl Southn Univ Hosps NHS Trust 09-10; Trust Chapl Univ Hosp Southn NHS Foundn Trust from 10. *The Vicarage, The Street, Lockerley, Romsey SO51 0JF* T: (01794) 340635 M: 07906-027042   E: suepitkin@minister.com

PITMAN, Mrs Janet Elizabeth. b 67. All SS Cen for Miss & Min 12. **d** 15. C Oldham St Paul and Werneth *Man* from 15. *Address temp unknown*

PITMAN, Jessica. b 62. Newton Park Coll Bath BEd 85. STETS 07. **d** 10 **p** 11. C Langport Area *B & W* from 10. *Vicarage, Huish Episcopi, Langport TA10 9QR* T: (010458) 251489   E: jessicapitman@aol.com

PITMAN, Roger Thomas. b 64. St Mich Coll Llan BTh 00. **d** 00 **p** 01. C Caerphilly *Llan* 00-02; C Coity w Nolton 02-07; P-in-c Llanharry 07-12; P-in-c Llangeinor and the Garw Valley from 12; Chapl Pontypridd and Rhondda NHS Trust 07-10. *The Vicarage, 2 Waun Wen, Bettws Road, Llangeinor, Bridgend CF32 8PH* T: (01656) 870280   E: vicar@the-vicarage.net

PITT, Mrs Beatrice Anne. b 50. I M Marsh Coll of Physical Educn Liv CertEd 71 Open Univ BA 01. Trin Coll Bris 80. **d** 82 **p** 97. C Rhyl w St Ann *St As* 82-86; CMS 86-92; Jt Co-ord Dioc Bible Schs Bukavu Zaïre 88-92; NSM Penycae *St As* 92-98; Hon Rep for CMS *St As* and *Ban* 93-98; NSM Killesher *K, E & A* 98-01; P-in-c Killinagh w Kiltyclogher and Innismagrath 98-01; P-in-c Firbank, Howgill and Killington *Bradf* 01-05; rtd 05. *20 Thornsbank, Sedbergh LA10 5LF* T: (01539) 622095 E: anne@pitt.euro1net.com

PITT, George. b 52. QUB BD 79 MTh 88. CITC 81. **d** 81 **p** 82. C Belfast St Mary *Conn* 81-86; CMS 86-92; Zaïre 88-92; V Penycae *St As* 92-98; I Killesher *K, E & A* 98-01; Educn Adv Ch of Ireland Bps' Appeal 01-03; PtO *Bradf* 04-06; Chapl HM Pris Moorland 06-13; rtd 13. *20 Thornsbank, Sedbergh LA10 5LF* T: (01539) 622095

PITT, Karen Lesley Finella. *See* TIMMIS, Karen Lesley Finella

PITT, Robert Edgar. b 37. Chich Th Coll 70. **d** 73 **p** 74. C Knowle *Bris* 73-77; C Wells St Cuth w Coxley and Wookey Hole *B & W* 77-81; TV Wellington and Distr 81-94;

V Burnham 94-02; Chapl Taunton and Somerset NHS Trust 94-02; rtd 02; PtO *Sarum* from 03. *Redmaye, 119 High Street, Burbage, Marlborough SN8 3AA* T: (01672) 810651

PITT, Canon Trevor. b 45. Hull Univ BA 66 MA 69 Open Univ DipEd 91. Linc Th Coll 68 Union Th Sem (NY) STM 70. **d** 70 **p** 71. C Sheff St Geo 70-74; TV Gleadless Valley 74-78; TR 78-79; P-in-c Elham *Cant* 79-82; V Elham w Denton and Wootton 82-91; Vice Prin Cant Sch of Min 81-91; Six Preacher Cant Cathl 85-91; Prin NEOC *Newc* 91-10; Hon Can Newc Cathl 91-10; PtO *York* from 91; *Leeds* from 91; rtd 10; Hon C Escomb *Dur* from 12; Hon C Etherley from 12; Hon C Witton Park from 12; Hon C Hamsterley and Witton-le-Wear from 12; PtO from 15. *Green View House, Hamsterley, Bishop Auckland DL13 3QF* T: (01388) 488898 E: trevorpitt@aol.com

PITT, Mrs Valerie. b 55. Liv Univ BA 77. STETS 02. **d** 05 **p** 06. NSM Oxshott *Guildf* 05-09; NSM Meole Brace *Lich* from 09. *4 Meole Hall Gardens, Shrewsbury SY3 9JS* T: (01743) 270102 E: valerie.pitt@trinitychurches.org

PITTARIDES, Renos. b 62. Surrey Univ BA 85. **d** 07 **p** 08. OLM Cobham and Stoke D'Abernon *Guildf* from 07. *46 Freelands Road, Cobham KT11 2ND* T/F: (01932) 887996 E: renosp@gmail.com

PITTIS, Canon Stephen Charles. b 52. Sheff Univ MA 01. Oak Hill Th Coll. **d** 76 **p** 77. C Win Ch Ch 76-79; Chapl Dorset Inst of HE and Bournemouth and Poole Coll of FE *Sarum* 79-84; V Woking St Paul *Guildf* 84-97; Dir of Faith Development *Win* 97-09; Dioc Missr and Can Res Win Cathl 09-11; Hon Can Win Cathl from 13; R Michelmersh and Awbridge and Braishfield etc from 11. *The Rectory, Braishfield Road, Braishfield, Romsey SO51 0PR* T: (01794) 368335

PITTS, Canon Evadne Ione (Eve). b 50. Qu Coll Birm. **d** 89 **p** 94. C Bartley Green *Birm* 89-93; Team Dn Kings Norton 93-94; TV 94-98; P-in-c Highters Heath 98-00; V 00-09; P-in-c Birchfield 09-14; V from 14; Hon Can Birm Cathl from 05. *Holy Trinity Vicarage, 213 Birchfield Road, Birmingham B20 3DG* T: 0121-356 4241 E: blackuhru@aol.com

PITTS, The Very Revd Michael James. b 44. Worc Coll Ox BA 66 Worc Coll of Educn MA 69. Qu Coll Birm 67. **d** 69 **p** 70. C Pennywell St Thos and Grindon St Oswald CD *Dur* 69-72; C Darlington H Trin 72-74; Chapl Dunkerque w Lille Arras etc Miss to Seamen *Eur* 74-79; V Tudhoe *Dur* 79-81; Chapl Helsinki w Moscow *Eur* 81-85; Chapl Stockholm 85-88; Hon Can Brussels Cathl 87-88; Hon Chapl Miss to Seafarers Canada from 88; R Montreal St Cuth 88-91; Dean Ch Ch Cathl Montreal 91-09; P-in-c Montreal St Ignatius from 09; rtd 09. *3279 rue Gariepy RR4, Sainte Julienne QC J0K 2T0, Canada* T: (001) (450) 834 2956 E: michael.pitts@worc.oxon.org

PITYANA, Prof Nyameko Barney. b 45. K Coll Lon BD 81 Cape Town Univ PhD 95 Trin Coll Hartford (USA) Hon DD 96. Ripon Coll Cuddesdon 82. **d** 82 **p** 83. C Woughton *Ox* 82-85; V Highters Heath *Birm* 85-88; Dir Progr to Combat Racism WCC Geneva *Eur* 88-92; Hon C 88-92; Sen Lect RS Cape Town Univ S Africa 93-95; Chair Human Rights Commission 95-01; Prin and Vice Chan UNISA 01-10; FKC 06; R Coll of Transfiguration Grahamstown from 11; Can of Prov from 11. *College of the Transfiguration, PO Box 77, Grahamstown, 6140 South Africa* T: (0027) (46) 622 3332 F: 622 3877 E: rector@cott.co.za

PIX, Mrs Sarah Anne Louise. b 71. Southn Univ BSc 92 Birkbeck Coll Lon MSc 97. Ridley Hall Cam 02. **d** 06 **p** 07. C W Slough *Ox* 06-08; C Britwell 08-09; TV Hampreston *Sarum* 09-15; TR from 15. *9 Pinewood Road, Ferndown BH22 9RW* T: (01202) 890798 E: revsarahpix@yahoo.co.uk

PIX, Stephen James. b 42. Ex Coll Ox BA 64 MA 68 Univ of Wales (Cardiff) LLM 97. Clifton Th Coll 66. **d** 68 **p** 69. C St Helens St Helen *Liv* 68-71; LtO *S'wark* 71-76; Hon C Wallington 76-84; V Osmotherley w E Harlsey and Ingleby Arncliffe *York* 84-89; V Ox St Mich w St Martin and All SS 89-01; rtd 01; PtO *St E* 01-07; *Ox* from 07. *10 Cadogan Park, Woodstock OX20 1UW* T: (01993) 812473

PIZZEY, Canon Lawrence Roger. b 42. Dur Univ BA 64. Westcott Ho Cam 65. **d** 67 **p** 68. C Bramford *St E* 67-71; Tutor Woodbridge Abbey 71-77; Asst Chapl Woodbridge Sch 71-77; P-in-c Flempton w Hengrave and Lackford *St E* 77-85; R Culford, W Stow and Wordwell 77-85; P-in-c Acton w Gt Waldingfield 85-89; V 89-95; P-in-c Sudbury and Chilton 95-98; R 98-07; RD Sudbury 96-06; Hon Can St E Cathl 00-07; rtd 07; PtO *St E* from 07. *9 Constable Road, Bury St Edmunds IP33 3UQ* T: (01284) 762863 E: lrp.sudbury@virgin.net

PLACE, Rodger Goodson. b 37. St Chad's Coll Dur BA 60. **d** 62 **p** 63. C Pontesbury I and II *Heref* 62-65; C Heref St Martin 65-68; V Ditton Priors 68-75; R Neenton 68-75; P-in-c Aston Botterell w Wheathill and Loughton 69-75; P-in-c Burwarton w N Cleobury 69-75; P-in-c Dacre w Hartwith *Ripon* 75-76; V 76-82; V Wyther 82-92; P-in-c Roundhay St Jo 92-97;

V 97-00; rtd 00; PtO *York* from 00. *72 Field Lane, Thorpe Willoughby, Selby YO8 9FL* T: (01757) 703174

PLACE, Thomas Richard. b 59. Ridley Hall Cam 93. **d** 93 **p** 94. C Huyton St Geo *Liv* 93-97; CF 97-07; Sen CF from 07. *c/o MOD Chaplains (Army)* T: (01264) 383430 F: 381824

PLACKETT, Miss Jane Louise. b 85. St Jo Coll Nottm 12. **d** 15. *131 Radbourne Street, Derby DE22 3BW* M: 07593-700999 E: revjplackett@gmail.com

PLAISTER, Keith Robin. b 43. K Coll Lon BD 65 AKC 65. **d** 66 **p** 67. C Laindon w Basildon *Chelmsf* 66-71; V Gt Wakering 71-78; V Gt Wakering w Foulness 78-90; C Witham 91-94; TV 94-99; P-in-c Sandon and E Hanningfield 99-08; rtd 08; PtO *Chelmsf* from 10. *118 Maldon Road, Great Baddow, Chelmsford CM2 7DH* T: (01245) 473135 E: keithplaister@hotmail.com

PLANT, Caroline Mary. b 56. Ripon Coll Cuddesdon 01. **d** 03 **p** 04. C Gnosall *Lich* 03-06; C Gnosall and Moreton 06-07; TV Penkridge 07-12; Asst Chapl Staffs Univ 12-15; rtd 15. *Address temp unknown* E: carolineplant@yahoo.co.uk

PLANT, Mrs Edith Winifred Irene (Ewith). b 31. Liv Univ BEd 71. Cranmer Hall Dur 81. **dss** 83 **d** 87. Countesthorpe w Foston *Leic* 83-86; Loughborough All SS and H Trin 86-90; Par Dn 87-90; Par Dn Thurnby Lodge 90-91; rtd 91; PtO *Leic* 91-96; *Ab* from 97. *c/o Mrs J Wallis, Upper Braikley Cottage, Methlick, Ellon AB41 7HD* T: (01651) 806209

PLANT, Miss Elizabeth Bowers. b 48. Westf Coll Lon BA 70 Man Univ PGCE 71. **d** 08 **p** 09. OLM Deane *Man* from 08. *25 Kintyre Drive, Bolton BL3 4PE* T: (01204) 63730 E: eplant@supanet.com

PLANT, Mrs Glenys. b 49. ALA 71. EMMTC 95. **d** 98 **p** 99. C Allestree *Derby* 98-01; rtd 01; PtO *Derby* from 01. *3 Stoodley Pike Gardens, Allestree, Derby DE22 2TN* T: (01332) 552697

PLANT, John Frederick. b 61. Man Univ BA 82 MEd 95. Qu Coll Birm 83. **d** 85 **p** 86. C Kersal Moor *Man* 85-88; Chapl Aston Univ *Birm* 88-94; TR Market Bosworth, Cadeby w Sutton Cheney etc *Leic* 94-00; P-in-c The Sheepy Gp 98-00; TR Bosworth and Sheepy Gp 00-12; P-in-c Nailstone and Carlton w Shackerstone 04-12; Ch Relns Manager Chr Aid from 12. *Brookfield Barn, Sibson Lane, Shenton, Nuneaton CV13 6DA* T: (01455) 212334

PLANT, Michael Ian. b 47. Man Univ MEd 85 GNSM 68. St Jo Coll Nottm 97. **d** 99 **p** 00. NSM St D Cathl 99-01; NSM Dewisland from 01. *Pencnwc Cottages, St Ishmael's, Castle Morris, Haverfordwest SA62 5ER* T: (01348) 841390

PLANT, Michelle. b 50. NEOC. **d** 08 **p** 11. NSM Burley *Leeds* from 08. *20 Lakeland Crescent, Leeds LS17 7PR* T: 0113-261 4757

PLANT, Nicholas. See PLANT, Richard George Nicholas

PLANT, Nicholas. b 58. MAAT 87. SAOMC 95. **d** 98 **p** 99. OLM W Slough *Ox* 98-04; OLM Burnham w Dropmore, Hitcham and Taplow 04-08; NSM Taplow and Dropmore 08-09; C The Cookhams 09-14; V from 14. *The Vicarage, Churchgate, Sutton Road, Cookham, Maidenhead SL6 9SP* T: (01628) 529183 E: fr.nick@ymail.com

PLANT, Richard. b 41. Open Univ BSc 93. Qu Coll Birm 88. **d** 90 **p** 91. C Skelmersdale St Paul *Liv* 90-93; R Golborne 93-00; R Hesketh w Becconsall *Blackb* 00-07; rtd 07; PtO *Blackb* from 07. *12 Granville Avenue, Hesketh Bank, Preston PR4 6AH* T: (01772) 815257 E: richard.plant1@btinternet.com

PLANT, Richard George Nicholas. b 45. Man Univ BA 67. Coll of Resurr Mirfield 68. **d** 71 **p** 72. C Cleckheaton St Jo *Wakef* 71-74; P-in-c Adel *Ripon* 74-78; V Ireland Wood 78-82; V Armley w New Wortley 82-92; R Garforth 92-08; rtd 08; PtO *York* from 08. *3 Holman Avenue, Garforth, Leeds LS25 1HU* T: 0113-287 6064 E: nick.plant@tiscali.co.uk

PLANT, Robert David. b 28. Birm Univ BSc 49 Ch Ch Coll Cant MA 98. St Deiniol's Hawarden 74. **d** 76 **p** 80. NSM Llandrillo-yn-Rhos *St As* 76-79; NSM St Nicholas at Wade w Sarre and Chislet w Hoath *Cant* 79-07; PtO 07-12. *4 Sandalwood Drive, St Nicholas-at-Wade, Birchington CT7 0PE* T: (01843) 847274

PLANT, Stephen John. b 64. Birm Univ BA 86 Fitzw Coll Cam PhD 93. ERMC 10. **d** 11 **p** 11. Dean Trin Hall Cam from 10; NSM Cambridge St Jas *Ely* from 11. *Trinity Hall, Cambridge CB2 1TJ* T: (01223) 241169 or 332548 M: 07824-835199 E: sjp27@cam.ac.uk

PLANT, Thomas Richard. b 79. St Andr Univ MA 01 Bris Univ MPhil 05 Selw Coll Cam PhD 13. Westcott Ho Cam 08. **d** 12 **p** 13. C Gt Berkhamsted, Gt and Lt Gaddesden etc *St Alb* from 12. *15 Bourne Road, Berkhamsted HP4 3JY* M: 07766-283546 E: hyperousios@googlemail.com

PLATT, Andrew Martin Robert. b 41. Oak Hill Th Coll 74. **d** 76 **p** 77. C St Alb St Paul *St Alb* 76-79; V Gazeley w Dalham and Moulton *St E* 79-85; V Gazeley w Dalham, Moulton and Kentford 85-86; RD Mildenhall 84-86; P-in-c Saxmundham 86-89; R 89-97; P-in-c Sudbury w Ballingdon and Brundon

97-98; V 98-04; rtd 04; Co Ecum Officer *Nor* 04-09; PtO *St E* from 04; *Nor* from 04. *21 Homefield Paddock, Beccles NR34 9NE* T: (01502) 717744

PLATT, Anne Cecilia. *See* HOLMES, Anne Cecilia

PLATT, Anthea Kate Helen. b 71. **d** 08 **p** 09. C Thorley *St Alb* 08-14. *Address temp unknown* E: antheaplatt@hotmail.com

PLATT, Damian Edward. b 82. Ox Brookes Univ BA 04. Oak Hill Th Coll BA 12. **d** 12 **p** 13. C Bispham *Blackb* 12-15. *89 Ashfield Road, Blackpool FY2 0EN* T: (01253) 595873 M: 07875-311929 E: damian@theplattfamily.org

PLATT, David. *See* PLATT, William David

PLATT, Mrs Jane Marie. b 54. Westhill Coll Birm CertEd 76 Open Univ BA 90. Qu Coll Birm 05. **d** 08 **p** 09. NSM Quinton Road W St Boniface *Birm* 08-15; PtO from 15. *39 Richmond Road, Rubery, Rednal, Birmingham B45 9UN* T: 0121-453 3035 E: janeplatt@onetel.com

PLATT, John Dendy. b 24. Magd Coll Cam BA 49 MA 55. Wells Th Coll 50. **d** 52 **p** 53. C Headley All SS *Guildf* 52-56; C Haslemere 56-58; R Skelton w Hutton-in-the-Forest *Carl* 59-71; rtd 89. *17 Primula Drive, Norwich NR4 7LZ* T: (01603) 504272

PLATT, John Emerson. b 36. Pemb Coll Ox BA 59 MA 65 DPhil 77 Hull Univ MTh 72. Cuddesdon Coll 59. **d** 61 **p** 62. C Adlington *Blackb* 61-64; C Sutton St Mich *York* 64-68; C Ox St Giles 68-71; Asst Chapl Pemb Coll Ox 68-69; Chapl 69-02; rtd 02. *Apple Tree Cottage, 2 Church Road, Wilmcote, Stratford-upon-Avon CV37 9XD* T: (01789) 770127

PLATT, Mrs Katherine Mary. b 29. Sheff Univ BA 51 ARIBA 51. Westcott Ho Cam 76. **dss** 79 **d** 87. Chesterton Gd Shep *Ely* 78-84; Whitton St Aug *Lon* 84-86; Dean of Women's Min 86-94; Hampton St Mary 86-94; Par Dn 87-94; rtd 94; PtO *Ches* 94-11. *Pine Cottage, Portloe, Truro TR2 5RB*

PLATT, Michael Robert. b 39. SS Coll Cam BA 61 MA 85 Nottm Univ PGCE 62. Cuddesdon Coll 62. **d** 64. C Far Headingley St Chad *Ripon* 64-65; Asst Master Belmont Coll Barnstaple 65-68; Asst Master Qu Coll Taunton 68-00; Ho Master 72-83; Hd Geography 89-00; rtd 00. *8 Court Hill, Taunton TA1 4SX* T/F: (01823) 270687

PLATT, William David. b 31. St Chad's Coll Dur BA 54. Coll of Resurr Mirfield 54. **d** 56 **p** 57. C Bethnal Green St Jo w St Simon *Lon* 56-60; C Pinner 60-65; V N Hammersmith St Kath 65-72; V Woodham *Guildf* 72-88; Chapl Community of St Mary V Wantage 88-96; rtd 96; NSM Blewbury, Hagbourne and Upton *Ox* 96-03. *14 Radley House, Marston Ferry Road, Oxford OX2 7EA* T: (01865) 556019

PLATTEN, Aidan Stephen George. b 76. Ripon Coll Cuddesdon BTh 03. **d** 03 **p** 04. C Woodbridge St Mary *St E* 03-06; Bp's Chapl *Glouc* 06-11; Hon Min Can Glouc Cathl 09-11; V St Marylebone St Mark Hamilton Terrace *Lon* from 11. *St Mark's Vicarage, Hamilton Terrace, London NW8 9UT* T: (020) 7328 4373

PLATTEN, Gregory Austin David. b 78. Worc Coll Ox BA 00 MA 08 Ox Univ MTh 05 Linc Coll Ox DPhil 13. Ripon Coll Cuddesdon 01. **d** 03 **p** 04. C St John's Wood *Lon* 03-07; Chapl Linc Coll and Hon C Ox St Mich w St Martin and All SS 07-13; V Friern Barnet All SS *Lon* from 13. *14 Oakleigh Park South, London N20 9JU* T: (020) 8445 0015 M: 07891-124478 E: gregory@priest.com

✣**PLATTEN, The Rt Revd Stephen George.** b 47. Lon Univ BEd 72 Trin Coll Ox BD 03 UEA Hon DLitt 03 Huddersfield Univ Hon DUniv 12 Hon FGCM 12. Cuddesdon Coll 72. **d** 75 **p** 76 **c** 03. C Headington *Ox* 75-78; Chapl and Tutor Linc Th Coll 78-83; Can Res Portms Cathl and Dir of Ords 83-89; Abp's Sec for Ecum Affairs *Cant* 90-95; Hon Can Cant Cathl 90-95; Dean Nor 95-03; Bp Wakef 03-14; rtd 14; R St Mich Cornhill w St Pet le Poer etc *Lon* from 14; Hon Asst Bp Lon from 14; Hon Asst Bp Newc from 14; Asst Bp S'wark from 14; Hon Can Musoma from 08. *73A Gloucester Place, London W1U 8JW* E: stephen.platten@icloud.com

PLATTIN, Miss Darleen Joy. b 63. Oak Hill Th Coll BA 94. ERMC 04. **d** 07 **p** 08. C Barnham Broom and Upper Yare *Nor* 07-10; P-in-c Easton, Colton, Marlingford and Bawburgh 10-14; P-in-c Gt and Lt Plumstead w Thorpe End and Witton from 14. *The Rectory, 9 Lawn Crescent, Thorpe End, Norwich NR13 5BP* E: darleenplattin@btinternet.com

PLATTS, Anthony Russell. b 41. Qu Coll Birm. **d** 08 **p** 09. NSM Hill *Birm* 08-11; PtO from 11. *14 Wheatcroft Close, Four Oaks, Sutton Coldfield B75 5SU* M: 07984-817564 E: a_platts1@sky.com

PLATTS, Mrs Hilary Anne Norrie. b 60. K Coll Lon BD 85 AKC 85 SRN 81. Ripon Coll Cuddesdon 86. **d** 88 **p** 94. C Moulsham St Jo *Chelmsf* 88-90; Chapl Reading Univ Ox 90-99; C Calcot 90-92; NSM Reading Deanery 99-06; PtO *Birm* 00-07; Chapl Birm Specialist Community Health NHS Trust 01-07; Chapl N Warks NHS Trust 03-07; PtO *Chelmsf* from 07;

Adv for Women's Min (Colchester Area) from 08; Chapl Colchester Hosp Univ NHS Foundn Trust from 09. *The Rectory, 7 Merlin End, Colchester CO4 3FW* E: hilaryplatts@googlemail.com

PLATTS, Timothy Caradoc. b 61. LMH Ox BA 83 MA 88 St Cross Coll Ox DPhil 88. Ripon Coll Cuddesdon 87. **d** 89 **p** 90. C Whitley Ch Ch *Ox* 89-95; P-in-c Earley St Nic 95-98; V 98-00; V Four Oaks *Birm* 00-07; P-in-c Elmstead *Chelmsf* 07-14; Chapl to Bp Colchester 07-14; P-in-c Greenstead w Colchester St Anne from 14. *The Rectory, 7 Merlin End, Colchester CO4 3FW* E: dogwalker2512@gmail.com

PLAXTON, Canon Edmund John Swithun. b 36. AKC 60. **d** 61 **p** 62. C Crofton Park St Hilda w St Cypr *S'wark* 61-65; C Coulsdon St Jo 65-69; V Forest Hill St Paul 69-80; V Belmont 80-93; V Lingfield and Crowhurst 93-01; Hon Can S'wark Cathl 97-01; rtd 01. *Tynymaes, Y Fron, Upper Llandwrog, Caernarfon LL54 7BW* T: (01286) 880188 E: edmundrachel@aol.com

PLAYER, Leslie Mark. b 65. Ridley Hall Cam 92. **d** 95 **p** 96. C Belper *Derby* 95-98; C Hamworthy *Sarum* 98-03; R W Downland from 03. *The Rectory, 97 Mill End, Damerham, Fordingbridge SP6 3HU* T: (01725) 518642 E: leslieplayer@hotmail.com

PLAYLE, Ms Merrin Laura. b 58. Univ of Wales (Swansea) BSc 79. Ridley Hall Cam 99. **d** 01 **p** 02. C Haslemere and Grayswood *Guildf* 01-05; V E Ham St Paul *Chelmsf* from 05. *St Paul's Vicarage, 227 Burges Road, London E6 2EU* T: (020) 8472 5531 E: merrin.playle@btopenworld.com

PLEDGER, Miss Alison Frances. b 56. Univ of Wales (Cardiff) BA 79 K Alfred's Coll Win PGCE 80. Linc Th Coll 89. **d** 91 **p** 94. Par Dn Soham *Ely* 91-94; C Ely 94-96; C Rusthall *Roch* 97-00; V Alkborough *Linc* from 00; P-in-c Flixborough w Burton upon Stather from 09. *The Vicarage, Back Street, Alkborough, Scunthorpe DN15 9JJ* T: (01724) 721126

PLEDGER, Mrs Nicola. b 55. Lon Bible Coll BA 94. SAOMC 99. **d** 01 **p** 02. C Ware Ch Ch *St Alb* 01-05; PtO 05-11; V Hitcham *Ox* from 11. *Hitcham Vicarage, 1 The Precincts, Burnham, Slough SL1 7HU* T: (01628) 602778 E: nicky@thepledgers.co.uk

PLESSIS, John Kenneth. b 69. Univ of Wales (Cardiff) BSc 91 BA 05 Univ of Wales (Swansea) PhD 03 PGCE 92. St Mich Coll Llan 03. **d** 05 **p** 06. C Haverfordwest St Mary and St Thos w Haroldston *St D* 05-08; C Abergavenny St Mary w Llanwenarth Citra *Mon* 08-10; PtO *St D* 11-12; P-in-c Llangennech and Hendy and Llwynhendy from 12. *57 Pendderi Road, Llanelli SA14 9PL* T: (01554) 821353 M: 07868-750228

PLIMLEY, Canon William. b 17. St Aid Birkenhead 50. **d** 52 **p** 53. C Norbury *Ches* 52-55; V Laisterdyke *Bradf* 55-83; RD Calverley 65-78; Hon Can Bradf Cathl 67-83; rtd 83; PtO *Leeds* from 83. *465 Bradford Road, Pudsey LS28 8ED* T: (01274) 664862

PLIMMER, Wayne Robert. b 64. St Chad's Coll Dur BA 85 Leeds Univ MA 07. St Steph Ho Ox 86. **d** 88 **p** 89. C Cockerton *Dur* 88-91; C Poulton-le-Fylde *Blackb* 91-93; V Darton *Wakef* 93-06; P-in-c Cawthorne 04-06; V Beeston *S'well* from 06. *The Vicarage, Middle Street, Beeston, Nottingham NG9 1GA* T: 0115-925 4571 E: wplimmer@tiscali.co.uk

PLOWMAN, Richard Robert Bindon. b 38. Solicitor 61. Ridley Hall Cam 76. **d** 78 **p** 79. C Combe Down w Monkton Combe *B & W* 78-81; C Combe Down w Monkton Combe and S Stoke 81-83; V Coxley w Godney, Henton and Wookey 83-03; RD Shepton Mallet 95-01; rtd 03; PtO *B & W* from 04. *Hyland House, Lower Rudge, Frome BA11 2QE* T: (01373) 831316

PLOWS, Jonathan. b 57. Warwick Univ BA 79 Homerton Coll Cam PGCE 80 Birkbeck Coll Lon MSc 85. STETS BA 07. **d** 07 **p** 08. NSM Salisbury St Thos and St Edm *Sarum* from 07. *171 Castle Road, Salisbury SP1 3RX* T: (01722) 331647 F: 410941 E: jonplows@aol.com

PLUCK, Richard. b 60. Southn Univ BTh 90. Aston Tr Scheme 84 Sarum & Wells Th Coll 86. **d** 90 **p** 91. C Harpenden St Nic *St Alb* 90-94; CF from 94. *c/o MOD Chaplains (Army)* F: 381824 T: (01264) 383430

PLUMB, Gordon Alan. b 42. Leeds Univ BA 64. Sarum & Wells Th Coll. **d** 82 **p** 83. C Biggleswade *St Alb* 82-86; TV Grantham *Linc* 86-95; P-in-c Saxby All Saints 95-97; R 97-07; P-in-c Bonby 95-97; V 97-07; P-in-c Horkstow 95-97; V 97-07; P-in-c S Ferriby 95-97; R 97-07; P-in-c Worlaby 95-97; V 97-07; rtd 07; PtO *Linc* from 08. *Ingham House, 45A Dam Road, Barton-upon-Humber DN18 5BT* T: (01652) 636445 E: gplumb2000@aol.com

PLUMB, Nicola Louise. *See* MOY, Nicola Louise

PLUMB, Capt Stephen Paul. b 59. **d** 15. NSM The Six *Cant* from 15. *7 Church Mews, The Street, Iwade, Sittingbourne ME9 8TH* T: (01795) 470418 E: captainplumby@btinternet.com

PLUMB, Stuart Peter. b 81. Ox Brookes Univ BA 04. Trin Coll Bris MA 14. **d** 14 **p** 15. C Kingston Hill St Paul *S'wark* from 14. *33A Queens Road, Kingston upon Thames KT2 7SF* M: 07598-335324 E: stuplumb@gmail.com

PLUMB, Miss Valerie Isabelle Dawn Frances. b 69. Ripon Coll Cuddesdon BTh 02. **d** 01 **p** 02. C Newport St Andr *Mon* 01-03; C Monmouth w Overmonnow etc 03-06; TV By Brook and Colerne w N Wraxall *Bris* 06-09; R Quantock Towers *B & W* from 09. *The Rectory, 11 Trendle Lane, Bicknoller, Taunton TA4 4EG* M: 07825-877722 E: revd_val@yahoo.co.uk

PLUMLEY, Paul Jonathan. b 42. St Jo Coll Nottm 71. **d** 74 **p** 75. C Mile Cross *Nor* 74-77; P-in-c Wickham Skeith *St E* 77-79; P-in-c Stoke Ash, Thwaite and Wetheringsett 77-79; Assoc Min Woodbridge St Jo 80-81; Chapl RAF 81-86; PtO *Roch* 86-95; R Hever, Four Elms and Mark Beech 95-00; Sen Chapl Maidstone and Tunbridge Wells NHS Trust 00-07; rtd 07; PtO *Roch* from 08; PV Roch Cathl from 12. *4 Cedar Ridge, Tunbridge Wells TN2 3NX* M: 07925-615601 T: (01892) 514499 E: pauljplumley@gmail.com *or* paul.plumley@tiscali.co.uk

PLUMMER, Angela. b 59. Linc Sch of Th and Min. **d** 13 **p** 14. *1 Blackthorn Close, Melbourne, Derby DE73 8LY* T: (01332) 863592 M: 07721-023339 E: aplummer@live.co.uk

PLUMMER, Miss Anne Frances. b 36. Bedf Coll Lon BA 57. S'wark Ord Course 79. **dss** 82 **d** 87 **p** 94. NSM Salfords *S'wark* 82-06; Dean MSE (Croydon) 97-02; PtO 06-07. *50 Park View Road, Salfords, Redhill RH1 5DN* T: (01293) 785852

PLUMMER, Canon Deborah Ann. b 49. St Hugh's Coll Ox BA 71 MA 75. St Alb Minl Tr Scheme 82. **dss** 85 **d** 87 **p** 94. Ickenham *Lon* 85-88; Par Dn 87-88; C Northolt St Mary 88-92; Chapl Lee Abbey 92-95; P-in-c Kintbury w Avington *Ox* 95-01; Lect Bolton St Pet *Man* 01-07; P-in-c Prestwich St Marg 07-14; C Prestwich St Gabr 10-14; AD Radcliffe and Prestwich 09-13; Hon Can Man Cathl 12-14; rtd 14; PtO *Man* from 15. *Meadow View, 7 Church Terrace, Berry Brow, Huddersfield HD4 7NB* M: 07939-916315 T: (01484) 667661

PLUMMER, Lee Richard. b 77. Liv Univ BA 98 Birm Univ PGCE 00. St Jo Coll Nottm LTh 10. **d** 10. C Newchapel *Lich* 10-14; TV Cen Telford from 14. *28 Bartholomew Road, Lawley Village, Telford TF4 2PW* M: 07590-606425 E: lee@leeandbeckyplummer.co.uk

PLUMMER, Mrs Susan Mary. b 44. **d** 14 **p** 15. NSM Darlington St Hilda and St Columba *Dur* from 14; NSM Darlington St Jo from 14. *24 Woodcrest Road, Darlington DL3 8EF* T: (01325) 255497 M: 07743-886158 E: cawood78@hotmail.com

PLUMPTON, Paul. b 50. Keble Coll Ox BA 72 MA 76. St Steph Ho Ox 72. **d** 74 **p** 75. C Tonge Moor *Man* 74-76; C Atherton 76-79; V Oldham St Jas 79-99; V Oldham St Jas w St Ambrose from 99. *The Vicarage, Yates Street, Oldham OL1 4AR* T: 0161-633 4441

PLUNKETT, Michael Edward. b 38. MBE 04. Leeds Univ BSc 61. Ely Th Coll 61. **d** 63 **p** 64. C Kirkby *Liv* 63-68; Lect Stockton-on-Tees 68-72; LtO *Dur* 72-73; TV Stockton 73-75; V Cantril Farm *Liv* 75-81; Soc Resp Officer 81-89; V Melling 81-91; TR Speke St Aid 91-04; rtd 04; PtO *Heref* from 04. *1 The Ridge, Bishops Castle SY9 5AB* T: (01588) 630078

PLUNKETT, Canon Peter William. b 30. Oak Hill Th Coll. **d** 61 **p** 62. C Fazakerley Em *Liv* 61-64; C St Helens St Mark 64-68; V Kirkdale St Paul N Shore 68-79; P-in-c Bootle St Mary w St Jo 77-79; V Bootle St Mary w St Paul 79-81; V Goose Green 81-89; V W Derby St Jas 89-98; Hon Can Liv Cathl 97-98; rtd 98. *50 Trinity Crescent, West Shore, Llandudno LL30 2PQ* T: (01492) 872109

PLYMING, Philip James John. b 74. Rob Coll Cam BA 96 St Jo Coll Dur BA 00 Edin Univ PhD 08. Cranmer Hall Dur 98. **d** 01 **p** 02. C Chineham *Win* 01-06; V Claygate *Guildf* from 06; RD Emly from 12. *The Vicarage, Church Road, Claygate, Esher KT10 0JP* T: (01372) 463603 E: philipplyming@holytrinityclaygate.org.uk

PLYMOUTH, Archdeacon of. *See* CHANDLER, The Ven Ian Nigel

PLYMOUTH, Suffragan Bishop of. *See* MACKINNEL, The Rt Revd Nicholas Howard Paul

PNEMATICATOS, Nicholas Peter Anthony. b 59. N Lon Univ BA 92 Lon Univ MA 93. Ripon Coll Cuddesdon 93. **d** 95 **p** 96. C Yeovil St Mich *B & W* 95-98; Chapl Yeovil Coll 95-96; Chapl RN 98-02; Chapl RAF 02-08; P-in-c Mill End and Heronsgate w W Hyde *St Alb* 08-10. *St Mary's Vicarage, 18 Neasden Lane, London NW10 2TS* M: 07703-566787 E: delvillewood@aol.com

POARCH, Canon John Chilton. b 30. Bris Univ BA 54. Ridley Hall Cam 54. **d** 56 **p** 57. C Swindon Ch Ch *Bris* 56-59; C Corsham 59-61; R Praslin Seychelles 61-63; V Brislington St Cuth *Bris* 63-69; Adn Seychelles 69-72; R St Paul's Cathl Mahé 69-72; V Warmley *Bris* 72-86; R Syston 72-86; RD Bitton

79-85; P-in-c 80-86; Hon Can Bris Cathl 82-95; P-in-c Langley Fitzurse 86-94; Dioc Dir of Ords 86-94; Dir Ord Tr 94-95; P-in-c Draycot Cerne 87-94; rtd 95; PtO *Bris* from 95; *B & W* 98-01; Officer for the Welfare of Rtd Mins Bris Adnry from 01; Dioc Convenor Rtd Clergy Assn from 01. *16 Norley Road, Bristol BS7 0HP* T: 0117-951 7970

POCOCK, Mrs Gillian Margaret. b 35. Nottm Univ BA 57. Cranmer Hall Dur 82. **dss** 83 **d** 87 **p** 94. Bearpark *Dur* 83-88; Hon Par Dn 87-88; Par Dn S Hetton w Haswell 88; Asst RD Dur 89-90; Chapl St Aid Coll Dur 89-93; Par Dn Esh *Dur* 90-92; P-in-c 92-99; P-in-c Hamsteels 97-99; P-in-c Langley Park 98-99; rtd 99; PtO *Dur* from 04. *11 Cooke's Wood, Broom Park, Durham DH7 7RL* T: 0191-386 1140 E: gillian.pocock@lineone.net

POCOCK, Lynn Elizabeth. b 48. Coll of Wooster Ohio BA 69 CertEd 71. Qu Coll Birm 73. **dss** 82 **d** 87 **p** 94. Par Dn Thorpe Hesley *Sheff* 87-92; NSM Ribbesford w Bewdley and Dowles *Worc* 92-03; PtO from 03. *2 Waterworks Road, Worcester WR1 3EX* T: (01905) 612634 E: lynn_pocock@yahoo.com

POCOCK, Canon Nigel John. b 47. Lon Univ BSc 68 Birm Univ MA 83 Lambeth STh 78. Oak Hill Th Coll 69. **d** 72 **p** 73. C Tunbridge Wells St Jas *Roch* 72-75; C Heatherlands St Jo *Sarum* 75-78; V Leic St Chris 78-83; R Camborne *Truro* 83-97; RD Carnmarth N 91-96; Hon Can Truro Cathl 92-97; V Old Windsor *Ox* 97-09; rtd 09. *23 Culm Valley Way, Uffculme, Cullompton EX15 3XZ* T: (01884) 849198 E: njpoc@tiscali.co.uk

PODGER, Richard Philip Champeney. b 38. K Coll Cam BA 61 MA 66. Cuddesdon Coll 62. **d** 64 **p** 65. C Doncaster St Geo *Sheff* 64-68; C Orpington All SS *Roch* 68-74; W Germany 76-88; Chapl Kassel *Eur* 83-88; TV Whitstable *Cant* 88-94; PtO 95-12; Chapl E Kent NHS and Soc Care Partnership Trust 02-06; Chapl Kent & Medway NHS and Soc Care Partnership Trust 06-10; PtO *S & B* from 12. *Dros y Sir, Pen Cantref, Cantref, Brecon LD3 8LT* T: (01874) 622160 E: podger@centrespace.freeserve.co.uk

POGMORE, Canon Edward Clement. b 52. Sarum & Wells Th Coll 76. **d** 79 **p** 80. C Calne and Blackland *Sarum* 79-82; TV Oakdale 82-89; Min Creekmoor LEP 82-89; Chapl Geo Eliot Hosp Nuneaton 89-94; Chapl Nuneaton Hosps 89-94; Chapl Geo Eliot Hosp NHS Trust Nuneaton 94-14; Chapl Co-ord for N Warks 94-14; PtO *Leic* 91-14; Hon Can Cov Cathl 00-14; rtd 14; Chapl Abbeyfield Binley *Cov* from 14. *1 Bowman Green, Burbage, Hinckley LE10 2QY* T: (01455) 611492 E: edpog@hotmail.com

POINTS, John David. b 43. Qu Coll Birm 78. **d** 80 **p** 81. C Wednesbury St Paul Wood Green *Lich* 80-85; V 93-01; V Wednesfield St Mary 85-93; TR Wednesfield 01-08; AD Wolverhampton 03-08; rtd 08; PtO *St As* from 09. *13 Oldcastle Avenue, Guilsfield, Welshpool SY21 9PA* T: (01938) 552092

POLASHEK, Miss Stella Christine. b 44. Leic Poly MA 85. EMMTC 92. **d** 95 **p** 96. NSM Appleby Gp *Leic* 95-08; NSM Woodfield 08-10; Chapl Leic Gen Hosp NHS Trust 99-00; Chapl Univ Hosps Leic NHS Trust 00-10; rtd 10; PtO *Leic* from 11. *85 Parkfield Crescent, Appleby Magna, Swadlincote DE12 7BW* T: (01530) 272547 E: stella.85@btinternet.com

POLE, David John. b 46. Bath Academy of Art BA 72. Trin Coll Bris 84. **d** 86 **p** 87. C Bris St Mary Redcliffe w Temple etc 86-90; V Alveston 90-98; V Alveston and Littleton-on-Severn w Elberton 98-15; C Pilning w Compton Greenfield 11-15; rtd 15. *Address temp unknown* E: david.pole@dsl.pipex.com

POLE, Francis John Michael. b 42. FRSA 64 MInstLM 00 CQSW 74 MCMI 99. St Jo Sem Wonersh 62. **d** 67 **p** 68. In RC Ch 67-75; NSM Walthamstow St Pet *Chelmsf* 75; NSM Penge Lane H Trin *Roch* 76-77; NSM Shirley St Jo *Cant* 77-79; Assoc Chapl The Hague *Eur* 79-83; V Norbury St Steph and Thornton Heath *Cant* 83-84; S'wark 85-00; Sen Dioc Police Chapl 95-00; Sen Chapl Sussex Police 00-03; Nat Co-ord Police Chapl 00-04; Sen Chapl Sussex Ambulance Service 04-06; Co-ord Chapl SE Coast Ambulance Service 06-12; TV Crawley *Chich* 00-12; Chapl to People at Work 00-12; Sen Chapl SE Coast Ambulance Service NHS Foundn Trust from 12; PtO *Chich* from 13. *35 Turnpike Place, Crawley RH11 7UA* T: (01293) 513264 M: 07764-752608 E: francis.pole@virgin.net

POLHILL, Mrs Christine. b 46. Nottm Coll of Educn CertEd 67 Qu Coll Birm BA 00. St Alb Minl Tr Scheme 81. **dss** 84 **d** 87 **p** 94. St Alb St Mary Marshalswick *St Alb* 84-94; Hon Par Dn 87-94; C Cottered w Broadfield and Throcking 94-96; P-in-c 96-99; C Ardeley 94-96; P-in-c 96-99; C Weston 94-96; PtO *Lich* 99-00; C Lich St Mich w St Mary and Wall 00-06; rtd 06; LtO *Lich* 06-12; PtO 12-13; Hon C Hints 13-14. *Little Hayes, Beaudesert Park, Cannock Wood, Rugeley WS15 4JJ* T: (01543) 674474 E: christine@reflectiongardens.org.uk

POLITT, Robert William. b 47. ARCM LGSM 68. Oak Hill Th Coll 73. **d** 76 **p** 77. C Bexleyheath St Pet *Roch* 76-82; TV Southgate *Chich* 82-90; Chapl N Foreland Lodge Sch Basingstoke 90-98; R Sherfield-on-Loddon and Stratfield Saye etc *Win* 98-13; P-in-c Bramley 10-13; rtd 13. *53 Somerset Road, Histon, Cambridge CB24 9JS*
E: 113225.103@compuserve.com

POLKINGHORNE, Canon John Charlton. b 30. KBE 97. Trin Coll Cam BA 52 PhD 55 MA 56 ScD 74 FRS 74. Westcott Ho Cam 79. **d** 81 **p** 82. NSM Chesterton St Andr *Ely* 81-82; C Bedminster St Mich *Bris* 82-84; V Blean *Cant* 84-86; Dean Trin Hall Cam 86-89; Pres Qu Coll Cam 89-96; Can Th Liv Cathl from 94; rtd 95; Six Preacher Cant Cathl 96-00; PtO *Ely* from 96. *74 Hurst Park Avenue, Cambridge CB4 2AF* T: (01223) 360743

POLKINHORN, Mrs Judith Edith Elizabeth. b 47. Wolv Univ MBA 04. ERMC 13. **d** 14 **p** 15. NSM Lordsbridge *Ely* from 14. *The Old Rectory, High Street, Harlton, Cambridge CB23 1ES* T: (01223) 262072 E: judypolkinhorn@gmail.com

POLL, Canon Martin George. b 61. Kent Univ BA 83. Ripon Coll Cuddesdon 84. **d** 87 **p** 88. C Mill Hill Jo Keble Ch *Lon* 87-90; Chapl RN 90-10; Prin Angl Chapl and Adn for the RN 10-12; QHC 10-12; Hon Can Portsm Cathl 11-12; Can Windsor and Chapl in Windsor Gt Park from 12. *1 The Cloisters, Windsor Castle, Windsor SL4 1NJ* T: (01753) 848713 E: martin.poll@stgeorges-windsor.org

POLLARD, Adrian. *See* POLLARD, James Adrian Hunter

POLLARD, Mrs Ann Beatrice. b 46. **d** 03 **p** 04. NSM Mirfield *Wakef* 03-10; NSM Dewsbury *Leeds* from 10. *9 Manor Drive, Mirfield WF14 0ER* T: (01924) 495322 M: 07751-630609 E: ann.pollard@o2.co.uk

POLLARD, Mrs Christine Beryl. b 45. NOC 86. **d** 89 **p** 94. Par Dn Ingrow w Hainworth *Bradf* 89-94; C Nuneaton St Nic *Cov* 94-98; P-in-c Bourton w Frankton and Stretton on Dunsmore etc 98-07; rtd 07; PtO *Cov* from 08. *9 Overberry Orchard, Leamington Spa CV33 9SJ* T: (01926) 832053 E: cbpollard@talktalk.net

POLLARD, Canon Clifford Francis. b 20. AKC 49. **d** 50 **p** 51. C Leominster *Heref* 50-53; C Luton St Mary *St Alb* 53-56; V Stopsley 56-60; Chapl Toc H (Kent and Sussex) 60-64; R Mersham *Cant* 64-68; Asst Dir of Educn 68-69; Dir of Educn 69-87; Hon Can Cant Cathl 72-91; rtd 87; PtO *Cant* 03-13. *The Red House Nursing Home, London Road, Canterbury CT2 8BN* T: (01227) 464171

POLLARD, David. b 55. LSE BSc 77. Trin Coll Bris 78. **d** 80 **p** 81. Canada 81-84; C-in-c Hillsfield and Monkspath LEP *Birm* 85-89; Crosslinks 89-93 and 93-95; Spain 89-94; V Doncaster St Jas *Sheff* 95-98; rtd 98. *6 Mulberry Way, Armthorpe, Doncaster DN3 3UE* T: (01302) 833404

POLLARD, David John Athey. b 44. ACP 74 Culham Coll Ox CertEd 69. St Jo Coll Nottm LTh 88. **d** 88 **p** 89. C Illogan *Truro* 88-91; R Roche and Withiel 91-95; TV Maidstone St Martin *Cant* 95-97; C Parkwood CD 95-97; R Lanreath *Truro* 97-99; V Pelynt 97-99; R Lanreath, Pelynt and Bradoc 99-03; rtd 03. *Melyn Brea, 11 Mill Hill, Lostwithiel PL22 0HB* T: (01208) 871541 E: david.pollard@totalise.co.uk

POLLARD, Eric John. b 43. Chich Th Coll 83. **d** 85 **p** 86. C Brighton St Matthias *Chich* 85-90; C E Grinstead St Swithun 90-96; C Hove 96-00; P-in-c Brighton St Matthias 00-13; rtd 13. *30 Pondsyde Court, Sutton Drove, Seaford BN25 3ET* E: eric.pollard@btinternet.com

POLLARD, James Adrian Hunter. b 48. St Jo Coll Nottm BTh 78. **d** 78 **p** 79. C Much Woolton *Liv* 78-81; CMS 81-84; V Toxteth Park Ch Ch *Liv* 85-90; CF 90-09; rtd 09; PtO *Sarum* 09-12; Hon C Upper Wylye Valley 12-14; PtO from 14. *Horwood House, 80 Boreham Road, Warminster BA12 9JW*

POLLARD, John Edward Ralph. b 40. ALCD 68. **d** 67 **p** 68. C Ollerton *S'well* 67-71; C Walton H Trin *Ox* 71-74; P-in-c Cuddington w Dinton 74-77; V Haddenham 74-77; V Kingsey 75-77; V Haddenham w Cuddington and Kingsey 77-85; RD Aylesbury 80-85; V Haddenham w Cuddington, Kingsey etc 85-87; V Furze Platt 87-96; rtd 97. *2 Waldren Close, Poole BH15 1XS* T: (01202) 681494

POLLARD, Mrs Judith Mary. b 56. Westcott Ho Cam 09. **d** 11 **p** 12. C Newark w Coddington *S'well* 11-14; C Gayton, Gayton Thorpe, E Walton, E Winch etc *Nor* 14-15; TV Ashwicken w Leziate, Bawsey etc from 15. *The Rectory, Watery Lane, Grimston, King's Lynn PE32 1BQ* M: 07852-257734 E: wotzpollard@aol.com

POLLARD, Matthew Rupert. b 66. St Jo Coll Nottm. **d** 03 **p** 04. C Huddersfield St Pet *Wakef* 03-07; Asst Chapl Huddersfield Univ 03-07; P-in-c Rastrick St Matt 07-08; P-in-c Rastrick St Jo 07-08; V Rastrick 08-13; R Bridlington Priory *York* from 13. *The Rectory, Church Green, Bridlington YO16 7JX* T: (01262) 672221 E: matthewrpollard@btinternet.com

POLLARD, Mrs Patricia Julie. b 46. Open Univ BA 97. Cant Sch of Min 93. **d** 96 **p** 97. NSM Eastling w Ospringe and Stalisfield

w Otterden *Cant* 96-04; rtd 04; PtO *Cant* from 04. *65 Princes Gardens, Margate CT9 3AS* T: (01843) 280814
E: norman.pollard@tesco.net

POLLARD, Roger Frederick. b 32. Sheff Univ BSc 52 K Coll Lon PGCE 55 Lanc Univ MA 78. Linc Th Coll 56. **d** 58 **p** 59. C Catford St Laur *S'wark* 58-63; Ghana 63-66; C Fulford *York* 66-67; C Camberwell St Geo *S'wark* 67; Asst Master Roch Valley Sch Milnrow 68-69; S Craven Sch Cross Hills 69-91; rtd 91; PtO *Bradf* 69-93; *B & W* 93-06. *Little Garth, Rectory Lane, Dowlish Wake, Ilminster TA19 0NX* T: (01460) 52594

POLLARD, Samuel David. b 84. Nottm Univ BA 06 MA 08. Trin Coll Bris MPhil 11. **d** 11 **p** 12. C Loughton St Mary *Chelmsf* 11-15; NSM from 15. *32 Longcroft Rise, Loughton IG10 3NB* E: samuel.d.pollard@gmail.com *or* sam@stmarysloughton.com

POLLARD, Stephen. b 59. Coll of Resurr Mirfield 96. **d** 98 **p** 99. C Lt Lever *Man* 98-02; P-in-c Westleigh St Pet 02-10; P-in-c Westleigh St Paul 08-10; P-in-c Rosebud w McCrae Australia from 10. *120 Fifth Avenue, Rosebud, Victoria 3939, Australia* E: fatherstephenpollard@googlemail.com

POLLARD (née RAMSBOTTOM), Mrs Susan Elizabeth. b 56. Trin Coll Bris BD 79. Qu Coll Birm 06. **d** 09 **p** 10. NSM Warndon St Nic *Worc* from 09. *5 Falmouth, Worcester WR4 0TE* T: (01905) 759214 E: suepollard2610@hotmail.com

POLLARD, Vaughan. b 59. Aston Tr Scheme 88 Trin Coll Bris 90. **d** 92 **p** 93. C Nailsea H Trin *B & W* 92-95; C Acomb St Steph and St Aid *York* 95-97; P-in-c Moldgreen *Wakef* 97-99; P-in-c Rawthorpe 97-99; V Moldgreen and Rawthorpe 99-07; C Spalding and Spalding St Paul *Linc* 07-11; V Clayton *Leeds* from 11; AD Bowling and Horton from 14. *The Vicarage, Clayton Lane, Clayton, Bradford BD14 6AX* T: (01274) 880373 E: pollard247@ntlworld.com

POLLINGER (née WHITFORD), Canon Judith. b 41. Ex Univ TCert 78 BEd 79. SWMTC 92. **d** 95 **p** 96. NSM St Endellion w Port Isaac and St Kew *Truro* 95-12; NSM St Minver 07-12; NSM N Cornwall Cluster from 12; Convenor Bp's Gp for Min of Healing 04-11; Hon Can Truro Cathl from 10; Preb St Endellion from 12. *4 Marshalls Way, Trelights, Port Isaac PL29 3TE* T: (01208) 880181 E: rev.judith@btinternet.com

POLLINGTON, Miss Ann Elizabeth Jane. b 56. Univ Coll Chich BA 00. Ripon Coll Cuddesdon 00. **d** 02 **p** 03. C Honiton, Gittisham, Combe Raleigh, Monkton etc *Ex* 02-07; P-in-c St Ippolyts *St Alb* 07-10; P-in-c Gt and Lt Wymondley 07-10; R St Ippolyts w Gt and Lt Wymondley from 10. *The Vicarage, Stevenage Road, St Ippolyts, Hitchin SG4 7PE* T: (01462) 457552 E: annpolly@freeuk.com

POLLIT, Preb Michael. b 30. Worc Coll Ox BA 54 MA 58. Wells Th Coll 54. **d** 56 **p** 57. C Cannock *Lich* 56-59; C Codsall 59-62; V W Bromwich St Pet 62-67; R Norton in the Moors 67-76; RD Leek 72-76; V Shrewsbury St Chad 76-87; V Shrewsbury St Chad w St Mary 87-95; Preb Lich Cathl 81-95; P-in-c Shrewsbury St Alkmund 91-95; rtd 95; PtO *Heref* from 96. *Pentreheyling House, Churchstoke, Montgomery SY15 6HU* T: (01588) 620273

POLLIT, Ruth Mary. *See* LILLINGTON, Ruth Mary

POLLITT, Graham Anthony. b 48. BA 79. Oak Hill Th Coll 76. **d** 79 **p** 80. C Rusholme H Trin *Man* 79-82; TV Southgate *Chich* 82-83; C Burgess Hill St Andr 83-86; Chapl St Martin's Coll of Educn *Blackb* 86-90; Chapl Cheltenham and Glouc Coll of HE 90-98; PtO *Glouc* 98-99; C Bispham *Blackb* 99-04; P-in-c Caton w Littledale from 04. *The Vicarage, 153 Brookhouse Road, Brookhouse, Lancaster LA2 9NX* T: (01524) 770300 E: grahamapollitt@gmail.com

POLLOCK, Christopher John. b 62. TCD BTh 89 QUB BD. CITC 86. **d** 89 **p** 90. C Agherton *Conn* 89-91; C Ballymoney w Finvoy and Rasharkin 91-93; I Derryvolgie 93-03; I Saintfield *D & D* from 03. *The Vicarage, 11 Lisburn Road, Saintfield, Ballynahinch BT24 7AL* T: (028) 9751 0286 E: chris.pollock3@btinternet.com

POLLOCK, Darren John. b 85. Cranmer Hall Dur 13. **d** 15. C Walton Breck *Liv* from 15. *1 Burnet Road, Liverpool L5 1XN* M: 07851-488922 E: darrenjaypollock@gmail.com

POLLOCK, Duncan James Morrison. b 54. QGM 75 MBE 95. Nottm Univ BCombStuds 83. Linc Th Coll 80. **d** 83 **p** 84. C Folkestone St Mary and St Eanswythe *Cant* 83-85; CF 85-98; R Broughton, Bossington, Houghton and Mottisfont *Win* 98-00; I Grousport *D & D* from 00. *22 Sandringham Drive, Bangor BT20 5NA* T: (028) 9146 4476 E: duncanjmpollock@btinternet.com

POLLOCK, James Colin Graeme. b 53. St Chad's Coll Dur BA 76. Ripon Coll Cuddesdon 77. **d** 78 **p** 79. C Hartlepool St Oswald *Dur* 78-81; C Hartlepool St Aid 81-84; V Dawdon 84-05; V Seaham Harbour 03-05; TV S Shields All SS 05-13; rtd 13; PtO *Dur* from 13. *25 Knocklofty Court, Belfast BT4 3NF*

POLOMSKI, Elias Robert Michael. b 42. **d** 85 **p** 86. In RC Ch 85-90; C Headington Quarry *Ox* 91-94; Chapl St Alb Abbey

St Alb 94-97; Chapl St Alb Sch 94-97; P-in-c Streatley w Moulsford *Ox* 97-03; C 03-04; P-in-c Streatley 04-07; rtd 07. *The Hermitage, 1 Bremilham Road, Malmesbury SN16 0DQ* T: (01666) 825607

POMERY, David John. b 45. SS Mark & Jo Coll Chelsea CertEd 67. Chich Th Coll 75. **d** 77 **p** 78. C Coseley Ch Ch *Lich* 77-79; C Stocksbridge *Sheff* 79-81; V Bentley 81-87; Asst Master Radlett Prep Sch 87-03; P-in-c Barton Bendish w Beachamwell and Shingham *Ely* 03-09; P-in-c Boughton 03-09; P-in-c Wereham 03-09; P-in-c Fincham 03-09; P-in-c Marham 03-09; P-in-c Shouldham 03-09; P-in-c Shouldham Thorpe 03-09; V Edstaston, Fauls, Prees, Tilstock and Whixall *Lich* 09-12; rtd 12. *c/o Mrs S Hall, 3 Broxbourne Gardens, Bentley, Doncaster DN5 0HJ* E: rev-djpomery@supanet.com

POND, Canon Geraldine Phyllis. b 53. SRN 74 HVCert 75. St Jo Coll Nottm MA 97. **d** 97 **p** 98. C Ancaster Wilsford Gp *Linc* 97-01; P-in-c Harlaxton Gp 01-07; Chapl Linc Distr Healthcare NHS Trust 01-07; P-in-c Ashbourne St Oswald w Mapleton *Derby* 07-14; V from 14; P-in-c Ashbourne St Jo from 07; P-in-c Clifton from 09; P-in-c Norbury w Snelston from 09; Asst Dir of Ords 08-09; Dioc Dir of Ords from 09; Hon Can Derby Cathl from 10. *The Vicarage, 61 Belle Vue Road, Ashbourne DE6 1AT* T: (01335) 343129 E: geraldine@geraldinepond.com

POND, Nigel Peter Hamilton. b 40. AKC 65. **d** 66 **p** 67. C E Dereham w Hoe *Nor* 66-69; C Chapl RN 69-85; TR Woughton *Ox* 85-93; Chapl Milton Keynes Gen Hosp 85-93; RD Milton Keynes *Ox* 90-93; R Olney w Emberton 93-97; R Olney 97-03; rtd 03. *11 Gippingstone Road, Bramford, Ipswich IP8 4DR* T: (01473) 741887 E: nigelphpond@talktalk.net

PONSONBY, Simon Charles Reuben. b 66. Bris Univ MLitt 96. Trin Coll Bris BA 94. **d** 95 **p** 96. C Thorpe Edge *Bradf* 95-98; Pastorate Chapl Ox St Aldate from 98. *St Aldate's Parish Centre, 40 Pembroke Street, Oxford OX1 1BP* T: (01865) 254800 F: 201543 E: simon.ponsonby@staldates.org.uk

PONT, Gordon John Harper. b 35. Glas Univ BSc 56 BD 65. Edin Th Coll 56. **d** 59 **p** 60. C Dunfermline *St And* 59-62; C Motherwell *Glas* 62-65; R Largs 65-68; Dioc Supernumerary *Bre* 68-71; Chapl Dundee Univ 68-73; R Dundee St Luke 71-74; NSM Dundee St Paul and Hon Chapl St Paul's Cathl Dundee 74-99; Dioc Sec 96-02; rtd 02. *27 Fishersview Court, Station Road, Pitlochry PH16 5AN* T: (01796) 472745 E: gordon.pont@btinternet.com

PONTEFRACT, Archdeacon of. *See* TOWNLEY, The Ven Peter Kenneth

PONTER, John Arthur. b 37. Univ of Wales (Abth) BA 61 Linacre Coll Ox BA 63 MA 68 UEA PhD 81. Wycliffe Hall Ox 61. **d** 63 **p** 64. C Gidea Park *Chelmsf* 63-67; C-in-c Colchester St Anne CD 67-69; V Colchester St Anne 69-72; Chapl UEA *Nor* 72-78; Chapl Chelmsf Cathl 78-79; Chapl Chelmsf Cathl Cen 78-84; V Moulsham St Jo *Chelmsf* 79-85; Dir Man Chr Inst and Chr Leadership Course 85-92; Educn Officer N Federation for Tr in Min 85-92; TR Stantonbury and Willen *Ox* 92-02; rtd 02. *3 The Croft, 43A East Street, Wareham BH20 4NW* T: (01929) 558286 E: ponter@msn.com

PONTIN, Colin Henry. b 37. Trin Coll Bris. **d** 83 **p** 84. C Downend *Bris* 83-86; C Riverside *Ox* 86-88; V Eton w Eton Wick and Boveney 88-90; TV Riverside 91-95; V Churt *Guildf* 95-02; rtd 02; PtO *Win* from 03. *22 Shearsbrook Close, Bransgore, Christchurch BH23 8HF* T: (01425) 673918 M: 07989-173259 E: colinpontin@lineone.net

POOBALAN, Canon Isaac Munuswamy. b 62. RGN 84 Edin Univ BD 90 MTh 97 Aber Univ MPhil 98. Edin Th Coll 91. **d** 94 **p** 95. C Edin St Pet 94-97; P-in-c Aberdeen St Clem *Ab* 97-01; R Aberdeen St Jo from 01; P-in-c Aberdeen St Pet from 04; Can St Andr Cathl from 06. *The Rectory, 15 Ashley Road, Aberdeen AB10 6RU* T: (01224) 591527 E: aipoobalan@btinternet.com *or* rector@st-johns-aberdeen.org

POODHUN, Canon Lambert David. b 30. Natal Univ BA 53. Edin Th Coll 54. **d** 56 **p** 57. C Durban St Aidan S Africa 56-60; P-in-c Pietermaritzburg St Paul 60-64; R 64-67; R Overport 67-76; Adn Durban 75-76; C Upton cum Chalvey *Ox* 77-80; Chapl Kingston Hosp Surrey 80-81; Chapl Tooting Bec Hosp Lon 81-84; Chapl Hurstwood Park Hosp Haywards Heath 84-01; Chapl St Fran Hosp Haywards Heath 84-94; Chapl Mid Sussex NHS Trust 94-01; Can and Preb Chich Cathl from 93; Hon C Haywards Heath St Rich from 01. *8 Nursery Close, Haywards Heath RH16 1HP* T: (01444) 440938 E: lambertpoodhun@aol.com

POOLE, Andrew John. b 52. EMMTC 98. **d** 01 **p** 02. NSM Scraptoft *Leic* 01-14. *64 Scalborough Close, Countesthorpe, Leicester LE8 5XH* T: 0116-277 4949 E: andrew@aptrainingonline.co.uk

POOLE, Clifford George. b 36. Keble Coll Ox BA 61 MA 65 Lon Univ PGCE 75. S'wark Ord Course 83. **d** 86 **p** 87. C W Dulwich All SS and Em *S'wark* 86-90; Chapl Luxembourg

Eur 90-02; rtd 02; P-in-c Alderton, Gt Washbourne, Dumbleton etc *Glouc* 02-05; TV Winchcombe 05-08; PtO *S'wark* from 09. *11 Berwyn Road, London SE24 9BD* T: (020) 8674 3369 E: poole_clifford@yahoo.co.uk

POOLE, David. b 54. **d** 02 **p** 04. OLM Chase Terrace *Lich* 02-12; PtO from 12. *435 Littleworth Road, Cannock WS12 1HZ* T: (01543) 422218 E: dave.poole54@sky.com

POOLE, Canon Denise June. b 49. Leic Univ BSc 70 Bradf and Ilkley Coll DipAdEd 85. NOC 90. **d** 93 **p** 94. C Horton and Bradf St Oswald Chapel Green 93-97; Chapl Co-ord Bradf Hosps NHS Trust 97-00; V Bradf St Aug Undercliffe 00-06; Dioc Dir of Ords 01-06; Bp's Dom Chapl 06-14; Hon Can Bradf Cathl from 07. *23 Leylands Lane, Bradford BD9 5PX* T: (01274) 401679 *or* 545414 F: 544831 E: denise.poole@bradford.anglican.org

POOLE, Edward John. b 53. Hull Univ BA 81 Heythrop Coll Lon MA 04. St Steph Ho Ox 81. **d** 83 **p** 84. C Stevenage St Andr and St Geo *St Alb* 83-86; Tutor St Paul's Th Coll Madagascar 86-88; V Weston and P-in-c Ardeley *St Alb* 88-96; P-in-c Cottered w Broadfield and Throcking 94-96; Chapl Bucharest w Sofia *Eur* 96-98; Chapl HM Pris Lewes 98-03; Chapl HM Pris Featherstone 03-09; R York, Beverley w Brookton and Quairading Australia 09-12; PtO *Heref* from 12. *Wyken Bungalow, Wyken, Worfield, Bridgnorth WV15 5NN* T: (01746) 716164 M: 07899-793805 E: john_poole_uk@yahoo.co.uk

POOLE, Helen Margaret. b 39. SRN. SWMTC. **d** 94 **p** 95. NSM Ludgvan *Truro* 94-97; NSM Paul 97-02; NSM St Buryan, St Levan and Sennen 02-04; rtd 04; PtO *Truro* 05-08; *Guildf* from 12. *12 Lansdown, Guildford GU1 2LY* T: (01483) 546234 E: helenbob@stlevan.eclipse.co.uk

POOLE, Ian Richard Morley. b 62. Birm Univ MB, ChB 85 MRCGP 90. St Jo Coll Nottm MTh 02. **d** 02 **p** 03. C Willenhall H Trin *Lich* 02-06; TV Bushbury from 06. *131 Taunton Avenue, Wolverhampton WV10 6PN* T: (01902) 788151 E: woodchipper@blueyonder.co.uk

POOLE, James Christopher. b 73. Peterho Cam BA 94 MA 98. Aston Tr Scheme 96 Wycliffe Hall Ox 97. **d** 00 **p** 01. C Wimbledon Park St Luke *S'wark* 00-04; Miss Partner Crosslinks 04-07; Kenya 05-07; C Cambridge H Sepulchre *Ely* 07-14; Exec Dir Wycliffe Bible Translators from 14; PtO *Ox* 14-15; NSM Ox St Ebbe w H Trin and St Pet from 15. *29A Wren Road, Oxford OX2 7SX* T: (01865) 513268 E: james@poolehouse.org

POOLE, Miss Joan Wendy. b 37. Sarum Dioc Teacher Tr Coll CertEd 57 Trin Coll Bris 86. **d** 87 **p** 94. Par Dn Longfleet *Sarum* 87-89; Par Dn Hamworthy 89-94; C 94-97; rtd 97; PtO *Sarum* from 97. *35 Borley Road, Poole BH17 7DT* T: (01202) 256377 E: jwendypoole@virginmedia.com

POOLE, John. *See* POOLE, Edward John

POOLE, Martin Bryce. b 59. Reading Univ BSc 80. St Jo Coll Nottm 81. **d** 87 **p** 88. NSM Tulse Hill H Trin and St Matthias *S'wark* 87-99; NSM Hove *Chich* 00-01; PtO 01-10; P-in-c Prestonville St Luke 10-13; V from 13. *St Luke's Vicarage, 64A Old Shoreham Road, Brighton BN1 5DD* T/F: (01273) 557772 E: martin@stlukesonline.co.uk

POOLE, Martin Ronald. b 59. Aston Univ BSc 81 Leeds Univ BA 86. Coll of Resurr Mirfield 84. **d** 87 **p** 88. C Sheff St Cath Richmond Road 87-90; C W Hampstead St Jas *Lon* 90-94; V Colindale St Matthias 94-06; V Munster Square Ch Ch and St Mary Magd from 06. *8 Laxton Place, London NW1 3PT* T: (020) 7388 3095 F: 08701-289048 E: martin@mpoole57.freeserve.co.uk

POOLE, Nigel John Graydon. b 53. **d** 15. C Penge St Jo *Roch* from 15. *37 Groveland Road, Beckenham BR3 3PU* T: (020) 8663 1344 M: 07849-609486 E: nigel_poole@hotmail.co.uk *or* nigel@penge-anglicans.org

POOLE, Peter William. b 35. St Pet Hall Ox BA 59 MA 63. Wells Th Coll 59. **d** 61 **p** 62. C Cheriton Street *Cant* 61-64; C Birchington w Acol 64-67; V Newington 67-73; P-in-c Lower Halstow 72-73; V Bearsted 73-76; V Lane End w Cadmore End *Ox* 84-89; R Chalfont St Giles 89-99; rtd 99; PtO *Guildf* from 99. *Primrose Cottage, St Nicholas Avenue, Cranleigh GU6 7AQ* T: (01483) 272703

POOLE, Richard Eric. b 65. Huddersfield Poly BEng 87. Trin Coll Bris BA 98. **d** 98 **p** 99. C Sandal St Helen *Wakef* 98-01; TV Southgate *Chich* from 01. *St Andrew's Vicarage, Weald Drive, Crawley RH10 6NU* T: (01293) 531828

POOLE, Roy John. b 26. Lon Univ BD 54. St Jo Coll Lon LTh 54. **d** 54 **p** 55. C Benwell St Aid *Newc* 54-57; Bush Brotherhood of St Paul Australia 57-59; C Warwick 59-61; R Bradford cum Beswick *Man* 61-66; Area Sec Chr Aid Dept BCC 66-68; Regional Supervisor (S and E England) Chr Aid 68-74; Exec Officer Angl Health and Welfare Services Australia 74-77; Gen Sec W Australia Coun of Ch Australia 77-83; LtO 84; R Carine w Cuncraig 85-91; rtd 91. *Unit 14, St Davids Retirement Centre, 17-19 Lawley Crescent, Mt Lawley, WA 6050, Australia* E: roy@poole.com.au

POOLE, Stuart. b 33. Lon Univ BScEng 55 Man Univ MSc 76 CEng 65 FIEE 85. **d** 91 **p** 92. NSM Cheadle *Ches* 91-03; PtO from 03. *1 Dene House, 3 Green Pastures, Stockport SK4 3RB* T/F: 0161-432 6426 E: stuart.poole33@tiscali.co.uk

POOLE, Wendy. *See* POOLE, Joan Wendy

POOLEY, Clifford Russell. b 48. Glos Univ BA 03. WEMTC 08. **d** 09 **p** 10. NSM Coberley, Cowley, Colesbourne and Elkstone *Glouc* 09-14; NSM Churn Valley from 14. *8A Salterley Grange, Leckhampton Hill, Cheltenham GL53 9QW* T: (01242) 243981 E: cliff.pooley@btinternet.com

POOLEY, Peter Owen. b 32. Kelham Th Coll 54. **d** 58 **p** 59. C Paddington St Mary Magd *Lon* 58-62; R Rockland St Mary w Hellington *Nor* 62-67; Asst Master Thos Lethaby Sch 67-70; St Phil Gr Sch Edgbaston 70-74; Lordswood Gr Sch 74-80; Hon C Edgbaston St Geo *Birm* 77-80; R Elton *Ely* 80-01; P-in-c Stibbington and Water Newton 80-01; R Elton w Stibbington and Water Newton 01-02; rtd 02; PtO *Linc* from 03. *1 Warrenne Keep, Stamford PE9 2NX* T: (01780) 751646 E: peterpooley@live.co.uk

POOLMAN, Alfred John. b 46. K Coll Lon BD 69 AKC 69. St Aug Coll Cant 69. **d** 70 **p** 71. C Headingley *Ripon* 70-74; C Moor Allerton 75-78; C Monk Bretton *Wakef* 78-80; V Copley and Chapl Halifax Gen Hosp 80-90; R Llanfynydd *St As* 90-06; P-in-c 06-10; rtd 11; PtO *St As* from 14. *The Rectory, Llanfynydd, Wrexham LL11 5HH* T: (01978) 762304 E: johnpoolman@btinternet.com

POOLMAN, Mrs Carole Margaret. b 53. St As & Ban Minl Tr Course 98. **d** 01 **p** 02. NSM Pontblyddyn *St As* 01-06; P-in-c 06-15; P-in-c Llanfynydd 10-14; P-in-c Treuddyn w Nercwys from 15. *The Rectory, Llanfynydd, Wrexham LL11 5HH* T: (01978) 762304 E: carole.poolman@tesco.net

POOLTON, Martin Ronald. b 60. SSC Kingston Poly BSc 81 Salford Univ MSc 83 Bp Grosseteste Coll PGCE 85 FRGS 81. Ripon Coll Cuddesdon 95. **d** 97 **p** 98. C Penzance St Mary w St Paul *Truro* 97-99; C Northampton St Matt *Pet* 99-01; R Jersey St Pet *Win* 01-14. *Address temp unknown* E: poolton@onetel.com

POON, Michael Nai-Chiu. b 53. Univ of BC BSc 75 MSc 77. Wycliffe Coll Toronto MDiv 80 DPhil 84. **d** 86 **p** 87. C St Steph Hong Kong Hong Kong 86-90; V Macau St Mark 90-99; P-in-c Morrison Chpl 90-04; Dir Cen for Story of Christianity Singapore Singapore 04-14; Hon Can Singapore from 07; PtO *Lon* from 14. *5 Avalon Close, London W13 0BJ* T: (020) 8998 4525 M: 07779-537601 E: mncpoon@gmail.com

POPE, Preb Charles Guy. b 48. AKC 70. St Aug Coll Cant 70. **d** 71 **p** 72. C Southgate Ch Ch *Lon* 71-74; C N St Pancras All Hallows 74-77; C Hampstead St Steph 74-77; V New Southgate St Paul 77-86; V Brookfield St Mary from 86; P-in-c Brookfield St Anne, Highgate Rise 88-99; AD S Camden 95-00; Preb St Paul's Cathl from 04. *St Mary's Vicarage, 85 Dartmouth Park Road, London NW5 1SL* T: (020) 7267 5941 F: 7482 2136 M: 07770-693435 E: guypope@blueyonder.co.uk

POPE, Donald Keith. b 35. Sarum & Wells Th Coll 81. **d** 76 **p** 77. Hon C Caerleon *Mon* 76-82; C 82-83; V Pontypool 83-86; R Grosmont and Skenfrith and Llangattock etc 86-98; RD Abergavenny 93-98; rtd 98. *1 Lancaster Drive, Lydney GL15 5SN*

POPE, Miss Elizabeth Mercy. b 51. Man Univ BSc 73 Ex Univ PGCE 74. Trin Coll Bris 99. **d** 01 **p** 02. C Bardsley *Man* 01-05; P-in-c Oldham St Paul 05-08; P-in-c Denton St Lawr from 08; C Audenshaw St Steph from 13; C Denton Ch Ch from 13; C Haughton St Anne from 13. *St Lawrence's Rectory, 131 Town Lane, Denton, Manchester M34 2DJ* T: 0161-320 4895 E: elizabeth@mpope.plus.com

POPE, Guy. *See* POPE, Charles Guy

POPE, Michael John. b 37. Sarum Th Coll 62. **d** 65 **p** 66. C Broseley w Benthall *Heref* 65-68; C Shrewsbury St Giles *Lich* 68-71; P-in-c Shrewsbury St Geo 71-75; V 75-79; V Gnosall 79-00; RD Eccleshall 92-00; rtd 00; PtO *Lich* from 01. *Rivendell, 2 Dark Lane, Broseley TF12 5LH* T: (01952) 883960

POPE, Michael Ronald. b 41. Bps' Coll Cheshunt 65. **d** 68 **p** 69. C Lyonsdown H Trin *St Alb* 68-72; C Seaford w Sutton *Chich* 72-76; R Hurstpierpoint 76-80; rtd 99. *34 Wilton Road, Shanklin PO37 7BZ* T: (01983) 863602

POPELY, David Charles. b 51. K Coll Lon BA 00. SEITE 00. **d** 03. NSM Catford St Laur *S'wark* 03-05. *121 Brynbrain Estate, Cwmllynfell, Swansea SA9 2WH* T: (01639) 831675 M: 07513-004579 E: davidpopely@googlemail.com

POPHAM, Neil Andrew. b 69. Trin Coll Ox BA 91 DPhil 96 MA 05 St Jo Coll Dur BA 05. Cranmer Hall Dur 03. **d** 05 **p** 06. C Quarry Bank *Worc* 05-07; C Brierley Hill 07-09; P-in-c Kirkby in Ashfield St Thos *S'well* 09-11; V from 11; P-in-c Kirkby in Ashfield from 15. *The Vicarage, 109 Diamond Avenue, Kirkby-in-Ashfield, Nottingham NG17 7LX* E: thepophams@talktalk.net

POPP, Miss Julia Alice Gisela. b 45. Univ of BC BA 71. St Jo Coll Nottm 78. **dss** 81 **d** 87 **p** 94. Woking St Mary *Guildf* 81-83; Hornsey Rise St Mary w St Steph *Lon* 83-87; Par Dn Hornsey Rise Whitehall Park Team 87-91; Par Dn Sutton St Nic *S'wark* 91-94; C 94-98; Missr Sutton Town Cen 91-98; TV Hackney Marsh *Lon* 98-05; rtd 05; PtO *Ely* from 06. *32 Regatta Court, Oyster Row, Cambridge CB5 8NS* T: (01223) 350164 E: j.popp@btinternet.com

POPPE, Andrew Nils. b 60. NE Lon Poly BSc 83. STETS 08. **d** 11 **p** 12. C Clarendon *Sarum* 11-15; V Cowes H Trin and St Mary *Portsm* from 15. *The Vicarage, Church Road, Cowes PO31 8HA* T: (01983) 292509 M: 07729-322616

POPPLETON, Julian George. b 63. St Chad's Coll Dur BA 85 PGCE 86 Surrey Univ BA 02. STETS 99. **d** 02 **p** 03. NSM Harnham *Sarum* from 02; Chapl K Edw VI Sch Southn from 02. *19 Thompson Close, Salisbury SP2 8QU* T: (01722) 334272 or (023) 8070 4561 E: julianpoppleton@gmail.com

POPPLEWELL, Andrew Frederick. b 53. St Jo Coll Dur BA 75. Wycliffe Hall Ox 76. **d** 78 **p** 79. C Clifton *York* 78-81; C Lich St Chad 82-84; V Laisterdyke *Bradf* 84-99. *Clifton, 210A Leeds Road, Eccleshill, Bradford BD2 3JU* T: (01274) 637651

PORT, Mrs Betty Anne. b 50. Univ of W Indies BA 71 Open Univ MA 93. STETS BA 10. **d** 10 **p** 11. NSM Preston w Sutton Poyntz, Littlemoor etc *Sarum* 10-14; NSM Wyke Regis from 14. *68 Mellstock Avenue, Dorchester DT1 2BQ* T: (01305) 263058 E: betty.port@which.net

PORTEOUS, Michael Stanley. b 35. S'wark Ord Course 70. **d** 73 **p** 74. C Barnes St Mich *S'wark* 73-76; Chapl Greycoat Hosp Sch 76-78; C Brighton Annunciation *Chich* 78-80; Chapl Ch Hosp Horsham 80-85; TV Moulsecoomb *Chich* 85-88; R W Blatchington 88-99; rtd 99; PtO *Chich* from 99. *15 Mariners Close, Shoreham-by-Sea BN43 5LU*

PORTER, Andrew William. b 69. Bris Univ BSc 91 BA 01 PGCE 94. Trin Coll Bris 98. **d** 01 **p** 02. C Ipsley *Worc* 01-04; V Fairfield *Liv* 04-10; P-in-c Liv St Phil w St Dav 08-10; V Liv All SS 11-13; V S'well H Trin from 13. *Holy Trinity Vicarage, Westhorpe, Southwell NG25 0NB* E: awporter9@gmail.com

PORTER, Anthony. *See* PORTER, David Anthony

✠**PORTER, The Rt Revd Anthony.** b 52. Hertf Coll Ox BA 74 MA 78 Fitzw Ho Cam BA 76 MA 80. Ridley Hall Cam 74. **d** 77 **p** 78 **c** 06. C Edgware *Lon* 77-80; C Haughton St Mary *Man* 80-83; P-in-c Bacup Ch Ch 83-87; V 87-91; R Rusholme H Trin 91-06; Hon Can Man Cathl 04-06; Suff Bp Sherwood *S'well* from 06; Hon Can S'well Minster from 06. *Dunham House, Westgate, Southwell NG25 0JL* T: (01636) 819133 F: 819085 E: bishopsherwood@southwell.anglican.org

PORTER, Barbara Judith. *See* JEAPES, Barbara Judith

PORTER, Brian Meredith. b 39. Monash Univ Aus BA 66 Trin Hall Cam BA 75 MA 79 New England Univ NSW BLitt 79 MLitt 85 ACT ThD 01. Cuddesdon Coll 68. **d** 68 **p** 71. C Kew Australia 68-69; K Sch Parramatta 70-73; Chapl Canberra Gr Sch 75-82; Chapl Ivanhoe Gr Sch 83-97; Sen Chapl Melbourne Gr Sch 98-05; Chapl Brighton Gr Sch from 05. *4 Fairholme Grove, Camberwell Vic 3124, Australia* T: (0061) (3) 9882 8740 E: bmporter@comcen.com.au

PORTER (née RICHARDSON), Mrs Catherine Elisabeth. b 75. Edge Hill Coll of HE BA 96 Trin Coll Bris BA 99 MA 01. SNWTP 07. **d** 08 **p** 09. NSM Fairfield *Liv* 08-10; NSM Liv All SS 11-13. *Holy Trinity Vicarage, Westhorpe, Southwell NG25 0NB* E: cathy.porter@bigfoot.com

PORTER, Damian Michael. b 66. Linc Th Coll BTh 92. **d** 92 **p** 93. C Pelsall *Lich* 92-96; V Greenlands *Blackb* 96-00; V St Annes St Anne 00-09; AD Kirkham 06-09; P-in-c Warton St Oswald w Yealand Conyers 09-11; V from 11; AD Tunstall from 14. *St Oswald's Vicarage, Warton, Carnforth LA5 9PG* T: (01524) 732946 E: fatherd@btinternet.com

PORTER, Canon David Anthony (Tony). b 34. Wycliffe Hall Ox 73. **d** 75 **p** 76. C Watford St Luke *St Alb* 75-78; C Worting *Win* 78-81; V Snettisham *Nor* 81-82; P-in-c Ingoldisthorpe 81-82; C Fring 81-82; R Snettisham w Ingoldisthorpe and Fring 82-84; Chapl Asst Colchester Gen Hosp 87-88; Chapl Maidstone Hosp 88-94; Chapl Mid Kent Healthcare NHS Trust 94-98; Hon Can Cant Cathl 97-98; rtd 98; PtO *Nor* from 98; *Ely* from 98. *The Greys, 12 Hawthorn Close, Watlington, King's Lynn PE33 0HD* T: (01553) 811301 E: daporter7985@btinternet.com

PORTER, David Michael. b 46. Nottm Univ BMedSci 80 BM 82 BS 82. EMMTC 94. **d** 97 **p** 98. NSM Edwinstowe *S'well* 97-99. *Gorsethorpe Cottage, Edwinstowe, Mansfield NG21 9HJ* T: (01623) 844657

PORTER, David Michael. b 37. Coll of Ripon & York St Jo BA 88. Ely Th Coll 61. **d** 64 **p** 65. C Clun w Chapel Lawn *Heref* 64-67; C Scarborough St Mary w Ch Ch, St Paul and St Thos *York* 67-69; C Fulford 69-71; V Strensall 71-78; Chapl Claypenny and St Monica's Hosps 78-91; V Easingwold w Raskelfe *York* 78-91; TR York All SS Pavement w St Crux and St Martin etc 91-97; R York All SS Pavement w St Crux and St Mich 97-02; rtd 02; PtO *York* from 02. *10 Hall Rise, Haxby, York YO32 3LP* T: (01904) 769823

PORTER, David Rowland Shelley. b 46. City of Liv Coll of HE CertEd 69. STETS 00. **d** 03 **p** 04. NSM Whitehawk *Chich* from 03. *33 Warleigh Road, Brighton BN1 4NT* T: (01273) 703499 E: davejanera@aol.com

PORTER, Howard. b 56. S Glam Inst HE CertEd 78. St Mich Coll Llan 99. **d** 01 **p** 02. C Maindee Newport *Mon* 01-05; TV Aberystwyth *St D* 05-09. *21 Gwalch y Penwaig, Barry CF62 5AG*

PORTER, James Richard. b 73. Lon Univ BMedSci 97 MB, BS 98. Oak Hill Th Coll MTh 05. **d** 05 **p** 06. C Cromer *Nor* 05-09; R W Horsley *Guildf* 09-15; V Cromer *Nor* from 15. *42 Cromwell Road, Cromer NR27 0BE* T: (01263) 512000 E: jamestherector@yahoo.co.uk *or* james.porter@cromer-church.org.uk

PORTER, John Dudley Dowell. b 33. St Edm Hall Ox BA 60 MA 61. Qu Coll Birm 57. **d** 59 **p** 60. C Londonderry *Birm* 59-62; C Tettenhall Regis *Lich* 62-65; Chapl RAF 65-69; V Wombourne *Lich* 69-75; V Rickerscote 75-81; P-in-c Chapel Chorlton 81-85; P-in-c Maer 81-85; P-in-c Whitmore 81-85; R Chapel Chorlton, Maer and Whitmore 85-92; TR Wednesfield 92-00; rtd 00; P-in-c Haughton St Anne *Man* 00-03; P-in-c Nord Pas de Calais *Eur* 04-06. *37 Rue Principale, 62130 Framecourt, France* T: (0033) 3 21 04 36 35 E: jddporter@hotmail.co.uk

PORTER, Miss Joy Dove. b 50. Lon Bible Coll BA 81 Lon Univ PGCE 83. Wycliffe Hall Ox 89. **d** 91 **p** 94. Par Dn Chalgrove w Berrick Salome *Ox* 91-92; Par Dn Chipping Norton 92-94; C 94-95; Hong Kong 96-97; P-in-c Rouen All SS and Chapl Rouen Miss to Seamen *Eur* 97-00; Hon C Warfield *Ox* 03-12; PtO from 12. *Warfield Church Office, Church Lane, Warfield, Bracknell RG42 6EG* T: (01344) 886900 E: admin@warfield.org.uk

PORTER, Malcolm Derek. b 53. BSc. NTMTC. **d** 05 **p** 06. C Woodford Wells *Chelmsf* 05-09; NSM from 10. *121 Beatyville Gardens, Ilford IG6 1JZ* T: (020) 8550 8161 E: thoseporters@aol.com

PORTER, Mrs Marie-Jeanne. b 60. EMMTC 95. **d** 98 **p** 99. NSM Warsop *S'well* 98-04. *Gorsethope Cottage, Edwinstowe, Mansfield NG21 9HJ* T: (01623) 844657

PORTER, Matthew James. b 69. Nottm Univ BA 90. Wycliffe Hall Ox BTh 93. **d** 96 **p** 97. C Dore *Sheff* 96-00; V Woodseats St Chad 00-09; C York St Mich-le-Belfrey 09-10; V from 10. *St Barnabas' Vicarage, Jubilee Terrace, York YO26 4YZ* T: (01904) 412057 M: 07985-645844 E: matthew.porter@belfrey.org

PORTER, Canon Michael Edward. b 44. Trin Coll Bris 75. **d** 77 **p** 78. C Corby St Columba *Pet* 77-81; C Rainham *Chelmsf* 81-82; TV 82-92; P-in-c S Hornchurch St Jo and St Matt 92-95; V Anerley *Roch* 95-09; TR 09; AD Beckenham 05-09; Hon Can Roch Cathl 09; rtd 09; PtO *Nor* from 10. *20 Park Lane, Wymondham NR18 9BG* T: (01953) 602708 E: mike@porterfamily.freeuk.com

PORTER, Nigel Jonathan. b 58. Sunderland Univ BEd 90 Portsm Univ MPhil 99 PhD 05. STETS MA 10. **d** 10 **p** 11. C Lower Sandown St Jo *Portsm* 10-14; PtO 14-15; P-in-c Niton from 15; P-in-c Whitwell from 15; P-in-c St Lawrence from 15; P-in-c Chale from 15. *Niton Rectory, Pan Lane, Niton, Ventnor PO38 2BT* M: 07533-394043 E: nigel.porter6@btinternet.com

PORTER, Raymond James. b 43. Worc Coll Ox BA 66 MA 70 Wycliffe Hall Ox MPhil 93 FRAS 93. **d** 06 **p** 07. Dir World Miss Studies Oak Hill Th Coll from 06; PtO *St Alb* from 07; *Ely* from 11. *24 Bevington Way, Eynesbury, St Neots PE19 2HQ* T: (01480) 211839 *or* (020) 8449 0467 M: 07976-753822 E: ray@wiradanuprojo.f2s.com *or* rayp@oakhill.ac.uk

PORTER, Mrs Susan Patricia June. b 53. STETS 00. **d** 03. NSM Wilton w Netherhampton and Fugglestone *Sarum* 03-05; NSM Sarum Cathl 05-08; PtO 08-09 and from 12; NSM Wilton w Netherhampton and Fugglestone 09-11. *24 Belle Vue Road, Salisbury SP1 3YG* T: (01722) 331314 E: rev.porter@tesco.net

PORTER, William Albert. b 28. Univ of NZ BA 51 MA 52. Coll of Resurr Mirfield 53. **d** 55 **p** 56. C Perry Barr *Birm* 55-58; V Port Chalmers New Zealand 59-61; V Warrington 61-62; Tutor St Jo Coll Suva Fiji 62-63; Asst Supt Melanesian Miss 62-64; Supt 64-67; Can and Prec H Trin Cathl Suva 65-67; C Wimbledon *S'wark* 68; Asst Chapl HM Pris Liv 69-70; Chapl HM Pris Brixton 70-74; Chapl HM Pris Long Lartin 74-79; Chapl HM Pris Liv 79-87; HM Pris Nor 87-90; P-in-c Sneinton St Matthias *S'well* 90-93; rtd 94; PtO *Glouc* from 01. *40 Duke Street, Cheltenham GL52 6BP* T: (01242) 262198

PORTER-BABBAGE, Michelle Louise. b 64. **d** 14 **p** 15. C Bourton-on-the-Water w Clapton etc *Glouc* from 14. *Phoenix House, Moore Road, Bourton-on-the-Water, Cheltenham GL54 2AZ* T: (01451) 821635 E: michellep-b@hotmail.com

PORTER-PRYCE, Ms Julia Frances. b 57. Man Univ BA 78 Leic Univ MPhil 94. NTMTC 93. **d** 96 **p** 97. C Stoke Newington Common St Mich *Lon* 96-99; C Is of Dogs Ch Ch and St Jo w St Luke 99-02; V De Beauvoir Town St Pet from 02; AD Hackney 09-14. *St Peter's Vicarage, 86 De Beauvoir Road, London N1 5AT* T: (020) 7254 5670 E: juliap@freeuk.com

PORTEUS, Canon James Michael. b 31. Worc Coll Ox BA 55 MA 58. Cuddesdon Coll. **d** 57 **p** 58. C Fleetwood St Pet *Blackb* 57-60; C Ox St Mary V 60-62; Staff Sec SCM Ox 60-62; Chapl Chicago Univ USA 62-65; Chapl Bryn Mawr, Haverford and Swarthmore Colls 62-65; Chapl Lon Univ 69-74; V Hampstead Garden Suburb 74-86; Chapl Arizona Univ USA 86-91; Min Livingston LEP *Edin* 91-96; rtd 96; P-in-c Portree *Arg* 96-05; Hon Can Cumbrae from 06; PtO *Truro* from 09. *Triskele, Rinsey, Ashton, Helston TR13 9TS* T: (01736) 761870

PORTEUS, Canon Robert John Norman. b 50. TCD BA 72 MA 76. CITC 75. **d** 75 **p** 76. C Portadown St Mark *Arm* 75-79; I Ardtrea w Desertcreat 79-83; I Annaghmore 83-98; I Derryloran from 98; Can Arm Cathl from 98; Preb from 01. *Derryloran Rectory, 13 Loy Street, Cookstown BT80 8PZ* T/F: (028) 8676 2261 E: rector@derryloran.com

PORTHOUSE, Canon John Clive. b 32. Lon Univ BD 58. Tyndale Hall Bris 55 Oak Hill Th Coll 58. **d** 60 **p** 61. C Leyton All SS *Chelmsf* 60-62; C Kendal St Thos *Carl* 62-64; V Flimby 64-68; V Sidcup St Andr *Roch* 68-74; V Beckenham St Jo 74-86; RD Beckenham 80-86; V Southborough St Pet w Ch Ch and St Matt 86-96; TR 96-97; Hon Can Roch Cathl 96-97; rtd 97; PtO *Carl* from 98; *Roch* from 11. *234 Ralph Perring Court, Stone Park Avenue, Beckenham BR3 3LX* T: (020) 3441 4259 E: clive.porthouse@talktalk.net

PORTHOUSE, Roger Gordon Hargreaves. b 39. Tyndale Hall Bris 66. **d** 69 **p** 70. C Wellington w Eyton *Lich* 69-71; C Cheadle *Ches* 71-75; R Frettenham w Stanninghall *Nor* 75-81; R Spixworth w Crostwick 75-81; V Hailsham *Chich* 81-04; RD Dallington 96-03; rtd 05. *19 Cornmill Gardens, Polegate BN26 5NJ* T: (01323) 487372 E: rporthouse@btclick.com

PORTLOCK, John Anthony. b 37. RIBA. WMMTC 96. **d** 99 **p** 00. NSM Lyddington w Stoke Dry and Seaton etc *Pet* 99-07; NSM Bulwick, Blatherwycke w Harringworth and Laxton 05-07; rtd 07; PtO *Pet* from 08. *7 Chestnut Close, Uppingham, Oakham LE15 9TQ* T: (01572) 823225 E: jandmportlock@gmail.com

PORTSDOWN, Archdeacon of. See GRENFELL, The Ven Joanne Woolway

PORTSMOUTH, Bishop of. See FOSTER, The Rt Revd Christopher Richard James

PORTSMOUTH, Dean of. See BRINDLEY, The Very Revd David Charles

PORTWOOD, Prof Derek. b 31. Keele Univ MA 69 PhD 79. ALCD 57. **d** 57 **p** 58. C Laisterdyke *Bradf* 57-60; C-in-c Westlands St Andr CD *Lich* 60-66; V Westlands St Andr 66-69; rtd 96; PtO *Ely* 96-00. *51 River Lane, Cambridge CB5 8HP* T/F: (01223) 311044

POSKITT, Mark Sylvester. b 63. Loughb Univ BSc 84. St Jo Coll Nottm MA 95. **d** 97 **p** 98. C Brigg, Wrawby and Cadney cum Howsham *Linc* 97-00; TV Howden *York* 00-09; P-in-c Barnsley St Edw *Leeds* from 09; P-in-c Gawber from 09. *The Vicarage, Church Street, Gawber, Barnsley S75 2RL* T: (01226) 207140 E: rev.markp@tiscali.co.uk

POSS, Steven Keith. b 78. St Mellitus Coll BA 13. **d** 13 **p** 14. NSM Leigh-on-Sea St Aid *Chelmsf* from 13. *16 Chenies Drive, Basildon SS15 4AE*

POST, David Charles William. b 39. Jes Coll Cam BA 61 MA 65. Oak Hill Th Coll 61. **d** 63 **p** 64. C Orpington Ch Ch *Roch* 63-66; C Fulwood *Sheff* 66-68; V Lathom *Liv* 68-75; V Poughill *Truro* 75-78; V Sherburn in Elmet *York* 79-91; P-in-c Kirk Fenton 84-85; V Thornthwaite cum Braithwaite and Newlands *Carl* 91-93; R Wheldrake w Thorganby *York* 93-04; P-in-c Elvington w Sutton on Derwent and E Cottingwith 03-04; rtd 04. *Cheviot, 5 Mayfield Crescent, Middle Rasen, Market Rasen LN8 3UA* T: (01673) 843388

POST, Oswald Julian. b 48. Derby Lonsdale Coll BEd 79. EMMTC. **d** 84 **p** 85. Travelling Sec Ruanda Miss 79-89; Hon C Hulland, Atlow, Bradley and Hognaston *Derby* 84-89; V Wormhill, Peak Forest w Peak Dale and Dove Holes 89-99; P-in-c Youlgreave, Middleton, Stanton-in-Peak etc 99-09; r-d 09; UK Ambassador AE Evangelisic Enterprise Ltd from 10; PtO *Lich* from 13. *1 Rose Cottage, Hulland Village, Ashbourne DE6 3EP* T: (01335) 370285 E: ossiepost@icloud.com

POSTILL, John Edward. b 35. Oak Hill Th Coll 64. **d** 67 **p** 68. C Southgate *Chich* 67-70; C Bowling St Jo *Bradf* 70-74; TV Winfarthing w Shelfanger *Nor* 74-79; R Slaugham *Chich* 79-97; C Busbridge and Hambledon *Guildf* 97-03; rtd 03; PtO *Guildf* from 04. *Dora Cottage, Beech Hill, Hambledon, Godalming GU8 4HL* T: (01428) 687968 E: j.e.postill@talktalk.net

POSTILL, Canon Richard Halliday. b 37. Hull Univ BSc 59. Westcott Ho Cam 66. **d** 68 **p** 69. C Wylde Green *Birm* 68-72; C Kingswinford St Mary *Lich* 72-76; V Yardley Wood *Birm* 76-86; V Acocks Green 86-02; AD Yardley 93-00; Hon Can Birm Cathl 99-02; rtd 02; PtO *Birm* from 03. *32 Longmore Road, Shirley, Solihull B90 3DY* T: 0121-744 6217
E: richardh@postill.fsbusiness.co.uk

POSTON, Jonathan David. b 59. Ches Coll of HE MTh 05. NOC 01. **d** 04 **p** 05. C Prestwich St Marg *Man* 04-10; PtO 10-14; NSM Matlock Bank and Tansley and Dethick, Lea and Holloway *Derby* 10-12; NSM Spondon 12-14; R Wingerworth from 14. *The Rectory, Longedge Lane, Wingerworth, Chesterfield S42 6PU* T: (01246) 279932 M: 07754-517797
E: jont.post@gmail.com

POTHEN, Canon Simon John. b 60. Westmr Coll Ox BA 86. Ripon Coll Cuddesdon 86. **d** 88 **p** 89. C Southgate Ch Ch *Lon* 88-91; C Tottenham St Mary 91-93; TV Gt Grimsby St Mary and St Jas *Linc* 93-96; R Friern Barnet St Jas *Lon* 96-02; V Pinner 02-07; Prec and Can Res Chelmsf Cathl from 07. *1A Harlings Grove, Chelmsford CM1 1YQ* T: (01245) 491599 M: 07939-523366 E: precentor@chelmsfordcathedral.org.uk

POTIPHER, John Malcolm Barry. b 42. St Alb Minl Tr Scheme 79. **d** 82 **p** 83. Chapl Herts Fire Brigade 82-91; NSM Chambersbury *St Alb* 82-84; NSM Hemel Hempstead 84-86; NSM Digswell and Panshanger 86-92; P-in-c Pirton 92-95; rtd 95; PtO *St Alb* from 95. *66 Peartree Lane, Welwyn Garden City AL7 3UH* T: (01707) 886953 E: jmbpot@ntlworld.com

POTTAGE, Timothy Lindsay. b 65. **d** 15. C Galmington *B & W* from 15. *Midfields, Comeytrowe Lane, Taunton TA1 5BJ* M: 07971-010710 E: timpottage@hotmail.com

POTTEN, Rosemary. b 48. **d** 13 **p** 14. OLM Barkingside H Trin *Chelmsf* from 13. *51 Greeleafe Drive, Barkingside, Ilford IG6 1LH*

POTTER, Mrs Anne Mary. b 57. Open Univ BA 92 Chich Coll PGCE 96. Qu Coll Birm 09. **d** 11 **p** 12. C Badsey w Aldington and Offenham and Bretforton *Worc* 11-15; TV Worcs W from 15; C Worc Dines Green St Mich and Crown E, Rushwick from 15. *Old Rectory, Brockamin, Leigh, Worcester WR6 5LA* M: 07783-711665 E: revannepotter@gmail.com

POTTER, Charles Elmer. b 42. Georgetown Univ (USA) BS 65 Valparaiso Univ JD 73. Wycliffe Coll Toronto MDiv 81. **d** 81 **p** 82. C Southport Ch Ch *Liv* 81-84; Chapl Lee Abbey 84-87; P-in-c Westmeadows and Bulla Australia 87-93; P-in-c Aldingham and Dendron and Rampside *Carl* 93-96; P-in-c Aldingham, Dendron, Rampside and Urswick 96-99; V Bexley St Mary *Roch* 99-07; rtd 07. *3/6 Granholm Grove, Melton West VIC 3337, Australia*
E: charles.potter@tiscali.co.uk

POTTER, The Ven Christopher Nicholas Lynden. b 49. Leeds Univ BA 71. St As Minl Tr Course 90. **d** 93 **p** 94. C Flint *St As* 93-96; V Llanfair DC, Derwen, Llanelidan and Efenechtyd 96-01; Dean and Lib St As Cathl 01-11; V St As 01-03; TR 03-11; R Caerwys and Bodfari 11-14; Adn St As 11-14; rtd 14; PtO *St As* from 14. *Bryn Celyn, Willow Street, Llangollen LL20 8HH* T: (01978) 861831 E: chris_potter@btinternet.com

POTTER, Clive Geoffrey. b 55. Aston Tr Scheme 88 Sarum & Wells Th Coll 90. **d** 92 **p** 93. C Epsom Common Ch Ch *Guildf* 92-97; TV Westborough 97-98; TR 98-07; V Milford from 07; RD Godalming from 12. *The New Vicarage, Milford Heath, Milford, Godalming GU8 5BX* T: (01483) 414710 E: milfordvicarage@gmail.com

POTTER, Desmond. b 54. St Paul's Coll Grahamstown 85. **d** 88 **p** 88. C Benoni S Africa 88-90; C Springs 90-91; C Linden 91-93; R Kempton Park 93-97; V Newton *Ches* 98-06; C Toowoomba Australia 06-08; R Callide Valley from 08. *76 Kariboe Street, PO Box 69, Biloela Qld 4715, Australia* T: (0061) (7) 4992 1545 F: 4992 3644 M: 41-975 5979
E: thesapotters@bigpond.com

POTTER, Graham Alec James. b 63. Middx Univ BSc 09. St Mellitus Coll BA 14. **d** 14 **p** 15. C Carl St Luke Morton from 14. *25 Wigton Road, Carlisle CA2 7BB* T: (01228) 595647 E: grahamaj.potter@btinternet.com

POTTER, Harry Drummond. b 54. Em Coll Cam BA 76 MA 79 MPhil 81 LLB 92 Barrister 93. Westcott Ho Cam 79. **d** 81 **p** 82. C Deptford St Paul *S'wark* 81-84; Chapl Selw Coll Cam 84-87; Chapl Newnham Coll Cam 84-87; Chapl HM Pris Wormwood Scrubs 87-88; Chapl HM YOI Aylesbury 88-93; NSM Camberwell St Giles w St Matt *S'wark* 93-03; PtO 03-07. *19 Dobell Road, London SE9 1HE* T: (020) 7067 1500 E: tuahousis@hotmail.com

POTTER, Canon James David. b 35. AKC 66. **d** 67 **p** 68. C Longbridge *Birm* 67-70; LtO 71-73; V N Harborne 73-78; V Smethwick H Trin w St Alb 78-83; V Blurton *Lich* 83-90; V Dordon *Birm* 90-98; RD Polesworth 91-96; Hon Can Birm Cathl 96-98; rtd 98; PtO *Birm* from 98. *49 Winstanley Road, Stechford, Birmingham B33 8UH* T: 0121-783 2734

POTTER, John Daniel. b 29. Sydney Univ BA 50. St Jo Coll Morpeth ThL 51. **d** 51 **p** 53. Australia 52-65; C High Harrogate Ch Ch *Ripon* 65-66; Chapl St Mary's Sch Wantage 66-68; Chapl St Jo Sch and NSM St Andr Cathl Singapore 68-71; OCM 68-71; Australia from 71; rtd 95; LtO *Eur* 95-97. *200 Castella Road, Toolangi Vic 3777, Australia* T: (0061) (3) 5962 9449

POTTER, John Dennis. b 39. Ealing Tech Coll. S Dios Minl Tr Scheme 92. **d** 94 **p** 95. NSM Box w Hazlebury and Ditteridge *Bris* 94-98; PtO *B & W* from 06. *87A Southdown Road, Bath BA2 1HL* T: (01225) 316656 M: 07745-873759 E: johndpotter@talktalk.net

POTTER, John Ellis. b 45. Sarum & Wells Th Coll 82. **d** 84 **p** 85. C Wootton Bassett *Sarum* 84-88; TV Swindon New Town *Bris* 88-96; V Milber *Ex* from 96. *St Luke's Vicarage, 10 Laburnum Road, Newton Abbot TQ12 4LQ* T: (01626) 365837

POTTER, Mrs Judith Anne. b 46. Rolle Coll CertEd 68. **d** 05 **p** 06. OLM Shere, Albury and Chilworth *Guildf* 05-12; NSM from 12; Chapl Birtley Ho Bramley 08-12. *3 Bank Terrace, Gomshall Lane, Shere, Guildford GU5 9HB* T: (01483) 203352 F: 202077 E: judyp@btopenworld.com

POTTER, Kenneth Benjamin. b 39. Open Univ BA GLCM. NEOC 84. **d** 87 **p** 88. NSM Ryton w Hedgefield *Dur* 87-95; P-in-c Harby w Thorney and N and S Clifton *S'well* 95-09; rtd 10. *Address withheld by request*
E: kenneth.b.potter@btinternet.com

POTTER, Mrs Linda. b 47. Cranmer Hall Dur 92. **d** 94 **p** 95. C Shildon w Eldon *Dur* 94-98; P-in-c Castleside 98-04; TR Gt Aycliffe 04-12; rtd 12; *Leeds* from 14. *32 Knaresborough Road, Harrogate HG2 7LU*

POTTER, Malcolm Emmerson. b 48. Bedf Coll Lon BSc 70. St Jo Coll Nottm. **d** 75 **p** 76. C Upton (Overchurch) *Ches* 76-78; CPAS Staff 78-84; Development Officer St Jo Coll Nottm 84-86; P-in-c Wellington All SS w Eyton *Lich* 86-95; V 95-06; Preb Lich Cathl 99-06; Membership Development Manager Age Concern 06-07; Chapl Shropshire Co Primary Care Trust 07-12; rtd 12. *2 Barns Green, Shrewsbury SY3 9QB* T: (01743) 641251 E: malcolmepotter@blueyonder.co.uk

POTTER, Neil John. b 63. **d** 12 **p** 13. NSM Redruth w Lanner and Treleigh *Truro* 12-15; NSM Camborne and Tuckingmill from 15. *Strawberry Bank, Carn, Stithians, Truro TR3 7AW* M: 07539-593684 E: neilpotter@talktalk.net

POTTER, The Ven Peter Maxwell. b 46. Univ of Wales (Swansea) BA 69 Univ of BC MA 71. Sarum & Wells Th Coll 83. **d** 85 **p** 86. C Bradford-on-Avon H Trin *Sarum* 85-88; C Harnham 88-91; P-in-c N Bradley, Southwick and Heywood 91-96; V Sale St Anne *Ches* 96-00; R Largs *Glas* 00-08; Chapl Berne w Neuchâtel *Eur* from 08; Adn Switzerland from 09. *St Ursula, Jubiläumsplatz 2, 3005 Berne, Switzerland* T: (0041) (31) 352 8567 F: 351 0548 E: peshar@bluewin.ch *or* berne@anglican.ch

POTTER, Phillip. b 54. Stirling Univ BA 75. Trin Coll Bris 82. **d** 84 **p** 85. C Yateley *Win* 84-88; V Haydock St Mark *Liv* 88-07; Dir Pioneer Min 07-14; C Haydock St Mark 07-09; P-in-c Southport St Phil and St Paul 12-14; Hon Can Liv Cathl 03-14; Abps' Missr and Team Ldr Fresh Expressions *Cant* from 14; NSM Bowdon *Ches* from 15. *Chapel House, Chester Road, Tabley, Knutsford WA16 0HN*

POTTER, Miss Sharon Jane. b 63. UEA BSc 96 K Coll Lon MSc 00 RGN 91. Dioc OLM tr scheme 00. **d** 04 **p** 05. OLM Ipswich All Hallows *St E* 04-06; OLM Ipswich St Helen, H Trin, and St Luke 07-12; R Bradfield St Clare, Bradfield St George etc from 12. *The Rectory, Howe Lane, Cockfield, Bury St Edmunds IP30 0HA* T: (01284) 828599 M: 07825-086063 E: revsharon@btinternet.com

POTTER, Simon Jonathan. b 76. Southn Univ BA 98 Ex Univ PGCE 99. Trin Coll Bris MA 14. **d** 14 **p** 15. C Ox St Andr from 14. *5 Squitchey Lane, Oxford OX2 7LD* T: (01865) 311212 E: simon.potter@standrewsoxford.org

POTTER, Stephen Michael. b 55. Oak Hill Th Coll 93. **d** 95 **p** 96. C Chesterfield H Trin and Ch Ch *Derby* 95-99; P-in-c S Normanton 99-01; R from 01. *The Rectory, Church Street, South Normanton, Alfreton DE55 2BT* T: (01773) 811273 E: stephen@potter55.fsnet.co.uk

POTTER, Timothy John. b 49. Bris Univ BSc 71. Oak Hill Th Coll 73. **d** 76 **p** 77. C Wallington *S'wark* 76-79; C Hampreston *Sarum* 79-81; TV Stratton St Margaret w S Marston etc *Bris* 81-87; P-in-c Hatfield Heath *Chelmsf* 87-89; P-in-c Sheering 87-89; R Hatfield Heath and Sheering 90-09; P-in-c Gt Hallingbury and Lt Hallingbury 06-09; RD Harlow 07-09; Hon Can Chelmsf Cathl 02-09; rtd 09. *Redcot, 91 High Street, Dunmow CM6 1AF* E: tim.potter1@btinternet.com

POTTERTON, David Steven. b 59. Ox Min Course 13. **d** 15. C Romsey *Win* from 15. *15 Mount Temple, Romsey SO51 5UW* M: 07827-994083 T: (01794) 501926 E: david.potterton@btinternet.com

POTTIER, Ronald William. b 36. S'wark Ord Course 73. **d** 76 **p** 77. NSM Lower Sydenham St Mich *S'wark* 76-98; NSM Sydenham All SS 98-05; PtO from 05. *12 Neiderwald Road, London SE26 4AD* T: (020) 8699 4375

POTTINGER, Justin Charles Edward. b 82. Keble Coll Ox BA 03 Ox Brookes Univ PGCE 04. STETS 05 Ripon Coll Cuddesdon 07. **d** 08 **p** 09. C Devizes St Jo w St Mary *Sarum* 08-11; Chapl Clayesmore Sch Blandford 11-14; V Red Post *Sarum* from 15. *The Vicarage, East Morden, Wareham BH20 7DW* T: (01929) 459244
E: redpostbenefice@gmail.com

POTTS, Heather Dawn. See BUTCHER, Heather Dawn

POTTS, James. b 30. K Coll Lon BD 56 AKC 56. **d** 57 **p** 58. C Brighouse *Wakef* 57-59; Tanganyika 59-64; Tanzania 64-71; C-in-c Athersley and New Lodge CD *Wakef* 71-73; V Athersley 73-77; V Madeley *Lich* 77-85; V Baswich 85-93; RD Stafford 88-95; rtd 93; PtO *Lich* from 95. *16A Christchurch Lane, Lichfield WS13 8BA* T: (01543) 418808

POTTS, Mrs Jill. b 46. Open Univ BA 89. STETS 02. **d** 05 **p** 06. NSM Corfe Mullen *Sarum* 05-07; NSM Grantham, Manthorpe *Linc* 07-13; rtd 13; PtO *Linc* from 13. *18 Dallygate, Great Ponton, Grantham NG33 5DP* T: (01476) 530361
E: jill@jpotts.me.uk

POTTS, Mrs Susan Pamela. b 54. Huddersfield Poly BA 76 Lanc Univ PGCE 77. ERMC 09. **d** 12 **p** 13. NSM Raddesley Gp *Ely* 12-14; NSM Three Rivers Gp from 14. *1A Station Road, Swaffham Bulbeck, Cambridge CB25 0NB* T: (01223) 813260
M: 07851-184295 E: susan.potts@scherzando.org *or* revd.sue@icloud.com

POULARD, Christopher. b 39. FCA 64. Ridley Hall Cam 82. **d** 84 **p** 85. C N Walsham w Antingham *Nor* 84-86; C Oulton Broad 86-90; TV Raveningham 90-94; R Raveningham Gp 94-99; RD Loddon 98-99; PtO *Chelmsf* from 99; rtd 06. *Cuddington, Colam Lane, Little Baddow, Chelmsford CM3 4SY* T: (01245) 224221 F: 221394 E: chris.poulard@virgin.net

POULSON, Anna Louise. b 73. Univ Coll Dur BA 94 K Coll Lon MA 97 PhD 06. Ridley Hall Cam 98. **d** 02 **p** 03. C Ealing St Mary *Lon* 02-06; Dioc Discretion 07; C Southall Green St Jo 11-14; V from 15. *St John's Vicarage, Church Avenue, Southall UB2 4DH* T: (020) 8571 3027 M: 07795-595915
E: annapoulson@btinternet.com

POULSON, Mark Alban. b 63. Bath Coll of HE BEd 86 Anglia Poly Univ MA 03. Ridley Hall Cam. **d** 00 **p** 01. C Alperton *Lon* 00-03; P-in-c Southall Green St Jo 03-06; V 06-14; Adv for Inter Faith Matters from 14; Abp's Sec for Inter-Relig Affairs *Cant* from 15. *Lambeth Palace, London SE1 7JU* T: (020) 7898 1247
E: mpoulson@btinternet.com

POULTNEY, Andrew Timothy. b 68. K Coll Lon MA 03. St Paul's Th Cen Lon 06. **d** 08 **p** 09. C Collier Row St Jas and Havering-atte-Bower *Chelmsf* from 08. *40 Kingston Road, Romford RM1 3NB* M: 07903-112599 T: (01708) 606030
E: andypoultney@deepernetworkchurch.com

POULTNEY, David Elis. b 73. Loughb Univ BEng 96 CEng 97. Trin Coll Bris 07. **d** 09 **p** 10. C Luton Lewsey St Hugh *St Alb* 09-13; C Bushey from 13. *60 Beechcroft Road, Bushey WD23 2JU* T: (01923) 805061
E: dave.poultney@outlook.com

POULTON, Arthur Leslie. b 28. K Coll Lon BA 53 AKC 53 BD 60 Leic Univ MA 85. Tyndale Hall Bris 53. **d** 55 **p** 56. C New Catton St Luke *Nor* 55-56; C Earlham St Anne 56-58; C Chorleywood Ch Ch *St Alb* 58-61; R E Barnet 61-64; Ches Coll of HE 64-87; Chapl 64-84; Sen Lect 66-87; Dir of Studies Course in Chr Studies *Chelmsf* 87-94; P-in-c Gt Canfield 87-94; rtd 94; PtO *Ches* from 96. *2 The Cloisters, Rhos on Sea, Colwyn Bay LL28 4PW* T: (01493) 549473

POULTON, Canon Ian Peter. b 60. Lon Univ BSc(Econ) 83 Open Univ BA 94. **d** 86 **p** 87. C Newtownards *D & D* 86-89; I Bright w Ballee and Killough 89-96; Relig Adv Downtown Radio 91-96; I Larne and Inver *Conn* 96-99; I Killiney Ballybrack *D & G* 99-10; I Clonenagh w Offerlane, Borris-in-Ossory etc *C & O* from 10; Can St Patr Cathl Dublin from 11. *Clonenagh Rectory, Portlaoise Road, Mountrath, Co Laois, Republic of Ireland* T: (00353) (57) 873 2146 E: poulton@oceanfree.net

POULTON, The Very Revd Katharine Margaret. b 61. Man Univ BA 83. **d** 87 **p** 91. C Bangor St Comgall *D & D* 87-91; C Seagoe 91-96; C Kilwaughter w Cairncastle and Craigy Hill *Conn* 96-99; C Greystones *D & G* 99-00; Bp's C Dublin St Geo and St Thos 00-10; Can Ch Ch Cathl Dublin 07-10; Dean Ossory *C & O* from 10; I Kilkenny w Aghour and Kilmanagh from 10; Can Leighlin Cathl from 10; Can Ferns Cathl from 14. *The Deanery, The Close, Coach Road, Kilkenny, Republic of Ireland* T: (00353) (56) 772 1516 F: 775 1817
E: katharinepoulton@gmail.com

POULTON, Neville John. b 48. STETS. **d** 02. NSM Portsea St Cuth *Portsm* 02-07. *18 Belgravia Road, Portsmouth PO2 0DX* T: (023) 9236 1104 M: 07768-661796

POUNCE, Alan Gerald. b 34. Lon Univ BSc 55. Wycliffe Hall Ox 57. **d** 59 **p** 60. C Wednesfield Heath *Lich* 59-61; C Heref St Pet w St Owen 61-63; R Gt w Lt Dunham *Nor* 63-69; Asst Master Windsor Boys' Sch 69-94; rtd 94; PtO *Ox* 69-99; LtO from 99. *38 Longdown Road, Sandhurst GU47 8QG* T: (01344) 772870

POUNCEY, Christopher Michael Godwin. b 52. Reading Univ BSc 74 Wycliffe Hall Ox BA 77 MA. SWMTC 03. **d** 04 **p** 05. NSM S Molton w Nymet St George, High Bray etc *Ex* from 04. *Brightley Barton, Umberleigh EX37 9AL* T: (01769) 540405 M: 07977-930045 E: cmgpouncey@hotmail.com

POUND, Canon Keith Salisbury. b 33. St Cath Coll Cam BA 54 MA 58. Cuddesdon Coll 55. **d** 57 **p** 58. C St Helier *S'wark* 57-61; Tr Officer Holloford Tr and Conf Cen Sheff 61-64; Warden 64-67; R S'wark H Trin 68-74; P-in-c Newington St Matt 68-74; R S'wark H Trin w St Matt 74-78; RD S'wark and Newington 73-78; TR Thamesmead 78-86; Sub-Dean Woolwich 84-86; RD Greenwich 85-86; Hon Can S'wark Cathl 85-86; Chapl Gen of Pris 86-93; Chapl to The Queen 88-03; Chapl HM Pris Grendon and Spring Hill 93-98; rtd 98; PtO *Chich* from 99. *1 Sinnock Square, Hastings TN34 3HQ* T: (01424) 428330

POUT, John. **d** 12 **p** 14. NSM Moreton-in-Marsh w Batsford, Todenham etc *Glouc* from 12. *12 Oriel Grove, Moreton-in-Marsh GL56 0ED*

POVEY, William Peter. b 36. JP 85. Man Univ MSc 82 MRCS 61 LRCP 61 FFPH 79 FRIPH HonFChS. NOC 90. **d** 93 **p** 94. Dioc Drug Liaison Officer *Ches* 93-01; NSM Latchford Ch Ch 93-00; NSM Daresbury 00-03; rtd 03; PtO *Ches* from 03; *Ex* from 04. *Applebrook House, 4 Trinnicks Orchard, Ugborough, Ivybridge PL21 0NX* T: (01752) 691654
E: povey.peter@googlemail.com

POW, Mrs Deborah Jayne. b 64. Trin Coll Bris 13. **d** 15. NSM Charlcombe w Bath St Steph *B & W* from 15. *The Close, Inglesbatch, Bath BA2 9DZ* E: debbie.pow@btinternet.com

POWDRILL, Penelope Anne. b 47. Lon Univ BSc 69 PGCE 71 Birm Univ MEd 77. WEMTC 10. **d** 11 **p** 12. OLM Goodrich, Marstow, Welsh Bicknor, Llangarron etc *Heref* from 11; OLM Wye Reaches Gp from 11. *Homebush, Lower Prospect Road, Osbaston, Monmouth NP25 3AS* T: (01600) 714096
E: pennypowdrill@btinternet.com

POWE, David James Hector. b 50. Wycliffe Hall Ox 88. **d** 90 **p** 91. C Ventnor St Cath *Portsm* 90-92; Chapl HM Pris Belmarsh 93-94 and 98-04; Chapl HM Pris Lewes 94-97; Chapl HM Pris Bris from 04. *The Chaplain's Office, HM Prison, Cambridge Road, Bristol BS7 8PS* T: 0117-372 3246 *or* 372 3100

POWELL, Canon Anthony James. b 51. Sarum & Wells Th Coll 78. **d** 79 **p** 80. C Larkfield *Roch* 79-83; C Leybourne 79-83; V Borough Green from 83; Hon Can Roch Cathl from 04. *The Vicarage, 24 Maidstone Road, Borough Green, Sevenoaks TN15 8BD* T/F: (01732) 882447

POWELL, Charles David. b 38. St Pet Coll Saltley CertEd 61 ACP 74. SAOMC 96. **d** 99 **p** 00. NSM Ampthill w Millbrook and Steppingley *St Alb* 99-04; PtO from 05; RD Ampthill 03-08. *33 Putnoe Heights, Bedford MK41 8EB* T: (01234) 345020 M: 07811-260675
E: rev.davidpowell@btinternet.com

POWELL, Christopher John. b 71. K Coll Lon BA 94 AKC 94. Coll of Resurr Mirfield 95. **d** 97 **p** 98. C Botley *Portsm* 97-01; C Portsea N End St Mark 01-05; P-in-c Clayton w Keymer *Chich* 05-13; R from 13. *The Rectory, 1 The Crescent, Hassocks BN6 8RB* T: (01273) 843570
E: christopher.powell123@btinternet.com

POWELL, Colin Arthur. b 32. Hatf Coll Dur BA 53. Oak Hill Th Coll 56. **d** 58 **p** 59. C Leyland St Andr *Blackb* 58-61; C Lancaster St Thos 61-64; C Tranmere St Cath *Ches* 64-65; R Cheetham Hill *Man* 65-81; TV Oldham 81-86; TV Rochdale 86-97; Chapl Rochdale Healthcare NHS Trust 94-97; rtd 97; PtO *Man* from 97. *103 Parsonage Road, Withington, Manchester M20 4NU* T: 0161-434 2409

POWELL, David. See POWELL, Charles David

POWELL, Mrs Diane. b 41. SWMTC 03. **d** 88 **p** 94. Hon C St Merryn *Truro* 88-92; Dn-in-c Gerrans w St Anthony in Roseland 92-94; P-in-c 94-00; Asst Chapl R Cornwall Hosps Trust 00-05; rtd 05; PtO *Truro* from 05. *Windsway, Sandy Common, Constantine Bay, Padstow PL28 8JL* T: (01841) 521610 E: diannick@msn.com

POWELL, Dudley John. b 44. Tyndale Hall Bris 65. **d** 69 **p** 70. C Blackb Sav 69-71; C Rodbourne Cheney *Bris* 71-74; P-in-c Kingsdown 74-79; V 79-80; V Stoke Gifford 80-90; TR 90-91; Ancient World Outreach Albania 91-03; PtO *Bris* 91-03; *Win* 03-13; rtd 09. *30 Homechurch House, 31 Purewell, Christchurch BH23 1EH* T: (01202) 481379
E: dudleyberat@tesco.net

POWELL, Eleanor Ann. b 55. Univ of Wales BA 82 Leeds Univ MA 06 Gwent Coll Newport CertEd 76. Qu Coll Birm 82. **d** 83 **p** 94. C Caereithin *S & B* 83-86; C Bishopston 86-88;

Dioc Children's Officer *Glouc* 88-94; Dioc Adv for Women's Min 94-01; P-in-c The Edge, Pitchcombe, Harescombe and Brookthorpe 94-00; V Churchdown St Jo 00-01; Hon Can Glouc Cathl 94-01; Chapl Univ Hosps Bris NHS Foundn Trust 01-06; Chapl N Glam NHS Trust from 06. *Park Farm Lodge, The Legar, Langattock, Crickhowell NP8 1HH* T: (01873) 811355 E: eleanor.powell@nglam-tr.wales.nhs.uk

POWELL, Elizabeth Mary. b 49. **d** 09 **p** 10. OLM The Bourne and Tilford *Guildf* 09-13; NSM from 13. *13 Woodcut Road, Wrecclesham, Farnham GU10 4QF* T: (01252) 725933 E: powellliz@hotmail.com

POWELL, Preb Frank. b 29. AKC 52. **d** 53 **p** 54. C Stockingford *Cov* 53-56; C Netherton St Andr *Worc* 56-60; P-in-c W Bromwich St Jo *Lich* 60-66; C W Bromwich Gd Shep w St Jo 60-66; V 66-69; V Bilston St Leon 69-76; P-in-c Hanbury 76-82; V Hanbury w Newborough 83-86; V Basford 86-92; Preb Lich Cathl 87-92; rtd 92; PtO *Ches* from 92. *39 Wright Court, London Road, Nantwich CW5 6SE* T: (01270) 618679 E: fjpowell1@gmail.com

POWELL, Gareth Stuart Aidan. b 78. Brunel Univ BA 00 Pemb Coll Cam MPhil 08 PhD 12. Westcott Ho Cam 07. **d** 11 **p** 12. C Solihull *Birm* 11-14; C Streatham Hill St Marg *S'wark* from 14. *4 Kirstall Road, London SW2 4HF* M: 07917-624177 E: frgarethpowell@me.com

POWELL, Gary Charles. b 62. UWIST BSc 84. Coll of Resurr Mirfield 92. **d** 95 **p** 96. C Roath *Llan* 95-00; V Llansawel, Briton Ferry 00-09; V Dafen *St D* 09-13; AD Cydweli 11-13; Chapl Hywel Dda Health Bd 11-13; P-in-c Gelligaer *Llan* from 13. *The Rectory, Church Road, Gelligaer, Hengoed CF82 8FW* T: (01443) 832119

POWELL, John. b 44. St Luke's Coll Ex CertEd 66 Univ of Wales (Lamp) MA 02. Glouc Sch of Min 81. **d** 84 **p** 85. NSM Stroud and Uplands w Slad *Glouc* 84-89; Chapl Eliz Coll Guernsey 89-92; C Llandudno *Ban* 92-93; TV 94-96; V Dwygyfylchi 96-02; V Cardigan w Mwnt and Y Ferwig w Llangoedmor *St D* 02-10; rtd 10; P-in-c Llangrannog w Llandysiliogogo w Penbryn *St D* 10-11; PtO 11-12; P-in-c Maenordeifi Gp 12-14; PtO from 14. *Crud yr Haul, 12 Maes y Dderwen, Cardigan SA43 1PE* T: (01239) 621512 E: parchjohnpowell@btinternet.com

POWELL, John Keith Lytton. b 52. S Dios Minl Tr Scheme 91. **d** 94 **p** 95. NSM Bridgwater H Trin *B & W* 94-97; P-in-c Hatch Beauchamp w Beercrocombe, Curry Mallet etc 97-02; P-in-c Staple Fitzpaine, Orchard Portman, Thurlbear etc 97-02; R Beercrocombe w Curry Mallet, Hatch Beauchamp etc 02-05; P-in-c Exford, Exmoor, Hawkridge and Withypool 05-09; P-in-c Middlezoy and Othery and Moorlinch 09-11; P-in-c Greinton 09-11; R Middlezoy w Othery, Moorlinch and Greinton from 11; Dioc Renewal Adv from 06. *The Vicarage, High Street, Othery, Bridgwater TA7 0QA* T: (01823) 698999 E: jill.powell3@googlemail.com

POWELL, Miss Katherine. b 56. Sydney Univ BSS 79. Wycliffe Hall Ox 84. **dss** 86 **d** 87 **p** 94. Broadwater St Mary *Chich* 86-87; Par Dn 87-91; Asst Chapl Ch Hosp Horsham 91-96; Chapl Glennie Sch Australia from 97. *The Glennie School, Herries Street, Toowoomba Qld 4350, Australia* T: (0061) (7) 4637 9359 *or* 4688 8808 F: 4688 8848 E: powellk@glennie.qld.edu.au

POWELL, Kelvin. b 49. Wycliffe Hall Ox 71. **d** 74 **p** 75. C Prescot *Liv* 74-77; C Ainsdale 77-79; V Bickershaw 79-85; R Hesketh w Becconsall *Blackb* 85-99; PtO *Leic* from 14. *19 Stuart Court, High Street, Kibworth, Leicester LE8 0LR*

POWELL, Laurence James. b 86. Win Univ BA 08. Ripon Coll Cuddesdon 10. **d** 13 **p** 14. C Strood St Nic w St Mary *Roch* from 13. *18 Honeypot Close, Rochester ME2 3DU* T: (01634) 716353 E: laurence.powell@me.com

POWELL, Mark. b 57. Bath Univ BSc 78 PhD 81. Ripon Coll Cuddesdon 84. BA MA 88. **d** 85 **p** 86. C Evesham *Worc* 85-88; V Exhall *Cov* 88-96; V Leavesden *St Alb* 96-00; V Ealing St Pet Mt Park *Lon* 00-11; V Melbourne, Ticknall, Smisby and Stanton *Derby* from 11. *The Vicarage, Church Square, Melbourne, Derby DE73 8JH* T: (01332) 864741 E: mark.powell4@btinternet.com

POWELL, Martin. b 57. St Steph Ho Ox BTh 00. **d** 00 **p** 01. C Caterham *S'wark* 00-03; V New Addington 03-14; R Aldingbourne, Barnham and Eastergate *Chich* from 14. *Field House, Church Road, Aldingbourne, Chichester PO20 3TT* T: (01243) 545404 E: frmartinpowell@gmail.com

POWELL, Michael. *See* POWELL, Eric Michael

POWELL, Canon Pamela. b 56. Univ of Wales BEd 79 Goldsmiths' Coll Lon MA 82. St As Minl Tr Course 00. **d** 03 **p** 04. C Wrexham *St As* 03-06; P-in-c Llansantffraid-ym-Mechain and Llanfechain 06-08; V 08-15; AD Llanfyllin 11-12; AD Caereinion and Llanfyllin 12-14; V Brymbo w Bwlchgwyn from 15; Dir Lay Min from 10; Chan St As Cathl from 14. *The Vicarage, 8 Whiteoaks, Bwlchgwyn, Wrexham LL11 5UJ* M: 07711-053565 T: (01978) 721083 E: pampowell@micro-plus-web.net

POWELL, Patricia Mary. b 36. STETS. **d** 03 **p** 04. NSM Woodford Valley *Sarum* 03-09; NSM Tidworth, Ludgershall and Faberstown 09-12; NSM Woodford Valley w Archers Gate from 13; NSM Amesbury from 13. *The Rectory, St George's Road, Tidworth SP9 7EW* T: (01980) 843730 E: patricia-powell@tiscali.co.uk

POWELL, Canon Ralph Dover. b 49. ARMCM 70. Chich Th Coll 71. **d** 74 **p** 75. C Coppenhall *Ches* 74-77; C Heref H Trin 77-80; V Crewe St Barn *Ches* from 80; Hon Can Ches Cathl from 14. *St Barnabas' Vicarage, West Street, Crewe CW1 3AX* T: (01270) 212418 E: robert.rc.pearson@btinternet.com

POWELL, Richard Penry. b 15. Dur Univ LTh 38. St Aid Birkenhead 34. **d** 38 **p** 39. C Brierley Hill *Lich* 38-42; C Derby St Chad 42-45; C Uttoxeter w Bramshall *Lich* 45-47; V Alton 47-60; V Bradley-in-the-Moors 48-60; R Drayton Bassett 60-64; Min Canwell CD 60-64; V Wrockwardine 64-80; V Uppington 64-80; rtd 80; PtO *Lich* from 80. *34 Herbert Avenue, Wellington, Telford TF1 2BS* T: (01952) 242528

POWELL, Robert John. b 65. Trin Coll Bris BA 92. **d** 92 **p** 93. C Biggin Hill *Roch* 92-95; C Edgware *Lon* 95-01; Area Sec SAMS (NW England and N Wales) 01-04; TV Upper Holloway *Lon* 04-12; V Whitehall Park 12-13; TR Furzedown *S'wark* from 13. *St James's Rectory, 236 Mitcham Lane, London SW16 6NT*

POWELL, Roger Roy. b 68. Thames Poly BSc 91. Ripon Coll Cuddesdon BTh 94. **d** 94 **p** 95. C Leic St Jas 94-98; C The Abbey Leic 98-00; TV 00-05; P-in-c Leic St Paul 01-05; Youth Chapl 98-05; P-in-c Ridgeway *Sarum* 05-10; R from 10. *The Rectory, 3 Butts Road, Chiseldon, Swindon SN4 0NN* T: (01793) 740369 E: revd.rpowell@btopenworld.com

POWELL, Stuart William. b 58. K Coll Lon BD 80 AKC 80. Ripon Coll Cuddesdon 86. **d** 88 **p** 89. C Horden *Dur* 88-90; C Northolt Park St Barn *Lon* 90-93; V Castle Vale St Cuth *Birm* 93-00; V Stockland Green 00-11; P-in-c Rough Hills *Lich* from 11; P-in-c Wolverhampton St Steph from 11. *St Martin's Vicarage, Dixon Street, Wolverhampton WV2 2BG* T: (01902) 341030 M: 07889-887358 P: 07336-734456 E: spowell.t21@btinternet.com

POWER, Alan Edward. b 26. Worc Coll Ox BA 50 MA 53. Lich Th Coll. **d** 57 **p** 58. C Summerfield *Birm* 57-60; C Oldbury 60-63; V Short Heath 63-97; rtd 97; PtO *Birm* 97-12. *8 Southam Drive, Sutton Coldfield B73 5PD* T: 0121-355 8923

POWER, Canon David Michael. b 56. BA 81 BEd. Oak Hill Th Coll. **d** 81 **p** 82. C Warblington w Emsworth *Portsm* 81-84; C-in-c Hartplain CD 84-88; V Hartplain 88-91; Adv in Evang 91-97; V Portsea St Cuth from 97; Hon Can Portsm Cathl from 13. *St Cuthbert's Vicarage, 2 Lichfield Road, Portsmouth PO3 6DE* T/F: (023) 9282 7071

POWER, Ivor Jonathan. b 43. Lambeth STh 87. CITC 66. **d** 69 **p** 70. C Dromore Cathl 69-71; C Enniscorthy *C & O* 71-74; I Youghal *C, C & R* 74-78; I Youghal Union 78-81; I Athlone w Benown, Kiltoom and Forgney *M & K* 81-98; Can Meath 87-98; Dir of Ords (Meath) 91-97; I Dublin Crumlin w Chapelizod *D & G* 98-08; Can Ch Ch Cathl Dublin 05-08; rtd 08. *62 Maudlin Street, Kilkenny, Republic of Ireland* T: (00353) (56) 779 0618

POWER, James Edward. b 58. Nottm Univ BSc 81 Leeds Univ BA 85. Coll of Resurr Mirfield 83. **d** 86 **p** 87. C Cadoxton-juxta-Barry *Llan* 86-89; Chapl Harrow Sch from 89; V Harrow St Mary *Lon* from 15. *35 West Street, Harrow HA1 3EG* T: (020) 8872 8234 E: jep@harrowschool.org.uk

POWER, Mrs Jeanette. b 57. Oak Hill Th Coll BA 81. **dss** 82 **d** 87 **p** 94. Warblington w Emsworth *Portsm* 82-84; Hartplain CD 84-87; Hon C Hartplain 87-91; Community Mental Health Chapl Havant and Petersfield from 91; NSM Wickham 93-97; NSM Portsea St Cuth from 97; Team Chapl Portsm Hosps NHS Trust from 01. *St Cuthbert's Vicarage, 2 Lichfield Road, Portsmouth PO3 6DE* T/F: (023) 9282 7071 E: jeanettepower@ntlworld.com

POWER, Mrs Lynn Diane. b 59. K Coll Lon BA 81 PGCE 82 AKC 81. STETS 10. **d** 13 **p** 14. NSM N Hants Downs *Win* from 13. *1 Alton Road, South Warnborough, Hook RG29 1RT* T: (01256) 861433 M: 07850-232995

POWER, Michael Andrew. b 61. Westcott Ho Cam. **d** 12 **p** 13. C Romford St Edw *Chelmsf* 12-15; V from 15. *St Edward's Vicarage, 15 Oaklands Avenue, Romford RM1 4DB* M: 07793-463640 E: mikeapower@aol.com

POWER, Richard Victor John. b 80. Oak Hill Th Coll 13. **d** 15. C Banbury St Paul *Ox* from 15. *10 Hardwick Park, Banbury OX16 1YD* M: 07925-394122 E: rvjpower@gmail.com

POWIS, Miss Amy Victoria. b 87. Reading Univ BA 08. Trin Coll Bris BA 14. **d** 14 **p** 15. C Shirley *Win* from 14. *16 Radway Road, Southampton SO15 7PW* T: (023) 8048 0365 E: amyvpowis@gmail.com

POWIS, Michael Ralph. b 63. St Jo Coll Nottm BTh 95. **d** 95 **p** 96. C Dibden *Win* 95-00; V Hedge End St Luke 00-09; Adult Discipleship and Evang Tr Officer 09-11; P-in-c Pokesdown

All SS from 11; P-in-c Bournemouth St Clem from 11. *All Saints' Vicarage, 14 Stourwood Road, Bournemouth BH6 3QP* T: (01202) 423747 E: mikepowischurch@gmail.com

POWLES, Charles Anthony. b 39. EAMTC. **d** 88 **p** 89. NSM Hemsby *Nor* 88-93; NSM Bradwell 01-07; PtO from 07. *94 Winifred Way, Caister-on-Sea, Great Yarmouth NR30 5PE* T: (01493) 720096 E: charles.powles@btinternet.com

POWLES, Michael Charles. b 34. Reading Univ BSc 56 Lon Univ PGCE 83. Qu Coll Birm. **d** 60 **p** 61. C Goodmayes All SS *Chelmsf* 60-65; C Surbiton St Matt *S'wark* 65-78; Lect Woolwich Coll 79-99; rtd 99. *Spring Cottage, 3 Rushett Close, Thames Ditton KT7 0UR* T: (020) 8398 9654

POWLEY, Miss Julia Hodgson. b 55. St Andr Univ MA 77 Anglia Ruskin Univ MA 10 FCA 80. Ridley Hall Cam 07. **d** 09 **p** 10. C Carl H Trin and St Barn 09-12; P-in-c Harrington from 12; P-in-c Distington from 12. *The Rectory, Rectory Close, Harrington, Workington CA14 5PN* T: (01946) 830215 M: 07765-217335 E: julia@powley.plus.com

POWLEY, Mark Thomas. b 75. Nottm Univ BA 96 Birm Univ PGCE 98. Wycliffe Hall Ox 01. **d** 03 **p** 04. C Addiscombe St Mary Magd w St Martin *S'wark* 03-06; C Hammersmith St Paul *Lon* 06-09; TV Leeds St Geo 10-15; Prin Yorks Min Course from 15. *34 Holmwood Avenue, Meanwood, Leeds LS6 4NJ* T: 0113-243 8498 E: principal@ymc.org.uk

POWLEY, Canon Robert Mallinson. b 39. Fitzw Coll Cam MA 65. Ridley Hall Cam 61. **d** 63 **p** 64. C Bermondsey St Mary w St Olave, St Jo etc *S'wark* 63-67; C Moseley St Anne *Birm* 67-69; LtO *Man* 72-77; Hon C Walshaw Ch Ch 77-88; V Prestwich St Gabr 88-94; Bp's Dom Chapl 88-94; P-in-c Hargrave *Ches* 94-05; Exec Officer Bd for Soc Resp 94-05; Hon Can Ches Cathl 00-05; rtd 05; PtO *Ban* 05-12. *39A Bentley Lane, Leeds LS6 4AJ* T: 0113-275 9876

POWNALL, Miss Hilary Frances. b 54. SEITE 08. **d** 11. NSM Eastbourne St Mary *Chich* from 11. *Foundlings, 34A Broomfield Street, Eastbourne BN20 8LQ* T: (01323) 411816 M: 07985-714201 E: hfpownall@hfpownall.plus.com

POWNALL, Lydia Margaret. *See* HURLE, Lydia Margaret

POWNALL, Stephen. b 56. St Jo Coll Nottm BA 02. **d** 02 **p** 03. C Herne Hill *S'wark* 02-06; TV Westborough *Guildf* from 06. *St Clare's Vicarage, 242 Cabell Road, Guildford GU2 8JW* T: (01483) 301349 E: stevep97@live.co.uk

POWNALL-JONES, Timothy William. b 79. Univ of Wales (Cardiff) BD 00 MTh 02. Trin Coll Bris 04. **d** 06 **p** 07. C Newark w Coddington *S'well* 06-10; Chapl N Notts Coll of FE 10-11; LtO from 10; Chapl Notts Healthcare NHS Trust from 15. *Rampton Hospital, Retford DN22 0PD* M: 07837-630005 E: t_pownall_jones@hotmail.com

POYNTZ, Jocelin Georgina Massey. b 58. Ridley Hall Cam. **d** 13 **p** 14. C Stanford-le-Hope w Mucking *Chelmsf* from 13. *Glebe House, Wharf Road, Stanford-le-Hope SS17 0BY* M: 07743-124181 E: jokey.poyntz@gmail.com

✠POYNTZ, The Rt Revd Samuel Greenfield. b 26. TCD BA 48 MA 51 BD 53 PhD 60 Ulster Univ Hon DLitt 95. TCD Div Sch Div Test 50. **d** 50 **p** 51 **c** 78. C Dublin St Geo and St Thos, Finglas and Free Ch *D & G* 50-52; C Bray 52-55; C Dublin St Michan w St Paul 55-59; Sec and Sch Insp Ch Educn Soc for Ireland 56-75; I Dublin St Steph *D & G* 59-67; I Dublin St Ann 67-70; I Dublin St Ann w St Steph 70-78; Adn Dublin 74-78; Bp C, C & R 78-87; Bp Conn 87-95; rtd 95. *3 The Gables, Ballinteer Road, Dundrum, Dublin 16, Republic of Ireland* T: (00353) (1) 296 6748

PRADELLA, Henry. b 54. St Mary's Coll Twickenham BEd 78. NTMTC 97. **d** 00 **p** 01. NSM Hainault *Chelmsf* 00-04; C Romford Gd Shep 04-06; R Rainham w Wennington from 06. *The Vicarage, 73 Lake Avenue, Rainham RM13 9SG* T: (01708) 559157 E: pradfam@tiscali.co.uk

PRAGNELL, John William. b 39. Lon Univ BD 65. Lambeth STh 87 LTh 88. **d** 65 **p** 66. C Bitterne Win 65-68; C Hatfield Hyde *St Alb* 68-73; Kuwait 73-75; Chapl Leavesden Hosp Abbots Langley 75-88; Chapl Abbots Langley Hosp *Nor* 75-88; Chapl Watford Gen Hosp 86-88; V St Alb St Steph *St Alb* 88-95; RD St Alb 91-95; P-in-c Copythorne *Win* 95-02; Dioc Ecum Officer 95-02; Hosp Chapl Adv (Bournemouth Adnry) 00-02; rtd 02; PtO *Sarum* 03-07. *10 Palmers Court, Southwell NG25 0JG*

PRAGNELL, Michael John. b 40. Down Coll Cam BA 62 PhD 65 MA 66 FIQA 81 MRSC CChem MSOSc 88. Ox NSM Course 81. **d** 84 **p** 85. NSM High Wycombe *Ox* 84-98; C Beercrocombe w Curry Mallet, Hatch Beauchamp etc *B & W* 98-05; rtd 05; PtO *B & W* from 05. *2 Listers Court, Listers Hill, Ilminster TA19 0DP* T: (01460) 54212 E: curatemjp@waitrose.com

PRAGNELL, The Very Revd Sandra Ann. b 53. Hull Univ BA 75 TCD BTh 01 Dub City Univ MA 04. CITC 98. **d** 01 **p** 02. C Castleknock and Mulhuddart w Clonsilla *D & G* 01-05; PV Ch Ch Cathl Dublin 03-05; I Dundalk w Heynestown *Arm* 05-12; I Ballymascanlan w Creggan and Rathcor 05-12; Dean

Limerick and Ardfert *L & K* from 12; I Limerick City from 12. *The Deanery, 7 Kilbane, Castletroy, Limerick, Republic of Ireland* T: (00353) (61) 338697 M: 87-265 8592 E: sandrapragnell@eircom.net

PRAILL, David William. b 57. York Univ BA 79 FRGS 90. Cranmer Hall Dur 81. **d** 82 **p** 83. C Digswell and Panshanger *St Alb* 82-84; CMS 84-89; Course Dir St Geo Coll Jerusalem 85-89; Dir McCabe Educn Trust 90-91; Dir St Luke's Hospice Harrow and Wembley 91-98; Chief Exec Help the Hospices from 98. *Hospice House, 34-44 Britannia Street, London WC1X 9JG* T: (020) 7520 8200 F: 7278 1021

PRANCE, Robert Penrose. b 47. Southn Univ BTh 73. Sarum & Wells Th Coll 69. **d** 72 **p** 73. C Gillingham and Fifehead Magdalen *Sarum* 72-76; P-in-c Edmondsham 76-80; P-in-c Woodlands 76-80; P-in-c Wimborne St Giles 76-80; P-in-c Cranborne 77-80; R Cranborne w Boveridge, Edmondsham etc 80-83; Chapl Sherborne Sch 83-93; Asst Dir of Ords *Sarum* 76-86; V Stoke Gabriel and Collaton *Ex* 93-99; Dep PV Ex Cathl 95-99; Chapl Shiplake Coll Henley 99-09; Chapl St Edm Sch Cant 09-10; rtd 10; PtO *Ox* from 09; *Sarum* from 11. *Hill House Rectory, Farnham, Blandford Forum DT11 8DE* T: (01725) 516974 E: robertprance@live.co.uk

PRASADAM, Canon Jemima. b 39. MBE 05. BD 61 BA 87. Cranmer Hall Dur 86. **d** 87 **p** 94. Par Dn Luton All SS w St Pet *St Alb* 87-94; C 94-96; P-in-c Lozells St Paul and St Silas *Birm* 96-07; V 07-09; P-in-c 09-14; rtd 09; Hon Can Birm Cathl 05-14; PtO from 14. *Address temp unknown*

PRASADAM, Madhu Smitha. b 64. Qu Coll Birm. **d** 03 **p** 04. C Blackheath *Birm* 03-07; V Hamstead St Paul from 07. *Hamstead Vicarage, 840 Walsall Road, Birmingham B42 1ES* T: 0121-357 8941

PRATT, Basil David. b 38. Ripon Hall Ox 64. **d** 67 **p** 68. C Lewisham St Jo Southend *S'wark* 67-68; C Caterham Valley 68-70; CF 70-93; PtO *Glas* from 08. *St Michael's, Bankend Road, Dumfries DG1 4AL* T: (01387) 267933

PRATT, Christine Fiona. *See* BLACKMAN, Christine Fiona

PRATT, Edward Andrew. b 39. Clare Coll Cam BA 61 MA 65. Clifton Th Coll 63. **d** 66 **p** 67. C Southall Green St Jo *Lon* 66-69; C Drypool St Columba w St Andr and St Pet *York* 69-71; P-in-c Radbourne *Derby* 71-74; R Kirk Langley 71-78; V Mackworth All SS 71-78; V Southsea St Simon *Portsm* 78-97; rtd 97; PtO *Sarum* from 97. *7 Bay Close, Swanage BH19 1RE*

PRATT, Mrs Janet Margaret. b 40. Herts Coll BEd 78. St Alb Minl Tr Scheme 78. **dss** 81 **d** 87 **p** 94. High Wych and Gilston w Eastwick *St Alb* 81-89; Hon Par Dn 87-89; Par Dn Histon *Ely* 89-94; C 94-97; Par Dn Impington 89-94; C 94-97; R Bardney *Linc* 97-07; rtd 07; PtO *Ely* from 08; *St Alb* from 08. *26 Stamford Avenue, Royston SG8 7DD* T: (01763) 243508 E: janetmpratt99@yahoo.com

PRATT, John. b 37. **d** 99 **p** 00. OLM St Enoder *Truro* 99-05; rtd 06. *Chyteg, Newquay Road, St Columb Road, St Columb TR9 6PY* T/F: (01726) 860747

PRATT, John Anthony. b 38. Selw Coll Cam BA 61 MA 65. Qu Coll Birm. **d** 66 **p** 67. C Harrow Weald All SS *Lon* 66-69; C St Pancras w St Jas and Ch Ch 69-74; C Saffron Walden w Wendens Ambo *Chelmsf* 74-75; TV Saffron Walden w Wendens Ambo and Littlebury 75-79; V St Mary-at-Latton 79-88; Chapl Princess Alexandra Hosp Harlow 82-88; RD Harlow *Chelmsf* 83-88; R Tolleshunt Knights w Tiptree and Gt Braxted 88-03; rtd 03; PtO *Cov* from 03. *2 Erica Drive, Whitnash, Leamington Spa CV31 2RS* T: (01926) 428609 E: j.a.pratt@btinternet.com

PRATT, Michael. *See* HARRIS, Michael

PRATT, The Ven Richard David. b 55. Linc Coll Ox BA 77 MA 81 Birm Univ PhD 01 Nottm Univ BCombStuds 84. Linc Th Coll 81. **d** 84 **p** 85. C Wellingborough All Hallows *Pet* 84-87; TV Kingsthorpe w Northampton St Dav 87-92; V Northampton St Benedict 92-97; Dioc Communications Officer *Carl* from 97; P-in-c Carl St Cuth w St Mary 97-08; Adn W Cumberland from 09; Hon Can Carl Cathl from 02. *50 Stainburn Road, Stainburn, Workington CA14 1SN* T: (01900) 66190 E: archdeacon.west@carlislediocese.org.uk

PRATT, Samuel Charles. b 40. ALAM 59. Oak Hill Th Coll 69. **d** 71 **p** 72. C Upper Holloway St Jo *Lon* 71-73; C Bucknall and Bagnall *Lich* 73-76; V Liv St Mich 76-80; Chapl R Liv Hosp 80-94; Chapl R Liv Univ Hosp NHS Trust 94-01; V Billinge *Liv* 01-06; rtd 06. *15 Billinge Road, Wigan WN5 9JW* T: (01942) 731346 M: 07957-367114 E: sp001f3678@blueyonder.co.uk

PRATT, Stephen Samuel. b 67. Univ Coll Ches BA 88 Keele Univ PGCE 89. Oak Hill Th Coll BA 00. **d** 00 **p** 01. C Goodmayes All SS *Chelmsf* 00-03; TV Chell *Lich* 03-07; P-in-c 07-08; V 08-15; CF(V) from 05. *The Rectory, 203 St Michael's Road, Stoke-on-Trent ST6 6JT* T: (01782) 838708 E: stephen_pratt@sky.com

PRATT, Canon William Ralph. b 47. Keble Coll Ox BA 69 MA 73. Linc Th Coll 70. **d** 72 **p** 73. C Ifield *Chich* 72-78; TV 78; C Brighton St Pet w Chpl Royal and St Jo 79-83; P-in-c Hove St Jo 83-87; Dioc Communications Officer 87-00; V Ringmer 00-14; Can and Preb Chich Cathl 90-14; rtd 14. *70 Harebeating Drive, Hailsham BN27 1JG* T: (01323) 442662 E: wrpratt@btinternet.com

PRATTEN, Miss Susan Avarina. b 60. Birm Univ BA 81 Univ Coll of Swansea PGCE 82. St Mich Coll Llan 10. **d** 12 **p** 13. C Caerphilly *Llan* 12-15; C Eglwysilan and Caerphilly from 15. *St Andrew's House, Troed-y-Bryn, Caerphilly CF83 2PX* M: 07979-742198 T: (029) 2088 0211 E: s.pratten@btinternet.com

PRECIOUS, Sally Joanne. *See* WRIGHT, Sally Joanne

PREECE, Barry Leslie. b 48. Lich Th Coll 68. **d** 71 **p** 72. C Ewell *Guildf* 71-74; C York Town St Mich 75-77; P-in-c Ripley 77-81; Chapl HM Det Cen Send 77-81; V Cuddington *Guildf* 81-88; V Cobham 88-03; R E and W Clandon 03-13; rtd 13; PtO *Cant* from 13. *43 Paxton Avenue, Hawkinge, Folkestone CT18 7GW* T: (01303) 894304 E: rev.preece@btinternet.com

PREECE, Canon Colin George. b 51. Bernard Gilpin Soc Dur 71 Chich Th Coll 72. **d** 75 **p** 76. C Upper Gornal *Lich* 75-78; C Wednesbury St Paul Wood Green 78-81; V Oxley 81-89; V Kennington *Cant* 89-03; RD E Charing 92-98; P-in-c Ashford 03-15; Hon Can Cant Cathl 08-15; rtd 15. *Bowood House, 2 Bishop Court, Colyton EX24 6RQ* T: (01297) 552154 E: colinpreece@btinternet.com

PREECE, Mrs Jill Annette. b 58. Bp Otter Coll BEd 79. SEITE 08. **d** 11 **p** 12. NSM Eastbourne St Elisabeth *Chich* from 11. *2 Osborne Road, Eastbourne BN20 8JL* T: (01323) 638020 M: 07742-655986

PREECE, Canon Mark Richard. b 61. St Paul's Coll Chelt BA 85. Linc Th Coll 85. **d** 87 **p** 88. C Coity w Nolton *Llan* 87-89; C Penarth w Lavernock 89-92; V Ewenny w St Brides Major 92-99; V Canton St Luke 99-02; TR Canton Cardiff from 02; AD Cardiff 08-13; Can Llan Cathl from 14. *Canton Rectory, 12 Thompson Avenue, Cardiff CF5 1EY* T/F: (029) 2056 2022 E: mp@mandm6162.plus.com

PREECE, Roger Martin Howell. b 64. Imp Coll Lon BSc 86 FRSA 96. St Steph Ho Ox BA 05 MA 10. **d** 06 **p** 07. C Marple All SS *Ches* 06-08; V Bowdon from 08. *The Vicarage, Church Brow, Bowdon, Altrincham WA14 2SG* T: 0161-928 2468 E: roger.preece@gmail.com

PREECE, Ronald Alexander. b 29. Lon Univ BD 56. ALCD 55. **d** 56 **p** 57. C Rusholme H Trin *Man* 56-59; Teacher Kidbrooke Sch Lon 59-60; Chapl Pernambuco Brazil 60-63; PtO *Cant* 63-70; Teacher Abp's Sch Cant 64-70; OMF 70-94; SW Regional Dir 76-94; rtd 94; PtO *Cant* from 98. *5 Tonford Lane, Canterbury CT1 3XU* T: (01227) 471061

PREMRAJ, Deborah Devashanthy. b 66. Bangalore Univ BSc 87 BEd 92 Serampore Univ BD 91. United Th Coll Bangalore 87. **d** 96 **p** 97. Deacon Vedal India 96-97; Presbyter Madurantakam 97-02; PtO *S'wark* 02-05; C Battersea Fields 05-06; Presbyter St Geo Cathl Chennai India from 06. *St George's Cathedral, 224 Cathedral Road, Chennai 600 086, India* T: (0091) (44) 2811 4261 E: premraj@csistgeorgescathedral.org

PREMRAJ, Dhanaraj Charles. b 63. Madras Univ BA 86 MA 88 Heythrop Coll Lon MTh 03. United Th Coll Bangalore BD 92. **d** 93 **p** 94. India 93-02; PtO *S'wark* 02-05; C Battersea Fields 05-06; Presbyter St Geo Cathl Chennai India from 06. *St George's Cathedral, 224 Cathedral Road, Chennai 600 086, India* T: (0091) (44) 2811 4261 E: premraj@csistgeorgescathedral.org

PRENTICE, Brian. b 40. St Jo Coll Nottm 81. **d** 83 **p** 84. C W Bromwich All SS *Lich* 83-86; C Tettenhall Wood 86-89; TV 89-90; V Essington 90-98; TR Willenhall H Trin 98-05; P-in-c Bentley 05; AD Wolverhampton 03-05; rtd 05; Chapl R Wolv Sch 05-14; PtO *Lich* from 05. *3 Hamilton Gardens, Bushbury, Wolverhampton WV10 8AX* T: (01902) 564603

PRENTICE, Mark Neil. b 73. Ex Univ BA 94. Wycliffe Hall Ox MTh 00. **d** 00 **p** 01. C Tulse Hill H Trin and St Matthias *S'wark* 00-04; C Langham Place All So *Lon* 04-13; P-in-c Ipswich St Jo *St E* from 13; P-in-c Ipswich St Andr from 14. *St John's Vicarage, Cauldwell Hall Road, Ipswich IP4 4QE* T: (01473) 721070 E: mark@stjohnsipswich.org.uk

PRENTICE, Paul Frederick. b 68. SEITE 04. **d** 07 **p** 08. C Bromley SS Pet and Paul *Roch* 07-10; P-in-c Orpington St Andr 10-15; V Cray Valley from 15. *The Vicarage, Anglesea Road, Orpington BR5 4AN* T: (01689) 823775 M: 07949-059993 E: paul.prentice2@btinternet.com

PRENTIS, Calvert Clayton. b 62. St Jo Coll Nottm 95. **d** 97 **p** 98. C Wood End *Cov* 97-00; TV Leeds St Geo *Ripon* 00-05; Asst Dioc Dir of Ords 02-05; P-in-c Huddersfield H Trin *Wakef* 05-07; V 07-12; Asst Dioc Dir of Ords 09-12; TR Horley *S'wark* from 12; Asst Dir of Ords Croydon Area from 13; Dioc

Minority Ethnic Voc Champion from 14. *4 Russell's Crescent, Horley RH6 7DN* T: (01293) 782218 M: 07940-293691 E: ccp@talktalk.net

PRENTIS, Richard Hugh. b 36. Ch Coll Cam BA 60 MA 64. Sarum Th Coll 69. **d** 71 **p** 72. C Bath Bathwick St Mary *B & W* 71-76; Bp's Dom Chapl *Lich* 76-80; PV Lich Cathl 76-80; V Longton St Mary and St Chad 80-84; V Shifnal 84-94; P-in-c Badger 84-85; P-in-c Ryton 84-85; P-in-c Beckbury 84-85; rtd 94. *23A The Close, Lichfield WS13 7LD* T: (01543) 411234

PRENTIS, Sharon Teresa. b 64. Cov Univ BA 93 Keele Univ MSc 97 Leeds Univ PhD 05 Sheff Univ MA 13. Yorks Min Course 10. **d** 13 **p** 14. NSM Redhill St Matt *S'wark* from 13. *4 Russell's Crescent, Horley RH6 7DN* T: (01293) 783509 E: sharon2serve@yahoo.co.uk

PRESCOTT, David Anthony. b 62. Univ of Wales (Lamp) BA 84 Coll of Ripon & York St Jo PGCE 85. Ripon Coll Cuddesdon MTh 07. **d** 07 **p** 08. C W Heref 07-10; TV Burrington, Chawleigh, Cheldon, Chulmleigh etc *Ex* 10-12; Chapl Warminster Sch from 12. *25 Church Street, Warminster BA12 8PJ* T: (01985) 220576 M: 07779-588619 E: dprescott@warminsterschool.org.uk

PRESCOTT, David John. b 51. St Kath Coll Liv BEd 73. NOC 00. **d** 03 **p** 04. C Southport Em *Liv* 03-07; P-in-c Birchwood 07-11; rtd 11. *90 Halsall Lane, Ormskirk L39 3AX* T: (01695) 574602 M: 07762-943138 E: prezzy@hotmail.co.uk

PRESCOTT, Thomas Robert. b 41. St Mich Coll Llan 93. **d** 95 **p** 96. C Abertillery w Cwmtillery w Six Bells *Mon* 95-99; V Llanhilleth 99-03; rtd 03. *70 Glandwr Street, Abertillery NP13 1TZ* T: (01495) 216782

PRESCOTT, William Allan. b 57. ACIS 87. Sarum & Wells Th Coll 91. **d** 93 **p** 94. C Horsell *Guildf* 93-98; R Guernsey St Sav *Win* 98-08; P-in-c Guernsey St Marguerite de la Foret 98-08; Chapl Guernsey Airport 08; R Compton, Hursley, and Otterbourne *Win* from 08. *The Rectory, Kiln Lane, Otterbourne, Winchester SO21 2EJ* T: (01962) 714551

PRESS, Richard James. b 45. Southn Univ CertEd 67. Sarum & Wells Th Coll 92. **d** 92 **p** 93. C Bradford-on-Avon H Trin *Sarum* 92-95; P-in-c Rowde and Poulshot 95-98; R Rowde and Bromham 98-01; Chapl Wilts and Swindon Healthcare NHS Trust 98-00; P-in-c Chickerell w Fleet *Sarum* 01-07; R 07-11; P-in-c Abbotsbury, Portesham and Langton Herring 09-11; rtd 11. *10 Carrick Close, Dorchester DT1 2SB* E: rjpress@gmail.com

PRESS, William John. b 72. QUB MEng 94 BTh. **d** 99 **p** 00. C Knockbreda *D & D* 99-03; C Dundonald 03-05; I Annalong 05-14; I Knockbreda from 14. *Knockbreda Rectory, 69 Church Road, Newtownbreda, Belfast BT8 7AN* T: (028) 9064 1493

PREST, Ms Deborah Ann. b 56. Leeds Univ BA 77 Ches Univ BTh 13 Man Univ PGCE 98. SNWTP 07. **d** 10 **p** 11. C Timperley *Ches* 10-14; P-in-c Greenlands *Blackb* from 14; P-in-c Blackpool St Paul from 14. *85 Salmesbury Avenue, Blackpool FY2 0PR* T: (01253) 353900 M: 07866-872625 E: deborahprest@icloud.com

PREST, Hilary Irene. **d** 15. NSM Bassaleg *Mon* from 15. *6 Silure Way, Langstone, Newport NP18 2NU* T: (01633) 412803 E: hilprest@aol.com

PRESTIDGE, Colin Robert. b 58. W Sussex Inst of HE BEd 86 Open Univ BA 01. STETS 01. **d** 04 **p** 05. NSM Crofton *Portsm* from 04; Asst Chapl E Hants Primary Care Trust from 04. *96 Titchfield Road, Stubbington, Fareham PO14 2JB* T: (01329) 664375 E: colin@prestidge.org.uk

PRESTNEY, Canon Patricia Christine Margaret. b 49. UEA BEd 94. Oak Hill Th Coll 84. **d** 87 **p** 94. NSM Lawford *Chelmsf* 87-95; Chapl Benenden Sch 95-97; Chapl St Jo Coll Ipswich 97-00; R Lawford *Chelmsf* 00-10; Hon Can Chelmsf Cathl 09-10; rtd 10; PtO *Chelmsf* 11-13; P-in-c Gt Bentley from 13; PtO from 15. *2 Cedar Way, Great Bentley, Colchester CO7 8LT* T: (01206) 255319 E: patprestney@yahoo.com or pat@saltshaker.co.uk

PRESTON, David Francis. b 50. BNC Ox BA 72 MA 78. St Steph Ho Ox 72. **d** 74 **p** 75. C Beckenham St Jas *Roch* 74-79; C Hockley *Chelmsf* 81-83; C Lamorbey H Redeemer *Roch* 83-89; V Gillingham St Barn 89-00; PtO 00-11. *103 High Street, Kirkcudbright DG6 4JG* T: (01557) 330650 E: d.preston.347@btinternet.com

PRESTON, Mrs Deborah Anne. b 46. GTCL 67. CBDTI 01. **d** 04 **p** 06. OLM Kirkby Lonsdale *Carl* 04-06; NSM Old Hutton and New Hutton and Crosscrake 06-10; NSM Kirkby Lonsdale from 10. *The Old Schoolhouse, Kirkby Lonsdale, Carnforth LA6 2DX* T: (015242) 72509 M: 07799-246380 E: nsm@therainbowparish.org

PRESTON, Donald George. b 30. St Alb Minl Tr Scheme 77. **d** 80 **p** 81. NSM Elstow *St Alb* 80-87; NSM Goldington 87-94; PtO 95-15. *106 Putnoe Street, Bedford MK41 8HJ* T: (01234) 267313

PRESTON, Frederick John. b 32. MBE 72. Oak Hill Th Coll 54. **d** 57 **p** 58. C Hove Bp Hannington Memorial Ch *Chich* 57-59; C-in-c Knaphill *Guildf* 60-62; CF 62-69 and 71-79; V Otterton *Ex* 69-71; NSM 79-84; Chapl ICS 84-89; rtd 89; PtO *Nor* 96-98; *Chich* from 98. *10 Cliff House, 57 Chesterfield Road, Eastbourne BN20 7NU* T: (01323) 638212

PRESTON, Jack. b 32. Th Ext Educn Coll 78. **d** 81 **p** 82. C Borrowdale Ch Ch Zimbabwe 81-85; C Mabelreign St Pet 85-87; C Belvedere St Eliz 87-94; C Harrismith St Jo S Africa 94-96; LtO Dio Harare Zimbabwe 96-09; PtO *Blackb* from 10. *14 Ravensthorpe, Astley Village, Chorley PR7 1XM* T: (01257) 234199

PRESTON, James Martin. b 31. Trin Coll Cam MA 55 Ch Ch Ox MA 57. Virginia Th Sem 57 S'wark Ord Course 87. **d** 88 **p** 88. NSM Blackheath Ascension *S'wark* 88-95; NSM Lewisham St Mary 95-97; NSM Catford St Laur 97-99; PtO *Chich* 99-08; *S'wark* from 08. *14 Curness Street, London SE13 6JY* T: (020) 8690 0993 E: prestonjm@btopenworld.com

PRESTON, John Michael. b 40. K Coll Lon BD 63 AKC 63 Lon Univ BA 81 Southn Univ PhD 91 Univ of Wales (Lamp) MA 09. St Boniface Warminster. **d** 65 **p** 66. C Heston *Lon* 65-67; C Northolt St Mary 67-72; Trinidad and Tobago 72-74; P-in-c Aveley *Chelmsf* 74-78; V 78-82; C Eastleigh *Win* 82-84; C-in-c Boyatt Wood CD 84-87; V W End 87-00; P-in-c Newton Valence, Selborne and E Tisted w Colemore 00-03; rtd 03; Chapl SSB from 03; PtO *Portsm* from 03; *Win* from 09. *10 Trent Way, Lee-on-the-Solent PO13 8JF* M: 07801-553233 E: john.preston1508@gmail.com

PRESTON, Mrs Junko Monica. b 38. Aoyama Gakuin Tokyo BA. **d** 92 **p** 93. C St Paul's Cathl Wellington New Zealand from 92. *60A Messines Road, Karori, Wellington 6012, New Zealand* T: (0064) (4) 476 7902

PRESTON, Martin. See PRESTON, James Martin

PRESTON, Michael Christopher. b 47. Hatf Coll Dur BA 68. Ripon Coll Cuddesdon 75. **d** 78 **p** 79. C Epsom St Martin *Guildf* 78-82; C Guildf H Trin w St Mary 82-86; V Epsom St Barn 86-14; rtd 14. *Address temp unknown* E: rev@m-c-preston.org.uk

PRESTON, Mrs Paula Ann. b 65. St Jo Coll Nottm 10. **d** 12 **p** 13. C Cambridge St Martin *Ely* from 12. *18 Langham Road, Cambridge CB1 3SE* E: mrspaulapreston@gmail.com

PRESTON, Reuben James. b 65. York Univ BSc 86 MEng 87 Birm Univ PGCE 97. Westcott Ho Cam 88. **d** 91 **p** 92. C Weoley Castle *Birm* 91-94; TV Malvern Link w Cowleigh *Worc* 94-96; PtO *Birm* 96-99; C Bordesley St Benedict 99-07; PtO *Portsm* 07-08; Hon C Portsea St Sav and Portsea St Alb 08; P-in-c Bridgemary and Chapl Bridgemary Community Sports Coll 08-11; Chapl HM Pris Kingston (Portsm) 08-11; V Hackney Wick St Mary of Eton w St Aug *Lon* from 11. *St Mary of Eton Church, Eastway, London E9 5JA* M: 07971-895897 T: (020) 8985 8462 E: rjp@reubenjamespreston.co.uk *or* vicar@stmaryofeton.org.uk

PRESTWOOD, James Anthony. b 78. York Univ BSc 99 K Coll Lon MA 03. St Mellitus Coll BA 11. **d** 11 **p** 12. C Tollington *Lon* 11-14; P-in-c Linc St Swithin from 14. *41 Mercer Drive, Lincoln LN1 1AG* E: jimprestwood@me.com

PRESTWOOD, Ms Jayne Marie. b 64. Man Univ BA 86 Nottm Univ MA 93. Linc Th Coll MA 94. **d** 94 **p** 95. C Reddish *Man* 94-98; Dioc Drugs Misuse Project Worker 98-00; P-in-c N Reddish 00-04; P-in-c Haughton St Anne 04-06; Tr Officer for Reader Tr 04-06; Vice Prin Dioc Reader and OLM Schemes 06-12; Chapl Man Univ from 12; Chapl Man Metrop Univ from 12; Chapl RNCM from 12. *354 Wilbraham Road, Manchester M21 0UX* E: jayne.prestwood@manchester.ac.uk

PRETT, Alan. b 39. **d** 05 **p** 06. OLM Styvechale *Cov* from 05. *Meikleour Lodge, Meikleour, Perth PH2 6DY* T: (01250) 883304 E: alanprett@btinternet.com

PRETTY, John Leslie. b 27. Wycliffe Hall Ox 61. **d** 63 **p** 64. C Bucknall and Bagnall *Lich* 63-67; C Abingdon w Shippon *Ox* 67-76; Warden Stella Carmel Conf Cen Haifa Israel 76-80; Dir Israel Trust of the Angl Ch and R Jerusalem 80-84; V S Kensington St Luke *Lon* 84-92; P-in-c S Kensington St Jude 88-92; rtd 92; Hon C Hordle *Win* 92-97; PtO 97-98; *Worc* 98-07. *16 Masefield Avenue, Ledbury HR8 1BW* T: (01531) 634881

PRICE, David Derek. b 53. St Edm Hall Ox BA 75 Southn Univ PhD 80. ERMC 07. **d** 10 **p** 11. NSM Aldenham, Radlett and Shenley St Alb from 10. *34 Vanda Crescent, St Albans AL1 5EX*

PRICE, David Gareth Michael. b 64. Ex Univ BA 86 Kent Univ MA 87 FSS. Wycliffe Hall Ox BTh 94. **d** 97 **p** 98. C Godalming *Guildf* 97-00; Min Elvetham Heath LEP 00-12; V Heatherlands St Jo *Sarum* from 12. *St John's Vicarage, 21 Crescent Road, Poole BH14 9AS* T: (01202) 740235 E: mail@pricefamilypoole.plus.com

PRICE, Canon David Rea. b 39. St Aid Birkenhead 61. **d** 63 **p** 64. C Green Street Green *Roch* 63-66; C Gillingham St Mary 66-69; C New Windsor St Jo *Ox* 69-72; V Winkfield 72-80; RD

Errislannan and Roundstone 91-93; Dean Tuam 93-96; I Tuam w Cong and Aasleagh 93-96; Adn Tuam and Can Tuam Cathl 96-06; I Omey w Ballynakill, Errislannan and Roundstone 96-06; rtd 06. *Oldchapel, Oughterard, Co Galway, Republic of Ireland* T/F: (00353) (91) 552126

PREWER, Dennis. b 30. Kelham Th Coll 50. **d** 54 **p** 55. C Stockport St Thos *Ches* 54-58; C Gt Grimsby St Mary and St Jas *Linc* 58-62; V Gt Harwood St Jo *Blackb* 62-64; V Scarcliffe *Derby* 64-70; Org Sec CECS 70-92; Dios Liv, Ban and St As 70-78; Dio Man 78-92; LtO *Ches* 70-92; PtO *Man* 78-96; rtd 92; PtO *Ches* from 92. *Address temp unknown*

PRICE, Alan John. b 48. Wilson Carlile Coll 69. **d** 08 **p** 08. P-in-c Charlesworth and Dinting Vale *Derby* 08-11; rtd 11; LtO *Mor* from 12. *2 Cloy Cottages, High Street, Fortrose IV10 8TA* T: (01381) 622438 M: 07785-723952 E: alan@alanprice.me.uk

PRICE, Alison Jane. See DOBELL, Alison Jane

PRICE, Alison Jean. b 50. Man Univ BSc 71 Open Univ MA 93 Kellogg Coll Ox DPhil 01 PGCE 89. Ox Min Course 05. **d** 08 **p** 09. NSM Marston w Elsfield Ox from 08; PtO from 12. *The Vicarage, Elsfield Road, Marston, Oxford OX3 0PR* T: (01865) 247034 M: 07792-460923 E: alisonjeanprice@gmail.com

PRICE, Mrs Alison Mary. b 48. K Alfred's Coll Win CertEd 69. **d** 01. Par Dn Magor *Mon* 01-11; PtO from 11. *Greenwillow, Church Road, Undy, Caldicot NP26 3EN* T: (01633) 880557

PRICE, Alun. b 60. Bradf Univ BSc 82 Loughb Univ MSc 88 Univ Coll Ches BTh 04 CSci. NOC 01. **d** 04 **p** 05. NSM Bramley *Sheff* 04-05; NSM Wath-upon-Dearne 05-07; P-in-c Wadworth w Loversall from 07; C Balby 11-12; P-in-c from 12. *The Vicarage, Vicarage Drive, Wadworth, Doncaster DN11 9AN* T: (01302) 851974 M: 07958-685393 E: fatheralun@hotmail.com *or* alun.price@sheffield.anglican.org

PRICE, Alun Huw. b 47. MBE 91. St D Coll Lamp. **d** 70 **p** 71. C Carmarthen St Dav *St D* 70-73; V Betws Ifan 73-77; CF 77-03. *Bryn Seion, Llyn y Fran Road, Llandysul SA44 4JW* T: (01559) 363954

PRICE, Anthony Ronald. b 49. Linc Coll Ox BA 71 MA 83 St Jo Coll Dur BA 78. **d** 79 **p** 80. C St Alb St Paul *St Alb* 79-81; C Wootton 81-85; C Lydiard Millicent w Lydiard Tregoz *Bris* 85-86; TV The Lydiards 86-91; V Marston *Ox* 91-95; V Marston w Elsfield from 95; RD Cowley 97-02. *The Vicarage, Elsfield Road, Marston, Oxford OX3 0PR* T: (01865) 247034 M: 07584-492225 E: tonyprice01@gmail.com

PRICE, Carol Ann. b 46. St Jo Coll Nottm 02. **d** 03 **p** 04. NSM Derby St Alkmund and St Werburgh 03-04; NSM Charlesworth and Dinting Vale 04-11; rtd 11; LtO *Mor* from 12. *2 Cloy Cottages, High Street, Fortrose IV10 8TA* T: (01381) 622438 M: 07787-522127 E: carol@carolprice.me.uk

PRICE, Christine. b 46. Leic Univ BA 94. EAMTC 98. **d** 01 **p** 02. C Jersey St Helier *Win* 01-06; NSM Jersey St Sav 10-15. *7 Le Geyt Close, La Rue de Deloraine, St Saviour, Jersey JE2 7NY* T: (01534) 737575 M: 07971-026711 E: christineriss@jerseymail.co.uk

PRICE, Mrs Christine Janice. b 45. Sarum & Wells Th Coll 83. **dss** 86 **d** 87 **p** 94. Roxbourne St Andr Lon 86-90; NSM 87-90; NSM Roxeth Ch Ch and Harrow St Pet 90-93; C Roxeth 93-96; C Costessey *Nor* 96-98; rtd 98; PtO *Nor* 98-05. *31 Russell Court, Chesham HP5 3JH* T: (01494) 773263 E: chrisjpri@aol.com

PRICE, Canon Clive Stanley. b 42. ALCD 69. **d** 69 **p** 70. C Chenies and Lt Chalfont *Ox* 69-75; R Upper Stour *Sarum* 75-79; C-in-c Panshanger CD *St Alb* 79-82; TV Digswell and Panshanger 82-86; P-in-c St Oswald in Lee w Bingfield *Newc* 86-07; Dioc Ecum Officer 86-07; Hon Can Newc Cathl 97-07; AD Bellingham 00-06; rtd 07. *Ubbanford Bank Cottage, Norham, Berwick-upon-Tweed TD15 2JZ* T: (01289) 382051

PRICE, David. b 27. Wycliffe Hall Ox 61. **d** 63 **p** 64. C Bucknall and Bagnall *Lich* 63-67; C Abingdon w Shippon *Ox* 67-76; Warden Stella Carmel Conf Cen Haifa Israel 76-80; Dir Israel Trust of the Angl Ch and R Jerusalem 80-84; V S Kensington St Luke *Lon* 84-92; P-in-c S Kensington St Jude 88-92; rtd 92; Hon C Hordle *Win* 92-97; PtO 97-98; *Worc* 98-07. *16 Masefield Avenue, Ledbury HR8 1BW* T: (01531) 634881

Bracknell 78-86; V Sunningdale 80-86; TR Wimborne Minster and Holt *Sarum* 86-96; R Wimborne Minster 96-01; RD Wimborne 88-98; Can and Preb Sarum Cathl 92-01; P-in-c Witchampton, Stanbridge and Long Crichel etc 00-01; Chapl Wimborne Hosp 86-01; rtd 01; PtO *Ex* 01-14; RD Aylesbeare 11-13; PtO *Sarum* from 14. *161 Sopwith Crescent, Wimborne EX8 2NW* T: (01202) 885488
E: rea@14broadway.eclipse.co.uk

PRICE, Canon David Trevor William. b 43. Keble Coll Ox BA 65 MA 69 MEHS 79 FRHistS 79 FSA 95. Sarum & Wells Th Coll 72. **d** 72 **p** 73. Lect Univ of Wales (Lamp) *St D* 70-87; Sen Lect 87-97; Chapl 79-80; Dean of Chpl 90-91; Public Preacher 72-86; Dioc Archivist 82-98; P-in-c Betws Bledrws 86-97; Hon Can St D Cathl 90-92; Can St D Cathl 92-00; V Cydweli and Llandyfaelog 97-00; P-in-c Myddle and Broughton *Lich* 00-08; P-in-c Loppington w Newtown 02-08; rtd 08; PtO *St As* from 01; *Lich* from 08; RD Wem and Whitchurch 14-15. *57 Kynaston Drive, Wem, Shrewsbury SY4 5DE* T: (01939) 234777 M: 07811-712911 E: williamprice@talktalk.net

PRICE, Dawson. b 31. OBE . Peterho Cam BA 52. Oak Hill NSM Course 88. **d** 91 **p** 92. NSM Harpenden St Nic *St Alb* 91-99; rtd 99; PtO *Win* 99-11. *8 Kimberley Close, Fair Oak, Eastleigh SO50 7EE* T: (023) 8069 2273

PRICE, Derek Henry. b 51. Trin Coll Bris BA 98. **d** 98 **p** 99. C Bayston Hill *Lich* 98-02; R Barrow St Paul *Carl* from 02. *St Paul's Rectory, 353 Abbey Road, Barrow-in-Furness LA13 9JY* T: (01229) 821546 E: dh.price@virgin.net

PRICE, Canon Derek William. b 27. St Pet Hall Ox BA 51 MA 55. Qu Coll Birm 51. **d** 53 **p** 54. C St Marylebone St Mark Hamilton Terrace *Lon* 53-57; C Stevenage *St Alb* 57-63; Jamaica 63-67; R Bridgham and Roudham *Nor* 67-80; R E w W Harling 69-80; Hon Can Nor Cathl 75-92; RD Thetford and Rockland 76-86; P-in-c Kilverstone 80-87; P-in-c Croxton 80-87; TR Thetford 80-87; R Castleacre w Newton, Rougham and Southacre 87-92; PtO 92-99 and from 00; P-in-c Easton w Colton and Marlingford 99-00. *Fourways, King's Road, Dereham NR19 2AG* T: (01362) 691660

PRICE, Chan Desmond. b 23. St D Coll Lamp BA 50. **d** 51 **p** 52. C Llwynypia *Llan* 51-52; C Ystradyfodwg 52-54; C Watford Ch Ch *St Alb* 54-56; Chapl RAF 56-68; R Dinas and Llanllawer *St D* 68-72; V Llandeilo Fawr w Llandyfeisant 72-79; V Llandeilo Fawr and Taliaris 79-91; Can St D Cathl 83-91; Chan 89-91; RD Llangadog and Llandeilo *St D* 90-91; rtd 91; Hon Can St D Cathl from 91. *24 Diana Road, Llandeilo SA19 6RS* T: (01558) 824039

PRICE, Canon Edward Glyn. b 35. Univ of Wales (Lamp) BA 55. Ch Div Sch of the Pacific (USA) BD 58. **d** 58 **p** 59. C Denbigh *St As* 58-65; V Llanasa 65-76; V Buckley 76-91; Dioc RE Adv 77-88; RD Mold 86-91; Can St As Cathl from 87; Preb and Sacr from 95; V Llandrillo-yn-Rhos 91-00; rtd 00; PtO *St As* from 09. *7 Rhodfa Criccieth, Bodelwyddan, Rhyl LL18 5WL* T: (01745) 571286

PRICE, Frank Lea. b 69. SS Coll Cam BA 92 Solicitor 96. Oak Hill Th Coll BA 99. **d** 99 **p** 00. C Hinckley H Trin *Leic* 99-04; C Cambridge H Sepulchre *Ely* 04-08; P-in-c Cambridge St Matt from 08. *St Matthew's Vicarage, 24 Geldart Street, Cambridge CB1 2LX* T: (01223) 363545 F: 512304
E: frankprice@stmatthews.uk.net

PRICE, Frederick Leslie. b 30. Oak Hill Th Coll 59. **d** 61 **p** 62. C Hougham in Dover Ch Ch *Cant* 61-64; R Plumbland and Gilcrux *Carl* 64-95; rtd 95; PtO *Carl* from 98. *1 Beech Hill, Oughterside, Wigton CA7 2QA* T: (016973) 20255

PRICE, Geoffrey David Gower. b 46. Oak Hill Th Coll. **d** 83 **p** 84. C Gt Baddow *Chelmsf* 83-86; C Hampreston *Sarum* 86-88; TV 88-93; P-in-c Drayton in Hales *Lich* 93-97; V 97-99; P-in-c Adderley and Moreton Say 93-97; R Ipswich St Helen, H Trin, and St Luke *St E* 99-05; V E Bedfont *Lon* 05-14; TV Cherwell Valley *Ox* from 14. *The Vicarage, 44 Forge Place, Fritwell, Bicester OX27 7QQ* T: (01869) 346262
E: geoffandhope@yahoo.com

PRICE, Gerald Andrew. b 31. NEOC. **d** 84 **p** 85. C Monkseaton St Mary *Newc* 84-87; V Cowgate 87-94; C Beltingham w Henshaw 94-96; C Haydon Bridge 94-96; rtd 96; PtO *Newc* from 96. *39 Primlea Court, Aydon Road, Corbridge NE45 5ES* T: (01434) 634919

PRICE, Glyn. See PRICE, Edward Glyn

PRICE, Gregory Philip. b 54. Cranmer Hall Dur. **d** 83 **p** 84. C Gt Crosby St Luke *Liv* 83-86; PtO *Derby* 12-13; *S'well* 12-15; V Tuxford w Weston, Markham Clinton etc from 15. *The Vicarage, 30 Lincoln Road, Newark NG22 0HP* M: 07850-182951 T: (01777) 872917
E: gregory.price1@btinternet.com

PRICE, Ian Arthur. b 57. Yorks Min Course 09. **d** 11 **p** 12. NSM Eckington and Ridgeway *Derby* from 11. *118 Shakespeare Crescent, Dronfield S18 1ND* T: (01246) 410892 M: 07929-716502 *or* 843017 E: ianaprice@btinternet.com

PRICE, Iorwerth Meirion Rupert. b 68. Univ of Wales (Lamp) BA 92 SOAS Lon MA 93 Greenwich Univ PGCE 97. SEITE 05 WEMTC 07. **d** 08 **p** 09. C Heref S Wye 08-10; C Woodford Valley w Archers Gate *Sarum* 10-12; CF (TA) 10-13; CF from 13. *c/o MOD Chaplains (Army)* F: 381824 T: (01264) 383430
E: iorwerthprice@btinternet.com

PRICE, Mrs Jean Amelia. b 44. SAOMC 99. **d** 02 **p** 03. OLM N Buckingham *Ox* 02-06; NSM Beercrocombe w Curry Mallet, Hatch Beauchamp etc *B & W* 06-11; rtd 11; NSM Dunster, Carhampton, Withycombe w Rodhuish etc *B & W* from 11. *Wydon, Marsh Street, Dunster, Minehead TA24 6PN* T: (01643) 822506 E: jean.price326@btinternet.com

PRICE, John Joseph. b 44. Ridley Hall Cam 89. **d** 92 **p** 93. C Glenfield *Leic* 92-97; Relig Affairs Adv BBC Radio Leics 93-97; Midl Regional Co-ord Crosslinks 97-05; NSM Werrington *Pet* 04-05; P-in-c Pet St Mark and St Barn 05-11; rtd 11; Chapl Peterborough and Stamford Hosps NHS Foundn Trust from 11. *Copper Beeches, 59A Peterborough Road, Castor, Peterborough PE5 7AL* T: (01733) 380025 M: 07729-360524
E: johnjprice@gmail.com

PRICE, Canon John Richard. b 34. Mert Coll Ox BA 58 MA 62. Westcott Ho Cam 58. **d** 60 **p** 61. C Man St Aid 60-63; C Bramley *Ripon* 63-67; V Leeds All Hallows w St Simon 67-74; P-in-c Wrangthorn 73-74; V Claughton cum Grange *Ches* 74-78; V Mottram in Longdendale w Woodhead 78-88; R Nantwich 88-99; RD Mottram 79-88; Hon Can Ches Cathl 86-99; rtd 99; PtO *Leeds* from 99. *21 Mill Croft, Cowling, Keighley BD22 0AJ* T: (01535) 637699

PRICE, Joseph Roderick. b 45. St Mich Coll Llan 74. **d** 75 **p** 76. C Fleur-de-Lis *Mon* 75-79; CF 79-99; Rtd Officer Chapl RAChD 99-05; Chapl Limassol St Barn Cyprus 06-08; rtd 08; PtO Cyprus and the Gulf from 08. *Flamingo Villa, Pine Bay Villas, PO Box 59426, Pissouri Village, 4607 Limassol, Cyprus* T: (00357) (25) 222213 M: 99-965663
E: rodberyl@cytanet.com.cy

PRICE, Julie Elizabeth. b 60. STETS. **d** 10 **p** 11. NSM Hambledon *Portsm* 10-14; NSM Warblington w Emsworth from 14. *39 Horndean Road, Emsworth PO10 7PU*

PRICE, Mrs Katherine Ann Magdalene. b 83. Mert Coll Ox BA 04 MA MSt 05 Sheff Univ BA 13. Coll of Resurr Mirfield 11. **d** 14 **p** 15. C Gt Grimsby St Mary and St Jas *Linc* from 14. *St Giles's Rectory, 44 Waltham Road, Grimsby DN33 2LX* E: katherine.price@grimsbyminster.co.uk

PRICE, Preb Lawrence Robert. b 43. LICeram 71. Cranmer Hall Dur 76. **d** 78 **p** 79. C Harlescott *Lich* 78-80; C Cheddleton 80-83; P-in-c Calton, Cauldon, Grindon and Waterfall 83-84; R 85-88; P-in-c Kingsley 95-00; R Kingsley and Foxt-w-Whiston 01-07; P-in-c 00-01; C Alton w Bradley-le-Moors and Oakamoor w Cotton 06-07; RD Cheadle 98-07; Preb Lich Cathl 00-08; rtd 08; P-in-c Cheddleton *Lich* 07-13; PtO from 13. *3 Beech Close, Leek ST13 7AF* E: preblrprice@btinternet.com

PRICE, Leslie. See PRICE, Frederick Leslie

PRICE, Canon Mari Josephine. b 43. St Hugh's Coll Ox BA 65 Ox Univ MA 69 DipEd 66. Llan Dioc Tr Scheme 93. **d** 97 **p** 98. NSM Lisvane *Llan* 97-02; NSM Roath 02-03; Hon Chapl Llan Cathl 03-14; Hon Can Llan Cathl 11-14. *23 Ty Draw Road, Roath, Cardiff CF23 5HB* T: (029) 2045 6757 M: 07850-019883 E: mari.price23@gmail.com

PRICE, Martin Randall Connop. b 45. Lon Univ BSc 71 Fitzw Coll Cam BA 75 MA 79 Univ of Wales (Swansea) PhD 02. Ridley Hall Cam 73. **d** 76 **p** 77. C Keynsham *B & W* 76-79; Ind Chapl *Sheff* 79-83; V Wortley 79-83; R Hook Norton w Gt Rollright, Swerford etc *Ox* 83-91; V Shiplake w Dunsden 91-03; P-in-c Harpsden 02-03; R Shiplake w Dunsden and Harpsden 03-09; rtd 09. *Coniston, 20 Eastfield Road, Ross-on-Wye HR9 5JY* T: (01989) 565975

PRICE (née ALDERTON), Mrs Mary Louise. b 54. Nottm Univ BSc 75 IPFA 87. EAMTC 02. **d** 05 **p** 06. NSM Melbourn *Ely* from 05; NSM Meldreth from 05. *4 Barrons Green, Shepreth, Royston SG8 6QN* T: (01763) 261569
E: mary@price10051.fsnet.co.uk

PRICE, Michael Graham. b 62. Ex Coll Ox BA 84. Linc Th Coll 84. **d** 86 **p** 87. C Salford St Phil w St Steph *Man* 86-90; R Man Gd Shep 90-95; V Netherton St Andr *Worc* 95-99; Chapl Bloxham Sch from 14 and from 14; PtO *Ox* from 14. *Bloxham School, Bloxham, Banbury OX15 4PQ* T: (01295) 720222

PRICE, Morris John. b 39. **d** 03 **p** 04. OLM Gt Wyrley *Lich* from 03. *42 Huthill Lane, Walsall WS6 6PB* T: (01922) 412846
E: normoss@talktalk.net

PRICE, Norman. See PRICE, William Norman

✠**PRICE, The Rt Revd Peter Bryan.** b 44. Redland Coll of Educn CertEd 66. Oak Hill Th Coll 72. **d** 74 **p** 75 **c** 97. C Portsdown *Portsm* 74-78; Chapl Scargill Ho 78-80; P-in-c Addiscombe St Mary *Cant* 80-81; V 81-84; V *S'wark* 85-88; Can Res and

Chan S'wark Cathl 88-92; Gen Sec USPG 92-97; Area Bp Kingston *S'wark* 97-02; Bp B & W 02-13; rtd 13. *4 Longways, Shaftesbury Road, Gillingham SP8 4ED*

PRICE, Peter Charles. b 27. Angl Th Coll (BC). **d** 61 **p** 62. Canada 61-66; St Mary-at-Latton *Chelmsf* 66-68; C Bearsted *Cant* 68-74; TV Ebbw Vale *Mon* 74-77; V Llanfihangel Crucorney w Oldcastle etc 77-87; V St Paul's Cathl St Helena 87-90; V Llanishen w Trellech Grange and Llanfihangel etc *Mon* 90-94; rtd 94; PtO *Heref* from 95. *1 Kynaston, Much Marcle, Ledbury HR8 2PD* T: (01531) 670687

PRICE, Rachel Anne. *See* JACKSON, Rachel Anne

PRICE, Ramon Philip. *See* PRICE, Gregory Philip

PRICE, Raymond Francklin. b 30. Wycliffe Hall Ox 61. **d** 62 **p** 63. C Bilston St Leon *Lich* 62-67; C Keighley *Bradf* 67-70; V Mangotsfield *Bris* 70-79; Ind Chapl *Birm* 79-86; C Birm St Martin 84-85; C Birm St Martin w Bordesley St Andr 85-86; V Edgbaston St Aug 86-99; rtd 99; PtO *Birm* 00-12. *35 Middle Park Road, Selly Oak, Birmingham B29 4BH* T: 0121-475 4458

PRICE, Roderick. *See* PRICE, Joseph Roderick

PRICE, Roland Kendrick. b 41. Cam Univ MA 64 Essex Univ PhD 69. SAOMC 92. **d** 95 **p** 96. NSM Cholsey *Ox* 95-97; Asst Chapl The Hague *Eur* 99-11; PtO 11-14; *Ox* from 14. *Bentinckstraat 129, 2582 ST Den Haag, The Netherlands* T: (0031) (15) 215 1871 *or* (70) 355 5359 F: 354 1023 E: rolandprice@ziggo.nl

PRICE, Stanley George. b 32. FRICS 69. Trin Coll Bris 84. **d** 85 **p** 86. C Newport w Longford and Chetwynd *Lich* 85-88; V Ipstones w Berkhamsytch and Onecote w Bradnop 88-97; rtd 98; PtO *B & W* 98-03 and from 08; P-in-c Rodney Stoke w Draycott 03-08. *St Aidan, Rectory Way, Lympsham, Weston-super-Mare BS24 0EN* T: (01934) 750323 E: stanley.price@btinternet.com

PRICE, Steven Albert. b 68. Brunel Univ BSc 90 CEng 95. Oak Hill Th Coll BTh 06. **d** 06 **p** 07. C New Borough and Leigh *Sarum* 06-09; C Loose *Cant* 09-11; P-in-c 11-14; V from 14. *The Vicarage, 17 Linton Road, Loose, Maidstone ME15 0AG* T: (01622) 745882 E: steveandhelenprice@yahoo.co.uk

PRICE, Timothy Fry. b 51. Clare St Jo Coll Nottm 85. **d** 87 **p** 88. C Church Stretton *Heref* 87-91; V Sinfin *Derby* 91-00; Regional Adv (SW) CMJ 00-03; Nat Field Co-ord 03-05; PtO *Glouc* 01-05; *B & W* 01-05; *Bris* 01-05; V Chaffcombe, Cricket Malherbie etc *B & W* from 06; PtO *Ex* 06-09. *The Vicarage, 3 Home Farm, Tatworth, Chard TA20 2SH* T: (01460) 220237 *or* T/F: 220404 E: pricetf@aol.com

PRICE, Victor John. b 35. Oak Hill Th Coll 62. **d** 65 **p** 66. C Rainham *Chelmsf* 65-70; V Dover St Martin *Cant* 70-78; V Madeley *Heref* 78-90; P-in-c Derby St Pet and Ch w H Trin 90-91; V 91-96; P-in-c Morley 96-00; P-in-c Smalley 96-00; rtd 00; PtO *S'well* from 00. *4 Holmefield, Farndon, Newark NG24 3TZ* T: (01636) 611788

PRICE, William. *See* PRICE, David Trevor William

PRICE, William Norman. b 52. GRNCM 73. NOC 86. **d** 89 **p** 90. C Lower Broughton Ascension *Man* 89-91; Min Can and Succ St E Cathl 92-96; Prec 94-96; V Par *Truro* 96-00; V Musbury *Blackb* 00-06; rtd 06; PtO *Man* from 06. *5 Lower Drake Fold, Westhoughton, Bolton BL5 2RE* T: 07071-299999 E: golfsierra999@rcsb.co.uk

PRICE-ROBERTS, Mervyn. b 29. Trin Coll Carmarthen TCert 51 Univ of Wales BEd 79. Ban Ord Course 84. **d** 87 **p** 88. NSM Bangor *Ban* 87-89; V Llandygai w Tregarth 89-97; rtd 97; PtO *Ban* from 97. *Pont Llan, Llanllechid, Bangor LL57 3LE* T: (01248) 605370

PRIDDIN, Emma. *See* YOUNG, Emma

PRIDDIN, Mrs Maureen Anne. b 46. Leeds Univ BA 67 Nottm Univ DipEd 68. EMMTC 82. **dss** 85 **d** 87 **p** 94. Mickleover St Jo *Derby* 85-11; Hon Par Dn 87-94; Hon C 94-06; P-in-c 06-11; Hon C Mickleover All SS 06-11; Dioc World Development Officer 87-90; rtd 11. *7 Portland Close, Mickleover, Derby DE3 9BZ* T: (01332) 513672 E: mpriddin@ntlworld.com

✠**PRIDDIS, The Rt Revd Anthony Martin.** b 48. CCC Cam BA 69 MA 73 New Coll Ox MA 75. Cuddesdon Coll 69. **d** 72 **p** 73 **c** 96. C New Addington *Cant* 72-75; Chapl Ch Ch Ox 75-80; TV High Wycombe *Ox* 80-86; P-in-c Amersham 86-90; R 90-96; RD 92-96; Hon Can Ch Ch 95-96; Suff Bp Warw and Hon Can Cov Cathl 96-04; Bp Heref 04-13; rtd 13; Hon Asst Bp Glouc from 14; PtO *Heref* from 15. *Round Oak Cottage, Bridstow, Ross-on-Wye HR9 6QJ* T: (01989) 218503 E: anthony@priddis.me

PRIDEAUX, Humphrey Grevile. b 36. CCC Ox BA 59 MA 63 Birm Univ CertEd 66 Lon Univ DipEd 73 Open Univ BA 87. Linc Th Coll 59. **d** 61 **p** 62. C Northampton St Matt *Pet* 61-62; C Milton *Portsm* 62-65; PtO *Birm* 65-66; Hd of RE Qu Mary's Gr Sch Walsall 66-69; Lect St Martin's Coll Lanc

69-80; PtO *Portsm* 80-86; Hon C Fareham H Trin 86-87; Hon C Bishop's Waltham 87-94; NSM P-in-c W Meon and Warnford 94-03. *6 Rectory Close, Alverstoke, Gosport PO12 2HT* T: (023) 9250 1794

PRIDGEON, Paul Garth Walsingham. b 45. Sussex Univ BA 69 CertEd. Glouc Sch of Min 87. **d** 87 **p** 88. NSM Cirencester *Glouc* 87-97; NSM Northleach w Hampnett and Farmington etc 97-03; PtO from 03. *4 Abbey Way, Cirencester GL7 2DT* T: (01285) 656860

PRIDIE, William Raleigh. b 49. Bris Univ BEd 72 ACP 82 FCollP 83. SWMTC 90. **d** 93 **p** 94. C Kingstone w Clehonger, Eaton Bishop etc *Heref* 93-96; P-in-c Kimbolton w Hamnish and Middleton-on-the-Hill 96-97; P-in-c Bockleton w Leysters 96-97; CME Officer 96-00; TV Leominster 97-00; R Fownhope w Mordiford, Brockhampton etc 00-10; rtd 11; PtO *Heref* from 11. *64 Bargates, Leominster HR6 8EY* E: wpridie365@waitrose.com

PRIDMORE, John Stuart. b 36. Nottm Univ BA 62 MA 67 Lon Inst of Educn PhD 00. Ridley Hall Cam 62. **d** 65 **p** 66. C Camborne *Truro* 65-67; Tutor Ridley Hall Cam 67-68; Chapl 68-71; Asst Chapl K Edw Sch Witley 71-75; Chapl 75-86; Tanzania 86-88; Angl Chapl Hengrave Hall Cen 88-89; C St Martin-in-the-Fields *Lon* 89-95; TR Hackney 95-03; R St John-at-Hackney 03-06; rtd 06. *Flat 2, 3 Palmeira Square, Hove BN3 2JA* T: (01273) 720654 E: john.pridmore@btinternet.com

PRIEST, Richard Mark. b 63. Oak Hill Th Coll BA 90. **d** 90 **p** 91. C Okehampton w Inwardleigh *Ex* 90-94; C Okehampton w Inwardleigh, Bratton Clovelly etc 94; CF from 94. *c/o MOD Chaplains (Army)* F: 381824 T: (01264) 383430

PRIEST, Richard Philip. b 52. WEMTC 08. **d** 10 **p** 11. NSM Frome Valley *Heref* from 10. *Idalilian, Burley Gate, Hereford HR1 3QS* T: (01432) 820170 M: 07717-132896 F: (01885) 490615 E: richard@allegro.co.uk

PRIESTLEY, Adam James. b 80. Wolv Univ BA 11. St Jo Coll Nottm MTh 15. **d** 14 **p** 15. C W Bessacarr *Sheff* from 14. *17 Carr Lane, Bessacarr, Doncaster DN4 7PX* M: 07883-851700 E: adampriestley@hotmail.co.uk *or* adam.priestley@sheffield.anglican.org

PRIESTLEY, Mandy. b 65. **d** 11 **p** 12. C Broughton w Loddington and Cransley etc *Pet* 11-13; C Shepton Mallet w Doulting *B & W* 13-15; C Ashwick w Oakhill and Binegar from 15. *The Rectory, Fosse Road, Oakhill, Radstock BA3 5HU* T: (01749) 840239 E: priestleymandy@mac.com

PRIESTLEY, Richard Allan. b 63. Ridley Hall Cam 07. **d** 09 **p** 10. C Broughton w Loddington and Cransley etc *Pet* 09-12; PtO 13; P-in-c Ashwick w Oakhill and Binegar *B & W* from 13; C Shepton Mallet w Doulting from 13. *The Rectory, Fosse Road, Oakhill, Radstock BA3 5HU* T: (01749) 840239 E: rpriestley@me.com

PRIESTLEY, Rosemary Jane. *See* LAIN-PRIESTLEY, Rosemary Jane

PRIESTNER, Hugh. b 45. Nottm Univ BTh 75. Linc Th Coll 71. **d** 75 **p** 76. C Seaton Hirst *Newc* 75-78; C Longbenton St Bart 78-81; P-in-c Glendale Gp 81-82; TV 83-88; Chapl Stafford Acute Hosps 88-89; Tr Co-ord W Cumberland Hosp 89-92; Chapl Fair Havens Hospice 94-98; Chapl Walsgrave Hosps NHS Trust 98-00; Chapl Team Ldr Univ Hosps Cov and Warks NHS Trust from 00; PtO *Cov* from 10. *Walsgrave General Hospital, Clifford Bridge Road, Coventry CV2 2DX* T: (024) 7696 7515 E: hugh.priestner@btinternet.com

PRIGG, Patrick John. b 53. K Coll Lon BD 82. Sarum & Wells Th Coll 89. **d** 92 **p** 93. C Wavertree St Mary *Liv* 92-96; Chapl Sandown Coll 92-96; P-in-c Glemsford, Hartest w Boxted, Somerton etc *St E* 96-99; R from 99. *The Rectory, 6 Lion Road, Glemsford, Sudbury CO10 7RF* T: (01787) 282164 E: revpat@glem-valley.org.uk

PRIME, David Alan. b 54. Chelt & Glouc Coll of HE BEd 98. Wesley Coll Bris 82. **d** 12. NSM Trellech and Penallt *Mon* from 12. *5 Badgers Dene, The Narth, Monmouth NP25 4QU* T: (01600) 860925 M: 07870-216995 E: prime.family@yahoo.com

PRIMROSE, David Edward Snodgrass. b 55. St Jo Coll Cam MA 80. Trin Coll Bris BA 92. **d** 87 **p** 92. Pakistan 87-89; C Glouc St Paul 92-96; R Badgeworth, Shurdington and Witcombe w Bentham 96-03; V Thornbury and Oldbury-on-Severn w Shepperdine 03-10; AD Hawkesbury 04-09; Dir Transforming Communities *Lich* from 10. *Hill House, Vicarage Lane, Bednall, Stafford ST17 0SE* E: primrose@blueyonder.co.uk

PRINCE, Alastair. b 76. Nottm Univ BSc 99 SS Coll Cam BTh 06. Westcott Ho Cam 03. **d** 06 **p** 07. C Toxteth Park Ch Ch and St Mich w St Andr *Liv* 06-09; V Croxteth Park from 09. *St Cuthbert's Vicarage, 1 Sandicroft Road, Liverpool L12 0LX* T: 0151-549 2202 M: 07732-489424 E: alastairprince@hotmail.com

PRINCE (née RUMBLE), Mrs Alison Merle. b 49. Surrey Univ BSc 71. Trin Coll Bris BA 89. **d** 89 **p** 94. Par Dn Willesden Green St Gabr *Lon* 89-91; Par Dn Cricklewood St Gabr and St Mich 92; Par Dn Herne Hill *S'wark* 92-94; C 94-95; Chapl Greenwich Healthcare NHS Trust 95-96; TV Sanderstead All SS *S'wark* 97-03; TV Kegworth, Hathern, Long Whatton, Diseworth etc *Leic* 04-09; rtd 09; PtO *Leic* from 13. *23 Grangefields Drive, Rothley, Leicester LE7 7ND*

PRINCE (née GRIFFITHS), Caroline Heidi Ann. b 66. Ex Univ BA 88. Linc Th Coll 90. **d** 90 **p** 97. C Newport St Woolos and Chapl St Woolos Cathl 90-94; C Abergavenny Deanery 94-96; TV Cwmbran 96-97; V Llantilio Crossenny w Penrhos, Llanvetherine etc 97-06; PtO *S & B* 11-15; P-in-c Llantilio Crossenny w Penrhos, Llanvetherine etc *Mon* from 15. *The Vicarage, LLantilio Crossenny, Abergavenny NP7 8SU* E: llantiliovicar@aol.com

PRINCE, Mrs Melanie Amanda. b 71. St D Coll Lamp BA 92 Univ of Wales (Cardiff) MPhil 93. St Mich Coll Llan 96. **d** 98 **p** 99. C Aberavon *Llan* 98-01; C Gabalfa 01-08; TV Llantwit Major 08-13; P-in-c Porthkerry and Rhoose from 13; Voc Adv from 13. *The Vicarage, 6 Milburn Close, Rhoose, Barry CF62 3EJ* T: (01446) 719734

PRINCE, Penelope Ann. b 46. SWMTC 96. **d** 99 **p** 00. NSM Halsetown *Truro* 99-02; P-in-c Breage w Godolphin and Germoe 02-12; rtd 12; Hon C Is of Scilly *Truro* from 13. *Address temp unknown* M: 07929-152234 T: (01752) 300331

PRING, Althon Kerrigan (Kerry). b 34. AKC 58. **d** 59 **p** 60. C Limehouse St Anne *Lon* 59-61; C Lt Stanmore St Lawr 61-64; C Langley Marish *Ox* 64-68; P-in-c Radnage 68-72; P-in-c Ravenstone w Weston Underwood 72-75; P-in-c Stoke Goldington w Gayhurst 72-75; R Gayhurst w Ravenstone, Stoke Goldington etc 75-85; P-in-c 85-86; RD Newport 78-80; TV Woughton 86-90; P-in-c Nash w Thornton, Beachampton and Thornborough 90-94; R 94-96; rtd 96; PtO *Ox* 99-07. *Kingsmead, 9 Malting Close, Stoke Goldington, Newport Pagnell MK16 8NX* T: (01908) 551345 E: kerriganpring@btinternet.com

PRINGLE, Cecil Thomas. b 43. TCD BA 65. CITC 66. **d** 66 **p** 67. C Belfast St Donard *D & D* 66-69; I Cleenish *Clogh* 69-80; I Cleenish w Mullaghdun 78-80; I Rossorry 80-08; P-in-c Drumkeeran w Templecarne and Muckross from 08; Preb Clogh Cathl 86-89; Adn Clogh 89-14. *35 Station Road, Derryscobe, Letterbreen, Enniskillen BT74 9FB* M: 07742-516188

PRINGLE, Graeme Lindsley. b 59. St Cath Coll Cam BA 81 MA 85. St Jo Coll Nottm 92. **d** 94 **p** 95. C Binley *Cov* 94-99; V Allesley Park and Whoberley 99-11; Dioc Projects and Communications Officer from 11; PtO from 11. *The Rectory, Spring Hill, Bubbenhall, Coventry CV8 3BD* E: graeme.pringle@covcofe.org

PRINGLE, Margaret Brenda. b 49. CITC. **d** 05 **p** 06. NSM Clogh w Errigal Portclare 05-13; NSM Carrickmacross w Magheracloone from 13. *Rawdeer Park, Clones, Co Monaghan, Republic of Ireland* T: (00353) (47) 51439 E: mrspringle@eircom.net

PRINGLE, Richard John. b 55. Lon Univ AKC 76 CertEd 77 Open Univ BA 84. Chich Th Coll 78. **d** 78 **p** 79. C Northampton St Matt *Pet* 78-81; C Delaval *Newc* 81-84; V Newsham from 84; RD Bedlington 93-94. *St Bede's Vicarage, Newcastle Road, Newsham, Blyth NE24 4AS* T/F: (01670) 352391

PRINS, Canon Stanley Vernon. b 30. TD 76. Dur Univ BSc 54 MA 69. Ripon Hall Ox 56. **d** 58 **p** 59. C Benwell St Jas *Newc* 58-61; Asst Chapl Newc Univ 61-65; CF (TA) from 64; C-in-c Whorlton H Nativity Chpl Ho Estate *Newc* 65-72; TV Whorlton 73-76; V Humshaugh 76-83; P-in-c Simonburn 82-83; P-in-c Wark 82-83; RD Bellingham 83-93; R Humshaugh w Simonburn and Wark 83-96; Hon Can Newc Cathl 88-96; rtd 96; PtO *Newc* from 96. *Woodside Cottage, Scrogwood, Bardon Mill, Hexham NE47 7AA* T: (01434) 344876

PRINT, Michael Guy. b 81. Sheff Univ BA 02. Wycliffe Hall Ox BTh 15. **d** 15. C Padiham w Hapton and Padiham Green *Blackb* from 15. *14 Bendwood Close, Padiham, Burnley BB12 8RT* E: michael.padihamparish@gmail.com

PRIOR, Adam Phillip. b 72. Cen Lancs Univ BA 94 K Coll Lon MA 05. Ridley Hall Cam. **d** 08 **p** 09. NSM Watford St Pet *St Alb* from 08. *57 Brighton Road, Watford WD24 5HN* M: 07931-896750 E: aprior@soulsurvivorwatford.co.uk

PRIOR, Carla. *See* VICENCIO PRIOR, Carla Alexandra

PRIOR, David Clement Lyndon. b 40. Trin Coll Ox BA 63 MA 66. Ridley Hall Cam 65. **d** 67 **p** 68. C Reigate St Mary *S'wark* 67-72; C Kenilworth Ch Ch S Africa 72-76; R Wynberg 76-79; Can Cape Town 76-79; C Ox St Aldate w H Trin 79-82; C Ox St Aldate w St Matt 82-84; USA 84-85; V Ches Square St Mich w St Phil *Lon* 85-95; P-in-c Mayfair Ch Ch 85-95; Public Preacher 95-97; P-in-c St Botolph without Aldersgate

97-00; rtd 05; PtO *Chich* from 05. *2 North Lane, Wiston, Steyning BN44 3DQ* T: (01903) 893566 E: dclraprior@hotmail.com

PRIOR (née CHIUMBU), Esther Tamisa. b 73. Univ of Zimbabwe BSc 95. Trin Coll Bris BA 02 MA 07. **d** 03 **p** 04. NSM Redland *Bris* 03-05; C Deptford St Jo w H Trin and Ascension *S'wark* 05-08; Chapl Blackheath Bluecoat C of E Sch 08-09; Chapl HM Pris Cookham Wood 10-11; TV Cove St Jo *Guildf* from 11. *Fircroft, 21 St John's Road, Farnborough GU14 9RL* T: (01252) 373301 E: esthertj@yahoo.com

PRIOR, Gregory Stephen. b 68. Geo Whitfield Coll S Africa BTh 90. **d** 95 **p** 96. In C of E in S Africa 95-01; Min for Miss Muswell Hill St Jas w St Matt *Lon* 01-04; P-in-c Wandsworth All SS *S'wark* 04-06; V from 06; AD Wandsworth from 13. *Wandsworth Vicarage, 11 Rusholme Road, London SW15 3JX* T: (020) 8788 7400 E: greg@wandsworthparish.co.uk

PRIOR, Canon Ian Graham. b 44. Lon Univ BSc(Econ) 71. Oak Hill Th Coll 78. **d** 80 **p** 81. C Luton Ch Ch *Roch* 80-83; TV Southgate *Chich* 83-93; V Burgess Hill St Andr 93-09; RD Hurst 98-04; Can and Preb Chich Cathl 03-09; rtd 09. *5 Chestnut Walk, Worthing BN13 3QL* T: (01903) 830127 E: ian@priorjane.wanadoo.co.uk

PRIOR, Ian Roger Lyndon. b 46. St Jo Coll Dur BA 68. Lon Coll of Div 68. **d** 70 **p** 71. C S Croydon Em *Cant* 70-73; PtO *S'wark* 73-85; Dir Overseas Personnel TEAR Fund 73-79; Dep Dir 79-83; Fin and Admin Dir CARE Trust and CARE Campaigns 85-92; Dir Careforce 92-12; NSM New Malden and Coombe *S'wark* 85-12; rtd 12; PtO *S'wark* from 12. *39 Cambridge Avenue, New Malden KT3 4LD* T: (020) 8949 0912 E: ianrlprior@gmail.com

PRIOR, James Murray. b 39. Edin Univ BCom 64. St And Dioc Tr Course 85. **d** 90 **p** 91. NSM Kirriemuir *St And* 90-02; NSM Forfar 90-02; NSM Dundee St Jo and Dundee St Ninian *Bre* 02-10; rtd 10. *Naughton Lodge, Balmerino, Newport-on-Tay DD6 8RN* T: (01382) 330132 E: ham.prior@tiscali.co.uk

PRIOR, Jonathan Roger Lyndon. b 74. Trin Coll Ox BA 95 MA 99 K Coll Lon PGCE 96. Wycliffe Hall Ox 07. **d** 09 **p** 10. C Elworth and Warmingham *Ches* 09-11; C Elworth 11-12; Chapl City of Lon Freemen's Sch from 12; C Ashtead *Guildf* from 12. *17 Loraine Gardens, Ashtead KT21 1PD* E: prior.jon@gmail.com *or* j.prior@yahoo.co.uk

PRIOR, Canon Kenneth Francis William. b 26. St Jo Coll Dur BA 49. Oak Hill Th Coll 46. **d** 49 **p** 50. C S Mimms Ch Ch *Lon* 49-52; C Eastbourne H Trin *Chich* 52-53; V Onslow Square St Paul *Lon* 53-65; V Hove Bp Hannington Memorial Ch *Chich* 65-70; R Sevenoaks St Nic *Roch* 70-87; Hon Can Roch Cathl 82-87; C-in-c Hampstead St Jo Downshire Hill Prop Chpl *Lon* 87-90; rtd 89; PtO *Ex* from 01. *22 Barnfield Road, Torquay TQ2 6TN* T: (01803) 606760

PRIOR, Matthew Thomas. b 74. Rob Coll Cam BA 97 MA 00. Trin Coll Bris BA 04 MA 05. **d** 05 **p** 06. C Deptford St Jo w H Trin and Ascension *S'wark* 05-08; P-in-c Borstal *Roch* 08-11; PtO *Guildf* 11-13; NSM Cove St Jo from 13; Chapl Abp Tenison's C of E High Sch Croydon 13-14; Adult Discipleship and Learning Adv *Guildf* from 15. *Fircroft, 21 St John's Road, Farnborough GU14 9RL* T: (01252) 373301 E: mprior36@gmail.com

PRIOR, Nigel John. b 56. Bris Univ BA 78 Chich Univ MA 09. Westcott Ho Cam 79. **d** 81 **p** 82. C Langley All SS and Martyrs *Man* 81-82; C Langley and Parkfield 82-84; C Bury St Jo w St Mark 84-87; R Man Clayton St Cross w St Paul 87-99; P-in-c Mark Cross *Chich* 99-00; V Mayfield from 99. *The Vicarage, High Street, Mayfield TN20 6AB* T: (01435) 873180 E: stdunstan@tiscali.co.uk

PRIOR, Stephen Kenneth. b 55. Rhode Is Coll (USA) BA 78. Wycliffe Hall Ox 79. **d** 82 **p** 83. C Aberavon *Llan* 82-85; P-in-c New Radnor and Llanfihangel Nantmelan etc *S & B* 85-86; R 86-90; V Llansamlet 90-94; P-in-c Chester le Street *Dur* 94-96; R 96-01; R Caldbeck, Castle Sowerby and Sebergham *Carl* 01-09; Dir of Ords 04-08; R Rushden St Mary w Newton Bromswold *Pet* from 09; RD Higham from 14. *The Rectory, Rectory Road, Rushden NN10 0HA* T: (01933) 312554 E: sprior@toucansurf.com

PRIOR-JONES, Mrs Christine Jane. b 51. Univ of Wales (Ban) BA 73. STETS 09. **d** 12 **p** 13. NSM Steep and Froxfield w Privett *Portsm* from 12. *5 Pine Walk, Liss GU33 7AT* T: (01730) 894040 M: 07952-702202 E: cpj@savoirmec.co.uk

PRIORY, Barry Edwin. b 44. Open Univ BA 81 FCIS. Qu Coll Birm 84. **d** 86 **p** 87. C Boldmere *Birm* 86-89; C Somerton w Compton Dundon, the Charltons etc *B & W* 89-93; R Porlock and Porlock Weir w Stoke Pero etc 93-08; RD Exmoor 97-03; rtd 08; PtO *B & W* from 08; Chapl Somerset Partnership NHS Foundation Trust from 09. *Dove Cottage, Moor Road, Minehead TA24 5RX* T: (01643) 706808 M: 07811-092416 E: barry.priory@btinternet.com

PRITCHARD, Andrew James Dunn. *See* PRITCHARD-KEENS, Andrew James Dunn

PRITCHARD, Antony Robin. b 53. Van Mildert Coll Dur BSc 74 SS Paul & Mary Coll Cheltenham CertEd 75. St Jo Coll Nottm. **d** 84 **p** 85. C Desborough *Pet* 84-87; C Rushden w Newton Bromswold 87-91; R Oulton St Mich *Nor* from 91. *The Rectory, Christmas Lane, Oulton, Lowestoft NR32 3JX* T: (01502) 565722 E: robinpritchard925@btinternet.com

PRITCHARD, Brian James. Open Univ BA 05 ACIS 85. SAOMC 99. **d** 01 **p** 02. NSM Newbury *Ox* 01-06; V Billingshurst *Chich* from 06; PtO *St D* from 05. *The Vicarage, East Street, Billingshurst RH14 9PY* T: (01403) 785303 *or* 782332 E: vicar.billingshurst@gmail.com

PRITCHARD, Brian James Pallister. b 27. CCC Cam BA 51 MA 66. Westcott Ho Cam 51. **d** 53 **p** 54. C Attercliffe w Carbrook *Sheff* 53-58; V New Bentley 58-60; Chapl Park Hill Flats Sheff 60-67; P-in-c Sheff St Swithun 67-72; V Welton *Linc* 72-92; RD Lawres 86-92; rtd 92; PtO *Derby* from 92. *Bridgeways, Milford Lane, Bakewell DE45 1DX* T: (01629) 813553

PRITCHARD, Mrs Carol Sandra. b 52. St Aid Coll Dur BA 74 Bris Univ PGCE 75. EAMTC 96. **d** 99 **p** 00. NSM Oulton St Mich *Nor* from 99. *The Rectory, Christmas Lane, Oulton, Lowestoft NR32 3JX* T: (01502) 565722 E: carolpritchard3@btinternet.com

PRITCHARD, Colin Wentworth. b 38. K Coll Lon 59 St Boniface Warminster 59. **d** 63 **p** 64. C Putney St Marg *S'wark* 63-67; C Brixton St Matt 67-70; C Milton *Portsm* 70-74; V Mitcham St Mark *S'wark* 74-82; R Long Ditton 82-94; V Earlsfield St Andr 94-03; RD Wandsworth 98-03; rtd 03. *38 Hartfield Road, Seaford BN25 4PW* T: (01323) 894899 E: colin.pritchard@gmx.co.uk

PRITCHARD, Mrs Coral. b 37. F L Calder Coll Liv TCert 58 Lanc Univ BA 97. CBDTI 99. **d** 02 **p** 03. OLM Stalmine w Pilling *Blackb* 02-07; NSM 07-11; rtd 11; PtO *Blackb* from 11. *Heyswood House, Head Dyke Lane, Pilling, Preston PR3 6SJ* T: (01253) 790335 E: coralpritchard@btinternet.com

PRITCHARD, Canon David Paul. b 47. Newc Univ BA 68 Em Coll Cam PGCE 69 LTCL 70 FRCO 72. Wycliffe Hall Ox 80. **d** 82 **p** 83. C Kidlington *Ox* 82-84; P-in-c Marcham w Garford 84-85; V 86-96; RD Abingdon 91-96; R Henley w Remenham 96-04; Can Res Ely Cathl 04-14; Vice Dean 08-12; Acting Dean 11-12; Pastor 08-14; rtd 15; PtO *Ely* from 14. *2 Chapel Lane, Little Downham, Ely CB6 2TN* T: (01353) 698831

PRITCHARD, John Anthony. b 74. Ripon Coll Cuddesdon BTh 07. **d** 07 **p** 08. C Gt Berkhamsted, Gt and Lt Gaddesden etc *St Alb* 07-11; C St Marylebone All SS *Lon* 11-13; P-in-c Upper Norwood St Jo *S'wark* from 13. *The Vicarage, 2 Sylvan Road, London SE19 2RX* T: (020) 8771 6686 E: johnapritchard@hotmail.co.uk

✠**PRITCHARD, The Rt Revd John Lawrence.** b 48. St Pet Coll Ox BA 70 MA 73 Dur Univ MLitt 93. Ridley Hall Cam 70. **d** 72 **p** 73 **c** 02. C Birm St Martin 72-76; Asst Dir RE *B & W* 76-80; Youth Chapl 76-80; P-in-c Wilton 80-88; Dir Past Studies Cranmer Hall Dur 89-93; Warden 93-96; Adn Cant and Can Res Cant Cathl 96-02; Suff Bp Jarrow *Dur* 02-07; Bp Ox 07-14; rtd 14; Hon Asst Bp Dur from 15. *42 Bolton Avenue, Richmond DL10 4BA* T: (01865) 208222

PRITCHARD, Jonathan Llewelyn. b 64. Edin Univ MA 87 Leeds Univ MA 89 PhD 99. Ripon Coll Cuddesdon 98. **d** 00 **p** 01. C Skipton H Trin *Bradf* 00-04; P-in-c Keighley All SS *Leeds* from 04; P-in-c Thwaites Brow from 06. *All Saints' Vicarage, 21 View Road, Keighley BD20 6JN* T: (01535) 665312 E: jon@thans.info

PRITCHARD, Miss Kathryn Anne. b 60. St Cath Coll Ox MA K Coll Lon MA 10. Cranmer Hall Dur. **d** 87. Par Dn Addiscombe St Mary *S'wark* 87-90; CPAS Staff 90-92; PtO *Cov* 92-95; Producer Worship Progr BBC Relig Broadcasting 94-99; Publicity Manager Hodder & Stoughton Relig Books 99-01; Commissioning and Product Development Manager Ch Ho Publishing 01-09. *Address temp unknown* E: kathryn.pritchard@churchofengland.org *or* pritchard.55@btinternet.com

PRITCHARD, Kenneth John. b 30. Liv Univ BEng 51. NW Ord Course 72. **d** 74 **p** 75. C Ches 74-78; Miss to Seamen 78-84; V Runcorn St Jo Weston *Ches* 78-84; V Gt Meols 84-98; rtd 98; PtO *Ches* from 99; *Liv* from 99. *13 Fieldlands, Scarisbrick, Southport PR8 5HQ* T: (01704) 514600 E: kjp@talk21.com

PRITCHARD, Malcolm John. b 55. Bradf Univ BA 85 CQSW 85. St Jo Coll Nottm 86. **d** 88 **p** 89. C Peckham St Mary Magd *S'wark* 88-93; V Luton St Matt High Town *St Alb* from 93. *St Matthew's Vicarage, 85 Wenlock Street, Luton LU2 0NN* T: (01582) 732320 E: b4mjp2c@ntlworld.com

PRITCHARD, Michael Owen. b 49. Trin Coll Carmarthen CertEd 71. St Mich Coll Llan 71. **d** 73 **p** 74. C Conwy w Gyffin *Ban* 73-76; TV Dolgellau w Llanfachreth and Brithdir etc 76-78; Dioc Children's Officer 77-86; V Betws y Coed and Capel Curig 78-83; V Betws-y-Coed and Capel Curig w Penmachno etc 83-86; CF (TAVR) from 79; Chapl Claybury

Hosp Woodford Bridge 86-96; Chapl Team Leader Forest Healthcare NHS Trust Lon 96-01; Chapl Team Leader NE Lon Foundn Trust 01-12; rtd 12. *1 St James Court, 71 Aldersbrook Road, London E12 5DL* T: (020) 8989 3813 M: 07852-194967 E: mopritchard@hotmail.com

PRITCHARD, Mrs Norma Kathleen. b 32. Birm Univ BA 53 CertEd 54. EMMTC 81. **dss** 84 **d** 87 **p** 94. Derby St Alkmund and St Werburgh 84-90; Par Dn 87-90; Par Dn Derby St Andr w St Osmund 90-94; C 94-96; Assoc Min Alvaston 96-02; rtd 02; PtO *S'wark* from 02; *Derby* from 02. *44 Evans Avenue, Allestree, Derby DE22 2EN* T: (01332) 557702 E: norma@allestreepark.plus.com

PRITCHARD, Peter Benson. b 30. FPhS 60 LCP 68 Univ of Wales (Lamp) BA 51 Lon Univ PGCE 68 DipEd 70 Liv Univ MEd 74 PhD 81. Ripon Hall Ox 55. **d** 58 **p** 59. C Wavertree H Trin *Liv* 58-60; C Sefton 60-61; C-in-c Thornton CD 61-64; Chapl Liv Coll Boys' Sch 64-70; Hon C Wavertree St Bridget *Liv* 70-89; Lect CF Mott Coll of Educn 70-76; Sen Lect Liv Coll of HE 76-83; Liv Poly 83-87; PtO *Liv* 90-96; *Ches* from 90; Chapl St Jo Hospice Wirral from 93; Tutor Open Univ 90-95; rtd 95. *68 Gleggside, West Kirby, Wirral CH48 6EA* T: 0151-625 8093

PRITCHARD, Peter Humphrey. b 47. Univ of Wales (Ban) BA 70 MA 98 Liv Univ PGCE 73. Qu Coll Birm 85. **d** 87 **p** 88. C Llanbeblig w Caernarfon and Betws Garmon etc *Ban* 87-90; R Llanberis w Llanrug 90-94; R Llanfaethlu w Llanfwrog and Llanrhuddlad etc 94-99; R Llanfair Mathafarn Eithaf w Llanbedrgoch 99-05; rtd 05. *4 Penlon Gardens, Bangor LL57 1AQ*

PRITCHARD, Simon Geraint. b 61. Coll of Ripon & York St Jo BA 85 Ex Univ PGCE 88. Cranmer Hall Dur 98. **d** 00 **p** 01. C Heysham *Blackb* 00-01; C Morecambe St Barn 01-03; C Standish 03-06; V Haigh and Aspull *Liv* 06-15; TV Wigan All SS from 15. *The Vicarage, Copperas Lane, Haigh, Wigan WN2 1PA* T: (01942) 830356 E: s.pritchard41@btinternet.com

PRITCHARD, Thomas James Benbow. b 47. St Paul's Coll Chelt CertEd 69 Univ of Wales (Cardiff) BEd 79 MSc 85 Ex Univ BTh 08. SWMTC 96. **d** 99 **p** 00. NSM St Enoder *Truro* 99-01; P-in-c Roche and Withiel 01-05; V Llangollen w Trevor and Llantysilio *St As* 05-06; P-in-c Mylor w Flushing *Truro* 06-07; rtd 07. *Suncot, Short Cross Road, Mount Hawke, Truro TR4 8DU* T: (01209) 891766 E: thms_pritchard@yahoo.co.uk

PRITCHARD, The Ven Thomas William. b 33. Keele Univ BA 55 DipEd 55 Univ of Wales (Cardiff) LLM 94. St Mich Coll Llan 55. **d** 57 **p** 58. C Holywell *St As* 57-61; C Ruabon 61-63; V 77-87; R Pontfadog 63-71; R Llanferres, Nercwys and Eryrys 71-77; Dioc Archivist 76-98; Can St As Cathl 84-98; RD Llangollen 86-87; Adn Montgomery 87-98; V Berriew and Manafon 87-98; rtd 98; PtO *St As* from 09. *4 Glynne Way, Hawarden, Deeside CH5 3NL* T: (01244) 538381

PRITCHARD-KEENS, Andrew James Dunn. b 57. Van Mildert Coll Dur BSc 79 Ch Ch Ox PGCE 80. Wycliffe Hall Ox 07. **d** 09 **p** 10. C Cogges and S Leigh *Ox* 09-12; C N Leigh 09-12; TV Wheatley 12-14; V Beckley, Forest Hill, Horton-cum-Studley and Stanton St John from 14; Chapl Thames Valley Police from 14. *The New Vicarage, Cox Lane, Stanton St John, Oxford OX33 1HW* T: (01865) 358340 M: 07944-522098 E: andrewjdp@yahoo.co.uk

PRITCHETT, Antony Milner. b 63. Kent Univ BA 86. Westcott Ho Cam 96. **d** 98 **p** 99. C Broughton Astley and Croft w Stoney Stanton *Leic* 98-02; V Gawber *Wakef* 02-08; Chapl Barnsley Hospice 02-08; P-in-c Pickering w Lockton and Levisham *York* 08-12; V from 12. *The Vicarage, Whitby Road, Pickering YO18 7HL* T: (01751) 472983 E: vicar@pickeringchurch.com

PRITCHETT, Mrs Beryl Ivy. b 48. Worc Coll of Educn TCert 69. WMMTC 02. **d** 05 **p** 06. NSM Brockmoor *Worc* 05-07; NSM Brierley Hill from 07. *7 Muirville Close, Wordsley, Stourbridge DY8 5NR* T: (01384) 271470 M: 07790-563479 E: berylpritchett@hotmail.com

PRIVETT, Peter John. b 48. Qu Coll Birm 75. **d** 78 **p** 79. C Moseley St Agnes *Birm* 78-81; V Kingsbury 81-87; P-in-c Dilwyn and Stretford *Heref* 87-90; Dioc Children's Adv 87-01; TV Leominster 90-98; NSM 98-05; Dioc Millennium Officer 98-01; PtO 05-07; *Cov* 07-09; C Rugby 09-13; C Rugby St Andr w St Pet and St John from 13. *166 Lower Hillmorton Road, Rugby CV21 3TJ* T: (01788) 570332 E: peter.privett@yahoo.co.uk

PROBART, Raymond. b 21. Sarum Th Coll 49. **d** 51 **p** 52. C Padiham *Blackb* 51-54; C Burnley St Pet 54-56; V Heyhouses 56-60; V Douglas 60-88; rtd 88; PtO *B & W* 88-98; *Glouc* from 03. *6 Capel Court, The Burgage, Prestbury, Cheltenham GL52 3EL* T: (01242) 235771

PROBERT, Beverley Stuart. b 42. **d** 01 **p** 02. OLM Canford Magna *Sarum* 01-12; rtd 13; PtO *Sarum* from 13. *Blaenafon, 102 Knights Road, Bournemouth BH11 9SY* T: (01202) 571731 E: bevprobert@tiscali.co.uk

PROBERT, Christopher John Dixon. b 54. Univ of Wales (Ban) BTh 95 MTh 97. St Mich Coll Llan 74. **d** 78 **p** 79. C Aberdare St Fagan *Llan* 78-79; C Cadoxton-juxta-Barry 79-81; R Llanfynydd *St As* 81-84; V Gosberton Clough and Quadring *Linc* 84-86; TV Coventry Caludon *Cov* 86-88; V Llanrhian w Llanhywel and Llanrheithan *St D* 88-91; V Tregaron w Ystrad Meurig and Strata Florida 91-93; Chapl and Tutor St D NSM Course Tregaron Hosp 91-93; V Betws-y-Coed and Capel Curig w Penmachno etc *Ban* 93-98; Warden of Readers 96-98; V Lt Drayton *Lich* 98-04; P-in-c North Hill and Lewannick *Truro* 04-10; C Lezant w Lawhitton and S Petherwin w Trewen 04-10; R Three Rivers 10-11; rtd 11. *La Haudiardière, 50640 Heusse, France* T: (0033) (2) 33 61 35 82
E: cjdprobert@gmail.com

PROBERT, Canon Edward Cleasby. b 58. St Cath Coll Cam BA 80 MA 84. Ripon Coll Cuddesdon BA 84. **d** 85 **p** 86. C Esher *Guildf* 85-89; V Earlsfield St Andr *S'wark* 89-94; V Belmont 94-04; Can Res and Chan Sarum Cathl from 04. *24 The Close, Salisbury SP1 2EH* T: (01722) 555193
E: chancellor@salcath.co.uk

PROCTER, Andrew David. b 52. St Jo Coll Ox BA 74 MA 86. Trin Coll Bris 74. **d** 77 **p** 78. C Barnoldswick w Bracewell *Bradf* 77-80; P-in-c Kelbrook 80-82; V Heaton St Barn 87-93; V Swanley St Paul *Roch* 93-07; R Shipbourne w Plaxtol from 07. *The Rectory, The Street, Plaxtol, Sevenoaks TN15 0QG* T: (01732) 811081 M: 07963-943524 E: a.procter@live.co.uk

PROCTER, Nicholas Jonathan. b 59. Liv Univ BVSc 84 MRCVS 84. LCTP 06. **d** 09 **p** 10. NSM Leyland St Jo *Blackb* 09-14; PtO 14-15; NSM Bamber Bridge St Aid from 15; NSM Walton-le-Dale St Leon from 15. *23 Regents Way, Euxton, Chorley PR7 6PG* T: (01257) 241927
E: n.r.procter@btinternet.com

PROCTER, Kenneth Noel. b 33. St Aid Birkenhead 61. **d** 63 **p** 64. C Oldham St Paul *Man* 63-66; C Davyhulme St Mary 66-69; V Norden w Ashworth 69-00; rtd 00. *4 Bankscroft, Hopwood, Heywood OL10 2NG* T: (01706) 364197

PROCTOR, Michael John. b 59. Cranmer Hall Dur 93. **d** 93 **p** 94. C Leatherhead *Guildf* 93-98; V Henlow and Langford *St Alb* 98-01; V Marton-in-Cleveland *York* 01-13; Min Coulby Newham LEP 03-13; V S Cave and Ellerker w Broomfleet from 13; RD Howden from 15. *The Vicarage, 10 Station Road, South Cave, Brough HU15 2AA* E: mike@stcuthbertmarton.org.uk

PROCTOR, Canon Michael Thomas. b 41. Ch Ch Ox BA 65 MA 67. Westcott Ho Cam 63. **d** 65 **p** 66. C Monkseaton St Mary *Newc* 65-69; Pakistan 69-72; C Willington *Newc* 72-77; TV 77-79; Ed Sec Nat Soc 79-84; P-in-c Roxwell *Chelmsf* 79-84; Bp's Ecum Officer 85-00; Dir of Miss and Unity 85-94; P-in-c Gt Waltham w Ford End 94-00; Hon Can Chelmsf Cathl 85-00; rtd 00; Dir Chelmsf Counselling Foundn from 00. *Claremont, South Street, Great Waltham, Chelmsford CM3 1DP* E: mtproctor@lineone.net

PROCTOR, Nicholas Jonathan. *See* PROCTER, Nicholas Jonathan

PROCTOR, Canon Noel. b 30. MBE 93. St Aid Birkenhead 62. **d** 64 **p** 65. C Haughton le Skerne *Dur* 64-67; R Byers Green 67-70; Chapl HM Pris Eastchurch 70-74; Chapl HM Pris Dartmoor 74-79; Chapl HM Pris Man 79-95; Hon Can Man Cathl 91-95; rtd 95; PtO *Man* from 95. *Mizpah, 64 Barton Road, Swinton, Manchester M27 5LP* T: 0161-794 6040

PROCTOR, Canon Susan Katherine. b 44. **d** 89 **p** 94. Par Dn Beighton *Sheff* 89-91; Par Dn Aston cum Aughton and Ulley 91-93; Par Dn Aston cum Aughton w Swallownest, Todwick etc 93-94; TV Aston cum Aughton w Swallownest and Ulley 01-02; TR 02-05; R Dinnington 96-01; AD Laughton 98-03; Hon Can Sheff Cathl 98-05; rtd 05. *69 Ings Mill Avenue, Clayton West, Huddersfield HD8 9QG* T: (01484) 866189 M: 07768-293588 E: sueproctor@lineone.net

PROFIT, David Hollingworth. b 17. Man Univ BA 38. Cuddesdon Coll 40. **d** 41 **p** 42. C Kings Heath *Birm* 41-43; S Africa from 43. *Braehead House, 1 Braehead Road, Kenilworth, 7708 South Africa* T: (0027) (21) 762 6041

PROSSER, Gillian Margaret. b 40. Lon Inst of Educn TCert 61. **d** 99. OLM Cwmbran *Mon* 99-10; PtO from 12. *25 Forest Close, Coed Eva, Cwmbran NP44 4TE* T: (01633) 866716

PROSSER, Hugh. *See* PROSSER, Richard Hugh Keble

PROSSER, Jean. b 40. MBE 10. Open Univ BA 84 Surrey Univ PhD 94. **d** 02 **p** 05. NSM Grosmont and Skenfrith and Llangattock etc *Mon* from 02; P-in-c from 09. *Yew Tree Farm, Llangattock Lingoed, Abergavenny NP7 8NS* T: (01873) 821405 E: revjean.prosser@btinternet.com

PROSSER, Canon Rhys. b 51. BA 74 Southn Univ BTh 83 Hull Univ MA 93 Bris Univ CertEd 75. Sarum & Wells Th Coll 77. **d** 80 **p** 81. C Wimbledon *S'wark* 80-83; C St Helier 83-88; TV Gt and Lt Coates w Bradley *Linc* 88-95; P-in-c Saxilby Gp 95-97; R 97-15; R Stow Gp 13-15; RD Corringham 00-13; Can and Preb Linc Cathl 03-15. *Address withheld by request* E: rs.prosser@virgin.net

PROSSER, Richard Hugh Keble. b 31. Trin Coll Cam BA 53 MA 57 Leeds Univ PGCE 63. Cuddesdon Coll 55. **d** 57 **p** 58. C Wigan All SS *Liv* 57-60; CR 62-87; St Aug Miss Penhalonga Zimbabwe 64-90; R Pocklington and Owsthorpe and Kilnwick Percy etc *York* 90-00; rtd 00; PtO *Sarum* from 02. *Address temp unknown*

PROSSER, Stephanie. b 42. Linc Th Coll 94. **d** 96 **p** 99. NSM Linc St Nic w St Jo Newport 96-99; NSM Saxilby Gp from 99. *The Vicarage, 69 Mill Lane, Saxilby, Lincoln LN1 2HN* T: (01522) 702427

PROTHERO, Brian Douglas. b 52. St Andr Univ MTheol 75 Dundee Univ CertEd 77. Linc Th Coll 84. **d** 86 **p** 87. C Thornbury *Glouc* 86-89; V Goodrington *Ex* 89-04; R Weybridge *Guildf* from 04; Chapl Sam Beare Hospice from 06. *The Rectory, 3 Churchfields Avenue, Weybridge KT13 9YA* T: (01932) 842566 M: 07715-364389
E: brian.prothero@talktalk.net

PROTHERO, David John. b 43. St Pet Coll Ox BA 66 MA 70. St Steph Ho Ox 68. **d** 70 **p** 71. C Kirkby *Liv* 70-72; C St Marychurch *Ex* 72-74; V Marldon 74-83; Chapl HM Pris Channings Wood 78-83; V Torquay St Martin Barton *Ex* 83-91; P-in-c Bath Bathwick *B & W* 91-93; R 93-12; rtd 12; Chapl Bath St Mary Magd Holloway *B & W* from 12. *12 Wellington Buildings, Bath BA1 4EP* T: (01225) 938595
E: david@djprothero.fsnet.co.uk

PROTHERO, John Martin. b 32. Oak Hill Th Coll 64. **d** 66 **p** 67. C Tipton St Martin *Lich* 66-69; C Wednesfield Heath 69-72; Distr Sec BFBS 72-85; LtO *S'well* 73-86; Hon C Gedling 73; V Willoughby-on-the-Wolds w Wysall and Widmerpool 86-97; rtd 98. *The Elms, Vicarage Hill, Aberaeron SA46 0DY* T: (01545) 570568

PROTHEROE, Canon Rhys Illtyd. b 50. St D Coll Lamp. **d** 74 **p** 75. C Pen-bre *St D* 74-76; C Carmarthen St Dav 76-78; V Llanegwad 78-79; V Llanegwad w Llanfynydd 79-82; V Gors-las 82-95; RD Dyffryn Aman 94-95; V Llan-llwch w Llangain and Llangynog from 95; Hon Can St D Cathl from 13. *The New Vicarage, Millbank Lane, Johnstown, Carmarthen SA31 3HW* T: (01267) 236805

PROTHEROE, Canon Robin Philip. b 33. St Chad's Coll Dur BA 54 MA 60 Nottm Univ MPhil 75 Ox Univ DipEd 62. **d** 57 **p** 58. C Roath *Llan* 57-60; Asst Chapl Culham Coll Abingdon 60-64; Sen Lect RS Trent (Nottm) Poly *S'well* 64-84; PtO 64-66; LtO 66-84; P-in-c Barton in Fabis 70-73; P-in-c Thrumpton 70-73; Dir of Educn *Bris* 84-98; Hon Can Bris Cathl 85-98; Capitular Can Bris Cathl 01-07; PtO 98-10; *Chich* from 10. *58 Stroudley Road, Brighton BN1 4BH* T: (01273) 687822
E: rpprotheroe@gmail.com

✠**PROUD, The Rt Revd Andrew John.** b 54. K Coll Lon BD 79 AKC 79 SOAS Lon MA 01. Linc Th Coll 79. **d** 80 **p** 81 **c** 07. C Stansted Mountfitchet *Chelmsf* 80-83; TV Borehamwood *St Alb* 83-90; C Bp's Hatfield 90-92; R E Barnet 92-01; Chapl Adis Ababa St Matt Ethiopia 02-07; Area Bp Ethiopia and Horn of Africa 07-11; Area Bp Reading *Ox* from 11. *Bishop's House, Tidmarsh Lane, Tidmarsh, Reading RG8 8HA* T: 0118-984 1216 F: 984 1218 E: bishopreading@oxford.anglican.org

PROUD, David John. b 56. Leeds Univ BA 77 Dur Univ CertEd 78. Ridley Hall Cam 85. **d** 88 **p** 89. C Lindfield *Chich* 88-91; TV Horsham 91-97; V Ware Ch Ch *St Alb* 97-10; RD Hertford and Ware 04-10; Chapl E Herts NHS Trust 97-00; Chapl E and N Herts NHS Trust 00-06; R Bedhampton *Portsm* from 10. *The Rectory, Bidbury Lane, Bedhampton, Havant PO9 3JG* T: (02392) 483103

PROUD, George. b 43. Newc Univ BDS 71 MB, BS 71 MD 81 FRCS. Lindisfarne Regional Tr Partnership 10. **d** 11 **p** 12. OLM Riding Mill *Newc* 11-14; rtd 14. *Cartref, Marchburn Lane, Riding Mill NE44 6DN* T: (01434) 682393 M: 07990-970202 E: george.proud.1@btinternet.com

PROUDFOOT (*née* BLACKBURN), Mrs Jane Elizabeth. b 66. Lanc Univ BA 88 St Martin's Coll Lanc PGCE 93 Leeds Univ BA 09. NOC 06. **d** 09 **p** 10. C Stockton Heath *Ches* 09-12; R Grappenhall from 12. *The Rectory, 17 Hill Top Road, Stockton Heath, Warrington WA4 2ED* T: (01925) 661546
E: revdproudfoot@hotmail.co.uk

PROUDLEY, Sister Anne. b 38. Edin Univ BSc 60. SAOMC 97. **d** 00 **p** 01. CSJB from 00; NSM Blackbird Leys *Ox* 00-04; LtO 04-11; Chapl to the Homeless 05-11; NSM Blenheim 11-12; PtO from 12. *Harriet Monsell House, Ripon College, Cuddesdon, Oxford OX44 9EX* E: annecsjb@csjb.org.uk

PROUDLOVE, Lee Jason. b 70. Lon Bible Coll BA 94. Trin Coll Bris MA 01. **d** 01 **p** 02. C Morden *S'wark* 01-04; CMS Philippines 05-08; P-in-c W Bridgford *S'well* 08-11; R from 11. *The Rectory, 86 Bridgford Road, West Bridgford, Nottingham NG2 6AX* T: 0115-981 1112 E: rector@stgilesparish.com

PROUDLOVE, Stephen. b 85. SS Coll Cam BA 02 MA 05. Ridley Hall Cam 12. **d** 14 **p** 15. C Ilkley All SS *Leeds* from 14. *3 Low Beck, Ilkley LS29 8UN* T: (01943) 601386 M: 07794-678268 E: curate@ilkleyallsaints.org.uk

PROUDMAN, Canon Colin Leslie John. b 34. K Coll Lon BD 60 MTh 63. Wells Th Coll 60. d 61 p 62. C Radlett *St Alb* 61-64; Canada from 64; Hon Can Toronto from 86; Dean Div Toronto Div Coll 90-92; rtd 97. *1802-77 Maitland Place, Toronto ON M4Y 2V6, Canada* T: (001) (416) 923 4235

PROUT, Mrs Joan. b 42. Gipsy Hill Coll of Educn TCert 63. d 97 p 98. OLM Whitton *Sarum* 97-06. *22 Ermin Close, Baydon, Marlborough SN8 2JQ* T: (01672) 540465
E: joan.prout@genie.co.uk

PROVOST, Ian Keith. b 47. CA Tr Coll IDC 73 Ridley Hall Cam 91. d 93 p 94. C Verwood *Sarum* 93-97; P-in-c Redlynch and Morgan's Vale 97-02; TV Plymstock and Hooe *Ex* 02-10; rtd 10. *8 Larkhall Rise, Plymouth PL3 6LY*
E: ian.provost17@gmail.com

PROWSE, Mrs Barbara Bridgette Christmas. b 41. R Holloway Coll Lon BA 62. d 91 p 94. C Kingsthorpe w Northampton St Dav *Pet* 91-97; V Northampton St Jas 97-02; rtd 02; PtO *Truro* from 02. *36 Carn Basavern, St Just, Penzance TR19 7QX* T: (01736) 787994 E: bbc@prowseb.freeserve.co.uk

PRUDOM, William Haigh. b 26. STh 79 APhS 81 Hull Univ MPhil 88. St D Coll Lamp 60. d 62 p 63. C Aylesford *Roch* 62-63; C Margate St Jo *Cant* 63-66; V Long Preston *Bradf* 66-73; C Darlington St Cuth *Dur* 73-75; V Ticehurst *Chich* 75-79; P-in-c Flimwell 78-79; V Ticehurst and Flimwell 79-81; R Spennithorne w Finghall and Hauxwell *Ripon* 81-91; rtd 91; PtO *Leeds* from 91. *9 Sydall's Way, Catterick Village, Richmond DL10 7ND* T: (01748) 818604

PRUEN, Edward Binney. b 56. K Coll Lon BD 77 AKC 77. St Jo Coll Nottm 78. d 79 p 80. C Kidderminster St Mary *Worc* 79-82; C Woking St Jo *Guildf* 82-84; Chapl Asst R Marsden Hosp 84-86; C Stapleford *S'well* 86-88; Min Winklebury CD *Win* 88; V Winklebury 88-93; Chapl Ld Mayor Treloar Coll Alton 93-09; Hon Can Win Cathl 05-09; Can Res S'well Minster 09-12; P-in-c St Columb Major *Truro* from 12; P-in-c St Mawgan w St Ervan and St Eval from 12. *The Rectory, West Street, St Columb TR9 6AE* T: (01637) 880252
E: edpruen@btconnect.com *or* edpruen@yahoo.co.uk

PRUST, Mrs Judith Ann. b 46. St Mich Coll Llan 05. d 07 p 13. NSM Llanrhaeadr ym Mochnant etc *St As* 07-15; PtO from 15. *Minffordd, Llangynog, Oswestry SY10 0HD* T: (01691) 860420
E: judithprust@yahoo.co.uk

PRYCE, Donald Keith. b 35. Man Univ BSc. Linc Th Coll 69. d 71 p 72. C Heywood St Jas *Man* 71-74; P-in-c 74-75; V 75-86; R Ladybarn 86-06; Chapl S Man Coll 87-06; Chapl Christie Hosp NHS Trust Man 93-06; rtd 06; PtO *Ches* from 06; *Man* from 06. *62 Belmont Road, Gatley, Cheadle SK8 4AQ* T: 0161-286 9985 E: donaldpryce@hotmail.com

PRYCE, Canon Robin Mark. b 60. Sussex Univ BA 82 Can Univ MA 94. Westcott Ho Cam 84 United Th Coll Bangalore 85. d 87 p 88. C W Bromwich All SS *Lich* 87-90; Chapl Sandwell Distr Gen Hosp 90; Chapl and Fell CCC Cam 90-02; Tutor 92-02; Dean of Chpl 96-02; V Smethwick *Birm* 02-06; Bp's Adv for Clergy CME from 06; Hon Can Birm Cathl from 11. *1 Colmore Row, Birmingham B3 2BJ* T: 0121-426 0430
E: m.pryce@birmingham.anglican.org

PRYCE, William Robert. b 28. MBE 91. d 79 p 80. NSM Leverstock Green *St Alb* 79-80; PtO *Sheff* 80-84; NSM Sheff St Barn and St Mary 84-90; NSM Alveley and Quatt *Heref* 91-93; PtO 93-03. *5 Wren Way, Bicester OX26 6UJ*

PRYCE-WILLIAMS, Jean. b 48. d 10 p 11. NSM Cumnor *Ox* from 10. *118 Oxford Road, Cumnor, Oxford OX2 9PQ* T: (01865) 865687 E: j.pryce-williams@pippins.myzen.co.uk

PRYKE, Jonathan Justin Speaight. b 59. Trin Coll Cam BA 80 MA 85. Trin Coll Bris BD 85. d 85 p 86. C Corby St Columba *Pet* 85-88; C Jesmond Clayton Memorial *Newc* from 88. *15 Lily Avenue, Newcastle upon Tyne NE2 2SQ* T: 0191-281 9854

PRYOR, Derek John. b 29. Lon Univ BD 63 Birm Univ MEd 74. Linc Th Coll 79 Chich Th Coll 79. d 80 p 81. Hon C Youlgreave *Derby* 80-82; Hon C Stanton-in-Peak 80-82; Hon C Ingham w Cammeringham w Fillingham *Linc* 82-87 and 92-99; Chapl Bp Grosseteste Coll Linc 83-84; Dioc Schs Officer *Linc* 87-92; rtd 92. *Walnut Cottage, Chapel Lane, Fillingham, Gainsborough DN21 5BP* T: (01427) 668276 F: 667956
E: john.pryor@btinternet.com

PRYOR, William Lister Archibald. b 39. Trin Coll Cam BA 67 MA 69 DipEd 68. Ox NSM Course 72. d 75 p 90. NSM Summertown *Ox* from 75; PtO *Nor* 93-04 and from 09. *23 Harbord Road, Oxford OX2 8LH* T/F: (01865) 515102

PRYS, Deiniol. b 53. Univ of Wales (Ban) BTh 91. St Mich Coll Llan 82. d 83 p 84. C Llanbeblig w Caernarfon and Betws Garmon etc *Ban* 83-86; TV Amlwch 86-88; V Llanerch-y-medd 89-92; R Llansadwrn w Llanddona and Llaniestyn etc 92-11; LtO from 11. *Bryn Celyn, Llansadwrn, Menai Bridge LL59 5SL* T: (01248) 810534 M: 07740-541316

PRYSE, Hugh Henry David. b 58. St Chad's Coll Dur BA 81 SS Coll Cam PGCE 82 K Coll Lon MA 96. St Steph Ho Ox 94. d 96 p 97. C Branksome St Aldhelm *Sarum* 96-00; Chapl St Edw Sch Poole 98-00; TV Hove *Chich* 00-05; R Ex St Jas from 05; Asst Dioc Dir of Ords from 09. *The Rectory, 45 Thornton Hill, Exeter EX4 4NR* T: (01392) 431297 *or* 420407
E: henry.pryse@blueyonder.co.uk

PRYSOR-JONES, John Glynne. b 47. Heythrop Coll Lon MA 94 Leeds Metrop Univ BSc 05 CQSW 73. Westcott Ho Cam 88. d 90 p 91. C Mitcham St Mark *S'wark* 90-93; V Dudley St Fran *Worc* 93-99; R Woodchurch *Ches* 99-01; Hd Past Care Services Chorley and S Ribble NHS Trust and Preston Acute Hosps NHS Trust 01-02; Hd Past Care Services Lancs Teaching Hosps NHS Trust 02-06. *Bryn-y-Mor, St John's Park, Penmaenmawr LL34 6NE* T: (01492) 622515

PRZESLAWSKI, Maria Christina. b 50. Nottm Univ MA 91. EMMTC 08. d 10 p 11. NSM Wilne and Draycott w Breaston *Derby* from 10. *9 Holmes Road, Breaston, Derby DE72 3BT* T: (01332) 874480 E: maria.9@btinternet.com

PRZYWALA, Karl Andrzej. b 63. Univ Coll Dur BA 85 Chas Sturt Univ NSW BTh 04. St Mark's Nat Th Cen Canberra 01. d 04 p 05. C Houghton le Spring *Dur* 04-05; C Chester le Street 05-07; P-in-c Whatton w Aslockton, Hawksworth, Scarrington etc *S'well* 07-11; V 11-14; R Vancouver H Trin Canada from 14. *908 - 1755 West 14th Avenue, Vancouver V6J 2J6, Canada* T: (001) (604) 731 3221 E: karl_sydney@yahoo.co.uk

PUCKRIN, Christopher. b 47. Oak Hill Th Coll. d 82 p 83. C Heworth H Trin *York* 82-84; C Sherburn in Elmet 84-85; P-in-c Kirk Fenton 85-86; P-in-c Kirkby Wharfe 85-86; V Kirk Fenton w Kirkby Wharfe and Ulleskelfe 86-87; C York St Mich-le-Belfrey 87-94; P-in-c Barnstaple *Ex* 94-97; TV 97-00; V Woodside *Ripon* 00-07; C Holbeck 07-09; V Bardsey 09-12; P-in-c 12-13; rtd 12. *38 Oxenford Court, Magdalene Close, Leeds LS16 6QJ* T: 0113-267 8584

PUDDEFOOT, John Charles. b 52. St Pet Coll Ox BA 74 Edin Univ BD 78. Edin Th Coll 76. d 78 p 79. C Darlington H Trin *Dur* 78-81; Ind Chapl *Chich* 81-84; Asst Master Eton Coll from 84; Hd Mathematics from 93. *Eton College, Windsor SL4 6DB* T: (01753) 671320 E: j.puddefoot@etoncollege.org.uk

PUDGE, Mark Samuel. b 67. K Coll Lon BD 90 AKC 90 Heythrop Coll Lon MA 99. Ripon Coll Cuddesdon 91. d 93 p 94. C Thorpe Bay *Chelmsf* 93-96; TV Wickford and Runwell 97-00; Management Consultant Citizens' Advice Bureau from 00; Hon C Paddington St Jo w St Mich *Lon* from 03. *Flat 2, 12 Connaught Street, London W2 2AF*

PUDNEY, Malcolm Lloyd. b 48. SEITE 99. d 01 p 02. NSM S Nutfield w Outwood *S'wark* 01-06; P-in-c Woodham Mortimer w Hazeleigh and Woodham Walter *Chelmsf* 06-10; P-in-c Lurgashall and N Chapel w Ebernoe *Chich* 10-13; rtd 13. *26 Cuckfield Crescent, Worthing BN13 2ED* M: 07860-464836
E: yenduptoo@madasafish.com

PUERTO RICO, Bishop of. *See* ALVAREZ VELAZQUEZ, The Rt Revd David Andres

PUGH, Geoffrey William. b 47. Ox Min Course 09. d 09 p 10. NSM Ruscombe and Twyford *Ox* 09-12; NSM Ruscombe and Twyford w Hurst from 12. *3 Willow Drive, Twyford, Reading RG10 9DD* T: 0118-934 5482 M: 07934-420303
E: revgeoff@familypugh.co.uk

PUGH, Harry. b 48. K Coll Lon BD 70 AKC 71 Lanc Univ MA 89. d 72 p 73. C Milnrow *Man* 72-75; P-in-c Rochdale Gd Shep 75-78; TV Rochdale 78-79; PtO *Liv* 79-82; C Darwen St Cuth *Blackb* 82-85; C Darwen St Cuth w Tockholes St Steph 85-86; V Burnley St Steph 86-93; R Hoole 93-01; P-in-c Porthleven w Sithney *Truro* 01-13; rtd 13. *32 Cowling Gardens, Menheniot, Liskeard PL14 3QJ*

PUGH, Lynda. b 49. Man Univ BSocSc 93 MA 96 PhD 04. Ripon Coll Cuddesdon 07. d 09 p 10. C Glen Gp *Linc* 09-12; P-in-c Ringstone in Aveland Gp from 12. *The Vicarage, 46A High Street, Morton, Bourne PE10 0NR* M: 07775-660081
E: dr.lynda.pugh@gmail.com

PUGH, Ronald Keith. b 32. Jes Coll Ox BA 54 MA 57 DPhil 57. Ripon Hall Ox 56. d 59 p 60. C Bournemouth St Mich *Win* 59-61; Asst Chapl Bryanston Sch 61-66; Chapl Cranleigh Sch Surrey 66-68; Lect K Alfred Coll Winchester 68-97; rtd 97; Hon Sec and Treas Win and Portsm Dioc Clerical Registry 97-06; PtO *Win* from 06. *6 Windermere Gardens, Alresford SO24 9NL* T: (01962) 732879 E: rk.pugh@btinternet.com

PUGH, Stephen Gregory. b . Southn Univ BEd 77. Linc Th Coll 85. d 87 p 88. C Harpenden St Nic *St Alb* 87-90; C Stevenage All SS Pin Green 90-93; V Stotfold and Radwell 93-00; V Gt Ilford St Marg and St Clem *Chelmsf* from 00. *The Vicarage, 70 Brisbane Road, Ilford IG1 4SL* T: (020) 8554 7542 M: 07910-395925 E: stephenpugh@waitrose.com

PUGH, Miss Wendy Kathleen. b 48. Newnham Coll Cam BA 69 MA 75. Trin Coll Bris 93. d 95 p 96. C Hailsham *Chich* 95-99;

C Frimley *Guildf* 99-07; Hon C Chertsey, Lyne and Longcross 07-12; rtd 13. *6 Friars Orchard, Salisbury SP1 2SY* T: (01722) 501443 E: wkpugh@aol.com

PUGMIRE, Canon Alan. b 37. Tyndale Hall Bris 61. **d** 64 **p** 65. C Islington St Steph w St Bart and St Matt *Lon* 64-66; C St Helens St Mark *Liv* 66-71; R Stretford St Bride *Man* 71-82; R Burnage St Marg 82-02; AD Heaton 88-98; Hon Can Man Cathl 98-02; rtd 02; PtO *Man* from 02. *20 Shortland Crescent, Manchester M19 1SZ* T: 0161-431 3476 E: alan.pugmire@tiscali.co.uk

PUGSLEY, Anthony John. b 39. ACIB. Oak Hill Th Coll 89. **d** 90 **p** 91. C Chadwell *Chelmsf* 90-94; P-in-c Gt Warley Ch Ch 94-01; V Warley Ch Ch and Gt Warley St Mary 01-04; rtd 04. *3 Southcliffe Court, Southview Drive, Walton on the Naze CO14 8EP* T: (01255) 850967 E: revtony@aol.com

PULESTON, Mervyn Pedley. b 35. K Coll Lon BD 60 AKC 60. **d** 61 **p** 62. C Gt Marlow *Ox* 61-65; P Missr Blackbird Leys CD 65-70; V Kidlington 70-85; R Hampton Poyle 70-85; TR Kidlington w Hampton Poyle 85-86; Chapl Geneva *Eur* 86-92; TV Dorchester *Ox* 92-00; rtd 00. *55 Benmead Road, Kidlington OX5 2DB* T: (01865) 372360 E: mpuleston@aol.com

PULFORD, Christopher. b 59. Pemb Coll Ox BA 81 MA 87. Trin Coll Bris 82. **d** 84 **p** 85. C Parr *Liv* 84-87; Chapl Berkhamsted Colleg Sch Herts 87-92; Development Dir React from 92. *c/o React, St Luke's House, 270 Sandycombe Road, Kew, Richmond TW9 3NA* T: (020) 8940 2575 F: 8940 2050

PULFORD, John Shirley Walter. b 31. Jes Coll Cam BA 55 MA 59. Cuddesdon Coll 55. **d** 57 **p** 58. C Blackpool St Steph *Blackb* 57-60; N Rhodesia 60-63; V Newington St Paul *S'wark* 63-68; C Seacroft *Ripon* 68-70; Chapl HM Pris Liv 70-72; Chapl HM Pris Linc 72-73; Student Cllr Linc Colls of Art and Tech 73-79; Cam Univ Counselling Service 79-96; Dir 82-96; rtd 96. *59 Cromer Road, North Walsham NR28 0HB* T: (01692) 404320

PULFORD, Canon Stephen Ian. b 25. Clifton Th Coll 53. **d** 56 **p** 57. C Heref St Jas 56-58; R Coberley w Cowley *Glouc* 58-94; P-in-c Colesborne 75-94; Hon Can Glouc Cathl 84-94; RD Cirencester 88-89; rtd 94; PtO *Glouc* from 94. *16 Bafford Grove, Charlton Kings, Cheltenham GL53 9JE* T: (01242) 524261

PULKO, Susan Helen. b 55. **d** 14 **p** 15. NSM Market Weighton *York* from 14. *Alpha Schloss, Station Road, Shiptonthorpe YO43 3PB* E: s.h.pulko@hull.ac.uk

PULLAN, Ben John. b 43. Univ of Wales (Cardiff) MSc(Econ) 83. Bris Minl Tr Scheme 74. **d** 77 **p** 78. NSM Westbury-on-Trym St Alb *Bris* 77-91; NSM Henleaze 91-03; NSM Bishopston and St Andrews from 05. *28 Hobhouse Close, Bristol BS9 4LZ* T: 0117-962 4190 E: ben@bpullan.wanadoo.co.uk

PULLAN, Lionel Stephen. b 37. Keble Coll Ox BA 58 MA 62 ARCO 58 FIST 77. Cuddesdon Coll 58. **d** 60 **p** 61. C Tranmere St Paul *Ches* 60-63; C Higher Bebington 63-64; PtO 64-70; Hon C Luton St Chris Round Green *St Alb* 70-72; Hon C Hitchin H Sav 72-73; Hon C Welwyn 73-75; Hon C Welwyn w Ayot St Peter 75-78; Hon C Kimpton w Ayot St Lawrence 78-82; Hon C Stevenage St Andr and St Geo 82-85; Deputation Appeals Org CECS 85-90; V Sundon *St Alb* 90-03; rtd 03; PtO *St Alb* from 03; Chapl ATC from 92. *139 Turnpike Drive, Luton LU3 3RB* T: (01582) 573236

PULLEN, Adam William. b 73. Univ of Wales (Abth) BSc 97. St Jo Coll Nottm 03. **d** 06 **p** 07. C Swansea St Pet *S & B* 06-09; C Swansea St Thos and Kilvey 09-10; I Ballisodare w Collooney and Emlaghfad *T, K & A* from 10; Dom Chapl to Bp Tuam from 12. *The Rectory, Ballisodare, Co Sligo, Republic of Ireland* T: (00353) (71) 913 3217 M: 87-682 9627 E: adam.pullen@googlemail.com

PULLEN, Frances Jill. b 54. Birm Univ MB, ChB 76. WEMTC 10. **d** 13 **p** 14. C St Weonards *Heref* from 13. *New House, Garway Hill, Hereford HR2 8EZ* T: (01981) 240032 E: franpullen@btinternet.com

PULLEN, James Stephen. b 43. Lon Univ BSc 64 PGCE 65 Linacre Coll Ox BA 68. St Steph Ho Ox 66. **d** 68 **p** 69. C Chorlton-cum-Hardy St Clem *Man* 68-71; C Doncaster St Leon and St Jude *Sheff* 72-73; Chapl St Olave's Gr Sch Orpington 73-75; Chapl Haileybury Coll 75-01; Second Master 99-01; V St Ives *Ely* 01-10; rtd 10. *12 Broad Leas, St Ives PE27 5QB* T: (01480) 300070 E: jspullen84@btinternet.com

PULLEN, Roger Christopher. b 43. Lon Univ BSc 65 PGCE 90. Wells Th Coll 65. **d** 67 **p** 68. C S w N Hayling *Portsm* 67-69; C Farlington 69-73; V Farington *Blackb* 73-80; V Chorley All SS 80-83; V Kingsley *Ches* 83-92; R Cilcain and Nannerch and Rhydymwyn *St As* 92-99; Dioc MU Admin *Guildf* 99-02; Hon C Bramley and Grafham 99-00; PtO 00-02; *Chich* from 03. *Ewhurst, 6 Chichester Way, Selsey, Chichester PO20 0PJ* T: (01243) 601684 M: 07989-732729 E: roger_pullen@lineone.net

PULLEN, Timothy John. b 61. BNC Ox BA 84 St Jo Coll Dur MA 96. Cranmer Hall Dur 93. **d** 96 **p** 97. C Allesley *Cov* 96-00; V Wolston and Church Lawford 00-08; Can Res Cov Cathl 08-13; Sub-Dean 10-13; R Wollaton *S'well* from 13. *St Leonard's Rectory, 143 Russell Drive, Nottingham NG8 2BD* M: 07974-007665 T: 0115-928 9963 E: pullen1961@gmail.com

PULLIN, Andrew Eric. b 47. Kelham Th Coll 67 Linc Th Coll 71. **d** 73 **p** 74. C Pershore w Pinvin, Wick and Birlingham *Worc* 73-77; TV Droitwich 77-80; V Woburn Sands *St Alb* 80-85; PtO *B & W* 85-87. *85 Weymouth Road, Frome BA11 1HJ* T: (01373) 472170 E: a.pullin78@talktalk.net

PULLIN, Canon Christopher. b 56. St Chad's Coll Dur BA 77 Heythrop Coll Lon MA 04. Ripon Coll Cuddesdon 78 Ch Div Sch of Pacific 79. **d** 80 **p** 81. C Tooting All SS *S'wark* 80-85; V New Eltham All SS 85-92; V St Jo in Bedwardine *Worc* 92-08; RD Martley and Worc W 03-08; Hon Can Worc Cathl 07-08; Can Res and Chan Heref Cathl from 08. *2 Cathedral Close, Hereford HR1 2NG* T: (01432) 341905 F: 374220 E: chancellor@herefordcathedral.org

PULLIN, Peter Stanley. b 29. MA MSc CEng. Trin Coll Bris 87. **d** 88 **p** 89. NSM Rugby *Cov* 88-90; NSM Aylesbeare, Rockbeare, Farringdon etc *Ex* 90-98; PtO 99-04; *B & W* from 05. *25 Ashley Road, Bathford, Bath BA1 7TT* T: (01225) 852050 E: pa.pullin@btinternet.com

PULLIN, Rebecca. *See* CLARKE, Kathleen Jean Rebecca

PULLIN, Mrs Sarah Anne. b 52. STETS. **d** 12 **p** 13. NSM Bris St Steph w St Jas and St Jo w St Mich etc 12-15. *344 Wokingham Road, Reading RG6 7DE* T: 0118-957 1057 E: sarahpullin@btinternet.com

PULLIN, Stephen James. b 66. S Bank Univ BEng 89 Open Univ MBA 98. Trin Coll Bris BA 04. **d** 04 **p** 05. C Soundwell *Bris* 04-07; P-in-c Stapleton 07-14; C Frenchay and Winterbourne Down 07-14; Bp's Adv for Deliverance Min 10-14; P-in-c Reading St Mary the Virgin *Ox* from 14; AD Reading from 14. *344 Wokingham Road, Reading RG6 7DE* M: 07866-700881 T: 0118-966 9165 E: stephenpullin@btinternet.com

PULLINGER, Mrs Catherine Ann. b 54. York Univ BA 76. Oak Hill Th Coll 91. **d** 93 **p** 97. NSM Luton St Paul *St Alb* 93-99; NSM Luton Lewsey St Hugh 99-11; P-in-c Woodside from 11. *52 Wheatfield Road, Luton LU4 0TR* T: (01582) 606996 F: 472726 E: cathy@pullinger.net

PULLINGER, Ian Austin. b 61. Oak Hill Th Coll. **d** 96 **p** 97. C Weston *Win* 96-00; TV The Ortons, Alwalton and Chesterton *Ely* 00-10; TV Alwalton and Chesterton 10-12; C-in-c Orton Goldhay CD 12-13; V Corby St Columba *Pet* from 13; RD Corby from 13. *St Columba's Vicarage, 157 Studfall Avenue, Corby NN17 1LG* T: (01536) 400225 E: ianpullinger@btinternet.com

PULLINGER, Peter Mark. b 53. Heythrop Coll Lon MA 97. Ridley Hall Cam 01. **d** 03 **p** 04. C Clapham Park St Steph *S'wark* 03-06; C Telford Park 06-07; TV Sutton 07-15; P-in-c Merstham, S Merstham and Gatton from 15. *All Saints' Vicarage, Battlebridge Lane, Merstham, Redhill RH1 3LH* M: 07796-956774 E: mark@pullinger.net *or* mplarksong@aol.co.uk

PULMAN, John. b 34. EMMTC 78. **d** 81 **p** 82. NSM Mansfield SS Pet and Paul *S'well* 81-83; C Mansfield Woodhouse 83-86; V Flintham 86-99; R Car Colston w Screveton 86-99; Chapl HM YOI Whatton 87-90; Chapl HM Pris Whatton 90-99; rtd 99; PtO *S'well* from 99; *Derby* from 00. *101 Ling Forest Road, Mansfield NG18 3NQ* T: (01623) 474707

PUMFREY (née CERRATTI), Canon Christa Elisabeth. b 54. Wycliffe Hall Ox 94. **d** 97 **p** 98. C Chipping Norton *Ox* 97-00; P-in-c Lavendon w Cold Brayfield, Clifton Reynes etc 00-08; R from 08; R Gayhurst w Ravenstone, Stoke Goldington etc from 08; Deanery Youth Co-ord from 00; AD Newport 06-12; Hon Can Ch Ch from 11. *The New Rectory, 7A Northampton Road, Lavendon, Olney MK46 4EY* T: (01234) 240013 E: christina.pumfrey@btinternet.com

PUNSHON, Carol Mary. *See* BRENNAN, Carol Mary

PUNSHON, George Wilson. b 30. Bris Univ BSc Michigan State Univ MSc DipEd. Ripon Hall Ox 71. **d** 73 **p** 74. C Knighton St Mary Magd *Leic* 73-76; V Donisthorpe and Moira w Stretton-en-le-Field 76-82; R Gt Bowden w Welham, Glooston and Cranoe 82-86; Zimbabwe 87-89 and 00-04; PtO *Pet* 96-00; V Ascension Is 97-98; Chapl Peterho Sch Marondera 00-04. *101 The Downs, Nottingham NG11 7EA*

PUNSHON, Canon Keith. b 48. JP . Jes Coll Cam BA 69 MA 73 Birm Univ MA 77. Qu Coll Birm 71. **d** 73 **p** 74. C Yardley St Edburgha *Birm* 73-76; Chapl Eton Coll 76-79; V Hill *Birm* 79-86; CF (TA) from 79; V S Yardley St Mich *Birm* 86-96; Can Res Ripon Cathl 96-14; rtd 14. *Address temp unknown*

PURCHAS, Canon Thomas. b 35. Qu Coll Birm 59. **d** 62 **p** 63. C Bp's Hatfield *St Alb* 62-71; R Blunham 71-78; P-in-c Tempsford 71-78; R Blunham w Tempsford and Lt Barford

78-80; R Wheathampstead 80-00; RD 92-99; Hon Can St Alb 99-00; rtd 00; RD Hitchin *St Alb* 00-02; PtO from 00. *14 Horn Hill, Whitwell, Hitchin SG4 8AS* T/F: (01438) 871668

PURDY, Canon John <u>David</u>. b 44. Leeds Univ BA 65 MPhil 76. Coll of Resurr Mirfield 72. **d** 75 **p** 76. C Marske in Cleveland *York* 75-78; C Marton-in-Cleveland 78-80; V Newby 80-87; V Kirkleatham 87-95; V Kirkbymoorside w Gillamoor, Farndale etc 95-09; RD Helmsley 99-09; rtd 09; P-in-c Fylingdales and Hawsker cum Stainsacre *York* 10-12; Can and Preb York Minster 98-12; PtO from 12. *Drewann, Westfields, Kirkbymoorside, York YO62 6AG* T: (01751) 431809
M: 07504-428713 E: david.purdy@virgin.net

PURNELL, Marcus John. b 75. Ridley Hall Cam 07. **d** 09 **p** 10. C Northampton St Benedict *Pet* 09-12; V Cottesmore and Burley, Clipsham, Exton etc from 12. *The Rectory, 38 Main Street, Cottesmore, Oakham LE15 7DJ* T: (01572) 813031
M: 07535-639915 E: revmarcuspurnell@gmail.com

PURSER, Alan Gordon. b 51. Leic Univ BSc 73. Wycliffe Hall Ox 74. **d** 77 **p** 78. C Beckenham Ch Ch *Roch* 77-81; TV Barking St Marg w St Patr *Chelmsf* 81-84; R Kensington S Africa 84-88; Min Hadley Wood St Paul Prop Chpl *Lon* 88-03; UK Team Ldr Crosslinks from 03. *18 Salmon Lane, London E14 7LZ* T: (020) 7702 8741 M: 07802-888439
E: apurser@crosslinks.org

PURSER, Alec. **d** 10 **p** 11. NSM Abbeyleix w Ballyroan etc *C & O* 10-14; P-in-c Stradbally w Ballintubbert, Coraclone etc from 14. *The Rectory, Main Street, Stradbally, Co Laois, Republic of Ireland* M: (00353) 87-923 2694 E: familypurser@eircom.net

PURSER, Jillian. b 14. NSM Cullompton, Willand, Uffculme, Kentisbeare etc *Ex* from 14. *Leigh House, 3 Fore Street, Uffculme, Cullompton EX15 3AN* T: (01884) 840432

PURVEY-TYRER, Neil. b 66. Leeds Univ BA 87 MA 88. Westcott Ho Cam 88. **d** 90 **p** 91. C Denbigh and Nantglyn *St As* 90-92; Chapl Asst Basingstoke Distr Hosp 92-95; TV Cannock *Lich* 95-99; V Northampton H Sepulchre w St Andr and St Lawr *Pet* 99-02; Dioc Co-ord for Soc Resp 99-03; TR Duston 02-08; Chapl St Andr Hosp Northn 08-12; Hd of Chapl from 12; Past Care and Counselling Adv *Pet* 10-13. *St Andrew's Healthcare, Billing Road, Northampton NN1 5DG* T: (01604) 616379
E: ntyrer@standrew.co.uk

PURVIS, Sandra Anne. *See* TAUSON, Sandra Anne

PURVIS, Canon Stephen. b 48. AKC 70. **d** 71 **p** 72. C Peterlee *Dur* 71-75; Dioc Recruitment Officer 75-79; V Stevenage All SS Pin Green *St Alb* 79-88; TR Borehamwood 88-00; RD Aldenham 94-98; V Leagrave 00-13; RD Luton 07-12; Hon Can St Alb 02-13; rtd 13; PtO *St Alb* from 13. *23 Almeda Road, Bristol BS5 8RY* T: 0117-967 0507
E: stephen.purvis@yahoo.co.uk

PURVIS-LEE, Lynn. b 58. St Jo Coll Dur BA 97. Cranmer Hall Dur 94. **d** 98 **p** 99. C Gt Aycliffe *Dur* 98-02; Chapl N Tees and Hartlepool NHS Trust 02-14; R Penhill *Leeds* from 14. *The Vicarage, Carperby, Leyburn DL8 4DQ*
E: lynnhome28@gmail.com

PUSEY, Canon Ian John. b 39. Sarum Th Coll 69. **d** 71 **p** 72. C Waltham Abbey *Chelmsf* 71-75; TV Stantonbury *Ox* 75-80; P-in-c Bletchley 80-84; R 84-00; RD Milton Keynes 96-00; P-in-c Lamp 00-06; AD Newport 04-06; Hon Can Ch Ch 06; rtd 06. *16 Gussiford Lane, Exmouth EX8 2SF*
T: (01395) 275549 E: ian.pusey@btinternet.com

PUTNAM, Mrs Gillian. b 43. WEMTC 00. **d** 02 **p** 03. NSM Milton *B & W* 02-09; NSM Milton and Kewstoke from 09. *6 Miller Close, Weston-super-Mare BS23 2SQ* T: (01934) 416917
E: gillianputnam@yahoo.co.uk

PUTNAM, Jeremy James. b 76. Ripon Coll Cuddesdon 09. **d** 11 **p** 12. C Portishead *B & W* 11-15; P-in-c Highertown and Baldhu *Truro* from 14. *All Saints' Vicarage, Tresawis Road, Truro TR1 3LD* M: 07477-921397 E: jeremyjputnam@gmail.com

PUTT, Thomas David. b 83. Loughb Univ BEng 05. Oak Hill Th Coll BA 11. **d** 11 **p** 12. C Kirk Ella and Willerby *York* 11-15; Chapl Yeovil Coll *B & W* from 15; C Yeovil w Kingston Pitney from 15. *Yeovil College, Mudford Road, Yeovil BA21 4DR* M: 07824-337885 T: (01935) 423921 E: tomputt@gmail.com

✠PWAISIHO, The Rt Revd William Alaha. b 48. OBE 04. Bp Patteson Th Coll (Solomon Is) 71. **d** 74 **p** 75 **c** 81. Solomon Is 74-76; New Zealand 78-79; Solomon Is 79-95; Dean Honiara 80-81; Bp Malaita 81-89; Hon Asst Bp Ches from 97; C Sale St Anne 97-99; R Gawsworth 99-14; R Gawsworth w North Rode from 14. *The Rectory, Church Lane, Gawsworth, Macclesfield SK11 9RJ* T: (01260) 223201 M: 07711-241625
E: bishop.gawsworth@virgin.net

PYBUS, Antony Frederick. b 54. Birm Univ BA 77. Cranmer Hall Dur 78. **d** 81 **p** 82. C Ches H Trin 81-84; C W Hampstead St Jas *Lon* 84-89; V Alexandra Park St Andr 89-93; V Alexandra Park from 93. *The Vicarage, 34 Alexandra Park Road, London N10 2AB* T: (020) 8883 3181 *or* 8444 6898
E: office@alexandrapark.org *or* vicar@alexandrapark.org

PYE, Alexander Frederick. b 61. St Mich Coll Llan 93. **d** 95 **p** 96. C Griffithstown *Mon* 95-97; P-in-c Bistre *St As* 97-99; P-in-c Penmaen and Crumlin *Mon* 99-00; V 00-02; R Govilon w Llanfoist w Llanelen 02-09; V Beguildy and Heyope and Llangynllo and Bleddfa *S & B* 09-12; V Swansea St Pet from 12. *235 Cockett Road, Cockett, Swansea SA2 0FH* T: (01792) 588152
E: aok13@btinternet.com

PYE, Canon Allan Stephen. b 56. Univ of Wales (Lamp) BA 78 Lanc Univ MPhil 86. Westcott Ho Cam 79. **d** 81 **p** 82. C Scotforth *Blackb* 81-85; C Oswaldtwistle All SS 85-87; V Wrightington 87-91; P-in-c Hayton St Mary *Carl* 91-93; V Hayton w Cumwhitton 93-98; RD Brampton 95-98; P-in-c Hawkshead and Low Wray w Sawrey 98-03; V Hawkshead and Low Wray w Sawrey and Rusland etc 03-06; V Keswick St Jo 06-15; P-in-c Cross Fell Gp from 15; Hon Can Carl Cathl from 97. *1 Low Farm, Langwathby, Penrith CA10 1NH*
E: stephen.pye@virgin.net

PYE, Mrs Gay Elizabeth. b 46. RN 67 RM 68. Trin Coll Bris BD 73. **d** 96 **p** 96. NSM Castle Church *Lich* 96-00; Asst Chapl HM Pris Stafford 96-97; Chapl HM Pris Shrewsbury 97-00; Regional Manager Bible Soc 00-06; NSM Upper Derwent *Carl* 06-15; rtd 15. *5 Thorneyfields Lane, Stafford ST17 9YS* M: 07901-837813 T: *or* (01768) 777238
E: gay.pye@gmail.com

PYE, James Timothy. b 58. Oak Hill Th Coll BA 90. **d** 90 **p** 91. C Normanton *Derby* 90-94; R Talke *Lich* 94-04; R Knebworth *St Alb* from 04. *The Rectory, 15 St Martin's Road, Knebworth SG3 6ER* T: (01438) 817396 E: jim@jimpye.plus.com

PYE, Joseph Terence Hardwidge. b 41. MRICS 64. Trin Coll Bris 70. **d** 73 **p** 74. C Blackb Ch Ch 73-76; OMF 77-90; Korea 77-90; V Castle Church *Lich* 90-06; rtd 06; PtO *Carl* from 07. *5 Thorneyfields Lane, Stafford ST17 9YS*
E: terry.pye@gmail.com

PYE, Michael Francis. b 53. New Coll Ox BA 75 MA 78 DPhil 78. STETS 97. **d** 00 **p** 01. C Fareham H Trin *Portsm* 00-07; V Portsea All SS from 07. *All Saints' Vicarage, 51 Staunton Street, Portsmouth PO1 4EJ* T: (023) 9287 2815
E: mike@pye229.freeserve.co.uk

PYE, Nicholas Richard. b 62. Univ Coll Lon BA 84 Man Univ PGCE 87 Anglia Poly Univ MA 03. Ridley Hall Cam 95. **d** 98 **p** 99. C Epsom Common Ch Ch *Guildf* 98-01; C Harrow Trin St Mich *Lon* 01-03; V Finchley St Paul and St Luke from 03. *St Paul's Vicarage, 50 Long Lane, London N3 2PU* T: (020) 8346 8729 E: revpye@xalt.co.uk

PYE, Mrs Paula Jayne. b 67. St Jo Coll Dur BA 09 RGN 90. Cranmer Hall Dur 07. **d** 09 **p** 10. C Cockermouth Area *Carl* 09-12; Chapl RN from 12. *Royal Naval Chaplaincy Service, Mail Point 1.2, Leach Building, Whale Island, Portsmouth PO2 8BY* T: (023) 9262 5055 F: 9262 5134 E: paula@cateam.org.uk

PYE, Robin. b 63. All SS Cen for Miss & Min 12. **d** 15. C Hale and Ashley *Ches* from 15. *134 Cecil Road, Hale, Altrincham WA15 9NU* M: 07794-122602 E: revrobinpye@gmail.com

PYE, Sandra Anne. *See* ELLISON, Sandra Anne

PYE, Stephen. *See* PYE, Allan Stephen

PYKE, Alan. b 37. Trin Coll Bris BA 87. **d** 87 **p** 88. C Ipswich St Mary at Stoke w St Pet *St E* 87-90; R The Creetings and Earl Stonham w Stonham Parva 90-98; C S Trin Broads *Nor* 98-02; rtd 03; PtO *Nor* 03-08; *Leic* from 14. *29 Stuart Court, High Street, Kibworth, Leicester LE8 0LR* T: 0116-279 0113
E: alan.pyke@o2.co.uk

PYKE, Barry John. b 62. Qu Mary Coll Lon BSc 84 Southn Univ BTh 94 Open Univ BA 96 FGS 84. Sarum & Wells Th Coll 91. **d** 94 **p** 95. C Bengeworth *Worc* 94-96; C Worc City St Paul and Old St Martin etc 96-99; R Chipping Ongar w Shelley *Chelmsf* 99-06; RD Ongar 04-06; R Hinderwell, Roxby and Staithes etc *York* from 06; RD Whitby from 13. *The Rectory, 1 The High Street, Hinderwell, Saltburn-by-the-Sea TS13 5JX* T: (01947) 840249 E: bpyke@care4free.net

PYKE, Mrs Marion. b 41. **d** 10 **p** 11. OLM Caversham Thameside and Mapledurham *Ox* from 10. *26 Priest Hill, Caversham, Reading RG4 7RZ* T: 0118-947 5834

PYKE, Richard Ernest. b 50. Sarum & Wells Th Coll. **d** 82 **p** 83. C Bushey *St Alb* 82-85; C Gt Berkhamsted 85-89; V St Alb St Mary Marshalswick 89-00; TR Bp's Hatfield 00-05; TR Bp's Hatfield, Lemsford and N Mymms from 05; RD Hatfield from 03. *The Rectory, 1 Fore Street, Hatfield AL9 5AN* T/F: (01707) 262072
E: richard50pyke@tiscali.co.uk

PYKE, Mrs Ruth Cheryl. b 56. Bath Coll of HE BA 78 W Lon Inst of HE PGCE 80. SAOMC 95. **d** 98 **p** 99. C Leavesden *St Alb* 98-02; C St Alb St Steph 02-06; P-in-c Caddington 06-12; Bedfordshire Area Children's Work Adv 06-12; Dioc Children's Work Adv 12-15. *St Albans Diocesan Office, 41 Holywell Hill, St Albans AL1 1HE* T: (01727) 818178 M: 07787-112376 E: cwa@stalbans.anglican.org

PYKE, Thomas Fortune. b 62. St Chad's Coll Dur BA 85 Fitzw Coll Cam BA 88. Ridley Hall Cam 86. **d** 89 **p** 90. C Hitchin *St Alb* 89-94; Chapl Aston Univ *Birm* 94-99; V Birm St Paul 99-06; Ind Chapl 01-06; Th Ecum Officer Birm Bd for Miss 01-06; V Is of Dogs Ch Ch and St Jo w St Luke *Lon* from 06. *Christ Church Vicarage, Manchester Road, London E14 3BN* T: (020) 7538 1766   M: 07753-616499
E: tom.pyke@parishiod.org.uk

PYLE, John Alan. b 31. Qu Coll Birm. **d** 69 **p** 70. C Fenham St Jas and St Basil *Newc* 69-72; C Monkseaton St Pet 72-74; C Morpeth 74-78; R Bothal 78-83; TV Willington 83-91; V Chollerton w Birtley and Thockrington 91-97; rtd 97; PtO *Newc* from 97. *37 Ullswater Drive, Killingworth, Newcastle upon Tyne NE12 6GX* T: 0191-268 6044

PYM, David Pitfield. b 45. Nottm Univ BA 65 Ex Coll Ox DPhil 68. Ripon Hall Ox 66. **d** 68 **p** 69. C Nottingham St Mary *S'well* 68-72; Chapl RN 72-76 and 79-84; Chapl Worksop Coll Notts 76-79; R Avon Dassett w Farnborough and Fenny Compton *Cov* 84-07; rtd 07; PtO *Ox* from 07; *Cov* from 08. *Sunrise, Bury Court Lane, Shotteswell, Banbury OX17 1JA* T: (01295) 738948   E: davidpym@lineone.net

PYMBLE, Adam Oliver James. b 79. **d** 11 **p** 12. C Lindfield *Chich* 11-14; C Clerkenwell St Mark *Lon* from 14. *157 Park Road, London N8 8JJ* E: adampymble@gmail.com

PYNE, Robert Leslie. b 51. Lanchester Poly Cov BA 72 Solicitor 75. Coll of Resurr Mirfield 76. **d** 79 **p** 80. C Clifton All SS w St Jo *Bris* 79-81; Bp's Dom Chapl *Ox* 81-84; TV High Wycombe 84-90; Chapl RN 90-11; rtd 11; PtO *S'wark* from 11. *Holy Trinity Vicarage, 59 Southend Crescent, London SE9 2SD* T: (020) 8850 1246   E: rlp1951@tiscali.co.uk

PYNE-BAILEY, Mrs Sarian Iyamide Remilekun. b 40. Sierra Leone Th Hall 99. **d** 03 **p** 05. Sierra Leone 06-10; PtO *Chelmsf* from 11. *10 Hibiscus Lodge, 1A Glenavon Road, London E15 4DT* T: (020) 8279 4221   M: 07415-995370
E: iyamidepb@ymail.com

PYNN, Catherine. b 45. Reading Univ BSc 67. SAOMC 93. **d** 96 **p** 97. NSM Caversham St Pet and Mapledurham etc *Ox* 96-03; NSM Aldermaston w Wasing and Brimpton 03-06; NSM Woolhampton w Midgham and Beenham Valance 05-06; Chapl Bradfield Coll Berks 00-06; NSM Kintbury w Avington *Ox* 06-11; NSM W Woodhay w Enborne, Hampstead Marshall etc 06-11; NSM Walbury Beacon 11-13; PtO from 13; *Win* from 13. *27 Silchester Road, Pamber Heath, Tadley RG26 3ED* T: 0118-970 1007   M: 07863-968624
E: cathy.pynn@btinternet.com

PYNN, David Christopher. b 47. Trin Coll Cam MA 70 Cam Inst of Educn CertEd 69. NOC 06. **d** 08 **p** 09. NSM Scalby *York* from 08; NSM Scarborough St Luke from 08; RD Scarborough from 11; NSM Cloughton and Burniston from 14; NSM Ravenscar and Staintondale from 14. *6 Stepney Drive, Scarborough YO12 5DH* T: (01723) 369687   M: 07980-922208
E: davidpynn12@aol.com

✠**PYTCHES, The Rt Revd George Edward David.** b 31. Bris Univ BA 54 Nottm Univ MPhil 84. Tyndale Hall Bris 51. **d** 55 **p** 56 **c** 70. C Ox St Ebbe 55-58; C Wallington *S'wark* 58-59; Chile 59-77; Suff Bp Valparaiso 70-72; Bp Chile, Bolivia and Peru 72-77; V Chorleywood St Andr *St Alb* 77-96; rtd 96; PtO *St Alb* from 96. *5 Churleswood Court, Shire Lane, Chorleywood, Rickmansworth WD3 5NH*

PYTCHES, Preb Peter Norman Lambert. b 32. Lon Univ BD 57 Bris Univ MLitt 67 Southn Univ PhD 81 K Coll Lon MA 00 Potchefstroom Univ MTh 03 Open Univ MPhil 06 Lambeth STh 74. Tyndale Hall Bris 53. **d** 57 **p** 58. C Heatherlands St Jo *Sarum* 57-61; C Cromer *Nor* 61-63; V Plymouth St Jude *Ex* 63-71; V Heatherlands St Jo *Sarum* 71-76; Dir Past Tr Oak Hill Th Coll 76-81; V Finchley Ch Ch *Lon* 81-91; AD Cen Barnet 86-91; V Forty Hill Jes Ch 91-97; Preb St Paul's Cathl 92-97; rtd 97; PtO *Lon* from 98. *25 Weardale Gardens, Enfield EN2 0BA* T/F: (020) 8366 5126
E: peterpytches@googlemail.com

Q

QUANTRILL, Mrs Sarah Ellen. b 67. Newnham Coll Cam BA 90 MA 93 UEA PGCE 92. Westcott Ho Cam 13. **d** 15. C Oulton Broad *Nor* from 15. *76 Westwood Avenue, Lowestoft NR33 9RL* T: (01986) 896991   E: sarah.quantrill@cantab.net

QUARMBY, David John. b 43. St Jo Coll Dur BA 64 Lon Univ CertEd 70 Man Univ MEd 89 Sheff Univ MA 99. Ridley Hall Cam 65. **d** 67 **p** 68. C Bournville *Birm* 67-71; V Erdington St Chad 71-73; LtO *Blackb* 73-83; PtO *Man* 83-90 and from 98; C Oldham St Paul 90-98; Hon C 98-14; Hon C Oldham St Paul and Werneth from 14; Cllr Huddersfield Poly 90-92; Huddersfield Univ 92-01; Prin Adult Psychotherapist Hyndburn Community Mental Health Team from 00; Sen Cllr Blackb and Darwen Primary Care Trust 01-08. *30 College Avenue, Oldham OL8 4DS* T: 0161-626 2771
E: david.quarmby@zen.co.uk

QUARTON, Robert Edward. b 43. Wilson Carlile Coll 64 EMMTC 84. **d** 87 **p** 88. C Gresley *Derby* 87-88; C Clay Cross 88-90; C N Wingfield, Clay Cross and Pilsley 90-91; R Darley 91-10; P-in-c S Darley, Elton and Winster 03-10; RD Wirksworth 03-08; rtd 10. *12 Blenheim Avenue, Swanwick, Alfreton DE55 1PQ* T: (01773) 605766
E: robertquarton@uwclub.net

QUASH, Canon Jonathan Ben. b 68. Peterho Cam BA 90 MA 94 PhD 99. Westcott Ho Cam 91. **d** 95 **p** 96. NSM Cambridge St Mary Less *Ely* 95-96; Asst Chapl Peterho Cam 95-96; Chapl Fitzw Coll Cam 96-99; Fell 98-99; Tutor Wesley Ho Cam 96-99; Fell and Dean Peterho Cam 99-07; Prof K Coll Lon from 07; Can Th Cov Cathl from 04; Can Th Bradf Cathl from 13. *King's College London, Strand, London WC2R 2LS* T: (020) 7848 2336 F: 7848 2255   E: ben.quash@kcl.ac.uk

QUAYLE, Margaret Grace. b 28. Gipsy Hill Coll of Educn TCert 48 Lon Univ BA 53 Liv Univ MPhil 78. **d** 98 **p** 99. OLM Gt Crosby St Luke *Liv* 98-03; PtO from 03. *Clwyd, 9 Myers Road West, Liverpool L23 0RS* T: 0151-924 1659

QUAYLE, Martin Stuart. b 60. Lon Hosp BDS 82 Birkbeck Coll Lon BA 98 Leeds Univ BA 08 Open Univ MA 11. Coll of Resurr Mirfield 06. **d** 08 **p** 09. C Basingstoke *Win* 08-11; PtO *Heref* 12-14; C Diddlebury w Munslow, Holdgate and Tugford from 14. *3 Stanway Barns, Stanway, Rushbury, Church Stretton SY6 7EF* T: (01584) 841840   M: 07976-664872
E: martinsq@btinternet.com

QUIBELL, Edward Villiers. b 71. Anglia Poly BSc 93 Hughes Hall Cam PGCE 94. Trin Coll Bris BA 03. **d** 03 **p** 04. C Swindon Ch Ch *Bris* 03-06; PtO *Lon* 06-08; TV Broadwater *Chich* 08-14; rtd 14. *9 Foster Lane, Ashington, Pulborough RH20 3PG* E: revted@hotmail.co.uk

QUIBELL, Mrs Susan Elizabeth. b 50. **d** 03 **p** 04. OLM Aldridge *Lich* from 03. *20 Summer Lane, Walsall WS4 1DS* T: (01922) 744205   E: s.quibell@googlemail.com

QUICK, Mrs Janet. b 42. **d** 12 **p** 13. OLM Whittington *Derby* from 12. *72 Highfield Lane, Chesterfield S41 8AY* T: (01246) 201701
E: janetquick@btopenworld.com

QUICK, John Michael. b 46. N Counties Coll Newc TCert 68 Birkbeck Coll Lon BSc 73 FRGS 70. SAOMC 97. **d** 00 **p** 01. OLM New Windsor *Ox* from 00. *White Roses, 45 York Road, Windsor SL4 3PA* T: (01753) 865557   M: 07977-754822
E: littlefrquick@aol.com

QUICK, Roger Aelfred Melvin Tricquet. b 55. Leeds Univ BA 79 BA 96 PGCE 81. Coll of Resurr Mirfield 94. **d** 96 **p** 97. C Chapel Allerton *Ripon* 96-00; C Ireland Wood 00-04; Chapl Strathallan Sch 04-11; R Pitlochry *St And* 11-13; R Kilmaveonaig 11-13; R Kinloch Rannoch 11-13; Chapl to the Homeless *Leeds* from 13. *St George's Crypt, Great George Street, Leeds LS1 3BR* T: 0113-245 9061   M: 07762-159047
E: chaplain@stgeorgescrypt.org.uk

QUIGLEY, Adam. **d** 03 **p** 04. NSM Castlerock w Dunboe and Fermoyle *D & R* from 03. *41 Queens Park, Coleraine BT51 3JS* T: (028) 7035 5191

QUIGLEY, Andrew. b 72. New Coll Ox BA 96 Bris Univ PGCE 98. St Jo Coll Nottm MTh 03. **d** 04 **p** 05. C Burbage w Aston Flamville *Leic* 04-07; TV Market Harborough and The Transfiguration etc from 07. *The Vicarage, 49 Ashley Road, Market Harborough LE16 7XD* T: (01858) 463441
E: a.quigley@ntlworld.com

QUIGLEY, Donna Maree. b 40. Ulster Univ BEd BTh. **d** 01 **p** 02. C Portadown St Columba *Arm* 01-03; I Derryvolgie *Conn* 04-09. *284 Tennent Street, Belfast BT13 3GG*
E: donna_quigley@yahoo.co.uk

QUIGLEY, John Christopher. b 41. Pontifical Lateran Univ STL 68. **d** 67 **p** 68. P-in-c N Bersted *Chich* 03-08; rtd 08; P-in-c Lyminster *Chich* from 11. *The Vicarage, The Paddock, Lyminster, Littlehampton BN17 7QH* M: 07792-718875
E: john.quigley4@btinternet.com

QUILL, Andrew Thomas Edward. b 67. Heriot-Watt Univ BArch 91. Uganda Chr Univ 05. **d** 05 **p** 07. Dioc Co-ord Community Health Empowerment Uganda 05-06;

C Drumragh w Mountfield *D & R* 06-09; I Kinawley w H Trin *K, E & A* from 09; Dioc Communications Officer from 10. *The Rectory, 144A Main Street, Cloghan, Derrylin, Enniskillen BT92 9LD* T: (028) 6774 8994 M: 07738-960707 E: quills155@btinternet.com *or* kinawley@kilmore.anglican.org

QUILL, John Stephen. b 51. Linc Th Coll 76. d 79 p 80. C Sawbridgeworth *St Alb* 79-81; C Watford Ch Ch 81-85; Dioc Soc Services Adv *Worc* 85-90; Adv to Bd of Soc Resp 90-95; PtO *St Alb* 07-14; Chapl R Masonic Sch for Girls Rickmansworth from 14; PtO *S & B* from 13. *35 Kingfisher Drive, Hemel Hempstead HP3 9DD* T: (01442) 266369 *or* 266369 *or* 773168 E: johnsquill@btopenworld.com

QUILL, Walter Paterson. b 35. MBE . d 60 p 61. C Glendermott *D & R* 60-63; I Kilbarron 63-66; I Kilcronaghan w Ballynascreen 66-81; I Derg w Termonamongan 81-07; Can Derry Cathl 89-07; Preb Howth St Patr Cathl Dublin 94-07; rtd 07; P-in-c Clondevaddock w Portsalon and Leatbeg *D & R* 09-11. *1 University Gardens, Coleraine BT52 1JT* T: (028) 7035 2114 E: wquill@btinternet.com

QUIN, David Christopher. b 42. SAOMC 97. d 00 p 01. NSM Blunham, Gt Barford, Roxton and Tempsford etc *St Alb* 00-06; rtd 06. *16 Beceshore Close, Moreton-in-Marsh GL56 9NB* T: (01608) 651571 M: 07867-664924 E: davidcquin@aol.com

QUIN, Eric Arthur. b 22. Magd Coll Cam BA 46 MA 48 Lon Univ BD 56. Bps' Coll Cheshunt 46. d 48 p 49. C Luton St Andr *St Alb* 48-50; C Barnoldswick w Bracewell *Bradf* 50-52; PC Bradf St Sav 52-57; P-in-c Gt w Lt Wymondley *St Alb* 57-58; P-in-c St Ippolyts 57-58; V 58-70; RD Hitchin 68-70; V Haynes 70-87; rtd 87; PtO *Ches* from 87. *Annabel's Cottage, 4 The Lydiate, Wirral CH60 8PR* T: 0151-342 8650

QUIN, John James Neil. b 31. Ox Univ MA DipEd 53. Qu Coll Birm 61. d 63 p 64. C Cannock *Lich* 63-68; V Sneyd Green 68-78; V Stafford St Paul Forebridge 78-90; TV Tettenhall Regis 90-98; PtO *Ex* from 00. *Watcombe House, 28 Barnpark Road, Teignmouth TQ14 8PN* T: (01626) 772525

QUINE, Christopher Andrew. b 38. St Aid Birkenhead 61. d 64 p 65. C Hunts Cross *Liv* 64-67; C Farnworth and C-in-c Widnes St Jo 67-71; V Clubmoor 71-78; V Formby H Trin 78-99; V Arbory and Santan *S & M* 99-03; rtd 03. *15 Sandringham Road, Formby, Liverpool L37 6EG* M: 07963-588332 E: chris.quine@googlemail.com

QUINE, David Anthony. b 28. Qu Coll Cam BA 52 MA 59. Ridley Hall Cam 53. d 55 p 56. C Beckenham Ch Ch *Roch* 55-59; C Normanton *Derby* 59-60; V Low Elswick *Newc* 60-66; V Houghton *Carl* 66-68; LtO *York* 68-71; Chapl Monkton Combe Sch Bath 71-85; rtd 85; PtO *Carl* from 85. *Briar Cragg, Gale Rigg, Ambleside LA22 0AZ* T: (01539) 433563

✠**QUINLAN, The Rt Revd Alan Geoffrey.** b 33. Kelham Th Coll 54. d 58 p 59 c 88. C Bedford Leigh *Man* 58-61; R Bloemfontein St Marg S Africa 61-68; R Sasolburg 68-70; R Parys 70-72; Warden CR and Chapl Grahamstown Coll 72-76; R Plumstead All SS 76-88; Can Cape Town 80-88; Suff Bp Cape Town (Cen Region) 88-98; rtd 98. *132 Woodley Road, Plumstead, Cape Town, 7800 South Africa* T/F: (0027) (21) 705 1452

QUINN, Canon Arthur Hamilton Riddel. b 37. TCD BA 60 MA 64 BD 67. d 61 p 62. C Belfast H Trin *Conn* 61-63; C Belfast St Mary Magd 63-64; Chapl Hull Univ *York* 64-69; Chapl Keele Univ *Lich* 69-74; P-in-c Keele 72-74; V Shirley

St Jo *Cant* 74-84; V *S'wark* 85-06; RD Croydon Addington 95-04; Hon Can S'wark Cathl 03-06; rtd 06; PtO *S'wark* from 06. *23 Eden Road, Croydon CR0 1BB* T: 020 8680 3049 E: quinncanon@btinternet.com

QUINN, Canon Derek John. b 55. TCD BTh 88. d 88 p 89. C Mossley *Conn* 88-91; I Cappagh w Lislimnaghan *D & R* from 91; Bp's Dom Chapl from 00; Dioc Warden of Readers from 04; Can Derry Cathl from 07. *Erganagh Rectory, 1 Erganagh Road, Omagh BT79 7SX* T: (028) 8224 2572

QUINN, Eugene Frederick. b 35. Allegheny Coll (USA) AB 57 Univ of California MA 66 MA 69 PhD 70. Vancouver Sch of Th 71. d 74 p 75. C Washington St Columba USA 74-75; and 78-81; Chapl Prague *Eur* 75-78; C Chevy Chase All SS USA 81-82; and 86-90; Chapl Nat Cathl Washington 81-82; and from 95; C Washington Epiphany 83 and 86-88; V Bowie St Jas 82-84; Chapl Warsaw *Eur* 93-95. *5702 Kirkside Drive, Chevy Chase MD 20815-7116, USA* E: efquinn@msn.com

QUINN, George Bruce. b 23. MBE 05. d 82 p 83. NSM Douglas St Ninian *S & M* 82-05. *85 Port-e-Chee Avenue, Douglas, Isle of Man IM2 5EZ* T: (01624) 674080

QUINN, John James. b 46. TCD BA 70 PhD 76. St Jo Coll Nottm. d 81 p 82. C Gorleston St Andr *Nor* 81-84; R Belton 84-90; R Burgh Castle 84-90; R Belton and Burgh Castle 90-10; rtd 10; PtO *Nor* from 10. *23 Wren Drive, Bradwell, Great Yarmouth NR31 8JW* T: (01493) 718634 E: johnjquinn@lineone.net

QUINN, Kenneth Norman. b 40. QUB BSc 62 CEng MICE. CITC 80. d 85 p 86. NSM Seapatrick *D & D* 85-09; rtd 09. *4 Knollwood, Seapatrick, Banbridge BT32 4PE* T: (028) 4062 3515 E: ken.quinn3@btinternet.com

QUINN, Marjorie. d 94 p 97. NSM Hawarden *St As* 94-05; LtO from 05. *21 Hawarden Way, Mancot, Deeside CH5 2EL* T: (01244) 531639

QUINN, Naomi. d 11 p 12. C Derg w Termonamongan *D & R* from 11. *75 Castlefin Road, Castlederg BT81 7EE* T: (028) 8167 1440 E: ncquinnw@yahoo.co.uk

QUINNELL, Peter Francis. b 48. St Steph Ho Ox 93. d 95 p 96. C Tewkesbury w Walton Cardiff *Glouc* 95-99; R Stratton, N Cerney, Baunton and Bagendon 99-08; AD Cirencester 06-08; R Whitewater *Win* 08-14; rtd 14; Hon C Tetbury, Beverston, Long Newnton etc *Glouc* 14-15; Hon C Avening w Cherington 14-15; TV Stroud Team from 15. *The Vicarage, 58 Cashes Green Road, Stroud GL5 4RA* E: quinnell708@btinternet.com

QUINT, Mrs Patricia Mary. b 51. Milton Keynes Coll of Ed CertEd 76 Open Univ BA 77 Lon Univ MA 99. St Alb Minl Tr Scheme 90. d 93 p 94. C Hertford St Andr *St Alb* 93-96; C Bromham w Oakley and Stagsden 96-00; V Stotfold and Radwell 00-14; rtd 14; PtO *St E* from 15. *Upper Church Cottage, Church Hill, Walpole, Halesworth IP19 9AX* T: (01986) 784565 E: revquint@hotmail.com

QUINTON, Rosemary Ruth. *See* BRABY, Rosemary Ruth

QUIREY, Mrs Edith. b 56. CITC 98. d 01 p 02. Aux Min Belfast St Mich *Conn* 01-05; P-in-c Belfast St Steph w St Luke 05-07; Bp's C 07-09; I 09-15; P-in-c Hodnet *Lich* from 15. *Address temp unknown* E: edith.quirey@tesco.net

QUIST, Ms Frances Buckurel. NTMTC BA 09. d 09 p 10. C E Ham w Upton Park and Forest Gate *Chelmsf* 09-12; P-in-c Matson *Glouc* from 12. *The Rectory, Matson Lane, Gloucester GL4 6DX* T: (01452) 522598 M: 07734-711929 E: francesquist@btinternet.com

R

✠**RABENIRINA, The Rt Revd Remi Joseph.** b 38. Antananarivo Univ LèsL 83. St Paul's Coll Ambatoharanana 61 St Chad's Coll Dur 64 Bossey Ecum Inst Geneva. d 67 p 68 c 84. Dn Toamasina St Jas Madagascar 67; T St Matt Pro-Cathl Antsiranana 68-73; R Ambohimangakely St Jo 73-84; Angl Chapl Antananarivo Univ 73-84; Bp Antananarivo 84-08; Abp Indian Ocean 95-05; rtd 08. *Fonenana Nirina I, Andranomahery, Anosiala, 105 Ambohidratrimo, Madagascar* T: (00261) (2) 247 4852 M: 3311-20827

RABIN, Peter David. b 62. Southlands Coll Lon BA 86. Aston Tr Scheme 88 Ripon Coll Cuddesdon BTh 93. d 93 p 94. C Hornsey St Mary w St Geo *Lon* 93-97; V Cricklewood St Pet 97-07; C S Ockendon and Belhus Park *Chelmsf* 07-13; TV Mardyke from 13. *The Rectory, North Road, South Ockendon RM15 6QJ* T: (01708) 855321 E: frrabin@sky.com

RABJOHNS, Alan. b 40. Leeds Univ BA 62. Coll of Resurr Mirfield 62. d 64 p 65. C Ashington *Newc* 64-67; C Upton

cum Chalvey *Ox* 67-76; V Roath St Sav *Llan* 76-08; AD Cardiff 03-08; rtd 08. *40 Cwmgelli Close, Treboeth, Swansea SA5 9BY* T: (01792) 561157

RABJOHNS, Benjamin Thomas. b 86. Ex Univ BA 07 Cardiff Univ BA 11. St Mich Coll Llan 08. d 11 p 12. C Aberavon *Llan* 11-14; TV from 14. *The Vicarage, 44 Ynys y Gored, Port Talbot SA13 2EB* T: (01639) 698878 E: b.t.rabjohns@gmail.com

RABLEN, Antony Ford. b 52. Hatf Coll Dur BA 74. St Jo Coll Nottm BA 81. d 82 p 83. C Clifton *York* 82-85; TV Marfleet 85-92; P-in-c Welton w Melton 92-00; TR Sutton St Jas and Wawne 00-05; Chapl R Brompton and Harefield NHS Trust 05-07; Chapl Oxon & Bucks Mental Health Partnership NHS Trust 05-11; Chapl NHS SW Essex Community Services 11-12; V Becontree St Cedd *Chelmsf* from 12; Chapl NE Lon Foundn Trust from 14. *St Cedd's Vicarage, 185 Lodge Avenue, Dagenham RM8 2HQ* M: 07713-122917 E: vicarstcedds@btinternet.com

RABLEN, Mrs Christine Mary. b 52. Trevelyan Coll Dur BA 74 Hull Univ BA 92 Leeds Univ MA 94. NOC 00. **d** 02 **p** 03. C Sutton St Mich *York* 02-05; V Roxbourne St Andr *Lon* 05-11; V Leyton St Mary w St Edw and St Luke *Chelmsf* from 11. *Leyton Vicarage, 4 Vicarage Road, London E10 5EA* T: (020) 8558 5766 E: christinerablen@dsl.pipex.com

RABY, Malcolm Ernest. b 47. St Jo Coll York BEd 73. NOC 81. **d** 84 **p** 85. NSM Chadkirk *Ches* 84-88; Consultant E England CPAS 88-94; C Ely 94-96; TV 96-98; Dioc Adv in Miss and Evang 98-13; P-in-c Over 98-13; P-in-c Long Stanton w St Mich 02-13; rtd 13; Hon C Leatherhead and Mickleham *Guildf* from 13. *The Rectory, London Road, Mickleham, Dorking RH5 6EB* T: (01372) 378335

RACE, Alan. b 51. Bradf Univ BTech 73 Birm Univ MA 82. Ripon Coll Cuddesdon 73. **d** 76 **p** 77. C Tupsley *Heref* 76-79; Asst Chapl Kent Univ *Cant* 79-84; Dir Studies S'wark Ord Course 84-94; R Aylestone St Andr w St Jas *Leic* 94-07; P-in-c Leic St Phil 07-11; Hon Can Leic Cathl 07-11; R Lee St Marg S'wark from 11. *St Margaret's Rectory, Brandram Road, London SE13 5EA* E: alan.race@ntlworld.com

RACE, Andrew James. b 68. Birm Univ BA 92 MA 93. Ripon Coll Cuddesdon MTh 15. **d** 15. C Littleover *Derby* from 15. *28 Earlswood Drive, Mickleover, Derby DE3 5GA*

RACE, Christopher Keith. b 43. St Paul's Coll Grahamstown 76. **d** 78 **p** 80. Angl Chapl Stellenbosch Univ S Africa 79-81; R Kalk Bay 81-83; P-in-c E Kalahari, Dioc Admin Botswana and Personal Asst to Abp Cen Africa 83-86; V Tanworth St Patr Salter Street *Birm* 86-96; P-in-c Rothiemurchus *Mor* 96-01; PtO *Glouc* 02-03; P-in-c Kemble, Poole Keynes, Somerford Keynes etc 03-04; R 04-06; Prin Tutor and Lect Cant Ch Ch Univ 06-08; rtd 08. *c/o the Revd S P Race, The Vicarage, Green Road, Dodworth, Barnsley S75 3RT* M: 07866-585973 E: ck.race@gmail.com

RACE, John Arthur. b 37. SAOMC 95. **d** 98 **p** 99. OLM Haddenham w Cuddington, Kingsey etc *Ox* 98-08; PtO from 08. *8 The Closes, Haddenham, Aylesbury HP17 8JN* T: (01844) 290180

RACE, Canon Stephen Peter. b 69. SS Hild & Bede Coll Dur BA 93. St Steph Ho Ox MTh 03. **d** 02 **p** 03. C Wigton *Carl* 02-05; V Dodworth *Leeds* 05-14; P-in-c Barnsley St Mary *Wakef* from 14; Asst Dioc Dir of Ords 05-09; Dir from 09; RD Barnsley *Leeds* from 09; Hon Can Wakef Cathl from 11. *22 Elmwood Way, Barnsley S75 1EY* E: stephen.race@westyorkshiredales.anglican.org

RACKLYEFT, Emma Joy. b 79. Univ Coll Chich BA 01. Wycliffe Hall Ox BTh 13. **d** 13 **p** 14. C Thame *Ox* from 13. *71 Seven Acres, Thame OX9 3JQ* M: 07837-845420 E: emma@theracklyefts.co.uk

RACTLIFFE, Dudley John. b 38. Man Univ BA 62. Ridley Hall Cam 63. **d** 66 **p** 67. C Radford *Cov* 66-68; C Haslemere *Guildf* 69-73; V Perry Beeches *Birm* 73-78; V Worle *B & W* 78-88; Dioc Ecum Officer and R Dowlishwake w Kingstone, Chillington etc 88-93; TR Swanage and Studland *Sarum* 93-01; rtd 01; PtO *B & W* from 02. *12 Sid Lane, Sidmouth EX10 9AN* T: (01395) 579712

RADCLIFFE, Canon Albert Edward. b 34. Lon Univ BD 63. St Aid Birkenhead Ch Div Sch of the Pacific (USA) 61. **d** 62 **p** 63. C Knotty Ash St Jo *Liv* 62-64; C Blundellsands St Nic 64-66; Chapl Haifa St Luke Israel 66-69; V Tonge w Alkrington *Man* 69-77; R Ashton St Mich 77-91; AD Ashton-under-Lyne 87-91; Can Res Man Cathl 91-00; rtd 00; PtO *Man* from 01. *26 St Chad's Road, Withington, Manchester M20 4WH* T: 0161-445 1327

RADCLIFFE, David Jeffrey. b 52. Linc Th Coll 77. **d** 79 **p** 80. C Poulton-le-Fylde *Blackb* 79-84; V Ingol 84-88; R Lowther and Askham *Carl* 88-96; R Lowther and Askham and Clifton and Brougham 96-06; R Upton-on-Severn, Ripple, Earls Croome etc *Worc* 06-11; P-in-c W Preston *Blackb* from 11. *St Michael's Vicarage, 2 Egerton Road, Ashton-on-Ribble, Preston PR2 1AJ* T: (01772) 726157 E: revjeffradcliffe@hotmail.co.uk

RADCLIFFE, Eileen Rose. b 54. Carl Dioc Tr Inst 92. **d** 95 **p** 96. NSM Gt Salkeld w Lazonby *Carl* 95-96; NSM Dacre 99-02; PtO 02-06; *Worc* 06-08; NSM Upton-on-Severn, Ripple, Earls Croome etc 08-11; PtO from 11; *Blackb* from 11. *St Michael's Vicarage, 2 Egerton Road, Ashton-on-Ribble, Preston PR2 1AJ* T: (01772) 726157

RADCLIFFE, James. b 75. Rob Coll Cam MA 98. Oak Hill Th Coll BA 08. **d** 08 **p** 09. C Hove Bp Hannington Memorial Ch *Chich* 08-13; R Lavant from 13. *The Rectory, Pook Lane, East Lavant, Chichester PO18 0AH* T: (01243) 527313 M: 07941-248213 E: therectoratlavant@gmail.com

RADCLIFFE, John Frederick. b 39. **d** 01 **p** 02. OLM Meltham *Leeds* from 01. *13 Orchard Close, Meltham, Huddersfield HD9 4EG* T: (01484) 348806 E: johnandenid@yahoo.com

RADCLIFFE, Robert Mark. b 63. Cranmer Hall Dur 05. **d** 08 **p** 09. C Welling *Roch* 08-11; P-in-c Erith St Jo 11-12; V from

12. St John's Church House, 100 Park Crescent, Erith DA8 3DZ T: (01322) 332555 E: markradcliffe@msn.com

RADCLIFFE, Mrs Rosemary. b 45. SWMTC 87. **d** 90 **p** 94. NSM Devoran *Truro* 90-93; Dn-in-c N Newton w St Michaelchurch, Thurloxton etc *B & W* 93-94; P-in-c 94-00; Chapl to the Deaf 93-96; P-in-c Whipton *Ex* 00-01; rtd 01; PtO *Truro* from 03. *76 Upland Crescent, Truro TR1 1NE* T: (01872) 273906

RADCLIFFE, Rosie. *See* RADCLIFFE, Eileen Rose

RADFORD, Mrs Janet. b 58. Chelt & Glouc Coll of HE BSc 00 RN 79. Ripon Coll Cuddesdon 11. **d** 14 **p** 15. NSM Harwell w Chilton *Ox* from 14; Chapl Ox Univ Hosps NHS Trust from 14. *1 The Croft, Marcham, Abingdon OX13 6NF* T: (01865) 391282 E: janradford58@yahoo.com

RADFORD, Vincent Arthur. b 45. Ches Coll of HE CertEd 69. **d** 05 **p** 06. OLM Westhoughton and Wingates *Man* 05-13; OLM Daisy Hill, Westhoughton and Wingates from 13. *64 Molyneux Road, Westhoughton, Bolton BL5 3EU* T: (01942) 790091 E: vincent.radford@ntlworld.com

RADLEY, Mrs Jean Frances. b 40. Man Univ RGN 62 Univ Coll Lon RSCN 65 Cen Lancs Univ BSc 95. **d** 00 **p** 01. OLM Kendal St Geo *Carl* 00-07; OLM Beacon from 07. *21 Gallowbarrow, Natland Road, Kendal LA9 7RU* T: (01539) 738046 M: 07714-020189 E: jeanradley@btconnect.com *or* rev.jean@beaconteam.org.uk

RADLEY, Richard Brian. b 68. St Jo Coll Nottm 02. **d** 04 **p** 05. C Utley *Bradf* 04-08; P-in-c Doncaster St Mary *Sheff* 09-10; P-in-c Wheatley Park 09-10; V Doncaster St Mary and St Paul 10-15; TV Billingham *Dur* from 15. *68 Wolviston Road, Billingham TS22 5ET* E: radley@radleyfamily.fsnet.co.uk

RADLEY, Stephen John. b 68. St Jo Coll Nottm BTh 96. **d** 96 **p** 97. C Boulton *Derby* 96-00; Chapl RAF from 00. *Chaplaincy Services (RAF), HQ Air Command, RAF High Wycombe HP14 4UE* T: (01494) 496800 F: 496343

RAE, Stephen Gordon. b 65. AGSM 87. Oak Hill Th Coll BA 09. **d** 09 **p** 10. C Danehill *Chich* 09-13; V Westgate St Jas *Cant* from 13. *The Vicarage, Orchard Gardens, Margate CT9 5JT* T: (01825) 700615 M: 07776-147212 E: stephen@raefamily.net

RAE SMITH, Tristram Geoffrey. b 57. Clare Coll Cam BA 79 MA 83 St Jo Coll Dur BA 04. Cranmer Hall Dur 02. **d** 04 **p** 05. C Bradford-on-Avon Ch Ch *Sarum* 04-08; C Westwood and Wingfield 04-08; R Camelot Par *B & W* from 08; C Bruton and Distr 08-12. *The Rectory, 6 The Close, North Cadbury, Yeovil BA22 7DX* T: (01963) 440585 M: 07751-306272

RAFFAY, Julian Paul. b 60. Stirling Univ BSc 84. Cranmer Hall Dur BA 90. **d** 90 **p** 91. C Adel *Ripon* 90-93; C Leeds Halton St Wilfrid 93-95; Asst Chapl S Derbys Mental Health NHS Trust 95-97; TV Gleadless *Sheff* 97-01; V Deepcar 01-07; Chapl Team Ldr Sheff Care Trust 07-14; Specialist Research Chapl Mersey Care NHS Trust from 14. *Chaplaincy, Mersey Care NHS Trust, Ashworth Hospital, Parkbourn, Liverpool L31 1HW* T: 0151-471 2608 E: julian.raffay@merseycare.nhs.uk

RAGAN, Mrs Jennifer Mary. b 39. Linc Th Coll 71. **dss** 80 **d** 87 **p** 94. Par Dn Hornchurch St Andr *Chelmsf* 87-88; Par Dn Ingrave St Steph CD 88-90; Par Dn Gt Parndon 90-94; C 94-99; TV 99-07; rtd 07; PtO *Chelmsf* from 07; *St E* from 07. *18 Holme Oaks Court, 50 Cliff Lane, Ipswich IP3 0PE* T: (01473) 213577 E: revjenniferragan@btinternet.com

RAGBOURNE, Miss Pamela Mary. b 27. CertEd 47. Dalton Ho Bris 53. **dss** 76 **d** 87 **p** 94. CPAS Staff 68-79; Tottenham St Jo *Lon* 79-81; Gt Cambridge Road St Jo and St Jas 82-84; Camberley St Paul *Guildf* 84-86; rtd 87; PtO *Glouc* 87-93 and 97-05; NSM Winchcombe, Gretton, Sudeley Manor etc 93-97. *14 Crispin Close, Winchcombe, Cheltenham GL54 5JY* T: (01242) 603489

RAGGETT, Anita Jane. b 56. NOC. **d** 07 **p** 08. C Gomersal *Wakef* 07-10; C Cleckheaton St Jo 08-10; P-in-c Lepton *Leeds* from 10; Chapl Huddersfield Univ from 10. *The Vicarage, 138 Wakefield Road, Lepton, Huddersfield HD8 0LU* T: (01484) 606126 E: anita.raggett061@btinternet.com

RAHI, Hakim Banta Singh. b 36. Union Bibl Sem Yavatmal BD 71. **d** 74 **p** 74. India 74-83; In URC 83-88; PtO *Birm* 88-93; Ecum Evang Asian Community 88-93. *Flat 5, 12 Taverners Gree, Birmingham B20 2JJ*

RAHILLY, Philip James. b 54. Univ of Wales (Cardiff) BD 86. Wycliffe Hall Ox 86. **d** 88 **p** 89. C Knightwick w Doddenham, Broadwas and Cotheridge *Worc* 88; C Martley and Wichenford, Knightwick etc 89-91; C Worc St Barn w Ch Ch 91-92; TV Kidderminster St Mary and All SS w Trimpley etc 92-95; P-in-c Childe Okeford, Okeford Fitzpaine, Manston etc *Sarum* 95-00; P-in-c Shilling Okeford 99-00; R Okeford 00-06; P-in-c Stogursey w Fiddington *B & W* 06-07; R Quantock Coast 07-11; rtd 11. *Address withheld by request*

RAI, Mrs Mary Anne. b 61. La Sainte Union Coll BTh 83 PGCE 84. Trin Coll Bris 85. **dss** 86 **d** 87 **p** 99. Bury St Edmunds St Mary *St E* 86-89; Par Dn 87-89; PtO 90-93;

Cov 94-99 and from 02; NSM Styvechale 99-01. *61 Malthouse Lane, Kenilworth CV8 1AD* T: (01926) 732223 E: maryrai777@gmail.com

RAIKES, Miss Gwynneth Marian Napier. b 51. Somerville Coll Ox MA 72 Lon Univ BD 81. Trin Coll Bris 79. **dss** 81 **d** 98 **p** 98. Asst Chapl Bris Poly 81-86; Beckenham Ch Ch *Roch* 86-00; C 98-00; Dean of Women and Oak Hill Th Coll 00-13; 14; PtO *Lon* 03-13; *Ely* from 07. *28 Pilgrims Way, Ely CB6 3DL* E: gmnrpilgrim@gmail.com

RAIKES, Canon Peter. b 37. St Mich Coll Llan 78. **d** 80 **p** 81. C Roath *Llan* 80-82; V Resolven 82-86; V Resolven w Tonna 86-92; RD Neath 89-01; V Skewen 92-02; Can Llan Cathl 97-02; rtd 02; PtO *Llan* from 04. *2 Kennedy Drive, Pencoed, Bridgend CF35 6TW* T: (01656) 862317

RAIKES, Robert Laybourne. b 32. Wells Th Coll 59. **d** 61 **p** 62. C Poplar All SS w St Frideswide *Lon* 61-66; C Grendon Underwood w Edgcott Ox 66-68; C Swan 68-71; V Whitchurch Canonicorum w Wooton Fitzpaine etc *Sarum* 71-81; P-in-c Branksome St Aldhelm 81-82; V 82-91; V Pitminster w Corfe *B & W* 91-92; rtd 92; Chapl Madeira *Eur* 93-95; PtO *Glouc* 95-98; Hon C Broadwell, Evenlode, Oddington, Adlestrop etc 98-01; LtO *Eur* from 02; PtO *Chelmsf* from 09; *S'wark* from 10. *The College of St Barnabas, Blackberry Lane, Lingfield RH7 6NJ* T: (01342) 872826

RAILTON, David James. b 66. Bradf Univ BPharm 89. EMMTC 06. **d** 08 **p** 09. C Melbourne, Ticknall, Smisby and Stanton *Derby* 08-11; V Hazelwood, Holbrook and Milford 11-15; Bp's Asst Chapl 11-15; V Blackwell All SS and Salutation *Dur* from 15. *The Vicarage, 104 Blackwell Lane, Darlington DL3 8QQ* E: davidrailton@gmail.com

RAILTON, John Robert Henry. b 45. Reading Univ BSc 68 PhD 82 FCIB 79. S Dios Minl Tr Scheme 82. **d** 85 **p** 86. NSM Wickham *Portsm* 85-89; C Bridgemary 89-90; V 90-96; TR Ridgeway *Sarum* 96-02; TR Whitton 02-08; rtd 08; P-in-c Purton *Bris* 11-12. *20 Baileys Way, Wroughton, Swindon SN4 9AH* T: (01793) 814162 E: john.railton@btinternet.com

RAILTON, Ray. b 44. ERMC 13. **d** 15. C Wellingborough St Barn *Pet* from 15. *101 Mill Road, Woodford, Kettering NN14 4HL* T: (01832) 732736 E: ray.railton@btinternet.com

RAILTON, Sandra. b 46. S Dios Minl Tr Scheme 82. **dss** 85 **d** 87 **p** 94. Catherington and Clanfield *Portsm* 85-86; Lee-on-the-Solent 86-89; C 87-89; Par Dn Burnham w Dropmore, Hitcham and Taplow *Ox* 89-94; TV Wallingford w Crowmarsh Gifford etc 94-98; TV Wallingford 98; Dioc Dir Ords (OLM) Berks 96-99; TV Ridgeway *Sarum* 98-02; Dioc Voc Adv 99-02; TV Whitton 02-08; RD Marlborough 04-08; rtd 08. *20 Baileys Way, Wroughton, Swindon SN4 9AH* T: (01793) 814162

RAILTON-CROWDER, Mrs Mary. b 51. Luton Univ BA 96 RN 72 RM 91 MIOSH 93. SAOMC 98. **d** 01 **p** 02. NSM Elstow *St Alb* 01-04; Chapl De Montford Univ 02-04; C Douglas All SS and St Thos *S & M* 04-07; P-in-c Birchencliffe *Wakef* 07-08; V Birkby and Birchencliffe from 08; RD Huddersfield 10-15. *The Vicarage, 4 Brendon Drive, Huddersfield HD2 2DF* T: (01484) 546966 E: revmrc@yahoo.com

RAINBIRD, Ms Ruth Patricia. b 40. SRN 62. **d** 01 **p** 02. OLM Limpsfield and Titsey *S'wark* 01-10; PtO from 10. *73 Stoneleigh Road, Oxted RH8 0TP* T: (01883) 713683 E: ruthrainbird@btinternet.com

RAINE, Alan. b 49. NEOC 92. **d** 95 **p** 96. NSM Jarrow *Dur* 95-05; Chapl S Tyneside Coll 95-05; V Leam Lane *Dur* from 05. *St Andrew's Vicarage, Winbrooke, Gateshead NE10 8HR* T: 0191-489 3042 E: alanraine49@aol.com

RAINE, David. b 58. Dur Univ MBA 96 Open Univ BA 96 MCIM 99 MCIPD 03. NEOC 01. **d** 04 **p** 05. NSM N Wearside *Dur* 04-06; NSM Millfield St Mary from 06; NSM Bishopwearmouth Gd Shep from 06. *5 Maydown Close, Sunderland SR5 3DZ* T: 0191-549 7262 E: davidraine@dunelm.org.uk

RAINE, Stephen James. b 49. Sheff Poly BA 80. NOC 85. **d** 86 **p** 87. C Cottingham *York* 86-90; V Dunscroft Ch Ch *Sheff* 90-92; V Dunscroft St Edwin 92-96; V Kettering St Mary *Pet* 96-08; P-in-c Ipswich St Mary at the Elms *St E* 08-14; Chapl Ipswich Hosp NHS Trust 08-14; rtd 14. *20 rue du Château, 16190 Montmoreau-St-Cybard, France* T: (0033) 5 45 61 74 43 E: evangelist24@hotmail.com

RAINER, John Charles. b 54. Ex Univ BA 76 CertEd 78 Hull Univ MBA 02. St Jo Coll Nottm 86. **d** 88 **p** 89. C Fletchamstead *Cov* 88-94; V Leic H Apostles 94-03; V Shipley St Pet *Leeds* from 03. *The Vicarage, 2 Glenhurst Road, Shipley BD18 4DZ* T: (01274) 584488 or 400381 E: john.rainer@bradford.anglican.org

RAINES, Mrs Gisela Rolanda. b 58. Groningen Univ Kandidaats 80. K Coll Lon BD 83. **dss** 84 **d** 87 **p** 94. Charlton St Luke w H Trin *S'wark* 84-87; Par Dn 87; Chapl Imp Coll Lon 87-91; Hon C Birch w Fallowfield *Man* 94-95; P-in-c Withington St Chris 95-03; C Man St Ann 03-10; R Withington St Paul from 10. *34 Mauldeth Road, Manchester M20 4WD* T: 0161-448 9431 E: revgisela@btinternet.com

RAINES, William Guy. b 46. Lon Univ BSc 69 MSc 70 Ox Univ BA 80. Ripon Coll Cuddesdon 78. **d** 81 **p** 82. C W Drayton *Lon* 81-84; C Charlton St Luke w H Trin *S'wark* 84-87; Chapl K Coll Lon 87-94; Chapl Imp Coll 91-94; P-in-c Birch w Fallowfield *Man* 94-95; R 95-12; rtd 12; PtO *Man* from 13. *34 Mauldeth Road, Manchester M20 4WD* T: 0161-448 9431 E: wraines@btinternet.com

RAINEY, Graeme Norman. b 66. Van Mildert Coll Dur BA 88 Reading Univ MA 01. Ridley Hall Cam 93. **d** 93 **p** 94. C Maltby *Sheff* 93-96; Chapl Reading Univ *Ox* 96-04; Chapl Downe Ho Sch Berks 04-10; Asst Chapl Roedean Sch Brighton from 11. *Roedean School, Roedean Way, Brighton BN2 5RQ* T: (01273) 667500

RAINFORD, Robert Graham. b 55. Lanc Univ CertEd 76 BEd 77. St Steph Ho Ox 81. **d** 83 **p** 84. C Burnley St Cath w St Alb and St Paul *Blackb* 83-86; C-in-c Hawes Side St Chris CD 86-89; V Hawes Side 89-03; P-in-c Marton Moss 01-03; AD Blackpool 00-03; Hon Can Blackb Cathl 01-03; Sen Chapl to Bp Dover *Cant* 03-05; P Admin Upper Chelsea H Trin *Lon* 05-08; Asst P 08-11; Asst P Upper Chelsea H Trin and St Sav from 11. *Holy Trinity Church, Sloane Street, London SW1X 9BZ* T: (020) 7730 7270 E: priest@holytrinitysloanesquare.co.uk

RAINSBURY, Mark James. b 56. NE Lon Poly BA 79. Oak Hill Th Coll BA 87. **d** 88 **p** 89. C Tonbridge St Steph *Roch* 88-95; C Hampreston *Sarum* 95-97; TV 97-99; PtO *Win* from 03. *Old Orchard, Church Lane, West Parley, Ferndown BH22 8TS* T: (01202) 590042

RAINSFORD, Peter John. b 31. FCP 72. Qu Coll Birm 75. **d** 77 **p** 78. Hon C Lich St Chad 77-81; C 82; C Coseley Ch Ch 82-84; V Wednesbury St Bart 84-91; Chapl Sandwell Distr Gen Hosp 89-91; rtd 91; PtO *Lich* from 91. *34 Pegasus Court, 155 Chester Road, Streetly, Sutton Coldfield B74 3NW* E: p.j.rainsford@tinyonline.co.uk

RAISTRICK, Brian. b 38. St Paul's Coll Chelt TCert 60 Ex Univ AdDipEd 68 Newc Univ MEd 76 UEA PhD 86. Westcott Ho Cam 92. **d** 93 **p** 94. C Haverhill w Withersfield, the Wrattings etc *St E* 93-95; P-in-c Horringer cum Ickworth 95-02; P-in-c Risby w Gt and Lt Saxham and Westley 99-02; P-in-c Chevington w Hargrave and Whepstead w Brockley 00-02; R Horringer 02; RD Thingoe 99-01; rtd 03; PtO *St E* from 03. *Greenways, Westwood, Great Barton, Bury St Edmunds IP31 2SF* T: (01284) 787372 or 747372 E: brian@raistrick.freeserve.co.uk

RAISTRICK, Mrs Tracey Ann. b 65. Coll of Resurr Mirfield 13. **d** 15. C Utley *Leeds* from 15. *10 Railway Street, Keighley BD20 6AQ.* M: 07761-483637 E: rev.tracey@outlook.com

RAISTRICK, Tulo Dirk. b 69. Jes Coll Ox BA 91. SEITE 08. **d** 11 **p** 12. C Telford Park *S'wark* 11-14; V Earlsdon *Cov* from 14. *St Barbara's Vicarage, 24 Rochester Road, Coventry CV5 6AG* M: 07552-948068 E: tulo.raistrick@hotmail.co.uk

RAITT, Derek. b 41. K Coll Lon BD 63 AKC 63. **d** 64 **p** 65. C Blackb St Jas 64-67; C Burnley St Pet 67-69; V Foulridge 69-74; V Euxton 74-91; V Penwortham St Mary 91-00; P-in-c Halton w Aughton 00-06; rtd 06; PtO *Blackb* from 06. *84 Lymm Avenue, Lancaster LA1 5HR* E: draitt@wightcablenorth.net

RAJ-SINGH, Reji. b 52. Sidney Webb Coll of Educn CertEd 79 N Lon Poly BEd 90 Heythrop Coll Lon MA SAOMC 02. **d** 05 **p** 06. NSM Paddington St Jas *Lon* 05-11; NSM Paddington St Mary Magd and St Pet from 11. *27 Kendal Steps, St Georges Fields, London W2 2YE* T: (020) 7262 4261 M: 07983-430050 E: reji4@btinternet.com

RAJA, John Christopher Joshva. b 65. Serampore Coll MTh 93 Leic Univ MA 96 New Coll Edin 96. **d** 93 **p** 94. India 93 95; Hon C Leic H Spirit 95-96; Hon C Edin H Cross 96-99; Tutor Qu Foundn Birm 00-12; R Curdworth, Middleton and Wishaw *Birm* from 12. *The Rectory, Glebe Fields, Curdworth, Sutton Coldfield B76 9ES* T: (01675) 470384 E: j.raja@queens.ac.uk or joshvajohn@yahoo.co.uk

RAJKOVIC, Michael. b 52. Sheff Univ BMet 74 MMet 75 PhD 79 St Jo Coll Nottm MA 95 Lon Bible Coll MPhil 03. Cranmer Hall Dur 93. **d** 95 **p** 96. C Harrow Weald All SS *Lon* 95-98; C Woodford Wells *Chelmsf* 98-02; V Bricket Wood *St Alb* from 02. *20 West Riding, Bricket Wood, St Albans AL2 3QP* T: (01923) 681107 E: mrajk30852@aol.com

RAJKUMAR, Peniel Jesudason Rufus. b 77. Sri Venkateswara Univ India BA 98 MA 02 BD 03. **d** 05 **p** 06. NSM Upper Holloway *Lon* 05-08; Tutor United Th Coll Bangalore from 08. *63 Millers Road, Benson Town Post, Bangalore, 560 046, India* E: rufus_peniel@rediffmail.com

RAKE, David John. b 47. Nottm Univ BA 68 PhD 73. Wycliffe Hall Ox 73. **d** 74 **p** 75. C Radcliffe-on-Trent *S'well* 74-77; P-in-c Upwell St Pet *Ely* 77-79; P-in-c Outwell 77-79; Chapl Warw Univ *Cov* 79-86; V Kenilworth St Nic 86-98; P-in-c Tintagel *Truro* 98-08; Bp's Adv on Spiritual Formation 98-03; Dioc Adv 03-08; rtd 08; PtO *Truro* from 09. *The Old Vicarage, Zennor, St Ives TR26 3BY* T: (01736) 796955

RALPH, Brian Charles. b 66. St Steph Ho Ox 89. **d** 92 **p** 93. C Yeovil St Mich *B & W* 92-95; TV St Jo on Bethnal Green *Lon* 95-01; P-in-c Bethnal Green St Barn 01-03; V from 03. *12 Chisenhale Road, London E3 5TG* T: (020) 7247 1448 *or* 8983 3426 *or* 8806 4130 E: brianralph@btinternet.com

RALPH, Ms Caroline Susan. b 60. Birm Univ BA 81 UWE LLM 98. Westcott Ho Cam 04. **d** 06 **p** 07. C Crediton, Shobrooke and Sandford etc *Ex* 06-10; V Harborne St Pet *Birm* 10-13; R Dunster, Carhampton, Withycombe w Rodhuish etc *B & W* from 13. *The Rectory, Church Lane, Carhampton, Minehead TA24 6NT* E: caroline@249ralph.eclipse.co.uk

RALPH, Canon Nicholas Robert. b 63. Lanc Univ BSc 85 Trin Coll Cam BA 91. Westcott Ho Cam 89. **d** 92 **p** 93. C Fareham H Trin *Portsm* 92-95; C Portsea St Cuth 95-96; V Hayling Is St Andr 96-03; V N Hayling St Pet 96-03; Hd Miss and Soc 03-06 and from 06; Hon Can Portsm Cathl 06-09; Can Res Portsm Cathl from 09. *101 St Thomas's Street, Portsmouth PO1 2HE* T: (023) 9289 9674 E: nick@ralphy.org *or* nick.ralph@portsmouth.anglican.org

RALPH, Richard Gale. b 51. Pemb Coll Ox BA 73 MA 78 DPhil 78 FRSA 90. S Dios Minl Tr Scheme 84. **d** 87 **p** 88. NSM St Leonards Ch Ch and St Mary etc *Chich* from 87; NSM St Pancras H Cross w St Jude and St Pet *Lon* 87-94; Prin Westmr Coll Ox 96-00. *St Alban, 11 The Mount, St Leonards-on-Sea TN38 0HR* T: (01424) 422722 E: wea@nildram.co.uk

RALPHS, Robert Brian. b 31. Qu Coll Birm 75. **d** 78 **p** 79. Hon C Wednesbury St Jo *Lich* 78-80; Hon C Wednesbury St Paul Wood Green 80-81; PtO 81-96 and from 97; Hon C W Bromwich Gd Shep w St Jo 96. *204 Bromford Lane, West Bromwich B70 7HX* T: 0121-553 0119

RALPHS, Sharon Ann. *See* SIMPSON, Sharon Ann

RAMBLE, Anugrah Daniel. b 82. **d** 06 **p** 07. India 06-09; Chapl Aston Univ and C Erdington *Birm* 10-14; V Hill from 14. *61 Mere Green Road, Sutton Coldfield B75 5BW* T: 0121-308 0074 M: 07530-973238 E: adramble@gmail.com *or* vicarstjameshill@gmail.com

RAMPTON, Paul Michael. b 47. St Jo Coll Dur BA 69 MA 73 K Coll Lon PhD 85 Westmr Coll Ox MTh 99. Wycliffe Hall Ox 72. **d** 73 **p** 74. C Folkestone H Trin w Ch Ch *Cant* 73-77; P-in-c Ringwould w Oxney 77-79; P-in-c Kingsdown 77-79; R Ringwould w Kingsdown 79-83; V Maidstone St Paul 83-88; V Maidstone St Martin 88-95; V Steyning *Chich* 95-12; R Ashurst 95-12; RD Storrington 99-03; rtd 12; Dioc Warden of Readers *Chich* from 12. *54 Greenacres, Shoreham-by-Sea BN43 5WY* T: (01273) 271488

RAMPTON, Canon Valerie Edith. b 41. Nottm Univ BSc 63 MSc 66 BA 79. Gilmore Course 78. **dss** 82 **d** 87 **p** 94. Sneinton St Chris w St Phil *S'well* 80-87; Par Dn 87-88; Par Dn Stapleford 88-93; Dioc Adv on Women in Min 90-01; Dn-in-c Kneesall w Laxton and Wellow 93-94; V 94-02; Hon Can S'well Minster 97-02; rtd 02; PtO *Linc* from 02; *S'well* from 02. *Tansy Cottage, Hillside, Beckingham, Lincoln LN5 0RQ* T: (01636) 626665 E: valerie.rampton@waitrose.com

RAMSARAN, Susan Mira. b 49. K Coll Lon BA 70 Univ Coll Lon MA 72 PhD 78. Ripon Coll Cuddesdon BA 92. **d** 93 **p** 94. C Selling w Throwley, Sheldwich w Badlesmere etc *Cant* 93-97; P-in-c Shipbourne *Roch* 97-99; P-in-c Plaxtol 97-99; R Shipbourne w Plaxtol 99-06; RD Shoreham 01-06; TR N Tyne and Redesdale *Newc* from 06; AD Bellingham from 06. *The Rectory, Bellingham, Hexham NE48 2JS* T: (01434) 220019 E: smramsaran@aol.com

RAMSAY, Canon Alan Burnett. b 34. AKC 62. **d** 63 **p** 64. C Clapham H Trin *S'wark* 63-67; C Warlingham w Chelsham and Farleigh 67-71; P-in-c Stockwell St Mich 71-78; V Lingfield 78-85; P-in-c Crowhurst 83-85; V Lingfield and Crowhurst 85-92; RD Godstone 88-92; V Mitcham St Mark 92-00; Hon Can S'wark Cathl 93-00; rtd 00; PtO *Cant* from 00; *S & B* from 10. *Kent House, 9 Scotton Street, Wye, Ashford TN25 5BU* T: (01233) 813730 E: aramsay@talktalk.net

RAMSAY, Preb Carl Anthoney St Aubyn. b 55. WMMTC 88. **d** 90 **p** 91. C Wednesfield Heath *Lich* 90-94; V Willenhall St Anne 94-03; V Pelsall from 03; Preb Lich Cathl from 04. *The Vicarage, 39 Hall Lane, Pelsall, Walsall WS3 4JN* T: (01922) 682098 E: spreeboy@talk21.com

RAMSAY, Christopher. b 68. St Jo Coll Dur BA 90. Wycliffe Hall Ox BTh 94. **d** 97 **p** 98. C Cricklewood St Gabr and St Mich *Lon* 97-01; P-in-c Southall St Geo 01-06; V from 06; AD Ealing from 10. *1 Lancaster Road, Southall UB1 1NP* T: (020) 8574 1876 E: christopher.ramsay@btinternet.com

RAMSAY, Eric Nicolson. b 29. **d** 94 **p** 95. C Forfar and Kirriemuir *St And* 94-99; C 00-09; Asst Chapl Gtr Athens *Eur* 99-00; LtO *St And* from 09. *4 Beechwood Place, Kirriemuir DD8 5DZ* T: (01575) 572029 E: ericaileenramsay@tinyworld.co.uk

RAMSAY, James Anthony. b 52. Wadh Coll Ox BA 75 MA. **d** 86 **p** 87. C Olney w Emberton *Ox* 86-89; V Blackbird Leys 89-02;

Chapl Bucharest w Sofia *Eur* 02-05; P-in-c Lt Ilford St Barn *Chelmsf* 05-10; V from 10; Chapl E Lon Univ from 05. *St Barnabas' Vicarage, Browning Road, London E12 6PB* T: (020) 8472 2777 E: ramsay.jas@gmail.com

RAMSAY, Kerry. *See* TUCKER, Kerry

RAMSAY, Max Roy MacGregor. b 34. Ball Coll Ox MA 58. Qu Coll Birm 82. **d** 84 **p** 85. C Hale *Ches* 84-86; C Nantwich 87; V Haslington w Crewe Green 87-91; P-in-c Dunham Massey St Marg and St Mark 92-95; rtd 95; PtO *Ches* from 95. *6 Comber Way, Knutsford WA16 9BT* T: (01565) 632362 E: mrm.ramsay@ntlworld.com

RAMSBOTTOM, David. b 60. **d** 12 **p** 13. NSM Crowthorne *Ox* from 12. *The Rectory, The Village, Finchampstead, Wokingham RG40 4JX*

RAMSBOTTOM, Mrs Julie Frances. b 54. Trevelyan Coll Dur BA 76. S'wark Ord Course 88. **d** 91 **p** 94. Par Dn Bray and Braywood *Ox* 91-94; C 94-97; R W Woodhay w Enborne, Hampstead Marshall etc 97-11; P-in-c Kintbury w Avington 05-11; R Finchampstead and California from 11; AD Sonning from 13. *The Rectory, The Village, Finchampstead, Wokingham RG40 4JX* T: 0118-973 6374 E: julie.ramsbottom@talk21.com

RAMSBOTTOM, Susan Elizabeth. *See* POLLARD, Susan Elizabeth

RAMSBURY, Area Bishop of. *See* CONDRY, The Rt Revd Edward Francis

RAMSDEN, Canon Arthur Stuart. b 34. Kelham Th Coll 56. **d** 61 **p** 62. C Featherstone *Wakef* 61-63; C Barnsley St Pet 63-67; V Charlestown 67-70; V Middlestown 70-77; V Purston cum S Featherstone 77-04; Hon Can Wakef Cathl 95-04; rtd 04; PtO *Sheff* from 12. *31 Barnsley Road, Cawthorne, Barnsley S75 4HW* T: (01226) 790696

RAMSDEN, Jenny. Yorks Min Course. **d** 14 **p** 15. NSM Morton St Luke *Leeds* from 14; NSM Riddlesden from 14. *16 Avondale Crescent, Shipley BD18 4QS* T: (01274) 783870 M: 07905-202201 E: j.ramsden@blueyonder.co.uk

✠**RAMSDEN, The Rt Revd Peter Stockton.** b 51. Univ Coll Lon BSc 74 Leeds Univ MA 92. Coll of Resurr Mirfield 74. **d** 77 **p** 78 **c** 07. C Houghton le Spring *Dur* 77-80; C S Shields All SS 80-83; Papua New Guinea 83-90 and 93-96; P-in-c Micklefield *York* 90-93; V Long Benton *Newc* 96-07; Bp Port Moresby 07-14; rtd 14; Hon Asst Bp Carl from 15. *4 Railway Cottages, Long Marton, Appleby-in-Westmorland CA16 6BY* T: (017683) 61175 E: bishopramsden@gmail.com

RAMSDEN, Raymond Leslie. b 49. Open Univ BA 86. **d** 78 **p** 79. C Greenhill St Jo *Lon* 78-85; C Staines St Mary and St Pet 85-90; V Hounslow St Steph from 90. *St Stephen's Vicarage, Parkside Road, Hounslow TW3 2BP* T: (020) 8570 3056 E: revrramsden@hotmail.com

RAMSDEN, Stuart. *See* RAMSDEN, Arthur Stuart

RAMSEY, Alan Edward. b 72. Wycliffe Hall Ox. **d** 08 **p** 09. C Ox St Aldate 08-11; PtO 13; C Ox St Mary V w St Cross and St Pet from 13. *24 Martin Court, Middle Way, Oxford OX2 7LF* E: alanramsey@yahoo.com

RAMSEY, Christopher John. b 76. St Jo Coll Nottm BA 07. **d** 07 **p** 08. C Saxmundham w Kelsale cum Carlton *St E* 07-10; V Gt Cornard from 10. *The Vicarage, 95 Bures Road, Great Cornard, Sudbury CO10 0JE* T: (01787) 376293 E: revchrisramsey@gmail.com

RAMSEY, Victoria. b 71. **d** 11 **p** 12. C Ex St Mark, St Sidwell and St Matt from 11. *23 Sylvan Road, Exeter EX4 6EW* E: toria@ramseys.org.uk

RAMSHAW, Marcus John. b 71. St Andr Univ MTheol 93 York Univ MA 94. Cranmer Hall Dur 94. **d** 96 **p** 97. C Hythe *Cant* 96-00; Chapl Down Coll Cam 01-03; NSM Cam St Edw *Ely* 03-10. *Address temp unknown* M: 07793-064455

RANCE, Mrs Eleanor Jane. b 72. K Coll Lon BA 93 AKC 93 St Jo Coll Dur MA 96. Cranmer Hall Dur 94. **d** 96 **p** 97. C Barnes *S'wark* 96-99; Chapl RAF 99-10; PtO *Blackb* 10-13; P-in-c Wylye and Till Valley *Sarum* 13; V Salisbury Plain from 14; RD Stonehenge from 15. *The Rectory, Chapel Lane, Shrewton, Salisbury SP3 4BX* T: (01980) 620580 E: reveleanorrance@gmail.com

RANDALL, Anthony. *See* RANDALL, James Anthony

RANDALL, Benjamin Thomas. b 84. St Andr Univ MA 06 Bradf Univ MA 08. Ridley Hall Cam 11. **d** 14 **p** 15. C Pudsey St Lawr and St Paul *Leeds* from 14. *18 West Park, Pudsey LS28 7SN* M: 07704-585435 E: benjamin.t.randall@hotmail.com

RANDALL, Bernard Charles. b 72. St Andr Univ MA 95 Edin Univ MSc 97 Man Univ PhD 04. St Steph Ho Ox BA 06. **d** 06 **p** 07. C Bury St Mary *Man* 06-07; C Atherton and Hindsford w Howe Bridge 07-09; C Sale St Paul *Ches* 09-11; Chapl Ch Coll Cam from 11. *Christ's College, Cambridge CB2 3BU* T: (01223) 334900 E: bernard.randall@hotmail.co.uk *or* bcr26@cam.ac.uk

RANDALL, Colin Antony. b 57. SS Paul & Mary Coll Cheltenham BEd 78. Trin Coll Bris BD 84. **d** 84 **p** 85. C Denton Holme *Carl* 84-87; C Brampton RD 87-90; R Hanborough and Freeland *Ox* 90-99; P-in-c Croglin *Carl* 99-09; P-in-c Holme Eden 99-05; P-in-c Wetheral w Warwick 99-05; R Holme Eden and Wetheral w Warwick 05-09; RD Brampton 05-09; Hon Can Carl Cathl 08-09; P-in-c Barrow *Ches* 09-10; R 10-14; Dioc Worship Adv 09-14; P-in-c Sevenhampton w Charlton Abbots, Hawling etc *Glouc* from 14. *The Rectory, Station Road, Andoversford, Cheltenham GL54 4LA* E: colinrandall@mac.com

RANDALL, Preb Colin Michael Sebastian. b 50. Aston Univ BSc 72. Qu Coll Birm 72. **d** 75 **p** 76. C Tonge w Alkrington *Man* 75-78; C Elton All SS 78-82; P-in-c Bridgwater H Trin *B & W* 82-86; V 86-90; V Bishops Hull 90-00; TR Wellington and Distr 00-12; Preb Wells Cathl 05-12; rtd 12. *16 The Rosemullion, Cliff Road, Budleigh Salterton EX9 6LA* E: colinms.randall@virgin.net

RANDALL, Elizabeth Nicola. *See* BILLETT, Elizabeth Nicola

RANDALL, Evelyn. b 49. **d** 10 **p** 11. NSM Dormansland *S'wark* 10-15; NSM Lingfield and Dormansland from 15. *58 Hickmans Close, Godstone RH9 8EB* T: (01883) 742751

RANDALL, Gareth John. b 49. Southn Univ BA 72 PGCE 73 ACP 80. Oak Hill Th Coll 90. **d** 93 **p** 94. Dir of Studies Dame Alice Owen's Sch Potters Bar 84-95; Dir of Personnel 95-00; Asst Hd 00-07; NSM S Mymms K Chas *St Alb* 93-98; NSM Potters Bar 98-07; P-in-c Dinard *Eur* from 07. *No 7 Résidence Victor Hugo, 6 ave Georges Clemenceau, 35800 Dinard, France* T: (0033) 2 99 46 77 00

RANDALL, Gordon Charles. b 58. STETS BA 11. **d** 11 **p** 12. NSM Chineham *Win* from 11. *37 Belvedere Gardens, Chineham, Basingstoke RG24 8GB* T: (01256) 364940 M: 07913-742208 E: gordon.randall@sky.com

RANDALL, Ian Neville. b 39. Oriel Coll Ox BA 62 MA 65. St Steph Ho Ox 62. **d** 65 **p** 66. C Perivale *Lon* 65-68; C Fulham St Jo Walham Green 68-73; C Cowley St Jas *Ox* 73-79; TV 79-82; V Didcot St Pet 82-93; P-in-c Clewer St Andr 93-04; rtd 04. *12 Westmead Road, Fakenham NR21 8BL* T: (01328) 862443

RANDALL, James Anthony. b 36. ACIB 69. Ridley Hall Cam 68. **d** 70 **p** 71. C Rusthall *Roch* 70-74; V Shorne 74-79; V Bexleyheath Ch Ch 79-89; R Stone 89-98; rtd 98; PtO *Roch* from 99. *6 Sandling Way, St Mary's Island, Chatham ME4 3AZ* T: (01634) 890603 E: randalltonshe@virgin.co.uk

RANDALL, Canon John Terence. b 29. St Cath Coll Cam BA 52 MA 59. Ely Th Coll 52. **d** 54 **p** 55. C Luton Ch Ch *St Alb* 54; C Dunstable 54-57; C Ely 57-60; C Market Deeping *Linc* 60-62; Area Sec (S Midl) UMCA 62-64; Area Sec USPG Birm and Cov 65-76; P-in-c Avon Dassett w Farnborough *Cov* 76-78; P-in-c Fenny Compton 76-78; R Avon Dassett w Farnborough and Fenny Compton 78-84; V New Bilton 84-94; RD Rugby 89-94; Hon Can Cov Cathl 93-94; rtd 94; PtO *Cov* from 94; *Pet* from 94; *Leic* from 96. *52 Cymbeline Way, Rugby CV22 6LA* T: (01788) 816659

RANDALL, Jonathan Aubrey. b 64. Bris Univ BSc 85. Ridley Hall Cam 04. **d** 06 **p** 07. C Hemingford Abbots and Hemingford Grey *Ely* 06-09; V Yaxley and Holme w Conington from 09; P-in-c Farcet Hampton 09-12. *The Vicarage, Church Street, Yaxley, Peterborough PE7 3LH* T: (01733) 240339 E: jon.randall@yfh.org.uk or vicar@saintpeters.co.uk

RANDALL, Julian Adrian. b 45. Open Univ BA 78 Stirling Univ MSc 94 St Andr Univ PhD 01 MCIPD. St Jo Coll Nottm 68. **d** 70 **p** 71. Asst P Mortlake w E Sheen *S'wark* 71-72; Asst P Welling 72-74; Asst P Tunbridge Wells H Trin w Ch Ch *Roch* 74-79; NSM Dunfermline *St And* 96-98; P-in-c Elie and Earlsferry 98-03; P-in-c Pittenweem 98-03; Asst P St Andrews St Andr 03-05; Dir Progr Business Sch St Andr Univ 03-05; Sen Lect Aber Univ *Ab* from 05. *Flat D, 10 Shearwater Crescent, Dunfermline KY11 8JX* T: (01382) 554546 E: jrandall@randall.co.uk or julian.randall@abdn.ac.uk

RANDALL, Kelvin John. b 49. JP 80. K Coll Lon BD 71 AKC 71 Birm Univ PGCE 72 Trin Coll Carmarthen MPhil 97 Univ of Wales (Ban) PhD 00. St Jo Coll Nottm 73. **d** 74 **p** 75. C Peckham St Mary Magd *S'wark* 74-78; C Portsdown *Portsm* 78-81; C-in-c Crookhorn CD Cen CD 81-82; R Bedhampton 82-90; Bp's Chapl for Post-Ord Tr 84-89; RD Havant 87-89; P-in-c Bournemouth St Jo w St Mich *Win* 90-94; V 94-97; Chapl Talbot Heath Sch Bournemouth 90-94; Research Fell Trin Coll Carmarthen 97-00; C Portswood St Denys *Win* 00-02; P-in-c from 02; Visiting Research Fell Glyndwr Univ from 10. *The Vicarage, 54 Whitworth Crescent, Southampton SO18 1GD* T: (023) 8067 2108 F: 8067 1757 E: st.denys@tiscali.co.uk

RANDALL, Mrs Lynda Lorraine. b 44. Sarum & Wells Th Coll 89. **d** 91 **p** 94. Par Dn Chesterton St Andr *Ely* 91-94; C 94-95; C Linton 95-96; TV 96-99; R Byfield w Boddington

and Aston le Walls *Pet* 99-10; rtd 10. *14 Smithland Court, Greens Norton, Towcester NN12 8DA* T: (01327) 350203 E: lynda@chrislyn.demon.co.uk *or* revlyn@uwclub.net

RANDALL, Miss Marian Sally. b 49. Trin Coll Bris 75. dss 80 **d** 87 **p** 94. Peckham St Mary Magd *S'wark* 80-83; Sutton Ch Ch 83-97; Par Dn 87-94; C 94-97; P-in-c S Merstham 97-08; rtd 08; PtO *Cant* 09-12; *S'wark* from 14. *4 Vision Place, 8 Oxford Road, Redhill RH1 1QE* T: (01737) 764169 E: marian.randall@btinternet.com

RANDALL, Martin Trevor. b 51. St Jo Coll Dur BA 74. Trin Coll Bris 74. **d** 77 **p** 78. C Ashton-upon-Mersey St Mary Magd *Ches* 77-80; C Everton St Sav w St Cuth *Liv* 80-82; V W Derby Gd Shep 82-91; P-in-c Toxteth Park Ch Ch 91-94; P-in-c Toxteth Park St Bede 91-94; V Toxteth Park Ch Ch w St Bede 95-97; Chapl HM Pris Altcourse 97-07; PtO *Liv* from 07. *37 Silver Leigh, Liverpool L17 5BL* T: 0151-727 2922 E: martin@randfam.demon.co.uk

RANDALL, Samuel Paul. b 59. Leeds Univ MA 90. Ridley Hall Cam 84. **d** 87 **p** 88. C Kingston upon Hull St Nic *York* 87-89; CF 89-93; TV Bramley *Ripon* 93-96; Dioc Ecum Officer *Dur* 97-01; P-in-c Holmside 97-01; Bp's Officer for Ch in the World *Bradf* 02-12; Hon Can Bradf Cathl 04-12; PtO *Pet* from 13; Dioc Ecum Officer from 13. *The Sundial House, 57 Main Street, Yarwell, Peterborough PE8 6PR* T: (01780) 784684 M: 07967-120070 E: sam.randall@peterborough-diocese.org.uk

RANDELL, David Peter. b 48. Trin Coll Bris BA 88. **d** 92 **p** 93. C Wells St Cuth w Wookey Hole *B & W* 92-95; TV Wellington and Distr 95-05; R Chenderit *Pet* 05-14; rtd 14; PtO *Pet* from 14. *10 Birch Close, Woodford Halse, Daventry NN11 3NF* T: (01327) 260538 E: revrandell@supanet.com

RANDELL, Phillip John. b 45. Lon Univ BD 73 CertEd. Linc Th Coll 67. **d** 68 **p** 69. C Henbury *Bris* 68-71; C Summertown *Ox* 71-73; C Liskeard w St Keyne *Truro* 73-75; Chapl Coll of SS Mark and Jo Plymouth 75-79; Tutor St Mark's Th Coll Dar es Salaam 80-82; R Alvescot w Black Bourton, Shilton, Holwell etc *Ox* 82-87; R St Gennys, Jacobstow w Warbstow and Treneglos *Truro* 87-97; rtd 97; PtO *Truro* from 01. *14 Merlin's Way, Tintagel PL34 0BP* T: (01840) 770559

RANDLE-BISSELL, Alexander Paul. b 71. **d** 12 **p** 13. C E Green *Cov* 12-15; P-in-c Pastrow *Win* from 15. *The Rectory, Chalkcroft Lane, Penton Mewsey, Andover CV4 9ZG* M: 07717-778853 E: revdalex@me.com

RANDOLPH-HORN, David Henry. b 47. Nottm Univ BA 69 CQSW 71 Leeds Beckett Univ PhD 15. Qu Coll Birm 80. **d** 82 **p** 83. C Hamstead St Paul *Birm* 82-84; V Aston St Jas 84-94; Hon C Leytonstone H Trin and St Aug Harrow Green *Chelmsf* 93-99; Sec Inner Cities Relig Coun 94-99; Assoc Dir Leeds Ch Inst 99-07; P-in-c Heptonstall *Wakef* 99-02; Hon C Farnley *Ripon* 03; Hon C Leeds St Marg and All Hallows from 07. *23 Spencer Place, Leeds LS7 4DQ* T: 0113-229 7546 E: davidhrh@ntlworld.com

RANGER, Keith Brian. b 34. Down Coll Cam BA 58 MA 63. Glas NSM Course 58. **d** 81 **p** 82. OMF Internat 81-99; Ethnic Min Co-ord 90-99; Hong Kong 81-89; PtO *Ches* 89-93 and from 99; *Man* 93-99; rtd 99. *144 Newton Street, Macclesfield SK11 6RW* T: (01625) 439184 E: keithcath@ranger144.fsnet.co.uk

RANKIN, John. *See* RANKIN, William John Alexander

RANKIN, Joyce. b 03 **p** 04. C Dublin St Ann and St Steph *D & G* 03-09; I Bailieborough w Knockbride, Shercock and Mullagh *K, E & A* from 09. *The Rectory, Baillieborough, Co Cavan, Republic of Ireland* M: (00353) (42) 966 6794 M: 87-895 8877 E: fejoycer@eircom.net

RANKIN, Stephen Brian. b 65. Salford Univ BSc 88. Trin Coll Bris 95. **d** 97 **p** 98. C Ashton-upon-Mersey St Mary Magd *Ches* 97-06; V from 06. *St Mary's Vicarage, 20 Beeston Road, Sale M33 5AG* T: 0161-973 5118 E: srankin@uk2.net

RANKIN, Canon William John Alexander. b 45. Van Mildert Coll Dur BA 68 Fitzw Coll Cam BA 73 MA 77. Westcott Ho Cam 71. **d** 74 **p** 75. C St John's Wood *Lon* 74-78; Chapl Clifton Coll Bris 78-86; P-in-c The Claydons *Ox* 86-91; R 91-93; R Clare w Poslingford, Cavendish etc *St E* 93-04; R Stour Valley 04-10; Hon Can *St E* Cathl 05-10; rtd 10; PtO *St E* from 10; *Pet* from 11. *12 Hawthorn Drive, Uppingham, Oakham LE15 9TA* T: (01572) 822180 E: elizabeth@rankin4736.fsnet.co.uk

RANKINE, Christopher Barry. b 66. Portsm Poly BA 88. Linc Th Coll BTh 93. **d** 93 **p** 95. C Farlington *Portsm* 93-96; C Alverstoke 96-98; C Romsey *Win* 98-00; P-in-c W Andover 00-09; TR Portway and Danebury 09-13; V Eastcote St Lawr *Lon* from 13. *The Vicarage, 2 Bridle Road, Pinner HA5 2SJ* T: (020) 3665 2029 M: 07766-475743 E: chris-eastcote@sky.com

RANN, Preb Harry Harvey. b 18. Sarum Th Coll 47. **d** 50 **p** 51. C Victoria Docks Ascension *Chelmsf* 50-52; C Christchurch *Win* 52-56; C Mill Hill Jo Keble Ch *Lon* 56-57; V Woolfold

Man 57-62; Dean's Chapl and PV Ex Cathl 62-77; Sacr 65-77; Succ 73-77; V Colyton *Ex* 77-84; R Colyton and Southleigh 84-86; RD Honiton 84-86; Preb Ex Cathl 84-87; TR Colyton, Southleigh, Offwell, Widworthy etc 86-87; rtd 87; PtO *Ex* from 87. *19 Betjeman Drive, Exmouth EX8 5ST* T: (01395) 265995

RANSFORD, Elizabeth Ann. b 49. Sussex Univ BSc 70 Leeds Univ MA 99 Whitelands Coll Lon PGCE 71. Cranmer Hall Dur 07. **d** 08 **p** 09. OLM York St Thos w St Maurice 08-13; NSM York St Mich-le-Belfrey from 13. *17 St Mary's, York YO30 7DD* T: (01904) 672332 M: 07525-210572 E: earansford@gmail.com

RANSOM, Adam John. b 85. Chich Univ BA 07. Coll of Resurr Mirfield 13. **d** 15. C Eastbourne Ch Ch and St Phil *Chich* from 15. *19 Hoad Road, Eastbourne BN22 8DX* T: (01323) 733700 E: curate@ccwithsp.org

RANSON, Canon Arthur Frankland. b 50. St Jo Coll Dur BA 73. Wycliffe Hall Ox 73. **d** 75 **p** 76. C Bare *Blackb* 75-78; C Scotforth 78-81; V Leyland St Ambrose 81-02; AD Leyland 96-02; P-in-c Blackb St Silas 02-15; Hon Can Blackb Cathl 00-15; rtd 15. *6 Hazlewood, Silverdale, Carnforth LA5 0TQ* E: arthur.ranson@ntlworld.com

RANYARD, Michael Taylor. b 43. Nottm Univ BTh 74. Linc Th Coll 71. **d** 74 **p** 75. C Sutton in Ashfield St Mary *S'well* 74-76; Hon C Lewisham St Mary *S'wark* 76-77; C Rushmere *St E* 77-79; R Hopton, Market Weston, Barningham etc 79-83; Chr Educn and Resources Adv *Dur* 83-93; Prin Adv to Dioc Bd of Educn *Blackb* 93-98; Asst P Blackb Cathl 98-99; rtd 99; PtO *Heref* from 99. *72 Wyedean Rise, Belmont, Hereford HR2 7XZ* T/F: (01432) 355452 E: smranyard@xalt.co.uk

RAO, Norma Ruoman. b 63. Westmr Coll Ox BTh 97 Anglia Ruskin Univ MA 05. Westcott Ho Cam 99. **d** 01 **p** 02. C Endcliffe *Sheff* 01-04; C Rotherham 04-08; R Rossington 08-15. *The Rectory, Sheep Bridge Lane, Rossington, Doncaster DN11 0EZ* T: (01302) 867597 E: norma.rao@btinternet.com

RAPHAEL, The Ven Timothy John. b 29. Leeds Univ BA 53. Coll of Resurr Mirfield. **d** 55 **p** 56. C Westmr St Steph w St Jo *Lon* 55-60; V Welling *S'wark* 60-63; New Zealand 63-72; Dean Dunedin 65-72; V St John's Wood *Lon* 72-83; AD Westmr St Marylebone 82-83; Adn Middx 83-96; rtd 96; PtO *Glouc* from 96. *121 Hales Road, Cheltenham GL52 6ST* T: (01242) 256075

RAPHOE, Archdeacon of. *See* HUSS, The Ven David Ian

RAPHOE, Dean of. *See* BARRETT, The Very Revd Kenneth Arthur Lambart

RAPKIN, Kevern. b 39. St D Coll Lamp BA 62 Univ of Wales BD 72. Lich Th Coll 63. **d** 65 **p** 66. C Hanley w Hope *Lich* 65-68; C Woodchurch *Ches* 68-70; C Abbots Langley *St Alb* 70-73; R Mt Pleasant Australia 73-80; R Rockingham and Safety Bay 80-90; R Lesmurdie 90-00; C Sholing *Win* 00-04; rtd 04; Australia from 04. *15 Gamage Way, Lockridge WA 6054, Australia* T: (0061) (8) 9377 0332

RAPLEY, Mrs Joy Naomi. b 41. Portsm Poly CertEd 63 Open Univ BA 79. Sarum & Wells Th Coll 87. **d** 89 **p** 94. Par Dn Welwyn Garden City *St Alb* 89-92; Chapl S Beds Community Healthcare Trust 92-98; C Wilbury *St Alb* 94-95; NSM St Mary's Bay w St Mary-in-the-Marsh etc *Cant* 98-02; NSM New Romney w Old Romney and Midley 98-02; Asst Chapl E Kent NHS and Soc Care Partnership Trust 99-02; P-in-c Clopton w Otley, Swilland and Ashbocking *St E* 02-08; PtO from 08. *26 Angela Close, Martlesham, Woodbridge IP12 4TG* T: (01473) 622922 E: revraps@aol.com

RAPSEY, Preb Peter Nigel. b 46. K Coll Lon BD 68 AKC 68. St Boniface Warminster. **d** 69 **p** 70. C Walton-on-Thames *Guildf* 69-73; C Fleet 73-77; P-in-c The Collingbournes and Everleigh *Sarum* 77-79; TV Wexcombe 79-84; R Wokingham St Paul *Ox* 84-93; Chapl Warminster Sch 93-96; V Frome Ch Ch *B & W* 96-04; P-in-c Evercreech w Chesterblade and Milton Clevedon 04-11; RD Frome 01-03; Dir of Ords 03-11; Preb Wells Cathl 04-11; rtd 11. *3A Saxon Close, Crediton EX17 3DS* T: (01363) 774068 E: peter.rapsey@btinternet.com

RASHBROOK, Alan Victor. b 42. S'wark Ord Course. **d** 75 **p** 76. Hon C Woking St Mary *Guildf* 75-83. *Hope Cottage, Robin Hood Lane, Sutton Green, Guildford GU4 7QG* T: (01483) 762760

RASON, Stuart Paul. Trin Coll Bris BA 08. **d** 08 **p** 09. C The Downs *Win* 08-12; Chapl RN from 12. *Royal Naval Chaplaincy Service, Mail Point 1.2, Leach Building, Whale Island, Portsmouth PO2 8BY* T: (023) 9262 5055 F: 9262 5134 E: stuartrason@hotmail.com

RASTALL, Preb Thomas Eric. b 19. St Aid Birkenhead 62. **d** 63 **p** 64. C Leek St Luke *Lich* 64-67; V Brown Edge 67-74; P-in-c Croxden 74-78; V Denstone 74-81; P-in-c Ellastone 78-81; V Denstone w Ellastone and Stanton 81-91; RD Uttoxeter 87-91; Preb Lich Cathl 89-91; rtd 91; PtO *Cov* 91-01. *10 Vicarage Close, Burton, Carnforth LA6 1NP* T: (01524) 782186

RATCLIFF, Canon David William. b 37. Edin Th Coll 59. **d** 62 **p** 63. C Croydon St Aug *Cant* 62-65; C Selsdon St Jo w St Fran 65-69; V Milton Regis St Mary 69-75; Hon Min Can Cant Cathl 75-91; Asst Dir of Educn 75-91; Dioc Adv in Adult Educn and Lay Tr 75-91; Hon Pres Protestant Assn for Adult Educn in Eur 82-88; Chapl Frankfurt-am-Main 91-98; Adn Scandinavia *Eur* 96-05; Chapl Stockholm w Gävle and Västerås 98-02; rtd 05; PtO *Cant* from 02. *9 The Orchards, Elham, Canterbury CT4 6TR* T: (01303) 840624 F: 840871

RATCLIFF, Paul Ronald. b 62. Univ Coll Lon BSc 83 Leic Univ MSc 84 PhD 89 FRAS MInstP. SEITE 05. **d** 09 **p** 10. C Cant St Martin and St Paul 09-12; R King's Wood from 12; AD W Bridge from 14. *The Vicarage, 3 Hambrook Close, Chilham, Canterbury CT4 8EJ* T: (01227) 730235 E: pr.ratcliff@googlemail.com

RATCLIFFE, Elizabeth Clare. b 65. Ox Min Course 12. **d** 15. C Reading Ch Ch *Ox* from 15. *Rose Cottage, Recreation Lane, Spencers Wood, Reading RG7 1EB* M: 07752-386707 E: liz-ratcliffe@live.co.uk

RATCLIFFE, Canon Michael David. b 43. Lon Univ BSc 65 Southn Univ PGCE 67 Lon Univ BA 75 Lanc Univ MA 84. Cranmer Hall Dur 75. **d** 77 **p** 78. C Blackpool St Thos *Blackb* 77-81; V Oswaldtwistle St Paul 81-10; RD Accrington 97-03; Hon Can Blackb Cathl 00-10; rtd 10; PtO *Blackb* from 10. *8 Stanhill Road, Oswaldtwistle, Accrington BB5 4PP* E: mratossy@tiscali.co.uk

RATCLIFFE, Nicholas Hugh Bernard. b 61. **d** 12 **p** 13. NSM Chartham *Cant* 12-14; NSM Chartham and Upper Hardres w Stelling 14-15; NSM Cliftonville from 15. *Address temp unknown* E: nhb.ratcliffe@btinternet.com

RATCLIFFE, Peter Graham Bruce. St Mich Coll Llan. **d** 08 **p** 09. C Carmarthen St Pet *St D* 08-09; C E Carmarthen 09-10; P-in-c Llanpumsaint w Llanllawddog 10-15; P-in-c Cilgerran w Bridell and Llantwyd and Eglwyswrw from 15. *The Rectory, Penllyn, Cilgerran, Cardigan SA43 2RZ* T: (01239) 612511 E: peter@revpeter.plus.com

RATCLIFFE, Mrs Roosevelta (Rosie). b 60. K Coll Lon BA 97 MA 99. SEITE 98. **d** 01 **p** 02. C Croydon St Matt *S'wark* 01-04; Hon C Sanderstead 05-06; Chapl S Lon and Maudsley NHS Foundn Trust 04-13; Chapl Imp Coll Healthcare NHS Trust from 13; PtO *S'wark* from 14. *The Bays, South Wharf Road, St Mary's Hospital, Praed Street, London W2 1NY* E: rosie@andrious.freeserve.co.uk

RATE, Susan. *See* LEIGHTON, Susan

RATHBAND, The Very Revd Kenneth William. b 60. Edin Univ BD 86. Edin Th Coll 82. **d** 86 **p** 87. C Dundee St Paul *Bre* 86-88; TV Dundee St Martin 88-89; C Edin SS Phil and Jas 90-91; R Alyth *St And* from 91; R Blairgowrie from 91; R Coupar Angus from 91; Dean St Andr from 07. *10 Rosemount Park, Blairgowrie PH10 6TZ* T: (01250) 872431 *or* 874583 E: krathband@btinternet.com *or* abcsaints@btinternet.com

RATHBONE, Mrs Elizabeth. b 51. Lon Univ MB, BS 76 MRCGP 80. WMMTC 03. **d** 03 **p** 04. C Tettenhall Regis *Lich* 03-06; TV 06-14; rtd 14; PtO *Heref* from 15. *2 Southall Paddocks, Billingsley, Bridgnorth WV16 6PF* T: (01746) 861049 E: rathboneer@gmail.com

RATHBONE, Mrs Isobel. b 48. Girton Coll Cam MA 70 Leeds Univ MA 02 Solicitor 81. NEOC 02. **d** 05 **p** 06. NSM Moor Allerton *Ripon* 05-08; NSM Hooe and Ninfield *Chich* 08-09; NSM Guiseley w Esholt *Bradf* 10-13; P-in-c Batheaston w St Cath *B & W* from 13. *99 North End, Bath BA1 7HA* M: 07775-656257 E: isobel.rathbone@lmh.ox.ac.uk

RATHBONE, Paul. b 36. BNC Ox BA 58 MA 62. Wycliffe Hall Ox 58. **d** 60 **p** 61. C Carl St Jo 60-63; C Heworth w Peasholme St Cuth *York* 63-68; V Thorganby w Skipwith and N Duffield 68-83; V Bishopthorpe and Acaster Malbis 83-01; rtd 01; PtO *York* from 01. *12 Whitelass Close, Thirsk YO7 1FG* T: (01845) 523347 E: paul2rathbone@btinternet.com

RATHBONE, Stephen Derek. b 61. Wycliffe Hall Ox. **d** 00 **p** 01. C W Kirby St Bridget *Ches* 00-03; P-in-c Rainow w Saltersford and Forest 03-10; V from 10. *The Vicarage, Pedley Hill, Rainow, Macclesfield SK10 5TZ* T: (01625) 572013 E: steve.rathbone@virgin.net

RATHGEN, David Guy Stanley. b 43. Cant Univ (NZ) BA 67 BTS 69 La Trobe Univ Vic BEd 96 Aus Catholic Univ MSocSc 01. **d** 69 **p** 70. C Highfield New Zealand 69-72; C Linwood 72-74; CMS 74-75; Chapl Versailles w Maisons-Laffitte *Eur* 75; Chapl Bordeaux St Nic France 76-77; Chapl All SS Cathl Khartoum Sudan 77-79; V Hoon Hay New Zealand 79-84; V Hokitika 84-89; Chapl Swinburne Univ Australia 90-93; Par P Hawthorn St Columb 90-91; V S Camberwell 91-00; V Healesville w Yarra Glen 00-04; rtd 04. *23 Plover Street, Cowes VIC 3922, Australia* T: (0061) (3) 5952 5136 M: 41-111 8706 E: drathgen@gotalk.net.au

RATTENBERRY, Christopher James. b 59. York Univ BA 80 Solicitor . St Jo Coll Nottm 91. **d** 93 **p** 94. C Porchester

S'well 93-98; P-in-c Daybrook 98-04; V 04-06; AD Nottm N 01-05; P-in-c Ravenshead 06-11; V from 11. *St Peter's Vicarage, 55 Sheepwalk Lane, Ravenshead, Nottingham NG15 9FD* T: (01623) 405203 E: chris.rattenberry@ntlworld.com

✠RATTERAY, The Rt Revd Alexander Ewen. b 42. Codrington Coll Barbados 61. **d** 65 **p** 66 **c** 96. C S Kirkby *Wakef* 66-68; C Sowerby St Geo 68-71; V Airedale w Fryston 71-80; Bermuda 80-08; Adn Bermuda 94-96; Bp Bermuda 96-08; rtd 08. *PO Box HM 2021, Hamilton HM CX, Bermuda* E: bishopratteray@ibl.bm

RATTIGAN, Canon Paul Damian. b 61. Reading Univ BSc 87 Liv Hope MA 00 Sussex Univ PGCE 88. Qu Coll Birm 93. **d** 95 **p** 96. C Parr *Liv* 95-99; P-in-c St Helens St Matt Thatto Heath 99-01; V 01-05; P-in-c Boldmere *Birm* 05-08; V 08-13; Can Res Liv Cathl from 13. *4 Cathedral Close, Liverpool L1 7BR* T: 0151-702 7233 E: paul.rattigan@liverpoolcathedral.org.uk

RATTUE, James. b 69. Ball Coll Ox BA 91 MA 04 Leic Univ MA 93. St Steph Ho Ox 03. **d** 05 **p** 06. C Weybridge *Guildf* 05-08 and 09; C Englefield Green 08-09; R Farncombe from 09. *The Rectory, 38 Farncombe Hill, Godalming GU7 2AU* T: (01483) 860709 M: 07952-615499 E: jamesrattue@hotmail.com

RAVALDE, Canon Geoffrey Paul. b 54. St Cuth Soc Dur BA 76 SS Coll Cam BA 86 MA 90 Lon Univ MTh 91 Barrister 78. Westcott Ho Cam 84. **d** 87 **p** 88. C Spalding St Mary and St Nic *Linc* 87-91; P-in-c Wigton *Carl* 91-92; V from 92; P-in-c Thursby from 10; RD Carl 95-00; Hon Can Carl Cathl from 96. *The Vicarage, Longthwaite Road, Wigton CA7 9JR* T: (016973) 42337 E: gpravalde@yahoo.co.uk

RAVEN, Ann. *See* GURNER, Margaret Ann

RAVEN, Canon Barry. b 48. Sarum & Wells Th Coll 69. **d** 72 **p** 73. C Henbury *Bris* 72-76; P-in-c S Marston w Stanton Fitzwarren 76-78; TV Stratton St Margaret w S Marston etc 78-80; P-in-c Coalpit Heath 80-84; V 84-91; R Ashley, Crudwell, Hankerton and Oaksey 91-13; P-in-c Ashton Keynes, Leigh and Minety 07-13; RD N Wilts 99-06; Hon Can Bris Cathl 12-13; rtd 13. *10 Springfields, Tetbury GL8 8EN* T: (01666) 505616 E: barry@deanery.org.uk

RAVEN, Charles Frank. b 58. Magd Coll Ox BA 80 MA 86 St Jo Coll Dur BA 87 ACIB 84. Cranmer Hall Dur 85. **d** 88 **p** 89. C Heckmondwike *Wakef* 88-92; TV Kidderminster St Jo and H Innocents *Worc* 92-02; Abp's Officer for Angl Communion Affairs Kenya from 12; PtO *Dur* from 13. *Anglican Church of Kenya, P.O. Box 40502-00100, Nairobi, Kenya* T: (00254) (20) 271 4755 M: 00254-716-835315 M: 07789-934836 E: charlesraven@gafcon.org

RAVEN, Margaret Ann. *See* GURNER, Margaret Ann

RAVEN, Margaret Hilary. b 45. Dur Univ BA 67 Man Univ MEd 73. Wesley Th Sem Washington MDiv 95. **d** 96 **p** 97. USA 96-01; Asst R Martinsburg Trin Ch 96-99; Assoc R Toms River Ch 99-00; PtO *Edin* 02-06; NSM Edin Ch Ch 06-12. *4 Warrender Crescent, Dunbar EH42 1LU* T: (01368) 860524 E: mthrraven@btopenworld.com

RAVEN, Tony. b 39. Garnett Coll Lon CertEd 65 CEng 72 MIET 72. SAOMC 94. **d** 97 **p** 98. NSM Lt Berkhamsted and Bayford, Essendon etc *St Alb* 97-01; P-in-c Lt Hadham w Albury 01-05; rtd 05; Hon C Hazelbury Bryan and the Hillside Par *Sarum* 07-11. *Address temp unknown* E: t_raven@btopenworld.com

RAVENS, David Arthur Stanley. b 30. Jes Coll Ox BA 53 MA 61 Lon Univ BD 63. Wells Th Coll 61. **d** 63 **p** 64. C Seacroft *Ripon* 63-70; TV 70-73; Teacher Sir Wm Borcase's Sch Marlow 73-87; rtd 95. *44 Arthursdale Grange, Scholes, Leeds LS15 4AW* T: 0113-273 6648

RAVENSCROFT, Avril Shirley. b 46. **d** 11 **p** 12. NSM Prestbury *Ches* from 11. *2 Castlegate Mews, Prestbury, Macclesfield SK10 4BP* T: (01625) 820041 E: avril.ravenscroft@zen.co.uk

RAVENSCROFT, The Ven Raymond Lockwood. b 31. Leeds Univ BA 53. Coll of Resurr Mirfield 54. **d** 55 **p** 56. C Goodwood S Africa 55-57; C St Jo Cathl Bulawayo S Rhodesia 57-59; R Francistown Bechuanaland 59-62; C St Ives *Truro* 62-64; V Falmouth All SS 64-68; V St Stephens by Launceston 68-73; P-in-c Launceston St Thos 68-73; V Launceston St Steph w St Thos 73-74; TR Probus, Ladock and Grampound w Creed and St Erme 74-88; RD Powder 77-81; Hon Can Truro Cathl 82-88; P-in-c St Erme 84-85; Adn Cornwall and Can Lib Truro Cathl 88-96; rtd 96; PtO *Truro* from 96; Fx from 00. *19 Montpelier Court, St David's Hill, Exeter EX4 4DP* T: (01392) 430607

RAWDING, Andrew. b 70. Cranmer Hall Dur 00. **d** 02 **p** 03. C Enfield St Andr *Lon* 02-05; Hon C Arm St Mark 05-07; Chapl RN 08-11; I Brackaville w Donaghendry and Ballyclog *Arm* from 11. *Holy Trinity Rectory, 82 Dungannon Road, Coalisland, Dungannon BT71 4HT* T: (028) 8774 0243 M: 07771-851838 E: andrewrawding@gmail.com *or* rector@coalisland.gmail.com

RAWDON-MOGG, Timothy David. b 45. St Jo Coll Dur BA 76. Cuddesdon Coll 75. **d** 77 **p** 78. C Wotton St Mary *Glouc* 77-80; C Ascot Heath *Ox* 80-82; V Woodford Halse w Eydon *Pet* 82-88; V Shrivenham w Watchfield and Bourton *Ox* 88-00; R Horsted Keynes *Chich* 00-08; rtd 08; PtO *Heref* from 12; *Lich* from 13. *Stone Cottage, The Bog, Minsterley, Shrewsbury SY5 0NJ* T: (01743) 792073

RAWE, Alan Charles George. b 29. ALCD 56. **d** 56 **p** 57. C W Kilburn St Luke w St Simon and St Jude *Lon* 56-59; Lect Watford St Mary *St Alb* 59-61; R Ore St Helen and St Barn *Chich* 61-69; R Moreton *Ches* 69-80; V Coppull *Blackb* 80-83; Miss to Seamen 83-94; Felixstowe Seafarers' Cen 88-94; rtd 94; PtO *Blackb* from 94. *15 Starfield Close, Lytham St Annes FY8 4QA* T: (01253) 733647

RAWLING, Miss Jane Elizabeth. b 51. Birm Univ BSc 73 St Jo Coll York CertEd 75. St Jo Coll Nottm 81. **dss** 84 **d** 87 **p** 94. Southsea St Jude *Portsm* 84-88; C 87-88; C St Paul's Cray St Barn *Roch* 88-91; Hon C from 91; SE Regional Co-ord BCMS Crosslinks 91-01; Sec for Bps' Selection Conf and CME Sec Min Division 01-07. *50 Batchwood Green, Orpington BR5 2NF* T: (01689) 817467

RAWLING, Preb Stephen Charles. b 43. Man Univ BSc 64 Bris Univ MSc 71. Sarum & Wells Th Coll 71. **d** 73 **p** 74. C Bris St Andr Hartcliffe 73-76; C Westlands St Andr *Lich* 76-79; R Darlaston St Lawr 79-90; TR Bloxwich 90-98; Preb Lich Cathl 07-08; rtd 08; PtO *Lich* 09-14. *31 Stowe Street, Lichfield WS13 6AQ* T: (01543) 262917

RAWLINGS, Canon Brenda Susan. b 48. Sussex Univ CertEd 69. Oak Hill Th Coll 85. **d** 87 **p** 94. Par Dn Green Street Green *Roch* 87-90; Par Dn Collier Row St Jas and Havering-atte-Bower *Chelmsf* 90-94; C Greenstead 94-98; R 98-00; TR Greenstead w Colchester St Anne 00-06; Hon Can Chelmsf Cathl 05-06; rtd 06; PtO *St E* from 07; *Nor* from 07. *10 Sorrel Drive, Thetford IP24 2YJ* T: (01842) 752881 E: rawlings327@btinternet.com

RAWLINGS, Elizabeth. b 66. Nottm Univ BSc 96 RGN 87. St Jo Coll Nottm 04. **d** 06 **p** 07. C Derby St Alkmund and St Werburgh 06-07; C Walbrook Epiphany 07-10; Min Hamilton CD *Leic* from 10; Warden Past Assts 11-14. *2 Cransley Close, Hamilton, Leicester LE5 1QQ* E: lizrawlings@btinternet.com

RAWLINGS, Helen. b 54. **d** 13. NSM Brighton Gd Shep Preston *Chich* from 13. *6 Beacon Hill, Ovingdean, Brighton BN2 7BN* T: (01273) 306266

RAWLINGS, The Ven John Edmund Frank. b 47. AKC 69. St Aug Coll Cant 69. **d** 70 **p** 71. C Rainham *Roch* 70-73; C Tattenham Corner and Burgh Heath *Guildf* 73-76; Chapl RN 76-92; V Tavistock and Gulworthy *Ex* 92-05; Chapl Kelly Coll Tavistock 93-02; RD Tavistock *Ex* 97-02; Preb Ex Cathl 99-14; Adn Totnes 06-14. *9 Rosemount Lane, Honiton EX14 1RJ* T: (01404) 43404 E: rawlingsl@btinternet.com

RAWLINGS, Canon Philip John. b 50. St Jo Coll Nottm BTh 83. **d** 83 **p** 84. C Blackley St Andr *Man* 83-87; C Halliwell St Pet 87-93; R Old Trafford St Bride 93-11; AD Stretford 98-05; Borough Dean Trafford 10-11; Interfaith Officer Oldham from 11; Hon Can Man Cathl from 04. *68 Dudley Road, Manchester M16 8DE* T: 0161-232 0413 E: philjr053@gmail.com

RAWLINGS, Susan. *See* RAWLINGS, Brenda Susan

RAWLINS, Clyde Thomas. b 28. **d** 02. NSM Leeds St Aid *Ripon* 02-11; NSM Leeds All So and St Aid from 11. *26 Gledhow Wood Close, Leeds LS8 1PN* T: 0113-266 7731

RAWLINSON, Curwen. b 32. MBE 73. Leeds Univ CertEd 55 Man Univ DipEd 56 Open Univ BA 80. Sarum Th Coll 59. **d** 61 **p** 62. C Wigan St Mich *Liv* 61-63; CF 63-78; Dep Asst Chapl Gen 78-80; Asst Chapl Gen 80-85; QHC 83-98; R Uley w Owlpen and Nympsfield *Glouc* 85-98; RD Dursley 89-96; rtd 98; PtO *Glouc* from 98; Sub Chapl HM Pris Glouc from 02. *Cark House, 6 Groves Place, Fairford GL7 4BJ* T: (01285) 711009

RAWLINSON, Preb James Nigel. b 56. Em Coll Cam BA 77 MB, BCh 80 FRCSE 86 FFAEM 98. WMMTC 95. **d** 98 **p** 99. NSM Bath Weston All SS w N Stoke and Langridge *B & W* from 98; PtO *Bris* from 98; Consultant Bris R Infirmary from 99; Preb Wells Cathl from 15. *Glen Boyd House, 38 Court View, Wick, Bristol BS30 5QP* T: 0117-303 9220 E: email@nigelrawlinson.co.uk

RAWLINSON, John. b 47. Guy's Hosp Medical Sch BSc 67 MB, BS 71 MRCS. EAMTC 89. **d** 92 **p** 93. NSM Tilbrook *Ely* 92-05; NSM Covington 92-05; NSM Catworth Magna 92-05; NSM Keyston and Bythorn 92-05; Chapl Chu Coll Cam from 98. *The Malt House, 42 Stonely, Huntingdon PE28 0EH* T: (01480) 860263 F: 861590 E: dingleberry@lineone.net *or* jr338@cam.ac.uk

RAWSON, Canon Michael Graeme. b 62. York Univ BA 84. St Steph Ho Ox BA 88. **d** 89 **p** 90. C Brighouse St Martin *Wakef*

89-92; C Brighouse and Clifton 92-93; V Gomersal 93-04; Bp's Dom Chapl and Publicity Officer 04-07; Can Res Wakef Cathl 07-14; Can Res S'wark Cathl from 14; Vice Dean S'wark from 14. *73 St George's Road, London SE1 6ER*
E: michael.rawson@southwark.anglican.org

RAY, Mrs Joanna Zorina. b 55. AIMLS 78 K Coll Lon BSc 77 Garnett Coll Lon PGCE 80 Lon Inst of Educn MA 92. S'wark Ord Course 84. **d** 87 **p** 94. NSM Carshalton *S'wark* 87-91; NSM Sutton New Town St Barn 91-93; NSM Knighton St Mary Magd *Leic* 93-94; C Leic H Spirit 94-98; Chapl for Deaf People 94-98; Chapl St Andr Hosp Northn 99-03; PtO *S'well* 04-12; *S'wark* from 12. *45 Sanderstead Court Avenue, South Croydon CR2 9AW* T: (020) 8405 0303 M: 07802-300799
E: revdjoannaray@gmail.com

RAY, John Mead. b 28. OBE 79. St Andr Univ MA 50 DipEd 51. CMS Tr Coll Chislehurst 60. **d** 70 **p** 71. Miss Partner CMS 70-95; C Sparkhill St Jo *Birm* 87-90; C Sparkbrook Em 87-90; C Sparkhill w Greet and Sparkbrook 90; Deanery Missr 90-95; rtd 95; PtO *Birm* 95-14. *190 Sarehole Road, Birmingham B28 8EF* T: 0121-777 6143 E: cath.john@blueyonder.co.uk

RAY, Robin John. b 44. Sarum & Wells Th Coll 72. **d** 74 **p** 75. C Bourne Valley *Sarum* 74-78; P-in-c Dilton's-Marsh 78-82; V 82-87; V Taunton Lyngford *B & W* 87-93; R Exford, Exmoor, Hawkridge and Withypool 93-04; ACORA Link Officer and Rural Affairs Officer 93-04; rtd 04; PtO *B & W* from 04; RD Glastonbury 09-11. *Leigholt Farm, Somerton Road, Street BA16 0SU* T: (01458) 841281 M: 07772-563597
E: robinray@btinternet.com

RAYBOULD, James Clive Ransford. b 37. Wolv Univ BSc 62 Anglia Poly Univ MBA 94 PhD 01. Cranmer Hall Dur 81. **d** 83 **p** 84. C Cannock *Lich* 83-86; P-in-c Leek Wootton *Cov* 86-89; Dioc Tr Adv 86-89; TV Cannock *Lich* 89; Assoc Lect Anglia Ruskin Univ *Chelmsf* from 90; rtd 00. *29 Greystones, Bromham, Chippenham SN15 2JT* T: (01380) 859623

✠**RAYFIELD, The Rt Revd Lee Stephen.** b 55. Southn Univ BSc 78 Lon Univ PhD 81 SOSc 95. Ridley Hall Cam 93. **d** 93 **p** 94 **c** 05. C Woodford Wells *Chelmsf* 93-97; P-in-c Furze Platt *Ox* 97-05; AD Maidenhead and Windsor 00-05; Suff Bp Swindon *Bris* from 05. *Mark House, Field Rise, Swindon SN1 4HP* T: (01793) 538654 F: 525181
E: bishop.swindon@bristoldiocese.org

RAYMENT, Andrew David. b 45. Univ of Wales (Lamp) BA 68 Univ of Wales (Abth) MA 70 Nottm Univ PhD 06. Ridley Hall Cam 78. **d** 80 **p** 81. C Costessey *Nor* 80-83; C Earlham St Anne 83-90; V Old Catton 90-96; PtO *Pet* 00-11; Min Partnership Development Officer 04-11; Adult Educn Officer (CME and Min Partnership) 05-11; rtd 11; P-in-c Ketton, Collyweston, Easton-on-the-Hill etc *Pet* from 11. *The Vicarage, 4 Edmonds Drive, Ketton, Stamford PE9 3TH* T: (01780) 729052
M: 07752-648537 E: andrew-rayment2010@hotmail.co.uk

RAYMENT, Mrs Helen Elizabeth. b 46. Keswick Hall Coll CertEd 67. EAMTC 92. **d** 95 **p** 96. NSM Old Catton *Nor* 95-96; PtO *Pet* 01-02; P-in-c Weedon Bec w Everdon and Dodford 02-03; V 03-11; rtd 11. *The Vicarage, 4 Edmonds Drive, Ketton, Stamford PE9 3TH* T: (01780) 729052
E: h.rayment@btinternet.com

RAYMER, Victoria Elizabeth. b 46. Wellesley Coll (USA) BA 68 Harvard Univ MA 69 JD 78 PhD 81. St Steph Ho Ox BA 86 Qu Coll Birm 88. **d** 89 **p** 94. Par Dn Bushey *St Alb* 89-94; C Eaton Socon 94-98; V Milton Ernest, Pavenham and Thurleigh 98-01; Dir Studies Westcott Ho Cam from 01. *1 Short Street, Cambridge CB1 1LB* T: (01223) 352922 or T/F: 741011
E: ver21@cam.ac.uk

RAYMOND, The Very Revd Walter. b 49. **d** 92 **p** 93. OGS from 93; C Willowdale All So Canada 92-94; Chapl H Trin Sch Toronto 94-99; Dean and R H Trin Cathl Quebec 99-07; Chapl Monte Carlo *Eur* from 08. *St Paul's House, 22 avenue de Grande-Bretagne, 98000 Monte Carlo, Monaco* T: (00377) 9330 7106 F: 9330 5039 E: wraymond@ogs.net

RAYMONT, Philip Richard. b 56. Univ of Qld BA 79 BEdSt 86 Melbourne Univ MEd 00 Cam Univ PhD 05 MACE. **d** 04 **p** 09. Asst Chapl Selw Coll Cam 04-07; PtO *Ely* 07-09; Sen Chapl Guildford Gr Sch Australia from 09. *Guildford Grammar, 11 Terrace Road, Guildford WA 6935, Australia* T: (0061) (8) 9377 9245 E: praymont@ggs.wa.edu.au

RAYNER, Canon George Charles. b 26. Bps' Coll Cheshunt 50. **d** 52 **p** 53. C Rowbarton *B & W* 52-56; V Taunton H Trin 56-63; Chapl Taunton and Somerset Hosp 60-63; V Lower Sandown St Jo *Portsm* 63-69; R Wootton 69-89; Hon Can Portsm Cathl 84-89; rtd 89; PtO *B & W* 89-92; *Portsm* from 98; P-in-c Six Pilgrims *B & W* 93-02. *The Bungalow, 1 Alresford Road, Shanklin PO37 6HX* T: (01983) 867304

RAYNER, Mrs Karen June. b 54. ERMC 08. **d** 11 **p** 12. NSM Ormesby St Marg w Scratby, Ormesby St Mich etc *Nor* 11-13; C Redenhall w Scole 13-15; P-in-c Martham and Repps w Bastwick, Thurne etc from 15. *3 Bowman Close, Playing Field Lane, Martham, Great Yarmouth NR29 4SS* M: 07787-715819
T: (01379) 741223 E: kjrayner23@hotmail.com

RAYNER, Michael John. b 55. Magd Coll Ox BA 78 DPhil 85. Ox Min Course 04. **d** 07 **p** 08. Dir Br Heart Foundn Health Promotion Research Gp from 94; NSM Ox St Matt from 07. *198 Marlborough Road, Oxford OX1 4LT* T: (01865) 289244 M: 07871-758745 E: mike.rayner@dph.ox.ac.uk

RAYNER, Paul Anthony George. b 39. Dur Univ BA 60 Lon Univ BD 68 Cape Town Univ MA 79. Lon Coll of Div 65. **d** 68 **p** 69. C Crookes St Thos *Sheff* 68-72; P-in-c Diep River St Luke S Africa 72-79; P-in-c S Shoebury *Chelmsf* 80-84; R 84-97; V Loughton St Mich 97-04; rtd 04; PtO *Chelmsf* from 04; *Eur* from 08. *36 Amberley Road, Buckhurst Hill IG9 5QW* T: (020) 8504 7434 E: prayner@globalnet.co.uk

RAYNER, Miss Rosemary Jane. b 54. ERMC 12. **d** 15. NSM Nor Lakenham St Jo and All SS and Tuckswood from 15. *7 St Andrew's Close, Poringland, Norwich NR14 7TB* T: (01508) 495650

RAYNER, Mrs Shirley Christine. b 54. SEITE BA 08. **d** 05 **p** 06. C S Croydon St Pet and St Aug *S'wark* 05-09; C Carew *St D* 09-11; TV 11-14; P-in-c Carew and Cosheston and Nash and Redberth 14; Dioc Lay Development Officer 11-14; rtd 14; PtO *St D* from 14. *2 Cooksyeat View, Kilgetty SA68 0UA* T: (01834) 810044 E: revshirley@btinternet.com

RAYNER, Stewart Leslie. b 39. St Jo Coll Dur BA 61 MA 73. Cranmer Hall Dur. **d** 67 **p** 68. C Whiston *Sheff* 67-70; C Doncaster St Geo 70-74; Chapl Doncaster R Infirmary 70-74; R Adwick-le-Street *Sheff* 74-85; V Totley 85-91; Asst Chapl Pastures Hosp Derby 91-94; Asst Chapl Kingsway Hosp Derby 91-94; Asst Chapl S Derby Mental Health Services 91-94; P-in-c Etwall w Egginton *Derby* 94-99; R 99-08; RD Longford 96-01; rtd 09. *26 Lawn Avenue, Etwall, Derby DE65 6JB* T: (01283) 736079
E: stewart.rayner37@googlemail.com

RAYNER-WILLIAMS, Gareth Wynn. b 67. St D Coll Lamp BA 88 Hull Univ MA 89 Trin Coll Carmarthen PGCE 06. Westcott Ho Cam 89. **d** 91 **p** 92. C Mold *St As* 91-93; TV Hawarden 93-95; Ecum Chapl Glam Univ *Llan* 95-99; Lect Cardiff Univ from 99; Dir Academic Studies St Mich Coll Llan 99-04; Vice-Prin 02-04; V Roath *Llan* 04-05; PtO from 05; Hd RS Hawthorn Comp Sch Pontypridd 06-08; Chapl Bp of Llan High Sch from 08; Hd RE from 12; Asst Hd Teacher from 15. *12 Fairwater Grove West, Llandaff, Cardiff CF5 2JQ* T: (029) 2056 9581
E: garethraynerwilliams@me.com *or* garethrw@icloud.com

RAYNES, Canon Andrew. b 60. R Holloway Coll Lon BA 83. Wycliffe Hall Ox 93. **d** 95 **p** 96. C Crowborough *Chich* 95-99; V Blackb Ch Ch w St Matt from 99; AD Blackb and Darwen from 03; Hon Can Blackb Cathl from 10. *The Vicarage, Brandy House Brow, Blackburn BB2 3EY* T: (01254) 56292
E: andrewraynes@btopenworld.com

RAYNHAM, Mrs Penelope Anne. b 44. SWMTC 97. **d** 00 **p** 01. OLM S Hill w Callington *Truro* 00-15; rtd 15. *Bramblings, Honicombe Corner, Harrowbarrow, Callington PL17 8JN* T: (01822) 833065 E: penny@bramvista.co.uk

RAYNOR, Duncan Hope. b 58. Ex Coll Ox MA 80 MA 82 Birm Univ PGCE 88 MLitt 93. Qu Coll Birm 82. **d** 84 **p** 85. C Kings Heath *Birm* 84-87; PtO from 87; Hd of RE Alderbrook Sch Solihull 88-94; Chapl K Edw Sch Birm from 94. *29 Edenhall Road, Quinton, Birmingham B32 1DA* T: 0121-684 3407 or 472 1672 E: dhr@kes.bham.sch.uk

RAYNOR, Lynn Mary. b 52. HCIMA 00. St Jo Coll Nottm 12. **d** 13 **p** 14. NSM Ravenshead *S'well* from 13. *18 Park Drive, Hucknall, Nottingham NG15 7LQ* T: 0115-953 5949 M: 07855-648410 E: rev.raynorshine@virginmedia.com

RAYNOR, Michael. b 53. Lanc Univ BA 74 MSc 75. Ripon Coll Cuddesdon BA 84 MA 99. **d** 85 **p** 86. C Gt Crosby St Faith *Liv* 85-88; V Warrington St Barn 88-97; V Orford St Andr from 97; AD Warrington 99-05; Hon Can Liv Cathl 03-05. *St Andrew's Vicarage, Poplars Avenue, Orford, Warrington WA2 9UE* T: (01925) 631903 E: mjraynor@care4free.net

RAZZALL, Charles Humphrey. b 55. Worc Coll Ox BA 76 MA 81 Qu Coll Cam BA 78. Westcott Ho Cam 76. **d** 79 **p** 80. C Catford (Southend) and Downham *S'wark* 79-83; V Crofton Park St Hilda w St Cypr 83-87; UPA Officer 87-92; TV Oldham *Man* 87-01; AD 92-99; Hon Can Man Cathl 98-01; R Coppenhall *Ches* from 01. *The Rectory, 198 Ford Lane, Crewe CW1 3TN* T: (01270) 215151
E: razzall@angelfields.eclipse.co.uk

REA, Andrew Humphreys. b 47. CQSW 73 Blackpool and Fylde Coll of Further Tech TCert 92 Cen Lancs Univ BA 96 CertEd 98. **d** 05 **p** 06. NSM Blackpool St Mark *Blackb* 05-07; PtO from 12. *35 Rowntree Avenue, Fleetwood FY7 7HE* E: ahrea2@yahoo.co.uk

REA, Simon William John. b 60. G&C Coll Cam MA Victoria Univ Wellington MA Liv Univ BTh 07 Univ of Wales (Ban)

PGCE. Ridley Hall Cam 02. **d** 04 **p** 05. C Moreton *Ches* 04-08; C Edgware *Lon* from 08. *St Peter's Vicarage, Stonegrove, Edgware HA8 8AB* M: 07905-699185 E: simonrea@gmx.net

READ, Andrew Gordon. b 40. Nottm Univ BA 69 MRICS 63 FRICS 86. Cuddesdon Coll 70. **d** 70 **p** 71. C E Retford *S'well* 70-72; C Woodthorpe 72-76; P-in-c Newark St Leon 76-78; PtO *Roch* 79-91. *The Gables, 148 Hastings Road, Battle TN33 0TW* T: (01424) 773044

READ, Benjamin Stanley. b 85. Univ of Wales (Cardiff) BA 07. St Mich Coll Llan BTh 12. **d** 12 **p** 13. C Carmarthen St Pet *St D* 12-14; C Carmarthen St Pet and Abergwili etc from 14. *St Peter's Clergy House, 10A The Parade, Carmarthen SA31 1LY* T: (01267) 780434

READ, Charles William. b 60. Man Univ BA 81 MPhil 95 Man Poly PGCE 82. St Jo Coll Nottm 86. **d** 88 **p** 89. C Oldham *Man* 88-90; C Urmston 90-94; P-in-c Broughton St Jas w St Clem and St Matthias 94-96; TV Broughton 96-99; Lect Cranmer Hall Dur 99-06; Dir Studies 00-06; Teacher Dur Sch 06; Vice-Prin and Dir Studies Nor Dioc Min Course 07-13; Reader Tr Co-ord from 13. *42 Heigham Road, Norwich NR2 3AU* T: (01603) 660824 *or* 632041
E: charlesread@norwich.anglican.org

READ, Geoffrey Philip. b 60. Bris Univ LLB 82 Spurgeon's Coll MTh 04. Wycliffe Hall Ox 85. **d** 88 **p** 89. C Dorking St Paul *Guildf* 88-92; TV Westborough 92-97; TR 97-98; Chapl Basle *Eur* 98-13; P-in-c Freiburg-im-Breisau 98-01; CMD Advr Colchester Area *Chelmsf* from 13; Public Preacher from 13. *Diocesan Office, 53 New Street, Chelmsford CM1 1AT* T: (01245) 294400 E: gread@chelmsford.anglican.org

READ, James Arthur. b 51. Nottm Coll of Educn BEd 74. EMMTC 84. **d** 87 **p** 88. C Weoley Castle *Birm* 87-91; C W Smethwick 91-92; TV Atherton *Man* 92-97; P-in-c Facit 97-00; V Whitworth w Facit 00-08; P-in-c Royton St Anne from 08; C Heyside from 12. *St Anne's Vicarage, St Anne's Avenue, Royton, Oldham OL2 5AD* T: 0161-652 3090
E: revjames.read@icloud.com

READ, John. b 33. Worc Coll Ox BA 56 MA 60. Chich Th Coll 56. **d** 58 **p** 59. C Babbacombe *Ex* 58-60; C Heavitree 60-63; V Swimbridge 63-69; V Ex St Matt 69-80; P-in-c Ex St Sidwell 79-80; R Ex St Sidwell and St Matt 80-83; Chapl Warneford Hosp Leamington Spa 83-89; Chapl S Warks Hosps 83-89; Chapl Dur and Chester le Street Hosps 89-95; Chapl Dryburn Hosp 89-95; rtd 95; NSM Tamworth *Lich* 95-98; PtO *Cov* from 02. *8 Newsholme Close, Warwick CV34 5XF* T: (01926) 411598

READ, John du Sautoy. CITC. **d** 66 **p** 67. V Choral Derry Cathl 66-67; Dean's V Derry Cathl 67; S Africa from 69. *8 Allison Road, Scottsville, 3209 South Africa* T: (0027) (33) 342 0262
E: woeber@lantic.net

READ, John Samuel. b 33. Fitzw Ho Cam BA 56. Clifton Th Coll 62. **d** 64 **p** 65. C Sneinton St Chris w St Phil *S'well* 64-67; C Huyton St Geo *Liv* 67-70; LtO *Blackb* 70-72; V Moldgreen *Wakef* 72-84; V Rawtenstall St Mary *Man* 84-91; Chapl Rossendale Gen Hosp 84-91; R Earsham w Alburgh and Denton *Nor* 91-98; P-in-c Ditchingham, Hedenham and Broome 94-98; rtd 98; PtO *Nor* from 98; *St E* from 98. *23 Kingston Drive, Beccles NR34 9RP* T: (01502) 712585

READ, Mrs Julie Margaret. b 61. Keble Coll Ox BA 82 Univ of Wales (Ban) PGCE 83. WEMTC 97. **d** 00 **p** 01. C Bishop's Castle w Mainstone, Lydbury N etc *Heref* 00-03; R Pembridge w Moor Court, Shobdon, Staunton etc 03-11; PtO 11-12; C Bredenbury 12-13; C Kingsland w Eardisland, Aymestrey etc 13; P-in-c from 13. *2 The Villas, Dilwyn, Hereford HR4 8HR* T: (01544) 319374 E: rev.julie@btinternet.com

READ, Maureen Elizabeth. b 52. Man Metrop Univ BEd 93 Ches Coll of HE BTh 99. NOC 95. **d** 98 **p** 99. NSM Leesfield *Man* 98-99; C 99-02; TV Heywood 02-09; V Meltham *Leeds* from 09. *The Vicarage, 150 Huddersfield Road, Meltham, Holmfirth HD9 4AL* T: (01484) 850050
E: maureen.read09@btinternet.com

READ, Michael Antony. b 75. Lanc Univ BA 99 St Jo Coll Dur BA 01. Cranmer Hall Dur 99. **d** 02 **p** 03. C Stanley *Liv* 02-05; P-in-c Lowton St Luke 05-11; P-in-c Sudden and Heywood All So *Man* from 11. *41 Harold Lees Road, Heywood OL10 4DW* T: (01706) 360693 E: revmikeread@yahoo.co.uk

READ, Nicholas George. b 51. Chelsea Coll Lon BSc 72 PhD 81. SEITE 97. **d** 00 **p** 01. NSM Beckenham St Jo *Roch* 00-03; P-in-c Penge Lane H Trin 03-09; V from 09. *Holy Trinity Vicarage, 64 Lennard Road, London SE20 7LX* T: (020) 8778 8113 M: 07904-317488 E: nicholas.read@diocese-rochester.org *or* hancompro@aol.com

READ, Nicholas John. b 59. OBE 99. Keble Coll Ox BA 81 MSc 82 MA 85. Ox Min Course 92. **d** 95 **p** 96. NSM Charlbury w Shorthampton *Ox* 95-98; Dir Rural Stress Information Network 96-00; Chapl for Agric *Heref* 98-11; Assoc from 11. *2 The Villas, Dilwyn, Hereford HR4 8HR* T: (01544) 319374

READ, Canon Robert Edgar. b 47. Kelham Th Coll 66. **d** 70 **p** 71. C Harton Colliery *Dur* 70-75; C Wilmslow *Ches* 76-80; V Gatley 80-92; V Offerton 92-06; RD Stockport 00-05; V Newton 06-07; P-in-c Gatley 07-10; V 10-14; Hon Can Ches Cathl 03-14; rtd 14. *10 Stanley Boughey Place, Nantwich CW5 6GQ* E: reread@btinternet.com

READ, Victor. b 29. Lon Univ BD 58. ALCD 57. **d** 58 **p** 59. C Wimbledon *S'wark* 58-61; C Lt Marlow *Ox* 61-64; V Wootton *Linc* 64-67; R Croxton 64-67; V Ulceby 64-67; V Linc St Pet in Eastgate w St Marg 67-73; V W Wimbledon Ch Ch *S'wark* 73-94; rtd 94; PtO *Pet* from 94. *27 Nightingale Drive, Towcester NN12 6RA* T: (01327) 352027

✠**READE, The Rt Revd Nicholas Stewart.** b 46. Leeds Univ BA 70. Coll of Resurr Mirfield 70. **d** 73 **p** 74 **c** 04. C Evington St Chad *Lich* 73-75; C Codsall 75-78; V Upper Gornal 78-82; V Mayfield *Chich* 82-88; RD Dallington 82-88; V Eastbourne St Mary 88-97; RD Eastbourne 88-97; Can and Preb Chich Cathl 90-97; Min The Hydneye CD 91-93; Adn Lewes and Hastings 97-04; Bp Blackb 04-12; rtd 12; Hon Asst Bp Eur from 13; Hon Asst Bp Chich from 13. *5 Warnham Gardens, Bexhill-on-Sea TN39 3SP*

READE, Richard Barton. b 66. Wolv Poly BA 88. Ripon Coll Cuddesdon BA 91 MA 97. **d** 92 **p** 93. C Wilnecote *Lich* 92-96; C Penkridge 96-98; P-in-c Basford 98-04; P-in-c Matlock Bank *Derby* 04-11; V Matlock Bank and Tansley from 11. *All Saints' Vicarage, Smedley Street, Matlock DE4 3JG* T: (01629) 584107 E: richardreade@btinternet.com

READER, Christine Sarah. b 44. STETS. **d** 00 **p** 01. NSM N Waltham and Steventon, Ashe and Deane *Win* 00-11; rtd 11; PtO *Win* from 11. *5 Church Farm Close, North Waltham, Basingstoke RG25 2BN* T: (01256) 397503

READER, John. b 53. Trin Coll Ox BA 75 MA 79 Man Univ MPhil 87 Univ of Wales (Ban) PhD 02. Ripon Coll Cuddesdon 76. **d** 78 **p** 79. C Ely 78-80; C Baguley *Man* 80-83; TV Kirkby Lonsdale *Carl* 83-86; V Lydbury N *Heref* 86-89; P-in-c Hopesay w Edgton 86-89; R Lydbury N w Hopesay and Edgton 89-90; Tutor Glouc Sch for Min 86-88; Vice-Prin 88-90; Dir Past Th Sarum & Wells Th Coll 90-92; P-in-c Elmley Lovett w Hampton Lovett and Elmbridge etc *Worc* 92-07; Assoc Tr and Educn Officer 92-02; Ind Chapl 01-07; P-in-c Chelford w Lower Withington and Dioc Rural Officer *Ches* 07-09; R Ironstone *Ox* from 09. *The Rectory, Church Street, Wroxton, Banbury OX15 6QE* T: (01795) 730346
E: drjohnreader@hotmail.co.uk

READER, The Ven Trevor Alan John. b 46. Lon Univ BSc 68 MSc 70 Portsm Poly PhD 72. S Dios Minl Tr Scheme 83. **d** 86 **p** 87. C Alverstoke *Portsm* 86-89; P-in-c Hook w Warsash 89-95; V 95-98; P-in-c Blendworth w Chalton w Idsworth 98-03; Dioc Dir NSM 98-03; Adn Is of Wight 03-06; Adn Portsdown 06-13; Bp's Liaison Officer for Pris 03-06; Bp's Liaison Officer for Hosps 06-13; rtd 13; PtO *Portsm* from 13. *54 David Newberry Drive, Lee-on-the-Solent PO13 8FE* M: 07826-846133 E: trevor.reader@hotmail.co.uk

READING, Glenn Thomas. b 76. Staffs Univ BSc 98. Ripon Coll Cuddesdon 07. **d** 09 **p** 10. C Horninglow *Lich* 09-13; TV Redditch Ch the K *Worc* from 13. *The Vicarage, 16 Church Road, Astwood Bank, Redditch B96 6EH* T: (01527) 894436 M: 07964-282278 E: glenn.reading@gmail.com

READING, Mrs Lesley Jean. b 49. GNSM 70 Trent Park Coll of Educn CertEd 71. NOC 98. **d** 01 **p** 02. NSM Eccles *Man* 01-05; P-in-c Heywood St Jas 05-11; rtd 11; PtO *Man* from 12. *21 Sunny Bower Street, Tottington, Bury BL8 3HL* T: (01204) 886108 E: readinglesley@hotmail.com

READING, Miss Siân Jacqueline Mary. b 64. Westcott Ho Cam 92. **d** 95 **p** 96. C Northampton St Alb *Pet* 95-98; TV Duston 98-05; P-in-c Gretton w Rockingham and Cottingham w E Carlton from 05. *The Vicarage, Station Road, Gretton, Corby NN17 3BU* T: (01536) 770237 E: sjmr216@btinternet.com

READING, Area Bishop of. *See* PROUD, The Rt Revd Andrew John

REAGON, Darrol Franklin. b 46. St Mich Coll Llan 74. **d** 76 **p** 77. C Llandrillo-yn-Rhos *St As* 76-78; C Hawarden 78-81; V Northwich St Luke and H Trin *Ches* 81-85; V Moulton *Linc* 85-91; V Scunthorpe Resurr 91-92; P-in-c Branston 92-94; R Branston w Nocton and Potterhanworth 94-07; rtd 07; PtO *Win* from 09. *17 Wessex Avenue, New Milton BH25 6NG* T: (01425) 613622 E: revddarrol@btinternet.com

REAKES, Richard Frank. b 68. STETS 02. **d** 05 **p** 06. NSM Shepton Mallet w Doulting *B & W* 05-09; NSM Evercreech w Chesterblade and Milton Clevedon 09-14; TV Bishop's Cleeve and Woolstone w Gotherington etc *Glouc* from 14. *The Rectory, 67 Malleson Road, Gotherington, Cheltenham GL52 9EX* E: reakes4@aol.com

REAKES-WILLIAMS, Gordon Martin. b 63. St Cath Coll Cam BA 86 MA 89 St Jo Coll Dur BA 90. Cranmer Hall Dur. **d** 91 **p** 92. C Harold Wood *Chelmsf* 91-94; Chapl Leipzig *Eur* from 95. *Hillerstrasse 3, 04109 Leipzig, Germany* T: (0049) (341) 302 7951 F: 215 3666 M: 177-240 4207 E: earwig@t-online.de

REALE, Mrs Kathleen. b 38. Carl Dioc Tr Course 83. **dss** 86 **d** 87 **p** 94. Dalston *Carl* 86-87; Par Dn 87-90; Par Dn Westward, Rosley-w-Woodside and Welton 87-90; Par Dn Thursby 89-90; Dn-in-c Gt Salkeld w Lazonby 90-94; P-in-c 94-97; rtd 97; PtO *Carl* from 98. *17 Caldew Drive, Dalston, Carlisle CA5 7NS* T: (01228) 711749

REANEY, Mrs Beverly Jane. b 58. Nottm Univ BA 81. S Wales Ord Course 00. **d** 03 **p** 04. NSM Llanharry *Llan* 03-11; NSM Llangynwyd w Maesteg 11-13; P-in-c Glyncorrwg and the Upper Afan Valley etc from 13. *12 Cwrt y Fedwen, Maesteg CF34 9GH* T: (01656) 734142
E: bjreaney1158@btinternet.com

REANEY, Christopher Thomas. b 60. Univ of Wales (Lamp) BA 82. St Mich Coll Llan. **d** 85 **p** 86. C Maindee Newport *Mon* 85-87; C Griffithstown 88-89; V Treherbert w Treorchy *Llan* 89-99; V Treorchy and Treherbert 99-02; R Llanfabon 02-11; V Troedrhiwgarth from 11. *12 Cwrt y Fedwen, Maesteg CF34 9GH* T: (01656) 734142
E: c.reaney350@btinternet.com

REAPER-BROWN, Graham Stanley. b 51. Sarum & Wells Th Coll 82. **d** 84 **p** 85. C Crediton and Shobrooke *Ex* 84-87; Chapl RAF 87-93 and 99-06; R Elgin w Lossiemouth *Mor* 93-98; R Castle Douglas *Glas* 98-99; Chapl Sherwood Forest Hosps NHS Trust 06-09; Chapl Univ Hosps Bris NHS Foundn Trust 09-11; rtd 11. *11 Severn Road, Shirehampton, Bristol BS11 9TE* T: 0117-3821 748 E: padregsbrown@aol.com

REARDON, Mrs Catherine Barbara. b 57. **d** 10 **p** 11. C Bradley and Fixby and Cowcliffe *Wakef* 10-13; V Erringden *Leeds* from 13. *The Vicarage, Brier Hey Lane, Mytholmroyd, Hebden Bridge HX7 5PJ* T: (01422) 883944
E: cathyreardon@virginmedia.com

REAST, Eileen Joan. *See* BANGAY, Eileen Joan

REAVLEY, Cedric. b 51. Lon Univ BPharm 73. **d** 05 **p** 06. OLM Burford w Fulbrook, Taynton, Asthall etc *Ox* from 05. *124 High Street, Burford OX18 4QR* T: (01993) 823957 F: 824887
E: cedric_reavley@lineone.net

RECORD, John. b 47. St Chad's Coll Dur BA 71. Westcott Ho Cam 71. **d** 73 **p** 74. C Paddington St Jo w St Mich *Lon* 73-75; C Witney *Ox* 75-78; P-in-c Lt Compton and Chastleton 78-80; R Lt Compton w Chastleton, Cornwell etc 80-83; V Hawkhurst *Cant* 83-97; RD W Charing 89-95; Hon Can Cant Cathl 96-97; P-in-c Devizes St Jo w St Mary *Sarum* 97-07; P-in-c Devizes St Pet 00-04; RD Devizes 98-07; Can and Preb Sarum Cathl 02-07; V Hammersmith St Pet *Lon* 07-14; rtd 15. *155 Watchfield Court, Sutton Court Road, London W4 4NE*

RECORD, Sister Marion Eva. b 25. MRCS 50 LRCP 50 Leeds Univ FFARCS 57 Lon Univ BD 79. **dss** 78 **d** 87 **p** 94. OHP from 72; Chapl Hull Univ *York* 72-78; Chapl York Univ 78-80; LtO 80-95; PtO from 95; rtd 96. *St Hilda's Priory, Sneaton Castle, Whitby YO21 3QN* T: (01947) 602079

REDDIN, Mrs Christine Emily. b 46. Essex Univ BA 67. STETS 01. **d** 04 **p** 05. NSM Burpham *Guildf* 04-10; rtd 11; PtO *Guildf* from 11. *The Corner House, Sutton Green Road, Guildford GU4 7QD* T: (01483) 714708 M: 07764-677898
E: c.reddin@sky.com

REDDING, Benjamin James. b 73. K Coll Lon BSc 94 PGCE 95. Oak Hill Th Coll BA 05. **d** 05 **p** 06. C Angmering *Chich* from 05. *7 Beech View, Angmering, Littlehampton BN16 4DE* T: (01903) 784459 E: benjamesredding@yahoo.co.uk

REDDING, Roger Charles. b 45. Chich Th Coll 87. **d** 89 **p** 90. C Yeovil St Mich *B & W* 89-93; P-in-c Salisbury St Mark *Sarum* 93-94; LtO 94-96; TV Chalke Valley 96-12; Chapl to Travelling People 02-12; rtd 12; PtO *Bris* from 02; *B & W* from 03; *Win* from 12. *46 Queen Street, Tintinhull, Yeovil BA22 8PQ* T: (0135) 825057 E: mail@rogerredding.co.uk

REDDINGTON, Gerald Alfred. b 34. S'wark Ord Course 76. **d** 79 **p** 79. NSM St Vedast w St Mich-le-Querne etc *Lon* 79-85; Dir Past Support Gp Scheme 83-86; Hon C St Marylebone All SS 85-90; PtO *Portsm* from 88; V Ealing St Barn *Lon* 90-99; rtd 99; PtO *Lon* from 02. *The Orange Tree, Madeira Road, Seaview PO34 5BA* T: (01983) 617026
E: rev.redd@btinternet.com

REDEYOFF, Neil Martyn. b 69. St Jo Coll Nottm BA 01. **d** 01 **p** 02. C Grange St Andr and Runcorn H Trin *Ches* 01-04; R Darfield *Sheff* 04-08; P-in-c Finningley w Auckley 08-10; R from 10; AD W Doncaster from 11. *The Rectory, Rectory Lane, Finningley, Doncaster DN9 3DA* T: (01302) 770240
E: neilredeyoff1@btinternet.com

REDFEARN, James Jonathan. b 62. Newc Univ BA 83 PGCE 89. Cranmer Hall Dur 95. **d** 95 **p** 96. C Kidsgrove *Lich* 95-97. *56 Holly Avenue, Jesmond, Newcastle upon Tyne NE2 2QA* T: 0191-281 9046 E: jaredfearn@compuserve.com

REDFEARN, Michael. b 42. Open Univ BA 78 Hull Univ MA 84 BA 86. St Aid Birkenhead 64. **d** 68 **p** 69. C Bury St Pet *Man* 68-71; C Swinton St Pet 71-74; Ind Chapl *Bris* 74-79 and 80-81; Ind Chapl Australia 79-80; Ind Chapl *York* 81-86;

V Southill and Course Dir St Alb Minl Tr Scheme 86-93; Dep Chapl HM Pris Wandsworth 94; Chapl HM YOI and Rem Cen Feltham 94-97; Chapl HM YOI Aylesbury 97-02; rtd 02; Asst Chapl Palma de Mallorca *Eur* 04-10. *26 Chardwar Gardens, Bourton-on-the-Water, Cheltenham GL54 2BL*
E: mandsfearn42@gmail.com

REDFEARN, Ms Tracy Anne. b 66. Heythrop Coll Lon BD 88. Ripon Coll Cuddesdon 91. **d** 93 **p** 94. C Haslemere *Guildf* 93-97; TV Gt Grimsby St Mary and St Jas *Linc* 97-00; P-in-c Legbourne 00-01; P-in-c Raithby 00-01; P-in-c Wold-Marsh Gp 00-01; V Legbourne and Wold Marsh 01-05; C Brumby 05-08; rtd 08. *674 Firskill Crescent, Sheffield S4 7DR*
E: tracy.redfearn@btopenworld.com

✣**REDFERN, The Rt Revd Alastair Llewellyn John.** b 48. Ch Ch Ox BA 70 MA 74 Trin Coll Cam BA 74 MA 79 Bris Univ PhD 01. Westcott Ho Cam 72 Qu Coll Birm 75. **d** 76 **p** 77 **c** 97. C Tettenhall Regis *Lich* 76-79; Tutor Ripon Coll Cuddesdon 79-87; Hon C Cuddesdon *Ox* 83-87; Can Res Bris Cathl 87-97; Dioc Dir Tr 91-97; Suff Bp Grantham *Linc* 97-05; Dean Stamford 98-05; Can and Preb Linc Cathl 00-05; Bp Derby from 05. *The Bishop's House, 6 King Street, Duffield, Belper DE56 4EU* T: (01332) 840132 E: bishop@bishopofderby.org

REDFERN, Lisa. b 67. All SS Cen for Miss & Min 12. **d** 15. NSM Broadheath *Ches* from 15. *Address withheld by request* T: 0161-976 5290 M: 07934-216667
E: lisaredfern2011@live.co.uk

REDFERN, Paul. b 48. Ulster Univ BA 88. CITC BTh 94. **d** 94 **p** 95. C Belfast St Aid *Conn* 94-97; I Belfast St Mark 97-03; I Kilbride from 03. *Kilbride Rectory, 7 Rectory Road, Doagh, Ballyclare BT39 0PT* T: (028) 9334 0225

REDFIELD, David Peter. b 80. Anglia Ruskin Univ BA 10. Ridley Hall Cam 07. **d** 10 **p** 11. C Grays Thurrock *Chelmsf* 10-12; C Corringham and Fobbing 12-14. *24 The Crosspath, Radlett WD7 8HN* E: frdavidredfield@gmail.com

REDGERS, Brian. b 42. St Jo Coll Dur BA 65 Keswick Hall Coll PGCE 75. Westcott Ho Cam 65. **d** 67 **p** 68. C Rushmere *St E* 67-73; LtO from 73. *44 Belvedere Road, Ipswich IP4 4AB* T: (01473) 273829

REDGRAVE, Christine Howick. b 50. AIAT 73. Trin Coll Bris 75. **dss** 78 **d** 87 **p** 94. Watford *St Alb* 78; 78-83; Par Dn Bracknell *Ox* 87-94; TV 94-96; P-in-c Woolhampton w Midgham and Beenham Valance 96-04; Asst Dir of Ords 95-04; Dir of Ords (Reading and Dorchester) 04-10; Hon Can Ch Ch 00-10; C Yoxmere *St E* 10-14; V from 14; RD Saxmundham from 12. *The Rectory, The Street, Darsham, Saxmundham IP17 3QA* T: (01728) 667095 E: redgrave460@btinternet.com

REDHEAD, Edward. b 30. St Deiniol's Hawarden 60. **d** 63 **p** 64. C Mottram in Longdendale w Woodhead *Ches* 63-67; V Rivington *Man* 67-72; V Bloxwich *Lich* 72-75; Hon C Lich St Chad 82-84; P-in-c Bromfield w Waverton *Carl* 84-85; V 85-90; P-in-c W Newton 84-85; V 85-90; R Harrington 90-93; rtd 93. *Tigh-na-Mara, 2-3 Caroy, Struan, Isle of Skye IV56 8FQ* T: (01470) 572338

REDHOUSE, Mark David. b 67. Oak Hill Th Coll BA 94. **d** 94 **p** 95. C Fulham St Mary N End *Lon* 94-96; C Hove Bp Hannington Memorial Ch *Chich* 96-01; V Horam 01-10; RD Dallington 04-07; V Eastbourne All So from 10. *All Souls Vicarage, 53 Susans Road, Eastbourne BN21 3TH* T: (01323) 727033 E: markredhouse@aol.com

REDKNAP, Clive Douglas. b 53. Trin Coll Bris BA 95. **d** 95 **p** 96. C Patcham *Chich* 95-00; C Wadhurst and Stonegate 00-03; P-in-c Hollington St Jo 03-05; V 05-10. *87 Seabourne Road, Bexhill-on-Sea TN40 2SS*

REDMAN, Anthony James. b 51. Reading Univ BSc 72 Anglia Ruskin Univ MA 05 FRICS 95. EAMTC 01. **d** 03 **p** 04. NSM Bury St Edmunds All SS w St Jo and St Geo *St E* 03-06; NSM Blackbourne from 06. *The Cottage, Great Livermere, Bury St Edmunds IP31 1JG* T: (01359) 269335 F: (01284) 704734
E: tony@theredmans.co.uk

REDMAN, Canon Douglas Stuart Raymond. b 35. MCIOB 64. Roch Th Coll 66. **d** 68 **p** 69. C Shortlands *Roch* 68-71; V 80-00; R Kingsdown 71-76; R Chatham St Mary w St Jo 76-80; RD Beckenham 90-00; Hon Can Roch Cathl 93-00; PtO from 00; rtd 00; PtO *Cant* from 01. *25 Hovendens, Sissinghurst, Cranbrook TN17 2LA* T/F: (01580) 714600

REDMAN, Julia Elizabeth Hithersay. *See* WHITE, Julia Elizabeth Hithersay

REDMAN, Michael John. b 52. St Jo Coll Ox BA 74 Solicitor 86. NTMTC 04. **d** 06 **p** 07. NSM St Marylebone St Paul *Lon* from 06. *8 Bryanston Mews West, London W1H 2DD* T: (020) 7723 7407 E: redman.michaelj@gmail.com

REDPARTH, Paul Robert. b 58. Open Univ BSc 97 K Coll Lon PhD 01. Westcott Ho Cam 04. **d** 06 **p** 07. C Roughey *Chich* 06-09; C Forest Row 09-11; P-in-c Kirdford from 11. *The Vicarage, Kirdford, Billingshurst RH14 0LU* T: (01403) 820605

REDSELL, Corin Michael. b 69. Homerton Coll Cam BEd 92. Ridley Hall Cam 09. **d** 11 **p** 12. C Lordsbridge *Ely* 11-15; NSM from 15. *Address withheld by request*
E: corinredsell@lordsbridge.org

REDSHAW, Mrs Alison Janet. b 56. EMMTC. **d** 10 **p** 11. NSM Crich and S Wingfield *Derby* 10-13; C and Missr for Retirement Communities Repton from 13. *7 Chapel Close, Blackwell, Alfreton DE55 5BL* T: (01773) 819673
M: 07522-265336 E: rev-alison-r@hotmail.co.uk

REDWOOD, Canon David Leigh. b 32. Glas Univ DipSW 78. Edin Th Coll 57. **d** 59 **p** 60. C Stirling *Edin* 59-61; C Glas Ch Ch 61-64; P-in-c Glas Ascension 64-66; R 66-69; R Hamilton 69-74; R Callander *St And* 74-76; Hon C 76-78; R Lochearnhead 74-76; R Killin 74-76; Hon C Doune 76-78; Hon C Aberfoyle 78-85; R Dunfermline 85-97; TR W Fife Team Min 85-97; Can St Ninian's Cathl Perth 90-97; Syn Clerk 93-97; rtd 97. *8 Strathmore Avenue, Dunblane FK15 9HX*
T/F: (01786) 825493 E: david.redwood1@btinternet.com

REDWOOD, Marion. b 47. **d** 00 **p** 09. NSM Abercarn and Cwmcarn *Mon* 00-13; NSM Lower Islwyn from 13. *30 John Street, Cwmcarn, Crosskeys, Newport NP11 7EH* T: (01495) 271910

REECE, Donald Malcolm Hayden. b 36. CCC Cam BA 58 MA 62. Cuddesdon Coll 58. **d** 60 **p** 61. C Latchford St Jas *Ches* 60-63; C Matlock and Tansley *Derby* 63-67; C-in-c Hackenthorpe Ch Ch CD 67-70; C Salisbury Cathl Rhodesia 70-73; V Leic St Pet 74-82; V Putney St Marg *S'wark* 82-91; Home Sec Coun for Chr Unity 92-97; Hon C Wandsworth St Anne *S'wark* 94-97; V Shepherd's Bush St Steph w St Thos *Lon* 97-04; rtd 04; PtO *Ox* from 05. *8 Lamarsh Road, Oxford OX2 0LD* T: (01865) 792678

REECE, Paul Michael. b 60. Southn Univ BA 81. Coll of Resurr Mirfield 83. **d** 85 **p** 86. C Borehamwood *St Alb* 85-89; C Potters Bar 89-92; R Lt Stanmore St Lawr *Lon* from 92; AD Harrow 97-02. *Whitchurch Rectory, St Lawrence Close, Edgware HA8 6RB* T: (020) 8952 0019 F: 8537 0547 M: 07860-690503
E: paul.reece@london.anglican.org

REECE, Roger Walton Arden. b 56. **d** 00 **p** 01. OLM Chadderton St Luke *Man* 00-04; OLM Chadderton St Matt w St Luke 04-08; NSM 08-09; C Ashton from 09; Chapl HM Pris Buckley Hall from 08. *HM Prison Buckley Hall, Buckley Hall Road, Rochdale OL12 9DP* T: (01706) 514300
M: 07904-078901 E: roger.reece@ntlworld.com

REED, Adam Michael Frederick. b 73. Humberside Univ BA 95. Cranmer Hall Dur 96. **d** 99 **p** 00. C Northallerton w Kirby Sigston *York* 99-03; R Middleton, Newton and Sinnington 03-11; V Saltburn-by-the-Sea from 11; V New Marske from 14. *The Vicarage, Greta Street, Saltburn-by-the-Sea TS12 1LS* T: (01287) 622007 E: bilpop@btinternet.com

REED, Alan Ronald. b 44. Sarum Th Coll 66. **d** 68 **p** 70. C Ifield *Chich* 68-71; C Perivale *Lon* 71-72; C Ruislip St Martin 72-75; C Burgess Hill St Jo *Chich* 76-78; V Shoreham Beach 78-80; V Roughey 80-97; C-in-c Rusper 84-86; V Hove St Barn and St Agnes 97-10; rtd 10; PtO *Nor* from 10. *Candlemass Lodge, 12 Clarendon Road, Fakenham NR21 9HG* T: (01328) 855919

REED, Canon Annette Susan. b 54. Birm Univ BA 76 CQSW 78. Qu Coll Birm 84. **d** 87 **p** 94. C Churchover w Willey *Cov* 89-92; C Clifton upon Dunsmore and Newton 89-92; C Walsgrave on Sowe 92-95; C Cov E 92-95; C Burbage w Aston Flamville *Leic* 95-98; C Hinckley St Mary 95-98; C The Sheepy Gp 98-00; TV Bosworth and Sheepy Gp 00-06; V The Paxtons w Diddington *Ely* from 06; RD St Neots from 07; Hon Can Ely Cathl from 14. *The Vicarage, 24 St James's Road, Little Paxton, St Neots PE19 6QW* T: (01480) 211048
E: rev.reed@btinternet.com

REED, Brian. b 43. Bris Univ BSc 65. Linc Th Coll 73. **d** 76 **p** 77. C S Ashford Ch Ch *Cant* 76-78; C Spring Park 78-83; V Barming Heath 83-13; rtd 13; PtO *Cant* from 14. *8 The Thatchers, Maidstone ME16 0XA* T: (01622) 298164
M: 07759-620502

REED, Christopher John. b 42. Selw Coll Cam BA 64 MA 68. Cranmer Hall Dur 64. **d** 67 **p** 68. C Gt Ilford St Andr *Chelmsf* 67-70; P-in-c Bordesley St Andr *Birm* 70-72; V 72-80; V Crofton St Paul *Roch* 80-98; V Yalding w Collier Street 98-08; RD Paddock Wood 01-06; rtd 08; PtO *Roch* from 09. *66 Willow Park, Otford, Sevenoaks TN14 5NG* T: (01959) 523439
E: rev.chris.reed@sky.com

REED, Colin. *See* REED, Matthew Colin

REED, Colin Bryher. b 58. York Univ BA 80 RGN 86. Ridley Hall Cam 93. **d** 95 **p** 96. C Grays North *Chelmsf* 95-99; Chapl Plymouth Hosps NHS Trust 99-02; Hd Chapl Services Norfolk and Nor Univ Hosp NHS Trust 02-09; Asst RD Ingworth *Nor* 10-11; TR High Oak, Hingham and Scoulton w Wood Rising from 11. *The Rectory, Attleborough Road, Hingham, Norwich NR9 4HP* M: 07773-360262
E: revcolinreed@computekmail.co.uk

REED, Colin Charles Gilmour. b 40. LCP 75 FCP 86 St Luke's Coll Ex TCert 63 La Trobe Univ Vic MA 94 ACT ThD 06. Tyndale Hall Bris 67. **d** 69 **p** 70. C Weston-super-Mare Ch Ch *B & W* 69-71; Asst Master St Andr Sch Turi Kenya 71-79; Chapl Brighton Coll Jun Sch 79-80; R Corrimal Australia 80-84; Educn Sec CMS 84-99; Lect Amani Inst Tanzania 99-06; Australia from 06; rtd 06. *7 Camden Street, Wingello NSW 2579, Australia* T: (0061) (2) 4884 4551
E: wendyreed2@hotmail.com *or* cwreed@cms.org.au

REED, David. *See* REED, Richard David

REED, Mrs Elizabeth Christine. b 43. Lon Bible Coll Lon Univ BD 65. WMMTC 95. **d** 97 **p** 98. NSM Ledbury *Heref* from 97; Chapl Bromsgrove Sch 99-06. *The Old Barn, Perrystone Hill, Ross-on-Wye HR9 7QX* T: (01989) 780439

REED, Ethel Patricia Ivy. *See* WESTBROOK, Ethel Patricia Ivy

REED, Mrs Gillian Yvonne. b 44. CBDTI 04. **d** 07 **p** 10. NSM Blackb St Thos w St Jude 07-09; NSM Blackb St Mich w St Jo and H Trin 07-09; NSM Ospringe Deanery 09-10; NSM Faversham *Cant* 10-14; NSM Preston next Faversham, Goodnestone and Graveney 14; rtd 14; PtO *Cant* from 14. *18 Four Horseshoes Park, Seasalter Road, Graveney, Faversham ME13 9DE* T: (01795) 534059 E: gill.pete@talktalk.net

REED, Harvey. *See* REED, William Harvey

REED, The Ven John Peter Cyril. b 51. BD 78 AKC 78. Ripon Coll Cuddesdon 78. **d** 79 **p** 80. C Croydon St Jo *Cant* 79-82; Prec St Alb Abbey *St Alb* 82-86; R Timsbury and Priston *B & W* 86-93; Chapl Rural Affairs Bath Adnry 87-93; P-in-c Ilminster w Whitelackington 93-94; TR Ilminster and Distr 94-99; Adn Taunton from 99. *2 Monkton Heights, West Monkton, Taunton TA2 8LU* T: (01823) 413315 F: 413384
E: adtaunton@bathwells.anglican.org

REED, John William. b 57. Sussex Univ BSc 79. NOC 95. **d** 97 **p** 98. C Padgate *Liv* 97-99; C Orford St Marg 99-01; V 01-08; P-in-c Golborne 08-13; TV Lowton and Golborne from 13. *St Thomas's Rectory, Church Street, Golborne, Warrington WA3 3TH* T: (01942) 728305
E: john.reed@liverpool.anglican.org

REED (née McCARTHY), Mrs Lorraine Valmay. b 52. Birm Univ CertEd 73 Univ of Wales (Ban) BA 95 MTh 97 LGSM 82. SNWTP 09. **d** 11 **p** 12. NSM Middlewich w Byley *Ches* from 11; Asst Dir of Ords from 14. *1 Douglas Close, Hartford, Northwich CW8 1SH* T: (01606) 781071 M: 07711-379339
E: reed.blackbird77@tiscali.co.uk

REED, Malcolm Edward. b 45. Graduate Soc Dur MSc 75. Yorks Min Course 08. **d** 10 **p** 11. NSM Hoylandswaine and Silkstone w Stainborough *Wakef* 10-14; NSM Ryhill *Leeds* from 14; Bp's Hon Asst Chapl from 11. *Clough Cottage, Cathill, Hoylandswaine, Sheffield S36 7JB* T: (01226) 767328
M: 07803-031199 E: cathillreed@btinternet.com

REED, Matthew Colin. b 50. Edin Univ BD 82. Edin Th Coll 72. **d** 84 **p** 85. C Edin St Pet 84-87; P-in-c Linlithgow 87-94; P-in-c Bathgate 87-91; Chapl HM YOI Polmont 91-94; R Motherwell *Glas* 94-97; R Wishaw 94-97; Hon Asst P Edin St Fillan 00-14; Chapl HM Pris Edin 02-14; Hon C Edin Old St Paul from 14; P-in-c Edin St Marg from 14. *39 Hardgreen Lane, Dalkeith EH22 3NA* T: (01316) 634971 M: 07526-836767
E: colinmcreed@aol.com

REED, Matthew Graham. b 68. Nottm Univ BEng 89 Roehampton Inst MSc 03. Ripon Coll Cuddesdon BA 92 MA 97. **d** 93 **p** 94. C Oxton *Ches* 93-97; TV Gt Marlow w Marlow Bottom, Lt Marlow and Bisham *Ox* 97-02; Hd Lon and SE Team Chr Aid 02-04; C and Community Dir 04-08; Marketing Dir 08-10; Chief Exec Officer Cystic Fibrosis Trust 10-12; Chief Exec Officer Children's Soc from 12. *The Children's Society, Edward Rudolf House, Margery Street, London WC1X 0JL* T: (020) 7841 4446
E: matthew.reed@childrenssociety.org.uk

REED, Canon Pamela Kathleen. b 38. EMMTC. **dss** 84 **d** 87 **p** 94. Cambridge Ascension *Ely* 84-88; Par Dn 87-88; Par Dn Cherry Hinton St Andr 88-90; C 91-95; C Teversham 91-95; V Chesterton St Geo 95-04; Hon Can Ely Cathl 00-04; rtd 04; PtO *Ely* from 04. *17 Woodland Road, Sawston, Cambridge CB22 3DT* T: (01223) 832571
E: pamk.reed@hotmail.com

REED, Richard David. b 32. K Alfred's Coll Win CertEd 54 Ex Univ MA 02. Trin Coll Carmarthen. **d** 91 **p** 92. NSM Dale and St Brides w Marloes *St D* 91-96; P-in-c Blisland w St Breward *Truro* 96-99; rtd 99; PtO *Truro* from 99; *St D* from 02. *5 Smokehouse Quay, Milford Haven SA73 3BD* T: (01646) 663819 E: davidreed456@btinternet.com

REED, Canon Robert Chase. b 47. Emerson Coll Boston (USA) BSc 70 TCD HDipEd 72. **d** 87 **p** 88. Aux Min Taney *D & G* 87-97; Res Hd Master Wesley Coll Dub 87-12; Succ St Patr Cathl Dublin 93-97; Treas St Patr Cathl Dublin 96-01; Prec St Patr Cathl Dublin from 01. *38 Clonard Drive, Dublin 16, Republic of Ireland* T: (00353) (1) 295 6595
E: canrcr@gmail.com

REED, Simon John. b 63. Trin Coll Ox BA 86 MA 90. Wycliffe Hall Ox BA 90. **d** 91 **p** 92. C Walton H Trin *Ox* 91-96; P-in-c Hanger Hill Ascension and W Twyford St Mary *Lon* 96-01; V from 01. *The Ascension Vicarage, Beaufort Road, London W5 3EB* T/F: (020) 8566 9920 E: coa@talktalk.net

REED, William Harvey. b 47. K Coll Lon BD 69 AKC 69. St Aug Coll Cant 69. **d** 70 **p** 71. C Stockton St Mark CD *Dur* 70-72; C Billingham St Cuth 72-76; C S Westoe 76-79; V Chilton Moor 79-87; R Hutton *Chelmsf* 87-95; V Hullbridge 95-10; C Rawreth w Rettendon 06-10; V Rettendon and Hullbridge 10-12; rtd 12; PtO *Nor* from 12. *117 Lloyds Avenue, Kessingland, Lowestoft NR33 7TT* T: (01502) 741881 E: whreed@btinternet.com

REEDER, Angela Lilian. b 53. **d** 99 **p** 00. OLM Eastington, Frocester, Haresfield etc *Glouc* 99-04; PtO from 04. *St Loy Cottage, West End, Stonehouse GL10 3SL* T: (01453) 827446

REEDER, Michael William Peter. b 58. William Carlile Coll 84. **d** 09 **p** 10. Chapl St Luke's Hospice Sheff from 07; Hon C Sheff Cathl from 09; Liturg Chapl to Bp Doncaster from 12. *St Luke's Hospice, Little Common Lane, Sheffield S11 9NE* T: 0114-236 9911 M: 07947-706256 E: m.reeder@hospicesheffield.co.uk

REES (née HOLDER), Ms Adèle Claire. b 76. Luton Univ BSc 97 Sheff Univ MTh 03. Ripon Coll Cuddesdon 04. **d** 07 **p** 08. C Hill *Birm* 07-10; C Hatcham St Jas *S'wark* from 10; Chapl Goldsmiths' Coll Lon from 10; Ecum Adv Woolwich Area from 13. *3 St Michael's Centre, Desmond Street, London SE14 6JF* T: (020) 8691 4335 M: 07841-640974 E: adelerees@yahoo.co.uk

REES, Andrew Richard Akeroyd. b 76. Sydney Univ BEc. Moore Th Coll Sydney BD. **d** 04 **p** 05. C Kellyville Australia 04-06; C Fulwood *Sheff* 07-13; R Wahroonga St Andr Australia from 13. *2 Water Street, Wahroonga NSW 2076, Australia* T: (0061) (2) 9489 3278 F: 9489 0836 E: office@standys.org.au

REES, Anthony John. b 49. St Jo Coll Dur BA 72 MA 77 Man Univ MEd 89 MPhil 07. **d** 74 **p** 75. C Smethwick St Matt w St Chad *Birm* 74-77; C Bolton St Pet *Man* 77-80; R Cheetham St Mark 80-88; V Mottram in Longdendale w Woodhead *Ches* 88-93; V Mottram in Longdendale 93-02; V Chirk *St As* 02-14; rtd 14; PtO *Blackb* from 14. *31 Redhills Road, Arnside, Carnforth LA5 0AR* T: (01524) 761478 E: tonyandmary75@btinternet.com

REES, Antony. See REES, Percival Antony Everard

REES, Canon Brian. b 48. McGill Univ Montreal BA 74 St Andr Univ BD 76 PhD 80. Montreal Dioc Th Coll 76. **d** 80 **p** 81. C Montreal St Jas and Chapl Concordia Univ Canada 80-82; R Rawdon Ch Ch 82-85; Chapl Bedford Sch 85-92; Hd Master Bedford Prep Sch 92-97; Hd Master Pilgrims' Sch from 97; Hon Can Win Cathl from 11. *The Pilgrims' School, 3 The Close, Winchester SO23 9LT* T: (01962) 854189 E: hmsecretary@pilgrims-school.co.uk

REES, Ceirion James. b 80. Glam Univ BA 01 Trin Coll Bris BA 10. St Mich Coll Llan 10. **d** 10 **p** 11. C Coity, Nolton and Brackla *Llan* 10-13; P-in-c Hirwaun from 13. *The Vicarage, 6 Redhill Close, Hirwaun, Aberdare CF44 9NZ* T: (01685) 813046

REES, Celia Pamela. b 48. St D Coll Lamp BA 70. **d** 98 **p** 99. OLM Leominster *Heref* from 98. *Rivendell, 50 Oldfields Close, Leominster HR6 8TL* T: (01568) 616581 or 612124

REES, Mrs Christine Deryn Irving. b 57. Nottm Univ BSc Sheff Univ MA. Qu Coll Birm. **d** 00 **p** 01. NSM Astwood Bank *Worc* 00-01; C 01-03; TV Dronfield w Holmesfield *Derby* 03-11; PtO from 11. *54 Wake Road, Sheffield S7 1HG* T: 0114-250 7619 E: revdchristine@btopenworld.com

REES, Christopher John. b 40. Dur Univ BA 62. Ridley Hall Cam 62. **d** 64 **p** 65. C Wilmslow *Ches* 64-70; C Birkenhead St Pet w St Matt 70-74; V Lostock Gralam 75-83; R Davenham 83-96; P-in-c Aldford and Bruera 96-05; rtd 05; PtO *Ches* from 05. *15 Chapel Close, Comberbach, Northwich CW9 6BA* T: (01606) 891366 E: christopherrees954@btinternet.com

REES, David Grenfell. b 18. St D Coll Lamp BA 40 Qu Coll Birm 42. **d** 43 **p** 44. C Llangeinor *Llan* 43-47; C Cadoxton-juxta-Barry 47-53; C St Andrews Major 53-59; V Dyffryn 60-84; rtd 84; PtO *Llan* from 84. *10 Tyn-yr-Heol Road, Bryncoch, Neath SA10 7EA* T: (01639) 644488

REES, David Richard. b 60. St Mich Coll Llan. **d** 84 **p** 85. C Llanstadwel *St D* 84-86; C Carmarthen St Dav 86-91; V Llanrhian w Llanhywel and Carnhedryn etc 91-99; V Spittal w Trefgarn and Ambleston w St Dogwells from 99. *The Vicarage, Spittal, Haverfordwest SA62 5QP* T: (01437) 741505 E: rev.rees@btinternet.com

REES, Ms Diane Eluned. b 61. Univ of Wales (Ban) BSc 82 Em Coll Cam PGCE 83 Univ of Wales (Swansea) MEd 87 CPsychol AFBPsS. St Jo Coll Nottm BTh 95 MA 96. **d** 96 **p** 97. C Hall Green St Pet *Birm* 96-00; P-in-c Bozeat w Easton Maudit *Pet* 00-03; C Putney St Mary *S'wark* 03-04; TV 04-05; Asst Dir of

Min and Tr *Roch* 06-09; PtO from 09; V Shoreham from 15; Chapl St Mich Sch Otford from 15. *The Vicarage, Station Road, Shoreham, Sevenoaks TN14 7SA* T: (01959) 522363 E: der314@live.co.uk *or* revdrdi@outlook.com

REES, Mrs Elizabeth Mary. b 14. C Mountain Ash and Miskin *Llan* 14-15; C Neath from 15. *The Vicarage, 6 Redhill Close, Hirwaun, Aberdare CF44 9NZ* T: (01685) 813046 E: lizrees@fastmail.net

REES, Miss Emma Louise. b 79. Univ of Wales (Abth) BTh 01. St Mich Coll Llan MTh 11. **d** 11 **p** 12. C Barry All SS *Llan* from 11. *4 Alwen Drive, Barry CF52 7LH* T: (01446) 401792 E: reverendemma@gmail.com

REES, Glyn. b 63. St Bede's Coll Umtata 85. **d** 87 **p** 87. C Turffontein S Africa 87-88; Chapl S African Defence Force 89-90; P-in-c Nigel 91-92; C Kempton Park and Edenvale 92-93; TR Secunda 94-98; R Brakpan 99-00; R Whitwell *Derby* 00-05; R Wodonga Australia from 05. *225 Beechworth Road, Wodonga VIC 3690, Australia* T/F: (0061) (2) 6024 2053 M: 43-851 9954 E: stjohnsw@bigpond.net.au

REES, Grenfell. See REES, David Grenfell

REES, Mrs Helen. b 78. Univ of Wales (Cardiff) BD 99 MTh 10. St Mich Coll Llan 07. **d** 09 **p** 10. NSM Penarth All SS *Llan* 09-10; NSM Llandrindod w Cefnllys and Disserth *S & B* 10-13; NSM Gowerton from 13; Dioc Dir of Educn from 11. *The Vicarage, 14 Church Street, Gowerton, Swansea SA4 3EA* T: (01792) 920946 E: helenrees78@gmail.com

REES, Ian Kendall. b 66. St Mich Coll Llan 98. **d** 00 **p** 01. C Barry All SS *Llan* 00-03; Assoc P Grangetown 03-05; P-in-c Pyle w Kenfig 05-10; R Llandrindod w Cefnllys and Disserth *S & B* 10-13; V Gowerton from 13; Bp's Officer for Lay Min from 14. *The Vicarage, 14 Church Street, Gowerton, Swansea SA4 3EA* T: (01792) 920946 E: ianrees66@gmail.com

REES, Jane Elizabeth. b 70. K Coll Lon BD 92. Westcott Ho Cam 12 ERMC 13. **d** 14 **p** 15. NSM Wisbech St Mary and Guyhirn w Ring's End etc *Ely* from 14. *40B West End, March PE15 8DL* E: revjanerees@gmail.com

REES, Jennifer Mary. See MORRELL, Jennifer Mary

REES, Joanna Mary. See STOKER, Joanna Mary

REES, John. See REES, Vivian John Howard

REES, John Nigel. b 58. Derby Lonsdale Coll BCombStuds 79 Coll of Ripon & York St Jo PGCE 80. STETS 03. **d** 06 **p** 07. NSM Broad Blunsdon and Highworth w Sevenhampton and Inglesham etc *Bris* 06-10; P-in-c Rowde and Bromham *Sarum* from 10. *The Rectory, High Street, Bromham, Chippenham SN15 2HA* T: (01380) 859646 M: 07912-503267 E: revjohnrees@btinternet.com

REES, Canon John Philip Walford. b 41. St D Coll Lamp BA 62 Linacre Coll Ox BA 64 MA 69 Univ of Wales (Cardiff) BD 72. Wycliffe Hall Ox 62. **d** 64 **p** 65. C Reading St Jo *Ox* 64-67; V Patrick *S & M* 67-68; C Pontypool *Mon* 68-70; Area Sec CMS Glouc, Heref and Worc 70-75; V Bream *Glouc* 75-91; Team Ldr Ichthus Chr Fellowship 91-96; TV Glyncorrwg w Afan Vale and Cymmer Afan *Llan* 96-99; R Llandogo and Tintern *Mon* 99-00; R Llandogo w Whitebrook Chpl and Tintern Parva 00-07; AD Monmouth 02-06; Hon Can St Woolos Cathl 05-07; rtd 07. *Sparrow Cottage, The Narth, Monmouth NP25 4QG* T: (01600) 869194

REES, Canon Judith Margaret. b 39. Southn Univ BTh 89. **dss** 86 **d** 87 **p** 94. Par Dn Sanderstead All SS *S'wark* 87; Dir Cottesloe Chr Tr Progr *Ox* 89-99; Par Dn Gt Horwood 89-91; Par Dn Winslow w Gt Horwood and Addington 91-94; C 94-99; RD Claydon 96-99; Hon Can Ch Ch 97-99; rtd 99; PtO *Sarum* from 01. *Sidney Cottage, 111 Lower Road, Salisbury SP2 9NH* T: (01722) 410050

REES, Leslie. b 49. Leeds Univ LLB 72. NOC 03. **d** 06 **p** 07. NSM Swinton H Rood *Man* 06-08; NSM Eccles 08-09; NSM Hanbury, Newborough, Rangemore and Tutbury *Lich* 09-14; P-in-c from 14; C Rolleston from 14; C Anslow from 14. *The New Vicarage, Church Lane, Hanbury, Burton-on-Trent DE13 8TF* T: (01283) 813357 E: leslie.rees@virgin.net

REES, Matthew Haydn Brinley. b 69. Wycliffe Hall Ox. **d** 03 **p** 04. C Ox St Aldate 03-06; C Ox St Clem 06-08; LtO 08-10; NSM Cowley St Jo from 10. *Redwood House, 276A Cowley Road, Oxford OX4 1UR* M: 07811-149305 E: matt@home-online.org *or* mrees@me.com

REES, Michael. See REES, Richard Michael

REES, Canon Michael Lloyd. b 51. St D Coll Lamp. **d** 74 **p** 75. C Cardigan w Mwnt and Y Ferwig *St D* 74-77; Min Can St D Cathl 77-81; TV Aberystwyth 81-83; Dioc Children's Adv 83-92; V Pen-boyr 83-88; V Henfynyw w Aberaeron and Llanddewi Aberarth 88-99; RD Glyn Aeron 95-99; V Gors-las 99-13; V Betws w Ammanford 13-15; AD Dyffryn Aman 07-14; Can St D Cathl 09-15; rtd 15; PtO *St D* from 15. *3 Clôs Y Drindod, Buarth Road, Aberystwyth SY23 1LR* M: 07972-602620 T: (01970) 627593 E: michaelrees2013@outlook.com *or* mlr1@hotmail.co.uk

REES (née CURREY), Mrs Pauline Carol. b 46. WMMTC 94. d 98 p 99. OLM Leominster *Heref* from 98. *Crossways Cottage, Leysters, Leominster HR6 0HR* T: (01568) 750300 *or* 612124 E: rees.crossways@btinternet.com

REES, Percival Antony Everard. b 35. Pemb Coll Ox BA 56 MA 59. Clifton Th Coll 58. d 60 p 61. C Heatherlands St Jo *Sarum* 60-65 and 69-70; India 65-69; V W Hampstead St Luke *Lon* 70-82; Lect Oak Hill Th Coll 82-86; V Enfield Ch Ch Trent Park *Lon* 87-00; rtd 00; PtO *Chelmsf* from 00. *10 Winchester Road, Frinton-on-Sea CO13 9JB* T: (01255) 852464

REES, Philip. See REES, John Philip Walford

REES, Canon Richard John Edward Williams. b 36. Univ of Wales (Lamp) BA 58. St Mich Coll Llan 58. d 60 p 61. C St Issells *St D* 60-64; C Llanedy 64-67; V Whitchurch w Solva and St Elvis 67-77; V Whitchurch w Solva and St Elvis w Brawdy etc 77-01; RD Dewisland and Fishguard 73-01; Can St D Cathl 87-01; Treas St D Cathl 97-01; rtd 01. *The Smithy, Cheriton, Stackpole, Pembroke SA71 5BZ* T: (01646) 672235

REES, Canon Richard Michael. b 35. St Pet Hall Ox BA 57 MA 61. Tyndale Hall Bris 57. d 59 p 60. C Crowborough *Chich* 59-62; C Clifton Ch Ch w Em *Bris* 62-64; V Clevedon Ch Ch *B & W* 64-72; V Cambridge H Trin *Ely* 72-84; Chief Sec CA 84-90; Can Res Ches Cathl 90-00; Vice-Dean 93-00; Dioc Missr *Ches* 90-00; Cheshire Co Ecum Officer 91-99; rtd 00; PtO *Nor* from 01. *65 Tennyson Avenue, King's Lynn PE30 2QJ* T: (01553) 691982 E: myrees@btinternet.com

REES, Ronald Benjamin Dennis. b 44. Univ of Wales (Ban) BTh 00. St Mich Coll Llan 00. d 00 p 01. C Llanbedrog w Llannor and Llangian *Ban* 00-02; P-in-c Llanllyfni 02-03; R 03-05; R Dolgellau w Llanfachreth and Brithdir etc 05-13; AD Ystumaner 10-13; rtd 13; PtO *Ban* from 14. *Llety'r Wennol, Botwnnog, Pwllheli LL53 8RA* T: (01758) 730737

REES, Mrs Sally Elizabeth. d 14. C Crickhowell *S & B* from 14. *Curlews, Tretower, Crickhowell, NP8 1RG* T: (01873) 811332 E: sallyrees50@gmail.com

REES, Stephen Philip. b 70. St Luke's Coll Ex BA. Oak Hill Th Coll BA 03. d 03 p 04. C Moreton-in-Marsh w Batsford, Todenham etc *Glouc* 03-06; P-in-c Lt Heath *St Alb* 06-12; V from 12. *The Vicarage, Thornton Road, Potters Bar EN6 1JJ* T: (01707) 654414 E: zipyzac@globalnet.com

REES, Miss Susan Mary. b 61. Univ of Wales (Cardiff) BSc 82 Ox Univ BTh 05. Ripon Coll Cuddesdon 00. d 02 p 03. C Penarth All SS *Llan* 02-05; C Roath 05-08; P-in-c Eglwysilan 08-14; P-in-c Pontyclun w Talygarn from 14; P-in-c Llanharry from 14. *The Vicarage, Heol Miskin, Pontyclun CF72 9AJ* T: (01443) 231166 E: susanmrees@hotmail.com

REES, Canon Vivian John Howard. b 51. Southn Univ LLB 72 Ox Univ BA 79 MA 84 Leeds Univ MPhil 84. Wycliffe Hall Ox 76. d 79 p 80. C Moor Allerton *Ripon* 79-82; Sierra Leone 82-86; LtO *Ox* from 86; Jt Dioc Reg from 98; Dep Prov Reg 98-00; Prov Reg from 00; Legal Adv ACC from 98; Hon Prov Can Cant Cathl from 01. *Oxford Diocesan Registry, 16 Beaumont Street, Oxford OX1 2LZ* T: (01865) 297214 F: 726274 E: jrees@wslaw.co.uk

REES, William David Cledwyn. b 25. FRGS 54 Qu Coll Cam BA 49 DipEd 50 MA 52 Univ of Wales MA 75 PhD 81. St Deiniol's Hawarden 63. d 65 p 66. Hon C Rhyl w St Ann *St As* 65-72; Chapl and Lect St Mary's Coll Ban 72-77; LtO *Ban* 72-77; Lect Ban Univ from 77; Chapl Univ of Wales (Ban) 77-84; Sec Dioc Schs Cttee 84-86. *Anwylfa, Fron Park Avenue, Llanfairfechan LL33 0AS* T: (01248) 680054

REES-JONES, Diana Mary. b 58. Ridley Hall Cam. d 07 p 08. C Ness Gp *Linc* 07-09; Asst Chapl Oundle Sch 09-13; PtO *Pet* 13-14; C Northampton St Giles from 14. *15 Honeysuckle Way, Northampton NN3 3QE* E: diana.reesjones@btinternet.com

REESE, Preb John David. b 49. Cuddesdon Coll 73. d 76 p 77. C Kidderminster St Mary *Worc* 76-81; Malaysia 81-85; V Bishop's Castle w Mainstone *Heref* 85-91; RD Clun Forest 87-91; V Tupsley 91-93; P-in-c Hampton Bishop and Mordiford w Dormington 91-93; V Tupsley w Hampton Bishop 93-08; RD Heref City 96-02; TR Heref S Wye 08-14; Preb Heref Cathl 96-14; rtd 14. *32 Burns Road, Leamington Spa CV32 7EL* T: (01926) 833389

REEVE, Canon Brian Charles. b 36. Lon Univ BSc 57 BD 60. Tyndale Hall Bris 58. d 61 p 62. C Eccleston St Luke *Liv* 61-63; C Upton (Overchurch) *Ches* 63-65; C Pemberton St Mark Newtown *Liv* 65-68; V Macclesfield Ch Ch *Ches* 68-74; V Stone Ch Ch *Lich* 74-84; RD Trentham 77-84; V Hoole *Ches* 84-94; Chapl Ches City Hosp 84-91; P-in-c Alderley *Ches* 94-01; Dioc Warden of Readers 94-00; Hon Can Ches Cathl 94-01; rtd 01; PtO *Ches* from 02; *Lich* from 09. *18 Mount Crescent, Stone ST15 8LR* T: (01785) 749178 E: reeveinleek@talktalk.net

REEVE, David Michael. b 44. St Cath Coll Cam BA 67 MA 71. Coll of Resurr Mirfield 68. d 70 p 71. C Willingdon *Chich* 70-73; C Hove All SS 73-76; C Moulsecoomb 76-80; R Singleton and V E and W Dean 80-90; R Hurstpierpoint 90-99; R Kingston Buci 99-05; rtd 05; PtO *Cant* from 06; Clergy Widows Officer Cant Adnry from 09. *11 Wells Avenue, Canterbury CT1 3YB* T: (01227) 478446

REEVE, John Richard. b 65. Southn Univ BA 86 La Sainte Union Coll PGCE 88. Ripon Coll Cuddesdon 95. d 97 p 98. C Hale w Badshot Lea *Guildf* 97-00; TV Totton *Win* from 00; P-in-c Copythorne from 11. *The Vicarage, Ringwood Road, Woodlands, Southampton SO40 7GX* T: (023) 8066 3267 E: johnreeve6@aol.com

REEVE, Kenneth John. b 42. Sarum & Wells Th Coll 91. d 93 p 94. C Thorpe St Matt *Nor* 93-96; P-in-c S Lynn 96-99; PtO 03-04; P-in-c Gt and Lt Ellingham, Rockland and Shropham etc 04-11; RD Thetford and Rockland 09-11; rtd 11. *Hillmora Cottage, Tabernacle Lane, Forncett St Peter, Norwich NR16 1LE* E: kenreeve@btinternet.com

REEVE, Michael. See REEVE, David Michael

REEVE, Richard Malcolm. b 64. Reading Univ BSc 85. Trin Coll Bris BA 92. d 92 p 93. C Northolt St Mary *Lon* 92-95; C Acton Green 95-98; V Hayes St Edm 98-08; TR Tettenhall Regis *Lich* from 08. *The Rectory, 2 Lloyd Road, Tettenhall, Wolverhampton WV6 9AU* T: (01902) 742801 E: richardmreeve@aol.com

REEVE, Richard Noel. b 29. MB, ChB. St Deiniol's Hawarden. d 84 p 85. Hon C Norton *Ches* 84-85; C Filey *York* 85-87; TV Brayton 87-90; rtd 90; PtO *Man* 90-93; Res Min Bicton, Montford w Shrawardine and Fitz *Lich* 97-99; PtO *Man* from 99. *Barn Cottage, Low House, New Hutton, Kendal LA8 0AZ* T: (01539) 730198

REEVE, Preb Roger Patrick. b 42. Fitzw Coll Cam BA 65 MA 68. Coll of Resurr Mirfield. d 67 p 68. C Barnstaple St Pet w H Trin *Ex* 67-74; V Ernesettle 74-78; V Braunton 78-05; RD Barnstaple 85-93 and 01-03; Preb Ex Cathl from 92; rtd 05. *27 Westacott Meadow, Barnstaple EX32 8QX* T: (01271) 326927 E: rogerreeve@cwcom.net

REEVE, Sally Ann. See EPPS, Sally Ann

REEVES, Christopher. b 30. Nottm Univ BA 53. Wells Th Coll 53. d 55 p 56. C Rowbarton *B & W* 55-59; C Cant St Greg 59-61; Chapl Schiedam Miss to Seamen *Eur* 61-67; V Brankgside H Trin *Chelmsf* 67-97; rtd 97; PtO *Truro* from 00. *3 Albany Close, Goonown, St Agnes TR5 0XE* T: (01872) 552976

REEVES, David Eric. b 46. Sarum Th Coll 68. d 71 p 72. C Guildf H Trin w St Mary 71-74; C Warmsworth *Sheff* 74-78; V Herringthorpe 78-90; V Cleveleys *Blackb* 90-12; RD Poulton 94-00; rtd 12. *443 North Drive, Thornton-Cleveleys FY5 3AP* T: (01253) 864636

REEVES, Donald St John. b 34. Qu Coll Cam BA 57 MA 61 Lambeth MLitt 03. Cuddesdon 62. d 63 p 64. C Maidstone All SS w St Phil *Cant* 63-65; Bp's Dom Chapl *S'wark* 65-68; V St Helier 69-80; R Westmr St Jas *Lon* 80-98; Dir Soul of Eur Project from 98; rtd 98; PtO *Ex* from 00. *The Coach House, Church Street, Crediton EX17 2AQ* T: (01363) 775100 F: 773911 E: donalreeve@aol.com

REEVES, Elizabeth Anne. See THOMAS, Elizabeth Anne

REEVES, George Edward Charles. b 70. Dundee Univ MA 92. St Jo Coll Nottm 11. d 13 p 14. C Ashton *Man* from 13. *1 Windmill Lane, Denton, Manchester M34 3RN* T: 0161-335 9675 M: 07905-449079 E: revgeorgereeves@outlook.com

REEVES, Gillian Patricia. b 46. S'wark Ord Course 87. d 90 p 94. Par Dn Shirley St Geo *S'wark* 90-94; C 94-96; C Caterham 96-98; TV 98-12; rtd 12. *24 Addisons Close, Croydon CR0 8DX* T: (020) 8776 1530

REEVES, Graham. b 65. Southn Univ BTh 94 Univ Coll Chich MA 04. Chich Th Coll 91. d 94 p 95. C Cardiff St Mary and St Steph w St Dyfrig etc *Llan* 94-95; C Roath 95-98; Chapl Sussex Weald and Downs NHS Trust 98-02; Chapl W Sussex Health and Soc Care NHS Foundn Trust 02-08; OSB from 11. *2 Abbotsbury, Bognor Regis PO21 4RX* T: (01243) 265209 E: graham.reeves@sussexpartnership.nhs.uk

REEVES, Mrs Helen Marie. b 68. SEITE 12. d 15. NSM Gravesend St Geo *Roch* from 15. *50 Water Mill Way, South Darenth, Dartford DA4 9BE* T: (01322) 866365

REEVES, John Graham. b 44. Kelham Th Coll 64. d 69 p 71. C Aston cum Aughton *Sheff* 69-71; C Ribbleton *Blackb* 72-74; C Cleveleys 74-75; P-in-c Huncoat 75-77; V 77-82; V Knuzden 82-92; V Sandylands 92-09; rtd 09. *51 Parkfield Drive, Lancaster LA1 4BT* T: (01524) 411299 E: revjgr@tiscali.co.uk

REEVES, Ms Karen Susan. b 56. Bris Univ BA 78. Ripon Coll Cuddesdon 02. d 05 p 07. C De Beauvoir Town St Pet *Lon* 05-06; C Islington St Jas w St Pet 06-08; Chapl Frimley Park Hosp NHS Foundn Trust 08-09; NSM Frimley *Guildf* 08-09; Chapl Milton Keynes Hosp NHS Foundn Trust 09-10; TV Coventry Caludon *Cov* 10-13; Min Stoke Aldermoor CD

13-15; P-in-c Moston St Jo *Man* from 15; P-in-c Moston St Chad from 15. *St Luke's Rectory, 173 Kenyon Lane, Manchester M40 5HS* E: karen.reeves6@btinternet.com *or* newvicar@gmail.com

REEVES, Mrs Katharine Vive. b 66. Derbys Coll of HE BEd 89. St Jo Coll Nottm 11. **d** 13 **p** 14. C Denton St Lawr *Man* from 13. *1 Windmill Lane, Denton, Manchester M34 3RN* T: 0161-335 9675 M: 07941-472864 E: katiereeves1@hotmail.co.uk

REEVES, Kenneth William. b 38. TCD 67. **d** 69 **p** 70. C Killowen *D & R* 69-70; I Ardara 70-75; TV Quidenham *Nor* 76-81; V Swaffham 81-86; Chapl Nor City Coll of F&HE 86-91; P-in-c Lakenham St Alb 86-91; rtd 92; PtO *Nor* 92-98 and from 05; P-in-c Trowse 99-03; P-in-c Nerja and Almuñécar *Eur* 03-04. *15 Morris Close, Stoke Holy Cross, Norwich NR14 8LL* T: (01508) 494583 E: revkenn@btinternet.com

REEVES, Maria Elizabeth Ann. *See* COULTER, Maria Elizabeth Ann

REEVES, Michael Richard Ewert. b 74. Girton Coll Cam MA 00. Oak Hill Th Coll 98. **d** 02 **p** 03. NSM Langham Place All So *Lon* 02-05; Th Adv UCCF 05-12. *Address temp unknown* E: mreeves@dsl.pipex.com

REEVES, Nicholas John Harding. b 44. Glos Univ BA 99 Nottm Univ MA 02. ALCD 69. **d** 69 **p** 70. C Upton (Overchurch) *Ches* 69-72; C Woodlands *Sheff* 72-74; C-in-c Cranham Park CD *Chelmsf* 74-79; V Cranham Park 79-88; R Aldridge *Lich* 88-02; Dioc Officer for Evang *Carl* 03-10; rtd 09; V Dacre *Carl* from 12. *Dacre Vicarage, 12 Keld Close, Stainton, Penrith CA11 0EJ* T: (01768) 890530 M: 07988-576736 E: the7reeves@aol.com

REGAN, Brian. b 46. MBIM 80. WMMTC 88. **d** 91 **p** 92. C Cov St Jo 91-94; V Tile Hill 94-09; rtd 09; PtO *Cov* from 09. *160 Ansley Road, Nuneaton CV10 8NU* T: (024) 7673 4240 M: 07766-721837 E: brianregan32@hotmail.com

REGAN, Gareth Douglas. b 78. St Jo Coll Nottm 11. **d** 13 **p** 14. C Penn Fields *Lich* from 13. *131 Church Road, Bradmore, Wolverhampton WV3 7EN* M: 07776-302261 E: gregan1978@gmail.com

REGAN, Noel Henry Likely. b 49. **d** 99 **p** 00. Aux Min Cloonclare w Killasnett, Lurganboy and Drumlease *K, E & A* 99-06; Dioc C and P-in-c Garrison w Slavin and Belleek *Clogh* 06-11; I Clogh w Errigal Portclare from 11. *10 Augher Road, Clogher BT76 0AD* T: (028) 8554 9797 M: 07825-569303 E: revnoelregan@hotmail.com

REGAN, Paul John. b 67. Southn Univ BA 88 PhD 96 St Jo Coll Dur BA 98. Cranmer Hall Dur 96. **d** 99 **p** 00. C St Alb St Pet *St Alb* 99-03; TV Smestow Vale *Lich* 03-09; Chapl Trevelyan Coll *Dur* 09-14; Chapl Dur Univ 09-14; C Dur St Oswald and Shincliffe 09-14; Tutor Cranmer Hall Dur from 14. *Cranmer Hall, St John's College, 3 South Bailey, Durham DH1 3RJ* T: 0191-334 3893 E: cran.udos@durham.ac.uk

REGAN, Philip. b 49. Qu Mary Coll Lon BSc MSc. Wycliffe Hall Ox 81. **d** 83 **p** 84. NSM Scotforth *Blackb* 83-89; P-in-c Combe St Nicholas w Wambrook *B & W* 89-01; V 01-08; P-in-c Whitestaunton 89-01; R 01-08; rtd 08; PtO *B & W* from 09. *1 Blackmoor Road, Wellington TA21 8ED* T: (01823) 662193 E: pregan@ukonline.co.uk

REGINALD, Brother. *See* BOX, Reginald Gilbert

REID, Alison Margaret. *See* WADSWORTH, Alison Margaret

REID, Amanda Joy. *See* MARRIOTT, Amanda Joy

REID, Andrew John. b 47. Birm Univ BEd 70 Man Univ MEd 76. S'wark Ord Course 88. **d** 88 **p** 89. NSM Westerham *Roch* 88-90; Chapl Abp Tenison's Sch Kennington 90-05; PtO *Roch* from 05. *12 Westways, Westerham TN16 1TT* T: (01959) 561428

REID, Andrew John. b 58. Thames Poly BA 90. Trin Coll Bris 09. **d** 11 **p** 12. C Chorleywood St Andr *St Alb* 11-15; PtO from 15. *Wick Cottage, 34 Quickley Lane, Chorleywood, Rickmansworth WD3 5AF* M: 07876-773387 E: revreidserving@gmail.com

REID, Andrew Kieran. b 67. Coll of SS Mark and Jo Plymouth BA 90. Trin Coll Bris 10. **d** 12 **p** 13. C Addlestone *Guildf* from 12. *96 Crockford Park Road, Addlestone KT15 2LR* M: 07799-883412 E: andy.reid@stpaulscofe.org

REID, Catherine Elizabeth. b 79. Hull Univ BA 00 MA 02 St Petersburg State Univ PhD 07. Coll of Resurr Mirfield 12. **d** 14 **p** 15. C Ingleby Barwick *York* from 14. *27 Berrington Gardens, Ingleby Barwick, Stockton-on-Tees TS17 0UH* E: crcatherinereid@gmail.com

REID, Christopher Jason. b 69. Glos Univ BA 08. Trin Coll Bris 01. **d** 03 **p** 04. C Woodley *Ox* 03-07; V Selby St Jas *York* from 07. *St James's Vicarage, 14 Leeds Road, Selby YO8 4HX* T: (01757) 702861 E: cjasonreid@hotmail.com

REID, Canon Colin Guthrie. b 30. **d** 56 **p** 57. C Kendal St Thos *Carl* 56-59; C Crosthwaite Keswick 59-60; R Caldbeck w Castle Sowerby 60-76; RD Wigton 69-70; P-in-c Sebergham 75; R Caldbeck, Castle Sowerby and Sebergham 76-93; Hon Can Carl Cathl 88-93; rtd 93; PtO *Carl* from 93. *Mellbreak, Longthwaite Road, Wigton CA7 9JR* T: (016973) 45625

REID, David Graham. b 78. Hatf Coll Dur BSc 00. Wycliffe Hall Ox BTh 09. **d** 09 **p** 10. C Ox St Ebbe w H Trin and St Pet from 09. *24 East Avenue, Oxford OX4 1XP* T: (01865) 430965 E: dave.reid@stebbes.org.uk

REID, Mrs Diane Mary. b 73. Lanc Univ BMus 94 Huddersfield Univ PGCE 98. Trin Coll Bris BA 04. **d** 04 **p** 05. C Reading St Agnes w St Paul and St Barn *Ox* 04-07; PtO *York* 11-12; Hon C Selby St Jas from 12. *St James's Vicarage, 14 Leeds Road, Selby YO8 4HX* T: (01757) 702861 E: dianem_clark@hotmail.com

REID, Donald. b 58. Glas Univ LLB 79 Pemb Coll Ox MPhil 81 Edin Univ BD 85. Edin Th Coll 82. **d** 85 **p** 86. C Greenock *Glas* 85-88; C Baillieston 88-91; R 91-95; C Glas St Serf 88-91; R 91-95; Chapl Glas Univ 89-00; Chapl Glas Caledonian Univ 89-00; Chapl Strathclyde Univ 89-00; TP Glas St Mary 95-00; Assoc P 00-04; C Edin St Jo from 04. *St Columbas Hospice, 15 Boswall Road, Edinburgh EH5 3RW* T: 07808-932458 T: (01315) 517706 E: dreid212@me.com *or* dreid@stcolumbashospice.org.uk

REID, Eileen. b 53. **d** 12 **p** 13. NSM Westward, Rosley-w-Woodside and Welton *Carl* from 12. *Ceardach, Brackenthwaite, Wigton CA7 8AS* T: (01697) 343089 E: ereid2002@yahoo.co.uk

REID, Gareth McEwan. b 82. Univ of Wales (Abth) BA 03. St Mich Coll Llan BTh 10. **d** 10 **p** 11. C Dewisland *St D* 10-13; P-in-c Llandysul w Bangor Teifi and Llanfairorllwyn etc from 13; Dioc Warden Ords 14-15. *The Vicarage, Tanyfron, Well Street, Llandysul SA44 4DR* T: (01559) 363874 E: garethmreid@googlemail.com

✥**REID, The Rt Revd Gavin Hunter.** b 34. OBE 00. K Coll Lon BA 56. Oak Hill Th Coll 56. **d** 60 **p** 61 **c** 92. C E Ham St Paul *Chelmsf* 60-63; C Rainham 63-66; Publications Sec CPAS 66-71; Hon C St Paul's Cray St Barn *Roch* 68-71; Ed Sec USCL 71-74; Hon C Woking St Jo *Guildf* 72-92; Sec for Evang CPAS 74-92; Consultant Missr CPAS and BMU Adv 90-92; Suff Bp Maidstone *Cant* 92-00; Six Preacher Cant Cathl 92-97; rtd 00; PtO *Nor* from 00; *St E* from 00; Hon Asst Bp St E from 08. *Furzefield, 17 Richard Crampton Road, Beccles NR34 9HN* T: (01502) 717042 F: 710739 M: 07941-770549 E: gavin@reids.org

REID, Geraldine Felicity (Jo). b 47. RGN 69. EMMTC 95. **d** 98 **p** 99. NSM Skellingthorpe w Doddington *Linc* 98-02; NSM Hykeham from 02. *Tol Peden, Monson Park, Skellingthorpe, Lincoln LN6 5UE* T: (01522) 828402 *or* 828403 E: tolpedn@ntlworld.com

REID, Gordon. *See* REID, William Gordon

REID, Herbert Alan. b 31. AKC 55. **d** 56 **p** 57. C Penwortham St Mary *Blackb* 56-59; C-in-c Penwortham St Leon CD 59-63; V Brierfield 63-72; V Warton St Paul 72-79; V Read in Whalley 79-98; rtd 98; PtO *Blackb* from 98. *Paslew House, 6 The Sands, Whalley, Blackburn BB7 9TL* T: (01254) 824620

REID, James. b 46. Strathclyde Univ BSc 69. WMMTC 88. **d** 91 **p** 92. C Attleborough *Cov* 91-95; V Walsall Pleck and Bescot *Lich* 95-99; TR Chell 99-06; rtd 06; PtO *Cov* from 08. *22 St Ives Way, Nuneaton CV11 6FR* T: (024) 7634 2264

REID, Jason. *See* REID, Christopher Jason

REID, Jo. *See* REID, Geraldine Felicity

REID, Joanne. b 68. St Mich Coll Llan 08. **d** 10 **p** 11. C Brize Norton and Carterton *Ox* 10-14; TV Savernake *Sarum* from 14. *The Vicarage, Church Street, Collingbourne Ducis, Marlborough SN8 3EL* T: (01264) 850385 E: jo.reid185@btinternet.com

REID, Kirrilee Anne. b 70. Canberra Univ BTh 06. St Mark's Coll Canberra. **d** 06 **p** 07. C Canberra St Jo Australia 06-07; C Chapman 09-10; Youth Min Course Co-ord Chas Stuart Univ 07-10; R Glencarse *Bre* from 10; Dioc Dir of Ord from 12; Dioc Min Officer from 14. *The Rectory, Glencarse, Perth PH2 7LX* T: (01738) 860386 M: 07745-737608 E: rector@allsaintsglencarse.org

REID, Lucinda Jane. b 57. Dur Univ BA 78. Ripon Coll Cuddesdon 79. **dss** 81 **d** 85 **p** 85. Birtley *Dur* 81-84; Canada from 84. *5551 West Saanich Road, Victoria BC V9E 2G1, Canada* E: lreid@uoguelpha.ca

REID, Miss Margaret Patricia. b 41. Hull Univ BSc 62 Leeds Univ MA 07. Yorks Min Course 09. **d** 10 **p** 11. NSM Ilkley All SS *Leeds* from 10. *1 Chestnut Close, Ilkley LS29 8PX* T: (01943) 609232 E: pat.reid29@btinternet.com

REID, Mark. b 47. **d** 07 **p** 08. NSM Glenavy w Tunny and Crumlin *Conn* 07-12; NSM Belfast Upper Falls from 12. *12B Carmavy Road, Nutts Corner, Crumlin BT29 4TF* T: (028) 9445 4725

REID, Mrs Pauline Ann. b 57. Anglia Ruskin Univ MA 10. EAMTC 00. **d** 03 **p** 04. C Silverstone and Abthorpe w Slapton etc *Pet* 03-07; P-in-c Raddesley Gp *Ely* 07-14; P-in-c Cley Hill Villages *Sarum* from 14; RD Heytesbury from 15. *The Rectory, 6 Homefields, Longbridge Deverill, Warminster BA12 7DQ* M: 07586-358162 T: (01985) 841290 E: revpauline@btinternet.com

REID, Peter Ivor. b 30. Qu Coll Cam BA 53 MA 72. St Mich Coll Llan 78. **d** 80 **p** 81. C Llantwit Major *Llan* 80-84; V Laleston w Tythegston and Merthyr Mawr 84-88; V Roath 88-98; rtd 98; PtO *Llan* from 04. *18 Woolaston Avenue, Cardiff CF23 5EZ* T: (029) 2075 3306

REID, Roderick Andrew Montgomery. b 80. Brunel Univ BSc 01 Trin Hall Cam BTh 10. Westcott Ho Cam 08. **d** 11 **p** 12. C Waltham H Cross *Chelmsf* 11-14; P-in-c Bocking St Mary from 14. *The Deanery, Deanery Hill, Braintree CM7 5SR* T: (01376) 324887 M: 07799-734898 E: rod.a.reid@gmail.com

REID, Stewart Thomas. b 45. Liv Hope MA 01. Oak Hill Th Coll 66. **d** 70 **p** 71. C Normanton *Derby* 70-73; C Leyland St Andr *Blackb* 73-78; V Halliwell St Luke *Man* 78-95; V Southport Ch Ch *Liv* from 95. *The Vicarage, 12 Gloucester Road, Southport PR8 2AU* T: (01704) 565120

REID, Canon William Gordon. b 43. Edin Univ MA 63 Keble Coll Ox BA 66 MA 72. Edin Th Coll 63 Cuddesdon Coll 66. **d** 67 **p** 68. C Edin St Salvador 67-69; Chapl and Tutor Sarum & Wells Th Coll 69-72; R Edin St Mich and All SS 72-84; Provost St Andr Cathl Inverness 84-87; Chapl Ankara *Eur* 87-89; Chapl Stockholm w Gävle and Västerås 89-92; V Gen to Bp Eur 92-02; Can Gib Cathl 92-98; Adn in Eur 96-98; P-in-c St Mich Cornhill w St Pet le Poer etc *Lon* 97-98; Dean Gib *Eur* 98-00; Adn Italy and Malta 00-03; Chapl Milan w Genoa and Varese 00-03; R Philadelphia St Clem USA from 04. *2013 Appletree Street, Philadelphia PA 19103-1409, USA* T: (001) (215) 563 1876 F: 563 7627 E: gordonrr@earthlink.net

REIDE, Susannah Louise Court. b 69. Clare Coll Cam BA 91. Trin Coll Bris BA 04. **d** 04 **p** 05. C Marlborough *Sarum* 04-08; TV Cowley St Jas *Ox* 08-11; PtO from 11. *96 Cricket Close, Oxford OX4 3DJ* T: (01865) 401439 E: sr@reide.plus.com

REIGATE, Archdeacon of. See KAJUMBA, The Ven Daniel Steven Kimbugwe

REILLY, Thomas Gerard. b 38. **d** 64 **p** 64. In RC Ch 64-73; Hon C Clapton Park All So *Lon* 73-76; Hon C Haggerston All SS 76-78; Hon C Walthamstow St Sav *Chelmsf* 79-85; P-in-c Forest Gate Em w Upton Cross 85-89; V 89-92; V Chaddesden St Phil *Derby* 92-01; RD Derby N 95-00; rtd 01; PtO *B & W* 01-12. *9 Fleming Way, Exeter EX2 4SE* E: grryreilly@yahoo.co.uk

REILY, Jacqueline Estelle. b 61. Oak Hill Th Coll BA 84. ERMC 08. **d** 11 **p** 12. C Rayleigh *Chelmsf* 11-14; Chapl Scargill Ho from 14. *Scargill House, Kettlewell, Skipton BD23 5HU* T: (01756) 761236 M: 07580-114641 E: admin@scargillmovement.org *or* jackie@reily.co.uk

REILY, Paul Alan. b 59. UEA BA 81. St Jo Coll Nottm MA 92. **d** 92 **p** 93. C Westcliff St Mich *Chelmsf* 92-96; P-in-c Barkingside St Cedd 96-98; V 98-01; V Leyton St Cath and St Paul 01-11; AD Waltham Forest 04-07; PtO 11-14. *Scargill House, Kettlewell, Skipton BD23 5HU* T: (01756) 761236 M: 07967-977115 E: paul@reily.co.uk

REINDORP, David Peter Edington. b 52. TD 05. Trin Coll Cam BA 82 MA 86 CQSW 77. Westcott Ho Cam 79. **d** 83 **p** 84. C Chesterton Gd Shep *Ely* 83-85; C Hitchin *St Alb* 85-88; R Landbeach and V Waterbeach *Ely* 88-97; OCM 88-97; CF(V) 92-12; RD Quy *Ely* 94-97; V Cherry Hinton St Jo 97-06; RD Cambridge 04-06; Hon Can Ely Cathl 05-06; V Chelsea All SS *Lon* from 06; AD Chelsea from 11. *2 Old Church Street, London SW3 5DQ* T: (020) 7352 5627 E: david.reindorp@talk21.com

REINDORP, Canon Michael Christopher Jullan. b 44. Trin Coll Cam BA 67 MA 70 K Coll Lon MA 99. Cuddesdon Coll 67 United Th Coll Bangalore 68. **d** 69 **p** 70. C Poplar *Lon* 69-74; V Chatham St Wm *Roch* 74-84; R Stantonbury *Ox* 84-87; TR Stantonbury and Willen 87-92; P-in-c Richmond St Mary w St Matthias and St Jo *S'wark* 92-95; TR 96-09; Hon Can S'wark Cathl 03-09; rtd 09; PtO *S'wark* from 11. *10 Alpha Road, Teddington TW11 0QG* T: (020) 8614 6800 E: julianreindorp@hotmail.co.uk

REISS, Prof Michael Jonathan. b 58. Trin Coll Cam BA 78 MA 82 PhD 82 PGCE 83 FIBiol 90 Open Univ MBA 02. EAMTC 87. **d** 90 **p** 91. Lect Cam Univ 88-94; Reader 94-00; NSM Comberton *Ely* 90-94; NSM Deanery of Bourn 94-96; NSM 99-00; P-in-c Boxworth and Elsworth w Knapwell 96-99; PtO 99-03; Prof Science Educn Inst of Educn Lon Univ from 01; NSM Toft w Caldecote and Childerley *Ely* 03-10; NSM Lordsbridge from 10. *Institute of Education, University of London, 20 Bedford Way, London WC1H 0AL* T: (020) 7947 9522 E: m.reiss@ioe.ac.uk

REISS, Canon Peter Henry. b 62. Hertf Coll Ox BA 85 MA 91 Natal Univ MA 95. St Jo Coll Nottm 95. **d** 95 **p** 96. C Sherwood *S'well* 95-00; TV Bestwood 00-03; V Bestwood Park w Rise Park 03-04; Tr Officer CME and Laity Development *Man* 04-06; Dir Discipleship and Min Tr from 06; Hon Can Man Cathl from 11. *Discipleship and Ministry Training, 5th Floor, Church House, 90 Deansgate, Manchester M3 2GJ* T: 0161-828 1455 F: 828 1485 E: preiss@manchester.anglican.org

REISS, Canon Robert Paul. b 43. Trin Coll Cam BA 67 MA 71 Lambeth PhD 12. Westcott Ho Cam 67. **d** 69 **p** 70. C St John's Wood *Lon* 69-73; Bangladesh 73; Chapl Trin Coll Cam 73-78; Selection Sec ACCM 78-85; Sen Selection Sec 83; TR Grantham *Linc* 86-96; RD 92-96; Adn Surrey and Hon Can Guildf Cathl 96-05; Can Westmr Abbey 05-13; rtd 13; Min and Tr Consultant *S'wark* from 13; PtO from 13. *35 Addington Square, London SE5 7LB* M: 07545-178192 E: bobreiss@hotmail.co.uk

REITH, Robert Michael. b 55. Oak Hill Th Coll BA 83. **d** 83 **p** 84. C Kendal St Thos *Carl* 83-87; C Leyland St Andr *Blackb* 87-92; V Leyland St Jo 92-94; TR Dagenham *Chelmsf* 94-03; V 03-14; rtd 14. *155 Woodward Road, Dagenham RM9 4SU* M: 07595-303023 E: mikereith@me.com

RELF-PENNINGTON, Mrs Catherine Prudence. b 56. Man Poly BSc 82 Sussex Univ MSc 87 Flinders Univ Aus BTh 00. Adelaide Coll of Div 96. **d** 00 **p** 01. C Glenelg Australia 00-01; NSM American Cathl Paris 01-02; C Is of Dogs Ch Ch and St Jo w St Luke *Lon* 02-03; C De Beauvoir Town St Pet 03-04; P-in-c Nazeing *Chelmsf* 05-11; P-in-c Roydon 05-09; R Adelaide St Mary Magd Australia 11-14; C Wymondham *Nor* from 14. *The Curatage, 43 Back Lane, Wymondham NR18 0LB* E: cpennington@fastmail.net

RENAUT, Vanessa Anne. See HERRICK, Vanessa Anne

RENDALL, Canon John Albert. b 43. Hull Univ BTh 84 MA 89. Ripon Hall Ox 65. **d** 68 **p** 69. C Southsea St Simon *Portsm* 68-71; C Wallington *S'wark* 71-77; P-in-c Rufforth w Moor Monkton and Hessay *York* 77-79; R 79-08; P-in-c Long Marston 77-79; R 79-08; RD New Ainsty 85-97; P-in-c Healaugh w Wighill, Bilbrough and Askham Richard 02-08; P-in-c Tockwith and Bilton w Bickerton 03-08; Can and Preb York Minster 94-08; Chapl Purey Cust Nuffield Hosp 82-04; rtd 08; PtO *York* from 09. *5 Wains Road, York YO24 2TP* T: (01904) 778764 E: canjohnrendall@aol.com

RENDALL, Richard John. b 54. Wadh Coll Ox BA 76 LLB 76 MA 92 Solicitor 78. Wycliffe Hall Ox 90. **d** 92 **p** 93. C Heswall *Ches* 92-98; R High Ongar w Norton Mandeville *Chelmsf* 98-04; R Broadwell, Evenlode, Oddington, Adlestrop etc *Glouc* from 04. *The Rectory, Broadwell, Moreton-in-Marsh GL56 0TU* T: (01451) 831866 E: rendalls@talk21.com

RENDELL, Jason. b 68. **d** 05 **p** 09. Chapl to Bp Stepney *Lon* 05-07; NSM Clerkenwell H Redeemer 06-07; NSM Clerkenwell St Mark 06-07; Min Can and Succ St Paul's Cathl 07-09; Min Can and Sacr St Paul's Cathl 09-13; Chapl to Bp Chich 13-14; V Kingsbury St Andr *Lon* from 14. *St Andrew's Vicarage, 28 Old Church Lane, London NW9 8RZ* T: (020) 8205 7447

RENDLE, Graham Barton. b 40. **d** 99 **p** 00. OLM Rougham, Beyton w Hessett and Rushbrooke *St E* 99-10; rtd 10; PtO *St E* from 10. *Appletrees, Bury Road, Beyton, Bury St Edmunds IP30 9AB* T: (01359) 270924

RENFREY, Edward Donald John-Baptist. b 53. ACT. **d** 76 **p** 77. C Naracoorte Australia 76-77; P-in-c Kingston w Robe 78-81; R 81-84; Chapl RN 84-99; Chapl R Aus Navy Australia from 99. *5/7 Bayview Street, Fannie Bay NT 0820, Australia* M: (8) 409-662823 E: edwardrenfrey@hotmail.com.au

RENGERT, Mrs Helen Caroline. b 70. Open Univ BSc 97 Anglia Ruskin Univ MA 14 RGN 92. ERMC 10. **d** 13 **p** 14. C Thorpe St Matt *Nor* from 13. *The Rectory, Buxton Road, Spixworth, Norwich NR10 3PR* T: (01603) 893848 E: helen.rengert@btinternet.com

RENGERT, Keith Alan Francis. b 67. RGN 92. Ripon Coll Cuddesdon 07. **d** 09 **p** 10. C N Walsham and Edingthorpe *Nor* 09-12; R Horsham St Faith, Spixworth and Crostwick from 12; Hon PV Nor Cathl from 14. *The Rectory, Buxton Road, Spixworth, Norwich NR10 3PR* T: (01603) 898258 M: 07796-607649 E: k.rengert@btinternet.com *or* rector@spixworthchurch.org.uk

RENISON, Canon Gary James. b 62. SS Hild & Bede Coll Dur BA 83. Ridley Hall Cam 84. **d** 86 **p** 87. C Stapenhill w Cauldwell *Derby* 86-89; C Cheadle Hulme St Andr *Ches* 89-92; Min Cheadle Hulme Em CD 92-95; P-in-c Bar Hill *Ely* 95-05; V Childwall All SS *Liv* from 05; Hon Can Liv Cathl from 11. *All Saints' Vicarage, Childwall Abbey Road, Liverpool L16 0JW* T: 0151-737 2169 E: vicar.allsaints@uwclub.net

RENNARD, Edward Lionel. b 51. CertEd 72 Nottm Univ BTh 80. Linc Th Coll 76. **d** 80 **p** 81. C Old Brumby *Linc* 80-82; C-in-c Gt Grimsby St Matt Fairfield CD 82-86; V Fairfield St Matt 86-88; V Hykeham 88-91; TR 91-00; TR Blyth Valley *St E* from 00. *The Rectory, Highfield Road, Halesworth IP19 8SJ* T: (01986) 872602 M: 07958-191975 E: edward.rennard@btinternet.com

RENNARD, Margaret Rose. b 49. CertEd 75. Linc Th Coll 76. **dss** 80 **d** 87 **p** 94. C Fairfield St Matt *Linc* 87-88; C Hykeham 88-00; Chapl HM Pris Morton Hall 91-00; Asst Chapl HM Pris Blundeston 00-01; Asst Chapl HM Pris Hollesley Bay from 01; Chapl Allington NHS Trust 00-01; PtO *St E* from 00. *The Rectory, Highfield Road, Halesworth IP19 8SJ* T: (01986) 872602 E: edward.rennard@btinternet.com

RENNIE, Iain Hugh. b 43. Ripon Coll Cuddesdon 88. **d** 90 **p** 91. C Poulton-le-Sands w Morecambe St Laur *Blackb* 90-94; V Hornby w Claughton 94-02; V Hornby w Claughton and Whittington etc 02-11; rtd 11; PtO *Blackb* from 11. *65 Ashton Drive, Lancaster LA1 2LQ* T: (01524) 382926

RENNIE, John Aubery. b 47. Lon Univ MB, BS 70 FRCS 75. SEITE 04. **d** 06 **p** 07. NSM Melbury *Sarum* 06-10; NSM Sherborne w Castleton, Lillington and Longburton 10-12; Deanery Missr Sherborne from 12. *Rectory House, 2 Fore Street, Evershot, Dorchester DT2 0JW* T: (01935) 83003 M: 07826-447432 E: johnrennie40@hotmail.com

RENNIE, Paul Antony. b 58. Heriot-Watt Univ BSc 82 Edin Univ LTh. **d** 87 **p** 88. C Nairn *Mor* 87-90; C Forres 87-90; C Edin St Pet 90-92; Dep Chapl HM Pris Leeds 92; Chapl HM YOI Hindley 93-95; Chapl HM Pris Liv 95-97; Chapl RAF from 97. *Chaplaincy Services (RAF), HQ Air Command, RAF High Wycombe HP14 4UE* T: (01494) 496800 F: 496343

RENNISON, Mrs Patricia Elinor. b 46. **d** 11 **p** 12. OLM Shilbottle *Newc* from 11. *8 The Crescent, Shilbottle, Alnwick NE66 2UU* T: (01665) 575686 E: patriciarennison983@btinternet.com

RENNIX, Raymond Latham. b 37. QUB BTh 02. CITC 00. **d** 03 **p** 04. NSM Killaney w Carryduff *D & D* 03-08; NSM Glencraig 08-12; rtd 12. *5 Brompton Court, Dromara, Dromore BT25 2DQ* T: (028) 9753 3167 M: 07977-584053 E: r.rennix@btinternet.com

RENSHAW, Mrs Anne-Marie Louise. b 71. St Hilda's Coll Ox MA 96 Fitzw Coll Cam BA 97. Ridley Hall Cam 95. **d** 98 **p** 99. C Norton *St Alb* 98-02; TV Borehamwood 02-05; TV Elstree and Borehamwood 05-11; P-in-c Tolleshunt Knights w Tiptree and Gt Braxted *Chelmsf* 11-13; TR Thurstable and Winstree from 13. *The Rectory, Rectory Road, Tiptree, Colchester CO5 0SX* T: (01621) 815260 E: amlrenshaw@btinternet.com

RENSHAW, Mrs Claire Louise. b 80. Yorks Min Course 12. **d** 15 **p** 15. C Knaresborough *Ripon* from 15. *6 Florin Drive, Knaresborough HG5 0WG* M: 07912-104442 E: claire.renshaw@sky.com

RENSHAW, David William. b 59. Oak Hill Th Coll BA 85. **d** 85 **p** 86. C Shawbury *Lich* 85-88; V Childs Ercall and R Stoke upon Tern 88-92; V Stoneleigh *Guildf* 92-97; RD Epsom 95-97; Chapl Scarborough and NE Yorks Healthcare NHS Trust 97-99; Chapl St Cath Hospice Scarborough 97-99; R Meppershall w Campton and Stondon *St Alb* 99-01; C Bedford St Andr 02; PtO *Chich* 05-06; Hon C Bexhill St Pet 06; TV Rye 09-11; P-in-c Lynch w Iping Marsh and Milland 11-12; R 12-14. *102 Wallace Avenue, Worthing BN11 5QA* E: renshaw221@btinternet.com

RENSHAW, Canon Susan Kathryn. b 55. Shenstone Coll of Educn CertEd 77. WMMTC 99. **d** 02 **p** 03. C Sedgley All SS *Worc* 02-05; C Gornal and Sedgley 05-06; V Eckington from 06; V Defford w Besford from 06; V Overbury w Teddington, Alstone etc from 06; RD Pershore from 11; Hon Can Worc Cathl from 15. *The Vicarage, Drakes Bridge Road, Eckington, Pershore WR10 3BN* T: (01386) 750203 E: revsusan@btinternet.com

RENSHAW, Timothy John. b 65. Trin Coll Carmarthen BA 86. St Jo Coll Nottm MA 97. **d** 97 **p** 98. C Calverton *S'well* 97-01; C Epperstone 97-01; C Gonalston 97-01; C Oxton 97-01; P-in-c Shireoaks 01-05; Dioc Adv on Notts Coalfield 01-05; Project Manager Cathl Breakfast and Archer Projects Sheff from 05. *The Cathedral, 4-7 East Parade, Sheffield S1 2ET* T: 0114-275 1650 or 279 7042

RENWICK, Canon Colin. b 30. St Aid Birkenhead. **d** 59 **p** 60. C Drypool St Columba w St Andr and St Pet *York* 59-62; C Wigan St Cath *Liv* 62-64; Min Thornton CD 64-77; V Thornton 77-97; RD Bootle 83-89; Hon Can Bauchi from 93; rtd 97; PtO *Ches* from 97. *27 Briar Drive, Heswall, Wirral CH60 5RN* T: 0151-342 3308

RENYARD, Christopher. b 52. Open Univ BA 87. Coll of Resurr Mirfield 81. **d** 84 **p** 85. C Heckmondwike *Wakef* 84-88; C Harpenden St Nic *St Alb* 88-95; Asst Chapl Salisbury Health Care NHS Trust 95-01; Chapl Team Ldr Salisbury NHS Foundn Trust 01-12; LtO *Sarum* from 12. *Pilsdon Manor, Pilsdon, Bridport DT6 5NZ* T: (01308) 868308 F: 868161

RENYARD, Paul Holmwood. b 42. K Coll Lon BD 65 AKC 65. **d** 66 **p** 67. C Croydon St Aug *Cant* 66-69; C Farnham *Guildf* 69-72; V Capel 72-78; Asst Dir RE 77-88; P-in-c Roch 78-83; Hon C Roch 78-83; V Holdenhurst *Win* 83-95; V Pennington 95-07; rtd 07; PtO *Win* from 07. *53 Scarf Road, Poole BH17 8QJ* T: (01202) 682460 E: renyard@tiscali.co.uk

RENZ, Thomas. b 69. Freie Theologische Akademie Giessen MA 93 Chelt & Glouc Coll of HE PhD 97. Coll of Resurr Mirfield 09. **d** 09 **p** 10. C Highgate St Mich *Lon* 09-12; R Monken Hadley from 12. *The Rectory, Hadley Common, Barnet EN5 5QD* T: (020) 8449 9441 M: 07933-073692 E: thomas.renz@gmail.com

REPATH, George David. b 43. Kellogg Coll Ox MSt 96. St D Coll Lamp. **d** 68 **p** 69. C Cardiff St Jo *Llan* 68-73; C Gt Stanmore *Lon* 73-77; V Stratfield Mortimer *Ox* 77-85; RD Bradfield 82-85; P-in-c Mortimer W End w Padworth 83-85; V Bray and Braywood 85-07; rtd 07. *8 Summerfields, Findon, Worthing BN14 0TU* T: (01903) 877366

REPATH, John Richard. b 48. St Mich Coll Llan 72. **d** 75 **p** 76. C Canton St Jo *Llan* 75-79; C Burghclere w Newtown and Ecchinswell w Sydmonton *Win* 80-83; R Bewcastle and Stapleton *Carl* 83-88; P-in-c Kirklinton w Hethersgill and Scaleby 86-88; R Bewcastle, Stapleton and Kirklinton etc 88-97; rtd 97; P-in-c New Galloway *Glas* from 97. *The Rectory, Kenbridge Road, New Galloway, Castle Douglas DG7 3RP* T: (01644) 420235 E: johnrepath@btinternet.com

REPTON, Suffragan Bishop of. See SOUTHERN, The Rt Revd Humphrey Ivo John

RESCH, Colin Ernst. b 67. Trin Coll Bris 04. **d** 06 **p** 07. C Highley w Billingsley, Glazeley etc *Heref* 06-10; P-in-c Stottesdon w Farlow, Cleeton St Mary etc 10-14; P-in-c Mountsorrel Ch Ch and St Pet *Leic* from 14. *Christ Church Vicarage, 4 Rothley Road, Mountsorrel, Loughborough LE12 7JU* E: colin@godstuff.org.uk

RESCH, Elizabeth Barbara. b 66. Edge Hill Coll of HE BEd 88. SEITE 10. **d** 13 **p** 14. NSM Sittingbourne w Bobbing *Cant* from 13. *88 Albany Road, Sittingbourne ME10 1EL* T: (01795) 473393 E: lizresch@me.com

RESCH, Michael Johann. b 63. NTMTC 96. **d** 99 **p** 00. C Cullompton, Willand, Uffculme, Kentisbeare etc *Ex* 99-03; P-in-c Sittingbourne H Trin w Bobbing *Cant* 03-12; TR Sittingbourne w Bobbing from 12; AD Sittingbourne from 15. *88 Albany Road, Sittingbourne ME10 1EL* T: (01795) 473393 M: 07967-771231 E: mikeresch@me.com

RESTALL, Miss Susan Roberta. b 45. MSc. Sarum & Wells Th Coll 79. **dss** 82 **d** 87 **p** 94. Dorchester *Sarum* 82-84; Portland All SS w St Pet 84-87; Par Dn 87; Team Dn Yate New Town *Bris* 87-94; TV 94-95; Chapl Birm Heartlands and Solihull NHS Trust 95-01; rtd 01; PtO *Birm* from 03. *12 Croft Road, Yardley, Birmingham B26 1SG* T: 0121-783 3325

REUSS, Nathanael. b 76. Ballarat Univ BSc 98. St Jo Coll Nottm MA(MM) 12. **d** 11 **p** 12. C Ripley *Derby* 11-13; C Brailsford w Shirley, Osmaston w Edlaston etc 13-14. *Address temp unknown* M: 07840-343525 E: nathanaelreuss@gmail.com

REVELEY, James Stewart. b 69. Goldsmiths' Coll Lon BMus 92. Ch Div Sch of the Pacific (USA) 95 Ripon Coll Cuddesdon BA 97. **d** 96 **p** 97. C Goldington *St Alb* 96-00; C Harpenden St Nic 00-04; V Boxmoor St Jo 04-13; V Bedford St Andr from 13. *St Andrew's Vicarage, 1 St Edmond Road, Bedford MK40 2NQ* T: (01234) 254234 E: revjumble@aol.com

REVELL, Patrick Walter Millard. b 32. Wells Th Coll 65. **d** 67 **p** 68. C Leic St Jas 67-74; V Quorndon 74-82; TR Camelot Par *B & W* 82-90; RD Cary and Bruton 90-96; V Castle Cary w Ansford 90-97; rtd 97; PtO *B & W* from 97; *Sarum* from 97. *10 Fairfield, Bristol Road, Sherborne DT9 4HG* T: (01935) 813083 E: patrickrevell@btinternet.com

REVERA, Susan Mary. See LEATHLEY, Susan Mary

REW, Eric Malcolm. b 63. UEA BSc 84 PGCE 89. Qu Coll Birm 98. **d** 00 **p** 01. C Shepshed *Leic* 00-04; TV Kingsthorpe *Pet* from 04; Chapl Northants Police from 07. *The Vicarage, 42 Fallow Walk, Northampton NN2 8DE* T: (01604) 843465 E: vicar@rewfamily.plus.com

REX, Keith Leslie Herbert. b 30. K Coll Lon and St Boniface Warminster AKC 53. **d** 55 **p** 56. C Shepton Mallet *B & W* 55-58; C Cheshunt *St Alb* 58-60; V Weston-super-Mare St Andr Bournville *B & W* 60-67; R Charlton Adam w Charlton Mackrell 67-69; rtd 90. *46 Petherton Gardens, Hengrove, Bristol BS14 9BS* T: (01275) 891574

REY, Joshua Barnabas. b 65. Ball Coll Ox MA 88. Ripon Coll Cuddesdon BA 11. **d** 12 **p** 13. C Streatham St Leon *S'wark* from 12. *49 Aldrington Road, London SW16 1TU* M: 07525-421681 E: mail@joshuarey.com

REYNISH, David Stuart. b 52. Nottm Univ BEd 75. Linc Th Coll 72. **d** 77 **p** 78. C Boston *Linc* 77-80; C Chalfont St Peter *Ox* 80-84; V Thursby *Carl* 84-88; R Iver Heath *Ox* 88-03; V Kelvedon and Feering *Chelmsf* 03-13; TR Bexhill St Pet *Chich* from 13. *The Rectory, Church Street, Bexhill-on-Sea TN40 2HE* T: (01424) 217203 E: frdavidreynish@tiscali.co.uk

REYNOLDS, Alan Martin. b 53. Sarum & Wells Th Coll 73. **d** 77 **p** 78. C Glan Ely *Llan* 77-84; V Pontyclun w Talygarn 84-97; PtO 97-04; *Mon* from 12. *The Orchards, Stow Hill, Newport NP20 4EA* T: (01633) 215841 E: martin.reynolds1@me.com

REYNOLDS, Alan Thomas William. b 43. Lon Univ BSc 64. Linc Th Coll 64. **d** 66 **p** 67. C Leic St Pet 66-70; C Huntington *York* 70-72; R Darliston Jamaica 72-76; V Stechford *Birm* 76-83; Chapl E Birm Hosp 76-83; P-in-c Hampton in Arden *Birm* 83-86; V 87-93; Chapl Parkway Hosp Solihull 83-93; V Moseley St Anne *Birm* 93-02; Chapl Moseley Hall Hosp Birm 93; Chapl Birm Specialist Community Health NHS Trust 94-02; V Kerry, Llanmerewig, Dolfor and Mochdre *St As* 02-08; AD Cedewain 03-08; rtd 08; PtO *Lich* from 08; *St As* from 09. *49 Gittin Street, Oswestry SY11 1DU*
T: (01691) 680416 E: robbie.reynolds1@btinternet.com

REYNOLDS, Mrs Angela Heather. b 44. Wye Coll Lon BSc 66 Birm Univ CertEd 67. EAMTC 94. **d** 97 **p** 98. NSM Barnham Broom *Nor* 97-99; C Easton w Colton and Marlingford 99-00; P-in-c Easton, Colton, Marlingford and Bawburgh 00-09; rtd 09; PtO *Nor* from 09; Hon PV Nor Cathl from 14. *26 Clickers Road, Norwich NR3 2DD* T: (01603) 402688
E: angord@btinternet.com

REYNOLDS, David Hammerton. b 39. St Jo Coll Dur BA 62. Qu Coll Birm 63. **d** 65 **p** 66. C N Ormesby *York* 65-68; C Hessle 68-71; V Sherburn in Elmet 71-79; V Fulford 79-87; Resp for Clergy In-Service Tr York Area 82-87; TV Bolventor *Truro* 87-90; TR Brayton *York* 90-06; RD Selby 04-06; rtd 06; PtO *Sheff* from 06; *York* from 08. *42A George Street, Snaith, Goole DN14 9HZ* T: (01405) 869352 E: dhrey@btopenworld.com

REYNOLDS, David James. b 48. St Jo Coll Dur BA 72 Lanc Univ MA 85. Cranmer Hall Dur 69. **d** 73 **p** 74. C Formby H Trin *Liv* 73-77; P-in-c Widnes St Paul 77-80; V Southport St Paul 80-87; P-in-c Mawdesley *Blackb* 87-91; R 91-14; P-in-c Croston and Bretherton 06-13; R 13-14; Chapl Derian Ho Children's Hospice 93-97; rtd 14; PtO *Blackb* from 14. *Holly Mount, Rufford Road, Bispham, Ormskirk L40 3SA* T: (01704) 821684
E: rectordavid@hotmail.co.uk

REYNOLDS, Mrs Emily Jane. b 84. Lanc Univ BA 05. Westcott Ho Cam 11. **d** 15. C Walsall St Luke *Lich* from 15. *11 The Cloisters, Walsall WS4 2AJ* M: 07964-598760

REYNOLDS, Gordon. b 42. Sarum & Wells Th Coll 71. **d** 72 **p** 73. C Tunstall *Lich* 72-74; USPG Zambia 75-88; C Southmead *Bris* 88-90; rtd 07. *78 William Bentley Court, Graiseley Lane, Wolverhampton WV11 1QW* T: (01902) 730381

REYNOLDS, Hannah Claire. b 67. Kingston Univ MBA 95. St Steph Ho Ox BTh 09. **d** 06 **p** 07. C Twickenham All Hallows *Lon* 06-09; P-in-c Hanworth All SS 09-13; P-in-c Didcot St Pet *Ox* from 13. *The Vicarage, 47A Newlands Avenue, Didcot OX11 8QA* T: (01235) 812114 M: 07981-981493
E: hcreynolds@hotmail.co.uk

REYNOLDS, Ms Helen Tracy. b 65. Huddersfield Univ BA. Cranmer Hall Dur 03. **d** 06 **p** 07. C Ryton *Dur* 06-11; Lect Newcastle Coll 11-13; TV N Wearside *Dur* from 13. *The Team Rectory, Rotherham Road, Sunderland SR5 5QS*
E: htracyr@gmail.com

REYNOLDS, Canon John Lionel. b 34. JP. Westmr Coll Ox MTh 00. Chich Th Coll 58. **d** 61 **p** 62. C Whitkirk *Ripon* 61-64; C Tong *Bradf* 64-68; V Chiseldon and Draycot Foliat *Sarum* 68-74; TR Ridgeway 74-76; RD Marlborough 74-76; V Calne and Blackland 76-89; RD Calne 77-84; Can and Preb Sarum Cathl 80-02; V Woodford Valley 89-02; rtd 02; PtO *Sarum* from 02; *Win* from 03. *St Edmund, 21 New Road, Romsey SO51 7LL* T: (01794) 516349 E: carolannreynolds@aol.com

REYNOLDS, Katharine Stirling McDonald. **d** 12 **p** 13. C Edin Old St Paul from 12. *41 Jeffrey Street, Edinburgh EH1 1DH* T: 0131-556 7702 M: 07563-188757 E: curate@ols.org.uk

REYNOLDS, Mandy Elizabeth. b 59. NTMTC 99. **d** 02 **p** 03. NSM Wembley St Jo *Lon* 02-04; C 04-15; R Alde River *St E* from 15. *The Rectory, Great Glemham Road, Stratford St Andrew, Saxmundham IP17 1LJ* T: (01728) 602846
E: revmandy.alderiver@yahoo.co.uk

REYNOLDS, Marion. b 49. Chelmer Inst of HE CertEd 84. STETS 04. **d** 06 **p** 07. NSM Quantock Towers *B & W* 06-07; NSM Shelswell *Ox* 07-11; P-in-c Pattishall w Cold Higham and Gayton w Tiffield *Pet* from 12. *The Rectory, 17 Church Street, Pattishall, Towcester NN12 8NB* T: (01327) 830573 M: 07834-062268 E: marion.reynolds2@btopenworld.com

REYNOLDS, Martin. *See* REYNOLDS, Alan Martin

REYNOLDS, Michael. *See* REYNOLDS, Richard Michael

REYNOLDS, Mrs Michelle Angela. b 70. Ridley Hall Cam 02. **d** 04 **p** 05. C Hoddesdon *St Alb* 04-07; TV Grays Thurrock *Chelmsf* from 07. *Wendover Vicarage, College Avenue, Grays RM17 5UW* T: (01375) 373468
E: michellea_reynolds@hotmail.com

REYNOLDS, Paul Andrew. b 57. BA 86. Trin Coll Bris 83. **d** 86 **p** 87. C Reading St Jo *Ox* 86-90; C Dorridge *Birm* 90-95; TV Riverside *Ox* 95-06; R Beercrocombe w Curry Mallet, Hatch Beauchamp etc *B & W* from 06. *The Rectory, Stoke St Mary, Taunton TA3 5BX* T: (01823) 444023

REYNOLDS, Paul Frederick. b 56. St Jo Coll Nottm 90. **d** 92 **p** 93. C Hyde St Geo *Ches* 92-96; P-in-c Delamere 96-00;

Asst Dir Par Support and Development 96-98; Acting Dir 98-00; V Handforth *Ches* 00-07; P-in-c Bramcote *S'well* 07-11; V from 11. *The Vicarage, Moss Drive, Bramcote, Beeston NG9 3NF* T: 0115-922 9600
E: vicar@bramcoteparishchurch.com

REYNOLDS, Philip Delamere. b 53. Leeds Univ CertEd 74 Nottm Univ BCombStuds 82. Linc Th Coll 79. **d** 82 **p** 83. C Huddersfield St Jo *Wakef* 82-85; C Barkisland w W Scammonden 85-87; P-in-c Skelmanthorpe *Leeds* from 87. *St Aidan's Vicarage, Radcliffe Street, Skelmanthorpe, Huddersfield HD8 9AF* T: (01484) 863232 E: life.draw@virgin.net

REYNOLDS, Raymond Ernest. b 29. Nottm Univ MPhil 89. Lambeth STh 84 CA Tr Coll 50 Chich Th Coll 58. **d** 60 **p** 61. C Leeds St Marg *Ripon* 60-62; C Beeston *S'well* 62-64; R Farnley *Ripon* 64-76; R Higham-on-the-Hill w Fenny Drayton *Leic* 76-81; R Higham-on-the-Hill w Fenny Drayton and Witherley 81-90; V Sutton *Ely* 90-94; R Witcham w Mepal 90-94; rtd 94; C Nantwich *Ches* 94-96; PtO from 96. *4 St Alban's Drive, Nantwich CW5 7DW* T: (01270) 623534

REYNOLDS, Richard Michael. b 42. St Steph Ho Ox 65. **d** 67 **p** 68. C Kidderminster St Mary *Worc* 67-70; Guyana 70-73; TV N Creedy *Ex* 73-80; R Holsworthy w Hollacombe 80-86; R Holsworthy w Hollacombe and Milton Damerel 86-12; Chapl N Devon Healthcare NHS Trust 94-12; rtd 12. *Blagrove, Germansweek, Beaworthy EX21 5BH*
T: (01837) 871226 E: michaelreynolds64@hotmail.co.uk

REYNOLDS, Roderick Bredon (Rory). b 58. Man Univ BA 80. Ripon Coll Cuddesdon 93. **d** 95 **p** 96. C Hitchin *St Alb* 95-98; C Stevenage St Andr and St Geo 98-00; P-in-c High Wych and Gilston w Eastwick 00-06; TV Plaistow and N Canning Town *Chelmsf* 06-10; Chapl S Lon and Maudsley NHS Foundn Trust 10-12; Chapl SW Lon and St George's Mental Health NHS Trust 12-13; Chapl St Geo Healthcare NHS Trust Lon from 13. *Address temp unknown* M: 07515-353456
E: roryreynolds@mac.com

REYNOLDS, Mrs Rosemary Joan. b 46. WMMTC 00. **d** 03 **p** 04. NSM Brandwood *Birm* from 03. *23 Chanston Avenue, Birmingham B14 5BD* T: 0121-444 7015
E: hello@frankandrosemary.freeserve.co.uk

REYNOLDS, Stephen Paul. b 46. **d** 08 **p** 09. NSM Cannock *Lich* 08-09; NSM Heath Hayes 09-13; NSM Cannock and Huntington from 13. *4 Harebell Close, Cannock WS12 3XA* T: (01543) 270940 E: stevereyno@tiscali.co.uk

REYNOLDS, Tracy. *See* REYNOLDS, Helen Tracy

RHOADES, Andrew Craig. b 56. Hatf Poly BSc 79 CEng 84 MIEE 84. St Jo Coll Nottm MTh 09. **d** 09 **p** 10. C Hexagon *Leic* 09-12; P-in-c Broom Leys from 12. *St David's Vicarage, 7 Greenhill Road, Coalville LE67 4RL* T: (01530) 834210 M: 07531-121145 E: acrhoades@cheerful.com

RHODES, Adrian Michael. b 48. K Coll Lon BD 71 AKC 71. Qu Coll Birm 71. **d** 72 **p** 73. C Bury St Jo *Man* 73-75; Chapl N Man Gen Hosp 75-77; C Crumpsall *Man* 75-77; Chapl Walsall Manor and Bloxwich Hosps 77-83; Chapl Walsall Gen Hosp 81-83; Chapl Man R Infirmary 83-94; Chapl St Mary's Hosp Man 83-94; Chapl Man R Eye Hosp 83-94; Chapl Cen Man Healthcare NHS Trust 94-00; PtO *Man* 00-08. *58 Errwood Road, Burnage, Manchester M19 2QH* T: 0161-224 1739
E: adrian@rhodes.net

RHODES, Mrs Amanda Louise. b 63. Leeds Univ BA 07. NOC 04. **d** 07 **p** 08. C Kippax w Allerton Bywater *Ripon* 07-11; P-in-c Lofthouse *Leeds* 11-15; TV Rothwell, Lofthouse, Methley etc from 15. *The Vicarage, 8 Church Farm Close, Lofthouse, Wakefield WF3 3SA* T: (01924) 823286 M: 07971-998621 E: revmac63@googlemail.com

RHODES, Ann. b 56. **d** 13 **p** 14. NSM Hackenthorpe *Sheff* from 13. *1 Ormes Meadow, Owlthorpe, Sheffield S20 6TE* T: 0114-247 8749 E: treble20jr@hotmail.com

RHODES, Anthony John. b 27. Mert Coll Ox BA 50 MA 53. St Steph Ho Ox 52. **d** 54 **p** 55. C Northampton St Alb *Pet* 54-57; C Oakham 57-60; P-in-c S Queensferry *Edin* 60-74; V Mitcham St Olave *S'wark* 74-81; V Owston *Linc* 81-92; V W Butterwick 81-92; rtd 92; PtO *Leic* from 14. *12 Stuart Court, High Street, Kibworth, Leicester LE8 0LR* T: 0116-279 3674

RHODES, Arthur. b 31. Dur Univ BA 58. Cranmer Hall Dur 57. **d** 59 **p** 60. C Kirkdale St Lawr *Liv* 59-61; C Litherland St Phil 61-64; V St Helens St Matt Thatto Heath 64-67; V Samlesbury *Blackb* 67-79; LtO 80-01; PtO from 01. *88 Deborah Avenue, Fulwood, Preston PR2 9HU* T: (01772) 712212

RHODES, Canon Benjamin. b 71. Portsm Univ BSc 93 Heythrop Coll Lon MA 10. Westcott Ho Cam 94. **d** 97 **p** 98. C Upminster *Chelmsf* 97-01; Asst Chapl Lewisham Hosp NHS Trust 01-05; Sen Chapl Barts and The Lon NHS Trust 05-08; Lead Chapl 08-10; Lead Chapl Tower Hamlets Primary Care Trust 08-10; Spiritual Care Lead and Chapl Team Ldr King's Coll Hosp NHS Foundn Trust from 10; NSM St Bart Less

Lon 05-07; Bp's Adv for Healthcare Chapl Stepney Area 08-10; Bp's Adv for Hosp Chapl *S'wark* from 15; Hon Can S'wark Cathl from 15. *The Chaplaincy, King's College Hospital, Denmark Hill, London SE5 9RS* T: (020) 3299 3522
E: benrhodes@nhs.net

RHODES, Mrs Caroline Laura. b 66. Bath Univ BPharm 87 K Coll Lon MSc 91. Ripon Coll Cuddesdon 08. **d** 10 **p** 11. C Allestree St Edm and Darley Abbey *Derby* 10-14; C Wirksworth 14-15; V Guilsfield w Buttington and Pool Quay *St As* from 15. *The Vicarage, Guilsfield, Welshpool SY21 9NF*
T: (01938) 554245 E: revcarolinerhodes@me.com

RHODES, Christine. *See* RHODES, Lois Christine

RHODES, David George. b 45. Univ of Wales (Abth) BA 66. Trin Coll Bris 83. **d** 85 **p** 86. C Brinsworth w Catcliffe *Sheff* 85-89; V Mortomley St Sav 89-90; V Mortomley St Sav High Green 90-99; V Totley 99-11; rtd 11; PtO *Sheff* from 11; rtd 11. *12 Sheards Close, Dronfield Woodhouse, Dronfield S18 8NJ*
T: (01246) 767838 E: drhodes@toucansurf.com

RHODES, Duncan. b 35. Leeds Univ BSc 56. **d** 93 **p** 94. OLM Saddleworth *Man* 93-05; rtd 05; PtO *Man* from 06. *Holden Cottage, 21 Spurn Lane, Diggle, Oldham OL3 5QP*
T: (01457) 872399 E: dunrhodes@aol.com

RHODES, Mrs Heather Margaret. b 32. **d** 88. Par Dn Purley St Mark *S'wark* 89-94; C 94-98; rtd 98; Hon C Purley St Mark *S'wark* 00-05; PtO from 05. *24 Highfield Road, Purley CR8 2JG*
T: (020) 8660 1486

RHODES, John. *See* RHODES, Anthony John

RHODES, John Andrew. b 61. Teesside Poly GRSC 82 Univ of Wales (Swansea) PhD 91. WEMTC 11. **d** 14. NSM Ledbury *Heref* from 14. *The Brainge Bungalow, Putley, Ledbury HR8 2RD*
T: (01531) 670442 E: john.a.rhodes@btinternet.com

RHODES, Jonathan Peter. b 69. Coll of Ripon & York St Jo BA 96. NOC 01. **d** 04 **p** 05. C High Harrogate Ch Ch *Ripon* 04-08; P-in-c Hartlepool St Aid and St Columba *Dur* 08-11; R Brotton Parva *York* from 11. *St Margaret's Rectory, 9 Crispin Court, Brotton, Saltburn-by-the-Sea TS12 2XL* T: (01287) 201961

RHODES, Mrs Laura Clare. b 82. Ripon Coll Cuddesdon 13. **d** 15. C Wilmslow *Ches* from 15. *3 Rydal Mews, 117 Manchester Road, Wilmslow SK9 2JH* M: 07875-657784
E: lauracrhodes@gmail.com

RHODES, Lois Christine. b 34. Lon Univ BSc 61. Glouc Sch of Min 84. **d** 87 **p** 94. NSM Weobley w Sarnesfield and Norton Canon *Heref* 87-92; NSM Letton w Staunton, Byford, Mansel Gamage etc 87-92; Chapl Asst Heref Hosps NHS Trust from 93. *Bellbrook, Bell Square, Weobley, Hereford HR4 8SE*
T: (01544) 318410 *or* (01432) 355444

RHODES, Matthew Ivan. b 66. Bris Univ BA 89 Birm Univ MPhil 95 PhD 05. Qu Coll Birm BD 93. **d** 94 **p** 95. C Willenhall H Trin *Lich* 94-97; Chapl Maadi St Jo Egypt 97-00; P-in-c Middleton *Birm* 00-07; P-in-c Wishaw 00-07; P-in-c Curdworth 05-07; R Curdworth, Middleton and Wishaw 07-11; P-in-c Maney 11; V from 11; AD Sutton Coldfield 06-13; Dioc Chapl MU from 11. *The Vicarage, Maney Hill Road, Sutton Coldfield B72 1JJ* T: 0121-354 2426
E: vicarofmaney@gmail.com

RHODES, Robert George. b 41. Man Univ BSc 62. Ripon Hall Ox 72. **d** 74 **p** 75. C Banbury *Ox* 74-77; TV 77-81; P-in-c Long Horsley and Adult Educn Adv *Newc* 81-86; TR Wolverton *Ox* 86-97; P-in-c Bledlow w Saunderton and Horsenden 97-98; TV Risborough 98-02; Warden of Readers 97-02; USPG Miss Belize 02-06; rtd 06; PtO *Derby* from 07. *3 China House Yard, St Mary's Gate, Wirksworth, Matlock DE4 4DQ*
T: (01629) 823623 E: bandjrhodes@hotmail.com

RHODES-WRIGLEY, James. b 35. AKC 59. **d** 60 **p** 61. C S Harrow St Paul *Lon* 60-66; V Hendon Ch Ch 66-71; V Northolt Park St Barn 71-92; rtd 92; Hon C Whyke w Rumboldswhyke and Portfield *Chich* from 96. *4 Gordon Avenue, Donnington, Chichester PO19 8QY* T: (01243) 781664

RHYDDERCH, David Huw. b 48. St Mich Coll Llan 70. **d** 73 **p** 74. C Gelligaer *Llan* 73-76; C Penarth All SS 76-78; V Resolven 78-81; V Ystrad Rhondda w Ynyscynon 81-93; RD Rhondda 89-93; R St Andrews Major w Michaelston-le-Pit 93-13; rtd 13; PtO *Llan* from 13. *34 Holly Road, Cardiff CF5 3HJ*
T: (029) 2055 5597

RICE, David. b 57. Nottm Univ BA 79. Ripon Coll Cuddesdon 80. **d** 82 **p** 83. C Cirencester *Glouc* 82-86; R Theale and Englefield *Ox* 86-00; TR Wallingford from 00. *The Rectory, 22 Castle Street, Wallingford OX10 8DW* T: (01491) 202188

RICE, Franklin Arthur. b 20. FRICS 49. St Alb Minl Tr Scheme 77. **d** 80 **p** 81. NSM Hoddesdon *St Alb* 80-84; PtO *Guildf* from 85. *27 Mead Court, 281 Station Road, Addlestone KT15 2PR* T: (01932) 846462

RICE, John Leslie Hale. b 38. Lon Univ BScEng 60 BD 68 FCMI. EMMTC 73. **d** 76 **p** 77. NSM Allestree St Nic *Derby* 76-90; LtO 90-08; PtO from 08. *14 Gisborne Crescent, Allestree, Derby DE22 2FL* T: (01332) 557222 E: j.rice.t21@btinternet.com

RICE, Peter Langford. b 49. STETS 97. **d** 00 **p** 01. NSM Salisbury St Fran and Stratford sub Castle *Sarum* 00-03; P-in-c W Highland Region *Arg* 03-08; LtO from 09. *The Old Manse, Lochgair, Argyll PA31 8SB* T: (01546) 886674
M: 07776-105279 E: boutflower@aol.com

RICE-OXLEY, John Richard. b 44. Keble Coll Ox BA 66 MA 69 Dur Univ MA 85. Lon Coll of Div 68. **d** 70 **p** 71. C Eastwood *S'well* 70-73; Youth Adv CMS 73-78; V Mansfield St Jo *S'well* 78-82; P-in-c Thornley *Dur* 82-85; P-in-c Darlington St Matt and St Luke 85-87; V 87-98; V Hornsea w Atwick *York* 98-06; P-in-c Aldbrough, Mappleton w Goxhill and Withernwick 05-06; rtd 06; PtO *York* from 07. *3 Bertie Close, Swinstead, Grantham NG33 4PW* E: richardriceoxley@gmail.com

RICE-OXLEY, Mrs Sylvia Jeanette Kathleen. b 48. **d** 08 **p** 09. C Aldbrough, Mappleton w Goxhill and Withernwick *York* 08-11; P-in-c 11-13; rtd 13. *3 Bertie Close, Swinstead, Grantham NG33 4PW* E: sylviariceoxley@gmail.com

RICH, Brian John. b 49. Reading Univ BSc 70. Guildf Dioc Min Course 94. **d** 97 **p** 98. OLM Stoke Hill *Guildf* 97-12; PtO *Win* 12-15. *2 Boon Way, Oakley, Basingstoke RG23 7BS*
T: (01256) 783111 E: btrich@talktalk.net

RICH, Canon Christopher Robin. b 49. LSE MSc(Econ) 95. Brasted Th Coll 70 Sarum & Wells Th Coll 72. **d** 74 **p** 75. C Sholing *Win* 74-76; C Southampton Maybush St Pet 76-79; R Fawley 79-90; Ind Chapl 83-90; Dir Soc Resp 90-99; Hon Can Win Cathl 96-99; Dir Soc Resp *Blackb* 99-05; *Guildf* 06-14; rtd 14. *Robins Cottage, Nightingale Road, Ash, Aldershot GU12 6DD*

RICH, Nicholas Philip. b 49. St Cuth Soc Dur BA 74 PGCE 75 Coll of Ripon & York St Jo CertEd 83. Linc Th Coll 86. **d** 88 **p** 89. C W Acklam *York* 88-91; Chapl St Geo Sch Harpenden 91-95; rtd 95. *36 Park Hill, Ampthill, Bedford MK45 2LP*
E: maggie.rich@phonecoop.coop

RICH, Paul Michael. b 36. OBE 87. Sarum Th Coll 62. **d** 65 **p** 66. C Woodbridge St Mary *St E* 65-68; C W Wycombe *Ox* 68-70; CF 70-88; LtO *S & B* 88-90; V Crondall and Ewshot *Guildf* 91-05; rtd 05; PtO *Win* 08-13. *The Firs, The Street, Binsted, Alton GU34 4PF* T: (01420) 525302

RICH, Peter Geoffrey. b 45. Oak Hill Th Coll 74. **d** 77 **p** 78. C Blackheath St Jo *S'wark* 77-80; C Surbiton St Matt 80-87; V St Alb St Luke *St Alb* 87-98; V Gravesend St Aid *Roch* 98-10; rtd 11; P-in-c Stone w Dinton and Hartwell *Ox* from 11. *10 Badgers Rise, Stone, Aylesbury HP17 8RR* T: (01296) 748068
E: angela_richuk@yahoo.co.uk

RICH, Thomas. b 52. St Jo Coll Nottm 86. **d** 88 **p** 89. C Netherton *Liv* 88-91; P-in-c Bootle Ch Ch 91-93; V from 93. *Christ Church Vicarage, 1 Breeze Hill, Bootle L20 9EY*
T: 0151-525 2565 M: 07958-784313
E: tom@richchurch.freeserve.co.uk

RICHARDS, Alan Grenville. b 41. Kelham Th Coll 64. **d** 69 **p** 70. C Northolt St Mary *Lon* 69-75; V Fatfield *Dur* 75-84; V Beighton *Sheff* 84-91; V Endcliffe 91-94; Deputation Appeals Org Children's Soc 94-98; rtd 06; Hon C Cheriton All So w Newington *Cant* 98-06; rtd 06; Hon C Cheriton All So w Newington and Cheriton St Martin *Cant* 06-07; PtO from 07. *7 Pike Close, Folkestone CT19 5UT* T: (01303) 243999

RICHARDS, Andrew David Thomas. b 55. St Jo Coll Dur BA 76 Roehampton Inst PGCE 84 FRSA 96. St Steph Ho Ox 76. **d** 78 **p** 79. C Shirley *Birm* 78-80; C Cowley St Jo *Ox* 80-82; PtO *Win* 84-88; *Sarum* 88-92; NSM Hazelbury Bryan and the Hillside Par 92-94; Chapl Rossall Sch Fleetwood 94-99; Chapl K Sch Ely 99-03; Sen Chapl and Hd RS Wellington Coll Berks 03-08; Chapl Duke of York's R Mil Sch Dover 08-12; rtd 12. *Les Quiaulins, Gentillaud, 16210 Médillac, France*
M: 07757-601244

RICHARDS, Anne. b 58. **d** 10 **p** 11. NSM N Hull St Mich *York* from 10; Chapl Abp Sentamu Academy Hull from 14. *42 Riplingham Road, Kirk Ella, Hull HU10 7TP* T: (01482) 655084 E: work@anne-richards.com

RICHARDS, Mrs Anne Maria. b 54. Wolv Poly CertEd 88 HCIMA 83. Qu Coll Birm 08. **d** 11 **p** 12. OLM Fletchamstead *Cov* from 11. *2 Farthing Walk, Coventry CV4 8GR* T: (024) 7646 8660 M: 07769-943019

RICHARDS, Anthony Francis. b 26. Edin Univ 45 Wadh Coll Ox BA 51 MA 54. Ridley Hall Cam 50. **d** 52 **p** 53. C Finchley Ch Ch *Lon* 52-55; C Maidenhead St Andr and St Mary *Ox* 55-59; Lect All Nations Chr Coll Ware 58-59; V High Wycombe Ch Ch *Ox* 59-63; P-in-c 63-66; V Terriers 63-73; USA 70-71; V Cinderford St Steph w Littledean *Glouc* 73-80; V Clacton St Paul *Chelmsf* 80-93; New Zealand 88-89; rtd 93. *Montrichards, Mont, 58230 Ouroux-en-Morvan, France*
T: (0033) 3 86 78 24 44 E: anthony.richards@libertysurf.fr

RICHARDS, Mrs April Deborah. b 42. Man Univ BSc 63. S Dios Minl Tr Scheme 82. **dss** 85 **d** 87 **p** 94. Catherington and Clanfield *Portsm* 85-89; C 87-89; C E Meon and Langrish

89-95; Chapl Portsm Hosps NHS Trust 92-95; P-in-c Blackmoor and Whitehill *Portsm* 95-98; V 98-05; RD Petersfield 99-04; rtd 05; PtO *Pet* 06-08; Hon C Brington w Whilton and Norton etc 08-12. *6 Burrows Vale, Brixworth, Northampton NN6 9US* T: (01604) 882230 E: aprilrichards@waitrose.com

RICHARDS, Brian. b 39. Open Univ BA 78 BSc 05. St Deiniol's Hawarden 94. **d** 94 **p** 94. C St Mellons and Michaelston-y-Fedw *Mon* 94-96; P-in-c Michaelston-y-Fedw 96-02; P-in-c Haarlem *Eur* 02-06; rtd 06; P-in-c Llangwm Uchaf and Llangwm Isaf w Gwernesney etc *Mon* 06-07. *32 Monnow Keep, Monmouth NP25 3EX* T: (01600) 772886

RICHARDS, Brian William. b 45. Spurgeon's Coll Lon BA 88 MTh 99. Guildf Dioc Min Course 01. **d** 03 **p** 04. NSM Howell Hill w Burgh Heath *Guildf* 03-14; rtd 14. *Address temp unknown*

RICHARDS, Christopher Mordaunt. b 40. New Coll Ox BA 63 MA 72 Bris Univ MB, ChB 72. Cuddesdon Coll 63. **d** 65 **p** 81. C Bris St Mary Redcliffe w Temple etc 65-66; PtO 66-72; Hon C Keynsham *B & W* 81-90; PtO 90-93. *4 St Ronans Avenue, Bristol BS6 6EP* T: 0117-974 4062

RICHARDS, Daniel James. b 40. St D Coll Lamp. **d** 66 **p** 67. C Kingswinford H Trin *Lich* 66-69; C Banbury *Ox* 69-71; C Aylesbury 71-73; C-in-c Stoke Poges St Jo Manor Park CD 73-78; R W Slough 78-80; R Ilchester w Northover, Limington, Yeovilton etc *B & W* 80-90; RD Ilchester 81-91; RD Martock 89-91; TR Bruton and Distr 90-97; R Axbridge w Shipham and Rowberrow 97-04; rtd 04; PtO *B & W* from 05; Co-ord Clergy Retirement and Widows' Officer from 06. *1 Quaperlake Street, Bruton BA10 0HA* T: (01749) 812386 E: revdanrich@btinternet.com

RICHARDS, Daniel Michael Hamilton. b 79. Man Univ BA 02. Cranmer Hall Dur 05. **d** 07 **p** 08. C Bury St Jo w St Mark *Man* 07-08; C Tonge w Alkrington 08-11; Chapl Cov Univ 11-13; P-in-c Braddan *S & M* 13-14; V from 14. *The Vicarage, Saddle Road, Braddan, Douglas, Isle of Man IM4 4LB* T: (01624) 675523 E: thecollar@outlook.com

RICHARDS, Canon David. b 30. Bris Univ BA 52. St Mich Coll Llan 52. **d** 54 **p** 55. C Llangynwyd w Maesteg *Llan* 54-56; Iran 57-61 and 62-66; C Skewen *Llan* 61-62; V Cwmbach 66-76; Warden of Ords 71-77; R Coity w Nolton 76-96; Can Llan Cathl 88-96; rtd 96; PtO *Llan* from 96; *Mon* from 96. *The Rectory, Butterwick Road, Freiston, Boston PE22 0LF*

RICHARDS, David Arnold. b 56. Wycliffe Hall Ox 76. **d** 81 **p** 82. C Skewen *Llan* 81-84; C Barking St Marg w St Patr *Chelmsf* 84-85; TV 85-90; Chapl Barking Hosp 87-88; P-in-c Stratford St Jo and Ch Ch w Forest Gate St Jas *Chelmsf* 90-97; V Stratford St Jo w Ch Ch from 97; P-in-c W Ham St Matt from 13. *Stratford Vicarage, 20 Deanery Road, London E15 4LP* T: (020) 8534 8388 *or* 8503 1913 E: office@stjohnse15.freeserve.co.uk

RICHARDS, David Gareth. b 60. Hull Univ BA 83. Qu Coll Birm 89. **d** 92 **p** 93. C Knowle *Birm* 92-96; Assoc R Edin St Paul and St Geo 96-00; R from 00. *10 Broughton Street, Edinburgh EH1 3RH* T: 0131-332 3904 *or* 556 1355 F: 556 0492 E: dave@pandgchurch.org.uk

RICHARDS, Mrs Delyth Anne. b 63. **d** 13 **p** 14. NSM Carmarthen St Dav *St D* from 13. *8 Hillside, Llanelli SA15 4ER* T: (01554) 755481 E: delyth.richards@icloud.org

RICHARDS, Dennis. b 48. St Mich Coll Llan 95. **d** 97 **p** 98. C Cwmbran *Mon* 97-00; TV 00-06; TV Caldicot 06-14; P-in-c from 14. *The Rectory, 19 Main Road, Portskewett, Caldicot NP26 5SG* T: (01291) 423378 E: den.richards@btinternet.com

RICHARDS, Mrs Glenys Heather. b 51. SEN 73. **d** 06 **p** 07. OLM Heatons *Man* 06-12. *32 Lomas Close, Manchester M19 1TE* E: ghr@f25.com

RICHARDS, Gwilym David Marshall. b 56. SEITE. **d** 09 **p** 10. NSM Southgate *Chich* from 09. *11 Duncton Close, Crawley RH11 0AX* T: (01293) 547809

RICHARDS, James Johnston. b 59. Solicitor 84 Lon Bible Coll BA 90 Dur Univ MA 97. Cranmer Hall Dur 90. **d** 92 **p** 93. C Harrow Trin St Mich *Lon* 92-95; C Kendal H Trin *Carl* 95-99; R Windermere from 99; RD from 10. *The Rectory, Longlands Road, Bowness-on-Windermere, Windermere LA23 3AS* T: (015394) 43063 E: rector@stmartin.org.uk

RICHARDS, Mrs Jane Susan. b 64. Univ of E Lon MSc 03. St Mellitus Coll BA 14. **d** 14 **p** 15. NSM S Woodham Ferrers *Chelmsf* from 14; NSM Woodham Ferrers and Bicknacre from 14. *7 Avondale Close, Rayleigh SS6 8NR* T: (01268) 771377 M: 07702-808408 E: janesrichards@aol.com

RICHARDS, Mrs Jane Valerie. b 43. Westf Coll Lon BA 64 Birm Univ CertEd 65. S Dios Minl Tr Scheme 84. **d** 87 **p** 94. NSM Locks Heath *Portsm* 87-90; Chapl Qu Alexandra Hosp Portsm 90-92; Chapl Portsm Hosps NHS Trust 92-95; Asst to RD Fareham *Portsm* 95-96; C Locks Heath 95-96; Chapl Southn Univ Hosps NHS Trust 96-03; rtd 03; PtO *Portsm* from 97; *Win* 03-06. *16 Lodge Road, Locks Heath, Southampton SO31 6QY* T: (01489) 573891 E: revjane.richards@btinternet.com

RICHARDS, Mrs Joanna Sue. b 67. Univ Coll Lon MSc 96. SEITE 11. **d** 14 **p** 15. C Cant St Martin and St Paul from 14. *44 Newton Road, Faversham ME13 8DZ* M: 07932-656876 E: jorichards123@btinternet.com *or* curate@martinpaul.org

RICHARDS, Preb John Francis. b 37. Dur Univ BA 61. Wells Th Coll 61. **d** 63 **p** 64. C Sherwood *S'well* 63-67; C Bishop-wearmouth St Mich *Dur* 67-69; C Egg Buckland *Ex* 69-75; CF (ACF) 72-02; V Plymouth St Jas Ham *Ex* 75-83; V Plympton St Mary 83-02; RD Plymouth Moorside 88-93 and 96-01; Preb Ex Cathl 91-07; rtd 02; Clergy Widow(er)s Officer *Ex* from 02. *24 Trewithy Drive, Plymouth PL6 5TY* T: (01752) 214442 E: jfr-sjr@blueyonder.co.uk

RICHARDS, John George. b 48. Qu Coll Birm 87. **d** 89 **p** 90. C Acocks Green *Birm* 89-92; TV Shirley 92-96; P-in-c Yardley Wood 96-00; V 00-13; rtd 13; PtO *Birm* from 13. *60 Alderney Gardens, Birmingham B38 8YW* T: 0121-603 0801 E: rev.johnrichards@btinternet.com

RICHARDS, John Henry. b 34. CCC Cam BA 57 MA 75. St Mich Coll Llan BD 77. **d** 77 **p** 78. C Llangynwyd w Maesteg *Llan* 77-79; C Cardiff St Jo 79-82; Asst Chapl Univ of Wales (Cardiff) 79-82; V Penmark w Porthkerry 82-83; R Stackpole Elidor w St Petrox *St D* 83-85; R St Petrox w Stackpole Elidor and Bosherston etc 85-99; rtd 99. *20 Williamson Street, Pembroke SA71 4ER* T: (01646) 672472

RICHARDS, John Michael. b 53. Coll of Ripon & York St Jo TCert 76 Open Univ BA 81. Cranmer Hall Dur 93. **d** 93 **p** 94. C Wath-upon-Dearne *Sheff* 93-95; R Warmsworth 95-01; R Sprotbrough 01-10; P-in-c Barningham w Hutton Magna and Wycliffe *Leeds* 10-15; P-in-c Gilling and Kirkby Ravensworth 10-15; AD Richmond from 12; rtd 15. *Peep-o-Day, Low Row, Richmond DL11 6PH* T: (01748) 886246 E: johnmr1953@talk21.com

RICHARDS, John William. b 29. Southn Univ BSc 55. Sarum & Wells Th Coll 78. **d** 81 **p** 82. NSM Woking St Mary *Guildf* 81-85; C Addlestone 85-87; C S Gillingham *Roch* 87-89; Hon C W Byfleet *Guildf* 91-95; rtd 94; PtO *Sarum* from 95. *16 Normandy Way, Poundbury Whitfield, Dorchester DT1 2PP* T: (01305) 251529

RICHARDS, Keith David. b 50. Didsbury Coll of Educn CertEd 72. S'wark Ord Course 79. **d** 82 **p** 83. NSM Walworth *S'wark* 82-85; Chapl Derbyshire Coll of HE 85-87; V Rottingdean *Chich* 87-93; TR Crawley 93-97; V Arundel w Tortington and S Stoke 97-07; RD Arundel and Bognor 04-07; Can and Preb Chich Cathl 07; V Selby Abbey *York* 07-10; P-in-c Hove St Barn and St Agnes *Chich* 10-13; RD Hove 11-13; rtd 13; P-in-c Durrington *Chich* from 14; P-in-c W Tarring from 15. *19 North Ham Road, Littlehampton BN17 7AR* T: (01903) 722942 E: keithdrichards@btinternet.com

RICHARDS, Kelvin. b 58. Univ of Wales (Abth) BSc 80 MA 88. Ripon Coll Cuddesdon BA 82. **d** 83 **p** 84. C Killay *S & B* 83-86; C Morriston 86-89; R Llangattock and Llangynidr 89-15; P-in-c The Beacons from 15; P-in-c Llyn Safaddan from 15; AD Crickhowell 02-14. *The Rectory, Talybont-on-Usk, Brecon LD3 7UX* T: (01874) 676141 E: kelvin.richards@btinternet.com *or* kelvin@beaconssafaddan.plus.com

RICHARDS, Llewelyn. b 15. St Deiniol's Hawarden 73. **d** 75 **p** 76. NSM Corwen and Llangar *St As* 75-85; Past Care Gwyddelwern 78-85; rtd 85. *Address temp unknown*

RICHARDS, Mrs Mary Edith. b 33. SWMTC 85. **d** 87 **p** 94. NSM Kea *Truro* 87-88; Asst Chapl Bris Poly 88-91; C E Clevedon and Walton w Weston w Clapton *B & W* 91-96; rtd 96; Hon C Probus, Ladock and Grampound w Creed and St Erme *Truro* from 97; Mental Health Chapl Cornwall Healthcare NHS Trust 97-01. *62 Midway Drive, Uplands Park, Truro TR1 1NQ* T: (01872) 277556

RICHARDS, Mischa Thomas Anthony. b 88. St Jo Coll Dur BA 10. St Steph Ho Ox 11. **d** 13 **p** 14. C Brighton St Martin w St Wilfrid and St Alban *Chich* from 13. *116 Brentwood Road, Brighton BN1 7ES* M: 07799-117890 E: mischa.richards@hotmail.co.uk

RICHARDS, Nigel. **d** 14 **p** 15. NSM Binfield *Ox* from 14. *6 Holton Heath, Bracknell RG12 9RX* T: (01344) 488274 E: richards-nigel1@sky.com

RICHARDS, Norman John. b 47. BSc. Ridley Hall Cam. **d** 83 **p** 84. C Luton St Fran *St Alb* 83-86; R Aspenden and Layston w Buntingford 86-95; P-in-c Westmill 94-95; R Aspenden, Buntingford and Westmill 95-08; rtd 09; Hon Chapl Stansted Airport *Chelmsf* from 09. *Gardners Cottage, Hare Street, Buntingford SG9 0DY* T: (01763) 289720 E: nrichardsvic@btinternet.com

RICHARDS, Rebecca Mary. b 66. **d** 14 **p** 15. C Stafford St Jo and Tixall w Ingestre *Lich* from 14. *19 John Street, Stafford ST16 3PJ* M: 07905-891869 E: beckyrichards@hotmail.co.uk

RICHARDS, Robert Graham. b 42. St Jo Coll Nottm 77. **d** 80 **p** 81. C Radipole and Melcombe Regis *Sarum* 80-83;

TV Billericay and Lt Burstead *Chelmsf* 84-91; UK Dir CMJ 91-95; Chief Exec Nat Bibl Heritage Cen Ltd Trust 95-97; C Chorleywood St Andr *St Alb* 97-00; Chapl Lee Abbey 02-05; rtd 05; PtO *Sarum* from 05. *33 Stowell Crescent, Wareham BH20 4PT* T: (01929) 552174 E: robandannar@tiscali.co.uk

RICHARDS, Simon Granston. b 47. St Jo Coll Nottm BTh 72 ALCD 72. **d** 72 **p** 73. C Waltham Abbey *Chelmsf* 72-77; TV Basildon St Martin w H Cross and Laindon etc 77-80; V Grayshott *Guildf* 80-88; V Eccleston Ch Ch *Liv* 88-92; V Berkeley w Wick, Breadstone and Newport *Glouc* 92-02; P-in-c Stone w Woodford and Hill 99-02; V Berkeley w Wick, Breadstone, Newport, Stone etc 02-05; RD Dursley 96-02; Chapl Severn NHS Trust 94-05; V Bisley, Chalford, France Lynch, and Oakridge *Glouc* 05-12; AD Bisley 06-08; rtd 12. *1 Wynyard Close, Leominster HR6 8HH* T: (01568) 616602 E: simon@granstonrichards.co.uk

RICHARDS, Stephen. b 51. Bris Univ BSc 72 Maria Grey Coll Lon PGCE 73 Birm Univ MEd 77. STETS 07. **d** 10 **p** 11. NSM Corfe Mullen *Sarum* from 10. *Trevilling, Blandford Road, Corfe Mullen, Wimborne BH21 3HH* T: (01202) 698567 M: 07801-461117 E: richards.steve@btinternet.com

RICHARDS, Stuart Anthony. b 70. K Coll Lon BA 92 AKC 92 Keble Coll Ox BA 97 MA 02. St Steph Ho Ox MTh 02. **d** 99 **p** 00. C Reading All SS *Ox* 99-02; C Solihull *Birm* 02-06; Deanery P Handsworth 06-07; CF from 07. *c/o MOD Chaplains (Army)* F: 381824 T: (01264) 383430

RICHARDS, Terence David. b 43. Trin Coll Carmarthen DipEd 64 Open Univ BA 73 Magd Coll Ox MSc 83. Ox Min Course 04. **d** 07 **p** 08. NSM Chenderit *Pet* 07-13; rtd 13; PtO *Pet* from 13; *Ox* from 15. *11 Portway Drive, Croughton, Brackley NN13 5NA* T: (01869) 811251 E: tasker1@btinternet.com

RICHARDS, Canon Thomas John Wynzie. b 25. St D Coll Lamp BA 49. **d** 51 **p** 52. C Llandybie *St D* 51-53; V 71-87; C Llandegai *Ban* 53-56; R Llanymawddwy 56-57; Chapl Nat Nautical Sch Portishead 57-71; RD Dyffryn Aman *St D* 78-85; Can St D Cathl 83-92; Treas St D Cathl 89-92; V Pencarreg and Llanycrwys 87-92; rtd 92. *Maes Teifi, Cwmann, Lampeter SA48 8DT* T: (01570) 423354

RICHARDS, Tony Benjamin. b 48. STETS. **d** 09 **p** 10. NSM Sandown Ch Ch *Portsm* from 09; NSM Lower Sandown St Jo from 09. *Abbotsford Lodge, Cliff Bridge, Shanklin PO37 6QJ* T: (01983) 863450

RICHARDS, Canon William Hughes. b 37. St D Coll Lamp BA 58. **d** 60 **p** 61. C Llandysul *St D* 60-63; C Llanelli 63-65; V Llanddewi Brefi w Llanbadarn Odwyn 65-73; V Pen-bre 73-83; V Llangunnor w Cwmffrwd 83-88; V Cardigan w Mwnt and Y Ferwig 88-99; V Cardigan w Mwnt and Y Ferwig w Llangoedmor 99-01; Can St D Cathl 89-01; Treas St D Cathl 01; rtd 01. *Hafan Godbaith, 6 Cwrt y Gloch, Peniel, Carmarthen SA32 7HW* T: (01267) 235995

RICHARDS, Canon William Neal. b 38. ALCD 63. **d** 63 **p** 64. C Otley *Bradf* 63-65; C Leamington Priors St Mary *Cov* 65-67; CMS 67-69; Kenya 69-74; Asst Provost and Can Res Nairobi 70-74; V Gt Malvern St Mary *Worc* 74-86; Chapl Kidderminster Health Distr 86-91; RD Kidderminster *Worc* 89-91; R Martley and Wichenford, Knightwick etc 91-01; rtd 01; PtO *Worc* from 01. *Bay Tree Cottage, 32 Pump Street, Malvern WR14 4LU* T: (01684) 569658 E: bill_jane@btinternet.com

RICHARDS, Ms Alison Mary. b 63. Leic Univ BSc 84 St Jo Coll Dur BA 09. Cranmer Hall Dur 07. **d** 09 **p** 10. C Spennymoor and Whitworth *Dur* 09-11; C Upper Skerne 11-13; P-in-c Blackhall, Castle Eden and Monkhesleden from 13; C Peterlee from 13. *The Rectory, The Crescent, Blackhall Colliery, Hartlepool TS27 4LE* T: 0191-586 4202 M: 07873-596164 E: arichardson2@btinternet.com

RICHARDSON, Andrew Edward John. b 75. St Andr Univ BD 97. TISEC 04. **d** 06 **p** 07. C Dundee St Mary Magd *Bre* 06-09; Hon Chapl Dundee Univ 07-09; TR Glas E End 09-15. *8A Amen Court, London EC4M 7BU* T: (020) 7248 6115 E: aejrichardson@hotmail.com

RICHARDSON, Andrew John. b 44. Ex Univ CertEd 69. Trin Coll Bris 83. **d** 82 **p** 83. Kenya 82-87; Dioc Educn Sec Maseno N 83-87; Chapl Brentwood Sch 88; Chapl Scarborough Coll 88-01; TV Parkham, Alwington, Buckland Brewer etc *Ex* 01-09; RD Hartland 03-09; rtd 09. *La Retraite, 3 Park Avenue, Bideford EX39 2QH* T: (01237) 478324 E: rev.andy-ros@care4free.net

RICHARDSON, Miss Ann. b 72. Leeds Univ BA 94. Trin Coll Bris BA 10. **d** 10 **p** 11. C Bromley St Mark *Roch* 10-14; V Gillingham H Trin from 14; RD Gillingham from 15. *Holy Trinity Vicarage, 2 Waltham Road, Gillingham ME8 6XQ* T: (01634) 231690 M: 07902-889718 E: ann_r@btinternet.com

RICHARDSON, Aubrey. See RICHARDSON, John Aubrey

RICHARDSON, Catherine Elisabeth. See PORTER, Catherine Elisabeth

RICHARDSON, Christopher Edward. b 72. STETS 12. **d** 15. C Alverstoke *Portsm* from 15. *36 Gomer Lane, Gosport PO12 2SA* M: 07584-308877 E: chrisrichardson100@gmail.com

RICHARDSON, Clive John. b 57. Oak Hill Th Coll BA 83 Bris Univ MA 00. **d** 83 **p** 84. C Woking St Pet *Guildf* 83-86; C Worplesdon 86-90; V Rowledge 90-03; V Rowledge and Frensham from 03. *The Vicarage, Church Lane, Rowledge, Farnham GU10 4EN* T: (01252) 792402 E: rowvicar@btinternet.com

RICHARDSON, David. b 71. Edin Univ MA 93 Stranmillis Coll PGCE 94 QUB PhD 98. CITC BTh 02. **d** 02 **p** 03. C Coleraine *Conn* 02-06; Chapl RAF from 06. *Chaplaincy Services (RAF), HQ Air Command, RAF High Wycombe HP14 4UE* T: (01494) 496800 F: 496343 E: richardsons05@hotmail.co.uk

RICHARDSON, David Anthony. b 41. Kelham Th Coll 57. **d** 66 **p** 67. C Tong *Bradf* 66-68; C Richmond St Mary *S'wark* 68-71; C Sanderstead All SS 71-74; TV 74-78; R Beddington 78-92; V Dormansland 92-98; RD Godstone 95-98; Assoc R Tucson St Phil in the Hills USA 98-03; R Lake Havasu City from 04. *3111 Silver Saddle Drive, Lake Havasu City AZ 86406-6284, USA* T: (001) (928) 855 5397 F: 855 2508 E: medart1@frontiernet.net

RICHARDSON, David John. b 50. MA LLB FCIArb. S'wark Ord Course. **d** 85 **p** 86. NSM S Croydon Em *S'wark* 85-06; PtO 06-13. *20 Hurst View Road, South Croydon CR2 7AG* T: (020) 8688 4947 *or* 8688 6676 E: richardsonhome@blueyonder.co.uk

RICHARDSON, The Very Revd David John Leyburn. b 46. Univ of Qld BA 69. St Barn Coll Adelaide ACT ThL 70 Melbourne Coll of Div BD 75. **d** 70 **p** 71. C Maryborough Australia 71-73; C Ipswich and C-in-c E Heights 74-75; PtO *Birm* 75-76; C Cambridge Gt St Mary w St Mich *Ely* 76-79; Tutor St Barn Th Coll Adelaide Australia 79-80; Sub-Warden 80-82; R St Lucia 82-88; R Adelaide Cathl 88-89; Dean Adelaide 89-99; Dean Melbourne 99-08; Abp Cant's Rep H See and Dir Angl Cen Rome 08-13; rtd 13; Hon Prov Can Cant Cathl from 10. *Adelaide Club, 165 North Terrace, Adelaide SA 5000, Australia*

RICHARDSON, Preb Douglas Stanley. b 23. Bps' Coll Cheshunt 55. **d** 57 **p** 58. C Hampton St Mary *Lon* 57-61; V W Twyford 61-69; V Notting Hill St Pet 69-78; V Staines St Pet 78-83; P-in-c Staines St Mary 81-83; V Staines St Mary and St Pet 83-92; AD Spelthorne 83-92; Preb St Paul's Cathl 92; rtd 92; PtO *Win* from 92. *22 Rooks Down Road, Badgers Farm, Winchester SO22 4LT* T: (01962) 863687

RICHARDSON, Edward John. b 39. Westmr Coll Ox MTh 98. Lich Th Coll 62. **d** 65 **p** 66. C Chessington *Guildf* 65-70; TV Trunch *Nor* 70-75; V Stoneleigh *Guildf* 75-79; PtO *S'wark* 92-94; Hon C Kingston All SS w St Jo 94-99; C 99-04; rtd 04; PtO *S'wark* from 04; P-in-c Burpham *Chich* 05-09; PtO *Guildf* from 09. *3 Westways, Epsom KT19 0PH* T: (020) 8393 3648 E: rev.johnrichardson@tiscali.co.uk

RICHARDSON (née WOOD), Elaine Mary. b 51. SRN 74. SEITE 00. **d** 03 **p** 04. C Hythe *Cant* 03-06; C Folkestone Trin 06-07; V Herne from 07; Jt AD Reculver from 12. *The New Vicarage, Herne Street, Herne Bay CT6 7HE* T: (01227) 370256 E: elaine.longview@virgin.net

RICHARDSON, Mrs Elizabeth Rosalind. b 54. STETS 05. **d** 08 **p** 09. NSM Ewell St Fran *Guildf* 08-11; TV Surrey Weald from 11. *54 The Street, Capel, Dorking RH5 5LE* T: (01306) 711260 E: liz@hostmyserver.co.uk

RICHARDSON, Canon Eric Hatherley Humphrey. b 12. Qu Coll Ox BA 35 MA 46. Westcott Ho Cam 35. **d** 36 **p** 37. C Stoke Newington St Mary *Lon* 36-39; S Africa from 39. *PO Box 2289, Cramerview, 2060 South Africa* T: (0027) (11) 787 7813 E: ceric@kon.co.za

RICHARDSON, Geoffrey Stewart. b 47. St Jo Coll Ox BA 69 MA 73. St Steph Ho Ox 70. **d** 72 **p** 73. C Roxbourne St Andr *Lon* 72-75; C Woodford St Barn *Chelmsf* 75-80; V Goodmayes St Paul 80-87; R Stow in Lindsey *Linc* 87-92; P-in-c Coates 87-92; P-in-c Willingham 87-92; R Stow Gp 92-01; RD Corringham 93-00; R Shaldon, Stokeinteignhead, Combeinteignhead etc *Ex* 01-12; rtd 12. *167 Westhill Road, Torquay TQ1 4NS*

RICHARDSON, Graeme James. b 75. Oriel Coll Ox BA 97. Ripon Coll Cuddesdon MPhil 02. **d** 03 **p** 04. C Hatfield Hyde *St Alb* 03-06; Chapl BNC Ox 06-14; V Harborne St Pet *Birm* from 14. *The Vicarage, Old Church Road, Harborne, Birmingham B17 0BB* T: 0121-681 5446 *or* 681 1940 E: parishoffice@stpeterharborne.org.uk

RICHARDSON, Hedley. See RICHARDSON, John Hedley

RICHARDSON, Mrs Jacqueline Ann. b 61. **d** 10 **p** 11. OLM Walton-on-Thames *Guildf* from 10. *61 Braycourt Avenue, Walton-on-Thames KT12 2BA* T: (01932) 228883 M: 07787-445272 E: jackie.richardson@uwclub.net

RICHARDSON, Canon James John. b 41. OBE 07. Hull Univ BA 63 Sheff Univ DipEd 64 FRSA 91. Cuddesdon Coll 66. **d** 69 **p** 70. C Wolverhampton St Pet *Lich* 69-72; P-in-c Hanley All SS 72-75; R Nantwich *Ches* 75-82; Hon Can Ripon Cathl 82-88; V Leeds St Pet 82-88; Exec Dir Coun of Chrs and Jews 88-92; P-in-c Brington w Whilton and Norton *Pet* 93-96; P-in-c Brington w Whilton and Norton and Brockhall 96; P-in-c Church Brampton, Chapel Brampton, Harleston etc 94-96; TR Bournemouth St Pet w St Swithun, H Trin etc *Win* 96-08; P-in-c Bournemouth St Aug 01-08; rtd 09; Hon C Sherborne w Castleton, Lillington and Longburton *Sarum* 09-14. *67 Acreman Street, Sherborne DT9 3PH* T: (01935) 814984 E: canonrichardson@btinternet.com

RICHARDSON, John. *See* RICHARDSON, Edward John

RICHARDSON, John. b 55. Lon Univ BEd BD Kent Univ MA. St Steph Ho Ox. **d** 83 **p** 84. C Thornbury *Glouc* 83-86; C Sheff St Cecilia Parson Cross 86-87; C Clacton St Jas *Chelmsf* 87-90; R Gt and Lt Tey w Wakes Colne and Chappel from 90. *The Rectory, Brook Road, Great Tey, Colchester CO6 1JF* T: (01206) 211481 E: revjohn.richardson@virgin.net

RICHARDSON, John. b 47. Linc Th Coll 78. **d** 80 **p** 81. C Keighley St Andr *Bradf* 80-83; V Hugglescote w Donington *Leic* 83-84; V Hugglescote w Donington-le-Heath and Ellistown 84-86; TR Hugglescote w Donington, Ellistown and Snibston 86-97; RD Akeley S 87-96; Chapl ATC 84-97; R Hallaton w Horninghold, Allexton, Tugby etc *Leic* 97-00; Rural Officer (Leic Adnry) 97-00; rtd 00; PtO *Pet* 04-05; P-in-c Fylingdales and Hawsker cum Stainsacre *York* 05-09; C Alton w Bradley-le-Moors and Denstone etc *Lich* from 09. *Address temp unknown* E: allsaints2012@btinternet.com

RICHARDSON, John. b 41. Qu Coll Birm 69. **d** 72 **p** 73. C Ormskirk *Liv* 72-74; C Doncaster St Geo *Sheff* 74-77; R Hemsworth *Wakef* 77-79; V Penallt *Mon* 79-85; R Amotherby w Appleton and Barton-le-Street *York* 85-89; P-in-c Hovingham 86-89; P-in-c Slingsby 86-89; TR Street 89-90; R Skelton w Shipton and Newton on Ouse 90-93; V Alsager St Mary *Ches* 93-96; V Grangetown *York* 96-00; V E Coatham 00-02; V Coatham and Dormanstown 02-04; P-in-c York St Lawr w St Nic 04-06; rtd 06; Chapl Castle Howard 06-13; PtO *York* from 06. *27 Park Road, Norton, Malton YO17 9DZ* T: (01653) 690146 E: johnrichardson02@aol.com

RICHARDSON, John Aubrey. b 33. NEOC 90. **d** 93 **p** 94. NSM Warkworth and Acklington *Newc* 93-03; PtO from 03. *Harvest Lodge, 27 Acklington Village, Morpeth NE65 9BL* T: (01670) 760761

RICHARDSON, John Hedley. b 45. Leeds Univ BA 72. Qu Coll Birm 72. **d** 74 **p** 75. C Chaddesden St Phil *Derby* 74-76; PtO 76-86; TV Old Brampton and Loundsley Green 86-91; R Caston w Griston, Merton, Thompson etc *Nor* 91-95; RD Breckland 94-99; P-in-c Hockham w Shropham Gp of Par 94-95; R Caston, Griston, Merton, Thompson etc 95-02; P-in-c Clifton St Jas *Sheff* 02-03; V 03-08; rtd 08; PtO *Nor* from 11. *2 Admirals Court, Swaffham PE37 7TE* T: (01760) 722698 E: hedleyrichardson@aol.com

✠**RICHARDSON, The Rt Revd John Henry.** b 37. Trin Hall Cam BA 61 MA 65. Cuddesdon Coll 61. **d** 63 **p** 64 **c** 94. C Stevenage *St Alb* 63-66; C Eastbourne St Mary *Chich* 66-68; V Chipperfield St Paul *St Alb* 68-75; V Rickmansworth 75-86; RD 77-86; V Bishop's Stortford St Mich 86-94; Hon Can St Alb 87-94; Suff Bp Bedford 94-02; rtd 02; Hon Asst Bp Carl from 03; Hon Asst Bp Newc from 03. *The Old Rectory, Bewscastle, Carlisle CA6 6PS* T: (01697) 748389

RICHARDSON, John Humphrey. b 33. Dur Univ BA 57. Chich Th Coll 57. **d** 59 **p** 60. C Bexhill St Barn *Chich* 59-61; C Stanmer w Falmer and Moulsecoomb 61-64; C Ifield 64-70; R Earnley and E Wittering 70-79; V Stamford All SS w St Pet *Linc* 79-81; R Stamford St Jo w St Clem 79-81; V Stamford All SS w St Jo 81-92; RD Aveland and Ness w Stamford 80-87; P-in-c Metheringham w Blankney 92-94; V Metheringham w Blankney and Dunston 94-98; rtd 98; PtO *Chich* from 99. *68 Bishopsgate Walk, Chichester PO19 6FQ* T: (01243) 536864

RICHARDSON, John Malcolm. b 39. Glas Univ MA 60 BD 63 Andover Newton Th Coll STM 65. Edin Th Coll 84. **d** 84 **p** 85. C Edin Old St Paul 84-86; R Leven *St And* 86-90; R Newport-on-Tay 90-96; R Tayport 90-96; R Forfar 96-07; Can St Ninian's Cathl Perth 93-07; rtd 07; LtO *St And* from 07. *14 Chewton Road, Thornton, Kirkcaldy KY1 4AZ* T/F: (01592) 775133 E: audrey.richardson@tesco.net

RICHARDSON, John Stephen. b 50. Southn Univ BA 71. St Jo Coll Nottm 72. **d** 74 **p** 75. C Bramcote *S'well* 74-77; C Radipole and Melcombe Regis *Sarum* 77-80; P-in-c Stinsford, Winterborne Came w Whitcombe etc 80-83; Asst Dioc Missr 80-83; V Nailsea Ch Ch *B & W* 83-90; Adv on Evang 86-90; Provost Bradf 90-00; Dean Bradf 00-01; V Wye w Brook and Hastingleigh etc *Cant* 01-09; P-in-c 04-09; C Mersham w Hinxhill and Sellindge 08-09; AD W Bridge 03-09; Chapl

Wye Coll Kent *Lon* 01-09; P-in-c Margate H Trin *Cant* 09-13; V from 13. *The Vicarage, 5 Devonshire Gardens, Cliftonville, Margate CT9 3AF* T: (01843) 294129 E: vicarjohnsrichardson@googlemail.com

RICHARDSON, Canon John Stuart. b 46. Trin Coll Ox BA 68 MA 71 DPhil 73 FRSE 96. **d** 79 **p** 80. NSM St Andrews St Andr *St And* 79-87; Chapl St Andr Univ 80-87; Prof Classics Edin Univ from 87; TV Edin St Columba from 87; Hon Can St Mary's Cathl from 00. *29 Merchiston Avenue, Edinburgh EH10 4PH* T: 0131-228 3094 E: j.richardson@ed.ac.uk

RICHARDSON, John Thandule. b 49. Bradf and Ilkley Coll BSc 80 Lanc Univ MA 97. CBDTI 94. **d** 97 **p** 98. NSM Lea *Blackb* 97-02; NSM Broughton 02-04; NSM Lanercost, Walton, Gilsland and Nether Denton *Carl* 04-05; PtO *Blackb* 06-09; C Preston Risen Lord 09-12; Chapl Preston Coll 09-11; TV Costa Blanca *Eur* 12-13. *Address temp unknown* T: (01943) 969402 E: johntr123@aol.com

RICHARDSON, Katherine Ruth. d 15. C Cirencester *Glouc* from 15. *Address temp unknown*

RICHARDSON, Laurence Leigh. b 71. Trin Coll Carmarthen BA 92 PGCE 93 Univ of Wales (Cardiff) BTh 97 FGMS 04. St Mich Coll Llan 94. **d** 97 **p** 98. C Carmarthen St Pet *St D* 97-01; Chapl Carmarthenshire Coll 99-01; P-in-c Abergwili w Llanfihangel-uwch-Gwili etc *St D* 01-03; V 03-09; TV E Carmarthen 09-10; TR 10-12; P-in-c Carmarthen St Pet 12-14; P-in-c Carmarthen St Pet and Abergwili etc from 14; AD Carmarthen from 09; CF(V) from 01. *St Peter's Vicarage, Church Street, Carmarthen SA31 1GW* T: (01267) 237117 E: landcat10a@aol.com *or* rector@stpeterscarmarthen.org

RICHARDSON, Mrs Linda Joan. b 58. Univ of Wales BSc 80. SAOMC 01. **d** 04 **p** 05. NSM W Wycombe w Bledlow Ridge, Bradenham and Radnage *Ox* from 04. *Long Acre, Greenend Road, Radnage, High Wycombe HP14 4BY* T: (01494) 484607 F: 484608 E: linda.richardson@long-acre.co.uk

RICHARDSON, Malcolm. *See* RICHARDSON, John Malcolm

RICHARDSON, Margaret. b 23. **d** 05. C Aberdeen St Pet *Ab* from 05. *19 Balnagask Place, Torry, Aberdeen AB11 9LP* T: (01224) 878632

RICHARDSON, Michael Arkley. b 38. Bris Univ BScEng 59 Open Univ BA 91. Clifton Th Coll 61. **d** 63 **p** 64. C Chich St Pancras and St Jo 63-68; TV Winfarthing w Shelfanger *Nor* 68-78; rtd 03; PtO *Nor* from 73. *Rectory Farm Barn, Church Lane, Banham, Norwich NR16 2HR* T: (01953) 888958 M: 07884-421977 E: richardson790@btinternet.com

RICHARDSON, Preb Neil. b 46. Southn Univ BTh 83. Sarum & Wells Th Coll 71. **d** 74 **p** 75. C Oldham St Mary w St Pet *Man* 74-77; C-in-c Holts CD 77-82; R Greenford H Cross *Lon* 82-13; Preb St Paul's Cathl 02-13; rtd 13; PtO *Chelmsf* from 14. *49 Notley Road, Braintree CM7 1HE* T: (01376) 329012

RICHARDSON, Canon Paul. b 58. Univ of Wales (Cardiff) BSc 80. Ridley Hall Cam 81. **d** 84 **p** 85. C Stanwix *Carl* 84-87; Ind Chapl 87-89; Staff P Dalton-in-Furness 87-89; V Marton Moss *Blackb* 89-95; P-in-c Prestwich St Gabr *Man* 95-00; Bp's Dom Chapl 95-00; V Westbury *Sarum* 00-02; TR White Horse 02-07; RD Heytesbury 04-07; R Devizes St Jo w St Mary from 07; Can and Preb Sarum Cathl from 07; RD Devizes 10-11 and from 15. *The Rectory, Brandon House, Potterne Road, Devizes SN10 5DD* T: (01380) 829616 E: paul.richardson8@btinternet.com

RICHARDSON, Pauline Kate. *See* JENKINS, Pauline Kate

RICHARDSON, Robin John. b 71. Bris Univ BA 01 Loughb Univ BEng 92 PGCE 93. Trin Coll Bris 98. **d** 01 **p** 02. C Sidmouth, Woolbrook, Salcombe Regis, Sidbury etc *Ex* 01-04; CF from 04. *c/o MOD Chaplains (Army)* F: 381824 T: (01264) 383430 E: strangways@xalt.co.uk

RICHARDSON, Simon James. b 51. Loughb Univ BSc 82 Nottm Univ MA 99. EMMTC 96. **d** 99 **p** 00. C Market Harborough and The Transfiguration etc *Leic* 99-02; C Loughborough All SS w H Trin 02-04; Chapl Loughb Univ 02-13; NSM Barrow upon Soar w Walton le Wolds from 13; NSM Wymeswold and Prestwold w Hoton from 13. *St Mary's Vicarage, 5 The Stockwell, Wymeswold, Loughborough LE12 6UF* T: (01509) 881764 E: s.j.richardson@lboro.ac.uk

RICHARDSON, Simon John. b 56. Univ of Wales (Ban) BA 77. Ridley Hall Cam 81. **d** 84 **p** 85. C Luton St Mary *St Alb* 84-88; C Middleton *Man* 88-91; Sweden from 91. *Enebacken, Racksätter, 732 97 Arboga, Sweden* T: (0046) (589) 70103

RICHARDSON, Simon Kay Caoimhin. b 74. St Jo Coll Dur BA 96 Cant Ch Ch Univ MA 10 QUB MTh 13. Wycliffe Hall Ox 01. **d** 03 **p** 04. C Folkestone Trin *Cant* 03-06; C Hillsborough *D & D* 06-08; I 08-11; C Holywood 11-14; I Glencraig from 14. *3 Seahill Road, Holywood BT18 0DA* T: (028) 9042 1691 M: 07875-514431 E: simonkcr@gmail.com

RICHARDSON, Miss Susan. b 58. Cranmer Hall Dur. **d** 87 **p** 94. Par Dn Stokesley *York* 87-91; Par Dn Beverley St Nic 91-94; P-in-c Cloughton 94-97; V Cloughton and Burniston w Ravenscar etc 97-99; V Middlesbrough St Oswald 99-10; P-in-c Middlesbrough St Chad 09-10; V Middlesbrough St Oswald and St Chad from 10; Tr Officer E Riding from 94. *St Oswald's Vicarage, Lambton Road, Middlesbrough TS4 2RG* T: (01642) 816156 E: sue.richardson3@btinternet.com

RICHBOROUGH, Suffragan Bishop of (Provincial Episcopal Visitor). *See* BANKS, The Rt Revd Norman

RICHERBY, Canon Glynn. b 51. K Coll Lon BD 73 AKC 73. St Aug Coll Cant 73. **d** 74 **p** 75. C Weston Favell *Pet* 74-78; Prec Leic Cathl 78-81; V Glen Parva and S Wigston 81-93; V Leic St Jas from 93; Dir Post-Ord Tr 86-95; Dir CME from 95; Hon Can Leic Cathl from 98. *St James the Greater Vicarage, 216 London Road, Leicester LE2 1NE* T: 0116-254 4113 E: vicar.stjames@ntlworld.com

RICHES, Canon John Kenneth. b 39. CCC Cam BA 61 MA 65. Kirchliche Hochschule Bethel 61 Westcott Ho Cam 62. **d** 65 **p** 66. C Costessey *Nor* 65-68; Chapl and Fell SS Coll Cam 68-72; Lect Glas Univ 72-86; Sen Lect 86-91; Prof Div and Bibl Criticism Glas Univ 91-02; Hon Research Prof from 03; LtO *Glas* from 85; Can St Mary's Cathl from 01. *Viewfield House, Balmore, Torrance, Glasgow G64 4AE* T: (01360) 620254 E: randj.riches@virgin.net *or* j.riches@divinity.gla.ac.uk

RICHES, Malcolm Leslie. b 46. St Jo Coll Nottm 92. **d** 94 **p** 95. C Swaythling *Win* 94-97; P-in-c Boldre w S Baddesley 97-01; V 01-03; V Ellingham and Harbridge and Hyde w Ibsley 03-11; rtd 11; Hon C Caldbeck, Castle Sowerby and Sebergham *Carl* from 11. *The Rectory, Brewery House, Caldbeck, Wigton CA7 8EW* T/F: (016974) 78233 M: 07968-139851 E: malcolm.l.riches@gmail.com

RICHES, Nichola. b 72. Homerton Coll Cam BEd 95 R Holloway & Bedf New Coll Lon MA 96. SEITE 05. **d** 08 **p** 09. NSM Purley St Mark and Purley St Swithun *S'wark* 08-11; PtO from 12. *5 Hambledon Road, Caterham CR3 5EZ*

RICHEUX, Marc Stephen. b 66. Man Univ BA 89. Trin Coll Bris BA 00. **d** 00 **p** 01. C Plumstead St Jo w St Jas and St Paul *S'wark* 00-04; V Streatham Park St Alb 04-12; TV Furzedown from 12. *St Alban's Vicarage, 5 Fayland Avenue, London SW16 1SR* T: (020) 8677 4521 *or* 8769 5415 E: mricheux@clara.co.uk

✤**RICHMOND, The Rt Revd Francis Henry Arthur.** b 36. TCD BA 59 MA 66 Strasbourg Univ BTh 60 Linacre Coll Ox MLitt 64. Wycliffe Hall Ox 60. **d** 63 **p** 64 **c** 86. C Woodlands *Sheff* 63-66; Chapl Sheff Cathl 66-69; V Sheff St Geo 69-77; Chapl Sheff Univ 74-77; Warden Linc Th Coll 77-86; Can and Preb Linc Cathl 77-86; Suff Bp Repton *Derby* 86-98; Hon Can Derby Cathl 86-98; rtd 98; Hon Asst Bp Ox from 99. *39 Hodges Court, Oxford OX1 4NZ* T: (01865) 790466

RICHMOND, Gordon Blazewood. b 33. Launde Abbey 77. **d** 79 **p** 80. C Leic St Paul 79-81; C Shepshed 81-84; V Ryhall w Essendine *Pet* 84-91; RD Barnack 89-91; V Gretton w Rockingham 91-98; rtd 98; PtO *Pet* from 98; *Leic* from 99. *Malvern, 2 Linwal Avenue, Houghton-on-the-Hill, Leicester LE7 9HD* T: 0116-241 7638

RICHMOND, Patrick Henry. b 69. Ball Coll Ox BA 90 Green Coll Ox MA 94 DPhil 94. Wycliffe Hall Ox BA 96. **d** 97 **p** 98. C Leic Martyrs 97-01; Chapl and Fell St Cath Coll Cam 01-07; Dean of Chpl 06-07; V Eaton Ch Ch *Nor* from 07. *161 Newmarket Road, Norwich NR4 6SY* T: (01603) 250844 E: phr@eatonparish.com

RICHMOND, Peter James. b 54. Cant Ch Ch Univ MSc 07 Ex Univ PGCE 95. St Jo Coll Nottm. **d** 80 **p** 81. C Ogley Hay *Lich* 80-83; C Trentham 83-85; P-in-c Wolverhampton St Jo 85-89; P-in-c Loppington w Newtown 89-93; P-in-c Edstaston 89-93; PtO *Ex* 94-95; P-in-c Weston Zoyland w Chedzoy *B & W* 95-03; Chapl Somerset Partnership NHS and Soc Care Trust 97-03; Lead Chapl E Kent NHS and Soc Care Partnership Trust 03-06; Lead Chapl Kent & Medway NHS and Soc Care Partnership Trust 06-13; Hon C St Nicholas at Wade w Sarre and Chislet w Hoath *Cant* 04-10; rtd 13; PtO *Cant* from 13. *41 The Rope Walk, Canterbury CT1 2FY* T: (01227) 379229

RICHMOND, Yvonne Lorraine. b 63. Sheff Univ MA 07. WEMTC 96. **d** 99 **p** 00. NSM Magor *Mon* 99-00; NSM Kenilworth St Jo *Cov* 00-05; Chapl for Evang Cov Cathl 05-06; Can Res for Miss 06-09; Can for Development Birm Cathl 09-10; PtO 10-13; *Lon* from 13; *S'wark* from 14. *112 Salcott Road, London SW11 6DG* T: (020) 7223 6310 E: ylrichmond@gmail.com

RICHMOND, Suffragan Bishop of. *See* SLATER, The Rt Revd Paul John

RICHMOND AND CRAVEN, Archdeacon of. *Vacant*

RICKARDS, Bruce Walter. b 69. NTMTC 98. **d** 01 **p** 02. NSM St Marg Lothbury and St Steph Coleman Street etc *Lon* 01-06; NSM Wimbledon *S'wark* 06-09; C from 09. *85A Toynbee Road, London SW20 8SJ* T: (020) 8540 4150 M: 07850-655102 E: byrickards@btinternet.com

RICKETTS, Allan Fenn. b 46. Open Univ BA 76. Cranmer Hall Dur 68. **d** 71 **p** 72. C Rowley Regis *Birm* 71-72; C The Quinton 72-74; C Brierley Hill *Lich* 74-77; TV Chelmsley Wood *Birm* 77-82; TV Ross w Brampton Abbotts, Bridstow and Peterstow *Heref* 82-88; R Linton w Upton Bishop and Aston Ingham 88-96; rtd 06. *13 Falaise Close, Ross-on-Wye HR9 5UT* T: (01989) 565077 E: allanricketts@fsmail.net

RICKETTS, Mrs Diane. b 54. NTMTC 98. **d** 01 **p** 02. NSM Nazeing and Roydon *Chelmsf* 01-06; R Laindon w Dunton 06-14; rtd 14. *8 Tots Gardens, Barrow Hill, Acton, Sudbury CO10 0DJ* E: revd_diane_ricketts@hotmail.com

RICKETTS, Canon Kathleen Mary. b 39. Southlands Coll Lon TCert 59 Univ of W Aus BA 79. Westcott Ho Cam 81. **dss** 83 **d** 87 **p** 94. All Hallows by the Tower etc *Lon* 83-88; C 87-88; C Hall Green Ascension *Birm* 88-91; Chapl Birm Children's Hosp 91-94; Chapl Birm Children's Hosp NHS Trust 94-99; Hon Can Birm Cathl 96-99; rtd 99; PtO *Birm* from 00. *22 Holly Drive, Birmingham B27 7NF* T: 0121-706 1087

RICKETTS, Mrs Linda Elizabeth. b 52. RNMH 85. EAMTC 98. **d** 01 **p** 02. C Loddon, Sisland, Chedgrave, Hardley and Langley *Nor* 01-05; V Gorleston St Mary from 05. *The Vicarage, 41 Nuffield Crescent, Gorleston, Great Yarmouth NR31 7LL* T: (01493) 661741 E: l.ricketts787@btinternet.com

RICKETTS, Miss Theresa Lesley. b 76. Greyfriars Ox BA 00 Kingston Univ PGCE 07 Cam Univ BTh 14. Westcott Ho Cam 12. **d** 14 **p** 15. C Weybridge *Guildf* from 14. *87 Greenlands Road, Weybridge KT13 8PS* T: (01932) 848784 M: 07949-769580 E: theresaricketts@hotmail.co.uk

RICKMAN, The Very Revd Peter Alan. b 68. Ripon Coll Cuddesdon BTh 97. **d** 97 **p** 98. C Bitterne Park *Win* 97-01; Chapl St Paul's Colleg Sch Hamilton New Zealand 01-04; Sub Chapl HM Pris Win 04-05; P-in-c Bransgore *Win* 05-09; P-in-c Bransgore and Hinton Admiral 09-12; Dean Hamilton New Zealand from 12. *Waikato Cathedral Church of St Peter, PO Box 338 (51 Victoria Street), Hamilton 3240, New Zealand* T: (0064) (7) 839 4683 F: 839 5849 M: 021-197-7788 E: dean@stpeter.org.nz *or* pizzarev@btinternet.com

RIDDEL, Robert John. b 37. CITC 65. **d** 68 **p** 69. C Derryloran *Arm* 68-74; I Keady w Armaghbreague and Derrynoose 74-80; I Cleenish w Mullaghdun *Clogh* 80-84; I Cleenish 80-84; I Fivemiletown 84-05; Can Clogh Cathl 91-05; Preb Donaghmore St Patr Cathl Dublin 95-05; rtd 05. *9 Coolcrannel Square, Maguiresbridge, Enniskillen BT94 4RE* T: (028) 6772 3199 E: riddel.r.j@btinternet.com

RIDDELL, Morris Stroyan. b 34. Lon Univ BD 69. Tyndale Hall Bris 57. **d** 60 **p** 60. C Mowbray S Africa 60-62; V Addington Ch Ch 62-63; V N Grimston w Wharram Percy and Wharram-le-Street *York* 63-67; V Kirby Grindalythe 63-67; P-in-c Weaverthorpe w Helperthorpe and Luttons 65-67; P-in-c Settrington 65-67; P-in-c Wintringham 65-67; P-in-c Thorpe Bassett 65-67; R Bris St Jo w St Mary-le-Port 67-70; Dir Bris Samaritans 67-70; Chapl HM Pris Long Lartin 71-74; Chapl HM Pris Brixton 74-78; Chapl Cane Hill Hosp Coulsdon 78-85; Chapl HM Rem Cen Latchmere Ho 85-89; rtd 95. *Flat 5, 30 Montpelier Crescent, Brighton BN1 3JJ* T: (01273) 329229

RIDDELSDELL, Canon John Creffield. b 23. Selw Coll Cam BA 47 MA 52 Lon Univ BD 70. Ridley Hall Cam 47. **d** 49 **p** 50. C Kilburn St Mary *Lon* 49-52; CMS Coast Miss Adv Dio Mombasa Kenya 52-59; V Malindi 59-62; Prin St Phil Bible Sch Maseno 62-71; Tutor St Paul's Th Coll Limuru 71-74; Prin 74-76; V Gt Ilford St Andr *Chelmsf* 77-88; rtd 88; PtO *Chelmsf* from 88. *Waverley, Mill Lane, Walton on the Naze CO14 8PE* T: (01255) 850213

RIDDING, George. b 24. Oriel Coll Ox BA 50 MA 57. Wells Th Coll 60. **d** 61 **p** 62. C Wear *Ex* 61-62; Chapl Ex Sch 62-64; India 64-68; Hd Master W Buckland Sch Barnstaple 68-78; USPG 78-82; P-in-c Broadhembury w Payhembury *Ex* 82-83; P-in-c Plymtree 82-83; R Broadhembury, Payhembury and Plymtree 83-89; rtd 89; PtO *Sarum* 89-09. *The College of St Barnabas, Blackberry Lane, Lingfield RH7 6NJ* T: (01342) 872821

RIDDING, William Thomas. b 54. Southn Univ BTh. Sarum & Wells Th Coll 80. **d** 83 **p** 84. C Verwood *Sarum* 83-86; TV Gillingham 86-01; RD Blackmore Vale 95-01; P-in-c Stalbridge 01-02; R Stalbridge and Stock 02-07; R Spire Hill from 07; C Hazelbury Bryan and the Hillside Par from 08; C Okeford from 08. *The Rectory, Church Hill, Stalbridge, Sturminster Newton DT10 2LR* T: (01963) 362859 E: williamridding@btinternet.com

RIDDLESTONE, Mrs Jennifer Jane. b 83. Warwick Univ BSc 05 St Jo Coll Dur BATM 15. Cranmer Hall Dur 12. **d** 15. C Egham *Guildf* from 15. *33 Grange Road, Egham TW20 9QP* E: jenn.riddlestone@gmail.com

RIDER, Andrew. b 62. Nottm Univ BTh 90 K Coll Lon MA 96 RMN 85. Aston Tr Scheme 85 St Jo Coll Nottm 87. **d** 90 **p** 91. C Luton Ch Ch *Roch* 90-93; C w resp for Clubhouse Langham Place All So *Lon* 93-03; P-in-c Spitalfields Ch Ch w All SS 03-04;

R from 04; AD Tower Hamlets from 12. *The Rectory, 2 Fournier Street, London E1 6QE* T: (020) 7247 0790 *or* 7247 7202
F: 7247 5921 E: arider@ccspitalfields.org

RIDER, Canon Dennis William Austin. b 34. St Aid Birkenhead 58. **d** 61 **p** 62. C Derby St Aug 61-64; C Sutton *Liv* 64-67; R Stiffkey w Morston, Langham Episcopi etc *Nor* 67-71; V Buxton w Oxnead 71-79; R Lammas w Lt Hautbois 72-79; R Gaywood, Bawsey and Mintlyn 79-91; RD Lynn 89-91; Hon Can Nor Cathl 90-99; R E Dereham and Scarning 91-98; TR 98-99; RD Dereham in Mitford 95-98; rtd 99; PtO *Nor* 01-08; C Litcham w Kempston, E and W Lexham, Mileham etc 08-09; C Gt and Lt Dunham w Gt and Lt Fransham and Sporle 08-09; C Foulsham, Guestwick, Stibbard, Themelthorpe etc 10-11. *37A Holt Road, Fakenham NR21 8BW*
T: (01328) 856018 E: dandprider@btinternet.com

RIDER, Geoffrey Malcolm. b 29. Selw Coll Cam BA 53 MA 56 Lon Inst of Educn PGCE 68. Coll of Resurr Mirfield 53. **d** 55 **p** 56. C S Elmsall *Wakef* 55-60; C Barnsley St Mary 60-63; V Cleckheaton St Jo 63-67; Public Preacher *S'wark* 67-92; rtd 92; Succ Kimberley Cathl S Africa 92-95; PtO *S'wark* 95-03; Chapl and Hon Min Can Ripon Cathl from 04. *35 Kirkby Road, Ripon HG4 2EY* T: (01765) 690517
E: geoffrey.rider@btinternet.com

RIDGE, Aubrey. b 25. Oak Hill Th Coll 67. **d** 68 **p** 69. C Gorleston St Andr *Nor* 68-70; C Hamworthy *Sarum* 70-75; P-in-c Pitsea *Chelmsf* 75-78; R 78-81; P-in-c Stoke Ash, Thwaite and Wetheringsett *St E* 81-85; P-in-c Bedingfield and Thorndon w Rishangles 81-85; P-in-c Thorndon w Rishangles, Stoke Ash, Thwaite etc 85-86; P-in-c Risby w Gt and Lt Saxham and Westley 86-90; rtd 90; PtO *Sarum* 90-93; Hon C Milford *Win* 93-96; PtO 96-99. *7 Cherry Tree Court, Station Road, New Milton BH25 6LP*

RIDGE, James Scott. b 77. Ex Univ BSc 99 Selw Coll Cam BTh 05. Westcott Ho Cam 02. **d** 05 **p** 06. C Halstead Area *Chelmsf* 05-09; C Bocking St Pet 09; Chapl HM Pris Chelmsf from 09. *HM Prison Chelmsford, 200 Springfield Road, Chelmsford CM2 6LQ* T: (01245) 552077
E: james.ridge@hmps.gsi.gov.uk

RIDGE, Michael Anthony. b 70. Collingwood Coll Dur BSc 91 Dur Sch of Educn PGCE 93. St Jo Coll Nottm 07. **d** 09. C Formby St Luke *Liv* 09-12; C Blundellsands St Mich 12-14; R Dorrigo Australia from 14. *39 Kurrajong Street, Dorrigo NSW 2453, Australia* T: (0061) (2) 6657 2015
E: michaelridge@hotmail.co.uk

RIDGEWAY, David. b 59. St Chad's Coll Dur BSc 80 Cam Univ CertEd 81. Ripon Coll Cuddesdon 84. **d** 87 **p** 88. C Kempston Transfiguration *St Alb* 87-90; C Radlett 90-95; P-in-c Heath and Reach 95-98; V 98-01; V St Alb St Steph 01-15; RD St Alb 05-15; V Castor w Upton and Stibbington and Water Newton, Marholm and Sutton *Pet* from 15. *St Stephen's Vicarage, 14 Watling Street, St Albans AL1 2PX*
T: (01727) 862598 F: 07092-109111
E: davidridgeway@btinternet.com

RIDGEWELL, Miss Mary Jean. b 54. Dur Univ BA 76 PGCE 77. Ridley Hall Cam 89. **d** 91 **p** 94. Par Dn Trowbridge St Jas *Sarum* 91-94; C 94-95; Chapl Lee Abbey 95-96; NSM Bradford Peverell, Stratton, Frampton etc *Sarum* 96-97; Chapl HM Pris and YOI Guys Marsh 97-12; rtd 12; PtO *Sarum* from 12. *Address temp unknown*

RIDGWAY, Mrs Janet Elizabeth Knight. b 40. St Alb Minl Tr Scheme 83. **dss** 86 **d** 87 **p** 94. Tring *St Alb* 86-87; Hon Par Dn 87-94; Hon C 94-05; rtd 05. *Barleycombe, Trooper Road, Aldbury, Tring HP23 5RW* T/F: (01442) 851303
E: rev.j.ridgway@breathemail.net

RIDGWELL, Graham Edgar Charles. b 46. LGSM 71 Open Univ BA 82 Leeds Univ MA 04. **d** 02 **p** 03. NSM Whitby w Aislaby and Ruswarp *York* 02-05; Hon TV Linton *Ely* 05-15; PtO *Chelmsf* from 15. *76 Swan Street, Sible Hedingham, Halstead CO9 3HT* E: gecridgwell@googlemail.com *or* ridgwell@onetel.com

RIDING, Pauline Alison. *See* BICKNELL, Pauline Alison

RIDINGS, Neil Arthur. b 66. Man Poly BEd 90. St Jo Coll Nottm 01. **d** 01 **p** 02. C Holyhead *Ban* 01-05; TV 05-07; R Valley w Llechylched and Caergeiliog 07-14; R Bro Cwyfan from 14. *The Rectory, London Road, Valley, Holyhead LL65 3DP*
T: (01407) 741242

RIDLEY, Alfred Forbes. b 34. Bps' Coll Cheshunt 62. **d** 65 **p** 66. C Prittlewell St Mary *Chelmsf* 65-69; R Paulerspury *Pet* 69-73; P-in-c Wicken 71-73; V W Haddon w Winwick 73-83; RD Brixworth 80-83; R Guernsey St Philippe de Torteval *Win* 83-92; R Guernsey St Pierre du Bois 83-92; R Blakesley w Adstone and Maidford etc *Pet* 92-99; rtd 99; PtO *Pet* 99-07. *36 Verona Court, Yeo Vale Road, Barnstaple EX32 7EN*
T: (01271) 327850

RIDLEY, Andrew Roy. b 55. St Pet Coll Ox BA 77. Ripon Coll Cuddesdon 78. **d** 79 **p** 80. C Bollington St Jo *Ches* 79-83;

V Runcorn St Mich 83-94; Dioc Chapl MU 92-98; RD Frodsham 94-98; V Helsby and Dunham-on-the-Hill 94-98; P-in-c Alvanley 94-98; R Whitchurch *Lich* 98-11; RD Wem and Whitchurch 01-06; V Barton under Needwood w Dunstall and Tatenhill from 11. *The Vicarage, 3 Church Lane, Barton under Needwood, Burton-on-Trent DE13 8HU* T: (01283) 712359
E: arceridley@btinternet.com

RIDLEY, David Gerhard. b 60. Southn Univ BSc 82 Bath Univ PGCE 83. Qu Coll Birm 91. **d** 93 **p** 94. C Faversham *Cant* 93-97; Min Folkestone St Aug CD 97-01; V Dover St Mary 01-13; P-in-c Whitfield w Guston 02-12; P-in-c Guston 13; AD Dover 06-11; R Eastry and Woodnesborough from 13. *The Rectory, Brook Street, Eastry, Sandwich CT13 0HR*
M: 07887-880272 E: davidridley@btopenworld.com

RIDLEY, Derek. b 40. Newc Univ BSc 74. Cranmer Hall Dur 75. **d** 78 **p** 79. C Upperby St Jo *Carl* 78-81; C Penrith w Newton Reigny 81; C Penrith w Newton Reigny and Plumpton Wall 81-82; TV 82-86; V Cadishead *Man* 86-99; R Asfordby and P-in-c Ab Kettleby Gp *Leic* 99-02; P-in-c Old Dalby and Nether Broughton 99-01; rtd 02; PtO *Carl* from 08. *32 Carleton Place, Penrith CA11 8LW* T: (01768) 890676

RIDLEY, Jay. b 41. Birm Univ BA 63. St Steph Ho Ox 63. **d** 65 **p** 66. C Woodford St Mary *Chelmsf* 65-67; C Prittlewell St Mary 67-70; C-in-c Dunscroft CD *Sheff* 70-74; Asst Chapl HM Pris Wormwood Scrubs 75-77; Chapl HM Rem Cen Ashford 77-84; Chapl HM YOI Feltham 84-91; Chapl HM Pris Ashwell 91-00; C Oakham, Hambleton, Egleton, Braunston and Brooke *Pet* 00; rtd 11. *11 Ramsay Hall, 9-13 Byron Road, Worthing BN11 3HN* T: (01903) 210224
E: jay.ridley@hotmail.co.uk

RIDLEY, Mrs Jennifer Mary. b 62. **d** 14 **p** 15. NSM Sudbury w Ballingdon and Brundon *St E* from 14. *67 Acton Lane, Sudbury CO10 1QW* T: (01787) 375974 E: jennie67mr@gmail.com

RIDLEY, Mrs Lesley. b 46. Cranmer Hall Dur 75. **dss** 78 **d** 87 **p** 94. Upperby St Jo *Carl* 78-81; Penrith w Newton Reigny and Plumpton Wall 81-86; Cadishead *Man* 86-99; Par Dn 94-99; C Asfordby and Ab Kettleby Gp *Leic* 99-02; rtd 02; PtO *Carl* from 08. *32 Carleton Place, Penrith CA11 8LW*
T: (01768) 890676

RIDLEY, Louise. *See* COLLINS, Louise Ridley

RIDLEY, Canon Michael Edward. b 37. Ex Univ MA 90. St Boniface Warminster AKC 62. **d** 63 **p** 64. C Chapel Allerton *Ripon* 63-67; C Epsom St Martin *Guildf* 67-70; C Claxby w Normanby-le-Wold etc *Linc* 70-72; V Leake 72-75; R Harlaxton w Wyville and Hungerton 75-80; R Stroxton 76-80; Dioc Stewardship Adv *Portsm* 80-86; P-in-c Rowlands Castle 80-82; C Blendworth w Chalton w Idsworth etc 83-86; TV N Creedy *Ex* 86-90; R W Downland *Sarum* 90-02; RD Chalke 92-97 and 98-00; Can and Preb Sarum Cathl 00-02; rtd 02; PtO *Truro* from 03. *6 Cole Moore Meadow, Tavistock PL19 0ES*
T: (01822) 610799

RIDLEY, Michael Laurence. b 59. BA 81. Ripon Coll Cuddesdon 81. **d** 83 **p** 84. C Bollington St Jo *Ches* 83-88; V Thelwall 88-95; V Weaverham 95-05; RD Middlewich 99-05; V Stockton Heath from 05. *12 Melton Avenue, Walton, Warrington WA4 6PQ* T: (01925) 261396
E: stocktonheathvicar@tiscali.co.uk

RIDLEY, Peter John. b 39. Keble Coll Ox BA 61. Tyndale Hall Bris 61. **d** 63 **p** 64. C Clifton Ch Ch w Em *Bris* 63-67; C Lambeth St Andr w St Thos *S'wark* 67-69; V W Hampstead St Cuth *Lon* 69-77; V Eynsham *Ox* 77-85; RD Woodstock 82-84; V Nicholforest and Kirkandrews on Esk *Carl* 85-96; P-in-c Knoyle, Semley and Sedgehill *Sarum* 96-04; rtd 04; PtO *Carl* from 05. *The Castle, Castle Street, Hilton, Appleby-in-Westmorland CA16 6LX* T/F: (017683) 51682

RIDLEY, Simon. b 33. Magd Coll Ox BA 54 MA 58 BD 66. Linc Th Coll 54. **d** 57 **p** 58. C St John's Wood *Lon* 57-60; Abp's Dom Chapl *Cant* 60-61; V N Wootton *B & W* 61-66; Lect Wells Th Coll 61-65; Hong Kong 66-70; TR Basingstoke *Win* 70-73; rtd 96; PtO *Cant* from 96. *Oxney House, The Street, Wittersham, Tenterden TN30 7ED* T: (01797) 270215

RIDLEY, Stephen James. b 57. St Pet Coll Ox MA 83 Dur Univ EdD. Ripon Coll Cuddesdon 80. **d** 82 **p** 83. C Heald Green St Cath *Ches* 82-85; Chapl Ches Coll 85-90; Dioc Press Officer 85-90; Chapl Birkenhead Sch Merseyside 90-96; LtO Ches 90-96; Chapl Barnard Castle Sch 96-14; Teacher Dur High Sch for Girls from 15; PtO *Dur* from 15. *Durham High School for Girls, Farewell Hall, South Road, Durham DH1 3TB*
T: 0191-384 3226

RIDLEY, Stewart Gordon. b 47. K Coll Lon AKC 72. St Aug Coll Cant 72. **d** 73 **p** 74. C Armley w New Wortley *Ripon* 73-77; C Hawksworth Wood 77-79; C Rothwell w Lofthouse 79-81; R Whitwood *Wakef* 81-87; R Ingoldmells w Addlethorpe *Linc* 87-92; RD Calcewaithe and Candleshoe 89-92; V Settle *Bradf* 92-05; C Bolton by Bowland w Grindleton 05-07; P-in-c Hurst Green and Mitton 05-07; P-in-c Waddington 05-07;

rtd 07; PtO *York* 09-14; Chapl S Tees Hosps NHS Trust 11-14; PtO *Leeds* 14-16. *18 Brough Meadows, Catterick, Richmond DL10 7LQ* T: (01748) 519359 M: 07952-584138 E: stewartridley@uwclub.net

RIDLEY, Vic. *See* RIDLEY, David Gerhard

RIDOUT, Canon Christopher John. b 33. K Coll Lon BD 57 AKC 57 MA 92. **d** 58 **p** 59. C Roxeth Ch Ch *Lon* 58-62; CMS 62-63; Kenya 63-75; C Gt Malvern St Mary *Worc* 75-79; R Bredon w Bredon's Norton 79-98; RD Pershore 91-97; Hon Can Worc Cathl 92-98; rtd 98; PtO *Glouc* from 98. *5 Belworth Drive, Hatherley, Cheltenham GL51 6EL* T: (01242) 231765

RIDYARD, Preb John Gordon. b 33. St Aid Birkenhead 59. **d** 62 **p** 63. C Lancaster St Mary *Blackb* 62-65; C Bushbury *Lich* 65-68; V Darlaston All SS 68-76; TV Wolverhampton St Mark 76-78; TV Wolverhampton 78-82; V Bishopswood 82-89; V Brewood 82-89; RD Penkridge 83-89; R Newcastle w Butterton 89-98; Preb Lich Cathl 82-03; rtd 98; PtO *Lich* 98-11. *Upper Flat, Vicars' Hall, Beacon Street, Lichfield WS13 7AD* T: (01543) 306297

RIEM, Canon Roland Gerardus Anthony. b 60. St Chad's Coll Dur BSc 82 Kent Univ PhD 86 Heythrop Coll Lon MA 99. St Jo Coll Nottm 86. **d** 89 **p** 90. C Deal St Leon and St Rich and Sholden *Cant* 89-92; Sen Chapl Nottm Univ *S'well* 92-98; Dir Min STETS 98-05; Can Res Win Cathl from 05. *5A The Close, Winchester SO23 9LS* T: (01962) 857216 *or* 857239 F: 857201 E: roland.riem@winchester-cathedral.org.uk

RIENSTRA, Bruce Elliott. b 59. Ohio Univ (USA) BA 83. St Jo Coll Nottm 11. **d** 13 **p** 14. C Warsop *S'well* from 13. *19 Wood Street, Warsop, Mansfield NG20 0AX* T: (01623) 845617 M: 07742-172333 E: b.e.rienstra@gmail.com

RIESS, Trevor William. b 54. Down Coll Cam MA 76 CertEd 77. St Jo Coll Nottm 84. **d** 86 **p** 87. C Stainforth *Sheff* 86-88; Chapl St Jas Choir Sch Grimsby 89; C Lowestoft and Kirkley *Nor* 89-90; TV 90-94; TV Lowestoft St Marg 94-95; Chapl Lothingland Hosp 90-95; V Gorleston St Mary *Nor* 95-05; P-in-c Scole, Brockdish, Billingford, Thorpe Abbots etc 05-11; R Gunton St Pet from 11. *The Rectory, 36 Gunton Church Lane, Lowestoft NR32 4LF* T: (01502) 511464 E: trevorriess@btinternet.com

RIGBY, Harold. b 34. Nottm Univ MA 56 St Cath Soc Ox BA 58 MA 62 Man Poly PGCE 77. Ripon Hall Ox 56. **d** 58 **p** 59. C Didsbury St Jas and Em *Man* 58-61; C Bury St Jo 61-64; P-in-c Lostock St Thos and St Jo 64-76; Hon C Davyhulme St Mary 76-79; Lic Preacher 79-10; PtO from 10. *17 Atwood Road, Didsbury, Manchester M20 0TA* T: 0161-445 7454

RIGBY, Joseph. b 37. Open Univ BA 72. Ox NSM Course. **d** 78 **p** 79. NSM Earley St Pet *Ox* 78-80; C Penzance St Mary w St Paul *Truro* 80-82; V Mevagissey 82-83; P-in-c St Ewe 83; R Mevagissey and St Ewe 83-90; rtd 90; PtO *Truro* 90-09; *Guildf* from 10. *Flat 5, Manormead, Tilford Road, Hindhead GU26 6RA* T: (01428) 601505

RIGBY, William. b 51. Leic Univ BSc(Econ) 72 Newc Poly BSc 82. Cranmer Hall Dur 86. **d** 88 **p** 89. C Morpeth *Newc* 88-92; R St John Lee 92-00; Chapl to the Deaf 92-08; P-in-c Chapel House 00-08; V Bywell and Mickley from 08. *Bywell Vicarage, Meadowfield Road, Stocksfield NE43 7PY* T: (01661) 842272 E: bill.rigby1@btopenworld.com

RIGELSFORD, Mrs Anne Catharina (Ank). b 44. EAMTC 99. **d** 02 **p** 03. NSM Cambridge H Cross *Ely* 02-06; NSM Cambridge Ascension from 06. *19 Clare Street, Cambridge CB4 3BY* T: (01223) 368150 M: 07932-846395 E: ank1@btinternet.com

RIGLIN, Keith Graham. b 57. Lon Inst of Educn BEd 80 Regent's Park Coll Ox BA 83 MA 86 Heythrop Coll Lon MTh 85 Birm Univ ThD 08 FRSA 09. Westcott Ho Cam 06. **d** 08 **p** 08. In Bapt Union 83-96; in URC 97-08; C Notting Dale St Clem w St Mark and St Jas *Lon* 08-11; PtO from 12; *S'wark* 12-13; *Arg* from 12; Chapl K Coll Lon from 12. *19 Queen Anne's Gardens, London W5 5QD* M: 07946-871850 E: kgr23@cam.ac.uk

RIGNEY, Mrs Cindy Joanne. b 65. Coll of Ripon & York St Jo BA 89. CBDTI 03. **d** 06 **p** 07. C Poulton Carleton and Singleton *Blackb* 06-10; P-in-c Dolphinholme w Quernmore and Over Wyresdale 10-11; V from 11; Asst Dir of Ords from 12. *St Mark's Vicarage, Dolphinholme, Lancaster LA2 9AH* T: (01524) 793125 E: revcinders@hotmail.co.uk

RIGNEY, The Very Revd James Thomas. b 59. Sydney Univ BA 82 MA 88 Pemb Coll Ox DPhil 95 CCC Cam BA 00 MA 04. Westcott Ho Cam 98. **d** 01 **p** 02. C Cambridge St Jas *Ely* 01-04; Chapl and Fell Magd Coll Cam 05-09; Dean Newcastle Australia from 09. *The Deanery, 46 Newcomer Street, Newcastle NSW 2300, Australia* E: jamesrigney@hotmail.com

RILEY, David Leo. b 51. S Bank Univ MSc 95. Dioc OLM tr scheme 97. **d** 00 **p** 01. NSM Bellingham St Dunstan *S'wark* from 00. *117 Whitefoot Lane, Bromley BR1 5SB* T: (020) 8516 4544 E: driley3020@aol.com

RILEY, John Graeme. b 55. St Jo Coll Dur BA 78. Trin Coll Bris 79. **d** 81 **p** 82. C Hensingham *Carl* 81-84; C Preston St Cuth *Blackb* 84-87; V Blackb Ch Ch w St Matt 87-98; Chapl Qu Park Hosp Blackb 87-94; V Shevington *Blackb* 98-04; V Euxton 04-14; R Gosforth w Nether Wasdale and Wasdale Head *Carl* from 14; V Beckermet St Jo and St Bridget w Ponsonby from 14. *The Rectory, Gosforth, Seascale CA20 1AZ* T: (01946) 725251 E: lesleyjohn.riley@gmail.com

RILEY, Canon John Martin. b 37. St D Coll Lamp BA 62. **d** 63 **p** 64. C Conwy w Gyffin *Ban* 63-68; P-in-c Llanfachraeth 68-70; TV Dolgellau, Llanfachreth, Brithdir etc 70-72; V Beddgelert and Dioc Youth Chapl 72-78; V Tywyn 78-82; V Tywyn w Aberdyfi 82-95; V Llanegryn w Aberdyfi w Tywyn 95-03; AD Ystumaner 87-03; Can Ban Cathl 90-97; Preb 97-03; rtd 03; PtO *Ban* from 03; AD Cyfeiliog and Mawddwy 10-12. *Llwyncelyn, Chapel Street, Corris, Machynlleth SY20 9SP* T: (01654) 761769

RILEY, The Very Revd Kenneth Joseph. b 40. OBE 03. Univ of Wales BA 61 Linacre Ho Ox BA 64 MA 68. Wycliffe Hall Ox 61. **d** 64 **p** 65. C Fazakerley Em *Liv* 64-66; Chapl Brasted Place Coll Westerham 66-69; Chapl Oundle Sch 69-74; Chapl Liv Cathl 74-75; Chapl Liv Univ 74-93; V Mossley Hill St Matt and St Jas 75-83; RD Childwall 82-83; Can Res and Treas Liv Cathl 83-87; Can Res and Prec Liv Cathl 87-93; Dean Man 93-05; rtd 05. *145 Turning Lane, Southport PR8 5HZ*

RILEY, Mrs Lesley Anne. b 54. Totley Thornbridge Coll TCert 75. Trin Coll Bris. dss 81 **d** 87 **p** 98. Hensingham *Carl* 81-84; Preston St Cuth *Blackb* 84-87; Hon Par Dn Blackb Ch Ch w St Matt 87-98; Asst Dir of Ords 96-00; Dir of Ords and Dir IME 4-7 00-05; Hon C Shevington 98-04; Hon C Whittle-le-Woods 06-07; Resources Co-ord Dioc Bd of Educn 07-14; NSM Gosforth w Nether Wasdale and Wasdale Head *Carl* from 14; NSM Beckermet St Jo and St Bridget w Ponsonby from 14. *The Rectory, Gosforth, Seascale CA20 1AZ* T: (01946) 725251 E: lesley.riley@uwclub.net

RILEY, Linda. *See* RILEY-DAWKIN, Linda

RILEY, Malcolm. b 84. **d** 14 **p** 15. C Mayfair Ch Ch *Lon* from 14. *Basement Flat, 3 John Street, London WC1N 2ES* M: 07929-208079 E: malcolm_100@hotmail.co.uk

RILEY, Martin. *See* RILEY, John Martin

RILEY, Martin Shaw. b 47. Selw Coll Cam BA 71 MA 75 Cam Univ CertEd 72. Sarum & Wells Th Coll 85. **d** 87 **p** 88. C Tuffley *Glouc* 87-91; Hon Min Can Glouc Cathl from 88; P-in-c Barnwood 91-94; V 94-99; P-in-c Highnam, Lassington, Rudford, Tibberton etc 99-04; R 04-06; Chapl Glos Hosps NHS Foundn Trust 06-12; rtd 12. *61 Kingsholm Road, Gloucester GL1 3BA* T: (01452) 417337

RILEY, Michael Charles. b 57. Ball Coll Ox BA 79 MA 83 Ex Univ CertEd 80. Edin Th Coll 84. **d** 86 **p** 87. C Newc St Geo 86-89; C Chiswick St Nic w St Mary *Lon* 89-90; V Chiswick St Paul Grove Park from 90. *St Paul's Vicarage, 64 Grove Park Road, London W4 3SB* T: (020) 8987 0312 E: michaelc.riley@virgin.net

RILEY, Preb Patrick John. b 39. Leeds Univ BA 62. Coll of Resurr Mirfield 62. **d** 64 **p** 65. C Rowbarton *B & W* 64-72; P-in-c Farleigh Hungerford w Tellisford 72-73; P-in-c Rode Major 72-73; R 73-85; RD Frome 78-85; V Glastonbury w Meare and W Pennard 85-01; Preb Wells Cathl 90-01; rtd 01; PtO *Sarum* from 02. *30 St James Street, Shaftesbury SP7 8HE* T: (01747) 850361

RILEY, Sidney David. b 43. Birm Univ BA. Ridley Hall Cam 69. **d** 71 **p** 72. C Herne Bay Ch Ch *Cant* 71-74; C Croydon St Sav 74-77; C-in-c Aylesham CD 77; P-in-c Aylesham 77-78; V 78-82; V Tudeley w Capel *Roch* 82-97; Asst Chapl Pembury Hosp Tunbridge Wells 83-86; P-in-c Morley St Paul *Wakef* 97-00; rtd 00; PtO *York* 07-09. *18 Wheatlands Drive, Beverley HU17 7HR*

RILEY, Canon William. b 24. St Aid Birkenhead 48. **d** 51 **p** 52. C Edgehill St Dunstan *Liv* 51-53; C Halsall 53-57; V Prestolee *Man* 57-62; P-in-c Ringley 60-62; R Tarleton *Blackb* 62-92; RD Leyland 84-89; Hon Can Blackb Cathl 90-92; rtd 92; PtO *Blackb* from 92. *114 Liverpool Road, Hutton, Preston PR4 5SL* T: (01772) 614267

RILEY-BRALEY, Robert James. b 57. Ch Ch Ox BA 82 MA 82 Down Coll Cam BA 83 MA 87 K Coll Lon MA 98 Surrey Univ PGCE 92. Ridley Hall Cam 81. **d** 84 **p** 85. C Thames Ditton *Guildf* 84-87; C Gravesend St Geo *Roch* 87-91; PtO *Lon* 91-92; *Blackb* 92-95; *S'wark* 95-00; C Stevenage St Mary Shephall w Aston St Alb 02-08; P-in-c Croxley Green St Oswald 08-12; V from 12. *St Oswald's Vicarage, 159 Baldwins Lane, Croxley Green, Rickmansworth WD3 3LL* T: (01923) 332244 E: ril.bral@virgin.net

RILEY-DAWKIN, Mrs Linda. b 67. St Jo Coll Nottm BA 00. **d** 00 **p** 01. C Ince Ch Ch *Liv* 00-06; Chapl Knowsley Community Coll 06-08; V Ditton St Mich w St Thos *Liv* from 08. *339 Ditchfield Road, Widnes WA8 8XR* T: 0151-420 4963 M: 07932-038443 E: revlin.riley@btinternet.com

RIMMER, Andrew Malcolm. b 62. Magd Coll Cam BA 84 MA 88. Wycliffe Hall Ox 86. **d** 88 **p** 89. C Romford Gd Shep *Chelmsf* 88-92; C Hazlemere *Ox* 92-97; V Crookhorn *Portsm* 97-05; TV Canford Magna *Sarum* from 05. *The Vicarage, 359 Sopwith Crescent, Wimborne BH21 1XQ* T: (01202) 883630 E: andy@rimmerteam.com

RIMMER, Canon David Henry. b 36. Ex Coll Ox BA 60 MA 65. Linc Th Coll 62. **d** 64 **p** 65. C Liv Our Lady and St Nic 64-66; C Daybrook *S'well* 66-69; Chapl St Mary's Cathl 69-71; R Kirkcaldy *St And* 71-78; R Haddington *Edin* 78-83; R Dunbar 79-83; R Edin Gd Shep 83-01; Hon C San St Mary's Cathl 98-01; rtd 01; LtO *Edin* from 01. *3 Southbank Court, Easter Park Drive, Edinburgh EH4 6SH* T: 0131-539 0283 E: rimmerdh@blueyonder.co.uk

RIMMER, Janet. *See* SPICER, Dorothy Janet Rosalind

RIMMER, Mrs Margaret. b 55. St Jo Coll Dur BA 05 SRN 77 SCM 78. Cranmer Hall Dur 00. **d** 02 **p** 03. C Aysgarth and Bolton cum Redmire *Ripon* 02-06; V Gt and Lt Ouseburn w Marton cum Grafton etc 06-10; P-in-c Lostock Hall and Farington Moss *Blackb* 10-12; V from 12. *St James's Vicarage, 76A Brownedge Road, Lostock Hall, Preston PR5 5AD* T: (01772) 463842 E: margaretrimmer.rev@gmail.com

RIMMER, Paul Nathanael. b 25. Jes Coll Ox BA 48 MA 50. Wycliffe Hall Ox 48. **d** 50 **p** 51. C Douglas St Thos *S & M* 50-52; C Windermere St Martin *Carl* 52-55; Ch of S India 55-59; V Marston *Ox* 59-90; RD Cowley 69-73; rtd 90. *32 Ulfgar Road, Wolvercote, Oxford OX2 8AZ* T: (01865) 352567

RIMMINGTON, Gerald Thorneycroft. b 30. Lon Univ BSc 56 PhD 64 Leic Univ MA 59 Nottm Univ MEd 72 PhD 75 FCP 66. **d** 76 **p** 78. C Sackville and Dorchester Canada 76-79; Prof of Educn Mt Allison Univ 76-79; LtO *Leic* 79-80; R Paston *Pet* 81-86; V Cosby *Leic* 86-90; Dir CME 87-90; R Barwell w Potters Marston and Stapleton 90-93; rtd 95; PtO *Leic* from 95; RD Guthlaxton I 03-04. *7 Beechings Close, Countesthorpe, Leicester LE8 5PA* T: 0116-277 7155

RINDL, Antony William. b 64. St Jo Coll Nottm 97. **d** 99 **p** 00. C Syston *Leic* 99-03; TV Colne and Villages *Blackb* 03-08; TR 08-13; P-in-c Brierfield 10-13; AD Pendle 05-13; V Watford *St Alb* from 13. *The Vicarage, 14 Cassiobury Drive, Watford WD17 3AB* T: (01923) 819152 E: tony.rindl@googlemail.com

RINGER, Philip James. b 47. Ox Min Course 88. **d** 91 **p** 92. NSM Chalfont St Peter *Ox* 91-95; P-in-c Lynton, Brendon, Countisbury, Lynmouth etc *Ex* 95-96; TV Combe Martin, Berrynarbor, Lynton, Brendon etc 96-03; Chapl Devon and Cornwall Constabulary 00-03; R Wriggle Valley *Sarum* 03-08; rtd 08; PtO *Sarum* from 08. *7 Wanderwell Farm Lane, Bridport DT6 4JW* T: (01308) 425774 E: philipringer@aol.com

RINGLAND, Tom Laurence. b 61. SS Hild & Bede Coll Dur BSc 83. Trin Coll Bris BA 89. **d** 89 **p** 90. C Southgate *Chich* 89-92; C Polegate 92-96; P-in-c Coalville and Bardon Hill *Leic* 96-98; V 98-06; TR Kirby Muxloe 06-15; C Desford and Peckleton w Tooley 13-15; R Desford and Kirby Muxloe from 15. *The Rectory, 6 Station Road, Kirby Muxloe, Leicester LE9 2EJ* T: 0116-238 6822 *or* 238 6811 E: tringland@aol.com

RINGROSE, Brian Sefton. b 31. Clare Coll Cam BA 54 MA 58 Lon Univ PGCE 55. Tyndale Hall Bris 56. **d** 58 **p** 59. C Ox St Ebbe 58-60; C Erith St Paul *Roch* 60-61; India 61-75; P-in-c Ox St Matt 75-78; Interserve (Scotland) 78-96; PtO *Glas* 78-96; rtd 96; LtO *Edin* 96-10. *14 Townsend Court, Priory Way, Malmesbury SN16 0FR* T: (01666) 822102 E: brian.ringrose@yahoo.co.uk

RINGROSE, The Ven Hedley Sidney. b 42. Open Univ BA 79. Sarum Th Coll 65. **d** 68 **p** 69. C Bishopston *Bris* 68-71; C Easthampstead *Ox* 71-75; V Glouc St Geo w Whaddon 75-88; RD Glouc City 83-88; Hon Can Glouc Cathl 86-09; V Cirencester 88-98; RD 89-97; Adn Cheltenham 98-09; rtd 10; PtO *Ox* from 11. *131 North Street, Calne SN11 0HL* T: (01249) 821215 E: hedleyringrose@talktalk.net

RINK, Pamela Rosemary. b 56. **d** 10 **p** 12. NSM E Malling, Wateringbury and Teston *Roch* from 10; Guardian Pilsdon at Malling Community 11-15. *27 Water Lane, West Malling ME19 6HH* T: (01732) 840061 E: pam.rink@gmail.com

RINTAMÄKI, Juha Matti Sakari. b 69. **d** 02. Chapl Finnish Ch in Lon from 03; LtO *S'wark* from 04. *The Finnish Church in London, 33 Albion Street, London SE16 7HZ* T: (020) 7237 1261 F: 7237 1245 M: 07768-870614 E: juha.rintamaki@finnishchurch.org.uk

RIOCH, Mrs Wenda Jean. b 35. Sarum & Wells Th Coll 84. **d** 87 **p** 94. Par Dn Basingstoke *Win* 87-91; Par Dn Catshill and Dodford *Worc* 91-94; C 94-98; TV Ottery St Mary, Alfington, W Hill, Tipton etc *Ex* 98-05; rtd 05; PtO *Win* from 08. *76 Gardeners Green, Shipton Bellinger, Tidworth SP9 7TA* T: (01980) 842334 E: wrioch@aol.com

RIORDAN, Sean Charles. b 67. Loughb Univ BA 89. St Jo Coll Nottm MA 98 LTh 99. **d** 99 **p** 00. C Ockbrook *Derby* 99-03; Asst Chapl Tervuren *Eur* 03-08; C Woodley *Ox* from 08. *171 Hurricane Way, Woodley, Reading RG5 4UH* T: 0118-375 3718 E: sean.riordan907@gmail.com

RIPLEY, Gordon. b 48. SWMTC 03. **d** 06 **p** 07. NSM Torquay St Matthias, St Mark and H Trin *Ex* 06-10; NSM Timsbury w Priston, Camerton and Dunkerton *B & W* from 10. *The Rectory, Skinners Hill, Camerton, Bath BA2 0PU* T: (01761) 470249 E: gordonripley@blueyonder.co.uk

RIPON, Dean of. *See* DOBSON, The Very Revd John Richard

RIPON, Suffragan Bishop of. *See* BELL, The Rt Revd James Harold

RISBRIDGER, Jeffrey Edward. b 58. K Alfred's Coll Win BA 80 PGCE 81. Ripon Coll Cuddesdon 12. **d** 14 **p** 15. C Waterloo St Jo w St Andr *S'wark* from 14. *Hill House, Old Church Lane, Farnham GU9 8HQ* M: 07711-019590 E: revjeffreyrisbridger@icloud.com

RISBY, John. b 40. Lambeth STh 82. Oak Hill Th Coll 64. **d** 67 **p** 68. C Fulham Ch Ch *Lon* 67-68; C Ealing St Mary 68-70; C Chitts Hill St Cuth 70-73; C Hove Bp Hannington Memorial Ch *Chich* 73-76; V Islington St Jude Mildmay Park *Lon* 76-82; P-in-c Islington St Paul Ball's Pond 78-82; V Mildmay Grove St Jude and St Paul 82-84; R Hunsdon w Widford and Wareside *St Alb* 84-05; RD Hertford 91-96; rtd 05; PtO *Chelmsf* from 06. *1 Pilgrim Close, Great Chesterford, Saffron Walden CB10 1QG* T: (01799) 530232 E: jjrisby@tiscali.co.uk

RISDON, Mrs Caroline Louise. b 79. Cape Town Univ BSocSc 01 Univ Coll Lon MA 11 Chu Coll Cam BTh 14. Westcott Ho Cam 12. **d** 14 **p** 15. C Greenwich St Alfege *S'wark* from 14. *88 Ashburnham Grove, London SE10 8UJ* M: 07899-916089 E: caroline.risdon@st-alfege.org.uk

RISDON, John Alexander. b 42. Clifton Th Coll 66. **d** 68 **p** 69. C Ealing Dean St Jo *Lon* 68-72; C Heref St Pet w St Owen 72-74; Ord Cand Sec CPAS and Hon C Bromley Ch Ch *Roch* 74-77; TV Cheltenham St Mary, St Matt, St Paul and H Trin *Glouc* 77-86; R Stapleton *Bris* 86-00; R Bedhampton *Portsm* 00-09; rtd 09. *10 St Margarets Road, Gloucester GL3 3BP* T: (01452) 372702 M: 07719-460991 E: sue.risdon@care4free.net

RISHTON, Mrs Tracy Jane. b 67. St Jo Coll Nottm 01. **d** 04 **p** 05. C Earby *Bradf* 04-07; C Kelbrook 04-07; C Cross Roads cum Lees 07-09; Area Missr S Craven Deanery 07-09. *Hovland, 4389 Vikesa, Norway* E: tracy@rishton.info

RITCHIE, Canon Angus William Mark. b 74. Magd Coll Ox BA 94 BPhil 96 MA 98. Westcott Ho Cam 96. **d** 98 **p** 99. C Plaistow and N Canning Town *Chelmsf* 98-02; TV 02-04; Dir Contextual Th Cen R Foundn of St Kath in Ratcliffe from 05; Fells' Chapl Magd Coll Ox from 05; Hon C Gt Ilford St Luke *Chelmsf* 05-08; Chapl E Lon Univ 08-11; Asst Chapl Keble Coll Ox 11-12; Hon C Bethnal Green St Pet w St Thos *Lon* 12-15; P-in-c St Geo-in-the-East w St Paul from 15; Hon Can Worc Cathl from 15. *The Royal Foundation of St Katharine, 2 Butcher Row, London E14 8DS* T: (020) 7790 3540 F: 7702 7603 E: director@theology-centre.org

RITCHIE, Brian Albert. b 34. Open Univ BA 80 Birm Univ MA 84. Qu Coll Birm 60. **d** 63 **p** 64. C S Leamington St Jo *Cov* 63-67; C-in-c Canley Cd 67-70; PtO 71-80; Hon C Cov H Trin 82-88; R Hatton w Haseley, Rowington w Lowsonford etc 88-97; rtd 97; PtO *Cov* from 98. *10 Margetts Close, Kenilworth CV8 1EN*

RITCHIE, David John Rose. b 48. St Jo Coll Dur BA 72. Cranmer Hall Dur. **d** 74 **p** 75. C Harold Wood *Chelmsf* 74-79; TV Ipsley *Worc* 79-84; Chapl Vevey w Château d'Oex and Villars *Eur* 84-93; V Stoke Bishop *Bris* 93-13; rtd 13. *The Old Stores, Forty Green, Lowbands, Redmarley, Gloucester GL19 3SL* E: davidritchie@live.co.uk

RITCHIE, Canon David Philip. b 60. Hatf Coll Dur BA 85. Wycliffe Hall Ox 85. **d** 87 **p** 88. C Chadwell *Chelmsf* 87-90; C Waltham H Cross 90-94; TV Becontree W 94-98; TR 98-01; Lay Tr Officer 01-11; C Lt Waltham 02-05; C Gt and Lt Leighs and Lt Waltham 05-11; Dir Lay Min Studies NTMTC 06-11; TR Gt Baddow *Chelmsf* from 11; Hon Can Chelmsf Cathl from 09. *The Rectory, 12 Church Street, Great Baddow, Chelmsford CM2 7HZ* E: dpritchie1@gmail.com

RITCHIE, Miss Jean. b 30. Lon Univ CertEd 51. Trin Coll Bris 77. **dss** 79 **d** 87 **p** 94. Ox St Ebbe w H Trin and St Pet 79-87; Par Dn 87-91; rtd 91; PtO *B & W* 91-94 and from 96; NSM Clevedon St Andr and Ch Ch 94-96. *63 Holland Road, Clevedon BS21 7YJ* T: (01275) 871762 E: jean.ritch@o2.co.uk

RITCHIE, June. *See* FAULKNER, June

RITCHIE, Philip. *See* RITCHIE, David Philip

RITCHIE, Philip Simon James. b 68. Man Univ BA 90 Sussex Univ MA 98 Leeds Univ MA 01 Man Metrop Univ PGCE 92. Coll of Resurr Mirfield 99. **d** 01 **p** 02. C Brighton St Nic *Chich* 01-04; P-in-c Chich St Wilfrid 04-08; P-in-c Hove 08-10;

V Hove All SS 10-15; V Cowley St Jo *Ox* from 15. *The Vicarage, 271 Cowley Road, Oxford OX4 2AJ* T: (01865) 242396
E: philipsj68@gmail.com

RITCHIE, Robert Peter. b 57. St Pet Coll Ox BA 81 St Jo Coll Cam MPhil 83. SEITE 97. **d** 00 **p** 01. NSM Kingston All SS w St Jo *S'wark* 00-11. *7 Gibbon Road, Kingston upon Thames KT2 6AD* T: (020) 8546 5964
E: robert@rsritchie.freeserve.co.uk

RITCHIE, Canon Samuel. b 31. Lon Coll of Div 65. **d** 67 **p** 68. C Westlands St Andr *Lich* 67-70; V Springfield H Trin *Chelmsf* 70-82; Chapl HM Pris Chelmsf 70-82; Chapl HM Pris Brixton 82-84; Chapl HM Pris Hull 84-86; Sen Chapl HM Prison Wymott 86-95; NW Area Chapl Co-ord 86-95; rtd 95; P-in-c Helmingham w Framsden and Pettaugh w Winston *St E* 96-97; PtO from 03. *10 Castle Rise, Hadleigh, Ipswich IP7 6JL*

RITCHIE, William James. b 62. TCD MA 84. CITC. **d** 86 **p** 87. C Enniscorthy w Clone, Clonmore, Monart etc *C & O* 86-89; Asst Chapl Alexandria Egypt 89-91; Bp's C Kells Gp *C & O* 91-92; I Kells Union *M & K* 92-99; Warden of Readers 93-97; Dioc Ecum Officer 97-99; Min Can St Patr Cathl Dublin 97-99; I Clondehorkey w Cashel *D & R* 99-00; I Dublin St Bart w Leeson Park *D & G* 00-04; I Tullow w Shillelagh, Aghold and Mullinacuff *C & O* 04-08; Warden of Readers 05-08; PtO *Lon* 08-12; P-in-c Newport All SS *Mon* 12-15; P-in-c Abertillery w Cwmtillery w Llanhilleth etc from 15. *The Vicarage, Church Street, Abertillery NP13 1DA* T: (01495) 440431
E: duwillo@yahoo.co.uk

RITSON, Canon Gerald Richard Stanley (Bill). b 35. CCC Cam BA 59 MA 63. Linc Th Coll 59. **d** 61 **p** 62. C Harpenden St Jo *St Alb* 61-65; C Goldington 65-69; R Clifton 69-76; Sec to Dioc Past Cttee and P-in-c Aldenham 76-87; Hon Can St Alb 80-87; Can Res St Alb 87-00; rtd 00; PtO *S'wark* from 00; *Lon* from 04. *97 Mitre Road, London SE1 8PT* T: (020) 7633 0012

RITTMAN, Mrs Margaret. b 52. C F Mott Coll of Educn CertEd 73 Trent Poly BEd 80. Ripon Coll Cuddesdon MA 11. **d** 11 **p** 12. NSM Knight's Enham and Smannell w Enham Alamein *Win* 11-13; NSM Martlesham w Brightwell *St E* from 13. *Address temp unknown* M: 07847-099374
E: mgtritt@me.com

RIVERINA, Bishop of. *See* GILLION, The Rt Revd Alan Robert

RIVERS, David John. b 51. St Jo Coll Nottm. **d** 84 **p** 85. C Woodthorpe *S'well* 84-88; C Hyson Green St Paul w St Steph 88; Asst Chapl Colchester Gen Hosp 89-91; Chapl Leeds Teaching Hosps NHS Trust 91-05; rtd 05; PtO *Leeds* from 05. *28 Palace Road, Ripon HG4 1ET* T: (01765) 606227
M: 07810-430245 E: woollrivers@msn.com

RIVETT, Canon Peter John. b 42. St Jo Coll Dur BA 71. Cranmer Hall Dur 68. **d** 72 **p** 73. C Newland St Jo *York* 72-76; TV Marfleet 76-82; V Oxhey All SS *St Alb* 82-93; TR Swanborough *Sarum* 93-98; TV Pewsey and Swanborough 98-01; USPG Zambia 01-07; Adn S Zambia 08-10; Hon Can Lusaka 10; rtd 10. *16 Birks Lane, Millhouse Green, Sheffield S36 9NB* T: (01226) 765829 E: peter.rivett280@btinternet.com

RIVIERE, Canon Jonathan Byam Valentine. b 54. Cuddesdon Coll. **d** 83 **p** 84. C Wymondham *Nor* 83-88; TV Quidenham 88-94; P-in-c Somerleyton w Ashby, Fritton and Herringfleet 94; R Somerleyton, Ashby, Fritton, Herringfleet etc 95-03; R Sandringham w W Newton and Appleton etc from 03; P-in-c Castle Rising 03-11; R from 11; P-in-c Hillington 03-11; R from 11; RD Heacham and Rising from 13; Dom Chapl to The Queen from 03; Chapl to The Queen from 07; Hon Can Nor Cathl from 14. *The Rectory, Sandringham PE35 6EH* T: (01485) 540587 E: rector.sandringham@gmail.com

RIVIERE, Mrs Tanagra June. b 41. S Dios Minl Tr Scheme 88. **d** 91. NSM Medstead w Wield *Win* 91-94; NSM Bishop's Sutton and Ropley and W Tisted 94-96. *The Drey, Paice Lane, Medstead, Alton GU34 5PT* T/F: (01420) 563330

RIX, Patrick George. b 30. Magd Coll Ox BA 54 MA 57 DipEd 55. Ridley Hall Cam 58. **d** 60 **p** 61. C Dur St Nic 60-62; Asst Chapl Wrekin Coll Telford 62-70; Asst Chapl Gresham's Sch Holt 70-80; Chapl Bloxham Sch 80-86; rtd 86; P-in-c Swanton Abbott w Skeyton *Nor* 89; PtO 89-08. *c/o Miss C Rix, 195 Earlham Road, Norwich NR2 3RQ*

ROACH, Jason O'Neale. b 77. Guy's Hosp Medical Sch BSc 98 K Coll Lon MB, BS 02 St Mary's Coll Twickenham MA 05. Oak Hill Th Coll MTh 10. **d** 10 **p** 11. C St Helen Bishopsgate w St Andr Undershaft etc *Lon* from 10. *11 Heron House, Searles Close, London SW11 4RJ* T: (020) 7223 0273
M: 07957-473507 E: joroach@gmail.com

ROACH, Kenneth Thomas. b 43. St Andr Univ BD 69 Fitzw Coll Cam BA 71 MA 76. Westcott Ho Cam 69. **d** 71 **p** 72. C Glas St Marg 71-73; CF 73-76; R Johnstone *Glas* 76-85; TR Bearsden 85-96; TR Bearsden w Milngavie 96-08; CF (TA) 86-08; rtd 08. *Flat 1, 3 St John's Court, Pollokshields, Glasgow G41 5ED* T: 0141-429 1064 M: 07774-814052
E: kenroach@freeuk.co.uk

ROACHE, Anthony. b 60. Nazarene Th Coll Man BA 78. **d** 99 **p** 00. C Bury St Mary *Man* 99-02; P-in-c Ringley w Prestolee 02-06; Voc Adv 04-06; CF(V) 03-06; CF from 06. *c/o MOD Chaplains (Army)* F: 381824 T: (01264) 383430
E: roachefamily@ntlworld.com

ROAKE, Anthony Richard Garrard. b 52. Keble Coll Ox BA 75 MA 80. Wycliffe Hall Ox 75. **d** 77 **p** 78. C Clifton *S'well* 77-80; V Lapley w Wheaton Aston *Lich* 80-86; V Bournemouth St Andr *Win* 86-98; V Fernhurst *Chich* 98-07; Chapl The Hague *Eur* 07-12; R Nailsea Ch Ch w Tickenham *B & W* from 12. *The Rectory, 1 Christ Church Close, Nailsea, Bristol BS48 1RT* T: (01275) 853187 E: tonyrgr@gmail.com

ROAN, Canon William Forster. b 21. St Chad's Coll Dur BA 47. **d** 49 **p** 50. C Barrow St Jas *Carl* 49-52; C-in-c Westf St Mary CD 52-57; V Westfield St Mary 58-61; R Greystoke 61-69; V Workington St Jo 70-86; Hon Can Carl Cathl 72-86; RD Solway 77-84; rtd 86; PtO *Carl* from 86. *41 Chiswick Street, Carlisle CA1 1HJ* T: (01228) 521756

ROBARTS, Mrs Freda Margaret. b 43. Open Univ BA 86. St As Minl Tr Course 98. **d** 04 **p** 06. NSM Berriew *St As* 04-06; P-in-c Llansilin w Llangadwaladr and Llangedwyn 06-09; rtd 09; PtO *St As* from 09. *Bryn Awel, Llanrhaedr ym Mochnant, Oswestry SY10 0DJ*

ROBB, Ian Archibald. b 48. K Coll Lon 68. **d** 72 **p** 73. C E Ham w Upton Park *Chelmsf* 72-74; C Leckhampton SS Phil and Jas w Cheltenham St Jas *Glouc* 74-79; P-in-c Cheltenham St Mich 79-90; V Lower Cam w Coaley 90-14; rtd 14. *St Bartholomew's Vicarage, 99 Fairmead, Cam, Dursley GL11 5JR* T: (01453) 542679 E: ia_jdr@lineone.net

ROBB, Robert Hammond Neill. b 46. Open Univ BA 89 Man Univ 66. St Deiniol's Hawarden 87. **d** 87 **p** 88. C Lache cum Saltney *Ches* 87-89; V Norley and Crowton 89-97; P-in-c Kingsley 95-97; V Norley, Crowton and Kingsley 97-98; V Neston 98-12; rtd 12. *70 Craithie Road, Vicars Cross, Chester CH3 5JL* T: (01244) 630802 E: celtic.robb@tiscali.co.uk

ROBB, Timothy Simon. b 72. Cant Univ (NZ) BMus 94 LTCL 94 Lon Bible Coll BTh 98. Trin Coll Bris MA 03. **d** 03 **p** 04. C Bedford Ch Ch *St Alb* 03-07; Chapl De Montford Univ 05-07; V Eaton Socon from 07. *St Mary's Vicarage, 34 Drake Road, Eaton Socon, St Neots PE19 8HS* T: (01480) 212219
E: vicar@eatonsocon.org

ROBBIE, James Neil. b 68. Strathclyde Univ BEng 90. Oak Hill Th Coll BTh 02. **d** 05 **p** 06. C Wolverhampton St Luke *Lich* 05-09; V W Bromwich H Trin from 09. *Holy Trinity Vicarage, 1 Burlington Road, West Bromwich B70 6LF* T: 0121-525 3595
E: rev.robbie@btinternet.com

ROBBINS, Angela Mary. *See* TOWNSHEND, Angela Mary

ROBBINS, David Ronald Walter. b 47. Sarum & Wells Th Coll 85. **d** 87 **p** 88. C Meir Heath *Lich* 87-89; C Collier Row St Jas and Havering-atte-Bower *Chelmsf* 89-93; C Tamworth *Lich* 93-97; P-in-c Hulland, Atlow, Kniveton, Bradley and Hognaston *Derby* 97-98; R 98-02; R Widford *Chelmsf* 02-12; rtd 12. *65 The Lawns, Rollston-on-Dove, Burton-on-Trent DE13 9DD* T: (01283) 814051
E: dave@therobbinsfamily.co.uk

ROBBINS, Mrs Janet Carey. b 41. LMH Ox BA 63 MA 95 Nôtre Dame Coll Bearsden PGCE 81. St D Dioc Tr Course 96. **d** 98 **p** 99. NSM Llanfihangel Ystrad and Cilcennin w Trefilan etc *St D* 98-01; NSM Quantock Towers *B & W* 02-03; rtd 03; Hon C Bro Teifi Sarn Helen *St D* 08-11; PtO 11-14. *Gothic House, 48 Bridge Street, Pershore WR10 1AT* T: (01386) 555709
E: revdjanet@tiscali.co.uk

ROBBINS, Martin Charles. b 68. Thames Valley Univ BA 91. Ripon Coll Cuddesdon BTh 00. **d** 00 **p** 01. C Thatcham *Ox* 00-03; CF 03-08; Chapl Heathfield Sch Ascot 08-11; Asst Chapl K Sch Cant from 11; Hon Min Can Cant Cathl from 12. *The King's School, 25 The Precincts, Canterbury CT1 2ES* T: (01227) 595501 E: mcr@kings-school.co.uk

ROBBINS, Peter Tyndall. b 25. Magd Coll Ox BA 46 MA 51. Westcott Ho Cam 48. **d** 50 **p** 51. C Bury St Paul *Man* 50-53; C Swinton St Pet 53-55; V Prestwich St Hilda 55-59; V Lower Halstow *Cant* 59-63; V Charing w Lt Chart 63-73; V Basing *Win* 73-83; V Kingsclere 83-90; rtd 90; PtO *Birm* 91-00; Asst RD Tamworth *Lich* 91-95; PtO from 95. *5 St John's Hospital, St John Street, Lichfield WS13 6PB* T: (01543) 415197
E: robbinspt@tiscali.co.uk

ROBBINS, The Ven Stephen. b 53. K Coll Lon BD 74 AKC 74. St Aug Coll Cant 75. **d** 76 **p** 77. C Tudhoe Grange *Dur* 76-80; C-in-c Harlow Green CD 80-84; V Gateshead Harlow Green 84-87; CF 87-97; Sen CF 97-01; Chapl R Memorial Chpl Sandhurst 01-02; Asst Chapl Gen 02-07; Dep Chapl Gen 07-09; Chapl Gen 08-11; Adn for the Army 04-11; QHC 05-11; Can and Preb Sarum Cathl 07-11; PtO from 11; Bp's Chapl from 12. *South Canonry, 71 The Close, Salisbury SP1 2ER* T: (01722) 334031 F: 413112
E: bishops.chaplain@salisbury.anglican.org

ROBBINS, Walter. b 35. d 72 p 73. Argentina 73-82; Adn N Argentina 80-82; C Southborough St Pet w Ch Ch and St Matt *Roch* 82-86; V Sidcup St Andr 86-95; V Grain w Stoke 95-00; rtd 00; PtO *Roch* from 00; *Cant* 01-09. *Mariners, Imperial Avenue, Minster on Sea, Sheerness ME12 2HG* T: (01795) 876588

ROBBINS-COLE, Adrian Peter. b 62. LSE BSc(Econ) 84 K Coll Lon MA 96. Ch Div Sch of the Pacific (USA) 90 Ripon Coll Cuddesdon BA 92. d 93 p 94. C S Dulwich St Steph *S'wark* 93-97; V Motspur Park 97-04; RD Merton 01-04; R Peterborough All SS USA from 04. *49 Concord Street, Peterborough NH 03458-1510, USA* T: (001) (603) 924 3202 E: allsaintsnh@verizon.net

ROBBINS-COLE, Ms Sarah Jane. b 68. Vermont Univ BA 90 K Coll Lon MA 00. Ch Div Sch of the Pacific (USA) 92 Ripon Coll Cuddesdon BA 95. d 95 p 96. C W Dulwich All SS *S'wark* 95-98; Chapl K Coll Sch Wimbledon 98-04; Hon C Motspur Park *S'wark* 98-04; Asst P Peterborough All SS USA from 04. *49 Concord Street, Peterborough NH 03458-1510, USA* T: (001) (603) 924 3202 E: allsaintsnh@verizon.net

ROBERT, Brother. See ATWELL, Robert Ronald

ROBERT HUGH, Brother. See KING-SMITH, Philip Hugh

ROBERTS, Aelwyn. See ROBERTS, Joseph Aelwyn

ROBERTS, Alan Moss. b 39. CEng 68 MIMechE 68 MIMarEST 68. St Jo Coll Nottm 77. d 79 p 80. C Bromsgrove St Jo *Worc* 79-83; C Edgbaston St Germain *Birm* 83-89; R Broadhembury, Payhembury and Plymtree *Ex* 89-06; rtd 06. *8 Oakleigh, Sheldon, Honiton EX14 4QT* T: (01404) 841358 E: alanmossroberts@lineone.net

ROBERTS, Allen. b 47. Trin Coll Ox MA 72 Warwick Univ MA 74 PhD 79 Wolv Univ LLM 99. Qu Coll Birm 06. d 07 p 09. NSM Tettenhall Regis *Lich* from 07. *11 Grosvenor Court, Lime Tree Avenue, Wolverhampton WV6 8HB* T: (01902) 765741 M: 07885-341540 E: allen.roberts1@btinternet.com

ROBERTS, Mrs Andrea Joan. b 46. Liv Poly AVLA 68 St Jo Coll Dur BA 73 PGCE 74. Cranmer Hall Dur 70 CBDTI 03. d 04 p 05. NSM Garstang St Thos *Blackb* 04-13. *35 Worcester Avenue, Garstang PR3 1FJ* T: (01995) 603787 E: andrea.j.roberts@btinternet.com

ROBERTS, Preb Andrew Alexander. b 49. Open Univ BA 75. Bp Otter Coll Certed 70 Sarum & Wells Th Coll 76. d 80 p 81. NSM Dorchester *Sarum* 80-85; C Swanage and Studland 85-87; TV 87-94; TR Bridgnorth, Tasley, Astley Abbotts, etc *Heref* 94-09; P-in-c Morville w Aston Eyre 08-09; P-in-c Acton Round 08-09; P-in-c Upton Cressett w Monk Hopton 08-09; RD Bridgnorth 05-09; Preb Heref Cathl 03-09; rtd 09. *Quayway Cottage, 2 Cliff Place, Swanage BH19 2PL* T: (01929) 424324 E: andyaroberts@talk21.com

ROBERTS, Andrew John. b 55. Newc Univ BA 77. EMMTC 00. d 03 p 04. NSM Church Langton cum Tur Langton etc *Leic* 03-07; Chapl HM Pris Linc from 07. *The Chaplains' Office, HM Prison, Greetwell Road, Lincoln LN2 4BD* T: (01522) 663090 E: andrewroberts28@aol.com

ROBERTS, Anne Judith. b 44. Certed 65 DipEd 78 Open Univ BA 82. S Dios Minl Tr Scheme 86. d 89 p 94. Hon Par Dn S Kensington H Trin w All SS *Lon* 89-92; NSM Barnes *S'wark* 92-14; S'wark OLM Scheme 98-04; PtO *S'wark* from 14. *5 Avenue Gardens, London SW14 8BP* T: (020) 8878 5642 M: 07715-041212 E: revjr@blueyonder.co.uk

ROBERTS, Mrs Anne Marie. b 55. York Univ BA 77. St Jo Coll Nottm 80 WMMTC 93. d 96 p 97. NSM Meole Brace *Lich* 96-08; Chapl Robert Jones/Agnes Hunt Orthopaedic NHS Trust 98-00; Chapl Prestfelde Sch Shrewsbury 99-08; Dioc Healing Adv *Carl* 09-13; Dioc Dir of Ords 10-11; Chapl N Cumbria Univ Hosps NHS Trust from 11. *2 The Abbey, Carlisle CA3 8TZ* T: (01228) 523026 or 523444 ext 4090

ROBERTS, Anthony. See ROBERTS, John Anthony Duckworth

ROBERTS, Barrie Moelwyn Antony. b 43. RN Coll Dartmouth 63 Trin Coll Carmarthen Certed 70 Birm Poly BA 83. Qu Coll Birm 00. d 04 p 05. NSM Bartley Green *Birm* 04-12; NSM Rowley Regis 12-13; PtO from 13. *34 Wheats Avenue, Harborne, Birmingham B17 0RJ* T: 0121-426 2501 E: b.roberts@lineone.net

ROBERTS, Barry. See ROBERTS, Ronald Barry

ROBERTS, Belinda Helen. d 15. NSM Haverfordwest *St D* from 15. *5 Foley Way, Haverfordwest SA61 1BX* E: cplroberts@yahoo.com

ROBERTS, Brian David. b 44. Ball Coll Ox BA 66 Univ of Wales (Ban) BTh 06 FRSA 00. d 03 p 04. OLM Guildf H Trin w St Mary 03-14; PtO from 14. *Risby, Upper Guildown Road, Guildford GU2 4EZ* T: (01483) 570556 F: (020) 7631 6224 M: 07979-766471 E: b.roberts44@ntlworld.com

ROBERTS, Bryan Richard. b 55. Univ of Wales (Cardiff) BD 80. St Mich Coll Llan 78. d 80 p 81. C Finham *Cov* 80-83; Asst Youth Officer *Nor* 83-86; R N and S Creake w Waterden 86-91; P-in-c E w N and W Barsham 86-91; Chapl Epsom Coll 91-01; Chapl Gresham's Sch Holt from 01. *10 Kelling Road, Holt NR25 6RT* T: (01263) 713234

ROBERTS, Carol Susan Butler. b 63. Univ of Wales (Ban) BA 84 MTh 99 MPhil 02 PhD 05. Ban Ord Course 06. d 07 p 08. NSM Bangor *Ban* 07-10; C 10-11; P-in-c Llanberis, Llanrug and Llandinorwig 11-15; V Bro Eryri from 15. *The Rectory, Church Road, Llanberis, Caernarfon LL55 4TF* T: (01286) 870514 E: parchcarolroberts@yahoo.co.uk

ROBERTS, Charles Richard Meyrick. b 53. Huddersfield Poly BA 75 ARCM 75. St Paul's Coll Grahamstown 89. d 92 p 92. C Lansdowne St Aidan S Africa 92-93; C Claremont St Sav 93-94; C Bath Abbey w St Jas *B & W* 94-98; P-in-c Chew Magna w Dundry 98-00; R Chew Magna w Dundry and Norton Malreward 00-10; R Chew Magna w Dundry, Norton Malreward etc from 10; P-in-c Chew Stoke w Nempnett Thrubwell from 03. *The Rectory, Tunbridge Close, Chew Magna, Bristol BS40 8SU* T: (01275) 332199 M: 07876-451376 E: chewrector@gmail.com

ROBERTS, Christopher Michael. b 39. Man Univ DipAE 79. Qu Coll Birm 62. d 64 p 65. C Milton next Gravesend Ch Ch *Roch* 64-68; C Thirsk w S Kilvington *York* 68-69; V Castleton *Derby* 69-75; TV Buxton w Burbage and King Sterndale 75-79; PtO 84-87; NSM Marple All SS *Ches* 87-90; Chapl Asst St Helens Hosp *Liv* 90-91; Chapl Asst Whiston Co Hosp Prescot 90-91; Chapl Asst Rainhill Hosp Liv 90-91; Chapl R United Hosp Bath 91-94; Chapl R United Hosp Bath NHS Trust 94-99; Sen Chapl Birm Children's Hosp NHS Trust 99-04; rtd 04; PtO *Birm* 04-12. *6 Myring Drive, Sutton Coldfield B75 7RZ* T: 0121-329 2547 E: chrismirob@aol.com

ROBERTS, Canon Cyril. b 41. St Deiniol's Hawarden. d 84 p 85. C Maltby *Sheff* 84-86; TR Gt Snaith 86-12; AD Snaith and Hatfield 03-11; Hon Can Sheff Cathl 05-12; rtd 12; PtO *Sheff* from 12; *York* from 13. *28 Broadacres, Carlton, Goole DN14 9NF* T: (01405) 947328 M: 07979-949485 E: cyrilroberts@hotmail.co.uk

ROBERTS, David. b 44. Ex Univ BA 65. St Steph Ho Ox 65. d 67 p 68. C Southwick St Columba *Dur* 67-72; C-in-c Southwick St Cuth CD 72-79; R Alyth *St And* 79-84; R Blairgowrie 79-84; R Coupar Angus 79-84; P-in-c Taunton St Jo *B & W* 84-13; rtd 09; Chapl Somerset Coll of Arts and Tech 84-10. *17 Henley Road, Taunton TA1 5BW* T: (01823) 284176 E: scat.chap@virgin.net

ROBERTS, David Alan. b 38. Open Univ BA 82. Ripon Hall Ox 71. d 73 p 74. C W Bridgford *S'well* 73-77; V Awsworth w Cossall 77-82; V Oxclose *Dur* 82-94; P-in-c New Seaham 94-04; rtd 04; PtO *Dur* from 13. *8 Hazel Road, Gateshead NE8 2EP* T: 0191-460 9919

ROBERTS, David Charles. b 53. Poly of Wales Certed 76 Open Univ BA 82 BA 93 Univ of Wales MEd 87. St Mich Coll Llan 96. d 98 p 99. C Whitchurch *Llan* 98-00; Chapl Univ of Wales Inst Cardiff 00-05; Mental Health Chapl Gwent Healthcare NHS Trust from 05. *6 Gwaun Llwyfen, Nelson, Treharris CF46 6HY* T: (01443) 450995

ROBERTS, Preb David Henry. b 38. St Chad's Coll Dur BA 60. Qu Coll Birm. d 62 p 63. C Stonehouse *Glouc* 62-65; C Hemsworth *Wakef* 65-69; V Newsome 69-76; R Pontesbury I and II *Heref* 76-03; RD Pontesbury 83-93; Preb Heref Cathl from 85; rtd 03; PtO *Heref* from 03. *14 Beaconsfield Park, Ludlow SY8 4LY* T: (01584) 878568 E: dhroberts@lineone.net

ROBERTS, Canon David John. b 36. Man Univ BSc 58. St D Coll Lamp 65. d 67 p 68. C Rhosllannerchrugog *St As* 67-70; R Cerrigydrudion w Llanfihangel Glyn Myfyr etc 75-76; R Llanrwst and Llanddoget 75-76; R LLanrwst 76-77; R Llanrwst and Llanddoget and Capel Garmon 77-84; RD Llanrwst 77-84; V Abergele 84-01; RD Rhos 94-00; Hon Can St As Cathl 95-96; Can Cursal St As Cathl 96-01; rtd 01; PtO *St As* from 09. *21 Lowther Court, Bodelwyddan, Rhyl LL18 5YG* T: (01745) 798604

ROBERTS, Mrs Deryn Anne. b 49. Nottm Univ TCert 70 BEd 71. SWMTC 04. d 07 p 08. C St Teath and Lanteglos by Camelford w Advent *Truro* 07-12; PtO 12-14; P-in-c Altarnon w Bolventor, Laneast and St Clether 14-15; C Boscastle w Davidstow 14-15; R Moorland Gp from 15. *The Rectory, Altarnun, Launceston PL15 7SJ* T: (01566) 880081 M: 07977-318589 E: stnonnas@gmail.com

ROBERTS, Canon Dewi. b 57. LWCMD 77 Cyncoed Coll CertEd 78. St Mich Coll Llan. d 84 p 85. C Clydach *S & B* 84-88; V Glantawe 88-94; V Loughor 94-06; V Gowerton 06-13; AD Llwchwr 10-13; R Ystradgynlais from 13; Can Res Brecon Cathl from 13. *The New Rectory, 2 Heol Eglwys, Ystradgynlais, Swansea SA9 1EY* T: (01639) 843200

ROBERTS, Canon Dewi James Llewelyn. b 63. United Th Coll Abth 83. d 96 p 97. C Llandudno *Ban* 96-02; C Bodedern w Llanfaethlu 99-02 and 99-02; V Newcastle Emlyn and Llandyfriog etc *St D* from 02; AD Emlyn from 12; Can St D Cathl from 13. *The Vicarage, Terra Cotta, Station Road, Newcastle Emlyn SA38 9BX* T: (01239) 710154 E: dewi44@googlemail.com

ROBERTS, Diane. b 45. Bris Univ CertEd 66 BEd 82. STETS 02. d 05 p 06. NSM Kinson and W Howe *Sarum* 05-13; NSM Salisbury St Mark and Laverstock 13-15; rtd 15; PtO *Sarum* from 15. *6 Herbert Road, Woodfalls, Salisbury SP5 2LF* T: (01725) 510894 E: robertsdiane1@aol.com

ROBERTS, Dilwyn Carey. b 38. St Deiniol's Hawarden 74. d 76 p 77. C Glanadda *Ban* 76-77; TV Amlwch w Rhosybol, Llandyfrydog etc 77-81; V Llanllechid 81-85; V Caerhun w Llangelynin w Llanbedr-y-Cennin 85-87 and 87-92; rtd 93; PtO *Ban* from 07. *67 St Georges Drive, Conwy LL31 9PR*

ROBERTS, Donald James. b 26. Sarum & Wells Th Coll 83. d 86 p 87. NSM Corfe Castle, Church Knowle, Kimmeridge etc *Sarum* 86-88 and 91-95; C Broadstone 88-91; rtd 91; PtO *Sarum* 95-98; *St E* from 01. *42 Priory Court, Nacton, Ipswich IP10 0JU* T: (01473) 711242

ROBERTS, Edward John Walford. b 31. Trin Coll Carmarthen CertEd. St D Dioc Tr Course. d 79 p 80. NSM Burry Port and Pwll *St D* 79-98; NSM Swansea St Jas *S & B* 98-02; LtO from 02. *Hen Parc Cottage, Hen Par Lane, Upper Killay, Swansea SA2 7JL*

ROBERTS, Edward Mark. b 68. d 07 p 08. OLM Droylsden St Mary *Man* 07-10; P-in-c Blackley St Paul from 10; P-in-c Blackley St Pet from 10. *14 Hill Lane, Blackley, Manchester M9 6PE* T: 0161-740 2124 E: eddie@eddieroberts.net

ROBERTS, Canon Edward Owen. b 38. K Coll Lon BD 63 AKC 63. d 64 p 65. C Auckland St Andr and St Anne *Dur* 64-67; C Cheltenham St Paul *Glouc* 67-68; Asst Master Colne Valley High Sch Linthwaite 69-71; V Meltham Mills *Wakef* 71-75; R Emley 75-88; RD Kirkburton 80-88; V Huddersfield H Trin 88-04; RD Huddersfield 89-99; Hon Can Wakef Cathl 92-04; rtd 04; PtO *York* from 04. *8 Montague Graham Court, Kidbrook Gardens, London SE3 0PD* T: (020) 8269 2422

ROBERTS, Mrs Elizabeth Rose. d 11 p 12. NSM Llanfihangel Ysgeifiog w Llangristiolus etc *Ban* 11-12; NSM Seintiau Braint a Chefni 12-14; NSM Bro Cadwaladr from 15. *10 Y Fron, Aberffraw, Ty Croes LL63 5EQ* T: (01407) 840605 E: cushlarose@btinternet.com

ROBERTS, Eric. b 40. Ban Ord Course 90 St Mich Coll Llan 92. d 93 p 94. Min Can Ban Cathl 93-97; R Llanllyfni 97-02; V Llandysul w Bangor Teifi and Llanfairollwyn etc *St D* 02-11; AD Emlyn 04-11; rtd 11; P-in-c Newborough w Llanidan w Llangeinwen etc *Ban* 11-14; C Bro Dwynwen from 15. *Gerallt, Erw Wen, Caeathro, Caernarfon LL55 2TW* T: (01286) 671861

ROBERTS, Erica Jane. b 59. MB, ChB MRCP. STETS. d 10 p 11. NSM Portswood Ch Ch *Win* from 10. *Brookvale Cottage, Highfield Lane, Southampton SO17 1NQ* T: (02380) 556887 E: erica@samotto.demon.co.uk

ROBERTS, Garry Peter. b 77. Ripon Coll Cuddesdon 12. d 14 p 15. C Fareham H Trin *Portsm* from 14. *9 Brookmeadow, Fareham PO15 5JH* M: 07554-142729 E: revdgarryroberts@btinternet.com

ROBERTS, Gillian Susan. b 54. d 13 p 14. C Napton-on-the-Hill, Lower Shuckburgh etc *Cov* from 13; C Priors Hardwick, Priors Marston and Wormleighton from 13. *Sycamore Lodge, Church Street, Stockton, Southam CV47 8JG* T: (01926) 815831 E: gillian@thebridgesgroup.org.uk

ROBERTS, Graham Miles. b 59. Open Univ BA 95. Trin Coll Bris 90. d 92 p 93. C Charles w Plymouth St Matthias *Ex* 92-96; Chapl Plymouth Univ 92-94; TV Liskeard, St Keyne, St Pinnock, Morval etc *Truro* 96-99; P-in-c Bournemouth St Andr *Win* 99-04; V from 04. *St Andrew's Vicarage, 53 Bennett Road, Bournemouth BH8 8QQ* T: (01202) 396022 E: graham_roberts@ntlworld.com

ROBERTS, Gregory Stephen. b 64. St Chad's Coll Dur BSc 86 PGCE 87 CPhys 95. Ripon Coll Cuddesdon 08. d 10 p 11. C Kettering SS Pet and Paul 10-14; Asst Chapl St Andr Healthcare 12-13; P-in-c Pet All SS from 14. *All Saints' Vicarage, 208 Park Road, Peterborough PE1 2UJ* E: gregroberts81@hotmail.com

ROBERTS, Gwyneth. *See* WATKINS, Gwyneth

ROBERTS, James. *See* ROBERTS, William James

ROBERTS, Jane Elizabeth. b 53. SEITE 98. d 01 p 02. NSM Mitcham Ascension *S'wark* from 01. *39 Castleton Road, Mitcham CR4 1NZ* T: (020) 8764 6423 M: 07790-703710 E: janeroberts@nasuwt.net

ROBERTS, Canon Janet Lynne. b 56. Trin Coll Bris 76. dss 82 d 87 p 94. Par Dn Huyton St Mich *Liv* 87-91; C Aughton Ch Ch 91-98; TV Parr 98-05; TR from 05; Hon Can Liv Cathl from 13. *St Nicholas' Vicarage, Nicholas Road, Liverpool L23 6TS* T: 0151-924 3551 E: rovingrector@btinternet.com

ROBERTS, Mrs Jasmine Cynthia. b 46. Cant Sch of Min 88. d 91. NSM Sandwich *Cant* 91-13; Asst Dir of Ords 02-09; PtO from 14. *The Rectory, Knightrider Street, Sandwich CT13 9ER* T/F: (01304) 613138 E: jasmineroberts@supanet.com

ROBERTS, Ms Jeanette. b 67. RMHN 00. Cranmer Hall Dur 07. d 09 p 10. C Todmorden *Wakef* 09-12; P-in-c Sowerby 12-13;

P-in-c Norland 12-13; V Ryburn *Leeds* from 13. *Sowerby Vicarage, Sowerby, Sowerby Bridge HX6 1JJ* T: (01422) 646371 E: revdjeanetteroberts@gmail.com

ROBERTS, Jennifer. *See* GRAY, Jennifer

ROBERTS, John Anthony Duckworth. b 43. K Coll Lon BD 65 AKC 65. St Boniface Warminster 65. d 66 p 67. C Wythenshawe Wm Temple Ch CD *Man* 66-69; C Bradford-on-Avon H Trin *Sarum* 69-72; Chapl Dauntsey's Sch Devizes 72-73; CF 73-77; P-in-c Verwood *Sarum* 77-81; V 81-86; V Clitheroe St Mary *Blackb* 86-97; R Paget St Paul Bermuda 97-03; rtd 03. *The Old Coach House, Forwood, Minchinhampton, Stroud GL6 9AB* T: (01453) 835811

ROBERTS, John Charles. b 50. Nottm Univ BA 71 Cam Univ BA 73. Westcott Ho Cam 71. d 73 p 74. C Newark St Mary *S'well* 73-77; Chapl RAF 77-93; LtO *Bris* 93-95. *Address temp unknown* E: robertsjohnr@aol.com

ROBERTS, John Charles Welch. b 39. UMIST BSc 60. Oak Hill NSM Course 91 SWMTC 92. d 94 p 95. NSM Washfield, Stoodleigh, Withleigh etc *Ex* from 94. *East Sidborough, Loxbeare, Tiverton EX16 8DA* T/F: (01884) 256302 E: john@sidborough.eclipse.co.uk

ROBERTS, Canon John Hugh. b 42. K Alfred's Coll Win CertEd 72 Open Univ BA 75. Wells Th Coll 65. d 67 p 68. C Wareham w Arne *Sarum* 67-70; C Twyford *Win* 70-72; Asst Teacher Rawlins Sch Leics 72-74; V Nassington w Yarwell *Pet* 74-77; Asst Teacher Sponne Sch Towcester 78-92; RD Brackley *Pet* 94-03; P-in-c Helmdon w Stuchbury and Radstone etc 93-03; P-in-c Weedon Lois w Plumpton and Moreton Pinkney etc 02-03; R Astwell Gp 03-05; Can Pet Cathl 01-05; rtd 05; PtO *Pet* from 05; Chapl to Retired Clergy and Clergy Widows' Officer 08-10. *Pimlico House, Pimlico, Brackley NN13 5TN* T: (01280) 850378 E: rev.roberts@virgin.net *or* johnpimlicohouse@gmail.com

ROBERTS, Canon John Mark Arnott. b 54. AKC 75 CertEd 76. Chich Th Coll 77. d 77 p 78. C Ashford *Cant* 77-82; V St Mary's Bay w St Mary-in-the-Marsh etc 82-91; R Sandwich 91-12; P-in-c Woodnesborough w Worth and Staple 04-12; P-in-c Eastry and Northbourne w Tilmanstone etc 10-12; R Sandwich and Worth from 12; AD Sandwich 00-06; Hon Can Cant Cathl from 03. *The Rectory, Knightrider Street, Sandwich CT13 9ER* T/F: (01304) 613138 E: revdmarkroberts@supanet.com

ROBERTS, Canon John Victor. b 34. St Edm Hall Ox BA 58 MA 62. Tyndale Hall Bris 58. d 60 p 61. C Southport Ch Ch *Liv* 60-62; C Pemberton St Mark Newtown 62-65; V Blackb Sav 65-71; Chapl Blackb and Lancs R Infirmary and Park Lee Hosp 65-71; V Parr *Liv* 71-73; TR 73-80; R Much Woolton 80-02; RD Childwall 84-89; AD Liv S 89-00; Hon Can Liv Cathl 95-02; rtd 02; PtO *Liv* from 02; Hon Chapl Liv Cathl from 04. *8 Cherry Vale, Liverpool L25 5PX* T/F: 0151-428 8290 E: canonjvr@hotmail.com

ROBERTS, John Victor. b 40. GIPE 61. Qu Coll Birm 83. d 85 p 86. C Ludlow *Heref* 85-89 and 92-93; P-in-c Coreley w Doddington 89-92; P-in-c Knowbury 89-92; TV Ludlow, Ludford, Ashford Carbonell etc 93-02; rtd 02; PtO *Heref* from 02. *Carwood, 16 Stretton Farm Road, Church Stretton SY6 6DX* T: (01694) 723164

ROBERTS, Jonathan Christopher. b 82. Reading Univ BA 09. Ripon Coll Cuddesdon BA 15. d 15. C Dorchester *Ox* from 15. *26 Windrush Road, Berinsfield, Wallingford OX10 7PF* M: 07980-929302 T: (01865) 872555 E: revjonroberts@gmail.com

ROBERTS, Jonathan George Alfred. b 60. Lon Univ BD 82 Dur Univ MA 93. Qu Coll Birm. d 84 p 85. C Shepshed *Leic* 84-86; C Braunstone 86-87; Dioc Youth Adv *Dur* 88-92; Nat Youth Officer Gen Syn Bd of Educn 92-94; P-in-c Washington *Dur* 94-95; R 95-99; Regional Co-ord for Community Work Assessment Consortium for the NE 99-03; Sen Lect Teesside Univ *York* 03-14; PtO *Dur* 99-14; *Newc* 01-14; *S'wark* from 14; Par Development Adv Woolwich Area from 14; P-in-c Camberwell St Mich w All So w Em from 15; Chapl Ark All SS Academy Camberwell from 15. *128 Bethwin Road, London SE5 0YY* M: 07530-003368 T: (020) 7701 2231 E: jonathan.roberts@southwark.anglican.org

ROBERTS, Jonathan Peter Higham. b 76. St Jo Coll Dur BA 97 PGCE 98. St Jo Coll Nottm 09. d 12 p 13. C Cotes Heath and Standon and Swynnerton etc *Lich* from 12. *The Rectory, Station Road, Cotes Heath, Stafford ST21 6RS* T: (01782) 791679 E: jonathanroberts@talktalk.net

ROBERTS, Joseph Aelwyn. b 18. Univ of Wales (Lamp) BA 40. St Mich Coll Llan 41. d 42 p 43. C Llanllyfni *Ban* 42-44; Min Can Ban Cathl 44-52; V Llandegai 52-88; Dioc Dir for Soc Work 73-88; rtd 88; PtO *Ban* from 88. *The Vicarage, Llandygai, Bangor LL57 4LA* T: (01248) 353711

ROBERTS, Judith. *See* ROBERTS, Anne Judith

ROBERTS, Judith. *See* ABBOTT, Judith

ROBERTS, Julie. b 52. **d** 12 **p** 13. NSM Oxenhope *Leeds* from 12; NSM Haworth 12-15; NSM Cross Roads cum Lees 12-15; NSM Haworth and Cross Roads cum Lees from 15. *Springfield Cottage, Hebden Bridge Road, Oxenhope, Keighley BD22 9SY* T: (01535) 645102

ROBERTS, Preb Kathleen Marie. b 50. Th Ext Educn Coll 94. **d** 00 **p** 01. S Africa 00-02; C Crediton, Shobrooke and Sandford etc *Ex* 03-05; P-in-c Black Torrington, Bradford w Cookbury etc 05-15; R from 15; RD Holsworthy 11-15; Dean of Women's Min from 15; Preb Ex Cathl from 15. *The Rectory, Black Torrington, Beaworthy EX21 5PU* T: (01409) 231279 E: robertskm8@aol.com

ROBERTS, Keith Mervyn. b 55. St Pet Coll Birm CertEd 76 LGSM 78 GMus 78. Qu Coll Birm 89. **d** 91 **p** 92. C Hall Green St Pet *Birm* 91-95; TV Warwick *Cov* 95-00; P-in-c Bishop's Tachbrook 00-09; Dir Communications 03-04 and 04-09; Relig Affairs Correspondent BBC W Midl 95-01; Presenter/Producer 01-09; Hon Can Cov Cathl 07-09; TR Godalming *Guildf* from 09. *The Rectory, Westbrook Road, Godalming GU7 1ET* T/F: (01483) 860594 E: mervynroberts@aol.com *or* mervyn.roberts@godalming.org.uk

ROBERTS, The Ven Kevin Thomas. b 55. Qu Coll Cam BA 78 MA 82 Nottm Univ BA 82. St Jo Coll Nottm 80. **d** 83 **p** 84. C Beverley Minster *York* 83-86; C Woodley St Jo the Ev *Ox* 86-91; V Meole Brace *Lich* 91-09; RD Shrewsbury 98-08; Preb Lich Cathl 02-08; Adn Carl and Can Res Carl Cathl from 09. *2 The Abbey, Carlisle CA3 8TZ* T: (01228) 523026 E: archdeacon.north@carlislediocese.org.uk

ROBERTS, Laurence James. b 51. Sussex Univ BEd 73. Sarum & Wells Th Coll 75. **d** 78 **p** 79. C Rotherhithe St Mary w All SS *S'wark* 78-81; Public Preacher 81-84; Ind Chapl 81-84; Hon P Nunhead St Silas 82-84; TV Plaistow *Chelmsf* 84-89; Chapl Newham Gen Hosp and Plaistow Hosp 84-96; Tutor Community Nursing Services 89-96; Tutor Westmr Past Foundn from 90; Lect E Lon Univ *Chelmsf* from 92. *40 Boleyn Road, London E7 9QE* T: (020) 8472 2430 E: laurence.roberts@virgin.net

ROBERTS, Canon Leanne Kelly. b 74. St Hilda's Coll Ox BA 95 MA 02 Em Coll Cam BA 01 MA 05 Hertf Coll Ox MSt 08. Westcott Ho Cam 99. **d** 02 **p** 03. C Hampton All SS *Lon* 02-05; Chapl Hertf Coll Ox 05-11; Voc Adv *Ox* 07-11; Chapl Ox and Bucks Mental Health Trust 10-11; Can Res and Treas S'wark Cathl from 11; Dioc Dir of Ords from 11. *Trinity House, 4 Chapel Court, London SE1 1HW* T: (020) 7939 9400 F: 7939 9468 E: leanne.roberts@southwark.anglican.org

ROBERTS, Miss Marguerite Mary Grace. b 43. Keswick Hall Coll CertEd 65 Sussex Univ BEd 74 UEA MA 86. EAMTC 97. **d** 00 **p** 01. Hon C Cambridge St Mark *Ely* from 00. *5 Eachard Road, Cambridge CB3 0HZ* T: (01223) 359167 E: associatevicar@trumpingtonchurch.org.uk

ROBERTS, Mark. *See* ROBERTS, John Mark Arnott

ROBERTS, Martin Meredith Edward. b 62. Univ of Wales (Abth) BSc 85. **d** 06 **p** 07. OLM Woodbridge St Jo and Bredfield *St E* 06-13; NSM from 13. *64 Victoria Road, Woodbridge IP12 1EL* T: (01394) 388140 E: martin.me.roberts@bt.com

ROBERTS, Martin Vincent. b 53. Birm Univ BA 76 MA 77 PhD 82 LRAM 72. Ripon Coll Cuddesdon 76. **d** 78 **p** 79. C Perry Barr *Birm* 78-81; Sen Chapl and Lect W Sussex Inst of HE 81-86; Leic Poly 86-92; Sen Chapl De Montfort Univ 92-95; TV Leic H Spirit 86-89; TR 89-95; V Baswich *Lich* 95-01; V Selly Oak St Mary *Birm* 01-08; rtd 08; PtO *Birm* from 08. *14 Hartley Place, Vicarage Road, Edgbaston, Birmingham B15 3HS* T: 0121-454 5180 E: martin@mroberts48.fsnet.co.uk

ROBERTS, Matthew Haigh. b 75. Trin & All SS Coll Leeds BA 96 Edge Hill Coll of HE PGCE 97. St Jo Coll Nottm 11. **d** 13 **p** 14. C Haydock St Mark *Liv* from 13. *303 Park Street, Haydock, St Helens WA11 0BG* T: (01744) 602641 E: revmatt28@gmail.com

ROBERTS, Mervyn. *See* ROBERTS, Keith Mervyn

ROBERTS, Michael Brian. b 46. Oriel Coll Ox BA 68 MA 72 St Jo Coll Dur BA 73. Cranmer Hall Dur 71. **d** 74 **p** 75. C St Helens St Helen *Liv* 74-76; C Goose Green 76-78; C Blundellsands St Nic 78-80; V Fazakerley St Nath 80-87; V Chirk *St As* 87-01; V Cockerham w Winmarleigh and Glasson *Blackb* 01-13; rtd 13; PtO *Blackb* from 13. *35 Worcester Avenue, Garstang PR3 1FJ* T: (01995) 603787 E: michaelroberts@btinternet.com

ROBERTS, Michael Frederick. b 46. Sarum Th Coll 86. **d** 88 **p** 89. C Reading St Matt *Ox* 88-91; NSM Douglas St Geo and St Barn *S & M* 91-93; V Malew 93-11; rtd 11. *Rose Cottage, St Mary's Road, Port Erin, Isle of Man IM9 6JL* E: revroberts@manx.net

ROBERTS, Michael Graham Vernon. b 43. Keble Coll Ox BA 65. Cuddesdon Coll 65 Ch Div Sch of the Pacific (USA) BD 67.

d 67 **p** 68. C Littleham w Exmouth *Ex* 67-70; Chapl Clare Coll Cam 70-74; V Bromley St Mark *Roch* 74-79; Tutor Qu Coll Birm 79-85; TR High Wycombe *Ox* 85-90; Vice-Prin Westcott Ho Cam 90-93; Prin 93-06; Hon Can Ely Cathl 04-06; rtd 06. *121 Milehouse Road, Plymouth PL3 4AG* E: michael.su.roberts@orange.fr

ROBERTS, Neil Charles. b 72. K Coll Lon BA 94 AKC 94 Kent Univ BA 10 Cant Ch Ch Univ MA 14 Homerton Coll Cam PGCE 95 FGMS 01. SEITE. **d** 10 **p** 11. C Bletchingley and Nutfield *S'wark* 10-14; V Steyning *Chich* from 14; R Ashurst from 14; Boarders' Chapl Steyning Gr Sch from 14. *The Vicarage, Vicarage Lane, Steyning BN44 3YQ* T: (01903) 879877 E: frneilroberts@gmail.com

ROBERTS, Nia Wyn. *See* MORRIS, Nia Wyn

ROBERTS, Nicholas John. b 47. Lon Univ BD 70 AKC 70 MTh 78 Surrey Univ MSc 93. St Aug Coll Cant 70. **d** 71 **p** 72. C Tividale *Lich* 71-74; C St Pancras H Cross w St Jude and St Pet *Lon* 74-76; C Camberwell St Giles *S'wark* 76-78; Chapl Ch Coll Cam 78-82; V Kingstanding St Luke *Birm* 82-85; Chapl St Chas Hosp Ladbroke Grove 85-96; Chapl Princess Louise Hosp Lon 85-96; Chapl Paddington Community Hosp 85-96; Chapl Cen Middx Hosp NHS Trust 96-99; Chapl St Mary's NHS Trust Paddington 99-04; Chapl CSC 04-10; rtd 10; PtO *S'wark* from 10. *183 Dukes Avenue, Richmond TW10 7YH* T: (020) 8940 5504 M: 07946-243660 E: n.roberts7@homecall.co.uk

ROBERTS, Mrs Patricia Frances. b 62. Roehampton Inst BEd 85. Trin Coll Bris 93. **d** 96 **p** 97. NSM Buckhurst Hill *Chelmsf* 96-99; NSM Gt Baddow 99-07; NSM W Swindon and the Lydiards *Bris* from 11. *The Vicarage, The Butts, Lydiard Millicent, Swindon SN5 3LR* T: (01793) 772417 E: tudorandtricia@btinternet.com

ROBERTS, Paul Carlton. b 57. Worc Coll Ox BA 78 MA 86 CertEd. St Jo Coll Nottm 84. **d** 87 **p** 88. C Hazlemere *Ox* 87-91; C Woodley St Jo the Ev 91-92; TV Woodley 92-03; R Coulsdon St Jo *S'wark* from 03. *The Rectory, 232 Coulsdon Road, Coulsdon CR5 1EA* T/F: (01737) 552152 E: rev.paul.c.roberts@gmail.com

ROBERTS, Paul John. b 60. Man Univ BA 82 PhD 91 Man Poly PGCE 83. St Jo Coll Nottm 83. **d** 85 **p** 86. C Burnage St Marg *Man* 85-88; Tutor Trin Coll Bris 88-00; V Cotham St Sav w St Mary and Clifton St Paul *Bris* 00-08; Hon Can Bris Cathl 06-08; Dean Non-Res Tr St Mich Coll Llan 09-10; Dir Angl Formation and Tutor Trin Coll Bris from 10. *Trinity College, Stoke Hill, Bristol BS9 1JP* T: 0117-908 0332 *or* 968 0267 E: paul.roberts@trinity-bris.ac.uk

ROBERTS, Paul Matthew. b 78. **d** 15. C Bartestree Cross *Heref* from 15. *The Beeches, Withington, Hereford HR1 3PX* M: 07735-430335 E: revdpaulroberts@gmail.com

ROBERTS, Peter Francis. b 59. N Illinois Univ BSc 81 Leeds Univ BA 87. Coll of Resurr Mirfield 85. **d** 88 **p** 89. C Leeds All So *Ripon* 88-92; Asst Dioc Youth Chapl 91-92; USPG Belize 92-94; V Collingham w Harewood *Ripon* 95-01; World Miss Officer 95-01; Chapl Dubai and Sharjah w N Emirates 01-03; R Merritt Is USA from 03. *PO Box 541025, Merritt Island FL 32953, USA* T: (001) (321) 452 5260 E: stlukes1@bellsouth.net

ROBERTS, Peter Reece. b 43. Chich Th Coll 73. **d** 75 **p** 76. C Cadoxton-juxta-Barry *Llan* 75-79; C Brixham w Churston Ferrers *Ex* 79-81; C Bexhill St Pet *Chich* 81-84; R Heene 84-14; RD Worthing 89-97; rtd 14; PtO *Chich* from 14. *7 Mayfair Court, 21 Parchment Street, Chichester, PO19 3RA* T: (01243) 778543 E: revp.roberts@btinternet.com

ROBERTS, Philip Alan. b 59. Chich Th Coll 85. **d** 88 **p** 89. C Friern Barnet St Jas *Lon* 88-93; C Farnham Royal w Hedgerley *Ox* 93-02; TV Southend *Chelmsf* from 02. *39 St John's Road, Westcliff-on-Sea SS0 7JY* T: (01702) 433327 E: p.a.roberts@talk21.com

ROBERTS, Philip Anthony. b 50. St Jo Coll Dur BA 73. Wycliffe Hall Ox 75. **d** 77 **p** 78. C Roby *Liv* 77-79; C Ainsdale 79-80; C Pershore w Pinvin, Wick and Birlingham *Worc* 80-83; Chapl Asst Radcliffe Infirmary Ox 83-88; John Radcliffe and Littlemore Hosps Ox 83-88; Chapl R Victoria Hosp Bournemouth 88-91; Chapl R Bournemouth Gen Hosp 88-91; Chapl Heref Co Hosp 91-94; Chapl Heref Hosps NHS Trust 94-12; rtd 12. *More House, More, Bishop's Castle SY9 5HH*

ROBERTS, The Ven Raymond Harcourt. b 31. CB 84. St Edm Hall Ox BA 54 MA 58. St Mich Coll Llan 54. **d** 56 **p** 57. C Bassaleg *Mon* 56-59; Chapl RNR 57-59; Chapl RN 59-84; Chapl of the Fleet and Adn for the RN 80-84; QHC 80-84; Hon Can Gib Cathl 80-84; Gen Sec JMECA 85-89; C Hale *Guildf* 85-89; Hon Chapl Llan Cathl 90-95; LtO from 95. *8 Baynton Close, Llandaff, Cardiff CF5 2NZ* T: (029) 2057 8044

ROBERTS, Miss Rebecca Mary. b 71. Glam Univ BA 92 Chelt & Glouc Coll of HE PGCE 93. Qu Coll Birm BA 02 MA 03. **d** 03 **p** 04. C Greenstead w Colchester St Anne

Chelmsf 03-06; PtO *Win* 06-10; NSM Southampton (City Cen) 10-13; V Harnham *Sarum* from 13. *The Vicarage, Old Blandford Road, Salisbury SP2 8DQ* M: 07727-154234
E: reverendbecky@gmail.com

ROBERTS, Canon Richard Stephanus Jacob (Steph). b 28. TCD BA 51 MA 57. TCD Div Sch Div Test 51. **d** 51 **p** 52. C Orangefield *D & D* 51-54; Miss to Seamen 51-94; Portuguese E Africa 51-65; Ceylon 65-68; Chapl Miss to Seamen Dublin 68-72; Chapl Miss to Seamen Southn 72-94; Sen Chapl Ch on the High Seas 72-94; Hon Can Win Cathl 82-94; rtd 94; PtO *Win* from 94. *25 Bassett Crescent West, Southampton SO16 7EB* T: (023) 8079 0734

ROBERTS, Ronald Barry. b 40. S Dios Minl Tr Scheme 80. **d** 83 **p** 85. NSM Wedmore w Theale and Blackford *B & W* 83-85; C Odd Rode *Ches* 85-87; V Eaton and Hulme Walfield 87-04; rtd 04; PtO *Ches* from 04. *Iona, 8 Belmont Avenue, Sandbach CW11 1BX* T: (01270) 766124 E: barryroberts@uwclub.net

ROBERTS, Mrs Rosamunde Mair. b 58. RN 80. STETS 98. **d** 01 **p** 02. C Farnham *Guildf* 01-04; C Fleet 04-08; V Lenborough *Ox* from 08. *The Vicarage, Thornborough Road, Padbury, Buckingham MK18 2AH* T: (01280) 813162
E: lenborough.vicar@gmail.com

ROBERTS, Mrs Rosanne Elizabeth. b 51. Glouc Sch of Min 85. **d** 88 **p** 94. NSM Charlton Kings St Mary *Glouc* 88-93; C Leckhampton SS Phil and Jas w Cheltenham St Jas 93-96; R Ashchurch 96-08; R Ashchurch and Kemerton 08-13; rtd 13. *25 Buckles Close, Charlton Kings, Cheltenham GL53 8QT* T: (01242) 248194 E: rosanne.roberts@btinternet.com

ROBERTS, Miss Sandra June. b 58. Univ Coll Ches BA 96. Qu Coll Birm 98. **d** 98 **p** 99. C Mold St *As* 98-01; V Llandrillo-yn-Edeirnion and Llandderfel from 01; P-in-c Betws Gwerful Goch w Llangwm w Llawrybetws from 05; AD Penllyn and Edeirnion 04-10. *The Vicarage, Llandrillo, Corwen LL21 0SW* T: (01490) 440224

ROBERTS, Mrs Sharon. b 56. **d** 11 **p** 12. OLM Amersham on the Hill *Ox* from 11. *25 Longfield Drive, Amersham HP6 5HD* T: (01494) 433853 E: robertsn1@btinternet.com

ROBERTS, Stephanus. *See* ROBERTS, Richard Stephanus Jacob

ROBERTS, Stephen Bradley. b 66. K Coll Lon BD 90 Heythrop Coll Lon MA 03 PhD 11. Wycliffe Hall Ox 89. **d** 91 **p** 92. C W Hampstead St Jas *Lon* 91-94; TV Uxbridge 94-98; Chapl Brunel Univ 98-04; Vice Prin St Mich Coll Llan 04-12; PtO *Llan* from 12. *122 Pwllmelin Road, Cardiff CF5 3NA*

ROBERTS, The Ven Stephen John. b 58. K Coll Lon BD 81 Heythrop Coll Lon MTh 99. Westcott Ho Cam. **d** 83 **p** 84. C Riverhead w Dunton Green *Roch* 83-86; C St Martin-in-the-Fields *Lon* 86-89; Warden Trin Coll Cen Camberwell 89-99; V Camberwell St Geo *S'wark* 89-99; RD Camberwell 97-99; Treas and Can Res S'wark Cathl 00-05; Sen Dioc Dir of Ords 00-05; Adn Wandsworth 05-15; P-in-c Upper Tooting H Trin w St Aug 10-11; Bp's Officer for Non-Stipendiary Clergy from 15; Public Preacher from 15; Hon Can S'wark Cathl from 15. *2 Alma Road, London SW18 1AB* T: (020) 8874 8567 *or* 8545 2440 F: 8545 2441
E: stephen.roberts@southwark.anglican.org

ROBERTS, Preb Susan Emma. b 60. La Sainte Union Coll BTh 93. St Steph Ho Ox 94. **d** 96 **p** 97. C Petersfield *Portsm* 96-00; P-in-c Ashprington, Cornworthy and Dittisham *Ex* 00-04; TV Totnes w Bridgetown, Berry Pomeroy etc 04-06; RD Totnes 03-06; TR Honiton, Gittisham, Combe Raleigh, Monkton etc from 06; RD Honiton 07-13; Preb Ex Cathl from 06. *The Rectory, Rookwood Close, Honiton EX14 1BH* T: (01404) 42925 E: revdsue@btinternet.com

ROBERTS, Sydney Neville Hayes. b 19. K Coll Lon 38. Cuddesdon Coll 45. **d** 47 **p** 48. C Aylesbury *Ox* 47-52; CF 52-69; R Theale w N Street *Ox* 69-76; R Theale and Englefield 76-85; rtd 85; PtO *Ox* from 89. *34 Stonebridge Road, Steventon, Abingdon OX13 6AU* T: (01235) 834777

ROBERTS, Mrs Sylvia Ann. b 40. Stockwell Coll Lon TCert 60. S Dios Minl Tr Scheme 81. **dss** 84 **d** 87 **p** 94. Crookhorn *Portsm* 84-88; Hon Par Dn Bedhampton 88-89; Par Dn Southampton (City Cen) *Win* 89-91; Team Dn 91-94; TV 94-96; V Merton St Jo *S'wark* 96-06; P-in-c Colliers Wood Ch Ch 01-06; rtd 06; PtO *Portsm* from 07. *16 Bramble Road, Petersfield GU31 4HL* E: sylkenco@hotmail.com

ROBERTS, Canon Tegid. b 47. **d** 87 **p** 88. LtO *Ban* 87-93; NSM Llandinorwig w Penisa'r-waen 93-99; LtO 99-00; Dioc Officer for Children and Schs from 00; Min Can Ban Cathl 00-05; V Llandwrog and Llanwnda 05-11; Hon Can Ban Cathl 07-11; Can Res 11-12; rtd 12; PtO *Ban* from 12. *Arwel, Llanrug, Caernarfon LL55 3BA* T: (01286) 870760
E: tr@roberts485.freeserve.co.uk

ROBERTS, Terry Harvie. b 45. Sarum & Wells Th Coll 87. **d** 89 **p** 90. C Weymouth H Trin *Sarum* 89-93; TV Basingstoke *Win* 93-98; P-in-c Win St Barn 98-10; rtd 10; PtO *Win* from 10. *1 Poulner Park, Ringwood BH24 1TZ* T: (01425) 470232

ROBERTS, Tudor Vaughan. b 58. Newc Univ BA 81. All Nations Chr Coll 91 Trin Coll Bris BA 94. **d** 96 **p** 97. C Buckhurst Hill *Chelmsf* 96-99; TV Gt Baddow 99-07; TV W Swindon and the Lydiards *Bris* from 07. *The Vicarage, The Butts, Lydiard Millicent, Swindon SN5 3LR* T: (01793) 772417
E: tudorandtricia@btinternet.com

ROBERTS, Tunde. *See* ROBERTS, Vincent Akintunde

ROBERTS, Vaughan Edward. b 65. Selw Coll Cam BA 88 MA 91. Wycliffe Hall Ox 89. **d** 91 **p** 92. C Ox St Ebbe w H Trin and St Pet 91-95; Student Pastor 95-98; R from 98. *St Ebbe's Rectory, 2 Roger Bacon Lane, Oxford OX1 1QE* T: (01865) 240438 E: vroberts@stebbes.org.uk

ROBERTS, Vaughan Simon. b 59. Univ of Wales (Ban) BA 80 Bath Univ PhD 99. McCormick Th Sem Chicago MA 82 Westcott Ho Cam 83. **d** 85 **p** 86. C Bourne *Guildf* 85-89; Chapl Phyllis Tuckwell Hospice Farnham 88-89; Chapl Bath Univ *B & W* 89-96; NSM Bath Ch Ch Prop Chpl 90-96; P-in-c 92-96; P-in-c Chewton Mendip w Ston Easton, Litton etc 96-03; Dioc Voc Adv 96-99; Dir of Ords 99-03; TR Warwick *Cov* from 03. *St Mary's Vicarage, The Butts, Warwick CV34 4SS* T/F: (01926) 492909 E: vaughan.roberts@btinternet.com

ROBERTS, Preb Vincent Akintunde (Tunde). b 55. Kingston Poly BA(Econ) 81. S'wark Ord Course. **d** 91 **p** 92. Hon C Brixton Road Ch Ch *S'wark* 91-96; C Mitcham St Barn 96-99; P-in-c Stoke Newington St Olave *Lon* 99-03; V from 03; P-in-c Stoke Newington St Andr 06-12; P-in-c Upper Clapton St Matt 08-12; Preb St Paul's Cathl from 07. *St Olave's Vicarage, Woodberry Down, London N4 2TW* T/F: (020) 8800 1374 E: tunde.roberts@talk21.com

ROBERTS, Vivian Phillip. b 35. Univ of Wales BD 78. St D Coll Lamp 57. **d** 60 **p** 61. C Cwmaman *St D* 60-64; R Puncheston, Lt Newcastle and Castle Bythe 64-72; V Brynamman 72-77; V Brynaman w Cwmllynfell 77-83; V Pen-bre 83-00; rtd 00. *40 New Road, Llanelli SA15 3DR* T: (01554) 755506

ROBERTS, William James (Jim). b 55. Lon Bible Coll BA 77 Hughes Hall Cam PGCE 78. NEOC 92. **d** 94 **p** 95. NSM York St Mich-le-Belfrey from 94; Chapl Pocklington Sch from 06. *12 Bishop's Way, York YO10 5JG* T: (01904) 413479 E: roberts.jim@talk21.com

ROBERTS, Wynne. b 61. Univ of Wales (Ban) BTh 92. Ridley Hall Cam 85. **d** 87 **p** 88. Min Can Ban Cathl and C Ban Cathl 87-90; V Ynyscynhaearn w Penmorfa and Porthmadog 90-94; TV Bangor 94-04; Chapl NW Wales NHS Trust from 99. *North West Wales NHS Trust, Ysbyty Gwynedd, Penrhosgarnedd, Bangor LL57 2PW* T: (01248) 384384 F: 370629
E: wynne.roberts@nww-tr.wales.nhs.uk

ROBERTSHAW, Mrs Eleanor Elizabeth Mary. b 77. Univ of Wales (Ban) BA 98 MTh 00 Leeds Univ MA 10 PGCE 99. Yorks Min Course 08. **d** 10 **p** 11. C Stainforth *Sheff* 10-13; TR Gt Snaith from 13. *The Orchard, Pontefract Road, Snaith, Goole DN14 9JS* M: 07718-123138 T: (01405) 860866 E: eleanor.robertshaw@sheffield.anglican.org

ROBERTSHAW, Canon John Sean. b 66. York St Jo Coll BA 12. Cranmer Hall Dur 90. **d** 93 **p** 94. C Morley St Pet w Churwell *Wakef* 93-96; TV Upper Holme Valley 96-01; TR *Leeds* from 01; CF (TA) from 98; Hon Can Wakef Cathl from 11. *The Vicarage, Kirkroyds Lane, New Mill, Holmfirth HD9 1LS* T/F: (01484) 683375 M: 07980-289727
E: revsean@tiscali.co.uk

ROBERTSHAW, Jonothan Kempster Pickard Sykes. b 41. AKC 65. **d** 66 **p** 67. C Perranzabuloe *Truro* 66-69; Miss to Seamen 69-76; Hong Kong 69-72; Namibia 73-76; TV Probus, Ladock and Grampound w Creed and St Erme *Truro* 76-79; TV N Hill w Altarnon, Bolventor and Lewannick 79-80; P-in-c Lansallos 80-84; R 84-96; P-in-c Talland 80-84; V 84-96; V Madron 96-01; P-in-c Gulval 99-01; V Gulval and Madron 01; rtd 01; Hon C Penzance St Mary w St Paul and St Jo *Truro* 09-11; Hon Chapl R Cornwall Hosps Trust from 09; Hon Chapl Miss to Seafarers from 09. *38 Treassowe Road, Penzance TR18 2AU* T: (01736) 330612

ROBERTSON, Ms Beverley Ann. b 57. Qu Coll Birm 98. **d** 01 **p** 02. C Sutton Coldfield H Trin *Birm* 01-05; C Portsea N End St Mark *Portsm* 05-06; TV 06-10; P-in-c Bromsgrove All SS *Worc* 10-12; C Catshill and Dodford 10-12; TV Bromsgrove from 12. *20 Burcot Lane, Bromsgrove B60 1AE* T: (01527) 578297 E: bev_robertson@yahoo.com

ROBERTSON, Brian Ainsley. b 50. Warwick Univ BSc 72. St Jo Coll Nottm 94. **d** 94 **p** 95. C Leic Martyrs 94-97; C Oadby 97-98; TV 98-02; P-in-c Ashby-de-la-Zouch St Helen w Coleorton 02-05; P-in-c Breedon cum Isley Walton and Worthington 03-05; TR Ashby-de-la-Zouch and Breedon on the Hill 05-14; RD NW Leics 07-11; rtd 14; PtO *Leic* from 14. *84 Highway Road, Leicester LE5 5RF* T: 0116-319 5676 E: barobertson105@gmail.com

ROBERTSON, Charles Kevin. b 64. Virginia Poly & State Univ BA 85 Dur Univ PhD 99. Virginia Th Sem MDiv 93. **d** 93 **p** 94.

P-in-c USA 93-96; NSM Neville's Cross St Jo CD *Dur* 96-97; NSM Esh 97-99; R Milledgeville St Steph USA from 99. *Box 309, Milledgeville GA 31059-0309, USA* E: rector@ststephensga.org

ROBERTSON, Charles Peter. b 57. Aston Tr Scheme 92 Linc Th Coll 94. **d** 96 **p** 97. C Holbeach *Linc* 96-99; C S Lafford 01-03; P-in-c 03-13; P-in-c Bicker 13-14; P-in-c Donington 13-14; P-in-c Swineshead 13-14; P-in-c Sutterton and Wigtoft 13-14; V Haven Gp from 14. *The Rectory, Church Lane, Swineshead, Boston PE20 3JA* T: (01205) 820223

ROBERTSON, David John. b 54. Sheff Univ BA 76. Ridley Hall Cam 77. **d** 79 **p** 80. C Downend *Bris* 79-83; C Yate New Town 83-85; TV 85-87; TV High Wycombe *Ox* 87-97; RD Wycombe 91-97; P-in-c Haley Hill *Wakef* 97-99; V Ovenden 97-11; V S Ossett *Leeds* from 11. *South Ossett Vicarage, 36 Manor Road, Ossett WF5 0AU* T: (01924) 263311 E: rev.d.robertson@gmail.com

ROBERTSON, Douglas Laurence. b 52. St Edm Hall Ox MA 75. SEITE 04. **d** 07 **p** 08. C Roch St Margaret 07-11; V Pembury from 11. *The Vicarage, 4 Hastings Road, Pembury, Tunbridge Wells TN2 4PD* T: (01892) 824761 E: dlrobertson@btinternet.com

ROBERTSON, Mrs Elizabeth Mary. b 60. Cam Univ BA 82 MA 86 ACA 85 FCA 95. SEITE 03. **d** 06 **p** 07. NSM Fawkham and Hartley *Roch* 06-13; NSM Ash from 13; NSM Ridley from 13. *58 Redhill Wood, New Ash Green, Longfield DA3 8QP* T: (01474) 874144 E: robertem@supanet.com

ROBERTSON, Fiona Jane. *See* GREGSON, Fiona Jane Robertson

ROBERTSON, Iain Michael. b 67. Trin Coll Bris 03. **d** 05 **p** 06. C E Clevedon w Clapton in Gordano etc *B & W* 05-09; TV Salter Street and Shirley *Birm* 09-11; P-in-c Heanton Punchardon w Marwood *Ex* 11-15; R Heanton Punchardon, Marwood and W Down from 15. *The Rectory, Heanton, Barnstaple EX31 4DG* T: (01271) 817448 E: reviain@hotmail.co.uk

ROBERTSON, Canon James Alexander. b 46. Ox Univ MTh 99. Sarum & Wells Th Coll 72. **d** 75 **p** 76. C Monkseaton St Pet *Newc* 75-78; C Prudhoe 78-79; TV Brayton *York* 79-84; V Redcar 84-93; V Selby Abbey 93-96; V Monkseaton St Pet *Newc* 96-11; AD Tynemouth 98-09; V Whittingham and Edlingham w Bolton Chapel 11-15; AD Alnwick 11-15; Hon Can Newc Cathl 05-15; rtd 15. *4 Greenrigg Place, Shiremoor, Newcastle upon Tyne NE27 0GA* E: jim.a.robertson@blueyonder.co.uk

ROBERTSON, James Macaulay. b 51. St Jo Coll Dur BA 73. Oak Hill Th Coll. **d** 00 **p** 01. C Holdenhurst and Iford *Win* 00-04; V Marden *Cant* 04-11; R Holwell, Ickleford and Pirton *St Alb* from 11. *The Vicarage, Crabtree Lane, Pirton, Hitchin SG5 3QE* T: (01462) 712230 E: revjr@btinternet.com

ROBERTSON, Jane Lesley. *See* TRENHOLME, Jane Lesley

ROBERTSON, Canon John Charles. b 61. St Pet Coll Ox BA 81 Trin Coll Cam BA 89. Ridley Hall Cam 87. **d** 90 **p** 91. C Kenilworth St Jo *Cov* 90-94; Chapl York Univ 94-00; V Grove *Ox* 00-12; RD Wantage 09-12; Dir Ecum Miss from 12; Hon Can Ch Ch from 11. *Address temp unknown*

ROBERTSON (née PEGG), Mrs Josephine Anne. b 51. Lon Univ CertEd 72 Ch Ch Coll Cant BSc 91. **d** 02 **p** 03. OLM Folkestone H Trin w Ch Ch *Cant* 02-06; Chapl Dover Coll 02-05; C Sandgate St Paul w Folkestone St Geo *Cant* 05-06; C Folkestone Trin 06-10; C Wingham w Elmstone and Preston w Stourmouth 10-12; C Canonry 12-15; PtO from 15. *100 Surrenden Road, Folkestone CT19 4AQ* M: 07905-954504 T: (01303) 277330 E: Jo.robertson1@btinternet.com

ROBERTSON, Kathryn. b 58. Leeds Univ BA 05. NOC 02. **d** 05 **p** 06. C Dewsbury *Wakef* 05-08; TV *Leeds* from 08. *The Vicarage, 68 Staincliffe Road, Dewsbury WF13 4ED* T: (01924) 438302 E: kathycurate@drobertson99.wanadoo.co.uk

ROBERTSON, Mrs Linda Margaret. b 51. Somerville Coll Ox BA 71 MA 76 Aber Univ MSc 72. STETS 00. **d** 03 **p** 04. NSM Ampfield *Win* 03-08; NSM Totton from 08; TV from 10. *35 Winnington, Fareham PO15 6HP* T: (01329) 239857 E: revlindarob@yahoo.co.uk

ROBERTSON, Canon Paul Struan. b 45. St Jo Coll Dur BA 73 Newc Univ Aus BEdSt 79 MA 95. **d** 72 **p** 73. C Chester le Street *Dur* 72-73; C Hamilton Australia 73-77; C Cessnock 77-79; R Scone 79-88; V Collierley w Annfield Plain *Dur* 88-89; R New Lambton Australia 89-10; AD Newc W 96-10; Lect St Jo Coll Morpeth 97-06; Can Newc Cathl 01-10; rtd 10. *40 Cromwell Street, New Lambton NSW 2305, Australia* T: (0061) (2) 4957 2795 E: paulstruanrobertson@gmail.com

ROBERTSON, Philip Stuart. b 55. Newc Univ BA 77 BArch 80. Oak Hill Th Coll BA 07. **d** 07 **p** 08. C Woking St Jo *Guildf* 07-11; V Wolverhampton St Jude *Lich* from 11; P-in-c Wolverhampton St Andr from 15. *St Jude's Vicarage, St Jude's Road, Wolverhampton WV6 0EB* T: (01902) 827214 E: philipsrobertson@virginmedia.com

ROBERTSON (née OWEN), Sally Ann. b 68. New Hall Cam BA 89. Ox Min Course 07. **d** 10 **p** 11. NSM Purley *Ox* 10-13; NSM Haydon Wick *Bris* from 13. *139 Thames Avenue, Swindon SN25 1PT* T: (01793) 724219 E: sally.robertson27@btinternet.com

ROBERTSON, Canon Scott. b 64. Edin Univ BD 90 Open Univ MA 02 Glas Univ PhD 08. Edin Th Coll 86. **d** 90 **p** 91. C Glas Gd Shep and Ascension 90-92; P-in-c 92-97; P-in-c Ardrossan 97-10; P-in-c Dalry 97-10; P-in-c Irvine St Andr LEP 97-10; R Glas St Marg from 10; Can St Mary's Cathl from 12. *The Rectory, 22 Monreith Road, Glasgow G43 2NY* T: 0141-632 3292 *or* 636 1131 E: revscottrobertson@btinternet.com

ROBERTSON, Mrs Sheila Jean. b 40. **d** 99 **p** 01. OLM Chase *Sarum* 99-09; rtd 09. *Church Mead, Harley Lane, Gussage All Saints, Wimborne BH21 5HD* T: (01258) 840182 E: ross@churchmead.wanadoo.co.uk

ROBERTSON, Stephen Andrew. b 60. Strathclyde Univ BSc 82. Trin Coll Bris 90. **d** 92 **p** 93. C Vange *Chelmsf* 92-96; R Creeksea w Althorne, Latchingdon and N Fambridge 96-06; R Downham w S Hanningfield 06-11; V Downham w S Hanningfield and Ramsden Bellhouse from 11. *The Rectory, Castledon Road, Downham, Billericay CM11 2LD* T: (01268) 710370 E: stephen.robertson15@btinternet.com

ROBERTSON, Stuart Lang. b 40. Glas Univ MA 63 Edin Univ MTh 97. St Jo Coll Nottm 72. **d** 75 **p** 76. C Litherland St Jo and St Jas *Liv* 75-78; C Edin St Thos 78-81; Chapl Edin Univ and C Edin St Pet 81-83; R Edin St Jas 83-91; Miss to Seamen 83-91; Crosslinks 91-05; Hon Chapl St Petersburg *Eur* 93-98; Chapl Warsaw 98-04; Asst Chapl Barcelona 04-05; rtd 05. *3 Pentland Villas, Juniper Green EH14 5EQ* T: 0131-453 4755 E: stur067@yahoo.co.uk

ROBERTSON, William Robert Wilson. b 48. Glas Univ MA 71 MPhil 74 Strathclyde Univ PGCE 72. TISEC 03. **d** 05 **p** 06. C Edin St Mich and All SS 05-08; Chapl Dioc Boys' Sch Kowloon Hong Kong from 08. *Diocesan Boys' School, 131 Argyle Street, Mongkok, Kowloon, Hong Kong, China* T: (00852) 2711 5191 *or* 2711 5192 E: bill.robertson1@tiscali.co.uk

ROBILLIARD (née DE GARIS), Mrs Juliette Elizabeth Charmaine. b 58. STETS 11. **d** 13 **p** 14. NSM Guernsey Ste Marie du Castel *Win* from 13; NSM Guernsey St Matt from 13. *Le Petit Gree, Torteval, Guernsey GY8 0RD* T: (01481) 264344 E: filiola@cwgsy.net

ROBINS, Christopher Charles. b 41. St Mich Coll Llan 66. **d** 68 **p** 69. C Bideford *Ex* 68-71; C Dawlish 71-74; V Laira 74-81; P-in-c Dodbrooke 81-83; P-in-c Churchstow w Kingsbridge 81-83; R Kingsbridge and Dodbrooke 83-06; rtd 07. *26 Brownings Walk, Ogwell, Newton Abbot TQ12 6YR* T: (01626) 331366

ROBINS, Canon Douglas Geoffrey. b 45. Open Univ BA 90. Ex & Truro NSM Scheme. **d** 81 **p** 83. NSM Kenwyn *Truro* 81-84; Public Preacher 84-00; NSM Truro St Paul and St Clem 00-04; P-in-c Gerrans w St Anthony-in-Roseland and Philleigh 04-08; P-in-c Veryan w Ruan Lanihorne from 08; Hon Can Truro Cathl from 09. *The Vicarage, Veryan, Truro TR2 5QA* T: (01872) 501618 E: fatherdougrobins@talktalk.net

ROBINS, Ian Donald Hall. b 28. K Coll Lon BD 51 AKC 51 Lanc Univ MA 74. **d** 52 **p** 53. C Heyhouses on Sea *Blackb* 52-55; C Clitheroe St Mary 55-57; V Trawden 57-67; Hd of RE St Chris C of E Sch Accrington 67-76; P-in-c Hugill *Carl* 76-82; Asst Advr for Educn 76-82; Chapl St Martin's Coll of Educn *Blackb* 82-86; V St Annes St Marg 86-91; rtd 91; PtO *Blackb* from 91; *Leeds* from 05. *33 Manorfields, Whalley, Clitheroe BB7 9UD* T: (01254) 824930

ROBINS, Mrs Mary Katherine. b 34. FRGS Bris Univ BSc 55 CertEd 56. St Alb Minl Tr Scheme. **dss** 84 **d** 87 **p** 94. N Mymms *St Alb* 84-92; Hon Par Dn 87-92; NSM Northaw 92-95; Hon C Westmr St Jas *Lon* 95-00; PtO *St Alb* from 95. *15 Bluebridge Road, Brookmans Park, Hatfield AL9 7UW* T: (01707) 656670 E: maryrob@eclipse.co.uk

ROBINS, Terrence Leslie. b 38. CEng 67 FIMechE 78. NOC 99. **d** 00 **p** 01. Bp's Advr for Elderly People in Res Care *Wakef* 98-01; Hon C Cumberworth, Denby and Denby Dale 00-03; P-in-c 03-08; rtd 08; PtO *Leeds* from 08. *Cruck Cottage, Cumberworth Lane, Denby Dale, Huddersfield HD8 8RU* T/F: (01484) 866000 E: robinslt@aol.com

ROBINS, Canon Wendy Sheridan. b 56. Lanc Univ BA 77. EAMTC 93. **d** 93 **p** 94. Dir Communications and Resources *S'wark* from 92; NSM Walthamstow St Pet *Chelmsf* 93-02; Hon C S'wark Cathl from 02; Hon Can S'wark Cathl from 08. *17 Hillcrest Road, London E17 4AP, or Trinity House, 4 Chapel Court, Borough High Street, London SE1 1HW* T: (020) 8523 0016 *or* 7403 8686 F: 7403 4770 E: wendy.s.robins@southwark.anglican.org

ROBINSON, Alan Booker. b 27. Keble Coll Ox BA 51 MA 56. Sarum Th Coll 51. **d** 53 **p** 54. C Leeds All So *Ripon* 53-56; C Ilkley St Marg *Bradf* 57-59; V Carlton *Wakef* 59-66; OCM

66-92; V Hooe *Ex* 66-95; RD Plympton 81-83; RD Plymouth Sutton 86-91; rtd 95; PtO *Leeds* from 95. *31 Dunmail Manor, Dunmail Avenue, Cults, Aberdeen AB15 9LW*
E: robalb@ntlworld.com

ROBINSON, Alison Jane. b 55. WEMTC 99. **d** 02 **p** 03. C Bishop's Cleeve *Glouc* 02-06; P-in-c Meysey Hampton w Marston Meysey and Castle Eaton 06-08; TV Fairford Deanery 09-10; rtd 10. *19 Marsh Drive, Cheltenham GL51 9LN*
T: (01242) 698759 M: 07773-721238
E: alicesonrobinson@virginmedia.com

ROBINSON, Andrew David. b 61. St Cath Coll Ox BA 84 MA 01 RMN 89. Trin Coll Bris 97. **d** 02 **p** 08. C Southmead *Bris* 02-03; C Kington St Michael and Chippenham St Paul w Hardenhuish etc 03-04; NSM Barlby and Riccall *York* 05-10; P-in-c Ledsham w Fairburn from 10. *The Vicarage, 11 Main Street, Ledston, Castleford WF10 2AA* T: (01977) 553591
M: 07896-506321 E: andrewrobinson9@hotmail.com

ROBINSON, Canon Andrew Nesbitt. b 43. AKC 67. **d** 68 **p** 69. C Balsall Heath St Paul *Birm* 68-71; C Westmr St Steph w St Jo *Lon* 71-75; Chapl Sussex Univ *Chich* 75-12; Chapl Brighton Poly 75-92; Chapl Brighton Univ 92-93; P-in-c Stanmer w Falmer 80-12; Can and Preb Chich Cathl 98-12; rtd 12. *Appleberry Cottage, Newhaven Road, Kingston, Lewes BN7 3NE*
T: (01273) 755797 E: goretti_uk@yahoo.co.uk

ROBINSON, Andrew Stephen. b 49. Lanc Univ BA 71 Worc Coll of Educn PGCE 72. St Mich Coll Llan 90. **d** 95 **p** 96. NSM Llangattock and Llangynidr *S & B* 95-04; P-in-c Llanfeugan w Llanthetty etc 04-14; P-in-c Llanfrynach and Cantref w Llanhamlach 13-14; rtd 14; PtO *S & B* from 14. *The Hollies, Station Road, Talybont-on-Usk, Brecon LD3 7JE*
T: (01874) 676584

✠**ROBINSON, The Rt Revd Anthony William.** b 56. CertEd. Sarum & Wells Th Coll. **d** 82 **p** 83 **c** 02. C Tottenham St Paul *Lon* 82-85; TV Leic Resurr 85-89; TR 89-97; RD Christianity N 92-97; P-in-c Belgrave St Pet 94-99; Hon Can Leic Cathl 94-97; Adn Pontefract *Wakef* 97-03; Suff Bp Pontefract 02-15 and from 14; Can Res Wakef Cathl 05-13. *Pontefract House, 181A Manygates Lane, Sandal, Wakefield WF2 7DR* T: (01924) 250781 E: bishop.tony@westyorkshiredales.anglican.org

ROBINSON, Arthur Robert Basil. b 32. ACP 67 St Jo Coll Dur BA 56 Bradf Univ MA 84. Wycliffe Hall Ox 56. **d** 58 **p** 59. C Pemberton St Mark Newtown *Liv* 58-62; CF 62-65; Asst Master Colne Valley High Sch Linthwaite 65-69; Asst Chapl HM Pris Man 69; Chapl HM Borstal Roch 69-74; Peru 74-77; V Golcar *Wakef* 77-83; Admin Sheff Fam Conciliation Service 84-91; Warden St Sampson's Cen York 91-00; rtd 00. *Morangie, 2A Brecksfield, Skelton, York YO30 1YD*
T: (01904) 470558

ROBINSON, Arthur William. b 35. Dur Univ BSc 60. Clifton Th Coll 60. **d** 62 **p** 63. C Ox St Clem 62-65; Chile 65-77; V Hoxton St Jo w Ch Ch *Lon* 78-88; TV Gateacre *Liv* 88-00; rtd 00; PtO *Liv* from 00. *86 Kingsthorne Park, Liverpool L25 0QS* T: 0151-486 2588 E: arthelrob@aol.com

ROBINSON, Brian John Watson. b 33. St Cath Coll Cam BA 56 MA 60. Westcott Ho Cam 57. **d** 58 **p** 59. C Whitworth w Spennymoor *Dur* 58-62; India 62-66; P-in-c Preston St Steph *Blackb* 66-70; P-in-c Preston St Jo 70-72; V Ashton-on-Ribble St Andr 72-79; LtO 79-82; V Preston St Jude w St Paul 82-97; Chapl N Tyneside Health Care NHS Trust 94-97; rtd 97; PtO *Blackb* from 97. *50 Greenacres, Fulwood, Preston PR2 7DB*
T: (01772) 861516 E: jandjrobbo@hotmail.co.uk

ROBINSON, Mrs Christine. b 50. Nottm Univ BA 71. EAMTC 01. **d** 04 **p** 05. NSM Prittlewell St Pet w Westcliff St Cedd *Chelmsf* 04-13; NSM Hadleigh St Jas from 13; NSM Hadleigh St Barn from 13. *Pasadena, St John's Road, Benfleet SS7 2PT* T: (01702) 557000 E: crrob75@aol.com

ROBINSON (née KILCOOLEY), Mrs Christine Margaret Anne. b 59. K Coll Lon BA 05. SEITE 06. **d** 07 **p** 08. C Notting Hill St Pet *Lon* 07-10; V Belmont from 10. *St Anselm's Vicarage, Ventnor Avenue, Stanmore HA7 2HU* T: (020) 8907 3186
E: xtinerob@googlemail.com

ROBINSON, Christopher Gordon. b 49. Ridley Hall Cam. **d** 82 **p** 83. C Stanton *St E* 82-85; C Lawshall 85-86; P-in-c Lawshall w Shimplingthorne and Alpheton 86-89; TV Oakdale *Sarum* 89-99; V Easton H Trin w St Gabr and St Lawr and St Jude *Bris* 99-05; C S Molton w Nymet St George, High Bray etc *Ex* 05-14; C Shirwell, Loxhore, Kentisbury, Arlington, etc 12-14; rtd 14. *22 John Street, Bargoed CF81 8PG*

ROBINSON, Christopher James. b 52. St Pet Coll Birm CertEd 74. OLM course 97. **d** 99 **p** 00. OLM Wilnecote *Lich* from 99. *55 Sycamore, Wilnecote, Tamworth B77 5HB*
T: (01827) 282331 E: chrisrobinson55@hotmail.co.uk

ROBINSON, Christopher Mark Scott. b 83. Warwick Univ BSc 04. Ridley Hall Cam 06. **d** 09 **p** 10. C S Hartismere *St E* 09-12; R Rattlesden w Thorpe Morieux, Brettenham etc from 12. *The Rectory, High Street, Rattlesden, Bury St Edmunds IP30 0RA* M: 07789-772024 E: tifferrobinson@gmail.com

ROBINSON, Daffyd Charles. b 48. Qu Coll Birm 77. **d** 80 **p** 85. C Abington *Pet* 80-82; C Immingham *Linc* 85-90; R Willoughby 90-13; rtd 13. *57 Weelsby Avenue, Grimsby DN32 0AU* T: (01472) 753862

ROBINSON, Mrs Danielle Georgette Odette. b 47. SEITE 98. **d** 01 **p** 02. NSM Reigate St Mary *S'wark* from 01; Chapl Surrey and Sussex Healthcare NHS Trust from 01; PtO *Chich* from 01. *1 Chandler Way, Dorking RH5 4GA*
T: (01306) 883947 *or* (01293) 600300 ext 3141
E: daniellerobinson@uwclub.net *or*
danielle.robinson@sash.nhs.uk

ROBINSON, David. *See* ROBINSON, Roy David

ROBINSON, David. b 42. Sarum & Wells Th Coll. **d** 82 **p** 83. C Billingham St Cuth *Dur* 82-86; V Longwood *Wakef* 86-94; C Athersley 94-97; P-in-c Brotherton 97-02; rtd 02; PtO *York* from 03. *5 High Street, Stanhope, Bishop Auckland DL13 2UP*

ROBINSON, Canon David Hugh. b 47. Linc Th Coll 76. **d** 79 **p** 80. C Bulkington *Cov* 79-82; C Whitley 82-87; Chapl Whitley, Gulson & Cov and Warks Hosp 82-87; Chapl Walsgrave Hosp Cov 87-97; Hon Can Cov Cathl 92-98; Succ 00-05; PtO *Cov* 97-00 and 05-07; P-in-c Cov St Mary 07-10; rtd 10; PtO *Ex* from 11. *23A Crockwells Road, Exminster, Exeter EX6 8DH* M: 07947-023888 T: (01392) 833135
E: drx2robinson@talktalk.net

ROBINSON, David Mark. b 55. Univ Coll Dur BSc 76 Leic Univ MA 80 CQSW 80. Cranmer Hall Dur 86. **d** 88 **p** 89. C Shipley St Pet *Bradf* 88-92; P-in-c Ingrow w Hainworth 92-97; V Bramhope *Ripon* 97-05; V Chapel Allerton *Leeds* from 05. *The Vicarage, Wood Lane, Chapel Allerton, Leeds LS7 3QF*
T: 0113-268 3072

ROBINSON, David Michael Wood. *See* WOOD-ROBINSON, David Michael

ROBINSON, Deborah Veronica. b 73. St Andr Univ MTheol 95 Hull Univ MA 97. NEOC 05. **d** 08 **p** 09. NSM Darlington St Hilda and St Columba *Dur* 08-13; NSM Coniscliffe from 13. *14 Yoredale Avenue, Darlington DL3 9AN* T: (01325) 265434
M: 07971-549439 E: deborah.robinson5@ntlworld.com

ROBINSON, Denis Hugh. b 53. SS Mark & Jo Univ Coll Plymouth CertEd 75. S Dios Minl Tr Scheme 88. **d** 91 **p** 92. NSM Bisley and W End *Guildf* from 91; Hd RS Gordon's Sch Woking 80-12; Asst Chapl 91-94; Chapl from 94. *2A Queen's Road, Bisley, Woking GU24 9AN* T: (01483) 522006 *or* (01276) 858084 E: steviedenrob@aol.com *or* drobinson@gordons.surrey.sch.uk

ROBINSON, Dennis Winston. b 42. QUB BScEng 68. CITC. **d** 88 **p** 89. NSM Mullavilly *Arm* 88-92; NSM Arm St Mark 92-95; C Portadown St Mark 95-98; I Aghavea *Clogh* 98-10; Preb Clogh Cathl 06-10; rtd 10. *Oakridge, 31 Snowhill Road, Beagho, Lisbellaw, Enniskillen BT94 5FY* T: (028) 6638 5858
E: dw.robinson@btopenworld.com

ROBINSON, Derek Charles. b 43. S'wark Ord Course 91. **d** 94 **p** 95. NSM Abbey Wood *S'wark* 94-13; PtO from 13. *19 Silverdale Road, Bexleyheath DA7 5AB* T: (01322) 523870

ROBINSON, Dorothy Ann. b 50. Cranmer Hall Dur 05. **d** 07 **p** 08. NSM Tynemouth Priory *Newc* from 07. *57 Millview Drive, North Shields NE30 2QD* T/F: 0191-257 0980
E: dottirobinson@hotmail.com

ROBINSON, Douglas. b 48. Nottm Univ BEd 70 Lon Univ BD 74 Union Th Sem Virginia MA 75. **d** 75 **p** 76. C Southport Ch Ch *Liv* 75-78; V Clubmoor 78-85; Chapl Epsom Coll 85-88; Chapl Dauntsey's Sch Devizes 89-95; PtO *Eur* from 95. *Im Grünen Weg 1, Hangen Wiesheim 55234, Germany* T: (0049) (6375) 941575 E: reverendrobinson@t-online.de

ROBINSON, Elizabeth Carole Lesley. b 67. CITC 99. **d** 02 **p** 03. Aux Min Clonfert Gp *L & K* 02-06; Aux Min Roscrea w Kyle, Bourney and Corbally 06-11; Dioc C 11-13; I Dublin Clontarf *D & G* from 13. *The Rectory, 15 Seafield Road West, Clontarf, Dublin 3, Republic of Ireland* M: 87-909 1561 T: (00353) (1) 833 1181 E: clontarf@dublin.anglican.org

ROBINSON, Eric Charles. b 47. Lon Univ BD 71 Lanc Univ MA 97. CBDTI 94. **d** 97 **p** 98. NSM Carl St Cuth w St Mary 97-99; C Kendal H Trin 99-01; P-in-c Arthuret 01-07; P-in-c Nicholforest and Kirkandrews on Esk 01-07; R Arthuret w Kirkandrews-on-Esk and Nicholforest 07-08; P-in-c Kendal H Trin 08-10; rtd 10; PtO *Carl* 10-13; C York H Trin Micklegate from 14. *3 Palmer Street, York YO1 7NF*

ROBINSON, Frank. *See* ROBINSON, John Francis Napier

ROBINSON, Gareth James. b 74. Sheff Univ BA 95 Sheff Hallam Univ PGCE 96. St Mellitus Coll 13. **d** 13 **p** 14. C Marple All SS *Ches* from 13. *57 Marple Road, Stockport SK2 5EL*
M: 07825-413430 E: gareth@glochurch.org

ROBINSON, George. b 27. Oak Hill Th Coll 59. **d** 61 **p** 62. C Branksome St Clem *Sarum* 61-64; Australia from 64; rtd 80. *24 Abingdon Road, Roseville NSW 2069, Australia*
T: (0061) (2) 9416 4330 F: 9416 9936
E: mandgrobinson@ozemail.com.au

ROBINSON, Mrs Hazel. b 61. RGN 83 RSCN 83. St Jo Coll Nottm 02. **d** 04 **p** 05. C Toton *S'well* 04-09; P-in-c Blidworth w Rainworth 09-11; V from 11. *The Vicarage, 27 St Peter's Drive, Rainworth, Mansfield NG21 0BE* T: (01623) 475135 E: haze.rob@btopenworld.com

ROBINSON, Canon Ian. b 57. Nottm Univ BTh 87 MA 97. Linc Th Coll 84. **d** 87 **p** 88. C Bottesford w Ashby *Linc* 87-90; TV 90-95; P-in-c Caistor w Clixby 95-00; P-in-c Grasby 95-00; P-in-c Searby w Owmby 95-00; V Caistor Gp from 00; RD W Wold from 01; Can and Preb Linc Cathl from 07. *3 Spa Top, Caistor, Market Rasen LN7 6RB* T: (01472) 851339 E: revianrobinson@tiscali.co.uk

ROBINSON, Ian Christopher. b 63. Hull Univ BSc 84 Leeds Univ MA 10 ACMA. Yorks Min Course 07. **d** 10 **p** 11. C New Malton *York* 10-13. *6 Pinfold Garth, Malton YO17 7XQ* T: (01653) 696566 M: 07538-239068 E: curate@stmichaelsmalton.org.uk

ROBINSON, Ian Morgan. b 53. Lanc Univ BA 08 CEng 86 MCIBSE 86. CBDTI 05. **d** 08 **p** 09. NSM Askrigg w Stallingbusk *Ripon* 08-12; NSM Hawes and Hardraw 09-12; R Bedale and Leeming and Thornton Watlass *Leeds* from 12. *The Rectory, North End, Bedale DL8 1AF* T: (01677) 422103 M: 07801-657988 E: revrobbo@btinternet.com

ROBINSON, James Edward. b 85. Univ of Wales (Swansea) BA 09 Linc Coll Ox MSt 10 St Jo Coll Cam BA 14. Westcott Ho Cam 12. **d** 15. C Grantham *Linc* from 15. *St John's Rectory, Station Road East, Grantham NG31 6HX* E: jrobinson@stwulframs.com

ROBINSON, Mrs Jane Hippisley. b 41. Somerville Coll Ox MA 66 K Coll Lon PGCE. S Dios Minl Tr Scheme 88. **d** 91. NSM Ealing St Pet Mt Park *Lon* 91-96; NSM N Acton St Gabr 96-00; PtO from 00. *40 Brentham Way, London W5 1BE* T: (020) 8991 0206

ROBINSON, Mrs Janet. b 34. Milton Keynes Coll of Ed CertEd 77 Open Univ BA 78. WMMTC 89. **d** 92 **p** 94. NSM Roade and Ashton w Hartwell *Pet* 92-94; NSM Potterspury, Furtho, Yardley Gobion and Cosgrove 94-99; rtd 99; PtO *Pet* 99-14. *73 Eastfield Crescent, Yardley Gobion, Towcester NN12 7TT* T: (01908) 542331 E: revjandrewrobinson@btinternet.com

ROBINSON, Jean. See CLARK, Jean Robinson

ROBINSON, Mrs Jean Anne. b 50. Lon Univ BPharm 72 MRPharmS 73 Southn Univ BTh 98. STETS 95. **d** 98 **p** 99. NSM Frimley *Guildf* 98-03; NSM Worplesdon 03-05; NSM Egham Hythe 05-07; C Woodham 07-14; Chapl Surrey and Borders Partnership NHS Trust 05-14; Chapl Alpha Hosp Woking 05-14; NSM E Clevedon w Clapton in Gordano etc *B & W* from 14. *5 Chestnut Grove, Clevedon BS21 7LA* T: (01275) 791807 E: revjar95@yahoo.co.uk

ROBINSON, Jennifer Elizabeth. See BAKER, Jennifer Elizabeth

ROBINSON, Joan. b 62. **d** 13 **p** 14. NSM Blaydon and Swalwell *Dur* from 13. *9 Rose Avenue, Whickham, Newcastle upon Tyne NE16 4NA* T: 0191-420 1572 E: jrdallas@hotmail.co.uk

ROBINSON, John Francis Napier (Frank). b 42. St Edm Hall Ox BA 64 MA 68. Clifton Th Coll 65. **d** 68 **p** 69. C Southport Ch Ch *Liv* 68-71; C Coleraine *Conn* 71-74; Deputation Sec (Ireland) BCMS 74-76; TV Marfleet *York* 76-81; V Yeadon St Jo *Bradf* 81-95; P-in-c Rounds Green *Birm* 95-00; V 00-02; rtd 02; PtO *S'well* from 03; *Derby* from 03. *61 Clumber Avenue, Beeston, Nottingham NG9 4BH* T: 0115-922 1704

ROBINSON, The Very Revd John Kenneth. b 36. K Coll Lon BD 61 AKC 61. **d** 62 **p** 63. C Poulton-le-Fylde *Blackb* 62-65; C Lancaster St Mary 65-66; Chapl HM Pris Lanc 65-66; Chapl St Jo Sch Singapore 66-68; V Colne H Trin *Blackb* 68-71; Dir Educn Windward Is 71-74; V Skerton St Luke *Blackb* 74-81; Area Sec (E Anglia) USPG 81-91; Hon Min Can St E Cathl 82-91; Chapl Gtr Lisbon *Eur* 91-00; Adn Gib 94-02; Can Gib Cathl 94-00; Dean Gib 00-03; rtd 03; PtO *Blackb* from 03. *9 Poplar Drive, Coppull, Chorley PR7 4LS* T: (01257) 470042

ROBINSON, John Leonard William. b 23. Lon Univ BA 50. Bps' Coll Cheshunt 50. **d** 52 **p** 53. C Victoria Docks Ascension *Chelmsf* 52-55; C Kilburn St Aug *Lon* 55-63; C Westmr St Jas 63-81; V Compton, the Mardens, Stoughton and Racton *Chich* 81-93; V Stansted 85-93; rtd 93; PtO *St Alb* 93-15; Lon 96-13. *19 Greenhill Park, Barnet EN5 1HQ* T: (020) 8449 3984

ROBINSON, Jonathan William Murrell. b 42. Univ of Wales (Lamp) MA 01. Sarum Th Coll 65. **d** 68 **p** 69. C Tooting All SS *S'wark* 68-71; C Bourne *Guildf* 71-76; Dir Grail Trust from 76; Dir Grail Trust Chr Community Cen Burtle *B & W* 78-82; Hon C Willesden Green St Gabr *Lon* 82-87; V Stoke St Gregory w Burrowbridge and Lyng *B & W* 82-90; Dir Grail Retreat Cen from 90; NSM Aymestrey and Leinthall Earles w Wigmore etc *Heref* 92-96; rtd 01; PtO *Heref* from 01; *St D* 05-07. *The Liberty, Poole Road, Arthurs Gate, Montgomery SY15 6QU* T: (01686) 668502

ROBINSON, Katharine Mary. See McATEER, Katharine Mary

ROBINSON, Kathryn Elizabeth. b 55. Hull Univ BA 76 K Coll Lon MSc 86 St Hilda's Coll Ox PGCE 77. NTMTC 03. **d** 05 **p** 06. NSM Leytonstone St Jo *Chelmsf* 05-12; PtO from 12. *54 Corbett Road, London E17 3JZ* T: (020) 8520 3771 E: kthrynrbnsn@aol.com

ROBINSON, Kenneth. See ROBINSON, John Kenneth

ROBINSON, Kenneth Borwell. b 37. Lon Univ BA 62. Ridley Hall Cam 68. **d** 70 **p** 71. C Walthamstow St Jo *Chelmsf* 70-74; P-in-c Becontree St Alb 74-78; P-in-c Heybridge w Langford 78-84; TV Horley *S'wark* 84-98; C Oxted and Tandridge 98-02; rtd 02; PtO *Portsm* from 03. *49 Osborne Road, East Cowes PO32 6RZ* T: (01983) 295736

ROBINSON, Kevan John. b 63. Chich Univ BA 09. SEITE 08. **d** 10 **p** 11. NSM Southbourne w W Thorney *Chich* 10-14; P-in-c E Dean, Singleton, and W Dean from 14; Chapl Chich Coll from 14. *The Rectory, Singleton, Chichester PO18 0EZ* T: (01243) 811213 M: 07757-122446 E: k.robinson275@btinternet.com

ROBINSON, Lesley. See ROBINSON, Elizabeth Carole Lesley

ROBINSON, Leslie. b 31. St Aid Birkenhead 56. **d** 59 **p** 60. C Hugglescote w Donington *Leic* 59-61; C Greenside *Dur* 61-63; C-in-c New Cantley CD *Sheff* 63-66; V Choral Heref Cathl 66-67; R Easton-on-the-Hill *Pet* 67-69; Hon Min Can Pet Cathl 68-69; C Weston-super-Mare St Jo *B & W* 69-70; V Winkleigh *Ex* 70-72; V Thorpe Acre w Dishley *Leic* 72-78; V Cloughton *York* 78-79; V Hedon w Paull 79-81; V Bywell *Newc* 81-86; V Wymeswold and Prestwold w Hoton *Leic* 86-97; rtd 97; PtO *Leic* 97-98. *16 Victoria Road, Oundle, Peterborough PE8 4AY* T: (01832) 275048

ROBINSON, Linda Ann. b 53. **d** 12 **p** 13. NSM Newington w Hull St Andr *York* from 12. *162 Meadowbank Road, Hull HU3 6XP* T: (01482) 352704 E: robinson.linda28@yahoo.co.uk

ROBINSON, Linda Anne. b 54. Westf Coll Lon BA 75 Man Univ MEd 05 Ches Univ DProf 15. Yorks Min Course. **d** 14 **p** 15. NSM Bedale and Leeming and Thornton Watlass *Leeds* from 14. *The Rectory, North End, Bedale DL8 1AF* T: (01677) 422889 M: 07736-771216 E: lindarobinson@talk21.com

ROBINSON, Miss Margaret. b 32. S'wark Ord Course 83. **dss** 86 **d** 87 **p** 94. Finsbury St Clem w St Barn and St Matt *Lon* 86-87; Par Dn St Giles Cripplegate w St Bart Moor Lane etc 87-94; C 94-95; rtd 95; PtO *Win* 95-00; *Portsm* from 00; Hon Chapl Win Cathl 98-00. *32 Madeline Road, Petersfield GU31 4AL* T: (01730) 268056

ROBINSON, Margaret Ann. b 50. **d** 10 **p** 11. NSM Erdington Ch the K *Birm* 10-14; PtO from 14; Hon Chapl Birm Children's Hosp NHS Trust from 13. *3 Hepburn Edge, Birmingham B24 9JW* T: 0121-439 7617 M: 07710-771979 E: m.robinson1010@googlemail.com

ROBINSON, Matthew Jamie. b 72. St Steph Ho Ox 13. **d** 15. C Sevenoaks St Jo *Roch* from 15. *14 Quakers' Hall Lane, Sevenoaks TN13 3TR* E: m.jrobinson@icloud.com

ROBINSON, Monica Dorothy. b 40. SAOMC 99. **d** 01 **p** 02. NSM Bedford St Andr *St Alb* 01-10. *Shoyswell, Radwell Road, Milton Ernest, Bedford MK44 1RY* T: (01234) 824366 E: mdrobinson@btopenworld.com

ROBINSON, Mrs Norma Georgina. b 57. Edge Hill Coll of HE BEd 78 RGN 03. SNWTP 10. **d** 12 **p** 13. NSM Hyde St Geo *Ches* 12-14; NSM Macclesfield St Jo w Henbury from 14. *St John's Vicarage, 25 Wilwick Lane, Macclesfield SK11 8RS* T: (01625) 424185 E: normarobins@aol.com

ROBINSON, Norman Leslie. b 50. Liv Univ BSc 71. Lon Bible Coll BA 78 Wycliffe Hall Ox 78. **d** 80 **p** 81. C Bebington *Ches* 80-83; C St Helens St Helen *Liv* 83-90; P-in-c Westward, Rosley-w-Woodside and Welton *Carl* from 90; P-in-c Thursby 98-10; P-in-c Caldbeck, Castle Sowerby and Sebergham from 10. *The Vicarage, Rosley, Wigton CA7 8AU* T: (016973) 43723 E: normalrevs@aol.com

ROBINSON, Oliver Patrick Kilcooley. b 88. Heythrop Coll Lon BA 10 MA 11. Wycliffe Hall Ox MTh 15. **d** 15. C Cricklewood St Gabr and St Mich *Lon* from 15. *31 Olive Road, London NW2 6TY* M: 07904-531036 E: opk.robinson@gmail.com

ROBINSON, Paul Andrew. b 68. Hull Univ MBA 09. **d** 09 **p** 10. OLM Royton St Anne *Man* 09-12; NSM Medlock Head from 12. *19 Dorchester Drive, Royton, Oldham OL2 5AU* T: 0161-628 9019 M: 07984-938393 E: paul@nomoreproblems.co.uk

ROBINSON, Paul Leslie. b 65. St Steph Ho Ox 95. **d** 97 **p** 98. C Upholland *Liv* 97-01; V Lydiate and Downholland 01-08; P-in-c Halsall 04-08; R Halsall, Lydiate and Downholland from 08. *The Vicarage, Church Lane, Lydiate, Liverpool L31 4HL* T: 0151-526 0512 E: frpaul.robinson@btopenworld.com

ROBINSON, Canon Paul Leslie. b 46. Dur Univ MA 67. Linc Th Coll 71. **d** 74 **p** 75. C Poynton *Ches* 74-76; C Prenton 76-78; V Seacombe 78-88; V Stalybridge St Paul 88-00; P-in-c Wallasey St Hilary 00-04; R 04-10; Urban Min Officer 96-00;

Hon Can Ches Cathl 98-10; P-in-c E and W Tilbury and Linford *Chelmsf* from 10. *37 Clyde Crescent, Rayleigh SS6 7SX* T: (01268) 963911 E: paul@canonrobinson.plus.com

ROBINSON, Paula Patricia. b 50. Man Univ MEd 83 TCD BTh 94. **d** 94 **p** 95. C Killala w Dunfeeny, Crossmolina, Kilmoremoy etc *T, K & A* 94-97; I Crosspatrick Gp *C & O* 97-00; R Leonardtown St Andr USA 00-09; P-in-c Tockwith and Bilton w Bickerton *York* 09-11; P-in-c Rufforth w Moor Monkton and Hessay 09-11; P-in-c Healaugh w Wighill, Bilbrough and Askham Richard 09-11; P-in-c Long Marston 09-11; PtO *Man* from 12. *Lea Court, 45 Heaton Moor Road, Stockport SK4 4PZ* E: revpaula@supanet.com

ROBINSON, Peter Charles. b 53. Open Univ BA 83. Oak Hill Th Coll 85. **d** 87 **p** 88. C Nottingham St Ann w Em *S'well* 87-89; C Worksop St Anne 89-92; V S Ramsey St Paul *S & M* 92-99; Can St German's Cathl 98-99; P-in-c Goostrey and Dioc Dir of Ords *Ches* 99-03; P-in-c Aldeburgh w Hazlewood *St E* 03-04; C Arbory *S & M* 05-06; V 06-13; C Santan 05-06; V 06-13; C Castletown 05-06; V 06-13; RD Castletown and Peel 08-12; Hon Can St German's Cathl 09-12; Can and Bp's Chapl 12-13; V Malton and Old Malton *York* from 13. *The Vicarage, 17 The Mount, Malton YO17 7ND*

ROBINSON, Peter Edward Barron. b 40. Open Univ BSc 99. Sarum & Wells Th Coll 76. **d** 78 **p** 79. C Petersfield w Sheet *Portsm* 78-82; R Bentworth and Shalden and Lasham *Win* 82-88; R W Horsley *Guildf* 88-00; rtd 00; PtO *B & W* from 01. *14 Lyndhurst Grove, Martock TA12 6HW* T: (01935) 824562 E: peter@robinson.co.uk

ROBINSON, The Ven Peter John Alan. b 61. St Jo Coll Cam BA 83 MA 87 St Jo Coll Dur BA 92 PhD 97. Cranmer Hall Dur 90. **d** 95 **p** 96. C N Shields *Newc* 95-99; P-in-c Byker St Martin 99-08; P-in-c Byker St Mich w St Lawr 01-08; Hon Can Newc Cathl 07-08; Adn Lindisfarne from 08. *4 Acomb Close, Morpeth NE61 2YH* T: (01670) 503810 F: 510469 E: p.robinson@newcastle.anglican.org

ROBINSON, Peter McCall. b 24. Worc Coll Ox BA 48 MA 50. Wells Th Coll 48. **d** 50 **p** 51. C Durban St Thos S Africa 50-54; C Stoke Poges *Ox* 55-57; Asst Chapl Michaelhouse Sch S Africa 57-58; V Ixopo 58-65; R Margate 65-71; V Payhembury *Ex* 71-79; R Cheriton w Tichborne and Beauworth *Win* 79-81; S Africa 81-82; V Marystowe, Coryton, Stowford, Lewtrenchard etc *Ex* 82-85; V Blackawton and Stoke Fleming 85-88; rtd 88; PtO *Ex* 89-09. *10 Culver House, Vicarage Road, Sidmouth EX10 8UF*

ROBINSON, Philip. b 38. S Dios Minl Tr Scheme 88. **d** 91 **p** 92. NSM Ickenham *Lon* 91-95; P-in-c 95-04; P-in-c Hayes St Anselm 98-99; P-in-c Harlington 98-00; AD Hillingdon 97-03; rtd 04; PtO *Eur* from 04; *Lon* from 04. *5 Preston Court, 4 Fairfield Road, Uxbridge UB8 1DQ* T: (01895) 200303 or (0033) (4) 93 04 75 11 E: philip@stjean.fslife.co.uk

ROBINSON, Philip John. b 50. St Luke's Coll Ex CertEd 71 Leeds Univ BA 07. NOC 04. **d** 06 **p** 07. NSM Macclesfield Team *Ches* 06-09; P-in-c Rostherne w Bollington 09-13; V from 13. *The Vicarage, Rostherne Lane, Rostherne Village, Knutsford WA16 6RZ* T: (01565) 830595 E: p.robinson233@btinternet.com

ROBINSON, Raymonde Robin. b 43. St Jo Coll Dur BA 66. Chich Th Coll 67. **d** 70 **p** 71. C Ealing St Barn *Lon* 70-72; C Pinner 72-75; C Clerkenwell H Redeemer w St Phil 75-80; TV Kingsthorpe w Northampton St Dav *Pet* 80-89; R Letchworth *St Alb* 89-95; V Noel Park St Mark *Lon* 95-06; rtd 06. *12 West Hill Street, Brighton BN1 3RR* T: (01273) 728778

ROBINSON, Richard Hugh. b 35. St Jo Coll Cam BA 58 MA 62. Ridley Hall Cam 58. **d** 60 **p** 81. C Cheadle Hulme St Andr *Ches* 60-62; Hon C Alvanley 62-64; PtO *York* 64-80; Hon C Elloughton and Brough w Brantingham 80-86; C 86-87; Ext Dir CMJ 87-88; NSM Appleby *Carl* 91-93; PtO 93-98; *York* 93-98; rtd 00; PtO *Ely* 01-04 and from 10. *26 Paradise Street, Cambridge CB1 1DR* T: (01223) 328833 F: 328838

ROBINSON, Robert James. **d** 14. Drumglass w Moygashel *Arm* 14-15; C Drumragh w Mountfield *D & R* from 15. *12 Crevenagh Road, Omagh BT79 0JE* T: (028) 8224 1527

ROBINSON, Canon Roger George. b 24. Qu Coll Cam BA 46 MA 50. Ridley Hall Cam 46. **d** 48 **p** 49. C Gorleston St Andr *Nor* 48-51; C Drypool St Andr and St Pet *York* 51-54; P-in-c Kingston upon Hull St Aid Southcoates 54-55; V 55-60; V Clifton 60-70; Chapl Clifton Hosp York 61-70; V Far Headingley St Chad *Ripon* 70-81; RD Headingley 72-81; Hon Can Ripon Cathl 81; R Drayton w Felthorpe *Nor* 81-91; rtd 91; PtO *Ripon* 91-13. *1A9 Mount St Josephs, Shire Oak Road, Leeds LS6 2DE*

ROBINSON, Ronald Frederick. b 46. Ian Ramsey Coll Brasted 72 Oak Hill Th Coll 74. **d** 76 **p** 77. C Bedhampton *Portsm* 77-79; C Portsea N End St Mark 79-82; V 90-92; R Rowner 82-90; PtO 93-02; P-in-c Bury and Houghton *Chich* 96-97; P-in-c Coldwaltham and Hardham 96-97; P-in-c Bury w Houghton and Coldwaltham and Hardham 97-98; V 98; Past Sec Ch Union 98-02; P-in-c Portsea Ascension *Portsm* 02-05; V 05-09; rtd 10; PtO *Portsm* 10-11. *28 Haleybridge Walk, Tangmere, Chichester PO20 2HG* T: (01243) 533768 E: fr.robinson@tiscali.co.uk

ROBINSON, Roy David. b 35. AKC 59. **d** 60 **p** 61. C Acocks Green *Birm* 60-62; C Shirley 62-65; C Haslemere *Guildf* 65-70; R Headley w Box Hill 70-85; V Hinchley Wood 85-00; rtd 00; PtO *Guildf* from 02. *1 Park Road, Slinfold, Horsham RH13 0SD* T: (01403) 791640

ROBINSON, Prof Simon John. b 51. Edin Univ MA 72 PhD 89 Ox Univ BA 77. Wycliffe Hall Ox 75. **d** 78 **p** 79. C Haughton le Skerne *Dur* 78-81; Chapl Asst N Tees Hosp Stockton-on-Tees 81-83; C Norton St Mary *Dur* 81-83; Chapl Heriot-Watt Univ *Edin* 83-90; R Dalmahoy 83-90; Chapl Leeds Univ *Ripon* 90-04; P-in-c Leeds Em 90-04; Prof Ethics Leeds Metrop Univ from 04; NSM Leeds City from 05. *42 Woodside Avenue, Meanwood, Leeds LS7 2UL* T: 0113-283 7440 M: 07931-916381 E: s.j.robinson@leedsmet.ac.uk

ROBINSON, Simon Joseph. b 67. Warwick Univ BA 89. STETS. **d** 12 **p** 13. C Freshford, Limpley Stoke and Hinton Charterhouse *B & W* 12-15; V Minehead from 15. *7 Paganel Road, Minehead TA24 5ET* M: 07825-925243 E: sijorobinson@me.com

ROBINSON, Steven Paul. b 65. Roehampton Univ BEd 89 Oak Hill Th Coll BA 05. St Mellitus Coll MA 13. **d** 10 **p** 11. C Perranzabuloe and Crantock w Cubert *Truro* 10-13; R St Illogan from 13. *The Rectory, Robartes Terrace, Illogan, Redruth TR16 4RX* T: (01209) 843938 M: 07813-324148 E: forchurch@hotmail.com

✣**ROBINSON, The Rt Revd Stuart Peter.** b 59. Moore Th Coll Sydney BTh 85. ACT. **d** 87 **p** 87 **c** 09. C Miranda Australia 87-89; Asst Min Doonside and Quakers Hill 89-91; C-in-c Quakers Hill 91-97; PtO *Ox* 96; Chapl Tervuren *Eur* 98-01; P-in-c Liège 98-00; Sen Assoc Ev Dept Evang Min Australia 01-09; R Chatswood 05-09; Bp Canberra and Goulburn from 09. *GPO Box 1981, Canberra ACT 2601, Australia* T: (0061) (2) 6248 0811 F: 6247 6829

ROBINSON, Mrs Teresa Jane. b 56. SAOMC 98. **d** 01 **p** 02. OLM The Cookhams *Ox* 01-08; NSM Maidenhead St Luke from 08; Angl Communion Office from 14. *7 Golden Ball Lane, Maidenhead SL6 6NW* T: (01628) 634107 E: terrie.robinson@anglicancommunion.org

ROBINSON, Tiffer. *See* ROBINSON, Christopher Mark Scott

ROBINSON, Timothy. b 56. Hull Univ BSc 78 Liv Univ PhD 83 St Jo Coll Dur BA 07 FGA 86. Cranmer Hall Dur 05. **d** 07 **p** 08. C Nantwich *Ches* 07-10; V Stalybridge St Paul 10-14; V Macclesfield St Jo w Henbury from 14. *St John's Vicarage, 25 Wilwick Lane, Macclesfield SK11 8RS* M: 07981-108779 T: (01625) 424185 or 612511 E: timrobbo@aol.com

ROBINSON, Timothy James. b 59. Middx Poly BA 84 Coll of Ripon & York St Jo PGCE 00. St Steph Ho Ox 88. **d** 91 **p** 92. C W Acklam *York* 91-95; P-in-c N Ormesby 95-96; V 96-99; Teacher Hall Garth Sch Middlesbrough 00-10; PtO *Ripon* 99-02; Tutor NEOC 02-09; P-in-c Helmsley *York* 10-11; V from 11; P-in-c Upper Ryedale 10-11; R from 11; RD N Ryedale from 11. *The Vicarage, Baxtons Road, Helmsley, York YO62 5HT* T: (01439) 770983 E: tim.robinson123@btinternet.com

ROBINSON, Miss Tracy. b 75. Univ of Zimbabwe BSc 98. Wycliffe Hall Ox 03 Ripon Coll Cuddesdon MA 09. **d** 09 **p** 10. C Fordingbridge and Breamore and Hale etc *Win* 09-13; Chapl Hants Hosps NHS Foundn Trust from 13. *Basingstoke and North Hants Hospital, Aldermaston Road, Basingstoke RG24 9NA* T: (01256) 473202

ROBINSON-MULLER, Mrs Ank. b 75. Radboud Univ Nijmegen MA 04. ERMC 07. **d** 09. C E Netherlands *Eur* 09-10; C Rotterdam from 10. *Ritthemsestraat 498, 4389 PA Vlissingen, The Netherlands* T: (0031) (118) 467063 E: ank_muller@yahoo.com *or* ank.muller@mtsmail.org

ROBOTTOM, David Leonard Douglas. b 40. Qu Coll Birm 80 Sarum & Wells Th Coll 81. **d** 83 **p** 84. C Uppingham w Ayston and Wardley w Belton *Pet* 83-87; TV Sidmouth, Woolbrook and Salcombe Regis *Ex* 87-91; TV Sidmouth, Woolbrook, Salcombe Regis, Sidbury etc 91-95; R Bradninch and Clyst Hydon 95-10; RD Cullompton 03-08; rtd 10. *86 Queen Elizabeth Drive, Crediton EX12 2EJ* T: (01363) 773028 E: su2312@eclipse.co.uk

ROBSON, Alan. *See* ROBSON, Gilbert Alan

ROBSON, Claire English. b 62. Middx Poly BEd 88. Westcott Ho Cam 96. **d** 99 **p** 00. C Dorchester *Sarum* 99-02; C Kilburn St Mary w All So and W Hampstead St Jas *Lon* 02-04; Min Can and Chapl St Paul's Cathl 04-09; C Bath Abbey w St Jas *B & W* from 09. *26 Castle Gardens, Bath BA2 2AN* T: (01225) 484469 E: clairerobson@clara.net

ROBSON, Gilbert Alan. b 30. St Pet Hall Ox BA 53 MA 57. Linc Th Coll 56. **d** 57 **p** 58. C Chatham St Mary w St Jo *Roch* 57-59;

Sub Warden Roch Th Coll 59-62; Min Can Roch Cathl 59-62; Bp's Dom Chapl 61-64; Chapl Roch Th Coll 62-64; R Wouldham *Roch* 62-64; Chapl Nor Coll of Educn 65-68; Sen Lect in Div 68-72; V Shotwick *Ches* 72-74; Dioc Dir of Ords 72-74; Bp's Dom Chapl 72-74; Hd of Div Eton Coll Windsor 74-89; R Wrotham *Roch* 89-95; rtd 95; PtO *Nor* from 95. *3 Staden Park, Trimingham, Norwich NR11 8HX* T: (01263) 834887

ROBSON, Howard. *See* ROBSON, John Howard

ROBSON, Preb Ian Leonard. b 32. K Coll Lon MA 00. Bps' Coll Cheshunt 61. **d** 63 **p** 64. C Croxley Green All SS *St Alb* 63-65; C Harpenden St Nic 65-68; V Redbourn 68-72; V Ashford St Matt *Lon* 72-77; V Kensington St Mary Abbots w St Geo 77-97; AD Kensington 94-97; Preb St Paul's Cathl 96-97; rtd 97; PtO *Chich* from 97. *Wepham Lodge, Wepham, Arundel BN18 9RA* T: (01903) 884667 E: robsonoblate@aol.com

ROBSON, James Edward. b 65. Pemb Coll Ox BA 88 Middx Univ PhD 05. Wycliffe Hall Ox 91. **d** 94 **p** 95. C Enfield Ch Ch Trent Park *Lon* 94-98; C Oakwood St Thos 98-00; Tutor Oak Hill Th Coll 00-09; Tutor Wycliffe Hall Ox 09-10; Sen Tutor from 10. *Wycliffe Hall, 54 Banbury Road, Oxford OX2 6PW* T: (01865) 274200

ROBSON, John Howard. b 60. Newc Univ BA 81 ACIB 87. Cranmer Hall Dur 98. **d** 00 **p** 01. C Hethersett w Canteloff w Lt and Gt Melton *Nor* 00-04; R Brooke, Kirstead, Mundham w Seething and Thwaite 04-13; V Littleport *Ely* from 13; RD Ely from 14. *St George's Vicarage, 30 Church Lane, Littleport, Ely CB6 1PS* T: (01353) 864695 E: therevhoward@btinternet.com

ROBSON, John Phillips. b 32. LVO 99. St Edm Hall Ox. AKC 58. **d** 59 **p** 60. C Huddersfield SS Pet and Paul *Wakef* 59-62; Asst Chapl Ch Hosp Horsham 62-65; Chapl 65-80; Sen Chapl Wellington Coll Berks 80-89; Chapl to RVO and Qu Chpl of the Savoy 89-02; Chapl to The Queen 93-02; rtd 02; Extra Chapl to The Queen from 02. *Charterhouse, Charterhouse Square, London EC1M 6AN* T: (020) 7253 1591

ROBSON, Mrs Julie. b 52. **d** 12 **p** 13. NSM Corbridge w Halton and Newton Hall *Newc* from 12. *Whinburn, 9 Alexandra Crescent, Hexham NE46 3AA* T: (01434) 603958 E: j-r@talktalk.net

ROBSON, Mrs Margery June. b 44. Darlington Tr Coll CertEd 65. St Steph Ho Ox 92. **d** 94 **p** 95. C Tuffley *Glouc* 94-98; V Darlington St Mark w St Paul *Dur* 98-03; Chapl Metro Cen Gateshead 03-06; rtd 06. *23 Carr House Mews, Consett DH8 6FD* T: (01207) 581270

ROBSON, Martin Douglas. b 62. St Andr Univ MTheol 85 Cam Univ PGCE 88 Edin Univ MTh 94. Edin Th Coll 92. **d** 94 **p** 95. C Perth St Ninian *St And* 94-97; P-in-c Lockerbie *Glas* 97-01; P-in-c Moffat 97-01; R Edin St Hilda 01-06; R Edin St Fillan 01-14; R Edin St Mich and All SS from 14. *203 Gilmore Place, Edinburgh EH3 9PN* T: 0131-923 1179 E: rector@stmichaelandallsaints.org

ROBSON, Nolan Daniel Rhyl. b 77. Bath Univ BSc 99 Sheff Univ DipArch 02. Oak Hill Th Coll BA 13. **d** 13 **p** 14. C Kilnhurst *Sheff* from 13. *4 Hoylake Drive, Swinton, Mexborough S64 8ST* M: 07740-700899 E: nolan@kilnhurst-st-thomas.org.uk

ROBSON, Pamela Jean. b 44. STETS 94. **d** 97 **p** 98. NSM W Ewell *Guildf* 97-01; P-in-c Wotton and Holmbury St Mary 02-14; rtd 14; PtO *St E* from 15. *Old Guildhall, The Street, Badwell Ash, Bury St Edmunds IP31 3DP* T: (01359) 258939 E: robsonpam@btinternet.com

ROBSON, Canon Patricia Anne. b 40. MBE 99. CertEd 60. SWMTC 85. **d** 87 **p** 94. Dioc Youth Officer *Truro* 87 92; Hon C Paul 87-92; Hon C Kenwyn St Geo 88-92; Dn-in-c St Enoder 92-94; P-in-c 94-05; P-in-c Newlyn St Newlyn 03-05; Hon Can Truro Cathl 98-05; RD Pydar 02-03; rtd 05; P-in-c St Goran w Caerhays *Truro* 06-09. *Mill Cottage, Mill Lane, Grampound, Truro TR2 4RU* T: (01726) 882366 E: intercelt@aol.com

ROBSON, Paul Coutt. b 37. Leeds Univ BA 60. Coll of Resurr Mirfield 63. **d** 64 **p** 65. C Stokesay *Heref* 64-66; C St Geo Cathl Cape Town S Africa 66-68; R Roodebloem All SS 68-70; Chapl HM Pris Man 70-71; Chapl HM Borstal Feltham 71-74; Chapl HM Borstal Hollesley Bay 74-78; Chapl HM Pris Grendon and Spring Hill 78-85; Chapl HM Pris Nor 85-92; Chapl HM YOI and Remand Cen Brinsford 92-99; rtd 99; PtO *Heref* 00-01 and from 04; P-in-c Wistanstow 01-04. *Pilgrims, Henley Common, Church Stretton SY6 6RS* T: (01694) 781221 E: smrpcr@lineone.net

ROBSON, Peter. b 58. Leeds Univ BEd 80. Cranmer Hall Dur 05. **d** 07 **p** 08. C Bishopwearmouth St Gabr *Dur* 07-11. *35 Charter Drive, Sunderland SR3 3PG* T: 0191-528 2848 E: peterpoprobson@aol.com

ROBSON, Peter Cole. b 45. Clare Coll Cam BA 66 MA 70 Oriel Coll Ox BLitt 69 MLitt 70. Coll of Resurr Mirfield 70. **d** 71 **p** 72. C Gt Grimsby St Mary and St Jas *Linc* 71-73; Chapl BNC

Ox 73-76; R Timsbury *B & W* 76-79; P-in-c Blanchland w Hunstanworth *Newc* 80-83; rtd 87. *c/o J W T Robson Esq, 54 Linkfield Road, Mountsorrel, Leicester LE12 7DL*

ROBSON, Thomas Iain. b 83. Ridley Hall Cam 10. **d** 13 **p** 14. C Angmering *Chich* from 13. *59 Greenwood Drive, Angmering, Littlehampton BN16 4JW* T: (01903) 369005 E: tomrobson83@gmail.com

ROBSON, William. b 34. FCIS 66 FCCA 80. Sarum & Wells Th Coll 77. **d** 79 **p** 80. C Lymington *Win* 79-81; CF 81-93; V Barton Stacey and Bullington etc *Win* 93-98; rtd 98; Hon C Knaresborough *Ripon* 98-01; PtO *Newc* 03-04; Hon C Barrow upon Soar w Walton le Wolds *Leic* 04-07; Hon C Wymeswold and Prestwold w Hoton 04-07. *27 St James Road, Scawby, Brigg DN20 9BD* T: (01652) 600922 M: 07914-829885 E: camble@greenbee.net

ROBUS, Keith Adrian. b 59. Heythrop Coll Lon MA 01 MHCIMA 82. Chich Th Coll 85. **d** 88 **p** 89. C Greenhill St Jo *Lon* 88-92; C Willesden St Matt 92-02; V N Acton St Gabr 02-09; Chapl RN from 09. *Royal Naval Chaplaincy Service, Mail Point 1-2, Leach Building, Whale Island, Portsmouth PO2 8BY* T: (023) 9262 5055 F: 9262 5134 E: keith.robus382@mod.uk *or* keith.robus@btinternet.com

ROBY, Richard James. b 33. Imp Coll Lon BSc 54 Lon Inst of Educn PGCE 55. St Alb Minl Tr Scheme 82. **d** 85 **p** 86. NSM Bushey *St Alb* 85-92; NSM Wootton 92-00; rtd 00; PtO *St Alb* from 00. *5 Powis Mews, Flitwick, Bedford MK45 1SU* T: (01525) 718529 E: richard.roby@ntlworld.com

ROCHDALE, Archdeacon of. *See* VANN, The Ven Cherry Elizabeth

ROCHE, Miss Alison Mary. b 70. Man Univ BSc 91 Nottm Univ PGCE 94. St Jo Coll Nottm MA 00. **d** 01 **p** 02. C Leic Martyrs 01-05; P-in-c Leic St Chris 05-09; V from 09. *9 Springfield Road, Leicester LE2 3BB* T: 0116-283 0510 M: 07918-642567 E: vicar@stchristophers.info

ROCHE, Barry Robert Francis. b 40. Lon Univ BD 66 Ox Univ MTh 93. Clifton Th Coll 63. **d** 68 **p** 69. C Beckenham Ch Ch *Roch* 68-72; C Chester le Street *Dur* 72-74; C-in-c N Bletchley CD *Ox* 74-78; R Luton Ch Ch *Roch* 78-92; Chapl All SS Hosp Chatham 78-92; TR Glascote and Stonydelph *Lich* 92-99; RD Tamworth 95-99; V Oulton Broad *Nor* 99-05; rtd 05; PtO *S & B* from 06. *24 Lakeside Close, Nantyglo, Ebbw Vale NP23 4EG* T: (01495) 311048

ROCHELL, Stephen Peter. b 56. Open Univ MA 95 Sheff Univ BA 14. Yorks Min Course 11. **d** 14 **p** 15. NSM Hartshead, Hightown, Roberttown and Scholes *Leeds* from 14. *55 Greenside Road, Mirfield WF14 0AU* T: (01924) 521121 M: 07707-763689 E: stephen.rochell@ntlworld.com

ROCHESTER, Thomas Robson. b 33. NEOC 85. **d** 90 **p** 91. NSM Glendale Gp *Newc* 90-03; rtd 03; PtO *Newc* from 03. *8 Grange View, Morpeth NE61 5PG* E: trochester2@aol.com

ROCHESTER, Archdeacon of. *See* BURTON JONES, The Ven Simon David

ROCHESTER, Bishop of. *See* LANGSTAFF, The Rt Revd James Henry

ROCHESTER, Dean of. *See* BEACH, Mark Howard Francis

ROCK, Mrs Jean. b 37. Gilmore Course 76. **dss** 79 **d** 87 **p** 97. Douglas St Matt *S & M* 79-81; Marown 81-83; Chapl Asst Oswestry and Distr Hosp 83-87; Oswestry St Oswald *Lich* 83-90; Par Dn 87-90; C-in-c Pont Robert and Pont Dolanog *St As* 90-97; V 97; rtd 97; PtO *Lich* from 99; *St As* from 09. *10 Wharf Cottages, Rhoswiel, Weston Rhyn, Oswestry SY10 7TD* T: (01691) 773766

ROCKALL, Miss Valerie Jane. b 42. City of Cov Coll CertEd 63. St Alb Minl Tr Scheme 78. **dss** 81 **d** 87 **p** 94. Asst Hd Wigginton Sch Tring 73-90; Boxmoor St Jo *St Alb* 81-87; NSM Hemel Hempstead 87-90; Par Dn Ampthill w Millbrook and Steppingley 90-93; Team Dn Southampton (City Cen) *Win* 93-94; TV 94-99; P-in-c Aveley and Purfleet *Chelmsf* 99-10; rtd 10. *29 Adams Way, Tring HP23 5DY* T: (01442) 891386 E: rockallv@aol.com

ROCKEY, Antony Nicolas. b 65. Kingston Poly BEng 89. CBDTI 02. **d** 05 **p** 06. C Cockermouth Area *Carl* 05-09; P-in-c Fernhurst *Chich* 09-11. *The Old Stables, Middle Stoke Farm, Holne, Newton Abbot TQ13 7SS*

ROCKS, James Anthony. b 82. Trin Coll Bris BA 10. **d** 11 **p** 12. C Stoke Gifford *Bris* 11-15. *8 Somerset Crescent, Stoke Gifford, Bristol BS34 8PP* M: 07786-034993 E: jimmy@st-michaels-church.org.uk

RODD, Philip Rankilor. b 60. Ex Univ BA 79 K Coll Lon PGCE 85. Ridley Hall Cam 03. **d** 05 **p** 06. C Heigham H Trin *Nor* 05-08; V Eaton *St Andr* from 08. *The Vicarage, 210 Newmarket Road, Norwich NR4 7LA* T: (01603) 455778

RODD, Susan Eleanor. b 49. **d** 10 **p** 11. NSM Whitton *Sarum* 10-14; TV from 14. *16 The Garlings, Aldbourne, Marlborough SN8 2DT* T: (01672) 541571 E: suerodd@btinternet.com

RODDY, Keith Anthony. b 67. Leic Univ BA 89. Oak Hill Th Coll BA 09. **d** 09 **p** 10. C Chesterton *Lich* 09-12; V Springfield H Trin *Chelmsf* from 12. *The Vicarage, 61 Hill Road, Chelmsford CM2 6HW* T: (01245) 359299 M: 07986-903110 E: keitharoddy@googlemail.com

RODE, Margaret Macdonald. b 46. **d** 08. NSM Hedsor and Bourne End *Ox* 08-11; NSM Chalfont St Peter 11-14; C Edin Ch Ch from 14. *3 Morningside Road, Edinburgh EH10 4DD* M: 07855-952237 E: maggie.rode@ntlworld.com

RODE, Nigel Stewart. b 46. **d** 08. NSM Chalfont St Peter *Ox* 08-14; C Edin Ch Ch from 14. *3 Morningside Road, Edinburgh EH10 4DD* M: 07855-952238 E: nigel.rode@ntlworld.com

RODEL, Mark Neil. b 71. Southn Univ BA 96. STETS 02. **d** 05 **p** 06. C Southsea St Jude *Portsm* 05-08; C Portsea St Luke 08-12; V Lady Bay w Holme Pierrepont and Adbolton *S'well* from 12; Tutor St Jo Coll Nottm from 12. *Lady Bay Vicarage, 121 Holme Road, West Bridgford, Nottingham NG2 5AG* M: 07590-208803

RODEN, Jo. *See* LOVERIDGE, Joan Margaretha Holland

RODEN, John Michael. b 37. St Jo Coll York CertEd 64 Open Univ BA 82 MA 92 York Univ DPhil 96. Ripon Hall *Ox* 71. **d** 73 **p** 74. C Saltburn-by-the-Sea *York* 73-77; Chapl St Pet Sch York 77-82; Warden Marrick Priory *Ripon* 83; Hon C Appleton Roebuck w Acaster Selby *York* 84-85; P-in-c 86-03; Youth Officer 86-91; Sen Chapl Selby Coalfield Ind Chapl 96-03; rtd 03; PtO *York* from 03. *Ebor Cottage, 8 Copmanthorpe Grange, Copmanthorpe, York YO23 3TN* T: (01904) 744826 E: j.m.roden@btinternet.com

RODEN, Canon Michael Adrian Holland. b 60. Birm Univ MA 03. Ripon Coll Cuddesdon 82. **d** 85 **p** 86. C S Lambeth St Anne and All SS *S'wark* 85-88; C Wandsworth St Paul 88-90; C Ox St Mary V w St Cross and St Pet 90-94; Chapl Wadh Coll Ox 90-94; R Steeple Aston w N Aston and Tackley *Ox* 94-02; TR Hitchin *St Alb* from 02; P-in-c St Paul's Walden from 10; RD Hitchin from 07; Hon Can St Alb from 14. *The Rectory, 21 West Hill, Hitchin SG5 2HZ* T: (01462) 434017 or 452758 E: michaelroden@btinternet.com

RODERICK, Philip David. b 49. Univ of Wales (Swansea) BA 70 Univ of Wales (Abth) BD 77 Lon Univ CertEd 71. Linc Th Coll 80. **d** 80 **p** 81. C Llanfair-is-gaer and Llanddeiniolen *Ban* 80-82; TV Holyhead w Rhoscolyn w Llanfair-yn-Neubwll 82-84; Chapl and Lect Th Univ of Wales (Ban) 84-88; Warden Angl Chapl Cen 84-88; Prin Bucks Chr Tr Scheme *Ox* 88-94; Dir Chiltern Chr Tr Progr 88-94; Dir Quiet Garden Trust from 92; Dir The Well Inst from 96; V Amersham on the Hill *Ox* 94-04; Ldr Contemplative Fire from 04; Bp's Adv in Spirituality *Sheff* 10-15; Chapl Whirlow Grange Conf Cen Sheff 10-15. *16 Chorley Avenue, Saltdean, Brighton BN2 8AQ* E: philiproderick@btinternet.com

RODFORD, Canon Brian George. b 50. Hatf Poly BEd 84. **d** 79 **p** 80. NSM St Alb St Steph *St Alb* 79-85; Chapl St Mary's Sch 81-90; Sen Teacher 83-90; Hon C Hendon St Mary and Golders Green *Lon* 85-90; Hon C Winchmore Hill H Trin 90-95; V Ponders End St Matt 95-02; Dir Chain Foundn Uganda from 02; Can All SS Cathl Kampala from 02; PtO *St Alb* 04-05. *Simon's Acre, 17 Pagasvlei Road, Constantia, 7806 South Africa* T: (0027) (21) 794 8940 or (01727) 850382 E: brodford_chain@hotmail.com

RODGER, Canon Raymond. b 39. Westmr Coll Ox MTh 93. Bps' Coll Cheshunt 62. **d** 63 **p** 64. C Frodingham *Linc* 63-66; Asst Chapl St Geo Hosp Lon 66-69; C Waltham *Linc* 69-73; V Nocton 73-86; P-in-c Potter Hanworth 74-86; P-in-c Dunston 77-86; RD Graffoe 81-92; Can and Preb Linc Cathl from 85; V Nocton w Dunston and Potterhanworth 86-92; Bp's Dom Chapl 92-05; Gen Preacher 92-05; rtd 05. *13 Lupin Road, Lincoln LN2 4GB* T: (01522) 536723 M: 07803-123975 E: canrod@hotmail.com

RODGERS, Alasdair Martin. b 75. Lon Bible Coll BA 96. St Mellitus Coll 12 St Jo Coll Nottm 13. **d** 15. C Bebington *Ches* from 15. *8 Rolleston Drive, Bebington, Wirral CH63 3DB* M: 07790-270060 E: al@kateandal.com

RODGERS, David. b 26. Sarum Th Coll 63. **d** 65 **p** 66. C Combe Down *B & W* 65-68; V Leigh Woods 68-76; R Wellow w Foxcote and Shoscombe 76-79; C Wells St Cuth w Coxley and Wookey Hole 79-82; P-in-c Wookey w Henton 79-82; V Ercall Magna *Lich* 82-89; V Rowton 82-89; RD Wrockwardine 84-88; rtd 89; PtO *B & W* from 98. *6 The Cloisters, South Street, Wells BA5 1SA*

RODGERS, Eamonn Joseph. b 41. QUB BA 63 PhD 70. TISEC 04. **d** 05 **p** 06. NSM Glas St Ninian 05-12; LtO from 12. *4 Albert Drive, Glasgow G73 3RT* T: 0141-583 6949 M: 07586-302613 E: eamonn.rodgers@ntlworld.com

RODGERS, Preb Frank Ernest. b 46. Tyndale Hall Bris 68. **d** 71 **p** 72. C Madeley *Heref* 71-74; C Littleover *Derby* 74-77; V Clodock and Longtown w Craswell and Llanveyno *Heref* 77-79; P-in-c St Margaret's w Michaelchurch Eskley and Newton 77-79; V Clodock and Longtown w Craswell, Llanveynoe etc 79-10; RD Abbeydore 90-96; Preb Heref Cathl 96-10; rtd 10. *Thorneyglatt Cottage, Didley, Hereford HR2 9DA* T: (01981) 570629

RODGERS, John Terence Roche. b 28. TCD BA 53 MA 57 ACII. Bps' Coll Cheshunt. **d** 57 **p** 58. C Templecorran *Conn* 57-60; C Derriaghy 60-61; C Antrim All SS 62-64; I Belfast St Steph 64-79; I Dunmurry 79-94; Can Belf Cathl 92-94; rtd 94. *8 Aberdelghy Park, Lambeg, Lisburn BT27 4QF* T: (028) 9266 0430

RODGERS, Richard Thomas Boycott. b 47. Lon Univ MB, BS 70 FRCS 81. St Jo Coll Nottm. **d** 77 **p** 78. C Littleover *Derby* 77-80; Lect Birm St Martin w Bordesley St Andr 89-90; PtO from 90; rtd 12. *63 Meadow Brook Road, Birmingham B31 1ND* T: 0121-476 0789

RODHAM, The Ven Morris. b 59. Hatf Coll Dur BA 81 St Jo Coll Dur PGCE 85. Trin Coll Bris MA 93. **d** 93 **p** 94. C New Milverton *Cov* 93-97; V Leamington Priors St Mary 97-10; RD Warwick and Leamington 06-09; Adn Missr from 10; Adn Warwick from 10. *Cathedral and Diocesan Office, 1 Hill Top, Coventry CV1 5AB* T: (02476) 521337 M: 07929-861233 E: morris.rodham@covcofe.org

RODLEY, Ian Tony. b 48. Open Univ BA 08. Qu Coll Birm 77. **d** 80 **p** 81. C Baildon and Dioc Children's Adv *Bradf* 80-85; V Bradf St Wilfrid Lidget Green 85-90; Chapl to the Deaf 88-90; V Otley 90-98; C Wolverton *Ox* 98-03; TR Bramley *Ripon* 03-13; rtd 13. *4 Beadon Avenue, Huddersfield HD5 8QZ* E: ianrod@clara.co.uk

RODLEY, James William Eric. b 66. SS Hild & Bede Coll Dur BA 86 ACA 89. St Steph Ho Ox BTh 11. **d** 09 **p** 10. C Pokesdown All SS and Bournemouth St Clem *Win* 09-13; P-in-c N Weald Bassett *Chelmsf* from 13; P-in-c Harlow St Mary Magd from 13. *The Vicarage, 3 Oaklands Drive, Harlow CM17 9BE* T: (01279) 451065 E: jwerodley@yahoo.co.uk

RODRIGUEZ, Luis Mario. b 64. Occidental Coll (USA) BA 86 S California Univ MA 93. St Steph Ho Ox MTh 99. **d** 98 **p** 99. C Battersea Ch Ch and St Steph *S'wark* 98-02; C Pimlico St Pet w Westmr Ch Ch *Lon* 02-05; PtO *S'wark* 07-08; R Hanford USA from 08. *510 N Douty Street, Hanford CA 93230, USA* T: (001) (559) 584 7706 F: 584 7710 E: luis@smeltern.com

RODRIGUEZ, Miguel. *See* SANCHEZ RODRIGUEZ, Miguel

RODRIGUEZ-VEGLIO, Francis Bonny. b 33. Sarum Th Coll 62. **d** 64 **p** 65. C Alnwick St Paul *Newc* 64-68; V Horton w Piddington *Pet* 68-79; P-in-c Preston Deanery 68-72; P-in-c Wootton w Quinton and Preston Deanery 72-79; CF (ACF) 75-82; TV Is of Scilly *Truro* 79-82; Hon Chapl Miss to Seamen 79-82; PtO *Pet* 86-88; C Leic Ch Sav 88-91; V Kirkwhelpington, Kirkharle, Kirkheaton and Cambo *Newc* 91-95. *Gemacq Cottage, 14 Daventry Road, Norton, Daventry NN11 2ND* T: (01327) 872030 E: francis.andree@tiscali.co.uk or andree@gemacq.co.uk

RODWELL, Barry John. b 39. Birm Univ CertEd 59 Cam Univ DipAdEd 77. Ridley Hall Cam 67. **d** 70 **p** 71. C Sudbury St Greg and St Pet *St E* 70-73; Hd RE Hedingham Sch 73-80; R Sible Hedingham *Chelmsf* 80-85; RE Adv 85-93; V Gt Burstead 93-00; rtd 00; PtO *Nor* 00-07. *The Nutshell, 11 Filbert Road, Loddon, Norwich NR14 6LW* T: (01508) 522949 E: nutshell@tesco.net

RODWELL, Mrs Helen. b 70. WEMTC. **d** 09 **p** 10. NSM Forest of Dean Ch Ch w English Bicknor *Glouc* from 09. *The Other House, English Bicknor, Coleford GL16 7PD* T: (01594) 860205 E: helen@otherhouse.fsnet.co.uk

RODWELL (née VINCENT), Mrs Jacqueline Margaret. b 59. Glos Univ BA 04. WEMTC 01. **d** 04 **p** 05. NSM Cheltenham St Mark *Glouc* 04-08; NSM Cheltenham Em w St Steph 08-09; NSM S Cheltenham 10-14. *Address temp unknown*

RODWELL, Canon John Stanley. b 46. Leeds Univ BSc 68 Southn Univ PhD 74. Cuddesdon Coll 71. **d** 74 **p** 75. Hon C Horfield H Trin *Bris* 74-75; Hon C Skerton St Luke *Blackb* 75-77; LtO from 77; Hon Can Blackb Cathl from 03. *7 Derwent Road, Lancaster LA1 3ES* T: (01524) 62726

ROE, Mrs Caroline Ruth. b 57. Birm Univ BA 80 PGCE 93. Wycliffe Hall Ox 81. **dss** 84 **d** 87 **p** 96. Olveston *Bris* 84-87; Par Dn 87; NSM Alveley and Quatt *Heref* 87-94; Bp's Voc Officer 90-94; Hon C Loughborough Em and St Mary in Charnwood *Leic* 97-98; C Hathern, Long Whatton and Diseworth w Belton etc 98-00; PtO 01-04; Chapl Univ Hosps Leic NHS Trust 04-07; Lead Chapl 07-13. *4 John's Lee Close, Loughborough LE11 3LH* T: (01509) 260217 or (01509) 0116 256 5487

ROE, Daniel Cameron. b 84. Ball Coll Ox BA 05. Oak Hill Th Coll MTh 10. **d** 10 **p** 11. C Clifton *York* 10-15. *5 Manor Park Close, York YO30 5UZ* T: (01904) 345746 M: 07778-572928 E: daniel.roe@balliol.oxon.org or daniel.c.roe@gmail.com

ROE, Frank Ronald. b 31. Brasted Th Coll Westcott Ho Cam 55. **d** 57 **p** 58. C S w N Hayling *Portsm* 57-61; Hong Kong 61-77; Sen Chapl St Jo Cathl 61-66; Asst Chapl 77; Sen Chapl Miss to

Seamen 66-69; Hon Chapl Miss to Seamen Australia 77-06; rtd 96. *2004-699 Cardero Street, Vancouver BC V6G E3H, Canada* T: (001) (604) 325 5591 E: revfrank@bigpond.com

ROE, Canon Joseph <u>Thorley</u>. b 22. AKC 49 DipAdEd Hull Univ PhD 90. K Coll Lon 46. **d** 50 **p** 51. C Methley *Ripon* 50-53; C Richmond 53-55; V Leeds Gipton Epiphany 55-60; C of E Youth Coun Tr Officer 60-64; Sec Youth Dept BCC 64-67; Prin Lect Bretton Hall Coll Wakef 67-74; Sec for Miss and Unity *Ripon* 74-78; Dioc Missr and Bp's Dom Chapl 75-78; Can Res Carl Cathl 78-82; Dioc Dir of Tr 78-82; Dioc Adult Educn Officer *Wakef* 82-88; Hon Can Wakef Cathl 83-88; Dir Educn 85-88; rtd 88; PtO *Wakef* 88-08. *2 Fosbrook House, 8 Clifton Drive, Lytham St Annes FY8 5RQ* T: (01253) 667032

ROE, Peter Harold. b 37. K Coll Lon BD 62 AKC 62. **d** 63 **p** 64. C Knowle St Barn *Bris* 63-65; C Leckhampton St Pet *Glouc* 65-68; V Shaw Hill *Birm* 68-73; V Hobs Moat 73-90; V Packwood w Hockley Heath 90-99; rtd 99; PtO *Blackb* from 99. *14 Worcester Avenue, Garstang, Preston PR3 1EY* T: (01995) 605775

ROE, Robert Henry. b 22. LCP 57. Westcott Ho Cam 72. **d** 74 **p** 75. Hd Master St Mary's Primary Sch Saffron Walden 74-83; NSM Saffron Walden w Wendens Ambo and Littlebury *Chelmsf* 75-86; PtO *Nor* from 86. *Larchmount, High Street, Cley, Holt NR25 7RG* T: (01263) 740369 E: robert.roe01@btinternet.com

ROE, Thorley. *See* ROE, Joseph Thorley

ROEMMELE, Canon Michael Patrick. b 49. TCD BA 72 MA 76. **d** 73 **p** 74. C Portadown St Columba *Arm* 73-77; C Drumachose *D & R* 77-80; Bahrain 79-83; Cyprus 79-83; Chapl RAF 83-00; CF 00-07; I Camus-juxta-Bann *D & R* from 07; Can Derry Cathl from 14. *30 Drumrane Road, Limavady BT49 9LB* T: (028) 7776 3554 M: 07977-239863 E: mproemmele@googlemail.com *or* macosquin@derry.anglican.org

ROESCHLAUB, Robert <u>Friedrich</u>. b 39. Purdue Univ BSc 63. Berkeley Div Sch MDiv 66. **d** 66 **p** 66. USA 66-77; Hon C Tilehurst St Cath *Ox* 78-79; Hon C Tilehurst St Mich 79-82; P-in-c Millom H Trin w Thwaites *Carl* 82-85; P-in-c Millom 85-89; R Dunstall w Rangemore and Tatenhill *Lich* 89-93; rtd 94; PtO *Carl* from 98; *Lich* from 02. *20 Pannatt Hill, Millom LA18 5DB* T: (01229) 772185

ROEST, Wilma. b 62. Utrecht Univ MA 88 Roehampton Inst PGCE 92. SEITE 96. **d** 99 **p** 00. C Merton St Mary *S'wark* 99-02; TV N Lambeth 02-06; P-in-c Balham St Mary and St Jo 06-10; V from 10; AD Tooting from 09. *St Mary's Vicarage, 218A Balham High Road, London SW12 9BS* T: (020) 8673 1188 E: vicar@stmarybalham.org.uk

ROFF, Andrew Martin. b 42. Bede Coll Dur BSc 65. Westcott Ho Cam 65. **d** 70 **p** 71. C Ches St Mary 70-73; Min Can Blackb Cathl 73-76; P-in-c Blackb St Jo 74-75; V Longton 76-81; Chapl Trin Coll Glenalmond 82-83; R Allendale w Whitfield *Newc* 83-92; V Gosforth St Nic 92-97; Dioc Supernumerary *Mor* 01-10 from 08. *Rowan Glen, Upper Braefindon, Culbokie, Dingwall IV7 8GY* T: (01349) 877762 E: martin@roff-rowanglen.co.uk

ROFF, Canon John Michael. b 47. St Chad's Coll Dur BSc 69. Westcott Ho Cam 70. **d** 72 **p** 73. C Lancaster St Mary *Blackb* 72-75; C Dronfield *Derby* 75-76; TV 76-80; TR N Wingfield, Pilsley and Tupton 80-85; V Ilkeston St Mary 85-90; V Stockport St Geo *Ches* 90-94; TR Stockport SW 94-00; RD Stockport 95-00; Dioc Ecum Officer 92-99; Hon Can Ches Cathl 98-00; Can Res Ches Cathl 00-04; rtd 04; PtO *Ches* from 05; *Blackb* from 05. *14 Westbourne Road, Lancaster LA1 5DB* T: (01524) 841621 E: roff@roff.org.uk

ROGAN, Canon John. b 28. St Jo Coll Dur BA 49 MA 51 Open Univ BPhil 81. **d** 54 **p** 55. C Ashton St Mich *Man* 54-57; C Sharrow St Andr *Sheff* 57-61; Ind Chapl 57-61; Sec C of E Ind Cttee 61-66; V Leigh St Mary *Man* 66-78; RD Leigh 71-78; Hon Can Man Cathl 75-78; Provost St Paul's Cathl Dundee 78-83; R Dundee St Paul 78-83; Soc Resp Adv *Bris* 83-93; Can Res Bris Cathl 83-93; rtd 93; PtO *Bris* from 93. *84 Concorde Drive, Bristol BS10 6PX* T: 0117-950 5803

ROGERS, Anne Frances. *See* ILSLEY, Anne Frances

ROGERS, Brian Robert. b 36. Open Univ BA 80. St Jo Coll Nottm 70. **d** 72 **p** 73. C Ealing St Mary *Lon* 72-74; C Greenside *Dur* 74-75; LtO 75-85; PtO *Lich* 85-95; rtd 97; PtO *Sarum* from 97. *71 Alderney Avenue, Poole BH12 4LP* T: (01202) 772103

ROGERS, Brian Victor. b 50. Trin Coll Bris 75. **d** 78 **p** 79. C Plumstead St Jo w St Jas and St Paul *S'wark* 78-83; P-in-c Gayton *Nor* 83-85; P-in-c Gayton Thorpe w E Walton 83-85; P-in-c Westacre 83-85; P-in-c Ashwicken w Leziate 83-85; R Gayton Gp of Par 85-91; R Rackheath and Salhouse 91-96; P-in-c Warmington, Tansor, Cotterstock and Fotheringhay *Pet* 96-97; V Warmington, Tansor and Cotterstock etc 97-15; rtd 15. *Gortatlea, Mastergeehy, Killarney, Kerry, Republic of Ireland* E: bvictorr@hotmail.co.uk

ROGERS, Christopher Antony. b 47. NOC 79. **d** 81 **p** 82. C Chesterfield SS Aug *Derby* 81-84; C Chaddesden St Phil 84-86; R Whitwell 86-95; V W Burnley All SS *Blackb* 95-01; V Ashford St Hilda *Lon* from 01. *St Hilda's Vicarage, 8 Station Crescent, Ashford TW15 3HH* T: (01784) 254237 *or* 245712 E: christopher.rogers@london.anglican.org

ROGERS, Christopher Ian. b 79. Trin Coll Bris BA 01. K Coll Lon MA 05. **d** 07 **p** 08. NSM Roxeth *Lon* 07-10; C Shadwell St Paul w Ratcliffe St Jas from 10; C Bromley by Bow All Hallows 10-14; P-in-c 14-15; R from 15. *All Hallows' Rectory, Devons Road, London E3 3PN* T: (020) 7538 9756 M: 07974-371418 E: revcrisrogers@me.com

ROGERS, Clive Trevor Thorne. b 49. SAOMC 02. **d** 05 **p** 06. NSM Beaconsfield *Ox* 05-11; PtO *Ex* from 11. *Leeward House, West Charleton, Kingsbridge TQ7 2AB* E: clive_rogers@btinternet.com

ROGERS, Clive <u>William</u>. b 62. Selw Coll Cam BA 83 MA 87 MEng 23 Southn Univ BTh 90. Chich Th Coll 87. **d** 90 **p** 91. C Leic St Aid 90-93; P-in-c Ryhall w Essendine *Pet* 93-94; LtO *Ely* 94-03; PtO 03-04; LtO *Sarum* 04-06; Hon C Forest and Avon from 06. *4 The Sidings, Downton, Salisbury SP5 3QZ* T: (01725) 512141 E: bill@billrogers.info

ROGERS, Cyril David. b 55. Birm Univ BA 76 BTheol. Sarum & Wells Th Coll 80. **d** 83 **p** 84. C Leagrave *St Alb* 83-87; TV Langtree *Ox* 87-97; R Ballaugh *S & M* 97-12; V Michael 97-12; R Andreas, Ballaugh, Jurby and Sulby from 12; RD Ramsey from 12; Can St German's Cathl from 12. *The Rectory, Ballacrosha, Ballaugh, Isle of Man IM7 5AQ* T: (01624) 897873

ROGERS, Damon. b 66. Cov Univ BEng 92 Wolv Univ PGCE 94 Warwick Univ BPhil 02. Cranmer Hall Dur 01. **d** 03 **p** 04. C Heigham St Thos *Nor* 03-06; R Freethorpe, Wickhampton, Halvergate etc 06-13; V Lowestoft St Andr from 13. *51 Beresford Road, Lowestoft NR32 2NQ* E: therogers5@ukonline.co.uk

ROGERS, Canon David. b 48. Univ of Wales (Ban) BA 69. Westcott Ho Cam 70. **d** 72 **p** 73. C Rainbow Hill and Tolladine *Worc* 72-75; C Astwood Bank w Crabbs Cross 75-79; V Cradley 79-90; V Beoley 90-08; RD Bromsgrove 00-06; TR Redditch H Trin 08-13; Hon Can Worc Cathl 07-13; rtd 13. *2 Chalmers Close, Worcester WR5 1SX* T: (01905) 729618 E: davidrogers@santiago.plus.com

ROGERS, David Alan. b 55. City of Lon Poly BA 77 MCIT 82. Linc Th Coll 88. **d** 90 **p** 91. C Kingston upon Hull St Nic *York* 90-93; P-in-c Kingston upon Hull St Mary 93-96; N Humberside Ind Chapl 93-02; Dir Leeds Ch Inst *Ripon* 02-04; Chief Officer Hull Coun for Voluntary Service 04-12; TR Marfleet *York* from 12. *33 Carden Avenue, Hull HU9 4RT*

ROGERS, The Ven David Arthur. b 21. Ch Coll Cam BA 47 MA 52. Ridley Hall Cam 47. **d** 49 **p** 50. C Stockport St Geo *Ches* 49-53; R Levenshulme St Pet *Man* 53-59; V Sedbergh *Bradf* 59-74; P-in-c Cautley w Dowbiggin 59-60; V 60-74; P-in-c Garsdale 59-60; V 60-74; V Sedbergh, Cautley and Garsdale 74-79; P-in-c Firbank, Howgill and Killington 73-77; RD Sedbergh 59-73; RD Ewecross 73-77; Hon Can Bradf Cathl 67-77; Adn Craven 77-86; rtd 86; LtO *Bradf* 86-06; PtO *Blackb* 87-06; *Carl* 89-06. *24 Towns End Road, Sharnbrook, Bedford MK44 1HY* T: (01234) 782650

ROGERS, David Barrie. b 46. S Dios Minl Tr Scheme 89. **d** 93. NSM Old Alresford and Bighton *Win* 93-96; Dep Warden Dioc Retreat Ho (Holland Ho) Cropthorne *Worc* 96-98; Warden Stacklands Retreat Ho W Kingsdown 98-03; Hon C Kingsdown *Roch* 98-03; Warden St Pet Bourne Cen 03-13; rtd 13. *16 Quay Road, Newton Abbott TQ12 2BU*

ROGERS, David Martyn. b 56. Univ of Wales (Lamp) BA 77 K Coll Lon BD 79 AKC 79 St Kath Coll Liv DipEd 86 Liv Univ BPhil 94 MA 07. Chich Th Coll 79. **d** 80 **p** 81. C Hockerill *St Alb* 80-85; PtO *St As* 85-87; C Kilburn St Mary *Lon* 87-90; V New Longton *Blackb* from 90; Chapl Lancs Constabulary from 90. *All Saints' Vicarage, Station Road, New Longton, Preston PR4 4LN* T: (01772) 613347

ROGERS, George Hutchinson. b 51. Windsor Univ Ontario BSW 75. Wycliffe Coll Toronto MDiv 78. **d** 78 **p** 78. C Victoria St Matthias Canada 78-81; R Cobble Hill and Cowichan Station 81-86; I Vancouver St Matthias 86-97; Hon C Vancouver St Helen 97-98; C Tonbridge SS Pet and Paul *Roch* 99-03; V Werrington *Pet* from 03. *The Vicarage, 51 The Green, Werrington, Peterborough PE4 6RT* T: (01733) 571649 E: george@revgeorgerogers.plus.com

ROGERS, George Michael Andrew. b 69. Yale Div Sch MDiv 95. **d** 99 **p** 99. C Brant Lake St Paul USA 99-00; C New York St Thos 00-03; C Pelham Ch Ch 03-10; C Staines *Lon* 10-13; P-in-c Milton next Sittingbourne *Cant* from 13; P-in-c Murston w Bapchild and Tonge from 13. *The Vicarage, Vicarage Road, Sittingbourne ME10 2BL* T: (01795) 472016 M: 07527-746060 E: george.rogers3@gmail.com

ROGERS, Ian Colin. b 73. Wolv Univ BA 95. Coll of Resurr Mirfield BA 99. **d** 00 **p** 01. C Lon Docks St Pet w Wapping St Jo 00-03; P-in-c Hammersmith St Luke 03-08; P-in-c Tangmere and Oving *Chich* 08-12; CF from 12. *c/o MOD Chaplains (Army)* F: 381824　T: (01264) 383430　E: fr.ianrogers@ntlworld.com

ROGERS, Jane. *See* ROGERS, Lady

ROGERS, The Very Revd John. b 34. Univ of Wales (Lamp) BA 55 Oriel Coll Ox BA 58 MA 61. St Steph Ho Ox 57. **d** 59 **p** 60. C Roath St Martin *Llan* 59-63; Br Guiana 63-66; Guyana 66-71; V Caldicot *Mon* 71-77; V Monmouth 77-84; RD 81-84; TR Ebbw Vale 84-93; RD Blaenau Gwent 86-93; Can St Woolos Cathl 88-93; Dean Llan 93-99; V Llandaff w Capel Llanilltern 93-99; rtd 99. *Fron Lodge, Llandovery SA20 0LJ*　T: (01550) 720089

ROGERS, John. b 61. St Jo Coll Nottm 03. **d** 05 **p** 06. C Otley *Bradf* 05-08; V Oakworth *Leeds* from 08. *The Vicarage, 18 Sunhurst Drive, Oakworth, Keighley BD22 7RG*　T: (01274) 408354　E: john.rogers@bradford.anglican.org

ROGERS, John Arthur. b 47. MBIM. Edin Dioc NSM Course 90. **d** 92. C Middlesbrough St Martin *York* 92-93; NSM The Trimdons *Dur* 00-05; NSM Upper Skerne 05-07; R Tilehurst St Mich *Ox* from 07. *Tilehurst Rectory, Routh Lane, Reading RG30 4JY*　T: 0118-941 1127　E: rogj8@aol.com

ROGERS, John Howard. b 47. Ripon Coll Cuddesdon. **d** 09 **p** 09. NSM Southgate Ch Ch *Lon* 09-12; NSM Highgate All SS from 12; NSM Highgate St Mich from 12. *48 Twisden Road, London NW5 1DN*　T: (020) 7485 6376　E: hrogers442@aol.com

ROGERS, John Robin. b 36. St Alb Minl Tr Scheme 78. **d** 81 **p** 82. NSM Digswell and Panshanger *St Alb* 81-84; C Welwyn w Ayot St Peter 85-92; R Wilden w Colmworth and Ravensden 92-99; rtd 99; PtO *St Alb* 99-02; *Heref* from 03. *37 The Birches, Shobdon, Leominster HR6 9NG*　T: (01568) 708903

ROGERS, John William Trevor. b 28. Qu Coll Birm. **d** 85 **p** 86. NSM Dunchurch *Cov* 85-95; PtO 95-07. *15 Hillyard Road, Southam, Leamington Spa CV47 0LD*　T: (01926) 813469

ROGERS, Mrs Kathleen. b 56. Open Univ BA 93 Leeds Univ BA 07. NOC 04. **d** 07 **p** 08. Sen Resources Officer *Liv* 93-09; NSM Formby H Trin 07-09; C 09-12; P-in-c Thornton and Crosby 12-13; V from 13. *The Rectory, Water Street, Thornton, Liverpool L23 1TB*

ROGERS, Canon Kathleen Anne. b 54. **d** 08　**p** 09. C Machynlleth w Llanwrin and Penegoes *Ban* 08-11; P-in-c 11-12; P-in-c Machynlleth w Corris w Llanwrin and Penegoes 12-14; P-in-c Bro Cyfeiliog a Mawddwy from 14. *30 Tregarth, Machynlleth SY20 8HU*　T: (01654) 702961　E: kathleenrogers@hotmail.co.uk

ROGERS, Canon Kenneth. b 33. Cuddesdon Coll 68. **d** 69 **p** 70. C Perranzabuloe *Truro* 69-71; C Truro St Paul 71-74; P-in-c Kenwyn St Geo 74-87; RD Powder 81-88; Hon Can Truro Cathl 87-98; TR Bodmin w Lanhydrock and Lanivet 87-98; RD Trigg Minor and Bodmin 89-93; rtd 98; PtO *Truro* from 98. *28 Lowen Court, Quay Street, Truro TR1 2GA*　T: (01872) 261169

ROGERS, Kevin. b 62. Ridley Hall Cam 13. **d** 15. C Parkstone St Luke *Sarum* from 15. *32 Penn Hill Avenue, Poole BH14 9LZ*　M: 07979-932241　E: damac@uwclub.net

ROGERS, Lady (Constance Jane). b 51. Lanchester Poly Cov BA 73. WEMTC 10. **d** 13　**p** 14. C Cusop w Blakemere, Bredwardine w Brobury etc *Heref* from 13. *Blakemere House, Blakemere, Hereford HR2 9JZ*　T: (01981) 500478　E: jane@blakemerehouse.myzen.co.uk

ROGERS, Leon James. b 83. St Andr Univ MTheol 06. Qu Coll Birm MA 09. **d** 09 **p** 10. C E Darlington *Dur* 09-12; P-in-c Hartlepool St Aid and St Columba from 12. *39 Chichester Close, Hartlepool TS25 2QT*　T: (01429) 871009　M: 07714-354771　E: lnrgrs@gmail.com

ROGERS, Leslie Peter. b 53. St Mellitus Coll BA 13. **d** 13 **p** 14. C Chelmsf Ascension 13-14; C Chelmsf Ascension w All SS from 14; Bp's Chapl from 15. *6 Riddiford Drive, Chelmsford CM1 2GB*　M: 07903-447236　T: (01245) 495101　E: revd.leslierogers@btinternet.com

ROGERS, Canon Llewelyn. Univ of Wales (Lamp) BA 59. St Mich Coll Llan. **d** 61 **p** 62. C Holywell *St As* 61-64; C Hawarden 64-70; R Bodfari 70-73; V Rhosymedre 73-78; V Llansantffraid-ym-Mechain 77-83; V Llansantffraid-ym-Mechain and Llanfechain 83-98; RD Llanfyllin 84-88; V Pont Robert, Pont Dolanog, Garthbeibio etc 98-01; Can St As Cathl 98-01; rtd 01; PtO *Lich* from 02. *17 Orchard Green, Llanymynech SY22 6PJ*　T: (01691) 839920

ROGERS, Mrs Lynne Rosemary. b 49. CITC 00. **d** 03 **p** 04. Aux Min Ferns w Kilbride, Toombe, Kilcormack etc *C & O* 03-06; Aux Min Gorey w Kilnahue, Leskinfere and Ballycanew 06-07; P-in-c New w Old Ross, Whitechurch, Fethard etc 07-11; NSM Chartham *Cant* 11-14; NSM Stone Street Gp 11-14; C Chartham and Upper Hardres w Stelling from 14. *The Rectory, Curtis Lane, Stelling Minnis, Canterbury CT4 6BT*　T: (01227) 709318　E: lynnerogers123@gmail.com

ROGERS, Canon Malcolm Dawson. b 63. SS Hild & Bede Coll Dur BA 84 Selw Coll Cam BA 88. Ridley Hall Cam 86. **d** 89 **p** 90. C Ipswich St Jo *St E* 89-93; CMS Russia 93-95; C Holloway St Mary Magd *Lon* 95-97; V 97-05; V Bury St Edmunds St Mary *St E* from 05; Hon Can St E Cathl from 13. *St Mary with St Peter Vicarage, 78 Hardwick Lane, Bury St Edmunds IP33 2RA*　T: (01284) 763416　E: malcolmrogers@onetel.com

ROGERS, Canon Malcolm Kenneth. b 72. Liv Inst of Educn BA 93. St Jo Coll Nottm MA 95 LTh 96. **d** 96 **p** 97. C W Derby St Luke *Liv* 96-00; V Huyton Quarry from 00; Hon Can Liv Cathl from 13. *St Gabriel's Vicarage, 2 St Agnes Road, Huyton, Liverpool L36 5TA*　T: 0151-489 2688　E: malcolm.rogers@huytondeanery.org

ROGERS, Mark James. b 64. Univ of Wales (Lamp) BA. Qu Coll Birm. **d** 89 **p** 90. C Dudley St Aug Holly Hall *Worc* 89-93; C Worc St Barn w Ch Ch 93-94; TV 94-97; USPG Belize 97-00; R Montreal St Columba Canada from 00. *4020 Hingston Avenue, Montreal QC H4A 2J7, Canada*　T: (001) (514) 486 1753　E: mrogers@montreal.anglican.ca

ROGERS, Martin Brian. b 53. **d** 92 **p** 93. OLM Collyhurst *Man* from 92. *8 Greenford Road, Crumpsall, Manchester M8 0NW*　T: 0161-740 4614

ROGERS, Maurice George Walden. b 23. AKC 51. **d** 52 **p** 53. C Bedford All SS *St Alb* 52-56; C Southfields St Barn *S'wark* 56-58; C Chingford SS Pet and Paul *Chelmsf* 58-61; V Gt Ilford St Luke 61-72; V Woodford St Barn 72-89; rtd 89; PtO *Chelmsf* from 89; *Win* 93-14. *The Coach House, 13 Bodorgan Road, Bournemouth BH2 6NQ*　T: (01202) 291034

ROGERS, Michael Andrew. b 47. OBE 91. FRAeS 96. Ripon Coll Cuddesdon. **d** 01 **p** 02. C Bromsgrove St Jo *Worc* 01-04; R Berrow w Pendock, Eldersfield, Hollybush etc 04-13; rtd 13. *York House, Wyche Lane, Bunbury, Tarporley CW6 9PD*　E: mandmrogers@btinternet.com

ROGERS, Michael Ernest. b 34. Sarum & Wells Th Coll 83. **d** 85 **p** 86. C Roehampton H Trin *S'wark* 85-88; V Ryhill *Wakef* 88-94; V S Elmsall 94-00; rtd 00; PtO *Derby* from 00. *The Willows, 49 Main Street, Weston-on-Trent, Derby DE72 2BL*　T: (01332) 700273　E: rogersm@talktalk.com

ROGERS, Michael Hugh Walton. b 52. K Coll Lon BD 73 AKC 73. St Aug Coll Cant 74. **d** 75 **p** 76. C Eastbourne St Andr *Chich* 75-78; C Uppingham w Ayston *Pet* 78-82; V Eye 82-90; R Cottesmore and Barrow w Ashwell and Burley 90-04; C 04-09; C Greetham and Thistleton w Stretton and Clipsham 01-05; P-in-c 05-09; C Empingham and Exton w Horn w Whitwell 06-09; RD Rutland 95-00; Can Pet Cathl 01-09; Bp's Adv for Min of Healing 05-09; P-in-c Ilfracombe SS Phil and Jas w W Down *Ex* 09-15; R Ilfracombe SS Phil and Jas from 15. *St James's Vicarage, Kingsley Avenue, Ilfracombe EX34 8ET*　T: (01271) 867499　E: mhwrogers@talktalk.net

ROGERS, Mrs Pamela Rose. b 46. Keswick Hall Coll CertEd 68. S Dios Minl Tr Scheme 92. **d** 95 **p** 96. NSM Axbridge w Shipham and Rowberrow *B & W* 95-11; Bp's Officer for Ord NSM (Wells Adnry) 02-11; rtd 11. *28 Beech Road, Shipham, Winscombe BS25 1SB*　T: (01934) 842685　E: pam.rogers@care4free.net

ROGERS, Mrs Patricia Anne. b 54. Lon Univ BD. Trin Coll Bris. **d** 87 **p** 94. Hon C Gayton Gp of Par *Nor* 87-91; Hon C Rackheath and Salhouse 91-96; Chapl to the Deaf 91-96; *Pet* 96-00; Visual Communications 00-11; TR Binsey *Carl* from 11. *The Vicarage, Torpenhow, Wigton CA7 1HT*　T: (016973) 71541　E: visiblecommunication@lineone.net

ROGERS, Pauline Ann. *See* GODFREY, Pauline Ann

ROGERS, Philip John. b 52. Univ of Wales CertEd 74 Nottm Univ BTh 79. St Jo Coll Nottm 76. **d** 79 **p** 80. C Stretford St Bride *Man* 79-84; P-in-c Plumstead St Jo w St Jas and St Paul *S'wark* 84-85; V from 85. *St John's Vicarage, 176 Griffin Road, London SE18 7QA*　T: (020) 8855 1827　E: philipjrogers@ukonline.co.uk

ROGERS (née PHILLIPS), Mrs Rebecca Jane. b 82. Birm Univ BA 04 Clare Coll Cam BTh 10. Ridley Hall Cam. **d** 10 **p** 11. C Childwall All SS *Liv* 10-15; P-in-c King's Lynn St Jo the Ev *Nor* from 15; C King's Lynn St Marg w St Nic from 15. *St John's Vicarage, Blackfriars Road, Ling's Lynn PE30 1NT*　M: 07764-747611　E: curate.allsaints@uwclub.net

ROGERS (née GOLDER), Mrs Rebecca Marie (Beki). b 71. Brunel Univ BA 94. Trin Coll Bris BA 02. **d** 02 **p** 03. C Short Heath *Birm* 02-05; Dir Faith Willesden Area *Lon* from 05; NSM Roxeth 05-10; NSM Bromley by Bow All Hallows from 10. *All Hallows' Rectory, Devons Road, London E3 3PN*　T: (020) 7538 9756　E: beki.rogers@hotmail.com

ROGERS, Richard Anthony. b 46. Ex Coll Ox BA 69. Qu Coll Birm 70. **d** 71 **p** 72. C Shirley *Birm* 71-74; Chapl Solihull Sch 74-78; Hon C Cotteridge *Birm* 78-84; Hon C Hill 84-93; Hd RE Kings Norton Girls' Sch 93-05; rtd 05; PtO *Birm* from 93. *4 Byron House, Belwell Place, Sutton Coldfield B74 4AY*　T: 0121-308 0310　E: richardrogers154@hotmail.com

ROGERS, Richard Jonathan. b 64. Trin Coll Bris BTh 96. **d** 96 **p** 97. C Carterton *Ox* 96-00; Crosslinks 00-03; PtO *B & W* 00-06. *Address temp unknown*

ROGERS, Canon Robert. b 42. Bernard Gilpin Soc Dur 66 St Aid Birkenhead 67 Ridley Hall Cam 69. **d** 70 **p** 71. C Childwall St Dav *Liv* 70-73; C Huntington *York* 73-76; TR Brayton 76-89; RD Selby 84-89; V New Malton 89-98; RD Bulmer and Malton 97-98; Asst Chapl York Health Services NHS Trust 98-99; Sen Chapl York Hosps NHS Foundn Trust 99-08; Can and Preb York Minster 03-08; rtd 08; PtO *York* from 08. *Tabgha, 9 Middlecave Drive, Malton YO17 7BB* T: (01653) 699469 E: bob.jacqui@btinternet.com

ROGERS, Robert Charles. b 55. St Pet Coll Birm CertEd 77 Warwick Univ MA 99. St Jo Coll Nottm 87. **d** 89 **p** 90. C Wellesbourne *Cov* 89-93; R Bourton w Frankton and Stretton on Dunsmore etc 93-97; Behaviour Support Teacher Warks LEA from 98; LtO *Cov* 98-07; NSM Rugby 07-13; NSM Rugby St Andr w St Pet and St John from 13. *18 Waring Way, Dunchurch, Rugby CV22 6PH* T: (01788) 817361 E: rob.rogers@talktalk.net

ROGERS, Robin. See ROGERS, John Robin

ROGERS, Ryder Rondeau. b 44. Lon Bible Coll 62. **d** 08 **p** 08. In Bapt Min 68-04; NSM Bride Valley *Sarum* from 08. *Stonehaven, 25 Bindbarrow Road, Burton Bradstock, Bridport DT6 4RG* T: (01308) 897780 E: ryder@ryderrogers.wanadoo.co.uk

ROGERS, Ms Sally Jean. b 54. Univ of Wales (Lamp) BA 77 Nottm Univ BTh 87. Linc Th Coll 84. **d** 87 **p** 94. Par Dn Bris St Mary Redcliffe w Temple etc 87-90; Par Dn Greenford H Cross *Lon* 90-94; C 94-96; TV Hemel Hempstead *St Alb* 96-02; Development Worker Changing Attitude 03-06; Chapl R Holloway and Bedf New Coll *Guildf* 06-10; R Petryal and Betws yn Rhos *St As* from 10. *The Rectory, Llanfairtalhaiarn, Abergele LL22 8ST* T: (01745) 720273

ROGERS, Sarah Ann. b 73. York Univ BSc 94 Univ of Wales (Cardiff) PhD 98. St Mich Coll Llan BA 09. **d** 09 **p** 10. C Caerphilly *Llan* 09-12; P-in-c Abercynon from 12. *The Vicarage, 67 Grovers Field, Abercynon, Mountain Ash CF45 4PQ* T: (01443) 740207 E: revdsarah@btinternet.com

ROGERS, Trevor. See ROGERS, John William Trevor

ROGERS, Canon Valentine Hilary. b 48. UCD BA 68. St Columban's Coll Navan 65. **d** 71 **p** 72. C Dandenong Australia 88-89; P-in-c Eltham 89-92; I 92-96; C Dublin Ch Ch Cathl Gp and PV Ch Ch Cathl Dublin 96-97; I Armadale H Advent Australia 98-09; I Aughaval w Achill, Knappagh, Dugort etc *T, K & A* from 09; Can Tuam Cathl from 14; Can Killala Cathl from 14. *The Rectory, Newport Road, Westport, Co Mayo, Republic of Ireland* T: (00353) (98) 25127 M: 87-147 5597 E: valandjorogers@gmail.com

ROGERS, William. See ROGERS, Clive William

ROGERS, William Arthur. b 41. Lon Univ BA 64 CertEd. Chich Th Coll 79. **d** 81 **p** 82. C Chandler's Ford *Win* 81-84; R Bentley and Binsted 84-94; P-in-c The Lulworths, Winfrith Newburgh and Chaldon *Sarum* 94-99; rtd 99; PtO *Win* from 13. *Greenways, 6 Shaves Lane, New Milton BH25 5DJ* T: (01425) 638751

ROGERS, William John. b 71. SEITE 07. **d** 10 **p** 11. C Wimbledon Park St Luke *S'wark* 10-14; V Fulham St Matt *Lon* from 14. *St Matthew's Vicarage, 2 Clancarty Road, London SW6 3AB* T: (020) 7731 3272 M: 07879-084321 E: william.j.rogers@btinternet.com

ROGERSON, Anthony Carroll. b 37. Trin Coll Ox BA 59 MA 63 MCIPD 92. SAOMC 96. **d** 98 **p** 99. NSM Radley and Sunningwell *Ox* 98-02; PtO from 02. *9 Selwyn Crescent, Radley, Abingdon OX14 3AW* T: (01235) 550214 E: ahrogerson@yahoo.co.uk

✠**ROGERSON, The Rt Revd Barry.** b 36. Leeds Univ BA 60 Bris Univ Hon LLD 93. Wells Th Coll 60. **d** 62 **p** 63 **c** 79. C S Shields St Hilda w St Thos *Dur* 62-65; C Bishopwearmouth St Nic 65-67; Lect Lich Th Coll 67-71; Vice-Prin 71-72; Lect Sarum & Wells Th Coll 72-74; V Wednesfield St Thos *Lich* 75-79; TR Wednesfield 79; Suff Bp Wolverhampton 79-85; Bp Bris 85-02; rtd 02; Hon Asst Bp *B & W* from 03. *Flat 2, 30 Albert Road, Clevedon BS21 7RR* T: (01275) 541964 E: barry.rogerson@blueyonder.co.uk

ROGERSON, Colin Scott. b 30. St Andr Univ MA 55. Edin Th Coll. **d** 57 **p** 58. C Byker St Ant *Newc* 57-59; C Newc St Geo 59-63; C Wooler 63-67; V Tynemouth St Aug 67-75; C Dur St Marg 75-88; P-in-c Hebburn St Jo 88-95; rtd 95; PtO *Dur* from 95. *6 Edlingham Road, Durham DH1 5YS* T: 0191-386 1956

ROGERSON, Canon Ian Matthew. b 45. Bede Coll Dur CertEd 67 Open Univ BA 76. Oak Hill Th Coll. **d** 83 **p** 84. C Haughton St Mary *Man* 83-86; V Ramsbottom St Andr 86-05; P-in-c Edenfield and Stubbins 04-05; TR Ramsbottom and Edenfield 05-10; AD Bury 96-05; Hon Can Man Cathl 04-10; rtd 10; PtO *Man* 10-14; *St D* from 10. *Cae Banc, Broadway, Laugharne, Carmarthen SA33 4NT* T: (01994) 427664

ROGERSON, Prof John William. b 35. Man Univ BD 61 DD 75 Linacre Ho Ox BA 63 MA 67 Aber Univ Hon DD 98 Friedrich Schiller Univ DrTheol 05 Freiburg Univ DrTheol 06. Ripon Hall Ox 61. **d** 64 **p** 66. C Dur St Oswald 64-67; Lect Th Dur Univ 64-75; Sen Lect 75-79; LtO *Dur* 67-79; *Sheff* from 79; Prof Bibl Studies Sheff Univ 79-96; Hd of Dept 79-94; Hon Can Sheff Cathl 82-95. *60 Marlborough Road, Sheffield S10 1DB* T: 0114-268 1426

ROLAND, Andrew Osborne. b 45. Mert Coll Ox BA 66 St Jo Coll Dur BA 84. Cranmer Hall Dur. **d** 84 **p** 85. C Streatham St Leon *S'wark* 84-87; C Kingston All SS w St Jo 87-94; P-in-c Hackbridge and Beddington Corner 94-06; V 06-15; rtd 15. *Address temp unknown*

ROLES, John William. b 54. Middx Poly BA 76 Whitelands Coll Lon PGCE 77. Ripon Coll Cuddesdon 11. **d** 12. NSM Ilfracombe, Lee, Woolacombe, Bittadon etc *Ex* from 12. *6 Adelaide Terrace, Ilfracombe EX34 9JR* T: (01271) 863350 M: 07791-256361 E: johnroles@talk21.com

ROLFE, Charles Edward. b 34. Wells Th Coll 68. **d** 70 **p** 71. C Bath Twerton-on-Avon *B & W* 70-79; TV Wellington and Distr 79-85; P-in-c Frome Ch Ch 85-89; V 89-94; Chapl Victoria Hosp Frome 85-94; Chapl St Adhelm's Hosp Frome 88-94; rtd 94; NSM Fordingbridge and Breamore and Hale etc *Win* 95-05; PtO from 05. *29 Ayleswade Road, Salisbury SP2 8DW* T: (01722) 335601 E: charles@rolfe14.freeserve.co.uk

ROLFE, Joseph William. b 37. Qu Coll Birm 78. **d** 81 **p** 82. NSM Tredington and Darlingscott w Newbold on Stour *Cov* 81-91; NSM Brailes from 91; NSM Sutton under Brailes from 91; NSM Shipston Deanery from 98. *35 Manor Lane, Shipston-on-Stour CV36 4EF* T: (01608) 661737

ROLFE, Paul Douglas. b 46. MIBC 90. NOC 90. **d** 93 **p** 94. C Urmston *Man* 93-96; V Lawton Moor 96-03; P-in-c Burnage St Nic 03-07; Sen Chapl Costa Blanca *Eur* 07-08; P-in-c Mellor *Blackb* 09-11; P-in-c Balderstone 09-11; rtd 12. *51A Westfield Lane, Scholes, Cleckheaton BD19 6DR* T: (01274) 690476 E: paul.d.rolfe@btinternet.com

ROLFE, Mrs Susan Margaret. b 58. Man Univ BA 81. ERMC 05. **d** 08 **p** 09. NSM Pet Ch Carpenter 08-11; NSM Paston 11-12; NSM Pet St Paul 13; rtd 13. *1 Woodfield Road, Peterborough PE3 6HD* T: (01733) 567509 E: susan.m.rolfe@btinternet.com

ROLLETT, Robert Henry. b 39. Leeds Univ BA 61 Leic Univ CertEd 62. Linc Th Coll 77. **d** 79 **p** 80. C Littleport *Ely* 79-82; P-in-c Manea 82-83; V 83-85; P-in-c Wimblington 82-83; R 83-85; V Thorney Abbey 85-93; P-in-c The Ramseys and Upwood 93-94; TR 94-99; rtd 99; P-in-c Scalford w Goadby Marwood and Wycombe etc *Leic* 99-00; PtO *Pet* 01-05. *2 Stockerston Crescent, Uppingham, Oakham LE15 9UB* T: (01572) 823685

ROLLINGS, Mrs Tina Petula. b 51. St Mellitus Coll 12. **d** 13 **p** 14. OLM Chingford SS Pet and Paul *Chelmsf* from 13. *25 Woodland Road, London E4 7ET* T: (020) 8523 7174 E: tinaprollings@aol.com

ROLLINS, David. b 65. De Montfort Univ BA 98. St Steph Ho Ox 99. **d** 01 **p** 02. C Leic St Aid 01-05; P-in-c Corringham *Chelmsf* 05-10; P-in-c Fobbing 05-10; R Corringham and Fobbing from 10. *The Rectory, Church Road, Corringham, Stanford-le-Hope SS17 9AP* T: (01375) 673074 E: drollins@btinternet.com

ROLLINS, Deborah Mary Rollins. See FLACH, Deborah Mary Rollins

ROLLINSON, James Christopher. b 50. **d** 13 **p** 14. NSM Carmarthen St Pet and Abergwili etc *St D* 13-14; C Cynwyl Elfed w Newchurch and Trelech a'r Betws from 14. *The Vicarage, Cynwyl Elfed, Carmarthen SA33 6TH* E: jim.rollinson@gmail.com

ROLLS, Caroline Louise. b 87. **d** 15. C Watford *St Alb* from 15. *8A Lammas Road, Watford WD18 0BA* M: 07474-080011 E: rollscaroline@yahoo.com

ROLLS, Miss Pamela Margaret. b 59. **d** 10 **p** 11. OLM Harwell w Chilton *Ox* from 10. *15 Elderfield Crescent, Chilton, Didcot OX11 0RY* T: (01235) 834475 E: pamrolls@tiscali.co.uk

ROLLS, Peter. b 40. Leeds Inst of Educn CertEd. NOC 80. **d** 83 **p** 84. NSM Meltham *Leeds* from 83. *14 Heather Road, Meltham, Huddersfield HD7 3EY* T: (01484) 340342 E: p.c.rolls@hotmail.com

ROLPH, Reginald Lewis George. b 29. Open Univ BA 74. Bps' Coll Cheshunt 55. **d** 58 **p** 59. C Perivale *Lon* 58-61; C Wokingham St Paul *Ox* 61-63; C Letchworth *St Alb* 63-78; PtO from 78; rtd 93. *22 Souberie Avenue, Letchworth Garden City SG6 3JA* T: (01462) 684596

ROLSTON, Cyril Willis Matthias. b 29. CITC 66. **d** 68 **p** 69. C Portadown St Mark *Arm* 68-71; I Loughgilly w Clare 71-81; Dir of Ords from 72; Asst Chapl Craigavon Area Hosp Gp Trust 80-96; I Moy w Charlemont *Arm* 81-96; Preb Arm Cathl

92-96; rtd 96; Chapl Armagh and Dungannon Health and Soc Services from 96. *19 Lower Parklands, Dungannon BT71 7JN* T: (028) 8772 5910 M: 07742-421886
E: cyril.rolston@btinternet.com

ROLT (*formerly SHARPLES*)**, Mrs Jean.** b 37. Padgate Coll of Educn TCert 58. **d** 04 **p** 05. NSM Gerrans w St Anthony-in-Roseland and Philleigh *Truro* 04-08; NSM St Just-in-Roseland and St Mawes 05-08; rtd 08. *Tregear Vean Farmhouse, St Mawes, Truro TR2 5AB* T: (01326) 270954 M: 07840-567933
E: revjeanrolt@mac.com

ROLTON, Patrick Hugh. b 49. Sarum & Wells Th Coll 72. **d** 74 **p** 75. C Roch 74-79; C Edenbridge 79-81; R N Cray 81-97; rtd 97. *71 The Grove, Sidcup DA14 5NG*

ROMANIS, Adam John Aidan. b 57. Pemb Coll Ox BA 78 MA 83. Westcott Ho Cam 81. **d** 84 **p** 85. C Northfield *Birm* 84-88; TV Seaton Hirst *Newc* 88-93; V Newc Ch Ch w St Ann 93-99; V Cowley St Jo *Ox* 99-14; V Perry Beeches *Birm* from 14. *St Matthew's Vicarage, 313 Beeches Road, Birmingham B42 2QR* T: 0121-360 2100 E: adam.romanis@btinternet.com

ROMANO, Paul. b 56. Glas Univ MA 77 LLB 79 Open Univ BA 91. TISEC. **d** 05. NSM Glas St Marg 05-11; R Glas St Ninian from 11. *St Ninian's Rectory, 32 Glencairn Drive, Glasgow G41 4PW* T: 0141-423 1247 E: paul.romano@btinternet.com

ROMO-GARCIA, Brother Gerardo. b 66. **d** 04 **p** 05. Mexico 04-07; SSF from 08; PtO *Cant* 09-12; *Birm* from 12. *St George's Rectory, 100 Bridge Street West, Birmingham B19 2YX* T: 0121-359 2000 E: amici_91401@hotmail.com

RONAYNE, Peter Henry. b 34. FCA 68. Oak Hill Th Coll 64. **d** 66 **p** 67. C Chesham St Mary *Ox* 66-69; C Worthing H Trin *Chich* 69-74; V Shoreditch St Leon w St Mich *Lon* 74-82; P-in-c Norwood St Luke *S'wark* 82-85; V 85-94; V W Norwood St Luke 94-99; RD Streatham 87-91; rtd 99; PtO *S'wark* 00-04. *54 Maywater Close, South Croydon CR2 0LS* T: (020) 8651 9743 M: 07951-083278 E: pronayne@onetel.com

RONCHETTI, Quentin Marcus. b 56. Ripon Coll Cuddesdon 79. **d** 80 **p** 81. C Eastbourne St Mary *Chich* 80-83; C Moulsecoomb 83-85; TV 85-90; V Findon Valley 90-97; V Shoreham Beach 97-07; V Midhurst 07-12; Chapl Costa Blanca *Eur* 12-15; Sen Chapl from 15. *Partida Cuxarret 20C, 03710 Calpe (Alicante), Spain* T: (0034) 965 874 166

RONGONG, Tembu Namderr. b 76. St Andr Univ MA 98 Aber Univ BTh 09. TISEC. **d** 06 **p** 07. C Dunfermline *St And* 06-08; R Edin SS Phil and Jas from 08. *5 Wardie Road, Edinburgh EH5 3QE* T: 0131-552 4300 *or* 552 7244
E: tembu.rongong@btinternet.com

ROOKE, James Templeman. b 43. Saltley Tr Coll Birm CertEd 65. EMMTC 79. **d** 84 **p** 85. NSM Bassingham *Linc* 84-89; NSM Hykeham 89-94; Sub Chapl HM Pris Morton Hall 94; P-in-c Borrowdale *Carl* 94-97; Chapl Keswick Sch 94-95; NSM Hykeham *Linc* 97-02; Sub Chapl HM Pris Morton Hall 97-00; CF (ACF) 00-08; NSM Swinderby *Linc* from 02. *The Chestnuts, Main Street, Norton Disney, Lincoln LN6 9JU* T: (01522) 788315

ROOKE, John George Michael. b 47. St Jo Coll Dur BA 72. Cranmer Hall Dur 71. **d** 74 **p** 75. C Skelmersdale St Paul *Liv* 74-78; TV Speke St Aid 78-81; Ind Chapl 81-85; V Knotty Ash St Jo 85-08; rtd 08. *c/o Fairway Golf Shops Ltd, Units 1 & 2, Victoria Forge, Victoria Street, Windermere LA23 1AD*

✠**ROOKE, The Rt Revd Patrick William.** b 55. Open Univ BA 85 TCD MPhil 04. Sarum & Wells Th Coll 75. **d** 78 **p** 79 **c** 11. C Mossley *Conn* 78-81; C Ballywalter 81-83; I Craigs w Dunaghy and Killagan 83-88; I Ballymore *Arm* 88-94; Asst Prov and Dioc Registrar 92-94; Hon V Choral Arm Cathl 93-94; I Agherton *Conn* 94-06; Preb and Can Conn Cathl 01-06; Adn Dalriada 05-06; Dean Arm and Keeper of Public Lib 06-11; Bp T, K & A from 11. *Bishop's House, Breaffy Woods, Castlebar, Co Mayo, Republic of Ireland* T: (00353) (94) 903 5703 E: bishop@tuam.anglican.org *or* rooke59@hotmail.com

ROOKWOOD, Colin John. b 40. TCD BA 64 MA 66 SS Mark & Jo Coll Chelsea PGCE 66. Clifton Th Coll 67. **d** 70 **p** 71. C Eccleston Ch Ch *Liv* 70-75; V Penge St Jo *Roch* 75-82; V Childwall All SS *Liv* 82-91; Chapl Bethany Sch Goudhurst 91-03; rtd 03; PtO *Roch* 01-10; *Ches* from 11. *2 Glenthorn Grove, Sale M33 3AG* T: 0161-962 0003 M: 07541-426440
E: colinrookwood120@btinternet.com

ROOKWOOD (*née TASH*)**, Elizabeth.** b 82. Leeds Univ BA 05. Cranmer Hall Dur 12. **d** 15. C Morpeth *Newc* from 15. *3 Stobhill Villas, Morpeth NE61 2SH* M: 07793-964392

ROOM, Canon Frederick John. b 24. St Jo Coll Ox BA 49 MA 53. Wells Th Coll 49. **d** 51 **p** 52. C Bradford cum Beswick *Man* 51-54; C Halliwell St Marg 54-56; C Farnham Royal *Ox* 56-58; C-in-c Farnham Royal S CD 58-70; TV Thetford *Nor* 70-89; Sen Ind Missr 75-89; Hon Can Nor Cathl 77-89; rtd 89; PtO *Nor* from 89. *41 Brakendon Close, Norwich NR1 3BX* T: (01603) 664315

ROOME, Mrs Alison Morag Venessa. b 48. Bp Lonsdale Coll TCert 71. EMMTC 98. **d** 01 **p** 02. NSM Alfreton *Derby* 01-07; P-in-c 05-07; NSM Belper Ch Ch w Turnditch from 07. *55 Dovedale Crescent, Belper DE56 1HJ* T: (01773) 825635 E: aliroome@lineone.net *or* alison@christchurchbelper.org.uk

ROOMS (*née JONES*)**, Mrs Karen Sheila Frances.** b 61. Bris Univ BA 82. St Jo Coll Nottm MTh 06. **d** 06 **p** 07. C Hyson Green and Forest Fields *S'well* 06-09; P-in-c Nottingham St Ann w Em 09-11; V from 11; AD Nottm S from 13. *St Ann's Vicarage, 17 Robin Hood Chase, Nottingham NG3 4EY* T: 0115-950 5471 E: vyumba@yahoo.co.uk

ROOMS, Canon Nigel James. b 60. Leeds Univ BSc 81 Nottm Univ MA 95 Birm Univ ThD 08 CEng 86 MIChemE 86. St Jo Coll Nottm 87. **d** 90 **p** 91. C Chell *Lich* 90-94; Min Moshi St Marg Tanzania 94-01; Dir Th Educn by Ext 94-01; Hon Can Arusha from 01; Dioc Dir of Tr *S'well* 02-07; Assoc Dir Practical Th 07-10; P-in-c Basford St Leodegarius 07-09; Dir Min and Miss from 10; C Bestwood Park w Rise Park from 10. *St Ann's Vicarage, 17 Robin Hood Chase, Nottingham NG3 4EY* T: 0115-950 5471 E: nigel.rooms@southwell.anglican.org

ROONEY, Andrew John. b 59. St Mellitus Coll 13. **d** 15. C Hammersmith H Innocents and St Jo *Lon* from 15. *Address temp unknown*

ROOSE-EVANS, James Humphrey. b 27. St Benet's Hall Ox BA 52 MA 56. **d** 81 **p** 81. NSM Kington and Weobley *Heref* 81-05; NSM Primrose Hill St Mary w Avenue Road St Paul *Lon* 82-97; PtO from 97; *Heref* 05-13; *S & B* 07-13. *26B Upper Park Road, London NW3 2UT* T: (020) 7586 6507
E: j.rooseevans@btinternet.com

ROOT, Preb John Brereton. b 41. Lon Univ BA 64 Em Coll Cam BA 66 MA. Ridley Hall Cam 64. **d** 68 **p** 69. C Harlesden St Mark *Lon* 68-73; C Lower Homerton St Paul 73-76; Chapl Ridley Hall Cam 76; Vice-Prin 76-79; V Alperton *Lon* 79-11; AD Brent 95-00; Preb St Paul's Cathl 01-11; rtd 11. *42 Newlyn Road, London N17 6RX* M: 07723-033831

ROOTES, William Brian. b 44. St And NSM Tr Scheme 88. **d** 91. NSM Auchterarder *St And* 91-97; NSM Muthill 91-97; Dioc Sec 98-00; Treas Action of Chs Together in Scotland 01-06; LtO *St And* from 06. *The School House, Fowlis Wester, Crieff PH7 3NL* T: (01764) 683772 E: w.rootes77@btinternet.com

ROOTHAM, Gerald Raymond. b 47. **d** 02 **p** 03. OLM Mattishall and the Tudd Valley *Nor* 02-10; C 10-14; rtd 15; PtO *Nor* from 15. *8 Burgh Lane, Mattishall, Dereham NR20 3QW* T: (01362) 858533 E: geraldrootham@outlook.com

ROPER, David John. b 53. St Steph Ho Ox 93. **d** 95 **p** 96. C Hunstanton St Mary w Ringstead Parva etc *Nor* 95-98; TV E Dereham and Scarning 98-00; R Barham w Bishopsbourne and Kingston *Cant* 00-08; C Nonington w Wymynswold and Goodnestone etc 00-08; AD E Bridge 01-08; P-in-c Broadstairs 08-11; R 11-14; AD Thanet 08-09; P-in-c St Peter-in-Thanet 10-11; Hon Min Can Cant Cathl 03-08; Hon Can Cant Cathl 08-14; R Falkland Is from 14. *PO Box 160, The Deanery, 17 Ross Road, Stanley, Falkland Islands FIQQ 1ZZ* T: (00500) 21100 E: christchurch@horizon.co.fk

ROPER, Glenn. b 51. York Univ MA 91 Caerleon Coll of Educn CertEd 73. **d** 04 **p** 05. NSM Ovenden *Leeds* from 04. *113 Meadow Drive, Halifax HX3 5JZ* T: (01422) 368086 E: glennroper@fsmail.net

ROPER, Mrs Joan. b 49. **d** 10 **p** 11. NSM Newport w Longford, and Chetwynd *Lich* 10-12; NSM Tong, Shifnal and Sheriffhales 12-13; NSM Gt and Lt Ouseburn w Marton cum Grafton etc *Leeds* from 13. *11 Back Lane, Whixley, York YO26 8BG*

ROPER, Michael Darwin Alston. b 66. Leeds Univ BA 03. Coll of Resurr Mirfield 01. **d** 03 **p** 04. C Mortlake w E Sheen *S'wark* 03-07; P-in-c Egham Hythe *Guildf* from 07. *St Paul's Vicarage, 214 Wendover Road, Staines TW18 3DF* T: (01784) 453625 E: gore_lodge@yahoo.co.uk

ROPER, Terence Chaus. b 35. K Coll Lon 56. St Boniface Warminster 59. **d** 60 **p** 61. C Forton *Portsm* 60-63; C Arlington St Alban USA 63-65; C Dallas St Thos 65-67; R Dallas Our Lady of Grace 67-73; R Irving Redeemer 73-76; R Dallas Transfiguration 76-99; R Philadelphia H Trin from 99. *1815 John F Kennedy Boulevard #2308, Philadelphia PA 19103-1731, USA* T: (001) (215) 587 6873 *or* 567 1267

ROSAMOND, Derek William. b 49. Linc Th Coll 87. **d** 89 **p** 90. C Coventry Caludon *Cov* 89-93; Urban Regeneration Chapl S Tyneside *Dur* 93-96; TV Sunderland 96-04; P-in-c Stockton St Paul 04-15; Community P SW Stockton 04-15; rtd 15. *28 Stoneybrough Lane, Thirsk YO7 2LS*
E: derekrosamond@hotmail.com

ROSBOROUGH, Mrs Rachel Claire. b 76. Anglia Poly Univ BA 00 Ches Univ MA 14. St Jo Coll Nottm 06. **d** 08 **p** 09. C Charlton Kings H Apostles *Glouc* 10-11; R Bourton-on-the-Water w Clapton etc from 11. *The Rectory, School Hill, Bourton-on-the-Water, Cheltenham GL54 2AW* T: (01451) 820386 E: rachelrosborough@hotmail.com

ROSCOE, David John. b 64. UEA BA 87 Selw Coll Cam BA 93. Aston Tr Scheme 89 Westcott Ho Cam 91. **d** 94 **p** 95. C Ditton St Mich *Liv* 94-98; TV Kirkby 98-99; V Wigan St Steph 99-03; Jt P-in-c Aspull and New Springs 02-03; V New Springs and Whelley and Chapl Wrightington Wigan and Leigh NHS Trust 03-10; P-in-c Feniscowles *Blackb* from 10; C Blackb St Fran and St Aid 13-14; P-in-c Feniscliffe from 14. *The Vicarage, 732 Preston Old Road, Feniscowles, Blackburn BB2 5EN* T: (01254) 201236

ROSCOE, Simon Nicolas. b 51. SEITE 02. **d** 04 **p** 06. C Whitstable *Cant* 04-05; C Faversham 05-09; V Southchurch Ch Ch *Chelmsf* from 09. *Christ Church Vicarage, 58 Colbert Road, Southend-on-Sea SS1 3BP* T: (01702) 582585 E: simonsccc@aol.com

ROSE, Andrew David. b 45. BA 81. Oak Hill Th Coll 78. **d** 81 **p** 82. C Northwood Em *Lon* 81-86; V Iver *Ox* 86-95; R Frinton *Chelmsf* 95-07; TV Washfield, Stoodleigh, Withleigh etc *Ex* 07-10; rtd 10; PtO *Chelmsf* from 14. *3 Corinda House, 14 Queens Road, Frinton-on-Sea CO13 9BL* T: (01255) 677238 E: andrewandjen@eclipse.co.uk

ROSE (née ARDLEY), Annette Susan. b 68. SEITE 01. **d** 04 **p** 05. C Barham w Bishopsbourne and Kingston *Cant* 04-07; P-in-c Wingham w Elmstone and Preston w Stourmouth 07-09; P-in-c New Eltham All SS *S'wark* 09-10; V from 10. *All Saints' Vicarage, 22 Bercta Road, London SE9 3TZ* T: (020) 8850 0374 E: revannette.rose@btinternet.com

ROSE, Anthony James. b 47. Trin Coll Bris BD 72. **d** 73 **p** 74. C Halliwell St Pet *Man* 73-76; CF 76-94; R Colchester Ch Ch w St Mary V *Chelmsf* 94-01; RD Colchester 98-01; P-in-c Boreham 01-06; rtd 06; PtO *Chelmsf* from 06. *30 The Mill Apartments, East Street, Colchester CO1 2QT* T: (01206) 616739 E: ajrose@dsl.pipex.com

ROSE, Anthony John. b 53. Birm Univ BA 79. Trin Coll Bris 84. **d** 86 **p** 87. C The Quinton *Birm* 86-90; R Abbas and Templecombe w Horsington *B & W* 90-98; V New Thundersley *Chelmsf* from 98. *St George's Vicarage, 89 Rushbottom Lane, Benfleet SS7 4DN* T: (01268) 792088 E: stgvicar@blueyonder.co.uk

ROSE, Canon Bernard Frederick. b 47. **d** 91 **p** 92. OLM Ipswich St Thos St E 91-09; P-in-c Somersham w Flowton and Offton w Willisham 09-15; P-in-c Ringshall w Battisford, Barking w Darmsden etc 09-15; Hon Can St E Cathl from 05; rtd 15; PtO *St E* from 15. *84 Chesterfield Drive, Ipswich IP1 6DN* T: (01473) 462390 E: holy-rose@supanet.com

ROSE, Christopher John. b 66. Edin Univ BSc 88. EAMTC 97. **d** 00 **p** 01. NSM Cambridge St Paul *Ely* 00-07; NSM All Hallows Lon Wall from 07. *6 Montreal Road, Cambridge CB1 3NP* T: (01223) 511241 *or* (020) 7588 8922 F: 566092 E: chris@amostrust.org

ROSE, Eve. b 63. Leeds Univ BA 85. Qu Coll Birm 99. **d** 01 **p** 02. C Seacroft *Ripon* 01-04; Chapl Hull and E Riding Community Health NHS Trust 04-06; Mental Health Chapl Humber Mental Health Teaching NHS Trust from 06; Hon C Hessle *York* 06-11. *Humber Mental Health NHS Trust, Beverley Road, Willerby, Hull HU10 6ED* T: (01482) 223191 F: 303900 M: 07771-851725

ROSE, Miss Geraldine Susan. b 47. Trin Coll Bris BD 78. **dss** 78 **d** 87 **p** 94. Tonbridge St Steph *Roch* 78-80; Littleover *Derby* 80-88; Par Dn 87-88; Par Dn Wombwell *Sheff* 88-94; C 94-96; rtd 96; PtO *Sheff* from 96. *5 Wheatcroft, Conisbrough, Doncaster DN12 2BL* T: (01709) 867761 E: sroserhodon@onetel.net.uk

ROSE, Harry. See ROSE, Lionel Stafford Harry

ROSE, Ms Helen Anita. b 63. STETS 09. **d** 12 **p** 13. C Shoreham Beach *Chich* 12-14; C New Shoreham and Shoreham Beach from 14. *17 Colvill Avenue, Shoreham-by-Sea BN43 5WN* T: (01273) 461551 M: 07971-779284 E: rosyrosy@tiscali.co.uk

ROSE, Ingrid Elizabeth. b 57. Univ of Wales (Abth) BA 78 DipEd 79. Trin Coll Carmarthen 84. **d** 87 **p** 01. NSM Ysbyty Cynfyn w Llantrisant and Eglwys Newydd *St D* 87-90 and 92-95; NSM to Adn Cardigan 00-03; NSM Grwp Bro Ystwyth a Mynach 03-13; PtO from 13. *Ystwyth Villa, Pontrhydygroes, Ystrad Meurig SY25 6DS* T: (01974) 282728 E: ingridrose@btinternet.com

ROSE, John Clement Wansey. b 46. New Coll Ox BA 71 MA 72. Ripon Hall Ox 70. **d** 72 **p** 73. C Harborne St Pet *Birm* 72-76; TV Kings Norton 76-81; V Maney 81-02; R Condover w Frodesley, Acton Burnell etc *Heref* 02-12; rtd 12; PtO *Lich* from 13. *32 Park Lane, High Ercall, Telford TF6 6AY* T: (01952) 770243

ROSE, Jonathan Graham. b 47. Leeds Univ BA 72 Birm Univ MEd 83 Ex Univ MA 08 FRSA 97 MCIPD 03. STETS 10. **d** 11 **p** 12. NSM Quantock Towers *B & W* from 11; RD Quantock from 15. *4 Bakers Orchard, Crowcombe Heathfield, Taunton TA4 4PA* T: (01984) 618715 M: 07969-008091 E: revjonrose@gmail.com

ROSE, Judith Barbara. b 51. TCert 72. SAOMC 96. **d** 99 **p** 00. OLM Stantonbury and Willen *Ox* 99-11; PtO from 11. *16 Runnymede, Giffard Park, Milton Keynes MK14 5QL* T/F: (01908) 618634

ROSE, The Ven Kathleen Judith. b 37. Lon Bible Coll BD 73 St Mich Ho Ox 64. **dss** 76 **d** 87 **p** 94. Leeds St Geo *Ripon* 76-81; Bradf Cathl 81-85; S Gillingham *Roch* 85-87; Par Dn 87-90; RD Gillingham 88-90; Bp's Dom Chapl 90-95; Asst Dir of Ords 90-95; Hon Can Roch Cathl 93-02; Acting Adn Tonbridge 95-96; Adn Tonbridge 96-02; rtd 02; PtO *B & W* from 03. *47 Hill Lea Gardens, Cheddar BS27 3JH* T: (01934) 741708 M: 07736-616382 E: rosegwyer@btinternet.com

ROSE, Lionel Stafford Harry. b 38. MBE 93. Wells Th Coll 69. **d** 71 **p** 72. C Minchinhampton *Glouc* 71-73; C Thornbury 73-75; R Ruardean 75-80; V Whiteshill 80-84; CF 84-93; Chapl HM Pris Kirkham 93-95; Chapl HM Pris Wymott 95-01; Chapl HM Pris Rye Hill 01; rtd 01; PtO *Ely* from 02. *4 Samian Close, Highfield, Caldecote, Cambridge CB23 7GP*

ROSE, Mrs Lynda Kathryn. b 51. Ex Univ BA 73 Barrister-at-Law (Gray's Inn) 81. Wycliffe Hall Ox BA 86. **d** 87 **p** 94. C Highfield *Ox* 87-88; C Ox St Clem 89-93; Dir Anastasis Min 93-99; NSM Ambrosden w Merton and Piddington *Ox* 94-99. *14 Scholar Mews, Marston Ferry Road, Oxford OX2 7GY* T: (01865) 554421 E: lyndarose2000@yahoo.co.uk

ROSE, Margaret. See FARR, Margaret

ROSE, Michael Mark. b 63. Hull Univ BA 04. Westcott Ho Cam 07. **d** 09 **p** 10. C Linc St Nic w St Jo Newport 09-10; C Boultham 10-12; V Carr Dyke Gp from 12. *The Vicarage, 6 Walcott Road, Billinghay, Lincoln LN4 4EH* M: 07846-601141 E: mikeredrose63@hotmail.com

ROSE, Mrs Pamela Inneen. b 49. Hull Univ BSc 71 Moray Ho Coll of Educn PGCE 72. **d** 06 **p** 07. OLM Stow Gp *Linc* from 06. *Daisy Cottage, 16-18 Grange Lane, Willingham by Stow, Gainsborough DN21 5LB* T: (01427) 787578 E: pamrose@worldshare.org.uk

ROSE, Canon Paul Rosamond. b 32. Trin Hall Cam BA 56 MA 60. Westcott Ho Cam 57. **d** 59 **p** 60. C Wandsworth St Anne *S'wark* 59-61; C Tormohun *Ex* 61-64; P-in-c Daramombe Rhodesia 64-67; Min Can, Prec and Sacr Pet Cathl 67-72; V Paddington St Jo w St Mich *Lon* 72-79; PV Westmr Abbey 74-79; Min Can and Prec Cant Cathl 79-84; V Rothwell w Orton *Pet* 84-87; R Rothwell w Orton, Rushton w Glendon and Pipewell 87-97; Can Pet Cathl 94-97; rtd 97; Heidelberg *Eur* 98; Chapl PtO *Pet* from 97; *Lon* from 98; *Eur* from 98; *Ely* from 03. *15 Standish Court, Campaign Avenue, Peterborough PE2 9RR* T: (01733) 553272 E: canons.rose@virgin.net

ROSE, Robert Alec Lewis. b 41. Man Univ BSc 64. Wycliffe Hall Ox 85. **d** 87 **p** 88. C Vange *Chelmsf* 87-91; C Langdon Hills 91-94; P-in-c Bentley Common 94-00; P-in-c Kelvedon Hatch 94-00; P-in-c Navestock 94-00; R Bentley Common, Kelvedon Hatch and Navestock 00-08; rtd 08; PtO *St E* from 09. *47 High Street, Wickham Market, Woodbridge IP13 0HE* T: (01728) 748199 E: robdaphnerose@btinternet.com

ROSE, Susan. See ROSE, Geraldine Susan

ROSE, Mrs Susan Margaret. b 59. Westmr Coll of Educn BEd 81. SAOMC 95. **d** 98 **p** 99. C N Petherton w Northmoor Green *B & W* 98-01; P-in-c 01-03; P-in-c N Newton w St Michaelchurch, Thurloxton etc 01-03; R Alfred Jewel 03-09; RD Sedgemoor 06-09; P-in-c Cheddar 09-11; P-in-c Rodney Stoke w Draycott 09-11; R Cheddar, Draycott and Rodney Stoke 11-15; RD Axbridge 14-15; Dir of Voc from 15; Dir IME 4-7 from 15. *25 Wood Close, Wells BA5 2GA* T: (01749) 938449 E: rev.suerose@virgin.net

ROSE, Miss Susan Mary. b 36. TCert 56. Dalton Ho Bris 68 Trin Coll Bris 74. **dss** 81 **d** 87 **p** 94. Brinsworth w Catcliffe *Sheff* 75-77; Scargill Ho 77-83; Netherthorpe *Sheff* 83-87; Tutor Trin Coll Bris 87-96; V Normanton *Wakef* 96-01; rtd 01; PtO *Sheff* from 01. *23 Kendal Vale, Worsborough Bridge, Barnsley S70 5NL* T: (01226) 771590

ROSE, Timothy Edward Francis. b 72. Univ of Wales (Cardiff) BD 93 MA 95 K Coll Lon PhD 98. Wycliffe Hall Ox MTh 03. **d** 01 **p** 02. C Jesmond H Trin and Newc St Barn and St Jude 01-04; Chapl R Holloway and Bedf New Coll *Lon* 04-06; C Farnham *Guildf* 06-09; P-in-c Stanford in the Vale w Goosey and Hatford *Ox* 09-12. *13 Nea Road, Christchurch BH23 4NA* M: 07709-722325 E: tefrose@gmail.com

ROSE, Timothy Mark. b 77. Luton Univ BA 98. St Mellitus Coll BA 10. **d** 10 **p** 11. C Upper Sunbury St Sav *Lon* 10-13; C Shepperton and Littleton from 13. *Littleton Rectory, Rectory Close, Shepperton TW17 0QE* M: 07966-031432

ROSE-CASEMORE, Claire Pamela. b 63. St Paul's Coll Chelt BA 84 St Luke's Coll Ex PGCE 85 Anglia Poly Univ MA 02. Ridley Hall Cam 95. **d** 97 **p** 98. Par Dn Kingsthorpe w Northampton St Dav *Pet* 97-98; C 98-01; TV Daventry, Ashby

St Ledgers, Braunston etc 01-10; P-in-c Bideford, Northam, Westward Ho!, Appledore etc *Ex* from 10. *The Rectory, Abbotsham Road, Bideford EX39 3AB* T: (01237) 475765 E: clairerc@btopenworld.com

ROSE-CASEMORE, John. b 27. Chich Th Coll. **d** 55 **p** 56. C Epsom Common Ch Ch *Guildf* 55-58; C Hednesford *Lich* 58-60; V Dawley 60-65; R Puttenham and Wanborough *Guildf* 65-72; R Frimley 72-83; RD Surrey Heath 76-81; R Ludgershall and Faberstown *Sarum* 83-86; R Tidworth, Ludgershall and Faberstown 86-92; rtd 92; PtO *Ex* from 93. *5 Culvery Close, Woodbury, Exeter EX5 1LZ* T: (01395) 233426

ROSE-CASEMORE, Miss Penelope Jane. b 56. Bris Univ CertEd 77 BEd 78. Westcott Ho Cam 83. **dss** 85 **d** 87 **p** 94. Waterloo St Jo w St Andr *S'wark* 85-87; Par Dn 87-88; Asst Chapl Gt Ormond Street Hosp for Sick Children *Lon* 88-90; Par Dn Balham St Mary and St Jo *S'wark* 90-94; C 94-96; Par Dn Upper Tooting H Trin 90-94; C 94-96; TV Clapham Team 96-01; V Clapham Ch Ch and St Jo from 02; AD Lambeth N 05-10; Dir Ords Kingston Area from 13. *Christchurch Vicarage, 39 Union Grove, London SW8 2QJ* T/F: (020) 7622 3552 E: penny@christchurchstjohn.com

ROSEDALE, John Richard. b 54. Leeds Univ BA 05. NOC 02. **d** 05 **p** 06. NSM Hadfield *Derby* 05-10; TV Saddleworth *Man* from 10. *Friarmere Vicarage, 1 Coblers Hill, Delph, Oldham OL3 5HT* T: (01457) 874209

ROSENTHAL, Canon James Milton. b 51. **d** 07 **p** 09. Dir Communications Angl Communion Office 89-09; NSM All Hallows by the Tower etc *Lon* 07-12; C Wantsum Gp *Cant* from 12. *The Vicarage, The Length, St Nicholas at Wade, Birchington CT7 0PW* M: 07742-856149 E: james.rosenthal@gmail.com

ROSENTHAL, Sheila. b 57. Warwick Univ BA 81 MA 95. Ripon Coll Cuddesdon 04. **d** 06 **p** 07. C Worc SE 06-09; Asst Chapl St Richard's Hospice Worc from 09; Chapl Worcs Primary Care Trust from 10. *Springwood Cottage, Bourton on the Hill, Moreton-in-Marsh GL56 9AE* T: (01386) 700530 E: mrsr@quista.net

ROSEWEIR, Clifford John. b 43. Glas Univ MA 64 MCIPD 81. S'wark Ord Course 83. **d** 84 **p** 85. NSM Redhill H Trin *S'wark* 84-89; P-in-c Croydon St Martin 89-92; PtO 92-93; Hon C Wallington 93-94; V Croydon Ch Ch 94-97; PtO from 06. *206 Bridle Road, Croydon CR0 8HL* T: (020) 8777 2820 M: 07850-480058 E: clifford@ascentiumhr.co.uk

ROSIE, James Robert. b 78. Leeds Univ BA 08. Coll of Resurr Mirfield 08. **d** 10 **p** 11. C Kingston upon Hull St Alb *York* 10-14; R Cheadle w Freehay *Lich* from 14. *The Rectory, Church Street, Cheadle, Stoke-on-Trent ST10 1HU* T: (01538) 753337 M: 07931-120897 E: james.rosie1@googlemail.com

✠**ROSIER, The Rt Revd Stanley Bruce.** b 28. Univ of W Aus BSc 48 Ox Univ BA 52 MA 56. Westcott Ho Cam 53. **d** 54 **p** 55 **c** 67. C Ecclesall *Sheff* 54-57; R Wyalkatchem Australia 57-64; R Kellerberrin 64-67; Can Perth 66-67; Adn Northam 67-70; Bp Willochra 70-87; Asst Bp 90-92; R Parkside Australia 87-94; rtd 94. *5A Fowler's Road, Glenunga SA 5064, Australia* T: (0061) (8) 8379 5213 E: bfrosier@senet.com.au

ROSINGH, Anna Clara Abena. *See* THOMASSON-ROSINGH, Anna Clara Abena

ROSKELLY, James Hereward Emmanuel. b 57. BSc ACSM 80. Cranmer Hall Dur 83. **d** 86 **p** 87. C Dunster, Carhampton and Withycombe w Rodhuish *B & W* 86-90; C Ealing St Mary *Lon* 90-93; Chapl R Marsden Hosp 93-95; CF 95-03; TV Rayleigh *Chelmsf* 03-10; R Dickleburgh and The Pulhams *Nor* from 10. *The Rectory, Station Road, Pulham Market, Diss IP21 4TE* T: (01379) 676256 M: 07989-442434 E: jamesroskelly@btinternet.com

ROSKILLY, John Noel. b 33. Man Univ MB, ChB 58 MRCGP 68. St Deiniol's Hawarden 74. **d** 75 **p** 76. NSM Bramhall *Ches* 75-86; V Capesthorne w Siddington and Marton 86-91; Dioc Dir of Counselling 89-93; Bp's Officer for NSM 87-93; NSM Macclesfield St Paul 92-93; rtd 93; PtO *Ches* from 93. *North View, Hawkins Lane, Rainow, Macclesfield SK10 5TL* T: (01625) 501014 E: johnliz.roskilly@gmail.com

ROSKROW, Mrs Pamela Mary. b 25. St Alb Minl Tr Scheme. **dss** 85 **d** 87 **p** 94. Digswell and Panshanger *St Alb* 85-90; Hon Par Dn 87-90; Hon Par Dn Gt Gaddesden 90-94; Hon C 94-95; Hon Par Dn Lt Gaddesden 92-94; Hon C 94-95; PtO 96-05. *Jevinda, 5 Phillips Terrace, North Roskear, Camborne TR14 8PJ* T: (01209) 711761

ROSS, Alexander. *See* ROSS, David Alexander

ROSS, Alexander John. b 84. Melbourne Univ BEd 08 BA 09 Melbourne Coll of Div BTh 10 Aus Catholic Univ MA 11. Ripon Coll Cuddesdon MTh 13. **d** 13 **p** 13. C S Yarra Ch Ch Australia 13-15; Asst Chapl Em Coll Cam from 15. *7 Green Street, Cambridge CB2 3JU* E: ajr211@cam.ac.uk

ROSS, Canon Anthony McPherson. b 38. OBE . Univ of Wales (Lamp) BA 60 Lon Univ BD 63. St Mich Coll Llan 60. **d** 61 **p** 62. C Gabalfa *Llan* 61-65; Chapl RN 65-93; QHC 89-93;

P-in-c Coln St Aldwyns, Hatherop, Quenington etc *Glouc* 93-95; V 95-08; RD Fairford 96-04; rtd 08; Bp's Adv on Deliverance Min *Glouc* from 08; Hon Can Glouc Cathl from 02. *Rowan Tree Cottage, Ampney Crucis, Cirencester GL7 5RY* T: (01285) 851410 E: tonyrosstssf468@gmail.com

ROSS (*nee* BENSON), Ashley Dawn. b 85. **d** 14 **p** 15. C Everton St Geo *Liv* from 14. *22 Calder Road, Liverpool L5 0RD* T: 0151-260 7397

ROSS, Mrs Audrey Ruth. b 42. Herts Coll BA 86. SAOMC 99. **d** 02 **p** 03. NSM Leavesden *St Alb* 02-06; NSM Storrington *Chich* from 06. *9 Longland Avenue, Storrington, Pulborough RH20 4HY* T: (01903) 746231 E: revross@supanet.com

ROSS, David Alexander. b 46. Oak Hill Th Coll 73. **d** 75 **p** 76. C Northwood Em *Lon* 75-80; R Eastrop *Win* 80-86; V Hove Bp Hannington Memorial Ch *Chich* 86-93; V Muswell Hill St Jas w St Matt *Lon* 93-07; rtd 07; Hon C S Tottenham St Ann *Lon* 07-11; PtO *Ox* from 11. *4 Glissard Way, Bradwell Village, Burford OX18 4XD* T: (01993) 824871 E: alexlynne.ross@googlemail.com

ROSS, Douglas. b 58. SEITE 12. **d** 15. NSM Salfords *S'wark* from 15. *Address temp unknown*

ROSS, Preb Duncan Gilbert. b 48. Lon Univ BSc 70. Westcott Ho Cam 75. **d** 78 **p** 79. C Stepney St Dunstan and All SS *Lon* 78-84; V Hackney Wick St Mary of Eton w St Aug 84-95; P-in-c Bow Common 95-03; V 03-13; Preb St Paul's Cathl 95-13; rtd 13. *37 Aberavon Road, London E3 5AR* E: duncan.ross5@btinternet.com

ROSS, Frederic Ian. b 34. Man Univ BSc 56. Westcott Ho Cam 58. **d** 62 **p** 63. C Oldham *Man* 62-65; Sec Th Colls Dept SCM 65-69; Teacher Man Gr Sch 69-84; V Shrewsbury H Cross *Lich* 84-02; rtd 02; PtO *Heref* from 02; *Lich* 02-14. *The Paddock, Plealey Road, Annscroft, Shrewsbury SY5 8AN* T: (01743) 860327

ROSS, Frederick Kenneth Wilson. b 29. **d** 99 **p** 00. C Margate S Africa 99-02; PtO *S & M* from 04. *116 Saddle Mews, Douglas, Isle of Man IM2 1HU* T: (01624) 672591 M: 07624-477279 E: kaross@manx.net

ROSS, Mrs Helen Jane. b 61. St Andr Univ BSc 84 Aber Univ DipEd 90 MTh 12 SOSc 10. TISEC 06. **d** 09 **p** 10. C Aberdeen St Clem *Ab* 09-12; R Prestwick *Glas* from 12. *St Ninian's Rectory, 56 Ayr Road, Prestwick KA9 1RR* T: (01292) 479582 E: rector@stniniansprestwick.org.uk

ROSS, Henry Ernest. b 40. NW Ord Course 70. **d** 73 **p** 74. NSM Litherland St Phil *Liv* 73-75; C Newton-le-Willows 75-77; P-in-c Walton St Luke 77-79; V 79-10; RD Walton 84-89; rtd 10. *Blue Haven, 46 Somerset Drive, Southport PR8 3SN* T: (01704) 571287 E: harry.ross@hotmail.co.uk

ROSS, John. b 41. Wells Th Coll 66. **d** 69 **p** 70. C Newc St Gabr 69-71; C Prudhoe 71-75; Hon C Shotley 75-87; Hon C Whittonstall 75-87; P-in-c Wallsend St Pet 93-94. *11 Weston Avenue, Whickham, Newcastle upon Tyne NE16 5TS* T: 0191-488 1546 E: rossj41@blueyonder.co.uk

ROSS, John Colin. b 50. Oak Hill Th Coll 84. **d** 86 **p** 87. C Stowmarket *St E* 86-89; C Wakef St Andr and St Mary 89-91; R Gt and Lt Whelnetham w Bradfield St George *St E* 91-94; V Newmarket All SS 94-02; V Erith St Paul *Roch* 02-04; P-in-c Combs and Lt Finborough *St E* 04-13; rtd 13; PtO *St E* from 14. *23 Pinner's Way, Bury St Edmunds IP33 3JN* T: (01284) 706776 M: 07904-124227 E: john@johnross.org

ROSS, Mrs Kirsty Leanne. b 88. Trin Coll Melbourne BTh 10 Qu Coll Ox PGCE 13. Ripon Coll Cuddesdon 11. **d** 13 **p** 13. C Toorak Australia from 13. *The Old Vicarage, 677 Punt Road, South Yarra VIC 3141, Australia* T: (0061) (4) 8146 3868 E: kirstylross@hotmail.com

ROSS, Malcolm Hargrave. b 37. Dur Univ BSc 58. Westcott Ho Cam 63. **d** 64 **p** 65. C Armley St Bart *Ripon* 64-67; USPG 67-71; Trinidad and Tobago 67-71; V New Rossington *Sheff* 71-75; Bp's Missr in E Lon 75-82; P-in-c Haggerston All SS 75-82; V Bedford Leigh *Man* 82-85; Area Sec USPG Bris and Glouc 85-90; Bp's Officer for Miss and Evang *Bris* 90-94; P-in-c Lacock w Bowden Hill 90-94; V Sherston Magna, Easton Grey, Luckington etc 94-06; rtd 06. *132 Larecombe Road, St Austell PL25 3EZ* E: m-eross@tiscali.co.uk

ROSS, Nicholas Martin. b 52. **d** 15. NSM Smethwick Resurr *Birm* from 15. *123 Willow Avenue, Birmingham B17 8HN* T: 0121-420 2901 E: nickmross@hotmail.co.uk

ROSS, Oliver Charles Milligan. b 58. Lon Univ BA 80 St Edm Ho Cam BA 85. Ridley Hall Cam 84. **d** 87 **p** 88. C Preston St Cuth *Blackb* 87-90; C Paddington St Jo w St Mich *Lon* 90-95; V Hounslow H Trin w St Paul and St Mary 95-96; P-in-c Isleworth St Mary 01-02; R St Olave Hart Street w All Hallows Staining etc from 06; P-in-c St Kath Cree from 06; P-in-c St Clem Eastcheap w St Martin Orgar from 12; P-in-c St Marg Pattens from 14; AD The City from 09. *St Olave's Rectory, 8 Hart Street, London EC3R 7NB* T: (020) 7702 0244 E: ocmross@mac.com *or* rector.stolave@mac.com

ROSS, Ms Rachel Anne. b 64. York Univ BSc 85 SS Coll Cam PGCE 86 Sheff Univ MA 97 Coll of Ripon & York St Jo MA 00. NOC 97. **d** 00 **p** 01. C Pendleton *Man* 00-04; P-in-c Salford Ordsall St Clem 03-04; P-in-c Salford St Ignatius and Stowell Memorial 03-04; R Ordsall and Salford Quays 04-07; P-in-c Loughborough All SS w H Trin *Leic* 07-08; R 08-14; Bp's NSM Officer 10-13; Chapl Qu Anne's Sch Caversham from 15; NSM Caversham Thameside and Mapledurham *Ox* from 15. *The Rectory, 20 Church Road, Caversham, Reading RG4 7AD* T: 0118-947 9505 M: 07884-371688
E: rachelross@tiscali.co.uk

ROSS, Canon Raymond John. b 28. Trin Coll Cam BA 52 MA 57. St Steph Ho Ox 52. **d** 54 **p** 55. C Clifton All SS *Bris* 54-58; C Solihull *Birm* 58-66; C-in-c Hobs Moat CD 66; V Hobs Moat 67-72; R Newbold w Dunston *Derby* 72-95; RD Chesterfield 78-91; Hon Can Derby Cathl 86-95; rtd 96; PtO *Derby* 96-09. *20 Stuart Court, High Street, Kibworth, Leicester LE8 0LR* T: (0116) 2793874

ROSS (née FAIRWEATHER), Mrs Sally Helen. b 69. St Hilda's Coll Ox BA 91. Cranmer Hall Dur 94. **d** 97 **p** 98. C Illingworth *Wakef* 97-01; Warden H Rood Ho and C Thirsk *York* 01-02; Chapl Northallerton Health Services NHS Trust 01-02; C Sheff St Mark Broomhill 02-04; Mental Health Chapl Sheff Care Trust from 04. *40 Bents Drive, Sheffield S11 9RP* T: 0114-235 1652 E: sh.ross@tiscali.co.uk

ROSS, Vernon. b 57. Portsm Poly BSc 79 RGN 86. Trin Coll Bris 89. **d** 91 **p** 92. C Fareham St Jo *Portsm* 91-94; P-in-c Witheridge, Thelbridge, Creacombe, Meshaw etc *Ex* 94-00; TR Barnstaple 00-08; P-in-c Fyfield, Moreton w Bobbingworth etc *Chelmsf* from 08. *6 Forest Drive, Fyfield, Ongar CM5 0TP* T: (01277) 899886 E: vross@chelmsford.anglican.org

ROSS-McCABE, Mrs Philippa Mary Seton. b 63. Natal Univ BA 83 HDipEd 86 Bris Univ BA 01. Trin Coll Bris 99. **d** 01 **p** 02. C Burpham *Guildf* 01-05; LtO 05-06; C Wisley w Pyrford 06-08; Tutor Local Min Progr from 06; Hon C Byfleet from 09. *The Rectory, 81 Rectory Lane, Byfleet, West Byfleet KT14 7LX* T: (01932) 342374 E: p.rossmccabe@btinternet.com

ROSS-McNAIRN, Jonathon Edward. b 73. Sheff Univ LLB 95 Solicitor 98. St Mellitus Coll BA 11. **d** 11 **p** 12. C Hucclecote *Glouc* 11-12; C Glouc St Geo w Whaddon 12-14; Chapl Trin Sch Teignmouth from 14. *Trinity School, Buckeridge Road, Teignmouth TQ14 8LY* T: (01626) 774138
E: jonathonrossm@yahoo.co.uk

ROSS, Dean of. *See* PETERS, The Very Revd Christopher Lind

✠**ROSSDALE, The Rt Revd David Douglas James.** b 53. Westmr Coll Ox MA 91 Surrey Univ MSc 01 K Coll Lon MSc 10. Chich Th Coll 80. **d** 81 **p** 82 **c** 00. C Upminster *Chelmsf* 81-86; V Moulsham St Luke 86-90; V Cookham *Ox* 90-00; RD Maidenhead 94-00; Hon Can Ch Ch 99-00; Suff Bp Grimsby *Linc* 00-13; rtd 13; Can and Preb Linc Cathl from 00; Hon Asst Bp Linc from 13. *Home Farm, Fen Lane, East Keal, Spilsby PE23 4AY* T: (01790) 752163
E: rossdale@btinternet.com

ROSSETER, Miss Susan Mary. b 46. Man Univ BA 67 Edin Univ DASS 71. St Jo Coll Nottm LTh 84. **d** 87 **p** 94. Par Dn Bromley Common St Aug *Roch* 87-88; C Pudsey St Lawr and St Paul *Bradf* 88-95; C Haughton le Skerne *Dur* 95-00; C Wilnecote *Lich* 00-11; rtd 11. *14 Meadowsway, Upton, Chester CH2 1HZ* E: s.rosseter@ntlworld.com

ROSSITER, Donald William Frank. b 30. **d** 80 **p** 81. NSM Abergavenny St Mary w Llanwenarth Citra *Mon* 80-96; NSM Govilon w Llanfoist w Llanelen 92-05; PtO from 05. *10 Meadow Lane, Abergavenny NP7 7AY* T: (01873) 855648

ROSSITER, Canon Gillian Alice. b 56. SRN 75 RSCN 75. NOC 98. **d** 01 **p** 02. C Neston *Ches* 01-06; P-in-c St Meols 06-09; V from 09; RD Wirral N 08-15; Hon Can Ches Cathl from 15. *The Vicarage, 1 Stanley Road, Hoylake, Wirral CH47 1HL* T: 0151-632 3897
E: stjohnthebaptist@uwclub.net

ROSSITER, Paul Albert. b 55. Leeds Univ BA 06. NOC 03. **d** 06 **p** 07. NSM Wallasey St Nic w All SS *Ches* 06-12; V Hoylake from 12. *The Vicarage, 1 Stanley Road, Hoylake, Wirral CH47 1HL* T: 0151-632 3897 E: p.a.rossiter@uwclub.net

ROSSITER, Raymond Stephen David. b 22. MBE 99. St Deiniol's Hawarden 75. **d** 76 **p** 77. NSM Sale St Anne *Ches* 76-90; PtO from 90; rtd 91. *Old Mill Farm, Station Road, Wrenbury, Nantwich CW5 8EX* T: (01270) 780939

ROSSLYN SMITH, Mrs Katherine Dorothy Nevill. b 40. STETS 97. **d** 00 **p** 01. NSM Tisbury *Sarum* 00-01; NSM Nadder Valley 01-03; NSM Chalke Valley 03-06; rtd 06. *The Old School House, Church Street, Bowerchalke, Salisbury SP5 5BE* T: (01722) 780011 E: kateinthevalley@yahoo.co.uk

ROSSLYN-SMITH, Mrs Kirsten Louise. b 73. Nottm Trent Univ BA 96. St Jo Coll Nottm MTh 05. **d** 05 **p** 06. C Tunbridge Wells St Jas *Roch* 05-10; V Stoke Hill *Guildf* from 10. *St Peter's Church House, 37 Hazel Avenue, Guildford GU1 1NP* T: (01483) 451908

ROSTILL, Brian. b 50. K Alfred's Coll Win BTh 00. Cranmer Hall Dur 01. **d** 03 **p** 04. C Knight's Enham and Smannell w Enham Alamein *Win* 03-07; P-in-c Boyatt Wood 07-09; V 09-12; Hon C Jersey St Mary from 12. *St Mary's Rectory, La Route de Ste Marie, Jersey JE3 3DB* T: (01534) 484678
E: rostill@tiscali.co.uk

ROSTRON, Derek. b 34. St Mich Coll Llan 65. **d** 67 **p** 68. C Morecambe St Barn *Blackb* 67-70; C Ribbleton 70-72; V Chorley All SS 72-79; C Woodchurch *Ches* 79-80; V Audlem 80-03; RD Nantwich 87-97; rtd 04; PtO *Lich* 04-06; *Ches* 04-06. *30 St Matthew's Drive, Derrington, Stafford ST18 9LU* T: (01785) 246349

ROTERS, Craig Lawrence. b 81. St Jo Coll Dur BA 03 Leeds Univ MA 10 Man Metrop Univ PGCE 06. Coll of Resurr Mirfield 08. **d** 10 **p** 11. C High Crompton *Man* 10-12; Shrine P and Pastor for Schs Shrine of Our Lady of Walsingham 12-13; C Holt w High Kelling Nor from 14. *New Bungalow, Lodge Farm, Norwich Road, Holt NR25 6SW* T: (01263) 710110
E: frcraig@runbox.com

ROTH, Jill Marie. b 61. Ox Min Course 07. **d** 10 **p** 11. NSM Flackwell Heath *Ox* from 10. *White Cottage, Hay Lane, Fulmer, Slough SL3 6HJ* T: (01753) 663181 M: 07985-945990 E: jillroth@dsl.pipex.com

ROTH, Johannes. b 66. Ridley Hall Cam. **d** 13 **p** 14. C Northwood Em *Lon* from 13. *64 Chester Road, Northwood HA6 1BH* M: 07722-128180
E: johannes.roth@btinternet.com

ROTHERHAM, Eric. b 36. Clifton Th Coll 63. **d** 67 **p** 68. C Gt Crosby St Luke *Liv* 67-69; C Sutton 69-71; V Warrington St Paul 72-79; LtO 79-80; PtO from 80; *Ches* from 80. *7 Paul Street, Warrington WA2 7LE* T: (01925) 633048

ROTHERY, Jean Helen. b 44. **d** 98 **p** 99. NSM Purley *Ox* 98-12; NSM Pangbourne w Tidmarsh and Sulham 12-14; PtO from 14. *Oak Lea, Tidmarsh Road, Tidmarsh, Reading RG8 8ER* T: 0118-984 3625

ROTHERY, Robert Frederick (Fred). b 34. Lon Coll of Div 67. **d** 69 **p** 70. C Burscough Bridge *Liv* 69-72; C Chipping Campden *Glouc* 72-75; P-in-c Didmarton w Oldbury-on-the-Hill and Sopworth 75-77; R Boxwell, Leighterton, Didmarton, Oldbury etc 77-83; R Stow on the Wold 83-00; RD Stow 90-99; rtd 00. *12 Phillips Road, Marnhull, Sturminster Newton DT10 1LF* T: (01258) 820668

ROTHWELL, Canon Bryan. b 60. St Edm Hall Ox BA 81 MA 85. Trin Coll Bris. **d** 85 **p** 86. C Carl St Jo 85-88; C Ulverston St Mary w H Trin 88-90; P-in-c Preston St Mary *Blackb* 90-96; P-in-c St John's in the Vale w Wythburn *Carl* 96-99; R St John's-in-the-Vale, Threlkeld and Wythburn 99-11; Warden Dioc Youth Cen 96-11; RD Derwent 05-10; TR Solway Plain from 11; Hon Can Carl Cathl from 08. *The Vicarage, Wigton Road, Silloth, Wigton CA7 4NJ* T: (016973) 31413 E: bryan@therothwells.co.uk

ROTHWELL, Edwin John. b 53. Lanc Univ BA 74 PhD 79. Sarum & Wells Th Coll 88. **d** 90 **p** 91. C Malvern Link w Cowleigh *Worc* 90-94; R Bowbrook N 94-00; Asst Chapl Swindon and Marlborough NHS Trust 00-03; Chapl E Somerset NHS Trust 03-14; Chapl Somerset Partnership NHS Foundation Trust from 14. *Somerset Partnership NHS Trust, Mallard Court, Express Park, Bristol Road, Bridgewater TA6 4RN* T: (01278) 432000 E: john.rothwell@sompar.nhs.uk

ROTHWELL, Mrs Emma. b 73. Liv Univ BSc Cam Univ MEd. ERMC. **d** 10 **p** 11. C Papworth *Ely* 10-13; Lect Cam Th Federation from 13; Dir Practical Th ERMC *Ely* from 14. *Cambridge Theological Federation, Wesley House, Jesus Lane, Cambridge CB5 8BQ* T: (01223) 741055 M: 07793-954603 E: emma.rothwell@ely.anglican.org

ROTHWELL, Steven. b 68. Roehampton Inst BA 99 Cam Univ MA 02. Westcott Ho Cam 00. **d** 02 **p** 03. C Chesterton Gd Shep *Ely* 02-06; R Gamlingay and Everton from 06. *The Rectory, 3A Stocks Lane, Gamlingay, Sandy SG19 3JP* T: (01767) 650568 E: s.rothwell3@btinternet.com

ROTHWELL-JACKSON, Christopher Patrick. b 32. St Cath Soc Ox BA 58 MA 61 Bris Univ PGCE 66. St Steph Ho Ox 55. **d** 59 **p** 60. C E Clevedon All SS *B & W* 59-62; C Midsomer Norton 62-65; Asst Teacher St Pet Primary Sch Portishead 66-68; Clevedon Junior Sch 68-72; Dep Hd Clevedon All SS Primary Sch 72-75; Hd Master Bp Pursglove Sch Tideswell 75-90; rtd 90; PtO *Ex* from 95. *Rosedale, Hookway, Crediton EX17 3PU* T: (01363) 772039

ROUCH, David Vaughan. b 36. Oak Hill Th Coll 67. **d** 69 **p** 70. C Denton Holme *Carl* 69-74; V Litherland St Jo and St Jas *Liv* 74-95; V Pemberton St Mark Newtown 95-06; P-in-c Wigan St Barn Marsh Green 03-06; rtd 06; PtO *Lich* from 07. *16 Parrs Lane, Bayston Hill, Shrewsbury SY3 0JS* T: (01743) 873800 E: drouchatjennyr@blueyonder.co.uk

ROUCH, The Ven Peter Bradford. b 66. BNC Ox MA 87 Peterho Cam MA 99 Man Univ PhD 05. Westcott Ho Cam 96. **d** 99

p 00. C E Dulwich St Jo *S'wark* 99-02; Jun Research Fell St Steph Ho Ox 02-04; Chapl St Jo Coll Ox 03-04; P-in-c Man Apostles w Miles Platting 05-11; Hon Research Fell Man Univ 07-11; Adn Bournemouth *Win* from 11. *Glebe House, 22 Bellflower Way, Chandler's Ford, Eastleigh SO53 4HN* T/F: (023) 8026 0955 E: peter.rouch@winchester.anglican.org

ROULSTON, Joseph Ernest. b 52. BNC Ox BA 74 MA 78 Lon Univ PhD 81 FRSC 86 FLS 94 FIBiol 01 FRCPath 01 CSci 04. Edin Dioc NSM Course 83. **d** 86 **p** 87. C Edin St Hilda 86-88; C Edin St Fillan 86-88; NSM Edin St Mich and All SS 88-97; Dioc Chapl Gen from 96; Assoc P Roslin (Rosslyn Chpl) 99-07; P-in-c from 07. *16 Summerside Street, Edinburgh EH6 4NU* T: 0131-554 6382 *or* 242 9225 M: 07903-969698 E: j.e.roulston@ed.ac.uk

ROUND, Keith Leonard. b 49. Sarum & Wells Th Coll 88. **d** 90 **p** 91. C Meir *Lich* 90-95; V Burslem St Werburgh from 95. *The Presbytery, Haywood Road, Stoke-on-Trent ST6 7AH* T: (01782) 837582

ROUND, Canon Malcolm John Harrison. b 56. Lon Univ BSc 77 BA 81. Oak Hill Th Coll. **d** 81 **p** 82. C Guildf St Sav w Stoke-next-Guildford 81-85; C Hawkwell *Chelmsf* 85-88; R Balerno *Edin* from 88; Hon Chapl Heriot-Watt Univ from 12; Can St Mary's Cathl from 10. *St Mungo's Ministry Centre, 46B Bavelaw Road, Balerno EH14 7AE* T: 0131-449 9907 E: malcolm.round@stmungos.org

ROUNDHILL, The Ven Andrew (John). b 65. CCC Cam BA 87. Ripon Coll Cuddesdon BTh 93. **d** 93 **p** 94. C Lancaster Ch Ch w St Jo and St Anne *Blackb* 93-97; Chapl Loretto Sch Musselburgh 97-02; Chapl Hong Kong Cathl 02-04; Sub-Dean 04-06; R Aspley w Albany Creek Australia 06-07; AD Brisbane NW 07-08; Adn Lilley from 08. *30 Ridley Road, Bridgeman Downs QLD 4035, Australia* T: (0061) (7) 3263 9254 *or* 3263 3518 E: rector@aspley-albanycreek.org.au

ROUNDTREE, James Clabern (Clay). b 75. Oklahoma Univ BFA 98 York Univ MA 00. St Steph Ho Ox BA 02. **d** 03 **p** 04. C Yarm *York* 03-07; V Ingleby Barwick from 07. *St Francis's House, Barwick Way, Ingleby Barwick, Stockton-on-Tees TS17 0WD* T: (01642) 760171 E: clayroundtree@hotmail.com

ROUNDTREE, Samuel William. b 19. TCD BA 42 MA 54. CITC 43. **d** 43 **p** 44. C Waterford Ch Ch & C O 44-47; I Tallow w Kilwatermoy 47-51; I Kiltegan w Stratford 51-62; I Rathvilly 60-62; Treas Leighlin Cathl 62-78; Preb Ossory Cathl 62-78; I Dunleckney 62-82; Chan Ossory and Leighlin Cathls 78-80; Prec Ossory and Leighlin Cathls 80-82; I New w Old Ross, Whitechurch, Fethard etc 82-88; Adn Ferns 86-88; rtd 88. *Greystones Nursing Home, Church Road, Greystones, Co Wicklow, Republic of Ireland*

ROUNTREE, The Ven Richard Benjamin. b 52. NUI BA 73. CITC 76. **d** 76 **p** 77. C Orangefield *D & D* 76-80; C Dublin Zion Ch *D & G* 80-83; I Dalkey St Patr 83-97; I Powerscourt w Kilbride from 97; Dioc Dir Decade of Evang 90-96; Can Ch Ch Cathl Dublin from 92; Treas Ch Ch Cathl Dublin from 04; Dioc Dir Lay Min 05-09; Adn Glendalough from 09. *Powerscourt Rectory, Enniskerry, Bray, Co Wicklow, Republic of Ireland* T/F: (00353) (1) 286 3534 M: 87-276 7564 E: rbrountree@gmail.com

ROUSE, Graham. b 58. Sheff City Coll of Educn CertEd 79 Leic Univ DipEd 84. Cranmer Hall Dur 90. **d** 92 **p** 93. C Longridge *Blackb* 92-96; P-in-c Fairhaven 96-97; V 97-07; P-in-c Blackpool St Mary 07-10; P-in-c S Shore St Pet 07-10; P-in-c S Shore H Trin 08-10; P-in-c from 10. *36 Canterbury Street, Chorley PR6 0LN* T: (01257) 265996 E: revg.rouse@btinternet.com

ROUSELL, Ian Douglas. b 64. Trin Coll Bris 11. **d** 13 **p** 14. C Keynsham *B & W* from 13. *37 Mayfields, Keynsham BS31 1BW* M: 07896-598830 E: idsj@btinternet.com

ROUT, Thomas. b 78. Univ Coll Lon BA 02. Wycliffe Hall Ox BA 10. **d** 11 **p** 12. C Rothley *Leic* 11-15; P-in-c Ipswich St Helen, H Trin, and St Luke *St E* from 14; Chapl Suffolk New Coll from 15. *The Rectory, 42 Clapgate Lane, Ipswich IP3 0RD* M: 07791-122331 E: tomrout@gmail.com

ROUTH, Canon Eileen Rosemary. b 41. Cant Sch of Min 82. **dss** 85 **d** 87 **p** 94. Folkestone St Sav *Cant* 85-90; Par Dn 87-90; Par Dn Woodnesborough w Worth and Staple 90-91; Dn-in-c 91-94; V 94-96; V Maidstone St Martin 96-99; Hon Can Cant Cathl 99; rtd 99; PtO *Cant* from 00. *121 Rough Common Road, Canterbury CT2 9DA* T: (01227) 464052

ROUTH, William John. b 60. Magd Coll Ox BA 81 MA 92. Ripon Coll Cuddesdon 93. **d** 95 **p** 96. C Longton *Blackb* 95-99; V Sutton Coldfield St Chad *Birm* 99-06; P-in-c 06-11; P-in-c Sutton Coldfield H Trin 06-11; R from 11. *Holy Trinity Rectory, 5 Broome Gardens, Sutton Coldfield B75 7JE* T: 0121-311 0474 E: john.routh@btinternet.com *or* john.routh.htsc@gmail.com

ROUTLEDGE, Christopher Joseph. b 78. Keele Univ BSc 99 SS Mark & Jo Univ Coll Plymouth PGCE 01. Oak Hill Th Coll BA 08. **d** 08 **p** 09. C Tiverton St Geo and St Paul *Ex* 08-12;

P-in-c Egg Buckland from 12; C Estover from 12; C Plymouth Crownhill Ascension from 12; C Bickleigh and Shaugh Prior from 12. *The Vicarage, 100 Church Hill, Eggbuckland, Plymouth PL6 5RD* T: (01752) 781564 E: chrisroutledge829@btinternet.com

ROUTLEDGE, Christopher Simon Bruce. b 73. Southn Univ BA 94. Ripon Coll Cuddesdon 09. **d** 11 **p** 12. C Northfleet and Rosherville *Roch* 11-15; V Bradwell and Porthill *Lich* from 15. *St Barnabas' Vicarage, Oldcastle Avenue, Newcastle ST5 8QG* T: (01474) 535814 M: 07837-177571 E: rev.chrisr73@gmail.com

ROW, Mrs Pamela Anne. b 54. Open Univ BA 86 MA 92 Homerton Coll Cam BEd 75. NOC 94. **d** 96 **p** 97. NSM Neston *Ches* 96-01; Chapl Heref Cathl Sch from 02; Min Can Heref Cathl from 04. *4 Harley Court, Hereford HR1 2NA* T: (01432) 363508 *or* 363522 F: 363525

ROWAN, Nicholas Edward. b 76. Essex Univ BA. Trin Coll Bris. **d** 06 **p** 07. C Rayleigh *Chelmsf* 06-10; TV from 10. *St Michael's House, 13 Sir Walter Raleigh Drive, Rayleigh SS6 9JB* T: (01268) 784426 E: nickrowan@btinternet.com

ROWBERRY, Christopher Michael. b 58. Univ of Wales (Lamp) MA 04 CQSW 85. Qu Coll Birm 94. **d** 96 **p** 97. C Lytchett Minster *Sarum* 96-00; TV Totton *Win* 00-10; V Hedge End St Jo from 10. *The Vicarage, Vicarage Drive, Hedge End, Southampton SO30 4DU* T: (01489) 789578 E: chrisrow@btopenworld.com

ROWBERRY, Mrs Karen. b 57. Ex Univ BEd 79. STETS 07. **d** 10 **p** 11. NSM Eastleigh *Win* 10-12; NSM Hedge End St Jo from 12. *The Vicarage, Vicarage Drive, Hedge End, Southampton SO30 4DU* T: (01489) 789578 M: 07976-232259 E: karenrow@btinternet.com

ROWBERRY, Michael James. b 46. Sussex Univ BA 74. Edin Th Coll 85. **d** 87 **p** 92. C Wolvercote w Summertown *Ox* 87-88; NSM Cov St Fran N Radford 91-95; PtO 95-98; C Doncaster Intake and Doncaster H Trin *Sheff* 98-00; C-in-c St Edm Anchorage Lane CD 00-06; C Doncaster St Geo 06-12; rtd 12. *5 Thorntree Close, Leicester LE3 9QS*

ROWBORY, Simon Michael. b 84. Grey Coll Dur BSc 06. Westcott Ho Cam 10. **d** 13 **p** 14. C Leic Martyrs from 13. *62 Ashleigh Road, Leicester LE3 0FB* M: 07771-963859 E: simon.rowbory@gmail.com

ROWE, Andrew Robert. b 64. Westmr Coll Ox BA 85 PGCE 86. Ridley Hall Cam 93. **d** 95 **p** 96. C Broadheath *Ches* 95-99; V E Ardsley *Wakef* 99-06; Chapl HM Pris Wakef 06-13; Chapl HM YOI Wetherby from 13. *HM Young Offender Institution, York Road, Wetherby LS22 5ED* T: (01937) 544200 E: andyrowe@uwclub.net

ROWE, Canon Bryan. b 50. Carl Dioc Tr Course 87. **d** 90 **p** 91. C Kells *Carl* 90-93; P-in-c Aspatria w Hayton 93-02; R Workington St Mich 02-15; P-in-c Distington 06-08; P-in-c Westfield St Mary 10-12; RD Solway 99-08 and 11-15; Hon Can Carl Cathl 99-15; rtd 15. *St Michael's Rectory, Dora Crescent, Workington CA14 2EZ* T: (01900) 602311 E: bryan.rowe@dsl.pipex.com

ROWE, Christine Elizabeth. b 55. Southn Univ BEd 77. Ripon Coll Cuddesdon 84. **dss** 86 **d** 87 **p** 94. Denham *Ox* 86-87; Par Dn 87-89; Par Dn Aylesbury 89 and 89-93; NSM Caversham St Jo 93-99; Chapl HM Pris Reading 93-98; Chapl MU 95-00; Chapl R Berks and Battle Hosps NHS Trust 96-00; P-in-c Vancouver St Thos Canada 00-01; R 01-04; Adn Burrard 04-06; R N Vancouver St Cath from 06. *1062 Ridgewood Drive, North Vancouver BC V7R 1H8, Canada* T: (001) (604) 987 6307 *or* 985 0666 F: 980 3868 E: stcatherinecr@aol.com

ROWE, David Brian. b 58. Trin Coll Bris 80. **d** 83 **p** 84. C Radipole and Melcombe Regis *Sarum* 83-86; C Cranham Park *Chelmsf* 86-88; Assoc Min and Par Missr Eastrop *Win* 88-92; P-in-c Arborfield w Barkham *Ox* 92-97; Asst Dioc Adv in Evang *S'well* 97-02; P-in-c Wilford 00-06; R 06-08; Warden Lee Abbey from 08. *Garden Lodge, Lee Abbey, Lynton EX35 6JJ* T: (01598) 752621 *or* 754204 F: 752619 E: warden@leeabbey.org.uk

ROWE, Geoffrey Lewis. b 44. Univ of Wales (Lamp) BA. Ripon Coll Cuddesdon 80. **d** 82 **p** 83. C Milber *Ex* 82-84; TV Withycombe Raleigh 84-90; R Clyst St Mary, Clyst St George etc 90-08; rtd 08. *Odle Hill Cottage, Abbotskerswell, Newton Abbot TQ12 5NW* T: (01626) 366143

ROWE, George William. b 36. K Alfred's Coll Win CertEd 64 BEd 82. **d** 07 **p** 08. NSM Week St Mary Circle of Par *Truro* 07-11. *Tanglewood, Long Park Drive, Widemouth Bay, Bude EX23 0AN* T: (01288) 361712 M: 07970-186038 E: george@rowe.gs.go-plus.net

ROWE, Miss Joan Patricia. b 54. Trin Coll Bris BA 87. **d** 88 **p** 94. C Radstock w Writhlington *B & W* 88-92; C Nailsea H Trin 92-96; P-in-c Shapwick w Ashcott and Burtle 96-07; Master St Jo Hosp Bath 07-09; PtO *Liv* 10-11; P-in-c Westbury *Heref* 11-13; P-in-c Worthen 11-13; P-in-c Yockleton 11-13;

R Westbury, Worthen and Yockleton from 13. *The Rectory, Westbury, Shrewsbury SY5 9QX* T: (01743) 885318 E: j.rowe91@btinternet.com

ROWE, John Goring. b 23. McGill Univ Montreal BA 48 BD 51 Selw Coll Cam BA 53. Montreal Dioc Th Coll LTh 51. d 51 p 52. C N Clarendon Canada 51; C Trumpington *Ely* 51-53; Hon C Bow Common *Lon* 53-84; rtd 88. *10 Cordelia Street, London E14 6DZ* T: (020) 7515 4681

ROWE, Mrs Pauline Frances. b 58. d 13 p 14. NSM Wigan All SS and St Geo *Liv* 13-15; NSM Wigan All SS from 15. *15 Calverhall Way, Ashton-in-Makerfield, Wigan WN4 9LB* T: (01942) 717029   M: 07783-570214 E: pauline.rowe2@btinternet.com

ROWE, Peter Anthony. b 46. Univ Coll Dur BA 68 Birkb Coll Lon MA 91 Heythrop Coll Lon MTh 02 St Andr Univ PhD 11 Barrister 78 Solicitor 85. SEITE 95. d 98 p 99. NSM Ashford *Cant* 98-03; PtO 04-13; C Maidstone St Mich from 13. *St Andrew's Vicarage, 416 Tonbridge Road, Maidstone ME16 9LW* E: peterrowe@madasafish.com

ROWE, Philip William. b 57. Southn Univ BSc 78 Lambeth STh 86. Trin Coll Bris 82. d 85 p 86. C Tooting Graveney St Nic *S'wark* 85-89; V Abbots Leigh w Leigh Woods *Bris* 89-96; V Almondsbury 96-98; P-in-c Littleton on Severn w Elberton 96-98; V Almondsbury and Olveston from 98; C Pilning w Compton Greenfield from 10; AD Bris W 00-06. *The Vicarage, 3 Sundays Hill, Almondsbury, Bristol BS32 4DS* T: (01454) 613223   E: office@stmaryssevernside.org.uk

ROWE, Shiela. *See* JOHNSON, Shiela

ROWE, The Ven Stephen Mark Buckingham. b 59. SS Mark & Jo Univ Coll Plymouth BA 81. Ripon Coll Cuddesdon 83. d 86 p 87. C Denham *Ox* 86-89; C Aylesbury 89-90; TV 90-93; V Caversham St Jo 93-00; Canada from 00; Sen Chapl Miss to Seafarers 00-01; P-in-c Surrey Epiphany Canada 01-02; R 02-07; Adn Fraser from 07. *1062 Ridgewood Drive, North Vancouver BC V7R 1H8, Canada* T: (001) (604) 987 6307 *or* T/F: 588 4511   E: rowesmb@aol.com

ROWE, Vanda Sheila. *See* PERRETT, Vanda Sheila

ROWELL, Canon Alan. b 50. Lon Univ BSc 71 AKC 71. Trin Coll Bris. d 75 p 76. C W Hampstead St Cuth *Lon* 75-78; C Camborne *Truro* 78-81; V Pendeen w Morvah 81-15; Hon Can Truro Cathl 03-15; rtd 15. *34 Penhaligon Court, Truro TR1 1YB* E: canonrowell@outlook.com

✠ROWELL, The Rt Revd Douglas **Geoffrey**. b 43. CCC Cam BA 64 MA 68 PhD 68 Keble Coll Ox DD 97. Cuddesdon Coll. d 68 p 69 c 94. Asst Chapl New Coll Ox 68-72; Chapl Keble Coll Ox 72-94; Wiccamical Preb Chich Cathl 81-01; Suff Bp Basingstoke *Win* 94-01; Bp Eur 01-13; rtd 13; Hon Asst Bp Chich from 13; Asst Bp Portsm from 15. *2 Roman Wharf, Chichester PO19 3RZ* T: (01243) 789867 E: geoffrey.rowell@btconnect.com

ROWELL, Mrs Gillian Margaret. b 56. Lon Bible Coll BA 96. SAOMC 97. d 99 p 00. NSM The Lee *Ox* 99-04; NSM Hawridge w Cholesbury and St Leonard 99-04; TV Cottesloe from 13. *The Rectory, 29 Mentmore Road, Cheddington, Leighton Buzzard LU7 0SD* E: gillrowell@tiscali.co.uk

ROWETT, David Peter. b 55. Univ Coll Dur BA 76. Ripon Coll Cuddesdon 82. d 84 p 85. C Yeovil *B & W* 84-88; C Yeovil St Mich 88-89; V Fairfield St Matt *Linc* 89-05; P-in-c Barton upon Humber 05-10; V from 10; R Saxby All Saints from 10; V Horkstow from 10; R S Ferriby from 10; RD Yarborough from 11. *The Vicarage, Beck Hill, Barton-upon-Humber DN18 5EY* T: (01652) 632202   E: david.rowett@aol.com

ROWETT, Mrs Margaret Pettigrew **Coupar**. b 33. Sarum & Wells Th Coll 84. dss 86 d 87 p 95. Widley w Wymering *Portsm* 86-88; C 87-88; Par Dn Plympton St Mary *Ex* 88-91; rtd 91; NSM St Mewan *Truro* 94-96; PtO from 97. *Epiphany Cottage, 9 Socotra Drive, Trewoon, St Austell PL25 5SQ* T: (01726) 71450

ROWLAND, Andrew John William. b 60. STETS 98. d 01 p 02. C Verwood *Sarum* 01-06; V W Moors from 06. *The Vicarage, 57 Glenwood Road, West Moors, Ferndown BH22 0EN* T: (01202) 893197   E: ajwrowland@tiscali.co.uk

ROWLAND, Prof Christopher Charles. b 47. Ch Coll Cam BA 69 MA 73 PhD 75. Ridley Hall Cam 72. d 75 p 76. Lect RS Newc Univ 74-79; Hon C Benwell St Jas 75-78; Hon C Gosforth All SS 78-79; Dean Jes Coll Cam 79-91; Asst Lect Div Cam Univ 83-85; Lect Div 85-91; LtO *Ely* 79-91; Prof of Exegesis of H Scripture Ox Univ from 91; Fell Qu Coll Ox from 91; Can Th Liv Cathl from 05. *Queen's College, Oxford OX1 4AW* T: (01865) 279120

ROWLAND, Ms Dawn Jeannette. b 38. RSCN 61 RGN 63. S'wark Ord Course 81. dss 84 d 87 p 94. Par Dn Croydon H Sav *S'wark* 84-89; NSM Riddlesdown 89-08; PtO from 08. *18 Le Personne Road, Caterham CR3 5SU*

ROWLAND, Jennifer Norah. b 48. Worc Coll of Educn CertEd 70 Open Univ BA 83 ACIB. WMMTC 96. d 99 p 00.

C Stratford-upon-Avon, Luddington etc *Cov* 99-03; P-in-c Ditton Priors w Neenton, Burwarton etc *Heref* 03-12; R 12-14; rtd 14. *19 Farnell Drive, Stratford-upon-Avon CV37 9DJ* T: (01789) 415548   E: jenny@rowland.entadsl.org

ROWLAND, Mrs June Mary. b 46. SRN 67. EMMTC 03. d 05 p 06. NSM Grantham *Linc* from 05; Chapl United Lincs Hosps NHS Trust from 06. *73 Harlaxton Road, Grantham NG31 7AE* M: 07710-455379   E: junerowlandhome@aol.com

ROWLAND, Matthew John. b 80. UWE BA 02 Bris Univ PGCE 03. Wycliffe Hall Ox 11. d 14. C Ex St Leon w H Trin from 14. *63 Cedars Road, Exeter EX2 4NB* M: 07818-422449 T: (01392) 286998   E: matt.rowland@stlens.org.uk

ROWLAND, Canon Robert William. b 51. Birm Univ BA 72. St Mich Coll Llan 72. d 74 p 75. C Connah's Quay St As 74; C Shotton 74-76; C Llanrhos 76-81; V Dyserth and Trelawnyd and Cwm from 81; AD St As 94-10; Hon Can St As Cathl 08-11; Can Cursal St As Cathl from 11. *The Vicarage, Dyserth, Rhyl LL18 6DB* T: (01745) 570750

ROWLAND, Sally Margaret. *See* MARCHANT, Sally Margaret

ROWLAND, Stanley George. b 48. Middx Univ BA 86. NTMTC 95. d 98 p 99. NSM Enfield St Geo *Lon* 98-02; C Grantham *Linc* 02-03; V Grantham, Earlesfield 03-11; P-in-c Grantham St Anne New Somerby and Spitalgate 10-11; rtd 11. *73 Harlaxton Road, Grantham NG31 7AE* E: sgrathome@aol.com

ROWLAND JONES, Sarah Caroline. b 59. LVO 93 OBE 97. Newnham Coll Cam BA 80 MA 84. St Jo Coll Nottm BTh 98. d 99 p 00. C Wrexham *St As* 99-02; S Africa 02-13; P-in-c Cardiff City Par *Llan* from 13. *16 Queen Anne Square, Cardiff CF10 3ED* T: (029) 2022 0136 E: sarahrowlandjones@churchinwales.org.uk

ROWLANDS, Mrs Alison Mary. b 51. d 06 p 07. OLM Redland *Bris* 06-12. *24 Northumberland Road, Bristol BS6 7BB* T: 0117-924 3528   M: 07749-044041 E: alisrow@blueyonder.co.uk

ROWLANDS, Alun Geoffrey. b 51. Open Univ MBA 02. d 12 p 13. OLM Mickleover All SS *Derby* 12-14; OLM Mickleover St Jo 12-14; OLM Mickleover from 14. *117 Western Road, Mickleover, Derby DE3 9GR* T: (01332) 517964 E: alunrowlands@btinternet.com

ROWLANDS, The Ven Emyr Wyn. b 42. St Mich Coll Llan 69. d 70 p 71. C Holyhead w Rhoscolyn *Ban* 70-71; C Holyhead w Rhoscolyn w Llanfair-yn-Neubwll 71-74; V Bodedern w Llechgynfarwy and Llechylched etc 74-88; R Machynlleth and Llanwrin 88-97; R Machynlleth w Llanwrin and Penegoes 97-10; AD Cyfeiliog and Mawddwy 96-10; Can Ban Cathl 97-03; Can and Preb Ban Cathl 03-10; Adn Meirionnydd 04-10; rtd 10; PtO *Ban* from 10. *2 Ffordd Meillion, Llangristiolus, Bodorgan LL62 5DQ* T: (01248) 750148

ROWLANDS, Forrest John. b 25. LSE BSc(Econ) 51. Chich Th Coll 54. d 56 p 57. C Hove St Phil *Chich* 56-58; C Haywards Heath St Wilfrid 58-62; R Kingston by Sea 62-74; rtd 90. *11 Granville Terrace, Yeadon, Leeds LS19 7UW* T: 0113-250 0208

ROWLANDS, Gareth Richard. b 70. Univ of Wales BA 93. St Steph Ho Ox BTh 93. d 96 p 97. C Shotton *St As* 96-00; TV Wrexham and Chapl Maelor Hosp 00-03; Chapl Co-ord Cheshire and Wirral Partnerships NHS Trust 03-05; Chapl Co-ord Ches and Ellesmere Port Hosps 03-05; Lead Chapl Princess Alexandra Hosp NHS Trust 05-07; Chapl Papworth Hosp NHS Foundn Trust from 07; Bp's Adv for Health Chapl *Ely* from 09. *Papworth Hospital, Papworth Everard, Cambridge CB23 3RE* T: (01480) 830541 E:.gareth.rowlands@papworth.nhs.uk

ROWLANDS, Graeme Charles. b 53. K Coll Lon BD 74 AKC 74. St Aug Coll Cant 75. d 76 p 77. C Higham Ferrers w Chelveston *Pet* 76-79; C Gorton Our Lady and St Thos *Man* 79-81; C Reading H Trin *Ox* 81-89; P-in-c Kentish Town St Silas *Lon* 89-92; V 92-98; P-in-c Haverstock Hill H Trin w Kentish Town St Barn 93-98; V Kentish Town St Silas and H Trin w St Barn from 98. *St Silas's House, 11 St Silas's Place, London NW5 3QP* T: (020) 7485 3727   E: ssmktw@gmail.com

ROWLANDS, Mrs Jacqueline Adèle. b 43. Golds Coll Lon CertEd 65 BEd 72 Heythrop Coll Lon MA 05. St Alb Minl Tr Scheme 82. dss 85 d 87 p 05. Bromham w Oakley *St Alb* 85-88; Par Dn 87-88; Par Dn Bromham w Oakley and Stagsden 88-89; PtO 04-05 and from 11; Hon C Bedford St Andr 05-11. *2A Rosemary Drive, Bromham, Bedford MK43 8PL* M: 07793-045203

ROWLANDS, Canon John Henry Lewis. b 47. Univ of Wales (Lamp) BA 68 Magd Coll Cam BA 70 MA 74 Dur Univ MLitt 86. Westcott Ho Cam 70. d 72 p 73. C Aberystwyth *St D* 72-76; Chapl Univ of Wales (Lamp) 76-79; Youth Chapl 76-79; Dir Academic Studies St Mich Coll Llan 79-84; Sub-Warden 84-88; Warden 88-97; Lect Univ of Wales (Cardiff) *Llan* 79-97; Asst Dean 81-83; Dean 93-97; Dean of Div 91-95; Dir of

Ords 85-88; V Whitchurch 97-02; TR from 02; Hon Can Llan Cathl 90-97; Can Llan Cathl from 97; Chan Llan Cathl from 02; Chapl Cardiff Community Healthcare NHS Trust from 97. *The Vicarage, 6 Penlline Road, Cardiff CF14 2AD*
T/F: (029) 2062 6072
E: office@parishofwhitchurch.freeserve.co.uk

ROWLANDS, Canon Joseph Haydn. b 36. Univ of Wales (Lamp) BA 61. **d** 63 **p** 64. C Llanfairisgaer *Ban* 63-68; R Maentwrog w Trawsfynydd 68-75; V Henfynyw w Aberaeron and Llanddewi Aberarth *St D* 75-80; R Trefdraeth *Ban* 80-84; V Llandysul *St D* 84-98; V Llandysul w Bangor Teifi and Llanfairollwyn etc 98-01; Hon Can St D Cathl 88-90; Can St D Cathl from 90; RD Emlyn 92-01; rtd 01. *1 Llys Ystrad, Johnstown, Carmarthen SA31 3PU* T: (01267) 222487

ROWLANDS, Kenneth Albert. b 41. MA DipAE. NW Ord Course 70. **d** 73 **p** 74. NSM Hoylake *Ches* 73-80; NSM Oxton 80-82; PtO 82-00; C Stoneycroft All SS *Liv* 92-94; V Mossley Hill St Barn 94-03; rtd 03; PtO *Ches* from 03. *77 Queens Avenue, Meols, Wirral CH47 0LT* T: 0151-632 3033

ROWLANDS, Marc Alun. b 62. Univ of Wales (Abth) BSc 84 St D Coll Lamp MPhil 89 PhD 95. Wycliffe Hall Ox 97. **d** 99 **p** 00. C Betws w Ammanford *St D* 99-01; C Carmarthen St Pet 01-02; P-in-c Llanpumsaint w Llanllawddog 02-05; TV Cwm Gwendraeth 06-10; TR Trisant from 10. *The Vicarage, 32A Heol y Bryn, Upper Tumble, Llanelli SA14 6DR* T: (01269) 841358
E: revdocrock@yahoo.com

ROWLANDS, Michael Huw. b 62. Birm Univ BA 85 Univ of Wales (Cardiff) BD 88. St Mich Coll Llan 85. **d** 88 **p** 89. C Penarth All SS *Llan* 88-91; V Martletwy w Lawrenny and Minwear etc *St D* 91-99; CF 99-02; P-in-c Nolton w Roch *St D* 02-04; R Nolton w Roch and St Lawrence w Ford etc from 04. *Calbern, Simpson Cross, Haverfordwest SA62 6EP* T: (01437) 710209

ROWLANDS, Robert. b 31. Roch Th Coll. **d** 68 **p** 69. C Hooton *Ches* 68-71; V Stretton 71-88; P-in-c Appleton Thorn and Antrobus 87-88; V Stretton and Appleton Thorn 88-00; rtd 00; PtO *Carl* from 01. *Uplands, Redhills Road, Arnside, Carnforth LA5 0AS* T: (01524) 761612

ROWLANDS, Simon David. b 66. **d** 99 **p** 00. C St Peter-in-Thanet *Cant* 99-03; Chapl Cant Ch Ch Univ 03-06; V Bridge *Cant* 07-13; P-in-c Faversham from 13; C The Brents and Davington w Oare and Luddenham 13-14; C Eastling w Ospringe and Stalisfield w Otterden 13-14; P-in-c The Brents and Davington from 14; P-in-c Ospringe from 14. *The Vicarage, 16 Newton Road, Faversham ME13 8DY* T: (01795) 532592

ROWLANDS, Mrs Valerie Christine. b 54. St As Minl Tr Course 99. **d** 02 **p** 03. NSM Llanbedr DC w Llangynhafal, Llanychan etc *St As* 02-04; Chapl St As Cathl 04-14; TV St As 06-14; V Llanrhaeadr-yng-Nghinmeirch and Prion w Nantglyn from 14. *The Rectory, Llandyrnog, Denbigh LL16 4LT* E: rowlands@hafoty.fsnet.co.uk

ROWLANDSON, Diana. b 56. **d** 13 **p** 14. NSM Gerrards Cross and Fulmer *Ox* from 13. *4 Criss Grove, Chalfont St Peter, Gerrards Cross SL9 9HG* T: (01753) 886049

ROWLES, Mrs Carol. b 51. **d** 06 **p** 07. NSM Worcester Park Ch Ch w St Phil *S'wark* from 06. *23 Delcombe Avenue, Worcester Park KT4 8NY* T: (020) 8330 2068

ROWLEY, Ms Anne Christine. b 50. Lanc Univ BA 96 Leeds Univ MA 10 Huddersfield Univ PGCE 99. Yorks Min Course 07. **d** 10 **p** 11. NSM Dunnington *York* 10-12; Chapl York Hosps NHS Foundn Trust from 12; NSM Rural E York 12-14; NSM York All SS Pavement w St Crux and St Mich 14; NSM York St Olave w St Giles 14; NSM York St Helen w St Martin 14; NSM York St Denys 14; Chapl York St Jo Univ from 14. *2 Lady Hewley's Cottages, St Saviourgate, York YO1 8NW* T: (01904) 651189 E: anne.christine@virgin.net

ROWLEY, Preb Christopher Francis Elmes. b 48. St Jo Coll Dur BA 70 St Luke's Coll Ex PGCE 71. St Steph Ho Ox 76. **d** 78 **p** 79. C Parkstone St Pet w Branksea and St Osmund *Sarum* 78-81; TV 82-85; P-in-c Chard Gd Shep Furnham *B & W* 85-89; P-in-c Dowlishwake w Chaffcombe, Knowle St Giles etc 88-89; R Chard, Furnham w Chaffcombe, Knowle St Giles etc 89-91; V Stoke St Gregory w Burrowbridge and Lyng 91-04; RD Taunton 01-04; TV Wellington and Distr 04-13; RD Tone 07-12; Preb Wells Cathl 09-13; rtd 13. *39 Cornlands, Sampford Peverell, Tiverton EX16 7UA* T: (01884) 799011
E: christoprowley@uwclub.net

ROWLEY, David Michael. b 39. NOC 87. **d** 90 **p** 91. C Stainland *Wakef* 90-93; V Hayfield *Derby* 93-99; P-in-c Chinley w Buxworth 98-99; V Glossop 99-04; RD 96-04; rtd 04; PtO *Derby* from 04. *8 Weavers Close, Belper DE56 0HZ*
T: (01773) 882690

ROWLEY, Jennifer Jane Elisabeth. b 61. LMH Ox BA 84 MA 92. EAMTC 99. **d** 02 **p** 03. C Kingsthorpe w Northampton St Dav *Pet* 02-04; C Kettering SS Pet and Paul 04-06; P-in-c Nettleham

Linc 06-13; P-in-c Welton and Dunholme w Scothern 10-13; R Selsdon St Jo w St Fran *S'wark* from 13. *St John's Rectory, Upper Selsdon Road, South Croydon CR2 8DD*
E: jennyrowley@waitrose.com

ROWLEY, John. b 47. **d** 05 **p** 06. OLM Mitford and Hebron *Newc* from 05. *Thistledene, Fulbeck, Morpeth NE61 3JU*
T: (01670) 515915 E: john_rowley1@btinternet.com

ROWLEY, Mrs Susan. b 49. **d** 01 **p** 02. OLM Fazeley *Lich* 01-11; rtd 11; PtO *Lich* from 12. *137 Reindeer Road, Fazeley, Tamworth B78 3SP* T: (01827) 250431 *or* 289414 E: s.rowley2@sky.com

ROWLEY-BROOKE, Marie Gordon. b 46. ARIAM 69. Ripon Coll Cuddesdon 00. **d** 02 **p** 03. C Leckhampton SS Phil and Jas w Cheltenham St Jas *Glouc* 02-05; I Nenagh *L & K* 05-15; Can Limerick Cathl 10-15; Treas Limerick Cathl 14-15; Treas 14-15; rtd 15; PtO *L & K* from 15. *Holly Cottage, Sallypark, Latteragh, Nenagh, Co Tipperary, Republic of Ireland* M: (00353) 85-147 4792 E: canonmarie@me.com

ROWLING, Canon Catherine. b 55. Man Poly BEd 77. Westcott Ho Cam 83 NEOC 85. **dss** 86 **d** 87 **p** 94. Gt Ayton w Easby and Newton-in-Cleveland *York* 86-89; Par Dn 87-89; Chapl Teesside Poly 89-92; Chapl Teesside Univ 92-96; Dioc Adv for Diaconal Mins 96-98; Dean of Women's Min 98-08; Co Dir of Ords 98-05; Dioc Dir of Ords 05-09; Dioc Moderator Reader Tr 99-04; Dir Reader Studies 05-09; Can and Preb York Minster 01-09; Prin Lindisfarne Regional Tr Partnership from 09; PtO *York* from 09. *The Rectory, Cemetery Road, Thirsk YO7 1PR*
T: (01845) 522258 M: 07714-052282
E: cathyrowling@dunelm.org.uk

ROWLING, Canon Richard Francis. b 56. BA. Westcott Ho Cam. **d** 84 **p** 85. C Stokesley *York* 84-87; C Stainton-in-Cleveland 87-90; V New Marske 90-96; V Wilton 92-96; P-in-c Ingleby Greenhow w Bilsdale Priory, Kildale etc 96-98; V 98-03; R Thirsk from 03; Abp's Adv for Rural Affairs from 98; RD Mowbray 04-14; Can and Preb York Minster from 10. *The Rectory, Cemetery Road, Thirsk YO7 1PR* T: (01845) 523183
E: richardrowling@dunelm.org.uk

ROWNTREE, Peter. b 47. St D Coll Lamp BA 68 Univ of Wales (Cardiff) MA 70. St Steph Ho Ox 70. **d** 72 **p** 73. C Stanwell *Lon* 72-75; C Northolt St Mary 75-79; Chapl Ealing Gen Hosp 79-83; Chapl Cherry Knowle Hosp Sunderland 83-87; Chapl Ryhope Hosp Sunderland 83-87; Chapl Ealing Gen Hosp 87-90; Chapl Ealing Hosp NHS Trust 91-94 and 94-99; Chapl W Lon Healthcare NHS Trust 94-99; Sen Co-ord Chapl Univ Coll Lon Hosps NHS Foundn Trust 99-08; rtd 08; PtO *Nor* from 08. *4 Chapel Court, Chapel Street, King's Lynn PE30 1EG*

ROWSELL, Canon John Bishop. b 25. Jes Coll Cam BA 49 MA 55. Ely Th Coll 49. **d** 51 **p** 52. C Hackney Wick St Mary of Eton w St Aug *Lon* 51-55; C Is of Dogs Ch Ch and St Jo w St Luke 55-56; C Reading St Mary V *Ox* 56-59; V Hightown *Wakef* 59-69; R Harlton *Ely* 69-81; V Haslingfield 69-81; V Methwold 81-95; RD Feltwell 81-95; R Northwold 82-95; Hon Can Ely Cathl 84-99; P-in-c Hockwold w Wilton 95-99; P-in-c Weeting 95-99; PtO from 00. *Reed House, High Street, Hilgay, Downham Market PE38 0LH* T: (01366) 387662

ROWSON, Frank. b 40. CEng 67 MIStructE 67. Sarum & Wells Th Coll 87. **d** 90 **p** 91. NSM Ore Ch Ch *Chich* 90-98; NSM Fairlight, Guestling and Pett 98-00; rtd 00; PtO *Chich* from 01. *149 Priory Road, Hastings TN34 3JD* T: (01424) 439802

ROWSON, Mrs Rhoda Lyn. b 63. RGN 86. Qu Coll Birm 06. **d** 09 **p** 10. NSM Coseley Ch Ch *Worc* 09-13; C Dudley 13-14; C Wordsley from 14. *25 Middleway Avenue, Stourbridge DY8 5NB* E: lyn63@blueyonder.co.uk

✠**ROWTHORN, The Rt Revd Jeffery William.** b 34. Ch Coll Cam BA 57 MA 62 Union Th Sem (NY) BD 61 Oriel Coll Ox BLitt 72 Berkeley Div Sch DD 87. Cuddesdon Coll 61. **d** 62 **p** 63 **c** 87. C Woolwich St Mary w H Trin *S'wark* 62-65; R Garsington *Ox* 65-68; Chapl and Dean Union Th Sem NY USA 68-73; Assoc Prof Past Th Yale and Berkeley Div 73-87; Suff Bp Connecticut 87-93; Bp in Charge Convocation of American Chs in Eur 94-01; Asst Bp Eur 95-01; Asst Bp Spain 97-01; Asst Bp Portugal 97-01; rtd 01. *17 Woodland Drive, Salem CT 06420-4023, USA* T: (001) (860) 859 3377
E: jefferyrowthorn@yahoo.com

ROXBY, Gordon George. b 39. Lon Univ BSc 61. Coll of Resurr Mirfield 61. **d** 63 **p** 64. C Fleetwood St Pet *Blackb* 63-66; C Kirkham 66-68; V Runcorn St Jo Weston *Ches* 68-78; R Moston St Chad *Man* 78-86; V Bury St Pet 86-99; AD Bury 86-96; Hon Can Man Cathl 97-99; V Sandiway *Ches* 99-05; Initial Minl Tr Officer 99-04; rtd 05; PtO *Ches* from 05. *16 St Joseph's Way, Nantwich CW5 6TE* T: (01270) 619898
E: gordon@roxbylife.org.uk

ROY, Jennifer Pearl. *See* DREW, Jennifer Pearl

ROYDEN, Canon Charles. b 60. Wycliffe Hall Ox BA 86 MA 91. **d** 87 **p** 88. C Bidston *Ches* 87-91; V N Brickhill and Putnoe *St Alb* 91-92; V Bedf St Mark from 93; Hon Can St Alb from 13. *The Vicarage, Calder Rise, Bedford MK41 7UY* M: 07973-113861
F: (01234) 342613 T: 309175 E: vicar@thisischurch.com

ROYDEN, Eric Ramsay. b 29. St Deiniol's Hawarden 75. **d** 77 **p** 78. Hon C Tranmere St Paul w St Luke *Ches* 77-81; C Eastham 81; V New Brighton All SS 81-95; P-in-c 95-97; rtd 95; PtO *Ches* 97-07. *84 Asgard Drive, Bedford MK41 0UT* T: (01234) 294496 E: eroyden@googlemail.com

ROYDEN, Ross Eric. b 55. Lon Bible Coll BA 77 Nottm Univ MTh 82. Wycliffe Hall Ox 79. **d** 81 **p** 82. C Moreton *Ches* 81-84; Chapl and Tutor Bedf Coll of HE *St Alb* 84-93; R Banchory *Ab* 93-00; R Kincardine O'Neil 93-00; V Kowloon Tong Ch Ch Hong Kong from 00. *Christ Church Vicarage, 2 Derby Road, Kowloon Tong, Kowloon, Hong Kong* T: (00852) 2338 4433 F: 2338 8422 E: rossroyden@aol.com

ROYLANCE, Mrs Margaret. b 47. St Mary's Coll Chelt CertEd 68. Cant Sch of Min 93. **d** 96 **p** 97. Chapl Ashford Sch 96-10; NSM Tenterden and Smallhythe *Cant* from 96; NSM Rother and Oxney from 13. *5 Southgate Road, Tenterden TN30 7BS* T: (01580) 762332 F: 765267 E: johnsroylance@btopenworld.com

ROYLE, Antony Kevan. b 50. Lon Univ BSc 71 FIA 76. Trin Coll Bris 76. **d** 79 **p** 80. C Chell *Lich* 79-82; C Leyland St Andr *Blackb* 82-86; V Blackb Sav 86-95; Chapl Blackb R Infirmary and Park Lee Hosp 86-95; Chapl E Lancs Hospice 86-95; TR Walton H Trin *Ox* 95-01; NSM Wendover Deanery from 01. *4 Darley Close, Aylesbury HP21 7EA* T: (01296) 582470 M: 07796-143905

ROYLE, Gillian Mary. *See* PAWSON, Gillian Mary

ROYLE, Michael Arthur. b 38. Univ of Wales (Ban) BSc 61. St Jo Coll Nottm 81. **d** 82 **p** 83. C Boulton *Derby* 82-85; C Belper 85-87; P-in-c Smalley and Morley 87-95; RD Heanor 89-94; V Charlesworth and Dinting Vale 95-02; rtd 02; PtO *Ches* from 02; *Derby* 03-13. *Kaiama, 55 Cross Lane, Marple, Stockport SK6 7PZ* T: 0161-427 6453 E: mroyle@eprimus.co.uk *or* mjroyle@talktalk.net

ROYLE, Canon Peter Sydney George. b 34. K Coll Lon BD 57 AKC 57. **d** 58 **p** 59. C St Helier *S'wark* 58-62; C Alice Springs Australia 62-63; R 63-68; Can Darwin 68; P-in-c Sydenham St Phil *S'wark* 69-72; V Leigh Park *Portsm* 72-85; RD Havant 77-82; V S w N Hayling 85-96; V S Hayling 96-97; Hon Can Portsm Cathl 95-97; rtd 97; PtO *Ex* 97-06; *Sarum* from 06. *12 Jackson Close, Devizes SN10 3AP* T: (01380) 720405 E: george.royle.1@btinternet.com

ROYLE, Canon Roger Michael. b 39. AKC 61 Lambeth MA 90. **d** 62 **p** 63. C Portsea St Mary *Portsm* 62-65; C St Helier *S'wark* 65-68; Succ S'wark Cathl 68-71; Warden Eton Coll Dorney Par Project *Ox* 71-74; Conduct Eton Coll 74-79; LtO *S'wark* 79-90; Chapl Ld Mayor Treloar Coll Alton 90-92; Hon C Froyle and Holybourne *Win* 90-92; Hon Can and Chapl S'wark Cathl 93-99; PtO from 99; rtd 04. *Address withheld by request*

ROYLE, Canon Stanley Michael. b 43. K Coll Lon BD 69 AKC 69 Man Univ MA 75. St Aug Coll Cant 71. **d** 72 **p** 73. C Timperley *Ches* 72-76; PtO 76-81; R Milton Abbas, Hilton w Cheselbourne etc *Sarum* 81-86; Dir of Ords 86-01; Adv on CME 86-98; Bp's Dom Chapl 98-01; LtO 01-08; Can and Preb Sarum Cathl 89-08; rtd 08; PtO *Sarum* 08-13; Hon C Spetisbury w Charlton Marshall etc 13-14; PtO from 14. *Three Firs, Blandford Road, Sturminster Marshall, Wimborne BH21 4AF* T: (01258) 857326 E: smroyle@sky.com

ROYSTON, Virginia Helen. b 53. Bris Univ BSc 76 MB, ChB 79. STETS 09. **d** 12 **p** 13. NSM Cotham St Sav w St Mary and Clifton St Paul *Bris* from 12. *14 Grove Avenue, Coombe Dingle, Bristol BS9 2RP* T: 0117-968 6622 M: 07813-692852 E: poppyr@tiscali.co.uk

RUAIIA, Bishop of. *See* MTETEMELA, The Rt Revd Donald Leo

RUCK, John. b 47. Bris Univ BSc 68 Birm Univ MPhil 92. All Nations Chr Coll MA 03. **d** 80 **p** 83. OMF Internat from 78; Indonesia 80-86 and 87-91; PtO *Birm* 86-87 and 91-98; Lect Crowther Hall CMS Tr Coll Selly Oak 00-04; CMS from 04. *121 Bournbrook Road, Birmingham B29 7BY* T: 0121-471 1573 E: johnanne@ruckja.freeserve.co.uk

RUDALL, Mark Edward. b 53. Regent's Park Coll Ox BA 80 MA 84. Ripon Coll Cuddesdon 00. **d** 01 **p** 02. In Bapt Min 80-00; C Wallingford *Ox* 01-03; Dioc Dir Communications *Guildf* 04-13; rtd 13; PtO *Win* 11-14. *108 Prospect Road, Farnborough GU14 8NS* T: (01252) 645486 M: 07779-654975 E: mark.rudall@ntlworld.com

RUDD, Carl Nigel. b 71. Salford Univ BSc 93 PhD 97. Trin Coll Bris BA 06. **d** 06 **p** 07. C Whitstable *Cant* 06-10; C Penn Fields *Lich* from 10. *100 Bellencroft Gardens, Wolverhampton WV3 8DU* T: (01902) 766929 E: carl.rudd@googlemail.com

RUDD, Colin Richard. b 41. AKC 64. **d** 65 **p** 66. C N Stoneham *Win* 65-70; V Rotherwick, Hook and Greywell 70-74; R Hook w Greywell 74-78; Toc H 78-89; V Buckland *Ox* 89-98; V Littleworth 89-98; R Pusey 89-98; R Gainfield 89-98; RD Vale of White Horse 96-99; rtd 99; PtO *B & W* from 06. *Alcudia, Bilbrook, Minehead TA24 6HE* T: (01984) 640021 E: colinrudd70@gmail.com

RUDD, Robert Arthur. b 33. ALCD 60. **d** 60 **p** 61. C Blackb Sav 60-63; C Huyton St Geo *Liv* 63-65; V Bickershaw 65-72; Asst Chapl HM Pris Liv 72-73; Birm 73-78; Parkhurst 78-86; Camp Hill 86-92; Chapl St Mary's Hosp Newport 92-95; rtd 95; PtO *Portsm* from 95. *The Elms, 13 Horsebridge Hill, Newport PO30 5TJ* T: (01983) 524415

RUDD, Mrs Sonia Winifred. b 44. Nottm Univ BSc 66 Leeds Univ MSc 68. Ox Min Course 92. **d** 94 **p** 95. NSM Ox St Andr 94-96; C Buckland 96-99; PtO *B & W* from 06. *Alcudia, Bilbrook, Minehead TA24 6HE* T: (01984) 640021 M: 07886-451743 E: soniarudd67@googlemail.com

RUDDICK, David Mark. b 76. Pemb Coll Cam BA 98 Homerton Coll Cam PGCE 99. Oak Hill Th Coll BA 09. **d** 09 **p** 10. C Elmswell *St E* 09-12; TV Morden *S'wark* from 12. *140 Stonecot Hill, Sutton SM3 9HQ* T: (020) 8330 6566 M: 07761-320736 E: davidruddick.online@googlemail.com

RUDDLE, Canon Donald Arthur. b 31. MBE 04. Linc Th Coll 64. **d** 66 **p** 67. C Kettering SS Pet and Paul 66-70; V Earlham St Anne *Nor* 70-79; V E Malling *Roch* 79-95; RD Malling 84-93; Hon Can Roch Cathl 88-95; Chapl Nord Pas de Calais *Eur* 95-98; rtd 98; PtO *Eur* from 98; *Cant* from 05. *Sycamore Lodge, 5 Windmill Lane, Faversham ME13 7GT* T: (01795) 533461 E: don.ruddle@talktalk.net

RUDDOCK, Brian John. b 45. Dur Univ BA 66 Nottm Univ MEd 91. Westcott Ho Cam 67. **d** 69 **p** 70. C Ross *Heref* 69-72; C Kettering SS Pet and Paul 72-75; P-in-c Colchester St Steph *Chelmsf* 75-77; TR Colchester St Leon, St Mary Magd and St Steph 77-84; R March St Pet *Ely* 84-89; R March St Mary 84-89; RD March 87-89; Bp's Officer for Unemployment *Sheff* 89-94; Resource and Development Officer Chs Community Work Alliance 96-02; LtO *Sheff* from 96; PtO *Sarum* from 07; rtd 09. *10 Holly Drive, Wick, Littlehampton BN17 6LB* T: (01903) 721467 E: brianjruddock@btinternet.com

RUDDOCK, Bruce. *See* RUDDOCK, Reginald Bruce

RUDDOCK, Charles Cecil. b 28. TCD Div Sch. **d** 57 **p** 58. C Belfast St Mary *Conn* 57-59; C Carnmoney 59-61; C Belfast St Aid 61-63; I Kiltegan w Rathvilly *C & O* 63-69; C Newtownards *D & D* 69-72; R Beaconsfield w Exeter Australia 72-77; R Sandford 77-83; I Mallow Union *C, C & R* 83-89; I Fenagh w Myshall, Aghade and Ardoyne *C & O* 89-95; Can Ossory and Leighlin Cathls 92-95; rtd 95; PtO *Glouc* 95-05. *11 Bevis Court, Bibra Lake, Perth WA 6163, Australia*

RUDDOCK, Canon Edgar Chapman. b 48. St Jo Coll Dur BA 70 MA 76. Cranmer Hall Dur 70. **d** 74 **p** 75. C Birm St Geo 74-78; R 78-83; Dir Tr Dio St Jo S Africa 83-86; P-in-c Mandini 86-87; Prov Dir Tr 88-91; Hon Can Zululand from 95; TR Stoke-upon-Trent *Lich* 91-02; Dir Internat Relns United Soc 03-14; Dep Gen Sec 05-14; rtd 14; PtO *Guildf* 04-14; *Win* from 15. *2 Talbot Road, Dibden Purlieu, Southampton SO45 4PP* T: (023) 8194 4047 E: edgar.ruddock@gmail.com

RUDDOCK, Kenneth Edward. b 30. TCD BA 52 QUB MTh 79. CITC 53 Div Test. **d** 53 **p** 54. C Ballymena *Conn* 53-56; C Belfast St Thos 56-60; I Tomregan w Drumlane *K, E & A* 60-68; I Belfast St Luke *Conn* 68-80; Miss to Seamen 80-96; I Whitehead and Islandmagee *Conn* 80-96; Can Lisburn Ch Ch Cathl 90-96; Dioc Info Officer from 90; Chan Conn Cathl 96; rtd 96; Dioc C *Conn* from 98. *24 Fourtowns Manor, Ahoghill, Ballymena BT42 1RS* T: (028) 2587 8966

RUDDOCK, Leonard William. b 58. CITC 90. **d** 94 **p** 95. NSM Roscrea w Kyle, Bourney and Corbally *L & K* 94-06; C Stillorgan w Blackrock *D & G* 06-08; I Blessington w Kilbride, Ballymore Eustace etc from 08. *The Rectory, 13 Ashton, Blessington, Co Wicklow, Republic of Ireland* T: (00353) (45) 865178 M: 87-764 3296 E: leonardruddock@gmail.com

RUDDOCK, Canon Reginald Bruce. b 55. AGSM 77. Chich Th Coll 80. **d** 83 **p** 84. C Felpham w Middleton *Chich* 83-86; C Portsea St Mary *Portsm* 86-88; P-in-c Barnes St Mich *S'wark* 88-95; Dir Angl Cen Rome 95-99; Hon Can American Cathl Paris from 96; Can Res Worc Cathl 99-04; Can Res Pet Cathl from 04; Liturg Officer 04-12; Chapl to The Queen from 08. *Precentor's Lodging, Minster Precincts, Peterborough PE1 1XX* T: (01733) 562828 *or* 355310 F: 355316 E: bruce.ruddock@peterborough-cathedral.org.uk

RUDEN, Lars Olav. b 43. **d** 00 **p** 01. OLM Bamford *Man* 00-05; P-in-c Healey 05-13; P-in-c Hamer 11-13; rtd 13; PtO *Man* from 13. *11 Dell Side Way, Rochdale OL12 6XX* M: 07743-509193 E: larsruden.norge@virgin.net

RUDGE, Colin. b 48. Open Univ BA 04. Wilson Carlile Coll 96 SEITE 08. **d** 10 **p** 11. C Hollington St Jo *Chich* 10-12; C Seaford w Sutton from 12. *St Luke's House, 16 Saltwood Road, Seaford BN25 3SP* T: (01323) 893391 M: 07967 778765 E: colin.rudge@gmail.com

RUDGE, Miss Susannah Mary. b 84. Trin Coll Ox BA 05 MA 10 Jes Coll Cam MPhil 10. Westcott Ho Cam 08. **d** 10 **p** 11. C Bournville *Birm* 10-15; R Upminster *Chelmsf* from 15.

The Rectory, 4 Gridiron Place, Upminster RM14 2BE T: (01708) 220174 E: susannah.rudge@gmail.com

RUDIGER, David John. b 42. MCMI 91. Ox Min Course 91. **d** 94 **p** 95. NSM Woughton *Ox* 94-11; rtd 11. *56 Kirtlington, Downhead Park, Milton Keynes MK15 9AZ* T: (01908) 668474 E: david@rudiger2.freeserve.co.uk

RUDKIN, Simon David. b 51. Bradf Univ BA 74 K Coll Lon BD 77 AKC 77. Coll of Resurr Mirfield 77. **d** 78 **p** 79. C Flixton St Mich *Man* 78-81; C Atherton 81-84; V Lever Bridge 84-91; P-in-c Pennington w Lindal and Marton *Carl* 91-96; P-in-c Pennington and Lindal w Marton and Bardsea 96-00; V Morland, Thrimby, Gt Strickland and Cliburn 00-09; P-in-c Kirkby Thore w Temple Sowerby and Newbiggin 04-07; P-in-c Bolton and Crosby Ravensworth 05-09; R Bedale and Leeming and Thornton Watlass *Ripon* 09-11; R The Thorntons and The Otteringtons *York* from 11; Chapl N Yorks Police from 11. *The Vicarage, 4 Endican Lane, Thornton le Moor, Northallerton DL7 9FB* T: (01609) 774413 E: sd.rudkin@btinternet.com

RUDMAN, Preb David Walter Thomas. b 48. Oak Hill Th Coll BD 72. **d** 72 **p** 73. C Plymouth St Jude *Ex* 72-75; C Radipole *Sarum* 76; C Radipole and Melcombe Regis 77; Warden St Geo Ho Braunton 77-03; R Georgeham *Ex* 88-03; Dioc Adv in Adult Tr 97-03; TV S Molton w Nymet St George, High Bray etc 03-13; Dioc Adv in OLM 03-13; Preb Ex Cathl 09-13; rtd 13. *Greendale Farm, Pill Lane, Barnstaple EX32 9EQ* E: rudman1604@gmail.com

RUE, Kenneth. TCD BBS 75. **d** 10 **p** 11. NSM Powerscourt w Kilbride *D & G* 10-11; NSM Wicklow w Killiskey from 11. *9 Kingston Crescent, Dundrum, Dublin 16, Republic of Ireland* T: (00353) (1) 298 9497 M: 87-276 6590 E: krue@eircom.net

RUEHORN, Eric Arthur. b 33. St Aid Birkenhead 58. **d** 61 **p** 62. C Harpurhey Ch Ch *Man* 61-65; V Roughtown 65-74; V Hawkshaw Lane 74-99; rtd 99; PtO *Man* from 00. *101 Bankhouse Road, Bury BL8 1DZ* T: 0161-761 3983

RUFF, Brian Chisholm. b 36. Lon Univ BD 66 ACA 60 FCA 70. Oak Hill Th Coll 63. **d** 67 **p** 68. C Cheadle *Ches* 67-72; Educn and Youth Sec CPAS 72-76; V New Milverton *Cov* 76-90; V Westbourne Ch Ch Chpl *Win* 90-01; rtd 02; PtO *Win* from 02; *Sarum* from 03. *19 Hardy Road, West Moors, Wimborne BH22 0EX* T: (01202) 868733 E: bcr@ruffys.fsnet.co.uk

RUFF, Michael Ronald. b 49. K Coll Lon BD 72 AKC 72 Ch Ch Coll Cant PGCE 77. St Aug Coll Cant 72. **d** 73 **p** 74. C Old Shoreham *Chich* 73-76; Chapl Ellesmere Coll 77-81; Chapl Grenville Coll Bideford 81-87; Chapl Stamford Sch 87-06; P-in-c Stamford St Mary and St Martin *Linc* 06-13; rtd 11. *3 Baxters Lane, Easton on the Hill, Stamford PE9 3NH* T: (01780) 766567

RUFFLE, Preb John Leslie. b 43. ALCD 66. **d** 66 **p** 67. C Eastwood *S'well* 66-70; C Keynsham w Queen Charlton *B & W* 70-75; P-in-c Weston-super-Mare Em 75; TV Weston-super-Mare Cen Par 75-84; V Yatton Moor 84-91; TR 91-98; P-in-c Chew Stoke w Nempnett Thrubwell 98-03; Dioc Adv in Past Care and Counselling 03-06; rtd 06; Preb Wells Cathl 97-13; PtO from 06. *52 Highbridge Road, Burnham-on-Sea TA8 1LN* T: (01278) 788322 E: john.ruffle01@btinternet.com

RUFFLE, Wendy Ann. b 45. **d** 10 **p** 11. C Tewkesbury w Walton Cardiff and Twyning *Glouc* from 10. *High Bank, Gambles Lane, Cleeve Hill, Cheltenham GL52 3QA* T: (01242) 674103 E: rev.wendy@me.com

RUFLI, Alan John. b 63. TCD BA 89. **d** 91 **p** 92. C Donaghcloney w Waringstown *D & D* 91-94; C Knock 94-95; I Rathcoole *Conn* 95-01; I Holmpatrick w Balbriggan and Kenure *D & G* 01-10; I Clondalkin w Rathcoole from 10. *St John's Rectory, 5 Monastery Road, Clondalkin, Dublin 22, Republic of Ireland* T: (00353) (1) 459 2160 M: 87-997 2401 E: rufrev@aol.com

RUGEN, Peter. b 60. Crewe & Alsager Coll BEd 86. Trin Coll Bris MA 00. **d** 00 **p** 01. C Shipley St Pet *Bradf* 00-04; P-in-c Riddlesden and Morton St Luke 04-08; P-in-c Norley, Crowton and Kingsley *Ches* 08-11; V from 11; RD Frodsham from 11. *St John's House, Pike Lane, Kingsley, Frodsham WA6 8EH* T: (01928) 787180 E: p.rugen@btinternet.com

RUGG, Andrew Philip. b 47. Kent Univ BA 82. Sarum & Wells Th Coll 83. **d** 85 **p** 86. C Harlesden All So *Lon* 85-90; TV Benwell *Newc* 90-97; V Weetslade 97-00; rtd 00; PtO *York* from 00. *2 Ellen Wilson Cottages, Lawrence Street, York YO10 3WP* M: 07980-390051

RUGG, Christopher James McTeer. b 75. St Jo Coll Dur BSc 97. Trin Coll Bris 06. **d** 08 **p** 09. C Week St Mary Circle of Par *Truro* 08-11; USA from 11. *4104 Tiffany Lane, Redding CA 96002, USA* T: (001) (503) 233 3833 E: cjmrugg@gmail.com

RUGG, Richard Edward. b 79. Oak Hill Th Coll BA 06 Trin Coll Bris 10. **d** 12 **p** 13. C Buckingham *Ox* from 12. *5 Chandos Close, Buckingham MK18 1AW* M: 07968-173365 E: richardrugg79@gmail.com

RUGMAN, Mrs Hazel. b 47. R Holloway Coll Lon BA 68 ACIS 89. NOC 01. **d** 03 **p** 04. NSM Sandbach *Ches* 03-06; NSM Crewe St Andr w St Jo from 06; NSM Crewe Ch Ch 07-13. *High Trees, 157 Sandbach Road North, Alsager, Stoke-on-Trent ST7 2AX* T: (01270) 876386 F: 883737 M: 07762-706120 E: hazelrugman@btinternet.com

✠**RUHUMULIZA, The Rt Revd Jonathan.** b 56. Makumira Univ Coll Tanzania BD 89. Butare Th Sch Rwanda 78. **d** 82 **p** 83 **c** 91. C Kigeme Rwanda 82-84; Manager and Chapl Kigeme High School 83-86; Manager and Chapl Kigeme Hosp 89-90; Manager and Chapl Kigeme High Sch 90-91; Asst Bp Butare 91-92; Prov Sec Rwanda 92-93; Asst Bp Kigali 93; Coadjutor Bp 93-95; Bp 95-97; Cameroon 98-04; C Droitwich Spa *Worc* 05-06; Hon Asst Bp Worc from 05; C Elmley Lovett w Hampton Lovett and Elmbridge etc 12-14; C Ombersley w Doverdale 12-14; C Hartlebury 12-14; PtO *Birm* from 13. *6 Riverside Way, Droitwich, Worcester WR9 8UP* T: (01905) 799329 E: bspjrmuliza@yahoo.co.uk

RUITERS, Canon Ivan John. b 61. Coll of Transfiguration Grahamstown 94. **d** 96 **p** 97. C Berea S Africa 96-00; R Maidstone 00-01; R Newlands 02-07; I Killesher *K, E & A* from 07; Can Kilmore Cathl from 14. *The New Rectory, 10 Mill Road, Tully, Enniskillen BT92 1FN* T: (028) 6634 8235 M: 07902-174219 E: ivanruiters@yahoo.com

✠**RUMALSHAH, The Rt Revd Munawar Kenneth (Mano).** b 41. Punjab Univ BSc 60 Serampore Coll BD 65 Karachi Univ MA 68 Homerton Coll Cam PGCE 88. Bp's Coll Calcutta 62. **d** 65 **p** 66 **c** 94. C H Trin Cathl Karachi Pakistan 65-69; C Roundhay St Edm *Ripon* 70-73; Area Sec and Asst Home Sec CMS 73-78; Educn Sec BCC 78-81; P-in-c Southall St Geo *Lon* 81-88; Lect Edwardes Coll Peshawar Pakistan 89-94; Bp Peshawar 94-99 and 03-07; Gen Sec USPG and Hon Asst Bp S'wark 99-03; rtd 07. *81 Bantry Road, Slough SL1 5FD* E: bishopmanodop@hotmail.com

RUMBALL, William Michael. b 41. Surrey Univ BSc 63 Hon BUniv 11 Birm Univ PhD 66 MA 11 Open Univ BA 75 MIM 66 MINucE 73 FIMMM 03. Wycliffe Hall Ox 78. **d** 80 **p** 81. C S Molton, Nymet St George, High Bray etc *Ex* 80-83; V S Hetton w Haswell *Dur* 83-90; V S Wingfield and Wessington *Derby* 90-99; rtd 99; Hon C Brailsford w Shirley and Osmaston w Edlaston *Derby* 01-03; PtO 03-10; *Lich* 08-10; *B & W* 10-14. *21 Capel Court, The Burgage, Prestbury, Cheltenham GL52 3EL* E: wm.rumball@gmail.com

RUMBLE, Alison Merle. *See* PRINCE, Alison Merle

RUMBOLD, Bernard John. b 43. **d** 73 **p** 75. Hon C Alotau Papua New Guinea 73-76; C Gt Burstead *Chelmsf* 76-77; Chapl RAF 77-93; Chapl HM Pris Featherstone 93-95; C Wordsley *Worc* 95-96; TV 96-99; Chapl Dudley Gp of Hosps NHS Trust 96-99; R Teme Valley N *Worc* 99-02; P-in-c Brompton Regis w Upton and Skilgate *B & W* 03-08; P-in-c Gt w Lt Tew and Over w Nether Worton *Ox* 08-10; rtd 11. *6 St David's Drive, Evesham WR11 2AU* E: bernardrumbold@btinternet.com

RUMBOLD, Graham Charles. b 44. Open Univ BA 79. S Dios Minl Tr Scheme 76. **d** 79 **p** 80. NSM Widley w Wymering *Portsm* 79-82; Chapl Cynthia Spencer Unit Manfield Hosp 82-94; Chapl Northampton Community Healthcare NHS Trust 94-01; Chapl Northants Healthcare NHS Trust 01-04; NSM Weston Favell *Pet* 93-95; NSM Northampton St Matt 98-12. *3 Calstock Close, Northampton NN3 3BA* T: (01604) 627389 E: graham.rumbold@yahoo.com

RUMENS, Canon John Henry. b 21. AKC 49. **d** 50 **p** 51. C Wareham w Arne *Sarum* 50-54; V Alderholt 54-59; R Salisbury St Edm 59-72; RD Salisbury 69-72; R Trowbridge H Trin 72-79; P-in-c Sturminster Marshall 79-83; V 83-85; Can and Preb Sarum Cathl 72-85; rtd 85; PtO *Sarum* from 85. *20 Constable Way, Salisbury SP2 8LN* T: (01722) 334716

RUMENS, Ms Katharine Mary. b 53. UEA BEd 76. Westcott Ho Cam 90. **d** 92 **p** 94. Par Dn E Ham w Upton Park and Forest Gate *Chelmsf* 92-94; C 94-95; C Waterloo St Jo w St Andr S'wark 95-00; Chapl S Bank Cen and Chapl Lon Weekend TV 95-00; R St Giles Cripplegate w St Bart Moor Lane etc *Lon* from 00. *The Rectory, 4 The Postern, Wood Street, London EC2Y 8BJ* T/F: (020) 7588 3013 T: 7638 1997 E: rumens@stgileschurch.com

RUMING, Canon Gordon William. b 27. Kelham Th Coll 45. **d** 52 **p** 53. C Baildon *Bradf* 52-55; C Prestbury *Glouc* 55-60; C Penzance St Mary *Truro* 60-61; R Calstock 61-92; Hon Can Truro Cathl 79-92; RD E Wivelshire 85-91; rtd 92; PtO *Truro* from 92; *Ex* from 99. *3 Derry Avenue, Plymouth PL4 6BH* T: (01752) 661986

RUMSEY, Andrew Paul. b 68. Reading Univ BA 89. Ridley Hall Cam MA 98. **d** 97 **p** 98. C Harrow Trin St Mich *Lon* 97-01; V Gipsy Hill Ch Ch *S'wark* 01-11; R Oxted and Tandridge 11-14; TR Oxted from 14. *The Rectory, 29 Chichele Road, Oxted RH8 0AE* T: (01883) 712955 E: andrew.rumsey@btinternet.com

RUMSEY, Ian Mark. b 58. Van Mildert Coll Dur BSc 79 St Jo Coll Dur BA 89. Cranmer Hall Dur 87. **d** 90 **p** 91. C Dalston *Carl* 90-94; C Wreay 92-94; TV Cockermouth w Embleton and Wythop 94-04; Adv for Post-Ord Tr 97-00; V Hurdsfield *Ches* 04-12; Par Development Officer from 12. *Church House, 5500 Daresbury Park, Daresbury, Warrington WA4 4GE* T: (01928) 718834 E: ian.rumsey@chester.anglican.org

RUNCORN, David Charles. b 54. BA 77. St Jo Coll Nottm 77. **d** 79 **p** 80. C Wealdstone H Trin *Lon* 79-82; Chapl Lee Abbey 82-87; C Ealing St Steph Castle Hill *Lon* 89-90; V 90-96; Dir Past and Evang Studies Trin Coll Bris 96-03; Dir Min Development *Lich* 03-08; Tutor St Jo Coll Nottm 08-12; Public Preacher *Glouc* from 12; Dioc Dir of Ords from 15. *9 College Green, Gloucester GL1 2LX* M: 07870-331537 E: davidruncorn@mac.com

RUNCORN, Jacqueline Ann. *See* SEARLE, Jacqueline Ann

RUNDELL, Simon Philip. b 67. Univ of N Lon BSc 95 Leeds Univ BA 01 RGN 90. Coll of Resurr Mirfield 99. **d** 01 **p** 02. C Southsea H Spirit *Portsm* 01-04; P-in-c Elson 04-09; V 09-12; P-in-c Bickleigh and Shaugh Prior *Ex* from 12; C Egg Buckland from 12; C Estover from 12; C Plymouth Crownhill Ascension from 12. *33 Leat Walk, Roborough, Plymouth PL6 7AT* E: simon@rundell.org.uk

RUNDLE, Mrs Beryl Rosemary. b 28. Bris Univ BA 49 CertEd 50. S Dios Minl Tr Scheme 83. **dss** 86 **d** 87. Tangmere *Chich* 86-87; Hon Par Dn 87-92; Boxgrove 86-87; Hon Par Dn 87-92; Hon Par Dn Eastbourne St Sav and St Pet 92-98; PtO *Portsm* from 98. *22 Sovereign Drive, Southsea PO4 8XX* T: (01705) 826859

RUNDLE, Hilary. *See* WONG, Hilary

RUNDLE, Nicholas John. b 59. Southn Univ BA 80. St Steph Ho Ox BTh 84. **d** 84 **p** 85. C E Preston w Kingston *Chich* 84-87; Chapl RAF 87-91; Assoc P Magill Australia 91-93; R Grange 93-98; R Hawthorn 98-02; Chapl and Past Care Co-ord Miss Australia from 03. *Mission Australia, PO Box 6626, Adelaide SA 5000, Australia* T: (0061) (8) 8370 3583 *or* 8223 5428 F: 8223 6425 M: 403-183005 E: rundlen@mission.com.au

RUNDLE, Penelope Anne. b 36. St Hugh's Coll Ox MA 59. S Dios Minl Tr Scheme 85. **d** 88 **p** 94. Hon Par Dn Mere w W Knoyle and Maiden Bradley *Sarum* 88-91; Hon Par Dn Upper Stour 91-94; Hon C 94-02; rtd 02; PtO *Sarum* 02-08. *7 Prospect Place, Ann Street, Salisbury SP1 2EA* T: (01722) 411774 E: peneloperundle@aol.com

RUNNACLES, Ms Jasmine Celine Leweston. b 47. Lon Bible Coll BA 75 RN 68. STETS 05. **d** 08 **p** 09. NSM Burpham *Guildf* from 08; Chapl N Surrey Primary Care Trust from 11. *Chydham Cottage, Maybury Hill, Woking GU22 8AF* T/F: (01483) 765239 M: 07774-171818 E: jclrunnacles@virginmedia.com

RUOFF, Mark Frederick John. b 76. K Coll Lon BA 98. St Mellitus Coll BA 15. **d** 15. C Onslow Square and S Kensington St Aug *Lon* from 15. *147 Lavenham Road, London SW18 5EP* M: 07919-403853 E: markfjruoff@gmail.com

RUSCHMEYER, Henry Cassell. b 44. Union Coll NY BA 66 Bank St Coll of Ed NY MEd 73 NY Univ MA 88. Gen Th Sem (NY) MDiv 78. **d** 78 **p** 79. USA 78-89 and from 97; NSM Wilton Place St Paul *Lon* 89-97. *2929 SE Ocean Boulevard Apt M9, Stuart FL 34996-2782, USA*

RUSCOE, Canon John Ernest. b 32. Dur Univ BA 57. Qu Coll Birm 57. **d** 59 **p** 60. C Jarrow St Paul *Dur* 59-63; C Whitburn 63-65; V S Hylton 65-10; Hon Can Dur Cathl 85-10; rtd 10; PtO *Dur* from 10. *17 Marina Avenue, Sunderland SR6 9AL* T: 0191-549 8371

RUSDELL-WILSON, Arthur Neville. b 43. Lon Univ BScEng 65 Linacre Coll Ox BA 70 MA 74. St Steph Ho Ox 68. **d** 71 **p** 72. C Whitton St Aug *Lon* 71-73; C Chiswick St Nic w St Mary 73-76; C Littlehampton St Jas *Chich* 76-81; C Littlehampton St Mary 76-81; C Wick 76-81; V Whitworth St Bart *Man* 81-88; V Shaw 88-98; rtd 03. *21 Fairview Avenue, Goring-by-Sea, Worthing BN12 4HT* T: (01903) 242561

RUSH, Paul Andrew. b 57. Lon Bible Coll BA 79 Anglia Poly Univ MA 01. Ridley Hall Cam 98. **d** 00 **p** 01. C Bar Hill *Ely* 00-03; Dioc Evang Officer *Leic* 03-06; Adv in Evang and Par Development *Bris* 06-13; C W Sheppey *Cant* from 13. *2 St Peter's Close, Minster on Sea, Sheerness ME12 3DD* T: (01795) 663661 M: 07906-118810 E: revdpaulrush@gmail.com

RUSH, Miss Shan Elizabeth. b 64. RGN 86 RSCN 86. Yorks Min Course 07. **d** 10 **p** 12. NSM Sheff St Mark Broomhill from 10; Chapl Bluebell Wood Children's Hospice from 14. *28 Rivelin Street, Sheffield S6 5DL* M: 07598-156817 E: shan.rush@sheffield.anglican.org

RUSHER, James Victor Francis. b 28. RMA. Ridley Hall Cam 58. **d** 60 **p** 61. C Kensington St Helen w H Trin *Lon* 60-63; C Edgbaston St Bart *Birm* 63-66; V Summerfield 66-71; V Knowle 71-82; PtO 82-12; Chapl Parkway Hosp Solihull 85-93; rtd 93. *4 Froxmere Close, Solihull B91 3XG* T: 0121-705 4514

RUSHFORTH, Colin Stephen. b 53. Chich Th Coll 74. **d** 77 **p** 78. C Moulsecoomb *Chich* 77-79; C Rumboldswyke 79-81; C Whyke w Rumboldswhyke and Portfield 81-82; V Friskney *Linc* 82-84; P-in-c Thorpe St Peter 82-84; TV Leic H Spirit 84-87; Chapl Leic R Infirmary 87-94; Chapl Leic R Infirmary NHS Trust 94-98; PtO *Leic* 08-12; P-in-c Sneinton St Steph w St Matthias *S'well* from 12; P-in-c Nottingham St Geo w St Jo from 12. *St George's Vicarage, Strome Close, Nottingham NG2 1HD* M: 07960-649191 E: colinrushforth@hotmail.co.uk

RUSHFORTH, Richard Hamblin. b 40. Keble Coll Ox BA 62 MA 71. Chich Th Coll 62. **d** 64 **p** 65. C St Leonards Ch Ch *Chich* 64-79; Org Sec Fellowship of St Nic 79-81; V Portslade St Nic and St Andr *Chich* 81-12; Min Portslade Gd Shep CD 88-89; rtd 12. *12 Upper Church Road, St Leonards-on-Sea TN37 7AT*

RUSHOLME, Susan. b 53. Leeds Univ BA 10. Yorks Min Course 07. **d** 10 **p** 11. NSM Chapel Allerton *Leeds* from 10. *71 Eaton Hill, Leeds LS16 6SE* T: 0113-261 2913 M: 07504-880199 E: revsue.rusholme@virginmedia.com

RUSHTON, Christopher John. b 54. JP 89. LBIPP 93. Qu Coll Birm 10. **d** 11 **p** 12. OLM Hartshill, Penkhull and Trent Vale *Lich* 11-14; NSM 14-15; P-in-c 15; Dioc Lay Min Adv from 12. *The School House, Vicarage Road, Hartshill, Stoke-on-Trent ST4 7NL* T: (01782) 410011 E: church@chrisrushton.co.uk

RUSHTON, David William. b 70. St Chad's Coll Dur BA 96. St Steph Ho Ox. **d** 98 **p** 99. C Hornsey St Mary w St Geo *Lon* 98-01; C Thamesmead *S'wark* 01-02; Asst Chapl King's Coll Hosp NHS Trust 02-04; Chapl King's Coll Hosp NHS Foundn Trust 04-10; Lead Chapl and Hospitaller Barts and The Lon NHS Trust 10-14; Lead Chapl R Free London NHS Foundn Trust from 14. *The Chaplaincy, Royal Free London NHS Foundn Trust, Royal Free Hospital, Pond Street, London NW3 2QG* T: (020) 7830 2742 *or* 3758 2000 ext 35085 E: davidrushton@nhs.net

RUSHTON, Canon James David. b 39. Dur Univ BA 61. Cranmer Hall Dur. **d** 64 **p** 65. C Upper Armley *Ripon* 64-67; C Blackpool Ch Ch *Blackb* 67-70; V Preston St Cuth 70-79; V Denton Holme *Carl* 79-96; P-in-c Preston All SS *Blackb* 96-00; V 00-04; AD Preston 98-03; Hon Can Blackb Cathl 00-04; rtd 04; PtO *Blackb* from 04. *1 Stable Mews, Fleetwood Road, Thornton-Cleveleys FY5 1SQ* T: (01253) 820402 E: james@jamesrushton.wanadoo.co.uk

RUSHTON, Ms Janet Maureen. b 46. Keele Univ BA 68 Leic Univ PGCE 69. Wycliffe Hall Ox BTh 94. **d** 94 **p** 95. C Harrow St Mary *Lon* 94-98; C Putney St Mary *S'wark* 98-02; P-in-c Wolvercote w Summertown *Ox* 02-07; P-in-c Summertown 07-11; rtd 11; PtO *Lon* from 11. *20 Harvard Court, Honeybourne Road, London NW6 1HJ* T: (020) 7431 4606 E: jan.rushton5@gmail.com

RUSHTON, Matthew John. b 75. St Anne's Coll Ox BA 96 MA 01 Linc Univ MA 13 Solicitor 01. Ripon Coll Cuddesdon 07. **d** 09 **p** 10. C Nettleham *Linc* 09-12; Hon PV Linc Cathl 11-12; Abp's Chapl *Cant* 12-13; Chapl to Bp Dover 12-13; C Cant St Dunstan w H Cross and Cant St Pet w St Alphege and St Marg etc 12-13; Prec Cant Cathl from 13. *Cathedral House, 11 The Precincts, Canterbury CT1 2EH* T: (01227) 762862 E: precentor@canterbury-cathedral.org

RUSHTON, Patricia Mary. *See* DUFFETT-SMITH, Patricia Mary

RUSHTON, Philip William. b 38. Open Univ BA 87. Clifton Th Coll 62. **d** 65 **p** 66. C Brixton St Paul *S'wark* 65-67; C Aldridge *Lich* 67-69; C Bushbury 69-71; Chapl Nat Nautical Sch Portishead 71-72; Chapl RAF 72-79; P-in-c Bolton on Swale *Ripon* 79-87; P-in-c The Cowtons 80-82; V 82-89; CF (TA) from 88; R Litcham, Kempston, Lexham, Mileham, Beeston etc *Nor* 89-95; P-in-c Tittleshall w Godwick 93-95; R Litcham w Kempston, E and W Lexham, Mileham etc 95-96; P-in-c Scole, Brockdish, Billingford, Thorpe Abbots etc 96-98; R 98-01; PtO *St E* from 00; rtd 01; PtO *Carl* from 01. *Helm Lea, Kirkby Thore, Penrith CA10 1UA* T/F: (017683) 61597 E: philipwrushton@hotmail.com

RUSHTON, The Ven Samantha Jayne. b 65. St Hilda's Coll Ox MA 87. Trin Coll Bris BA 05. **d** 05 **p** 06. C Highworth w Sevenhampton and Inglesham etc *Bris* 05-08; C Broad Blunsdon 05-08; Dioc Adv for Lic Min 08-15; C Chippenham St Paul w Hardenhuish etc 08-15; C Kington St Michael 08-15; Warden of Readers 11-15; AD Chippenham 13-15; Adn Cleveland *York* from 15. *48 Langbaurgh Road, Hutton Rudby, Yarm TS15 0HL* T: (01642) 660451 M: 07906-376036

RUSHTON, Mrs Susan Elizabeth. b 44. Univ of Wales (Cardiff) BA 65. Bris Sch of Min 83. **dss** 86 **d** 87 **p** 94. Westbury-on-Trym H Trin *Bris* 86-91; Hon Par Dn 87-91; C Wotton St Mary *Glouc* 91-94; P-in-c Frampton Cotterell *Bris* 94-07; Chapl United Bris Healthcare NHS Trust 94-98; P-in-c Iron Acton *Bris* 98-07; rtd 07; PtO *York* from 08. *9 Lime Avenue, Heworth, York YO31 1BT* T: (01904) 410363 E: susan.rushton@onetel.net

RUSHTON, Mrs Valerie Elizabeth Wendy. b 40. Birm Univ BSocSc 62. WMMTC 86. **d** 89 **p** 94. C Nuneaton St Nic *Cov* 89-93; C Stockingford 93-96; TV Watling Valley *Ox* 96-01; rtd 02; PtO *Ox* from 02. *106 Moreton Road, Buckingham MK18 1PW* T: (01280) 824942

RUSK, The Very Revd Frederick John. b 28. QUB BA 50 TCD 52. **d** 53 **p** 54. C Ballymoney w Finvoy and Rasharkin *Conn* 53-56; C Belfast St Nic 56-59; I Broomhedge 59-65; RE Insp 64-66; I Belfast St Simon *Conn* 65-78; I Ballymena w Ballyclug 78-88; I Belfast St Nic 88-98; Preb Conn Cathl 84-86; Treas Conn Cathl 86-90; Prec Conn Cathl 90; Chan Conn Cathl 90-95; Dean Conn 95-98; rtd 98. *28 Banbridge Road, Lurgan, Craigavon BT66 7EQ* T: (028) 3832 9763

RUSK, Canon Michael Frederick. b 58. Cam Univ BA MA Dur Univ MA 98. Westcott Ho Cam 81. **d** 84 **p** 85. C Altrincham St Geo *Ches* 84-87; Chapl Collingwood Coll Dur 87-90; Lect Dur Univ 89-99; C-in-c Neville's Cross St Jo CD 90-99; TR Oadby *Leic* from 99; RD Gartree II 00-13; RD Gartree I 07-13; Hon Can Leic Cathl from 06. *The Rectory, 31 Hill Field, Oadby, Leicester LE2 4RW* T: 0116-271 2135
E: m.f.rusk@leicester.anglican.org

RUSS, Canon Timothy John. b 41. AKC 64. Sarum Th Coll 66. **d** 66 **p** 67. C Walthamstow St Pet *Chelmsf* 66-70; C Epping St Jo 70-73; C Stepney St Dunstan and All SS *Lon* 73-75; Youth Officer 75-79; Tutor YMCA Nat Coll Walthamstow 79-84; Hon C St Botolph Aldgate w H Trin Minories *Lon* 82-89; Selection Sec ACCM 84-89; Dir St Marylebone Healing and Counselling Cen 89-92; Gen Sec Inst of Relig and Medicine 89-92; Hon C Hoxton St Anne w St Columba *Lon* 90-92; P-in-c St Dennis *Truro* 92-06; Par Development Adv 92-99; Dioc Dir Minl Tr 99-06; Hon Can Truro Cathl 01-06; rtd 06. *Russet Cottage, 26 St Francis Meadow, Mitchell, Newquay TR8 5DB* T: (01872) 519142 E: timruss@tesco.net

RUSSELL, Adrian Camper. b 45. Chich Th Coll 79. **d** 81 **p** 82. C Marton *Blackb* 81-84; C Haslemere *Guildf* 84-85; V Hartlepool H Trin *Dur* 85-89; P-in-c Cornforth 89-94; R Auchterarder and Muthill *St And* 94-97; P-in-c Kenton Ascension *Newc* 97-07; rtd 07. *23 Lambley Avenue, North Shields NE30 3SL* T: 0191-280 9552 E: acr26682@blueyonder.co.uk

RUSSELL, Alexandra Blaise. b 58. St Steph Ho Ox 96. **d** 98 **p** 99. C Gt Bookham *Guildf* 98-03; R Long Ditton 03-07; PtO *Win* 07-08; P-in-c Pennington from 08. *The Vicarage, 29 Ramley Road, Lymington SO41 8HF* T: (01590) 610963
E: alexblaiserussell@gmail.com

RUSSELL, Andrea. b 64. K Coll Lon LLB 86 Nottm Univ BA 04 MA 05 PhD 10. EMMTC 08. **d** 10 **p** 11. C Sherwood *S'well* 10-12; Dir of Studies St Jo Coll Nottm 12-14. *Address temp unknown*

RUSSELL, Ms Anne. b 66. Man Univ BA(Econ) 88. LCTP 06. **d** 11 **p** 12. C Kendal H Trin *Carl* 11-14; TR Bentham, Burton-in-Lonsdale, Chapel-le-Dale etc *Bradf* from 14. *The Vicarage, 1 Moons Acre, Bentham, Lancaster LA2 7BL* M: 07528-572072
E: curatekpc@gmail.com

✠**RUSSELL, The Rt Revd Anthony John.** b 43. St Chad's Coll Dur BA 65 Trin Coll Ox DPhil 71. Cuddesdon Coll 65. **d** 70 **p** 71 **c** 88. C Hilborough w Bodney *Nor* 70-73; P-in-c Preston-on-Stour w Whitchurch *Cov* 73-76; P-in-c Atherstone on Stour 73-76; V Preston on Stour and Whitchurch w Atherstone 77-88; Can Th Cov Cathl 77-88; Chapl Arthur Rank Cen 73-82; Dir 83-88; Chapl to The Queen 83-88; Area Bp Dorchester *Ox* 88-00; Bp Ely 00-10; rtd 10; Hon Asst Bp Ox from 11. *Lye Hill House, Holton, Oxford OX33 1QF* T: (01865) 876415

RUSSELL, The Ven Brian Kenneth. b 50. Trin Hall Cam BA 73 MA 76 Birm Univ MA 77 PhD 83. Cuddesdon Coll 74. **d** 76 **p** 77. C Redhill St Matt *S'wark* 76-79; Dir Studies NEOC 79-83; P-in-c Merrington *Dur* 79-83; Dir of Studies and Lect Linc Th Coll 83-86; Selection Sec and Sec Cttee for Th Educn ABM 86-93; Bp's Dir for Min *Birm* 93-05; Adn Aston 05-14; Hon Can Birm Cathl 99-14; Sen Chapl Oslo w Bergen, Trondheim and Stavanger *Eur* from 14; PtO *Birm* from 14. *Harald Hårfagres Gate 2, Apartment 52, 0363 Oslo, Norway* M: 99-472987 T: (0047) 22 692274 E: b-russell5@sky.com

RUSSELL, Brian Robert. b 61. QUB BA BD 92. CITC. **d** 85 **p** 86. C Dublin Drumcondra w N Strand *D & G* 85-87; C Carrickfergus *Conn* 87-90; I Kilmegan w Maghera *D & D* 90-96; I Bailieborough w Knockbride, Shercock and Mullagh K, *E & A* 96-00; I Kilbarron w Rossnowlagh and Drumholm *D & R* from 00. *The Rectory, Lisminton, Ballintra, Co Donegal, Republic of Ireland* T/F: (00353) (74) 973 4025
E: banderussell@eircom.net

RUSSELL, Bruce Harley. b 57. Ch Ch Ox BA 79 Roehampton Inst PGCE 80. Ripon Coll Cuddesdon. **d** 99 **p** 00. C Bracknell *Ox* 99-03; TV Langley Marish from 03. *St Francis's Vicarage, 21 Lynward Avenue, Slough SL3 7BJ* T: (01753) 557150
E: bhrussell@supanet.com

RUSSELL, Canon Christopher Ian. b 68. St Jo Coll Dur BA 91 St Edm Coll Cam MPhil 96. Ridley Hall Cam 93. **d** 96 **p** 97. C Deptford St Jo w H Trin *S'wark* 96-99; Soul Survivor Watford *St Alb* 99-01; C Reading St Mary the Virgin *Ox* 01-14; V Reading St Laur from 15; Hon Can Ch Ch from 13; Abp's Adv for Evang and Witness *Cant* from 13. *9 Mansfield Road, Reading RG1 6AL* T: 0118-956 0559
E: chris@belindarussell.freeserve.co.uk

RUSSELL, Clive Phillip. b 61. Ridley Hall Cam 04. **d** 06 **p** 07. C High Ongar w Norton Mandeville *Chelmsf* 06-09; V Grays North from 09. *St John's Vicarage, 8A Victoria Avenue, Grays RM16 2RP* T: (01375) 372101 E: russell-mail@tiscali.co.uk

RUSSELL, David John. b 57. Sarum & Wells Th Coll BTh 94. **d** 94 **p** 95. C Glouc St Geo w Whaddon 94-98; P-in-c Wickwar w Rangeworthy 98-01; R Wickwar, Rangeworthy and Hillesley 02-11; R Charfield and Kingswood w Wickwar etc from 11. *The Rectory, 75 High Street, Wickwar, Wotton-under-Edge GL12 8NP* T: (01454) 294267 E: davidrussell@gmx.com

RUSSELL, David John Timothy. b 75. Oak Hill Th Coll. **d** 09 **p** 10. C Padiham w Hapton and Padiham Green *Blackb* 09-13; V Woodford *Ches* from 13. *The Vicarage, 531 Chester Road, Woodford, Stockport SK7 1PR* T: 0161-439 2286
E: drjaz@hotmail.com

RUSSELL, David Robert. b 43. Brasted Th Coll 66 Sarum Th Coll 68. **d** 70 **p** 71. C Leintwardine *Heref* 70-73; C Bridgnorth w Tasley 73-75; R Lockridge and Eden Hill Australia 75-80; R Bellevue and Darlington 80-87; Asst Chapl Dept of Corrective Services 87-93; Sen Chapl 93-95; R Carlisle and Rivervale 95-03; E Deanery Miss Development 03-04; R Kondinin and Corrigin 05-08; rtd 08. *Unit 403, 34 Robinson Street, Inglewood WA 6052, Australia* T: (0061) (8) 6106 1070 M: 42-754 5560 E: davrobruss@virginbroadband.com.au

RUSSELL, Canon Derek John. b 30. St Pet Hall Ox BA 54 MA 58. Qu Coll Birm 54. **d** 56 **p** 57. C Boxley *Cant* 56-59; C Whitstable All SS 59-63; Chapl HM Pris Wormwood Scrubs 63-65; Chapl HM Pris Stafford 65-69; Chapl HM Pris Pentonville 70; Chapl HM Pris Wormwood Scrubs 71-89; SE Regional Chapl 74-81; Chapl HM Rem Cen Latchmere Ho 74-77; Asst Chapl Gen of Pris 81-83; Dep 83-90; Hon Can Cant Cathl 86-90; rtd 90; PtO *Cant* from 90. *25 Pier Avenue, Whitstable CT5 2HQ* T: (01227) 276654

RUSSELL, Ms Elizabeth Marilyn Vivia. b 50. LRAM 70 GRSM 72. Westcott Ho Cam 95. **d** 97 **p** 98. C Alton St Lawr *Win* 97-01; C St Martin-in-the-Fields *Lon* 01-08; P-in-c S Kensington H Trin w All SS from 08; Dir of Ords Two Cities Area from 08. *5 Aldwyn House, Davidson Gardens, London SW8 2HX* T: (020) 7498 5623 E: erussell101@btinternet.com

RUSSELL, Eric Watson. b 39. FCA 76. Clifton Th Coll 66. **d** 69 **p** 70. C Kinson *Sarum* 69-73; C Peckham St Mary Magd *S'wark* 73-77; TV Barking St Marg w St Patr *Chelmsf* 77-82; V Kells St Paul and St Silas *Birm* 82-95; RD Aston 89-94; P-in-c Barston and C Knowle 95-04; I Kells Union *M & K* 04-09; rtd 09; PtO *St E* from 15. *96 Abbot Road, Bury St Edmunds IP33 3UN* T: (01284) 489861 E: ericandjoan@uwclub.net

RUSSELL, Gary William Algernon. b 64. Ripon Coll Cuddesdon 04. **d** 06 **p** 07. C Harpenden St Nic *St Alb* 06-09; P-in-c St Alb St Mary Marshalswick 09-14; rtd 14. *33 Suffolk House, 31-33 Suffolk Road, Bournemouth BH2 6AT*
E: moreteavicar@hotmail.co.uk

RUSSELL, The Ven Harold Ian Lyle. b 34. Lon Coll of Div ALCD 59 BD 60. **d** 60 **p** 61. C Iver *Ox* 60-63; C Fulwood *Sheff* 63-67; V Chapeltown 67-75; RD Tankersley 73-75; V Nottingham St Jude *S'well* 75-89; AD Nottingham Cen 86-89; Hon Can S'well Minster 88-89; Adn Cov 89-00; rtd 01; Chapl to The Queen 97-04; PtO *S'well* from 01. *5 Old Acres, Woodborough, Nottingham NG14 6ES* T: 0115-965 3543

RUSSELL, Ms Isoline Lucilda (Lyn). b 41. **d** 03 **p** 04. OLM Camberwell St Giles w St Matt *S'wark* 03-11; PtO from 11. *124 Hindman's Road, London SE22 9NH* T: (020) 8299 4431
E: therusselfamily@fsmail.net

RUSSELL, James Anthony Tomkins. b 67. Oak Hill Th Coll BA 99. **d** 99 **p** 00. C Chadwell *Chelmsf* 99-03; C Patcham *Chich* 03-07; P-in-c N Mundham w Hunston and Merston from 07. *The Rectory, Church Lane, Hunston, Chichester PO20 1AJ* T: (01243) 782003 E: russell.j760@gmail.com

RUSSELL, Canon Janet Mary. b 53. Univ of Wales BSc 74 BArch 76. Ox Min Course 91. **d** 94 **p** 95. C Watlington w Pyrton and Shirburn *Ox* 94-97; C Icknield 97-98; TV Wallingford 98-05; Par Development Adv (Berks) 05-11; Dir Miss *S & B* from 11; Hon Can Brecon Cathl from 12. *The Rectory, Talybont-on-Usk, Brecon LD3 7UX* T: (01874) 665460
E: janetrussell@churchinwales.org.uk

RUSSELL, Canon John Arthur. b 29. AKC 62. **d** 63 **p** 64. C Fareham H Trin *Portsm* 63-67; R Greatham w Empshott 67-79; V Ham St Andr *S'wark* 79-87; P-in-c Battersea St Luke 87-92; V 92-96; Hon Can S'wark Cathl 95-96; rtd 97; PtO

S'wark 97-03. *10 Emden House, Barton Lane, Headington, Oxford OX3 9JU* E: jarussell@ya.com

RUSSELL, John Bruce. b 56. Ripon Coll Cuddesdon. **d** 95 **p** 96. C Newport Pagnell w Lathbury and Moulsoe *Ox* 95-98; P-in-c Wing w Grove 98-03; AD Mursley 02-03; PtO *St Alb* 08-10; TV Gt Berkhamsted, Gt and Lt Gaddesden etc from 10. *St John's Vicarage, Pipers Hill, Great Gaddesden, Hemel Hempstead HO1 3BY* T: (01442) 214898
E: john_russell@live.co.uk

RUSSELL, John Graham. b 35. G&C Coll Cam BA 58 MA 62. Westcott Ho Cam 59. **d** 61 **p** 62. C Durleigh *B & W* 61-66; C Bridgwater St Mary w Chilton Trinity 61-66; C Far Headingley St Chad *Ripon* 66-72; P-in-c Leeds St Matt Lt London 72-79; V Rowley Regis *Birm* 79-84; V Hall Green Ascension 84-95; Deanery P Warley Deanery 95-00; rtd 01; PtO *Birm* from 01. *1 Stapylton Avenue, Harborne, Birmingham B17 0BA* T: 0121-426 4529 E: pmr@russellp21.fsnet.co.uk

RUSSELL, John Richard. b 53. Westmr Coll Ox MTh 01 FRSA 02. Spurgeon's Coll 77 Ripon Coll Cuddesdon 01. **d** 01 **p** 02. Hon C St Mary le Strand w St Clem Danes *Lon* 01-02; Chapl RAF 02-08; PtO *Chelmsf* from 09. *32 Feeches Road, Southend-on-Sea SS2 6TD* T: (01702) 300978

RUSSELL, Canon Jonathan Vincent Harman. b 43. K Coll Lon 68. **d** 69 **p** 70. C Addington *Cant* 69-73; C Buckland in Dover w Buckland Valley 73-76; P-in-c Selling 76-85; P-in-c Throwley w Stalisfield and Otterden 79-85; R Selling w Throwley, Sheldwich w Badlesmere etc 85-95; Hon Min Can Cant Cathl 83-94; RD Ospringe 90-95; P-in-c Elham w Denton and Wootton 95-01; V 01-08; Hon Can Cant Cathl 94-08; rtd 08; PtO *Cant* from 08. *Kirkella, Goodwin Road, St Margaret's Bay, Dover CT15 6ED* T: (01304) 852811 M: 07702-314865 E: jvhrussell@btinternet.com

RUSSELL, Jonathan Wingate. b 55. Newc Univ BSc 76. St Jo Coll Nottm BA 83. **d** 84 **p** 85. C Southsea St Jude *Portsm* 84-87; P-in-c Shorwell w Kingston 87-92; V 92-06; P-in-c Gatcombe 87-92; R 92-06; P-in-c Chale 89-92; R 92-06; RD W Wight 96-01; R Allendale w Whitfield *Newc* from 06; AD Hexham from 11. *The Rectory, 16 Forstersteads, Allendale, Hexham NE47 9AS* T/F: (01434) 618607
E: rector@allendalechurch.co.uk

RUSSELL, Lyn. *See* RUSSELL, Isoline Lucilda

RUSSELL, Madeleine. b 41. Pargau Teacher Tr Coll Switzerland TDip 62. **d** 04 **p** 05. NSM Halifax H Trin and St Jude *Leeds* from 04. *Hillcroft, 12 Westborough Drive, Halifax HX2 7QN*

RUSSELL, Mrs Marion. b 54. Glas Univ BEd 75 Jordanhill Coll Glas TCert 75. CBDTI 03. **d** 06 **p** 07. NSM Altham w Clayton le Moors *Blackb* 06-10; Chapl Trin Academy Halifax 10-12; C Huddersfield St Pet *Leeds* 12-14; V Rastrick from 14. *1 Vicarage Gardens, Rastrick, Brighouse HD6 3HD*
E: revd.marion@gmail.com

RUSSELL, Martin Christopher. b 48. St Jo Coll Dur BA 70. Coll of Resurr Mirfield 72. **d** 74 **p** 75. C Huddersfield St Pet *Wakef* 74-77; Trinidad and Tobago 78-85; V S Crosland *Wakef* 86-00; P-in-c Helme 86-00; P-in-c Halifax H Trin 00-02; P-in-c Halifax St Jude 00-02; V Halifax H Trin and St Jude 02-13; rtd 13. *Hillcroft, 12 Westborough Drive, Halifax HX2 7QN*

RUSSELL, Michael John. b 38. Clifton Th Coll 68. **d** 68 **p** 69. C Cranham Park CD *Chelmsf* 68-70; C Bucknall and Bagnall *Lich* 70-77; P-in-c Tintwistle *Ches* 77-79; V 79-86; New Zealand from 86; rtd 03. *144 Winchester Street, Ashhurst 4810, New Zealand* T: (0064) (6) 326 8547

RUSSELL, Canon Neil. b 47. EMMTC 78. **d** 81 **p** 82. NSM Wyberton *Linc* 81-84; C 84-85; V Frampton 85-93; Agric Chapl and Countryside Officer 88-93; P-in-c Stamford All SS w St Jo 93-97; V 97-08; RD Aveland and Ness w Stamford 00-06; Warden Sacrista Prebend Retreat Ho *S'well* 08-10; Can and Preb Linc Cathl 02-10; rtd 10; PtO *Dur* from 11. *Clare Cottage, 4 The Paddocks, Gainford, Darlington DL2 3GA* T: (01325) 733140 M: 07730-403630
E: canonneilrussell@yahoo.co.uk

RUSSELL, Mrs Noreen Margaret. b 39. Man Univ BA 60 Lon Univ PGCE 61 BD 66. WMMTC 90. **d** 91 **p** 94. NSM Swynnerton and Tittensor *Lich* 91-97; C Draycott-le-Moors w Forsbrook 97-06; rtd 06; PtO *Lich* from 06. *40 Old Road, Barlaston, Stoke-on-Trent ST12 9EQ* T: (01782) 372992

RUSSELL, The Ven Norman Atkinson. b 43. Chu Coll Cam BA 65 MA 69 Lon Univ BD 70. Lon Coll of Div 67. **d** 70 **p** 71. C Clifton Ch Ch w Em *Bris* 70-74; C Enfield Ch Ch Trent Park *Lon* 74-77; R Harwell w Chilton *Ox* 77-84; P-in-c Gerrards Cross 84-88; P-in-c Fulmer 85-88; R Gerrards Cross and Fulmer 88-98; Hon Can Ch Ch 95-98; RD Amersham 96-98; Adn Berks 98-13; rtd 13; PtO *Ox* from 13. *47A Theobalds Way, Frimley, Camberley GU16 9RF*

RUSSELL, Peter Richard. b 60. Ch Ch Coll Cant BA 99. SEITE 02. **d** 05 **p** 06. NSM Margate All SS and Westgate St Sav

Cant 05-08; Chapl St Lawr Coll Ramsgate from 09. *St Lawrence College, College Road, Ramsgate CT11 7AE* T: (01843) 572900
E: minnisbay@hotmail.com

RUSSELL, Richard Alexander. b 44. Univ of Wales (Abth) BA 65 McMaster Univ Ontario MA 67 Bris Univ MA 73 PGCE 74 MEd 76. Trin Coll Bris 79. **d** 82 **p** 83. C Hartlepool St Paul *Dur* 82-85; P-in-c Bath Widcombe *B & W* 85-88; V 88-00; rtd 00; PtO *B & W* from 09. *76 Waterside Way, Radstock, Bath BA3 3YQ.* T: (01761) 433217 E: richardandjan@yokel.org.uk

RUSSELL, Roger Geoffrey. b 47. Worc Coll Ox BA 69 MA 73. Cuddesdon Coll 70. **d** 72 **p** 73. C Anlaby Common St Mark *York* 72-75; C Wilton Place St Paul *Lon* 75-86; R Lancing w Coombes *Chich* 86-12; RD Worthing 97-05; rtd 13. *32 Lime Grove, Angmering, Littlehampton BN16 4HA*

RUSSELL, Canon William Warren. b 52. QUB BSocSc 74. CITC 74. **d** 77 **p** 78. C Agherton *Conn* 77-79; C Lisburn Ch Ch Cathl 79-83; I Magheradroll *D & D* from 83; Treas Dromore Cathl from 08; Dioc C from 11. *The Rectory, 18 Church Road, Ballynahinch BT24 8LP* T: (028) 9756 2289 M: 07810-222906 E: rev_wwrussell@hotmail.com

RUSSELL GRANT, Julia Rosalind. b 45. **d** 11 **p** 12. OLM Layer de la Haye and Layer Breton w Birch etc *Chelmsf* 11-13; OLM Thurstable and Winstree 13-15; NSM from 15. *8 Heath House, Crayes Green, Layer Breton, Colchester CO2 0PN* T: (01206) 330235 E: church@hatfield-broad-oak.net

RUSSELL-SMITH, Mark Raymond. b 46. New Coll Edin MTh 91 St Jo Coll Dur BA 71. BA 71 Cranmer Hall Dur. **d** 72 **p** 73. C Upton (Overchurch) *Ches* 72-75; C Deane *Man* 75-77; UCCF Travelling Sec 77-80; LtO *York* 78-81; BCMS Kenya 81-92; P-in-c Slaidburn *Bradf* 92-11; P-in-c Long Preston w Tosside 97-11; rtd 11; PtO *York* from 12. *11 Osprey Close, York YO24 2YE* T: (01904) 792154 E: mars4654@uwclub.net

RUST, Mrs Alison Theresa (Tessa). b 56. Auckland Univ BA 76. St Mellitus Coll BA 11. **d** 11 **p** 12. C W Ealing St Jo w St Jas *Lon* 11-14; Chapl Heathrow Airport from 14. *14 Gloucester Road, London W5 4JB* T: (020) 8567 1047 M: 07979-627714
E: tessa@gtrust.fsnet.co.uk

RUST, Jonathan Kenneth. b 62. Reading Univ BSc 84. Ridley Hall Cam. **d** 00 **p** 01. C Holloway St Mary Magd *Lon* from 00. *The Vicarage, 55 Lough Road, London N7 8RH* T: (020) 7607 8585 E: j.rust@tiscali.co.uk

RUSTED, Mrs Mary Elizabeth. b 44. **d** 00 **p** 01. OLM Mildenhall *St E* 00-10; rtd 10; PtO *St E* from 10. *3 Ford Close, West Row, Bury St Edmunds IP28 8NR* T: (01638) 715054
E: maryrusted@hotmail.com

RUSTELL, Canon Anthony Christopher. b 77. Ch Ch Ox BA 98 MSt 01 MA 02 Keble Coll Ox DPhil 07. St Steph Ho Ox 98. **d** 01 **p** 02. NSM Ox St Barn and St Paul 01-04; P-in-c N Hinksey and Wytham 04-10; P-in-c Ox St Frideswide w Binsey 09-10; R Osney 10-11; Dir Minl Tr *Llan* 11-14; P-in-c Tongwynlais 11-14; Can Res Portsm Cathl from 14; Hd Miss, Discipleship and Min from 14. *1 Pembroke Close, Portsmouth PO1 2NX* T: (023) 9282 3300 E: acrustell@btinternet.com

RUTHERFORD, Anthony Richard. b 37. Culham Coll Ox TCert 62 Sussex Univ MA 77. S'wark Ord Course 83. **d** 86 **p** 87. Hon C Tunbridge Wells St Luke *Roch* 86-88; C Bromley SS Pet and Paul 88-90; V Wragby *Linc* 90-94; Asst Min Officer 90-94; V Penge Lane H Trin *Roch* 94-02; rtd 02; PtO *Roch* from 03. *6 Ashley Gardens, Tunbridge Wells TN4 8TY* T: (01892) 541009 E: arrutherford@f2s.com

RUTHERFORD, Daniel Fergus Peter. b 65. Hatf Coll Dur BA 86 CertEd 87. Ridley Hall Cam 88. **d** 90 **p** 91. C Harold Wood *Chelmsf* 90-94; C Hove Bp Hannington Memorial Ch *Chich* 94-97; Chapl City of Lon Freemen's Sch 97-11; Chapl Strathallan Sch 12-15; Asst Hd (Past) Dulwich Prep Sch Cranbrook from 15. *Dulwich Preparatory School, Coursehorn, Golford Road, Cranbrook TN17 3NP* T: (01580) 712179
E: drutherford@dcpskent.org

RUTHERFORD, Emma Christine. Ulster Univ BA. St Jo Coll Nottm MTh. **d** 11 **p** 12. C Coleraine *Conn* 12-13; Dioc C from 13. *20 Kinnegar Roads, Donaghadee BT21 0EZ* M: 07753-117838 E: revecr@gmail.com

✠**RUTHERFORD, The Rt Revd Graeme Stanley.** b 43. Cranmer Hall Dur BA 77 MA 78 ACT 66. **d** 66 **p** 67 **c** 00. C Bendigo Cathl Australia 66-70; V Pyramid Hill 70-73; C Holborn St Geo w H Trin and St Bart *Lon* 73-74; C Dur St Nic 74-77; R Kyabram Australia 77-82; I Malvern 82-87; I Camberwell St Jo 87-00; Can Melbourne Cathl 91-00; Asst Bp Newcastle 00-08; rtd 08. *3/68 Campbell Road, Hawthorn East VIC 3123, Australia* T: (0061) (3) 9813 4185 M: 40-837 4847
E: gcruth@bigpond.com

RUTHERFORD, Ian William. b 46. Univ of Wales (Lamp) BA 68. Cuddesdon Coll 68. **d** 70 **p** 71. C Gosforth All SS *Newc* 70-72; C Prestbury *Glouc* 73-76; Chapl RN 76-93; CMP from 93; TV Redruth w Lanner and Treleigh *Truro* 93-94; V Paulsgrove

Portsm 94-99; V Leeds Belle Is St Jo and St Barn *Ripon* 99-11; rtd 11; PtO *Portsm* from 11. *Flat 12, 27-29 St Simons Road, Southsea PO5 2QE* E: fatherian@onetel.com

RUTHERFORD, Janet Elizabeth. b 37. S'wark Ord Course 86. **d** 89. NSM Plaistow St Mary *Roch* 89-90; NSM Linc St Botolph 91-93. *6 Ashley Gardens, Tunbridge Wells TN4 8TY* T: (01892) 541009

RUTHERFORD, Canon John Bilton. b 23. Qu Coll Birm 49. **d** 52 **p** 53. C Newc H Cross 52-57; C Longbenton St Bart 57-60; V High Elswick St Phil 60-66; V Walker 66-74; I Benwell St Jas 74-81; Hon Can Newc Cathl 80-90; V Lesbury w Alnmouth 81-90; RD Alnwick 86-89; PtO from 90; rtd 90. *68 Worcester Way, Woodlands Park, Wideopen, Newcastle upon Tyne NE13 6JD* T: 0191-236 4785

RUTHERFORD, Peter George. b 34. Nor Ord Course 73. **d** 76 **p** 77. NSM New Catton Ch Ch *Nor* 76-79; NSM Eaton 79-80; NSM Nor St Steph 81-92; PtO 92-94 and from 99; P-in-c Earlham St Mary 94-99; RD Nor S 98-99; rtd 99. *126 Colman Road, Norwich NR4 7AA* T/F: (01603) 457629 E: petergrutherford@btinternet.com

RUTHERFORD, Peter Marshall. b 57. St Andr Univ MTheol 81 Ulster Univ MA 96. CITC 83. **d** 83 **p** 84. C Stormont *D & D* 83-85; CF 85-01; Asst Chapl Gen 01-02; Asst Chapl Milan w Genoa and Varese *Eur* 03-04; I Castlepollard and Oldcastle w Loughcrew etc *M & K* 04-10; I Julianstown and Colpe w Drogheda and Duleek from 10; Dioc Dir of Ords from 05; Warden of Readers from 12. *The Rectory, Laytown Road, Julianstown, Co Meath, Republic of Ireland* T: (00353) (41) 982 9831 E: peterrutherford@me.com

RUTHERFORD (née ERREY), Ms Rosalind Elisabeth. b 52. St Hugh's Coll Ox BA 74 Surrey Univ BA 02 Goldsmiths' Coll Lon PGCE 78. STETS 99. **d** 02 **p** 03. C Earley St Pet *Ox* 02-06; TV Basingstoke *Win* from 06. *45 Beaconsfield Road, Basingstoke RG21 3DG* T: (01256) 464616 E: revrosalind@btinternet.com

RUTLEDGE, Canon Christopher John Francis. b 44. Lon Univ BSc 67 Univ of Wales MPhil 94 PhD 99 TCert 80. Sarum Th Coll 67. **d** 70 **p** 71. C Birm St Pet 70-73; C Calne and Blackland *Sarum* 73-76; P-in-c Derry Hill 76-78; V 78-81; P-in-c Talbot Village 81-82; V 82-10; Can and Preb Sarum Cathl 95-10; Chapl Talbot Heath Sch Bournemouth 04-09; rtd 10; PtO *Sarum* from 10. *48 Wollaton Road, Ferndown BH22 8QY* T: (01202) 895116 E: christopher.rutledge@talktalk.net

RUTLEDGE, Francis George. b 62. TCD BA 83 BTh 90. **d** 86 **p** 87. C Holywood *D & D* 86-89; C Willowfield 89-91; I Kilmakee *Conn* 91-97; I Carrigrohane Union *C, C & R* 97-04; I Donacavey w Barr *Clogh* 04-05; Bp's C Bangor Primacy *D & D* from 05. *4 Glendowan Way, Bangor BT19 7SP* T: (028) 9185 9731 E: francis.rutledge@btinternet.com

RUTT, Mrs Celia Mary Avril. b 43. Cranmer Hall Dur. **d** 02 **p** 03. NSM Heworth H Trin *York* 02-05; NSM Acomb St Steph and St Aid 05-09; NSM Clifton 09-11; rtd 11; PtO *York* from 11. *226 Shipton Road, York YO30 5RZ* T: (01904) 627384 E: celia.rutt@tiscali.co.uk

RUTT-FIELD, Benjamin John. b 48. Chich Th Coll. **d** 90 **p** 91. C Wickford and Runwell *Chelmsf* 90-94; V Goodmayes St Paul 94-14; rtd 14. *33 Hillcourt Avenue, London N12 8EY* E: b.ruttfield@btinternet.com

RUTTER, Canon Allen Edward Henry (Claude). b 28. Qu Coll Cam BA 52 MA 56. Cranmer Hall Dur. **d** 59 **p** 60. C Bath Abbey w St Jas *B & W* 59-60; C E Dereham w Hoe *Nor* 60-64; R Cawston 64-69; Chapl Cawston Coll 64-69; P-in-c Felthorpe w Haveringland *Nor* 64-69; R Gingindhlovu S Africa 69-73; P-in-c Over and Nether Compton, Trent etc *Sarum* 73-80; RD Sherborne 77-87; P-in-c Oborne w Poyntington 79-80; P-in-c Queen Thorne 80-96; Can and Preb Sarum Cathl 86-96; rtd 96; PtO *B & W* 98-99 and from 00; P-in-c Thorncombe w Winsham and Cricket St Thomas 99; C Chard and Distr 99-00. *Home Farm, Chilson, South Chard, Chard TA20 2NX* T: (01460) 221368

RUTTER, Graham Piers. b 77. St Jo Coll Dur BSc 98 PhD 03 Liv Univ MSc 99. St Jo Coll Nottm 06. **d** 08 **p** 09. C Wellington All SS w Eyton *Lich* 08-12; P-in-c Swadlincote *Derby* from 12; C Hartshorne and Bretby from 13; RD Repton from 13. *The Vicarage, Church Street, Swadlincote DE11 8LF* T: (01283) 214583 E: gprutter@gmail.com

RUTTER, John Edmund Charles. b 53. Qu Coll Cam MA 76. St Jo Coll Nottm MA 93. **d** 93 **p** 94. C Penge St Jo *Roch* 93-97; Bp's C Bangor Primacy *D & D* 97-04; I Glenavy w Tunny and Crumlin *Conn* from 04. *The Vicarage, 30 Crumlin Road, Glenavy, Crumlin BT29 4LG* T/F: (028) 9442 2361 E: glenavy@connor.anglican.org

RUTTER, John Smiles. b 49. Hertf Coll Ox BA 71 PGCE 72. NEOC 02. **d** 07 **p** 08. NSM Ripon H Trin *Leeds* from 07; NSM Ripon Cathl from 11. *17 Church Lane, Ripon HG4 2ES* T: (01765) 605638

RUTTER, Martin Charles. b 54. Wolv Poly BSc 75 Southn Univ BTh 81. Sarum & Wells Th Coll 76. **d** 79 **p** 80. C Cannock *Lich* 79-82; C Uttoxeter w Bramshall 82-86; V W Bromwich St Jas 86-97; P-in-c W Bromwich St Paul 89-97; V W Bromwich St Jas w St Paul 97-02; RD W Bromwich 94-02; V Gt Barr from 02; RD Walsall from 10. *St Margaret's Vicarage, Chapel Lane, Great Barr, Birmingham B43 7BD* T: 0121-357 1390

RUTTER, Michael. b 75. Trin Coll Bris BA 06 Coll of Resurr Mirfield 99. **d** 07 **p** 08. C Dudley Wood *Worc* 07-10; TV Halas 10-15; V Darby End and Netherton from 15. *The Vicarage, Highbridge Road, Netherton, Dudley DY2 0HT* T: (01384) 237264 E: fr.mike.rutter@gmail.com

RUTTER, Michael John. b 58. **d** 10 **p** 11. NSM York St Paul 10-13; C Philadelphia St Thos *Sheff* from 13. *31 Barkers Road, Sheffield S7 1SD* E: mike@rutterworld.com *or* mike.rutter@sheffield.anglican.org

RUTTER, Ronald. b 47. SS Hild & Bede Coll Dur TCert 71 Open Univ BA 81 CMath MIMA. CBDTI. **d** 00 **p** 01. NSM Heversham and Milnthorpe *Carl* 00-11; PtO from 11. *Ellerslie, Woodhouse Lane, Heversham, Milnthorpe LA7 7EW* T/F: (015395) 64260 E: ron_rutter@hotmail.com

RUXTON, Charles. b 58. Van Mildert Coll Dur BSc 79 CGeol FGS MCIWEM. **d** 06 **p** 07. OLM Meole Brace *Lich* 06-12; NSM from 12. *New Place, Westbury, Shrewsbury SY5 9RY* T: (01743) 891636 E: c.ruxton@btinternet.com

RWANDA, Archbishop of. *See* KOLINI, The Most Revd Emmanuel Musaba

RYALL, John Francis Robert. b 30. New Coll Ox BA 52 MA 57. Westcott Ho Cam 52. **d** 54 **p** 55. C Petersfield w Sheff *Portsm* 54-56; C Portsea St Mary 56-62; C Warblington w Emsworth 62-65; C Freshwater 65-67; R Frating w Thorrington *Chelmsf* 67-73; R Gt Yeldham 74-76; P-in-c Lt Yeldham 75-76; R Gt w Lt Yeldham 76-80; P-in-c Thorley *Portsm* 80-82; P-in-c Shalfleet 80-82; V 82-95; V Calbourne w Newtown 82-95; rtd 95; PtO *Portsm* from 95. *Weald House, Main Road, Wellow, Yarmouth PO41 0SZ* T: (01983) 760783

RYALL, Michael Richard. b 36. TCD BA 58 MA 65 HDipEd 66. TCD Div Sch Div Test 58. **d** 58 **p** 59. C Dublin St Geo and St Thos, Finglas and Free Ch *D & G* 58-62; CF 62-65 and 68-90; CF (TAVR) 67-68; C Dublin Rathmines *D & G* 65-66; R Yardley Hastings, Denton and Grendon etc *Pet* 90-01; rtd 01; PtO *St D* from 07; P-in-c Mayland *Chelmsf* 08-12. *44 Great North Road, Milford Haven SA73 2NA* T: (01646) 697157 M: 07968-111258 E: michaelryall@waitrose.com

RYALLS, Craig James. b 74. Bris Univ BA 96 Peterho Cam BA 01. Ridley Hall Cam 99. **d** 02 **p** 03. C Bearsted w Thurnham *Cant* 02-06; C Woking Ch Ch *Guildf* 06-14; R Fisherton Anger *Sarum* from 14. *St Paul's Rectory, Fisherton Street, Salisbury SP2 7QW* T: (01722) 331003 E: craig.ryalls@gmail.com

RYAN, Alan John. b 57. SWMTC. **d** 09 **p** 10. C Fremington, Instow and Westleigh *Ex* 09-11; C Whitchurch 11-13; P-in-c Winterborne Valley and Milton Abbas *Sarum* from 13. *The Rectory, North Street, Winterborne Stickland, Blandford Forum DT11 0NL* T: (01258) 880482 E: alanryan1957@btinternet.com

RYAN, Barbara. b 56. **d** 12 **p** 13. NSM Hessle *York* from 12. *40 Valentine Close, Hull HU4 7DN* T: (01482) 646482 E: barbara@hullcc.gov.uk *or* beegee96@hotmail.com

RYAN, David Peter. b 64. Aston Univ BSc 86. Linc Th Coll BTh 94. **d** 94 **p** 95. C Horsforth *Ripon* 94-97; C Bedale 97-98; P-in-c Startforth and Bowes and Rokeby w Brignall 98-00; V 00-04; P-in-c Warndon St Nic *Worc* 04-13; Chapl Worcs Acute Hosps NHS Trust from 13; Dioc Ecum Officer *Worc* from 04. *The Alexandra Hospital, Woodrow Drive, Redditch B98 7UB* T: (01527) 503030 E: davidryannow@netscapeonline.co.uk

RYAN, Graham William Robert (Gregg). b 51. CITC 90. **d** 93 **p** 94. NSM Clonsast w Rathangan, Thomastown etc *M & K* 93-97; Dioc Communications Officer 96-97; Press Officer from 97; Dioc C *M & K* from 97. *Millicent Hall, Millicent South, Sallins, Naas, Co Kildare, Republic of Ireland* T: (00353) (45) 879464 F: 875173 E: gregg.ryan@irishrail.ie

RYAN, James Francis. b 47. Surrey Univ BSc. St Jo Coll Nottm. **d** 83 **p** 84. C Littleover *Derby* 83-86; C Chipping Sodbury and Old Sodbury *Glouc* 86-89; V Pype Hayes *Birm* 89-99; R W Winch w Setchey, N Runcton and Middleton *Nor* 99-12; rtd 12. *30 Rook Way, Horsham RH12 5FR*

RYAN, Canon Maureen. **d** 98 **p** 99. C Tuam w Cong and Aasleagh *T, K & A* from 98; Preb Kilmactalway St Patr Cathl Dublin 01-09; Can Tuam Cathl from 05; Provost Tuam from 13; Can Killala Cathl from 13. *Marshal's Park, Rinville, Oranmore, Galway, Republic of Ireland* T/F: (00353) (91) 794599 E: ryans@iol.ie

RYAN, Robert Lloyd. b 65. Warwick Univ BA 87. SEITE 05. **d** 08 **p** 09. C Roch Cathl 08-12; NSM Gillingham St Mark 12-15; NSM E Greenwich *S'wark* from 15. *37 Becquerel Court, West Parkside, London SE10 0QQ* M: 07595-354067 E: rob.ryan@mac.com

RYAN, Roger John. b 47. Lon Bible Coll BA 79 Surrey Univ MA 00 St Pet Coll Ox DPhil 06 Univ Coll Lon MA 09. Oak Hill Th Coll 79. **d** 80 **p** 81. C Luton St Fran *St Alb* 80-83; R Laceby *Linc* 83-88; V Summerstown *S'wark* from 88. *St Mary's Vicarage, 46 Wimbledon Road, London SW17 0UQ* T: (020) 8946 9853 E: rogerryan307@hotmail.com

RYAN, Canon Stephen John. b 49. Univ of Wales (Swansea) BA 70. Sarum & Wells Th Coll 70. **d** 73 **p** 74. C Llantrisant *Llan* 73-77; V Treherbert w Treorchy 77-89; Youth Chapl 80-85; RD Rhondda 84-89; V Aberdare St Fagan 89-02; RD Cynon Valley 97-02; TR Neath from 02; Can Llan Cathl from 02; AD Neath 04-10. *The Rectory, 23 London Road, Neath SA11 1LE* T: (01639) 644612 E: rectorneath@btinternet.com

RYCRAFT, Andrew George. b 48. Ox Brookes Univ BA 12 FRICS 94. Wycliffe Hall Ox 02 SAOMC 04. **d** 06 **p** 07. NSM Ray Valley *Ox* 06-07 and 09-15; P-in-c Exning St Martin w Landwade *St E* from 15. *The Vicarage, 1 New River Green, Exning, Newmarket CB8 7HS* E: andrew.rycraft@gmail.com

RYCRAFT, Mrs Rosemary Ives Stewart. b 49. Westmr Coll Ox BTh 00 SRN 72 SCM 74. SAOMC 00. **d** 03 **p** 04. NSM New Marston *Ox* 03-07; TV Aylesbury 07-11; PtO 11-12; C Mildenhall *St E* from 12. *The Vicarage, 2 Oak Drive, Beck Row, Bury St Edmunds IP28 8UA* T: (01638) 711538 E: rosemary.rycraft@btinternet.com

RYCROFT, Alistair John. b 79. St Cath Coll Ox BA 01 Fitzw Coll Cam BA 08 Ox Brookes Univ PGCE 02. Ridley Hall Cam 06. **d** 09 **p** 10. C York St Mich-le-Belfrey 09-13; C York St Thos w St Maurice 14-15; P-in-c from 15. *157 Haxby Road, York YO31 8JL* T: (01904) 341979

RYDER, Canon Derek Michael. b 36. St Cath Coll Cam BA 60 MA 64. Tyndale Hall Bris 61. **d** 63 **p** 64. C Hampreston *Sarum* 63-66; Asst Chapl Brentwood Sch 66-72; Chapl Ipswich Sch 72-77; Home Sec CMJ 77-87; TR Wexcombe *Sarum* 87-99; RD Pewsey 89-99; Can and Preb Sarum Cathl 97-99; rtd 99; PtO Ox from 00; *Sarum* from 00. *31 The Green, Calne SN11 8DJ* T: (01249) 821797

RYDER, Jennifer Ann. *See* HAYNES, Jennifer Ann

RYDER, John Merrick. b 55. Natal Univ BA 75 BA 77. St Pet Coll Natal 81. **d** 82 **p** 83. S Africa 84-88; St Helena 88-91; C Havant *Portsm* 91-95; P-in-c Godshill 95-99; V from 99; P-in-c Wroxall 99-02. *The Vicarage, Church Hill, Godshill, Ventnor PO38 3HY* T: (01983) 840895 E: johnmryder@btinternet.com

RYDER, Lisle Robert Dudley. b 43. Selw Coll Cam BA 68 MA 72. Sarum Th Coll 69. **d** 71 **p** 72. C Lowestoft St Marg *Nor* 71-75; Chapl Asst Oxon Area HA 76-79; C Littlehampton St Jas *Chich* 79-85; C Littlehampton St Mary 79-85; C Wick 79-85; Chapl Worc R Infirmary 85-94; Chapl Worc R Infirmary NHS Trust 94-00; Chapl Worcs Acute Hosps NHS Trust 00-03; Hon Can Worc Cathl 89-04; P-in-c Pyworthy, Pancrasweek and Bridgerule *Ex* 04-08; rtd 08. *Little Appleton, 3 Lumley Terrace, Newton le Willows, Bedale DL8 1SS* T: (01677) 450180 E: lisleryder@gmail.com

RYDER, Oliver Hugh Dudley. b 74. UEA BA 98. Ridley Hall Cam 05. **d** 07 **p** 08. C Tollington *Lon* 07-10; C Kensal Rise St Mark and St Martin 10-11; V Kensal Rise St Mark from 11. *Kensal Rise Vicarage, 93 College Road, London NW10 5EU* T: (020) 8969 4598 M: 07963-580242 E: oliver.ryder@gmail.com

RYDER-WEST, Keith. b 63. Sunderland Poly BSc 86 Leeds Univ BTh 95. Chich Th Coll 92 Coll of Resurr Mirfield. **d** 95 **p** 96. C Rawmarsh w Parkgate *Sheff* 95-96; C Armley w New Wortley *Ripon* 96-99; V Altofts *Wakef* 99-06; V Sheff St Cecilia Parson Cross from 06; P-in-c Sheff St Leon Norwood from 14. *St Leonard's Vicarage, 93 Everingham Road, Sheffield S5 7LE* E: keith.ryder-west@sheffield.anglican.org

RYDINGS, Donald. b 33. Jes Coll Ox BA 57 MA 61. Linc Th Coll 57. **d** 59 **p** 60. C Poulton-le-Fylde *Blackb* 59-62; C Ox St Mary V 62-66; Staff Sec SCM 62-66; C-in-c Bourne End

St Mark CD *Ox* 66-74; R Hedsor and Bourne End 74-76; P-in-c Gt Missenden w Ballinger and Lt Hampden 76-93; RD Wendover 79-89; V Gt Missenden w Ballinger and Lt Hampden 93-02; rtd from 02. *16 Marroway, Weston Turville, Aylesbury HP22 5TQ* T: (01296) 612281

RYELAND, John. b 58. K Coll Lon BD 80 AKC 80 Lon Sch of Th MA 09. Linc Th Coll 80. **d** 81 **p** 82. C Enfield St Jas *Lon* 81-84; C Coulsdon St Andr *S'wark* 84-87; C-in-c Ingrave St Steph CD *Chelmsf* 87-97; Dir Chr Healing Miss from 97. *8 Cambridge Court, 210 Shepherd's Bush Road, London W6 7NJ* T: (020) 7603 8118 F: 7603 5224 E: chm@healingmission.org

RYLANCE, Wendy Sheila. b 52. Lon Univ MB, BS 78 MRCGP 82 DRCOG 89. WEMTC 11. **d** 13 **p** 14. NSM Highley w Billingsley, Glazeley etc *Heref* from 13. *Roughton Farmhouse, Roughton, Bridgnorth WV15 5HE* T: (01746) 716399 M: 07523-352210 E: wendyrylance@aol.com

RYLANDS, Preb Amanda Craig. b 52. Homerton Coll Cam CertEd 75. Trin Coll Bris 83. **dss** 85 **d** 87 **p** 94. Chippenham St Andr w Tytherton Lucas *Bris* 85-87; Par Dn Stockport St Geo *Ches* 87-91; Par Dn Acton and Worleston, Church Minshull etc 91-94; C 94-97; Dioc Adv for Min Among Children 95-97; NSM Langport Area *B & W* 97-98 and 99-01; TV 98-99; Asst Dioc Voc Adv 00-01; PtO *Ex* 02-03; C Tedburn St Mary, Whitestone, Oldridge etc 04-05; Dioc Dir of Ords 05-09; Bp's Adv for Women in Min 06-09; Preb Ex Cathl 08-09; PtO *Lich* 10-13; NSM Shrewsbury St Chad, St Mary and St Alkmund from 13; Rep for Women in Min Shrewsbury Area from 13; SSM Officer from 13. *Athlone House, 68 London Road, Shrewsbury SY2 6PG* T: (01743) 235867

✠**RYLANDS, The Rt Revd Mark James.** b 61. SS Hild & Bede Coll Dur BA 83. Trin Coll Bris BA 87. **d** 87 **p** 88 **c** 09. C Stockport St Geo *Ches* 87-91; V Acton and Worleston, Church Minshull etc 91-97; TR Langport Area *B & W* 97-02; Dioc Missr and Can Res Ex Cathl 02-09; Area Bp Shrewsbury *Lich* from 09. *Athlone House, 68 London Road, Shrewsbury SY2 6PG* T: (01743) 235867 F: 242296 E: bishop.shrewsbury@lichfield.anglican.org

RYLETT, Adam Geoffrey. b 78. Southn Univ MEng 00 Ox Brookes Univ BA 04. Trin Coll Bris 10. **d** 12 **p** 13. C S Croydon Em *S'wark* 12-15; C Barnes from 15. *Address temp unknown* M: 07595-345480 E: adam@rylett.co.uk

RYLEY, Canon Patrick Macpherson. b 30. Pemb Coll Ox BA 54 Lon Univ BD 56. Clifton Th Coll 54. **d** 56 **p** 57. C Ox St Clem 56-59; Burma 60-66; Kenya 68-75; V Lynn St Jo *Nor* 76-92; V King's Lynn St Jo the Ev 92-95; RD Lynn 78-83; Hon Can Nor Cathl 90-95; rtd from 95; PtO *Bradf* 95-11. *12 Green End, Denton, Manchester M34 7PU*

RYLEY, Timothy Patrick. b 64. Man Univ BA 86. St Jo Coll Nottm MA 93. **d** 93 **p** 94. C Pendlebury St Jo *Man* 93-97; P-in-c Norris Bank 97-01; Age Concern from 01; PtO *Man* from 09. *12 Green End, Denton, Manchester M34 7PU*

RYMER, David John Talbot. b 37. Chich Th Coll 63. **d** 66 **p** 67. C Tuffley *Glouc* 66-69; Rhodesia 69-79; P-in-c S Kensington St Jude *Lon* 79-82; V 82-88; P-in-c Ambergate *Derby* 88-91; P-in-c Heage 88-91; R Ambergate and Heage 91-96; P-in-c Findern 96-01; V 01-03; P-in-c Willington 96-01; V 01-03; rtd from 00; PtO *Derby* from 03. *2 Glebe Close, Long Lane, Dalbury Lees, Ashbourne DE6 5BJ* T: (01332) 824165 E: david.rymer@amserve.net *or* dfrymer@yahoo.co.uk

RYRIE, Alexander Crawford. b 30. Edin Univ MA 52 BD 55 Glas Univ MLitt 75. New Coll Edin 52 Union Th Sem (NY) STM 56. **d** 83 **p** 83. Hon C Edin St Mary 83-85; R Jedburgh 85-95; rtd from 95. *Boisils, Bowden, Melrose TD6 0ST* T: (01835) 823226 E: sandyryrie@googlemail.com

RYRIE, Mrs Isabel. b 31. Edin Univ MA 51 Glas Univ MEd 70 ABPsS 73 CPsychol 88. **d** 89 **p** 94. Bp's Dn *Edin* 89-91; NSM Edin St Mary 91-98; rtd from 98. *Boisils, Bowden, Melrose TD6 0ST* T: (01835) 823226 E: isabel.ryrie@btinternet.com

S

SABAN, Ronald Graham Street. b 28. Bps' Coll Cheshunt 60. **d** 62 **p** 63. C Maidstone St Martin *Cant* 62-66; C Croydon St Sav 66; rtd 94. *34 Kingsway, Caversham, Reading RG4 6RA* T: 0118-947 9454

SABELL, Michael Harold. b 42. Open Univ BA 78 Surrey Univ MSc. Sarum & Wells Th Coll 77. **d** 80 **p** 81. NSM Shirley *Win* 80-82; NSM Finham *Cov* 82-85; Chapl to the Deaf *Win* 81-82; PtO *Cov* 82-85; *Sheff* 85-89; *Lich* 89-96; *St Alb* 96-01; P-in-c Gt and Lt Wymondley 96-01; R Ingoldsby *Linc* 01-04; R Old Somerby 01-04; R Ropsley 01-04; R Sapperton w Braceby

01-04; rtd 04; PtO *Lich* 05-08 and from 10; P-in-c Muchalls *Bre* 08-10; PtO *S & B* from 12. *35 Charlemont Avenue, West Bromwich B71 3BY* T: 0121-588 6185 E: michaelhsabell@btinternet.com

SABEY-CORKINDALE, Charmaine Clare. b 58. SROT 87. SAOMC. **d** 02 **p** 03. NSM St Ippolyts *St Alb* 02-03; C Hitchin 03-05; TV 05-13. *5 Lavender Way, Hitchin SG5 2LU* T: (01462) 435497

SABINE WILLIS, Anthony Charles. *See* WILLIS, Anthony Charles Sabine

SACH, Andrew. b 75. Oak Hill Th Coll. **d** 07. C St Helen Bishopsgate w St Andr Undershaft etc *Lon* from 07. *St Helen's Church, Great St Helen's, London EC3A 6AT* T: (020) 7283 2231

SACHS, Andrew James. b 73. Reading Univ BSc 94 Kingston Univ PGCE 96. Wycliffe Hall Ox BTh 05. **d** 05 **p** 06. C Upper Sunbury St Sav *Lon* 05-08; C E Twickenham St Steph 08-12; P-in-c Colchester St Jo *Chelmsf* from 12. *St John's Vicarage, Evergreen Drive, Colchester CO4 0HU* T: (01206) 843232 M: 07808-886996 E: andyvanessasachs@gmail.com

SACKLEY (née WITT), Mrs Caroline Elizabeth. b 51. Surrey Univ BSc 04. STETS 02. **d** 05 **p** 06. C Graffoe Gp *Linc* 05-08; P-in-c W Meon and Warnford *Portsm* 08-12; rtd 12; P-in-c The Vendée *Eur* from 13. *L'etravy, 53140 St Cyr en Pail, France* E: revcarosack1@gmail.com

SACRE, Phillip Daniel. b 83. Essex Univ BSc 04. Oak Hill Th Coll BA 14. **d** 14 **p** 15. C Gt Clacton *Chelmsf* from 14. *2 Reigate Avenue, Clacton-on-Sea CO16 8FB* E: phillip.sacre@gmail.com

SADDINGTON, Mrs Jean. b 53. Bournemouth Univ BSc 02 Cant Ch Ch Univ PGCE 04. STETS 05. **d** 08 **p** 12. NSM Dorchester *Sarum* 08-14; NSM Dorchester and the Winterbournes from 14. *The Rectory, Martinstown, Dorchester DT2 9JZ* E: jean.saddington@hotmail.co.uk

SADGROVE, The Very Revd Michael. b 50. Ball Coll Ox BA 71 MA 75. Trin Coll Bris 72. **d** 75 **p** 76. LtO *Ox* 75-77; Tutor Sarum & Wells Th Coll 77-82; Vice-Prin 80-82; V Alnwick *Newc* 82-87; Vice-Provost, Can Res and Prec Cov Cathl 87-95; Provost Sheff 95-00; Dean Sheff 00-03; Dean Dur from 03. *The Deanery, The College, Durham DH1 3EQ* T: 0191-384 7500 F: 386 4267 E: michael.sadgrove@durhamcathedral.co.uk

SADLER, Ann Penrith. *See* IRVINE, Ann Penrith

SADLER, The Ven Anthony Graham. b 36. Qu Coll Ox BA 60 MA 64. Lich Th Coll 60. **d** 62 **p** 63. C Burton St Chad *Lich* 62-65; V Rangemore and Dunstall 65-72; V Abbots Bromley 72-79; V Pelsall 79-90; RD Walsall 82-90; P-in-c Uttoxeter w Bramshall 90-97; P-in-c Stramshall 90-97; P-in-c Kingstone w Gratwich 90-97; P-in-c Checkley 90-97; P-in-c Marchington w Marchington Woodlands 90-97; P-in-c Leigh 93-97; TR Uttoxeter Area 97; Adn Walsall 97-04; Preb Lich Cathl 87-04; rtd 04; PtO *St As* from 09. *Llidiart Newydd, Llanrhaeadr-ym-Mochnant, Oswestry SY10 0ED* T: (01691) 780276

SADLER, Canon John Ernest. b 45. Nottm Univ BTh 78. Linc Th Coll 74. **d** 78 **p** 79. C Brampton St Thos *Derby* 78-81; TV Coventry Caludon *Cov* 81-85; V Newc St Phil and St Aug 86-94; P-in-c Newc Epiphany 94-99; PtO from 00; Ch Development Worker 01-12; Hon Can Newc Cathl 08-12; rtd 12. *2 Southlands, Great Whittington, Newcastle upon Tyne NE19 2HS* T: (01434) 672145 E: jjsadler@btinternet.com

SADLER, Michael Stuart. b 57. Wycliffe Hall Ox 78. **d** 81 **p** 82. C Henfynyw w Aberaeron and Llanddewi Aberarth *St D* 81-88; V Llanddewi Rhydderch w Llangattock-juxta-Usk etc *Mon* 88-09; V Llandeilo Fawr and Taliaris *St D* from 09. *The New Vicarage, Thomas Terrace, Llandeilo SA19 6NN*

SAFFORD, Jeremy. b 66. Ox Brookes Univ BA 02. Ridley Hall Cam 08. **d** 09 **p** 10. C Collingtree w Courteenhall and Milton Malsor *Pet* 09-11; C Salcey 11-12; C Grange Park LEP 12; R Burton Latimer from 12; Dioc Healing Adv from 12. *The Rectory, Preston Court, Burton Latimer, Kettering NN15 5LR* T: (01536) 660797 M: 07512-856732 E: jez.saffprd@uwclub.net

SAGE, Canon Andrew George. b 58. Univ Coll Chich BA 99. Chich Th Coll 83. **d** 85 **p** 86. C Rawmarsh w Parkgate *Sheff* 85-87; C Fareham SS Pet and Paul *Portsm* 87-89; C Southsea H Spirit 89-91; P-in-c Nuthurst *Chich* 91-93; R 93-95; V Hangleton 95-04; Chapl Worthing and Southlands Hosps NHS Trust 01-02; Chapl W Sussex Health and Soc Care NHS Trust 02-04; V Blackpool St Steph *Blackb* from 04; Warden Whalley Abbey 08-10; Hon Can Blackb Cathl from 08. *The Vicarage, St Stephen's Avenue, Blackpool FY2 9RB* T: (01253) 351484 E: andrewsage@aol.com

SAGE, Canon Jesse. b 35. Trin Hall Cam BA 61 MA 65. Chich Th Coll 61. **d** 63 **p** 64. C Feltham *Lon* 63-67; C Port Elizabeth St Mary S Africa 67; P-in-c Port Elizabeth Ch the K and St Mark 68-72; R Abbas and Temple Combe *B & W* 72-75; R Abbas and Templecombe w Horsington 76-77; Chapl Agric and Rural Soc in Kent *Cant* 78-95; Hon Can Cant Cathl 90-95; R Gonubie St Martin by the Sea S Africa 96-00; P-in-c Komga St Paul 98-00; rtd 00; Hon Can Grahamstown from 02. *25 Shapway Road, Evercreech, Shepton Mallet BA4 6JT* T: (01749) 831649 M: 07955-251312 E: jesse.sage1935@gmail.com

SAGOVSKY, Canon Nicholas. b 47. CCC Ox BA 69 St Edm Ho Cam PhD 81. St Jo Coll Nottm BA 73. **d** 74 **p** 75. C Newc St Gabr 74-77; C Cambridge St Mary w St Mich *Ely* 81; Vice-Prin Edin Th Coll 82-86; Dean of Chpl Clare Coll Cam 86-97; Wm Leech Prof Fell Newc Univ 97-02; Liv Hope Univ Coll 02-04; Can Westmr Abbey 04-11; rtd 11; PtO *S'wark* from 12. *92 Tyndale Mansions, Upper Street, London N1 2XG* T: (020) 7682 3287

SAID, Yazeed. b 75. Hebrew Univ Jerusalem BA 96 CCC Cam BA 99 MA 03 MPhil 05 PhD 10. Westcott Ho Cam 97. **d** 99 **p** 01. Chapl Ch Ch Sch Nazareth Israel 99-00; Chapl to Bp Jerusalem 00-02; C St Geo Cathl 00-04; Acting Dean 02-04; Asst Chapl CCC Cam 04-08; PtO *Ely* from 08. *Faculty of Religious Studies, 3520 University Street, Montreal QC H3A 2A7, Canada* E: yazeed.said@gmx.net *or* yazid.said@mcgill.ca

SAIET, Timothy Robin. b 65. Wycliffe Hall Ox 06. **d** 08 **p** 09. NSM Ealing St Paul *Lon* 08-11; Chapl Philo Trust 11-14; V Hildenborough *Roch* from 14. *The Vicarage, 194 Tonbridge Road, Hildenborough, Tonbridge TN11 9HR* T: (01732) 833596 M: 07973-136968 E: timsaiet@btinternet.com

SAINSBURY, Peter Donald. b 67. K Coll Lon MA 04. Ridley Hall Cam 98. **d** 00 **p** 01. C Longfleet *Sarum* 00-04; Chapl Glos Univ 04-08; V Summerfield *Birm* from 08. *Christ Church Vicarage, 64 Selwyn Road, Birmingham B16 0SW* T: 0121-454 2689 E: vicar@christchurchsummerfield.org

✠**SAINSBURY, The Rt Revd Roger Frederick.** b 36. Jes Coll Cam BA 58 MA 62. Clifton Th Coll. **d** 60 **p** 61 **c** 91. C Spitalfields Ch Ch w All SS *Lon* 60-63; Missr Shrewsbury Ho Everton *Liv* 63-74; P-in-c Everton St Ambrose w St Tim 67-74; Warden Mayflower Family Cen Canning Town *Chelmsf* 74-81; P-in-c Victoria Docks St Luke 78-81; V Walsall *Lich* 81-87; TR 87-88; Adn W Ham *Chelmsf* 88-91; Area Bp Barking 91-02; Moderator Ch's Commn for Racial Justice 99-02; rtd 02; Hon Asst Bp B & W from 03. *Abbey Lodge, Battery Lane, Portishead, Bristol BS20 7JD* T: (01275) 847082 E: bishoproger.abbey@btopenworld.com

SAINT, David Gerald. b 45. Sarum & Wells Th Coll 72. **d** 75 **p** 76. C Wellingborough All Hallows *Pet* 75-79; R Kislingbury w Rothersthorpe 79-83; V Kings Heath 83-85; Relig Progr Producer BBC Radio Northn from 85; PtO *Pet* 86-14; rtd 10. *71 Stanwell Way, Wellingborough NN8 3DD* T: (01933) 675995 E: words@davidsaint.co.uk

ST ALBANS, Archdeacon of. *See* SMITH, The Ven Jonathan Peter

ST ALBANS, Bishop of. *See* SMITH, The Rt Revd Alan Gregory Clayton

ST ALBANS, Dean of. *See* JOHN, The Very Revd Jeffrey Philip Hywel

ST ANDREWS, DUNKELD AND DUNBLANE, Bishop of. *See* CHILLINGWORTH, The Most Revd David Robert

ST ANDREWS, DUNKELD AND DUNBLANE, Dean of. *See* RATHBAND, The Very Revd Kenneth William

ST ASAPH, Archdeacon of. *See* LOMAS, The Ven John Derrick Percy

ST ASAPH, Bishop of. *See* CAMERON, The Rt Revd Gregory Kenneth

ST ASAPH, Dean of. *See* WILLIAMS, The Very Revd Nigel Howard

ST DAVIDS, Archdeacon of. *See* WIGHT, The Ven Dennis Marley

ST DAVIDS, Bishop of. *See* EVANS, The Rt Revd John Wyn

ST DAVIDS, Dean of. *See* LEAN, The Very Revd David Jonathan Rees

ST EDMUNDSBURY AND IPSWICH, Bishop of. *See* SEELEY, The Rt Revd Martin Alan

ST EDMUNDSBURY, Dean of. *See* WARD, The Very Revd Frances Elizabeth Fearn

ST GERMANS, Suffragan Bishop of. *See* GOLDSMITH, The Rt Revd Christopher David

ST HELENA, Bishop of. *See* FENWICK, The Rt Revd Richard David

ST JOHN NICOLLE, Jason Paul. b 66. Mert Coll Ox BA 88 Called to the Bar (Inner Temple) 95. Ripon Coll Cuddesdon 01. **d** 04 **p** 05. C Kidlington w Hampton Poyle *Ox* 04-08; R The Churn from 08; AD Wallingford from 12; AD Wantage from 13. *The Rectory, Church End, Blewbury, Didcot OX11 9QH* T: (01235) 850267

SALA, Kuabuleke Meymans. b 68. **d** 08 **p** 09. C Edmonton All SS w St Mich *Lon* from 08. *60 Tillotson Road, London N9 9AH* T: (020) 8887 9369 E: smeymans@hotmail.com

SALEH, Mrs Carey Jane. b 62. Sheff Univ BA 94 RGN 83. Qu Coll Birm 11. **d** 13 **p** 14. C Bromsgrove *Worc* from 13. *2 Verona Road, Bromsgrove B60 2SS* M: 07933-744107 E: careysaleh@gmail.com

SALES, Joel Peter. b 85. **d** 14 **p** 15. C Teddington St Mark and Hampton Wick *Lon* from 14. *7 River Reach, Teddington TW11 9QL* M: 07825-162158 E: joel@talk21.com

SALES, Canon Patrick David. b 43. K Coll Lon AKC 68 BD 74 Kent Univ MA 00. **d** 69 **p** 70. C Maidstone All SS w St Phil *Cant* 69-71; C Maidstone All SS w St Phil and H Trin 71-72; C Chart next Sutton Valence 72-74; C Birchington w Acol 75-77; V Boughton under Blean w Dunkirk 77-83; V Herne 83-03; P-in-c St Nicholas at Wade w Sarre and Chislet w Hoath 98-03; TV Whitstable 03-06; Hon Min Can Cant Cathl 83-01; Hon Can Cant Cathl 01-06; RD Reculver 86-92; AD 01-06; Dioc Adv in Liturgy 00-06; rtd 06. *The Well House, South Lane, Dallington, Heathfield TN21 9NJ* T: (01435) 830194 M: 07803-257283 E: patrick@sales64.freeserve.co.uk

SALFORD, Archdeacon of. *See* SHARPLES, The Ven David John

SALISBURY, Anne Ruth. b 37. Dalton Ho Bris 63. **d** 87 **p** 94. C Harrow Trin St Mich *Lon* 87-98; C Paddington Em and W Kilburn St Luke w St Simon and St Jude 99-03; rtd 03. *c/o Crockford, Church House, Great Smith Street, London SW1P 3AZ* M: 07986-868667

SALISBURY, Harold Gareth. b 21. St Pet Hall Ox BA 42 MA 46. Wycliffe Hall Ox 42. **d** 44 **p** 45. C Pet St Mark 44-46; India 47-63; Lect Bp's Coll Calcutta 47-49; Chapl St Andr Cathl Nasik 49-51; Chapl Aurangabad 51-53; Chapl Thana and Agripada 53-57; Chapl Union Th Coll Poona 58-62; V Norham *Newc* 63-70; V Duddo 63-70; V Norham and Duddo 70-78; V Snaith *Sheff* 78-86; P-in-c Cowick 78-86; TR Gt Snaith 86; rtd 86; PtO *Pet* from 87. *33 Nightingale Drive, Towcester NN12 6RA* T: (01327) 353674 E: gareth.salisbury@btopenworld.com

SALISBURY, Peter Brian Christopher. b 58. UMIST BSc 80 MBCS 85. Sarum & Wells Th Coll BTh 92. **d** 92 **p** 93. C Stanmore *Win* 92-95; V Chilworth w N Baddesley 95-05; V Lymington from 05; AD Lyndhurst from 13. *The Vicarage, Grove Road, Lymington SO41 3RF* T: (01590) 673847

SALISBURY, Canon Roger John. b 44. Lon Univ BD 67. Lon Coll of Div 66. **d** 68 **p** 69. C Harold Wood *Chelmsf* 68-73; V Dorking St Paul *Guildf* 73-82; R Rusholme H Trin *Man* 82-90; TR Gt Chesham *Ox* 90-06; RD Amersham 98-04; Hon Can Ch Ch 02-06; C Langham Place All So *Lon* 06-11; rtd 11; Sec Ch Patr Trust from 06; Sec Peache Trustees from 11. *6 Church Street, Widcombe, Bath BA2 6AZ* T: (01225) 489076 E: rogerandhilda.salisbury@gmail.com

SALISBURY, Canon Tobias. b 33. Em Coll Cam BA 60. Ripon Hall Ox 60. **d** 62 **p** 63. C Putney St Mary *S'wark* 62-65; C Churchdown St Jo *Glouc* 65-67; V Urchfont w Stert *Sarum* 67-73; R Burton Bradstock w Shipton Gorge and Chilcombe 73-79; P-in-c Long Bredy w Lt Bredy and Kingston Russell 75-79; TR Bride Valley 79-86; V Gt and Lt Bedwyn and Savernake Forest 86-97; Can and Preb Sarum Cathl 92-98; rtd 98; PtO *B & W* from 98. *Anfield, Hayes Lane, Compton Dundon, Somerton TA11 6PB* T: (01458) 274459

SALISBURY, Bishop of. *See* HOLTAM, The Rt Revd Nicholas Roderick

SALISBURY, Dean of. *See* OSBORNE, The Very Revd June

SALLADIN, James. b 77. Regent Coll Vancouver MTh 07. Fuller Th Sem California. **d** 08 **p** 08. C Vancouver St Jo Canada 08-11; C Muswell Hill St Jas w St Matt *Lon* from 11. *67 St James Lane, London N10 3QY*

SALMON, Alan Clive. b 63. Bris Univ BA 84. St Mich Coll Llan 84. **d** 86 **p** 87. C Llanelli *St D* 86-88; C Roath St German *Llan* 88-90; V Nevern and Y Beifil w Eglwyswrw and Meline etc *St D* 90-92; In RC Ch 92-99; PtO *S'wark* 99-00; Hon C Lavender Hill Ascension etc 00-01; TP Glas E End 01-03; P-in-c Mathry w St Edren's and Grandston etc *St D* 08-12. *Abbey of Our Lady and St John, Abbey Road, Beech, Alton GU34 4AP* T: (01420) 562145 M: 07763-133775

SALMON, Canon Andrew Ian. b 61. St Jo Coll Nottm BTh 88. **d** 88 **p** 89. C Collyhurst *Man* 88-92; P-in-c Pendleton St Ambrose 92-95; TV Pendleton 95-99; TR 99-04; P-in-c Salford Sacred Trin and St Phil from 04; AD Salford 06-13; Borough Dean Salford from 13; Hon Can Man Cathl from 10. *St Philip's Rectory, 6 Encombe Place, Salford M3 6FJ* T: 0161-834 2041 E: rev.andy@btinternet.com

SALMON, Andrew Meredith Bryant. b 30. Jes Coll Cam BA 54 MA 58. Ridley Hall Cam 54. **d** 56 **p** 57. C Enfield Ch Ch Trent Park *Lon* 56-58; Chapl Monkton Combe Sch Bath 58-71; Chapl Milton Abbey Sch Dorset 71-89; TV Bride Valley *Sarum* 89-96; rtd 97; PtO *Sarum* from 97. *1 Barnhill Road, Wareham BH20 5BD* T: (01929) 554039

SALMON, Anthony James Heygate. b 30. CCC Ox BA 53 MA 57. Cuddesdon Coll 54. **d** 56 **p** 57. C S Norwood St Mark *Cant* 56-59; S Africa 59-69; Chapl USPG Coll of the Ascension Selly Oak 69-74; P-in-c Frinsted w Wormshill and Milstead *Cant* 74-78; R Harrietsham 74-85; P-in-c Ulcombe 81-85; V Chobham w Valley End *Guildf* 85-95; rtd 95; PtO *St Alb* from 95. *24 Elmwood, Welwyn Garden City AL8 6LE* T: (01707) 333694

SALMON, Mrs Constance Hazel. b 25. R Holloway Coll Lon BSc 46. Lon Bible Coll 66 Gilmore Course 71. **dss** 80 **d** 87 **p** 96. Sidcup St Andr *Roch* 80-88; NSM 87-88; PtO 88-96; NSM Eynsford w Farningham and Lullingstone from 96. *43 Old Mill Close, Eynsford, Dartford DA4 0BN* T: (01322) 866034

SALMON, Jonathan. b 66. Univ Coll of Swansea BSc(Econ) 88 Sussex Univ MA 95 MPhil 95. Wycliffe Hall Ox 01. **d** 03 **p** 04. C Bowling St Jo *Bradf* 03-07; P-in-c Earley Trin *Ox* 07-14; V from 14. *Trinity Church House, 15 Caraway Road, Earley, Reading RG6 5XR* T: 0118-986 9798 M: 07840-494072 E: jonathansalmon@sky.com

SALMON, Mrs Margaret. b 37. Leeds Univ BA 59 CertEd 60. SWMTC 85. **d** 88 **p** 94. NSM Yelverton, Meavy, Sheepstor and Walkhampton *Ex* from 88. *5 Manor Park, Dousland, Yelverton PL20 6LX* T: (01822) 853310 E: peggy@littlegidding.eclipse.co.uk

SALMON, Mark Harold. b 62. Trin Coll Bris. **d** 00 **p** 01. C Bath Weston All SS w N Stoke and Langridge *B & W* 00-04; P-in-c Harlescott *Lich* 04-07; V from 07; RD Shrewsbury from 13. *Harlescott Vicarage, Meadow Farm Drive, Shrewsbury SY1 4NG* T: (01743) 362883 E: mark.salmon@xalt.co.uk

SALMON, Michael John. b 77. **d** 13. NSM Bishopston and St Andrews *Bris* from 13. *67 Thomas Baines Road, London SW11 2HH* M: 07779-107841 E: Michaelsalmon@mac.com *or* Michael@it-games.co.uk

SALMON, Paul Richard. b 59. **d** 06 **p** 07. OLM Humberston *Linc* from 06. *70 Tetney Road, Humberstone, Grimsby DN36 4JJ* T: (01472) 814550 E: paulsal@stayfree.co.uk

SALMON, Philip John. b 63. Oak Hill Th Coll 96. **d** 98 **p** 99. C Kington w Huntington, Old Radnor, Kinnerton etc *Heref* 98-02; TV Radipole and Melcombe Regis *Sarum* from 02. *The Vicarage, 74 Field Barn Drive, Weymouth DT4 0EF* T: (01305) 778995 M: 07771-688226 E: vicar@emmanuelwey.co.uk

SALMON, Richard Harold. b 35. Fitzw Ho Cam BA 57. Clifton Th Coll 57. **d** 59 **p** 60. C Blackheath Park St Mich *S'wark* 59-61; C St Alb St Paul *St Alb* 61-63; OMF 63-65; C Telok Anson St Luke Malaysia 63-65; V Kuanton Pehang Epiphany 65-75; P-in-c March St Wendreda *Ely* 75-76; R 76-85; V Congresbury w Puxton and Hewish St Ann *B & W* 85-00; rtd 00; PtO *Truro* 00-01; *B & W* from 02. *2 Wisteria Avenue, Hutton, Weston-super-Mare BS24 9QF* T: (01934) 813750 M: 07966-038543 E: richardandhelensalmon@gmail.com

SALMON, William John. b 50. Lon Univ BSc 72 DipEd 73. Cranmer Hall Dur 76. **d** 79 **p** 80. C Summerstown *S'wark* 79-81; C Hampreston *Sarum* 81-86; V Sundon *St Alb* 86-90; Dep Chapl HM Young Offender Inst Glen Parva 90-91; Chapl HM Pris Whitemoor 91-95; Chapl HM Pris Blundeston 95-04 and 07-14; Chapl HM Pris Belmarsh 04-07. *Address temp unknown*

SALMON, Mrs Yvonne Delysia. b 40. Cant Sch of Min 00. **d** 03 **p** 04. OLM Boughton Monchelsea *Cant* 03-10; PtO from 11. *Elderden Farm Cottage, Maidstone Road, Staplehurst, Tonbridge TN12 0RN* T: (01622) 842598 E: y.salmon@tesco.net

SALOP, Archdeacon of. *See* THOMAS, The Ven Paul Wyndham

SALT, Canon David Christopher. b 37. Univ of Wales (Lamp) BA 59. Sarum Th Coll 59. **d** 61 **p** 62. C Kidderminster St Mary *Worc* 61-66; Ind Chapl 66-72; R Knightwick w Doddenham, Broadwas and Cotheridge 72-82; Chapl Worc Coll of HE 72-82; V Redditch St Steph *Worc* 82-02; P-in-c Tardebigge 84-88; RD Bromsgrove 91-00; Hon Can Worc Cathl 92-02; r-d 02; PtO *Worc* 03-12; *Cov* 05-12; *Sarum* from 12. *21 Cook Road, Aldbourne, Marlborough SN8 2EG* E: mill@gmail.com

SALT, David Thomas Whitehorn. b 32. K Coll Lon AKC 56 BD 57. **d** 57 **p** 58. Chapl Torgil Girls' Sch Aoba New Hebrides 57-59; Warden Catechist Coll Lolowai 59-63; Prin St Andr Coll Guadalcanal Solomon Is 63-66; C Hawley H Trin *Guildf* 66-68; V Shelf *Bradf* 68-73; R Checkendon *Ox* 73-81; RD Henley 78-84; TR Langtree 81-84; V Hungerford and Denford 84-89; Chapl Hungerford Hosp 84-89; P-in-c Harpsden *Ox* 89-95; Gen Sec Melanesian Miss 89-95; rtd 95; PtO *Sarum* 95-05; *Guildf* from 06; *Win* 06-12. *12 Heather Court, Heather Way, Hindhead GU26 6AN* T: (01428) 609352 E: dtwsalt@gmail.com

SALT, Jeremy William. b 61. St Mellitus Coll. **d** 11 **p** 12. NSM Ingatestone w Fryerning *Chelmsf* 11-15; P-in-c Buckden w the Offords *Ely* from 15; Dioc Social Justice Co-ord from 15. *Address temp unknown* E: jes1@salt1970.wanadoo.co.uk

✠**SALT, The Rt Revd John William.** b 41. Kelham Th Coll 61. **d** 66 **p** 67 **c** 99. C Barrow St Matt *Carl* 66-70; C Mohale's Hoek Lesotho 70-71; Asst Chapl St Agnes Sch Teyateyaneng 71-72; C Maseru Cathl 73-77; S Africa 77-99; OGS from 81; Dean Eshowe Cathl and Adn S Zululand S Africa 89-99; Superior OGS 96-05; Bp St Helena 99-11; rtd 11; Hon Asst Bp Nor from 11. *Palmers, 5 Common Place, Walsingham NR22 6BW* T: (01328) 820823 E: jsalt@ogs.net

SALT, Neil. b 64. Univ of Wales (Ban) BA 85 New Coll Edin BD 89 Man Metrop Univ BSc 97. Edin Th Coll 86. **d** 89 **p** 90. C Stretford All SS *Man* 89-93; V Smallbridge and Wardle 93-94; PtO *Wakef* 94-01; Hon C Ripponden and Barkisland w W Scammonden 01-06; Chapl Rishworth Sch Ripponden 02-05; V Thornton-le-Fylde *Blackb* 06-11; P-in-c from 14. *10 Egerton Road, Ashton-on-Ribble, Preston PR2 1AJ* T: (01772) 769858 E: nsalt292@gmail.com

SALTER, Arthur Thomas John. b 34. TD 88. AKC 60. **d** 61 **p** 62. C Ealing St Pet Mt Park *Lon* 61-65; C Shepherd's Bush St Steph w St Thos 65-66; C Holborn St Alb w Saffron Hill St Pet 66-70; P-in-c Barnsbury St Clem 70-77; P-in-c Islington St Mich

70-77; V Pentonville St Silas w All SS and St Jas 70-00; CF (TAVR) from 75; Gen Sec Angl and E Chs Assn from 76; Chmn from 90; P-in-c St Dunstan in the West *Lon* 79-99; rtd 00. *1 St James's Close, Bishop Street, London N1 8PH* T: (020) 7359 0250

SALTER, Christopher. *See* SALTER, Nigel Christopher Murray

SALTER, David Whitton. b 69. Bris Univ BEng 90. Trin Coll Bris 06. **d** 08 **p** 09. C Eynsham and Cassington *Ox* 08-11; TV Chipping Norton from 11. *6 The Grange, Kingham, Chipping Norton OX7 6XY* T: (01608) 658852 M: 07768-582285 E: david.w.salter@btinternet.com

SALTER, George Alfred. b 25. TCD BA 47 MA. CITC 49. **d** 49 **p** 50. C Rathdowney *C & O* 49-51; C Cork St Luke *C, C & R* 51-53; I Fermoy Union 53-55; I Cork St Luke w St Ann 55-73; Can Ross Cathl 69-88; Can Cork Cathl 69-88; Treas Cork Cathl 88-94; I Cork St Luke Union 73-94; Preb Tymothan St Patr Cathl Dublin 88-94; rtd 94. *Mount Vernon House, 66 Wellington Road, Cork, Republic of Ireland* T: (00353) (21) 450 6844

SALTER, Janet Elizabeth. b 48. Leeds Univ CertEd 69. SWMTC 92. **d** 95 **p** 98. C Coleshill *Birm* 95-97; Hon C St Dennis *Truro* 97-00; TV Gillingham *Sarum* 00-04; V Stour Vale 04-11; rtd 11. *6 Maple Close, St Columb TR9 6SL* T: (01637) 881552 E: vicarjan@tiscali.co.uk

SALTER, John. *See* SALTER, Arthur Thomas John

SALTER, Canon John Frank. b 37. Dur Univ BA 62. Cranmer Hall Dur 62. **d** 64 **p** 65. C Bridlington Priory *York* 64-67; Travelling Sec IVF 67-70; V Stoughton *Guildf* 70-02; RD Guildf 89-94; Hon Can Guildf Cathl 99-02; rtd 03; PtO *Guildf* from 03. *7 Aldershot Road, Guildford GU2 8AE* T: (01483) 511165 E: j.salter@btinternet.com

SALTER, Canon John Leslie. b 51. AKC 76 Heythrop Coll Lon MA 05. Coll of Resurr Mirfield 77. **d** 78 **p** 79. C Tottenham St Paul *Lon* 78-82; P-in-c Castle Vale *Birm* 82-83; TV Curdworth w Castle Vale 83-90; V Castle Vale St Cuth 90-92; V Wantage *Ox* from 93; AD 01-08; Hon Can Ch Ch from 06. *The Vicarage, The Cloisters, Wantage OX12 8AQ* T: (01235) 762214

SALTER, Nigel Christopher Murray. b 46. Loughb Univ BTech. Ripon Coll Cuddesdon 79. **d** 81 **p** 82. C Glouc St Aldate 81-84; C Solihull *Birm* 84-88; V Highters Heath 88-97; Asst Chapl Greenwich Healthcare NHS Trust 97-01; Asst Chapl Qu Eliz Hosp NHS Trust 01-03; P-in-c Leaton and Albrighton w Battlefield *Lich* 03-06; rtd 06; PtO *Win* from 12. *4 Maple Close, Alton GU34 2AY* T: (01420) 85412 E: chris@princehal.freeserve.co.uk

SALTER, Roger John. b 45. Trin Coll Bris 75. **d** 79 **p** 80. C Bedminster St Mich *Bris* 79-82; C Swindon Ch Ch 82-84; V Bedminster Down 84-89; P-in-c Northwood *Portsm* 89-93; P-in-c W Cowes H Trin 89-92; V Cowes H Trin and St Mary 92-94; USA from 94; rtd 10. *1300 Panorama Drive, Vestavia Hill AL 35216-3032, USA* T: (001) (1) 205 7967 E: salter.roger@gmail.com

SALTMARSH, Philip. b 71. Keele Univ MA 03 RN 93. SNWTP 08. **d** 11 **p** 12. NSM Grassendale *Liv* 11-14; NSM C Liv All SS from 14. *19 Lockerby Road, Liverpool L7 0HG* M: 07715-397390 E: philsaltmarsh@aol.com

SALTWELL, Ms Kathleen. b 48. Edin Univ BD 00 Cam Univ MA 02. Westcott Ho Cam 00. **d** 02 **p** 03. C Worc SE 02-06; Teacher Amity Foundn China from 07. *The Amity Foundation, 71 Hankou Road, Gulou, Nanjing, Jiangsu, China 210008* T: (0086) (25) 8326 0800 E: kathsaltwell@tiscali.co.uk

SALWAY, Canon Donald Macleay. b 31. St Pet Hall Ox BA 54 MA 59. Oak Hill Th Coll 54. **d** 56 **p** 57. C Holloway St Mary w St Jas *Lon* 56-67; V Cambridge St Phil *Ely* 67-81; V Mile Cross *Nor* 81-96; RD Nor N 89-95; Hon Can Nor Cathl 91-96; rtd 96; PtO *B & W* from 96; C Langport Area 98-00. *2 Hodges Barton, Somerton TA11 6QD* T: (01458) 274640 E: donald.salway@btinternet.com

SAMBROOK, Kenneth Henry. b 42. NOC 04. **d** 05 **p** 06. NSM Wistaston *Ches* from 05. *6 Westfield Drive, Wistaston, Crewe CW2 8ES* T: (01270) 662455 E: revd.ken@stmaryswistaston.org.uk

SAMMÉ, Raymond Charles. b 50. Anglia Poly Univ MA 03 St Andr Univ MLitt 08 CBiol 80 MSB 80. Oak Hill Th Coll 85. **d** 87 **p** 88. C Holmer w Huntington *Heref* 87-90; C Derby St Alkmund and St Werburgh 90-93; V Romford Gd Shep *Chelmsf* 93-08; P-in-c Swanley St Paul *Roch* from 08. *3 Holt Close, Sidcup DA14 5EQ* T: (020) 8302 5491 E: ray.samme@btinternet.com

SAMMON, Canon Helen Mary. b 57. Newnham Coll Cam MA 79 Bris Univ MB, ChB 82 MRCGP 98. WEMTC 00. **d** 03 **p** 04. NSM Painswick, Sheepscombe, Cranham, The Edge etc *Glouc* 03-07; P-in-c Tuffley 07-12; Public Preacher from 12; Hon Can Glouc Cathl from 13. *Diocese of Western Tanganyika, PO Box 13, Kasulu, Tanzania* E: helen.sammon@gmail.dom *or* helen.sammon@doctors.org.uk

SAMMONS, Elizabeth Mary. *See* SLATER, Elizabeth Mary

SAMPLE, Mrs Fiona Jean. b 55. **d** 08 **p** 09. OLM Bolam w Whalton and Hartburn w Meldon *Newc* 08-14; NSM from 14; OLM Nether Witton 08-14; NSM from 14. *South Middleton, Scots Gap, Middleton, Morpeth NE61 4EB* T: (01670) 774245 M: 07905-207117

SAMPSON, Brian Andrew. b 39. **d** 94 **p** 95. C Glemsford, Hartest w Boxted, Somerton etc *St E* 94-96; C Pentlow, Foxearth, Liston and Borley *Chelmsf* 96-97; P-in-c 97-03; P-in-c N Hinckford 03-04; C 04-09; rtd 09. *4 Friars Court, Edgworth Road, Sudbury CO10 2TG* T: (01787) 371529 E: captainbrianca@waitrose.co.uk

SAMPSON, Clive. b 38. St Jo Coll Cam BA 61 MA 64. Ridley Hall Cam 63. **d** 65 **p** 66. C Tunbridge Wells St Jo *Roch* 65-69; Travelling Sec Scripture Union 69-79; V Maidstone St Luke *Cant* 79-94; rtd 98. *108 Bure Homage Gardens, Christchurch BH23 4DR* T: (01425) 279029

SAMPSON, Desmond William John. b 25. FRICS 60. Roch Th Coll 63. **d** 65 **p** 66. C Hythe *Cant* 65-70; V Alkham w Capel le Ferne and Hougham 70-76; V Wingham w Elmstone and Preston w Stourmouth 76-86; RD E Bridge 81-86; C Hythe 86-91; rtd 91; PtO *Cant* from 91. *25 Albert Road, Hythe CT21 6BP* T: (01303) 268457

SAMPSON, Gail Sampson. *See* SMITH, Gail Sampson

SAMPSON, Miss Gemma Marie. b 75. Coll of Resurr Mirfield 13. **d** 15. C Hartlepool St Aid and St Columba *Dur* from 15. *22 Fulbeck Close, Harlepool TS25 5TU* M: 07780-675322 E: gemma.sampson@virgin.net

SAMPSON, Julian Robin Anthony. b 78. St D Coll Lamp BA 00. St Steph Ho Ox 01. **d** 03. C Notting Hill All SS w St Columb *Lon* 03-04; C Staines and Asst Chapl HM Pris Bronzefield 04-07; Chapl HM Pris Birm 07-13; V Handsworth St Mich *Birm* from 13; P-in-c Birm Bp Latimer w All SS from 14. *20 Soho Avenue, Birmingham B18 5LB* T: 0121-554 3521 E: jrasampson@yahoo.co.uk *or* vicarhandsworth@hotmail.com

SAMPSON, Mrs Susan Ann. b 57. Bedf Coll Lon BA 81 St Mary's Coll Twickenham PGCE 98. Ripon Coll Cuddesdon 09. **d** 11 **p** 12. C Haywards Heath Ascension *Chich* 11-15; P-in-c Stowe *Ox* from 15; Asst Chapl Stowe Sch from 15. *Barons Barn, Casemore Farm, Preston Bissett MK18 4DP* M: 07780-907467 T: (01280) 848173 E: sue@suesabode.freeserve.co.uk

SAMPSON, Terence Harold Morris. b 41. ACA 64 FCA 75. Bps' Coll Cheshunt 64. **d** 67 **p** 68. C Penrith St Andr *Carl* 67-72; V Carl St Barn 72-80; TR Carl H Trin and St Barn 80-84; Chapl Cumberland Infirmary 83-84; R Workington St Mich *Carl* 84-01; Hon Can Carl Cathl 89-01; RD Solway 90-95; PtO from 02; *Eur* from 03. *Edificio Balcon de San Miguel, Avenida de Alicante 17/19, 03193 San Miguel de Salinas (Alicante), Spain* T: (0034) 677 237 496 M: 07775-683275 E: terenceandmargaret@hotmail.co.uk

SAMS, Mrs Jacqueline. b 53. Open Univ BA 82 St Osyth Coll of Educn CertEd 74. NTMTC BA 10. **d** 10 **p** 11. NSM Colchester Ch Ch w St Mary V *Chelmsf* 10-14; PtO from 14. *17 Chestnut Avenue, Colchester CO2 0AL* T: (01206) 530586 E: jackie.sams@ymail.com

SAMS, Michael Charles. b 34. FCA 62. Ox NSM Course 81. **d** 84 **p** 85. NSM Abingdon *Ox* 84-92 and 99-04; P-in-c Shippon 92-99; PtO from 04. *23 Chancery Avenue, Abingdon OX14 2NZ* T: (01235) 529084 E: michael-gwenda@uwclub.ne

SAMS, Raymond Victor. b 51. Goldsmiths' Coll Lon TCert 73. ERMC 03. **d** 06 **p** 07. NSM Colchester Ch Ch w St Mary V *Chelmsf* 06-10; P-in-c Cressing w Stisted and Bradwell etc 10-15; rtd 15. *18 Munnings Road, Colchester CO3 4QG* T: (01206) 560691 E: theolikon@googlemail.com

SAMSON, Hilary Lynn. b 50. SWMTC. **d** 03 **p** 04. NSM St Agnes and Mithian w Mount Hawke *Truro* 03-06; P-in-c St Enoder from 06; P-in-c Newlyn St Newlyn from 06; RD Pydar from 13. *The Rectory, Penhale View, My Lords Road, Fraddon, St Columb TR9 6LX* T: (01726) 860514 E: hilarysamson@lineone.net

SAMSON, Mrs Susan Mary. b 52. Southn Univ BA 73. **d** 09 **p** 10. OLM Sittingbourne w Bobbing *Cant* from 09. *11 Adelaide Drive, Sittingbourne ME10 1YB* T: (01795) 478635 E: suesamson@sky.com

SAMUEL, Adrian Frank Graham. b 68. Essex Univ BA 94 PhD 02 Warwick Univ MA 95. NTMTC 04. **d** 07 **p** 08. C Twickenham St Mary *Lon* 07-10; Chapl Cheltenham Coll from 12. *Cheltenham College, Bath Road, Cheltenham GL53 7LD* T: (01242) 265600 M: 07766-664345 E: adriansamuel@msn.com

SAMUEL, Alwin John. b 55. **d** 81 **p** 83. Pakistan 81-03; Interfaith Worker and Dioc Adv *Ox* 03-05; Inter Faith Adv Cowley Deanery 05-11. *63 Copperfields, High Wycombe HP12 4AN* M: 07956-882588

SAMUEL, Brother. *See* DOUBLE, Richard Sydney

SAMUEL, Fiaz. *See* SAMUEL, Luther Fiaz

SAMUEL, Kerry Jay. b 71. Nottm Univ BA 92 Hughes Hall Cam PGCE 93 K Coll Lon PhD 07. NTMTC 05. **d** 07 **p** 08. C Twickenham St Mary *Lon* 07-10; PtO *Glouc* 13-15; Chapl Cheltenham Coll from 13; Chapl All SS Academy Cheltenham from 13. *Chandos Lodge, Thirlestaine Road, Cheltenham GL53 7AA* M: 07717-470403 E: kerrysamuel@hotmail.com

✠**SAMUEL, The Most Revd Kunnumpurathu Joseph.** b 42. Union Bibl Sem Yavatmal BRE 68 Texas Chr Univ MDiv 86. **d** 68 **c** 90. Ch of S India from 68; Bp E Kerala from 90; Moderator Ch of S India 99-04. *CSI Bishop's House, Melukavumattom PO, Kottayam 686 652, Kerala State, India* T: (0091) (482) 291026 F: 291044

SAMUEL, Luther Fiaz. b 47. Karachi Univ BA 83. St Thos Th Coll Karachi BTh 88. **d** 88 **p** 89. Pakistan 88-96; Oman 96-03; PtO *Lich* 03-04; NSM Walsall St Matt 15; Minority Ethnic Angl Concerns Officer 04-05; Asian Missr 05-13; rtd 13; PtO *Lich* from 15. *27 Roebuck Road, Walsall WS3 1AH* M: 07901-718371 E: revlfs@hotmail.com

SAMUEL, Mrs Mary Rose. b 42. Newc Univ BA 65 CQSW 67. STETS 95. **d** 98 **p** 99. C Waltham on the Wolds, Stonesby, Saxby etc *Leic* 98-01; P-in-c Wymondham w Edmondthorpe, Buckminster etc 01-04; R S Framland 04-08; rtd 08; Hon C Wymeswold and Prestwold w Hoton and Barrow upon Soar w Walton le Wolds *Leic* 08-11. *13A Lenham Road West, Rottingdean, Brighton BN2 7GJ* T: (01273) 958693 E: mary.rosesamuel@tiscali.co.uk

SAMUEL, Oliver Harold. b 53. **d** 05 **p** 07. OLM Old Trafford St Bride *Man* from 05. *115 Northumberland Road, Old Trafford, Manchester M16 9PY* T: 0161-876 5055

SAMUEL, Stuart. b 48. AKC 70. St Aug Coll Cant 70. **d** 71 **p** 72. C Golcar *Wakef* 71-77; V Brampton St Mark *Derby* 77-79; P-in-c Hathern *Leic* 79-83; R Hathern, Long Whatton and Diseworth 83-90; R Hathern, Long Whatton and Diseworth w Belton etc 90-97; RD Akeley E 92-96; P-in-c Waltham on the Wolds, Stonesby, Saxby etc 97-02; P-in-c Wymondham w Edmondthorpe, Buckminster etc 97-01; P-in-c High Framland Par 97-01; P-in-c Helpringham w Hale *Linc* 02-10. *6 Seabank Road, Rhyl LL18 1EA* E: stuart@marymag.freeserve.co.uk

SAMUELS, Canon Ann Elizabeth. b 51. Birm Univ BA 73 CertEd 74. Trin Coll Bris 85. **d** 87 **p** 94. Par Dn Moreton *Ches* 87-91; Par Dn Halton 91-94; C 94-03; Bp's Adv for Women in Min 94-96; Asst Dir of Ords 96-03; RD Frodsham 99-03; Chapl Halton Gen Hosp NHS Trust 99-00; Chapl N Cheshire Hosps NHS Trust 01-03; V Higher Bebington *Ches* 03-14; Hon Can Ches Cathl 01-14; rtd 14. *The Vicarage, 47 Ardern Lea, Alvanley, Frodsham WA6 9EQ*

SAMUELS, Canon Christopher William John. b 42. AKC 66. **d** 67 **p** 68. C Kirkholt *Man* 67-72; C-in-c Houghton Regis St Thos CD *St Alb* 72-76; R Tarporley *Ches* 76-83; R Ches St Mary 83-05; RD Ches 95-02; Hon Can Ches Cathl 97-05; rtd 05; Chapl to The Queen 01-12; LtO *St As* from 05; PtO *Ches* from 07. *Riversleigh House, Station Road, Rossett, Wrexham LL12 0HE* T: (01244) 579021 M: 07929-420423 E: cwjsamuels@gmail.com

SAMUELS, Raymond John. b 49. Qu Mary Coll Lon BSc 73 Essex Univ CertEd 74. Trin Coll Bris 85. **d** 87 **p** 88. C Moreton *Ches* 87-91; V Halton 91-02; Dioc Dir of Ords 03-14; rtd 14; V Alvanley *Ches* from 14. *The Vicarage, 47 Ardern Lea, Alvanley, Frodsham WA6 9EQ*

SAMWAYS, Denis Robert. b 37. Leeds Univ BA 62. Coll of Resurr Mirfield 62. **d** 64 **p** 65. C Clun w Chapel Lawn *Heref* 64-69; C Pocklington w Yapham-cum-Meltonby, Owsthorpe etc *York* 69-71; C Millington w Gt Givendale 69-71; R Hinderwell w Roxby 71-76; Hon C 80-91; Hon C Loftus 76-80; V Boosbeck w Moorsholm 91-95; R Kirby Misperton w Normanby, Edston and Salton 95-02; rtd 02. *7 High Street, Gatehouse of Fleet, Castle Douglas DG7 2HR* T: (01557) 814095

SAMWAYS, John Feverel. b 44. BA. Trin Coll Bris 81. **d** 83 **p** 84. C Patcham *Chich* 83-86; C Ox St Aldate w St Matt 86-94; R Ox St Matt 95-97; TR Keynsham *B & W* 97-09; rtd 09; PtO *B & W* from 10. *9 Newland Gardens, Frome BA11 1PN* T: (01373) 454047 E: john.samways28@btinternet.com

✠**SAN SI HTAY, The Most Revd Samuel.** BA. **d** 67 **c** 89. Asst Pastor Indaw Burma 67-69; P-in-c Mawbi 70-76; Prin H Cross Coll 76-91; Asst Bp Yangon 91-93; Gen Sec Myanmar 93-01; Abp Myanmar and Bp Yangon from 01. *Bishopscourt, 140 Pyidaungsu Yeiktha Road, Dagon, Yangon 11191, Myanmar* T: (0095) (1) 246813 F: 251405 E: cpm.140@mptmail.net.mm

✠**SANANA, The Rt Revd Rhynold Ewaruba.** b 39. Newton Th Coll 60 St Barn Coll Adelaide 71 St Aug Coll Cant 75. **d** 67 **p** 67 **c** 76. Papua New Guinea 67-72, 73-90 and from 92; Asst P Dogura Cathl 67-69; Asst P Popondetta Resurr 69-70; St Barn

Coll Adelaide Australia 72-73; Dean Dogura and Adn E Region 74-76; Asst Bp New Guinea 76-77; Bp Dogura 77-89; Asst P Lakenham St Mark *Nor* 90-92; rtd 99. *Diocesan Office, PO Box 26, Popondetta, Oro Province, Papua New Guinea*

SANCHEZ RODRIGUEZ, Miguel. b 66. Deusto Univ MA 95. Coll of Resurr Mirfield 12. **d** 14 **p** 15. C Elland *Leeds* from 14. *St Michael's House, 50 Victoria Road, Elland HX5 0QA* M: 07761-501229 E: msanrod@gmail.com

SANDAY, Robert Ward. b 55. Sarum & Wells Th Coll 89. **d** 91 **p** 92. C Swindon Ch Ch *Bris* 91-94; V Lyddington and Wanborough and Bishopstone etc 94-00; Chapl to the Deaf Portsm and *Win* from 00; V Southampton Lord's Hill and Lord's Wood 10-15; P-in-c Hound from 15; C Bursledon from 15; C Hamble le Rice from 15. *1 Tangmere Drive, Southampton SO16 8GY* T: (023) 8073 1091 E: robertsandays@talktalk.net

SANDBERG, Canon Peter John. b 37. Lon Univ LLB 59. Lon Coll of Div 67. **d** 69 **p** 70. C Hailsham *Chich* 69-72; C Billericay St Mary *Chelmsf* 72-77; TV Billericay and Lt Burstead 77-83; R Thundersley 83-02; RD Hadleigh 90-00; Hon Can Chelmsf Cathl 00-02; rtd 02; PtO *Chelmsf* from 02. *Hethersett, School Road, Pentlow, Sudbury CO10 7JR* T: (01787) 281006 E: peterandcelia@talktalk.net

SANDELLS-REES, Kathy Louise. *See* JONES, Kathy Louise

SANDER, Thomas William. b 87. Westcott Ho Cam. **d** 11 **p** 12. C Sharnbrook, Felmersham and Knotting w Souldrop *St Alb* 11-14; V Flamstead and Markyate Street from 14. *The Vicarage, 50 Trowley Hill Road, Flamstead, St Albans AL3 8EE* E: thomas.william.sander@gmail.com

SANDER-HEYS, Mrs Jemma Joan. b 79. Ex Univ BA 02 Sheff Univ BA 11. Coll of Resurr Mirfield 09. **d** 12 **p** 13. C R Wootton Bassett *Sarum* 12-15; TV Gt Yarmouth *Nor* from 15. *1 Osborne Avenue, Great Yarmouth NR30 4EE* M: 07811-480438 E: jemmajsanders@hotmail.com

SANDERCOCK, Deborah Sharon Agnes. b 62. Coll of Ripon & York St Jo BSc 84 Man Metrop Univ MSc 96 Crewe & Alsager Coll PGCE 87. SNWTP 09. **d** 12 **p** 13. C Chadderton St Matt w St Luke *Man* from 12. *30 St George's Square, Chadderton, Oldham OL9 9NY* T: 0161-688 5441 M: 07871-760107

SANDERS, Mrs Alexandra Jane. b 58. Ex Univ BA 80 Leeds Univ MA 09. NOC 06. **d** 09 **p** 10. NSM Tarporley *Ches* 09-12; C Acton and Worleston, Church Minshull etc 11-12; V Mellor from 12. *The Vicarage, 51 Church Road, Mellor, Stockport SK6 5LX* T: 0161-427 1203 M: 07813-326313 E: revalex@sky.com

SANDERS, Diana Faye. b 46. Auckland Univ MA 68 LSE PhD 75 Anglia Ruskin Univ PhD 10. Westcott Ho Cam 02. **d** 04 **p** 05. NSM Cottenham *Ely* 04-08; P-in-c Farley Hill St Jo *St Alb* 08-11; rtd 11; PtO *Ely* from 11. *48 Tenison Manor, Cottenham, Cambridge CB24 8XL* T: (01954) 205420 E: sandersdianaf@gmail.com

SANDERS, Graham Laughton. b 32. Kelham Th Coll 52. **d** 56 **p** 57. C Glouc St Paul 56-60; India 61-68; V Heaton St Martin *Bradf* 68-76; V Gt Waltham *Chelmsf* 76-79; V Gt Waltham w Ford End 79-87; Sec Dioc Liturg Cttee 78-87; TR Guiseley w Esholt *Bradf* 87-94; rtd 97. *c/o M J P Sanders Esq, Beachborough School, Westbury Manor, Westbury, Brackley NN13 5LB* M: 07808-123165 E: sanders966@btinternet.com

SANDERS, Canon Hilary Clare. b 57. Hull Univ BA 79 UEA CertEd 81. EAMTC 83. **dss** 85 **d** 87 **p** 94. Haverhill w Withersfield, the Wrattings etc *St E* 85-87; Hon Par Dn Melton 87-94; Hon C 94-99; Dioc Dir Educn (Schools) 88-99; P-in-c Earl Soham w Cretingham and Ashfield 99-05; P-in-c Boulge w Burgh, Grundisburgh and Hasketon 05-13; R Carlford from 13; Dioc Adv for Women's Min from 10; RD Woodbridge from 11; Hon Can St E Cathl from 04. *The Rectory, Woodbridge Road, Grundisburgh, Woodbridge IP13 6UF* T: (01394) 735182 E: revclaresanders@tiscali.co.uk

SANDERS, James Alexander. b 29. **d** 65 **p** 66. Australia 65-78 and from 81; C Enfield St Jas *Lon* 78-81; rtd 94. *Apt 8, 82 Sandy Bay Road, Battery Point TAS 7004, Australia*

SANDERS, Mrs Marion. b 14. NSM Barnstaple *Ex* from 14. *3 Westaway Close, Barnstaple EX31 1RU* T: (01271) 346003

SANDERS, Canon Mark. b 57. Hull Univ BA 79 Cam Univ BA 82. Westcott Ho Cam 80. **d** 83 **p** 84. C Haverhill w Withersfield, the Wrattings etc *St E* 83-87; P-in-c Melton 87-91; R 91-98; Dioc Dir Post-Ord Tr 97-14; Asst Dioc Dir of Ords 98-99; Dioc Dir of Ords 99-14; Dioc Dir of CME 99-01; R Framlingham w Saxtead from 14; RD Loes from 15; Hon Can St E Cathl from 01; RD Loes from 15. *The Rectory, Framlingham, Woodbridge IP13 9BJ* T: (01728) 768875 E: revmarksanders@tiscali.co.uk

SANDERS, Michael Barry. b 45. Fitzw Coll Cam BA 67 MA 71 Lon Univ BD 71. St Jo Coll Nottm 68 Lon Coll of Div. **d** 71 **p** 72. C Ashtead *Guildf* 71-74; Chapl St Jo Coll Cam 75-79; V Dorridge *Birm* 79-89; TR Walsall *Lich* 89-01; Preb Lich

Cathl 97-01; Chapl The Hague *Eur* 01-07; P-in-c Kemble, Poole Keynes, Somerford Keynes etc *Glouc* 07-12; rtd 12. *1 Rowena Cade Avenue, Cheltenham GL50 2LA* T: (01242) 515631 E: mbsanders45@gmail.com

SANDERS, Nigel Wilding. b 29. Mert Coll Ox MA 55. Ox Min Course 91. **d** 92 **p** 93. NSM Maidenhead St Andr and St Mary *Ox* 92-97; NSM Furze Platt 97-04; rtd 04; PtO *B & W* from 05. *48 Hapil Close, Sandford, Winscombe BS25 5AA* T: (01934) 820136 M: 07976-715626 E: nigelisan@btinternet.com

SANDERS, Mrs Nora Irene. b 29. Lon Univ BA 50 CertEd 51. WMMTC 74. **dss** 78 **d** 87 **p** 94. Dorridge *Birm* 78-90; Par Dn 87-90; rtd 90; Hon C Tanworth *Birm* 94-96; PtO 96-15. *Woodstock, 14 Duchess Road, Osbaston, Monmouth NP25 3HT* T: (01600) 715819

SANDERS (née SHAW), Mrs Pamela Joyce. b 54. Liv Univ BA 76. WEMTC 02. **d** 05 **p** 06. C Leominster *Heref* 05-09; R Crathorne *York* from 09; V Kirklevington w Picton, and High and Low Worsall from 09. *The Vicarage, 2 Langbaurgh Road, Hutton Rudby, Yarm TS15 0HL* T: (01642) 700223 E: pam.notsaunders@googlemail.com

SANDERS, Roderick David Scott. b 58. Southn Univ BA 80 CertEd 81. Cranmer Hall Dur 85. **d** 88 **p** 89. C Luton St Mary *St Alb* 88-93; P-in-c Clovelly and Woolfardisworthy and Buck Mills *Ex* 93-94; TV Parkham, Alwington, Buckland Brewer etc 94-98; NSM Cove St Jo *Guildf* 98-03; NSM Guildf Ch Ch w St Martha-on-the-Hill 03-10; Asst Chapl HM Pris Wandsworth from 13. *HM Prison Wandsworth, PO Box 757, London SW18 3HS* T: (020) 8588 4000 M: 07720-85646 E: rod.sanders@ntlworld.com

SANDERS, Susan Rachel. *See* COLLINGRIDGE, Susan Rachel

SANDERS, Canon Wendy Elizabeth. b 49. Carl Dioc Tr Course 87. **d** 90 **p** 94. NSM Bampton w Mardale *Carl* 90-92; C Walney Is 92-94; C Stanwix 94-98; TV Chippenham St Paul w Hardenhuish etc *Bris* 98-03; TV Kington St Michael 98-03; RD Chippenham 99-03; TR Cockermouth Area *Carl* 03-14; Hon Can Carl Cathl 10-14; rtd 14; RD Derwent *Carl* from 11. *23 Lowscales Drive, Cockermouth CA13 9DR* T: (01900) 823269

SANDERS, William John. b 48. Liv Inst of Educn BA 80. Wycliffe Hall Ox 81. **d** 83 **p** 84. C Netherton *Liv* 83-87; P-in-c Wavertree St Bridget 87-97; V Wavertree St Bridget and St Thos 97-14; P-in-c from 14; rtd 14. *The Vicarage, 35 Ashfield, Wavertree, Liverpool L15 1EY* T: 0151-733 1117 E: billandalice@virginmedia.com

SANDERSON, Colin James. b 54. Univ of Wales (Cardiff) MA 95 SEN 76 RGN. St Mich Coll Llan 85. **d** 87 **p** 88. C Merthyr Dyfan *Llan* 87-90; C Cadoxton-juxta-Barry 90-91; V Llangeinor 91-99; LtO 04-10; V Congleton St Jas *Ches* from 10; Chapl Mid Cheshire Hosps Trust 11-12; Lead Chapl from 12. *St James's Vicarage, 116 Holmes Chapel Road, Congleton CW12 4NX* T: (01260) 408203 *or* (01270) 255141 M: 07713-742365 E: cjsanderson2005@hotmail.com

SANDERSON, Daniel. b 40. AKC 66. **d** 67 **p** 68. C Upperby St Jo *Carl* 67-72; V Addingham 72-75; V Ireleth w Askam 75-02; C Dalton-in-Furness and Ireleth-with-Askam 02-05; Hon Can Carl Cathl 95-05; RD Furness 01-04; rtd 05. *52 Parklands Drive, Askam-in-Furness LA16 7JP* T: (01229) 463018

SANDERSON, Canon Gillian. b 47. Cranmer Hall Dur 80. **dss** 82 **d** 87 **p** 94. Allesley *Cov* 82-86; Warwick 86-00; C 87-94; TV 94-00; Hon Can Cov Cathl 94-00; PtO from 00. *17 Marlborough Drive, Leamington Spa CV31 1XY* T: (01926) 459749 M: 07714-193776 E: gillian@sanderson17.orangehome.co.uk

SANDERSON, John Paul. *See* SANDERSON, Paul John

SANDERSON, Paul. b 59. Univ of Wales (Abth) BSc 80 Ches Coll of HE PGCE 81 Man Univ MEd 92. **d** 05 **p** 06. OLM Bury St Jo w St Mark *Man* 05-10; OLM Walmersley Road, Bury from 10. *261 Walmersley Road, Bury BL9 6NX* T: 0161-764 3452 E: paul261@fsmail.net

SANDERSON, Paul John. b 67. Maryvale Inst BDiv 04. Ushaw Coll Dur 86 Ripon Coll Cuddesdon 14. **d** 04 **p** 04. In RC Ch 04-11; C Warton St Paul *Blackb* from 15. *22 Rydal Avenue, Freckleton, Preston PR4 1DJ* M: 07969-428757 E: sandyson1967@hotmail.com

SANDERSON, Canon Peter Oliver. b 29. St Chad's Coll Dur BA 52. **d** 54 **p** 55. C Houghton le Spring *Dur* 54-59; R Linstead Jamaica 59-63; Chapl RAF 63-67; P-in-c Winksley cum Grantley and Aldfield w Studley *Ripon* 67-68; V 68-74; V Leeds St Aid 74-84; Can and Provost St Paul's Cathl Dundee 84-91; R Dundee St Paul 84-91; Lib from 91; rtd 94; Interim Dean Trin Cathl Iowa 05-06; Asst to the Dean 06-07. *410 Brentwood Drive, Alamogordo NM 88310-5439, USA* E: petersanderson@q.com

SANDERSON, Scott. b 42. Oak Hill Th Coll. **d** 82 **p** 83. C Galleywood Common *Chelmsf* 82-88; P-in-c Newport w Widdington 88-92; V Newport 92-98; V Walton le Soken 98-05; rtd 05; PtO *Chelmsf* from 07. *The Bungalow, 2 Captains Road, West Mersea, Colchester CO5 8QS* T: (01206) 385571 E: scott.sanderson@lineone.net

SANDERSON, Timothy. b 68. York Univ BSc 89 Glos Univ BA 03 St Jo Coll Dur MATM 09. Cranmer Hall Dur 07. **d** 09 **p** 10. C Jesmond H Trin *Newc* from 09; C Newc St Barn and St Jude from 09. *36 St Julien Gardens, Newcastle upon Tyne NE2 2QX* T: 0191-281 9452 M: 07592-720879 E: tim@htj.org.uk

SANDES, Denis Lindsay. b 46. CITC BTh 86. **d** 89 **p** 90. C Bandon Union *C, C & R* 89-92; I Kells Gp *C & O* 92-07; Can Leighlin Cathl 03-07; I Omey w Ballynakill, Errislannan and Roundstone *T, K & A* 07-13; Can Tuam Cathl 08-11; Provost Tuam 10-13; rtd 13. *Ballyhasty, Cloughjordan, Co Tipperary, Republic of Ireland* T: (00353) (76) 604 5868 M: 86-647 5056 E: revdlsandes@gmail.com

SANDFORD, Nicholas Robert. b 63. Kent Univ BA 84 Univ of Wales (Cardiff) BD 87. St Mich Coll Llan 84. **d** 87 **p** 88. C Neath w Llantwit *Llan* 87-90; C Cardiff St Jo 90-94; R Cilybebyll 94-97; Chapl HM Pris Swansea 95-97; Chapl HM Pris Parc (Bridgend) 97-04; Chapl HM Pris Usk and Prescoed 04-13; Chapl HM Pris Swansea from 13; PtO *Llan* from 14. *HM Prison Swansea, 200 Oystermouth Road, Swansea SA1 3SR* T: (01792) 485300

SANDFORD, Paul Richard. b 47. Em Coll Cam BA 69 MA 73. Wycliffe Hall Ox 72. **d** 75 **p** 76. C Upper Holloway St Pet *Lon* 75-77; C Finchley St Paul Long Lane 77-81; Ind Chapl *Newc* 81-88; TV Cramlington 81-88; TV Dronfield *Derby* 88-90; TV Dronfield w Holmesfield 90-02; P-in-c Sinfin 02-10; V 10-14; RD Derby S 02-10; rtd 14; PtO *Derby* from 14. *4 Dawlish Court, Alvaston, Derby DE24 0QZ* E: prsandford@ntlworld.com

SANDHAM, Daniel Paul. b 82. St Chad's Coll Dur BA 05. St Steph Ho Ox BA 09 MA 14. **d** 09 **p** 10. C Hendon St Mary and Ch Ch *Lon* 09-12; V Brownswood Park from 12. *St John's Vicarage, 2A Gloucester Drive, London N4 2LW* T: (020) 8809 6111 E: danielsandham@hotmail.com

SANDHAM, Shaun Graham. b 60. Cranmer Hall Dur 02. **d** 04 **p** 05. C Workington St Mich *Carl* 04-08; TV Sutton St Jas and Wawne *York* 08-12; V Sutton Park 12-15; P-in-c Wawne 13-15; P-in-c Kells *Carl* from 15. *The Vicarage, Cliff Road, Whitehaven CA28 9ET* M: 07787-575884 T: (01946) 693933 E: shaunsandham@gmail.com

SANDHAM, Stephen McCourt. b 41. K Coll Lon BD 65 AKC 65. **d** 66 **p** 67. C Stockton St Pet *Dur* 66-69; C Bishopwearmouth Gd Shep 69-71; C Bishopwearmouth St Mich w St Hilda 71-75; V Darlington St Mark w St Paul 75-82; P-in-c Sunderland St Chad 82-87; R Shincliffe 87-98; P-in-c 98-06; rtd 06; Chapl Sherburn Hosp Dur 98-07; PtO *Dur* from 07. *21 Hill Meadows, High Shincliffe, Durham DH1 2PE* E: stephensandham@yahoo.co.uk

SANDIFORD, Mrs Christine Krogh. b 44. Smith Coll (USA) BA 66 Man Univ PGCE 87. SNWTP 11. **d** 12 **p** 13. OLM Didsbury St Jas and Em *Man* from 12. *330 Lapwing Lane, Manchester M20 6UW* T: 0161-434 1343 E: cksandiford@hotmail.com

SANDOM, Miss Carolyn Elizabeth. b 63. Homerton Coll Cam BEd 85. Wycliffe Hall Ox BTh 93. **d** 94. C St Helen Bishopsgate w St Andr Undershaft etc *Lon* 94-96; C Cambridge H Sepulchre *Ely* 96-05; NSM Tunbridge Wells St Jo *Roch* from 11. *57 Green Way, Tunbridge Wells TN2 3HJ* T: (01892) 671629 E: carrie.sandom@stjohnstw.org

SANDOVER, Cherry Elizabeth. St Mellitus Coll 14. **d** 15. NSM Leigh St Clem *Chelmsf* from 15. *7B Victoria Drive, Leigh-on-Sea SS9 1SF*

SANDS, Colin Robert. b 38. JP 84. Ches Coll of HE CertEd 64. NOC 82. **d** 85 **p** 86. Hd Master St Andr Magull Primary Sch 80-00; NSM Bootle Ch Ch *Liv* 85-94; NSM Maghull 94-01; rtd 01; PtO *Carl* 01-07 and from 12; *Liv* 01-12. *12 Beacon Park, Penrith CA11 7UB* T: (01768) 863968

SANDS, Nigel Colin. b 39. Dur Univ BA 64 MA 68. Oak Hill Th Coll 65. **d** 67 **p** 68. C Skelmersdale St Paul *Liv* 67-71; C Childwall All SS 71-72; V Wavertree St Bridget 72-78; P-in-c Welford w Wickham and Gt Shefford *Ox* 78-86; P-in-c Boxford w Stockcross and Speen 84-86; R Welford w Wickham and Gt Shefford, Boxford etc 86-09; rtd 09; PtO *Ox* from 09. *Applemead, Chilton Way, Hungerford RG17 0JR* T: (01488) 680618

SANDS, William James. b 55. Nottm Univ LTh 83 Birm Univ MA 99. St Jo Coll Nottm 80. **d** 83 **p** 84. C St Mary-at-Latton *Chelmsf* 83-86; R Mvurwi Zimbabwe 86-87; C-in-c Barkingside St Cedd *Chelmsf* 87-89; C Woodford St Mary w St Phil and St Jas 87-89; P-in-c Elmsett w Aldham *St E* 89-92; P-in-c Kersey w Lindsey 89-92; R Esigodini Zimbabwe 92-96; Sub Dean

Harare 97; Chapl Algarve *Eur* 98-00; V Castle Bromwich St Clem *Birm* 00-09; P-in-c Yardley St Edburgha 09-11; V from 11. *49 Vicarage Road, Yardley, Birmingham B33 8PH*
E: williamsands123@btinternet.com

SANER-HAIGH, Robert James. b 73. Birm Univ BA 94 MPhil 98. Wycliffe Hall Ox BA 04 MA 08. **d** 05 **p** 06. C Appleby *Carl* 05-07; Bp's Dom Chapl and C Dalston w Cumdivock, Raughton Head and Wreay 07-10; Officer for IME 4-7 07-08; Dir of Ords 08-10; P-in-c Kendal H Trin from 10. *Holy Trinity Vicarage, 2 Lynngarth Drive, Kendal LA9 4JA* T: (01539) 729403
E: vicar@kendalparishchurch.co.uk

SANGSTER, Andrew. b 45. K Coll Lon BD 67 AKC 67 BA 71 MA 84 Lon Inst of Educn MPhil 93 LLB 97 UEA PhD 14 FCollP. St Boniface Warminster. **d** 69 **p** 70. C Aylesford *Roch* 69-72; C Shirley *Win* 73-76; V Woolston 76-79; Prov Youth Chapl Ch in Wales 79-82; Chapl Collegiate Sch New Zealand 82-89; Chapl Eton Coll 89-92; Hd Master St Edm Sch Hindhead 92-96; Hd Thos Day Schs Lon 96-99; V Ormesby St Marg w Scratby, Ormesby St Mich etc *Nor* 99-04; Chapl Bromley Coll 04-10; rtd 10; PtO *Nor* 10-15; Bp's Officer for Retired Clergy from 15; Hon PV Nor Cathl from 14. *10 Harvey Lane, Norwich NR7 0BQ* T: (01603) 437402
E: asangster666@btinternet.com

SANKEY, Julian. b 52. Qu Coll Ox BA 74 MA 79. St Jo Coll Nottm 84. **d** 86 **p** 87. C New Barnet St Jas *St Alb* 86-89; C Mansfield SS Pet and Paul *S'well* 89-94; Chapl St Luke's Hospice Sheff 94-07. *29 Grindlow Close, Sheffield S14 1PE* T: 0114-264 9988

SANKEY, Terence Arthur Melville. b 51. Trin Coll Bris 87. **d** 89 **p** 90. C Chalke Valley W *Sarum* 89-93; NSM Chalke Deanery 93-15; Chapl HM Pris Dorchester 99-13; rtd 15. *Address temp unknown* E: terry@rookhaye.freeserve.co.uk

SANLON, Peter Thomas. b 80. Wycliffe Hall Ox BA 01 St Cath Coll Cam MPhil 07 PhD 10. Ridley Hall Cam 05. **d** 10 **p** 11. C S Tottenham St Ann *Lon* 10-13; Lect Oak Hill Th Coll 10-13; V Tunbridge Wells St Mark *Roch* from 13. *The Vicarage, 1 St Mark's Road, Tunbridge Wells TN2 5LT* T: (01892) 526069 M: 07961-053781 E: petersanlon@gmail.com

SANSBURY, Canon Christopher John. b 34. Peterho Cam BA 57 MA. Westcott Ho Cam 58. **d** 59 **p** 60. C Portsea N End St Mark *Portsm* 59-63; C Weeke *Win* 63-71; V N Eling St Mary 71-78; R Long Melford *St E* 78-00; P-in-c Lawshall w Shimplingthorne and Alpheton 98-00; Hon Can St E Cathl 97-00; rtd 00; PtO *St E* from 00. *2 Deacon's Close, Lavenham, Sudbury CO10 9TT* T: (01787) 248068

SANSOM, John Reginald. b 40. St Jo Coll Nottm 73. **d** 75 **p** 76. C Ipswich St Marg *St E* 75-79; P-in-c Emneth *Ely* 79-85; P-in-c Hartford 85-86; TV Huntingdon 86-91; R Sawtry 91-97; R Sawtry and Glatton 97-99; TV Ely 99-05; rtd 05; PtO *Ely* from 06. *37 St Ovins Green, Ely CB6 3AW* T: (01353) 614913 E: johnjudysansom@ntlworld.com

SANSOM, Canon Michael Charles. b 44. Bris Univ BA 66 St Jo Coll Dur PhD 74. Cranmer Hall Dur 68. **d** 72 **p** 73. C Ecclesall *Sheff* 72-76; LtO *Ely* 76-88; Dir of Studies Ridley Hall Cam 76-88; Vice-Prin 79-88; Dir of Ords *St Alb* 88-10; Can Res St Alb 88-10; rtd 10. *101 Churchfields Drive, Bovey Tracey, Newton Abbot TQ13 9QZ* T: (01626) 836773
E: michaelsansom123@btinternet.com

SANSOM, Robert Arthur. b 29. St Aid Birkenhead 60. **d** 62 **p** 63. C Sutton in Ashfield St Mary *S'well* 62-65; V Holbrooke *Derby* 65-70; R North Saanich St Andr and H Trin Canada 70-80; R Oak Bay St Mary 80-84; R Saanichton St Mary 84-89; rtd 89. *1-9871 Resthaven Drive, Sidney BC V8L 3E9, Canada*

SANSUM, Canon David Henry. b 31. Bris Univ BA 52 MA 63. St Aid Birkenhead 54. **d** 56 **p** 57. C Henleaze *Bris* 56-59; C Stratton St Margaret 59-60; C Stoke Bishop 60-64; V Stechford *Birm* 64-76; V Ashbourne St Oswald w Mapleton *Derby* 76-98; P-in-c Fenny Bentley, Thorpe and Tissington 77-83; V Ashbourne St Jo 81-98; RD Ashbourne 91-98; Hon Can Derby Cathl 95-98; rtd 98; PtO *Glouc* from 98; *Bris* from 98. *Greenleaze, Main Road, Easter Compton, Bristol BS35 5SQ* T: (01454) 632563

SANTANA, Levy. *See* CAMPOS DE SANTANA, Levy Henrique

✠**SANTER, The Rt Revd Mark.** b 36. Qu Coll Cam BA 60 MA 64 Lambeth DD 99. Westcott Ho Cam. **d** 63 **p** 64 **c** 81. Tutor Cuddesdon Coll 63-67; C Cuddesdon *Ox* 63-67; Fell and Dean Clare Coll Cam 67-72; Tutor 68-72; Prin Westcott Ho Cam 73-81; Hon Can Win Cathl 78-81; Area Bp Kensington *Lon* 81-87; Bp Birm 87-02; rtd 02; Hon Asst Bp Worc from 02 and Birm from 03. *81 Clarence Road, Kings Heath, Birmingham B13 9UH* T: 0121-441 2194

SANTORINI, Melanie Yvonne. b 62. St Aid Coll Dur BA 84 Victoria Univ (BC) MA 85 Hertf Coll Ox DPhil 89. WMMTC 91. **d** 94 **p** 95. C Penn *Lich* 94-97; TV Cen Wolverhampton 97-09; rtd 10. *Pantyffynnon, Penrhyncoch, Aberystwyth SY23 3EX* M: 07748-304925

✠**SANTOS DE OLIVEIRA, The Most Revd Orlando. c** 97. Bp S Brazil from 97; Primate of Brazil 03-06. *Caxia Postal 11.510, Teresópolis, Porto Alegre, RS, 90870-970, Brazil* T: (0055) (51) 3318 6200 *or* 3318 6031 E: osoliveira@ieab.org.br

SANTRA, Jagat Ranjan. b 54. Utkal Univ BA 74 Serampore Univ BD 81 MTh 88. **d** 00 **p** 00. NSM Edin Old St Paul 00-06; Lect Union Bibl Sem Pune India from 06. *Union Biblical Seminary, PO Box 1425, Bibwewadi, Pune, India* T: (0091) (20) 2421 8670 F: 2421 5471 T: (0091) (20) 2421 1747 *or* 2421 1203
E: jagat_s@hotmail.com

SANTRAM, Philip James. b 27. MA Delhi Univ BSc 48 Serampore Univ BD 53. Bp's Coll Calcutta 49. **d** 52 **p** 54. India 52-66; Lect Bp's Coll Calcutta 61-65; R Delhi St Martin 65-66; R H Trin and Gurgaon Epiphany 65-66; Ethiopia 66-68; C Horton *Bradf* 68-71; C Whitley Ch Ch *Ox* 71-72; P Missr Tilehurst St Mary CD 72-76; V Tilehurst St Mary 76-78; R Lakefield Canada 78-82; R Chomedey-Bordeaux 82-97; rtd 97; Hon C Oakville Epiphany Canada from 00. *2336 Adirondak Trail, Oakville ON L6M 0E9, Canada* T: (001) (905) 827 6327 E: rpsantram@aol.com

SAPWELL, Mrs Lynette Lilian. b 51. Sussex Univ BEd 73 Middx Univ BA 03. NTMTC 00. **d** 03 **p** 04. NSM Rochford *Chelmsf* 03-07; P-in-c Appleton *Ox* from 07; P-in-c Besselsleigh from 07. *The Rectory, Oakesmere, Appleton, Abingdon OX13 5JS* T: (01865) 862458 E: lynsapwell@sky.com

SARALIS, Preb Christopher Herbert. b 34. Univ of Wales BA 54 St Cath Coll Ox BA 56 MA 60. Wycliffe Hall Ox. **d** 57 **p** 58. C Abergavenny St Mary w Llanwenarth Citra *Mon* 57-61; C Bridgwater St Mary w Chilton Trinity *B & W* 61-65; V Berrow 65-72; R Berrow and Breane 72-76; RD Burnham 72-76; V Minehead 76-92; RD Exmoor 80-86; Preb Wells Cathl 84-92; V Bowey Tracey SS Pet, Paul and Thos w Hennock *Ex* 92-99; rtd 99; PtO *B & W* from 99. *1 Broadway Road, Horton, Ilminster TA19 9RX* T: (01460) 52416
E: christophersaralis@talktalk.net

SARAPUK, Susan. b 59. Lon Univ BA 80 Univ of Wales PGCE 81. St Mich Coll Llan. **d** 90 **p** 97. C Morriston *S & B* 90-94; C Swansea St Pet 94-97; P-in-c Llangyfelach 97-98; V 98-02; C Sketty 02-08. *13 Edison Crescent, Clydach, Swansea SA6 5JF* T: (01792) 843521

SARGANT, John Raymond. b 38. CCC Cam BA 61 MA 70. Westcott Ho Cam 64 Harvard Div Sch 66. **d** 67 **p** 68. C Croydon St Jo *Cant* 67-72; Sec Zambia Angl Coun 72-75; P-in-c Bradford-on-Avon Ch Ch *Sarum* 76-81; V 81-90; TV Marlborough 90-03; Dioc Inter-Faith Adv 90-00; Can and Preb Sarum Cathl 92-01; rtd 03. *48 Summerhill Road, Lyme Regis DT7 3DT* T: (01297) 445922

✠**SARGEANT, The Rt Revd Frank Pilkington.** b 32. St Jo Coll Dur BA 55. Cranmer Hall Dur 57. **d** 58 **p** 59 **c** 84. C Gainsborough All SS *Linc* 58-62; C Gt Grimsby St Jas 62-66; V Hykeham 66-73; Dir In-Service Tr and Adult Educn *Bradf* 73-84; Can Res Bradf Cathl 73-77; Adn Bradf 77-84; Suff Bp Stockport *Ches* 84-94; Bp at Lambeth (Hd of Staff) *Cant* 94-99; rtd 99; Hon Asst Bp Eur 99-07; PtO *Ches* from 99. *32 Brotherton Drive, Trinity Gardens, Salford M3 6BH* T: 0161-839 7045 E: franksargeant68@hotmail.com

SARGEANTSON, Kenneth William. b 30. **d** 90 **p** 91. NSM The Marshland *Sheff* 90-93; NSM Goole 93-97; PtO 97-06; NSM The Marshland from 06; Hon Chapl Miss to Seafarers from 95. *97 High Street, Swinefleet, Goole DN14 8AH* T: (01405) 704256
E: kensargeantson@yahoo.co.uk

SARGENT, Miss Ann. b 65. **d** 98 **p** 99. C Bris St Andr Hartcliffe 98-01; P-in-c Flax Bourton *B & W* 01-09; P-in-c Barrow Gurney 01-09; P-in-c Long Ashton 05-09; R Long Ashton w Barrow Gurney and Flax Bourton from 09. *The Vicarage, 7 Church Lane, Long Ashton, Bristol BS41 9LU* T: (01275) 393109

SARGENT, Benjamin Charles. b 83. K Coll Lon BA 05 MA 07 AKC 05 Ox Univ DPhil 11. Wycliffe Hall Ox MTh 09. **d** 09 **p** 10. C Warblington w Emsworth *Portsm* 09-13; P-in-c Bransgore and Hinton Admiral *Win* from 13; Research Fell Wycliffe Hall Ox from 11. *The Vicarage, Ringwood Road, Bransgore, Christchurch BH23 8JH* T: (01425) 672850 M: 07990-695830 E: benjamin.sargent@wycliffe.ox.ac.uk *or* vicar@bransgore.org

SARGENT, Charles Edward. b 68. K Coll Lon BD 89 Leeds Univ MA 96. Coll of Resurr Mirfield 94. **d** 96 **p** 97. C Notting Dale St Clem w St Mark and St Jas *Lon* 96-00; P-in-c S Kensington St Aug 00-04; Chapl Imp Coll 00-04; Chapl Brunel Univ 04-10; PtO *S'wark* from 11. *4 Spinnakers, Pentire Avenue, Newquay TR7 1TT* T: (01637) 859934 E: charles.sargent@priest.com

SARGENT, David Gareth. b 63. Sheff Univ BA 85 St Jo Coll Dur BA 96. Cranmer Hall Dur 93. **d** 96 **p** 97. C Norbury *Ches* 96-01; V Hooton 01-06; TR Penrith w Newton Reigny and Plumpton Wall *Carl* from 06; RD Penrith from 14. *The Rectory, 3 Lamley Gardens, Penrith CA11 9LR* T: (01768) 863000
E: revdave.sargent@talk21.com

SARGENT, Mrs Janet. b 54. **d** 07 **p** 08. OLM Birchencliffe *Wakef* 07-08; OLM Birkby and Birchencliffe *Leeds* from 08. *11 Kirkwood Drive, Huddersfield HD3 3WA* T: (01484) 650390

SARGENT, Miss Philippa Mary. b 68. Oriel Coll Ox MA 94. Ripon Coll Cuddesdon 13. **d** 15. C Kempsey and Severn Stoke w Croome d'Abitot *Worc* from 15. *9 Plovers Rise, Kempsey, Worcester WR5 3SA* M: 07963-273221 E: philippa.sargent@me.com

SARGENT, Preb Richard Henry. b 24. Man Univ BA 50. Ridley Hall Cam 50. **d** 52 **p** 53. C Rusholme H Trin *Man* 52-54; C Cheadle *Ches* 54-59; V Cheadle Hulme St Andr 59-67; V Bushbury *Lich* 67-73; V Castle Church 73-89; RD Stafford 81-88; Preb Lich Cathl 87-89; rtd 89; PtO *Lich* from 90. *57 Deanshill Close, Stafford ST16 1BW* T: (01785) 605335

SARGISSON, Conrad Ralph. b 24. Keble Coll Ox BA 46 MA 50. Wells Th Coll 48. **d** 50 **p** 51. C Charlton Kings St Mary *Glouc* 50-53; C Prestbury 53-55; V St Briavels 55-58; V Lanteglos by Fowey *Truro* 58-62; V Penzance St Mary 62-73; RD Penwith 72-73; V Westbury-on-Trym H Trin *Bris* 73-79; P-in-c Blisland w St Breward *Truro* 79-83; V Mylor w Flushing 83-91; rtd 91; PtO *Heref* 91-93; P-in-c St Hilary w Perranuthnoe *Truro* 93-96; PtO from 96. *8 Halgavor Park, Bodmin PL31 1DL* T: (01208) 264938

SARMEZEY, George Arpad. b 61. Qu Mary Coll Lon BA 83 Goldsmiths' Coll Lon PGCE 86. Westcott Ho Cam 89. **d** 92 **p** 93. C Eastville St Anne w St Mark and St Thos *Bris* 92-94; C Stratton St Margaret w S Marston etc 94-97; Asst Chapl Northn Gen Hosp NHS Trust 97-00; Sen Chapl from 00. *Northampton General Hospital, Billing Road, Northampton NN1 5BD* T: (01604) 545773 *or* 634700 F: 544608 E: george.sarmezey@ngh.nhs.uk

SARUM, Archdeacon of. *See* JEANS, The Ven Alan Paul

SARVANANTHAN, Sudharshan. b 70. Trin Coll Bris 06. **d** 08 **p** 09. C Heart of Eden *Carl* 08-12; P-in-c Clifton, Dean and Mosser from 12; Network Youth Ch Ldr from 12; C Brigham, Gt Broughton and Broughton Moor *Carl* from 14. *The Vicarage, 1 Clifton Gardens, Great Clifton, Workington CA14 1TT* T: (01900) 603886 M: 07889-454428 E: rev.sudharshan@googlemail.com

SASADA, Benjamin John. b 33. EAMTC. **d** 82 **p** 83. NSM Dickleburgh, Langmere, Shimpling, Thelveton etc *Nor* 82-88; PtO *St E* from 84; NSM Diss *Nor* 88-95; P-in-c Dickleburgh, Langmere, Shimpling, Thelveton etc 95-99; rtd 99; PtO *Nor* from 99. *The Grange, Walcott Green, Diss IP22 5SS* T: (01379) 642174 E: benjamin@sasada2.freeserve.co.uk

SASSER, Howell Crawford. b 37. Maryland Univ BA 72 Geo Mason Univ Virginia MA 74 Westmr Coll Ox MTh 97. Washington Dioc Course 75. **d** 77 **p** 78. W Germany 77-80; Somalia 80-83; Cyprus 84-92; Chapl Montreux w Gstaad *Eur* 92-97; Chapl Oporto 97-05; Ab Gib 02-05; Bp's Chapl and Research Asst 05-06; rtd 06. *11944 Artery Drive, Fairfax VA 22030-6710, USA* T: (001) (703) 631 0466

SATKUNANAYAGAM, Kuhan. b 76. St Jo Coll Dur BSc 01 BA 11 Univ of E Lon MSc 06 PsychD 08. Cranmer Hall Dur 09. **d** 11 **p** 12. C Leatherhead and Mickleham *Guildf* 11-15; C Long Ditton from 15. *The Rectory, 3 Church Meadow, Long Ditton, Surbiton KT6 5EP* M: 07957-293907 T: (020) 8398 1583 E: kuhan@dunelm.org.uk

SATTERLY, Gerald Albert. b 34. Lon Univ BA 56 Ex Univ Hon BA. Wycliffe Hall Ox 58. **d** 60 **p** 61. C Southborough St Pet *Roch* 60-63; C S Lyncombe *B & W* 63-66; V Sheff St Barn 66-69; R Adwick-le-Street 69-73; V Awre and Blakeney *Glouc* 73-82; P-in-c Newnham 80-82; V Newnham w Awre and Blakeney 82-90; R Instow *Ex* 90-98; V Westleigh 90-98; rtd 98; PtO *Ex* from 98. *31 Gracey Court, Woodland Road, Broadclyst, Exeter EX5 3GA*

SAUL, Norman Stanley. b 30. St Aid Birkenhead 51. **d** 54 **p** 55. C S Shore H Trin *Blackb* 54-57; C Poulton-le-Fylde 57-59; PC Freckleton 59-66; V Blackb St Luke 66-68; V Barton 68-72; V Foxdale *S & M* 72-77; V Maughold 77-90; CF (ACF) 80-86; rtd 90; PtO *Blackb* from 90. *15 Croft Meadow, Bamber Bridge, Preston PR5 8HX* T: (01772) 314475

SAUNDERS, Alan William. b 67. St Mellitus Coll. **d** 13 **p** 14. C Halliwell St Pet *Man* from 13. *9 Capitol Close, Bolton BL1 6LU* T: (01204) 219617 M: 07767-643444 E: alan@alongside.me.uk

SAUNDERS, Andrew Vivian. b 44. Leeds Univ BA 65. Coll of Resurr Mirfield 66. **d** 68 **p** 69. C Goodmayes St Paul *Chelmsf* 68-71; C Horfield H Trin *Bris* 71-75; C Oldland 75-77; Ind Chapl *B & W* 77-80; P-in-c Buckland Dinham w Elm, Orchardleigh etc 77-78; P-in-c Buckland Dinham 78-80; V Westfield 80-90; R Clutton w Cameley 90-99; C Christchurch *Win* 99-05; rtd 05; PtO *B & W* from 06. *8 Mill House Court, Willow Vale, Frome BA11 1BG* T: (01373) 467683 E: andrew@asaunders15.fsnet.co.uk

SAUNDERS, Barry. *See* SAUNDERS, John Barry

SAUNDERS, Brian Gerald. b 28. Pemb Coll Cam BA 49 MA 53. Cuddesdon Coll 63. **d** 66 **p** 67. NSM Gt Berkhamsted *St Alb* 66-87; P-in-c Lt Gaddesden 87-92; rtd 92; PtO *Ox* 92-94; *St Alb* 92-02; *Pet* from 95; *Linc* from 01; Hon C Newton Longville w Stoke Hammond and Whaddon *Ox* 94-01. *2 Bruce Close, Lincoln LN2 1SL* T: (01522) 523193

SAUNDERS, Canon Bruce Alexander. b 47. St Cath Coll Cam BA 68 MA 72. Cuddesdon Coll 68. **d** 71 **p** 72. C Westbury-on-Trym H Trin *Bris* 71-74; Hon C Clifton St Paul 74-78; Asst Chapl Bris Univ 74-78; TV Fareham H Trin *Portsm* 78-84; TR Mortlake w E Sheen *S'wark* 84-97; RD Richmond and Barnes 89-94; Can Missr for Ch in Soc 97-03; Can Res S'wark Cathl 03-14; Sub Dean 12-14; C-in-c Bermondsey St Hugh CD *S'wark* 03-14; rtd 14. *10 Reedley Road, Bristol BS9 3ST*

SAUNDERS, David. b 28. Keble Coll Ox BA 50 MA 59. Cuddesdon Coll 51. **d** 53 **p** 54. C Mexborough *Sheff* 53-56; C Sheff St Cuth 56-60; V New Bentley 60-67; V Grimsby All SS *Linc* 67-78; V Caistor w Clixby 78-88; P-in-c Grasby 78-94; Chapl Caistor Hosp 78-94; P-in-c Searby w Owmby *Linc* 79-94; V Dunholme 88-92; P-in-c Welton and Dunholme w Scothern 92-94; rtd 94; PtO *Linc* from 94. *2 Oundle Close, Washingborough, Lincoln LN4 1DR* T: (01522) 793164

SAUNDERS, Gareth John McKeith. b 73. St Andr Univ BD 93 Edin Univ MTh 99. TISEC 99. **d** 99 **p** 00. C Inverness St Andr *Mor* 99-03; C Edin St Salvador and Edin Gd Shep 03-06; LtO *St And* from 07; Hon C St Andrews All SS from 10. *45 Lindsay Berwick Place, Anstruther KY10 3YP* T: (01333) 310140 M: 07732-356123 E: gareth@garethjmsaunders.co.uk

SAUNDERS, Geoffrey David. b 51. Bris Univ BSc 73. **d** 01 **p** 02. OLM Rockland St Mary w Hellington, Bramerton etc *Nor* 01-07; NSM 07-11; rtd 11; PtO *Nor* from 12. *13 The Street, Rockland St Mary, Norwich NR14 7ER* T: (01508) 538550 E: geoffsaunders@waitrose.com

SAUNDERS, Graham Howard. b 53. Hatf Poly BSc 77. Trin Coll Bris BA 86. **d** 86 **p** 87. C Birm St Martin w Bordesley St Andr 86-89; C Olton 89-96; TV Bedminster *Bris* 96-02; P-in-c Farnham Royal w Hedgerley *Ox* 02-08; R from 08. *The Rectory, Victoria Road, Farnham Common, Slough SL2 3NJ* T: (01753) 643233 F: 644130

SAUNDERS, Ivor John. b 37. Wolv Poly CQSW 81. **d** 04 **p** 05. OLM Wolverhampton St Jude *Lich* from 04. *34 Wrottesley Road, Wolverhampton WV6 8SF* T: (01902) 751162 E: ivor.wendy@talktalk.net

SAUNDERS, James Benedict John. b 72. St Aid Coll Dur BA 93 St Jo Coll Cam PhD 97 St Jo Coll Dur BA 00. Cranmer Hall Dur 98. **d** 01 **p** 02. C Sole Bay *St E* 01-04; P-in-c Teigh w Whissendine and Market Overton *Pet* 04-09; Asst Chapl HM Pris Ashwell 04-07; Chapl Uppingham Sch from 09. *Pentire, 48 High Street West, Uppingham, Oakham LE15 9QD* T: (01572) 829934 E: jbjs@uppingham.co.uk

SAUNDERS, Mrs Joan Mary (Jo). b 44. Univ Coll Lon BA 66 PGCE 67. EAMTC 00. **d** 03 **p** 04. NSM Gt and Lt Casterton w Pickworth and Tickencote *Pet* 03-05; P-in-c from 09; P-in-c Castle Bytham w Creeton *Linc* 05-09; Hon C Ketton, Collyweston, Easton-on-the-Hill etc *Pet* from 09. *Mellstock, Bourne Road, Essendine, Stamford PE9 4LH* T: (01780) 480479 E: revjosaunders@live.co.uk

SAUNDERS, John Barry. b 40. Chich Th Coll. **d** 83 **p** 84. C St Breoke *Truro* 83-84; C St Breoke and Egloshayle 84-87; V Treverbyn 87-96; RD St Austell 91-96; V Perranzabuloe 96-03; rtd 03; PtO *Truro* from 04. *48 Cormorant Drive, St Austell PL25 3BA* T: (01726) 71994

SAUNDERS, Canon John Michael. b 40. Brasted Th Coll 66 Clifton Th Coll 68. **d** 70 **p** 71. C Homerton St Luke *Lon* 70-74; C Bushey 74-81; P-in-c Horsmonden *Roch* 91-97; Area Sec (SE England) SAMS 91-97; V Gillingham St Mark *Roch* 97-08; rtd 08. *The Rectory, Drayton Road, Newton Longville, Milton Keynes MK17 0BH* T: (01908) 647694 E: jandjsaunders@aol.com

SAUNDERS, Kenneth John. b 35. Linc Th Coll 73. **d** 75 **p** 76. C Boultham *Linc* 75-79; V Swinderby 79-87; V Cherry Willingham w Greetwell 87-95; P-in-c S Kelsey Gp 95-98; P-in-c N Kelsey 95-98; P-in-c Kelsey Gp 98-00; rtd 00; PtO *Linc* from 01. *Pew End, 17 Wentworth Drive, Dunholme, Lincoln LN2 3UH* T: (01673) 862930

SAUNDERS, Malcolm Walter Mackenzie. b 34. Em Coll Cam BA 58 MA 62. Wycliffe Hall Ox 58. **d** 60 **p** 61. C Northampton St Giles *Pet* 60-63; C Northampton St Alb 63-66; V Corby St Columba 66-84; Nat Dir Evang Explosion 84-91; V Ketton *Pet* 91-92; R Ketton w Tinwell 92-01; rtd 01; PtO *Pet* from 01. *35 Main Street, Barrowden, Oakham LE15 8EQ* T: (01572) 747036 E: malcom.saunders@squiffle.net

SAUNDERS, Mrs Margaret Rose. b 49. Newnham Coll Cam BA 71 St Jo Coll York PGCE 72. St Alb Minl Tr Scheme 85. **d** 88 **p** 94. Hon Par Dn Gt Berkhamsted *St Alb* 88-90; Hon Chapl

Asst Gt Ormond Street Hosp for Sick Children Lon 88-90; Asst Chapl Aylesbury Vale HA 90-92; Chapl Milton Keynes Gen NHS Trust 92-98; Chapl Milton Keynes Community NHS Trust 92-98; C Newport Pagnell w Lathbury and Moulsoe Ox 98-01; TV Grantham Linc 01-02; P-in-c Grantham, Manthorpe 02-04; Chapl United Lincs Hosps NHS Trust 01-14; rtd 14; Gen Preacher Linc from 05. 2 Bruce Close, Lincoln LN2 1SL T: (01522) 523193 E: margar3t.saunders@gmail.com

SAUNDERS, Mark Richard. See VASEY-SAUNDERS, Mark Richard

SAUNDERS, Martin Paul. b 54. K Coll Lon BD 76 AKC 76 Univ of Northumbria at Newc DipSW 96. Westcott Ho Cam 77. d 78 p 79. C Seaton Hirst Newc 78-81; Regional Chapl Hong Kong Miss to Seamen 81; C Egglescliffe Dur 81-82; Chapl to Arts and Recreation 81-84; C Jarrow Dur 82-84; TV 84-88; V Southwick St Columba 88-94; PtO from 94. 55 The Meadows, Burnopfield, Newcastle upon Tyne NE16 6QW T: (01207) 271242 M: 07710-325197 E: martinsaunders@derwentheights.freeserve.co.uk

SAUNDERS, Martyn Leonard John. b 69. Magd Coll Cam MEng 92. Wycliffe Hall Ox BA 97. d 98 p 99. C Quinton Road W St Boniface Birm 98-02; TV Barnsbury Lon 02-10; V Chatham St Phil and St Jas Roch from 10. The Vicarage, 139 Sussex Drive, Walderslade, Chatham ME5 0NR T: (01634) 861108

SAUNDERS, Michael. b 38. Charing Cross Hosp Medical Sch MB, BS 62 FRCPEd 74 FRCP 78 MSOSc 84. NEOC 82. d 84 p 85. LtO York 84-92; Tutor NEOC 84-93; NSM Stokesley York 92-93; C Ripon Cathl 93-95; PtO York from 93; NSM Gt and Lt Ouseburn w Marton cum Grafton etc Ripon 95-02; NSM Masham and Healey Leeds from 02. College Grove, 2 College Lane, Masham, Ripon HG4 4HE T: (01765) 688306 M: 07711-567160 E: michael.saunders@btinternet.com

SAUNDERS, Michael Walter. b 58. Grey Coll Dur BSc 79 CChem MRSC 84. Wycliffe Hall Ox 86. d 89 p 90. C Deane Man 89-93; TV Eccles 93-02; Chapl Eccles Sixth Form Coll 96-02; Dioc Adv on Evang Man 98-02; C Yateley and Eversley Win 02-06; P-in-c Darby Green 05-06; V Darby Green and Eversley from 06. The Rectory, Glaston Hill Road, Eversley, Hook RG27 0LX T: 0118-973 6595 E: mikethevicar@thesaunders.plus.com

SAUNDERS, Moira Ruth Forbes. b 76. Birm Univ BA 99. Ridley Hall Cam 02. d 04 p 05. C Welling Roch 04-08; NSM Aldershot H Trin Guildf 09-12; PtO 13-15; V Hazelwell Birm from 15. St Mary Magdalen's Vicarage, 316 Vicarage Road, Kings Heath, Birmingham B14 7NN E: therevsemail@gmail.com or hazelwellvicar@gmail.com

SAUNDERS, Canon Reginald Frederick. b 15. St And NSM Tr Scheme 76. d 79 p 79. NSM Perth St Ninian St And from 79; NSM Stanley from 79; Hon Can St Ninian's Cathl Perth from 04. Kincarrathie House, Pitcullen Crescent, Perth PH2 7XH

SAUNDERS, Canon Richard Charles Hebblethwaite. b 17. Qu Coll Ox BA 40 MA 42. Westcott Ho Cam 41. d 42 p 43. C Darnall Sheff 42-45; India 46-49; V Thornton-le-Street w Thornton-le-Moor etc York 49-52; V Eastwood Sheff 52-62; V Bris St Ambrose Whitehall 62-75; P-in-c Easton All Hallows 65-68; TR E Bris 75-77; P-in-c Colerne 77-82; P-in-c N Wraxall 77-82; RD Chippenham 80-82; Hon Can Bris Cathl 82; rtd 82; Hon C Honiton, Gittisham, Combe Raleigh, Monkton etc Ex 85-12. 28 Yonder Close, Ottery St Mary EX11 1HE T: (01404) 811049 E: rsaunders17@yahoo.com

SAUNDERS, Richard George. b 54. BNC Ox BA 76 MA 81. St Jo Coll Nottm 82. d 85 p 86. C Barrow St Mark Carl 85-89; C Cranham Park Chelmsf 89-97; TV Kinson Sarum 97-00; TR Kinson and W Howe 00-12; V Sheet Portsm from 12. Sheet Vicarage, 2 Pulens Lane, Petersfield GU31 4DB T: (01730) 263673

SAUNDERS, Ronald. b 37. St Pet Coll Birm CertEd 62 Memorial Univ Newfoundland CertEd 80 Columbia Univ MA 82 PhD 87 ACP 67. Sarum Th Coll 69. d 68 p 70. LtO Malawi 68-70; C Blantyre 71-72; C Kensington St Mary Abbots w St Geo Lon 72-73; C Bournemouth St Fran Win 73-75; I Twillingate Canada 75-76; LtO 77-81; C Gt Marlow Ox 81-82; Area Org Leprosy Miss 82-85; V Penycae St As 85-87; TV Wrexham 87-89; LtO Ox 90-91; Chapl Morden Coll Blackheath 91-97; Master Wyggeston's Hosp Leic 97-03; P-in-c Nerja and Almuñécar Eur 05-07. Barrio San Isidro 92, 18830 Huescar (Granada), Spain E: ron1937uk@hotmail.co.uk

SAUNDERS, Sheila Lilian. b 42. d 03 p 04. OLM Walworth St Pet S'wark 03-07; NSM 07-12; rtd 12; PtO S'wark from 12. 9 Wooler Street, London SE17 2ED T: (020) 7252 5045 E: sheila.saunders3@btopenworld.com

SAUNDERS (née CORNWALL), Valerie Cecilia. b 40. Bedf Coll Lon BSc 62 Lon Inst of Educn PGCE 63. Scottish Chs Open Coll 96. d 03 p 04. NSM Dingwall Mor from 03; NSM Strathpeffer from 03. Chessbury, 12 Firthview, Dingwall IV15 9PF T: (01349) 865445 M: 07747-066993 E: valeriestj@btopenworld.com

SAUNDERS, Ms Wendy Jennifer. b 49. S'wark Ord Course 86. d 95 p 96. C Thamesmead S'wark 95-98; P-in-c Eltham St Sav from 98. St Saviour's Vicarage, 98 Middle Park Avenue, London SE9 5JH T: (020) 8850 6829 M: 07802-603754 E: wendy.saunders@sunday.surfaid.org

SAUNT, James Peter Robert. b 36. Chich Th Coll 73. d 75 p 76. C Portland All SS w St Pet Sarum 75-78; P-in-c Bratton 78-81; V 81-94; Chapl HM Pris Erlestoke 80-94; P-in-c Oldbury Sarum 94-99; R 99-01; rtd 01; PtO Sarum from 02. Elms, Waddon, Portesham, Weymouth DT3 4ER T: (01305) 871553

SAUSBY, John Michael. b 39. AKC. d 63 p 64. C Crosland Moor Wakef 63-65; C Halifax St Jo Bapt 65-67; V Birkby 67-77; V Holmfirth 77-89; TR Upper Holme Valley 89-01; rtd 01; PtO Leeds from 04. 15 River Holme View, Brockholes, Huddersfield HD9 7BP T: (01484) 667228

SAVAGE, Andrew Michael. b 67. Wye Coll Lon BSc 89 Cranfield Inst of Tech MSc 91. Wycliffe Hall Ox 93. d 96 p 97. C Ecclesall Sheff 96-99; TV Kirk Ella and Willerby York 99-06; Chapl Kingham Hill Sch from 06. Kingham Hill School, Kingham, Chipping Norton OX7 6TH T: (01608) 658999

SAVAGE, Canon Christopher Marius. b 46. Hull Univ MA 94 FRSA 99. Bps' Coll Cheshunt 66 Qu Coll Birm 68. d 70 p 71. C Battersea St Luke S'wark 70-75; TV Newbury Ox 75-80; R Lich St Mary w St Mich 80-85; V Chessington Guildf 85-91; Ind Chapl Win 91-00; Chapl Basingstoke Coll of Tech 91-00; V Newc Ch Ch w St Ann 00-07; Team Ldr Chapl to People at Work in Cam Ely 07-12; rtd 12; PtO Sarum from 12. 22 Burcombe Lane, Wilton, Salisbury SP2 0ES M: 07788-741489

SAVAGE, Helen. b 55. Birm Univ BA 76 Dur Univ BA 82 MA 90 Newc Univ MLitt 83 Dur Univ PhD 05. Cranmer Hall Dur 80. d 83 p 84. C Newc St Gabr 83-86; Adult Educn Adv 86-94; V Bedlington 94-00; PtO 09-15; V Slaley, Healey and Whittonstall from 15; R Blanchland w Hunstanworth and Edmundbyers etc from 15. Slaley Vicarage, Hexham NE47 0AA T: (01434) 673609 E: helensavage1@gmail.com

SAVAGE, Mrs Hilary Linda. b 48. RGN 71 RM 86. WMMTC 89. d 92 p 94. C Quinton Road W St Boniface Birm 92-96; P-in-c Edgbaston SS Mary and Ambrose 96-01; V 01-02; TV Cramlington Newc 02-10; R Eckington and Ridgeway Derby 10-14; rtd 14; PtO Ban from 14. Ein ty Noddfa, 4 Belle Vue, Ffestiniog, Blaenau Ffestiniog LL41 4NU T: (01766) 762383 E: hilarysavage@hotmail.com

SAVAGE, Mrs Jennifer Anne. b 52. CertEd 73. NOC 96. d 99 p 00. C Haworth Bradf 99-02; R 02-09; P-in-c Cross Roads cum Lees 07-09; P-in-c Thornton in Lonsdale w Burton in Lonsdale 09-13; P-in-c Steeton Leeds from 13. The Vicarage, 2 Halsteads Way, Steeton, Keighley BD20 6SN T: (01535) 657537 E: revdjenny@aol.com or jenny.savage@bradford.anglican.org

SAVAGE, John. b 48. Bris Univ BEd 76. SWMTC 94. d 97 p 98. C Falmouth K Chas Truro 97-00; P-in-c Mabe 00-13; Chapl Miss to Seafarers 00-07; rtd 13. 1 Willow Close, Mylor Bridge, Falmouth TR11 5SG T: (01326) 259739

SAVAGE, Jonathan Mark. b 57. Kingston Poly BSc 79 MSc 89 Roehampton Inst PGCE 80. Ridley Hall Cam 94. d 96 p 97. C Ely 96-99; TV Huntingdon 99-07; C Gt w Lt Stukeley 04-07; TV Huntingdon w the Stukeleys 07-12; Chapl HM Pris Lowdham Grange from 12. HM Prison Lowdham Grange, Lowdham, Nottingham NG14 7DA T: 0115-966 9200

SAVAGE, Michael Atkinson. b 33. St Pet Hall Ox BA 57 MA 61. Tyndale Hall Bris 57. d 59 p 60. C Rugby St Matt Cov 59-62; C Welling Roch 62-66; V Bowling St Steph Bradf 66-73; V Ben Rhydding 73-92; RD Otley 87-92; TR Quidenham Nor 92-97; R Quidenham Gp 97-99; rtd 99; PtO Leeds from 00. 42 Hollins Lane, Utley, Keighley BD20 6LT T: (01535) 606790 E: damsav@talktalk.net

SAVAGE, Paul Andrew. b 78. Univ of Wales (Ban) BA 00. St Jo Coll Nottm 10. d 12 p 13. C Bawtry w Austerfield and Misson S'well 12-15; C Bawtry w Austerfield, Misson, Everton and Mattersey from 15. 12 Dalton Grove, Bawtry, Doncaster DN10 6XS T: (01302) 719727 E: pashfish@gmail.com

SAVAGE, Paul James. b 58. Liv Univ BA 81. Wycliffe Hall Ox 88. d 91 p 92. C Litherland St Phil Liv 91-94; CMS from 94. CMS, PO Box 1799, Oxford OX4 9BN T: 08456-201799

SAVEGE, Timothy Michael. b 38. d 00 p 01. OLM Blyth Valley St E 00-05; OLM Bury St Edmunds St Mary 05-09; PtO Chelmsf from 09. 2 Chequer Square, Bury St Edmunds IP33 1QZ T: (01284) 728041 E: tim.savege@btinternet.com

SAVIDGE, Graham John. b 47. Univ of Wales (Ban) BSc 69 PhD 78. CITC 89. d 92 p 94. LtO D & D 92-10; NSM Down Cathl 94-97; NSM Lecale Gp 97-10; PtO from 10. 7 Cedar Grove, Ardglass, Downpatrick BT30 7UE T: (028) 4484 1501

SAVIGEAR, Miss Elfrida Beatrice. b 49. Wye Coll Lon BSc 71 Bath Univ MSc 85 Lambeth STh 94. Ridley Hall Cam 91. d 93 p 94. C Ross w Brampton Abbotts, Bridstow, Peterstow etc

Heref 93-97; P-in-c Butlers Marston and the Pillertons w Ettington Cov 97-99; P-in-c Alderminster and Halford 97-99; P-in-c Bicknoller w Crowcombe and Sampford Brett B & W 99-00; P-in-c Stogumber w Nettlecombe and Monksilver 99-00; R Quantock Towers 00-08; C Darlington H Trin Dur 08-11; rtd 11; Hon C Beaminster Area Sarum from 11. Manderley, Dodhams Lane, Bridport DT6 3DY T: (01308) 424031 E: elfsavigear@btinternet.com

SAVILL, David. b 27. TD 69 and Bar 75. Em Coll Cam BA 49 MA 52. Ridley Hall Cam 50. d 52 p 53. Chapl St E Cathl 52-54; C St Martin-in-the-Fields Lon 54-57; V Sunbury 57-67; V Heston 67-73; Hon C Mettingham w Ilketshall St John St E 73-79; Hon C Mettingham 79-80; Chapl Felixstowe Coll 80-90; rtd 90; PtO B & W 90-11; St E from 11. 14 St Anne's Close, Beccles NR34 9SD T: (01502) 716380 E: david.savill886@btinternet.com

SAVILLE, Andrew. b 66. Worc Coll Ox BA 92 MA 92 Cov Univ PhD 00. Wycliffe Hall Ox. d 95 p 96. C Tonbridge SS Pet and Paul Roch 95-99; NSM Bromley Ch Ch 99-03; Dir Bromley Chr Tr Cen 99-03; C Fordham Chelmsf 03-10; V Laleham Lon from 10; Ad Spelthorne from 14. The Vicarage, The Broadway, Laleham, Staines TW18 1SB T: (01784) 455524 E: andy@savilles.org.uk

SAVILLE, Canon Edward Andrew. b 47. Leeds Univ CertEd 70 Open Univ BA 75. Carl Dioc Tr Inst. d 90 p 91. C Accrington St Jo w Huncoat Blackb 90-93; C Standish 93-95; V Brierfield 95-09; P-in-c 09-10; Hon C 10-13; AD Pendle 98-05 and from 13; Lead Officer Dioc Bd for Soc Resp from 09; Hon Can Blackb Cathl from 11. The Vicarage, 5 Reedley Farm Close, Reedley, Burnley BB10 2RB T/F: (01282) 613235 M: 07912-227144 E: ed.saville@blackburn.anglican.org

SAVILLE (née McCULLAGH), Mrs Elspeth Jane Alexandra. b 68. Man Univ BSc 90. Wycliffe Hall Ox BTh 95. d 95 p 96. C Huddersfield H Trin Wakef 95-98; NSM Tonbridge SS Pet and Paul Roch 98-99; NSM Bromley Ch Ch 99-03; NSM Fordham Chelmsf 03-07. The Vicarage, The Broadway, Laleham, Staines TW18 1SB T: (01784) 455524

SAVILLE, Mrs Margaret. b 46. SWMTC 93. d 94 p 95. C Over St Chad Ches 94-98; V Crewe All SS and St Paul 98-05; P-in-c Helsby and Dunham-on-the-Hill 05-12; V 12; rtd 12; Hon C Devoran Truro 12-15; Hon C Feock 12-15. Address temp unknown T: (01872) 863116 E: thesavilles@tiscali.co.uk

SAWLE, Martin. b 49. Dundee Univ LLB 70 Solicitor 74. NOC 87. d 90 p 91. NSM Longton Blackb 90-92; P-in-c Hoghton 92-04; PtO from 04. 11 Newtown, Kelvedon, Colchester CO5 9PB E: martin@sawleandco.com

SAWREY, Paul Andrew. b 79. d 12 p 13. Pioneer Min King's Cross Lon from 12. KXC Office, Ground Floor, York House, 207-221 Pentonville Road, London N1 9UZ T: (020) 3432 5396 E: paul@kxc.org.uk

SAWYER, Andrew William. b 49. AKC 71 St Aug Coll Cant 71. d 72 p 73. C Farnham Guildf 72-75; C Dawlish Ex 75-78; R Colkirk w Oxwick, Whissonsett and Horningtoft Nor 78-82; R Colkirk w Oxwick w Pattesley, Whissonsett etc 82-90; V Hungerford and Denford Ox 90-15; rtd 15. 22 Lowdale Lane, Sleights, Whitby YO22 5BU T: (01947) 229123

SAWYER, Derek Claude. b 33. ALCD 58. d 58 p 59. C Kirby Muxloe Leic 58-60; C Braunstone 60-65; R Vacoas St Paul Mauritius 65-68; V Knighton St Mich Leic 68-82; Chapl Kifissia Eur 82; LtO Glouc 85-87; V Glouc St Aldate 87-01; rtd 01; R Capisterre w Dieppe St Kitts-Nevis 01-08; LtO 09; P-in-c Roseau w Portsmouth Dominica 09-11. Rawlins Ground, St Paul's Village, St Kitts, St Kitts and Nevis T: (001) (869) 466 2773 E: derekcsawyer@gmail.com

SAWYER, James Thomas Lawrence. b 66. ERMC 12. d 15. NSM Baldock w Bygrave and Weston St Alb from 15. 53 Bearton Road, Hitchin SG5 1UF T: (01462) 435437

SAX, Ms Katharine Margaret. b 50. Ripon Coll Cuddesdon. d 03 p 06. NSM Pokesdown All SS and Southbourne St Chris Win 04-05; C Swaythling 06-09; Ecum Officer (Wilts Area) Sarum 09-11; P-in-c Churchill and Langford B & W from 11. Park View, Maysmead Lane, Langford, Bristol BS40 5HX T: (01934) 862180 M: 07733-442476 E: kate@kinkiizi.fsnet.co.uk

✠SAXBEE, The Rt Revd John Charles. b 46. Bris Univ BA 68 St Jo Coll Dur PhD 74. Cranmer Hall Dur 68. d 72 p 73. C Compton Gifford Ex 72-77; P-in-c Weston Mill 77-80; V 80-81; TV Cen Ex 81-87; Jt Dir SWMTC 81-92; Preb Ex Cathl 88-92; Adn Ludlow Heref 92-01; Preb Heref Cathl 92-01; P-in-c Wistanstow 92-94; P-in-c Acton Scott 92-94; Suff Bp Ludlow 94-01; Bp Linc 01-11; rtd 11; PtO St D from 11. 22 Shelley Road, Priory Park, Haverfordwest SA61 1RX T: (01437) 768918

SAXBY, Canon Martin Peter. b 52. St Jo Coll Dur BA 77. Cranmer Hall Dur 74. d 78 p 79. C Peckham St Mary Magd S'wark 78-81; C Ramsey Ely 81-84; P-in-c Mattishall w

Mattishall Burgh Nor 84-89; P-in-c Welborne 84-89; P-in-c Yaxham 84-89; R Mattishall w Mattishall Burgh, Welborne etc 89-90; V Rugby St Matt Cov 90-07; V Rugby W 08-13; RD Rugby 06-13; Healthy Churches Development Mentor from 13; Hon Can Cov Cathl from 11; PtO from 13. St George's Vicarage, St John's Avenue, Rugby CV22 5HR F: 07053-480079 T: (024) 7652 1323 M: 07944-670288 E: martin.saxby@covcofe.org

SAXBY, Canon Steven Michael Paul. b 70. Fitzw Coll Cam BA 98 MA 02 Heythrop Coll Lon MA 05 Univ Coll Lon MA 08. Aston Tr Scheme 92 Linc Th Coll 94 Westcott Ho Cam 95. d 98 p 01. C E Ham w Upton Park and Forest Gate Chelmsf 98-00; C Barking St Marg w St Patr 00-02; Waltham Forest Deanery Development Worker 02-07; NSM Walthamstow 02-03; V Walthamstow St Pet 03-09; P-in-c Walthamstow St Barn and St Jas Gt 09-14; V from 14; P-in-c Walthamstow St Sav 11-13; RD Waltham Forest 07-12; Exec Officer Lon Chs Soc Action from 13; Hon Can Manila Philippines from 14. St Barnabas' Vicarage, St Barnabas Road, London E17 8JZ T: (020) 8520 5323 E: stevensaxby@btinternet.com

SAXTON, James. b 54. Lanc Univ BEd 77 Hull Univ MEd 85. Linc Th Coll 84. d 86 p 87. C Moor Allerton Ripon 86-90; C Knaresborough 90-92; TV Seacroft 92-95; V Ireland Wood 95-00; TV Becontree S Chelmsf 02-09; C Camberwell St Geo S'wark 09-12; Chapl S Lon and Maudsley NHS Foundn Trust 09-12; rtd 12. 11 Stannier Way, Watnall, Nottingham NG16 1GL E: james.saxton@talktalk.net

SAYER, Penelope Jane. b 59. Newc Univ BA 80 Open Univ BA 93. SEITE 04. d 07 p 08. NSM Upper St Leonards St Jo Chich 07-10; TR Becontree S Chelmsf from 10. St Alban's Vicarage, Vincent Road, Dagenham RM9 6AL T: (020) 8595 1042 M: 07729-372996 E: penny.st.john@btinternet.com

SAYER, Simon Benedict. b 59. Man Univ BA 07. St Steph Ho Ox MTh 11. d 10 p 11. C Hollinwood and Limeside Man 10-13; V Tipton St Jo Lich from 13; CMP from 13. St John's Vicarage, Upper Church Lane, Tipton DY4 9ND M: 07754-100845 T: 0121-679 7510 E: simonsayer@me.com

SAYER, Vivienne Rosina. d 15. C Newcastle Emlyn and Llandyfriog etc St D from 15. Llys Tefi, 9 Heol y Gof, Newcastle Emlyn SA38 9HN E: vrsayer@yahoo.co.uk*

SAYER, Canon William Anthony John. b 37. St Mich Coll Llan 60. d 64 p 65. C Gorleston St Andr Nor 64-67; P-in-c Witton w Ridlington 67-71; P-in-c Honing w Crostwight 67-71; V Bacton w Edingthorpe 67-71; CF 71-84; Miss to Seafarers from 84; R Holkham w Egmere w Warham, Wells and Wighton Nor 84-02; RD Burnham and Walsingham 87-92; Hon Can Nor Cathl 97-02; rtd 02; PtO Nor from 02. Greenway Lodge, Mill Road, Wells-next-the-Sea NR23 1RF T: (01328) 711224

SAYERS, Karen Jane. See GARDINER, Karen Jane

SAYERS, Simon Philip. b 59. Cam Univ MA 81. Oak Hill Th Coll 83. d 85 p 86. C Alperton Lon 85-89; C Hornsey Rise Whitehall Park Team 89-90; TV 90-96; Min Panshanger CD St Alb 96-02; R Warblington w Emsworth Portsm from 02; Hon Can Portsm Cathl from 14. The Rectory, 20 Church Path, Emsworth PO10 7DP T: (01243) 372428 E: simonsayers@hotmail.com

SAYERS, Susan. See HILL, Susan

SAYLE, Philip David. b 61. Nottm Univ BA 98. St Jo Coll Nottm 92. d 94 p 95. C Helston and Wendron Truro 94-97; R St Stephen in Brannel 97-00; R Kenwyn w St Allen 00-06; V Upton Ascension Ches from 06. 49 Heath Road, Upton, Chester CH2 1HT T: (01244) 381181 E: parish_sayle@me.com

SAYWELL, Philip. b 33. Linc Th Coll 57. d 60 p 61. C Stepney St Dunstan and All SS Lon 60-63; C Calstock Truro 63-66; V Lanteglos by Fowey 66-73; Iran 73-77; R Cockley Cley w Gooderstone Nor 78-81; V Didlington 78-81; R Gt and Lt Cressingham w Threxton 78-81; R Hilborough w Bodney 78-81; R Oxborough w Foulden and Caldecote 78-81; UAE 81-84; PtO Chich 84-88; Nat Co-ord (UK) SOMA UK 85-88; rtd 93; PtO B & W from 11. Riverside, Exford, Minehead TA24 7PX T: (01643) 831619 E: riverside@psaywell.plus.com

SCAIFE, Andrew. b 50. Ex Coll Ox BA 73 MA 76. Wycliffe Hall Ox 74. d 77 p 78. C Everton St Geo Liv 77-81; P-in-c Liv St Mich 81; TV St Luke in the City 81-86; V Litherland St Phil 86-96; Sen Chapl Cheshire and Wirral Partnerships NHS Trust from 96. Arrowe Park Hospital, Upton, Wirral CH49 5PE T: 0151-632 0646 or 678 5111 ext 2275 E: andrew.scaife@whnt.nhs.uk

SCAMMAN (née BEWES), Mrs Helen Catherine. b 71. Leeds Univ BA 94 York Univ PGCE 95 Cam Univ BA 01. Ridley Hall Cam 99. d 02 p 03. C Win Ch Ch 02-06; NSM 06-07; PtO Ely 07-10; Blackb 10-14; NSM Lancaster St Thos from 14. St Thomas's Vicarage, 33 Belle Vue Terrace, Lancaster LA1 4TY T: (01524) 590410 E: helenscamman@yahoo.co.uk

SCAMMAN, Jonathan Leitch. b 73. St Andr Univ MA 96 Ex Coll Ox MPhil 98 Cam Univ BA 01. Ridley Hall Cam 99. **d** 02 **p** 03. C Win Ch Ch 02-07; C Cambridge St Barn *Ely* 07-10; P-in-c Lancaster St Thos *Blackb* 10-11; V from 11. *St Thomas's Vicarage, 33 Belle Vue Terrace, Lancaster LA1 4TY* T: (01524) 590410 E: scampersons@yahoo.com

SCAMMAN, Peter Fletcher. b 80. SS Hild & Bede Coll Dur MEng 03. Oak Hill Th Coll BA 09. **d** 10 **p** 11. C Ox St Andr 10-14; C Fulwood *Sheff* from 14. *18 Fulney Road, Sheffield S11 7EW* M: 07917-714939 E: petescamman@hotmail.com

SCAMMELL, Frank. b 56. Cam Univ MA. St Jo Coll Nottm BA 83. **d** 82 **p** 83. C Stapenhill w Cauldwell *Derby* 82-86; TV Swanage and Studland *Sarum* 86-92; Min Southgate LEP *St E* 92-03; V Stoughton *Guildf* from 03; RD Guildf from 11. *Stoughton Vicarage, 3 Shepherds Lane, Guildford GU2 9SJ* T: (01483) 560560 E: frankpippa@hotmail.com

SCANLAN, Helen Tracy. b 66. Dioc OLM tr scheme 06. **d** 09 **p** 10. NSM Heaton Reddish *Man* 09-11; C Heatons 11-12; TV from 12. *6 Glenfield Road, Stockport SK4 2QP* T: 0161-432 2989 E: helen.scanlan@btinternet.com

SCANLON, Geoffrey Edward Leyshon. b 44. Coll of Resurr Mirfield. **d** 76 **p** 77. C Beamish *Dur* 76-79; C-in-c Bishopwearmouth St Mary V w St Pet CD 79-81; V Laurens Epiphany USA 81-85; V Columbia St Dav 85-87; R Danville H Trin 87-09; rtd 09. *2910 Stone Creek Boulevard, Urbana IL 61802-9420, USA* T: (001) 217) 344 1174

SCANTLEBURY, James Stanley. b 48. St Jo Coll Dur BA 69 Heythrop Coll Lon MTh 80. Westcott Ho Cam 70. **d** 72 **p** 73. C Upperby St Jo *Carl* 72-75; C Guildf H Trin w St Mary 75-77; Order of St Aug 77-86; Chapl Austin Friars Sch Carl 80-86; Chapl Mayfield Coll E Sussex 86-88; Chapl H Trin Sch Halifax 88-90; NSM Ripponden *Wakef* 88-90; V Torpenhow *Carl* 91-94; V Allhallows 91-94; V Falmouth All SS *Truro* 94-98; V Harden and Wilsden *Bradf* 98-02; rtd 03. *5 Westhill Avenue, Cullingworth, Bradford BD13 5BB* T: (01535) 272980

SCARD, Mrs Linda Joyce. b 52. STETS 11. **d** 14 **p** 15. NSM N Hants Downs *Win* from 14. *Adams Farm, The Street, North Warnborough, Hook RG29 1BL* M: 07801-089717 T: (01256) 704835 E: linda.scard@btinternet.com

SCARGILL, Christopher Morris. b 57. UEA BA 79 York Univ MA 81 Leeds Univ CertEd 81 Nottm Univ BTh 89. Linc Th Coll 86. **d** 89 **p** 90. C Desborough and Brampton Ash w Dingley and Braybrooke *Pet* 89-92; C Buxton w Burbage and King Sterndale *Derby* 92-93; TV 93-98; V Ipstones w Berkhamsytch and Onecote w Bradnop *Lich* 98-09; RD Alstonfield 08-09; Local Min Adv (Stafford) 07-09; Sen Chapl Torrevieja *Eur* 09-14; V S Anston w St Thos *Blackb* from 14. *The Vicarage, 2 St Thomas Road, Lytham St Annes FY8 1JL* T: (01253) 723750 E: revdcms@gmail.com

SCARGILL, Mrs Claire Frances. b 49. Birkbeck Coll Lon BSc 83 Heythrop Coll Lon MA 06. St Mellitus Coll 13. **d** 14 **p** 15. OLM Mistley w Manningtree and Bradfield *Chelmsf* from 14. *5 Rosewood Park, Mistley, Manningtree CO11 1UA* T: (01206) 392018 M: 07714-752100 E: cscargill@yahoo.co.uk

SCARISBRICK, Mrs Helen. b 60. Sheff Univ BA 81 Sheff Poly PGCE 82 Ches Coll of HE BTh 99. NOC 97. **d** 99 **p** 00. C Norbury *Ches* 99-03; P-in-c Cheadle Heath 03-07; C Edgeley and Cheadle Heath 07-09; V Broadheath from 09. *The Vicarage, Lindsell Road, West Timperley, Altrincham WA14 5NX* T: 0161-928 4820 E: helenscarisbrick@btinternet.com

SCARLATA, Mark. b 72. **d** 13 **p** 14. NSM Cambridge St Mark *Ely* from 13. *10 Roseford Road, Cambridge CB4 2HD* T: (01223) 977345 or 655399 E: mwscar@gmail.com

SCARR, Mrs Hazel Anne. b 44. SAOMC. **d** 00 **p** 01. NSM Adderbury w Milton *Ox* 00-04; NSM Chadlington and Spelsbury, Ascott under Wychwood 04-05; NSM Hardington Vale *B & W* 05-07; NSM Hook Norton w Gt Rollright, Swerford etc *Ox* 07-10; PtO from 11. *Betula House, Barford Road, Bloxham, Banbury OX15 4EZ* T: (01295) 720022 E: revhazel@yahoo.co.uk

SCARTH, John Robert. b 34. Leeds Univ BSc 55 CertEd. Cranmer Hall Dur 63. **d** 65 **p** 66. C Dewsbury All SS *Wakef* 65-68; V Shepley 68-72; Asst Master Kingston-upon-Hull Gr Sch 72-78; St Mary's C of E Sch Hendon 78-81; V Ossett cum Gawthorpe *Wakef* 81-88; R Tarrington w Stoke Edith, Aylton, Pixley etc *Heref* 88-96; rtd 96; PtO *Wakef* 96-09; S'wark from 10. *3 Russet Drive, Croydon CR0 7DS* M: 07867-505615 E: jorobscarth@gmail.com

SCEATS, Preb David Douglas. b 46. Ch Coll Cam BA 68 MA 72 Bris Univ MA 71. Clifton Th Coll 68. **d** 71 **p** 72. C Cambridge St Paul *Ely* 71-74; Lect Trin Coll Bris 74-83; V Shenstone *Lich* 83-86; Dioc Tr Officer 86-91; P-in-c Colton 86-90; Dir Local Min Development 91-98; Warden of Readers 91-96; C Lich St Chad 94-98; Dioc Board of Min Team Ldr 96-98; Preb Lich Cathl 96-98; Prin NTMTC 99-07; Preb St Paul's Cathl 02-07; P-in-c Selkirk *Edin* 07-11; rtd 11; Hon C Selkirk *Edin* from 11.

Nether Dalgleish, Selkirk TD7 5HZ T: (01750) 62269 E: dsceats@gmail.com *or* d-sceats@sky.com

SCHAEFER, Carl Richard. b 67. Coll of Resurr Mirfield 91. **d** 94 **p** 95. C Ribbleton *Blackb* 94-98; V Blackb St Thos w St Jude 98-08; P-in-c Blackb St Mich w St Jo and H Trin 03-08; V Goldthorpe w Hickleton *Sheff* from 08. *Goldthorpe Presbytery, Lockwood Road, Goldthorpe, Rotherham S63 9JY* T: (01709) 898426 E: carl@schaeferc.freeserve.co.uk

SCHAFER, Isabella. b 49. **d** 13 **p** 14. OLM Ashton-in-Makerfield St Thos *Liv* from 13. *56 Belvedere Road, Ashton-in-Makerfield, Wigan WN4 8RU* T: (01942) 717300

SCHARF, Brian Howard. b 39. Alberta Univ BA 60. Trin Coll Toronto 60 Coll of Resurr Mirfield 61. **d** 63 **p** 65. C Vancouver St Faith Canada 63-65; C Broadstairs *Cant* 65-68. *3236 Robinson Road, North Vancouver BC V7J 3E9, Canada* T: (001) (604) 987 0219 E: brianscharf@shaw.ca

SCHARIAH, Canon Zechariah. b 43. Zürich Univ BD 87. Baptist Th Sem Rueschlikon 83. **d** 93 **p** 93. Chapl to Miss to Minorities from 93; PtO *Eur* from 95; Can Dar-es-Salaam from 00. *Schaubhus 7, 6020 Emmenbrücke, Switzerland* E: karibumade@hotmail.com

SCHATZ, Stefani. b 62. Mills Coll Oakland (USA) BA 84. Episc Div Sch Cam Mass MDiv 01. **d** 01 **p** 02. C Hermosa Beach USA 01-04; C Brookline All SS 04-06; PtO *Man* 06-07; TV Gorton and Abbey Hey 07-08; R Reno Trin USA from 08. *1644 Shadow Wood Road, Reno NV 89523-1244, USA* T: (001) (775) 329 4279 E: stefani@trinityreno.org

SCHEFFER (née SQUIRES), Mrs Rachel Louise. b 79. Coll of Ripon & York St Jo BA 00. Ripon Coll Cuddesdon MA 07. **d** 07 **p** 08. C Alnwick *Newc* 07-12; C Monkseaton St Pet 13-15; P-in-c Stamfordham w Matfen from 15; Dioc Development Officer for Youth Work from 15. *St Mary's Vicarage, Stamfordham, Newcastle upon Tyne NE18 0QQ* T: (01661) 886853 E: rlsscheffer@gmail.com

SCHEMANOFF, Ms Natasha Anne. b 50. CertEd 71. **d** 96 **p** 97. C Freshford, Limpley Stoke and Hinton Charterhouse *B & W* 96-99; TV Worle 99-00; V Kewstoke w Wick St Lawrence 00-07; Bp's Adv for Racial Justice 00-07; rtd 07; PtO *Truro* from 97. *Hallane End, 4 The Terrace, Lostwithiel PL22 0DT* T: (01208) 871330

SCHILD, John. b 38. ALCD 64. **d** 64 **p** 65. C Cheltenham Ch Ch *Glouc* 64-67; Area Sec CMS Sheff and S'well 67-73; Area Sec CMS Chelmsf and St Alb 73-76; V Lt Heath *St Alb* 76-88; R Bedford St Pet w St Cuth 88-94; P-in-c King's Walden and Offley w Lilley 94-98; V 98-03; rtd 03. *Trenarren, St Cleer, Liskeard PL14 5DN* T: (01579) 347047 E: john@schild.demon.co.uk

SCHLEGER, Ms Maria Francesca. b 57. LSE BA 78 SS Coll Cam BA 84 MA 89. Westcott Ho Cam 82. **dss** 85 **d** 87 **p** 94. De Beauvoir Town St Pet *Lon* 85-90; Par Dn 87-90; Team Dn Bow H Trin and All Hallows 90-94; Dean of Women's Min (Stepney Area) 90-94; PtO *Birm* 94-98; NSM Stepney St Dunstan and All SS *Lon* 99-03; Chapl Mildmay Miss Hosp 03-12; PtO *Lon* from 12. *75 Lansdowne Drive, London E8 3EP* T: (020) 7683 0051 E: schleger@waitrose.com

SCHLOSS, Sandra. b 63. **d** 13 **p** 14. NSM Addiscombe St Mildred *S'wark* from 13. *, 87 Harcourt Road, Thornton Heath CR7 6BZ*

SCHLUTER, Nathaniel David. b 71. Pemb Coll Ox BA 93 MA 97 Green Coll Ox DPhil 98. Wycliffe Hall Ox BA. **d** 00 **p** 01. C Gerrards Cross and Fulmer *Ox* 00-05; Prin Johannesburg Bible Coll S Africa from 05; PtO *Ox* from 14. *PO Box 374, Auckland Park, 2006 South Africa* E: info@johannesburgbiblecollege.org

SCHMIDT, Canon Karen Rosemarie. b 48. Surrey Univ BSc 70 Solicitor 76. STETS 96. **d** 99 **p** 00. NSM Lee-on-the-Solent *Portsm* 99-05; P-in-c Purbrook 05-06; V 06-09; rtd 09; Bp's Dom Chapl *Portsm* 09-12; Hon C Brighstone and Brooke w Mottistone 13-14; Hon C Shorwell w Kingston 13-14; Hon C Chale 13-14. *31 Truscott Avenue, Swindon SN25 2GR* M: 07990-518541 T: (01793) 753457 E: karenrschmidt@yahoo.co.uk

SCHNAAR, Howard William. b 71. Wilson Carlile Coll 95. **d** 08 **p** 15. C Worthing H Trin w Ch Ch *Chich* 08-11; TV Southgate from 11. *21 Anglesey Close, Crawley RH11 9HG* T: (01293) 530339 E: howard-schnaar@o2.co.uk

SCHNYDER, Mrs Cécile. b 76. Ausbildungs Schule Bern BA 97 Roehampton Univ MA 10. Westcott Ho Cam BTh 15. **d** 15. C Sutton *S'wark* from 15. *37 St Barnabas Road, Sutton SM1 4NS* E: cecile.schnyder@cantab.net

SCHOFIELD, Andrew Thomas. b 47. K Coll Lon BD 70 AKC 71 PGCE 72. St Aug Coll Cant 70. **d** 81 **p** 82. C Whittlesey *Ely* 81-84; C Ramsey 84-87; P-in-c Ellington, Grafham, Easton and Spaldwick w Barham and Woolley 87-94; R March St Jo 94-05; P-in-c Duxford 05-09; P-in-c Hinxton 05-09; P-in-c Ickleton

05-09; rtd 09; P-in-c Beetham *Carl* 09-12. *Holker House, Whittington, Carnforth LA6 2NX* T: (01524) 274391
E: atschofield@outlook.com

SCHOFIELD, David Leslie. b 40. MISM 89. EMMTC 98. **d** 01 **p** 02. NSM Derby St Mark 01-04; P-in-c Dukinfield St Luke *Ches* 07-12; rtd 12. *72 Bromley Cross Road, Bromley Cross, Bolton BL7 9LT* T: (01204) 303137 E: fatherschofield@aim.com

SCHOFIELD, Gary. b 64. Ripon Coll Cuddesdon 97. **d** 99 **p** 00. C Exhall *Cov* 99-02; V Wales *Sheff* from 02; P-in-c Harthill and Thorpe Salvin from 08; P-in-c Todwick 12-13; AD Laughton 11-14. *The Vicarage, Manor Road, Wales, Sheffield S26 5PD* T: (01909) 771111 E: gary.schofield@sheffield.anglican.org

SCHOFIELD, John Martin. b 47. Selw Coll Cam BA 69 MA 73. St Steph Ho Ox 70. **d** 72 **p** 73. C Palmers Green St Jo *Lon* 72-75; C Friern Barnet St Jas 75-80; V Luton St Aug Limbury *St Alb* 80-89; V Biddenham and Dir CME 89-94; Dir Minl Tr *Guildf* 94-99; Can Res Guildf Cathl 95-99; PtO 03-05; Dir Dioc Min Course 05-09; rtd 09. *81 Pickmere Road, Sheffield S10 1GZ* E: johnscho@ntlworld.com

SCHOFIELD, John Verity. b 29. Jes Coll Ox BA 52 MA 56. Cuddesdon Coll 53. **d** 55 **p** 56. C Cirencester *Glouc* 55-59; R Stella *Dur* 59-67; Kenya 67-69; Asst Chapl St Paul's Sch Barnes 69-70; Chapl 71-80; Australia 81-83; Gen Sec Friends of Elderly & Gentlefolk's Help 83-94; PtO *Sarum* from 83; rtd 94. *Bishops Barn, Foots Hill, Cann, Shaftesbury SP7 0BW* T: (01747) 853852

SCHOFIELD, Canon Nigel Timothy. b 54. Dur Univ BA 76 Nottm Univ BCombStuds 83 FRCO. Linc Th Coll 80. **d** 83 **p** 84. C Cheshunt *St Alb* 83-86; TV Colyton, Southleigh, Offwell, Widworthy etc *Ex* 86-94; V Seaton 94-03; P-in-c Beer and Branscombe 01-03; V Seaton and Beer 03-06; RD Honiton 99-03; Can Res Chich Cathl from 06. *4 Vicars Close, Chichester PO19 1PT* T: (01243) 813589
E: precentor@chichestercathedral.org.uk

SCHOFIELD, Ruth Elizabeth. b 65. Imp Coll Lon BEng 87. STETS 06. **d** 09 **p** 10. NSM Botley, Curdridge and Durley *Portsm* 09-12; TV Fareham H Trin from 12; Asst Chapl Portsm Hosps NHS Trust from 11. *The Vicarage, 2 Hillson Drive, Fareham PO15 6PF* M: 07738-858909
E: revrschofield@gmail.com

SCHOFIELD, Ms Sarah. b 70. Man Univ BA 95. Qu Coll Birm 95. **d** 97 **p** 98. C Longsight St Luke *Man* 97-02; Tutor (Man Ho) Westcott Ho Cam 00-04; P-in-c Gorton St Phil *Man* 02-06; P-in-c Abbey Hey 04-06; TV Cen Wolverhampton *Lich* from 06; Rep for Women in Min Wolverhampton Area from 15. *All Saints' Church, c/o The Workspace, All Saints Road, Wolverhampton WV2 1EL* M: 07500-780494
T: (01902) 452584 E: revsarah@hotmail.co.uk

SCHOFIELD, Simon Whitworth. b 64. Birm Univ BA 88. SNWTP 10. **d** 13 **p** 14. NSM Stretford St Matt *Man* from 13. *20 Langshaw Street, Manchester M16 9LR* T: 0161-227 8285 M: 07761-636751 E: simon_schodog@yahoo.co.uk

SCHOFIELD, Timothy. *See* SCHOFIELD, Nigel Timothy

SCHOFIELD, Mrs Victoria Louise. b 56. Liv Poly BSc 88 Liv Univ PGCE 91. Wycliffe Hall Ox BTh 05. **d** 02 **p** 03. C Hattersley *Ches* 02-05; P-in-c Runcorn St Mich 05-06; V from 06. *145 Greenway Road, Runcorn WA7 4NR* T: (01928) 500993
E: vicki_schofield@hotmail.com

SCHOLEFIELD, Mrs Judith Lenore. b 45. RN 66 Open Univ BA 97. WEMTC 99. **d** 04 **p** 05. OLM Ledbury *Heref* from 04. *Oakland Lodge, The Homend, Ledbury HR8 1AR* T: (01531) 632279

SCHOLES, Ms Victoria Prichard. b 68. Man Univ BSc 89. St Jo Coll Nottm 97. **d** 00 **p** 01. C Macclesfield St Jo *Ches* 00-02; NSM 02-03; PtO from 03. *87B Gawsorth Road, Macclesfield SK11 8UF* T: (01625) 425049

SCHOLEY, Michael. b 45. **d** 10. NSM Staincross *Leeds* from 10. *8 Croft Close, Mapplewell, Barnsley S75 6FN* T: (01226) 386173 E: michael.scholey@virgin.net

SCHOLLAR, Canon Pamela Mary. b 39. Southn Univ DipEd 80. S Dios Minl Tr Scheme 89. **d** 92 **p** 94. NSM Bournemouth St Andr *Win* 92-94; NSM Pokesdown St Jas 94-09; Hon Can Win Cathl 02-09; PtO from 10. *22 Bethia Road, Bournemouth BH8 9BD* T: (01202) 397925 E: schollar@ukgateway.net

SCHOLZ, Terence Brinsley. b 44. St Martin's Coll Lanc MA 98. CBDTI 94. **d** 97 **p** 98. NSM St Annes St Thos *Blackb* 97-01; NSM Broughton 01-02; PtO 02-04; NSM Freckleton 04-12; rtd 12; PtO *Blackb* from 12. *14 Further Ends Road, Freckleton, Preston PR4 1RL* T: (01772) 632966 M: 07989-931909
E: tbscholz@btinternet.com

SCHOOLING, Bruce James. b 47. Rhodes Univ BA 73. St Paul's Coll Grahamstown 76. **d** 76 **p** 77. C Rondebosch St Thos S Africa 76-79; C St Geo Cathl Cape Town 79-83; R Malmesbury 83-86; C Wanstead St Mary *Chelmsf* 87-90; V Leigh-on-Sea St Jas 90-04; PtO from 05; rtd 07. *249 Woodgrange Drive, Southend-on-Sea SS1 2SQ* T: (01702) 613429
M: 07710-208476 E: b.schooling@btinternet.com

SCHRIMSHAW, Angela Anna Violet. b 51. SRN 73 SCM 76 Hull Univ BSc 98. NEOC 01. **d** 04 **p** 05. NSM Welton w Melton *York* from 04. *22 Bricknell Avenue, Hull HU5 4JS* T: (01482) 446609 E: schrim@schrim.karoo.co.uk

SCHRODER, Edward Amos. b 41. Cant Univ (NZ) BA 64. Cranmer Hall Dur. **d** 67 **p** 68. C St Marylebone All So w SS Pet and Jo *Lon* 67-71; Dean Gordon Coll and C Hamilton Ch Ch USA 71-76; Can Missr and Asst to Bp Florida 76-79; R Orange Park Grace Ch 79-86; R San Antonio Ch Ch 86-00; Chapl Amelia Plantation Chpl 00-06; rtd 06. *15 Hickory Lane, Amelia Island FL 32034-5064, USA* T: (001) (904) 277 6752 F: 277 8323 E: tschroder@ameliachapel.com

SCHRYVER, Mrs Linda Jean. b 56. Ch Ch Coll Cant BSc 00. SEITE 00. **d** 03 **p** 04. NSM Willesborough *Cant* 03-09. *2 Church Cottages, Canterbury Road, Godmersham, Canterbury CT4 7DS* T: (01227) 730750 M: 07768-566372
E: linda.schryver@mariecurie.org.uk

SCHULD DE VERNY, Dietrich Gustave. *See* Schuld, DE VERNY, David Dietrich

SCHUMAN, Andrew William Edward. b 73. Birm Univ BA 95 MSc 96 Bris Univ PhD 00 FRGS 02. Trin Coll Bris BA 03 MA 04. **d** 04 **p** 05. C Shirehampton *Bris* 04-08; C Bris Ch the Servant Stockwood 08-13; P-in-c Brislington St Chris from 13; Partnership P Bris S from 08. *23 First Avenue, Bristol BS4 4DU* T: 0117-909 4235 E: andrewschuman@me.com

SCHÜNEMANN, Canon Bernhard George. b 61. K Coll Lon BD 86 AKC 86 LRAM 83. Ripon Coll Cuddesdon 88. **d** 90 **p** 91. C Kirkby *Liv* 90-93; C St Martin-in-the-Fields *Lon* 93-97; Chapl Br Sch of Osteopathy 93-97; P-in-c Littlemore *Ox* 97-06; V S Dulwich St Steph *S'wark* from 06; Dir Ords Woolwich Area from 13; Hon Can Tamale Ghana from 13. *St Stephen's Vicarage, 111 College Road, London SE21 7HN* T: (020) 8693 3797 or 8766 7281 F: 8693 7194
E: schunemann@btinternet.com

SCHUTTE, Ms Margaret Ann. b 50. Natal Univ BA 71. SAOMC. **d** 04 **p** 05. C Overbury w Teddington, Alstone etc *Worc* 04-07; Chapl HM Pris Hewell from 07. *HM Prison Hewell, Hewell Lane, Redditch B97 6QS* T: (01527) 785000
E: schuttefamily@tesco.net

SCHWIER, Paul David. b 55. **d** 96 **p** 97. OLM Pulham Market, Pulham St Mary and Starston *Nor* 96-99; OLM Dickleburgh and The Pulhams from 99. *Street Farm, Pulham Market, Diss IP21 4SP* T: (01379) 676240 E: schwier1@aol.com

SCHWIER, Peter Andrew. b 52. **d** 91 **p** 92. NSM Fressingfield, Mendham, Metfield, Weybread etc *St E* 91-13; NSM Sancroft from 13. *Valley Farm, Metfield, Harleston IP20 0JZ* T: (01379) 586517

SCLATER, Jennifer. b 44. TISEC. **d** 02 **p** 04. Par Dn Elgin w Lossiemouth *Mor* 02-04; NSM from 04. *17 Larchfield, Colquhoun Street, Helensburgh G84 8JG* M: 07950-830017 E: jenny@sclater.com

SCLATER, John Edward. b 46. Nottm Univ BA 68 St Edm Hall Ox CertEd 71. Cuddesdon Coll 69. **d** 71 **p** 72. C Bris St Mary Redcliffe w Temple etc 71-75; Chapl Bede Ho Staplehurst 75-79; Chapl Warw Sch 79; P-in-c Offchurch *Cov* 79-80; Belgium 81-89; Willen Priory 89-91; C Linslade *Ox* 91-94; P-in-c Hedsor and Bourne End 94-02; rtd 02; PtO *B & W* from 03. *3 East Court, South Horrington Village, Wells BA5 3HL* T: (01749) 671349 M: 07896-893432
E: john.jes007@yahoo.co.uk

SCOBIE, Geoffrey Edward Winsor. b 39. Bris Univ BSc 62 MSc 68 Birm Univ MA 70 Glas Univ PhD 78 FRSA 96 AFBPsS. Tyndale Hall Bris 62. **d** 65 **p** 66. C Summerfield *Birm* 65-66; C Moseley St Anne 66-67; Lect Psychology Glas Univ 67-04; Hon C Glas St Silas 70-83; P-in-c 83-84; Hon R 84-85; TR 85-86; Team Chapl 86-88; Hon Asst Team Chapl 88-99; Assoc P Bishopbriggs 99-08; P-in-c Lenzie 06-09. *3 Norfolk Crescent, Bishopbriggs, Glasgow G64 3BA* T: 0141-722 2907
E: gscobie@ntlworld.com

SCOONES, Roger Philip. b 48. Trin Coll Bris. **d** 82 **p** 83. C Childwall All SS *Liv* 82-85; Bradf Cathl 85-90; V Congleton St Pet *Ches* 90-96; P-in-c Congleton St Steph 94-96; R Stockport St Mary from 96; PtO *Man* from 14. *St Mary's Rectory, 24 Gorsey Mount Street, Stockport SK1 4DU* T: 0161-429 6564 *or* 480 1815 F: 429 6564
E: roger@scoones9.freeserve.co.uk

SCORER, Canon John Robson. b 47. Westcott Ho Cam 73. **d** 75 **p** 76. C Silksworth *Dur* 75-78; C Newton Aycliffe 78-82; V Sherburn 82-83; V Sherburn w Pittington 83-89; P-in-c Croxdale 89-93; Chapl Dur Constabulary 89-11; Chapl Dur Police Tr Cen 93-05; Hon Can Dur Cathl 04-11; rtd 11; PtO *Dur* from 11. *45 Norwich Road, Durham DH1 5QA*

SCOTCHMER, Michael Leslie. b 48. **d** 14 **p** 15. OLM Chingford St Anne *Chelmsf* from 14. *142 Kings Avenue, Woodford Green IG8 0JQ* T: (020) 8504 7497 M: 07802-483147
E: mls@milesconsulting.co.uk

SCOTFORD, Bethan Lynne. b 44. Univ of Wales (Cardiff) BA 67 PGCE 68. St As Minl Tr Course 95. **d** 99 **p** 00. Fieldworker (Wales) USPG 98-11; C Guilsfield w Pool Quay *St As* 99-02; V Corwen w Llangar, Glyndyfrdwy etc 02-11; rtd 11; PtO *St As* from 11. *7 Fairview Avenue, Guilsfield, Welshpool SY21 9NE* T: (01938) 555153 M: 07802-656607 E: bscotford@toucansurf.com

SCOTLAND, Nigel Adrian Douglas. b 42. McGill Univ Montreal MA 71 Aber Univ PhD 75 CertEd 75 Bris Univ MLitt 85. Gordon-Conwell Th Sem MDiv 70 Lon Coll of Div ALCD 66 LTh 74. **d** 66 **p** 67. C Harold Wood *Chelmsf* 66-69; USA 69-70; R Lakefield Canada 70-72; LtO *Ab* 72-75; Chapl and Lect St Mary's Coll Cheltenham 75-79; Sen Lect 77-79; Chapl and Sen Lect Coll of SS Paul and Mary Cheltenham 79-84; NSM Cheltenham St Mark *Glouc* 85-92; Field Chair RS Cheltenham and Glouc Coll of HE 89-01; Field Chair Glos Univ 01-05; Prin Lect 96-08; Research Fell from 08; PtO *Glouc* from 92; Tutor Trin Coll Bris from 06; LtO *Bris* from 07; Tutor Bris Univ from 09. *8 The Rowans, Woodmancote, Cheltenham GL52 4RL* T: (01242) 676969 E: nigel.scotland@btopenworld.com

SCOTLAND, Primus of the Episcopal Church in. See CHILLINGWORTH, The Most Revd David Robert

SCOTT, Adam. b 47. TD 78 OBE 08. Ch Ch Ox BA 68 MA 72 City Univ MSc 79 St Andr Univ PhD 10 Barrister 72 FRSA 95 CEng 81 MIET 81 FIEE 94. S'wark Ord Course 73. **d** 75 **p** 76. MSE Blackheath Park St Mich *S'wark* from 75; Dean for MSE, Woolwich from 90; Prof Fell St Andr Univ *St And* 96-97; Sen Res Fell from 98; PtO from 96. *19 Blackheath Park, London SE3 8RW* T: (020) 8852 3286 F: 8852 6247 E: adam.scott@btinternet.com

SCOTT, Preb Allan George. b 39. Man Univ BA 61. Coll of Resurr Mirfield 61. **d** 63 **p** 64. C Bradford cum Beswick *Man* 63-66; P-in-c 66-72; Hon C Bramhall *Ches* 72-74; Hon C Tottenham St Jo *Lon* 74-76; Hon C Bush Hill Park St Steph 76-79; R Stoke Newington St Mary 79-02; P-in-c Brownswood Park 95-97; Preb St Paul's Cathl 91-04; rtd 04. *8 West Hackney House, 15 Northwold Road, London N16 7HJ* T: (020) 7923 0153 E: allangscott@gmail.com

SCOTT, Andrew Charles Graham. b 28. Mert Coll Ox BA 57 MA. Wells Th Coll 57. **d** 59 **p** 60. C Rugby St Andr *Cov* 59-64; Chapl RN 64-68; C Prenton *Ches* 68-71; V Tow Law *Dur* 71-81; RD Stanhope 77-81; V Bampton w Clanfield *Ox* 81-95; rtd 95; PtO *Ex* from 95. *99 Speedwell Crescent, Plymouth PL6 5SZ* T: (01752) 773570

SCOTT, Barrie. b 63. Birm Univ BA 85 Goldsmiths' Coll Lon PGCE 86. St Steph Ho Ox 93. **d** 95 **p** 96. C Tilehurst St Mich *Ox* 95-98; PtO *Birm* 98-15; V Perry Barr from 15. *The Vicarage, Church Road, Perry Barr, Birmingham B42 2LB* M: 07841-202408 T: 0121-356 7998 E: vicar@st-johns-perry-barr.org.uk

SCOTT, Basil John Morley. b 34. Qu Coll Cam BA 59 Banaras Hindu Univ MA 65. Ridley Hall Cam 58. **d** 60 **p** 61. C Woking St Pet *Guildf* 60-63; India 63-83; TR Kirby Muxloe *Leic* 83-89; Asian Outreach Worker (Leic Martyrs) 89-95; Derby Asian Chr Min Project 95-00; rtd 00; PtO *Ely* from 00. *14 Scotsdowne Road, Trumpington, Cambridge CB2 9HU* T: (01223) 476565 E: basil.scott2@ntlworld.com

SCOTT, Mrs Beryl May. b 28. Lon Univ BD 91 Westmr Coll Ox MTh 00. **d** 02 **p** 04. NSM Dalbeattie *Glas* from 02. *Islecroft House, Mill Street, Dalbeattie DG5 4HE* T: (01556) 610283 E: berylm.scott@virgin.net

SCOTT, Charles Geoffrey. b 32. St Jo Coll Cam BA 54 MA 58. Cuddesdon Coll 56. **d** 58 **p** 59. C Brighouse *Wakef* 58-61; C Bathwick w Woolley *B & W* 61-64; V Frome Ch Ch 64-78; R Winchelsea *Chich* 78-93; R Winchelsea and Icklesham 93-95; rtd 95; PtO *Chich* from 95. *Hickstead, Main Street, Iden, Rye TN31 7PT* T: (01797) 280096

SCOTT, Christopher John Fairfax. b 45. Magd Coll Cam BA 67 MA 71. Westcott Ho Cam 68. **d** 70 **p** 71. C Nor St Pet Mancroft 70-73; Chapl Magd Coll Cam 73-79; V Hampstead Ch Ch *Lon* 79-94; rtd 00. *49 St Barnabas Road, Cambridge CB1 2BX* T: (01223) 359421

SCOTT, Canon Christopher Michael. b 44. SS Coll Cam BA 66 MA 70. Cuddesdon Coll 66. **d** 68 **p** 69. C New Addington *Cant* 68-73; C Westmr St Steph w St Jo *Lon* 73-78; V Enfield St Mich 78-81; V Effingham w Lt Bookham *Guildf* 81-87; R Esher 87-98; RD Emly 91-96; R Bude Haven and Marhamchurch *Truro* 98-08; Hon Can Truro Cathl 03-08; rtd 08. *Lantyan, Poughill, Bude EX23 9EU* T: (01288) 350741 E: chriscott98@yahoo.co.uk

SCOTT, Christopher Stuart. b 48. Surrey Univ BA 92 MBPsS 92. Sarum & Wells Th Coll 79. **d** 81 **p** 82. C Enfield Chase St Mary *Lon* 81-82; C Coalbrookdale, Iron-Bridge and Lt Wenlock *Heref* 82-86; P-in-c Breinton 86-89; Chapl Hickey's Almshouses

Richmond 89-01; PtO *S'wark* from 06; Chapl Richmond Charities' Almshouses from 08. *164 Sheen Road, Richmond TW9 1XD* T: (020) 8940 6560

SCOTT, Claude John. b 37. Qu Mary Coll Lon BSc 60 PhD 64 Lon Inst of Educn PGCE 61 FRSA 94. EAMTC 88. **d** 91 **p** 92. NSM Heigham H Trin *Nor* 91-98; PtO from 98. *26 The Pastures, Blakeney, Holt NR25 7LY* T: (01263) 740573 E: cjscott@talktalk.net

SCOTT, Colin. b 32. Dur Univ BA 54. Coll of Resurr Mirfield 58. **d** 60 **p** 61. C Wallsend St Pet *Newc* 60-64; C Seaton Hirst 64-68; C Longbenton St Bart 68-70; V Benwell St Aid 70-77; V Sleekburn 77-89; P-in-c Cambois 77-88; V Longhoughton w Howick 89-96; rtd 96; PtO *Newc* from 96. *Pele Cottage, Hepple, Morpeth NE65 7LH* T: (01669) 640258

SCOTT, David. b 40. Rhodes Univ BA 63. St Paul's Coll Grahamstown LTh 65. **d** 65 **p** 66. C Pietermaritzberg St Pet S Africa 66-67; C Durban N St Martin-in-the-Fields 68; R Harding 69; R Newcastle H Trin 70-75; R Bellair 76-78; R Kabega Park All SS 79-87; Chapl Port Elizabeth Univ 88-91; TV Cheltenham St Mark *Glouc* 92-96; R Swanscombe *Roch* 96-10; rtd 10; PtO *Roch* from 11. *103 Hillside Avenue, Gravesend DA12 5QN* T: (01474) 248735 M: 07949-069019 E: scottrev@uwclub.net

SCOTT, David. *See* SCOTT, Timothy David

SCOTT, Canon David Victor. b 47. St Chad's Coll Dur BA 69 Lambeth DLitt 08. Cuddesdon Coll 69. **d** 71 **p** 72. C St Mary-at-Latton *Chelmsf* 71-73; Chapl Haberdashers' Aske's Sch Elstree 73-80; V Torpenhow *Carl* 80-91; V Allhallows 80-91; R Win St Lawr and St Maurice w St Swithun 91-10; Warden Sch of Spirituality Win 91-10; Hon Can Win Cathl 02-10; rtd 10; Hon Fell Win Univ from 05. *2 Sunnyside, Kendal LA9 7DJ* T: (01539) 728650 E: scott.d.v@live.com

SCOTT (formerly WOOD), **Mrs Elizabeth Jane.** b 51. Ch Ch Coll Cant DipEd 73. NEOC 98. **d** 01 **p** 02. C Denton *Newc* 01-04; V N Sunderland and Beadnell 04-11; V Monkseaton St Pet 11-15; AD Tynemouth 14-15; Developing Discipleship Officer Lindisfarne Regional Tr Partnership from 15. *St Michael's Vicarage, Howling Lane, Alnwick NE66 1DH* T: (01665) 603078 E: jane.wood14@btinternet.com

SCOTT, Mrs Erica Jane. b 58. Trin Coll Bris BA 02. **d** 02 **p** 03. C Ilminster and Distr *B & W* 02-05; C Nailsea Ch Ch w Tickenham 05-07; P-in-c Whitchurch *Bris* 07-08; PtO *S & M* 09-12; Chapl K Wm's Coll Is of Man from 12. *King William's College, Castletown, Isle of Man IM9 1TP* T: (01624) 820400 E: rev.erica@manx.net

SCOTT, Francis Richard. b 63. St Jo Coll Dur BA 85 Selw Coll Cam PGCE 86. St Jo Coll Nottm MA 02. **d** 00 **p** 01. C Huntington *York* 00-03; TV 03-09; V Swanland from 09. *The Vicarage, St Barnabas Drive, Swanland, North Ferriby HU14 3RL* T: (01482) 631271 E: fandfscott@aol.com *or* francis@stbchurch.org

SCOTT, Gary James. b 61. Edin Univ BD 87. Edin Th Coll 85. **d** 87 **p** 88. C Edin St Cuth 87-90; R Peebles 90-96; P-in-c Innerleithen 92-96; R Penicuik 96-98; R W Linton 96-98; Sen Chapl ACF 98-08; Hd Master Tweedbank Sch 06-10; CF from 10. *c/o MOD Chaplains (Army)* M: 07710-600953 T: (01264) 383430 F: 381824 E: shamrock.racing@btinternet.com

SCOTT, Geoffrey. *See* SCOTT, Charles Geoffrey

SCOTT, Canon Gordon. b 30. Man Univ BA 51. St Jo Coll Dur 51. **d** 53 **p** 54. C Monkwearmouth St Andr *Dur* 53-55; C Stranton 55-56; C Chester le Street 56-59; V Marley Hill 59-62; Chapl Forest Sch Snaresbrook 62-66; Chapl Dunrobin Sch Sutherland 66-72; Chapl Pocklington Sch York 72-74; V Barton w Pooley Bridge *Carl* 74-80; RD Penrith 79-82; P-in-c Lazonby 80; R Gt Salkeld w Lazonby 80-90; Hon Can Carl Cathl 83-94; P-in-c Patterdale 90-94; rtd 94; PtO *Carl* 94-97 and from 08. *48 Lakeland Park, Keswick CA12 4AT* T: (017687) 75862

SCOTT, Guy Charles. b 61. Coll of Resurr Mirfield. **d** 00 **p** 01. C Abington *Pet* 00-03; P-in-c Mullion *Truro* 03-07; C Cury and Gunwalloe 03-07; R Is of Scilly 07-10; P-in-c Biggleswade *St Alb* 10-13; V from 13. *The Vicarage, Shortmead Street, Biggleswade SG18 0AT* T: (01767) 312243 E: g.c.scott@btinternet.com

SCOTT, Mrs Helen Ruth. b 59. Surrey Univ BA 97 K Coll Lon MA 99 SRN 81 RM 85. S'wark Ord Course 89. **d** 92 **p** 94. NSM Richmond St Mary w St Matthias and St Jo *S'wark* 92-01; Chapl Hickey's Almshouses Richmond 01-08; PtO *S'wark* from 08; Chapl Ch Sch Richmond 09-13. *164 Sheen Road, Richmond TW9 1XD* T: (020) 8940 6560

SCOTT, Ian Michael. b 25. Bris Univ BA 50 Leic Univ DipEd 51 Open Univ MA 99. Bps' Coll Cheshunt 52. **d** 53 **p** 54. C Rotherhithe St Mary w All SS *S'wark* 53-55; C Lavender Hill Ascension 55-59; C Camberwell St Mich w All So w Em 59-60; C Kettering St Mary *Pet* 60-63; V Haverstock Hill

H Trin w Kentish Town St Barn *Lon* 63-93; rtd 93; PtO *Nor* 93-96. *Los Molinos 8, 03726 Benitachell (Alicante), Spain* T: (0034) 965 741 342 E: ian_benitachell@yahoo.co.uk

SCOTT, Mrs Inez Margaret Gillette. b 26. St Alb Minl Tr Scheme 76. **dss** 79 **d** 87 **p** 94. Preston w Sutton Poyntz, Littlemoor etc *Sarum* 83-86; Dorchester 86-96; Par Dn 87-88; NSM 88-96; rtd 88; PtO *Sarum* 96-08. *14 Came View Road, Dorchester DT1 2AE* T: (01305) 267547
E: pandiscott@googlemail.com

SCOTT, James Alexander Gilchrist. b 32. Linc Coll Ox BA 56 MA 60. Wycliffe Hall Ox 56. **d** 58 **p** 59. C Shipley St Paul *Bradf* 58-61; Abp's Dom Chapl *York* 61-65; Brazil 65-68; V Grassendale *Liv* 68-77; V Thorp Arch w Walton *York* 77-89; RD Tadcaster 78-86; Chapl HM Pris Rudgate 77-82; Askham Grange 82-87; V Kirk Ella *York* 89-92; TR 92-97; rtd 97; PtO *York* from 98. *2 Keld Close, Pickering YO18 9NJ* T: (01751) 476226

SCOTT, James William. b 39. S Dios Minl Tr Scheme 84. **d** 88 **p** 89. NSM Bremhill w Foxham and Hilmarton *Sarum* 88-94; NSM Derry Hill w Bremhill and Foxham 94-09. *14 Bremhill, Calne SN11 9LA* T: (01249) 813114
E: james@bremhill.force9.co.uk

SCOTT, Jane. *See* SCOTT, Elizabeth Jane

SCOTT, Canon Janice Beasant. b 44. Cam Th Federation MA 08 MCSP 66. EAMTC 89. **d** 92 **p** 94. NSM Fakenham w Alethorpe *Nor* 92-95; C Eaton 95-99; R Dickleburgh and The Pulhams 99-09; RD Redenhall 03-06; PtO 09-13; P-in-c Trowse from 13; Hon Can Nor Cathl from 08. *19 Ipswich Grove, Norwich NR2 2LU* T: (01603) 396744 M: 07450-480023
E: rockingrector@gmail.com

SCOTT, John. *See* SCOTT, William John

SCOTT, John. b 54. QUB BD 79. CITC 80. **d** 81 **p** 82. C Willowfield *D & D* 81-83; C Newtownards 83-85; I Kilskeery w Trillick *Clogh* 85-90; LtO *D & D* 90-96; I Bright w Ballee and Killough 96-01; PtO from 01. *Ash Tree House, Moor Road, Ballyward, Castlewellan BT31 9TY* T: (028) 4065 0908
E: john@ashtreehouse.net

SCOTT, John. b 54. Heriot-Watt Univ BA 76 Leeds Univ BA 97 Heythrop Coll Lon MA 05. Coll of Resurr Mirfield 95. **d** 97 **p** 98. C Bethnal Green St Matt w St Jas the Gt *Lon* 97-00; Asst Chapl Qu Mary and Westf Coll 97-00; C Heston 00-04; Inter-Faith Adv 00-05; USA 06-11; PtO *Win* 06-08; rtd 11. *Lakeview, Church Street, St Mary Bourne, Andover SP11 6BN* T: (01264) 738972 M: 07889-977593
E: absalom1662@yahoo.co.uk

SCOTT, John Eric. b 16. St Cath Coll Ox BA 38 MA 42 FSA. Ripon Hall Ox 39. **d** 40 **p** 41. C Heworth St Alb *Dur* 40-43; C Gateshead St Mary 43-45; Chapl and Sacr Ch Ch *Ox* 45-47; Ho Master Forest Sch Snaresbrook 55-81; P-in-c St Mich Cornhill w St Pet le Poer etc *Lon* 81-85; rtd 85. *17 Harman Avenue, Woodford Green IG8 9DS* T: (020) 8505 7093

SCOTT, John Harold. b 46. Univ of Wales (Cardiff) BSc 69. St Steph Ho Ox 69. **d** 72 **p** 73. C Skewen *Llan* 72-74; C Port Talbot St Theodore 74-77; P-in-c Bedlinog 77-78; V 78-85; R Penderyn w Ystradfellte and Pontneathvaughan *S & B* 85-04; R Penderyn Mellte 04-12; P-in-c 12-14. *20 The Pines, Hirwaun, Aberdare CF44 9QW* M: 07711-961667
E: jhs46@tesco.net

SCOTT, John Peter. b 47. Open Univ BA 80. Lambeth STh 81 K Coll Lon 69 St Aug Coll Cant 74. **d** 75 **p** 76. C Dartford St Alb *Roch* 75-78; C-in-c Goring-by-Sea *Chich* 78-81; Chapl Wells Hosp 81-86; Chapl Meare Manor Hosp 81-86; CF (TAVR) 82-90; Chapl Pangbourne Coll 86-90; Min Reigate St Phil CD *S'wark* 90-92; P-in-c Reigate St Phil 92-14; Chapl St Bede's Ecum Sch Reigate 90-13; rtd 14; PtO *S'wark* from 14. *5 Haine Close, Horley RH6 9SU* E: johnpeterscott@gmail.com

SCOTT, John Vickers. b 48. Open Univ BA 88 MCIOB 81. CBDTI 02. **d** 05 **p** 06. NSM Penwortham St Leon *Blackb* 05-09; P-in-c Chipping and Whitewell 09-15; rtd 15; PtO *Blackb* from 15. *10 Cuerden Rise, Lostock Hall, Preston PR5 5YD* M: 07875-895354 T: (01772) 335555
E: frjohn.chipping@btinternet.com

SCOTT (née GOLDIE), Canon Katrina Ruth. b 76. Fitzw Coll Cam BA 97 MPhil 00 MA 01. Westcott Ho Cam 98. **d** 00 **p** 01. C Cov E 00-04; V Willenhall 04-15; Dioc Adv for Women's Min 06-10; Dean Women's Min 10-15; Hon Can Cov Cathl 10-15; R The Guitings, Cutsdean, Farmcote etc *Glouc* from 15; AD N Cotswold from 15. *The Rectory, Copse Hill Road, Lower Slaughter, Cheltenham GL54 2HY* E: krgscott@hotmail.com

SCOTT, Keith Brounton de Salve. b 55. QUB BD. **d** 83 **p** 84. C Belfast St Matt *Conn* 83-87; I Ardclinis and Tickmacrevan w Layde and Cushendun 87-01; CMS 02-09; P-in-c Rathkeale w Askeaton, Kilcornan and Kilnaughtin *L & K* from 09. *The Rectory, Church Street, Askeaton, Co Limerick, Republic of Ireland* T: (00353) (61) 398647 E: kbs16355@gmail.com *or* rathkeale@limerick.anglican.org

SCOTT, Kenneth James. b 46. Bris Univ BA 68. Trin Coll Bris 71. **d** 73 **p** 74. C Illogan *Truro* 73-76; C Camberley St Paul *Guildf* 76-81; R Bradford Peverell, Stratton, Frampton etc *Sarum* 81-08; RD Dorchester 95-99; rtd 08; PtO *St E* from 09. *2 Fir Close, Wickham Market, Woodbridge IP13 0UB* T: (01728) 747232 E: kenscott@surfaid.org

SCOTT, Kevin Francis. b 51. Peterho Cam MA Mert Coll Ox DPhil 76 CChem MRSC. Wycliffe Hall Ox BA 83. **d** 83 **p** 84. C Ox St Ebbe w H Trin and St Pet 83-86; P-in-c Prestonpans *Edin* 86-93; R Musselburgh 86-93; R Edin SS Phil and Jas 93-08. *Kirklands, Craigend Road, Stow, Galashiels TD1 2RJ* T: 0131-208 0402 E: drkfs@aol.com

SCOTT, Kevin Peter. b 43. Coll of Resurr Mirfield 93. **d** 93 **p** 94. C Rushall *Lich* 93-97; P-in-c Goldenhill 97-10; rtd 10; PtO *Lich* from 12. *532 Turnhurst Road, Packmoor, Stoke-on-Trent ST7 4QB* T: (01782) 784141

SCOTT, Kevin Willard. b 53. Open Univ BA 96 Glos Univ MA 03. Linc Th Coll 92. **d** 92 **p** 93. C Walton-on-Thames *Guildf* 92-97; R Matson *Glouc* 97-03; RD Glouc City 01-03; V Malden St Jo *S'wark* from 03; AD Kingston 05-09; Chapl MU from 12. *5 Vicarage Close, Worcester Park KT4 7LZ* T: (020) 8337 8830 E: kevinwscott@btinternet.com

SCOTT, Lester Desmond Donald. NUI BA 89. CITC BTh 92. **d** 92 **p** 93. C Killeshandra w Killegar and Derrylane *K, E & A* 92-95; C Kilmore w Ballintemple 92-95; I Fenagh w Myshall, Aghade and Ardoyne *C & O* from 95. *The Glebe House, Ballon, Co Carlow, Republic of Ireland* T/F: (00353) (59) 915 9367 M: 87-250 4322 E: lesterscott@oceanfree.net

SCOTT (née CURRELL), Mrs Linda Anne. b 62. K Alfred's Coll Win BEd 84. Trin Coll Bris BA 92. **d** 92 **p** 94. Par Dn Tunbridge Wells St Mark *Roch* 92-94; C 94-97; TV Walthamstow *Chelmsf* 97-02; PtO 02-04; S'wark 05-14. *42 High Street, Yatton, Bristol BS49 4HJ* T: (01934) 838960 M: 07823-324979
E: scottlindatim@aol.com

SCOTT, Mrs Lissa Melanie. b 58. Birm Univ BA 79 PGCE 80. SAOMC 98. **d** 01 **p** 02. C Risborough *Ox* 01-06; Chapl Bucks Hosps NHS Trust 05-07; TV Monkwearmouth *Dur* 07-11; V Heighington and Darlington St Matt and St Luke from 11. *The Vicarage, 15 East Green, Heighington, Newton Aycliffe DL5 6PP* T: (01325) 312134
E: lissaandtom@btinternet.com

SCOTT, Canon Malcolm Kenneth Merrett. b 30. ACA 53 FCA 64. Clifton Th Coll 56. **d** 58 **p** 59. C Highbury Ch Ch *Lon* 58-60; CMS 60-61; Uganda 61-74; V Sunnyside w Bourne End *St Alb* 74-90; V Clapham 90-95; rtd 95; PtO *Lich* 96-14. *10 The Ring, Little Haywood, Stafford ST18 0TP* T: (01889) 881464

SCOTT, Nicholas Charles Andrew. b 74. Univ of Wales (Ban) BD 95. Westcott Ho Cam 97. **d** 99 **p** 00. C Ryde H Trin and Swanmore St Mich *Portsm* 99-01; C Burbage w Aston Flamville *Leic* 01-04; PtO *Cov* 04-08; NSM Willenhall 08-15. *The Rectory, Copse Hill Road, Lower Slaughter, Cheltenham GL54 2HY* E: ncascott@hotmail.com

SCOTT, Paul Malcolm. b 57. Sheff City Poly BA 79 CPFA 85. Ripon Coll Cuddesdon 98. **d** 00 **p** 01. C N Shields *Newc* 00-03; V Shiremoor 03-12; V Alnwick from 12. *St Michael's Vicarage, Howling Lane, Alnwick NE66 1DH* T: (01665) 602184
E: paulscott1957@btinternet.com

SCOTT, Mrs Pauline Claire Michalak. b 55. St Anne's Coll Ox BA 77 MA 82 Dur Univ PGCE 78. TISEC 98. **d** 01 **p** 02. NSM Papworth *Ely* 01-05; TV Ely 05-09; P-in-c Alresford *Chelmsf* 09-10; P-in-c Gt Bentley and Frating w Thorrington 09-10; V Alresford and Frating w Thorrington from 10. *The Rectory, St Andrew's Close, Alresford, Colchester CO7 8BL* T: (01206) 822088 M: 07855-395840 E: paulinecm.scott@tiscali.co.uk

SCOTT, Peter Crawford. b 35. Ch Ch Ox BA 56 MA 61. Cuddesdon Coll 60. **d** 62 **p** 63. C Broseley w Benthall *Heref* 62-66; P-in-c Hughenden *Ox* 66-71; C Hykeham *Linc* 71-73; P-in-c Stottesdon *Heref* 73-76; Australia from 76; rtd 97. *33 Church Street, Coleraine Vic 3315, Australia* F: (0061) (3) 5575 2491

SCOTT, Peter James Douglas Sefton. b 59. OBE 03. Edin Univ BD 83. Edin Th Coll 81. **d** 83 **p** 84. C Helensburgh *Glas* 83-86; C-in-c Glas St Oswald 86-89; R 89-91; Chapl RN 91-15; rtd 15; NSM Midi-Pyrénées and Aude *Eur* from 15. *Les Mayrins, 46000 Cahors, France* T: (0033) 5 65 23 62 30
E: peterscott@live.com

SCOTT, Peter Lindsay. b 29. Keble Coll Ox BA 54 MA 58. Linc Th Coll 54. **d** 56 **p** 57. C Weston-super-Mare St Sav *B & W* 56-59; C Knowle H Nativity *Bris* 59-61; P-in-c Glas St Pet 61-63; V Heap Bridge *Man* 63-73; V Rochdale St Geo w St Alb 73-86; R Droylsden St Andr 86-94; rtd 94; PtO *Man* from 94. *2 Chancel Place, Rochdale OL16 1FB* T: (01706) 523270

SCOTT, Prof Peter Manley. b 61. Birm Univ BA 83 MA 84 Bris Univ PhD 91. All SS Cen for Miss & Min 12. **d** 14 **p** 15. NSM

Old Trafford St Jo *Man* from 14. *40 Brookleigh Road, Manchester M20 4RX* T: 0161-445 0774 M: 07932-688503 E: peter.m.scott@dsl.pipex.com

SCOTT, Ruth. *See* SCOTT, Helen Ruth

SCOTT, Sara Rosamund. b 49. Portsm Poly BSc 70 Plymouth Poly MPhil 74. SEITE 97. **d** 00 **p** 01. NSM Rotherhithe H Trin *S'wark* 00-04; NSM Sydenham H Trin and St Aug 04-14; PtO from 14. *53 Sprules Road, London SE24 2NL* T: (020) 7639 6311 F: 7639 1842 E: sarascott@btinternet.com

SCOTT, Simon James. b 65. Ch Ch Ox BA 87 MA 90. Wycliffe Hall Ox 87. **d** 91 **p** 92. C Cheadle All Hallows *Ches* 91-95; Scripture Union 95-98; C Cambridge H Sepulchre *Ely* 98-05; R Lt Shelford from 05. *The Rectory, 2 Manor Road, Little Shelford, Cambridge CB22 5HF* T: (01223) 841998 M: 07739-984323 E: simonjscott1965@btinternet.com

SCOTT, The Ven Terence. b 56. QUB BSc 77. CITC 77. **d** 80 **p** 81. C Ballymena w Ballyclug *Conn* 80-83; C Antrim All SS 83-85; P-in-c Connor w Antrim St Patr 85-88; I Magherafelt *Arm* from 88; Hon V Choral Arm Cathl 95-06; Can Arm Cathl from 06; Adn Arm from 14. *The Rectory, 1 Churchwell Lane, Magherafelt BT45 6AL* T: (028) 7963 2365 M: 07590-894529 E: terryscott123@btinternet.com

SCOTT, Canon Theresa Anne. b 53. Bris Univ BSc 75 Lon Univ PGCE 76. Ox Min Course 89. **d** 92 **p** 94. NSM Wickham Bishops w Lt Braxted *Chelmsf* 92-93; NSM Drayton St Pet (Abingdon) *Ox* 94-01; NSM Convenor (Berks) 97-01; Bp's Officer for NSM 98-01; Bp's Adv for Women in Ord Min 01-05; P-in-c Hurley and Stubbings 01-02; V Burchetts Green 02-08; AD Maidenhead and Windsor 05-07; TR Bicester w Bucknell, Caversfield and Launton 08-13; Hon Can Ch Ch 05-13; rtd 13; PtO *Ox* from 13. *24 High Street, Thame OX9 2BZ* T: (01844) 218730 E: theresa.scott@driftway.co.uk

SCOTT, Timothy Charles Nairne. b 61. Ex Univ BA 83. Westcott Ho Cam 84. **d** 87 **p** 88. C Romford St Edw *Chelmsf* 87-89; Community Priest 89-94; P-in-c Leytonstone H Trin and St Aug Harrow Green 94-97; V 97-02; Educn and Tr Adv (Bradwell Area) 02-04; R S'wark Ch Ch 04-13; PtO 13-14; TR Yatton Moor *B & W* from 14. *42 High Street, Yatton, Bristol BS49 4HJ* E: timcnscott@gmail.com

SCOTT, Timothy David. b 68. Girton Coll Cam BA 89 Warw Univ PGCE 91. Ridley Hall Cam 13. **d** 15. C Romford Gd Shep *Chelmsf* from 15. *470 Mawney Road, Romford RM7 8QB* T: (01708) 762159 M: 07766-793959 E: davescott@thegoodshepherd.org.uk

SCOTT, Trevor Ian. b 57. Culham Coll Ox CertEd 79. EAMTC 97. **d** 98 **p** 99. NSM Waltham H Cross *Chelmsf* from 98. *Hartland Villas, 208 High Road, Broxbourne EN10 6QF* T: (01992) 420376 *or* 450321 E: trevor.scott2@ntlworld.com

SCOTT, William. b 20. MBE 97. St Chad's Coll Dur BA 46 Leeds Univ DipEd 53. **d** 60 **p** 61. CR 60-99; C Wolborough w Newton Abbot *Ex* 60-63; Chapl St Cath Sch Bramley 63-67; Chapl St Mary and St Anne's Sch Abbots Bromley 67-76; PtO *Cant* 77-90; Chapl Boulogne-sur-Mer w Calais and Lille *Eur* 87-90; Chapl Lille 90-97; rtd 97; PtO *Eur* from 97. *42 Westgate Court Avenue, Canterbury CT2 8JR* T: (01227) 456277

SCOTT, William John. b 46. MBE 14. TCD BA 70. CITC. **d** 71 **p** 72. C Bangor St Comgall *D & D* 71-74; C Holywood 74-80; Dioc Min of Healing Team from 75; I Carnalea 80-90; N Ireland Wing Chapl ATC from 80; I Seapatrick *D & D* 90-11; Treas Dromore Cathl 02-08; Adn Dromore 05-11; rtd 11. *11 Lord Moira Park, Ballynahinch BT24 8TF* T: (028) 9756 4851 M: 07803-147751 E: john@scottsfamily.co.uk

SCOTT, Preb William Sievwright. b 46. CVO 14. Edin Th Coll 67. **d** 70 **p** 71. C Glas St Ninian 70-73; C Bridgwater St Fran *B & W* 73-77; R Shepton Beauchamp w Barrington, Stocklinch etc 77-81; P-in-c Cossington and Woolavington 82-84; Chapl Community of All Hallows Ditchingham 84-91; V Pimlico St Mary Bourne Street *Lon* 91-02; P-in-c Pimlico St Barn 97-01; V 01-02; AD Westmr St Marg 97-04; Preb St Paul's Cathl from 00; Chapl to RVO and Qu Chpl of the Savoy 02-07; Chapl to The Queen 03-07; Sub-Dean HM Chpls R and Dep Clerk of the Closet 07-15; Sub-Almoner and Dom Chapl to The Queen 07-15; rtd 15; PtO *Lon* from 15. *13 Kylestrome House, Cundy Street, London SW1W 9JT* M: 07941-470399 T: (020) 7730 6920 E: bournebill@btinternet.com

SCOTT-BROMLEY, Mrs Deborah Joan. b 58. Surrey Univ BA 01 Open Univ BA 96 K Coll Lon MA 11 AKC 12. STETS 98. **d** 01 **p** 02. C Hale w Badshot Lea *Guildf* 01-05; V Bordon from 05. *St Mark's Vicarage, 58 Forest Road, Bordon GU35 0BP* T: (01420) 477550 M: 07855-704849 E: zadoka.rev@virgin.net

SCOTT-DEMPSTER, Canon Colin Thomas. b 37. Em Coll Cam BA 65 MA 68. Cuddesdon Coll 64. **d** 66 **p** 67. C Caversham *Ox* 66-69; Chapl Coll of SS Mark and Jo Chelsea 69-73; V Chieveley w Winterbourne and Oare *Ox* 73-02; RD Newbury

77-98; Hon Can Ch Ch 90-02; rtd 02; PtO *St And* from 10. *Old Faskally House, Killiecrankie, Pitlochry PH16 5LG* T: (01796) 473575 E: colin@faskally25.freeserve.co.uk

SCOTT-GARNETT, Linda. b 44. **d** 07 **p** 08. NSM Bermondsey St Hugh CD *S'wark* 07-14; PtO from 14. *1 Strood House, Manciple Street, London SE1 4LR* T: (020) 7642 1367 M: 07425-135804 E: revlindasg@gmail.com

SCOTT-HAMBLEN, Shane. b 66. Webster Univ (USA) BMus 89 St Thos Aquinas Univ Rome STB 94 MA 96 STL 96. **d** 94 **p** 95. C Staines St Mary and St Pet *Lon* 97-99; USA from 99; R Highlands St Mary from 02. *The Episcopal Church of St Mary, 1 Chestnut Street, Cold Spring NY 10516, USA* T: (001) (845) 265 2539

SCOTT-THOMPSON, Ian Mackenzie. b 57. Ch Ch Ox BA 78. St Jo Coll Nottm BA 82. **d** 83 **p** 84. C Hartley Wintney, Elvetham, Winchfield etc *Win* 83-85; C Bitterne 85-89; V Iford 89-99; P-in-c Holdenhurst 95-99; TR Cove St Jo *Guildf* 99-06; RD Aldershot 03-06; V Wonersh w Blackheath 06-10; P-in-c Marks Tey and Aldham *Chelmsf* from 10. *The Rectory, Church Lane, Marks Tey, Colchester CO6 1LW* T: (01206) 215772 E: ian.scott-thompson@virgin.net

SCRACE, Canon David Peter. b 46. Sarum & Wells Th Coll 79. **d** 81 **p** 82. C Abbots Langley *St Alb* 81-85; TV Chippenham St Paul w Hardenhuish etc *Bris* 85-91; P-in-c Harnham *Sarum* 91-99; V 99-11; RD Salisbury 93-98; Can and Preb Sarum Cathl 10-11; rtd 11; C Budleigh Salterton, E Budleigh w Bicton etc *Ex* 12-14. *14 Roselands, Sidmouth EX10 8PD* T: (01395) 708239 E: d.scrace@btopenworld.com

SCRAGG, Michael John. b 39. Griffith Univ Brisbane BA 93 MA 01 Jas Cook Univ Townsville BCommWelf 97. St Fran Coll Brisbane 73. **d** 74 **p** 75. C Camp Hill w Carina Australia 74-77; C Chesterton Gd Shep *Ely* 77-79; C Maryborough Australia 79-80; V Biggenden 80-85; Chapl Wolstone Park Hosp 85-91; P-in-c Taroom 91-96; C Willunga w Seaford Ecum Miss 96-97; PtO 97-98; rtd 98; PtO Brisbane Australia 98-05; Guardian Community of the Epiphany 05-15. *Clarendon Spence, 18/79 Spence Street, PO Box 5143, Cairns QLD 4870, Australia* M: (0061) 40-905 0606

SCRASE-FIELD, Edward Fraser Austin Longmer. b 76. Aber Univ BSc 98 Man Univ PhD 04 Cam Univ BA 07. Ridley Hall Cam 05. **d** 08 **p** 09. C Denton Holme *Carl* 08-11; C Cheadle *Ches* from 11. *1 Warren Avenue, Cheadle SK8 1NB* T: 0161-915 9849 M: 07730-514074

SCREECH, Prof Michael. b 26. Ordre national du Mérite 83 Chevalier Légion d'Honneur 92. Univ Coll Lon BA 50 Birm Univ DLitt 59 Univ Coll Lon DLitt 82 All So Coll Ox MA 84 DLitt 90 Ex Univ Hon DLitt 93 Geneva Univ Hon DD 98 FBA 81 FRSL 87. Ox Min Course 92. **d** 93 **p** 94. NSM Ox St Giles and SS Phil and Jas w St Marg 93-02; PtO from 02; Extraordinary Fell Wolfs Coll Ox from 93; Chapl and Fell All So Coll Ox 01-03. *5 Swanston Field, Whitchurch on Thames, Reading RG8 7HP* T/F: 0118-984 2513

✠**SCREECH, The Rt Revd Royden.** b 53. K Coll Lon BD 74 AKC 74. St Aug Coll Cant 75. **d** 76 **p** 77 **c** 00. C Hatcham St Cath *S'wark* 76-80; V Nunhead St Antony 80-87; P-in-c Nunhead St Silas 82-87; RD Camberwell 83-87; V New Addington 87-94; Selection Sec ABM 94-97; Sen Selection Sec Min Division Abps' Coun 97-00; Suff Bp St Germans *Truro* 00-11; rtd 12. *61 Edgcumbe Road, St Austell PL25 5DX* E: royscreech@yahoo.com

SCRINE, Ralph. b 19. Bris Univ BA 40 Fitzw Ho Cam BA 46 MA 60 Lon Univ MPhil 81. Westcott Ho Cam 45. **d** 46 **p** 47. C Moorfields *Bris* 46-51; P-in-c Biddestone w Slaughterford 51-52; P-in-c Lockleaze CD 52-60; V St Jas Less 60-65; Chapl Eliz Coll Guernsey 60-65; Lect Div Ch Ch Coll Cant 65-68; Chapl Ch Ch Coll of HE Cant 68-75; Sen Lect Ch Ch Coll Cant 68-84; rtd 84; PtO *Cant* 84-03. *6 Oaklands, Orchard Rise, Groombridge, Tunbridge Wells TN3 9RX* T: (01892) 861577

✠**SCRIVEN, The Rt Revd Henry William.** b 51. Sheff Univ BA 72. St Jo Coll Nottm 73. **d** 75 **p** 76 **c** 95. C Walkergate H Trin *Lon* 75-79; SAMS Argentina 79-82; USA 82-83; SAMS Spain 84-90; Chapl Madrid w Bilbao *Eur* 90-95; Suff Bp Eur 95-02; Dean Brussels 95-97; Dir of Ords 97-02; Suff Bp Pittsburgh USA 02-08; Miss Dir for S America SAMS / CMS from 09; Hon Asst Bp Ox from 09; Hon Asst Bp Win from 13. *16 East St Helen Street, Abingdon OX14 5EA* T: (01235) 536607 *or* (01865) 787500 E: henry.scriven@cms-uk.org

SCRIVEN, Hugh Alexander. b 59. Trin Coll Cam BA 80. Cranmer Hall Dur 81. **d** 84 **p** 85. C Pudsey St Lawr and St Paul *Bradf* 84-87; C Madeley *Heref* 87-91; TV 91-00; V Edgbaston St Germain *Birm* from 00. *St Germain's Vicarage, 180 Portland Road, Birmingham B16 9TD* T: 0121-429 3431

SCRIVENER, John Glenfield (Glen). b 78. Ball Coll Ox BA 96. Oak Hill Th Coll BTh 07. **d** 07 **p** 08. C Eastbourne All So *Chich* 07-11; Evang Revival Media from 11. *84 Susans Road, Eastbourne BN21 3TH* T: (01323) 644054 M: 07876-031734 E: glen@christthetruth.org.uk

SCRIVENER, Margaret Thelma. b 69. RN. STETS. **d** 12 **p** 13. NSM E Win from 12. *21 Westwood Gardens, Chandlers Ford, Eastleigh SO53 1FN* T: (023) 8026 3471
E: marscriv@gmail.com

SCRIVENER, Robert Allan. b 54. Nottm Univ BEd 78 Hull Univ BTh 98 De Montfort Univ Leic MA 99 Huddersfield Univ BA 03. Linc Th Coll 79. **d** 80 **p** 81. C Sherwood *S'well* 80-83; C Burghclere w Newtown and Ecchinswell w Sydmonton *Win* 83-86; TV Hemel Hempstead *St Alb* 86-93; V Kingston upon Hull St Nic *York* 93-03; V Mansfield Woodhouse *S'well* from 03. *The Vicarage, 7 Butt Lane, Mansfield Woodhouse, Mansfield NG19 9JS* T: (01623) 621875
E: allan.scrivener@virginmedia.com

SCRIVENS, Mrs Elaine. b 53. TCert 74 Man Univ BEd 75. NEOC. **d** 00 **p** 01. NSM E Coatham *York* 00-02; NSM Coatham and Dormanstown 02-04; Chapl Ven Bede Sch Ryhope 04-10; P-in-c Bishop's Tachbrook *Cov* from 10. *The Vicarage, 24 Mallory Road, Bishops Tachbrook, Leamington Spa CV33 9QX* T: (01926) 426922

SCROGGIE, Mrs Felicity Marie-Louise. b 62. Pemb Coll Ox BA 86 St Andr Univ MPhil 87. STETS BTh 99. **d** 99 **p** 00. C Brondesbury St Anne w Kilburn H Trin *Lon* 99-02; V Sudbury St Andr 02-13; AD Brent 10-13; TR Kidlington w Hampton Poyle *Ox* from 13. *The Rectory, 19 Mill Street, Kidlington OX5 2EE* T: (01865) 372230

SCULLY, Hazel Mary. RGN SCM. **d** 01 **p** 02. Aux Min Portarlington w Cloneyhurke, Lea etc *M & K* 01-06; Chapl Wilson's Hosp Sch Multyfarnham from 06; NSM Mullingar, Portnashangan, Moyliscar, Kilbixy etc from 11. *Wilson's Hospital School, Multyfarnham, Co Westmeath, Republic of Ireland* T: (00353) (44) 937 1115 M: 87-281 3956

SCULLY, Kevin John. b 55. NIDA BDA 96. St Steph Ho Ox 91. **d** 93 **p** 94. C Stoke Newington St Mary *Lon* 93-97; C Stepney St Dunstan and All SS 97-00; Dir of Ords and Voc Adv 97-00; P-in-c Bethnal Green St Matt w St Jas the Gt 00-02; R from 02. *St Matthew's Rectory, Hereford Street, London E2 6EX* T/F: (020) 7739 7586 E: kevin.scully@london.anglican.org

SCURR, David. b 54. Wilson Carlile Coll 98 SAOMC 05. **d** 05 **p** 06. C Thatcham *Ox* 05-08; P-in-c Farndon and Coddington *Ches* 08-12; V from 12. *The Vicarage, Church Lane, Farndon, Chester CH3 6QD* T/F: (01829) 270270
E: david.scurr@tinyworld.co.uk

SCUTTER, Canon James Edward. b 36. OBE 91. AKC 59 St Boniface Warminster 59. **d** 60 **p** 61. C Tilbury Docks *Chelmsf* 60-63; Bechuanaland 63-65; Rhodesia 65-70; New Zealand 70-79; Singapore 79-81; New Zealand from 81; Prin Chapl NZ Defence Force 84-91; QHC from 84; Hon Can Wellington from 87. *32 Waitaheke Road, RD1, Otaki 5581, New Zealand* T: (0064) (4) 364 3260
E: jandhscutter@asiaonline.net.nz

SEABOURNE (née PEARSON), Mrs Joanna Ruth. b 76. St Hilda's Coll Ox BA 97 PGCE 98 St Jo Coll Dur BA 05 MA 09. Cranmer Hall Dur 03. **d** 06 **p** 07. C Leeds St Geo *Ripon* 06-10; TV *Leeds* from 10; P-in-c Woodhouse and Wrangthorn from 12. *Kirkstall Vicarage, Leeds LS5 3HF*
E: joanna.seabourne@stgeorgesleeds.org.uk

SEABRIGHT, Mrs Elizabeth Nicola. b 52. SRN 73. WEMTC 01. **d** 04 **p** 05. NSM Ledbury *Heref* from 04; PtO *Worc* from 05. *The Grove Cottage, Fromes Hill, Ledbury HR8 1HP* T: (01531) 640252 M: 07977-016683 E: revdnick@gmail.com

SEABROOK, Alan Geoffrey. b 43. ALCD 65. **d** 66 **p** 67. C Bethnal Green St Jas Less *Lon* 66-70; C Madeley *Heref* 70-73; V Girlington *Bradf* 74-80; P-in-c Abdon w Clee St Margaret *Heref* 80-83; R Bitterley 80-83; P-in-c Cold Weston 80-83; P-in-c Hopton Cangeford 80-83; P-in-c Stoke St Milburgh w Heath 80-83; R Bitterley w Middleton, Stoke St Milborough etc 83-08; RD Ludlow 01-05; rtd 08. *Penhope House, Ballhurst, Bromyard HR7 4EF* T: (01885) 482184

SEABROOK, Alistair William. b 78. CCC Ox BA 99 MA 03. Oak Hill Th Coll MTh 06. **d** 06 **p** 07. C The Ortons, Alwalton and Chesterton *Ely* 06-09; C Elton w Stibbington and Water Newton 06-09; C Gladesville Australia from 09. *1/33B The Strand, Boronia Park NSW 2111, Australia* T: (0061) (2) 9817 2631 E: alistair_seabrook@yahoo.co.uk

SEABROOK, Paul. b 60. Univ of Wales (Cardiff) BA 81 Nottm Univ PGCE 82. Ridley Hall Cam 01. **d** 03 **p** 04. C Wimborne Minster *Sarum* 03-07; R Taverham *Nor* from 07. *The Rectory, 173 Taverham Road, Taverham, Norwich NR8 6SG* T: (01603) 868217 E: seabrooktribe@telco4u.net

SEABROOK, Penelope Anne. b 56. Hertf Coll Ox BA 77 K Coll Lon MA 98. SEITE 00. **d** 03 **p** 04. C Southfields St Barn *S'wark* 03-08; NSM 03-07; C Fulham All SS *Lon* from 08. *8 Deodar Road, London SW15 2NN* M: 07985-108541
E: pennyseabrook@hotmail.com

SEABROOK, The Ven Richard Anthony. b 68. Southn Univ BTh 92. Chich Th Coll 92. **d** 92 **p** 93. C Cottingham *York*

92-94; C Hawley H Trin *Guildf* 94-98; V Hockley *Chelmsf* 98-05; R Benalla Australia 05-09; R Mount Barker from 09; Adn The Murray 09-14; Adn The Murray-Riverland from 14; Dioc Admin The Murray 10-13. *PO Box 220, Mount Barker SA 5251, Australia* T: (0061) (8) 8398 2232
E: frras@blackwater.org.au

SEACH, Gregory John. b 65. Sydney Univ BA 88 DipEd 88 Clare Coll Cam PhD 09. Trin Coll Melbourne BD 02. **d** 02 **p** 02. C Camberwell St Jo Australia 02-04; PtO *Ely* 05-08; Dean Clare Coll Cam from 08. *Clare College, Cambridge CB2 1TL* T: (01223) 333240 E: gjs32@cam.ac.uk

SEAFORD, The Very Revd John Nicholas. b 39. Dur Univ BA 67. St Chad's Coll Dur 68. **d** 68 **p** 69. C Bush Hill Park St Mark *Lon* 68-71; C Stanmore *Win* 71-73; V N Baddesley 73-76; V Chilworth w N Baddesley 76-78; V Highcliffe w Hinton Admiral 78-93; RD Christchurch 90-93; Hon Can Win Cathl 93-05; Dean Jersey and R Jersey St Helier 93-05; Angl Adv Channel TV 93-05; Chapl Jersey Airport 98-00; Chapl HM Pris La Moye 03-05; rtd 05; PtO *Sarum* from 05; *Win* 05-14. *Claremont, Buffetts Road, Sturminster Newton DT10 1DZ* T: (01258) 471479

SEAGO, Timothy Paul. b 59. Ripon Coll Cuddesdon 06. **d** 08 **p** 09. C Marlborough *Sarum* 08-12; P-in-c Totteridge *St Alb* from 12. *St Andrew's Vicarage, 78 Greenway, London N20 8EJ* M: 07772-809136 E: timseago@btinternet.com

SEAGRAVE, Katherine Victoria. b 81. Wycliffe Hall Ox. **d** 09 **p** 10. C Balham Hill Ascension *S'wark* 09-13; C Ox St Aldate from 13. *St Aldate's Parish Centre, 40 Pembroke Street, Oxford OX1 1BP* T: (01865) 254800 M: 07905-342802
E: kate.seagrave@staldates.org.uk

SEAL, Canon Nicholas Peter. b 57. Ex Univ BA. Linc Th Coll 81. **d** 83 **p** 84. C Wareham *Sarum* 83-87; Chapl K Alfred Coll *Win* 87-91; V Stanmore 91-01; P-in-c Win St Matt 01-10; R from 10; RD Win 99-07; Chapl Peter Symonds Coll Win from 01; Hon Can Win Cathl from 13. *The Rectory, 44 Cheriton Road, Winchester SO22 5AY* T/F: (01962) 854849
E: peter.seal@ntlworld.com

SEAL, Philip Trevor. b 32. AKC 55. **d** 56 **p** 57. C Godalming *Guildf* 56-60; C Tamworth *Lich* 60-61; R Lich St Chad 61-73; Chapl HM Youth Cust Cen Swinfen Hall 66-73; R Shere *Guildf* 74-88; RD Cranleigh 76-81; V Abbotsbury, Portesham and Langton Herring *Sarum* 88-97; rtd 97; PtO *Ex* 01-08. *11 Wyatts Lane, Wareham BH20 4NH* T: (01929) 551471

SEAL (formerly MILLER), Mrs Rosamund Joy. b 56. R Holloway Coll Lon BSc 77 Whitelands Coll Lon PGCE 80. EMMTC 89. **d** 94 **p** 96. NSM Grantham *Linc* 94-96; C Stamford All SS w St Jo 96-00; C Spalding St Mary and St Nic 00-05; P-in-c Moulton 05-13; V Holbeach from 13; RD Elloe E from 09; RD Elloe W 09-13. *The Vicarage, 5 Church Street, Holbeach, Spalding PE12 7LL* T: (01406) 424989
E: rosamund@sealatmoulton.co.uk

SEAL, William Christopher Houston. b 50. Occidental Coll (USA) BA 72. Ch Div Sch of the Pacific (USA) MDiv 81. **d** 81 **p** 82. USA 81-88 and from 94; R Etton w Helpston *Pet* 88-94. *The Rectory, 171 Grove Street, Nevada City CA 95959-2601, USA* T: (001) (530) 265 8836

SEALE, William Arthur. b 62. NUI BA 84. CITC. **d** 87 **p** 88. C Drumragh w Mountfield *D & R* 87-90; I 01-14; I Drumgath w Drumgooland and Clonduff *D & D* 90-01; I Kells Union *M & K* from 14. *The Rectory, Mullingar Road, Kells, Co Meath, Republic of Ireland* T: (00353) (46) 929 3626

SEALY, Canon Gordon William Hugh. b 27. Leeds Univ BA 53 MA 64. Coll of Resurr Mirfield 53. **d** 55 **p** 56. C Greenford H Cross *Lon* 55-58; Br Honduras 58-68; R Tarrant Gunville, Tarrant Hinton etc *Sarum* 68-74; V Leic St Paul 74-96; Hon Can Leic Cathl 86-96; rtd 96. *12 Kingfisher Court, West Bay, Bridport DT6 4HQ* T: (01308) 422045

SEALY, Stephen. b 52. K Coll Lon BD 86 AKC 86. Linc Th Coll 86. **d** 88 **p** 89. C Botley *Portsm* 88-91; Min Can and Prec Cant Cathl 91-96; V Pembury *Roch* 96-04; V Sidcup St Jo from 04; AD Sidcup 08-14. *St John's Vicarage, 13 Church Avenue, Sidcup DA14 6BU* T/F: (020) 8300 0383
E: sealynk@btconnect.com

SEAMAN, Christopher Robert. b 34. St Jo Coll Ox BA 58 MA 74 Solicitor 62. Ox Min Course 92 SAOMC 94. **d** 95 **p** 96. NSM Watlington w Pyrton and Shirburn *Ox* 95-97; NSM Icknield 97-98; PtO 98-99 and from 05; Hon C Shippon 99-04. *5 Curtyn Close, Abingdon OX14 1SE* T: (01235) 520380

SEAMAN, John. *See* SEAMAN, Robert John

SEAMAN, Miss Miranda Kate. b 66. Univ Coll Lon BSc 88 Solicitor 90. EAMTC 02. **d** 05 **p** 06. NSM S Weald *Chelmsf* 05-08; NSM Ingatestone w Fryerning 08-10; NSM Downham w S Hanningfield 10-11; NSM Downham w S Hanningfield and Ramsden Bellhouse from 11. *54 High Street, Stock, Ingatestone CM4 9BW* T: (01277) 841921 *or* 210021 M: 07909-522763 E: seaman-young@tiscali.co.uk

SEAMAN, Canon Paul Robert. b 61. Bp Grosseteste Coll BEd 82. Chich Th Coll 83. **d** 86 **p** 87. C Tilehurst St Mich *Ox* 86-91; TV Moulsecoomb *Chich* 91-95; R Whyke w Rumboldswhyke and Portfield 95-06; V E Grinstead St Mary from 06; Can and Preb Chich Cathl from 14. *St Mary's Vicarage, Windmill Lane, East Grinstead RH19 2DS* T: (01342) 323439

SEAMAN (née HEWLINS), Mrs Pauline Elizabeth. b 47. Lon Univ BD 68 AKC. Ox Min Course 93. **d** 96 **p** 97. NSM Radley and Sunningwell *Ox* 96-99; NSM Shippon 99-09; P-in-c 06-09; Chapl SS Helen and Kath Sch Abingdon 96-04; Chapl SW Oxon Primary Care Trust 05-07; PtO *Ox* from 09. *5 Curtyn Close, Abingdon OX14 1SE* T: (01235) 520380

SEAMAN, Robert John. b 44. Glos Univ BA 04 Newland Park Teacher Tr Coll DipEd 69 ACP 84. EAMTC 84. **d** 84 **p** 85. NSM Downham Market w Bexwell *Ely* 84-90; V Southea w Murrow and Parson Drove 90-97; V Guyhirn w Ring's End 90-97; V Newnham w Awre and Blakeney *Glouc* 97-08; AD Forest N 04-08; Hon C Whitwick, Thringstone and Swannington *Leic* 08-11; rtd 11; PtO *Leic* from 11; *Pet* from 11. *6 Hiawatha, Wellingborough NN8 3SH* T: (01933) 382165 E: shipmates2@hotmail.co.uk

SEAMER, Stephen James George. b 50. AKC 73. Ridley Hall Cam 74. **d** 75 **p** 76. C Rustington *Chich* 75-78; C Bulwell St Jo *S'well* 78-79; P-in-c Camber and E Guldeford *Chich* 79-80; TV Rye 80-83; V Knowle *Birm* 83-87; Assoc Chapl Brussels Cathl 87-88; P-in-c Tervuren 88-94; Chapl 94-98; P-in-c Liège 90-98; V Tonbridge SS Pet and Paul *Roch* 98-06; Chapl Düsseldorf *Eur* 06-14; rtd 14; PtO *Nor* from 15. *The Eyrie, 6 Suffield Court, Mill Road, Cromer NR27 0BH* T: (01263) 479616 E: cromerclifftops@gmail.com

SEAR, Benjamin William. b 84. Southn Univ BSc 07. Oak Hill Th Coll BA 15. **d** 15. C Patcham *Chich* from 15. *78A Mackie Avenue, Brighton BN1 8RB* E: benjamin.w.sear@gmail.com

SEAR, Mrs Julie Anne Caradoc. b 61. Trin Coll Bris 08. **d** 10 **p** 11. C Ashington, Washington and Wiston w Buncton *Chich* 10-13; R Hartfield w Coleman's Hatch from 13. *The Rectory, Church Street, Hartfield TN7 4AG* M: 07840-021909 E: julie.sear@googlemail.com

SEAR, Peter Lionel. b 49. Ex Univ BA 72. Linc Th Coll 72. **d** 74 **p** 75. C Sheldon *Birm* 74-77; C Caversham *Ox* 77-81; C Caversham St Pet and Mapledurham etc 81-85; TR Thatcham 85-98; V Castle Cary w Ansford *B & W* 98-00; rtd 00; PtO *B & W* from 03. *Plumtree Cottage, 1 Rodmore Road, Evercreech, Shepton Mallet BA4 6JL* T: (01749) 838843 E: peter@knowlecottage.eclipse.co.uk

SEAR, Terence Frank. b 39. LDS 62 Univ Coll Lon BDS 63. Portsm Dioc Tr Course 88. **d** 89. NSM Ryde H Trin *Portsm* 89-98; NSM Swanmore St Mich w Havenstreet 89-92; NSM Swanmore St Mich 92-98; NSM Wroxall 99-00; NSM Godshill 99-01; PtO from 02. *34 Whitehead Crescent, Wootton Bridge, Ryde PO33 4JF* T: (01983) 883560

SEARE, Mrs Janice Mae. b 48. SEN. STETS 99. **d** 02 **p** 03. NSM Holdenhurst and Iford *Win* from 02. *Wood Farm, Holdenhurst Village, Bournemouth BH8 0EE* T: (01202) 302468 F: 391281

SEARL, John. b 37. Southn Univ BSc 58 Edin Univ PhD 69. **d** 00 **p** 01. NSM Edin St Cuth 00-03; Asst P Poolewe and Kishorn *Mor* 05-08; LtO from 08. *Tulach Ard, Badachro, Gairloch IV21 2AA* T: (01445) 741231 E: johnsearl@btinternet.com

SEARLE, Alan Mansfield. b 47. SEITE 04. **d** 07 **p** 08. NSM E Malling, Wateringbury and Teston *Roch* from 07. *6 Cobbs Close, Wateringbury, Maidstone ME18 5NJ* T: (01622) 814443 E: alan.searle8@btinternet.com

SEARLE, Anthony Miles. b 76. Univ of Wales (Abth) BSc 98 PGCE 99 SS Coll Cam BTh 10. Westcott Ho Cam 98. **d** 10 **p** 11. C Bishop's Stortford St Mich *St Alb* 10-13; Chapl Oundle Sch from 13. *Oundle School, Great Hall, New Street, Oundle, Peterborough PE8 4GH* T: (01832) 277122 M: 07785-357562 E: asearle76@googlemail.com

SEARLE, Charles Peter. b 20. Selw Coll Cam BA 48 MA 53. Ridley Hall Cam. **d** 50 **p** 51. C Becontree St Mary *Chelmsf* 50-53; P-in-c Bedford St Jo *St Alb* 53-56; R 56-60; V Weston-super-Mare Ch Ch *B & W* 60-70; V Woking Ch Ch *Guildf* 70-85; rtd 85; PtO *Ex* 85-07. *59 Alexandra Road, Windsor SL4 1HZ* E: asearle@dialstart.net

SEARLE, David William. b 37. MASI 89 ACIOB 98. **d** 99 **p** 00. OLM E Bergholt and Brantham *St E* 99-07; rtd 07; PtO *St E* from 07. *46 Chaplin Road, East Bergholt, Colchester CO7 6SR* T: (01206) 298932

SEARLE, Canon Hugh Douglas. b 35. St Cath Coll Cam BA 59 MA 63 Cranfield Inst of Tech MSc 85. Oak Hill Th Coll 59. **d** 61 **p** 62. C Islington H Trin Cloudesley Square *Lon* 61-64; Chapl HM Pris Lewes 64-65; Chapl HM Borstal Roch 65-69; Chapl HM Youth Cust Cen Hollesley Bay Colony 70-74; Chapl HM Pris Parkhurst 74-78; P-in-c Barton *Ely* 78-84; V 84-00; P-in-c Coton 78-84; R 84-00; RD Bourn 81-92; Hon Can Ely Cathl 97-00; rtd 00; PtO *Ely* from 00. *38 Field End, Witchford, Ely CB6 2XE* T: (01353) 659749 E: hugdoug@talktalk.net

SEARLE, The Ven Jacqueline Ann. b 60. Whitelands Coll Lon BEd 82 Bris Univ MA 01. Trin Coll Bris 90. **d** 92 **p** 94. Par Dn Roxeth *Lon* 92-94; C Ealing St Steph Castle Hill 94-96; Tutor and Dean of Women Trin Coll Bris 96-03; P-in-c Littleover *Derby* 03-04; V 04-12; RD Derby S 10-12; Hon Can Derby Cathl 11-12; Adn Glouc from 12; Can Res Glouc Cathl from 12. *2 College Green, Gloucester GL1 2LR* T: (01452) 835594 E: archdglos@glosdioc.org.uk

SEARLE, Canon John Francis. b 42. OBE 98. Lon Univ MB, BS 66 FRCA 70 FRSocMed 84. SWMTC 92. **d** 95 **p** 96. NSM Ex St Leon w H Trin 95-03; Assoc Staff Member SWMTC from 03; PtO *Truro* from 03; Can Res Ex Cathl from 15. *Belle Isle Lodge, Belle Isle Drive, Exeter EX2 4RY* T: (01392) 432153 M: 07814-712921 E: j.f.searle@btinternet.com

SEARLE, Mark Robin. b 73. Cen Sch Speech & Drama BA 94. Trin Coll Bris BA 03. **d** 03 **p** 04. C Cant St Mary Bredin 03-07; C Ashtead *Guildf* 07-10; P-in-c Upton *Ex* from 10. *Upton Rectory, Furzehill Road, Torquay TQ1 3JG* T: (01803) 201119 E: revmarksearle@gmail.com

SEARLE, Michael Westran. b 47. Leeds Univ LLB 68. Cuddesdon Coll 69. **d** 71 **p** 72. C Norton St Mary *Dur* 71-74; C Westbury-on-Trym H Trin *Bris* 74-77; V Bedminster Down 77-84; V Bris Ch the Servant Stockwood 84-88; Dir of Tr *York* 88-00; R Dunnington 00-07; rtd 07. *Lamorna Vean, Lamorna, Penzance TR19 6NY* T: (01736) 810218 E: msearle@yorktrain.demon.co.uk

SEARLE, Peter. *See* SEARLE, Charles Peter

SEARLE, Philip Robert. b 67. Westcott Ho Cam. **d** 95 **p** 96. C Plymstock *Ex* 95-97; C Plymstock and Hooe 97-98; TV Stoke-upon-Trent *Lich* 98-10; PtO from 10. *164 Vicarage Gardens, Plymouth PL5 1LJ* E: phil.hairetic@hotmail.co.uk

SEARLE-BARNES, Albert Victor. b 28. Sheff Univ MA 48 Lon Univ BD 53. ALCD 53. **d** 53 **p** 54. C Iver *Ox* 53-55; C Attenborough w Bramcote *S'well* 55-59; C Bramcote 55-59; R Cratfield w Heveningham and Ubbeston *St E* 59-64; R Wick w Doynton *Bris* 64-70; PtO 70-72; V Downend 73-78; V Market Rasen *Linc* 78-86; R Linwood 79-86; V Legsby 79-86; R Green's Norton w Bradden *Pet* 86-88; V Hambledon *Portsm* 88-92; rtd 92; PtO *Glouc* 92-09. *30 Gracey Court, Woodland Road, Exeter EX5 3GA* T: (01392) 462613

SEARLE-BARNES, Belinda Rosemary. b 51. Lon Univ MA 93 ARCM 72 GRSM 73. Sarum Th Coll 93. **d** 96 **p** 97. NSM Pimperne, Stourpaine, Durweston and Bryanston *Sarum* 96-00; Asst Par Development Adv 98-00; Asst Chapl Bryanston Sch 98-00; TV Southampton (City Cen) *Win* 00-04; Chapl Godolphin Sch 04-07; P-in-c Winslow w Gt Horwood and Addington *Ox* 07-08; R 08-14; rtd 14. *The Studio, Main Road, East Boldre, Brockenhurst SO42 7WD* T: (01590) 611233 E: belinda@searle-barnes.com

SEARS, Helen. *See* THAKE, Helen

SEARS, Jacqueline Isabella. SRN 69. NTMTC 95. **d** 99 **p** 00. NSM Hanwell St Mellitus w St Mark *Lon* 99-03; Asst Chapl Essex Rivers Healthcare NHS Trust 03-04; Chapl 04-06; C Ipswich St Matt *St E* 04-06; C Triangle, St Matt and All SS 06-10; rtd 10; PtO *St E* from 10. *4 Woodward Close, Ipswich IP2 0EA* T: (01473) 214125 M: 07984-077990 E: jackie@jbsears.com

SEARS, Jeanette. b 59. Man Univ BA 80 PhD 84 Lon Univ PGCE 85. Wycliffe Hall Ox 90. **d** 92 **p** 94. NSM Ox St Aldate 92-96; PtO *Lon* 98-01; *Ox* 01-04; Tutor Trin Coll Bris 04-11; PtO *Bris* from 04. *Address temp unknown* M: 07950-047476

SEARS, Michael Antony. b 50. Birm Univ BSc 71 PGCE 72. Linc Th Coll 78. **d** 80 **p** 81. C Willenhall H Trin *Lich* 80-83; C Caldmore 83-84; P-in-c 84-86; V 86-89; Abp Ilsley RC Sch Birm 89-97; TV Solihull *Birm* 98-02; R Castle Bromwich SS Mary and Marg 02-07; R Wroxham w Hoveton and Belaugh *Nor* 07-13. *Address temp unknown*

SEATON, Christopher Charles. b 54. St Andrews Major w Michaelston-le-Pit *Llan* 10-15; C Cadoxton-juxta-Barry from 15. *13 Hillside Close, Barry CF63 2QP* T: (01446) 747541 E: chris.c.seaton@fsmail.net

SEATON, Canon James Bradbury. b 29. Ch Coll Cam BA 53 MA 57. Westcott Ho Cam 53. **d** 55 **p** 56. C Derby St Werburgh 55-58; C Darlington St Cuth *Dur* 58-64; V Preston on Tees 64-72; TV Stockton H Trin 72; TV Cen Stockton 73-75; R Anstey *Leic* 75-89; RD Sparkenhoe III 81-88; Hon Can Leic Cathl 87-94; R Market Harborough Transfiguration 89-94; rtd 94; PtO *Glouc* from 94. *6 Saxon Grange, Sheep Street, Chipping Campden GL55 6BY* T: (01386) 841753

SEATON-BURN, Paul Simon. b 70. Ex Univ BA 92. St Jo Coll Nottm MTh 06. **d** 06 **p** 07. C Broughton w Loddington and Cransley etc *Pet* 06-09; P-in-c Desborough, Brampton Ash, Dingley and Braybrooke 09-11; P-in-c Chagford, S Tawton, Drewsteignton etc *Ex* 11-13; TR Chagford, Gidleigh, Throwleigh etc from 13. *The Rectory, Chagford, Newton Abbot TQ13 8BW* T: (01647) 432880 E: paulsburn@btinternet.com

SEBER, Derek Morgan. b 43. Man Poly MA 87 Man Metrop Univ MPhil 96. Oak Hill Th Coll 71. **d** 73 **p** 74. C Collyhurst *Man* 73-76; C Radcliffe St Thos and St Jo 76-77; Ind Missr 77-89; P-in-c Hulme St Geo 77-83; Hon C Moss Side St Jas w St Clem 83-96; Project Officer Linking Up 89-96; Lic Preacher *Man* 90-96; P-in-c Cheetham St Jo 97; P-in-c Thornton Hough *Ches* 97-05; V 05-08; Ind Chapl 97-05; rtd 08; PtO *Ches* 08-12; *Blackb* from 12. *3 Castle Park, Hornby, Lancaster LA2 8SB* T: (015242) 22011 E: derek.seber@sky.com

SECCOMBE, Marcus John. b 34. Oak Hill Th Coll 60. **d** 63 **p** 64. C Woodthorpe *S'well* 63-67; C Doncaster St Mary *Sheff* 67-72; V Owston 72-90; R Rossington 90-99; rtd 99; PtO *Sheff* from 99. *39 Marlborough Road, Doncaster DN2 5DF* T: (01302) 321505 E: mark@secco9.freeserve.co.uk

SECOMBE, Preb Frederick Thomas. b 18. St D Coll Lamp BA 40 St Mich Coll Llan 40. **d** 42 **p** 43. C Swansea St Mark *S & B* 42-44; C Knighton 44-46; C Machen *Mon* 46-49; C Newport St Woolos 49-52; Chapl St Woolos Hosp Newport 49-52; V Llanarth w Clytha, Llansantffraed and Bryngwyn *Mon* 52-54; R Machen and Rudry 54-59; V Swansea St Pet *S & B* 59-69; R Hanwell St Mary *Lon* 69-83; AD Ealing W 78-82; Preb St Paul's Cathl 81-83; rtd 83. *30 Westville Road, Penylan, Cardiff CF23 5AG* T: (029) 2048 3978

SECRETAN, Ms Jenny Ruth. b 54. St Aid Coll Dur BA 76 Ex Univ PGCE 77 Dur Univ MA 97. Linc Th Coll 81 Cranmer Hall Dur 83. **dss** 84 **d** 87 **p** 94. Asst Chapl Newc Poly 84-86; Sunderland St Chad *Dur* 84-86; Bordesley St Oswald *Birm* 86-91; Par Dn 87-91; Assoc Soc Resp Officer *Dur* 92-95; PtO 95-99; *Newc* 95-99. *14 Southwood Gardens, Newcastle upon Tyne NE3 3BU*

SEDANO, Juan Antonio. b 55. Centro de Discipulado Lima 85. **d** 88 **p** 88. Peru 88-90; Crosslinks 91-94; SAMS from 95; NSM Ingrave St Steph CD *Chelmsf* from 95. *5 The Chase, Middle Road, Ingrave, Brentwood CM13 3QT* T: (01277) 810907 E: esedano@btinternet.com

SEDDON, Mrs Carol Susan. b 44. ARCM 63 GNSM 66 Man Univ CertEd 67. Ripon Coll Cuddesdon. **d** 05 **p** 06. NSM Alsager St Mary *Ches* 05-08; Asst Chapl HM YOI Stoke Heath 05-08; V Northwich St Luke and H Trin *Ches* from 08. *1 Tall Trees Close, Northwich CW8 4YA* T: (01606) 74632 M: 07973-737038 E: carol_seddon@hotmail.com

SEDDON, Ernest Geoffrey. b 26. Man Univ MA 85 ARIBA 51. St Deiniol's Hawarden 80. **d** 80 **p** 81. C Dunham Massey St Marg *Ches* 80-83; P-in-c Warburton 82-87; P-in-c Dunham Massey St Mark 85-86; V 86-92; rtd 92; PtO *Ches* from 92. *7 Colwyn Place, Llandudno LL30 3AW* T: (01492) 547639 *or* 642107

SEDDON, Philip James. b 45. Jes Coll Cam BA 68 MA 71 Birm Univ MPhil 01. Ridley Hall Cam 67. **d** 70 **p** 71. C Tonge w Alkrington *Man* 70-74; CMS Nigeria 74-78; Lect St Jo Coll Nottm 78-79; LtO *Ely* 79-85; Chapl Magd Coll Cam 79-85; Lect Bibl Studies Selly Oak Colls 86-00; LtO *Birm* 87-05; Lect Th Birm Univ 00-05; Dir Min STETS 05-10; rtd 10. *6 Beech Close, Porton, Salisbury SP4 0NP* T: (01980) 619104 E: philipjseddon@gmail.com

SEDEN, Martin Roy. b 47. Man Univ MSc Salford Univ PhD. EMMTC 79. **d** 82 **p** 83. NSM Knighton St Mary Magd *Leic* 82-07; NSM Rutland Deanery *Pet* from 08. *60 Leicester Road, Uppingham, Oakham LE15 9SD* T: (01572) 822244 M: 07806-940407 E: rseden@gmail.com

SEDGEWICK, Clive Malcolm. b 56. Loughb Univ BSc 78 UEA MA 92 PGCE 79. SAOMC 00. **d** 04 **p** 05. NSM High Harrogate Ch Ch *Ripon* 04-13; P-in-c Bardsey *Leeds* from 13. *The Vicarage, Woodacre Lane, Bardsey, Leeds LS17 9DG* M: 07903-326053 E: clivesedgewick@yahoo.com

SEDGLEY, Mrs Jean. b 41. Open Univ BA 03 Whitelands Coll Lon CertEd 63. S Dios Minl Tr Scheme 92. **d** 95 **p** 96. NSM Haywards Heath St Wilfrid *Chich* 95-01; NSM Cuckfield 01-09; rtd 09. *25 Pasture Hill Road, Haywards Heath RH16 1LY* T: (01444) 413974 E: jean@sedgley.org

SEDGLEY, Canon Timothy John. b 42. St Jo Coll Ox BA 63 MA 68. Westcott Ho Cam 64. **d** 66 **p** 67. C Nor St Pet Mancroft 66-70; V Costessey 70-79; RD Nor N 75-79; V Walton-on-Thames *Guildf* 79-05; RD Emly 86-91; Hon Can Guildf Cathl 86-05; Dir OLMs and NSMs 93-05; rtd 05. *6 St Paul's Court, Moreton-in-Marsh, Gloucester GL56 0ET* T: (01608) 652696 E: timsedgley@hotmail.com

SEDGWICK, Jonathan Maurice William. b 63. BNC Ox BA 85 MA 89 Leeds Univ BA 88. Coll of Resurr Mirfield 86. **d** 89 **p** 90. C Chich St Paul and St Pet 89-91; Dean of Div and Chapl Magd Coll Ox 91-94; PtO *S'wark* 97-99; Hon C E Dulwich St Jo 99-11; Hon C Walworth St Chris 11-14; P-in-c S'wark St Geo w St Alphege and St Jude from 14. *2nd Floor Flat, St Alphege House, 2 Pocock Street, London SE1 0BJ* M: 07585-113773 E: jonathan@woodvale46.tiscali.co.uk

SEDGWICK, Canon Peter Humphrey. b 48. Trin Hall Cam BA 70 Dur Univ PhD 83. Westcott Ho Cam 71. **d** 74 **p** 75. C Stepney St Dunstan and All SS *Lon* 74-77; P-in-c Pittington *Dur* 77-79; Lect Th Birm Univ 79-82; Hon C The Lickey *Birm* 79-82; Th Consultant for NE Ecum Gp *Dur* 82-88; Lect Th Hull Univ 88-94; Abp's Adv on Ind Issues *York* 88-94; Vice-Prin Westcott Ho Cam 94-96; Asst Sec Abps' Coun Bd for Soc Resp 96-04; NSM Pet St Barn 96-98; Prin St Mich Coll Llan from 04; Can Llan Cathl from 06. *Church House, Grand Avenue, Cardiff CF5 4HX* T: (029) 2067 9833 E: peter.sedgwick2@btinternet.com

SEDLMAYR, Peter. b 53. Univ Coll Chich BA 01. **d** 04. NSM Littlehampton and Wick *Chich* from 04. *83 Joyce Close, Wick, Littlehampton BN17 7JG* T: (01903) 714968 M: 07941-921263 E: peterpaul@sedlmayr83.freeserve.co.uk

SEEAR, Ms Louise. b 57. St Mary's Coll Dur BA 78. Ripon Coll Cuddesdon 09. **d** 12 **p** 13. NSM N Lambeth *S'wark* 12-15; Asst Chapl King's Coll Hosp NHS Foundn Trust from 13. *49 Voltaire Road, London SW4 6DD* T: (020) 7498 7917 M: 07813-615150 E: louise.seear@virgin.net

SEED, Richard Edward. b 55. UNISA BTh 86 Westmr Coll Ox MEd. Kalk Bay Bible Inst S Africa. **d** 80 **p** 81. S Africa 80-85 and 87-89; Zimbabwe 85-87; Asst Chapl Kingham Hill Sch Oxon 89-90; C Beckenham Ch Ch *Roch* 90-95; Chapl Düsseldorf *Eur* 96-00; CMS from 00. *CMS, PO Box 1799, Oxford OX4 9BN* T: 08456-201799

SEED, The Ven Richard Murray Crosland. b 49. Leeds Univ MA 91. Edin Th Coll 69. **d** 72 **p** 73. C Skipton Ch Ch *Bradf* 72-75; C Baildon 75-77; Chapl HM Det Cen Kidlington 77-80; TV Kidlington *Ox* 77-80; V Boston Spa *York* 80-99; P-in-c Newton Kyme 84-85; P-in-c Clifford 89-99; P-in-c Thorp Arch w Walton 98-99; Chapl Martin House Hospice for Children Boston Spa 85-99; RD New Ainsty *York* 97-99; Adn York 99-12; R York H Trin Micklegate 00-12; rtd 12; PtO *York* from 14. *Mill Cottage, Main Street, Allerston, Pickering YO18 7PG* T: (01723) 859011

SEED, Susan Mary. b 61. **d** 14 **p** 15. C Lancaster Ch Ch *Blackb* from 14. *55 Masonfield Crescent, Lancaster LA1 3SR* T: (01524) 39157

SEEL, Richard Malcolm. b 45. **d** 04 **p** 05. OLM Bacton w Edingthorpe w Witton and Ridlington *Nor* 04-07; OLM Happisburgh, Walcott, Hempstead w Eccles etc 04-07; NSM Loddon, Sisland, Chedgrave, Hardley and Langley from 07. *31 Hillside, Chedgrave, Norwich NR14 6HZ* T: (01508) 521938 M: 07711-069680 E: richard@emerging-church.org

SEELEY, Jutta. See BRUECK, Jutta

✠**SEELEY, The Rt Revd Martin Alan.** b 54. Jes Coll Cam BA 76 MA 79. Ripon Coll Cuddesdon 76 Union Th Sem (NY) STM 78. **d** 78 **p** 79 **c** 15. C Bottesford w Ashby *Linc* 78-80; USA 80-90; Selection Sec ABM 90-96; Sec for Continuing Minl Educn 90-96; V Is of Dogs Ch Ch and St Jo w St Luke *Lon* 96-06; Prin Westcott Ho Cam 06-15; Hon Can Ely Cathl 08-15; Bp St E from 15; Hon Asst Bp Ely from 15. *The Bishop's House, 4 Park Road, Ipswich IP1 3ST* T: (01473) 252829 E: mas209@cam.ac.uk

SEEVARATNAM, Mohan Surenda. b 64. St Mellitus Coll 12. **d** 15. NSM W Harrow *Lon* from 15. *64 Wilson Gardens, Harrow HA1 4DZ* M: 07975-973982 E: barakams@aol.com

SEGAL, Mrs Marie. b 57. Leeds Univ BEd 78. NTMTC BA 07. **d** 07 **p** 08. NSM Gt Ilford St Andr *Chelmsf* 07-10; P-in-c 10-13; V from 13; AD Redbridge from 15. *St Andrew's Vicarage, St Andrew's Road, Ilford IG1 3PE* T: (020) 8554 9791 M: 07787-188449 E: segal.marie@btinternet.com

SEGGAR, Jennifer Mary. b 63. Open Univ PGCE 01. **d** 05 **p** 06. OLM Bildeston w Wattisham and Lindsey, Whatfield etc *St E* 05-09; C Sudbury and Chilton 09-11; P-in-c Bramford from 11. *The Vicarage, Vicarage Lane, Bramford, Ipswich IP8 4AE* T: (01473) 748914 E: jmseggar@aol.com

SEGGIE, Ms Karen Angela. b 75. Roehampton Univ BA 13. Ripon Coll Cuddesdon MTh 15. **d** 15. C Milton next Gravesend Ch Ch *Roch* from 15; C Gravesend St Aid from 15; C Gravesend H Family w Ifield from 15. *28 The Sandpipers, Gravesend DA12 5QB* T: (01474) 362654 E: karenseggie16@gmail.com

SEGRAVE-PRIDE, Mrs Philippa Louise. b 73. Westhill Coll Birm BTh 96. Ripon Coll Cuddesdon 97. **d** 99 **p** 00. C Harborne St Pet *Birm* 99-02; TV Tring *St Alb* 02-04; TV Bp's Hatfield, Lemsford and N Mymms 04-09; P-in-c Harpenden St Jo 09-12; V 12-13; Canada from 13. *1281 Durant Drive, Coquitlam, British Columbia V3B 6K8, Canada* T: (001) (778) 838 3122 E: philippa@segrave.net

SELBY, Benjamin. b 75. Ripon Coll Cuddesdon 08. **d** 10 **p** 12. C Clifton *S'well* 10-12. *Lower Brackendale Farm, Tithby Road, Bingham, Nottingham NG13 8GQ* T: (01949) 831386 M: 07527-994313 E: bselbyrev@aol.com

SELBY, Canon Carole Janis. b 50. Chelsea Coll of Physical Educn CertEd 71 Sussex Univ BEd 72 K Coll Lon MA 03. Westcott Ho Cam 93. **d** 95 **p** 96. C Worc St Barn w Ch Ch 95-99; Min Turnford St Clem CD *St Alb* 99-08; TV Cheshunt from 08; RD 04-12; Hon Can St Alb from 13. *St James Vicarage, St James Road, Goffs Oak, Waltham Cross EN7 6TP* T: (01707) 872328 E: c_selby@talk21.com

✠**SELBY, The Rt Revd Peter Stephen Maurice.** b 41. St Jo Coll Ox BA 64 MA 67 Episc Th Sch Cam Mass BD 66 K Coll Lon PhD 75 Birm Univ Hon DD 07. Bps' Coll Cheshunt 66. **d** 66 **p** 67 **c** 84. C Queensbury All SS *Lon* 66-69; C Limpsfield and Titsey *S'wark* 69-77; Assoc Dir of Tr 69-73; Vice-Prin S'wark Ord Course 70-72; Asst Dioc Missr *S'wark* 73-77; Dioc Missr *Newc* 77-84; Can Res Newc Cathl 77-84; Suff Bp Kingston *S'wark* 84-91; Area Bp 91-92; Wm Leech Prof Fell Dur Univ 92-97; Asst Bp Dur and Newc 92-97; Bp Worc 97-07; Hon Prof Univ Coll Worc from 98; Bp HM Pris 01-07; rtd 07; Pres Nat Coun Ind Monitoring Boards from 08; Hon Asst Bp Portsm 08-11; Hon Asst Bp S'wark from 11; Visiting Prof K Coll Lon from 08. *57 Girton Road, London SE26 5DJ* T: (020) 3538 0220 E: peterselby@onetel.com

SELBY, Philip James. b 82. Oak Hill Th Coll 12. **d** 15. C Buxton Trin Prop Chpl *Derby* from 15. *63 Park Road, Buxton SK17 6SN* M: 07910-321576 E: philandruthselby@gmail.com

SELBY-BOOTHROYD, Richard George. b 46. SWMTC. **d** 09 **p** 10. NSM St Illogan *Truro* 09-11; NSM Lyneham w Bradenstoke *Sarum* from 11; P-in-c from 15; NSM R Wootton Bassett *Sarum* 11-15; NSM Woodhill from 11. *The Vicarage, The Green, Lyneham, Chippenham SN15 4PD* T: (01249) 890675 E: selbyboothroyd@btinternet.com

SELBY, Suffragan Bishop of. *See* THOMSON, The Rt Revd John Bromilow

SELDON, Francis Peter. b 58. St Jo Coll Nottm 98. **d** 00 **p** 01. C Styvechale *Cov* 00-02; C Cheylesmore 02-04; V 04-11; V Chilvers Coton w Astley from 11. *Chilvers Coton Vicarage, Coventry Road, Nuneaton CV11 4NJ* T: (024) 7638 3010 or 7634 6413

SELF, Canon David Christopher. b 41. Toronto Univ BSc 62 MA 64 K Coll Lon BD 68 AKC 68. **d** 69 **p** 70. C Tupsley *Heref* 69-73; Chapl Dur Univ 73-78; TV Southampton (City Cen) *Win* 78-84; TR Dunstable *St Alb* 84-95; RD 90-91; TR Bris St Paul's 95-06; RD Bris City 98-99; AD City 99-03; Hon Can Bris Cathl 99-06; rtd 06. *3 Shannon Court, Thornbury, Bristol BS35 2HN* T: (01454) 418006 E: david@dcself.plus.com

SELF, John Andrew. b 47. Trin Coll Bris 74 CMS Tr Coll Crowther Hall 76. **d** 81 **p** 83. CMS Pakistan 77-91; Assoc V Bath Weston All SS w N Stoke *B & W* 91-92; V Sparkhill St Jo *Birm* from 92. *St John's Vicarage, 15 Phipson Road, Birmingham B11 4JE* T/F: 0121-449 2760 T: 753 1415 E: john.self@stjohnsparkhill.org.uk

SELF, Peter Allen. b 41. S Dios Minl Tr Scheme 84. **d** 87 **p** 98. NSM Wilton *B & W* 87-91; NSM Taunton Lyngford 91-96; Asst Chapl Taunton and Somerset NHS Trust 96-08; rtd 08; PtO *B & W* from 08. *20 Dyers Close, West Buckland, Wellington TA21 9JU* T: (01823) 663408 F: 663448

SELFE, John Ronald. b 41. EMMTC 85. **d** 95 **p** 96. OLM Mid Marsh Gp *Linc* from 95. *Bookend, 236 Eastgate, Louth LN11 8DA* T: (01507) 603809 E: john.dorothyselfe@tiscali.co.uk

SELL, Grace. b 39. RN 63. Sarum & Wells Th Coll BTh 91. **d** 91 **p** 94. C Helston and Wendron *Truro* 91-95; Chapl Havering Hosps NHS Trust 95-01; Chapl Barking Havering and Redbridge Hosps NHS Trust 01-02; NSM Rush Green *Chelmsf* 98-02; Bp Barking's Adv for Hosp Chapl 99-02; NSM Gt Burstead 06-08; P-in-c Farnleigh 08-11; PtO *Ely* from 12. *21 New Court, Church Road, Cambridge CB4 1EF* E: graceswift@hotmail.com

SELLER, Prof Mary Joan. b 40. Qu Mary Coll Lon BSc 61 Lon Univ PhD 64 DSc 82. S'wark Ord Course 89. **d** 91 **p** 94. NSM Hurst Green *S'wark* 91-10; PtO from 10. *11 Home Park, Oxted RH8 0JS* T: (01883) 715675 E: mary.seller@kcl.ac.uk

SELLER, Timothy John. b 46. Qu Mary Coll Lon BSc 67 Lon Univ PhD 71. **d** 08 **p** 09. OLM Ewhurst *Guildf* from 08. *Kerne Hus, Walliswood, Dorking RH5 5RD* T: (01306) 627548 M: 07845-192041 E: t.seller@dsl.pipex.com

SELLERS, Canon Anthony. b 48. Southn Univ BSc 71 PhD 76. Wycliffe Hall Ox 84. **d** 86 **p** 87. C Luton St Mary *St Alb* 86-90; V Luton St Paul from 90; Hon Can St Alb from 12. *St Paul's Vicarage, 37A Arthur Street, Luton LU1 3SG* T: (01582) 481796 E: tsellers@route56.co.uk

SELLERS, George William. b 35. NOC. **d** 89 **p** 90. NSM Rothwell *Ripon* 89-05; rtd 05. *16 Thornegrove, Rothwell, Leeds LS26 0HP* T: 0113-282 3522

SELLERS, Robert. b 58. Coll of Resurr Mirfield 90. **d** 92 **p** 93. C Wotton St Mary *Glouc* 92-95; TV Redruth w Lanner and Treleigh *Truro* 95-98; P-in-c Devoran 98-03; Bp's Dom Chapl 98-03; R Fountains Gp *Ripon* 03-11; TR Withycombe Raleigh *Ex* from 11; RD Aylesbeare 13-14. *The Rectory, 74 Withycombe Village Road, Exmouth EX8 3AE* T: (01395) 270206 E: fr.robertsellers@btinternet.com

SELLERS, Mrs Rosalind April. b 48. Liv Univ MA 77. SWMTC 06. **d** 09 **p** 11. NSM Cannington, Otterhampton, Combwich and Stockland *B & W* 09-10; NSM Puriton and Pawlett from 10. *1 St Mary's Crescent, North Petherton, Bridgwater TA6 6RA* T: (01278) 661279 M: 07794-666247 E: rosalind.sellers@virgin.net

SELLERS, Warren John. b 43. Bp Otter Coll Chich TCert 73 W Sussex Inst of HE DipAdEd 88. K Coll Lon 63 Sarum Th Coll 65. **d** 68 **p** 69. C Guildf H Trin w St Mary 68-72; Hon C Chich St Paul and St Pet 72-73; C Epping St Jo *Chelmsf* 73-76; Hon C Pulborough *Chich* 76-90; Hon C Fleet *Guildf* 90-92; Teacher 73-89; Waltham Abbey St Lawr and H Cross Schs Essex 73-76; Pulborough St Mary, Easeboure & Bp Tuffnell Schs 76-89; Hd Teacher St Pet Jun Sch Farnborough 90-92; TV Upper Kennet *Sarum* 92-95; TR 95-03; rtd 03. *71 Bay Crescent, Swanage BH19 1RD* E: wjandmjs27@btinternet.com

SELLEY, Paul Edward Henry. b 47. Bris Univ BEd 70 ALCM 67 LTCL 87. Sarum Th Coll 93. **d** 96 **p** 97. C Swindon Dorcan *Bris* 96-00; V Ashton Keynes, Leigh and Minety 00-07; rtd 07. *5 Miles Gardens, Weymouth DT3 5NH* T: (01305) 814948 E: paul.selley@which.net *or* selley306@btinternet.com

SELLGREN, Eric Alfred. b 33. AKC 61. **d** 62 **p** 63. C Ditton St Mich *Liv* 62-66; V Hindley Green 66-72; V Southport St Paul 72-80; Warden Barn Fellowship Winterborne Whitchurch 80-86; V The Iwernes, Sutton Waldron and Fontmell Magna *Sarum* 86-98; rtd 98; PtO *Sarum* from 98. *19 Savoy Court, Shaftesbury SP7 8BN* T: (01747) 853327

SELLICK, Peter James. b 67. Wadh Coll Ox BA 89. Edin Th Coll BD 94. **d** 94 **p** 95. C Kippax w Allerton Bywater *Ripon* 94-97; C Stanningley St Thos 97-02; C W Bromwich All SS *Lich* 02-12; Ind Chapl Black Country Urban Ind Miss 02-12; Development Dir Chs and Ind Gp Birm and Solihull from 12; PtO *Lich* from 15. *41 Wheatley Road, Oldbury B68 9HW* T: 0121-423 4334 E: peters@birmingham.anglican.org

SELLIN, Deborah Mary. b 64. St Andr Univ MA 86. STETS 04. **d** 07 **p** 08. NSM Guildf St Sav 07-10; V Wonersh w Blackheath from 10; RD Cranleigh from 15. *The Vicarage, The Street, Wonersh, Guildford GU5 0PG* T: (01483) 890453 E: d.sellin@ntlworld.com *or* vicar@wonershchurch.org.uk

SELLIX, Mrs Pamela Madge. b 47. Lon Univ BA 68 PGCE 68. SWMTC 00. **d** 04 **p** 05. NSM Saltash *Truro* from 04. *Farthings, Quarry Road, Pensilva, Liskeard PL14 5NT* T: (01579) 363464

SELLORS, Glenys Margaret. b 43. NOC. **d** 07 **p** 08. NSM Offerton St Alb and Stockport St Thos *Ches* from 07. *36 Brookside Avenue, Stockport SK2 5HR* T: 0161-483 0359 E: glenys.sellors@virgin.net

SELMAN, Laura. **d** 15. C Surbiton St Andr and St Mark *S'wark* from 15. *Address temp unknown*

SELMAN, Michael Richard. b 47. Sussex Univ BA 68 Bris Univ MA 70. Coll of Resurr Mirfield 71. **d** 73 **p** 74. C Hove All SS *Chich* 73-74; C Horfield H Trin *Bris* 74-78; P-in-c Landkey *Ex* 78-79; C Barnstaple and Goodleigh 78-79; TV Barnstaple, Goodleigh and Landkey 79-82; TR 82-84; P-in-c Sticklepath 83-84; TR Barnstaple 85; RD 83-85; TR Cen Ex 85-00; Chapl Aquitaine *Eur* 00-08; Partnership P E Bris 08-12; rtd 12. *1 Millwey Court, Axminster EX13 5GD* M: 07735-499920 E: revmichael.selman@gmail.com

SELMES, Brian. b 48. Nottm Univ BTh 74 Dur Univ MA 97. Linc Th Coll 70. **d** 74 **p** 75. C Padgate *Liv* 74-77; C Sydenham St Bart *S'wark* 77-80; Chapl Darlington Memorial and Aycliffe Hosps 80-98; Co-ord Chapl S Durham Healthcare NHS Trust 98-02; Sen Chapl Co Durham and Darlington NHS Foundn Trust 02-12; rtd 12; PtO *Dur* from 15. *56 West Crescent, Darlington DL3 7PR* T: (01325) 359688

SELVARATNAM, Christian Nathan. b 68. Warwick Univ BSc 90. Cranmer Hall Dur 06. **d** 08 **p** 09. NSM York St Mich-le-Belfrey from 08. *11/12 Minster Yard, York YO1 7HH* T: (01904) 624190 M: 07773-784728 E: christian.selvaratnam@gmail.com

SELVEY, Canon John Brian. b 33. Dur Univ BA 54. Cuddesdon Coll 56. **d** 58 **p** 59. C Lancaster St Mary *Blackb* 58-61; C Blackb Cathl 61-65; Cathl Chapl 64-65; V Foulridge *Blackb* 65-69; V Walton-le-Dale 69-82; V Cleveleys 82-89; Hon Can Bloemfontein Cathl from 88; V Slyne w Hest *Blackb* 89-97; Hon Can Blackb Cathl 93-97; rtd 97; PtO *Carl* from 98. *Low Quietways, Borrowdale Road, Keswick CA12 5UP* T: (01768) 773538

SELWOOD, Michael. b 40. Oak Hill Th Coll BA 91. **d** 91 **p** 92. Canada 91-95; P-in-c Sherborne, Windrush, the Barringtons etc *Glouc* 95-07; rtd 07. *17 Croft Holm, Moreton-in-Marsh GL56 0JH* T: (01608) 812384 E: 106631.11@compuserve.com

SELWOOD, Timothy John. b 45. Lon Univ LLB 66. Sarum Th Coll. **d** 83 **p** 84. NSM Colbury *Win* 83-85; NSM Copythorne and Minstead 85-90; PtO from 98. *1 St Nicholas Rise, Headbourne Worthy, Winchester SO23 7SY* T: (01962) 880928 E: tim_selwood@btinternet.com

SELWYN, David Gordon. b 38. Clare Coll Cam BA 62 MA 66 DD New Coll Ox MA 66 MEHS. Ripon Hall Ox 62. **d** 64 **p** 65. C Ecclesall *Sheff* 64-65; Asst Chapl New Coll Ox 65-68; Lect Univ of Wales (Lamp) *St D* 68-98; Reader 98-05; PtO *St D* 68-05. *62A Swiss Valley, Llanelli SA14 8BT* T: (01554) 773983

SEMPER, The Very Revd Colin Douglas. b 38. Keble Coll Ox BA 62. Westcott Ho Cam 61. **d** 63 **p** 64. C Guildf H Trin w St Mary 63-67; Sec ACCM 67-69; Producer Relig Broadcasting Dept BBC 69-75; Overseas Relig Broadcasting Org BBC 75-79; Hd Relig Progr BBC Radio 79-82; Hon Can Guildf Cathl 80-82; Provost Cov 82-87; Can and Treas Westmr Abbey 87-97; Steward 87-90; rtd 97; PtO *Sarum* 97-03; Hon C Rowledge and Frensham *Guildf* 03-06. *Beech House, 1 Twycross Road, Godalming GU7 2HH* T: (01483) 422790 E: sempers@freezone.co.uk

SEMPER, Jocelyn Rachel. *See* WALKER, Jocelyn Rachel

SEMPLE, Henry Michael. b 40. K Coll Lon BSc 62 Birkbeck Coll Lon PhD 67 CMath FIMA FCMI FRSA. S Dios Minl Tr Scheme. **d** 87 **p** 88. NSM Steyning *Chich* 87-91; PtO *Guildf* 87-91; *Linc* 92-93; NSM Linc Cathl 93-99; TR Headley All SS *Guildf* 99-02; R 02-10; rtd 10; PtO *Guildf* from 10; *Chich* from 11. *12 St Michael's Road, Worthing BN11 4SD* T: (01903) 520691 E: michael.semple@hotmail.co.uk

SEMPLE, Studdert Patrick. b 39. TCD BA 66. CITC 66. **d** 67 **p** 68. C Orangefield *D & D* 67-70; USA 70-71; I Stradbally *C & O* 71-82; Ch of Ireland Adult Educn Officer 82-88; I Donoughmore and Donard w Dunlavin *D & G* 88-96; Bp's C Dublin St Geo and St Thos 96-99; Chapl Mountjoy Pris 96-99; Chapl Mater Hosp 96-99; rtd 99. *49 Richmond Park, Monkstown, Co Dublin, Republic of Ireland* T: (00353) (1) 214 0843 E: pat.semple@gmail.com

SEN, Arani. b 61. R Holloway Coll Lon BA 84 St Martin's Coll Lanc PGCE 86 Open Univ MA 94 Fitzw Coll Cam BA 98 MA 02. Ridley Hall Cam 96. **d** 99 **p** 00. C Mildmay Grove St Jude and St Paul *Lon* 99-02; C-in-c Southall Em CD 02-06; V Southall Em 06-08; V Upper Armley *Leeds* from 08; AD Armley from 13. *22 Hill End Crescent, Leeds LS12 3PW* T: 0113-263 8788 E: revaranisen@gmail.com

SENIOR, Brian Stephen. b 55. Brighton Coll of Educn CertEd 76. Oak Hill Th Coll 91. **d** 93 **p** 94. C Hildenborough *Roch* 93-98; TV Tunbridge Wells St Jas w St Phil 98-04; V Tunbridge Wells St Phil 04-15; RD Tunbridge Wells 07-15. *St Philip's Vicarage, Birken Road, Tunbridge Wells TN2 3TE* T: (01892) 512071 *or* 531031 E: brian.senior@diocese-rochester.org

SENIOR, David John. b 47. Oak Hill Th Coll. **d** 82 **p** 83. C Market Harborough *Leic* 82-85; TV Marfleet *York* 85-91; R Desford and Peckleton w Tooley *Leic* 91-96; P-in-c Hall Green Ascension *Birm* 96-99; V 99-12; P-in-c Gospel Lane St Mich 97-03; AD Shirley 10-12; rtd 12; Hon C Londesborough Wold *York* 12-15; Hon C Pocklington Wold 12-15. *20 Wheatlands Close, Pocklington, York YO42 2UT* T: (01759) 305196 E: davidsenior3@gmail.com

SENIOR, David Norman. b 59. St Mellitus Coll 12. **d** 15. NSM Howell Hill w Burgh Heath *Guildf* from 15. *65 Higher Drive, Banstead SM7 1PW* T: (020) 8786 7733 M: 07710-313749 E: david@saintpauls.co.uk

SENIOR, Mrs Lisa Elaine. b 65. Leeds Univ BA 09. NOC 06. **d** 09 **p** 10. C Dewsbury *Leeds* 09-14; R Colne *Blackb* from 14. *The Rectory, 30 Grenfell Gardens, Colne BB8 9PL* T: (01282) 869420 E: lisasenior24@fsmail.net

SENIOR, Patrick Nicolas Adam. b 63. Univ of Wales (Ban) BA 86. Trin Coll Bris BA 94. **d** 94 **p** 95. C Derringham Bank *York* 94-98; V Brownhill *Leeds* 98-14; R Burnley St Pet and St Steph *Blackb* from 14. *The Rectory, 30 Grenfell Gardens, Colne BB8 9PL* T: (01282) 869420 E: patrick.senior@sky.com

✠**SENTAMU, The Most Revd and Rt Hon John Tucker Mugabi.** b 49. Makerere Univ Kampala LLB 71 Selw Coll Cam BA 76 MA MPhil 79 PhD 84. Ridley Hall Cam. **d** 79 **p** 79 **c** 96. Chapl HM Rem Cen Latchmere Ho 79-82; C Ham St Andr *S'wark* 79-82; C Herne Hill St Paul 82-83; P-in-c Tulse Hill H Trin 83-84; V Upper Tulse Hill St Matthias 83-84; V Tulse Hill H Trin and St Matthias 85-96; P-in-c Brixton Hill St Sav 87-89; Hon Can S'wark Cathl 93-96; Area Bp Stepney *Lon* 96-02; Bp Birm 02-05; Abp York from 05. *Bishopthorpe Palace, Bishopthorpe, York YO23 2GE* T: (01904) 707021 F: 709204 E: office@archbishopofyork.org

SENTAMU BAVERSTOCK, Mrs Grace Kathleen Nabanja. b 75. Nottm Univ BA 96 Selw Coll Cam BTh 10. Ridley Hall Cam 06. **d** 10 **p** 11. C Watford St Luke *St Alb* 10-14; V Leagrave from 14. *St Luke's Vicarage, High Street, Luton LU4 9JY* E: gracesenba@gmail.com

SEPHTON, Mrs Jacqueline Ann Driscoll. b 46. RGN 67. **d** 10 **p** 11. OLM Stoke by Nayland w Leavenheath and Polstead *St E* 10-13; NSM from 13. *12 Highlands Road, Hadleigh, Ipswich IP7 5HU* T: (01473) 810072 E: jackie.sephton@tiscali.co.uk

SEPHTON, John. b 43. **d** 01 **p** 02. OLM Newburgh w Westhead *Liv* from 01; Asst Chapl HM Pris Risley 02-09. *37 Brighouse Close, Ormskirk L39 3NA* T: (01695) 576774 E: johnsephton@postmaster.co.uk

SEPPALA, Christopher James. b 59. St Jo Coll Dur BA 82 Ch Ch Coll Cant CertEd 92. Chich Th Coll 83. **d** 85 **p** 86. C Whitstable *Cant* 85-88; C S Ashford Ch Ch 88-91; PtO from 01. *2 The Briars, Long Reach Close, Whitstable CT5 4QF* T: (01227) 282622 E: xpristopheros@netscapeonline.co.uk

SERBUTT, Rita Eileen. b 33. Man Univ BA 54 Univ of Wales (Cardiff) DipEd 56 FRSA 94. Dioc OLM tr scheme 98. **d** 01 **p** 02. OLM Balham St Mary and St Jo *S'wark* from 01; PtO from 05. *56 Manville Road, London SW17 8JL* T: (020) 8767 8383 E: eileen.serbutt@virgin.net

SERGEANT, John Richard Arthur. b 43. K Coll Dur BA 65 Newc Univ DipEd 66 DAES 87. **d** 06 **p** 07. OLM Cullercoats St Geo *Newc* 06-13; rtd 13. *5 Jedburgh Close, North Shields NE29 9NU* T: 0191-259 1752 E: sergeantjra@aol.com

SERGENT, Jean-Luc James. b 78. St Mellitus Coll 12. **d** 15. C The Hague *Eur* from 15. *Address temp unknown*

SERJEANT, Frederick James. b 28. Lon Inst of Educn BEd 77. AKC 53 St Boniface Warminster 53. **d** 54 **p** 55. C Leytonstone St Marg w St Columba *Chelmsf* 54-58; C Parkstone St Pet w Branksea *Sarum* 58-59; V Reigate St Luke S Park *S'wark* 59-65; V Battersea St Pet 65-71; C-in-c Battersea St Paul 67-71; V W Mersea *Chelmsf* 71-73; P-in-c E Mersea 71-73; R W w E Mersea 73-75; rtd 93. *9 Howard Close, Bothenhampton, Bridport DT6 4SR* T: (01308) 424510

SERJEANT, Mrs Heather Faith. b 60. Stirling Univ BSc 80 Ox Univ BTh 04. Ripon Coll Cuddesdon 00. **d** 02 **p** 03. C Caversham St Pet and Mapledurham *Ox* 02-06. *4A The Mount, Caversham, Reading RG4 7RU* T: 0118-947 2729 E: heatherserjeant@aol.com

SERJEANTSON, John Cecil Mylles. b 36. Bp's Univ Lennoxville BA 63 McGill Univ Montreal BD 66. Montreal Dioc Th Coll LTh 66. **d** 66 **p** 67. C Westmount St Matthias Canada 66-68; R Huntingdon w Ormstown 68-72; C Gt and Lt Driffield *York* 72-76; V Bilton St Pet 76-79; R Brome Canada 79-01; rtd 01. *103 St Patrick Boulevard, Cowansville QC J2K 1M4, Canada* T: (001) (450) 263 0454

SERMON, Michael John. b 61. Univ of Cen England in Birm ACIB 85. Qu Coll Birm BA 98 MA 99. **d** 99 **p** 00. C W Heath *Birm* 99-03; V Blackheath from 03; P-in-c Rounds Green from 11. *St Paul's Vicarage, 83 Vicarage Road, Halesowen B62 8HX* T: 0121-559 1000 E: mike@mikesermon.co.uk

SERTIN, John Francis. b 22. Fitzw Ho Cam BA 50 MA 54. Tyndale Hall Bris. **d** 45 **p** 46. C Sidcup Ch Ch *Roch* 45-47; Chapl Fitzw Ho Cam 47-50; C-in-c St Paul's Cray St Barn CD *Roch* 50-59; V Chitts Hill St Cuth *Lon* 59-62; Sec Ch Soc 62-67; P-in-c Woburn Square Ch Ch *Lon* 67-76; R Holborn St Geo w H Trin and St Bart 67-80; R Donyatt w Horton, Broadway and Ashill *B & W* 80-92; rtd 92; PtO *B & W* 92-02; *Win* 05-14. *23 Birstan Gardens, Andover SP10 4NY* T: (01264) 334544

SERTIN, Jonathan. **d** 14 **p** 15. NSM Earlsfield St Andr *S'wark* from 14. *Address temp unknown*

SERVANT, Canon Alma Joan. b 51. Nottm Univ BA 76. Westcott Ho Cam 83. **dss** 85 **d** 87 **p** 94. Ordsall *S'well* 85-88; Par Dn 87-88; Par Dn Man Whitworth 88-94; TV 94-96; Chapl Man Poly 88-92; Chapl Man Metrop Univ 92-96; P-in-c Heaton Norris St Thos 96-00; P-in-c Hulme Ascension 00-05; R 05-14; C Man Cathl 14-15; C Man St Ann 14-15; Hon Can Man Cathl 02-15; rtd 15; PtO *Man* from 15. *The Rectory, Royce Road, Hulme, Manchester M15 5FQ* T: 0161-226 5568

SERVANTE, Kenneth Edward. b 29. AKC 55. **d** 56 **p** 57. C Chaddesden St Phil *Derby* 56-58; C Brampton St Thos 58-61; C Whitfield 61-63; V Derby St Paul 63-70; V Elmton 70-81; P-in-c Winster 81-82; P-in-c Elton 81-82; R S Darley, Elton and Winster 82-94; rtd 94; PtO *Derby* from 94. *13 Chestnut Avenue, Belper DE56 1LY* T: (01773) 820513

SESSFORD, Canon Alan. b 34. Bps' Coll Cheshunt 65. **d** 66 **p** 67. C Highcliffe w Hinton Admiral *Win* 66-69; C Minehead *B & W* 70; C Chandler's Ford *Win* 70-73; V Burton and Sopley 73-00; RD Christchurch 93-98; Hon Can Win Cathl 98-00; rtd 00; PtO *Win* from 00; Chapl R Bournemouth and Christchurch Hosps NHS Trust from 01. *4 Benson Close, Bransgore, Christchurch BH23 8HX* T: (01425) 673412

SETTERFIELD, Nicholas Mark. b 63. Colchester Inst of Educn BA 89. St Steph Ho Ox 89. **d** 92 **p** 93. C Prestbury *Glouc* 92-96; R Letchworth *St Alb* 96-03; V Northampton St Matt *Pet* from 03. *St Matthew's Vicarage, 30 East Park Parade, Northampton NN1 4LB* T: (01604) 604412 E: vicar@stmatthews-northampton.org.uk

SETTIMBA, John Henry. b 52. Nairobi Univ BSc 78 Leeds Univ MA 91. Pan Africa Chr Coll BA 78. **d** 78 **p** 80. Kenya 78-81; Uganda 81-85; C Allerton *Bradf* 86-87; C W Ham *Chelmsf* 87-91; C-in-c Forest Gate All SS 91-94; P-in-c 94-96; TV Hackney *Lon* 96-02; rtd 07. *63 Belvedere Court, Upper Richmond Road, London SW15 6HZ* T: (020) 8789 8376

SEVILLE, Thomas Christopher John. b 57. Trin Hall Cam MA 80. Coll of Resurr Mirfield 87. **d** 89 **p** 90. C Knowle *Bris* 89-93; CR from 93. *House of the Resurrection, Stocks Bank Road, Mirfield WF14 0BN* T: (01924) 483315
E: tseville@mirfield.org.uk

SEWARD, Jolyon Frantom. b 57. Univ of Wales (Cardiff) BA 81. Chich Th Coll 83. **d** 86 **p** 87. C Llanblethian w Cowbridge and Llandough etc *Llan* 86-88; C Newton Nottage 88-93; Dioc Children's Officer 88-98; V Penyfai w Tondu 93-01; TV Heavitree and St Mary Steps *Ex* from 01. *St Lawrence's Vicarage, 36 Lower Hill Barton Road, Exeter EX1 3EH* T: (01392) 466302 *or* 677152 E: frjolyon@eurobell.co.uk

SEWARD, Nicholas. b 70. Imp Coll Lon BEng 91 St Jo Coll Dur BA 96 MA 98. Cranmer Hall Dur 94. **d** 98 **p** 99. C Bearsted w Thurnham *Cant* 98-02; Chapl and Hd RS Magd Coll Sch Ox 02-08; Hd Kingham Hill Sch from 08. *Kingham Hill School, Kingham, Chipping Norton OX7 6TH* T: (01608) 658999
E: n.seward@kingham-hill.oxon.sch.uk

SEWELL, Andrew. *See* SEWELL, John Andrew Clarkson

SEWELL, Canon Andrew William. b 61. Nottm Univ BSc 83. St Jo Coll Nottm 93. **d** 93 **p** 94. C Adel *Ripon* 93-96; C Far Headingley St Chad 96-98; Asst Dioc Missr 96-98; P-in-c Otham w Langley *Cant* 98-01; R 01-10; P-in-c Maidstone St Paul from 10; AD Maidstone from 10; Hon Can Cant Cathl from 11. *St Paul's Vicarage, 130 Boxley Road, Maidstone ME14 2AH* T: (01622) 691926 E: andrew@asewell.plus.com

SEWELL, Barry. *See* SEWELL, John Barratt

SEWELL, Canon Elizabeth Jill. b 56. Reading Univ BSc 77. Trin Coll Bris BA 97. **d** 97 **p** 98. C Rothley *Leic* 97-01; TV Market Harborough and The Transfiguration etc 01-07; RD Gartree I 06-07; TR Knaresborough *Ripon* 07-13; P-in-c Nidd 11-13; Can Res Ripon Cathl from 13. *16 Primrose Drive, Ripon HG4 1EY* T: (01765) 608545 E: ejsewell@btinternet.com

SEWELL, John Andrew Clarkson. b 58. Aston Tr Scheme 93 Ripon Coll Cuddesdon 95. **d** 97 **p** 98. C Horsham *Chich* 97-99; C Cleobury Mortimer w Hopton Wafers etc *Heref* 99-01; R 01-03; TV Ludlow, Ludford, Ashford Carbonell etc 03-04; Chapl Shropshire's Community NHS Trust 03-04; Lead Chapl ChAT (Weston-super-Mare Chapl About Town) *B & W* from 05; Hon C Weston super Mare St Jo 06-07; P-in-c Westbury sub Mendip w Easton 07-09; Min Can Bris Cathl from 15. *Chaplaincy About Town, 67 Meadow Street, Weston-super-Mare BS23 1QL* T: (01934) 643533
E: enquiries@westonchat.org.uk *or* andy.sewell@tiscali.co.uk

SEWELL, John Barratt (Barry). b 39. St Bart Hosp Medical Coll MB, BS 63. Ridley Hall Cam. **d** 92 **p** 93. C Ulverston St Mary w H Trin *Carl* 92-94; Asst Chapl R Cornwall Hosps Trust 94-98; Chapl 98-99; P-in-c Gerrans w St Anthony-in-Roseland and Philleigh *Truro* 00-03; rtd 03; PtO *Truro* from 04. *Greenacre, Zelah, Truro TR4 9HS* T: (01872) 540747
E: barry@cleswyth.freeserve.co.uk

SEWELL, Jonathan William. b 60. Lanc Univ BA 82 BTh 86. Linc Th Coll 83. **d** 86 **p** 87. C Ilkeston St Mary *Derby* 86-89; C Enfield Chase St Mary *Lon* 89-92; Dioc Youth Officer *Win* 92-97; P-in-c Headington St Mary *Ox* 98-10; V 10-11; PtO *York* 12-13; Chapl HM Pris Kirklevington Grange and HM Pris Northallerton 13; Chapl HM Pris Garth 13-14; PtO *Blackb* from 14. *Address temp unknown* E: jsailox@gmail.com

SEWELL, Peter Alexis. b 35. Lon Univ BSc 61 PhD 67 FRSC 86. Cyprus & Gulf Ord Course 92. **d** 94 **p** 95. Cyprus and the Gulf 94-97; NSM Ormskirk *Liv* 97-01; PtO from 01. *Shakelady Hey, Sandy Lane, Lathom, Ormskirk L40 5TU* T/F: (01695) 572095

SEWELL, Richard Michael. b 62. Birm Univ BA 84. SEITE 99. **d** 02 **p** 03. C Putney St Mary *S'wark* 02-05; TV Wimbledon 05-10; TR Barnes from 10. *The Rectory, 25 Glebe Road, London SW13 0DZ* E: sewell4321@btinternet.com

SEWELL, Robin Warwick. b 42. Trin Coll Bris 80. **d** 82 **p** 83. C Hinckley H Trin *Leic* 82-85; C Broadwater St Mary *Chich* 85-89; Chapl Barcelona *Eur* 89-02; V Braintree St Paul *Chelmsf* 02-12; rtd 12; PtO *Chelmsf* from 12. *59 Mountbatten Road, Braintree CM7 9EY* E: robinsewell1@tiscali.co.uk

SEWELL, Miss Sarah Frances. b 61. Wycliffe Hall Ox 87. **d** 91 **p** 94. C Binley *Cov* 91-94; Asst Chapl Derriford Hosp Plymouth 94-96; Chapl Stoke Mandeville Hosp NHS Trust 96-00; Chapl R Marsden NHS Foundn Trust 00-05; Chapl Team Ldr Epsom and St Helier Univ Hosps NHS Trust 05-07; Sen Co-ord Chapl 07-13; Lead Chapl from 13; C Sutton *S'wark* from 14. *Chaplains' Office, St Helier Hospital, Rythe Lane, Carshalton SM5 1AA* T: (020) 8296 2000
E: sarah.sewell@esth.nhs.uk

SEXTON, Canon Michael Bowers. b 28. SS Coll Cam BA 52 MA 56. Wells Th Coll 52. **d** 54 **p** 55. C Miles Platting St Luke *Man* 54-57; C Bradford cum Beswick 57-58; C-in-c Oldham St Chad Limeside CD 58-62; R Filby w Thrigby w Mautby *Nor* 62-72; P-in-c Runham 67-72; P-in-c Stokesby w Herringby 68-72; R Hethersett w Canteloff 72-85; V Ketteringham 73-84; RD Humbleyard 81-86; Hon Can Nor Cathl 85-93; R Hethersett w Canteloff w Lt and Gt Melton 85-86; V Hunstanton St Mary w Ringstead Parva, Holme etc 86-93; rtd 94; PtO *Nor* from 94. *3 Forge Close, Poringland, Norwich NR14 7SZ* T: (01508) 493885

SEYMOUR, Dom Anthony Nicholas. b 39. QUB BA 61. **d** 96 **p** 97. Community of Our Lady and St John 86-01; PtO *Win* from 01. *Abbey of Our Lady and St John, Abbey Road, Beech, Alton GU34 4AP* T: (01420) 562145 *or* 563575 F: 561691

SEYMOUR, Brian Anthony. b 45. **d** 07 **p** 08. OLM Ottershaw *Guildf* 07-15; rtd 15. *50 Rowtown, Addlestone KT15 1HQ*
T: (01932) 705260 E: brianandchrisseymour@yahoo.co.uk

SEYMOUR, David. b 43. Kelham Th Coll 60. **d** 68 **p** 69. C Cowley St Jas *Ox* 68-73; TV Lynton, Brendon, Countisbury, Lynmouth etc *Ex* 73-77; C-in-c Luton (Princes Park) CD *Roch* 78-79; V Rosherville 79-90; rtd 90. *3 Fosbrooke House, 8 Clifton Drive, Lytham St Annes FY8 5RQ* E: markbeech@boltblue.com

SEYMOUR, Canon David Raymond Russell. b 56. Keble Coll Ox BA 79 MA 88. St Steph Ho Ox 79. **d** 81 **p** 82. C Tilehurst St Mich *Ox* 81-85; TV Parkstone St Pet w Branksea and St Osmund *Sarum* 85-91; V Bradford-on-Avon Ch Ch 91-01; P-in-c Sturminster Newton and Hinton St Mary 01-02; V Sturminster Newton, Hinton St Mary and Lydlinch from 02; C Hazelbury Bryan and the Hillside Par from 08; C Okeford from 08; RD Blackmore Vale from 08; Can and Preb Sarum Cathl from 13. *The Vicarage, Church Street, Sturminster Newton DT10 1DB* T: (01258) 471276 E: drrseymour@hotmail.co.uk

SEYMOUR, Ian. *See* SEYMOUR, Robert Ian

SEYMOUR, John. b 73. Bris Univ BSc 95 MB, ChB 98 Heythrop Coll Lon MA 03 Trin Coll Cam BA 05. Westcott Ho Cam 03. **d** 06 **p** 07. C Poplar *Lon* 06-09; Chapl Twyford C of E High Sch Acton from 09. *41 Leighton Road, London W13 9EL*
T: (020) 8930 9305 E: john.seymour@london.anglican.org

SEYMOUR, John Anthony. b 46. SWMTC. **d** 08 **p** 09. NSM Carbis Bay w Lelant *Truro* 08-11; P-in-c 11-13; rtd 13. *5 Station Hill, Lelant, St Ives TR26 3DJ* E: tonyseymour@talktalk.net

SEYMOUR, Canon John Charles. b 30. Oak Hill Th Coll 51 and 55 Wycliffe Coll Toronto 54. **d** 57 **p** 58. C Islington St Andr w St Thos and St Matthias *Lon* 57-60; C Worthing St Geo *Chich* 60-63; V Thornton *Leic* 63-70; R Kirby Muxloe 70-81; TR 81-83; RD Sparkenhoe I 83-88; R Market Bosworth w Shenton 83-87; TR Market Bosworth, Cadeby w Sutton Cheney etc 87-93; RD Sparkenhoe W 89-92; Hon Can Leic Cathl 82-93; rtd 93. *56 Wyggeston Hospital, Hinkley Road, Leicester LE3 0UX* T: 0116-254 8295
E: jams56@btinternet.com

SEYMOUR, Nicholas. *See* SEYMOUR, Anthony Nicholas

SEYMOUR, Paul Edward. b 62. Humberside Univ BA 92. St Jo Coll Nottm 01. **d** 03 **p** 04. C Ingleby Barwick *York* 03-07; C Hatfield Hyde *St Alb* 07-10; P-in-c Stevenage All SS Pin Green 10-13; V from 13. *All Saints' Vicarage, 100 Derby Way, Stevenage SG1 5TJ* T: (01438) 358108 M: 07815-729831
E: revpaulseymour@btinternet.com

SEYMOUR, Robert Ian. b 63. Ox Min Course 08. **d** 11 **p** 12. OLM Wokingham St Sebastian *Ox* 11-15; NSM from 15. *24 Booth Drive, Finchampstead, Wokingham RG40 4HL*
T: 0118-973 1857 E: ian.seymour@btinternet.com

SEYMOUR-JONES, Michael D'Israeli. b 37. **d** 09. OLM Shiplake w Dunsden and Harpsden *Ox* 09-12; PtO from 13. *6 Heathfield Close, Binfield Heath, Henley-on-Thames RG9 4DS* T: 0118-947 8632 E: m.seymour_jones@btinternet.com

SEYMOUR-WHITELEY, Ms Alison. b 51. City of Lon Poly MA 90 Homerton Coll Cam PGCE 95. CITC 04. **d** 07 **p** 08. LtO *Clogh* 07-11; Chapl HM Pris Morton Hall 11-12; Chapl Notts Healthcare NHS Trust 12-15; P-in-c Templemore w Thurles and Kilfithmone *C & O* from 15. *The Rectory, Roscrea Road, Templemore, Co Tipperary, Republic of Ireland* T: (00353) (504) 31175 E: alisonsw@hotmail.co.uk

SEYMOUR-WHITELEY, Richard Dudley. b 59. Leic Poly BSc 80. Linc Th Coll 82. **d** 85 **p** 86. C Bushey *St Alb* 85-89; C Stevenage St Mary Shephall w Aston 89-93; P-in-c Blunham w Tempsford and Lt Barford 93-99; P-in-c The Stodden Churches 99-01; I Grey Abbey w Kircubbin *D & D* 01-06; I Galloon w Drummully and Sallaghy *Clogh* 06-11; P-in-c Bilsthorpe *S'well* 11-15; P-in-c Farnsfield 11-15; P-in-c Eakring 11-15; P-in-c Kirklington w Hockerton 11-15; P-in-c Maplebeck 11-15; P-in-c Winkburn 11-15; I Rathdowney w Castlefleming, Donaghmore etc *C & O* from 15. *The Rectory, Roscrea Road, Templemore, Co Tipperary, Republic of Ireland* T: (00353) (504) 31175

SHACKELL, Daniel William. b 42. d 95 p 96. Dir Spires Cen S'wark 93-06; OLM Streatham St Leon S'wark 95-99; LtO 99-06; rtd 07; PtO Sarum from 09. Wynways, 146 West Bay Road, Bridport DT6 4AZ T: (01308) 426514 M: 07818-808249 E: danshackell@hotmail.com

SHACKELL, Kenneth Norman. b 26. S'wark Ord Course 66. d 69 p 70. NSM Greenwich St Alfege w St Pet and St Paul S'wark 69-95; PtO Sarum 95-03. 17 Portman Drive, Child Okeford, Blandford Forum DT11 8HU T/F: (01258) 861583

SHACKERLEY, The Very Revd Albert Paul. b 56. K Coll Lon MA 97 Sheff Univ PhD 07. Chich Th Coll 91. d 93 p 94. C Harlesden All So Lon 93-96; P-in-c Chelmsf All SS 96-98; V 98-02; Can Res Sheff Cathl 02-09; Vice Dean 05-09; V Doncaster St Geo 10-14; Hon Can Sheff Cathl 10-14; Dean Brecon S & B from 14. The Cathedral Office, Cathedral Close, Brecon LD3 9DP T: (01874) 623857 E: paul_shackerley@btinternet.com

SHACKLADY, Mrs Thelma. b 38. Liv Univ BA 60. St Alb Minl Tr Scheme 89. d 92 p 94. NSM Luton St Andr St Alb 92-96; NSM Luton All SS w St Pet 96-03; PtO from 03. 45 Lilly Hill, Olney MK46 5EZ T: (01234) 712997 E: bill.shacklady@virgin.net

SHACKLEFORD, Richard Neal. b 40. Univ of Denver BA 64 Univ of N Colorado MA 74. St Steph Ho Ox 84. d 86 p 87. C Poulton-le-Fylde Blackb 86-88; Can St Jo Cathl Colorado USA 88-92; C Denver St Mich 92-96; R Lindenhurst St Boniface from 96. 100 46th Street, Lindenhurst NY 11747-2009, USA T: (001) (631) 957 2666 F: 957 2665

SHACKLETON, Canon Alan. b 31. Sheff Univ BA 53. Wells Th Coll 54. d 56 p 57. C Ladybarn Man 56-58; C Bolton St Pet 58-61; V Middleton Junction 61-70; V Heywood St Luke 70-84; AD Rochdale 82-92; Hon Can Man Cathl 84-97; V Heywood St Luke w All So 85-86; TV Rochdale 86-91; TR 91-97; rtd 97; PtO Man from 97. 28 Taunton Avenue, Rochdale OL11 5LD T: (01706) 645335 E: alan@shackletong.demon.co.uk

SHACKLETON, Anthea. b 42. d 07. OLM Ravensthorpe and Thornhill Lees w Savile Town Wakef 07-10; OLM Ossett and Gawthorpe Leeds from 10. 8 Trinity View, Ossett WF5 9NZ T: (01924) 276488 M: 07815-445757 E: ant.shack@btinternet.com

SHACKLETON, Ian Roderick. b 40. St Fran Coll Brisbane 69. d 72 p 72. C Toowoomba Australia 72-74; P-in-c Milmerran 74-75; R 75-78; C Birch St Agnes Man 79-80; P-in-c Newton Heath St Wilfrid and St Anne 80-87; NSM W Derby St Jo Liv 87-90; C 90-94; P-in-c Southport St Luke 94-05; Asst Chapl HM Pris Liv 94-05; rtd 06; PtO Cant from 06. 31 The Shrubbery, Walmer, Deal CT14 7PZ T: (01304) 379773

SHACKLEY, Prof Myra Lesley. b 49. Southn Univ BA 70 PhD 75 Nottm Univ MA 99 FRGS. EMMTC 96. d 99 p 00. NSM Ordsall S'well 99-02; Dioc Tourism Adv 02-08; PV S'well Minster 02-06; P-in-c N and S Muskham 06-08; P-in-c Averham w Kelham 06-08; Hon C Spofforth w Kirk Deighton Leeds 08-15; Hon Can Ripon Cathl from 13. The Rectory, Church Lane, Spofforth, Harrogate HG3 1AF T: (01937) 590770 M: 07889-691504

SHAFTO, Robert James. b 38. Univ of Wales (Ban) BTh 06 Heythrop Coll Lon MA 10 FCA 61. OLM course 96. d 99 p 00. NSM W Dulwich All SS S'wark 99-07; rtd 07; PtO S'wark from 08. 46 Cedar Close, London SE21 8HX T: (020) 8761 7395 E: bob@shafto46.wanadoo.co.uk

SHAHZAD, Sulaiman. b 60. BA. Oak Hill Th Coll BA 93. d 96 p 97. C Winchmore Hill St Paul Lon 96-00; TV Digswell and Panshanger St Alb 00-10; V Bostall Heath Roch from 10. St Andrew's Parsonage, 276 Brampton Road, Bexleyheath DA7 5SF T: (020) 8303 9332 E: sulishahzad@tiscali.co.uk

SHAKESHAFT, Mrs Petra Jayne. b 60. Anglia Ruskin Univ BA 97 Cam Univ BTh 14. Westcott Ho Cam 12. d 14 p 15. C Cherry Hinton St Jo Ely from 14. 20 Paddock Way, Sawston, Cambridge CB22 3JS T: (01223) 510387 M: 07847-307416 E: petra_paul.shakeshaft@ntlworld.com

SHAKESPEARE, James Douglas Geoffrey. b 71. Fitzw Coll Cam BA 93 MA 97 Man Univ MA 96. Westcott Ho Cam 97. d 99 p 00. C Cherry Hinton St Jo Ely 99-02; Bp's Chapl and Policy Adv Leic 02-05; P-in-c Birstall and Wanlip 05-09; V 09-10; NSM Market Harborough and The Transfiguration etc 10-11; TV from 11. The Vicarage, Dingley Road, Great Bowden, Market Harborough LE16 7ET T: (01858) 469109 E: jshakespeare@btinternet.com

SHAKESPEARE, Steven. b 68. CCC Cam BA 89 PhD 94. Westcott Ho Cam 93. d 96 p 97. C Cambridge St Jas Ely 96-99; V Endcliffe and Chapl Sheff Hallam Univ 99-03; Chapl Liv Hope Univ from 03. Anglican Chaplaincy, Hope Park, Taggart Avenue, Liverpool L16 9JD T: 0151-291 3545 E: shakess@hope.ac.uk

SHAMBROOK, Roger William. b 46. Sarum & Wells Th Coll 78. d 83 p 84. OSP 76-82; C Southbourne St Kath Win 83-86; TV Bridport Sarum 86-01; Chapl Bridport Community Hosp 86-94; Chapl Dorset Community NHS Trust 94-01; P-in-c Torre All SS Ex 01-12; rtd 12. Sticklepath Cottage, 22 North Street, Ottery St Mary EX11 1DR T: (01404) 812697

SHAND, Brian Martin. b 53. Univ Coll Lon BA 76 PhD 82. St Steph Ho Ox 85. d 87 p 88. C Uxbridge St Marg Lon 87-88; C Uxbridge 88-90; C Worplesdon Guildf 90-94; Relig Affairs Producer BBC Radio Surrey 90-94; V Weston Guildf 94-01; V Witley 01-14; rtd 14. 21 Parliament Court, Parliament Hill, London NW3 2TS

SHANKS, Canon Robert Andrew Gulval. b 54. Ball Coll Ox BA 75 G&C Coll Cam BA 79 Leeds Univ PhD 90. Westcott Ho Cam 77. d 80 p 81. C Potternewton Ripon 80-83; C Stanningley St Thos 84-87; Lect Leeds Univ 87-91; Teaching Fell Lanc Univ Blackb 91-95; Research Fell in Th Cheltenham and Glouc Coll of HE 95-96; NSM Leeds City Ripon 95-96; P-in-c Upper Ryedale and CME Officer Cleveland Adnry York 97-04; Can Res Man Cathl 04-14; rtd 14. 39 Derwent Mews, York YO10 3DN T: (01904) 500253 E: ragshanks@hotmail.com

SHANNON, Mrs Annette Denise. b 61. Hatf Poly BSc 83 Anglia Poly Univ CertEd 99. ERMC 05. d 08 p 09. C St Edm Way St E 08-11; R Sproughton w Burstall, Copdock w Washbrook etc from 11. The Rectory, Glebe Close, Sproughton, Ipswich IP8 3BQ T: (01473) 807674 E: revannettes@aol.com

SHANNON, Helen Louise. b 68. NTMTC 07. d 10 p 12. C Woodside Park St Barn Lon from 10. 24 Stable Walk, London N2 9RD T: (020) 8883 7450 M: 07866-507609 E: helenshannon@stbarnabas.co.uk

SHANNON, The Ven Malcolm James Douglas. b 49. TCD BA 72 MA 75. CITC 75. d 75 p 76. C Clooney D & R 75-78; I Kilcolman w Kiltallagh, Killorglin, Knockane etc L & K 78-09; Adn Ardfert and Aghadoe 88-09; Adn Limerick 04-09; Treas Limerick Cathl 88-09; Dir of Ords 91-09; rtd 09. Cloonfad More, Carrick-on-Shannon, Co Leitrim, Republic of Ireland

SHANNON, Canon Trevor Haslam. b 33. Selw Coll Cam BA 57 MA 61 Lon Univ BD 69. Westcott Ho Cam 57. d 59 p 60. C Moss Side Ch Ch Man 59-62; V Woolfold 62-66; Chapl Forest Sch Snaresbrook 66-80 and 87-88; V Gt Ilford St Marg Chelmsf 88-90; TR Gt Ilford St Clem and St Marg 90-96; V 96-99; RD Redbridge 90-95; Hon Can Chelmsf Cathl 93-99; rtd 99; PtO Nor from 00. Honeysuckle Cottage, Clubbs Lane, Wells-next-the-Sea NR23 1DP T: (01328) 711409 E: tshannon409@btinternet.com

SHARKEY, Philip Michael. b 50. York Univ BA 73 MA 08 CQSW 78. ERMC 06. d 08 p 09. NSM Shingay Gp Ely 08-13; NSM Duxford from 13; NSM Hinxton from 13; NSM Ickleton from 13. 23 Cherry Drive, Royston SG8 7DL T: (01763) 221284 M: 07917-619124 E: sharkey_phil@yahoo.co.uk

SHARLAND, Canon Marilyn. b 40. City of Birm Coll CertEd 61. Oak Hill Th Coll 84. dss 86 d 87 p 94. Barkingside St Laur Chelmsf 86-88; Hon Par Dn Hucclecote Glouc 88-89; C Coney Hill 89-98; P-in-c Tuffley 99-99; V 99-06; Hon Can Glouc Cathl 02-06; rtd 06. 51 Lynmouth Road, Hucclecote, Gloucester GL3 3JD

SHARP, Alfred James Frederick. b 30. Oak Hill Th Coll 62. d 64 p 65. C Hanley Road St Sav w St Paul Lon 64-68; P-in-c Leverton Linc 68-84; Chapl Pilgrim Hosp Boston 76-84; P-in-c Benington w Leverton Linc 84; V Ch Broughton w Boylestone amd Sutton on the Hill Derby 84-89; R Ch Broughton w Barton Blount, Boylestone etc 89-94; rtd 94. 54 Edgefield, Weston, Spalding PE12 6RQ T: (01406) 370376

SHARP, Canon Andrew Timothy. b 58. K Alfred's Coll Win BA 79. Wycliffe Hall Ox 82. d 85 p 86. C Scarborough St Mary w Ch Ch and H Apostles York 85-89; C Luton St Fran St Alb 89-90; V 90-98; P-in-c Guernsey St Jo Win 98-01; V 01-13; Vice-Dean Guernsey 01-07; Hon Can Win Cathl 11-13; Can Emer Win Cathl from 13; rtd 13. The Flat, Presbyterian Church, 32 Townsend Street, Belfast BT13 2ES

SHARP, Mrs Barbara Elaine. b 52. Open Univ BA 84. Ripon Coll Cuddesdon 01. d 03 p 04. C Timperley Ches 03-06; P-in-c Lostock Gralam 06-11; V Sale St Paul from 11. St Paul's Vicarage, 28 Kilvert Drive, Sale M33 6PN T: 0161-973 1042 E: revbarb@hotmail.co.uk

SHARP, Brian Phillip. b 48. Cant Sch of Min 85. d 88 p 89. C S Ashford Ch Ch Cant 88-92; C St Laur in Thanet 92-96; V Margate St Jo 96-13; P-in-c Margate All SS 09-13; rtd 13; PtO Cant from 14. 32 The Hawthorns, Broadstairs CT10 2NG T: (01843) 579871 E: brianthevic@yahoo.co.uk

SHARP, Canon David Malcolm. b 33. Hertf Coll Ox BA 56 MA 59. Cuddesdon Coll 56. d 58 p 59. C Bris St Mary Redcliffe w Temple 58-65; V Henleaze 65-75; V Nor St Pet Mancroft 75-82; R Nor St Pet Mancroft w St Jo Maddermarket 82-98; Hon Can Nor Cathl 86-98; Dioc Eur Contact 91-09;

rtd 98; PtO *Nor* from 98. *The Pines, Field Lane, Fakenham NR21 9QX* T: (01328) 864121 E: dmsharp22@btinternet.com

SHARP, Harold. b 41. JP 90. FCCA 76. CITC 03. **d** 06 **p** 07. NSM Larne and Inver and Glynn w Raloo *Conn* 06-15; rtd 15. *110 Dreen Road, Cullybackey, Ballymena BT42 1EE* T: (028) 2588 0461 E: sharpharold@aol.com

SHARP, Mrs Hazel Patricia. b 39. Qu Eliz Coll Lon BSc 61. SWMTC 05. **d** 06 **p** 07. NSM St Merryn and St Issey w St Petroc Minor *Truro* 06-09; rtd 09; PtO *B & W* 10-11; Chapl Somerset Partnership NHS Foundation Trust from 11. *22 Bekynton Avenue, Wells BA5 3NF* T: (01749) 674397 E: hh.psharp@btinternet.com

SHARP, Mrs Heather Karin. b 48. **d** 04 **p** 05. OLM Blackrod *Man* 04-10; PtO from 10. *27 Hill Lane, Blackrod, Bolton BL6 5JW* T: (01204) 693609 E: heathersharp@hotmail.com

SHARP, James Michael. b 65. Ox Brookes Univ BA 00. STETS 08. **d** 11 **p** 12. C Southbourne St Kath *Win* 11-15; C Moordown from 15. *Parson's Lodge, 17 Linwood Road, Bournemouth BH9 1DW* M: 07584-077847 E: revjamessharp@gmail.com

SHARP (née BROWN), Mrs Jane Madeline. b 54. **d** 97 **p** 98. C Aylestone St Andr w St Jas *Leic* 97-00; NSM Knighton St Mary Magd 00-08; NSM Leic St Jas from 08; Chapl Leic Coll of FE from 14. *10 St Mary's Road, Leicester LE2 1XA* T: 0116-270 6002 E: a.sharp53@ntlworld.com

SHARP, Mrs Janice Anne. b 54. Aston Tr Scheme 91 NOC 93. **d** 96 **p** 97. C Skipton H Trin *Bradf* 96-00; V Buttershaw St Paul 00-02; Chapl Hull and E Yorks Hosps NHS Trust from 02; Hon C Patrington w Hollym, Welwick and Winestead *York* 07-14; Hon C Easington w Skeffling, Keyingham, Ottringham etc from 14. *The Hull Royal Infirmary, Anlaby Road, Hull HU3 2JZ* T: (01482) 328541

SHARP, Nicholas Leonard. b 64. Grey Coll Dur BA 85. St Jo Coll Nottm MA 95. **d** 95 **p** 96. C Oakwood St Thos *Lon* 95-99; TV N Farnborough *Guildf* 99-05; Chapl Farnborough Sixth Form Coll 01-05; P-in-c Lt Amwell *St Alb* 05-08; TV Hertford from 08. *The Vicarage, 17 Barclay Close, Hertford Heath, Hertford SG13 7RW* T: (01992) 589140 E: nicthevic@gmail.com

SHARP, Philip Paul Clayton. b 66. Open Univ BSc 97. Trin Coll Bris 04. **d** 06 **p** 07. C Liskeard and St Keyne *Truro* 06-11; P-in-c St Martin w Looe from 11; C Duloe, Herodsfoot, Morval and St Pinnock from 11; RD W Wivelshire from 13. *The Rectory, St Martin, Looe PL13 1NX* T: (01503) 263070 E: ppsharp@tiscali.co.uk

SHARP, Preb Robert. b 36. FLCM 58. St Aid Birkenhead 64. **d** 67 **p** 68. C Shipley St Paul *Bradf* 67-70; C-in-c Thwaites Brow CD 70-74; V Thwaites Brow 74-77; P-in-c Alberbury w Cardeston *Heref* 77-78; V 78-87; V Ford 77-87; V Claverley w Tuckhill 87-97; RD Bridgnorth 89-96; Preb Heref Cathl 91-97; rtd 97; PtO *Heref* 97-99 and 01-12; C Stoke Lacy, Moreton Jeffries w Much Cowarne etc 99-00. *62 Biddulph Way, Ledbury HR8 2HN* T: (01531) 631972

SHARP, Miss Sarah Elizabeth. b 67. Bp Otter Coll Chich BA 89 Anglia Poly Univ MA 00 K Coll Lon MA 11 Coll of Ripon & York St Jo PGCE 90. Westcott Ho Cam 98. **d** 00 **p** 01. C Ross *Heref* 00-03; R Lower Windrush *Ox* 03-13; V Bodicote from 13. *2 The Rydes, Bodicote, Banbury OX15 4EJ* T: (01295) 250282 E: s550sharp@btinternet.com

SHARP, Trevor Andrew. b 63. Westcott Ho Cam. **d** 14 **p** 15. C St Mary-at-Latton *Chelmsf* from 14. *31 Denby Grange, Harlow CM17 9PZ* M: 07970-284332 E: trevorann@hotmail.co.uk *or* revtrev08@gmail.com

SHARPE, Canon Bruce Warrington. b 41. JP 88. Ely Th Coll 62 St Steph Ho Ox 64. **d** 65 **p** 66. C Streatham St Pet *S'wark* 65-67; C Castries St Lucia 67-68; Hon C Leic St Matt and St Geo 68-69; Hon C Catford St Laur *S'wark* 69-70; Hon C Deptford St Paul 70-75; Hon C Lamorbey H Redeemer *Roch* 76-83; Hon C Sidcup St Andr 88-99; Locum Chapl Morden Coll Blackheath 08-08; PtO *Roch* 83-88; *Lon* 97-06; *Ex* from 09; *S'wark* 98-10; *Roch* 99-01; Hon Can Bickley 01-11; Windward Is from 01. *Walnut Cottage, Upper Braddons Hill Road, Torquay TQ1 1QE* E: canonbruce1@aol.com

SHARPE, Cecil Frederick. b 23. Edin Th Coll 52. **d** 54 **p** 55. C Falkirk *Edin* 54-56; C Kings Norton *Birm* 56-58; V Withall 58-80; PtO 80-12; rtd 88. *c/o R J S Palmer Esq, 5 Belton Close, Hockley Heath, Solihull B94 6QU*

SHARPE, David Francis. b 32. Ex Coll Ox BA 56 MA 59. St Steph Ho Ox 57. **d** 60 **p** 61. C Hunslet St Mary and Stourton *Ripon* 60-63; C Notting Hill St Jo *Lon* 63-68; V Haggerston St Mary w St Chad 68-78; P-in-c Haggerston St Aug 73-78; V Haggerston St Chad 78-83; V Mill Hill St Mich 83-98; rtd 98; Chapl St Raphaël *Eur* 98-02; PtO *Lon* 02-13; *S'wark* from 11. *10 Up, The Quadrangle, Morden College, London SE3 0PW* T: (020) 8853 5104 E: davidsharpe32@waitrose.com

SHARPE, Derek Martin Brereton (Pip). b 29. Birkbeck Coll Lon BA 60. NEOC 90. **d** 90 **p** 91. NSM Scarborough St Luke *York*

90-92; Asst Chapl Scarborough Distr Hosp 90-92; P-in-c Sherburn and W and E Heslerton w Yedingham *York* 92-99; Hon C Buckrose Carrs 99; rtd 99; PtO *York* from 00. *Byland Lodge, 68A Low Moorgate, Rillington, Malton YO17 8JW* T: (01723) 759063

SHARPE, Gerard John. b 23. Westcott Ho Cam. **d** 64 **p** 65. C Thetford St Cuth w H Trin *Nor* 64-70; V Holme *Ely* 70-76; R Conington 70-76; V Holme w Conington 76-93; R Glatton 74-93; RD Yaxley 82-88; rtd 93; PtO *Ely* 93-00. *24 St Margaret's Road, Girton, Cambridge CB3 0LT* T: (01223) 574246

SHARPE, Mrs Jennifer Louise. b 74. St Jo Coll Nottm BA 15. **d** 15. C Mansfield St Jo w St Mary *S'well* from 15. *St Mary's Vicarage, Bancroft Lane, Mansfield NG18 5LZ* E: jenniesharpe2305@gmail.com

SHARPE, Miss Joan Valerie. b 33. EMMTC 73. **dss** 84 **d** 88 **p** 94. Hon Par Dn Warsop *S'well* 88-94; Hon C 94-98; rtd 98; PtO *S'well* from 04. *1 Forest Court, Eakring Road, Mansfield NG18 3DP* T: (01623) 424051

SHARPE, Canon John Edward. b 50. St Jo Coll Dur BSc 72. Cranmer Hall Dur 73. **d** 76 **p** 77. C Woodford Wells *Chelmsf* 76-79; C Ealing St Mary *Lon* 79-83; Min Walsall St Martin *Lich* 83-87; TV Walsall 87-96; R Glenfield *Leic* 96-15; AD Sparkenhoe E 03-11; Hon Can Leic Cathl 10-15; rtd 15. *18 Bramble Chase, Bishops Cleeve, Cheltenham GL52 8WN* T: (01242) 677057 E: jesharpe1@btinternet.com

SHARPE, The Ven Kenneth William. b 40. Univ of Wales (Lamp) BA 61. Sarum Th Coll 61. **d** 63 **p** 64. C Hubberston *St D* 63-71; TV Cwmbran *Mon* 71-74; Dioc Children's Adv 72-82; Dioc Youth Chapl 74-82; V Dingestow and Llangovan w Penyclawdd and Tregare 74-82; V Newport St Mark 82-97; Chapl Alltyryn Hosp Gwent 83-97; RD Newport *Mon* 93-97; Can St Woolos Cathl 94-08; Adn Newport 97-08; rtd 08. *27 Incline Way, Saundersfoot SA69 9LX* T: (01834) 813674

SHARPE, Mrs Margaret Joy. b 43. Qu Coll Birm. **d** 09 **p** 10. OLM Bilton *Cov* 09-12; NSM from 12. *60 Cymbeline Way, Bilton, Rugby CV22 6LA* T: (01788) 810794

SHARPE, Mrs Margaret Therèsa. b 48. Man Univ BEd 70. Cranmer Hall Dur 72 WMMTC 90. **d** 91 **p** 94. C W Bromwich H Trin *Lich* 91-96; Asst Chapl Glenfield Hosp NHS Trust Leic 96-99; Chapl 99-00; Chapl Univ Hosps Leic NHS Trust 00-04; Chapl Team Ldr 04-12; rtd 12; PtO *Leic* from 13. *18 Bramble Chase, Bishops Cleeve, Cheltenham GL52 8WN* T: (01242) 677057 E: mtsharpe@btinternet.com

SHARPE, Peter Richard. b 55. Salford Univ BSc 76 ACIB 81. STETS 98. **d** 01 **p** 02. C Ex St Jas 01-04; R S Hill w Callington *Truro* 04-12; C St Ive and Pensilva w Quethiock 09-12; P-in-c Linkinhorne and Stoke Climsland 10-12; RD E Wivelshire 11-12; P-in-c St Keverne from 12; P-in-c St Ruan w St Grade and Landewednack from 12. *The Vicarage, Lemon Street, St Keverne, Helston TR12 6NG* T: (01326) 280999 E: peter@petersharpe.net

SHARPE, Pip. *See* SHARPE, Derek Martin Brereton

SHARPE, Richard Gordon. b 48. Birm Univ BA 69. St Jo Coll Nottm BA 74. **d** 75 **p** 76. C Hinckley H Trin *Leic* 75-78; C Kingston upon Hull H Trin *York* 78-85; Chapl Marston Green Hosp Birm 85-88; Chapl Chelmsley Hosp Birm 86-88; TV Chelmsley Wood *Birm* 85-88; P-in-c Dosthill 88-93; V 93-97; R Desford and Peckleton w Tooley *Leic* 97-12; rtd 12. *65 West End, Kirkbymoorside, York YO62 6AD* T: (01751) 431364 E: sharpeblackhorse@aol.com

SHARPE, Canon Roger. b 35. TCD BA 60 MA 63. Qu Coll Birm 60. **d** 62 **p** 63. C Stockton H Trin *Dur* 62-64; C Oakdale St Geo *Sarum* 64-68; V Redlynch and Morgan's Vale 68-86; RD Alderbury 82-86; V Warminster St Denys 86-88; R Upton Scudamore 86-88; V Horningsham 86-88; R Warminster St Denys, Upton Scudamore etc 88-95; Can and Preb Sarum Cathl 89-00; RD Heytesbury 89-95; Chmn Dioc Assn for Deaf 91-98; P-in-c Corsley *Sarum* 92-95; TR Cley Hill Warminster 95-00; rtd 00; PtO *Sarum* from 01. *Woodside, Bugmore Lane, East Grimstead SP5 3SA* T: (01722) 712753

SHARPE, William Wilberforce. b 62. **d** 05 **p** 06. NSM Brixton St Matt w St Jude *S'wark* 05-10; NSM Tulse Hill H Trin and St Matthias from 10; Chapl Guy's and St Thos' NHS Foundn Trust from 08. *1D Lovelace Road, London SE21 8JY* T/F: (020) 8761 8539 M: 07956-546394 E: sharpeww@aol.com

SHARPLES, Angela (Ella). b 65. **d** 07 **p** 08. C Timperley *Ches* 07-09; C Congleton 09-11; Hon C Astbury and Smallwood 11-14. *Address temp unknown* E: ella_sharples@hotmail.com

SHARPLES, Catherine Ruth. b 70. Nottm Univ BSc 92 Nottm Trent Univ PhD 96. Trin Coll Bris 11. **d** 13 **p** 14. C Stevenage St Pet Broadwater *St Alb* from 13. *90 Ferrier Road, Stevenage SG2 0NZ* M: 07505-459157 E: kate.sharples@ymail.com

SHARPLES, David. b 41. Linc Th Coll 71. **d** 73 **p** 74. C Reddish *Man* 73-75; C Prestwich St Mary 76-78; V Ashton St Jas 78-86;

V Hope St Jas 86-06; rtd 06; PtO *Man* 06-08. *18 Holly Avenue, Worsley, Manchester M28 3DW* T: 0161-950 8675

SHARPLES, The Ven David John. b 58. Lon Univ BD 81 AKC 81. Coll of Resurr Mirfield. **d** 82 **p** 83. C Prestwich St Mary *Man* 82-87; V Royton St Anne 87-02; AD Tandle 94-02; Dir of Ords from 02; Hon Can Man Cathl from 06; Adn Salford from 09. *2 The Walled Gardens, Swinton, Manchester M27 0FR* T: 0161-794 2401   F: 794 2411
E: ddo@bishopscourt.manchester.anglican.org

SHARPLES, Derek. b 35. SS Paul & Mary Coll Cheltenham CertEd 57 Liv Univ DipEd 63 Man Univ MEd 66 Bath Univ PhD 72 Open Univ BA 79 FCollP 86. WMMTC 83. **d** 86 **p** 87. NSM Malvern H Trin and St Jas *Worc* 86-90; C St Jo in Bedwardine 90-92; R Belbroughton w Fairfield and Clent 92-00; rtd 00; PtO *Worc* from 00. *Witton, 16 Moorlands Road, Malvern WR14 2UA* T: (01684) 575742
E: witton@btinternet.com

SHARPLES, Ella. *See* SHARPLES, Angela

SHARPLES, Gregory Stephen. b 80. **d** 14 **p** 15. C S Widnes *Liv* from 14. *St Mary's Vicarage, St Mary's Road, Widnes WA8 0DN* M: 07730-512603   E: gregorysharples@hotmail.com

SHARPLES, Jean. *See* ROLT, Jean

SHARPLES, Jonathan David. b 65. Lon Bible Coll BA 95. Wycliffe Hall Ox 03. **d** 05 **p** 06. C Ashton-upon-Mersey St Mary Magd *Ches* 05-09; R Astbury and Smallwood 09-14. *Address temp unknown* E: jonsharples@hotmail.com

SHARPLES, Susan Margaret. *See* WEBSTER, Susan Margaret

SHARPLEY, The Ven Roger Ernest Dion. b 28. Ch Ch Ox BA 52 MA 56. St Steph Ho Ox 52. **d** 54 **p** 55. C Southwick St Columba *Dur* 54-60; V Middlesbrough All SS *York* 60-81; P-in-c Middlesbrough St Hilda w St Pet 64-72; P-in-c Middlesbrough St Aid 79; V 79-81; RD Middlesbrough 70-81; Can and Preb York Minster 74-81; V St Andr Holborn *Lon* 81-92; Adn Hackney 81-92; rtd 92; PtO *Dur* from 92; Chapl Grey Coll Dur 96-01. *2 Hill Meadows, High Shincliffe, Durham DH1 2PE* T: 0191-386 1908

SHAVE, Norman Rossen. b 60. G&C Coll Cam BA 82 MA 95 Newc Univ MB, BS 85 MRCGP 90. Cranmer Hall Dur 98. **d** 00 **p** 01. C Preston on Tees *Dur* 00-03; C Preston-on-Tees and Longnewton 03-04; V Norton St Mary 04-12; P-in-c Stockton St Chad 04-12; P-in-c Stranton from 12. *The Vicarage, 34A Westbourne Road, Hartlepool TS25 5RE* T: (01429) 233609

SHAW, Alan Taylor. b 52. Sarum & Wells Th Coll 88. **d** 90 **p** 91. C Beeston *Ripon* 90-93; C Stanningley St Thos 93-96; TV Seacroft 96-98; V Ryhill *Wakef* 98-02; rtd 03; PtO *Leeds* from 04. *65 Hollingthorpe Avenue, Hall Green, Wakefield WF4 3NP* T: (01924) 255210

SHAW, Alan Walter. b 41. TCD BA 63 BAI 63 Chu Coll Cam MSc 66. **d** 94 **p** 95. NSM Drumcliffe w Kilnasoolagh *L & K* 94-97; NSM Kenmare w Sneem, Waterville etc 97-09; Can Limerick Cathl 07-09; rtd 09. *22 Ceann Mara Court, Pairc na Gloine, Kenmare, Co Kerry, Republic of Ireland* M: 87-678 8700 E: shawa@eircom.net

✠**SHAW, The Rt Revd Alexander Martin.** b 44. AKC 67. **d** 68 **p** 69 **c** 04. C Glas St Oswald 68-70; C Edin Old St Paul 70-75; Chapl K Coll Cam 75-77; C St Marylebone All SS *Lon* 77-78; R Dunoon *Arg* 78-81; Succ Ex Cathl 81-83; Dioc Miss and Ecum Officer 83-89; TV Can Res 83-87; Can Res St E Cathl 89-04; Prec 96-04; Bp Arg 04-09; rtd 09; Hon Asst Bp Ex from 10. *11 Russell Terrace, Exeter EX4 4HX* T: (01392) 663511 M: 07801-549615   E: alexandermartin.shaw@virgin.net

SHAW, Mrs Alison Barbara. b 55. Open Univ BA 92. SWMTC 98. **d** 01 **p** 02. NSM St Breoke and Egloshayle *Truro* 01-03; C Bodmin w Lanhydrock and Lanivet 03-05; TV 05-10; TV Devonport St Boniface and St Phil *Ex* 10-14; V Devonport St Boniface from 14. *The Vicarage, 1 Normandy Way, Plymouth PL5 1SW* T: (01752) 369140   E: alishaw2001@yahoo.co.uk

SHAW, Andrew James. b 54. MBE 12. York Univ MA 97 Cumbria Univ BA 10. LCTP 07. **d** 10 **p** 11. NSM Fleetwood St Dav and Fleetwood St Pet *Blackb* 10-13; NSM Waterside Par 13-15; V from 15; NSM Stalmine w Pilling 13-15; V from 15. *St Mary's Vicarage, Burnley Road, Trawden, Colne BB8 8PN* M: 07876-571978   E: shaw-family@tiscali.co.uk

SHAW, Andrew Jonathan. b 50. Wycliffe Hall Ox 85. **d** 87 **p** 88. C Witton w Brundall and Braydeston *Nor* 87-89; C Brundall w Braydeston and Postwick 89-90; C Grayswood *Guildf* 90-91; P-in-c 91-99; Chapl RN Sch Haslemere 90-96; V Hendon St Paul Mill Hill *Lon* from 99. *St Paul's Vicarage, Hammers Lane, London NW7 4EA* T: (020) 8959 1856 *or* T/F: 8906 3793 E: parishoffice@stpaulsmillhill.freeserve.co.uk

SHAW, Anne. *See* MORRIS, Anne

SHAW, Ms Anne Lesley. b 50. SRN SCM. Linc Th Coll 77. **dss** 80 **d** 87 **p** 94. Camberwell St Luke *S'wark* 80-85; Chapl Asst R Lon Hosp (Whitechapel) 85-90; Chapl Lewisham Hosp 90-94;

Chapl Hither Green Hosp 90-94; Chapl Sydenham Childrens Hosp 90-94; Chapl Lewisham Hosp NHS Trust 94-10; rtd 10; PtO *S'wark* 11-13; *Cant* from 14. *54 Nutcroft Road, London SE15 1AF* T: (020) 7639 4031 E: shawpowell@hotmail.co.uk

SHAW, Anne Patricia Leslie. b 39. MB, BS 63 MRCS 63 LRCP 63. Qu Coll Birm 79. **dss** 81 **d** 87 **p** 94. Pinner *Lon* 81-84; Rickmansworth *St Alb* 84-09; NSM 87-09; rtd 09; PtO *St Alb* from 09. *37 Sandy Lodge Road, Moor Park, Rickmansworth WD3 1LP* T: (01923) 827663 E: anneshaw@doctors.net.uk

SHAW, Anthony Keeble. b 36. K Alfred's Coll Win CertEd 60 Birkbeck Coll Lon CPsychol 98. SWMTC 78. **d** 81 **p** 82. Hd Teacher Wolborough C of E Primary Sch 73-87; NSM E Teignmouth *Ex* 81-83; NSM Highweek and Teigngrace 83-87; Sub Chapl HM Pris Channings Wood 85-87; C Southbourne St Kath *Win* 87-89; Teaching 89-96; NSM Regent's Park St Mark *Lon* 93-96; P-in-c Winthorpe and Langford w Holme *S'well* 96-01; Dioc Chief Insp of Schs 96-01; rtd 01; PtO *Win* from 01. *Manlea Cottage, Centre Lane, Everton, Lymington SO41 0JP* T: (01590) 645451

SHAW, Clive Ronald. b 54. UEA BA 75 Lanc Univ MA 07 Hatf Coll Dur PGCE 76. CBDTI 99. **d** 02 **p** 03. C Westfield St Mary *Carl* 02-06; V Aspatria w Hayton and Gilcrux 06-14; P-in-c Millom from 14. *The Vicarage, St George's Road, Millom LA18 4JE* T: (01229) 772889 E: clivershaw@btinternet.com

SHAW, Craig Lee. b 72. Newc Univ LLB 94. Cranmer Hall Dur 12. **d** 14 **p** 15. C Penkridge *Lich* from 14. *31 Nursery Drive, Penkridge, Stafford ST19 5SJ* T: (01785) 713319 M: 07443-505615   E: craigls72@btinternet.com

SHAW, David George. b 40. Lon Univ BD 64 MA 03. Tyndale Hall Bris 58. **d** 65 **p** 66. C Kirkdale St Lawr *Liv* 65-68; C Bebington *Ches* 68-70; V Swadlincote *Derby* 70-75; R Eyam 75-04; rtd 04. *9 North Fields, Sturminster Newton DT10 1FD* T: (01258) 473797 E: berdav@btinternet.com

SHAW, Canon David Michael. b 61. Univ Coll Dur BA 83 Bris Univ BA 97. Trin Coll Bris 91. **d** 93 **p** 94. C Wotton-under-Edge w Ozleworth and N Nibley *Glouc* 93-97; P-in-c Jersey St Clem *Win* 97-98; R from 98; Can Mombasa from 11. *The Rectory, La rue du Presbytere, St Clement, Jersey JE2 6RB* T: (01534) 851992 E: shawhome@jerseymail.zzn.com

SHAW, David Parlane. b 32. CITC. **d** 69 **p** 70. Bp's C Lower w Upper Langfield *D & R* 69-75; R Chedburgh w Depden and Rede *St E* 75-78; R Chedburgh w Depden, Rede and Hawkedon 79-82; R Desford *Leic* 82-83; R Desford and Peckleton w Tooley 84-91; P-in-c Ramsden Crays w Ramsden Bellhouse *Chelmsf* 91-95; rtd 95; PtO *Leic* from 95. *95 Manor Road, Desford, Leicester LE9 9JQ* T: (01455) 821243 E: dshaw3234@btinternet.com

SHAW, David Thomas. b 45. Open Univ BA 78. WMMTC 87. **d** 90 **p** 91. C Sheldon *Birm* 90-93; R Chelmsley Wood 93-02; TR Broughton Astley and Croft w Stoney Stanton *Leic* 02-10; rtd 10; PtO *Cov* from 11. *39 Orchard Way, Stretton on Dunsmore, Rugby CV23 9HP* T: (024) 7654 2036 E: davidshaw139@btinternet.com

SHAW, Dennis Alfred Arthur. b 24. Wells Th Coll 64. **d** 65 **p** 66. C Redditch St Steph *Worc* 65-70; R Addingham *Bradf* 70-92; rtd 92; PtO *Leeds* from 92. *67 Crowther Avenue, Calverley, Pudsey LS28 5SA* T: (01274) 611746

SHAW, Elaine Rosemary. *See* MILLS, Elaine Rosemary

SHAW, Mrs Felicity Mary. b 46. UEA BSc 67 MSc 68. NOC 88. **d** 91 **p** 94. Par Dn Benchill *Man* 91-94; C 94-95; TV E Farnworth and Kearsley 95-98; TR 98-03; V Woodhall *Bradf* 03-07; rtd 07; PtO *Man* from 08. *99 Pennine Road, Horwich, Bolton BL6 7HW* T: (01204) 696851 E: rev.fmshaw@tesco.net

SHAW, Gerald Oliver. b 32. K Coll Lon 56. **d** 60 **p** 61. C Burnley St Cuth *Blackb* 60-62; C Heysham 62-65; C-in-c Oswaldtwistle All SS CD 65-66; V Oswaldtwistle All SS 66-69; Chapl Leavesden Hosp Abbots Langley 69-75; Chapl Broadmoor Hosp Crowthorne 75-88; C Easthampstead *Ox* 88-92; P-in-c Beech Hill, Grazeley and Spencers Wood 92-97; rtd 97; LtO *Ox* from 99; PtO *Win* 02-13. *1 Mortimer House Cottage, Mortimer Lane, Mortimer, Reading RG7 3PR* T: 0118-933 3660

SHAW, Graham. b 44. Worc Coll Ox BA 65. Cuddesdon Coll. **d** 69 **p** 70. C Esher *Guildf* 69-73; R Winford *B & W* 73-78; Chapl Ex Coll Ox 78-85; R Farnborough *Roch* 88-95; rtd 04. *21 Ulster Court, Albany Park Road, Kingston upon Thames KT2 5SS*

SHAW, Graham Lister. b 81. Fitzw Coll Cam BA 04. Wycliffe Hall Ox 05. **d** 07 **p** 08. C Camberley St Paul *Guildf* 07-11; V Ches Ch Ch from 11. *57 Black Diamond Park, Chester CH1 3EW* T: (01244) 325302 E: glshaw@gmail.com *or* graham.shaw@christchurchchester.com

SHAW, Canon Grahame David. b 44. Lich Th Coll 65. **d** 68 **p** 69. C Grange St Andr *Ches* 68-73; TV E Runcorn w Halton 73-74; TV Thamesmead *S'wark* 74-79; V Newington St Paul 79-13; S'wark Adnry Ecum Officer 90-13; RD S'wark and

Newington 96-02; Hon Can S'wark Cathl 99-13; rtd 13. *2 St Peter's Close, Pimperne, Blandford Forum DT11 8UZ* E: grahame@leat.org.uk

SHAW, Gregory. b 66. Chu Coll Cam MA 90 MEng 89. Ripon Coll Cuddesdon 09. **d** 12 **p** 13. NSM Yardley Hastings, Denton and Grendon etc *Pet* 12-15; C Earls Barton from 15. *114 Birchfield Road, Northampton NN1 4RH* T: (01604) 459954 E: gregnshaw@hotmail.com

SHAW, Mrs Irene. b 45. Gilmore Course 80 NEOC 82. **dss** 83 **d** 87 **p** 94. Elloughton and Brough w Brantingham *York* 83-86; Westborough *Guildf* 86-88; C 87-88; C Shottermill 88-91; C Lamorbey H Redeemer *Roch* 91-97; V Belvedere All SS 97-02; TV Em TM *Wakef* 02-05; rtd 05; PtO *York* from 07. *26 Brereton Close, Beverley HU17 7QE* T: (01482) 871095

SHAW, Prof Jane Alison. b 63. Ox Univ BA 85 MA 91 Harvard Div Sch MDiv 88 Univ of California Berkeley PhD 94. SAOMC 96. **d** 97 **p** 98. Fell Regent's Park Coll Ox 94-01; Dean 98-01; Hon Cathl Chapl Ch Ox 00-10; Fell, Chapl and Dean of Div New Coll Ox 01-10; NSM Ox St Mary V w St Cross and St Pet 97-01; Hon Can Ch Ox 05-10; Can Th Sarum Cathl 07-10; Dean Grace Cathl San Francisco USA 10-14; Dean Relig Life and Prof RS Stanford Univ from 14. *Office for Religious Life, Memorial Church, 450 Serra Mall, Stanford CA 94305-2037, USA* T: (001) (650) 723 1762 E: janeshaw@stanford.edu

SHAW, Miss Jane Elizabeth. b 47. New Hall Cam BA 68 MA 72 Brunel Univ MPhil 79. NEOC 98. **d** 01 **p** 02. NSM Moor Allerton *Ripon* 01-05; Presbyter Bp Rockey Chpl Raiwind Pakistan 06-11; NSM Upper Wylye Valley *Sarum* from 11. *Manor Farm House, Corton, Warminster BA12 0SZ* T: (01985) 850141 E: shawjane2005@gmail.com

SHAW, Mrs Jane Louise Claridge. b 66. Birm Poly BA 87. WMMTC 00. **d** 03 **p** 04. C Ironbridge *Birm* 03-07; V Dosthill from 07. *The Vicarage, 1 Church Road, Dosthill, Tamworth B77 1LU* T: (01827) 281349 E: louiseshaw6@yahoo.co.uk

SHAW, Mrs Janet Elaine. b 53. EMMTC 94. **d** 97 **p** 98. C Cleveleys *Blackb* 97-01; P-in-c Blackpool St Paul 01-03; V 03-12; rtd 12; PtO *Blackb* from 13. *10 Rossall Promenade, Thornton-Cleveleys FY5 1LP*

SHAW, Mrs Jayne. St Mich Coll Llan. **d** 08 **p** 09. NSM Tonyrefail w Gilfach Goch *Llan* 08-12; NSM Coity, Nolton and Brackla 12-14; NSM Coity, Nolton and Brackla w Coychurch from 14. *1 Cae Rhedyn, Coity, Bridgend CF35 6AQ* E: jayne@cnb-parish.org.uk

SHAW, John Boyde. b 52. St Jo Coll Nottm BA 00. **d** 00 **p** 01. C Gorleston St Andr *Nor* 00-04; P-in-c Rockland St Mary w Hellington, Bramerton etc 04-06; R from 06. *The Rectory, 2 Rectory Lane, Rockland St Mary, Norwich NR14 7EY* T: (01508) 538619 E: revjohnshaw@gmail.com

SHAW, Jonathan. *See* SHAW, Andrew Jonathan

SHAW, Judith Ann. b 52. Nottm Univ BA 74 PhD 90 York Univ MA 92. SEITE 11. **d** 13 **p** 14. NSM Rother and Oxney *Cant* from 13; NSM Tenterden and Smallhythe from 14. *Banks House, Smallhythe Road, Tenterden TN30 7NG* T: (01580) 763468 E: shawmalthouse@aol.com

SHAW, Keith Arthur. b 51. **d** 10 **p** 11. NSM Baswich *Lich* from 10; Chapl S Staffs Healthcare NHS Trust from 10. *3 Newhall Gardens, Cannock Road, Cannock WS11 5EA* T: (01543) 572255 E: keith.shaw@sssft.nhs.uk

SHAW, Kenneth James. b 36. St Jo Coll Nottm 85 Edin Th Coll 88. **d** 87 **p** 89. NSM Troon *Glas* 87-89; C Glas St Mary 89-90; R Lenzie 90-01; Warden of Readers 96-01; rtd 01; Hon C Glas St Mary 02-06; LtO from 08. *19 Mailerbeg Gardens, Moodiesburn, Glasgow G69 0JP* T: (01236) 873987 E: kenneth.shaw5@virginmedia.com

SHAW, Louise. *See* SHAW, Jane Louise Claridge

SHAW, Malcolm. b 46. Trin Coll Bris. **d** 01 **p** 02. C Bolsover *Derby* 01-05; R Brimington 05-10; P-in-c Chelford w Lower Withington *Ches* 10-13; rtd 13. *85 Rochester Crescent, Crewe CW1 5YQ* M: 07713-624005 E: malcolmshaw238@btinternet.com

SHAW, Malcolm Roy. b 47. Lon Univ BA 69 CQSW 76. NEOC 03. **d** 05 **p** 06. NSM Hunmanby w Muston *York* 05-08; NSM Rufforth w Moor Monkton and Hessay 08-13; NSM Long Marston 08-13; NSM Healaugh w Wighill, Bilbrough and Askham Richard 08-13; NSM Tockwith and Bilton w Bickerton 08-13; NSM N Ainsty 13; V from 13. *32 Westfield Road, Tockwith, York YO26 7PY* T: (01423) 359003 E: revroytockwith@btinternet.com

SHAW, Mrs Margaret Ann. b 58. Bp Otter Coll Chich BA 80 SS Paul & Mary Coll Cheltenham PGCE 81. EAMTC 00. **d** 03 **p** 04. C Langdon Hills *Chelmsf* 03-06; TV Basildon St Andr w H Cross from 06; RD Basildon from 10. *St Andrew's Vicarage, 3 The Fremnells, Basildon SS14 2QX* T: (01268) 520516 E: sh.ma@btinternet.com

SHAW, Martin. *See* SHAW, Alexander Martin

SHAW, Michael. *See* SHAW, Ralph Michael

SHAW, Michael Howard. b 38. Leeds Univ BSc 61. Linc Th Coll 64. **d** 66 **p** 67. C W Hartlepool St Paul *Dur* 66-68; Asst Master Stockbridge Co Sec Sch 68; Totton Coll 69; Gravesend Boys' Gr Sch 70-72; Maidstone Gr Sch 72-94; PtO *Roch* from 70; *Cant* 70-15; rtd 03. *11 Knights Croft, New Ash Green, Longfield DA3 8HT*

SHAW, Neil Graham. b 61. St Jo Coll Nottm LTh 91. **d** 91 **p** 92. C Leamington Priors St Paul *Cov* 91-95; TV Bestwood *S'well* 95-99; Chapl HM YOI Thorn Cross 99-01; Chapl HM Pris Hindley 01-07; Chapl HM Pris Liv 07-14; TV Warrington E *Liv* from 14. *18 Arpley Street, Warrington WA1 1NZ* T: (01925) 821555 M: 07432-157443 E: rev.ngs1@gmail.com

SHAW, Norman William. b 46. Open Univ BA 94. **d** 13 **p** 14. OLM Glossop *Derby* from 13. *32 Duke Street, Glossop SK13 8DU* T: (01457) 867493

SHAW, Pamela Joyce. *See* SANDERS, Pamela Joyce

SHAW, Peter Anthony. b 49. **d** 10 **p** 11. NSM Burwash *Chich* 10-14; NSM Bexhill St Pet 14-15; NSM Wrockwardine Deanery *Lich* from 15. *The Vicarage, Eaton Constantine, Shrewsbury SY5 6RF* E: pandsjshaw@clara.co.uk

SHAW, Peter Haslewood. b 17. Pemb Coll Cam BA 39 MA 65. Worc Ord Coll 65. **d** 67 **p** 68. C S Kensington St Jude *Lon* 67-69; V Alderney *Win* 69-78; V Disley *Ches* 78-82; rtd 82; Chapl Athens w Kifissia, Patras and Corfu *Eur* 82-85; Hon C Las Palmas 84-85; Hon C Breamore *Win* 85-89; PtO *Pet* from 07. *24 Hanover Court, Dulverton TA22 9HZ* T: (01398) 323740

SHAW, Ralph. b 38. Man Univ MEd 70. Sarum & Wells Th Coll 78. **d** 80 **p** 81. C Consett *Dur* 80-84; P-in-c Tanfield 84-88; V 88-97; R S Shields St Aid and St Steph 97-05; rtd 05. *10 Shipley Court, Gateshead NE8 4EZ* T: 0191-420 5137

SHAW, Ralph Michael. b 45. DipAdEd. Lich Th Coll 68. **d** 70 **p** 71. C Dewsbury All SS *Wakef* 70-75; TV Redcar w Kirkleatham *York* 75-76; Dioc Youth Officer St Alb 76-91; Chief Exec Jo Grooms 91-08; Team Ldr Workplace Min *St Alb* 08-10; rtd 10; PtO *St Alb* from 10. *18 Wyton, Welwyn Garden City AL7 2PF* T: (01707) 321813 E: revmshaw@yahoo.co.uk

SHAW, Richard. b 46. **d** 89 **p** 90. NSM Porchester *S'well* 89-91; NSM Daybrook 04-06; P-in-c Basford St Aid 06-11; P-in-c Basford St Leodegarius 09-11; V Basford St Leodegarius and St Aid from 11. *The Vicarage, 152 Perry Road, Nottingham NG5 1GL* T: 0115-960 2418

SHAW, Preb Richard Tom. b 42. AKC 69. St Aug Coll Cant 69. **d** 70 **p** 71. C Dunston St Nic *Dur* 70-73; C Maidstone All SS w St Phil and H Trin *Cant* 73-75; Chapl RN 75-79; V Barrow-on-Humber *Linc* 79-83; V Linc St Faith and St Martin w St Pet 83-91; V Clun w Bettws-y-Crwyn and Newcastle *Heref* 91-11; P-in-c Hopesay 98-02; rtd 11; RD Clun Forest *Heref* 94-05 and 08-11; Preb Heref Cathl 02-11. *The Granary, Newcastle Court, Newcastle, Craven Arms SY7 8QL* E: richard@rick-shaw.co.uk

SHAW, Robert Christopher. b 34. Man Univ BA BD. Union Th Sem (NY) STM. **d** 82 **p** 83. C Wragby w Sharlston *Wakef* 82-83; C Scissett St Aug 83-85; R Cumberworth w Denby Dale 85-90; P-in-c Denby 85-90; R Bolton w Ireby and Uldale *Carl* 90-95; rtd 95; PtO *York* from 95. *Stonecroft, Sproxton, York YO62 5EF* T: (01439) 770178

SHAW, Canon Robert William. b 46. Lon Univ BD 69. St Aug Coll Cant 69. **d** 70 **p** 71. C Hunslet St Mary and Stourton *Ripon* 70-71; C Hunslet St Mary 71-74; C Hawksworth Wood 74-76; R Stanningley St Thos 76-84; V Potternewton 84-94; V Manston 94-02; P-in-c Beeston Hill H Spirit 02-04; P-in-c Hunslet Moor St Pet and St Cuth 02-04; V Beeston Hill and Hunslet Moor 04-11; Hon Can Ripon Cathl 08-11; rtd 11. *23 St Chad's Rise, Leeds LS6 3QE* E: bobshaw46@hotmail.co.uk

SHAW, Mrs Rosemary Alice. b 44. CertEd 65 CQSW 78 Heythrop Coll Lon MA 96 MA 04. S'wark Ord Course 87. **d** 89 **p** 94. Par Dn Walworth *S'wark* 89-92; Par Dn E Dulwich St Jo 92-95; NSM 95-96; Eileen Kerr Mental Health Fell Maudsley Hosp 95-96; Chapl King's Healthcare NHS Trust 96-01; Sen Chapl Guy's and St Thos' NHS Foundn Trust 02-07; Chapl from 13; Hon C E Dulwich St Jo *S'wark* 96-12; Hon C Peckham St Sav 12-14; PtO from 14. *19 Scutari Road, London SE22 0NN* T: (020) 8693 6325 M: 07731-693247 E: rosemary.shaw1@ntlworld.com

SHAW, Roy. *See* SHAW, Malcolm Roy

SHAW, Mrs Sarah. **d** 14 **p** 15. C Edin St Cuth from 14. *Top Floor, 32 Manor Place, Edinburgh EH3 7EB* T: 0131-225 9688

SHAW, Stewart James. b 64. Wilson Carlile Coll 97 NTMTC BA 07. **d** 07 **p** 08. C Hounslow H Trin w St Paul and St Mary *Lon* 07-09; Chapl RAF from 09. *Chaplaincy Services (RAF), HQ Air Command, RAF High Wycombe HP14 4UE* T: (01494) 496800 F: 496343 E: stewchaplain82@blueyonder.co.uk

SHAW, Ms Susan Patricia. **d** 15. NSM Newmarket All SS *St E* from 15. *21 Spurling Close, Cheveley, Newmarket CB8 9RJ* T: (01638) 730526 E: suoverpond@yahoo.co.uk

SHAW, Wendy Jane. b 54. Shenstone Coll of Educn CertEd 75 Man Univ MEd 90. EAMTC 01. **d** 05 **p** 06. C Thurton *Nor* 05-08; Bp's Officer for Visual Arts from 08. *The Rectory, 2 Rectory Lane, Rockland St Mary, Norwich NR14 7EY* T: (01508) 537045 M: 07830-306384 E: wendyjane.shaw@virgin.net

SHAW, William John. Edin Coll of Art BSc 96 Bradf Univ MSc 97 Internat Chr Coll BA 10. TISEC 10. **d** 12 **p** 13. Chapl St Mary's Cathl from 12. *32 (GF2) Manor Place, Edinburgh EH3 7EB* T: 0131-225 9688 M: 07749-256547 E: chaplain@cathedral.net

SHAYLER-WEBB, Peter. b 57. Bath Univ BSc 81 BArch 83. Ripon Coll Cuddesdon 93. **d** 95 **p** 96. C Bedford St Paul *St Alb* 95-99; C Dorking w Ranmore *Guildf* 99-04; R Sherwood Australia from 04. *PO Box 107, Sherwood Qld 4075, Australia* T: (0061) (7) 3278 2498 *or* 3379 3437 F: 3278 2048 E: psw5957@bigpond.net.au

SHEA, Martyn Paul Leathley. b 66. City Univ BSc 89. Wycliffe Hall Ox. **d** 00 **p** 01. C Ches Square St Mich w St Phil *Lon* 00-03; C Stamford St Geo w St Paul *Linc* 03-08; P-in-c Jersey St Mark *Win* 08-10; V from 10. *The Vicarage, St Mark's Road, St Helier, Jersey JE2 4LY* T: (01534) 720595 M: 07976-869467 E: associaterector@stgeorgeschurch.net

SHEAD, John Frederick Henry. b 38. ACP 74 FCP 81. Westcott Ho Cam 72. **d** 74 **p** 75. Hd Master Thaxted Co Primary Sch 70-85; Hon C Thaxted *Chelmsf* 74-85; C Saffron Walden w Wendens Ambo and Littlebury 86-88; P-in-c Wethersfield w Shalford 88-96; P-in-c Finchingfield and Cornish Hall End 94-96; V Finchingfield and Cornish Hall End etc 96-04; RD Braintree 95-00; rtd 04. *57 Kenworthy Road, Braintree CM7 1JJ* T: (01376) 321783 E: j.shead@tiscali.co.uk

SHEARCROFT, Sister Elizabeth Marion. b 57. SRN 76. **d** 94 **p** 95. NSM Margate H Trin *Cant* 94-98; Chapl Thanet Healthcare NHS Trust 94-98; Chapl E Kent Hosps NHS Trust 99-02; C Kendal H Trin *Carl* 02-05; V Streatham Immanuel and St Andr *S'wark* from 05. *Immanuel Vicarage, 51A Guildersfield Road, London SW16 5LS* T: (020) 8764 5103 E: liz@thekingfishery.co.uk

SHEARD, Andrew Frank. b 60. York Univ BA 81. St Jo Coll Nottm 92. **d** 94 **p** 95. C Uxbridge *Lon* 94-96; TV 96-99; P-in-c 99-01; TR from 01. *St Margaret's Vicarage, 72 Harefield Road, Uxbridge UB8 1PL* T: (01895) 237853 *or* 258766 F: 812194 E: andrewf.sheard@btinternet.com

SHEARD, Gillian Freda. *See* COOKE, Gillian Freda

SHEARD, Preb Michael Rowland. b 42. K Coll Lon BA Man Univ PhD. **d** 95 **p** 95. World Miss Officer Lich 86-09; TV Willenhall H Trin *Lich* 95-09; Preb Lich Cathl 99-09; rtd 09. *9 Queen Street, Kirton Lindsay, Gainsborough DN21 4NS* T: (01652) 648846 M: 07711-541983 E: michael.sheard@btinternet.com

SHEARER, John Frank. b 35. Ex Univ BSc 60. Tyndale Hall Bris 62. **d** 63 **p** 64. C Blackheath St Jo *S'wark* 63-67; R Nuffield *Ox* 67-06; rtd 06. *Denbeigh Spring Gardens, Oak Street, Lechlade GL7 3AY* T: (01367) 252806

SHEARLOCK, The Very Revd David John. b 32. FRSA 91 Birm Univ BA 55. Westcott Ho Cam 56. **d** 57 **p** 58. C Guisborough *York* 57-60; C Christchurch *Win* 60-64; V Kingsclere 64-71; V Romsey 71-82; Dioc Dir of Ords 77-82; Hon Can Win Cathl 78-82; Dean Truro 82-97; R Truro St Mary 82-97; Chapl Cornwall Fire Brigade 91-97; rtd 98; PtO *Sarum* from 98. *3 The Tanyard, Shadrack Street, Beaminster DT8 3BG* T: (01308) 863170 E: dshearlock@toucansurf.com

SHEARN, Andrew William. b 43. Ex Univ BA 65. WMMTC 04. **d** 06 **p** 07. NSM Wellesbourne *Cov* 06-09; NSM Studley 10-13; NSM Spernall, Morton Bagot and Oldberrow 10-13; NSM Arden Marches from 13. *32 Birmingham Road, Alcester B49 5EP* T: (01789) 763348 E: andy_shearn@hotmail.com

SHEARS, Canon Michael George Frederick. b 33. Pemb Coll Cam BA 57 MA 68. St Steph Ho Ox 57. **d** 59 **p** 60. C Grantham St Wulfram *Linc* 59-68; R Waltham 68-80; R Barnoldby le Beck 74-80; RD Haverstoe 78-80; V Soham *Ely* 80-99; RD Fordham 83-95; Hon Can Ely Cathl 94-99; rtd 99; PtO *Nor* from 00. *Woodcutter's Cottage, 19 High Street, Wicklewood, Wymondham NR18 9QE* T: (01953) 605535 E: woodcutterscottage@btinternet.com

SHEATH, Allan Philip. b 48. SWMTC 95. **d** 98 **p** 99. NSM Tiverton St Pet and Chevithorne w Cove *Ex* 98-03; C Honiton, Gittisham, Combe Raleigh, Monkton etc 03-04; TV 04-11; C Tiverton St Andr from 12. *11 Fairfield, Sampford Peverell, Tiverton EX16 7DE* T: (01884) 820136 E: allan.sheath@gmail.com

SHEDD, Mrs Christine Elizabeth. b 49. City of Birm Coll CertEd 70 St Jo Coll York MA 02. NOC 02. **d** 04 **p** 05. C Thornton St Jas *Bradf* 04-07; TV Oakenshaw, Wyke and Low Moor 07-12; V Low Moor and Oakenshaw 12-13; Warden of Readers 09-13; rtd 14; PtO *Leeds* from 14. *84 New Road, Huddersfield HD5 0HR* T: (01484) 511071 M: 07814-958919 E: c.shedd@btinternet.com

SHEDDEN, Mrs Valerie. b 56. Ripon Coll of Educn CertEd 77. Cranmer Hall Dur 81. **dss** 84 **d** 87 **p** 94. Tudhoe Grange *Dur* 84-85; Whitworth w Spennymoor 85-91; Par Dn 87-91; Par Dn E Darlington 91-94; P-in-c Bishop Middleham 94-00; Dioc RE Adv 94-00; V Heworth St Mary 00-10; AD Gateshead 06-10; P-in-c Consett from 10. *The Vicarage, 10 Aynsley Terrace, Consett DH8 5NF* T: (01207) 500996 E: val.shedden@talk21.com

SHEEHAN, Patrick Edward Anthony. b 37. Campion Ho Middx 58 English Coll Lisbon 62. **d** 67 **p** 69. C Clapham H Spirit *S'wark* 73-75; P-in-c Wimbledon 75-77; R Balga Good Shep Australia 77-80; R Melville H Cross 80-85; Chapl R Newcastle Hosp 85-91; Chapl Jo Junter Hosp 91-97; R Terrigal 97-01; rtd 01. *22 Abby Crescent, Ashmore Qld 4214, Australia* T: (0061) (7) 5564 7064

SHEEHAN, Miss Rachel Margaret. b 89. Cranmer Hall Dur. **d** 15. C Liv All SS from 15. *Address temp unknown*

SHEEHY, Jeremy Patrick. b 56. Magd Coll Ox BA 78 MA 81 New Coll Ox DPhil 90. St Steph Ho Ox 78. **d** 81 **p** 82. C Erdington St Barn *Birm* 81-83; C Small Heath St Greg 83-84; Dean Div, Fell and Chapl New Coll Ox 84-90; V Leytonstone St Marg w St Columba *Chelmsf* 90-96; P-in-c Leytonstone St Andr 93-96; Prin St Steph Ho Ox 96-06; TR Swinton and Pendlebury *Man* from 06; AD Eccles 11-13. *St Peter's Rectory, Vicarage Road, Swinton, Manchester M27 0WA* T: 0161-794 1578

SHEEN, David Kenneth. b 70. Cov Univ BSc 95 Univ of Wales (Cardiff) BA 04 MA 08. St Mich Coll Llan 01. **d** 04 **p** 05. C Cowbridge *Llan* 04-07; C Penarth and Llandough 07-10; P-in-c Pwllgwaun and Llanddewi Rhondda 10-14; Warden of Readers 10-14; Chapl Cardiff Univ from 14. *The Anglican Chaplaincy, 61 Park Place, Cardiff CF10 3AT* T: (029) 2023 2550 E: sheend2@cardiff.ac.uk *or* dks101@mac.com

SHEEN, Canon John Harold. b 32. Qu Coll Cam BA 54 MA 58. Cuddesdon Coll 56. **d** 58 **p** 59. C Stepney St Dunstan and All SS *Lon* 58-62; V Tottenham St Jo 62-68; V Wood Green St Mich 68-78; P-in-c Southgate St Mich 77-78; R Kirkbride *S & M* 78-97; Chapl Ramsey Cottage Hosp 80-98; V Lezayre St Olave Ramsey *S & M* 80-98; RD Ramsey 88-97; Can St German's Cathl 91-98; Dir of Ords 93-01; rtd 98; PtO *S & M* from 99. *Kentraugh Mill, Colby, Isle of Man IM9 4AU* T: (01624) 832406

SHEERAN, Antony. b 58. Birm Poly BA 80. SEITE 02. **d** 05 **p** 06. NSM Mildmay Grove St Jude and St Paul *Lon* 05-09; NSM Dalston St Mark w St Bart 09-10. *26 Harcombe Road, London N16 0SA* T: (020) 7275 9190 M: 07881-811586 E: tony.sheeran@hotmail.com

SHEFFIELD, Julia. b 55. MCSP 78 SRP 78. NTMTC BA 05. **d** 05 **p** 06. NSM Yiewsley *Lon* 05-09; Chapl Mid-Essex Hosp Services NHS Trust 09-12; Lead Chapl from 12. *Latton Vicarage, The Gowers, Harlow CM20 2JP* T: (01279) 423609 *or* (01245) 514069 E: julishef@hotmail.co.uk *or* julia.sheffield@meht.nhs.uk

SHEFFIELD, Michael Julian. b 53. Brentwood Coll of Educn CertEd. Sarum & Wells Th Coll 76. **d** 79 **p** 80. C Locks Heath *Portsm* 79-83; C Ryde All SS 83-86; P-in-c Ryde H Trin 86-92; V 92-96; P-in-c Swanmore St Mich w Havenstreet 86-92; V Swanmore St Mich 92-96; V W Leigh 96-04; V Waterlooville from 04. *The Vicarage, 5 Deanswood Drive, Waterlooville PO7 7RR* T: (023) 9226 2145 M: 07818-031902 E: mikejs99@hotmail.com

SHEFFIELD AND ROTHERHAM, Archdeacon of. *See* CHAMBERLAIN, The Ven Malcolm Leslie

SHEFFIELD, Bishop of. *See* CROFT, The Rt Revd Steven John Lindsey

SHEFFIELD, Dean of. *See* BRADLEY, The Very Revd Peter Edward

SHEGOG, Preb Eric Marshall. b 37. City Univ MA 88. Lich Th Coll 64. **d** 65 **p** 66. C Benhilton *S'wark* 65-68; Asst Youth Adv 68-70; V Abbey Wood 70-76; Chapl Sunderland Town Cen 76-83; C Bishopwearmouth St Mich w St Hilda *Dur* 76-83; Hd Relig Broadcasting IBA 84-90; PtO *Lon* 85-90; *St Alb* 85-89; Hon C Harpenden St Nic 89-97; Dir Communications for C of E 90-97; Dir Communications *Lon* 97-00; Preb St Paul's Cathl 97-00; Acting Dioc Gen Sec 99; rtd 00; PtO *St Alb* from 00. *The Coach House, 7A High Street, Clophill, Bedford MK45 4AB* T: (01525) 864868

SHEHADI, Nabil Faouzi. b 58. Wycliffe Hall Ox 00. **d** 02 **p** 03. C Cobbold Road St Sav w St Mary *Lon* 02-05; V Internat Congregation Beirut All SS Lebanon from 05. *All Saints' Church, PO Box 11-2211, Riad El Solh, Beirut 1107 2100, Lebanon* T: (00961) (4) 530551 E: nabilshehadi@hotmail.com

SHELDON, Jennifer Christine. b 43. K Coll Lon BA 99. NTMTC 00. **d** 02 **p** 03. NSM Poplar *Lon* from 02. *23 Lancaster Drive, London E14 9PT* T: (020) 7538 2375 *or* 7538 9198 F: 7538 1551 E: jensheldon@aol.com

SHELDON, Jonathan Mark Robin. b 59. Cam Univ MA 83. Ridley Hall Cam 81. **d** 83 **p** 84. C Dulwich St Barn *S'wark*

83-86; C Worle *B & W* 86-88; V Chesterton St Andr *Ely* 88-97. *21 Chancery Lane, Thrapston, Kettering NN14 4JL* T: (01832) 731173 E: jsheldon@agnet.co.uk

SHELDON, Martin David. b 67. Sussex Univ BA 89. St Jo Coll Nottm MTh 01. **d** 01 **p** 02. C Milton *Win* 01-05; V Lightwater *Guildf* 05-11; Chapl RAF from 11. *Chaplaincy Services (RAF), HQ Air Command, RAF High Wycombe HP14 4UE* T: (01494) 496800 F: 496343 E: martinsheldon@me.com *or* martin.sheldon102@mod.uk

SHELDRAKE, Philip John William. b 74. Bedfordshire Univ BA 96. Trin Coll Bris BA 11. **d** 11 **p** 12. C Maidstone St Faith *Cant* 11-15; TV Gt Baddow *Chelmsf* from 15. *St Paul's Vicarage, 124 Beehive Lane, Chelmsford CM2 9SH* T: (01245) 269026 E: revdphilsheldrake@gmail.com

SHELDRAKE, Mrs Varlie Ivy. b 39. SRN 64 SCM 65. **d** 03 **p** 04. OLM E w W Harling, Bridgham w Roudham, Larling etc *Nor* 03-09; rtd 09; PtO *Nor* from 09. *12 Kemp's Barns, Garboldisham Road, East Harling, Norwich NR16 2TS* T: (01953) 717404 E: varlie@eastharling.com

SHELLEY, Catherine Jean. b 65. Down Coll Cam BA 88 MA 93 Man Univ PhD 11 Barrister 91 Solicitor 00. Westcott Ho Cam 08. **d** 10 **p** 11. C Kersal Moor *Man* 10-12; C W Didsbury and Withington St Chris 12-13; Chapl Birm Univ from 13. *35 Westhill Close, Birmingham B29 6QQ* T: 0121-414 7000 M: 07711-611201 E: revdrcath@gmail.com

SHELLEY, Derrick Sydney David. b 38. Lon Univ LLB 60 AKC 65. Linc Th Coll 66. **d** 68 **p** 69. C Weybridge *Guildf* 68-72; Chapl Red Bank Schs 71-76; PtO *Blackb* 76-96; rtd 96; PtO *Truro* 96-03; *Lich* 04-09; *Blackb* from 11. *57 Kenilworth Road, Lytham St Annes FY8 1LB* T: (01253) 780298 E: notatmyage@ntlworld.com

SHELLEY, Robin Arthur. b 34. CEng MIMechE. St Jo Coll Nottm 85. **d** 87 **p** 88. C Countesthorpe w Foston *Leic* 87-90; V Enderby w Lubbesthorpe and Thurlaston 90-00; rtd 00; PtO *Leic* 00-03; *York* from 02. *10 West Leys Park, Swanland, North Ferriby HU14 3LS* T: (01482) 637063 E: robin@shelley10.karoo.co.uk

SHELLEY, Rupert Harry. b 78. Bris Univ BSc 00. Wycliffe Hall Ox BTh 10. **d** 10 **p** 11. C Wimbledon Em Ridgway Prop Chpl *S'wark* 10-14; Ldr Forres Holidays Titus Trust from 14; PtO *Ox* from 15. *Forres, 12 Lime Tree Mews, 2 Lime Walk, Oxford OX3 7DZ* T: (01865) 766155 M: 07956-914123 E: info@forresholidays.org *or* rupertshelley@hotmail.com

SHELTON, Ian Robert. b 52. BEd 74 Lon Univ MA 79. Ripon Coll Cuddesdon BA 81 MA 90. **d** 82 **p** 83. C Wath-upon-Dearne w Adwick-upon-Dearne *Sheff* 82-86; TV Grantham *Linc* 86-93; P-in-c Waltham 93-97; R 97-11; P-in-c Barnoldby le Beck 93-97; R 97-11; RD Haverstoe 01-11; RD Grimsby and Cleethorpes 10-11; Can and Preb Linc Cathl 05-11; V Rowley Regis *Birm* from 11; AD Warley from 13. *St Giles' Vicarage, 192 Hanover Road, Rowley Regis, Warley B65 9EQ* T: 0121-559 1251 E: ianshelton232@hotmail.co.uk

SHELTON, Ms Pauline Mary. b 52. K Coll Lon BA 73. NOC 96. **d** 99 **p** 00. C Baswich *Lich* 99-02; TV Stoke-upon-Trent 02-06; Dioc OLM Course Ldr 06-10; Prin OLM and Reader Tr from 10. *Dray Cottage, Cheadle Road, Draycott, Stoke-on-Trent ST11 9RQ* T: (01782) 388834 E: rev.pauline@virgin.net

SHEMILT, Lisa. b 69. St Jo Coll Nottm 03. **d** 05 **p** 06. C Walton St Jo *Derby* 05-13; P-in-c Morley w Smalley and Horsley Woodhouse 13-14; V Morley and Smalley from 14; Dir Studies Initial Reader Tr from 13. *80 Main Road, Smalley, Ilkeston DE7 6EF* T: (01332) 880380 E: revlisashemilt@hotmail.co.uk

SHENTON, Canon Brian. b 43. Chich Th Coll 73. **d** 75 **p** 76. C Mill Hill Jo Keble Ch *Lon* 75-78; C New Windsor *Ox* 78-81; TV 81-82; P-in-c Cherbury 82-83; V Calcot 83-89; R Reading St Mary the Virgin 89-13; P-in-c Reading St Matt 96-00; RD Reading 95-13; Hon Can Ch Ch 98-13; rtd 13. *73 Watlington Street, Reading RG1 4RQ* M: 07710-490250 E: canon@waitrose.com

SHENTON, David. b 57. Aston Tr Scheme 91 Ripon Coll Cuddesdon 93. **d** 95 **p** 96. C Thurmaston *Leic* 95-98; C Melton Mowbray 98-99; TV 99-01; PtO *Linc* 08-10; C Gt Grimsby St Mary and St Jas 10-11; TV 11-12; P-in-c Grantham St Anne New Somerby and Spitalgate 12-14; P-in-c Grantham, Earlesfield 12-14; V S Grantham from 14. *St Anne's Vicarage, Harrowby Road, Grantham NG31 9ED* E: davidshenton257@btinternet.com

SHEPHARD, Brian Edward. b 34. Magd Coll Cam BA 56 MA 60 Ox Univ CertEd 71. Wycliffe Hall Ox 58. **d** 60 **p** 61. C Wigan St Cath *Liv* 60-62; C Kidderminster St Geo *Worc* 62-65; Lect CA Tr Coll Blackheath 65-70; Lect Hamilton Coll of Educn 70-77; Chapl Buchan Sch Castletown 77-88; Tutor Wilson Carlile Coll of Evang 88-89; C Andreas St Jude *S & M* 89-91; C Jurby 89-91; V Lezayre 91-02; rtd 02; PtO *S & M* from 02. *Keayn Ard, Queens Road, Port St Mary, Isle of Man IM9 5EP* T: (01624) 833315 E: kyriosvoskos@manx.net

SHEPHARD, Nicola Monica. b 82. Ox Brookes Univ BA 04 Clare Coll Cam BTh 12. Ridley Hall Cam 09. **d** 12 **p** 13. C Dorridge *Birm* from 12. *2 Hurst Green Road, Bentley Heath, Solihull B93 8AE* T: (01564) 772385 *or* 775652 E: revnicolashephard@gmail.com

SHEPHEARD-WALWYN, John. b 16. Oriel Coll Ox BA 38 MA 44. Wells Th Coll 38. **d** 40 **p** 42. C Roch St Pet w St Marg 41-44; C Lamorbey H Redeemer 44-49; C Edenbridge 49-56; V Rosherville 56-61; R Horwood and V Westleigh *Ex* 61-78; P-in-c Harberton w Harbertonford 78-82; rtd 82; PtO *Bris* 82-05. *5 Holly Road, Bramhall, Stockport SK7 1HH* T: 0161-439 9458

SHEPHERD, Canon Anthony Michael. b 50. Em Coll Cam BA 72 MA 76. Westcott Ho Cam 72. **d** 74 **p** 75. C Folkestone St Mary and St Eanswythe *Cant* 74-79; Bp's Dom Chapl *Ripon* 79-87; Dioc Communications Officer 79-87; V High Harrogate St Pet *Leeds* 87-15; Hon Can Ripon Cathl from 99; Chapl to The Queen from 09; rtd 15. *3 Heatherdale Mews, Summerbridge, Harrogate HG3 4BQ* T: (01423) 500901 E: ashepherd@talktalk.net

SHEPHERD, Mrs Bridget Clare. b 76. Open Univ BSc 01 K Coll Lon MA 04. Trin Coll Bris BA 08. **d** 08 **p** 09. C S Croydon Em *S'wark* 08-14; V Lee Gd Shep w St Pet from 14. *The Vicarage, 47 Handen Road, London SE12 8NR* M: 07833-031258 E: shoesunbagsaddict@gmail.com

SHEPHERD, Christopher Francis Pleydell. b 44. St Steph Ho Ox 68. **d** 69 **p** 70. C Milber *Ex* 69-72; C Ex St Thos 72-74; TV Ilfracombe, Lee and W Down 74-78; TV Ilfracombe, Lee, W Down, Woolacombe and Bittadon 78-80; P-in-c Tregony w St Cuby and Cornelly *Truro* 80-83; V 83-96; rtd 04. *2 Cherry Meadow, Cheriton Fitzpaine, Crediton EX17 4JX* T: (01363) 866896

SHEPHERD, Mrs Clare Frances. b 75. Cov Univ BA 02. St Mellitus Coll BA 15. **d** 15. C Shottermill *Guildf* from 15. *33 Sunvale Avenue, Haslemere GU27 1PJ* M: 07825-551412 E: clare.f.shepherd@me.com

SHEPHERD, David. b 42. St Jo Coll Dur BA 65 MA 68 MLitt 76. Edin Th Coll 66. **d** 68 **p** 69. Chapl St Paul's Cathl Dundee 68-79; Chapl Dundee Univ 73-79; R Dundee St Mary Magd from 79; Hon Chapl Abertay Univ from 01; Chapl NHS Tayside from 09. *14 Albany Terrace, Dundee DD3 6HR* T: (01382) 223510 E: meadowsidecrime@btinternet.com

SHEPHERD, David Mark. b 59. Reading Univ BA 81 Nottm Univ BTh 86. Linc Th Coll 83. **d** 86 **p** 87. C Wilmslow *Ches* 86-89; C Bromborough 89-92; V Leasowe 92-97; V Oxhey St Matt *St Alb* from 97. *The Vicarage, St Matthew's Close, Eastbury Road, Watford WD19 4ST* T: (01923) 241420 E: davidshepherd@matts52.fsnet.co.uk

SHEPHERD, Ernest John Heatley. b 27. TCD BA 48 BD 53. **d** 50 **p** 51. C Belfast St Mary Magd *Conn* 50-54; I Whitehouse 54-96; Can Conn Cathl 86-90; Co-ord Aux Min 87-96; Treas Conn Cathl 90; Prec Conn Cathl 90-96; rtd 96. *15 Downshire Gardens, Carrickfergus BT38 7LW* T: (028) 9336 2243

SHEPHERD, Miss Jayne Elizabeth. b 57. Reading Univ BA 78. Cranmer Hall Dur 79. **dss** 82 **d** 87 **p** 94. Wombourne *Lich* 82-85; Harlescott 85-90; Par Dn 87-90; Chapl Asst Qu Medical Cen Nottm Univ Hosp NHS Trust 90-97; Asst Chapl Cen Notts Healthcare NHS Trust 90-97; Chapl Pet Hosps NHS Trust 97-02; Chapl St Helens and Knowsley Hosps NHS Trust 02-08; V Knutsford St Cross *Ches* 08-15; P-in-c Alsager St Mary from 15. *St Mary's Vicarage, 37 Eaton Road, Alsager, Stoke-on-Trent ST7 2BQ* T: (01270) 875748 E: j.shepherd57@hotmail.com

SHEPHERD, Joan Frances Fleming. See STENHOUSE, Joan Frances Fleming

SHEPHERD, The Very Revd John Harley. b 42. Melbourne Univ BA 64 Union Th Sem (NY) MSacMus 73 St Cath Coll Cam PhD 84. Trin Coll Melbourne ThL 66. **d** 67 **p** 68. C W Footscray Australia 67-68; C Brunswick 69-70; C Stretford St Matt *Man* 71; Asst P Sayville Long Is USA 72-77; C Cherry Hinton St Andr *Ely* 78-80; Chapl Ch Ch Ox 80-88; Chapl Univ W Australia 88-90; Dean Perth from 90. *St George's Cathedral, 38 St George's Terrace, Perth WA 6000, Australia* T: (0061) (8) 9325 5766 *or* 9322 7265 F: 9325 5242 E: thedean@perthcathedral.org

SHEPHERD, John Martin. b 68. St Jo Coll Cam BA 90. Oak Hill Th Coll BA 96. **d** 96 **p** 97. C Rusholme H Trin *Man* 96-00; SAMS Brazil 00-03; TV Gt Chesham *Ox* from 03. *14A Manor Way, Chesham HP5 3BG* T: (01494) 771471 E: john@theshepherds.org.uk

SHEPHERD, Canon John Michael. b 42. BNC Ox BA 63 MA 72. Coll of Resurr Mirfield 64. **d** 66 **p** 67. C Clapham H Spirit *S'wark* 66-69; C Kingston All SS 69-72; V Upper Tooting H Trin 73-80; V Wandsworth St Paul 80-90; P-in-c Mitcham SS Pet and Paul 90-92; V 92-97; RD Merton 96-97; V Battersea St Luke 97-07; RD Battersea 01-04; Hon Can S'wark

Cathl 01-07; rtd 07; PtO *Portsm* from 08. *36 Lawrence Road, Southsea PO5 1NY* T: (023) 9283 7387
E: johnmshepherd36@gmail.com

SHEPHERD, Mrs Julie Margaret. b 37. **d** 03 **p** 04. OLM Halliwell *Man* 03-08; PtO from 08. *Apple Cottage, 16 Grove Street, Bolton BL1 3PG* T: (01204) 844508 M: 07742-667903
E: julie.shepherd@care4free.net

SHEPHERD, Keith Frederick. b 42. EMMTC 86. **d** 89 **p** 90. NSM Stocking Farm *Leic* 89-93; NSM Church Langton w Tur Langton, Thorpe Langton etc 93-99; TV Syston 99-07; rtd 07; PtO *Leic* from 07. *57 Fielding Road, Birstall, Leicester LE4 3AG* T: 0116-267 4172 E: keithshepherd55@btinternet.com

SHEPHERD, Mrs Pauline. b 53. Stockwell Coll of Educn TCert 73. WMMTC 00. **d** 03 **p** 04. C Walsall Pleck and Bescot *Lich* 03-08; P-in-c Yoxall 08; rtd 09; PtO *Lich* from 10. *7 Vicar's Close, Lichfield WS13 7LE* T: (01543) 418451
M: 07814-680304 E: p.shepherd140@btinternet.com

SHEPHERD, Canon Peter William. b 48. Reading Univ BA 71 Lon Univ BD 80 Brighton Poly MPhil 87 Lanc Univ MA 94 Open Univ PhD 04. Chich Th Coll 77. **d** 80 **p** 81. NSM Eastbourne St Sav and St Pet *Chich* 80-82; NSM Clitheroe St Mary *Blackb* 82-14; LtO from 14; Hd Master Wm Temple Sch Preston 83-88; Hd Master Canon Slade Sch Bolton 89-06; rtd 06; PtO *Man* 89-12; Hon Can Man Cathl from 06. *Homestead, Eastham Street, Clitheroe BB7 2HY* T/F: (01200) 425053
E: pws.canonslade@btconnect.com

✠**SHEPHERD, The Rt Revd Ronald Francis.** b 26. Univ of BC BA 48. AKC 52 St Jo Coll Winnipeg Hon DD 89. **d** 52 **p** 53 **c** 85. C Westmr St Steph w St Jo *Lon* 52-57; Canada from 57; Dean Edmonton 65-70; Dean Montreal 70-82; Bp BC 85-92; rtd 92; Hon V St Barn Miss San Diego USA 95-00. *Easter Hill, 110 Ensilwood Road, Salt Spring Island BC V8K 1N1, Canada* T: (001) (250) 537 1399

SHEPHERD, Stephen. b 54. All SS Cen for Miss & Min 12. **d** 15. NSM Whitworth w Facit *Man* from 15. *93 Rugby Road, Rochdale OL12 0DZ* T: (01706) 661572 E: stephenshep38@gmail.com

SHEPHERD, Thomas. b 52. Man Univ BA 79 Didsbury Coll Man PGCE 83 SRN 74. NOC 92. **d** 95 **p** 96. C Baguley *Man* 95-99; C Timperley *Ches* 99-03; V Sale St Paul 03-08; V Sandbach from 08. *The Vicarage, 15 Offley Road, Sandbach CW11 1GY* T: (01270) 762379 E: vicar@sandbachchurch.co.uk

SHEPHERD, Timothy Roy. b 34. Selw Coll Cam BA 58. Linc Th Coll 62. **d** 64 **p** 65. C Selly Oak St Mary *Birm* 64-67; C Stockland Green 67-72; V Perry Common 72-76; V Holton-le-Clay *Linc* 76-84; V Habrough Gp 84-93; P-in-c Uffington 93-95; R Uffington Gp 95-99; rtd 99; PtO *Pet* 99-01; *Linc* 00-01. *Chapelside, Chapel Hill, Wootton, Woodstock OX20 1DX* T: (01993) 813319

SHEPHERDSON, Mrs Maria Thérèse. b 65. STETS. **d** 07 **p** 08. C Warmley, Syston and Bitton *Bris* 07-11; P-in-c Upper Kennet *Sarum* 11-13; R from 13. *The Rectory, 27 High Street, Avebury, Marlborough SN8 1RF* T: (01672) 539643
E: mariashepherdson@rocketmail.com

SHEPPARD, Derrick Richard Adam. b 44. **d** 07 **p** 08. OLM Quidenham Gp *Nor* 07-15; P-in-c Guiltcross from 15. *Orchard House, Back Street, Garboldisham, Diss IP22 2SD* T: (01953) 681445 E: derrick.sheppard@btconnect.com

SHEPPARD, Evelyn Anne Frances. b 46. **d** 08 **p** 09. OLM Hanbury, Newborough, Rangemore and Tutbury *Lich* 08-14; NSM Anslow and Rolleston 14-15; PtO from 15. *Melbourne House, Knightsfield Road, Hanbury, Burton-on-Trent DE13 8TH* T: (01283) 575551
E: frances@melbourne-house.com

SHEPPARD, Ian Arthur Lough. b 33. Sarum & Wells Th Coll 71. **d** 74 **p** 75. C Bishop's Cleeve *Glouc* 74-77; Chapl RAF 77-81; V Gosberton *Linc* 81-87; V Leven Valley *Carl* 87-90; Deputation and Gen Appeals Org Children's Soc 90-98; rtd 98. *57 Seymour Grove, Eaglescliffe, Stockton-on-Tees TS16 0LE* T: (01642) 791612 E: ials@btopenworld.com

SHEPPARD, Canon Martin. b 37. Hertf Coll Ox BA 61 MA 65. Chich Th Coll 63. **d** 65 **p** 66. C N Hull St Mich *York* 65-68; C Hove St Jo *Chich* 68-71; V Heathfield St Rich 71-77; V New Shoreham and Old Shoreham 77-94; TR Rye 94-03; RD 95-02; Can and Preb Chich Cathl 02-03; rtd 03; PtO *Chich* from 03. *62 St Pancras Road, Lewes BN7 1JG* T: (01273) 474999

SHEPPARD, Norman George. b 32. Wolv Teacher Tr Coll CertEd 73. St D Coll Lamp 57. **d** 59 **p** 60. C Burry Port and Pwll *St D* 59-64; SAMS Chile 64-68; C Madeley *Heref* 68-69; Asst Master Madeley Court Sch 73-75; Gilbert Inglefield Sch Leighton Buzzard 75-80; USPG 80-81; Argentina from 80; rtd 95. *Doering 528, Capilla del Monte 5184, Provincia de Cordoba, Argentina*

SHEPPARD, Roger Malcolm. b 47. Aston Univ MBA 86 Wolv Poly PGCE 88 Solicitor 74. WMMTC 98. **d** 01 **p** 02. NSM Castle Vale w Minworth *Birm* 01-07; NSM Four Oaks 08-13;

P-in-c Wylde Green from 13; CF(V) from 07. *193 Dower Road, Sutton Coldfield B75 6SY* T: 0121-682 3976 *or* 308 8850
E: rmsheppard@hotmail.co.uk

SHEPPARD, Mrs Susan. b 59. Ex Univ BA 80 MA 99 SS Hild & Bede Coll Dur PGCE 81. SWMTC 95. **d** 98 **p** 99. NSM Stoke Canon, Poltimore w Huxham and Rewe etc *Ex* 98-01; Chapl St Pet High Sch Ex 99-06; Tutor SWMTC from 05; NSM Brampford Speke, Cadbury, Newton St Cyres etc *Ex* from 08. *Autumn Haze, Rewe, Exeter EX5 4HA* T/F: (01392) 841284
E: suesheppard@supanet.com

SHEPTON, Robert Leonard McIntyre. b 35. Jes Coll Cam BA 58 MA 61. Oak Hill Th Coll 59. **d** 61 **p** 62. C Weymouth St Jo *Sarum* 61-63; Boys' Ldr Cam Univ Miss Bermondsey 63-66; Warden Ox-Kilburn Club 66-69; Chapl St D Coll Llandudno 69-77; Chief Instructor Carnoch Outdoor Cen 77-80; Chapl Kingham Hill Sch Oxon 80-92; rtd 92. *Innisfree, Duror, Appin PA38 4DA* T: (01631) 730437 F: 730382
E: bob@innisfree.free-online.co.uk

SHER, Falak. b 65. Coll of Resurr Mirfield. **d** 07 **p** 08. C Radcliffe *Man* 07-10; TV Gorton and Abbey Hey 10-14; P-in-c Chorlton-cum-Hardy St Werburgh from 14; P-in-c Hulme Ascension from 14; C Whalley Range St Edm and Moss Side etc from 14. *St Werburgh's Rectory, 388 Wilbraham Road, Manchester M21 0UH* T: 0161-881 1742 M: 07930-573624
E: falakfalak@hotmail.com

SHERBORNE, Archdeacon of. *See* TAYLOR, The Ven Paul Stanley

SHERBORNE, Area Bishop of. *See* KINGS, The Rt Revd Graham Ralph

SHERBOURNE, Gloria. b 49. STETS 00. **d** 03 **p** 04. NSM Jersey St Brelade *Win* 03-10; Asst Chapl Jersey Gp of Hosps 03-04 and 05-10. *11 Iter Court, Bow, Crediton EX17 6BZ* T: (01363) 881240 E: gsherbourne@gmail.com

SHERCLIFF, Elizabeth Ann. b 56. Salford Univ BSc 79 Open Univ MA 96. St Jo Coll Nottm 08. **d** 09 **p** 10. Dir of Studies for Readers *Ches* from 09; NSM Marple All SS 09-10; NSM Bredbury St Barn 10-11; NSM Gee Cross 11-13. *56 Ernocroft Road, Marple Bridge, Stockport SK6 5DY* M: 07515-633856
E: lizshercliff@hotmail.com

SHERDLEY, Mrs Margaret Ann. b 46. Ches Coll of HE BTh 03. NOC 00. **d** 03 **p** 04. NSM Fellside Team *Blackb* 03-14; Chapl Myerscough Coll 06-11; rtd 11; PtO *Blackb* from 15. *Home Barn, Hollowforth Lane, Woodplumpton, Preston PR4 0BD* T: (01772) 691101 M: 07931-592787 E: m.sherdley@sky.com

SHERIDAN, Andrew Robert (Drew). b 61. Edin Univ MA 83 Jordanhill Coll Glas PGCE 86. TISEC 95. **d** 98 **p** 99. C Glas St Mary 98-01; R Greenock from 01; P-in-c Gourock from 06. *The Rectory, 96 Finnart Street, Greenock PA16 8HL* T: (01475) 732441 E: drew@frsheridan.fsnet.co.uk

SHERIDAN, Mrs Deborah Jane. b 47. Kent Univ BA 69 ALA 73. WMMTC 90. **d** 93 **p** 94. NSM Lich St Chad 93-03; NSM The Ridwares and Kings Bromley from 03; Voc Educn Officer from 06; Chapl St Giles Hospice Lich 98-14. *45 High Grange, Lichfield WS13 7DU* T: (01543) 264363 *or* 416595
E: d.sheridan@postman.org.uk

SHERIDAN, Peter. b 37. Saltley Tr Coll Birm CertEd 59 Leic Poly BEd 82. NOC 89. **d** 92 **p** 93. NSM Braunstone *Leic* 92-95; NSM Ratby cum Groby 95-98; NSM Newtown Linford 95-98; TV Bradgate Team 98-00; PtO 00-01 and 06-14; NSM Woodhouse, Woodhouse Eaves and Swithland 01-06. *16 Turnpike Way, Markfield LE67 9QT* T: (01530) 245166

SHERIDAN, Stephen Anthony. b 62. RMN 87. SEITE 04. **d** 07 **p** 08. NSM Bexhill St Pet *Chich* 07-08; NSM Stone Cross St Luke w N Langney 08-12; NSM Shotton *St As* 12-13. *26 Newry Court, Chester CH2 2AZ* M: 07871-727743
E: steveasheridan@btinternet.com

SHERIFF (née WORRALL), Canon Suzanne. b 63. Trin Coll Bris BA 86. **d** 87 **p** 94. Par Dn Kingston upon Hull St Nic *York* 87-91; Par Dn Kingston upon Hull St Aid Southcoates 91-94; C 94-96; TV Marfleet 96-00; TR 00-07; V Tadcaster w Newton Kyme 07-14; P-in-c Kirk Fenton w Kirkby Wharfe and Ulleskelfe 10-14; V Tadcaster from 14; Can and Preb York Minster from 01. *The Vicarage, 78 Station Road, Tadcaster LS24 9JR* T: (01937) 833394 E: sue.sheriff@virgin.net

SHERLOCK, Mrs Barbara Lee Kerney. b 48. Dur Univ PhD 07. Westcott Ho Cam. **d** 05 **p** 06. C Norton St Mary and Stockton St Chad *Dur* 05-07; P-in-c Newport and Widdington *Chelmsf* 07-11; V Barrow *St E* from 11. *The Rectory, Barrow, Bury St Edmunds IP29 5BA* T: (01284) 811675
E: barbara_sherlock@btinternet.com

SHERLOCK, Charles Patrick. b 51. New Coll Ox BA 73 MA 76 Open Univ MA 00. Ripon Coll Cuddesdon 75. **d** 77 **p** 78. C Ashtead *Guildf* 77-81; Ethiopia 81-82; Chapl Belgrade w Zagreb *Eur* 82-84; USPG Ethiopia 84-91; R Dollar *St And* 91-97; Bursar Fistula Hosp Ethiopia 97-00; P-in-c Crieff *St And* 01-04; R 04-07; P-in-c Comrie 01-04; R 04-07; P-in-c Lochearnhead 01-04; R 04-07; PtO 07-13; Assoc Chapl Addis Ababa St Matt Ethiopia 07-13; P-in-c Hilborough w Bodney *Nor* from 13;

P-in-c Oxborough w Foulden and Caldecote from 13; P-in-c Cockley Cley w Gooderstone from 13; P-in-c Didlington from 13. *The Rectory, Elm Place, Gooderstone, King's Lynn PE33 9BX*
T: (01366) 327053 M: 07740-981951
E: cpsherlock@msn.com

SHERLOCK, Canon Thomas Alfred. b 40. Aux Course 87. **d** 90 **p** 91. NSM Kilmallock w Kilflynn, Kilfinane, Knockaney etc *L & K* 90-94; C Templemore w Thurles and Kilfrithmone *C & O* 95-98; I 98-00; I Castlecomer w Colliery Ch, Mothel and Bilboa 00-11; Preb Ossory Cathl 05-11; rtd 11; Chapl Kingston Coll Mitchelstown from 13. *Castlequarter, Kildorrery, Co Cork, Republic of Ireland* T: (00353) (22) 40677 M: 86-810 4463
E: hazelsherlock@eircom.net

SHERMAN, Cornelia. b 70. STETS 06. **d** 09 **p** 10. C Portchester *Portsm* 09-13; P-in-c Purbrook from 13; C Crookhorn from 13; C Portsdown from 13. *The Vicarage, Marrels Wood Gardens, Purbrook, Waterlooville PO7 5RS* T: connie.27@hotmail.co.uk

SHERRATT, David Arthur. b 60. Univ of Wales (Lamp) BA 82 Leeds Univ BA 91. Coll of Resurr Mirfield 92. **d** 92 **p** 93. C St Jo on Bethnal Green *Lon* 92-95; C W Hampstead St Jas 95-98; V Abbey Wood *S'wark* from 98. *St Michael's Vicarage, 1 Conference Road, London SE2 0YH* T: (020) 8311 0377

SHERRATT, Richard John. b 84. Newc Univ BA 05 Liv Jo Moores Univ MSc 08. Wycliffe Hall Ox BA 13. **d** 14 **p** 15. C Heswall *Ches* from 14. *The Croft, 5 Croftsway, Wirral CH60 9JP*
E: richard.sherratt@theology.oxon.org

SHERRED, Peter William. b 47. Kent Univ BA 69. SEITE 96. **d** 99 **p** 00. NSM Dover St Mary *Cant* 99-02; PtO from 02. *Copthorne, Dover Road, Guston, Dover CT15 5EN* T: (01304) 203548
F: 206950 E: copthorne@talk21.com

SHERRING, Patrick. b 55. Trent Park Coll of Educn BEd 78 CertEd 77. Ridley Hall Cam 95. **d** 97 **p** 98. C Leyton St Mary w St Edw and St Luke *Chelmsf* 97-01; P-in-c Ingatestone w Buttsbury 01-04; V Ingatestone w Fryerning from 04; P-in-c Margaretting w Mountnessing and Buttsbury from 15. *The Rectory, 1 Rectory Close, Fryerning Lane, Ingatestone CM4 0DB*
T: (01277) 352562
E: patrick.sherring@ingatestoneparishchurch.org.uk

SHERRING, Toby Bruce. b 76. Ex Univ BA 97 St Luke's Coll Ex PGCE 98. St Steph Ho Ox MTh 04. **d** 02 **p** 03. C W Derby St Jo *Liv* 02-05; Chapl St Hilda's Sch for Girls Perth Australia from 06. *St Hilda's, Bay View Terrace, Mosman Park WA 6012, Australia* T: (0061) (8) 9285 4100

SHERRINGTON, Penelope. b 51. Kent Univ BA 11. SEITE 08. **d** 11 **p** 12. Chapl Gt Ormond Street Hosp NHS Foundn Trust from 11; NSM Godstone and Blindley Heath *S'wark* 11-14; NSM Bletchingley and Nutfield from 14. *Little Granta, Godstone Road, Bletchingley, Redhill RH1 4PL* T: (01883) 744991 E: martinpenny012000@yahoo.com

SHERSBY, Brian Alfred. b 41. Clifton Th Coll 68. **d** 71 **p** 72. C Stoughton *Guildf* 71-74; C Heref St Pet w St Owen 75-79; V Earlham St Mary *Nor* 79-91; R Murston w Bapchild and Tonge *Cant* 91-07; rtd 07. *4 Blenheim Gardens, Chichester PO19 7XE*

SHERWIN, Canon David Royston. b 56. St Jo Coll Nottm 84. **d** 89 **p** 90. C Conisbrough *Sheff* 89-95; V Wheatley Park and Dioc Adv for Evang 95-01; P-in-c Martley and Wichenford, Knightwick etc *Worc* 01-08; TR Worcs W from 09; RD Martley and Worc W from 15; Hon Can Worc Cathl from 15. *The Rectory, Martley, Worcester WR6 6QA* T/F: (01886) 888664
E: davidwin56@aol.com

SHERWIN, Mrs Jane. b 41. Sarum Th Coll 93. **d** 96 **p** 97. NSM Brightling, Dallington, Mountfield etc *Chich* 96-02; P-in-c Waldron 02-09; rtd 09; PtO *St E* from 10. *Treetops at Merlins, Uckfield Road, Ringmer, Lewes BN8 5RU* T: (01273) 812173
E: jane.sherwin@virgin.net

SHERWIN, Canon Margaret Joyce. b 65. NOC BTh 99. **d** 99 **p** 00. C Litherland St Phil *Liv* 99-03; V Hindley Green from 03; P-in-c Hindley St Pet from 15; AD Wigan from 08; Hon Can Liv Cathl from 08. *3 Green Lane, Hindley Green, Wigan WN2 4HN* T: (01942) 255833 E: mjsherwin@btinternet.com

SHERWIN, Miss Margaret Miriam. b 32. dss 83 **d** 87 **p** 94. Holborn St Alb w Saffron Hill St Pet *Lon* 83-88; Par Dn 87-88; Par Dn Highgate St Mich 88-93; rtd 93; Hon C Purbrook *Portsm* 93-99; PtO from 99. *16 Lombard Court, Lombard Street, Portsmouth PO1 2HU* T: (023) 9283 8429

SHERWIN, Mrs Philippa Margaret. b 46. Lon Univ BDS 70 LDS 70. **d** 99 **p** 00. OLM Queen Thorne *Sarum* 99-08; rtd 08; PtO *Sarum* from 08. *Haycroft, Sandford Orcas, Sherborne DT9 4RP* T: (01963) 220380 E: pm.sherwin@btinternet.com

SHERWOOD, David Charles. b 56. LRPS 94. WEMTC 98. **d** 01 **p** 02. C Taunton Lyngford *B & W* 01-05; P-in-c Hemyock w Culm Davy, Clayhidon and Culmstock *Ex* 05-11; P-in-c Ashburton, Bickington, Buckland in the Moor etc from 11. *The Rectory, Copperwood Close, Ashburton, Newton Abbot TQ13 7JQ* T: (01364) 652968 E: revdcs@yahoo.co.uk

SHERWOOD, David James. b 45. Univ of Wales (Cardiff) LLM 94 Solicitor 69. St Steph Ho Ox 81. **d** 83 **p** 84. C Westbury-on-Trym H Trin *Bris* 83-85; C Corringham *Chelmsf* 85-87; V Hullbridge 87-94; V Kenton *Lon* 94-06; rtd 06. *130 St Helens Road, Hastings TN34 2EJ* T: (01424) 719768
M: 07891-783719 E: canddsherwood@aol.co.uk

SHERWOOD, Canon Ian Walter Lawrence. b 57. TCD BA 80. **d** 82 **p** 84. C Dublin St Patr Cathl Gp 82-83; Chapl Billinge Hosp Wigan 83-86; C Orrell *Liv* 83-86; Chapl Bucharest w Sofia *Eur* 86-89; Chapl Istanbul w Moda from 89; Can Malta Cathl from 97. *c/o FCO (Istanbul), King Charles Street, London SW1A 2AH* T: (0090) (212) 251 5616 F: 243 5702
E: parson@tnn.net

SHERWOOD, Mrs Jane. b 62. Ripon Coll Cuddesdon 05. **d** 07 **p** 08. NSM Ox St Matt from 07. *36 Canning Crescent, Oxford OX1 4XB* T: (01865) 250672 *or* 251616
E: jane@sherwoodz.plus.com

SHERWOOD, Kenneth Henry. b 37. CITC 90. **d** 93 **p** 94. NSM Malahide w Balgriffin *D & G* 93-96 and from 04; NSM Castleknock and Mulhuddart w Clonsilla 96-97; NSM Leighlin w Grange Sylvae, Shankill etc *C & O* 97-04. *6 Beverton Way, Donabate, Co Dublin, Republic of Ireland* T: (00353) (1) 843 5287 E: kensherwood07@eircom.net

SHERWOOD, Canon Nigel John Wesley. b 58. CITC 86. **d** 86 **p** 87. C Kilmore w Ballintemple, Kildallan etc *K, E & A* 86-89; I Tullow w Shillelagh, Aghold and Mullinacuff *C & O* 89-95; I Arklow w Inch and Kilbride *D & G* from 95; Sec SPCK Glendalough from 98; Can Ch Ch Cathl Dublin from 13. *The Rectory, Emoclew Road, Arklow, Co Wicklow, Republic of Ireland*
T: (00353) (402) 32439

SHERWOOD, Suffragan Bishop of. *See* PORTER, The Rt Revd Anthony

SHEWAN, Alistair Boyd. b 44. Open Univ BA 83 BSc 95. Edin Th Coll 63. **d** 67 **p** 68. Prec St Andr Cathl Inverness 67-69; C Shepherd's Bush St Steph w St Thos *Lon* 70-72; Hon C Edin St Mich and All SS 73-75; PtO 75-81; Hon C Edin Old St Paul 81-86; NSM Edin St Columba 87-91; Asst Dioc Supernumerary from 91; C Edin St Ninian 95-08. *Limegrove, High Street, Gifford, Haddington EH41 4QU* T: (01620) 810402

SHEWAN, James William. b 36. Sarum Th Coll 61. **d** 63 **p** 64. C Rainbow Hill St Barn *Worc* 63-64; C Newton Aycliffe *Dur* 64-66; C Harton 66-69; V S Moor 69-72; CF 72-77; CF(V) from 81; P-in-c Benwell St Aid *Newc* 77-79; V Longhoughton w Howick 79-88; V Spittal and Scremerston 88-00; RD Norham 96-00; rtd 00; PtO *Newc* 00-04; Hon C Norham and Duddo 04-08; Hon C Cornhill w Carham 04-08; Hon C Branxton 04-08. *16 Chatton Mill Hill, Chatton, Alnwick NE66 5PA*

SHEWRING (née SMITH), Mrs Susan Helen. b 51. Univ of Cen England in Birm BEd 87 Warwick Univ PGDE 90. WMMTC 01. **d** 04 **p** 05. NSM Billesley Common *Birm* 04-07; Asst Chapl Univ Hosp Birm NHS Foundn Trust 07-14; rtd 14; PtO *Birm* from 14. *48 St Helens Road, Solihull B91 2DA*
T: 0121-448 1846 M: 07914-434058
E: sue_shewring@yahoo.co.uk

SHIELD, Barry Graham. b 39. Univ of Qld BA 79 Univ of New England DipEd 83 MLitt 86 Kent Univ MA 95 Washington Univ PhD 00. **d** 83 **p** 84. Australia 83-00 and from 01; P-in-c Haselbury Plucknett, Misterton and N Perrott *B & W* 00-01. *107 Molesworth Street, Tenterfield NSW 2372, Australia*
T: (0061) (2) 6736 1405 E: barryshield1@bigpond.com

SHIELD, Mrs Christine Ann. b 54. Lindisfarne Regional Tr Partnership 13. **d** 15. NSM Warkworth and Acklington *Newc* from 15. *Godric's Hollow, 18 Watershaugh Road, Warkworth, Morpeth NE65 0TX* T: (01665) 711141
E: christineannshield@googlemail.com

SHIELD, Graham Friend. b 63. Ripon Coll Cuddesdon. **d** 00 **p** 01. C Camborne *Truro* 00-03; P-in-c St Mawgan w St Ervan and St Eval 03-11; C St Columb Major w St Wenn 09-11; R Washburn and Mid-Wharfe *Leeds* from 13. *The Rectory, Stainburn Lane, Leathley, Otley LS21 2LH* M: 07980-524774
T: 0113-203 7754 E: leathleyrectory@btinternet.com

SHIELDS, Dennis. b 41. Brighton Coll of Educn CertEd 72 Brighton Poly DipEd 84 Roehampton Inst MA 87. **d** 05 **p** 06. NSM Meltham *Leeds* from 05. *11 The Hollow, Meltham, Holmfirth HD9 5LA* T: (01484) 850074 F: 326222
M: 07974-146120 E: dennis_shields@btinternet.com

SHIELDS, Mrs Jennifer Jill. b 39. Heref Coll of Educn CertEd 74. SAOMC 99. **d** 02 **p** 03. OLM Lenborough *Ox* 02-11; PtO from 11. *8 West Furlong, Padbury, Buckingham MK18 2BP*
T: (01280) 814474

SHIELDS, Canon Michael Penton. b 30. Bps' Coll Cheshunt. **d** 64 **p** 65. C Kingsbury St Andr *Lon* 64-67; C Friern Barnet All SS 67-69; V Colindale St Matthias 69-76; V Sevenoaks St Jo *Roch* 76-95; RD Sevenoaks 84-95; Chapl Sevenoaks Hosp 78-94; Chapl St Mich Sch Otford 90-95; Hon Can Roch Cathl

94-95; rtd 95; CMP from 79; Hon PV Roch Cathl 96-05; PtO from 05. *The College of St Barnabas, Blackberry Lane, Lingfield RH7 6NJ* T: (01342) 872870
E: pentonhook007@gmail.com

SHIELS, Rosalinde Cameron. *See* WALSER, Rosalinde Cameron

SHILL, Kenneth Leslie. b 49. Leic Univ BA 70 Lon Univ BD 73. Ridley Hall Cam 75. **d** 77 **p** 78. C Harborne Heath *Birm* 77-83; V Mansfield St Jo *S'well* 83-93; Bp's Adv on Healing 89-93; Chapl Amsterdam w Heiloo *Eur* 93-95; TR Bath Twerton-on-Avon *B & W* 95-04; V Arnold *S'well* 04-15; TV S Cheltenham *Glouc* from 15. *25 Hatherley Court Road, Cheltenham GL51 3AG* T: (01242) 461784 E: kshill@sky.com

SHILLAKER, Mrs Christine Frances. b 39. Gilmore Ho 74. **dss** 86 **d** 87 **p** 94. Par Dn Colchester St Leon, St Mary Magd and St Steph *Chelmsf* 87-89; Par Dn Colchester, New Town and The Hythe 89-94; C 94-96; P-in-c Ramsey w Lt Oakley 96-02; rtd 02; PtO *Chelmsf* from 02. *21 Nelson Road, Colchester CO3 9AP* T: (01206) 570234
E: jcshillaker@ntlworld.com

SHILLAKER, John. b 34. K Coll Lon BD 60 AKC 60. **d** 61 **p** 62. C Bush Hill Park St Mark *Lon* 61-65; C Milton *Win* 65-69; C-in-c Moulsham St Luke CD *Chelmsf* 69-78; V Moulsham St Luke 78-85; P-in-c Colchester St Leon, St Mary Magd and St Steph 85-86; R 86-89; R Colchester, New Town and The Hythe 89-96; rtd 96; PtO *Chelmsf* from 02. *21 Nelson Road, Colchester CO3 9AP* T: (01206) 570234 M: 07889-816264
E: jcshillaker@ntlworld.com

SHILLING, Ms Audrey Violet. b 26. Dur Univ BA 69. CA Tr Coll 51 Cranmer Hall Dur 66. **d** 87 **p** 94. NSM Gillingham H Trin *Roch* 87-93; NSM Rainham 94-96; PtO 96-10; *Guildf* from 10. *Flat 14, Manormead, Tilford Road, Hindhead GU26 6RA* T: (01428) 601514
E: audrey@shillinga.freeserve.co.uk

SHILLINGFORD, Brian. b 39. Lich Th Coll 65. **d** 68 **p** 69. C Lewisham St Swithun *S'wark* 68-71; C Godstone 71-75; TV Croydon St Jo *Cant* 75-81; TV N Creedy *Ex* 81-93; TR 93-05; rtd 05. *Lyndbank, Albert Road, Crediton EX17 2BZ* T: (01363) 877221 E: brianandkajshil@aol.com

SHILLINGTON, Maureen Lesley. *See* BROWELL, Maureen Lesley

SHILSON-THOMAS, Mrs Annabel Margaret. b 60. Jes Coll Ox BA 82. Westcott Ho Cam 87. **d** 89 **p** 98. Par Dn Sydenham St Bart *S'wark* 89-93; Journalist CAFOD 95-03; Hon C Kingston All SS w St Jo *S'wark* 97-98; PtO *Ely* 00-03; Chapl Anglia Poly Univ 03-04; C Kingston All SS w St Jo *S'wark* 04-05; Spirituality Consultant CAFOD from 05; C Cambridge Gt St Mary w St Mich *Ely* 07-15. *28 Fulbrooke Road, Cambridge CB3 9EE* T: (01223) 729475 E: ams94@cam.ac.uk

SHILSON-THOMAS, Canon Hugh David. b 64. Ex Coll Ox BA 86 MA 98 K Coll Lon MA 99. Westcott Ho Cam 87. **d** 89 **p** 90. C Sydenham All SS *S'wark* 89-92; C Lower Sydenham St Mich 89-92; Ecum Chapl Kingston Univ 93-98; Chapl Rob Coll Cam 98-03; Nat Adv for HE/Chapl Abps' Coun 03-08; Chapl and Dean of Chpl Selw Coll Cam from 08; Chapl Newnham Coll Cam from 08; Chapter Can Ely Cathl from 10. *28 Fulbrooke Road, Cambridge CB3 9EE* T: (01223) 729475 *or* 335846 E: hds21@cam.ac.uk

SHILVOCK, Geoffrey. b 47. Univ of Wales (Lamp) BA 69. Sarum Th Coll 70. **d** 72 **p** 73. C Kidderminster St Mary *Worc* 72-78; P-in-c Gt Malvern Ch Ch 78-85; V Wolverley and Cookley 85-12; RD Kidderminster 95-01; rtd 12. *7 Marsh Grove, Kidderminster DY10 2HS* T: (01562) 228996
E: geoffshilvock@hotmail.com

SHIMWELL, Robert John. b 46. ARCM 65. Trin Coll Bris 75. **d** 78 **p** 79. C Richmond H Trin and Ch Ch *S'wark* 78-79; C Cullompton and Kentisbeare w Blackborough *Ex* 79-81; V S Cave and Ellerker w Broomfleet *York* 81-87; Chapl Lee Abbey 87-88; R Glas St Silas 88-94; V Upton (Overchurch) *Ches* 94-05; RD Wirral N 97-98; Hon Can Ches Cathl 02-05; V Lee St Mildred *S'wark* 05-11; rtd 11; PtO *S'wark* from 11; *Roch* from 12. *83 Waylands, Swanley BR8 8TN* T: (01322) 838579
E: rob@shimwell.org

SHIN, Beom Jin (Stephen). b 80. Kyung Hee Univ Korea BA 03 Univ Coll Lon MSc 08. St Steph Ho Ox 08. **d** 11 **p** 12. C Banbury *Ox* from 15. *38 Hightown Road, Banbury OX16 9BT* T: (01295) 550369 M: 07830-707012
E: bjmonani@gmail.com

SHINE, Canon Ann Aisling. RGN SCM. **d** 03 **p** 04. Aux Min Dublin Drumcondra w N Strand *D & G* 03-05; Aux Min Clondalkin w Rathcoole from 05; Can Ch Ch Cathl Dublin from 10. *1 Roselawn Grove, Castleknock, Dublin 15, Republic of Ireland* T: (00353) (1) 820 1797 M: 87-239 7902
E: aislingshine@hotmail.com

SHINER, Michael Joseph. b 21. Chich Th Coll 51. **d** 53 **p** 54. C Weymouth H Trin *Sarum* 53-56; V Stanbridge w Tilsworth *St Alb* 56-63; V Powerstock w W Milton, Witherstone and

N Poorton *Sarum* 67-73; V Knutsford St Cross *Ches* 73-75; Area Sec Age Concern Cornwall 75-86; Co Org W Sussex 80-86; rtd 86. *55 Tennyson Drive, Malvern WR14 2UL* T: (01684) 563269

SHINKINS, Pamela Mhairi. b 41. Leeds Univ BSc 62 Open Univ BA 84. TISEC 05. **d** 07 **p** 08. LtO *Mor* from 08. *Homelea, 7 Blair, Poolewe, Achnasheen IV22 2LP* T: (01445) 781346
E: pam.shinkins@btinternet.com

SHINN, William Raymond. b 22. Sarum & Wells Th Coll 71. **d** 73 **p** 74. C Letchworth St Paul *St Alb* 73-75; C Dunstable 76-78; TV 78-80; V Luton St Chris Round Green 80-88; rtd 88; PtO *St Alb* from 88. *31 Coleridge Close, Hitchin SG4 0QX* T: (01462) 641883

SHINTON, Bertram David. b 41. WMMTC 95. **d** 98 **p** 99. NSM Broseley w Benthall, Jackfield, Linley etc *Heref* 98-12. *Gestiana, Woodlands Road, Broseley TF12 5PU* T: (01952) 882765 *or* (01952) 0121-311 2104

SHIPLEY, Christopher John. b 44. Leeds Univ BSc 65 MSc 70 BA 72. Coll of Resurr Mirfield 70. **d** 73 **p** 74. C Preston St Jo *Blackb* 73-77; Chapl Lancs (Preston) Poly 75-77; V Blackb St Mich w St Jo 77-81; P-in-c Blackb H Trin 78-81; V Blackb St Mich w St Jo and H Trin 81-82; V Walthamstow St Pet *Chelmsf* 82-85; Gen Sec Mary Feilding Guild Lon 85-86; Org Waltham Forest Coun for Voluntary Service 86-89; Gen Sec Hull 89-91; Dir Grimsby and Cleethorpes 91; Teacher Upbury Manor High Sch Gillingham 92-94; Hd of Science 94-02; Teacher Whitstable Community Coll 02-03; Hd of Science Cheyne Middle Sch Sheerness 03-09; Team Ldr Science Is of Sheppey Academy 09-10; C Minster-in-Sheppey *Cant* 10-12; C Sheerness H Trin w St Paul 10-12; C Queenborough 10-12; C W Sheppey 12-14; C Eastchurch w Leysdown and Harty 10-12; P-in-c 12-14; R from 14. *The Rectory, Warden Road, Eastchurch, Sheerness ME12 4EJ* T: (01795) 880205
E: chrisshply@googlemail.com

SHIPLEY, June Patricia. *See* ASQUITH, June Patricia

SHIPLEY, Canon Stephen Edwin Burnham. b 52. Univ Coll Dur BA 74. Westcott Ho Cam 85. **d** 87 **p** 88. C Ipswich St Marg *St E* 87-90; P-in-c Stuntney *Ely* 90-95; Min Can, Prec and Sacr Ely Cathl 90-95; Producer Worship Progr BBC Relig Broadcasting from 95; LtO *Derby* from 96; Hon Can Derby Cathl from 09. *21 Devonshire Road, Buxton SK17 6RZ* T: (01298) 78383 M: 07808-403812 E: stephen.shipley@bbc.co.uk

SHIPP, Miss Elizabeth Ann. b 81. Leic Univ BA 02 Ox Brookes Univ MA 09. Ripon Coll Cuddesdon BA 06. **d** 07 **p** 08. C Wymondham *Nor* 07-11; Bp's Chapl *Worc* from 11; Min Can Worc Cathl from 12. *The Old Palace, Deansway, Worcester WR1 1AH* T: (01905) 731603 M: 07554-013547
E: lizzie.shipp@cofe-worcester.org.uk

SHIPP, Linda Mary. b 49. Cranmer Hall Dur 00. **d** 02 **p** 03. Chapl among Deaf People *York* from 02; C Kirkleatham 02-05; V Whorlton w Carlton and Faceby from 05. *Whorlton Vicarage, 18 Church Lane, Swainby, Northallerton DL6 3EA* T: (01642) 701777 F: 706131 M: 07970-908517
E: revlmshipp@btinternet.com

SHIPP, Patricia Susan. *See* HOLLINS, Patricia Susan

SHIPP, Susan. *See* HOLLINS, Patricia Susan

SHIPTON, Canon Andrew James. b 60. Leeds Univ BA 82 Univ of Northumbria at Newc MEd 99 Leeds Univ MPhil 06. Cranmer Hall Dur 83. **d** 85 **p** 86. C Fishponds St Jo *Bris* 85-88; C Gosforth All SS *Newc* 88-91; V Long Benton St Mary 91-96; Chapl Northumbria Univ 96-06; TV Ch the King 06-07; TR 07-14; V Gosforth All SS from 14; Dioc Development Officer for Youth Work from 06; Hon Can Newc Cathl from 07. *All Saints' Vicarage, 33 Brackenfield Road, Newcastle upon Tyne NE3 4DX* T: 0191-284 5540 E: andrewshipton085@aol.com

SHIPTON, Miss Eileen Kay. b 81. Cardiff Univ BMus 03. St Mellitus Coll 12. **d** 15. C Chertsey, Lyne and Longcross *Guildf* from 15. *The Manse, 25 Abbey Road, Chertsey KT16 8AL* M: 07891-953164 E: eils@stpeterschertsey.org

SHIPTON, Linda Anne. *See* GREEN, Linda Anne

SHIPTON, (née WILSON), Mrs Marjorie Jayne. b 59. Hull Univ BA 80 Leeds Univ MA 01 K Alfred's Coll Win PGCE 81. Cranmer Hall Dur 85. **dss** 86 **d** 87 **p** 94. Ormesby *York* 86-89; Par Dn 87-89; Chapl Asst Newc Gen Hosp 89-91; Chapl 91-95; Dep Hd Chapl Newcastle upon Tyne Hosps NHS Foundn Trust from 95; NSM Whorlton *Newc* 94-97. *Royal Victoria Infirmary, Queen Victoria Road, Newcastle upon Tyne NE1 4LP* T: 0191-232 5131 *or* 266 6172

SHIRES, Alan William. b 36. Lon Univ BA 60. Oak Hill Th Coll 57. **d** 61 **p** 62. C York St Paul 61-64; C Southgate *Chich* 64-67; V Doncaster St Mary *Sheff* 67-75; PtO *Portsm* 75-96; Student Counsellor Portsm Poly 75-88; Hd Student Services Portsm Poly 88-96; rtd 96. *15 Broomfield Road, Admaston, Wellington TF5 0AR*

SHIRLEY, Gary Ronald. b 57. Wilson Carlile Coll 96 SWMTC 06. **d** 09 **p** 10. C Devonport St Budeaux *Ex* 09-12; C Yelverton,

809

Meavy, Sheepstor and Walkhampton from 12. *The Rectory, Tor View, Horrabridge, Yelverton PL20 7RE* T: (01822) 854239 E: gary.shirley2@btinternet.com

SHIRLEY, Valerie Joy. b 42. **d** 96 **p** 97. OLM Sydenham H Trin *S'wark* 96-07; OLM Sydenham H Trin and St Aug 07-12; PtO from 12. *9 Faircroft, 5 Westwood Hill, London SE26 6BG* T: (020) 8778 2551 E: valshirley@btinternet.com

SHIRRAS, The Ven Edward Scott. b 37. St Andr Univ BSc 61. Clifton Th Coll 61. **d** 63 **p** 64. C Surbiton Hill Ch Ch *S'wark* 63-66; C Jesmond Clayton Memorial *Newc* 66-68; CPAS 68-75; Hon C Wallington *S'wark* 69-75; V Roxeth Ch Ch *Lon* 75-82; V Roxeth Ch Ch and Harrow St Pet 82-85; AD Harrow 82-85; Adn Northolt 85-92; V Win Ch Ch 92-01; rtd 01; PtO *Ox* 01-02 and from 09; P-in-c Marcham w Garford 02-09. *4 Culham Close, Abingdon OX14 2AS* T: (01235) 553129 E: epshirras@aol.com

SHIRRAS, Mrs Pamela Susan. b 41. St Andr Univ BSc 62 Brunel Univ PGCE 80. Wycliffe Hall Ox 04. **d** 05 **p** 06. NSM Marcham w Garford *Ox* 05-09; PtO *Ox* 09; NSM Abingdon 09-11; PtO from 11. *4 Culham Close, Abingdon OX14 2AS* T: (01235) 553129 E: epshirras@aol.com

SHIRRAS, Rachel Joan. *See* COLLINS, Rachel Joan

SHIRVILL, Lee. b 68. St Mark's Coll Canberra BTh 07. **d** 07 **p** 08. C Alstonville Australia 07-09; P-in-c 09-14; TR Kinson and W Howe *Sarum* from 14. *St Andrew's Rectory, 51 Millhams Road, Bournemouth BH10 7LJ* E: lrshirvill@gmail.com

SHOCK, Rachel Alexandra. b 63. Nottm Trent Univ LLB 94. EMMTC 95. **d** 98 **p** 00. NSM Radford All So w Ch Ch and St Mich *S'well* 98-99; NSM Lenton Abbey 99-02; NSM Wollaton 02-08; Chapl Development Worker from 06. *1 May Avenue, Wollaton, Nottingham NG8 2NE*

SHOESMITH (*née* HALL), Mrs Judith Frances. b 64. SS Coll Cam BA 85 MA 89 MEng 94 BTh 02 CEng 97. Ridley Hall Cam 99. **d** 02 **p** 03. C Drayton in Hales *Lich* 02-05; LtO *Liv* 05-11; TV Walthamstow *Chelmsf* from 11. *11 Sylvan Road, London E17 7QR* M: 07505-126167 E: frances@walthamstowchurch.org.uk

SHOESMITH, Ms Kathia Andree. b 64. Leeds Univ BA 08 RN 98. Coll of Resurr Mirfield 06. **d** 08 **p** 09. C Ripponden and Barkisland w W Scammonden *Wakef* 08-11; V Bradshaw and Holmfield *Leeds* from 11. *The Vicarage, Pavement Lane, Bradshaw, Halifax HX2 9JJ* T: (01422) 244330 E: zen27915@zen.co.uk

SHOKRALLA, Adel Salah Makar. b 75. Ain Shams Univ Cairo BSc 96. Alexandria Sch of Th 05 Trin Coll Bris MA 10. **d** 10. C Heavitree and St Mary Steps *Ex* 10-12; CMS Egypt from 12. *38 Brocks Drive, Fairlands, Guildford GU3 3NQ* M: 07503-903323 E: adel@shokralla.org

SHONE, The Very Revd John Terence. b 35. Selw Coll Cam BA 58 MA 64 Newc Univ MA 92. Linc Th Coll 58. **d** 60 **p** 61. C St Pancras w St Jas and Ch Ch *Lon* 60-62; Chapl Aber Univ *Ab* 62-68; Chapl St Andr Cathl 62-65; V Gt Grimsby St Andr and St Luke *Linc* 68-69; Chapl Stirling Univ *St And* 69-80; R Bridge of Allan 69-86; P-in-c Alloa 77-85; Can St Ninian's Cathl Perth 80-89; P-in-c Dollar 81-86; Dean St Andr 82-89; Research and Development Officer 86-89; Dioc Supernumerary *St And* 86-89; TV Cullercoats St Geo *Newc* 89-00; rtd 00; LtO *St And* from 00; Hon C Alloa 00-09. *33D Grange Road, Alloa FK10 1LR* T: (01259) 721388 E: j.shone267@aol.com

SHONE, Miss Ursula Ruth. b 34. Stirling Univ BA 75 Open Univ BPhil 88. **dss** 81 **d** 86 **p** 94. Bridge of Allan *St And* 81-85; Lochgelly 85-87; Chapl Cov Cathl 87-90; Ind Chapl 87-90; Par Dn Ainsdale *Liv* 90-94; Dioc Science Adv 90-99; C Ainsdale 94-96; C Childwall St Dav 96-99; rtd 99; NSM Brechin *Bre* 00-12. *5 Abbotsford Court, Kelso TD5 7SQ* T: (01573) 224210 E: u.shone@btinternet.com

SHOOTER, Philippa Margaret. b 49. Hull Univ BA 70 Nottm Univ MA 72 CQSW 72. NOC 04. **d** 06 **p** 07. NSM Fence-in-Pendle and Higham *Blackb* 06-11; Hon C Coppull and Coppull St Jo 11-13; rtd 13; PtO *York* from 13. *23 Nelson Street, Bridlington YO15 3BJ* T: (01262) 424802 E: philippashooter@btinternet.com

SHOOTER, Robert David. b 44. Lon Univ BSc 70 Lanc Univ MA 94 CQSW 72 LRAM 92. NOC 99. **d** 02 **p** 03. NSM Brierfield *Blackb* 02-04; NSM Briercliffe 04-09; PtO 09-13; *York* from 13. *23 Nelson Street, Bridlington YO15 3BJ* T: (01262) 424802 E: robertshooter@btinternet.com

SHOOTER, Ms Susan. b 58. Nottm Univ BA 81 PGCE 82. St Jo Coll Nottm MA 96. **d** 96 **p** 98. C Dartford H Trin *Roch* 96-97; C Crayford 97-00; V Bostall Heath 00-09. *131 Pengelly, Delabole PL33 9AT* T: (01840) 213645 M: 07929-496942 E: shooter160@btinternet.com

SHORT, Brian Frederick. b 29. St Jo Coll Nottm 70. **d** 72 **p** 73. C Walton *St E* 72-75; P-in-c Barking w Darmsden and Gt Bricett 75-78; P-in-c Ringshall w Battisford and Lt Finborough 75-78; TV Nor St Pet Parmentergate w St Jo 78-88; R Winfarthing w Shelfanger w Burston w Gissing etc 88-90; rtd 90; PtO *Nor* from 92. *31 Nursery Gardens, Blofield, Norwich NR13 4JE* T: (01603) 712396

SHORT, Bryan Raymond. b 37. Bris Univ BSc 59 CertEd 60. Dioc OLM tr scheme 00. **d** 02 **p** 03. OLM Kirkheaton *Wakef* 02-09; PtO *Leeds* from 09. *12 Bankfield Lane, Kirkheaton, Huddersfield HD5 0JG* T: (01484) 425832 E: bryan@b-s-short.fsnet.co.uk

SHORT, Ms Clare. b 50. Leic Univ BA 72 St Mary's Coll Twickenham PGCE 73. S Dios Minl Tr Scheme 89. **d** 92 **p** 94. NSM Horsham *Chich* 92-99; PtO *Newc* from 04. *Hedgelea, South Road, Lowick, Berwick-upon-Tweed TD15 2TX* T: (01289) 389222

SHORT, David Keith. Nottm Univ MSci 01 Chu Coll Cam BTh 13 Warwick Univ PGCE 04. Ridley Hall Cam 10. **d** 13 **p** 14. C Chorleywood Ch Ch *St Alb* from 13. *Address withheld by request* E: office@cccw.org.uk

SHORT, Eileen. b 45. Ex Univ BA 66. NOC 93. **d** 96 **p** 97. NSM Castleton Moor *Man* 96-98; NSM Chorlton-cum-Hardy St Clem 98-00; NSM Baguley 00-10; PtO from 10. *2 Netherwood Road, Northenden, Manchester M22 4BQ*

SHORT, Geoffrey Martin. b 57. OBE 04. Ripon Coll Cuddesdon 82. **d** 85 **p** 86. C Heref St Martin 85-87; C Oxton *Ches* 87-88; Asst P Manila H Trin Philippines 06-08; C Cullercoats St Geo *Newc* 09-12; TV Ch the King from 12. *St Columba's Vicarage, West View, Wideopen, Newcastle upon Tyne NE13 6NH* T: 0191-236 7780 E: geoffshort2557@gmail.com

SHORT, Mrs Heather Mary. b 50. LWCMD 71 Cardiff Coll of Educn CertEd 72. WEMTC 98. **d** 01 **p** 02. C Heref S Wye 01-05; P-in-c Bodenham, Felton and Preston Wynne 05-12; P-in-c Marden w Amberley and Wisteston 05-12; P-in-c Sutton St Nicholas w Sutton St Michael 05-12; R Maund Gp from 12. *The Vicarage, Bodenham, Hereford HR1 3JX* T: (01568) 797370

SHORT, Canon John Timothy. b 43. Kelham Th Coll 63. **d** 68 **p** 69. C St Marylebone Ch Ch w St Barn *Lon* 68-70; C Southgate Ch Ch 70-72; P-in-c Mosser and Dioc Youth Officer *Carl* 72-78; R Heyford w Stowe Nine Churches *Pet* 78-87; V Northampton St Jas 87-96; RD Wootton 88-96; TR Kingsthorpe w Northampton St Dav 96-08; Can Pet Cathl 97-08; rtd 08; PtO *Pet* from 09. *11 Cytringan Close, Kettering NN15 6GW* T: (01536) 310633 E: jtimshort@btinternet.com

SHORT, Kenneth Arthur. b 33. Tyndale Hall Bris 64. **d** 67 **p** 68. C E Twickenham St Steph *Lon* 67-71; C Paddock Wood *Roch* 71-74; SE Area Sec BCMS 74-82; Hon C Sidcup Ch Ch *Roch* 74-82; V Tollington Park St Mark w St Anne *Lon* 82-86; V Holloway St Mark w Em 86-89; R Alfold and Loxwood *Guildf* 89-98; rtd 98; PtO *Roch* from 00; *Lon* 02-13. *10 Montague Graham Court, Kidbrooke Gardens, London SE3 0PD* T: (020) 8858 8033 E: jukebox.short@btinternet.com

SHORT, Martin Peter. b 54. Peterho Cam BA 77 MA 81. Wycliffe Hall Ox 77. **d** 79 **p** 80. C Shipley St Pet *Bradf* 79-82; C Becontree St Mary *Chelmsf* 82-86; V Bolton St Jas w St Chrys *Bradf* 86-92; Dioc Communications Officer 92-98; C Otley 92-98; Hd Media Tr Communications Dept Abps' Coun 98-05; Hon C and Hon Chapl Bradf Cathl 98-05; Chapl to Bp Dover *Cant* 05-12; Hon Min Can Cant Cathl 06-12; R Stow on the Wold, Condicote and The Swells *Glouc* from 12. *The Rectory, Sheep Street, Stow on the Wold, Cheltenham GL54 1AA* T: (01451) 830607

SHORT, Martin Ronald. b 57. Crewe & Alsager Coll CertEd 78 Leic Univ BEd 85. St Jo Coll Nottm 93. **d** 93 **p** 94. C Frankby w Greasby *Ches* 93-97; TV Horwich and Rivington *Man* 97-02; TV Turton Moorland 02-08; P-in-c Rawtenstall St Mary from 08; P-in-c Constable Lee from 08; Borough Dean Rossendale 10-13; AD Rossendale 13-15. *St Paul's Vicarage, Hollin Lane, Rawtenstall, Rossendale BB4 8HT* T: (01706) 215585 E: martin.short1@btopenworld.com

SHORT, Canon Michael John. b 38. Univ of Wales (Lamp) BA 59. Sarum Th Coll 59. **d** 61 **p** 62. C Swansea St Nic *S & B* 61-64; C Oystermouth 64-69; V Merthyr Vale w Aberfan *Llan* 69-82; RD Merthyr Tydfil 76-82; R Caerphilly 82-08; RD 83-04; Can Llan Cathl 89-08; Prec 02-08; rtd 08; PtO *Llan* from 10. *238 Abercynon Road, Abercynon, Mountain Ash CF45 4LU* T: (01443) 742650 M: 07831-742515

SHORT, Neil Robert. b 58. Loughb Univ BSc 81 St Jo Coll Dur BA 86. Cranmer Hall Dur 83. **d** 86 **p** 87. C Whitfield *Derby* 86-90; C Bradf St Aug Undercliffe 90-96; V Burscough Bridge *Liv* 96-07; Pioneer Min Toxteth 07-09; V St Jas in the City from 09. *8 Lady Chapel Close, Liverpool L1 7BZ* T: 0151-708 8559 E: neil@theshorts.go-plus.net

SHORT, Mrs Patricia Ann (Pip). b 41. K Coll Lon BA 62 AKC 62. **d** 00 **p** 01. NSM Etwall w Egginton *Derby* 00-10; NSM Ashbourne St Jo from 10; NSM Ashbourne St Oswald w

Mapleton from 10; NSM Clifton from 10; NSM Norbury w Snelston from 10; Chapl Asst Derby Hosps NHS Foundn Trust from 00; PtO *Lich* 05-09 and from 14. *Ivy Cottage, 19 Monk Street, Tutbury, Burton-on-Trent DE13 9NA* T: (01283) 813640 *or* (01332) 347141 M: 07711-823082 F: (01283) 814373
E: pip.short@derbyhospitals.nhs.uk *or* pipshort@talktalk.net

SHORT, Robert Leslie. b 48. Em Coll Cam BA 70 MA 76. Wycliffe Hall Ox 87. **d** 92 **p** 92. Mexico 92-93; Chapl Repton Sch Derby 93-04; P-in-c Ibiza *Eur* 04-13; rtd 13; PtO *Eur* from 13. *49 Manton Crescent, Beeston, Nottingham NG9 2GD*

SHORT, Stephen Timothy. b 71. Cheltenham & Glouc Coll of HE BA 96. Ripon Coll Cuddesdon 05. **d** 07 **p** 08. C Tewkesbury w Walton Cardiff and Twyning *Glouc* 07-11; P-in-c Clowne *Derby* 11-13; C Barlborough and Renishaw 11-13; R Barlborough and Clowne from 13. *The Rectory, Church Street, Barlborough, Chesterfield S43 4EP* T: (01246) 813569 M: 07801-357612
E: stephen.short71@btinternet.com

SHORT, Timothy. *See* SHORT, John Timothy

SHORT, Vincent Charles. b 57. Oak Hill Th Coll 95. **d** 97 **p** 98. C Chatham St Phil and St Jas *Roch* 97-01; V Istead Rise 01-11; V New Beckenham St Paul from 11. *St Paul's Vicarage, Brackley Road, Beckenham BR3 1RB* T: (020) 8650 3400
E: vcshort@o2.co.uk *or* vince.short@diocese-rochester.org

SHORTER, Mrs Anne Roberta. b 56. Edin Univ BA 77 Cam Univ BTh 09. Westcott Ho Cam 07. **d** 09 **p** 10. C Brackley St Pet w St Jas 09-12; P-in-c Stanground *Ely* 13; P-in-c Farcet 13; V Stanground and Farcet from 13. *38 Riverside Mead, Peterborough PE2 8JN* T: (01733) 707059
E: anne.shorter@btinternet.com

SHORTER, Robert Edward. b 48. Ripon Coll Cuddesdon 89. **d** 91 **p** 92. C Braunton *Ex* 91-94; C Bishopsnympton, Rose Ash, Mariansleigh etc 94-96; TV 96-98; P-in-c E w W Harptree and Hinton Blewett *B & W* 98-03; Dioc Ecum Officer 98-03; rtd 03. *Pen-y-Bryn, Dolau, Llandrindod Wells LD1 5TW* T: (01597) 850132 E: robertshorter@live.co.uk

SHORTHOUSE, Raymond Trevor. b 34. Warwick Univ DPhil 00 DipAdEd. Ridley Hall Cam 68. **d** 70 **p** 71. C Gt Ilford St Andr *Chelmsf* 70-73; C Ludlow *Heref* 73-75; P-in-c Cressage w Sheinton 76-80; P-in-c Harley w Kenley 76-80; P-in-c Denby *Derby* 80-84; Adult Educn Officer 80-85; RD Heanor 83-84; V Chellaston 84-88; P-in-c Breadsall 88-98; Dioc Dir of Studies 88-96; rtd 98; P-in-c Symondsbury *Sarum* 99-04. *19 Orchard Drive, Minsterley, Shrewsbury SY5 0DG*
E: justin@shorthouse.netlineuk.net

SHOTLANDER, Lionel George. b 27. Cant Univ (NZ) BA 49 MA 51. **d** 51 **p** 52. New Zealand 51-58 and 60-74; C Southsea St Pet *Portsm* 58-60; V Curdridge 74-85; R Durley 79-85; V Twyford and Owslebury and Morestead *Win* 85-91; rtd 91; PtO *Win* from 91; *Portsm* from 91. *Cambria, High Street, Shirrell Heath, Southampton SO32 2JN* T: (01329) 832353

SHOTTER, The Very Revd Edward Frank. b 33. Univ of Wales (Lamp) BA 58 FRSocMed 74 Hon FRCP 07. St Steph Ho Ox 58. **d** 60 **p** 61. C Plymouth St Pet *Ex* 60-62; Inter-Colleg Sec SCM (Lon) 62-66; PtO *Lon* 62-69; Dir Lon Medical Gp 63-89; Chapl Lon Univ Medical Students 69-89; Dir Inst of Medical Ethics 74-89; Preb St Paul's Cathl 77-89; Dean Roch 89-03; rtd 03; PtO *St E* from 04. *Hill House, School Road, Westhall, Halesworth IP19 8QZ* T: (01502) 575364
E: deanemeritus@hotmail.co.uk

SHOULER, Mrs Margaret Fiona. b 55. Nottm Univ BEd 78. St Jo Coll Nottm MTh 03. **d** 01 **p** 02. C Sherwood *S'well* 01-06; P-in-c Selston 06-11; V from 11. *The Vicarage, 58 Church Lane, Selston, Nottingham NG16 6EW* T: (01773) 813777
E: fionashouler@hotmail.com

SHOULER, Simon Frederic. b 54. Pemb Coll Cam MA 79 FRICS 89. EMMTC 82. **d** 85 **p** 86. NSM Asfordby *Leic* 85-89; LtO from 89. *1 West End, Long Clawson, Melton Mowbray LE14 4PE* T: (01664) 822698
E: oldmanorhouse@shoulers.co.uk

SHOWERS, Cyril. b 64. Fourah Bay Coll Freetown BA 89. SEITE 09. **d** 12 **p** 13. NSM N Dulwich St Faith *S'wark* from 12. *66 Galleywall Road, London SE16 3PB* T: (020) 7237 3431 M: 07951-762440 E: cyril_showers@yahoo.com

SHREEVE, The Ven David Herbert. b 34. St Pet Hall Ox BA 57 MA 61. Ridley Hall Cam 57. **d** 59 **p** 60. C Plymouth St Andr *Ex* 59-64; V Bermondsey St Anne *S'wark* 64-71; V Eccleshill *Bradf* 71-84; RD Calverley 78-84; Hon Can Bradf Cathl 83-84; Adn Bradf 84-99; rtd 99; PtO *Leeds* from 99 and 00-14. *26 Kingsley Drive, Harrogate HG1 4TJ* T: (01423) 886479

SHREEVES, Keir Laurence. b 82. Brunel Univ BA 04. St Mellitus Coll BA 13. **d** 13 **p** 14. C Turnham Green Ch Ch *Lon* from 13. *64A Grove Park Road, London W4 3SB*
E: keir.shreeves@gmail.com

SHREWSBURY, Preb Michael Buller. b 30. St Jo Coll Dur BA 54. Linc Th Coll 54. **d** 56 **p** 57. C Salford St Phil w St Steph *Man* 56-60; Chapl RN 60-63; Chapl HM Pris Pentonville 64-67; Bermuda 67-70; V Dalston H Trin w St Phil *Lon* 70-86; AD Hackney 79-84; Preb St Paul's Cathl 86-92; R Stepney St Dunstan and All SS 86-92; rtd 92; PtO *Lon* from 92. *Flat 1, 150 Wapping High Street, London E1W 3PH* T: (020) 7480 5479 E: mike.shrewsbury@btinternet.com

SHREWSBURY, Area Bishop of. *See* RYLANDS, The Rt Revd Mark James

SHRIMPTON, Mrs Sheila Nan. b 32. Qu Mary Coll Lon BA 54 LSE CertSS 55. St Chris Coll Blackheath 57. **dss** 83 **d** 87 **p** 94. LtO *B & W* 83-90; NSM Barkston and Hough Gp *Linc* 90-97; Asst Local Min Officer 90-97; C Brant Broughton and Beckingham 97-98; P-in-c Churchstanton, Buckland St Mary and Otterford *B & W* 98-02; rtd 02; PtO *B & W* from 03. *2 King William Mews, Church Street, Curry Rivel, Langport TA10 0HD* T: (01458) 259293 E: nanshrimpton@virgin.net

SHRINE, Robert Gerald. b 44. Birm Univ BA 65 Lanc Univ MA 74 Open Univ BA 80 Univ of Zambia PGCE 70. St Jo Coll Nottm MA 97. **d** 97 **p** 98. C Blackpool St Thos *Blackb* 97-99; Dioc Chapl among Deaf People *Bradf* and *Wakef* 99-13; rtd 13. *7 Russell Hall Lane, Queensbury, Bradford BD13 2AJ* T: (01274) 818280 F: 889006 E: bob.shrine@btinternet.com

SHRINE, Mrs Susan Elaine Walmsley. b 56. NOC. **d** 02 **p** 03. C Bradshaw and Holmfield *Wakef* 02-04; TV Shelf w Buttershaw St Aid *Bradf* 04-10; P-in-c Queensbury *Leeds* 10-15; V *Bradf* from 15. *7 Russell Hall Lane, Queensbury, Bradford BD13 2AJ* T: (01274) 818280 F: 889006
E: sue.shrine780@btinternet.com

SHRISUNDER, Romita Jones. b 78. Kolhapur Univ India BSc 98 Leeds Univ BA 03 MA 10. St Steph Ho Ox 04. **d** 06 **p** 07. C Brighouse and Clifton *Wakef* 06-09; V Chaddesden St Phil w Derby St Mark from 11. *St Philip's Vicarage, Taddington Road, Chaddesden, Derby DE21 4JU* T: (01332) 660072
E: romitashrisunder@yahoo.com

SHUFFLEBOTHAM, Alastair Vincent. b 32. Nottm Univ CSocSc 57. Lich Th Coll 63. **d** 65 **p** 66. C W Kirby St Bridget *Ches* 65-69; V Tranmere St Paul 69-71; V Tranmere St Paul w St Luke 71-78; V Neston 78-97; rtd 97; PtO *St As* from 09. *Y-Clystyrau, 5 Tan-y-Bryn, Llanbedr Dyffryn Clwyd, Ruthin LL15 1AQ* T: (01824) 704619

SHUKER, Linda Kathleen. b 56. Imp Coll Lon BSc 77 PhD 81. St Jo Coll Nottm 05. **d** 07 **p** 08. C Rothley *Leic* 07-11; R Birling, Addington, Ryarsh and Trottiscliffe *Roch* from 11. *The Vicarage, Birling Road, Ryarsh, West Malling ME19 5LS* T: (01732) 842249 E: dlshuker@aol.com

SHUKMAN, Ann Margaret. b 31. Girton Coll Cam BA 53 MA 58 LMH Ox DPhil 74. WMMTC 80. **dss** 84 **d** 92 **p** 94. Steeple Aston w N Aston and Tackley *Ox* 84-96; NSM 92-96; rtd 96; PtO *Ox* from 96; Hon C Dumfries *Glas* from 01. *Elshieshields Tower, Lockerbie DG11 1LY* T: (01387) 810280
E: ann.shukman@virgin.net *or* revann@stjohnsdumfries.org

SHULER, Patricia Ann Margaret. b 52. Anglia Ruskin Univ MA 08 Univ of Wales (Ban) BTh 08. Ridley Hall Cam 02. **d** 05 **p** 06. C Ipswich St Aug *St E* 05-09; C Woodbridge St Jo and Bredfield 09-12; P-in-c Martlesham w Brightwell 12-15; rtd 15. *16 Merton Drive, Chester CH4 7PQ*
E: tricia.shuler@gmail.com

SHUTT, Anthony John. b 57. Brunel Univ BSc 79. Trin Coll Bris 87. **d** 89 **p** 90. C Epsom St Martin *Guildf* 89-95; P-in-c Send from 95. *St Mary's Vicarage, Vicarage Lane, Send, Woking GU23 7JN* T: (01483) 222193 E: tony@tonyshutt.co.uk

SHUTT, Laurence John. b 42. MPS 64 MRPharmS 88. St Steph Ho Ox 87 Llan Dioc Tr Scheme 80. **d** 84 **p** 85. NSM Whitchurch *Llan* 84-87; C Llanishen and Lisvane 88-90; V Middlestown *Wakef* 90-97; P-in-c Arnside *Carl* 97-04; Chapl RNR 89-04; rtd 04. *PO Box 59448, Pissouri, 4607 Limassol, Cyprus* T: (00357) 2522 2507 M: (00357) 9913 9416
E: shasting@cytanet.com.cy

SHUTT, Nicholas Stephen. b 58. Qu Mary Coll Lon LLB 80 Solicitor 83. SWMTC 91. **d** 94 **p** 95. NSM Yelverton, Meavy, Sheepstor and Walkhampton *Ex* from 94; P-in-c from 08. *12 Blackbrook Close, Walkhampton, Yelverton PL20 6JF* T: (01822) 854653 E: nick.shutt@dsl.pipex.com

SIBANDA, Melusi Francis. b 72. Univ of Zimbabwe BSc 96 BA 99 St Martin's Coll Lanc MA 06. Bp Gaul Th Coll Harare 97. **d** 98 **p** 99. C Bulawayo Cathl Zimbabwe 98-01; R Bulawayo St Marg 01-03; C Colne and Villages *Blackb* 03-06; P-in-c Rednal *Birm* 06-12; V from 12; AD Kings Norton from 12. *St Stephen's Vicarage, Edgewood Road, Rednal, Birmingham B45 8SG* T: 0121-453 3347 M: 07887-745427
E: melusi.sibanda@gmail.com

SIBBALD, Olwyn Eileen. *See* MARLOW, Olwyn Eileen

SIBLEY, Jonathan Paul Eddolls. b 55. Newc Univ BA 77. Westcott Ho Cam 78 Ripon Coll Cuddesdon 85. **d** 87 **p** 88. C Waltham Cross *St Alb* 87-90; C Chalfont St Peter *Ox* 90-96; P-in-c Sulhamstead Abbots and Bannister w Ufton Nervet

96-02; P-in-c Sutton St Mary *Linc* 02-11; V Long Sutton w Lutton etc from 11. *The Vicarage, Market Place, Long Sutton, Spalding PE12 9JJ* T/F: (01406) 362033
E: jonathan.sibley3@btinternet.com

SIBLEY, Peter Linsey. b 40. Selw Coll Cam BA 61 MA 63. Oak Hill Th Coll 79. **d** 81 **p** 82. C Crofton *Portsm* 81-84; TV Cheltenham St Mark *Glouc* 84-93; P-in-c Tewkesbury H Trin 93-96; V 96-05; RD Tewkesbury and Winchcombe 97-02; rtd 05. *14 Griffiths Avenue, Cheltenham GL51 7BH*
T: (01242) 514640 E: sibglos@aol.com

SIBSON, Canon Edward John. b 39. Brasted Th Coll 61 St Aid Birkenhead 63. **d** 65 **p** 66. C Gt Parndon *Chelmsf* 65-69; C Saffron Walden 69-72; P-in-c Colchester St Leon 72-77; TV Colchester St Leon, St Mary Magd and St Steph 77-80; Ind Chapl 72-80; V Layer de la Haye 80-90; R Chipping Ongar w Shelley 90-98; RD Ongar 94-98; P-in-c High and Gd Easter w Margaret Roding 98-04; P-in-c Gt Canfield w High Roding and Aythorpe Roding 02-04; Hon Can Chelmsf Cathl 01-04; rtd 04; PtO *Chelmsf* from 04. *73 Thaxted Road, Saffron Walden CB11 3AG* T: (01799) 520007
E: ejohnsibson@btinternet.com

SIBSON, Canon Robert Francis. b 46. Leeds Univ CertEd 68. Sarum & Wells Th Coll 78. **d** 80 **p** 81. C Watford St Mich *St Alb* 80-83; TV Digswell and Panshanger 83-90; V Biggleswade 90-02; Chapl Bedford and Shires Health and Care NHS Trust 94-02; RD Biggleswade *St Alb* 96-01; V Sawbridgeworth 02-12; Hon Can St Alb 98-12; rtd 12; PtO *Ely* from 13. *35 High Street, Offord D'Arcy, St Neots PE19 5RF*
T: (01480) 812756 M: 07711-705081
E: robert.sibson@btinternet.com

SICHEL, Stephen Mackenzie. b 59. UEA BA 80 Birm Univ MA 95. Ripon Coll Cuddesdon 87. **d** 90 **p** 91. C Tettenhall Regis *Lich* 90-95; C Camberwell St Giles w St Matt *S'wark* 95-01; P-in-c Brixton St Matt 01-02; P-in-c Brixton St Matt w St Jude 02-13; V from 13; AD Lambeth N 10-12. *The Vicarage, 5 St Matthew's Road, London SW2 1ND* T/F: (020) 7733 9605
E: sichel@freenet.co.uk

SIDDALL, Canon Arthur. b 43. Lanc Univ MA 81 Surrey Univ PGCE 94 MCMI 96. ALCD 67. **d** 67 **p** 68. C Formby H Trin *Liv* 67-70; C Childwall All SS 70-72; CMS 72-77; Chapl Chittagong Ch Ch Bangladesh 74-77; V Clitheroe St Paul Low Moor *Blackb* 77-82; V Blackb St Gabr 82-90; Dep Gen Sec Miss to Seamen 90-93; Hon C Leatherhead *Guildf* 93-96; V Chipping and Whitewell *Blackb* 96-04; Rural Chapl 03-04; Chapl Naples w Sorrento, Capri and Bari *Eur* 04-07; Chapl Montreux w Anzere, Gstaad and Monthey 07-09; Adn Italy and Malta 05-09; Adn Switzerland 07-09; rtd 09. *24 Shaw Crescent, Liverpool L37 8DA*

SIDDLE, Michael Edward. b 33. Dur Univ BA 54. St Aid Birkenhead 55. **d** 57 **p** 58. C Fazakerley *Em Liv* 57-59; C Farnworth 59-62; V Swadlincote *Derby* 62-70; Distr Sec (Northd and Dur) BFBS 70-72; Yorkshire 72-82; V Bamber Bridge St Aid *Blackb* 82-87; V Horsforth *Ripon* 87-00; rtd 00; PtO *Leeds* from 00. *28 Carr Bridge Drive, Cookridge, Leeds LS16 7JY* T: 0113-261 0498 M: 07941-209069
E: mirisiddle@aol.com

SIDEBOTHAM, Canon Stephen Francis. b 35. Qu Coll Cam BA 58 MA 80. Linc Th Coll 58. **d** 60 **p** 61. C Bitterne Park *Win* 60-64; Hong Kong 64-83; Dean 76-83; Adn 78-83; Chapl Gravesend and N Kent Hosp 83-94; R Gravesend St Geo *Roch* 83-94; RD Gravesend 91-94; P-in-c Rosherville 91-94; Acorn Chr Foundn from 94; rtd 97; PtO *Ox* 97-98. *87 Aston Abbotts Road, Weedon, Aylesbury HP22 4NH* T: (01296) 640098

SIDEBOTTOM, Andrew John. See GRACE, Andrew John

SIDEBOTTOM, Susan. b 60. Yorks Min Course. **d** 09 **p** 10. NSM Chesterton *Lich* from 09. *18 Leech Avenue, Newcastle ST5 7PN*

SIDWELL, Elizabeth Sarah. b 57. Girton Coll Cam BA 79 MA 83 Univ of Wales (Swansea) MSc 94. Ripon Coll Cuddesdon 08. **d** 10 **p** 11. C Wells St Cuth w Wookey Hole *B & W* 10-14; PtO 14-15; R Bredenbury *Heref* from 15. *The Rectory, Bredenbury, Bromyard HR7 4TF* T: (01885) 482737
E: essidwell@yahoo.ie

SIEBERT, Mrs Rosemary Clare. b 48. Solicitor 03. SEITE 99. **d** 08 **p** 09. NSM Folkestone St Mary, St Eanswythe and St Sav *Cant* from 08. *35 Warren Way, Folkestone CT19 6DT*
T: (01303) 244114 M: 07763-330113
E: rsiebert@btinternet.com

SIEJKOWSKI, Piotr Jan. See ASHWIN-SIEJKOWSKI, Piotr Jan

SIGRIST, Mrs Catherine Mary. b 55. Westcott Ho Cam. **d** 07 **p** 08. C Cheriton St Martin *Cant* 07-10; C Cheriton All So w Newington 07-10; R Ringwould w Kingsdown and Ripple etc from 10; Dir of Ords from 10. *The Rectory, Upper Street, Kingsdown, Deal CT14 8BJ* T: (01304) 373951
E: catherine.sigrist@btinternet.com

SIGRIST, Richard Martin. b 46. Bernard Gilpin Soc Dur 67 Sarum Th Coll 68. **d** 71 **p** 72. C Yeovil St Mich *B & W* 71-74;

Chapl RN 74-84; TV Sidmouth, Woolbrook and Salcombe Regis *Ex* 84-86; TR 86-91; TR Sidmouth, Woolbrook, Salcombe Regis, Sidbury etc 91-94; RD Ottery 90-94; USA 94-99; P-in-c Devonport St Bart *Ex* 99-02; V 02-07; V Devonport St Bart and Ford St Mark 08-11; RD Plymouth Devonport 01-11; rtd 11; PtO *B & W* from 11. *4 Brue Crescent, Burnham-on-Sea TA8 1LR* T: (01278) 780135 E: rmsigrist@hotmail.com

SIGSWORTH, David. b 61. York Univ BA 82 K Coll Lon MMus 83 Lon Inst of Educn PGCE 84. Trin Coll Bris 12. **d** 14 **p** 15. C Gt Bookham *Guildf* from 14. *19 The Lorne, Bookham, Leatherhead KT23 4JY* T: (01372) 454023
E: sherdave@dsigsworth1.wanadoo.co.uk

SILCOCK, Donald John. b 30. AKC 59. **d** 60 **p** 61. C Hackney St Jo *Lon* 60-63; C-in-c Plumstead Wm Temple Ch Abbey Wood CD *S'wark* 63-68; C Felpham w Middleton *Chich* 68-74; R Ightham *Roch* 74-84; R Cliffe at Hoo w Cooling 84-92; RD Strood 85-91; rtd 92; PtO *Chich* from 92. *Puck's House, 26 Ancton Way, Bognor Regis PO22 6JN* T: (01243) 582589

SILINS, Jacqueline. See JOHNSON, Jacqueline

SILK, Canon Ian Geoffrey. b 60. Pemb Coll Cam BA 81 MA 85. Trin Coll Bris BA 89. **d** 89 **p** 90. C Linc St Giles 89-93; P-in-c Linc St Geo Swallowbeck 93-98; V from 98; PV Linc Cathl from 01; Can and Preb Linc Cathl from 07. *St George's Vicarage, 87 Eastbrook Road, Lincoln LN6 7EW* T: (01522) 870881

SILK, John Arthur. b 52. Selw Coll Cam BA 73 MA 77 K Coll Lon MTh 80. Westcott Ho Cam 75. **d** 77 **p** 78. C Banstead *Guildf* 77-80; C Dorking w Ranmore 80-84; R Ringwould w Kingsdown *Cant* 84-95; V Thames Ditton *Guildf* 95-14; rtd 14. *Southolme, Church Street, Milborne Port, Sherborne DT9 5DJ*
E: johnsilk@tiscali.co.uk

SILK, Richard Trevor. b 67. St Steph Ho Ox 01. **d** 03 **p** 04. C St Marychurch *Ex* 03-06; P-in-c Bovey Tracey St Jo w Heathfield 06-09; V Hamilton Ch Ch Australia 09-12; P-in-c Devonport St Bart and Ford St Mark *Ex* from 12. *St Bartholomew's Vicarage, 13 Outland Road, Plymouth PL2 3BZ* T: (01752) 562623 M: 07507-662627
E: fr.richard@bigpond.com

SILK, Stuart Charles. b 76. SS Mark & Jo Univ Coll Plymouth BA 99. Oak Hill Th Coll BA 10. **d** 10 **p** 11. C Southbourne w W Thorney *Chich* 10-13; C Lindfield from 13. *66 Finches Gardens, Lindfield RH16 2PB* M: 07866-487535
T: (01444) 483547 E: stuartcsilk@gmail.com

SILK, Timothy James. b 73. Ox Brookes Univ BSc 96. Oak Hill Th Coll BA 99. **d** 99 **p** 00. C Stamford St Geo w St Paul *Linc* 99-02; C Arborfield w Barkham *Ox* 02-07; Ireland Team Ldr Crosslinks 07-11; C Kill *D & G* 08-11; P-in-c Bris St Phil and St Jacob w Em 11-14; V from 14. *Parish Office, St Philip and St Jacob Church, Tower Hill, Bristol BS2 0ET* T: 0117-929 3386
E: timsilk@pipnjay.org

SILKSTONE, Thomas William. b 27. St Edm Hall Ox BA 51 MA 55 BD 67. Wycliffe Hall Ox 51. **d** 53 **p** 54. C Aston SS Pet and Paul *Birm* 53-56; Div Master Merchant Taylors' Sch Crosby 56-62; Lect K Alfred's Coll Win 62-65; Sen Lect 65-75; Prin Lect 75-85; LtO *Win* 62-85; PtO *Truro* from 82; rtd 92. *Trevalyon, Lansallos, Looe PL13 2PX* T: (01503) 72110

SILLER, Canon James Robert William. b 44. Pemb Coll Ox BA 65 MA 70. Westcott Ho Cam 67. **d** 70 **p** 71. C Spring Grove St Mary *Lon* 70-73; C Leeds St Pet *Ripon* 73-77; P-in-c Leeds City 73-77; V Gilling and Kirkby Ravensworth 77-82; P-in-c Middleton Tyas and Melsonby 77-82; R Farnley 82-94; V Potternewton 94-05; Hon Can Ripon Cathl 99-05; rtd 05; PtO *York* from 06. *1 Sandhill Oval, Leeds LS17 8EB* T: 0113-268 0014

SILLETT, Angela Veronica Isabel. See BERNERS-WILSON, Angela Veronica Isabel

SILLEY, Andrew. b 85. Wycliffe Hall Ox 12. **d** 15. C Corby Epiphany w St Jo *Pet* from 15. *13 Honiton Gardens, Corby NN18 8BW* M: 07791-086899 E: andrewsilley@msn.com

SILLEY, Canon Michael John. b 48. Ripon Coll Cuddesdon 82. **d** 84 **p** 85. C Frodingham *Linc* 84-87; V Ingham w Cammeringham w Fillingham 87-96; R Aisthorpe w Scampton w Thorpe le Fallows etc 87-96; RD Lawres 92-96; P-in-c N w S Carlton 93-96; P-in-c Brigg 96-97; V Brigg, Wrawby and Cadney cum Howsham 97-04; RD Yarborough 01-02; Bp's Dom Chapl 05-12; Gen Preacher 05-12; Can and Preb Linc Cathl 09-13; rtd 12; PtO *Linc* from 13. *46 Windsor Way, Broughton, Brigg DN20 0EL* T: (01652) 651055
E: michael.silley@virginmedia.com

SILLIS, Andrew Keith. b 66. Wolv Poly BSc 87. Aston Tr Scheme 91 Westcott Ho Cam 93. **d** 96 **p** 97. C Boyne Hill *Ox* 96-99; C Hayes St Nic CD *Lon* 99-00; C-in-c 00-05; V N Hayes St Nic 05-09; V Cuddington *Guildf* 09-12; Chapl Bonn w Cologne *Eur* from 12. *Koblenzerstrasse 85, 53177 Bonn, Germany* T: (0049) (228) 3681 6598 M: 170-693 5538
E: asillis@aol.com

SILLS, Eric Keith. b 41. NW Ord Course 75. d 78 p 79. C Blackpool St Steph *Blackb* 78-82; V Huncoat 82-86; V Blackpool St Wilfrid 86-95; V Fleetwood St Dav 95-06; Dioc Chapl MU 99-06; rtd 06; PtO *Blackb* from 06. *23 Fernwood Avenue, Thornton-Cleveleys FY5 5EU* T: (01253) 865449
E: ksillis@stdavid.freeserve.co.uk *or* ksillis@fsnet.co.uk

SILLITOE, William John. b 37. Lich Th Coll 67. d 69 p 70. C Ettingshall *Lich* 69-71; C March St Jo *Ely* 72-74; P-in-c Kennett 74-77; V Fordham St Pet 74-77; V Castle Bromwich St Clem *Birm* 77-00; rtd 00; PtO *Birm* 00-04; *Lich* from 15. *St Clement's Croft, 11 Wood Green Road, Wednesbury WS10 9AX* T: 0121-505 5954 E: rmwfort34.freeserve.co.uk

SILLS, Canon Peter Michael. b 41. Nottm Univ BA 63 LLM 68 Kent Univ PhD 00 Barrister 76. S'wark Ord Course 78. d 81 p 82. C W Wimbledon Ch Ch *S'wark* 81-85; P-in-c Barnes H Trin 85-93; Wandsworth Adnry Ecum Officer 90-93; V Purley St Mark 93-00; Can Res Ely Cathl 00-08; rtd 08; PtO *Chich* from 08. *The Coach House, Keymer Road, Hassocks BN6 8JR* T: (01273) 842760

SILVA, Peter John. b 47. Rhodes Univ BA 73 HDipEd 77 BEd 79. St Paul's Coll Grahamstown 68. d 74 p 74. C Bloemfontein Cath S Africa 74-75; Chapl Dioc Sch for Girls Grahamstown 75-79; Lect Rhodes Univ 79-81; Dir Academic Support Services Natal Univ 81-85; Regional Manager Performance and Educn 86; Dir Tape Aids for the Blind 87; R Overport Ch Ch 88-89; Chapl Dioc Sch for Girls Grahamstown 89-95; Dir Educn Projects Grahamstown Foundn 95-98; TV Abingdon *Ox* 99-02; Chief Exec Officer Peers Early Educn Partnership 02-11; P-in-c Gt w Lt Tew and Over w Nether Worton *Ox* 11-13; rtd 12; PtO *Ox* from 13. *Woodford Bridge Cottage, Banbury Road, Enstone, Chipping Norton OX7 4AA* M: 07980-264472
E: silvapete@gmail.com

SILVERMAN, Prof Bernard Walter. b 52. Jes Coll Cam BA 73 MA 76 PhD 78 ScD 89 Southn Univ BTh 00 FRS 97. STETS 97. d 99 p 00. Prof Statistics Bris Univ 93-03; Prof Statistics Ox Univ from 03; Master St Pet Coll Ox 03-09; Hon C Cotham St Sav w St Mary and Clifton St Paul *Bris* 99-05; LtO *Ox* 05-09; Hon C Ox St Giles and SS Phil and Jas w St Marg 09-15; PtO from 15. *St Margaret's Church, 19 St Margaret's Road, Oxford OX2 6RX*
E: bernard.silverman@smithschool.ox.ac.uk

SILVERSIDES, Mark. b 51. Lon Univ BD 73. St Jo Coll Nottm 74. d 76 p 77. C Hornchurch St Andr *Chelmsf* 76-80; P-in-c Becontree St Thos 80-85; TR Becontree W 85-86; CPAS Staff 86-92; New Media Producer from 92. *15 Glenhurst Drive, Whickham, Newcastle upon Tyne NE16 5SH* T: 0191-488 1937 E: msilversides@ambitnewmedia.com

SILVERTHORN, Alan. b 37. St Mich Coll Llan 62. d 65 p 66. C Machen and Rudry *Mon* 65-71; V New Tredegar 71-83; V Llanfrechfa and Llanddewi Fach w Llandegfeth 83-04; rtd 04. *14 Davies Street, Ystrad Mynach, Hengoed CF82 8AD* T: (01443) 816649

SILVESTER, Christine. b 51. WMMTC 02. d 05 p 06. NSM Walsall Wood *Lich* 05-08; NSM Shelfield and High Heath from 08; Chapl R Wolv Hosps NHS Trust 08-14. *31 Field Lane, Pelsall, Walsall WS4 1DN* E: silvesterchristine@hotmail.com

SILVESTER, David. b 59. Qu Mary Coll Lon BSc 80 Nottm Univ BCombStuds 85. Linc Th Coll 82. d 85 p 86. C Walthamstow St Mary w St Steph *Chelmsf* 85-90; TV Barking St Marg w St Patr 90-96; V Mildmay Grove St Jude and St Paul *Lon* 96-08; AD Islington 03-07; TR Hackney Marsh 08-11; V Studley *Cov* 11-13; P-in-c Spernall, Morton Bagot and Oldberrow 11-13; R Arden Marches from 13; AD Alcester from 14. *The Vicarage, 3 Manor Mews, Manor Road, Studley B80 7NA*
E: dsilve5737@aol.com

SILVESTER, Canon Stephen David. b 59. Chu Coll Cam BA 80 MA 83 Man Univ PGCE 82. St Jo Coll Nottm 88. d 91 p 92. C Nottingham St Jude *S'well* 91-96; V Gamston and Bridgford 96-08; AD W Bingham 04-07; P-in-c Nottingham St Nic 08-11; R from 11; P-in-c Sneinton St Chris w St Phil 10-14; Hon Can S'well Minster from 13. *37 Lyme Park, West Bridgford, Nottingham NG2 7TR* T: 0115-982 0407

SIM, David Hayward. b 29. Qu Coll Birm 57. d 59 p 60. C Foleshill St Laur *Cov* 59-62; C Kenilworth St Nic 62-64; V Devonport St Aubyn *Ex* 64-69; V Frampton *Linc* 69-74; V Gainsborough St Geo 74-82; V Sturminster Newton and Hinton St Mary *Sarum* 82-89; R Stock and Lydlinch 82-89; Dorchester 89-94; Chapl HM Pris Dorchester 89-94; rtd 95; PtO *Sarum* from 95. *12 Eldridge Close, Dorchester DT1 2JS* T: (01305) 269262

SIMCOX, Stephen Roy. b 59. Ridley Hall Cam 02. d 04 p 05. C The Ramseys and Upwood *Ely* 04-07; P-in-c Tyseley *Birm* 07-10; V from 10; P-in-c Sparkbrook Ch Ch 07-13. *St Edmund's Vicarage, 277 Reddings Lane, Tyseley, Birmingham B11 3DD* T: 0121-777 2433 E: stevesimcox@me.com

SIMESTER, Paul Stephen. b 57. Oak Hill Th Coll 97. d 99 p 00. C Bransome Park All SS *Sarum* 99-03; TV Wareham 03-07. *27 Weyman's Avenue, Bournemouth BH10 7JR* T: (01202) 574995 E: psimester@hotmail.com *or* paul@church2.freeserve.co.uk

SIMISTER, Norman Harold. b 39. Bris Univ BSc 60. d 93 p 94. OLM Wainford *St E* 93-09; PtO from 10. *Romaine, 1 School Road, Ringsfield, Beccles NR34 8NZ* T: (01502) 715549

SIMM, Michael Keith. b 63. Trin Coll Bris BA. d 00 p 01. C Ipswich St Matt *St E* 00-03; C Gorleston St Andr *Nor* from 03. *283 Lowestoft Road, Gorleston, Great Yarmouth NR31 6JW* T: (01493) 667914 E: mike_simm@talk21.com

SIMMONDS, David Brian. b 38. Selw Coll Cam BA 62 MA 66 Heidelberg Univ 62. Ridley Hall Cam 63. d 65 p 66. C Newcastle w Butterton *Lich* 65-69; V Branston 69-97; RD Tutbury 95-97; rtd 97; PtO *Pet* 97-00 and 04-10; P-in-c Easton on the Hill, Collyweston w Duddington etc 00-02; Hon C Ketton, Collyweston, Easton-on-the-Hill etc 03-04. *8 Plover Road, Essendine, Stamford PE9 4UR* T: (01780) 751967
E: david937@sky.com

SIMMONDS, Edward Alan. b 32. St Edm Hall Ox MA 60. Ripon Coll Cuddesdon 88. d 89 p 90. NSM Ox St Mich w St Martin and All SS 89-92; NSM Ox St Mary V w St Cross and St Pet 92-94; Chapl Lugano *Eur* 94-98; rtd 98; PtO *Ex* from 98. *Rokesdown, Higher Duryard, Pennsylvania Road, Exeter EX4 5BQ* T: (01392) 270311 E: asimmonds@eclipse.co.uk

SIMMONDS, Paul Andrew Howard. b 50. Nottm Univ BSc 73. Trin Coll Bris 75. d 78 p 79. C Leic H Trin w St Jo 78-82; SW Regional Co-ord CPAS 83-86; Hd Adult Tr and Resources CPAS 86-95; Hon C Wolston and Church Lawford *Cov* from 89; Dioc Miss Adv 95-03; Research Dir Forward Vision 03-05; Team Ldr Foundations21 BRF from 05; Ind Chapl *Cov* from 08. *31 John Simpson Close, Wolston, Coventry CV8 3HX* T: (024) 7654 3188 E: paul@workcare.org

SIMMONDS, Canon Paul Richard. b 38. AKC 63. d 64 p 65. C Newington St Mary *S'wark* 64-67; C Cheam 68-73; P-in-c Stockwell Green St Andr 73-87; V 87-03; Hon Can S'wark Cathl 97-03; rtd 03. *Timbers, 37 Ocean Drive, Ferring, Worthing BN12 5QP* T: (01903) 242679 E: paulangela@hotmail.com

SIMMONDS, Robert John. b 58. Aston Tr Scheme 92 Ripon Coll Cuddesdon 94. d 96 p 97. C Southampton Thornhill St Chris *Win* 96-00; TV Basingstoke 00-05; Chapl Co-ord HM Pris Peterborough 05-08; Chapl W Lon Mental Health NHS Trust 08-11; Sen Chapl R Berks NHS Foundn Trust from 11. *Royal Berkshire Hospital, London Road, Reading RG1 5AN* T: 0118-322 5111 E: bob.simmonds@royalberkshire.nhs.uk

SIMMONDS, Robert William. b 52. Nottm Univ BTh 77. Linc Th Coll 72. d 80 p 81. C Roehampton H Trin *S'wark* 80-83; TV Hemel Hempstead *St Alb* 83-90; V S Woodham Ferrers *Chelmsf* 90-94; rtd 94; PtO *Cant* 03-06; *Blackb* 10-14; *Cant* from 14. *70 Wynn Road, Whitstable CT5 2JN* T: (01227) 634919 E: bobwsimmonds@tiscali.co.uk

SIMMONDS, William Francis. b 63. Qu Mary Coll Lon BSc 85 Warwick Univ MSc 86 PhD 91. WEMTC 10. d 13 p 14. C Ledbury *Heref* from 13. *6 Frome Brook Road, Ledbury HR8 2FH* T: (01531) 635796 M: 07720-654280
E: wfsimmonds@btopenworld.com

SIMMONS, Mrs Ann. b 56. WMMTC 04. d 07 p 08. C Blackheath *Birm* 07-11; V Dordon from 11; AD Polesworth from 14. *The Vicarage, Watling Street, Dordon, Tamworth B78 1TE* T: (01827) 892294 E: annbsimmons@aol.com

SIMMONS, Barry Jeremy. b 32. Leeds Univ BA 54 MA 62. Ridley Hall Cam 61. d 63 p 64. C Buttershaw St Aid *Bradf* 63-65; Jamaica 65-68; V Earby *Bradf* 68-73; Hong Kong 73-74; Bahrain 75-79; Chapl Luxembourg *Eur* 80-91; V Shoreham *Roch* 91-00; rtd 00; PtO *Glouc* from 01; *Worc* from 01. *Touchdown, 57 Griffin Close, Stow on the Wold, Cheltenham GL54 1AY* T: (01451) 831637

SIMMONS, Bernard Peter. b 26. CA Tr Coll 48 S'wark Ord Course 86. d 88 p 88. C Chatham St Wm *Roch* 88-91; rtd 91; P-in-c Underriver and Seal St Lawr *Roch* 91-95; PtO *Pet* 95-11. *5 Sycamore Drive, Desborough, Kettering NN14 2YH* T: (01536) 763302 E: mail@petersimmons.me.uk

SIMMONS, Canon Brian Dudley. b 35. Master Mariner. St Steph Ho Ox 62. d 64 p 65. C Bournemouth St Pet *Win* 64-67; Miss to Seamen 67-71; Hon C Milton next Gravesend w Denton *Roch* 67-70; Hon C Gravesend St Geo 70-71; V Lamorbey H Trin 71-90; R Hever w Mark Beech 90-93; P-in-c Four Elms 90-93; R Hever, Four Elms and Mark Beech 93-94; V Langton Green 94-01; Hon Can Roch Cathl 91-01; rtd 01; PtO *Roch* from 04. *17 Chancellor House, Mount Ephraim, Tunbridge Wells TN4 8BT* T: (01892) 617262
E: canonsimmons@gmail.com

SIMMONS, Canon Christopher John. b 49. Mert Coll Ox MA 77. NEOC 88. d 90 p 91. C Kirkleatham *York* 90-93; P-in-c Barlby 93-95; V Barlby and Riccall 95-02; RD Derwent 98-01; R Pocklington and Owsthorpe and Kilnwick Percy etc

02-08; P-in-c Burnby 06-08; P-in-c Londesborough 06-08; P-in-c Nunburnholme and Warter and Huggate 06-08; P-in-c Shiptonthorpe and Hayton 06-08; P-in-c Skirlaugh w Long Riston, Rise and Swine 08-12; C Brandesburton and Leven w Catwick 11-12; RD N Holderness 09-11; Can and Preb York Minster 08-12; rtd 12; Hon C Brandesburton and Leven w Catwick *York* 12-13. *22 Valebrook, Hexham NE46 2BL*
E: chris@csimmons.plus.com

SIMMONS, Eric. b 30. Leeds Univ BA 51. Coll of Resurr Mirfield 51. **d** 53 **p** 54. C Chesterton St Luke *Ely* 53-57; Chapl Keele Univ *Lich* 57-61; CR from 63; Warden Hostel of the Resurr Leeds 66-67; Superior CR 74-87; R Foundn of St Kath in Ratcliffe 89-92; Prior St Mich Priory 93-97; rtd 98. *House of the Resurrection, Stocks Bank Road, Mirfield WF14 0BN*
T: (01924) 494318   F: 490489

SIMMONS, Gary David. b 59. Trin Coll Bris BA 86. **d** 87 **p** 88. C Ecclesfield *Sheff* 87-90; Min Stapenhill Immanuel CD *Derby* 90-95; V Stapenhill Immanuel 97-98; R Slaugham *Chich* 98-10; P-in-c Staplefield Common 08-10; R Slaugham and Staplefield Common from 10; RD Cuckfield from 11. *The Rectory, Brighton Road, Handcross, Haywards Heath RH17 6BU*
T: (01444) 400221

SIMMONS, Godfrey John. b 39. Open Univ BA 81. St And NSM Tr Scheme 71 Edin Th Coll 77. **d** 74 **p** 74. Dioc Supernumerary *St And* 74-75 and 80-81; C Strathtay and Dunkeld 75-77; C Bridge of Allan and Alloa 77-80; Asst Chapl Stirling Univ 77-80; Chapl 80; Min Crieff, Muthill and Comrie 80-81; R 81-85; Chapl HM Pris Perth 80-85; R Kirkwall and Stromness *Ab* 85-91; R Strichen 91-94; R Longside, Old Deer and Peterhead 91-92; Chapl HM Pris Peterhead 91-94; Miss to Seafarers 85-02; Hon Chapl (Scotland) 85-90; Hon Area Chapl (Scotland) 90-94; Chapl Supt Mersey Miss to Seafarers 94-02; TV Ch the K *Dur* 02-06; rtd 06; PtO *Glas* from 07; Hon C Dumfries from 09. *11/13 High Street, Lochmaben, Lockerbie DG11 1NG*   T: (01387) 810490
E: joandjohnsimmons@aol.com *or*
revjohn@stjohnsdumfries.org

SIMMONS, John. b 53. Carl Dioc Tr Course 82. **d** 85 **p** 86. C Wotton St Mary *Glouc* 85-88; P-in-c Amberley 88-92; R Burton Latimer *Pet* 92-98; RD Kettering 94-98; R Paston 98-01; V Irchester 01-15; rtd 15. *Address temp unknown*

SIMMONS, John Graham. b 54. Westf Coll Lon BSc 75 Man Univ PGCE 76. NOC 89. **d** 92 **p** 93. C Thame w Towersey *Ox* 92-97; R Heydon, Gt and Lt Chishill, Chrishall etc *Chelmsf* 97-05; V Chadderton Ch Ch *Man* from 05. *The Vicarage, Block Lane, Chadderton, Oldham OL9 7QB*   T: 0161-652 2950
E: vicar@chadderton.plus.com

SIMMONS, John Harold. b 46. FCCA. Sarum & Wells Th Coll 86. **d** 89 **p** 90. NSM The Iwernes, Sutton Waldron and Fontmell Magna *Sarum* 89-01; NSM Iwerne Valley from 01; RD Milton and Blandford from 13. *Fourways, Frog Lane, Iwerne Courtney, Blandford Forum DT11 8QL*   T: (01258) 860515
E: john@fourways.plus.com

SIMMONS, Mrs Margaret Irene. b 49. Cov Univ BSc 02 RGN RSCN. **d** 08 **p** 09. NSM Leam Valley *Cov* 08-10; NSM Hillmorton from 10; P-in-c from 12. *The Vicarage, 18 Hoskyn Close, Rugby CV21 4LA*   T: (01788) 576253

SIMMONS, Ms Marion. b 45. NOC 95. **d** 98 **p** 99. NSM Stoneycroft All SS *Liv* 98-99; C 00-01; TV Fazakerley Em 01-08; TR 08-14; rtd 14. *1 Rainbow Drive, Melling, Liverpool L31 1BY*
E: marionstpauls@aol.com

SIMMONS, Canon Maurice Samuel. b 27. St Chad's Coll Dur BA 50 Newc Univ MA 99 MPhil 02. **d** 52 **p** 53. C S Shields St Hilda *Dur* 52-58; Youth Chapl 54-60; R Croxdale 58-81; Soc and Ind Adv to Bp Dur 61-70; Gen Sec Soc Resp Gp 70-75; Hon Can Dur Cathl from 71; Sec Dioc Bd for Miss and Unity 75-82; V Norton St Mary *Dur* 81-92; RD Stockton 85-92; rtd 92; PtO *Dur* from 04. *39 Claypath Court, Durham DH1 1QE*
T: 0191-384 7493   E: m.simmons.1@btinternet.com

SIMMONS, Peter. *See* SIMMONS, Bernard Peter

SIMMONS, Peter Maurice. b 51. ERMC 10. **d** 11 **p** 12. C Kettering Ch the King *Pet* 11-15; V Penn Street *Ox* from 15. *The Vicarage, Penn Street, Amersham HP7 0PX*   M: 07824-618875
E: revpeter@live.co.uk

SIMMONS, Richard Andrew Cartwright. b 46. Trin Coll Bris 73. **d** 75 **p** 76. C Worting *Win* 75-80; R Six Pilgrims *B & W* 80-92; R Bincombe w Broadwey, Upwey and Buckland Ripers *Sarum* from 92. *The Rectory, 526 Littlemoor Road, Weymouth DT3 5PA*   T: (01305) 812542   E: rac_simmons@lineone.net

SIMMS, Miss Melanie Laura. b 73. Trin Coll Bris 06. **d** 08 **p** 09. C Southway *Ex* 08-13; C Rainham *Roch* from 13. *60 Childscroft Road, Rainham, Gillingham ME8 7SN*
E: revmelaniesimms@hotmail.com

SIMMS, William Michael. b 41. Open Univ BA 87 BSc 01 ACIS 70 MCIPD 75. NEOC 84. **d** 87 **p** 88. C Croft and

Eryholme and Middleton Tyas and Melsonby *Ripon* 87-88; C Headingley 88-90; C Richmond w Hudswell and C-in-c Downholme and Marske 90-93; V Hawes and Hardraw 93-09; rtd 09. *56 Ronaldshay Drive, Richmond DL10 5BW*
T: (01748) 826702

SIMON, Brother. *See* BROOK, Peter Geoffrey

SIMON, David Sidney. b 49. Univ of Wales (Abth) BSc(Econ) 70 Hull Univ MA 83 Lanc Univ MA 05. NEOC 84. **d** 87 **p** 88. NSM Beverley St Mary *York* 87-94; NSM Beverley Deanery 94-98; Lect Humberside Coll of HE 87-90; Humberside Poly 90-92; Humberside Univ *York* 92-96; Lincs and Humberside Univ 96-98; Admin Rydal Hall *Carl* 98-01; PtO 01-02; NSM Cartmel Peninsula 02-14; Dioc Officer for NSM 08-14; rtd 14; Lect Halifax *Leeds* from 14. *25 Winterbutlee Grove, Todmorden OL14 7QU*   T: (01706) 810336
E: d.simon@halifaxminster.org.uk

SIMON, Fiona Elizabeth. b 64. Bradf Univ BEng 86. STETS 06. **d** 09 **p** 10. C Stoke-next-Guildf 09-13; PtO 13-14; P-in-c New Haw from 14. *149 Woodham Lane, New Haw, Addlestone KT15 3NJ*   T: (01932) 343187   M: 07810-160254
E: fionasimon1964@gmail.com

SIMON, Frederick Fairbanks. b 42. Ripon Coll Cuddesdon 74. **d** 77 **p** 78. C Cheddleton *Lich* 77-79; C Woodley St Jo the Ev *Ox* 79-82; V Spencer's Wood 82-85; P-in-c Steventon w Milton 85-87; Chapl Grenville Coll Bideford 87-95; rtd 96; PtO *Ex* 96-04. *Fairview Cottage, Link Road, Pillowell, Lydney GL15 4QY*
T: (01594) 560308

SIMON, Haydn Henry England. *See* ENGLAND-SIMON, Haydn Henry

✠**SIMON, The Rt Revd Oliver.** b 45. Dur Univ BA 67 Sussex Univ MA 68 Sheff Univ MMinTheol 94 Lon Univ DMin 09. Cuddesdon Coll 69. **d** 71 **p** 72 **c** 12. C Kidlington *Ox* 71-74; C Bracknell 74-78; V Frodsham *Ches* 78-88; R Easthampstead *Ox* 88-00; Chapl Ripon Coll Cuddesdon 00-05; Chapl Community of St Mary V Wantage 00-05; Chapl Pemb Coll Ox 03-04; TV Rugby *Cov* 05-10; OLM Officer and Dir Studies 06-10; OLM Tutor Qu Foundn Birm 07-10; rtd 10; Dir Studies Dio Mauritius 10-12; Bp Antsiranana 12-15. *Colcombe Mill Cottage, Colyton EX24 6EU*   T: (01297) 552870
E: oliversimon@dunelm.org.uk

SIMONS, Miss Christine. b 40. RGN 62 RM 64 RHV 69. St Jo Coll Nottm 82. **dss** 84 **d** 87 **p** 94. Claygate *Guildf* 84-87; C Camberley St Paul 87-93; NSM 93-99; C Woking Ch Ch 99-05; rtd 05; PtO *Guildf* from 05. *25 Kingsway, Blackwater, Camberley GU17 0JW*   T: (01276) 503174
E: chris@spaceagenow.co.uk

SIMONS, Preb John Trevor. b 34. Lon Univ BD 67. ALCD 66. **d** 67 **p** 68. C Becontree St Mary *Chelmsf* 67-71; V Cranham Park 71-78; P-in-c Nailsea N Trin *B & W* 78-83; R 83-97; Sen Asst P 97-99; Preb Wells Cathl 90-99; rtd 99; Nat Dir Crosswinds Prayer Trust from 97; PtO *B & W* from 99. *1 Gilmore Road, Weston-super-Mare BS22 8JG*   T: (01934) 221537   E: john@crosswinds.org.uk

SIMONSON, Canon Juergen Werner Dietrich. b 24. Lon Univ BD 52. ALCD 52. **d** 52 **p** 53. C W Kilburn St Luke w St Simon and St Jude *Lon* 52-56; Nigeria 57-63; Chapl CMS Tr Coll Chislehurst 64-65; Vice-Prin 65-67; Prin 67-69; V Putney St Marg *S'wark* 69-81; RD Wandsworth 74-81; Hon Can S'wark Cathl 75-90; R Barnes St Mary 81-90; rtd 90; PtO *Win* from 90. *Elm Cottage, Horseshoe Lane, Ibthorpe, Andover SP11 0BY*   T: (01264) 736381   E: juergens@tiscali.co.uk

SIMPER, Rachel Dawn. *See* WATTS, Rachel Dawn

SIMPKINS, Canon Lionel Frank. b 46. UEA BSc 68 Lambeth STh 77. St Jo Coll Nottm LTh 74. **d** 73 **p** 74. C Leic H Apostles 73-77; C Bushbury *Lich* 77-80; V Sudbury w Ballingdon and Brundon *St E* 80-96; Chapl Sudbury Hosps 80-96; RD Sudbury *St E* 88-96; V Ipswich St Aug 96-12; Warden of Readers 03-10; Hon Can St E Cathl 94-12; rtd 12; PtO *St E* from 12. *Poplar House, 64A Nowton Road, Bury St Edmunds IP33 2BU*
T: (01284) 725108   E: lionelsimpkins@hotmail.com

SIMPKINS, Matthew Jonathan. b 78. Oriel Coll Ox BA 99 MA 08 Essex Univ PGCE 08. Ripon Coll Cuddesdon MPhil 15. **d** 15. C Wickford and Runwell *Chelmsf* from 15. *32 Wallace Drive, Wickford SS12 9LZ*   T: (01268) 765524
E: revdmatthewsimpkins@gmail.com

SIMPKINS, Susan Carol. b 58. St Steph Ho Ox 03. **d** 05. NSM Ruislip St Martin *Lon* 05-11; PtO 12-13. *70 Park Avenue, Ruislip HA4 7UJ*   T: (01895) 630170   M: 07742-912664
E: sue.simpkins@btopenworld.com

SIMPSON, Alan Eric. b 52. Ch Ch Ox BA 73 MA 77 Birm Univ PhD 77 Dur Univ MA 01 CPhys 77 MInstP 77. Cranmer Hall Dur 96. **d** 98 **p** 99. C Long Benton *Newc* 98-02; P-in-c Cresswell and Lynemouth 02-06; V from 06. *The Vicarage, 33 Till Grove, Ellington, Morpeth NE61 5ER*   T: (01670) 860242
E: fr.alan@talk21.com

SIMPSON, Alan James. b 78. Yorks Min Course 13. **d** 15. NSM Burnage St Nic *Man* from 15. *Manchester Diocesan Board of Finance, Church House, 90 Deansgate, Manchester M3 2GH*
T: 0161-828 1419   M: 07553-371162
E: alansimpson@manchester.anglican.org

SIMPSON, Alexander. b 31. Oak Hill Th Coll 74. **d** 76 **p** 77. Hon C Lower Homerton St Paul *Lon* 76-81; Hon C Homerton St Barn w St Paul 81-85; TV Hackney Marsh 85-87; V Kensington St Helen w H Trin 87-97; rtd 97; PtO *Derby* 01-07; *Nor* from 08. *2 Ferndale Close, Norwich NR6 5SD*
T: (01603) 443412

SIMPSON, The Very Revd Alison Jane. b 60. St Andr Univ BSc 83 BD 86 Princeton Univ MTh 87. **d** 99 **p** 99. C Ellon *Ab* 99-02; R Huntly *Mor* 02-09; R Keith 02-09; R Aberchirder 02-09; P-in-c Fochabers 04-09; R Nairn from 09; Can St Andr Cathl Inverness from 09; Dean Mor from 14. *The New Rectory, 3 Queen Street, Nairn IV12 4AA* T: (01667) 452458 M: 07548-230745   E: revalison433@btinternet.com *or* dean@moray.anglican.org

SIMPSON, Andrew. b 48. Liv Univ BEng 69. Sarum Th Coll 83. **d** 86 **p** 87. NSM Canford Magna *Sarum* 86-15; PtO from 15. *17 Sopwith Crescent, Wimborne BH21 1SH* T: (01202) 883996
E: andrew.simpson6@virgin.net

SIMPSON, Andrew Charles. b 65. NEOC 06. **d** 09 **p** 10. C Hessle *York* 09-12; V Skirlaugh, Catwick, Long Riston, Rise, Swine w Ellerby from 12. *The Vicarage, Church Lane, Skirlaugh, Hull HU11 5EU* T: (01964) 564634
E: andrew617simpson@hotmail.com

SIMPSON, Aron Brian. b 77. St Jo Coll Nottm 09. **d** 12 **p** 13. C Bakewell, Ashford w Sheldon and Rowsley *Derby* from 12. *West Lawn, 2 Aldern Way, Bakewell DE45 1AJ* T: (01629) 813736   M: 07951-564132 E: aron.simpson@me.com

SIMPSON, Catherine Jane. d 14. Castledawson *D & R* 14-15; C Seapatrick *D & D* from 15. *Address temp unknown*

SIMPSON, Charles Michael. b 38. St Cath Coll Cam MA 63 Campion Hall Ox MA 65 Heythrop Coll Lon STL 69 K Coll Lon PhD 71. **d** 68 **p** 69. Lect Th Lon Univ 72-84; Chapl Prince of Peace Community Greenwich 85-87; Retreat Dir St Beuno's Clwyd 87-91; P-in-c Selkirk *Edin* 91-94; P-in-c Offchurch *Cov* 94-96; Warden Offa Retreat Ho and Dioc Spirituality Adv 94-00; P-in-c Stoke Canon, Poltimore w Huxham and Rewe etc *Ex* 00-04; Dioc Adv in Adult Tr 00-04; rtd 04; PtO *Cov* from 05. *10 Applemede, Silverton, Exeter EX5 4JX*
E: michaelandsharon@shepherdsway.wanadoo.co.uk

SIMPSON, Christine. b 43. **d** 07 **p** 08. OLM Drayton in Hales *Lich* 07-14; NSM Cheswardine, Childs Ercall, Hales, Hinstock etc from 14. *18 Mortimer Road, Buntingsdale Park, Market Drayton TF9 2EP* T: (01630) 638794
E: christine@simpson12.plus.com

SIMPSON, Colin George. b 63. Birm Univ BA 11. Qu Coll Birm 06. **d** 08 **p** 09. C Astwell Gp *Pet* 08-11; P-in-c Brigstock w Stanion and Lowick and Sudborough from 11; P-in-c Weldon w Deene 11-14. *The Rectory, 12 Church Street, Brigstock, Kettering NN14 3EX* T: (01536) 373965
E: revcolinsimpson@btinternet.com

SIMPSON, David Charles Edward. b 51. NEOC 02. **d** 05 **p** 06. NSM York St Chad 05-09; PtO 09-12; NSM York All SS Pavement w St Crux and St Mich from 12; NSM York St Helen w St Martin from 12; NSM York St Denys from 12; NSM York St Olave w St Giles from 12. *98 Brunswick Street, York YO23 1ED* T: (01904) 635085
E: david@simpson5000.fslife.co.uk

SIMPSON, David John. b 61. Univ Coll Dur BA 85 Univ Coll Lon MA 11. Sarum & Wells Th Coll 89. **d** 91 **p** 92. C Selby Abbey *York* 91-94; C Romsey *Win* 94-97; Chapl Southn Univ 97-05; Chapl RN from 05. *Royal Naval Chaplaincy Service, Mail Point 1-2, Leach Building, Whale Island, Portsmouth PO2 8BY* T: (023) 9262 5055   F: 9262 5134
E: davidsimpson23@hotmail.co.uk

SIMPSON, Derek John. b 59. Oak Hill Th Coll BA 89. **d** 89 **p** 90. C Alperton *Lon* 89-95; TR Brentford from 95; AD Hounslow 02-15. *The Rectory, 3 The Butts, Brentford TW8 8BJ* T: (020) 8568 6502 *or* 8568 7442
E: derek.simpson@btinternet.com

SIMPSON, Eleanor Elizabeth Mary. *See* ROBERTSHAW, Eleanor Elizabeth Mary

SIMPSON, Mrs Elizabeth Ann. b 59. Lon Bible Coll BA 80 Trin Coll Bris 84. **dss** 86 **d** 97 **p** 98. Thornbury *Glouc* 86-87; Beckenham Ch Ch *Roch* 87-90; Heydon, Gt and Lt Chishill, Chrishall etc *Chelmsf* 90-93; Shirwell, Loxhore, Kentisbury, Arlington, etc *Ex* 93-97; NSM S Molton w Nymet St George, High Bray etc 97-99; C 99-03; P-in-c W Buckingham *Ox* 03-11; R from 11. *The Vicarage, Orchard Place, Westbury, Brackley NN13 5JT* T: (01280) 704964   E: revliz@o2.co.uk

SIMPSON, Geoffrey Sedgwick. b 32. Hamilton Coll (NY) BA 54 Wisconsin Univ MA Pemb Coll Cam PhD 70. Gen Th Sem

---

(NY) STB 57. **d** 57 **p** 57. USA 57-77; Chapl Birm Univ 77-80; V Shoreham *Roch* 80-90; TR Street *York* 90-02; rtd 02; PtO *Sarum* 03-14. *The Laurels, Queen Street, Yetminster, Sherborne DT9 6LL* T: (01935) 872915

SIMPSON, Mrs Georgina. b 46. Westmr Coll Ox BTh 93 Birm Univ MA 95 DipEd 98. SAOMC 95. **d** 97 **p** 98. NSM Littlemore *Ox* 97-98; C Ox St Giles and SS Phil and Jas w St Marg 98-09; Hon C from 12; PtO 09-12. *85 Church Road, Sandford-on-Thames, Oxford OX4 4YA* T: (01865) 775160
E: georgio-simpson1@gmail.com

SIMPSON, Herbert. b 20. Carl Dioc Tr Course. **d** 82 **p** 83. NSM Barrow St Aid *Carl* 82; NSM Barrow St Jo 82-90; rtd 90; PtO *Carl* 90-07. *Address temp unknown*

SIMPSON, Mrs Janet Mary. b 42. New Coll Edin LTh 94. EAMTC 99. **d** 00 **p** 01. C Aldringham w Thorpe, Knodishall w Buxlow etc *St E* 00-03; R Elmsett w Aldham, Hintlesham, Chattisham etc 03-06; rtd 06. *Ferfoot Residential Home, Old Hardenhuish Lane, Chippenham SN14 6HH* T: (01249) 658677
E: revjanelmsett@tiscali.co.uk

SIMPSON, Jill. b 53. **d** 13 **p** 14. NSM Ferring *Chich* from 13. *Greensward, 64 Lime Tree Avenue, Worthing BN14 0DP*
T: (01903) 872746

SIMPSON, The Very Revd John Arthur. b 33. OBE 01. Keble Coll Ox BA 56 MA 60. Clifton Th Coll 56. **d** 58 **p** 59. C Low Leyton *Chelmsf* 58-59; C Orpington Ch Ch *Roch* 59-62; Tutor Oak Hill Th Coll 62-72; V Ridge *St Alb* 72-79; P-in-c 79-81; Dir of Ords and Post-Ord Tr 75-81; Hon Can St Alb 77-79; Can Res St Alb 79-81; Adn Cant and Can Res Cant Cathl 81-86; Dean Cant 86-00; rtd 00; PtO *Cant* from 01. *Flat D, 9 Earls Avenue, Folkestone CT20 2HW* T: (01303) 211868

SIMPSON, Canon John Bernard. b 40. St Paul's Coll Chelt CertEd 62 Ox Univ MTh 95 ACP 66. **d** 93 **p** 93. In URC 63-93; Asst to RD Lothingland *Nor* 93-94; RD 99-10; C Hopton w Corton 93-94; P-in-c 94-99; TR Lowestoft St Marg 99-10; Hon Can Nor Cathl 01-10; rtd 10; P-in-c Publow w Pensford, Compton Dando and Chelwood *B & W* from 10. *The Rectory, Old Road, Pensford, Bristol BS39 4BB* T: (01761) 490227 M: 07905-013183 E: canonjohn145@btinternet.com

SIMPSON, Canon John Lawrence. b 33. DL 04. SS Coll Cam BA 55 MA 59 ARCM 60 UWE Hon MMus. Wells Th Coll 63. **d** 65 **p** 66. Chapl Win Cathl 65-66; C Win St Bart 65-69; Chapl Repton Sch Derby 69-71; Hd of RE Helston Sch 71-78; P-in-c Curry Rivel *B & W* 79-80; R Curry Rivel w Fivehead and Swell 80-86; V Tunbridge Wells K Chas *Roch* 86-89; Can Res Bris Cathl 89-99; rtd 99; PtO *B & W* from 00. *Yardes Cottage, Windmill Hill, Ilminster TA19 9NT* T: (01823) 480593
E: simpson.yardes@virgin.net

SIMPSON, John Peter. b 39. ALCD 66. **d** 66 **p** 67. C Woodside *Ripon* 66-69; C Burnage St Marg *Man* 69-72; V Rochdale Deeplish St Luke 72-80; R Lamplugh w Ennerdale *Carl* 80-04; rtd 04. *8 Queens Avenue, Seaton, Workington CA14 1DN*
T: (01900) 604215 E: revpetersim@supanet.com

SIMPSON, John Raymond. b 41. Univ of S Aus DipEd 92. Chich Th Coll 65. **d** 67 **p** 68. C Scarborough St Martin *York* 67-71; C Grangetown 71-72; Youth Chapl Bermuda 72-75; C Lewisham St Mary *S'wark* 76; C Albany Australia 76-78; R Carey Park 78-84; Chapl RAAChD 77-84; Chapl RAN 84-90; Chapl RAAF 90-99; Asst P Grace Cathl San Francisco USA 99-00; Chapl RANSR Australia from 00. *44/19 Oakleigh Drive, Erskine Grove, Erskine WA 6210, Australia* T: (0061) (8) 9586 4144 E: simpsonjohnr@googlemail.com

SIMPSON, John Verrent. b 68. Univ of Wales (Cardiff) BScEcon 93. Ripon Coll Cuddesdon BTh 98. **d** 98 **p** 99. C Cardiff St Jo *Llan* 98-00; C Cen Cardiff 00-01; C Upper Chelsea H Trin *Lon* 01-04; P-in-c Lt Missenden *Ox* from 05. *The Vicarage, Little Missenden, Amersham HP7 0RA* T: (01494) 862008 M: 07919-551614 E: vicar@lmchurch.org

SIMPSON, Kevin Gordon. b 54. QPM 02. Univ of Wales BEd 96 MCIPD 94. St Mich Coll Llan. **d** 02 **p** 03. NSM Llantwit Fardre *Llan* from 02. *95 St Anne's Drive, Pontypridd CF38 2PB*
T: (01443) 207033   M: 07870-397494
E: k.g.simpson@btinternet.com

SIMPSON, Miss Margery Patricia. b 36. SRN 57 SCM 59. Oak Hill Th Coll BA 86. **dss** 86 **d** 87 **p** 94. Rodbourne Cheney *Bris* 86-87; Par Dn 87-90; Par Dn Warmley 90-94; C Warmley, Syston and Bitton 94-95; TV Yate New Town 95-96; rtd 97; PtO *Sarum* 97-04; *Carl* from 05. *19 Wentworth Park, Stainburn, Workington CA14 1XP* T: (01900) 61523

SIMPSON, Mark Lawrence. b 73. Oak Hill Th Coll BA 03. **d** 03 **p** 04. C Leyland St Andr *Blackb* from 03. *45 Westgate, Leyland PR25 2LX* T: (01772) 622446
E: mark.simpson@standrewsleyland.org.uk

SIMPSON, Martha Grace. b 83. **d** 14 **p** 15. C Chipping Norton *Ox* from 14. *15 Cross Leys, Chipping Norton OX7 5HG* M: 07828-921518 E: martha.simpson@stmaryscnorton.com

SIMPSON, Matthew John. b 76. Nottm Univ BA 95 Leic Univ MA 01. St Jo Coll Nottm 11. **d** 13 **p** 14. C The Quinton *Birm* from 13. *6 Birch Walk, Oldbury B68 0ET* M: 07522-586254
E: mattsimpson365@hotmail.com *or* revmattsimpson@gmail.com

SIMPSON, Michael. *See* SIMPSON, Charles Michael

SIMPSON, Peter. *See* SIMPSON, John Peter

SIMPSON, Peter Richard. b 53. Univ Coll Lon BSc(Econ) 74 Qu Mary Coll Lon MSc 75 FRSocMed 09. **d** 97. In RC Ch 97-11; NSM St Andr Cathl Inverness from 12. *26 Westfield Brae, Westhill, Inverness IV2 5TL* T: (01463) 798075
M: 07710-123202 E: prs1@waitrose.com

SIMPSON, Philip Alexander. b 54. Keele Univ BA 79 CQSW 79 Sunderland Univ MSc 03. CMS Tr Coll Selly Oak 85. **d** 89 **p** 07. CMS from 85; Pakistan 85-98; Regional Dir for Eurasia from 98; PtO *Guildf* 06-07; NSM Woking Ch Ch from 07. *CMS, PO Box 1799, Oxford OX4 9BN* T: 08456-201799
E: phil.simpson@cms-uk.org

SIMPSON, Rachel Victoria. b 89. Ban Univ BD 11. St Mich Coll Llan 11. **d** 13 **p** 14. C Llantwit Major *Llan* from 13. *The Rectory, 1 Rectory Drive, St Athan, Barry CF62 4PD* T: (01446) 751241 E: rachelvsimpson@hotmail.co.uk

SIMPSON, Raymond James. b 40. Lon Coll of Div ALCD 63 LTh 74. **d** 63 **p** 64. C Longton St Jas *Lich* 64-68; C Upper Tooting H Trin *S'wark* 68-71; BFBS Distr Sec E Anglia 71-77; C-in-c Bowthorpe CD *Nor* 78-84; V Bowthorpe 84-96; PtO *Newc* from 96; Guardian Community of Aid and Hilda from 96. *White House, Fenkle Street, Holy Island, Berwick-upon-Tweed TD15 2SR* T: (01289) 389145
E: raysimpson@ndirect.co.uk

SIMPSON, Richard Lee. b 66. Keble Coll Ox BA 88 MPhil 91 Westmr Coll Ox PGCE 89. Wycliffe Hall Ox 91. **d** 93 **p** 94. C Newc St Gabr 93-97; P-in-c Jesmond H Trin 97-06; P-in-c Newc St Barn and St Jude 97-06; P-in-c Brancepeth *Dur* from 06; Dir IME 4-7 Dur and Newc 06-09; Dir IME 4-7 Lindisfarne Regional Tr Partnership from 09. *The Rectory, Brancepeth, Durham DH7 8EL* T: 0191-380 0440 M: 07867-802671
E: ricksimpson300@btinternet.com

SIMPSON, Canon Robert Charles. b 46. Ridley Hall Cam. **d** 85 **p** 86. C Eastwood *S'well* 85-88; V Yardley St Cypr Hay Mill *Birm* 88-93; P-in-c Newent and Gorsley w Cliffords Mesne *Glouc* 93-95; R 95-05; Dioc Ecum Officer 04-05; P-in-c Glouc St Jas and All SS 05-10; V Glouc St Jas and All SS and Ch Ch 10-12; AD Glouc City 08-11; Hon Can Glouc Cathl 10-12; rtd 12; PtO *Glouc* 12-13; C St Briavels w Hewelsfield from 13. *27 Ryelands Road, Bream, Lydney GL15 6LD* T: (01594) 560202
E: revrobertcsimpson@blueyonder.co.uk

SIMPSON, Robert David. b 61. Fitzw Coll Cam BA 83 MA 87 Bris Univ MLitt 94. Trin Coll Bris 85. **d** 87 **p** 88. C Beckenham Ch Ch *Roch* 87-90; C Heydon w Gt and Lt Chishill *Chelmsf* 90; C Chrishall 90; C Elmdon w Wendon Lofts and Strethall 90; C Heydon, Gt and Lt Chishill, Chrishall etc 91-93; TV Shirwell, Loxhore, Kentisbury, Arlington, etc *Ex* 93-97; TR S Molton w Nymet St George, High Bray etc 97-03. *The Vicarage, Orchard Place, Westbury, Brackley NN13 5JT* T: (01280) 782893
E: revsimpson@supanet.com

SIMPSON, Robert John. NUU MA PGCE. **d** 03 **p** 04. NSM Ballymoney w Finvoy and Rasharkin *Conn* 03-08; NSM Ballywillan from 08. *28 Willowfield Park, Coleraine BT52 1RE* T: (028) 7035 8552 E: robert@robertheather.fsnet.co.uk

SIMPSON, Robert Theodore. b 34. Linc Coll Ox BA 58 MA 61 K Coll Lon PhD 71 UNISA MEd 85. Chich Th Coll 58. **d** 60 **p** 61. C Ellesmere Port *Ches* 60-63; CR 63-66; S Africa 68-88; Prin St Pet Coll 72-75; Pres Federal Th Sem 73-75; Sen Lect Th Swaziland Univ 83-87; Assoc Prof Th 87-88; Chapl and Lect Coll of SS Mark and Jo Plymouth 88-90; Tutor Simon of Cyrene Th Inst 90-92; PtO *S'wark* 91-92; P-in-c Shadwell St Paul w Ratcliffe St Jas *Lon* 92-01; rtd 01. *36 Whitton Dene, Hounslow TW3 2JT* E: theo@cologon.org

SIMPSON, Canon Roger Westgarth. b 51. Lon Univ BSc 72. St Jo Coll Nottm 77. **d** 79 **p** 80. C St Marylebone All So w SS Pet and Jo *Lon* 79-85; R Falkland and St Geo 85-95; R Vancouver H Trin Canada 95-99; V York St Mich-le-Belfrey 99-10; C 10-13; Abp's Evangelist from 10; Hon C York St Barn from 14; Can and Preb York Minster from 10. *22 Bishopfields Drive, York YO26 4WN* T: (01904) 654214 *or* 628539
E: rogerwestgarthsimpson@gmail.com

SIMPSON, Samuel. b 26. TCD BA 55 MA 69 Div Test 56. TCD Div Sch. **d** 56 **p** 57. C Coleraine *Conn* 56-60; I Donagh w Cloncha and Clonmany *D & R* 60-64; I Ballyscullion 64-81; Can Derry Cathl 78-96; I Errigal w Garvagh 81-96; Adn Derry 89-96; rtd 96. *53 Magheramenagh Drive, Atlantic Road, Portrush BT56 8SP* T: (028) 7082 4292

SIMPSON (née RALPHS), Mrs Sharon Ann. b 55. St Mary's Coll Dur BA 77. Cranmer Hall Dur 81. **dss** 83 **d** 87 **p** 94. Caverswall *Lich* 83-87; Par Dn 87-89; Asst Dioc Officer for Minl Tr *St As* 90-91; NSM Selkirk *Edin* 91-94; C Offchurch *Cov* 94-96;

Warden Offa Retreat Ho and Dioc Spirituality Adv 94-00; C Stoke Canon, Poltimore w Huxham and Rewe etc *Ex* 00-04; Dioc Adv in Adult Tr 00-04; rtd 04; PtO *Cov* from 05. *10 Applemede, Silverton, Exeter EX5 4JX*
E: michaelandsharon@shepherdsway.wanadoo.co.uk

SIMPSON, Mrs Susan Fiona. b 67. Herts Univ BSc 89. ERMC 09. **d** 11 **p** 12. C Soham and Wicken *Ely* 11-14; V Somersham w Pidley and Oldhurst and Woodhurst from 14. *The Rectory, Rectory Lane, Somersham, Huntingdon PE28 3EL*
M: 07775-828745 T: (01487) 840676
E: susan.charlotte@googlemail.com

SIMPSON, Mrs Susie Alexandra. b 58. Hertf Coll Ox BA 81. St Steph Ho Ox BA 98. **d** 99 **p** 00. C High Wycombe *Ox* 99-03; TV 03-08; Chapl HM YOI Roch 09-10; Chapl HM Pris Isis from 10. *HM Prison Isis, 1 Belmarsh Road, London SE28 0EB* T: (020) 8331 4400 E: susie.simpson@hmps.gsi.gov.uk

SIMPSON, Theodore. *See* SIMPSON, Robert Theodore

SIMPSON, Ursula Lucy. b 51. St Anne's Coll Ox MA 73 Leeds Univ MA 05. NOC 02. **d** 05 **p** 06. NSM York St Paul 05-10; P-in-c York St Barn from 10. *22 Bishopfields Drive, York YO26 4WN* T/F: (01904) 654214
E: u.simpson@btinternet.com *or* ulsimpson@gmail.com

SIMPSON-GRAY, Lennox George (Rickey). b 64. S Bank Univ BA 93 FCMA 96. ERMC 11. **d** 14 **p** 15. NSM Hemel Hempstead *St Alb* from 14. *22 Bennetts End Close, Hemel Hempstead HP3 8DT* T: (01442) 204935 M: 07985-169243
E: rev-rick@outlook.com

SIMS, Bernard David. b 40. Bath Univ BSc 66. Ox Min Course 91. **d** 94 **p** 95. NSM Beedon and Peasemore w W Ilsley and Farnborough *Ox* 94-98; TV Blakenall Heath *Lich* 98-10; rtd 10; PtO *Lich* from 10. *2 March Way, Walsall WS9 8SG* E: sims@beechdale.fsnet.co.uk

SIMS, The Ven Christopher Sidney. b 49. Wycliffe Hall Ox 74. **d** 77 **p** 78. C Walmley *Birm* 77-80; V Yardley St Cypr Hay Mill 80-88; V Stanwix *Carl* 88-96; RD Carl 89-95; Hon Can Carl Cathl 91-95; P-in-c Bassenthwaite, Isel and Setmurthy 96-00; P-in-c Bolton w Ireby and Uldale 96-00; P-in-c Allhallows 96-00; P-in-c Torpenhow 96-00; TR Binsey 00-03; V Shrewsbury H Cross *Lich* 03-09; RD Shrewsbury 08-09; Adn Walsall 09-14; rtd 14. *25 Kingsland Bridge Mansions, Murivance, Shrewsbury SY1 1JF* E: ven.csims@gmail.com

SIMS, James Henry. b 35. St Jo Coll Nottm 87. **d** 89 **p** 91. NSM Bangor Abbey *D & D* 89-93; C Holywood 93; Bp's C Kilbroney 93-01; Min Can Belf Cathl 99-09; P-in-c Clonallon w Warrenpoint *D & D* 01-09; Can Dromore Cathl 03-09; rtd 09. *7 Prior's Lea, Holywood BT18 9QW* T: (028) 9042 4360
E: jim.sims321@tiscali.co.uk

SIMS, Jane Ann. **d** 15. NSM Malpas *Mon* from 15. *20 Cory Park, Llantarnam, Cwmbran NP44 3HE* T: (01633) 763805 E: peter-sims@hotmail.com

SIMS, Mrs Julia Mary Heaton. b 56. STETS 04. **d** 07 **p** 08. NSM Winscombe and Sandford *B & W* 07-11; Past Co-ord St Monica Trust Sandford Station from 11; PtO *B & W* 11-15; NSM Banwell from 15. *7 Round Oak Grove, Cheddar BS27 3BW* T: (01934) 740120 M: 07875-340291
E: jms125@hotmail.co.uk

SIMS, Ruth. b 62. **d** 06 **p** 07. NSM Alveley and Quatt *Heref* from 06. *Church Farm House, Alveley, Bridgnorth WV15 6ND*

SIMS, Vickie Lela. b 56. Iowa State Univ BA 79. Ripon Coll Cuddesdon 00. **d** 02 **p** 03. C Grantham *Linc* 02-05; P-in-c Coulsdon St Andr *S'wark* 05-11; V 11-14; Jt Dir of IME Croydon Area 09-14; Chapl Milan w Lake Como and Genoa *Eur* from 14. *via Solferino 17, 20121 Milano, Italy* T: (0039) (02) 655 2258 E: allsaintspriest@hotmail.com *or* simstabbat@hotmail.com

SIMS-WILLIAMS, Robert James Alden (Robin). b 79. Trin Hall Cam MEng 02 MA 05 BTh 12. Westcott Ho Cam 10. **d** 13 **p** 14. C Paddington St Jo w St Mich *Lon* from 13. *2nd Floor Flat, 12A Connaught Street, London W2 2AF* M: 07812-167292 E: robin@cantab.net

SINCLAIR, Andrew John McTaggart. b 58. Ex Univ BA 80. Westcott Ho Cam 81. **d** 84 **p** 85. C Aston cum Aughton and Ulley *Sheff* 84-87; C Rotherham 87-88; TV Edin Old St Paul 88-93; Hon Angl Chapl Edin Univ and Moray Ho Coll 89-93; TV Dunstable *St Alb* 93-00; V Verwood *Sarum* from 00. *The Vicarage, 34 Dewlands Way, Verwood BH31 6JN* T: (01202) 822298 *or* 813256 E: ansinclair@aol.com

SINCLAIR, Canon Arthur Alfred. b 46. **d** 87 **p** 89. Hon C St Andr Cathl Inverness 87-92; C 93-97; Chapl Asst Inverness Hosp 87-89; Dioc Chapl *Mor* 87-89; NSM Culloden St Mary-in-the-Fields 89-92; P-in-c 93-12; P-in-c Inverness St Jo 93-12; Edin Th Coll 92-93; Chapl Raigmore Hosp NHS Trust Inverness from 93; Can St Andr Cathl Inverness 05-12; rtd 12; LtO *Mor* from 12. *Rose Cottage, 8A Southside Place, Inverness IV2 3JF* T: (01463) 716288
E: arthurasinclair@btinternet.com

SINCLAIR, Colin. b 30. **d** 84 **p** 85. NSM Ramoan w Ballycastle and Culfeightrin *Conn* 84-92. *4 Bushfoot Cottages, Portballintrae, Bushmills BT57 8RN* T: (028) 2073 1551

✠**SINCLAIR, The Rt Revd Gordon Keith.** b 52. Ch Ch Ox MA. Cranmer Hall Dur. **d** 84 **p** 85 **c** 08. C Summerfield *Birm* 84-88; V Aston SS Pet and Paul 88-01; AD Aston 00-01; Hon Can Birm Cathl 00-01; V Cov H Trin 01-07; Suff Bp Birkenhead *Ches* from 07. *Bishop's Lodge, 67 Bidston Road, Prenton CH43 6TR* T: 0151-652 2741 F: 651 2330
E: bpbirkenhead@chester.anglican.org

SINCLAIR, Jane Elizabeth Margaret. b 56. St Hugh's Coll Ox BA 78 MA 80. St Jo Coll Nottm BA 82. **dss** 83 **d** 87 **p** 94. Herne Hill St Paul *S'wark* 83-86; Chapl and Lect St Jo Coll Nottm 86-93; Can Res Sheff Cathl 93-03; Hon Can Sheff Cathl 03-07; V Rotherham 03-07; Adn Stow and Lindsey *Linc* 07-14; Can Steward Westmr Abbey from 14. *2 Little Cloister, London SW1P 3PL* T: (020) 7654 4815
E: jane.sinclair@westminster-abbey.org

SINCLAIR, Canon John Robert. b 58. Oak Hill Th Coll 90. **d** 92 **p** 93. C Ponteland *Newc* 92-96; V Long Benton St Mary 96-01; V Newburn 01-11; AD Newc W 07-11; Hon Can Newc Cathl 08-11; Can Res Newc Cathl from 11; Dioc Adv in Local Evang from 11. *16 Towers Avenue, Newcastle upon Tyne NE2 3QE* T: 0191-281 0714 M: 07746-743857
E: johnsinclair247@aol.com

SINCLAIR, Keith. *See* SINCLAIR, Gordon Keith

✠**SINCLAIR, The Rt Revd Maurice Walter.** b 37. Nottm Univ BSc 59 Leic Univ PGCE 60. Tyndale Hall Bris 62 Nashotah Ho Hon DD 01. **d** 64 **p** 65 **c** 90. C Boscombe St Jo *Win* 64-67; SAMS 67-02; Argentina 67-78; Personnel Sec 79-83; Asst Gen Sec 83-84; Prin Crowther Hall CMS Tr Coll Selly Oak 84-90; Bp N Argentina 90-02; Primate of S Cone 95-02; rtd 02; Hon Asst Bp Birm from 02. *55 Selly Wick Drive, Birmingham B29 7JQ* T: 0121-471 2617 E: mandg@sinclair401.fsnet.co.uk

SINCLAIR, Michael David Bradley. b 42. NOC Coll of Resurr Mirfield. **d** 97 **p** 98. NSM Settrington w N Grimston, Birdsall w Langton *York* 97-99; R W Buckrose 99-08; rtd 08; NSM Helmsley and Upper Ryedale *York* 09-13; P-in-c Lastingham w Appleton-le-Moors, Rosedale etc 13-15. *Witham Cottage, Langton, Malton YO17 9QP* T: (01653) 658360
E: mdbsinclair@tiscali.co.uk

SINCLAIR, Nigel Craig. b 65. Teesside Poly BA 87 St Jo Coll Dur BA 93 Coll of Ripon & York St Jo MA 00. Cranmer Hall Dur BA 93. **d** 94 **p** 95. C Marton-in-Cleveland *York* 94-97; TV Thirsk 97-02; V Pannal w Beckwithshaw *Ripon* 02-13; AD Harrogate 09-13; TR Abbeylands *Leeds* from 13. *St Margaret's Vicarage, Hall Park Avenue, Horsforth, Leeds LS18 5LY* T: 0113-258 2481 E: nigelsinclair@btinternet.com

SINCLAIR, Peter. b 44. Oak Hill Th Coll. **d** 88 **p** 89. C Darlington H Trin *Dur* 88-91; C-in-c Bishop Auckland Woodhouse Close CD 91-98; P-in-c Consett 98-09; rtd 09; PtO *Dur* from 11. *16 Deanery View, Lanchester, Durham DH7 0NH*

SINCLAIR, Peter Monteith. b 52. St Andr Univ BSc 73. NEOC. **d** 01 **p** 02. NSM Darlington St Cuth *Dur* 01-05; Hon Min Can Dur Cathl 05-12; V Woodhorn w Newbiggin *Newc* from 12. *The Vicarage, 34A Front Street, Newbiggin-by-the-Sea NE64 6PS* T: (01670) 817220 E: peter@psld.co.uk

SINCLAIR, Reginald William. b 53. Wolv Poly BSc 77 CEng MIMechE. Man OLM Scheme 04. **d** 07 **p** 08. OLM Atherton and Hindsford w Howe Bridge *Man* 07-09; TV from 09; Borough Dean Wigan from 13. *Bumbles, 23 Millers Lane, Atherton, Manchester M46 9BW* T: (01942) 892996
M: 07707-419642 E: reg.sinclair@tiscali.co.uk

SINDALL, Canon Christine Ann. b 42. ALA 69. EAMTC 84. **d** 87 **p** 94. NSM Sutton *Ely* 87-89; C Cambridge Ascension 89-94; TV 94-96; R Cheveley 96-07; R Ashley w Silverley 96-07; V Kirtling 96-07; V Wood Ditton w Saxon Street 96-07; RD Linton 01-07; Hon Can Ely Cathl 01-07; rtd 07. *9 East Moor, Longhoughton, Alnwick NE66 3JB* T: (01665) 572247
E: csindall@btinternet.com

SINES, Abigail. **d** 14. Glenageary *D & G* 14-15; C Dublin Ch Ch Cathl Gp from 15. *Address temp unknown*

SINGAPORE, Bishop of. *See* CHEW, John Hiang Chea

SINGH, Balwant. b 32. BA 60. Saharanpur Th Coll 50. **d** 53 **p** 58. India 53-67 and 71-73; Hon C Handsworth St Jas *Birm* 67-71; Hon C N Hinksey Ox 73-80; LtO 80-81; Hon C S Hinksey 82-05; PtO from 05. *Address temp unknown* T: (01865) 459621

SINGH, Graham Andrew. b 77. Huron Coll Ontario BA 00 LSE MSc 01. Ridley Hall Cam 06. **d** 08 **p** 09. C W Hampstead Trin *Lon* 08-10; PtO Kensington Area 10-13; Canada from 13. *54 Hilldale Crescent, Guelph ON N1G 4B9, Canada*

SINGH, Jonathan James. b 72. Bp Grosseteste Coll BA 96 Drew Univ New Jersey DMin 12. Ripon Coll Cuddesdon 97. **d** 00 **p** 01. C Spalding St Mary and St Nic *Linc* 00-02; C Sanderstead St Mary *S'wark* 02-03; P-in-c 03-05; TV Sanderstead 05-06; V E Crompton *Man* 06-09; R Broughty Ferry *Bre* 09-11; Chapl

St Mich Hospice Harrogate 11-13; Bereavement Support Worker from 13; PtO *Leeds* 13-14; NSM Ripon Cathl from 14; PtO *York* from 14. *The Vicarage, Knaresborough Road, Bishop Monkton, Harrogate HG3 3QQ* T: (01765) 676298
E: revdrjonathansingh@gmail.com

SINGH, Thomas Balwant. b 62. Westmr Coll Ox BTh 98. Wycliffe Hall Ox 98. **d** 00 **p** 01. C Houghton Regis *St Alb* 00-04; V Biscot from 04. *The Vicarage, 161 Bishopscote Road, Luton LU3 1PD* T: (01582) 579410
E: thomassingh@hotmail.com

SINGH, Timon Balwant. b 60. Ripon Coll Cuddesdon. **d** 08 **p** 09. C Waterlooville *Portsm* 08-12; P-in-c Bellingham St Dunstan *S'wark* from 12. *St Dunstan's Vicarage, 5 Gramsci Way, London SE6 3HA* E: timon_ox@hotmail.com

SINGH, Vivian Soorat. b 30. Trin Coll Cam BA MA 53. Westcott Ho Cam 54. **d** 55 **p** 56. C Yardley Wood *Birm* 55-57; C Birm St Paul 57-59; Asst Master Framlingham Coll 59-72; Chapl 60-72; Chapl Wymondham Coll 72-75; Dep Hd Litcham High Sch 75-88; rtd 88; PtO *Nor* from 88. *Manor Cottage, Wendling Road, Longham, Dereham NR19 2RD* T: (01362) 687382

SINGLETON, David Brinley. b 59. St Steph Ho Ox. **d** 00 **p** 01. C Soham *Ely* 00-01; C Soham and Wicken 02-04; P-in-c Capel St Mary w Lt and Gt Wenham *St E* 04-08; R 08-13; RD Samford 10-13; R Bansfield from 13. *The Rectory, Church Road, Wickhambrook, Newmarket CB8 8XH* T: (01440) 821029
E: brinsingleton@btinternet.com

SINGLETON, Kenneth Miller. b 58. Oak Hill Th Coll 89. **d** 91 **p** 92. C Grove *Ox* 91-95; P-in-c Ashbury, Compton Beauchamp and Longcot w Fernham 95-99; C Kirkheaton *Wakef* 99-04. *34 Arlington Way, Huddersfield HD5 9TF* T: (01484) 319592 E: kensingleton@hotmail.com

SINNAMON, William Desmond. b 43. TCD BA 65 MA 80 MPhil 95. CITC 66. **d** 66 **p** 67. C Seapatrick *D & D* 66-70; C Arm St Mark w Aghavilly 70-74; V Choral Arm Cathl 73-74; I Ballinderry 75-80; I Dublin St Patr Cathl Gp 80-83; Preb Tipperkevin St Patr Cathl Dublin 80-83; I Taney *D & G* 83-11; Can St Patr Cathl Dublin 91-11; Treas St Patr Cathl Dublin 91-96; Chan St Patr Cathl Dublin 96-11; rtd 11. *3 Botanic Avenue, Glasnevin, Dublin 9, Republic of Ireland* T: (00353) (1) 444 1616

SINTON, Bernard. b 43. Leic Univ BSc 66. Sarum & Wells Th Coll 87. **d** 90 **p** 91. NSM Horsham *Chich* from 90. *The Vicarage, Red Lane, Shipley, Horsham RH13 8PH* T: (01403) 741238

SINTON, Mrs Patricia Ann. b 41. RGN 62 SCM 64. STETS 95. **d** 98 **p** 99. NSM Horsham *Chich* 98-01; P-in-c Shipley from 01. *The Vicarage, Red Lane, Shipley, Horsham RH13 8PH* T: (01403) 741238 E: pa.sinton@tesco.net

SINTON, Vera May. b 43. Somerville Coll Ox BA 65 MA 69 Bris Univ CertEd 66. Trin Coll Bris 79. **dss** 81 **d** 87 **p** 94. Broxbourne w Wormley *St Alb* 81-87; Hon Par Dn 87; Tutor All Nations Chr Coll Ware 81-87; Chapl St Hilda's Coll Ox 87-90; Tutor Wycliffe Hall Ox 87-98; NSM Ox St Clem 99-09; Tutor Ox Cen for Youth Min 01-04; rtd 09; PtO *Ox* from 09. *Rookhurst, West End, Gayle, Hawes DL8 3RT* T: (01969) 666948 E: vera@vsinton.co.uk

SIRCAR, Deepak Debchandan. b 46. Lon Hosp BDS 72 Leeds Univ BA 06. NOC 03. **d** 06 **p** 07. NSM Doncaster St Geo *Sheff* 06-10; NSM Bath Widcombe *B & W* 10-13; P-in-c Barnby Dun *Sheff* from 13. *The Vicarage, Stainforth Road, Barnby Dun, Doncaster DN3 1AA* M: 07768-830393
E: deepaksircar@btinternet.com

SIRR, John Maurice Glover. b 42. TCD BA 63. CITC 65. **d** 65 **p** 66. C Belfast St Mary *Conn* 65-68; C Finaghy 68-69; I Drumcliffe w Lissadell and Munninane *K, E & A* 69-87; Preb Elphin Cathl 81-87; Dean Limerick and Ardfert *L & K* 87-11; I Limerick City 87-11; Chapl Limerick Pris 87-11; rtd 11. *17A Knockhill, Ennis Road, Limerick, Republic of Ireland* T: (00353) (61) 277372 M: 87-254 1121 E: msirr@iol.ie

SISTIG, Andreas. b 75. St Geo Th Sem Frankfurt 96. **d** 04 **p** 05. C Hillcrest S Africa 04-08; C Fleet *Guildf* 08-14; V Bagshot from 14. *43 Church Road, Bagshot GU19 5EQ* M: 07595-542143 T: (01276) 473348

SISTIG (née STEWART), Mrs Jennifer Jane. b 71. Urban Univ Rome STB 00. St Jos Th Inst Cedara BTh 00. **d** 99 **p** 00. C Kirby-Hilton S Africa 99-00; C Scottsville 00-01; R Woodlands-Montclair-cum-Yellowwood Park 01-05; R Hillcrest 05-08; NSM Fleet *Guildf* from 08; Chapl St Geo Sch Ascot from 10; Chapl Frimley Park Hosp NHS Foundn Trust from 13; PtO *Ox* from 12. *43 Church Road, Bagshot GU19 5EQ* M: 07546-120844 T: (01276) 473348
E: jennifer@parishoffleet.org.uk

SITCH, Keith Frank. b 40. Ex Univ BA 63 Lon Univ MA 95. S'wark Ord Course 72. **d** 75 **p** 76. NSM Romford St Edw *Chelmsf* 75-78; NSM Kidbrooke St Jas *S'wark* 78-10; PtO from 10. *92 Kidbrooke Park Road, London SE3 0DX* T: (020) 8856 3843 E: keith.sitch@btinternet.com

SITWELL, Mrs Mary Elizabeth. b 49. Brighton Coll of Educn DipEd 71 Sussex Univ BEd 72. **d** 03 **p** 12. NSM Bishopstone *Chich* 03-06; NSM Alfriston w Lullington, Litlington and W Dean 06-09; Chapl Roedean Sch Brighton 03-09; rtd 09; NSM Iford w Kingston and Rodmell *Chich* 12-13; NSM Iford w Kingston and Rodmell and Southease from 13. *49 Fitzgerald Avenue, Seaford BN25 1AZ* T: (01323) 892424
E: isla.sitwell@btinternet.com

SIU, Leslie. b 87. City Univ BSc 09. Wycliffe Hall Ox BA 14. **d** 15. C Westlands St Andr *Lich* from 15. *40 Eleanor Crescent, Newcastle ST5 3SA 40 Eleanor Crescent, Newcastle ST5 3SA* M: 07732-878076 E: anglican.leslie@gmail.com

SIVILL, David. **d** 14. OLM Atherton and Hindsford w Howe Bridge *Man* from 14. *Address temp unknown*

SIVYER, Steven Robert. b 74. SEITE 12. **d** 15. C Marden *Cant* from 15. *12 Lime Close, Marden, Tonbridge TN12 9EQ* E: steven@sivyer.org.uk

SIXSMITH, David. b 39. Lon Univ BD 66. **d** 97 **p** 98. NSM Castleacre w Newton, Rougham and Southacre *Nor* 97-99; OLM Narborough w Narford 97-99; OLM Pentney St Mary Magd w W Bilney 97-99; OLM Westacre 97-99; C Hunstanton St Mary w Ringstead Parva etc 99-01; P-in-c Foulsham w Hindolveston and Guestwick 01-06; P-in-c N Elmham w Billingford and Worthing 02-05; rtd 06; PtO *Nor* from 06. *Old Mill Cottage, Broadmeadow, Castle Acre, King's Lynn PE32 2BU* T: (01760) 755703
E: david.sixsmith@hotmail.co.uk

SIZER, Stephen Robert. b 53. Sussex Univ BA Ox Univ MTh 94. Trin Coll Bris 80. **d** 83 **p** 84. C St Leonards St Leon *Chich* 83-86; C Guildf St Sav w Stoke-next-Guildford 86-89; R Stoke-next-Guildf 89-97; V Virginia Water from 97. *Christ Church Vicarage, Callow Hill, Virginia Water GU25 4LD* T/F: (01344) 842374 M: 07970-789549
E: stephen.sizer@btinternet.com *or* stephen@sizers.org

SKELDING, Mrs Hazel Betty. b 25. LGSM 66 CertEd 45. Gilmore Course 80. **dss** 83 **d** 87 **p** 94. Hinstock and Sambrook *Lich* 83-84; Asst Children's Adv RE 86-91; Hon Par Dn Alderbury Team *Sarum* 91-94; C 94-96; rtd 96; PtO *Sarum* 96-01; *Truro* 01-06. *308 Grafton Road, Thames 3500, New Zealand* T: (0064) (7) 868 3231

SKELLEY, Mrs Janice Ann. b 66. St Jo Coll Nottm 04. **d** 06 **p** 07. C Barnard Castle w Whorlton *Dur* 06-08; C Hedworth 09-12; rtd 12; PtO *Dur* from 13. *15 Langford Drive, Boldon Colliery NE35 9LJ* T: 0191-680 5040 E: jas66@hotmail.com

SKELTON, Beresford. b 52. St Chad's Coll Dur BA 74. Chich Th Coll 74. **d** 76 **p** 77. CMP from 77; C Byker St Ant *Newc* 76-80; C Newc St Jo 80-82; Chapl Asst Newc Gen Hosp 80-81; Chapl Asst Freeman Hosp Newc 81-82; V Cresswell and Lynemouth *Newc* 82-88; P-in-c Millfield St Mary *Dur* 88-93; V from 93; P-in-c Bishopwearmouth Gd Shep from 04. *St Mary Magdalene's Vicarage, Wilson Street, Sunderland SR4 6HJ* T/F: 0191-565 6318

SKELTON (née BOXER), Mrs Caroline Victoria. b 46. Bradf Univ BA 69. Yorks Min Course 09. **d** 11 **p** 12. NSM Baildon *Leeds* from 11. *2 Highfield Mews, Baildon, Shipley BD17 5PF* T: (01274) 582224 E: caroline.skelton2@gmail.com

SKELTON, Dennis Michael. b 33. K Coll Lon BSc 55. NEOC 76. **d** 79 **p** 80. NSM Pennywell St Thos and Grindon St Oswald CD *Dur* 79-84; V Heathercleugh 84-99; V St John in Weardale 84-99; V Westgate 84-99; rtd 99; PtO *Dur* from 99. *52 Vicarage Close, New Silksworth, Sunderland SR3 1JF* T: 0191-523 7135

SKELTON, Melvyn Nicholas. b 38. St Pet Coll Ox BA 61 MA 65 Selw Coll Cam BA 63 MA 68. Ridley Hall Cam 62. **d** 64 **p** 65. C St Marychurch *Ex* 64-66; C Bury St Edmunds St Mary *St E* 66-69; Hon C 69-78; LtO 78-08; PtO from 09. *Milburn House, The Street, Moulton, Newmarket CB8 8RZ* T: (01638) 750563

SKEPPER, Mrs Suzanne Jayne. b 63. Trin Coll Bris BA 09. **d** 09 **p** 10. C Wotton St Mary *Glouc* 09-13; V Twigworth, Down Hatherley, Norton, The Leigh etc from 13. *The Rectory, Tewkesbury Road, Twigworth, Gloucester GL2 9PQ* M: 07981-429259 E: suzanne.skepper@hotmail.co.uk

SKIDMORE, Iaen Macdonald. b 58. SNWTP 11. **d** 13 **p** 14. C Marown, Foxdale and Baldwin *S & M* from 13. *11 Oak Road, Ballawattleworth Estate, Peel, Isle of Man IM5 1WB* T: (01624) 842220 M: 07624-403945 E: iaenskidmore@manx.net

SKIDMORE (née CANNINGS), Karen Rachel. b 75. Nottm Univ BA 96. Ridley Hall Cam 04. **d** 06 **p** 07. C Pitsmoor Ch Ch *Sheff* 06-10; P-in-c Herringthorpe 10-15; V from 15. *The Vicarage, 493 Herringthorpe Valley Road, Rotherham S60 4LB* T: (01709) 836052 E: karen.skidmore@yahoo.co.uk *or* karen.skidmore@sheffield.anglican.org

SKIDMORE, Michael Anthony. b 38. **d** 98 **p** 99. NSM Rainworth and Blidworth *S'well* 98-00; P-in-c Basford St Leodegarius 00-05; P-in-c Willoughby-on-the-Wolds w Wysall and Widmerpool 05-07; NSM Carlton-in-the-Willows, Porchester

and Woodthorpe 07-09; rtd 09. *11 Graveney Gardens, Arnold, Nottingham NG5 6QW* T: 0115-926 0773
E: mike.skidmore@breathemail.net

SKIDMORE, Mrs Sheila Ivy. b 36. **d** 87 **p** 94. Hon Par Dn Leic Resurr 87-91; Par Dn Clarendon Park St Jo w Knighton St Mich 91-94; TV 94-01; rtd 01; PtO *Leic* from 01. *15 School Lane, Birstall, Leicester LE4 4EA* T: 0116-267 3318
E: skidmore010@btinternet.com

SKIDMORE, Simon Peter. b 88. Univ of Wales (Ban) BD 10. Trin Coll Bris 12. **d** 14 **p** 15. C Wednesbury St Bart *Lich* from 14. *The Rectory, 1 Hollies Drive, Wednesbury WS10 9EQ* M: 07919-800533 E: skiders180@hotmail.co.uk

SKILLEN, John Clifford Tainish. b 50. NUU BA 72 MA 82 TCD BTh 89 QUB DipEd 73. CITC 86. **d** 89 **p** 90. C Bangor Abbey *D & D* 89-92; I Kilwarlin Upper w Kilwarlin Lower 92-96; I Finaghy *Conn* 96-09; Asst Ed *The Church of Ireland Gazette* from 99; Bp's Sen Dom Chapl *Conn* from 08. *25 Berkeley Hall Square, Lisburn BT27 5TB* T: (028) 9267 0257 M: 07740-553926 E: st-polycarp@utvinternet.com

SKILLING, Graham. b 53. **d** 12 **p** 13. NSM Kendal H Trin *Carl* from 12. *7 Danes Road, Staveley, Kendal LA8 9PW* T: (01539) 822695 E: gr36939@yahoo.co.uk

SKILLINGS, Martyn Paul. b 46. St Chad's Coll Dur BA 68. Linc Th Coll 68. **d** 70 **p** 71. C Stanley *Lich* 70-72; C Warrington St Elphin 72-75; Ind Chapl 75-76; V Surfleet *Linc* 88-92; V Burton St Chad *Lich* 92-08; R Calton, Cauldon, Grindon, Waterfall etc 08-12; RD Alstonfield 10-11; rtd 12; PtO *Lich* 13-14; P-in-c Outwell *Ely* from 14; P-in-c Upwell St Pet from 14. *18 Main Road, Friday Bridge, Wisbech PE14 0HJ* M: 07887-854525 E: paul_skillings@talktalk.net

SKILTON, The Ven Christopher John. b 55. Magd Coll Cam BA 76 MA 80. Wycliffe Hall Ox 77. **d** 80 **p** 81. C Ealing St Mary *Lon* 80-84; C New Borough and Leigh *Sarum* 84-88; TV Gt Baddow *Chelmsf* 88-95; TR Sanderstead All SS *S'wark* 95-04; P-in-c Sanderstead St Mary 02-04; RD Croydon S 00-04; Adn Lambeth 04-13; P-in-c Kennington St Mark 08-09; Adn Croydon from 13. *St Matthew's House, 100 George Street, Croydon CR0 1PE* T: (020) 8256 9630 F: 8256 9631
E: christopher.skilton@southwark.anglican.org

SKILTON, Joseph Laurence. b 41. Univ of Wales TCert 64 Murdoch Univ Aus BA 90 Aus Pacific Coll MA 93. St Mich Coll Llan. **d** 70 **p** 71. C Bicester *Ox* 71-73; C Shrewsbury St Chad *Lich* 73-76; V W Bromwich St Phil 76-80; Australia from 80; rtd 06. *11 Tillbrook Street, Glen Forrest WA 6071, Australia* T: (0061) (8) 9298 9454 *or* 6188 6024 E: pax2u2@gmail.com

SKINGLEY, Christopher George. b 49. K Coll Lon MA 98. Oak Hill Th Coll BA 90 Qu Coll Birm. **d** 00 **p** 01. C Enfield St Jas *Lon* 00-03; V Ramsgate St Mark *Cant* 03-15; rtd 15. *18 Royal Native Way, Whitstable CT5 4UE* T: (01227) 272508
E: chris.skingley@btinternet.com

✠**SKINNER, The Rt Revd Brian Antony.** b 39. Reading Univ BSc 60. Tyndale Hall Bris 66. **d** 67 **p** 68 **c** 77. C Woking St Pet *Guildf* 67-70; Chile 70-86; Adn Valparaiso 76-77; Suff Bp Valparaiso 77-86; C Chorleywood St Andr St Alb 87-96; V Iver Ox 96-06; rtd 06. *10 Benton Drive, Chinnor OX39 4DP* T: (01844) 353504 E: skinnerofiver@go-plus.net

SKINNER, Mrs Elaine Teresa (Terri). b 55. Bath Univ BSc 78. EMMTC 99. **d** 02 **p** 03. NSM Whitwick St Jo the Bapt *Leic* 02-05; NSM Thorpe Acre w Dishley 05-10; P-in-c Leic St Theodore from 10. *St Theodore's House, 4 Sandfield Close, Leicester LE4 7RE* M: 07810-241381
E: terri.skinner@btopenworld.com

SKINNER, Graeme John. b 57. Southn Univ BSc 79. Trin Coll Bris BA 86. **d** 86 **p** 87. C Bebington *Ches* 86-90; V Ashton-upon-Mersey St Mary Magd 90-06; V Upton (Overchurch) from 06. *The Vicarage, 20 Church Road, Upton, Wirral CH49 6JZ* T: 0151-677 4810 E: graeme@stm-upton.org.uk

SKINNER, Mrs Jane Mary. b 59. Leeds Univ BA 81. Cranmer Hall Dur 82. **dss** 84 **d** 87 **p** 94. Chatham St Phil and St Jas *Roch* 84-87; Hon Par Dn Church Coniston *Carl* 87-91; Hon Par Dn Torver 87-91; NSM Dalton-in-Furness 91-97; Chapl HM Pris Haverigg 92-97; Chapl Carl Hosps NHS Trust 97-01; Chapl N Cumbria Acute Hosps NHS Trust 01-02; TV Carl H Trin and St Barn 98-02; Hon C W Swindon and the Lydiards *Bris* 02-09; Chapl Swindon and Marlborough NHS Trust 03-10; NSM Golden Cap Team *Sarum* 09-10; TV from 10. *The Vicarage, 4 Dragons Hill, Lyme Regis DT7 3HW* T: (01297) 443763 E: sjmskinners@btinternet.com

SKINNER, Mrs Jean. b 47. Univ of Northumbria at Newc BA 03 RN 68 RM 70. NEOC 93. **d** 96 **p** 97. NSM Ch the King *Newc* 96-03; NSM Newc St Thos Prop Chpl from 03; NSM City Cen Chapl 03-06; Dioc Child Protection Adv from 07; NSM Newc Cathl from 12. *32 Easedale Avenue, Melton Park, Newcastle upon Tyne NE3 5TB* T: 0191-236 3474
E: revjeanskinner@yahoo.com

SKINNER, Preb John Cedric. b 30. Bris Univ BA 55. Tyndale Hall Bris 55. **d** 57 **p** 58. C St Leonard Ex 57-62; Univ Sec IVF 62-68; V Guildf St Sav 68-76; R Stoke next Guildf St Jo 74-76; R Guildf St Sav w Stoke-next-Guildford 76-84; R Ex St Leon w H Trin 84-98; Chapl R W of England Sch for the Deaf 84-98; Preb Ex Cathl 92-98; rtd 98; PtO Ex from 00. *386 Topsham Road, Exeter EX2 6HE* T: (01392) 876540

SKINNER, John Richard. b 45. NOC 84. **d** 87 **p** 88. C Allerton *Liv* 87-90; C Huyton St Mich 90-97; P-in-c Fairfield 97-03; rtd 04. *30 Duke Street, Formby, Liverpool L37 4AT* T: (01704) 874899

SKINNER, John Timothy. b 55. Linc Th Coll 79. **d** 81 **p** 82. C Newton Aycliffe *Dur* 81-82; PtO *Newc* 95-01; Bermuda from 01. *St John's Church, PO Box HM 1856, Hamilton HM HX, Bermuda* T: (001441) 292 6802

SKINNER, Leonard Harold. b 36. K Coll Lon BD 62 AKC 62. **d** 63 **p** 64. C Hackney Wick St Mary of Eton w St Aug *Lon* 63-66; C Palmers Green St Jo 66-70; V Grange Park St Pet 70-80; TV Hanley H Ev *Lich* 80-86; Chapl Sunderland Poly *Dur* 86-92; Chapl Sunderland Univ 92-93; P-in-c Hebburn St Oswald 93-01; rtd 01; PtO *Newc* from 01. *28 Brighton Grove, Whitley Bay NE26 1QH* T: 0191-251 4891

SKINNER, Maurice Wainwright. b 30. St Jo Coll Ox BA 53 MA 59 FRSC 70. Ox NSM Course. **d** 86 **p** 87. NSM Furze Platt *Ox* 86-94; NSM Hurley and Stubbings 94-00; rtd 00; PtO *Ox* from 00. *133 Beverley Gardens, Maidenhead SL6 6ST* T: (01628) 624875

SKINNER, Michael Thomas. b 39. Open Univ BA 88 BA 90 Heythrop Coll Lon MA 11. S'wark Ord Course 73. **d** 78 **p** 79. NSM Orpington St Andr *Roch* 78-82; P-in-c 99-09; NSM Orpington All SS 82-99; Assoc Bp's Officer for NSMs 90-98; Bp's Officer for NSMs *Roch* 98-09; rtd 09; PtO *Roch* from 09; *Lon* from 11; S'wark 02-05 and from 16. *16 Ambleside Gardens, South Croydon CR2 8SF* T: (020) 8239 1973
E: mikeskinner2@virginmedia.com

SKINNER, Mrs Nicola Jayne. b 70. Birm Univ BA 92. Cuddesdon Coll MTh. **d** 98 **p** 99. C Bartley Green *Birm* 98-01; Assoc Min Aurora Trin Ch Canada 01-06; P-in-c King City All SS from 06. *All Saints Church, 12935 Keele Street, King City ON L4G 1R3, Canada* T: (001) (905) 833 5432 F: 833 2597

SKINNER, Paul Anthony. b 35. RD. Sarum Th Coll. **d** 09 **p** 10. NSM Sixpenny Handley w Gussage St Andrew etc *Sarum* from 09. *11 The Parsonage, Sixpenny Handley, Salisbury SP5 5QJ* T: (01785) 552785 E: paulofpaskin@rya-online.net

SKINNER, Raymond Frederick. b 45. St Jo Coll Dur BA 67 Dur Univ MA 93. Cranmer Hall Dur. **d** 70 **p** 71. C High Elswick St Paul *Newc* 70-76; V Newbottle *Dur* 76-87; Ind Chapl 81-87; RD Houghton 84-87; Chapl Oman 87-90; TR Morden *S'wark* 90-13; rtd 13; Public Preacher *S'wark* from 13. *6 Lawrence Avenue, Bidborough, Tunbridge Wells TN4 0XB* T: (01892) 525913 E: skinhicks@aol.com

SKINNER, Stephen John. b 52. Bris Univ BSc St Jo Coll Dur BA Dur Univ MLitt AIA. Cranmer Hall Dur. **d** 83 **p** 84. C Chatham St Phil and St Jas *Roch* 83-87; P-in-c Torver *Carl* 87-90; R 90-91; P-in-c Church Coniston 87-90; V 90-91; V Dalton-in-Furness 91-97; TR Carl H Trin and St Barn 97-02; TR W Swindon and the Lydiards *Bris* 02-09; TR Golden Cap Team *Sarum* from 09. *The Vicarage, 4 Dragons Hill, Lyme Regis DT7 3HW* T: (01297) 443763 E: sjmskinners@btinternet.com

SKINNER, Terri. *See* SKINNER, Elaine Teresa

SKIPPER, Kenneth Graham. b 34. St Aid Birkenhead 65. **d** 68 **p** 69. C Newland St Aug *York* 68-71; C Newby 71-74; V Dormanstown 74-78; V Aldbrough, Mappleton w Goxhill and Withernwick 79-89; R Londesborough 89-96; R Burnby 90-96; R Nunburnholme and Warter 90-96; V Shiptonthorpe w Hayton 90-96; rtd 96. *18 Elder Crescent, Bowmore, Isle of Islay PA43 7HU* T: (01496) 810321 M: 07776-373057
E: kgschurch@googlemail.com

SKIPPON, Kevin John. b 54. St Steph Ho Ox 78. **d** 81 **p** 82. C Gt Yarmouth *Nor* 81-84; C Kingstanding St Luke *Birm* 84-86; V Smethwick SS Steph and Mich 86-92; Chapl Derbyshire R Infirmary 92-94; Chapl Derbyshire R Infirmary NHS Trust 94-98; Chapl Derby Hosps NHS Foundn Trust 98-04 and 04-08; C Upminster *Chelmsf* 09-14; Chapl St Andr Healthcare 09-13; Chapl Havering Primary Care Trust 09-13; rtd 14. *Beech Cottage, 25 Banks Head, Bishops Castle SY9 5JL* T: (01588) 630777 E: kevin.skippon@asitis.me.uk

SKIPWORTH, Nicola Rachael. b 72. Southn Inst BA 95. Trin Coll Bris BA 01. **d** 01 **p** 02. C Bassaleg *Mon* 01-05; TV High Wycombe *Ox* 05-13; TV Carew *St D* 13-14; P-in-c Pembroke Dock from 14. *The Rectory, Church Street, Pembroke Dock SA72 6AR* T: (01646) 687825 M: 07720-201173
E: revnicky@btinternet.com

SKIRROW, Paul Richard. b 52. Hull Univ BA 82 Ches Coll of HE MTh 00. NOC 97. **d** 00 **p** 01. C St Luke in the City *Liv* 00-03; V Ditton St Mich w St Thos 03-07; Asst Dir CME 03-07; rtd 07; PtO *Ely* from 10. *Ferrar House, Little Gidding, Huntingdon PE28 5RJ* T: (01832) 293383 E: paulskirrow@googlemail.com

SKLIROS, Michael Peter. b 33. Clare Coll Cam BA 57 MA 62. Ridley Hall Cam 57. **d** 59 **p** 60. C Hornchurch St Andr *Chelmsf* 59-61; Asst Chapl Denstone Coll Uttoxeter 61-65; Chapl RAF 65-77; P-in-c Stowmarket *St E* 77-78; LtO 78-85; C Gt Finborough w Onehouse and Harleston 85-91; P-in-c 91; R Gt and Lt Bealings w Playford and Culpho 91-96; rtd 96; Hon Asst to Bp Brandon Canada 03-11. *2 Gordon Road, Oundle, Peterborough PE8 4LD* T: (01832) 358546
E: pifont2@gmail.com

SKOYLES, John Alan. b 32. Breakspear Coll 50 Christleton Hall 53. **d** 58 **p** 59. In RC Ch 59-80; Soc worker 80-99; NSM The Hydneye *Chich* 99-00; C Kenton, Mamhead, Powderham, Cofton and Starcross *Ex* 00-01. *18 Bodiam Crescent, Eastbourne BN22 9HQ* T: (01323) 504358

SKRINE, Charles Walter Douglas. b 75. Qu Coll Ox BA 98. Oak Hill Th Coll BA 03. **d** 03 **p** 04. C St Helen Bishopsgate w St Andr Undershaft etc *Lon* from 03. *73 Victoria Park Road, London E9 7NA* T: (020) 7283 2231
E: charles@cwdskrine.freeserve.co.uk

SKUBLICS, Ernest. b 36. Sant' Anselmo Univ Rome STB 62 Ottawa Univ MTh 64 STL 64 Nijmegen Univ DrTheol 67. **d** 73 **p** 73. R Whitewood Canada 73-76; Chapl Manitoba Univ 76-77; Soc Worker 77-86; Registrar and Asst Prof Manitoba Univ 86-90; Assoc Dir Inst for Th Studies Seattle Univ USA 90-93; Dean Graduate Sch Mt Angel Sem Oregon 93-00; C Hawley H Trin *Guildf* 04-07; rtd 07; PtO *Bradf* 08-11. *Broadfield House, Dent, Sedbergh LA10 5TG* T: (015396) 25296
E: eskublics1@freeuk.com

SKUCE, Canon David. b 56. NUU BSc 79 QUB PGCE 80 TCD BTh 89. CITC 87. **d** 89 **p** 90. C Templemore *D & R* 89-92; I Kilbarron w Rossnowlagh and Drumholm 92-99; I Urney w Sion Mills 99-06; Bp's Dom Chapl 94-06; I Maguiresbridge w Derrybrusk *Clogh* from 06; Preb Donaghmore St Patr Cathl Dublin from 11; Preb Clogh Cathl from 11. *The Rectory, 15 Drumgoon Road, Drumgoon, Maguiresbridge, Enniskillen BT94 4PB* T: (028) 6772 1250

SKUSE, Anne Martha. CITC. **d** 09 **p** 10. NSM Kilmocomogue *C, C & R* from 09. *Westlands, Crossmahon, Bandon, Co Cork, Republic of Ireland* T: (00353) (23) 8884 4306 M: 86-023 9699
E: anneskuse@eircom.net

SLACK, Michael. b 53. St Jo Coll Dur BA 74 Lon Univ PGCE 79 RGN 83. St Steph Ho Ox 74. **d** 76 **p** 77. C Wolverhampton St Steph *Lich* 76-77; NSM Bywell *Newc* 89-93; TV Cullercoats St Geo 93-98; TR 98-05. *Address temp unknown*

SLACK, Mrs Moira Elizabeth. b 52. Brunel Univ BTech 74 Leeds Univ BA 06. NOC 03. **d** 06 **p** 07. C Heaton Ch Ch *Man* 06-09; P-in-c Stretford All SS 09-14; C Bolton St Pet w St Phil from 14. *50 Devonshire Road, Bolton BL1 4PQ* T: (01204) 841865
E: moslack@btinternet.com

SLADDEN, Daniel John. b 69. K Coll Cam BA 91 MA 95. Yorks Min Course. **d** 12 **p** 13. NSM Ingleby Barwick *York* from 12. *27 Front Street, Sowerby, Thirsk YO7 1JQ* T: (01845) 527793
E: dan@sladden.com

SLADDEN, John David. b 49. RN Eng Coll Plymouth BSc 74 St Edm Coll Cam MA 86. Ridley Hall Cam 80. **d** 83 **p** 84. C St Bees *Carl* 83-85; PtO *Lich* 85-87; Miss Co-ord Down to Earth Evangelistic Trust 85-87; V Doncaster St Jas *Sheff* 87-94; PtO *Ely* from 07. *9 Teal Close, Chatteris PE16 6PR* T: (01354) 694097 E: jds25@cantab.net

SLADE, Canon Adrian Barrie. b 47. K Alfred's Coll Win DipEd 68. St Jo Coll Nottm BTh 73 ALCD 72. **d** 73 **p** 74. C Streatham Immanuel w St Anselm *S'wark* 73-76; C Chipping Barnet *St Alb* 76-78; C Chipping Barnet w Arkley 78-80; V Sundon 80-85; Soc Resp Officer *Glouc* 86-12; Hon Can Glouc Cathl 91-12; rtd 12. *16 Conway Road, Hucclecote, Gloucester GL3 3PL* T: (01452) 372468 E: glossr@star.co.uk

SLADE, Alfred Laurence. b 12. ACII. Roch Th Coll 67. **d** 69 **p** 70. NSM Cliftonville *Cant* 69-71; NSM Westgate St Jas 71-75; PtO *Sarum* 75-81; *Cant* 81-93. *21 McKinlay Court, The Parade, Birchington CT7 9QG* T: (01843) 46882

SLADE, Michael John. b 55. Trin Coll Bris 94. **d** 96 **p** 97. C Blagdon w Compton Martin and Ubley *B & W* 96-99; V Winscombe and Sandford 99-10; RD Locking 05-08; V Chollerton w Birtley and Thockrington *Newc* from 10. *The Vicarage, Chollerton, Hexham NE46 4TF* T: (01434) 681721
E: chollertonvicar@gmail.com

SLADEN, Mrs Katharine Anne. b 78. Dur Univ BA 99 Leic Univ MSc 04. St Mellitus Coll BA 11. **d** 11. C Easthampstead *Ox* 11-12; Hon C Westminster St Jas the Less *Lon* 12-13. *19B Sussex Street, London SW1V 4RR* M: 07941-939141
E: kate@popvote.co.uk

SLATER, Andrew Kenneth. b 62. Reading Univ BA 84 PGCE 85 Open Univ MA 99. ERMC 10. **d** 13 **p** 14. NSM Wymondham *Nor* from 13. *The Battle, 110 Norwich Road, Attleborough NR17 2JY* T: (01953) 455046 M: 07850-924575
E: slatera@wymondhamhigh.co.uk

SLATER, Canon Ann. b 46. Somerville Coll Ox BA 67 MA 71. WMMTC 92. **d** 95 **p** 96. C Northampton St Benedict *Pet* 95-99; TV Daventry, Ashby St Ledgers, Braunston etc 99-05; R Heyford w Stowe Nine Churches and Flore etc 05-14; RD Daventry 08-13; Can Pet Cathl 10-14; rtd 14; PtO *Pet* from 15. *34 Millway, Northampton NN5 6ES*   T: (01604) 586014
E: ann.slater@btinternet.com

SLATER, Carol Ann. *See* COSLETT, Carol Ann

SLATER, Christopher Richard. b 69. Oak Hill Th Coll BA 08. **d** 08. C Rock Ferry *Ches* 08-12; C Tranmere St Cath 08-12; V Rock Ferry from 12. *The Vicarage, St Peter's Road, Birkenhead CH42 1PY*   T: 0151-645 1622   M: 07899-807507
E: slater.cr@btinternet.com

SLATER, David. *See* SLATER, Philip David

SLATER (née SAMMONS), Mrs Elizabeth Mary. b 71. RN 94 RHV 98. Wycliffe Hall Ox 03. **d** 05 **p** 06. C Stoke Gifford *Bris* 05-09; PtO from 09. *20 Railton Jones Close, Stoke Gifford, Bristol BS34 8BF* E: wizsammons@hotmail.com

SLATER, Ian Stuart. b 47. St Jo Coll Nottm BA 07. **d** 04 **p** 05. NSM Gt Horton *Bradf* 04-11; P-in-c 11-12; C Fairweather Green *Leeds* 12-14. *Stable Cottage, 5 The Drive, Denholme, Bradford BD13 4DY*   T: (01274) 831437
E: revianslater@gmail.com

SLATER, James Richard David. b 61. New Univ of Ulster BA 83 TCD BTh 89 Univ of Ulster MA 92. CITC 86. **d** 89 **p** 90. C Clooney w Strathfoyle *D & R* 89-93; I Aghadowey w Kilrea 93-05; I Cumber Upper w Learmount from 05; Bp's Dom Chapl from 07. *The Rectory, 91 Cumber Road, Claudy, Londonderry BT47 4JA*   T: (028) 7133 7883

SLATER, John Ralph. b 38. Kent Univ BA 90. Linc Th Coll 71. **d** 73 **p** 74. C S Hackney St Mich w Haggerston St Paul *Lon* 73-74; C Leytonstone St Marg w St Columba *Chelmsf* 74-77; C Whitstable All SS w St Pet *Cant* 77-80; V Gt Ilford St Alb *Chelmsf* 80-83; V Clipstone *S'well* 83-87; rtd 87. *4 Rowena Road, Westgate-on-Sea CT8 8NQ*   T: (01227) 831593

SLATER, Mark Andrew. b 56. ARCS 79 Imp Coll Lon BSc 79. Ridley Hall Cam 87. **d** 89 **p** 90. C Northampton St Giles *Pet* 89-92; C Stopsley *St Alb* 92-93; C-in-c Bushmead CD 93-99; V St Alb St Luke from 99; RD St Alb from 15. *St Luke's Vicarage, 46 Cell Barnes Lane, St Albans AL1 5QJ*   T: (01727) 865399
F: 865399   E: mark.slater@saint-lukes.co.uk

SLATER, Paul John. b 73. St Jo Coll Nottm 10. **d** 12 **p** 13. C Skirbeck H Trin *Linc* from 12. *17 Linley Drive, Boston PE21 7EJ*   M: 07863-164134   E: paul.slaterclan@sky.com

✠**SLATER, The Rt Revd Paul John.** b 58. CCC Ox MA 83 St Jo Coll Dur BA 83. Cranmer Hall Dur 81. **d** 84 **p** 85 **c** 15. C Keighley St Andr *Bradf* 84-88; P-in-c Cullingworth and Dir Dioc Foundn Course 88-93; Bp's Personal Exec Asst 93-95; Warden of Readers 92-96; R Haworth *Bradf* 95-01; Bp's Officer for Min and Miss *Leeds* 01-15; Adn Craven *Bradf* 05-14; Adn Richmond and Craven *Leeds* 14-15; Suff Bp Richmond from 15. *4 Borrowdale Court, 5 Clifton Drive, Menston, Ilkley LS29 6FZ*   E: paul.slater@westyorkshiredales.anglican.org

SLATER, Capt Philip. b 55. Wilson Carlile Coll 76. **d** 12. Asst Chapl RN from 12. *Royal Naval Chaplaincy Service, Mail Point 1.2, Leach Building, Whale Island, Portsmouth PO2 8BY*   T: (023) 9262 5055   F: 9262 5134

SLATER, Canon Philip David. b 27. K Coll Lon 58. **d** 60 **p** 61. C Havant *Portsm* 60-67; C Leigh Park 68-69; Hants Co RE Adv 69-74; Gosport and Fareham RE Adv 74-82; Hon C Bishop's Waltham *Portsm* 76-82; V Bulford, Figheldean and Milston *Sarum* 82-93; RD Avon 85-95; Can and Preb Sarum Cathl 91-95; V Avon Valley 93-95; rtd 95; V of Close Sarum Cathl 95-02; Chapl Godolphin Sch 95-04; PtO *Sarum* from 05; *Win* 06-14. *102 Coombe Road, Salisbury SP2 8BD*   T: (01722) 332529
E: voc@salcath.co.uk

SLATER, Robert Adrian. b 48. St Jo Coll Nottm 76. **d** 79 **p** 80. C Bedworth *Cov* 79-82; TV Billericay and Lt Burstead *Chelmsf* 82-88; V Rounds Green *Birm* 88-94; rtd 07. *11 Lewis Road, Birmingham B30 2SU*   T: 0121-689 2721
E: robslater@freeuk.com

SLATER, Thomas Ernest. b 37. Chelsea Coll Lon TCert 60 Lon Univ BD 71. ALCD 66. **d** 67 **p** 68. C Bootle Ch Ch *Liv* 67-72; C Stapleford *S'well* 72-75; Supt Tower Hamlets Miss 75-77; Hon C Stepney St Pet w St Benet *Lon* 78-79; Asst Chapl The Lon Hosp (Whitechapel) 79-83; Chapl 83-89; NSM Poplar *Lon* 89-92 and 94-02; PtO *Lon* 92-94; rtd 02. *11 Elgin House, Cordelia Street, London E14 6EG*   T: (020) 7987 4504
E: allsaints.poplar@tiscali.co.uk

SLATER, Victoria Ruth. b 59. Hertf Coll Ox BA 82 MA 87 Selw Coll Cam BA 89 MA 94. Westcott Ho Cam 86. **d** 89 **p** 94. Chapl Asst Man R Infirmary 89-90; Chapl 90-94; Chapl St Mary's Hosp Man 90-94; Chapl Ox Radcliffe Hosp NHS Trust 94-97; Chapl Sir Michael Sobell Ho Palliative Care Unit 97-05; Asst Soc Resp Adv *Ox* 05-07; Chapl Care Co-ord N Lon Hospice 07-08; Research and Development Officer Ox

Cen for Ecclesiology and Practical Th 09-13. *Address temp unknown*

SLATER, Preb William Edward. b 51. Aston Tr Scheme 85 Oak Hill Th Coll 87. **d** 89 **p** 90. C Balderstone *Man* 89-94; V Newchapel *Lich* from 94; RD Stoke N 99-08 and from 12; Preb Lich Cathl from 08. *The Vicarage, 32 Pennyfield Road, Newchapel, Stoke-on-Trent ST7 4PN*   T: (01782) 782837
E: willslater@tinyworld.co.uk

SLATTER, Barrie John. b 44. Nottm Univ BSc 66 FRICS 97. Dioc OLM tr scheme 97. **d** 00 **p** 01. OLM Hundred River *St E* 00-03; C Alde River 03-06; R 06-14; rtd 14; PtO *St E* from 14. *Moor Farm Barn, Kings Lane, Sotherton, Beccles NR34 8AF*
T: (01986) 872100   M: 07802-924738
E: barrie.rectory@btinternet.com

SLATTERY, Maurice Michael. b 43. Southlands Coll Lon TCert 73 Lon Inst of Educn BEd 74. S'wark Ord Course 91. **d** 94 **p** 95. NSM Malden St Jas *S'wark* 94-97; NSM Niton, Whitwell and St Lawrence *Portsm* 97-99; NSM Selsdon St Jo w St Fran *S'wark* 99-03; PtO *Portsm* 03-04 and 07-08 and from 09; P-in-c St Lawrence 04-06; NSM Clayton w Keymer *Chich* 08-09; P-in-c Burpham from 13; P-in-c Poling from 13. *The Vicarage, Burpham, Arundel BN18 9RJ*
E: mauricemslattery@hotmail.com

SLAUGHTER, Clive Patrick. b 36. St Paul's Coll Grahamstown. **d** 77 **p** 78. S Africa 77-87; R Thorley w Bishop's Stortford H Trin *St Alb* 87-90; R Thorley 90-01; RD Bishop's Stortford 96-01; rtd 01; PtO *St Alb* 01-03; P-in-c Much Hadham 03-04; P-in-c Braughing w Furneux Pelham and Stocking Pelham 04-05. *53 High Street, Hunsdon, Ware SG12 8QB*
T: (01279) 844955   E: clive.slaughter@virgin.net

SLAVIC, Jean-Sacha (Sacha). b 68. **d** 12 **p** 13. NSM Foleshill St Laur *Cov* 12-14; NSM Cov Cathl from 15; Chapl Bablake Sch Cov from 14. *1 Crown Green, Coventry CV6 6FA*
T: (024) 7627 1200   M: 07714-288352

SLAYEN, Karen Elizabeth. b 59. **d** 12 **p** 13. OLM Atherton and Hindsford w Howe Bridge *Man* from 12. *51 Treen Road, Astley, Tyldesley, Manchester M29 7HD*   T: (01942) 891154
M: 07966-643950   E: karenslayen@aol.com

SLEDGE, The Ven Richard Kitson. b 30. Peterho Cam BA 52 MA 57. Ridley Hall Cam 52. **d** 54 **p** 55. C Compton Gifford *Ex* 54-57; C Ex St Martin, St Steph, St Laur etc 57-63; V Dronfield *Derby* 63-76; TR 76-78; RD Chesterfield 72-78; Adn Huntingdon *Ely* 78-96; R Hemingford Abbots 78-89; Hon Can Ely Cathl 78-99; rtd 96; Bp's Dom Chapl *Ely* 96-99; Retired Clergy Officer 98-07; Asst (Huntingdon/Pet Area) from 07; PtO from 99. *7 Budge Close, Brampton, Huntingdon PE28 4PL*   T: (01480) 380284 *or* (01353) 662749
F: (01480) 437789   E: rksledge@supanet.com

SLEDGE, Canon Timothy Charles Kitson. b 64. Coll of Ripon & York St Jo BA 87 York Univ MA 88. Trin Coll Bris. **d** 95 **p** 96. C Huddersfield St Thos *Wakef* 95-98; V Luddenden w Luddenden Foot 98-03; P-in-c Sowerby 02-03; Dioc Miss Enabler *Pet* 03-08; V Romsey *Win* from 08; AD 13; Hon Can Win Cathl from 14. *The Vicarage, Church Lane, Romsey SO51 8EP*   T: (01794) 513125   E: vicarofromsey@gmail.com

SLEE, John Graham. b 51. Brunel Univ BTech 73. Oak Hill Th Coll 85. **d** 87 **p** 88. C St Columb Minor and St Colan *Truro* 87-91; R St Mawgan w St Ervan and St Eval 91-02; RD Pydar 93-95; P-in-c St Just-in-Roseland and St Mawes 02-07; rtd 07; PtO *Ox* from 08. *4 Mill View House, Aalborg Place, Lancaster LA1 1AU*   E: john@nbepiphany.co.uk

SLEEMAN, Matthew Timothy. b 68. St Cath Coll Cam BA 90 MA 95 PhD 96 K Coll Lon PhD 07. Wycliffe Hall Ox BA 97 MA 07. **d** 99 **p** 00. C Eynsham and Cassington *Ox* 98-02; PtO *Lon* 03-06; *St Alb* from 03; Oak Hill Th Coll from 06. *Oak Hill College, Chase Side, London N14 4PS*   T: (020) 8449 0467

SLEGG, John Edward. b 36. St Pet Coll Ox BA 62 MA 66. Ridley Hall Cam 62. **d** 64 **p** 65. C Perranzabuloe *Truro* 64-66; CF 66-86; V Lyminster and Poling *Chich* 86-05; rtd 06. *4 Bakers Meadow, Billingshurst RH14 9GG*   T: (01403) 784362

SLEIGHT, Gordon Frederick. b 47. AKC 69. St Aug Coll Cant 69. **d** 70 **p** 71. C Boston *Linc* 70-74; P-in-c Louth St Mich and Stewton 74; TV Louth 74-81; V Crosby 81-95; P-in-c Nettleham 95-97; V 97-05; RD Lawres 04-05; rtd 05; LtO *Mor* from 05. *Elderbank, Stoer, Lochinver, Lairg IV27 4JE*
T: (01571) 855207   E: gsassynt@gmail.com

SLENNETT, Mrs Jane Alison. b 57. St Mich Coll Llan. **d** 08. NSM Aberavon *Llan* from 08. *42 Carlton Place, Porthcawl CF36 3ET*
T: (01656) 784840   E: deacon@parishofaberavon.com

SLIM, David Albert. b 49. Westhill Coll Birm CertEd 72. Linc Th Coll 90. **d** 90 **p** 91. C Walmley *Birm* 90-93; R Marchwiel and Isycoed *St As* 93-03; TV Wrexham 03-08; Chapl Ellesmere Coll 08-15; rtd 15. *Caradoc, Shotton Lane, Harmer Hill, Shrewsbury SY12 9BE*   T: (01939) 291174
E: rev.david.slim@btinternet.com

SLIPPER, Charles Callan. b 55. Lanc Univ BA 77 PhD 84. S Dios Minl Tr Scheme 91. **d** 93 **p** 94. Focolare Movement from 77;

NSM N Acton St Gabr *Lon* 93-96. *138 Parkway, Welwyn Garden City AL8 6HP*   T: (01707) 339242
E: callanslipper@btconnect.com

SLIPPER, Robert James. b 64. St Jo Coll Cam BA 87 MA 91. Wycliffe Hall Ox BA 92. d 92 p 93. C Southgate *Chich* 92-95; C Stoughton *Guildf* 95-00; V Terrington St Clement *Ely* from 00. *The Vicarage, 27 Sutton Road, Terrington St Clement, King's Lynn PE34 4PQ*   T: (01553) 828430   E: rjslipper@dsl.pipex.com

SLOAN, William. b 49. Lanc Univ CertEd 78 BEd 79 Cumbria Univ MA 11. CBDTI 04. d 07 p 08. NSM Croston and Bretherton *Blackb* 07-10; NSM Hoole 10-11; PtO 11-13; NSM Hesketh w Becconsall 13-15; rtd 15; NSM *Blackb* from 15. *5 Red House Lane, Eccleston, Chorley PR7 5RH*   T: (01257) 453665 M: 07721-923001 E: billsloan5@btinternet.com

SLOANE, Andrew Leslie. b 53. St Edm Hall Ox MA 76 Nashotah Ho Wisconsin MTS 78 Hon DD 05. Ripon Coll Cuddesdon 76. d 78 p 79. C Schenectady St Geo USA 78-81; C New York St Mary V 82-89; R Sheboygan 89-98; R Washington St Paul 98-13; C Wilton Place St Paul *Lon* from 13. *Flat 7, 32-33 Wilton Place, London SW1X 8SH*   T: (020) 7201 9996
E: andrewsloane@spkb.org

SLOANE, Niall James. b 81. TCD BA 03. CITC 03. d 05 p 06. C Agherton *Conn* 05-07; C Taney *D & G* 07-12; I Killiney H Trin from 12; Min Can St Patr Cathl Dublin from 08; Abp's Dom Chapl *D & G* from 08. *Holy Trinity Rectory, Killiney Road, Killiney, Co Dublin, Republic of Ireland*   T: (00353) (1) 285 2695 E: rector.htkilliney@dublin.anglican.org

SLOGGETT, Donald George. b 49. Trin Coll Bris 81. d 83 p 84. C Horfield H Trin *Bris* 83-86; C Highworth w Sevenhampton and Inglesham etc 86-88; P-in-c Upavon w Rushall *Sarum* 88-90; R Upavon w Rushall and Charlton 90-01; R Stoulton w Drake's Broughton and Pirton etc *Worc* from 01. *The Rectory, Manor Farm, Stoulton, Worcester WR7 4RS*   T: (01905) 840528 E: donsloggett@zetnet.co.uk

SLOW, Leslie John. b 47. Liv Univ BSc 68 MSc 69. NOC 77. d 80 p 81. NSM Gt Horton *Bradf* 80-07; PtO *York* from 08. *21 Mile End Park, Pocklington, York YO42 2TH*   T: (01759) 303888 E: les@theslows.plus.com

SLUMAN, Richard Geoffrey Davies. b 34. St Jo Coll Ox BA 68 MA 68. Sarum Th Coll 68. d 70 p 71. C Gt Yarmouth *Nor* 70-73; V Churchdown *Glouc* 73-82; P-in-c Blockley w Aston Magna 82-83; V Blockley w Aston Magna and Bourton on the Hill 83-94; rtd 94; PtO *Cov* 94-10. *21 Manor Farm Road, Tredington, Shipston-on-Stour CV36 4NZ*   T: (01608) 662317

SLUSAR (née WOODLEY), Priscilla Elizabeth. b 54. Univ of Wales (Abth) BA 75 Homerton Coll Cam PGCE 76. Westcott Ho Cam 08. d 10 p 11. C Codsall *Lich* 10-14; R Bernwode *Ox* from 14. *The Vicarage, 7 High Street, Brill, Aylesbury HP18 9ST*   T: (01494) 238325   M: 07812-851839 E: priscillaslusar@fsmail.net

SLY, Canon Christopher John. b 34. Selw Coll Cam BA 58 MA 62. Wycliffe Hall Ox. d 60 p 61. C Buckhurst Hill *Chelmsf* 60-64; V Berechurch 64-75; V Southend St Sav Westcliff 75-87; R Wickham Bishops w Lt Braxted 87-99; RD Witham 87-96; Hon Can Chelmsf Cathl 93-99; rtd 99. *Ludlow Cottage, Church Lane, Little Leighs, Chelmsford CM3 1PQ*   T: (01245) 361489

SLYFIELD, Mrs Margaret Medi. b 61. Linc Sch of Th and Min 11. d 14 p 15. NSM Buxton w Burbage and King Sterndale *Derby* from 14. *Old Shoe Shop, Queen Street, Tideswell, Buxton SK17 8JT*   T: (01298) 871478 E: mmslyfield@yahoo.co.uk

SMAIL, Richard Charles. b 57. CCC Ox BA 80 MA 83. Ox Min Course 90. d 93 p 95. NSM Keble Coll Ox 93-96; Chapl, Fell and Lect BNC Ox 97-02; PtO *Ox* 02-05; P-in-c Rousham from 05. *Top Flat, 256 Abingdon Road, Oxford OX1 4S P*   T: (01865) 245553   E: richardsmail@supanet.com

SMAILES, Ian Collingwood. b 46. Brighton Poly BSc 71. NTMTC BA 07. d 07 p 08. NSM Laleham *Lon* from 07. *Gadebridge House, 211 Thames Side, Staines TW18 1UF*   T: (01784) 461195 E: ianandrosalind@gmail.com

SMALE, Frederick Ronald. b 37. K Coll Lon BD 60 AKC 60. d 61 p 62. C Bearsted *Cant* 61-64; C Fishponds St Mary *Bris* 64-69; V Hartlip *Cant* 69-71; P-in-c Stockbury w Bicknor and Huckinge 69-71; V Hartlip w Stockbury 71-75; R River 75-85; V Birchington w Acol and Minnis Bay 85-00; rtd 00; PtO *Cant* from 01. *28 Margate Road, Broomfield, Herne Bay CT6 7BL*   T: (01227) 283880

SMALE, Ian Keith. b 53. Wycliffe Hall Ox 98. d 00 p 01. C Overton w Laverstoke and Freefolk *Win* 00-04; P-in-c E Dean w Friston and Jevington *Chich* 04-06; R 06-08; P-in-c Overton w Laverstoke and Freefolk *Win* from 08; P-in-c N Waltham and Steventon, Ashe and Deane from 11. *The Rectory, 54 Lordsfield Gardens, Overton, Basingstoke RG25 3EW*   T: (01256) 770207   E: iansue.smale@btinternet.co.uk

SMALE, Ian Stuart. b 49. d 07. NSM Chich Cathl from 07. *9 Canal Place, Chichester PO19 8DR*   M: 07973-747694

SMALE, Mrs Irene Euphemia. b 52. Chich Univ BA Win Univ MA. d 14. C Chich St Pancras and St Jo from 14. *Diocesan Church House, 211 New Church Road, Hove BN3 4ED*   T: (01273) 421021   M: 07980-617584
E: irene.smale@chichester.anglican.org

SMALING, Christopher James. b 72. Bath Univ BSc 93 K Coll Lon PGCE 95. STETS 11. d 14 p 15. NSM Aldersbrook *Chelmsf* from 14. *84 St James Road, London E15 1RN*   M: 07977-564035

SMALL, David Binney. b 39. Brasted Th Coll 61 Westcott Ho Cam 63. d 65 p 66. C Milton *Portsm* 65-69; CF 69-92; R Wickwar w Rangeworthy *Glouc* 92-97; RD Hawkesbury 94-97; rtd 97; PtO *Glouc* from 97; Sub Chapl HM Pris Glouc 98-01. *6 Malvern Drive, Thornbury, Bristol BS35 2HY*

SMALL, Gordon Frederick. b 41. St Jo Coll Nottm 77. d 79 p 80. C Belper *Derby* 79-84; NSM Matlock Bath 90-91; C Ripley 91-93; TV Bucknall and Bagnall *Lich* 93-98; Assoc P Deal St Leon w St Rich and Sholden etc *Cant* 98-06; rtd 06. *10 Elmer Close, Malmesbury SN16 9UE*   T: (01666) 823722 E: gordon.small1@btopenworld.com

SMALL, Marcus Jonathan. b 67. Univ of Wales (Ban) BD 94 St Jo Coll Dur MA 13. Ripon Coll Cuddesdon 94. d 96 p 97. C Moseley St Mary *Birm* 96-99; TV Wenlock *Heref* 99-05; R Eardisley w Bollingham, Willersley, Brilley etc from 05; RD Kington and Weobley 12-14. *Church House, Church Road, Eardisley, Hereford HR3 6NN*   T: (01544) 327440 E: rector@eardisleygroup.org.uk

SMALL, Mrs Shirley Maureen. b 45. WEMTC. d 09 p 10. NSM Pontesbury I and II *Heref* from 09. *Nills Farm House, Habberley Road, Pontesbury, Shrewsbury SY5 0TN*   T: (01743) 791885

SMALL, Simon William. b 57. Cuddesdon Coll. d 98 p 99. C Kidderminster St Mary and All SS w Trimpley etc *Worc* 98-01; Chapl to Bp Dudley 01-07; PtO from 08; Chapl Abbey Ho Retreat Glastonbury *B & W* from 11. *The Coach House, Abbey House Retreat, Chilkwell Street, Glastonbury BA6 8DH*   T: (01458) 835503   E: simon@simonsmall.info

SMALLDON, The Ven Keith. b 48. Open Univ BA 76 Newc Univ MA 94. St Mich Coll Llan. d 71 p 72. C Cwmbran *Mon* 71-73; C Chepstow 73-75; Dioc Youth Adv *Bradf* 75-79; P-in-c Woolfold *Man* 82-85; Dioc Youth and Community Officer 82-90; P-in-c Thursby *Carl* 90-94; Dir of Clergy Tr 90-94; TR Daventry, Ashby St Ledgers, Braunston etc *Pet* 94-98; Chapl Danetre Hosp 94-98; TR Llantwit Major *Llan* 98-03; Can Res Brecon Cathl 03-11; Dioc Dir of Min 03-11; P-in-c Swansea St Barn 08-11; Adn St D 11-13; P-in-c Steynton 11-13; rtd 13; PtO *Ox* from 13. *41 Horsham Close, Banbury OX16 1XP*   T: (01295) 269281   E: keithsmalldon@btinternet.com

SMALLEY, The Very Revd Stephen Stewart. b 31. Jes Coll Cam BA 55 MA 58 PhD 79. Eden Th Sem (USA) BD 57 Ridley Hall Cam. d 58 p 59. C Portman Square St Paul *Lon* 58-60; Chapl Peterho Cam 60-63; Dean 62-63; Lect RS Ibadan Univ Nigeria 63-69; Lect Th Man Univ 70-77; Can Res and Prec Cov Cathl 77-87; Vice-Provost 86-87; Dean Ches 87-01; rtd 01; PtO *Glouc* from 02. *The Old Hall, The Folly, Longborough, Moreton-in-Marsh GL56 0QS*   T: (01451) 830238   E: stephen@sssss.fsworld.co.uk

SMALLMAN, Miss Margaret Anne. b 43. Hull Univ BSc 64 Bris Univ CertEd 65. St Jo Coll Nottm. dss 83 d 87 p 94. Bromsgrove St Jo *Worc* 83-88; Par Dn 87-88; Par Dn Stoke Prior, Wychbold and Upton Warren 88-90; Team Dn Tettenhall Wood *Lich* 91-94; TV 94-99; P-in-c W Bromwich H Trin 99-08; C W Bromwich Gd Shep w St Jo 99-08; RD W Bromwich 04-08; rtd 08; PtO *Lich* 08-09; Hon C Wellington All SS w Eyton from 09. *10 St Agatha's Close, Telford TF1 3QP*   T: (01952) 253643 E: mas@msmallman.fsnet.co.uk

SMALLMAN, The Ven Wilhelmina Tokcumboh. b 56. Cen Sch Speech & Drama BEd 88 Middx Univ BA 06. NTMTC 03. d 06 p 08. C S Harrow St Paul *Lon* 06-07; C Gt Stanmore 07-10; TV Barking *Chelmsf* 10-13; Adn Southend from 13. *459 Rayleigh Road, Benfleet SS7 3TH*   T: (01268) 779345 E: minaexp@hotmail.com *or* a.southend@chelmsford.anglican.org

SMALLS, Peter Harry. b 34. FCCA. d 97 p 98. OLM Castleacre w Newton, Rougham and Southacre *Nor* 97-99; OLM Narborough w Narford 97-99; OLM Pentney St Mary Magd w W Bilney 97-99; OLM Westacre 97-99; OLM Narborough w Narford and Pentney 99-02; PtO from 03; *St E* from 07. *Windward, Drapers Lane, Ditchingham, Bungay NR35 2JW*   T: (01986) 894667   E: peter@smalls6740.freeserve.co.uk

SMALLWOOD, Simon Laurence. b 58. St Jo Coll Dur BSc 80. Cranmer Hall Dur 89. d 92 p 93. C Stapenhill w Cauldwell *Derby* 92-96; TV Dagenham *Chelmsf* 96-03; V Becontree St Geo from 03. *The Vicarage, 86 Rogers Road, Dagenham RM10 8JX*   T: (020) 8593 2760   E: thesmallies@ntlworld.com

SMART, Barry Anthony Ignatius. b 57. Lanc Univ BEd 79. St Steph Ho Ox 85. d 88 p 89. C Wantage *Ox* 88-91;

C Abingdon 91-93; TV 93-95; C Princes Risborough w Ilmer 95-97; C Kingstanding St Luke *Birm* 97-00; V Small Heath 00-09; Chapl Compton Hospice 09-13; V Kingstanding St Luke *Birm* from 13. *The Clergy House, 49 Caversham Road, Birmingham B44 0LW* T: 0121-354 3281 M: 07952-663872
E: frbarrysmart@yahoo.co.uk

SMART, Mrs Carol. b 45. SSF SRN 67. S Dios Minl Tr Scheme 89. d 92 p 94. Chapl Isle of Wight Healthcare NHS Trust 92-99; NSM Shorwell w Kingston *Portsm* 99-02; NSM Gatcombe 92-02; NSM Chale 92-02; PtO from 02. *20 Sydney Close, Shide, Newport PO30 1YG* T: (01983) 526242
E: revcarolsmart@tiscali.co.uk

SMART, Gillian Mary. b 52. All SS Cen for Miss & Min 12. d 15. OLM Horwich and Rivington *Man* from 15. *18 Grosvenor Way, Horwich, Bolton BL6 6DJ* T: (01204) 486271
E: g.m.smart@btinternet.com

SMART, Harry Gavin. b 67. St D Coll Lamp BA 90 Sheff Hallam Univ MA 06. Westcott Ho Cam 90. d 94 p 95. C Thirsk *York* 94-97; C Sheff St Leon Norwood 97-99; Mental Health Chapl Sheff Care Trust 99-06; Lead Mental Health Chapl Lincs Partnership NHS Foundn Trust 07-13. *Address temp unknown*
E: harry.smart@lpft.nhs.uk

SMART, Canon Haydn Christopher. b 38. Wells Th Coll 66. d 69 p 70. C Hillmorton *Cov* 69-72; C Duston *Pet* 72-75; V Woodford Halse 75-79; V Woodford Halse w Eydon 79-82; V Wellingborough All SS 82-92; RD Wellingborough 87-92; V Longthorpe 92-03; Can Pet Cathl 92-03; RD Pet 96-01; rtd 03; P-in-c Madeira *Eur* 03-06; PtO *Pet* from 06; Chapl to Retired Clergy and Clergy Widows' Officer from 08. *4 Silvester Road, Castor, Peterborough PE5 7BA* T: (01733) 380460
E: havenincastor@btinternet.com

SMART, Mrs Hilary Jean. b 42. SOAS Lon BA 63. EMMTC 85. d 88 p 94. Par Dn Walsall Pleck and Bescot *Lich* 88-94; TV Sheff Manor 94-02; Bp's Ecum Officer 94-02; rtd 02; Chapl Compton Hospice 02-06. *77 Denton Drive, West Bridgford, Nottingham NG2 7FS* T: 0115-923 1097

SMART, John Francis. b 36. Keble Coll Ox BA 59 MA 69. Cuddesdon Coll 59. d 61 p 66. C Cannock *Lich* 61-63; Hon C Gt Wyrley 63-66; C Wednesfield St Thos 66-70; V Brereton 70-85; R E Clevedon and Walton w Weston w Clapton *B & W* 85-02; Chapl Southmead Health Services NHS Trust 85-99; Chapl N Bris NHS Trust 99-02; rtd 02; P-in-c Hatherleigh, Meeth, Exbourne and Jacobstowe *Ex* 05-07. *Sunnymead, Ford Cross, South Zeal, Okehampton EX20 2JL* T: (01837) 840233
E: jandrsmart@btinternet.com

SMART, Lorraine Ann. St Mellitus Coll 14. d 15. OLM Loughton St Mich *Chelmsf* from 15. *30 Stonards Hill, Loughton IG10 3EG* T: (020) 8502 2017

SMART, Neil Robert. b 61. Bris Univ BVSc 84. Ridley Hall Cam 01. d 03 p 04. C Shirley *Win* 03-07; P-in-c Brockenhurst 07-11; V from 11; P-in-c Boldre w S Baddesley 09-11; V from 11. *The Vicarage, Meerut Road, Brockenhurst SO42 7TD* T: (01590) 623309 E: somesmarts@btopenworld.com

SMART, Richard Henry. b 23. Lon Univ BA 51. Oak Hill Th Coll. d 53 p 54. C Bedworth *Cov* 53-56; C New Malden and Coombe *S'wark* 56-59; V Hanley Road St Sav w St Paul *Lon* 59-71; V Plumstead All SS *S'wark* 71-88; rtd 88; PtO *Chich* from 88. *2 Annington Road, Eastbourne BN22 8NG* T: (01323) 726850

SMART, Russell Martin. b 79. Moorlands Coll BA 06 Anglia Ruskin Univ MA 11. Ridley Hall Cam 09. d 11 p 12. C Romford Gd Shep *Chelmsf* 11-15; C N Farnborough *Guildf* from 15. *3 Forth Close, Farnborough GU14 9NZ* T: (01252) 540810 E: russ@goodshepherdchurch.org.uk

SMEATON, William Brian Alexander. b 37. CITC 69. d 71 p 72. C Belfast St Luke *Conn* 71-81; I Tullyaughnish w Kilmacrennan and Killygarvan *D & R* 81-02; Bp's Dom Chapl 87-02; Can Raphoe Cathl 88-02; Dioc Radio Officer 90-02; rtd 02. *Bearna Ghaoithe, Drumcavney, Trentagh, Letterkenny, Co Donegal, Republic of Ireland* M: 74-913 7917
E: smeaton@indigo.ie

SMEDLEY, Christopher John. b 62. Trent Poly BSc 90. St Jo Coll Nottm MA 98. d 98 p 99. C Cotmanhay *Derby* 98-02; R Wilne and Draycott w Breaston from 02. *The Rectory, 68 Risley Lane, Breaston, Derby DE72 3AU* T: (01332) 872242
E: smedley7@btinternet.com

SMEDLEY, Paul Mark. b 59. Bris Univ BA 80 Lanc Univ MA 81. S Dios Minl Tr Scheme 89. d 92 p 93. NSM Acton St Mary *Lon* 92-08; PtO from 08. *12 Baldwin Gardens, London W3 6HH* T: (020) 8993 5527 *or* 8932 8497 F: 8932 8315
E: paul@planningforum.co.uk

SMEETON (*née* GRESHAM), Mrs Karen Louise. b 75. Hull Univ LLB 96. Ripon Coll Cuddesdon BA 01. d 02 p 03. C Leesfield *Man* 02-05; V Hamer 05-11; P-in-c Spotland 11-13; C Oakenrod and Bamford 11-13; V Spotland and Oakenrod from 13. *13 Brooklands Court, Rochdale OL11 4EJ*
E: therevdk-smeeton@yahoo.co.uk

SMEETON, Nicholas Guy. b 74. Trin Hall Cam MA 99. Ripon Coll Cuddesdon BA 03. d 04 p 05. C Ashton Ch Ch *Man* 04-07; P-in-c Oldham St Steph and All Martyrs 07-11; TV Oldham 07-11; V Coldhurst and Oldham St Steph from 11. *13 Brooklands Court, Rochdale OL11 4EJ*
E: frnicksmeeton@gmail.com

SMEJKAL, Yenda Marcel. b 68. Van Mildert Coll Dur BA 97. Coll of Resurr Mirfield 97. d 99 p 00. C S Shields All SS *Dur* 99-03; TV N Wearside 03-04; P-in-c Sundon *St Alb* from 04; P-in-c Luton St Sav from 12. *St Mary's Vicarage, 1 Selina Close, Luton LU3 3AW* T: (01582) 583076
E: yenda.smejkal@virgin.net

SMETHAM, Abigail Laura. See THOMPSON, Abigail Laura

SMETHURST, David Alan. b 36. Lon Univ BD 60 Man Univ MPhil 84. Tyndale Hall Bris 57. d 61 p 62. C Burnage St Marg *Man* 61-63; P-in-c Whalley Range St Marg 63-65; R Haughton St Mary 65-74; R Ulverston St Mary w H Trin *Carl* 74-87; Dean Hong Kong 87; Dir Acorn Chr Healing Trust Resource Cen 88-93; V Epsom St Martin *Guildf* 93-00; RD Epsom 97-00; rtd 01; PtO *Carl* from 01. *3 Friars Ground, Kirkby-in-Furness LA17 7YB* T/F: (01229) 889725
E: friarsground@yahoo.com

SMETHURST, Gordon McIntyre. b 40. Man Univ BA 62 BD 69. Wells Th Coll 70. d 70 p 71. C Sandal St Helen *Wakef* 70-73; P-in-c Whitwood and Smawthorpe 73-75; Hd RE Goole Gr Sch 75-79; S Hunsley Sch Melton 80-00; V Anlaby Common St Mark *York* 00-03; P-in-c Roos and Garton w Tunstall, Grimston and Hilston 03-07; rtd 07. *43 Ebor Manor, Keyingham, Hull HU12 9SN* M: 07817-434209
E: revsmev@hotmail.com

SMILLIE, Linda Barbara. b 46. Oak Hill Th Coll 85. d 87 p 94. Par Dn Holloway St Mary w St Jas *Lon* 87-88; Par Dn Holloway St Mary Magd 88-90; Chapl W End Stores 90-91; C Holloway St Mark w Em 90-91; Hon C Islington St Mary 92-94; C-in-c Southall Em CD 95-01; rtd 01; PtO *Ox* 01-04; Hon C Hanger Hill Ascension and W Twyford St Mary *Lon* 04-07. *20 Wyvern Place, Warnham, Horsham RH12 3QU* T: (01403) 273788 E: rsmillie@freenetname.co.uk

SMITH, Adrian Paul. b 73. Ches Coll of HE BA 94. Cranmer Hall Dur 07. d 09 p 10. C Mablethorpe w Trusthorpe *Linc* 09-12; R Spring Line Gp from 12; R Owmby Gp from 12. *The Rectory, Main Street, Hackthorn, Lincoln LN2 3PF* T: (01673) 860464
E: aksmith96@btinternet.com

SMITH, Aidan John. b 54. Leic Univ BA 76 Man Univ MBA 81. STETS 04. d 07 p 08. NSM St Martin Ludgate *Lon* 07-13; NSM Pinner from 13. *4 Terrilands, Pinner HA5 3AJ* T: (020) 3226 0061 E: smithanddenny@hotmail.com

✠**SMITH, The Rt Revd Alan Gregory Clayton.** b 57. Birm Univ BA 78 MA 79 Univ of Wales (Ban) PhD 02. Wycliffe Hall Ox 79. d 81 p 82 c 01. C Pudsey St Lawr *Bradf* 81-82; C Pudsey St Lawr and St Paul 82-84; Chapl Lee Abbey 84-90; TV Walsall *Lich* 90-97; Dioc Missr 90-97; Adn Stoke 97-01; Area Bp Shrewsbury 01-09; Bp St Alb *St Alb* from 09. *Abbey Gate House, 4 Abbey Mill Lane, St Albans AL3 4HD* T: (01727) 853305
F: 846715 E: bishop@stalbans.anglican.org

SMITH, Alan Leonard. b 51. Madeley Coll of Educn CertEd 72. Trin Coll Bris 93. d 95 p 96. C Taunton St Mary *B & W* 95-98; V Taunton Lyngford 98-07; RD Taunton 04-06; V Chatham St Steph *Roch* 07-14; RD Roch 11-14; rtd 14. *4 Elm Grove Drive, Dawlish EX7 0EU* T: (01626) 439983
E: revdalansmith@yahoo.co.uk

SMITH, Alan Pearce Carlton. b 20. Trin Hall Cam BA 40 MA 45 LLB 46. Westcott Ho Cam 76. d 78 p 79. NSM Cherry Hinton St Jo *Ely* 78-82; P-in-c Madingley and Dry Drayton 82-83; P-in-c Swaffham Bulbeck 84-88; rtd 88; PtO *Ely* 88-03 and from 07. *38 Alpha Road, Cambridge CB4 3DG* T: (01223) 358124

SMITH, Alan Thomas. b 35. Open Univ BA 78 Sussex Univ DipEd 79. Ridley Hall Cam 82. d 84 p 85. C Bedworth *Cov* 84-89; R Carlton Colville w Mutford and Rushmere *Nor* 89-97; rtd 97; PtO *Nor* from 01. *17 St Martins Gardens, New Buckenham, Norwich NR16 2AX* T: (01953) 860550
M: 07811-229493

SMITH, Alec John. b 29. AKC 53. d 54 p 55. C Charlton Kings St Mary *Glouc* 54-56; C-in-c Findon Valley CD *Chich* 56-57; V Viney Hill *Glouc* 57-65; V Churchdown St Jo 65-66; V Bishop's Cannings *Sarum* 66-69; CF 69-88; V Douglas St Thos *S & M* 88-92; rtd 92; PtO *S & M* 92-05. *17 Saddle Mews, Douglas, Isle of Man IM2 1JA* T: (01624) 670093

SMITH, Alexander Montgomery. b 36. TCD BA 59 MA 64 BD 65. TCD Div Sch Div Test 60. d 61 p 62. C Knock *D & D* 61-64; C Belfast St Thos *Conn* 64-66; Lect St Kath Coll Liv 66-69; Sen Lect 69-98; Asst Chapl St Kath Coll Liv 66-69; Chapl 69-80; NSM Allerton *Liv* 80-98; NSM Christchurch *Win* from 98. *Priory Cottage, 4 Quay Road, Christchurch BH23 1BU* T: (01202) 476103

SMITH, Andrew. b 84. Southn Univ BSc 06 K Coll Lon MA 12. Wycliffe Hall Ox 06. **d** 09 **p** 10. C Lymington *Win* 09-13; P-in-c Bitterne Park from 13. *Bitterne Park Vicarage, 7 Thorold Road, Southampton SO18 1HZ* E: revandysmith@gmail.com

SMITH, Andrew Clifford. b 67. Ridley Coll Melbourne BMin 00. **d** 01 **p** 01. C Clayton All SS Australia 01-03; C Gainsborough and Morton *Linc* 03-06; TV 06-08; P-in-c Woodhall Spa Gp 08-14; P-in-c Mt Dandelong Australia from 14. *PO Box 148, Kalorama VA 3766, Australia*

SMITH, Andrew Graham. b 81. St Mellitus Coll BA 14. **d** 14 **p** 15. C Basildon St Andr w H Cross *Chelmsf* from 14. *12 Holden Gardens, Basildon SS14 3LF* M: 07743-870851 E: basildon.andrew@gmail.com

SMITH, Andrew John. b 59. Birm Univ BSc 80 PhD 81. WMMTC 89. **d** 91 **p** 92. C Lower Mitton *Worc* 91-92; C Stourport and Wilden 92-95; TV Redditch, The Ridge 95-05; P-in-c Redditch St Steph 02-05; Ind Chapl 95-05; Chapl Redditch and Bromsgrove Primary Care Trust 01-05; V W Bromwich All SS *Lich* 05-15; RD W Bromwich 08-13; TR March *Ely* from 15. *St Peter's Rectory, 54 High Street, March PE15 9JR* E: andrew.marchurch@gmail.com

SMITH, Andrew John. b 46. Lon Univ BScEng 67 PhD 71 Bath Univ MEd 88 CEng 96 MIET 96. Coll of Resurr Mirfield 74. **d** 76 **p** 77. C Swindon New Town *Bris* 76-78; C Southmead 78-79; PtO 79-91; rtd 11. *15 Dyrham Close, Bristol BS9 4TF* T: 0117-942 8594 E: a3-smith@blueyonder.co.uk

SMITH, Andrew John. b 53. Loughb Univ BTech 74. Lon Bible Coll 95 St Jo Coll Nottm MA 98. **d** 99 **p** 00. C Hailsham *Chich* 99-02; P-in-c Worc St Mich 02-03; TV Almondbury w Farnley Tyas *Wakef* 03-07; V Woolston New Zealand 07-11; C Remuera St Aidan 13-14; Jt P-in-c St Heliers Bay 14-15; from 15. *59B Wakeman Street, Pahiatua 4910, New Zealand* M: 21-0251 5716 E: ajsinz211@gmail.com

SMITH, Andrew John. b 37. Leeds Univ BA 61. Coll of Resurr Mirfield 61. **d** 63 **p** 64. C W Hackney St Barn *Lon* 63-65; Dir and Chapl Northorpe Hall Trust Yorkshire 65-72; Warden Ox Ho Bethnal Green 72-78; Dir and Chapl The Target Trust 78-86; P-in-c Gt Staughton *Ely* 86-88; Norfolk DTI Educn Adv 88-91; PtO *Ex* 92-96 and from 98; C Widecombe-in-the-Moor, Leusdon, Princetown etc 96-97; rtd 97. *Mountjoy, Rilla Mill, Callington PL17 7NT*

SMITH, Andrew Lewis. b 60. Bris Univ BSc 83 CEng 88 MIET 88. Trin Coll Bris BA 11. **d** 11 **p** 12. C E Dean w Friston and Jevington *Chich* 11-15; R Fetcham *Guildf* from 15. *The Rectory, 10A The Ridgeway, Fetcham, Leatherhead KT22 9AZ* M: 07974-795343 E: revandrewsmith@hotmail.com

SMITH, Andrew Perry Langton. b 56. Sheff City Poly BSc 79 Imp Coll Lon MSc 80. Trin Coll Bris 89. **d** 91 **p** 92. C Littleover *Derby* 91-95; TV Walsall *Lich* 95-09; Ind Chapl Black Country Urban Ind Miss from 95; Hon C Walsall St Paul and Walsall Pleck and Bescot 05-09; Ecum Dean Telford Chr Coun from 10; RD Telford from 12. *St Matthew's Vicarage, St George's Road, Donnington, Telford TF2 7NJ* T: (01952) 604239 E: andysmith@telfordchristiancouncil.co.uk

SMITH, Angela Elisabeth. b 53. Southn Univ BA 75 Bp Grosseteste Coll PGCE 76. WEMTC 03. **d** 06 **p** 07. NSM Matson *Glouc* 06-09; NSM Glouc St Geo w Whaddon 09-15; NSM N Cheltenham from 15. *The Rectory, Tatchley Lane, Prestbury, Cheltenham GL52 3DQ* T: (01242) 512348

SMITH, Mrs Angela Royston. b 64. Portsm Poly BA 86 DipArch 89. Wycliffe Hall Ox 11 11. **d** 14 **p** 15. C Win Ch Ch from 14. *21 Nursery Gardens, Winchester SO22 5DT* M: 07754-877575 T: (01962) 854454 E: angierosiesmith@gmail.com *or* angie.smith@ccwinch.org.uk

SMITH, Mrs Anita Elisabeth. b 57. Westhill Coll Birm BEd 79. Trin Coll Bris 85. **d** 88 **p** 94. Par Dn Bermondsey St Anne *S'wark* 88-92; Par Dn Brockley Hill St Sav 92-94; C 94-99; Miss Partner CMS Kenya 99-14; P-in-c Banbury St Hugh *Ox* from 14. *St Hugh's Vicarage, 4 Longfellow Road, Banbury OX16 9LB* T: (01295) 369021 E: anita.smith.nbi@gmail.com

SMITH, Ann Veronica. b 38. Doncaster Coll of Educn DipEd. Edin Dioc NSM Course 88. **d** 95 **p** 96. NSM S Queensferry *Edin* 95-99; NSM Falkirk 99-10; rtd 10; LtO *Edin* from 10. *16 Mannerston, Linlithgow EH49 7ND* T: (01506) 834361

SMITH *(née* JENNINGS), **Mrs Anne.** b 41. CertEd 63 STh. Gilmore Ho 65. **dss** 71 **d** 87 **p** 94. Dn-in-c Hillock *Man* 87-88; Chapl Wakef Cathl 88-96; P-in-c Whitwell *Derby* 96-00; V Mansfield Woodhouse *S'well* 00-01; rtd 01; PtO *Carl* 02-05; *Blackb* from 05; *Bradf* 05-11. *20 Bendwood Close, Padiham, Burnley BB12 8RT* T: (01282) 660523

SMITH, Anthony Cyril. b 40. K Coll Lon 65. **d** 69 **p** 70. C Crewkerne *B & W* 69-71; C Crewkerne w Wayford 71-74; TV Hemel Hempstead *St Alb* 74-76; Asst Chapl K Coll Taunton

76-80; Chapl 80-02; rtd 02; PtO *B & W* from 03. *1 Castle Street, Stogursey, Bridgwater TA5 1TG* T: (01278) 733577

SMITH, Anthony James. b 57. FCA Sheff Univ BA. Ridley Hall Cam 83. **d** 86 **p** 87. C Woking St Pet *Guildf* 86-90; C Reigate St Mary *S'wark* 90-94; CMS Kenya 94-00; Finance Team Ldr World Vision UK 00-05; NSM Walton Milton Keynes *Ox* 10-12; PtO *Win* from 12; Hd of Resource Development from 13. *The Brambles, Homestead Road, Medstead, Alton GU34 5PW* M: 07521-222886 E: anthony.smith@winchester.anglican.org

SMITH, Antoinette. b 47. NTMTC 95. **d** 98 **p** 99. NSM Chigwell and Chigwell Row *Chelmsf* 98-02; TV 02-10; V Blackmore and Stondon Massey 10-15; RD Ongar 10-13; rtd 15; PtO *Pet* from 15. *The Maples, 10 Northampton Road, Orlingbury, Northampton NN14 1JF* E: reverend@tonismith.freeserve.co.uk

SMITH, Miss Audrey. b 47. S'wark Ord Course 89. **d** 92 **p** 94. NSM Croydon St Aug *S'wark* 92-98; P-in-c Redmarley D'Abitot, Bromesberrow w Pauntley etc *Glouc* 98-00; PtO 05-06; NSM Newent and Gorsley w Cliffords Mesne 06-08; Chapl Hartpury Coll 06-08; NSM Brampton St Thos *Derby* 08-10; rtd 10. *Rose Cottage, Cotton Mill Hill, Holymoorside, Chesterfield S42 7EJ* T: (01246) 569632

SMITH, Mrs Audrey Isabel. b 20. Lon Univ. Qu Coll Birm IDC 79. **dss** 84 **d** 87 **p** 94. NSM Kingston All SS w St Jo *S'wark* 87-95; PtO *Truro* 95-08. *31 Copes Gardens, Truro TR1 3SN* T: (01872) 261813

SMITH, Austin John Denyer. b 40. Worc Coll Ox BA 62. Cuddesdon Coll 64. **d** 66 **p** 67. C Shepherd's Bush St Steph w St Thos *Lon* 66-69; C W Drayton 69-72; Chapl Sussex Univ *Chich* 72-79; V Caddington *St Alb* 79-06; rtd 06. *209 Bedford Road, Hitchin SG5 2UE* T: (01462) 437433 E: ajdsmith@waitrose.com

SMITH, Mrs Barbara Ann. b 56. SNWTP 07. **d** 10 **p** 11. NSM Liv St Chris Norris Green from 10. *25 Meadow Lane, Liverpool L12 5EA* T: 0151-226 3534 M: 07957-963546 E: basmith@blueyonder.co.uk

SMITH, Mrs Barbara Jean. b 39. Bris Univ BA 62 Surrey Univ PGCE 93. S'wark Ord Course 83. **dss** 86 **d** 87 **p** 94. Hon Dss Chislehurst St Nic *Roch* 86; Hon Par Dn 87-90; Hon C Wrecclesham *Guildf* 90-94; Hon C Herriard w Winslade and Long Sutton etc *Win* 94-99; P-in-c 99-03; P-in-c Newnham w Nately Scures w Mapledurwell etc 99-03; rtd 03; PtO *Portsm* 06-07; *Roch* from 08. *15 The Ridings, Paddock Wood, Tonbridge TN12 6YA* T: (01892) 833564 E: barbarajeansmith@tiscali.co.uk

SMITH, Mrs Barbara Mary. b 47. Doncaster Coll of Educn CertEd 68. Cranmer Hall Dur 82. **dss** 85 **d** 87 **p** 94. Par Dn Beverley St Nic *York* 87; NSM S'wark H Trin w St Matt 89-90; Ind Chapl Teesside *York* 91-95; Hon C Middlesbrough St Chad 94-95; PtO *St Alb* 96-02; Locum Chapl Anglia Poly Univ *Ely* 96-98; TV Linton 00-04; rtd 04; PtO *Dur* from 10. *38 Second Street, Bradley Bungalows, Consett DH8 6JX*

SMITH, Canon Barry. b 41. Univ of Wales (Lamp) BA 62 Fitzw Ho Cam BA 64 MA 68 Man Univ MPhil 91. Ridley Hall Cam. **d** 65 **p** 66. C Rhyl w St Ann *St As* 65-70; Chapl Scargill Ho 70-72; C Flint *St As* 72-74; V Broughton 74-86; Dioc Ecum Officer 82-86; RD Wrexham 82-86; TR 86-95; Can Cursal St As Cathl 86-95; Chan 95; PtO *S'wark* 97-02. *1 Acorn Keep, Rowhills, Farnham GU9 9BL* T: (01252) 322111

SMITH, Barry Roy. b 46. STETS. **d** 00 **p** 04. NSM Blendworth w Chalton w Idsworth *Portsm* 00-05; Asst Chapl Portsm Hosps NHS Trust 03-05; Team Chapl from 05; PtO *Portsm* 05-07 and from 09; NSM Blendworth w Chalton w Idsworth 07-09. *298 Milton Road, Cowplain, Waterlooville PO8 8JP* T: (023) 9226 5620 E: barry.roy.smith@googlemail.com

SMITH, Beverley Anne. b 56. Univ of Wales Coll of Medicine MSc 97 RN 78 RM 80 RHV 87 Univ of Wales PGCE 00. St Mich Coll Llan. **d** 05 **p** 06. NSM Whitchurch *Llan* 05-11; NSM Mynyddislwyn *Mon* 11-13. *3 Solva Avenue, Cardiff CF14 0NP* M: 07841-707525 E: beverleyatciw@btinternet.com

SMITH, The Ven Brian. b 44. Westmr Coll Ox MTh 95. Sarum & Wells Th Coll 71. **d** 74 **p** 75. C Pennywell St Thos and Grindon St Oswald CD *Dur* 74-77; Chapl RAF 77-95; P-in-c Keswick St Jo *Carl* 95-96; V 96-05; RD Derwent 98-05; Hon Can Carl Cathl 99-05; Adn of Man *S & M* 05-11; V Douglas St Geo 05-11; rtd 11. *The Coach House, The Street, Westward, Wigton CA7 8AF* T: (01697) 345396 E: brian.smith157@btinternet.com

✠**SMITH, The Rt Revd Brian Arthur.** b 43. Edin Univ MA 66 Fitzw Coll Cam BA 68 MA 72 Jes Coll Cam MLitt 73. Westcott Ho Cam 66. **d** 72 **p** 73 **c** 93. Tutor and Lib Cuddesdon Coll 72-75; Dir of Studies Ripon Coll Cuddesdon 75-78; Sen Tutor 78-79; C Cuddesdon *Ox* 76-79; Dir Tr *Wakef* 79-87; P-in-c Halifax St Jo 79-85; Hon Can Wakef Cathl 81-87; Adn Craven

Bradf 87-93; Suff Bp Tonbridge *Roch* 93-01; Hon Can Roch Cathl 93-01; Bp Edin 01-11; rtd 11; LtO *Edin* from 11. *Flat E, 2A Dean Path, Edinburgh EH4 3BA* T: 0131-220 6097
E: bishopsmith@btinternet.com

SMITH, Brian Godfrey. b 24. Chich Th Coll 63. **d** 65 **p** 66. C Newc H Cross 65-68; C Redcar *York* 68-72; C Kirkleatham 68-72; V Wortley-de-Leeds *Ripon* 72-76; Chapl Costa del Sol E *Eur* 76-82; Chapl Estoril 82-84; V Worfield *Heref* 84-89; rtd 89; PtO *Heref* from 92. *2 Pineway, Lodge Farm, Bridgnorth WV15 5DT* T: (01746) 764088

SMITH, Brian Michael. b 42. Kelham Th Coll 69. **d** 69 **p** 70. C Somers Town *Lon* 70-74; C Stamford Hill St Jo 74-75; C Stamford Hill St Bart 75-84; P-in-c Edmonton St Pet w St Martin 84-92; V 92-07; rtd 07. *9 Derwent Gardens, Derwent Avenue, Matlock DE4 3LX* T: (01629) 56559
E: bms@sple.freeserve.co.uk

SMITH, Canon Bridget Mary. b 46. Bp Otter Coll CertEd 67. S Dios Minl Tr Scheme 88. **d** 91 **p** 94. C Pet H Spirit Bretton 91-95; P-in-c Silverstone and Abthorpe w Slapton 95-03; R Silverstone and Abthorpe w Slapton etc 03-09; Warden of Past Assts 00-06; Can Pet Cathl 01-09; rtd 09. *2 Merryweather Close, Southwell NG25 0BN* T: (01636) 812215
E: quickvic@lineone.net

SMITH, Carl Alexander. b 82. Glos Univ BA 05. Trin Coll Bris 13. **d** 13 **p** 14. C Burgess Hill St Andr *Chich* from 13. *9 Pendean, Burgess Hill RH15 0DW* M: 07816-979665
E: john8vs50@yahoo.co.uk

SMITH, Canon Carol. b 55. SEITE 01. **d** 04 **p** 05. C Epping Distr *Chelmsf* 04-07; Chapl Epping Forest Primary Care Trust 05-07; V Moulsham St Luke *Chelmsf* from 07; P-in-c Moulsham St Jo from 13; C Galleywood Common from 13; C Widford from 13; Hon Can Chelmsf Cathl from 13. *St Luke's House, 26 Lewis Drive, Chelmsford CM2 9EF* T: (01245) 354479
E: carolrev@gotadsl.co.uk

SMITH, Mrs Catherine Eleanor Louise. b 52. SAOMC 99. **d** 02 **p** 03. NSM Denham *Ox* 02-05; NSM Penn Street 05-15; NSM Beaconsfield from 15; Chapl Heatherwood & Wexham Park Hosps NHS Foundn Trust from 05. *24 Westfield Road, Beaconsfield HP9 1EF* T/F: (01494) 670389

SMITH, Mrs Charlene. b 79. Coll of Resurr Mirfield 12. **d** 14 **p** 15. C Meltham *Leeds* from 14. *4 Pavilion Way, Meltham, Holmfirth HD9 5QW* E: charlene.smith1979@gmail.com

SMITH, Charles Henry Neville. b 31. Nottm Univ BA 52 MA 65. Sarum Th Coll 55. **d** 57 **p** 58. C Thirsk w S Kilvington *York* 57-60; C Linthorpe 60-61; V Danby 61-66; Chapl United Camb Hosps 66-76; Chapl Lanc Moor Hosp 76-84; Hon Can Blackb Cathl 81-84; Asst Sec Gen Syn Hosp Chapl Coun 84-88; Hon C Lee St Marg *S'wark* 84-88; Chapl Guy's Hosp Lon 88-96; rtd 96; Hon Chapl S'wark Cathl from 96. *57 Belmont Park, London SE13 5BW* T: (020) 8318 9993 E: revnev@talktalk.net

SMITH, Canon Charles Rycroft. b 46. Sarum & Wells Th Coll 76. **d** 78 **p** 79. C Heref St Martin 78-81; C Southampton Maybush St Pet *Win* 81-83; R The Candover Valley 83-99; RD Alresford 90-99; P-in-c Guernsey St Andr 99-01; R 01-07; Vice-Dean Guernsey 02-07; P-in-c Beaulieu and Exbury and E Boldre 07-14; rtd 14; Hon Can Win Cathl from 14; PtO *Heref* from 15. *Hope Cottage, 25B New Street, Ledbury HR8 2EA* T: (01531) 631104 E: rycs006@gmail.com

SMITH, Charles Septimus. b 23. Bris & Glouc Tr Course. **d** 79 **p** 80. NSM Bris St Agnes and St Simon w St Werburgh 79-86; C 86-87; C Bris St Paul's 87-89; rtd 89. *2476 Barcella Crescent, Mississauga ON L5K 1E2, Canada*

SMITH, Mrs Christine. b 46. NOC 94. **d** 97 **p** 98. C Salterhebble All SS *Wakef* 97-01; P-in-c Siddal 01-06; V Cornholme and Walsden 06-11; rtd 11. *38 Horley Green Road, Claremount, Halifax HX3 6AS* T: (01422) 301681
E: c.waltonsmith@talktalk.net

SMITH, Christine Lydia. *See* CARTER, Christine Lydia

SMITH, Mrs Christine Mary. b 53. Ox Min Course 13. **d** 15. NSM E Win from 15. *Pilgrim Cottage, Stoke Charity, Winchester SO21 3PF* T: (01962) 760309
E: smith.stokecharity@gmail.com

SMITH, The Ven Christopher Blake Walters. b 63. Univ of Wales (Cardiff) BMus 84 BD 88 LLM 95. St Mich Coll Llan 85. **d** 88 **p** 89. C Aberdare *Llan* 88-93; V Tongwynlais 93-00; Dioc Dir Post-Ord Tr 95-05; Dom Chapl Bp Llan and Warden of Ords 01-07; Chapl to Abp Wales 03-07; Adn Morgannwg from 06; P-in-c Cwmbach from 07; Metrop Can from 04. *The Heights, Nant y Groes Drive, Tirfounder Road, Aberdare CF44 0BE* T: (01685) 378455
E: archdeacon.morgannwg@churchinwales.org.uk

SMITH, Canon Christopher Francis. b 46. K Coll Lon BD 68 AKC 68. St Aug Coll Cant 69. **d** 70 **p** 71. C Norwood All SS *Cant* 70-72; Asst Chapl Marlborough Coll 72-76; C Deal St Leon w Sholden *Cant* 77-81; P-in-c Benenden 81-83; V 83-07; P-in-c Sandhurst w Newenden 04-07; Hon Can Cant

Cathl 03-07; AD Tenterden 05-07; Chapl Benenden Sch 81-92; Chapl Benenden Hosp 91-07; rtd 07; PtO *Cant* from 07. *34 Richmond Road, Whitstable CT5 5PH* T: (01227) 266569
E: christopherfrancissmith@yahoo.co.uk

SMITH, Christopher James. b 72. Newc Univ BSc 94. Wycliffe Hall Ox BTh 01. **d** 02 **p** 03. C Cambridge H Trin *Ely* 02-04; Assoc R Manchester Zion Ch USA 04-08; R Chevening *Roch* from 09. *Chevening Rectory, Homedean Road, Chipstead, Sevenoaks TN13 2RU* T: (01732) 453555
E: revcjsmith@gmail.com

SMITH, Christopher Matthew. b 67. New Coll Ox BA 89 MA 93 Homerton Coll Cam PGCE 90 LLB 07. St Steph Ho Ox BA 94. **d** 95 **p** 96. C Wantage *Ox* 95-99; Dom Chapl to Bp Horsham *Chich* 99-01; V Beckenham St Mich w St Aug *Roch* 01-11; V Holborn St Alb w Saffron Hill St Pet *Lon* from 11. *St Alban's Clergy House, 18 Brooke Street, London EC1N 7RD* T: (020) 7405 1831 F: 7430 2551

SMITH, Canon Christopher Milne. b 44. Selw Coll Cam BA 66. Cuddesdon Coll 67. **d** 69 **p** 70. C Liv Our Lady and St Nic 69-74; TV Kirkby 74-81; R Walton St Mary 81-91; Can Res Sheff Cathl 91-02; V Doncaster St Geo 02-10; Bp's Adv on the Paranormal 97-10; Hon Can Sheff Cathl 03-10; rtd 10; PtO *Sheff* from 10; Chapl to The Queen 04-14. *14 Ravensdowne, Berwick-upon-Tweed TD15 1HX* T: (01289) 330375
E: smith@rev.cm.fsnet.co.uk

SMITH, Clifford. b 31. St Aid Birkenhead 59. **d** 61 **p** 62. C Limehouse St Anne *Lon* 61-63; C Ashtead *Guildf* 63-66; R Bromley All Hallows *Lon* 66-76; V Hillsborough and Wadsley Bridge *Sheff* 76-89; V Stainforth 89-96; rtd 96; Hon C Hurst *Ox* 97-12; Hon C Ruscombe and Twyford w Hurst from 12. *33 King Street Lane, Winnersh, Wokingham RG41 5AX* T: 0118-978 9453

SMITH, Clive Leslie. b 50. Leeds Univ BA 72 MA 03 Ch Coll Liv PGCE 73. Coll of Resurr Mirfield 75. **d** 77 **p** 78. C Goldington *St Alb* 77-81; C Cheshunt 81-84; V Watford St Pet 84-89; Chapl Leavesden Hosp Abbots Langley 89-94; Chapl St Alb and Hemel Hempstead NHS Trust 94-00; Chapl W Herts Hosps NHS Trust 00-01; Sen Chapl Doncaster and Bassetlaw Hosps NHS Foundn Trust 01-14; rtd 14; PtO *S'well* from 02. *4 Hampson Gardens, Edenthorpe, Doncaster DN3 2TN* T: (01302) 881351 E: clivelsmith@outlook.co.uk

SMITH, Colin. b 39. MBE. Open Univ BA 80 LRSC 65 CChem 88 FRSC 88. NEOC 94. **d** 97 **p** 98. NSM Jesmond H Trin and Newc St Barn and St Jude 97-08; rtd 08. *1 Cayton Grove, Newcastle upon Tyne NE5 1HL* T: 0191-267 9519
E: colinandevelyn@btopenworld.com

SMITH, Colin Graham. b 59. Hatf Poly BA 82 CQSW 82. Trin Coll Bris BA 88. **d** 88 **p** 89. C Bermondsey St Jas w Ch Ch *S'wark* 88-92; V Brockley Hill St Sav 92-99; Miss Partner CMS Kenya 99-13; PtO *Ox* from 14. *St Hugh's Vicarage, 4 Longfellow Road, Banbury OX16 9LB* T: (01295) 369021

SMITH, Colin Richard. b 53. Liv Poly BA 80 Liv Univ MTD 83. Oak Hill Th Coll 84. **d** 86 **p** 87. C Ormskirk *Liv* 86-89; V Wigan St Cath 89-94; C St Helens St Helen 94-99; TV 99-10; P-in-c St Helens St Mark 06-10; TV St Helens Town Cen 10-15; rtd 15. *Address temp unknown*

SMITH, Mrs Corinne Anne. b 52. St Andr Univ MTheol 91. SAOMC 95. **d** 97. C Abingdon *Ox* 97-02; Chapl Pemb Coll Ox 02-03; Chapl Ox Radcliffe Hosps NHS Trust 03-07; Chapl Portsm Hosps NHS Trust 07-12; Chapl Sue Ryder - Nettlebed Hospice from 12. *Sue Ryder Home for Palliative Care, Joyce Grove, Nettlebed, Henley-on-Thames RG9 5DF* T: (01491) 641384
E: corinne.smith@vizzavi.net

SMITH, Craig Philip. b 61. Sheff City Poly BA 86. St Jo Coll Nottm 90. **d** 93 **p** 94. C Bramley and Ravenfield w Hooton Roberts etc *Sheff* 93-97; C Rainham w Wennington *Chelmsf* 97-00; TV Gainsborough and Morton *Linc* 00-03; V Catshill and Dodford *Worc* 03-07; New Zealand from 07. *PO Box 64, Culverden, North Canterbury 7345, New Zealand* T: (0064) (3) 315 8210

SMITH, Daniel Bradley. b 69. Harris Man Coll Ox BTh 05. St Steph Ho Ox 04. **d** 06 **p** 07. C Bexhill St Pet *Chich* 06-11; R W Blatchington from 11. *St Peter's Rectory, 23 Windmill Close, Hove BN3 7LJ* T: (01273) 732459
E: db.smith@alumni.oxon.net

SMITH, Darren John Anthony. b 62. Nottm Univ BCombStuds 84. Linc Th Coll 84. **d** 86 **p** 87. C Leic Ascension 86-90; C Curdworth w Castle Vale *Birm* 90; C Castle Vale St Cuth 90-91; C Kingstanding St Luke 91-92; P-in-c 92-93; V 93-08; P-in-c Kingstanding St Mark 01-02; Gen Sec ACS from 08. *Gordon Browning House, 8 Spitfire Road, Birmingham B24 9PB* T: 0121-382 5533 F: 382 6999
E: fr.smith@additionalcurates.co.uk

SMITH, David. *See* SMITH, Terence David

SMITH, David Earling. b 35. AKC 60. **d** 61 **p** 62. C Knebworth *St Alb* 61-63; C Chipping Barnet 64-66; C S Ormsby w Ketsby,

Calceby and Driby *Linc* 66-69; R Claxby w Normanby-le-Wold 69-74; R Nettleton 69-74; R S Kelsey 69-74; R N Owersby w Thornton le Moor 69-74; R Stainton-le-Vale w Kirmond le Mire 69-74; V Ancaster 74-79; Warden and Chapl St Anne Bedehouses Linc 79-89; C Linc Minster Gp 79-89; rtd 89; PtO *Linc* 90-02. *17 Egerton Road, Lincoln LN2 4PJ* T: (01522) 510336 E: david@limani17.fsnet.co.uk

✠**SMITH, The Rt Revd David James.** b 35. AKC 58 FKC 99. **d** 59 **p** 60 **c** 87. C Gosforth All SS *Newc* 59-62; C Newc St Fran 62-64; C Longbenton St Bart 64-68; V Longhirst 68-75; V Monkseaton St Mary 75-82; RD Tynemouth 80-82; Hon Can Newc Cathl 81-87; Adn Lindisfarne 81-87; V Felton 82-83; Suff Bp Maidstone *Cant* 87-92; Bp HM Forces 90-92; Bp Bradf 92-02; rtd 02; Hon Asst Bp York from 02; Hon Asst Bp Eur from 02. *34 Cedar Glade, Dunnington, York YO19 5QZ* T: (01904) 481225 E: david@djmhs.force9.co.uk

SMITH, Canon David John. b 32. Goldsmiths' Coll Lon BA 76 LSE MSc 79. Lon Coll of Div 68. **d** 70 **p** 71. C Clerkenwell St Jas and St Jo w St Pet *Lon* 70-73; P-in-c Penge St Paul *Roch* 74-78; V 78-89; RD Beckenham 86-89; Chapl Bromley and Sheppard's Colls 90-97; PtO *S'wark* 90-97; Dioc Clergy Widows and Retirement Officer *Roch* 90-97; Hon Can Roch Cathl 95-97; rtd 98; PtO *St Alb* from 98; *Lon* from 99. *13 Park Way, Rickmansworth WD3 7AU* T: (01923) 775963

SMITH, Canon David Robert. b 54. Southn Univ BSc 75 Loughb Univ MSc 86 CEng 84 MRAeS 84. WEMTC 02. **d** 05 **p** 06. C Matson *Glouc* 05-09; P-in-c Glouc St Geo w Whaddon 09-12; V 12-15; AD Glouc City 11-15; TR N Cheltenham from 15; Hon Can Glouc Cathl from 14. *The Rectory, Tatchley Lane, Prestbury, Cheltenham GL52 3DQ* T: (01242) 512348 E: draesmith2@btinternet.com

SMITH, David Roland Mark. b 46. Dur Univ BA 68 ACP 78 FRSA 87. Edin Th Coll 68. **d** 70 **p** 71. C Southwick St Columba *Dur* 70-74 and 81-82; Asst Chapl Univ of Wales (Cardiff) *Llan* 74-76; Hon C E Bris 76-78; Hon C Filton 78-79; Min Leam Lane CD *Dur* 80-81; Co-ord Chapl Service Sunderland Poly 81-86; Chapl Birm Univ 86-95; Chapl Heathrow Airport *Lon* 95-00; rtd 00; Chapl Wolv Airport *Lich* 00-09. *5 The Keepings Residential Care Home, 12 Priory Road, Dudley DY1 4AD* T: (01384) 259540

SMITH, David Roy. b 74. Westcott Ho Cam 10. **d** 12 **p** 13. C Thorpe St Andr *Nor* from 12. *9 Pine Road, Norwich NR7 9LE* T: (01603) 433053

SMITH, David Stanley. b 41. Ox NSM Course. **d** 84 **p** 85. NSM Burghfield *Ox* 84-86; NSM Stratfield Mortimer 86-88; NSM Mortimer W End w Padworth 86-88; C St Breoke and Egloshayle *Truro* 88-93; V Penwerris 93-07; rtd 07; PtO *Ox* 09-10. *Emmaus, 1 Webster Close, Reading RG2 8BF* T: 0118-987 2597

SMITH, David Watson. b 31. Sarum Th Coll 63. **d** 65 **p** 66. C W Wimbledon Ch Ch *S'wark* 65-69; C Cheam 69-74; V Haslington *Ches* 74-83; V Haslington w Crewe Green 83-87; V Daresbury 87-98; rtd 98; PtO *Pet* from 98. *4 Wakefield Way, Nether Heyford, Northampton NN7 3LU* T: (01327) 341561 E: rev.dw.smith@freeuk.com

SMITH, Canon David William. b 46. Sarum Th Coll 70. **d** 72 **p** 73. C Stokesley *York* 72-75; C Edin St Mich and All SS 75-77; R Galashiels 77-85; R Yarm *York* 85-00; TR Whitby w Ruswarp 00-15; P-in-c Fylingdales and Hawsker cum Stainsacre 03-05; Can and Preb York Minster from 05; rtd 15. *4 Harker Close, Yarm TS15 9TT*

SMITH, Deborah Jane. b 62. Newc Poly BA 83. STETS 00. **d** 03 **p** 04. C Dorchester *Sarum* 03-07; R Wyke Regis from 07. *The Rectory, 1 Portland Road, Weymouth DT4 9ES* T/F: (01305) 784649 M: 07870-560354 E: revdebsmith@gmail.com

SMITH, Mrs Deborah Louise. b 56. WEMTC 02 NOC 03. **d** 05 **p** 06. C Honley *Wakef* 05-07; Chapl HM Pris and YOI New Hall 05-07; NSM Woolston New Zealand 07-11; Chapl Nelson Hosps 11-12; C Remuera St Aidan 13-14; Jt P-in-c St Heliers Bay 14-15; from 15. *59B Wakeman Street, Pahiatua 4910, New Zealand* E: dlsinz@xtra.co.nz

SMITH, Mrs Decia Jane. b 47. ALAM 66. WMMTC 92. **d** 95 **p** 96. C Edgbaston St Germain *Birm* 95-99; P-in-c Abbots Leigh w Leigh Woods *Bris* 00-12; rtd 12. *4 Kingsmill, Bristol BS9 1BZ* T: 0117-968 3511 E: revdecia@yahoo.co.uk

SMITH, Declan. *See* SMITH, Godfrey Declan Burfield

SMITH, Denis Richard. b 53. MA. St Jo Coll Nottm 83. **d** 85 **p** 86. C Hersham *Guildf* 85-88; C Thatcham *Ox* 88-91; V Shefford *St Alb* 91-02; P-in-c Tilehurst St Cath *Ox* 02-07; V Tilehurst St Cath and Calcot from 07. *The Vicarage, Wittenham Avenue, Tilehurst, Reading RG31 5LN* T: 0118-942 7786 E: revdenissmith@hotmail.com

SMITH, Mrs Denise. b 46. Didsbury Coll of Educn CertEd 67. **d** 08 **p** 09. OLM Goodshaw and Crawshawbooth *Man* from 08. *122 Goodshaw Lane, Rossendale BB4 8DD* T: (01706) 830251 M: 07954-645212 E: mrsbucket122@btinternet.com

SMITH, Dennis Austin. b 50. Lanc Univ BA 71 Liv Univ PGCE 72. NW Ord Course 74. **d** 77 **p** 78. NSM Seaforth *Liv* 77-83; NSM Gt Crosby St Faith 77-83; Hon C 83-98; Hon C Gt Crosby St Faith and Waterloo Park St Mary from 98; Asst Chapl Merchant Taylors' Sch Crosby 79-83; Chapl from 83. *16 Fir Road, Liverpool L22 4QL* T: 0151-928 5065

SMITH, Derek Arthur. b 38. Chich Th Coll 63. **d** 66 **p** 67. C Cheadle *Lich* 66-70; C Blakenall Heath 70-72; P-in-c 76-77; TR 77-86; V Knutton 72-76; R Lich St Mary w St Mich 86-96; P-in-c Wall 90-96; R Lich St Mich w St Mary and Wall 96-98; V W Bromwich St Andr w Ch Ch 98-02; rtd 02; PtO *Lich* from 02. *20 Tiverton Drive, West Bromwich B71 1DA* T: 0121-525 0260

SMITH, Derek Arthur Byott. b 26. Hull Univ MA 89. S Dios Minl Tr Scheme 78. **d** 81 **p** 82. NSM Wimborne Minster and Holt *Sarum* 81-83; C Northampton St Alb *Pet* 83-85; Ind Chapl *York* 85-89; P-in-c Kingston upon Hull St Mary 88-89; P-in-c Newington w Dairycoates 89-93; rtd 93; PtO *York* from 93. *107 Cardigan Road, Bridlington YO15 3LP* T: (01262) 678852 E: dabs@talktalk.net

SMITH, Derek Graham. b 52. St Cath Coll Cam BA 74 MA 77. Westcott Ho Cam 74. **d** 76 **p** 77. C Weymouth H Trin *Sarum* 76-79; P-in-c Bradpole 79; TV Bridport 79-84; R Monkton Farleigh, S Wraxall and Winsley 84-98; TR Melksham 98-09; C Atworth w Shaw and Whitley 07-09; C Broughton Gifford, Gt Chalfield and Holt 07-09; RD Bradford 01-08; Chapl Wilts and Swindon Healthcare NHS Trust 00-02; Can and Preb Sarum Cathl 03-09; Chapl Limassol St Barn from 09. *PO Box 51494, 3506 Limassol, Cyprus* T: (00357) (25) 362713 E: stbac@spidernet.com.cy

SMITH, Diana Linnet. b 47. Sheff Univ BSc 69 Goldsmiths' Coll Lon MA 83 Trin Coll Carmarthen PhD 99. EAMTC 02. **d** 03 **p** 04. C Oundle w Ashton and Benefield w Glapthorn *Pet* 03-06; R Brundall w Braydeston and Postwick *Nor* 06-12; rtd 12; PtO *Pet* 13-15; Hon C Guilsborough and Hollowell and Cold Ashby etc from 15. *The Vicarage, 2 Church Road, Spratton, Northampton NN6 8HR*

SMITH, Donald Edgar. b 56. Oak Hill Th Coll 89. **d** 91 **p** 92. C Holloway St Mark w Em *Lon* 91-92; C Tollington 92-95; TV W Ealing St Jo w St Jas 95-08; R Frinton *Chelmsf* from 08. *The Rectory, 22 Queens Road, Frinton-on-Sea CO13 9BL* T: (01255) 674664 E: donthevic@btinternet.com

✠**SMITH, The Rt Revd Donald Westwood.** b 28. Edin Th Coll 54 St D Coll Lamp 50. **d** 54 **p** 55 **c** 90. Asst Dioc Supernumerary *Ab* 54-55; Chapl St Andr Cathl 55-56; Canada 56-57; R Longside *Ab* 57-65; Mauritius 65-85; P-in-c St Geo-in-the-East St Mary *Lon* 85-86; Seychelles 86-87; Madagascar 87-99; Bp Toamasina 90-99. *Avenue Cote d'Emeraude, Morcellement Raffray, Albion, Mauritius* T: (00230) 238 5966 E: tighdhonuil@hotmail.com

SMITH, Edward George. b 61. Surrey Univ BSc 82 Cov Univ MSc 95. Ox Min Course 06. **d** 09 **p** 10. NSM Aynho and Croughton w Evenley etc *Pet* 09-11; NSM Chenderit 11-14; R Cogenhoe and Gt and Lt Houghton w Brafield from 14. *The Rectory, Church Street, Cogenhoe, Northampton NN7 1LS* M: 07740-909756 T: (01604) 891166 E: eddie.smith@talk21.com

SMITH, Elaine Joan. *See* GARRISH, Elaine Joan

SMITH, Ms Elizabeth. b 46. Liv Inst of Educn CertEd 67 Heythrop Coll Lon BD 76 Lon Univ MPhil 84. Westcott Ho Cam 90. **d** 92 **p** 94. Par Dn Moulsham St Jo *Chelmsf* 92-94; C 94-96; V Westcliff St Andr 96-00; V Sedgley St Mary *Worc* 00-09; rtd 09. *2 Buckstone Close, Leeds LS17 5EU* E: revdeliz@aol.com

SMITH, Elizabeth Anne. *See* ETHERINGTON, Elizabeth Anne

SMITH, Miss Elizabeth Jane. b 50. Birm Univ BA 72. Trin Coll Bris 88. **d** 90 **p** 94. C Lowestoft and Kirkley *Nor* 90-94; TV Rugby *Cov* 94-01; C Shepton Mallet w Doulting *B & W* 01-03; R 03-10; Chapl Mendip Primary Care Trust 01-06; Chapl Somerset Primary Care Trust 06-10; rtd 10. *19 Alcock Crest, Warminster BA12 8AE* E: revdlizsmith@btinternet.com

SMITH, Canon Elizabeth Marion. b 52. ACA 76 FCA 82. Carl Dioc Tr Inst 91. **d** 94 **p** 95. C Appleby *Carl* 94-98; P-in-c Hesket-in-the-Forest and Armathwaite 98-04; P-in-c Skelton and Hutton-in-the-Forest w Ivegill 98-04; R Inglewood Gp 04-12; RD Penrith 06-09; Hon Can Carl Cathl 08-12; rtd 13. *Tanglewood, Cumwhinton, Carlisle CA4 8DL* T: (01228) 560310 E: revdesmith@hotmail.com

SMITH, Esther. b 65. Trin Coll Bris. **d** 13 **p** 14. C Bath Walcot *B & W* from 13. *5 The Linleys, Bath BA1 2XE* M: 07742-011936 E: esmith21@blueyonder.co.uk

SMITH, Eustace. b 20. St Pet Hall Ox BA 43 MA 46. Wycliffe Hall Ox 43. **d** 46 **p** 46. C Tiverton St Pet *Ex* 46-47; C Clenston S'well 47-49; C Aston SS Pet and Paul *Birm* 49-53; V Bermondsey St Anne *S'wark* 53-59; V Buckminster w Sewstern *Leic* 59-74; V Buckminster w Sewstern, Sproxton and Coston

74-82; R Algarkirk *Linc* 82-88; V Fosdyke 82-88; rtd 89; PtO *Leic* 89-00. *32 Wadsworth Way, Measham, Swadlincote DE12 7ER* T: (01530) 273765

SMITH (*née* DAVIS), **Felicity Ann.** b 40. Bris Univ MB, ChB 63. Qu Coll Birm 83. **dss** 86 **d** 87 **p** 94. NSM Dioc Bd for Soc Resp *Cov* 86-96; NSM Leamington Spa H Trin from 96. *14 Oakwood Grove, Warwick CV34 5TD* T: (01926) 492452 E: felicity@fandi.me.uk

SMITH, Felix Arran Jerome. b 87. Edin Univ MA 11. Ripon Coll Cuddesdon MTh 13. **d** 13 **p** 15. C Dundee St Paul *Bre* 13-14; C Coplow *Leic* from 14. *20A Weare Close, Billesdon, Leicester LE7 9DY* M: 07818-407114 E: linkyandloola@yahoo.com

SMITH, Frances Mary. See KNIGHT, Frances Mary

SMITH, Francis Christian Lynford. b 36. Padgate Coll of Educn TCert 59. Cuddesdon Coll 72. **d** 74 **p** 75. C Catford St Laur *S'wark* 74-79; P-in-c Vacoas St Paul Mauritius 79-80; Chapl Dulwich Coll 81-91; Chapl St Mich Univ Sch Victoria Canada from 91; rtd 01. *Apartment 403, 2626 Blackwood Street, Victoria BC V8T 3W3, Canada* T: (001) (250) 598 3459 E: smudge4147@hotmail.com

SMITH, Francis Malcolm. b 44. Open Univ BA 82 FCMI ACIB 69. EAMTC 90. **d** 93 **p** 94. NSM Prittlewell *Chelmsf* 93-08; PtO from 08. *24 St Augustine's Avenue, Southend-on-Sea SS1 3JH* T: (01702) 586680 F: 291166 E: franksmith44@hotmail.com

SMITH, Canon Frank. b 39. Nottm Univ CertEd 65 Open Univ BA 76. Paton Congr Coll Nottm 61 Cuddesdon Coll 69. **d** 69 **p** 70. C Davyhulme St Mary *Man* 69-72; PC Peak Forest and Wormhill *Derby* 72-78; R W Hallam and Mapperley 78-85; V Henleaze *Bris* 85-01; RD Clifton 93-99; Hon Can Bris Cathl 99-01; rtd 01; PtO *Derby* from 01. *4 Hall Court, The Village, West Hallam, Ilkeston DE7 6GS* T: 0115-944 3474

SMITH, Mrs Gabrielle Lynette Claire. b 49. St Aid Coll Dur BA 70 ARCM 73. SAOMC 95. **d** 98 **p** 99. NSM Gt Marlow w Marlow Bottom, Lt Marlow and Bisham *Ox* from 98. *29 Bovingdon Heights, Marlow SL7 2JR* T: (01628) 482923 E: gabrielle.smith@btopenworld.com

SMITH (*née* SAMPSON), **Ms Gail Sampson.** b 49. Towson State Univ (USA) BA 85. Virginia Th Sem MDiv 93. **d** 93 **p** 94. Assoc R Ellicott City St Jo USA 93-99; PtO *S'wark* 00-01; Hon C Kew St Phil and All SS w St Luke 01-02 and 06-07; The Netherlands 02-06; C Chatham St Chris USA from 07. *35 Skyline Drive, Chatham MA 02633, USA* E: ukrevgss@aol.com

SMITH, Gareth Hugh St John. b 45. FCA 69. SEITE BA 06. **d** 06 **p** 07. NSM Tunbridge Wells St Phil *Roch* 06-08. *Lavender House, Moor Hall Drive, Ninfield, Battle TN33 9JT* M: 07780-907066 E: gareth.smith@diocese-rochester.org

SMITH, Gary Russell. b 56. Southn Univ BTh 94 Ox Brookes Univ DipEd 02. Cuddesdon Coll 94. **d** 96 **p** 97. C Southampton Maybush St Pet *Win* 96-00. *Soar Valley College, Gleneagles Avenue, Leicester LE4 7GY* T: 0116-266 9625

SMITH, Gavin Craig. b 71. Ridley Hall Cam 02. **d** 04 **p** 05. C Heatons *Man* 04-07; CF from 07. *c/o MOD Chaplains (Army)* T: (01264) 383430 F: 381824 M: 07919-354796 E: gavinsmith1971@hotmail.com

SMITH, Geoffrey. b 45. Bernard Gilpin Soc Dur 65 Sarum Th Coll 66. **d** 69 **p** 70. C Hatfield *Sheff* 69-71; C Bolton St Pet *Man* 71-74; V Lt Hulton 74-78; P-in-c Newc St Andr and Soc Resp Adv Newc 78-87; Hon Can Newc Cathl 84-87; Dir Cen for Applied Chr Studies 87-91; Team Ldr Home Office Birm Drug Prevention Unit 91-93; Public Preacher *Birm* 87-93; C Brampton and Farlam and Castle Carrock w Cumrew *Carl* 93-96; ACUPA Lnk Officer 94-96; Can Res Bradf Cathl 96-00; Nat Dir Toc H 00-07; PtO *Ox* 00-02; Hon C Biddenham *St Alb* 02-07; rtd 07; PtO *Carl* from 07; *Eur* from 07. *30 Waters Meet, Warwick Bridge, Carlisle CA4 8RT* T: (01228) 560981 *or* (01228) 05602-231702 E: geoffsmith1@btinternet.com

SMITH, Canon Geoffrey Cobley. b 30. Bps' Coll Cheshunt 63. **d** 65 **p** 66. C Hockerill *St Alb* 65-68; C Evesham *Worc* 68-72; V Walberswick w Blythburgh *St E* 72-85; RD Halesworth 81-85; R Newmarket St Mary w Exning St Agnes 85-00; RD Mildenhall 86-00; Hon Can St E Cathl 87-00; rtd 00; PtO *St E* from 00. *78 Eastgate Street, Bury St Edmunds IP33 1YR* T: (01284) 731061

SMITH, Geoffrey Keith. b 37. Lon Coll of Div 57. **d** 60 **p** 61. C Leek St Luke *Lich* 60-63; C Trentham 63-66; V Lilleshall 66-84; P-in-c Sheriffhales w Woodcote 83-84; V Lilleshall and Sheriffhales 84-87; P-in-c Haughton 87-91; R Derrington, Haughton and Ranton 91-03; RD Stafford 95-03; rtd 03; PtO *Lich* from 03. *19 Meadow Drive, Haughton, Stafford ST18 9HU* T: (01785) 259076

SMITH, Geoffrey Raymond. b 49. AKC 71. St Aug Coll Cant 71. **d** 72 **p** 73. C Hendon St Alphage *Lon* 72-75; C Notting Hill St Mich and Ch Ch 75-78; P-in-c Isleworth St Fran 78-83; P-in-c Chipping Ongar *Chelmsf* 83-84; R 84-86; R Shelley 84-86; R Chipping Ongar w Shelley 86-89; RD Ongar 88-89;

P-in-c Harlow St Mary Magd 89-90; V 90-98; R Woodford St Mary w St Phil and St Jas 98-08; TR Loughton St Jo 08-09; R 09-15; rtd 15. *44 Beuzeville Avenue, Hailsham BN27 3PB*

SMITH, George Frederick. b 35. AKC 59. **d** 60 **p** 61. C Radford *Cov* 60-64; C Kenilworth St Nic 64-67; V Burton Dassett 67-71; OCM 67-71; CF 71-74; V Lapley w Wheaton Aston *Lich* 74-80; V Gt Wyrley 80-90; V Shareshill 90-95; rtd 95. *Brantome, North Road, Lampeter SA48 7JA*

SMITH, Georgina Leah. See HOLDING, Georgina Leah

SMITH, Gerald. b 36. Sarum Th Coll 61. **d** 63 **p** 64. C Menston w Woodhead *Bradf* 63-66; Chapl RAF 66-70; C Hoylake *Ches* 70-72; R Inverurie *Ab* 72-74; R Kemnay 72-74; TV Hucknall Torkard *S'well* 74-75; R Falkland Is 75-78; V Luddenden w Luddenden Foot *Wakef* 79-86; V Scopwick Gp *Linc* 86-94; P-in-c Leasingham 94-96; rtd 96; PtO *Ex* from 96; *Truro* from 00. *Ivy Cottage, Woolsery, Bideford EX39 5QS* T/F: (01237) 431298

SMITH, Mrs Gillian. b 55. EAMTC 02. **d** 05 **p** 06. NSM Burwell w Reach *Ely* 05-09; P-in-c Potton w Sutton and Cockayne Hatley *St Alb* 09-13; R from 13. *The Rectory, Hatley Road, Potton, Sandy SG19 2RP* T: (01767) 260782 E: gillsmith.pot@gmail.com

SMITH, Mrs Gillian Angela. b 39. RGN 60 RM 62. All Nations Chr Coll IDC 65. **d** 94 **p** 95. NSM Haydock St Mark *Liv* 94-96; PtO *Ely* 96-02; Hon C Milton *Win* 02-03; PtO *Ely* 03-11; *Chelmsf* 04-11; *York* from 11. *3 Belvedere Mansions, Lonsdale Road, Scarborough YO11 2QU* T: (01723) 448560 E: rev.gill@outlook.com

SMITH, Gillian Carol. See HUBBARD, Gillian Carol

SMITH, Godfrey Declan Burfield. b 42. TCD BA 64 MA 67 PGCE 65. Sarum Th Coll. **d** 69 **p** 70. Zambia 70-75; PtO *D & G* 81-02; S Regional Sec (Ireland) CMS 81-99; Overseas Sec 87-93; Miss Personnel Sec 93-99; I Donoughmore and Donard w Dunlavin *D & G* 02-11; rtd 11. *Moelvra, 1 Marlborough Road, Glenageary, Co Dublin, Republic of Ireland* M: 87-298 7364 E: declansmith14@gmail.com

SMITH, Graeme Richard. b 65. Leeds Univ BA 87 MA 91 Birm Univ PhD 97. Qu Coll Birm 87. **d** 89 **p** 90. C Daventry *Pet* 89-92; PtO *Birm* 92-97; Lect Th Westmr Coll Ox 97-00; Co Ecum Officer *Ox* 97-00; Sen Lect Ox Brookes Univ 00-02; Dean Non-Res Tr St Mich Coll Llan 04-08; Sen Lect Chich Univ from 08. *37 Middleton Hall Road, Birmingham B30 1AB* T: 0121-459 0565

SMITH, Graham. See SMITH, John Graham

SMITH, Graham. b 39. Univ of Wales (Ban) CertEd 60 Lon Univ DipEd 75. **d** 01 **p** 02. OLM Upper Holme Valley *Wakef* 01-05; NSM E Richmond *Ripon* 05-08; rtd 08. *15 Church Street, Denby Village, Ripley DE5 8PA* T: (01332) 881324 M: 07918-025346 E: graham.smith50@btopenworld.com *or* gsmith370@btinternet.com

SMITH, Graham Arthur James. b 43. MRICS 68. STETS 98 Coll of Resurr Mirfield 01. **d** 01 **p** 02. NSM Broadstone *Sarum* 01-06; NSM Christchurch *Win* 06-10; rtd 10; PtO *Sarum* from 10. *5 Durlston Road, Poole BH14 8PQ* M: 07710-328685 E: fr.graham.smith@talk21.com

SMITH, The Very Revd Graham Charles Morell. b 47. St Chad's Coll Dur BA 74. Westcott Ho Cam 74. **d** 76 **p** 77. C Tooting All SS *S'wark* 76-80; TV Thamesmead 80-87; TR Kidlington w Hampton Poyle *Ox* 87-97; RD Ox 89-95; TR Leeds City *Ripon* 97-04; Hon Can Ripon Cathl 97-04; Dean Nor 04-13; rtd 13. *Blacksmith's Cottage, Church Street, Ashreigney, Chulmleigh EX18 7LP* T: (01769) 520824 M: 07798-916321 E: graham@gcmsmith.org.uk

SMITH, Graham David Noel. b 37. Oak Hill Th Coll 72. **d** 73 **p** 74. C Southborough St Pet w Ch Ch and St Matt *Roch* 73-76; C Bedworth *Cov* 76-79; R Treeton *Sheff* 79-84; V Riddlesden *Bradf* 84-96; RD S Craven 91-96; rtd 96; Hon C Addingham All SS *Bradf* 97-03; PtO *Leeds* from 03. *26 Hawthorne Grove, Burley in Wharfdale, Ilkley LS29 7RF* T: (01943) 864754 E: graham.smith@bradford.anglican.org

SMITH, Graham John. b 31. **d** 75 **p** 76. NSM Devonport St Mark Ford *Ex* 75-81; NSM Plympton St Maurice 81-90; V Ernesettle 90-03; P-in-c 03-08; rtd 08. *15 Abingdon Road, Plymouth PL4 6HZ* T: (01752) 603812 M: 07974-815552 E: fathergrahamsmith@hotmail.com

SMITH, Graham John. b 60. RN Eng Coll Plymouth BScEng 84. Trin Coll Bris BA 90 St Jo Coll Nottm MA 00. **d** 90 **p** 91. C Herne *Cant* 90-93; Chapl RN 93-96; C Henfield w Shermanbury and Woodmancote *Chich* 96-98; Chapl Sussex Police 96-98; Chapl Portsm Hosps NHS Trust 98-00; P-in-c Cosham and Chapl Highbury Coll of FE Portsm 00-05; CME Officer *Portsm* 03-05; PtO from 06. *18 Poynings Place, Portsmouth PO1 2PB* T: (023) 9229 1239 M: 07970-826160 E: gjsmith@first-web.co.uk

SMITH, Graham Russell. b 60. New Coll Ox BA 81 MA 89 Lon Univ BD 89. Qu Coll Birm 02. **d** 04 **p** 05. C Yardley St Edburgha *Birm* 04-08; TV Bushbury *Lich* from 08. *The*

Good Shepherd Vicarage, 17 Goodyear Avenue, Wolverhampton WV10 9JX T: (01902) 731713 M: 07746-994186
E: grakiew@talktalk.net

SMITH, Grahame Clarence. b 32. Lich Th Coll 58. **d** 60 **p** 61. C New Sleaford *Linc* 60-63; R Tydd 63-76; V Barholm w Stowe 76-81; V Tallington 76-81; R Uffington 76-81; P-in-c W Deeping 76-77; R 77-81; R Uffington 81-92; rtd 92; PtO *Linc* 92-95. *Keeper's Cottage, Careby Road, Aunby, Stamford PE9 4EG* T: (01780) 66386

SMITH, Greg Peter. b 60. Warwick Univ BA 86 Qu Coll Birm BA 99. WMMTC 97. **d** 99 **p** 00. C Binley *Cov* 99-04; p-in-c E Green from 04. *St Andrew's Vicarage, Church Lane, Eastern Green, Coventry CV5 7BX* T: (024) 7642 2856
E: gregsmith31760@aol.com

SMITH, Gregory James. *See* CLIFTON-SMITH, Gregory James

SMITH, Mrs Gwendoline Anne. b 52. K Coll Lon BA 97. SEITE 97. **d** 99 **p** 00. C Erith St Paul *Roch* 99-02; V Hadlow 02-12; RD Paddock Wood 10-12; TV Bideford, Northam, Westward Ho!, Appledore etc *Ex* from 12. *The Rectory, Weare Giffard, Bideford EX39 4QP* T: (01237) 429468
E: gwensmith1252@gmail.com

SMITH, Miss Hannah Joy. b 82. Sheff Univ BA 03 K Coll Lon MA 10. St Mellitus Coll 08. **d** 12 **p** 13. C Leeds City from 12. *Holy Trinity Vicarage, 28 Hawksworth Avenue, Leeds LS5 3PN* T: 0113-245 2036 M: 07766-997287
E: hannah.smith@leedsminster.org

SMITH, Harold. *See* SMITH, Robert Harold

SMITH, Harold. b 20. Qu Coll Birm 77. **d** 80 **p** 81. NSM Gravelly Hill *Birm* 80-85; NSM Duddeston w Nechells 85-93; PtO from 93. *37 Dovey Tower, Duddeston Manor Road, Birmingham B7 4LE* T: 0121-682 9417

SMITH, Harvey Jefferson. b 19. AMCT 39 FIEE 38 FIMechE 52 FIPlantE 67 ACIArb 78. St Alb Minl Tr Scheme 81. **d** 88 **p** 97. NSM Hemel Hempstead *St Alb* 88-92 and 95-00; PtO 92-95 and from 00. *43 Garland Close, Hemel Hempstead HP2 5HU* T: (01442) 266377

SMITH, Sister Hazel Ferguson Waide. b 33. Univ Coll Lon BA 55. **dss** 64 **d** 87. CSA 58-77; St Etheldreda's Children's Home Bedf 64-85; Bedford St Paul *St Alb* 85-92; Par Dn 87-92; rtd 92; PtO *St Alb* from 92; *Ox* 93-00; Assoc Sister CSA from 03. *Paddock House, 6 Linford Lane, Willen, Milton Keynes MK15 9DL* T/F: (01908) 397267 M: 07789-654881
E: hazel.s35@ukonline.co.uk

SMITH, Henry Robert. b 41. Lanchester Poly Cov BSc 66. Qu Coll Birm 75. **d** 78 **p** 79. Hon C Hillmorton *Cov* 78-81; LtO *S'well* 81-85; Hon C Radcliffe-on-Trent and Shelford etc 85-89; C Sutton in Ashfield St Mary 89-92; P-in-c Forest Town 92-98; P-in-c Babworth w Sutton-cum-Lound 98-02; P-in-c Scofton w Osberton 98-02; R Babworth w Sutton-cum-Lound and Scofton etc 02-06; rtd 06. *61 Eldon Street, Tuxford, Newark NG22 0LG* T: (01777) 872819 E: bobsmith@dircon.co.uk

SMITH, Howard Alan. b 46. St Jo Coll Dur BA 73. Cranmer Hall Dur. **d** 74 **p** 75. C Brighton St Matthias *Chich* 74-77; C Henfield w Shermanbury and Woodmancote 77-80; R Northiam 80-87; Chapl St Ebba's Hosp Epsom 87-94; Chapl Qu Mary's Hosp Carshalton 87-94; Chapl Merton and Sutton Community NHS Trust 94-99; Chapl Epsom and St Helier Univ Hosps NHS Trust 99-08; rtd 08; PtO *S'wark* from 08; Chapl Wandsworth Primary Care Trust 10-13. *72 Park Lane, Wallington SM6 0TL* T: (020) 8643 3300
E: howard_a_smith2003@yahoo.co.uk

SMITH, Howard Gilbert. b 48. Leeds Univ BA 69. St Steph Ho Ox BA 71 MA 75 Ridley Hall Cam 72. **d** 73 **p** 74. C Wallsend St Luke *Newc* 73-76; C Farnworth and Kearsley *Man* 76-77; P-in-c Farnworth All SS 77-78; TV E Farnworth and Kearsley 78-82; V Belfield 82-93; V Leesfield 93-04; V Northallerton w Kirby Sigston *York* 04-13; rtd 13; PtO *York* from 13. *7 West End, Stokesley, Middlesbrough TS9 5BL* T: (01642) 205980
E: howardgsmith@tiscali.co.uk

SMITH, Howard Vincent. b 48. Trin Coll Bris 09. **d** 11 **p** 12. OLM Winterbourne *Bris* from 11; OLM Coalpit Heath 12-13; OLM Frampton Cotterell and Iron Acton from 12; OLM Frenchay and Winterbourne Down from 12. *15 Winchcombe Road, Frampton Cotterell, Bristol BS36 2AG* T: (01454) 773817 M: 07504-435443 E: revd.hvs@gmail.com

SMITH, Ian. b 62. Qu Coll Birm. **d** 14 **p** 15. C Edgbaston St Germain *Birm* from 14. *410 Gillott Road, Birmingham B16 9LP* M: 07841-615945 T: 0121-247 2839
E: iansmith@34hotmail.com *or* ian@stgermains.org.uk

SMITH, Canon Ian. b 62. Hull Univ BA 83 Man Univ MA 09. Oak Hill Th Coll BA 88. **d** 88 **p** 89. C W Hampstead St Luke *Lon* 88-90; C Woking St Pet *Guildf* 90-95; V Leyland St Jo *Blackb* 95-02; C Goole *Sheff* 02-03; P-in-c Sheff St Paul 03-12; R Warmsworth from 12; Hon Can Sheff Cathl from 12. *Warmsworth Rectory, 187 Warmsworth Road, Doncaster DN4 0TW* T: (01302) 853324
E: ian.smith@sheffield.anglican.org

SMITH, Canon Ian Walker. b 29. Leeds Univ BA 52. Coll of Resurr Mirfield 52. **d** 54 **p** 55. C Moulsecoomb *Chich* 54-61; Chapl K Sch Cant 61-62; C Crawley *Chich* 62-79; TV 79-81; R Clenchwarton *Ely* 81-94; RD Lynn Marshland 84-94; Hon Can Ely Cathl 88-94; PtO *Nor* 88-94; rtd 94; PtO *Ely* from 94. *27 Jubilee Drive, Dersingham, King's Lynn PE31 6YA* T: (01485) 540203

SMITH, Irene Lillian. b 47. **d** 99 **p** 00. OLM Moston St Chad *Man* from 99; OLM Moston St Jo from 11; OLM Newton Heath from 11. *1 Walmersley Road, Manchester M40 3RS* T: 0161-682 5927 E: irenel.smith@ukgateway.net

SMITH, Mrs Irene Mary. b 43. Shenstone Coll of Educn CertEd 64 Lon Univ BD 77. OLM course 96. **d** 99 **p** 00. OLM Uttoxeter Area *Lich* from 99. *16 Teanhurst Close, Tean, Stoke-on-Trent ST10 4NN* T: (01538) 722975
E: irene.smith0@btinternet.com

SMITH, Irene Victoria. *See* WATKINS, Irene Victoria

SMITH, James. *See* SMITH, Michael James

SMITH, James. *See* SMITH, Philip James

SMITH, James. b 26. NEOC 76. **d** 79 **p** 80. NSM Seaton Hirst *Newc* 79-82; NSM Cresswell and Lynemouth 82-88; NSM Cambois 88-93; rtd 93; PtO *Newc* from 93. *140 Pont Street, Ashington NE63 0PX* T: (01670) 816557

SMITH, James Edward. b 30. Chich Th Coll 57. **d** 58 **p** 59. C Ellesmere Port *Ches* 58-61; C W Bromwich All SS *Lich* 61-63; Chapl RN 63-65; V Walton St Jo *Liv* 65-71; V Anfield St Columba 71-79; V Altcar 79-92; rtd 92; PtO *Linc* 93-02. *The Hollies, 43 Carlton Road, Bassingham, Lincoln LN5 9HB* T: (01522) 788260

SMITH, James Harold. b 31. Ch Coll Tasmania ThL 61. **d** 61 **p** 61. Australia 61-63 and 66-85 and 92-94; Canada 64-65; Chapl St Chris Hospice Lon 86-87; Asst Chapl Brook Gen Hosp Lon 87-92; Asst Chapl Greenwich Distr Hosp Lon 87-92; PtO *S'wark* 94-07. *Poplar Cottage, 80 Charlton Road, London SE7 7EY* T: (020) 8858 4692

SMITH, James Henry. b 32. St Aid Birkenhead. **d** 65 **p** 66. C Wigan St Cath *Liv* 65-68; V Parkfield in Middleton *Man* 68-77; V Bolton Breightmet St Jas 77-97; rtd 97; PtO *Liv* from 97. *Flat 4, 14A Cropton Road, Formby, Liverpool L37 4AD* T: (01704) 833682

SMITH, Janet. *See* SMITH, Patricia Janet

SMITH, Janice Lilian. b 51. Open Univ BSc 98. NOC 98. **d** 01 **p** 02. NSM Yeadon St Jo *Bradf* 01-06; P-in-c Bramhope *Leeds* from 06; P-in-c Ireland Wood *Ripon* 09-12. *The Vicarage, 26 Leeds Road, Bramhope, Leeds LS16 9BQ* T: 0113-203 7523
E: revjanice.smith@tiscali.co.uk

SMITH, Canon Jeffry Bradford. b 56. Pitzer Coll BA 82. Ripon Coll Cuddesdon 83 Ch Div Sch of the Pacific (USA) MDiv 85. **d** 86 **p** 87. C Visalia USA 86-87; C Frimley *Guildf* 87-91; R E and W Clandon 91-03; Chapl HM Pris Send 94-96; Chapl HM Pris Channings Wood 03-04; Bermuda 04-09; TV Glendale Gp *Newc* 09-14; rtd 14; R Coldstream *Edin* from 15. *20 Tenter Hill, Wooler NE71 6DG* E: honesmith@talk21.com

SMITH, Mrs Jennifer Pamela. b 63. Girton Coll Cam BA 85 MA 88. Oak Hill Th Coll BA 91. **d** 91 **p** 94. C Rawdon *Bradf* 91-93; Chapl Bradf Cathl 93-96; P-in-c Kelbrook 96-00; Asst Chapl Airedale NHS Trust 01-07; Chapl Airedale NHS Foundn Trust from 07. *24 Greenacres, Skipton BD23 1BX* T: (01756) 790852 *or* (01535) 294088
E: jenny.smith@bradford.anglican.org

SMITH, Jeremy John Hawthorn. b 52. Birm Univ BSc 73 Lanc Univ MA 97. CBDTI 94. **d** 97 **p** 98. NSM Long Marton w Dufton and w Milburn *Carl* 97-00; NSM Hesket-in-the-Forest and Armathwaite 00-04; NSM Skelton and Hutton-in-the-Forest w Ivegill 00-04; NSM Ainstable 00-04; NSM Inglewood Gp 04-12. *Tanglewood, Cumwhinton, Carlisle CA4 8DL* T: (01228) 560310

SMITH, Jeremy Victor. b 60. Keble Coll Ox BA 82. Chich Th Coll 83. **d** 85 **p** 86. C Alton St Lawr *Win* 85-88; C W Hampstead St Jas *Lon* 88-93; V St Geo-in-the-East St Mary 93-97. *18 The Grange, Grange Road, London W4 4DE* T: (020) 8742 7104

SMITH, Jesse Lee. b 70. Man Univ BA 93 Nottm Univ MA 96. Linc Th Coll 94 Westcott Ho Cam 95. **d** 96 **p** 97. C Gomersal *Wakef* 96-00; C Penarth All SS *Llan* 00-02; TV Cen Cardiff 02-03; V Hartlepool H Trin *Dur* 03-08; V Caerau w Ely *Llan* from 08. *The Vicarage, Cowbridge Road West, Cardiff CF5 5BQ* T: (029) 2056 32564 E: jls4hart@yahoo.co.uk

SMITH, John. *See* SMITH, Stephen John

SMITH, John. b 64. Bournemouth Univ BA 92 Leeds Metrop Univ MSc 01 Leeds Univ BA 10 Huddersfield Univ CertEd 89. Yorks Min Course 08. **d** 10 **p** 11. C Idle *Bradf* 10-14; V Pannal w Beckwithshaw *Leeds* from 14. *St Robert's Vicarage, 21 Crimple Meadows, Pannal, Harrogate HG3 1EL* T: (01423) 391514 M: 07772-165722 E: jrs.smith@talktalk.net

SMITH, John Alec. b 37. Lon Coll of Div ALCD 62 BD 63. **d** 63 **p** 64. C Cromer *Nor* 63-66; C Barking St Marg *Chelmsf* 66-69; V Attercliffe *Sheff* 69-75; P-in-c Sheff St Barn and St Mary 76-78; V 78-89; Ind Chapl 78-89; RD Ecclesall 80-85; TR Chippenham St Paul w Hardenhuish etc *Bris* 89-00; V Kington St Michael 89-00; rtd 00. *82 Victoria Road, Bidford-on-Avon, Alcester B50 4AR* T: (01789) 772072

SMITH, John Bartlett. b 50. St Chad's Coll Dur BA 73 ACIPD. Cuddesdon Coll 73. **d** 76 **p** 77. C Heref St Martin 76-86; NSM Isleworth St Mary *Lon* 86-89; NSM Millom *Carl* 89-92; NSM Balham St Mary and St Jo *S'wark* 92-04; PtO *Ox* 10-14. *91 Willowbourne, Fleet GU51 5BP* M: 07769-990391
E: j29bs@yahoo.com

SMITH, John Denmead. b 44. Keble Coll Ox BA 65 MA 69 St Jo Coll Ox DPhil 71. Coll of Resurr Mirfield 72. **d** 75 **p** 76. NSM Win St Lawr and St Maurice w St Swithun 75-80; Chapl Win Coll 75-04; Sen Chapl 04-06; rtd 06; Lect Uganda Chr Univ Mukono from 06. *56D North Bar Without, Beverley HU17 7AB* T: (01482) 865513 E: jds1000@gmail.com

SMITH, John Ernest. b 52. St Andr Univ MTheol 77. Wycliffe Hall Ox 78. **d** 79 **p** 80. C Bermondsey St Mary w St Olave, St Jo etc *S'wark* 79-87; P-in-c Whyteleafe 87-97; RD Caterham 96-98; P-in-c Merstham and Gatton 98-10; TR Merstham, S Merstham and Gatton 10-12; P-in-c Hoo St Werburgh *Roch* from 12. *The Vicarage, Vicarage Lane, Hoo, Rochester ME3 9BB* T: (01634) 250291 E: revjohn.e.smith@btinternet.com

SMITH, John Graham. b 32. **d** 78 **p** 79. NSM Hordle *Win* 78-00; rtd 00; PtO *Win* from 00. *3 Marryat Road, New Milton BH25 5LW* T: (01425) 615701 E: rev.smith@ukgateway.net

SMITH, John Lawrence. b 43. Birm Univ BSc 65. Linc Th Coll 67. **d** 70 **p** 71. C Frodingham *Linc* 70-75; TV Gt Grimsby St Mary and St Jas 75-83; V Wolverhampton St Andr *Lich* 83-12; rtd 12; PtO *Ox* from 14. *75 Courtington Lane, Bloxham, Banbury OX15 4HS* T: (01295) 721709

SMITH, Canon John Leslie. b 44. Trin Coll Cam BA 65 MA 71. Ripon Coll Cuddesdon 79. **d** 81 **p** 82. C Ollerton *S'well* 81-84; P-in-c Farndon and Thorpe 84-88; P-in-c Winthorpe and Langford w Holme 88-95; Dioc Chief Insp of Schs 88-95; Dir of Educn *Pet* 95-99; P-in-c Cottingham w E Carlton 97-99; P-in-c Gretton w Rockingham and Cottingham w E Carlton 99; Dir of Educn *Roch* 99-10; Hon Can Roch Cathl 04-10; P-in-c Bredgar w Bicknor and Frinsted w Wormshill etc *Cant* 05-10; rtd 10; PtO *S'well* from 10. *Whiteways, Low Road, Besthorpe, Newark NG23 7HJ* T: (01636) 894277
E: revcanjohn.smith@googlemail.com

SMITH, John Malcolm. b 36. ACIB 60. NOC 81. **d** 84 **p** 85. NSM Bury St Pet *Man* 84-06; PtO from 06. *46 Ajax Drive, Bury BL9 8EF* T: 0161-766 8378

SMITH, John Roger. b 36. Dur Univ BA 59. Tyndale Hall Bris 59. **d** 61 **p** 62. C Chaddesden St Mary *Derby* 61-63; C Gresley 63-66; V Burton Ch Ch *Lich* 66-76; V Doncaster St Mary *Sheff* 76-92; R Barnburgh w Melton on the Hill etc 92-01; rtd 01; PtO *Leeds* from 02. *2 Fieldhead Drive, Cross Hills, Keighley BD20 7RJ* T: (01535) 634062

SMITH, John Simon. b 46. Middx Hosp MB, BS 70 FRCGP 91. Ripon Coll Cuddesdon 05. **d** 06 **p** 07. NSM Kettering SS Pet and Paul from 06. *34 Poplars Farm Road, Barton Seagrave, Kettering NN15 5AG* T: (01536) 513786
E: john@poplarsfarm.org

SMITH, John Sydney. b 36. Lanc Univ MA 97 ALA 59 FLA 68 FISM 82. CBDTI 94. **d** 97 **p** 98. NSM Arthuret, Nicholforest and Kirkandrews on Esk *Carl* 97-02; rtd 02; PtO *Carl* from 01. *The Jays, 3 White House, Walton, Brampton CA8 2DJ* T: (016977) 41114 E: johnandjill.thejays@btinternet.com

SMITH, John Thomas. b 29. Keele Univ DASE 72 Wolv Poly MPhil 81 PhD 87. WMMTC 87. **d** 91 **p** 92. NSM Drayton in Hales *Lich* 91-96; NSM Cheswardine, Childs Ercall, Hales, Hinstock etc 96-98; rtd 98; PtO *Lich* 98-11. *Red Bank House, Market Drayton TF9 1AY* T: (01630) 652302

SMITH, John Thompson. b 30. Wycliffe Hall Ox 64. **d** 66 **p** 67. C Walsall *Lich* 66-69; V Stoke Prior *Worc* 69-75; Asst Gen Sec Red Triangle Club 75-85; R Trendring and Lt Bentley w Beaumont cum Moze *Chelmsf* 85-89; R Fairstead w Terling and White Notley etc 89-92; Chapl Heath Hosp Tendring 85-92; rtd 92; PtO *B & W* from 92. *1 Harvey Close, Weston-super-Mare BS22 7DW* T: (01934) 514256

SMITH, John Trevor. b 47. GGSM. Coll of Resurr Mirfield 74. **d** 77 **p** 78. C Loughton St Jo *Chelmsf* 77-80; C Ruislip St Martin *Lon* 80-84; P-in-c Southall Ch Redeemer 84-91; V Kingsbury St Andr 91-13; rtd 13; PtO *Nor* from 13. *1 All Saints Street, King's Lynn PE30 5AD* T: (01553) 775250
E: johntsmith23@btinternet.com

SMITH, John William. b 51. EAMTC 00. **d** 03 **p** 04. NSM Erpingham w Calthorpe, Ingworth, Aldborough etc *Nor* 03-06; P-in-c Roughton and Felbrigg, Metton, Sustead etc 06-15; rtd 15. *18 Pound Lane, Aylsham, Norwich NR11 6DR* T: (01263) 734761 E: ajksmith@btinternet.com

SMITH, Jonathan Paul. b 60. Univ of Wales (Lamp) BA 81. Wycliffe Hall Ox 82. **d** 84 **p** 85. C Baglan *Llan* 84-88; C Gabalfa 88-90; R Llangammarch w Llanganten and Llanlleonfel etc *S & B* 90-01; Dioc Missr 95-01; R Denbigh *St As* 01-15; AD 09-14; from 15. *Llwyn, 3 Craigmillar Road, Wrexham LL12 7AR* T: (01978) 350797
E: plwyfdinbych@googlemail.com

SMITH, The Ven Jonathan Peter. b 55. K Coll Lon BD 77 AKC 77 Cam Univ PGCE 78. Westcott Ho Cam 79. **d** 80 **p** 81. C Gosforth All SS *Newc* 80-82; C Waltham Abbey *Chelmsf* 82-85; Chapl City Univ *Lon* 85-88; R Harrold and Carlton w Chellington *St Alb* 88-97; Chapl Beds Police 90-97; V Harpenden St Jo *St Alb* 97-08; RD Wheathampstead 99-04; Adn St Alb from 08. *6 Sopwell Lane, St Albans AL1 1RR* T: (01727) 818121 E: archdstalbans@stalbans.anglican.org

SMITH, Joseph Paul Tobias George. b 73. Ox Univ BTh 95 Ex Univ MA 97. **d** 08 **p** 09. OLM Talbot Village *Sarum* 08-11; NSM Branksome St Aldhelm from 11. *16 Southlea Avenue, Bournemouth BH6 3AB* T: (01202) 424148
E: smithjoe91264316@aol.com

SMITH, Joyce Mary. b 52. Lon Hosp BDS 74 Nottm Univ MMedSc 77 Lon Univ PhD 84 MCCDRCS 89. EAMTC. **d** 00 **p** 01. C Harlow St Mary and St Hugh w St Jo the Bapt *Chelmsf* 00-02; C Waltham H Cross 02-03; TV 03-10; NSM from 10; RD Epping Forest 10-13; RD Epping Forest and Ongar from 13; Chapl St Clare Hospice 10-14. *2 Takeley Close, Waltham Abbey EN9 1QH* T: (01992) 733655 E: revdjoyces@sky.com

SMITH, Miss Judith. b 74. SS Coll Cam BA 95 MA 98 PGCE 97. Trin Coll Bris BA 09. **d** 09 **p** 10. C Beeston *Ripon* 09-13; TV Abbeylands *Leeds* from 13. *St Mary's Vicarage, 50 Cragside Walk, Leeds LS5 3QE* T: 0113-258 2923
E: revjudesmith@gmail.com

SMITH, Julian William. b 64. Liv Univ BSc 85. Trin Coll Bris BA 93. **d** 93 **p** 94. C Henfynyw w Aberaeron and Llanddewi Aberarth *St D* 93-97; V Llansantffraed and Llanbadarn Trefeglwys etc 97-05; V Llansantffraed w Llanrhystud and Llanddeiniol from 05. *The Vicarage, 11 Maes Wyre, Llanrhystud SY23 5AH* T: (01974) 202336 E: julian.debs@tiscali.co.uk

SMITH, Julie Lesley. b 64. **d** 14 **p** 15. C Saltburn-by-the-Sea *York* from 14. *10 Allendale Tee, New Marske, Redcar TS11 8HN* E: jls446439@gmail.com

SMITH, Mrs Justine Lydia. b 69. **d** 12 **p** 13. C Elloughton and Brough w Brantingham *York* from 12. *14 Aspen Walk, Welton, Brough HU15 1TB* T: (01430) 431449
E: mjandsmith@googlemail.com or justinesmith2288@gmail.com

SMITH, Mrs Katharine Emma. b 85. Pemb Coll Cam MEng 08. Ridley Hall Cam 11. **d** 14. C Battersea St Pet and St Paul *S'wark* from 14. *24 Parma Crescent, London SW11 1LT* M: 07814-601366 E: katesmith@gmail.com

SMITH, Mrs Katherine Jane. b 42. Sussex Univ BA 65. **d** 07 **p** 08. NSM Battersea St Luke *S'wark* 07-12; rtd 12; PtO *S'wark* from 12. *74 Alfriston Road, London SW11 6NW* T: (020) 7228 3079 M: 07747-874970
E: katherine.smith42@btopenworld.com

SMITH, Keith. b 46. ACIB. S Dios Minl Tr Scheme 85. **d** 87 **p** 88. NSM W Worthing St Jo *Chich* 87-94; NSM Maybridge 94-96; C Durrington 96-01; V Pagham 01-11; rtd 11. *20 Trent Road, Worthing BN12 4EL* T: (01903) 534498
E: keith_smith_99@yahoo.com

SMITH, Kenneth Robert. b 48. K Coll Lon BD 75 AKC 75. St Aug Coll Cant 75. **d** 76 **p** 77. C Birtley *Dur* 76-80; V Lamesley 80-90; R Whitburn 90-13; rtd 13. *105 Sidecliffe Road, Sunderland SR6 9JR* T: 0191-549 7700

SMITH, Kenneth Victor George. b 37. ALCD 61 Lon Univ BD 62. **d** 62 **p** 63. Hon C Bromley Common St Aug *Roch* 62-66; Hon C Streatham Immanuel w St Anselm *S'wark* 66-68; PtO 68-78; Chapl Whitgift Sch and Ho Croydon 78-97; Hon C Sanderstead All SS *S'wark* 78-91; Hon C Croydon St Jo 91-97; rtd 02. *Bridle Ways, Haling Grove, South Croydon CR2 6DQ* T: (020) 8680 4460

SMITH, Kevin. b 66. Westmr Coll Ox BA 89. Chich Th Coll 90. **d** 92 **p** 93. C Worksop Priory *S'well* 92-96; V New Cantley *Sheff* 96-03; P-in-c Horden *Dur* 03-06; V from 06. *The Vicarage, 4 Stapylton Drive, Peterlee SR8 4HY* T: 0191-586 7110
E: ks.horden@btinternet.com

SMITH, Laurence Robert. b 91. UEA BA 12. Ridley Hall Cam 12. **d** 15. C Bury St Edmunds St Mary St E from 15. *18 Vinery Road, Bury St Edmunds IP33 2JR* M: 07909-331350
E: revlaurencesmith@gmail.com

SMITH, Laurence Sidney. b 37. Sarum & Wells Th Coll 70. **d** 73 **p** 74. C Surbiton St Matt *S'wark* 73-77; C Horley 76-81; V W Ewell *Guildf* 81-90; V W Byfleet 90-02; rtd 02; PtO *Glouc* from 03. *Candlemill Cottage, Millbank, George Street, Nailsworth, Stroud GL6 0AG* T: (01453) 836432

SMITH, Lawrence Paul. b 51. Southn Univ BTh 81 Ch Ch Coll
Cant CertEd 72. Chich Th Coll 76. **d** 79 **p** 80. C Margate St Jo
Cant 79-84; R Eythorne and Elvington w Waldershare etc
84-97; Par Min Development Adv Kensington Area Lon 97-09;
NSM Isleworth St Fran 00-09; P-in-c 05-09; TR Northfleet
and Rosherville Roch from 09; P-in-c Perry Street from 14.
St Botolph's Vicarage, The Hill, Northfleet, Gravesend DA11 9EU
T: (01474) 566400 E: lawrence.smith@diocese-rochester.org

SMITH, Lewis Shand. b 52. Aber Univ MA 74 Edin Univ BD 78
FRSA 00. Edin Th Coll 74. **d** 77 **p** 78. C Wishaw Glas 77-79;
P-in-c 79-80; C Motherwell 77-79; P-in-c 79-80; R Lerwick and
Burravoe Ab 80-00; Can St Andr Cathl 93-00; R Dumfries Glas
00-05; Miss to Seamen 80-00; LtO Edin from 08. Sandview,
Bigton, Shetland ZE2 9JA M: 07785-744610
E: shand.smith@talk21.com

SMITH, Mrs Linda Jean. b 61. Ripon Coll Cuddesdon 97. **d** 99
p 00. C St Martin w Looe Truro 99-03; P-in-c Talland 03-09;
C Lanreath, Pelynt and Bradoc 03-09; TV Langtree Ox from
09. The Vicarage, Reading Road, Woodcote, Reading RG8 0QX
T: (01491) 680979

SMITH, Linnet. See SMITH, Diana Linnet

SMITH, Miss Lorna Cassandra. b 43. Open Univ BA 76. Cant
Sch of Min 82. **dss** 86 **d** 87 **p** 94. Birchington w Acol and
Minnis Bay Cant 86-92; Par Dn 87-92; C Addlestone Guildf
92-97; V Englefield Green 97-05; rtd 05; PtO Guildf from 05;
Lon 08-13. 39 Simons Walk, Englefield Green, Egham TW20 9SJ
T: (01784) 470800 E: revlcs@aol.com

SMITH, Mrs Lorna Rosalind. b 53. Oak Hill NSM Course 89.
d 92 **p** 94. NSM Squirrels Heath Chelmsf 92-94; NSM Stanford-
le-Hope w Mucking 94-97; P-in-c Fobbing 97-04; P-in-c
Tillingham 04-15; rtd 15. 33 Latchingdon Road, Cold Norton
CM3 6JG T: E: lornads24@aol.com

SMITH, Lydia Jane. b 63. St Mellitus Coll BA 13. **d** 13 **p** 14.
C Saffron Walden and Villages Chelmsf from 13. 42 De Vigier
Avenue, Saffron Walden CB10 2BN
E: lydiasmith73@googlemail.com

SMITH, Lynford. See SMITH, Francis Christian Lynford

SMITH (née THORNTON), Magdalen Mary. b 69. Warwick Univ
BA 90. Qu Coll Birm BD 95. **d** 96 **p** 97. C Kirkby Liv 96-98;
C Birm St Martin w Bordesley St Andr 00-03; NSM Tilston and
Shocklach Ches 03-08; C Wilmslow from 08; Asst Dir of Ords
12-14; Dioc Dir of Ords from 14. The Rectory, 15 Parkway,
Wilmslow SK9 1LS T: (01625) 524717 or 520309
E: revmagssmith@btinternet.com

SMITH, Margaret Elizabeth. b 46. Bretton Hall Coll CertEd 67.
NOC 85. **d** 88 **p** 94. Hon Par Dn Battyeford Wakef 88-89; Hon
C Mirfield 89-91; Chapl HM Pris and YOI New Hall 90-95;
Dn-in-c Flockton cum Denby Grange Wakef 91-94; P-in-c
94-96; V Scholes 96-01; P-in-c Buckden Ely 01-05; P-in-c
Offord D'Arcy w Offord Cluny 01-05; R Buckden w the
Offords 05-06; rtd 06; PtO Leeds from 06. 9 Bobbin Mill Court,
Steeton, Keighley BD20 6PU T: (01535) 654721
E: memagsmith@tesco.net

SMITH, Mrs Marion Elizabeth. b 51. Bris Univ CertEd 73 Middx
Univ BA 99. NTMTC. **d** 98 **p** 99. NSM Cowley Lon 98-00;
P-in-c Harlington 00-08; R from 08. The Rectory, St Peter's Way,
Hayes UB3 5AB T: (020) 8759 9569 M: 07803-617509
E: marion.smith@tiscali.co.uk

SMITH, Mark Andrew. b 59. UNISA BA 86. St Paul's Coll
Grahamstown 85 **d** 86 **p** 86. P Port Elizabeth St Mary Magd S
Africa 88-89; R Cradock St Pet 89-92; R Alexandra Plurality 93;
Chapl St Andr Coll Grahamstown 94-01; Chapl Denstone
Coll Uttoxeter 02-07; NSM Alton w Bradley-le-Moors and
Oakamoor w Cotton Lich 06-07; NSM Denstone w Ellastone
and Stanton 06-07; NSM Mayfield 06-07; Chapl K Coll
Taunton from 07. King's College, South Road, Taunton TA1 3LA
T: (01823) 328211 or 328137
E: masmith@kings-taunton.co.uk

SMITH, Mark David. See LAYNESMITH, Mark David

SMITH, Mark Gordon Robert Davenport. b 56. St Jo Coll Dur
BA 77. Ridley Hall Cam 78. **d** 80 **p** 81. C Sheff St Jo 80-83;
C Brightside w Wincobank 83-86; V Kimberworth Park 86-91;
Consultant NE England CPAS 91-98; Nat Co-ord Cert in Evang
Studies (CA) 98-04; Chapl for Deaf People Derby 04-15;
V Rawdon Leeds from 15; Min in Deaf Community from 15.
The Vicarage, Layton Avenue, Rawdon, Leeds LS19 6QQ
M: 07702-269608 T: 0113-391 0389
E: mail@revmarksmith.com or mark@deafchurch.co.uk

SMITH, Mark Graham. b 63. Ex Univ BA 86 Lanc Univ PhD 03.
Westcott Ho Cam 87. **d** 90 **p** 91. C Cottingham York 90-92;
C Guisborough 92-94; Sen Chapl St Martin's Coll Blackb
94-98; V Ashton-on-Ribble St Mich w Preston St Mark 98-03;
V Scotforth 03-10; Dioc World Development Adv 00-10; P-in-c
Vale of Belvoir Leic 10-14; PtO 14-15. Address temp unknown
E: mark-smith23@sky.com

SMITH, Mark Peter. b 61. Reading Univ BA 82 Open Univ BA 93
MA 97 Liv Univ MTh 02 Keele Univ PGCE 84. NOC 99. **d** 02
p 03. C Wingerworth Derby 02-06; TV Ex St Thos and Em
06-09; P-in-c Kingsteignton and Teigngrace 09-15; V from 15.
The Vicarage, Daws Meadow, Kingsteignton, Newton Abbot
TQ12 3UA T: (01626) 355127
E: mark@mpsosb1.demon.co.uk

SMITH, Mark Stephen. b 84. Peterho Cam BA 05 PGCE 06
MA 10 MPhil 12. Ridley Hall Cam 08. **d** 12 **p** 13. C Lt Shelford
Ely 12-15; Chapl Peterho Cam 12-15; Chapl Ch Coll Cam
from 15; LtO Ely from 15. 59 Church Road, Hauxton, Cambridge
CB22 5HS T: (01223) 874194 E: mss53@cam.ac.uk or
m.s.smith.02@cantab.net

SMITH, Mark Winton. b 60. St Jo Coll Dur BA 81 Barrister-at-
Law (Middle Temple) 82. SEITE 01. **d** 04 **p** 05. NSM E
Wickham S'wark from 04. 16 Watersmeet Way, London
SE28 8PU T/F: (020) 8310 5063 E: revdmarksmith@aol.com

SMITH, Martin David. b 52. Hull Univ BA 75 LTCL. Cuddesdon
Coll 75. **d** 78 **p** 79. C Brentwood St Thos Chelmsf 78-80;
C Reading St Giles Ox 80-91; R Colkirk w Oxwick w Pattesley,
Whissonsett etc Nor 91-95; P-in-c Gt and Lt Ryburgh w
Gateley and Testerton 94-95; P-in-c Hempton and Pudding
Norton 94-95; P-in-c Nor St Pet Parmentergate w St Jo 95-03;
R Nor St Jo w St Julian 03-13; rtd 13. 67 Sunny Grove, Norwich
NR5 0EJ T: (01603) 742396 E: frmartinsmith@clara.net

SMITH, Martin Lee. b 47. Worc Coll Ox BA 68 MA 72.
Cuddesdon Coll 68. **d** 70 **p** 71. C Digswell St Alb 70-71;
C Cheshunt 71-73; PtO Ox 74-80; SSJE 76-02; USA from 81;
rtd 12. 1245 4th Street SW E-208, Washington DC 20024,
USA E: martin.l.smith@worldnet.att.net

SMITH, Martin Stanley. b 53. Univ of Wales (Abth) BScEcon 75.
STETS. **d** 99 **p** 00. NSM Woking Ch Ch Guildf from 99.
Brackenlea, 11 Heather Close, Horsell, Woking GU21 4JR
T: (01483) 714307 E: martin.wokingmiffs@googlemail.com

SMITH, Canon Martin William. b 40. K Coll Lon BD 63 AKC 63.
d 64 **p** 65. C Ashford St Hilda CD Lon 64-67; R Labuan Sabah
Malaysia 67-69; R Likas Sabah 69-71; V Lakenham St Mark Nor
72-85; V N Walsham w Antingham 85-01; P-in-c Neatishead,
Barton Turf and Irstead 94-95; RD Tunstead 91-96; RD St Benet
96-99; Hon Can Nor Cathl 93-05; V Wymondham 01-05;
rtd 06; PtO Nor from 06. Dragon House, 72 Besthorpe Road,
Attleborough NR17 2NQ T: (01953) 456003
E: smithdragonhouse@btinternet.com

SMITH, Martyn. b 52. CertEd 73. Oak Hill Th Coll BA 81. **d** 81
p 82. C Halliwell St Pet Man 81-86; V Cambridge St Martin
Ely 86-89; Vineyard Chr Fellowship from 89. M V Centre,
1 Belmont House, Deakins Park, Blackburn Road, Egerton, Bolton
BL7 9RP T: 08452-303321
E: admin@manchestervineyard.co.uk

SMITH, Megan Rachel. b 70. Man Univ MB, ChB 94 Liv Univ
MTh 00 Univ of Wales Coll of Medicine MSc 04 MRCP 97
FRCPCH 05. EMMTC 06. **d** 07 **p** 08. NSM Wilford S'well
07-12; V Lenton from 12; Asst Chapl Nottm Univ from 12. The
Vicarage, 35A Church Street, Nottingham NG7 2FF T: 0115-998
9306 E: megansmith@doctors.net.uk or
vicar@lentonparish.org.uk

SMITH, Melvyn. See SMITH, William Melvyn

SMITH, Merrick Thomas Jack. b 37. CEng 65 MCIBSE 65. Oak
Hill NSM Course 90. **d** 92 **p** 93. NSM Isleworth St Mary Lon
92-94; PtO Birm 94-96; NSM Warfield Ox 96-98; TV
Wallingford 98-01; P-in-c Tredington and Darlingscott w
Newbold on Stour Cov 01-03; rtd 03; PtO Sarum from 03;
P-in-c Ilsington Ex 06-11; PtO Truro from 11; Ex from 13.
4 Lendon Way, Winkleigh EX19 8JS
E: smith.merrick@btinternet.com

SMITH, Michael. b 54. Matlock Coll of Educn CertEd 76 Nottm
Univ BEd 77. Ridley Hall Cam 87. **d** 89 **p** 90. C Ilkeston
St Mary Derby 89-92; TV Wirksworth 92-98; RD 97-98;
V Ashbourne St Oswald w Mapleton 98-04; P-in-c Ashbourne
St Jo 98-04; rtd 09. 4 Montford Road, Worksop S81 7RY
E: mikesmith@belton77.wanadoo.co.uk

SMITH, Canon Michael David. b 57. BA 80. St Steph Ho Ox 81.
d 83 **p** 84. C Beaconsfield Ox 83-87; V Wing w Grove 87-92;
R Farnham Royal w Hedgerley 92-01; P-in-c Cookham 01-03;
V The Cookhams 03-13; AD Maidenhead and Windsor 11-13;
Can Res York Minster from 13. 4 Minster Yard, York YO1 7JD
T: (01904) 557211

SMITH, Michael David. b 68. Westmr Th Cen 11 Trin Coll
Bris 13. **d** 15. C Cheltenham Ch Ch Glouc from 15. Hilltops,
10 Chapel Lane, Woodmancote, Cheltenham GL52 9HT
T: (01242) 672392 M: 07909-363037
E: mdsmith.email@gmail.com

SMITH, Michael Edward. b 69. MCIM. STETS 08. **d** 11 **p** 12.
C Chandler's Ford Win 11-14; V Hatch Warren and
Beggarwood from 14. 29 Lapin Lane, Basingstoke RG22 4XH
M: 07799-730362 E: frmichael.smith@gmail.com

SMITH, Michael Ian Antony. b 69. Warwick Univ BSc 91. Oak Hill Th Coll BA 95. **d** 95 **p** 96. C Cheadle *Ches* 95-98; C Hollington St Leon *Chich* 98-01; C Hartford *Ches* 01-04; V from 04. *The Vicarage, 7 The Green, Hartford, Northwich CW8 1QA* T: (01606) 77557 *or* 872255
E: mike@stjohnshartford.org

SMITH, Michael James. b 47. AKC 69. St Aug Coll Cant 70. **d** 71 **p** 72. C Corby St Columba *Pet* 71-78; V Collierley *Dur* 78-80; CPAS Evang 83-90; rtd 12. *Freshfields, Mutton Hall Hill, Heathfield TN21 8NL*

SMITH, Michael John. b 47. Kelham Th Coll 65. **d** 71 **p** 72. C Cov St Mary 71-75; Chapl RN 75-90; CF 90-95; R Lynch w Iping Marsh and Milland *Chich* 95-03; RD Midhurst 98-03; Community Chapl Bielefeld Station Germany 03-12; rtd 13. *36 Sherwin Road, Stapleford, Nottingham NG9 8PQ*
E: revmjsmith@hotmail.com

SMITH, Michael Keith John. b 66. Thames Poly BSc 88. Linc Th Coll BTh 95. **d** 95 **p** 96. C Birch St Agnes w Longsight St Jo w St Cypr *Man* 95-99; TV Pendleton 99-06; P-in-c Lower Kersal 03-06; Bp's Chapl and Policy Adv *Leic* 06-14; R Caversham Thameside and Mapledurham *Ox* from 14. *The Rectory, 20 Church Road, Caversham, Reading RG4 7AD* T: 0118-947 9505 E: mkjsmith@btinternet.com

SMITH, Michael Raymond. b 36. Qu Coll Cam BA 59 MA 63 ARCM 56 ARCO 56. Cuddesdon Coll 64. **d** 65 **p** 66. C Redcar *York* 65-70; V Dormanstown 70-73; Prec Worc Cathl 73-77; TR Worc St Barn w Ch Ch 77-83; RD Worc E 79-83; V Eskdale, Irton, Muncaster and Waberthwaite *Carl* 83-87; Chapl Uppingham Sch 87-93; P-in-c Stoke Lacy, Moreton Jeffries w Much Cowarne etc *Heref* 93-01; Dioc Schs Officer 93-01; rtd 01; PtO *Heref* 04-12; *Mon* from 10. *Upper House, Grosmont, Abergavenny NP7 8EP* T: (01981) 240790
E: michael.smith365@btinternet.com

SMITH, Michael Richard Guy. b 55. Man Univ BA 77. Ripon Coll Cuddesdon 88. **d** 90 **p** 91. C Wallasey St Hilary *Ches* 90-93; C Howden *York* 93-94; TV 94-97; V Gt and Lt Driffield 04-10; RD Harthill 08-10; Chapl Puerto de la Cruz Tenerife *Eur* 10-14; P-in-c Nailsworth w Shortwood, Horsley etc *Glouc* 14-15; V from 15. *The Vicarage, 3 Vicarage Gardens, Nailsworth, Stroud GL6 0QS* M: 07840-260182 E: mike.davica@sky.com

SMITH, Neville. *See* SMITH, Charles Henry Neville

SMITH, Preb Olwen. b 44. Birm Univ BA 66. Selly Oak Coll 67. **d** 87 **p** 94. Ind Chapl Black Country Urban Ind Miss *Lich* 84-98; TV Cen Wolverhampton 94-10; Preb Lich Cathl 99-10; rtd 10; PtO *Lich* 10-12; *Ox* from 14. *75 Courtington Lane, Bloxham, Banbury OX15 4HS* T: (01295) 721709
E: smitholwen@btinternet.com

SMITH, Mrs Pamela Christina. b 46. SAOMC 97. **d** 00 **p** 01. NSM Ironstone Ox and Chapl Kath Ho Hospice 00-10; PtO *Ox* from 10. *15 Park View Road, Witney OX28 1GA* T: (01993) 834801 E: pamela.p.c.smith@btinternet.com

SMITH, Miss Pamela Frances. b 44. St Mary's Coll Chelt TCert 65. WEMTC 91. **d** 94 **p** 95. NSM Badgeworth, Shurdington and Witcombe w Bentham *Glouc* 94-02; NSM The Lavingtons, Cheverells, and Easterton *Sarum* 02-05; C E Clevedon w Clapton in Gordano etc *B & W* 05-08; rtd 08. *25 Glebe Farm Court, Up Hatherley, Cheltenham GL51 3EB* E: pfsmith@freeuk.com

SMITH, Ms Pamela Jane Holden. b 56. Warwick Univ BA 78 Lon Inst of Educn PGCE 82. Qu Coll Birm BA 04. **d** 04 **p** 05. C Coventry Caludon *Cov* 04-08; NSM 04-06; PtO from 08; Web Pastor i-church *Ox* from 08. *34 Styvechale Avenue, Coventry CV5 6DX* T: (024) 7667 2893 E: rev.pam.smith@gmail.com *or* webpastor@i-church.org

SMITH, Mrs Patricia. b 48. **d** 10 **p** 11. NSM Silsden *Leeds* from 10. *34 Lower Park Green, Silsden, Keighley BD20 9QE* T: (01535) 653740 E: pat@smithcorner.co.uk

SMITH, Ms Patricia Janet. b 45. Oak Hill Th Coll 87. **d** 89 **p** 90. Canada 89-02; V Charminster and Stinsford *Sarum* from 02; P-in-c Bradford Peverell, Stratton, Frampton etc from 09; RD Dorchester from 09. *The Vicarage, Mill Lane, Charminster, Dorchester DT2 9QP* T: (01305) 262477
E: plumsmith18@googlemail.com

SMITH, Patricia Joanna. **d** 12 **p** 13. C Dumbarton *Glas* 12-14; C Johnstone from 14; C Renfrew from 14. *21 Macleod Drive, Helensburgh G84 9QS* T: (01436) 671091
E: patsmithcurate@gmail.com

SMITH, Paul. b 52. **d** 98 **p** 99. OLM Leominster *Heref* from 98. *32 The Meadows, Leominster HR6 8RF* T: (01568) 615862 *or* 612124

SMITH, Paul. b 48. STETS 99. **d** 02 **p** 03. NSM Copthorne *Chich* 02-12; rtd 12. *7 Heather Close, Copthorne, Crawley RH10 3PZ* T: (01342) 714308 E: heatherclose@freenet.co.uk

SMITH, Paul Aidan. b 59. Birm Univ BA 82. Wycliffe Hall Ox 82. **d** 85 **p** 86. C Selly Park St Steph and St Wulstan *Birm* 85-88; C Kensal Rise St Mark and St Martin *Lon* 88-91; V Water

Eaton *Ox* 91-00; TR Hale w Badshot Lea *Guildf* 00-02; TV Stantonbury and Willen *Ox* 02-09; TR from 09. *2 Hooper Gate, Willen, Milton Keynes MK15 9JR* T: (01908) 606689 M: 07930-308644 E: paul_a_smith@bigfoot.com

SMITH, Paul Allan. b 66. Ch Coll Cam BA 88 MA 00 PhD 94. WMMTC 98 Ripon Coll Cuddesdon 99. **d** 00 **p** 01. C Moseley St Mary *Birm* 00-03; P-in-c Tilston and Shocklach *Ches* 03-08; Officer for Initial Min Tr 03-08; R Wilmslow from 08. *The Rectory, 15 Parkway, Wilmslow SK9 1LS* T: (01625) 524717 *or* 520309 E: revpaulsmith@btinternet.com

SMITH, Paul Andrew. b 55. St Chad's Coll Dur BA 76. Chich Th Coll 78. **d** 80 **p** 81. C Habergham Eaves St Matt *Blackb* 80-83; C Ribbleton 83-86; V Rishton 86-05; RD Whalley 95-01; R Cottingham *York* from 05; AD Cen and N Hull from 10. *The Rectory, Hallgate, Cottingham HU16 4DD* T: (01482) 847668 E: dreadnoughtfam@aol.com

SMITH, Paul Anthony. b 66. Ripon Coll Cuddesdon. **d** 00 **p** 01. C Prestwood and Gt Hampden *Ox* 00-05; P-in-c W Leigh *Portsm* 05-06; V 06-10; TV Abingdon *Ox* from 10. *St Michael's Vicarage, Faringdon Road, Abingdon OX14 1BG* T: (01235) 534654 E: paul315smith@btinternet.com

SMITH, Preb Paul Gregory. b 39. Ex Univ BA 61. St Steph Ho Ox 61. **d** 63 **p** 64. C Walthamstow St Mich *Chelmsf* 63-66; C Devonport St Mark Ford *Ex* 66-69; C Hemel Hempstead St Alb 69-71; TV 71-83; R Bideford *Ex* 83-96; TR Bideford, Northam, Westward Ho!, Appledore etc 96; Chapl Bideford and Torridge Hosps 83-96; P-in-c Ex St Jas 96-98; R 98-03; rtd 03; Preb Ex Cathl from 95. *Valrose, Broad Lane, Appledore, Bideford EX39 1ND* T: (01237) 423513
E: fatherpaulsmith@aol.com

SMITH, Mrs Paula Mary. b 57. Sheff Poly BA 79 Qu Coll Birm BA 06. WMMTC 03. **d** 06 **p** 07. C Walsall *Lich* 06-10; P-in-c Donnington Wood from 10; Min Development Adv (Salop) from 10. *St Matthew's Vicarage, St George's Road, Donnington, Telford TF2 7NJ* T: (01952) 604239
E: revdpaula@hotmail.co.uk

SMITH, Mrs Pauline Frances. b 37. Bris Univ BA 58 Lon Univ CertEd 59. Sarum & Wells Th Coll 87. **d** 90 **p** 94. C Cobham *Guildf* 90-96; P-in-c Lower Wylye and Till Valley *Sarum* 96-97; TV Wylye and Till Valley 97-03; RD Stonehenge 01-03; rtd 03; PtO *Glouc* from 04. *267B London Road, Charlton Kings, Cheltenham GL52 6YG* T: (01242) 222810
E: panda.smith@talktalk.net

SMITH, Mrs Pauline Patricia. **d** 14 **p** 15. C Coity, Nolton and Brackla w Coychurch *Llan* from 14. *The Rectory, 9 Heol Cae Tyla, Coychurch, Bridgend CF35 5HR* T: (01656) 645876
E: pauline.930smith@btinternet.com

SMITH (formerly FLEMING), Penelope Rawling. b 43. Glas Univ MA 63. Westcott Ho Cam 87. **d** 89 **p** 94. C Bourne *Guildf* 89-94; R Wotton and Holmbury St Mary 94-01; RD Dorking 99-01; Dioc Voc Adv 94-01; R Gt Bookham 01-07; rtd 07. *Westrip Farm House, Redhouse Lane, Westrip, Stroud GL6 6HA* T: (01453) 757296

SMITH, Peter. b 49. Ex Univ BSc 69 PGCE 73. Carl Dioc Tr Course. **d** 82 **p** 83. NSM Kendal H Trin *Carl* from 82. *55 Empson Road, Kendal LA9 5PR* T: (01539) 721467
E: rev.p.smith@btinternet.com

SMITH, Peter. b 36. Keele Univ BA 60. Cuddesdon Coll 73. **d** 75 **p** 76. C Shrewsbury St Chad *Lich* 75-80; V Burton St Chad 80-90; P-in-c Berwick w Selmeston and Alciston *Chich* 90-91; R 91-02; rtd 02; PtO *Sarum* from 03. *40 Homefield, Child Okeford, Blandford Forum DT11 8EN* T: (01258) 861833

SMITH, Peter Alexander. *See* GRAYSMITH, Peter Alexander

SMITH, Peter Denis Frank. b 52. Local Minl Tr Course. **d** 81 **p** 83. OLM Camberwell St Mich w All So w Em *S'wark* 81-95; OLM Croydon St Jo 95-04; PtO from 10. *57 Alton Road, Croydon CR0 4LZ* T: (020) 8406 3557
E: peter.smith59@live.co.uk

SMITH, Peter Francis Chasen. b 28. Leeds Univ BA 54. Coll of Resurr Mirfield 54. **d** 56 **p** 57. C E Dulwich St Clem *S'wark* 56-59; C Sutton St Nic 59-62; C-in-c Wrangbrook w N Elmsall CD *Wakef* 62-68; Chapl St Aid Sch Harrogate 68-85; P-in-c Lower Nidderdale *Ripon* 85-93; rtd 93; PtO *Leeds* from 93; *York* from 95. *Clematis Cottage, Main Street, Kilburn, York YO61 4AH* T: (01347) 868394 E: peter.f.c.smith@btinternet.com

SMITH, Peter Harold. b 53. Cumbria Univ BA 13. LCTP 07. **d** 10 **p** 11. NSM Euxton *Blackb* 10-15; C Chorley St Pet from 15. *St Peter's Vicarage, Harpers Lane, Chorley PR6 0HT* M: 07412-624931 T: (01257) 433308
E: vicarstpeter@gmail.com

SMITH, Peter Henry. b 62. Bris Univ BA 83. SEITE 96. **d** 99 **p** 00. C Romford St Edw *Chelmsf* 99-02; V Aldersbrook 02-10; TR Waltham H Cross from 10. *The Rectory, Highbridge Street, Waltham Abbey EN9 1DG* T: (01992) 701352
E: peterhxsmith@aol.com

SMITH, Peter Howard. b 57. St Jo Coll Dur BSc 78 Selw Coll Cam BA 82 MA 85. Ridley Hall Cam 80. **d** 83 **p** 84. C Welling *Roch* 83-87; C Hubberston w Herbrandston and Hasguard etc *St D* 87-88; C Hubberston 89-91; V Canley *Cov* 91-00; V Burney Lane *Birm* 00-06; P-in-c 06-07; P-in-c Ward End 06-07; P-in-c Bordesley Green 06-07; V Ward End w Bordesley Green from 07; AD Yardley and Bordesley 05-12. *Christ Church Vicarage, Burney Lane, Birmingham B8 2AS* T: 0121-783 7455 E: peter@ccbl.org.uk

SMITH, Peter Howard. b 55. St Andr Univ MTheol 78. Trin Coll Bris 78. **d** 79 **p** 80. C Handforth *Ches* 79-82; C Eccleston St Luke *Liv* 82-85; V Leyton St Paul *Chelmsf* 85-91; V Darwen St Barn *Blackb* 91-99; TR Bushbury *Lich* 99-06; R Hawkwell *Chelmsf* from 06. *The Rectory, Ironwell Lane, Hawkwell, Hockley SS5 4JY* T: (01702) 200620 E: peterhsmith@talktalk.net

SMITH, Peter James. b 23. K Coll Lon 49. **d** 53 **p** 54. C Atherton *Man* 53-55; C Wokingham All SS *Ox* 55-56; C Doncaster St Geo *Sheff* 56-59; V Whitgift w Adlingfleet 59-62; Chapl Highcroft Hosp Birm 62-71; C Wolborough w Newton Abbot *Ex* 71-74; C Furze Platt *Ox* 74-78; Travelling Sec Ch Coun for Health and Healing 78-81; P-in-c Bisham *Ox* 82-90; rtd 90; NSM Hindhead *Guildf* 90-96; PtO 96-97; *Portsm* 97-07. *37 St Mary's Square, Gloucester GL1 2QT* T: (01452) 330842

SMITH, Peter Michael. b 28. Open Univ BA 75. K Coll Lon 52. **d** 56 **p** 57. C Pokesdown St Jas *Win* 56-59; C Weeke 59-63; V Hutton Roof *Carl* 63-69; V Barrow St Aid 69-72; V Preston Patrick 72-93; rtd 93; Chapl to the Deaf and Hard of Hearing *Carl* from 93; PtO from 93. *7 Green Road, Kendal LA9 4QR* T: (01539) 726741   M: 07973-224289 E: peter@smith687.freeserve.co.uk

SMITH, Philip David. b 55. Shoreditch Coll Lon BEd 78. Oak Hill Th Coll BA 98. **d** 98 **p** 99. C Cheltenham St Mary, St Matt, St Paul and H Trin *Glouc* 98-03; TV Cheltenham St Mark from 03. *3 Deacon Close, Cheltenham GL51 3NY* T: (01242) 528567

SMITH, Philip Hathway. b 66. St Andr Univ MTheol 88. Coll of Resurr Mirfield 90. **d** 92 **p** 93. C Shrewsbury St Giles w Sutton and Atcham *Lich* 92-94; C Clayton 94-97; TV Hanley H Ev 97-02; C Croydon St Mich w St Jas *S'wark* 02-04; P-in-c Sydenham All SS from 04. *All Saints' Vicarage, 41 Trewsbury Road, London SE26 5DP* T: (020) 8778 3065

SMITH, Philip James. b 60. Imp Coll Lon BScEng 82 Fitzw Coll Cam BA 94. Ridley Hall Cam 92. **d** 95 **p** 96. C Aldborough w Boroughbridge and Roecliffe *Ripon* 95-99; V 99-15; V E Bedfont *Lon* from 15. *9 Hatton Road, Bedfont, Feltham TW14 9JR* M: 07786-087389 E: revpsmith@gmail.com

SMITH, Philip James. b 32. St Alb Minl Tr Scheme. **d** 82 **p** 83. NSM Radlett *St Alb* 82-85; C 85-89; V Codicote 89-99; RD Hatfield 95-01; rtd 99; PtO *St Alb* from 00. *34 Cherry Tree Rise, Walkern, Stevenage SG2 7JL* T: (01438) 861951

SMITH, Philip Lloyd Cyril. b 22. Ch Coll Cam BA 47 MA 49. Wycliffe Hall Ox 47. **d** 49 **p** 50. C St Helens St Helen *Liv* 49-52; C Woking St Jo *Guildf* 52-56; R Burslem St Jo *Lich* 56-83; P-in-c Burslem St Paul 82-83; R Burslem 83-86; rtd 86; PtO *Sheff* 86-01. *Upper Treasurer's House, 42 Bromley College, London Road, Bromley BR1 1PE* T: (020) 8290 1566

SMITH, Philip Raymond. b 56. ERMC 08. **d** 11 **p** 12. NSM Farndon w Thorpe, Hawton and Cotham *S'well* 11-14; NSM E Trent from 14. *Dart Cottage, 4 Lancaster Road, Coddington, Newark NG24 2TA* T: (01636) 703305   M: 07532-164314 E: dartcottage@btinternet.com

SMITH, Mrs Priscilla Elizabeth. b 48. Open Univ BSc 93 Nottm Univ MA 08. **d** 12 **p** 13. OLM Horncastle Gp *Linc* from 12. *Evergreen, Upland Close, Horncastle LN9 5AR* T: (01507) 524611 M: 07798-695950 E: priscilla.smith926@btinternet.com

SMITH, Rachel Ross. *See* ROSS, Rachel Anne

SMITH, Raymond Charles William. b 56. K Coll Lon BD 78 AKC 78. Coll of Resurr Mirfield 79. **d** 80 **p** 81. C Iffley *Ox* 80-83; C Wallingford w Crowmarsh Gifford etc 83-86; V Tilehurst St Mary 86-96; TR Haywards Heath St Wilfrid *Chich* 96-08; V from 08. *The Rectory, St Wilfrid's Way, Haywards Heath RH16 3QH* T: (01444) 413300

SMITH, Canon Raymond Douglas. b 31. TCD BA 53 MA 56 BD 56. **d** 54 **p** 55. C Belfast St Mich *Conn* 54-56; C Ballymacarrett St Patr *D & D* 56-58; CMS Tr Coll Chislehurst 58-60; Kenya (CMS) 60-71; Asst Gen Sec (Hibernian) CMS 71-74; Gen Sec CMS 74-86; CMS Ireland 76-86; Hon Can N Maseno from 78; I Powerscourt w Kilbride and Annacrevy *D & G* 86-96; Can Ch Ch Cathl Dublin 94-96; rtd 96. *Glencarrig Lodge, Kindlestown Upper, Delgany, Co Wicklow, Republic of Ireland* T: (00353) (1) 287 3229

SMITH, Raymond Frederick. b 28. Lon Univ BSc 51 Leeds Univ MA 65. Oak Hill Th Coll 51. **d** 53 **p** 54. C Toxteth Park St Philemon *Liv* 53-56; C Halliwell St Pet *Man* 56-58; V Denton and Weston *Bradf* 58-66; V Normanton *Wakef* 66-81; RD Chevet 73-81; R Moreton *Ches* 81-90; rtd 90; PtO *Lich* 03-13; *St As* from 09. *Cornerways, Station Road, Llanymynech SY22 6EG* T: (01691) 839294

SMITH, Raymond George Richard. b 38. Univ of Wales (Ban) BSc 61 MSc 65. WMMTC 91. **d** 94 **p** 95. NSM Edgmond w Kynnersley and Preston Wealdmoors *Lich* 94-97; Chapl Princess R Hosp NHS Trust Telford 95-03; V Llandegfan w Llandysilio *Ban* 03-08; rtd 09; PtO *Ban* 09-14; AD Tindaethwy from 11. *41 Cae Mair, Beaumaris LL58 8YN* T: (01248) 810032

SMITH, Richard Harwood. b 34. Sarum Th Coll 57. **d** 59 **p** 60. C Kington w Huntington *Heref* 59-62; C Georgetown St Phil Br Guiana 62-64; C Kitty 64-65; V Mackenzie Guyana 65-69; C Broseley w Benthall *Heref* 69-70; Area Sec USPG Heref and Worc 70-76; R Wigmore Abbey *Heref* 76-84; V Eye w Braiseworth and Yaxley *St E* 84-96; P-in-c Bedingfield 84-96; P-in-c Occold 84-96; rtd 96. *33 Broad Street, Leominster HR6 8DD* T: (01568) 610676

SMITH, Canon Richard Ian. b 46. Jes Coll Ox BA 69 MA 80. Ripon Hall Ox 69. **d** 70 **p** 71. C Eston *York* 70-76; TV E Ham w Upton Park and Forest Gate *Chelmsf* 76-80; R Crook *Dur* 80-86; V Stanley 80-86; V Billingham St Cuth 86-11; AD Stockton 92-01; Hon Can Dur Cathl 98-11; rtd 11; PtO *Dur* from 11. *The Garth, 21A Upper Garth Gardens, Guisborough TS14 6HA* T: (01287) 205012 E: richardismith57@hotmail.com

SMITH, Richard Keith. b 44. St Jo Coll Nottm. **d** 84 **p** 85. C Wirksworth w Alderwasley, Carsington etc *Derby* 84-87; R Hulland, Atlow, Bradley and Hognaston 87-96; P-in-c Long Compton, Whichford and Barton-on-the-Heath *Cov* 96-08; P-in-c Wolford w Burmington 97-08; P-in-c Cherington w Stourton 97-08; P-in-c Barcheston 97-08; R S Warks Seven Gp 08-09; RD Shipston 05-09; rtd 09; PtO *Cov* from 09. *12 Moreton Close, Stratford-upon-Avon CV37 7HB* T: (01789) 296712 E: rkvjsmith@gmail.com

SMITH, Richard Michael. b 52. Lon Univ BA 74. EAMTC 79. **d** 82 **p** 83. NSM Cambridge Ascension *Ely* 82-84; C Rainham *Roch* 84-88; V Southborough St Thos 88-96; P-in-c Lake *Portsm* 96-99; V 99-06; P-in-c Shanklin St Sav 96-99; V 99-06; V Southsea 06-15; rtd 15. *Address temp unknown*

SMITH, Robert Alfred William. b 53. **d** 08 **p** 09. OLM Withington St Paul *Man* from 08. *61 Burnside Drive, Burnage, Manchester M19 2NA* T: 0161-225 2509 E: bob.smith@sumojo.co.uk

SMITH, Robert Harold. b 23. Lon Univ BA 49. Oak Hill Th Coll 46. **d** 50 **p** 51. C Nottingham St Ann *S'well* 50-52; C-in-c Elburton CD *Ex* 52-57; V Lowestoft Ch Ch *Nor* 57-67; R Upton *Ex* 67-80; R Bressingham *Nor* 80-81; P-in-c N w S Lopham 80-81; P-in-c Fersfield 80-81; R Bressingham w N and S Lopham and Fersfield 81-87; rtd 87; PtO *Nor* from 87. *22 St Walstan's Road, Taverham, Norwich NR8 6NG* T: (01603) 861285

✠**SMITH, The Rt Revd Robin Jonathan Norman.** b 36. Worc Coll Ox BA 60 MA 64. Ridley Hall Cam 60. **d** 62 **p** 63. **c** 90. C Barking St Marg *Chelmsf* 62-67; Chapl Lee Abbey 67-72; V Chesham St Mary *Ox* 72-80; RD Amersham 79-82; TR Gt Chesham 80-90; Hon Can Ch Ch 88-90; Suff Bp Hertford *St Alb* 90-01; rtd 01; Hon Asst Bp St Alb *St Alb* from 02. *7 Aysgarth Road, Redbourn, St Albans AL3 7PJ* T/F: (01582) 791964 E: bprobin@no7.me.uk

SMITH, Rodney Frederic Brittain. b 37. Jes Coll Cam BA 61 MA 64. St Steph Ho Ox 87. **d** 88 **p** 89. NSM Rainworth *S'well* 88-89; C Basford St Aid 89-91; C Sneinton St Cypr 91-94; P-in-c Sneinton St Matthias 94-96; V 96-02; P-in-c Sneinton St Steph w St Alb 01-02; rtd 02. *43 Cyprus Road, Nottingham NG3 5EB* T: 0115-962 0378

SMITH, Roger. *See* SMITH, Thomas Roger

SMITH, Roger. *See* SMITH, John Roger

SMITH, Roger Owen. b 50. Univ of Wales (Abth) BA 72 St Chad's Coll Dur CertEd 73 FRGS. S'wark Ord Course 84. **d** 87 **p** 88. NSM Nunhead St Antony w St Silas *S'wark* 87-91; NSM Forest Hill St Aug 91-98; NSM Crofton Park St Hilda w St Cypr 91-98; NSM Brockley Hill St Sav 91-98; NSM Camberwell St Giles w St Matt 98-00; PtO *Cant* 01-07; NSM Folkestone Trin from 07. *22 Wear Bay Road, Folkestone CT19 6BN* T: (01303) 259896

SMITH, Canon Roger Stuart. b 41. Chich Th Coll 65. **d** 66 **p** 67. C Garforth *Ripon* 66-70; C Hilborough Gp *Nor* 70-73; TV 73-78; V Mendham w Metfield and Withersdale *St E* 78-89; P-in-c Fressingfield w Weybread and Wingfield 88-89; R Fressingfield, Mendham, Metfield, Weybread etc 90-91; RD Hoxne 86-91; R Kelsale-cum-Carlton, Middleton, Theberton etc 91-01; C Yoxmere Conf 01-04; RD Saxmundham *St E* 96-03; Hon Can *St E* Cathl 97-04; rtd 04; PtO *St E* from 04. *Rookery Nook, Wash Lane, St Margaret South Elmham, Harleston IP20 0PQ* T: (01986) 782465 E: canonroger@middleton3112.freeserve.co.uk

SMITH, Roger William. b 48. Imp Coll Lon BSc 70. EAMTC. **d** 00 **p** 01. NSM Rothwell w Orton, Rushton w Glendon and Pipewell *Pet* 00-11; PtO *Eur* from 11. *14 rue du Parc, 34480 Autignac, France* T: (0033) 4 99 57 07 81 E: rogerwilliamsmith@gmail.com

SMITH, Ronald Eric. b 43. EMMTC 93. **d** 93 **p** 94. NSM Wingerworth *Derby* 93-99; NSM Newbold w Dunston 99-01; NSM Loundsley Green 01-05; rtd 05; PtO *Derby* from 05; *York* from 06. *20 Oak Tree Lane, Haxby, York YO32 2YH* T: (01904) 767691 E: revronsmith@btinternet.com

SMITH, Canon Ronald James. b 36. Linc Th Coll 73. **d** 75 **p** 76. C Bilborough St Jo *S'well* 75-78; P-in-c Colwick 78-81; R 81-85; P-in-c Netherfield 78-81; V 81-85; C Worksop Priory 85-90; TV Langley and Parkfield *Man* 90-95; P-in-c Barton w Peel Green 95-01; Hon Can Tamale from 01; rtd 01; PtO *Man* 01-08; *Ches* from 03. *12 Bramhall Drive, Holmes Chapel, Crewe CW4 7EJ* T: (01477) 544072 E: annevicarage01@sky.com

SMITH, Ronald William. b 45. St Jo Coll York CertEd 67. Chich Th Coll 70. **d** 73 **p** 74. C Scarborough St Martin *York* 73-76; C Stainton-in-Cleveland 76-80; V E Coatham 80-89; V Brookfield 89-10; rtd 10; PtO *York* from 11. *85 High Street, Marske by the Sea, Redcar TS11 6JL* T: (01642) 282241 E: ronald.smith180@ntlworld.com *or* revronsmith@ntlworld.com

SMITH, Canon Rowan Quentin. b 43. AKC 66. **d** 67 **p** 68. C Matroosfontein S Africa 67-69; C Bonteheuwel 70; C Plumstead All SS 71-72; P-in-c Grassy Park 72-77; CR 77-88; Chapl Cape Town Univ S Africa 88-90; Prov Exec Officer 90-95; Dean Cape Town 96-10; rtd 10. *30 Balers Way, Sunset Beach, Cape Town, 7441 South Africa*

SMITH, Preb Roy Leonard. b 36. Clifton Th Coll 63. **d** 66 **p** 67. C Clapham St Jas *S'wark* 66-70; C Kennington St Mark 70-74; C-in-c Southall Em CD *Lon* 74-83; V Stonebridge St Mich 83-06; Preb St Paul's Cathl 96-06; rtd 06; Hon C Kensal Rise St Mark and St Martin *Lon* 06-11; PtO from 11. *4 Biko House, 2 Barry Road, London NW10 8DW* T: (020) 8961 7312 E: prebroy@yahoo.co.uk

SMITH, Royston. b 55. EMMTC 87. **d** 90 **p** 91. NSM Shirland *Derby* 90-94; NSM Ashover and Brackenfield 95-00; LtO 00-11; NSM Walton St Jo from 11. *Kirkdale Cottage, Greenfield Lane, Milltown, Ashover, Chesterfield S45 0HT* T: (01246) 590975 E: royston@kirkdalecottage.freeserve.co.uk

SMITH, Ruth. *See* YOUNG, Vivienne Ruth

SMITH, Rycroft. *See* SMITH, Charles Rycroft

SMITH, Mrs Sally Anne. b 63. Ches Univ BA 13 RN 85. St Jo Coll Nottm 07. **d** 09 **p** 10. C Stone St Mich and St Wulfad w Aston St Sav *Lich* 09-12; C Hanley H Ev 12-13; TV from 13; Dioc Officer for Vulnerable Adults from 12. *Hanley Rectory, 35 Harding Road, Stoke-on-Trent ST1 3BQ* T: (01782) 791213 M: 07962-025659 E: revsally6@aol.com

SMITH, Sarah Anne Louise. *See* PIX, Sarah Anne Louise

SMITH, Scott Anthony. b 73. K Alfred's Coll Win BA 99. Trin Coll Bris 08. **d** 10 **p** 11. C Clevedon St Andr and Ch Ch *B & W* 10-13; C Beckenham St Jo *Roch* from 13. *91 The Grove, West Wickham BR4 9LA* M: 07810-810313 E: smithscott@hotmail.com

SMITH, Mrs Sharon. b 56. ERMC 13. **d** 15. NSM Caddington *St Alb* from 15. *185 Farley Hill St Jo* from 15. *183 Cutenhoe Road, Luton LU1 3NQ*

SMITH, Mrs Shirley Ann. b 46. RSCN 68 RM 82 RGN 84 RHV 86. Sarum & Wells Th Coll 89. **d** 93 **p** 94. C Totton *Win* 93-96; Chapl Portsm Hosps NHS Trust 96-98; V Lord's Hill *Win* 98-01; TV Beaminster Area *Sarum* 01-05; rtd 05; PtO *Sarum* 05-08; P-in-c Hazelbury Bryan and the Hillside Par 08-11; P-in-c Okeford 08-11; PtO *B & W* 11-12; Chapl Yeovil Distr Hosp NHS Foundn Trust from 12. *2 Franklyn Place, Kingsbury Episcopi, Martock TA12 6AZ* T: (01935) 508013 E: shirleywinch@aol.com

SMITH, Stephen. b 60. Coll of Resurr Mirfield 02. **d** 04 **p** 05. C Burnley St Cath w St Alb and St Paul *Blackb* 04-07; C St Annes St Anne 07-10; PtO from 10. *7 Gayle Way, Accrington BB5 0JX* M: 07898-301807 E: stephen.smith6@o2.co.uk

SMITH, Stephen. b 53. CQSW 78. Sarum & Wells Th Coll 87. **d** 89 **p** 90. C Redcar *York* 89-92; C Leeds St Aid *Ripon* 92-96; R Lanteglos by Camelford w Advent *Truro* 96-99; Chapl Hull and E Yorks Hosps NHS Trust 99-01; V Leeds St Marg and All Hallows *Ripon* 08-14; AD Headingley 09-13; P-in-c Mabe *Truro* from 14. *The Vicarage, Church Road, Mabe Burnthouse, Penryn TR10 9HN* T: (01326) 617628 E: revstevesmith53@gmail.com

SMITH, Stephen John. b 46. Kelham Th Coll 65. **d** 69 **p** 70. C Warsop *S'well* 69-73; C Heaton Ch Ch *Man* 73-75; V Bolton St Bede 75-78; R Bilborough w Strelley *S'well* 78-84; R E Leake 84-92; P-in-c Costock 84-92; P-in-c Rempstone 84-92; P-in-c Stanford on Soar 84-92; R E and W Leake, Stanford-on-Soar, Rempstone etc 92-97; RD W Bingham 92-97; V Swaffham *Nor* 97-11; C Gt and Lt Dunham w Gt and Lt Fransham and Sporle 03-11; RD Breckland 02-06; Chapl NW Anglia Healthcare NHS Trust 99-11; rtd 11. *388A Dysart Road, Grantham NG31 7LY* T: (01476) 560801 E: s-smith102@sky.com

SMITH, Stephen John. b 55. Lon Univ BD 80. Trin Coll Bris 77. **d** 81 **p** 82. C Fulham St Matt *Lon* 81-86; C Stoke Gifford *Bris* 86-90; TV 90-01; rtd 01; PtO *Bris* from 01. *47 Saxon Way, Bradley Stoke, Bristol BS32 9AR* T: (01454) 616429 E: steve@revsmith.freeserve.co.uk

SMITH, Canon Stephen John Stanyon. b 49. Sussex Univ BA 81 Birm Univ MSocSc 83. Westcott Ho Cam 83. **d** 85 **p** 86. C Four Oaks *Birm* 85-89; Asst P Cheyenne River Reservation USA 89-91; Miss P Rosebud Reservation 91-94; Assoc R Ivoryton and Essex 94-98; Can St Paul's Cathl Buffalo 98-04; Asst P Buffalo St Andr from 04. *3105 Main Street, Buffalo NY 14214, USA* T: (001) (716) 834 9337 F: 836 0558 E: sjsmith6@buffalo.edu

SMITH, Stephen Thomas. b 55. Westcott Ho Cam 95. **d** 97 **p** 98. C Kempston Transfiguration *St Alb* 97-01; C Bromham w Oakley and Stagsden 01-05; TV Elstow from 05. *St Michael's Vicarage, Falda Road, Bedford MK42 0EH* T: (01234) 266920

SMITH, Steven Barnes. b 60. Cov Poly BA 83 Leeds Univ BA 86 MSc 02. Coll of Resurr Mirfield 84. **d** 87 **p** 88. C Darlington St Mark w St Paul *Dur* 87-89; C Prescot *Liv* 89-91; V Hindley Green 91-96; Asst Chapl Havering Hosps NHS Trust 96-98; Hd Multi-Faith Chapl Chelsea and Westmr Hosp NHS Foundn Trust 98-07; PtO *Lon* 07-13. *9 Walham Grove, London SW6 1QP* T: (020) 7385 1348 E: sbsmith01@aol.com

SMITH, Steven Gerald Crosland. b 48. Linc Th Coll 82. **d** 84 **p** 85. Chapl St Jo Sch Tiffield 84-87; C Towcester w Easton Neston *Pet* 84-87; P-in-c Kings Heath 87-89; V 89-93; TV N Creedy *Ex* 93-06; TR 06-13; RD Cadbury 02-13; rtd 13. *5 Melhuish Close, Witheridge, Tiverton EX16 8AZ* E: stevengcsmith@aol.com

SMITH, Susan. b 48. FInstD 87. Ox Min Course 93. **d** 96 **p** 97. C Burnham w Dropmore, Hitcham and Taplow *Ox* 96-00; TV Whitton *Sarum* 00-02; TV W Slough *Ox* 02-08; V Cippenham 08-13; rtd 13; PtO *Ox* from 13. *Easter Cottage, 36 Britwell Road, Burnham, Slough SL1 8AG* T: (01628) 603046 E: suzone@hotmail.co.uk

SMITH, Miss Susan Ann. b 50. Bris Univ BA 72 St Jo Coll York PGCE 73. Ripon Coll Cuddesdon 97. **d** 99 **p** 00. C Swaffham *Nor* 99-02; R King's Beck 02-12; rtd 12; PtO *Nor* from 13. *9 Eagle Close, Erpingham, Norwich NR11 7AW* T: (01263) 761497 E: s.497@btinternet.com

SMITH, Mrs Susan Elizabeth. b 53. Man Univ BSc 94 Brunel Univ MSc 98. SEITE 05. **d** 08 **p** 09. NSM Reigate St Mark *S'wark* 08-12; NSM Hoo St Werburgh *Roch* from 12. *The Vicarage, Vicarage Lane, Hoo, Rochester ME3 9BB* T: (01634) 250291

SMITH, Susan Helen. *See* SHEWRING, Susan Helen

SMITH, Mrs Susan Jennifer. b 52. MCIPD 90. SAOMC 94. **d** 97 **p** 98. C Ascot Heath *Ox* 97-01; P-in-c Flixton St Mich *Man* 01-10; P-in-c Altcar and Hightown *Liv* 10-14; P-in-c Hightown from 14. *79 Greenloons Drive, Formby, Liverpool L37 2LX* T: (01704) 833856 E: saxoncross@btinternet.com

SMITH, Mrs Susan Penelope Zoë. b 61. Ox Min Course 12. **d** 15. C Weston Turville *Ox* from 15. *Address temp unknown*

SMITH, Terence. b 38. Brunel Univ BSc 79 Cranfield Inst of Tech MSc 80. Tyndale Hall Bris 67. **d** 69 **p** 70. C Cheylesmore *Cov* 69-71; C Leamington Priors St Paul 71-74; V Halliwell St Paul *Man* 74-75; Lect Uxbridge Coll 81-86; R Medstead w Wield *Win* 86-99; P-in-c Kennington *Ox* 99-03; V 03-08; rtd 08. *15 Grove Road, Seaford BN25 1TP* E: ter.s@btinternet.com

SMITH, Terence David. b 59. **d** 02. NSM Myddle *Lich* 02-08; NSM Broughton 02-08; NSM Loppington w Newtown 02-08; NSM Wem from 08; NSM Lee Brockhurst from 08. *Lamorna, Scholars' Lane, Loppington, Shrewsbury SY4 5RE* M: 07703-183034

SMITH, Terrence Gordon. b 34. TD 83. MCSP 58 SRN 60. St Mich Coll Llan 68. **d** 70 **p** 71. C Gelligaer *Llan* 70-73; CF (TA) 72-99; C Aberavon *Llan* 73-75; V Pontlottyn w Fochriw 75-77; V Kenfig Hill 77-84; V Dyffryn 84-99; rtd 99. *1 Gnoll Crescent, Neath SA11 3TF*

SMITH, Canon Thomas Roger. b 48. Cant Sch of Min 77. **d** 80 **p** 81. NSM Folkestone St Sav *Cant* 80-82; NSM Lyminge w Paddlesworth, Stanford w Postling etc 82-85; Chapl Cant Sch of Min 82-91; R Biddenden and Smarden *Cant* 86-91; TR Totnes, Bridgetown and Berry Pomeroy etc *Ex* 91-96; P-in-c Haslingden w Grane and Stonefold *Blackb* 96-98; V 98-15; P-in-c Musbury 07-15; AD Accrington 03-13; Hon Can Blackb Cathl 08-15; rtd 15; PtO *Blackb* from 15. *150 Southwood Drive, Accrington BB5 2TU* T: (01254) 237581 E: rsmith9456@aol.com

SMITH, Timothy. b 58. Trin Coll Bris 00. **d** 02 **p** 03. C Warminster Ch Ch *Sarum* 02-06; P-in-c Plymouth St Jude *Ex* from 06. *St Jude's Vicarage, Knighton Road, Plymouth PL4 9BU* T: (01752) 224178 E: timmy.smith@virgin.net

SMITH, Timothy Brian. b 62. Brisbane Coll BA(Theol) 92. **d** 92 **p** 92. Coffs Harbour Australia 92-94; C Heald Green St Cath *Ches* 94-96; R Mid Richmond Australia 96-01; P-in-c Belmont

St Steph from 01. *42 Regent Street, Belmont Vic 3216, Australia* T: (0061) (3) 5243 2557 M: 412-673152 E: timsandy@turboweb.net.au

SMITH, Toni. *See* SMITH, Antoinette

SMITH, Trevor Andrew. b 60. St Jo Coll Dur BA 86. Cranmer Hall Dur 83. **d** 87 **p** 88. C Guisborough *York* 87-90; C Northallerton w Kirby Sigston 90-95; R Middleton, Newton and Sinnington 95-01; Chapl St Luke's Hospice Plymouth from 01. *St Luke's Hospice, Stamford Road, Plymouth PL9 9XA* T: (01752) 401172 *or* 316868 F: 481878

SMITH, Trevor Bernard. b 33. Culham Coll of Educn CertEd 70 Ox Poly BEd 82. Oak Hill Th Coll 61. **d** 64 **p** 65. C Bispham *Blackb* 64-66; C Chesham St Mary *Ox* 66-68; PtO 90-94; rtd 96. *126 The Broadway, Herne Bay CT6 8HA* T: (01227) 362665

SMITH (*née* **WOOD), Mrs Valerie Rosemary.** b 53. Warwick Univ BA 74. WEMTC 06. **d** 09 **p** 10. NSM Highley w Billingsley, Glazeley etc *Heref* from 09. *20 Yew Tree Grove, Highley, Bridgnorth WV16 6DG* T: (01746) 861966 E: keithandvals@aol.com

SMITH, Mrs Virginia Jane. b 41. Nottm Univ BSc 63. Guildf Dioc Min Course 04. **d** 09 **p** 10. NSM Surrey Weald *Guildf* 09-13; rtd 13; PtO *Guildf* from 13. *Dove Cottage, 14 The Paddock, Westcott, Dorking RH4 3NT* T: (01306) 885349 E: virginia.smith@smartemail.co.uk

SMITH, Walter. b 37. Westcott Ho Cam 67. **d** 69 **p** 70. C N Hull St Mich *York* 69-72; C Whitby 72-74; V Newington w Dairycoates 74-77; P-in-c Skipton Bridge 77; P-in-c Baldersby 77; TV Thirsk 77-88; P-in-c Topcliffe w Dalton and Dishforth 82-87; V Lythe w Ugthorpe 88-97; rtd 97; PtO *York* 98-11. *102 Upgang Lane, Whitby YO21 3JW* T: (01947) 605456

SMITH, Miss Wendy Hamlyn. b 41. ALA 70 Open Univ BA 85. Ridley Hall Cam 85. **d** 87 **p** 94. C Stroud H Trin *Glouc* 87-90 and 91-92; Australia 90-91; Team Dn Stoke-upon-Trent *Lich* 92-94; TV 94-97; V Pheasey 97-02; P-in-c Barlaston 02-06; Chapl Douglas Macmillan Hospice Blurton 04-06; rtd 07; PtO *Lich* 07-11; *Portsm* from 11. *Flat 3, 47 Monkton Street, Ryde PO33 2BB*

SMITH, Mrs Wendy Patricia. b 60. **d** 10 **p** 11. OLM Walton and Trimley *St E* 10-13; NSM from 13. *12A Langley Avenue, Felixstowe IP11 2NA* T: (01394) 211755 M: 07708-597808 E: grannysmith57@hotmail.co.uk

SMITH, William Manton. b 64. Univ of Wales (Abth) LLB 85 St Jo Coll Dur PGCE 90. United Th Coll Abth BD 89 St Jo Coll Nottm 91. **d** 93 **p** 94. C Coventry Caludon *Cov* 93-97; V Exhall 97-09; TR Coventry Caludon from 09. *Stoke Rectory, 365A Walsgrave Road, Coventry CV2 4BG* T: (024) 7663 5731 *or* 7644 3691 E: wms.smith@btinternet.com

SMITH, Canon William Melvyn. b 47. K Coll Lon BD 69 AKC 69 PGCE 70. St Aug Coll Cant 71. **d** 71 **p** 72. C Kingswinford H Trin *Lich* 71-73; Hon C Coseley Ch Ch 73-74; C Wednesbury St Paul Wood Green 75-78; V Coseley St Chad 78-91; TR Wordsley 91-93; RD Himley 83-93; TR Wordsley *Worc* 93-96; RD Himley 93-96; Stewardship and Resources Officer 97-10; Hon Can Worc Cathl 03-10; Asst Chapl Palma de Mallorca *Eur* 10-12; rtd 12. *14 Beech Tree Close, Kingswinford DY6 7DR* T: (01384) 357062 E: wmelsmith@blueyonder.co.uk

SMITH-CAMERON, Canon Ivor Gill. b 29. Madras Univ BA 50 MA 52. Coll of Resurr Mirfield. **d** 54 **p** 55. C Rumboldswyke *Chich* 54-58; Chapl Imp Coll Lon 58-72; Dioc Missr S'wark 72-92; Can Res S'wark Cathl 72-94; C Battersea Park All SS 92-94; Hon C 94-96; Hon C Battersea Fields 96-05; Co-ord All Asian Chr Consultation 92-93; rtd 94; Chapl to The Queen 95-99; PtO *S'wark* from 05. *24 Holmewood Gardens, London SW2 3RS* T: (020) 8678 8977 E: ivorsmithcameron@yahoo.co.uk

SMITHAM, Ann. *See* HOWELLS, Elizabeth Ann

SMITHSON, Michael John. b 47. Newc Univ BA 68 Lon Univ BD 79 Dur Univ PGCE FRGS. Trin Coll Bris 76. **d** 79 **p** 80. C S Mimms Ch Ch *Lon* 79-81; Support and Public Relations Sec UCCF 82-84; R Frating w Thorrington *Chelmsf* 84-88; V Portsea St Luke *Portsm* 88-04. *1 Owen House, Whitcombe Gardens, Portsmouth PO3 6BL* M: 07802-482584

SMITHSON, Philip George Allan. b 55. Bede Coll Dur TCert 82 Open Univ BA 82. **d** 07 **p** 08. OLM Monkwearmouth *Dur* from 07. *2 Sea View Gardens, Sunderland SR6 9PN* E: philipsmithson@talktalk.net

SMITHURST, Jonathan Peter. b 54. FInstLEx 81. EMMTC 91. **d** 94 **p** 95. NSM Bramcote S'well 94-03; NSM Attenborough 03-06; AD Beeston 99-06; P-in-c Everton, Mattersey, Clayworth and Gringley 06-11; V 11-14; AD Bassetlaw and Bawtry 09-14; P-in-c Attenborough 14; V from 14; Dioc Ecum Officer from 14. *Vale Cottage, 19 Church Lane, Attenborough, Nottingham NG9 6AS* T: 0115-925 9602 E: office@attenboroughchurch.org.uk

SMITS, Eric. b 29. **d** 61 **p** 62. C Thornaby on Tees St Paul *York* 61-66; R Brotton Parva 66-98; rtd 98. *7 Pikes Nurseries, Ludham, Great Yarmouth NR29 5NW* T: (01692) 678156

SMOUT, Francis David James. b 36. TD. **d** 03 **p** 04. NSM Eyemouth *Edin* from 03. *Benedict House, Coldingham, Eyemouth TD14 5NE* T: (01890) 771220 E: davidsmout007@btinternet.com

SMOUT, Canon Michael John. b 37. St Pet Coll Ox BA 61 MA 75 Lon Univ BD 64. Lon Coll of Div 62. **d** 64 **p** 65. C Toxteth Park St Philemon w St Silas *Liv* 64-69; C Everton St Sav 69-70; Missr E Everton Gp of Chs 70-74; V Everton St Sav w St Cuth *Liv* 74-79; R Aughton St Mich 79-02; RD Ormskirk 82-89; AD 89-02; Hon Can Liv Cathl 92-02; rtd 02. *4 Victoria Road, Aughton, Ormskirk L39 5AU* T: (01695) 423054

SMYTH, Anthony Irwin. b 40. TCD BA 63 MA 66. Clifton Th Coll 64. **d** 66 **p** 67. C Worthing St Geo *Chich* 66-69; SAMS Chile 70-75; Dir Th Educn Valparaiso 72-75; C Woodley St Jo the Ev *Ox* 75-80; V St Leonards St Ethelburga *Chich* 80-93; R Stopham and Fittleworth 93-05; rtd 05; PtO *Chich* from 05; *Portsm* from 05. *20 Grenehurst Way, Petersfield GU31 4AZ* T: (01730) 260370 E: anthony.smyth@btinternet.com

SMYTH, Elizabeth. *See* LEAVER, Lucinda Elizabeth Jane

SMYTH, Canon Gordon William. b 47. Open Univ BA. St Jo Coll Nottm 81. **d** 83 **p** 84. C St Keverne *Truro* 83-86; V Landrake w St Erney and Botus Fleming 86-95; RD E Wivelshire 94-95; V Highertown and Baldhu 95-14; rtd 14; Hon Can Truro Cathl from 06. *3 Carnon Valley, Carnon Downs, Truro TR3 6LG* T: (01872) 870743 E: gordonsmyth58@gmail.com

SMYTH, Kenneth James. b 44. TCD BA 67 MA 72. **d** 68 **p** 69. C Bangor Abbey *D & D* 68-71; C Holywood 71-74; I Gilnahirk 74-82; I Newtownards w Movilla Abbey 82-88; I Newtownards 89-11; Preb Wicklow St Patr Cathl Dublin 93-11; rtd 11. *3 Mount Royal, Bangor BT20 3BG* T: (028) 9145 8706 E: kennethjsmyth@o2.co.uk

SMYTH, Lucinda Elizabeth Jane. *See* LEAVER, Lucinda Elizabeth Jane

SMYTH, Peter Charles Gordon. b 72. Univ of Wales (Ban) BA 94 TCD BTh 98. CITC. **d** 98 **p** 99. C Stillorgan w Blackrock *D & G* 98-01; R Thunder Bay St Mich Canada from 01. *2 Sydney Street, Thunder Bay ON P7B 1P7, Canada* T: (001) (807) 767 4711 F: 768 0382 E: stmichaelsch@tbaytel.net

SMYTH, Peter Frederick. b 58. SNWTP. **d** 10 **p** 11. C Prescot *Liv* 10-13; TV Kirkby from 13. *St Andrew's Vicarage, 9 Redwood Way, Liverpool L33 4DU* M: 07847-456025

SMYTH, Robert Andrew Laine (Brother Anselm). b 30. Trin Coll Cam BA 53 MA 59 Lon Univ PGCE 60 DipEd 65. **d** 79 **p** 80. SSF from 53; Min Prov Eur Prov SSF 79-91; LtO *Linc* 84-92; P-in-c Cambridge St Benedict *Ely* 92-93; V 93-00; rtd 00; PtO *Worc* from 08. *Glasshampton Monastery, Shrawley, Worcester WR6 6TQ* T: (01299) 896345 E: anselmsssf@franciscans.org.uk

SMYTH, Roderick. **d** 13 **p** 14. C Belfast Malone St Jo *Conn* from 14. *53 Chippendale Avenue, Bangor BT20 4PX* T: (028) 9146 6102 M: 07973-464785 E: rsmyth6582@btinternet.com

SMYTH, Trevor Cecil. b 45. Chich Th Coll 66. **d** 69 **p** 70. C Cookridge H Trin *Ripon* 69-73; C Middleton St Mary 73-75; C Felpham w Middleton *Chich* 75-78; P-in-c Wellington Ch Ch 78-80; V 80-86; P-in-c W Wittering *Chich* 86; R W Wittering and Birdham w Itchenor 86-94; PtO 00; TV Withycombe Raleigh *Ex* 01-15; Hon C E Blatchington and Bishopstone *Chich* from 15. *St Andrew's House, 14 Marine Drive, Seaford BN25 2RS* T: (01323) 892972

SMYTH, William Richard Stephen. b 56. Cape Town Univ BA 77. **d** 90 **p** 92. S Africa 90-07; C Ballyholme *D & D* 09-12; I Kilmore and Inch from 12. *The Rectory, 22 Church Road, Crossgar, Downpatrick BT30 9HR* T: (028) 4483 0371 E: stephensmyth17@gmail.com

SMYTHE, Mrs Angela Mary. b 53. St Jo Coll Nottm 85. **d** 87 **p** 94. Par Dn Forest Town S'well 87-90; Dn-in-c Pleasley Hill 90-94; V 94-03; AD Mansfield 98-03; P-in-c Sneinton St Chris w St Phil 03-08; Chapl Qu Eliz Sch and Samworth Ch Academy 08-13; rtd 13. *Happy Days, 1A Main Street, Palterton, Chesterfield S44 6UJ* E: angiesmythe@aol.com *or* angie.smythe1@sky.com

SMYTHE, Peter John Francis. b 32. Lon Univ LLB 56 Barrister-at-Law (Middle Temple) 76. Wells Th Coll 56. **d** 58 **p** 59. C Maidstone All SS *Cant* 58-62; V Barrow St Jo *Carl* 62-65; V Billesdon w Goadby and Rolleston *Leic* 65-71; rtd 97. *The Gables, 16 Geraldine Road, Malvern WR14 3PA* T: (01684) 573266

SNAITH, Bryan Charles. b 33. Univ of Wales BSc 55. St Mich Coll Llan 61. **d** 61 **p** 62. C Bargoed w Brithdir *Llan* 61-62; C Llanishen and Lisvane 62-71; Ind Chapl *Dur* 71-76; *Worc* 76-81; P-in-c Stone 76-81; C Chaddesley Corbett 77-81; TV Colchester St Leon, St Mary Magd and St Steph *Chelmsf* 81-86; Ind Chapl 81-03; rtd 03; PtO *Chelmsf* from 04.

4 Wren Close, Stanway, Colchester CO3 8ZB T: (01206) 767793
E: bryansnaith-colchester@msn.com

SNAPE, Gary John Stanley. b 50. STETS. **d** 05 **p** 06. NSM Fareham H Trin *Portsm* 05-09; NSM Whiteley CD 09-12; PtO from 12. *51 Crescent Road, Locks Heath, Southampton SO31 6PE* T: (01489) 589205 E: gary.snape1@ntlworld.com

SNAPE, Harry. b 21. Qu Coll Birm 76. **d** 78 **p** 79. NSM Highters Heath *Birm* 78-82; NSM Stirchley 82-84; TV Corby SS Pet and Andr w Gt and Lt Oakley 84-89; rtd 89; PtO *Chich* 89-05. *16 Capel Court, The Burgage, Prestbury, Cheltenham GL52 3EL* T: (01242) 513289

SNAPE, Mrs Lorraine Elizabeth. b 52. STETS. **d** 02 **p** 07. NSM Titchfield *Portsm* 02-06; C-in-c Whiteley CD 06-12; PtO from 12. *51 Crescent Road, Locks Heath, Southampton SO31 6PE* T: (01489) 589205

SNAPE, Paul Anthony Piper. b 44. **d** 98 **p** 99. OLM Tettenhall Wood and Perton *Lich* 98-10; PtO from 10. *24 Windsor Gardens, Castlecroft, Wolverhampton WV3 8LY* T: (01902) 763577 E: p-snape44@tiscali.co.uk

SNARE, Peter Brian. b 39. Cape Town Univ BSc 63. SEITE 99. **d** 02 **p** 03. NSM Dymchurch w Burmarsh and Newchurch *Cant* 02-09; NSM New Romney w Old Romney and Midley 07-09; NSM St Mary's Bay w St Mary-in-the-Marsh etc 07-09; PtO from 09. *35 Shepherds Walk, Hythe CT21 6PW* T: (01303) 269242 *or* (020) 7320 1701 E: peter.snare@btinternet.com

SNARES, Ian. b 68. Brunel Univ BEng 91. Ridley Hall Cam 09. **d** 11 **p** 12. C Ilfracombe, Lee, Woolacombe, Bittadon etc *Ex* 11-15; C Ilfracombe SS Phil and Jas w W Down 11-15; V Cowplain *Portsm* from 15. *The Vicarage, Padnell Road, Waterlooville PO8 8DZ* M: 07971-798191 T: (023) 9225 1603 E: iansnares@gmail.com

SNASDELL, Canon Antony John. b 39. St Chad's Coll Dur BA 63. **d** 65 **p** 66. C Boston *Linc* 65-70; Hon C Worksop Priory *S'well* 71-82; P-in-c Gt Massingham *Nor* 82-84; P-in-c Lt Massingham 82-84; P-in-c Harpley 82-84; R Gt and Lt Massingham and Harpley 84-91; R Thorpe St Andr 91-04; Hon Can Nor Cathl 03-04; rtd 04; PtO *Nor* from 05. *1 Speedwell Road, Wymondham NR18 0XQ* T: (01953) 857509

SNEARY, Michael William. b 38. Brentwood Coll of Educn CertEd 71 Open Univ BA 79. Ely Th Coll 61. **d** 64 **p** 65. C Loughton St Jo *Chelmsf* 64-67; Youth Chapl 67-70; Hon C Ingrave 70-71; Teacher Harold Hill Gr Sch Essex 71-74; Ivybridge Sch 74-76; Coombe Dean Sch Plymouth 76-03; rtd 03. *The Lodge, 1 Lower Port View, Saltash PL12 4BY*

✠**SNELGROVE, The Rt Revd Donald George.** b 25. TD 72. Qu Coll Cam BA 48 MA 53 Hull Univ Hon DD 97. Ridley Hall Cam. **d** 50 **p** 51 **c** 81. C Oakwood St Thos *Lon* 50-53; C Hatch End St Anselm 53-56; V Dronfield *Derby* 56-62; CF (TA) 60-73; V Hessle York 63-70; RD Hull 67-70 and 81-90; Can and Preb York Minster 69-81; Adn E Riding 70-81; R Cherry Burton 70-78; Suff Bp Hull 81-94; rtd 94; Hon Asst Bp Linc from 95. *c/o J Snelgrove Esq, Kilncroft, Tile Kiln Lane, Hemel Hempstead HP3 8NQ* E: donaldsnelgrove@aol.com

SNELL, Mrs Brigitte. b 43. BA 85. EAMTC 86. **d** 89 **p** 94. NSM Cambridge Gt St Mary w St Mich *Ely* 89-91; Par Dn Cambridge St Jas 91-94; C 94-95; V Sutton 95-03; R Witcham w Mepal 95-03; rtd 03; PtO *Ely* from 05. *45 London Road, Harston, Cambridge CB22 7QQ* T: (01223) 872839 E: brigittesnell@gmail.com

SNELL, Colin. b 53. Trin Coll Bris 94. **d** 96 **p** 97. C Martock w Ash *B & W* 96-00; TV Wilton 00-08; V Galmington from 08. *St Michael's House, 1 Comeytrowe Lane, Taunton TA1 5PA* T: (01823) 326525

SNELLGROVE, Canon Martin Kenneth. b 54. City Univ BSc 77 CEng 80 MICE 84. Aston Tr Scheme 85 Ridley Hall Cam 87. **d** 89 **p** 90. C Four Oaks *Birm* 89-92; TV Wrexham *St As* 92-01; R Hope 01-13; AD Hawarden 03-10; V Corwen w Llangar w Glyndyfrdwy etc from 13; AD Penllyn and Edeirnion from 13; Can Cursal St As Cathl from 13. *The Rectory, Ffordd Ty Cerrig, Corwen LL21 9RP* T: (01490) 413520

SNELLING, Brian. b 40. **d** 69 **p** 70. C Slough *Ox* 69-72; C Hoole *Ches* 72-76; V Millbrook 76-80; V Homerton St Luke *Lon* 80-90; R Marks Tey w Aldham and Lt Tey *Chelmsf* 90-98; V Stebbing w Lindsell 98-04; V Stebbing and Lindsell w Gt and Lt Saling 04-05; rtd 05; PtO *Chelmsf* from 06. *69 Reynmead Close, West Mersea, Colchester CO5 8DN* T: (01206) 383717 E: revbrians@aol.com

SNELLING, Stephen Thomas. b 47. City of Lon Poly BA 73. SEITE 08. **d** 10 **p** 11. NSM Seal SS Pet and Paul *Roch* 10-11; NSM Nantwich *Ches* from 12. *Silverhurst, 16 Holly Place, Wistaston, Nantwich CW5 6NG* T: (01270) 668858 M: 07775-833824 E: curate@silverhurst.co.uk

SNELSON, William Thomas. b 45. Ex Coll Ox BA 67 Fitzw Coll Cam BA 69 MA 75. Westcott Ho Cam 67. **d** 69 **p** 70. C Godalming *Guildf* 69-72; C Leeds St Pet *Ripon* 72-75;

V Chapel Allerton 75-81; V Bardsey 81-93; Dioc Ecum Officer 86-93; W Yorkshire Ecum Officer *Bradf* 93-97; Gen Sec Chs Together in England 97-08; rtd 08; Development Officer Angl Cen Rome from 08; PtO *Leeds* from 09. *6 Abbey Crags Way, Knaresborough HG5 8EF* T: (01423) 862660 M: 07917-663250 E: developmentuk@anglicancentre.it

SNOOK, Hywel Geraint. b 77. Aston Univ BSc 99 Leeds Univ BA 04. Coll of Resurr Mirfield 02. **d** 05 **p** 06. C Marton *Blackb* 05-06; C Chorley St Laur 06-09; P-in-c Lt Drayton *Lich* from 09; Chr Discipleship Adv Shrewsbury Area from 15. *The Vicarage, 1 Christ Church Copse, Christ Church Lane, Market Drayton TF9 1DY* T: (01630) 652801 E: hywel.snook@tiscali.co.uk

SNOOK, Mrs Margaret Ann. b 41. S Dios Minl Tr Scheme. **d** 91 **p** 94. NSM Keynsham *B & W* 91-04; Chapl Univ Hosps Bris NHS Foundn Trust from 91; PtO *B & W* from 04. *32 Hurn Lane, Keynsham, Bristol BS31 1RS* T: 0117-986 3439 M: 07802-944528 E: snook926@btinternet.com

SNOW, Campbell Martin Spencer. b 35. JP 75. Roch Th Coll 65. **d** 67 **p** 68. C Dover St Mary *Cant* 67-72; C Birchington w Acol 72-74; V Reculver 74-80; P-in-c New Addington 80-81; V 81-84; V *S'wark* 85-87; P-in-c Caterham Valley 87-99; CF (ACF) 84-87; CF (TA) 87-92; OCM 92-95; rtd 99; PtO *S'wark* from 99; Widows' Officer 99-04. *28 The Crossways, Merstham, Redhill RH1 3NA* T: (01737) 643388 E: csnow@talktalk.net

SNOW, Frank. b 31. Lon Univ BD 57. **d** 83 **p** 84. Hon C Tweedmouth *Newc* 83-86; Hon C Berwick H Trin 86-89; Hon C Berwick St Mary 86-89; Hon C Berwick H Trin and St Mary 89-90; R Gt Smeaton w Appleton Wiske and Birkby etc *Ripon* 90-97; rtd 97; PtO *Leeds* from 97; *Sheff* from 02. *18D Abbey Lane Dell, Sheffield S8 0BZ* T: 0114-327 5067 E: frank@fcrsnow.freeserve.co.uk

✠**SNOW, The Rt Revd Martyn James.** b 68. Sheff Univ BSc 89. Wycliffe Hall Ox BTh 95. **d** 95 **p** 96 **c** 13. C Brinsworth w Catcliffe and Treeton *Sheff* 95-97; CMS Guinea 98-01; V Pitsmoor Ch Ch *Sheff* 01-10; P-in-c Stocksbridge 07-08; AD Ecclesfield 07-10; Adn Sheff and Rotherham 10-13; Suff Bp Tewkesbury *Glouc* from 13. *Bishop's House, Church Road, Staverton, Cheltenham GL51 0TW* T: (01452) 835563 E: bshptewk@glosdioc.org.uk

SNOW, Miss Patricia Margaret. b 21. Dub Bible Coll 45 St Mich Ho Ox 51. **dss** 72 **d** 87 **p** 96. W Ham *Chelmsf* 72-83; Acomb St Steph and St Aid *York* 78-83; rtd 83; NSM Northfleet *Roch* 96-01; PtO 01-13. *5 Dulverton Hall, Esplanade, Scarborough YO11 2AR*

SNOW, Peter David. b 37. St Jo Coll Cam BA 61 MA 67. Ridley Hall Cam 62. **d** 64 **p** 65. C Kingshurst *Birm* 64-66; C Santa Barbara All SS USA 67-71; Can Missr for Youth Los Angeles 71-75; R Jackson St Jo 75-81; Asst R Bellevue Resurr 81-85; R Redmond H Cross 89-01; rtd 01; P-in-c Edmonds SS Hilda and Patr USA 02-03. *927 36th Avenue, Seattle WA 98122-5216, USA* T: (001) (206) 329 3784 E: peterorlisa@cs.com

SNOW, Richard John. b 57. Bris Univ BSc 80 K Coll Lon MA 05. **d** 90 **p** 91. C Preston Plucknett *B & W* 90-95; TV Stratton St Margaret w S Marston etc *Bris* 95-02; R Box w Hazlebury and Ditteridge 02-07; TR Kirkby Lonsdale *Carl* from 07. *The Rectory, Vicarage Lane, Kirkby Lonsdale, Carnforth LA6 2BA* T: (01524) 272044 E: rector@therainbowparish.org

SNOWBALL, Miss Deborah Jane. b 67. Middx Poly BEd 90. Ripon Coll Cuddesdon 02. **d** 04 **p** 05. C Sawbridgeworth *St Alb* 04-07; P-in-c Rickmansworth 07-12; V from 12; RD from 11. *The Vicarage, Bury Lane, Rickmansworth WD3 1ED* T: (01923) 772627 E: vicar@stmarysrickmansworth.org.uk

SNOWBALL, Dorothy Margaret. b 52. Sunderland Univ BA 98. NEOC 98. **d** 01 **p** 02. NSM Heworth St Mary *Dur* 01-07; P-in-c Eighton Banks from 07. *2 Oval Park View, Felling, Gateshead NE10 9DS* T: 0191-469 5059 E: dsnowball@talk21.com

SNOWBALL, Michael Sydney. b 44. Dur Univ BA 70 MA 72. Cranmer Hall Dur. **d** 72 **p** 73. C Stockton St Pet *Dur* 72-75; C Dunston St Nic 75-77; C Dunston 77-78; C Darlington St Jo 78-81; V Chilton 81-91; V Brompton w Deighton *York* 91-09; rtd 09; PtO *York* from 10. *36 Woodhall Close, Marske-by-the-Sea, Redcar TS11 6AJ* T: (01642) 271147 E: mickthevic@aol.com

SNOWDEN, Miss Alice Isabel Glass. b 55. Lanc Univ BA 77 Humberside Coll of Educn PGCE 84. Ripon Coll Cuddesdon 91. **d** 94 **p** 95. C Mirfield *Wakef* 94-97; TV Guiseley w Esholt *Bradf* 97-02; V Bankfoot 02-09; P-in-c Leeds All So *Ripon* 09-11; TV Leeds All So and St Aid 11-15; rtd 14. *2 Westfield Farm, Westfield Drive, Ossett WF5 0QT* E: sobachenki@ntlworld.com

SNOWDEN (née HALL), Mrs Elizabeth. b 58. Plymouth Poly BSc 79 Birm Univ BA 01 Lon Inst of Educn PGCE 80. Qu Coll Birm 98. **d** 01 **p** 02. C Burntwood *Lich* 01-04; C and Youth Work Co-ord Ogley Hay 04-10; P-in-c Bestwood Em w St Mark *S'well* 10-11; V from 11; AD Nottm N from 13. *Emmanuel*

Vicarage, 10 Church View Close, Arnold, Nottingham NG5 9QP
T: 0115-920 8879   M: 07973-824934
E: revesnowden@yahoo.co.uk

SNUGGS, Canon David Sidney. b 49. Keble Coll Ox BA 71 PGCE 72 MA 75. S Dios Minl Tr Scheme 89. **d** 92 **p** 93. C Bitterne *Win* 92-96; V Fair Oak 96-14; Hon Can Win Cathl 11-14; rtd 14; PtO *Win* from 14. *13 Cranbourne Park, Hedge End, Southampton SO30 0NX* M: 07875-733323
E: david@sttoms.co.uk

SNYDER, Miss Susanna Jane. b 78. Em Coll Cam BA 00 MA 05. Qu Coll Birm BA 04. **d** 05 **p** 06. C Brownswood Park and Stoke Newington St Mary *Lon* 05-08; PtO *Ox* 08-10; USA 10-14; PtO *Ox* from 14. *103 High Street, Wheatley, Oxford OX33 1XP* M: 07904-769559 E: susannajsnyder@gmail.com

SNYDER GIBSON, Catherine. *See* GIBSON, Catherine Snyder

SOADY, Canon Mark. b 60. Univ of Wales BTh RMN 84. St Mich Coll Llan 96. **d** 96 **p** 97. C Tenby *St D* 96-99; TV 99-03; Min Can St Woolos Cathl 03-08; P-in-c Newport All SS and Chapl Univ of Wales (Newport) 08-12; V Abergavenny St Mary w Llanwenarth Citra from 12; P-in-c Abergavenny H Trin from 12; AD Abergavenny from 14; CF(V) from 98; Can St Woolos Cathl from 14. *St Mary's Vicarage, Monk Street, Abergavenny NP7 5ND* T: (01873) 853168 M: 07968-753978
E: vicar@stmarys-priory.org

SOAR, Angela Margaret. *See* PATERSON, Angela Margaret

SOAR, Martin William. b 54. Wye Coll Lon BSc 78. Wycliffe Hall Ox 86. **d** 88 **p** 89. C Henfynyw w Aberaeron and Llanddewi Aberarth *St D* 88-91; C Hubberston 91-93; P-in-c Low Harrogate St Mary *Ripon* 93-95; V 95-06; Chapl Old Swinford Hosp Sch Stourbridge from 06; C Kinver and Enville *Lich* from 10. *7 Wrekin Drive, Stourbridge DY9 7HB*
E: soars@blueyonder.co.uk *or* msoar@oshsch.com

✠**SOARES, The Rt Revd Fernando da Luz.** b 43. Univ of Porto. **d** 71 **p** 72 **c** 80. Bp Lusitanian Ch from 80; Hon Asst Bp Eur from 95. *Rua Elias Garcia 107-1 Dto, 4430-091 Vila Nova de Gaia, Portugal* T: (00351) (22) 375 4646 F: 375 2016
E: fernandols@netc.pt *or* ilcae@mail.telepac.pt

SOBCZAK, Mrs Susan Clare. b 49. WEMTC 10. **d** 13 **p** 14. NSM Nailsworth w Shortwood, Horsley etc *Glouc* from 13. *1 Byways, Horsley, Stroud GL6 0PP* T: (01453) 833526
E: suesobczak@gmail.com

SOCHON, David Lomas Philipe. b 40. Univ Coll Lon BA 62. **d** 07 **p** 08. OLM Newton Flotman, Swainsthorpe, Tasburgh, etc *Nor* 07-15; RD Depwade 09-13; rtd 15; PtO *St E* from 15; *Nor* from 15. *Greenacre, Stone Street, Spexhall, Halesworth IP19 0RN* T: (01986) 781151
E: davidsochon@googlemail.com

SODADASI, David Anand Raj. b 63. Osmania Univ Hyderabad BCom 85 MA 99 Union Bibl Sem Pune BD 95 Univ of Wales PhD 12. United Th Coll Bangalore MTh 00. **d** 01 **p** 02. C Jabalpur Cathl India 01-04; Lect Leonard Th Coll 00-04; PtO *Ox* 04-05; NSM Ray Valley 05-10; R Cusop w Blakemere, Bredwardine w Brobury etc *Heref* from 10. *The Rectory, Cusop, Hay-on-Wye, Hereford HR3 5RF* T: (01497) 821656
E: anandsodadasi@hotmail.co.uk

SODOR AND MAN, Bishop of. *See* PATERSON, The Rt Revd Robert Mar Erskine

SOER, Patricia Kathleen Mary. b 40. Hull Coll of Educn CertEd 61. **d** 99 **p** 00. OLM Deptford St Jo w H Trin *S'wark* 99-06; OLM Deptford St Jo w H Trin and Ascension 06-10; PtO from 10. *350 Wood Vale, London SE23 3DY* T: (020) 8699 4616 E: pat@sjht.org.uk

SOFIELD, Martin. b 60. **d** 02 **p** 03. OLM Clifton *Man* 02-10; NSM Ardrossan *Glas* 10-11; R from 11; NSM Dalry 10-11; R from 11; NSM Irvine St Andr LEP 10-11; I from 11. *St Andrew's Rectory, 31 Milgarholm Avenue, Irvine KA12 0EL* M: 07710-428896 T: (01294) 278341
E: martin.sofield@btinternet.com

SOGA, Hector Ian. b 47. Glas Univ MA 70 BMus 78 PhD 90 Selw Coll Cam BA 72 MA 76. St And NSM Tr Scheme 87. **d** 88 **p** 89. NSM Dollar St And 88-14. *25 Mitchell Court, Dollar FK14 7BF* T: (01259) 740303

SOKANOVIC (née HARRIS), Mrs Mary Noreen Cecily. b 58. Suffolk Coll BA 97 RGN 79 RN 96. EAMTC 02. **d** 05 **p** 06. NSM Whitton and Thurleston w Akenham *St E* 05-10; Bp's Chapl from 10. *Bishop's House, 4 Park Road, Ipswich IP1 3ST* T: (01473) 252829 *or* (01449) 766137
E: mary.sokanovic@cofesuffolk.org *or* marysokanovic@gmail.com

SOKOLOWSKI (née MAHON), Mrs Stephanie Mary. b 56. Liv Univ BSc 80 SRN 80 K Coll Lon BA 00. S'wark Ord Course 91. **d** 94 **p** 95. C Warlingham w Chelsham and Farleigh *S'wark* 94-97; C Godstone and Blindley Heath 97-04; C Shere, Albury and Chilworth *Guildf* from 07. *The Vicarage, Brook Road, Chilworth, Guildford GU4 8ND* T: (01483) 534293
M: 07731-783924 E: ssokolowski@btinternet.com

SOLMAN, Mrs Fiona Barbara. b 53. SRN 75 RSCN 75 RHV 80. STETS 03. **d** 06 **p** 07. C Cottesmore and Barrow w Ashwell and Burley *Pet* 06-09; C Empingham and Exton w Horn w Whitwell 06-09; C Greetham and Thistleton w Stretton and Clipsham 06-09; R Etwall w Egginton *Derby* from 09. *Etwall Rectory, Rectory Court, Main Street, Etwall, Derby DE65 6LP* T: (01283) 732349 E: fionasolman@aol.com

SOMASUNDRAM, Ian Mark. b 81. Man Univ MEng 04 Jes Coll Cam PhD 10. Oak Hill Th Coll BA 15. **d** 15. C Hebburn St Jo *Dur* from 15. *St Oswald's Vicarage, St Oswald's Road, Hebburn NE31 1HR* M: 07742-319151
E: ian.m.somasundram@gmail.com

SOMERS-EDGAR, Carl John. b 46. Otago Univ BA 69. St Steph Ho Ox 72. **d** 75 **p** 76. C Northwood H Trin *Lon* 75-79; C St Marylebone All SS 79-82; V Liscard St Mary w St Columba *Ches* 82-85; V Caversham St Pet New Zealand 85-11; rtd 11. *32 Cole Street, Caversham, Dunedin 9012, New Zealand* T: (0064) (3) 487 9877 E: paratus@xtra.co.nz

SOMERS HESLAM, Peter. *See* HESLAM, Peter Somers

SOMERVILLE, David. b 58. QUB BEd. **d** 00 **p** 01. C Lisburn Ch Ch *Conn* 00-03; I Drumgath w Drumgooland and Clonduff *D & D* 03-13; I Richhill *Arm* from 13. *15 Annareagh Road, Richhill, Armagh BT61 9JT* T: (028) 3887 0798
M: 07811-916825 E: revds@btinternet.com

SOMERVILLE, John William Kenneth. b 38. St D Coll Lamp 60. **d** 63 **p** 64. C Rhosllannerchrugog *St As* 63-67; C Llangystennin 67-70; V Gorsedd 70-76; V Gorsedd w Brynford and Ysgeifiog 77-02; RD Holywell 96-02; rtd 02; PtO *St As* from 09. *15 Bryn Marl Road, Mochdre, Colwyn Bay LL28 5DT*

SOMMERVILLE, Prof Robert Gardner. b 27. Glas Univ MB 50 ChB 50 MD 60 FRCPGlas 67 Lon Univ FRCPath 68. **d** 96 **p** 96. NSM Blairgowrie *St And* 96-97; NSM Coupar Angus 96-97; NSM Alyth 96-97; P-in-c Killin 97-99; PtO 99-01; P-in-c Tayport 01-09; rtd 09; LtO *St And* from 09. *Monkmyre, Myreriggs Road, Coupar Angus, Blairgowrie PH13 9HS* T/F: (01828) 627131 E: rsommerville120@btinternet.com

SONG, James. b 32. Lon Coll of Div 57. **d** 60 **p** 61. C Virginia Water *Guildf* 60-63; C Portman Square St Paul *Lon* 63-66; V Matlock Bath *Derby* 66-76; V Woking St Jo *Guildf* 76-94; RD Woking 87-92; rtd 94; PtO *Guildf* from 94. *Ash House, Churt, Farnham GU10 2JU* T/F: (01428) 714493

SONG, Leonardo. b 60. Angl Th Coll Seoul BA. Angl Th Sem Seoul MDiv. **d** 91 **p** 93. Korea 91-03; Fell Crowther Hall CMS Tr Coll Selly Oak 03-04; Consultant CMS 05-06; Chapl Angl Korean Community *Lon* from 07. *268C New Cross Road, London SE14 5PL* T: (020) 7732 2377 M: 07834-831022
E: leonardosong@hotmail.com

SOOSAINAYAGAM, Xavier. b 50. Sri Lanka Nat Sem BPh 73 St Paul's Sem Trichy BTh 77 S'wark Ord Course 89. **d** 76 **p** 77. In RC Ch 76-89; C Streatham St Leon *S'wark* 89-94; C Merton St Jas 94-97; V Croydon H Sav 97-13; rtd 13. *Address temp unknown* M: 07789-567842

SOPER, Jonathan Alexander James. b 64. Univ Coll Dur BA 85. Wycliffe Hall Ox 94. **d** 96 **p** 97. C Bath Weston All SS w N Stoke and Langridge *B & W* 96-00; C Bryanston Square St Mary w St Marylebone St Mark *Lon* 00-04; LtO *Ex* from 07. *Church Office, 22 Southernhay West, Exeter EX1 1PR* T: (01392) 434311 E: jon@enc.uk.net

SOPHIANOU, Neofitos Anthony. b 47. Sarum & Wells Th Coll 86. **d** 88 **p** 89. C St Peter-in-Thanet *Cant* 88-91; PtO *St Alb* 97-99; C Stevenage St Nic and Graveley 99-03; PtO 03-04; V Wheatley Park *Sheff* 04-07; V Goole 07-11; R Sprotbrough 11-14; Bp's Urban Adv 05-14; rtd 14; PtO *Sheff* from 14; Ecum Officer Doncaster Adnry from 15. *7 Victoria Avenue, Hatfield, Doncaster DN7 6QG* T: (01302) 459403
E: sophianou@virginmedia.com

SORENSEN, Ms Anna Katrine Elizabeth. b 58. Man Univ BA 82 MPhil 94 Open Univ PGCE 95. Ripon Coll Cuddesdon 83. **d** 87 **p** 94. Par Dn Ashton H Trin *Man* 87-88; Asst Chapl St Felix Sch Southwold 89-90; Chapl 90-99; Hon Par Dn Reydon *St E* 89-92; Hon Par Dn Blythburgh w Reydon 92-94; Hon C 94-99; C Gislingham and Thorndon 99-03; P-in-c Billingborough Gp *Linc* from 03. *The Vicarage, 13 High Street, Billingborough, Sleaford NG34 0QG* T: (01529) 240750
M: 07932-031479 E: anna_sor@yahoo.com

SOTONWA, Canon Oladapo Oyegbola. b 56. Ibadan Univ Nigeria BEd 79 MEd 81 PhD 86. Immanuel Coll Ibadan 91. **d** 94 **p** 95. C Italupe Em Nigeria 94-95; V Egbeba All SS 95-03; V Simeon Ashiru Mem Ch 03-04; V Odogbondu St Pet 04-05; Hon Can Ijebu from 05; PtO *S'wark* 06-07; Hon C W Dulwich Em 07-11; Hon C S'wark H Trin w St Matt 11; Chapl HM Pris Nor from 11. *Address temp unknown* T: (01603) 708600 M: 07983-630658 E: oladaposotonwa@yahoo.co.uk

SOTONWA, Thomas Bamidele Adegboyega. b 78. Ambrose Alli Univ Nigeria BMLS 05 Middx Univ MSc 11. **d** 05 **p** 06.

Nigeria 05-13; PtO *Birm* from 13. *20 Manor Road, Aston, Birmingham B6 6QT* M: 07837-421941
E: sotzi2002@gmail.com

SOULSBY, Canon Michael. b 36. Dur Univ BSc 57. Westcott Ho Cam 61. **d** 62 **p** 63. C Selly Oak St Mary *Birm* 62-66; C Kings Norton 66-72; TV 73-76; TR Sutton *Liv* 76-88; RD Prescot 84-88; P-in-c Orton Longueville *Ely* 88-96; RD Yaxley 92-02; TR The Ortons, Alwalton and Chesterton 96-04; Hon Can Ely Cathl 94-04; rtd 04; PtO *Ely* from 05; *Pet* from 14. *8 Leiston Court, Eye, Peterborough PE6 7WL* T: (01733) 221124
E: m.soulsby@talk21.com

SOULT, Mrs Pamela Elizabeth. b 46. SNWTP. **d** 09 **p** 10. NSM Over Peover w Lower Peover *Ches* 09-11; NSM Goostrey w Swettenham from 11. *The Tower House, The Courtyard, Swettenham, Congleton CW12 2JZ* T: (01477) 571844
E: pamelasoult@aol.com

SOUNDY, Mrs Philippa Clare. b 60. BNC Ox BA 81. St Mellitus Coll BA 10. **d** 10 **p** 11. CMS from 10; NSM Amersham on the Hill *Ox* 10-14; NSM Hawridge w Cholesbury and St Leonard from 14. *3 Hoppers Way, Great Kingshill, High Wycombe HP15 6EY* T: (01494) 714161 M: 07791-226162
E: pippasoundy@hotmail.co.uk *or* pippasoundy@btinternet.com

SOUPER, Patrick Charles. b 28. K Coll Lon BD 55 AKC 55. **d** 57 **p** 58. Chapl Derby City Hosp 57-62; Chapl Derby Cathl 57-62; Asst Chapl Lon Univ 62-64; C St Marylebone w H Trin 64-65; Chapl St Paul's Sch Barnes 65-70; Lect in Educn Southn Univ 70-87; rtd 87. *Prines, Box 3726, 74100 Rethymno, Crete, Greece* T: (0030) (831) 31521 F: 31903 E: pigiaki@phl.uoc.gr

SOUPPOURIS, Ms Gail Camilla. b 52. Essex Univ BA 75. SEITE 02. **d** 05 **p** 06. C W Wickham St Fran and St Mary *S'wark* 05-08; P-in-c Shoreham Beach *Chich* 08-14; rtd 14. *The Rotyngs, Rottingdean, Brighton BN2 7DX* M: 07950-665051 T: (01273) 240420 E: reverend.gail@gmail.com

SOURBUT, Catherine Ann. b 67. Bath Univ BA 91 MSc 93 PhD 97. STETS MA 07. **d** 07 **p** 08. C Saltford w Corston and Newton St Loe *B & W* 07-11; P-in-c Bath St Barn w Englishcombe from 11. *The Vicarage, Mount View, Southdown, Bath BA2 1JX* E: vicar@englishcombe.net

SOURBUT, Preb Philip John. b 57. Cam Univ BA MA. Cranmer Hall Dur BA. **d** 85 **p** 86. C Springfield All SS *Chelmsf* 85-88; C Roxeth Ch Ch and Harrow St Pet *Lon* 88-91; P-in-c Bath St Sav *B & W* 91-93; R Bath St Sav w Swainswick and Woolley 93-98; V Cullompton and R Kentisbeare w Blackborough *Ex* 98-01; TR Cullompton, Willand, Uffculme, Kentisbeare etc 01-09; Dioc Voc Development Officer 09-15; Tutor SWMTC 09-15; C Ex St Mark, St Sidwell and St Matt 09-15; Dioc Dir Miss and Min from 15; Preb Ex Cathl from 15. *The Old Deanery, The Cloisters, Cathedral Close, Exeter EX1 1HS* T: (01392) 294903 E: philip.sourbut@exeter.anglican.org

SOUTER, Ruth Rosemary. b 55. Dur Univ BEd 77. EMMTC 00. **d** 03 **p** 04. C Braunstone Park CD *Leic* 03-07; V Erdington Ch the K *Birm* from 07. *St Margaret's Vicarage, Somerset Road, Erdington, Birmingham B23 6NQ* T: 0121-373 9209
E: ruthsouter@yahoo.com

SOUTER, William Ewen Logan. b 66. Em Coll Cam BA 88 Univ Coll Lon PhD 93. Trin Coll Bris BA 94 MA 97. **d** 97 **p** 98. C Harborne Heath *Birm* 97-01; TV Horsham *Chich* 01-11; PtO *Llan* from 13. *89 Claude Road, Cardiff CF24 3QD* T: (029) 2115 4631 M: 07807-384350 E: willsouter@hotmail.co.uk

SOUTH, Gerald. b 45. **d** 09 **p** 10. NSM Limpsfield and Tatsfield *S'wark* from 09. *Clouds, Ricketts Hill Road, Tatsfield, Westerham TN16 2NB* T: (01959) 577598 E: gp.south@btopenworld.com

SOUTH, Gillian. *See* HARWOOD, Gillian

SOUTH EAST ASIA, Archbishop of. *See* CHEW, The Most Revd John Hiang Chea

SOUTH INDIA, Moderator of the Church of. *See* SUGANDHAR, The Most Revd Badda Peter

SOUTHALL, Colin Edward. b 36. Lich Th Coll 63. **d** 65 **p** 82. C Wylde Green *Birm* 65-67; PtO 68-73; *Pet* 73-81; Hon C Linc St Faith and St Martin w St Pet 82-85; Hon C Gt Glen, Stretton Magna and Wistow etc *Leic* 85-93; Chapl Asst Leic R Infirmary 93-96; Hon C Fleckney and Kilby *Leic* 96-98; PtO from 99. *1 Spinney View, Great Glen, Leicester LE8 9EP* T: 0116-259 2959
E: csouthall959@btinternet.com

SOUTHAMPTON, Suffragan Bishop of. *See* FROST, The Rt Revd Jonathan Hugh

SOUTHEE, Mrs Sandra Margaret. b 43. EAMTC 97. **d** 00 **p** 01. NSM Galleywood Common *Chelmsf* 00-02; NSM Moulsham St Jo 02-06; Asst Chapl Mid-Essex Hosp Services NHS Trust 01-06; PtO *Chelmsf* 06-07; NSM Gt Baddow 07-12; rtd 12; PtO *Chelmsf* from 12. *6 Hampton Road, Chelmsford CM2 8ES* T: (01245) 475456 E: sandysouthee@hotmail.co.uk

SOUTHEND, Archdeacon of. *See* LOWMAN, The Ven David Walter

✠**SOUTHERN, The Rt Revd Humphrey Ivo John.** b 60. Ch Ch Ox BA 82 MA 86. Ripon Coll Cuddesdon 83. **d** 86 **p** 87 **c** 07. C Rainham *Roch* 86-90; C Walton St Mary *Liv* 90-92; C Walton-on-the-Hill 92; V Hale *Guildf* 92-96; TR 96-97; TR Hale w Badshot Lea 97-99; Dioc Ecum Officer 92-99; TR Tisbury *Sarum* 99-01; TR Nadder Valley 01-07; RD Chalke 00-07; Can and Preb Sarum Cathl 06-07; Suff Bp Repton *Derby* 07-15; Warden of Readers 09-15; Prin Ripon Coll Cuddesdon from 15; Asst Bp Ox from 15. *Ripon College, Cuddesdon, Oxford OX44 9EX* T: (01865) 877400 E: principal@rcc.ac.uk

SOUTHERN, John Abbott. b 27. Leeds Univ BA 47. Coll of Resurr Mirfield. **d** 51 **p** 52. C Leigh St Mary *Man* 51-55; C Gt Grimsby St Jas *Linc* 55-58; V Oldham St Jas *Man* 58-60; V Haigh *Liv* 60-75; V Pemberton St Jo 75-98; rtd 98; PtO *Liv* from 00. *145 Moor Road, Orrell, Wigan WN5 8SJ* T: (01942) 732132

SOUTHERN, Mrs Lindsay Margaret. b 70. Univ of Wales (Abth) BA 01 Reading Univ PGCE 04 St Jo Coll Dur BA 08. Cranmer Hall Dur 06. **d** 08 **p** 09. C Kirklington w Burneston and Wath and Pickhill *Ripon* 08-12; V Catterick *Leeds* from 12. *The Vicarage, High Green, Catterick, Richmond DL10 7LN* E: revlindsay@btinternet.com

SOUTHERN, Paul Ralph. b 48. Oak Hill Th Coll 85. **d** 87 **p** 88. C Chadwell Heath *Chelmsf* 87-91; P-in-c Tolleshunt D'Arcy w Tolleshunt Major 91-01; V Tolleshunt D'Arcy and Tolleshunt Major 01-08; rtd 08; PtO *Chelmsf* from 08. *12 Guisnes Court, Back Road, Tolleshunt D'Arcy, Maldon CM9 8TW* T: (01621) 860380

SOUTHERN BRAZIL, Bishop of. *See* SANTOS DE OLIVEIRA, Orlando

SOUTHERN CONE OF AMERICA, Primate of. *See* VENABLES, The Most Revd Gregory James

SOUTHERTON, Kathryn Ruth. *See* TRIMBY, Kathryn Ruth

SOUTHERTON, Canon Peter Clive. b 38. MBE 01. Univ of Wales (Lamp) BA 59. Qu Coll Birm. **d** 61 **p** 62. C Llandrillo-yn-Rhos *St As* 61-68; Bermuda 68-71; V Esclusham *St As* 72-82; V Prestatyn 82-04; Hon Can St As Cathl 96-04; rtd 04; PtO *St As* from 09. *6 Llwyn Mesen, Prestatyn LL19 8NS* T: (01745) 853176

SOUTHEY, George Rubidge. b 34. St Mich Coll Llan 84. **d** 86 **p** 87. C Hessle *York* 86-89; P-in-c Scarborough St Columba 89-92; V 92-99; rtd 99; PtO *Glouc* 00-06. *9 Smokey Glade, Doreen Vic 3754, Australia* T: (0061) (3) 9717 5717 M: 43-833 9877 E: george.southey@bigpond.com

SOUTHGATE, Mrs Clair Mary. b 67. Trin Coll Bris 09. **d** 11 **p** 12. OLM Box w Hazlebury and Ditteridge *Bris* from 11; OLM Colerne w N Wraxall from 11. *6 Queens Square, Box, Corsham SN13 8EA* T: (01225) 743970 M: 07917-117644
E: meddling@tiscali.co.uk

SOUTHGATE, Graham. b 63. GIBiol 85 NE Surrey Coll of Tech PhD 89. Ripon Coll Cuddesdon BTh 93. **d** 93 **p** 94. C Tisbury *Sarum* 93-97; TV Chalke Valley 97-03; R Bratton, Edington and Imber, Erlestoke etc 03-11; TR Nadder Valley from 11. *The Rectory, Shaftesbury Road, Fovant, Salisbury SP3 5JA* T: (01722) 714826 E: grahamsouthgate63@hotmail.com

SOUTHGATE, Patricia. b 44. **d** 03 **p** 04. OLM Parkstone St Pet and St Osmund w Branksea *Sarum* from 03. *60 Orchard Avenue, Poole BH14 8AJ* T: (01202) 745081
E: patsouthgate@btinternet.com

SOUTHGATE, Stephen Martin. b 61. Lanc Univ BA 83 St Martin's Coll Lanc PGCE 84. Cranmer Hall Dur 96. **d** 98 **p** 99. C Witton *Ches* 98-01; R Backford and Capenhurst from 01. *The Vicarage, Grove Road, Mollington, Chester CH1 6LG* T: (01244) 851071 E: bchvicarage@btinternet.com

SOUTHWARD, Douglas Ambrose. b 32. St Jo Coll Nottm LTh 74 FBS 02. ALCD 57. **d** 57 **p** 58. C Otley *Bradf* 57-61; C Sedbergh 61-63; C Cautley w Dowbiggin 61-63; C Garsdale 61-63; PV Lich Cathl 63-65; V Hope *Derby* 65-72; V Crosby Ravensworth *Carl* 72-82; V Bolton 74-82; Sec Dioc Past and Redundant Chs Uses Cttees 78-82; RD Appleby 78-82; Hon Can Carl Cathl 81-95; R Asby 81-82; V Hawkshead and Low Wray w Sawrey 82-98; P-in-c Windermere St Jo 84-89; RD Windermere 84-89; P-in-c Satterthwaite 94-95; rtd 98; PtO *Carl* from 98. *Hawthorn House, Town End, Witherslack, Grange-over-Sands LA11 6RL* T: (01539) 552078

SOUTHWARD, Canon James Fisher. b 57. St Martin's Coll BEd 80. Chich Th Coll 83. **d** 86 **p** 87. C Woodford St Barn *Chelmsf* 86-89; TV Crawley *Chich* 89-95; V Higham and Merston *Roch* from 95; RD Strood 02-12; Hon Can Roch Cathl from 09. *The Vicarage, Hermitage Road, Higham, Rochester ME3 7NE* T/F: (01634) 717360
E: james.southward@diocese-rochester.org

SOUTHWARK, Archdeacon of. *See* STEEN, The Ven Jane Elizabeth

SOUTHWARK, Bishop of. *See* CHESSUN, The Rt Revd Christopher Thomas James

SOUTHWARK, Dean of. *See* NUNN, The Very Revd Andrew Peter

SOUTHWELL, Peter John Mackenzie. b 43. New Coll Ox BA 64 MA 68. Wycliffe Hall Ox 66. **d** 67 **p** 68. C Crookes St Thos *Sheff* 67-70; Lect Sheff Univ 67-70; Sen Tutor Wycliffe Hall Ox 70-08; Chapl and Lect Qu Coll Ox 82-10; rtd 10; LtO *Ox* from 10. *The Queen's College, Oxford OX1 4AW* T: (01865) 279120　E: peter.southwell@queens.ox.ac.uk

SOUTHWELL AND NOTTINGHAM, Bishop of. *See* WILLIAMS, The Rt Revd Paul Gavin

SOWDEN, Charles William Bartholomew. b 47. **d** 97 **p** 98. OLM Saxonwell *Linc* 97-06; NSM Metheringham w Blankney and Dunston 06-09; P-in-c Wyberton from 09; P-in-c Frampton from 09. *The Rectory, Church Lane, Wyberton, Boston PE21 7AF*　T: (01205) 353593 E: charles.sowden1@btinternet.com

SOWDEN, Geoffrey David. b 57. Kingston Poly BA 79. Wycliffe Hall Ox 95. **d** 97 **p** 98. C Ware Ch Ch *St Alb* 97-02; V Highworth w Sevenhampton and Inglesham etc *Bris* from 02; P-in-c Broad Blunsdon from 05. *The Vicarage, 10 Stonefield Drive, Highworth, Swindon SN6 7DA*　T: (01793) 765554 E: the.sowdens@btinternet.com

SOWDON, Henry Lewis Malcolm. b 37. TCD BA. Bps' Coll Cheshunt. **d** 64 **p** 65. C Newport w Longford *Lich* 64-66; C Caverswall 66-69; Chapl Clayesmore Sch Blandford 69-72; Hon C Hornsey Ch Ch *Lon* 72-80; Chapl Gordon's Sch Woking 80-86; TV Hodge Hill *Birm* 86-91; PtO 91-12; rtd 02. *157 Heathfield Road, Birmingham B19 1JD*　T: 0121-240 3557

SOWERBUTTS, Alan. b 49. Sheff Univ BSc 70 PhD 73 Qu Coll Cam BA 75 MA 79. Westcott Ho Cam 74. **d** 76 **p** 77. C Salesbury *Blackb* 76-80; V Lower Darwen St Jas 80-84; V Musbury 84-93; P-in-c Brindle 93-98; Sec Dioc Adv Cttee for the Care of Chs 93-98; V Read in Whalley 98-14; rtd 14; PtO *Man* from 14; *Blackb* from 14. *9 Hapton Way, Rossendale BB4 8QG*　T: (01706) 219279

SOWERBUTTS, Philip John. b 67. Ches Coll of HE BEd 89 Edge Hill Coll of HE PGCE 99. Oak Hill Th Coll BA 03. **d** 03 **p** 04. C Kirk Ella and Willerby *York* 03-07; V Castle Church *Lich* from 07. *Castle Church Vicarage, 18 Castle Bank, Stafford ST16 1DJ*　T: (01785) 223673　M: 07910-606876 E: vicar@castlechurch.org.uk

SOWERBY, Geoffrey Nigel Rake. b 35. St Aid Birkenhead 56. **d** 60 **p** 61. C Armley St Bart *Ripon* 60-63; Min Can Ripon Cathl 63-65; V Thornthwaite w Thruscross and Darley 65-69; V Leeds All SS 69-73; V Leyburn w Bellerby 73-81; R Edin Old St Paul 81-86; V Hawes and Hardraw *Ripon* 86-92; Dioc Adv in Deliverance Min 91-92; rtd 92; PtO *Dur* from 92; *Leeds* from 92. *25 Greendale Court, Bedale DL8 1FB*　T: (01677) 425860　M: 07749-229189 E: geoffreynsowerby@btinternet.com

✤**SOWERBY, The Rt Revd Mark Crispin Rake.** b 63. K Coll Lon BD 85 AKC 85 Lanc Univ MA 94. Coll of Resurr Mirfield 85. **d** 87 **p** 88　**c** 09. C Knaresborough *Ripon* 87-90; C Darwen St Cuth w Tockholes St Steph *Blackb* 90-92; V Accrington St Mary 92-97; Chapl St Chris High Sch Accrington 92-97; Chapl Victoria Hosp Accrington 92-97; Asst Dir of Ords *Blackb* 93-96; Voc Officer and Selection Sec Min Division 97-01; V Harrogate St Wilfrid *Ripon* 01-04; TR 04-09; Asst Dir of Ords 05-09; Area Bp Horsham *Chich* from 09. *Bishop's House, 21 Guildford Road, Horsham RH12 1LU*　F: 217349 E: bishop.horsham@chichester.anglican.org

SOWTER, Colin Victor. b 35. Ball Coll Ox BA 56 MA 59 DPhil 60. Oak Hill NSM Course 88. **d** 91 **p** 92. NSM Cranleigh *Guildf* 91-93; NSM Wonersh 93-98; NSM Wonersh w Blackheath 98-05; rtd 05; PtO *Guildf* from 05. *Hollycroft, Grantley Avenue, Wonersh Park, Guildford GU5 0QN*　T: (01483) 892094　F: 892894　E: colin.sowter@btopenworld.com

SOWTON, Mrs Alison. b 62. Qu Coll Birm. **d** 09 **p** 10. C Oxhey All SS *St Alb* 09-13; TV Melksham *Sarum* from 13. *St Andrew's Vicarage, 33 Church Lane, Melksham SN12 7EF*　T: (01225) 434113　M: 07739-712548　E: alisonsowton@live.com

SOX, Harold David. b 36. N Carolina Univ BA 58. Union Th Sem (NY) MDiv 61. **d** 61 **p** 61. USA 61-74; Hon C Richmond St Mary *S'wark* 74-79; Hon C Richmond St Mary w St Matthias and St Jo 79-82; Hon C Kensington St Mary Abbots w St Geo *Lon* 82-84 and 89-93; PtO 84-89; Hon C Beedon and Peasemore w W Ilsley and Farnborough *Ox* 93-94; PtO 93-97; *S'wark* 97-04. *20 The Vineyard, Richmond TW10 6AN*　T: (020) 8940 0094

SPACKMAN (née MORRISON), Mrs Ailsa. b 40. Qu Univ Kingston Ontario BA 82. Montreal Dioc Th Coll. **d** 83 **p** 85. Canada 83-95; Dn Caspe 83-85; I Malbay Miss Par 85-92; Chapl Drummondville Penitentiary 92-93; rtd 93; PtO *Ex* from 99. *Cofton Lodge, Cofton Hill, Cockwood, Exeter EX6 8RB* T: (01626) 891584

SPACKMAN, Canon Peter John. b 37. Southn Univ BSc 60. Westcott Ho Cam 65. **d** 66 **p** 67. C Boxmoor St Jo *St Alb* 66-69; C Alnwick St Paul *Newc* 69-72; C-in-c Stewart Town Jamaica

72-74; I Sept-Iles Canada 74-77; R Baie Comeau 77-80; R Gaspe 80-92; Adn Gaspe 88-92; R Richmond and Hon Can Quebec Canada 92-94; PtO *Ex* 95-97; Hon C Kenton, Mamhead, Powderham, Cofton and Starcross 97-02; PtO from 02. *Cofton Lodge, Cofton Hill, Cockwood, Exeter EX6 8RB* T: (01626) 891584　E: spackman1@btinternet.com

SPAIGHT, Robert George. b 45. Ridley Hall Cam. **d** 84 **p** 85. C St Columb Minor and St Colan *Truro* 84-87; C Worksop St Jo *S'well* 87-89; V Barlings *Linc* 89-13; rtd 13. *The Forge, Cross Roads, Riby, Grimsby DN37 8NH*　T: (01469) 569768

SPANKIE, Mrs Susan Jane. b 61. SCRTP 12. **d** 15. C Hanborough and Freeland *Ox* from 15. *Address temp unknown*

SPANNER, Handley James. b 51. Lanchester Poly Cov BSc 73 BA. Oak Hill Th Coll 82. **d** 85 **p** 86. C Cov H Trin 85-89; V Rye Park St Cuth *St Alb* 89-01; V Colney Heath St Mark 01-12; rtd 12. *79 Old Manor Road, Rustington, Littlehampton BN16 3QF*　E: jamesspanner@aol.com

SPARGO, Anne Elizabeth. b 51. Newnham Coll Cam MB 76 BChir 77 MA 79. WEMTC 03. **d** 06 **p** 07. NSM Frampton on Severn, Arlingham, Saul etc *Glouc* 06-10; P-in-c from 10. *Ashleigh House, The Street, Frampton on Severn, Gloucester GL2 7ED*　T: (01452) 741147　E: anne.spargo@btinternet.com

SPARHAM, Canon Anthony George. b 41. St Jo Coll Dur BA 69. Cranmer Hall Dur 66. **d** 71 **p** 72. C Bourne *Linc* 71-74; TV Tong *Bradf* 74-76; V Windhill 76-81; Dioc Dir of Educn *St E* 82-85; V Goostrey *Ches* 85-99; R Wilmslow 99-08; Dir Lay Tr 85-90; Jt Dir Lay Tr 90-97; Hon Can Ches Cathl 94-08; rtd 08; PtO *Ches* from 08; *Lich* 08-11 and from 14; Hon C Whittington and W Felton w Haughton 11-14. *The Rectory, Threadneedle Street, West Felton, Oswestry SY11 4LE* T: (01691) 610586　E: tony.sparham@virgin.net

SPARKES, Mrs Lynne. b 55. Chelt & Glouc Coll of HE BEd 96. WEMTC 06. **d** 09 **p** 10. NSM Barnwood *Glouc* 09-12; C Gt Malvern Ch Ch *Worc* 13-14; TV Malvern Chase from 14. *137 Madresfield Road, Malvern WR14 2HD* E: lynnesparkes@googlemail.com

SPARKS, Ian. b 59. Lanc Univ BSc(Econ) 81. Cranmer Hall Dur 94. **d** 96 **p** 97. C Bowdon *Ches* 96-00; V Chelford w Lower Withington 00-06; P-in-c Macclesfield St Jo 06-14; P-in-c Luddenden w Luddenden Foot *Leeds* from 14; C Ryburn from 14. *The Vicarage, 50 Carr Field Drive, Luddenden, Halifax HX2 6RJ*　E: iansparks5@googlemail.com

SPARROW, Miss Elisabeth Joy. b 70. Nottm Univ BEng 94. Qu Coll Birm 11. **d** 11 **p** 12. C Bartley Green *Birm* 11-15; P-in-c Bridgwater St Jo *B & W* from 15. *St John's Vicarage, Blake Place, Bridgwater TA6 5BA*　T: (01278) 422540 E: lis.sparrow@gmail.com *or* revlisstjohnbridgewater@gmail.com

SPARROW, Michael Kenneth. St Jo Coll Dur BA 74. Coll of Resurr Mirfield 74. **d** 75 **p** 76. C N Hinksey *Ox* 75-78; C Portsea St Mary *Portsm* 78-85; V Midsomer Norton w Clandown *B & W* 85-93; Chapl Schiedam Miss to Seafarers *Eur* 93-03; Chapl Mombasa Kenya 04-12; P-in-c N Ockendon *Chelmsf* from 14. *52 Birch Crescent, South Ockendon RM15 6TZ* T: (01708) 859598 *or* 671717　E: mksparrow13@gmail.com

SPEAKMAN, Anthony Ernest. b 40. **d** 71 **p** 72. C Newtown w Llanllwchaiarn w Aberhafesp *St As* 71-72; C Holywell 72-75; C St Marylebone w H Trin *Lon* 75-77; V Camberwell St Phil and St Mark *S'wark* 77-80; LtO *Lon* 94-96; NSM Kensington St Jo 96-05. *6A Park Place Villas, London W2 1SP*　T: (020) 7723 8920

SPEAKMAN, Joseph Frederick. b 26. NW Ord Course 75. **d** 78 **p** 79. NSM Wallasey St Hilary *Ches* 78; C 79-82; V Marthall w Over Peover 82-91; rtd 91; PtO *Ches* from 91. *1 Kinnaird Court, Cliff Road, Wallasey CH44 3AX*　T: 0151-637 0109 E: revjoe1@virginmedia.com

SPEAR, Andrew James Michael. b 60. Dur Univ BA 81. Ridley Hall Cam 83. **d** 86 **p** 87. C Haughton le Skerne *Dur* 86-90; C Eastbourne H Trin *Chich* 90-95; C Patcham 95-02; V Oldland *Bris* from 02; P-in-c Longwell Green from 13. *Oldland Vicarage, Grangeville Close, Longwell Green, Bristol BS30 9YJ*　T: 0117-932 7178 *or* 932 3291 E: andrewjmspear@hotmail.com

SPEAR, Miss Jennifer Jane. b 53. Westhill Coll Birm BEd 76. Trin Coll Bris 82. **dss** 84 **d** 87 **p** 95. Reading St Jo *Ox* 84-90; Par Dn 87-90; Hon Par Dn Devonport St Barn *Ex* 90-91; Hon Par Dn Devonport St Mich 90-91; Par Dn Plymstock 91-94; C 94-97; TV Plymstock and Hooe 97-11; rtd 11. *69 Plymstock Road, Plymouth PL9 7PD*　T: (01752) 405202 E: jenniferspear@amserve.com

SPEAR, John Cory. b 33. Open Univ BA 87. Ridley Hall Cam 68. **d** 70 **p** 71. C Gerrards Cross *Ox* 70-73; TV Washfield, Stoodleigh, Withleigh etc *Ex* 73-79; R Instow 79-90; V Westleigh 79-90; R Hartland 82-89; V Pilton w Ashford 90-97; TR Barnstaple 97-99; rtd 99; PtO *Ex* from 00. *Abbots Lodge, Abbotsham Court, Abbotsham, Bideford EX39 5BH* T: (01237) 476607

SPEAR, Sylvia Grace. b 36. St Chris Coll Blackheath 60. **dss** 76 **d** 87 **p** 94. S Wimbledon H Trin and St Pet *S'wark* 76-80; Lee Gd Shep w St Pet 80-95; Par Dn 87-94; C 94-95; rtd 95; PtO *Nor* from 95. *19 Grovelands, Ingoldisthorpe, King's Lynn PE31 6PG* T: (01485) 543469

SPEARS, Reginald Robert Derek. b 48. Trin Coll Ox BA 72 MA 75. Cuddesdon Coll 72. **d** 75 **p** 76. C Hampton All SS *Lon* 75-79; C Caversham *Ox* 79-81; C Caversham St Pet and Mapledurham etc 81-84; V Reading St Matt 84-94; V Earley St Pet 94-14; rtd 14; PtO *Ox* from 14. *Address temp unknown* T: 0118-926 2009 E: derekspears@compuserve.com

SPECK, Ms Jane Elisabeth. b 72. Univ of Cen England in Birm BA 94 St Jo Coll Dur BA 01 MA 02. Cranmer Hall Dur 98. **d** 02 **p** 03. C Stourport and Wilden *Worc* 02-05; C N Lambeth *S'wark* 05-11; Chapl K Coll Lon from 05; Dir Ords Kingston Area from 13. *11 Wilkinson Street, London SW8 1DD* T: (020) 7582 4915 E: janespeck@hotmail.com

SPECK, Preb Peter William. b 42. Univ of Wales (Ban) BSc 64 Birm Univ BA 66 MA 71 Lambeth DM 12. Qu Coll Birm 64. **d** 67 **p** 68. C Rhosddu *St As* 67-71; C Wrexham 71-72; Asst Chapl United Sheff Hosps 72-73; Chapl N Gen Hosp Sheff 73-79; Chapl R Free Hosp Lon 79-95; Hon Sen Lect Sch of Med 87-95; Preb St Paul's Cathl 92-95; Chapl Southn Univ Hosps NHS Trust 95-02; rtd 02; Public Preacher *Win* from 02; Visiting Fell Southn Univ from 02; Hon Sen Research Fell and Hon Sen Lect K Coll Lon from 02. *22 The Harrage, Romsey SO51 8AE* T: (01794) 516937

SPECK, Raymond George. b 39. Oak Hill Th Coll 64. **d** 67 **p** 68. C Stretford St Bride *Man* 67-70; C Roxeth Ch Ch *Lon* 70-74; V Woodbridge St Jo *St E* 74-85; R Jersey St Ouen w St Geo *Win* 85-98; rtd 98; PtO *Win* from 98. *Rosevale Lodge, rue du Craslin, St Peter, Jersey JE3 7BU* T: (01534) 634987

SPEDDING, Clare. See FRYER-SPEDDING, Clare Caroline

SPEDDING, Geoffrey Osmond. b 46. Hull Univ BA 67 Fitzw Coll Cam BA 69 MA BD. **d** 70 **p** 71. C Bradf Cathl 70-73; C Sutton St Jas and Wawne *York* 73-76; TV Preston St Jo *Blackb* 76-82; TV Yate New Town *Bris* 82-87; TR Bestwood *S'well* 87-94; V Ravenshead 94-04; rtd 04; Estate Manager Scargill Ho 06-08; P-in-c Cullingworth *Bradf* 08-09; Hon C E Richmond *Ripon* 09-12. *Mokes Barn, Wainstalls, Halifax HX2 7TR*

SPEDDING, William Granville. b 39. Tyndale Hall Bris BD 60. **d** 62 **p** 63. C Man Albert Memorial Ch 62-65; Hd RE Whitecroft Sch Bolton 65-71; Co-ord Humanities Hayward Sch Bolton 71-93; PtO *Man* 65-67 and from 02; NSM New Bury 67-79; NSM Bolton St Paul w Em 79-86; NSM Pennington 86-02. *26 Milverton Close, Lostock, Bolton BL6 4RR* T: (01204) 841248 E: granvillespedding@ntlworld.com

SPEEDY (née BRINDLEY), Mrs Angela Mary. b 44. Oak Hill Th Coll 93 NOC 99. **d** 00 **p** 01. C Handforth *Ches* 00-03; R Whaley Bridge 03-05; rtd 05; Hon C Barthomley *Ches* from 07. *The Rectory, Rushy Lane, Barthomley, Crewe CW2 5PE* T: (01270) 877112

SPEEDY, Canon Darrel Craven. b 35. St Chad's Coll Dur BA 57. Wells Th Coll 57. **d** 59 **p** 60. C Frodingham *Linc* 59-63; V Heckington w Howell 63-71; V Barton upon Humber 71-79; R Tain *Mor* 79-85; Dioc Sec 82-85; Can St Andr Cathl Inverness 83-85; Syn Clerk 83-85; R Whaley Bridge *Ches* 85-01; RD Chadkirk 88-95; Hon Can Ches Cathl from 96; rtd 01; P-in-c Barthomley *Ches* from 01. *The Rectory, Rushy Lane, Barthomley, Crewe CW2 5PE* T: (01270) 877112 E: darrel.speedy@btopenworld.com

SPEEKS, Mark William. b 62. Ex Univ BA 82 Ex Coll Ox MSt 83 Yale Univ MDiv 02. **d** 02 **p** 02. C Los Angeles St Alban USA 02-03; NSM Kilburn St Mary w All So and W Hampstead St Jas *Lon* 04-08; NSM St Botolph Aldgate w H Trin Minories 08-10; CF from 10; NSM Belsize Park *Lon* from 10; NSM S Hampstead St Sav from 10. *c/o MOD Chaplains (Army)* T: (01264) 383430 F: 381824 M: 07843-518063 E: mspeeks@acuitycapital.co.uk

SPEERS, Canon Samuel Hall. b 46. TCD BA 70 MA 75. Cuddesdon Coll 70. **d** 73 **p** 74. C Boreham Wood All SS *St Alb* 73-76; Madagascar 76-88; Hon Can Antananarivo from 85; R S Lafford *Linc* 88-02; RD Lafford 96-02; TR Chipping Barnet *St Alb* 02-13; rtd 13; Hon C Chingford SS Pet and Paul *Chelmsf* from 13. *Old Church House, 1A Priory Avenue, London E4 8AA* T: (020) 8529 3738 E: hall.speers@talk21.com

SPELLER, Shaun Lawrence. b 65. Birm Poly BA 88. Ripon Coll Cuddesdon 11. **d** 13 **p** 14. C Harpenden St Nic *St Alb* from 13. *86 Tuffnells Way, Harpenden AL5 3HG* M: 07922-129361

SPENCE, Beth Ann. b 65. Smith Coll (USA) BA 87 St Hilda's Coll Ox MA 90. SAOMC 02. **d** 05 **p** 06. C Cowley St Jas *Ox* 05-08; PtO Sydney Australia from 08. *3/159 Victoria Road, Bellevue Hill NSW 2023, Australia* T: (0061) (2) 9389 1603 M: 423-104101 E: beth.a.spence@googlemail.com

SPENCE, Ms Catherine Anita. b 64. St Mary's Coll Dur BSc 85 MSc 88. Ox Min Course 06. **d** 10 **p** 11. NSM Earley Trin *Ox*

10-14; NSM Loddon Reach from 14. *Little Haddon, Swallowfield Street, Swallowfield, Reading RG7 1QX* F: 0118-975 3463 M: 07885-593103 T: 988 3595 E: cath@hineni.plus.com

SPENCE, David Royston. b 80. St Jo Coll Cam MA 06 PhD 06. Trin Coll Bris 10. **d** 13 **p** 14. C Shill Valley and Broadshire *Ox* from 13. *School House, Filkins, Lechlade GL7 3JJ* T: (01367) 860071 M: 07754-299275 E: david.r.spence@gmail.com

SPENCE, Graham Barry. **d** 13 **p** 14. C Ballymore *Arm* from 14. *30 The Mount, Tandragee, Craigavon BT62 2AP* M: 07955-370308 E: grahamspence@btinternet.com

SPENCE, James Knox. b 30. Worc Coll Ox BA 55 MA 58. Ridley Hall Cam. **d** 57 **p** 58. C W Hampstead Trin *Lon* 57-60; C Ox St Ebbe w St Pet 61-64; Cand Sec CPAS 64-68; V Reading Greyfriars *Ox* 68-78; C St Helen Bishopsgate w St Andr Undershaft etc *Lon* 78-82; P-in-c Gt Baddow *Chelmsf* 82-86; V 86-88; TR 88-95; rtd 95; Hon C Wallingford *Ox* from 96. *15 High Street, Wallingford OX10 0BP* T: (01491) 826814 E: jim@spence15.plus.com

SPENCE, Michael James. b 62. Sydney Univ BA 85 LLB 87 St Cath Coll Ox DPhil 96. St Steph Ho Ox. **d** 06 **p** 07. NSM Cowley St Jas *Ox* 06-08; Vice-Chan Sydney Univ Australia from 08. *Vice-Chancellor's Office, Quadrangle A14, University of Sydney, NSW 2006, Australia* T: (0061) (2) 9351 5051 or 9389 1603 M: 401-693506 E: vice-chancellor@vcc.usyd.edu.au

SPENCE, Mrs Moira Joan. b 44. SAOMC 96. **d** 01 **p** 02. OLM Risborough *Ox* 01-06; NSM Ewenny w St Brides Major *Llan* from 07. *Ty Bara, 33 Main Road, Ogmore-by-Sea, Bridgend CF32 0PD*

SPENCE, Canon Philip Arthur. b 39. Lon Univ BD 71 Open Univ BA 76. Westcott Ho Cam 78. **d** 78 **p** 79. C Walthamstow St Pet *Chelmsf* 78-80; Dioc Adv on Evang 80-87; Dep Dir Dept of Miss (Evang Division) 80-85; P-in-c Greensted 80-86; Asst Dir of Miss and Unity 85-87; R Greensted-juxta-Ongar w Stanford Rivers 86-87; V Cambridge St Mark *Ely* 87-95; Chapl Wolfs Coll Cam 87-95; Relig Adv Anglia TV 91-95; V Pet St Jo 95-01; Warden and Can Res Pet Cathl 97-01; Can Pet Cathl 01-06; P-in-c Preston and Ridlington w Wing and Pilton 01-06; Adult Educn Officer 01-05; rtd 06; PtO *Pet* from 06. *20 Bayley Close, Uppingham, Oakham LE15 9TG* T: (01572) 820199 E: monica.spence@virgin.net

SPENCE, Susan Karen. See WELLER, Susan Karen

SPENCELEY, Douglas. b 49. Edin Univ MA 70 SS Mark & Jo Univ Coll Plymouth PGCE 71. ERMC 07. **d** 09 **p** 10. NSM Arthingworth, Harrington w Oxendon and E Farndon *Pet* 09-12; NSM Maidwell w Draughton, Lamport w Faxton 09-12; Bp's V for Ch Schs from 12; NSM Billing from 12. *1 Russet Drive, Little Billing, Northampton NN3 9TF* T: (01604) 407977 E: dspenceley@lineone.net

SPENCELEY, Haydon du Garde. b 84. Nottm Univ BA 06 Leeds Univ MA 09. St Jo Coll Nottm 11. **d** 14 **p** 15. C Northampton Em *Pet* from 14. *24 The Nurseries, Northampton NN1 5HN* T: (01604) 244391 M: 07985-973773 E: haydon.spenceley@gmail.com

SPENCELEY, Malcolm. b 40. Open Univ BA 92 Dur Inst of Educn CertEd 72. Cranmer Hall Dur 78. **d** 80 **p** 81. C Redcar *York* 80-85; V Middlesbrough Ascension 85-93; V Newby 93-05; rtd 05; PtO *York* from 06. *6 Tameside, Stokesley, Middlesbrough TS9 5PE* T: (01642) 710443

SPENCER, Andrew. b 47. St Matthias Coll Bris BEd 70 Univ of Wales (Ban) BTh 05. **d** 04 **p** 05. Moderator for Reader Tr *Guildf* 01-06; OLM Busbridge and Hambledon from 04; Tutor Local Min Progr from 07. *24 Park Road, Godalming GU7 1SH* T: (01483) 416333 E: andy.spencer@bhcgodalming.org

SPENCER, Antony Wade. b 50. Ridley Hall Cam 92. **d** 94 **p** 95. C Bury St Edmunds St Geo *St E* 94-96; PtO 96-97; C Rougham, Beyton w Hessett and Rushbrooke 97-99; TV Mildenhall 99-07; Dir Past Development Harborne Heath *Birm* 07-11; C from 11. *74 Croftdown Road, Birmingham B17 8RD* T: 0121-426 6228 M: 07704-324444 E: antonyspencer@stjohns-church.co.uk

SPENCER, Miss Christine Patricia. b 66. Man Univ BSc 02. St Steph Ho Ox 13. **d** 15. C Storrington *Chich* from 15. *38 Howard Road, Horsham RH13 6AB* T: (01403) 261020 M: 07980-617588 E: christine.spencer66@gmail.com

SPENCER, Christopher Graham. b 61. Magd Coll Cam BA 83 MA 87 Bath Univ MSc 84. St Jo Coll Nottm 93. **d** 93 **p** 94. C Ore St Helen and St Barn *Chich* 93-97; V Deal St Geo *Cant* from 97. *The Vicarage, 8 St George's Road, Deal CT14 6BA* T: (01304) 372587 E: chris.spencer@stgdeal.org

SPENCER, Christopher Stuart. b 84. Bournemouth Univ BSc 05. St Jo Coll Nottm 08. **d** 12. C Southbroom *Sarum* 12-14. *22 Grampian Close, Oldland Common, Bristol BS30 8QA* M: 07792-098249 T: 0117-932 8726 E: chris_spencer2000@yahoo.co.uk

SPENCER, David William. b 43. EAMTC 80. **d** 81 **p** 82. NSM Wisbech St Aug *Ely* 81-84; C Whittlesey 84-86; R Upwell

Christchurch 86-90; R March St Pet and March St Mary 90-98; TV Stanground and Farcet 98-01; V Farcet 01-04; V Farcet Hampton 04-08; rtd 08; PtO *Ely* 08-10; P-in-c Elton w Stibbington and Water Newton 10-12. *10 Hemingford Crescent, Peterborough PE2 8LL* E: davidspencer@freezone.co.uk

SPENCER, Derek Kenneth. b 67. St Jo Coll Nottm BA 98. **d** 03 **p** 05. Storrington Deanery Youth Missr *Chich* 01-06; C Steyning 05-06; P-in-c Sullington and Thakeham w Warminghurst 07-15; R from 15. *The Rectory, The Street, Thakeham, Pulborough RH20 3EP* T: (01798) 813121 M: 07734-330678 E: noba@btinternet.com

SPENCER, Mrs Gail. b 57. STETS. **d** 03 **p** 04. NSM Wilton w Netherhampton and Fugglestone *Sarum* 03-06; NSM Radcliffe-on-Trent and Shelford *S'well* 06-07; Chapl Qu Medical Cen Nottm Univ Hosp NHS Trust from 07. *2 Gatcombe Close, Radcliffe-on-Trent, Nottingham NG12 2GG* T: 0115-933 6068 E: gailespencer@yahoo.co.uk

SPENCER, Geoffrey. b 50. Open Univ BA 84 Nottm Univ CertEd 78 ALCM 76. Linc Th Coll 85. **d** 87 **p** 88. C Skegness and Winthorpe *Linc* 87-90; V Heckington 90-93; P-in-c Bottesford and Muston *Leic* 93-98; P-in-c Harby, Long Clawson and Hose 94-98; P-in-c Barkestone w Plungar, Redmile and Stathern 94-98; RD Framland 97-98; PtO *Leic* 03-05; Lic Preacher 05-06; P-in-c Church Langton cum Tur Langton etc *Leic* 07-10; P-in-c Mundford w Lynford *Nor* 10-11; P-in-c Ickburgh w Langford 10-11; P-in-c Cranwich 10-11; P-in-c W Tofts and Buckenham Parva 10-11; rtd 11; PtO *Leic* 11-14; *Linc* 11-14; *Birm* 12-14; P-in-c Kelsey Gp *Linc* from 14. *The Rectory, Grange Lane, North Kelsey, Market Rasen LN7 6EZ* T: (01652) 679494 M: 07512-849976 E: geoffreyspencer@pobroadband.co.uk

SPENCER, George. b 56. Cam Univ BA 77 MA 83 Leeds Metrop Univ DipSW 01. Coll of Resurr Mirfield 80. **d** 83 **p** 84. C Edin Old St Paul 83-85; P-in-c Edin St Ninian 85-92; Chapl Asst St Helens and Knowsley Hosps NHS Trust 92-93; Chapl 93-96; Chapl Calderdale and Huddersfield NHS Foundn Trust from 12; PtO *Leeds* from 08. *Chaplaincy, Huddersfield Royal Infirmary, Acre Street, Huddersfield HD3 3EA* T: (01484) 342092 E: george.spencer@cht.nhs.uk

SPENCER, Canon Gilbert Hugh. b 43. Lon Univ BD 67. ALCD 66. **d** 67 **p** 68. C Bexleyheath Ch Ch *Roch* 67-73; C Bexley St Jo 73-76; P-in-c Bromley St Jo 76-78; V 78-81; R Chatham St Mary w St Jo 81-91; V Minster-in-Sheppey *Cant* 91-09; P-in-c Queenborough 99-05; AD Sittingbourne 94-00, 03-04 and 06-09; Hon Can Cant Cathl 99-09; Chapl Sheppey Community Hosp 91-98; Chapl Thames Gateway NHS Trust 98-09; rtd 09; PtO *Cant* from 09; Retirement Officer (Ashford Adnry) from 11. *75 Acorn Close, Kingsnorth, Ashford TN23 3HR* T: (01233) 501774 M: 07961-545934 E: gilbert_spencer@hotmail.com

SPENCER, Gordon Thomas. b 45. ACA 68. STETS 03. **d** 06 **p** 07. NSM W Tarring *Chich* from 06. *8 Thakeham Close, Goring-by-Sea, Worthing BN12 5BA* T: (01903) 243998 E: gordon.spencer8@btinternet.com

SPENCER, Graham Lewis. b 48. St Jo Coll Nottm 80. **d** 82 **p** 83. C Leic St Anne 82-85; P-in-c Frisby-on-the-Wreake w Kirby Bellars 85-86; TV Melton Gt Framland 86-93; V Upper Wreake 93-99; V Glen Magna cum Stretton Magna etc 99-05; rtd 05; PtO *Leic* from 05. *18 Chetwynd Drive, Melton Mowbray LE13 0HU* T: (01664) 564266 E: grahamandtrish@talktalk.net

SPENCER, Ian John. b 61. Qu Coll Birm 03. **d** 05 **p** 06. C Gt Malvern St Mary *Worc* 05-08; Warden Dioc Retreat Ho (Holland Ho) Cropthorne from 08. *Holland House, Main Street, Cropthorne, Pershore WR10 3NB* T: (01386) 860330 E: ian.spencer@hollandhouse.org

SPENCER, Joan. b 50. **d** 98 **p** 99. OLM Nor St Mary Magd w St Jas from 98. *94 Mousehold Avenue, Norwich NR3 4RS* T: (01603) 404471 E: revjoan@virginmedia.com

SPENCER, John Edward. b 36. Bris Univ BA 60. Tyndale Hall Bris 60. **d** 61 **p** 62. C St Helens St Mark *Liv* 61-64; Japan 65-70; Area Sec CMS *Leic* and Pet 70-71; Warden and Chapl Rikkyo Japanese Sch Rudgwick 71-73; Hd Master and Chapl Pennthorpe Sch Rudgwick 74-96; NSM Rudgwick *Chich* 95-96; rtd 96; PtO *Chich* 96-98; *Guildf* 96-98; Hd Master Ardingly Coll Jun Sch Haywards Heath 97-98; Chapl Rowcroft Hospice Torquay 99-01; Hon C Bovey Tracey SS Pet, Paul and Thos w Hennock *Ex* 99-13. *19 Lamsey Lane, Heacham, King's Lynn PE31 7LA* T: (01485) 572029 E: jhnspncr@btinternet.com

SPENCER, Mrs Margot Patricia Winifred. b 48. Coll of St Matthias Bris CertEd 69. STETS 98. **d** 01 **p** 02. NSM Wonersh w Blackheath *Guildf* 01-05; NSM Busbridge and Hambledon from 05. *24 Park Road, Godalming GU7 1SH* T: (01483) 416333 E: margotspencer@bhcgodalming.org

SPENCER, Peter Roy. b 40. CertEd. Sarum & Wells Th Coll 72. **d** 74 **p** 75. C Northampton St Alb *Pet* 74-77; TV Cov E 77-90;

V Erdington St Barn *Birm* 90-02; TR Erdington 02-07; Chapl John Taylor Hospice Birm 90-07; rtd 07; PtO *Birm* from 07. *15 Poplar Road, Smethwick B66 4AW* T: 0121-429 4514

SPENCER, Richard Dennis. b 50. Imp Coll Lon BSc 71. NTMTC 93. **d** 96 **p** 97. C Leek and Meerbrook *Lich* 96-00; P-in-c Shrewsbury H Trin w St Julian 00-10; V 10-15; TV Saffron Walden and Villages *Chelmsf* from 15. *The Vicarage, Radwinter Road, Ashdon, Saffron Walden CB10 2ET* T: (01799) 584171 E: rdspencer@virgin.net

SPENCER, Richard Hugh. b 62. Univ of Wales (Cardiff) LLB 84 BD 88 Bris Univ MA 92. St Mich Coll Llan 85. **d** 88 **p** 89. C Barry All SS *Llan* 88-90; Asst Chapl Univ of Wales (Cardiff) 90-92; Lect NT Studies 92-98; Tutor St Mich Coll Llan 92-98; R Llangenni and Llanbedr Ystrad Yw w Patricio *S & B* 98-00; Dir Post-Ord Tr 00; TV Cowbridge *Llan* 02-03; NSM 03-04; Hd of Th Trin Coll Carmarthen 03-04; P-in-c Kenfig Hill *Llan* 04-10; P-in-c Cardiff Ch Ch Roath Park 10-13; Dioc Dir of Ords 10-11. *11 Clos-y-Talcen, Pen-y-Fai, Bridgend CF31 4BU* T: (01656) 715579 E: rhspencer@outlook.com

SPENCER, Richard William Edward. b 33. FSCA 66. WMMTC 78. **d** 81 **p** 82. NSM The Lickey *Birm* 81-83; Area Sec (Warks and W Midl) Chr Aid 83-93; PtO *Birm* 84-91 and 95-98; *Worc* from 95; *Cov* 85-93; *Heref* from 98. *Honey Hedge, 165 Godiva Road, Leominster HR6 8TB* T: (01568) 620097

SPENCER, Robert. b 48. St Jo Coll Nottm. **d** 93 **p** 94. NSM Ellon *Ab* 93-95 and 99-09; NSM Cruden Bay 93-95; NSM Fraserburgh w New Pitsligo 95-99; P-in-c Oldmeldrum from 09. *12 Riverview Place, Ellon AB41 9NW* T: (01358) 723193 F: (01224) 248515 E: revbob.spencer@btinternet.com

SPENCER, Roy Primett. b 26. Oak Hill Th Coll 50. **d** 53 **p** 54. C Bedford St Pet *St Alb* 53-55; C Luton Ch Ch 55-58; C Nottingham St Mary *S'well* 58-60; V Middlestown *Wakef* 60-61; Chapl Crumpsall Hosp Man 61-66; R Fleet *Linc* 66-69; V Accrington St Paul *Blackb* 69-78; V Woodplumpton 78-83; P-in-c Preston St Luke 83-89; P-in-c Preston St Luke and St Oswald 89-90; Chapl Preston Hosp N Shields 83-91; rtd 91; PtO *Blackb* from 91. *5 Hollywood Avenue, Penwortham, Preston PR1 9AS* T: (01772) 743783

SPENCER, Canon Stephen Christopher. b 60. Ball Coll Ox BA 82 DPhil 90. Edin Th Coll 88. **d** 90 **p** 91. C Harlesden All So *Lon* 90-93; P-in-c Nyamandhlovu Zimbabwe 93-99; R Bulawayo All SS 96-99; V Caton w Littledale *Blackb* 99-03; Dep Prin CBDTI 99-03; Tutor NOC 03-08; Tutor Yorks Min Course 08-12; Co-ord Yorks Regional Tr Partnership 08-10; P-in-c Brighouse and Clifton *Wakef* 10; V 11-14; Tutor Yorks Min Course from 14; Hon Can Musoma from 13. *Yorkshire Ministry Course, The Mirfield Centre, Stocks Bank Road, Mirfield WF14 0BW* T: (01924) 481925 F: 481922 E: stephenspencer8@me.com

SPENCER, Stephen Nigel Howard. b 53. Pemb Coll Ox BA 75 MA 03 Jes Coll Cam PGCE 76. Trin Coll Bris 80. **d** 82 **p** 83. C Partington and Carrington *Ches* 82-85; C Brunswick *Man* 85-88; Chapl UEA *Nor* 88-92; rtd 92; PtO *Nor* 92-95. *259 Wellbrook Way, Girton, Cambridge CB3 0GL* T: (01223) 277238 E: howard.spencer@btinternet.com

SPENCER, Stephen Robert. b 61. NTMTC BA 08. **d** 08 **p** 09. C Langdon Hills *Chelmsf* 08-11; V Eastwood from 11. *The Vicarage, Eastwoodbury Lane, Southend-on-Sea SS2 6UH* T: (01702) 525272 E: revsteve.spencer@btinternet.com

SPENCER, Steven Christopher. b 47. RGN 69. NTMTC 98. **d** 98 **p** 99. NSM Chatham St Phil and St Jas *Roch* from 98; Asst Chapl Medway NHS Foundn Trust 04-09; Lead Chapl from 09. *Medway Hospital, Windmill Road, Gillingham ME7 5NY* T: (01634) 830000 ext 5414 E: steven.spencer@medway.nhs.uk

SPENCER, Canon Susan. b 47. EMMTC 87. **d** 90 **p** 94. Par Dn Cotgrave *S'well* 90-94; C 94-98; P-in-c Rolleston w Fiskerton, Morton and Upton 98-10; Asst Warden of Readers 98-07; AD S'well 07-10; Jt AD S'well and Newark 08-09; Hon Can S'well Minster 08-10; rtd 10. *15 Cherry Avenue, Branston, Lincoln LN4 1UY* T: (01522) 823947 E: suespencer47@googlemail.com

SPENCER, Mrs Susan Lesley. b 55. **d** 00 **p** 01. OLM Middleton and Thornham *Man* from 00. *1 Westbrook Close, Rochdale OL11 2XY* T: (01706) 350668 E: suespencer@bigfoot.com

SPENCER, Sylvia. **d** 98. Chapl Grampian Univ Hosp NHS Trust 98-01. *Address temp unknown*

SPENCER-THOMAS, Canon Owen Robert. b 40. MBE 08. Lon Univ BSc(Soc) 70 Westmr Coll Lon DLitt 10 LGSM 96 MRTvS 76. Westcott Ho Cam 70. **d** 72 **p** 73. C S Kensington St Luke *Lon* 72-76; Lect RS S Kensington Inst 74-76; Dir Lon Chs Radio Workshop & Relig Producer BBC 76-78; Relig Producer Anglia TV 78-95; LtO *Lon* 76-87; NSM Cambridge Ascension *Ely* 87-07; Chapl St Jo Coll Sch Cam 93-98; Chapl St Bede's Sch Cam 96-97; Chapl Ch Coll Cam 97-01; Dioc Dir of Communications *Ely* 02-07; Bp's Press Officer 07-11; Hon

Can Ely Cathl 04-11; PtO from 11. *52 Windsor Road, Cambridge CB4 3JN* T: (01223) 358448
E: owenst@btinternet.com

SPERRING, Clive Michael. b 43. Oak Hill Th Coll 71. **d** 75 **p** 76. C Hawkwell *Chelmsf* 75-78; C-in-c Gt Baddow 78-82; Asst P Kohimarama New Zealand 82-85; V Orakei St Jas from 86. *132 Gowing Drive, Meadowbank, Auckland 1072, New Zealand* T: (0064) (9) 528 4400 E: cmsperring@vodafone.co.nz

SPICER, David John. b 52. Sussex Univ BA 76 Lon Univ MTh 78. Westcott Ho Cam 77. **d** 79 **p** 80. C E Dulwich St Jo *S'wark* 79-82; C Richmond St Mary w St Matthias and St Jo 82-87; V Lewisham St Swithun 87-91; Chapl Community of All Hallows Ditchingham from 91. *St Edmund's House, All Hallows Convent, Ditchingham, Bungay NR35 2DZ* T: (01986) 892139

SPICER (formerly RIMMER), Dorothy Janet Rosalind. b 49. Cen Sch of Art Lon BA 72 Middx Poly ATD 74 E Lon Univ MA 98. Westcott Ho Cam. **d** 00 **p** 01. C Notting Hill St Jo and St Pet *Lon* 00-02; V Totternhoe, Stanbridge and Tilsworth *St Alb* 02-11; rtd 11; PtO *St Alb* from 11. *Sewell Manor, Sewell, Dunstable LU6 1RP* T: (01582) 690125
E: revjanetspicer@btinternet.com

SPICER, Leigh Edwin. b 56. Birm Univ MA 02. Sarum & Wells Th Coll 78. **d** 81 **p** 82. C Harborne St Pet *Birm* 81-83; C Bloxwich 83-87; Chapl RAF 87-11; PtO *S & B* from 12. *Dolyfelin, Llanbister Road, Llandrindod Wells LD1 6SP* T: (01597) 851109

SPICER, Nicolas. b 61. Univ of Wales (Lamp) BA 84. Coll of Resurr Mirfield 84. **d** 86 **p** 87. C Westbury-on-Trym H Trin *Bris* 86-89; C Willesden Green St Andr and St Fran *Lon* 89-93; Chapl Asst Charing Cross Hosp Lon 93-94; Asst Chapl Hammersmith Hosps NHS Trust 94-97; R Ardleigh and The Bromleys *Chelmsf* 97-07; P-in-c Worksop Priory *S'well* 07-11; V from 11; P-in-c Worksop St Paul from 13. *The Vicarage, Cheapside, Worksop S80 2HX* T: (01909) 472180
E: vicar@worksoppriory.co.uk

SPICER, Robert Robin. b 39. FCA 68. SAOMC 94. **d** 97 **p** 98. NSM Riverside *Ox* 97-01; NSM Beaconsfield 01-07. *16 Hayse Hill, Windsor SL4 5SZ* T: (01753) 864697
E: spicerrevrob@aol.com

SPIERS, Canon Peter Hendry. b 61. St Jo Coll Dur BA 82. Ridley Hall Cam 83. **d** 86 **p** 87. C W Derby St Luke *Liv* 86-90; TV Everton St Pet 90-95; V Everton St Geo 95-05; P-in-c Gt Crosby St Luke 05-13; V from 13; Hon Can Liv Cathl from 06. *St Luke's Vicarage, Liverpool Road, Crosby, Liverpool L23 5SE* T: 0151-924 1737 E: pete@spiersfamily.eclipse.co.uk

SPIERS, Philip John. b 55. Reading Univ BSc 76. Ripon Coll Cuddesdon 10. **d** 13 **p** 14. NSM Darby Green and Eversley *Win* from 13. *Copse Mead, Vicarage Lane, Hound Green, Hook RG27 8LF* T: 0118-932 6073 M: 07771-505350
E: spiersjohn@talk21.com

SPIKIN, Simon John Overington. b 48. Nottm Univ BTh 74 K Coll Lon MTh 80 Univ of Wales (Lamp) MA 11. Linc Th Coll 70. **d** 75 **p** 76. C Sawbridgeworth *St Alb* 75-79; C Odiham w S Warnborough and Long Sutton *Win* 79-81; R Dickleburgh w Thelveton w Frenze and Shimpling *Nor* 81-82; P-in-c Dickleburgh w Thelveton, Frenze, Shimpling etc 81-82; R Dickleburgh, Langmere, Shimpling, Thelveton etc 82-96; rtd 96; PtO *Cant* 01-12. *Marley Court, Kingston, Canterbury CT4 6JH* T: (01227) 832405

SPILLER, Canon David Roger. b 44. St Jo Coll Dur BA 70 Fitzw Coll Cam BA 72 MA 76 Nottm Univ DipAdEd 80. Ridley Hall Cam 70. **d** 73 **p** 74. C Bradf Cathl 73 77; C Stratford on Avon w Bishopton *Cov* 77-80; Chapl Geo Eliot Hosp Nuneaton 80-90; V Chilvers Coton w Astley *Cov* 80-90; RD Nuneaton 84-90; Prin Aston Tr Scheme 90-97; C Kings Norton *Birm* 98-99; C Shirley 99-00; Dir of Min and Dioc Dir of Ords *Cov* 00-11; Hon Can Cov Cathl 04-11; rtd 11; PtO *Cov* from 12. *Pear Tree Cottage, Wick Road, Little Comberton, Pershore WR10 3EG* T: (01386) 710725 E: rogerspiller@btinternet.com

SPILMAN, Derrick Geoffrey. b 27. North Th Coll 61. **d** 63 **p** 64. C Dover St Mary *Cant* 63-67; CF 67-71; Canada from 71; rtd 92. *5398 Walter Place, Burnaby BC V5G 4K2, Canada* T: (001) (604) 294 6816

SPILSBURY, Stephen Ronald Paul. b 39. Nottm Univ BSc 69 MPhil 72 Bris Univ PhD 99. Linc Th Coll 71. **d** 64 **p** 65. In RC Ch 64-71; C Cricklade w Latton *Bris* 72-75; P-in-c Swindon All SS 76-81; V Lawrence Weston 81-95; RD Westbury and Severnside 89-91; rtd 99; PtO *Bris* from 03. *10 Woodside Grove, Bristol BS10 7RF* T: 0117-959 1079
E: paulspilsbury@btinternet.com

SPINDLER, Miss Jane Diana. b 54. Southn Univ BA 75 CertEd 76. Wycliffe Hall Ox 87. **d** 89 **p** 94. C Bishopsworth *Bris* 89-93; C Brislington St Luke 93-94; rtd 95; PtO *Bris* from 95. *143 Highridge Road, Bishopsworth, Bristol BS13 8HT* T: 0117-935 8137

SPINK, Mrs Diana. b 40. Ex Univ BA 63 PGCE 64. SAOMC 97. **d** 00 **p** 01. NSM Hemel Hempstead *St Alb* 00-10; rtd 10; PtO *St Alb* from 10. *39 Garland Close, Hemel Hempstead HP2 5HU* T: (01442) 262133 M: 07808-184321
E: diana2spink@hotmail.com

SPINKS, Prof Bryan Douglas. b 48. St Chad's Coll Dur BA 70 BD 79 K Coll Lon MTh 72 Dur Univ DD 88 Yale Univ Hon MA 98 FRHistS 85. **d** 75 **p** 76. C Witham *Chelmsf* 75-78; C Clacton St Jas 78-79; Chapl Chu Coll Cam 80-97; Affiliated Lect Div Cam Univ 82-97; Prof Liturg Studies Yale Univ and Fell Morse Coll 98-07; Prof Past Th Yale Univ from 07; PtO *Ely* from 02. *27 Egypt Lane, Clinton CT 06413, USA*
E: bryan.spinks@yale.edu *or* bryspinkus@aol.com

SPINKS, Christopher George. b 53. Oak Hill Th Coll BA 88. **d** 88 **p** 89. C Hove Bp Hannington Memorial Ch *Chich* 88-92; Travelling Sec UCCF 92-95; Itinerant Min 95-98; Chapl Martlets Hospice Hove 98-11; TV Hove *Chich* 99-10; V Polegate from 11. *Church Office, St John's Church, Church Road, Polegate BN26 5BX* T: (01323) 483259
E: chrisgspinks@hotmail.com

SPINKS, John Frederick. b 40. Westmr Coll Ox MTh 97. Oak Hill Th Coll 79. **d** 82 **p** 83. NSM Roxbourne St Andr *Lon* 82-89; C Northwood H Trin 89-93; P-in-c Greenhill St Jo 93-96; V 96-04; rtd 04; PtO *Lon* from 04; *Ox* from 04; *St Alb* from 04. *Woodpecker Cottage, 232 Northwood Road, Harefield, Uxbridge UB9 6PT* T: (01895) 822477 M: 07711-635199
E: woodpecker232@tiscali.co.uk

SPITTLE, Christopher Bamford. b 74. St Jo Coll Dur BA 95. Ridley Hall Cam 97. **d** 99 **p** 00. C Netherton *Liv* 99-03; TR Sutton 03-11; P-in-c Skelmersdale St Paul from 11. *The Vicarage, Church Road, Skelmersdale WN8 8ND* T: (01695) 722087

SPITTLE, Robin. b 57. St Jo Coll Nottm 84. **d** 86 **p** 87. C Ipswich St Fran St E 86-91; Min Shotley St Mary CD 91-92; R Shotley 92-99; P-in-c Copdock w Washbrook and Belstead 93-99; V Kesgrave from 99. *4 Wades Grove, Kesgrave, Ipswich IP5 2EF* T: (01473) 805091 E: robin.spittle@talktalk.co.uk

SPIVEY, Colin. b 35. ACII 61. Oak Hill Th Coll 74. **d** 76 **p** 77. C Egham *Guildf* 76-79; C Edgware *Lon* 79-83; R Haworth *Bradf* 83-95; Sub Chapl HM Pris Leeds 94-99; V Thorpe Edge *Bradf* 95-00; rtd 01; PtO *Leeds* from 01. *2 Woodhill View, Wetherby LS22 6PP* T: (01937) 581508 E: ca.spivey@virgin.net

SPOKES, David Lawrence. b 57. Nottm Univ BCombStuds 85. Linc Th Coll 82. **d** 85 **p** 86. C Rushall *Lich* 85-89; TV Thornaby on Tees *York* 89-93; R Yardley Hastings, Denton and Grendon etc *Pet* 02-14; Rural Adv Northn Adnry 05-14; P-in-c Howden-le-Wear and Hunwick *Dur* from 14; P-in-c Willington and Sunnybrow from 14. *The Rectory, Willington, Crook DL15 0DE* T: (01388) 747914 E: mail@davidspokes.com

SPOKES, Keith John. b 29. EAMTC. **d** 84 **p** 85. NSM Bury St Edmunds St Mary *St E* 84-89; P-in-c Helmingham w Framsden and Pettaugh w Winston 89-92; rtd 93; PtO *St E* from 93. *34 Southgate House, Rougham Road, Bury St Edmunds IP33 2RN* T: (01284) 706742

SPONG, Bennett Jarod. b 49. Coll of Charleston (USA) BA 74 Thames Poly PGCE 87. **d** 05 **p** 06. OLM Charlton *S'wark* from 05. *10 Mayhill Road, London SE7 7JQ* T: (020) 8853 4457
E: bjspong@hotmail.com

SPONG, Mrs Hilary Vida. b 44. Ex Univ BTh 09. SWMTC 06. **d** 09 **p** 10. NSM St Stythians w Perranarworthal and Gwennap *Truro* 09-12; NSM Feock 11-12; NSM Devoran 11-12; NSM Perranzabuloe and Crantock w Cubert 12-14; rtd 14. *Nansough Manor, Ladock, Truro TR2 4PB* T: (01726) 883315
M: 07855-781134 E: hilaryspong@sent.com

SPONG, Terence John. *See* MESLEY-SPONG, Terence John

SPOONER, Anthony Patrick David. b 45. Univ Coll of Rhodesia Univ Coll of Nyasaland BA 68. Linc Th Coll 71. **d** 74 **p** 75. C Glynde, W Firle and Beddingham *Chich* 74-77; Rhodesia 77-80; Zimbabwe 80-86; P-in-c Clacton St Jas *Chelmsf* 86-90; V 90-12; rtd 12. *St Martin of Tours, 9 Page Road, Clacton-on-Sea CO15 3AE* E: revapdspooner@aol.com

SPRAGGETT, Miss Agnes Louise. b 29. Bp Otter Coll *Chich* TCert 55. CBDTI 06. **d** 06 **p** 07. NSM Embsay w Eastby *Bradf* 06-11; PtO *Leeds* from 11. *16 Millholme Rise, Embsay, Skipton BD23 6NU* T: (01756) 793575 E: loutin@talktalk.net

SPRATT, Robert Percival. b 31. MBE 08. FCIOB MRSPH ACABE. Carl Dioc Tr Inst 84. **d** 87 **p** 88. NSM Kendal St Thos *Carl* 87-89; Chapl HM Pris Preston 89-96; Dir Miss to Pris from 96; Asst Chapl HM Pris Wymott 97-04; Sessional Chapl HM Pris Lanc 04-06; Asst Chapl HM Pris Haverigg from 06; PtO *Blackb* from 96; *Carl* from 97. *Missions to Prisons, PO Box 37, Kendal LA9 6GF* T/F: (01539) 720475 E: bob@greenstones.org.uk

SPRAY, Canon Charles Alan Francis Thomas. b 27. Lon Univ BScEng 51 ARSM 51. Ridley Hall Cam 57. **d** 59 **p** 60. C Chich St Pancras and St Jo 59-63; V Shipley 63-69; R Ore St Helen and St Barn 70-85; V Burgess Hill St Andr 85-93; Can and Preb

Chich Cathl 88-93; rtd 93; PtO *Chich* from 93. *The College of St Barnabas, Blackberry Lane, Lingfield RH7 6NJ*

SPRAY, John William. b 29. Sarum & Wells Th Coll 71. **d** 73 **p** 74. C Clayton *Lich* 73-77; V Hartshill 77-82; P-in-c Aston 82-83; P-in-c Stone St Mich 82-83; P-in-c Stone St Mich w Aston St Sav 83-84; R 84-90; rtd 90; PtO *Lich* from 90. *2 Belvoir Avenue, Trentham, Stoke-on-Trent ST4 8SY* T: (01782) 644959

SPRAY, Mrs Josephine Ann. b 44. Nottm Coll of Educn TCert 65. SAOMC 95. **d** 98 **p** 99. NSM Watford St Mich *St Alb* 98-02; P-in-c Turvey 02-10; rtd 11; PtO *St Alb* from 11. *121 High Street, Olney MK46 4EF* T: (01234) 713726 E: jo-spray@sky.com

SPRAY, Mrs Karen Patricia. b 55. **d** 06 **p** 07. NSM Littleham w Exmouth *Ex* 06-07; C Honiton, Gittisham, Combe Raleigh, Monkton etc 07-09; P-in-c Clyst St Mary, Clyst St George etc 09-13; C Lympstone and Woodbury w Exton 09-13; C Aylesbeare, Rockbeare, Farringdon etc 09-13; V Aylesbeare, Clyst St George, Clyst St Mary etc from 13. *The Rectory, 40 Clyst Valley Road, Clyst St Mary, Exeter EX5 1DD* T: (01392) 877400 E: church@revdkaren.org.uk

SPRAY, Richard Alan. b 43. EMMTC 85. **d** 88 **p** 89. NSM Cotgrave *S'well* 88-96; P-in-c Barton in Fabis 96-01; P-in-c Thrumpton 96-01; P-in-c Kingston and Ratcliffe-on-Soar 96-01; P-in-c Blyth 01-02; P-in-c Scrooby 01-02; V Blyth and Scrooby w Ranskill 02-10; AD Bawtry 06-09; rtd 11; PtO *Sheff* from 12. *Thorn Lea, Mattersey Road, Ranskill, Retford DN22 8ND* T: (01777) 816048 M: 07971-637670 E: revrich@talktalk.net

SPREADBRIDGE, Alison Margaret. b 50. Open Univ BSc 96. SEITE 04. **d** 07 **p** 08. C Dartford St Edm *Roch* 07-11; P-in-c Gillingham H Trin 11-13; rtd 13. *3 Wheal Regent Park, Carlyon Bay, St Austell PL25 3SP* T: (01726) 825178 M: 07979-013559 E: a.spreadbridge9@btinternet.com

SPREADBRIDGE, Paul Andrew. b 49. Greenwich Univ CertEd 02 Kent Univ BA 05. SEITE 99. **d** 98 **p** 03. In RC Ch 98-01; NSM Chatham St Steph *Roch* 02-04; C Orpington All SS 04-07; V Bexley St Mary 07-11; R Chelsfield 11-13; P-in-c Charlestown *Truro* from 13; P-in-c Par from 13. *3 Wheal Regent Park, Carlyon Bay, St Austell PL25 3SP* T: (01726) 825178 E: paul.spreadbridge@btinternet.com

SPREADBURY, Joanna Mary Magdalen. b 65. Magd Coll Ox BA 90 MA 93 K Coll Lon PhD 99. Westcott Ho Cam MA 99. **d** 99 **p** 00. C Watford St Mich *St Alb* 99-03; C Leavesden 03-06; V Abbots Langley from 06. *The Vicarage, 6 High Street, Abbots Langley WD5 0AS* T: (01923) 263013

SPREADBURY, John Graham. b 59. **d** 99 **p** 00. OLM Billingborough Gp *Linc* from 99. *Osbourne House, 3-5 Low Street, Billingborough, Sleaford NG34 0QJ* T: (01529) 240440

SPREDBURY, Mary Jane. b 59. Open Univ BA 99. STETS 03. **d** 06 **p** 07. NSM Acton St Mary *Lon* from 06. *6 St Catherine's Court, Bedford Road, London W4 1UH* M: 07803-759886 T: (02) 8995 8879 E: spredbury@btinternet.com

SPRENT, Michael Francis (Brother Giles). b 34. Ex Coll Ox BA 58 MA 62. Kelham Th Coll 58. **d** 61 **p** 62. C Plaistow St Andr *Chelmsf* 61-63; SSF from 61; Papua New Guinea 65-69; Hilfield Friary 69-74, 77-78, 97-02, 03-04 and from 12; Alnmouth Friary 74-76; Sweden 76-77; TV High Stoy *Sarum* 77-78; Harbledown Friary 78-82; Solomon Is 83-97; Zimbabwe 02-03; Stepney Friary 05-08; Canning Town Friary 08-12; PtO *Sarum* from 12. *Society of St Francis, The Friary, Hilfield, Dorchester DT2 7BE* T: (01300) 341345 E: gilesssf@franciscans.org.uk

SPRIGGS, John David Robert. b 36. BNC Ox BA 58 MA 63. S'wark Ord Course 73. **d** 75 **p** 76. LtO *Ox* 75-97; Chapl Pangbourne Coll 95-97; PtO *Linc* from 97. *Glen House, Great Ponton Road, Boothby Pagnell, Grantham NG33 4DH* T: (01476) 585756

SPRINGATE, Paul Albert Edward. b 48. Oak Hill Th Coll 81. **d** 83 **p** 84. C Pennycross *Ex* 83-87; TV Sileby, Cossington and Seagrave *Leic* 87-96; Chapl and Warden Harnhill Healing Cen 96-13; Bp's Adv on Healing *Glouc* 03-13; rtd 13. *111 North Home Road, Cirencester GL7 1DU* M: 07748-846164

SPRINGER, Richard Kevin. b 76. Middx Univ BA 98 Birkbeck Coll Lon MSc 06 Cam Univ BTh 13. Westcott Ho Cam 11. **d** 13 **p** 14. C De Beauvoir Town St Pet *Lon* from 13. *The Basement Flat, 306A Amhurst Road, London N16 7UE* M: 07730-597513 E: richardspringer@hotmail.co.uk

SPRINGETT, The Ven Robert Wilfred. b 62. Nottm Univ BTh 89 Lon Univ MA 92. Linc Th Coll 86. **d** 89 **p** 90. C Colchester

St Jas, All SS, St Nic and St Runwald *Chelmsf* 89-92; C Basildon St Martin w Nevendon 92-94; P-in-c Belhus Park and S Ockendon 94-01; RD Thurrock 98-01; R Wanstead St Mary w Ch Ch 01-10; AD Redbridge 08-10; Hon Can Chelmsf Cathl 08-10; Adn Cheltenham *Glouc* from 10. *Abbey Cottage Stables, 1 Gloucester Road, Tewkesbury GL20 5SS* T: (01684) 300067 E: archdchelt@glosdioc.org.uk

SPRINGETT, Simon Paul. b 56. Warwick Univ LLB 78. Wycliffe Hall Ox 78. **d** 81 **p** 82. C Harlow St Mary and St Hugh w St Jo the Bapt *Chelmsf* 81-84; C Gt Clacton 84-86; R Rayne 86-91; Chapl RN 91-14; Chief Exec Officer Aggie Weston's from 14; Chapl RNR from 14; PtO *Portsm* from 14. *Castaway House, 311 Twyford Avenue, Portsmouth PO2 8RN* T: (023) 9265 0505 E: simon.springett@aggies.org.uk

SPRINGFORD, Patrick Francis Alexander. b 45. Wycliffe Hall Ox 71. **d** 74 **p** 75. C Finchley Ch Ch *Lon* 74-79; CF 79-06; Rtd Officer Chapl RAChD 06-12; PtO *Cant* from 13. *12 De Burgh Hill, Dover CT17 0BS* T: (01304) 332492 E: patrick.springford@live.co.uk

SPRINGTHORPE, Canon David Frederick. b 47. Open Univ BA. AKC 72. **d** 73 **p** 74. C Dartford St Alb *Roch* 73-77; C Biggin Hill 77-80; R Ash 80-89; R Ridley 80-89; R Eynsford w Farningham and Lullingstone 89-94; V Barnehurst 94-04; RD Erith 98-04; R Keston 04-12; Hon Can Roch Cathl 02-12; rtd 12; PtO *Roch* from 12; *Cant* from 13. *38 Alvis Avenue, Herne Bay CT6 8AR* T: (01227) 219853 E: david.springthorpe@btopenworld.com

SPROATS, Mrs Beverley Louise. b 73. St Cath Coll Ox BA 94 MA 98 Cam Univ BTh 13. Ridley Hall Cam 11. **d** 13 **p** 14. C Yeadon *Leeds* from 13. *37 Millbank, Yeadon, Leeds LS19 7AY* M: 07986-937329 E: beverleysproats@gmail.com

SPROSTON, Bernard Melvin. b 37. Cranmer Hall Dur 77. **d** 79 **p** 80. C Westlands St Andr *Lich* 79-82; P-in-c Heage *Derby* 82-87; V Heath 87-02; rtd 02; PtO *Derby* from 02. *2 Upwood Close, Holmehall, Chesterfield S40 4UP* T: (01246) 207401 E: bernel@hotmail.co.uk

SPROULE, Gerald Norman. b 26. TCD Div Sch. **d** 60 **p** 61. C Monaghan w Tydavnet and Kilmore *Clogh* 60-62; I Cleenish 62-68; I Magheracross 68-73; Admin Sec (Ireland) BCMS 73-79; I Belfast St Aid *Conn* 79-86; I Magherally w Annaclone D & D 86-94; rtd 94. *4 Hilden Park, Lisburn BT27 4UG* T: (028) 9260 1528

SPRY, Miss Elisabeth Roselie. b 47. Open Univ BA 82. **d** 06 **p** 07. OLM Stratton St Mary w Stratton St Michael etc *Nor* from 06. *13 Whitehouse Drive, Long Stratton, Norwich NR15 2TD* T: (01508) 530478 E: erspry@yahoo.co.uk

SPURGEON, Michael Paul. b 53. MIEx. Linc Th Coll 83. **d** 85 **p** 86. C Lillington *Cov* 85-89; C Min Can Ripon Cathl 89-95; R Lower Nidderdale *Leeds* from 95. *Lower Nidderdale Rectory, 6 Old Church Green, Kirk Hammerton, York YO26 8DL* T: (01423) 331142 E: lowernidderdale@aol.com

SPURIN, Canon Richard Mark. b 28. Peterho Cam BA 52 MA 60. Wycliffe Hall Ox 54. **d** 55 **p** 56. C Foleshill St Laur *Cov* 55-58; C Atherstone 58-60; CMS 60-61; Kenya 61-73; C-in-c Ewell St Paul Howell Hill CD *Guildf* 73-82; V Netherton *Liv* 82-86; V Brandwood *Birm* 86-91; C Padiham *Blackb* 91-93; Hon Can Nambale Cathl Kenya from 92; rtd 93; PtO *Blackb* 93-11. *11 Rosemount Avenue, Burnley BB11 2JU* T: (01282) 421402

SPURR, Andrew. b 58. St Jo Coll Dur BA 80. Qu Coll Birm 82. **d** 93 **p** 94. C Rainham *Roch* 93-96; C Stansted Mountfitchet *Chelmsf* 96; C Stansted Mountfitchet w Birchanger and Farnham 97; R 97-06; V Evesham w Norton and Lenchwick *Worc* from 06. *Church House, Market Place, Evesham WR11 4RW* T: (01386) 446219 E: vicar@eveshamparish.com

SPURRELL, John Mark. b 34. CCC Ox BA 57 MA 61 FSA 87. Linc Th Coll 58. **d** 60 **p** 61. C Tilbury Docks *Chelmsf* 60-65; C Boston *Linc* 65-76; R Stow in Lindsey 76-85; P-in-c Willingham 76-85; P-in-c Coates 76-85; P-in-c Brightwell w Sotwell *Ox* 85-97; rtd 97; PtO *B & W* from 97. *10 The Liberty, Wells BA5 2SU* T: (01749) 678966 M: 07929-725502 E: mspurrell@gmail.com

SPURRIER, Richard Patrick Montague. b 25. Bris Univ BA 59. Wycliffe Hall Ox 59. **d** 61 **p** 62. C S Lyncombe *B & W* 61-63; C Weston St Jo 63-64; rtd 90. *48 Longford Road, Melksham SN12 6AU* T: (01225) 707419

SPURWAY, Christine Frances. b 54. Cuddesdon Coll 96. **d** 98 **p** 99. C Coulsdon St Andr *S'wark* 98-02; P-in-c Riddlesdown 02-05; V from 05; RD Croydon S from 04. *St James's Vicarage, 1B St James's Road, Purley CR8 2DL* T: (020) 8660 5436

SQUIRE, Geoffrey Frank. b 36. Ex & Truro NSM Scheme. **d** 83 **p** 84. NSM Barnstaple *Ex* 83-98; NSM Swimbridge w W Buckland and Landkey from 98. *Little Cross, Northleigh Hill, Goodleigh, Barnstaple EX32 7NR* T: (01271) 344935

SQUIRE, Humphrey Edward. b 29. St Chad's Coll Dur BA 55. Coll of Resurr Mirfield. **d** 57 **p** 58. C Newbold w Dunston *Derby* 57-59; C Thorpe St Andr *Nor* 59-61; Zanzibar 61-63; C

Whittington *Derby* 63-64; R Drayton *Nor* 64-75; Chapl Dover Coll 75-83; TV Wareham *Sarum* 83-94; rtd 94; PtO *Sarum* from 94. *La Retraite, Burbidge Close, Lytchett Matravers, Poole BH16 6EG* T: (01202) 623204

SQUIRES, John Anthony. b 50. CPFA 78. LCTP. **d** 08 **p** 09. OLM Waterside Par *Blackb* from 08. *11 Carr Lane, Hambleton, Poulton-le-Fylde FY6 9BA* T: (01253) 701895 M: 07704-659556 E: squiresja@aol.com

SQUIRES, John Wallace Howden. b 45. Sydney Univ BA 67 DipEd 68 MTh 97 PhD 05 Lon Univ BD 75. Moore Th Coll Sydney ThL 74. **d** 76 **p** 76. C Normanhurst Australia 76-78; C Luton St Mary *St Alb* 78-79; Chapl Home of Divine Healing Crowhurst 79-80; C-in-c Putney Australia 80-82; R Longueville 83-97; Dir Inst for Values Univ of NSW 97-02; Dir Aus Human Rights Cen Univ of NSW 03-05. *22 Moorehead Street, Redfern NSW 2016, Australia* T: (0061) (2) 9690 0206 *or* 9385 3637 F: 9385 1778 M: 41-822 6976 E: j.squires@unsw.edu.au

SQUIRES, The Ven Malcolm. b 46. St Chad's Coll Dur BA 72. Cuddesdon Coll 72. **d** 74 **p** 75. C Headingley *Ripon* 74-77; C Stanningley St Thos 77-80; V Bradshaw *Wakef* 80-85; V Ripponden 85-89; V Barkisland w W Scammonden 85-89; V Mirfield 89-96; TR Wrexham *St As* 96-02; Hon Can St As Cathl 00-01; Adn Wrexham 01-10; R Llandegla 02-10; Bp's Chapl 10-11; Can Cursal St As Cathl 10-11; rtd 11; PtO *St As* from 11. *1A Penrhyn Park, Penrhyn Bay, Llandudno LL30 3HW* T: (01492) 544560 M: 07966-200894 E: malcolm@squires1a.plus.com

SQUIRES, Rachel Louise. *See* SCHEFFER, Rachel Louise

SSERUNKUMA, Michael Wilberforce. b 54. Trin Coll Bris BA 90. Bp Tucker Coll Mukono. **d** 77 **p** 78. Uganda 77-87; C Gabalfa *Llan* 90-94; TV Cyncoed *Mon* 94-95; R Canton St Jo *Llan* 95-01; Asst Chapl R Berks and Battle Hosps NHS Trust 01-02; Chapl Team Ldr R Berks NHS Foundn Trust 02-10; Hd Past Care W Middx Univ Hosp NHS Trust from 10. *West Middlesex University Hospital, Twickenham Road, Isleworth TW7 6AF* T: (020) 8560 2121

STABLES, Katharine Ruth. b 45. R Holloway Coll Lon BA 67. WMMTC 90. **d** 93 **p** 94. NSM Knutton *Lich* 93-05; NSM Silverdale and Alsagers Bank 93-96; Soc Resp Officer 96-99; Officer for NSMs 03-05; P-in-c Startforth and Bowes and Rokeby w Brignall *Ripon* 05-09; rtd 10; PtO *Dur* from 10. *15 Greenbank, Eggleston, Barnard Castle DL12 0BQ* T: (01833) 650006 E: kruth@btopenworld.com

STACE, Michael John. b 44. Open Univ BA 80. SEITE 94. **d** 97 **p** 98. NSM Cant St Dunstan w H Cross 97-01; NSM Cant All SS 01-06; P-in-c 06-14; rtd 14; PtO *Cant* from 15. *124 St Stephen's Road, Canterbury CT2 7JS* T: (01227) 451169 F: 455627 M: 07831-174900 E: michaelstace31@gmail.com

STACEY, Gillian. *See* STILL, Gillian

STACEY, Graham John. b 68. Lon Bible Coll BA 97. Ripon Coll Cuddesdon 05. **d** 08 **p** 09. C Beedon and Peasemore w W Ilsley and Farnborough *Ox* 08-10; C E Downland 10-11; PtO from 12. *The Vicarage, Church Street, Shipton-under-Wychwood, Chipping Norton OX7 6BP* T: (01993) 830257 M: 07753-687389 E: graham@thestaceys.tv

STACEY, Mrs Kate Elizabeth. b 73. Lon Bible Coll BTh 97. Ripon Coll Cuddesdon 05. **d** 08 **p** 09. C E Downland *Ox* 08-11; V Wychwood from 11. *The Vicarage, Church Street, Shipton-under-Wychwood, Chipping Norton OX7 6BP* T: (01993) 832514 E: kate@wychwoodbenefice.org.uk

STACEY, La. *See* STACEY, Rosalind Ruth

STACEY, Nicolas David. b 27. St Edm Hall Ox BA 51 MA 55. Cuddesdon Coll 51. **d** 53 **p** 54. C Portsea N End St Mark *Portsm* 53-58; Bp's Dom Chapl *Birm* 58-59; R Woolwich St Mary w H Trin *S'wark* 59-68; Borough Dean Greenwich 65-68; Dep Dir Oxfam 68-70; PtO *Ox* 68-71; P-in-c Selling *Cant* 76-78; PtO 79-84 and from 90; Six Preacher Cant Cathl 84-89; rtd 92. *The Old Vicarage, Selling, Faversham ME13 9RD* T: (01227) 752833 F: 752889 E: nicolas@nstacey.fsnet.co.uk

STACEY, Mrs Rosalind Ruth (La). b 54. New Hall Cam MA 81 Bulmershe Coll of HE PGCE 94. Ripon Coll Cuddesdon 09. **d** 11 **p** 12. C Easthampstead *Ox* 11-14; V Eton w Eton Wick, Boveney and Dorney from 14. *The Vicarage, 69A Eton Wick Road, Eton Wick, Windsor SL4 6NE* T: (01753) 852268 E: revlastacey@gmail.com

STACEY (née O'BRIEN), Mrs Shelagh Ann. b 55. RGN 83 Bedf Coll Lon BSc 77. NOC 89. **d** 92 **p** 94. Par Dn S Elmsall *Wakef* 92-94; C 94-95; C Carleton 95-97; P-in-c 97-99; C E Hardwick 95-97; P-in-c 97-99; V Carleton and E Hardwick *Leeds* from 99. *The Vicarage, 10 East Close, Pontefract WF8 3NS* T: (01977) 702244

STACEY, Timothy Andrew. b 58. Imp Coll Lon BSc 79 York Univ PGCE 83. St Jo Coll Nottm 94. **d** 94 **p** 95. C Chorleywood Ch Ch *St Alb* 94-99; P-in-c Chalfont St Giles *Ox* 99-08; R 08-13;

Chapl Bucks New Univ 99-13; Teacher Abbey Sch Reading from 13. *26 Sunny Bank, Widmer End, High Wycombe HP15 6PA* T: (01494) 715194 E: timstacey@ntlworld.com

STACEY, The Very Revd Victor George. b 44. NUI BA 69 QUB MTh. CITC 72. **d** 72 **p** 73. C Derriaghy *Conn* 72-76; C Knock *D & D* 76-79; I Ballymacarrett St Martin 79-86; I Dublin Santry w Glasnevin *D & G* 86-94; I Dun Laoghaire 95-12; Bp's Dom Chapl 90-12; Prov and Dioc Registrar 95-12; Preb Maynooth St Patr Cathl Dublin 97-12; Dean St Patr Cathl Dublin from 12. *The Deanery, Upper Kevin Street, Dublin 8, Republic of Ireland* T: (00353) (1) 475 5449 *or* 453 9472 E: dean@stpatrickscathedral.ie

STACY, Christine Rosemary. b 49. UEA BSc 70 Keswick Hall Coll PGCE 71 Univ of Wales (Ban) MSc 75 Northumbria Univ PhD 94. **d** 10 **p** 11. OLM Upper Coquetdale *Newc* from 10. *Ovenstone, Sharperton, Morpeth NE65 7AT* T: (01669) 640382 E: rosie.stacy@virgin.net

STAFF, Mrs Jean. b 44. CertEd 64. EMMTC 81. **dss** 84 **d** 87 **p** 94. Old Brumby *Linc* 84-88; C 87-88; C Gainsborough St Geo 88-91; Dn-in-c 91-94; P-in-c 94-96; P-in-c Haxey 96-97; P-in-c Owston 96-97; V Haxey 97-04; V Owston 97-04; rtd 04. *5 South Furlong Croft, Epworth, Doncaster DN9 1GB* T: (01427) 871422

STAFF, Susan. *See* JACKSON, Susan

STAFFORD, Christopher James. b 67. Birm Univ BSc 88 PhD 92. St Jo Coll Nottm MA 98. **d** 99 **p** 00. C Westbrook St Phil *Liv* 99-03; R Newchurch w Croft 03-14; TV Newton from 14. *All Saints' Vicarage, 243 Crow Lane East, Newton-le-Willows WA12 9UB* T: (01925) 271421 E: cjstaff@surfaid.org

STAFFORD, David George. b 45. Qu Coll Birm 75. **d** 77 **p** 78. C Chesterfield SS Aug *Derby* 77-80; C Ranmoor *Sheff* 80-83; V Bolton-upon-Dearne 83-11; rtd 11. *4 Rylestone Court, Sheffield S12 4NJ* T: 0114-248 0993 E: davidstaffordbod@yahoo.co.uk

STAFFORD, Canon John Ingham Henry. b 31. TCD BA 52 MA 58. **d** 53 **p** 55. C Clonallon *D & D* 53-56; C Belfast Malone St Jo *Conn* 56-59; Australia 59-64; Min Can Down Cathl 64-68; Hd of S Ch Miss Ballymacarrett 68-73; I Bright w Killough *D & D* 73-83; C Bangor Primacy 83-92; Can Down Cathl 90-92; I Urney w Sion Mills *D & R* 92-98; rtd 98. *14 Cleland Park North, Bangor BT20 3EN* T: (028) 9145 6311 M: 07709-978874 E: jihsscp@yahoo.co.uk

STAFFORD, Matthew Charles. b 73. Wilson Carlile Coll 94 Ripon Coll Cuddesdon 99. **d** 99 **p** 00. C High Wycombe *Ox* 99-02; P-in-c Wrockwardine Wood *Lich* 02-04; R Oakengates and Wrockwardine Wood 04-15; TR Wenlock *Heref* from 15. *The Rectory, 1 New Road, Much Wenlock TF13 6EQ* M: 07889-376865 T: (01952) 727396 E: revmatthewstafford@gmail.com

STAFFORD, Canon Richard William. b 46. Ringsent Tech Inst TCert 69. CITC 96. **d** 99 **p** 00. NSM Annagh w Drumgoon, Ashfield etc *K, E & A* 99-07; P-in-c Drumgoon 07-12; Can Kilmore Cathl from 08. *12 Cherrymount, Keadue Lane, Cavan, Co Cavan, Republic of Ireland* T: (00353) (49) 437 1173 M: 87-240 4630 E: rwstafford@yahoo.com

STAFFORD, Area Bishop of. *See* ANNAS, The Rt Revd Geoffrey Peter

STAFFORD-WHITTAKER, William Paul. b 69. Chich Th Coll 91. **d** 94 **p** 95. C Brighton Resurr *Chich* 94-97; C Holborn St Alb w Saffron Hill St Pet *Lon* 97-02; V Stanwell 02-14; USA from 14. *The Rectory, 222 8th Street NE, Washington DC 20002-6106, USA* T/F: (001) (202) 546 1746

STAGG, Jeremy Michael. b 47. Leeds Univ BSc 69 Fontainebleau MBA 77 Southn Univ BTh 94. Sarum & Wells Th Coll 90. **d** 92 **p** 93. C Basing *Win* 92-96; P-in-c Barton, Pooley Bridge and Martindale *Carl* 96-99; Hon CMS Rep 96-99; C Burgh-by-Sands and Kirkbampton w Kirkandrews etc *Carl* 99-00; C Barony of Burgh 00-01; P-in-c Distington 01-05; Dioc Past Sec 00-05; TR Cheswardine, Childs Ercall, Hales, Hinstock etc *Lich* 05-10; RD Hodnet 06-11; rtd 10; PtO *Lich* from 11. *27 Fishers Lock, Newport TF10 7ST* T: (01952) 813735

STAGG, Roy Ernest. b 48. **d** 01 **p** 02. OLM Birchington w Acol and Minnis Bay *Cant* 01-04; OLM St Laur in Thanet 04-05. *7 Minster Road, Acol, Birchington CT7 0JB* T: (01843) 841551 M: 07802-406066 E: roystagg@hotmail.co.uk

STAGG, Russell James. b 69. SEITE 08. **d** 11 **p** 12. NSM Haggerston St Chad *Lon* 11-12; C Holborn St Alb w Saffron Hill St Pet 12-15; P-in-c Roughey *Chich* from 15. *52 Shepherds Way, Horsham RH12 4LX* M: 07834-735002 T: (01403) 274297 E: father.russell@me.com

STAINER, David John. b 58. RCM BMus 80. St Mellitus Coll BA 11. **d** 11 **p** 12. NSM Collier Row St Jas and Havering-atte-Bower *Chelmsf* from 11. *29 Cormorant Walk, Hornchurch RM12 5HE* T: (01708) 550053 M: 07870-820314 E: davidjstainer@hotmail.com

STAINER, Helene Lindsay. b 59. SWMTC 01. **d** 04 **p** 05. NSM Ivybridge w Harford *Ex* 04-09; P-in-c Milverton w Halse and Fitzhead *B & W* 09-10; R Milverton w Halse, Fitzhead and Ash Priors from 10. *The Vicarage, Parsonage Lane, Milverton, Taunton TA4 1LR* T: (01823) 400305 E: helenestainer@aol.com

STAINER, Canon Richard Bruce. b 62. Anglia Ruskin Univ MA 09. Linc Th Coll 92. **d** 94 **p** 95. C N Walsham w Antingham *Nor* 94-97; R Cogenhoe and Gt and Lt Houghton w Brafield *Pet* 97-14; RD Wootton 01-07; V Higham Ferrers w Chelveston from 14; Can Pet Cathl from 12. *The Vicarage, Wood Street, Higham Ferrers, Rushden NN10 8DL* T: (01933) 314750 *or* 426202 E: canon.stainer@gmail.com

STAINES, Edward Noel. b 26. Trin Coll Ox BA 48 BSc 49 MA 52 MSc 85. Chich Th Coll 51 57. **d** 57 **p** 58. C Eastbourne St Mary *Chich* 57-61; V Amberley w N Stoke 61-70; V Forest Row 70-75; V Bexhill St Aug 75-79; TR Ovingdean w Rottingdean and Woodingdean 79-85; V Rottingdean 85-86; Chapl Gtr Lisbon *Eur* 88; Chapl Marseille 90; rtd 90; PtO *Worc* 86-09. *16 Conningsby Drive, Pershore WR10 1QX* T: (01386) 554382

STAINES, Michael John. b 28. Trin Coll Ox BA 52 MA 56. Wells Th Coll 62. **d** 64 **p** 65. C Southwick St Mich *Chich* 64-67; TV Harling Gp *Nor* 67-73; P Missr S Chilterns Gp *Ox* 74-75; R W Wycombe w Bledlow Ridge, Bradenham and Radnage 76-93; RD Wycombe 83-87; rtd 93; PtO *Heref* 93-13; *Worc* 93-06. *6 Walnut Close, Stoke Mandeville, Aylesbury HP22 5UG*

STAINSBY, Alan. b 48. NEOC 01. **d** 04 **p** 05. NSM Hart w Elwick Hall *Dur* 04-06; NSM Haswell, Shotton and Thornley from 06. *6 Church View, Shotton Colliery, Durham DH6 2YD* T: 0191-526 5200 E: astainsbyshotton@aol.com

STALEY, Andrew. b 50. Rhode Is Univ BA 83. Westcott Ho Cam 01. **d** 04 **p** 05. C Bridport *Sarum* 04-08; TV Nadder Valley from 08. *The Rectory, Park Road, Tisbury, Salisbury SP3 6LF* T: (01747) 870312 E: rev.staley@googlemail.com

STALEY, John Colin George. b 44. Hull Univ MA 83. Wycliffe Hall Ox 68. **d** 71 **p** 72. C Tinsley *Sheff* 71-73; C Slaithwaite w E Scammonden *Wakef* 73-75; V Wakef St Andr and St Mary 75-80; Warden Scargill Ho 80-82; P-in-c Macclesfield St Pet *Ches* 82-85; TV Macclesfield Team 85-99; Sen Ind Chapl 86-99; Hon Ind Chapl 99-02; PtO from 10. *Greenhills, Swanscoe, Rainow, Macclesfield SK10 5SZ* T: (01625) 421296 M: 07824-736383 E: jjstaley@hotmail.co.uk

STALKER, Harry. b 47. **d** 04 **p** 05. OLM Felixstowe SS Pet and Paul *St E* 04-12; NSM Nacton and Levington w Bucklesham etc from 12. *2 Ascot Drive, Felixstowe IP11 9DW* T: (01394) 210826 F: 210663 M: 07710-221275 E: aitchess@clara.net

STALKER, William John. b 49. NOC 89. **d** 91 **p** 92. C Formby H Trin *Liv* 91-94; V Stoneycroft All SS 94-03; Chapl R Liv Univ Hosp NHS Trust 94-03; P-in-c Lowton St Mary *Liv* 03-13; TR Lowton and Golborne 13-14; rtd 14. *Hilltop House, Oubas Hill, Ulverston LA12 7LB*

STALLARD, John Charles. b 34. Selw Coll Cam BA 58 MA 62. Ripon Hall Ox 62. **d** 64 **p** 65. C Hall Green Ascension *Birm* 64-66; C Sutton Coldfield H Trin 66-68; C-in-c Brandwood CD 68-71; Chapl Dame Allan's Schs Newc 71-74; V Warley Woods *Birm* 75-84; TR Droitwich *Worc* 84-87; P-in-c Dodderhill 84-87; TR Droitwich Spa 87-94; V Pennsett 94-00; rtd 00; PtO *St D* 00-07; *St As* from 09. *Craigievar, Abbey Road, Llangollen LL20 8SN* T: (01978) 860654 E: greengates@breathemail.net

STALLARD, Mary Kathleen Rose. b 67. Selw Coll Cam BA 88 Lon Inst of Educn PGCE 90. Qu Coll Birm 91. **d** 93 **p** 97. C Newport St Matt *Mon* 93-96; P-in-c Ysbyty Cynfyn w Llantrisant and Eglwys Newydd *St D* 96-97; V 97-02; Min Can and Chapl St As Cathl 02-03; Can Res St As Cathl 03-11; Dir of Ords and Co-ord of Minl Formation St As 10-11; Chapl St Jos High Sch Wrexham from 11. *The Vicarage, Abbey Road, Llangollen LL20 8SN* T: (01978) 860231

STALLEY, Brian Anthony. b 38. Oak Hill Th Coll 60. **d** 63 **p** 64. C Summerstown *S'wark* 63-70; Surrey BFBS Sec 70-73; Manager Action Cen BFBS 73-76; R Branston *Linc* 76-91; rtd 91; PtO *Linc* from 91. *6 Sunningdale Grove, Washingborough, Lincoln LN4 1SP* T: (01522) 794164 F: 794663 M: 07941-508445 E: brian@bstalley.freeserve.co.uk

STAMFORD, Brian. b 37. **d** 91 **p** 92. CMS Uganda 88-95; P-in-c North Hill and Lewannick Truro 95-03; P-in-c Altarnon w Bolventor, Laneast and St Clether 03-07; rtd 07; PtO *Pet* from 08. *2 William Dalby House, South Street, Oakham LE15 6HY* T: (01572) 723493 E: brianstamford@btopenworld.com

STAMFORD, Dean of. *See* WARRICK, The Very Revd Mark

STAMP, Andrew Nicholas. b 44. Ex Univ BA 67. Sarum Th Coll 67. **d** 69 **p** 70. C S Beddington St Mich *S'wark* 69-73; Tutor Sarum & Wells Th Coll 73-76; Chapl RN 76-81; C-in-c W Leigh CD *Portsm* 81-82; V W Leigh 82-87; R Botley 87-95; V Curdridge and R Durley 94-95; P-in-c Compton, the Mardens, Stoughton and Racton *Chich* 95-08; P-in-c Stansted 95-08; Tutor Bp Otter Coll Chich 95-98; Dioc Rural Officer

Chich 00-08; rtd 08; Hon C Arlington, Berwick, Selmeston w Alciston etc *Chich* 11-13. *36 Up Marden, Chichester PO18 9JR* T: (01243) 535010 E: revastamp@aol.com

STAMP, Canon Ian Jack. b 47. Aston Tr Scheme 82 NOC 83. **d** 86 **p** 87. C Tonge w Alkrington *Man* 86-89; V Heywood St Marg 89-98; P-in-c Heywood St Luke w All So 96-98; TR Heywood 98-01; V Bury St Jo w St Mark 01-10; V Walmersley Road, Bury 10-12; Borough Dean Bury 10-12; Hon Can Man Cathl 11-12; rtd 12; PtO *Man* from 12. *10 Unity Crescent, Heywood OL10 3DW* T: (01706) 367788 E: ianstamp@tiscali.co.uk

STAMP, Philip Andrew. b 53. Linc Th Coll 86. **d** 88 **p** 89. C Barton w Peel Green *Man* 88-91; R Blackley H Trin from 91; P-in-c Lightbowne from 04. *Holy Trinity Rectory, Goodman Street, Manchester M9 4BW* T: 0161-205 2879

STAMP, Richard Mark. b 36. St Chad's Coll Dur BA 60. **d** 62 **p** 63. Australia 62-69 and from 72; C Greenhill St Jo *Lon* 69-72; rtd 01. *127 Hilda Drive, RMB Ravenswood, Harcourt Vic 3453, Australia* T/F: (0061) (3) 5435 3576 E: stamp@netcon.net.au

STAMPER, Dawn Caroline. b 62. **d** 14 **p** 15. NSM Willesborough w Sevington *Cant* from 14. *Malthouse Farm, Rock Hill Road, Egerton, Ashford TN27 9EB*

STAMPS, Canon Dennis Lee. b 55. Biola Univ (USA) BA 78 Trin Evang Div Sch (USA) MDiv 83 MA 87 Dur Univ PhD 95. Westcott Ho Cam 90. **d** 92 **p** 93. C Olveston w Aust *Bris* 92-96; Dir WMMTC 96-01; Dean Qu Coll Birm 01-02; Can Res St Alb *St Alb* 02-12; Minl Development Officer 02-12; Dir Min 11-12; R Harpenden St Nic from 12. *The Rectory, 9 Rothamsted Avenue, Harpenden AL5 2DD* T: (01582) 712202 E: dstampsuk@aol.com

✠**STANAGE, The Rt Revd Thomas Shaun.** b 32. Pemb Coll Ox BA 56 MA 60 Nashotah Ho Wisconsin Hon DD 86. Cuddesdon Coll 56. **d** 58 **p** 59 **c** 78. C Gt Crosby St Faith *Liv* 58-61; Min Orford St Andr CD 61-63; V Orford St Andr 63-70; S Africa from 70; Dean Kimberley 75-78; Suff Bp Johannesburg 78-82; Bp Bloemfontein 82-97; rtd 97; Acting Lect Th Univ of the Free State from 97. *PO Box 13598, Noordstad, Bloemfontein, 9301 South Africa* T: (0027) (51) 436 7282

✠**STANCLIFFE, The Rt Revd David Staffurth.** b 42. Trin Coll Ox BA 65 MA 68 Lambeth DD 04. Cuddesdon Coll 65. **d** 67 **p** 68 **c** 93. C Armley St Bart *Ripon* 67-70; Chapl Clifton Coll Bris 70-77; Dir of Ords and Can Res Portsm Cathl 77-82; Provost Portsm 82-93; Bp Sarum 93-10; rtd 10; Hon Asst Bp Eur from 11; Hon Asst Bp Dur from 13. *Butts House, 15 The Butts, Stanhope, Bishop Auckland DL13 2UQ* T: (01388) 526912 E: david.stancliffe@hotmail.com

STAND, Andrew George. b 68. St Jo Coll Dur BA 06. Cranmer Hall Dur 04. **d** 06 **p** 07. C Bromsgrove St Jo *Worc* 06-09; TV Gornal and Sedgley from 09. *The Vicarage, 35 Eve Lane, Dudley DY1 3TY* T: (01902) 883467

STANDEN, David Charles. b 68. K Coll Lon BA 91 AKC 91 PGCE 92 Lon Univ PhD 00. Westcott Ho Cam 01. **d** 03 **p** 04. C Prittlewell *Chelmsf* 03-07; P-in-c Stratton and Launcells *Truro* 07-11; P-in-c Bude Haven and Marhamchurch 09-11; R Edin St Mich and All SS 11-13; Chapl K Edw Sch Witley from 13. *King Edward's School, Petworth Road, Wormey, Godalming GU8 5SG* T: (01428) 686700 E: d.c.standen@btinternet.com

STANDEN, Mark Jonathan. b 63. LMH Ox BA 85 Cam Univ BA 94 Barrister 86. Ridley Hall Cam 92. **d** 95 **p** 96. C Sevenoaks St Nic *Roch* 95-99; R Angmering *Chich* from 99; RD Arundel and Bognor from 08. *The Rectory, Rectory Lane, Angmering, Littlehampton BN16 4JU* T: (01903) 784979

STANDEN McDOUGAL, Canon John Anthony Phelps. b 33. AKC 58. **d** 59 **p** 60. C Ipswich St Marg *St E* 59-63; C Bury St Edmunds St Mary 63-65; C Wadhurst *Chich* 65-70; C Tidebrook 65-70; R Tollard Royal w Farnham *Sarum* 70-81; P-in-c Gussage St Michael and Gussage All Saints 71-76; R 76-81; RD Milton and Blandford 81-86; R Tollard Royal w Farnham, Gussage St Michael etc 82-86; Can and Preb Sarum Cathl 86-94; TR Bride Valley 86-94; rtd 94; PtO *Sarum* from 94. *Silverbridge Cottage, North Chideock, Bridport DT6 6LG* T: (01297) 489408

STANDING, Victor. b 44. Lon Univ BMus 66 Clare Coll Cam PGCE 68 FRCO 67. Ripon Coll Cuddesdon 75. **d** 78 **p** 79. C Wimborne Minster *Sarum* 78-80; TV Wimborne Minster and Holt 80-83; R Ex St Sidwell and St Matt 83-94; Dep PV Ex Cathl 83-01; Chapl R Devon and Ex Hosp 83-94; Chapl W of England Eye Infirmary Ex 83-94; P-in-c Tedburn St Mary, Whitestone, Oldridge etc *Ex* 94-96; P-in-c Dunsford and Doddiscombsleigh 95-96; P-in-c Cheriton Bishop 95-96; TR Tedburn St Mary, Whitestone, Oldridge etc 96-01; RD Kenn 97-01; V New Shoreham and Old Shoreham *Chich* 01-11; rtd 11; P-in-c Shanklin St Blasius *Portsm* 11-15. *23 Abnalls Croft, Lichfield WS13 7BP* T: (01543) 418890 E: victor@victorstanding.plus.com

STANDISH, Derrick Edgar. b 41. Univ of Wales (Lamp) BA 67. Wycliffe Hall Ox 68. **d** 68 **p** 69. C Brynmawr *S & B* 68-69; C Morriston 69-74; V Merthyr Cynog and Dyffryn Honddu 74-76; R Llanwenarth Ultra *Mon* 76-83; V Abersychan and Garndiffaith 83-91. *7 Intermediate Road, Brynmawr, Ebbw Vale NP23 4SF* T: (01495) 312183

STANDRING, Rupert Benjamin Charles. b 68. Pemb Coll Ox BA 90 MA 99 Cam Univ BA 94. Ridley Hall Cam 92. **d** 95 **p** 96. C Bromley Ch Ch *Roch* 95-99; Tutor Cornhill Tr Course 99-04; Hon C W Hampstead St Luke *Lon* 99-04; PtO 04-05; Min Mayfair Ch Ch 05-09; Lic Preacher 09-10; P-in-c Fulham St Pet 10-11; V from 11. *56 Langthorne Street, London SW6 6JY* T: (020) 7385 4950 E: rupert.standring@googlemail.com

STANES, The Ven Ian Thomas. b 39. Sheff Univ BSc 62 Linacre Coll Ox BA 65 MA 69. Wycliffe Hall Ox 63. **d** 65 **p** 66. C Leic H Apostles 65-69; V Broom Leys 69-76; Warden Marrick Priory *Ripon* 76-82; Officer Miss, Min and Evang Willesden Area *Lon* 82-92; CME Officer 82-92; Preb St Paul's Cathl 89-92; Adn Loughborough *Leic* 92-05; rtd 05. *192 Bath Road, Bradford-on-Avon BA15 1SP* T: (01225) 309036

STANESBY, Derek Malcolm. b 31. Leeds Univ BA 56 Man Univ MEd 75 PhD 84 SOSc. Coll of Resurr Mirfield 56. **d** 58 **p** 59. C Lakenham St Jo *Nor* 58-61; C Welling *S'wark* 61-63; V Bury St Mark *Man* 63-67; R Ladybarn 67-85; Can and Steward Windsor 85-97; rtd 97; PtO *Leic* from 00; *Pet* 00-07. *32 Elizabeth Way, Uppingham, Oakham LE15 9PQ* T: (01572) 821298

STANFORD, Mrs Emma Joanne. b 72. Qu Coll Birm 08. **d** 11 **p** 12. C Wordsley *Worc* 11-14; P-in-c Coseley Ch Ch from 14; P-in-c Sedgley St Mary from 14. *The Vicarage, 40 Church Road, Bilston WV14 8YB* E: emma.stanford@blueyonder.co.uk

STANFORD, Canon Mark Roger. b 59. Cranmer Hall Dur 96. **d** 98 **p** 99. C Aughton Ch Ch *Liv* 98-02; TV Toxteth St Philemon w St Gabr and St Cleopas 02-11; TR 11-12; AD Toxteth and Wavertree 06-12; Chapl St Hilda's Priory and Sch Whitby 03-12; P-in-c Formby H Trin *Liv* 12-14; V Formby H Trin and Altcar from 14; Hon Can Liv Cathl from 06. *Holy Trinity Vicarage, 2A Brows Lane, Liverpool L37 3HZ* T: (01704) 386464 E: mark-stanford@hotmail.co.uk

STANFORD, Timothy Charles. b 61. **d** 11 **p** 12. C Walton Breck *Liv* 11-13; P-in-c Worksop St Jo *S'well* from 13. *St John's Vicarage, 1B Shepherds Avenue, Worksop S81 0JD* E: tcs227@gmail.com

STANGHAN, Eileen. b 40. Whitelands Coll Lon CertEd 75. **d** 98 **p** 99. OLM Reigate St Phil *S'wark* 98-10; PtO from 10. *20 Saxon Way, Reigate RH2 9DH* T: (01737) 240920 *or* (01293) 430043

STANIER, Robert Sebastian. b 75. Magd Coll Ox BA 98 Selw Coll Cam BA 05. Westcott Ho Cam 03. **d** 06 **p** 07. C Perry Hill St Geo w Ch Ch and St Paul *S'wark* 06-09; Chapl Abp Tenison's Sch Kennington 09-13; Hon C N Lambeth and S Lambeth St Anne and All SS *S'wark* 09-13; V Surbiton St Andr and St Mark from 13. *The Vicarage, St Mark's Hill, Surbiton KT6 4LS* T: (020) 8399 0639 E: robertstanier@btinternet.com

STANIFORD, Canon Doris Gwendoline. b 43. Gilmore Course IDC 79. **dss** 80 **d** 87 **p** 94. Par Dn Durrington *Chich* 87-89; Chich Th Coll 83-89; C Crawley and Chapl Crawley Gen Hosp 89-97; Dioc Voc Adv and Chapl St Cath Hospice Crawley 92-97; Asst Dir of Ords *Chich* 97-12; C Southwick St Mich 97-99; TV Ifield 99-12; Can and Preb Chich Cathl 08-12; rtd 12. *28 Beechside, Crawley RH10 6TL*

STANIFORTH, Julian Martin. b 56. Aston Univ BSc 82 MCIMA 93. SEITE 07. **d** 10 **p** 11. C Herne *Cant* 10-14; V The Six from 14. *The Vicarage, Church Lane, Newington, Sittingbourne ME9 7JU* T: (01795) 227329 M: 07879-626115 E: julian.staniforth@gmail.com

STANLEY, Arthur Patrick. b 32. TCD BA 54 Div Test 55 MA 64. **d** 55 **p** 56. C Waterford H Trin *C & O* 55-57; CF 58-74; Dep Asst Chapl Gen 74-83; USA 84-04; rtd 94; PtO *B & W* from 05. *9 Westbourne Court, Cooden Drive, Bexhill-on-Sea TN39 3AA* T: (01424) 539307 E: patnpaddy@hotmail.com

STANLEY, Baden Thomas. b 68. TCD BA 91. CITC BTh 94. **d** 94 **p** 95. C Seapatrick *D & D* 94-98; I Bray *D & G* from 98. *The Rectory, Church Road, Bray, Co Wicklow, Republic of Ireland* T/F: (00353) (1) 286 2968 M: 87-948 4407 E: christchurchbray@gmail.com

STANLEY, Canon John Alexander. b 31. OBE 99. Tyndale Hall Bris. **d** 56 **p** 57. C Preston All SS *Blackb* 56-60; C St Helens St Mark *Liv* 60-63; V Everton St Cuth 63-70; P-in-c Everton St Sav 69-70; V Everton St Sav w St Cuth 70-74; V Huyton St Mich from 74; Hon Can Liv Cathl from 87; AD Huyton 89-02; Chapl to The Queen 93-01. *The Vicarage, Bluebell Lane, Liverpool L36 7XA* T: 0151-449 3900 F: 480 6002 M: 07740-621833 E: huytonchurch@btconnect.com

STANLEY, Canon Nicola Vere. b 56. Surrey Univ BA 07 MCIPD 83. STETS 99. **d** 02 **p** 03. C Bedford Park *Lon* 02-06;

V Twickenham All Hallows 06-14; Asst Dir of Ords Kensington Area 04-14; Can Res, Prec and Sacr Bris Cathl from 14. *Bristol Cathedral, College Green, Bristol BS1 5TJ* T: 0117-926 4879 E: canon.precentor@bristol-cathedral.co.uk

STANLEY, Patrick. *See* STANLEY, Arthur Patrick

STANLEY, Canon Simon Richard. b 44. Wells Th Coll 66. **d** 69 **p** 70. C Foleshill St Laur *Cov* 69-71; C Hessle *York* 71-75; P-in-c Flamborough 75-80; R Dunnington 80-92; P-in-c York St Barn 92-99; P-in-c York St Chad 99-14; P-in-c York All SS Pavement w St Crux and St Mich 03-09; P-in-c York St Denys 04-09; Relig Progr Producer BBC Radio York 94-03; rtd 09; P-in-c York St Chad 09-14; Can and Preb York Minster 05-14; PtO from 14. *69 Temple Avenue, York YO10 3RS* M: 07946-466364 E: simonstanley@clara.net

STANLEY-SMITH, James. b 29. Hatf Coll Dur BA 54 DipEd 55. S Dios Minl Tr Scheme 81. **d** 84 **p** 85. C Bournemouth St Jo w St Mich *Win* 84-87; R Hale w S Charford 87-94; rtd 94; PtO *Win* from 94. *10 Rownhams Way, Rownhams, Southampton SO16 8AE* T: (023) 8073 2529 E: jstanley-smith@cwcom.net

STANNARD, Miss Beryl Elizabeth. b 36. SRN 62 SCM 64. Oak Hill Th Coll BA 92. **d** 92 **p** 94. Par Dn Streatham Park St Alb *S'wark* 92-94; C 94-96; C Gerrards Cross and Fulmer *Ox* 96-01; rtd 01; PtO *Ox* from 02. *20 Wey Lane, Chesham HP5 1JH* T: (01494) 774715

STANNARD, Brian. b 46. MICE 71 MIStructE 71. Cranmer Hall Dur 86. **d** 88 **p** 89. C Burnage St Marg *Man* 88-91; V Walmersley 91-03; TV Westhoughton and Wingates 03-04; rtd 04. *63 Portland Street, Southport PR8 5AF* T: (01704) 534632 E: brian@stannardrev.fsnet.co.uk

STANNARD, The Ven Colin Percy. b 24. TD 66. Selw Coll Cam BA 47 MA 49. Linc Th Coll 47. **d** 49 **p** 50. C St E Cathl 49-52; C-in-c Nunsthorpe CD *Linc* 52-55; CF (TA) 53-67; V Barrow St Jas *Carl* 55-64; V Upperby St Jo 64-70; R Gosforth 70-75; RD Calder 70-75; P-in-c Natland 75-76; V 76-84; RD Kendal 75-84; Hon Can Carl Cathl 75-84; Can Res Carl Cathl 84-93; Adn Carl 84-93; rtd 93; PtO *Carl* from 93. *Flat 4, Manormead, Tilford Road, Hindhead GU26 6RA*

STANNARD, Canon Peter Graville. b 59. Univ of Wales (Abth) BSc(Econ) 81. St Steph Ho Ox BA 85 MA 86. **d** 86 **p** 87. C Worksop Priory *S'well* 86-89; Prin St Nic Th Coll Ghana 89-96; Hon Can Koforidua from 93; TR Shelf w Buttershaw St Aid *Bradf* 96-99; P-in-c Heaton Norris St Thos *Man* 00-02; TV Heatons 02-08; P-in-c S Shields St Hilda w St Thos *Dur* 08-12; P-in-c S Shields St Aid and St Steph 08-12; C Houghton le Spring 12-13; rtd 13; PtO *Dur* from 13. *8 Dunscar, Houghton le Spring DH4 5FF* E: frpeter@blueyonder.co.uk

STANNING (née CROMPTON), Mrs Gillian Kay. b 65. Univ of Wales (Ban) BA 86 Homerton Coll Cam PGCE 87. SNWTP 07. **d** 10 **p** 11. C Norley, Crowton and Kingsley *Ches* 10-13; V Sandbach Heath w Wheelock from 13. *The Heath Vicarage, School Lane, Sandbach CW11 2LS* M: 07840-627725 E: g.stanning@btinternet.com

STANTON, Ms Angela. b 59. Loughb Univ BSc 80 Ch Coll Liv PGCE 81. Westcott Ho Cam 03. **d** 05 **p** 06. C Atherton and Hindsford w Howe Bridge *Man* 05-08; P-in-c Reddish from 08; Hon Assoc Dioc Dir of Ords from 10; Borough Dean Stockport from 13. *St Elisabeth's Rectory, 28 Bedford Street, Stockport SK5 6DJ* T: 0161-432 3033 E: angiestanton27@yahoo.co.uk

STANTON, Miss Barbara. b 51. Whitelands Coll Lon TCert 72 Lon Univ BD 86. WMMTC 89. **d** 92 **p** 94. NSM Hinckley St Mary *Leic* 92-97; P-in-c Husbands Bosworth w Mowsley and Knaptoft etc 97-06; P-in-c Arnesby w Shearsby and Bruntingthorpe 02-06; Bp's Ecum Adv 97-03; Dioc Rural Officer 03-06; R Bildeston w Wattisham and Lindsey, Whatfield etc *St E* 06-14; P-in-c Chilton Cantelo, Ashington, Mudford, Rimpton etc *B & W* 14-15; R from 15. *The New Rectory, Camel Street, Marston Magna, Yeovil BA22 8DD* E: b.stanton150@btinternet.com

STANTON, Canon David John. b 60. St Andr Univ MTheol 82 Ex Univ MA 00 FSAScot 89 FRSA 98. Ripon Coll Cuddesdon 83. **d** 85 **p** 86. C Beckenham St Geo *Roch* 85-88; Asst Chapl Shrewsbury Sch 88-90; Hon C Shrewsbury All SS w St Mich *Lich* 88-90; P-in-c Abbotskerswell *Ex* 90-94; Chapl Plymouth Univ *Ex* 90-94; P-in-c Bovey Tracey St Jo, Chudleigh Knighton etc 94-99; V Bovey Tracey St Jo w Heathfield 99-05; Dioc Voc Adv 95-05; Warden of Readers 96-03; Acting Dioc Dir of Ords 03-05; RD Moreton 98-05; Can Prec and Can Past Worc Cathl 05-13; Can and Treas Westmr Abbey from 13. *1 Little Cloister, London SW1P 3PL* T: (020) 7654 4804 F: 7654 4811 E: david.stanton@westminster-abbey.org

STANTON, Gregory John. b 47. Sarum & Wells Th Coll 84. **d** 86 **p** 87. C Willenhall H Trin *Lich* 86-89; C Plympton St Mary *Ex* 89-91; V Milton Abbot, Dunterton, Lamerton etc 91-13; rtd 13; P-in-c Bovey Tracey St Jo w Heathfield *Ex* from 13. *St John's Vicarage, Newton Road, Bovey Tracey, Newton Abbot TQ13 9BD* E: gjstanton31@hotmail.com

STANTON, Miss Julie Elizabeth. b 59. Matlock Coll of Educn CertEd 80. EMMTC 00. **d** 03 **p** 04. NSM Matlock Bath and Cromford *Derby* 03-11. *35 Intake Lane, Cromford, Matlock DE4 3RH* T: (01629) 822653 F: 760903 M: 07769-748276 E: revjs@hotmail.com

STANTON, Ms Karen Janis. b 55. NOC 00. **d** 03 **p** 04. C Withington St Paul *Man* 03-04; C Urmston 04-07; TV Wythenshawe 07-12; R Kinver and Enville *Lich* from 12. *The Rectory, Vicarage Drive, Kinver, Stourbridge DY7 6HJ* T: (01384) 872556 M: 07814-254744 E: kaz@thestantons.me.uk

STANTON, Richard Oliver. b 90. Pemb Coll Cam BA 11 MA 15 MPhil 12. Westcott Ho Cam 12. **d** 15. C Attleborough w Besthorpe *Nor* from 15. *39 Cedar Drive, Attleborough NR17 2EX* T: (01953) 456732 E: richard_stanton@btinternet.com

STANTON-HYDE, Mrs Marjorie Elizabeth. b 37. TCert 58. Cranmer Hall Dur 86. **d** 88 **p** 94. Par Dn Elmley Lovett w Hampton Lovett and Elmbridge etc *Worc* 88-91; Par Dn Wilden 88-91; Par Dn Hartlebury 88-91; Dn-in-c 91-92; P-in-c 94-97; R 97-98; rtd 98; Hon C Gt Malvern St Mary *Worc* 99-02; Warden Jes Hosp Cant 02-05; Chapl Worcs Community and Mental Health Trust 05-12. *4 Severn Drive, Malvern WR14 2SZ* T: (01684) 569589 E: marjemoto@gmail.com

STANTON-SARINGER, Maurice Charles. b 49. Bris Univ BSc 71 PGCE 72 Fitzw Coll Cam BA 77 MA 81. Ridley Hall Cam 75. **d** 78 **p** 79. C Gerrards Cross *Ox* 78-80; C Bletchley 80-83; Chapl Stowe Sch 83-91; R Sherington w Chicheley, N Crawley, Astwood etc *Ox* 91-06; RD Newport 95-04; TR Loddon Reach 06-13; rtd 13; PtO *Ox* from 13. *23 Western Avenue, Buckingham MK18 1LJ* E: saringer@btinternet.com

STANWAY, Peter David. b 48. K Coll Lon BD 71. St Aug Coll Cant 72. **d** 73 **p** 74. C Maidstone All SS w St Phil and H Trin *Cant* 73-77; Canada 77-84; C Waterlooville *Portsm* 84-87; R Laughton w Ripe and Chalvington *Chich* 87-90; Chapl Witney Community Hosp 90-91; C Wheatley w Forest Hill and Stanton St John *Ox* 91-92; C Cowley St Jas 93-02; rtd 02. *22 Collywood, Kennington, Oxford OX1 5NF* T: (01865) 739342

STAPLE, Miss Patricia Ann. b 54. Birm Univ BA 75. St Steph Ho Ox 00. **d** 02 **p** 05. C Dartmouth and Dittisham *Ex* 02-04; C Colyton, Musbury, Southleigh and Branscombe 04-07; V Athelney *B & W* from 07. *Athelney Vicarage, Stoke Road, North Curry, Taunton TA3 6HN* T: (01823) 490255 M: 07731-931683 E: triciastaple1@btinternet.com

STAPLEFORD, Robin Duncan. b 62. Aston Tr Scheme 92 St Jo Coll Nottm 94. **d** 96 **p** 97. C Evington *Leic* 96-99; TV Vale of Belvoir 00-08; R Upper Wensum Village Gp *Nor* from 08. *The Rectory, Market Hill, Colkirk, Fakenham NR21 7NU* T: (01328) 864128 E: staple@tiscali.co.uk

STAPLES, David. b 35. Jes Coll Ox BA 59 MA 63 BD 75. Linc Th Coll 59. **d** 61 **p** 62. C Kettering St Andr *Pet* 61-64; C Doncaster St Geo *Sheff* 64-66; Dioc Youth Chapl 66-71; V Mexborough 71-83; Chapl Montagu Hosp Mexborough 71-83; RD Wath *Sheff* 77-83; Hon Can Sheff Cathl 80-83; V W Haddon w Winwick *Pet* 83-88; RD Brixworth 83-89; V W Haddon w Winwick and Ravensthorpe 88-00; ACUPA Link Officer 90-00; rtd 00; PtO *Linc* from 00. *1 Sycamore Close, Bourne PE10 9RS* T: (01778) 423121

STAPLES, Jeffrey Joseph. b 61. St Jo Coll Nottm 97. **d** 99 **p** 00. C Prenton *Ches* 99-03; P-in-c Wallasey St Nic 03-04; P-in-c New Brighton All SS 03-04; V Wallasey St Nic w All SS from 04. *St Nicholas' Vicarage, 22 Groveland Road, Wallasey CH45 8JY* T: 0151-639 3589 E: jeffstaples4@hotmail.com

STAPLES, John Michael. b 45. STETS 94. **d** 97 **p** 98. C Tisbury *Sarum* 97-01; P-in-c Barford St Martin, Dinton, Baverstock etc 00-01; TV Nadder Valley 01-08; C Fovant, Sutton Mandeville and Teffont Evias etc 06-08; rtd 08; PtO *Sarum* from 08. *Crabstone Cottage, Locarno Road, Swanage BH19 1HY* T: (01929) 421715 E: john_staples@btinternet.com

STAPLES, John Wedgwood. b 42. Hertf Coll Ox BA 64 MA. Wycliffe Hall Ox 64. **d** 66 **p** 67. C Yardley St Edburgha *Birm* 66-69; C Knowle 69-74; R Barcombe *Chich* 74-81; V Old Windsor *Ox* 81-96; P-in-c Pangbourne w Tidmarsh and Sulham 96-99; R 99-07; rtd 07; PtO *Win* from 07. *6 Douglas Road, Bournemouth BH6 3ER* T: (01202) 425859 E: revd_john@yahoo.com

STAPLES, Canon Peter Brian. b 38. Bps' Coll Cheshunt 66. **d** 68 **p** 69. C Birkdale St Jas *Liv* 68-71; C Sevenoaks St Jo *Roch* 71-74; V Tweslothan *Truro* 74-80; V Truro St Paul and St Clem 80-02; Hon Can Truro Cathl 98-02; rtd 02; PtO *St E* from 03. *25 Osmund Walk, Bury St Edmunds IP33 3UU* T: (01284) 760620

STAPLETON, The Very Revd Henry Edward Champneys. b 32. MBE 09. FSA 74 Pemb Coll Cam BA 54 MA 58. Ely Th Coll 54. **d** 56 **p** 57. C York St Olave w St Giles 56-59; C Pocklington w Yapham-cum-Meltonby, Owsthorpe etc 59-61; R Seaton Ross w Everingham and Bielby and Harswell 61-67; RD Weighton 66-67; R Skelton by York 67-75; V Wroxham w Hoveton *Nor* 75-81; P-in-c Belaugh 76-81; Can Res and Prec Roch Cathl 81-88; Dean Carl 88-98; rtd 98; PtO *Leeds* from 98; *York* from 03. *Rockland House, 20 Marsh Gardens, Honley, Huddersfield HD9 6AF* T: (01484) 666629

STAPLETON, Leonard Charles. b 37. Chich Th Coll 75. **d** 77 **p** 78. C Crayford *Roch* 77-81; C Lamorbey H Redeemer 81-83; V Belvedere St Aug 83-89; V Beckenham St Jas 89-02; rtd 02; PtO *Roch* 03-04; *Win* from 04. *14 Howlett Close, Lymington SO41 9LA* T: (01590) 679414

STAPLETON, Robert Michael Vorley. b 25. ALCD 51. **d** 51 **p** 52. C Plymouth St Andr *Ex* 51-56; Chapl RN 56-60; C Surbiton St Matt *S'wark* 60-64; R Chenies and Lt Chalfont *Ox* 64-87; P-in-c Latimer w Flaunden 86-87; R Chenies and Lt Chalfont, Latimer and Flaunden 87-92; rtd 92. *Woodside, Swannaton Road, Dartmouth TQ6 9RL* T: (01803) 832972

STAPLETON, Robert Vauvelle. b 47. St Jo Coll Dur BA 70. Cranmer Hall Dur. **d** 71 **p** 72. C Moreton *Ches* 71-73; C Monkwearmouth All SS *Dur* 73-76; C Stranton 76-79; P-in-c Kelloe 79-86; V New Shildon 86-96; R Stoke Albany w Wilbarston and Ashley etc *Pet* 96-04; P-in-c Somborne w Ashley *Win* 04-12; Dioc Rural Officer 04-12; rtd 12; PtO *York* from 12. *14 St Mary's Way, Thirsk YO7 1BS* T: (01845) 522676 E: robertstapleton@hotmail.com

STARBUCK, Francis Tony. b 36. Kelham Th Coll 57. **d** 61 **p** 62. C Mansfield St Mark *S'well* 61-63; C Clifton H Trin CD 63-64; C Didcot *Ox* 67-71; P Missr California CD 71-75; R Barkham 74-75; V Hagbourne 75-82; V Maidenhead St Luke 82-87; V Te Puke St Jo New Zealand 87-96; Can Waiapu 90-94; V Clevedon All So 96-01; rtd 01; Chapl Selwyn Oaks Papakura New Zealand from 01. *16 Selwyn Oaks, 21 Youngs Road, Papakura 2110, New Zealand*

STARES, Canon Brian Maurice William. b 44. St Deiniol's Hawarden 74. **d** 74 **p** 75. C Risca *Mon* 74-77; V Newport St Steph and H Trin 77-87; V Fleur-de-Lis 87-92; Chapl HM Pris Belmarsh 92-93; Chapl HM YOI Dover 93-98; Feltham 98-99; V Bishton *Mon* 99-09; Hon Can St Woolos Cathl 07-09; rtd 09; P-in-c Las Palmas *Eur* from 14. *Los Porches 1-16, Calle Inglaterra 5, 35100 Playa del Ingles, Gran Caneria, Spain*

STARES, Mrs Olive Beryl. b 33. Sarum Th Coll 83. **dss** 86 **d** 87 **p** 94. Crofton *Portsm* 86-87; Hon C 87-01; rtd 01. *62 Mancroft Avenue, Hill Head, Fareham PO14 2DD* T: (01329) 668540

STARK, Mrs Beverley Ann. b 52. Bp Otter Coll CertEd 73 EMMTC 92. **d** 92 **p** 94. Par Dn Bulwell St Jo *S'well* 92-94; C 94-97; TV Bestwood 97-03; V Bestwood Em w St Mark 03-04; R Ironstone Villages *Leic* from 04; RD Framland 06-11. *The Rectory, 23 Melton Road, Waltham on the Wolds, Melton Mowbray LE14 4AJ* T: (01664) 464600 E: beverley.stark@ntlworld.com

STARK, John Jordan. b 40. Hull Univ BA 62. St Chad's Coll Dur. **d** 64 **p** 65. C Buxton *Derby* 64-67; C Wolborough w Newton Abbot *Ex* 67-74; R Belstone 74-79; P-in-c Plymouth St Gabr 79-80; V 80-10; rtd 10. *11 Warwick Orchard Close, Plymouth PL5 3NZ* T: (01752) 787132

STARK, Margaret Alison. b 46. Univ of Wales BA 70 BA 71. St Mich Coll Llan. **d** 90 **p** 97. C Llanishen and Lisvane *Llan* 90-93; C Llanishen 93-94; C Aberavon 94-98; R Llanfabon 98-01; rtd 01; PtO *Llan* from 04. *6 Alexandra House, Beach Road, Penarth CF64 1FN* T: (029) 2070 1303

STARK, Michael. b 35. Dur Univ BSc 56 SEN 58. Chich Th Coll 58. **d** 60 **p** 61. C Middlesbrough St Paul *York* 60-64; C S Bank 64-66; R Skelton in Cleveland 66-74; P-in-c Upleatham 66-67; R 67-74; Asst Chapl HM Pris Wormwood Scrubs 74-76; Liv 75-76; Chapl HM Pris Featherstone 76-83; Ex 83-89; Leic 89-97; rtd 97; PtO *Leic* 99-12; *S'well* from 99; P-in-c Rotterdam *Eur* 04-06. *28 St Peter's Road, Leicester LE2 1DA*

STARK TOLLER, Peter Sheridan. b 74. Pemb Coll Ox BA 96 MA Nottm Univ PGCE 97. Wycliffe Hall Ox 11. **d** 13 **p** 14. C Dibden *Win* from 13. *2 Corsair Drive, Dibden, Southampton SO45 5UF* M: 07758-006578 E: peter@starktoller.co.uk

STARKEY, Gerald Dennis. b 34. Qu Coll Birm 79. **d** 82 **p** 83. C Wilnecote *Lich* 82-86; Min Stoke-upon-Trent 86-90; P-in-c W Bromwich St Pet 90-00; rtd 00; PtO *Lich* 01-14. *6 Hazelwood Drive, Wednesfield, Wolverhampton WV11 1SH* T: (01902) 726252

STARKEY, Michael Stuart. b 63. LMH Ox BA 85 Nottm Univ BTh 92 MA 93. St Jo Coll Nottm 90. **d** 93 **p** 94. C Ealing St Mary *Lon* 93-95; C Brownswood Park 95-97; P-in-c 97-01; V Twickenham Common H Trin 01-09; V Kennington St Mark *S'wark* 09-11; V Llanidloes w Llangurig *Ban* 11-13; Can Ban Cathl 12-13; Tutor Wilson Carlile Coll of Evang from 14; PtO *Man* from 14. *1 Princess Court, 38 Circular Road, Manchester M20 3LP* T: 0161-434 6306 M: 07870-281055 E: revstarkey@yahoo.co.uk

STARKEY, Ms Naomi Ernestine. b 65. LMH Ox BA 86. St Seiriol Cen 11. d 14 p 15. NSM Bro Cyfeiliog a Mawddwy *Ban* 14-15; C Bro Enlli from 15. *Y Ficerdy, Aberdaron, Pwllheli LL53 8BP* E: naomi.starkey@gmail.com

STARKEY, Naomi Faith Ezitt (Ness). b 61. Lanc Univ BSc 97 MA 02 Leeds Univ MA 07 RGN 83 RM 85. NOC 04. d 07 p 08. C Broughton *Blackb* 07-10; LtO from 10; C Braunschweig Germany 10-11; V Ingol *Blackb* from 12. *St Margaret's Vicarage, 1A St Margaret's Close, Ingol, Preston PR2 3ZU* T: (01772) 727208 E: ness.starkey@yahoo.co.uk

STARKEY, Patrick Robin. b 37. d 64 p 65. C Tonbridge SS Pet and Paul *Roch* 64-68; Asst Chapl Sherborne Sch 68-72; Scripture Union 73-85; rtd 99. *14 Heol Twrch, Lower Cwmtwrch, Swansea SA9 2TD*

STARKEY, Simon Mark. b 36. Liv Univ BA 78 MA 96. Clifton Th Coll 63. d 66 p 67. C Ox St Ebbe w St Pet 66-72; Community Chapl CPAS Kirkdale 72-75; TV Toxteth Park St Bede *Liv* 75-78; P-in-c 78-80; V 80-90; RD Toxteth 81-89; Chapl Ches Coll of HE 90-96; TV St Luke in the City *Liv* 96-03; rtd 03; PtO *Liv* from 03. *23 Merlin Street, Liverpool L8 8HY* T: 0151-709 0208

STARKEY, Susan Anne. b 52. St Jo Coll Nottm. d 97 p 98. C Watford St Luke *St Alb* 97-02; C Oxhey All SS 02-04; V Findern *Derby* from 04; V Willington from 04. *The Vicarage, 66 Castle Way, Willington, Derby DE65 6BU* T: (01283) 703928 E: susan.starkey@btopenworld.com

STARKINGS, Susan Anne. b 52. Kent Univ BSc 82 Sheff City Poly MSc 90 Punjab Univ PhD 93. SEITE 08. d 11 p 12. NSM G7 Benefice *Cant* 11-14; C King's Wood from 14. *The Forge, Godmersham Park, Godmersham, Canterbury CT4 7DT* T: (01227) 730925 E: sue.starkings@btinternet.com

STARNES, Peter Henry. b 19. St Jo Coll Cam BA 42 MA 47 Ch Ch Coll Cant PGCE 72 LTCL 74. Linc Th Coll 42. d 44 p 45. C Gillingham *Sarum* 44-50; C St Peter-in-Thanet *Cant* 50-52; CF 52-55; Hon CF from 55; R Hothfield *Cant* 56-60; V Westwell 56-65; R Eastwell w Boughton Aluph 60-65; rtd 84. *Whitebeams, High Halden, Ashford TN26 3LY* T: (01233) 850245

STARNS, Helen Edna. *See* PATTEN, Helen Edna

STARR, Michael Richard. b 43. Sarum Th Coll 65. d 68 p 69. C Plymouth St Pet *Ex* 68-72; C Blackpool St Paul *Blackb* 72-74; V Burnley St Cuth 74-79; C Eastbourne St Mary *Chich* 79-84; P-in-c Eastbourne Ch Ch 84-87; V 87-88; R Guernsey Ste Marie du Castel *Win* 88-01; V Guernsey St Matt 94-01; Vice-Dean Guernsey 99-01; P-in-c Win St Bart 01-08; rtd 09; PtO *Win* from 09. *62 Beresford Road, Chandler's Ford, Eastleigh SO53 2LY* T: (023) 8036 1505 E: michael_starr@hotmail.co.uk

STARRS, Lindsey Carolyn. b 49. Alsager Coll of Educn CertEd 70 Liv Inst of HE BEd 85. Ripon Coll Cuddesdon 00. d 02 p 03. C Penkridge *Lich* 02-06; TV N Creedy *Ex* from 06. *The Rectory, Church Street, Morchard Bishop, Crediton EX17 6PJ* T: (01363) 877221 E: starrs@lstarrs.fsnet.com

STARTIN, Nicola Gail. b 57. K Coll Lon LLB 79. St Steph Ho Ox 88. d 90 p 96. C Wellingborough All SS *Pet* 90-92; NSM Pyle w Kenfig *Llan* 94-95; Asst Chapl Mid Kent Healthcare NHS Trust 95-97; Chapl HM Pris E Sutton Park 97-00; Chapl HM Pris Haslar 00-02; Chapl Haslar Immigration Removal Cen from 02. *Haslar Immigration Removal Centre, 2 Dolphin Way, Gosport PO12 2AW* T: (023) 9260 4047 E: nicola.startin@hmps.gsi.gov.uk

STATHAM, Brian Edward. b 55. K Coll Lon MA AKC 76. St Steph Ho Ox 77. d 78 p 79. C Ches H Trin 78-81; C Birkenhead Priory 81-82; TV 82-86; V Newton 86-91; SSF 91-94; TV Horsham *Chich* 95-99; Chapl Horsham Gen Hosp 95-99; TV Ches 99-03; P-in-c Stockport St Matt 03-07; C Edgeley and Cheadle Heath 07-10; V Milton *Lich* from 10. *The Vicarage, Baddeley Green Lane, Stoke-on-Trent ST2 7EY* T: (01782) 534062 E: brianstatham@aol.com

STATHAM, John Francis. b 31. Kelham Th Coll 51. d 56 p 57. C Ilkeston St Mary *Derby* 56-58; C New Mills 58-59; V 69-81; C Newbold w Dunston 59-62; PC Ridgeway 62-69; RD Glossop 78-81; R Matlock 81-89; R Killamarsh 89-93; rtd 93; PtO *Derby* from 93; S'well from 93. *33 Ackford Drive, The Meadows, Worksop S80 1YG* T: (01909) 476031

STATHER, Thomas William John. b 79. Van Mildert Coll Dur BSc 00. St Steph Ho Ox BTh 04. d 04 p 05. C Colchester St Jas and St Paul w All SS etc *Chelmsf* 04-08; P-in-c Tunstall *Lich* 08-10; V Goldenhill and Tunstall from 10. *Christ Church Vicarage, 26 Stanley Street, Tunstall, Stoke-on-Trent ST6 6BW* T: (01782) 838288 E: john_stather@hotmail.com

STATON, Preb Geoffrey. b 40. Wells Th Coll 64. d 66 p 67. C Wednesfield St Thos *Lich* 66-69; C Cannock 69-72; V Cheddleton 72-82; RD Leek 77-82; V Harlescott 82-90; TR Penkridge 90-05; rtd 05; C Colton, Colwich and Gt Haywood *Lich* 05-10; C Abbots Bromley, Blithfield, Colton, Colwich etc 11-13; Preb Lich Cathl 87-10; PtO from 13. *5 Hunters Close, Great Haywood, Stafford ST18 0GF* T: (01889) 882081 M: 07971-016494 E: geoffrey.staton@virgin.net

STATTER, Ms Deborah Hilary. b 55. d 00 p 01. OLM Everton St Pet *Liv* 00-02; OLM Everton St Pet w St Chrys 02-04; C 04-08; P-in-c Netherton 08-14; TR from 14. *St Oswald's Vicarage, 183 St Oswald's Lane, Bootle L30 5SR* T: 0151-525 1882 M: 07952-105466

STAUNTON, Mrs Mary Provis. b 52. Leic Univ BSc 74. EMMTC 05. d 07 p 08. NSM Mickleover All SS *Derby* 07-14; NSM Mickleover St Jo 07-14; NSM Mickleover from 14. *165A Pastures Hill, Littleover, Derby DE23 4AZ* T: (01332) 510264 E: mps52@staunton.force9.co.uk

STAVELEY-WADHAM, Robert Andrew. b 43. ACII. Ridley Hall Cam 79. d 81 p 82. C Saffron Walden w Wendens Ambo and Littlebury *Chelmsf* 81-84; P-in-c Austrey and Warton *Birm* 84-87; PtO *Chich* 87-02; Ely 88-96; P-in-c Tillington *Chich* 02-07; P-in-c Duncton 02-07; P-in-c Upwaltham 02-07; rtd 07. *2 Little Bognor Cottage, Little Bognor, Fittleworth, Pulborough RH20 1JT* T: (01798) 865668 E: bobswpic@aol.com

STAVERT, Miss Rachel Louise. b 66. Coll of Ripon & York St Jo BEd 88. Cranmer Hall Dur 10. d 12 p 13. C Penrith w Newton Reigny and Plumpton Wall *Carl* from 12. *18 Skirsgill Close, Penrith CA11 8QF* T: (01768) 744687 M: 07813-962740 E: revrachstav@gmail.com

STAVROU, Stephen Francis. b 83. St Jo Coll Cam BA 05 MA 09 Peterho Cam MPhil 09. Westcott Ho Cam 07. d 09 p 10. C Bedford Park *Lon* 09-13; Succ S'wark Cathl from 13; Chapl K Coll Lon from 13. *St Paul's Vicarage, 54 Kipling Street, London SE1 3RU* T: (020) 7367 6705 M: 07801-551592 E: stephen.stavrou@southwark.anglican.org

STAYNINGS, Margaret Rose. b 42. d 13 p 14. PtO *Bris* from 13. *5 Cotman Walk, Bristol BS7 9UG* T: 0117-935 4540 M: 07542-191959 E: davenmar@hotmail.co.uk

STAYTE, Miss Samantha Mary. b 71. Ex Coll Ox BA 92 MPhil 02 Ex Univ PGCE 95. Westcott Ho Cam 10. d 13 p 14. C Summertown *Ox* from 13. *15 Aldrich Road, Oxford OX2 7SS* E: samanthastayte@hotmail.com

STAZIKER, Catherine. b 61. Hull Univ BA 84 Anglia Ruskin Univ BA 13. Westcott Ho Cam 10. d 12 p 13. C Millhouses H Trin *Sheff* 12-15; C Abbeydale St Jo 12-15; C Abbeydale and Millhouses from 15. *6 Kenwell Drive, Sheffield S17 4PJ* T: 0114-235 1144 M: 07968-316812 E: catherinestaziker@btinternet.com

STEACY, William Leslie. b 59. UCD BAgrSc 82 MAgrSc 88 TCD BTh 06. CITC 03. d 06 p 07. C Dunboyne and Rathmolyon *M & K* 06-10; I Kingscourt w Syddan from 10. *The Rectory, Kingscourt, Co Cavan, Republic of Ireland* T: (00353) (42) 966 7255 E: williamsteacy@eircom.net

STEAD, Canon Andrew Michael. b 63. BA 84 Heythrop Coll MA 12. Coll of Resurr Mirfield 84. d 87 p 88. C Wellingborough All Hallows *Pet* 87-90; Chapl St Alb Abbey *St Alb* 90-94; Chapl Aldenham Sch Herts 94-04 and 12-13; Ho Master 01-08; Teacher 08-13; PtO *St Alb* 04-12; NSM St Alb Abbey 05-13; Can Res Lich Cathl and Chapl Lich Cathl Sch from 13. *8 The Close, Lichfield WS13 7LD* E: rev.amstead@gmail.com

STEAD, Christopher Andrew. b 86. Leeds Univ LLB 07 Barrister (Middle Temple) 08. Oak Hill Th Coll 11. d 15. C Grange Park St Pet *Lon* from 15. *5 Ruston Gardens, London N14 4PF* M: 07974-895751 E: christopher_stead@hotmail.co.uk

STEAD, Philip John. b 60. Sheff Univ LLB 82 City of Lon Poly ACII 85. Linc Th Coll 95. d 95 p 96. C Warsop S'well 95-99; P-in-c Forest Town from 99; P-in-c Mansfield Oak Tree Lane from 07; P-in-c Mansfield St Lawr from 13. *The Vicarage, Old Mill Lane, Forest Town, Mansfield NG19 0EP* T: (01623) 622177

STEAD, Timothy James. b 60. Ex Univ BSc 82. St Steph Ho Ox 93. d 95 p 97. C Broseley w Benthall, Jackfield, Linley etc *Heref* 95-99; TV Haywards Heath St Wilfrid *Chich* 99-07; P-in-c Headington Quarry Ox 07-10; V from 10; AD Cowley from 14. *The Vicarage, 46 Quarry Road, Headington, Oxford OX3 8NU* T: (01865) 307939 or 762931 E: tim_stead@btinternet.com

STEADMAN, Mrs Gloria Ann. b 44. STETS BA 04. d 04 p 05. NSM Farington Portsm 04-08; NSM W Leigh 08-15; PtO from 15. *Lane End House, 63 Glamorgan Road, Waterlooville PO8 0TS* T: (023) 9259 5561 E: gloria_nembles@yahoo.co.uk

STEADMAN, Mark John. b 74. Southn Univ LLB 95 Ch Coll Cam BA 01 MA 05 Barrister-at-Law (Inner Temple) 96. Westcott Ho Cam 99. d 02 p 03. C Portsea St Mary *Portsm* 02-05; P-in-c Camberwell St Phil and St Mark *S'wark* 05-12; AD Bermondsey 08-11; Bp's Chapl from 11. *Trinity House, 4 Chapel Court, London SE1 1HW* T: (020) 7939 9422 E: mark.steadman@southwark.anglican.org

STEADMAN, Mrs Wendy Anne Eleanor. b 35. Somerville Coll Ox BA 56 MA 61. d 06 p 07. NSM Lache cum Saltney *Ches* from 06. *32 Curzon Park South, Chester CH4 8AB* T: (01244) 682989 E: waesteadman@btinternet.com

STEADMAN-ALLEN, Miss Barbara. b 53. Birm Univ BMus 77 Spurgeon's Coll Lon MTh 00 Trent Park Coll of Educn

CertEd 74 ARCM 83. Cranmer Hall Dur 88. **d** 90 **p** 94. C Chessington *Guildf* 90-94; C Chertsey 94-99; P-in-c Mickleham 99-01; C Leatherhead and Mickleham 01-04; Chapl Box Hill Sch 99-04; TV Surrey Weald *Guildf* from 04. *The Vicarage, Horsham Road, Holmwood, Dorking RH5 4JX*
T: (01306) 889118   M: 07817-006254   E: revdbsa@gmail.com

STEADY, Miss Vilda May. b 51. Linc Th Coll 87. **d** 89 **p** 94. Par Dn Cannock *Lich* 89-91; Par Dn Hammerwich 91-94; C 94-95; Asst Chapl Eastbourne Hosps NHS Trust 95-97; Chapl Luton and Dunstable Hosp NHS Foundn Trust 97-01; Sen Chapl Jas Paget Healthcare NHS Trust 01-11; rtd 11. *4 Cliff Cottages, Warren Road, Hopton, Great Yarmouth NR31 9BN*

STEAR, Michael Peter Hutchinson. b 47. Goldsmiths' Coll Lon TCert 68. Wycliffe Hall Ox 71. **d** 74 **p** 75. C Streatham Vale H Redeemer *S'wark* 74-77; C-in-c Ramsgate St Mark *Cant* 77-82; V 82-83; Min Jersey St Paul Prop Chpl *Win* 83-94; TR Radipole and Melcombe Regis *Sarum* 94-00; Chapl Weymouth Coll 94-97; rtd 00; PtO *Sarum* from 01. *Flat 3, 5 Widcombe Street, Poundbury, Dorchester DT3 6BH*

STEAR, Mrs Patricia Ann. b 38. Birm Univ BSc 60. **d** 97 **p** 98. OLM Bradford Peverell, Stratton, Frampton etc *Sarum* 97-09; rtd 09; PtO *Sarum* from 09. *Westwood House, Bradford Peverell, Dorchester DT2 9SE* T: (01305) 889227   F: 889718
E: patstear@saqnet.co.uk

STEBBING, Christopher Henry. b 64. G&C Coll Cam MEng 87 MA 90. Cranmer Hall Dur 98. **d** 00 **p** 01. C Malin Bridge *Sheff* 00-04; V Sheff St Jo 04-12; Dir IME 4-7 08-12; V Lodge Moor St Luke from 12. *St Luke's House, 18 Blackbrook Road, Sheffield S10 4LP* T: 0114-230 3538
E: chris.stebbing@sheffield.anglican.org

STEBBING, Michael Langdale (Nicolas). b 46. Univ of Zimbabwe BA 68 UNISA MTh 86. Coll of Resurr Mirfield. **d** 74 **p** 75. C Borrowdale *Carl* 74-75; P-in-c Chikwaka Rhodesia 76-77; S Africa 79-86; CR from 80. *House of the Resurrection, Stocks Bank Road, Mirfield WF14 0BN* T: (01924) 494318
E: nstebbing@mirfield.org.uk

STEDMAN, Barrie John. b 49. **d** 00 **p** 01. OLM Mildenhall *St E* 00-07. *The Cottage, Tudor Grange, Poy Street Green, Rattlesden, Bury St Edmunds IP30 0RX* T: (01638) 750505
M: 07864-076896   E: barriestedman@aol.com

STEDMAN, Preb Michael Sydney. b 34. MRICS 58. Clifton Th Coll 62. **d** 65 **p** 66. C Lindfield *Chich* 65-68; C Gt Baddow *Chelmsf* 68-73; TV Ashby w Thurton, Claxton and Carleton *Nor* 73-75; P-in-c 75-85; TV Rockland St Mary w Hellington 73-75; P-in-c 75-85; TV Framingham Pigot 73-75; P-in-c 75-85; TV Bramerton w Surlingham 73-75; P-in-c 75-85; TV Bergh Apton w Yelverton 73-75; P-in-c 75-85; RD Loddon 78-85; R Church Stretton *Heref* 85-99; RD Condover 88-96; Preb Heref Cathl 94-99; rtd 99; PtO *St E* from 00. *44 The Mowbrays, Framlingham, Woodbridge IP13 9DL*
T: (01728) 724479   E: michael@stedmanm.freeserve.co.uk

STEDMAN, Robert Alfred. b 24. Qu Coll Birm 50. **d** 52 **p** 53. C Portchester *Portsm* 52-55; V Brighton St Anne *Chich* 55-61; V Salehurst 61-76; R Newhaven 76-90; rtd 90; PtO *Chich* 90-99. *12 Lady Wootton's Green, Canterbury CT1 1NG*

STEED, Christopher Denis. b 55. Lon Univ BD 92 Bris Univ MSc 03 Ex Univ PGCE 01 EdD 05. Sarum Th Coll 05. **d** 06 **p** 07. C Yatton Moor *B & W* 06-10; P-in-c Combe Martin, Berrynarbor, Lynton, Brendon etc *Ex* 11-15; TR Totton *Win* from 15. *The Rectory, 92 Salisbury Road, Totton, Southampton SO40 3JA* M: 07704-138433   T: (023) 8184 3308
E: chrissteed@uwclub.net

STEED, The Ven Helene. b 70. Uppsala Univ MDiv 95. Past Inst Uppsala 95. **p** 96. C Stora Melby Sweden 96-97; TV Essunga 97-04; Dean's V Cork Cathl 04-08; I Clones w Killeevan *Clogh* from 08; Preb Clogh Cathl from 11; Adn Clogh from 14. *The Rectory, Scotshouse, Clones, Co Monaghan, Republic of Ireland* T: (00353) (47) 56962   M: 86-860 3112
E: helenesteed@yahoo.com

STEEL, Coralie Mary. b 47. Bedf Coll Lon BA 69 Solicitor 73. St Mich Coll Llan 98. **d** 01 **p** 02. NSM Llangunnor w Cwmffrwd *St D* 01-12; rtd 12; PtO *St D* from 12. *Llwyn Celyn, 24 Picton Terrace, Carmarthen SA31 3BX* T: (01267) 236369

STEEL, Graham Reginald. b 51. Cam Univ MA. Trin Coll Bris 80. **d** 83 **p** 84. C Gt Parndon *Chelmsf* 83-86; C Barking St Marg w St Patr 86-89; P-in-c Westcliff St Cedd 89-96; P-in-c Prittlewell St Pet 92-96; Chapl Southend Health Care NHS Trust 89-92; V Prittlewell St Pet w Westcliff St Cedd *Chelmsf* 96-07; P-in-c S Trin Broads *Nor* 07-08; R from 08. *The Rectory, Main Road, Fleggburgh, Great Yarmouth NR29 3AG* T: (01493) 368210   E: grahamsteel@tiscali.co.uk

STEEL, Leslie Frederick. b 34. Webster Univ Geneva MA 88. St Jo Coll Auckland 57 LTh 65. **d** 59 **p** 60. C Roslyn New Zealand 59-62; V Waimea Plains 62-69; CF 70-73; Singapore 72-73; V Dunstan New Zealand 74-81; Adn Otago 77-82; V Anderson's Bay and Chapl Police Force 82-86; Can Dunedin

Cathl 82-85; Adn Dunedin 85-86; Hon C Geneva *Eur* 87-90; Chapl Lausanne 90-97; PtO *Pet* 98-99; P-in-c Potterspury, Furtho, Yardley Gobion and Cosgrove 99-02; R Potterspury w Furtho and Yardley Gobion etc 02-04; rtd 04. *14 Kaspar Street, Warkworth 0910, New Zealand* T: (0064) (9) 422 2560
E: ehsteel@xtra.co.nz

STEEL, Norman William. b 53. Sarum & Wells Th Coll 85. **d** 87 **p** 88. C S Woodham Ferrers *Chelmsf* 87-91; R Woolavington w Cossington and Bawdrip *B & W* 91-99; P-in-c Pitminster w Corfe 99-02; Chapl Richard Huish Coll Taunton 99-05; PtO *B & W* 02-05. *28 Wilton Street, Taunton TA1 3JR*
T: (01823) 368161   E: norman.steel@sky.com

STEEL, Richard John. b 57. Dur Univ BA 79 Cam Univ MA 86 Edin Univ MTh 97. Ridley Hall Cam 81. **d** 84 **p** 85. C Hull St Jo Newland *York* 84-87; Relig Broadcasting Officer *Derby* 88-92; Dioc Communications Officer *Blackb* 92-97; Communication Dir CMS 97-05; NSM Stoke-next-Guildf 00-05; R Kirkheaton *Leeds* from 05; RD Almondbury *Wakef* 06-14; AD *Leeds* from 14. *The New Rectory, Church Lane, Kirkheaton, Huddersfield HD5 0BH* T: (01484) 532410
E: richard.steel@ntlworld.com

STEEL, Thomas Molyneux. b 39. Man Univ BA 61. Ripon Hall Ox 61. **d** 63 **p** 64. C Newc H Cross 63-66; P-in-c Man St Aid 66-71; R Failsworth St Jo 71-79; P-in-c Farnham Royal *Ox* 79-81; P-in-c Hedgerley 80-81; R Farnham Royal w Hedgerley 81-91; V Prescot *Liv* 91-03; rtd 03; PtO *Lon* from 04. *20 Barnet Way, London NW7 3BH* T: (020) 8906 0271
E: t.steel@virgin.net

STEELE, Alan Christopher. b 63. Cape Town Univ BA 85 Univ of Zimbabwe BA 91. Gaul Ho Harare 89. **d** 91 **p** 93. C Harare St Mary Magd Zimbabwe 91-93; C Harare St Luke 93-95; Chapl Ruzawi Sch 96-99; CF from 99. *c/o MOD Chaplains (Army)* F: 381824   T: (01264) 383430

STEELE, Alan Lindsay. b 44. **d** 09 **p** 10. OLM Billingborough Gp *Linc* from 09. *7 Paddock Estate, Horbling, Sleaford NG34 0PQ* T: (01529) 240602

STEELE, Derek James. b 53. St Jo Coll Nottm. **d** 97 **p** 98. Aux Min Ballywillan *Conn* 97-12; NSM Armoy w Loughguile and Drumtullagh from 13. *106 Mountsandel Road, Coleraine BT52 1TA* T: (028) 7035 1633

STEELE, Edwin Harry. b 80. Mattersey Hall BA 05. Ridley Hall Cam 06. **d** 08 **p** 09. C Ecclesall *Sheff* 08-11; P-in-c Greenhill from 11. *St Peter's Vicarage, Reney Avenue, Sheffield S8 7FN*
T: 0114-327 3103   E: edwinharrysteele@gmail.com *or* harry@saintpeters.co

STEELE, The Ven Gordon John. b 55. Kent Univ BA 76 Worc Coll Ox BA 82 MA 87. Coll of Resurr Mirfield 82. **d** 84 **p** 85. C Greenhill St Jo *Lon* 84-88; TV Uxbridge 88-94; V Northampton St Alb *Pet* 94-01; V Pet St Jo 01-12; RD Pet 04-10; Adn Oakham from 12; Can Pet Cathl from 04. *Diocesan Office, The Palace, Minster Precincts, Peterborough PE1 1YB*
T: (01733) 887017
E: archdeacon.oakham@peterborough-diocese.org.uk

STEELE, Keith Atkinson. b 28. CEng MIMechE FInstMC. Qu Coll Birm Oak Hill Th Coll 80. **d** 81 **p** 82. NSM Westoning w Tingrith *St Alb* 81-87; NSM Chalgrave 87-88; P-in-c 88-96; RD Dunstable 91-96; PtO from 96. *Mariner's Lodge, Church Road, Westoning, Bedford MK45 5JW* T: (01525) 714111

STEELE, Peter Gerald. b 44. Bournemouth Tech Coll BSc 67 Essex Univ MSc 69. Sarum & Wells Th Coll 91. **d** 93 **p** 94. C Beaminster Area *Sarum* 93-97; P-in-c Aldermaston w Wasing and Brimpton *Ox* 97-08; P-in-c Woolhampton w Midgham and Beenham Valance 05-08; R Aldermaston and Woolhampton 08-10; AD Bradfield 07-10; rtd 10. *11 Mayfield Way, Ferndown BH22 9HP* T: (01202) 895927
E: p.steele343@btinternet.com

STEELE, Canon Terence. b 54. Linc Th Coll 85. **d** 87 **p** 88. C New Sleaford *Linc* 87-90; V Cowbit 90-95; P-in-c Burgh le Marsh 95-97; V 97-06; P-in-c Orby 95-97; V 97-06; P-in-c Bratoft w Irby-in-the-Marsh 95-97; R 97-06; P-in-c Welton-le-Marsh w Gunby 95-97; R 97-06; R Burgh Gp from 06; RD Calcewaithe and Candleshoe from 05; Can and Preb Linc Cathl from 07. *The Vicarage, Glebe Rise, Burgh le Marsh, Skegness PE24 5BL* T: (01754) 810216   E: father.terry@btclick.com

STEELE-PERKINS, Mrs Barbara Anita. b 46. Whitelands Coll Lon CertEd 68 Spurgeon's Coll MTh 98. STETS 99. **d** 01 **p** 02. Tutor Local Min Progr *Guildf* from 95; NSM Wisley w Pyrford 01-04; NSM Haslemere and Grayswood from 04. *Church House, Church Close, Grayswood, Haslemere GU27 2DB*
T: (01428) 656504   E: barbarasteeleperkins@tiscali.co.uk

STEEN, The Ven Jane Elizabeth. b 64. Newnham Coll Cam BA 88 MA 90 PhD 92. Westcott Ho Cam 93. **d** 96 **p** 97. C Chipping Barnet w Arkley *St Alb* 96-99; Chapl and Personal Asst to Bp S'wark 99-05; Hon Chapl S'wark Cathl 00-05; Chan and Can Th and Dir Min Tr 05-13; Adn S'wark from 13. *2 Harmsworth Mews, London SE11 4SQ* T: (020) 7820 8079 *or* 7939 9449   E: jane.steen@southwark.anglican.org

STEER, Norman William. b 35. MBE 00. SRN 57. EAMTC 01. d 03 p 04. NSM Dickleburgh and The Pulhams *Nor* 03-14; PtO from 14. *Brook Cottage, Harleston Road, Starston, Harleston IP20 9NL* T: (01379) 854245 M: 07941-473255
E: norman@nandrsteer.com

STEER, Simon Morrison. b 58. York Univ BA 81. Princeton Th Sem MDiv 87 Westmr Th Sem (USA) PhD 02. d 12 p 13. Chapl Abingdon Sch from 12; NSM N Abingdon *Ox* from 12. *29 Park Road, Abingdon OX14 1DA* T: (01235) 536529
E: simon.steer@abingdon.org.uk

STEIN, Ms Ann Elizabeth. b 57. Loughb Univ BSc 78 Liv Hope MA 01. NOC 05. d 07 p 08. C Ormskirk *Liv* 07-11; P-in-c Abram from 11; P-in-c Bickershaw from 11. *The Vicarage, 1 Vicarage Gardens, Abram, Wigan WN2 5SA* T: (01942) 865647 E: revannstein@yahoo.com

STEINBERG, Eric Reed (Joseph). b 65. Trin Coll Bris BA 94. d 94 p 95. C Chigwell and Chigwell Row *Chelmsf* 94-99; Dir Y2000 99-00; Dir Jews for Jesus UK 00-05; Dir CMS from 05; PtO *Ox* from 12. *47 New Bridge Street, Witney OX18 1YA* T: 08456-201799 E: kosherjoe@mac.com

STELL, Peter Donald. b 50. Leeds Univ 74 Southn Univ BA 81 Man Univ 93 MInstM. Sarum & Wells Th Coll 78. d 81 p 82. C Rothwell w Lofthouse *Ripon* 81-85; TV Brayton *York* 85-87; Chapl Asst Leybourne Grange Hosp W Malling 87-88; Chapl Asst Kent, Sussex and Pembury Hosps Tunbridge Wells 87-88; C Spalding St Jo w Deeping St Nicholas *Linc* 87-93; Chapl S Lincs HA Mental Handicap Unit 88-93; Chapl HM Pris Liv 93-94; Chapl HM Pris Wayland 94-99; Chapl HM Pris Grendon and Spring Hill 99-02; Chapl HM Pris Rye Hill 02-05; Chapl HM Pris N Sea Camp 05-13; Chapl Thorpe Hall Hospice from 14. *Thorpe Hall Hospice, Thorpe Road, Peterborough PE3 6LW* T: (01733) 330060 E: peter.stell@suerydercare.org

STENHOUSE, Joan Frances Fleming. b 45. RGN 66. Ab Dioc Tr Course 82. dss 84 d 86 p 94. Ellon and Cruden Bay *Ab* 84-97; NSM 86-97; Bp's Chapl for Tr and Educn 95-97; Asst P Cuminestown 97-00; C Nova Scotia St Martin Canada from 00. *27 Birch Grove, Upper Tantallon NS B3Z 1L1, Canada* E: jstenhouse@bwr.eastlink.ca

STENTIFORD, Canon Pauline Cecilia Elizabeth. b 48. EAMTC 98. d 00 p 01. NSM Gt and Lt Bealings w Playford and Culpho *St E* 00-03; P-in-c 03-13; RD Woodbridge 05-11; Hon Can St E Cathl 08-13; rtd 14; PtO *St E* from 14. *Sheepstor, Boyton, Woodbridge IP12 3LH* T: (01394) 411469
E: pauline@stentiford.com

STEPHEN, Canon Kenneth George. b 47. Strathclyde Univ BA 69 Edin Univ BD 72. Edin Th Coll 69. d 72 p 73. C Ayr *Glas* 72-75; R Renfrew 75-80; R Motherwell 80-93; R Wishaw 80-93; R Kilmarnock 93-06; R Dalbeattie 06-14; Syn Clerk 87-12; Can St Mary's Cathl 87-12; Hon Can St Mary's Cathl 12-14; rtd 14. *32 Dalmellington Road, Ayr KA7 3PY*
E: kenstephen253@btinternet.com

STEPHEN, Robert. b 63. Lon Bible Coll BA 85 Westmr Coll Ox MTh 97 FSAScot 01. EMMTC 03. d 04 p 05. In Bapt Min 85-97; NSM Burbage w Aston Flamville *Leic* 04-15; Chapl K Henry VIII Sch Cov 07-15; R Handsworth St Mary *Birm* from 15. *The Rectory, 228 Hamstead Road, Handsworth, Birmingham B20 2RB* M: 07957-312892 T: 0121-554 3407
E: rector@handsworthstmary.org

STEPHENI, Frederick William. b 28. TD 73. FSAScot 81 FRSA 82 Cranfield Inst of Tech MSc 82. Lambeth STh 83 Qu Coll Birm 54. d 55 p 56. C Arnold *S'well* 55-57; P-in-c 57-58; P-in-c Hucknall Torkard 58-59; Chapl Stoke-on-Trent City Gen Hosp 59-62; Chapl N Staffs R Infirmary Stoke-on-Trent 59-62; CF (TA) 60-88; Chapl K Coll Hosp Lon 62-63; R Cotgrave *S'well* 63-76; V Owthorpe 63-76; Chapl Addenbrooke's Hosp Cam 76-88; LtO *Ely* 76-99; rtd 88; PtO *York* from 00. *64A Scarborough Road, Norton, Malton YO17 8AE* T: (01653) 694995

STEPHENS, Anthony Wayne. b 54. Surrey Univ BSc 80. St Jo Coll Nottm 02. d 04 p 05. C Preston w Sutton Poyntz, Littlemoor etc *Sarum* 04-08; Pioneer Min Weymouth Town Cen 08-13; P-in-c S Hill w Callington *Truro* from 13; P-in-c Linkinhorne from 13; Chapl Duchy Coll from 15. *The Rectory, Stoke Climsland, Callington PL17 8NZ* T: (01579) 371496
E: revtonystephens@icloud.com

STEPHENS, Canon Archibald John. b 15. Selw Coll Cam BA 37 MA 44. Wells Th Coll 46. d 47 p 48. C Gt Malvern St Mary *Worc* 47-50; Nigeria 50-68 and 70-71; Hon Can Ondo 57-71; Hon Can Owerri from 71; C Swindon Ch Ch *Bris* 68-70; C-in-c Ash Vale CD *Guildf* 71-72; V Ash Vale 72-77; P-in-c Thursley 77-82; rtd 82; PtO *Guildf* 85-06. *26 Cruse Close, Sway, Lymington SO41 6AY* T: (01590) 682097
E: resfernhill@aol.com

STEPHENS, Canon Harold William Barrow. b 47. Lon Univ BEd 71. S Dios Minl Tr Scheme 80. d 82 p 83. NSM Heytesbury

and Sutton Veny *Sarum* 82-83; NSM Bishopstrow and Boreham 83-91; Dep Hd Master Westwood St Thos Sch Salisbury 91-99; P-in-c Market Lavington and Easterton *Sarum* 99-03; P-in-c W Lavington and the Cheverells 02-03; R The Lavingtons, Cheverells, and Easterton 03-07; TR Dorchester 07-13; P-in-c The Winterbournes and Compton Valence 09-13; Can and Preb Sarum Cathl 09-13; rtd 13; PtO *Sarum* from 13. *40 Ashley Place, Warminster BA12 9QJ*
E: harold.stephens627@btinternet.com

STEPHENS, James Charles. b 62. d 91 p 92. C Kilcolman w Kiltallagh, Killorglin, Knockane etc *L & K* from 91. *Kilderry, Miltown, Co Kerry, Republic of Ireland* T: (00353) (66) 976 7735 M: 87-052 9107 E: stiofain.s@gmail.com *or* stephens.j@temmler.eu

STEPHENS, Mrs Jean. b 46. St As Minl Tr Course. d 89 p 97. NSM Gwernaffield and Llanferres *St As* 89-02 and 04-09; NSM Hawarden 02-04; NSM Cilcain, Gwernaffield, Llanferres etc 09-12; rtd 13; PtO *St As* from 14. *Noddfa, Pen y Fron Road, Pantymwyn, Mold CH7 5EF* T: (01352) 740037

STEPHENS, Jill. *See* STEPHENS, Rosemary Jill

STEPHENS, Mrs Joan. b 38. d 00 p 01. OLM Irlam and Cadishead *Man* 09-12; rtd 12; PtO *Man* from 12. *77 Baines Avenue, Irlam, Manchester M44 6AS* T: 0161-775 7538

STEPHENS, Mrs Joanna Louise. b 69. St Jo Coll Nottm BA 08. d 08 p 09. C Bramcote *S'well* 08-10; C Attenborough 10-12; C Toton 10-12; TV Hucknall Torkard from 12. *The Vicarage, 63 Ruffs Drive, Hucknall, Nottingham NG15 6JG* T: 0115-963 3640 M: 07890-385133 E: joke.stephens@talktalk.net

STEPHENS, John. *See* STEPHENS, Archibald John

STEPHENS, John Michael. b 29. MRICS 52. Lich Th Coll 62. d 64 p 65. C Birchington w Acol *Cant* 64-70; V Tovil 70-79; V Brabourne w Smeeth 79-94; RD N Lympne 87-94; rtd 94; PtO *York* from 94. *Southacre, Kirby Mills, Kirkbymoorside, York YO62 6NR* T: (01751) 432766

STEPHENS (née FLIPPANCE), Canon Kim Sheelagh May. b 64. RGN 85 RM 88. Trin Coll Bris 97. d 99 p 00. C Alderbury Team *Sarum* 99-01; C Clarendon 01-02; Chapl Salisbury NHS Foundn Trust 02-13; Chapl Team Ldr from 13; Can and Preb Sarum Cathl from 15. *The Chaplains' Office, Salisbury District Hospital, Salisbury SP2 8BJ* T: (01722) 336262
E: chaplains.department@salisbury.nhs.uk

STEPHENS, Martin Nicholas. b 64. Brunel Univ BSc 88 Nottm Univ MTh 01. St Jo Coll Nottm 99. d 01 p 02. C Newchapel *Lich* 01-04; TV Bucknall from 04. *St John's Parsonage, 28 Greasley Road, Stoke-on-Trent ST2 8JE* T: (01782) 542861

STEPHENS, Michael. *See* STEPHENS, John Michael

STEPHENS, Paul. b 53. AGSM 73 Newton Park Coll Bath PGCE 74. Trin Coll Bris 91. d 93 p 94. C S Molton w Nymet St George, High Bray etc *Ex* 93-97; R Norton Fitzwarren *B & W* 97-99; Chapl St Aug Sch Taunton 97-99; Chapl Monkton Combe Sch Bath 99-08; P-in-c Winford w Felton Common Hill *B & W* from 08. *The Rectory, 4 Parsonage Lane, Winford, Bristol BS40 8DG* T: (01275) 474636

STEPHENS, Paul John. b 74. Ridley Hall Cam 09. d 11 p 12. C Forest Row *Chich* 11-14; C Southgate from 14. *1 Southgate Road, Crawley RH10 6BL* M: 07879-864611 T: (01293) 320094 E: revpaulstephens@hotmail.com

STEPHENS, Mrs Penny Clare. b 60. St Anne's Coll Ox BA 83 Lon Inst of Educn PGCE 85. Oak Hill Th Coll. d 99 p 00. C Turnham Green Ch Ch *Lon* 99-03; P-in-c Brasted *Roch* 03-10; PtO from 10. *The Oast House, Forest Farm, Pembury Road, Tonbridge TN11 0ND* T: (01732) 358208
E: pennystephens@btinternet.com

STEPHENS, Canon Peter John. b 42. Oriel Coll Ox BA 64 MA 67. Clifton Th Coll 63. d 68 p 68. C Lenton *S'well* 68-71; C Brixton Hill St Sav *S'wark* 71-73; P-in-c 73-82; TV Barnham Broom *Nor* 82-89; V Gorleston St Mary 89-94; RD Flegg (St Yarmouth) 92-94; P-in-c High Oak 94-97; RD Humbleyard 95-98; C Hingham w Wood Rising w Scoulton 96-97; TR High Oak, Hingham and Scoulton w Wood Rising 97-05; Hon Can Nor Cathl 99-05; rtd 05; PtO *St Alb* from 12. *15 Church Row, Wootton, Bedford MK43 9HQ* T: (01234) 765403 M: 07768-425349 M: 07973-322513
E: peterstephens@aol.com

STEPHENS, Preb Peter Stanley. b 33. ALCD 59. d 59 p 60. C Paignton St Paul Preston *Ex* 59-64; V Buckland Monachorum 64-74; RD Tavistock 70-74; V Compton Gifford 74-85; RD Plymouth Sutton 83-86; Preb Ex Cathl 84-05; TR Plymouth Em w Efford 85-86; R Thurlestone w S Milton 86-98; rtd 98. *Headland View, 14 Court Park, Thurlestone, Kingsbridge TQ7 3LX* T/F: (01548) 560891

STEPHENS, Mrs Rebecca Louise. b 76. Birm Univ BSc 97 PGCE 98. Qu Coll Birm 12. d 14 p 15. C Coleshill *Birm* from 14; C Maxstoke from 14. *Address withheld by request*
E: beckystephens17@gmail.com

STEPHENS, Richard William. b 37. Dur Univ BSc 62. Cranmer Hall Dur 62. **d** 64 **p** 65. C Hensingham *Carl* 64-67; C Norbury *Ches* 67-71; R Elworth and Warmingham 71-79; V Bootle St Matt *Liv* 79-89; P-in-c Litherland St Andr 79-83; P-in-c Failsworth H Trin *Man* 89-93; R 93-02; P-in-c Oldham St Barn 01-02; AD Oldham 99-02; rtd 02; Hon C Dalbeattie *Glas* from 02. *Cloverstone, 3 Craignair Street, Dalbeattie DG5 4AX* T: (01556) 610627 E: revrstephens@btinternet.com

STEPHENS, Robert Charles. b 46. Nottm Trent Univ BA 03. EMMTC 08. **d** 10 **p** 11. NSM Daybrook *S'well* 10-13; NSM Bulwell St Jo from 13. *1 Leyland Close, Toton, Nottingham NG9 6HB* T: 0115-973 5418 M: 07757-422260 E: r.c.stephens@btinternet.com

STEPHENS, Mrs Rosemary Jill. b 46. SRN 68. WEMTC 96. **d** 08 **p** 13. NSM Goodrich, Marstow, Welsh Bicknor, Llangarron etc *Heref* from 08; NSM Wye Reaches Gp from 08. *Sunnyside Cottage, Coppett Hill, Goodrich, Ross-on-Wye HR9 6JG* T: (01600) 890975 E: jill.stephens1@btinternet.com

STEPHENS, Canon Simon Edward. b 41. OBE 97. Qu Coll Birm PhD 80. Bps' Coll Cheshunt 63. **d** 67 **p** 68. C Cov St Mark 67-71; C Lillington 71-76; C-in-c Canley CD 76-79; V Canley 79-80; Chapl RN 80-97; Asst Chapl Menorca *Eur* 97-98; Chapl 98-99; Chapl Moscow 99-14; Hon Can Malta Cathl 01-14; rtd 14. *119 Hoe Court, Citadel Road, Plymouth PL1 2RN* T: (01752) 660728 E: apokosar@gmail.com

STEPHENS, Mrs Susanne Hilary. b 44. St Jo Coll Nottm. Guildf Dioc Min Course. **d** 00 **p** 01. OLM Camberley St Paul *Guildf* 00-14; PtO from 14. *St Paul's Church, Crawley Ridge, Camberley GU15 2AD* T: (01276) 700210 E: sue-stephens3@hotmail.com

STEPHENS, Mrs Tessa. b 74. Leeds Univ BA 97. St Jo Coll Nottm MTh 10. **d** 10 **p** 11. C Hipswell *Ripon* 10-14; C Linthorpe *York* from 14; Chapl Teesside Univ from 14. *35 Adcott Road, Middlesbrough TS5 7ER* M: 07944-302344 E: tessa.stephens@btinternet.com

STEPHENS, David. b 76. Huddersfield Univ BMus 98. Qu Coll Birm 12. **d** 14 **p** 15. C Darwen St Pet *Blackb* from 14. *St Matthew's Vicarage, Harriet Street, Burnley BB11 4JH* T: (01282) 424849 E: frdavidstephenson@gmail.com

STEPHENSON, David John. b 65. Bris Univ BSc(Soc) 87 Dur Univ BA 91. Cranmer Hall Dur 92. **d** 92 **p** 93. C Whickham *Dur* 92-94; C Sunderland Pennywell St Thos 94-97; V Stockton St Jo and Stockton St Jas 99-06; V W Dulwich All SS *S'wark* from 06; P-in-c Streatham Hill St Marg from 14; AD Lambeth S from 13. *All Saints' Vicarage, 165 Rosendale Road, London SE21 8LN* T: (020) 8670 0826 E: vicar@all-saints.org.uk

STEPHENSON, Canon Eric George. b 41. Bede Coll Dur CertEd 63. Qu Coll Birm. **d** 66 **p** 67. C Wakef St Jo 66-69; C Seaham w Seaham Harbour *Dur* 69-73; C Cockerton 73-75; LtO 75-85; V E Boldon 85-08; AD Jarrow 92-01; Hon Can Dur Cathl 93-08; rtd 08; Chapl to The Queen 02-11; PtO *Dur* from 14. *39 Haversham Park, Sunderland SR5 1HW* T: 0191-549 5278 E: ericgstephenson@googlemail.com

STEPHENSON, Ian Clarke. b 24. Tyndale Hall Bris 52. **d** 56 **p** 57. C Bedworth *Cov* 56-58; C Edgware *Lon* 58-65; R Biddulph Moor *Lich* 65-70; Hon C Biddulph 70-88; Hon C Burslem 85-88; New Zealand from 87; rtd 89. *5 Arthur Terrace, Balclutha 9230, New Zealand* T: (0064) (3) 418 2657 E: clarkeia@es.co.nz

STEPHENSON, James Alexander. b 77. Hatf Coll Dur BSc 00 Ox Univ BTh 15. Ripon Coll Cuddesdon 09. **d** 11 **p** 12. Chapl Canford Sch and C N Poole Ecum Team *Sarum* 11-12; PtO *Ox* 13; Zambia from 13; Chapl St Paul's Colleg Sch Hamilton New Zealand from 15. *St Paul's Collegiate School, 77 Hukanui Road, Hamilton, New Zealand* M: 07709-865590 E: jxstevo@hotmail.com

STEPHENSON, Mrs Jane Eleanor. b 50. Leeds Univ BA 72 PGCE 73. **d** 05 **p** 06. NSM Bunbury and Tilstone Fearnall *Ches* 05-09; P-in-c Tilston and Shocklach 09-13; R from 13; Educn and Tr Officer 07-09; Past Worker Tr Officer 06-10. *The Mount, Hobb Hill, Tilston, Malpas SY14 7DU* T: (01829) 250249 or 250628 E: stephenson256@btinternet.com

STEPHENSON, John Joseph. b 35. St Jo Coll Dur BA 74. Qu Coll Birm 75. **d** 76 **p** 77. C Whitworth w Spennymoor *Dur* 76-79; V Eppleton 79-96; rtd 96; PtO *Dur* from 96. *5 Snackgate Lane, Heighington Village, Newton Aycliffe DL5 6RG*

STEPHENSON (née BRYAN), Judith Claire. b 57. Aston Univ BSc 79 PhD 82 Trent Poly PGCE 83. St Jo Coll Nottm BTh 94 LTh 95. **d** 95 **p** 96. C Wolverhampton St Matt *Lich* 95-99; Chapl Hull Univ *York* 99-08; Chapl W Lon YMCA 08-14; PtO *Lon* from 14. *Ground Floor Flat B, 25 Montpelier Road, London W5 2QT* T: (020) 8991 9134 E: stephenson414@btinternet.com

STEPHENSON, Juliet. b 69. St Jo Coll Dur BA 05. Cranmer Hall Dur 03. **d** 05 **p** 06. C Retford *S'well* 05-08; V Newnham w

Awre and Blakeney *Glouc* 08-13; V Chapel House *Newc* from 13. *44 Queensbury Drive, North Walbottle, Newcastle upon Tyne NE15 9XF* T: 0191-229 0436 E: juliet_stephenson@hotmail.com

STEPHENSON, Canon Martin Woodard. b 55. St Cath Coll Cam BA 77 MA 82. Westcott Ho Cam 78. **d** 81 **p** 82. C Eastleigh *Win* 81-85; C Ferryhill *Dur* 85-87; Asst Dir of Ords 87-89; Chapl St Chad's Coll 87-89; TR Clarendon Park St Jo w Knighton St Mich *Leic* 89-98; P-in-c Hall Green St Pet *Birm* 98-99; V from 99; Warden of Readers from 08; Hon Can Birm Cathl from 14. *St Peter's Vicarage, 33 Paradise Lane, Birmingham B28 0DY* T: 0121-777 1935 E: martin.stephenson@cantab.net

STEPHENSON, Norman Keith. b 62. St Jo Coll Cam MA 88 Strathclyde Univ MBA 91. NEOC 04. **d** 07 **p** 08. NSM Kingston upon Hull H Trin *York* 07-08; NSM Ealing St Pet Mt Park *Lon* 08-13; PtO from 13. *Ground Floor Flat B, 25 Montpelier Road, London W5 2QT* T: (020) 8991 9134 M: 07880-602577 E: n.k.stephenson@btinternet.com

STEPHENSON, Canon Robert. b 36. St Chad's Coll Dur BA 58. **d** 60 **p** 61. C Whickham *Dur* 60-63; C Gateshead St Mary 63-65; PC Low Team 65-67; R Stella 67-74; V Comberton *Ely* 74-04; RD Bourn 94-97; P-in-c Dry Drayton 97-01; Hon Can Ely Cathl 01-04; rtd 04; PtO *Ely* from 04. *1 Porthmore Close, Highfields, Caldecote, Cambridge CB23 7ZR* T: (01954) 210638 E: robert@stephenson.wanadoo.co.uk or robert1pc@yahoo.co.uk

STEPHENSON, Simon George. b 44. St Jo Coll Dur BA 67. Trin Coll Bris 74. **d** 76 **p** 77. C Hildenborough *Roch* 76-82; C Bishopsworth *Bris* 82-85; C-in-c Withywood CD 85-90; TV Wreningham *Nor* 90-97; P-in-c Tasburgh w Tharston, Forncett and Flordon 94-97; TV High Oak, Hingham and Scoulton w Wood Rising 98-05; rtd 05; Asst Chapl HM Pris Wayland 98-09; PtO *Nor* from 09. *7 Swanton Avenue, Dereham NR19 2HJ* T: (01362) 699537 E: paulineandsimon@talktalk.net

STEPNEY, Area Bishop of. *See* NEWMAN, The Rt Revd Adrian

STERLING, Anne. *See* HASELHURST, Anne

STERLING, John Haddon. b 40. Pemb Coll Cam BA 62 MA 66. Cuddesdon Coll 63. **d** 65 **p** 66. C Pretoria Cathl S Africa 65-69; LtO Natal 69-70; Chapl Bris Cathl 71-74; Member Dioc Soc and Ind Team 71-74; Ind Chapl *Linc* 74-87; *Ripon* 87-92; TV Hanley H Ev and Min in Ind *Lich* 92-97; P-in-c Hixon w Stowe-by-Chartley 97-02; P-in-c Fradswell, Gayton, Milwich and Weston 97-02; TR Mid Trent 02-06; rtd 06; PtO *Lich* from 07. *10 Newquay Avenue, Stafford ST17 0EB* T: (01785) 662870

STERRY, Christopher. b 54. K Coll Lon BD 77 AKC 77. Episc Sem Austin Texas 78 St Jo Coll Nottm 79. **d** 80 **p** 81. C Huddersfield St Jo *Wakef* 80-84; V Middlestown 84-89; Chapl and Tutor NOC 89-94; Lect Ches Coll of HE 93-94; NSM Padgate *Liv* 92-94; Bp's Dom Chapl *Blackb* 94-97; Chapl Whalley Abbey 94-97; Warden 97-04; V Whalley 97-09; P-in-c Sabden and Pendleton 07-09; C Colne and Villages 09-12; P-in-c Huntley and Longhope, Churcham and Bulley *Glouc* from 12; C Abenhall w Mitcheldean from 12; C Westbury-on-Severn w Flaxley, Blaisdon etc from 12; Warden of Readers from 13. *The Rectory, 56 Byfords Road, Huntley, Gloucester GL19 3EL* M: 07855-607824 E: chrisforestedge@gmail.com

STERRY, Mrs Susan Helen. St Mellitus Coll 13. **d** 14 **p** 15. NSM Gt Ilford St Andr *Chelmsf* from 14. *56 Manor Road, Romford RM1 2RD* T: (01708) 756143 E: sue.sterry@btinternet.com

STERRY, Timothy John. b 34. Oriel Coll Ox BA 58 MA 62. Wycliffe Hall Ox 58. **d** 60 **p** 61. C Cromer *Nor* 60-64; Chapl Oundle Sch 64-72; Teacher Cheam Prep Sch 72-75; Hd Master Temple Grove Sch E Sussex 75-80; Team Ldr Scripture Union Independent Schs 81-99; rtd 00; PtO *Sarum* from 02. *24 Barn Road, Broadstone BH18 8NJ* T: (01202) 699299 E: tim@sterry.org

STEVEN, Canon David Bowring. b 38. AKC 64. **d** 64 **p** 65. C Grantham St Wulfram *Linc* 64-68; C Kimberley St Cypr S Africa 68-71; R Mafeking 71-75; C Bramley *Ripon* 76-77; V Sutton Valence w E Sutton and Chart Sutton *Cant* 77-82; P-in-c Littlebourne 82-86; Warden of Readers 82-86; V Mansfield Woodhouse *S'well* 86-98; P-in-c Mullion *Truro* 98-03; RD Kerrier 01-03; rtd 03; Hon Can Truro Cathl 03-07; PtO from 03. *5 Guinea Port Parc, Wadebridge PL27 7BY* T: (01208) 815393

STEVEN, Canon James Henry Stevenson. b 62. CCC Cam BA 84 MA 87 St Jo Coll Dur BA 87 K Coll Lon PhD 99. Cranmer Hall Dur 84. **d** 87 **p** 88. C Welling *Roch* 87-91; C Bournemouth St Jo w St Mich *Win* 91-94; TV Bournemouth St Pet w St Swithun, H Trin etc 94-00; Chapl Bournemouth and Poole Coll of FE 94-00; Tutor Trin Coll Bris 00-08; Lect K Coll Lon 08-11; Dir Liturgy and Worship Sarum Coll from 11; Can Th *Glouc* from 14. *Sarum College, 19 The Close, Salisbury SP1 2EE* T: (01722) 424800 E: jsteven@sarum.ac.uk

STEVEN, Richard John. b 54. Oak Hill Th Coll BA 99. **d** 99 **p** 01. C Bluff Pt Australia 00-03; P-in-c Horsmonden *Roch* 04-09; Chapl HM Pris Blantyre Ho 05-09; Australia 09-11; P-in-c Herstmonceux and Wartling *Chich* from 11. *The Rectory, West End, Herstmonceux, Hailsham BN27 4NY* T: (01323) 833124 E: ra_steven@hotmail.com

STEVENETTE, John Maclachlan. b 30. St Pet Coll Ox MA 60. Ripon Hall Ox 60. **d** 61 **p** 62. C Newhaven *Chich* 61-66; R Lynch w Iping Marsh 66-74; R Birdham w W Itchenor 74-78; R Byfleet *Guildf* 78-86; V Whittlesey *Ely* 86-90; TR Whittlesey and Pondersbridge 91; R Itchen Valley *Win* 91-99; rtd 99; PtO *Bris* from 00. *35 Ballard Chase, Abingdon OX14 1XQ* T: (01235) 526706

STEVENETTE, Canon Simon Melville. b 62. Hull Univ BA 83. Wycliffe Hall Ox 84. **d** 87 **p** 88. C Carterton *Ox* 87-90; C Keynsham *B & W* 90-91; TV 91-98; Chapl Keynsham Hosp Bris 92-98; V Swindon Ch Ch *Bris* from 98; AD Swindon from 11; Hon Can Bris Cathl from 13. *Christ Church Vicarage, 26 Cricklade Street, Swindon SN1 3HG* M: 07880-710172 F: (01793) 529166 T: 522832 E: simon@stevenette.freeserve.co.uk

STEVENS, Alan Robert. b 55. Warwick Univ BA 77. St Jo Coll Nottm 87. **d** 89 **p** 90. C Ex St Leon w H Trin 89-92; TV Rugby *Cov* 92-97; P-in-c N w S Kilworth and Misterton *Leic* 97-00; PtO from 13. *23 Catesby Road, Rugby CV22 5JJ* T: (01788) 330177 E: hattersbarmyarmy@googlemail.com

STEVENS, Andrew. *See* STEVENS, John David Andrew

STEVENS, Canon Andrew Graham. b 54. BEd MA. Coll of Resurr Mirfield. **d** 83 **p** 84. C Leigh Park *Portsm* 83-87; TV Brighton Resurr *Chich* 87-94; V Plumstead St Nic *S'wark* from 94; Hon Can S'wark Cathl from 14. *St Nicholas's Vicarage, 64 Purrett Road, London SE18 1JP* T: (020) 8854 0461 F: 8265 5065 E: frandrew@dircon.co.uk

STEVENS, Anne Helen. b 62. Warwick Univ BA 82 Fitzw Coll Cam BA 90 MA 94 Heythrop Coll Lon MTh 99. Ridley Hall Cam 88. **d** 91 **p** 94. Par Dn E Greenwich Ch Ch w St Andr and St Mich *S'wark* 91-94; Chapl Trin Coll Cam 94-99; P-in-c Battersea St Mich *S'wark* 99-07; V 07-12; Dir Readers' Tr 99-12; Hon Can S'wark Cathl 05-12; V St Pancras w St Jas and Ch Ch *Lon* from 12; Dean of Women's Ministry Edmonton Area from 15. *St Pancras Vicarage, 6 Sandwich Street, London WC1H 9PL* T: (020) 7388 1630

STEVENS, Anthony Harold. b 46. CEng 71 MIStructE 71 FIStructE 87 MICE 75 FICE 92. St Mich Coll Llan 94. **d** 95 **p** 96. C Cardiff St Jo *Llan* 95-98; TV Cowbridge 98-01; R Eglwysilan 01-08; R Gelligaer 08-12; AD Caerphilly 04-10; rtd 13; PtO *Llan* from 13; *Mon* from 13. *2 Falcon Grove, Penarth CF64 5FB* T: (029) 2070 7745 E: revtonystevens@sky.com

STEVENS, Brian Henry. b 28. Oak Hill Th Coll. **d** 69 **p** 70. C Chadwell *Chelmsf* 69-75; V Penge Ch Ch w H Trin *Roch* 75-85; V St Mary Cray and St Paul's Cray 85-93; rtd 93; PtO *Cant* from 93. *53 Middle Deal Road, Deal CT14 9RG* T: (01304) 379494

STEVENS, Brian Henry. b 45. Open Univ BA 80. S Dios Minl Tr Scheme 81. **d** 84 **p** 85. NSM S Malling *Chich* 84-86; C Langney 86-87; TV Wolverton *Ox* 87-88; V Welford w Sibbertoft and Marston Trussell *Pet* 88-91; V Hardingstone and Horton and Piddington 91-11; Chapl Northants Police 06-11; rtd 11. *2C Manor Road, Great Billing, Northampton NN2 6QJ* M: 07710-207201 E: fr.brian@talktalk.net

STEVENS, David John. b 45. Bris Univ BA 67. Clifton Th Coll. **d** 70 **p** 71. C Ex St Leon w H Trin 70-75; P-in-c Lt Burstead *Chelmsf* 75-77; TV Billericay and Lt Burstead 77-81; P-in-c Illogan *Truro* 81-83; R St Illogan 83-96; RD Carnmarth N 96; V Highworth w Sevenhampton and Inglesham etc *Bris* 96-01; P-in-c Constantine *Truro* 01-10; RD Kerrier 03-10; rtd 10; PtO *Truro* from 10; RD Penwith from 14. *Bede House, Primrose Hill, Goldsithney, Penzance TR20 9JR* T: (01736) 719090

STEVENS, David Lynne. b 59. Poly of Wales BA 81 York St Jo Coll MA 06. NOC 99. **d** 02 **p** 03. C Horsforth *Ripon* 02-06; Chapl Abbey Grange High Sch 04-06; P-in-c Potternewton *Leeds* 06-15; AD Allerton 13-15; V Doncaster St Geo *Sheff* from 15. *The Vicarage, 98 Thorne Road, Doncaster DN2 5BJ* M: 07963-060911 T: (01302) 325668 E: davidstev1@aol.com

STEVENS, Douglas George. b 47. Lon Univ BA 69. Westcott Ho Cam 69. **d** 72 **p** 73. C Portsea St Geo CD *Portsm* 72-75; C Portsea N End St Mark 75-79; Chapl NE Lon Poly *Chelmsf* 79-83; C-in-c Orton Goldhay CD *Ely* 83-87; V Elm 87-91; V Coldham 87-91; V Friday Bridge 87-91; R Woodston 91-98; P-in-c Fletton 94-98; rtd 98. *28 Francis Gardens, Peterborough PE1 3XX* T: (01733) 755430

STEVENS, Miss Gillian. b 51. K Alfred's Coll Win CertEd 72. EAMTC 98. **d** 01 **p** 02. C March St Mary and March St Pet *Ely* 01-03; C Whittlesey, Pondersbridge and Coates 03-05; TV from 05. *8 The Grove, Whittlesey, Peterborough PE7 2RF* T/F: (01733) 202563 E: gill.stevens8@btinternet.com

STEVENS, James Anthony. b 47. Worc Coll Ox MA 69. Trin Coll Bris 78. **d** 80 **p** 81. C Heref St Pet w St Owen and St James; C Lowestoft and Kirkley *Nor* 84-85; TV 85-89; V Dorridge *Birm* 89-05; AD Shirley 02-05; R Sarratt and Chipperfield *St Alb* 05-12; rtd 12; PtO *Roch* from 13. *17 Prospect Park, Southborough, Tunbridge Wells TN4 0EQ* T: (01892) 670954 E: revjim@virginmedia.com

STEVENS, Jane. *See* KRAFT, Jane

STEVENS, Janice Hazel. b 42. **d** 00 **p** 01. Chapl S Lon and Maudsley NHS Foundn Trust 00-07; Hon C Warlingham w Chelsham and Farleigh *S'wark* 00-12; rtd 12; PtO *S'wark* 12-13. *7 Harrow Road, Warlingham CR6 9EY* T: (01883) 626308

STEVENS, John David Andrew. b 44. Wycliffe Hall Ox. **d** 68 **p** 69. C Standish *Blackb* 68-71; C Stonehouse *Glouc* 71-76; P-in-c E Coker w Sutton Bingham and Closworth *B & W* 76-77; P-in-c Barwick 76-77; TV Yeovil 77-80; R Chewton Mendip w Ston Easton, Litton etc 80-94; R Quantoxhead 94-07; RD Quantock 95-01; rtd 07; PtO *B & W* from 07. *Amberwell, Holywell Road, Edington, Bridgwater TA7 9LE* T: (01278) 722327 E: andrewstevens@zetnet.co.uk

STEVENS, Martin Leonard. b 35. St Jo Coll Dur BA 60 MA 72. Oak Hill Th Coll 60. **d** 62 **p** 63. C Low Elswick *Newc* 62-65; C S Croydon Em *Cant* 65-69; Hon C 69-74; S England Deputation Sec *ICM* 69-74; V Felling *Dur* 74-84; NSM Ches Square St Mich w St Phil *Lon* 92-96; rtd 95; Hon C Cullompton and Kentisbeare w Blackborough *Ex* 96-01; PtO *Cov* from 03. *11 Foxes Way, Warwick CV34 6AX* T: (01926) 490864 E: martin.stevens6@sky.com

STEVENS, Matthew. b 80. Cam Univ BTh 07. Ridley Hall Cam 04. **d** 07 **p** 08. C Reading St Mary the Virgin *Ox* 07-11; Chapl RAF from 11. *Chaplaincy Services (RAF), HQ Air Command, RAF High Wycombe HP14 4UE* T: (01494) 496800 F: 496343 E: rev.mattstevens@googlemail.com

STEVENS, Michael John. b 37. St Cath Coll Cam BA 63. Coll of Resurr Mirfield 63. **d** 65 **p** 66. C Poplar All SS w St Frideswide *Lon* 65-71; Asst Chapl The Lon Hosp (Whitechapel) 71-74; Chapl St Thos Hosp Lon 75-96; Hospitaller St Barts Hosp Lon 96-05; P-in-c St Bart Less *Lon* 96-99; V 99-05; rtd 05; PtO *Chelmsf* 03-10. *The Oaks, Toogoods Way, Nursling, Southampton SO16 0XL* T: (023) 8073 2234

STEVENS, Norman William. b 38. St Chad's Coll Dur BA 61. **d** 63 **p** 99. C Wingate Grange *Dur* 63-64; NSM Ansty and Shilton *Cov* from 99; PtO from 08. *60 Clinton Lane, Kenilworth CV8 1AT* T: (01926) 858090 *or* (024) 7622 7597 E: norstevens@hotmail.com

STEVENS, Canon Olive. b 48. Ex Univ BA 04. SWMTC 01. **d** 04 **p** 05. C Camborne *Truro* 04-13; C Redruth w Lanner and Treleigh 11-14; TV 14-15; R Camborne and Tuckingmill from 15; RD Carnmarth N from 08; Hon Can Truro Cathl from 14. *Hideaway, The Square, Portreath, Redruth TR16 4LA* T: (01209) 842372 E: olivestevens@aol.com

STEVENS, Penelope Ann. *See* PRINCE, Penelope Ann

STEVENS, Peter David. b 36. MRICS. Oak Hill Th Coll 79. **d** 81 **p** 82. C Branksome St Clem *Sarum* 81-87; R Moreton and Woodsford w Tincleton 87-98; rtd 98; Hon C Hordle *Win* 98-02; PtO 02-12. *15 Brough Lane, Crossways, Dorchester DT2 8WU* T: (01305) 852135 E: peterstevens181@btinternet.com

STEVENS, Philip Terence. b 55. MBE 07. Man Univ BSc 76 Lon Univ BD 81 St Jo Coll Dur MA 86. Cranmer Hall Dur 81. **d** 83 **p** 84. C Withington St Paul *Man* 83-86; C Middleton 86-88; V Saddleworth 88-92; V Sheff St Paul 93-96; TR Sheff Manor 96-00; PtO 00-06; *Newc* 06-08; *B & W* 09-10; P-in-c Bleadon and Weston-super-Mare St Andr Bournville 10-13; PtO *York* from 13; P-in-c Laceby and Ravendale Gp *Linc* 14; P-in-c Keelby Gp 14; V Wolds Gateway Group from 14. *The Rectory, 4 Cooper Lane, Laceby, Grimsby DN37 7AX* T: (01472) 753602 M: 07914-357544 E: philiptstevens@gmail.com

STEVENS, Miss Rebecca Claire. St Mich Coll Llan. **d** 14 **p** 15. C Bedwas w Machen w Michaelston-y-Fedw w Rudry *Mon* from 14. *The Rectory, Rectory Gardens, Machen, Caerphilly CF83 8SU* E: rebeccaclairestevens@gmail.com

STEVENS, Richard William. b 36. AKC 59. St Boniface Warminster 59. **d** 60 **p** 61. C Greenhill St Jo *Lon* 60-63; Chapl RAF 63-79; CF 79-01; rtd 01; PtO *Cant* 02-10. *The Old Vicarage, Stockbury, Sittingbourne ME9 7UN* T: (01795) 844891

STEVENS, Robin George. b 43. Leic Univ BA 65. Cuddesdon Coll 74. **d** 74 **p** 75. C Hemel Hempstead *St Alb* 74-77; Chapl K Coll Sch Wimbledon 77-03; TV Wimbledon *S'wark* 98-09; rtd 09; PtO *S'wark* 11-13; *Sarum* from 13. *329 Wimbledon Park Road, London SW19 6NS* T: (020) 8788 4308

STEVENS, Mrs Sara-Jane. b 72. Southn Univ BEd 97. SEITE 12. **d** 15. C Worthing St Matt *Chich* from 15. *42 Pavilion Road, Worthing BN14 7EF* M: 07786-851565 E: bands.stevens@icloud.com

STEVENS, Simon Mark. b 72. Lon Univ BD Cam Univ MPhil. STETS 00. **d** 01 **p** 02. C Sholing *Win* 01-05; Chapl Southn Univ 05-10; Chapl Loughb Univ *Leic* 10-15; C Leic Resurr from 15. *445A Loughborough Road, Birstall, Leicester LE4 4BH* T: 0116-267 3290 E: simon.m.stevens@btinternet.com

STEVENS, Mrs Susan Ann. b 46. Lon Univ BEd 85. St Mich Coll Llan. **d** 07 **p** 08. NSM Bargoed and Deri w Brithdir *Llan* 07-10; NSM Gelligaer 10-12; rtd 13; PtO *Llan* from 13. *2 Falcon Grove, Penarth CF64 5FB* T: (029) 2070 7745 E: salutsue@aol.com

STEVENS, Mrs Susan Marjorie Earlam. b 52. RGN 74. WMMTC 97. **d** 00 **p** 01. NSM Harborne St Faith and St Laur *Birm* 00-02; NSM Publow w Pensford, Compton Dando and Chelwood *B & W* 03-12; Chapl R United Hosp Bath NHS Trust 06-12; rtd 12. *Woollard Place, Woollard, Pensford, Bristol BS39 4HU* T: (01761) 490898 E: smestevens@hotmail.co.uk

STEVENS, Thomas Walter. b 33. Bps' Coll Cheshunt. **d** 65 **p** 66. C Newc St Matt w St Mary 65-69; C Wallsend St Luke 69-70; C Cranford *Lon* 70-87; C Fulwell St Mich and St Geo 87-90; C Teddington SS Pet and Paul and Fulwell 90-91; rtd 92; PtO *S'wark* 92-13. *23A Samos Road, London SE20 7UQ* T: (020) 8776 7960

✠**STEVENS, The Rt Revd Timothy John.** b 46. Selw Coll Cam BA 68 MA 72. Ripon Coll Cuddesdon 75. **d** 76 **p** 77 **c** 95. C E Ham w Upton Park and Forest Gate *Chelmsf* 76-80; TR Canvey Is 80-88; Dep Dir Cathl Cen for Research and Tr 82-84; Bp's Urban Officer 87-91; Hon Can Chelmsf Cathl 87-91; Adn W Ham 91-95; Suff Bp Dunwich *St E* 95-99; Bp Leic 99-15; rtd 15. *62 Horringer Road, Bury St Edmunds IP33 2DR* T: (01284) 768321 M: 07860-692258 E: tjs46@icloud.com

STEVENSON, Canon Alastair Rice. b 42. Open Univ BA 78. Ripon Coll Cuddesdon 78. **d** 80 **p** 81. C Bexhill St Pet *Chich* 80-82; C Brighton St Matthias 82-84; C Swindon Ch Ch *Bris* 84-87; Bp's Soc and Ind Adv 87-97; P-in-c Swindon All SS w St Barn 97-01; V 01-11; P-in-c Swindon St Aug 04-11; Hon Can Bris Cathl 02-11; rtd 11. *17 Kelly Gardens, Swindon SN25 4YH* M: 07880-710172 T: (01793) 336587 E: al@stair.me.uk

STEVENSON, Canon Andrew James. b 63. IEng AMICE MIAT. SWMTC 94. **d** 97 **p** 98. NSM Highertown and Baldhu *Truro* 97-08; NSM Mylor w Flushing from 08; Hon Can Truro Cathl from 15. *31 Nansavallon Road, Truro TR1 3JU* T: (01872) 241880 E: theblackstuff@sky.com

STEVENSON, Beaumont. *See* STEVENSON, Frank Beaumont

STEVENSON, Bernard Norman. b 57. Kent Univ BA 78 Fitzw Coll Cam BA 81 MA 86. Ridley Hall Cam. **d** 82 **p** 83. C Mortlake w E Sheen *S'wark* 82-84; C Kensal Rise St Martin *Lon* 84-88; C Headstone St Geo 88-90; V Worfield *Heref* 90-95; R Hutton *B & W* 95-07; RD Locking 04-05. *13 Godolphin Road, Long Rock, Penzance TR20 8JW* T: (01736) 711692 E: bstevenson@clara.net

STEVENSON, Brian. *See* STEVENSON, Robert Brian

STEVENSON, Brian. b 34. JP 66. NW Ord Course 76. **d** 79 **p** 80. C Padiham *Blackb* 79-82; V Clitheroe St Paul Low Moor 82-89; V Blackb St Silas 89-01; rtd 01; PtO *Blackb* from 01. *1 Chatburn Close, Great Harwood, Blackburn BB6 7TL* T: (01254) 885051

STEVENSON, Christopher James. b 43. TCD BA 65 MA 73 Em Coll Cam BA 69 MA 73. Westcott Ho Cam 68. **d** 70 **p** 71. C Newc H Cross 70-72; C Arm St Mark w Aghavilly 72-73; C Dublin Crumlin *D & G* 73-76; Hon Clerical V Ch Ch Cathl Dublin 75-76; C-in-c Appley Bridge All SS CD *Blackb* 76-82; P-in-c Appley Bridge 82-91; Bp's C Cloonclare w Killasnett, Lurganboy and Drumlease *K, E & A* 91-12; rtd 12. *7 Merchants Quarter, Cathcart Square, 14 Dublin Road, Enniskillen BT74 6HJ* T: (028) 6632 8512 M: 07982-262862

STEVENSON, David Andrew. b 60. Trin Coll Bris BA 92. **d** 92 **p** 93. C Nottingham St Sav *S'well* 92-96; P-in-c Darlaston All SS and Ind Chapl Black Country Urban Ind Miss *Lich* 96-00; C Darlaston St Lawr 99-00; TV Broadwater *Chich* 00-08; P-in-c Eastwood *S'well* from 08; P-in-c Brinsley w Underwood from 09. *The Rectory, 5A Woodland Way, Eastwood, Nottingham NG16 3BU* T: (01773) 710770

STEVENSON, David Eugene. b 66. Luton Univ BA 02. St Steph Ho *Ox* 06. **d** 08 **p** 09. C Nor St Jo w St Julian 08-11; P-in-c Watford St Jo *St Alb* 11-13; V from 13. *St John's Vicarage, 9 Monmouth Road, Watford WD1 1QW* T: (01923) 25775 M: 07980-315534 E: rev.davidstevenson@googlemail.com

STEVENSON, Donald Macdonald. b 48. Lon Univ BSc(Econ) 70 Leeds Univ MA 72 Univ of Wales (Abth) PGCE 73 Warwick Univ MEd 78 MBACP 11. Oak Hill Th Coll BA 88. **d** 88 **p** 89. C Gt Malvern St Mary *Worc* 88-92; Chapl Bedford Sch 92-98; Sen Chapl 96-98; PtO *St Alb* 99-02; rtd 13. *94 Curlew Crescent, Bedford MK41 7HZ* T: (01234) 217013 E: don_xmcds9@gmx.co.uk

STEVENSON, Elizabeth. *See* STEVENSON, Margaret Elizabeth Maud

STEVENSON, Canon Frank Beaumont. b 39. Duke Univ (USA) BA 61 MInstGA. Episc Th Sch Harvard MDiv 64. **d** 64 **p** 64. USA 64-66; Zambia 66-68; Lect Th Ox Univ from 68; Bp's Tr Officer *Ox* 69-70; Chapl Keble Coll Ox 71-72; Chapl Oxon Mental Healthcare NHS Trust 75-07; Officer for CME *Ox* from 90; Dioc Adv Past Care from 90; Hon Can Ch Ch from 98. *The School House, Wheatley Road, Stanton St John, Oxford OX33 1ET* T: (01865) 351635 E: beaumont.stevenson@btinternet.com

STEVENSON, Gerald Ernest. b 35. S'wark Ord Course 80. **d** 83 **p** 84. NSM Eltham Park St Luke *S'wark* 83-88; Asst Chapl HM Pris Wormwood Scrubs 88-98; PtO *S'wark* 88-99; rtd 99; Hon C Eltham St Barn *S'wark* from 99. *7 Moira Road, London SE9 1SJ* T: (020) 8850 2748

STEVENSON, Graham. **d** 14 **p** 15. NSM Stamford Hill St Thos *Lon* from 14. *Address temp unknown*

STEVENSON, Hugh. *See* STEVENSON, Richard Hugh

STEVENSON, James Christian William. b 79. New Coll Ox BA 00. Trin Coll Bris 05. **d** 07 **p** 08. C Henbury *Bris* 07-10; P-in-c Bishopston and St Andrews from 10. *7 Kings Drive, Bishopston, Bristol BS7 8JW* T: 0117-373 8450 E: revjamesstevenson@yahoo.co.uk

STEVENSON, John. b 39. Glas Univ MA 64 Jordan Hill Coll Glas TCert 65. St Jo Coll Nottm Edin Th Coll. **d** 87 **p** 88. NSM Moffat *Glas* 87-92; P-in-c Eastriggs 92-95; P-in-c Gretna 92-95; P-in-c Langholm 92-95; Israel 95-01; P-in-c Thurso and Wick *Mor* 01-06; rtd 06; LtO *Glas* from 07. *Hoppertitty, Beattock, Moffat DG10 9PJ* T: (01683) 300164 M: 07588-342060 E: hoppertitty@msn.com

STEVENSON, John William. b 44. Salford Univ BSc 66 UNISA BTh 89. St Paul's Coll Grahamstown 84. **d** 87 **p** 87. C St Mary's Cathl Johannesburg S Africa 87-88; R Bezuidenhout Valley 88-93; V Broom Leys *Leic* 93-11; rtd 11; PtO *Pet* from 12. *5 Roman Way, Daventry NN11 0RW* T: (01327) 700119 E: johnandrene@btinternet.com

STEVENSON, The Ven Leslie Thomas Clayton. b 59. TCD BA MPhil. **d** 83 **p** 84. C Dundela St Mark *D & D* 83-87; I Kilmore and Inch 87-92; R Donaghadee 92-99; I Portarlington w Cloneyhurke, Lea etc *M & K* from 99; Can Meath from 08; Can Kildare Cathl from 08; Adn Meath from 09; Adn Kildare from 09. *The Rectory, Portarlington, Co Laois, Republic of Ireland* T/F: (00353) (57) 864 0117 E: lesliestevenson@eircom.net

STEVENSON, Miss Margaret Elizabeth Maud. b 49. Stranmillis Coll CertEd 70 Ulster Univ BEd 86. CITC 07. **d** 10 **p** 11. NSM Drumglass w Moygashel *Arm* from 10. *1 Derrycaw Lane, Portadown, Craigavon BT62 1TW* T: (028) 3885 1503 E: elizabethstevenson431@btinternet.com

STEVENSON, Michael Richard Nevin. b 52. Univ Coll Lon MA 77. CITC. **d** 86 **p** 87. C Clooney w Strathfoyle *D & R* 86-89; CF 89-12; I Bunclody w Kildavin, Clonegal and Kilrush *C & O* from 12. *The Rectory, Ryland Road, Bunclody, Co Wexford, Republic of Ireland* T: (00353) (53) 937 7652 E: bunclody@ferns.anglican.org

STEVENSON, Miss Pamela Mary. b 35. CQSW 74. **d** 97 **p** 98. OLM Mitcham Ascension *S'wark* 97-05; PtO from 05; Retirement Officer Kingston Area from 08. *7 Robin Hood Close, Mitcham CR4 1JN* T: (020) 8764 8331 M: 07702-928204 E: revpam@tesco.net

STEVENSON, Peter John. b 70. Southn Univ BSc 91 MSc 93. Wycliffe Hall Ox 00. **d** 02 **p** 03. C Watford St Luke *St Alb* 02-06; TV Hemel Hempstead from 06. *The Vicarage, 436 Warners End Road, Hemel Hempstead HP1 3QF* T: (01442) 251897

STEVENSON, Richard Hugh. b 45. Ex Univ BA 68 Bexley Hall Rochester NY DMin 83. Westcott Ho Cam 68. **d** 70 **p** 71. C Millhouses H Trin *Sheff* 70-74; Chapl Hong Kong Cathl 74-80; R Fairport St Luke USA 81-91; R Kenwood St Patr from 91. *610 Los Alamos, Santa Rosa CA 95409-4413, USA* T: (001) (707) 833 4228 E: stpatskenwood@aol.com

STEVENSON, Robert. b 52. UWIST BSc 73 Cant Ch Ch Univ MA 11 MRTPI 78 MCIM 89. SEITE 03. **d** 05 **p** 06. NSM Woodnesborough w Worth and Staple *Cant* 05-12; NSM Eastry and Woodnesborough from 12; Managing Dir Dioc Architects from 11. *The Old Rectory, 5 Cowper Road, Deal CT14 9TW* T: (01304) 366003 E: rev.rob.stevenson@btinternet.com

STEVENSON, Canon Robert Brian. b 40. QUB BA 61 Qu Coll Cam BA 67 MA 71 Pemb Coll Ox BA 69 BD 76 MA 76 Birm Univ PhD 70. Cuddesdon Coll 69. **d** 70 **p** 71. C Lewisham St Jo Southend *S'wark* 70-73; C Catford (Southend) and Downham 73-74; Lect and Dir Past Studies Chich Th Coll 74-81; Acting Vice-Prin 80-81; V W Malling w Offham *Roch* 81-10; RD Malling 93-02; Hon Can Roch Cathl 98-10; rtd 10; PtO *Roch* from 10. *Michaelmas Cottage, Stan Lane, West Peckham, Maidstone ME18 5JT* T: (01622) 817693 E: woolystevenson@yahoo.co.uk

STEVENSON, Sheila Reinhardt. *See* SWARBRICK, Sheila Reinhardt

STEVENSON, Trevor Donald. b 59. TCD Div Sch BTh. **d** 91 **p** 92. C Magheralin w Dollingstown *D & D* 91-95; CMS Uganda 95-98; Dir Fields of Life from 98; I Crinken *D & G* from 11. *Tree Tops, Brides Glen Road, Shankill, Dublin 18, Republic of Ireland* T/F: (00353) (1) 282 0150 M: 87-981 2025 E: trevor.stevenson@fieldsoflife.org

STEVENSON TATE, Ms Lynne Margaret. b 54. Open Univ BA 96. Yorks Min Course 06. **d** 12 **p** 13. NSM Farsley *Leeds* from 12. *6 Providence Street, Farsley, Pudsey LS28 5AZ* T: 0113-255 4677   M: 07749-424557 E: lynnestevensontate@gmail.com

STEVENTON, Canon June Lesley. b 61. Aston Tr Scheme 86 Sarum & Wells Th Coll BTh 91. **d** 91 **p** 94. Par Dn Chatham St Steph *Roch* 91-94; C 94-96; PtO *York* 96-97; *Liv* 97-00; V Abram 00-10; V Bickershaw 00-10; P-in-c Winwick 10-15; R from 15; P-in-c Burtonwood 14-15; V from 15; Hon Can Liv Cathl from 06. *The Rectory, Golborne Road, Winwick, Warrington WA2 8SZ* T: (01925) 632760 E: june.steventon123@btinternet.com

STEVENTON, Kenneth. b 59. Cuddesdon Coll 94. **d** 96 **p** 97. C Spalding St Mary and St Nic *Linc* 96-99; R Sutterton, Fosdyke, Algarkirk and Wigtoft 99-05; P-in-c Evenwood *Dur* 05-09; P-in-c Ingleton from 05; P-in-c Staindrop from 05. *St Mary's Vicarage, 7 Beechside, Staindrop, Darlington DL2 3PE* T: (01833) 660237 E: revken@freeuk.co.uk

STEVINSON, Harold John Hardy. b 34. Selw Coll Cam BA 57 MA 61. Qu Coll Birm. **d** 59 **p** 60. C Bris St Mary Redcliffe w Temple 59-63; C Caversham *Ox* 63-73; Soc Resp Officer *Dur* 74-82; Sec Dioc Bd for Miss and Unity 82-88; P-in-c Croxdale *Dur* 82-88; P-in-c Leamington Hastings and Birdingbury *Cov* 88-96; rtd 96; PtO *Cov* 96-00; *Glouc* from 96. *8 Greenways, Winchcombe, Cheltenham GL54 5LG* T: (01242) 602195

STEVINSON, Mrs Josephine Mary. b 25. STh 56. Cranmer Hall Dur 86. **dss** 86 **d** 87 **p** 94. Croxdale *Dur* 86-87; LtO 87-88; *Cov* 88-96; NSM Leamington Hastings and Birdingbury 94-96; rtd 96; PtO *Glouc* from 96. *8 Greenways, Winchcombe, Cheltenham GL54 5LG* T: (01242) 602195

STEWARD, Mrs Linda Christine. b 46. NE Lon Poly CQSW 82. S'wark Ord Course 85. **d** 88 **p** 94. NSM E Ham w Upton Park and Forest Gate *Chelmsf* 88-91; Chapl Newham Healthcare NHS Trust Lon 91-98; NSM Plaistow *Chelmsf* 91-96; NSM Plaistow and N Canning Town 96-98; P-in-c Rawreth w Rettendon 98-06; rtd 06. *2 Belfairs Park Close, Leigh-on-Sea SS9 4TR* T: (01702) 525638 E: steward_linda@hotmail.com

STEWARDSON, Enid Joyce. b 53. **d** 11 **p** 12. OLM Heath Hayes *Lich* 11-15; PtO from 15. *Highfield House, 20 Highfield Road, Cannock WS12 2DX* T: (01543) 279817 E: joycestewa@aol.com

STEWART, Alan. See STEWART, Hugh Alan

STEWART, Alan Valentine. b 47. Univ Coll Galway BA 98. **d** 97 **p** 98. NSM Mullingar, Portnashangan, Moyliscar, Kilbixy etc *M & K* 97-00; NSM Clane w Donadea and Coolcarrigan 00-05; NSM Dunboyne and Rathmolyon from 05. *Casteway, Baltrasna, Ashbourne, Co Meath, Republic of Ireland* T: (00353) (1) 835 0997 *or* 814 0297   M: 87-179 3197 E: casteway@hotmail.com *or* alan.stewart@fas.ie

STEWART, Alice Elizabeth. b 42. **d** 00 **p** 01. C Cloughfern *Conn* from 00. *3 Fergus Court, Carrickfergus BT38 8HT* T: (028) 9336 5721

STEWART, Alistair Charles. b 60. St Andr Univ MA 83 Birm Univ PhD 92. Qu Coll Birm 86. **d** 89 **p** 90. C Stevenage St Andr and St Geo *St Alb* 89-92; C Castle Vale St Cuth *Birm* 92-93; Lect Codrington Coll Barbados 93-97; C Hanley H Ev *Lich* 97-98; Prof Gen Th Sem NY USA 98-01; V Bridge Par *Sarum* 01-10; C Sherborne w Castleton, Lillington and Longburton 10-12; TV Upton cum Chalvey *Ox* from 13. *St Peter's Vicarage, 52 Montem Lane, Slough SL1 2QJ* T: (01753) 520725

STEWART (*née* BARBER), Mrs Anne Louise. b 71. QUB BA 93 PGCE 94. CITC 97. **d** 00 **p** 01. NSM Belfast Malone St Jo *Conn* 00-09; NSM Finaghy 09-11; I from 11. *St George's Rectory, 6 Royal Lodge Park, Belfast BT8 7YP* T: (028) 9070 1350 *or* 9029 2980   M: 07724-067547 E: stewartrevslb@yahoo.com

STEWART, Miss Betty. b 25. S'wark Ord Course 91. **d** 93 **p** 94. NSM Wandsworth Common St Mary *S'wark* 93-95; NSM Hampton Hill *Lon* 95-05. *71 Ormond Drive, Hampton TW12 2TL* T: (020) 8979 2069

STEWART, Ms Brenda Alice. b 60. ERMC. **d** 09 **p** 10. C Abbots Ripton w Wood Walton *Ely* 09-12; C Kings Ripton 09-12; C Houghton w Wyton 09-12; P-in-c W Leightonstone from 12. *The Rectory, Church Lane, Brington, Huntingdon PE28 5AE* E: bas@con-brio.com

STEWART, Brian. b 59. TCD BTh 91. CITC 88. **d** 91 **p** 92. C Ballywillan *Conn* 91-94; I Belfast St Geo from 94. *St George's Rectory, 6 Royal Lodge Park, Belfast BT8 7YP* T: (028) 9070 1350 M: 07902-792080

STEWART, Charles. b 55. St Jo Coll Cam BA 77 MA 81 CertEd 79. Wycliffe Hall Ox 85. **d** 87 **p** 88. C Bowdon *Ches* 87-90; C Bath Abbey w St Jas *B & W* 90-94; Can Res, Prec and Sacr Win Cathl 94-06; V Walton-on-Thames *Guildf* 06-15; P-in-c Christchurch *Win* from 15. *The Vicarage, 13A Church Street, Christchurch BH23 1BW* E: canonstewart@tiscali.co.uk

STEWART, Charles Michael. b 50. Ball Coll Ox MA 82 K Coll Lon BA 05 AKC 05 MA 07 FCA 82. Ripon Coll Cuddesdon 06. **d** 07 **p** 08. NSM Leatherhead and Mickleham *Guildf* 07-11. *Rickstones, Punchbowl Lane, Dorking RH5 4BN* T: (01306) 884153   M: 07936-524152 E: mikestewart999@btinternet.com

STEWART, Ms Dorothy Elaine. b 51. Man Metrop Univ BA 93 Bradf Univ MA 98. Coll of Resurr Mirfield 08. **d** 10 **p** 11. C Potternewton *Leeds* 10-14; V Fairweather Green *Bradf* from 14. *The Vicarage, Ings Way, Bradford BD8 0LU* M: 07826-107049 E: dotelartuna@hotmail.com

STEWART, Hugh Alan. b 67. Lon Inst BA 91 Middx Univ BA 03. NTMTC 00. **d** 03 **p** 04. C Gt Stanmore *Lon* 03-06; P-in-c Hertford St Andr *St Alb* 06-08; P-in-c Hertingfordbury 06-08; TV Hertford from 08. *St Andrew's Rectory, 7 Elizabeth Close, Hertford SG14 2DB* T: (01992) 582726 E: h.alanstewart@tiscali.co.uk

STEWART, Ian Guild. b 43. Edin Th Coll 89. **d** 84 **p** 85. NSM Dundee St Mary Magd *Bre* 84-87; NSM Dundee St Jo 87-90; C 90-92; NSM Dundee St Martin 87-90; C 90-92; R Montrose 92-08; P-in-c Inverbervie 92-08; Can St Paul's Cathl Dundee 01-08; Dean Bre 07-08; rtd 08; Hon Can St Paul's Cathl Dundee from 08; LtO *Edin* from 11. *36 Forbes Road, Edinburgh EH10 4ED* T: 0131-466 8405

STEWART, James. See STEWART, Malcolm James

STEWART, James. b 32. Div Hostel Dub. **d** 69 **p** 70. C Belfast St Donard *D & D* 69-72; C Dundonald 72-74; I Rathmullan w Tyrella 74-80; I Belfast St Clem 80-97; I Moy w Charlemont *Arm* 97-04; rtd 04. *25 Barnish Road, Kells, Ballymena BT42 3PA* T: (028) 2589 8787   M: 07833-791790 E: revj.stewart@subfish.com

STEWART, Canon James Patrick. b 55. Keele Univ BA 77 Birm Univ MA 78. Ridley Hall Cam 86. **d** 88 **p** 89. C Boulton *Derby* 88-91; C Cove St Jo *Guildf* 91-92; TV 92-97; TR Tunbridge Wells St Jas w St Phil *Roch* 97-04; V Tunbridge Wells St Jas from 04; RD Tunbridge Wells 99-07; Hon Can Roch Cathl from 05. *The Vicarage, 12 Shandon Close, Tunbridge Wells TN2 3RE* T: (01892) 530687 *or* 521703 E: jpstewart4@googlemail.com

STEWART, James William. b 71. Selw Coll Cam BA 92 MA 96 Anglia Ruskin Univ MA 12. Westcott Ho Cam 09 Yale Div Sch 10. **d** 11 **p** 12. C Gt Yarmouth *Nor* 11-14; Bp's Chapl from 14; Hon PV Nor Cathl from 14. *The Vicarage, St Martin at Palace Plain, Norwich NR3 1RW* M: 07986-839583   T: (01603) 614172 E: bishops.chaplain@dioceseofnorwich.org

STEWART, Mrs Janet Margaret. b 41. Roehampton Inst CertEd 62. Cranmer Hall Dur 67. **d** 87 **p** 94. Hon Par Dn Oulton Broad *Nor* 87-94; Hon C 94-97; Chapl Lowestoft Hosp 94-97; PtO *B & W* 97-98; C Quidenham Gp *Nor* 98-01; Asst Chapl Norfolk and Nor Univ Hosp NHS Trust from 00. *30 St Joseph's Road, Sheringham NR26 8JA* T: (01263) 824497

STEWART, Jennifer Jane. See SISTIG, Jennifer Jane

STEWART, John. b 39. Oak Hill Th Coll 75. **d** 77 **p** 78. C Accrington Ch Ch *Blackb* 77-79; TV Darwen St Pet w Hoddlesden 79-86; R Coppull St Jo 86-04; rtd 04; PtO *Blackb* 05-11. *83 Regents Way, Euxton, Chorley PR7 6PG*

✠**STEWART, The Rt Revd John Craig.** b 40. Ridley Coll Melbourne LTh 64. **d** 65 **p** 66 **c** 84. C Prospect Australia 65-67; C Mt Gambier 67-68; C Crawley *Chich* 68-70; Australia 70-74; I Frankston 74-79; Gen Sec CMS Vic 79-84; Asst Bp Melbourne 84-01; W Region 84-91; N Region 91-94; E Region 94-01; V Gen 88-01; R Woodend 01-04; rtd 04. *PO Box 928, Bacchus Marsh Vic 3440, Australia* T: (0061) (3) 5367 0081 E: bishopjcstewart@bigpond.com

STEWART, Canon John Wesley. b 52. QUB BD 76 TCD 76. **d** 77 **p** 78. C Seagoe *D & D* 77-79; C Lisburn Ch Ch *Conn* 79-85; I Ballybay w Mucknoe and Clontibret *Clogh* 85-90; I Derryvullen S w Garvary from 90; Bp's Dom Chapl 95-00; Glebes Sec from 95; Dioc Registrar from 98; Exam Can Clogh Cathl 98-00; Preb from 00. *The Rectory, 2 Ballylucas Road, Tullyharney, Enniskillen BT74 4PR* T: (028) 6638 7236 E: jva.stewart@hotmail.co.uk

STEWART, Keith Malcolm Morris. b 45. **d** 08 **p** 09. OLM Stalybridge *Man* 08-14; PtO from 14; *Ches* from 14. *6 Hillside Close, Weston, Crewe CW2 5FZ* T: (01270) 829044

STEWART, Kim Deborah. See MATHERS, Kim Deborah

STEWART, Louise. See STEWART, Anne Louise

STEWART, Malcolm James. b 44. TR 78. York Univ BA 66 K Coll Lon MA 68 Lon Inst of Educn PGCE 69 Solicitor 79. NEOC 89. **d** 93 **p** 94. NSM Upper Nidderdale *Ripon* 93-95; C Fountains Gp 95-98; V Catterick 98-03; P-in-c Culmington w Onibury, Bromfield etc *Heref* 03-06; TV Ludlow 06-10; RD 07-10; rtd 10. *3 Leadon Place, Ledbury HR8 2GD* T: (01531) 630237

STEWART, Marcus Patrick Michael. b 66. Ox Univ BA 89 MSc 93 Cam Univ BA 92. Ven English Coll Rome 89 Westcott Ho Cam 96. **d** 98 **p** 99. C Headington *Ox* 98-00; Hon C S Hinksey 00-01; CF 01-04; Chapl RN 04-07; PtO *Cant* 08-09; Chapl HM Pris Elmley 09-10; Hon C St Peter-in-Thanet *Cant* 09-10; Chapl Kent Police 09-10; Lead Chapl Peterborough and Stamford Hosps NHS Foundn Trust 10-12; Chapl Pilgrims Hospice Thanet 12-15; Chapl E Kent Hosps NHS Trust from 15. *Kent and Canterbury Hospital, Ethelbert Road, Canterbury CT1 3NG* M: 07948-218521 T: (01227) 864095
E: marcus.stewart@pilgrimshospices.org

STEWART, Maxwell Neville Gabriel. b 33. Essex Univ MA 68 Hertf Coll Ox BA 58 MA 59. Wycliffe Hall Ox 58. **d** 60 **p** 61. C Perry Beeches Birm 60-62; Chapl Rosenberg Coll St Gallen 62-64; PtO *Chelmsf* 64-70; Warden Leics Poly 70-92; De Montfort Univ Leic 92-93; Hon C Leic St Mary 74-79; rtd 93; PtO *Leic* from 79. *25 Sidney Court, Norwich Road, Leicester LE4 0LR*

STEWART, Michael. *See* STEWART, Charles Michael

STEWART, Michael. b 65. St Jo Coll Nottm LTh 89. **d** 89 **p** 90. C Ealing St Paul *Lon* 89-93; P-in-c N Wembley St Cuth 93-98; V 98-02; Assoc P Abbotsford Canada from 02. *St Matthew's Anglican Church, 2010 Guilford Drive, Abbotsford BC, V2S 5R2, Canada* T: (001) (604) 853 2416
E: mikes@stmatthewsanglicanchurch.com

STEWART, Ms Monica Frances Ethel. b 35. RGN 57 RM 59. **d** 08 **p** 12. NSM Stamford Hill St Thos *Lon* from 08. *2 The Heights, 165 Mountview Road, London N4 4JU* T: (020) 8340 4746 M: 07947-026297
E: monica.f.stewart@googlemail.com

STEWART, Canon Raymond John. b 55. TCD BA 79 MA 82. CITC Div Test 77. **d** 79 **p** 80. C Clooney *D & R* 79-82; I Dunfanaghy 82-87; I Gweedore Union 85-87; Dioc Youth Adv 83-87; Bp's Dom Chapl 85-87; I Castledawson 87-03; I Tamlaght O'Crilly Upper w Lower from 03; Ed D & R Dioc News 89-93; Dioc Glebes Sec *D & R* from 93; Stewardship Adv from 98; Can Derry Cathl from 99. *Hervey Hill Rectory, 16 Hervey Hill, Kilrea, Coleraine BT51 5TT* T/F: (028) 2954 0296 M: 07761-585412
E: raymondandpatricia@herveyhill.wanadoo.co.uk

STEWART, Stephen John. b 62. Oak Hill Th Coll. **d** 99 **p** 00. C Mile Cross *Nor* 99-04; TV Cove St Jo *Guildf* from 04. *Southwood Vicarage, 15 The Copse, Farnborough GU14 0QD* T: (01252) 513422 E: stevestewartce@hotmail.com

STEWART, Susan Catherine. *See* BELL, Susan Catherine

STEWART, Susan Theresa. b 58. NOC 01. **d** 04 **p** 05. C Lodge Moor St Luke *Sheff* 04-08; V Mosborough from 08. *The Vicarage, 25 Kelgate, Mosborough, Sheffield S20 5EJ* T: 0114-248 6518 M: 07966-695095

STEWART, William James. b 58. Ulster Poly BA 82 Spurgeon's Coll Lon MTh 10. CITC 80. **d** 83 **p** 84. C Glenageary *D & G* 83-86; Rostrevor Renewal Cen 86-87; I Naas w Kill and Rathmore *M & K* 87-93; Min Dublin Ch Ch Cathl Gp 93-04; CORE (St Cath Ch) 93-04; Min Can St Patr Cathl Dublin 00-04; LtO Cashel, Waterford and Lismore *C & O* 08-11; V Loddon, Sisland, Chedgrave, Hardley and Langley *Nor* 11-12. *Address temp unknown* M: 07582-873183
E: willijstewart@yahoo.co.uk

STEWART, William Jones. b 32. Trin Hall Cam BA 55 MA 59 Cam Univ CertEd 56. Edin Th Coll 67. **d** 69 **p** 69. Chapl St Ninian's Cathl Perth 69-71; Bp's Dom Chapl *Ox* 71-75; V Lambourn 75-03; P-in-c Lambourne Woodlands 83-03; P-in-c Eastbury and E Garston 83-03; rtd 04. *9 Ascott Way, Newbury RG14 2FH* T: (01635) 580244
E: stewart.clan4@btopenworld.com

STEWART-DARLING, Fiona Lesley. b 58. Kingston Poly GRSC 79 Lon Univ PhD 82 K Coll Lon MA 99. Trin Coll Bris BA 91. **d** 91 **p** 94. C Cirencester *Glouc* 91-94; Chapl Cheltenham and Glouc Coll of HE 94-97; Chapl Portsm Univ 97-04; Hon Chapl Portsm Cathl 97-04; Bp's Chapl in Docklands *Lon* from 04; PV Westmr Abbey from 13. *143 New Atlas Wharf, 3 Arnhem Place, London E14 3ST* T: (020) 7477 1073 M: 07739-461090
E: fiona.stewart-darling@london.anglican.org

STEWART ELLENS, Gordon Frederick. *See* ELLENS, Gordon Frederick Stewart

STEWART SMITH, Mrs Alison Mary. b 74. St Andr Univ MA 96 St Jo Coll Dur BA 15 Homerton Coll Cam PGCE 97. Cranmer Hall Dur 13. **d** 15. C Swaledale *Ripon* from 15. *Mill House, Swale Hall Lane, Grinton, Richmond DL11 6HL* T: (01748) 884635 E: alisonmstewartsmith@gmail.com

STEWART-SYKES, Teresa Melanie. b 64. Bris Univ BA 85. Qu Coll Birm 87. **d** 89. Par Dn Stevenage St Andr and St Geo *St Alb* 89-92; PtO *Birm* 92-93; Barbados 93-97; C Meir Heath

Lich 97-98; USA 98-01; NSM Dorchester *Sarum* 12-14; NSM Dorchester and the Winterbournes from 14. *1 Mithras Close, Dorchester DT1 2RF* T: (01305) 266472
E: tstewartsykes@blandfordschool.org.uk

STIBBE, Mrs Hazel Mary. **d** 99 **p** 00. NSM Wolverhampton St Andr *Lich* 99-02; LtO *St As* 03-08; rtd 08; PtO *St As* from 09. *Braemar, Kerry Street, Montgomery SY15 6PG* T: (01686) 668912

STIBBE, Mark William Godfrey. b 60. Trin Coll Cam BA 83 MA 86 Nottm Univ PhD 88. St Jo Coll Nottm 83. **d** 86 **p** 87. C Stapleford *S'well* 86-90; C Crookes St Thos *Sheff* 90-93; Lect Sheff Univ 90-97; V Grenoside *Sheff* 93-97; V Chorleywood St Andr *St Alb* 97-09; Ldr Father's Ho Trust 09-12. *Address temp unknown* E: markstibbe@aol.com

STICKINGS, James Edmund de Garis. b 76. Magd Coll Ox BA 98 MA 08. Ripon Coll Cuddesdon 08. **d** 12 **p** 13. C Headington Quarry *Ox* from 12. *53 Downside Road, Headington, Oxford OX3 8HR* T: (01865) 742046 M: 07804-624488 E: stickingsjames@gmail.com

STICKLAND, David Clifford. b 44. Surrey Univ BA 01 CPFA 68 MAAT 77 FCCA 80. STETS 98. **d** 01 **p** 02. NSM Greatham w Empshott and Hawkley w Prior's Dean *Portsm* 01-05; NSM Petersfield and Buriton 05-10; rtd 10; PtO *Portsm* from 11. *14 Captains Row, Portsmouth PO1 2TT* M: 07836-282561
E: david_stickland.t21@btinternet.com

STICKLAND, Geoffrey John Brett. b 42. Open Univ BSc 96. St D Coll Lamp. **d** 66 **p** 67. C Aberavon H Trin *Llan* 66-69; C-in-c Llanrumney CD *Mon* 69-72; C Tetbury w Beverston *Glouc* 72-75; V Hardwicke 75-82; R Hardwicke, Quedgeley and Elmore w Longney 82-98; V Quedgeley 98-11; rtd 11. *19 Tai Cae Mawr, Llanwrtyd Wells LD5 4RJ* T: (01591) 610701 E: geoffstickland@googlemail.com

STICKLEY (née BRAGG), Mrs Annette Frances. b 44. Chich Th Coll 97. **d** 00. NSM Worth *Chich* 00-06; PtO from 06. *14 Elmstead Park Road, West Wittering, Chichester PO20 8NQ* T: (01243) 514619 E: annettestickley@talktalk.net

STIDOLPH, Canon Robert Anthony. b 54. GBSM 76 ARCM 75 FRSA 92. St Steph Ho Ox 77. **d** 80 **p** 80. C Hove All SS *Chich* 80-84; TV Brighton Resurr 84-87; Chapl Cheltenham Coll 87-94; Sen Chapl and Hd RS Wellington Coll Berks 94-01; Chapl and Asst Master Radley Coll 01-05; Hon Can Ch Ch *Ox* 00-04; P-in-c Worth, Pound Hill and Maidenbower *Chich* 05-10; Chapl Peterho Zimbabwe 10-14; Chapl Llandovery Coll from 14. *Llandovery College, Llandovery SA20 0EE* T: (01550) 723000 E: anthony.stidolph@hotmail.co.uk

STIFF, Canon Derrick Malcolm. b 40. Lich Th Coll 69. **d** 72 **p** 73. C Cov St Geo 72-75; R Benhall w Sternfield *St E* 75-79; P-in-c Snape w Friston 75-79; V Cartmel *Carl* 79-87; R Sudbury and Chilton *St E* 87-94; P-in-c Lavenham 94-95; P-in-c Preston 94-95; R Lavenham w Preston 95-03; Min Can St E Cathl 90-00; Hon Can St E Cathl 00-03; RD Lavenham 95-03; rtd 03; PtO *St E* from 03; *Sarum* from 03. *8 Keats Close, Saxmundham IP17 1WJ* T: (01728) 652964
E: canonstiff@hotmail.com

STILEMAN, William Mark Charles. b 63. Selw Coll Cam BA 85 MA 89 PGCE 86. Wycliffe Hall Ox. **d** 91 **p** 92. C Ox St Andr 91-95; TV Gt Chesham 95-03; P-in-c Maidenhead St Andr and St Mary 03-04; V from 04. *St Mary's Vicarage, 14 Juniper Drive, Maidenhead SL6 8RE* T: (01628) 624908
E: will.stileman@stmarysmaidenhead.org

STILL, Colin Charles. b 35. Selw Coll Cam BA 67 MA 71 United Th Sem Dayton STM 69. Cranmer Hall Dur 67. **d** 69 **p** 70. C Drypool St Columba w St Andr and St Pet *York* 69-72; Abp's Dom Chapl 72-75; Recruitment Sec ACCM 76-80; P-in-c Ockham w Hatchford *Guildf* 76-80; R 80-90; Can Missr and Ecum Officer 80-90; PtO *Chich* from 92; rtd 96. *Flat 9, 16 Lewes Crescent, Brighton BN2 1GB* T: (01273) 686014

STILL (née STACEY), Mrs Gillian. b 53. SWMTC 94. **d** 97 **p** 98. NSM Peter Tavy, Mary Tavy, Lydford and Brent Tor *Ex* 97-06; C Abbotskerswell from 06; Chapl Rowcroft Hospice Torquay from 01. *The Vicarage, Church Path, Abbotskerswell, Newton Abbot TQ12 5NY* T: (01626) 334445 *or* (01803) 210829 M: 07971-412511 E: gillstill@yahoo.co.uk

STILL, Jonathan Trevor Lloyd. b 59. Ex Univ BA 81 Qu Coll Cam BA 84 MA 88. Westcott Ho Cam 82. **d** 85 **p** 86. C Weymouth H Trin *Sarum* 85-88; Chapl for Agric *Heref* 88-93; V N Petherton w Northmoor Green *B & W* 93-00; V The Bourne and Tilford *Guildf* 00-11; RD Farnham 05-10; V Buckland Newton, Cerne Abbas, Godmanstone etc *Sarum* from 11. *The Vicarage, 4 Back Lane, Cerne Abbas, Dorchester DT2 7JW* T: (01300) 341251 E: cernevicar@gmail.com

STILL, Kenneth Donald. b 37. St Aid Birkenhead 64. **d** 67 **p** 95. C Ainsdale *Liv* 67-68; C Kirkby 68-69; C Sutton 96-98; TV 98-03; rtd 03. *The Cottage, Wash Road, Kirton, Boston PE20 1QG* T: (01205) 724043

STILWELL, Malcolm Thomas. b 54. Coll of Resurr Mirfield 83. **d** 86 **p** 87. C Workington St Mich *Carl* 86-90; P-in-c Flimby

90-93; PtO 93-95; NSM Westfield St Mary 95-11; NSM Workington St Jo from 11. *18 Moorfield Avenue, Workington CA14 4HJ* T: (01900) 66757 E: info@thestilwellstudio.co.uk

STILWELL, Mrs Susan May. b 59. Herts Univ MA 96. ERMC 08. **d** 11 **p** 12. NSM Bp's Hatfield, Lemsford and N Mymms *St Alb* from 11. *42 Barleycroft Road, Welwyn Garden City AL8 6JU* T: (01707) 338304 E: susan.stilwell@clara.co.uk

STILWELL, Timothy James. b 65. Birm Univ BA 87. Wycliffe Hall Ox 96. **d** 98 **p** 99. C Clifton Ch Ch w Em *Bris* 98-02; C Hammersmith St Paul *Lon* 02-05; V Fulham St Dionis from 05; AD Hammersmith and Fulham from 15. *St Dionis' Vicarage, 18 Parson's Green, London SW6 4UH* T: (020) 7731 1376 E: tim@stdionis.org.uk

STIMPSON, Nigel Leslie. b 60. St Martin's Coll Lanc BA 92 Lanc Univ MA 99. Coll of Resurr Mirfield 94. **d** 94 **p** 95. C Heyhouses on Sea *Blackb* 94-96; C Torrisholme 96-99; V Ravensthorpe and Thornhill Lees w Savile Town *Wakef* 99-05; TR Ribbleton *Blackb* 05-12; R 12-13; Chapl Gtr Lisbon *Eur* 13-14; Asst Chapl Palma de Mallorca from 14. *St Philip and St James, Nuñez de Balboa 6, Son Armadans, 07014 Palma de Mallorca* T: (0034) 971 737 279 E: nigel.stimpson13@gmail.com

STINSON, Andrew James. b 80. Newc Univ MEng 04 St Jo Coll Dur BA 11. Cranmer Hall Dur 09. **d** 12 **p** 13. C Oxton *Ches* 12-15; R Barrow from 15; Dioc Worship Adv from 15. *The Rectory, Mill Lane, Great Barrow, Chester CH3 7JF* M: 07847-948976 T: (01829) 740263 E: revandystinson@gmail.com

STIRLING, Canon Christina Dorita (Tina). b 48. Lon Univ BEd 73. Wycliffe Hall Ox 87. **d** 89 **p** 94. Par Dn Thame w Towersey *Ox* 89-94; C 94-98; P-in-c Brill, Boarstall, Chilton and Dorton 98; R Bernwode 98-13; AD Aylesbury 05-10; Hon Can Ch Ch 09-13; rtd 13; PtO *Ox* from 13. *The Rectory, Stone, Aylesbury HP17 8RZ* T: (01296) 747587 E: tina.stirling@btinternet.com

STIRLING TROY, Mrs Margaret Ann. b 63. St Hilda's Coll Ox BA 85 MA. STETS 10. **d** 13 **p** 14. C Farncombe *Guildf* from 13. *10 Dormers Close, Godalming GU7 2QX* T: (01483) 428733 E: mstirling1@hotmail.co.uk

STIRZAKER, Maureen Ann. b 51. **d** 08 **p** 09. NSM Chadderton St Matt w St Luke *Man* 08-11; NSM Aberdour *St And* from 11; NSM Burntisland from 11; NSM Inverkeithing from 11. *4 Morayvale, Aberdour, Burntisland KY3 0XE* T: (01383) 861283 E: stirzaker776@btinternet.com

STOBART, Stuart Malcolm. b 64. Glos Univ BA 07. Yorks Min Course 07. **d** 09 **p** 10. C Clayton *Bradf* 09-12; P-in-c Hellifield *Leeds* 12-15; P-in-c Long Preston w Tosside 12-15; V Hellifield and Long Preston from 15. *Kellwell House, Kendal Road, Hellifield, Skipton BD23 4HE* T: (01729) 851511 M: 07545-631387 E: stuart.stobart@yahoo.co.uk

STOBER, Brenda Jacqueline. b 57. Liv Univ BSc 79 Leeds Univ BA 08 Lanc Univ PGCE 80. NOC 04. **d** 07 **p** 08. C Southport Em *Liv* 07-11; C Wavertree H Trin 11-13; V Denton *Newc* from 13. *The Vicarage, Dunblane Crescent, Newcastle upon Tyne NE5 2BE* T: 0191-267 2058 M: 07812-471269 E: jackstober@yahoo.co.uk

STOCK, Edward Christopher James. b 85. Heythrop Coll Lon BA 12. Ridley Hall Cam 12. **d** 14 **p** 15. C Eastwood *Chelmsf* from 14. *215 Green Lane, Leigh-on-Sea SS9 5QN* M: 07838-156835 E: eddstock@hotmail.com

STOCK, Lionel Crispian. b 58. Nottm Univ BTh 94 ACMA 85 ACIS 94. Linc Th Coll 91. **d** 94 **p** 95. C Preston w Sutton Poyntz, Littlemoor etc *Sarum* 94-97; P-in-c Stalbridge 97-00; Hon C Hillingdon All SS *Lon* 01-04; NSM Kendal H Trin *Carl* 04-10; PtO *Win* 10-12; Min Can Win Cathl 12-13; PtO *Eur* 10-13; P-in-c W Meon and Warnford *Portsm* from 13. *The Rectory, Doctors Lane, West Meon, Petersfield GU32 1LR* T: (01730) 829266 M: 07814-935715 E: revlstock@hotmail.com

STOCK, Nigel. See STOCK, William Nigel

STOCK, Miss Ruth Vaughan. b 51. Birkbeck Coll Lon BA 79 MA 85. Wycliffe Hall Ox 91. **d** 93 **p** 94. Par Dn Toxteth St Philemon w St Gabr and St Cleopas *Liv* 93-94; C 94-97; TV 97-10; TV St Luke in the City 10-13; C from 13. *St Michael's Church Flat, Upper Pitt Street, Liverpool L1 5DB* E: ruthstock@ymail.com

STOCK, The Very Revd Victor Andrew. b 44. OAM 02. AKC 68 FRSA 95. **d** 69 **p** 70. C Pinner *Lon* 69-73; Chapl Lon Univ 73-79; R Friern Barnet St Jas 79-86; R St Mary le Bow w St Pancras Soper Lane etc 86-02; P-in-c St Mary Aldermary 87-98; Dean Guildf 02-12; rtd 12. *62 Bramwell House, Churchill Gardens, London SW1V 3DS* T: (020) 7828 4921 E: vastock@btinternet.com

✠**STOCK, The Rt Revd William Nigel.** b 50. St Cuth Soc Dur BA 72. Ripon Coll Cuddesdon. **d** 76 **p** 77 **c** 00. C Stockton St Pet *Dur* 76-79; Papua New Guinea 79-84; V Shiremoor *Newc*

85-91; TR N Shields 91-98; RD Tynemouth 92-98; Hon Can Newc Cathl 97-98; Can Res Dur Cathl 98-00; Chapl Grey Coll Dur 99-00; Suff Bp Stockport *Ches* 00-07; Bp St E 07-13; Bp at Lambeth *Cant* from 13; Hon Asst Bp S'wark from 13; Bp Falkland Is from 14; Bp HM Forces from 14. *Lambeth Palace, London SE1 7JU* T: (020) 7898 1200

STOCKBRIDGE, Alan Carmichael. b 33. MBE 89. Keble Coll Ox BA 55 MA 62. Wycliffe Hall Ox 66. **d** 68 **p** 69. CF 68-78 and 82-92; Chapl Reading Sch 78-82; R Harrietsham w Ulcombe *Cant* 92-98; rtd 98; PtO *Eur* from 00; *Cant* from 09. *Albrecht Dürerstrasse 4, 96106 Ebern, Germany* T/F: (0049) (9531) 942799 E: erikastockbridge@aol.com

STOCKER, David William George. b 37. Bris Univ BA 58 CertEd. Qu Coll Birm 59. **d** 60 **p** 61. C Sparkhill St Jo *Birm* 60-64; C Keighley *Bradf* 64-66; V Grenoside *Sheff* 66-83; V Sandbach *Ches* 83-01; rtd 01; PtO *Ches* from 01. *18 Mill Bridge Close, Crewe CW1 5DZ* T: (01270) 212865 E: david_stocker06@tiscali.co.uk

STOCKER, John Henry. b 48. Cov Univ BSc 71 Sheff Univ BEd 81 ACP 88. St Mich Coll Llan 01. **d** 04 **p** 05. NSM E Radnor *S & B* 04-06; NSM Irfon Valley 06-09; rtd 09; PtO *S & B* from 10. *1 Tai Cae Mawr, Llanwrtyd Wells LD5 4RJ* T: (01592) 610231 M: 07891-086631

STOCKER, Rachael Ann. See KNAPP, Rachael Ann

STOCKING, Clifford Brian. b 67. Trin Coll Bris 08. **d** 10 **p** 11. C Hadlow *Roch* 10-13; P-in-c March St Wendreda *Ely* 13-15; P-in-c March St Jo 13-15; TV March from 15. *St Wendreda's Rectory, 21 Wimblington Road, March PE15 9QW* T: (01732) 851655 M: 07941-062637 E: clifford2567@gmail.com

STOCKITT, Robin Philip. b 56. Liv Univ BA 77 Crewe & Alsager Coll PGCE 78. Ridley Hall Cam 95. **d** 97 **p** 98. C Billing *Pet* 97-01; P-in-c Freiburg-im-Breisau *Eur* 01-14; Asst Chapl Basle 01-14; I Donagheady *D & R* from 14. *The Rectory, 33 Longland Road, Dunamanagh, Strabane BT82 0PH* T: (028) 7139 8017 M: 07538-243138 E: robin.stockitt@gmail.com

STOCKLEY, Mrs Alexandra Madeleine Reuss. b 43. Cranmer Hall Dur 80 Carl Dioc Tr Inst. **dss** 84 **d** 87 **p** 94. Upperby St Jo *Carl* 84-89; Par Dn 87-89; Dn-in-c Grayrigg, Old Hutton and New Hutton 90-94; P-in-c 94-95; P-in-c Levens 95-03; rtd 03; PtO *Carl* from 03. *Crowberry, Ulpha, Broughton-in-Furness LA20 6DZ* T: (01229) 716875

STOCKPORT, Suffragan Bishop of. See LANE, The Rt Revd Elizabeth Jane Holden

STOCKS, Simon Paul. b 68. Rob Coll Cam BA 89 MA 93 Man Univ PhD 11. Trin Coll Bris BA 03 MPhil 06. **d** 04 **p** 05. C Coulsdon St Jo *S'wark* 04-07; Hon C 07-13; Hon C Purley Ch Ch from 13; Tutor SEITE from 11. *316 Coulsdon Road, Coulsdon CR5 1EB* T: (01737) 553190 E: simon@spstocks.freeserve.co.uk

STOCKTON, Canon Ian George. b 49. Selw Coll Cam BA 72 MA 76 Hull Univ PhD 90. St Jo Coll Nottm PGCE 74. **d** 75 **p** 76. C Chell *Lich* 75-78; C Trentham 78-80; R Dalbeattie *Glas* 80-84; P-in-c Scotton w Northorpe *Linc* 84-88; Asst Local Min Officer 84-88; Local Min Officer and LNSM Course Prin 88-97; TR Monkwearmouth *Dur* 97-11; Can Res and Chan Blackb Cathl from 11. *St Francis House, St Francis Road, Blackburn BB2 2TZ* T: (01254) 200720 E: ian.stockton@blackburncathedral.co.uk

STODDART, David Easton. b 36. K Coll Dur BSc 60 PhD 66 CEng 66 MIMechE 66 FCMI 72 FIQA 76. WEMTC 92. **d** 95 **p** 96. OLM Stroud H Trin *Glouc* 95-99; OLM Woodchester and Brimscombe 99-00; NSM 00-08; Jt Angl Chapl Severn NHS Trust 99-05; Jt Angl Chapl Glos Primary Care Trust 05-11; rtd 11; PtO *Glouc* from 08. *Woodstock, Hampton Green, Box, Stroud GL6 9AD* T: (01453) 885338 E: stoddart@david-isabel.co.uk

STOKE-ON-TRENT, Archdeacon of. See PARKER, The Ven Matthew John

STOKER, Andrew. b 64. Coll of Ripon & York St Jo BA 86. Coll of Resurr Mirfield 87. **d** 90 **p** 91. C Horton *Newc* 90-92; C Clifford *York* 92-96; P-in-c March St Wendreda 96-98; P-in-c Ryther 96-98; P-in-c Wistow 96-98; R Cawood w Ryther and Wistow 98-04; P-in-c York St Clem w St Mary Bishophill Senior 04-05; R York St Clem w St Mary Bishophill from 05. *13 Nunthorpe Avenue, York YO23 1PF* T: (01904) 624425

STOKER, Canon Howard Charles. b 62. Linc Th Coll BTh 93. **d** 93 **p** 94. C Hessle *York* 93-96; C Richmond w Hudswell *Ripon* 96-99; C Downholme and Marske 96-99; R Holt w High Kelling *Nor* from 99; RD Holt 05-11; Hon Can Nor Cathl from 13. *The Rectory, 11 Church Street, Holt NR25 6BB* T: (01263) 712048 F: 711397 E: holtrectory@tiscali.co.uk

STOKER, Canon Joanna Mary. b 57. Leic Univ BA 79 Nottm Univ BCombStuds 83. Linc Th Coll 80. **dss** 83 **d** 87 **p** 94. Greenford H Cross *Lon* 83-87; Par Dn 87-89; Par Dn Farnham Royal w Hedgerley *Ox* 89-92; Dn-in-c Seer Green and Jordans 92-94; P-in-c 94-97; TV Stantonbury and Willen 97-03;

TR Basingstoke *Win* from 03; Hon Can Win Cathl from 08. *The Rectory, Church Street, Basingstoke RG21 7QT* T: (01256) 326654 E: jostoker@dsl.pipex.com

STOKES, Canon Andrew John. b 38. G&C Coll Cam BA 60 MA 64. Ripon Hall Ox 60. **d** 62 **p** 63. C Northampton All SS w St Kath *Pet* 62-65; C Endcliffe *Sheff* 65-68; Ind Missr 65-68; Sen Ind Chapl 69-74; P-in-c Bridport *Sarum* 75-79; TR 79-80; V Holbeach Marsh *Linc* 82-88; Bp's Dom Chapl 88-92; Can Res and Prec Linc Cathl 92-03; rtd 03; PtO *Linc* from 03. *2 Lupin Road, Lincoln LN2 4GD* T: (01522) 537595 E: andrew.stokes@ntlworld.com

STOKES, Colin Arthur (Ted). b 59. Birm Univ BDS 82. WEMTC 00. **d** 03 **p** 04. NSM Bromyard *Heref* 03-08; NSM Bromyard and Stoke Lacy from 09. *Solmor Paddocks, Linley Green Road, Whitbourne, Worcester WR6 5RE* T: (01886) 821625

STOKES, David Francis Robert. b 53. Lon Inst of Educn PGCE 76 Peterho Cam MA 81 Trin Coll Bris BA 87 St Jo Coll Dur MATM 03. Cranmer Hall Dur 01. **d** 03 **p** 04. C Salisbury St Mark *Sarum* 03-08; Asst Chapl Salisbury NHS Foundn Trust 08-10; CMS Argentina from 10. *Misión Anglicana, Salta S/N, Ingeniero Juárez, 3636 Formosa, Argentina* T: (0054) (3711) 420265 E: ds.stokes@tiscali.co.uk

STOKES (née VASTENHOUT), Mrs Jeannetta Hermina. b 62. St Jo Coll Nottm BA 07. **d** 07 **p** 08. C Newport w Longford, Chetwynd and Forton *Lich* 07-11; P-in-c Worfield *Heref* from 11; RD Bridgnorth from 15. *The Vicarage, Hallon, Worfield, Bridgnorth WV15 5JZ* T: (01746) 716698 M: 07985-923202 E: jeannetta.stokes@btopenworld.com

STOKES, Miss Mary Patricia. b 39. St Hilda's Coll Ox BA 62 MA 66 Lanc Univ MA 80 Bris Univ CertEd 63. EMMTC 78. **d** 87 **p** 94. Par Dn Pheasey *Lich* 87-93; C Walton-on-Thames *Guildf* 93-05; rtd 05; PtO *Guildf* from 05. *21 Brittain Road, Walton-on-Thames KT12 4LR* T: (01932) 248945 E: mstokes@gotadsl.co.uk

STOKES, Michael John. b 34. Lich Th Coll 63. **d** 65 **p** 66. C Worplesdon *Guildf* 65-68; Chapl RAF 68-84; Asst Chapl-in-Chief RAF 84-89; QHC 87-95; V Chesterton w Middleton Stoney and Wendlebury *Ox* 89-95; RD Bicester and Islip 90-95; Chapl Kyrenia St Andr Cyprus 95-00; rtd 00; PtO *Ox* from 00. *4 Bicester House, Kings End, Bicester OX26 6DT* T: (01869) 389078

STOKES, Roger Sidney. b 47. Clare Coll Cam BA 68 MA 72. Sarum & Wells Th Coll 69. **d** 72 **p** 73. C Keighley *Bradf* 72-74; C Bolton St Jas w St Chrys 74-78; V Hightown *Wakef* 78-85; Dep Chapl HM Pris Wakef 85-87; Chapl HM Pris Full Sutton 87-89; PtO *Wakef* 92-95; P-in-c Carlinghow 95-99; P-in-c Bedford St Martin *St Alb* 99-14; rtd 14; PtO *St Alb* from 14. *88 Sovereigns Quay, Bedford MK40 1TF* T: (01234) 261812 E: r.s.stokes.65@cantab.net

STOKES, Canon Simon Colin. b 62. Nene Coll Northn BSc 83. Ridley Hall Cam 89. **d** 92 **p** 93. C New Catton Ch Ch *Nor* 92-96; P-in-c King's Lynn St Jo the Ev 96-06; P-in-c Bowthorpe 06-11; Chapl Coll of W Anglia 01-06; R Sprowston w Beeston *Nor* from 11; Hon Can Nor Cathl from 06. *The Vicarage, 2 Wroxham Road, Norwich NR7 8TZ* T: (01603) 426492 E: simon@simonstokes.co.uk

STOKES, Simon Jeremy. b 63. St Anne's Coll Ox BA 86 MA 90 Mass Inst of Tech SM 88 Univ of Wales (Cardiff) LLM 97 Solicitor 92. NTMTC BA 08. **d** 08 **p** 09. NSM Clerkenwell H Redeemer *Lon* 08-13; NSM St Marylebone St Cypr from 13. *10 Pensioners Court, Charterhouse, Charterhouse Square, London EC1M 6AU* M: 077220-48110 E: frsstokes@googlemail.com

STOKES, Ted. *See* STOKES, Colin Arthur

STOKES, Terence Harold. b 46. Open Univ BA 89. Sarum & Wells Th Coll 71. **d** 73 **p** 74. C Blakenall Heath *Lich* 73-75; C Walsall Wood 75-78; C Northampton St Alb *Pet* 78-81; TV Swinton St Pet *Man* 81-85; V Daisy Hill 85-92; rtd 09; PtO *Blackb* 09-12; Hon C Chorley St Laur from 12; PtO *Man* from 13. *17 St John's Court, Chorley Road, Westhoughton, Bolton BL5 3WG* M: 07899-040781 E: revthstokes@aim.com

STOKES, Preb Terence Walter. b 34. Bps' Coll Cheshunt 62. **d** 64 **p** 65. C Wanstead St Mary *Chelmsf* 64-67; C St Alb Abbey 67-70; Asst Dir RE *B & W* 70-75; Youth Chapl 70-75; P-in-c Yeovil 75-77; TV 77-82; TR Wellington and Distr 82-99; RD Tone 89-96; Preb Wells Cathl 90-99; rtd 99; PtO *B & W* 99-10; *Win* from 10. *16 Tadfield Road, Romsey SO51 5AJ* T: (01794) 518396

STOKES-HARRISON, David Neville Hurford. b 41. FCA 65 FCCA 67 FInstM 68. Qu Coll Birm 97. **d** 00 **p** 01. NSM Walsall *Lich* 00-07; NSM Edgmond w Kynnersley and Preston Wealdmoors from 07; NSM Tibberton w Bolas Magna and Waters Upton from 07. *The Rectory, Mill Lane, Tibberton, Newport TF10 8NL* T: (01952) 551063 E: stokesharrison@btinternet.com

STOKOE, Prof Rodney James Robert. b 20. Dur Univ BSc 46 BA 48. Crozer Th Sem Pennsylvania ThM 67 Atlantic Sch of Th Halifax (NS) Hon DD 87. **d** 49 **p** 50. C W Hartlepool St Paul *Dur* 49-53; R Edin Ch Ch 53-57; P-in-c Bishopwearmouth St Gabr *Dur* 57-60; Prof Div K Coll NS Canada 60-71; Prof Past Th Atlantic Sch Th NS 71-85; rtd 85. *Fergus Hall C61, 378 Young Street, Truro NS B2N 7H2, Canada* T: (001) (902) 843 8076 E: rodstokoe20@yahoo.ca

STOKOE, Wayne Jeffrey. b 56. Coll of Resurr Mirfield 94. **d** 96 **p** 97. C Sheff St Cath Richmond Road 96-99; V Edlington 99-09; P-in-c Doncaster H Trin 09-10; P-in-c New Cantley 09-10; V from 10. *St Hugh's House, Levet Road, Doncaster DN4 6JQ* T: (01302) 371256 E: wjs56@live.co.uk

STOLTZ, Christopher Barry. b 76. St Olaf Coll Minnesota BA 99. Concordia Th Sem Indiana MDiv 03. **d** 06 **p** 07. C Highgate St Mich *Lon* 06-09; Chapl Trin Coll Cam 09-14; Min Can and Sacr Westmr Abbey from 14. *The Chapter Office, 20 Dean's Yard, London SW1P 3PA* T: (020) 7654 4855 E: christopher.stoltz@westminster-abbey.org

STONE, Adrian Gordon. b 68. Trent Poly BSc 89 Nottm Univ PGCE 92. St Jo Coll Nottm 01. **d** 03 **p** 04. C Bayston Hill *Lich* 03-06; V Stafford St Jo and Tixall w Ingestre from 06. *St John's Vicarage, Westhead Avenue, Stafford ST16 3RP* T: (01785) 253493 M: 07739-043709 E: adrian@the-stone-family.net

STONE, Albert John. b 44. Loughb Univ BTech 67 BSc. Sarum & Wells Th Coll 83. **d** 85 **p** 86. C Plymstock *Ex* 85-88; P-in-c Whitestone 88-92; P-in-c Oldridge 88-92; P-in-c Holcombe Burnell 88-92; R Tedburn St Mary, Whitestone, Oldridge etc 93-94; P-in-c Yarcombe w Membury and Upottery 94; P-in-c Cotleigh 94; V Yarcombe, Membury, Upottery and Cotleigh 95-99; P-in-c Bampton, Morebath, Clayhanger and Petton 99-10; rtd 10. *9 Castle Park, Hemyock, Cullompton EX15 3SA* T: (01823) 681459 E: ajstone@orpheusmail.co.uk

STONE, Christopher. *See* STONE, John Christopher

STONE, Christopher John. b 49. Lanc Univ MA 89 Keele Univ MA 92. Lambeth STh 84 Linc Th Coll 78. **d** 81 **p** 82. C Bromley St Mark *Roch* 81-84; R Burgh-by-Sands and Kirkbampton w Kirkandrews etc *Carl* 84-89; Chapl N Staffs R Infirmary Stoke-on-Trent 89-93; Co-ord Staff Support Services N Staffs Hosp 93-09; rtd 09. *Coppers Nest, Fore Street, Milton Abbot, Tavistock PL19 0PA* T: (01822) 870721 E: stonecj49@btinternet.com

STONE, Christopher Martyn Luke. b 78. Glam Univ BA 99. St Steph Ho Ox 99. **d** 02 **p** 03. C Merthyr Tydfil Ch Ch *Llan* 02-07; TV Bassaleg *Mon* 07-13; TR from 13. *The Vicarage, 1 Church View, Caerphilly Road, Bassaleg, Newport NP10 8ND* T: (01633) 378354 E: vicchris78@sky.com

STONE, Canon David Adrian. b 56. Oriel Coll Ox BA 78 MA 83 BM, BCh 83. Wycliffe Hall Ox 85. **d** 88 **p** 89. C Holborn St Geo w H Trin and St Bart *Lon* 88-91; C S Kensington St Jude 91-93; V 93-02; AD Chelsea 96-02; TR Newbury *Ox* 02-10; Can Res and Prec Cov Cathl from 10; Sub-Dean from 14. *55 Cotswold Drive, Coventry CV3 6EZ* M: 07973-215927 E: david@dandb.org.uk

STONE, Elizabeth Karen Forbes. *See* FORBES STONE, Elizabeth Karen

STONE, The Ven Godfrey Owen. b 49. Ex Coll Ox BA 71 MA 75 W Midl Coll of Educn PGCE 72. Wycliffe Hall Ox BA 78. **d** 81 **p** 82. C Rushden w Newton Bromswold *Pet* 81-87; Dir Past Studies Wycliffe Hall Ox 87-92; TR Bucknall and Bagnall *Lich* 92-02; RD Stoke 98-02; Adn Stoke 02-13; P-in-c Edensor 04-07; rtd 13; PtO *Ox* from 14. *12 William Lucy Way, Oxford OX2 6EQ*

STONE, Ian Matthew. b 72. Ox Univ BTh 08. Ripon Coll Cuddesdon 03. **d** 05 **p** 06. C Hammersmith St Pet *Lon* 05-08; V Queensbury All SS 08-14; R Gt Stanmore from 14. *14 Chambers Walk, Stanmore HA7 4FN* T: (020) 8954 3876 E: rector@stjohnschurchstanmore.org.uk

STONE, Jeffrey Peter. b 34. Nottm Univ TCert 72 BEd 73. Lich Th Coll 58. **d** 61 **p** 62. C Newark St Mary *S'well* 61-65; C Sutton in Ashfield St Mich 65-69; Robert Smyth Sch Market Harborough 72-89; R Waltham on the Wolds, Stonesby, Saxby etc *Leic* 90-96; rtd 96; PtO *Leic* from 99. *71 Redland Road, Oakham LE15 6PH* T: (01572) 756842

STONE, John. *See* STONE, Albert John

STONE, John Anthony. b 46. Univ of Wales (Lamp) MA 05. St Chad's Coll Dur BA 68. **d** 69 **p** 70. C New Addington *Cant* 69-72; C Tewkesbury w Walton Cardiff *Glouc* 72-76; C-in-c Dedworth CD *Ox* 76-82; V Dedworth 82-86; TV Chipping Barnet w Arkley *St Alb* 86-95; R Baldock w Bygrave 95-03; R Ches H Trin 03-11; rtd 11; PtO *St As* from 12; *Ban* from 14. *4 Carpenter Avenue, Llandudno LL30 1YW* E: jastone@dunelm.org.uk

STONE, Canon John Christopher. b 53. Newc Univ BA 74 Birkbeck Coll Lon MA 77 MSTSD 74 LGSM 73 MIPR FRSA.

Oak Hill NSM Course 89. **d** 92 **p** 93. NSM Southfleet *Roch* 92-07; Dioc Communications Officer 96-03; Chapl Univ of Greenwich 98-99; Hon Can Roch Cathl from 02; Bp's Dom Chapl 03-07; Bp's Media Adv 03-07; Bp's Communications Consultant from 07; R Gravesend St Geo from 07. *St George's Rectory, 54 The Avenue, Gravesend DA11 0LX* T: (01474) 534965 E: chris.stone@rochester.anglican.org

STONE, Martyn. *See* STONE, Christopher Martyn Luke

STONE, Matthew. *See* STONE, Ian Matthew

STONE, Michael Graham. b 33. FBCS. S Dios Minl Tr Scheme. **d** 83 **p** 84. NSM Chich St Paul and St Pet 83-95; NSM Chich 95-98; rtd 98; PtO *Chich* from 98. *125 Cedar Drive, Chichester PO19 3EL* T: (01243) 784484

STONE, Michael John. b 33. Trin Hall Cam MA 56 LLB 58. EAMTC 78. **d** 80 **p** 81. NSM Whitton and Thurleston w Akenham *St E* 80-84; NSM Westerfield and Tuddenham w Witnesham 84-95; Dioc Chr Stewardship Adv 93-95; P-in-c Coddenham w Gosbeck and Hemingstone w Henley 95-98; Asst P 98-02; Asst P Crowfield w Stonham Aspal and Mickfield 98-02; Dioc Voc Adv 95-99; rtd 02; PtO *St E* from 02. *10 Coppice Close, Melton, Woodbridge IP12 1RX* T: (01394) 385810 E: emjaystone@aol.com

STONE, Nigel John. b 57. Bedf Coll Lon BSc 82 Lon Bible Coll MA 95. St Jo Coll Nottm 82. **d** 85 **p** 86. C Battersea Park St Sav *S'wark* 85-87; C Battersea St Sav and St Geo w St Andr 87-89; P-in-c Brixton St Paul 89-92; V 92-97; Adult Educ and Tr Officer 97-09; Dioc Olympic Adv 10-12; Par Support P Kingston Area 10-13; Hon Chapl S'wark Cathl 97-13; V Mitcham St Mark from 13. *St Mark's Vicarage, Locks Lane, Mitcham CR4 2JX* T: (020) 8648 2397 *or* 8640 1035 E: nigelstone@btinternet.com

STONE, Peter Jonathan Michael. b 71. Ripon Coll Cuddesdon 08. **d** 10 **p** 11. C Charminster and Stinsford *Sarum* 10-14; TV Bridport from 14. *The Vicarage, 5 Garden Close, Bridport DT6 3AJ* M: 07971-425889 T: (01308) 426459 E: revpetestone@yahoo.co.uk *or* peter.stone9@virginmedia.com

STONE, Philip William. b 58. Ridley Hall Cam 85. **d** 88 **p** 89. C Hackney Marsh *Lon* 88-97; V Kensal Rise St Mark and St Martin 97-04; TR 04-10; AD Brent 03-10; Dir Scargill Ho from 10. *Scargill House, Kettlewell, Skipton BD23 5HU* T: (01756) 761240 E: philstone@freenet.co.uk

STONEBANKS, David Arthur. b 34. Louvain Univ Belgium MA 70. Coll of Resurr Mirfield 64. **d** 66 **p** 67. C Burgess Hill St Jo *Chich* 66-68; Chapl City Univ *Lon* 70-73; Chapl Strasbourg w Stuttgart and Heidelberg *Eur* 73-80; Chapl Geneva 80-86; Chapl Zürich w St Gallen and Winterthur 86-89; R Horsted Keynes *Chich* 89-99; rtd 99; PtO *S'wark* from 01. *42 Home Park, Oxted RH8 0JU* T: (01883) 732339

STONEHOLD, Wilfred Leslie. b 33. St Luke's Coll Ex TCert 71. **d** 99 **p** 00. OLM Harlescott *Lich* 99-06; PtO from 06. *19 Wendsley Road, Harlescott Grange, Shrewsbury SY1 3PE* T: (01743) 369237

STONES, Preb John Graham. b 49. Southn Univ BSc 72. SWMTC 91. **d** 94 **p** 95. C Okehampton w Inwardleigh, Bratton Clovelly etc *Ex* 94-97; TV Sidmouth, Woolbrook, Salcombe Regis, Sidbury etc 97-04; R Church Stretton *Heref* 04-07; TR Teignmouth, Ideford w Luton, Ashcombe etc *Ex* 07-14; Preb Ex Cathl 13-14; rtd 14. *23 Ashleigh Road, Honiton EX14 1TD* E: gandmstones@btinternet.com

STONESTREET, George Malcolm. b 38. MBE 05. AKC 61. **d** 62 **p** 63. C Leeds St Pet *Ripon* 62-64; C Far Headingley St Chad 64-67; V Askrigg w Stallingbusk 67-82; V Bramley 82-85; TR 85-94; V Eskdale, Irton, Muncaster and Waberthwaite *Carl* 94-03; rtd 03; PtO *Carl* from 09. *Northside, Grange, Keswick CA12 5UQ* T: (01768) 777671 E: malcolm@dip.edi.co.uk

STONHAM, Mrs Emma Jane. b 60. Southn Univ BA 00. Ripon Coll Cuddesdon 10. **d** 12 **p** 13. C E Grinstead St Swithun *Chich* 12-15; C New Fishbourne from 15. *19 Mill Close, Chichester PO19 3JW* T: (01342) 311021 M: 07403-114365 E: estonham@yahoo.co.uk

STONIER, Mrs Mary. b 56. **d** 09 **p** 10. OLM Crowle Gp *Linc* from 09. *28 Windsor Road, Crowle, Scunthorpe DN17 4ES* T: (01724) 710900 E: mary.stonier@tiscali.co.uk

STOODLEY, Peter Bindon. b 47. Linc Th Coll 89. **d** 91 **p** 92. C Holbeck *Ripon* 91-94; P-in-c Osmondthorpe St Phil 94-99; V Sowerby Bridge *Wakef* 99-09; rtd 09; PtO *Wakef* 09-11; Hon C Bolton St Jas w St Chrys *Leeds* from 11; Hon C Wrose from 11; PtO from 12. *8 Beechwood Drive, Bradford BD6 3AG* E: maverick.stoodley@tiscali.co.uk

STORDY, Richard Andrew. b 64. St Jo Coll Ox BA 86 Univ of Wales MTh 10 Barrister 86. Cranmer Hall Dur BA 97. **d** 98 **p** 99. C Gt Horton *Bradf* 98-02; V Chapeltown *Sheff* from 02; AD Ecclesfield 10-14. *St John's Vicarage, 23 Housley Park, Chapeltown, Sheffield S35 2UE* T: 0114-257 0966 M: 07812-924926 E: rick@rastordy.plus.com

STOREY, Earl. *See* STOREY, William Earl Cosbey

STOREY, Gerard Charles Alfred. b 57. Thames Poly BSc 80 Lon Univ PhD 84 GRSC 80. Wycliffe Hall Ox 84. **d** 87 **p** 88. C Broadwater *Chich* 87-92; TV 92-95; Chapl Northbrook Coll of Design and Tech 90-95; Oman 95-99; P-in-c Guernsey H Trin *Win* 99-01; V 01-07; P-in-c Bream *Glouc* 07-12; V 12-14; Tanzania from 14; Public Preacher *Glouc* from 14. *80 Evelyn Avenue, Ruislip HA4 8AS* E: gerardstorey@yahoo.co.uk

STOREY, Canon Michael. b 36. Chich Th Coll 73. **d** 75 **p** 76. C Illingworth *Wakef* 75-78; V Rastrick St Jo 78-87; V Crosland Moor 87-06; Hon Can Wakef Cathl 00-06; rtd 06; PtO *Leeds* from 07. *198 Healey Wood Road, Brighouse HD6 3RW* T: (01484) 713663 E: mickthevic@googlemail.com

✠**STOREY, The Most Revd Patricia Louise.** b 60. TCD MA 83. CITC BTh 94. **d** 97 **p** 98 **c** 13. C Ballymena w Ballyclug *Conn* 97-00; C Glenavy w Tunny and Crumlin 00-04; I Londonderry St Aug *D & R* 04-13; Bp M & K from 13. *Bishop's House, Moyglare, Maynooth, Co Kildare, Republic of Ireland* T: (00353) (1) 628 9825 *or* 629 2163 E: patriciastorey56@yahoo.co.uk *or* bishop@meath.anglican.org

STOREY, Timothy. b 60. Trin Coll Bris 92. **d** 94 **p** 95. C Bath Weston St Jo w Kelston *B & W* 94-98; C Shirley *Win* 98-03; R Blandford Forum and Langton Long *Sarum* 03-14; TR Cen Telford *Lich* from 14. *The Rectory, 20 Burlington Close, Dawley, Telford TF4 3TD* T: (01952) 595915 E: revtimstorey@gmail.com

STOREY, William Earl Cosbey. b 58. Kent Univ BA MPhil. CITC. **d** 82 **p** 83. C Drumglass w Moygashel *Arm* 82-86; I Crinken *D & G* 86-96; I Glenavy w Tunny and Crumlin *Conn* 98-04; Dioc Communications Officer *D & R* from 07. *Bishop's House, Moyglare, Maynooth, Co Kildare, Republic of Ireland* T: (00353) (1) 628 9354 *or* 628 9825 E: dco@derry.anglican.org *or* earl@topstorey.org

STORK BANKS, Daniel John. b 78. Reading Univ MBA 11 Univ of Wales (Abth) BScEcon 02. Ripon Coll Cuddesdon 13. **d** 15. C Cheswardine, Childs Ercall, Hales, Hinstock etc *Lich* from 15. *The Vicarage, Childs Ercall, Market Drayton TF9 2DA* M: 07825-951659 E: danstorkbanks@gmail.com

STORY, Victor Leonard. b 45. St Mark & St Jo Coll Lon TCert 66 Brighton Poly BSc 74 LIMA 74. Ripon Coll Cuddesdon 80. **d** 81 **p** 82. C Evesham *Worc* 81-85; P-in-c Ilmington w Stretton on Fosse and Ditchford *Cov* 85-90; P-in-c Ilmington w Stretton-on-Fosse etc 90-96; Chapl Vlissingen (Flushing) Miss to Seamen *Eur* 96-97; Chapl Rotterdam Miss to Seafarers 97-99; Rotterdam 99; R Gt w Lt Milton and Gt Haseley *Ox* 99-15; rtd 15. *66 Rowell Way, Chipping Norton OX7 5BD* E: victor.story@btinternet.com

STOTE, Mrs Judith Ann. b 50. Qu Coll Birm 07. **d** 09 **p** 10. OLM Studley *Cov* 09-12; NSM 12-13; NSM Spernall, Morton Bagot and Oldberrow 12-13; NSM Arden Marches 13-15; rtd 15; PtO *Cov* from 15. *The Paddocks, Birmingham Road, Mappleborough Green, Studley B80 7DJ* T: (01527) 852515 E: judy@ardenmarches.com

STOTE, Mrs Pamela Anne. b 49. Dudley Coll of Educn TCert 70 Open Univ BA 83. WMMTC 97. **d** 00 **p** 01. NSM Cov St Geo 00-03; NSM Whitley 03-13; P-in-c 05-13; rtd 13; PtO *Cov* 14-15; NSM Allesley Park and Whoberley from 15. *22 Chetwode Close, Coventry CV5 9NA* M: 07905-230924

STOTER, David John. b 43. MBE 02. K Coll Lon AKC 66. **d** 67 **p** 68. C Reading St Giles *Ox* 67-71; C Luton Lewsey St Hugh *St Alb* 71-73; Chapl Chelsea and Westmr Hosp Lon 73-79; Convenor of Chapls Notts Distr HA 79-94; Chapl Univ Hosp Nottm 79-94; Chapl Nottm Gen Hosp 79-02; Sen Chapl Qu Medical Cen Nottm Univ Hosp NHS Trust 94-02; Sen Chapl Notts Healthcare NHS Trust 94-02; Manager Chapl and Bereavement Services 94-02; R Gedling *S'well* 02-06; rtd 06; OCM 06-08; PtO *St And* 06-08; Hon C Nettlebed w Bix, Highmoor, Pishill etc *Ox* 08-10; PtO *Ches* from 11. *7 Wentworth Drive, Bramhall, Stockport SK7 2LQ* T: 0161-285 1702 E: david.stoter@yahoo.co.uk

STOTESBURY, Robert John. **d** 06 **p** 07. NSM Ferns w Kilbride, Toombe, Kilcormack etc *C & O* 06-10; NSM Enniscorthy w Clone, Clonmore, Monart etc from 10. *Croneyhorn, Carnew, Arklow, Co Wicklow, Republic of Ireland* T: (00353) (53) 942 6300 M: 87-988 2507 E: rstotesbury@hotmail.com

STOTT, Andrew David. b 61. NOC 03. **d** 05 **p** 06. C Walton Breck *Liv* 05-09; P-in-c W Derby St Luke 09-14; TR 4Saints Team from 14. *St Luke's Vicarage, Princess Drive, Liverpool L14 8XG* T: 0151-259 8125 M: 07510-222374 E: andrew@stott401.fsnet.co.uk

STOTT, Antony. b 21. Bps' Coll Cheshunt 53. **d** 55 **p** 56. Australia 55-62; V Longbridge Deverill w Hill Deverill *Sarum* 62-66; V Bratton 66-74; R Marnhull 74-81; P-in-c Broad Chalke and Bower Chalke 81; P-in-c Ebbesbourne Wake w

Fifield Bavant and Alvediston 81; P-in-c Berwick St John 81; V Chalke Valley W 81-87; rtd 87; PtO *Ex* from 87. *29 Gracey Court, Woodland Road, Broadclyst, Exeter EX5 3GA* E: revtony1@aol.com

STOTT, Christopher John. b 45. Lon Univ BD 68. Tyndale Hall Bris. **d** 69 **p** 70. C Croydon Ch Ch Broad Green *Cant* 69-72; Ethiopia 73-76; Area Sec (SW) BCMS 76-78; Tanzania 78-85; R Harwell w Chilton *Ox* 85-10; RD Wallingford 91-95; rtd 10; PtO *Ox* from 10. *1 Dibleys, Blewbury, Didcot OX11 9PT* E: cjstott@freenetname.co.uk

STOTT, Mrs Debra Ann. b 60. Univ of Wales (Ban) BA 81 Open Univ BSc 00. All SS Cen for Miss & Min 12. **d** 14 **p** 15. NSM Moreton *Ches* from 14. *20 Broomleigh Close, Wirral CH63 2RH* T: 0151-608 3364 M: 07879-851796 E: debbi.stott@outlook.com

STOTT, Eric. b 36. ALCD 62. **d** 62 **p** 63. C Penn Fields *Lich* 62-65; C Normanton *Derby* 65-71; R Lower Broughton St Clem w St Matthias *Man* 71-79; V Chadderton Em 79-01; rtd 01; PtO *Glouc* from 01. *21 Laynes Road, Hucclecote, Gloucester GL3 3PU* T: (01452) 534492

STOTT, Gary. b 69. Leeds Univ BA 92 St Jo Coll Dur MA 99. Cranmer Hall Dur 97. **d** 99 **p** 00. C Farnley *Ripon* 99-03; V Manston 03-06; Care Cen Manager St Geo Crypt Leeds 06-07; Chief Exec Officer 07-09; Dep Chairman Create Foundn from 09. *The Create Foundation, Moor View, Leeds LS11 9NF* T: 0113-394 6120 E: gary.stott@createfoundation.co.uk

STOTT, Jonathan. b 69. **d** 07 **p** 07. NSM Cheltenham H Trin and St Paul *Glouc* 07-09; PtO from 09. *29 Brizen Lane, Cheltenham GL53 0NG* T: (01242) 228894 E: jonathan@glenfall.org.uk

STOTT, Jonathan Robert. b 67. Ripon Coll Cuddesdon 99. **d** 01 **p** 02. C Anfield St Columba *Liv* 01-05; V Dovecot 05-10; Chapl HM Pris Risley 10; P-in-c Dovecot *Liv* 10-13; TR Lowton and Golborne from 15. *St Luke's Vicarage, 246 Slag Lane, Lowton, Warrington WA3 2ED* E: frjonathan@btinternet.com

STOTT, Nicholas. b 73. **d** 12 **p** 13. C Onslow Square and S Kensington St Aug *Lon* 12-14; PtO *S'wark* 12-14; Zimbabwe from 14. *Address temp unknown* E: nickstott73@gmail.com

STOTT, Miss Teresa. b 57. Linc Th Coll 94. **d** 94 **p** 95. C Lee-on-the-Solent *Portsm* 94-97; C Spalding St Jo w Deeping St Nicholas *Linc* 97-98; P-in-c Freiston w Butterwick 98-99; R Freiston w Butterwick and Benington 99-03; R Freiston, Butterwick w Bennington, and Leverton 03-04; C-in-c Cleethorpes St Fran CD 04-09; TV Gt and Lt Coates w Bradley 09-11; Chapl Matthew Humberston Sch 04-11; Chapl St Andr Hospice Grimsby 06-11; Chapl Whiteley Village *Guildf* 11-15; V Skerton St Luke *Blackb* from 15. *St Luke's Vicarage, Slyne Road, Lancaster LA1 2HU* T: (01524) 389038 E: stott145@btinternet.com

STOTT, Victoria. Wycliffe Hall Ox. **d** 09 **p** 10. C Battersea Rise St Mark *S'wark* 09-14; Zimbabwe from 14. *Address withheld by request* E: vicstott@gmail.com

STOW, John Mark. b 51. Selw Coll Cam BA 73 MA 77. Linc Th Coll 76. **d** 78 **p** 79. C Harpenden St Jo *St Alb* 78-82; TV Beaminster Area *Sarum* 82-87; P-in-c Hawkchurch 87-88; P-in-c Marshwood Vale 87-88; TR 88-91; Past Co-ord Millfield Jun Sch 93-98; Manager Somerset Rural Youth Project 99-12; Regional Development Manager Learning SW from 12; PtO *B & W* 09-13; Hon C Somerton w Compton Dundon, the Charltons etc 13. *14 The Fields, Mere, Warminster BA12 6EA* E: stowjm@gmail.com

STOW, Peter John. b 50. Oak Hill Th Coll. **d** 89 **p** 90. C Forest Gate St Mark *Chelmsf* 89-94; V from 94. *St Mark's Vicarage, 41A Tylney Road, London E7 0LS* T: (020) 8555 2988 E: saintmarks@clara.net *or* pj.stow@btinternet.com

STOW, Archdeacon of. *See* SINCLAIR, Canon Jane Elizabeth Margaret

STOWE, Brian. b 32. Trin Coll Cam BA 55 BA 56 MA 59. Ridley Hall Cam 55. **d** 57 **p** 58. C New Catton St Luke *Nor* 57-59; Chapl R Masonic Sch Bushey 59-70; Tutor Rickmansworth Sch Herts 70-71; Chapl Alleyn's Foundn Dulwich 71-75; Hon C Dulwich St Barn *S'wark* 71-75; Chapl Ellerslie Sch Malvern 75-92; Chapl Malvern Coll 92-93; TV Malvern Link w Cowleigh *Worc* 93-94; rtd 95; P-in-c Malvern St Andr *Worc* 95-96; PtO 96-12. *22 Stuart Court, Kibworth, Leicester LE8 0LR* M: 07792-515307 E: bandmstowe2@onetel.com

STOWE, Mrs Katharine Elizabeth. b 78. Birm Univ BA 01 PGCE 02 Trin Coll Cam BA 06. Westcott Ho Cam 04. **d** 07 **p** 08. C Salter Street and Shirley *Birm* 07-11; Bp's Dom Chapl from 11. *East Wing, Bishop's Croft, Old Church Road, Harborne, Birmingham B17 0BE* T: 0121-427 1163 E: bishopschaplain@birmingham.anglican.org

STOWE, Nigel James. b 36. Bris Univ BSc 57. Clifton Th Coll 59. **d** 61 **p** 62. C Ware Ch Ch *St Alb* 61-64; C Reigate St Mary *S'wark* 64-67; V Islington St Jude Mildmay Park *Lon* 67-75; V

Penn Street *Ox* 75-01; rtd 01. *27 Snowdrop Way, Widmer End, High Wycombe HP15 6BL* T: (01494) 717496

STOWE, Canon Rachel Lilian. b 33. Qu Coll Birm 79. **dss** 83 **d** 87 **p** 94. Dean w Yelden, Melchbourne and Shelton *St Alb* 82-87; Pertenhall w Swineshead 82-87; Bp's Officer for NSMs and Asst Dir of Ords 87-93; rtd 93; NSM The Stodden Churches *St Alb* 87-96; Hon Can St Alb 92-96; Convenor Dioc Adv Gp for Chr Healing *Ripon* 98-03; PtO *Leeds* from 97; York from 98. *Preston Cottage, East Cowton, Northallerton DL7 0BD* T/F: (01325) 378173 M: 07860-618600 E: rachel@stowe2106.freeserve.co.uk

STOWELL, Ms Jody. b 75. Spurgeon's Coll BD 09. Ridley Hall Cam 09. **d** 11 **p** 12. C Harrow Weald All SS *Lon* 11-14; V Harrow Weald St Mich from 14. *74 Bishop Ken Road, Harrow HA3 7HR* M: 07940-269148 E: revjody@virginmedia.com

STRACHAN, Donald Philip Michael. b 37. St D Coll Lamp 60. **d** 62 **p** 63. C Aberdeen St Mary *Ab* 62-64; P-in-c Aberdeen St Paul 64-66; Chapl St Andr Cathl 65-68; Itinerant Priest *Mor* 68-73; R Coatbridge *Glas* 73-85; Chapl HM Pris Glas (Barlinnie) 84-87; Dioc Supernumerary *Glas* 85-94; rtd 94; PtO *Arg* 87-06; LtO from 06. *Reul na Mara, Claddach Kirkibost, Isle of North Uist HS6 5EP* T: (01876) 580392

STRACHAN, Mrs Gillian Lesley. b 44. Furzedown Coll of Educn TCert 65 Open Univ BA 77 Hatf Poly MA 87. EAMTC 03. **d** 06 **p** 07. C Aquitaine *Eur* 06-10; Asst Chapl from 10. *La Gravette, 24150 Bayac, France* T/F: (0033) 5 53 58 12 58 M: 6 76 39 25 15 E: gillstrachan@wanadoo.fr

STRAFFORD, Mrs Elizabeth. b 52. **d** 09 **p** 10. NSM Dur N 09-15. *Address temp unknown*

STRAFFORD, Nigel Thomas Bevan. b 53. Univ of Wales (Lamp) BA 80. Sarum & Wells Th Coll 80. **d** 82 **p** 94. C Kidderminster St Mary *Worc* 82; C Kidderminster St Mary and All SS, Trimpley etc 82-83; Hon C Stockton St Mark *Dur* 84-86; Asst P Longwood *Wakef* 86-94; V Athersley 94-97; P-in-c Ferrybridge 97-03; P-in-c Holme and Seaton Ross Gp *York* 03-04; R 04-13; rtd 13; PtO *Dur* from 14. *5 High Street, Stanhope, Bishop Auckland DL13 2UP* T: (01388) 526405

STRAIN, Christopher Malcolm. b 56. Solicitor Southn Univ LLB 77. Wycliffe Hall Ox 83. **d** 86 **p** 87. C Werrington *Pet* 86-89; C Broadwater *Chich* 89-94; TV Hampreston *Sarum* 94-00; P-in-c Parkstone St Luke 00-03; V from 03. *The Vicarage, 2 Birchwood Road, Parkstone, Poole BH14 9NP* T: (01202) 741030 E: cmstrain@tiscali.co.uk

STRAIN, John Damian. b 49. Keele Univ BA 72 Birkbeck Coll Lon MSc 83 PhD 89 AFBPsS 89. STETS BTh 00. **d** 00 **p** 01. NSM Hindhead *Guildf* 00-03; NSM Churt and Hindhead 03-09; Work Economy and Business Adv 08-12; P-in-c Compton, the Mardens, Stoughton and Racton *Chich* 09-12; P-in-c Stansted 09-12; V Octagon from 12. *The Vicarage, Compton, Chichester PO18 9HD* T: (023) 9263 1252 E: octagonvicar@btinternet.com

STRAINE, Gillian Kathleen. b 79. Imp Coll Lon BSc 00 PhD 05. Ripon Coll Cuddesdon BA 08. **d** 09 **p** 10. C Kidlington w Hampton Poyle *Ox* 09-13. *All Saints' Vicarage, 14 Oakleigh Park South, London N20 9JU* T: (020) 8445 0015 M: 07747-010249 E: gillian.straine@btinternet.com

STRANACK, The Very Revd David Arthur Claude. b 43. Chich Th Coll 65. **d** 68 **p** 69. C Forest Gate St Edm *Chelmsf* 68-69; C Colchester St Jas, All SS, St Nic and St Runwald 69-74; V Brentwood St Geo 74-82; V Nayland w Wiston *St E* 82-99; R Hadleigh 99-02; V Hadleigh, Layham and Shelley 02-08; Dean Bocking 99-08; RD Hadleigh 99-07; Hon Can St E Cathl 94-08; rtd 08; PtO *St E* from 08. *12 Sandy Lane, Sudbury CO10 7HG* T: (01787) 881657

STRANACK, Canon Richard Nevill. b 40. Leeds Univ BA 63. Coll of Resurr Mirfield 63. **d** 65 **p** 66. C Bush Hill Park St Mark *Lon* 65-68; C Brighton St Martin *Chich* 68-72; P-in-c Toftrees w Shereford *Nor* 72-74; V 74-81; P-in-c Pensthorpe 72-74; R 74-81; V Hempton and Pudding Norton 72-81; RD Burnham and Walsingham 78-81; V Par *Truro* 81-94; P-in-c St Blazey 87-91; Hon Chapl Miss to Seafarers from 81; V Stratton and Launcells *Truro* 94-06; RD Stratton 02-05; Chapl Cornwall Healthcare NHS Trust 97-02; Chapl N and E Cornwall Primary Care Trust 02-06; rtd 06; P-in-c Duloe, Herodsfoot, Morval and St Pinnock *Truro* 06-08; Hon Can Truro Cathl 98-08. *8 Sunwine Place, Exmouth EX8 2SE* T: (01395) 225638 E: rnstranack@yahoo.co.uk

STRAND, Mrs Christine Ann. b 56. Yorks Min Course 13. **d** 15. NSM Bridlington Priory *York* from 15. *Ranamana, Georgian Way, Bridlington YO15 3TB* T: (01262) 679056 E: christine@thestrands.plus.com

STRAND, Matthew David. b 87. Northumbria Univ BSc 08. St Jo Coll Nottm MA 12. **d** 12 **p** 13. C Linthorpe *York* from 12. *23 Linden Grove, Middlesbrough TS5 5NF* M: 07825-585965 E: matthewstrand@hotmail.com

STRAND, Mrs Sarah Elizabeth. b 90. Ex Univ BA 11 St Jo Coll Cam BA 13 MA 14. Cranmer Hall Dur 11. **d** 14 **p** 15. C Stokesley w Seamer *York* from 14. *23 Linden Grove, Middlesbrough TS5 5NF* T: (01642) 828329 E: revsarahstrand@outlook.com

STRANG, Martin Guthrie. b 55. Bris Univ BSc 76 Paisley Coll of Tech MSc 83 MIMechE 85. St Jo Coll Nottm 07. **d** 09 **p** 10. C Trowell, Awsworth and Cossall *S'well* 09-12; P-in-c Stafford St Paul Forebridge *Lich* 12-13; P-in-c Castle Town 12-13; V Stafford St Paul and St Thos from 13. *St Thomas's Vicarage, Doxey, Stafford ST16 1EQ* T: (01785) 258796 M: 07908-995450 E: mstrang12@btinternet.com

STRANGE, Canon Alan Michael. b 57. Pemb Coll Ox BA 79 MA 89. Wycliffe Hall Ox BA 84. **d** 84 **p** 85. C York St Paul 84-87; Asst Chapl Brussels Cathl 87-91; Assoc Chapl 91-95; P-in-c Heigham H Trin *Nor* 95-99; R from 99; RD Nor S from 09; Hon Can Nor Cathl from 10. *The Rectory, 17 Essex Street, Norwich NR2 2BL* T: (01603) 622225 E: rector@trinitynorwich.org *or* big1al@ntlworld.com

STRANGE, Malcolm. b 58. Westmr Coll Ox MTh 95. Sarum & Wells Th Coll 82. **d** 85 **p** 86. C Seaton Hirst *Newc* 85-88; C Ridgeway *Sarum* 88-89; TV 89-91; TV Newbury *Ox* 91-98; TR Bideford, Northam, Westward Ho!, Appledore etc *Ex* 98-01; RD Hartland 99-01. *Address withheld by request*

✠**STRANGE, The Rt Revd Mark Jeremy.** b 61. Aber Univ LTh 82. Linc Th Coll 87. **d** 89 **p** 90 **c** 07. C Worc St Barn w Ch Ch 89-92; V Worc St Wulstan 92-98; R Elgin w Lossiemouth *Mor* 98-07; P-in-c Dufftown 04-07; P-in-c Aberlour 04-07; Can St Andr Cathl Inverness 00-07; Syn Clerk 03-07; Bp Mor from 07. *Bishop's House, St John's, Arpafeelie, North Kessock, Inverness IV1 3XD* T: (01463) 819900 E: bishop@moray.anglican.org

STRANGE, Canon Peter Robert. b 48. Univ Coll Lon BA 69 Ex Coll Ox BA 71 MA 76. Cuddesdon Coll 71. **d** 72 **p** 73. C Denton *Newc* 72-74; C Newc St Jo 74-79; Chapl for Arts and Recreation 79-90; R Wallsend St Pet 79-86; Can Res Newc Cathl 86-11; Angl Adv Tyne Tees TV 90-10; Asst Dioc Dir of Ords Newc 94-98; rtd 11. *4 Woodthorne Road, Jesmond, Newcastle upon Tyne NE2 3PB* T: 0191-284 4468 M: 07712-594950 E: p.strange119@btinternet.com

STRANGE, Preb Robert Lewis. b 45. Sarum & Wells Th Coll 72. **d** 74 **p** 75. C Walthamstow St Barn and St Jas Gt *Chelmsf* 74-77; C Wickford 77-80; P-in-c Treverbyn *Truro* 80-83; V 83-86; Asst Stewardship Adv 82-96; V Newlyn St Pet 86-10; Preb Trehaverock 94-10; rtd 10; Hon Chapl Miss to Seafarers from 86. *Michaelmas, Lelant Downs, Hayle TR27 6NJ* E: robert.sarov@tiscali.co.uk

STRANGE, The Ven William Anthony. b 53. Qu Coll Cam BA 76 MA 80 K Alfred's Coll Win CertEd 77 Ox Univ DPhil 89. Wycliffe Hall Ox 79. **d** 82 **p** 83. Tutor Wycliffe Hall Ox 82-87; C Aberystwyth *St D* 87; TV 87-91; V Llandeilo Fawr and Taliaris 91-96; Hd of Th and RS Trin Coll Carmarthen 96-01; V Carmarthen St Pet *St D* 03-09; AD Carmarthen 06-09; V Pencarreg and Llanycrwys from 09; Adn Cardigan from 09. *The Vicarage, Cwmann, Lampeter SA48 8DU* T: (01570) 422385 E: archdeacon.cardigan@churchinwales.org.uk

STRANRAER-MULL, The Very Revd Gerald Hugh. b 42. AKC 69. St Aug Coll Cant 69. **d** 70 **p** 71. C Hexham *Newc* 70-72; C Corbridge w Halton 72; R Ellon *Ab* 72-08; R Cruden Bay 72-08; Can St Andr Cathl 81-08; Dean Ab 88-08; P-in-c Peterhead 02-04; rtd 08; P-in-c Strathnairn St Paul *Mor* 09-12; Hon C Inverness St Mich from 11. *7S The Cairns, Muir of Ord IV6 7AT* T: (01463) 870986 E: stranraermull@btinternet.com

STRAPPS, Canon Robert David. b 28. St Edm Hall Ox BA 52 MA 56. Wycliffe Hall Ox 52. **d** 54 **p** 55. C Low Leyton *Chelmsf* 54-57; C Ox St Aldate w H Trin 57-60; V Sandal St Helen *Wakef* 60-94; RD Chevet 81-93; Hon Can Wakef Cathl 92-94; rtd 94; PtO *Wakef* 94-98; *Glouc* from 94; *Worc* from 94. *Brookside, Hill Road, Kemerton, Tewkesbury GL20 7JN* T: (01386) 725515

STRASZAK, Edmund Norman. b 57. Coll of Resurr Mirfield 88. **d** 90 **p** 91. C Adlington *Blackb* 90-93; C Harrogate St Wilfrid and St Luke *Ripon* 93-95; V Chorley All SS *Blackb* from 95. *All Saints' Vicarage, Moor Road, Chorley PR7 2LR* T: (01257) 265665 E: edmund1@talktalk.net

STRATFORD, Mrs Anne Barbara. Southn Univ CertEd 58 Ox Univ MTh 99. Qu Coll Birm 88. **d** 91 **p** 94. Officer Dioc Bd of Soc Resp (Family Care) *Lich* 85-97; NSM Kinnerley w Melverley and Knockin w Maesbrook 91-95; Chapl Robert Jones and Agnes Hunt Orthopaedic Hosp 95-97; NSM Maesbury *Lich* 95-96; P-in-c 96-97; Chapl Moreton Hall Sch from 96; P-in-c Ford *Heref* 97-02; V 02-05; P-in-c Alberbury w Cardeston 97-02; V 02-05; rtd 05; PtO *Lich* from 05; *St As* from 05. *Pentre Cleddar, Hengoed, Oswestry SY10 7AB* T: (01691) 650469

STRATFORD, David. b 46. **d** 98 **p** 99. OLM Ditton St Mich w St Thos *Liv* 98-11. *96 Clincton View, Widnes WA8 8RW* T: 0151-423 4912

STRATFORD, Niall. CITC. **d** 09. NSM Killiney Ballybrack *D & G* from 09. *8 Hermitage Downs, Grange Road, Rathfarnham, Dublin 16, Republic of Ireland* T: (00353) (1) 493 7535

STRATFORD, Terence Stephen. b 45. Chich Th Coll 67. **d** 69 **p** 70. C Old Shoreham *Chich* 69-73; C New Shoreham 69-73; C Uckfield 73-75; C Lt Horsted 73-75; C Isfield 73-75; P-in-c Waldron 76-80; R 80-82; V Blacklands Hastings Ch Ch and St Andr 82-89; P-in-c Ovingdean 89-95; Dioc Ecum Officer 89-95; P-in-c Staplefield Common 95-00; Sussex Ecum Officer 95-01; V Ferring *Chich* 00-08; C New Shoreham and Old Shoreham 08-11; P-in-c Kingston Buci 11-15; Hon C New Shoreham and Shoreham Beach from 15; RD Hove from 14. *The Vicarage, West Beach, Shoreham-by-Sea BN43 5LF* T: (01273) 453768 E: terry.stratford@yahoo.co.uk

STRATFORD, The Ven Timothy Richard. b 61. York Univ BSc 82 Sheff Univ PhD 08. Wycliffe Hall Ox 83. **d** 86 **p** 87. C Mossley Hill St Matt and St Jas *Liv* 86-89; C St Helens St Helen 89-91; Bp's Dom Chapl 91-94; V W Derby Gd Shep 94-03; TR Kirkby 03-12; Adn Leic from 12. *46 Southernhay Road, Leicester LE2 3TJ* T: 0116-270 4441 E: tim.stratford@leccofe.org

STRATHIE, Duncan John. b 58. Heythrop Coll Lon MA 02. Cranmer Hall Dur BA 95. **d** 97 **p** 98. C Yateley *Win* 97-01; V Kempshott 01-07; Min Tr Officer 07-14; Dioc Convenor of Voc Advisers 03-14; Co-ord for Learning and Discipleship *Sarum* from 14. *Church House, Crane Street, Salisbury SP1 2QB* T: (01722) 411922 E: duncan@strathie.net

STRATON, Christopher James. b 46. **d** 93 **p** 94. Chapl Miss to Seamen S Africa 93-96; Asst P Gingindlovu All SS 97-99; R 99-00; P-in-c Tyldesley w Shakerley *Man* 00-06; TV Astley, Tyldesley and Mosley Common 06-11; rtd 11. *2 Scarisbrick Court, Scarisbrick New Road, Southport PR8 6QF* E: chrisstraton@hotmail.co.uk

STRATTA, Antony Charles. b 36. ACIS. S'wark Ord Course 82. **d** 85 **p** 86. C Southborough St Pet w Ch Ch and St Matt *Roch* 85-88; R Gt Mongeham w Ripple and Sutton by Dover *Cant* 88-96; rtd 96; PtO *St E* from 96. *Well House, The Great Yard, Rougham Green, Bury St Edmunds IP30 9JP* T: (01284) 386140 E: antonystratta@btinternet.com

STRATTON, Mrs Anne Margaret. b 58. JP 98. Nottm Univ BEng 79. EMMTC 03. **d** 06 **p** 07. NSM Bradgate Team *Leic* 06-10; P-in-c Belper *Derby* 10-13; V from 13. *St Peter's Vicarage, 6 Chesterfield Road, Belper DE56 1FD* T: (01773) 821323 M: 07773-076555 *or* 839560 E: rev.annestratton@btinternet.com

STRATTON, Henry William. b 39. Bris Univ CertEd 74 BEd 75. Glouc Sch of Min 80. **d** 83 **p** 84. NSM Cainscross w Selsley *Glouc* 83-87; C Odd Rode *Ches* 87-92; V Runcorn H Trin 92-96; V Lostock Gralam 96-05; rtd 05; PtO *Ches* from 05. *10 The Beeches, Great Sutton, Ellesmere Port CH66 4UJ* T: 0151-339 3715 E: harry@hstratton.fsnet.co.uk

STRATTON, John Jefferies. b 27. Bps' Coll Cheshunt 53. **d** 55 **p** 56. C Watford St Mich *St Alb* 55-60; C Stevenage 60-65; R Cottered w Broadfield and Throcking 65-82; RD Buntingford 75-82; V S Mimms St Mary and Potters Bar *Lon* 82-84; V Potters Bar *St Alb* 85-94; P-in-c Flamstead 94-96; rtd 94; PtO *B & W* from 97. *17 The Fairways, Sherford, Taunton TA1 3PA* T: (01823) 330564 E: john@stratton10.orangehome.co.uk

STRAUGHAN, Prof Keith. b 60. Imp Coll Lon BSc 81 Lon Univ PhD 87 Imp Coll Lon ARCS 81 CPhys 87 MInstP 87 Trin Coll Cam BA 97 MA 00. Westcott Ho Cam 94. **d** 97 **p** 98. C Abbots Langley *St Alb* 97-00; Fell SS Coll Cam 00-08; Chapl 00-03; Dean 03-05; Sen Tutor 05-08; Dean Univ Cen Milton Keynes from 08; NSM Milton Keynes *Ox* from 11. *University Campus Milton Keynes, 502 Avebury Boulevard, Milton Keynes MK9 3HS* T: (01582) 743070 E: keith.straughan@ucmk.ac.uk

STRAW, Mrs Juliet Lesley. b 49. Univ of Wales (Ban) BA 70 Leeds Univ PGCE 71. SAOMC 00. **d** 03 **p** 04. NSM Stratfield Mortimer and Mortimer W End etc *Ox* 03-10; P-in-c Wymering *Portsm* from 10; P-in-c Cosham from 10. *Wymering Vicarage, Medina Road, Portsmouth PO6 3NH* T: (023) 9238 1836 E: juliet.straw@btinternet.com

STRAWBRIDGE, Jennifer Ruth. b 78. Washington & Lee Univ BA 01 Ox Univ MSt 02. Virginia Th Sem MDiv 04. **d** 04 **p** 04. C New Haven Ch Ch USA 04-05; C Arlington St Mary 05-09; Asst Chapl Keble Coll Ox 09-10; Chapl from 10. *Keble College, Parks Road, Oxford OX1 3PG* T: (01865) 272725 E: jennifer.strawbridge@keble.ox.ac.uk

STREATER, David Arthur. b 33. Oak Hill Th Coll 67. **d** 68 **p** 69. C Lindfield *Chich* 68-71; S Africa 71-86; R Kingham w Churchill, Daylesford and Sarsden *Ox* 86-91; Dir Ch Soc 91-98; Sec Ch Soc Trust 91-96; rtd 98; P-in-c Odell *St Alb* 98-03. *16 Linden Avenue, West Cross, Swansea SA3 5LE* T: (01792) 406849 E: monty@ukgateway.net

STREATFEILD, Peter Michael Fremlyn. b 53. Newc Univ BSc 77 St Jo Coll Dur BA 03. Cranmer Hall Dur 00. **d** 03 **p** 04.

C Solway Plain *Carl* 03-08; TV Binsey from 08. *The Vicarage, Bassenthwaite, Keswick CA12 4QH* T: (017687) 76198 E: petermfs@hotmail.com

STREET, Anthony James. b 57. Trin Coll Bris 79. **d** 85 **p** 87. SAMS 85-95; C Temuco H Trin Chile 85-87; V Temuco St Matt 87-95; P-in-c Warley *Wakef* 96-99; V *Leeds* 99-14; P-in-c Halifax St Hilda 10-14; R Sawley *Derby* from 14. *The Rectory, 561 Tamworth Road, Long Eaton, Nottingham NG10 3FB* T: 0115-973 4900 E: familiastreet@btinternet.com

STREET, David. b 72. St Jo Coll Nottm. **d** 10 **p** 11. C Bucknall *Lich* 10-13; TV from 13. *12 Tansey Close, Bucknall, Stoke-on-Trent ST2 9QX* T: (01782) 283934 E: revdavestreet@gmail.com

STREET, Matthew Graham. b 61. Regent's Park Coll Ox BA 83. Wycliffe Hall Ox 99. **d** 01 **p** 02. C Combe Down w Monkton Combe and S Stoke *B & W* 01-05; P-in-c Peasedown St John w Wellow 05-10; V Peasedown St John w Wellow and Foxcote etc from 10. *The Vicarage, 18 Church Road, Peasedown St John, Bath BA2 8AA* T: (01761) 432293 F: 08701-307814 M: 07762-794371 E: mgstreet@me.com

STREET, Peter Jarman. b 29. K Coll Lon BD 59 AKC 59. **d** 59 **p** 60. C Highters Heath *Birm* 59-60; C Shirley 60-62; Lect Cheshire Coll of Educn 62-66; St Pet Coll of Educn Birm 66-70; RE Adv Essex Co Coun 70-92; Hon C Gt Dunmow *Chelmsf* 71-85; Sen Insp RE and Humanities 74-92; R Gt w Lt Yeldham *Chelmsf* 85-92; RD Belchamp 90-92; rtd 92; PtO *Chelmsf* from 92. *18 Jubilee Court, Great Dunmow CM6 1DY* T: (01371) 876871

STREET, Philip. b 47. Lon Univ BPharm 68. NW Ord Course 75. **d** 78 **p** 79. C Heaton St Barn *Bradf* 78-81; C Evington *Leic* 82-84; R Wymondham w Edmondthorpe, Buckminster etc 84-88; V Gosberton Clough and Quadring *Linc* 88-95; Asst Local Min Officer 88-95; V Buttershaw St Paul *Bradf* 95-99; P-in-c Gt and Lt Casterton w Pickworth and Tickencote *Pet* 99-04; R 04-09; P-in-c Empingham and Exton w Horn w Whitwell 02-06; rtd 09; PtO *Pet* from 09. *35 Foundry Walk, Thrapston, Kettering NN14 4LS* T: (01832) 731661 or 734267 E: p.street08@btinternet.com

STREETE, Peter William. b 44. **d** 13 **p** 14. OLM Thurstable and Winstree *Chelmsf* from 13. *86 School Road, Copford, Colchester CO6 1BX* T: (01206) 210457 M: 07791-906912 E: revd.peterstreete@gmail.com

STREETER, Brian Thomas. b 68. Reading Univ BSc 89. Ridley Hall Cam 05. **d** 08 **p** 09. C Windermere St Mary and Troutbeck *Carl* 08-12; Par Missr 13-15; P-in-c Egton-cum-Newland and Lowick and Colton *Carl* from 15. *The Vicarage, Penny Bridge, Ulverston LA12 7RQ* M: 07505-048736 T: (01229) 861668 E: streeter787@btinternet.com

STREETER, Christine Mary. *See* HADDON-REECE, Christine Mary

STREETER, David James. b 42. Pemb Coll Cam BA 64 MA 68. Qu Coll Birm 65. **d** 67 **p** 68. C Saffron Walden *Chelmsf* 67-71; C Shrub End 71-73; R Rayne 73-79; V Highams Park All SS 79-82; P-in-c Stradbroke w Horham and Athelington *St E* 82-87; R Stradbroke, Horham, Athelington and Redlingfield 87-12; RD Hoxne 91-00; rtd 12; PtO *St E* from 13. *Doggets Farm, New Street, Stradbroke, Eye IP21 5JG* T: (01379) 384869 M: 07798-784179 E: davidstreeter@suffolkonline.net

STREETING, John William. b 52. Cam Inst of Educn CertEd 74 Birm Univ BEd 77 Anglia Poly Univ MA 99 FGMS 98 FRSA 98. St Steph Ho Ox 90. **d** 92 **p** 93. C Upminster *Chelmsf* 92-95; C Chingford SS Pet and Paul 95-97; Assoc V Chelsea St Luke and Ch Ch *Lon* 97-03; V Sheerness H Trin w St Paul *Cant* 03-10; P-in-c 10; P-in-c Queenborough 05-10; AD Sittingbourne 04-06; P-in-c Axminster, Chardstock, All Saints etc *Ex* 10-15; TR from 15. *The Rectory, Church Street, Axminster EX13 5AQ* T: (01297) 598213 E: axrector@talktalk.net

STRETCH, Richard Mark. b 53. **d** 93 **p** 94. OLM Stowmarket *St E* 93-13; NSM from 13. *91 Kipling Way, Stowmarket IP14 1TS* T: (01449) 676219

STRETTON, Reginald John. b 37. Man Univ BSc 62 Nottm Univ PhD 65 MRPharmS 63 CBiol 70 MSB 70. EMMTC 88. **d** 91 **p** 92. NSM Loughb Gd Shep *Leic* 91-94; P-in-c Burrough Hill Pars 94-02; rtd 02; PtO *Leic* from 02; *S'well* 02-14; *Derby* 05-14. *19 Paddock Close, Quorn, Loughborough LE12 8BJ* T: (01509) 412935 E: reginaldstretton@btinternet.com

STRETTON, Robert John. b 45. Kelham Th Coll. **d** 69 **p** 70. C Hendon *Dur* 69-73; C Middlesbrough St Thos *York* 73-77; OSB 77-78; V Brandon *Dur* 78-85; SSM from 85; LtO *Dur* 85-91; Tr in Evang Ch in Wales 91-94; PtO *S'wark* 94-01; Lesotho 01-05; PtO *S'wark* from 14. *86B Vassall Road, London SW9 6JA* E: ssmlondon@yahoo.co.uk

STREVENS, Brian Lloyd. b 49. St Jo Coll Dur BA 70. Ripon Hall Ox 70. **d** 73 **p** 74. C Old Trafford St Jo *Man* 73-76; C Bolton St Pet 76-78; Org Sec Southn Coun of Community Service 78-92; PtO *Win* 82-86 and 92-95 and from 01; Hon C

Bitterne Park 86-92; Hon C N Stoneham 95-01. *186 Hill Lane, Southampton SO15 5DB* T: (023) 8033 3301 E: hq@scaccs.org.uk

STREVENS, Richard Ernest Noel. b 34. Nottm Univ BA 60. Linc Th Coll 60. **d** 62 **p** 63. C St Botolph Aldgate w H Trin Minories *Lon* 62-66; C Ealing St Steph Castle Hill 66-68; Hon C St Botolph without Bishopgate 68-76; V Clent *Worc* 76-86; V Pirbright *Guildf* 86-00; PtO *Ex* 69-98 and 00-13; rtd 00. *11 George Law Court, Anchorfields, Kidderminster DY10 1PZ* T: (01562) 227026

STRIBLEY, William Charles Harold. b 29. SWMTC 84. **d** 87 **p** 88. NSM Kenwyn St Geo *Truro* 87-92; NSM Truro St Paul and St Clem 92-98; PtO from 99. *54 Chirgwin Road, Truro TR1 1TT* T: (01872) 272958

STRICKLAND (née CUTTS), Mrs Elizabeth Joan Gabrielle. b 61. St Jo Coll Dur BA 83. Westcott Ho Cam 87. **d** 90 **p** 94. C Cayton w Eastfield *York* 90-92; NSM Biggin Hill *Roch* 93-96; PtO *Ox* 96-00; *Ely* 00-02; P-in-c Holywell w Needingworth 02-07. *Windswept, Holywell, St Ives PE27 4TQ* T: (01480) 495275 or 460107 E: epstrickland@ukonline.co.uk

STRICKLAND, Jonathan Edward Tully. b 56. Westf Coll Lon BSc 78. Ridley Hall Cam 00. **d** 02 **p** 03. C Margate H Trin *Cant* 02-06; P-in-c Bawtry w Austerfield and Misson *S'well* 07-11; V 11-15; V Bawtry w Austerfield, Misson, Everton and Mattersey from 15. *The Vicarage, Martin Lane, Bawtry, Doncaster DN10 6NJ* T: (01302) 710298 E: strickers@tesco.net

STRIDE, Clifford George. b 58. Win Univ BA 11. STETS 08. **d** 11 **p** 12. NSM Ampfield, Chilworth and N Baddesley *Win* from 11. *4 Dibble Drive, North Baddesley, Southampton SO52 9NF* T: (023) 8073 9835 E: cgstride@btinternet.com

STRIDE, Clifford Stephen. b 21. Ex & Truro NSM Scheme. **d** 81 **p** 82. NSM Chulmleigh *Ex* 81-83; NSM Hardham *Chich* 87-93; NSM Coldwaltham and Hardham 93-97; NSM Bury w Houghton and Coldwaltham and Hardham 97-05. *Ambleside, Sandy Lane, Watersfield, Pulborough RH20 1NF* T: (01798) 831851

STRIDE, John David. b 46. Ex Univ BSc 68. Oak Hill Th Coll 86. **d** 88 **p** 89. C Ashtead *Guildf* 88-96; V Lodge Moor St Luke *Sheff* 96-11; rtd 11; PtO *Sheff* from 11. *11 Blenheim Mews, Sheffield S11 9PR* T: 0114-235 6220 E: john@jonjax.net

STRIDE, John Michael. b 48. Oak Hill Th Coll BA 77. **d** 80 **p** 81. C Edmonton All SS *Lon* 80-82; C Edmonton All SS w St Mich 82-83; C Wembley St Jo 83-85; P-in-c Hockering *Nor* 85-89; R Hockering, Honingham, E and N Tuddenham 89-91; V Tuckswood 91-93; Chapl HM Pris Leeds 93-94; Chapl HM Pris Littlehey 94-96; V Heeley *Sheff* 96-99; TR Heeley and Gleadless Valley 99-04; AD Attercliffe 02-04; V Goole 04-06; Chapl Combined Courts 06-11; Hon C Darfield 07-11; V Ludham, Potter Heigham, Hickling and Catfield *Nor* from 11. *The Vicarage, Norwich Road, Ludham, Great Yarmouth NR29 5QA* E: johnmo@mojnst.plus.com

STRIKE, Maurice Arthur. b 44. FRSA 66. Sarum & Wells Th Coll 85. **d** 87 **p** 88. C Chippenham St Andr w Tytherton Lucas *Bris* 87-91; R Corfe Castle, Church Knowle, Kimmeridge etc *Sarum* 91-04; R Guernsey St Philippe de Torteval *Win* 04-13; R Guernsey St Pierre du Bois 04-13; rtd 13; PtO *Nor* from 13; *Win* from 13. *The Flint House, 49 Mundesley Road, Overstrand, Cromer NR27 0NB* T: (01263) 576805 E: mstrike@hotmail.co.uk

STRINGER, Adrian Nigel. b 60. Univ of Wales (Cardiff) BD 82 Lanc Univ PGCE 83. Sarum & Wells Th Coll 86. **d** 88 **p** 89. C Barrow St Matt *Carl* 88-92; TV Westhoughton *Man* 92-94; I Inver w Mountcharles, Killaghtee and Killybegs *D & R* 94-96; V Tuckingmill *Truro* 96-01; Chapl R Alexandra and Albert Sch Reigate 01-03; I Desertlyn w Ballyeglish *Arm* from 03. *The Rectory, 24 Cookstown Road, Moneymore, Magherafelt BT45 7QF* T: (028) 8674 8200 E: blackdogmaverick@yahoo.co.uk

STRINGER, Harold John. b 36. Peterho Cam BA 58. Ripon Hall Ox 62. **d** 64 **p** 65. C Hackney St Jo *Lon* 64-68; C Roehampton H Trin *S'wark* 68-71; P-in-c Southampton St Mich w H Rood, St Lawr etc *Win* 71-73; TV Southampton (City Cen) 73-82; Ind Chapl 77-82; V Notting Hill St Jo *Lon* 82-87; V Notting Hill St Pet 82-87; V Notting Hill St Jo and St Pet 87-01; AD Kensington 98-01; rtd 02; PtO *Lon* from 03. *56 Mountfield Road, London W5 2NQ* T: (020) 8998 8049 E: mail@haroldandchristina.co.uk

STRINGER, Canon John Roden. b 33. AKC 61. **d** 62 **p** 63. C Auckland St Helen *Dur* 62-63; C Roehampton *Cro* 63-67; V Cassop cum Quarrington 67-88; RD Sedgefield 84-88; V Lumley 88-98; Hon Can Dur Cathl 88-98; rtd 98; PtO *Dur* 98-03. *4 Darwin Road, Walsall WS2 7EW* T: (01922) 649243

STROEBEL, Mrs Stephanie Suzanne. b 47. Middx Univ BA 06. NTMTC 03. **d** 06 **p** 07. NSM Ashingdon w S Fambridge *Chelmsf* 06-08; NSM S Woodham Ferrers 08-10; P-in-c

Woodham Mortimer w Hazeleigh 10-15; P-in-c Woodham Walter 10-15; rtd 15; PtO *Chelmsf* from 15. *27 Orchard Avenue, Hockley SS5 5BA* M: 07930-105163 T: (01702) 200901
E: s.stroebel135@gmail.com

STRØMMEN, Mrs Mary Natasha. b 52. Kent Univ BA 73 Bp Otter Coll Chich PGCE 74. EAMTC 00. **d** 03 **p** 04. NSM Oslo w Bergen, Trondheim and Stavanger *Eur* from 03. *Lykkestien 4, 7053 Ranheim, Norway* T: (0047) 7391 3281
E: mary.strommen@c2i.net

STRONG, Christopher Patteson. b 43. Ridley Hall Cam. **d** 83 **p** 84. C Dalton-in-Furness *Carl* 83-87; V Wootton *St Alb* 87-02; RD Elstow 94-02; R Fowlmere, Foxton, Shepreth and Thriplow *Ely* 02-08; rtd 08. *Kiln Farm, Priory Road, Campton, Shefford SG17 5PG* T: (01462) 819274
E: christopherpstrong@hotmail.com

STRONG, John. *See* STRONG, William John Leonard

STRONG, Canon John David. b 34. Cuddesdon Coll 59. **d** 61 **p** 62. C Gosforth All SS *Newc* 61-65; Chapl Malvern Coll 65-71; R Welford w Weston on Avon *Glouc* 72-79; V Nailsworth 79-01; RD Tetbury 83-00; Hon Can Glouc Cathl 91-01; rtd 01. *Glebe House, The Meads, Leighterton, Tetbury GL8 8UW* T: (01666) 890236
E: canondavid@penshouse.freeserve.co.uk

STRONG (formerly BULMAN), Ms Madeline Judith. b 61. K Coll Lon BD AKC Lon Metrop Univ MA. **dss** 86 **d** 87 **p** 94. Shepperton *Lon* 86-88; Par Dn 87-88; Par Dn Brentford 88-94; C 94-96; V Cobbold Road St Sav w St Mary 96-04; Dean of Women's Min 99-02; Chapl Stamford Ho Secure Unit 02-04; Spiritual Cllr PROMIS 04-07; PtO *Cant* 04-10; Hon C Stone Street Gp 10-13. *Address temp unknown* M: 07973-954802
E: expressiveart@idnet.uk

STRONG, Matthew John. b 60. Lon Univ BA 81 Cam Univ BA 84 MA 89. Ridley Hall Cam 82. **d** 85 **p** 86. C Houghton *Carl* 85-89; C Hirwaun *Llan* 89-91; V Troedyrhiw w Merthyr Vale 91-95; Tutor Llan Ord Course 91-95; PtO *Birm* from 14. *22 Birch Lane, Oldbury B68 0NZ* T: 0121-421 5978

STRONG, Rowan Gordon William. b 53. Victoria Univ Wellington BA 76 Edin Univ PhD 92 Melbourne Coll of Div ThM 88. St Jo Coll (NZ) LTh 80. **d** 77 **p** 78. C Kapiti New Zealand 77-83; C Palmerston N St Pet 79-81; V Shannon 81-83; Assoc P E Hill Australia 83-89; NSM Edin Old St Paul 89-92; Tutor Edin Univ 91-92; Lect Murdoch Univ Australia from 92; Sen Lect from 02. *150 George Street, East Fremantle WA 6158, Australia* T: (0061) (8) 9339 0643 *or* 9360 6470 F: 9360 6480 M: 439-988896
E: r.strong@murdoch.edu.au

STRONG, Capt William John Leonard. b 44. CA Tr Coll 64 Chich Th Coll 87. **d** 89 **p** 90. C Mayfield *Chich* 89-92; C Seaford w Sutton 92-94; V Crawley Down All SS 94-97; rtd 01. *21 Carroll Close, Poole BH12 1PL* M: 07944-670125

STROUD, David Alan. b 74. Kent Univ BA 96 Ch Ch Coll Cant PGCE 95. Westcott Ho Cam 02. **d** 04 **p** 05. C Liss *Portsm* 04-08; Asst Chapl Cant Ch Ch Univ from 08. *Canterbury Christ Church University, North Holmes Road, Canterbury CT1 1QU* T: (01227) 767700 E: david.stroud@canterbury.ac.uk

STROWGER, Mrs Patricia. b 45. Surrey Univ BA 06. STETS 01. **d** 04 **p** 05. NSM The Lavingtons, Cheverells, and Easterton *Sarum* 04-11; C The Cannings and Redhorn 11-12; rtd 12. *60 High Street, Littleton Panell, Devizes SN10 4ES* T: (01380) 860650

✠**STROYAN, The Rt Revd John Ronald Angus.** b 55. St Andr Univ MTheol 76. Qu Coll Birm 81 Bossey Ecum Inst Geneva 82. **d** 83 **p** 84 **c** 05. C Cov E 83-87; V Smethwick St Matt w St Chad *Birm* 87-94; V Bloxham w Milcombe and S Newington *Ox* 94-05; AD Deddington 02-05; Suff Bp Warw *Cov* from 05. *Warwick House, 139 Kenilworth Road, Coventry CV4 7AF* T: (024) 7641 2627 F: 7641 5254
E: bishop.warwick@covcofe.org

STRUDWICK, Mrs Caroline Mary Easdeale. b 55. STETS 12. **d** 15. NSM Upper Itchen *Win* from 15. *Corvus Cottage, South Street, Ropley, Alresford SO24 0DY* T: (01962) 773093
E: carolinestrudwick@carolinestrudwick.co.uk

STRUDWICK, Canon Vincent Noel Harold. b 32. Nottm Univ BA 59 DipEd Lambeth DD 09. Kelham Th Coll 52. **d** 59 **p** 60. Tutor Kelham Th Coll 59-63; Sub-Warden 63-70; C Crawley *Chich* 70-73; Adult Educn Adv 73-77; R Fittleworth 73-77; Planning Officer for Educn Milton Keynes 77-80; Dir of Educn *Ox* 80-89; Hon Can Ch Ch from 82; Continuing Minl Educn Adv 85-89; Dir Dioc Inst for Th Educn 89-97; Prin Ox Min Course 89-94; Prin SAOMC 94-96; Fell and Tutor Kellogg Coll Ox 94-00; C Aylesbury *Ox* 97-98. *31 The Square, Brill, Aylesbury HP18 9RP* T: (01844) 237748
E: vincent.strudwick@conted.ox.ac.uk

STRUGNELL, John Richard. b 30. Lon Univ BA 52 Leeds Univ MA 61 Univ of Qld PhD 77. Wells Th Coll 54. **d** 56 **p** 57.

C Leeds Halton St Wilfrid *Ripon* 56-59; C Moor Allerton 59-62; Australia from 65; rtd 95. *231 Grandview Road, Pullenvale Qld 4069, Australia* T: (0061) (7) 3374 1776

STRUTT, Peter Edward. b 40. SAOMC 94. **d** 97 **p** 98. NSM Penn Street *Ox* 97-02; PtO from 02. *59 King's Ride, Penn, High Wycombe HP10 8BP* T: (01494) 812418

STRUTT, Preb Susan. b 45. Glouc Sch of Min 87. **d** 90 **p** 94. NSM Eye, Croft w Yarpole and Lucton *Heref* 90-94; C Leominster 94-96; Hon Chapl RAF 94-96; P-in-c Bosbury w Wellington Heath etc *Heref* 96-98; TV Ledbury 98-14; Dioc Adv on Women in Min 99-03; Preb Heref Cathl 07-14; rtd 14. *Address temp unknown* E: suestrutt@strutts.fsnet.co.uk

STUART, Angus Fraser. b 61. Bedf Coll Lon BA 83 K Coll Lon PhD 91 St Jo Coll Dur BA 92. Cranmer Hall Dur 90. **d** 93 **p** 94. C Twickenham St Mary *Lon* 93-96; Sen Chapl Bris Univ 96-05; Hon C Bris St Mich and St Paul 96-98; P-in-c 98-99; P-in-c Cotham St Sav w St Mary and Clifton St Paul 99-00; Hon C 00-05; I W Vancouver St Fran in the Wood Canada from 05. *4773 South Piccadilly, West Vancouver BC V7W 1J8, Canada* T: (001) (604) 922 3531

STUART, Sister Ann-Marie Lindsay. b 41. Westmr Coll Lon CertEd 69 Kent Univ BA 80 Univ of Wales (Lamp) MA 03. Franciscan Study Cen 76. **d** 99 **p** 00. NSM Sherborne w Castleton and Lillington *Sarum* 99-01; TV Golden Cap Team 01-05; TR 05-08; rtd 08; Hon C Crosslacon *Carl* 08-11; NSM Brigham, Gt Broughton and Broughton Moor 11-12; Dioc Adv for Spirituality 09-12; PtO *Truro* 13-14; *Sarum* from 14. *The Hermitage, 67 Acreman Street, Sherborne DT9 3PH* T: (01935) 817718 E: mail@revams.plus.com

STUART, Brother. *See* BURNS, Stuart Mainland

STUART, Christopher John. b 74. Keble Coll Ox BA 95 MA 04 Loughb Univ MSc 98 St Jo Coll Dur BA 05 MA 06 PhD 13. Cranmer Hall Dur 03. **d** 06 **p** 07. C Pershore w Pinvin, Wick and Birlingham *Worc* 06-09; P-in-c St Jo in Bedwardine from 09; C Worc St Clem and Lower Broadheath from 13. *St John's Vicarage, 143 Malvern Road, Worcester WR2 4LN* T: (01905) 429773 E: chris.stuart@orangehome.co.uk

STUART, Francis David. b 32. Barrister-at-Law Lon Univ BA 54 AKC 57. Ridley Hall Cam 62. **d** 64 **p** 65. C Addiscombe St Mildred *Cant* 64-67; Chapl RN 67-71; LtO *Liv* 76-80; TV Oldham *Man* 84-89; Chapl Oldham and Distr Gen Hosp 84-89; Chapl Oldham R Infirmary 86-89; Chapl R Oldham Hosp 89-94; Chapl Oldham NHS Trust 94-98; rtd 97; PtO *Man* 00-03. *17 rue de la Villeneuve, 56150 Baud, France* T: (0033) 2 97 51 11 38 E: davidetpam@orange.fr

STUART, Canon Herbert James. b 26. CB 83. TCD BA 48 MA 55. **d** 49 **p** 50. C Sligo Cathl 49-53; C Dublin Rathmines *D & G* 53-55; Chapl RAF 55-73; Asst Chapl-in-Chief RAF 73-80; Chapl-in-Chief and Adn for the RAF 80-83; Can and Preb Linc Cathl 81-83; R Cherbury *Ox* 83-87; PtO *Glouc* 87-97; *Ox* 87-96; rtd 91. *1 Abbot's Walk, Lechlade GL7 3DB* T: (01367) 253299

✠**STUART, The Rt Revd Ian Campbell.** b 42. New England Univ (NSW) BA 70 CertEd 70 Melbourne Univ DipEd 77 MA 92 MACE 72 FAIM 91. St Barn Coll Adelaide 84. **d** 85 **p** 85 **c** 92. Australia 85-99; Asst Bp N Queensland 96-99; Chapl Liv Hope Univ from 99; Hon Asst Bp Liv from 99. *The Chaplaincy, Liverpool Hope, Hope Park, Taggart Avenue, Liverpool L16 9JD* T: 0151-291 3547 F: 291 3873 E: stuarti@hope.ac.uk

STUART-BLACK, Veronica. *See* CAROLAN, Veronica

STUART-BOURNE, Mrs Rona. b 67. Surrey Univ BSc 89. Ripon Coll Cuddesdon 09. **d** 11 **p** 12. C Freshwater and Yarmouth *Portsm* 11-12; C Portsea St Luke 12-13; C Southsea St Pet 12-13; C Southsea St Luke and St Pet 13-14; C Greatham w Empshott and Hawkley w Prior's Dean from 14. *The Vicarage, Hawkley, Liss GU33 6NF* T: (01730) 827459
E: revrona@gmail.com

STUART-LEE, Nicholas Richard. b 54. Wycliffe Hall Ox. **d** 83 **p** 84. C Costessey *Nor* 83-85; TV Dewsbury *Wakef* 85-90; R Rowlands Castle *Portsm* 90-00; V Nottingham St Jude *S'well* 00-03; TR Thame *Ox* 03-07. *69 Harefields, Oxford OX2 8NR* T: (01865) 511044 E: nrsl@ciloros.fsnet.co.uk

STUART-MARTIN, Rosanna. b 60. Bris Univ BA 81. Wycliffe Hall Ox 89. **d** 92 **p** 94. Par Dn Stanford in the Vale w Goosey and Hatford *Ox* 92-94; C 94-96; C Abingdon 96-00; PtO 00-04; P-in-c Uffington, Shellingford, Woolstone and Baulking 04-14; PtO from 15. *7 Limetrees, Chilton, Didcot OX11 0HW* T: (01235) 821861

STUART-SMITH, David. b 36. St Pet Coll Ox BA 61 MA 65. Tyndale Hall Bris. **d** 63 **p** 64. C Tooting Graveney St Nic *S'wark* 63-67; C Richmond H Trin 67-70; LtO 70-74; NSM Canonbury St Steph *Lon* 70-74; Travelling Sec IVF 70-74; Bangladesh 74-79; V Clapham Park St Steph *S'wark* 79-95; RD Streatham 83-87; Chapl Wye Coll Kent 95-99; Chapl Wye Campus Imp Coll *Lon* 99-01; P-in-c Wye w Brook *Cant* 95-01;

P-in-c Hastingleigh 00-01; rtd 01; PtO *Cant* 01-07; *Lon* from 07. *42 Rennie Court, 11 Upper Ground, London SE1 9LP* T: (020) 7261 1866

STUART-WHITE, The Ven William Robert. b 59. Ox Univ BA. Trin Coll Bris BA. **d** 86 **p** 87. C Upper Armley *Ripon* 86-91; P-in-c Austrey *Birm* 91-92; P-in-c Warton 91-92; V Austrey and Warton 92-98; R Camborne *Truro* 98-06; P-in-c Stoke Climsland 06-09; P-in-c Linkinhorne 06-09; P-in-c St Breoke and Egloshayle 09-12; Hon Can Truro Cathl 09-12; Adn Cornwall from 12. *10 The Hayes, Bodmin Road, Truro TR1 1FY* T: (01872) 242374 E: bill@truro.anglican.org

STUBBINGS, Mrs Paulette Joanne. b 71. Kent Univ BA 92. SEITE 12. **d** 15. C Boughton under Blean w Dunkirk and Hernhill *Cant* from 15. *35 Douglas Avenue, Whitstable CT5 1RT* E: paulettejstubbings@gmail.com

STUBBS, Ian Kirtley. b 47. Man Univ DipAE 90. Kelham Th Coll 66. **d** 70 **p** 71. C Chandler's Ford *Win* 70-75; C Farnham Royal *Ox* 75-80; Ind Chapl 75-80; *Man* 81-86; TV Oldham 81-86; TR Langley and Parkfield 86-88; Community Work Officer Dioc Bd of Soc Resp 88-90; Dir Laity Development 90-96; Nat Adv in Adult Learning C of E Bd of Educn 97-02; V Stalybridge *Man* 02-11; P-in-c Glossop *Derby* 11-14; V from 14; C Hadfield 11-14; C Charlesworth and Dinting Vale 11-14; V Dinting Vale from 14. *The Vicarage, Church Street South, Glossop SK13 7RU* M: 07712-451710 T: (01457) 237841 E: iks1647@gmail.com

STUBBS, Stanley Peter Handley. b 23. Lon Univ BD 52 Lille 3 Univ MèsL 82. Ely Th Coll 55. **d** 55 **p** 56. C Fletton *Ely* 55-58; Hon Min Can Pet Cathl 56-58; C Hounslow Heath St Paul *Lon* 58-63; CF (TA) 59-78; V Northampton St Alb *Pet* 63-76; R Brondesbury Ch Ch and St Laur *Lon* 76-93; rtd 93; PtO *Lon* from 93. *3 Westbury Lodge Close, Pinner HA5 3FG* T: (020) 8868 8296 E: peter.stubbsuk@gmail.com

STUBBS, Canon Trevor Noel. b 48. AKC 70. St Aug Coll Cant 73. **d** 74 **p** 75. C Heckmondwike *Wakef* 74-77; C Warwick Australia 77-80; V Middleton St Cross *Ripon* 80-89; R Wool and E Stoke *Sarum* 89-95; TR Bridport 95-09; RD Lyme Bay 06-09; rtd 09; Admin Bp Gwynne Th Coll Sudan from 09; LtO *Sarum* from 09; Can and Preb Sarum Cathl from 03. *15 Cleeve Grove, Keynsham, Bristol BS31 2HF* T: 0117-986 9664 E: revtrev.stubbs@gmail.com

STUBENBORD, Jess William. b 48. BA 72. Trin Coll Bris 75. **d** 78 **p** 79. C Cromer *Nor* 78-82; C Gorleston St Mary 82-85; P-in-c Saxthorpe and Corpusty 85-89; P-in-c Blickling 86-89; R Saxthorpe w Corpusty, Blickling, Oulton etc 89-93; P-in-c Mulbarton w Kenningham 93-97; P-in-c Mulbarton w Bracon Ash, Hethel and Flordon 94-97; P-in-c Wreningham 95-97; R Mulbarton w Bracon Ash, Hethel and Flordon 98-13; rtd 13; PtO *Nor* from 13. *Haven Cottage, 13 Cromer Road, Overstrand, Cromer NR27 0NT* T: (01263) 578230 E: jess.stubenbord@btinternet.com

STUCKES, Preb Stephen. b 62. Trin Coll Bris BA 99. **d** 96 **p** 97. C Dunster, Carhampton and Withycombe w Rodhuish *B & W* 96-00; V Alcombe from 00; RD Exmoor from 09; Preb Wells Cathl from 12. *The Vicarage, 34 Manor Road, Minehead TA24 6EJ* T: (01643) 703285 E: stephen1962@btinternet.com

STUCKEY, Mrs Ann Marie. b 54. STETS 10. **d** 13 **p** 14. NSM Seaton and Beer *Ex* from 13. *7 West Acres, Seaton EX12 2HP* T: (01297) 23016 M: 07814-078710 E: stuckey777@btinternet.com

STUDD, John Eric. b 34. Clare Coll Cam BA 58 MA 62. Coll of Resurr Mirfield 58. **d** 60 **p** 61. C Westmr St Steph w St Jo *Lon* 60-65; 4335-69; Hon C Kensington St Mary Abbots w St Geo *Lon* 70-71; P-in-c Monks Risborough *Ox* 72-77; P-in-c Gt and Lt Kimble 72-77; C Aylesbury 78; Chapl to the Deaf 78-82; Chapl Hants, Is of Wight and Channel Is Assn for Deaf 82-91; Chapl to the Deaf *Win* 91-99; PtO *Guildf* 82-96; *Portsm* 82-99; rtd 99. *28 Elgin Way, Flagstaff Hill SA 5159, Australia* T: (0061) (8) 8370 4707 F: 8370 6517 E: jonea@senet.com.au

STUDDERT-KENNEDY, Canon Andrew Geoffrey. b 59. Ch Ch Ox BA 80 MA 86. Ripon Coll Cuddesdon BA 88. **d** 89 **p** 90. C Wimbledon *S'wark* 89-94; V Norbury St Oswald 94-02; RD Croydon N 99-02; TR Marlborough *Sarum* from 02; RD from 09; Can and Preb Sarum Cathl from 12. *The Rectory, 1 Rawlingswell Lane, Marlborough SN8 1AU* T: (01672) 514357 *or* 512357 E: andrewsk1959@btinternet.com

STUDDERT-KENNEDY, Canon Christopher John. b 22. BNC Ox BA 49 MA 53. Wells Th Coll 49. **d** 51 **p** 52. C Bermondsey St Mary w St Olave and St Jo *S'wark* 51-54; C Clapham H Trin 54-56; V Putney St Marg 56-66; R Godstone 66-91; RD 76-88; Hon Can S'wark Cathl 80-91; rtd 91; PtO *Chich* from 91. *Orchard House, The Street, Washington, Pulborough RH20 4AS* T: (01903) 892774

STUDHOLME, Muriel Isabel. b 25. **d** 96. NSM Bromfield w Waverton *Carl* 96-02; NSM Solway Plain from 02. *Yew Tree Cottage, Dundraw, Wigton CA7 0DP* T: (01697) 342506

STURCH, Richard Lyman. b 36. Ch Ch Ox BA 58 MA 61 DPhil 70 Open Univ BSc 06. Ely Th Coll. **d** 62 **p** 63. C Hove All SS *Chich* 62-65; C Burgess Hill St Jo 65-66; C Ox St Mich w St Martin and All SS 67-68; Tutor Ripon Hall Ox 67-71; Lect Univ of Nigeria 71-74; Lect Lon Bible Coll 75-80; TV Wolverton *Ox* 80-86; R Islip w Charlton on Otmoor, Oddington, Noke etc 86-01; rtd 01. *35 Broomfield, Stacey Bushes, Milton Keynes MK12 6HA* T: (01908) 316779 E: rsturch@fsmail.net

STURROCK, Marian Elizabeth. b 46. Westmr Coll Ox BTh 97. St Mich Coll Llan 97. **d** 99 **p** 00. C Swansea St Pet *S & B* 99-03; Chapl Swansea NHS Trust 00-03; R Thundersley *Chelmsf* from 03. *St Peter's Rectory, Church Road, Thundersley, Benfleet SS7 3HG* T: (01268) 566206 E: mariansturrock@sky.com

STURT, Mrs Rachel Caroline. b 60. Open Univ BSc 03 RGN 81. STETS 08. **d** 11 **p** 12. NSM Wrecclesham *Guildf* 11-15; PtO from 15. *14 Arthur Road, Farnham GU9 8PB* T: (01252) 710968 E: rachelsturt@btopenworld.com

STURT, Rock André Daniel. b 56. Liv Univ BSc 79 Lon Univ CertEd 80. Oak Hill Th Coll BA 88. **d** 88 **p** 89. Chapl St Bede's Sch Cam 88-90; Par Dn Cambridge St Martin *Ely* 88-90; C 90-91; P-in-c Alwalton and Chesterton 91-96; TV The Ortons, Alwalton and Chesterton 96-03; R Gravesend St Geo *Roch* 03-06; Chapl HM YOI Roch 13-14; Chapl HM Pris Pentonville from 14; PtO *Roch* from 15. *HM Prison Pentonville, Caledonian Road, London N7 8TT* T: (020) 7023 7000 M: 07866-867179 E: sturtrock672@gmail.com

STUTZ, Ms Sally Ann. b 64. Univ of Wales BSc 88 Leeds Metrop Univ MSc 93 Birm Univ BD 95 SRD 90. Qu Coll Birm 93. **d** 96 **p** 97. C Middleton St Mary *Ripon* 96-00; C Wilmslow *Ches* 00-03; Dioc Worship Adv 00-03; PtO from 03. *1 Arundel Close, Knutsford WA16 9BZ* T: (01565) 650919 E: sally.stutz@stutzsanyal.fsnet.co.uk

STYLER, Jamie Cuming. b 36. Sarum & Wells Th Coll 70. **d** 72 **p** 73. C Whipton *Ex* 72-75; C Paignton St Jo 76-78; V Topsham 78-88; V Plymouth St Simon 88-01; Chapl Plymouth Community Services NHS Trust 94-01; rtd 01; PtO *Ex* from 01. *Drey House, 27 Langham Way, Ivybridge PL21 9BX* T: (01752) 691592

STYLES, Charlie Adam Mark. b 81. St Hild Coll Dur BA 04. Oak Hill Th Coll 06. **d** 09 **p** 10. C Britwell *Ox* 09-11; C Stoke Poges 11-13; P-in-c Lutterworth w Cotesbach and Bitteswell *Leic* from 13. *The Rectory, Coventry Road, Lutterworth LE17 4SH* E: charliestyles@dunelm.org.uk

STYLES, Christopher James. b 60. Univ Coll Lon BA 94. Wycliffe Hall Ox 10. **d** 12 **p** 13. C Chich St Pancras and St Jo from 12. *62 Swanfield Drive, Chichester PO19 6UD* T: (01243) 775189 M: 07990-433020 E: cjstyles@talk21.com

STYLES, Canon Lawrence Edgar. b 19. AM 88. Pemb Coll Cam BA 48 MA 52. Ridley Hall Cam. **d** 50 **p** 51. C Bishop's Stortford St Mich *St Alb* 50-53; V Tyldesley w Shakerley *Man* 53-60; Australia from 60; Can Melbourne 82-86; rtd 86. *25 Carson Street, Kew VIC 3101, Australia* T/F: (0061) (3) 9853 9749 E: lstyles@co31.aone.net.au

STYLES, Mary Elise. b 60. Southn Univ BM 85 Univ Coll Lon MSc 97 Anglia Ruskin Univ BA 12. ERMC 09. **d** 12 **p** 13. C Rome *Eur* from 12. *via del Babuino 153, 00187 Rome, Italy* T: (0039) (06) 3600 1881 E: styles@alice.it

SUART, Geoffrey Hugh. b 49. Man Univ BSc 70 Nottm Univ PGCE 71. Oak Hill Th Coll. **d** 83 **p** 84. C Ogley Hay *Lich* 83-86; TV Wenlock *Heref* 86-90; TR Kirby Muxloe *Leic* 90-04; RD Sparkenhoe E 99-03; R Snettisham w Ingoldisthorpe and Fring *Nor* 04-14; Chapl Norfolk Hospice 11-14; rtd 14. *285 Station Road, Bagworth, Coalville LE67 1BL* E: geoffsuart.t21@btinternet.com

SUCH, Colin Royston. b 62. UEA LLB 83. Ripon Coll Cuddesdon 94. **d** 97 **p** 98. C Streetly *Lich* 97-00; P-in-c Wednesfield St Greg 00-04; V Rushall from 04; P-in-c Walsall St Pet 08-13. *Rushall Vicarage, 10 Tetley Avenue, Walsall WS4 2HE* T: (01922) 624677

SUCH, Howard Ingram James. b 52. Southn Univ BTh 81 Lon Univ MA 97. Sarum & Wells Th Coll 77. **d** 81 **p** 82. C Cheam *S'wark* 81-84; Prec Cant Cathl 84-91; V Borden 91-03; Hon Min Can Cant Cathl 84-03; AD Sittingbourne 00-03; Can Res and Prec Sheff Cathl 03-07; Warden St Barn Coll Lingfield *S'wark* from 07; Superior Soc of Retreat Conductors 05-11; PtO *Roch* from 10. *The Lodge, The College of St Barnabas, Blackberry Lane, Lingfield RH7 6NJ* T: (01342) 872805 E: warden@collegeofstbarnabas.com

SUCH, Miss Nicola Jane. b 73. Roehampton Inst BA 95. Trin Coll Bris 12. **d** 14 **p** 15. C Wroughton *Bris* from 14. *49 Perry's Lane, Wroughton, Swindon SN4 9AZ* E: nzuri@hotmail.co.uk

SUCH, Paul Nigel. b 52. FGA 72 BTh 84. Chich Th Coll 79. **d** 84 **p** 85. C Handsworth St Andr *Birm* 84-87; C Rugeley *Lich* 87-88; TV 88-91; R Longton 91-02; R Cov St Jo 02-14; rtd 14. *11 Borrowdale Close, Coventry CV6 2LQ* T: (024) 7633 4990

SUCH, Royston Jeffery. b 46. Solicitor Univ Coll Lon LLB 67. Sarum & Wells Th Coll 83. **d** 83 **p** 84. NSM Ringwood *Win* 83-90; R Bishop's Sutton and Ropley and W Tisted 90-14; rtd 14. *The Drey, Paice Lane, Medstead, Alton GU34 5PT* T: (01420) 563330

SUCKLING, Keith Edward. b 47. CChem FRSC Darw Coll Cam PhD 71 Liv Univ BSc 87 DSc 89. Oak Hill NSM Course 91. **d** 94 **p** 95. NSM Digswell and Panshanger *St Alb* 94-14; P-in-c Fraserburgh *Ab* from 14. *6 Crimond Court, Fraserburgh AB43 9QW* E: keith.suckling@cantab.net

SUDAN, Archbishop of the Episcopal Church of the. *See* MARONA, The Most Revd Joseph Biringi Hassan

SUDBURY, Archdeacon of. *See* JENKINS, The Ven David Harold

SUDDABY, Susan Eveline. b 43. Bedf Coll of Educn CertEd 64. S'wark Ord Course 93. **d** 96 **p** 97. NSM Rusthall *Roch* 96-00; C Northfleet 00-02; PtO 03-06; P-in-c N Chapel w Ebernoe *Chich* 06-08; rtd 08; PtO *Chich* from 08. *54 Garden Wood Road, East Grinstead RH19 1JX* T: (01342) 313042

SUDELL, Philip Henry. b 61. Thames Poly BScEng 84 Lon Univ PGCE 85. Wycliffe Hall Ox 89. **d** 92 **p** 93. C Worthing Ch the King *Chich* 92-96; C Muswell Hill St Jas w St Matt *Lon* 96-05; LtO from 05; P-in-c Chitts Hill St Cuth from 14; AD W Haringey from 14. *163 Colney Hatch Lane, London N10 1HA* T: (020) 8883 7417 E: philip.sudell@gracech.org.uk

SUDRON, David Jeffrey. b 78. Univ Coll Dur BA 99 MA 00. St Steph Ho Ox 01. **d** 03 **p** 04. C Gt Grimsby St Mary and St Jas *Linc* 03-08; Min Can Dur Cathl 08-12; R Wallsend St Pet and St Luke *Newc* from 12. *The Rectory, North Terrace, Wallsend NE28 6PY* T: 0191-262 3723 E: david.sudron@dunelm.org.uk

SUDWORTH, Frank. b 43. Open Univ BA 92. Oak Hill Th Coll. **d** 78 **p** 79. C Deane *Man* 78-81; C Worksop St Jo *S'well* 82-85; V Wollaton Park 85-90; P-in-c Lenton Abbey 85-86; V 86-90; V Upper Armley *Ripon* 90-97; RD Armley 92-95; Dep Chapl HM Pris Liv 97-98; P-in-c Low Moor H Trin *Bradf* 98-03; V Low Moor 03; P-in-c Oakenshaw, Wyke and Low Moor 06-07; rtd 07; PtO *Blackb* from 07. *12 Brampton Avenue, Thornton-Cleveleys FY5 2JY* T: (01253) 858377

SUDWORTH, Richard John. b 68. Leeds Univ LLB 90 Spurgeon's Coll MTh 05. Qu Coll Birm 05. **d** 10 **p** 11. C Sparkbrook Ch Ch and Tyseley *Birm* 10-13; P-in-c Sparkbrook Ch Ch from 13; Tutor Qu Foundn Birm from 13. *65 Arden Road, Acocks Green, Birmingham B27 6AH* T: 0121-243 4832 M: 07891-635664 E: suddy@blueyonder.co.uk

SUDWORTH, Timothy Mark. b 70. St Martin's Coll Lanc BA 93 K Coll Lon MA 03. St Paul's Th Cen Lon 06. **d** 08 **p** 09. NSM Egham *Guildf* from 08; Chapl Strode's Coll from 08. *25 Mead Close, Egham TW20 8JA* T: (01784) 437935 E: timsudworth@btinternet.com *or* tim@stjohnsegham.com

SUEKARRAN, Robert Patrick. b 84. Bradf Univ BSc 06 St Jo Coll Dur BA 15 Keele Univ PGCE 08. Cranmer Hall Dur 12. **d** 15. C Strensall *York* from 15. *1 Whin Close, Strensall, York YO32 5ZD* T: (01904) 269880 M: 07944-592355 E: robert_suekarran@hotmail.com

SUFFERN, Richard William Sefton. b 57. Reading Univ BSc 79. Trin Coll Bris 88. **d** 90 **p** 91. C Radipole and Melcombe Regis *Sarum* 90-94; TV Cheltenham St Mark *Glouc* 94-99; R Whitnash *Cov* from 99. *St Margaret's Rectory, 2 Church Close, Whitnash, Leamington Spa CV31 2HJ* T: (01926) 425070 E: rwss@talktalk.net

SUFFOLK, Archdeacon of. *See* MORGAN, The Ven Ian David John

SUGANDHAR, The Most Revd Badda Peter. b 43.. Bp Medak from 01; Moderator Ch of S India from 04. *145 MacIntyre Road, Secunderabad, Andhra Pradesh 500 003, India* 1/F: (0091) (40) 783 3151

SUGDEN, Charles Edward. b 59. Magd Coll Cam PGCE 82 MA 83. Trin Coll Bris 89. **d** 91 **p** 92. C Gidea Park *Chelmsf* 91-94; TV Melksham *Sarum* 94-01; NSM Poole 02-08; V Locks Heath *Portsm* from 08. *The Vicarage, 125 Locks Heath Park Road, Locks Heath, Southampton SO31 6LY* E: cesthevicar28@hotmail.com

SUGDEN, Canon Christopher Michael Neville. b 48. St Pet Coll Ox BA 70 MA 74 Nottm Univ MPhil 74 Westmr Coll Ox PhD 88. St Jo Coll Nottm 72. **d** 74 **p** 75. C Leeds St Geo *Ripon* 74-77; Assoc P Bangalore St Jo India 77-83; LtO *Ox* from 83; Can St Luke's Cathl Jos Nigeria from 00; Exec Dir Ox Cen for Miss Studies 01-04; Exec Sec Angl Mainstream Internat from 04. *Anglican Mainstream International, 21 High Street, Eynsham, Oxford OX29 4HE* T: (01865) 883388 E: csugden@anglican-mainstream.net

SULLIVAN, Mrs Charlotte Lucy. b 66. ERMC 12. **d** 15. C Aquitaine *Eur* from 15. *Address temp unknown*

SULLIVAN, Canon Julian Charles. b 49. Lon Univ BSc 74 CertEd 75. Wycliffe Hall Ox 80. **d** 83 **p** 84. C Southall Green St Jo *Lon* 83-87; C Wells St Cuth w Wookey Hole *B & W* 87-90; V Sheff St Barn and St Mary 90-91; V Sheff St Mary w Highfield Trin 91-95; V Sheff St Mary Bramall Lane from 95; P-in-c Endcliffe 04-07; Hon Can Sheff Cathl from 01; AD Ecclesall 01-06; Bp's Urban Adv from 05. *St Mary's Vicarage, 42 Charlotte Road, Sheffield S1 4TL* T: 0114-272 4987 E: jandvsullivan@blueyonder.co.uk

SULLIVAN, Mrs Linda Mary. b 45. **d** 14 **p** 15. OLM Malmesbury w Westport and Brokenborough *Bris* from 14; OLM Corston w Rodbourne from 14. *Address temp unknown*

SULLIVAN, The Ven Nicola Ann. b 58. SRN 81 RM 84. Wycliffe Hall Ox BTh 95. **d** 95 **p** 96. C Earlham St Anne *Nor* 95-99; Assoc V Bath Abbey w St Jas *B & W* 99-02; Chapl R Nat Hosp for Rheumatic Diseases NHS Trust 99-02; Bp's Chapl and Past Asst *B & W* 02-07; Sub-Dean and Preb Wells Cathl 03-07; Adn Wells and Can Res Wells Cathl from 07. *6 The Liberty, Wells BA5 2SU* T: (01749) 685147 E: adwells@bathwells.anglican.org

SULLIVAN, Trevor Arnold. b 40. CITC 69. **d** 70 **p** 71. C Lurgan Ch the Redeemer *D & D* 71-72; C Tralee w Kilmoyley, Ballymacelligott etc *L & K* 72-75; Irish Sch of Ecum 75-77; Ind Chapl *D & G* 77-80; I Ematris *Clogh* 80-84; I Aughrim w Ballinasloe etc *L & K* 84-07; Can Limerick and Killaloe Cathls 89-07; rtd 07. *5 Dunlo Quay, Harbour Road, Ballinasloe, Co Galway, Republic of Ireland* M: 87-241 2194

SULLY, Andrew Charles. b 67. Southn Univ BA 88 Birm Univ MPhil 95. Qu Coll Birm 90. **d** 93 **p** 94. C Maindee Newport *Mon* 93-96; V Llanfihangel w Llanafan and Llanwnnws etc *St D* 96-02; TV St As 03-06; PV St As Cathl 02-06; V Llangollen w Trevor and Llantysilio from 06; AD Llangollen 10-12. *The Vicarage, Abbey Road, Llangollen LL20 8SN* T: (01978) 860231

SULLY, Mrs Christine Ann. b 43. Sussex Univ BA 95. Linc Sch of Th and Min 10. **d** 11. NSM Corringham and Blyton Gp *Linc* 11-14; NSM Glentworth Gp 11-14; NSM Trentcliffe Gp from 14. *6 Lancaster Green, Hemswell Cliff, Gainsborough DN21 5TQ* T: (01427) 667351 M: 07951-897393 E: chrisasully@talktalk.net

SULTAN, Pervaiz. b 55. Punjab Univ BSc 75 Ox Cen for Miss Studies PhD 97. Gujranwala Th Sem MDiv 80. **d** 80 **p** 84. Sec for Chr Educn Lahore Pakistan 81-89; Lect St Thos Th Coll Karachi 89-11; Vice Prin 93-95; Prin 95-11; V Murree H Trin 84-85; Assoc V Lahore St Andr 86-89; V Karachi 90-93; 06-10; P-in-c Highgate *Birm* 11-13; Chapl St Alb Academy 11-13; Prin St Thos Th Coll Karachi Pakistan from 13. *St Thomas' Theological College, Abdullah Hardin Road, Karachi 75530, Pakistan* T: (0092) (21) 3521 4707 E: pervaizsultan35@yahoo.com

SUMARES, Manuel. b 43. Stonehill Coll USA BA 66 Dominican Coll of Philosophy and Th Ottawa BPh 74 Catholic Univ of Portugal PhD 84 Westmr Coll Ox BTh 99. **d** 97 **p** 99. Hon Asst Chapl Oporto *Eur* 97-05; P-in-c 05-12. *Casa do Bárrio-Monsul, P-Póvoa de Lanhoso 4830, Portugal* T: (00351) (253) 993067 E: op14089@mail.telepac.pt

SUMMERS, Alexander William Mark. b 75. Leic Univ BA 98 MA 00 Fitzw Coll Cam BTh 09 Open Univ PGCE 01. Westcott Ho Cam 07. **d** 09 **p** 10. C Chingford SS Pet and Paul *Chelmsf* 09-12; P-in-c Walthamstow St Mich 12-13; V from 13; AD Waltham Forest from 15. *The Vicarage, 9 Palmerston Road, London E17 6PQ* T: (020) 8509 3895 M: 07434-918410 E: awm.summers@icloud.com

SUMMERS, Graham. b 50. SCRTP 12. **d** 15. C Penn and Tylers Green *Ox* from 15. *Address temp unknown*

SUMMERS, Jeanne. *See* SUMMERS, Ursula Jeanne

SUMMERS, John Ewart. b 35. MIMechE 66 Ex Univ MA 95. ALCD 69. **d** 69 **p** 70. C Fulham St Matt *Lon* 69-72; Chapl RN 72-81; V Devonport St Barn *Ex* 81-98; V Devonport St Mich and St Barn 98-00; rtd 00; PtO *Ex* from 00. *Box Cottage, Aish, South Brent TQ10 9JH* T: (01364) 72976

SUMMERS (née PASCOE), Mrs Lorraine Eve. b 51. SAOMC 98. **d** 01 **p** 02. NSM Sandon, Wallington and Rushden w Clothall *St Alb* 01-06; P-in-c Kimpton w Ayot St Lawrence 06-14; Asst Chapl E and N Herts NHS Trust 06-14; rtd 14; PtO *Nor* from 15. *Trafoi, Banham Road, Kenninghall, Norwich NR16 2ED* T: (01953) 888389

SUMMERS, Neil Thomas. b 58. Roehampton Inst BA 93 K Coll Lon MA 94 St Mary's Coll Strawberry Hill PGCE 95. SEITE 97. **d** 00 **p** 01. NSM Richmond St Mary w St Matthias and St Jo *S'wark* 00-14; TV from 14. *2 Ravensbourne Road, Twickenham TW1 2DH* T: (020) 8892 8313 M: 07540-974702 E: neil.summers@richmondteamministry.org

SUMMERS, Paul Anthony. b 53. St Jo Coll York CertEd 75. Coll of Resurr Mirfield 77. **d** 80 **p** 81. C Manston *Ripon* 80-83; Min Can and Prec Ripon Cathl 83-88; Chapl Univ Coll of Ripon and York St Jo 84-88; V Whitkirk *Ripon* 88-95; R Lower Wharfedale 95-00; AD Harrogate 98-00; rtd 04; PtO *Bradf* 05-10; Hon C Addingham *Leeds* from 10. *16 Beacon Street, Addingham, Ilkley LS29 0QX* T: (01943) 839552 M: 07747-131731 E: paulsummers65@hotmail.com

SUMMERS, Canon Raymond John. b 41. Univ of Wales TCert 63 Open Univ BA 75. St Mich Coll Llan 77. d 77 p 78. NSM Mynyddislwyn *Mon* 77-81; NSM Abercarn 81-82; P-in-c 82-89; V 89-91; V Mynyddislwyn 91-95; TR 95-08; RD Bedwellty 93-04; Can St Woolos Cathl 01-08; rtd 08. *12A Maple Gardens, Risca, Newport NP11 6AR* T: (01633) 613676

SUMMERS, Stephen Bruce. b 63. St Andr Univ MTheol 95 Chich Univ PhD 08. STETS 98. d 00 p 01. C Bishop's Waltham *Portsm* 00-02; R Farlington 02-09; Prin Local Min Progr *Guildf* from 09. *Diocesan House, Quarry Street, Guildford GU1 3XG* T: (01483) 790319
E: steve.summers@cofeguildford.org.uk

SUMMERS, Preb Ursula Jeanne. b 35. Birm Univ BA 56 Liv Univ CertEd 57. Glouc Sch of Min. dss 85 d 87 p 94. Fownhope *Heref* 85-87; Hon C 87; Brockhampton w Fawley 85-87; Hon C 87; C Marden w Amberley and Wisteston 88-94; P-in-c 94-02; RD Heref Rural 93-99; P-in-c Wellington w Pipe-cum-Lyde and Moreton-on-Lugg 96-02; Preb Heref Cathl 96-02; rtd 02; PtO *Heref* from 02. *33 St Botolph's Green, Leominster HR6 8ER* T: (01568) 617456
E: rolandandjeanne@yahoo.co.uk

SUMNER, Angela Diane. b 56. Brighton Poly BSc 78 Sussex Univ PGCE 92 Coll of SS Mark and Jo Plymouth MA 02 MRPharmS. SWMTC 10. d 12 p 13. NSM Totnes w Bridgetown, Berry Pomeroy etc *Ex* from 12; Asst Chapl S Devon Healthcare NHS Foundn Trust 12-13; Chapl from 13. *9 Wayside, Brixham TQ5 8PY* T: (01803) 853959
E: angela.sumner@talk21.com

SUMNER, Preb Gillian Mansell. b 39. St Anne's Coll Ox BA 61 MA 65 MLitt 76. Wycliffe Hall Ox BA 85. dss 86 d 87 p 94. Ox St Andr 86-91; Hon C 87-91; Tutor Wycliffe Hall Ox 86-89; Prin Ox Area Chr Tr Scheme 89-91; Vice-Prin Ox Min Course 89-91; Assoc Prin 91-94; Hon C Kirtlington w Bletchingdon, Weston etc *Ox* 91-94; Hon Can Ch Ch 94; Local Min Officer *Heref* 95-02; P-in-c Wistanstow 95-98; Preb Heref Cathl from 97; Adv for NSM 02-05; rtd 05. *Black Venn, Reeves Lane, Stanage, Knighton LD7 1NA* T: (01547) 530281
E: gandmsumner@compuserve.com

SUMNER, John Gordon. b 46. CCC Cam BA 68 MA 72. Ridley Hall Cam 69. d 72 p 73. C Liskeard w St Keyne *Truro* 72-75; C Caversham *Ox* 75-81; V Swallowfield 81-93; Asst Chapl Reading Univ 81-93; C Glastonbury w Meare *B & W* 93-04; Ldr Quest Community 93-08; Chapl Laslett's *Worc* 04-08; Hon C Worcs W from 08; Bp's Adv on New Relig Movements from 08. *The Rectory, Church Road, Clifton-on-Teme, Worcester WR6 6DJ* T: (01886) 812483 E: cliftonrectory@wwrt.org.uk

SUMNERS, Ms Cristina Jordan. b 47. Vassar Coll (NY) BA 73 BNC Ox MPhil 85. Princeton Th Sem 73 Gen Th Sem (NY) MDiv 76. d 78 p 82. Asst to R San Antonio St Dav USA 80-90; P-in-c Rockport Trin by Sea 90-91; Asst Chapl K Edw Sch Witley 93-95; PtO *Guildf* 93-96; NSM Guildf H Trin w St Mary 97-02; Educn Officer 98-00; USA from 02. *NDCBU 5798, Taos NM 87571, USA*

SUMPTER, Guy. b 60. Leic Univ BA 01 PhD 08. Ripon Coll Cuddesdon 09. d 11 p 12. C Brentwood St Thos *Chelmsf* 11-14; R Eye *St E* from 14. *The Vicarage, 41 Castle Street, Eye IP23 7AW* T: (01379) 871986 E: fatherguy@btinternet.com

SUMPTER, Timothy Mark. b 62. St Jo Coll Nottm BTh 95 MA 98. d 95 p 96. C Ockbrook *Derby* 95-98; C Wallington S'wark 98-01; V Ockbrook *Derby* from 01; CF (TA) from 09. *74 The Ridings, Ockbrook, Derby DE72 3SF* T: (01332) 820084 M: 07900-023122 E: tmsumpter@btinternet.com

SUMSION, Paul Henry. b 74. UMIST BSc 97. Trin Coll Bris BA 03 MA 06. d 04 p 05. C Hawkshaw Lane *Man* 04-08; P-in-c 08; C Holcombe 04-08; P-in-c 08; R Holcombe and Hawkshaw from 09; Chapl Bury Coll of FE 05-07; CF (TA) from 11. *St Mary's Vicarage, Bolton Road, Hawkshaw, Bury BL8 4JN* T: (01204) 888060 E: paul@holcombehawkshaw.org

SUNDERLAND, Christopher Allen. b 52. BA 75 St Pet Coll Ox MA 80 DPhil 80. Trin Coll Bris 84. d 86 p 87. C Stratton St Margaret w S Marston etc *Bris* 86-90; V Barton Hill St Luke w Ch Ch 90-98; RD Bris City 94-98; PtO from 98; Research Assoc Churches' Coun for Ind & Soc Resp from 98. *50 Guest Avenue, Emersons Green, Bristol BS16 7GA* T/F: 0117-957 4652
E: csunderland@pavilion.co.uk

SUNDERLAND, Wendy Jillian. b 47. d 99 p 00. OLM Bury St Edmunds St Mary *St E* 99-08; rtd 08. *9 Crown Street, Bury St Edmunds IP33 1QU* T: (01284) 766883
E: wendy.sunderland@btinternet.com

SUNDERLAND, Archdeacon of. *See* BAIN, The Ven John Stuart

SUNLEY, Carol. b 49. Leeds Univ BA 12. Yorks Min Course 10. d 12. NSM N Ormesby *York* from 12. *21 Norfolk Crescent, Middlesbrough TS3 0LZ* T: (01642) 503468
E: pcsunley@ntlworld.com *or* carol.sunley@trinitycentre.org

SUNLEY, Denis John. b 50. d 02. OLM Cannock *Lich* 02-09; OLM Cannock and Huntington 09-15; Chapl Walsall Hosps

NHS Trust from 10. *22 Huntsman's Rise, Huntington, Cannock WS12 4PH* T: (01543) 570572 E: dsunley@bigfoot.com

SURMAN, Malcolm Colin. b 48. Birm Univ CertEd 72 Southn Univ BTh 88 Worc Univ BA 12. Sarum & Wells Th Coll 76. d 78 p 79. C Basingstoke *Win* 78-81; P-in-c Alton All SS 81-85; V 85-01; Chapl N Hants Loddon Community NHS Trust 84-01; P-in-c Burton and Sopley *Win* 01-14; rtd 14; PtO *Ox* from 15. *31 Van Diemens Close, Chinnor OX39 4QE*
T: (01844) 761717 E: mcsurman@me.com

SURREY, Mrs Maureen. b 53. Man OLM Scheme 98. d 01 p 03. OLM Davyhulme Ch Ch *Man* 01-02; OLM Walkden and Lt Hulton 03-09; OLM Flixton St Jo from 09. *56 Abingdon Road, Urmston, Manchester M41 0GN* T: 0161-748 3961
E: sidandmo@hotmail.com

SURREY, Archdeacon of. *See* BEAKE, The Ven Stuart Alexander

SURRIDGE, Mrs Hilary Ann. b 69. Leic Poly BSc 90. Ripon Coll Cuddesdon 10. d 12 p 13. C Fenn Lanes Gp *Leic* 12-15; Chapl De Montfort Univ from 15. *St Mary's House, 90B Netherley Road, Hinckley LE10 0RF* T: (01455) 233064
E: hilary@surridge.plus.com

SURRIDGE, Jonathan Mark. b 67. Leic Poly BSc 88. Ripon Coll Cuddesdon 10. d 12 p 13. C Hinckley St Mary *Leic* from 12. *St Mary's House, 90B Netherley Road, Hinckley LE10 0RF*
T: (01455) 233064 E: jonathan@surridge.plus.com

SURTEES, Brian Lawrence. b 44. CQSW. NTMTC. d 01 p 02. NSM Hatfield Heath and Sheering *Chelmsf* 01-05; NSM Tye Green w Netteswell 05-08; NSM Chipping Ongar w Shelley 08-13; NSM Harlow Town Cen w Lt Parndon from 13. *13 Bowes Drive, Ongar CM5 9AU* T: (01277) 363607
E: bsurtees@seetrus.com

SURTEES, Timothy John de Leybourne. b 31. G&C Coll Cam BA 54 MA 58. Westcott Ho Cam 54. d 56 p 57. C Guisborough *York* 56-59; C Grantham St Wulfram *Linc* 59-61; V Cayton w Eastfield *York* 61-72; R Cheam *S'wark* 72-96; rtd 96; PtO *Heref* from 96. *39 Campbell Road, Hereford HR1 1AD* T: (01432) 371654

SUTCH, The Ven Christopher David. b 47. TD 92. AKC 69. St Aug Coll Cant 69. d 70 p 71. C Bris St Andr Hartcliffe 70-75; C Swindon Dorcan 75-78; TV 78-79; P-in-c Alveston 79-83; V 83-89; RD Westbury and Severnside 86-89; CF (TA) 80-03; TR Yate New Town *Bris* 89-99; RD Stapleton 95-99; V Cainscross w Selsley *Glouc* 99-07; AD Stonehouse 04-07; Chapl Costa del Sol E *Eur* 07-13; Adn Gib 08-13; rtd 13. *5 Mostham Place, Brockworth, Gloucester GL3 4BA*

SUTCH, Canon Christopher Lang. b 21. Oriel Coll Ox BA 47 MA 47. Cuddesdon Coll 47. d 49 p 50. C Westbury-on-Trym H Trin *Bris* 49-53; V Bedminster Down 53-58; V Hanham 58-74; R Brinkworth w Dauntsey 74-86; RD Malmesbury 79-85; Hon Can Bris Cathl 82-86; rtd 86; Hon C E Bris 86-91; PtO 91-08; *Glouc* 01-08. *14 Queen Anne Court, Quedgeley, Gloucester GL2 4JY* T: (01452) 690040

SUTCLIFFE, Crispin Francis Henry. b 48. Keble Coll Ox BA 69. Sarum & Wells Th Coll 73. d 74 p 75. C Truro St Paul 74-77; C St Jo Cathl Umtata S Africa 77-80; P-in-c Treslothan *Truro* 80-85; V 85-91; R Ilchester w Northover, Limington, Yeovilton etc *B & W* 91-11; rtd 11. *57 Wilbert Road, Beverley HU17 0AJ* T: (01482) 864674

SUTCLIFFE, Howard Guest. b 44. Fitzw Coll Cam BA 66 MA 70 Birm Univ MA 75. Westcott Ho Cam 73. d 74 p 75. C Chorlton-cum-Hardy St Clem *Man* 74-77; Chapl Chetham's Sch of Music 77-80; V Oldham St Paul *Man* 80-94; Co-ord Werneth and Freehold Community Development Project 94-06; PtO 94-09; rtd 09; Hon C Saddleworth *Man* 09-14. *The Vicarage, Station Road, Uppermill, Oldham OL3 6HQ* T: (01457) 872412 E: howardguestsutcliffe@waitrose.com

SUTCLIFFE, Ian. b 31. Surrey Univ BSc 69. Qu Coll Birm 61. d 63 p 65. C W Wimbledon Ch Ch *S'wark* 63-65; C Battersea St Phil 65-66; C Kingston Hill St Paul 71-73; LtO *Carl* 75-96; rtd 96. *42 Hill Street, Arbroath DD11 1AB*

SUTCLIFFE, John Leslie. b 35. Liv Univ BA 56. Sarum Th Coll 58. d 60 p 61. C Lytham St Cuth *Blackb* 60-62; C Altham w Clayton le Moors 62-65; C-in-c Penwortham St Leon CD 65-71; Ind Chapl *Liv* 71-74; V Orford St Andr 74-79; V Burnley St Cuth *Blackb* 79-88; Bp's Adv on UPA *Ripon* 88-94; Hon C Leeds Gipton Epiphany 88-94; I Carrickmacross w Magheracloone *Clogh* 94-01; rtd 01; PtO *Blackb* from 02; *Leeds* from 13. *1 Beckside, Barley, Burnley BB12 9JZ* T: (01282) 449687 E: sutcliffe287@btinternet.com

SUTCLIFFE, Peter John. b 58. BA. Linc Th Coll. d 82 p 83. C Skipton Ch Ch *Bradf* 82-85; C Tettenhall Regis *Lich* 85-86; TV 86-89; TV Warwick *Cov* 89-93; Relig Producer BBC Radio Cov and Warks 89-93; V Burley in Wharfedale *Bradf* 93-03; RD Otley 97-02; P-in-c Yeadon St Andr 03-06; V Lightcliffe *Wakef* 06-09; V Lesbury w Alnmouth *Newc* 09-11; V Longhoughton w Howick 09-11; rtd 11. *29 Oaky Balks, Alnwick NE66 2QE* E: peter.sutcliffe@btinternet.com

SUTCLIFFE, Richard John. b 67. ACMA 03. Ripon Coll Cuddesdon 09. **d** 12 **p** 13. NSM Hurstbourne Priors, Longparish etc *Win* from 12. *2 Applegate, St Mary Bourne, Andover SP11 6DT* T: (01264) 738288 M: 07976-672733 E: rev.sutcliffe@btinternet.com

SUTER, Canon Richard Alan. b 48. Rhodes Univ BA 72 St Jo Coll Dur BA 74. Cranmer Hall Dur 72. **d** 75 **p** 76. C Darlington H Trin *Dur* 75-77; C Wrexham *St As* 77-82; R Llansantffraid Glan Conwy and Eglwysbach 82-87; V Broughton 87-92; RD Wrexham 90-97; V Rossett 92-04; V Holt, Rossett and Isycoed 04-09; V Rossett and Isycoed 09-11; Hon Can St As Cathl 11; rtd 11; PtO *St As* from 11. *64 Leaches Lane, Mancot, Deeside CH5 2BL* T: (01244) 534374 E: etsuterra1@gmail.com

SUTHERLAND, Alistair Campbell. b 31. Lon Univ BSc 50 Ex Univ BA 77 CEng MIET. Wycliffe Hall Ox 77. **d** 78 **p** 79. C Nottingham St Jude *S'well* 78-81; R Barton in Fabis 81-96; P-in-c Thrumpton 81; V 81-96; RD W Bingham 87-92; Dioc Adv on Ind Soc 92-96; NSM Gotham 93-96; NSM Kingston and Ratcliffe-on-Soar 93-96; rtd 96; PtO *Ex* 99-05; *S'wark* 88-01. *36 Pyrton Lane, Watlington OX49 5LX* T: (01491) 612705

SUTHERLAND, Mrs Elaine Anita. b 64. EMMTC 95 Moorlands Bible Coll 86. **d** 10 **p** 11. C Leic H Trin w St Jo from 10. *1 Anthony Drive, Thurnby, Leicester LE7 9RA* T: 0116-241 7109 M: 07747-466865 E: elainesutherland@fsmail.net

SUTHERLAND, Canon Mark Robert. b 55. Univ of NZ LLB 77 Lon Inst of Educn MA 95. Ripon Coll Cuddesdon 82. **d** 85 **p** 86. C Pinner *Lon* 85-88; C Sudbury St Andr 88-91; Chapl Maudsley Hosp Lon 91-94; Chapl Bethlem R Hosp Beckenham 91-94; Chapl Bethlem and Maudsley NHS Trust Lon 94-99; Presiding Chapl S Lon and Maudsley NHS Foundn Trust 99-10; Can Pastor Trin Cathl Phoenix USA from 10. *Trinity Cathedral, 100 West Roosevelt Street, Phoenix AZ 85003-1406, USA* T: (001) (602) 254 7126 F: 495 6612

SUTHERLAND, Robert. b 78. Newc Univ BA 00 St Jo Coll Dur MA 09 SS Hild & Bede Coll Dur PGCE 01. Cranmer Hall Dur 05 Coll of Resurr Mirfield 08. **d** 09 **p** 10. C Morley *Wakef* 09-12; V Mixenden and Illingworth *Leeds* from 12. *37 Hops Lane, Halifax HX3 5FB* T: (01422) 353929 E: robb@priest.com

SUTHERLAND, Sophie Louisa. b 65. **d** 12 **p** 13. NSM Chevening *Roch* from 12. *Brasted Place, High Street, Brasted, Westerham TN16 1JE* T: (01959) 565611 M: 07962-136673 E: sophie.sutherland@gmail.com

SUTTIE, Miss Jillian. b 53. ERMC. **d** 08 **p** 09. NSM Colney Heath St Mark *St Alb* from 08. *51 West Riding, Bricket Wood, St Albans AL2 3QE* T: (01923) 662772

SUTTLE, Neville Frank. b 38. Reading Univ BSc 61 Aber Univ PhD 64. **d** 76 **p** 77. NSM Penicuik *Edin* from 76. *44 St James's Gardens, Penicuik EH26 9DU* T/F: (01968) 673819

SUTTON, Charles Edwin. b 53. Bris Univ CertEd 76 BEd 77 Birkbeck Coll Lon MSc 00 PhD 07. Ripon Coll Cuddesdon 77. **d** 80 **p** 81. C Stanwix *Carl* 80-84; Warden Marrick Priory *Ripon* 84-88; Fell Birkbeck Coll Lon 00-10; PtO *Bris* 12-13; NSM Clifton All SS w St Jo 13-15; V from 15; Bp's Adv for SSM from 14. *All Saints' Vicarage, 68 Pembroke Road, Clifton, Bristol BS8 3ED* M: 07785-912663 E: charles.sutton@org-edge.com

SUTTON, Christopher David. b 69. Kent Univ BSc 90 FIA 93. SEITE 11. **d** 14 **p** 15. NSM Slaugham and Staplefield Common *Chich* from 14. *Coppers, 19A Denmans Lane, Lindfield, Haywards Heath RH16 2LA* M: 07903-068366 E: christopher.sutton@yahoo.co.uk

SUTTON, Colin Phillip. b 51. Birm Univ BA 73. Chich Th Coll 73. **d** 75 **p** 76. C Penarth All SS *Llan* 75-77; C Roath 77-80; C Caerau w Ely 80-84; V Rhydyfelin 84-04; V Fairwater from 04. *St Peter's Parsonage, 211 St Fagans Road, Cardiff CF5 3DW* T: (029) 2056 2551

SUTTON, David John. b 49. St Mich Coll Llan 97. **d** 99 **p** 00. C Maesglas and Duffryn *Mon* 99-05; Chapl Paphos Cyprus 05; R Luton Ch Ch *Roch* from 06. *Luton Rectory, Capstone Road, Chatham ME5 7PN* T: (01634) 843780

SUTTON, David Robert. b 49. Birm Univ BA 69 Ox Univ CertEd 72. St Steph Ho Ox 70. **d** 72 **p** 73. C Clitheroe St Mary *Blackb* 72-75; C Fleetwood St Pet 75-78; V Calderbrook *Man* 78-88; V Winton 88-08; Chapl Salford Mental Health Services NHS Trust 92-08; Chapl Gtr Man W Mental Health NHS Foundn Trust from 08; PtO *Man* from 14. *The Chaplaincy, Knowsley Building, Bury New Road, Prestwich, Manchester M25 3BL* T: 0161-772 3833 M: 07770-737887 E: david.sutton@gmw.nhs.uk

SUTTON, Eves. *See* SUTTON, Peter Eves

SUTTON, James William. b 41. Oak Hill Th Coll 81. **d** 84 **p** 85. NSM Chorleywood St Andr *St Alb* 84-06; PtO *Eur* from 06. *1A Mediterranean Terrace, Library Ramp, Gibraltar* T: (00350) 200 46796 E: sutton@gibtelecom.net

SUTTON, Jeremy John Ernest. b 60. Ridley Hall Cam 83. **d** 86 **p** 87. C Seacombe *Ches* 86-88; C Northwich St Luke and H Trin 88-90; TV Birkenhead Priory 90-94; V Over St Chad 94-01; V Dunham Massey St Marg and St Mark from 01. *St Margaret's Vicarage, Dunham Road, Altrincham WA14 4AQ* T/F: 0161-928 1609 E: jerrysutton@fsmail.net

SUTTON, Canon John. b 47. St Jo Coll Dur BA 70. Ridley Hall Cam 70. **d** 72 **p** 73. C Denton St Lawr *Man* 72-77; R 77-82; V High Lane *Ches* 82-88; V Sale St Anne 88-96; V Timperley 96-12; RD Bowdon 03-12; Hon Can Ches Cathl 01-12; rtd 12. *11 Broad Road, Sale M33 2AE* T: 0161-973 6265 E: jfsuttontimp@aol.com

SUTTON, John Stephen. b 33. Em Coll Cam BA 57 MA 61. Wycliffe Hall Ox 57. **d** 59 **p** 60. C Dagenham *Chelmsf* 59-62; C Bishopwearmouth St Gabr *Dur* 62-63; V Over Kellet *Blackb* 63-67; V Darwen St Barn 67-74; V Walthamstow St Jo *Chelmsf* 74-84; V Stebbing w Lindsell 84-98; RD Dunmow 94-98; rtd 98; PtO *Chich* from 98. *20 Firwood Close, Eastbourne BN22 9QL* T: (01323) 504654

SUTTON, Canon John Wesley. b 48. Rolle Coll CertEd 71. All Nations Chr Coll. **d** 76 **p** 77. Chile 76-77; Peru 79-84; Area Sec SAMS 84-88; Youth Sec 88-91; Personnel Sec and Asst Gen Sec 91-03; Gen Sec 03-09; Dir Strategic Partnerships and Miss Nationwide Chr Trust 09-10; C Hornchurch St Andr *Chelmsf* 10-14; rtd 14; Hon Can Peru from 93. *Apt 1D, Block A Royal Golf, Sev Ballesteros, Mijas Costa, 29649 Málaga, Spain* E: johnsutton2104@gmail.com

✠**SUTTON, The Rt Revd Keith Norman.** b 34. Jes Coll Cam BA 58 MA 62. Ridley Hall Cam. **d** 59 **p** 60 **c** 78. C Plymouth St Andr *Ex* 59-61; Chapl St Jo Coll Cam 62-67; Chapl Bp Tucker Coll Uganda 68-72; Prin Ridley Hall Cam 73-78; Suff Bp Kingston *S'wark* 78-84; Bp Lich 84-03; rtd 03. *Room 21, Manormead, Tilford Road, Hindhead GU26 6RA*

SUTTON, Kingsley Edwin. b 70. TCD BTh 94. **d** 97 **p** 98. C Belfast St Matt *Conn* 97-99; C Willowfield *D & D* 99-02; I Newry from 02. *Glebe House, 1 Windsor Avenue, Newry BT34 1EQ* T: (028) 3026 2621 E: rev.sutton@gmail.com

SUTTON, Mrs Monica Rosalind. b 48. Sheff Hallam Univ MSc 99 Leeds Univ BA 09. Yorks Min Course. **d** 09 **p** 10. NSM Sheff St Cuth from 09. *4 Cyprus Terrace, Sheffield S6 3QH* T: 0114-232 3559 E: monica_r_sutton@yahoo.com

SUTTON, The Ven Peter Allerton. b 59. Ex Univ BA 85. Linc Th Coll 85. **d** 87 **p** 88. C Fareham H Trin *Portsm* 87-90; C Alverstoke 90-93; Chapl HM Pris Haslar 90-93; V Lee-on-the-Solent *Portsm* 93-12; Warden of Readers 96-00; RD Gosport 06-09; Hon Can Portsm Cathl 09-12; Adn Is of Wight from 12; IME Officer from 12. *5 The Boltons, Wootton Bridge, Ryde PO33 4PB* T: (01983) 884432 E: adiow@portsmouth.anglican.org

✠**SUTTON, The Rt Revd Peter Eves.** b 23. CBE 90. Wellington Univ (NZ) BA 45 MA 47. NZ Bd of Th Studies LTh 48. **d** 47 **p** 48 **c** 65. C Wanganui New Zealand 47-50; C Bethnal Green St Jo w St Simon *Lon* 50-51; C Bp's Hatfield *St Alb* 51-52; V Berhampore New Zealand 52-58; V Whangarei 58-62; Adn Waimate 62-64; Dean Dunedin 64-65; Bp Nelson 65-90; Acting Primate of New Zealand 85-86; rtd 90. *3 Ngatiawa Street, Nelson 7010, New Zealand* T/F: (0064) (3) 546 6591 E: bishop.sutton@xtra.co.nz

SUTTON, Philip Frank. b 55. SAOMC 92. **d** 95 **p** 96. NSM Akeman *Ox* 95-00; Chapl Ox Radcliffe Hosps NHS Trust 96-00; Sen Chapl R United Hosp Bath NHS Trust 00-07; Dioc Adv Hosp Chapl *Ox* 04-07; Chapl Team Ldr Ox Radcliffe Hosps NHS Trust 07-12; Chapl Team Ldr Ox Univ Hosps NHS Trust from 12. *John Radcliffe Hospital, Headley Way, Headington, Oxford OX3 9DU* T: (01865) 857921 E: philip.sutton@orh.nhs.uk

SUTTON, Richard Alan. b 39. Reading Univ BSc 61. Wycliffe Hall Ox 70. **d** 72 **p** 73. C Galleywood Common *Chelmsf* 72-76; Pakistan 76-79; C Walsall St Martin *Lich* 79-83; V Barton Hill St Luke w Ch Ch *Bris* 83-89; V Sidcup Ch Ch *Roch* 89-95; rtd 95; PtO *Roch* 95-98. *30 Mill Road Avenue, Angmering, Littlehampton BN16 4HS* T: (01903) 856721

SUTTON, Richard John. b 45. Lon Inst of Educn CertEd 68. St Alb Minl Tr Scheme 77 Linc Th Coll 81. **d** 82 **p** 83. C Royston *St Alb* 82-87; C Bp's Hatfield 87-95; P-in-c Kempston and Biddenham 95-05; P-in-c Rackheath and Salhouse *Nor* 05-08; rtd 08; PtO *Nor* from 08. *Augusta Cottage, 1 Old School Court, Upper Sheringham, Sheringham NR26 8UA* T: (01263) 821918 E: suttonsea@greenbee.net

SWABEY, Brian Frank. b 44. BA. Oak Hill Th Coll 79. **d** 82 **p** 83. C Clapham St Jas *S'wark* 82-84; C Wallington 84-88; Chapl Mt Gould Hosp Plymouth 88-89; V Plymouth St Jude *Ex* 88-92; Chapl RN 92-99; V Penn Fields *Lich* 99-01; rtd 01; PtO *Ex* 01-09. *30 Treskewes Estate, St Keverne, Helston TR12 6RA* T: (01326) 281168 E: brian@swabey.org

SWABY, Anthony. *See* SWABY, Leward Anthony Woodrow

SWABY, Desrene. b 42. SEITE 00. **d** 03 **p** 04. NSM S'wark St Geo w St Alphege and St Jude 03-09; NSM Camberwell St Mich w All So w Em from 09. *36 Gabriel House, 10 Odessa Street, London SE16 7HQ* T: (020) 7231 9834

SWABY, Keith Graham. b 48. Southn Univ BA 75. St Steph Ho Ox 75. **d** 77 **p** 78. C Lt Stanmore St Lawr *Lon* 77-80; C Hove All SS *Chich* 80-83; TV Haywards Heath St Wilfrid 83-95; C Clayton w Keymer 95-02; rtd 02. *3 Lonsdale Court, Penrith CA11 8LD* T: (01768) 862453

SWABY, Leward Anthony Woodrow. b 60. Trin Coll Bris 86 Ripon Coll Cuddesdon 89. **d** 92 **p** 93. C Wembley St Jo *Lon* 92-95; C Northampton St Matt *Pet* 95-97; TV Kingsthorpe w Northampton St Dav 97-01; Asst Chapl Worcs Acute Hosps NHS Trust 01-05; P-in-c Willenhall St Anne *Lich* 05-09; Asst Chapl HM Pris Brinsford 06-09; P-in-c Bilstrope *S'well* 09-10; P-in-c Eakring 09-10; P-in-c Farnsfield 09-10; P-in-c Kirklington w Hockerton 09-10; P-in-c Maplebeck 09-10; P-in-c Winkburn 09-10; PtO *Lich* 11-12; Lead Chapl E Sussex Healthcare NHS Trust from 12. *East Sussex Healthcare NHS Trust, St Annes House, 729 The Ridge, St Leonards-on-Sea TN37 7RD* T: (01424) 755255
E: leward.anthony.swaby@esht.nhs.uk

SWADLING, Pamela Grace. b 45. SEITE 08. **d** 10. NSM Middleton *Chich* 10-14; NSM Clymping and Yapton w Ford from 14. *66 Lane End Road, Middleton-on-Sea, Bognor Regis PO22 6LT* T: (01243) 587979
E: pam_swadling@hotmail.co.uk

SWAIN, David Noel. b 36. Wellington Univ (NZ) BA 63 MA 66. Coll of Resurr Mirfield 65. **d** 67 **p** 68. C Clapham H Trin *S'wark* 67-70; C Paraparaumu New Zealand 70-72; Chapl Victoria Univ Wellington 72-75; P-in-c Hermitage *Ox* 75-76; P-in-c Hampstead Norris 75-76; V Hermitage w Hampstead Norreys 76-80; TR Hermitage and Hampstead Norreys, Cold Ash etc 80-82; R Bingham *S'well* 82-94; rtd 94; PtO *S'well* 94-07; *Ox* 08-14. *33 Sheppard's College, London Road, Bromley BR1 1PF*
E: swain936@btinternet.com

SWAIN, John Edgar. b 44. Lich Th Coll 67. **d** 69 **p** 70. C E Dereham w Hoe *Nor* 69-73; V Haugh *Linc* 73-74; R S Ormsby w Ketsby, Calceby and Driby 73-74; R Harrington w Brinkhill 73-74; R Oxcombe 73-74; R Ruckland w Farforth and Maidenwell 73-74; R Somersby w Bag Enderby 73-74; R Tetford and Salmonby 73-74; R Belchford 73-74; V W Ashby 73-74; C Attleborough *Nor* 74-78; P-in-c Oxford Cen w Eastwood & Princeton Canada 78-84; P-in-c Oldcastle w Colchester N 84-90; P-in-c Kirton w Falkenham *St E* 90-95; Chapl Suffolk Constabulary 90-01; P-in-c Gt and Lt Whelnetham w Bradfield St George 95-01; P-in-c Lawshall w Shimplingthorne and Alpheton 98-01; R Wawa w White River and Hawk Junction Canada 01-09; rtd 09. *70 Mosher Road, RR #2, Iron Bridge ON POR 1HO, Canada* E: jswain@ontera.net

SWAIN, Canon John Roger. b 29. Fitzw Ho Cam BA 55 MA 59. Bps' Coll Cheshunt 55. **d** 57 **p** 58. C Headingley *Ripon* 57-60; C Moor Allerton 60-65; V Wyther 65-75; V Horsforth 75-86; P-in-c Roundhay St Edm 86-88; V 88-95; RD Allerton 89-94; Hon Can Ripon Cathl 89-95; rtd 95; PtO *Leeds* from 05. *3 Harlow Court, Park Avenue, Leeds LS8 2JH* T: 0113-246 1274

SWAIN, Preb Peter John. b 44. Sarum & Wells Th Coll 86. **d** 88 **p** 89. C Beaminster Area *Sarum* 88-92; P-in-c W Newton and Bromfield w Waverton *Carl* 92-98; Member Rural Life and Agric Team 93-96; Ldr 96-98; RD Solway *Carl* 95-98; Hon Can Carl Cathl 96-98; TR Leominster *Heref* 98-05; RD 98-05; Preb Heref Cathl 03-05; rtd 05; PtO *Heref* from 12. *10 Market Hall Street, Kington HR5 3DP* T: (01544) 230999
E: pandpswain@btinternet.com

SWAIN, Mrs Sharon Juanita. b 46. Sussex Univ BA 75 CertEd 76 Heythrop Coll Lon MA 04. Glouc Sch of Min 81. **dss** 84 **d** 87 **p** 94. Upton St Leonards *Glouc* 84-88; C 87-88; Children's Officer *Worc* 88-95; Min Can Worc Cathl 94-95; V Hanley Castle, Hanley Swan and Welland 95-01; R E Bergholt and Brantham *St E* 01-06; RD Samford 01-06; TR Solway Plain *Carl* 06-10; rtd 10; C Carew *St D* 13-14. *Selemat, Jameston, Tenby SA70 8QJ* T: (01834) 871381 E: rev.s.swain@googlemail.com

SWAINE, Judith Ann. b 55. STETS. **d** 09 **p** 10. Gosport Deanery C Portsea All SS *Portsm* 09-13; PtO *Win* from 13; Chapl HM Pris Is of Wight from 14. *HM Prison Albany, 55 Parkhurst Road, Newport PO30 5RS* T: (01983) 556573

SWAINSON, Norman. b 38. Salford Univ MSc 75. St Jo Coll Nottm 77. **d** 79 **p** 80. C Levenshulme St Pet *Man* 79-84; R Jarrow Grange *Dur* 84-97; rtd 97; PtO *Ches* from 98. *176 George Street, Compstall, Stockport SK6 5JD* T: 0161-449 0551

SWALES, David James. b 58. Warwick Univ BA 79. Cranmer Hall Dur 81. **d** 84 **p** 85. C Ecclesshill *Bradf* 84-88; C Prenton *Ches* 88-92; V Oakworth *Bradf* 92-00; V Bolton St Jas w St Chrys 00-09; V Haughley w Wetherden and Stowupland *St E* from 09. *The Vicarage, The Folly, Haughley, Stowmarket IP14 3NS* T: (01449) 675503 M: 07806-785714
E: haughley.benefice@btinternet.com

SWALES, Peter. b 52. ACIB 78 Open Univ BA 99. Ridley Hall Cam 85. **d** 87 **p** 88. C Allestree *Derby* 87-91; P-in-c Horsley 91-99; RD Heanor 97-99; V Heckmondwike *Wakef* 99-03; V Chellaston *Derby* 03-10; rtd 10. *18 Kerry Drive, Smalley, Ilkeston DE7 6ER* T: (01332) 881752
E: pasta.swales@gmail.com

SWALLOW, Mrs Alice Gillian. b 51. Birm Univ BA 72 CertEd 73. NEOC 82. **dss** 84 **d** 87 **p** 94. Morpeth *Newc* 84-86; Uttoxeter w Bramshall *Lich* 86-88; Par Dn 87-88; Par Dn Rocester 88; Chapl to the Deaf *Man* 88-90; Par Dn Goodshaw and Crawshawbooth 88-93; C Barkisland w W Scammonden *Wakef* 93-95; V Ripponden 95-97; rtd 97; PtO *Leeds* from 02. *22 Scholes Lane, Scholes, Cleckheaton BD19 6NR* T: (01274) 875529
E: jill_swallow@yahoo.co.uk

SWALLOW, John Brian. b 36. Trent Poly 78. **d** 84 **p** 85. C Cleveleys *Blackb* 84-87; V Blackpool St Mich 87-93; P-in-c Burnley St Steph 93-98; V 98-01; RD Burnley 97-00; rtd 01; PtO *Dur* from 01. *6 Chichester Walk, Haughton-le-Skerne, Darlington DL1 2SG*

SWALLOW, Judith Hazel. *See* KENWORTHY, Judith Hazel

SWAN, Duncan James. b 65. Imp Coll Lon BSc 88 SS Coll Cam BA 91 MA 95 K Coll Lon MA 04. Ridley Hall Cam 89. **d** 92 **p** 93. C Stevenage St Andr and St Geo *St Alb* 92-95; C Harpenden St Nic 95-99; V Redbourn 99-06; TR Caterham *S'wark* from 06; AD from 11. *The Rectory, 5 Whyteleafe Road, Caterham CR3 5EG* T: (01883) 373083
E: duncpen@hotmail.com

SWAN, Owen. b 28. ACP 71. Edin Th Coll 56. **d** 59 **p** 60. C Lewisham St Jo Southend *S'wark* 59-64; CF (TA) from 60; V Richmond St Luke *S'wark* 64-82; C-in-c Darlington St Hilda and St Columba CD *Dur* 82-84; R Feltwell *Ely* 84-87; R Holywell w Needingworth 87-97; rtd 97; P-in-c Gt Staughton *Ely* 97-02; P-in-c Hail Weston and Southoe 00-02; PtO from 02; *St E* 02-13. *Primrose Cottage, Hawes Lane, Norton, Bury St Edmunds IP31 3LS* T: (01359) 231108

SWAN, Philip Douglas. b 56. Wye Coll Lon BSc 78 Qu Coll Cam MA 81 CertEd 81. St Jo Coll Nottm 86. **d** 88 **p** 89. C Birm St Martin w Bordesley St Andr 88-92; C Selly Park St Steph and St Wulstan 92-96; P-in-c The Lickey 96-98; V 98-10; Dir World Miss *Lich* from 10; C Penn 12-14; C Hanley H Ev from 14. *Christ Church Vicarage, 10 Emery Street, Stoke-on-Trent ST6 2JJ* E: swan@lickey30.freeserve.co.uk

SWAN, Preb Ronald Frederick. b 35. St Cath Coll Cam BA 59 MA. Coll of Resurr Mirfield. **d** 61 **p** 62. C Staveley *Derby* 61-65; Chapl Lon Univ 65-72; C St Martin-in-the-Fields 72-77; V Ealing St Barn 77-88; V Ealing St Steph Castle Hill 81-88; AD Ealing E 84-88; V Harrow St Mary 88-97; AD Harrow 89-94; Preb St Paul's Cathl 91-06; Master R Foundn of St Kath in Ratcliffe 97-06; rtd 06. *8 Moat Lodge, London Road, Harrow HA1 3LU* T: (020) 8864 4625
E: ronaldswan@btinternet.com

SWANBOROUGH, Alan William. b 38. Southn Univ BEd 75. Sarum & Wells Th Coll 77. **d** 80 **p** 81. NSM Ventnor H Trin *Portsm* 80-85; NSM Ventnor St Cath 80-85; Chapl Upper Chine Sch Shanklin 85-94; Chapl Ryde Sch w Upper Chine 94-03; NSM Shanklin St Blasius *Portsm* 91-10; P-in-c 93-10; rtd 10; PtO *Portsm* from 10. *6 The Cambria, 32 Broadway, Sandown PO36 9BY* T: (01983) 402686
E: a.swanborough38@btinternet.com

SWANEPOEL, David John. b 41. Rhodes Univ BA 62 UNISA BA 64 BTh 84. **d** 75 **p** 76. S Africa 75-94; Dean George 85-89; NSM Hellingly and Upper Dicker *Chich* 94-99. *Providence House, Coldharbour Road, Upper Dicker, Hailsham BN27 3QE* T: (01323) 843887

SWANN, Ms Anne Barbara. b 49. St Mich Coll Llan BTh 07 MTh 08. **d** 08 **p** 09. Hon C Peterston-super-Ely w St Brides-super-Ely *Llan* 08-10; PtO 10-12; C Glan Ely 12-15; rtd 14; PtO *Llan* from 15. *19 Fairways Crescent, Cardiff CF5 3DZ* T: (029) 2056 2641 M: 07810-798465 E: revdanne@live.co.uk

SWANN, Antony Keith. b 34. St Aid Birkenhead 58. **d** 61 **p** 62. C Bilston St Leon *Lich* 61-66; Sierra Leone 66-70; V W Bromwich St Phil *Lich* 70-75; Nigeria 76-78; R Church Lench w Rous Lench and Abbots Morton *Worc* 78-88; Chapl HM Pris Coldingley 88-90; Chapl HM Pris Leyhill 91-97; rtd 97; P-in-c Kemble, Poole Keynes, Somerford Keynes etc *Glouc* 97-02; PtO 03-15; *Llan* from 15. *43 Park Avenue, Whitchurch, Cardiff CF14 7AP*

SWANN, Deborah Jane. b 68. St Jo Coll Dur BA 89 Brunel Univ MSc 01 DipCOT 92. St Mich Coll Llan 08. **d** 10 **p** 11. C Gwersyllt *St As* 10-12; PtO from 14. *St Matthew's Vicarage, 114 Church Road, Buckley CH7 3JN* M: 07583-275053 T: (01244) 550645 E: debjswann@gmail.com

SWANN, Edgar John. b 42. TCD BA 66 MA 70 BD 77 HDipEd 80. CITC 68. **d** 68 **p** 69. C Crumlin *Conn* 68-70; C Howth *D & G* 70-73; I Greystones 73-08; Can Ch Ch Cathl Dublin 90-08; Adn Glendalough 93-08; rtd 09. *Noah's Ark,*

4 Mount Haven, New Road, Greystones, Co Wicklow, Republic of Ireland T: (00353) (1) 255 7572 M: 87-255 7032
E: edgarjswann@eircom.net

SWANN, Frederick David. b 38. **d** 69 **p** 70. C Lurgan Ch the Redeemer *D & D* 69-77; I Ardmore w Craigavon 77-79; I Comber 79-85; I Drumglass w Moygashel *Arm* 85-06; Can Arm Cathl 96-06; Preb Arm Cathl 98-01; Treas Arm Cathl 01-06; rtd 06; P-in-c Tubbercurry w Killoran *T, K & A* from 14. *Branchfield, Ballymote, Co Sligo, Republic of Ireland* T: (00353) (71) 919 7097 E: derickswann@eircom.net

SWANN, Paul David James. b 59. Ch Ch Ox BA 81 MA 88. St Jo Coll Nottm 87. **d** 90 **p** 91. C Old Hill H Trin *Worc* 90-94; V 94-02; C Worc City and Chapl Worc Tech Coll 02-09; rtd 09. *26 Knotts Avenue, Worcester WR4 0HZ* T: (01905) 619339
E: pdjswann@gmail.com

SWANNACK, David Joseph. b 65. **d** 11 **p** 12. C Frodingham and New Brumby *Linc* 11-15; V Messingham from 15; P-in-c Scotter w E Ferry from 15; P-in-c Scotton w Northorpe from 15. *The Rectory, Church Lane, Scotter, Gainsborough DN21 3RZ* T: (01724) 647789 E: daveswannack@gmail.com

SWANSEA AND BRECON, Bishop of. *See* DAVIES, The Rt Revd John David Edward

SWANTON, John Joseph. b 61. Bradf and Ilkley Coll BA 84 Univ of Wales (Ban) BTh 10 MCIH 89. S Dios Minl Tr Scheme 92. **d** 95 **p** 96. NSM Shalford *Guildf* 95-99; NSM Compton w Shackleford and Peper Harow 99-11; TV S Cotswolds *Glouc* 11-14; TR from 14. *The Rectory, Ampney Crucis, Cirencester GL7 5RY* T: (01285) 851309 E: john@swanton.plus.com

SWARBRICK (*née* PITE), Mrs Sheila Reinhardt. b 60. St Jo Coll Dur BA 82 Nottm Univ MA 98. Oak Hill Th Coll BA 88. **d** 88 **p** 94. Par Dn Derby St Aug 88-92; C Brampton St Thos 92-95; PtO *St Alb* 95-96; P-in-c The Stodden Churches 96-98; Chapl Papworth Hosp NHS Trust 98-99; TV Braunstone *Leic* 99-02; P-in-c 02-07; PtO *Ex* 07-08; Hon C Cen *Ex* 08-14; P-in-c from 14; Asst Chapl R Devon and Ex NHS Foundn Trust from 09. *7 Lower Kings Avenue, Exeter EX4 6JT* T: (01392) 438866
E: sheila.pite@cooptel.net

SWARBRIGG, David Cecil. b 42. TCD BA 64 MA 67. **d** 65 **p** 66. C Lisburn Ch Ch *Conn* 65-67; C Thames Ditton *Guildf* 72-76; Chapl Hampton Sch Middx 76-97; rtd 97. *39 Harefield, Hinchley Wood, Esher KT10 9TY* T: (020) 8398 3950

SWART-RUSSELL, Phoebe. b 58. Cape Town Univ BA 79 MA 82 DPhil 88. Ox NSM Course 89. **d** 90 **p** 94. C Riverside *Ox* 90-95; Hon C Chenies and Lt Chalfont, Latimer and Flaunden 96-00. *The Rectory, Latimer, Chesham HP5 1UA* T: (01494) 762281

SWARTZ, Clifford Robert. b 71. Trin Coll Connecticut BA 92 Trin Coll Cam BA 99. Ridley Hall Cam 97. **d** 00 **p** 01. C Kirk Ella *York* 00-03; Regional Dir FOCUS USA 03-11; Hon C Tariffville Trin Ch 03-11; P-in-c St Bees *Carl* 11-12; V from 12; Chapl St Bees Sch 11-15. *The Vicarage, Priory Close, St Bees CA27 0DR* T: (01946) 822279 E: clifford.swartz@gmail.com

SWARTZ, The Very Revd Oswald Peter Patrick. b 53. St Paul's Coll Grahamstown 76. **d** 80 **p** 80. C Welkom St Matthias S Africa 80-81; R Heidedal 81-87; R Mafikeng 87-92; Adn Mafikeng 89-92; Bp's Exec Officer Kimberley and Kuruman 93-94; Sub-Dean Kimberley 94-96; Dioc Sec and Bp's Exec Officer 96-00; Can Kimberley from 93; USPG 01-06; Hon Chapl S'wark Cathl 01-06; Dean Pretoria from 06. *St Alban's Cathedral, PO Box 3053, Pretoria, 0001 South Africa* T/F (0027) (12) 322 7670 T: 348 4955
E: cathedral@mail.ngo.za

SWAYNE, Jeremy Michael Deneys. b 41. Worc Coll Ox BA 63 BM, BCh 67 MRCGP 71 FFHom 91. **d** 00 **p** 01. NSM Fosse Trinity *B & W* 00-04; P-in-c 04-05; rtd 05; PtO *B & W* from 05. *Tanzy Cottage, Rimpton, Yeovil BA22 8AQ* T: (01935) 850031 E: jem.swayne@btinternet.com

SWAYZE, Margaret. b 69. **d** 11 **p** 12. OLM Diss *Nor* from 11. *32 Croft Lane, Diss IP22 4NA* T: (01379) 644701
E: maggiecroftlane@live.co.uk

SWEATMAN, John. b 44. Open Univ BA 89. Bernard Gilpin Soc Dur 67 Oak Hill Th Coll 68. **d** 71 **p** 72. C Rayleigh *Chelmsf* 71-73; C Seaford w Sutton *Chich* 73-77; Chapl RN 77-82; CF 82-85; V Hellingly and Upper Dicker *Chich* 85-90; Hon C Mayfield 95-96; P-in-c Malborough w S Huish, W Alvington and Churchstow *Ex* 96-02; V Ash w Westmarsh *Cant* 02-11; P-in-c Wingham w Elmstone and Preston w Stourmouth 10-11; AD E Bridge 08-11; rtd 11; PtO *Cant* from 12. *2 Pennington Close, Westbere, Canterbury CT2 0HL* E: johnsrev@btinternet.com

SWEED, John William. b 35. Bernard Gilpin Soc Dur 58 Clifton Th Coll 59. **d** 62 **p** 63. C Shrewsbury St Julian *Lich* 62-64; C Sheff St Jo 64-70; V Doncaster St Jas 70-79; V Hatfield 79-00; RD Snaith and Hatfield 84-93; rtd 00; PtO *Sheff* from 00. *21 The Oval, Tickhill, Doncaster DN11 9HF* T: (01302) 743293

SWEENEY, Andrew James. b 61. Wycliffe Hall Ox 96. **d** 96 **p** 97. C Bladon w Woodstock *Ox* 96-99; C Coleraine *Conn*

99-02; V Cogges and S Leigh *Ox* 02-12; V N Leigh 09-12; AD Witney 07-08; I Ballymoney w Finvoy and Rasharkin *Conn* from 12. *The Rectory, 4 Queen Street, Ballymoney BT53 6JA* M: 07720-472556 T: (028) 2766 2149
E: ballymoneyrector@sky.com

SWEENEY, Andrew John. b 59. Ripon Coll Cuddesdon 09. **d** 11 **p** 12. C Clapham Ch Ch and St Jo *S'wark* 11-15; P-in-c Hythe *Cant* from 15. *The Vicarage, Oak Walk, Hythe CT21 5DN* T: (01303) 266217 E: vicarofhythe@gmail.com

SWEENEY, Robert Maxwell. b 38. Ch Ch Ox BA 63 MA 66 Birm Univ MA 78. Cuddesdon Coll 63. **d** 65 **p** 66. C Prestbury *Glouc* 65-68; C Handsworth St Andr *Birm* 68-70; Asst Chapl Lancing Coll 70-73; V Wotton St Mary *Glouc* 74-79; V Ox St Thos w St Frideswide and Binsey 79-03; Chapl Magd Coll Ox 82-88; rtd 03. *22 Park House, 39 Park Place, Cheltenham GL50 2RF* T: (01242) 254028

SWEENEY, William David. b 89. St Jo Coll Nottm BA 13. **d** 14. C Ex St Thos and Em from 14. *13 Sydney Road, Exeter EX2 9AJ* T: (01392) 926357 M: 07909-830621
E: revwillsweeney@aol.co.uk

SWEET, Miss Lynette Jessica. b 59. Kent Univ BA 80. Westcott Ho Cam 03. **d** 05 **p** 06. C Wilton w Netherhampton and Fugglestone *Sarum* 05-09; P-in-c Marthall *Ches* 09-14; Chapl David Lewis Cen for Epilepsy 09-14; Chapl HM Pris Risley from 14. *HM Prison Risley, Warrington Road, Risley, Warrington WA3 6BP* T: (01925) 733000
E: lynettesweet753@btinternet.com

SWEET, Mrs Margaret Adelaide. b 33. Open Univ BA 75 UEA MA 83 FCollP 83 FRSA 89. St Steph Ho Ox BTh 05. **d** 06 **p** 07. NSM Stratford-upon-Avon, Luddington etc *Cov* 06-13; PtO from 13. *5 Broad Street, Stratford-upon-Avon CV37 6HN* T: (01789) 297395 E: sweetmargaret@btinternet.com

SWEET, Reginald Charles. b 36. Open Univ BA 74. Ripon Hall Ox 61. **d** 62 **p** 63. C Styvechale *Cov* 62-65; Chapl RN 65-69 and 74-93; R Riddlesworth w Gasthorpe and Knettishall *Nor* 69-74; R Brettenham w Rushford 69-74; PtO 93-96; Chapl Miss to Seamen 96-99; rtd 99; Chapl St Cross Hosp 99-12; Master from 12. *The Chaplain's Lodge, The Hospital of St Cross, St Cross Road, Winchester SO23 9SD* T: (01962) 853525
M: 07889-375085

SWEET, Preb Vaughan Carroll. b 46. Aston Univ BSc 69 MSc 70. Linc Th Coll 89. **d** 91 **p** 92. C Uttoxeter w Bramshall *Lich* 91-95; P-in-c Hadley 95-98; V 98-07; P-in-c Wellington Ch Ch 03-07; V Hadley and Wellington Ch Ch 07-11; RD Telford 00-11; RD Telford Severn Gorge *Heref* 00-03; Preb Lich Cathl 05-11; rtd 12; PtO *Lich* from 12. *Brynhaul, High Street, Llanfair Caereinion, Welshpool SY21 0QX* E: v.sweets@virginmedia.com

SWEETING, David Charles. b 67. Nottm Univ BSc 89. STETS 04. **d** 08 **p** 09. C Holbeach *Linc* 08-12; V Glen Gp from 12. *The Vicarage, 19 Spalding Road, Pinchbeck, Spalding PE11 3UD* T: (01775) 725698 M: 07973-841799
E: david@davidsweeting.orangehouse.co.uk

SWEETING, Paul Lee. b 68. Lanc Univ BSc 90 St Martin's Coll Lanc PGCE 92. Cranmer Hall Dur BA 99. **d** 99 **p** 00. C Blackb St Gabr 99-03; R Falkland Is 03-06; Chapl Sedbergh Sch from 06; Chapl RAuxAF from 15. *Greenrigg, Loftus Hill, Sedbergh LA10 5SQ* M: 07794-737886
E: sweeting.paul@googlemail.com

SWEETMAN (*née* BURNIE), Ms Judith. b 57. Leic Univ BA 79 Anglia Ruskin Univ BA 07. Westcott Ho Cam 05. **d** 07 **p** 08. C Coggeshall w Markshall *Chelmsf* 07-10; P-in-c Boxford, Edwardstone, Groton etc *St E* from 10. *The Rectory, School Hill, Boxford, Sudbury CO10 5JT* T: (01787) 210091
E: rvdjudithboxriver@btinternet.com

SWENSSON, Sister Gerd Inger. b 51. Lon Univ MPhil 85 Uppsala Univ 70. **dss** 74 **d** 87. In Ch of Sweden 74-75; Notting Hill *Lon* 75-77; CSA from 75; Abbey Ho Malmesbury *Bris* 77-79; R Foundn of St Kath in Ratcliffe 79-81; Notting Hill All SS w St Columb *Lon* 81-84; Kensington St Mary Abbots w St Geo 85-89; C Bedford Park 91-95; Sweden from 95. *Christens Gård, Pl 8, St Slågarp, S-231 95 Trelleborg, Sweden* T/F: (0046) (40) 487059 M: 708-743994
E: tedeum@mail.bip.net

SWIFT, Ainsley Laird. b 56. Liv Univ BEd 80. Ripon Coll Cuddesdon. **d** 94 **p** 95. C Prescot *Liv* 94-98; TV New Windsor *Ox* 98-01; P-in-c 01-15; TR from 15. *The Vicarage, Hermitage Lane, Windsor SL4 4AZ* T: (01753) 858720 or 855447
F: 860839 E: ainsley@swift9485.fsnet.co.uk

SWIFT, Andrew Christopher. b 87. K Coll Lon LLB 08. St Steph Ho Ox BTh 12. **d** 12 **p** 13. C Hendon St Mary and Ch Ch *Lon* 12-15; C Smallthorne *Lich* from 15. *Address temp unknown* M: 07792-809334 E: frandrew@hendonparish.org.uk

SWIFT, The Very Revd Andrew Christopher. b 68. Edin Univ BEng 90 Aber Univ MSc 97. Ripon Coll Cuddesdon BTh 05. **d** 07 **p** 08. C Glouc Sch Cath 07-10; P-in-c Dunoon *Arg* from 10;

P-in-c Tighnabruaich 10-11; P-in-c Rothesay from 10; Dean Arg from 12. *The Rectory, Kilbride Road, Dunoon PA23 7LN* T: (01369) 702444 E: rev.andrew@familyswift.org.uk

SWIFT, Christopher James. b 65. Hull Univ BA 86 Man Univ MA 95 Sheff Univ PhD 06. Westcott Ho Cam 89. **d** 91 **p** 92. C Longton *Blackb* 91-94; TV Chipping Barnet w Arkley *St Alb* 94-97; Chapl Wellhouse NHS Trust 97-98; Chapl Dewsbury Health Care NHS Trust 98-01; Hd Chapl Services Leeds Teaching Hosps NHS Trust from 01. *The Chaplaincy, St James's University Hospital, Beckett Street, Leeds LS9 7TF* T: 0113-206 4658 M: 07786-510292 E: chris.swift@nhs.uk

SWIFT, Christopher John. b 54. Linc Coll Ox BA 76 MA Selw Coll Cam BA 80. Westcott Ho Cam 79. **d** 81 **p** 82. C Portsea N End St Mark *Portsm* 81-84; C Alverstoke 84-87; V Whitton SS Phil and Jas *Lon* 87-94; R Shepperton 94-08; R Shepperton and Littleton from 08; AD Spelthorne 98-04. *The Rectory, Church Square, Shepperton TW17 9JY* T/F: (01932) 220511 E: christopher.swift@london.anglican.org

SWIFT, Grace. *See* SELL, Grace

SWIFT, Ian John Edward. b 46. NTMTC 99. **d** 02 **p** 03. NSM Basildon St Martin *Chelmsf* 02-06; C Vange 06-11; Ind Chapl 06-11; Chapl Essex Police 06-11; P-in-c Crosscrake *Carl* from 11. *The Vicarage, Shyreakes Lane, Crosscrake, Kendal LA8 0AB* T: (015395) 60333 M: 07725-037680 E: ijeswift@googlemail.com

SWIFT, Jessica Suzanne. b 75. Univ of New Brunswick BSc 99. Wycliffe Hall Ox 99. **d** 02 **p** 03. C Islington St Mary *Lon* 02-05; C Mildmay Grove St Jude and St Paul 05-09; C Barnsbury from 09; Stepney Area from 14. *306B Amhurst Road, London N16 7UE* T: (020) 7923 0114 M: 07812-676240 E: swift_jessica@hotmail.com

SWIFT, Ms Pamela Joan. b 47. Liv Univ BSc 68. NEOC 85. **d** 88 **p** 94. Par Dn Bermondsey St Jas w Ch Ch *S'wark* 88-91; Par Dn Middleton St Cross *Ripon* 91-92; C Leeds All So and Dioc Stewardship Adv 92-95; TR Bramley 95-99; Miss Adv USPG Blackb, Bradf, Carl and Wakef 99-01; Hon C Kildwick *Bradf* 99-01; R and Community P Glas St Matt 01-05; rtd 05; Hon C Lanercost, Walton, Gilsland and Nether Denton *Carl* 06-10; Chapl N Cumbria Acute Hosps NHS Trust 06-08; PtO *Newc* 11-14; Chapl Northumbria Healthcare NHS Foundn Trust 14-15; P-in-c Glazebury w Hollinfare *Liv* from 15. *10 Hesnall Close, Glazebury, Warrington WA3 5PB* M: 07833-938843 E: pam.swift@tiscali.co.uk

SWIFT, Richard Barrie. b 33. Selw Coll Cam BA 58 MA 64. Ripon Hall Ox. **d** 60 **p** 61. C Stepney St Dunstan and All SS *Lon* 60-64; C Sidmouth St Nic *Ex* 64-72; P-in-c W Hyde St Thos *St Alb* 72-77; V Mill End 72-77; V Mill End and Heronsgate w W Hyde 77-82; V Axminster *Ex* 82-83; P-in-c Chardstock 82-83; P-in-c Combe Pyne w Rousdon 82-83; TR Axminster, Chardstock, Combe Pyne and Rousdon 83-94; rtd 94; PtO *Ex* from 94. *28 Gracey Court, Broadclyst, Exeter EX5 3GA* T: (01392) 469436

SWIFT, Sarah Jane. b 65. St Aid Coll Dur BSc 88 Nottm Univ MA 10. St Jo Coll Nottm 05. **d** 06 **p** 07. C Wealdstone H Trin *Lon* 06-10; Chapl Chr Healing Miss from 10. *8 Cambridge Court, 210 Shepherd's Bush Road, London W6 7NJ* T: (020) 7603 8118 E: sarah@healingmission.org

SWIFT, Stanley. b 47. Open Univ BA 86 ACIS 71. Linc Th Coll 71. **d** 74 **p** 75. C Heaton St Barn *Bradf* 74-77; C Bexhill St Pet *Chich* 77-81; R Crowland *Linc* 81-86; RD Elloe W 82-86; R Upminster *Chelmsf* 86-95; P-in-c N Ockendon 94-95; V Rush Green 95-02; V Gt Burstead 02-11; V Gt Burstead w Ramsden Crays 11-13; rtd 13. *16 Mariners Way, Maldon CM9 6YW* T: (01621) 859955 E: stanswift@hotmail.com

SWINBANK, Mrs Anne Jennifer. b 52. SS Paul & Mary Coll Cheltenham BA 90. St Steph Ho Ox 08. **d** 09. NSM N Cheltenham *Glouc* from 09. *5 Priory Mews, Sidney Street, Cheltenham GL52 6DJ* T: (01242) 700128 E: jennifer.swinbank@northchelt.org.uk

SWINDELL, Anthony Charles. b 50. Selw Coll Cam BA 73 MA 77 Leeds Univ MPhil 77 PhD 00 Lambeth DD 12. Ripon Hall Ox 73. **d** 75 **p** 76. C Hessle *York* 75-78; P-in-c Litlington w W Dean *Chich* 78-80; Adult Educn Adv E Sussex 78-80; TV Heslington *York* 80-81; Chapl York Univ 80-81; R Harlaxton *Linc* 81-91; RD Grantham 85-90; R Jersey St Sav *Win* 91-15; PtO *Nor* 93-96; rtd 15. *Address temp unknown* E: anthonyswindell@aol.co.uk

SWINDELL, Brian. b 35. St Jo Coll Nottm 86. **d** 88 **p** 89. C Wombwell *Sheff* 88-91; V Brinsworth w Catcliffe 91-93; TR Brinsworth w Catcliffe and Treeton 93-99; rtd 99; PtO *S'well* from 04. *36 Wasdale Close, West Bridgford, Nottingham NG2 6RG* T: 0115-914 1125

SWINDELL, Richard Carl. b 45. Didsbury Coll Man CertEd 67 Open Univ BA 73 Leeds Univ MEd 86. NOC 79 Qu Coll Birm 77. **d** 82 **p** 83. Hd Teacher Moorside Jun Sch 78-96; NSM Halifax St Aug *Wakef* 82-92; NSM Huddersfield H Trin

Leeds from 92; Family Life and Marriage Officer *Wakef* 96-02; Bp's Adv for Child Protection 02-14; Leeds from 14. *13 Moor Hill Court, Laund Road, Salendine Nook, Huddersfield HD3 3GQ* T: (01484) 640473 M: 07946-761364 E: rswin25004@aol.com

SWINDELLS, Jonathan Reid. b 66. Bp Otter Coll Chich BA 90 Cam Univ PGCE 93 Leeds Univ BA 02. Coll of Resurr Mirfield 00. **d** 02 **p** 03. C Sherborne w Castleton and Lillington *Sarum* 02-05; TV Hove *Chich* 05-10; V Hove St Andr 10-12; R W Wittering and Birdham w Itchenor from 12. *The Rectory, Pound Road, West Wittering, Chichester PO20 8AJ* M: 07790-430070 E: jonathanswindellsrector@gmail.com

SWINDELLS, Philip John. b 34. St Edm Hall Ox BA 56 MA 60. Ely Th Coll 56. **d** 58 **p** 59. C Upton cum Chalvey *Ox* 58-62; C Bishops Hull St Jo *B & W* 62-66; C Stevenage St Geo *St Alb* 66-71; V Stevenage All SS Pin Green 71-78; R Clophill 78-00; P-in-c Upper w Lower Gravenhurst 83-93; P-in-c Shillington 96-99; rtd 00; PtO *Ely* from 00. *21 Wertheim Way, Huntingdon PE29 6UH* T: (01480) 436886 M: 07980-093219 E: philip.swindells@btinternet.com

SWINDELLS, Mrs Tracy Jane. b 67. Open Univ BA 01 Warwick Univ MA 09 Man Metrop Univ PGCE 03. LCTP 10. **d** 12 **p** 13. NSM Lostock Hall and Farington Moss *Blackb* 12-14; NSM Leyland St Jas from 14. *Cock Robin Cottage, 164 Longmeanygate, Midge Hall, Leyland PR26 6TD* T: (01772) 424552 M: 07855-538585 E: revtswindells@aol.com

SWINDLEHURST, Canon Michael Robert Carol. b 29. Worc Coll Ox BA 52 MA 56. Cuddesdon Coll 61. **d** 63 **p** 64. C Havant *Portsm* 63-66; C Hellesdon *Nor* 66-69; V Brightlingsea *Chelmsf* 69-95; Miss to Seamen 69-95; RD St Osyth *Chelmsf* 84-94; Hon Can Chelmsf Cathl 89-95; rtd 95; PtO *Chelmsf* from 95; *St Alb* 95-98. *9 Radwinter Road, Saffron Walden CB11 3HU* T: (01799) 513788

SWINDON, Suffragan Bishop of. *See* RAYFIELD, The Rt Revd Lee Stephen

SWINHOE, John Robert. b 58. **d** 10 **p** 14. NSM Horton *Newc* from 10; NSM Blyth St Mary from 15; Chapl Northd Fire and Rescue Service from 11. *St Benedict's Vicarage, Brierley Road, Blyth NE24 5PP* T: (01670) 544495 E: johnswinhoe19@gmail.com

SWINHOE, Terence Leslie. b 49. Man Univ BA 71 PGCE 72 Lon Univ BD 95. NOC. **d** 84 **p** 85. C Harborne St Pet *Birm* 84-87; V Warley *Wakef* 87-96; V Rastrick St Matt 96-06; P-in-c Greetland and W Vale *Leeds* 06-14; rtd 14. *6 Bent Lea, Huddersfield HD2 1QW* T: (01484) 429767 E: swinfam@aol.com

SWINN, Gerald Robert. b 40. Leeds Univ BSc 60 Lon Univ BD 70. Oak Hill Th Coll 63. **d** 66 **p** 67. C Weston-super-Mare Ch Ch *B & W* 66-69; C Harefield *Lon* 70-72; LtO *Sarum* from 72. *7 Whittcompton Road, Broadstone BH18 8HY* T: (01202) 249782 E: geraldswinn@ntlworld.com

SWINN, Philip Daniel. b 65. Oak Hill Th Coll BA 01. **d** 01 **p** 02. C Harpenden St Nic *St Alb* 01-04; TV Bp's Hatfield 04-05; TV Bp's Hatfield, Lemsford and N Mymms 05-10; R Cowra Australia from 10. *The Rectory, 131 Taragala Street, Cowra NSW 2794, Australia* E: pd_swinn@swinns.com

SWINNEY, Shawn Douglas. b 76. Oak Hills Chr Coll (USA) BA 01 Regent Coll Vancouver MA 04. Ox Min Course 07. **d** 09 **p** 10. NSM Gerrards Cross and Fulmer *Ox* 09-13; C Surbiton Hill Ch Ch *S'wark* from 13. *19 Dennan Road, Surbiton KT6 7RY* M: 07508-078058 T: (020) 8090 4008 E: shawnswinney@hotmail.com *or* shawn.swinney@ccsurbiton.org

SWINTON, Garry Dunlop. b 59. SS Mark & Jo Univ Coll Plymouth BA 81 CertEd 82. Ripon Coll Cuddesdon 85. **d** 88 **p** 89. C Surbiton St Andr and St Mark *S'wark* 88-92; Succ S'wark Cathl 92-97; P-in-c Wandsworth St Faith 97-01; Chapl YMCA Wimbledon 97-01; Chapl Greycoat Hosp Sch from 01; Chapl Westmr City Sch from 01; PV Westmr Abbey from 06. *4 Greenham Close, London SE1 7RP* T: (020) 7261 9321 M: 07961-422033 E: garry.swinton1@btinternet.com

SWIRES-HENNESSY, Matthew. b 81. Lon Sch of Th BA 06. Wycliffe Hall Ox MTh 10. **d** 09 **p** 10. C Luton St Fran *St Alb* 09-12; C N Farnborough *Guildf* from 12. *27 Church Road East, Farnborough GU14 6QJ* M: 07803-928006 E: revd.msh@googlemail.com

SWITHINBANK, Kim Stafford. b 53. SS Coll Cam BA 77 MA 79. Cranmer Hall Dur 78. **d** 80 **p** 81. C Heigham H Trin *Nor* 80-83; Chapl Monkton Combe Sch Bath 83-85; C Langham Place All So *Lon* 85-89; R Stamford St Geo w St Paul *Linc* 90-02; Chapl NW Anglia Healthcare NHS Trust 90-02; V Falls Ch Virginia USA 02-05; Dir Alpha Network 05-07; V Muswell Hill St Jas w St Matt *Lon* 08-13. *Corner Cottage, Littleton Drew, Chippenham SN14 7NB* M: 07891-615984

SWITHINBANK, Mrs Penelope Jane. b 53. St Andr Univ MTheol 74 Hughes Hall Cam PGCE 75. Ridley Hall Cam 00.

d 02 **p** 03. Dir Connections Falls Ch Virginia USA 02-07; R Johns Island Ch of our Sav 07-08; Chapl St Mellitus Coll *Lon* from 08. *Corner Cottage, Littleton Drew, Chippenham SN14 7NB* M: 07870-497365 E: penelope.swithinbank@st-james.org.uk

SWITZERLAND, Archdeacon of. *See* POTTER, The Ven Peter Maxwell

SWORD, Bernard James. b 46. **d** 04 **p** 05. NSM Millbrook *Ches* 04-07; P-in-c Bredbury St Barn 07-14; rtd 15. *17 Woodlands Park, Wash Lane, Allostock, Knutsford WA16 9LG* M: 07866-446681 E: bernardsword1@aol.com

SWYER, David Martin. b 64. Univ of Wales (Abth) BA 87 PGCE 89. St Mich Coll Llan 89. **d** 91 **p** 92. C Killay *S & B* 91-93; C Newton St Pet 93-95; R Albourne w Sayers Common and Twineham *Chich* 95-13. *22 Marchants Road, Hurstpierpoint BN6 9UU*

SWYER (née HARRIS), Canon Rebecca Jane. b 67. Univ of Wales (Lamp) BA 88 Univ of Wales (Cardiff) MPhil 93. St Mich Coll Llan 89. **d** 91. C Sketty *S & B* 91-95; PtO *Chich* 95-02; LtO from 02; Lect Th Chich Univ 97-09; Min Development Officer *Chich* from 09; Can and Preb Chich Cathl from 10; Dir Dept Apostolic Life from 15. *22 Marchants Road, Hurstpierpoint BN6 9UU* T: (01273) 425695 E: rebecca.swyer@chichester.anglican.org

SWYNNERTON, Brian Thomas. b 31. JP 77. Ox Univ Inst of Educn 56 NY Univ BA 74 PhD 75 FRGS 62 LCP 62. Lich Th Coll 67. **d** 69 **p** 70. C Swynnerton *Lich* 69-71; CF (TAVR) 70-80; C Eccleshall *Lich* 71-74; C Croxton w Broughton 74-80; Chapl and Lect Stafford Coll 80-84; Chapl Naples w Sorrento, Capri and Bari *Eur* 84-85; PtO *Lich* 85-11; Chapl Rishworth Sch Ripponden 85-88; Chapl Acton Reynald Sch Shrewsbury 88-96; Chapl Telford City Tech Coll from 96. *Hales Farm, Market Drayton TF9 2PP* T: (01630) 657156

SYDNEY, Archbishop of. *See* DAVIES, Glenn Naunton

SYER, Mrs Angela. b 48. ARCM 69 Philippa Fawcett Coll CertEd 71. Qu Coll Birm. **d** 00 **p** 01. C Oakdale *Sarum* 00-04; P-in-c Coxley w Godney, Henton and Wookey *B & W* 04-13; rtd 13; PtO *Sarum* from 13. *The Old Inn, Stalbridge Weston, Sturminster Newton DT10 2LA* T: (01963) 362830 E: angelasyer@hotmail.com

SYKES, Alan Roy. b 53. Sheff Univ BA 75. Dioc OLM tr scheme 05. **d** 08 **p** 09. NSM Richmond St Mary w St Matthias and St Jo *S'wark* from 08. *251 King's Road, Kingston upon Thames KT2 5JH* T: (020) 8549 3887 E: alan.sykes10@btinternet.com

SYKES, Christine Virginia. b 43. **d** 07 **p** 08. NSM Castle Church *Lich* from 07. *18 Delamere Lane, Stafford ST17 9TL* T: (01785) 240529 E: curate@castlechurch.co.uk

SYKES, Mrs Clare Mary. b 61. Open Univ BA 10. WEMTC 93. **d** 96 **p** 97. C Tupsley w Hampton Bishop *Heref* 96-01; NSM Bromyard and Stanford Bishop, Stoke Lacy, Moreton Jeffries w Much Cowarne etc 01-08; NSM Bromyard and Stoke Lacy 09-12; RD Bromyard 05-12; R Osney *Ox* from 12. *Osney Rectory, 81 West Way, Oxford OX2 9JY* T: (01865) 242345 E: revclare@btinternet.com

SYKES, Cynthia Ann. b 41. **d** 05 **p** 06. OLM Em TM *Leeds* from 05. *The Old Dairy, Parkhead Farm, Birdsedge, Huddersfield HD8 8XW* T: (01484) 603894

SYKES, Mrs Emma Caroline Mary. b 75. Warwick Univ BA 96. St Jo Coll Nottm 06. **d** 08 **p** 09. C Birm St Martin w Bordesley St Andr 08-14; PtO 14-15; Hon C Boldmere from 15. *159 Boldmere Road, Sutton Coldfield B73 5UL* T: 0121-354 3130 M: 07859-066510 E: emmarsykes@hotmail.com

SYKES, Gerald Alfred. b 58. Univ of Wales (Abth) BSc 79 PhD 83 Univ of Wales (Cardiff) BD 98. St Mich Coll Llan 95. **d** 98 **p** 99. C Cardigan w Mwnt and Y Ferwig w Llangoedmor *St D* 98-01; P-in-c Brechfa w Abergorlech etc 01-08; P-in-c Alverthorpe *Leeds* from 08; P-in-c Westgate Common from 08. *The Vicarage, St Paul's Drive, Wakefield WF2 0BT* T: (01924) 383724 E: sykesga@bigfoot.com

SYKES, Graham Timothy Gordon. b 59. ACIB 89. St Jo Coll Nottm BTh 92. **d** 92 **p** 93. C Kington w Huntington, Old Radnor, Kinnerton etc *Heref* 92-95; C Breinton 95-97; TV W Heref 97-98; Dioc Co-ord for Evang 95-01; V Bromyard 01-08; P-in-c Stanford Bishop, Stoke Lacy, Moreton Jeffries w Much Cowarne etc 01-08; V Bromyard and Stoke Lacy 09-12; Bp's Dom Chapl *Ox* from 13. *Oxford Diocesan Church House, North Hinksey Lane, Botley, Oxford OX2 0NB* T: (01865) 208221 *or* 242345 E: graham.sykes@oxford.anglican.org

SYKES, Ian. b 44. Leic Univ DipEd. Bris Bapt Coll 64 Ripon Coll Cuddesdon 84. **d** 85 **p** 86. In Bapt Min 64-84; C Headington *Ox* 85-88; TV Bourne Valley *Sarum* 88-97; R Peter Tavy, Mary Tavy, Lydford and Brent Tor *Ex* 97-07; Hon C 07-10; PtO *Win* from 11. *Forge Cottage, East End, Damerham, Fordingbridge SP6 3HQ* T: (01725) 518635 E: iansforgery@btinternet.com

SYKES, James Clement. b 42. Keble Coll Ox BA 64 MA 71. Westcott Ho Cam 65. **d** 67 **p** 68. C Bishop's Stortford St Mich

St Alb 67-71; Chapl St Jo Sch Leatherhead 71-73; Bermuda 74-79; V Northaw *St Alb* 79-87; Chapl St Marg Sch Bushey 87-98; R Guernsey St Sampson *Win* 99-07; rtd 07; PtO *Win* from 07. *Petit Robinet, Rue de Bouverie, Castel, Guernsey GY5 7UA* T: (01481) 256381 M: 07781-111459 E: jimandsue@cwgsy.net

SYKES, Miss Jean. b 45. Leeds Univ BA 66 Bris Univ CertEd 67. Ripon Coll Cuddesdon 86. **d** 88 **p** 94. C N Huddersfield *Wakef* 88-91; Team Dn 91-93; TV Kippax w Allerton Bywater *Ripon* 93-13; AD Whitkirk 05-09; rtd 13. *21 Dearne Hall Road, Barugh Green, Barnsley S75 1LU* T: (01226) 388709

SYKES, Jeremy Gordon. b 63. Hull Univ BA 85. St Alb Minl Tr Scheme 92 Ripon Coll Cuddesdon 97. **d** 99 **p** 00. C Ipswich St Mary-le-Tower *St E* 99-02; P-in-c Briston w Burgh Parva and Melton Constable *Nor* 02-06; P-in-c Briston, Burgh Parva, Hindolveston etc from 06; RD Holt from 11. *The Vicarage, 1 Grange Close, Briston, Melton Constable NR24 2LY* T: (01263) 860280 E: jeremy@sykes-uk.com

SYKES, Jeremy Jonathan Nicholas. b 61. Girton Coll Cam BA 83 MA 86. Wycliffe Hall Ox 88 MA 91. **d** 89 **p** 90. C Knowle *Birm* 89-92; Asst Chapl Oakham Sch 92-98; Chapl Giggleswick Sch 98-06; Hd Master Gt Walstead Sch 06-10; Chapl Hurstpierpoint Coll from 10. *Hurstpierpoint College, College Lane, Hurstpierpoint, Hassocks BN6 9JS* T: (01273) 836889 E: jeremy.sykes@hppc.co.uk

SYKES, Canon John. b 39. Man Univ BA 62. Ripon Hall Ox 61. **d** 63 **p** 64. C Heywood St Luke *Man* 63-67; C Bolton H Trin 67-71; Chapl Bolton Colls of H&FE 67-71; R Reddish *Man* 71-78; V Saddleworth 78-87; TR Oldham 87-04; Hon Can Man Cathl 91-04; rtd 04; PtO *Man* from 04; Chapl to The Queen 95-09. *53 Ivy Green Drive, Springhead, Oldham OL4 4PR* T: 0161-678 6767 E: j.sykes@rdplus.net

SYKES, John Harold. b 50. Van Mildert Coll Dur BA 71 K Coll Lon BD 73 AKC 74 MTh 75 Linc Coll Ox MSc 89 ALAM 71 FRSA 92. S'wark Ord Course 75. **d** 09 **p** 09. NSM Ashburnham w Penhurst *Chich* from 09. *Woodlands, Dorothy Avenue, Cranbrook TN17 3AL* T: (01580) 712793

SYKES, Margaret. b 48. CITC 03. **d** 06 **p** 07. NSM Ardamine w Kiltennel, Glascarrig etc *C & O* 06-10; NSM Ferns w Kilbride, Toombe, Kilcormack etc 10-13; P-in-c Baltinglass w Ballynure etc 13-15; P-in-c New w Old Ross, Whitechurch, Fethard etc from 15. *The Rectory, College Road, New Ross, Co Wexford, Republic of Ireland* M: (00353) 87-640 7627 E: margaretsykes@eircom.net

SYKES, Sandra. b 51. St Mellitus Coll 13. **d** 14 **p** 15. OLM Gt and Lt Leighs and Lt Waltham *Chelmsf* from 14; OLM Gt Waltham w Ford End from 15; OLM The Chignals w Mashbury from 15. *41 Brickbarns, Great Leighs, Chelmsford CM3 1JJ* T: (01245) 362701 E: sandra.sykes59@btinternet.com

SYLVESTER, Jeremy Carl Edmund. b 56. Cape Town Univ BA 78 HDipEd 79. Coll of Resurr Mirfield 84. **d** 87 **p** 88. C St Cypr Cathl Kimberley S Africa 87-89; C Ganyesa 89-92; Chapl Informal Settlements Johannesburg 92-96; P-in-c Stoke Newington St Olave *Lon* 96-98; TV Plymouth Em, St Paul Efford and St Aug *Ex* 98-01; CMS 01-06; V Nether w Upper Poppleton *York* from 06. *The Vicarage, 15 Nether Way, Upper Poppleton, York YO26 6JQ* T: (01904) 789522 E: jeremysylvester@btinternet.com

SYMCOX, Ms Caroline Jane. b 80. Keble Coll Ox BA 01 MSt 02 MLitt 10. Ripon Coll Cuddesdon 09. **d** 11 **p** 12. C Amersham *Ox* 11-14; TV S Cotswolds *Glouc* from 14. *The Vicarage, The Croft, Fairford GL7 4BB* M: 07811-212370 T: (01285) 712467 E: carolinesymcox@googlemail.com

SYMES, Andrew John Barrington. b 66. Magd Coll Cam BA 88 MA 92. All Nations Chr Coll 90. **d** 00 **p** 00. C Walmer St Jo S Africa 00-02; Dir Ext Progr Bible Inst E Cape 02-06; P-in-c Kings Heath *Pet* 07-13; C Northampton St Giles 07-13; Exec Sec Angl Mainstream Internat from 13; PtO *Ox* 13-14; C Fyfield w Tubney and Kingston Bagpuize from 14. *79 Laurel Drive, Southmoor, Abingdon OX13 5DJ* T: (0185) 883388 M: 07921-921324 E: andrew.symes1@ntlworld.com *or* asymes@anglican-mainstream.net

SYMES-THOMPSON, Hugh Kynard. b 54. Peterho Cam BA 76 MA 81. Cranmer Hall Dur. **d** 79 **p** 80. C Summerfield *Birm* 79-82; C Harlow New Town w Lt Parndon *Chelmsf* 82-83; Australia 84-89; TV Dagenham *Chelmsf* 89-95; R Cranfield and Hulcote w Salford *St Alb* from 95; Chapl Cranfield Univ from 02. *The Rectory, Court Road, Cranfield, Bedford MK43 0DR* T: (01234) 750214 E: revhugh@symes-thom.freeserve.co.uk

SYMINGTON, Patricia Ann. *See* TURNER, Patricia Ann

SYMMONS, Roderic Paul. b 56. Chu Coll Cam BA 77 MA 81 Oak Hill Th Coll BA 83 Fuller Th Sem California DMin 90. **d** 83 **p** 84. C Ox St Aldate w St Matt 83-88; LtO LA USA 89-90; R Ardingly *Chich* 90-99; RD Cuckfield 95-99; P-in-c Redland *Bris* 99-14; V from 14; Tutor Trin Coll Bris 99-10;

AD City *Bris* from 14. *Redland Vicarage, 151 Redland Road, Bristol BS6 6YE*   T: 0117-946 4691   F: 946 6862
E: rod@redland.org.uk

SYMON, Canon John Francis Walker. b 26. Edin Univ MA 50. Edin Th Coll 50. **d** 52 **p** 53. C Edin St Cuth 52-56; CF 56-59; R Forfar *St And* 59-68; R Dunblane 68-85; Can St Ninian's Cathl Perth 74-91; Can Emer St Andr from 00; Chapl Trin Coll Glenalmond 85-91; rtd 91; P-in-c Killin *St And* 95-98. *20 Cromlix Crescent, Dunblane FK15 9JQ*   T: (01786) 822449
E: johnsymon123@btinternet.com

SYMON, Canon Roger Hugh Crispin. b 34. St Jo Coll Cam BA 59. Coll of Resurr Mirfield 59. **d** 61 **p** 62. C Westmr St Steph w St Jo *Lon* 61-66; P-in-c Hascombe *Guildf* 66-68; Chapl Surrey Univ 66-74; V Paddington Ch Ch *Lon* 74-78; V Paddington St Jas 78-79; USPG 80-87; Abp Cant's Acting Sec for Angl Communion Affairs 87-94; Can Res Cant Cathl 94-02; rtd 02; PtO *Glouc* from 02. *5 Bath Parade, Cheltenham GL53 7HL*   T: (01242) 700645
E: rogersymon@blueyonder.co.uk

SYMONDS, Alan Jeffrey. b 56. Ridley Hall Cam 93. **d** 95 **p** 96. C Bath St Luke *B & W* 95-99; R Abbas and Templecombe w Horsington 99-06; P-in-c Somerton w Compton Dundon, the Charltons etc from 06. *Rosemount, Sutton Road, Somerton TA11 6QP*   T: (01458) 272029
E: somerton.vicar@btinternet.com

SYMONDS, James Henry. b 31. Ripon Hall Ox 67. **d** 69 **p** 70. C Southampton (City Cen) *Win* 69-71; CF 71-78 and 79-90; P-in-c Arrington *Ely* 78-79; P-in-c Orwell 78-79; P-in-c Wimpole 78-79; P-in-c Croydon w Clopton 78-79; CF (R of O) 90-96; rtd 96; P-in-c Coughton, Spernall, Morton Bagot and Oldberrow *Cov* 99-02; PtO *Lich* from 00; *Cov* from 02. *Thimble*

Cottage, Kings Coughton, Alcester B49 5QD   T: (01789) 764609
E: jim.marie@btinternet.com

SYMONS, Stewart Burlace. b 31. Keble Coll Ox BA 55 MA 59. Clifton Th Coll 55. **d** 57 **p** 58. C Hornsey Rise St Mary *Lon* 57-60; C Gateshead St Geo *Dur* 60-61; C Patcham *Chich* 61-64; R Stretford St Bride *Man* 64-71; V Waterloo St Jo *Liv* 71-83; R Ardrossan *Glas* 83-96; C-in-c Irvine St Andr LEP 83-96; Miss to Seamen 83-96; rtd 96; PtO *Carl* from 96. *8 Carlingdale, Burneside, Kendal LA9 6PW*   T: (01539) 728750

SYMONS, Mrs Susannah Mary. b 59. LMH Ox BA 81 La Sainte Union Coll PGCE 94. STETS 02. **d** 05 **p** 06. C Nadder Valley *Sarum* 05-09; TV Beaminster Area 09-11; R Bradeley, Church Eaton, Derrington and Haughton *Lich* from 11. *The Rectory, Rectory Lane, Haughton, Stafford ST18 9HU*   T: (01785) 780608
E: sue.symons@btinternet.com

SYMS, Richard Arthur. b 43. Ch Coll Cam BA 66 MA 71. Wycliffe Hall Ox 66. **d** 68 **p** 69. C New Eltham All SS *S'wark* 68-72; Chapl to Arts and Recreation *Dur* 72-73; C Hitchin St Mary *St Alb* 73-76; TV Hitchin 77-78; PtO 78-97; P-in-c Datchworth 97-03; rtd 03; PtO *Lon* from 03; *St Alb* from 03. *8 Lytton Fields, Knebworth SG3 6AZ*   T: (01438) 811933
M: 07900-241470   E: richard.syms@sky.com

SYNNOTT, The Ven Alan Patrick Sutherland. b 59. **d** 85 **p** 86. C Lisburn Ch Ch *Conn* 85-88; CF 88-95; I Galloon w Drummully *Clogh* 95-01; I Monkstown *Conn* 01-04; PtO 04-09; I Skreen w Kilmacshalgan and Dromard *T, K & A* from 09; Adn Killala from 10; Can Killala Cathl from 10; Can Achonry Cathl from 10; Dioc Dir of Ords from 12; Can Tuam Cathl from 13. *The Rectory, Skreen, Co Sligo, Republic of Ireland* T: (00353) (71) 916 6941   M: 86-848 4924
E: alan.synnott@yahoo.ie *or* skreen@killala.anglican.org

T

TABER-HAMILTON, Nigel John. b 53. Univ of Wales (Ban) BA 75. Qu Coll Birm Ch Div Sch of Pacific 77. **d** 78 **p** 81. C W Wimbledon Ch Ch *S'wark* 78-79; C Berkeley St Mark USA 79-81; C Bloomington H Trin 81-90; and 92-94; Interim R Crawfordsville St Jo 90-91; Interim R New Harmony St Steph 91-92; V Seymour All SS 94-00; R St Aug in-the-Woods from 00. *PO Box 11, Freeland WA 98249, USA*   T: (001) (360) 331 4887   F: 331 4822   E: rector@whidbey.com

TABERNOR, Brian Douglas. b 43. **d** 07 **p** 08. OLM Brereton and Rugeley *Lich* from 07. *31 Ashtree Bank, Rugeley WS15 1HN* T: (01889) 804587   E: brian.tabernor@ntlworld.com

TABOR, James Hugh. b 63. Univ of W Aus BA 85. Ripon Coll Cuddesdon BTh 06. **d** 04 **p** 05. C Alverstoke *Portsm* 04-07; Chapl RN from 07. *Royal Naval Chaplaincy Service, Mail Point 1-2, Leach Building, Whale Island, Portsmouth PO2 8BY* T: (023) 9262 5055   F: 9262 5134

TABOR, John Tranham. b 30. Ball Coll Ox BA 56 MA 58. Ridley Hall Cam 55. **d** 58 **p** 59. C Lindfield *Chich* 58-62; Tutor Ridley Hall Cam 62-63; Chapl 63-68; Warden Scargill Ho 68-75; R Berkhamsted St Mary *St Alb* 75-96; rtd 96; PtO *St Alb* from 96; *Ox* 99-00. *1 The Downs, Aldbourne, Marlborough SN8 2RZ*   T: (01672) 540640
E: johnttabor@yahoo.co.uk

TAFT, Mrs Janet Anne. b 59. Sheff Univ BA 80 Wolv Univ PGCE 82. Wycliffe Hall Ox 06. **d** 08 **p** 09. NSM Abingdon *Ox* 08-12; Chapl SS Helen and Kath Sch Abingdon 10-13; C Warfield from 13. *Flores House, Goughs Lane, Bracknell RG12 2JS*   M: 07929-543626   E: janet.taft@ntlworld.com *or* janettaft@warfield.org.uk

TAGGART, Terence. b 57. Linc Univ BA 13. Linc Sch of Th and Min 09. **d** 13 **p** 14. NSM Fen and Hill Gp *Linc* 13-15; P-in-c Stornoway *Arg* from 15; P-in-c Eorropaidh from 15. *St Peter's House, 10 Springfield Road, Stornoway HS1 2PT* M: 07768-219984   E: terry_t_2000_uk@yahoo.co.uk

TAGGART, Canon William Joseph. b 54. **d** 85 **p** 86. C Belfast St Mich *Conn* 85-90; I Belfast St Kath from 90; Dioc Registrar from 06; Can Conn Cathl from 12. *St Katharine's Rectory, 24 Lansdowne Road, Belfast BT15 4DB*   T: (028) 9077 7647
E: belfast.stkatharine@connor.anglican.org

TAGUE, Russell. b 59. Aston Tr Scheme 90 Linc Th Coll 92. **d** 94 **p** 95. C Astley *Man* 94-97; Chapl HM YOI Swinfen Hall 97-00; Chapl HM Pris Risley 00-05; TV Kirkby *Liv* 05-08; R Arthuret w Kirkandrews-on-Esk and Nicholforest *Carl* from 08. *Arthuret Rectory, 1 Arthuret Drive, Longtown, Carlisle CA6 5SG*   T: (01228) 791338   E: taguejosh@yahoo.co.uk

TAILBY, Ms Jane Dorothy. b 56. Culham Coll of Educn BEd 79. WEMTC 01. **d** 04 **p** 05. NSM Frampton Cotterell and Iron

Acton *Bris* 04-09; NSM Winterbourne and Frenchay and Winterbourne Down 08-09; TV Nadder Valley *Sarum* from 09. *The Vicarage, 11A Tyndale's Meadow, Dinton, Salisbury SP3 5HU* T: (01722) 717883   E: jdtailby@aol.com

TAILBY, Peter Alan. b 49. Chich Th Coll 83. **d** 85 **p** 86. C Stocking Farm *Leic* 85-88; C Knighton St Mary Magd 88-90; P-in-c Thurnby Lodge 90-98; P-in-c W Molesey *Guildf* 98-05; V from 05. *The Vicarage, 518 Walton Road, West Molesey KT8 2QF* T: (020) 8979 3846   E: ptailby@supanet.com

TAINTON, Mrs Carol Anne. b 50. EMMTC 96. **d** 99 **p** 00. NSM Gamston and Bridgford *S'well* 99-03; P-in-c Lowdham w Caythorpe, and Gunthorpe 03-04; V from 04. *The Vicarage, 12 Old Tannery Drive, Lowdham, Nottingham NG14 7PS* T: 0115-966 5922   E: revcaroltainton@ukonline.co.uk

TAIT, James Laurence Jamieson. b 47. Cranmer Hall Dur 78. **d** 80 **p** 81. C Heyside *Man* 80-81; C Westhoughton 81-84; R Aldingham and Dendron and Rampside *Carl* 84-88; V Flookburgh 88-92; V Hunterville New Zealand 92-94; V Palmerston N from 94. *PO Box 5134, Terrace End, Palmerston North 4441, New Zealand*   T: (0064) (6) 358 9134 *or* T/F 358 5403   E: stpeters@inspire.net.nz

TAIT, Philip Leslie. b 52. Ex Univ BA 73 Hull Univ PGCE 74. NEOC 87. **d** 90 **p** 91. NSM Osbaldwick w Murton *York* 90-92; Chapl and Hd RS Berkhamsted Sch Herts 93-97; P-in-c Woodhorn w Newbiggin *Newc* 98; Chapl HM Pris Wolds 98-00; Chapl R Russell Sch Croydon 00-05; Chapl Hurstpierpoint Coll 05-07; TV Upper Skerne *Dur* 07-13; P-in-c Cheveley *Ely* from 13. *The Rectory, 132 High Street, Cheveley, Newmarket CB8 9DG*   E: philiptait548@btinternet.com

TAIT (née DAVIS), Canon Ruth Elizabeth. b 39. St Andr Univ MA 62 Moray Ho Coll of Educn DipEd 63. Moray Ord Course 89. **dss** 90 **d** 94 **p** 95. Chapl w Lossiemouth *Mor* 90-96; C 94-96; NSM Dufftown *Ab* 96-03; C Forres *Mor* 96-98; NSM Aberlour 98-03; Dioc Dir of Ords 02-08; NSM Elgin w Lossiemouth 04-08; LtO *Mor* from 10; Hon Can St Andr Cathl Inverness from 03. *Benmore, Burnbank, Birnie, Elgin IV30 8RW*   T: (01343) 862808
E: ruth.e.tait@btinternet.com

TAIT, Ms Valerie Joan. b 60. Open Univ BA 96 SRN 82 RSCN 82. Trin Coll Bris 99. **d** 01 **p** 02. C W Heref 01-06; P-in-c Ford 06-13; P-in-c Gt Wollaston 10-13; P-in-c Alberbury w Cardeston 06-13; V Ford, Gt Wollaston and Alberbury w Cardeston from 13. *The Vicarage, Ford, Shrewsbury SY5 9LZ* T: (01743) 850254

TALBOT, Alan John. b 23. BNC Ox BA 49 MA 55. Coll of Resurr Mirfield 49. **d** 51 **p** 52. C Hackney Wick St Mary of Eton w St Aug *Lon* 51-54; C Portsea St Sav *Portsm* 54-63; Chapl

St Jo Coll Chidya Tanzania 63-65; P-in-c Namakambale 65-68; V Stepney St Aug w St Phil *Lon* 69-78; V Twickenham All Hallows 78-86; rtd 88; PtO *S'wark* from 88. *46 Brandon Street, London SE17 1NL* T: (020) 7703 0719

TALBOT, Derek <u>Michael</u>. b 55. St Jo Coll Dur BSc 77. St Jo Coll Nottm 84. **d** 87 **p** 88. C Rushden w Newton Bromswold *Pet* 87-90; C Barton Seagrave w Warkton 90-95; V Kettering Ch the King 95-02; V Northwood Em *Lon* from 02; P-in-c Northolt St Jos 13-14; AD Harrow 02-07; Dir of Ords Willesden Area from 10. *Emmanuel Vicarage, 3 Gatehill Road, Northwood HA6 3QB* T: (01923) 828914 *or* 845203 F: 845209 M: 07767-763715 E: mike.talbot@lineone.net *or* mike.talbot@ecn.org.uk

TALBOT (*née* **THOMSON), Mrs Elizabeth Lucy.** b 74. Lanc Univ BA 96 Bris Univ BA 00 MA 01. Trin Coll Bris 98. **d** 01 **p** 02. C Bitterne *Win* 01-05; Chapl Dean Close Sch Cheltenham from 05. *Dean Close School, Shelburne Road, Cheltenham GL51 6HE* T: (01242) 258000 M: 07977-115923 E: libby@thomson74.fslife.co.uk

TALBOT, George Brian. b 37. Qu Coll Birm 78. **d** 80 **p** 81. C Heref St Martin 80-83; R Bishop's Frome w Castle Frome and Fromes Hill 83-90; P-in-c Acton Beauchamp and Evesbatch w Stanford Bishop 83-90; R Burstow *S'wark* 90-02; rtd 02. *14 Locksash Close, West Wittering, Chichester PO20 8QP* T: (01243) 512454

TALBOT, James Edward. b 85. St Cuth Soc Dur BA 07. Trin Coll Bris 11. **d** 14 **p** 15. C Woodford Wells *Chelmsf* from 14. *55B Montalt Road, Woodford Green IG8 9RS* T: (020) 8505 4077 M: 07746-133438 E: james@asww.org.uk

TALBOT, John <u>Herbert</u> **Boyle.** b 30. TCD BA 51 MA 52. CITC 52. **d** 53 **p** 54. C Dublin St Pet *D & G* 53-57; Chan Vicar St Patrick's Cathl Dub 56-61; C Dublin Zion Ch *D & G* 57-61; Chapl Asst St Thos Hosp Lon 61-64; Min Can and Sacr Cant Cathl 64-67; R Brasted *Roch* 67-84; R Ightham 84-95; P-in-c Shipbourne 87-91; RD Shoreham 89-95; rtd 95; PtO *Roch* from 01. *12 Waterlakes, Edenbridge TN8 5BX* T: (01732) 865729 E: jbtalbot@waitrose.com

TALBOT, Mrs June Phyllis. b 46. Ripon Coll of Educn CertEd 67. NEOC 88. **d** 91 **p** 94. NSM Cleadon *Dur* 91-97; Dioc Voc Adv from 94; NSM Bishopwearmouth St Gabr from 97. *66 Wheatall Drive, Whitburn, Sunderland SR6 7HQ* T: 0191-529 2265

TALBOT, Mair Josephine. See McFADYEN, Mair Josephine

TALBOT, Mrs Marian. b 25. Qu Coll Birm 76. **dss** 78 **d** 87 **p** 94. Droitwich *Worc* 78-87; Par Dn Droitwich Spa 87-88; Chapl Droitwich Hosp 83-88; Asst Chapl Alexandra Hosp Redditch 88-98; PtO *Worc* 88-98; rtd 98; PtO *Truro* from 00. *Number Ten, The Fairway, Mawnan Smith, Falmouth TR11 5LR* T: (01326) 250035

TALBOT, Michael. See TALBOT, Derek Michael

TALBOT, Simon George Guy. b 79. Reading Univ BSc 01. Oak Hill Th Coll BA 07. **d** 07 **p** 08. C Ipswich St Marg *St E* 07-10; C Plymouth Em, St Paul Efford and St Aug *Ex* 10-11; TV from 11. *28A Sefton Avenue, Plymouth PL4 7HB* T: (01752) 245813 E: simon@thetalbots.org.uk

TALBOT, Sister Susan Gabriel. b 46. Leeds Univ BA 69 Man Poly CertEd 70 Man Univ PhD 00. NOC 91. **d** 94 **p** 95. C Wythenshawe St Martin *Man* 94-98; P-in-c Cheetham St Jo 98-02; LtO 02-04; C Wilmslow *Ches* 04-05; Dioc Adv Healing 06-08; NSM Bowdon 06-11. *34 Eaton Road, Bowdon, Altrincham WA14 3EH* T: 0161-233 0630 E: susangabriel@btinternet.com

TALBOT-PONSONBY, Preb Andrew. b 44. Coll of Resurr Mirfield 66. **d** 68 **p** 70. C Radlett *St Alb* 68-70; C Salisbury St Martin *Sarum* 70-73; P-in-c Acton Burnell w Pitchford *Heref* 73-80; P-in-c Frodesley 73-80; P-in-c Cound 73-80; Asst Dioc Youth Officer 73-80; P-in-c Bockleton w Leysters 80-81; V 81-92; P-in-c Kimbolton w Middleton-on-the-Hill 80-81; V Kimbolton w Hamnish and Middleton-on-the-Hill 81-92; P-in-c Wigmore Abbey 92-96; R 97-98; RD Leominster 97-98; Public Preacher 98-14; Warden of Readers 02-12; Preb Heref Cathl from 87; rtd 09; Retired Clergy Officer *Heref* from 13; PtO from 14. *The Old Barn, Cleeve Lane, Ross-on-Wye HR9 7TB* T: (01989) 565003 E: andrew@talbot-ponsonby.org

TALBOT-PONSONBY, Preb Gillian. b 50. Sarum & Wells Th Coll 89. **d** 91 **p** 94. C Leominster *Heref* 91-92; NSM Wigmore Abbey 92-98; Public Preacher from 98; Asst Dioc Adv on Women in Min 99-03; Dioc Adv from 03; Preb Heref Cathl from 14. *The Old Barn, Cleeve Lane, Ross-on-Wye HR9 7TB* T: (01989) 565003 E: jill@talbot-ponsonby.org

TALBOTT, Brian <u>Hugh</u>. b 34. RD 78. St Pet Hall Ox BA 57 MA 64. Westcott Ho Cam. **d** 59 **p** 60. C Newc H Cross 59-61; C Newc St Jo 61-64; Chapl RNR 63-91; Chapl Barnard Castle Sch 64-71; Chapl Bishop's Stortford Coll 71-96; Hon C Bishop's Stortford St Mich *St Alb* 71-96; rtd 96; PtO *B & W*

from 96; Acting Chapl Wells Cathl Sch 97-98. *Four Seasons, Milton Lane, Wookey Hole, Wells BA5 1DG* T: (01749) 679678 E: talbott@talktalk.net

TALBOTT, Scott Malcolm. b 55. SAOMC 00. **d** 03 **p** 04. NSM Watford St Andr *St Alb* 03-10; PtO from 10. *Elmhurst, 40 Berks Hill, Chorleywood, Rickmansworth WD3 5AH* T: (01923) 282370 M: 07802-244877 E: scott.talbott@talk21.com

TALBOTT, Simon John. b 57. Pontifical Univ Maynooth BD 81. **d** 81 **p** 82. In RC Ch 81-87; C Headingley *Ripon* 88-91; V Gt and Lt Ouseburn w Marton cum Grafton 91-97; Chapl Qu Ethelburga's Coll York 91-97; P-in-c Markington w S Stainley and Bishop Thornton *Ripon* 97-01; AD Ripon 97-01; P-in-c Epsom St Martin *Guildf* 01-02; V 02-13; Chapl Univ for the Creative Arts 06-13; P-in-c Gt Shelford *Ely* from 13. *The Vicarage, 12 Church Street, Great Shelford, Cambridge CB22 5EL* T: (01223) 847068 M: 07740-665210 E: s.talbott@virgin.net

TALING, Johannes Albert (<u>Hans</u>). b 59. St Jo Coll Nottm 93. EAMTC 00. **d** 02 **p** 03. C Littleborough *Man* 02-05; P-in-c N Buckingham *Ox* 05-08; R from 08. *The Rectory, South Hall, Maids Moreton, Buckingham MK18 1QD* T: (01280) 813246 E: taling@btinternet.com

TALKS, David. b 57. Trin Hall Cam BA 78 MA 81. Trin Coll Bris BA 06. **d** 06 **p** 07. C Colchester St Jo *Chelmsf* 06-11; P-in-c Lynchmere and Camelsdale *Chich* from 11. *The Vicarage, School Road, Camelsdale, Haslemere GU27 3RN* T: (01428) 652108 M: 07867-808207 E: rev.dave@btinternet.com *or* lynchcam.vicarage@btinternet.com

TALLANT, John. b 45. Edin Th Coll 86. **d** 88 **p** 89. C Cayton w Eastfield *York* 88-90; C N Hull St Mich 90-91; V Scarborough St Sav w All SS 91-93; V Fleetwood St Nic *Blackb* 93-99; P-in-c Sculcoates St Paul w Ch Ch and St Silas *York* 99-03; P-in-c Hull St Mary Sculcoates 99-03; P-in-c Hull St Steph Sculcoates 99-03; V Woldsburn 03-11; P-in-c Dunscroft St Edwin *Sheff* 11-15; rtd 15. *8 Pomona Way, Driffield YO25 6YH* E: john.tallant@homecall.co.uk

TALLINN, Dean of. See PIIR, Gustav Peeter

TALLON, Jonathan Robert Roe. b 66. Rob Coll Cam BA 88 MA 92 Nottm Univ MPhil 07. St Jo Coll Nottm BTh 94. **d** 97 **p** 98. C Bury St Jo w St Mark *Man* 97-01; P-in-c Cadishead 01-08; V 08-09; Tutor N Bapt Learning Community from 09. *Luther King House, Brighton Grove, Manchester M14 5JP* T: 0161-249 2546 E: jonathan.tallon@northern.org.uk

TALLOWIN (*née* BOUDIER), Mrs Rosemary. b 57. St Mellitus Coll BA 11. **d** 11 **p** 12. C Colchester St Mich Myland *Chelmsf* 11-14; TV Harwich Peninsula from 14. *The Vicarage, Church Hill, Ramsey, Harwich CO12 5EU* T: (01255) 880291 E: rosie.tallowin@btinternet.com

TAME, Mrs Helene Louise. b 63. ERMC 12. **d** 15. C St Neots *Ely* from 15. *Address temp unknown*

TAMPLIN, Peter Harry. b 44. Sarum & Wells Th Coll 71. **d** 73 **p** 74. C Digswell *St Alb* 73-76; C Chesterton St Luke *Ely* 76-82; V Chesterton St Geo 82-95; R Durrington *Sarum* 95-07; r-d 07. *1 Gathorne Road, Bristol BS3 1LR* T: 0117-963 9628 E: phtamplin@yahoo.co.uk

TAMPLIN, Roger Ian. b 41. K Coll Lon BD 63 AKC 63. St Boniface Warminster 60. **d** 64 **p** 65. C St Helier *S'wark* 64-68; C Camberwell St Giles 68-72; C Tanga St Aug Tanzania 72-73; P-in-c Brent Pelham w Meesden *St Alb* 74-78; P-in-c Anstey 75-78; rtd 01. *31 Shackleton Spring, Stevenage SG2 9DF* T: (01438) 316031 E: roger.tamplin@ntlworld.com

TAMS, Paul William. b 56. Huddersfield Poly CertEd 77. EAMTC 87. **d** 90 **p** 91. NSM Mildenhall *St E* 90-93; NSM Brandon and Santon Downham w Elveden etc from 93. *38 Raven Close, Mildenhall, Bury St Edmunds IP28 7LF* T: (01638) 715475 E: paultams@lineone.net

TAN (*née* MITCHELL), Mrs Sarah Rachel. b 79. Birm Univ BA 00 Fitzw Coll Cam BA 04. Westcott Ho Cam 02. **d** 05 **p** 06. C Reddal Hill St Luke *Worc* 05-08; Chapl HM Pris Wayland 08-13; PtO *Ely* from 08. *Address withheld by request* E: sarah@icklesarah.fsnet.co.uk

TANCOCK, Steven John. b 73. Westmr Coll Ox BTh 01. St Steph Ho Ox 02. **d** 04 **p** 05. C Wincanton and Pen Selwood *B & W* 04-09; C Warren Park and Leigh Park *Portsm* 09-14. *29 Marshfield Road, Minehead TA24 6AH* T: (01643) 704847 E: rev.steve@btinternet.com

TANN, Canon David John. b 31. K Coll Lon BD 57 AKC 57. **d** 58 **p** 59. C Wandsworth St Anne *S'wark* 58-60; C Sholing *Win* 60-64; Asst Chapl Lon Univ 64-65; C Fulham All SS 65-68; Hon C 72-82; LtO 68-72; Teacher Godolphin and Latymer Sch Hammersmith 68-73; Ealing Boys Gr Sch 69-73; Hd of RE Green Sch Isleworth 73-82; V Dudley St Jas *Worc* 82-95; Chapl Burton Road Hosp Dudley 83-95; Hon Can Worc Cathl 90-95; RD Dudley 93-95; rtd 95; PtO *Lon* from 97. *75 Parkview Court, Fulham High Street, London SW6 3LL* T: (020) 7736 6018

TANNER, Preb Alan John. b 25. OBE 97. SS Coll Cam 43 Linc Coll Ox BA 52 MA 65. Coll of Resurr Mirfield 52. **d** 54 **p** 55. C Hendon St Mary *Lon* 54-58; V S Harrow St Paul 58-60; Dir Coun for Chr Stewardship 60-65; Dir Lay Tr 65-71; Sec Coun for Miss and Unity 65-80; V St Nic Cole Abbey *Lon* 66-78; Sec Gtr Lon Chs' Coun 76-83; P-in-c St Ethelburga Bishopgate *Lon* 78-85; R St Botolph without Bishopgate 78-97; P-in-c All Hallows Lon Wall 80-97; Bp's Ecum Officer 81-97; AD The City 90-97; Preb St Paul's Cathl 91-97; P-in-c St Clem Eastcheap w St Martin Orgar 93-97; P-in-c St Sepulchre w Ch Ch Greyfriars etc 93-97; P-in-c St Kath Cree 93-97; P-in-c Smithfield St Bart Gt 94-95; rtd 97; Preacher Charterhouse 73-00; PtO *Lon* 00-13; *B & W* 01-02; *Cant* from 03. *The White House, Derringstone Hill, Barham, Canterbury CT4 6QD* T: (01227) 830356

TANNER, Canon Frank Hubert. b 38. St Aid Birkenhead 63. **d** 66 **p** 67. C Ipswich St Marg *St E* 66-69; C Mansfield SS Pet and Paul *S'well* 69-72; V Huthwaite 72-79; Chapl to the Deaf 79-92; Hon Can S'well Minster 90-92; Chapl Northn and Rutland Miss to the Deaf 92-01; rtd 01; PtO *Truro* from 03. *The Tamarisks, Trenow Lane, Perranuthnoe, Penzance TR20 9NY* T: (01736) 719426 E: franktanner@lineone.net

TANNER, Leonard John. **d** 03 **p** 04. C Taney *D & G* 03-07; I Tullow from 07; Dioc Dir Lay Min from 09; Chan V St Patr Cathl Dublin 07-11. *Tullow Rectory, Brighton Road, Carrickmines, Dublin 18, Republic of Ireland* T: (00353) (1) 289 3154 M: 86-302 1376 E: tanner1@eircom.net

TANNER, Canon Mark Simon Austin. b 70. Ch Ch Ox BA 92 MA 96 St Jo Coll Dur BA 98 Liv Univ MTh 05. Cranmer Hall Dur 95. **d** 98 **p** 99. C Upton (Overchurch) *Ches* 98-01; V Doncaster St Mary *Sheff* 01-07; V Ripon H Trin 07-11; AD Ripon 09-11; Warden Cranmer Hall Dur from 11; Vice-Prin St Jo Coll Dur from 11; Hon Can Dur Cathl from 15. *St John's College, 3 South Bailey, Durham DH1 3RJ* T: 0191-334 3500 F: 334 3501 E: m.s.a.tanner@durham.ac.uk

TANNER, Canon Mark Stuart. b 59. Nottm Univ BA 81. Sarum & Wells Th Coll. **d** 85 **p** 86. C Radcliffe-on-Trent *S'well* 85; C Radcliffe-on-Trent and Shelford etc 85-88; C Bestwood 88-89; TV 89-93; Bp's Research Officer 93-97; P-in-c S'well H Trin 93-98; V 98-13; AD S'well 01-06; Hon Can S'well Minster 07-13; V Hartley Wintney, Elvetham, Winchfield etc *Win* from 13. *The Vicarage, Church Lane, Hartley Wintney, Hook RG27 8DZ* T: (01252) 842670 E: mark.tanner@tesco.net

TANNER, Martin Philip. b 54. Univ Coll Lon BSc(Econ) 75. Ridley Hall Cam 79. **d** 82 **p** 83. C Bitterne *Win* 82-85; C Weeke 85-88; V Long Buckby w Watford *Pet* 88-96; P-in-c Desborough 96-97; R Desborough, Brampton Ash, Dingley and Braybrooke 97-08; P-in-c Drayton in Hales *Lich* from 08; RD Hodnet from 14; OCM from 09. *The Vicarage, Mount Lane, Market Drayton TF9 1AQ* T: (01630) 652527 E: mp.tanner@btinternet.com

TANSILL, Canon Derek Ernest Edward. b 36. Univ of Wales (Lamp) BA 61. Ripon Hall Ox 61. **d** 63 **p** 64. C Chelsea St Luke *Lon* 63-67; C-in-c Saltdean CD *Chich* 67-69; V Saltdean 69-73; V Billingshurst 73-82; R Bexhill St Pet 82-85; RD Battle and Bexhill 84-86; V Horsham 85-86; TR 86-06; RD 77-82 and 85-93; Can and Preb Chich Cathl from 81; Chapl Chich Cathl from 06. *5 The Chantry, Canon Lane, Chichester PO19 1PZ* T: (01243) 775596 E: derek@tansill.plus.com

TANSWELL, Stuart Keith. b 79. Reading Univ BSc 01. Ripon Coll Cuddesdon BTh 08. **d** 08 **p** 09. C St Blazey and Luxulyan and Tywardreath w Tregaminion *Truro* 08-11; V N Holmwood *Guildf* from 11. *The Vicarage, Willow Green, North Holmwood, Dorking RH5 4JB* T: (01306) 882135 E: stuart@tanswell.net or vicar@stjohns-northholmwood.info

TANZANIA, Archbishop of. *See* MOKIWA, The Most Revd Valentino

TAPHOUSE, Bryan George. b 50. STETS 95. **d** 98 **p** 99. NSM Romsey *Win* from 98. *2 Campion Drive, Romsey SO51 7RD* T: (01794) 516022

TAPLIN, John. b 35. St Alb Minl Tr Scheme 78. **d** 81 **p** 82. NSM Knebworth *St Alb* 81-88; R Lt Hadham w Albury 88-00; rtd 00; PtO *St E* from 00. *77 Hepworth Road, Stanton, Bury St Edmunds IP31 2UA* T: (01359) 250212 E: johntaplin@supanet.com

TAPLIN, Kim. b 58. Lon Bible Coll BA 79 Homerton Coll Cam PGCE 81 Regent's Park Coll Ox MTh 03. S Dios Minl Tr Scheme 94 Regent's Park Coll Ox MTh 03. **d** 94 **p** 95. C Sholing *Win* 94-97; P-in-c Rendcomb *Glouc* 97-00; Chapl Rendcomb Coll Cirencester 97-00; Chapl Clifton Coll Bris 01-13; V Clifton All SS w St Jo *Bris* 14-15; Chapl Malvern St Jas Girls' Sch from 15. *20 Manby Road, Malvern WR14 3BB* E: kimtaplin@tesco.net

TAPLIN, Stewart Tennent Eaton. b 46. Melbourne Univ BEd 92 MEd 97. ACT ThL 69. **d** 72 **p** 73. C Reservoir Australia 72-74; C Stocking Farm *Leic* 74-76; LtO *Carl* 76-77; Chapl Yarra Valley Sch Australia 78-82; PtO Melbourne 83-85; Asst Chapl St Mich Gr Sch 86-91; C Mornington 91-93; Chapl Tintern Girls' Gr Sch from 94. *2 Boston Street, Ashwood Vic 3147, Australia* T: (0061) (3) 9888 3328 *or* 9845 7777 F: 9845 7710 M: 40-208 0366 E: staplin@tintern.vic.edu.au

TAPPER, Canon John A'Court. b 42. FCA 64. Sarum & Wells Th Coll 89. **d** 91 **p** 92. C Ashford *Cant* 91-94; P-in-c Folkestone H Trin w Ch Ch 94-96; V 96-06; P-in-c Sandgate St Paul w Folkestone St Geo 01-06; V Folkestone Trin 06-07; AD Elham 00-05; Hon Can Cant Cathl 06-07; rtd 07; PtO *Cant* 07-08 and from 12; Retirement Officer (Maidstone Adnry) 07-08; Hon C Cranbrook 08-12. *Mill Cottage, Mill Lane, Sissinghurst, Cranbrook TN17 2HX* T: (01580) 713836 E: johnliztapper@tesco.net

TAPPIN, Andrew Peter. b 65. **d** 13 **p** 14. NSM New Clee *Linc* from 13. *210 Legsby Avenue, Grimsby DN32 0LB*

TARGETT, Kenneth. b 28. Qu Coll Birm 54. **d** 57 **p** 58. C Mansfield Woodhouse *S'well* 57-59; C Skipton Ch Ch *Bradf* 59-62; V Bradf St Jo 62-65; PtO 65-82; Australia 82-87; V Old Leake w Wrangle *Linc* 87-94; rtd 94; PtO *Linc* from 00. *The Sloop, Sea Lane, Old Leake, Boston PE22 9JA* T: (01205) 871991 E: ken@thesloop.fsnet.co.uk

TARIQ, Mark. b 81. Wycliffe Hall Ox BTh 12. **d** 12 **p** 13. C Liss *Portsm* from 12. *13 Kelsey Close, Liss GU33 7HR* M: 07554-001153 E: mark.tariq@me.com

TARLETON, Canon Peter. b 46. TCD BA 72 MA 80 HDipEd 77. TCD Div Sch Div Test 73. **d** 73 **p** 74. C Cork St Luke w St Ann *C, C & R* 73-75; C Dublin Drumcondra *D & G* 75-77; I Limerick City *L & K* 77-82; I Drumgoon w Dernakesh, Ashfield etc *K, E & A* 82-85; Chapl HM YOI Hindley 85-89; Chapl HM Pris Lindholme 89-99; Hon Can Sheff Cathl 98-99; Chapl HM Pris Leeds 99-06; Chapl Lancs Teaching Hosps NHS Trust 08-11; Co-ord Chapl Southport and Ormskirk NHS Trust 11; I Killeshin w Cloydagh and Killabban *C & O* from 11; Can Ossory Cathl from 15. *The Rectory, Maidenhead, Ballickmoyler, Co Carlow, Republic of Ireland* T: (00353) (59) 862 5321 E: peter.tarleton@hotmail.co.uk

TARLING, Matthew Paul. b 79. Nottm Univ MEng 03. Oak Hill Th Coll BA 09. **d** 09 **p** 10. C Blaydon and Swalwell *Dur* 09-13; V Spennymoor and Whitworth from 13. *30 Jubilee Close, Spennymoor DL16 6GA* T: (01388) 327603 M: 07714-212374 E: revmatttarling@gmail.com

TARLING, Preb Paul. b 53. Oak Hill Th Coll BA. **d** 85 **p** 86. C Old Hill H Trin *Worc* 85-89; V Walford w Bishopswood *Heref* 89-90; P-in-c Goodrich w Welsh Bicknor and Marstow 89-90; R Walford and St John w Bishopswood, Goodrich etc 90-96; RD Ross and Archenfield 95-96; P-in-c Kington w Huntington, Old Radnor, Kinnerton etc 96-00; R 00-08; RD Kington and Weobley 02-07; Preb Heref Cathl 07-08; rtd 08; PtO *S & B* from 11. *1 Alexandra Road, Llandrindod Wells LD1 5LT* T: (01597) 822615 E: revpt@yahoo.com

TÄRNEBERG, Helene. *See* STEED, Helene

TARPER, Miss Ann Jennifer. b 47. SRN 71 Nottm Univ BCombStuds 82. Linc Th Coll 79. **dss** 83 **d** 87 **p** 96. Par Dn Witham *Chelmsf* 87-90; Min and Educn Adv to Newmarch Gp Min *Heref* 90-93; PtO 93-95; Dep Chapl HM Pris Dur 95-97; Chapl HM Pris Foston Hall 97-00; PtO *York* 97-02; C W End *Win* 02-05; V Slade Green *Roch* from 05. *St Augustine's Vicarage, Slade Green Road, Erith DA8 2HX* T: (01322) 332669 *or* 346258

TARR, James Robert. b 39. Bps' Coll Cheshunt 64. **d** 67 **p** 68. C Wortley-de-Leeds *Ripon* 67-69; C Hunslet St Mary and Stourton St Andr 70-73; V Moorends *Sheff* 73-77; V Cross Stone *Wakef* 77-83; V Chilworth w N Baddesley *Win* 83-90; V Andover St Mich 90-93; V W Andover 93-00; Chapl Mojácar *Eur* 00-02; rtd 02. *Les Couardes, 16350 Le Vieux-Cerier, France* T: (0033) 5 45 30 00 39

TARRAN, Mrs Susan Ann. b 63. CPFA 92. ERMC 08. **d** 11 **p** 12. NSM Bishop's Stortford *St Alb* 11-12; NSM Hockerill from 12. *47 Church Manor, Bishop's Stortford CM23 5AF* M: 07970-952228 E: su.tarran@ntlworld.com

TARRANT, Canon Ian Denis. b 57. G&C Coll Cam BA MA. St Jo Coll Nottm 81. **d** 84 **p** 85. C Ealing St Mary *Lon* 84-87; CMS Democratic Republic of Congo 88-98; Can Boga from 97; Sen Angl Chapl Nottm Univ *S'well* 98-09; R Woodford St Mary w St Phil and St Jas *Chelmsf* from 09. *The Rectory, 8 Chelmsford Road, London E18 2PL* T: (020) 8504 7981 E: rector@stmaryswoodford.org.uk

TARRANT, John Michael. b 38. St Jo Coll Cam BA 59 MA 63 Ball Coll Ox BA 62 MA 76. Ripon Hall Ox 60. **d** 62 **p** 63. C Chelsea All SS *Lon* 62-65; Chapl and Lect St Pet Coll Saltley 66-70; Belize 70-74; V Forest Row *Chich* 75-87; PtO *Heref* 93-99; NSM Ross 99-00; P-in-c Guilsborough w Hollowell and Cold Ashby *Pet* 00-08; Jt P-in-c Cottesbrooke w Gt Creaton and Thornby

00-08; P-in-c W Haddon w Winwick and Ravensthorpe 03-08; P-in-c Spratton 07-08; rtd 08. *16 Windsor Road, Salisbury SP2 7DX* T: (01722) 340058
E: thetarrants16w@btinternet.com

TARREN, Eileen. b 46. Cranmer Hall Dur. **d** 02 **p** 03. NSM Shadforth and Sherburn *Dur* 02-13; Chapl Sherburn Hosp Dur from 13. *Shincliffe House, Sherburn Hospital, Durham DH1 2SE*

TARRIS, Canon Geoffrey John. b 27. Em Coll Cam BA 50 MA 55. Westcott Ho Cam 51. **d** 53 **p** 54. C Abbots Langley *St Alb* 53-55; Prec St E Cathl 55-59; V Bungay H Trin w St Mary 59-72; RD S Elmham 65-72; V Ipswich St Mary le Tower 72-78; V Ipswich St Mary le Tower w St Lawr and St Steph 78-82; Hon Can St E Cathl 74-82; Can Res St E Cathl 82-93; Dioc Dir of Lay Min 82-87; Warden of Readers 82-87; Dioc Dir of Ords 87-93; rtd 93; PtO *Nor* 93-12; *St E* from 93; Hon PV Nor Cathl 94-12. *53 The Close, Norwich NR1 4EG* T: (01603) 622136

TARRIS, Philip Geoffrey. b 54. Univ of Wales (Swansea) BSc 76 Lon Univ MSc 78. ERMC. **d** 10 **p** 11. NSM Gt Dunmow and Barnston *Chelmsf* 10-14; P-in-c The Sampfords and Radwinter w Hempstead from 14. *1 Hydes Gate Cottages, Thaxted, Dunmow CM6 3QB* T: (01799) 586570
E: ptarris@btinternet.com

TARRY, Canon Gordon Malcolm. b 54. Leeds Univ BSc 75 Lon Bible Coll BA 83. Ridley Hall Cam. **d** 85 **p** 86. C Gt Ilford St Andr *Chelmsf* 85-89; C Rainham 89-92; C Rainham w Wennington 92-93; V Gt Ilford St Jo 93-06; RD Redbridge 01-06; TR Barking St Marg w St Patr 06-11; V Leigh-on-Sea St Aid from 11; Hon Can Chelmsf Cathl from 05. *St Aidan's Vicarage, 78 Moor Park Gardens, Leigh-on-Sea SS9 4PY*
T: (01702) 512531 E: gordontarry@yahoo.co.uk

TASH, Elizabeth. See ROOKWOOD (*née* TASH), Elizabeth

TASH, Stephen Ronald. b 56. Warw Univ BEd 79. WMMTC 88. **d** 91 **p** 92. C Studley *Cov* 91-95; P-in-c Salford Priors 95-09; Dioc Youth Officer 95-00; P-in-c Temple Grafton w Binton 00-09; P-in-c Exhall w Wixford 03-09; V Fulford *York* 09-11; rtd 14. *16 Eclipse Road, Alcester B49 5EH*
E: stevetash@aol.com

TASKER, Harry Beverley. b 41. BA 76. Wycliffe Hall Ox 64. **d** 67 **p** 68. C Withington St Paul Man 66-71; C Bingley All SS *Bradf* 71-72; Chapl RAF 72-76; R Publow w Pensford, Compton Dando and Chelwood *B & W* 76-84; V Long Ashton 84-04; RD Portishead 86-91; rtd 04. *The Malthouse, Manor Court, Manor Lane, Ettington, Stratford-upon-Avon CV37 7TW*
T: (01789) 748290

TASSELL, Mrs Stella Venetia. b 39. RGN 60 RNT 63 RMN 66 RHV 72. **d** 01 **p** 02. OLM Woodham *Guildf* 01-09; PtO *Leeds* from 10. *72 Sandy Lane, Woking GU22 8BH* T: (01483) 762944
M: 07790-521567 E: stella.tassell@btinternet.com

TATE, David. b 44. Open Univ BA 78 CIPFA 70. **d** 02 **p** 03. OLM N w S Wootton *Nor* 02-14; PtO from 14. *36 The Birches, South Wootton, King's Lynn PE30 3JG* T: (01553) 672474
E: revdavidtate@talktalk.net

TATE, Denis Steven. b 53. Lanc Univ MA 76. LCTP 09. **d** 11 **p** 12. NSM Ellel w Shireshead *Blackb* from 11. *13 Meadowside, Lancaster LA1 3AQ* E: tated@ripley.lancs.sch.uk

TATE, Mrs Harriet Jane. b 62. Hull Univ BA 84. **d** 02 **p** 03. OLM Heatons *Man* 02-10; Lic Preacher from 10. *70 Winchester Drive, Stockport SK4 2NU* T: 0161-431 7051
E: harriettate@supanet.com

TATE, James. b 56. Oak Hill Th Coll 93. **d** 95 **p** 96. C Hammersmith St Simon *Lon* 95-98; C N Hammersmith St Kath 98-99; P-in-c from 99. *St Katherine's Vicarage, Primula Street, London W12 0RF* T: (020) 8746 2213 or 8743 3951
E: jim@stkats.wanadoo.com

TATE, John Robert. b 38. Dur Univ BA 61 MA 71. Cranmer Hall Dur. **d** 70 **p** 71. C Bare *Blackb* 70-73; V Over Darwen St Jas 73-81; V Caton w Littledale 81-98; rtd 98; PtO *Blackb* from 98. *19 Clifton Drive, Morecambe LA4 6SR*
T: (01524) 832844

TATE, Pauline Marilyn. b 42. Westcott Ho Cam 05. **d** 07 **p** 08. NSM Gt w Lt Addington and Woodford *Pet* 07-12; NSM Irthlingborough 11-12; NSM Irthlingborough, Gt Addington, Lt Addington etc from 13. *2 Manor Close, Great Addington, Kettering NN14 4BU* T: (01536) 330740 M: 07803-455700
E: revd.pauline@nenecrossings.org.uk

TATE, Robert John Ward. b 24. St Jo Coll Morpeth ThL 48. **d** 49 **p** 50. Australia from 49; Chapl RN 53-79; QHC 76-79; rtd 79. *58 Skye Point Road, Carey Bay NSW 2283, Australia* T: (0061) (2) 4959 2921

TATE, Toby James. b 74. Univ of Wales (Abth) BSc 96 Sheff Univ MEd 00 Warwick Univ PGCE 97. Ripon Coll Cuddesdon 11. **d** 13 **p** 14. C Triangle, St Matt and All SS *St E* from 13. *19 Dales View Road, Ipswich IP1 4HJ* T: (01473) 809429
E: tobyjtate@gmail.com

TATHAM, Andrew Francis. b 49. Grey Coll Dur BA 71 K Coll Lon PhD 84 AKC 88 FBCartS 96. S'wark Ord Course 89. **d** 92

p 93. NSM Headley w Box Hill *Guildf* 92-02; TV Ilminster and Distr *B & W* 02-10; V Isle Valley 10-14; RD Crewkerne and Ilminster 07-12; RD Ilminster 12-14; rtd 14; Hon C Quantock Coast *B & W* from 14. *61 West Street, Watchet TA23 0BH*
T: (01984) 633331 E: aftatham@btinternet.com

TATTERSALL, John Hartley. b 52. Ch Coll Cam BA 73 MA 76 FCA 89. SEITE 04. **d** 07 **p** 08. NSM Wykeham *Ox* from 07. *Abingdon House, Park Lane, Swalcliffe, Banbury OX15 5EU*
T: (01295) 780283 M: 07711-733978 E: jhtatters@aol.com

TATTON-BROWN, Canon Simon Charles. b 48. Qu Coll Cam BA 70 MA 78 Man Univ CQSW 72. Coll of Resurr Mirfield 78. **d** 79 **p** 80. C Ashton St Mich *Man* 79-82; P-in-c Prestwich St Gabr 82-87; V 87-88; Bp's Dom Chapl 82-88; TR Westhoughton 88-96; TR Westhoughton and Wingates 97-00; V Chippenham St Andr w Tytherton Lucas Bris 00-13; RD Chippenham 03-06; Hon Can Bris Cathl 11-13; rtd 14. *259 Bloomfield Road, Bath BA2 2BA* T: (01225) 835404
M: 07891-898412 E: simon@tattonbrown.myzen.co.uk

TATTUM, Ian Stuart. b 58. N Lon Poly BA 79 Fitzw Coll Cam BA 89. Westcott Ho Cam 87. **d** 90 **p** 91. C Beaconsfield *Ox* 90-94; C Bushey *St Alb* 94-96; P-in-c Pirton 96-01; P-in-c St Ippolyts 00-06; P-in-c Lt and Lt Wymondley 01-06; P-in-c Southfields St Barn *S'wark* 06-11; V from 11. *St Barnabas' Vicarage, 146A Lavenham Road, London SW18 5EP* T: (020) 8480 2290 E: iantattum@gmail.com

TATTUM, Ruth Margaret. See LAMPARD, Ruth Margaret

TATUM, Mrs Josephine Gayle. b 56. St Jo Coll Nottm BATM 12. **d** 12 **p** 13. C Nottingham St Nic *S'well* from 12. *55 St Austell Drive, Nottingham NG11 7BT* T: 0115-846 5760
M: 07504-018386 E: josephinetatum@gmail.com

TAULTY, Mrs Eileen. b 45. **d** 03. OLM Pemberton St Mark Newtown *Liv* 03-07; OLM Marsh Green w Newtown 08-14; OLM Newtown from 14. *38 Alexandra Crescent, Wigan WN5 9JP* T: (01942) 208021

TAUNTON, Archdeacon of. See REED, The Ven John Peter Cyril

TAUNTON, Suffragan Bishop of. See MAURICE, The Rt Revd Peter David

TAUSON (*née* PURVIS), Ms Sandra Anne. b 56. Univ Coll Ches BTh 01. NOC 98. **d** 01 **p** 02. C Blackpool St Jo *Blackb* 01-06; P-in-c Gt Harwood 06-08; Chapl Pennine Acute Hosps NHS Trust from 08; V Chorley St Pet *Blackb* 11-14; PtO *Man* from 15. *Trust Headquarters, North Manchester General Hospital, Delaunays Road, Manchester M8 5RB* T: 0161-624 0420
M: 07967-136992

TAVERNER, Lorraine Dawn. See COLAM, Lorraine Dawn

TAVERNOR (*née* LLOYD), Mrs Eileen. b 50. FIBMS 74. NOC 88. **d** 91 **p** 94. C Heref St Martin w St Fran 91-95; P-in-c Bucknell w Chapel Lawn, Llanfair Waterdine etc 95-01; V 01-09; rtd 09; PtO *Heref* 09-15. *Froglands, Rosemary Lane, Leintwardine, Craven Arms SY7 0LP* T: (01547) 540365

TAVERNOR, William Noel. b 16. Lich Th Coll 37. **d** 40 **p** 41. C Ledbury *Heref* 40-43; C Kidderminster St Mary *Worc* 43-46; V Bettws-y-Crwyn w Newcastle *Heref* 46-50; V Upton Bishop 50-57; V Aymestrey and Leinthall Earles 57-65; P-in-c Shobdon 58-65; V Canon Pyon w Kings Pyon and Birley 65-88; rtd 88; PtO *Heref* from 97. *Vine Cottage, Kingsland, Leominster HR6 9QS* T: (01568) 708817

TAVINOR, The Very Revd Michael Edward. b 53. Univ Coll Dur BA 75 Em Coll Cam CertEd 76 K Coll Lon MMus 77 AKC 77 ARCO 77 Univ of Wales (Lamp) MTh 10. Ripon Coll Cuddesdon BA 81 MA 86. **d** 82 **p** 83. C Ealing St Pet Mt Park *Lon* 82-85; Min Can, Prec and Sacr Ely Cathl 85-90; P-in-c Stuntney 87-90; V Tewkesbury w Walton Cardiff *Glouc* 90-99; P-in-c Twyning 98-99; V Tewkesbury w Walton Cardiff and Twyning 99-02; Hon Can Glouc Cathl 97-02; Dean Heref from 02. *The Deanery, Cathedral Close, Hereford HR1 2NG*
T: (01432) 374203 F: 374220 E: dean@herefordcathedral.org

TAWN, Andrew Richard. b 61. Trin Coll Cam BA 83 Ox Univ BA 88. Ripon Coll Cuddesdon 86. **d** 89 **p** 90. C Dovecot *Liv* 89-93; TV Dorchester *Ox* 93-98; Student Supervisor Cuddesdon Coll 93-98; R Addingham *Bradf* 98-12; Dir Clergy Development *Leeds* from 12; PtO from 13. *The Vicarage, Morton Lane, East Morton, Keighley BD20 5RS* T: (01274) 567898
E: a.tawn@btinternet.com

TAYLER, Jeremy Charles. b 78. LSE BSc 00 Birkbeck Coll Lon MA 06. Westcott Ho Cam 13. **d** 15. C St John's Wood *Lon* from 15. *3 Cochrane Street, London NW8 7PA*
E: jeremyctayler@gmail.com *or* curate.stjohnswood@london.anglican.org

TAYLER, Raymond James. b 38. K Alfred's Coll Win TCert 74. SWMTC 98. **d** 01 **p** 02. NSM Málaga *Eur* 01-07. *Casa Palomero, Oficina de Correos, 29714 Salares (Málaga), Spain* T: (0034) 952 030 461 E: rjtayler@yahoo.co.uk

TAYLER, Mrs Wendy Christine. b 76. **d** 13 **p** 14. C Neath *Llan* from 13. *Little Haven, Lewis Road, Neath SA11 1DJ*
T: (01639) 760060 E: wcsanderson@hotmail.co.uk

TAYLEUR, Mrs Gillian Sarah. b 61. Bedf Coll Lon BSc 82. OLM course 05. **d** 08 **p** 09. NSM Herne Hill *S'wark* from 08. *27 Finsen Road, London SE5 9AX* T: (020) 7737 1991
E: gill@hernehillparish.org

TAYLOR, Alan Clive. b 48. Southn Univ BTh 79 DipEd 73. Sarum Th Coll 69. **d** 74 **p** 75. C Watford St Pet *St Alb* 74-78; C Broxbourne w Wormley 78-83; Chapl to the Deaf 83-91; V Shefford 83-91; R Portishead *B & W* 91-02; TR 02-08; rtd 08. *Larkhill, The Green, Dauntsey, Chippenham SN15 4HY*
T: (01666) 511169 E: padreact@btinternet.com

TAYLOR, Alan Gerald. b 33. Roch Th Coll 61 St Aid Birkenhead 61. **d** 63 **p** 64. C W Bridgford *S'well* 63-66; C E w W Barkwith *Linc* 66-69; V E Stockwith 69-76; V Morton 69-76; Countryside Officer 69-88; R Ulceby w Fordington 76-88; R Willoughby w Sloothby w Claxby 76-88; R Woolpit w Drinkstone *St E* 88-98; Rural Min Adv from 88; rtd 98; PtO *St E* from 01. *5 Finch Close, Stowmarket IP14 5BQ*
T: (01449) 614078

TAYLOR, Canon Alan Leonard. b 43. Chich Th Coll 67. **d** 69 **p** 70. C Walton St Mary *Liv* 69-73; C Toxteth St Marg 73-75; V Stanley 75-83; V Leeds St Aid *Ripon* 84-11; V Leeds Richmond Hill 06-11; TR Leeds All So and St Aid 11-12; Hon Can Ripon Cathl 97-12; AD Allerton 08-12; rtd 13. *Marsh Bank Cottage, Frampton Roads, Frampton, Boston PE20 1AY*
T: (01205) 722693

TAYLOR, Mrs Alison Isabella. b 76. **d** 10 **p** 11. C Sparkhill St Jo *Birm* 10-12; V Alperton *Lon* from 12. *The Vicarage, 34 Stanley Avenue, Wembley HA0 4JB* T: (020) 8902 1729
E: tayloriali@googlemail.com

TAYLOR, Andrew David. b 58. Regent's Park Coll Ox BA 81 MA 86 Toronto Univ MDiv 92 K Coll Lon MTh 95 FRSA 08. Westcott Ho Cam 85. **d** 87 **p** 89. C Leckhampton St Phil and Jas w Cheltenham St Jas *Glouc* 87-91; P-in-c Swindon w Uckington and Elmstone Hardwicke 92-93; C Highgate St Mich *Lon* 94-97; Chapl R Holloway and Bedf New Coll *Guildf* 97-03; Public Preacher 04; PtO 05-13; C Englefield Green 13; Research Fell Ox Cen for Christianity and Culture from 12; Chapl Downe Ho Sch Berks from 15. *Hammer House, 30 High Street, Sunningdale, Ascot SL5 0NG* T: (01344) 870319
E: andrew.taylor@regents.ox.ac.uk

TAYLOR, Andrew John. b 58. Aston Univ MBA 94 Azusa Pacific Univ (USA) MA 02 K Coll Lon DMin 10 Cam Univ BTh 12. Ridley Hall Cam 10. **d** 12 **p** 13. C Cambridge St Barn *Ely* from 12. *17 Rustat Avenue, Cambridge CB1 3PF* T: (01223) 519526 *or* 241171 M: 07403-671440 E: andrew.taylor@stbs.org.uk *or* andrew.connie@gmail.com

TAYLOR, Ann. *See* TAYLOR, Margaret Ann

TAYLOR, Ms Anne Elizabeth. b 68. Ulster Univ BSc 91 MA 99. CITC BTh 94. **d** 94 **p** 95. C Dublin Rathfarnham *D & G* 94-14; Chapl Adelaide and Meath Hosp Dublin 01-03; Abp's Dom Chapl *D & G* 03-14; Children's Min Officer Sunday Sch Soc of Ireland 05-14; V Formby St Pet *Liv* from 14. *St Peter's Vicarage, Cricket Path, Formby, Liverpool L37 7DP* T: (01704) 873369
E: revannetaylor@gmail.com

TAYLOR, Arthur Alfred. b 32. Univ Coll Ox MA 56. Ox NSM Course 80. **d** 83 **p** 84. NSM Monks Risborough *Ox* 83-96; NSM Aylesbury Deanery from 96. *9 Place Farm Way, Monks Risborough, Princes Risborough HP27 9JJ* T: (01844) 347197

TAYLOR, Miss Averil Mary. b 36. Sarum Dioc Tr Coll TCert 56 Westmr Coll Ox TCert (Mus) 66. WEMTC 99. **d** 00 **p** 01. OLM Longden and Annscroft w Pulverbatch *Heref* 00-08. *Sheaves, Lyth Bank, Lyth Hill, Shrewsbury SY3 0BE* T/F: (01743) 872071

TAYLOR, Avril Fiona. b 58. NEOC 02. **d** 05 **p** 06. NSM Byker St Silas *Newc* from 05. *20 Percy Gardens, Gateshead NE11 9RY*
T: 0191-420 7983 E: avriltaylor@blueyonder.co.uk

TAYLOR, Brian. b 42. St Deiniol's Hawarden 78. **d** 80 **p** 81. C Mold *St As* 80-84; V Bagillt 84-08; rtd 08; PtO *St As* from 09. *13 Bryn Awel, Pentre Halkyn, Holywell CH8 8JB*
T: (01352) 780744 M: 07803-305956
E: brian@prayers.freeserve.co.uk

TAYLOR, Brian. b 61. St Mich Coll Llan 91. **d** 94 **p** 95. C Aberdare *Llan* 94-97; V Cwmparc 97-07; V Pen Rhondda Fawr 07-13; PtO from 14. *12 Plas Cleddau, Barry CF62 7FG*
E: frbtaylor@talktalk.net

TAYLOR, Brian. b 38. Bris Univ BA 60 Liv Univ BA 70 Southn Univ MA 90. Ridley Hall Cam 60. **d** 66 **p** 66. Chapl Victoria Coll Ondo Nigeria 66-72; PtO *Derby* 74-78; Chapl Newbury Coll 76-94; P-in-c Shaw cum Donnington *Ox* 89-90; R 90-08; rtd 08; PtO *Ox* from 08; *Derby* from 15. *Fairview House Barn, The Moor, Tideswell, Buxton SK17 8LR* M: 07925-126761
E: brian_harker_taylor@yahoo.co.uk

TAYLOR, Brian John Chatterton. b 30. Trin Hall Cam BA 53 Kent Univ MA 57 Melbourne Univ BEd 66 Lon Univ MA 78. Westcott Ho Cam 53. **d** 55 **p** 56. C Leigh St Jo *Man* 55-57; C Ashton Ch Ch 57-58; Australia from 58; Miss to Seamen 58-60; Vic State High Schs 60-71; Sen Lect Toorak Teachers' Coll 72-80; Prin Lect Inst of Cath Educn 80-88; Co-ord RE

Tintern Angl Girls' Gr Sch 89-93; Supernumerary Asst Redhill St Geo from 90. *21 One Chain Road, Merricks North VIC 3926, Australia* T/F: (0061) (3) 5989 7564 M: 408-250630
E: sumptonv@surf.net

TAYLOR, Mrs Bryony Ruthellen. b 77. Leeds Univ BA 99 MA 05 St Jo Coll Dur BA 14. Cranmer Hall Dur 12. **d** 14 **p** 15. C Houghton le Spring *Dur* from 14. *St Andrew's Vicarage, Chilton Moor, Houghton le Spring DH4 6LU* M: 07960-735352
E: bryony.taylor@gmail.com

TAYLOR, Charles Derek. b 36. Trin Hall Cam BA 59 MA 62. Ripon Hall Ox 59. **d** 61 **p** 62. C Nottingham All SS *S'well* 61-64; C Binley *Cov* 64-67; C Stoke 67-70; R Purley *Ox* 70-74; V Milton *B & W* 74-93; RD Locking 86-87 and 90-93; V Wells St Cuth w Wookey Hole 93-98; rtd 98; PtO *Roch* from 00. *5 Banner Farm Road, Tunbridge Wells TN2 5EA*
T: (01892) 526825 E: c.derektaylor5@yahoo.co.uk

TAYLOR, The Very Revd Charles William. b 53. Selw Coll Cam BA 74 MA 78. Cuddesdon Coll 74. **d** 76 **p** 77. C Wolverhampton *Lich* 76-79; Chapl Westmr Abbey 79-84; V Stanmore *Win* 84-90; R N Stoneham 90-95; Can Res and Prec Lich Cathl 95-07; Dean Pet from 07. *The Deanery, Minster Precincts, Peterborough PE1 1XS* T: (01733) 562780 F: 897874
E: deanpetoffice@aol.com

TAYLOR, Christopher Drewett. b 58. Qu Coll Birm 06. **d** 09 **p** 10. C Shepshed and Oaks in Charnwood *Leic* 09-13; Chapl Loughb Univ from 13. *Brockington Building, Loughborough University, Loughborough LE11 3TU* T: (01509) 223742
M: 07946-763257 E: christaylor36beacon@msn.com or c.taylor2@lboro.ac.uk

TAYLOR, Christopher Vincent. b 47. Cranmer Hall Dur 94. **d** 96 **p** 97. C Kendal St Geo *Carl* 96-99; TV Wheatley *Ox* 99-03; TV Leeds City *Ripon* 03-06; rtd 06; Hon C Beacon *Carl* from 08. *78 Windermere Road, Kendal LA9 5EZ* T: (01539) 727424
E: christaylor156@btinternet.com

TAYLOR, Colin John. b 66. Witwatersrand Univ BCom 87 BTh 94. Wycliffe Hall Ox MTh 97. **d** 97 **p** 98. C Denton Holme *Carl* 97-01; Bp's Dom Chapl 01-06; Dir CME 1-4 00-06; V Felsted and Lt Dunmow *Chelmsf* from 06. *The Vicarage, Bury Chase, Felsted, Dunmow CM6 3DQ* T: (01371) 820242
E: ctaylor585@googlemail.com

TAYLOR, Canon David. b 53. St Jo Coll Dur BA 74 PGCE 75 Liv Univ MTh 04. Sarum & Wells Th Coll 91. **d** 93 **p** 94. C Cheadle Hulme All SS *Ches* 93-97; V Macclesfield St Jo 97-05; RD Macclesfield 03-05; TR Congleton from 05; RD 08-13; Hon Can Ches Cathl from 09. *2 Hartley Gardens, Congleton CW12 3WA* T: (01260) 273182
E: ctprector@hotmail.co.uk

TAYLOR, David Christopher Morgan. b 56. Leeds Univ BSc 77 Univ Coll Lon PhD 80 Univ Coll Ches MEd 96 SOSc MSB. NOC 91. **d** 94 **p** 95. Tutor Liv Univ from 86; NSM Waterloo Ch Ch and St Mary 94-99; P-in-c Altcar 98-00; NSM Altcar and Hightown 03-14; NSM Formby H Trin and Altcar from 14. *20 Liverpool Road, Formby, Liverpool L37 4BW*
T: (01704) 873304 F: 0151-794 5337 E: dcmt@liverpool.ac.uk *or* taylordcm@aol.com

TAYLOR, Derek. *See* TAYLOR, Charles Derek

TAYLOR, The Very Revd Derek John. b 31. Univ of Wales (Lamp) BA 52 Fitzw Ho Cam BA 54 MA 58 Ex Univ CertEd 70. St Mich Coll Llan 54. **d** 55 **p** 56. C Newport St Paul *Mon* 55-59; CF (TA) 57-59 and 62-64; CF 59-62; V Bettws *Mon* 62-64; V Exminster *Ex* 64-70; Hd of RE Heathcote Sch Tiverton 70-71; W Germany 71-75; Chapl R Russell Sch Croydon 75-79; Chapl St Andr C of E High Sch Croydon 79-84; P-in-c Croydon St Andr *Cant* 79-81; R 81-84; Chapl Bromsgrove Sch 84-89; Provost St Chris Cathl Bahrain 90-97; Hon Chapl Miss to Seamen 90-97; NSM Droitwich Spa *Worc* 97-99; P-in-c Bearsden w Milngavie *Glas* 00-03; PtO *Worc* 04-11. *22 Coxwold View, Wetherby LS22 7PU* M: 07904-205669
E: dervaltaylor@talktalk.net

TAYLOR, Elizabeth. *See* TAYLOR, Mary Elizabeth

TAYLOR, Garry Kenneth. b 53. Edin Univ BMus 75 Southn Univ BTh 81 Ch Ch Coll Cant PGCE 95. Sarum & Wells Th Coll 76. **d** 79 **p** 80. C Southsea H Spirit *Portsm* 79-82; C Croydon St Jo *Cant* 82-84; C *S'wark* 85-86; V Choral *S'well* Minster 86-90; V Portsea St Alb *Portsm* 90-94; NSM Hamble le Rice *Win* 96-97; P-in-c Southampton St Jude 97-04; V Highcliffe w Hinton Admiral 04-09; V Highcliffe 09-15. *The Vicarage, 33 Nea Road, Christchurch BH23 4NB* T: (01425) 272761
E: garrykt@aol.com

TAYLOR, George James Trueman. b 36. Ripon Hall Ox 66. **d** 69 **p** 70. C Wavertree H Trin *Liv* 69-73; V Newton-le-Willows 73-79; V Stoneycroft All SS 79-83; V Haigh 83-04; Jt P-in-c Aspull and New Springs 02-03; rtd 04. *228 Wigan Road, Aspull, Wigan WN2 1DU* T: (01942) 830430

TAYLOR, Canon Gordon. b 46. AKC 68. St Aug Coll Cant 69. **d** 70 **p** 71. C Rotherham *Sheff* 70-74; P-in-c Brightside St Thos 74-79; P-in-c Brightside St Marg 77-79; V Brightside St Thos

and St Marg 79-82; R Kirk Sandall and Edenthorpe 82-91; V Beighton 91-96; V Goole 96-03; AD Snaith and Hatfield 98-03; V Tickhill w Stainton 03-11; Hon Can Sheff Cathl 93-11; rtd 11; PtO *Sheff* from 11. *96 Whitton Close, Doncaster DN4 7RD* T: (01302) 533249
E: gordon.taylor809@btinternet.com

TAYLOR, Graham Smith. b 70. TISEC 98. **d** 01 **p** 02. C Ellon, Cruden Bay and Peterhead *Ab* 01-04; P-in-c 04-06; R Aberdeen St Mary 06-14; Dioc Dir Ords 06-14; Can St Andr Cathl 08-14; R Aberdeen St Clem 09-12; R Perth St Jo *St And* from 14. *St John's Rectory, 23 Comely Bank, Perth PH2 7HU* M: 07773-482174 T: (01738) 245922
E: revgraham@tiscali.co.uk

TAYLOR, Hilary Elizabeth. *See* EVANS, Hilary Elizabeth

TAYLOR, Hugh Nigel James. b 43. MCMI FInstD. NTMTC 04. **d** 06 **p** 07. NSM Loughton St Mary *Chelmsf* 06-14; PtO from 14. *4 Twentyman Close, Woodford Green IG8 0EW* T/F: (020) 8504 8901 M: 07770-365255
E: hughnj@btinternet.com *or* hugh@stmarysloughton.com

✠**TAYLOR, The Rt Revd Humphrey Vincent.** b 38. Pemb Coll Cam BA 61 MA 66 Lon Univ MA 70. Coll of Resurr Mirfield 61. **d** 63 **p** 64 **c** 91. C N Hammersmith St Kath *Lon* 63-64; C Notting Hill St Mark 64-66; USPG Malawi 67-71; Chapl Bp Grosseteste Coll Linc 72-74; Sec Chapls in HE Gen Syn Bd of Educn 75-80; Gen Sec USPG 80-91; Sec Miss Progr 80-84; Hon Can Bris Cathl 86-91; LtO *S'wark* 89-91; Suff Bp Selby *York* 91-03; rtd 03; Hon Asst Bp Glouc 03-13; Hon Asst Bp Worc from 03. *10 High Street, Honeybourne, Evesham WR11 7PQ* T: (01386) 834846 E: humanne.taylor@virgin.net

TAYLOR, Iain William James. b 41. **d** 03 **p** 04. OLM Cant St Pet w St Alphege and St Marg etc 03-11; rtd 11; PtO *Cant* from 12. *30 Deans Mill Court, The Causeway, Canterbury CT1 2BF* T: (01227) 457711

TAYLOR, Ian. b 53. Saltley Tr Coll Birm CertEd 75. **d** 95 **p** 96. OLM Heywood *Man* 95-10; OLM Sudden and Heywood All So from 10. *818A Edenfield Road, Rochdale OL12 7RB* T: (01706) 355738

TAYLOR, Mrs Jacqueline Margaret. b 56. Trin Coll Bris 02. **d** 04 **p** 05. C Bath St Luke *B & W* 04-08; Chapl Univ Hosps Bris NHS Foundn Trust 08-13; P-in-c Kingsbridge and Dodbrooke *Ex* from 13. *Dodbrooke Rectory, Church Street, Kingsbridge TQ7 1NW* E: jtaylor808@btinternet.com

TAYLOR, James. *See* TAYLOR, Nigel James

TAYLOR, James Charles. b 81. Fitzw Coll Cam BA 03 MA 07. Oak Hill Th Coll BA 11. **d** 12 **p** 13. C W Hampstead St Luke *Lon* from 12. *40 Ingham Road, London NW6 1DE* E: james.taylor@cantab.net

TAYLOR, Jamie Alexander Franklyn. b 73. Kent Univ BA 95. Westcott Ho Cam. **d** 98 **p** 99. C Walton-on-Thames *Guildf* 98-02; C St Peter-in-Thanet *Cant* 02-08; Chapl E Kent NHS and Soc Care Partnership Trust 03-06; Chapl Kent & Medway NHS and Soc Care Partnership Trust 06-08; V Sonning *Ox* from 08. *The Vicarage, Thames Street, Sonning, Reading RG4 6UR* T: 0118-969 3298 E: revjaft@yahoo.co.uk

TAYLOR, Jane Suzanne. b 54. Ex Univ BA 73. SEITE 96. **d** 99 **p** 00. NSM Knaphill w Brookwood *Guildf* 99-00; C Frimley Green and Mytchett 00-04; PtO *Ex* from 04. *Rocknell Manor Farm, Westleigh, Tiverton EX16 7ES* T: (01884) 829000
E: janetaylor@millhouseretreats.co.uk

TAYLOR (*née* MAYOR), Mrs Janet Hilary. b 55. St Martin's Coll Lanc BA 96 Open Univ PGCE 98. LCTP 10. **d** 11 **p** 12. NSM Chorley St Laur *Blackb* 11-15; NSM Croston, Bretherton and Mawdesley w Bispham from 15. *Woodlands, Highfield Road, Croston, Leyland PR26 9HH* T: (01772) 603155
E: janet55@hotmail.co.uk

TAYLOR, Jason Victor. b 71. Lon Bible Coll BTh 01 St Jo Coll Dur MA 03. Cranmer Hall Dur 01. **d** 03 **p** 04. C Ripley *Derby* 03-07; TV Drypool *York* 07-13; Chapl Abp Sentamu Academy Hull 09-13; P-in-c Brampton *Ely* from 13; C E Leightonstone from 14. *The Rectory, 15 Church Road, Brampton, Huntingdon PE28 4PF* T: (01480) 453341 M: 07825-408351
E: revjasontaylor@gmail.com

TAYLOR, Miss Jean. b 37. Nottm Univ TCert 58. St Andr Coll Pampisford 62. **dss** 68 **d** 00 **p** 01. CSA 62-79; E Crompton *Man* 79-97; Chadderton St Luke 97-04; OLM 00-04; OLM Chadderton St Matt w St Luke 04-05; Warden Jes Hosp Cant 05-08; PtO *Cant* from 05. *7 Chantry Court, St Radigund's Street, Canterbury CT1 2AD* T: (01227) 761652

TAYLOR, Mrs Jennifer Anne. b 53. Sussex Univ BEd 75 Surrey Univ BA 01 Win Univ MA 09. STETS 98. **d** 01 **p** 02. Chapl Salisbury Cathl Sch from 01; NSM Salisbury St Thos and St Edm *Sarum* 01-09; NSM Chalke Valley 09-13; TV from 13. *27 Viking Way, Salisbury SP2 8TA* T/F: (01722) 503081
E: geoffrey.taylor5@ntlworld.com

TAYLOR, Sister Jennifer Mary. b 41. CA Tr Coll IDC 65. **dss** 77 **d** 87 **p** 07. CA from 65; Chapl Asst HM Pris Holloway 75-79;

Ho Mistress Ch Hosp Sch Hertf 78-79; Chapl Asst Rtd Officer Chapl RAChD 80-90; Germany 90-96; rtd 96; PtO *Eur* from 96; *Nor* 06-07 and from 11; Hon C Dereham and Distr 07-11. *4 Eckling Grange, Norwich Road, Dereham NR20 3BB* T: (01362) 692547

TAYLOR, Jeremy Christopher. b 75. Birm Univ BA 97. Oak Hill Th Coll BA 07. **d** 07 **p** 08. C Chell *Lich* 07-10; P-in-c Enderby w Lubbesthorpe and Thurlaston *Leic* from 10. *The Rectory, 16A Desford Road, Leicester LE9 7TE* T: (01455) 888679 M: 07787-514058 E: juneandjerry@btinternet.com

TAYLOR, Joanna Beatrice. *See* NEARY, Joanna Beatrice

TAYLOR, John. b 58. Aston Tr Scheme 94 Ripon Coll Cuddesdon 96. **d** 98 **p** 99. C Southport Em *Liv* 98-03; V Hindley All SS 03-09; R Yanchep Australia from 09. *2 Lagoon Drive, Yanchep WA 6035, Australia* T: (0061) (8) 9561 1357 *or* T/F 9561 1421 E: revj-tay@bigpond.com

TAYLOR, John Alexander. b 54. S Dios Minl Tr Scheme 89. **d** 92 **p** 93. NSM Abbotts Ann and Upper and Goodworth Clatford *Win* 92-99; PtO 99-00; NSM Hatherden w Tangley, Weyhill and Penton Mewsey 00-02; NSM W Andover 02-09; NSM Portway and Danebury 09-13. *256 Weyhill Road, Andover SP10 3LR* T: (01264) 359160 E: john@w256.fsnet.co.uk

TAYLOR, Canon John Andrew. b 53. Linc Th Coll 86. **d** 88 **p** 89. C Stanley *Liv* 88-91; V Wigan St Jas w St Thos 91-04; AD Wigan W 99-04; Hon Can Liv Cathl 03-04; V Prescot from 04; AD Huyton from 06; Hon Can Liv Cathl from 07. *The Vicarage, Vicarage Place, Prescot L34 1LA* T: 0151-426 6719

✠**TAYLOR, The Rt Revd John Bernard.** b 29. KCVO 97. Ch Coll Cam BA 50 MA 54 Jes Coll Cam 52 Hebrew Univ Jerusalem 54. Ridley Hall Cam 55. **d** 56 **p** 57 **c** 80. C Morden *S'wark* 56-59; V Henham *Chelmsf* 59-64; V Elsenham 59-64; Sen Tutor Oak Hill Th Coll 64-65; Vice-Prin 65-72; V Woodford Wells *Chelmsf* 72-75; Dioc Dir of Ords 72-80; Adn W Ham 75-80; Bp St Alb *St Alb* 80-95; Ld High Almoner 88-97; rtd 95; Hon Asst Bp Ely from 95; Hon Asst Bp Eur from 98. *22 Conduit Head Road, Cambridge CB3 0EY* T: (01223) 313783 E: john.taylor6529@ntlworld.com

TAYLOR, Canon John Michael. b 30. St Aid Birkenhead 56. **d** 59 **p** 60. C Chorley St Jas *Blackb* 59-62; C Broughton 62-64; Chapl St Boniface Coll Warminster 64-68; V Altham w Clayton le Moors *Blackb* 68-76; RD Accrington 71-76; Can Res Blackb Cathl 76-96; Tutor CBDTI 88-96; rtd 96; PtO *Blackb* 96-11. *8 Fosbrooke House, Clifton Drive, Lytham St Annes FY8 5RQ*

✠**TAYLOR, The Rt Revd John Mitchell.** b 32. Aber Univ MA 54. Edin Th Coll 54. **d** 56 **p** 57 **c** 91. C Aberdeen St Marg *Ab* 56-58; R Glas H Cross 58-64; R Glas St Ninian 64-73; R Dumfries and Chapl Dumfries and Galloway R Infirmary 73-91; Can St Mary's Cathl 79-91; Bp Glas 91-98; rtd 98; Hon Asst Bp Glas from 99. *85 Lord Lyell Drive, Kirriemuir DD8 4LF* E: j.taylor897@btinternet.com

TAYLOR, John Porter. b 48. Ex Univ BA 71 MA 76. Cranmer Hall Dur 93. **d** 93 **p** 94. C Ossett cum Gawthorpe *Wakef* 93-96; R Crofton 96-02; Chapl Mid Yorks Hosps NHS Trust 03-06; Chapl Oakham Sch 06-13; rtd 13; PtO *Pet* 13-14; Hon C Empingham, Edith Weston, Lyndon, Manton etc from 14. *24 Main Street, Empingham, Oakham LE15 8PS* T: (01780) 460735 E: jpt100948@gmail.com

TAYLOR, John Ralph. b 48. St Jo Coll Nottm BTh 74. **d** 74 **p** 75. C Clitheroe St Jas *Blackb* 74-77; C Kidsgrove *Lich* 77-79; C Hawkwell *Chelmsf* 79-82; V Linc St Geo Swallowbeck 82-92; rtd 92. *16 Rosedale Close, Cherry Willingham, Lincoln LN3 4RE*

✠**TAYLOR, Canon John Rowland.** b 29. OBE 74. St Mich Coll Llan 57. **d** 58 **p** 59. C Caerau St Cynfelin *Llan* 58-59; C Aberdare 59-61; Chapl Miss to Seamen 61-88; Dar-es-Salaam Tanzania 61-73; Adn Dar-es-Salaam 65-73; V-Gen 67-73; Hon Can Dar-es-Salaam from 73; V Bangkok Ch Ch Thailand 73-84; Chapl Rotterdam w Schiedam *Eur* 84-88; V Warnham *Chich* 88-98; rtd 98; PtO *Chich* 98-00; P-in-c Streat w Westmeston 00-07. *11 The Cedars, St George's Park, Ditchling Road, Burgess Hill RH15 0GR* T: (01444) 232232
E: canonjohn@btinternet.com

TAYLOR, Jonathan Paul. b 74. Birm Univ BEng 97 Birm Chr Coll BA 05. Trin Coll Bris 07. **d** 11 **p** 12. C Coventry Caludon Cov 11-14; V Binley from 14. *St Bartholomew's Vicarage, 68 Brandon Road, Binley, Coventry CV3 2JF*
E: jonandsu@gmail.com

TAYLOR, Joseph Robin Christopher. b 34. St Aid Birkenhead 58. **d** 61 **p** 62. C Aldershot St Mich *Guildf* 61-64; C Fleet 64-68; R Manaton *Ex* 69-74; R N Bovey 69-74; V Dawlish 74-87; P-in-c Christow, Ashton, Trusham and Bridford 87-88; R 88-95; PtO 95-98; *St E* from 98; rtd 99. *24 Edwin Panks Road, Hadleigh, Ipswich IP7 5JL* T: (01473) 824262

TAYLOR, Julia Mary. *See* CODY, Julia Mary

TAYLOR, Kane Matthew. b 70. Open Univ BSc 04. Wycliffe Hall Ox 09. **d** 11 **p** 12. C Kettering St Andr *Pet* 11-14; P-in-c

Weldon w Deene from 14. *The Rectory, 13 School Lane, Weldon, Corby NN17 3JN* E: kane.taylor@hotmail.co.uk *or* kane.taylor@virgin.net

TAYLOR, Kelvin John. b 53. Portsm Univ CertEd 94 BA 96. Trin Coll Bris 02. **d** 04 **p** 05. C Overton w Laverstoke and Freefolk *Win* 04-08; V Kempshott from 08. *The Vicarage, 171 Kempshott Lane, Kempshott, Basingstoke RG22 5LF* T: (01256) 356400

TAYLOR, Kingsley Graham. b 55. Univ of Wales (Cardiff) BD 93. St Mich Coll Llan 90. **d** 93 **p** 94. C Llanelli *St D* 93-97; V Whitland w Cyffig and Henllan Amgoed etc from 97. *The Vicarage, North Road, Whitland SA34 0BH* T: (01994) 240494 E: ktaylor559@aol.com

TAYLOR, Lee Anthony. b 77. Univ of Wales (Lamp) BA 02 Win Univ MA 12. Ripon Coll Cuddesdon 10. **d** 12 **p** 13. C Leigh-on-Sea St Marg *Chelmsf* 12-15; C Leigh St Clem from 15. *38 Flemming Avenue, Leigh-on-Sea SS9 3AW* T: (01702) 826221 E: frleetaylor@hotmail.co.uk

TAYLOR, Luke Alastare John. b 68. Brunel Univ BA 97. Oak Hill Th Coll BA 00. **d** 00 **p** 01. C Hanworth St Rich *Lon* 00-04; C E Twickenham St Steph 04-10; C Dedworth and Clewer St Andr *Ox* 10-12; C Sunningdale 11-12; R Binfield from 12. *The Rectory, Terrace Road North, Binfield, Bracknell RG42 5JG* T: (01344) 454406 M: 07939-526361 E: lukeandgissy@talktalk.net

TAYLOR, Lynda Brigid. b 45. Man Univ BA Cam Univ PhD. ERMC. **d** 10 **p** 11. NSM Chesterton St Geo *Ely* from 10. *47 Montague Road, Cambridge CB4 1BU* T: (01223) 575172 E: lynda_and_nigel_taylor@ntlworld.com

TAYLOR, Lyndon John. b 49. St Mich Coll Llan 92. **d** 95 **p** 96. NSM Swansea St Nic *S & B* 95-99; C Llwynderw 99-01; V Waunarllwydd 01-06; V Clydach 08-14; rtd 14; PtO *Mon* from 14; *Llan* from 15. *85 Pen yr Alltwen, Alltwen, Pontardawe, Swansea SA8 3EA* T: (01792) 934999

TAYLOR, Lynne. b 51. Sheff Univ BMet 73 Salford Univ PhD 80. Man OLM Scheme 98. **d** 01 **p** 02. OLM Turton Moorland *Man* 01-11; rtd 11; PtO *Man* from 11; *Blackb* from 14. *56 Station Road, Turton, Bolton BL7 0HA* T: (01204) 852551 E: innoveras@hotmail.co.uk

TAYLOR, Margaret Ann. b 46. **d** 98 **p** 99. OLM Newcastle w Butterton *Lich* from 98. *12 Silverton Close, Bradwell, Newcastle ST5 8LU* T: (01782) 660174 E: revanntaylor@yahoo.co.uk

TAYLOR, Marian Alexandra. b 62. Newc Univ BA 85. Qu Coll Birm 89. **d** 91 **p** 96. C Earls Barton *Pet* 91-93; NSM Wellingborough St Barn 95-96; NSM Beaumont Leys *Leic* 96-97; PtO *Pet* 99-00; NSM Kingsthorpe w Northampton St Dav 00-04; TV 04-09. *Braeburn, Applewood Close, Belper DE56 1TH* E: marian.taylor62@ntlworld.com

TAYLOR, Mark Frederick. b 62. N Ireland Poly BA 84. CITC. **d** 87 **p** 88. C Ballymacarrett St Patr *D & D* 87-90; C Dundela St Mark 90-93; I Kilmore and Inch 93-02; I Whitehead and Islandmagee *Conn* from 02. *St Patrick's Rectory, 74 Cable Road, Whitehead, Carrickfergus BT38 9SJ* T/F: (028) 9337 3300

TAYLOR, Mark John. b 73. St Andr Univ MTheol 99. Coll of Resurr Mirfield 01. **d** 03 **p** 04. C N Meols *Liv* 03-07; TV Sutton from 07. *40 Eaves Lane, St Helens WA9 3UB* E: mtaylor@mirfield.org.uk

TAYLOR, Martyn Andrew Nicholas. b 66. **d** 96 **p** 97. C Stamford St Geo w St Paul *Linc* 96-03; R from 03; P-in-c Stamford Ch Ch 11-15. *St George's Rectory, 16 St George's Square, Stamford PE9 2BN* T: (01780) 757343 *or* 481800 E: rector@stgeorgeschurch.net

TAYLOR, Mrs Mary Elizabeth. b 39. **d** 01 **p** 02. OLM Parr *Liv* from 01. *16 Hignett Avenue, St Helens WA9 2PJ* T: (01744) 21086

TAYLOR, Matthew. b 62. NTMTC. **d** 11 **p** 12. C Rushden St Mary w Newton Bromswold *Pet* from 11. *36 Meadow Sweet Road, Rushden NN10 0GA* T: (01933) 311164 E: matt_t_taylor@btinternet.com

TAYLOR, Mrs Maureen. b 36. Lon Bible Coll BTh 90 MA 94. **d** 97 **p** 98. NSM Borehamwood *St Alb* 97-00; NSM Radlett 00-05; PtO from 06. *57A Loom Lane, Radlett WD7 8NX* T: (01923) 855197

TAYLOR, Michael. *See* TAYLOR, John Michael

TAYLOR, Michael Alan. b 47. Bris Univ CertEd 70 Lon Univ BD 85. Trin Coll Bris 72. **d** 76 **p** 77. C Chilwell *S'well* 76-79; Chapl RAF 79-87; New Zealand from 87. *31 Kiteroa Place, Cashmere, Christchurch 8022, New Zealand* T: (0064) (3) 352 331 8440 E: strategic@chch.planet.org.nz

TAYLOR, Michael Allan. b 50. Nottm Univ BTh 80. St Jo Coll Nottm 76. **d** 80 **p** 81. C Bowling St Jo *Bradf* 80-82; C Otley 82-85; P-in-c Low Moor St Mark 85-92; P-in-c Bris St Andr w St Bart 92-96. *19 Alexander Place, Abercanaid, Merthyr Tydfil CF48 1SJ* T: (01443) 691481 E: micktaylor61@gmail.com

TAYLOR, Michael Andrew James. b 40. Univ Coll Ches BTh 96. **d** 99 **p** 00. NSM Halliwell *Man* 99-11; TV 03-11; rtd 11; PtO *Man* from 11. *123 Smithills Dean Road, Bolton BL1 6JZ* T: (01204) 491503

TAYLOR, Michael Barry. b 38. Bps' Coll Cheshunt 63. **d** 65 **p** 66. C Leeds St Cypr Harehills *Ripon* 65-68; C Stanningley St Thos 68-70; V Hunslet Moor St Pet and St Cuth 70-78; V Starbeck 78-00; rtd 00; PtO *Leic* from 00. *11 Aulton Crescent, Hinckley LE10 0XA* T: (01455) 442218

TAYLOR, Michael Frank Chatterton. b 30. St Aid Birkenhead 59. **d** 61 **p** 62. C Knighton St Jo *Leic* 61-65; V Briningham *Nor* 65-86; R Melton Constable w Swanton Novers 65-86; P-in-c Thornage w Brinton w Hunworth and Stody 85-86; R Lyng w Sparham 86-90; R Elsing w Bylaugh 86-90; R Lyng, Sparham, Elsing and Bylaugh 90-95; RD Sparham 92-95; rtd 95; PtO *Portsm* from 95. *The Rhond, 33 Station Road, St Helens, Ryde PO33 1YF* T/F: (01983) 873531 M: 07989-274848 E: mfct@tesco.net

TAYLOR, Michael John. b 50. **d** 07 **p** 08. OLM Went Valley *Wakef* 07-11; NSM Pontefract St Giles *Leeds* from 11. *19 Windsor Rise, Pontefract WF8 4PZ* T: (01977) 702824 M: 07968-932135 E: michael@darringtonchurch.com

TAYLOR, Canon Michael Joseph. b 49. Gregorian Univ Rome STB 72 PhL 74 Birm Univ MA 81 Nottm Univ PhD 05. English Coll Rome 67. **d** 72 **p** 73. In RC Ch 72-83; Hon C Newport Pagnell w Lathbury *Ox* 83-85; Hon C Newport Pagnell w Lathbury and Moulsoe 85-86; TV Langley Marish 86-90; Vice Prin EMMTC *S'well* 90-97; Prin 97-06; R Gedling from 06; P-in-c Lambley from 11; Hon Can S'well Minster from 00. *The Rectory, Rectory Drive, Gedling, Nottingham NG4 4BG* T: 0115-961 3214

TAYLOR, Michael Laurence. b 43. Ch Coll Cam BA 66 MA 70 CertEd 72 MPhil 90 ARCM 68. Cuddesdon Coll 66. **d** 68 **p** 69. C Westbury-on-Trym H Trin *Bris* 68-72; Asst Chapl Wellington Coll Berks 72-76; C St Helier *S'wark* 76-78; TV Bedminster *Bris* 78-82; P-in-c Chippenham St Andr w Tytherton Lucas 82-88; V 88-89; Dioc Ecum Officer *B & W* 89-90; P-in-c Rodney Stoke w Draycott 89-90. *The Paddock, Wells Road, Rodney Stoke, Cheddar BS27 3UU* T: (01749) 870684 E: mendipadvolacy@btinternet.com

TAYLOR, Michael Noel. b 40. Leeds Univ BSc 62 PGCE 63. EMMTC 95. **d** 98 **p** 99. NSM Woodthorpe *S'well* 98-02; NSM Gedling Deanery 02-03; NSM Epperstone, Gonalston, Oxton and Woodborough from 03; NSM Calverton from 03. *16 Church Meadow, Calverton, Nottingham NG14 6HG* T: 0115-847 3718 F: 912 7671 M: 07713-125771 E: michael.taylor21@ntlworld.com

TAYLOR, Michael Stewart. b 58. St Mich Coll Llan BTh 91. **d** 91 **p** 92. C Llangunnor w Cwmffrwd *St D* 91-94; V Llansantffraed and Llanbadarn Trefeglwys etc 94-97; P-in-c Jersey St Andr *Win* 97-99; V from 99. *The Vicarage, St Andrew's Road, First Tower, St Helier, Jersey JE2 3JG* T/F: (01534) 734975 E: vicarmike@gmail.com

TAYLOR, Mrs Monica. b 39. **d** 06 **p** 07. OLM Wyke *Guildf* 06-09; PtO Ox from 09. *Glifada, Guildford Road, Normandy, Guildford GU23 2AR* T: (01483) 234927 E: mrsmonicataylor@hotmail.com

TAYLOR, Nancy. b 49. SRN 70 SCM 72. Ox Min Course 88. **d** 91 **p** 94. Chapl Asst Stoke Mandeville Hosp Aylesbury 91-94; Asst Chapl Aylesbury Vale Community Healthcare NHS Trust 94-97; NSM Weston Turville *Ox* 91-99; PtO 99-14; *Ely* 98-07; Chapl Kneesworth Ho Hosp from 98. *Kneesworth House Hospital, Old North Road, Bassingbourn, Royston SG8 5JP* T: (01763) 255700

TAYLOR, Neil Andrew. b 56. ERMC 13. **d** 15. NSM Chigwell and Chigwell Row *Chelmsf* from 15. *9 Cheltenham Gardens, Loughton IG10 3AW*

TAYLOR, Canon Nicholas Hugh. b 63. Cape Town Univ BA 83 MA 87 Dur Univ PhD 91 Ox Univ MTh 07. **d** 96 **p** 97. Lect and Chapl Univ of Swaziland 95-98; Chapl St Mich Sch Manzini 96-98; Sen Lect Africa Univ Zimbabwe 98-01; Can Th Mutare Cathl from 99; Dioc Dir Th Educn Manicaland 99-01; R Penhalonga 00-01; Assoc Prof Pretoria Univ S Africa 02-04; R Pretoria St Hilda 02-03; R Pretoria N St Mary 03; Hon C Smithfield St Bart *Glas* Lon 04; Research Fell Univ of Zululand S Africa from 04; Hon Tutor Ripon Coll Cuddesdon 04-05; K Coll Lon 06; PtO *Nor* from 04; *Ox* 05-07; R Clarkston *Glas* from 09; Tutor TISEC from 10. *St Aidan's Rectory, 8 Golf Road, Clarkston, Glasgow G76 7LZ* T: 0141-638 3080 M: 07944-091132 E: nicholas.h.taylor@btconnect.com

TAYLOR, Preb Nicholas James. b 46. St Chad's Coll Dur BA 67. **d** 69 **p** 70. C Beamish *Dur* 69-74; C Styvechale *Cov* 74-77; P-in-c Wilmcote w Billesley 77-79; P-in-c Aston Cantlow 77-79; V Aston Cantlow and Wilmcote w Billesley 79-87; V Cov St Fran N Radford 87-97; RD Cov N 93-97; V Wilton *B & W* 97-11; Preb Wells Cathl 08-11; rtd 11. *50 Summerlands Park Avenue, Ilminster TA19 9BT* T: (01460) 929392 M: 07761-437505 E: nickruthtaylor@gmail.com

TAYLOR, Nicholas John. b 48. Leeds Univ BSc 69. St Mich Coll Llan BTh 09. **d** 09 **p** 10. NSM Griffithstown *Mon* 09-13; NSM Panteg and Griffithstown from 13. *Panteg Rectory, The Highway, New Inn, Pontypool NP4 0PH* M: 07860-507258 T: (01495) 763724 E: njt.littlebarton@btinternet.com

TAYLOR, Nigel James. b 73. Lanc Univ BA 94. Trin Coll Bris BA 11. **d** 11 **p** 12. C Risborough *Ox* 11-15; C Idle *Leeds* from 15. *92 Town Lane, Bradford BD10 8PJ* M: 07749-816265 E: revdjimtaylor@gmail.com

TAYLOR, Nigel Roy. b 63. Keele Univ MA 01 RGN 86 RMN 89. Qu Coll Birm 10. **d** 12 **p** 13. C Walsall St Paul *Lich* 12-15; C Walsall St Luke 12-15; TV Kidderminster Ismere *Worc* from 15; Ind Chapl from 15. *42 Woodlands Road, Cookley, Kidderminster DY10 3TL* E: nigelr.taylor@btinternet.com

TAYLOR, Nigel Thomas Wentworth. b 60. Bris Univ BA 82 Ox Univ BA 86. Wycliffe Hall Ox 84. **d** 87 **p** 88. C Ches Square St Mich w St Phil *Lon* 87-91; C Roxeth Ch Ch and Harrow St Pet 91-93; TV Roxeth 93-97; V S Mimms Ch Ch from 97; AD Cen Barnet 04-09. *Christ Church Vicarage, St Albans Road, Barnet EN5 4LA* T: (020) 8449 0942 *or* 8449 0832 E: nigel.taylor@london.anglican.org

TAYLOR, Mrs Noelle Rosemary. b 58. NTMTC 02. **d** 05 **p** 06. C St Mary-at-Latton *Chelmsf* 05-08; TV St Parndon 08-14; V 14-15; P-in-c Chipping Ongar w Shelley from 15. *The Rectory, Shakletons, Ongar CM5 9AT* T: (01277) 362173 E: noelletaylor@hotmail.com

TAYLOR, Norman. b 26. CCC Cam BA 49 MA 52. Cuddesdon Coll 49. **d** 51 **p** 52. C Clitheroe St Mary *Blackb* 51-54; C Pontesbury I and II *Heref* 54-55; R Lt Wilbraham *Ely* 55-71; Chapl St Faith's Sch Cam 71-86; Hon C Chesterton St Andr *Ely* 87-91; rtd 91; PtO *Sarum* 91-09; *York* from 11. *Brook House, West End, Ampleforth, York YO62 4DY* T: (01439) 787199

TAYLOR, Norman Adrian. b 48. Ho of Sacred Miss 64 St D Coll Lamp 70. **d** 73 **p** 74. C Fleur-de-Lis *Mon* 73-75; C W Drayton *Lon* 75-79; C-in-c Hayes St Edm CD 79-85; V Hayes St Edm 85-87; V Pilton w Ashford *Ex* 87-89; V Sidley *Chich* 89-02; Chapl Hastings and Rother NHS Trust 00-02; V Durrington *Chich* 02-13; rtd 13. *7 Guernsey Road, Ferring, Worthing BN12 5PN* T: (01903) 245939 E: frnormantaylor@gmail.com

TAYLOR, Mrs Patricia Anne. b 56. TCD BTh 05. CITC 03. **d** 05 **p** 06. C Wicklow w Killiskey *D & G* 05-10; TV Smestow Vale *Lich* 10-13; rtd 13; PtO *Lich* from 13; *Leeds* from 14. *2 Poplar Avenue, Shafton, Barnsley S72 8PU* E: patricia.taylor@gmail.com

TAYLOR, Patricia Mary. b 52. Goldsmiths' Coll Lon BEd 80. Wycliffe Hall Ox 06. **d** 09 **p** 10. NSM Upper Holloway *Lon* 09-12; NSM Hornsey Rise 12-13; NSM Wandsworth St Mich w St Steph *S'wark* from 13. *4 Anatola Road, London N19 5HN* T: (020) 7272 8990 E: p.taylor2410@btinternet.com

TAYLOR, Patrick James. b 72. Magd Coll Cam BA 96 MA 99 MEng 96. Ripon Coll Cuddesdon BA 00. **d** 01 **p** 02. C Kenilworth St Nic *Cov* 01-05; TV Solihull *Birm* 05-14; R Stratford-upon-Avon, Luddington etc *Cov* from 14. *The Vicarage, 7 Old Town, Stratford-upon-Avon CV37 6BG* T: (01789) 266316 E: vicar@stratford-upon-avon.org

TAYLOR, Paul. b 63. RGN 85. Sarum & Wells Th Coll 92 Linc Th Coll BTh 95. **d** 95 **p** 96. C Boultham *Linc* 95-98; C Ditton St Mich w St Thos *Liv* 98-00; V Bickerstaffe and Melling 00-06; TV N Meols 06-08; rtd 08; Chapl St Helens and Knowsley Hosps NHS Trust from 13. *139 Sussex Road, Southport PR8 6AF* T: (01704) 500617 E: joandpaultaylor@talktalk.net

TAYLOR, Paul Frank David. b 60. Leic Poly BSc 84 MRICS 87. Trin Coll Bris BA 91. **d** 91 **p** 92. C Edin St Thos 91-94; C Kempshott *Win* 94-98; C-in-c Hatch Warren CD 98-01; V Salisbury St Fran and Stratford sub Castle *Sarum* from 01; C Bourne Valley from 09; RD Salisbury from 14. *The Vicarage, 52 Park Lane, Salisbury SP1 3NP* T: (01722) 333762 E: plaj.taylor52@btopenworld.com

TAYLOR, Paul Jeremy. b 72. Brunel Univ BSc 96. Ridley Hall Cam 02. **d** 04 **p** 05. C Longfleet *Sarum* 04-08; V Hordle *Win* from 08. *The Vicarage, Stopples Lane, Hordle, Lymington SO41 0HX* T: (01425) 614428 M: 07776-425621 E: pjtaylorsurfing@hotmail.com

TAYLOR, Paul Michael. b 66. EMMTC 03. **d** 05 **p** 05. C Derby St Pet and Ch Ch w H Trin 05-07; P-in-c Brailsford w Shirley and Osmaston w Edlaston 07-09; R Brailsford w Shirley, Osmaston w Edlaston etc from 09. *The Rectory, Church Lane, Brailsford, Ashbourne DE6 3BX* T: (01335) 361239 E: paul@fiveofthebest.org.uk

TAYLOR, The Ven Paul Stanley. b 53. Ox Univ BEd 75 MTh 98. Westcott Ho Cam. **d** 84 **p** 85. C Bush Hill Park St Steph *Lon* 84-88; Asst Dir Post Ord Tr Edmonton Episc Area 87-94; Dir Post Ord Tr 94-00 and 02-04; V Southgate St Andr *Lon* 88-97; V Hendon St Mary 97-01; V Hendon St Mary and Ch Ch 01-04; AD W Barnet 00-04; Adn Sherborne *Sarum*

from 04; Can and Preb Sarum Cathl from 04. *Aldhelm House, West Stafford, Dorchester DT2 8AB* T: (01305) 269074 *or* (01202) 659427 M: 07796-691203 E: adsherborne@salisbury.anglican.org *or* pstaylor53@gmail.com

TAYLOR, Pauline Frances. b 58. LCTP 11. **d** 14. OLM Broughton *Blackb* from 14. *29 Goodwood Avenue, Fulwood, Preston PR2 9TZ* T: (01772) 774634 E: pauline.hair@btinternet.com

TAYLOR, Peter. b 51. St Jo Coll Cam BA 72 MA 76. Ridley Hall Cam 73. **d** 76 **p** 77. C Roch 76-79; PtO *Ely* 79-99 and 05-06; NSM Downham 99-05; P-in-c Coveney from 06; RD Ely 09-14; Bp's Adv for Self-Supporting Min 10-14. *Gravel Head Farm, Downham Common, Little Downham, Ely CB6 2TY* T: (01353) 698714 F: 699107 E: peter@taylormonroe.co.uk

TAYLOR, Canon Peter David. b 47. Liv Univ BEd 74 Man Univ MEd 78 Lanc Univ MA 88. NOC 78. **d** 81 **p** 82. C Formby H Trin *Liv* 81-84; V Stoneycroft All SS 84-91; Chapl St Kath Coll 91-96; Dioc RE Field Officer 91-96; Dioc Dir of Educn *Leic* 96-09; Hon Can Leic Cathl 98-09; Dir Operations Ch Academy Services Ltd *Pet* 09-11; PtO *Leic* from 09; rtd 11. *87 Main Street, Humberstone, Leicester LE5 1AE* T: 0116-220 1461 *or* (01733) 566575 E: peter.tay1947@gmail.com

TAYLOR, Peter David. b 38. FCA. NOC 77. **d** 80 **p** 81. C Penwortham St Mary *Blackb* 80-84; V Farington 84-92; V Euxton 92-04; rtd 04; PtO *Blackb* from 04. *33 Aspendale Close, Longton, Preston PR4 5LJ* T: (01772) 614795

TAYLOR, The Ven Peter Flint. b 44. Qu Coll Cam BA 65 MA 69. Lon Coll of Div BD 70. **d** 70 **p** 71. C Highbury New Park St Aug *Lon* 70-73; C Plymouth St Andr w St Paul and St Geo *Ex* 73-77; V Ironville *Derby* 77-83; P-in-c Riddings 82-83; R Rayleigh *Chelmsf* 83-96; Chapl HM YOI Bullwood Hall 85-90; RD Rochford *Chelmsf* 89-96; Adn Harlow 96-09; rtd 09. *5 Springfield Terrace, Springfield Road, South Brent TQ10 9AP* T: (01364) 73427 E: peterftaylor@lineone.net

TAYLOR, Peter John. b 71. St Andr Univ MA 94 Sussex Univ PGCE 99. Oak Hill Th Coll BA 05. **d** 05 **p** 06. C Boscombe St Jo *Win* 05-09; P-in-c Heatherlands St Jo *Sarum* 09-11; V 11. *49 Alexandra Crescent, Bromley BR1 4EX*

TAYLOR, Peter John. b 40. Oak Hill Th Coll 62. **d** 65 **p** 66. C St Paul's Cray St Barn *Roch* 65-69; C Woking St Jo *Guildf* 69-77; R Necton w Holme Hale *Nor* 77-94; R Necton, Holme Hale w N and S Pickenham 95-05; RD Breckland 86-94; Hon Can Nor Cathl 98-03; rtd 05; PtO *Nor* from 05. *5 Starling Close, Aylsham, Norwich NR11 6XG* T: (01263) 731964

TAYLOR, Peter Joseph. b 41. Bps' Coll Cheshunt 66. **d** 68 **p** 69. C Wollaton *S'well* 68-71; C Cockington *Ex* 71-74; V Broadhembury 74-79; V Broadhembury w Payhembury 79-81; V Gt Staughton *Ely* 81-86; V Gt Paxton and R Offord D'Arcy w Offord Cluny 86-01; Chapl HM YOI Gaynes Hall 81-91; rtd 01; PtO *Ely* from 01. *9 Park Way, Offord Cluny, St Neots PE19 5RW* T: (01480) 811662 E: peter.taylor9@talktalk.net

TAYLOR, Mrs Rachel Sara. b 60. Univ Coll Lon BA 81. SEITE 98. **d** 01 **p** 02. C Wimbledon *S'wark* 01-05; V Motspur Park from 05. *The Vicarage, 2 Douglas Avenue, New Malden KT3 6HT* T: (020) 8942 3117 E: rachel@taylortalk.fsnet.co.uk

TAYLOR, Ralph Urmson. Tulsa Univ 64 Man Coll of Educn DipEd 74 TCert 82. Kelham Th Coll. **d** 56 **p** 57. C Redcar *York* 57-59; C Bridlington Quay H Trin 59-62; C Sewerby w Marton 60-62; Asst P Tulsa H Trin USA 62-65; Chapl Holland Hall Sch 65-93; rtd 93; Sacr Tulsa H Trin USA 93-02. *43 East Cliffe, Lytham St Annes FY8 5DX*

TAYLOR, Raymond. b 34. Lon Coll of Div 62. **d** 65 **p** 66. C Pennington *Man* 65-70; P-in-c Wombridge *Lich* 70-80; R S Normanton *Derby* 80-88; RD Alfreton 86-88; V Youlgreave, Middleton, Stanton-in-Peak etc 88-98; rtd 99; PtO *Derby* from 98. *4 Jeffries Avenue, Crich, Matlock DE4 5DU* T: (01773) 856845

TAYLOR, Raymond George. b 39. Bucknell Univ BS 59 Univ of Penn MS 65 EdD 66 Penn State Univ MPA 77 Maine Univ MBA 85. Episc Th Sch Cam Mass BD 62. **d** 62 **p** 63. C Chestnut Hill St Martin USA 62-66; V Warwick St Mary 70-77; Assoc P Smithfield St Paul 87-90; Assoc P Oriental St Thos 90-00; Superintendent of Schs Maine 77-86; Prof N Carolina State Univ 86-01; P-in-c Málaga *Eur* 04-06. *Cortijo Moya, 29710 Periana (Málaga), Spain* T/F: (0034) 609 885 479 M: 650 780 087 E: cortijomoya@terra.es

TAYLOR, Raymond Montgomery. b 43. Oak Hill Th Coll 77. **d** 80 **p** 81. Hon C Cricklewood St Pet *Lon* 80-85; Hon C Golders Green 85-87; V New Southgate St Paul 87-00; AD Cen Barnet 96-00; V Thaxted *Chelmsf* 00-13; rtd 13; PtO *Chelmsf* from 13. *2 Crescent Close, Dunmow CM6 1DE* T: (01371) 874809 E: scribendi@live.co.uk

TAYLOR, Richard Godfrey. b 73. Pemb Coll Cam MA 99. Oak Hill Th Coll BA 00. **d** 00 **p** 01. C Brunswick *Man* 00-04;

C Aldridge *Lich* 04-09; V Clapham Common St Barn *S'wark* from 09. *The Vicarage, 8 Lavender Gardens, London SW11 1DL* T: (020) 7223 5953 E: fatboytaylor@gmail.com

TAYLOR, Richard John. b 46. Ripon Coll Cuddesdon 85. **d** 85 **p** 86. C Moseley St Mary *Birm* 85-87; V Kingsbury 87-91; TR Hodge Hill 91-03; P-in-c 03-05; R Weston super Mare St Jo *B & W* from 05; RD Locking from 08. *The Rectory, Cecil Road, Weston-super-Mare BS23 2NF* T: (01934) 623399

TAYLOR, Preb Richard John. b 21. Kelham Th Coll 38. **d** 45 **p** 46. C Tunstall Ch Ch *Lich* 45-48; C Uttoxeter w Bramshall 48-52; V Croxden 52-57; V Willenhall H Trin 57-68; R Edgmond 68-77; V Streetly 77-87; Preb Lich Cathl 78-87; rtd 87; PtO *Lich* from 87. *15 Covey Close, Lichfield WS13 6BS* T: (01543) 268558

TAYLOR, Robert Ian. b 68. St Jo Coll Nottm. **d** 08 **p** 09. C Buttershaw St Paul *Bradf* 08-12; Chapl Bradf Academy from 08. *52 Bowling Park Drive, East Bowling, Bradford BD4 7ES* T: (01274) 788722 E: robtlr@aol.com

TAYLOR, Robert Stirling. b 62. Ball Coll Ox BA 83 Leeds Univ PhD 88 Nottm Trent Univ PGCE 93. Cranmer Hall Dur 00. **d** 02 **p** 03. C Mansfield St Jo *S'well* 02-04; C Eastwood 04-06; Chapl Loughb Univ *Leic* 06-09; R Kingsland w Eardisland, Aymestrey etc *Heref* 10-12; V Goole *Sheff* from 12. *7 Salisbury Avenue, Goole DN14 5JW* T: (01405) 449049 E: vicarofgoole@sky.com

TAYLOR, Robin. *See* TAYLOR, Joseph Robin Christopher

TAYLOR, Roger James Benedict. b 42. Glouc Sch of Min 89 WMMTC 95. **d** 96 **p** 97. NSM Cromhall w Tortworth and Tytherington *Glouc* 96-99; P-in-c Wistanstow *Heref* 99-01; Min Can Brecon Cathl 01-07; rtd 07. *9 Jubilee Close, Bidford-on-Avon, Alcester B50 4ED* E: roger.taylor36@btinternet.com

TAYLOR, Canon Roland Haydn. b 29. St Chad's Coll Dur BA 53. **d** 55 **p** 56. C N Gosforth *Newc* 55-58; C Barnsley St Mary *Wakef* 58-61; V Brotherton 61-68; V Purston cum S Featherstone 68-76; RD Pontefract 74-94; R Badsworth 76-97; Hon Can Wakef Cathl 81-97; rtd 97. *57 Fairview, Carleton, Pontefract WF8 3NU* T: (01977) 796564

TAYLOR, Rosemary Edith. b 47. Nottm Univ MA 04 RGN 68 RHV 71. EMMTC 01. **d** 04 **p** 05. NSM Bassingham Gp *Linc* 04-08; P-in-c Sibsey w Frithville 08-13; V from 13; P-in-c Brothertoft Gp 10-13; V from 13. *The Vicarage, Vicarage Lane, Sibsey, Boston PE22 0RT* T: (01205) 751674 E: natuna@btopenworld.com

TAYLOR, Roy. b 63. Ex Coll Ox BA 86 Ox Univ MA 89 York Univ PGCE 87 Univ of Wales (Cardiff) BD 97. St Mich Coll Llan 95. **d** 97 **p** 98. C Guisborough *York* 97-99; Chapl Rossall Sch Fleetwood 99-02; V Dolphinholme w Quernmore and Over Wyresdale *Blackb* 02-08; Chapl Geneva *Eur* 08-13; Chapl Tenerife Sur 13-15. *Address temp unknown*

TAYLOR, Canon Roy Partington. b 33. Birm Univ BA 54 PGCE 55 Bulmershe Coll of HE MPhil 87. SAOMC 96. **d** 98 **p** 99. NSM Hurley and Stubbings *Ox* 98-02; NSM Burchetts Green 02-03; PtO from 03; Lect Bp Hannington Inst Kenya 01-02; Prin 04; Hon Can Taita Taveta from 08. *16 Highfield Road, Maidenhead SL6 5DF* T: (01628) 625454 E: roy_taylor16@btopenworld.com

TAYLOR, Roy William. b 37. Ch Coll Cam BA 61 MA 64. Clifton Th Coll 61. **d** 63 **p** 64. C Blackb Sav 63-66; C Hensingham *Carl* 66-68; CMS Taiwan 69-79; TV Bushbury *Lich* 79-85; OMF 85-93; Hon C Wolverhampton St Jude *Lich* 93-94; P-in-c Torquay St Jo and Ellacombe *Ex* 94-99; R Instow and V Westleigh 99-03; RD Hartland 01-03; rtd 03. *31 Shore Road, Millisle, Newtownards BT22 2BT* T: (028) 9186 2769

TAYLOR, Simon Dominic Kent. b 69. Surrey Univ BSc 90 W Sussex Inst of HE PGCE 91 Sussex Univ MA(Ed) 99. Trin Coll Bris BA 01. **d** 01 **p** 02. C Southgate *Chich* 01-04; TV 04-10; Dioc Officer for Emerging Leadership 04-10; R Busbridge and Hambledon *Guildf* from 10. *Busbridge Rectory, Old Rectory Gardens, Godalming GU7 1XB* T: (01483) 421267 E: simon.taylor@bhcgodalming.org

TAYLOR, Canon Simon John. b 72. Worc Coll Ox BA 94 MPhil 96 MA 99 DPhil 00. St Mich Coll Llan 00 Ven English Coll Rome 01. **d** 02 **p** 03. C Cotham St Sav w St Mary and Clifton St Paul *Bris* 02-06; P-in-c Bris St Mary Redcliffe w Temple etc 06-12; CMD Officer and Can Res Derby Cathl from 12. *149 Church Road, Quarndon, Derby DE22 5JA* T: (01332) 341201 *or* 388650 E: simon.taylor@derby.anglican.org

TAYLOR, Simon Wheldon. b 62. **d** 12 **p** 13. NSM Tunbridge Wells St Phil *Roch* from 12. *September Cottage, Monks Lane, Wadhurst TN5 6EN* T: (01892) 782043 M: 07970-716163 E: st@cloisters.com

TAYLOR, Stephen Charles. b 53. St Edm Hall Ox BA 75 Ex Univ PGCE 78. WEMTC 05. **d** 08 **p** 09. NSM Highnam, Lassington, Rudford, Tibberton etc *Glouc* 08-13; P-in-c Westbury-on-Severn w Flaxley, Blaisdon etc from 13. *Address withheld by request* T: (01452) 760756 E: stevewillstay@gmail.com

TAYLOR, Stephen Gordon. b 35. Bris Univ BA 60. Ridley Hall Cam 60. **d** 62 **p** 63. C Gt Baddow *Chelmsf* 62-65; C Portsdown *Portsm* 65-69; P-in-c Elvedon *St E* 69-70; R 70-75; P-in-c Eriswell 69-70; R 70-75; P-in-c Icklingham 69-70; R 70-75; Chapl St Felix Sch Southwold 75-77; R Lt Shelford w Newton *Ely* 77-96; rtd 96; PtO *Ely* from 96. *15 Church Close, Whittlesford, Cambridge CB22 4NY* T: (01223) 830461 E: sgt707@btinternet.com

TAYLOR, Stephen Graham. b 77. St Jo Coll Nottm. **d** 08 **p** 09. C Sparkhill St Jo *Birm* 08-12; C Alperton *Lon* from 12. *The Vicarage, 34 Stanley Avenue, Wembley HA0 4JB* T: (020) 8902 1729 M: 07702-814456 E: vicarsteve@googlemail.com

TAYLOR, Stephen James. b 48. Chich Th Coll 70. **d** 73 **p** 74. C Tottenham St Paul *Lon* 73-76; St Vincent 78-85; Grenada 85-88; C-in-c Hammersmith SS Mich and Geo White City Estate CD *Lon* 88-96; AD Hammersmith 92-96; P-in-c Hammersmith St Luke *Lon* 94-96; USPG Brazil 96-98; PtO *Lon* from 14. *12 Bletchley Court, Wenlock Street, London N1 7NX* T: (020) 7253 8629 E: stephentaylor2001@hotmail.com

TAYLOR, Stephen Mark. b 65. City Univ BSc 87 Lon Univ PGCE 90. NTMTC 95. **d** 98 **p** 99. Chapl Bp Stopford's Sch Enfield 98-02 and 03-06; NSM Enfield Chase St Mary *Lon* 98-02; PtO *Eur* 02-03; C Hornsey St Mary w St Geo *Lon* 03-06; P-in-c March St Jo *Ely* 06-08; Hon Asst Dir of Ords 07-08; P-in-c Enfield St Mich *Lon* 08-13; V from 13. *The Vicarage, 2 Gordon Hill, Enfield EN2 0QP* T: (020) 8363 1063 M: 07711-559107 E: stephen.taylor@london.anglican.org

TAYLOR, The Ven Stephen Ronald. b 55. MBE 09. Dur Univ MA 99. Cranmer Hall Dur 80. **d** 83 **p** 84. C Chester le Street *Dur* 83-87; V Newbottle 87-92; V Stranton 92-00; TR Sunderland 00-07; Provost Sunderland Minster 07-11; Hon Can Dur Cathl 06-11; Adn Maidstone *Cant* from 11; Hon Can Rift Valley Tanzania from 00; Hon Fell Sunderland Univ *Dur* from 09. *The Archdeaconry, 4 Redcliffe Lane, Penenden Heath, Maidstone ME14 2AG* T: (01622) 200221 E: staylor@archdeacmaid.org

TAYLOR, Stewart. b 51. Cranmer Hall Dur 74. **d** 77 **p** 78. C Norwood St Luke *S'wark* 77-81; C Surbiton Hill Ch Ch 81-91; V Cambridge St Phil *Ely* from 91. *St Philip's Vicarage, 252 Mill Road, Cambridge CB1 3NF* T: (01223) 247652 *or* 414775 E: vicar@stphilipschurch.org.uk

TAYLOR, Canon Stuart Bryan. b 40. St Chad's Coll Dur BA 64. **d** 66 **p** 67. C Portsea N End St Mark *Portsm* 66-70; C Epsom St Martin *Guildf* 70-76; Chapl Clifton Coll Bris 76-88; Dir Bloxham Project 88-93; Chapl Giggleswick Sch 93-95; Bp's Officer for Miss and Evang *Bris* 96-01; Bp's Adv for Past Care for Clergy and Families 01-10; Hon Min Can Bris Cathl 02-04; Chapl Bris Cathl Sch 01-09; Hon Can Bris Cathl 04-10; rtd 10; PtO *B & W* from 12. *62 Providence Lane, Long Ashton, Bristol BS41 9DN* T: (01275) 393625 M: 07974-316489 E: sbtbristol@gmail.com

TAYLOR, Mrs Susan Mary. b 51. Ex Univ LLB 73 St Anne's Coll Ox BCL 75 Solicitor 78. SEITE 03. **d** 06 **p** 07. NSM Barkingside St Laur *Chelmsf* 06-12; Chapl Evelina Children's Hosp from 12; Chapl Guy's and St Thos' NHS Foundn Trust from 13; PtO *S'wark* from 10; *Chelmsf* from 12. *Norwood, North End, Buckhurst Hill IG9 5RA* T: (020) 8504 9867 *or* 7188 7188 E: suetaylorthorne@aol.com

TAYLOR, Mrs Teresa Mary. b 53. SRN 76 SCM 78. WEMTC 98. **d** 02 **p** 03. NSM Kingswood *Bris* 02-12; Chapl Freeways Trust from 07; P-in-c Mangotsfield *Bris* 12-13; V from 13. *19 Hicks Avenue, Emersons Green, Bristol BS16 7HA* E: revtmt@blueyonder.co.uk

TAYLOR, Thomas. b 33. Sarum & Wells Th Coll 77. **d** 80 **p** 81. NSM Heatherlands St Jo *Sarum* 80-82; TV Kinson 82-88; TV Shaston 88-98; Chapl Westmr Memorial Hosp Shaftesbury 88-98; rtd 98; PtO *Sarum* from 98. *10 Hanover Lane, Gillingham SP8 4TA* T: (01747) 826569

TAYLOR, Thomas. b 42. St Jo Coll Dur BA 64 Leeds Univ MA 02. Linc Th Coll 64. **d** 66 **p** 67. C Clitheroe St Mary *Blackb* 66-69; C Skerton St Luke 69-71; C-in-c Penwortham St Leon CD 71-72; V Penwortham St Leon 72-78; R Poulton-le-Sands 78-81; P-in-c Morecambe St Lawr 78-81; R Poulton-le-Sands w Morecambe St Laur 81-85; Chapl Lord Wandsworth Coll Hook 85-92; V Walton-le-Dale *Blackb* 92-94; P-in-c Samlesbury 92-94; V Walton-le-Dale St Leon w Samlesbury St Leon 95-96; RD Leyland 94-96; Hon C Tarleton 03-11; Hon C Rufford and Tarleton 11-12. *52 Hesketh Lane, Tarleton, Preston PR4 6AQ* T: (01772) 813871 E: rustichouse@bigfoot.com

TAYLOR, Timothy Robert. b 62. W Midl Coll of Educn BEd 87 Cumbria Univ BA 10. LCTP 07. **d** 10 **p** 11. NSM Egremont and Haile *Carl* from 10. *42 Abbey Vale, St Bees CA27 0EF* T: (01946) 822255 E: timothy@trtaylor.co.uk

TAYLOR, William Austin. b 36. Linc Th Coll 65. **d** 67 **p** 68. C Tyldesley w Shakerley *Man* 67-71; R Cheetham St Mark 71-79; TR Peel 79-90; AD Farnworth 83-90; V Pelton

Dur 90-96; rtd 96; PtO *Man* 96-08. *36 Tynesbank, Worsley, Manchester M28 8SL* T: 0161-790 5327

TAYLOR, Willam Goodacre Campbell. See CAMPBELL-TAYLOR, William Goodacre

TAYLOR, Canon William Henry. b 56. Kent Univ BA 79 Lon Univ MTh 81 Lanc Univ MPhil 87 SOAS Lon PhD 10 FRAS 80. Westcott Ho Cam. **d** 83 **p** 84. C Maidstone All SS and St Phil w Tovil *Cant* 83-86; Abp's Adv on Orthodox Affairs 86-88; C St Marylebone All SS *Lon* 86-88; Chapl Guy's Hosp Lon 88; CMS Jordan 88-91; V Ealing St Pet Mt Park *Lon* 91-00; AD Ealing 93-98; Dean Portsm 00-02; P-in-c Notting Hill St Jo and St Pet *Lon* 02-03; V Notting Hill St Jo from 03; Hon Can Manila Philippines from 13. *St John's Vicarage, 25 Ladbroke Road, London W11 3PD* T: (020) 7727 3439 *or* T/F 7727 4262 E: vicar@stjohnsnottinghill.com

TAYLOR, William Richard de Carteret Martin. b 33. CCC Cam MA 57. Westcott Ho Cam 58. **d** 59 **p** 60. C Eastney *Portsm* 59-63; Chapl RN 63-67 and 70-87; V Childe Okeford *Sarum* 67-70; V Manston w Hamoon 67-70; QHC from 83; TR Tisbury *Sarum* 87-89; Chapl Hatf Poly *St Alb* 89-92; Chapl Herts Univ 92-98; rtd 98; PtO *Ely* from 00. *7 West Street, St Neots PE19 1AH* E: bill.taylor2@talktalk.net

TAYLOR, Capt William Thomas. b 61. Rob Coll Cam BA 83 BA 90. Ridley Hall Cam 88. **d** 91 **p** 92. C Bromley Ch Ch *Roch* 91-95; C St Helen Bishopsgate w St Andr Undershaft etc *Lon* 95-98; R from 98; R St Pet Cornhill from 01. *The Old Rectory, Merrick Square, London SE1 4JB* T: (020) 7378 8186

TAYLOR-COOK, Andrew. b 62. ERMC. **d** 08 **p** 09. C Wirksworth *Derby* 08-12; Chapl amongst Deaf People *Derby* 11-13; *Pet* 12-15; C Guilsborough and Hollowell and Cold Ashby etc 13-15; P-in-c Codnor *Derby* from 15; P-in-c Horsley and Denby from 15; P-in-c Loscoe from 15; P-in-c Horsley Woodhouse from 15. *The Vicarage, 20 Codnor Denby Lane, Codnor, Ripley DE5 9SN* T: (01604) 846690 M: 07840-848123 E: andrewtc@btinternet.com

TAYLOR-KENYON (née THOMPSON), Louise Margaret. b 61. Clare Coll Cam BA 83 MA 07 Homerton Coll Cam PGCE 84 Leeds Univ MA 07. NOC 04. **d** 07 **p** 08. C Skipton H Trin *Bradf* 07-10; C Skipton Ch Ch w Carleton 07-10; C Embsay w Eastby 10-14; V from 14; CME Officer from 10. *The Vicarage, 21 Shires Lane, Skipton BD23 6SB* T: (01756) 798057 M: 07545-235362 E: louise.taylor-kenyon@bradford.anglican.org

TEAGUE, Gaythorne Derrick. b 24. MBE 05. Bris Univ MB, ChB 49 MRCGP 53. **d** 74 **p** 75. NSM Bris St Andr Hartcliffe 74-86; PtO *B & W* from 86. *Innisfree, Bell Square, Blagdon, Bristol BS40 7UB* T: (01761) 462671 M: 07909-690983

TEAL, Andrew Robert. b 64. Birm Univ BA 85 PhD 06 Ox Brookes Univ PGCE 05 Pemb Coll Ox MA 08. Ripon Coll Cuddesdon 86. **d** 88 **p** 89. C Wednesbury St Paul Wood Green *Lich* 88-92; TV Sheff Manor 92-97; Asst Post-Ord Tr Officer 93-98; Tutor Ripon Coll Cuddesdon 92-97; V Tickhill w Stainton *Sheff* 97-02; Warden of Readers 98-02; Hd of Th Plater Coll 02-03; Hd of Th and Past Studies 03-05; Chapl Pemb Coll Ox from 05; Fell from 08; Lect Ripon Coll Cuddesdon from 08; Warden SLG from 09; Lect Th Ox Univ from 07. *Pembroke College, Oxford OX1 1DW* T: (01865) 286276 F: 276418 E: andrew.teal@theology.ox.ac.uk

TEALE, Adrian. b 53. Univ of Wales (Abth) BA 74 CertEd 77 MA 80 Univ of Wales (Cardiff) MTh 89. Wycliffe Hall Ox 78. **d** 80 **p** 81. C Betws w Ammanford *St D* 80-84; V Brynaman w Cwmllynfell from 84; RD Dyffryn Aman 95-01. *Y Dalar Deg, 10 Bryn Road, Upper Brynamman, Ammanford SA18 1AU* T: (01269) 822275 E: tinkerteale@googlemail.com

TEAR, Jeremy Charles. b 67. Westmr Coll Ox BA 89 Birm Univ MA 99 MCIPD 94. Aston Tr Scheme 95 Qu Coll Birm 97. **d** 99 **p** 00. C Timperley *Ches* 99-03; V Macclesfield St Paul 03-10; C Caversham Thameside and Mapledurham *Ox* from 10. *St John's Vicarage, St John's Road, Caversham, Reading RG4 5AN* T: 0118-946 2884 E: revjtear@btinternet.com

TEARE, Adrian Jeremy. b 79. Van Mildert Coll Dur BA 01 G&C Coll Cam BA 10. Westcott Ho Cam 08. **d** 12. C Tottenham St Paul *Lon* 12-13; C Kilburn St Mary w All So and W Hampstead St Jas 13-14; C Palmers Green St Jo from 14. *20 Powell House, 4 Dunstan Mews, Enfield EN1 1GF* E: adrianjteare@hotmail.com

TEARE, Mrs Marie. b 46. Open Univ BA 81 RSCN 65. NOC 95. **d** 98 **p** 99. C Brighouse and Clifton *Wakef* 98-01; V Waggoners *York* 01-08; RD Harthill 02-08; rtd 08; PtO *York* from 08. *Mayfield Bungalow, Easingwold Road, Huby, York YO61 1HN* T: (01347) 811565 E: marie.teare@btinternet.com

TEARE, Canon Robert John Hugh. b 39. Bris Univ BSc 62. Coll of Resurr Mirfield 67. **d** 70 **p** 71. C Fareham SS Pet and Paul *Portsm* 70-73; Chapl K Alfred Coll *Win* 73-78; V Pokesdown St Jas 78-82; R Winnall 82-06; RD Win 89-99; Hon Can Win Cathl 92-06; rtd 06; Chapl CSMV 06-09; PtO *Ox* 09-11; P-in-c

Hanney, Denchworth and E Challow 11-12; PtO from 12. *29 Elizabeth Drive, Wantage OX12 9YA* T: (01235) 770966 E: robertteare@googlemail.com

TEARNAN, John Herman Janson. b 37. Bris Univ BSc 59. Kelham Th Coll 62. **d** 66 **p** 67. C Kettering SS Pet and Paul 66-71; LtO 71-85; PtO *St Alb* 82-85; *Pet* 85-94; Chapl HM YOI Wellingborough 89-90; Chapl HM YOI Glen Parva 90-94; Guyana 94-03; rtd 03; PtO *Pet* from 05. *14 Rectory Walk, Barton Seagrave, Kettering NN15 6SP* T: (01536) 510629 E: jaytee1937@btinternet.com

TEASDALE, Keith. b 56. Cranmer Hall Dur 86. **d** 88 **p** 89. C Crook *Dur* 88-92; V Dunston 92-10; AD Gateshead W 00-10; V Carl St Cuth w St Mary from 10; P-in-c Carl St Aid and Ch Ch from 12. *St Cuthbert's Vicarage, 20 St Aidan's Road, Carlisle CA1 1LS* T: (01228) 810599 *or* 521982 E: ktcarlisle@hotmail.co.uk

TEASDEL, David Charles. b 77. Coll of Resurr Mirfield 05. **d** 08 **p** 09. C Ouzel Valley *St Alb* 08-11; TV Staveley and Barrow Hill *Derby* 11-14; P-in-c Altofts *Wakef* from 14; P-in-c Sharlston from 14. *The Vicarage, 72A Church Road, Normanton WF6 2QG* E: fatherdavidteasdel@gmail.com

TEATHER, Andrew James. b 75. Leeds Univ BA 09. Yorks Min Course 07. **d** 09 **p** 10. C Preston St Jo and St Geo *Blackb* 09-13; V Willesden St Matt *Lon* from 13. *St Matthew's Vicarage, 77 St Mary's Road, London NW10 4AU* T: (020) 8965 3748 E: andrewteather@gmail.com

TEBBOTH, Mrs Jennifer Mary. b 61. Ox Min Course 12. **d** 15. C Chalfont St Giles, Seer Green and Jordans *Ox* from 15. *Address temp unknown*

TEBBS, Richard Henry. b 52. Southn Univ BTh. Sarum & Wells Th Coll 75. **d** 78 **p** 79. C Cinderhill *S'well* 78-82; C Nor St Pet Mancroft w St Jo Maddermarket 82-85; TV Bridport *Sarum* 85-94; TR Yelverton, Meavy, Sheepstor and Walkhampton *Ex* 94-08; P-in-c Frankley *Birm* 08-13; R from 13. *The Rectory, Frankley Green, Birmingham B32 4AS* T: 0121-476 2246 E: frankleychurch@btinternet.com

TEBBUTT, Canon Christopher Michael. b 55. ACA CTA. St Jo Coll Nottm BA 99. **d** 96 **p** 97. C Catherington and Clanfield *Portsm* 96-00; P-in-c Southbroom *Sarum* 00-07; V 07-09; TR Canford Magna from 09; RD Wimborne from 11; Can and Preb Sarum Cathl from 12. *The Rectory, Canford Magna, Wimborne BH21 3AF* T: (01202) 882270 M: 07917-190307 E: rector@canfordparish.org

TEBBUTT, Sandra Eileen. b 56. FBDO 78. STETS 96. **d** 99 **p** 00. NSM Blendworth w Chalton w Idsworth *Portsm* 99-00; Chapl Wilts and Swindon Healthcare NHS Trust 00-05; Regional Manager Bible Soc from 05; NSM Southbroom *Sarum* 04-09; NSM Canford Magna from 10. *The Rectory, Canford Magna, Wimborne BH21 3AF* T: (01202) 883382 E: sandra.tebbutt@biblesociety.org.uk

TEBBY, Ms Janet Elizabeth. b 52. Open Univ BA 88 Lady Spencer Chu Coll of Educn CertEd 73. ERMC 05. **d** 08 **p** 09. NSM Wootton w Quinton and Preston Deanery *Pet* 08-12; TV Oakham, Ashwell, Braunston, Brooke, Egleton etc from 12. *The Rectory, 3 Paddock Close, Whissendine, Oakham LE15 7HW* T: (01664) 474596 E: jtebby@gmail.com

TEDD, Christopher Jonathan Richard. See HOWITZ, Christopher Jonathan Richard

TEECE, David. b 54. MIET. **d** 06 **p** 07. OLM Normanton *Wakef* 06-07; NSM Stanley 07-10 and from 13; NSM Ackworth *Wakef* 10-13. *61 Fairway, Normanton WF6 1SE* T: (01924) 891326 M: 07757-263627 E: david.teece@btconnect.com

TEED, John Michael. b 44. Middx Univ BA 04. NTMTC 01. **d** 04 **p** 05. NSM Hanworth All SS *Lon* 04-07; NSM Staines 07-10; PtO *Ex* 10-12; NSM Dawlish 12-15; NSM Kenton, Mamhead, Powderham, Cofton and Starcross 12-15. *47 West Cliff Road, Dawlish EX7 9DZ* T: (01626) 865466 M: 07702-244078 E: johnteed@sky.com

TEGALLY, Narinder Jit Kaur. b 57. RGN 93. SAOMC 99. **d** 02 **p** 03. NSM Welwyn Garden City *St Alb* 02-05; Asst Chapl R Free Hampstead NHS Trust 05-07; Sen Chapl Guy's and St Thos' NHS Foundn Trust 07-12; PtO *St Alb* 05-12; TV Beaconsfield *Ox* from 12. *St Thomas's House, Mayflower Way, Beaconsfield HP9 1UF* T: (01494) 670460 M: 07940-580859 E: narindertegally@hotmail.com

TEGGARTY, Samuel James Karl. b 53. Dundee Univ BSc 77. CITC 98. **d** 01 **p** 02. NSM Newry *D & D* 01-03; NSM Kilkeel from 03. *79 Knockchree Avenue, Kilkeel, Newry BT34 4BP* T: (028) 4176 9076 E: karl.teggarty@btinternet.com

TEGGIN, John. b 26. **d** 83 **p** 84. NSM Dublin Sandford w Milltown *D & G* 84-93; Dir Leprosy Miss 86-96. *Apartment 4, 69 Strand Road, Sandymount, Dublin 4, Republic of Ireland* T: (00353) (1) 261 1792

TELEN, Salvador Roberto Sabornido. b 66. **d** 89. C Notting Hill St Jo *Lon* 05-10; Hon C Walthamstow St Sav *Chelmsf* 12-13; P-in-c 13-14; V from 14; Hon C Walthamstow St Barn

and St Jas Gt 12-13. *St Saviour's Vicarage, 210 Markhouse Road, London E17 8EP* T: (020) 8520 2036
E: father.telen@btinternet.com

TELFER, Andrew Julian. b 68. Essex Univ BA 94. Wycliffe Hall Ox BTh 97. **d** 97 **p** 98. C Skelmersdale St Paul *Liv* 97-01; C Ashton-in-Makerfield St Thos 01-03; V Whiston from 03. *The Vicarage, 90 Windy Arbor Road, Prescot L35 3SG* T: 0151-426 6329

TELFER, Canon Frank Somerville. b 30. Trin Hall Cam BA 53 MA 58. Ely Th Coll 53. **d** 55 **p** 56. C Liv Our Lady and St Nic 55-58; Chapl Down Coll Cam 58-62; Bp's Chapl *Nor* 62-65; Chapl Kent Univ *Cant* 65-73; Can Res Guildf Cathl 73-95; rtd 96; PtO *Nor* from 96. *Holbrook, Glandford, Holt NR25 7JP* T: (01263) 740586 E: fandjtelfer@btinternet.com

TELFORD, Alan. b 46. St Jo Coll Nottm. **d** 83 **p** 84. C Normanton *Derby* 83-86; TV N Wingfield, Pilsley and Tupton 86-90; TV N Wingfield, Clay Cross and Pilsley 90-92; P-in-c Oakwood 92-94; V Leic St Chris 94-05; P-in-c Leic St Theodore 05-09; rtd 09. *2 Springfield Cottage, Newmarket Lane, Clay Cross, Chesterfield S45 9AR* T: (01246) 866988 M: 07854-937449 E: atelford@talktalk.net

TELFORD, Ms Carolin Judith. b 57. Victoria Univ Wellington BA 78. SEITE 02. **d** 05 **p** 06. NSM Lee St Aug *S'wark* 05-07; Chapl St Cuth Coll Epsom New Zealand from 07. *St Cuthbert's College, PO Box 26020, Epsom, Auckland 1344, New Zealand*

TELFORD, John Anthony. b 72. Oak Hill Th Coll BA 96. **d** 13 **p** 14. C Anlaby St Pet *York* from 13; C Anlaby Common St Mark from 13. *St Mark's Vicarage, 1055 Anlaby Road, Hull HU4 7PP* T: (01482) 575232 M: 07956-100383 E: john.telfs@gmail.com *or* telfordj@btinternet.com

TELFORD, Richard Francis. b 46. K Coll Lon 65. **d** 69 **p** 70. C Barkingside H Trin *Chelmsf* 69-72; C Wickford 72-77; P-in-c Romford St Jo 77-80; V 80-82; PtO 93-96; rtd 08. *Juglans, The Street, Wattisfield, Diss IP22 1NS* E: richard_telford@hotmail.com

TELLINI, Canon Gianfranco. b 36. Gregorian Univ Rome DTh 65. Franciscan Sem Trent 57. **d** 61 **p** 61. In RC Ch 61-66; C Mill Hill Jo Keble Ch *Lon* 66; C Roxbourne St Andr 66-67; Lect Sarum Th Coll 67-69; Sen Tutor Sarum & Wells Th Coll 69-74; Vice-Prin Edin Th Coll 74-82; Lect Th Edin Univ 74-95; R Pittenweem *St And* 82-85; R Elie and Earlsferry 82-85; R Dunblane 85-98; Can St Ninian's Cathl Perth from 90; rtd 99; PtO *St And* from 04. *53 Buchan Drive, Dunblane FK15 9HW* T: (01786) 823281 E: giantellini@mac.com

TEMBEY, David. b 51. **d** 96 **p** 97. NSM Whitehaven *Carl* 96-00; NSM Holme Cultram St Cuth 00-02; NSM Holme Cultram St Mary 00-02; NSM Bromfield w Waverton 00-02; TV Solway Plain 02-15; V Marske in Cleveland *York* from 15. *The Vicarage, 6 Windy Hill Lane, Marske-by-the-Sea, Redcar TS11 7BN* T: (01642) 473119 E: tembey@btinternet.com

TEMPERLEY, Robert Noble. b 29. JP. St Jo Coll York CertEd 50 ACP 52 Dur Univ DAES 62. NEOC 85. **d** 88 **p** 88. NSM Ryhope *Dur* 88-97; rtd 98; PtO *Dur* from 97. *18 Withernsea Grove, Ryhope, Sunderland SR2 0BU* T: 0191-521 1813

TEMPLE, Mrs Sylvia Mary. b 48. Ex Univ BA 70 Univ of Wales (Abth) PGCE 71. St D Dioc Tr Course 93. **d** 94 **p** 97. NSM Tenby *St D* 94-99; C 99-00; V Martletwy w Lawrenny and Minwear etc 00-05. *Llwyn Onn, Trafalgar Road, Tenby SA70 7DW*

TEMPLE-WILLIAMS, Alexander. **d** 04 **p** 05. C Pontypool *Mon* 04-09; TV Cyncoed from 09. *40 Felbrigg Crescent, Pontprennau, Cardiff CF23 8SE* T: (029) 2054 0955

TEMPLEMAN (*née* WILLIAMS), Mrs Ann Joyce. b 50. St Hugh's Coll Ox BA 72 MA 75 PGCE 73. Cranmer Hall Dur 03. **d** 05 **p** 06. Headmistress Dur High Sch for Girls 98-11; NSM Peterlee *Dur* 05-11; P-in-c Theale and Englefield *Ox* from 11. *The Rectory, Englefield Road, Theale, Reading RG7 5AS* T: 0118-930 2759 M: 07877-659156 E: anntempleman@live.co.uk

TEMPLEMAN, Peter Morton. b 49. Ch Ch Ox BA 71 MA 75. Wycliffe Hall Ox MA 75. **d** 76 **p** 77. C Cheltenham St Mary, St Matt, St Paul and H Trin *Glouc* 76-79; Chapl St Jo Coll Cam 79-84; P-in-c Finchley St Paul Long Lane *Lon* 84-85; P-in-c Finchley St Luke 84-85; V Finchley St Paul and St Luke 85-99; V Peterlee *Dur* 99-11; C Theale and Englefield *Ox* from 11. *The Rectory, Englefield Road, Theale, Reading RG7 5AS* T: 0118-930 2759

TEMPLETON, Iain McAllister. b 57. St Andr Coll Drygrange 80. **d** 85 **p** 86. In RC Ch 85-92; NSM Dornoch *Mor* 95; P-in-c Kirriemuir *St And* 95-99; R Eccleston *Blackb* 99-09; V Walsall St Andr *Lich* from 09. *St Andrew's Vicarage, 119 Hollyhedge Lane, Walsall WS2 8PZ* T: (01922) 721658 E: fatheriain@aol.com

TEN WOLDE, Christine Caroline. b 57. **d** 99 **p** 00. NSM Llanegryn w Aberdyfi w Tywyn *Ban* 99-12; NSM Tywyn w Llanegryn w Aberdyfi w Pennal 12-13; NSM Bro Ystumanner from 13. *Abergroes, Aberdovey LL35 0RE* T: (01654) 767047 F: 767572 M: 07977-108438 E: curate@stpeterschurch.org.uk

TENNANT, Cyril Edwin George. b 37. Keble Coll Ox BA 59 MA 63 Lon Univ BD 61 Ex Univ MA 03 Univ of Wales PhD 11. Clifton Th Coll 59. **d** 62 **p** 63. C Stapleford *S'well* 62-65; C Felixstowe SS Pet and Paul *St E* 65-69; V Gipsy Hill Ch Ch *S'wark* 69-84; V Lee St Mildred 84-90; P-in-c Lundy Is *Ex* 90-92; V Ilfracombe SS Phil and Jas w W Down 90-01; rtd 01; PtO *Ex* 01-06; *Ox* 06-08 and from 12. *27 Harvest Way, Witney OX28 1BX* T: (01993) 778977 E: candc.tennant@virgin.net

TER HAAR, Roger Edward Lound. b 52. QC 92. Magd Coll Ox BA 73. **d** 06 **p** 07. OLM Bramley and Grafham *Guildf* from 06. *Howicks, Hurlands Lane, Dunsfold, Godalming GU8 4NT* T: (020) 7797 8100 E: terhaar@crownofficechambers.com

TERESA, Sister. *See* WHITE, Teresa Joan

TERRANOVA, Jonathan Rossano (Ross). b 62. Sheff Poly BA 85. Oak Hill Th Coll BA 88. **d** 88 **p** 89. C Carl St Jo 88-91; C Stoughton *Guildf* 91-94; R Ditton *Roch* from 94; RD Malling 02-07. *The Rectory, 2 The Stream, Ditton, Maidstone ME20 6AG* T: (01732) 842027

TERRELL, Richard Charles Patridge. b 43. Wells Th Coll 69. **d** 71 **p** 72. C Shepton Mallet *B & W* 71-76; P-in-c Drayton 76-77; P-in-c Muchelney 76-77; TV Langport Area 78-82; P-in-c Tatworth 82-89; V 89-96; R W Coker w Hardington Mandeville, E Chinnock etc 96-09; rtd 09; PtO *B & W* from 09. *2 Hamdon View, Norton sub Hamdon, Stoke-sub-Hamdon TA14 6SE* T: (01935) 881330 M: 07736-836004 E: richard.terrell@homecall.co.uk

TERRETT, Mervyn Douglas. b 43. AKC 65. **d** 66 **p** 67. C Pet St Mary Boongate 66-69; C Sawbridgeworth *St Alb* 69-74; V Stevenage H Trin 74-85; PtO from 86; rtd 08. *Red Roofs, 20 Woodfield Road, Stevenage SG1 4BP* T: (01438) 720152 E: a-top@tiscali.co.uk

TERRY, Canon Christopher Laurence. b 51. Heythrop Coll Lon MA 09 FCA 80. St Alb Minl Tr Scheme. **d** 83 **p** 84. Hon C Dunstable *St Alb* 83-89; C Abbots Langley 89-92; TV Chambersbury 92-99; Chapl Abbot's Hill Sch Herts 96-99; R Southwick St Mich *Chich* 99-03; RD Hove 00-03; Finance and Admin Sec Min Division Abps' Coun 04-09; TR Gt Yarmouth *Nor* from 09; RD from 11; Hon Can Nor Cathl from 13. *The Rectory, Town Wall Road, Great Yarmouth NR30 1DJ* T: (01493) 842915 E: gyteamrector@btinternet.com

TERRY, Colin Alfred. b 49. Trin Coll Bris 98. **d** 00 **p** 01. C Bexleyheath Ch Ch *Roch* 00-03; V Belvedere All SS 03-10; Chapl Bromley Coll 10-12; P-in-c Lamorbey H Redeemer *Roch* from 12; AD Sidcup from 14. *Holy Redeemer Vicarage, 64 Day's Lane, Sidcup DA15 8JR* T: (020) 8300 1508 E: colin.terry.49@btinternet.com

TERRY, Darcy. *See* CHESTERFIELD-TERRY, John Darcy Francis Malcolm

TERRY, Ms Helen Barbara. b 58. Keele Univ BA 80 ATCL 98. Ripon Coll Cuddesdon 01. **d** 03 **p** 04. C Cainscross w Selsley *Glouc* 03-07; C Minchinhampton 07-08. *The Lodge, Shepherds Well, Rodborough Common, Stroud GL5 5DD* T: (01453) 873645

TERRY, Mrs Hilary June. b 45. SEITE 08. **d** 11. NSM Uckfield *Chich* 11-15; rtd 15. *11 St Saviours, Framfield Road, Uckfield TN22 5AS* T: (01825) 767793 M: 07947-923513 E: june.terry@tiscali.co.uk

TERRY, Ian Andrew. b 53. St Jo Coll Dur BA 74 St Jo Coll York PGCE 75 St Mary's Coll Twickenham MA 99 Surrey Univ PhD 05. Coll of Resurr Mirfield 78. **d** 80 **p** 81. C Beaconsfield *Ox* 80-83; C N Lynn w St Marg and St Nic *Nor* 83-84; Chapl and Hd RE Eliz Coll Guernsey 84-89; Chapl St Jo Sch Leatherhead 89-92; R Bisley and W End *Guildf* 92-02; Asst Chapl HM Pris Coldingley 99-02; Dioc Dir of Educn *Heref* 02-08; Hon TV W Heref 03-08; Chapl St Edm Sch Cant 08-09; TR Bournemouth Town Cen *Win* from 09. *St Peter's Rectory, 18 Wimborne Road, Bournemouth BH2 6NT* T/F: (01202) 554058 E: ianterry@live.co.uk

TERRY, James Richard. b 74. Linc Coll Ox BA 95. Oak Hill Th Coll BA 03. **d** 03 **p** 04. C Harold Wood *Chelmsf* 03-07; NSM Blackb Ch Ch w St Matt 07-13; V Tranmere St Cath *Ches* from 13. *St Catherine's Vicarage, 39 Westbank Road, Birkenhead CH42 7JP* T: 0151-652 7379 E: james_terry1@hotmail.com

TERRY, John Arthur. b 32. S'wark Ord Course. **d** 66 **p** 67. C Plumstead All SS *S'wark* 66-69; C Peckham St Mary Magd 69-72; V Streatham Vale H Redeemer 72-80; R Sternfield w Benhall and Snape *St E* 80-84; V Stevenage St Mary Shephall *St Alb* 84-86; V Stevenage St Mary Shephall w Aston 86-90; V Cople w Willington 90-97; Chapl Shuttleworth Agric Coll 90-97; rtd 97; PtO *St E* from 98; *Nor* 98-04; *Ely* from 03. *2 Kestrel Drive, Brandon IP27 0UA* T: (01842) 812055 E: jterry83@hotmail.com

TERRY, John Darcy Francis Malcolm. *See* CHESTERFIELD-TERRY, John Darcy Francis Malcolm

TERRY, John Michael. b 56. Ex Univ BSc 78 Southn Univ MSc 88 Anglia Ruskin Univ BA 09 CEng 93 MIMarEST 93. Ridley Hall Cam 06. **d** 09 **p** 10. NSM Fareham St Jo *Portsm* 09-13;

NSM Hook w Warsash from 13; Jt P-in-c from 14. *The Vicarage, 113 Church Road, Warsash, Southampton SO31 9GF* M: 07979-815026 E: mike.revsterry@btinternet.com

TERRY, June. *See* TERRY, Hilary June

TERRY, Justyn Charles. b 65. Keble Coll Ox BA 86 St Jo Coll Dur BA 95 K Coll Lon PhD 03. Cranmer Hall Dur 92. **d** 95 **p** 96. C Paddington St Jo w St Mich *Lon* 95-99; V Kensington St Helen w H Trin 99-05; Assoc Prof Trin Episc Sch for Min USA 05-08; Dean and Pres from 08. *Trinity Episcopal School for Ministry, 311 Eleventh Street, Ambridge PA 15003-2302, USA* T: (001) (800) 874 8754 E: jterry@tesm.edu

TERRY, Lydia Patricia Maud. b 44. Open Univ BSc 00. **d** 08 **p** 09. OLM Lydd *Cant* 08-13; NSM Brookland, Fairfield, Brenzett w Snargate etc 13-14; rtd 14; PtO *Cant* from 14. *5 Eastern Road, Lydd, Romney Marsh TN29 9EE* T: (01797) 320218

TERRY, Marc David. b 78. Trin Coll Bris 08. **d** 10 **p** 11. C Margate H Trin *Cant* 10-14; C Aylesham w Adisham and Nonington from 15. *The Rectory, Dorman Avenue North, Aylesham, Canterbury CT3 3BL* M: 07734-857820 T: (01304) 840471 E: revmarcterry@gmail.com

TERRY (née LEONARD), Mrs Nicola Susan. b 61. Keele Univ BA 85. Ridley Hall Cam 07. **d** 09 **p** 10. NSM Alverstoke *Portsm* 09-13; NSM Hook w Warsash from 13; Jt P-in-c from 14. *The Vicarage, 113 Church Road, Warsash, Southampton SO31 9GF* E: revnsterry@btinternet.com

TERRY, Stephen John. b 49. K Coll Lon BD 72 AKC 74. **d** 75 **p** 76. C Tokyngton St Mich *Lon* 75-78; C Hampstead St Steph w All Hallows 78-81; V Whetstone St Jo 81-89; TR Aldrington *Chich* 89-07; R from 07. *The Rectory, 77 New Church Road, Hove BN3 4BB* T: (01273) 737915 F: 206348 E: stephenterry@aldrington.wanadoo.co.uk

TESTA, Luigi Richard Frederick. b 30. EMMTC. **d** 85 **p** 86. NSM Castle Donington and Lockington cum Hemington *Leic* 85-95; PtO from 95. *50 Huntingdon Drive, Castle Donington, Derby DE74 2SR* T: (01332) 814671

TETLEY, Brian. b 38. St Jo Coll Dur BA 82 ACA 62 FCA 72. Cranmer Hall Dur 80. **d** 83 **p** 84. C Chipping Sodbury and Old Sodbury *Glouc* 83-86; Chapl and Succ Roch Cath 86-89; R Gravesend H Family w Ifield 89-93; Tutor Westcott Ho Cam 93-94 and 95-96; Tutor Ridley Hall and Prec Ely Cathl 95; C Duxford, Hinxton and Ickleton 97; PtO 98-99; NSM Worc Cathl 00-03; rtd 03; PtO *Worc* 03-08; *Ox* from 08. *23 Cripley Road, Oxford OX2 0AH* T: (01865) 250209 E: briantetley@btinternet.com

TETLEY, Miss Carol Ruth. b 61. Ches Coll of HE BA 84. NEOC 06. **d** 09 **p** 10. NSM Anlaby St Pet *York* 09-13; NSM Anlaby Common St Mark 11-13; NSM Hessle from 13; Chapl Hull and E Yorks Hosps NHS Trust from 13. *27 Cranberry Way, Hull HU4 7AQ* T: (01482) 351644 E: carol_tetley@lineone.net *or* caroltetley@crt61.karoo.co.uk

TETLEY, The Ven Joy Dawn. b 46. St Mary's Coll Dur BA 68 Leeds Univ CertEd 69 St Hugh's Coll Ox BA 75 MA 80 Dur Univ PhD 88. NW Ord Course 77. **dss** 77 **d** 87 **p** 94. Bentley *Sheff* 77-79; Buttershaw St Aid *Bradf* 79-80; Dur Cathl 80-83; Lect Trin Coll Bris 83-86; Chipping Sodbury and Old Sodbury *Glouc* 83-86; Dn Roch Cathl 87-89; Hon Can 90-93; Assoc Dir of Post Ord Tr 87-88; Dir Post Ord Tr 88-93; Hon Par Dn Gravesend H Family w Ifield 89-93; Prin EAMTC *Ely* 93-99; Adn Worc and Can Res Worc Cathl 99-08; rtd 08; PtO *Ox* from 08. *23 Cripley Road, Oxford OX2 0AH* T: (01865) 250209 E: briantetley@btinternet.com

TETLEY, Matthew David. b 61. Bucks Coll of Educn BSc 83. Sarum & Wells Th Coll BTh 89. **d** 87 **p** 88. C Kirkby *Liv* 87-90; C Hindley St Pet 90-93; TV Whorlton *Newc* 93-96; V Newbiggin Hall 96-01; P-in-c Longhorsley and Hebron 01-06; Chapl HM Pris Acklington 01-06 and from 08; Chapl HM Pris Frankland 06-08. *HM Prison Acklington, Morpeth NE65 9XF* T: (01670) 762300 E: matthew.tetley@hmps.gsi.gov.uk

TETLOW, John. b 46. St Steph Ho Ox 73. **d** 76 **p** 77. C Stanwell *Lon* 76-77; C Hanworth All SS 77-80; C Somers Town 80-83; TV Wickford and Runwell *Chelmsf* 83-90; P-in-c Walthamstow St Mich 90-96. *6A Bushwood, London E11 3AY* T: (020) 8989 9076 E: johntetlow@tiscali.co.uk

TETLOW, Richard Jeremy. b 42. Trin Coll Cam MA 66 Goldsmiths' Coll Lon CQSW 74. Qu Coll Birm 81. **d** 83 **p** 84. C Birm St Martin 83-85; C Birm St Martin w Bordesley St Andr 85-88; V Birm St Jo Ladywood 89-01; V Ladywood St Jo and St Pet 01-08; rtd 08; PtO *Birm* from 08. *26 Sovereign Way, Moseley, Birmingham B13 8AT* T: 0121-449 4892

TETZLAFF, Mrs Geraldine Vivienne. b 59. St Jo Coll Nottm 10. **d** 12 **p** 13. C Macclesfield Team *Ches* from 12. *7 Brocklehurst Way, Macclesfield SK10 2HY* T: (01625) 617680 E: gerri.tetzlaff@gmail.com

TETZLAFF, Silke. b 67. Friedrich Schiller Univ 87 K Coll Lon BA 97 AKC 97 Anglia Poly Univ MA 01. Westcott Ho Cam 99. **d** 01 **p** 02. C Leagrave *St Alb* 01-05; TV Baldock w Bygrave and Weston 05-11; C Sandon, Wallington and Rushden w Clothall 10-11; R Staplehurst *Cant* from 11. *The New Rectory, High Street, Staplehurst, Tonbridge TN12 0BJ* T: (01580) 891258 E: silke.tetzlaff@btinternet.com

TEVERSON, Ms Nicola Jane. b 65. SEITE. **d** 05 **p** 06. C Bromley St Mark *Roch* 05-09; PtO from 09. *The Farm House, Blackness Lane, Keston BR2 6HR* E: nicky.teverson@btinternet.com

TEWKESBURY, Suffragan Bishop of. *See* SNOW, The Rt Revd Martyn James

THACKER, Christine Mary. b 44. Simon Fraser Univ BC BA 90. Vancouver Sch of Th MDiv 93. **d** 92 **p** 93. R Kitimat Ch Ch Canada 93-00; C Boultham *Linc* 00-09; rtd 10; PtO *Nor* from 10. *c/o Cherrytree Chocolates, 9 High Street, Hunstanton PE36 5AB* E: christine.thacker@virginmedia.com

THACKER, Ian David. b 59. Univ of Wales (Lamp) MA 13. Oak Hill Th Coll BA 91. **d** 91 **p** 92. C Illogan *Truro* 91-94; C Eglwysilan *Llan* 94-96; TV Hornsey Rise Whitehall Park Team *Lon* 96-97; TV Upper Holloway 97-01; Chapl HM YOI Huntercombe and Finnamore 01-11; Chapl HM Pris Huntercombe from 11. *HM Prison Huntercombe, Huntercombe Place, Nuffield, Henley-on-Thames RG9 5SB* T: (01491) 632212 M: 07864-095435 E: ian.thacker@hmps.gsi.gov.uk

THACKER, Jonathan William. b 53. Lon Univ BA 74. Linc Th Coll 76. **d** 79 **p** 80. C Bromyard *Heref* 79-82; C Penkridge w Stretton *Lich* 82-87; V Brothertoft Gp *Linc* 87-96; RD Holland W 92-95; P-in-c Crosby 96-01; V from 01; RD Manlake from 11; RD Is of Axholme from 11; Chapl Scunthorpe and Goole Hosps NHS Trust 99-01. *St George's Vicarage, 87 Ferry Road, Scunthorpe DN15 8LY* T/F (01724) 843328 T: 843336 E: jo@han195.freeserve.co.uk

THACKRAY, John Adrian. b 55. Southn Univ BSc 76 ACIB 84. Coll of Resurr Mirfield 81. **d** 84 **p** 85. C Loughton St Jo *Chelmsf* 84-87; Chapl Bancroft's Sch Woodford Green 87-92; Sen Chapl K Sch Cant 92-01; Chapl Abp's Sch Cant 01-02; Hon Min Can Cant Cathl 93-15; Sen Chapl K Sch Roch 02-15; Hon PV Roch Cathl 02-15; P-in-c Ipswich St Mary at the Elms *St E* from 15. *The Vicarage, 68 Blackhorse Lane, Ipswich IP1 2EF* T: 07780-613754 E: thereverendfather@hotmail.com

THACKRAY, William Harry. b 44. Leeds Univ CertEd 66. Chich Th Coll 70. **d** 73 **p** 74. C Sheff St Cuth 73-76; C Stocksbridge 76-78; P-in-c Newark St Leon *S'well* 79-80; TV Newark w Hawton, Cotham and Shelton 80-82; V Choral S'well Minster 82-85; V Bawtry w Austerfield 85; P-in-c Misson 85; V Bawtry w Austerfield and Misson 86-93; RD Bawtry 90-93; P-in-c Balderton 93-03; P-in-c Coddington w Barnby in the Willows 98-03; V Biggleswade *St Alb* 03-09; RD 07-09; rtd 09; Hon C Lower Swale *Leeds* 09-14; PtO *York* from 14. *The Vicarage, 11 Meadow Drive, Scruton, Northallerton DL7 0QW* T: (01609) 748245 E: vicar@the-thackrays.eclipse.co.uk

THAKE (née SEARS), Ms Helen. b 50. Birm Coll of Educn CertEd 71. Qu Coll Birm 96. **d** 98 **p** 99. C Hadley *Lich* 98-01; C Cannock 01-06; Chapl HM Pris Swinfen Hall 06-07; Chapl HM Pris Foston Hall from 07. *HM Prison Foston Hall, Foston, Derby DE65 5EN* T: (01283) 584300 E: helen.thake@btinternet.com

THAKE, Preb Terence. b 41. ALCD 65. **d** 66 **p** 67. C Gt Faringdon w Lt Coxwell *Ox* 66-70; C Aldridge *Lich* 70-73; V Werrington 73-82; Chapl HM Det Cen Werrington Ho /3-82; TR Chell *Lich* 82-94; Chapl Westcliff Hosp 82-94; RD Stoke N *Lich* 91-94; V Colwich w Gt Haywood 94-00; P-in-c Colton 95-00; R Colton, Colwich and Gt Haywood 00-04; RD Rugeley 98-06; Preb Lich Cathl 94-10; Dioc Environmental Adv *Derby* from 12; rtd 04; PtO *Lich* from 15. *9 Rowan Court, Belper DE56 1SJ* E: tthake@tiscali.co.uk *or* terry.thake@btinternet.com

THATCHER, Ms Catherine Mary. b 72. Em Coll Cam MA 97 City Univ MSc 01 Cam Univ BTh 14 ACCA 98. Westcott Ho Cam 12. **d** 14 **p** 15. C Bradf Cathl from 14. *Bradford Cathedral, 1 Stott Hill, Bradford BD1 4EH* T: (01274) 777720

THATCHER, Stephen Bert. b 58. Greenwich Univ PGCE 03. St Jo Coll Nottm LTh 87 ALCD 87. **d** 87 **p** 88. C Bargoed and Deri w Brithdir *Llan* 87-89; C Llanishen and Lisvane 89-91; V Llanwnda, Goodwick w Manorowen and Llanstinan *St D* 91-95; P-in-c Coberley, Cowley, Colesbourne and Elkstone *Glouc* 95-96; Dioc Rural Adv 95-96; R New Radnor and Llanfihangel Nantmelan etc *S & B* 96-00; Dioc Tourism Officer 96-99; Dioc Chs and Tourism Rep 97-00; CF from 00. *c/o MOD Chaplains (Army)* F: 381824 T: (01264) 383430 E: stephen.thatcher2@btopenworld.com

THAWLEY, The Very Revd David Laurie. b 24. St Edm Hall Ox BA 47 MA 49. Cuddesdon Coll 49. **d** 51 **p** 52. C Bitterne Park *Win* 51-56; C-in-c Andover St Mich CD 56-60; Australia from

60; Can Res Brisbane 64-72; Dean Wangaratta 72-89; rtd 89. *Lavender Cottage, 2 Bond Street, North Caulfield VIC 3161, Australia* T: (0061) (3) 9571 0513 M: 407-811870
E: dthawley@bigpond.com

THAYER, Andrew Richard. b 68. Univ of Texas at Dallas BFA Univ of the S MDiv 04. **d** 04 **p** 05. C San Antonio St Mark USA 04-06; C Corpus Christi St Bart 06-09; NSM Chase *Ox* 10-14; R Montgomery Ascension USA from 14. *315 Clanton Avenue, Montgomery AL 36104, USA* T: (001) (334) 263 5529 F: 263 6411 E: andythay@gmail.com

THAYER, Michael David. b 52. Sarum & Wells Th Coll 77. **d** 80 **p** 81. C Minehead *B & W* 80-85; Chapl RN 85-89; TV Lowestoft and Kirkley *Nor* 89-92; Chapl St Helena Hospice Colchester 92-97; Chapl HM Pris Acklington 99-01; Chapl HM Pris Erlestoke 01-03; R S Tawton and Belstone *Ex* 03-07; P-in-c Highweek from 07. *The Rectory, 15 Stoneleigh Close, Newton Abbot TQ12 1QZ* T: (01626) 201436
E: rmhthayer@yahoo.co.uk

THEAKER, David Michael. b 41. **d** 68 **p** 69. C Folkingham w Laughton *Linc* 68-71; C New Cleethorpes 71-74; P-in-c Gt Grimsby St Andr and St Luke 74-77; P-in-c Thurlby 77-79; PtO *Ely* from 00. *11 Willow Way, Hauxton, Cambridge CB22 5JB* T: (01223) 873132 E: the-theakers@issue-forth.com

THEAKER, John Henry. b 42. MBE 01. WEMTC 05. **d** 08 **p** 09. NSM Leominster *Heref* 08-12; PtO from 12. *Monkland House, Monkland, Leominster HR6 9DE* T: (01568) 720472 M: 07796-595664 E: theaker958@btinternet.com

THEAKSTON, Canon Sally Margaret. b 62. UEA BSc 84 K Coll Lon MA 94. Ripon Coll Cuddesdon BA 89. **d** 89 **p** 94. Par Dn Hackney *Lon* 89-93; Par Dn Putney St Mary *S'wark* 93-94; C 94-96; Chapl RN 96-02; TR Gaywood *Nor* 02-09; TR Dereham and Distr from 09; RD Dereham in Mitford 10-13; P-in-c Shipdham w Bradenham from 14; Hon Can Nor Cathl from 10. *The Rectory, 1 Vicarage Meadows, Dereham NR19 1TW* T: (01362) 693680 M: 07904-070654 E: stheakston@aol.com

THELWALL, The Ven John Berry. b 49. Univ of Wales (Ban) BD 72. Qu Coll Birm 73. **d** 73 **p** 74. C Minera *St As* 73-80; Dioc Youth Chapl 78-86; V Gwernaffield and Llanferres 80-93; Chapl Clwyd Fire Service 88-94; RD Mold *St As* 91-95; TR Hawarden 93-02; Can Cursal St As Cathl 95-02; Prec 98-02; Adn Montgomery *St As* 02-12; V Berriew 03-12; rtd 12; PtO *St As* from 13. *O'r Diwedd, 2 Bryn Road, Bryn-y-Baal, Mold CH7 6RY*

THEOBALD, Graham Fitzroy. b 43. ALCD 67. **d** 67 **p** 68. C Crookham *Guildf* 67-71; C York Town St Mich 71-74; V Wrecclesham 74-83; Chapl Green Lane Hosp 74-81; R Frimley *Guildf* 83-85; Chapl Frimley Park Hosp 83-85; PtO *Ox* 90-92; C Easthampstead 92-97; Chapl E Berks NHS Trust 92-03; rtd 03; PtO *Ox* 03-12; Hon C Ruscombe and Twyford w Hurst from 12. *50 Viking, Bracknell RG12 8UL* T: (01344) 428525 M: 07721-408740
E: witsend50@waitrose.com

THEOBALD, John Walter. b 43. St Aid Birkenhead 62. **d** 65 **p** 66. C Hindley All SS *Liv* 65-68; C Beverley Minster *York* 68-71; R Loftus 71-86; P-in-c Carlin How w Skinningrove 73-86; Dep Chapl HM Pris Leeds 86-89; Chapl HM Pris Rudgate 89-93; Thorp Arch 89-93; Leeds 93-97; V Leeds St Cypr Harehills *Ripon* 97-01; rtd 01; P-in-c Swillington *Ripon* 01-05; PtO *York* from 14. *8 Inverness Road, Garforth, Leeds LS25 2LS* T: 0113-286 6706

THEOBALD, Susan Ann. b 61. La Sainte Union Coll BEd 83. STETS 07. **d** 10 **p** 11. C Southsea St Jude *Portsm* 10-14; P-in-c Ryde St Jo Oakfield and H Trin from 14. *The New Rectory, Pitts Lane, Ryde PO33 3SU* E: theobald.sue.79@gmail.com

THEODOSIUS, James William Fletcher. b 73. Univ of Wales (Cardiff) BA 94 Selw Coll Cam BA 04 MA 08 Sussex Univ DPhil 09 Cant Ch Ch Univ Coll PGCE 96. Westcott Ho Cam 02. **d** 05 **p** 06. C Chich St Paul and Westhampnett 05-09; Dir Reader Tr SWMTC 09-15; V Kettlewell w Conistone, Hubberholme etc *Bradf* from 15. *The Vicarage, Westgate, Kettlewell, Skipton BD23 5QU*
E: upperwharfedale@westyorkshiredales.anglican.org

THETFORD, Suffragan Bishop of. *See* WINTON, The Rt Revd Alan Peter

THEWLIS, Andrew James. b 64. Man Univ BSc 86. Cranmer Hall Dur 87. **d** 90 **p** 91. C Walshaw Ch Ch *Man* 90-95; P-in-c Jersey St Jo *Win* 95-98; R from 98. *The Rectory, La rue des Landes, St John, Jersey JE3 4AF* T: (01534) 861677 M: 07797-723828 E: athewlis@jerseymail.co.uk

THEWLIS, Brian Jacob. b 24. Melbourne Univ BA 49. Coll of Resurr Mirfield 52. **d** 53 **p** 54. C Wednesbury St Jas *Lich* 53-57; Chapl K Coll Auckland New Zealand 57-61; C Sidley *Chich* 59-67; I Reservoir St Geo Australia 61-68; I Malvern St Paul 68-82; I Beaumaris St Mich 82-87; I Frankston St Paul 87-94; rtd 94. *41 Sixth Street, Parkdale Vic 3194, Australia* T: (0061) (3) 9587 3095

THEWLIS, Canon John Charles. b 49. Van Mildert Coll Dur BA 70 PhD 75. NOC 78. **d** 81 **p** 82. NSM Hull St Mary Sculcoates *York* 81-83; C Spring Park *Cant* 83-84; C Spring Park All SS *S'wark* 85-86; V Eltham Park St Luke 86-01; R Carshalton from 01; Hon Can S'wark Cathl from 14. *The Rectory, 2 Talbot Road, Carshalton SM5 3BS* T: (020) 8647 2366
E: rector@jctclerk.demon.co.uk

THEWSEY, Robert Sydney. b 65. Ripon Coll Cuddesdon 99. **d** 01 **p** 02. C Chorlton-cum-Hardy St Clem *Man* 01-04; P-in-c Stretford All SS 04-08; P-in-c Boscastle w Davidstow *Truro* 08-15; R Boscastle and Tintagel Gp from 15; RD Stratton from 11. *The Rectory, Forrabury, Boscastle PL35 0DJ* T: (01840) 250359 E: robert.thewsey@btinternet.com

THICKE, James Balliston. b 43. Sarum & Wells Th Coll 74. **d** 77 **p** 78. C Wareham *Sarum* 77-80; TV 80-83; Dioc Youth Adv *Dur* 83-87; C Portishead *B & W* 87-90; V Westfield 90-08; RD Midsomer Norton 98-04; Chapl Norton Radstock Coll of FE 00-08; rtd 08; PtO *B & W* from 09. *11 Welton Grove, Midsomer Norton, Radstock BA3 2TS* T: (01761) 411905
M: 07971-943654 E: jamesballiston@hotmail.com

✠**THIRD, The Rt Revd Richard Henry McPhail.** b 27. Em Coll Cam BA 50 MA 55 Kent Univ Hon DCL 90. Linc Th Coll 50. **d** 52 **p** 53 **c** 76. C Mottingham St Andr w St Alban *S'wark* 52-55; C Sanderstead All SS 55-59; V Sheerness H Trin w St Paul *Cant* 59-67; V Orpington All SS *Roch* 67-76; RD Orpington 73-76; Hon Can Roch Cathl 74-76; Suff Bp Maidstone *Cant* 76-80; Suff Bp Dover 80-92; rtd 92; Hon Asst Bp B & W from 92. *c/o Ms H Third, 110 Gilmore Place, Edinburgh EH3 9PL*

THIRLWELL, Miss Margaret. b 36. Bris Univ BA 59 St Aid Coll Dur DipEd 61. **d** 03 **p** 04. OLM Binfield *Ox* 03-09; PtO from 09. *70 Red Rose, Binfield, Bracknell RG42 5LD* T: (01344) 423920 E: margaret@mthirlwell.fsnet.co.uk

THIRTLE, Ms Lucy Rachel. b 62. Ex Univ BA 85. Cranmer Hall Dur 97. **d** 99 **p** 00. C Basingstoke *Win* 99-04; P-in-c Kingsclere 04-06; P-in-c Ashford Hill w Headley 04; V Kingsclere and Ashford Hill w Headley 06-15; Hon C Ray Valley *Ox* from 15. *3 The Rise, Islip, Kidlington OX5 2TG* M: 07769-854387
E: lucythirtle1@hotmail.co.uk

THISELTON, Prof Anthony Charles. b 37. Lon Univ BD 59 K Coll Lon MTh 64 Sheff Univ PhD 77 Dur Univ DD 93 Lambeth DD 02 FBA 10 FKC 10. Oak Hill Th Coll 58. **d** 60 **p** 61. C Sydenham H Trin *S'wark* 60-63; Tutor Tyndale Hall Bris 63-67; Sen Tutor 67-70; Lect Bibl Studies Sheff Univ 70-79; Sen Lect 79-85; Prof Calvin Coll Grand Rapids USA 82-83; Special Lect Th Nottm Univ 86-88; Prin St Jo Coll Nottm 86-88; Prin St Jo Coll w Cranmer Hall Dur 88-92; Prof Chr Th Nottm Univ from 92; Can Th Leic Cathl from 94; Can Th S'well Minster from 00. *Department of Theology, Nottingham University, University Park, Nottingham NG7 2RD* T: 0115-951 5852 F: 951 5887 E: thiselton@ntlworld.com

THISTLETHWAITE, Canon Nicholas John. b 51. Selw Coll Cam BA 73 MA 77 PhD 80. Ripon Coll Cuddesdon BA 78 MA 83. **d** 79 **p** 80. C Newc St Gabr 79-82; Chapl G&C Coll Cam 82-90; LtO *Ely* 82-90; V Trumpington 90-99; Can Res and Prec Guildf Cathl from 99; Sub-Dean from 06. *3 Cathedral Close, Guildford GU2 7TL* T/F (01483) 569682 T: 547865
E: precentor@guildford-cathedral.org

THISTLEWOOD, Michael John. b 31. Ch Coll Cam BA 53 MA 57. Linc Th Coll 54. **d** 56 **p** 57. C N Hull St Mich *York* 56-59; C Scarborough St Mary 59-61; V Kingston upon Hull St Jude w St Steph 61-67; V Newland St Aug 67-72; Asst Master Bemrose Sch Derby 72-80; V Derby St Andr w St Osmund 80-82; LtO *Ox* 84-95; rtd 88; PtO *Carl* 88-98; *Derby* 98-05; *Carl* 05-08 and from 09. *44 Blackhall Croft, Blackhall Road, Kendal LA9 4UU*

THODAY, Margaret Frances. b 38. **d** 03 **p** 04. OLM Roughton and Felbrigg, Metton, Sustead etc *Nor* 03-08; PtO from 08. *Flat 3, 4 Norwich Road, Cromer NR27 0AX* T: (01263) 510945

THODY, Charles Michael Jackson. b 62. Linc Th Coll BTh 94. **d** 94 **p** 95. C Immingham *Linc* 94-97; P-in-c Leasingham and Cranwell 97-01; P-in-c Bishop Norton, Waddingham and Snitterby 01-03; Chapl Doncaster and S Humber Healthcare NHS Trust 03-03; Chapl Notts Healthcare NHS Trust 03-09; Chapl Rotherham, Doncaster and S Humber NHS Trust 09-11; Sen Chapl N Lincs and Goole Hosps NHS Trust from 12. *Chaplaincy, Scunthorpe General Hospital, Cliff Gardens, Scunthorpe DN15 7BH* T: (01724) 282282

THOM, Alastair George. b 60. G&C Coll Cam BA 81 MA 84 ACA 86. Ridley Hall Cam 88. **d** 91 **p** 92. C Lindfield *Chich* 91-94; C Finchley St Paul and St Luke *Lon* 94-98; P-in-c W Kilburn Em Harrow Road 98-13; V W Kilburn St Luke and Harrow Road Em from 13; AD Westmr Paddington 06-11. *The Vicarage, 19 Macroom Road, London W9 3HY* T: (020) 8962 0294 E: alastairthom@yahoo.co.uk

THOM, Christopher Henry. b 43. **d** 03 **p** 04. NSM Loose *Cant* from 03. *Wierton Grange, Back Lane, Boughton Monchelsea, Maidstone ME17 4JR* T: (01622) 744833
E: chthom@ukonline.co.uk

THOM, James. b 31. St Chad's Coll Dur BA 53. **d** 57 **p** 58. C Middlesbrough St Thos *York* 57-60; C Hornsea and Goxhill 60-62; C S Bank 62-63; V Copmanthorpe 63-75; V Coxwold 75-77; V Coxwold and Husthwaite 77-87; RD Easingwold 77-82; Spiritual Dir York Angl Cursillo 86-93; P-in-c Topcliffe 87-93; rtd 93; PtO *York* from 93; *Leeds* from 93. *34 Hell Wath Grove, Ripon HG4 2JT* T: (01765) 605083

THOMAS, Adrian Leighton. b 37. Univ of Wales (Lamp) BA 62 Univ of Wales (Cardiff) PGCE 73. St D Coll Lamp. **d** 63 **p** 64. C Port Talbot St Theodore *Llan* 63-70; V Troedrhiwgarth 70-73; C Sandhurst *Ox* 73-77; V Streatley 77-84; P-in-c Moulsford 81-84; V Streatley w Moulsford 84-90; P-in-c Sutton Courtenay w Appleford 90-00; V 00-02; AD Abingdon 96-02; rtd 02; P-in-c Lugano *Eur* 02-06. *13 The Birches, Goring, Reading RG8 9BW* T: (01491) 872696
E: adrianleighton.thomas@gmail.com

THOMAS, Alan. *See* THOMAS, Thomas Alan

THOMAS, Aled Huw. b 59. Univ of Wales (Abth) BD 81. St Mich Coll Llan 84. **d** 85 **p** 86. C Llandeilo Fawr and Taliaris *St D* 85-86; P-in-c Llangrannog and Llandysiliogogo 86-88; Chapl RAF 88-92; R Ystradgynlais *S & B* 92-94; CF 94-08; Sen CF 08-10; V St Dogmael's w Moylgrove and Monington w Meline *St D* 10-11; V St Dogmael's and Monington and Nevern etc 11-12; rtd 12. *40 Lakeside Avenue, Llandrindod Wells LD1 5NT* T: (01597) 822594 E: padrealed@googlemail.com

THOMAS, The Ven Alfred James Randolph. b 48. St D Coll Lamp. **d** 71 **p** 72. C Cydweli and Llandyfaelog *St D* 71-74; C Carmarthen St Dav 74-76; TV Aberystwyth 76-81; V Betws w Ammanford 81-90; RD Dyffryn Aman 90-93; V Carmarthen St Pet and Chapl Carmarthenshire NHS Trust 93-02; Can St D Cathl 96-02; V Bronllys w Llanfilo *S & B* 02-06; P-in-c Llanfrynach and Cantref w Llanhamlach 06-13; Adn Brecon 03-13; rtd 13; PtO *S & B* from 13; *St D* from 13. *Llwyncelyn, 10 Clos y Wennol, Porthyrhyd, Carmarthen SA32 8BD* T: (01267) 275871

THOMAS, Andrew Herbert Redding. b 41. Lon Coll of Div 66. **d** 69 **p** 70. C Cromer *Nor* 69-72; Holiday Chapl 72-76; R Grimston w Congham *Nor* 76-83; R Roydon All SS 76-83; C-in-c Ewell St Paul Howell Hill CD *Guildf* 83-89; V Howell Hill 89-95; RD Epsom 93-95; TR Beccles St Mich *St E* 95-04; P-in-c Worlingham w Barnby and N Cove 98-01; rtd 04; PtO *St E* from 04; *Nor* from 04. *9A Corner Street, Cromer NR27 9HW* T: (01263) 515091 E: ahrthomas@waitrose.com

THOMAS, Andrew John. b 62. Univ of Wales (Abth) BSc 84 ACA 87. ERMC 04. **d** 07 **p** 08. NSM Stevenage H Trin *St Alb* from 07; NSM Officer Hertford Adnry from 14. *1 Ash Drive, St Ippolyts, Hitchin SG4 7SJ* T: (01462) 421647
E: ajt250762@aol.com

THOMAS, Andrew Nigel. b 75. Ox Brookes Univ BA 13. Westcott Ho Cam 08. **d** 10 **p** 11. C The Cookhams *Ox* 10-13; Chapl RN 13-14; R Dulverton w Brushford, Brompton Regis etc *B & W* from 14. *The Vicarage, High Street, Dulverton TA22 9DW* T: (01398) 323018 E: and73w@me.com

THOMAS, Andrew Robert. b 80. G&C Coll Cam BA 03. Oak Hill Th Coll BA 09. **d** 09 **p** 10. C Angmering *Chich* 09-12; C Cambridge St Matt *Ely* from 12. *112 Sturton Street, Cambridge CB1 2QF* T: (01223) 301048 M: 07786-376615
E: andythomas196@yahoo.co.uk

THOMAS, Anne Valerie. *See* NOBLE, Anne Valerie

THOMAS, Canon Barry Wilfred. b 41. Univ of Wales (Cardiff) BD 75. St Mich Coll Llan 72. **d** 75 **p** 76. C Porthmadog *Ban* 75-78; V Llanegryn and Llanfihangel-y-Pennant etc 78-82; TR Llanbeblig w Caernarfon and Betws Garmon etc 82-94; Sec Dioc Coun for Miss and Unity 81-94; Can Ban Cathl 89-94; Chapl Monte Carlo *Eur* 95-00; V Llanfihangel Ystrad and Cilcennin w Trefilan etc *St D* 00-06; rtd 06. *46 Munich House, Heol Glan Rheidol, Cardiff CF10 5NS* T: (01765) 600519 M: 07763-477230

THOMAS, Bernard. *See* THOMAS, Edward Bernard Meredith

THOMAS, Bernard. *See* THOMAS, Elwyn Bernard

THOMAS, Brian. *See* THOMAS, David Brian

THOMAS, Bryan. b 36. Univ of Wales (Abth) BA 59. St Deiniol's Hawarden 68. **d** 70 **p** 71. C Llangynwyd w Maesteg *Llan* 70-72; V Cwmllynfell *St D* 72-76; V Gors-las 76-82; R Yarnbury *Sarum* 82-97; TR Wylye and Till Valley 97-02; RD Wylye and Wilton 94-98; rtd 02; PtO *Sarum* from 03; *B & W* from 05. *11 Ebble Crescent, Warminster BA12 9PF* T: (01985) 300519 M: 07763-477230

THOMAS, The Ven Charles Edward (Ted). b 27. Univ of Wales (Lamp) BA 51. Coll of Resurr Mirfield 51. **d** 53 **p** 54. C Ilminster w Whitelackington *B & W* 53-56; Chapl St Mich Coll Tenbury 56-57; C St Alb St Steph *St Alb* 57-58; V Boreham Wood St Mich 58-66; R Monksilver w Brompton Ralph and Nettlecombe *B & W* 66-74; P-in-c Nettlecombe 68-69; R S Petherton w The Seavingtons 74-83; RD Crewkerne 77-83; Adn Wells, Can Res and Preb Wells Cathl 83-93; rtd 93; PtO *St D* from 93. *Geryfelin, Pentre, Tregaron SY25 6JG* T: (01974) 298102

THOMAS, Charles Leslie. b 58. Qu Coll Birm 09. **d** 11 **p** 12. C Sevenhampton w Charlton Abbots, Hawling etc *Glouc* 11-15; V Worc St Wulstan from 15. *The Vicarage, Cranham Drive, Worcester WR4 9PA* T: (01905) 754385
E: coln.river.curate@gmail.com

THOMAS, Charles Moray Stewart Reid. b 53. BNC Ox BA 74 MA 79. Wycliffe Hall Ox 75. **d** 78 **p** 79. C Bradf Cathl 78-81; C Barnsbury St Andr and H Trin w All SS *Lon* 81-90; TV Barnsbury 90-99; Chapl Lon Goodenough Trust 99-08; V Grayshott *Guildf* from 08. *The Vicarage, 10 Vicarage Gardens, Grayshott, Hindhead GU26 6NH* T: (01428) 606703
E: moray@thethomases.org.uk

THOMAS, Chloe Ann Mary. b 60. GMusRNCM 83. Ripon Coll Cuddesdon 07. **d** 09 **p** 10. C Knighton St Mary Magd *Leic* 09-13; P-in-c Brixworth w Holcot *Pet* from 13. *The Vicarage, Station Road, Brixworth, Northampton NN6 9DF* T: (01604) 882014 M: 07801-886736 E: chloe.thomas5@btinternet.com

THOMAS, Clive Alexander. b 49. Open Univ BA 77 St Luke's Coll Ex CertEd 71. STETS 94. **d** 97 **p** 99. NSM Southwick St Mich *Chich* 97-01; C Bridport *Sarum* 01-04; TV Shaston 04-09; TR Shaftesbury 09-14; rtd 14. *2 Marlborough Park, Ilfracombe EX34 8JB* T: (01271) 600089
E: rev.clive@btinternet.com

✠**THOMAS, The Rt Revd David.** b 42. Keble Coll Ox BA 64 MA 66 MA 67. St Steph Ho Ox 64. **d** 67 **p** 68 **c** 96. C Hawarden *St As* 67-69; Tutor St Mich Coll Llan 69-70; Chapl 70-75; Sec Ch in Wales Liturg Commn 70-75; Vice-Prin St Steph Ho Ox 75-79; Prin 82-87; V Chepstow *Mon* 79-82; LtO 82-87; V Newton St Pet *S & B* 87-96; Can Brecon Cathl 94-96; RD Clyne 96; Asst Bp to Abp Wales 96-08; rtd 08. *65 Westland Avenue, West Cross, Swansea SA3 5AH*

THOMAS, David. b 49. **d** 08 **p** 09. NSM Barnes *S'wark* 08-12; PtO 12-14; Asst Chapl Richmond Charities' Almshouses from 14. *8 Church Estate Almshouses, Richmond TW9 1UX* T: (020) 8948 4188 E: david@dthomas91.fsnet.co.uk

THOMAS, David Brian. b 45. MIEEE. St D Dioc Tr Course 82. **d** 85 **p** 86. NSM Llandysul *St D* 85-87; NSM Lampeter Pont Steffan w Silian 88-92; NSM Lampeter and Ultra-Aeron 92-96; P-in-c Llanfihangel Genau'r-glyn and Llangorwen 96-97; V 97-10; AD Llanbadarn Fawr 00-10; rtd 10. *5 Willowdene, St Martin's Road, Gobowen, Oswestry SY10 7GA* T: (01691) 662629 E: dbrianthomas@yahoo.com

THOMAS, David Edward. b 60. Univ of Wales (Lamp) BA 83. St Mich Coll Llan 85. **d** 86 **p** 87. C Killay *S & B* 86-89; P-in-c Newbridge-on-Wye and Llanfihangel Brynpabuan 89-90; V 90-91; V Brecon St David w Llanspyddid and Llanilltyd 91-09; V Glasbury and Llowes w Clyro and Betws from 09. *The Vicarage, 4 The Birches, Glasbury, Hereford HR3 5NW* T: (01497) 847156 E: thomas3693@btinternet.com

THOMAS, David Geoffrey. b 37. Univ of Wales (Cardiff) BA 58. Launde Abbey 70 Qu Coll Birm 71. **d** 71 **p** 72. Hon C Fenny Drayton *Leic* 71-75; Chapl Community of the H Family Baldslow *Chich* 75-77; PtO *Chich* 77-79; P-in-c Mill End and Heronsgate w W Hyde *St Alb* 79-81; Sen Lect Watford Coll 82-91; R Walgrave w Hannington and Wold and Scaldwell *Pet* 91-01; rtd 01; PtO *Pet* 01-06. *1 Cypress Close, Desborough, Kettering NN14 2XU* T/F: (01536) 763749

THOMAS, The Very Revd David Glynne. b 41. Dur Univ BSc 63. Westcott Ho Cam 64. **d** 67 **p** 68. C St John's Wood *Lon* 67-70; Min Can St Alb *St Alb* 70-72; Chapl Wadh Coll Ox 72-75; C Ox St Mary V w St Cross and St Pet 72-75; Bp's Dom Chapl 75-78; P-in-c Burnham 78-82; TR Burnham w Dropmore, Hitcham and Taplow 82-83; R Coolangatta Australia 83-86; R Toowoomba 86-87; Can Res Worc Cathl 87-99; Dean Brisbane 99-03; Chapl to Abp Brisbane 03-06; rtd 06. *173 Edgewater Village, 171 David Low Way, Bli Bli QLD 4560, Australia* T: (0061) (7) 5450 8224 E: davidthomas@westnet.com.au

THOMAS, David Godfrey. b 50. St Chad's Coll Dur BA 71 Fitzw Coll Cam BA 74 MA 78. Westcott Ho Cam 72. **d** 75 **p** 76. C Kirkby *Liv* 75-78; TV Cov E 78-88; TR Canvey Is *Chelmsf* 88-92; R Wivenhoe 92-09; R Shenfield from 09. *The Rectory, 41 Worrin Road, Shenfield, Brentwood CM15 8DH* T: (01277) 220360 E: davidthomas50@tiscali.co.uk

THOMAS, David John. b 34. Univ of Wales (Swansea) St D Coll Lamp. St D Dioc Tr Course 85. **d** 88 **p** 89. NSM Cwmaman *St D* 88-96; Public Preacher 96-11; PtO from 11. *9 New School Road, Garnant, Ammanford SA18 1LL* T: (01269) 823936

THOMAS, Prof David Richard. b 48. BNC Ox BA 71 MA 74 Fitzw Coll Cam BA 75 MA 80 Lanc Univ PhD 83. Ridley Hall Cam 73 Qu Coll Birm 79. **d** 80 **p** 81. C Anfield St Columba *Liv*

80-83; C Liv Our Lady and St Nic w St Anne 83-85; Chapl CCC Cam 85-90; V Witton *Blackb* 90-93; Bp's Adv on Inter-Faith Relns 90-93; Lect Cen for Study of Islam and Chr-Muslim Relns Selly Oak 93-04; Sen Lect Birm Univ 99-04; Reader 04-07; Prof Christianity and Islam from 07; PtO *Derby* 05-11; LtO from 11; Hon Can Th Derby Cathl from 11. *Department of Theology and Religion, University of Birmingham, Edgbaston, Birmingham B15 2TT* T: 0121-415 8373
E: d.r.thomas.1@bham.ac.uk

THOMAS, David Ronald Holt. b 28. Lich Th Coll 55. **d** 58 **p** 59. C Uttoxeter w Bramshall *Lich* 58-61; C Hednesford 61-66; R Armitage from 66; RD Rugeley 88-94. *The Rectory, Hood Lane, Armitage, Rugeley WS15 4AG* T: (01543) 490278
E: davidthomas015@btinternet.com

THOMAS, Canon David Thomas. b 44. St Cath Coll Cam BA 66 MA 70. Cranmer Hall Dur. **d** 71 **p** 72. C Chorlton-cum-Hardy St Clem *Man* 71-74; Chapl Salford Tech Coll 74-79; P-in-c Pendleton St Thos *Man* 75-77; V 77-80; TR Gleadless *Sheff* 80-90; RD Attercliffe 86-90; V Benchill *Man* 90-99; TV Wythenshawe 99-00; AD Withington 99-00; P-in-c Stretford St Matt 00-09; Hon Can Man Cathl 09; rtd 09; PtO *Man* from 09; *Carl* from 10. *31 Sun Street, Ulverston LA12 7BX* T: (01229) 585900 E: tom-hil@talk21.com

THOMAS, Dorothy Judith. b 47. Univ of Wales (Cardiff) BA 68. Princeton Th Sem MDiv 94 MTh 96 San Francisco Th Sem DMin 01. **d** 03 **p** 04. NSM Wargrave w Knowl Hill *Ox* 03-07; PtO from 09. *7 Cranbourne Hall, Drift Road, Winkfield, Windsor SL4 4FG* T: (01344) 891699 E: djudthomas@hotmail.com

THOMAS (née THOMSON), Mrs Dorothy Lucille. b 39. Univ of Wales (Lamp). **d** 00 **p** 10. OLM Pontnewydd *Mon* from 00. *Raldoro, Mount Pleasant Road, Pontnewydd, Cwmbran NP44 1BD* T: (01633) 771353

THOMAS, Edward. *See* THOMAS, Charles Edward

THOMAS, Edward Bernard Meredith. b 21. Leeds Univ BA 44 Univ of Qld BEd 68 BD 72. Coll of Resurr Mirfield 47. **d** 49 **p** 50. C St Mary-at-Lambeth *S'wark* 49-54; C Portsea N End St Mark *Portsm* 54-56; V Portsea All SS 56-64; R Woolloongabba Australia 64-72; PtO Brisbane 72-78; Miss Chapl 78-92; rtd 92. *33 Highfield Street, Durack QLD 4077, Australia* T: (0061) (7) 3372 3517 M: 41-622 7121
E: bernard_thomas@iinet.net.au

THOMAS, Edward Walter Dennis. b 32. St Mich Coll Llan 61. **d** 63 **p** 64. C Loughor *S & B* 63-69; V Ystradfellte 69-74; V Dukinfield St Mark and St Luke *Ches* 74-04; Chapl Gtr Man Police from 77; OCM 88-00; rtd 04; PtO *Ches* from 04; *Man* from 04. *16 Boyd's Walk, Dukinfield SK16 4TW* T: 0161-330 1324 E: revewdt@aol.com

THOMAS, Canon Eirwyn Wheldon. b 35. St Mich Coll Llan 58. **d** 61 **p** 62. C Glanadda *Ban* 61-67; R Llantrisant and Llandeusant 67-75; V Nefyn w Tudweiliog w Llandudwen w Edern 75-01; Can Ban Cathl 97-01; rtd 01; PtO *St As* from 09. *11 Wenfro Road, Abergele LL22 7LE* T: (01745) 823587

THOMAS (née REEVES), Mrs Elizabeth Anne. b 65. Sheff Univ BA 67 PGCE 75. SWMTC 87. **d** 90 **p** 94. Par Dn Stoke Damerel *Ex* 90-93; Dioc Children's Adv *Bradf* 93-01; Par Dn Baildon 93-94; C 94-96; P-in-c Denholme Gate 96-01; P-in-c Tuxford w Weston and Markham Clinton *S'well* 01-08; rtd 08. *The Lyrics, 113 The Oval, Retford DN22 7SD* T: (01777) 700047
E: l.a.thomas@btinternet.com

THOMAS, The Ven Elwyn Bernard. b 45. Univ of Wales (Swansea) BSc 68. St Mich Coll Llan BD 71. **d** 71 **p** 72. C Aberdare St Fagan *Llan* 71-74; C Merthyr Dyfan 74-76; R Dowlais 76-86; V Llangynwyd w Maesteg 86-00; Can Llan Cathl 98-00; Adn St As 00-11; R Llandyrnog and Llangwyfan 00-11; P-in-c 11-14; rtd 11. *11 Cae Glas, Trefnant, Denbigh LL16 5UB* T: (01745) 731732 E: bernardthomas@aol.com

THOMAS, Ernest Keith. b 49. St Mich Coll Llan 73. **d** 76 **p** 77. C Swansea St Gabr *S & B* 76-79; C Killay 79-81; Prec Kimberley Cathl S Africa 81-84; R Kimberley St Aug 84-92; R Kimberley St Alb 89-92; Can Kimberley Cathl 86-92; V Aberdare *Llan* 93-96; Sub-Dean Bloemfontein Cathl S Africa 96-10; R Welkom from 10. *PO Box 231, Welkom, 9460 South Africa* T: (0027) (57) 352 3497 *or* 352 5664 F: 352 2272 M: 83-709 0976 E: stmatt@global.co.za

THOMAS, Mrs Gabrielle Rachael. b 74. Bris Univ BA 95 Ches Univ MTh 13. St Jo Coll Nottm 11. **d** 15. C Teddington St Mary w St Alb *Lon* from 15. M: 07710-479047
E: inthedivine@gmail.com

THOMAS, Gareth David. b 75. Sheff Univ BA 96 Ches Univ PGCE 03. All SS Cen for Miss & Min 10. **d** 13 **p** 14. C Ches St Paul from 13; C Huntington from 13; Chapl Ches Univ from 14. *6 Jesmond Road, Chester CH1 4EQ* T: (01244) 374697
E: g-thomas@hotmail.co.uk

THOMAS, Gareth Mark. b 72. Cranmer Hall Dur. **d** 10 **p** 11. C Atherton and Hindsford w Howe Bridge *Man* 10-13; TV Daisy Hill, Westhoughton and Wingates from 13. *30 Lower Leigh Road, Westhoughton, Bolton BL5 2EH* T: (01942) 819569 M: 07814-166016 E: garethmthomas@hotmail.co.uk

THOMAS, Geoffrey. *See* THOMAS, David Geoffrey

THOMAS, Geoffrey Brynmor. b 34. K Coll Lon BA 56 AKC 56. Ridley Hall Cam 58. **d** 60 **p** 61. C Harlow New Town w Lt Parndon *Chelmsf* 60-65; V Leyton All SS 65-74; V Haley Hill *Wakef* 74-82; R The Winterbournes and Compton Valence *Sarum* 82-89; TV Cheltenham St Mark *Glouc* 89-92; P-in-c Dowdeswell and Andoversford w the Shiptons etc 92-95; RD Northleach 92-95; rtd 95; PtO *B & W* from 96. *48 Riverside Walk, Midsomer Norton, Bath BA3 2PD* T: (01761) 414146
E: gbt34@btinternet.com

THOMAS, Canon Geoffrey Heale. b 29. St Mich Coll Llan 58. **d** 60 **p** 61. C Llansamlet *S & B* 60-63; Nigeria 63-67; V Swansea St Nic *S & B* 67-80; CF (TA) 72; V Oystermouth *S & B* 80-98; Hon Can Brecon Cathl 92-96; Can Brecon Cathl 97-98; rtd 98. *19 Ffordd Dryden, Killay, Swansea SA2 7PA* T: (01792) 206308

THOMAS, George. b 46. Leeds Univ BEd 69. Cranmer Hall Dur 75. **d** 78 **p** 79. C Highfield *Liv* 78-83; V Chorley St Jas *Blackb* 83-02; P-in-c Blackb St Gabr 02-08; rtd 08; PtO *Blackb* from 08. *80 Severn Drive, Walton-le-Dale, Preston PR5 4TE* T: (01772) 330152

THOMAS, Glyn. b 36. Lon Univ BPharm 61. St Deiniol's Hawarden 80. **d** 82 **p** 83. C Rhyl w St Ann *St As* 83-85; R Llanycil w Bala and Frongoch and Llangower etc 85-03; RD Penllyn 96-03; rtd 03; PtO *St As* from 09. *Blaen-y-Coed, 7 Lon Helyg, Abergele LL22 7JQ* T: (01745) 827725

THOMAS, Gordon Herbert. b 43. Guildf Dioc Min Course 00. **d** 00 **p** 01. OLM Cove St Jo *Guildf* 00-13; rtd 13. *13 Tay Close, Farnborough GU14 9NB* T: (01252) 512347
E: gh.thomas27@btinternet.com

THOMAS, Greville Stephen. b 64. Qu Coll Birm 94. **d** 96 **p** 97. C Hillingdon All SS *Lon* 96-99; C Acton Green 99-04; P-in-c Northolt St Mary 04-06; R 06-14; V Sudbury St Andr from 14. *St Andrew's Vicarage, 956 Harrow Road, Wembley HA0 2QA* T: (020) 8904 4016 E: greville.thomas@london.anglican.org

THOMAS, Canon Harald Daniel. b 34. FInstTT. **d** 97 **p** 05. Par Dn Pontnewydd *Mon* from 97; Hon Can St Woolos Cathl from 10. *Raldoro, Mount Pleasant Road, Pontnewydd, Cwmbran NP44 1BD* T: (01633) 771353

THOMAS, Miss Hilary Faith. b 43. Ex Univ BA 65 Southn Univ PGCE 66. Trin Coll Bris 90. **d** 94 **p** 95. C Yeovil w Kingston Pitney *B & W* 94-98; V Brislington St Luke *Bris* 98-07; rtd 07; PtO *B & W* 09-12; NSM Mark w Allerton 12-14. *Brierley, Lower North Street, Cheddar BS27 3HH* T: (01934) 742207
E: hilarythomas@uwclub.net

THOMAS, Hugh Vivian. b 57. Kingston Poly LLB 80 Barrister-at-Law (Lincoln's Inn) 86. SEITE 02. **d** 05 **p** 06. NSM Knockholt w Halstead *Roch* 05-12; P-in-c St Marg Pattens *Lon* 12-14; NSM St Mich Cornhill w St Pet le Poer etc from 14. *5 The Meadows, Halstead, Sevenoaks TN14 7HD* T: (01959) 532664
E: hughvthomas@btopenworld.com

THOMAS, Canon Huw Glyn. b 42. MBE 07. St D Coll Lamp BA 62 Linacre Coll Ox BA 65 MA 69. Wycliffe Hall Ox 62. **d** 65 **p** 66. C Oystermouth *S & B* 65-68; Asst Chapl Solihull Sch 68-69; Chapl and Hd Div 69-73; Selection Sec ACCM 73-78; C Loughton St Jo *Chelmsf* 73-77; V Bury St Jo *Man* 78-83; V Bury St Jo w St Mark 83-86; Dir of Ords 82-87; Can Res and Treas Liv Cathl 87-95; USPG 95-06; Chapl Addis Ababa Ethiopia 95-97; Provost All SS Cathl Cairo 97-01; Can from 01; Prin Edwardes Coll Peshawar Pakistan 01-06; rtd 06; Hon Sen Fell Liv Hope Univ from 07; PtO *Lon* 07-12; *Blackb* 12-14; P-in-c Overton from 14. *St Helen's Vicarage, Chapel Lane, Overton, Morecambe LA3 3HU* T: (01524) 858234 M: 07981-114255 E: huwapglyn@gmail.com

THOMAS, Ian Melville. b 50. Jes Coll Ox BA 71 MA 75. St Steph Ho Ox 71. **d** 73 **p** 74. PV St D Cathl 73-77; Chapl RAF 77-95; Command Chapl RAF 95-00; V Llanelli *St D* 01-02; TR 02-06; R Eccleston and Pulford *Ches* 06-15; rtd 15. *43 The Verlands, Cowbridge CF71 7BY* T: (01446) 773567
E: ospreys427@live.co.uk

THOMAS, Ian William. b 53. Bedf Coll of Educn CertEd 74. Ox Min Course 89. **d** 92 **p** 93. NSM Fenny Stratford *Ox* from 92. *5 Laburnum Grove, Bletchley, Milton Keynes MK2 2JW* T: (01908) 644457

THOMAS, Canon Idris. b 48. St D Coll Lamp. **d** 71 **p** 72. C Llanbeblig w Caernarfon and Betws Garmon etc *Ban* 71-75; P-in-c Llanaelhaiarn 75-77; R Llanaelhaearn w Clynnog Fawr 77-11; RD Arfon 93-00; AD 02-04; Hon Can Ban Cathl 99-11; rtd 11; PtO *Ban* from 11. *Glanrafon, Deiniol Road, Deiniolen, Caernarfon LL55 3LL* T: (01286) 872135

THOMAS, Irene Jean. b 42. **d** 04 **p** 05. OLM E Wickham *S'wark* 04-12; rtd 12; PtO *S'wark* from 12; *Cant* from 12. *South Wings, 264A Reculver Road, Herne Bay CT6 6RR* T: (01227) 369531 E: irene.thomas5@virginmedia.com

THOMAS, Jeffrey. d 15. C Llansadwrn w Llanwrda and Manordeilo *St D* from 15. *Address temp unknown*

THOMAS, Jeffrey Malcolm. d 10 **p** 12. C Morriston *S & B* 10-11; C Swansea St Thos and Kilvey 12-14; P-in-c Porth Newydd *Llan* from 14. *4 Kimberley Way, Porth CF39 9HS*
E: jeffreymthomas61@yahoo.com

THOMAS, Canon Jennifer Monica. b 58. Wilson Carlile Coll 79 Sarum & Wells Th Coll 91. **d** 93 **p** 94. Par Dn Wandsworth St Paul *S'wark* 93-94; C 94-97; V Forest Hill 97-02; V Mitcham Ascension from 02; Hon Can S'wark Cathl from 14. *The Vicarage, Sherwood Park Road, Mitcham CR4 1NE*
T: (020) 8764 1258

THOMAS, Jeremy Paul. b 63. Lanc Univ BSc 87. Trin Coll Bris 04. **d** 06 **p** 07. C Aughton Ch Ch *Liv* 06-10; P-in-c Ashton-in-Makerfield St Thos 10-15; V from 15. *The Vicarage, 18 Warrington Road, Ashton-in-Makerfield, Wigan WN4 9PL*
T: (01942) 727275 E: vicar@stthomasstluke.org.uk

THOMAS, Canon John Herbert Samuel. b 34. Pemb Coll Cam BA 57 MA 64. St Mich Coll Llan 57. **d** 58 **p** 59. C Port Talbot St Theodore *Llan* 58-60; C Llantwit Major and St Donat's 60-67; P-in-c Barry All SS 67-74; V Dinas and Penygraig w Williamstown 74-85; V Pontypridd St Cath 85-90; V Pontypridd St Cath w St Matt 90-99; RD Pontypridd 90-99; Can Llan Cathl 95-99; rtd 99; PtO *Llan* from 04. *Ty Canon, Salisbury Road, Abercynon, Mountain Ash CF45 4NU*
T: (01443) 742577

THOMAS, John <u>Roger</u>. Trin Coll Carmarthen BA. St Mich Coll Llan. **d** 03 **p** 04. C Cardigan w Mwnt and Y Ferwig w Llangoedmor *St D* 03-06; P-in-c Crymych Gp 06-07; V 07-11; V Llansadwrn w Llanwrda and Manordeilo from 11. *The Vicarage, Llanwrda SA19 8HD* T: (01550) 777343
E: vicar.llanwrda@gmail.com

THOMAS, John Thurston. b 28. Univ of Wales (Swansea) BSc 48 DipEd 49 Leeds Univ PhD 58 CChem FRSC 65. Glouc Sch of Min 88. **d** 90 **p** 91. NSM S Cerney w Cerney Wick and Down Ampney *Glouc* 90-96; PtO 96-01; *S & B* from 01. *4 Nicholl Court, Mumbles, Swansea SA3 4LZ* T: (01792) 360098

THOMAS, Jonathan Mark Gutteridge. b 66. Southn Univ BSc 88. Trin Coll Bris BA 10. **d** 10 **p** 11. C Cranleigh *Guildf* 10-14; P-in-c Woking St Pet from 14. *66 Westfield Road, Woking GU22 9NG* M: 07804-196876

THOMAS, Judith. *See* THOMAS, Dorothy Judith

THOMAS, Julian <u>Mark</u>. b 48. Liv Univ BA 05. SWMTC 00. **d** 03 **p** 04. C Okehampton w Inwardleigh, Bratton Clovelly etc *Ex* 03-07; C Essington *Lich* 07-12; rtd 12; PtO *Lich* from 13. *9 New Minster House, Bird Street, Lichfield WS13 6PR*
T: (01543) 253319 E: mark.thomas108@o2.co.uk

THOMAS, Mrs June Marion. b 31. Univ of Wales BA 53 DipEd 54. NEOC 83. **dss** 86 **d** 87 **p** 94. Stockton St Pet *Dur* 86-89; Hon Par Dn 87-89; NSM Stockton St Mark 89-94; P-in-c 94-01; rtd 01; PtO *Dur* from 01. *50 Brisbane Grove, Stockton-on-Tees TS18 5BP* T: (01642) 582408

THOMAS, Mrs Karen Rosemary. b 53. Qu Coll Birm 04. **d** 06 **p** 07. C Glenfield *Leic* 06-10; TV Woodfield 10-12; rtd 12; PtO *Leic* from 14. *17 Barry Drive, Kirby Muxloe, Leicester LE9 2HG* E: karen.thomas7@sky.com

THOMAS, Katie. b 71. **d** 14 **p** 15. C Stoke-next-Guildf from 14. *35 Woking Road, Guildford GU1 1QD*

THOMAS, Keith. *See* THOMAS, Ernest Keith

THOMAS, Keith. b 55. Southlands Coll Lon TCert 80. NOC 92. **d** 95 **p** 96. NSM Knuzden *Blackb* 95-98; NSM Darwen St Pet w Hoddlesden 98-04; Tullyallan Sch Darwen 99-04; NSM Turton Moorland *Man* from 04. *20 Duxbury Street, Darwen BB3 2LA*
T: (01254) 776484

THOMAS, Kimberley Ann. b 59. Cranmer Hall Dur 02. **d** 04 **p** 05. C Chesterton *Lich* 04-07; V Stretton w Claymills from 07. *The Vicarage, Church Road, Stretton, Burton-on-Trent DE13 0HD* T: (01283) 564435
E: vicar@stmarys-stretton.org.uk

THOMAS, Leighton. *See* THOMAS, Adrian Leighton

THOMAS, Canon Leslie Richard. b 45. Lon Coll of Div 65. **d** 69 **p** 70. C Knotty Ash St Jo *Liv* 69-72; C Sutton 72-74; TV 74-77; V Banks 77-82; V Gt Crosby All SS 82-92; P-in-c Marthall and Chapl David Lewis Cen for Epilepsy *Ches* 92-02; V Bickerton, Bickley, Harthill and Burwardsley 02-10; RD Malpas 04-10; Hon Can Ches Cathl 07-10; rtd 10. *7 Fairhaven Road, Southport PR9 9UJ* T: (01704) 227511 E: sandstone@tesco.net

THOMAS, Mark. *See* THOMAS, Julian Mark

THOMAS, Preb Mark Wilson. b 51. Dur Univ BA 72 Hull Univ MA 89. Ripon Coll Cuddesdon 76. **d** 78 **p** 79. C Chapelthorpe *Wakef* 78-81; C Seaford w Sutton *Chich* 81-84; V Gomersal *Wakef* 84-92; TR Almondbury w Farnley Tyas 92-01; RD Almondbury 93-01; Hon Can Wakef Cathl 99-01; P-in-c Shrewsbury St Chad w St Mary *Lich* 01-07; V Shrewsbury St Chad, St Mary and St Alkmund 07-13; RD Shrewsbury 09-13; Preb Lich Cathl 11-13; rtd 13; PtO *Lich* from 14. *25 The Crescent, Town Walls, Shrewsbury SY1 1TH* T: (01743) 343761

THOMAS, Martin Russell. b 66. Edin Univ BMus 88 UEA PhD 13 LRSM 02. Ripon Coll Cuddesdon BTh 05. **d** 03 **p** 04. C Wymondham *Nor* 03-06; P-in-c Fulham St Andr *Lon* 06-07; V 07-11; Can Res St E Cathl 11-12; P-in-c Kennington Park St Agnes *S'wark* 12-13; TR Plaistow and N Canning Town *Chelmsf* from 14. *The Rectory, 19 Abbey Street, London E13 8DT*
M: 07460-257103 T: (020) 7473 2809
E: fathermartinthomas@gmail.com

THOMAS, Sister Mary Josephine. b 30. Ripon Dioc Tr Coll TCert 50 Carl Dioc Tr Course 88. **d** 90 **p** 94. NSM Hawes Side *Blackb* 90-93; NSM St Annes St Marg 93-00; PtO from 00. *112 St Andrew's Road North, Lytham St Annes FY8 2JQ*
T: (01253) 728016

THOMAS, Michael Longdon Sanby. b 34. Trin Hall Cam BA 55 MA 60. Wells Th Coll 56. **d** 58 **p** 59. C Sandal St Helen *Wakef* 58-60; Chapl Portsm Cathl 60-64; V Shedfield 64-69; V Portchester 69-98; rtd 98. *188 Castle Street, Portchester, Fareham PO16 9QH* T/F: (023) 9242 0416
E: thomasfamily73@cwtv.net

THOMAS, Michael Rosser David. b 74. Kent Univ BA 96. St Steph Ho Ox BTh 02. **d** 02 **p** 03. C Aberavon *Llan* 02-05; Min Can Brecon Cathl 05-08; Succ from 08; P-in-c Brecon St Mary w Llanddew 08-11; P-in-c Brecon St Mary 11-13; Bp's Chapl from 14. *The Almonry, Cathedral Close, Brecon LD3 9DP*
T: (01874) 622972
E: chaplain.swanbrec@churchinwales.org.uk

THOMAS, Moray. *See* THOMAS, Charles Moray Stewart Reid

THOMAS, Nigel Bruce. b 63. Univ of Wales BD 91. St Jo Coll Nottm MA 98. **d** 97 **p** 98. C Millom *Carl* 97-02; R Bentham *Bradf* 02-07; P-in-c St Breoke and Egloshayle *Truro* 07-08; TR Carew *St D* 08-12. *14 Westgate Court, Pembroke SA71 4LF*
E: thomas-tribe@hotmail.co.uk

THOMAS, Nigel Clayton. b 52. Leeds Univ BA 76 Univ of Wales (Cardiff) PGCE 77. ERMC 08. **d** 11 **p** 12. C Madrid *Eur* from 11. *Rincon de Andalucia 3, Majadahonda el Real, 28410 Madrid, Spain* T: (0034) 918 527 276 M: 663 665 703
E: nigelthomasnta@gmail.com

THOMAS, Ms Pamela Sybil. b 38. Ripon Coll Cuddesdon 88. **d** 90 **p** 94. Par Dn Preston w Sutton Poyntz, Littlemoor etc *Sarum* 90-94; C 94-96; P-in-c Weymouth St Edm 96-05; P-in-c Abbotsbury, Portesham and Langton Herring 97-08; Chapl Westhaven Hosp Weymouth 96-08; rtd 08; Hon C Cullompton, Willand, Uffculme, Kentisbeare etc *Ex* from 08. *5 Cotters Close, Kentisbeare, Cullompton EX15 2DJ*
T: (01884) 266741 E: rev.thomas@btinternet.com

THOMAS, Canon Patrick Hungerford Bryan. b 52. St Cath Coll Cam BA 73 MA 77 Leeds Univ BA 78 Univ of Wales PhD 82. Coll of Resurr Mirfield 76. **d** 79 **p** 80. C Aberystwyth *St D* 79-81; C Carmarthen St Pet 81-82; R Llangeitho and Blaenpennal w Betws Leucu etc 82-84; Warden of Ords 83-86; R Brechfa w Abergorlech etc 84-01; V Carmarthen St Dav from 01; Can St D Cathl from 00. *St David's Vicarage, 4 Penllwyn Park, Carmarthen SA31 3BU* T: (01267) 234183
E: canon.patrick@yahoo.co.uk

THOMAS, Paul Richard. b 75. Univ of Wales (Cardiff) BA 96 MA 99 Hon ARAM 12. Ripon Coll Cuddesdon BA 01 MA 06. **d** 02 **p** 03. C Wanstead St Mary w Ch Ch *Chelmsf* 02-06; C St Marylebone w H Trin *Lon* 06-11; V Paddington St Jas from 11; Chapl St Marylebone C of E Sch 08-11; Chapl R Academy of Music *Lon* 08-12. *St James's Vicarage, 6 Gloucester Terrace, London W2 3DD* T: (020) 7262 1265
M: 07967-753671 E: vicar@stjamespaddington.org.uk

THOMAS, Canon Paul Robert. b 42. OBE 02. NOC. **d** 82 **p** 83. C Hull St Jo Newland *York* 82-84; P-in-c Rowley 84-87; Soc Resp Officer Hull 84-87; R Rowley w Skidby 87-88; TR Barking St Marg w St Patr *Chelmsf* 88-93; Gen Sec and Admin St Luke's Hosp for Clergy 93-03; Can and Preb Chich Cathl 98-03; P in O 99-12; rtd 03; PtO *Nor* 03-14; P-in-c Erpingham w Calthorpe, Ingworth, Aldborough etc from 14. *The Rectory, School Road, Erpingham, Norwich NR11 7QY*
E: synergyatwork@aol.com

THOMAS, The Ven Paul Wyndham. b 55. Oriel Coll Ox BA 76 BTh 78 MA 80. Wycliffe Hall Ox 77. **d** 79 **p** 80. C Llangynwyd w Maesteg *Llan* 79-85; TV Langport Area *B & W* 85-90; P-in-c Thorp Arch w Walton *York* 90-93; Clergy Tr Officer 90-04; V Nether w Upper Poppleton 93-04; P-in-c Castle Town *Lich* 04-11; RD Stafford 05-11; Local Par Development Adv Stafford Area 10-11; Adn Salop from 11; P-in-c Forton from 11. *The Vicarage, Tong, Shifnal TF11 8PW*
T: (01902) 372622

THOMAS, Peter. *See* UNGOED-THOMAS, Peter

THOMAS, Peter James. b 53. Lon Univ BSc 75. Trin Coll Bris 77. **d** 80 **p** 81. C Hucclecote *Glouc* 80-84; C Loughborough Em *Leic* 84-85; TV Parr *Liv* 85-92; V Eckington and Defford w Besford *Worc* 92-05; RD Pershore 00-05; P-in-c Norton sub Hamdon, W Chinnock, Chiselborough etc *B & W* from 05;

P-in-c Stoke sub Hamdon from 12; RD Ivelchester 07-13. *The Rectory, Cat Street, Chiselborough, Stoke-sub-Hamdon TA14 6TT* T: (01935) 881202 E: pthomas5@aol.com

THOMAS, Peter Rhys. b 37. TCD BA 59 MA 72 MInstPkg MCIPD. **d** 72 **p** 73. C Tuam w Cong, Ballinrobe and Aasleagh *T, K & A* 73-75; I 75-77; C Bingley All SS *Bradf* 77-79; V Shelf 79-81; Producer Relig Broadcasting Viking Radio 81-84; P-in-c Croxton *Linc* 81-82; P-in-c Ulceby 81-82; P-in-c Wootton 81-82; P-in-c Ulceby Gp 82; V 82-84; R E and W Tilbury and Linford *Chelmsf* 84-89; I Celbridge w Straffan and Newcastle-Lyons *D & G* 89-93; I Youghal Union *C, C & R* 93-99; Dioc Communications Officer (Cork) 95-99; Can Cork Cathl 97-99; Preb Cloyne Cathl 97-99; rtd 99; Rep Leprosy Miss Munster from 00. *Abina Cottage, Ballykenneally, Ballymacoda, Co Cork, Republic of Ireland* T/F: (00353) (24) 98082 E: prthomas@iol.ie

THOMAS, Peter Wilson. b 58. K Coll Lon BD 80 AKC 80. Ripon Coll Cuddesdon 80. **d** 82 **p** 83. C Stockton St Pet *Dur* 82-85; TV Solihull *Birm* 85-90; V Rednal 90-05; Chapl MG Rover 95-05; P-in-c Balsall Common 05-10; V from 10. *St Peter's House, Holly Lane, Balsall Common, Coventry CV7 7EA* T/F: (01676) 532721 E: frpeter@uwclub.net

THOMAS, Canon Philip Harold Emlyn. b 41. Cant Univ (NZ) BA 64 MA 77 Dur Univ PhD 82. Melbourne Coll of Div BD 68. **d** 68 **p** 69. C Adelaide H Trin Australia 68-71; LtO Dio Christchurch New Zealand 71-77; Fell and Chapl Univ Coll Dur 77-83; V Heighington *Dur* 84-10; AD Darlington 94-00; Hon Can Dur Cathl 07-10; rtd 10. *2 Gloucester Street, Cirencester GL7 2DG* E: philip.thomas7@btinternet.com

THOMAS, Philip John. b 52. Liv Poly BSc 74 Leeds Poly 77. Trin Coll Bris 94. **d** 96 **p** 97. C Skelton w Upleatham *York* 96-97; C Acomb St Steph and St Aid 97-01; V Woodthorpe *S'well* 01-14; V Cinderhill from 15 and from 14. *Christ Church Vicarage, 587 Nuthall Road, Nottingham NG8 6AD* T: 0115-970 8151

THOMAS, Ramon Lorenzo. b 44. Victoria Univ Wellington BCA 73 Mass Inst of Tech MSc 80 CA 73. Oak Hill Th Coll 89. **d** 97 **p** 98. NSM Yateley *Win* 97-99; Chairman Judah Trust from 99; PtO *Chich* from 10. *58 Rock Gardens, Bognor Regis PO21 2LF* T: (01243) 825523 E: judahtrust@aol.com

THOMAS, Randolph. *See* THOMAS, Alfred James Randolph

THOMAS, Rhys. *See* THOMAS, Peter Rhys

THOMAS, Richard Frederick. b 24. Qu Coll Cam BA 45 MA 49. Ridley Hall Cam 47. **d** 49 **p** 50. C S Croydon Em *Cant* 49-51; Chapl and Ho Master Haileybury Coll 51-67; Hd Master Angl Ch Sch Jerusalem 67-73; Ho Master Bp Luffa Sch Chich 74-80; Hon C Chich St Pancras and St Jo 78-80; R N Mundham w Hunston and Merston 80-89; PtO *Portsm* from 89; C Stansted and Compton, the Mardens, Stoughton and Racton *Chich* 96-00; rtd 00; PtO *Chich* from 00. *16 Brent Court, Emsworth PO10 7JA* T: (01243) 430613 M: 07947-518314 E: thomasrb@ntlworld.com

THOMAS, Richard Nathan. b 76. Ch Ch Coll Cant BA 98. Ridley Hall Cam 11. **d** 13 **p** 14. C Ealing St Paul *Lon* from 13. *15A Erlesmere Gardens, London W13 9TZ* M: 07786-132897 E: richnthomas@gmail.com

THOMAS, Richard Paul. b 50. MIPR. Wycliffe Hall Ox 74. **d** 76 **p** 77. C Abingdon w Shippon *Ox* 76-80; R Win All SS w Chilcomb and Chesil 80-88; Dioc Communications Officer Win 83-89; Ox 89-07. *71B St Thomas Street, Wells BA5 2UY* T: (01749) 671478

THOMAS, Robert Graham. b 53. G&C Coll Cam BA 75 MA 79 Imp Coll Lon PhD 78 CEng 82 FIMechE 93. SAOMC 04. **d** 06 **p** 07. C Bathampton w Claverton *B & W* 06-10; P-in-c Trowbridge St Jas and Keevil *Sarum* 10-11; R from 11; Chapl Wilts Coun from 11. *The Rectory, Union Street, Trowbridge BA14 8RU* T: (01225) 350647 E: rob.thomas@cantab.net

THOMAS, Robin. b 27. St Steph Ho Ox 89. **d** 89 **p** 90. NSM Clifton All SS w St Jo *Bris* 89-94; P-in-c Tintagel *Truro* 94-97; rtd 97; PtO *Truro* from 97. *22 Hendra Vean, Truro TR1 3TU* T: (01872) 271276

THOMAS, Preb Roderick Charles Howell. b 54. LSE BSc 75. Wycliffe Hall Ox 91. **d** 93 **p** 94. C Plymouth St Andr w St Paul and St Geo *Ex* 93-95; C Plymouth St Andr and Stonehouse 95-99; P-in-c Elburton 99-05; V from 05; Preb Ex Cathl from 12. *St Matthew's Vicarage, 3 Sherford Road, Plymouth PL9 8DQ* T: (01752) 402771 E: roderick.t@virgin.net

THOMAS, Roger. *See* THOMAS, John Roger

THOMAS, Russen William. b 30. Univ of Wales (Lamp) BA 55. St Mich Coll Llan 55. **d** 57 **p** 58. C Newport St Jo Bapt *Mon* 57-59; C Pembroke Dock *St D* 59-62; R St Florence and Redberth 62-69; V Newport St Julian *Mon* 69-79; V Stratton *Truro* 79-88; RD 83-88; V Lanteglos by Fowey 88-91; Hon Chapl Miss to Seafarers from 88; rtd 92; Chapl Playa de Las Americas Tenerife *Eur* 93-97; PtO *Cov* 97-06; *B & W* from 06. *Ruslin, Stratton Road, Bude EX23 8AQ* T: (01288) 355342 M: 07801-473862 E: wen.rus@virgin.net

THOMAS, Mrs Ruth Alison Mary. b 57. York Univ BA 79 Dur Univ PGCE 80 MA 96. NEOC 07. **d** 09 **p** 10. NSM Dur St Giles from 09; NSM Shadforth and Sherburn 09-12; PtO from 12. *68 Gilesgate, Durham DH1 1HY* T: 0191-386 0402 M: 07855-236063 E: ruththomas.durham@gmail.com

THOMAS, Mrs Sally. **d** 14 **p** 15. NSM Howell Hill w Burgh Heath *Guildf* from 14. *2 Kilcorral Close, Epsom KT17 4HX* T: (01372) 724391 E: sallyt@stpauls.co.uk

THOMAS, Mrs Sheila Mary Witton. b 49. STETS 06. **d** 09 **p** 10. NSM Marnhull *Sarum* 09-14; rtd 14; PtO *Sarum* from 15. *5 Burtonhayes, Burton Street, Marnhull, Sturminster Newton DT10 1PR* T: (01258) 820469 M: 07748-974806 E: sheila2is@yahoo.co.uk

THOMAS, Simon Jonathan Francklin. b 51. Sheff Univ BA 72 Nottm Univ BA 78 Open Univ MA 02. St Jo Coll Nottm 76. **d** 80 **p** 80. SAMS 80-82 and 83-95; Peru 80-82; Bolivia 83-95; C Camberwell All SS *S'wark* 82; C Ashtead *Guildf* 96-06; rtd 06. *4 Masefield Road, Harpenden AL5 4JN* T: (01582) 462227 E: simonjfthomas@aol.com

THOMAS, Sonia Patricia. *See* BARRON, Sonia Patricia

THOMAS, Stefan Carl. b 67. Kent Univ BA 02 MA 04. SEITE 08. **d** 10 **p** 12. NSM Broadstairs *Cant* from 10; Chapl Chatham and Clarendon Gr Sch Federation from 12. *195 Bradstow Way, Broadstairs CT10 1AX* T: (01843) 861724 E: slazz@btinternet.com

THOMAS, Preb Stephen Blayney. b 35. St D Coll Lamp BA 62. Bp Burgess Hall Lamp. **d** 63 **p** 64. C Ledbury *Heref* 63-67; C Bridgnorth w Tasley 67-68; C Clun w Chapel Lawn, Bettws-y-Crwyn and Newcastle 68-73; C Clungunford w Clunbury and Clunton, Bedstone etc 68-73; V Worfield 73-84; RD Bridgnorth 81-83; R Kingsland 84-96; P-in-c Eardisland 84-96; P-in-c Aymestrey and Leinthall Earles w Wigmore etc 84-96; R Kingsland w Eardisland, Aymestrey etc 97-99; Preb Heref Cathl 85-01; rtd 99; PtO *Heref* from 00; *Worc* from 00. *28 Castle Close, Burford, Tenbury Wells WR15 8AY* T: (01584) 819642 E: stephenbbthomas@btinternet.com

THOMAS, Canon Stuart Grahame. b 54. Pemb Coll Cam BA 77 MA 81 ATCL 97. Ridley Hall Cam 85. **d** 87 **p** 88. C Guildf H Trin w St Mary 87-91; V Churt 91-94; V Ewell St Fran 94-14; Dioc Ecum Officer 99-07; RD Epsom 07-14; R Frimley from 14; Hon Can Guildf Cathl from 12. *The Rectory, 3 Parsonage Way, Frimley, Camberley GU16 8HZ* T: (01276) 23309 E: revstuart.thomas@btinternet.com

THOMAS, Miss Susan. b 58. City of Liv Coll of HE BA 80 PGCE 81. SNWTP 10. **d** 13 **p** 14. C Formby H Trin and Altcar *Liv* from 13. *19 Hampton Road, Formby, Liverpool L37 6EJ* T: (01704) 398990 E: thomass1109@aol.com

THOMAS, Susan Linda. b 60. SEITE 08. **d** 11 **p** 12. NSM Coulsdon St Jo *S'wark* from 11. *40 West Hill, South Croydon CR2 0SA*

THOMAS, Canon Sydney Robert. b 44. Univ of Wales (Swansea) BA 65 MA 83. St D Coll Lamp LTh 67. **d** 67 **p** 68. C Llanelli *St D* 67-77; V Pontyberem 77-01; TR Cwm Gwendraeth 01-08; RD Cydweli 94-05; Can St D Cathl 94-08; Chan St D Cathl 01-03; Treas St D Cathl 03-08; rtd 09. *40 Waungoch, Upper Tumble, Llanelli SA14 6BX* T: (01269) 841677 E: sydvic@sydvic.plus.com

THOMAS, Thomas. b 68. Selw Coll Cam BA 90. Wycliffe Hall Ox 91. **d** 93 **p** 94. C Much Woolton *Liv* 93-97; V Carr Mill 97-10; C Springfield *Birm* 10-11; P-in-c 11-15; V from 15. *St Christopher's Vicarage, 172 Woodlands Road, Springfield, Birmingham B11 4ET* M: 07980-650801 T: 0121-702 2745 E: tom172thomas@btinternet.com

THOMAS, Thomas Alan. b 37. K Coll Lon BD 60 AKC 60. St Boniface Warminster 60. **d** 61 **p** 62. C Washington *Dur* 61-65; C Bishopwearmouth St Mary V w St Pet CD 65-70; V Ruishton w Thornfalcon *B & W* 70-82; R Hutton 82-94; V Frome Ch Ch 94-96; Chapl Victoria Hosp Frome 94-96; R Camerton w Dunkerton, Foxcote and Shoscombe *B & W* 96-00; rtd 00; PtO *B & W* from 00. *12 Farrington Way, Farrington Gurney, Bristol BS39 6US* T: (01761) 453434

THOMAS, Thomas John Samuel. b 21. St D Coll Lamp BA 48. **d** 49 **p** 50. C Dafen and Llwynhendy *St D* 49-50; Chapl RAF 52-77; QHC 73-85; V Horsham *Chich* 77-85; rtd 85; PtO *St D* from 85. *1 Glynhir Road, Llandybie, Ammanford SA18 2TA* T: (01269) 850726

THOMAS, Timothy Charles Rank. b 75. Trin Coll Bris. **d** 14 **p** 15. C Walkden and Lt Hulton *Man* from 14. *4 Mort Fold, Little Hulton, Manchester M38 9GY*

THOMAS, Virginia Jacqueline. b 48. UEA BA 70. Yale Div Sch MDiv 97. **d** 00 **p** 01. NSM Chelsea St Luke and Ch Ch *Lon* 00-04; NSM W Brompton St Mary w St Pet 04-06; P-in-c 05-06; P-in-c W Brompton St Mary w St Peter and St Jude 06-10; V 10-14; rtd 14; V Gt w Lt Tew and Heythrop *Ox* from 14. *The Vicarage, New Road, Great Tew, Chipping Norton OX7 4AG* T: (01608) 683584 E: ginnytea@googlemail.com

THOMAS, Vivian Ivor. b 52. S Bank Univ MSc 95 Regent Coll Vancouver MCS 97 K Coll Lon PhD 02. **d** 08 **p** 09. NSM Hammersmith St Paul *Lon* from 08. *76 Rannoch Road, London W6 9SP* T: (020) 7384 5954 M: 07767-777891
E: vivian.thomas@btinternet.com

THOMAS, William George. b 29. JP. Birm Univ BA 50 CertEd 51 FRSA. EAMTC 82. **d** 85 **p** 86. NSM Brampton *Ely* 85-87; NSM Bluntisham w Earith 87-89; P-in-c Foxton 89-95; rtd 95; PtO *Ely* from 95. *3 The Paddock, Bluntisham, Huntingdon PE28 3NR* T: (01487) 842057
E: w.thomas57@btopenworld.com

THOMAS, The Ven William Jordison. b 27. K Coll Cam BA 50 MA 55. Cuddesdon Coll 51. **d** 53 **p** 54. C Byker St Ant *Newc* 53-56; C Berwick H Trin 56-59; V Alwinton w Holystone and Alnham 59-70; V Alston cum Garrigill w Nenthead and Kirkhaugh 70-80; P-in-c Lambley w Knaresdale 72-80; RD Bamburgh and Glendale 81-83; P-in-c St Glendale Gp 80-83; Adn Northd and Can Res Newc Cathl 83-92; rtd 92; PtO *Newc* from 92. *20 Robert Adam Court, Bondgate Without, Alnwick NE66 1PH* T: (01665) 602644

THOMAS, The Ven William Phillip. b 43. Lich Th Coll 68. **d** 70 **p** 71. C Llanilid w Pencoed *Llan* 70-74; C Pontypridd St Cath 74-76; V Tonyrefail 76-84; Youth Chapl 78-80; RD Rhondda 81-84; R Neath w Llantwit 84-98; Adn Llan 97-08; V Caerau w Ely 98-00; rtd 09; PtO *Llan* from 09. *102 Heol Croesty, Pencoed, Bridgend CF35 5LT* T: (01656) 865969

THOMAS, Wilson Hugo. b 40. **d** 01 **p** 05. Barbados 01-05; NSM Frimley *Guildf* 05-07. *3B Ansell Road, Frimley GU16 8BS* T: (01276) 681652 E: wilsonthomas56@googlemail.com

THOMAS ANTHONY, Brother. See DEHOOP, Thomas Anthony

THOMASSON, Keith Duncan. b 69. St Pet Coll Ox BA 91 MA 97 Lon Inst of Educn PGCE 92. Ripon Coll Cuddesdon BA 01 Bossey Ecum Inst Geneva. **d** 02 **p** 03. C Lancaster St Mary w St John and St Anne *Blackb* 02-04; C Longridge 04-06; Partnership P E Bris 06-11; Chapl Hants Colleg Sch 11-14; Hon C Romsey *Win* 11-14; Sen Chapl Alabaré Christian Care Centres from 14. *6 Albany Road, Romsey SO51 8EE* T: (01794) 516209 E: romseyabbeycayfm@phonecoop.coop

THOMASSON-ROSINGH, Mrs Anna Clara Abena (Anne Claar). b 74. Ede Chr Coll BEd 97 Utrecht Univ MA 01 Man Univ PhD 09. Leiden Protestant Sem 98 Bossey Ecum Inst Geneva 01. **d** 14 **p** 15. Remonstrant Min 02-14; C Clarendon *Sarum* from 14. *6 Albany Road, Romsey SO51 8EE* T: (01794) 516209 E: acthomasson-rosingh@stets.ac.uk

THOMPSON (née SMETHAM), Abigail Laura. b 75. K Coll Lon BMus 97 Clare Coll Cam BA 05. Westcott Ho Cam 03. **d** 06 **p** 07. C Sheff Manor 06-10; P-in-c Clifton St Jas 10-15; V from 15; Dean of Women's Min from 15. *Clifton Vicarage, 10 Clifton Crescent North, Rotherham S65 2AS* T: (01709) 363082 M: 07947-475073 E: rev.abi.thompson@gmail.com *or* abi.thompson@sheffield.anglican.org

THOMPSON, Adrian David. b 68. Univ of Wales (Abth) BSc 93 PhD 97 Bris Univ PGCE 98. Wycliffe Hall Ox 93. **d** 05 **p** 06. C Blackb St Gabr 05-08; Chapl Abp Temple Sch Preston 09-11; TV Cockermouth Area *Carl* from 11; C Gt Broughton from 14. *The Rectory, Lorton Road, Cockermouth CA13 9DU* T: (01900) 821288 *or* 829926
E: adrian.cockermouth@gmail.com *or* adrian@cateam.org.uk

THOMPSON, Alan. b 61. Qu Coll Birm 04. **d** 07 **p** 08. C Saltley and Washwood Heath *Birm* 07-14; V from 14. *9 Old Oscott Hill, Birmingham B44 9SR* T: 0121-350 8847
E: frathompson@btinternet.com

THOMPSON, Andrew. **d** 13 **p** 14. NSM Belfast St Donard *D & D* 13-14; C Donaghcloney w Waringstown from 14. *The Curatage, 51 Main Street, Donaghcloney, Craigavon BT66 7LR* T: (028) 3882 0064 M: 07803-062874
E: andrew7hompson@yahoo.co.uk

THOMPSON, Canon Andrew David. b 68. MBE 11. Poly of Wales BSc 90 Nottm Univ MA 03. Wycliffe Hall Ox 98. **d** 00 **p** 01. C Oakwood *Derby* 00-04; Asst Chapl UAE 05-06; Chapl Kuwait 06-10; Chapl Abu Dhabi St Andr UAE from 10; Hon Can Bahrain from 11. *St Andrew's, PO Box 262, Abu Dhabi, United Arab Emirates* T: (00971) 2446 1361
E: andythompson1968@swissmail.org

THOMPSON, Mrs Angela Lorena Jennifer. b 44. SAOMC 96. **d** 99 **p** 00. NSM Chalfont St Giles *Ox* 99-12; rtd 12; PtO *Ox* from 12. *3 The Leys, Chesham Bois, Amersham HP6 5NP* T: (01494) 726654 E: angelalj70@hotmail.com

THOMPSON, Canon Anthony Edward. b 38. Bris Univ BA 61. Ridley Hall Cam 61. **d** 63 **p** 64. C Peckham St Mary Magd *S'wark* 63-66; SAMS Paraguay 67-72; C Otley *Bradf* 72-75; TV Woughton *Ox* 75-82; P-in-c Lower Nutfield *S'wark* 82-02; V S Nutfield w Outwood 02-03; RD Reigate 91-93; Local Min Adv Croydon Episc Area 93-03; Hon Can S'wark Cathl 03; rtd 03; PtO *Chich* from 04. *3 The Curlews, Shoreham-by-Sea BN43 5UQ* T: (01273) 440182
E: tonythompsonsbs@hotmail.com

THOMPSON, Athol James Patrick. b 34. St Paul's Coll Grahamstown 72. **d** 74 **p** 75. S Africa 74-83; P-in-c Dewsbury St Matt and St Jo *Wakef* 84; TV Dewsbury 84-93; Chapl Staincliffe and Dewsbury Gen Hosps Wakef 84-90; Chapl Dewsbury and Distr Hosp 90-93; V Shiregreen St Jas and St Chris *Sheff* 93-99; rtd 99; PtO *Sheff* from 99. *109 Park Avenue, Chapeltown, Sheffield S35 1WH* T: 0114-245 1028

THOMPSON, Canon Barry Pearce. b 40. St Andr Univ BSc 63 Ball Coll Ox PhD 66 Hull Univ MA 82. NW Ord Course 76. **d** 79 **p** 80. C Cottingham *York* 79-82; V Swine 82-83; Lect Th Hull Univ 83-88; Ind Chapl *York* 83-85; Abp's Adv on Ind Issues 85-88; Can Res Chelmsf Cathl 88-98; Treas and Can Windsor 98-02; rtd 02; PtO *York* from 03. *28 Herriot Way, Thirsk YO7 1FL* M: 07768-515790
E: barry.thompson10@btopenworld.com

THOMPSON, Benjamin Joseph Peter. b 79. Trin Coll Cam BA 00 MA 04. Oak Hill Th Coll MTh 12. **d** 12 **p** 13. C Moreton-in-Marsh w Batsford, Todenham etc *Glouc* from 12. *32 Croft Holm, Moreton-in-Marsh GL56 0JH* M: 07912-675561 E: bjpthompson@hotmail.com

THOMPSON, Brian. b 34. MRICS 65 FRICS 75. St Jo Coll Nottm 81. **d** 84 **p** 85. C Bletchley *Ox* 84-87; V Sneyd Green *Lich* 87-99; rtd 99; PtO *Lich* from 12. *14 Stuart Court, High Street, Kibworth, Leicester LE8 0LR* T: 0116-319 7523
E: thompson.brian48@gmail.com

THOMPSON, Carrie Julia Lucy Jadwiga. b 77. Keble Coll Ox BA 99 MA 04. St Steph Ho Ox MA 06. **d** 04 **p** 05. C Camberwell St Giles w St Matt *S'wark* 04-08; V Forton *Portsm* from 08; Chapl St Vincent Sixth Form Coll from 08. *The Vicarage, 10 Spring Garden Lane, Gosport PO12 1HY* T: (023) 9250 3140 E: mother.carrie@btinternet.com

THOMPSON, Daniel Edward John. b 75. Staffs Univ BA 97 Birkbeck Coll Lon MA 06 Brighton Univ PGCE 08. **d** 14 **p** 15. C Hadleigh, Layham and Shelley *St E* from 14. *42 Oxford Drive, Hadleigh, Ipswich IP7 6AY* T: (01473) 827926
E: tbfspace@hotmail.com

THOMPSON, David. See THOMPSON, John David

THOMPSON, David Arthur. b 37. Clifton Th Coll. **d** 69 **p** 70. C Finchley Ch Ch *Lon* 69-72; C Barking St Marg w St Patr *Chelmsf* 72-75; TV 75-81; V Toxteth Park St Clem *Liv* 81-91; TR Parr 91-03; rtd 03; PtO *Sarum* 03-10. *Calm Haven, 21 Arklow Drive, Hale Village, Liverpool L24 5RN* T: 0151-425 2012

THOMPSON, David John. b 64. Cranmer Hall Dur 92. **d** 95 **p** 96. C Poulton-le-Sands w Morecambe St Laur *Blackb* 95-99; V Farington Moss 99-02; V Lea 02-09; Warden Past Assts 06-09; P-in-c Ringley w Prestolee *Man* 09-10; TV Farnworth, Kearsley and Stoneclough 10-13; V Walmersley Road, Bury from 13. *St John's Vicarage, 270 Walmersley Road, Bury BL9 6NH* T: 0161-764 3412 E: dvjt@yahoo.com

THOMPSON, David Simon. b 57. Aston Univ BSc 82 MRPharmS 83. STETS 01. **d** 04 **p** 05. NSM Bournemouth H Epiphany *Win* from 04. *15 Cheriton Avenue, Bournemouth BH7 6SD* T: (01202) 426764 M: 07763-052009
E: david_iford@hotmail.com

THOMPSON, Derrick Lionel. b 65. Trin Coll Bris 13. **d** 15. NSM S Norwood H Innocents *S'wark* from 15. *Address temp unknown*

THOMPSON, Edward Ronald Charles. b 25. AKC 51. **d** 52 **p** 53. C Hinckley St Mary *Leic* 52-54; Asst Master St Geo Upper Sch Jerusalem 54-55; Chapl St Boniface Coll Warminster 56-59; R Hawkchurch w Fishpond *Sarum* 59-63; V Camberwell St Mich w All So w Em *S'wark* 63-67; P-in-c St Mary le Strand w St Clem Danes *Lon* 67-74; R 74-93; rtd 93; PtO *S'wark* from 95. *3 Woodsyre, Sydenham Hill, London SE26 6SS* T: (020) 8670 8289 E: woodsyre@btinternet.com

THOMPSON, Ms Eileen Carol. b 46. Lon Univ BA 69. New Coll Edin MTh 92. **d** 96 **p** 97. Par Dn Dhaka St Thos Bangladesh 96-97; Presbyter Madras H Cross w St Mich India 97-99; Presbyter in charge Madras St Mary 99-02; V Pallikunu St Geo and Palla Ch Ch 02-04; Min Livingston LEP *Edin* 04-13; rtd 13. *4/2 Saxe Coburg Terrace, Edinburgh EH3 5BU* T: 0131-315 4928 E: eileencthompson@gmail.com

THOMPSON, Elizabeth Gray McManus. **d** 06 **p** 07. NSM Garrison w Slavin and Belleek *Clogh* 06-07; NSM Rossorry 07-09; NSM Enniskillen 09-11; Bp's C Aghalurcher w Tattykeeran, Cooneen etc 11-13; NSM Donagh w Tyholland and Errigal Truagh from 13. *En-Rimmon, 6 Tullylammy Road, Irvinestown, Enniskillen BT94 1RN* T: (028) 6862 8258
E: thompson.clogher@btinternet.com

THOMPSON, Frederick Robert. b 15. Dur Univ LTh 40. St Aug Coll Cant 37. **d** 40 **p** 41. C Northampton Ch Ch *Pet* 40-44; C Maidstone All SS *Cant* 44-46; India 46-57; Area Sec (Dios Birm and Lich) SPG 57-64; V Tutbury *Lich* 64-80; rtd 80; PtO *Sarum* from 80. *1 Panorama Road, Poole BH13 7RA* T: (01202) 700735

THOMPSON, Garry John. b 49. Qu Coll Birm. **d** 96 **p** 97. C Wilnecote *Lich* 96-99; V Lapley w Wheaton Aston and

P-in-c Blymhill w Weston-under-Lizard 99-09; R Watershed 09-11; R Clifton Campville w Edingale and Harlaston 11-15; P-in-c Elford 11-15; P-in-c Thorpe Constantine 11-15; R Mease Valley from 15. *The Rectory, 32 Main Street, Clifton Campville, Tamworth B79 0AP* T: (01827) 373257
E: garry@garrythompson2.wanadoo.co.uk

✠**THOMPSON, The Rt Revd Geoffrey** Hewlett. b 29. Trin Hall Cam BA 52 MA 56. Cuddesdon Coll 52. **d** 54 **p** 55 **c** 74. C Northampton St Matt *Pet* 54-59; V Wisbech St Aug *Ely* 59-66; V Folkestone St Sav *Cant* 66-74; Area Bp Willesden *Lon* 74-79 and 79-85; Bp Ex 85-99; rtd 99; Hon Asst Bp Carl from 99. *Low Broomrigg, Warcop, Appleby-in-Westmorland CA16 6PT* T: (01768) 341281

THOMPSON, Geoffrey Peter. b 58. St Pet Coll Ox BA 80 MA 82. SEITE 99. **d** 02 **p** 03. C Cheam *S'wark* 02-06; C Croydon St Jo 06-11; P-in-c Norbury St Steph and Thornton Heath from 11. *St Stephen's Vicarage, 9 Warwick Road, Thornton Heath CR7 7NH* T: (020) 8684 3820 E: gtchurch@waitrose.com

THOMPSON, Preb Gordon Henry Moorhouse. b 41. Univ of Wales LLM 95. K Coll Lon 63 St Boniface Warminster 66. **d** 67 **p** 68. C Leominster *Heref* 67-70; C Whitton w Greete and Hope Bagot 70-74; TV 74-89; C Burford III w Lt Heref 70-74; TV 74-89; C Tenbury Wells 70-74; TV 74-89; TV Burford I, Nash and Boraston 74-89; RD Ludlow 83-89; Preb Heref Cathl 85-97; rtd 89; PtO *Heref* 89-03. *The Poplars, Bitterley Village, Ludlow SY8 3HQ* T: (01584) 891093

THOMPSON, Harold Anthony. b 41. NOC 84. **d** 87 **p** 88. C Leeds Belle Is St Jo and St Barn *Ripon* 87-90; V Leeds St Cypr Harehills 90-96; V Shadwell 96-06; rtd 06. *551 Shadwell Lane, Leeds LS17 8AP* T: 0113-266 5913
E: haroldthompson41@hotmail.com

THOMPSON, Hewlett. *See* THOMPSON, Geoffrey Hewlett

THOMPSON, Ian David. b 51. Hull Univ BSc 72. NOC 94. **d** 97 **p** 98. C Blackley St Andr *Man* 97-00; P-in-c 00-06; R Burnage St Marg from 06. *St Margaret's Rectory, 250 Burnage Lane, Manchester M19 1FL* T: 0161-432 1844
E: iandthompson@talktalk.net

THOMPSON, Ian George. b 60. SEITE 99. **d** 02 **p** 03. NSM Walworth St Pet *S'wark* 02-05; NSM Dulwich St Clem w St Pet 05-07; Chapl HM Pris Pentonville 07-11; Chapl HM YOI Wetherby 11-13; Chapl HM Pris Coldingley from 13. *HM Prison Coldingley, Shaftesbury Road, Bisley, Woking GU24 9EX* T: (01483) 344300 M: 07985-582257
E: ian.thompson@hmps.gsi.gov.uk

THOMPSON, James. b 37. Coll of Resurr Mirfield 64. **d** 67 **p** 68. C Shieldfield Ch Ch *Newc* 67-69; C Hendon *Dur* 69-74; V Gateshead St Chad Bensham 74-85; R Easington 85-90; Chapl Thorpe Hosp Easington 85-90; V Cassop cum Quarrington *Dur* 90-06; rtd 06; PtO *Dur* from 06. *43 Heathfield, Sunderland SR2 9EW* T: 0191-522 9490

THOMPSON, Jeremy James Thomas. b 58. Sunderland Univ BEd 92. Cranmer Hall Dur 94. **d** 96 **p** 97. C Bedlington *Newc* 96-00; P-in-c Choppington 00-02; V 02-08; R St John Lee from 08; V Warden w Newbrough from 08. *St John Lee Rectory, Acomb, Hexham NE46 4PE* T: (01434) 600268
E: revjjtt@gmail.com

THOMPSON, John David. b 40. Lon Univ BD 65 Ch Ch Ox DPhil 69. St Steph Ho Ox 65. **d** 67 **p** 68. C Solihull *Birm* 67-71; C Biddestone w Slaughterford *Bris* 71-73; Lect Sarum & Wells Th Coll 71-72; C Yatton Keynell *Bris* 71-73; C Castle Combe 71-73; V Braughing *St Alb* 74-77; R Digswell 77-82; TR Digswell and Panshanger 82-98; rtd 00. *11 Russell Street, Boddam, Peterhead AB42 3NG* T: (01779) 472680

THOMPSON, Canon John Michael. b 47. Nottm Univ BTh 77. Linc Th Coll 73. **d** 77 **p** 78. C Old Brumby *Linc* 77-80; C Grantham 80-81; TV 81-84; V Holton-le-Clay 84-94; V Holton-le-Clay and Tetney 94-97; R Humshaugh w Simonburn and Wark *Newc* 97-14; Hon Can Newc Cathl 11-14; rtd 14. *2 Woodside Avenue, Corbridge NE45 5EL*

THOMPSON, John Turrell. b 57. Sheff Univ BA(Econ) 79 Southn Univ BTh 88. Sarum & Wells Th Coll 83. **d** 86 **p** 87. C Tavistock and Gulworthy *Ex* 86-90; TV Pinhoe and Broadclyst 90-95; P-in-c Northam w Westward Ho! and Appledore 95-96; TV Bideford, Northam, Westward Ho!, Appledore etc 96-00; rtd 00; PtO *Ex* from 00. *Brambles Patch, 39 Westermore Drive, Roundswell, Barnstaple EX31 3XU*

THOMPSON, John Wilfrid. b 44. CA Tr Coll 66 St Deiniol's Hawarden 84. **d** 85 **p** 86. C Rhyl w St Ann *St As* 85-87; R Fritwell w Souldern and Ardley w Fewcott *Ox* 87-97. *19 Tangmere Close, Bicester OX26 4YZ* T: (01869) 601082
M: 07813-997491 E: thompsonjohnwilfrid@sky.com

THOMPSON (née LILLIE), Mrs Judith Virginia. b 44. LMH Ox BA 66 Essex Univ MA 73 Univ of E Africa DipEd 67. Gilmore Course IDC 82. **dss** 82 **d** 87 **p** 94. Hon Par Dn E Bris 87-95; Chapl HM Rem Cen Pucklechurch 87-91; Chapl Asst

Southmead Hosp Bris 91-95; C Knowle St Barn *Bris* 95-02; Bp's Adv for Past Care for Clergy and Families 97-00; Community Th St Mich Coll Llan 00-05; Dir In-House Tr 02-05; Chapl Worcs Acute Hosps NHS Trust 05-09; rtd 09. *Grove Cottage, Barton Lane, Mere, Warminster BA12 6JA* T: (01747) 860553
E: judithvthompson@aol.com

THOMPSON, Kevin. b 55. Sheff Univ BEd 77. Oak Hill Th Coll. **d** 89 **p** 90. C Brinsworth w Catcliffe *Sheff* 89-92; V Kimberworth Park 92-97; V Grenoside 97-98; PtO from 98. *30 Arnold Avenue, Charnock, Sheffield S12 3JB* T: 0114-239 6986 E: kevin.thompson10@virgin.net

THOMPSON, Livingstone Anthony. b 59. Univ of W Indies BA 82 Irish Sch of Ecum MPhil 00 TCD PhD 03. McCormick Th Sem Chicago MA(TS) 89. **d** 83 **p** 90. Jamaica 83-05; CITC 05-06. *83 Hermitage Glen, Kells, Co Meath, Republic of Ireland* T: (00353) (46) 929 3861 M: 86-373 7135

THOMPSON, Louise Margaret. *See* TAYLOR-KENYON, Louise Margaret

THOMPSON, Mark William. b 52. St Jo Coll Nottm 77. **d** 81 **p** 82. C Barnsbury St Andr and H Trin w All SS *Lon* 81-84; C Addiscombe St Mary *Cant* 84; C *S'wark* 85-87; V Thorpe Edge *Bradf* 87-94; Chapl Colchester Hosp Univ NHS Foundn Trust from 94. *Colchester General Hospital, Turner Road, Colchester CO4 5JL* T: (01206) 747474 or 742513
E: mark.thompson@essexrivers.nhs.uk

THOMPSON, Martin Eric. b 52. FCCA. Trin Coll Bris 95. **d** 97 **p** 98. C Heref St Pet w St Owen and St Jas 97-01; P-in-c Huntley and Longhope *Glouc* 01-02; R Huntley and Longhope, Churcham and Bulley 03-05; P-in-c Worfield *Heref* 05-10; V Twigworth, Down Hatherley, Norton, The Leigh etc *Glouc* 10-13; rtd 13; PtO *Heref* from 14. *1 Church Close, Ross-on-Wye HR9 5HS* T: (01989) 565575
E: revmthompson123@btinternet.com *or* mandft@hotmail.co.uk

THOMPSON, Canon Matthew. b 68. CCC Cam BA 90 MA 94 MPhil 94. Ridley Hall Cam 91. **d** 94 **p** 95. C Hulme Ascension *Man* 94-97; C Langley and Parkfield 97-98; TV 98-00; P-in-c Man Clayton St Cross w St Paul 00-08; AD Ardwick 03-08; P-in-c Bolton St Pet 08-11; P-in-c Bolton St Phil 08-11; V Bolton St Pet w St Phil from 11; Borough Dean Bolton from 10; Hon Can Man Cathl from 12. *35 Sherbourne Road, Bolton BL1 5NN* T: (01204) 845332
E: vicar@boltonparishchurch.co.uk

THOMPSON, Mervyn Patrick. b 59. Wilson Carlile Coll 84 Coll of Resurr Mirfield 90. **d** 92 **p** 93. C Sheff St Cath Richmond Road 92-95; V Thurnscoe St Hilda 95-06; P-in-c Thurnscoe St Helen 99-06; R Thurnscoe 06-11; TR S Shields All SS *Dur* from 11. *The Rectory, Tyne Terrace, South Shields NE34 0NF* T: 0191-456 1851

THOMPSON, Michael. b 49. NEOC 83. **d** 86 **p** 87. C Ashington *Newc* 86-88; C Ponteland 88-91; TV Newc Epiphany 91-98; P-in-c Choppington 98-99; P-in-c Woldingham *S'wark* 99-02; TV Caterham 02-03; TV Saffron Walden w Wendens Ambo, Littlebury etc *Chelmsf* 03-08; R N Hartismere *St E* 08-14; RD Hartismere 13-14; TV Upper Skerne *Dur* from 14. *St Alban's Vicarage, Trimdon Grange, Trimdon Station TS29 6EX*
T: (01429) 883032 E: frmichael.thompson@btinternet.com

THOMPSON, Michael Bruce. b 53. N Carolina Univ BA 75 Dallas Th Sem ThM 79 Virginia Th Sem 79 Ch Coll Cam PhD 88. **d** 80 **p** 81. Asst Min New Bern N Carolina 80-83; Chair Youth and Evang and Renewal in E Carolina 81-83; Lect Greek Cam Univ 87-88; Lect St Jo Coll Nottm 88-95; Lect NT and Dir of Studies Ridley Hall Cam 95-00; Vice-Prin from 00. *Ridley Hall, Ridley Hall Road, Cambridge CB3 9HG* T: (01223) 746580 E: mbt2@cam.ac.uk

THOMPSON, Michael John. b 39. Cam Univ MA. **d** 00 **p** 01. OLM Badgeworth, Shurdington and Witcombe w Bentham *Glouc* 00-06. *Cornerways, 1 Church Lane, Shurdington, Gloucester GL51 4TJ* T: (01242) 862467 E: mthompson123@aol.com

THOMPSON, Mrs Michelle. b 68. Man Univ BA 89. Ripon Coll Cuddesdon 90. **d** 92 **p** 94. Par Dn Leigh St Mary *Man* 92-94; Asst Chapl HM Pris Full Sutton 95-97; V York St Hilda 97-00; Dir Reader Tr and Local Min Development *Man* 00-03; Chapl HM Pris Styal 04-13; Chapl Wrightington Wigan and Leigh NHS Trust from 13. *35 Sherbourne Road, Bolton BL1 5NN* T: (01204) 845332

THOMPSON, Canon Neil Hamilton. b 48. SS Hild & Bede Coll Dur BEd 72 Leic Univ MA 75. S'wark Ord Course 77 Ven English Coll Rome. **d** 80 **p** 81. C Merton St Mary *S'wark* 80-82; C Dulwich St Barn 82-84; V Shooters Hill Ch Ch 84-87; V S Dulwich St Steph 87-96; Ldr Post Ord Tr Woolwich Area 94-96; R Limpsfield and Titsey 96-08; Can Res and Prec Roch Cathl from 08. *Easter Garth, The Precinct, Rochester ME1 1SX* T: (01634) 405265 *or* 810063 F: 401410
E: precentor@rochestercathedral.org

THOMPSON, Patricia. b 60. SRN. NEOC 94. **d** 97 **p** 98. NSM Sunderland St Chad *Dur* from 97; Voc Adv from 99; PtO from 15. *11 Friarsfield Close, Chapelgarth, Sunderland SR3 2RZ* T: 0191-522 7911

THOMPSON, Patrick Arthur. b 36. Dur Univ BA 59. Qu Coll Birm. **d** 61 **p** 62. C W Wickham St Fran *Cant* 61-65; C Portchester *Portsm* 65-68; C Birchington w Acol *Cant* 68-71; V S Norwood St Mark 71-77; P-in-c Norbury St Oswald 77-81; V *S'wark* 81-93; V Sutton New Town St Barn 93-00; rtd 00; LtO *Mor* 00-03 and from 10; Resident P Grantown-on-Spey 04-10. *Rose Cottage, 2 Market Street, Forres IV36 1EF* T: (01309) 675917

THOMPSON, Paul. b 65. TCD BA 87. CITC 87. **d** 89 **p** 90. C Orangefield w Moneyreagh *D & D* 89-92; I Dromara w Garvaghy 92-97; I Ramoan w Ballycastle and Culfeightrin *Conn* 97-00; Dep Chapl HM Pris Liv 00-01; Chapl HM YOI Portland 01-13; Chapl HM Pris Erlestoke from 14. *HM Prison, Erlestoke House, Erlestoke, Devizes SN10 5TU* T: (01380) 814250 ext 4494 E: paul.thompson08@hmps.gsi.gov.uk

THOMPSON, Paul. b 58. Ox Univ BA. Ripon Coll Cuddesdon 80. **d** 83 **p** 84. Chapl Fazakerley Hosp Liv 83-86; C Kirkby *Liv* 83-86; TV 86-89; Ind Chapl 86-89; Chapl Kirkby Coll of FE 86-89; CF 89-01; Chapl Epsom Coll from 01. *Epsom College, Epsom KT17 4JQ* T: (01372) 821288 E: s-chaplain@epsomcollege.org.uk

THOMPSON, Paul Noble. b 54. Univ of Wales (Cardiff) BMus 77 Univ of Wales (Ban) MPhil 04 Glyndwr Univ PhD 13. Coll of Resurr Mirfield. **d** 80 **p** 81. C Bargoed and Deri w Brithdir *Llan* 80-83; C Whitchurch 83-84; V Porth w Trealaw 84-90; V Llanharan w Peterston-super-Montem 90-97; Hon C Barry All SS 97-01; Dioc Youth Chapl 90-01; V Lisvane 01-09; Chapl Univ of St Mark and St Jo *Ex* 09-14; Dioc Dir of Ords *Mon* from 14; C St Woolos Cathl from 14. *St Mark's Vicarage, 7 Gold Tops, Newport NP20 4PH* T: (01633) 252046 E: revpaulthompson@btinternet.com

THOMPSON, Pauline. *See* WILLCOX, Pauline

THOMPSON, Peter Alrick. b 79. QUB BA 01 TCD MPhil 03 ARIAM 99 FLCM 09. CITC 01. **d** 03 **p** 04. C Clooney w Strathfoyle *D & R* 03-06; I Donaghmore w Upper Donaghmore *Arm* from 06; Hon V Choral Arm Cathl from 06; Succ from 11; Dioc Liturg Officer from 09. *St Michael's Rectory, 66 Main Street, Castlecaulfield, Dungannon BT70 3NP* T: (028) 8776 1214 M: 07732-856306 E: donaghmore@armagh.anglican.org

THOMPSON, Canon Peter Ross. b 26. St Jo Coll Cam BA 47 MB, BChir 50. Tyndale Hall Bris. **d** 60 **p** 61. C New Malden and Coombe *S'wark* 60-61; BCMS Burma 61-66; R Slaugham *Chich* 66-72; V Polegate 72-92; Can and Preb Chich Cathl 91-92; rtd 92; PtO *Guildf* from 92. *Tregenna, Barley Mow Lane, Knaphill, Woking GU21 2HX* T: (01483) 480595

THOMPSON, Mrs Rachel Mary. b 65. Roehampton Inst BA 87 Rolle Coll PGCE 88 Nottm Univ MA 08. EMMTC 04. **d** 07 **p** 08. NSM Wilne and Draycott w Breaston *Derby* 07-11; NSM Kirk Hallam 11-14; Missr Erewash Deanery 14-15. *Address temp unknown* T: M: 07925-001400 E: rev.rach@gmail.com

THOMPSON, Raymond Craigmile. b 42. Man Univ BTh. **d** 84 **p** 85. C Clooney *D & R* 84-86; I Urney w Sion Mills 86-92; I Derryvullen N w Castlearchdale *Clogh* 92-05; Chapl to Bp Clogh 02-05; Can Clogh Cathl 03-05; Dean Clogh 05-09; I Clogh w Errigal Portclare 05-09; rtd 09. *En-Rimmon, 6 Tullylammy Road, Irvinestown, Enniskillen BT94 1RN* T: (028) 6862 8258

THOMPSON, Richard Brian. b 60. Sheff Poly BSc 83. Ripon Coll Cuddesdon 86. **d** 89 **p** 90. C Thorpe Bay *Chelmsf* 89-92; V Rushmere *St E* 92-97; Dep Chapl HM Pris Nor 97-98; Chapl HM Pris Wayland 98-01; Chapl HM Pris Hollesley Bay 01-06; Chapl HM Pris Whitemoor 06-08; Chapl HM Pris Hollesley Bay and HM Pris and YOI Warren Hill 08-13; Chapl HM Pris Peterborough from 13. *HM Prison, Saville Road, Peterborough PE3 7PD* T: (01733) 217500 E: richard.thompson02@hmps.gsi.gov.uk

THOMPSON, Robert Craig. b 72. Univ Coll Dur BA 92. Westcott Ho Cam 94. **d** 96 **p** 97. C Wigan All SS *Liv* 96-00; P-in-c Ladybrook *S'well* 00-05; P-in-c Bengeo *St Alb* 05-08; TV Hertford from 08. *The Rectory, Byde Street, Hertford SG14 3BS* T: (01992) 413691 E: revrobert@tiscali.co.uk

THOMPSON, Robert George. b 71. K Coll Cam BA 93 MA 97. Ripon Coll Cuddesdon MTh 95. **d** 97 **p** 98. C Ruislip St Martin *Lon* 97-01; Chapl Parkside Community NHS Trust Lon 01-09; Chapl R Brompton and Harefield NHS Trust from 09; Hon C Holland Park *Lon* 09-15; Hon C Notting Dale St Clem w St Mark and St Jas from 15. *Chaplain's Office, Royal Brompton Hospital, Sydney Street, London SW3 6NP* T: (020) 7352 8121 ext 4740 E: r.thompson2@rbht.nhs.uk

THOMPSON, Roger Quintin. b 63. K Coll Lon BA 85 AKC 85 Nottm Univ PGCE 86 MA 96. Aston Tr Scheme 92 St Jo Coll

Nottm 94. **d** 96. C Easton H Trin w St Gabr and St Lawr and St Jude *Bris* 96-00; C Lisburn Ch Ch Cathl 00-04; I Kilwaughter w Cairncastle and Craigy Hill 04-15; Partnership Co-ord CMS Ireland from 15. *Address temp unknown* E: rqtfi@btinternet.com

THOMPSON, Ross Keith Arnold. b 53. Sussex Univ BA 75 Bris Univ PhD 82. Coll of Resurr Mirfield 80. **d** 82 **p** 83. C Knowle *Bris* 82-85; TV E Bris 85-94; V Bristol St Aid w St Geo 94-95; V Knowle St Barn and H Cross Inns Court 95-02; Tutor St Mich Coll Llan 02-05; rtd 09. *Grove Cottage, Barton Lane, Mere, Warminster BA12 6JA* T: (01747) 860553

THOMPSON, Ruth Jean. *See* GOSTELOW, Ruth Jean

THOMPSON, Mrs Shanthi Hazel Peiris. b 67. Cranmer Hall Dur 07. **d** 09 **p** 10. C Kirkby Lonsdale *Carl* 09-13; P-in-c Staveley, Ings and Kentmere from 13. *The Vicarage, Kentmere Road, Staveley, Kendal LA8 9PA* T: (01539) 821267 M: 07931-446025 E: staveleyvicarage@gmail.com

THOMPSON, Stephen Peter. b 45. Lon Univ BSc 67 Lon Inst of Educn PGCE 71 K Coll Lon BD 77 AKC 77 SOAS Lon BA 82 Poona Univ MPhil 85 PhD 87 FRAS 91. Ripon Coll Cuddesdon. **d** 00. NSM Bedford Park *Lon* 00-01; NSM Isleworth St Fran 01-08; PtO from 08. *12 Minsterley Avenue, Shepperton TW17 8QT* T: (01932) 781805 E: revdocstephen@gmail.com

THOMPSON, Thomas Michael. b 46. **d** 11 **p** 12. NSM Silverton, Butterleigh, Bickleigh and Cadeleigh *Ex* from 11. *Gable Cottage, Bickleigh, Tiverton EX16 8RD* T: (01884) 855309 M: 07866-133640 E: tmdfthompson@uwclub.net

THOMPSON, Timothy Charles. b 51. Lon Univ BSc 73 AKC. Westcott Ho Cam 75. **d** 78 **p** 79. C Ipswich St Mary at Stoke w St Pet etc *St E* 78-81; Ind Chapl *Nor* 81-88; C Lowestoft and Kirkley 81-83; TV 83-88; V Coney Hill *Glouc* 88-94; P-in-c Caister *Nor* 94-00; R from 00. *The Rectory, Rectory Close, Caister-on-Sea, Great Yarmouth NR30 5EG* T: (01493) 720287 E: tim@timthompson.plus.com

THOMPSON, Canon Timothy William. b 47. Bris Univ CertEd 70 Open Univ BA 78. EMMTC. **d** 88 **p** 89. C Scartho *Linc* 88-91; V Haxey 91-95; P-in-c Surfleet 95-00; Asst Local Min Officer 95-00; RD Elloe W 98-00; P-in-c Linc St Pet-at-Gowts and St Andr 00-09; P-in-c Linc St Botolph 00-09; RD Christianity 02-08; rtd 09; Can and Preb Linc Cathl from 02. *16 Nocton Park Road, Nocton, Lincoln LN4 2BE* T: (01526) 320171 M: 07885-238813 E: timwthompson@btinternet.com

THOMPSON, Canon Tom Malcolm. b 38. Dur Univ BA 60 Man Univ MPhil 93. Bps' Coll Cheshunt 60. **d** 62 **p** 63. C Standish *Blackb* 62-65; C Lancaster St Mary 65-67; V Chorley All SS 67-72; V Barrowford 72-78; RD Pendle 75-78; R Northfield *Birm* 78-82; RD Kings Norton 79-82; V Longton *Blackb* 82-94; RD Leyland 89-94; V Nunthorpe *York* 94-03; Can and Preb York Minster 98-03; RD Stokesley 00-03; rtd 03; PtO *Carl* from 03; *Blackb* from 08. *Wainstones, 6 Greengate Crescent, Levens, Kendal LA8 8QB* T: (015395) 61409

THOMPSON-McCAUSLAND, Marcus Perronet. b 31. Trin Coll Cam BA 54 MA 60. Coll of Resurr Mirfield 57. **d** 59 **p** 60. C Perry Barr *Birm* 59-65; V Rubery 65-72; R Cradley *Heref* 72-82; P-in-c Storridge 72-82; P-in-c Mathon 72-82; P-in-c Castle Frome 72-82; Hon C Camberwell St Giles *S'wark* 82-87; Hon C Lydbury N *Heref* 88-89; Hon C Lydbury N w Hopesay and Edgton 89-94; Hon C Wigmore Abbey 95-01; PtO from 01. *18 Watling Street, Leintwardine, Craven Arms SY7 0LW* T: (01547) 540228

THOMPSON-VEAR, John Arthur. b 76. Sunderland Univ BA 98. St Steph Ho Ox BA 02 MA 06. **d** 03 **p** 04. C Plymouth Crownhill Ascension *Ex* 03-06; Chapl RN 06-08; TV Harrogate St Wilfrid *Ripon* 08-11; CF(V) from 10. *22 Park House Green, Harrogate HG1 3HW* T: (01423) 709432 M: 07799-215148 E: frjohnx@gmail.com

THOMPSTONE, Canon John Deaville. b 39. BNC Ox BA 63 MA 67. Ridley Hall Cam 63. **d** 65 **p** 66. C Hoole *Ches* 65-68; C Fulwood *Sheff* 68-71; V Skirbeck H Trin *Linc* 71-77; V Shipley St Pet *Bradf* 77-91; RD Airedale 82-88; V Poynton *Ches* 91-04; Hon Can Ches Cathl 02-04; rtd 04. *Greyfriars, Broadway Road, Childswickham, Broadway WR12 7HP* T: (01386) 852930 E: greyfriars@homecall.co.uk

THOMSETT, Murray Richard. b 32. MBKSTS. Oak Hill Th Coll 91. **d** 92 **p** 93. NSM Whitton SS Phil and Jas *Lon* 92-96; NSM Hampton All SS 96-02; Chapl Terminal 4 Heathrow Airport 96-12; rtd 12. *27 Coombe Road, Hampton TW12 3PB* T: (020) 8979 7549 E: murrayt@nildram.co.uk

THOMSON, Alexander Keith. b 38. Cranmer Hall Dur BA 63. **d** 64 **p** 65. C Middleton *Man* 64-68; Chapl Rannoch Sch Perthshire 68-72; P-in-c Kinloch Rannoch *St And* 68-72; Asst Chapl Oundle Sch 72-94; LtO *Pet* 73-94; Chapl Laxton Sch 88-94; PtO *Pet* 94-01; rtd 98. *School House Cottage, Alderley Road, Chelford, Macclesfield SK11 9AP* T: (01625) 860996

THOMSON, Andrew Maitland. b 43. CA(Z) 67. Westcott Ho Cam 78. **d** 80 **p** 81. C Harre Cathl Zimbabwe 80-82; R Kadoma and P-in-c Chegutu 82-87; R Malborough St Paul Harare 87-92; P-in-c E w N and W Barsham *Nor* 92-95; P-in-c N and S Creake w Waterden 92-94; P-in-c Sculthorpe w Dunton and Doughton 92-94; R N and S Creake w Waterden, Syderstone etc 95-11; rtd 11; C E w W Rudham, Helhoughton etc *Nor* from 11. *3 Charles Road, Fakenham NR21 8JX* T: (01328) 862557 E: pandathomson@btinternet.com

THOMSON, Mrs Anja. b 58. STETS. **d** 12 **p** 13. NSM Fishponds St Mary *Bris* from 12. *1 Dundridge Gardens, Bristol BS5 8SZ* T: 0117-967 0779 M: 07742-968633 E: anjathomson@btinternet.com

THOMSON, Bruce. *See* THOMSON, Sydney Bruce

THOMSON, Canon Celia Stephanie Margaret. b 55. LMH Ox MA 83 Birkbeck Coll Lon MA 87 K Coll Lon MA 94. Sarum & Wells Th Coll 89. **d** 91 **p** 94. Par Dn Southfields St Barn *S'wark* 91-94; C 94-95; V W Wimbledon Ch Ch 95-03; Tutor SEITE 95-00; Voc Adv Lambeth Adnry 96-00; Can Res Glouc Cathl from 03. *3 Miller's Green, Gloucester GL1 2BN* T: (01452) 415824 E: cthomson@gloucestercathedral.org.uk

THOMSON, Christopher Grant. b 71. Cam Univ BTh 07. Westcott Ho Cam 05. **d** 07 **p** 08. C Bletchingley and Nutfield *S'wark* 07-11; P-in-c Kenley from 11; P-in-c Purley St Barn from 11; Asst Dir of Ords Croydon Area from 13. *The Vicarage, 3 Valley Road, Kenley CR8 5DJ* T: (020) 8660 6981 E: revdthomson@btinternet.com

✠**THOMSON, The Rt Revd David.** b 52. Keble Coll Ox MA 78 DPhil 78 Selw Coll Cam BA 80 MA 84 FRSA 06 FSA 08 FRHistS 08. Westcott Ho Cam 78. **d** 81 **p** 82 **c** 08. C Maltby *Sheff* 81-84; TV Banbury *Ox* 84-94; Sec Par and People 84-93; TR Cockermouth w Embleton and Wythop *Carl* 94-02; Adn Carl and Can Res Carl Cathl 02-08; Suff Bp Huntingdon *Ely* from 08. *14 Lynn Road, Ely CB6 1DA* T: (01353) 662137 F: 669357 M: 07771-864550 E: bishop.huntingdon@ely.anglican.org

THOMSON, David Francis. b 54. Salford Univ BA 81 CPFA 84. NOC 05. **d** 07 **p** 08. NSM New Bury w Gt Lever *Man* 07-10; P-in-c Ainsworth from 10; C Bury St Mary from 13. *The Vicarage, Ainsworth Hall Road, Ainsworth, Bolton BL2 5RY* T: (01204) 398567 M: 07970-461907 E: thomsondf@hotmail.com

THOMSON, Dorothy Lucille. *See* THOMAS, Dorothy Lucille

THOMSON, Canon Elizabeth Jane. b 64. Univ Coll Ox MA 85 DPhil 89 Trin Coll Cam BA 02 Moray Ho Coll of Educn PGCE 90. Westcott Ho Cam 00. **d** 03 **p** 04. C Pilton w Croscombe, N Wootton and Dinder *B & W* 03-07; TV Witney *Ox* 07-14; Can Missr Derby Cathl from 14. *22 Kedleston Road, Derby DE22 1GU* T: (01332) 208995 E: missioner@derbycathedral.org

THOMSON, Elizabeth Lucy. *See* TALBOT, Elizabeth Lucy

THOMSON, Glyn Douglas. b 48. **d** 13 **p** 14. NSM 4Saints Team *Liv* from 13. *82 Eaton Gardens, Liverpool L12 3HW* T: 0151-228 7880 E: glyn.thomson@yahoo.co.uk

THOMSON, James. b 39. St Andr Coll Melrose 58 Episc Sem Austin Texas 88. **d** 62 **p** 63. C Oklahoma City All So USA 89-90; R Oklahoma St Matt 90-95; Assoc R Oklahoma H Trin 95-05; P-in-c Pittenweem *St And* 06-09; P-in-c Elie and Earlsferry 06-09; rtd 09; LtO *St And* 09-11; P-in-c Fraserburgh *Ab* 11-12. *41A South Street, St Andrews KY16 9QR* T: (01334) 479645 E: jim39@talktalk.net

THOMSON, James Maclaren. b 69. Grey Coll Dur BA 91 Univ Coll Lon MA 93. Wycliffe Hall Ox BA 99. **d** 00 **p** 01. C Oulton Broad *Nor* 00-04; V Chatteris *Ely* 04-13; Hon C from 13; Chapl Qu Eliz Hosp King's Lynn NHS Foundn Trust from 13. *The Vicarage, Church Lane, Chatteris PE16 6JA* T: (01354) 692173 E: james@chatteris.org

✠**THOMSON, The Rt Revd John Bromilow.** b 59. York Univ BA 81 Wycliffe Hall Ox BA 84 MA 91 Nottm Univ PhD 01. **d** 85 **p** 86 **c** 14. C Ecclesall *Sheff* 85-89; Tutor St Paul's Coll Grahamstown S Africa 89-92; Asst P Grahamstown St Bart 90-92; Asst Lect Rhodes Univ 91-92; V Doncaster St Mary *Sheff* 93-01; Dir Min 01-14; Hon Can Sheff Cathl 01-14; Suff Bp Selby *York* from 14. *Bishop's House, York Road, Barlby, Selby YO8 5JP* T: (01757) 429982 E: bishopofselby@yorkdiocese.org

THOMSON, Julian Harley. b 43. AKC 70. St Aug Coll Cant 70. **d** 71 **p** 72. C Wellingborough All Hallows *Pet* 71-74; Min Can, Prec and Sacr Ely Cathl 74-80; P-in-c Stuntney 76-80; V Arrington 80-91; R Croydon w Clopton 80-91; R Orwell 80-91; R Wimpole 80-91; V Linton 91-96; R Bartlow 91-96; P-in-c Castle Camps 91-96; TR Linton 96-01; RD 99-01; rtd 01; PtO *Nor* from 01. *Lavender Cottage, 7 Abbey Road, Great Massingham, King's Lynn PE32 2HN* T: (01485) 520721 E: thomson5816@btinternet.com

THOMSON, Keith. *See* THOMSON, Alexander Keith

THOMSON, Mark Stephen. b 57. Glas Univ MA 78. Ridley Hall Cam 10. **d** 12 **p** 13. C Market Deeping *Linc* 12-15; C Uffington Gp from 15. *16 Church Street, Deeping St James, Peterborough PE6 8HD* T: (01778) 348394

THOMSON, Matthew James. b 63. Nottm Univ BA 92. St Jo Coll Nottm 92. **d** 95 **p** 96. C Cosham *Portsm* 95-98; C Nailsea Ch Ch w Tickenham *B & W* 98-01; V Congresbury w Puxton and Hewish St Ann from 01; Bp's Healing Adv from 01. *The Vicarage, Station Road, Congresbury, Bristol BS49 5DX* T: (01934) 833126 E: revmatthomson@hotmail.com

THOMSON, Monica Anne. b 38. **d** 06 **p** 07. *9 Broomfields Road, Appleton, Warrington WA4 3AE* T: (01925) 604235 E: jomo.tomsky@ntlworld.com

THOMSON, Canon Richard Irving. b 32. Oak Hill Th Coll 57. **d** 60 **p** 61. C Kingston upon Hull H Trin *York* 60-63; C S Croydon Em *Cant* 63-66; V Shoreditch St Leon *Lon* 66-73; Chapl Vevey w Château d'Oex and Villars *Eur* 73-78; V Reigate St Mary *S'wark* 78-97; Hon Can S'wark Cathl 90-97; rtd 97; PtO *Win* 97-14. *Little Heathfield, Forest Front, Dibden Purlieu, Southampton SO45 3RG* T: (023) 8084 9613 E: richardithomson@compuserve.com

THOMSON, Richard William Byars. b 60. Birm Univ BA 86. Ripon Coll Cuddesdon 86. **d** 88 **p** 89. C Moulsecoomb *Chich* 88-90; P-in-c Kirriemuir *St And* 90-94; P-in-c Piddletrenthide w Plush, Alton Pancras etc *Sarum* 94-02; P-in-c Milborne St Andrew w Dewlish 94-02; Chapl Milton Abbey Sch Dorset 02-12; P-in-c Boxwell, Leighterton, Didmarton, Oldbury etc *Glouc* from 12. *Withymore Vicarage, Old Down Road, Badminton GL9 1EU* T: (01454) 219236 E: r.thomson@live.co.uk

THOMSON, Robert Douglass. b 37. Lon Univ TCert 61 Newc Univ DAES 70 Dur Univ BEd 75. NEOC 76. **d** 79 **p** 80. NSM Shincliffe *Dur* 79-98; Chapl St Aid Coll Dur 93-99; PtO *Dur* from 99. *11 Hill Meadows, High Shincliffe, Durham DH1 2PE* T: 0191-386 3358

THOMSON, Robin Alexander Stewart. b 43. Ch Coll Cam MA 69 K Coll Lon MTh 72. SEITE 94. **d** 96 **p** 97. NSM Wimbledon Em Ridgway Prop Chpl *S'wark* 96-02 and 10-13; NSM Tooting Graveney St Nic 02-10; PtO from 13. *2 Coppice Close, London SW20 9AS* T: (020) 8540 7748 *or* 8770 9717 F: 8770 9747

THOMSON, Canon Ronald. b 24. Leeds Univ BA 49. Coll of Resurr Mirfield 49. **d** 51 **p** 52. C Sunderland *Dur* 51-54; C Attercliffe w Carbrook *Sheff* 54-57; V Shiregreen St Hilda 57-73; RD Ecclesfield 72-73; V Worsbrough St Mary 73-88; RD Tankersley 75-85; Hon Can Sheff Cathl 77-88; rtd 88; PtO *Sheff* 88-15. *4 St Mary's Garden, Worsbrough, Barnsley S70 5LU* T: (01226) 203553

THOMSON, Sydney Bruce. b 49. Fuller Th Sem California MA 91 ThM 92 Stirling Univ MLitt 98. Ox Min Course 05. **d** 07 **p** 08. C Worcs W *Worc* 07-10; TV Leominster *Heref* from 10. *The New Vicarage, Kimbolton, Leominster HR6 0EJ* T: (01568) 615295 E: beagle67@btinternet.com

THOMSON, Wendy Leigh. b 64. Trin W Univ Vancouver BA 87. Wycliffe Hall Ox BTh 99. **d** 00 **p** 01. C Oulton Broad *Nor* 00-04; C Chatteris *Ely* 04-13; V from 13. *The Vicarage, Church Lane, Chatteris PE16 6JA* T: (01354) 692173 E: wendy@chatteris.org

THOMSON, Mrs Winifred Mary. b 35. St Mary's Coll Dur BA 57 MA 58. Qu Coll Birm 79. **dss** 82 **d** 87 **p** 94. Leic H Spirit 82-86; Oadby 86-92; Par Dn 87-92; rtd 93; PtO *Leic* from 94. *140 Knighton Church Road, Leicester LE2 3JJ* T: 0116-270 5863

THOMSON GIBSON, Thomas. *See* GIBSON, Thomas Thomson

THOMSON-GLOVER, Canon William Hugh. b 28. Trin Hall Cam BA 52 MA 56. Cuddesdon Coll 52. **d** 54 **p** 55. C Stepney St Dunstan and All SS *Lon* 54-58; C Tiverton St Andr *Ex* 58-60; P-in-c 60-63; Chapl Clifton Coll Bris 63-69; V Bris Lockleaze St Mary Magd w St Fran 70-76; P-in-c Sherston Magna w Easton Grey 76-81; P-in-c Luckington w Alderton 76-81; V Sherston Magna, Easton Grey, Luckington etc 81-93; P-in-c Foxley w Bremilham 84-86; RD Malmesbury 88-93; Hon Can Bris Cathl 91-93; rtd 93; PtO *Ex* from 93. *Woodgate Farm House, Woodgate, Culmstock, Cullompton EX15 3HW* T: (01884) 841465

THORBURN, Guy Douglas Anderson. b 50. Trin Coll Ox BA 74 MA 78. Ridley Hall Cam. **d** 83 **p** 84. C Putney St Marg *S'wark* 83-87; R Moresby *Carl* 87-97; V Gt Clacton *Chelmsf* from 97; C Harwich Peninsula from 15; AD St Osyth from 07; AD Harwich from 15. *St John's Vicarage, Valley Road, Clacton-on-Sea CO15 4AR* T: (01255) 421483 E: revguy.thorburn@virgin.net

THORBURN, Simon Godfrey. b 51. Newc Univ BSc 73 Fitzw Coll Cam BA 77 MA 81 Sheff Univ MMinTheol 97. Westcott Ho Cam 75. **d** 78 **p** 79. C Stafford *Lich* 78-82; C Tettenhall Regis 82-83; TV 83-90; Soc Resp Officer *S'wark* 90-97; V Edgbaston St Geo *Birm* 97-09; AD Edgbaston 03-08; Chapl St Geo Sch Edgbaston 99-08; V Oswestry *Lich* from 09;

R Rhydycroesau from 09. *The Vicarage, Penylan Lane, Oswestry SY11 2AJ* T: (01691) 653467 E: simon@thorburns.plus.com

THORESEN, Ms Alveen Fern. b 46. Avondale Coll NSW BA(Ed) 69 Newc Univ Aus BA 76 New England Univ NSW MA 82. SAOMC 96. **d** 01 **p** 02. NSM Caversham St Pet and Mapledurham *Ox* 01-10; NSM Boxwell, Leighterton, Didmarton, Oldbury etc *Glouc* from 10. *The Rectory, The Meads, Leighterton, Tetbury GL8 8UW* T: (01666) 890548 E: alveen@waitrose.com

THORIUS, Mrs Lynn Christine. b 51. Newc Univ DAES 85. Yorks Min Course 08. **d** 11 **p** 12. NSM E Richmond *Leeds* 11-14; Bp's Chapl and Policy Adv *Leic* from 14. *11 Bedford View, Leeds LS16 6DL* M: 07788-862397 E: rlthorius@tiscali.co.uk

THORLEY, Canon Barry. b 44. Westcott Ho Cam 70. **d** 73 **p** 74. C Camberwell St Giles *S'wark* 73-76; C Moseley St Mary *Birm* 76-78; V Birchfield 78-83; V Brixton St Matt *S'wark* 84-89; C Greenwich St Alfege 96-00; C Thamesmead 00-01; TR 01-06; rtd 06; Hon Can Zanzibar from 04. *St Benet's Chapel, PO Box 104, Nkawie-Toase, Ghana* E: thorleybarry@yahoo.co.uk

THORLEY, Mrs Mary Kathleen. b 53. OBE 00. Univ of Wales (Swansea) BA 74 Glos Coll of Educn PGCE 75. St Mich Coll Llan 99. **d** 02 **p** 03. NSM Carmarthen St Pet *St D* 02-05; NSM Carmarthen St Dav 05-12. *Bryn Heulog, Heol Penllanffos, Carmarthen SA31 2HL* T: (01267) 235927

THORN (formerly KINGS), Mrs Jean Alison. b 63. RGN 85 Heythrop Coll Lon MTh. Cranmer Hall Dur BA 90. **d** 91 **p** 93. Chapl Bris Poly 91-92; Chapl UWE 92-95; Hon C Bris Lockleaze St Mary Magd w St Fran 91-95; C Fishponds All SS 95-96; Hon C 96-97; V Bris Ch the Servant Stockwood 97-01; Hon C Whitchurch 01-04. *The Rectory, Church Street, Burton Bradstock, Bridport DT6 4QS* T: (01308) 898799 E: jean@jeanandbob.demon.co.uk

THORN, Kevan. b 67. CBDTI 03. **d** 06 **p** 07. NSM Blackpool H Cross *Blackb* 06-10; NSM Kirkham from 10. *16 Bannistre Close, Lytham St Annes FY8 3HS* T: (01253) 713088 F: 08707-621548 E: kevanthorn@btopenworld.com

THORN, Mrs Pamela Mary. b 46. Brentwood Coll of Educn BEd 78. EAMTC 01. **d** 04 **p** 05. NSM Waterbeach *Ely* from 04. *31 Lode Avenue, Waterbeach, Cambridge CB25 9PX* T: (01223) 864262 M: 07989-491557 E: pamandtrevorthorn@btinternet.com

THORN, Peter. b 50. Man Poly BEd 79. Ridley Hall Cam 82. **d** 84 **p** 85. C Aughton Ch Ch *Liv* 84-87; C Skelmersdale St Paul 87-90; Dioc Children's Officer 87-92; P-in-c Croft w Southworth 90-92; C Streatley *St Alb* 92-95; R Blofield w Hemblington *Nor* 95-96; P-in-c 96-99; Assoc Dioc Dir of Tr 97-99; V Sheff St Bart 99-01; P-in-c Shotley *St E* 01-07; P-in-c Tweedmouth *Newc* 07-09; P-in-c Claydon and Barham *St E* 09-15; C Gt and Lt Blakenham w Baylham and Nettlestead 09-15; rtd 15; P-in-c Flixton St Jo *Man* from 15. *St John's Vicarage, Irlam Road, Urmston, Manchester M41 6AP* M: 07810-363291 E: peterthorn15@hotmail.com

THORN, Simon Alexander. b 66. Bris Univ BSc 89 PhD 92 FLS 98 FCollP 96. Ox Min Course 06. **d** 09 **p** 10. NSM Abingdon *Ox* 09-12; NSM Hermitage 12-14; Chapl Downe Ho Sch Berks 11-14; Chapl Win Coll from 15. *57 Kingsgate Street, Winchester SO23 9PF* M: 07714-194591 T: (01962) 868291

THORNALLEY, Graham Paul. b 70. Coll of Resurr Mirfield 05. **d** 07 **p** 08. C Brumby *Linc* 07-09; C Frodingham 09-11; TV Howden *York* from 11. *The New Vicarage, Portington Road, Eastrington DN14 7QE* T: (01430) 410096 E: gthornalley@tiscali.co.uk

THORNBURGH, Richard Hugh Perceval. b 52. Sarum & Wells Th Coll. **d** 84 **p** 85. C Broadstone *Sarum* 84-87; TV Beaminster Area 87-95; TV Hanley H Ev *Lich* 96-01; R S Elmham and Ilketshall *St E* from 01; C Bungay from 14. *Parsonage House, Low Street, Ilketshall St Margaret, Bungay NR35 1QZ* T/F: (01986) 781345 E: rhpt@pharisaios.co.uk

THORNBURY, Peter Dawson. b 43. Open Univ BA 84 TCD BTh 93. CITC 90. **d** 93 **p** 94. C Annagh w Drumgoon, Ashfield etc *K, E & A* 93-96; I Clondehorkey w Cashel *D & R* 96-98; I Mevagh w Glenalla 96-98; Bp's C Kilsaran w Drumcar, Dunleer and Dunany *Arm* 98-06; I Aghaderg w Donaghmore and Scarva *D & D* 06-13; rtd 13. *Le Guirzout, 56110 Gourin, France* T: (0033) 2 97 34 27 73 E: wildthornp@gmail.com

THORNBY, Mrs Janet. b 40. **d** 06 **p** 07. OLM Cheriton All So w Newington *Cant* 06-10; PtO from 10. *11 Peene Cottages, Peene, Folkestone CT18 8BB* T: (01303) 271267 E: thornbyrobjan@aol.com

THORNDIKE, Benjamin Robert. b 77. Leeds Metrop Univ BA 99 Trin & All SS Coll Leeds PGCE 02. Oak Hill Th Coll 11. **d** 13 **p** 14. C Arborfield w Barkham *Ox* from 13. *Church Office, The Rectory, Church Lane, Arborfield, Reading RG2 9HZ* T: 0118-976 0285 E: ben@abch.org.uk

THORNE, Mrs Anita Dawn. b 46. Trin Coll Bris 84. **dss** 86 **d** 87 **p** 94. Asst Chapl Bris Poly 86-88; Par Dn Olveston 88-94; P-in-c 94-96; P-in-c Portland All SS w St Pet *Sarum* 96-05; P-in-c Clutton w Cameley *B & W* 05-10; R Clutton w Cameley, Bishop Sutton and Stowey 10-12; rtd 12. *2 Armada Way, Dorchester DT1 2TL* T: (01305) 265118 E: thorne391@btinternet.com

THORNE, Mrs Anne. b 55. SWMTC 95. **d** 98 **p** 99. C Crediton and Shobrooke *Ex* 98-01; C Beer and Branscombe 01-03; C Seaton and Beer 03-06; P-in-c Braunton from 06. *The Vicarage, Church Street, Braunton EX33 2EL* T: (01271) 815330 E: vicarthorne@aol.com

THORNE, Mrs Margaret. b 58. Kingston Poly BA 79 Heythrop Coll Lon MA 02 LGSM 78. Ox Min Course 05. **d** 08 **p** 09. C Earley St Pet *Ox* 08-12; V Headington St Mary 12-15; R Chinnor, Sydenham, Aston Rowant and Crowell from 15. *The Rectory, High Street, Chinnor OX3 9EY* M: 07512-951780 T: (01844) 354626 E: maggie53thorne@gmail.com

THORNE, Mrs Marie Elizabeth. b 47. EMMTC 83. **dss** 86 **d** 87 **p** 94. Cleethorpes *Linc* 86-90; C 87-90; C Brigg 90-96; P-in-c New Waltham 96-00; V 00-07; R Gt w Lt Massingham, Harpley, Rougham etc *Nor* 07-11; rtd 11. *46 Westward Ho, Grimsby DN34 5AE* E: m.e.thorne@btinternet.com

THORNETT, Joan. b 38. **d** 07 **p** 09. OLM Stickney Gp *Linc* 07-12. *93 Boston Road, Spilsby PE23 5HH* T: (01790) 754151

THORNEWILL, Canon Mark Lyon. b 25. ALCD 56. **d** 56 **p** 58. C-in-c Bradf Cathl 56-59; C-in-c Otley 59-62; R Lifton *Ex* 62-66; R Kelly w Bradstone 62-66; Dir Past Care Norton Hosps Louisville USA 69-84; Hon Can Louisville Cathl from 70; rtd 90. *116 East Campbell Street, Frankfort KY 40601-3508, USA* T: (001) (502) 696 9274 E: markthornewill@gmail.com

THORNEYCROFT, Preb Pippa Hazel Jeanetta. b 44. Ex Univ BA 65. WMMTC 85. **d** 88 **p** 94. NSM Albrighton *Lich* 88-90; NSM Beckbury, Badger, Kemberton, Ryton, Stockton etc 90-96; P-in-c Shareshill 96-09; P-in-c Essington 07-09; Dioc Adv for Women in Min 93-00; Preb Lich Cathl 99-09; RD Penkridge 01-05; rtd 09; C Tettenhall Wood and Perton *Lich* 10-12; C Hadley and Wellington Ch Ch from 12; Chapl to The Queen 01-14. *Manor Cottage, 21 High Street, Albrighton, Wolverhampton WV7 3JB* T: (01902) 375523 M: 07970-869011 E: pippa@thorneycroft.plus.com

THORNILEY, Richard James Gordon. b 56. Portsm Poly BA 78. St Jo Coll Nottm MTh 95. **d** 97 **p** 98. C Bowbrook S *Worc* 97-01; R Church Lench w Rous Lench and Abbots Morton etc from 01. *The Rectory, Station Road, Harvington, Evesham WR11 8NJ* T: (01386) 870527 E: richardgill@rthorniley.fsnet.co.uk

THORNLEY, David Howe. b 43. Wycliffe Hall Ox 77. **d** 79 **p** 80. C Burgess Hill St Andr *Chich* 79-83; P-in-c Amberley w N Stoke 83-84; P-in-c Parham and Wiggonholt w Greatham 83-84; V Amberley w N Stoke and Parham, Wiggonholt etc 84-92; P-in-c S w N Bersted 92-99; V 99-08; rtd 08. *Spinnaway Cottage, Church Hill, Slindon, Arundel BN18 0RD* M: 07941-834920

THORNLEY, Edward Charles. b 84. Ex Univ BA 05 Anglia Ruskin Univ MA 10. Westcott Ho Cam 08 Yale Div Sch 09. **d** 10 **p** 11. C Dereham and Distr *Nor* 10-13; C St Marylebone w H Trin *Lon* from 13; Chapl St Marylebone C of E Sch from 13; Chapl R Academy of Music from 13. *Flat 5, 38 Nottingham Place, London W1U 5NU* M: 07709-674615 E: edward.thornley@gmail.com

THORNLEY, Nicholas Andrew. b 56. St Jo Coll Nottm BTh 81. **d** 81 **p** 84. C Frodingham *Linc* 81-84; P-in-c Belton 84-85; V 85-90; V Horncastle w Low Toynton 90-98; V High Toynton 98; R Greetham w Ashby Puerorum 98; RD Horncastle 94-98; TR Gainsborough and Morton 98-11; Can and Preb Linc Cathl 98-11; P-in-c Broughton and Duddon *Carl* from 11. *The Vicarage, Broughton-in-Furness LA20 6HS* T: (01229) 716305 E: nickthornley@btconnect.com

THÖRNQVIST, Miss Karin Elisabet. b 41. Uppsala Univ 64 BD 83. **p** 84. Sweden 84-97 and 98-07; C Skegness and Winthorpe *Linc* 97-98; Gen Preacher from 07. *Address temp unknown*

THORNS, Mrs Joanne. b 64. Sunderland Univ BSc 86 MRPharmS. Cranmer Hall Dur 97. **d** 99 **p** 00. C Norton St Mary *Dur* 99-04; C Stockton St Chad 02-04; TV Dur N 04-14; Regional Officer NE Chs Acting Together from 14. *25 Barnard Close, Durham DH1 5XN* T: 0191-386 8049 E: nechurchesactingtogether@gmail.com

THORNTON, Darren Thomas. b 68. Wilson Carlile Coll 90 EAMTC 00. **d** 02 **p** 03. C E Dereham and Scarning *Nor* 02-05; P-in-c Nor St Giles 05-13; V from 13; Chapl UEA from 05; RD Nor E from 14. *St Giles's Vicarage, 44 Heigham Road, Norwich NR2 3AU* T: (01603) 623724 E: d.thornton@uea.ac.uk

THORNTON, David John Dennis. b 32. Kelham Th Coll 52. **d** 56 **p** 57. C New Eltham All SS *S'wark* 56-58; C Stockwell Green St Andr 58-62; V Tollesbury *Chelmsf* 62-74; P-in-c Salcot

Virley 72-74; V Kelvedon 74-00; rtd 00; PtO *Nor* 01-07. *The Old Stable, 24 Pauls Lane, Overstrand, Cromer NR27 0PE* T: (01263) 579279

THORNTON, Mrs Diana Rachel. b 64. Mert Coll Ox MA 86. SEITE 03. **d** 06 **p** 07. C S Wimbledon H Trin and St Pet *S'wark* 06-09; C Cobham and Stoke D'Abernon *Guildf* 09-12; PtO from 12; Chapl St Mark's C of E Academy Mitcham from 13. *Ranworth Cottage, Sheath Lane, Oxshott, Leatherhead KT22 0QU* E: revdianathornton@gmail.com

THORNTON, Dominic Oskari. b 83. Westcott Ho Cam 12. **d** 15. C Salisbury St Thos and St Edm *Sarum* from 15. *Address temp unknown*

THORNTON, Howard Deyes. b 52. Canadian Th Sem MA 99. **d** 01 **p** 03. NSM Hanborough and Freeland *Ox* 01-02; C Luton St Mary *St Alb* 02-04; Chapl Luton Univ 01-06; Chapl Bedfordshire Univ 06-07; TR Cowley St Jas *Ox* 07-14; Canada from 14. *Address temp unknown*

THORNTON, John. b 26. St Edm Hall Ox BA 53 MA 57. Westcott Ho Cam 53. **d** 55 **p** 56. C Woodhall Spa *Linc* 55-58; C Glouc St Steph 58-60; C Wotton St Mary 60-62; P-in-c Gt Witcombe 62-63; R 63-91; Chapl HM Pris Glouc 82-91; rtd 91; PtO *Glouc* from 91. *17 Manor Gardens, Barnwood Road, Gloucester GL4 3JY* T: (01452) 619775

THORNTON, Magdalen Mary. *See* SMITH, Magdalen Mary

THORNTON, Richard Oliver. b 41. St Paul's Coll Chelt CertEd 63. **d** 11. NSM Nettleham *Linc* from 11. *45 High Street, Nettleham, Lincoln LN2 2PL* T: (01522) 821161 E: richard.thornton1@ntlworld.com

THORNTON, Timothy Charles Gordon. b 35. Ch Ch Ox BA 58 MA 61. Linc Th Coll 60. **d** 62 **p** 63. C Kirkholt CD *Man* 62-64; Tutor Linc Th Coll 64-68; Chapl 66-68; Fiji 69-73; Chapl Brasted Place Coll Westerham 73-74; Can Missr *Guildf* 74-79; P-in-c Hascombe 74-79; V Chobham w Valley End 79-84; V Spelsbury and Chadlington *Ox* 84-87; V Chadlington and Spelsbury, Ascott under Wychwood 87-00; rtd 00; PtO *Carl* from 01. *The Old Cottage, Warcop, Appleby-in-Westmorland CA16 6NX* T: (017683) 41239

⊕**THORNTON, The Rt Revd Timothy Martin.** b 57. Southn Univ BA 78 K Coll Lon MA 97. St Steph Ho Ox 78. **d** 80 **p** 81 **c** 01. C Todmorden *Wakef* 80-82; P-in-c Walsden 82-85; Lect Univ of Wales (Cardiff) *Llan* 85-87; Chapl 85-86; Sen Chapl 86-87; Bp's Chapl *Wakef* 87-91; Dir of Ords 88-91; Bp's Chapl *Lon* 91-94; Dep P in O 92-01; Prin NTMTC 94-98; V Kensington St Mary Abbots w St Geo *Lon* 98-01; AD Kensington 00-01; Area Bp Sherborne *Sarum* 01-08; Bp Truro from 08. *Lis Escop, Feock, Truro TR3 6QQ* T: (01872) 862657 F: 862037 E: bishop@truro.anglican.org

THOROGOOD, Preb John Martin. b 45. Birm Univ BA 68 PGCE 69. Ox NSM Course 82. **d** 85 **p** 86. NSM Sunningdale *Ox* 85-90; Chapl St Geo Sch Ascot 88-90; TV Camelot Par *B & W* 90-97; V Evercreech w Chesterblade and Milton Clevedon 97-03; RD Cary and Bruton 96-03; R Dulverton and Brushford 03-10; P-in-c Brompton Regis w Upton and Skilgate 08-10; R Dulverton w Brushford, Brompton Regis etc 10-13; RD Exmoor 05-09; Preb Wells Cathl 07-13; rtd 13. *Holden Cottage, 2 West Street, Withycombe, Minehead TA24 6PX* T: (01984) 641745 E: johntvicar@btinternet.com

THOROLD, Alison Susan Joy. *See* HEALY, Alison Susan Joy

THOROLD, Jeremy Stephen. b 59. **d** 04 **p** 05. OLM Gainsborough and Morton *Linc* 04-07; NSM Lanteglos by Camelford w Advent and St Teath *Truro* 07-09; P-in-c Menheniot and St Ive and Pensilva w Quethiock 09-11; Bp's Dom Chapl from 11; Minl Development Review Admin 10-14; Bp's Adv for Deliverance Min from 14. *Lis Escop, Feock, Truro TR3 6QQ* T: (01872) 862657 F: 862037 E: chaplain@truro.anglican.org

THOROLD, Canon John Stephen. b 35. Bps' Coll Cheshunt 61. **d** 63 **p** 64. C Cleethorpes *Linc* 63-70; V Cherry Willingham w Greetwell 70-77; P-in-c Firsby w Gt Steeping 77-79; R 79-86; R Aswardby w Sausthorpe 77-86; R Halton Holgate 77-86; R Langton w Sutterby 77-86; V Spilsby w Hundleby 77-86; R Lt Steeping 79-86; R Raithby 79-86; V New Sleaford 86-01; RD Lafford 87-96; Can and Preb Linc Cathl 98-01; rtd 01; PtO *Linc* from 01. *8 Ashwood Close, Horncastle LN9 5HA* T: (01507) 526562

THOROLD, Trevor Neil. b 63. Hull Univ BA 87. Ripon Coll Cuddesdon 88. **d** 89 **p** 90. C W Bromwich St Andr w Ch Ch *Lich* 89-93; Res Min Oswestry 93-97; P-in-c Petton w Cockshutt, Welshampton and Lyneal etc 97-05; Local Min Adv (Shrewsbury) 97-05; RD Ellesmere 98-02. *66B High Street, Wem, Shrewsbury SY4 5DR*

THORP, Adrian. b 55. Clare Coll Cam BA 77 MA 80 Lon Univ BD 80. Trin Coll Bris 77. **d** 80 **p** 81. C Kendal St Thos *Carl* 80-83; C Handforth *Ches* 83-86; V Siddal *Wakef* 86-91; V Bishopwearmouth St Gabr *Dur* 91-05; C Upper Skerne

05-07; R Blaydon and Swalwell from 07. *St Cuthbert's Rectory, Shibdon Road, Blaydon-on-Tyne NE21 5AE* T: 0191-414 2720 E: ahthorp@btinternet.com

THORP, Mrs Alison Claire. b 63. Kingston Poly BSc 85 Nottm Univ MA 10. EMMTC 06. **d** 09 **p** 10. NSM Bosworth and Sheepy Gp *Leic* 09-13; Chapl Geo Eliot Hosp NHS Trust Nuneaton 12-14; Chapl Burton Hosps NHS Foundn Trust from 14; PtO *Leic* from 13. *Culloden Farm, Gopsall, Atherstone CV9 3QJ* T: (01530) 270350 E: alisonthorp@btconnect.com

THORP, Mrs Helen Mary. b 54. Bris Univ BA 75 MA(Theol) 77 Dur Univ MA 98. Trin Coll Bris 78. **d** 87 **p** 94. NSM Siddal *Wakef* 87-91; NSM Bishopwearmouth St Gabr *Dur* 91-05; NSM Upper Skerne 05-07; NSM Blaydon and Swalwell from 07; Voc Adv 93-05; Tutor Cranmer Hall Dur from 98. *St Cuthbert's Rectory, Shibdon Road, Blaydon-on-Tyne NE21 5AE* T: 0191-414 2720 E: h.m.thorp@durham.ac.uk

THORP, Mrs Maureen Sandra. b 47. Man OLM Scheme 92. **d** 95 **p** 96. OLM Heywood *Man* 95-01; P-in-c Shore and Calderbrook 01-06; V Tonge w Alkrington 06-15; Borough Dean Rochdale 10-12; rtd 15; PtO *Man* from 15. *Address temp unknown* E: thorpmaureen@aol.com

THORP, Norman Arthur. b 29. Tyndale Hall Bris 63. **d** 65 **p** 66. C Southsea St Jude *Portsm* 65-68; C Braintree *Chelmsf* 68-73; P-in-c Tolleshunt D'Arcy w Tolleshunt Major 73-75; V 75-83; R N Buckingham *Ox* 83-95; RD Buckingham 90-95; rtd 95; PtO *Ox* 97-00. *27 Baisley Gardens, Napier Street, Bletchley, Milton Keynes MK2 2NE* T: (01908) 370221

THORP, Roderick Cheyne. b 44. Ch Ch Ox BA 65 MA 69. Ridley Hall Cam 66. **d** 69 **p** 70. C Reading Greyfriars *Ox* 69-73; C Kingston upon Hull St Martin *York* 73-76; C Heworth H Trin 76-79; C-in-c N Bletchley CD *Ox* 79-86; TV Washfield, Stoodleigh, Withleigh etc *Ex* 86-96; RD Tiverton 91-96; P-in-c Dolton 96-00; P-in-c Iddesleigh w Dowland 96-00; P-in-c Monkokehampton 96-00; rtd 00; P-in-c Etton w Dalton Holme *York* 00-08; PtO from 09. *4 Stonegate Court, Stonegate, Hunmanby, Filey YO14 0NZ* T: (01723) 892628 E: aranjay@freeuk.com *or* aranjay@phonecoop.coop

THORP, Stephen Linton. b 62. Trin Coll Bris BA 92. **d** 92 **p** 93. C Knutsford St Jo and Toft *Ches* 92-96; TV Newton Tracey, Horwood, Alverdiscott etc *Ex* 96-06; R Necton, Holme Hale w N and S Pickenham *Nor* from 06. *The Rectory, School Road, Necton, Swaffham PE37 8HT* T: (01760) 722021 E: slthorp@btinternet.com

THORP, Susannah Ruth. b 83. Jes Coll Cam BA 05 MA 09. Wycliffe Hall Ox MTh 10. **d** 08 **p** 09. C Preston-on-Tees and Longnewton *Dur* 08-12; C Stockton 08-12; C Billingham 12-13; P-in-c Doxford St Wilfrid from 13; Chapl St Jo Coll Dur from 13. *2 Whitebark, Sunderland SR3 2NX* T: 0191-522 7639

THORP, Timothy. b 65. St Steph Ho Ox BTh 93. **d** 96 **p** 97. C Jarrow *Dur* 96-99; P-in-c N Hylton St Marg Castletown 99-02; C Felpham and Missr Arundel and Bognor *Chich* 02-07; C Arundel w Tortington and S Stoke 07-08; P-in-c Ernesettle *Ex* 08-11; P-in-c Whitleigh 08-11; C Honicknowle 08-11; P-in-c Plymouth Crownhill Ascension from 11. *The Vicarage, 33 Tavistock Road, Plymouth PL5 3AF* T: (01752) 417618 E: fathertimt@bigfoot.com

THORPE, Ben Michael. b 85. De Montfort Univ BSc 06 Cam Univ BTh 13. Ridley Hall Cam 10. **d** 13 **p** 14. C Deal St Geo *Cant* from 13. *35 Church Path, Deal CT14 9TH* E: benthorpe85@gmail.com

THORPE, Preb Christopher David Charles. b 60. Cov Poly BA 83. Ripon Coll Cuddesdon 85. **d** 88 **p** 89. C Norton *St Alb* 88-92; TV Blakenall Heath *Lich* 92-99; TR Bilston 99-08; V Shifnal and Sheriffhales from 08; P-in-c Tong from 11; Preb Lich Cathl from 07. *The Vicarage, Manor Close, Shifnal TF11 9AJ* T: (01952) 463694 E: chris@christthorpe.org

THORPE, Donald Henry. b 34. St Aid Birkenhead 57. **d** 60 **p** 61. C Mexborough *Sheff* 60-64; C Doncaster St Leon and St Jude 64-67; V Doncaster Intake 67-74; V Millhouses H Trin 74-85; Prec Leic Cathl 85-89; TR Melton Gt Framland 89-93; rtd 93; PtO *Sheff* from 93; *S'well* from 93. *18 All Hallows Drive, Tickhill, Doncaster DN11 9PP* T: (01302) 743129 E: dsthorpe1@tiscali.co.uk

THORPE, Canon Kerry Michael. b 51. Oak Hill Th Coll BD 78. **d** 78 **p** 79. C Upton (Overchurch) *Ches* 78-81; C Chester le Street *Dur* 81-84; V Fatfield 84-93; V Margate H Trin *Cant* 93-98; C 98-09; Dioc Missr 06-11; Min Harvest New Angl Ch 10-11; Dioc Miss and Growth Adv *Cant* from 11; Hon Can Cant Cathl from 08. *22 St Martin's Close, Canterbury CT1 1QG* T: (01227) 459401 E: kthorpe@diocant.org

THORPE, Lynne Gail. b 62. Dioc OLM tr scheme 99. **d** 02 **p** 03. OLM Ipswich St Jo *St E* 02-06. *31 King Edward Road, Ipswich IP3 9AN* T: (01473) 717833

THORPE, Martin Xavier. b 66. Collingwood Coll Dur BSc 87 Bris Univ MPhil 00 GRSC 87. Trin Coll Bris BA 94. **d** 94 **p** 95. C Ravenhead *Liv* 94-98; TV Sutton 98-02; V Westbrook St Phil 02-11; P-in-c Westbrook St Jas 11-14; TV Warrington W from

14; Asst Dir CME from 01. *St James's Vicarage, 302 Hood Lane North, Great Sankey, Warrington WA5 1UQ* T: (01925) 492631 E: martinel.thorpe@talk21.com *or* martin.cme1-4@talk21.com

THORPE, Michael William. b 42. Lich Th Coll 67. **d** 70 **p** 71. C Walthamstow St Mich *Chelmsf* 70-71; C Plaistow St Andr 71; P-in-c Plaistow St Mary 72-74; TV Gt Grimsby St Mary and St Jas *Linc* 74-78; Chapl Grimsby Distr Hosps 78-83; Chapl Roxbourne Hosp Harrow 83-87; Chapl Northwick Park Hosp Harrow 83-87; Chapl Harrow Hosp 83-87; Chapl St Geo Hosp Linc 87-92; Chapl Linc Co Hosp Gp 87-92; Chapl Ipswich Hosp NHS Trust 92-00; rtd 00. *Moselle Cottage, 68 Lacey Street, Ipswich IP4 2PH* T: (01473) 421850

THORPE, Richard Charles. b 65. Birm Univ BSc 87. Wycliffe Hall Ox 93. **d** 96 **p** 97. C Brompton H Trin w Onslow Square St Paul *Lon* 96-05; P-in-c Shadwell St Paul w Ratcliffe St Jas 05-10; R from 10; P-in-c Bromley by Bow All Hallows 10-14. *St Paul's Rectory, 298 The Highway, London E1W 3DH* T: (020) 7481 2883 *or* 7680 2772 E: ric.thorpe@stpaulsshadwell.org

THREADGILL, Steven Alan. b 59. Cant Univ (NZ) BA 84 MA 88 Christchurch Teachers' Coll Dip Teaching 88. STETS MA 08. **d** 08 **p** 09. C Lee-on-the-Solent *Portsm* 08-11; C Bundaberg Australia from 11. *8 Hodgetts Court, Bundaberg QLD 4670, Australia* T: (0061) (7) 4151 2621 *or* 4151 3128 M: 40-769 3897 E: steventhreadgill@yahoo.co.uk

THRELFALL, Mrs Christine Emily. b 66. SNWTP. **d** 13 **p** 14. C W Bolton *Man* from 13. *Throstle House, Moss Lea, Bolton BL1 6PL* M: 07966-681335

THRELFALL-HOLMES, Miranda. b 73. Ch Coll Cam BA 95 MA 97 Univ Coll Dur PhD 00 St Jo Coll Dur BA 02. Cranmer Hall Dur 00. **d** 03 **p** 04. C Newc St Gabr 03-06; Chapl and Fell Univ Coll Dur 06-12; Interim Prin Ustinov Coll Dur 11-12; V Belmont and Pittington *Dur* from 12. *Belmont Vicarage, Broomside Lane, Durham DH1 2QW* T: 0191-386 1545 E: miranda@threlfall-holmes.net

THROSSELL, John Julian. b 30. Nottm Univ BSc 53 Syracuse Univ PhD 56. Oak Hill Th Coll 72. **d** 75 **p** 76. NSM Wheathampstead *St Alb* 75-82; V Codicote 82-88; NSM Halesworth w Linstead, Chediston, Holton etc *St E* 89-95; rtd 91. *1A Sharpe's Hill, Barrow, Bury St Edmunds IP29 5BY* T: (01284) 810314

THROUP, Ms Caroline Elizabeth. b 64. St Cath Coll Cam BA 86 MA 90 Man Univ MBA 94 Ches Univ MTh 13. St Jo Coll Nottm 08. **d** 10 **p** 11. C Burnage St Marg *Man* 10-13; R Levenshulme from 13. *St Andrew's Rectory, 27 Errwood Road, Levenshulme M19 2PN* T: 0161-283 5897 E: caroline.throup@ntlworld.com

THROWER, Clive Alan. b 41. Sheff Univ BSc 62 CEng 90. EMMTC 76. **d** 79 **p** 80. C Derby Cathl 79-86; C Spondon 86-91; Soc Resp Officer 86-91; Faith in the City Link Officer 88-91; Dioc Rural Officer 91; P-in-c Ashford w Sheldon 91; V Ashford w Sheldon and Longstone 92-07; Dioc Rural and Tourism Officer 96-07; RD Bakewell and Eyam 04-07; rtd 07; PtO *Derby* from 07. *Longstone House, 5 Vernon Green, Bakewell DE45 1DT* T: (01629) 814863 E: clive@thrower.org.uk

THROWER, The Very Revd Martin Charles. b 61. EAMTC 95. **d** 98 **p** 99. NSM Ipswich St Bart *St E* 98-01; NSM Bury St Edmunds All SS w St Jo and St Geo 01-03; P-in-c Gt and Lt Whelnetham w Bradfield St George 03-04; P-in-c Lawshall 03-04; P-in-c Hawstead and Newton w Stanningfield etc 03-04; R St Edm Way 04-09; RD Lavenham 05-09; V Hadleigh, Layham and Shelley from 09; Dean Bocking from 09; RD Hadleigh from 10. *The Deanery, Church Street, Hadleigh, Ipswich IP7 5DT* T: (01473) 822218 E: martin.thrower@btinternet.com

THROWER, Philip Edward. b 41. Kelham Th Coll 61. **d** 66 **p** 67. C Hayes St Mary *Lon* 66-69; C Yeovil *B & W* 69-71; C Shirley St Jo *Cant* 71-77; P-in-c S Norwood St Mark 77-81; V 81-84; V S'wark 85-97; V Malden St Jas 97-07; rtd 07; PtO *S'wark* from 07. *243 Chipstead Way, Banstead SM7 3JN* T: (01737) 218306

THRUSH, Margaret. b 37. St Mary's Coll Dur BA 60. Cranmer Hall Dur BA 96. **d** 97 **p** 98. NSM Houghton le Spring *Dur* 97-03; NSM Pittington, Shadforth and Sherburn 03-05; rtd 05; PtO *Dur* from 06. *45 Highgate, Durham DH1 4GA* T: 0191-386 1958

THUBRON, Thomas William. b 33. Edin Th Coll 62. **d** 65 **p** 66. C Gateshead St Mary *Dur* 65-66; C Shildon 66-67; E Pakistan 68-71; Bangladesh 71-80; V Wheatley Hill *Dur* 80-87; V Dur St Giles 87-98; rtd 98; PtO *Dur* from 04. *The Old Vicarage, Gable Terrace, Wheatley Hill, Durham DH6 3RA* T: (01429) 823940

THURBURN-HUELIN, David Richard. b 47. St Chad's Coll Dur BA 69 Ex Univ MA 98. Westcott Ho Cam 69. **d** 71 **p** 72. C Poplar *Lon* 71-76; Chapl Liddon Ho Lon 76-80; R Harrold and Carlton w Chellington *St Alb* 81-88; V Goldington 88-95; Dir OLM *Truro* 95-00; P-in-c Shipston-on-Stour w Honington

and Idlicote *Cov* 01-05; R 05-12; rtd 12; PtO *Cov* from 13. *19 The Firs, Lower Quinton, Stratford-upon-Avon CV37 8TJ* T: (01789) 720967 E: d.r.thurburnhuelin@homecall.co.uk

THURGILL, Sally Elizabeth. b 60. **d** 02 **p** 03. OLM Mattishall and the Tudd Valley *Nor* from 02. *3 Dereham Road, Yaxham, Dereham NR19 1RF* T: (01362) 692745 E: csmsthurgill@ukonline.co.uk

THURLOW, Mrs Heather. b 49. **d** 14. NSM Dewsbury *Leeds* from 14. *31 Old Mill View, Dewsbury WF12 9QJ* E: heather.thurlow@hotmail.co.uk

THURLOW, Ms Judith Mary Buller. b 44. Ch Ch Coll Cant CertEd 63 Natal Univ DipEd 78 BTh 94 MTh 00. **d** 95 **p** 96. C Port Shepstone St Kath S Africa 95-98; C Durban St Paul 99-00; C Orpington All SS *Roch* 00-02; R Kingsdown 02-14; rtd 14. *Address temp unknown* M: 07949-272106 E: judiththurlow@ukgateway.net

THURSTON-SMITH, Trevor. b 59. Chich Th Coll 83. **d** 86 **p** 87. C Rawmarsh w Parkgate *Sheff* 86-87; C Horninglow *Lich* 87-91; Chapl for People affected by HIV *Leic* 05-11; P-in-c Broughton Astley and Croft w Stoney Stanton 11-14; V Wigston from 14. *8 Harrogate Way, Wigston LE18 3YB* E: trevor@thursmith.co.uk

THURTELL, Canon Victoria Ann. b 59. St Jo Coll Dur BSc 82 Univ of Wales (Lamp) BA 11 PGCE 96. STETS 02. **d** 05 **p** 06. C Chickerell w Fleet *Sarum* 05-08; TV Dorchester 08-14; TV Dorchester and the Winterbournes 14-15; Can Res and Prec Ex Cathl from 15. *12 Cathedral Close, Exeter EX1 1EZ* T: (01392) 259329 E: precentor@exeter-cathedral.org.uk

TIBBO, George Kenneth. b 29. Reading Univ BA 50 MA 54. Coll of Resurr Mirfield 55. **d** 57 **p** 58. C W Hartlepool St Aid *Dur* 57-61; V Darlington St Mark 61-73; V Darlington St Mark w St Paul 73-75; R Crook 75-80; V Stanley 76-80; V Oldham St Chad Limeside *Man* 80-87; V Hipswell *Ripon* 87-95; OCM 90-95; rtd 95; P-in-c Nidd *Ripon* 95-01; PtO 02-04; Hon C Saddleworth *Man* 04-10; Hon C Denshaw 10-14; PtO *Dur* from 14. *14 Greenside, Greatham, Hartlepool TS25 2HQ* T: (01429) 682854

TIBBOTT (née VINE), Mrs Carolyn Ann. b 63. Anglia Poly Univ BSc 04. NTMTC BA 07. **d** 07 **p** 08. C Gidea Park *Chelmsf* 07-11; V Broomfield from 11. *Broomfield Vicarage, 10 Butlers Close, Chelmsford CM1 7BE* T: (01245) 440318 E: ctibbott@hotmail.com

TIBBS, Canon John Andrew. b 29. AKC 53. **d** 54 **p** 55. C Eastbourne St Mary *Chich* 54-57; S Africa 57-62; C Bourne *Guildf* 62-64; Swaziland 64-68; V Sompting *Chich* 69-73; R Ifield 73-78; TR 78-83; V Elstow *St Alb* 83-89; rtd 90; Chapl Bedf Gen Hosp 90-95; Hon Can St Alb *St Alb* 91-95; PtO from 00. *19 Adelaide Square, Bedford MK40 2RN* T: (01234) 308737

TIBBS, Simon John. b 71. **d** 08 **p** 09. C Edin Old St Paul 08-11; Lect Coll of Transfiguration Grahamstown S Africa 11-12; PtO *St Alb* 12-13; P-in-c Gt Crosby St Faith and Waterloo Park St Mary *Liv* 13-14; C from 14. *65 Fazakerley Road, Liverpool L9 2AJ* E: tibbs.simon@googlemail.com

TICE, Richard Ian. b 66. Bris Univ BA 88. Wycliffe Hall Ox BTh 94. **d** 94 **p** 95. C Langham Place All So *Lon* from 94. *12 De Walden Street, London W1G 8RN* T: (020) 7580 8954 *or* 7580 3522 E: ricospa-grace@allsouls.org

TICKLE, Robert Peter. St Chad's Coll Dur BA 74. St Steph Ho Ox 74. **d** 76 **p** 77. *5 Bramley Court, Orchard Lane, Harrold, Bedford MK43 7BG* T: (01234) 721417

TICKNER, Canon Colin de Fraine. b 37. Chich Th Coll. **d** 66 **p** 67. C Huddersfield SS Pet and Paul *Wakef* 66-68; C Dorking w Ranmore *Guildf* 68-74; V Shottermill 74-91; RD Godalming 89-91; R Ockley, Okewood and Forest Green 91-97; Hon Can Guildf Cathl 96-97; rtd 97; Adv for Past Care *Guildf* 97-12; Chapl St Cath Sch Bramley 97-12; PtO *Guildf* 12-14. *11 Linersh Drive, Bramley, Guildford GU5 0EJ* T: (01483) 898161 E: colin.tickner@sky.com

TICKNER, Canon David Arthur. b 44. MBE 89. AKC 67. **d** 69 **p** 70. C Thornhill Lees *Wakef* 69-71; C Billingham St Aid *Dur* 71-74; TV 74-78; CF 78-98; PtO *Guildf* 96-98; R Heysham *Blackb* 98-13; Hon Can Blackb Cathl 12-13; rtd 13; P-in-c Turners Hill *Chich* from 13. *The Vicarage, Church Road, Turners Hill, Crawley RH10 4PB* T: (01342) 715278 E: david.tickner@tesco.net

TIDESWELL, Mrs Lynne Maureen Ann. b 49. NOC 02. **d** 05 **p** 06. NSM Stoke-upon-Trent *Lich* 05-10; NSM Knutton from 10; P-in-c from 14. *14 High Lane, Cheddleton Heath Road, Leek ST13 7DY* T: (01538) 361134 E: vicarsrest@talktalk.net

TIDSWELL, David Alan. b 42. CEng 73 FIEE 84 Univ Coll Chich BA 03. St Steph Ho Ox 99. **d** 00 **p** 01. NSM Forest Row *Chich* 00-07; P-in-c Fairwarp 07-10; P-in-c High Hurstwood from 07. *Manapouri, Hammerwood Road, Ashurst Wood, East Grinstead RH19 3SA* T: (01342) 822808 E: datidswell@btinternet.com

TIDY, John Hylton. b 48. AKC 72 St Aug Coll Cant 72. **d** 73 **p** 74. C Newton Aycliffe *Dur* 73-78; V Auckland St Pet 78-84; V Burley in Wharfedale *Bradf* 84-92; Dean Jerusalem 92-97; V Surbiton St Andr and St Mark *S'wark* 97-05; RD Kingston 00-05; Israel 05-06; P-in-c Miami Beach All So USA from 06. *5455 Alton Road, Miami Beach FL 33140-2016, USA* T: (001) (305) 538 2244 E: parishoffice@allsoulsmiamibeach.org

TIERNAN, Paul Wilson. b 54. Man Univ BA 76. Coll of Resurr Mirfield 77. **d** 79 **p** 80. C Lewisham St Mary *S'wark* 79-83; V Sydenham St Phil from 83. *St Philip's Vicarage, 122 Wells Park Road, London SE26 6AS* T: (020) 8699 4930

TIESEMA-SAMSOM, Mrs Astrid Leonore. b 61. Anglia Ruskin Univ BA 13. ERMC 09. **d** 13 **p** 14. C Harwich Peninsula *Chelmsf* from 13. *19 Beacon Hill Avenue, Harwich CO12 3NR* T: (01255) 504322 E: altsamsom@hotmail.com

TIGHE, Derek James. b 58. Ox Univ BTh 11. Ripon Coll Cuddesdon 05. **d** 07 **p** 08. C Wimborne Minster *Sarum* 07-12; V Dorking w Ranmore *Guildf* from 12. *St Martin's Vicarage, Westcott Road, Dorking RH4 3DN* T: (01306) 882875 E: revd.derek.tighe@btinternet.com

TIGWELL, Brian Arthur. b 36. S'wark Ord Course 74. **d** 77 **p** 78. C Purley St Mark *S'wark* 77-80; TV Upper Kennet *Sarum* 80-85; V Devizes St Pet 85-99; Wilts Adnry Ecum Officer 88-99; RD Devizes 92-98; rtd 99; PtO *Sarum* from 01; *B & W* from 04. *7 Green Lane, Devizes SN10 5BL* T: (01380) 738219

TILBY, Canon Angela Clare Wyatt. b 50. Girton Coll Cam BA 72 MA 76. Cranmer Hall Dur 77. **d** 97 **p** 98. Tutor Westcott Ho Cam 97-11; Vice-Prin 01-06; Hon C Cherry Hinton St Jo *Ely* 97-06; V Cambridge St Benedict 07-11; CMD Officer and Can Res Ch Ch *Ox* from 11. *33A Vicarage Road, Oxford OX1 4RD* T: (01865) 241233 M: 07966-132045 E: angela.tilby@tilby@chch.ox.ac.uk

TILDESLEY, Edward William David. b 56. SS Hild & Bede Coll Dur BEd 79. SAOMC 93. **d** 96 **p** 97. Chapl Shiplake Coll Henley 96-99; NSM Emmer Green *Ox* 96-99; Chapl Oakham Sch 99-00; TV Dorchester *Ox* 00-05; C Aldershot St Mich *Guildf* 05-08; rtd 08; NSM Wyke Regis *Sarum* from 12; Chapl HM Pris Dorchester from 13. *Address withheld by request* E: etildesley@home.gb.com

TILL, Barry Dorn. b 23. Jes Coll Cam BA 49 MA 49. Westcott Ho Cam 48. **d** 50 **p** 51. C Bury St Mary *Man* 50-53; Fell Jes Coll Cam 53-60; Chapl 53-56; Dean 56-60; Dean Hong Kong 60-64; Attached Ch Assembly 64-65; Prin Morley Coll Lon 66-87; Dir Baring Foundn 87-92; rtd 92. *44 Canonbury Square, London N1 2AW* T: (020) 7359 0708

TILLBROOK, Richard Ernest. b 50. St Mark & St Jo Coll Lon CertEd 71 ACP 76. NTMTC 96. **d** 99 **p** 00. Hd RE Davenant Foundn Sch Loughton 71-03; NSM High Laver w Magdalen Laver and Lt Laver etc *Chelmsf* 99-03; V Colchester St Barn from 03. *St Barnabas' Vicarage, 13 Abbot's Road, Colchester CO2 8BE* T: (01206) 797481 M: 07818-440530 E: fathercap@hotmail.com

TILLER, Edgar Henry. b 22. Ex Univ CertEd 69 Open Univ BA 78 ACP 71. Wells Th Coll 57. **d** 59 **p** 60. C Weston-super-Mare St Jo *B & W* 59-62; V Stoke Lane and Leigh upon Mendip 62-67; Asst Master Chaddiford Sch Barnstaple 69-81; PtO *Ex* 67-05; *Llan* from 06; rtd 95. *42 Llys Pegasus, Ty Glas Road, Llanishen, Cardiff CF14 5ER*

TILLER, The Ven John. b 38. Ch Ch Ox BA 60 MA 64 Bris Univ MLitt 72. Tyndale Hall Bris 60. **d** 62 **p** 63. C Bedford St Luke *St Alb* 62-65; C Widcombe *B & W* 65-67; Tutor Tyndale Hall Bris 67-71; Chapl 67-71; Lect Trin Coll Bris 71-73; P-in-c Bedford Ch Ch *St Alb* 73-78; Chief Sec ACCM 78-84; Hon Can St Alb *St Alb* 79-84; Can Res Heref Cathl 84-04; Chan 84-02; Dioc Dir of Tr *Heref* 91-00; Adn Heref 02-04; rtd 05; Local Miss and Min Adv (Shrewsbury Area) *Lich* 05-09; Hon C Meole Brace 09; PtO from 10. *2 Pulley Lane, Bayston Hill, Shrewsbury SY3 0JH* T: (01743) 873595 E: canjtiller@aol.com

TILLETT, Leslie Selwyn. b 54. Peterho Cam BA 75 MA 79 Leeds Univ BA 80. Coll of Resurr Mirfield 78. **d** 81 **p** 82. C W Dulwich All SS and Em *S'wark* 81-85; R Purleigh, Cold Norton and Stow Maries *Chelmsf* 85-93; R Beddington *S'wark* 93-05; R Wensum Benefice *Nor* 05-14; RD Sparham 08-13; P-in-c Flegg Coastal Benefice from 14. *The Rectory, Somerton Road, Winterton-on-Sea, Great Yarmouth NR29 4AW* T: (01493) 393430 E: selwyn@tillett.org.uk

TILLETT, Luke David. b 88. Rob Coll Cam BTh 10. Ridley Hall Cam 07. **d** 10 **p** 11. C Guisborough *York* 10-15; Chapl to Bp Beverley from 15. *Holy Trinity Rectory, 81 Micklegate, York YO1 6LE* E: lukedavidtillett@googlemail.com

TILLETT, Michael John Arthur. b 57. Ridley Hall Cam 96. **d** 98 **p** 99. C Framlingham w Saxtead *St E* 98-01; P-in-c Stoke by Nayland w Leavenheath and Polstead 01-03; R 03-10; RD Hadleigh 07-10; R Ipswich St Helen, H Trin, and St Luke 10-13. *Address temp unknown* M: 07531-940870 E: revtillett@aol.com

TILLETT, Miss Sarah Louise. b 59. Regent Coll Vancouver MCS 00. Wycliffe Hall Ox 01. **d** 03 **p** 03. C Knowle *Birm* 03-07; P-in-c Bloxham w Milcombe and S Newington *Ox* 07-14. *Ebenezer Chapel, High Street, Great Rollright, Chipping Norton OX7 5RH* M: 07764-608796 E: sarah02tillett@gmail.com

TILLETT, Selwyn. *See* TILLETT, Leslie Selwyn

TILLEY, Canon David Robert. b 38. Kelham Th Coll 58. **d** 63 **p** 64. C Bournemouth St Fran *Win* 63-67; C Moulsecoomb *Chich* 67-70; C Ifield 70-75; TV Warwick *Cov* 76-85; P-in-c Alderminster and Halford 85-96; Dioc Min Tr Adv 85-90; CME Adv 90-04; Assoc Min Willenhall 96-04; Hon Can Cov Cathl 03-04; rtd 04; PtO *Cov* from 04. *17 Coventry Road, Baginton, Coventry CV8 3AD* T/F: (024) 7630 2508 E: david.tilley1@homecall.co.uk

TILLEY, Elizabeth Anne. b 45. Bris Univ BA 67 PGCE 68. All Nations Chr Coll 72 Lon Bible Coll MA 89. **d** 07 **p** 08. OLM Wonersh w Blackheath *Guildf* from 07. *9 Hullmead, Shamley Green, Guildford GU5 0UF* T: (01483) 891730 E: etilley945@btinternet.com

TILLEY, James Stephen. b 55. St Jo Coll Nottm BTh 84. **d** 84 **p** 85. C Nottingham St Jude *S'well* 84-88; C Chester le Street *Dur* 88-92; Tr and Ed CYFA (CPAS) 92-94; Hd 94-02; PtO *Cov* 92-06; *Bris* from 06; C Nailsea H Trin *B & W* from 06. *29 Vynes Way, Nailsea, Bristol BS48 2UG* T: (01275) 543332 F: 545803 M: 07971-563229 E: steve.tilley@htnailsea.org.uk

TILLEY, Peter Robert. b 41. Bris Univ BA 62. Sarum & Wells Th Coll 77. **d** 79 **p** 80. C Wandsworth St Paul *S'wark* 79-82; V Mitcham St Mark 82-91; RD Merton 89-91; R Walton St Mary *Liv* 91-92; TR Walton-on-the-Hill 92-98; rtd 98; P-in-c Ghent *Eur* 98-10; P-in-c Knokke 08-10; PtO *Lon* from 11. *15 Edinburgh Close, Uxbridge UB10 8RA* T: (01895) 905529 E: peter.tilley@blueyonder.co.uk

TILLIER, Preb Jane Yvonne. b 59. New Hall Cam BA 81 PhD 85. Ripon Coll Cuddesdon BA 90. **d** 91 **p** 94. Par Dn Sheff St Mark Broomhill 91-94; C 94-95; Chapl Glouc Cathl 95-97; P-in-c Madeley *Lich* 97-03; P-in-c Betley 02-03; PtO 03-04; Chapl and Team Ldr Douglas Macmillan Hospice Blurton 04-08; P-in-c Barlaston *Lich* 08-14; Min Development Adv Stafford Area 10-14; Dioc Adv for Women in Min from 11; Bp's Adv for Past Care and Wellbeing from 14; Preb Lich Cathl from 11. *10 Plantation Park, University of Keele, Keele, Newcastle ST5 5NA* T: (01782) 639720 E: jane@atherton-tillier.co.uk

TILLMAN, Miss Mary Elizabeth. b 43. S Dios Minl Tr Scheme 86. **d** 89 **p** 95. NSM Bridgemary *Portsm* 89-93; NSM Portsea All SS 93-13; PtO from 13; Adv in Min to People w Disabilities from 93. *3 Fareham Road, Gosport PO13 0XL* T: (01329) 232589

TILLOTSON, Simon Christopher. b 67. Lon Univ BA 90 Trin Coll Cam BA 93 MA 96. Ridley Hall Cam 91. **d** 94 **p** 95. C Paddock Wood *Roch* 94-98; C Ormskirk *Liv* 98-00; V Aylesford *Roch* 00-07; TV Whitstable *Cant* from 07. *The Vicarage, Church Street, Whitstable CT5 1PG* T: (01227) 272308 M: 07946-527471 E: tillotsons@gmail.com

TILLYER, Preb Desmond Benjamin. b 40. Ch Coll Cam BA 63 MA 67. Coll of Resurr Mirfield 64. **d** 66 **p** 67. C Hanworth All SS *Lon* 66-70; Chapl Liddon Ho Lon 70-74; V Pimlico St Pet w Westmr *Lon* 74-06; AD Westmr St Marg 85-92; Preb St Paul's Cathl 01-06; rtd 06; PtO *Nor* from 06. *85 Claremont House, 14 Aerodrome Road, London NW9 5NW* T: (020) 8457 1246 E: montclare85@btinternet.com

TILSON, Canon Alan Ernest. b 46. TCD. **d** 70 **p** 71. C Londonderry Ch Ch *D & R* 70-73; I Inver, Mountcharles and Killaghtee 73-79; I Leckpatrick w Dunnalong 79-89; Bermuda 89-05; Hon Can Bermuda Cathl 96-05; I Tullyaughnish w Kilmacrennan and Killygarvan *D & R* 05-10; rtd 10. *The Brambles, 2 Rinclevan, Dunfanaghy, Co Donegal, Republic of Ireland* T: (00353) (74) 910 0729 E: canonalan@eircom.net

TILSTON, Derek Reginald. b 27. NW Ord Course. **d** 73 **p** 74. NSM Bury St Mark *Man* 73-77; NSM Holcombe 77-82; NSM Bury St Jo 82-83; NSM Bury St Jo w St Mark 83-84; C Bramley *Ripon* 85-87; TV 87-90; R Tendring and Lt Bentley w Beaumont cum Moze *Chelmsf* 90-92; rtd 93; PtO *St E* 93-11. *Room 6, Manormead, Tilford Road, Hindhead GU26 6RA*

TILT, Dawn Caroline. b 59. Llan Ord Course. **d** 99 **p** 00. NSM Pyle w Kenfig *Llan* 99-00; NSM Ewenny w St Brides Major 00-04; Chapl HM Pris Parc (Bridgend) from 04. *HM Prison Parc, Heol Hopcyn John, Bridgend CF35 6AP* T: (01656) 300200 E: thetilts@hotmail.com

TILTMAN, Canon Alan Michael. b 48. Selw Coll Cam BA 70 MA 74. Cuddesdon Coll 71. **d** 73 **p** 74. C Chesterton Gd Shep *Ely* 73-77; C Preston St Jo *Blackb* 77-79; Chapl Lancs (Preston) Poly 77-79; TV Man Whitworth 79-86; Chapl Man Univ (UMIST) 79-86; V Urmston *Man* 86-99; Dir CME 99-03; C Salford Sacred Trin and St Phil 99-02; V Buckley *St As* 04-14; Chan St As Cathl 13-14; rtd 14; PtO *St As* from 14. *The Vicarage, Church Street, Rhosymedre, Wrexham LL14 3EA* T: (01978) 824087 E: a.tiltman@zoo.co.uk

TILTMAN, Mrs Katherine Joan. b 53. St Hugh's Coll Ox MA 74 Man Metrop Univ MSc 02. St Mich Coll Llan 09. **d** 11 **p** 12. C Wrexham *St As* 11-14; C Ruabon and Rhosymedre 14; V from 14. *The Vicarage, Church Street, Rhosymedre, Wrexham LL14 3EA* T: (01978) 824087 M: 07753-230644 E: katetiltman@hotmail.com

TIMBRELL, Keith Stewart. b 48. Edin Th Coll 72. **d** 74 **p** 75. C Chorley St Pet *Blackb* 74-77; C Altham w Clayton le Moors 77-79; Chapl Whittingham Hosp Preston 79-95; Trust Chapl Dorset HealthCare University NHS Foundn Trust 95-08; rtd 08; PtO *Win* from 10. *9 Whitecross Close, Poole BH17 9HN* T: (01202) 604985 M: 07788-907965 E: clerigo@btinternet.com

TIMINGS, Mrs Julie Elizabeth. b 54. **d** 10 **p** 11. C Sleaford *Linc* 10-14; V Elloe Stone from 14. *The Vicarage, 34 Church Lane, Moulton, Spalding PE12 6NP* M: 07931-387186

TIMMINS, Susan Katherine. b 64. Leic Univ BScEng 85 MICE 91. St Jo Coll Nottm MTh 94. **d** 96 **p** 97. C Iver Ox 96-00; P-in-c Pendlebury St Jo *Man* 00-06; V 06-15; Hon Assoc Dioc Dir of Ords 10-15; PtO from 15; Nigeria from 15. *Address temp unknown* E: susanktimmins@aol.com

TIMMIS (née PITT), Mrs Karen Lesley Finella. b 62. Lon Univ BA 84. Chich Th Coll BTh 94. **d** 94 **p** 95. C Walton-on-the-Hill *Liv* 94-98; P-in-c Warrington St Barn 98-00; V from 00. *The Vicarage, 73 Lovely Lane, Warrington WA5 1TY* T: (01925) 633556

TIMOTHY, Miss Bronwen Doris (Bonnie). b 57. Sheff City Poly BSc 81 Univ of Wales (Cardiff) PGCE 82. St Mich Coll Llan 99. **d** 02 **p** 03. C Tenby *St D* 02-04; C Lampeter and Llanddewibrefi Gp 04-06; V Llanfihangel-ar-arth w Capel Dewi from 06. *Y Ficerdy, Llanfihangel-ar-Arth, Pencader SA39 9HU* T: (01559) 384858 M: 07773-645694 E: bronwentimothy@yahoo.com

TIMS, Brian Anthony. b 43. Solicitor 64. STETS 95. **d** 98 **p** 99. NSM Whitchurch w Tufton and Litchfield *Win* 98-02; NSM Shipton Bellinger 02; PtO 06-13; Ox from 13. *Fern Bank, Bere Court Road, Pangbourne, Reading RG8 8JT* T: 0118-984 2335 E: brian@timsfamily.com

TINGAY, Kevin Gilbert Xavier. b 43. Sussex Univ BA 79. Chich Th Coll 79. **d** 80 **p** 81. C W Tarring *Chich* 80-83; TV Worth 83-90; R Bradford w Oake, Hillfarrance and Heathfield *B & W* 90-01; RD Tone 96-01; P-in-c Camerton w Dunkerton, Foxcote and Shoscombe 01-10; Bp's Inter Faith Officer 01-10; Bp's Adv for Regional Affairs 01-10; rtd 10; PtO *B & W* from 10. *82B Keyford, Frome BA11 1JJ* T: (01373) 455778 M: 07719-320507 E: kgxt@btinternet.com

TINKER, Christopher Graham. b 78. Collingwood Coll Dur BA 00. Wycliffe Hall Ox 02. **d** 04 **p** 05. C Houghton *Carl* 04-08; NSM Terrington St Clement *Ely* 08-13; R Bradwell *Nor* from 13. *The Rectory, Church Walk, Bradwell, Great Yarmouth NR31 8QQ* T: (01493) 663219 E: christinkerwork@aol.co.uk

TINKER, Melvin. b 55. Hull Univ BSc Ox Univ MA. Wycliffe Hall Ox 80. **d** 83 **p** 84. C Wetherby *Ripon* 83-85; Chapl Keele Univ *Lich* 85-90; V Cheadle All Hallows *Ches* 90-94; V Hull St Jo Newland *York* from 94. *St John's Vicarage, Clough Road, Hull HU6 7PA* T: (01482) 343658 E: melvin@tink.karoo.co.uk *or* tink@tink.karoo.co.uk

TINNISWOOD, Ms Louise. b 71. Staffs Univ BA 96 Cliff Coll MA 11 Huddersfield Univ PGCE 97. St Jo Coll Nottm 10. **d** 12 **p** 13. C Finningley w Auckley *Sheff* 12-15. *18 Farringdon Drive, New Rossington, Doncaster DN11 0UT* T: (01302) 860169 M: 07989-862189 E: louise.tinniswood@talktalk.net

TINNISWOOD, Robin Jeffries. b 41. K Coll Lon BScEng 64. Wells Th Coll 67. **d** 70 **p** 71. C Yeovil St Mich *B & W* 70-72; C Gt Marlow Ox 72-74; C Christow, Ashton, Trusham and Bridford *Ex* 74-77; P-in-c Ex St Paul 77; TV Heavitree w Ex St Paul 78-79; TV Ifield *Chich* 79-85; P-in-c *S'wark* 98-01; P-in-c Cury and Gunwalloe w Mawgan *Truro* 01-03. *Flat 4, 1 Pine Gardens, Horley RH6 7RA*

TINSLEY, Bernard Murray. b 26. Nottm Univ BA 51. Westcott Ho Cam 51. **d** 53 **p** 54. C Rotherham *Sheff* 53-56; C Goole 56-58; V Thorpe Hesley 58-61; R Alverdiscott w Huntshaw *Ex* 61-78; R Newton Tracey 61-78; R Beaford and Roborough 67-78; V St Giles in the Wood 67-78; V Yarnscombe 67-78; R Newton Tracey, Alverdiscott, Huntshaw etc 78-88; RD Torrington 81-86; rtd 88; PtO *Ex* 88-08. *The Grange, Grange Road, Bideford EX39 4AS* T: (01237) 471414

TINSLEY, Derek. b 31. ALCM 65 BTh 93 PhD 97. NW Ord Course 73. **d** 76 **p** 77. C Gt Crosby St Faith *Liv* 76-80; V Wigan St Anne 80-85; V Colton w Satterthwaite and Rusland *Carl* 85-93; rtd 93; PtO *Liv* from 93. *Lyndale, 43 Renacres Lane, Ormskirk L39 8SG*

TINSLEY, Preb Derek Michael. b 35. Lon Coll of Div ALCD 66 LTh. **d** 66 **p** 67. C Rainhill *Liv* 66-68; C Chalfont St Peter Ox 68-73; P-in-c Maids Moreton w Foxcote 73-74; P-in-c Akeley w

Leckhampstead 73-74; P-in-c Lillingstone Dayrell w Lillingstone Lovell 73-74; R N Buckingham 74-82; RD Buckingham 78-82; P-in-c Alstonfield *Lich* 82-84; P-in-c Butterton 82-84; P-in-c Warslow and Elkstones 82-84; P-in-c Wetton 82-84; V Alstonfield, Butterton, Warslow w Elkstone etc 85-95; RD Alstonfield 82-95; Preb Lich Cathl 91-98; V Cheddleton 95-98; Chapl St Edward's Hosp Cheddleton 96-98; rtd 98; PtO *Lich* from 98; *Derby* from 98. *3 Windsor Close, Manor Green, Ashbourne DE6 1RJ* T: (01335) 346226 E: derekm.tinsley@btinternet.com

TIPLADY, Janet. b 56. Liv Univ BEd 79 St Kath Coll Liv TCert 78. ERMC 10. **d** 12 **p** 13. NSM Warboys w Broughton and Bury w Wistow *Ely* from 12. *22 Locksgate, Somersham, Huntingdon PE28 3HZ* T: (01487) 840193 M: 07713-099346 E: janet.tiplady@gmail.com

TIPLADY, Peter. b 42. Dur Univ MB, BS 65 MRCGP 72 FFPHM 86. Carl Dioc Tr Course 86. **d** 89 **p** 90. NSM Wetheral w Warwick *Carl* 89-05; NSM Holme Eden and Wetheral w Warwick 05-10; PtO from 10. *Meadow Croft, Wetheral, Carlisle CA4 8JG* T: (01228) 561611 E: peter.tiplady@me.com

TIPP (formerly NORTHERN), Mrs Elaine Joy. b 54. Leic Univ BSc 75. SEITE 00. **d** 03 **p** 04. C Snodland All SS w Ch Ch *Roch* 03-08. *14 Church Road, Murston, Sittingbourne ME10 3RU* T: (01795) 472574 E: 2xp@talktalk.net

TIPP, James Edward. b 45. Heythrop Coll Lon MA 93. Oak Hill Th Coll 73. **d** 75 **p** 76. C St Mary Cray and St Paul's Cray *Roch* 75-78; C Southborough St Pet w Ch Ch and St Matt 78-82; R Snodland All SS w Ch Ch 82-08; RD Cobham 96-08; Hon Can Roch Cathl 01-08; rtd 08. *14 Church Road, Murston, Sittingbourne ME10 3RU* T: (01795) 472574 E: 2xp@talktalk.net

TIPPER, Michael William. b 38. Hull Univ BSc 59 MSc 61. Em Coll Saskatoon 72. **d** 73 **p** 74. Canada 73-77 and 79-80 and 83-88 and from 91; R Amcotts *Linc* 77-79; V Aycliffe *Dur* 80-83; V Kneesall w Laxton and Wellow *S'well* 88-91; rtd 98. *106 Purdue Court West, Lethbridge AB T1K 4R8, Canada*

TIPPING, Canon Brenda Margaret. b 44. N Lon Univ CQSW 85 Dur Univ MA 96. SAOMC 96. **d** 99 **p** 00. NSM Stevenage St Andr and St Geo *St Alb* 99-05; P-in-c S Mymms and Ridge 05-13; V 13-14; Chapl among Deaf People 05-14; NSM Officer Hertford Adnry 06-14; Hon Can St Alb 12-14; rtd 14. *250 Grace Way, Stevenage SG1 5AJ* E: ken@tipping1941.freeserve.co.uk

TIPPING, Canon John Woodman. b 42. AKC 65. **d** 66 **p** 67. C Croydon St Sav *Cant* 66-70; C Plaistow St Mary *Roch* 70-72; V Brockley Hill St Sav *S'wark* 72-83; P-in-c Sittingbourne St Mary *Cant* 83-86; V 86-94; P-in-c Mersham w Hinxhill 94-03; P-in-c Mersham w Hinxhill and Sellindge 03-07; P-in-c Sevington 94-07; P-in-c Brabourne w Smeeth 95-00; AD N Lympne 95-02; Hon Can Cant Cathl 03-07; rtd 07; PtO *St E* from 08. *5 Peace Place, Thorpeness, Leiston IP16 4NA* T: (01728) 454165 E: jwtipping@talk21.com

TIPPLE, Neil. b 58. Loughb Univ BTech 81 Aston Univ MSc 86. WMMTC 04. **d** 04 **p** 05. C Cov E 04-08; V Haywards Heath Ascension *Chich* from 08. *Ascension Vicarage, 1 Redwood Drive, Haywards Heath RH16 4ER* T: (01444) 416262 M: 07792-198451 E: ginandwhisky@aol.com

TIRWOMWE, Stephen Warren. b 46. TCert 73 Bp Tucker Coll Mukono BD 88 Open Univ MA 94 Leeds Univ MA 01. **d** 81 **p** 82. Dioc Youth Worker and Educn Sec Kigezi Uganda 81-85; Dioc Missr 88-92; Dep Prin Bp Barham Div Coll 92-97; C Osmondthorpe St Phil *Ripon* 97-02; Dioc Miss Co-ord Kigezi Uganda 02-11; rtd 11. *Abaho Ahurira, PO Box 1091, Kabale, Uganda* T: (00256) (77) 870467 E: swtirwomwe@hotmail.com

TISDALE, Mark-Aaron Buchanan. b 67. Pittsburgh Univ BA 94. Westcott Ho Cam 00. **d** 02 **p** 03. C Norton *St Alb* 02-05; P-in-c Clifton and Southill 05-11; Chapl St Edm Sch Cant 11-12; C Finchampstead and California *Ox* from 12; CF (ACF) from 10. *California Vicarage, Vicarage Close, Finchampstead, Wokingham RG40 4JW* T: 0118-327 9724 E: mark-aaron@finchampstead.co.uk

TISSINGTON, Irene Frances. b 50. EMMTC 03. **d** 06 **p** 07. NSM Harworth *S'well* 06-10; LtO from 10. *14 Station Avenue, Ranskill, Retford DN22 8LF* T: (01777) 818923 M: 07856-892759 E: irene@itissington.freeserve.co.uk

TITCOMB, Mrs Claire. b 35. SAOMC 95. **d** 98 **p** 99. OLM Witney Ox from 98; Assoc P for Min Development from 01. *30 Beech Road, Witney OX28 6LW* T: (01993) 771234 E: claireoyt@clara.net

TITCOMBE, Peter Charles. *See* JONES, Peter Charles

TITFORD, Richard Kimber. b 45. UEA BA 67. Ripon Coll Cuddesdon 78. **d** 80 **p** 80. C Middleton *Man* 80-83; P-in-c Edwardstone w Groton and Lt Waldingfield *St E* 83-90 and 95-02; R 90-94; P-in-c Boxford 00-02; C Assington w Newton Green and Lt Cornard 00-02; R Boxford, Edwardstone, Groton etc 02-03; rtd 03; PtO *St E* from 03; *S'wark* 10-13; *Chelmsf* from 13. *2 Chestnut Mews, Friars Street, Sudbury CO10 2AH* T/F: (01787) 880303 E: titford@keme.co.uk

TITLEY, Canon David Joseph. b 47. Ex Univ BSc Surrey Univ PhD. Wycliffe Hall Ox. d 82 p 83. C Stowmarket *St E* 82-85; C Bloxwich *Lich* 85-90; TV 90-95; V Prees and Fauls 95-00; V Clacton St Paul *Chelmsf* 00-13; Hon Can Chelmsf Cathl 12-13; rtd 13; PtO *Chelmsf* from 14. *34 Turner Avenue, Lawford, Manningtree CO11 2LG* T: (01206) 396462

TITLEY, Canon Robert John. b 56. Ch Coll Cam BA 78 MA 82 K Coll Lon PhD 95. Westcott Ho Cam. d 85 p 86. C Lower Sydenham St Mich *S'wark* 85-88; C Sydenham All SS 85-88; Chapl Whitelands Coll of HE 88-94; V W Dulwich All SS 94-06; RD Streatham 04-05; Dioc Dir of Ords and Can Res and Treas S'wark Cathl 06-10; Hon Can S'wark Cathl 10-15; TR Richmond St Mary w St Matthias and St Jo 10-15. *The Vicarage, Ormond Road, Richmond TW10 6TH* T: (020) 8940 0362 E: robert.titley@richmondteamministry.org

TIVEY, Nicholas. b 65. Liv Poly BSc 89. Ridley Hall Cam 91. d 94 p 95. C Bromborough *Ches* 94-97; TV Walton H Trin *Ox* 97-01; Chapl HM Pris Wayland 01-08; Chapl Nor Sch 08-14; Chapl Harrow Sch from 14. *4 Kennett House, Harrow Park, Harrow HA1 3JE* T: (020) 8872 7235 M: 07733-099792 E: nt@harrowschool.org.uk

TIZZARD, Peter Francis. b 53. Oak Hill Th Coll 88. d 90 p 91. C Letchworth St Paul w Willian *St Alb* 90-95; I Drumkeeran w Templecarne and Muckross *Clogh* 95-00; P-in-c Ramsgate Ch Ch *Cant* 00-02; V from 02. *24 St Mildred's Avenue, Ramsgate CT11 0HT* T: (01843) 853732

TOAN, Robert Charles. b 50. Oak Hill Th Coll. d 84 p 85. C Upton (Overchurch) *Ches* 84-87; V Rock Ferry 87-99; RD Birkenhead 97-99; V Plas Newton 99-06; P-in-c Ches Ch Ch 03-06; V Plas Newton w Ches Ch Ch 07-09; RD Ches 02-08; Cambodia from 09. *c/o Ben Toan Esq, 123 Hope Farm Road, Great Sutton, Ellesmere Port CH66 2TJ* T: 0151-347 9220 E: bob.toan@xaltmail.com

TOASE, Mrs Catherine Jane. b 56. Yorks Min Course 13. d 15. NSM Easingwold w Raskelf *York* from 15. *The Priory, Raskelf Road, Easingwold, York YO61 3JY* T: (01347) 821659 E: catherine.toase@yahoo.co.uk

TOBIN, Rebecca Louise. b 75. St Martin's Coll Lanc BA 00 Newc Univ MA 12 Sheff Univ BA 14. Coll of Resurr Mirfield 12. d 14 p 15. C The Boldons *Dur* from 14. *10 Churchdown Close, Boldon Colliery NE35 9HA* E: mthrrebecca@outlook.com

TOBIN, Richard Francis. b 44. CertEd. Chich Th Coll 76. d 78 p 79. C W Leigh CD *Portsm* 78-79; C Halstead St Andr w H Trin and Greenstead Green *Chelmsf* 79-87; Youth Chapl 82-87; V S Shields St Simon *Dur* 87-04; V Ipswich All Hallows *St E* 04-09; rtd 09; PtO *Chelmsf* from 10; *St E* from 12. *18 Greenside Drift, South Shields NE33 3ND* E: pringing@hotmail.com

TOBIN, Robert Benjamin. b 70. Harvard Univ AB 93 TCD MPhil 98 Mert Coll Ox DPhil 04 Em Coll Cam BA 07 MA 11 Ox Univ MA 11. Westcott Ho Cam 04. d 07 p 08. C Beaconsfield *Ox* 07-09; Chapl Harvard Univ USA 09-10; Chapl Oriel Coll Ox from 10. *Oriel College, Oxford OX1 4EW* T: (01865) 276580 E: robert.tobin@oriel.ox.ac.uk

TOBIN, Mrs Vanessa Joanne. b 69. Wolv Univ BA 90 Univ of Cen England in Birm PGCE 92. Qu Coll Birm 13. d 15. C Wednesfield *Lich* from 15. *21 New Street, Merry Hill, Wolverhampton WV3 7NW* T: (01902) 340632 M: 07854-773432

TODD, Andrew George. b 67. Coll of Resurr Mirfield 13. d 15. C Barbourne *Worc* from 15. *1 Chacewater Avenue, Worcester WR3 7AW* T: (01905) 611979

TODD, Canon Andrew John. b 61. Univ Coll Dur BA 84 K Coll Lon MPhil 98 Cardiff Univ PhD 09. Coll of Resurr Mirfield 85. d 87 p 88. C Thorpe St Andr *Nor* 87-91; Chapl K Alfred Coll *Win* 91-94; Sen Asst P E Dereham and Scarning *Nor* 94-97; Dir Studies EAMTC *Ely* 94-01; Vice-Prin 97-01; CME Officer *St E* 01-06; Can Res St E Cathl 01-06; Sub Dean 04-06; Dean Chapl Studies St Mich Coll Llan from 06; Hon Research Fell Cardiff Univ *Llan* from 07. *St Michael and All Angels' College, 54 Cardiff Road, Llandaff, Cardiff CF5 2YJ* T: (029) 2083 8001 or 2056 3379 F: 2083 8008 M: 07785-560558 E: ajt@stmichaels.ac.uk

TODD, Catherine Frances. b 61. Surrey Univ BSc 84 Westmr Coll Ox BTh 99 RGN 84 RM 86. EAMTC 96. d 99 p 00. NSM Sutton and Witcham w Mepal *Ely* 99-01; C Horringer *St E* 01-03; R 03-07; Chapl HM Pris Erlestoke 07-10; Chapl HM Pris Glouc 10-11; Chapl HM Pris Leyhill from 11. *HM Prison Leyhill, Wotton-under-Edge, Gloucester GL12 8BT* T: (01454) 264000 E: catherine.todd@hmps.gsi.gov.uk

TODD, Clive. b 57. Open Univ BSc 04 Linc Univ MA 11. Linc Th Coll 89. d 91 p 92. C Consett *Dur* 91-93; C Bensham 93-95; P-in-c S Hetton w Haswell 95-98; R Ebchester and

V Medomsley 98-04; P-in-c S Lawres Gp *Linc* 04-09; RD Lawres 06-07; P-in-c Thanington *Cant* 09-13; Dir of Ords 09-13; R Lower Swale *Leeds* from 13. *The Rectory, Manor Lane, Ainderby Steeple, Northallerton DL7 9PY* E: clive.todd1@btinternet.com

TODD, David Alan. b 70. Napier Univ Edin BSc 92. Oak Hill Th Coll BA 12. d 12 p 13. C Normanton *Derby* from 12. *23 Nevinson Drive, Littleover, Derby DE23 1GX* T: (01332) 765834 M: 07801-720023 E: david.todd@stgiles-derby.org.uk

TODD, Edward Peter. b 44. Cranmer Hall Dur 86. d 88 p 89. C Hindley All SS *Liv* 88-91; P-in-c Wigan St Steph 91-96; V 96-98; P-in-c N Meols 98-03; TR 03-05; rtd 05; P-in-c Scarisbrick *Liv* 10-12. *1B Nixons Lane, Southport PR8 3ES* E: revtodd@btopenworld.com

TODD, George Robert. b 21. Sarum & Wells Th Coll 74. d 76 p 77. Hon C Wellington and Distr *B & W* 76-86; PtO 86-06. *15 John Grinter Way, Wellington TA21 9AR* T: (01823) 662828

TODD, Ian Campbell. b 68. Westcott Ho Cam. d 04 p 05. C Scotforth *Blackb* 04-08; TV Hitchin *St Alb* from 09. *Holy Saviour Vicarage, St Anne's Road, Hitchin SG5 1QB* T: (01462) 456140 E: iancamtodd@googlemail.com

TODD, Jeremy Stephen Bevan. b 69. Trin Coll Bris BA 92. d 97 p 98. C Tufnell Park St Geo and All SS *Lon* 97-99; PtO 03-07; *S'wark* 07-13. *Address temp unknown* E: jeremytodd@me.com

TODD, Joy Gertrude. b 28. Ox Univ MTh 99. d 90 p 94. OLM Guildf H Trin w St Mary 90-99; PtO from 99. *165 Stoke Road, Guildford GU1 1EY* T: (01483) 567500

TODD, Michael Edward. b 62. Brighton Poly BA 84 Surrey Univ PGCE 85. SEITE 96 Ven English Coll Rome 98. d 99 p 05. C Farnham *Guildf* 99-00; Chapl Surrey Inst Art and Design 99-00; Development Officer Surrey Univ *Guildf* 00-02; Progr Manager and Lect Croydon Coll 02-05; Dep Dir City and Islington Coll 05-07; Hon C Camberwell St Giles w St Matt *S'wark* 04-05; Hon C Newington St Mary from 05; Hd of Sch S Thames Coll 07-10; Chapl Trin Sch Lewisham 11-14; Par Partnerships Manager Children's Soc from 15. *1 William Dyce Mews, London SW16 6AW* T: (020) 8677 7328 M: 07946-701279 E: mikeytodd@hotmail.com

TODD, Nicholas Stewart. b 61. Open Univ BA 03 MA 08. Wycliffe Hall Ox 94. d 96 p 97. C Gt Wyrley *Lich* 96-99; V Leaton and Albrighton w Battlefield 99-02; R Holbrook, Stutton, Freston, Woolverstone etc *St E* 02-06; CF from 06. *c/o MOD Chaplains (Army)* F: 381824 T: (01264) 383430 E: nick@toddsrus.org

TODD, Canon Norman Henry. b 19. PhC Lon Univ BPharm 42 Fitzw Ho Cam BA 50 MA 55 Nottm Univ PhD 78. Westcott Ho Cam 50. d 52 p 53. C Aspley *S'well* 52-54; Chapl Westcott Ho Cam 55-58; V Arnold *S'well* 58-65; V Rolleston w Morton 65-69; Can Res S'well Minster 65-69; R Elston w Elston Chapelry 71-76; R E Stoke w Syerston 72-76; V Sibthorpe 72-76; Bp's Adv on Tr 76-83; C Averham w Kelham 76-80; V Rolleston w Morton 80-83; P-in-c Upton 80-83; V Rolleston w Fiskerton, Morton and Upton 83-88; Hon Can S'well Minster 82-88; rtd 88; PtO S'well from 88; Abps' Adv for Bps' Min 88-94. *17 Woodville Drive, Sherwood, Nottingham NG5 2GZ* E: n.todd1@ntlworld.com

TODD, Canon William Moorhouse. b 26. Lich Th Coll 54. d 57 p 58. C W Derby St Mary *Liv* 57-61; V Liv St Chris Norris Green 61-97; Hon Can Liv Cathl 92-97; rtd 97; PtO *Liv* from 97. *3 Haymans Grove, West Derby, Liverpool L12 7LD* T: 0151-256 1712

TOLHURST, David. b 72. Cranmer Hall Dur 07. d 09 p 10. C Middleton St George *Dur* 09-13; C Sadberge 09-13; V Silksworth from 13. *St Matthew's Vicarage, Silksworth Road, New Silksworth, Sunderland SR3 2AA* T: 0191-523 9932 E: revtolhurst@btinternet.com

TOLL, Brian Arthur. b 35. Ely Th Coll 62 Linc Th Coll 64. d 65 p 66. C Cleethorpes *Linc* 65-68; C Hadleigh w Layham and Shelley *St E* 69-72; R Claydon and Barham 72-86; P-in-c Capel w Lt Wenham 86-94; P-in-c Holton St Mary w Gt Wenham 87-91; R Capel St Mary w Lt and Gt Wenham 94-96; P-in-c Ipswich St Mary at the Elms 96-01; Bp's Adv on Deliverance and Exorcism 89-97; rtd 01; PtO *St E* from 01. *39 Derwent Road, Ipswich IP3 0QR* T: (01473) 424305 E: batoll@ntlworld.com

TOLLEFSEN VAN DER LANS, Alida Thadden Maria (Alja). b 50. Utrecht Univ 89. St Steph Ho Ox 96. d 98 p 99. C Bramhall *Ches* 98-02; V Knutsford St Cross 02-07; Utrecht Old Catholic Ch *Eur* 07-12; Chapl E Netherlands from 12. *Wilhelminapark 27, 3581 NG Utrecht, The Netherlands* T: (0031) (30) 251 7511 E: alja.tollefsen@xs4all.nl

TOLLER, Peter Sheridan. *See* STARK TOLLER, Peter Sheridan

TÖLLER, Elizabeth Margery. b 53. Leeds Univ BA 75. Ripon Coll Cuddesdon 84. d 87 p 00. Asst Chapl Leeds Gen Infirmary 87-90; PtO *Nor* 90-91; Chapl Lt Plumstead Hosp 92-93; Chapl Co-ord HM Pris Nor 93-95; Chapl Gt Yarmouth

Coll 96-99; PtO S'wark 99-00; Hon C Wandsworth St Paul from 00; Hon Asst Chapl St Chris Hospice Lon 03-10. *St Paul's Vicarage, 116 Augustus Road, London SW19 6EW* T: (020) 8788 2024 E: mtoller@gmx.de

TÖLLER, Heinz Dieter. b 52. NEOC 86. **d** 87 **p** 88. C Leeds Gipton Epiphany *Ripon* 87-90; R Coltishall w Gt Hautbois and Horstead *Nor* 90-99; V Wandsworth St Paul S'wark from 99; AD Wandsworth 05-13. *St Paul's Vicarage, 116 Augustus Road, London SW19 6EW* T: (020) 8788 2024 F: 08702-843237 M: 07941-291120 E: htoller@gmail.com

TOLLEY, Canon George. b 25. Lon Univ BSc 45 MSc 48 PhD 52 Sheff Univ Hon DSc 83 Open Univ Hon DUniv 84 Hon DSc 86 FRSC CBIM. Linc Th Coll 65. **d** 67 **p** 68. C Sharrow St Andr *Sheff* 67-90; Hon Can Sheff Cathl 76-98. *74 Furniss Avenue, Sheffield S17 3QP* T: 0114-236 0538

TOLWORTHY, Canon Colin. b 37. Chich Th Coll 64. **d** 67 **p** 68. C Hulme St Phil *Man* 67-70; C Lawton Moor 70-71; C Hangleton *Chich* 72-76; V Eastbourne St Phil 76-87; V Hastings H Trin 87-10; Can and Preb Chich Cathl 03-10; rtd 10. *The Charterhouse, Charterhouse Square, London EC1M 6AN* T: (020) 7250 0119 E: colintolworthy@gmx.com

TOMALIN, Stanley Joseph Edward. b 66. Oak Hill Th Coll BA 93. **d** 96 **p** 97. C Bitterne *Win* 96-00; C Hailsham *Chich* 00; P-in-c Hawkswood CD 01-05; V Hawkswood 05-11; C Hailsham from 11; RD Dallington 07-14. *Harmers Hay House, 1 Barn Close, Hailsham BN27 1TL* T: (01323) 846680 E: stantomalin@gmail.com

TOMBS, Kenneth Roberts. b 42. Open Univ BA 84. S Dios Minl Tr Scheme 92. **d** 95 **p** 96. Dep Hd Twyford C of E High Sch Acton 86-97; Chapl 98-02; rtd 02; NSM Ickenham *Lon* 95-12; PtO from 12. *91 Burns Avenue, Southall UB1 2LT* T: (020) 8574 3738 E: ken.tombs@btinternet.com

TOME DA SILVA, Carlos Alberto. b 76. **d** 01 **p** 01. Brazil 01-04; C Risca *Mon* 04-05; C Bassaleg 05-06; CF from 06. *c/o MOD Chaplains (Army)* F: 381824 T: (01264) 383430 E: betome@hotmail.com

TOMKINS, Ian James. b 60. Univ of Wales (Cardiff) LLB 81 Aston Business Sch MBA 90. Ridley Hall Cam. **d** 00 **p** 01. C Bourton-on-the-Water w Clapton *Glouc* 00-04; P-in-c Broxbourne w Wormley *St Alb* 04-07; R 07-10; Adv for Minl Support *Bris* from 10; Hon C Stoke Gifford from 11. *33 Fernbank Road, Bristol BS6 6PX* T: 0117-330 7454 E: ian-tomkins@lineone.net *or* ian.tomkins@bristoldiocese.org

TOMKINS, James Andrew. b 66. R Holloway & Bedf New Coll Lon BA 88. SAOMC 01. **d** 04 **p** 06. C Lavendon w Cold Brayfield, Clifton Reynes etc *Ox* 04-05; C Risborough 05-08; TV from 08. *The Rectory, Mill Lane, Monks Risborough, Princes Risborough HP27 9JE* T: (01844) 275944 E: jamestomkins@btinternet.com

TOMKINS, Jocelyn Rachel. *See* WALKER, Jocelyn Rachel

TOMKINS, Justin Mark. b 71. Chu Coll Cam BA 93 MA 97 PhD 98. Trin Coll Bris BA 10 MPhil 12. **d** 11 **p** 12. C Longfleet *Sarum* from 11. *43 Kingston Road, Poole BH15 2LR* T: (01202) 338721 E: email@justintomkins.org *or* justin.tomkins@smlpoole.org.uk

TOMKINS, Simon Charles Ross. b 83. St Jo Coll Dur BA 06 Cam Univ BA 12. Ridley Hall Cam 10. **d** 13 **p** 14. C Lt Shelford *Ely* from 13. *79 Hauxton Road, Little Shelford, Cambridge CB22 5HJ*

TOMKINSON, Linda Margaret. b 76. QUB BD 97 St Jo Coll Dur MATM 13. Cranmer Hall Dur 10. **d** 12 **p** 13. C Blackpool St Jo *Blackb* from 12. *122 Park Road, Blackpool FY1 4ES* T: (01253) 753993 M: 07784-325537 E: revlindam@hotmail.co.uk

TOMKINSON, Raymond David. b 47. Ox Brookes Univ MA 10 SRN 71 MSSCh 72. EAMTC 86. **d** 89 **p** 90. NSM Chesterton St Geo *Ely* 89-91; C Sawston 91-93; C Babraham 91-93; P-in-c Wimbotsham w Stow Bardolph and Stow Bridge etc 93-94; R 94-00; RD Fincham 94-97; Dir Old Alresford Place *Win* 00-06; P-in-c Old Alresford and Bighton 00-06; rtd 06; PtO *Leic* from 07; *Pet* from 07; Chapl Ripon Coll Cuddesdon from 09. *8 Uppingham Road, Oakham LE15 6JD* T: (01572) 756844 E: raymondtomkinson@btinternet.com

✠**TOMLIN, The Rt Revd Graham Stuart.** b 58. Linc Coll Ox BA 80 MA 83 Ex Univ PhD 96. Wycliffe Hall Ox BA 85. **d** 86 **p** 87 **c** 15. C Ex St Leon w H Trin 86-89; Chapl Jes Coll Ox 89-94; Tutor Wycliffe Hall Ox 89-98; Vice-Prin 98-05; Prin St Paul's Th Cen *Lon* 05-15; Dean St Mellitus Coll 07-15; Area Bp Kensington from 15. *Dial House, Riverside, Twickenham TW1 3DT* M: 07929-048720 T: (020) 7932 1180 E: graham.tomlin@stmellitus.org

TOMLIN, Keith Michael. b 53. Imp Coll Lon BSc 75. Ridley Hall Cam 77. **d** 80 **p** 81. C Heywood St Jas *Man* 80-83; C Rochdale 83-84; TV 84-85; Chapl Rochdale Tech Coll 83-85; R Benington w Leverton *Linc* 85-99; R Leverton 99-01; Chapl HM Pris N Sea Camp 97-01; P-in-c Fotherby *Linc* 01-06; Louthesk Deanery Chapl 06-10; rtd 13. *Address withheld by request* E: keithtomlin@live.co.uk

TOMLINE, Stephen Harrald. b 35. Dur Univ BA 57. Cranmer Hall Dur. **d** 61 **p** 62. C Blackley St Pet *Man* 61-66; V Audenshaw St Steph 66-90; V Newhey 90-01; rtd 01; PtO *Carl* from 01. *3 Humphrey Cottages, Stainton, Kendal LA8 0AD* T: (01539) 560988

TOMLINSON, Anne Lovat. b 56. Edin Univ MA 78 PhD 85 MTh 98. St Jo Coll Nottm 84. **d** 93. Tutor TISEC 93-02; Dir Past Studies 98-00; Dioc Dir of Ords *Edin* 02-05; Prov Local Collaborative Min Officer 02-08; Min Development Officer *Glas* from 09. *3 Bright's Crescent, Edinburgh EH9 2DB* T/F: 0131-668 1322 M: 07729-054417 E: mdo.gg@btinternet.com

TOMLINSON, Barry William. b 47. Clifton Th Coll 72. **d** 72 **p** 73. C Pennington *Man* 72-76; SAMS 76-80; Chile 77-80; C-in-c Gorleston St Mary CD *Nor* 80; V Gorleston St Mary 80-88; Chapl Jas Paget Hosp Gorleston 81-87; P-in-c Gt w Lt Plumstead *Nor* 88-89; R Gt w Lt Plumstead and Witton 89-93; R Gt and Lt Plumstead w Thorpe End and Witton 93-98; Chapl Lt Plumstead Hosp 88-94; Chapl Norwich Community Health Partnership NHS Trust 94-95; RD Blofield *Nor* 96-98; V Margate H Trin *Cant* 98-99; R Roughton and Felbrigg, Metton, Sustead etc *Nor* 99-02; PtO 02-10; P-in-c Brinton, Briningham, Hunworth, Stody etc from 10. *12 Heath Road, Sheringham NR26 8JH* T: (01263) 820266 M: 07796-243436 E: barrywtomlinson@gmail.com

TOMLINSON, David Robert. b 63. Open Univ BA 07 St Jo Coll Dur BA 09. Cranmer Hall Dur 07. **d** 09 **p** 10. C Shildon *Dur* 09-13; P-in-c from 13. *St John's Vicarage, 1A Burnie Gardens, Shildon DL4 1ND* M: 07546-596079 E: smileydavid63@gmail.com

TOMLINSON, David Robert. b 60. Kent Univ BSc 82 Chelsea Coll Lon PGCE 83 Jes Coll Cam BA 92 MA 96. Ridley Hall Cam 90. **d** 93 **p** 94. C Godalming *Guildf* 93-98; V Grays North *Chelmsf* 98-08; RD Thurrock 03-08; TR Saffron Walden w Wendens Ambo, Littlebury etc 08-11; TR Saffron Walden and Villages from 12; RD Saffron Walden from 09. *The Rectory, 17 Borough Lane, Saffron Walden CB11 4AG* T: (01799) 500947 E: rector@stmarryssaffronwalden.org

TOMLINSON, David William. b 48. Lon Bible Coll MA 95 Westcott Ho Cam 97. **d** 97 **p** 98. NSM W Holloway St Luke *Lon* 97-00; P-in-c 00-01; V from 01. *St Luke's Vicarage, Penn Road, London N7 9RE* T/F: (020) 7607 1504 E: revdavetomlinson@hotmail.com

TOMLINSON, Eric Joseph. b 45. Lich Th Coll 70 Qu Coll Birm 72. **d** 73 **p** 74. C Cheadle *Lich* 73-76; C Sedgley All SS 77-79; V Ettingshall 79-94; V Horton, Lonsdon and Rushton Spencer 94-12; rtd 12; PtO *Lich* 12-13. *4 Burgis Close, Cheddleton, Leek ST13 7NR* T: (01538) 361151

TOMLINSON, Frederick William. b 58. Glas Univ MA 80 Edin Univ BD 83. Edin Th Coll 80. **d** 83 **p** 84. C Cumbernauld *Glas* 83-86; C Glas St Mary 86-88; R Edin St Hilda 88-01; R Edin St Fillan 88-01; R Edin St Pet from 01; Syn Clerk from 06. *3 Bright's Crescent, Edinburgh EH9 2DB* T/F: 0131-667 6224 E: fredwtomlinson@gmail.com *or* rector@stpetersedinburgh.org

TOMLINSON, Helen. b 53. **d** 07 **p** 08. OLM Stretford All SS *Man* 07-12; NSM Blackley St Paul from 12. *Address temp unknown*

TOMLINSON, Canon Ian James. b 50. Hull Univ MA 90 Ox Univ MTh 01 K Coll Lon DThMin 12. AKC 72 St Aug Coll Cant 72. **d** 73 **p** 74. C Thirsk w S Kilvington and Carlton Miniott etc *York* 73-76; C Harrogate St Wilfrid *Ripon* 76-79; R Appleshaw, Kimpton, Thruxton, Fyfield etc *Win* from 79; Dioc Adv in Past Care and Counselling from 01; Hon Can Win Cathl from 04. *The Rectory, Ragged Appleshaw, Andover SP11 9HX* T: (01264) 772414 F: 771302 E: ian@raggedappleshaw.freeserve.co.uk

TOMLINSON, Mrs Jean Mary. b 32. K Coll Lon BEd 75. S Dios Minl Tr Scheme 84. **d** 87 **p** 94. Hon Par Dn Spring Park All SS S'wark 87-92; Chapl HM YOI Hatfield 92-98; PtO S'well from 92. *6 Cheyne Walk, Bawtry, Doncaster DN10 6RS* T: (01302) 711281

TOMLINSON (née MILLS), Canon Jennifer Clare. b 61. Trin Hall Cam BA 82 MA 86. Ridley Hall Cam 88. **d** 91 **p** 94. C Busbridge *Guildf* 91-95; C Godalming 95-98; NSM Grays North *Chelmsf* 98-08; NSM Saffron Walden w Wendens Ambo, Littlebury etc 08-11; NSM Saffron Walden and Villages from 12; Par Development Adv (Colchester Area) from 11; Bp's Adv on Women's Min from 11; Chapl Thurrock Primary Care Trust 99-08; Hon Can Chelmsf Cathl from 12. *The Rectory, 17 Borough Lane, Saffron Walden CB11 4AG* T: (01799) 500757 *or* (01708) 740385 E: jtomlinson@chelmsford.anglican.org

TOMLINSON, John Howard. b 54. Newc Univ BSc 76 MICE 83. Chich Th Coll 91. **d** 93 **p** 94. C Blewbury, Hagbourne and Upton *Ox* 93-96; C Cowley St Jas 96-97; TV 97-04; TR Upper Wylye Valley *Sarum* 04-15; RD Heytesbury 07-13; rtd 15. *11 Castle Mews, Folkestone CT20 2BU* E: johntomlinson73@gmail.com

TOMLINSON, John William Bruce. b 60. Univ of Wales (Abth) BA 82 Man Univ MA 90 Birm Univ PhD 08 Nottm Trent Univ PGCE 11 FRHistS 14. Hartley Victoria Coll 87 Mar Thoma Th Sem Kottayam 90 Linc Th Coll 91. **d** 92 **p** 93. In Methodist Ch 90-91; C Sawley *Derby* 92-95; P-in-c Man Victoria Park 95-98; Dioc CUF Officer 95-98; Chapl St Anselm Hall Man Univ 96-98; V Shelton and Oxon *Lich* 98-04; Ecum Co-ord for Miss and Chief Exec Officer Lincs Chapl Services *Linc* 04-06; PtO 08-14; V Carrington *S'well* from 14. *The Vicarage, 6 Watcombe Circus, Nottingham NG5 2DT* T: 0115-962 1291 M: 07983-134597 E: dr.pelican@hotmail.co.uk

TOMLINSON, Martyn Craig. b 78. Coll of Resurr Mirfield 13. **d** 15. C Barnsley St Mary *Wakef* from 15. *The Vicarage, 186 Racecommon Road, Barnsley S70 6JY* T: (01226) 958449 M: 07523-260707 E: fr.craig@outlook.com

TOMLINSON, Matthew Robert Edward. b 61. St Chad's Coll Dur BA 83 Univ of Wales (Cardiff) BD 94. St Mich Coll Llan 92. **d** 94 **p** 95. C Abergavenny St Mary w Llanwenarth Citra *Mon* 94-96; PV Llan Cathl and Chapl Llan Cathl Sch 96-00; V Edgbaston St Aug *Birm* from 00. *St Augustine's Vicarage, 44 Vernon Road, Birmingham B16 9SH* T/F: 0121-454 0127 M: 07989-915499 E: jm.tomlinson@blueyonder.co.uk

TOMLINSON, Stuart. b 51. **d** 12 **p** 13. OLM Hawes Side and Marton Moss *Blackb* from 12. *1A Chatham Avenue, Lytham St Annes FY8 2RT* T: (01253) 726657 M: 07707-414135 E: clothesofsand@hotmail.co.uk

TOMPKINS, April. b 51. Man Univ BEd 75. EMMTC 05. **d** 07 **p** 08. NSM Belper *Derby* from 07. *8 Derwent Grove, Alfreton DE55 7PB* T: (01773) 835122 E: april_tompkins@hotmail.com

TOMPKINS, David John. b 32. Oak Hill Th Coll 55. **d** 58 **p** 59. C Northampton St Giles *Pet* 58-61; C Heatherlands St Jo *Sarum* 61-63; V Selby St Jas and Wistow *York* 63-73; V Retford St Sav *S'well* 73-87; P-in-c Clarborough w Hayton 84-87; V Kidsgrove *Lich* 87-90; V Tockwith and Bilton w Bickerton *York* 90-97; rtd 97; PtO *Pet* 00-03. *49 Wentworth Drive, Oundle, Peterborough PE8 4QF* T: (01832) 275176

TOMPKINS, Janet. b 45. **d** 11 **p** 12. OLM Mablethorpe w Trusthorpe *Linc* from 11; OLM Sutton, Huttoft and Anderby from 11. *Brigadoon, 51 Rutland Road, Mablethorpe LN12 1EN* T: (01507) 478078

TOMPKINS, Michael John Gordon. b 35. JP 76. Man Univ BSc 58 MPS 59. NOC 82. **d** 85 **p** 86. C Abington *Pet* 85-87; TV Daventry 87-92; P-in-c Braunston 87-92; TV Daventry, Ashby St Ledgers, Braunston etc 92-93; R Paston 93-98; rtd 00; PtO *Ches* from 98. *19 Clarendon Close, Chester CH4 7BL* T: (01244) 659147 E: michaeltompkins@onetel.com

TOMPKINS, Peter Michael. b 58. Open Univ BA 92 SS Hild & Bede Coll Dur CertEd 79. St Jo Coll Nottm MA 96. **d** 96 **p** 97. C Bromfield w Waverton *Carl* 96-99; R Woldsburn *York* 99-01; TV E Farnworth and Kearsley *Man* 01-05; P-in-c Laceby and Ravendale Gp *Linc* 05-11; P-in-c Brough w Stainmore, Musgrave and Warcop *Carl* 11-13. *Address temp unknown* E: revtompkins@btinternet.com

TOMS, Elizabeth Jane. b 66. **d** 13 **p** 14. C Crondall and Ewshot *Guildf* from 13; Chapl Frimley Health NHS Foundn Trust from 15. *48 Danvers Drive, Church Crookham, Fleet GU52 0UD* T: (01252) 810624

TOMS, Sheila Patricia. b 33. Cam Univ TCert 54 Univ of Wales (Cardiff) BEd 77. Llan Ord Course 90. **dss** 91 **d** 94 **p** 97. Canton St Luke *Llan* 91-94; NSM Peterston-super-Ely w St Brides-super-Ely 94-00; P-in-c Newport St Paul *Mon* 00-06; PtO 07-13; P-in-c Goetre w Llanover 13-14; PtO from 14. *26 Fairfax View, Raglan, Usk NP15 2DR* T: (01291) 690250 E: sheilaptoms@btinternet.com

TONBRIDGE, Archdeacon of. *See* MANSELL, The Ven Clive Neville Ross

TONBRIDGE, Suffragan Bishop of. *See* CASTLE, The Rt Revd Brian Colin

TONES, Kevin Edward. b 64. Hertf Coll Ox BA 85. Ridley Hall Cam 88. **d** 91 **p** 92. C Warmsworth *Sheff* 91-92; C Thorne 92-96; V Greasbrough 96-11; C Kimberworth, Rawmarsh w Parkgate and Kimberworth Park 10-11; rtd 11; PtO *Dur* from 11. *40A Blakelock Road, Hartlepool TS25 5PG* T: (01429) 265625 E: kevt@worshiptrax.co.uk

TONGE, Brian. b 36. St Chad's Coll Dur BA 58. Ely Th Coll 59. **d** 61 **p** 62. C Fleetwood St Pet *Blackb* 61-65; Chapl Ranby Ho Sch Retford 65-69; Hon C Burnley St Andr w St Marg *Blackb* 69-97; rtd 97; PtO *Blackb* from 97. *50 Fountains Avenue, Simonstone, Burnley BB12 7PY* T: (01282) 776518

TONGE, The Very Revd Lister. b 51. K Coll Lon AKC 74 Loyola Univ Chicago MPS 95. St Aug Coll Cant 74. **d** 75 **p** 76. C Liv Our Lady and St Nic w St Anne 75-78; C Johannesburg Cathl S Africa 78-79; CR 79-91; LtO *Wakef* 83-91; PtO *Man* 89-94;

USA 93-95; PtO *Liv* 95-96; Chapl Community of St Jo Bapt from 96; Chapl Ripon Coll Cuddesdon 05-09; LtO Newark USA from 08; Chapl New Coll Ox 10-11; Dean Mon from 12; V Newport St Woolos 12-14; V Newport St Woolos w St Mark from 14. *The Deanery, 105 Stow Hill, Newport NP2 4ED* T: (01633) 259627 E: listertonge@gmail.com

TONGE, Malcolm. b 53. Lancs Poly BA 74 FCA 77. NEOC 00. **d** 03 **p** 04. NSM Brookfield *York* 03-07; NSM Ingleby Barwick 07-08; NSM Lower Swale *Leeds* from 08. *8 Meadow Court, Scruton, Northallerton DL7 0QU* E: malcolm.tonge@huntsman.com

TONGUE, Charles Garth. b 32. **d** 01 **p** 01. P-in-c Strontian and Kinlochmoidart *Arg* 01-13. *The Old Smiddy, Anaheilt, Strontian, Acharacle, Argyll PH36 4JA* T: (01967) 402467 M: 07766-463127

TONGUE, Canon Paul. b 41. St Chad's Coll Dur BA 63. **d** 64 **p** 65. C Dudley St Edm *Worc* 64-69; C Sedgley All SS *Lich* 69-70; V Amblecote *Worc* 70-07; Chapl Dudley Gp of Hosps NHS Trust 93-07; Hon Can Worc Cathl 93-07; RD Stourbridge 96-01; rtd 07; PtO *Worc* from 09. *99 Woolhope Road, Worcester WR5 2AP* T: (01905) 352052 E: paul_tongue@sky.com

TONKIN, The Ven David Graeme. b 31. Univ of NZ LLB 56 LLM 57 Barrister-at-Law. Coll of Resurr Mirfield 57. **d** 59 **p** 60. C Hackney Wick St Mary of Eton w St Aug *Lon* 59-62; Chapl Worksop Coll Notts 62-68; LtO *S'well* 63-68; Jordan 68-74; New Zealand from 74; Can St Pet Cathl Waikato 88-89; Adn Waitomo 89-98; rtd 93. *Box 91, Owhango, New Zealand* T/F: (0064) (7) 895 4738

TONKIN, Mrs Jacqueline Anne. b 50. Open Univ BSc 02 DipSW 02. Yorks Min Course. **d** 11 **p** 12. NSM Langtoft w Foxholes, Butterwick, Cottam etc *York* from 11; NSM Gt and Lt Driffield from 12. *Hunmanset Lodge, Back Street, Langtoft, Driffield YO25 3TD* T: (01377) 267321 E: jacki.tonkin1@btinternet.com

TONKIN, Canon Richard John. b 28. Lon Coll of Div ALCD 59 BD 60. **d** 60 **p** 61. C Leic Martyrs 60-63; C Keynsham *B & W* 63-66; V Hinckley H Trin *Leic* 66-74; RD Sparkenhoe II 71-74; R Oadby 74-84; V Leic H Apostles 84-93; Hon Can Leic Cathl 83-93; rtd 93; PtO *Leic* from 93. *39 Shackerdale Road, Wigston, Leicester LE8 1BQ* T: 0116-281 2517

TONKINSON, Canon David Boyes. b 47. K Coll Lon BD 71 AKC 71. St Aug Coll Cant 71. **d** 72 **p** 73. C Surbiton St Andr *S'wark* 72-74; C Selsdon St Jo w St Fran *Cant* 75-81; V Croydon St Aug *Cant* 81-84; V Croydon St Aug *S'wark* 85-89; C Easthampstead and Ind Chapl *Ox* 89-96; Chapl Bracknell Coll 93-96; Soc Resp Adv *Portsm* 96-02; Hon Can Portsm Cathl 96-02; Ind Chapl *Win* 02-08; Hon C Heckfield w Mattingley and Rotherwick 06-07; Hon C Hook and Heckfield w Mattingley and Rotherwick 07-08; Soc Resp Partnership Development Officer *Guildf* 08-11; rtd 11. *17 Squirrel Close, Sandhurst GU47 9DL* E: david.tonkinson@o2.co.uk

TOOBY, Anthony Albert. b 58. Sarum & Wells Th Coll 89. **d** 91 **p** 92. C Warsop *S'well* 91-95; C Ollerton w Boughton 95-98; V Girlington *Bradf* 98-10; P-in-c Mancetter *Cov* from 10. *The Vicarage, Quarry Lane, Mancetter, Atherstone CV9 1NL* T: (01827) 713266 E: tonytooby@virginmedia.com

TOOGOOD, Mrs Gillian Mary. b 58. Ridley Hall Cam 08. **d** 10 **p** 11. C Brentford *Lon* 10-13; Lic Preacher Kensington Area from 13; V Feltham from 14. *5 Fulmer Way, London W13 9XQ* M: 07936-793362 T: (020) 8567 1299 E: gill.toogood@tiscali.co.uk

TOOGOOD, John Peter. b 73. Leeds Univ BA 95. Ripon Coll Cuddesdon 98. **d** 00 **p** 01. C Sherborne w Castleton and Lillington *Sarum* 00-03; P-in-c Chieveley w Winterbourne and Oare *Ox* 03-10; R E Downland from 10. *The Vicarage, Church Lane, Chieveley, Newbury RG20 8UT* T: (01635) 247566 E: edownlandrector@gmail.com

TOOGOOD, Katie Leanne. b 80. Leic Univ BSc 02 Man Metrop Univ PGCE 04. Ripon Coll Cuddesdon 11. **d** 14 **p** 15. C Louth *Linc* from 14. *24 Grosvenor Road, Louth LN11 0BB* M: 07447-478048 E: kltoogood@yahoo.com

TOOGOOD, Ms Melanie Lorraine. b 57. K Coll Lon BD 78 AKC 78. Ripon Coll Cuddesdon 94. **d** 96 **p** 97. C Shepperton *Lon* 96-99; C Greenford H Cross 99-04; P-in-c Tufnell Park St Geo and All SS 04-06; V from 06. *St George's Vicarage, 72 Crayford Road, London N7 0ND* T: (020) 7700 0383 E: melanietoogood@tesco.net *or* melanie@toogood.info

TOOGOOD, Noel Hare. b 32. Birm Univ BSc 54. Wells Th Coll 59. **d** 61 **p** 62. C Rotherham *Sheff* 61-65; C Darlington St Jo *Dur* 65-70; V Burnopfield 70-81; P-in-c Roche *Truro* 81-84; P-in-c Withiel 81-84; R Roche and Withiel 84-91; RD St Austell 88-91; V Madron 91-96; rtd 96; PtO *Portsm* from 97. *Acorn Cottage, Oakhill Road, Seaview PO34 5AP*

TOOGOOD, Robert Charles. b 45. AKC 70. St Aug Coll Cant 70. **d** 71 **p** 72. C Shepperton *Lon* 71-74; C Kirk Ella *York* 74-76; P-in-c Levisham w Lockton 76-81; P-in-c Ebberston w

Allerston 76-81; R Kempsey and Severn Stoke w Croome d'Abitot *Worc* 81-92; V Bramley *Win* 92-10; rtd 10; PtO *Win* from 10. *14 Huntsmead, Alton GU34 2SE* T: (01420) 87007

TOOGOOD, Robert Frederick. b 43. St Paul's Coll Chelt CertEd 65 Open Univ BA 74. Trin Coll Bris 93. **d** 95 **p** 96. C Southbroom *Sarum* 95-99; TV Langport Area *B & W* 99-04; rtd 04; PtO *Ox* from 05; *Sarum* from 05. *49 Barrow Close, Marlborough SN8 2BE* T: (01672) 511468
E: bob@toogood12.wanadoo.co.uk

TOOKE, Mrs Sheila. b 44. EAMTC 89. **d** 91 **p** 94. NSM March St Wendreda *Ely* 91-95; P-in-c Upwell Christchurch 95-97; P-in-c Welney 95-97; P-in-c Manea 95-97; R Christchurch and Manea and Welney 97-03; rtd 03; PtO *Ely* from 03. *The Haven, 21 Wisbech Road, March PE15 8ED* T: (01354) 652844
E: stooke@havenmarch.plus.com

TOOKEY, Preb Christopher Tom. b 41. AKC 67. **d** 68 **p** 69. C Stockton St Pet *Dur* 68-71; C Burnham *B & W* 71-77; R Clutton w Cameley 77-81; V Wells St Thos w Horrington 81-06; RD Shepton Mallet 86-95; Chapl Bath and West Community NHS Trust 95-06; Preb Wells Cathl 90-11; rtd 06; PtO *B & W* from 06. *47 Drake Road, Wells BA5 3LE* T: (01749) 676006 E: christophertookey@talktalk.net

TOOLEY, Norman Oliver. b 27. Roch Th Coll. **d** 65 **p** 66. C Gravesend St Mary *Roch* 65-68; C Ormskirk *Liv* 68-73; Chapl Merseyside Cen for the Deaf 73-78; C Bootle Ch Ch *Liv* 78-80; C W Ham *Chelmsf* 80-86; Chapl RAD 86-92; rtd 92; PtO *Roch* 92-98. *30 Blackbrook Lane, Bromley BR2 8AY*

TOOMBS, Ian Melvyn. b 39. Hull Univ BA 64 MSc 90 FCIPD 93. Ripon Coll Cuddesdon 07. **d** 07 **p** 08. NSM Alton St Lawr *Win* 07-09; PtO from 11. *31 Princess Drive, Alton GU34 1QE* T: (01420) 88130

TOON, John Samuel. b 30. Man Univ BA. Bps' Coll Cheshunt 64. **d** 65 **p** 66. C Newark St Mary *S'well* 65-67; C Clewer St Andr *Ox* 67-69; R Osgathorpe *Leic* 70-72; C Maidstone All SS w St Phil and H Trin *Cant* 76-78; Canada 73-76 and from 78; rtd 95; Hon C Portage la Prairie St Mary Canada 95-02; P-in-c N Peace Par 02-05; R Oshawa Gd Shep from 05. *St George's Residence, Unit 104, 505 Simcoe Street South, Oshawa ON L1H 4J9, Canada* T: (001) (905) 571 5976
E: fathertoon@rogers.com

TOOP, Preb Allan Neil. b 49. St Alb Minl Tr Scheme 79 Linc Th Coll 82. **d** 83 **p** 84. C Kempston Transfiguration *St Alb* 83-87; C Ludlow *Heref* 87-92; P-in-c Stokesay and Sibdon Carwood w Halford 92-01; P-in-c Acton Scott 96-01; RD Condover 96-00; V Minsterley 01-13; R Habberley 01-13; P-in-c Hope w Shelve 07-13; R Minsterley, Habberley and Hope w Shelve 13-15; Preb Heref Cathl 06-15; rtd 15. *The Rectory, 15 Brookside, Bicton, Shrewsbury SY3 8EP* T: (01743) 851375

TOOP, Mrs Mary-Louise. b 55. Glouc Sch of Min 90. **d** 04 **p** 05. Dir of Ords *Heref* 00-15; NSM Minsterley 04-13; NSM Habberley 04-13; NSM Hope w Shelve 04-13; NSM Minsterley, Habberley and Hope w Shelve 13-15; Preb Heref Cathl 12-15; P-in-c Bicton, Montford w Shrawardine and Fitz *Lich* from 15. *The Rectory, 15 Brookside, Bicton, Shrewsbury SY3 8EP*
T: (01743) 851375 E: maryloutoop@lineone.net

TOOTH, Nigel David. b 47. RMN 69. Sarum & Wells Th Coll 71. **d** 74 **p** 75. C S Beddington St Mich *S'wark* 74-77; C Whitchurch *Bris* 77-83; TV Bedminster 83-87; Chapl Dorchester Hosps 87-94; Chapl Herrison Hosp Dorchester 87-94; Chapl W Dorset Gen Hosps NHS Trust 94-11; rtd 11. *5 Hope Terrace, Martinstown, Dorchester DT2 9JN*
T: (01305) 889576 E: nigeltooth@hotmail.co.uk

TOOVEY, Rupert William. b 66. **d** 10 **p** 11. NSM Storrington *Chich* 10-15; NSM Steyning from 15; NSM Ashurst from 15. *31 Downsview Avenue, Storrington, Pulborough RH20 4PS*

TOPALIAN, Canon Berj. b 51. Sheff Univ BA 72 PhD 77. Sarum Th Coll 95. **d** 97 **p** 98. NSM Clifton Ch Ch w Em *Bris* 97-98; C Bris St Mich and St Paul 98-99; C Cotham St Sav w St Mary and Clifton St Paul 99-01; V Pilning w Compton Greenfield 01-08; Chapl St Monica Home Westbury-on-Trym from 08; Hon Min Can Bris Cathl 04-11; Hon Can Bris Cathl from 11. *Gate Lodge, St Monica Home, Cote Lane, Bristol BS9 3UN*
T: 0117-949 4020 E: berj.topalian@st.monicatrust.org.uk

TOPHAM, Benjamin Mark. b 84. Cliff Coll BA 05. Ridley Hall Cam 13. **d** 14 **p** 15. C Chalfont St Peter *Ox* from 14. *The Parsonage, Oval Way, Gerrards Cross SL9 8PZ* T: (01753) 880171 M: 07736-953127 E: ben.topham@csp-parish.org.uk

TOPLEY (née BRANCHE), Caren Teresa. b 59. Avery Hill Coll BEd 81. SEITE 94. **d** 97 **p** 98. NSM Arlesey w Astwick *St Alb* 97-99; NSM Clifton and Southill from 99. *7 Fairfax Close, Clifton, Shefford SG17 5RH* T: (01462) 615499
E: topley@ntlworld.com

TOPPING, Kenneth Bryan Baldwin. b 27. Bps' Coll Cheshunt 58. **d** 59 **p** 60. C Fleetwood St Pet *Blackb* 59-63; V Ringley *Man* 63-70; V Cleator Moor w Cleator *Carl* 70-91; rtd 92; PtO *Blackb* 92-07. *28 Glebelands, Corbridge NE45 5DS* T: (01434) 634944

TOPPING, Roy William. b 37. MBE 92. S Dios Minl Tr Scheme 91. **d** 92 **p** 93. Bahrain 89-94; Chapl Miss to Seamen Milford Haven 94-99; rtd 99; PtO *Sarum* from 00. *7 Lady Down View, Tisbury, Salisbury SP3 6LL* T: (01747) 871909

TORDOFF, Donald William. b 45. Nottm Univ BA 69. Qu Coll Birm 69. **d** 71 **p** 72. C High Harrogate Ch Ch *Ripon* 71-75; C Moor Allerton 75-80; V Bilton 80-92; R Spennithorne w Finghall and Hauxwell 92-01; rtd 01; PtO *Leeds* from 02; *York* from 10. *4 Weavers Green, Northallerton DL7 8FJ*
T: (01609) 760155 E: don@tordoffs.eclipse.co.uk

TORDOFF (née PARKER), Mrs Margaret Grace. b 40. SRN 65 SCM 67. Cranmer Hall Dur 81. dss 83 **d** 87 **p** 94. Bilton *Ripon* 83-87; C 87-92; Chapl Spennithorne Hall 92; NSM Spennithorne w Finghall and Hauxwell 92-00; rtd 00; PtO *M & K* from 00; *Leeds* from 00; *York* from 10. *4 Weavers Green, Northallerton DL7 8FJ* T: (01609) 760155
E: margaret@tordoffs.eclipse.co.uk

TORR, Stephen Charles. b 81. Birm Univ BA 05 PhD 12. Ridley Hall Cam 10. **d** 12 **p** 13. C Wilnecote *Lich* 12-13; C Abbots Bromley, Blithfield, Colton, Colwich etc from 13. *Little Haywood Vicarage, Main Road, Little Haywood, Stafford ST18 0TS* M: 07764-578583 E: stephentorr99@gmail.com

TORRENS, Marianne Rose. *See* ATKINSON, Marianne Rose

TORRENS, Robert Harrington. b 33. Trin Coll Cam BA 56 MA 61. Ridley Hall Cam 56. **d** 58 **p** 59. C Bromley SS Pet and Paul *Roch* 58-60; C Aylesbury *Ox* 60-63; V Eaton Socon *St Alb* 63-73; LtO 73-75; V Pittville All SS *Glouc* 75-84; Chapl Frenchay Hosp Bris 84-94; Chapl Manor Park Hosp Bris 84-94; Chapl St Pet Hospice Bris 94-98; P-in-c Chippenham *Ely* 98-01; P-in-c Snailwell 98-01; PtO from 01; *St E* from 01. *68 Barons Road, Bury St Edmunds IP33 2LW* T: (01284) 752075
E: torrensatkinson@aol.com

TORRY, Malcolm Norman Alfred. b 55. St Jo Coll Cam BA 76 MA 80 K Coll Lon MTh 79 LSE MSc 96 Lon Univ BD 78 PhD 90 BA 01 BSc 10. Cranmer Hall Dur 79. **d** 80 **p** 81. C S'wark H Trin w St Matt 80-83; C S'wark Ch Ch 83-88; Ind Chapl 83-88; V Hatcham St Cath 88-96; V E Greenwich Ch Ch w St Andr and St Mich 96-97; TR E Greenwich 97-13; TV 13-14; RD Greenwich Thameside 98-01; rtd 14; PtO *S'wark* from 15. *286 Ivydale Road, London SE15 3DF*
T: (020) 7635 7916 E: malcolm@torry.org.uk

TOSTEVIN, Alan Edwin John. b 51. Trin Coll Bris BA 86. **d** 86 **p** 87. C Hildenborough *Roch* 86-89; TV Ipsley *Worc* 89-06; rtd 06; PtO *Worc* from 06. *Bowling Green Cottage, Hanley Road, Malvern WR14 4HZ* T: (01684) 561468
E: artostevin@gmail.com

TOTNES, Archdeacon of. *See* DETTMER, The Ven Douglas James

TOTNEY (née YATES), Mrs Jennifer Clare. b 83. Trin Coll Cam BA 04 MA 05 Selw Coll Cam BA 08. Westcott Ho Cam 06. **d** 09 **p** 10. C White Horse *Sarum* 09-12; TV Vale of Pewsey from 12. *The Rectory, Church Street, Pewsey SN9 5DL* T: (01672) 562886
E: jennifer.totney@gmail.com

TOTTEN, Andrew James. b 64. MBE 01. QUB BA 87 TCD BTh 90 Univ of Wales (Cardiff) MTh 07. CITC. **d** 90 **p** 91. C Newtownards *D & D* 90-94; CF from 94. *c/o MOD Chaplains (Army)* F: 381824 T: (01264) 383430
E: andrewjtotten@hotmail.com

TOTTERDELL, Preb Rebecca Helen. b 57. Lon Bible Coll BA 80 MA 99. Oak Hill Th Coll 88. **d** 91 **p** 94. Par Dn Broxbourne w Wormley *St Alb* 91-94; C 94-95; C Stevenage St Nic and Graveley 95-99; P-in-c Benington w Walkern 99-08; Asst Dir of Ords 03-08; Bp's Adv for Women in Min 03-07; Asst Dioc Dir of Ords *Ex* 09-10; Dioc Dir of Ords from 10; Hon C Bovey Tracey SS Pet, Paul and Thos w Hennock from 09; Preb Ex Cathl from 14. *The Bishop's Office, The Palace, Palace Gate, Exeter EX1 1HY* T: (01392) 477702
E: ddo@exeter.anglican.org

TOTTLE, Nicola Rachael. *See* SKIPWORTH, Nicola Rachael

TOUCHÉ-PORTER, The Most Revd Carlos. Bp Mexico from 01; Presiding Bp from 04. *San Jeronimo #117, Angel CP 01000, Del Alvaro Obregón, DF, Mexico* T: (0052) (55) 5616 3193 F: 5616 2205 E: diomex@avantel.net

TOUCHSTONE, Grady Russell. b 32. Univ of S California 51. Wells Th Coll 63. **d** 65 **p** 66. C Maidstone St Mich *Cant* 65-70; USA from 70; rtd 95. *1069 South Gramercy Place, Los Angeles CA 90019-3634, USA* T: (001) (323) 731 5822 F: 731 5880

TOULMIN, Miles Roger. b 74. BNC Ox BA 95. Wycliffe Hall Ox BA 06. **d** 07 **p** 08. C Brompton H Trin w Onslow Square St Paul *Lon* 07-11; C Onslow Square and S Kensington St Aug 11-14; Malaysia from 14. *Address temp unknown*

TOURNAY, Ms Corinne Marie Eliane Ghislaine. b 57. Louvain Univ Belgium Lic 82 STB 90 MA 90. Cuddesdon Coll 92. **d** 94 **p** 95. C Redhill St Jo *S'wark* 94-98; V Brockley St Pet from 98. *St Peter's Vicarage, Wickham Way, London SE4 1LT* T: (020) 8469 0013

TOVAR, Gillian Elaine. See NICHOLLS, Gillian Elaine

TOVEY, John Hamilton. b 50. Cant Univ (NZ) BA 72. St Jo Coll Nottm 78. **d** 80 **p** 81. C Hyson Green *S'well* 80-83; C Cashmere New Zealand 83-85; Chapl Christchurch Cathl 85-89; P-in-c Amuri 89-90; V 90-94; C Johnsonville and Churton Park 94-96; P-in-c Churton Park 96-00; V Wainuiomata from 00. *117 Main Road, Wainuiomata, Lower Hutt 5014, New Zealand* T: (0064) (4) 478 4099 F: 478 4087 E: john.tovey@xtra.co.nz

TOVEY, Phillip Noel. b 56. Lon Univ BA 77 Lon Bible Coll BA 83 Nottm Univ MPhil 88 Lambeth STh 95 Ox Brookes Univ PhD 06. St Jo Coll Nottm 85. **d** 87 **p** 88. C Beaconsfield *Ox* 87-90; C Banbury 90-91; TV 91-95; Chapl Ox Brookes Univ 95-98; P-in-c Holton and Waterperry w Albury and Waterstock 95-97; TV Wheatley 97-98; Dioc Tr Officer from 98; Dir Reader Tr from 04; NSM Wootton and Dry Sandford from 05; Lect Ripon Coll Cuddesdon from 04. *20 Palmer Place, Abingdon OX14 5LZ* T: (01235) 527077 E: phillip.tovey@oxford.anglican.org

TOVEY, Canon Ronald. b 27. AKC 51. **d** 52 **p** 53. C Glossop *Derby* 52-55; C Chorlton upon Medlock *Man* 55-57; C Hulme St Phil 55-57; C Hulme St Jo 55-57; C Hulme H Trin 55-57; Malawi 57-69; Lesotho 69-85; Adn S Lesotho 77-85; Hon Can Lesotho 85-92; R Reddish *Man* 85-92; rtd 92; PtO *Pet* 92-07; *Linc* 99-02. *86 Kings Road, Oakham LE15 6PD* T: (01572) 770628 E: ronshir@tovey2.fsnet.co.uk

TOWELL, Alan. b 37. Sarum & Wells Th Coll 86 WMMTC 87. **d** 89 **p** 90. C Boultham *Linc* 89-93; P-in-c Scunthorpe Resurr 93-97; rtd 97. *154 Upper Eastern Green Lane, Coventry CV5 7DN* T: (024) 7646 1881

TOWERS, Canon David Francis. b 32. G&C Coll Cam BA 56 MA 60. Clifton Th Coll 56. **d** 58 **p** 59. C Gresley *Derby* 58-63; V Brixton St Paul *S'wark* 63-75; V Chatteris *Ely* 75-87; RD March 82-87; Hon Can Ely Cathl 85-87; R Burnley St Pet *Blackb* 87-97; rtd 97; PtO *Leeds* from 99. *9 West View, Langcliffe, Settle BD24 9LZ* T: (01729) 825803

TOWERS, John Keble. b 19. Keble Coll Ox BA 41 MA 57. Edin Th Coll 41. **d** 43 **p** 44. Chapl Dundee St Paul *Bre* 43-47; India 47-62; R Edin Ch Ch-St Jas 62-71; V Bradf St Oswald Chapel Green 71-78; P-in-c Holme Cultram St Mary *Carl* 78-80; V 80-85; rtd 85; PtO *Glas* 85-92; Hon C Moffat 92-00. *Braeburn Home, 35 Inverleith Terrace, Edinburgh EH3 5NU* T: 0131-332 7227

TOWERS, Patrick Leo. b 43. AKC 68 Hull Univ CertEd 69. **d** 74 **p** 75. Japan 74-81; TV Bourne Valley *Sarum* 81-83; Dioc Youth Officer 81-83; Chapl Oundle Sch 83-86; I Rathkeale w Askeaton and Kilcornan *L & K* 86-89; I Nenagh 89-00; Can Limerick, Killaloe and Clonfert Cathls 97-00; Provost Tuam *T, K & A* 00-09; Can Tuam Cathl 00-09; I Galway w Kilcummin 00-09; rtd 09. *Doonwood, Mountbellew, Co Galway, Republic of Ireland* T: (00353) (90) 968 4547 M: 86-814 0649 E: towers.patrick@gmail.com

TOWLER, David George. b 42. Cranmer Hall Dur 73. **d** 76 **p** 77. C Newbarns w Hawcoat *Carl* 76-80; V Huyton St Geo *Liv* 80-98; V Newburgh w Westhead 98-07; AD Ormskirk 01-06; Hon Can Liv Cathl 03-07; rtd 07. *7 Padstow Close, Southport PR9 9RX* E: davidtowler@postmaster.co.uk

TOWLER, John Frederick. b 42. Surrey Univ PhD 05. Bps' Coll Cheshunt 62. **d** 66 **p** 67. C Lowestoft St Marg *Nor* 66-71; R Horstead 71-77; Warden Dioc Conf Ho Horstead 71-77; Prec and Min Can Worc Cathl 77-81; rtd 02; Hon C Fordingbridge and Breamore and Hale etc *Win* 06-12; PtO from 12. *24 Oak Road, Alderholt, Fordingbridge SP6 3BL* T: (01425) 656595 M: 07940-855952 E: cjtptners@talktalk.net

TOWLSON, George Eric. b 40. NOC 80. **d** 83 **p** 84. NSM Wakef St Andr and St Mary 83-84; NSM Ox St Mich w St Martin and All SS 84-86; PtO 86-87; NSM Hoar Cross w Newchurch *Lich* 87-93; C Wednesbury St Paul Wood Green 93-01; rtd 01; PtO *Lich* from 01. *58 Church Lane, Barton under Needwood, Burton-on-Trent DE13 8HX* T: (01283) 713673

TOWNEND, John Philip. b 52. Southn Univ BTh 95. Sarum & Wells Th Coll 89. **d** 91 **p** 92. C Sherborne w Castleton and Lillington *Sarum* 91-95; P-in-c Wool and E Stoke 95-98; Sacr and Chapl Westmr Abbey 98-01; P-in-c Brightwalton w Catmore, Leckhampstead etc *Ox* 01-10; P-in-c Beedon and Peasemore w W Ilsley and Farnborough 05-10; R W Downland from 10. *The Old Rectory, Church Street, Great Shefford, Hungerford RG17 7DU* T: (01488) 648164 E: jptownend@btinternet.com

TOWNEND, Lee Stuart. b 65. St Jo Coll Dur MA 08. Cranmer Hall Dur 96. **d** 98 **p** 99. C Buxton w Burbage and King Sterndale *Derby* 98-01; V Loose *Cant* 01-08; P-in-c Ilkley All SS *Bradf* 08-12; Ch Growth Officer Chesterfield Adnry *Derby* from 12. *The Vicarage, Curbar Lane, Curbar, Calver, Hope Valley S32 3YF* T: (01332) 388668 E: leethevicar@gmail.com

TOWNER, Andrew Paul John. b 76. Bris Univ BSc 98 Surrey Univ Roehampton PGCE 02. Oak Hill Th Coll MTh 07. **d** 07. C St Helen Bishopsgate w St Andr Undershaft etc *Lon* 07-10; C Beckenham Ch Ch *Roch* 10-14; P-in-c Houghton *Carl* from 14. *12 Brunstock Close, Carlisle CA3 0HL* T: (01228) 810076 or 515972 M: 07956-569983 E: andrew@hkchurch.org.uk

TOWNER, Colin David. b 39. St Pet Coll Ox BA 61 MA 65 Lon Univ BD 63 ARCM 72 LRAM 73. Tyndale Hall Bris 61. **d** 64 **p** 65. C Southsea St Simon *Portsm* 64-67; C Penge St Jo *Roch* 67-70; V Leic St Chris 70-74; Hon C Southsea St Jude *Portsm* 75-82; PtO 86-90 and 00-01 and from 12; C Southsea St Pet 01-03; P-in-c 03-07; P-in-c Portsea St Luke 05-07; rtd 07; PtO *Ely* 08-12. *10 Ophir Road, Portsmouth PO2 9EN* E: sctowner@btinternet.com

TOWNER, Preb Paul. b 51. Bris Univ BSc 72 BTh 81. Oak Hill Th Coll 78. **d** 81 **p** 82. C Aspley *S'well* 81-84; R Gt Hanwood *Heref* 84-99; RD Pontesbury 93-99; P-in-c Heref St Pet w St Owen and St Jas 99-11; V from 11; RD Heref City 07-10; RD Heref Rural 07-10; RD Heref from 10; Preb Heref Cathl from 96. *The Vicarage, 102 Green Street, Hereford HR1 2QW* T: (01432) 273676 E: preb.paul@btinternet.com

TOWNLEY, The Ven Peter Kenneth. b 55. Sheff Univ BA 78. Ridley Hall Cam 78. **d** 80 **p** 81. C Ashton Ch Ch *Man* 80-83; C-in-c Holts CD 83-88; R Stretford All SS 88-96; V Ipswich St Mary-le-Tower *St E* 96-08; RD Ipswich 01-08; Hon Can St E Cathl 03-08; Adn Pontefract *Leeds* from 08. *The Vicarage, Kirkthorpe Lane, Kirkthorpe, Wakefield WF1 5SZ* T/F (01924) 896327 T: 434459 F: 364834 E: peter.townley@westyorkshiredales.anglican.org

TOWNLEY, Robert Keith. b 44. TCD MPhil 04. St Jo Coll Auckland LTh 67. **d** 67 **p** 68. C Devonport H Trin New Zealand 67-70; C Lisburn Ch Ch *Conn* 71-74; C Portman Square St Paul *Lon* 75-80; Dean Ross and I Ross Union *C, C & R* 82-94; Chan Cork Cathl 82-94; Dean Kildare and I Kildare w Kilmeague and Curragh *M & K* 95-06; Chapl Defence Forces 95-06; rtd 06; LtO *Arm* from 06. *10 Beresford Row, Armagh BT61 9AU* T: (028) 3752 5667

TOWNLEY, Roger. b 46. Man Univ BSc York Univ MSc. St Deiniol's Hawarden 82. **d** 84 **p** 85. C Longton *Blackb* 84-88; V Penwortham St Leon 88-92; V Wrightington 92-11; Chapl Wrightington Hosp NHS Trust 92-01; Chapl Wrightington Wigan and Leigh NHS Trust 01-11; rtd 11. *10 Hosey Road, Sturminster Newton DT10 1QP* T: (01258) 471900 E: r.townley@talk21.com

TOWNROE, Canon Edward John. b 20. St Jo Coll Ox BA 42 MA 48 FKC 59. Linc Th Coll 42. **d** 43 **p** 44. C Sunderland *Dur* 43-48; Chapl St Boniface Coll Warminster 48-56; Warden 56-69; LtO *Sarum* 48-93; PtO 93; Can and Preb Sarum Cathl 69-93; rtd 85. *St Boniface Lodge, Church Street, Warminster BA12 8PG* T: (01985) 212355

TOWNS, Ms Claire Louise. b 69. Portsm Poly BA 90 Univ of Wales (Cardiff) MSc 93 St Jo Coll Nottm MA 01. EMMTC 06. **d** 07 **p** 08. C Beeston *S'well* 07-12; V Swanmore St Barn *Portsm* from 12. *The Vicarage, Church Road, Swanmore, Southampton SO32 2PA* T: (01489) 808968 M: 07766-541152 E: clairetowns@googlemail.com

TOWNSEND, Allan Harvey. b 43. WMMTC 89. **d** 92 **p** 93. NSM Fenton *Lich* 92-96; C Tividale 96-98; P-in-c Saltley and Shaw Hill *Birm* 98-06; P-in-c Washwood Heath 01-06; V Saltley and Washwood Heath 06-09; rtd 09; PtO *Lich* 09-10 and from 11; C Wolstanton 10; PtO *Birm* from 14. *5 The Croft, Stoke-on-Trent ST4 5HT* T: (01782) 416333

TOWNSEND, Anne Jennifer. b 38. Lon Univ MB, BS 60 MRCS 60 LRCP 60. S'wark Ord Course 88. **d** 91 **p** 94. NSM Wandsworth St Paul *S'wark* 91-08; Chapl Asst St Geo Hosp Lon 91-92; Dean MSE *S'wark* 93-99; PtO 08-13; *Roch* from 13. *3 Bromley College, London Road, Bromley BR1 1PE* T: (020) 8460 3869 E: revdrannetow@yahoo.co.uk

TOWNSEND, Christopher Robin. b 47. St Jo Coll Nottm. **d** 74 **p** 75. C Gt Horton *Bradf* 74-77; C Heaton St Barn 77-78; C Wollaton *S'well* 78-80; V Slaithwaite w E Scammonden *Leeds* from 80. *The Vicarage, Station Road, Slaithwaite, Huddersfield HD7 5AW* T/F: (01484) 842748 E: robin.townsend@homecall.co.uk

TOWNSEND, Derek William. b 52. Fitzw Coll Cam BA 74 Man Univ PhD 89. St Jo Coll Nottm 91. **d** 91 **p** 92. C Hazlemere *Ox* 91-95; TV Banbury 95-98; V Banbury St Paul 98-01; PtO from 11. *24 Lower Lodge Lane, Hazlemere, High Wycombe HP15 7AT* T: (01494) 715964 M: 07855-015519 E: bill.townsend@tiscali.co.uk

TOWNSEND, Mrs Diane Rosalind. b 45. Stockwell Coll of Educn CertEd 66 K Alfred's Coll Win BEd 88. Sarum Th Coll 93. **d** 96 **p** 97. NSM Botley, Durley and Curdridge *Portsm* 96-00; NSM Buriton 00-05; NSM Portsea N End St Mark 05-10; TV 06-10; rtd 10; PtO *Portsm* from 10. *9 Daisy Lane, Locks Heath, Southampton SO31 6RA* T: (01489) 574092 E: dirobdaisy@aol.com

TOWNSEND, Gary. b 65. Trin Coll Bris. **d** 00 **p** 01. C Minster-in-Sheppey *Cant* 00-04; C Tonbridge SS Pet and Paul *Roch* 04-10; V Henham and Elsenham w Ugley *Chelmsf* from 10. *The Vicarage, Carters Lane, Henham, Bishop's Stortford CM22 6AQ* T: (01279) 850281 M: 07719-876452
E: gary.townsend@heuchurch.co.uk

TOWNSEND, Canon John Clifford. b 24. St Edm Hall Ox BA 48 MA 49. Wells Th Coll. **d** 50 **p** 51. C Machen *Mon* 50-51; C Usk and Monkswood w Glascoed Chpl and Gwehelog 51-55; R Melbury Osmond w Melbury Sampford *Sarum* 55-60; Chapl RNVR 57-58; Chapl RNR 58-75; V Branksome St Aldhelm *Sarum* 60-70; R Melksham 70-73; TR 73-80; Can and Preb *Sarum* Cathl 72-90; RD Bradford 73-80; P-in-c Harnham 80-81; V 81-90; RD Salisbury 80-85; rtd 90; PtO *Sarum* from 90. *49 Hascombe Court, Somerleigh Road, Dorchester DT1 1AG* T: (01305) 261384

TOWNSEND, John Elliott. b 39. ALCD 63. **d** 64 **p** 65. C Harold Wood *Chelmsf* 64-68; C Walton St E 68-72; V Kensal Rise St Martin *Lon* 72-83; V Hornsey Ch Ch 83-98; V Forty Hill Jes Ch 98-06; rtd 06; PtO *Chelmsf* from 06. *4 Harper Way, Rayleigh SS6 9NA* T: (01268) 780938
E: johnetbar@internet.com

TOWNSEND, Peter. b 35. AKC 63. **d** 64 **p** 65. C Norbury St Oswald *Cant* 64-67; C New Romney w Hope 67-69; C Westborough *Guildf* 69-74; P-in-c Wicken *Pet* 74-87; R Paulerspury 74-84; P-in-c Whittlebury w Silverstone 82-84; V Whittlebury w Paulerspury 84-87; V Greetham and Thistleton w Stretton and Clipsham 87-01; rtd 01; PtO *Pet* 01-08; *Leic* from 04. *26 King's Road, Oakham LE15 6PD* T: (01572) 759286 E: peterlinda1@hotmail.co.uk

TOWNSEND, Peter. b 37. Open Univ BA 87. Wells Th Coll 67. **d** 69 **p** 70. C Desborough *Pet* 69-72; C Bramley *Ripon* 72-75; C-in-c Newton Hall LEP *Dur* 75-80; P-in-c Newton Hall 80-81; V Hartlepool St Luke 81-03; rtd 03; PtO *Dur* from 03. *348 Stockton Road, Hartlepool TS25 2PW* T: (01429) 291651
E: townsendfamgo@ntlworld.com

TOWNSEND, Philip Roger. b 51. Sheff Univ BA 78. Trin Coll Bris 78. **d** 80 **p** 81. C W Streatham St Jas *S'wark* 80-85; C Ardsley *Sheff* 85-88; V Crookes St Tim from 88; AD Hallam 05-12. *St Timothy's Vicarage, 152 Slinn Street, Sheffield S10 1NZ* T: 0114-266 1745 E: vicar@sttims.org.uk

TOWNSEND, Canon Robert William. b 68. Univ of Wales (Ban) BA 90. St Mich Coll Llan BTh 93. **d** 93 **p** 95. C Dolgellau w Llanfachreth and Brithdir etc *Ban* 93-94; Min Can Ban Cathl 94-96; P-in-c Amlwch 96-97; R 97-99; R Llanfair-pwll and Llanddaniel-fab etc 99-03; P-in-c Llanilar w Rhostie and Llangwyryfon etc *St D* 03-06; Dioc Schools Officer 03-06; R Llanberis, Llanrug and Llandinorwig *Ban* 06-11; P-in-c Llandwrog and Llanwnda 11-12; P-in-c Uwch Gwyrfai Beuno Sant 12-13; AD Arfon from 12; Dioc Dir of Educn 10-15; Dioc Communications Officer 12-15; Dioc Dir of Communication from 15; C Bro Eryri from 15; Hon Can Ban Cathl from 12. *12 Llys y Waun, Waunfawr, Caernarfon LL55 4ZA* T: (01286) 650262 M: 07855-492006
E: robert@gwedd.io

TOWNSEND, Robin. See TOWNSEND, Christopher Robin
TOWNSEND, William. See TOWNSEND, Derek William

TOWNSHEND (formerly WEAVER), Angela Mary. b 48. WMMTC 92. **d** 95 **p** 96. C Hill *Birm* 95-99; V Hamstead St Paul 99-06; AD Handsworth 05-06; Hon Can Birm Cathl 05-06; Can Res Guildf Cathl 06-11; C-in-c Bath Ch Ch Prop Chpl *B & W* 11-15; PtO *Guildf* from 15. *16 Kings Road, Shalford, Guildford GU4 8JU* M: 07791-551824
E: angelatownshend@btinternet.com

TOWNSHEND, Charles Hume. b 41. St Pet Coll Ox BA 64 MA 69. Westcott Ho Cam 64. **d** 66 **p** 67. C Warlingham w Chelsham and Farleigh *S'wark* 66-75; R Old Cleeve, Leighland and Treborough *B & W* 75-85; R Bishops Lydeard w Bagborough and Cothelstone 85-95; V N Curry 95-06; rtd 06. *Mutterings, Church Road, Colaton Raleigh, Sidmouth EX10 0LW* T: (01395) 567460

TOWNSHEND, David William. b 57. Lon Univ PGCE 80 Ox Univ MA 85. Cranmer Hall Dur 81. **d** 84 **p** 85. C Barking St Marg w St Patr *Chelmsf* 84-87; Canada from 87. *225 Colonel Douglas Crescent, Brockville ON K6V 6W1, Canada*

TOWNSHEND, Edward George Hume. b 43. Pemb Coll Cam BA 66 MA 70. Westcott Ho Cam 68. **d** 70 **p** 71. C Hellesdon *Nor* 70-74; Ind Chapl 74-81; TV Lowestoft St Marg 74-78; TV Lowestoft and Kirkley 79-81; V Stafford St Jo *Lich* 81-85; P-in-c Tixall w Ingestre 81-85; V Stafford St Jo and Tixall w Ingestre 85-87; R Lich St Chad 87-99; RD Lich 94-99; P-in-c Hammerwich 94-99; C Hamstead St Paul *Birm* 99-02; Chapl Birm Airport 00-05; Sen Ind Chapl 02-05; rtd 05; PtO *Birm* 05-06. *16 Kings Road, Shalford, Guildford GU4 8JU* M: 07931-928114 E: dryfly57@hotmail.com

TOY, Elizabeth Margaret. b 37. CQSW 77. Oak Hill NSM Course 85. **d** 88 **p** 94. NSM Hildenborough *Roch* 88-07; PtO from 08. *2 Francis Cottages, London Road, Hildenborough, Tonbridge TN11 8NQ* T: (01732) 833886
E: liz.toy@diocese-rochester.org

TOY, Canon John. b 30. Hatf Coll Dur BA 53 MA 62 Leeds Univ PhD 82 FSA 13. Wells Th Coll 53. **d** 55 **p** 56. C Newington St Paul *S'wark* 55-58; S Sec SCM 58-60; Chapl Ely Th Coll 60-64; Chapl Gothenburg w Halmstad and Jönköping *Eur* 65-69; Asst Chapl St Jo Coll York 69-72; Sen Lect 72-79; Prin Lect 79-83; Can Res and Chan York Minster 83-99; rtd 99; PtO *Eur* from 99; *S'well* from 03. *Dulverton Hall, Esplanade, Scarborough YO11 2AR* T: (01723) 340115
E: jtoy19@talktalk.net

TOYNBEE, Claire Louise. See ALCOCK, Claire Louise

TOYNE, Mrs Marian Elizabeth Christine. b 63. Rolle Coll BA 84 Swansea Coll of Educn PGCE 85. Linc Sch of Th and Min 11. **d** 14 **p** 15. NSM Frodingham and New Brumby *Linc* from 14. *Glebe Farmhouse, Tunnel Road, Wrawby, Brigg DN20 8SF* E: marian.toyne@live.co.uk

TOZE, Lissa Melanie. See GIBBONS, Lissa Melanie
TOZE, Lissa Melanie. See SCOTT, Lissa Melanie

TOZE, Stephen James. b 51. Birm Univ BA 79. Qu Coll Birm 76 Westcott Ho Cam 93. **d** 93 **p** 94. C Leominster *Heref* 93-94; R Gt Brickhill w Bow Brickhill and Lt Brickhill *Ox* 94-02; Rural Officer Buckm Adnry 95-02; V Wilshamstead and Houghton Conquest *St Alb* from 02; Ecum Officer Buckm Adnry from 13. *The Vicarage, 15 Vicarage Lane, Wilstead, Bedford MK45 3EU* T: (01234) 740423

TRACEY, Mrs Caroline Patricia. b 56. SNWTP 10. **d** 13 **p** 14. OLM Horwich and Rivington *Man* from 13. *82 Pennine Road, Horwich, Bolton BL6 7HW* T: (01204) 692303
E: caroline@archangelos.co.uk

TRACEY, Gareth Paul. b 81. K Alfred's Coll Win BA 03. St Jo Coll Nottm 06. **d** 09 **p** 10. C Roby *Liv* 09-11; C Eccleston 11-13; V Colney Heath St Mark *St Alb* from 13. *St Mark's Vicarage, St Mark's Close, Colney Heath, St Albans AL4 0NQ* M: 07880-928644 E: gaztherev@googlemail.com

TRACEY-MacLEOD, Talisker Isobel. b 81. St Andr Univ MA 03. Ripon Coll Cuddesdon BTh 11. **d** 11 **p** 12. C Hove All SS *Chich* from 11. *The Parsonage, Blatchington Road, Hove BN3 3TA* T: (01273) 778938 E: revd@alathea.org.uk

TRAFFORD, Peter. b 39. Chich Th Coll. **d** 83 **p** 84. C Bath Bathwick *B & W* 83-86; Chapl RN 86-90; P-in-c Donnington *Chich* 90-99; V Jarvis Brook 99-04; rtd 04. *26 Bourne Way, Midhurst GU29 9HZ* T: (01730) 815710

TRAFFORD-ROBERTS, Rosamond Jane. b 40. Qu Coll Birm BA. **d** 95 **p** 96. C Ledbury *Heref* 95-00; Lect St Botolph Aldgate w H Trin Minories *Lon* 00-05; Chapl Ho of St Barn-in-Soho 03-05; rtd 05; PtO *Lon* from 05. *47C St George's Square, London SW1V 3QN* T: (020) 7828 1122 M: 07736-335959
E: revdros@hotmail.com

TRAILL, Geoffrey Conway. b 58. Ridley Coll Melbourne BA 82 BTh 87. **d** 85 **p** 85. Australia 85-87 and from 88; C Shrub End *Chelmsf* 87-88. *1 Albert Street, Point Lonsdale Vic 3225, Australia* T: (0061) (3) 5258 4624 M: 412-381225 F: 5258 4623
E: gtraill@optusnet.com.au

TRAIN, Paul Michael. b 57. Stellenbosch Univ BChD 82. SEITE 03. **d** 06 **p** 07. NSM Loughton St Jo *Chelmsf* 06-10. *5 Monkchester Close, Loughton IG10 2SN* T: (020) 8508 2937
E: ungaaz@aol.com

TRAINOR, Mrs Lynn Joanna. b 65. Bris Univ BSc 87 Ex Univ PGCE 89. SAOMC 99. **d** 02 **p** 03. C Ascot Heath *Ox* 02-06. *5 Lavender Row, King Edward's Rise, Ascot SL5 8QR* T: (01344) 890577 E: lynn@lynnie.co.uk

TRANTER, John. b 51. St Jo Coll Nottm. **d** 00 **p** 01. C Gt Wyrley *Lich* 00-04; V Altham w Clayton le Moors *Blackb* 04-14; R Chelsfield *Roch* from 14; AD Orpington from 15. *The Rectory, Skibbs Lane, Orpington BR6 7RH* T: (01689) 825749
E: revjohnt@talktalk.net or rector@stmartinchelsfield.org.uk

TRANTER, Stephen. b 61. Lanc Univ BA 81 RGN 87 RM 89. Trin Coll Bris BA 99. **d** 99 **p** 00. C Blackpool St Thos *Blackb* 99-03; P-in-c Blackb St Jas 03-10; P-in-c Blackb St Steph 04-10; Chapl Univ Hosps of Morecambe Bay NHS Trust 10-12; P-in-c Ellel w Shireshead *Blackb* 11-12; OLM Officer *Man* from 12. *Diocese of Manchester, Church House, 90 Deansgate, Manchester M3 2GH* T: 0161-828 1400 M: 07528-309954
E: stephentranter@msn.com

TRAPNELL, Mrs Hazel Joan. b 45. Trin Coll Bris. **d** 12 **p** 13. OLM Stoke Bishop *Bris* from 12. *30 Hazelwood Court, Hazelwood Road, Bristol BS9 1PU* T: 0117-968 7190
E: hazeltrapnell@blueyonder.co.uk

TRAPNELL, Miss Sandra. b 51. SEN 73 SRN 79 RGN 87. **d** 08 **p** 09. OLM W Derby Gd Shep *Liv* from 08. *70 Ince Avenue, Anfield, Liverpool L4 7UX* M: 07999-715201

TRAPNELL, Canon Stephen Hallam. b 30. G&C Coll Cam BA 53 MA 57 Virginia Th Sem BD 56 MDiv 70 Hon DD 02. Ridley Hall Cam 53. **d** 56 **p** 57. C Upper Tulse Hill St Matthias *S'wark* 56-59; C Reigate St Mary 59-61; V Richmond Ch Ch 61-72; P-in-c Sydenham H Trin 72-80; R Worting *Win* 80-92; Field Officer Decade of Evang 92-96; Can Shyogwe (Rwanda) from 93; rtd 96; PtO *Sarum* from 93; *Win* 96-14. *Yew Tree House, Mill Lane, Shalbourne, Marlborough SN8 3XA*
T: (01672) 870460 E: steptrap@btinternet.com

TRASK, Imtiaz Ashley. b 58. **d** 13 **p** 14. NSM Frant w Eridge *Chich* from 13. *The Rectory, Church Street, Cowden, Edenbridge TN8 7JE* M: 07891-262975 E: imtiazat@hotmail.co.uk

TRASK, Mrs Marion Elizabeth. b 54. Leic Univ BSc 75 Brunel Univ PGCE 76. Moorlands Bible Coll 82 Oak Hill Th Coll 93. **d** 96 **p** 97. C Bermondsey St Mary w St Olave, St Jo etc *S'wark* 96-00; C Peckham St Mary Magd 00-04; P-in-c Cowden w Hammerwood *Chich* from 10. *The Rectory, Church Street, Cowden, Edenbridge TN8 7JE* T: (01342) 850221
E: m.traskcwhd@btinternet.com

TRASLER, Canon Graham Charles George. b 44. Ch Ch Ox BA 65 MA 69. Cuddesdon Coll 66. **d** 68 **p** 69. C Gateshead St Mary *Dur* 68-71; P-in-c Monkwearmouth St Pet 71-79; R Bentley and Binsted *Win* 79-84; R New Alresford w Ovington and Itchen Stoke 84-01; RD Alresford 99-01; P-in-c Stockbridge and Longstock and Leckford 01-03; R 03-09; Hon Can Win Cathl 05-09; rtd 09; PtO *Win* from 09. *30 Cole Close, Andover SP10 4NL* T: (01264) 359843 M: 07810-693910
E: costadelanton@gmail.com

TRATHEN, Paul Kevin. b 68. York Univ BA 91 MA 93 Jordanhill Coll Glas PGCE 94 Middx Univ BA 03. NTMTC 00. **d** 03 **p** 04. C Wickford and Runwell *Chelmsf* 03-07; P-in-c Rawreth w Rettendon 07-10; P-in-c Rawreth 10-11; Dioc Adv for Faith in the Public Square 11-12; V Walthamstow St Pet from 12. *121 Forest Rise, Walthamstow, London E17 3PW* T: (020) 8509 8901 M: 07871-584997
E: ptrathen@chelmsford.anglican.org

TRAVERS, Canon Colin James. b 49. St Pet Coll Ox BA 70 MA 74. Ridley Hall Cam 70. **d** 72 **p** 73. C Hornchurch St Andr *Chelmsf* 72-75; Youth Chapl 75-77; C Aldersbrook 75-77; V Barkingside St Laur 77-82; V Waltham Abbey 82-88; V S Weald 88-95; Co-ord NTMTC and Hon C Gt Warley and Ingrave St Nic 95-98; P-in-c Gt Canfield w High Roding and Aythorpe Roding 98-02; V Theydon Bois 02-09; Hon Can Chelmsf Cathl 01-09; rtd 09; PtO *Ely* from 10. *7 Springhead Lane, Ely CB7 4QY* T: (01353) 659732 E: colin@travers.name

TRAVERS, John William. b 48. Open Univ BA 84 Hull Univ MA 86. Linc Th Coll 75. **d** 78 **p** 79. C Headingley *Ripon* 78-81; TV Louth *Linc* 81-89; P-in-c Shingay Gp *Ely* 89; R 90-95; V Hamble le Rice *Win* 95-12; rtd 13. *Los Falcones 3, D3-10 Los Balandros, Palm Mar, Arona 38632, Tenerife*
E: jwtravers@gmail.com

TRAVES, Stephen Charles. b 44. Sheff City Coll of Educn CertEd 66 Open Univ BA 79. NOC 96. **d** 99 **p** 00. NSM Barnsley St Pet and St Jo *Wakef* 99-02; NSM Cudworth 02-07; NSM Lundwood 02-04; PtO *Leeds* from 07; *Eur* from 08. *La Barrière, 24230 Vélines, France* T: (0033) 5 53 57 53 72
E: stephen.traves@orange.fr

TRAYNOR, Neil Owen. b 70. Worc Coll Ox BA 91 MA 94 Leeds Univ BA 11 Reading Univ PGCE 94. Coll of Resurr Mirfield 09. **d** 11 **p** 12. C Barnsley St Mary *Wakef* 11-13; Bp's Dom Chapl *Leeds* 13-14; TV Witney *Ox* from 14. *4 Maidley Close, Witney OX28 1ER*

TRAYNOR, Nigel Martin Arthur. b 58. St Jo Coll Nottm 94. **d** 96 **p** 97. C Wellington All SS w Eyton *Lich* 96-00; P-in-c Pype Hayes *Birm* 00-02; TV Erdington from 02; AD Aston from 12. *St Mary's Vicarage, 1162 Tyburn Road, Birmingham B24 0TB* T: 0121-373 3534 E: nigelt6@msn.com or revnigel@yahoo.co.uk

TREACY, Richard James. b 74. Aber Univ BD Univ of Wales (Cardiff) MTh 99. **d** 98 **p** 99. C Hillsborough *D & D* 98-02. *14 Downshire Crescent, Hillsborough BT26 6DD* T: (028) 9268 3098 M: 07917-854222 E: richard.treacy@btinternet.com

TREANOR, Canon Desmond Victor. b 28. St Jo Coll Dur BA 53 MA 59. **d** 54 **p** 55. C Oakwood St Thos *Lon* 54-57; C Sudbury St Andr 57-59; V Lansdown *B & W* 59-66; V Derby St Werburgh 66-68; V Leic St Anne 68-75; V Humberstone 75-86; Hon Can Leic Cathl 78-93; P-in-c Leic St Eliz Nether Hall 81-86; RD Christianity N 82-86; R Gt Bowden w Welham, Glooston and Cranoe 86-93; RD Gartree I 88-93; rtd 93; PtO *Leic* from 93. *5 Brookfield Way, Kibworth, Leicester LE8 0SA* T: 0116-279 2750

TREANOR, Terence Gerald. b 29. St Jo Coll Ox BA 52 MA 56. Wycliffe Hall Ox 52. **d** 54 **p** 55. C Hornsey Ch Ch *Lon* 54-57; C Cambridge H Trin *Ely* 57-60; V Doncaster St Mary *Sheff* 60-66; Chapl Oakham Sch 66-94; rtd 94; PtO *Leic* 94-12; *Linc* 94-99. *35 Glebe Way, Oakham LE15 6LX* T: (01572) 757495

TREANOR, Timothy Lyons Victor. b 62. St Jo Coll Cam BA 83 MA 87 K Coll Lon MA 95 Cranfield Univ MSc 01. Ripon Coll Cuddesdon BTh 08. **d** 08 **p** 09. C Tavistock and Gulworthy *Ex* 08-10; C Ottery St Mary, Alfington, W Hill, Tipton etc 10-13; TR Wellington and Distr *B & W* from 13. *The Rectory, 72 High Street, Wellington TA21 8RF* T: (01823) 662248
E: tlvtreanor@btinternet.com

TREASURE, Canon Andrew Stephen. b 51. Oriel Coll Ox BA 73 MA 77. St Jo Coll Nottm BA 76. **d** 77 **p** 78. C Beverley Minster *York* 77-81; C Cambridge H Trin *Ely* 81-84; C Cambridge H Trin w St Andr Gt 84-85; V Eccleshill *Bradf* 85-98; P-in-c Bradf St Oswald Chapel Green 98-04; P-in-c Horton 98-04; V Lt Horton *Leeds* from 04; C Bowling St Steph 05-15; Hon Can Bradf Cathl from 04; C Bankfoot and Bowling St Steph from 15. *St Oswald's Vicarage, Christopher Street, Bradford BD5 9DH* T: (01274) 522717 E: stephen.treasure@bradford.anglican.org

TREASURE, Geoffrey. b 39. Hatf Coll Dur BA 61 Univ of Wales (Cardiff) DipEd 62. Oak Hill NSM Course 90. **d** 93 **p** 94. NSM Forty Hill Jes Ch *Lon* 93-95; Consultant SW England CPAS 95-02; PtO *B & W* 95-04; P-in-c Stoke St Gregory w Burrowbridge and Lyng 04-07; rtd 07; PtO *B & W* from 07. *Gable Cottage, West Lyng, Taunton TA3 5AP* T: (01823) 490458
E: geofftreasure@googlemail.com

TREASURE, Stephen. *See* TREASURE, Andrew Stephen

TREBY, David Alan. b 47. FIBMS 72 Bris Poly MSc 90. St Jo Coll Nottm MA 95. **d** 95 **p** 96. C Camborne *Truro* 95-00; V Stoke Gabriel and Collaton *Ex* 00-12; rtd 12. *28 Ham Meadow, Marnhull, Sturminster Newton DT10 1LR* T: (01258) 820678
E: dave@treby.freeserve.co.uk

TREDENNICK, Canon Angela Nicolette. b 38. SRN 62 SCM 63. S'wark Ord Course 87. **d** 90 **p** 94. NSM Charlwood *S'wark* 90-92; Par Dn Roehampton H Trin 92-94; C 94-97; RD Wandsworth 95-97; V Redhill St Matt 97-06; RD Reigate 00-03; Hon Can S'wark Cathl 05-06; rtd 06; Hon C Godstone and Blindley Heath *S'wark* 06-09; PtO from 09. *The Old Curiosity Shop, Chapel Road, Smallfield, Horley RH6 9NW* T: (01342) 843570 E: rev.nicky@btinternet.com

TREDWELL, Mrs Samantha Jane. b 69. Nottm Trent Univ BEd 92. EMMTC 00. **d** 03 **p** 04. C Skegby w Teversal *S'well* 03-07; TV Newark w Coddington from 07. *Christ Church Vicarage, Boundary Road, Newark NG24 4AJ* T: (01636) 704969

TREE, Robin Leslie. b 46. Brunel Univ MSc 00 Univ of Wales (Lamp) MTh 10. S Dios Minl Tr Scheme 89. **d** 92 **p** 93. NSM St Leonards Ch Ch and St Mary *Chich* 92-95; NSM Hastings H Trin 95-98; TV Bexhill St Pet 98-01; V Hampden Park 01-10; P-in-c The Hydneye 08-10; V Hampden Park and The Hydnye 10-11; rtd 11. *30 The Links, St Leonards-on-Sea TN38 0UW* T: (01424) 552275 M: 07967-954411
E: frrobin.tree@btinternet.com

TREEBY, Stephen Frank. b 46. Man Univ LLB 67 Lambeth STh 01. Cuddesdon Coll 69 Bangalore Th Coll 70. **d** 71 **p** 72. C Ashbourne St Oswald w Mapleton *Derby* 71-74; C Boulton 74-76; Chapl Trowbridge Coll *Sarum* 76-79; TV Melksham 79-87; V Dilton's-Marsh 87-01; Chapl Westbury Hosp 87-91; Chapl Wilts and Swindon Healthcare NHS Trust 92-01; R Spetisbury w Charlton Marshall etc *Sarum* 01-11; rtd 11. *5 Walnut Road, Honiton EX14 2UG* T: (01404) 548715
E: stephentreeby@hotmail.com

TREETOPS, Ms Jacqueline. b 47. NEOC 83. **dss** 86 **d** 87 **p** 94. Low Harrogate St Mary *Ripon* 86-87; C Roundhay St Edm 87-95; C Potternewton 95-97; rtd 97; PtO *Leeds* from 01. *43 Lincombe Bank, Leeds LS8 1QG* T: 0113-237 0474

TREFUSIS, Charles Rodolph. b 61. Hull Univ BA 83. Wycliffe Hall Ox 85. **d** 90 **p** 91. C Blackheath St Jo *S'wark* 90-94; V Purley Ch Ch from 94. *The Vicarage, 38 Woodcote Valley Road, Purley CR8 3AJ* T: (020) 8660 1790 E: ctrefusis@aol.com

TREGALE, Diane Ruth. b 68. Spurgeon's Coll MTh 05. St Jo Coll Nottm 07. **d** 08 **p** 09. C Wilford *S'well* 08-11; C Sherborne w Castleton, Lillington and Longburton *Sarum* from 11; Chapl Gryphon Sch Sherborne from 11. *69 Granville Way, Sherborne DT9 4AT* T: (01935) 815820 E: diane@tregale.co.uk

TREGALE, John Ernest. b 69. Ex Univ BSc 90 Sheff Univ MA 01. St Jo Coll Nottm 05. **d** 08 **p** 09. C Wilford *S'well* 08-11; C Sherborne w Castleton, Lillington and Longburton *Sarum* from 11. *69 Granville Way, Sherborne DT9 4AT* T: (01935) 815820 E: jono@tregale.co.uk

TREGENZA, Matthew John. b 69. Univ of Wales (Lamp) BA 92 BA(Theol) 08 SS Coll Cam PGCE 93 Lon Univ MA 01 FRGS 96. Westcott Ho Cam 01. **d** 03 **p** 04. C Marnhull *Sarum* 03-06; TV Mynyddislwyn *Mon* 06-08; P-in-c Blackwood 08-12; R Bishop's Lydeard w Lydeard St Lawrence etc *B & W* from 12. *The Rectory, Church Street, Bishops Lydeard, Taunton TA4 3AT* T: (01823) 432935 E: matthew.tregenza@gmail.com

TREGUNNO, Timothy Frederick. b 79. St Andr Univ MTheol 02. St Steph Ho Ox 04. **d** 06 **p** 07. C St Leonards

Ch Ch and St Mary *Chich* 06-10; P-in-c Turners Hill 10-12; Chapl Heathfield Sch Ascot from 12. *Heathfield School, London Road, Ascot SL5 8BQ* T: (01344) 898343 E: frtimt@yahoo.co.uk

TREHARNE, David Owen. b 73. Univ of Wales (Cardiff) BMus 94 MPhil 06 Bris Univ MEd 04 Bris Coll PGCE 00. Trin Coll Bris 94. **d** 99 **p** 04. NSM Bassaleg *Mon* 99-00; C Caerphilly *Llan* 04-08; P-in-c Porthkerry and Rhoose 08-12; Dioc Voc Adv 08-12; V Tidenham w Beachley and Lancaut *Glouc* from 12; P-in-c St Briavels w Hewelsfield from 12. *Tidenham Vicarage, Gloucester Road, Tutshill, Chepstow NP16 7DH* T: (01291) 760034 E: dtrevd@aol.com

TRELENBERG, Olaf. b 72. Ridley Hall Cam 06. **d** 08 **p** 09. C Scotforth *Blackb* 08-12; P-in-c Sandiacre *Derby* 12-14; R from 14. *St Giles's Rectory, Church Drive, Sandiacre, Nottingham NG10 5EE* T: 0115-939 7163 M: 07877-357332 E: olaf@talktalk.net

TRELLIS, The Very Revd Oswald Fitz-Burnell. b 35. Chich Th Coll 73. **d** 74 **p** 75. C Chelmsf All SS 74-79; C-in-c N Springfield CD 79-85; V Heybridge w Langford 85-94; Dean Georgetown Guyana 94-02; P-in-c Doddinghurst and Mountnessing *Chelmsf* 02-04; P-in-c Doddinghurst 04-05; rtd 06; *The Chelmsf* from 06. *31 Douglas Matthew House, White Lyons Road, Brentwood CM14 4YT* T: (01277) 215954

TREMBATH, Martyn Anthony. b 65. Leeds Univ BA 86. Ripon Coll Cuddesdon 88. **d** 90 **p** 91. C Bodmin w Lanhydrock and Lanivet *Truro* 90-91; C St Erth 92-96; C Phillack w Gwithian and Gwinear 94-96; C Hayle 94-96; Asst Chapl R Free Hampstead NHS Trust 96-98; Sen Chapl R Cornwall Hosps Trust 98-10; NSM Godrevy *Truro* 08-10; TR 10-13; Hon Can Truro Cathl 09-13; Chapl Luton and Dunstable Hosp NHS Foundn Trust from 13; PtO *Ox* from 14. *The Chaplaincy, Luton and Dunstable Hospital, Lewsey Road, Luton LU4 0DZ* T: 08451-270127 E: godrevy-tr@hotmail.co.uk

TREMELLING, Peter Ian. b 53. Ex & Truro NSM Scheme 94. **d** 96 **p** 98. NSM St Illogan *Truro* 96-12. *38 Rosewarne Park, Higher Enys Road, Camborne TR14 0AG* T: (01209) 710518 E: reverendpeter@tesco.net

TREMLETT, The Ven Andrew. b 64. Pemb Coll Cam BA 86 MA 90 Qu Coll Ox BA 88 MA 95 Ex Univ MPhil 96 Liv Univ PGCE 03. Wycliffe Hall Ox 86. **d** 89 **p** 90. C Torquay St Matthias, St Mark and H Trin *Ex* 89-92; Miss to Seamen 92-94; Asst Chapl Rotterdam *Eur* 92-94; Chapl 94-95; TV Fareham H Trin *Portsm* 95-98; Bp's Dom Chapl 98-03; V Goring-by-Sea *Chich* 03-08; Can Res Bris Cathl 08-10; Can Westmr Abbey and R Westmr St Marg from 10; Adn Westmr from 14. *5 Little Cloister, Westminster Abbey, London SW1P 3PL* T: (020) 7654 4806 E: andrew.tremlett@westminster-abbey.org

TREMLETT, The Ven Anthony Frank. b 37. Ex & Truro NSM Scheme 78. **d** 81 **p** 82. C Southway *Ex* 81-82; P-in-c 82-84; V 84-88; RD Plymouth Moorside 86-88; Adn Totnes 88-94; Adn Ex 94-02; rtd 02. *57 Great Berry Road, Crownhill, Plymouth PL6 5AY* T: (01752) 240052 E: tremlettaf@aol.com

TREMTHTHANMOR, Ms Chrys Mymmir Evnath Tristan. b 66. Univ of California BA 88. St Mich Coll Llan BA 05 MPhil 07. **d** 06 **p** 07. C Coity, Nolton and Brackla *Llan* 06-10; TV Daventry, Ashby St Ledgers, Braunston etc *Pet* from 10. *31 Newbury Drive, Daventry NN11 0WQ* T: (01327) 707925 E: vicarwelton@o2.co.uk

TRENCHARD, Hubert John. b 26. S Dios Minl Tr Scheme. **d** 83 **p** 84. NSM Sturminster Marshall *Sarum* 83-87; NSM Blandford Forum and Langton Long 87-96. *20 Chapel Gardens, Blandford Forum DT11 7UY* T: (01258) 455516

TRENCHARD, Paul Charles Herbert Anstiss. b 53. Liv Univ LLB 76. St Steph Ho Ox 77. **d** 80 **p** 81. C Torquay St Martin Barton *Ex* 80-84; R Ashprington, Cornworthy and Dittisham 84-92; R Barnwell w Tichmarsh, Thurning and Clapton *Pet* 92-04. *19 Place du Terreau, 71400 Autun, France* E: trenchard.paul@orange.fr

TRENDALL, Matthew James. b 72. Oriel Coll Ox BA 93 MA 98. Trin Coll Bris BA 10. **d** 10 **p** 11. C Redland *Bris* 10-13; P-in-c Walton Milton Keynes *Ox* 13-14; R from 14. *The Rectory, Walton Road, Wavendon, Milton Keynes MK17 8LW* T: (01908) 582839 M: 07947-150396 E: aliseandmatt@talktalk.net

TRENDALL, Peter John. b 43. Oak Hill Th Coll 66. **d** 69 **p** 70. C Beckenham Ch Ch *Roch* 69-73; C Bedworth *Cov* 73-76; V Hornsey Rise St Mary *Lon* 76-82; P-in-c Upper Holloway St Steph 80-82; V Hornsey Rise St Mary w St Steph 82-84; TR Walthamstow St Mary w St Steph *Chelmsf* 84-85 and 85-93; P-in-c Chigwell 93-94; TR Chigwell and Chigwell Row 94-08; PtO *St E* from 08. *22 The Crescents, Reydon, Southwold IP18 6RT* T: (01502) 722962 M: 07731-854650 E: peter.trendall@btinternet.com

TRENDER, Lawrence. b 37. Bps' Coll Cheshunt 64. **d** 66 **p** 67. C Petersham *S'wark* 66-71; C Malden St Jo 71-73; R Thornham Magna w Thornham Parva *St E* 73-81; R Thornhams Magna

and Parva, Gislingham and Mellis 81-87; P-in-c Mellis 73-81; P-in-c Gislingham 73-81; RD Hartismere 85-87; R Skipsea w Ulrome and Barmston w Fraisthorpe *York* 92-01; rtd 01; PtO *York* from 01. *Stone Cottage, 5 Far Lane, Bewholme, Driffield YO25 8EA* T: (01964) 533020

TRENHOLME (née ROBERTSON), Mrs Jane Lesley. b 54. Man Univ BSc 76 Leeds Univ BA 06. NOC 03. **d** 06 **p** 07. NSM Northowram *Wakef* 06-08; C Tong *Leeds* 08-14; C Laisterdyke *Bradf* 08-10; P-in-c *Leeds* 10-14. *Stretchgate, Rookes Lane, Halifax HX3 8PU* T: (01274) 693392 M: 07771-823281 E: jltrenholme@hotmail.co.uk

TRENHOLME, William Nicholas David. b 85. Grey Coll Dur MSci 08. Oak Hill Th Coll BA 13. **d** 13 **p** 14. C Wollaston w Strixton and Bozeat etc *Pet* from 13. *6 Hinwick Road, Wollaston, Wellingborough NN29 7QT* M: 07712-627243 E: nick.trenholme@gmail.com

TRENIER, Andrew Peter Christopher. b 80. Univ of Wales (Swansea) BScEcon 02. Ripon Coll Cuddesdon BA 11. **d** 12 **p** 13. C Derby Cathl 12-15; R Chingford SS Pet and Paul *Chelmsf* from 15. *The Rectory, 2 The Green Walk, London E4 7ER* M: 07786-868615 T: (020) 8529 1291 E: andytrenier@gmail.com *or* fr.andy@parishofchingford.org.uk

TRESIDDER, Alistair Charles. b 65. Qu Coll Ox BA 88. Cranmer Hall Dur 93. **d** 93 **p** 94. C Limehouse *Lon* 93-98; V W Hampstead St Luke from 98. *St Luke's Vicarage, 12 Kidderpore Avenue, London NW3 7SU* T: (020) 7794 2634 *or* 7431 6317 E: alistair@alistairtresidder.wanadoo.co.uk

TRETHEWEY, The Ven Frederick Martyn. b 49. Lon Univ BA 70 Lambeth STh 79. Oak Hill Th Coll 75. **d** 78 **p** 79. C Tollington Park St Mark w St Anne *Lon* 78-82; C Whitehall Park St Andr Hornsey Lane 82-87; TV Hornsey Rise Whitehall Park Team 87-88; V Brockmoor *Lich* 88-93; V Worc 93-01; Chapl Russells Hall Hosp Dudley 88-91; Chapl Dudley Gp of Hosps NHS Trust 92-01; RD Himley *Worc* 96-01; Hon Can Worc Cathl 99-01; Adn Dudley 01-13; rtd 13; P-in-c Brittany *Eur* from 13. *4 rue des Bandes Mavieux, 56460 La Chapelle Caro, France* E: fred@trethewey.org.uk

TRETHEWEY, Richard John. b 74. Jes Coll Ox MA 02. Wycliffe Hall Ox BA 02. **d** 02 **p** 03. C Biddulph *Lich* 02-06; C Knowle *Birm* from 06. *46 Crabmill Close, Knowle, Solihull B93 0NP* T: (01564) 201010 M: 07759-650572 E: richard@trethewey.org.uk

TRETT, Peter John. b 44. **d** 97 **p** 98. OLM High Oak, Hingham and Scoulton w Wood Rising *Nor* 97-14; PtO from 14. *Holly House, 35 Plough Lane, Hardingham, Norwich NR9 4AE* T: (01953) 850369 E: trett@nnbus.co.uk

TREVELYAN, Mrs Rosemary Elizabeth. b 43. Ex Univ CertEd 64 Open Univ BA 91. **d** 11. NSM Washingborough w Heighington and Canwick *Linc* from 11. *9 Canterbury Drive, Washingborough, Lincoln LN4 1SJ* T: (01522) 827874 E: rtrev911@hotmail.com

TREVITHICK, Janet Anne. b 54. **d** 13 **p** 14. NSM Titchfield *Portsm* from 13. *34 Vicarage Lane, Fareham PO14 2LA* T: (01329) 668957 E: janettrevithick@m8n.com

TREVOR, Canon Charles Frederic. b 27. Sarum Th Coll 54. **d** 56 **p** 57. C Sutton in Ashfield St Mich *S'well* 56-58; C Birstall *Leic* 58-61; V Prestwold w Hoton 61-66; V Thornton in Lonsdale w Burton in Lonsdale *Bradf* 66-74; V Kirkby Malham 74-85; P-in-c Coniston Cold 81-85; Hon Can Bradf Cathl 85-92; V Sutton 85-92; RD S Craven 86-91; rtd 92; PtO *Leeds* from 92. *6 Elbolton Flats, Hebden Road, Skipton BD23 5LH* T: (01756) 752640

TREW, Mrs Ann Patricia. b 58. Ripon Coll Cuddesdon. **d** 00 **p** 01. C Hambleden Valley *Ox* 00-03; P-in-c Hedsor and Bourne End 03-08; R 08-12; PtO *Portsm* 13-14; C S Hayling 14-15; PtO from 15. *Address temp unknown* E: aptrew@gmail.com

TREW, Jeremy Charles. b 66. Univ of Wales (Abth) BSc 89 Leeds Univ MSc 92. St Jo Coll Nottm MA 94. **d** 97 **p** 98. C Roundhay St Edm *Ripon* 97-01; P-in-c Spofforth w Kirk Deighton 01-07; V Seaton and Beer *Ex* from 07; RD Honiton from 13. *The Vicarage, Colyford Road, Seaton EX12 2DF* T: (01297) 20391 E: jeremytrew@hotmail.com

TREW, Robin Nicholas. b 52. UWIST BSc 74 Open Univ MA 01. St Jo Coll Nottm 87. **d** 89 **p** 90. C Cov H Trin 89-93; V Snitterfield w Bearley 93-02; R Allesley from 02; AD Cov N from 10. *The Rectory, Rectory Lane, Allesley, Coventry CV5 9EQ* T: (024) 7640 2006 E: robtrew@lineone.net

TREWEEK, Guy Matthew. b 65. LSE BSc(Econ) 87 Peterho Cam BA 07 MA 12. Westcott Ho Cam 05 Yale Div Sch 07. **d** 08 **p** 09. C Hammersmith St Pet *Lon* 08-11; P-in-c St Andr-by-the-Wardrobe w St Ann, Blackfriars 11-15; P-in-c St Jas Garlickhythe w St Mich Queenhithe etc 11-15. *Bishopscourt, Pitt Street, Gloucester GL1 2BQ* E: guy.treweek@london.anglican.org

✠**TREWEEK (née MONTGOMERY), The Rt Revd Rachel.** b 63. Reading Univ BA 85. Wycliffe Hall Ox BTh 94. **d** 94 **p** 95 **c** 15. C Tufnell Park St Geo and All SS *Lon* 94-99; V Bethnal Green St Jas Less 99-06; CME Officer 99-06; Adn Northolt 06-11; Adn Hackney 11-15; Bp Glouc from 15. *Bishopscourt, Pitt Street, Gloucester GL1 2BQ* T: (01452) 835512

TREWEEKS, Mrs Angela Elizabeth. b 35. Gilmore Ho IDC 59. **dss** 59 **d** 87 **p** 94. Chapl St Nic Hosp Newc 87; Hon C Newc St Geo 87-89; Chapl St Mary's Hosp Stannington 92-95; Hon C Rothbury Newc 94-96; rtd 95; PtO Newc from 96. *The Nook, Pondicherry, Rothbury, Morpeth NE65 7YS* T: (01669) 620393

TRICK, Matthew John Harvey. Univ of Wales (Abth) BSc 02. St Mich Coll Llan BTh 08. **d** 08 **p** 09. C Cowbridge *Llan* 08-10; C Aberavon 10-11; TV 11-14; P-in-c Cambourne *Ely* from 14. *The Vicarage, 97 Broad Street, Great Cambourne, Cambridge CB23 6DH* T: (01954) 712882 M: 07793-823406 E: matthew.trick@me.com

TRICKETT, Canon Judith. b 50. Open Univ BA 00. St Jo Coll Nottm 89. **d** 91 **p** 94. Par Dn Kimberworth *Sheff* 91-93; Dn-in-c Worsbrough Common 93-94; V 94-01; V Herringthorpe 01-10; R Firbeck w Letwell 10-15; V Woodsetts 10-15; Hon Can Sheff Cathl 08-15; rtd 15; Hon C Harthill and Thorpe Salvin *Sheff* from 15. *The Rectory, 4A Barker Hades Road, Letwell, Worksop S81 8DF* T: (01909) 540193 M: 07974-404831 E: judith.trickett493@btinternet.com

TRICKETT, Stanley Mervyn Wood. b 27. Lich Th Coll 64. **d** 66 **p** 67. C Kington w Huntington *Heref* 66-70; P-in-c Old Radnor 70-81; P-in-c Knill 70-81; V Shrewton *Sarum* 81-97; P-in-c Winterbourne Stoke 81-92; RD Wylye and Wilton 85-89; rtd 97; PtO *Sarum* from 97. *3 Oakwood Grove, Alderbury, Salisbury SP5 3BN* T: (01722) 710275

TRICKETT, Preb Susan. b 42. JP 89. S Dios Minl Tr Scheme 91. **d** 94 **p** 95. NSM Combe Down w Monkton Combe and S Stoke *B & W* 94-99; Dean Women Clergy and V High Littleton 99-05; Preb Wells Cathl 00-12; rtd 05; PtO *B & W* from 05. *Granville House, Tyning Road, Combe Down, Bath BA2 5ER* T: (01225) 833007 M: 07949-512380 E: susitrickett@me.com

TRICKEY, Christopher Jolyon. b 57. Jes Coll Cam BA 79 MA 83 Barrister-at-Law 80. Trin Coll Bris BA 90. **d** 90 **p** 91. C Chesham Bois *Ox* 90-93; R Busbridge *Guildf* 94-98; P-in-c Hambledon 97-98; R Busbridge and Hambledon 98-09; Chapl Godalming Coll 01-09; R Nailsea H Trin *B & W* from 09. *The Rectory, 10 Ilminster Close, Nailsea, Bristol BS48 4YU* T: (01275) 790845 E: jolyon.trickey@htnailsea.org.uk

TRICKEY, Mrs Frances Anne. b 59. Keele Univ BA 81 Lon Inst of Educn PGCE 82 W Univ BA 11. STETS 08. **d** 11 **p** 12. NSM Wraxall *B & W* from 11. *The Rectory, 10 Ilminster Close, Nailsea, Bristol BS48 4YU* T: (01275) 790845 E: francestrickey@hotmail.co.uk

TRICKEY, The Very Revd Frederick Marc. b 35. Dur Univ BA 62. Cranmer Hall Dur. **d** 64 **p** 65. C Alton St Lawr *Win* 64-68; V Win St Jo cum Winnall 68-77; Angl Adv Channel TV from 77; R Guernsey St Martin *Win* 77-02; P-in-c Sark 02-03; Dean Guernsey 95-03; Hon Can Win Cathl 95-03; rtd 03; PtO *Win* from 03. *L'Esperance, La Route des Camps, St Martin, Guernsey GY4 6AD* T: (01481) 238441

TRICKLEBANK, Steven. b 56. Nottm Univ BTh 88 Keele Univ MA 97. Linc Th Coll 85. **d** 88 **p** 89. C Ditton St Mich *Liv* 88-91; C Wigan All SS 91-93; Chapl Aintree Hosps NHS Trust *Liv* 93-97; C-in-c St Edm Anchorage Lane CD *Sheff* 97-00; Chapl Doncaster R Infirmary and Montagu Hosp NHS Trust 97-00; V Stocksbridge *Sheff* 00-04; P-in-c Streatham Ch Ch *S'wark* 04-05; P-in-c Streatham Hill St Marg 04-05; V Streatham Ch Ch from 05. *Christ Church Vicarage, 3 Christchurch Road, London SW2 3ET* T: (020) 8674 5723 E: steventricklebank@hotmail.com

TRIFFITT, Jonathan Paul. b 74. St Jo Coll Nottm BA 03. **d** 03 **p** 04. C W Kilburn St Luke w St Simon and St Jude *Lon* 03-06; C Paddington Em Harrow Road 03-06; C Sherborne w Castleton etc and Chapl Gryphon Sch Sherborne 06-10; V Southbroom *Sarum* 10-15; RD Devizes 11-15; R Blandford Forum and Langton Long from 15. *The Rectory, 2 Portman Place, Blandford Forum DT11 7DG* T: (01258) 480092 E: jonathan.triffitt@btinternet.com

TRIGG, Jeremy Michael. b 51. Open Univ BA 88. Ripon Coll Cuddesdon 80. **d** 81 **p** 82. C Roundhay St Edm *Ripon* 81-84; C Harrogate St Wilfrid and St Luke 84-87; TV Pocklington Team *York* 87-90; R Rowley w Skidby 90-97; TV Wolverton *Ox* 97-98; R 98-11; P-in-c Rothwell *Leeds* 11-15; TR Rothwell, Lofthouse, Methley etc from 15. *The Vicarage, Beech Grove, Rothwell, Leeds LS26 0EF* T: 0113-282 0341 E: jeremy.trigg@btinternet.com

TRIGG, Preb Jonathan David. b 49. Ex Coll Ox BA 71 MA 75 Dur Univ PhD 92. Cranmer Hall Dur BA 82. **d** 83 **p** 84. C Enfield St Andr *Lon* 83-87; V Oakwood St Thos 87-96; AD Enfield 92-96; V Highgate St Mich from 96; P-in-c Highgate All SS 09-14; C from 14; AD W Haringey 00-06; Dir of Ords Edmonton Area from 08; Preb St Paul's Cathl from 10. *The Vicarage, 10 The Grove, London N6 6LB* T: (020) 8347 5124 *or* 8340 7279 F: 8348 4635 E: jdtrigg@gmail.com

TRIGLE, Alan Neil. b 61. St Mellitus Coll 12. **d** 15. C Kensal Town St Thos w St Andr and St Phil *Lon* from 15. *Address temp unknown*

TRILL, Barry. b 42. Chich Th Coll 65. **d** 68 **p** 69. C W Hackney St Barn *Lon* 68-73; TV Is of Dogs Ch Ch and St Jo w St Luke 73-78; P-in-c Hastings All So *Chich* 78-79; V 79-99; rtd 99. *17 School Place, Bexhill-on-Sea TN40 2PX* T: (01424) 217765

TRILL, Victor Alfred Mansfield. b 21. St Deiniol's Hawarden. **d** 81 **p** 82. Hon C Prestbury *Ches* 81-83; Hon C Church Hulme 83-85; V Marbury 85-90; rtd 90; PtO *Ches* from 90. *82 Rosedale Avenue, Liverpool L23 0UQ*

TRIM, Elizabeth Ann. See VARLEY, Elizabeth Ann

TRIMBLE, Eleanor Louise. b 69. Man Metrop Univ BSc 97. Yorks Min Course. **d** 09 **p** 10. C Old Trafford St Jo *Man* 09-13; P-in-c Man Apostles w Miles Platting from 13. *Church of the Apostles Rectory, Ridgway Street, Manchester M40 7FY* T: 0161-948 4197 M: 07887-601451 E: eleanor.trimble@btinternet.com

TRIMBLE, Canon John Alexander. b 33. Lon Univ BD 65. Edin Th Coll 55. **d** 58 **p** 59. C Glas St Mary 58-60; C Edin St Jo 60-65; R Baillieston *Glas* 65-69; R Falkirk *Edin* 69-86; R Troon *Glas* 86-98; Can St Mary's Cathl 91-98; rtd 98; PtO *Newc* from 98. *4 Hencotes Mews, Hexham NE46 2DZ* T: (01434) 603032

TRIMBLE, Thomas Henry. b 36. TCD BTh 90. CITC 79. **d** 82 **p** 83. C Seapatrick *D & D* 82-85; I Magheracross *Clogh* 85-90; Bp's Appeal Sec 89-90; I Donegal w Killymard, Lough Eske and Laghey *D & R* 90-01; Can Raphoe Cathl 93-01; rtd 01. *Tyrone House, Tullycullion, Co Donegal, Republic of Ireland* T: (00353) (74) 974 0706 E: harry.trimble@virgin.net

TRIMBY (née SOUTHERTON), Kathryn Ruth. b 66. Univ of Wales (Lamp) BA 88. Sarum & Wells Th Coll 90. **d** 92 **p** 97. C Connah's Quay *St As* 92-97; R Halkyn w Caerfallwch w Rhesycae 97-04; I Tubbercurry w Killoran *T, K & A* 04-14; Can Achonry Cathl 11-14; Can Tuam Cathl 13-14; R Llanyblodwel, Llanymynech, Morton and Trefonen *Lich* from 14. *The Rectory, Rectory Lane, Pant, Oswestry SY10 9RA* T: (01691) 831211 E: kathsoutherton@hotmail.com

TRIMMER, Penelope Marynice. See DRAPER, Penelope Marynice

TRINDER, Miss Gillian Joyce. b 68. Birm Univ BA 90 Bp Grosseteste Coll PGCE 91. Westcott Ho Cam 09. **d** 11 **p** 12. C Whitkirk *Ripon* 11-13; C Starbeck *Leeds* 13-14. *Address temp unknown*

TRIPLOW, Keith John. b 44. Selw Coll Cam BA 66 MA 70. Chich Th Coll 70. **d** 72 **p** 73. C Ipswich All Hallows *St E* 72-76; C Dartford H Trin *Roch* 76-78; V Fyfield w Tubney and Kingston Bagpuize *Ox* 78-08; rtd 08. *5 Hyde Road, Denchworth, Wantage OX12 0DR* T: (01235) 868915

TRIST, Richard McLeod. b 55. Univ of NSW BSEd 76. Ridley Coll Melbourne BTh 86. **d** 87 **p** 87. C Camberwell St Jo Australia 87-88; P-in-c Cranbourne 88-91; I 91-92; Sen Assoc Min Kew St Hilary 93-96; C Langham Place All So *Lon* 97-01; V Camberwell St Mark Australia from 01; AD Camberwell 03-05. *1 Canterbury Road, Camberwell Vic 3124, Australia* T: (0061) (3) 9897 1532 *or* 9882 3776 F: 9882 6514 E: richard.trist@bigpond.com *or* stmarksc@bigpond.com

TRISTRAM, Canon Catherine Elizabeth. b 31. Somerville Coll Ox BA 53 MA 57. **dss** 83 **d** 87 **p** 94. Holy Is *Newc* 84-01; Hon C 87-01; Hon Can Newc Cathl 94-01; PtO from 01. *4 Lewins Lane, Holy Island, Berwick-upon-Tweed TD15 2SB* T: (01289) 389306

TRISTRAM, Geoffrey Robert. b 53. K Coll Lon BA 76 Pemb Coll Cam BA 78 MA 80. Westcott Ho Cam 77. **d** 79 **p** 80. C Weymouth H Trin *Sarum* 79-82; C Gt Berkhamsted *St Alb* 83-85; OSB 85-99; Asst Chapl Oundle Sch 86-88; Sen Chapl 88-91; R Welwyn w Ayot St Peter *St Alb* 91-99; Chapl Qu Victoria Hosp and Danesbury Home 91-99; SSJE USA from 99. *SSJE, 980 Memorial Drive, Cambridge MA 02138, USA* T: (001) (617) 876 3037

TRISTRAM, Canon Michael Anthony. b 50. Solicitor 76 Ch Coll Cam BA 72 MA 76. Ripon Coll Cuddesdon 79. **d** 82 **p** 83. C Stanmore *Win* 82-85; R Abbotts Ann and Upper and Goodworth Clatford 85-92; V Pershore w Pinvin, Wick and Birlingham *Worc* 92-03; Hon Can Worc Cathl 00-03; Can Res Portsm Cathl 03-15. *51 High Street, Portsmouth PO1 2LU* T: (023) 9273 1282 F: 9289 2964 E: michael.tristram@portsmouthcathedral.org.uk

TRIVASSE, Keith Malcolm. b 59. Man Univ BA 81 CertEd 82 MPhil 90 Dur Univ MA 98. Qu Coll Birm 84. **d** 86 **p** 87. C Prestwich St Marg *Man* 86-88; C Orford St Marg *Liv* 88-90; TV Sunderland *Dur* 90-91; P-in-c N Hylton St Marg Castletown

91-95; R Bothal and Pegswood w Longhirst *Newc* 95-97; P-in-c Bury Ch King *Man* 01-11; P-in-c Bury St Paul 01-03; C Bury, Roch Valley 11-15; rtd 15. *St Paul's Vicarage, Fir Street, Bury BL9 7QG* T: 0161-761 6991 E: keith.trivasse@care4free.net

TRIVASSE, Ms Margaret. b 59. Dur Univ BA 80 MA 97 New Coll Dur PGCE 01 Liv Univ MTh 05. NOC 01. **d** 04 **p** 05. NSM Radcliffe *Man* 04-08; NSM Prestwich St Gabr from 08. *114 Valley Mill Lane, Bury BL9 9BY* T: 0161-258 0649 E: margtriv@yahoo.co.uk

TRODDEN, Michael John. b 54. K Coll Lon BD 77 AKC 77 CertEd. Wycliffe Hall Ox 79. **d** 80 **p** 81. C Woodford St Mary w St Phil and St Jas *Chelmsf* 80-87; V Aldborough Hatch 87-96; R Ampthill w Millbrook and Steppingley *St Alb* from 96. *The Rectory, 10 Church Avenue, Ampthill, Bedford MK45 2PN* T: (01525) 402320

TROLLOPE, David Harvey. b 41. BSc 63. Lon Coll of Div 66. **d** 68 **p** 69. C Bermondsey St Jas w Ch Ch *S'wark* 68-71; CMS Namibia 71-72; Uganda 72-77; Kenya 77-82; V Gt Crosby St Luke *Liv* 82-04; rtd 04; PtO *Ches* from 04. *26 White House Lane, Heswall, Wirral CH60 1UQ* T: 0151-342 2648 E: davidtrollope@btinternet.com

TROMANS, Judith Anne. See OLIVER, Judith Anne

TROMANS, Kevin Stanley. b 57. St Martin's Coll Lanc BEd 79 St Jo Coll Dur MA 12 MA 11. Aston Tr Scheme 90 Coll of Resurr Mirfield 92. **d** 94 **p** 95. C Rawdon *Bradf* 94-96; C Woodhall 96-98; V Liversedge w Hightown *Wakef* 98-02; V Bierley *Bradf* 02-07; Chapl Co Durham and Darlington NHS Foundn Trust 07-12; Sen Chapl from 12; CF(V) from 08. *University Hospital Durham, North Road, Durham DH1 5TW* T: 0191-333 2183 E: kevin.tromans@cddft.nhs.uk

TROMBETTI, Lynda Joan. b 52. **d** 03 **p** 04. OLM Dorking w Ranmore *Guildf* 03-11; NSM 11-12; Chapl Epsom and St Helier Univ Hosps NHS Trust 05-12; PtO *Portsm* from 15. *Mead Cottage, Pilgrims Way, Westhumble, Dorking RH5 6AP* T: (01306) 884360 M: 07968-629364 E: theflyingtrombetti@talktalk.net

TROOD, James William. b 68. Cov Poly BSc 90 St Jo Coll Dur PGCE 91. St Jo Coll Nottm MTh 02. **d** 02 **p** 03. C Anchorsholme *Blackb* 02-06; TV Glascote and Stonydelph *Lich* 06-15; RD Tamworth 09-14; P-in-c Walsall St Matt from 15. *The Rectory, 48 Jesson Road, Walsall WS1 3AX* M: 07939-587208 E: rector@stmatthewswalsall.co.uk

TROTT, Stephen. b 57. Hull Univ BA 79 Fitzw Coll Cam BA 83 MA 87 Univ of Wales (Cardiff) LLM 03 FRSA 86. Westcott Ho Cam 81. **d** 84 **p** 85. C Hessle *York* 84-87; C Kingston upon Hull St Alb 87-88; R Pitsford w Boughton *Pet* from 88; Sec CME 88-93; Chapl Pitsford Sch from 91; RD Brixworth *Pet* from 15. *The Rectory, Humfrey Lane, Boughton, Northampton NN2 8RQ* T: (01604) 845655 M: 07712-863000 F: 07053-406290 E: revstrott@btinternet.com

TROTTER, Harold Barrington (Barry). b 33. Sarum Th Coll 64. **d** 66 **p** 67. C Salisbury St Fran *Sarum* 66-69; Dioc Youth Officer 69-72; V Horton and Chalbury 69-73; R Frenchay *Bris* 73-81; V Henbury 81-99; rtd 99; PtO *Ex* 00-02; *Glouc* from 02. *14 Butlers Mead, Blakeney GL15 4EH* T: (01594) 510176

TROUT, Keith. b 49. Trin Coll Bris 90. **d** 92 **p** 93. C Pudsey St Lawr and St Paul *Bradf* 92-97; V Burley *Leeds* 97-14; rtd 14; P-in-c Burley Leeds from 14. *St Matthias Vicarage, 271 Burley Road, Leeds LS4 2EL* T: 0113-278 5872 or 230 4408 E: keithtrout03@stmatthias.co.uk

TROWSDALE, James Andrew. b 61. Yorks Min Course 13. **d** 15. NSM Burton Fleming w Fordon, Grindale etc *York* from 15. *Dale Farm, Weaverthorpe, Malton YO17 8EX* T: (01944) 738147 E: jamestrowsdale@hotmail.co.uk

TRUBY, Canon David Charles. b 57. Ba 79. Linc Th Coll 79. **d** 82 **p** 83. C Stanley *Liv* 82-85; C Hindley St Pet 85-90; R Brimington *Derby* 90-98; Can Res Derby Cathl 98-03; TR Wirksworth from 03; RD from 08; Hon Can Derby Cathl from 04. *The Rectory, Coldwell Street, Wirksworth, Matlock DE4 4FB* T: (01629) 824707 or 822858 E: david.truby@btinternet.com

TRUDGETT, Raymond John. b 46. Wilson Carlile Coll 86. **d** 04 **p** 05. Port Chapl and C Aqaba SS Pet and Paul Jordan 04-07; Chapl Medway and Thames Ports *Roch* 07-11; PtO *Cant* 07-11; *Chelmsf* 07-11; rtd 11; PtO *Nor* from 11. *9 Holly Road, Lowestoft NR32 3NH* T: (01502) 583668 E: trudgett831@btinternet.com

TRUDGILL, Harry Keith. b 25. LCP 54 Leeds Univ DipEd 49 Lon Univ BD 61. St Deiniol's Hawarden 76. **d** 76 **p** 76. In Methodist Ch 58-75; C Glas St Marg 76-78; R Lenzie 78-86; rtd 86; PtO *Leeds* from 86. *10 Wharfe View, Grassington, Skipton BD23 5NL* T: (01756) 752114

TRUMAN, Miss Catherine Jane. b 64. Coll of Ripon & York St Jo BEd 88. St Jo Coll Nottm 01. **d** 03 **p** 04. C Owlerton *Sheff* 03-06; Hd Academic Progr Wilson Carlile Coll of Evang from 06. *Wilson Carlile College of Evangelism, 50 Cavendish Street, Sheffield S3 7RZ* T: 0114-278 7020 E: j.truman@churcharmy.org.uk

TRUMAN, Miss Charlotte Jane. b 71. Birm Univ BPhil 96. Westcott Ho Cam 96. **d** 99 **p** 00. C High Harrogate Ch Ch *Ripon* 99-03; P-in-c Oulton w Woodlesford 03-06; Chapl HM YOI Northallerton 06-09; Chapl HM Pris and YOI New Hall from 09. *HM Prison and Young Offender Institution New Hall, New Hall Way, Flockton, Wakefield WF4 4XX* T: (01924) 803000 E: charlotte.truman@hmps.gsi.gov.uk

TRUMPER, Roger David. b 52. Ex Univ BSc 74 K Coll Lon MSc 75 Ox Univ BA 80 MA 85. Wycliffe Hall Ox 78. **d** 81 **p** 82. C Tunbridge Wells St Jo *Roch* 81-84; C Slough *Ox* 84-87; TV Shenley and Loughton 87-88; TV Watling Valley 88-93; R Byfleet *Guildf* 93-05; TV Sidmouth, Woolbrook, Salcombe Regis, Sidbury etc *Ex* from 05. *All Saints' Vicarage, All Saints' Road, Sidmouth EX10 8ES* T: (01395) 515963 E: roger.thetrumpers@virgin.net

TRUNDLE, Christopher Philip. b 85. Trin Coll Cam BA 07 MA 10 PGCE 08. Coll of Resurr Mirfield 08. **d** 10 **p** 11. C Tottenham St Paul *Lon* 10-12; C Pimlico St Gabr 12-13; P-in-c Clerkenwell H Redeemer 13-14; V from 14; P-in-c Clerkenwell St Mark 13-14; V from 14. *The Clergy House, 24 Exmouth Market, London EC1R 4QE* T: (020) 7837 1861 E: chris.trundle@gmail.com *or* holyredeemerstmark@tiscali.co.uk

TRURO, Bishop of. See THORNTON, The Rt Revd Timothy Martin

TRURO, Dean of. See BUSH, The Very Revd Roger Charles

TRUSS, Canon Charles Richard. b 42. Reading Univ BA 63 Linacre Coll Ox BA 66 MA 69 K Coll Lon MPhil 79. Wycliffe Hall Ox 64. **d** 66 **p** 67. C Leic H Apostles 66-69; C Hampstead St Jo *Lon* 69-72; V Belsize Park 72-79; V Wood Green St Mich 79-82; TR Wood Green St Mich w Bounds Green St Gabr etc 82-85; R Shepperton 85-94; V Waterloo St Jo w St Andr *S'wark* 94-08; RD Lambeth 95-05; Hon Can S'wark Cathl 01-08; Sen Chapl Actors' Ch Union 04-08; rtd 08; PtO *S'wark* from 08; *Guildf* from 10. *12 Camden Cottages, Church Walk, Weybridge KT13 8JT* T: (01932) 702317 E: richard.truss@btinternet.com

TRUSTRAM, Canon David Geoffrey. b 49. Pemb Coll Ox BA 71 MA 76 Qu Coll Cam BA 73 MA 77. Westcott Ho Cam 74. **d** 75 **p** 76. C Surbiton St Mark *S'wark* 75-77; C Surbiton St Andr and St Mark 77-78; C Richmond St Mary w St Matthias and St Jo 78-82; P-in-c Eastry *Cant* 82-88; R Eastry and Northbourne w Tilmanstone etc 88-90; Chapl Eastry Hosp 82-90; V Tenterden St Mildred w Smallhythe *Cant* 90-10; P-in-c Tenterden St Mich 07-10; Hon Can Cant Cathl 96-10; AD Tenterden 99-05; rtd 10; PtO *Cant* from 11. *Hensmead, New Road, Headcorn, Ashford TN27 9SE* T: (01622) 892480 M: 07811-874806 E: trustram@btinternet.com

TSANG, Wing Man. b 52. Lon Univ BSc 74 MPhil 84 MCB 88 MRCPath 88 FRCPath 96. STETS 99. **d** 02 **p** 03. C Merthyr Tydfil Ch Ch *Llan* 02-05; TV Broadwater *Chich* from 05. *67 Normandy Road, Worthing BN14 7EA* M: 07961-839018 E: wing2699@hotmail.com

TSIPOURAS, John George. b 38. Trin Coll Bris 76. **d** 78 **p** 79. C Cheadle Hulme St Andr *Ches* 78-82; V Hurdsfield 82-03; rtd 03; P-in-c W Heath *Birm* 04-05; PtO *Cov* from 04; *Birm* from 06. *5 Ashfurlong Close, Balsall Common, Coventry CV7 7QA* T: (01676) 534048 E: john@tsipouras.org.uk

TUAM, Archdeacon of. See HASTINGS, The Ven Gary Lea

TUAM, Dean of. See GRIMASON, The Very Revd Alistair John

TUAM, KILLALA AND ACHONRY, Bishop of. See ROOKE, The Rt Revd Patrick William

TUAM, Provost of. See RYAN, Canon Maureen

TUBBS, Preb Brian Ralph. b 44. AKC 66. **d** 67 **p** 68. C Ex St Thos 67-72; TV Sidmouth, Woolbrook and Salcombe Regis 72-77; R Ex St Jas 77-96; RD Christianity 89-95; V Paignton St Jo and Chapl S Devon Healthcare NHS Foundn Trust 96-09; Preb Ex Cathl 95-09; rtd 09. *58 Dorset Avenue, Exeter EX4 1ND* T: (01392) 200506 E: brtubbs@virginmedia.com

TUBBS, Gary Andrew. b 59. Univ of Wales (Swansea) BA 82 Bris Univ MSc 84 Bris Poly PGCE 84. Oak Hill Th Coll. **d** 00 **p** 01. C Stanwix *Carl* 00-02; C Carl H Trin and St Barn 02-08; P-in-c Pennington and Lindal w Marton and Bardsea from 08. *Trinkeld Vicarage, Main Road, Swarthmoor, Ulverston LA12 0RZ* T: (01229) 583174 E: gary.tubbs@hotmail.co.uk

TUBBS, Peter Alfred. b 22. G&C Coll Cam BA 48 MA 53. Linc Th Coll 55. **d** 57 **p** 58. C Tettenhall Regis *Lich* 57-60; C Wellington Ch Ch 60-64; Asst Chapl Keele Univ 63-69; V Cardington *St Alb* 69-85; RD Elstow 77-82; C Sandy 85-89; rtd 89; PtO *St Alb* from 89. *24 Dulverton Hall, Esplanade, Scarborough YO11 2AR* T: (01723) 340124

TUCK, Canon Andrew Kenneth. b 42. Kelham Th Coll 63. **d** 68 **p** 69. C Poplar *Lon* 68-74; TV 74-76; V Walsgrave on Sowe *Cov* 76-90; R Farnham *Guildf* 90-12; Chapl Surrey Hants Borders NHS Trust 90-05; Chapl Surrey and Borders Partnership NHS Trust 05-12; RD Farnham *Guildf* 00-05; Hon Can Guildf Cathl 09-12; rtd 12; PtO *Guildf* 12-13; Dioc Spiritual Direction Co-ord from 14. *7 Forge Close, Farnham GU9 9PX* T: (01252) 716119

TUCK, David John. b 36. St Cath Coll Cam BA 61 MA 65. Cuddesdon Coll 61. **d** 63 **p** 64. C Holt and Kelling w Salthouse *Nor* 63-68; Zambia 68-73; V Sprowston *Nor* 73-84; R Beeston St Andr 73-84; RD Nor N 81-84; V Pinner *Lon* 84-01; rtd 01; PtO *Lon* 02-04; *St Alb* from 04; Hon C N Harrow St Alb *Lon* from 04. *119 High Street, Northwood HA6 1ED* T: (01923) 825806   M: 07443-576905 E: dandtuck@btinternet.com

TUCK, Gillian. b 40. SRN 64 SCM 66. Llan Dioc Tr Scheme 93. **d** 97 **p** 98. NSM Pontypridd St Cath w St Matt *Llan* 97-01; P-in-c Pontypridd St Matt and Cilfynydd 01-05; NSM Pontypridd St Matt and Cilfynydd w Llanwynno 05-08; rtd 08. *4 Maes Glas, Coed y Cwm, Pontypridd CF37 3EJ* T: (01443) 791049

TUCK, Nigel Graham. b 57. Chich Th Coll 82. **d** 85 **p** 86. C Port Talbot St Theodore *Llan* 85-87; C Llantrisant 87-90; TV Duston *Pet* 90-95; C Aldwick *Chich* 95-98; C-in-c N Bersted CD 98-00; V N Bersted 01-02; rtd 02. *1 Yr Arglawdd, Heathwood Road, Cardiff CF14 4GH*

TUCK, Ralph Thomas. b 42. Worc Coll Ox BA 64 Bris Univ CertEd 66. NOC 87. **d** 90 **p** 91. NSM S Crosland *Wakef* 90-93; NSM Helme 90-93; PtO 93-05. *48 Kirkwood Drive, Huddersfield HD3 3WJ*

TUCK, Canon Ronald James. b 47. S'wark Ord Course 75. **d** 78 **p** 79. C Upper Holloway St Pet w St Jo *Lon* 78-81; P-in-c Scottow and Swanton Abbott w Skeyton *Nor* 81-88; R Bradwell 88-12; Hon Can Nor Cathl 10-12; rtd 12; PtO *Nor* from 12. *5 Gosford Heights, 47 Gosford Road, Beccles NR34 9SP* T: (01502) 717273   E: revtuck@btinternet.com

TUCKER, Andrew Michael. b 64. K Coll Lon BD 87. Wycliffe Hall Ox 93. **d** 95 **p** 96. C Moreton *Ches* 95-96; C Poynton 96-99; C Poulgate *Chich* 99-02; C-in-c Lower Willingdon St Wilfrid CD 03-12; Chapl Fujairah Cyprus and the Gulf 13-15; PtO *St Alb* 15; R Ellon *Ab* from 15; R Cruden Bay from 15. *The Rectory, St Mary on the Rock, South Road, Ellon AB41 9NP*

TUCKER, Canon Anthony Ian. b 50. CA Tr Coll 73 S'wark Ord Course 81. **d** 85 **p** 86. NSM E Ham w Upton Park and Forest Gate *Chelmsf* 85-86; NSM S'well H Trin 86-90; C Rolleston w Fiskerton, Morton and Upton 90-93; P-in-c Teversal 93-96; Chapl Sutton Cen 93-96; P-in-c Norwell w Ossington, Cromwell and Caunton 96-04; Dioc Tourism Adv 96-04; V Balderton and Barnby-in-the-Willows from 04; AD Newark 00-12; Jt AD Newark and S'well 08-12; Hon Can S'well Minster from 08. *The Vicarage, Main Street, Balderton, Newark NG24 3NN* T: (01636) 704811   E: tonytucker57@gmail.com

TUCKER, Ms Catherine Jane. b 62. Birkbeck Coll Lon BA 97 Jes Coll Cam MPhil 11. Westcott Ho Cam 09. **d** 11 **p** 12. C Forest Hill w Lower Sydenham *S'wark* 11-14; V Croydon H Sav from 14. *The Vicarage, 115 St Saviour's Road, Croydon CR0 2XF* M: 07709-618063   T: (020) 3784 3017 E: holysav@hotmail.com

TUCKER, Desmond Robert. b 29. Bris Sch of Min 83. **d** 86 **p** 87. C Bris St Mich 86-88; P-in-c 88-94; rtd 94; PtO *Bris* from 94. *48 Cranbrook Road, Bristol BS6 7BT* T: 0117-373 5584

TUCKER, Douglas Greening. b 17. St Aid Birkenhead 49. **d** 52 **p** 53. C Jesmond Clayton Memorial *Newc* 52-56; C Fenham St Jas and St Basil 56-58; V Cowgate 58-62; V Elsham *Linc* 62-85; V Worlaby 62-85; V Bonby 73-85; rtd 85; PtO *Newc* 85-02. *Balintore, 4 Kilrymont Place, St Andrews KY16 8DH* T: (01334) 476738

TUCKER, Mrs Gillian Mary. b 57. Bris Poly BEd 79. WEMTC 04. **d** 07 **p** 08. NSM Sharpness, Purton, Brookend and Slimbridge *Glouc* from 07. *Hinton Cottage, Hinton, Berkeley GL13 9HZ* T: (01453) 811105

TUCKER, Ian Malcolm. b 46. S Dios Minl Tr Scheme 86. **d** 89 **p** 90. NSM Pill w Easton in Gordano and Portbury *B & W* 89-95; C Frome St Jo and St Mary 95-99; TV Redruth w Lanner and Treleigh *Truro* 99-04; P-in-c Par and Hon Chapl Miss to Seafarers 04-11; rtd 11. *4 Priory Road, Portbury, Bristol BS20 7TH* E: iandm@btinternet.com

TUCKER, Jill. b 47. UMIST BSc 68 MSc 69 PhD 77. Qu Coll Birm 05. **d** 06 **p** 07. NSM Ilmington w Stretton-on-Fosse etc *Cov* 06-09; NSM Shipston-on-Stour w Honington and Idlicote from 09; AD Shipston from 09; Dean of Self-Supporting Min from 11. *The Old House, Back Lane, Oxhill, Warwick CV35 0QN* T: (01295) 680663   F: 688193   M: 07973-994800 E: revjill.tucker@tiscali.co.uk

TUCKER, John Yorke Raffles. b 24. Magd Coll Cam BA 49 MA 56. Westcott Ho Cam 49. **d** 51 **p** 52. C Shadwell St Paul w Ratcliffe St Jas *Lon* 51-54; C Preston Ascension 54-58; V S Hackney St Mich 58-67; V Belmont 67-78; V Sunbury 78-89; rtd 89; PtO *Ex* 89-93; *B & W* from 93. *3 Beauchamp Gardens, Hatch Beauchamp, Taunton TA3 6SD* T: (01823) 481543   E: johnandlesley.tucker@btinternet.com

TUCKER (née RAMSAY), Kerry. b 59. Heythrop Coll Lon MA 94. Westcott Ho Cam 92. **d** 94 **p** 96. C Westville St Eliz S Africa

95-96; C Charlton St Luke w H Trin *S'wark* 96-99; C Cambridge Gt St Mary w St Mich *Ely* 99-04; V Sunninghill Ox 04-08; P-in-c S Ascot 07-08; PtO from 08; Hon C Byfleet *Guildf* 09-10; Hon C E Horsley and Ockham w Hatchford and Downside 10-14. *Diocesan House, Quarry Street, Guildford GU1 3XG* E: kerrytux@tiscali.co.uk

TUCKER, Michael. b 33. **d** 84 **p** 85. NSM Sawston *Ely* 84-87; C Ely 87-90; P-in-c Barton Bendish w Beachamwell and Shingham 90-98; P-in-c Wereham 90-98; rtd 98; PtO *Nor* 99-04; *Ely* from 00. *119 The Beach, Snettisham, King's Lynn PE31 7RB* T: (01485) 544660

TUCKER, Canon Michael Owen. b 42. Lon Univ BSc 66 Surrey Univ PhD 69. Glouc Sch of Min 81. **d** 84 **p** 85. NSM Uley w Owlpen and Nympsfield *Glouc* 84-92; P-in-c Amberley 92-09; Dioc NSM Officer 94-09; Hon Can Glouc Cathl 98-09; RD Stonehouse 99-04; rtd 09. *18 Bownham Mead, Rodborough Common, Stroud GL5 5DZ* T: (01453) 873352 E: mike@tuckers.org.uk

TUCKER, Nicholas Harold. b 41. Reading Univ BSc 66. NOC 90. **d** 93 **p** 94. NSM Ilkley All SS *Bradf* 93-98; P-in-c Uley w Owlpen and Nympsfield *Glouc* 98-06; rtd 06; NSM Nailsworth w Shortwood, Horsley etc *Glouc* 07-08. *29 The Chipping, Tetbury GL8 8EU* T: (01666) 503188   E: nick@tucker141.fsnet.co.uk

TUCKER, Nicholas John Cuthbert. b 74. Birm Univ BSc 96. Oak Hill Th Coll MTh 04. **d** 04 **p** 05. C Bebington *Ches* 04-07; Research Fell Oak Hill Th Coll 07-15; PtO *St Alb* 08-15; V Edgbaston St Bart *Birm* from 15. *The Vicarage, 1B Arthur Road, Edgbaston, Birmingham B15 2UW*   M: 07957-566714 E: njctucker@hotmail.com

TUCKER, Richard Parish. b 51. Cam Univ BA 72 MA 76 Lon Univ BD 83. Wycliffe Hall Ox 80. **d** 83 **p** 84. C Wellington w Eyton *Lich* 83-84; C Walsall 84-88; TV Dronfield *Derby* 88-90; TV Dronfield w Holmesfield 90-98; V Sutton Coldfield St Columba *Birm* from 98. *St Columba's Vicarage, 280 Chester Road North, Sutton Coldfield B73 6RR* T: 0121-354 5873 E: richardtucker@tiscali.co.uk

TUCKER, Stephen Reid. b 51. New Coll Ox BA 72 MA 76. Ripon Coll Cuddesdon. **d** 77 **p** 78. C Hove All SS *Chich* 77-80; Lect Chich Th Coll 80-86; V Portsea St Alb *Portsm* 86-90; Chapl and Dean of Div New Coll Ox 90-95; P-in-c Ovingdean *Chich* 96-01; Bp's Adv on CME 96-01; V Hampstead St Jo *Lon* from 01; AD N Camden from 14. *The Vicarage, 14 Church Row, London NW3 6UU* T: (020) 7435 0553 *or* 7794 5808 E: stucker957@btinternet.com

TUCKER, Preb Susan. b 53. Stockwell Coll of Educn CertEd 74. **d** 97 **p** 98. C Taunton St Andr *B & W* 97-01; V Bishops Hull 01-10; RD Taunton 06-10; Chapl St Marg Hospice Taunton 01-07; R Chard St Mary w Combe St Nicholas, Wambrook etc *B & W* from 10; RD Ilminster from 14; Preb Wells Cathl from 15. *The Vicarage, Forton Road, Chard TA20 2HJ* T: (01460) 62320   E: suetucker99@btinternet.com

TUCKER, Vivian Clive Temple. b 39. Univ of Wales (Swansea) BSc 60 Univ of Wales DipEd 61. St As Minl Tr Course 93. **d** 96 **p** 97. NSM Gresford w Holt *St As* 96-04; NSM Holt, Rossett and Isycoed 04-09; rtd 09; PtO *St As* from 09. *8 Snowdon Drive, Ty Gwyn, Wrexham LL11 2UY* T: (01978) 359226

TUCKETT, Prof Christopher Mark. b 48. Qu Coll Cam MA 71 Lanc Univ PhD 79. Westcott Ho Cam 71. **d** 75 **p** 76. C Lancaster St Mary *Blackb* 75-77; Chapl and Fell Qu Coll Cam 77-79; Lect NT Man Univ 79-89; Sen Lect 89-91; Prof Bibl Studies 91-96; Lect NT Ox Univ 96-00; Prof NT Studies 00-13; rtd 13; PtO *Ox* from 13. *1 Wallingford Road, Cholsey, Wallingford OX10 9LQ* T: (01491) 659091 E: christopher.tuckett@theology.ox.ac.uk

TUCKETT, Ms Katherine Ann. b 76. Selw Coll Cam MA 98. SEITE 10. **d** 13 **p** 14. C Merton Priory *S'wark* from 13. *Holy Trinity Church, 234 Broadway, London SW19 1SB* M: 07890-397296   E: kate_tuckett@yahoo.co.uk

TUCKWELL, Jonathan David. b 77. St Jo Coll Cam MEng 00 MA 02. Oak Hill Th Coll BA 11. **d** 11 **p** 12. C Cambridge St Andr Less *Ely* from 11. *48 College Fields, Woodhead Drive, Cambridge CB4 1YZ* T: (01223) 420143   M: 07785-576939 E: jon@jon-ruth.co.uk

TUCKWELL, Richard Graham. b 46. SS Mark & Jo Univ Coll Plymouth TCert 67 Open Univ BA. **d** 07 **p** 08. NSM Tarvin *Ches* 07-09; P-in-c Alvanley 09-12; V 12-14; rtd 14. *Iddesleigh, 5 Walkers Lane, Tarporley CW6 0BX* T: (01829) 732732 M: 07713-485318   E: richard.tuckwell@googlemail.com

TUDGE, Paul Quartus. b 55. Leeds Univ BEd 78. Cranmer Hall Dur 84. **d** 87 **p** 88. C Roundhay St Edm *Ripon* 87-90; C Leeds City 91; V Woodside 91-99; Warden of Readers 96-99; V Ilkley All SS *Bradf* 99-08; RD Otley 02-08; P-in-c Farsley 08-11; V from 11; RD Calverley 10-14; AD N Bradford from 14. *The Vicarage, 9 St John's Avenue, Farsley, Pudsey LS28 5DN* T: 0113-257 0059   E: paul.tudge@bradford.anglican.org

TUDGEY, Stephen John. b 51. Nottm Univ BTh 81 Westmr Coll Ox MTh 00. St Jo Coll Nottm LTh 81. **d** 81 **p** 82.

C Grays Thurrock *Chelmsf* 81-83; C Madeley *Heref* 84-87; R Chilcompton w Downside and Stratton on the Fosse *B & W* 87-03; P-in-c Falmouth K Chas *Truro* from 03; Hon Chapl Miss to Seafarers from 04. *The Rectory, 19 Trescobeas Road, Falmouth TR11 2JB* T: (01326) 319141 E: steve.tudgey@btinternet.com

TUDOR, David Charles Frederick. b 42. Sarum Th Coll 70. **d** 73 **p** 74. C Plymouth St Pet *Ex* 73-75; C Reddish *Man* 75-78; P-in-c Hamer 78-80; V Goldenhill *Lich* 80-87; V Meir 87-91; Chapl Asst Nottm City Hosp 91-94; Chapl Cen Sheff Univ Hosps NHS Trust 94-96; V Nottingham St Geo w St Jo *S'well* 96-04; rtd 05; PtO *S'well* from 05; *Derby* 05-13. *102 St Albans Road, Nottingham NG6 9HG* T: 0115-975 0184 M: 07811-866348

TUDOR, David St Clair. b 55. K Coll Lon BD 77 AKC 77 K Coll Lon MTh 89. Ripon Coll Cuddesdon 77. **d** 78 **p** 79. C Plumstead St Nic *S'wark* 78-80; C Redhill St Matt 80-83; C-in-c Reigate St Phil CD 83-87; Asst Sec Gen Syn Bd for Miss and Unity 87-88; PtO *S'wark* 94-97; TV Canvey Is *Chelmsf* 97-00; TR from 00; AD Hadleigh from 08. *St Nicholas House, 210 Long Road, Canvey Island SS8 0JR* T: (01268) 682586 E: dstudor@tiscali.co.uk

TUFFIN, Mrs Gillian Patricia. b 43. S Dios Minl Tr Scheme 91. **d** 94 **p** 95. C Gidea Park *Chelmsf* 94-98; TV Stoke-upon-Trent *Lich* 98-01; Admin and Prayer Co-ord Shalom Chr Healing Cen from 02; NSM Northolt Park St Barn *Lon* 02-08; PtO from 08. *76 Stowe Crescent, Ruislip HA4 7SS* T: (020) 8864 5394 E: g.tuffin@btopenworld.com

TUFNELL, Andrew Stephen Goodwin. b 83. Univ of Wales (Cardiff) BSc 05 PGCE 06. Ridley Hall Cam 12. **d** 15. C Gamston and Bridgford *S'well* from 15. *9 Fountains Close, West Bridgford, Nottingham NG2 6LL* M: 07779-639507 E: a.tufnell@gmail.com

TUFFNELL, Nigel Owen. b 65. Teesside Poly BSc 90 UEA MSc 01. St Jo Coll Nottm 87. **d** 94 **p** 95. C Guisborough *York* 94-97; P-in-c Northwold *Ely* 97-98; P-in-c Stoke Ferry w Wretton 97-98; P-in-c Whittington 97-98; R Northwold and Wretton w Stoke Ferry etc 98-03; Bp's Adv on Environmental Issues 02-03; TR Kegworth, Hathern, Long Whatton, Diseworth etc *Leic* 03-06; PtO *Nor* 10; Hon C Hopton w Corton 10-12; P-in-c Scole, Brockdish, Billingford, Thorpe Abbots etc 12-14; P-in-c Redenhall, Harleston, Wortwell and Needham 12-14; R Redenhall w Scole from 14; RD Redenhall from 15. *The Rectory, 10 Swan Lane, Harleston IP20 9AN* T: (01379) 308905 E: rector.redenhallscole@hotmail.co.uk

TUFNELL, Edward Nicholas Pember. b 45. Chu Coll Cam MA 68. St Jo Coll Nottm BA 73. **d** 73 **p** 74. C Ealing St Mary *Lon* 73-76; BCMS Tanzania 76-88; P-in-c Lt Thurrock St Jo *Chelmsf* 89-91; V Grays North 91-98; Chapl Thurrock Community Hosp Grays 89-98; P-in-c Bourton-on-the-Water w Clapton *Glouc* 98-05; R Bourton-on-the-Water w Clapton etc 05-11; AD Stow 09-10; rtd 11. *Karibuni, 37 Harrold Priory, Bedford MK41 0SD* T: (01234) 215440 M: 07816-123470 E: e.tufnell1979@btinternet.com

TUFNELL, Michael. b 81. Imp Coll Lon BEng 05. St Mellitus Coll MA 10. **d** 10 **p** 11. C Enfield Ch Ch Trent Park *Lon* 10-14; C Turnham Green Ch Ch from 14. *48 Park Drive, London W3 8NA* M: 07977-139544 E: michaeltufnell@gmail.com

TUFT, Preb Patrick Anthony. b 31. Selw Coll Cam BA 56 MA 60. Edin Th Coll 56. **d** 58 **p** 59. C Keighley *Bradf* 58-63; PV Chich Cathl 63-68; Min Can St Paul's Cathl 68-74; Hon Min Can St Paul's Cathl 74-94; V Chiswick St Nic w St Mary 74-06; PV Westmr Abbey 74-79; AD Hounslow *Lon* 87-93; P-in-c Chiswick St Paul Grove Park 88-90; Preb St Paul's Cathl 95-06; rtd 07. *68 Worple Road, Isleworth TW7 7HU* T: (020) 8581 3014 M: 07768-892099 E: patrick@tuft.tv

TUGWELL, Elizabeth Ann. b 36. SWMTC. **d** 94 **p** 95. NSM Ludgvan *Truro* 94-97; NSM St Hilary w Perranuthnoe 94-97; PtO 99-05; P-in-c Portpatrick *Glas* 05-08; P-in-c Stranraer 05-10; rtd 10. *Address temp unknown*

TULK, Giles David. b 65. Leeds Univ BA 86. ERMC 06. **d** 09 **p** 10. C Stansted Mountfitchet w Birchanger and Farnham *Chelmsf* 09-11; C Bocking St Mary 11-13; TR Albury, Braughing, Furneux Pelham, Lt Hadham etc *St Alb* from 13. *The Rectory, High Street, Much Hadham SG10 6DA* T: (01279) 842609 E: gtulk@waitrose.com

TULL, Preb Christopher Stuart. b 36. Hertf Coll Ox BA 60 MA 64. Oak Hill Th Coll 60. **d** 62 **p** 63. C Stoodleigh *Ex* 62-71; C Washfield 62-71; TV Washfield, Stoodleigh, Withleigh etc 71-74; RD Tiverton 74-75; R Bishops Nympton w Rose Ash 75-77; V Mariansleigh 75-77; TR Bishopsnympton, Rose Ash, Mariansleigh etc 77-99; RD S Molton 80-87 and 95-99; Preb Ex Cathl 84-99; rtd 99; PtO *B & W* from 04. *The Old Smithy, Challacombe, Barnstaple EX31 4TU* T: (01598) 763201

TULLETT, Paul Budworth. b 71. Lanc Univ BSc 92 Birm Univ MBA 00 Anglia Ruskin Univ BA 09. Ridley Hall Cam 07. **d** 09 **p** 10. C Taunton St Mary *B & W* 09-13; V Water Orton *Birm*

from 13. *The Vicarage, Vicarage Lane, Water Orton, Birmingham B46 1RX* M: 07581-544978 E: paulof3decades@hotmail.com

TULLETT, Peter Watts. b 46. Qu Coll Birm 92. **d** 94 **p** 95. C Worle *B & W* 94-96; Chapl HM YOI Portland 96-01; PtO *B & W* 02-04 and from 07; Hon C Uphill 04-06. *2 Ferry Lane, Lympsham, Weston-super-Mare BS24 0BT* T: (01934) 814284 M: 07803-330395 E: peter@valmagnolia.plus.com

TULLOCH, Richard James Anthony. b 52. Wadh Coll Ox BA 74 Selw Coll Cam BA 79. Ridley Hall Cam 76. **d** 79 **p** 80. C Morden *S'wark* 79-83; C Jesmond Clayton Memorial *Newc* 83-94; V New Borough and Leigh *Sarum* 94-11; TR Eden, Gelt and Irthing *Carl* from 11. *St Martin's Vicarage, Main Street, Brampton CA8 1SH* T: (016977) 41304 E: rjatulloch@gmail.com

TULLOCH, Yvonne. *See* RICHMOND, Yvonne Lorraine

TULLY, David John. b 56. St Jo Coll Dur BA 77 Nottm Univ PGCE 78. Ridley Hall Cam 81. **d** 84 **p** 85. C Gosforth St Nic *Newc* 84-86; C Newburn 86-90; TV Whorlton 90-96; V 96-00; R Gateshead Fell *Dur* 00-09; R Chester le Street from 09. *The Rectory, Lindisfarne Avenue, Chester le Street DH3 3PT* T: 0191-388 4027 E: david.tully@tesco.net

TULLY, Janet Florence. b 43. **d** 03 **p** 04. OLM Margate St Jo *Cant* 03-08; PtO *Nor* from 09. *4 Westgate Court, Wymondham NR18 0PX* M: 07866-839275

TUNBRIDGE, Genny Louise. b 64. Clare Coll Cam BA 85 St Cross Coll Ox DPhil 93. Qu Coll Birm BD 95. **d** 96 **p** 97. C Boston *Linc* 96-00; Lect 00-01; Prec Chelmsf Cathl 01-06; Can Res Chelmsf Cathl 02-06; V Gosforth All SS *Newc* 06-13; rtd 13; PtO *Birm* from 15. *The Old Rectory, 80 Hodge Hill Common, Birmingham B36 8AG* M: 07891-610868 E: genny.tunbridge@gmail.com

TUNGAY, Michael Ian. b 45. Oak Hill Th Coll 70. **d** 73 **p** 74. C Fulham St Mary N End *Lon* 73-75; C Hammersmith St Simon 76-79; P-in-c 79-84; PtO *S'wark* 09-11. *7 Lily Close, London W14 9YA* T: (020) 8748 3151 E: miketungay@uk2.net

TUNLEY, Timothy Mark. b 61. Ridley Hall Cam 89. **d** 92 **p** 93. C Aldborough w Boroughbridge and Roecliffe *Ripon* 92-95; C Knaresborough 95-98; V Swaledale 98-05; TV Seacroft 05-09; Dioc Adv for NSM 03-08; Chapl Miss to Seafarers from 09. *109 Avalon Gardens, Linlithgow Bridge, Linlithgow EH49 7PL* M: 07581-625941 T: (01506) 842629 E: timothy.tunley@mtsmail.org

TUNNICLIFFE, Mrs Jean Sarah. b 36. RGN 69. Glouc Sch of Min 89. **d** 92 **p** 94. NSM Dixton *Heref* 92-05; PtO from 05. *Bryn Awelon, 21 Ridgeway, Wyesham, Monmouth NP25 3JX* T: (01600) 714115

TUNNICLIFFE, Canon Martin Wyndham. b 31. Keele Univ BA 56. Qu Coll Birm 59. **d** 60 **p** 61. C Castle Bromwich SS Mary and Marg *Birm* 60-65; V Shard End 65-73; R Over Whitacre w Shustoke 73-78; V Tanworth 78-98; RD Solihull 89-94; Hon Can Birm Cathl 91-98; rtd 98; PtO *Birm* from 98. *202 Ralph Road, Shirley, Solihull B90 3LE* T/F: 0121-745 6522 E: martin@ralph202.wanadoo.co.uk

TUNNICLIFFE, Mrs Siv. b 33. Stockholm Univ MPhil 58. SAOMC 94. **d** 97 **p** 98. OLM Wingrave w Rowsham, Aston Abbotts and Cublington *Ox* 97-12; OLM Wing w Grove 04-12; OLM Cottesloe from 12. *Baldway House, Wingrave, Aylesbury HP22 4PA* T/F: (01296) 681374 E: siv.baldwayhouse@virgin.net

TUNSTALL, Barry Anthony. b 29. Sarum Th Coll 53. **d** 55 **p** 56. C Croxley Green All SS *St Alb* 55-58; C Apsley End 58-63; V N Mymms 63-81; R Kirkby Overblow *Ripon* 81-94; rtd 94; PtO *B & W* from 01. *23 Mondyes Court, Wells BA5 2QX* T: (01749) 677004 E: btunstall49@btinternet.com

TUPLING, Mrs Catherine Louise. b 74. Westhill Coll Birm BTh 96. Wycliffe Hall Ox 01. **d** 03 **p** 04. C Belper *Derby* 03-07; P-in-c Hathersage w Bamford and Derwent 07-08; P-in-c Hathersage w Bamford and Derwent and Grindleford 08-13; V Dore *Sheff* from 13. *The Vicarage, 51 Vicarage Lane, Dore, Sheffield S17 3GY* T: 0114-236 3335 E: katie.tupling@sheffield.anglican.org

TUPPER, Michael Heathfield. b 20. St Edm Hall Ox BA 41 MA 46. Ridley Hall Cam 41. **d** 43 **p** 44. C Win Ch Ch 43-45; Chapl Monkton Combe Sch Bath 45-48; Asst Chapl Shrewsbury Sch 48-59 and 60-79; Kenya 59-60; Hon C Bayston Hill *Lich* 80-98; rtd 98; PtO *Lich* 99-08. *9 Eric Lock Road, Bayston Hill, Shrewsbury SY3 0HQ* T: (01743) 722674

✠**TUREI, The Most Revd William Brown.** b 24. BTS 76. **d** 49 **p** 50 **c** 92. C Tauranga New Zealand 49-52; V Whangaro Pastorate 52-59; V Te Puke Tauranga Miss Distr 59-64; V Ruatoki Whakatane Pastorate 64-70; V Turanga Pastorate 70-74; V Phillipstown and Maori Missr 74-81; V Waipatu-Moteo Pastorate 81-84; Chapl Napier Pris 84-88; Taonga Whakamana Mahi Minita 89-92; den Tairawhiti 87-92; Bp in Tairawhiti 92-05; Bp Aotearoa from 05; Abp New Zealand from 06. *PO Box 568, Gisborne, New Zealand* T: (0064) (6) 867 8856 F: 867 8859

TURLEY, Debra. b 67. Oak Hill Th Coll BA 91. LCTP 07. **d** 10 **p** 11. C Utley *Leeds* 10-15; V Taunton Lyngford *B & W* from 14. *62 Eastwick Road, Taunton TA2 7HD*
E: debbi.turley@sky.com

✠**TURNBULL, The Rt Revd Anthony Michael Arnold.** b 35. CBE 03 DL 05. Keble Coll Ox BA 58 MA 62 Dur Univ Hon DD 03. Cranmer Hall Dur. **d** 60 **p** 61 **c** 88. C Middleton *Man* 60-61; C Luton w E Hyde *St Alb* 61-65; Dir of Ords *York* 65-69; Abp's Dom Chapl 65-69; Chapl York Univ 69-76; V Heslington 69-76; Chief Sec CA 76-84; Can Res Roch Cathl 84-88; Adn Roch 84-88; Bp Roch 88-94; Bp Dur 94-03; rtd 03; Hon Asst Bp Cant and Eur from 03. *67 Strand Street, Sandwich CT13 9HN* T: (01304) 611389
E: amichaelturnbull@yahoo.co.uk

TURNBULL, Brian Robert. b 43. Chich Th Coll 71. **d** 74 **p** 75. C Norbury *St Phil Cant* 74-76; C Folkestone St Sav 76-77; Hon C Tong *Lich* 83-88; C Jarrow *Dur* 88-89; V 89-94; P-in-c Hartlepool St Oswald 94-96; V 96-04; rtd 04; PtO *Dur* from 05. *50 The Chare, Leazes Square, Newcastle upon Tyne NE1 4DD* T: 0191-221 2312
E: frbrian@turnbull23.freeserve.co.uk

TURNBULL, James Awty. b 28. Solicitor Bradf Univ HonDLaws 97. Cranmer Hall Dur 89. **d** 89 **p** 90. NSM Bolton Abbey *Bradf* 89-98; PtO *Leeds* from 98. *Deerstones Cottage, Deerstones, Skipton BD23 6JB*

TURNBULL, Michael. *See* TURNBULL, Anthony Michael Arnold

TURNBULL, Michael Francis. b 62. Liv Univ BTh 99. NOC 95. **d** 98 **p** 99. C Birkenhead Ch Ch *Ches* 98-02; P-in-c Leasowe 02-08; R Wistaston from 08; Asst Warden of Readers from 04. *The Rectory, 44 Church Lane, Wistaston, Crewe CW2 8HA* T: (01270) 665742 *or* 567119 M: 07595-908644
E: mfturnbull@gmail.com

TURNBULL, Michael Peter. b 56. SEITE 09. **d** 12. NSM Sidley *Chich* from 12. *17 Knebworth Road, Bexhill-on-Sea TN39 4JH* T: (01424) 221948 M: 07864-628081
E: mpt@michaelturnbull.co.uk

TURNBULL, Peter Frederick. b 64. SS Mark & Jo Univ Coll Plymouth BA 85. Sarum & Wells Th Coll BTh 91. **d** 91 **p** 92. C Upper Norwood All SS *S'wark* 91-95; Chapl HM Pris Dorchester 95-98; C Dorchester *Sarum* 95-98; NSM Melbury 98-99; C Maltby *Sheff* 99-02; TV 02-08; TV Crosslacon Carl from 08. *The Vicarage, Trumpet Road, Cleator CA23 3EF* T: (01946) 810510 E: pfturnbull@gmail.com

TURNBULL, Richard Duncan. b 60. Reading Univ BA 82 St Jo Coll Dur BA 92 Dur Univ PhD 97 Ox Univ MA 05 MICAS 85 FRHistS. Cranmer Hall Dur 90. **d** 94 **p** 95. C Portswood Ch Ch *Win* 94-98; V Chineham 98-05; Prin Wycliffe Hall Ox 05-12; Dir Cen for Enterprise, Markets and Ethics from 12. *16A Woodstock Road East, Begbroke, Kidlington OX5 1RG* T: (01865) 371358 E: richard.turnbull@theceme.org

TURNBULL, Mrs Sally Elizabeth. b 55. Bp Grosseteste Coll BEd 78. **d** 11 **p** 12. OLM Owmby Gp *Linc* from 11. *Sunnymede, Faldingworth Road, Spridlington, Market Rasen LN8 2DF* T: (01673) 862764 E: supersonicsal55@gmail.com

TURNER, Alan James. b 40. Oak Hill Th Coll BA 81. **d** 81 **p** 82. C Bradley *Wakef* 81-84; C Sandal St Helen 84-86; P-in-c Sibley *Leic* 86-87; TR Sileby, Cossington and Seagrave 87-94; R Hollington St Leon *Chich* 94-01; R Frant w Eridge 01-08; rtd 08; PtO *York* from 10. *4 The Limes, Helmsley, York YO62 5DT* T: (01439) 771957
E: alanturner3040@btinternet.com

TURNER, Alan Roy. b 51. Sheff Univ BA 96 MA 99. EMMTC. **d** 00 **p** 01. C Bladon w Woodstock *Ox* 00-03; Chapl Cokethorpe Sch Witney 01-03; TV Brize Norton and Carterton *Ox* 03-09; P-in-c Stonesfield w Combe Longa from 09. *The Rectory, Brook Lane, Stonesfield, Witney OX29 8PR* T: (01993) 898552 M: 07777-670006
E: r.turner131@btinternet.com

TURNER, Albert Edward. b 41. Glouc Sch of Min 83. **d** 89 **p** 90. C Woodford St Mary w St Phil and St Jas *Chelmsf* 89-91; R Greatworth and Marston St Lawrence etc *Pet* 91-99; R Somersham w Pidley and Oldhurst *Ely* 99-02; rtd 02; PtO *St Alb* from 04. *83 Horslow Street, Potton, Sandy SG19 2NX* T: (01767) 260566 M: 07950-097525 E: aet546@hotmail.com *or* eddie.turner@bedfordhospital.nhs.net

TURNER, Alison Joan. b 66. EAMTC. **d** 97 **p** 98. PtO *Chelmsf* 97-01; PV Ex Cathl from 04. *Address temp unknown* M: 07958-276651

TURNER, Andrew John. b 52. St Jo Coll Nottm. **d** 83 **p** 84. C Framlingham w Saxtead *St E* 83-86; P-in-c Badingham w Bruisyard and Cransford 86-88; P-in-c Dennington 86-88; R Badingham w Bruisyard, Cransford and Dennington 88-91; Chapl RAF 91-12; rtd 12. *2 Spitfire Row, St Eval, Wadebridge PL27 7TF* T: (01841) 540947
E: a.turner682@btinternet.com

TURNER, Ann. *See* TURNER, Patricia Ann

TURNER, Mrs Ann Elizabeth Hamer. b 38. Ex Univ BA 59 PGCE 60. Trin Coll Bris 84. **dss** 86 **d** 87 **p** 94. Bath St Luke *B & W* 86-91; Hon C 87-91; Chapl Dorothy Ho Foundn 89-91; C Bath Twerton-on-Avon *B & W* 91-94; TV 94-96; rtd 98; PtO *Ex* 00-06; Hon C Ottery St Mary, Alfington, W Hill, Tipton etc from 06. *4 Beech Park, West Hill, Ottery St Mary EX11 1UH* T: (01404) 813476

TURNER, Anthony John. b 49. St Mich Coll Llan 89. **d** 91 **p** 92. C Coity w Nolton *Llan* 91-95; R Castlemartin w Warren and Angle etc *St D* 95-04; TV Monkton 04-07; TV Cwmbran *Mon* 07-13; OCM 95-01; rtd 13; PtO *Llan* from 13. *14 Dol Nant Dderwen, Bridgend CF31 5AA* T: (01656) 750713

TURNER, The Ven Antony Hubert Michael. b 30. FCA 63. Tyndale Hall Bris 54. **d** 56 **p** 57. C Nottingham St Ann *S'well* 56-58; C Cheadle *Ches* 58-62; V Macclesfield Ch Ch 62-68; LtO *S'wark* 68-74; Home Sec BCMS 68-74; V Southsea St Jude *Portsm* 74-86; P-in-c Portsea St Luke 75-80; RD Portsm 79-84; Hon Can Portsm Cathl 85-86; Adn Is of Wight 86-96; rtd 96; PtO *Portsm* from 96. *15 Avenue Road, Hayling Island PO11 0LX* T: (023) 9246 5881

TURNER, Benjamin John. b 45. CEng MICE. NOC 82. **d** 85 **p** 86. C Worsley *Man* 85-88; V Elton St Steph 88-95; Asst P Greystoke, Matterdale, Mungrisdale etc *Carl* 95-98; TV Gd Shep TM 98-01; Asst Chapl Leeds Teaching Hosps NHS Trust 01-02; Chapl 02-07; rtd 07; PtO *Leeds* from 09. *40 Nightingale Walk, Bingley BD16 3QB* T: (01274) 568035

TURNER, Carl Francis. b 60. St Chad's Coll Dur BA 81. St Steph Ho Ox 83. **d** 85 **p** 86. C Leigh-on-Sea St Marg *Chelmsf* 85-88; C Brentwood St Thos 88-90; TV Plaistow 90-95; P-in-c 95-96; TR Plaistow and N Canning Town 96-01; Prec and Can Res Ex Cathl 01-14; R New York St Thos USA from 14. *1 West 53rd Street, New York, NY 10019, USA* T: (001) (212) 757 7013 F: 977 6582 E: rector@saintthomaschurch.org

TURNER, Carlton John. b 79. Univ of W Indies BA 05 Qu Coll Birm MA 09. **d** 05 **p** 06. C Bahamas St Greg Bahamas 05-06; C S Beach All SS & Asst Chapl Main Hosp 06-08; C Nassau Calvery Hill 08-10; TV Bloxwich *Lich* from 10. *6 Cresswell Crescent, Walsall WS3 2UW*

TURNER, Charles Maurice Joseph. b 13. **d** 79 **p** 80. NSM Brislington St Luke *Bris* 79-83; NSM Bris Ch Ch w St Ewen and All SS 83-84; NSM Bris St Steph w St Nic and St Leon 83-84; NSM City of Bris 84-89; PtO 89-98. *31 Eagle Road, Bristol BS4 3LQ* T: 0117-977 6329

TURNER, Mrs Christine. b 42. EMMTC. **d** 94 **p** 95. Asst Chapl Qu Medical Cen Nottm Univ Hosp NHS Trust 94-97; NSM Hickling w Kinoulton and Broughton Sulney *S'well* 94-97; NSM Cotgrave 97-99; P-in-c Willoughby-on-the-Wolds w Wysall and Widmerpool 99-04; rtd 04; PtO *Ox* from 12. *The Rosarie, Milcombe, Banbury OX15 4RS* T: (01295) 722330 E: revd.christine@care4free.net

TURNER, Christopher Gilbert. b 29. New Coll Ox BA 52 MA 55. Ox Min Course 91. **d** 92 **p** 93. NSM Hook Norton w Gt Rollright, Swerford etc *Ox* from 92. *Rosemullion, High Street, Great Rollright, Chipping Norton OX7 5RQ* T: (01608) 737359

TURNER, Christopher James Shepherd. b 48. Ch Ch Ox BA 70 MA 74. Wycliffe Hall Ox 71. **d** 74 **p** 75. C Rusholme H Trin *Man* 74-78; C Chadderton Ch Ch 78-80; V 80-89; V Selly Park St Steph and St Wulstan *Birm* 89-99; P-in-c Locking *B & W* 99-05; Chapl Weston Hospice 99-05; P-in-c The Quinton *Birm* 05-09; R 09-11; AD Edgbaston 08-10; PtO from 11. *10 Presthope Road, Birmingham B29 4NJ* T: 0121-603 7916
E: chris@quintonchurch.co.uk

TURNER, Christopher Matthew. b 68. Brunel Univ BSc 90. Cranmer Hall Dur 01. **d** 03 **p** 04. C Hykeham *Linc* 03-06; P-in-c Mid Marsh Gp 06-14; R from 14; P-in-c Saltfleetby 06-14; V from 14; P-in-c Theddlethorpe 06-14; R from 14. *The Rectory, 37 Tinkle Street, Grimoldby, Louth LN11 8SW* T: (01507) 327735 E: c.turner@which.net

TURNER, Mrs Claire Elizabeth. b 76. Plymouth Univ BA 99. Qu Coll Birm 08. **d** 11 **p** 12. C Wednesfield *Lich* 11-14; P-in-c Rubery *Birm* from 14. *St Chad's Vicarage, 126A New Road, Rubery, Rednal, Birmingham B45 9JA* M: 07748-998227 T: 0121-439 2153 E: revclaireturner@gmail.com

TURNER, Colin Peter John. b 42. Clifton Th Coll 63. **d** 66 **p** 67. C Kinson *Sarum* 66-68; C York St Paul 68-72; Org Sec (SE Area) CPAS 73-78; TV Radipole and Melcombe Regis *Sarum* 78-87; R Radstock w Writhlington *B & W* 90-07; R Kilmersdon w Babington 90-07; RD Midsomer Norton 04-07; rtd 07; PtO *B & W* from 07. *12 Gainsborough Rise, Trowbridge BA14 9HX* E: colinpjt@blueyonder.co.uk

TURNER, Derek John. b 54. Univ of Wales (Ban) BSc 81 PhD 86. St Jo Coll Nottm. **d** 87 **p** 88. C Pelsall *Lich* 87-91; C Stratford-on-Avon w Bishopton *Cov* 91-99; R Leire w Ashby Parva and Dunton Bassett *Leic* 00-06; rtd 06; PtO *Win* from 07. *The Parsonage, La Rue du Crocquet, St Brelade, Jersey JE3 8BZ* M: 07713-832676 E: frderek@cesmail.net

TURNER, Dominic. b 75. Essex Univ BA 08. St Jo Coll Nottm 12. **d** 14 **p** 15. C Harlow Town Cen w Lt Parndon *Chelmsf* from 14. *92 Ram Gorse, Harlow CM20 1PZ* M: 07533-484009
E: info@domturner.com

TURNER, Donald. b 29. S'wark Ord Course. **d** 71 **p** 72. C Hounslow St Steph *Lon* 71-76; Hon C Isleworth St Jo 76-78; C Brighton St Pet w Chpl Royal *Chich* 78-80; C Brighton St Pet w Chpl Royal and St Jo 80-85; P-in-c St Leonards SS Pet and Paul 85-87; V 87-91; rtd 91; Hon C Malborough w S Huish, W Alvington and Churchstow *Ex* 93-98; Chapl Las Palmas *Eur* 98-01; PtO *Ex* from 02. *15 Coombe Meadows, Chillington, Kingsbridge TQ7 2JL* T: (01548) 531440

TURNER, Dylan Lawrence. b 72. Goldsmiths' Coll Lon BMus 96 SS Coll Cam BTh 08. Westcott Ho Cam 06. **d** 08 **p** 09. C Strood St Nic w St Mary *Roch* 08-12; P-in-c Longfield from 12. *The Rectory, 67 Main Road, Longfield DA3 7PQ* T: (01474) 702201 M: 07779-225810 E: dylan.turner@cantab.net

TURNER, Edgar. *See* TURNER, Robert Edgar

TURNER, Edward. *See* TURNER, Albert Edward

TURNER, Edward Nicholas. b 80. Birm Univ BA 01 Anglia Ruskin Univ MA 08. Westcott Ho Cam 06. **d** 08 **p** 09. C Winchmore Hill St Paul *Lon* 08-11; V Edmonton St Aldhelm 11-14; V Southgate St Andr from 14. *St Andrew's Vicarage, 184 Chase Side, London N14 5HN* T: (020) 8886 7523 M: 07788-782646 E: edd.turner@expertit.net

TURNER, Canon Edward Robert. b 37. Em Coll Cam BA 62 BTh 66 MA 67. Westcott Ho Cam 64. **d** 66 **p** 67. C Salford St Phil w St Steph *Man* 66-69; Chapl Tonbridge Sch 69-81; Adv for In-Service Tr *Roch* 81-89; Dir of Educn 81-96; Can Res Roch Cathl 81-00; Vice-Dean 88-00; Dioc Adv on Community Affairs 96-00; Consultant Rochester 2000 Trust and Bp's Consultant on Public Affairs 00-02; rtd 02; PtO *Nor* from 01. *Glebe House, Church Road, Neatishead, Norwich NR12 8BT* T: (01692) 631295 E: aandeturner@broadlandnet.co.uk

TURNER, Mrs Eileen Margaret. b 45. Goldsmiths' Coll Lon TCert 66 Ches Coll of HE MTh 02. NOC 90. **d** 93 **p** 94. Par Dn Sandal St Cath *Wakef* 93-94; C 94-96; P-in-c Hammerwich *Lich* 96-02; Dir Ext Studies St Jo Coll Nottm 02-10; rtd 10; PtO *Sheff* from 11. *1 Holly Court, Endcliffe Vale Road, Sheffield S10 3DS* T: 0114-268 2282 M: 07774-623769 E: eileenmturner@gmail.com

TURNER, Mrs Elaine. b 58. Birm Univ BSc 79 CEng 84 MICE 84 MIStructE 85. **d** 04 **p** 05. OLM Walesby *Linc* from 04. *Rose Cottage, Normanby-le-Wold, Market Rasen LN7 6SS* T: (01673) 828142 E: elaine-turner58@supanex.com

TURNER, Miss Elizabeth Jane. b 67. Leeds Univ BEng 88. Trin Coll Bris 93. **d** 96 **p** 97. C Eccles *Man* 96-00; P-in-c Barrow *Ches* 00-08; Dioc Ecum Officer 00-08; R Thurstaston from 08; Dioc Ecum Officer from 08. *Thurstaston Rectory, 77 Thingwall Road, Wirral CH61 3UB* T: 0151-648 1816
E: rector@thurstaston.org.uk

TURNER, Canon Frederick Glynne. b 30. Univ of Wales (Lamp) BA 52. St Mich Coll Llan 52. **d** 54 **p** 55. C Aberaman *Llan* 54-60; C Oystermouth *S & B* 60-64; V Abercynon *Llan* 64-71; V Ton Pentre 71-73; TR Ystradyfodwg 73-77; R Caerphilly 77-82; V Whitchurch 82-96; Can Llan Cathl 84-96; Prec 95-96; rtd 96; PtO *Llan* from 96. *83 Newborough Avenue, Llanishen, Cardiff CF14 5DA* T: (029) 2075 4443

TURNER, Miss Gaynor. b 44. LNSM course 93. **d** 96 **p** 97. NSM Salford Sacred Trin *Man* 96-99; Asst Chapl among Deaf People from 96; Lic Preacher 99-07; PtO 07-15; NSM Broughton from 15. *19 Ellesmere Avenue, Worsley, Manchester M28 OAU*

TURNER, Geoffrey. b 51. Selw Coll Cam BA 75 MA 78 PGCE 75. NOC 90. **d** 93 **p** 94. C E Crompton *Man* 93-96; C Heywood St Luke w All So 96-98; TV Heywood 98-01; TR 01-08; TR Worsley from 08; C Swinton H Rood from 13. *St Mark's Rectory, Walkden Road, Worsley, Manchester M28 2WH* T: 0161-799 6082 E: gt1951@btinternet.com

TURNER, Geoffrey Edwin. b 45. Aston Univ BSc 68 Newc Univ MSc 69 PhD 72. Cranmer Hall Dur BA 74. **d** 75 **p** 76. C Wood End *Cov* 75-79; V Huyton Quarry *Liv* 79-86; Press and Communications Officer *Ely* 86-94; P-in-c Gt w Lt Abington 86-94; P-in-c Hildersham 86-94; V Letchworth St Paul w Willian *St Alb* 94-01; P-in-c Willingham *Ely* 01-02; R 02-08; P-in-c Rampton 01-02; R 02-08; rtd 08; PtO *Leeds* from 09. *8 Wayside Crescent, Harrogate HG2 8NJ* T: (01423) 885668 E: geoffrey168@btinternet.com

TURNER, Geoffrey James. b 46. St Deiniol's Hawarden 85. **d** 87 **p** 88. C Loughor *S & B* 87-89; C Swansea St Pet 89-90; R New Radnor and Llanfihangel Nantmelan etc 90-96; V Ystalyfera 96-07; RD Cwmtawe 00-06; V Loughor 07-13; rtd 13; PtO *S & B* from 13. *35 Tawe Park, Ystradgynlais, Swansea SA9 1GU* T: (01639) 841760
E: geoffrey.turner2@sky.com

✠**TURNER, The Rt Revd Geoffrey Martin.** b 34. Oak Hill Th Coll 60. **d** 63 **p** 64 **c** 94. C Tonbridge St Steph *Roch* 63-66;

C Heatherlands St Jo *Sarum* 66-69; V Derby St Pet 69-73; V Chadderton Ch Ch *Man* 73-79; R Bebington *Ches* 79-93; Hon Can Ches Cathl 89-93; RD Wirral N 89-93; Adn Ches 93-94; Suff Bp Stockport 94-00; rtd 00; PtO *Ches* from 00; Hon Asst Bp Ches from 02. *23 Lang Lane, West Kirby, Wirral CH48 5HG* T: 0151-625 8504

TURNER, Gerald Garth. b 38. Univ of Wales (Lamp) BA 61 St Edm Hall Ox BA 63 MA 67 Man Univ PhD 11. St Steph Ho Ox 63. **d** 65 **p** 66. C Drayton in Hales *Lich* 65-68; Chapl Prebendal Sch Chich 68-70; PV Chich Cathl 68-70; C Forest Row 70-72; V Hope *Derby* 72-78; Prec Man Cathl 78-86; Can Res Man Cathl 78-86; R Tattenhall and Handley *Ches* 86-04; rtd 04; PtO *S'well* from 04; *Ches* from 15. *75 London Road, Nantwich CW5 6LN* T: (01270) 749415
E: ggarthturner@hotmail.com

TURNER, Graham Colin. b 55. Bradf Univ BTech. Oak Hill Th Coll BA 81. **d** 81 **p** 82. C Upper Armley *Ripon* 81-86; V Bordesley Green *Birm* 86-05; AD Yardley and Bordesley 00-05; TR Macclesfield Team *Ches* 05-15; Chapl HM Pris Garth from 15. *HM Prison Garth, Ulnes Walton Lane, Leyland PR26 8NE* T: (01772) 443300
E: grahamcturner@hotmail.com

TURNER, Mrs Heather Winifred. b 43. Open Univ BA 08 Win Univ MA 13 SRN 65. Cant Sch of Min 89. **d** 90 **p** 94. Par Dn Orpington All SS *Roch* 90-93; Chapl to the Deaf 93-00; P-in-c Wrotham 95-01; TV E Dereham and Scarning *Nor* 01-02; rtd 02; PtO *Nor* 02-04; C Darsham *St E* 04-06; C Middleton cum Fordley and Theberton w Eastbridge 04-06; C Westleton w Dunwich 04-06; C Yoxford, Peasenhall and Sibton 04-06; C Blyth Valley 06-07; TV 07; PtO from 07; *Cov* from 08; Chapl Shakespeare Hospice from 14. *Shakespeare Hospice, Church Lane, Shottery, Stratford-upon-Avon CV37 9UL* T: (01789) 266852 E: revhwturner@gmail.com

TURNER, Henry John Mansfield. b 24. Magd Coll Cam BA 45 MA 48 BD 12 Man Univ PhD 85. Westcott Ho Cam 48. **d** 50 **p** 51. C Crosby *Linc* 50-52; C Chorlton upon Medlock *Man* 52-55; Inter-Colleg Sec SCM (Man) 52-55; C Leigh St Mary *Man* 55-57; V Rochdale Gd Shep 57-62; India 63-67; V Becontree St Geo *Chelmsf* 67-71; R Weeley 71-79; Chapl St Deiniol's Lib Hawarden 79-80; Sub-Warden 80-86; PtO *Chelmsf* from 86; Hon C St Botolph without Bishopgate *Lon* from 87. *Merrywood, 25 Fourth Avenue, Frinton-on-Sea CO13 9DU* T: (01255) 677554

TURNER, James Alfred. b 34. MCIPS 76. Ox Min Course 91. **d** 94 **p** 95. NSM Kidlington w Hampton Poyle *Ox* 94-06; PtO from 06. *11 St Mary's Close, Kidlington, Oxford OX5 2AY* T: (01865) 375562

TURNER, James Henry. b 51. NOC 99. **d** 02 **p** 03. NSM Middleton St Cross *Ripon* 02-13; NSM Beeston *Leeds* from 13. *38 Acre Crescent, Middleton, Leeds LS10 4DJ* T: 0113-277 2681 E: jameshpturner@aol.com

TURNER, Jane. *See* TURNER, Elizabeth Jane

TURNER, Jessica Mary. b 60. SS Coll Cam BA 81 PGCE 82. Trin Coll Bris 88. **d** 91 **p** 94. Par Dn Preston Em *Blackb* 91-94; C Bamber Bridge St Aid 94-95; Chapl Preston Acute Hosps NHS Trust 95-98; Chapl Blackpool Victoria Hosp NHS Trust 98-03; Chapl Blackpool, Fylde and Wyre Hosps NHS Trust 03-05; Hon Can Blackb Cathl 02-05; Chapl Ox Radcliffe Hosps NHS Trust 06-12; PtO *Ox* from 12. *33 Mayfield Road, Farmoor, Oxford OX2 9NY* T: (01865) 864435 M: 07966-016399
E: jessicatu@btinternet.com

TURNER, John. *See* TURNER, Henry John Mansfield

TURNER, John David Maurice. b 22. Keble Coll Ox BA 45 MA 48. Ripon Hall Ox 69. **d** 70 **p** 71. C Crowthorne *Ox* 70-73; V Cropredy w Gt Bourton 73-79; V Cropredy w Gt Bourton and Wardington 80-83; PtO 83-03; *Pet* 83-03; rtd 87. *16 Stuart Court, High Street, Kibworth, Leicester LE8 OLR* T: (01858) 881378

TURNER, John William. b 43. Sheff Univ BSc 73. Wycliffe Hall Ox 86. **d** 88 **p** 89. C Clayton *Bradf* 88-91; C Horton 91-92; V Bankfoot 92-01; V Holland-on-Sea *Chelmsf* 01-05; rtd 05. *20 Grantley Drive, Harrogate HG3 2ST* T: (01423) 545994
E: john.turner15@virgin.net

TURNER, Mrs Karen Lesley. b 48. ERMC. **d** 08 **p** 09. NSM Langelei *St Alb* 08-15; PtO 15; NSM S Mymms and Ridge from 15. *The Vicarage, 6 Hamilton Close, South Mimms, Potters Bar EN6 3PG* T: (01707) 658651 E: karenlfturner@icloud.com

TURNER, Canon Keith Howard. b 50. Southn Univ BA 71. Wycliffe Hall Ox 72. **d** 75 **p** 76. C Enfield Ch Ch Trent Park *Lon* 75-79; C Chilwell *S'well* 79-83; P-in-c Linby w Papplewick 83-90; R 90-15; Hon Can *S'well* Minster 02-13. *The Rectory, Main Street, Linby, Nottingham NG15 8AE* T: 0115-963 2346
E: k.h.turner@btopenworld.com

TURNER, Keith Stanley. b 51. ACIB 80. NTMTC 96. **d** 99 **p** 00. C S Hornchurch St Jo and St Matt *Chelmsf* 99-12; rtd 12; PtO *Chelmsf* from 12. *16 Wells Gardens, Rainham RM13 7LU* T: (01708) 554274 E: revkeitht@ntlworld.com

TURNER, Kevin Louis Sinclair. b 60. St Jo Coll Nottm BA 00. **d** 00 **p** 01. C Mount Pellon *Wakef* 00-03; P-in-c Sowerby 03-05; Evang Adv Croydon Area Miss Team *S'wark* 05-08. *Address temp unknown*

TURNER, Lawrence John. b 43. Kelham Th Coll 65. **d** 70 **p** 71. C Lower Gornal *Lich* 70-73; C Wednesbury St Paul Wood Green 73-74; C Porthill 75-77; C Wilton *York* 77-80; P-in-c 80-82; R Jersey St Martin *Win* 82-10; rtd 10; PtO *Win* 10-14; Chmn Miss to Seafarers from 82. *10 Le Clos de Gouray, Gorey Village Main Road, Grouville, Jersey JE3 9EP* T: (01534) 854294 E: ljturner@jerseymail.co.uk

TURNER, Leslie. b 29. NE Lon Poly BSc 87. Cranmer Hall Dur 50 St Aid Birkenhead 51. **d** 54 **p** 55. C Darwen St Cuth *Blackb* 54-56; C Haslingden w Grane and Stonefold 56-59; V Oswaldtwistle St Paul 59-65; Chapl Belmont and Henderson Hosp Sutton 65-71; St Ebba's Hosp Epsom 65-71; Qu Mary's Carshalton 67-71; Chapl Princess Marina Hosp Northn 71-87; Chapl St Crispin's Hosp Northn 71-87; Chapl Northn Gen Hosp 87-94; Chapl Manfield Hosp Northn 87-94; Chapl St Edm Hosp Northn 87-94; rtd 94; PtO *Pet* from 94. *20 Banbury Close, Northampton NN4 9UA* T: (01604) 769233

TURNER, Mrs Lorraine Elizabeth. b 67. Brunel Univ BSc 90 Open Univ MA 96. Cranmer Hall Dur 01. **d** 03 **p** 04. C Birchwood *Linc* 03-06; TV Louth from 06; P-in-c Legbourne and Wold Marsh from 06; Chapl United Lincs Hosps NHS Trust 07-13. *The Rectory, 37 Tinkle Street, Grimoldby, Louth LN11 8SW* T: (01507) 327735 *or* 327667 E: lorraine.t@which.net

TURNER, Mark. b 60. Aston Tr Scheme 87 Sarum & Wells Th Coll BTh 92. **d** 92 **p** 93. C New Sleaford *Linc* 92-94; C Bottesford and Muston *Leic* 94-98; C Harby, Long Clawson and Hose 94-98; C Barkestone w Plungar, Redmile and Stathern 94-98; P-in-c Thurnby Lodge 98-00; C Aylestone Park CD 00-03; P-in-c Areley Kings *Worc* 03-05; R from 05; RD Stourport 06-07 and from 13. *14 Dunley Road, Stourport-on-Severn DY13 0AX* T: (01299) 829557 E: revturner@tinyworld.co.uk

TURNER, Mark Roy James. b 79. All SS Cen for Miss & Min 13. **d** 15. NSM Burton and Shotwick *Ches* from 15. *20 The Birches, Neston CH64 3SB* T: 0151-353 8177 M: 07469-893264 E: ddowirral@yahoo.co.uk

TURNER, Martin John. b 34. Trin Hall Cam BA 55 MA 59. Cuddesdon Coll 58. **d** 60 **p** 61. C Rugby St Andr *Cov* 60-65; C Cov Cathl 65-68; USA 68-70; V Rushmere *St E* 70-82; V Monkwearmouth St Pet *Dur* 82-90; V Bathford *B & W* 90-99; rtd 99; PtO *B & W* 00-07; *Truro* from 97. *Hallane End, 4 The Terrace, Lostwithiel PL22 0DT* T: (01208) 871330 M: 07929-231167 E: turnerschemanoff@aol.com

TURNER, Mrs Maureen. b 55. Leeds Univ BA 78 MA 01. St Jo Coll Nottm 84. **d** 87 **p** 94. Par Dn Darlaston St Lawr *Lich* 87-91; C Stratford-on-Avon w Bishopton *Cov* 91-98; Chapl Myton Hamlet Hospice 98-01; NSM Leire w Ashby Parva and Dunton Bassett *Leic* 00-06; Chapl Team Ldr Univ Hosps Leic NHS Trust 01-07; Chapl Team Ldr Jersey Gp of Hosps from 07. *Chaplain's Office, General Hospital, Gloucester Street, St Helier, Jersey JE1 3QS* T: (01534) 622000

TURNER, Maurice. *See* TURNER, Charles Maurice Joseph

TURNER, Maurice William. b 27. Sarum Th Coll 53. **d** 56 **p** 57. C Thornhill *Wakef* 56-60; V Gawber 60-71; V Alverthorpe 71-74; V Shelton and Oxon *Lich* 74-81; V Leaton 81-82; P-in-c Battlefield w Albrighton 81-82; V Leaton and Albrighton w Battlefield 82-92; rtd 92; PtO *Lich* from 93; *Heref* from 96. *10 Melbourne Rise, Bicton Heath, Shrewsbury SY3 5DA* T: (01743) 352667

TURNER, Michael Andrew. b 34. K Coll Cam BA 59 MA 62. Cuddesdon Coll 59. **d** 61 **p** 62. C Luton St Andr *St Alb* 61-64; V 70-77; C-in-c Northolt St Jos *Lon* 64-70; PtO *St Alb* 77-93; Dep Hd and Chapl Greycoat Hosp Sch 86-93; P-in-c Shilling Okeford *Sarum* 93-99; Chapl Croft Ho Sch Shillingstone 93-99; rtd 99; PtO *Sarum* from 99; V of Close Sarum Cathl 02-07; Dioc Retirement Officer from 08. *12 Berkshire Road, Harnham, Salisbury SP2 8NY* T: (01722) 504000 E: sarum.turners@ntlworld.com

TURNER, Michael John Royce. b 43. St Jo Coll Dur BA 65. Chich Th Coll 65. **d** 67 **p** 68. C Hodge Hill *Birm* 67-71; C Eling, Testwood and Marchwood *Win* 71-72; TV 72-77; R Kirkwall *Ab* 77-85; R Drumlithie *Bre* from 85; R Drumtochty from 85; R Fasque from 85; R Laurencekirk from 85. *Beattie Lodge, Laurencekirk AB30 1HJ* T/F: (01561) 377380 E: mjrturner@btinternet.com

TURNER, Canon Nicholas Anthony. b 51. Clare Coll Cam BA 73 MA 77 Keble Coll Ox BA 77 MA 81. Ripon Coll Cuddesdon 76. **d** 78 **p** 79. C Stretford St Matt *Man* 78-80; Tutor St Steph Ho Ox 80-84; V Leeds Richmond Hill *Ripon* 84-91; Offg Chapl RAF and V Ascension Is 91-96; Can Th St Helena Cathl from 94; V Raynes Park St Sav *S'wark*

96-01; P-in-c Broughton, Marton and Thornton *Bradf* 01-02; R *Leeds* from 02. *The Rectory, 7 Roundell Drive, West Marton, Skipton BD23 3UL* T: (01282) 842332 E: nicholas.turner@bradford.anglican.org

TURNER (née SYMINGTON), Canon Patricia Ann. b 46. SRN 68 RMN 71 SCM 72. St Steph Ho Ox 82. **dss** 84 **d** 87. Buttershaw St Aid *Bradf* 84-87; TM Manningham 87-91; Ascension Is 91-96; Par Dn Raynes Park St Sav *S'wark* 96-01; Par Dn Broughton, Marton and Thornton *Leeds* from 01; RD Skipton from 05; Assoc Dioc Dir of Ords from 04; Hon Can Bradf Cathl from 09. *The Rectory, 7 Roundell Drive, West Marton, Skipton BD23 3UL* T: (01282) 842332 E: ann.turner@bradford.anglican.org

TURNER, Peter Carpenter. b 39. Oak Hill Th Coll 63. **d** 66 **p** 67. C Chadwell *Chelmsf* 66-69; C Braintree 69-73; R Fyfield 73-87; P-in-c Moreton 77-83; P-in-c Fyfield and Moreton w Bobbingworth 83-87; C-in-c Bobbingworth 82-83; P-in-c Willingale w Shellow and Berners Roding 84-87; V E Ham St Geo 87-04; rtd 04; PtO *Lon* from 05. *9 Llandovery House, Chipka Street, London E14 3LE* T: (020) 7987 5902 E: detox.uk@btinternet.com *or* petercturner@btinternet.com

TURNER, The Ven Peter Robin. b 42. CB 98 DL 07. St Luke's Coll Ex PGCE 70 Open Univ BA 79 Westmr Coll Ox MTh 96 AKC 65. St Boniface Warminster 65. **d** 66 **p** 67. C Crediton *Ex* 66-69; PtO 69-70; Chapl RAF 70-88; Asst Chapl-in-Chief RAF 88-95; Chapl-in-Chief RAF 95-98; QHC 92-98; Can and Preb Linc Cathl 95-98; Chapl Dulwich Coll 98-02; Bp's Dom Chapl *S'well* 02-07; Hon Can S'well Minster 02-12; Chapl for Sector Min 07-12; rtd 12. *12 Chimes Meadow, Southwell NG25 0GB* T: (01636) 812250 M: 07990-633137 E: pr.turner@lineone.net

TURNER, Philip. b 54. **d** 11 **p** 12. NSM Gt Sankey *Liv* 11-14; NSM Warrington W 14-15; Chapl Warrington and Halton Hosps NHS Foundn Trust from 14; NSM Gateacre *Liv* from 15. *147 Cradley, Widnes WA8 7PN* T: 0151-424 0037 E: birdcycle1954@sky.com

TURNER, Ms Philippa Anne. b 64. Trevelyan Coll Dur BA 86 Yale Univ MDiv 88. **d** 94 **p** 95. Chapl New York Hosp USA 91-95; Assoc P New York Ch of Heavenly Rest 95-08; Chapl R Veterinary Coll *Lon* from 08; Chapl R Free and Univ Coll Medical Sch from 08; PtO *St Alb* from 12. *15 Ormonde Mansions, 106A Southampton Row, London WC1B 4BP* T: (020) 7242 2574 *or* 7468 5145 M: 07525-234382 E: pturner@rvc.ac.uk

TURNER, Ricky Ronald. b 84. Middx Univ BA 05 Goldsmiths' Coll Lon PGCE 06. Qu Coll Birm 11. **d** 14 **p** 15. C Oxhey All SS *St Alb* from 14. *14 The Hoe, Watford WD19 5AY* E: rickyturner@ntlworld.com

TURNER, Canon Robert Edgar. b 20. TCD BA 42 MA 51. Linc Th Coll 44. **d** 45 **p** 46. C Kings Heath *Birm* 45-51; Min Can Belf Cathl 51-63; Dean of Res QUB 51-58; Bp's Dom Chapl *D & D* 56-67; I Belfast St Geo *Conn* 58-90; Can Belf Cathl 71-76; Preb Clonmethan St Patr Cathl Dublin 76-90; Dioc Registrar *Conn* 82-06; Prin Registrar from 06; rtd 90. *19 Cricklewood Park, Belfast BT9 5GU* T: (028) 9066 3214 F: 9058 6843 E: returner@ntlworld.com *or* registrar@connor.anglican.org

TURNER, Canon Roger Dyke. b 39. Trin Coll Bris 79. **d** 81 **p** 82. C Clevedon St Andr and Ch Ch *B & W* 81-85; R Freshford, Limpley Stoke and Hinton Charterhouse 85-88; V Kenilworth St Jo *Cov* 88-04; RD Kenilworth 90-98; Hon Can Cov Cathl 00-04; rtd 04; PtO *Birm* 04-05; *Cov* from 04; P-in-c Barston *Birm* 05-11; PtO from 12. *15 Caesar Road, Kenilworth CV8 1DL* T: (01926) 734330

TURNER, Roy. *See* TURNER, Alan Roy

TURNER, Ms Ruth Carpenter. b 63. Anglia Ruskin Univ BA 09 LLCM 83 GLCM 84. Ridley Hall Cam 07. **d** 09 **p** 10. C Brampton St Thos *Derby* 09-13; TV Dronfield w Holmesfield from 13. *11 Rothay Close, Dronfield Woodhouse, Dronfield S18 8PR* T: (01246) 416893 M: 07855-714538 E: ruthturner2632@btinternet.com

TURNER, St John Alwin. b 31. Dur Univ BA 57 MA 61. Cranmer Hall Dur. **d** 59 **p** 60. C W Hartlepool St Paul *Dur* 59-62; C S Shore H Trin *Blackb* 62-65; V Huncoat 65-67; Org Sec CMS Ripon and York 67-72; V Harrogate St Mark *Ripon* 72-94; rtd 96; PtO *Linc* from 01. *2 The Tilney, Whaplode, Spalding PE12 6UW* T: (01406) 371390

TURNER, Stewart Gordon. b 54. Ex Univ BTh 06. SWMTC 03. **d** 06 **p** 07. NSM Falmouth All SS *Truro* 06-09; C Mawnan 09-13; P-in-c from 13; C Budock 09-13; P-in-c Constantine from 11. *The Vicarage, Chalbury Heights Brill, Constantine, Falmouth TR11 5UR* T: (01326) 340259 E: stewart.turner@tiscali.co.uk

TURNER, Susan Mary. b 58. Man Univ BA 89. NOC 89. **d** 92 **p** 94. NSM Balderstone *Man* 92-93; NSM E Crompton 93-94; Hon C 94-96; Chapl Man Coll of Arts and Tech 92-96; Asst

Chapl S Man Univ Hosps NHS Trust 96-97; Chapl Burnley Health Care NHS Trust 97-03; Chapl Cen Man/Man Children's Univ Hosp NHS Trust 02-12; rtd 12; PtO *Man* from 12. *St Mark's Rectory, Walkden Road, Worsley, Manchester M28 1UY* T: 0161-799 6082

TURNER, Sylvia Jean. b 46. Lon Univ 72 Open Univ BA 77. Westcott Ho Cam 93. **d** 95 **p** 96. C Whitstable *Cant* 95-99; R Wigmore Abbey *Heref* 99-09; P-in-c Pontesbury I and II 09-11; rtd 11. *Wheelwrights, Witton, Ludlow SY8 3DB* T: (01584) 890586 E: sylvia.turner@virgin.net

TURNER, Tina. b 60. St Jo Coll Nottm BA 02. **d** 02 **p** 03. C Halifax All So and St Aug *Wakef* 02-05; C S Beddington and Roundshaw *S'wark* 05-06; TV Warlingham w Chelsham and Farleigh 06-08. *Address temp unknown*

TURNER, Valerie Kay. b 50. SS Paul & Mary Coll Cheltenham BEd 72. WMMTC 97 Wycliffe Hall Ox 99. **d** 00 **p** 01. C Cheltenham St Luke and St Jo *Glouc* 00-04; P-in-c Forest of Dean Ch Ch w English Bicknor 04-12; P-in-c Lydbrook 04-05; rtd 12; PtO *Heref* from 12. *2 River Meadows, Hereford HR1 1TB* T: (01432) 273697 E: valmark@btinternet.com

TURNER, Vivien. b 53. **d** 13. NSM Banstead *Guildf* from 13. *10 Monks Road, Banstead SM7 2EP* T: (01737) 352060 E: vturner@waitrose.com

TURNER-CALLIS, Mrs Gillian Ruth. b 79. Aber Univ BD 03. Wycliffe Hall Ox MTh 05. **d** 05 **p** 06. C Shepshed and Oaks in Charnwood *Leic* 05-08; TR Kegworth, Hathern, Long Whatton, Diseworth etc 08-15; R W Hallam and Mapperley w Stanley *Derby* from 15. *The Rectory, The Village, West Hallam, Ilkeston DE7 6GR* T: 0115-944 5784 M: 07838-881307 E: gill@thets.demon.co.uk

TURNER-LOISEL, Mrs Elizabeth Anne. b 57. Lanc Univ BA 79 MA 80 York Univ PGCE 81. EMMTC 96. **d** 99 **p** 00. Chapl Nat Sch Hucknall 99-04; P-in-c Annesley w Newstead *S'well* 04-11; V 11-14; Hon Can S'well Minster 13-14; V Hatfield *Sheff* from 14; AD Snaith and Hatfield from 14. *The Vicarage, 2 Vicarage Close, Hatfield, Doncaster DN7 6HN* T: (01302) 459110 E: revd.liz@gmail.com

TURNHAM, Mrs Dominique Emma. b 90. Homerton Coll Cam BA 11 MA 15. St Steph Ho Ox 13. **d** 15. C Dereham and Distr *Nor* from 15. *15 George Eliot Way, Dereham NR19 1EX* M: 07788-278684 E: dominiqueturnham@gmail.com

TURNOCK, Geoffrey. b 38. Leeds Univ BSc 61 PhD 64 MSOSc. EMMTC 84. **d** 87 **p** 88. NSM Oadby *Leic* 87-00; NSM Okeford *Sarum* 00-04; PtO from 04. *10 Billingsmoor Lane, Poundbury, Dorchester DT1 3WT* T: (01305) 757177 E: gturnock384@btinternet.com

TURP, Paul Robert. b 48. Oak Hill Th Coll BA 79. **d** 79 **p** 80. C Southall Green St Jo *Lon* 79-83; V Shoreditch St Leon w St Mich 83-88 and from 00; TR Shoreditch St Leon and Hoxton St Jo 88-00. *The Vicarage, 36 Hoxton Square, London N1 6NN* T: (020) 7739 2063 E: paul@shoreditch0.demon.co.uk

TURPIN, Christine Lesley. b 63. Westcott Ho Cam. **d** 09 **p** 10. C Bredon w Bredon's Norton *Worc* 09-12; P-in-c Worc St Wulstan 12-14. *Address temp unknown*

TURPIN, Canon John Richard. b 41. St D Coll Lamp BA 63 Magd Coll Cam BA 65 MA 70. Cuddesdon Coll 65. **d** 66 **p** 67. C Tadley St Pet *Win* 66-71; V Southampton Thornhill St Chris 71-85; V Ringwood 85-10; Hon Can Win Cathl 99-10; rtd 10; PtO *Win* from 10. *111 Beaufort Road, Bournemouth BH6 5AU* T: (01202) 421321 E: john.turpin4@btinternet.com

TURPIN, Raymond Gerald. b 35. **d** 97 **p** 98. OLM Brockley Hill St Sav *S'wark* 97-05; PtO from 05; Retirement Officer Woolwich Area from 08. *60 Bankhurst Road, London SE6 4XN* T: (020) 8690 6877 *or* 8311 2000 E: rayturpin@talktalk.net

TURRELL, Peter Charles Morphett. b 47. **d** 01 **p** 02. NSM Carshalton Beeches *S'wark* 01-15; PtO from 15. *62 Stanley Park Road, Carshalton SM5 3HW* T: (020) 8669 0318 E: peterturrell@btinternet.com

TURRELL, Stephen John. b 35. S'wark Ord Course. **d** 83 **p** 84. NSM W Wickham St Jo *Cant* 83-84; NSM Addington *S'wark* 85-92; NSM Blendworth w Chalton w Idsworth *Portsm* 92-97; PtO 97-01; NSM Storrington *Chich* 01-06; rtd 06. *29 Timberlands, Storrington, Pulborough RH20 3NF* T: (01903) 741272

TURTON, Douglas Walter. b 38. Kent Univ BA 77 Surrey Univ MSc 90 Univ of Wales (Ban) DPhil 04. Oak Hill Th Coll 77. **d** 78 **p** 79. C Cant St Mary Bredin 78-80; P-in-c Thornton Heath St Paul 80-81; V 81-84; V *S'wark* 85-91; R Eastling w Ospringe and Stalisfield w Otterden *Cant* 91-00; rtd 00; PtO *Cant* from 14. *16 Weatherall Close, Dunkirk, Faversham ME13 9UL* T: (01227) 752244

TURTON, Neil Christopher. b 45. Wycliffe Hall Ox 77. **d** 79 **p** 80. C Guildf Ch Ch 79-83; C Godalming 83-86; V Wyke 86-92; R Frimley 92-02; RD Surrey Heath 97-02; V Bay Head All SS USA 02-14. *719 Burnt Tavern Road, Point Pleasant NJ 08742-4022, USA* E: neilturton@comcast.net

TURVILLE, Mrs Janet Elizabeth. b 59. Matlock Coll of Educn BEd 82. Ripon Coll Cuddesdon 11. **d** 12 **p** 13. C Wirksworth *Derby* from 12. *57 Yokecliffe Drive, Wirksworth, Matlock DE4 4PF* T: (01629) 820049 M: 07963-959541 E: janetturville@hotmail.co.uk *or* janet.turville@btinternet.com

TUSCHLING, Ruth Mary Magdalen. b 65. Freiburg Univ MA 94 CCC Cam PhD 04. Westcott Ho Cam BA 97. **d** 98 **p** 99. C Hampstead St Jo *Lon* 98-01; PtO *Ely* 02-04; OSB 04-08; Warden Offa Retreat Ho and Dioc Spirituality Adv *Cov* 08-12; Dioc Spirituality Adv *Portsm* from 12. *50 Penny Street, Portsmouth PO1 2NL* T: (023) 9281 5044 E: florinequals@googlemail.com

✠**TUSTIN, The Rt Revd David.** b 35. Magd Coll Cam BA 57 MA 61 Lambeth DD 98. Cuddesdon Coll 58. **d** 60 **p** 61 **c** 79. C Stafford St Mary *Lich* 60-63; C St Dunstan in the West *Lon* 63-67; Asst Gen Sec C of E Coun on Foreign Relns 63-67; V Wednesbury St Paul Wood Green *Lich* 67-71; V Tettenhall Regis 71-79; RD Trysull 76-79; Suff Bp Grimsby *Linc* 79-00; Can and Preb Linc Cathl 79-00; rtd 00; Hon Asst Bp Linc from 01. *The Ashes, Tunnel Road, Wrawby, Brigg DN20 8SF* T/F: (01652) 655584 E: tustindavid@hotmail.com

TUTTON, Canon John Knight. b 30. Man Univ BSc 51. Ripon Hall Ox 53. **d** 55 **p** 56. C Tonge w Alkrington *Man* 55-57; C Bushbury *Lich* 57-59; R Blackley St Andr *Man* 59-67; R Denton Ch Ch 67-95; Hon Can Man Cathl 90-95; rtd 95; Hon C Exminster and Kenn *Ex* 96-01; PtO from 01. *2 Hescane Park, Cheriton Bishop, Exeter EX6 6JP* T: (01647) 24651 E: johnktutton@onetel.com

✠**TUTU, The Most Revd Desmond Mpilo.** b 31. UNISA BA K Coll Lon BD MTh FKC 78. St Pet Rosettenville LTh. **d** 60 **p** 61 **c** 76. S Africa 60-62; C Golders Green St Alb *Lon* 62-65; C Bletchingley *S'wark* 65-66; S Africa 67-70; Lesotho 70-72; Assoc Dir Th Educn Fund WCC 72-75; C Lee St Aug *S'wark* 72-75; Dean Johannesburg 75-76; Bp Lesotho 76-78; Asst Bp Johannesburg 78-85; Bp Johannesburg 85-86; Abp Cape Town 86-96; rtd 96. *PO Box 1092, Milnerton, 7435 South Africa* T: (0027) (21) 552 7524 F: 552 7529 E: info@tutu.org.za

TWADDELL, Canon William Reginald. b 33. TCD 61. **d** 62 **p** 63. C Belfast Whiterock *Conn* 62-65; I Loughgilly w Clare *Arm* 65-71; I Milltown 71-84; I Portadown St Mark 84-01; Preb Arm Cathl 88-96; Treas Arm Cathl 96-98; Prec Arm Cathl 98-01; rtd 01. *Tea Cottage, 19 Birches Road, Portadown BT62 1LS* T: (028) 3885 2520 E: reggie.twaddell@hotmail.co.uk

TWEDDLE, Christopher Noel. b 66. Auckland Univ BA 93. St Jo Coll Auckland. **d** 92 **p** 93. New Zealand 92-97; C Maindee Newport *Mon* 97-98; P-in-c Discovery Bay Hong Kong 98-00; V New Lynn New Zealand 00-05; Chapl St Pet Sch Cam from 06. *St Peter's School, Private Bag 884, Cambridge, New Zealand* T: (0064) (7) 827 9888 M: 27-454 1306 E: chaplain@stpeters.school.nz

TWEDDLE, David William Joseph. b 28. Dur Univ BSc 50 Open Univ BA 97 ATCL 56. Wycliffe Hall Ox 54. **d** 56 **p** 57. C Darlington H Trin *Dur* 56-60; P-in-c Prestonpans *Edin* 60-63; PV Linc Cathl 63-65; C Pet St Jo 65-71; Hon Min Can Pet Cathl 68-93; V Southwick w Glapthorn 71-83; P-in-c Benefield 80-83; R Benefield and Southwick w Glapthorn 83-93; RD Oundle 84-89; rtd 94; PtO *Ely* 94-07. *6 Barton Square, Ely CB7 4DF* T: (01353) 614393

TWEED, Andrew. b 48. Univ of Wales (Cardiff) BA 69 Trin Coll Carmarthen MA 97. St Deiniol's Hawarden. **d** 81 **p** 84. NSM Llandrindod w Cefnllys *S & B* 81-86; NSM Llandrindod w Cefnllys and Disserth from 87. *Gwenallt, Wellington Road, Llandrindod Wells LD1 5NB* T: (01597) 823671 E: andrewtweed1@aol.com

TWEEDIE-SMITH, Ian David. b 60. Newc Univ BA 83. Wycliffe Hall Ox 83. **d** 85 **p** 86. C Hatcham St Jas *S'wark* 85-89; C Bury St Edmunds St Mary *St E* 89-02; TV Woking St Pet *Guildf* 02-12; P-in-c Purton *Bris* 12-14; V from 14. *The Vicarage, 2 Kingsacre, Hyde Lane, Purton, Swindon SN5 4DU* T: (01793) 770077 E: vicarage@stmaryspurton.org.uk

TWEEDY, Andrew Cyril Mark. b 61. Man Univ BA(Econ) 81. SAOMC 98. **d** 01 **p** 02. C Carterton Ox 01-03; C Brize Norton and Carterton 03-04; V Bromham w Oakley and Stagsden St Alb 04-08; Chapl Barcelona *Eur* 08-14; R Lower Windrush Ox from 14. *The Rectory, Main Road, Stanton Harcourt, Witney OX29 5RP* E: revdrew61@gmail.com

TWEEDY, Richard Walpole. b 67. **d** 12 **p** 13. C Worcs W *Worc* from 12. *Wichenford Oak, Wichenford, Worcester WR6 6YY* T: (01886) 888544

TWIDELL, Canon William James. b 30. St Mich Coll Llan 58. **d** 60 **p** 61. C Tonge w Alkrington *Man* 60-63; C High Wycombe All SS *Ox* 63-65; P-in-c Elkesley w Bothamsall *S'well* 65-66; V Bury St Thos *Man* 66-72; V Daisy Hill 72-84; R Flixton St Mich 84-00; AD Stretford 88-98; Hon Can Man

Cathl 97-00; rtd 00; PtO *Man* from 00; *Ches* from 00. *11 Mercer Way, Nantwich CW5 5YD* T: (01270) 620328

TWIGG, Mrs Allison Latka. b 70. Nene Coll Northn BEd 93. Ripon Coll Cuddesdon 13. **d** 15. C Weston Favell *Pet* from 15. *5 Kestrel Close, Weston Favell, Northampton NN3 3JG* M: 07759-835011 E: allisontwigg@sky.com

TWINING, Kathryn. b 60. Westcott Ho Cam. **d** 07 **p** 08. C Greenwich St Alfege *S'wark* 07-09; C New Addington 09-11; PtO *Guildf* from 14. *The Small House, Summersbury Hall, Summersbury Drive, Shalford, Guildford GU4 8JJ* M: 07763-739007 E: mk.twining@cantab.net

TWINLEY, David Alan. b 70. Ox Univ BTh 00 Heythrop Coll Lon MA 10. St Steph Ho Ox 97. **d** 00 **p** 01. C Saffron Walden w Wendens Ambo, Littlebury etc *Chelmsf* 00-03; V Bury w Houghton and Coldwaltham and Hardham *Chich* from 03; RD Petworth from 10. *The Vicarage, Church Lane, Bury, Pulborough RH20 1PB* T: (01798) 839057 E: frdavid@twinley.me.uk

TWISLETON, John Fiennes. b 48. St Jo Coll Ox BA 69 MA 73 DPhil 73. Coll of Resurr Mirfield 73. **d** 76 **p** 77. C New Bentley *Sheff* 76-79; P-in-c Moorends 79-80; V 80-86; USPG 86-90; Prin Alan Knight Tr Cen Guyana 87-90; V Holbrooks *Cov* 90-96; Edmonton Area Missr *Lon* 96-01; Dioc Adv for Miss and Renewal *Chich* 01-09; C Haywards Heath St Rich 01-09; R Horsted Keynes from 09. *The Rectory, Station Road, Horsted Keynes, Haywards Heath RH17 7ED* T: (01825) 790317 E: john@twisleton.co.uk

TWISLETON, Peter. b 50. Linc Th Coll. **d** 84 **p** 85. C Bodmin w Lanhydrock and Lanivet *Truro* 84-87; C Par 87-90; R St Breoke and Egloshayle 90-93; R Bude Haven and Marhamchurch 93-97; V Horbury w Horbury Bridge *Wakef* 98-07; P-in-c Seaham Harbour and Dawdon *Dur* 07; V from 08. *The Vicarage, Maureen Terrace, Seaham SR7 7SN* T: 0191-581 3385

TWISS, Dorothy Elizabeth. Gilmore Ho 68 Linc Th Coll 70. **d** 87 **p** 94. Chapl Asst RAF 78-91; TV Pewsey *Sarum* 91-95; Chapl HM Pris Drake Hall 95-01; Chapl HM Pris Ford 01-03; rtd 03; PtO *Portsm* from 05. *41 Rosecott, Havant Road, Horndean, Waterlooville PO8 0XA* M: 07929-650284 E: dorothy.twiss311@btinternet.com

TWITCHEN, Ruth Kathleen Frances. *See* BUSHYAGER, Ruth Kathleen Frances

TWITTY, Miss Rosamond Jane. b 54. Univ of Wales (Ban) BSc 75 CertEd 76. Trin Coll Bris BA 89. **d** 90 **p** 94. Par Dn Lt Thurrock St Jo *Chelmsf* 90-94; C 94-95; C Upper Armley *Ripon* 95-08; TV Langport Area *B & W* 08-14; C from 14. *The Vicarage, 1 New Street, Long Sutton, Langport TA10 9JW* T: (01458) 241260 E: jane.twitty_team.langport@btinternet.com

TWOHIG, Brian Robert. b 48. La Trobe Univ Vic BA 77 PhD 86. St Mich Th Coll Crafers 70. **d** 72 **p** 73. Australia 72-78 and 80-82; C Leatherhead *Guildf* 78-80; TV New Windsor *Ox* 82-92; V Sheff St Cuth 92-97; rtd 97; PtO *Chich* from 99. *26A Bloomsbury Street, Brighton BN2 1HQ* T: (01273) 270481

TWOMEY, David James Benedict. b 87. Sheff Univ BSc 08 Northumbria Univ PGCE 09. **d** 14 **p** 15. C Cullercoats St Geo *Newc* from 14. *2 Seacombe Avenue, North Shields NE30 3DR* E: david.twomey@ymail.com

TWOMEY, Canon Jeremiah Francis (Derry). b 50. Man Poly BA 83 Univ of Wales (Ban) PGCE 85. NEOC 92. **d** 94 **p** 95. C Beverley St Nic *York* 94-96; V Anlaby Common St Mark 96-99; Ind Chapl *Newc* 99-05; V Bedlington from 05; P-in-c Cambois and Sleekburn from 13; AD Bedlington 09-12; Hon Can Newc Cathl from 15. *The Vicarage, 21 Church Lane, Bedlington NE22 5EL* T: (01670) 829220 E: derrytwomey@aol.com

TWOMEY, Jeremiah Thomas Paul. b 46. CITC 87. **d** 87 **p** 88. C Derryloran *Arm* 87-90; I Brackaville w Donaghendry and Ballyclog 90-97; I Mohill w Farnaught, Aughavas, Oughteragh etc *K, E & A* 97-00; Bp's C Belfast Whiterock *Conn* 00-08. *Cornerstone House, 443-445 Springfield Road, Belfast BT12 7DL* E: ptwomey@esatclear.ie

TWYFORD, Canon Arthur Russell. b 36. ALCD 60. **d** 60 **p** 61. C Speke All SS *Liv* 60-64; R Maids Moreton w Foxcote *Ox* 64-72; Asst Dioc Youth Officer 64-70; P-in-c Lillingstone Dayrell w Lillingstone Lovell 70-72; V Desborough *Pet* 72-88; P-in-c Brampton Ash w Dingley 73-77; P-in-c Braybrook 73-77; R Brampton Ash w Dingley and Braybrooke 77-88; RD Kettering 79-87; Can Pet Cathl 81-95; R Stanwick w Hargrave 88-95; rtd 95; PtO *Pet* 95-07. *chemin des Fées, 46250 Cazals, France* T: (0033) 5 65 21 66 93 E: artwyford@aol.com

TWYNAM, Mrs Susan Elizabeth. b 59. Bath Coll of HE BEd 81. SEITE 06. **d** 09 **p** 10. NSM Sidcup St Jo *Roch* 09-13; NSM Bexleyheath Ch Ch from 13. *6 Williams Way, Dartford DA2 7WF* T: (01322) 559501 E: susantwynam@btconnect.com

TYDEMAN, Rosemary. *See* WILLIAMS, Rosemary

TYE, Dominic Geoffrey Bernard. b 43. Lanc Univ BA 70 PhD 75. Kelham Th Coll 62. **d** 67 **p** 68. SSM 66-78; C Lancaster St Mary *Blackb* 67-70; Lect Kelham Th Coll 70-73; Chapl Woden Hosp Australia 75-76; Teacher Lancaster 78-84; Hd Sixth Form Fleetwood Sch 84-87; Dep Hd Lancaster Girls Gr Sch 87-90; Hd Thorncliffe Sch Barrow-in-Furness 90-97; Co-ord Cen Educn Leadership Man Univ 98-02; rtd 08. *St Cland, Stockley Lane, Glapwell, Chesterfield S44 5NA* T: (01246) 769680 E: member@dtye.freeserve.co.uk

TYE, Eric John. b 37. St Alb Minl Tr Scheme 78. **d** 81 **p** 82. NSM Rushden St Mary w Newton Bromswold *Pet* 81-07; PtO from 07. *29 Kingsmead Park, Bedford Road, Rushden NN10 0NF* T: (01933) 353274 E: johnchristye@tiscali.co.uk

TYE, John Raymond. b 31. Lambeth STh 64 Linc Th Coll 66. **d** 68 **p** 69. C Crewe St Mich *Ches* 68-71; C Wednesfield St Thos *Lich* 71-76; P-in-c Petton w Cockshutt 76-79; P-in-c Hordley 79; P-in-c Weston Lullingfield 79; R Petton w Cockshutt and Weston Lullingfield etc 79-81; V Hadley 81-84; R Ightfield w Calverhall 84-89; V Ash 84-89; R Calton, Cauldon, Grindon and Waterfall 89-96; RD Alstonfield 95-96; rtd 96; PtO *Lich* 05-14. *38 Aston Street, Wem, Shrewsbury SY4 5AU* T: (01939) 236218

TYERS, Canon John Haydn. b 31. Lon Univ BSc 51 Open Univ BA 00. Ridley Hall Cam 53. **d** 55 **p** 56. C Nuneaton St Nic *Cov* 55-58; C Rugby St Andr 58-62; V Cov St Anne 62-70; TR Cov E 70-71; V Keresley and Coundon 71-78; V Atherstone 78-85; P-in-c Pleshey *Chelmsf* 85-91; Warden Pleshey Retreat Ho 85-91; Hon Can Chelmsf Cathl 86-91; P-in-c Ash *Lich* 91-96; P-in-c Ightfield w Calverhall 91-96; rtd 96; PtO *Heref* 97-08; *Leic* 09-14. *30 Stuart Court, High Street, Kibworth, Leicester LE8 0LR* T: 0116-279 3093

TYERS, Philip Nicolas. b 56. St Jo Coll Nottm BTh 84. **d** 84 **p** 85. C Rugby St Matt *Cov* 84-88; TV Cov E 88-95; P-in-c Preston St Matt *Blackb* 95-96; TR Preston Risen Lord 96-06; Co-ord Chapl HM Pris Leeds 06-07; Co-ord Chapl HM Pris Wymott from 07. *HM Prison Wymott, Ulnes Walton Lane, Leyland PR26 8LW* T: (01772) 442000 E: philip.tyers@hmps.gsi.gov.uk

TYLDESLEY, Mrs Vera. b 47. Man Coll of Educn BEd 80. **d** 98 **p** 99. OLM Pendlebury St Jo *Man* from 98. *7 Kingsway, Swinton, Manchester M27 4JU* T: 0161-736 3845

TYLER, Canon Alan William. b 60. Ridley Hall Cam 84. **d** 86 **p** 87. C Bedwellty *Mon* 86-89; C St Mellons and Michaelston-y-Fedw 89-92; V Abersychan and Garndiffaith 92-97; Chapl Glan Hafren NHS Trust 97-99; Sen Chapl Gwent Healthcare NHS Trust from 99; Can St Woolos Cathl from 08. *The Royal Gwent Hospital, Cardiff Road, Newport NP20 2UB* T: (01633) 234263 *or* 871457 E: alan.tyler@gwent.wales.nhs.uk

TYLER, Alison Ruth. b 51. Keele Univ BA 74 CQSW 78. S'wark Ord Course 93. **d** 95 **p** 96. NSM Hatcham St Cath *S'wark* 95-99; Dep Chapl HM Pris Brixton 99-02; Chapl HM Pris Wormwood Scrubs 02-07; Learning and Development Manager HM Pris Service Chapl from 07; Hon Chapl S'wark Cathl from 06; PtO from 06; *Cov* from 08. *Chaplaincy HQ, Post Point 3.08, 3rd Floor Red Zone, Clive House, 70 Petty France, London SW1H 9HD* T: 03000-475193 *or* (020) 7207 0756 F: 03000-476822/3 E: alison.tyler01@hmps.gsi.gov.uk *or* ar.tyler@ntlworld.com

TYLER, Andrew. b 57. Univ of Wales (Lamp) BA 79 Warw Univ MA 80 Man Univ BD 83. Coll of Resurr Mirfield 83. **d** 87 **p** 88. C Glen Parva and S Wigston *Leic* 87-90; C Didcot All SS *Ox* 90-92; Asst Chapl Chu Hosp Ox 92-93; NSM Caversham St Andr Ox 93-97; Co-ord Tr Portfolio (Berks) 96-97; P-in-c Nor St Giles 97-99; P-in-c Nor St Mary Magd w St Jas 99-00; V 00-08; Hon C Eaton Ch Ch 09-12; C Cawston w Booton and Brandiston etc 12-15; PtO from 15. *Address withheld by request* M: 07768-581679 E: xatyler@aol.com

TYLER, Brian Sidney. b 32. MIPI 79. Chich Th Coll 62. **d** 64 **p** 65. C Brighton St Mich *Chich* 64-69; C-in-c Southwick St Pet 69-75; PtO 80; NSM Brighton Resurr 93-94; Chapl St Dunstan's Hosp Brighton 93-95; C Brighton St Matthias *Chich* 95-02; Hon C 02-05; rtd 02; PtO *Chich* from 05. *318 Ditchling Road, Brighton BN1 6JG* T: (01273) 559292

TYLER, Charles Stewart. **d** 14 **p** 15. OLM Mease Valley *Lich* from 14. *Orchard House, 4 Woodland View, Chilcote, Swadlincote DE12 8DP* T: (01827) 373248 E: stewart.tyler6@btinternet.com

TYLER, David Stuart. b 69. Hull Univ BSc 91 ACA 94. Wycliffe Hall Ox 01. **d** 03 **p** 04. C Ashby-de-la-Zouch St Helen w Coleorton *Leic* 03-05; C Ashby-de-la-Zouch and Breedon on the Hill 05-07; P-in-c Hanborough and Freeland *Ox* 07-11; R from 11; AD Woodstock from 12. *The Rectory, Swan Lane, Long Hanborough, Witney OX29 8BT* T: (01993) 881270 E: revdavidtyler@googlemail.com

TYLER (née FOSTER), Mrs Frances Elizabeth. b 55. Linc Th Coll 81. **dss** 84 **d** 87 **p** 94. Hampton All SS *Lon* 84-87; Par Dn Brentford 87-91; NSM Walsgrave on Sowe *Cov* from 91; Dioc Adv for Women's Min 97-05; Chapl S Warks Gen Hosps NHS Trust from 08. *The Vicarage, 4 Farber Road, Coventry CV2 2BG* T: (024) 7661 5152 E: revftyler@aol.com

TYLER, Mrs Gaynor. b 46. Univ of Wales (Abth) BA 68. S'wark Ord Course 87. **d** 90 **p** 94. NSM Reigate St Luke S Park *S'wark* 90-97; Deanery NSM Maelienydd *S & B* 97-04; NSM Cwmdauddwr w St Harmon and Llanwrthwl 04-05; NSM Llanwrthwl w St Harmon, Rhayader, Nantmel etc 05-06; PtO from 06. *Dyffryn Farm, Llanwrthwl, Llandrindod Wells LD1 6NU* T: (01597) 811017

TYLER, John Thorne. b 46. Selw Coll Cam BA 68 MA 71. Sarum & Wells Th Coll 70. **d** 72 **p** 73. C Frome St Jo *B & W* 72-74; Chapl Richard Huish Coll Taunton 74-93; Hon C Stoke St Gregory w Burrowbridge and Lyng *B & W* 77-93; P-in-c Shepton Beauchamp w Barrington, Stocklinch etc 93-94; TV Ilminster and Distr 94-98; rtd 99; Hon C Quantock Towers *B & W* 99-01; P-in-c Stogursey w Fiddington 01-06; PtO 06-09; C Chard St Mary w Combe St Nicholas, Wambrook etc 09-10; PtO from 11. *24 Ganges Close, Fivehead, Taunton TA3 6PG* T: (01460) 281574 E: tyleruk@tiscali.co.uk

TYLER, Malcolm. b 56. Kent Univ BSc 77 Cam Univ BA 84. Ridley Hall Cam 82. **d** 85 **p** 86. C Twickenham St Mary *Lon* 85-88; C Acton St Mary 88-91; V Walsgrave on Sowe *Cov* from 91; AD Cov E 07-14. *The Vicarage, 4 Farber Road, Coventry CV2 2BG* T: (024) 7661 5152 *or* 7661 8845 E: stmaryssowe@aol.com

TYLER, Paul Graham Edward. b 58. Cranmer Hall Dur. **d** 83 **p** 84. C Stranton *Dur* 83-86; C Collierley w Annfield Plain 86-89; V Esh and Hamsteels 89-92; Chapl HM Pris Frankland from 09. *HM Prison Frankland, Brasside, Durham DH1 5YD* T: 0191-332 3000

TYLER, Samuel John. b 32. Lon Univ BD 57. Oak Hill Th Coll 57. **d** 58 **p** 59. C W Ham All SS *Chelmsf* 58-61; V Berechurch 61-64; R Aythorpe w High and Leaden Roding 64-72; PtO 73-74; P-in-c Gt Ilford St Jo 74-76; V 76-92; rtd 92. *85 Glynde Way, Southend-on-Sea SS2 4TT* T: (01702) 580503

TYLER, Stewart. *See* TYLER, Charles Stewart

TYLER (née WAITE), Mrs Sheila Margaret. b 25. SRN 47. Trin Coll Bris 71. **dss** 79 **d** 87 **p** 94. Hon Par Dn Henleaze *Bris* 87-94; Hon C 94-95; Chapl Stoke Park and Purdown Hosps Stapleton 88-90; PtO *B & W* 95-00; *Bris* 95-08; *Chich* 01-02. *6 Gracey Court, Woodland Road, Broadclyst, Exeter EX5 3GA* T: (01392) 462872

TYNDALL, Daniel Frank. b 61. Aston Tr Scheme 90 Sarum & Wells Th Coll BTh 93. **d** 93 **p** 94. C Wolverhampton *Lich* 93-96; C Bris St Mary Redcliffe w Temple etc 96-01; V Earley St Nic *Ox* 01-08; P-in-c Caversham St Pet and Mapledurham 08-10; P-in-c Caversham St Jo 08-10; R Caversham Thameside and Mapledurham 10-13; V Bris St Mary Redcliffe w Temple etc from 13. *The Vicarage, 10 Redcliffe Parade West, Bristol BS1 6SP* T: 0117-929 1962 E: dftyndall@gmail.com

TYNDALL, Mrs Elizabeth Mary. b 30. St Andr Univ MA 51 Hughes Hall Cam CertEd 52. Qu Coll Birm 81. **dss** 83 **d** 87 **p** 94. Rugby *Cov* 83-87; Par Dn Feltham *Lon* 87-91; rtd 92; NSM Vale of White Horse Deanery *Ox* 93-03. *c/o The Revd D F Tyndall, 10 Redcliffe Parade West, Bristol BS1 6SP*

TYNDALL, Jeremy Hamilton. b 55. Birm Univ MPhil 01. St Jo Coll Nottm BTh 81 LTh 81. **d** 81 **p** 82. C Oakwood St Thos *Lon* 81-84; C Upper Holloway St Pet w St Jo 84-87; TV Halewood *Liv* 87-96; P-in-c Yardley St Edburgha *Birm* 96-99; V 99-01; R Eugene St Thos USA 01-08; Dean Den Convocation 06-08; TR Cove St Jo *Guildf* from 08. *The Rectory, 55 Cove Road, Farnborough GU14 0EX* T: (01252) 544544 E: rector@parishofcove.org.uk

TYNDALL, Canon Simon James. b 54. LSE BSc(Econ) 77 Lon Univ PGCE 82 Open Univ MA 98. St Jo Coll Nottm 88. **d** 90 **p** 91. C Yeovil w Kingston Pitney *B & W* 90-94; V Rastrick St Jo *Wakef* 94-01; TR Chippenham St Paul w Hardenhuish etc *Bris* 01-13; V Kington St Michael 01-13; AD Chippenham 08-13; Hon Can Bris Cathl 11-13; Chapl Tervuren *Eur* from 13. *26 Dennenlaan, 3080 Tervuren, Belgium* T: (0032) (2) 767 3435 E: simon@tyndall.plus.com *or* simon.tyndall@stpaulstervuren.be

TYNDALL, Canon Timothy Gardner. b 25. Jes Coll Cam BA 50. Wells Th Coll 50. **d** 51 **p** 52. C Warsop *S'well* 51-55; R Newark St Leon 55-60; V Sherwood 60-75; P-in-c Bishopwearmouth St Mich w St Hilda *Dur* 75-85; RD Wearmouth 75-85; Hon Can Dur Cathl 83-90; Chief Sec ACCM 85-90; rtd 90; PtO *Lon* from 90; *S'wark* from 90. *Flat 16, 2B Bollo Lane, London W4 5LE* T: (020) 8994 4516

TYNEY, Canon James Derrick. b 33. TCD. **d** 62 **p** 63. C Ballynafeigh St Jude *D & D* 62-64; C Bangor St Comgall 64-69; I Clonallon w Warrenpoint 69-75; I Groomsport 75-00; Can Belf Cathl 93-00; Dioc Registrar *D & D* 95-00; rtd 00. *27 Sandringham Drive, Bangor BT20 5NA* T: (028) 9145 5670

TYRER, Ms Jayne Linda. b 59. Goldsmiths' Coll Lon BA 81 CertEd 82. Sarum & Wells Th Coll 85. **d** 87 **p** 95. C Rochdale *Man* 87-88; Par Dn Heywood St Luke w All So 88-91; Hon Par Dn Burneside *Carl* 91-07; Hon Par Dn Beacon from 07; Chapl Kendal Hosp 91-94; Chapl Westmorland Hosps NHS Trust 94-98; Chapl Univ Hosps of Morecambe Bay NHS Trust from 98. *St Oswald's Vicarage, Burneside, Kendal LA9 6QX* T: (01539) 722015 E: jayne.tyrer@wgh.mbht.nhs.uk

TYRER, Neil. *See* PURVEY-TYRER, Neil

TYRÉUS, Per Jonas Waldemar (Peter). b 45. Uppsala Univ 66. **p** 71. Sweden 71-00; C Pelton *Dur* 00-03; C Chester le Street 03-11; rtd 11. *27 Castle Riggs, Chester le Street DH2 2DL* E: petertyreus@googlemail.com

TYRREL, John Cockett. b 16. Qu Coll Cam BA 38 MA 42. Ridley Hall Cam 38. **d** 40 **p** 41. C Southall H Trin *Lon* 40-43; Chapl RNVR 43-46; S Africa 46-50; Australia from 50; rtd 81. *20/58 Shackleton Circuit, Mawson ACT 2607, Australia* T: (0061) (2) 6286 1317

TYRRELL, The Very Revd Charles Robert. b 51. SRN 73 Open Univ BA 80. Oak Hill Th Coll 74. **d** 77 **p** 78. C Halewood *Liv* 77-80; C St Helens St Helen 80-83; V Banks 83-88; Can Wellington New Zealand 88-94; Dean Nelson from 94. *The Deanery, 365 Trafalgar Street, Nelson 7010, New Zealand* T: (0064) (3) 548 8574 *or* 548 1008 E: charlest@nelsonanglican.org.nz

TYRRELL, John Patrick Hammond. b 42. Cranmer Hall Dur 62. **d** 65 **p** 66. C Edin St Jo 65-68; Chapl RN 68-72; Chapl St John's Cathl Hong Kong 72-74; 78-82; Area Sec SE Asia SOMA UK 78-82; V Westborough *Guildf* 74-78; C Yateley *Win* 82-83; C-in-c Darby Green CD 83-88; V Darby Green 88-96; V Chineham 96-97; rtd 02; PtO *Linc* from 06. *5 Blacksmith's Court, Metheringham, Lincoln LN4 3YQ* T: (01526) 322147 E: john_tyrrell42@hotmail.com

TYRRELL, Stephen Jonathan. b 39. Sheff Univ BA 62. Clifton Th Coll. **d** 65 **p** 66. C Rodbourne Cheney *Bris* 66-68; C Lillington *Cov* 68-72; P-in-c Bishop's Itchington 73-78; V 78-86; V Kingston upon Hull St Nic *York* 86-92; TV Cheltenham St Mary, St Matt, St Paul and H Trin *Glouc* 92-04; rtd 04; PtO *Glouc* from 05. *96A Fosseway Avenue, Moreton-in-Marsh GL56 0EA* T: (01608) 812350

TYSOE, James Raymond. b 19. Qu Coll Birm 70. **d** 75 **p** 76. NSM Cov E 75-85; NSM Cov Cathl 85-87; PtO *Glouc* from 87. *Wisma Mulia, Bridge Road, Frampton on Severn, Gloucester GL2 7HE* T: (01452) 740890

TYSON, Mrs Frances Mary. b 44. Reading Univ BScAgr 68 Wolv Univ PGCE 91. St Jo Coll Nottm 01. **d** 02 **p** 03. NSM Walsall *Lich* 02-07; NSM Portswood Ch Ch *Win* from 07. *26 Reynolds Road, Southampton SO15 5GS*

TYSON, Mrs Nigella Jane. b 44. RGN 66 Kent Univ BA 95. SEITE 96. **d** 97 **p** 98. NSM Aylesham w Adisham, Nonington w Wymynswold and Goodnestone etc *Cant* 97-00; P-in-c Kingsland w Eardisland, Aymestrey etc *Heref* 00-04; R 04-09; rtd 09. *Fairview, Stoke Prior, Leominster HR6 0NE* T: (01568) 760610 E: revnigella@sky.com

TYSON, Canon William Edward Porter. b 25. St Cath Coll Cam BA 49 MA 52. Ridley Hall Cam 49. **d** 51 **p** 52. C Wilmslow *Ches* 51-54; C Astbury 54-57; V Macclesfield St Pet 57-62; V Over Tabley 62-70; V High Legh 62-70; CF (TA) 64-91; V Church Hulme *Ches* 70-91; Chapl Cranage Hall Hosp 70-91; Hon Can Ches Cathl 82-91; RD Congleton 85-90; rtd 91; PtO *Ches* from 91; *Carl* from 91. *59 Kirkhead Road, Allithwaite, Grange-over-Sands LA11 7DD*

TYSON, Canon William Edward Porter. b 25. St Cath Coll Cam BA 49 MA 52. Ridley Hall Cam 49. **d** 51 **p** 52. C Wilmslow *Ches* 51-54; C Astbury 54-57; V Macclesfield St Pet 57-62; V Over Tabley 62-70; V High Legh 62-70; CF (TA) 64-91; V Church Hulme *Ches* 70-91; Chapl Cranage Hall Hosp 70-91; Hon Can Ches Cathl 82-91; RD Congleton 85-90; rtd 91; PtO *Ches* from 91; *Carl* from 91. *59 Kirkhead Road, Allithwaite, Grange-over-Sands LA11 7DD*

U

UDAL, Canon Joanna Elizabeth Margaret. b 64. SS Hild & Bede Coll Dur BSc 86. Ripon Coll Cuddesdon BTh 94. **d** 97 **p** 98. C Whitton St Aug *Lon* 97-00; Asst to Abp Sudan 00-09; Abp's Sec for Angl Communion Affairs *Cant* 09-14; Chapl S'wark Cathl from 11. *4 York Square, London E14 7LU* T: (020) 7790 8525

UDDIN, Mohan. b 52. Sussex Univ BA 74 PGCE 75 Lon Bible Coll MA 87 PhD 98 Anglia Poly Univ MA 02. Ridley Hall Cam 99. **d** 03 **p** 04. C Hornchurch St Andr *Chelmsf* 03-07; PtO 08-11; *Win* 09-12; TV Newbury *Ox* 10-13; rtd 13; PtO *Win* from 13. *247 Oceana Boulevard, Lower Canal Walk, Southampton SO14 3JG* M: 07515-386301
E: mohan.uddin@btopenworld.com

UFFINDELL, David Wilfred George. b 37. Qu Coll Birm 72. **d** 75 **p** 76. NSM Harlescott *Lich* 75-07; PtO 08-14. *13 Kenley Avenue, Heath Farm, Shrewsbury SY1 3HA* T/F: (01743) 352029
E: revuffindell@talktalk.net

UFFINDELL, Harold David. b 61. Down Coll Cam MA 87. Wycliffe Hall Ox BA 86 MA 91 Oak Hill Th Coll 86. **d** 87 **p** 88. C Kingston Hill St Paul *S'wark* 87-91; C Surbiton St Matt 91-98; V Sunningdale *Ox* from 98; AD Bracknell from 12. *The Vicarage, Sidbury Close, Sunningdale, Ascot SL5 0PD* T: (01344) 620061 E: davidvffindell@btconnect.com

UGANDA, Archbishop of. *See* OROMBI, The Most Revd Henry Luke

UGWUNNA, The Ven Sydney Chukwunma. b 45. Nebraska Wesleyan Univ BSc 67 Univ of Nebraska, Linc MSc 70 Wayne State Univ PhD 79. Virginia Th Sem MDiv 96. **d** 96 **p** 97. C Alexandria Resurrection USA 96-97; C Knaresborough *Ripon* 98-02; Dean Trin Th Coll and Adn Umuahia Nigeria 03-06; R Alexandria Meade Memorial Ch USA 06-08; Visiting P Washington Cathl 09-10; R Earleville St Steph 10-11. *189 New Haw Road, Addlestone KT15 2DP*
E: revugwunna@gmail.com

ULLMANN, Clair. *See* FILBERT-ULLMANN, Clair

ULOGWARA, Canon Obinna Chiadikobi. b 68. Univ of Nigeria BA(Ed) 98 Lagos Univ MEd 03. Trin Coll Umuahia 87. **d** 90 **p** 91. V Ahiara H Trin Nigeria 90-05; Chapl Secondary Schs Dio Mbaise 90-93; V Irete St Pet 93-95; Chapl Secondary Schs Dio Owerri 94-99; V Egbeada Em 99; V Sari Iganmu St Phil 00-01; V Igbobi St Steph 01-05; Hon Chapl to Abp Lagos 01-05; C Dublin Whitechurch *D & G* 05-10; Bp's C Dublin St Geo and St Thos from 10. *St George's Rectory, 96 Lower Drumcondra Road, Dublin 9, Republic of Ireland* T: (00353) (1) 830 0160 M: 87-247 6339
E: binagwara@yahoo.com

UMPLEBY, Mark Raymond. b 70. Trin Coll Bris BA 99. **d** 99 **p** 00. C Birstall *Wakef* 99-02; TV N Huddersfield 02-06; Dioc Voc Adv 04-06; Chapl David Young Community Academy Leeds 06-13; PtO *Leeds* from 14; C Batley St Thos *Wakef* from 14; C Hanging Heaton from 14. *St Thomas's Vicarage, 16 Stockwell Drive, Batley WF17 5PA* E: markumpleby@hotmail.com

UNDERDOWN, Margaret Jean (Meg). b 49. Univ of Wales (Abth) BSc 70. St Mich Coll Llan 06. **d** 08 **p** 09. Chapl HM Pris Cardiff 03-13; C Cathays *Llan* from 13. *Address temp unknown*

UNDERDOWN, Steven. b 52. Hull Univ BSc 75 CertEd 76 K Coll Lon PhD 02. **d** 88 **p** 04. CSWG 82-02; Chapl Brighton and Sussex Univ Hosps NHS Trust 03-15; NSM Hove *Chich* 03-09; P-in-c Hove St Patr 09-15; Chapl Burrswood Chr Hosp *Roch* from 15. *May Cottage, Burrswood, Groombridge, Tunbridge Wells TN3 9PU* M: 07981-423973
E: steven.underdown@hotmail.com

UNDERHILL, Robin. b 31. Marymount Coll California BA 89 Woodbury Univ California BSc 90. Claremont Sch of Th MA 92. **d** 93 **p** 94. Asst P Beverly Hills All SS USA 93-00; Pastor San Fernando St Simon 00-01; P-in-c Stranraer and Portpatrick *Glas* 01-04; Sec for Scotland Miss to Seafarers 04-10; rtd 10; Hon Can St Andr Cathl from 10. *Tigh Ban, Hightae, Lockerbie DG11 1JN* T: (01387) 811112 M: 07800-798483
E: mts_scotland@onetel.com

UNDERHILL, Stanley Robert. b 27. Cant Sch of Min. **d** 82 **p** 83. C New Addington *Cant* 82-84; C Cannock *Lich* 84-86; TV 86-88; R Dymchurch w Burmarsh and Newchurch *Cant* 88-92; rtd 92; Chapl Menorca *Eur* 92-94; PtO *Cant* 94-04; *Lon* 05-13. *Charterhouse, Charterhouse Square, London EC1M 6AN* T: (020) 7490 5059 M: 07970-954958 E: stanunder@aol.com

UNDERWOOD, Adrian Anthony. b 67. **d** 02 **p** 03. C Sparkhill w Greet and Sparkbrook *Birm* 02-06; C Selly Park St Steph and

St Wulstan 06-10; rtd 10. *11 Weoley Park Road, Selly Park, Birmingham B29 6QY* T: 0121-537 2151 M: 07954-140326
E: adrianandsarah@blueyonder.co.uk

UNDERWOOD, Miss Anne Frances. b 58. Ox Min Course 12. **d** 15. C Bushey *St Alb* from 15. *6 Church Walk, Bushey WD23 3BW*

UNDERWOOD, Brian. b 35. Dur Univ BA 57 Keble Coll Ox PGCE 76 Dur Univ MA 72. Clifton Th Coll 57. **d** 59 **p** 60. C Blackpool Ch Ch *Blackb* 59-61; C New Malden and Coombe S'wark 61-64; Travel Sec Pathfinders 64-68; Chapl Chantilly *Eur* 68-69; Home Sec CCCS 69-71; P-in-c Gatten St Paul *Portsm* 71-72; Chapl Lyon w Grenoble and Aix-les-Bains *Eur* 72-75; Asst Chapl Trent Coll Nottm 76-80; Chapl Qu Eliz Gr Sch Blackb 80-85; R Bentham St Jo *Bradf* 85-92; V St Alb Ch Ch 92-00; rtd 00; PtO *St Alb* 00-14; *Guildf* from 15. *2 Coombe Court, Station Approach, Tadworth KT20 5AL*

UNDERWOOD, Charles Brian. b 23. Leeds Univ BA 48 CertEd. Coll of Resurr Mirfield 48. **d** 50 **p** 51. C Tilehurst St Mich *Ox* 50-53; C Leic St Paul 53-54; Youth Chapl 54-61; V Leic St Geo 57-59; R Harby 59-61; New Zealand 61-62; Dioc Youth Chapl *Bradf* 63-72; R Carleton-in-Craven 63-76; V Twyning *Glouc* 76-88; RD Tewkesbury 81-88; rtd 88; PtO *Glouc* from 00. *3 Brampton Cottages, Brampton Valley Lane, Brampton, Northampton NN6 8GA* T: (01604) 850743

UNDERWOOD, David Richard. b 47. AKC 69 St Osyth Coll of Educn PGCE 72. St Aug Coll Cant 69. **d** 70 **p** 92. C Witham *Chelmsf* 70-71; Teacher 71-82; Hd Teacher Gt Heath Sch Mildenhall 82-91; NSM Chevington w Hargrave and Whepstead w Brockley *St E* 82-91; Par Dn Haverhill w Withersfield, the Wrattings etc 91-92; TV 92-94; P-in-c Bury St Edmunds St Jo 94-99; RD Thingoe 95-99; P-in-c Bury St Edmunds St Geo 98-99; Dioc Dir of Educn 99-04; Hon Can St E Cathl 03-04; rtd 07. *1 Fishers Way, Godmanchester, Huntingdon PE29 2XE* T: (01480) 411293 E: davidunderwood2@aol.com or davidunderwood2@btinternet.com

UNDERWOOD, John Alan. b 40. Glos Coll of Arts & Tech BSc 88 Ox Poly CertEd 84 MBCS 74. SAOMC 96. **d** 99 **p** 00. OLM Eynsham and Cassington *Ox* 99-10; PtO from 10. *17 Witney Road, Eynsham, Oxford OX29 4PH* T: (01865) 881254 or 301305 F: 301301 E: junderw549@aol.com

UNDERWOOD, Mrs Susannah Lucy. b 72. Westmr Coll Ox BTh 98. ERMC 05. **d** 08 **p** 09. C Stevenage H Trin *St Alb* 08-11; TV Welwyn from 11. *The Rectory, Brook Bridge Lane, Datchworth, Knebworth SG3 6SU* T: (01438) 817183
E: team.vicar@welwyn.org.uk

UNGOED-THOMAS, Peter. b 27. Pemb Coll Ox BA 51 MA 67. St Mich Coll Llan. **d** 60 **p** 61. C Llangeinor *Llan* 60-64; I Dublin Donnybrook *D & G* 64-66; RAChD 67-70; Chapl Leigh C of E Schs 70-74; C Leigh St Mary *Man* 70-74; Lect Warley Coll 74-86; PtO *Birm* 75-00; St D from 75; Lect Sandwell Coll of F&HE from 86; rtd 94. *93 Heol Felin-Foel, Llanelli SA15 3JQ* T: (01554) 741067

UNITED STATES OF AMERICA, Presiding Bishop of. *See* JEFFERTS SCHORI, The Most Revd Katharine

✠UNO, The Most Revd James Toru. c 98. Bp Kita Kanto 98-02; Bp Osaka from 02; Primate of Nippon Seikokai 02-06. *2-1-8 Matsuzaki-cho, Abeno-ku, Osaka 545-0053, Japan* T: (0081) (6) 621 2179 F: 621 3097 E: osaka@nskk.org

UNSWORTH, Philip James. b 41. UEA BEd 82 Nottm Coll of Educn CertEd 63 Nottm Univ DipEd 72. EAMTC 94. **d** 97 **p** 98. NSM Hethersett w Canteloff w Lt and Gt Melton *Nor* 97-00; P-in-c Blofield w Hemblington 00-06; rtd 06; PtO *Nor* from 06. *55 Campbell Close, Hunstanton PE36 5PJ* T: (01485) 532436

UNSWORTH, Thomas Foster. b 28. Lon Univ BA 56. Lich Th Coll 60. **d** 62 **p** 63. C Northfield *Birm* 62-64; C The Lickey 64-66; V Forcett *Ripon* 66-68; V Bellerby and Leyburn 68-69; V Leyburn w Bellerby 69-73; Chapl Whittingham Hosp Preston 73-79; V Freckleton *Blackb* 79-83; V S Yardley St Mich *Birm* 83-86; V Sutton w Carlton and Normanton upon Trent etc *S'well* 86-90; Chapl from 90; St Raphaël *Eur* 90-97; PtO *Cant* from 99. *31 Broadlands Avenue, New Romney TN28 8JE* T: (01797) 361922

UNWIN, Barry. b 70. Sheff Univ BA 91. Oak Hill Th Coll BA 05. **d** 05 **p** 06. C Hebburn St Jo *Dur* 05-09; C Jarrow Grange 05-09; P-in-c New Barnet St Jas *St Alb* 09-13; V from 13. *St James' Vicarage, 11 Park Road, Barnet EN4 9QA* T: (020) 8449 4043
E: barryunwin@gmail.com

UNWIN, Christopher Michael Fairclough. b 31. Dur Univ BA 57. Linc Th Coll 65. **d** 67 **p** 68. C S Shields St Hilda w St Thos *Dur* 67-73; R Tatsfield *S'wark* 73-81; RE Adv to Ch Secondary Schs 73-81; V Newc St Gabr 81-96; RD Newc E 96; rtd 96; PtO *Dur* from 96; *Newc* from 96. *2 The Cottage, West Row, Greatham, Hartlepool TS25 2HW* T: (01429) 872781

UNWIN, The Ven Kenneth. b 26. St Edm Hall Ox BA 48 MA 52. Ely Th Coll 49. **d** 51 **p** 52. C Leeds All SS *Ripon* 51-55; C Dur St Marg 55-59; V Dodworth *Wakef* 59-69; V Royston 69-73; V Wakef St Jo 73-82; Hon Can Wakef Cathl 80-82; RD Wakef 80-81; Adn Pontefract 82-92; rtd 92; PtO *Bradf* 92-10; *Leeds* from 92. *2 Rockwood Close, Skipton BD23 1UG* T: (01756) 791323

UNWIN, Michael. *See* UNWIN, Christopher Michael Fairclough

UPCHURCH, Sarah Louise. b 66. **d** 12 **p** 13. NSM Ardingly *Chich* from 12. *66 Silver Birches, Haywards Heath RH16 3PD* T: (01444) 414808

UPHILL, Ms Ann Carol. b 54. Westcott Ho Cam 95. **d** 97 **p** 98. C Strood St Nic w St Mary *Roch* 97-01; R Footscray w N Cray 01-14; rtd 14. *46 St Leonard's Rise, Orpington BR6 9NB* M: 07802-883121 T: (01689) 637515 E: ann.uphill@uwclub.net

UPHILL, Keith Ivan. b 35. Keble Coll Ox BA 70 MA 74. Wycliffe Hall Ox 67. **d** 70 **p** 71. C Maghull *Liv* 70-73; V Wroxall *Portsm* 73-77; TV Fareham H Trin 77-82; C Havant 82-84; P-in-c Merton St Jo *S'wark* 84-85; V 85-95; rtd 95; PtO *Portsm* from 95. *20 Wilby Lane, Anchorage Park, Portsmouth PO3 5UF* T: (023) 9266 6998

UPTON, Anthony Arthur. b 30. Leic Univ MA 97 PhD 03. Wells Th Coll 61. **d** 63 **p** 64. C Milton *Portsm* 63-67; Chapl RN 67-83; V Foleshill St Laur *Cov* 83-91; rtd 91; PtO *Cov* from 91. *Redlands Bungalow, Banbury Road, Lighthorne CV35 0AH*

UPTON, Ms Caroline Tracey. b 67. Lon Univ BMus 90 Edin Univ BD 94. Edin Th Coll 91. **d** 94 **p** 95. C Edin St Martin 94-96; Hon C Edin St Pet 97-99; C 99-01; Chapl Lothian Univ Hosps NHS Trust from 01. *10 (3F1) Montagu Terrace, Edinburgh EH3 5QX* T: 0131-552 0731 *or* 536 0144 E: carrie.upton@luht.scot.nhs.uk

UPTON, Mrs Christina Phoebe. b 61. Man Univ MB, ChB 85 Ches Univ MTh 04 MRCPsych 93. NOC 06. **d** 08 **p** 09. C W Kirby St Bridget *Ches* 08-12; R Ches H Trin from 12. *The Rectory, 50 Norris Road, Chester CH1 5DZ* T: (01244) 372721 E: tina.upton@tesco.net

UPTON, Christopher Martin. b 53. Bp Grosseteste Coll CertEd 74. EAMTC 94. **d** 97 **p** 98. NSM Gorleston St Andr *Nor* 97-05; NSM Bradwell from 05. *27 Curlew Way, Bradwell, Great Yarmouth NR31 8QX* T: (01493) 668184 E: rev.martin.upton@talk21.com

UPTON, Clement Maurice. b 49. Linc Th Coll 88. **d** 90 **p** 91. C Northampton St Alb *Pet* 90-93; V Laxey and Lonan *S & M* 93-96; V Hipswell *Ripon* 96-01; V Wellingborough St Andr *Pet* 01-10; Chapl Northants Police 05-10; rtd 10; PtO *Leic* from 15. *1 Stamford Drive, Coalville LE67 4TA* T: (01530) 839946 E: sheclem26@yahoo.co.uk

UPTON, Canon Julie. b 61. Ripon Coll Cuddesdon 87. **d** 88 **p** 94. C Kirkstall *Ripon* 88-91; Par Dn E Greenwich Ch Ch w St Andr and St Mich *S'wark* 91-94; C 94; PtO 01-03; *St E* 02-03; NSM Manningham *Bradf* 03-04; TV Bramley *Ripon* 04-10; P-in-c Sheff Manor 10-12; TR from 12; Hon Can Sheff Cathl from 14. *St Aidan's Vicarage, 4 Manor Lane, Sheffield S2 1UF* T: 0114-272 4676 E: julie.upton1@googlemail.com

UPTON, Martin. *See* UPTON, Christopher Martin

UPTON, Michael Gawthorne. b 29. AKC 53. **d** 54 **p** 55. C Middleton *Man* 54-57; C Plymouth St Andr *Ex* 57-59; Dep Dir of Educn *Cant* 59-63; Hon C Riverhead *Roch* 63-70; Youth Chapl 63-70; LtO *Ex* 70-94; Chr Aid Area Sec (Devon and Cornwall) 70-94; Chr Aid SW Region Co-ord 73-89; rtd 94; PtO *Ex* 94-09. *Otter Dell, Harpford, Sidmouth EX10 0NH* T: (01395) 568448

UPTON, Mrs Susan Dorothy. b 53. Bp Grosseteste Coll CertEd 74 Nottm Univ BEd 75. EAMTC 99. **d** 02 **p** 03. NSM Bradwell *Nor* from 02. *27 Curlew Way, Bradwell, Great Yarmouth NR31 8QX* T: (01493) 668184 E: sue-upton@talk21.com

UPTON-JONES, Peter John. b 38. Selw Coll Cam BA 63 MA 67 Liv Univ CertEd 64. NOC 90. **d** 92 **p** 93. NSM Formby H Trin *Liv* 92-00; P-in-c Lezayre St Olave Ramsey *S & M* 00-03; V 03-08; P-in-c Kirkbride 00-03; R 03-08; rtd 08; PtO *S & M* from 09. *Clock Cottage, Glen Road, Colby, Isle of Man IM9 4NT* T: (01624) 830216 E: peteru_j@hotmail.com

UREN, Malcolm Lawrence. b 37. AKC 63. **d** 64 **p** 65. C Cant St Martin w St Paul 64-67; C Falmouth K Chas *Truro* 67-71; V St Blazey 71-79; P-in-c Tuckingmill 79-83; V 83-89; V Launceston St Steph w St Thos 89-92; V St Stephen by Launceston 92-96; rtd 00; PtO *Truro* from 00. *17 Forth An Tewennow, St Mary's Gardens, Phillack, Hayle TR27 4QE* T: (01736) 756619 E: malcolm.uren1@btinternet.com

URMSON-TAYLOR, Ralph. *See* TAYLOR, Ralph Urmson

✠**URQUHART, The Rt Revd David Andrew.** b 52. Ealing Business Sch BA 77. Wycliffe Hall Ox 82. **d** 84 **p** 85 **c** 00. C Kingston upon Hull St Nic *York* 84-87; TV Drypool 87-92; V Cov H Trin 92-00; Hon Can Cov Cathl 99-00; Suff Bp Birkenhead *Ches* 00-06; Bp Birm from 06. *Bishop's Croft, Old Church Road, Birmingham B17 0BG* T: 0121-427 1163 F: 426 1322 E: bishop@birmingham.anglican.org

URQUHART, Canon Edmund Ross. b 39. Univ Coll Ox BA 62 MA 68. St Steph Ho Ox 62. **d** 64 **p** 65. C Milton *Win* 64-69; C Norton *Derby* 69-73; V Bakewell 73-05; RD Bakewell and Eyam 95-04; Hon Can Derby Cathl 02-05; rtd 05; PtO *Derby* from 05; *Lich* 08-14. *1 Hambleton Close, Ashbourne DE6 1NG* T: (01335) 346454 E: edmund991@btinternet.com

URQUHART, Ian Garnham. b 46. Univ Coll Lon LLB 71. Wycliffe Hall Ox 98. **d** 99 **p** 00. C Barnston *Ches* from 99. *8 Antons Road, Wirral CH61 9PT* T: 0151-648 1512 F: 648 2402 M: 07770-823373 E: ian@papintalo.co.uk

URSELL, David John. b 45. MRAC 70. SWMTC 92. **d** 95 **p** 96. NSM Dolton *Ex* from 95; Rural Convenor from 95. *Aller Farm, Dolton, Winkleigh EX19 8PP* T: (01805) 804414 *or* 804737 E: ursell@farmersweekly.net

URSELL, Canon Philip Elliott. b 42. Univ of Wales BA 66 Ox Univ MA 82 Nashotah Ho Wisconsin DD 08. St Steph Ho Ox 66. **d** 68 **p** 69. C Newton Nottage *Llan* 68-71; Asst Chapl Univ of Wales (Cardiff) 71-77; Chapl Wales Poly 74-77; LtO *Llan* 77-07; Chapl Em Coll Cam 77-82; Prin Pusey Ho 82-03; Warden Ascot Priory 85-13; LtO *Ox* 82-13; Can Rio Grande 99; PtO *Llan* from 15. *273 Hayes Apartments, The Hayes, Cardiff CF10 1BZ* T: (029) 2132 8359 E: peu@cantab.net

✠**URWIN, The Rt Revd Lindsay Goodall.** b 56. Heythrop Coll Lon MA 03 Nashotah Ho Wisconsin Hon DD 11. Ripon Coll Cuddesdon 77. **d** 80 **p** 81 **c** 93. C Walworth *S'wark* 80-83; V N Dulwich St Faith 83-88; Dioc Missr *Chich* 88-93; Area Bp Horsham 93-09; Can and Preb Chich Cathl 93-09; P Admin Shrine of Our Lady of Walsingham 09-15; Hon Asst Bp Nor from 09; OGS from 91; Provost Woodard Corp (S Division) 06-15; R Brunswick Ch Ch Australia from 15; Bp for Angl Schs Melbourne from 15. *8 Glenlyon Road, Brunswick, Vic 3056, Australia* T: (0061) 39-380 1064 E: lindsayurwin1@gmail.com

USHER, George. b 30. Univ of Wales (Swansea) BSc 51. St Deiniol's Hawarden 73. **d** 75 **p** 76. NSM Clun w Chapel Lawn *Heref* 75-78; NSM Clun w Chapel Lawn, Bettws-y-Crwyn and Newcastle 79-80; C Shrewsbury St Giles *Lich* 80-83; C Shrewsbury St Giles w Sutton and Atcham 83-84; R Credenhill w Brinsop and Wormsley etc *Heref* 84-98; rtd 98; PtO *Ex* from 02. *1 Trinity Court, The Esplanade, Sidmouth EX10 8BE* T: (01395) 513889 E: georgeusher@clara.net

✠**USHER, The Rt Revd Graham Barham.** b 70. Edin Univ BSc 93 CCC Cam BA 95 MA 00. Westcott Ho Cam 93 St Nic Th Coll Ghana 96. **d** 96 **p** 97 **c** 14. C Nunthorpe *York* 96-99; V N Ormesby 99-04; R Hexham *Newc* 04-14; AD 06-11; Suff Bp Dudley *Worc* from 14; Hon Can Kumasi Ghana from 07. *Bishop's House, Bishop's Walk, Cradley Heath B64 7RH* T: 0121-550 3407 F: 550 7340

USHER, Robin Reginald. b 50. AKC 74. St Aug Coll Cant 75. **d** 76 **p** 77. C Hulme Ascension *Man* 76-80; P-in-c Newall Green St Fran 80-85; C Atherton 85-87; TV 87-90; V Leigh St Jo 90-99; Chapl Wigan and Leigh Health Services NHS Trust 93-99; V Milnrow *Man* from 99. *The Vicarage, 40 Eafield Avenue, Milnrow, Rochdale OL16 3UN* T: (01706) 642988 M: 07410-686484 E: robin.usher@zen.co.uk

UTTIN, Suzanne. *See* GRINDROD, Suzanne

UTTLEY, Mrs Valerie Gail. b 43. Man Univ BA 64. NOC 80. **dss** 83 **d** 87 **p** 94. Otley *Bradf* 83-87; Hon Par Dn 87-89; Par Dn Calverley 89-92; Ind Chapl *Ripon* 92-97; C Kirkstall 95-97; V Lofthouse 97-10; rtd 10. *1 Victoria Terrace, Alnwick NE66 1RE* E: gailuttley@yahoo.co.uk

UZOIGWE, Austin Chuks. b 64. Qu Coll Birm 13. **d** 15. C Mardyke *Chelmsf* from 15. *All Saints Vicarage, Foyle Drive, South Ockendon RM15 5HF* M: 07778-135998 E: austin.uzoigwe@gmail.com

V

VACCARO, Mrs Alexandra. b 64. Qu Coll Birm 07. **d** 10 **p** 11. NSM Kidderminster St Mary and All SS w Trimpley etc *Worc* 10-15; NSM Kidderminster Ismere from 15. *18 Batham Road, Kidderminster DY10 2TN* T: (01562) 515894
E: alexvaccaro@fsmail.net

VAIL, David William. b 30. Dur Univ BA 56 Sheff Univ DipEd 71. Oak Hill Th Coll 56. **d** 58 **p** 59. C Toxteth Park St Bede *Liv* 58-61; Kenya 61-77; Chapl Versailles *Eur* 77-82; Gen Sec Rwanda Miss 82-88; V Virginia Water *Guildf* 88-96; rtd 96; PtO *Ox* from 98. *36 Silverthorne Drive, Caversham, Reading RG4 7NS* T: 0118-954 6667

VAIZEY, Martin John. b 37. AKC 64. **d** 65 **p** 66. C Bishopwearmouth Gd Shep *Dur* 65-69; C Darlington H Trin 69-72; V Easington Colliery 72-80; C-in-c Bishopwearmouth St Mary V w St Pet CD 80-85; V Sunderland Springwell w Thorney Close 85-88; R Witton Gilbert 88-96; P-in-c Wingate Grange 96-99; V Wheatley Hill and Wingate w Hutton Henry 99-07; rtd 07; PtO *Dur* from 13. *Elmside, 2 Etherley Lane, Bishop Auckland DL14 7QR* T: (01388) 450093

VALE, Thomas Stanley George. b 52. Chich Th Coll 85. **d** 87 **p** 88. C Leic St Phil 87-90; C Knighton St Mary Magd 90-93; P-in-c Leic St Chad 93-97; V 97-01; V Blackfordby and Woodville from 01. *The Vicarage, 11 Vicarage Close, Blackfordby, Swadlincote DE11 8AZ* T: (01283) 211310
E: tvale@webleicester.co.uk

VALENTINE, Derek William. b 24. S'wark Ord Course 65. **d** 68 **p** 69. NSM Battersea St Luke S'wark 68-77; NSM Fenstanton *Ely* 77-88; PtO *Bradf* 88-96. *Address withheld by request*

VALENTINE, Hugh William James. b 56. Bradf Univ BA 83 CQSW. S'wark Ord Course 86. **d** 89 **p** 90. NSM Stoke Newington Common St Mich *Lon* 89-92; NSM Westmr St Jas from 92; Bps' Adv in Child Protection Stepney and Two Cities Areas from 96; Bp's Adv in Child Protection *Ox* 96-05. *The Clerk's House, 127 Kennington Road, London SE11 6SF* T: (020) 7735 3138   M: 07760-176704
E: mail@hughvalentine.net

VALENTINE, Jeremy Wilfred. b 38. NW Ord Course 76. **d** 79 **p** 80. C Cundall *Ripon* 79-81; TV Huntington *York* 82-87; V Sand Hutton 87-08; P-in-c Whitwell w Crambe, Flaxton and Foston 01-08; RD Buckrose and Bulmer and Malton 98-02; rtd 08; PtO *York* from 08. *5 Sand Hutton Court, Sand Hutton, York YO41 1LU* T: (01904) 468443   F: 468670
E: jeremyvalentine38@hotmail.co.uk

VALENTINE, John Harvey. b 63. Ch Ch Ox BA 85 MA 85. Ridley Hall Cam BA 92. **d** 93 **p** 94. C Heigham H Trin *Nor* 93-97; C Ches Square St Mich w St Phil *Lon* 97-00; C Brompton H Trin w Onslow Square St Paul 00-02; P-in-c Holborn St Geo w H Trin and St Bart 02-09; R from 09. *13 Doughty Street, London WC1N 2PL* T: (020) 7404 9606 *or* 7404 4407   F: 7831 0588   M: 07736-066091   E: john.valentine@sgtm.org

VALENTINE, Mrs Katherine Anne. b 58. Newc Poly BA 80 Anglia Ruskin Univ MA 12. ERMC 03. **d** 06 **p** 07. C Haughley w Wetherden and Stowupland *St E* 06-10; P-in-c Pakenham w Norton and Tostock from 10; C Badwell and Walsham from 15. *The Orwell, Woolpit Road, Norton, Bury St Edmunds IP31 3LU* T: (01359) 235095
E: katherine@kavalentine.plus.com

VALIANT, Mrs Lesley Jean. b 51. Whitelands Coll Lon CertEd 74 Univ Coll Chich BA 99. STETS 99. **d** 01 **p** 02. NSM Bedhampton *Portsm* 01-04; C Southsea St Jude 04-06; Asst to RD Portsm 04-06; TV Pewsey and Swanborough *Sarum* 06-09; TV Modbury, Bigbury, Ringmore, Kingston etc *Ex* 11-13; PtO *Cant* from 14; Chapl MU from 14. *27 Cliffe Avenue, Margate CT9 5DU* T: (01843) 293964   M: 07751-168228
E: ljvaliant@gmail.com

VALLENTE-KERR, Susan Fiona. b 77. St Martin's Coll Lanc BA 98 Ch Ch Coll Cant PGCE 00 Moorlands Coll MA 08. St Mellitus Coll 08. **d** 11 **p** 12. C Frindsbury w Upnor and Chattenden *Roch* from 11. *85 Rivenhall Way, Hoo, Rochester ME3 9GF* M: 07875-349029   E: suziqvk@yahoo.co.uk

VALLINS, Canon Christopher. b 43. Hon FRSocMed 06. Lich Th Coll 63. **d** 66 **p** 67. C Cuddington *Guildf* 66-70; C Aldershot St Mich 70-73; V W Ewell 73-81; R Worplesdon and Chapl Merrist Wood Coll of Agric and Horticulture 81-89; RD Guildf 86-89; Chapl Epsom Health Care NHS Trust 89-99; Hd Past Care Epsom and St Helier Univ Hosps NHS Trust 99-07; Bp's Adv on Healing *Guildf* 97-07; Bp's Adv for Hosp Chapl from 07; Hon Can Guildf Cathl from 01; PtO S'wark from 07.

Little Watermead, Reigate Road, Hookwood, Horley RH6 0HD T: (01293) 824188   F: 823282   M: 07917-337920
E: chrisvallins@yahoo.com

VALLIS, Brett Paul Stanley. b 72. G&C Coll Cam BA 93 St Jo Coll Dur BA 01. Cranmer Hall Dur 99. **d** 02 **p** 03. C Monkseaton St Mary *Newc* 02-05; P-in-c Fatfield *Dur* 05-10; V 10-11; Chapl Dur High Sch for Girls from 11. *26 Kipling Way, Crook DL15 9AJ* E: revbrettvallis@yahoo.co.uk

VAN BEVEREN (née FORBES), Mrs Susan Margaret. b 64. St Hugh's Coll Ox BA 85 MA 89. Trin Th Sch Melbourne 95. **d** 96 **p** 96. Ind Chapl Inter-Ch Trade and Ind Miss Australia 96-99; NSM Amsterdam w Den Helder and Heiloo *Eur* 00-03; Officer for Miss in Work and Economic Life *Ox* 03-07; Dioc Adv 08-13; NSM S Ascot 07-09; NSM Sunninghill and S Ascot 09-13; PtO from 14; Chapl Heatherwood & Wexham Park Hosps NHS Foundn Trust from 14. *27 Cottesmore, Bracknell RG12 7YL* E: susanvanbeveren@gmail.com

VAN BLERK, Etienne. b 68. Pretoria Univ BA 88 Stellenbosch Univ BTh 92 Lebanese American Univ BA 96. Ox Min Course 07. **d** 09 **p** 10. C Bicester w Bucknell, Caversfield and Launton *Ox* 09-11; C Walton H Trin 11-13; Chapl Rossall Sch Fleetwood from 13. *3 Newell Court, Rossall School, Broadway, Fleetwood FY7 8JW* T: (01253) 774201   M: 07795-985942
E: etiennevanblerk@btinternet.com

VAN CARRAPIETT, Timothy Michael James. b 39. Chich Th Coll 60. **d** 63 **p** 64. C Sugley *Newc* 63-65; C Newc St Fran 65-69; P-in-c Wrangbrook w N Elmsall CD *Wakef* 69-74; P-in-c Flushing *Truro* 74-75; P-in-c Mylor w Flushing 75-76; P-in-c St Day 76-82; R Aldrington *Chich* 82-87; V Bexhill St Barn 87-01; rtd 01; PtO *St E* 01-13; *Chelmsf* from 08. *The College of St Barnabas, Blackberry Lane, Lingfield RH7 6NJ*

VAN CULIN, Canon Samuel. b 30. OBE. Princeton Univ AB 52. Virginia Th Sem DB 55 Hon DD 77 Gen Th Sem NY Hon DD 83. **d** 55 **p** 56. USA 55-83; Sec Gen Angl Communion Office 83-94; Hon C All Hallows by the Tower etc *Lon* 89-04; Hon Can Cant Cathl 83-94; Hon Can Ibadan from 83; Hon Can Jerusalem from 84; Hon Can S Africa from 89; Hon Can Honolulu from 91; rtd 94; Hon Can Nat Cathl USA from 04. *3900 Watson Place, NW B-5D, Washington DC 20016, USA* T: (001) (202) 537 6200

VAN D'ARQUE, Christopher Simon Wayne. b 62. St Jo Coll Dur BA 99. Cranmer Hall Dur. **d** 99 **p** 00. C Letchworth St Paul w Willian *St Alb* 99-02; C Westminster St Jas the Less *Lon* 02-03; V W Bessacarr *Sheff* 03-10; V Walton St Jo *Derby* 10-13; Chapl Sheff Teaching Hosps NHS Foundn Trust 13-15; Chapl Doncaster and Bassetlaw Hosps NHS Foundn Trust from 15. *Chaplaincy, Doncaster Royal Infirmary, Armthorpe Road, Doncaster DN2 5LT* T: (01302) 381484
E: wordsmith.twentyone@zoho.com

VAN DE KASTEELE, Peter John. b 39. Magd Coll Cam BA 61 MA 65. Clifton Th Coll 61. **d** 63 **p** 64. C Eastbourne H Trin *Chich* 63-66; C N Pickenham w S Pickenham etc *Nor* 66-70; R Mursley w Swanbourne and Lt Horwood *Ox* 70-80; Admin Sec Clinical Th Assn from 83; Gen Dir 88-99; PtO *Glouc* from 83; Hon C Westcote w Icomb and Bledington 88-89; rtd 99. *St Mary's House, Church Westcote, Chipping Norton OX7 6SF* T: (01993) 830193

van de WEYER, Robert William Bates. b 50. Lanc Univ BA 76. S'wark Ord Course 78. **d** 81 **p** 82. Warden Lt Gidding Community 77-98; Hon C Gt w Lt Gidding and Steeple Gidding *Ely* 81-83; P-in-c 83-93; P-in-c Winwick 83-93; P-in-c Hamerton 83-93; P-in-c Upton and Copmanford 83-93; PtO from 93. *4 Copse Way, Cambridge CB2 8BJ*
E: robert@vandeweyer.co.uk

VAN DEN BERG, Jan Jacob. b 56. Sarum & Wells Th Coll 86. **d** 88 **p** 89. C Glouc St Aldate 88-91; C Ollerton w Boughton S'well 91-95; P-in-c Scrooby 95-00; P-in-c Blyth 97-00; C Brampton and Farlam and Castle Carrock w Cumrew *Carl* 00-02; TV Eden, Gelt and Irthing 02-05; P-in-c Rockcliffe and Blackford from 05. *The Vicarage, Rockcliffe, Carlisle CA6 4AA* T: (01228) 674209   F: 672006   E: jan@vandenberg.fsnet.co.uk

VAN DEN BERGH, Victor Michael Cornelius. b 53. ALBC 92. Ridley Hall Cam 02. **d** 03 **p** 04. C Tamworth *Lich* from 03. *St Francis's Vicarage, Masefield Drive, Tamworth B79 8JB* T: (01827) 65926   M: 07770-900712
E: vic_vdb@btinternet.com

van den HOF, Ariadne Rolanda Magdalena. b 71. Univ of Wales (Cardiff) MTh 96 Leiden Univ MA 05. Old Cath Sem

Amersfoort 90 St Mich Coll Llan 98. **d** 99 **p** 00. C Dolgellau w Llanfachreth and Brithdir etc *Ban* 99-01; Min Can Ban Cathl 01-02; P-in-c Trefdraeth w Aberffraw, Llangadwaladr etc 02-03; R 03-06; R Llanffestiniog w Blaenau Ffestiniog etc 06-11; Rural Life Co-ord 04-11; V Shooters Hill Ch Ch *S'wark* from 11. *Christ Church Vicarage, 1 Craigholm, Shooters Hill, London SE18 3RR* T: (020) 8856 5858 E: armvandenhof@gmail.com
VAN DER HART, William Richard. b 76. Homerton Coll Cam BEd 99. Wycliffe Hall Ox BTh 04. **d** 04 **p** 05. C Bryanston Square St Mary w St Marylebone St Mark *Lon* 04-08; TV Roxeth 08-11; V W Harrow 11-14; C Onslow Square and S Kensington St Aug from 14. *20 Alderbury Road, London SW13 9BU* M: 07968-132129
E: william.vanderhart@htb.org.uk
VAN DER LELY, Janice Kay. b 55. Sheff Univ BA 76 Dur Univ PhD 79 Webster Univ (USA) MA 05 Ox Brookes Univ MA 10. Ripon Coll Cuddesdon 08. **d** 09 **p** 10. C Cirencester *Glouc* 09-12; V Thornbury and Oldbury-on-Severn w Shepperdine from 12. *The Vicarage, 27 Castle Street, Thornbury, Bristol BS35 1HQ* T: (01454) 412731 M: 07595-270438
E: janvanderlely@gmail.com
van der LINDE, Herbert John. b 43. Rhodes Univ BA 66. Coll of Resurr Mirfield. **d** 68 **p** 69. C Kingston St Luke *S'wark* 68-75; C Chipping Campden w Ebrington *Glouc* 75-78; V Cheltenham St Pet 78-84; V Bussage 84-13; rtd 13. *Amen Corner, 18 Waylands, Cricklade, Swindon SN6 6BT* T: (01793) 759026
VAN DER PUMP, Charles Lyndon. b 25. FRCM. S'wark Ord Course 86. **d** 88 **p** 89. NSM Primrose Hill St Mary w Avenue Road St Paul *Lon* 88-02; PtO from 02. *48 Canfield Gardens, London NW6 3EB* T/F: (020) 7624 4517
E: office@smvph.freeserve.co.uk
VAN DER TOORN, Canon Stephne. b 53. Natal Univ BA 73 Stellenbosch Univ HDipEd 75. Th Ext Educn Coll. **d** 93 **p** 95. NSM Pretoria St Mary S Africa 93-01; C Fawley *Win* 01-07; R E Bergholt and Brantham *St E* from 07; Hon Can St E Cathl from 13. *The Rectory, Rectory Lane, Brantham, Manningtree CO11 1PZ* T: (01206) 392646
E: revsteph3@vodafoneemail.co.uk
van der VALK, Jesse. b 59. Nottm Univ BTh 84 Birm Univ MPhil 88 Avery Hill Coll PGCE 85. St Jo Coll Nottm 81. **d** 88 **p** 89. C Droitwich Spa *Worc* 88-92; V Hartshead and Hightown *Wakef* 92-96; R Woolwich St Mary w St Mich *S'wark* from 96; USPG (Lon Volunteers and Co-workers Team) from 97. *The Rectory, 43 Rectory Place, London SE18 5DA* T: (020) 8465 7307 *or* 8316 4338 E: jessevdvalk@aol.com
VAN KOEVERING, Mrs Helen Elizabeth Parsons. b 60. SS Hild & Bede Coll Dur BA 82 Trin Coll Bris MPhil 99. S Wales Ord Course 01. **d** 02 **p** 03. C Bettws *Mon* 02-03; Bp's Sec Niassa Mozambique from 03. *CP 264, Lichinga, Niassa, Mozambique* T/F: (00258) 712 0735 E: mark@koev.freeserve.co.uk *or* diocese.niassa@teledata.mz
✠**VAN KOEVERING, The Rt Revd Mark Allan.** b 57. Michigan State Univ BSc 79 MSc 85. Trin Coll Bris BA 99. **d** 99 **p** 00 **c** 03. C Bettws *Mon* 99-01; P-in-c 01-03; Bp Niassa Mozambique from 03. *Diocese do Niassa, CP 264, Lichinga, Niassa, Mozambique* T/F: (00258) 712 0735
E: mark@koev.freeserve.co.uk *or* diocese.niassa@teledata.mz
VAN KRIEKEN VANNERLEY, David. See VANNERLEY, David van Krieken
VAN LEER, Samuel Wall. b 67. Virginia Univ BA 90 California Univ MA 91 St Jo Coll Dur BA 01. Cranmer Hall Dur 99. **d** 02 **p** 03. C Berne w Neuchâtel *Eur* 02-05; Chapl E Netherlands 05-11; Hon Asst Chapl Utrecht w Zwolle from 11. *Tussenkoelen 16, 9753 KX Haren, The Netherlands* T: (0031) (50) 785 0703
VAN LEEUWEN, Canon Dirk Willem. b 45. Utrecht Univ LLD 71. Th Faculty Brussels 71 S'wark Ord Course 80. **d** 82 **p** 83. Asst Chapl Brussels Cathl 82-84; Chapl Haarlem 84-93; Chapl Antwerp St Boniface 94-06; Assoc Chapl 06-07; Chapl Charleroi 94-00; P-in-c Ypres 97-99; P-in-c Leuven 98-99; Can Brussels Cathl 96-07; Chapl Knokke 01-07; P-in-c Ostend 01-06; P-in-c Bruges 01-03; V Gen to Bp Eur 02-07; Adn NW Eur 05-07; rtd 08. *Koningin Elisabethlei 6, Box 22, 2018 Antwerp, Belgium* T: (0032) (3) 238 3162 E: dirk.vanleeuwen@scarlet.be
VAN ROSSUM, Paul Anthony. b 53. Sheff Univ BScTech 74 Birm Univ PGCE 75 Open Univ MA 92. Trin Coll Bris 09. **d** 12 **p** 13. OLM Almondsbury and Olveston *Bris* from 12. *18 Townsend Lane, Almondsbury, Bristol BS32 4EQ* T: (01454) 626160
E: paulvanrossum@gmail.com
VAN STRAATEN, Christopher Jan. b 55. Bris Univ BA 77 Natal Univ HDipEd 78. Oak Hill Th Coll 90. **d** 92 **p** 93. C Woodley Ox 92-96; V Gillingham St Aug *Roch* 96-07; V Aylesford from 07. *The Vicarage, Vicarage Close, Aylesford ME20 7BB* T: (01622) 717434 E: chris.vanstraaten@diocese-rochester.org
van WENGEN, Rosemary Margaret. b 38. Westf Coll Lon BA 60 Univ of Leiden MA 77 PhD 81. SEITE 98. **d** 01 **p** 02. NSM

Benenden *Cant* 01-10; NSM Sandhurst w Newenden 04-10; NSM Benenden and Sandhurst 10-11; PtO from 11. *Beach House, Grange Road, St Michaels, Tenterden TN30 6EF* T: (01580) 764857 F: 761405 E: r.vanwengen@tiscali.co.uk
VAN ZANDBERGEN, Karen. See BURNETT-HALL, Karen
VANE, Benjamin Christopher George. b 81. Bath Univ BSc 03. Oak Hill Th Coll BA 15. **d** 15. C Oakwood St Thos *Lon* from 15. *22 Curthwaite Gardens, Enfield EN2 7LN* M: 07967-602513 E: ben.vane@gmail.com
VANN, The Ven Cherry Elizabeth. b 58. ARCM 78 GRSM 80. Westcott Ho Cam 86. **d** 89 **p** 94. Par Dn Flixton St Mich *Man* 89-92; Chapl Bolton Inst of F&HE 92-98; Par Dn Bolton St Pet 92-94; C 94-98; TV E Farnworth and Kearsley 98-04; TR 04-08; Chapl among Deaf People 98-04; AD Farnworth 05-08; Adn Rochdale from 08. *57 Melling Road, Oldham OL4 1PN* T: 0161-678 1454 F: 678 1455
E: archrochdale@manchester.anglican.org
VANNERLEY, David van Krieken. b 50. Kent Univ BA 78 MPhil 07 Cant Ch Ch Univ MA 11 Ch Ch Coll Cant CertEd 71. SEITE 00. **d** 05 **p** 06. NSM St Laur in Thanet *Cant* 05-13; PtO *Roch* from 13; *Cant* 13-14; TV Whitstable from 14; Chapl Kent Critical Incident Chapl Service from 10. *The Rectory, 69 Swalecliffe Court Drive, Whitstable CT5 2NF* T: (01227) 792826 E: vannerley@aol.com
VANNOZZI, Peter. b 62. Lon Univ BA 83 Heythrop Coll Lon MA 06. Ripon Coll Cuddesdon BA 86 MA 91. **d** 87 **p** 88. C Kenton *Lon* 87-90; C Fleet *Guildf* 90-93; V Northwood Hills St Edm *Lon* 93-97; AD Harrow 95-97; V S Dulwich St Steph *S'wark* 97-05; RD Dulwich 02-05; Can Res Wakef Cathl 05-07; V Hampton Hill *Lon* from 07. *The Vicarage, 46 St James's Road, Hampton TW12 1DQ* T/F: (020) 8979 2069
E: vicar@stjames-hamptonhill.org.uk
VANSTON, The Ven William Francis Harley. b 24. TCD BA 48 MA 52. **d** 48 **p** 49. C Belfast St Mary *Conn* 48-51; C Dublin Rathfarnham *D & G* 51-58; I Narraghmore w Fontstown and Timolin 58-65; I Arklow 65-67; I Arklow w Inch 67-73; I Arklow w Inch and Kilbride 73-89; RD Rathdrum 77-89; Adn Glendalough 83-89; rtd 89. *128 Brabazon House, 2 Gilford Road, Sandymount, Dublin 4, Republic of Ireland* T: (00353) (1) 260 8882
VANSTONE, Preb Walford David Frederick. b 38. Open Univ BA 81. AKC 69. **d** 70 **p** 71. C Feltham *Lon* 70-75; TV E Runcorn w Halton *Ches* 75-80; V Grange St Andr 80-82; V Hampton All SS *Lon* 82-05; P-in-c Teddington SS Pet and Paul and Fulwell 99-00; AD Hampton 95-03; Preb St Paul's Cathl 99-05; Chapl Richmond Coll 02-05; rtd 05; PtO *Lon* from 05. *13 Lammas Close, Staines TW18 4XT* E: wvanstone@aol.com
VARAH, Canon Paul Hugh. b 46. St Deiniol's Hawarden 83. **d** 85 **p** 86. C Prestatyn *St As* 85-87; P-in-c Hawarden 87-88; TV 88-89; V Esclusham 89-96; V Connah's Quay 96-13; Can Cursal St As Cathl 08-13; rtd 13; PtO *St As* from 14. *4 New Road, Dobshill, Deeside CH5 3LU* T: (01244) 540728
E: paulhvarah@gmail.com
VARGESON, Canon Peter Andrew. b 53. Wycliffe Hall Ox 85. **d** 87 **p** 88. C Yateley *Win* 87-92; V Bursledon from 92; AD Eastleigh 99-06 and from 09; P-in-c Hound from 07; Hon Can Tororo Uganda from 99. *The Vicarage, School Road, Bursledon, Southampton SO31 8BW* T: (023) 8040 2821 *or* 8040 6021
E: peter.vargeson@ukgateway.net
VARLEY (née TRIM), Elizabeth Ann. b 52. Homerton Coll Cam BEd 75 Van Mildert Coll Dur PhD 85 St Jo Coll Dur BA 96. NEOC 94. **d** 96 **p** 97. C Sedgefield *Dur* 96-99; Dir Post-Ord Tr Stepney Area *Lon* 99-02; V Hipswell *Ripon* 02-07; Hon Can Ripon Cathl 05-07; R Bacton w Wyverstone, Cotton and Old Newton etc *St E* 07-15; C Bro Arwystli *Ban* from 15. *The Vicarage, Trefeglwys Road, Llanidloes SY18 6HZ* M: 07922-012703 E: liz_varley@btinternet.com
VARLEY, Robert. b 36. St Jo Coll Cam BA 57 MA 64 Man Poly PGCE 92. NW Ord Course 71. **d** 74 **p** 75. C Wallasey St Hilary *Ches* 74-77; V Rock Ferry 77-81; PtO *Man* 82-83; Hon C E Farnworth and Kearsley 83-86; Hon C Walkden Moor 86-87; C 87-89; V Lt Hulton 89-90; PtO from 97. *66 Normanby Road, Worsley, Manchester M28 7TS* T: 0161-790 8420
VARNEY, Peter David. b 38. Univ Coll Dur BA 61 MA 64. Qu Coll Birm 61. **d** 64 **p** 65. C Newington St Paul *S'wark* 64-66; C Camberwell St Mich w All So w Em 66-67; PtO Kuching Malaysia 67-68; Hon C Croxley Green All SS *St Alb* 69; Asst Sec Gen Syn Bd for Miss and Unity 69-72; PtO *Roch* 69-72 and 74-84; Asst Chapl CSJB 72-73; Asst Sec Chrs Abroad 74-79; Dir Bloxham Project 84-86; PtO *Cant* 84-85; S'wark 85-86; P-in-c Thornage w Brinton w Hunworth and Stody *Nor* 87-88; P-in-c Briningham 87-88; C Melton Constable w Swanton Novers 87-88; PtO from 88; Chapl Yare and Norvic Clinics and

St Andr Hosp Nor 90-95; rtd 03. *280 The Pavilion, St Stephens Road, Norwich NR1 3SN* T: (01603) 760838
E: varney@waitrose.com

VARNEY, Stephen Clive. b 59. Qu Mary Coll Lon BSc 80 Sussex Univ MSc 82 Southn Univ BTh 88. Sarum & Wells Th Coll 83. **d** 86 **p** 87. C Riverhead w Dunton Green *Roch* 86-91; V Bostall Heath 91-99; V Bromley St Mark from 99. *St Mark's Vicarage, 51 Hayes Road, Bromley BR2 9AE* T: (020) 8460 6220 M: 07961-117578

VARNHAM, Gerald Stanley. b 29. Sarum & Wells Th Coll 74. **d** 77 **p** 78. Hon C Portchester *Portsm* 77-86; PtO 88-99. *15 Southampton Road, Fareham PO16 7DZ* T: (01329) 234182

VARNON, Nicholas Charles Harbord. b 45. St Luke's Coll Ex CertEd 71 Open Univ BA 83 BPhil 91 MA 94 Univ of Wales MPhil 00. St Mich Coll Llan **d** 93 **p** 94. C Pontypridd St Cath w St Matt *Llan* 93-97; P-in-c Sutton St Nicholas w Sutton St Michael *Heref* 97-04; P-in-c Withington w Westhide 97-04; P-in-c Weybourne Gp *Nor* 04-06; R N Elmham, Billingford, Bintree, Guist etc from 06; CF (ACF) from 00. *The Rectory, 48 Holt Road, North Elmham, Dereham NR20 5JQ* T: (01362) 668030 E: nchv@btinternet.com

VARQUEZ, Leo Bacleon. b 61. St Andr Th Sem Manila 82. **d** 86 **p** 86. P St Andr Philippines 86-91; P St Isidore 92-94; SSF 95-99; NSM Edin St Jo 98-99; NSM Mill End and Heronsgate w W Hyde *St Alb* 99-00; Asst Chapl HM Pris Featherstone 00-02; C Hednesford *Lich* 00-04; C Kingstanding St Luke *Birm* 04-06; Asst Chapl Univ Coll Lon Hosps NHS Foundn Trust 06-08; Chapl Univ Hosp of N Staffs NHS Trust from 08. *University Hospital of North Staffs, Newcastle Road, Stoke-on-Trent ST4 6QG* T: (01782) 676400 E: leo.varquez@uhns.nhs.uk

VARTY, John Eric. b 44. Tyndale Hall Bris 68. **d** 71 **p** 72. C Barrow St Mark *Carl* 71-74; C Cheadle *Ches* 74-82; V Cheadle All Hallows 82-89; V Alsager Ch Ch 89-06; rtd 06; Chapl to Bp Stockport *Ches* 07-14; C Acton and Worleston, Church Minshull etc 12-14. *14 Gowy Close, Alsager, Stoke-on-Trent ST7 2HX* T: (01270) 877360
E: john.varty@homecall.co.uk

VARTY, Robert. b 46. LRAM. Sarum & Wells Th Coll 84. **d** 86 **p** 87. C Plympton St Mary *Ex* 86-89; TV Northam w Westward Ho! and Appledore 89-95; P-in-c Wigginton *St Alb* 95-00; TV Tring 95-00; rtd 00; PtO *Ex* 01-04; Clergy Widow(er)s Officer 02-04; PtO *Eur* from 05. *La Butte, 61110 Bellou-sur-Huisne, France* T: (0033) 2 33 25 55 64
E: varty.robert@wanadoo.fr

VASBY-BURNIE, Timothy Roy. b 79. Trin Coll Cam MA 00. Wycliffe Hall Ox BTh 07. **d** 07 **p** 08. C Stone Ch Ch and Oulton *Lich* 07-10; V Wednesbury St Bart from 10. *The Vicarage, 4 Little Hill, Wednesbury WS10 9DE* T: 0121-556 0378
E: tim@timvb.plus.com

VASETHE, Sister Veronica. b 69. Solomon Is Coll of HE CertEd 87. Trin Coll Bris BA 12. **d** 11 **p** 12. NSM Ham St Andr *S'wark* from 11. *St Michael's Convent, 56 Ham Common, Richmond TW10 7JH* T: (020) 8940 8711 F: 8948 5525 M: 07898-267660 E: veronica@sistersofthechurch.org.uk

VASEY, Arthur Stuart. b 37. Qu Coll Birm 68. **d** 71 **p** 72. C Shelf *Bradf* 71-73; Australia 74-76; Chapl St Jo Hosp Linc 76-79; P-in-c Tanfield *Dur* 79-84; C Birtley 84-85; C Middlesbrough St Thos *York* 85-86; rtd 02. *Glen Esk, 3 Quarry Bank, Malton YO17 7HA*

VASEY, Mrs Janet Mary. b 41. Margaret McMillan Coll of Educn CertEd 62. Local Minl Tr Course 11. **d** 11. NSM Gt Grimsby St Mary and St Jas *Linc* from 11. *34 Western Outway, Grimsby DN34 5EX* T: (01472) 753145 E: jan.vasey@btinternet.com

VASEY-SAUNDERS, Mrs Leah Beverley. b 77. Huddersfield Univ BMus 98 St Jo Coll Dur BA 03. Cranmer Hall Dur 00. **d** 03 **p** 04. C Whorlton *Newc* 03-04; Hon C Newc St Geo 05-08; TV Cannock *Lich* 08-09; TV Cannock and Huntington 09-10; V Heath Hayes 10-11; C Hednesford 08-11; PtO *S'well* 12-13; P-in-c Harworth from 13. *The Vicarage, Tickhill Road, Harworth, Doncaster DN11 8PD* T: (01302) 744157
E: leah@vasey-saunders.co.uk

VASEY-SAUNDERS, Mark Richard. b 74. Coll of Ripon & York St Jo BA 95 St Jo Coll Dur BA 00. Cranmer Hall Dur 98. **d** 01 **p** 02. C Ponteland *Newc* 01-04; Chapl Newc Univ 04-08; PtO *Lich* 10-11; TV Retford Area *S'well* from 11. *The Vicarage, Tickhill Road, Harworth, Doncaster DN11 8PD* T: (01302) 744157 E: mark@vasey-saunders.co.uk

VASTENHOUT, Jeannetta Hermina. *See* STOKES, Jeannetta Hermina

VAUGHAN, Canon Andrew Christopher James. b 61. Univ of Wales (Lamp) BA 82. Linc Th Coll 84. **d** 84 **p** 85. C Caerleon *Mon* 84-86; C Magor w Redwick and Undy 86-88; Ind Chapl 84-94; Linc Ind Miss from 94; Can and Preb Linc Cathl from 05. *4 Grange Close, Canwick, Lincoln LN4 2RH* T/F: (01522) 528266 M: 07702-468549 E: vaughanlim@tesco.net

VAUGHAN, Andrew Kenneth. b 64. MCIOB 01. Ridley Hall Cam 04. **d** 07 **p** 08. C Chislehurst Ch Ch *Roch* 07-11; V Istead Rise from 11. *The Vicarage, Upper Avenue, Istead Rise, Gravesend DA13 9DA* T: (01474) 832403 M: 07977-154809
E: andrewvaughan@akv64s.com

VAUGHAN, Brian John. b 38. Lich Th Coll 65. **d** 68 **p** 69. C Fisherton Anger *Sarum* 68-70; C Wareham w Arne 70-73; Asst P Mt Lawley Australia 73; R Dalwallinu 73-76; R Morawa 75-78; Field Officer Bible Soc of W Australia 78-81; Assoc P Mt Lawley 82-86; R Pinjarra 86-96; R Manjimup 96-00; rtd 00. *Milborne, 6 Steeple Retreat, Busselton WA 6280, Australia* T: (0061) (8) 9751 1225 E: sherton38@optusnet.com.au

VAUGHAN, Carole Ann. b 47. Leeds Univ CertEd 68. STETS 95. **d** 98 **p** 99. NSM Oakley w Wootton St Lawrence *Win* from 98. *The Rectory, 9 The Drive, Oakley, Basingstoke RG23 7DA* T: (01256) 780825 E: carole@cjvaughan.co.uk

VAUGHAN, Miss Catherine Margaret. b 64. Bp Grosseteste Coll BEd 88 Moorlands Coll BA 05. STETS MA 12. **d** 12 **p** 13. C Bath Twerton-on-Avon *B & W* from 12. *20A Bellotts Road, Bath BA2 3RT* M: 07879-498474

VAUGHAN, Charles Jeremy Marshall. b 52. Man Univ BSc 75. St Jo Coll Nottm 83. **d** 85 **p** 86. C Epsom Common Ch Ch *Guildf* 85-88; C Woking Ch Ch 88-93; R Worting *Win* 93-07; R Winklebury and Worting 07-10; R Oakley w Wootton St Lawrence from 10. *The Rectory, 9 The Drive, Oakley, Basingstoke RG23 7DA* T: (01256) 780825
E: jeremy@cjvaughan.co.uk

VAUGHAN, Craig. d 12. NSM Newton Nottage *Llan* from 12. *Address temp unknown*

VAUGHAN, Idris Samuel. b 46. Sarum Th Coll 70. **d** 72 **p** 73. C Workington St Jo *Carl* 72-76; C Foley Park *Worc* 76-79; V Hayton St Mary *Carl* 79-85; Chapl Asst Univ Hosp Nottm 85-90; Chapl Asst Nottm Gen Hosp 85-90; Chapl Stafford Distr Gen Hosp 90-94; Chapl Chase Hosp Cannock 90-94; Chapl Mid Staffs Gen Hosps NHS Trust 94-06; rtd 06; P-in-c Lanzarote *Eur* 06-10. *43 Silkmore Crescent, Stafford ST17 4JL*

VAUGHAN, Jeffrey Charles. b 45. S'wark Ord Course 85. **d** 88 **p** 89. NSM Tottenham St Paul *Lon* 88-91; C Hendon St Alphage 91-95; V Enfield SS Pet and Paul from 95. *The Vicarage, 177 Ordnance Road, Enfield EN3 6AB* T: (01992) 719770 F: (020) 8292 8456

VAUGHAN, Jeremy. *See* VAUGHAN, Charles Jeremy Marshall

VAUGHAN, Patrick Handley. b 38. TCD BA 60 BD 65 Selw Coll Cam BA 62 MA 66 Nottm Univ PhD 88. Ridley Hall Cam 61. **d** 63 **p** 64. Min Can Bradf Cathl 63-66; Uganda 67-73; P-in-c Slingsby *York* 74-77; Tutor NW Ord Course 74-77; P-in-c Hovingham *York* 74-77; Prin EMMTC *S'well* 77-90; Hon Can Leic Cathl 87-90; Assoc Lect Open Univ from 94. *113 Upperthorpe Road, Sheffield S6 3EA* T: 0114-272 2675
E: patrickvaughan38@yahoo.co.uk

✠**VAUGHAN, The Rt Revd Peter St George.** b 30. Selw Coll Cam BA 55 MA 59 BNC Ox MA 63. Ridley Hall Cam. **d** 57 **p** 58 **c** 89. C Birm St Martin 57-63; Chapl Ox Pastorate 63-67; Asst Chapl BNC Ox 63-67; V Galle Face Ch Ch Ceylon 67-72; Prec H Trin Cathl Auckland New Zealand 72-75; Prin Crowther Hall CMS Tr Coll Selly Oak 75-83; Adn Westmorland and Furness *Carl* 83-89; Hon Can Carl Cathl 83-89; Area Bp Ramsbury *Sarum* 89-98; Can and Preb Sarum Cathl 89-98; rtd 98; Hon Asst Bp Bradf 98-01; Hon Can Bradf Cathl 98-01; PtO *Glouc* 01-06; Hon Asst Bp Glouc 06-11; Hon Asst Bp Bris from 02. *Willowbrook, Downington, Lechlade GL7 3DL* T: (01367) 252216

VAUGHAN, Preb Roger Maxwell. b 39. AKC 62. **d** 63 **p** 64. C W Bromwich All SS *Lich* 63-65; C Wolverhampton 65-70; V Tunstall Ch Ch 70-79; V Abbots Bromley 79-86; P-in-c Blithfield 85-86; V Abbots Bromley w Blithfield 86-93; V Stafford St Jo and Tixall w Ingestre 93-04; Preb Lich Cathl 99-04; rtd 04; PtO *Lich* from 04. *51 Crestwood Drive, Stone ST15 0LW* T: (01785) 812192
E: salrog.vaughan@btinternet.com

VAUGHAN, Trevor. b 41. TD 91. Cen Lancs Univ BA 91. Linc Th Coll 66. **d** 69 **p** 70. C Wyken *Cov* 69-72; C Stratford-on-Avon w Bishopton 72-73; P-in-c Monks Kirby w Withybrook and Copston Magna 73-75; P-in-c Wolvey, Burton Hastings and Stretton Baskerville 73-77; P-in-c Withybrook w Copston Magna 73-77; V Heyhouses *Blackb* 77-80; CF (TA) from 79; V Chorley St Geo *Blackb* 80-83; R Bolton by Bowland w Grindleton *Bradf* 83-89; V Settle 89-91; R Broughton, Marton and Thornton 91-00; V Morecambe St Barn *Blackb* 00-03; P-in-c Sabden and Pendleton 03-06; rtd 06. *3 Westmount Close, Ripon HG4 2HU* T: (01765) 605591

VAUGHAN-WILSON, Jane Elizabeth. b 61. Magd Coll Ox MA 87. Cranmer Hall Dur. **d** 89 **p** 94. Par Dn Ormesby *York* 89-93; Dn-in-c Middlesbrough St Agnes 93-94; P-in-c 94-95; TV Basingstoke *Win* 95-03; PtO *Truro* from 03; Dioc Dir of Ords from 14. *4 Tolver Road, Penzance TR18 2AG* T: (01736) 351825

VAYRO, Mark Shaun. b 66. Aston Tr Scheme 88 Linc Th Coll BTh 93. d 93 p 94. C Northampton St Mich w St Edm *Pet* 93-96; TV Duston 96-98; V Elm and Friday Bridge w Coldham *Ely* 98-01. *125 Spalding Road, Pinchbeck, Spalding LN11 3UE*

VAZ, Stanley Hubert. b 62. St Jo Coll Nottm 09. d 11 p 12. C Stretton w Claymills *Lich* 11-15; P-in-c Rocester and Croxden w Hollington from 15. *The Vicarage, Church Lane, Rocester, Uttoxeter ST14 5JZ* M: 07803-054057
E: vaz9301@gmail.com

VEEN, Keith Henry. b 46. d 01 p 02. OLM Croydon St Pet *S'wark* 01-02; OLM Croydon Ch Ch from 02. *91 The Ridgeway, Croydon CR0 4AH* T: (020) 8688 3565
E: keithveen@veenco.fsnet.co.uk

VELLACOTT, Peter Graham. b 38. EAMTC 90. d 93 p 94. NSM Framlingham w Saxtead *St E* 93-95; NSM Brandeston w Kettleburgh 95-99; NSM Easton 95-99; P-in-c Brandeston w Kettleburgh and Easton 99-07; rtd 07; PtO *St E* from 07. *Soham House, Brandeston, Woodbridge IP13 7AX*
T: (01728) 685423

VENABLES, Deborah. b 70. d 12 p 13. NSM Presteigne w Discoed, Kinsham, Lingen and Knill *Heref* from 12. *17 Caenbrook Meadow, Presteigne LD8 2NE* T: (01544) 267663
E: revdebbiev@aol.com

✠**VENABLES, The Most Revd Gregory James.** b 49. Lon Univ CertEd 74. d 84 p 84 c 93. SAMS from 77; Paraguay 78-90; C Rainham *Chelmsf* 90-92; C Rainham w Wennington 92-93; Aux Bp Peru and Bolivia 93-95; Bp Bolivia 95-00; Asst Primate of S Cone 95-02; Bp Coadjutor Argentina 00-02; Dioc Bp from 02; Presiding Bp of S Cone from 01. *Rioja 2995, B1636DMG - Olivos, Provincia de Buenos Aires, Argentina* T: (0054) (11) 4799 7124 E: bpgreg@ciudad.com.ar

VENABLES, Canon Margaret Joy. b 37. Bp Otter Coll CertEd 57. S Dios Minl Tr Scheme 86. d 89 p 94. NSM Wilton *B & W* 89-91; C Taunton St Andr 91-97; P-in-c Haynes *St Alb* 97-03; P-in-c Clophill 00-03; R Campton, Clophill and Haynes 03-06; RD Shefford 01-06; Hon Can St Alb 05-06; rtd 06; P-in-c Barnack w Ufford and Bainton *Pet* 06-10; PtO from 10. *The Cottage, Millstone Lane, Barnack, Stamford PE9 3ET* T: (01780) 749127 E: margsv@waitrose.com *or* margaretvenables@gmail.com

VENABLES, Philip Richard Meredith. b 58. Magd Coll Ox BA 79 CertEd 80. Wycliffe Hall Ox 85. d 88 p 89. C Gillingham St Mark *Roch* 88-93; V Penge St Jo 93-07; R Bebington *Ches* 07-12; V Whittle-le-Woods *Blackb* from 12. *The Vicarage, Preston Road, Whittle-le-Woods, Chorley PR6 7PS* T: (01257) 241291 E: philip.venables@ntlworld.com

VENEZUELA, Bishop of. *See* GUERRERO, The Rt Revd Orlando

VENN, Richard Frank. b 49. Leeds Univ BSc 72 Strathclyde Univ PhD 77 CChem FRSC 97. Ridley Hall Cam 04. d 05 p 06. C Margate H Trin *Cant* 05-08; P-in-c Len Valley from 08. *The Vicarage, Old Ashford Road, Lenham, Maidstone ME17 2PX* T: (01622) 858195 M: 07970-288669 E: pic@lvb.org.uk

VENNELLS, Ms Paula Anne. b 59. Bradf Univ BA 81 FRSA 88. SAOMC 02. d 05 p 06. NSM Bromham w Oakley and Stagsden *St Alb* from 05. *Rushey Ford House, West End Road, Kempston, Bedford MK43 8RU* T: (01234) 851594 M: 07786-174638
E: paula@rusheyford.freeserve.co.uk

✠**VENNER, The Rt Revd Stephen Squires.** b 44. DL 09. Birm Univ BA 65 Linacre Coll Ox BA 67 MA 71 Lon Univ PGCE 72 Birm Univ Hon DD 09 Cant Ch Ch Univ DUniv 10. St Steph Ho Ox 65. d 68 p 69 c 94. C Streatham St Pet *S'wark* 68-71; C Streatham Hill St Marg 71-72; C Balham Hill Ascension 72-74; V Clapham St Pet 74-76; Bp's Chapl to Overseas Students 74-76; P-in-c Studley *Sarum* 76; V 76-82; V Weymouth H Trin 82-94; RD Weymouth 88-93; Can and Preb Sarum Cathl 89-94; Suff Bp Middleton *Man* 94-99; Suff Bp Dover *Cant* 99-09; rtd 09; Bp Falkland Is 11-14; Bp HM Forces 09-14; Hon Asst Bp Eur from 11; Hon Asst Bp St Alb *St Alb* from 13. *81 King Harry Lane, St Albans AL3 4AS* M: 07980-743628 T: (01727) 831704 E: stephen@venner.org.uk

VENNING, Miss Alice Helen. b 83. St Mellitus Coll 12. d 15. C Blenheim *Ox* from 15. *73 Heath Lane, Bladon, Woodstock OX20 1RZ* M: 07966-977157 E: alice.venning@gmail.com

VENNING, Nigel Christopher. b 50. K Coll Lon BD 75 AKC 75. St Aug Coll Cant 75. d 76 p 77. C Minehead *B & W* 76-80; C Fawley *Win* 80-83; P-in-c Whitestaunton and Combe St Nicholas w Wambrook *B & W* 83-89; R Staplegrove 89-01; P-in-c Norton Fitzwarren 00-01; R Staplegrove w Norton Fitzwarren 01-03; R Blackdown 03-05; RD Taunton 96-01; r-d 05; PtO *B & W* from 05. *Crispin House, 5 Mendip Edge, Weston-super-Mare BS24 9JF* T: (01934) 814112
E: nigelvenning@hotmail.com

VENTON, Kathryn Magdelana. *See* LAWRIE, Kathryn Magdalena

VERE NICOLL, Charles Fiennes. b 55. Solicitor 79. SAOMC 96. d 99 p 00. NSM Basildon w Aldworth and Ashampstead *Ox*

99-08; PtO 08-10; *Lon* from 10. *Ashvine, Westridge, Highclere, Newbury RG20 9RY* M: 07768-238128 E: cvn@cvnsbh.com

VEREKER, Jennifer Lesley. b 45. Totley Hall Coll CertEd 66. WMMTC 96. d 99 p 00. NSM Rugby *Cov* 99-03; TV Gt and Lt Coates w Bradley *Linc* 03-08; rtd 08; PtO *St E* from 08. *Laurelwood, Thurston Road, Great Barton, Bury St Edmunds IP31 2PW* T: (01359) 234413 E: j.vereker@btinternet.com

VEREY, Christopher Douglas. b 46. St Chad's Coll Dur BA 68 MA 70. Ripon Coll Cuddesdon 02. d 04 p 05. NSM Yate New Town *Bris* 04-09. *2 The Green, Heathend, Wotton-under-Edge GL12 8AR* E: chrisverey@tiscali.com.uk

VERHEY, Shawn Gordon. b 59. Ottawa Univ BA 88 Liv Univ BTh 03. NOC 00. d 04 p 05. NSM Southport SS Simon and Jude w All So *Liv* 04-07; Asst Chapl HM Pris Garth 04-07; Chapl HM YOI Thorn Cross from 07. *HM Young Offender Institution, Thorn Cross, Arley Road, Appleton, Warrington WA4 4RL* T: (01925) 805100 E: vrhshawn@aol.com

VERNON, Bryan Graham. b 50. Qu Coll Cam BA 72 MA 76. Qu Coll Birm 73. d 75 p 76. C Newc St Gabr 75-79; Chapl Newc Univ 79-91; Lect Health Care Ethics from 91; Chmn Newc Mental Health Trust 91-94; PtO from 94. *34 Queens Road, Jesmond, Newcastle upon Tyne NE2 2PQ* T: 0191-281 3861
E: b.g.vernon@ncl.ac.uk

VERNON, John Christie. b 40. Imp Coll Lon BScEng 62. Linc Th Coll 63. d 65 p 66. C Barnard Castle *Dur* 65-69; CF 69-90; Asst Chapl Gen 90-92; Chapl Ellesmere Coll 92-99; PtO *Lich* 99-01; NSM Ellesmere Deanery 01-05 and 06-08; P-in-c Petton w Cockshutt, Welshampton and Lyneal etc 05-06; RD Ellesmere 02-08; PtO from 08. *The Drift House, Lake House Mews, Grange Road, Ellesmere SY12 9DE* T: (01691) 623765 M: 07778-312226 E: john@jvernon.go-plus.net

VERNON, Canon Matthew James. b 71. Collingwood Coll Dur BSc 93 Fitzw Coll Cam BA 96 MA 98. Westcott Ho Cam 94. d 97 p 98. C Guildf H Trin w St Mary 97-01; Chapl St Jo Cathl and P-in-c Pokfulam Em Hong Kong 01-09; Can Res St E Cathl from 09; Sub Dean from 12. *2 Abbey Precincts, Bury St Edmunds IP33 1RS* T: (01284) 701472
E: canon.pastor@stedscathedral.co.uk

VERNON, Robert Leslie. b 47. Sarum & Wells Th Coll 73. d 76 p 77. C Hartlepool St Luke *Dur* 76-79; C Birm St Geo 79-82; V Bordesley Green 82-86; Dioc Youth Officer *Carl* 86-89; P-in-c Holme 86-89; Dioc Youth Adv *Newc* 89-95; V Ulgham and Widdrington 95-01; P-in-c Pokesdown St Jas *Win* 01-12; P-in-c Boscombe St Andr 09-12; rtd 12. *Killard, Doonbeg, Co Clare, Republic of Ireland* E: revbobvernon@hotmail.com

VERNON-YORKE, Mrs Suzanne. b 74. Huddersfield Univ BA 96. St Jo Coll Nottm 99. d 03 p 04. C Wrose *Bradf* 03-06; Chapl Ripley St Thos C of E High Sch Lanc *Blackb* 06-11; Peru 11-12; Chapl and Dep Warden Lee Abbey Internat Students' Club Kensington 13-14; Chapl Bradf Univ from 14; Miss P Bradf Adnry from 14; Hon Can Bradf Cathl from 15. *Desmond Tutu House, 2 Ashgrove, Bradford BD7 1BN*
E: chocsxxx@hotmail.com

VERSCHOYLE, Dermot Henry. b 48. d 13 p 14. NSM Merrow *Guildf* from 13. *1 Chatfield Drive, Guildford GU4 7XP* T: (01483) 533449

VERWEY, Mrs Eileen Susan Vivien. b 41. Open Univ BA 78 BA 93 Goldsmiths' Coll Lon PGCE 82. WEMTC 03. d 05 p 06. NSM Burghill *Heref* from 05; NSM Stretton Sugwas from 05; NSM Pipe-cum-Lyde and Moreton-on-Lugg from 05. *Mill Croft House, Staunton-on-Wye, Hereford HR4 7LW* T: (01981) 500626

VESEY, Nicholas Ivo. b 54. Bris Univ BSc 73. Cranmer Hall Dur 95. d 97 p 98. C Tunbridge Wells St Mark *Roch* 97-01; V New Catton St Luke w St Aug *Nor* 01-14; Chapl Aspen Chpl Colorado USA from 14. *77 Meadowood Drive, Aspen CO 81611, USA* T: (001) (970) 925 7184 E: nicholas@vesey.net

VESSEY, Canon Andrew John. b 45. Bp Otter Coll CertEd 67. Sarum & Wells Th Coll 84. d 86 p 87. C Framlingham w Saxtead *St E* 86-89; V Catshill and Dodford *Worc* 89-94; P-in-c Areley Kings 94-95; R 95-02; RD Stourport 00-02; TV Kidderminster St Jo and H Innocents 02-05; TR Cen Swansea *S & B* 05-10; Hon Can Brecon Cathl 10; rtd 10; PtO *Nor* from 10; *St E* from 10. *3 The Laurels, Fressingfield, Eye IP21 5NZ* T: (01379) 588389 E: andrew.vessey@btinternet.com

VESSEY, Peter Allan Beaumont. b 36. ALCD 65. d 64 p 65. C Rayleigh *Chelmsf* 64-67; C Cambridge H Trin *Ely* 67-71; V Kingston upon Hull St Aid Southcoates *York* 71-80; V Swanwick and Pentrich *Derby* 80-94; PtO from 94; rtd 96; PtO *Portsm* from 15. *3 Scarthin Terrace, Scarthin, Cromford, Matlock DE4 3QF* T: (01629) 825572
E: pnuvessey@hotmail.co.uk

VESTERGAARD, David Andrew. b 64. Reading Univ BSc 86. Wycliffe Hall Ox 97. d 99 p 00. C Chadderton Ch Ch *Man* 99-02; V Wednesfield Heath *Lich* 02-13; AD Wolverhampton 07-11; RD 11-13; Preb Lich Cathl 12-13; R Bebington *Ches* from 13. *The Rectory, Church Road, Bebington, Wirral CH63 3EX* E: david@vestergaard.co.uk

VETTERS, Miss Shirley Jacqueline Margaret. b 34. S'wark Ord Course 85. **d** 88 **p** 94. NSM E Ham w Upton Park and Forest Gate *Chelmsf* 88-91; C Birm St Martin w Bordesley St Andr 91-04; Chapl to the Markets 91-04; rtd 04; PtO *Chelmsf* 05-13. *32 Seeds Lane, Walsall WS8 6HU* T: (01543) 379668

VEVERS, Canon Geoffrey Martin. b 51. Oak Hill Th Coll. **d** 82 **p** 83. C Wealdstone H Trin *Lon* 82-84; C Harrow Trin St Mich 84-88; V Wandsworth St Steph *S'wark* 88-96; V Battersea Fields from 96; RD Battersea 04-10; Hon Can S'wark Cathl from 06. *St Saviour's Vicarage, 351A Battersea Park Road, London SW11 4LH* T: (020) 7498 1642

VIBERT (née GREEN), Imogen Elizabeth. b 73. Birm Univ BA 96 Cam Univ BTh 02. Westcott Ho Cam 99. **d** 02 **p** 03. C Poplar *Lon* 02-06; Hon C Upper Clapton St Matt 06-12; Hon C Stamford Hill St Thos 06-12; Chapl St Sav and St Olave's Sch Newington from 12; Chapl S'wark Cathl from 13. *St Saviour's and St Olave's School, New Kent Road, London SE1 4AN* T: (020) 7407 1843
E: imogen@vibert.wannadoo.co.uk

VIBERT, Simon David Newman. b 63. Oak Hill Th Coll BA 89. **d** 89 **p** 90. C Houghton *Carl* 89-92; C-in-c Buxton Trin Prop Chpl *Derby* 92-99; V Wimbledon Park St Luke *S'wark* 99-07; Vice Prin Wycliffe Hall Ox 07-12; Acting Prin 12-13; Dir Sch of Preaching from 08. *Wycliffe Hall, 54 Banbury Road, Oxford OX2 6PW* T: (01865) 274200
E: simon.vibert@wycliffe.ox.ac.uk

VICENCIO PRIOR, Mrs Carla Alexandra. b 70. Bath Univ BSc 93 SSEES Lon MA 97 Ches Univ MTh 15. St Jo Coll Nottm 12. **d** 15. C Kirk Hallam *Derby* from 15. *10 Orlando Court, Chellaston, Derby DE73 5BJ* T: (01332) 703407
M: 07767-087530 E: carlavp@talktalk.net

VICKERMAN, Canon John. b 42. Chich Th Coll 69. **d** 72 **p** 73. C Horbury *Wakef* 72-76; C Elland 76-78; V Glass Houghton 78-89; V Bruntcliffe 89-96; V King Cross 96-11; RD Halifax 00-06; Hon Can Wakef Cathl 02-11; rtd 11. *6 St Barnabas, Newland, Malvern WR13 5AX* T: (01684) 563741
E: john.vickerman42@gmail.com

VICKERS (née CONWAY), Mrs Catherine Mary. b 61. Newc Univ BA 82 Leeds Univ PGCE 83. NEOC 03. **d** 06 **p** 07. C Bedale and Leeming *Ripon* 06-08; C Bedale and Leeming and Thornton Watlass 08-10; R Stourdene Gp *Cov* from 10. *The Vicarage, Old Warwick Road, Ettington, Stratford-upon-Avon CV37 7SH* T: (01789) 748137 E: cathvickers@hotmail.com

VICKERS, Dennis William George. b 30. RIBA 72 York Univ MA 91 IHBC 99. Glouc Th Course 83. **d** 86 **p** 87. NSM Stokesay *Heref* 86-88; NSM Bucknell w Chapel Lawn, Llanfair Waterdine etc 88-92; NSM Wigmore Abbey 93-01; PtO from 01. *Address temp unknown*

VICKERS, Donald. b 48. Edge Hill Coll of HE DASE 80 Univ of Wales (Ban) MEd 87. NOC 07. **d** 00 **p** 01. NSM Leigh St Mary *Man* 00-05; NSM Westleigh St Pet 05-12; Asst Chapl HM Pris Man 00-12; rtd 12; PtO *Man* from 12. *21 Broom Way, Westhoughton, Bolton BL5 3TZ* T: (01942) 815193
M: 07768-492581 E: don@dvickers20.freeserve.co.uk

VICKERS, Mrs Janice Audrey Maureen. b 56. **d** 96 **p** 97. OLM Woking Ch Ch *Guildf* 96-06; OLM Ottershaw from 06. *7 Langdale Close, Woking GU21 4RS* T: (01483) 720873
E: bobjan@bjvickers.eclipse.co.uk

VICKERS, Mrs Mary Janet. b 57. Westmr Coll Ox MTh 97. St Jo Coll Nottm BTh 85. **dss** 85 **d** 87 **p** 99. Worc City St Paul and Old St Martin etc 85-89; Par Dn 87-89; World Miss Officer Worc 89-92; USPG 92-00; LtO *Eur* 95-99; PtO from 99; PtO Adnry of the Army from 97; NSM Cheswardine, Childs Ercall, Hales, Hinstock etc *Lich* 99-01; NSM Wrecclesham *Guildf* 01-02; NSM Pimperne, Stourpaine, Durweston and Bryanston *Sarum* 03-05; NSM Hipswell *Ripon* 05-06; NSM W Andover *Win* 07-09; NSM Portway and Danebury 09-10; Ind Chapl *Linc* from 10. *The Rectory, 1A The Avenue, Healing, Grimsby DN41 7NA* T: (01472) 883481 M: 07730-972403
E: vickers983@btinternet.com

VICKERS, Michael. b 60. Cranmer Hall Dur BA 98. **d** 98 **p** 99. C Monkwearmouth *Dur* 98-00; C Kowloon St Andr Hong Kong 00-07; V Cranham Park *Chelmsf* from 07. *St Luke's Vicarage, 201 Front Lane, Upminster RM14 1LD* T: (01708) 222562 F: 223253 E: revmichaelvickers@gmail.com

✠**VICKERS, The Rt Revd Michael Edwin.** b 29. Worc Coll Ox BA 56 MA 56. Cranmer Hall Dur. **d** 59 **p** 60 **c** 88. C Bexleyheath Ch Ch *Roch* 59-62; Chapl Lee Abbey 62-67; V Hull St Jo Newland *York* 67-81; AD Cen and N Hull 72-81; Can and Preb York Minster 81-88; Adn E Riding 81-88; Area Bp Colchester *Chelmsf* 88-94; rtd 94; Hon Asst Bp Blackb 94-13. *137 Canalside, Redhill RH1 2FH* T: (01737) 642984
E: micjan@tiscali.co.uk

VICKERS, Peter. b 56. St Jo Coll Nottm LTh 85. **d** 85 **p** 86. C Worc St Barn w Ch Ch 85-88; TV Kidderminster St Mary and All SS w Trimpley etc 88-92; Ind Chapl 88-92; CF 92-11;

RD Grimsby and Cleethorpes *Linc* 11-13; RD Haverstoe 11-13; Ind Chapl from 13. *The Rectory, 1A The Avenue, Healing, Grimsby DN41 7NA* T: (01472) 885807
E: revd.p.vickers@hotmail.co.uk

VICKERS, Peter George. b 41. Local Minl Tr Course 90. **d** 93 **p** 94. OLM Cobham *Guildf* 93-04; OLM Cobham and Stoke D'Abernon 04-11; rtd 11; PtO *Guildf* from 11. *24 Station Road, Stoke D'Abernon, Cobham KT11 3BN* T: (01932) 862497
E: revpgv@googlemail.com

VICKERS, Randolph. b 36. Newc Univ MA 93 FCIM FInstD. St Alb Minl Tr Scheme 77. **d** 80 **p** 82. NSM Hitchin *St Alb* 80-87; NSM Luton Lewsey St Hugh 87-89; NSM Shotley *Newc* 89-01; rtd 01; PtO *Newc* from 01; *Dur* from 14. *4 The Paddock, Stocksfield NE43 7PH* T/F: (01661) 842364
E: rvickers@christian-healing.com

VICKERSTAFF, John Joseph. b 60. Dur Univ BEd 82 Teesside Univ BA 84 MA 86 MPhil 88 ARCO 92. Westcott Ho Cam 97. **d** 97 **p** 98. C Halesworth w Linstead, Chediston, Holton etc *St E* 97-99; C Blyth Valley 99-00; TV Ch the King *Newc* 00-05; P-in-c Doveridge, Scropton, Sudbury etc *Derby* 05-10; C Alkmonton, Cubley and Marston Montgomery 07-10; R S Dales from 11. *The Rectory, Main Road, Sudbury, Ashbourne DE6 5HS* T: (01283) 585098 E: grumpy.revs@tiscali.co.uk

VICKERY, Jonathan Laurie. b 58. Bretton Hall Coll BEd 80. Wycliffe Hall Ox 81. **d** 84 **p** 85. C Gorseinon *S & B* 84-86; P-in-c Whitton and Pilleth and Cascob etc 86-87; R 87-91; V Crickhowell w Cwmdu and Tretower 91-02; P-in-c Downend *Bris* 02-07; V from 07. *Christ Church Vicarage, Shrubbery Road, Bristol BS16 5TB* T: 0117-908 9868
E: vicar@christchurchdownend.com

VICKERY, Robin Francis. b 48. K Coll Lon BD 73 AKC 73. **d** 74 **p** 75. C Clapham St Jo *S'wark* 74-77; C Clapham Ch Ch and St Jo 75-77; C Reigate St Luke S Park 77-79; Hon C Clapham H Spirit 80-87 and 02-10; Hon C Clapham Team 87-01; Hon C N Lambeth from 10. *13 Chelsham Road, London SW4 6NR* T: (020) 7622 4792

VIDAL-HALL, Roderic Mark. b 37. Sheff Univ BSc 60. Lich Th Coll 62. **d** 64 **p** 65. C Ilkeston St Mary *Derby* 64-67; C Nether and Over Seale 67-70; C Chellaston 70-84; C Marchington w Marchington Woodlands *Lich* 84-97; C Kingstone w Gratwich 85-97; TV Uttoxeter Area 97-01; rtd 01. *Le Perhou, 22630 Saint-Juvat, France* T: (0033) 2 96 88 16 34 E: mark@vidalhall.co.uk

VIGARS, Anthony Roy. b 54. St Jo Coll Dur BA 75. Trin Coll Bris 77. **d** 78 **p** 79. C Barking St Marg w St Patr *Chelmsf* 78-81; C Littleover *Derby* 81-84; C-in-c Stapenhill Immanuel CD 84-90; V Meltham *Wakef* 90-97; C Reading St Jo *Ox* 97-06; rtd 07; PtO *Ox* 07-08; *Ex* from 09. *15 Edgcumbe Drive, Tavistock PL19 0ET* T: (01822) 610539 E: vigars@lineone.net

VIGEON, Canon Owen George. b 28. Peterho Cam BA 52 MA 57. Ely Th Coll 52. **d** 54 **p** 55. C Barrow St Luke *Carl* 54-58; Chapl St Jo Coll York 58-61; V Burnley St Steph *Blackb* 61-69; V Bilsborrow and Asst Dir RE 69-73; V St Annes St Thos 74-85; RD Fylde 80-85; R Halton w Aughton 85-93; Hon Can Blackb Cathl 92-93; rtd 93; PtO *Worc* 93-04; *Cov* from 04. *10 Hall Lane, Coventry CV2 2AW* T: (024) 7661 1712
E: owenvig@virginmedia.com

VIGERS, Neil Simon. b 62. K Coll Lon BD 84 MTh 87. Linc Th Coll 88. **d** 90 **p** 91. C Chelsea St Luke and Ch Ch *Lon* 90-93; C Staines St Mary and St Pet 93-96; P-in-c Hook *Win* 96-02; R 02-07; PtO *Guildf* from 14. *St Andrew's House, 16 Tavistock Crescent, London W11 1AP* T: (020) 7313 3900 F: 7313 3999

VIGERS, Patricia Anne. b 31. Lon Inst of Educn TCert 53. **d** 99 **p** 00. OLM Betchworth and Buckland *S'wark* 99-06; PtO from 06. *5 Normanton, Buckland Road, Reigate RH2 9RQ* T: (01737) 243698

VIGOR, Ms Margaret Ann. b 45. Ripon Coll Cuddesdon 85. **d** 87 **p** 96. Chapl Asst All SS Convent Ox 87-89; Par Dn Basildon St Martin w Nevendon *Chelmsf* 89-91; NSM Billingham St Cuth *Dur* 96-11; rtd 11; PtO *Dur* from 10. *15 Mitchell Street, Hartlepool TS26 9EZ* T: (01429) 867458

VILES, Joan Mary. b 47. **d** 13 **p** 14. NSM Thornes *Leeds* from 13. *4 Thornes Moor Close, Wakefield WF2 8QA* T: (01924) 383564
E: joan.viles@blueyonder.co.uk

VILLAGE, Andrew. b 54. Collingwood Coll Dur BSc 75 Edin Univ PhD 80 Bris Univ PhD 03. Trin Coll Bris BA 92. **d** 92 **p** 93. C Northampton St Giles *Pet* 92-95; R Middleton Cheney w Chacombe 95-04; Dir Cen for Min Studies Univ of Wales (Ban) 04-07; Lect York St Jo Univ from 07; PtO *York* from 08. *York St John University, Lord Mayor's Walk, York YO31 7EX* T: (01904) 876723 M: 07749-484425
E: a.village@yorksj.ac.uk

VILLER, Canon Allan George Frederick. b 38. EAMTC 78. **d** 81 **p** 82. NSM Ely 81-85; V Emneth 85-92; V Littleport 92-03; RD Ely 98-03; rtd 03; Hon Can Ely Cathl 01-06; Hon C Barton Bendish w Beachamwell etc 03-06; PtO *Ely* from 06; *Nor* from 07. *41 Westfields, Narborough, King's Lynn PE32 1SX* T/F: (01760) 337633 E: allan@viller.net

VINCE, Mrs Barbara Mary Tudor. b 29. St Alb Minl Tr Scheme 79. **dss** 82 **d** 87 **p** 94. Northwood H Trin Lon 82-86; Belmont 86-89; Par Dn 87-89; rtd 90. 10 Risinghill Close, Northwood HA6 3PH

VINCE, David Eric. b 59. Birm Univ BA 81 Nottm Univ BCombStuds 85 Goldsmiths' Coll Lon PGCE 90. Linc Th Coll 82. **d** 85 **p** 86. C Gt Malvern St Mary Worc 85-88; C All Hallows by the Tower etc Lon 88-90; Min St Giles Cripplegate w St Bart Moor Lane etc 90-92; R Salwarpe and Hindlip w Martin Hussingtree Worc 92-97; R Willersey, Saintbury, Weston-sub-Edge etc Glouc 97-03; P-in-c Quinton 02-03; R Mickleton, Willersey, Saintbury etc 03-06; RD Campden 01-06; PtO 06-07; Worc 06-07; CF from 07. c/o MOD Chaplains (Army) F: 381824 T: (01264) 383430

VINCENT, Preb Alfred James. b 30. Bris Univ BA 54 Lon Univ BD 56. Tyndale Hall Bris 50. **d** 54 **p** 55. C Shrewsbury St Julian Lich 54-56; C Camborne Truro 56-59; V Kenwyn 59-68; LtO St Alb 68; Lect Qu Coll Birm 68-70; LtO Birm 68-70; V Bordesley St Oswald 70-76; V S Shields St Hilda w St Thos Dur 76-84; Hon Chapl Miss to Seafarers from 79; V Bude Haven Truro 84-89; R Bude Haven and Marhamchurch 89-92; RD Stratton 88-92; Preb St Endellion 90-95; rtd 92; P-in-c Chacewater Truro 92-95; PtO from 95. 5 Raymond Road, Redruth TR15 2HD T: (01209) 219263

VINCENT, Christopher Robin. b 30. Sarum Th Coll 57. **d** 60 **p** 61. C Frome St Jo B & W 60-64; V Puxton w Hewish St Ann and Wick St Lawrence 64-70; V Buckland Dinham w Elm 70-71; V Buckland Dinham w Elm, Orchardleigh etc 71-77; P-in-c Frome H Trin 77-90; Chapl St Adhelm's Hosp Frome 77-88; RD Frome B & W 85-89; V Kewstoke w Wick St Lawrence 90-94; rtd 94; PtO B & W from 94. Willows Edge, 2 Westwood Close, Weston-super-Mare BS22 6JU T: (01934) 517425

VINCENT, David Cyril. b 37. Selw Coll Cam BA 60 MA 64. Coll of Resurr Mirfield 60. **d** 62 **p** 63. C Cheetwood St Alb Man 62-65; C Lawton Moor 65-67; V Wandsworth Common St Mary S'wark 67-84; RD Tooting 75-80; R Stoke D'Abernon Guildf 84-02; rtd 02; PtO B & W from 04. 29 North Street, Stoke-sub-Hamdon TA14 6QS T: (01935) 825438 E: dajovincent@btinternet.com

VINCENT, Jacqueline Margaret. See RODWELL, Jacqueline Margaret

VINCENT, James. See VINCENT, Alfred James

VINCENT, John Leonard. b 61. Univ of Wales (Lamp) BA 83 Southn Univ BTh 87 Cardiff Univ MTh 14. Chich Th Coll 84. **d** 87 **p** 88. C Hampton All SS Lon 87-90; C Shepperton 90-95; V Whitton SS Phil and Jas 95-03; CF from 03. c/o MOD Chaplains (Army) F: 381824 T: (01264) 383430 E: padrejohn@live.co.uk

VINCENT, Michael Francis. b 48. CertEd 70 Open Univ BA 83. Sarum & Wells Th Coll 85. **d** 87 **p** 88. C Nuneaton St Mary Cov 87-90; C Stockingford 90-91; P-in-c 91-99; V 99-14; rtd 14. 11 Elmcroft Road, North Kilworth, Lutterworth LE17 6HX E: mick@vincent4850.freeserve.co.uk

VINCENT, Robin. See VINCENT, Christopher Robin

VINCENT, Roy David. b 54. Chich Th Coll 81. **d** 83 **p** 84. C Atherton Man 83-86; V E Crompton 86-95; P-in-c Burwash Chich 95-00; R 00-04; rtd 04; PtO Carl 05-11; Mor from 12. 24 Stewart Street, Portgordon, Buckie AB56 5QT T: (01542) 834705

VINCENT, Stephen Alan. b 74. Dundee Univ BSc 98 Cam Univ BTh 11. Westcott Ho Cam 08. **d** 11 **p** 12. C Newcastle w Butterton Lich 11-14. 40 Eleanor Crescent, Newcastle ST5 3SA T: (01782) 638054 M: 07795-031587 E: revstevevincent@gmail.com

VINCER, Ms Louise Claire. b 69. Roehampton Inst BA 90 Edin Univ MTh 93. Westcott Ho Cam 97. **d** 00 **p** 01. C Waltham H Cross Chelmsf 00-04; C Perry Hill St Geo w Ch Ch and St Paul S'wark 04-06; C Bermondsey St Anne and St Aug 06-11; C Bermondsey St Jas w Ch Ch and St Crispin 06-11; Community P N Lincs Linc 11-13; Developing Discipleship Progr Co-ord from 14. The Rectory, 49 Park Drive, Grimsby DN32 0EG T: (01472) 351815 E: louise.vincer@lincoln.anglican.org

VINE, Carolyn Ann. See TIBBOTT, Carolyn Ann

VINE, James David. b 67. Brighton Univ BSc 95. St Steph Ho Ox. **d** 00 **p** 01. C Eastbourne St Mary Chich 00-03; V Stone Cross St Luke w N Langney from 03. The Vicarage, 8 Culver Close, Eastbourne BN23 8EA T: (01323) 764473 E: jamesdavidvine@gmail.com

VINE, John. b 24. Keble Coll Ox BA 45 MA 50. St Steph Ho Ox 45. **d** 48 **p** 49. C Hackney Wick St Mary of Eton w St Aug Lon 48-50; C Holborn St Alb w Saffron Hill St Pet 50-53; Chapl Ely Th Coll 53-56; Vice-Prin Ely Th Coll 56-60; Hon C St Leonards Ch Ch Chich 60-62; Chapl Lich Th Coll 62-67; R Wrington B & W 67-69; V Earl's Court St Cuth w

St Matthias Lon 69-11; rtd 12. 26 College Lane, East Grinstead RH19 3LY

VINE, Michael Charles. b 51. Worc Coll Ox BA 73 MA 80. Cuddesdon Coll 73. **d** 76 **p** 77. C Wallsend St Luke Newc 76-79; C Denton 79-81; V Sugley 81-91; V Shiremoor 91-02; R Wallsend St Pet and St Luke 02-11; rtd 11. 26 Percy Street, North Shields NE30 4HA T: 0191-257 4711 E: vinemichael@freeuk.co.uk

VINE, Canon Neville Peter. b 54. K Coll Lon BD 80 AKC 80. Linc Th Coll 80. **d** 81 **p** 82. C Peterlee Dur 81-86; Chapl Peterlee Coll 84-86; V Auckland St Pet Dur 86-89; PtO 89-91; R Easington 91-99; R Easington, Easington Colliery and S Hetton 99-03; AD Easington 98-03; V Auckland St Andr and St Anne 03-14; V Bishop Auckland from 14; AD Auckland from 03; Hon Can Dur Cathl from 03. 4 Conway Grove, Bishop Auckland DL14 6AF T: (01388) 604397 E: neville.vine@btinternet.com

VINER, Canon Leonard Edwin. b 20. Univ Coll Dur BA 43. St Aug Coll Cant 38. **d** 43 **p** 44. C W Molesey Guildf 43-45; Miss Likoma Nyasaland 46-52; Warden St Andr Th Coll Likoma 52-56; and 58-60; C Roxbourne St Andr Lon 56-58; Chapl St Mich Teacher Tr Coll Malindi Malawi 60-64; Warden St Andr Th Coll Mponda's 64-67; P-in-c Malindi 67-69; R Zomba 69-71; Hon Can S Malawi from 71; R Honing w Crostwight Nor 71-75; P-in-c E Ruston 71-73; V 73-75; P-in-c Witton w Ridlington 71-73; V 73-75; C Corby Epiphany w St Jo Pet 75-79; V Brigstock w Stanion 79-86; rtd 86; Asst Chapl Lisbon Eur 86-87; Chapl Tangier 87-89; PtO Pet from 90. 38 High Street, Brigstock, Kettering NN14 3HA T: (01536) 373104

VINEY, Arthur William. b 32. BEd. S Dios Minl Tr Scheme. **d** 82 **p** 83. NSM Clayton w Keymer Chich 82-86; NSM Streat w Westmeston 86-94; rtd 94; PtO Chich from 94. 3 The Almshouses of the Holy Name, Brighton Road, Hurstpierpoint, Hassocks BN6 9EF T: (01273) 832570 E: a.viney@btopenworld.com

VINEY, Christopher William. b 54. All SS Cen for Miss & Min 13. **d** 14 **p** 15. NSM Newton w Flowery Field Ches from 14. 7 Rochester Close, Dukinfield SK16 5DG T: 0161-303 1244 M: 07880-343804 E: chrisviney@me.com

VINEY, Peter. b 43. Ox NSM Course. **d** 76 **p** 77. NSM High Wycombe Ox from 76. 76 Westmead, Princes Risborough HP27 9HS T: (01844) 275461

VIRDEN, Richard. b 40. K Coll Lon BSc 61 Univ Coll Lon MSc 62 PhD 66. **d** 04 **p** 05. OLM N Tyne and Redesdale Newc from 04. Ingram Cottage, West Woodburn, Hexham NE48 2SB T: (01434) 270334 E: richard.virden@ncl.ac.uk

VIVASH, Peter Henry. b 57. Hockerill Coll of Educn CertEd 78 CQSW 85. Cranmer Hall Dur 90. **d** 92 **p** 93. C Malpas Men 92-95; R Bettws 95-01; P-in-c Upper Derwent Carl from 01; Dioc Rep CMS from 01; Warden of Readers Carl from 05. Thornthwaite Vicarage, Braithwaite, Keswick CA12 5RY T: (01768) 778243 E: peter.vivash@dsl.pipex.com

VIVIAN, Adrian John. b 42. K Coll Lon BD 65 AKC 66. St Denys Warminster 62. **d** 66 **p** 67. C Bromley St Andr Roch 66-69; C Egg Buckland Ex 69-73; PtO 73-84; P-in-c Newton Ferrers w Revelstoke 84-87. 9 Munro Avenue, Yealmpton, Plymouth PL8 2NQ

VIVIAN, Thomas Keith. b 27. St Jo Coll Cam BA 48 MA 52. St Deiniol's Hawarden 76. **d** 80 **p** 81. Hd Master Lucton Sch Leominster 62-85; LtO Heref 80-85; P-in-c Chew Stoke w Nempnett Thrubwell B & W 85-88; R 88-97; P-in-c Norton Malreward 85-88; R 88-97; RD Chew Magna 92 97; rtd 97; PtO Heref from 97; B & W from 97. Timberley, Sidmouth Road, Lyme Regis DT7 3ES T: (01297) 443547

VIVIAN, Victor Ivan. b 38. Nottm Poly LLB 87. EMMTC 91. **d** 94 **p** 95. NSM Bestwood S'well 94-99; Korea 99-03; rtd 03; PtO S'well from 03. 12 Deepdale Road, Wollaton, Nottingham NG8 2FU T: 0115-928 3954 E: vicvivian@yahoo.com

VLACH, Jane Elizabeth. b 64. Man Univ BA 87 BPI 88 MRTPI. STETS 07. **d** 11 **p** 12. C Guildf H Trin w St Mary 11-15; V Witley from 15. Witley Vicarage, Petworth Road, Witley, Godalming GU8 5LT

✠**VOBBE, The Rt Revd Joachim Gerhard.** b 47. **p** 72 **c** 95. Chapl Cologne Utrecht Old Catholic Ch Eur 72-74; Chapl Düsseldorf W Germany 74-77; R Blumberg 77-82; R Offenbach Germany 82-95; Bp Bonn from 95; Hon Asst Bp Eur from 99. Gregor-Mendel-Strasse 28, D-53115 Bonn, Germany T: (0049) (228) 232285 F: 238314 E: ordinariat@alt-katholisch.de

VOCKINS, Preb Michael David. b 44. OBE 96. Univ of Wales (Abth) BSc 69. Glouc Sch of Min 85. **d** 88 **p** 89. NSM Cradley w Mathon and Storridge Heref 88-14; PtO from 14; RD Ledbury 02-13; PtO Worc from 88; Chapl Heref Sixth Form Coll 05-09; Bp's Adv for SSM Heref 06-15; Preb Heref Cathl from 09. Birchwood Lodge, Birchwood, Storridge, Malvern WR13 5EZ T: (01886) 884366 E: mdvockins@btinternet.com

VOGT, Charles William Derek. b 36. Ex Univ BA 07. EMMTC 83. **d** 86 **p** 87. NSM Ilkeston H Trin *Derby* 86-87; C Derby St Anne and St Jo 87-90; TV Staveley and Barrow Hill 90-95; P-in-c Hasland 95-96; R 97-01; P-in-c Temple Normanton 95-96; V 97-01; rtd 01; PtO *Ex* from 01. *54 Old Bakery Close, Exeter EX4 2UZ* T: (01392) 271943

VOGT, Robert Anthony. b 25. Jes Coll Cam BA 50 MA 54. S'wark Ord Course 60. **d** 63 **p** 64. C Sutton New Town St Barn *S'wark* 63-67; C Kidbrooke St Jas 67-72; V Wood End *Cov* 72-80; RD Cov E 77-80; R Kidbrooke St Jas *S'wark* 80-85; TR 85-90; rtd 90; PtO *S'wark* from 90. *15 Serica Court, 154 Greenwich High Road, London SE10 8NZ* T: (020) 8853 3430 E: bobvogt@hotmail.co.uk

VOLLAND, Michael John. b 74. Northumbria Univ BA 96 K Coll Lon MA 04 Dur Univ DThM 13. Ridley Hall Cam 04. **d** 06 **p** 07. Pioneer Min Glouc City 06-09; C Glouc Cathl 07-09; Dir Miss Cranmer Hall Dur from 09; P Missr E Dur Miss Project from 14; AD Easington *Dur* from 14; CF (ACF) from 13. *St John's College, 3 South Bailey, Durham DH1 3RJ* T: 0191-334 3866 E: m.j.volland@durham.ac.uk

VOLTZENLOGEL, Timothy John. b 60. St Jo Coll Dur BA 81. Wycliffe Hall Ox BTh 00. **d** 00 **p** 01. C Eastbourne All SS *Chich* 00-04; V Church Langley *Chelmsf* 04-11; V Bexhill St Steph *Chich* from 11. *The Vicarage, 67 Woodsgate Park, Bexhill-on-Sea TN39 4DL* T: (01424) 211186 E: tim@timv.freeserve.co.uk

VON FRAUNHOFER, Nicola. d 14. NSM Wandsworth St Paul *S'wark* from 14. *Address temp unknown*

VOOGHT, Canon Michael George Peter. b 38. St Pet Hall Ox BA 61 MA 65. Chich Th Coll 61. **d** 63 **p** 64. C E Dulwich St Jo *S'wark* 63-66; C Prestbury *Glouc* 66-72; R Minchinhampton 72-85; RD Stonehouse 79-85; V Thornbury 85-02; Hon Can Glouc Cathl 86-02; rtd 02; PtO *Glouc* from 03. *62 High Street, Thornbury, Bristol BS35 2AN* T: (01454) 414915

VOSS, Mrs Philomena Ann. b 35. Edge Hill Coll of HE CertEd 55. St Alb Minl Tr Scheme 87 EAMTC 95. **d** 96 **p** 97. NSM Tye Green w Netteswell *Chelmsf* 96-03; NSM Ware St Mary *St Alb* 03-06; PtO from 06. *21 Queen's Road, Hertford SG13 8AZ* T: (01992) 554676 E: annvoss@tesco.net

VOST, Mrs Jane. b 62. **d** 04 **p** 08. OLM Radcliffe *Man* 04-10; OLM Radcliffe St Andr 10-13; PtO from 13; Chapl Wrightington Wigan and Leigh NHS Trust from 12. *43 Laurel Avenue, Bolton BL3 1AS* T: (01204) 559161

VOTH HARMAN, Karin. b 65. Virginia Univ BA 87 Sussex Univ MA 93 PhD 99. Westcott Ho Cam 09. **d** 11 **p** 12. NSM King's Cliffe, Bulwick and Blatherwycke etc *Pet* from 11; NSM Ketton, Collyweston, Easton-the-Hill etc from 13. *Headmaster's House, Spring Back Way, Uppingham, Oakham LE15 9TT* T: (01572) 822688 M: 07971-936253 E: karinvoth@hotmail.com

VOUSDEN, Canon Alan Thomas. b 48. K Coll Lon BSc 69. Qu Coll Birm. **d** 72 **p** 73. C Orpington All SS *Roch* 72-76; C Belvedere All SS 76-80; R Cuxton and Halling 80-86; V Bromley St Mark 86-98; Chapl Bromley Hosp 86-94; Chapl Bromley Hosps NHS Trust 94-98; V Rainham *Roch* 98-10; RD Gillingham 00-10; Bp's Dom Chapl 10-13; Hon Can Roch Cathl 99-13; rtd 13; PtO *Roch* from 13. *3 Fartherwell Avenue, West Malling ME19 6NG* E: alanvousden@btinternet.com

VOWLES, Ms Patricia. b 50. S'wark Ord Course 84. **d** 87 **p** 94. USPG 70-91; NSM Nunhead St Antony w St Silas *S'wark* 87-91; Par Dn Newington St Mary 91-94; Par Dn Camberwell St Mich w All So w Em 91-94; V 94-06; Chapl Cautley Ho Chr Cen 06-10; C Croydon St Jo *S'wark* from 11. *Church House, Barrow Road, Croydon CR0 4EZ* T: (020) 8688 7006 M: 07709-253496 E: patricia.vowles@yahoo.com

VOWLES, Canon Peter John Henry. b 25. Magd Coll Ox BA 50 MA 55. Westcott Ho Cam 50. **d** 52 **p** 53. C Kings Heath *Birm* 52-56; C Huddersfield St Pet *Wakef* 56-57; V Perry Beeches *Birm* 57-64 and 64-72; R Cottingham *York* 72-83; R Man St Ann 83-91; Hon Can Man Cathl 83-91; rtd 91; PtO *Man* from 91. *10 Redshaw Close, Manchester M14 6JB* T: 0161-257 2065

VROLIJK, Paul Dick. b 64. Delft Univ of Tech MSc 88. Trin Coll Bris BA 03 PhD 08. **d** 04 **p** 05. NSM Stoke Gifford *Bris* 04-08; Chapl Aquitaine *Eur* 09-15; Sen Chapl and Chan Brussels Cathl from 15. *Rue Capitaine Crespel 29, B-1050 Brussels, Belgium* T: (0032) (2) 511 7183 E: paul.vrolijk@gmail.com

VROOM, Richard Adriaan. d 88 p 88. Utrecht Old Catholic Ch *Eur* 88-07; V Llanegryn w Aberdyfi w Tywyn *Ban* 07-12; V Tywyn w Llanegryn w Aberdyfi w Pennal 12-13; V Bro Ystumanner from 13. *The Vicarage, Tywyn LL36 9BF* T: (01654) 712549 E: ravroom@mac.com

✠**VUNAGI, The Most Revd David.** b 50. Univ of the S Pacific DipEd 76 Univ of Papua New Guinea BEd 83. St Jo Coll Auckland BTh 91 Vancouver Sch of Th MTh 98. **d** 92 **p** 92 **c** 01. Lect Bp Patteson Th Coll Kohimarama Solomon Is 92-93; Prin Selwyn Coll 93-96; Asst P Vancouver St Anselm Canada 96-98; Solomon Is from 98; Prin Selwyn Coll 99; Miss Sec 00; Bp Temotu 01-09; Abp Melanesia and Bp Cen Melanesia from 09. *Selwyn College, PO Box 253, Honiara, Solomon Islands* T: (00677) 21892 *or* 26101 F: 21098 E: dvunagi@comphq.org.sb

VYE, Mrs Georgina Ann. b 57. SWMTC 06. **d** 09 **p** 10. C Littleham w Exmouth and Lympstone and Woodbury w Exton *Ex* 09-10; C Ex St Thos and Em 10-14; C Chard St Mary w Combe St Nicholas, Wambrook etc *B & W* from 14. *57 Caraway Close, Chard TA20 1HP* M: 07954-413984 E: g.vye@btinternet.com

VYVYAN, Michael David. b 78. **d** 15. C Camberwell St Phil and St Mark *S'wark* from 15. *138 Friary Road, London SE15 5UW* M: 07946-709274 E: mdvyvyan@gmail.com

---

W

✠**WABUKALA, The Most Revd Eliud.** b 51. St Paul's Coll Limuru 85 Wycliffe Coll Toronto 91. **d** 88 **c** 96. Canada 91-94; Lect St Paul's Th Coll Limuru 94-96; Bp Bungoma 96-09; Abp Kenya from 09. *PO Box 40502, Nairobi 00100, Kenya* T: (00254) (2) 714753 F: 718442 E: archoffice@swiftkenya.com

WADDELL, James William Boece. b 74. Trin Coll Bris 06. **d** 08 **p** 09. C Slaugham *Chich* 08-11; C Slaugham and Staplefield Common 11-12; USA 12-13; V Leyton St Cath and St Paul *Chelmsf* from 13. *The Vicarage, 2B Fairlop Road, London E11 1BL* T: (020) 8558 4607 M: 07813-872871 E: jim@thecornerstone.org.uk

WADDELL, Peter Matthew. b 75. Keble Coll Ox BA 96 Fitzw Coll Cam MPhil 98 PhD 02. Westcott Ho Cam 98. **d** 02 **p** 03. C Oxton *Ches* 02-04; Chapl SS Coll Cam 05-10; Past Dean 10-12; Dean of Chpl Win Univ from 12. *The University of Winchester, Sparkford Road, Winchester SO22 4NR* T: (01962) 827246 E: chaplaincy@winchester.ac.uk *or* peterwaddell@rocketmail.com

WADDINGTON, Gary Richard. b 69. St Chad's Coll Dur BSc 91 Heythrop Coll Lon MA 05. St Steph Ho Ox BTh 96. **d** 96 **p** 97. C Southsea H Spirit *Portsm* 96-00; V Paulsgrove 00-10; TR Harrogate St Wilfrid *Leeds* from 10. *St Wilfrid's Vicarage, 51B Kent Road, Harrogate HG1 2EU* T: (01423) 503259 M: 07920-464818 E: frgaryw@btinternet.com

WADDINGTON-FEATHER, John Joseph. b 33. Leeds Univ BA 54 Keele Univ PGCE 74 FRSA 87. St Deiniol's Hawarden 75. **d** 77 p 78. NSM Longden and Annscroft w Pulverbatch *Heref* 77-03; Chapl Asst HM Pris Shrewsbury 77-09; Sudan 84-85; Chapl Prestfelde Sch Shrewsbury 86-96; Ed The Poetry Church 95-08; PtO *Lich* 99-09; *Heref* 03-13. *Fair View, Old Coppice, Lyth Bank, Shrewsbury SY3 0BW* T/F: (01743) 872177 E: john@feather-books.com

WADE, Canon Andrew John. b 50. Trin Coll Bris. **d** 86 **p** 87. C St Keverne *Truro* 86-89; TV Probus, Ladock and Grampound w Creed and St Erme 89-92; V Constantine 92-00; P-in-c Ludgvan 00-01; P-in-c Marazion 00-01; P-in-c St Hilary w Perranuthnoe 00-01; R Ludgvan, Marazion, St Hilary and Perranuthnoe 01-08; RD Penwith 03-08; TR Probus, Ladock and Grampound w Creed and St Erme from 08; Hon Can Truro Cathl from 08; Rural Link Officer from 12. *The Sanctuary, Wagg Lane, Probus, Truro TR2 4JX* T: (01726) 882746 E: andrewsanctuary@aol.com

WADE, Christopher John. b 54. Trent Poly BSc 81 MRICS 82 ACIArb 88. Aston Tr Scheme 88 Trin Coll Bris. **d** 92 **p** 93. C Barnsley St Geo *Wakef* 92-95; C Whittle-le-Woods *Blackb* 95-99; P-in-c Bulwell St Jo *S'well* 99-03; Dir Heavenfire Min from 03. *46 Hastings Avenue, Whitley Bay NE26 4AG* T: 084516-65277 E: chris@heavenfire.org

WADE, Canon David Peter. b 65. St Jo Coll Nottm LTh 92. **d** 92 **p** 93. C Victoria Docks Ascension *Chelmsf* 92-95; P-in-c Victoria Docks St Luke 95-97; V from 97; AD Newham 07-15; Hon Can Chelmsf Cathl from 08. *The Vicarage, 16A Ruscoe Road, London E16 1JB* T: (020) 7476 2076 E: davenicky@hotmail.com

WADE, Geoffrey Adrian. b 61. Ripon Coll Cuddesdon. **d** 01 **p** 02. C Worc City St Paul and Old St Martin etc 01-02; C Wordsley 02-04; TV Ilminster and Distr *B & W* 04-10; V Winsmoor from 10. *The Rectory, Shepton Beauchamp, Ilminster TA19 0LP* T: (01460) 240228
E: begw1@greenbee.net

WADE, Mrs Mary Ruth. b 70. Leeds Univ BA 92 Wolv Univ PGCE 94. Qu Coll Birm 10. **d** 12 **p** 13. C Albrighton, Boningale and Donington *Lich* 12-15; V from 15. *The Vicarage, High Street, Albrighton, Wolverhampton WV7 3EQ* T: (01902) 373486 M: 07857-039641 E: albrightoncurate@gmail.com

WADE, Walter. b 29. Oak Hill Th Coll 64. **d** 66 **p** 67. C Denton Holme *Carl* 66-69; V Jesmond H Trin *Newc* 69-78; R Moresby *Carl* 78-87; P-in-c Langdale 87-94; Member Rural Life and Agric Team 93-94; rtd 94; PtO *Carl* from 94. *Manor Cottage, Fellside, Caldbeck, Wigton CA7 8HA* T: (016974) 78214

WADEY, Ms Rachel Susan. b 71. Lanc Univ BA 94 Ox Univ BA 98. St Steph Ho Ox 95. **d** 98 **p** 99. C Poulton-le-Fylde *Blackb* 98-01; C Blackpool H Cross 01-03; V Skerton St Chad 03-09; Chapl Prospect Park Hosp Reading from 09. *Prospect Park Hospital, Honey End Lane, Tilehurst, Reading RG30 4EJ* T: 0118-960 5000 E: rachel.wadey@talktalk.net

WADGE, Alan. b 46. Grey Coll Dur BA 68 MA 72. St Chad's Coll Dur. **d** 70 **p** 71. C Cockerton *Dur* 70-74; C Whitworth w Spennymoor 74-75; P-in-c Shipton Moyne w Westonbirt and Lasborough *Glouc* 75-80; Chapl Westonbirt Sch 75-80; V Dean Forest H Trin *Glouc* 80-83; Chapl Gresham's Sch Holt 83-91; R Ridgeway *Ox* 91-11; RD Wantage 95-01; rtd 11; PtO *Sarum* from 12. *8 Underhill, Mere, Warminster BA12 6LU*
E: alanwadge@hotmail.com

WADHAM, Canon Philip Andrew. b 41. Saltley Tr Coll Birm CertEd 70 Bradf Univ MA 92. Vancouver Sch of Th BTh 80. **d** 79 **p** 80. Canada 80-82; Ecuador 82-85; R Virden Canada 85-88; Area Sec USPG Wakef and Bradf 88-92; R W Coast Miss Canada 94-97; Regional Miss Co-ord 97-06; rtd 06; P-in-c Sooke Canada from 06. *4544 Rocky Point Road, Victoria BC V9C 4E4, Canada* T: (001) (250) 391 7436
E: pwadham@telus.net

WADLAND, Douglas Bryan. b 33. K Coll Dur BA 61 CQSW 62. Oak Hill Th Coll 90. **d** 91 **p** 92. NSM Cowley *Lon* 91-93; Asst Chapl Hillingdon Hosp NHS Trust 91-93; P-in-c Wembley St Jo *Lon* 93-00; Chapl Cen Middx Hosp NHS Trust 93-00; rtd 00; Kenya 01-03; Hon C Alperton *Lon* 03-09; PtO from 09. *55 Copthall Road East, Uxbridge UB10 8SE* T: (01895) 613904
E: wadland@lizbryan.freeserve.co.uk

WADMAN, Vera Margaret. b 51. EAMTC 97. **d** 00 **p** 01. NSM Burnham *Chelmsf* 00-02; NSM Creeksea w Althorne, Latchingdon and N Fambridge 02-09; NSM Creeksea from 09; P-in-c from 10. *Fernlea Cottage, 8 Fernlea Road, Burnham-on-Crouch CM0 8EJ* T: (01621) 783963
E: vera.wadman@allsaintscreeksea.org.uk

WADSWORTH (née REID), Mrs Alison Margaret. b 36. Bris Univ CertEd 57. **d** 97 **p** 98. OLM Cley Hill Warminster *Sarum* 97-06. *2 Saxon's Acre, Warminster BA12 8HT* T: (01985) 212510
E: awap@blueyonder.co.uk

WADSWORTH, Andrew James. b 56. St Jo Coll Dur BA 79 Cam Univ CertEd 80 Lambeth STh 95 FRSA 99. Sarum & Wells Th Coll 84 Chich Th Coll 86. **d** 87 **p** 88. NSM Forest Row and E Grinstead St Swithun *Chich* 87-89; C Shrewsbury St Chad w St Mary *Lich* 89-91; TV Honiton, Gittisham, Combe Raleigh, Monkton etc *Ex* 91-97; V Bulkington w Shilton and Ansty *Cov* 97-06; P-in-c Bognor *Chich* 06-07, V from 07. *St Wilfrid's Vicarage, 17 Victoria Drive, Bognor Regis PO21 2RH* T: (01243) 821965 E: rev.andrew@wadswortha.fsnet.co.uk

WADSWORTH, Andrew John. b 67. Reading Univ BSc 88 MRICS 90. Wycliffe Hall Ox 99. **d** 01 **p** 02. C Plymouth St Andr and Stonehouse *Ex* 01-05; C Enfield Ch Ch Trent Park *Lon* 05-13; C Grange Park St Pet from 13. *2 Firs Lane, London N21 2HU* T: (020) 8441 6444
E: awadsworth@waddy20.freeserve.co.uk

WADSWORTH, Jean. b 44. St Jo Coll Dur BA 71. Cranmer Hall Dur 85. **d** 87 **p** 94. Par Dn Thamesmead *S'wark* 87-92; Par Dn Rotherhithe H Trin 92-94; C 94-98; V New Eltham All SS 98-08; RD Eltham and Mottingham 01-05; rtd 08. *2 Peak Coach House, Cotmaton Road, Sidmouth EX10 8SY*

WADSWORTH, Canon Michael Philip. b 43. Qu Coll Ox BA 65 MA 68 DPhil 75 Cam Univ PhD 78. Ripon Hall Ox 67. **d** 70 **p** 71. C Sutton St Mich *York* 70-73; Lect Sussex Univ *Chich* 73-78; Hon C Hove St Jo 75-78; Fell and Chapl SS Coll Cam 78-81; Dir Th Studies 79-81; CF (TA) from 80; C Ditton St Mich *Liv* 81; TV 82-84; Dioc Lay Tr Officer 83-89; V Orford St Marga 84-89; V Haddenham *Ely* 89-98; V Wilburton 89-98; RD Ely 94-98; P-in-c Gt Shelford 98-01; Hon Can Ely Cathl 96-01; rtd 01; PtO *Ely* from 01; *Linc* from 01. *9 Eastgate, Sleaford NG34 7DL* T: (01529) 304251

WADSWORTH, Peter Richard. b 52. Qu Coll Ox BA 73 MA 77. Cuddesdon Coll 74 English Coll Rome 76. **d** 77 **p** 78. C High Wycombe *Ox* 77-81; C Farnham Royal w Hedgerley 81-84; Dioc Ecum Officer *Portsm* 84-90; V E Meon 84-96; V Langrish 84-96; V Elson 96-04; RD Gosport 96-02; V St Alb St Sav *St Alb* from 04. *St Saviour's Vicarage, 25 Sandpit Lane, St Albans AL1 4DF* T: (01727) 851526
E: peter.wadsworth52@ntlworld.com

WADSWORTH, Roy. b 37. NEOC 89. **d** 89 **p** 90. NSM Alne *York* from 89; Ind Chapl 94-03; rtd 02. *Address temp unknown*

WAGGETT, Geoffrey James. b 49. Sarum & Wells Th Coll 83. **d** 85 **p** 86. C Newton Nottage *Llan* 85-88; TV Glyncorrwg w Afan Vale and Cymmer Afan 88-89; R 89-99; V Glyncorrwg and Upper Afan Valley 99-00; TR Ebbw Vale *Mon* 00-13; TV Upper Ebbw Valleys from 13. *The Rectory, Eureka Place, Ebbw Vale NP23 6PN* T: (01495) 301723

WAGSTAFF (née JONES), Ms Alison. b 40. K Coll Dur BA 63 Man Univ CertEd 64. TISEC 95. **d** 98 **p** 99. C Edin St Cuth 98-00; Assoc P Edin St Columba from 00; Chapl St Columba's Hospice 01-05. *27 Cambridge Gardens, Edinburgh EH6 5DH* T: 0131-554 6702 M: 07766-383117

WAGSTAFF, Canon Andrew Robert. b 56. K Coll Lon BD 79 AKC 79. Coll of Resurr Mirfield 81. **d** 83 **p** 84. C Newark w Hawton, Cotham and Shelton *S'well* 83-86; C Dublin St Bart w Leeson Park *D & G* 86-89; V Nottingham St Geo w St Jo *S'well* 89-95; V Worksop Priory 95-06; Chapl Antwerp St Boniface *Eur* from 06; Hon Can from 12. *Grétrystraat 39, 2018 Antwerp, Belgium* T: (0032) (3) 239 3339 E: chaplain@boniface.be

WAGSTAFF, The Ven Christopher John Harold. b 36. St D Coll Lamp BA 62. **d** 63 **p** 64. C Queensbury All SS *Lon* 63-68; V Tokyngton St Mich 68-73; V Coleford w Staunton *Glouc* 73-83; RD Forest S 76-82; Adn Glouc 83-00; Hon Can Glouc Cathl 83-00; Hon Can St Andr Cathl Njombe (Tanzania) from 93; rtd 00; PtO *Glouc* from 00. *Karibuni, Collafield, Littledean, Cinderford GL14 3LG* T: (01594) 825282

WAGSTAFF, Miss Joan. b 33. Gilmore Ho. **dss** 75 **d** 87 **p** 94. Ellesmere Port *Ches* 86-87; Par Dn 87-93; rtd 93; PtO *Ches* from 93. *41 Heywood Road, Great Sutton, South Wirral CH66 3PS* T: 0151-348 0884

WAGSTAFF, Ms Julie. b 48. Univ of Wales (Swansea) BA 93. St Mich Coll Llan 10. **d** 13 **p** 15. NSM Waunarllwydd *S & B* from 13. *14 Bethania Road, Clydach, Swansea SA6 5DE* T: (01792) 845426 E: juliewagstaff1948@gmail.com

WAGSTAFF, Michael. b 59. R Holloway Coll Lon BA 81. Coll of Resurr Mirfield 86. **d** 89 **p** 90. C Worksop Priory *S'well* 89-92; C Ab Kettleby Gp *Leic* 92-94; TV Leic Resurr 94-00; Dioc Soc Resp Officer *Sheff* 00-08; Chapl RN from 08. *Royal Naval Chaplaincy Service, Mail Point 1-2, Leach Building, Whale Island, Portsmouth PO2 8BY* T: (023) 9262 5055 F: 9262 5134

WAGSTAFF, Robert William. b 36. Edin Th Coll 61. **d** 63 **p** 64. C Harringay St Paul *Lon* 63-64; C Mill Hill Jo Keble Ch 64-69; NSM N Lambeth *S'wark* 70-80; NSM Wilden *Worc* 80-92; NSM Stourport and Wilden 92-97; NSM Hartlebury 80-97; NSM Ombersley w Doverdale 80-97; C Shrawley, Witley, Astley and Abberley 98-02; rtd 02; PtO *Worc* from 02. *The Red House, Quarry Bank, Hartlebury, Kidderminster DY11 7TE* T: (01299) 250883

WAGSTAFFE, Eric Herbert. b 25. St Aid Birkenhead 55. **d** 57 **p** 58. C Harpurhey Ch Ch *Man* 57-60; R 60-69; V Pendlebury St Jo 69-84; V Hoghton *Blackb* 84-91; rtd 91; PtO *Blackb* 91-02; *Man* from 95. *3 Chelwood Close, Bolton BL1 7LN* T: (01204) 596048

WAIKATO, Bishop of. See HARTLEY, Helen-Ann Macleod

WAIN, Phillip. b 54. Aston Tr Scheme 89 Linc Th Coll 93. **d** 93 **p** 94. C Witton *Ches* 93-97; R Lea Gp *Linc* 97-14 and from 14; RD Corringham from 13. *The Rectory, 18 Gainsborough Road, Lea, Gainsborough DN21 5HZ* T: (01427) 613188

WAINAINA, Canon Francis Samson Kamoko. b 51. St Jo Coll Dur MA 89. Oak Hill Th Coll BA 84. **d** 84 **p** 85. Kenya 84-88; C Upton (Overchurch) *Ches* 89-92; V Ellesmere St Pet *Sheff* 92-95; V York St Mich-le-Belfrey 95-01; V Starbeck *Leeds* from 01; Hon Can Ripon Cathl from 12. *The Vicarage, 78 High Street, Harrogate HG2 7LW* T: (01423) 546477 *or* 889162 E: francis.wainaina@talktalk.net

✠**WAINE, The Rt Revd John.** b 30. KCVO 96. Man Univ BA 51. Ridley Hall Cam 53. **d** 55 **p** 56 **c** 75. C W Derby St Mary *Liv* 55-58; C Sutton 58-60; V Ditton St Mich 60-64; V Southport H Trin 64-69; V Kirkby 69-71; TR 71-75; Suff Bp Stafford *Lich* 75-78; Preb Lich Cathl 75-78; Bp St E 78-86; Bp Chelmsf 86-96; Clerk of the Closet 89-96; rtd 96; PtO *St E* from 96; Hon Asst Bp St E from 08. *Broadmere, Ipswich Road, Grundisburgh, Woodbridge IP13 6TJ* T: (01473) 738296 E: bpjohn@jwaine.mail1.co.uk

WAINE, The Very Revd Stephen John. b 59. Westcott Ho Cam 81. **d** 84 **p** 85. C Wolverhampton *Lich* 84-88; Min Can and Succ St Paul's Cathl 88-93; V Romford St Edw

Chelmsf 93-10; P-in-c Romford St Jo 02-10; Adn Dorset *Sarum* 10-15; Can and Preb Sarum Cathl 10-15; Dean Chich from 15. *The Deanery, Canon Lane, Chichester PO19 1PX* T: 812484 *or* (01243) 812494
E: dean@chichestercathedral.org

WAINWRIGHT, John Pounsberry. b 42. St Steph Ho Ox 64. **d** 66 **p** 67. C Palmers Green St Jo *Lon* 66-70; C Primrose Hill St Mary w Avenue Road St Paul 70-71; P-in-c St John's Wood All SS 71-73; V Hendon All SS Childs Hill from 73. *All Saints' Vicarage, Church Walk, London NW2 2TJ* T: (020) 7435 3182

WAINWRIGHT, Kevin Frank. b 46. Linc Th Coll 73. **d** 75 **p** 76. C Stand *Man* 75-78; C Radcliffe St Thos and St Jo 78-80; V Kearsley Moor 80-13; rtd 13; PtO *Man* from 13. *216 Oldham Road, Middleton, Manchester M24 2JZ*

WAINWRIGHT, Malcolm Hugh. b 47. Man Univ BA 68 Nottm Univ MA 89. St Jo Coll Nottm MA 98. **d** 98 **p** 99. NSM Cotgrave and Owthorpe *S'well* 98-02; P-in-c Plumtree and Tollerton 02-09; Hon C Burton Fleming w Fordon, Grindale etc *York* 09-11; P-in-c Skelton w Shipton and Newton on Ouse from 11. *The Rectory, Church Lane, Skelton, York YO30 1XT* T: (01904) 471351 E: malcolm@mhwainwright.eclipse.co.uk

WAINWRIGHT, Mrs Margaret Gillian. b 45. Qu Mary Coll Lon BA 68. EAMTC 00. **d** 03 **p** 04. NSM Combs and Lt Finborough *St E* 03-05; NSM The Creetings and Earl Stonham w Stonham Parva 05-11; rtd 11. *The Cottage, Elmswell Road, Wetherden, Stowmarket IP14 3LN* T: (01359) 242653
E: margwain@btopenworld.com

WAINWRIGHT, Martin John. b 69. Loughb Univ BEng 92. Trin Coll Bris BA 98. **d** 98 **p** 99. C Chislehurst Ch Ch *Roch* 98-02; V Camberley St Mary *Guildf* 02-10; V Howell Hill w Burgh Heath from 10. *St Paul's Vicarage, 17 Northey Avenue, Sutton SM2 7HS* T: (020) 8224 9927
E: martin.wainwright@ntlworld.com *or* martinw@saintpauls.co.uk

WAINWRIGHT, Pauline Barbara. *See* FLORANCE, Pauline Barbara

WAINWRIGHT, Peter Anthony. b 45. K Coll Lon BD 73 MRICS 67. Ridley Hall Cam 73. **d** 75 **p** 76. C Ashtead *Guildf* 76-79; V Woking St Paul 79-84; PtO *Ox* 87-92 and 03-05; P-in-c Harston w Hauxton and Newton *Ely* 05-10; rtd 10; PtO *Ox* from 10. *19 Rosebery Avenue, High Wycombe HP13 7AL* M: 07814-835528 T: (01494) 267913
E: rev@peterwainwright.plus.com

WAINWRIGHT, Robert James David. b 86. St Jo Coll Dur BA 07 Ch Ch Ox MSt 08 DPhil 11. Wycliffe Hall Ox BA 14. **d** 15. C Burford w Fulbrook, Taynton, Asthall etc *Ox* from 15. *The Parsonage, 20 Oxford Road, Burford OX18 4NR* M: 07799-262056 E: robert.wainwright@chch.oxon.org

WAINWRIGHT, Robert Neil. b 52. NEOC 99. **d** 02 **p** 03. NSM Barlby and Riccall *York* 02-05; NSM Selby Abbey 05-12; TV Tenby *St D* from 12; Dioc Lay Development Officer from 14. *The Vicarage, Penally, Tenby SA70 7PN* T: (01834) 849459 M: 07768-390060 E: robbwain@gmail.com

WAITE, Daniel Alfred Norman. b 42. **d** 04 **p** 05. OLM Gorleston St Andr *Nor* 04-12; PtO from 12. *15 Laburnum Close, Bradwell, Great Yarmouth NR31 8JB* T: (01493) 664591
E: djwaite@btinternet.com

WAITE, Julian Henry. b 47. Open Univ BA 98. Brasted Th Coll 68 Ridley Hall Cam 70. **d** 72 **p** 73. C Wollaton *S'well* 72-76; C Herne Bay Ch Ch *Cant* 76-79; P-in-c Mersham 79-87; Chapl Wm Harvey Hosp Ashford 79-87; V Marden *Cant* 87-93; Chapl HM Pris Blantyre Ho 90-93; Chapl HM Pris Swaleside 01-12; rtd 12; PtO *Cant* from 12. *31 Shearwater, Maidstone ME16 0DW* T: (01622) 664957

WAITE, Robin Derek. b 59. **d** 05 **p** 06. NSM Derringham Bank *York* 05-06; NSM Woldsburn from 06. *Mulberry Cottage, Parklands Drive, North Ferriby HU14 3EU* T: (01482) 631162
E: rojaw@freezone.co.uk

WAITE, Sheila Margaret. *See* TYLER, Sheila Margaret

WAIYAKI, Canon Jennie. b 34. MBE 88. ALA 64. NEOC 89. **d** 92 **p** 94. NSM Ulgham and Widdrington *Newc* 92-97; Chapl MU 96-02; Chapl Northumbria Healthcare NHS Foundn Trust from 97; NSM Longhorsley and Hebron *Newc* 97-04; Hon Can Newc Cathl from 02. *Address temp unknown*

WAIZENEKER, Ms Ann Elizabeth. b 56. Southn Univ BSc 78. SEITE 05. **d** 08 **p** 09. C Chich St Paul and Westhampnett 08-12; P-in-c New Shoreham 12-14; V New Shoreham and Shoreham Beach from 14; P-in-c Old Shoreham 12-15. *The Vicarage, Church Street, Shoreham-by-Sea BN43 5DQ* T: (01273) 965303 E: annwaizeneker@aol.com

WAKE, Colin Walter. b 50. Oriel Coll Ox BA 72 MA. Cuddesdon Coll 74. **d** 75 **p** 76. C Sandhurst *Ox* 75-78; C Faversham *Cant* 79-80; TV High Wycombe *Ox* 80-89; R Weston Favell *Pet* 89-06; Chapl St Jo Hosp Weston Favell 89-06; rtd 06. *35 Greenhill, Royal Wootton Bassett, Swindon SN4 8EH* E: c.w.wake@talk21.com

WAKEFIELD, Allan. b 31. Qu Coll Birm 72. **d** 74 **p** 75. C Kingsthorpe w Northampton St Dav *Pet* 74-77; TV Clifton *S'well* 77-81; V Bilborough St Jo 81-85; R Bere Ferrers *Ex* 85-91; R Mevagissey and St Ewe *Truro* 91-96; rtd 96; PtO *Truro* 96-98; Hon C Malborough w S Huish, W Alvington and Churchstow *Ex* 98-02; PtO from 01. *4 Eden Cottages, Exeter Road, Ivybridge PL21 0BL* T: (01752) 698724

WAKEFIELD, Andrew Desmond. b 55. K Coll Lon BD 77 AKC 77. Coll of Resurr Mirfield 77. **d** 78 **p** 79. C Mitcham Ascension *S'wark* 78-81; C Putney St Mary 81-86; TV Wimbledon 86-91; Ind Chapl from 90; Dioc Urban Missr 91-97; P-in-c S Wimbledon St Andr 91-97; V from 97. *105 Hartfield Road, London SW19 3TJ* T: (020) 8542 6566 E: andrew.d.wakefield@btopenworld.com

WAKEFIELD, Anne Frances. b 58. St Aid Coll Dur BSc 79 Sheff Univ PGCE 80. NTMTC 94. **d** 97 **p** 98. NSM Danbury *Chelmsf* 97-98; NSM Sherburn w Pittington *Dur* 98-01; Asst Chapl HM Pris Dur 01-03; Chapl HM YOI Northallerton 03-05; Chapl HM Pris Low Newton 05-08; P-in-c Stamford Bridge Gp *York* 09-12; R from 12; RD S Wold from 12. *The Rectory, 8 Viking Road, Stamford Bridge, York YO41 1BR* T: (01759) 371264 E: fran.wakefield@btopenworld.com

WAKEFIELD, David Geoffrey. b 43. AMIC 90. S'wark Ord Course 84. **d** 87 **p** 88. C Addiscombe St Mildred *S'wark* 87-89; C Reigate St Luke S Park 89-93; Chapl HM Pris Bullingdon 93-96; Chapl HM Pris Ranby 96-99; P-in-c Flintham *S'well* 99-08; P-in-c Car Colston w Screveton 99-08; Chapl HM Pris Whatton 99-03; rtd 08; PtO *York* from 08. *5 Manor Gardens, Hunmanby, Filey YO14 0PT* T: (01723) 891212 M: 07754-219741 E: d.g.wakefield@hotmail.co.uk

WAKEFIELD, David Kenneth. b 64. Ridley Hall Cam 02. **d** 04 **p** 05. C Bures w Assington and Lt Cornard *St E* 04-07; P-in-c Burlingham St Edmund w Lingwood, Strumpshaw etc *Nor* 07-09; R from 09. *The Rectory, Barn Close, Lingwood, Norwich NR13 4TS* T: (01603) 713880 E: rev.wake@btinternet.com

WAKEFIELD, Frances. *See* WAKEFIELD, Anne Frances

WAKEFIELD, Gavin Tracy. b 57. Van Mildert Coll Dur BSc 78 Sheff Univ CertEd 80 Kent Univ PhD 98. St Jo Coll Nottm 83. **d** 86 **p** 87. C Anston *Sheff* 86-89; C Aston cum Aughton and Ulley 89-91; TV Billericay and Lt Burstead *Chelmsf* 91-98; Dir Miss and Past Studies Cranmer Hall Dur 98-08; Dir Tr, Miss and Min *York* from 09; NSM Stamford Bridge Gp from 13. *The Rectory, 8 Viking Road, Stamford Bridge, York YO41 1BR* T: (01759) 371264 *or* (01904) 699504
E: gavin.wakefield@yorkdiocese.org

WAKEFIELD, Kenneth. b 54. St Jo Coll Dur BA 95. BA 95 Cranmer Hall Dur. **d** 95 **p** 96. C E and W Leake, Stanford-on-Soar, Rempstone etc *S'well* 95-98; TV Launceston *Truro* 98-03; P-in-c Boyton, N Tamerton, Werrington etc 03-08; R from 08. *The Rectory, 12 Dicna Close, St Giles-on-the-Heath, Launceston PL15 9SH*

WAKEFIELD, Mark Jeremy. b 55. York Univ BA 77. NTMTC BA 07. **d** 07 **p** 08. NSM Primrose Hill St Mary w Avenue Road St Paul *Lon* from 07. *15 Evangelist Road, London NW5 1UA* T: (020) 7267 8202 M: 07899-668493
E: mark.wakefield@blueyonder.co.uk

WAKEFIELD, Peter. b 48. St Jo Coll Nottm BTh 72 ALCD 72. **d** 72 **p** 73. C Hinckley H Trin *Leic* 72-75; C Kirby Muxloe 75-78; V Barlestone 78-85; TV Padgate *Liv* 85-88; V Quinton w Marston Sicca *Glouc* 91-97; rtd 97. *295 Leach Green Lane, Rednal, Birmingham B45 8EB* T: 0121-453 6979
E: pete.wakefield@orange.fr

WAKEFIELD, Dean of. *See* GREENER, The Very Revd Jonathan Desmond Francis

WAKEFIELD, Suffragan Bishop of. *See* ROBINSON, The Rt Revd Anthony William

WAKEHAM, Miss Ellen Liesel. b 82. York Univ BA 04 CCC Cam BA 08. Westcott Ho Cam 06 Yale Div Sch 08. **d** 09 **p** 10. C Frodingham *Linc* 09-12; Chapl St Gabr Coll Camberwell from 12; Hon C Kennington St Jo w St Jas *S'wark* from 12. *St Gabriel's College, Langton Road, London SW9 6UL* T: (020) 7793 3901 E: ellenwakeham@me.com

WAKEHAM-DAWSON, Andrew Whistler. b 65. Wye Coll Lon BSc 87 Open Univ PhD 94. STETS 98. **d** 01 **p** 02. NSM Paddington St Sav *Lon* 01-04; Chapl RAF from 04. *Chaplaincy Services (RAF), HQ Air Command, RAF High Wycombe HP14 4UE* T: (01494) 496800 F: 496343

WAKELIN, Brian Roy. b 53. Westf Coll Lon BSc 74. STETS 96. **d** 99 **p** 00. NSM Win Ch Ch from 99. *11 Elm Court, Elm Road, Winchester SO22 5BA* T: (01962) 868679

WAKELING, Canon Bruce. b 50. Lon Univ BA 74. Westcott Ho Cam 74. **d** 77 **p** 78. C Weymouth H Trin *Sarum* 77-82; TV Oakdale 82-89; R Clopton w Otley, Swilland and Ashbocking *St E* 89-98; V Rushmere from 98; Hon Can St E Cathl from 14. *The Vicarage, 253 Colchester Road, Rushmere, Ipswich IP4 4SH* T: (01473) 270976

WAKELING, Miss Faith Georgina. b 65. Anglia Ruskin Univ BA 10. Westcott Ho Cam 08. **d** 10 **p** 11. C Loughton St Jo *Chelmsf* 10-14; C Plaistow and N Canning Town from 14. *St Martin's Vicarage, 34 St Martin's Avenue, London E6 3DX* M: 07837-968967 E: faithwakeling@gmail.com

WAKELING, Hugh Michael. b 42. Cape Town Univ BSc 63 CEng 82 FIChemE 94. Wycliffe Hall Ox 71. **d** 74 **p** 75. C Kennington St Mark *S'wark* 74-78; C Surbiton Hill Ch Ch 78-80; NSM Richmond H Trin and Ch Ch 80-84; NSM California *Ox* 85-89 and 00-07; NSM Arborfield w Barkham 89-00; LtO from 07. *61 Roycroft Lane, Finchampstead, Wokingham RG40 4HN* T: 0118-973 4078

WAKELING, Mrs Joan. b 44. Hockerill Coll Cam CertEd 65. S'wark Ord Course 76. **dss** 79 **d** 90 **p** 94. Surbiton Hill Ch Ch S'wark 79-80; Richmond H Trin and Ch Ch 80-84; California *Ox* 84-89; Arborfield w Barkham 89-00; NSM 90-00; Chapl Luckley-Oakfield Sch Wokingham 90-05; NSM Finchampstead *Ox* 00-05; P-in-c Raglan w Llandenny and Bryngwyn *Mon* 05-14; rtd 14; PtO *Heref* from 14. *28 Pound Meadow, Ledbury HR8 2EU* T: (01531) 633188 E: revdjwakeling@gmail.com

WAKELING, Rayner Alan. b 58. Portsm Poly BSc 79 Bris Univ PGCE 80. St Steph Ho Ox. **d** 01 **p** 02. C Willesden Green St Andr and St Fran *Lon* 01-05; V Greenhill St Jo 05-11; V Pentonville St Silas w All SS and St Jas from 11. *St Silas House, 45 Cloudesley Road, London N1 0EL* T: (020) 7278 1101 E: raynerwakeling@hotmail.com

WAKELY, Edna Clare. **d** 12 **p** 14. C Dublin Drumcondra w N Strand *D & G* 12-14; C Limerick City *L & K* from 14. *50 Ballinvoher, Father Russel Road, Dooradoyle, Limerick, Republic of Ireland* T: (00353) (61) 302038 *or* 310293 M: 86-357 4917 E: ednawakely@hotmail.com

WAKELY, Marcus. b 40. Solicitor 62 FRSA 88. EMMTC 84. **d** 87 **p** 88. NSM Carrington *S'well* 87-91; C Worksop Priory 91-95; V Sheff St Matt 95-01; rtd 01. *16 Park House Gates, Nottingham NG3 5LX* T: 0115-960 9038

WAKELY, Roger. b 42. St Paul's Coll Chelt CertEd. S'wark Ord Course 67. **d** 70 **p** 71. C Ealing St Mary *Lon* 70-76; Chapl Bp Wand Sch Sunbury-on-Thames 76-82; R Gaulby *Leic* 82-87; V Galleywood Common *Chelmsf* 87-95; Warden of Ords 89-95; rtd 95; PtO *Chelmsf* 95-99; Ex 99-09. *5 Summerlands Court, Heavitree Road, Exeter EX1 2LY*

WAKELY, Simon Nicolas. b 66. K Alfred's Coll Win BA 88. St Jo Coll Nottm 89. **d** 92 **p** 93. C Wymondham *Nor* 92-95; P-in-c Babbacombe *Ex* 95-08; rtd 08. *29 Studley Road, Torquay TQ1 3JN* T: (01803) 431016 M: 07801-536181 E: finbar@tesco.net

WAKEMAN, Canon Hilary Margaret. b 38. EAMTC. **dss** 85 **d** 87 **p** 94. Heigham St Thos *Nor* 85-90; C 87-90; C Nor St Mary Magd w St Jas 90-91; Dn-in-c Norwich Over-the-Water Colegate St Geo 90-91; Team Dn Norwich Over-the-Water 91-94; TV 94-96; Hon Can Nor Cathl 94-96; I Kilmoe Union *C, C & R* 96-01; Dir of Ords 99-01; rtd 01. *Skeagh, Schull, Co Cork, Republic of Ireland* T: (00353) (28) 28263 E: hilary.wakeman@gmail.com

WAKERELL, Richard Hinton. b 55. Qu Coll Birm 81. **d** 84 **p** 85. C Gillingham St Mary *Roch* 84-87; C Kingswinford St Mary *Lich* 87-93; V Rickerscote 93. *Address temp unknown*

WALDEN, Alan Howard. b 64. Bris Univ BSc 86 Lon Business Sch MBA 93. Trin Coll Bris BA 09. **d** 09 **p** 10. C Frimley *Guildf* 09-12; P-in-c Madeley *Heref* from 12. *St Michael's Vicarage, Church Street, Madeley, Telford TF7 5BN* T: (01952) 586645 M: 07957-773043 E: ahwalden@gmail.com

✠**WALDEN, The Rt Revd Graham Howard.** b 31. Univ of Qld BA 52 MA 54 Ch Ch Ox BLitt 60 MLitt 80. St Fran Coll Brisbane ThL 54. **d** 54 **p** 55 **c** 81. C W Hackney St Barn *Lon* 54-56; C Poplar St Sav w St Gabr and St Steph 57-58; PtO *Ox* 55-59; Australia from 59; Adn Ballarat 70-89; Bp in Hamilton 81-84; Asst Bp 84-89; Bp The Murray 89-01; rtd 01. *13 O'Connor Place, Dubbo NSW 2380, Australia* T: (0061) (2) 6884 0883

WALDEN, Mrs Jane. b 55. Cartrefle Coll of Educn CertEd 76 Chelt & Glouc Coll of HE BA 01. WEMTC 02. **d** 05 **p** 06. NSM Minchinhampton *Glouc* 05-09; NSM Minchinhampton w Box and Amberley 09-12; V Brockworth from 12. *The Vicarage, 42 Court Road, Brockworth, Gloucester GL3 4ET* T: (01452) 862114 E: jane_walden@hotmail.com

WALDEN, John Edward Frank. b 38. FInstSMM. Oak Hill Th Coll 67. **d** 69 **p** 70. C Rainham *Chelmsf* 69-73; P-in-c Bris H Cross Inns Court 73-78; Conf and Publicity Sec SAMS 78-81; Hon C Southborough St Pet w Ch Ch and St Matt *Roch* 78-81; Exec Sec Spanish and Portuguese Ch Aid Soc 80-81; Hon C Tonbridge St Steph *Roch* 81-84; R Earsham w Alburgh and Denton *Nor* 84-89; PtO from 01; rtd 03. *2 Wentworth Drive, Harrogate HG2 7LA* T: (01603) 746062 E: revjohnw@googlemail.com

WALDSAX, Mrs Heather. b 58. Bris Univ BA 79 PGCE 80. STETS 06. **d** 08 **p** 09. NSM Canford Magna *Sarum* from 08. *60 Floral Farm, Canford Magna, Wimborne BH21 3AU* T: (01202) 889269 E: heather@waldsax.net

WALE (née BROWN), Wendy Anne. b 71. Homerton Coll Cam BEd 89. Trin Coll Bris 09. **d** 11 **p** 12. C Summerfield and Edgbaston St Germain *Birm* 11-14; Chapl Wadham Coll Ox 14-15; PtO from 14. *1 Exeter Farm Barns, Cassington Road, Yarnton, Kidlington OX5 1QB* M: 07825-288779 E: wendyannebrown@googlemail.com

WALES, David Neville. b 55. Rhodes Univ BA 78 Open Univ BSc 01. Coll of Resurr Mirfield 80. **d** 82 **p** 83. Zimbabwe 82-88; C Linslade *Ox* 89-91; P-in-c Weston Turville 91-07; R from 07; Voc Adv from 99. *The Rectory, Church Walk, Weston Turville, Aylesbury HP22 5SH* T: (01296) 613212 M: 07889-964287 E: d.wales512@btinternet.com

WALES, Mrs Janet Mary. b 56. Rhodes Univ MA 80 CTABRSM 98. Ox Min Course 11. **d** 14 **p** 15. OLM Ellesborough, The Kimbles and Stoke Mandeville *Ox* from 14. *The Rectory, Church Walk, Weston Turville, Aylesbury HP22 5SH* T: (01296) 612936 E: janetwales@gmail.com

WALES, Stephen Francis. b 70. Leic Univ BSc 93 Leeds Univ BA 07. Coll of Resurr Mirfield 05. **d** 07 **p** 08. C Carrington *S'well* 07-10; TV Retford Area 10-13; V St Gluvias *Truro* from 13. *The Vicarage, St Gluvias, Penryn TR10 9LQ* E: steve.wales301@btinternet.com

WALES, Archbishop of. See MORGAN, The Most Revd Barry Cennydd

WALFORD, Mrs Angela. b 44. Whitelands Coll Lon CertEd 76. S Dios Minl Tr Scheme 85. **d** 92 **p** 94. NSM Boyatt Wood *Win* 92-99; Asst Chapl Epsom and St Helier Univ Hosps NHS Trust 99-07; PtO *S'wark* 07-13. *58 Wolseley Road, Mitcham Junction, Mitcham CR4 4JQ* T: (020) 8646 2841

WALFORD, David. b 45. S'wark Ord Course 75. **d** 78 **p** 79. NSM Hackbridge and N Beddington *S'wark* 78-83; C Fawley *Win* 83-87; C-in-c Boyatt Wood CD 87-90; V Boyatt Wood 90-97; rtd 97; PtO *S'wark* 98-02; Assoc P S Beddington and Roundshaw 00-07; Hon Chapl Epsom and St Helier NHS Trust 00-03; Asst Chapl Epsom and St Helier Univ Hosps NHS Trust 03-10; PtO *S'wark* 10-13. *58 Wolseley Road, Mitcham Junction, Mitcham CR4 4JQ* T: (020) 8646 2841 E: wols@tinyworld.co.uk

WALFORD, David John. b 47. St Luke's Coll Ex CertEd 68 AKC 71. St Aug Coll Cant 71. **d** 72 **p** 73. C Oxton *Ches* 72-77; C Neston 77-80; V Backford and Youth Chapl 80-81; C Woodchurch 81; Chapl Fulbourn Hosp Cam 82; Chapl N Man Gen Hosp 82-85; Distr Chapl in Mental Health Ex HA 85-87; Chapl Manager R Devon and Ex Hosp (Wonford) 87-94; Chapl Manager R Devon and Ex NHS Foundn Trust 94-07; rtd 07; Chapl Ex Hospiscare from 08. *Barnhayes Farm, Whimple, Exeter EX5 2UD* T: (01404) 822863

WALFORD, Frank Roy. b 35. Birm Univ MB, ChB 58. Qu Coll Birm 78. **d** 80 **p** 81. Hon C Walsall Pleck and Bescot *Lich* 80-85; Chr Healing Cen Bordon 85-88; Dep Medical Dir St Wilfrid's Hospice Chich from 88; PtO *Chich* from 88. *15 Grove Road, Chichester PO19 8AR* T: (01243) 533947 E: ronowal@aol.com

WALFORD, James Nicholas. b 80. Bris Univ BSc 02. Wycliffe Hall Ox 11. **d** 14 **p** 15. C Clifton Ch Ch w Em *Bris* from 14. *89 Kings Drive, Bishopston, Bristol BS7 8JQ* M: 07852-674317 E: jimw@emmanuelbristol.org.uk

WALFORD, Mrs Marion Gladys. b 54. NTMTC BA 08. **d** 08 **p** 09. C Canvey Is *Chelmsf* 08-12; TV from 12. *37 Ruskol Road, Canvey Island SS8 9QN* T: (01268) 698991 E: revmarion@google.com

WALFORD, Robin Peter. b 46. Qu Coll Birm 75. **d** 78 **p** 79. C Radcliffe-on-Trent *S'well* 78-81; TV Newark w Hawton, Cotham and Shelton 81-84; P-in-c Forest Town 84-92; Co-ord Chapl Leeds Community and Mental Health Services 92-97; PtO *Leeds* from 97. *15 Oaklands Drive, Adel, Leeds LS16 8NZ* T: 0113-281 7251 E: robin.walford@btinternet.com

WALKER, Alan Robert Glaister. b 52. K Coll Cam BA 76 MA 79 New Coll Ox MA 84 Poly Cen Lon LLB 91 Heythrop Coll Lon MTh 93 Univ of Wales LLM 96. St Steph Ho Ox 82. **d** 84 **p** 85. C St John's Wood *Lon* 84-86; Chapl Poly Cen Lon 87-92; Chapl Univ of Westmr 92-94; Chapl Univ Ch Ch the K 87-94; V Hampstead Garden Suburb from 94. *The Vicarage, 1 Central Square, London NW11 7AH* T/F: (020) 8455 7206 M: 07956-491037 E: fatherwalker@aol.com

WALKER, Canon Allen Ross. b 46. Portsm Univ BA 94 MA 98. Chich Th Coll 86. **d** 88. C Cosham *Portsm* 88-91; Chapl Portsm Mental Health Community 91-97; Dn Portsm Deanery 91-97; Community Chapl Burnham and Slough Deanery *Ox* 97-12; AD Burnham and Slough 05-12; Hon Can Ch Ch 08-12; rtd 12. *8 Marksmead, Drimpton, Beaminster DT8 3RZ* E: mrarwalker@aol.com

WALKER, Mrs Amanda Frances. b 62. Cen Sch Speech & Drama BSc 85 Univ Coll Lon MSc 94 Qu Coll Birm BA 09. WMMTC 06. **d** 09 **p** 10. C Stafford *Lich* 09-12; V Streetly from 12. *All Saints' Vicarage, 2 Foley Church Close, Sutton Coldfield B74 3JX* T: 0121-353 5875 M: 07811-326204
E: revdmandywalker@btinternet.com

WALKER, Andrew David. b 84. BSc 06. Trin Coll Bris BA 10. **d** 11 **p** 12. C S Dales *Derby* 11-15; R Eckington and Ridgeway from 15. *The Rectory, 17 Church Street, Eckington, Sheffield S21 4BG* T: (01246) 432196 E: adwalker2@googlemail.com

WALKER, Andrew Stephen. b 58. St Chad's Coll Dur BA 80 Heythrop Coll Lon MA 99. St Steph Ho Ox 83. **d** 85 **p** 86. C Fareham SS Pet and Paul *Portsm* 85-87; C St John's Wood *Lon* 87-93; V Streatham St Pet *S'wark* 93-98; PtO *Bris* 98-00; *S'wark* 98-09; R St Edm the King and St Mary Woolnoth etc *Lon* 00-10; P-in-c Lewes St Mich and St Thos at Cliffe w All SS *Chich* 09-14; NSM Brighton St Mich and St Paul from 14; C St Marylebone w H Trin *Lon* from 15. *15 Pelham Square, Brighton BN1 4ET* M: 07931-745853
E: andrew.walker@operamail.com

WALKER, Ms Angela Jean. b 55. St Jo Coll Nottm 03. **d** 05 **p** 06. C Kempshott *Win* 05-09; P-in-c Cobham w Luddesdowne and Dode *Roch* from 10. *The Vicarage, Battle Street, Cobham, Gravesend DA12 3DB* T: (01474) 814332
E: ahiangel@aol.com

WALKER, Canon Anthony Charles St John. b 55. Trin Coll Ox MA 80. Wycliffe Hall Ox 78. **d** 81 **p** 82. C Bradf Cathl 81-84; C Nottingham St Ann w Em *S'well* 84-88; V Retford St Sav 88-01; TR Retford 02-11; TR Retford Area from 11; AD Retford 00-09; Hon Can S'well Minster 04-11. *St Saviour's Vicarage, 31 Richmond Road, Retford DN22 6SJ* T/F: (01777) 703800
E: tony@tonywalker.f9.co.uk

WALKER, Arthur Daniel. b 60. Nene Coll Northn BA 86 St Martin's Coll Lanc PGCE 90 Leeds Univ BA 10. Yorks Min Course 07. **d** 10 **p** 11. C Northallerton w Kirby Sigston *York* 10-14; V Birkenshaw w Hunsworth *Leeds* from 14. *The Vicarage, 6 Vicarage Gardens, Birkenshaw, Bradford BD11 2EF* E: arthur.walkerwalker@btinternet.com

WALKER (née JEYES), Mrs Caroline Helen. b 58. Wye Coll Lon BSc 81 Anglia Ruskin Univ MA 11. ERMC 08. **d** 10 **p** 11. NSM Desborough, Brampton Ash, Dingley and Braybrooke *Pet* 10-13; Chapl Kettering Gen Hosp NHS Trust 10-13; R Hardington Vale *B & W* from 13. *The Rectory, Vicarage Lane, Norton St Philip, Bath BA2 7LY* T: (01373) 834258
E: carolinehwalker@btinternet.com

WALKER, Ms Cherie Pauline. b 57. LCTP 12. **d** 15. C Broughton *Blackb* from 15. *3 The Turnpike, Fulwood, Preston PR2 3NT*

WALKER, Christina. b 52. **d** 08 **p** 09. NSM Birkenshaw w Hunsworth *Leeds* from 08. *Upper Chatts Farm, Cliff Hollins Lane, East Brierley, Bradford BD4 6RH* T: (01274) 670551
E: tinalet@hotmail.com

WALKER, Christopher James Anthony. b 43. Sarum & Wells Th Coll 85. **d** 87 **p** 88. Hon C Durrington *Sarum* 87-89; CF 87-98; PtO *Win* from 99. *Horseshoe Meadow Farm, Cholderton, Salisbury SP4 0ED* T: (01980) 629234
E: horseshoewalkers@supanet.com

WALKER, Christopher John. b 52. ALA 74. Chich Th Coll 75. **d** 78 **p** 79. C Reading All SS *Ox* 78-82; C Stony Stratford 82-84; C Wokingham All SS 84-90; V Headington St Mary 90-98; R S w N Moreton, Aston Tirrold and Aston Upthorpe 98-05; C Abingdon 05-07; rtd 07. *25 Coralberry Drive, Weston-super-Mare BS22 6SQ* T: (01934) 707959 E: rwalker1202@aol.com

WALKER, Christopher John Deville. b 42. St Jo Coll Dur BA 69. Westcott Ho Cam 69. **d** 71 **p** 72. C Portsea St Mary *Portsm* 71-75; C Saffron Walden w Wendens Ambo and Littlebury *Chelmsf* 75-77; C St Martin-in-the-Fields *Lon* 77-80; V Riverhead w Dunton Green *Roch* 80-89; V Chatham St Steph 89-97; R Chislehurst St Nic 97-05; rtd 05; PtO *Heref* from 05; *Lich* 06-07; Hon C Shrewsbury St Chad, St Mary and St Alkmund 07-13; PtO 13-14. *2 Springbank, Shrewsbury Road, Church Stretton SY6 6HA* T: (01694) 723444
E: chris@riberac.force9.co.uk

WALKER, Daniel. *See* WALKER, Arthur Daniel

WALKER, Canon David. b 48. Linc Th Coll 71. **d** 74 **p** 75. C Arnold *S'well* 74-77; C Crosby *Linc* 77-79; V Scrooby *S'well* 79-86; V Sutton in Ashfield St Mary 86-94; P-in-c Sutton in Ashfield St Mich 89-94; TR Birkenhead Priory *Ches* 94-05; RD Birkenhead 99-05; R Bromborough 05-13; Hon Can Ches Cathl 03-13; rtd 13. *12 Mead Court, Newcastle upon Tyne NE12 9RF* E: dave.walker48@outlook.com

WALKER, David Andrew. b 76. Van Mildert Coll Dur BSc 97. Oak Hill Th Coll MTh 07. **d** 07 **p** 08. C Cheadle All Hallows *Ches* 07-11; V Finchley Ch Ch *Lon* from 11. *Christ Church Vicarage, 616 High Road, London N12 0AA* T: (020) 8445 2532 M: 07980-360408 E: davasarahwava@yahoo.co.uk

WALKER, Canon David Andrew. b 52. St Andr Univ MTheol 75 MA Hull Univ MPhil 00. Linc Th Coll 79. **d** 81 **p** 82. C Hessle *York* 81-84; C N Hull St Mich 84-86; V from 86; AD Cen and N Hull 99-10; RD Hull 00-10; Can and Preb York Minster from 01. *St Michael's Vicarage, 214 Orchard Park Road, Hull HU6 9BX* T: (01482) 803375 E: david@stmichaelsnorthhull.org

WALKER, David Gilmour. b 73. Plymouth Univ BA 96. Wycliffe Hall Ox 07. **d** 09 **p** 10. C Brompton H Trin w Onslow Square St Paul *Lon* 09-11; C Onslow Square and S Kensington St Aug from 11. *3 Holy Trinity Church House, Brompton Road, London SW7 2RW* M: 07807-876525 E: davidgwalker@hotmail.co.uk

WALKER, Canon David Grant. b 23. Bris Univ BA 49 Ball Coll Ox DPhil 54 FSA 60 FRHistS 62. **d** 62 **p** 62. NSM Swansea St Mary w H Trin *S & B* 62-86; Chapl and Lect Univ of Wales (Swansea) 62; Sen Lect 63-82; Dir Post-Ord Tr 65-93; Can Brecon Cathl from 72; Prec Brecon Cathl 79-90; Chan Brecon Cathl 90-93; Chapl Univ of Wales (Swansea) 75-76; Dir of In-Service Tr from 77; P-in-c Caereithin 86-87. *52 Eaton Crescent, Swansea SA1 4QN* T: (01792) 472624

WALKER, David Ian. b 41. Bernard Gilpin Soc Dur 64 Bps' Coll Cheshunt 65. **d** 68 **p** 69. C Todmorden *Wakef* 68-72; V Rastrick St Jo 72-77; V Crosland Moor 77-86; R Kirton in Lindsey w Manton *Linc* 86-99; R Grayingham 86-99; V Clee 99-06; OCM 88-06; rtd 07; PtO *Linc* from 07; Asst Chapl N Lincs and Goole Hosps NHS Trust 08-11. *48 Pretymen Crescent, New Waltham, Grimsby DN36 4PB* T: (01472) 826958
E: davidian8@virginmedia.com

WALKER, David John. b 47. St Jo Coll Nottm 88. **d** 90 **p** 91. C Strood St Fran *Roch* 90-94; V Larkfield from 94. *The Vicarage, 206 New Hythe Lane, Larkfield, Maidstone ME20 6PT* T/F: (01732) 843349 E: david.walker@diocese-rochester.org

WALKER, David Meuryn. b 44. Bris Univ BSc 66 Nottm Univ PGCE 67. NOC 97. **d** 00 **p** 01. NSM Wakef St Jo 00-02; NSM Horbury Junction *Leeds* from 02. *188 Stanley Road, Wakefield WF1 4AE* T: (01924) 210797 M: 07775-583764
E: meuryn@blueyonder.co.uk

✠**WALKER, The Rt Revd David Stuart.** b 57. K Coll Cam MA 81. Qu Coll Birm. **d** 83 **p** 84 **c** 00. C Handsworth *Sheff* 83-86; TV Maltby 86-91; Ind Chapl 86-91; V Bramley and Ravenfield 91-95; R Bramley and Ravenfield w Hooton Roberts etc 95-00; Hon Can Sheff Cathl 00; Suff Bp Dudley *Worc* 00-13; Bp Man from 13. *Bishopscourt, Bury New Road, Salford M7 4LE* T: 0161-792 2096 F: 792 6826
E: bishop.david@manchester.anglican.org

WALKER, Derek Fred. b 46. Trin Coll Bris 71. **d** 74 **p** 75. C St Paul's Cray St Barn *Roch* 74-78; C Rushden w Newton Bromswold *Pet* 78-80; R Kirkby Thore w Temple Sowerby and Newbiggin *Carl* 80-83; V Coppull *Blackb* 83-87; V New Ferry *Ches* 87-96; R Akeman *Ox* 96-11; rtd 11; PtO *Nor* from 13. *34 Valley Rise, Dersingham, King's Lynn PE31 6PT* T: (01485) 541124

WALKER, Duncan Andrew. b 59. **d** 90 **p** 91. C Gorseinon *S & B* 90-91; C Morriston 92-94; V Llanelli Ch Ch *St D* 94-98; V Swansea St Jas *S & B* 98-11; V Pyle w Kenfig *Llan* from 11. *The Vicarage, Pyle Road, Pyle, Bridgend CF33 6PG* T: (01656) 740500

✠**WALKER, The Rt Revd Edward William Murray (Dominic).** b 48. DL 14. AKC 73 Heythrop Coll Lon MA 97 Brighton Univ Hon DLitt 98 Univ of Wales LLM 05. **d** 72 **p** 72 **c** 97. CGA 67-83; C Wandsworth St Faith *S'wark* 72-73; Bp's Dom Chapl 73-76; R Newington St Mary 76-85; RD S'wark and Newington 80-85; OGS from 83; Superior 90-96; V Brighton St Pet w Chpl Royal and St Jo *Chich* 85-86; P-in-c Brighton St Nic 85-86; TR Brighton St Pet and St Nic w Chpl Royal 86-97; RD Brighton 85-97; Can and Preb Chich Cathl 85-97; Area Bp Reading *Ox* 97-03; Bp Mon 03-13; rtd 13; Hon Asst Bp *S & B* from 13. *2 St Vincent's Drive, Monmouth NP25 5DS* T: (01600) 772151
E: dwalker.ogs@btinternet.com

WALKER, Mrs Elizabeth. b 42. CQSW 85. NEOC 91. **d** 94 **p** 00. NSM Stockton St Chad *Dur* 94-08; rtd 08; PtO *Dur* from 08. *29 Bramble Road, Stockton-on-Tees TS19 0NQ* T: (01642) 615332

WALKER, Canon Elizabeth Margaret Rea. b 49. Ch Ch Coll Cant CertEd 70. S'wark Ord Course 89. **d** 92 **p** 94. NSM Ash and Ridley *Roch* 92-97; Chapl St Geo Sch Gravesend 92-97; P-in-c Burham and Wouldham *Roch* 97-05; P-in-c Platt 05-12; V 12-15; Assoc Dir of Ords 97-15; Hon Can Roch Cathl 09-15; rtd 15. *The Vicarage, Comp Lane, Platt, Sevenoaks TN15 8NR* T: (01732) 885482 M: 07931-356502
E: revliz.walker@btinternet.com

WALKER, Gavin Russell. b 43. FCA 78. Coll of Resurr Mirfield 76. **d** 78 **p** 79. C Wakef St Jo 78-81; C Northallerton w Kirby Sigston *York* 81-83; V Whorlton w Carlton and Faceby 83-85; P-in-c Brotherton *Wakef* 85-89; V Earl's Heaton 89-97; TV Dewsbury 97-99; TV Egremont and Haile *Carl* 99-04; rtd 04; PtO *Carl* from 05. *4 South Parade, Seascale CA20 1PZ* T: (019467) 29463 M: 07986-505886 E: staffa@lineone.net

WALKER, Geoffrey. *See* WALKER, Philip Geoffrey

WALKER, Gerald Roger. b 41. K Coll Lon BD 67 AKC 67. **d** 68 **p** 69. C High Elswick St Phil *Newc* 68-70; C Goring-by-Sea *Chich* 70-75; R Selsey 75-81; V Hove St Andr Old Ch 81-91; V Copthorne 91-95; rtd 95; NSM Streat w Westmeston *Chich* 95-99; PtO *S'wark* from 00; *Guildf* 00-15. *1 Glebe Cottages, Newdigate, Dorking RH5 5AA* T: (01306) 631587 E: clergyoncall@btinternet.com

WALKER, Canon Harvey William. b 26. Edin Univ MA 52. St Steph Ho Ox 58. **d** 60 **p** 61. C Newc St Matt w St Mary 60-64; V 64-94; Hon Can Newc Cathl 80-94; rtd 95; PtO *Newc* from 95. *21 Grosvenor Drive, Whitley Bay NE26 2JP* T: 0191-252 1858

WALKER, Mrs Hazel. b 47. Coll of Ripon & York St Jo MA 01. NOC 97. **d** 00 **p** 01. NSM Crofton *Leeds* from 01; Asst Chapl SW Yorks Mental Health NHS Trust 04-07. *30 Heron Drive, Sandal, Wakefield WF2 6SW* T: (01924) 259687 *or* 327319 E: hazel.walker60@btinternet.com

WALKER, Hugh. *See* WALKER, John Hugh

WALKER, Ian Richard Stevenson. b 51. Univ of Wales (Lamp) BA 73. Qu Coll Birm. **d** 76 **p** 77. C Stainton-in-Cleveland *York* 76-79; C Fulford 79-81; C Kidderminster St Mary *Worc* 81-82; TV Kidderminster St Mary and All SS, Trimpley etc 82-86; R Keyingham w Ottringham, Halsham and Sunk Is *York* 86-98; RD S Holderness 94-98; R Scartho *Linc* 98-08; P-in-c Epworth Gp 08-12; R from 12. *St Andrew's Rectory, 16 Belton Road, Epworth, Doncaster DN9 1JL* T: (01427) 873790 E: irsw@btinternet.com

WALKER, Jane. b 65. All SS Cen for Miss & Min. **d** 14 **p** 15. NSM Man Cathl from 14. *Address withheld by request* M: 07967-665161

WALKER, Jane Elizabeth. d 14. NSM Sherwood *S'well* from 14. *22 Mellors Road, Arnold, Nottingham NG5 8HD* E: jane.walker943@ntlworld.com

WALKER, Mrs Jane Louise. b 63. STETS 03. **d** 06 **p** 07. NSM Alton All SS *Win* 06-09; Chapl Phyllis Tuckwell Hospice Farnham from 10; NSM Rowledge and Frensham *Guildf* from 11. *The Vicarage, The Street, Frensham, Farnham GU10 3DT* T: (01420) 88730 E: revjwalker@btconnect.com

WALKER, Mrs Jillian Francesca. b 41. **d** 99 **p** 00. OLM Blackbourne St *E* 99-11; PtO from 11. *The Woolpack, Bury Road, Ixworth, Bury St Edmunds IP31 2HX* T: (01359) 230776 E: digger.walker@mac.com

WALKER (née SEMPER), Canon Jocelyn Rachel. b 64. Univ of Wales (Ban) BA 85 Man Univ PGCE 86. NOC 98. **d** 01 **p** 02. C Chadderton St Matt *Man* 01-04; Chapl Asst Salford R Hosps NHS Trust 04-07; P-in-c Maidstone St Martin *Cant* 07-14; Voc Officer from 14; Dioc Dir of Ords from 13; Hon Can Cant Cathl from 14. *St Mary's Vicarage, Taswell Street, Dover CT16 1SE* E: joss.walker@tiscali.co.uk

WALKER, Canon John. b 51. Aber Univ MA 74 Edin Univ BD 78. Edin Th Coll 75. **d** 78 **p** 79. C Broughty Ferry *Bre* 78-81; P-in-c Dundee St Jo 81-85; Ind Chapl 83-88; R Dundee St Luke 85-95; R Alford *Ab* 95-02; R Inverurie from 95; R Auchindoir from 95; P-in-c Kemnay from 95; Syn Clerk from 08; Can St Andr Cathl from 01. *The Rectory, St Mary's Place, Inverurie AB51 3NW* T: (01467) 620470 E: jwcan@tiscali.co.uk *or* jwcan@btinternet.com

WALKER, John Anthony Patrick. b 58. Kent Univ PhD 12. Trin Coll Bris BA 86. **d** 86 **p** 87. C Canford Magna *Sarum* 86-90; TV Glyncorrwg w Afan Vale and Cymmer Afan *Llan* 90-96; Hd of RE Wentworth High Sch Eccles 97-99; Community Chapl and C Gorton St Phil *Man* 00-03; P-in-c Oldham St Paul 03-04; PtO 04-07; Chapl 07-12; Hon C Maidstone St Martin 12-14; TR Dover Town from 15; AD Dover from 15. *St Mary's Vicarage, Taswell Street, Dover CT16 1SE* M: 07980-692813 E: johnwalker_uk@btinternet.com

WALKER, John David. b 44. St Jo Coll Dur BA 76. Cranmer Hall Dur 77. **d** 77 **p** 78. C Heworth H Trin *York* 77-81; P-in-c Allerthorpe and Barmby on the Moor w Fangfoss 81-83; TV Pocklington Team 84-89; P-in-c Hovingham 89; TV Street 89-92; R Dunnington 92-99; V Thorne *Sheff* 99-03; rtd 03; PtO *York* from 03. *9 Bishop Blunt Close, Hessle HU13 9NJ* T: (01482) 642110 E: john.d.walker@btinternet.com

WALKER, John Frank. b 53. Leeds Univ BEd 76 Ripon Coll of Educn CertEd 75. NW Ord Course 78. **d** 81 **p** 82. NSM Whitkirk *Ripon* 81-82; C 82-85; V Sutton Courtenay w Appleford *Ox* 85-90; Dioc Children's Adv *S'wark* 90-94; V Walworth St Jo from 94; Youth and Children's Officer Woolwich Episc Area 95-99. *St John's Vicarage, 18 Larcom Street, London SE17 1NQ* T: (020) 7703 4375

WALKER, John Howard. b 47. Brasted Th Coll 67 Clifton Th Coll 69. **d** 72 **p** 73. C Upton (Overchurch) *Ches* 72-76; Asst Chapl Liv Univ 76-79; V Everton St Chrys 79-82; C Parr Mt 83-86; SAMS 86-94; Area Sec (NE and E Midl) SAMS 86-89;

Paraguay 89-94; V Calverley *Bradf* 95-12; rtd 12; Hon C Leeds St Geo from 12. *103 Harehills Avenue, Leeds LS8 4HU* T: 0113-249 6239 M: 07903-836806 E: john.h.walker@btinternet.com

WALKER, John Hugh. b 34. K Coll Lon BD 57 AKC 57 K Coll Lon MTh 75 MA 85 Lon Inst of Educn PGCE 68. St Boniface Warminster 57. **d** 58 **p** 59. C Southend St Alb *Chelmsf* 58-61; V Gt Ilford St Alb 61-67; PtO 67-68; Hon C Forest Gate St Edm 68-74; PtO *Cant* 75-82 and 87-12; R Dymchurch w Burmarsh and Newchurch 82-87; rtd 94. *14 Danes Court, Dover CT16 2QE* T: (01304) 202233

WALKER, Canon John Percival. b 45. CITC 68. **d** 71 **p** 72. C Belfast St Clem *D & D* 71-74; C Magheraculmoney *Clogh* 74-78; C Lisburn St Paul *Conn* 78-81; I Belfast St Ninian 81-88; I Belfast St Mary w H Redeemer 88-12; Preb Conn Cathl 98-12; Treas Conn Cathl 04-12; rtd 12. *4 Sprucefield Court, Lisburn BT27 5UL* M: 07835-866914 E: walkerjohnpercival@googlemail.com

WALKER, John Richard. *See* WALKER, Richard John

WALKER, Judith Anne. *See* WALKER-HUTCHINSON, Judith Anne

WALKER, Julie Lorraine. b 68. Liv Univ BTh 05 Ches Univ MTh 09. St Jo Coll Nottm 10. **d** 12 **p** 13. C Wybunbury and Audlem w Doddington *Ches* 12-15; V Haslington w Crewe Green from 15. *The Vicarage, 163 Crewe Road, Haslington, Crewe CW1 5RL* M: 07581-540435 T: (01270) 582388 E: juleswalker68@gmail.com

WALKER, Keith. b 48. Linc Th Coll 82. **d** 84 **p** 85. C Whickham *Dur* 84-87; C Trimdon Station 87; P-in-c 87-89; V 89-90; R Penshaw 90-98; P-in-c Shiney Row 92-95; P-in-c Herrington 93-95; rtd 98; Hon C Jersey St Brelade *Win* 01-03; PtO *Dur* from 03. *16 Westfields, School Aycliffe, Newton Aycliffe DL5 6PX*

WALKER, Canon Lesley Ann. b 53. Westmr Coll Ox MTh 00. S Dios Minl Tr Scheme 85. **d** 88 **p** 94. Par Dn Oakdale *Sarum* 88-92; Team Dn Bridgnorth, Tasley, Astley Abbotts, etc *Heref* 92-94; TV 94-03; Vice-Prin OLM Tr Scheme *Cant* 03-04; PtO 06-07; R Meneage *Truro* 07; RD Kerrier from 10; Hon Can Truro Cathl from 15. *The Rectory, St Martin, Helston TR12 6BU* T: (01326) 231971 E: walker53@btopenworld.com

WALKER, Mrs Linda Joan. b 47. **d** 04 **p** 05. OLM Blurton *Lich* 04-11; OLM Blurton and Dresden from 11. *6 Thackeray Drive, Blurton, Stoke-on-Trent ST3 2HE* T: (01782) 324895 E: linda.walker910@ntlworld.com

WALKER, Marcus Dian Dennison. b 59. WEMTC 04. **d** 07 **p** 08. NSM Churchdown St Jo and Innsworth *Glouc* 07-11; NSM Hardwicke and Elmore w Longney 11-14. *16 Meadowleaze, Gloucester GL2 0PN* T: (01452) 557560 M: 07732-966174 E: marcus-walker@blueyonder.co.uk

WALKER, Margaret (Mother Lucy Clare). b 37. Guildf Dioc Min Course 99. **d** 01 **p** 02. CSP from 88; Mother Superior from 06; NSM Aldershot St Mich *Guildf* 01-04; NSM Chertsey, Lyne and Longcross 04-07; LtO from 07; PtO *Blackb* from 12. *33 Fosbrooke House, 8 Clifton Drive, Lytham St Annes FY8 5RQ* T: (01253) 667004 E: reverendmother@stpetersconvent.co.uk

WALKER, Mrs Margaret Joy. b 44. Westhill Coll Birm TCert 66 Newc Univ MA 93. CA Tr Coll 80. **dss** 86 **d** 87 **p** 94. Hon Par Dn Monkwearmouth St Andr *Dur* 87; Hon Par Dn Chester le Street 87-93; Hon Chapl Wells Cathl 93-01; PtO *Cant* 02-05; NSM Stone Street Gp 05-11; AD W Bridge 09-11; PtO 11-13. *Address temp unknown* E: margiwalker@uwclub.net

WALKER, Mrs Marion Joyce. b 52. **d** 08 **p** 09. NSM Triangle, St Matt and All SS *St E* 08-12; NSM Ipswich St Aug 12-14; PtO from 14. *33 Hardwick Close, Rushmere St Andrew, Ipswich IP4 5XB* T: (01473) 729860 E: mwalker278@btinternet.com

WALKER, Mark Alexander (Marcus). b 81. Oriel Coll Ox BA 02 MA 08 MSt 04. Ripon Coll Cuddesdon MA 10. **d** 11 **p** 12. C Winchmore Hill St Paul *Lon* 11-14; Assoc Dir Angl Cen Rome from 14. *Anglican Cen, Palazzo Doria Pamphilj, Piazza del Collegio Romano 2, 00186 Rome, Italy* T: (0039) (06) 678 0302 E: associate.director@anglicancentre.it

WALKER, Lt Col Mark George. b 68. Univ of New England BProfStud 00 Canberra Univ MDefStud 00 Chas Sturt Univ NSW BTheol 07. **d** 06 **p** 07. C Albany St Jo Australia 06-08; PtO Perth 09-11; C Balga w Mirrabooka 09-11; NSM Frampton on Severn, Arlingham, Saul etc *Glouc* 11; PtO *B & W* from 11; Bris from 11; Ox from 11; *Sarum* from 11; *Worc* from 11. *Ashleigh House, The Street, Frampton-on-Severn, Gloucester GL2 7ED* M: 07580-756141 E: markwalker68@me.com

WALKER, Martin John. b 52. Linc Coll Ox BA 73 PGCE 74 St Jo Coll Dur BA 78. Cranmer Hall Dur. **d** 79 **p** 80. C Harlow New Town w Lt Parndon *Chelmsf* 79-81; C Dorchester *Ox* 81-83; Chapl Bath Coll of HE 83-89; TV Southampton (City Cen) *Win* 89-91; Adv in RE and Resources *Sarum* 91-92; Hon C Northolt St Mary *Lon* 92-00; Chapl Bancroft's Sch Woodford Green 92-99; Chapl St Helen's Sch Northwood from 99; Chapl

Wellingborough Sch from 00. *Marsh House, Wellingborough School, Irthlingborough Road, Wellingborough NN8 2BX*
T: (01933) 277271 E: revmjwalker@yahoo.com

WALKER, Meuryn. *See* WALKER, David Meuryn

WALKER, Michael John. b 39. St D Coll Lamp BA 61. St Aid Birkenhead 61. **d** 63 **p** 64. C Clifton *York* 63-66; C Marfleet 66-69; V Salterhebble St Jude *Wakef* 69-83; V Llangollen w Trevor and Llantysilio *St As* 83-93; RD Llangollen 87-93; V Kerry and Llanmerewig and Dolfor 93-01; RD Cedewain 97-01; rtd 01; PtO *Ban* 01-11. *41 Oldfields Close, Leominster HR6 8TL* T: (01568) 617472
E: margaret@margretw46.plus.com

WALKER, Canon Nigel Maynard. b 39. ALCD 66. **d** 67 **p** 68. C Southsea St Jude *Portsm* 67-70; C Addington S Africa 70-73; R 73-76; C Abingdon w Shippon *Ox* 76-80; V Upton (Overchurch) *Ches* 80-94; Chapl Brussels and Chan Brussels Cathl 94-04; P-in-c Leuven 02-04; rtd 05; PtO *Cant* 05-10; *Eur* from 05; *Portsm* from 10; *Win* from 10; *Chich* from 12; *Guildf* from 13. *12 The Sands, Whitehill, Bordon GU35 9QW*
T: (01420) 477323 E: nigelmwalker@gmail.com

WALKER, Mrs Pamela Sarah. b 52. Somerville Coll Ox BA 73 MA 77 St Jo Coll Dur BA 78. Cranmer Hall Dur 76. **dss** 79 **d** 87 **p** 94. Harlow New Town w Lt Parndon *Chelmsf* 79-81; Dorchester *Sarum* 82-83; Bath St Bart *B & W* 85-88; Hon Par Dn 87-88; Par Dn Warmley *Bris* 88-89; Par Dn Bitton 88-89; Par Dn Southampton (City Cen) *Win* 89-92; Par Dn Northolt St Mary *Lon* 92-94; R 94-04; R Corfe Mullen *Sarum* from 04. *The Rectory, 32 Wareham Road, Corfe Mullen, Wimborne BH21 3LE* T: (01202) 692129 E: fmw202@btinternet.com

WALKER, Paul Gary. b 59. Lon Univ BD. St Jo Coll Nottm 82. **d** 84 **p** 85. C Bowling St Steph *Bradf* 84-87; C Tong 87-90; P-in-c Oakenshaw cum Woodlands 90-97; V Wrose 97-13; P-in-c Bolton St Jas w St Chrys 10-13; RD Calverley 01-09. *Address temp unknown* E: paulwalker71@blueyonder.co.uk

WALKER, Paul Laurence. b 63. St Chad's Coll Dur BA 84. Chich Th Coll BTh 90. **d** 88 **p** 89. C Shildon w Eldon *Dur* 88-91; C Barnard Castle w Whorlton 91-93; C Silksworth 93-96; C-in-c Moorside St Wilfrid CD 96-99; V Norton St Mary 99-04; Chapl Manager Tees and NE Yorks NHS Trust from 04; PtO *Dur* from 04. *St Luke's Hospital, Marton Road, Middlesbrough TS4 3AF* T: (01642) 516068
E: paul.walker@tney.northy.nhs.uk

WALKER, Paulette Winifred. b 47. **d** 08 **p** 09. OLM Swinderby *Linc* from 09. *Shepherd's Pasture, 3 Chancery Close, Lincoln LN6 8SD* T: (01522) 520225 E: pwalker03@talktalk.net

WALKER, Canon Pauline Ann. b 51. Open Univ BA 87. St As Minl Tr Course 88. **d** 93 **p** 97. NSM Bistre *St As* 93-99; C 99-04; V Llay 04-11; V LLay, Rossett and Isycoed from 11; Can Cursal St As Cathl from 12. *The Vicarage, First Avenue, Llay, Wrexham LL12 0TN* T: (01978) 852262
E: pawalker200@btinternet.com

WALKER, Pauline Jean. b 49. St Hild Coll Dur BSc 72 Homerton Coll Cam PGCE 73. St Jo Coll Nottm MA 96. **d** 96 **p** 97. C Bitterne *Win* 96-01; CMS 01-10; CMS-Africa Rep S Sudan from 10. *Trucker's Ghyll, Horsham Road, Handcross, Haywards Heath RH17 6DT* M: 07928-010864

WALKER, Mrs Pepita. b 44. **d** 07 **p** 08. OLM Kemble, Poole Keynes, Somerford Keynes etc *Glouc* 07-11; NSM 11-14; rtd 14. *Woodstock, Frampton Mansell, Stroud GL6 8JE* T: (01285) 760211 E: pepita@pepitawalker.co.uk

WALKER, Percival. *See* WALKER, John Percival

WALKER, Peter Anthony. b 57. Pemb Coll Cam BA 79 MA 83 St Jo Coll Dur BA 86. Cranmer Hall Dur 84. **d** 87 **p** 88. C Chesham Bois *Ox* 87-90; Chapl Bradf Cathl 90-93; TV W Swindon and the Lydiards *Bris* 93-99; V Keresley and Coundon *Cov* 99-10; P-in-c Bidford-on-Avon 10-12; V 12-15; P-in-c Exhall w Wixford 10-15; P-in-c Salford Priors 10-15; P-in-c Temple Grafton w Binton 10-15; R Heart of England from 15. *The Vicarage, 5 Howard Close, Bidford-on-Avon, Alcester B50 4EL* T: (01789) 772217

WALKER, Canon Peter Anthony Ashley. b 46. Chich Th Coll 67. **d** 70 **p** 71. C Stamford Hill St Thos *Lon* 70-74; C Bethnal Green St Matt 74-77; V Hackney Wick St Mary of Eton w St Aug 77-84; Warden Rydal Hall *Carl* 84-95; P-in-c Rydal 84-95; P-in-c Porthleven w Sithney *Truro* 95-01; RD Kerrier 96-01; Can Res Truro Cathl 01-11; P-in-c Feock 01-10; Chapl Is of Scilly 10-12; rtd 12. *Ryancot, Wansford Meadows, Gorran Haven, St Austell PL26 6HU*
T: (01726) 843621 E: peter.walker2@btinternet.com

WALKER, Peter Jeffrey. b 46. Kelham Th Coll 65. **d** 70 **p** 71. C Middlesbrough All SS *York* 70-75 and 77-78; SSF 75-77; C-in-c Badsworth *Wakef* 78-82; V Athersley 82-86; SSM 86-88; PtO *Dur* 88-89; V Hartlepool H Trin 89-95; Dep Chapl HM Pris Birm 95-96; Chapl HM Pris Moorland 96-01; Full Sutton 01-04; Co-ord Chapl HM Pris Ford 04-05; Chapl 06-11; P-in-c Ferrybridge and Brotherton *Wakef* 05-06; rtd 11; OGS

from 01; PtO *Portsm* from 14. *38 Glynde Crescent, Bognor Regis PO22 8HT* T: (01293) 822067

WALKER, Peter Ronald. b 50. Southn Univ BA 72 K Alfred's Coll Win PGCE 73. WMMTC 02. **d** 05 **p** 06. NSM Hadley and Wellington Ch Ch *Lich* 05-10; Chapl Shrewsbury and Telford NHS Trust 09-10; TV Rhos-Cystennin *St As* from 10; PtO *Ban* from 14. *The Rectory, Glyn y Marl Road, Llandudno Junction LL31 9NS* T: (01492) 583579
E: peter@walker1592.fsnet.co.uk

WALKER, Peter Sidney Caleb. b 50. St Mich Th Coll Crafers 76. **d** 80 **p** 81. C Devonport Australia 80-81; P-in-c Fingal Valley 81-84; R E Devonport and Spreyton 84-88; R Swallow *Linc* 88-94; R Selworthy, Timberscombe, Wootton Courtenay etc *B & W* 94-01; Chapl Costa del Sol W *Eur* 01-04; R Coxheath, E Farleigh, Hunton, Linton etc *Roch* 05-12; P-in-c Offwell, Northleigh, Farway, Cotleigh etc *Ex* from 12. *The Rectory, Offwell, Honiton EX14 9SB* T: (01404) 831193
E: peterdiana@talktalk.net

WALKER, Canon Peter Stanley. b 56. SRN RMN Nottm Univ BCombStuds. Linc Th Coll 80. **d** 83 **p** 84. C Woodford St Barn *Chelmsf* 83-86; C Brentwood St Thos 86-88; V Colchester St Barn 88-94; P-in-c Colchester St Jas, All SS, St Nic and St Runwald 94-96; R Colchester St Jas and St Paul w All SS etc from 96; Hon Can Chelmsf Cathl from 09. *The Rectory, 76 East Hill, Colchester CO1 2QW* T: (01206) 866802 F: 799444
M: 07867-972231 E: fatherpeter@walkerssc.freeserve.co.uk

WALKER, Prof Peter William Leyland. b 61. CCC Cam BA 82 MA 86 PhD 87 Ox Univ DPhil 96. Wycliffe Hall Ox 87. **d** 89 **p** 90. C Tonbridge SS Pet and Paul *Roch* 89-93; Fell Tyndale Ho Cam 93-96; Tutor Wycliffe Hall Ox 96-12; Hon C Abingdon *Ox* 97-06; Prof Bibl Studies Trin Sch for Min USA from 12. *311 11th Street, Ambridge PA 15003, USA* T: (001) (724) 266 3838

WALKER, Canon Philip Geoffrey. b 47. St Jo Coll Dur BA 70 Oriel Coll Ox BA 72 MA 76 Newc Univ MA 93 Bris Univ PhD 01. Ripon Hall Ox 70. **d** 74 **p** 75. C Sheff St Geo 74-77; C Cambridge Gt St Mary w St Mich *Ely* 77-81; V Monkwearmouth St Andr *Dur* 81-87; R Chester le Street 87-93; RD Chester-le-Street 89-93; Dioc Missr *B & W* 93-01; Can Res Wells Cathl 94-01; Prin OLM Tr Scheme *Cant* 02-05; Prin Whitelands Coll Roehampton Univ 05-12; rtd 12. *Brook House Farm, 6 Main Street, Ebberston, Scarborough YO13 9NS* T: (01723) 850703 E: drgeoffrey.walker@virgin.net

WALKER, Philip Kingsley. b 47. Ox Univ BA 70. St Mich Coll Llan. **d** 90 **p** 91. C Maindee Newport *Mon* 90-92; C Llanmartin 92-94; V Bishton 94-98; R Panteg 98-03; R Panteg w Llanfihangel Pontymoile 03-07; rtd 07. *Glan Aber, Lon Isallt, Trearddur Bay, Holyhead LL65 2UP*

WALKER, Richard David. b 45. Hull Univ BSc 68. S Dios Minl Tr Scheme 92. **d** 95 **p** 96. NSM Horfield St Greg *Bris* 95-98; NSM Lawrence Weston and Avonmouth 98-00; Chapl HM Pris Leic 00-01; Chapl HM Pris Usk and Prescoed 01-03; Hon C Cromhall, Tortworth, Tytherington, Falfield etc *Glouc* 04-07. *Ford House, Bronllys Road, Talgarth, Brecon LD3 0HH* T: (01874) 712292 E: richard-walker@live.co.uk

WALKER, Richard John. b 67. Humberside Coll of Educn BSc 88 Leeds Univ MSc(Eng) 97 St Jo Coll Dur BA 04 St Jo Coll Nottm MA 14. Cranmer Hall Dur 02. **d** 04 **p** 05. C Scarborough St Mary w Ch Ch and H Apostles *York* 04-08; V Elloughton and Brough w Brantingham 08-13; V Beverley St Nic from 13; Asst Dioc Dir of Ords from 13. *St Nicholas' Vicarage, 72 Grovehill Road, Beverley HU17 0ER* T: (01482) 881458
E: revrichardjwalker@gmail.com

WALKER, Richard Mainprize. b 43. Keele Univ BA DipEd. Wycliffe Hall Ox 84. **d** 86 **p** 87. C Guildf Ch Ch 86-90; V Bradley St Martin *Lich* 90-05; rtd 05. *10 Rockland Park, Largs KA30 8HB* E: richardandcelia@btinternet.com

WALKER, Richard Mark. b 63. York Univ BSc 84. St Jo Coll Nottm MA 00. **d** 00 **p** 01. C Ben Rhydding *Bradf* 00-04; P-in-c Yeadon St Jo 04-08; V Yeadon from 08. *St John's Vicarage, Barcroft Grove, Yeadon, Leeds LS19 7XZ* T: 0113-250 2272
E: richard.walker@bradford.anglican.org

WALKER, Rie. *See* WALKER, Cherie Pauline

WALKER, Roger. *See* WALKER, Gerald Roger

WALKER, Mrs Ruth. b 51. MAAT 95. **d** 03 **p** 04. OLM Camberley St Mary *Guildf* from 03. *73 Verran Road, Camberley GU15 2ND* T: (01276) 503551 E: tandr.walker@ntlworld.com

WALKER (née APPLETON), Mrs Ruth Elizabeth. b 58. St Jo Coll Dur BA 79 Hughes Hall Cam PGCE 80. St Jo Coll Nottm 86. **d** 88 **p** 94. Par Dn Princes Risborough w Ilmer *Ox* 88-90; C and Congr Chapl Bradf Cathl 90-93; C The Lydiards *Bris* 93-94; NSM W Swindon and the Lydiards 94-96; C Swindon St Jo and St Andr 96-98; PtO 98-99; C Keresley and Coundon *Cov* 99-10; AD Cov N 04-10; C Bidford-on-Avon 10-15; C Exhall w Wixford 10-15; C Salford Priors 10-15; C Temple Grafton w Binton 10-15; C Heart of England from 15. *The Vicarage, 5 Howard Close, Bidford-on-Avon, Alcester B50 4EL* T: (01789) 772217

WALKER, Sharon Anne. b 60. Derby Univ BA 99. St Jo Coll Nottm. **d** 02 **p** 03. C Greetham and Thistleton w Stretton and Clipsham *Pet* 02-05; C Cottesmore and Barrow w Ashwell and Burley 02-05; P-in-c Pet St Mary Boongate 05-10; R Street w Walton *B & W* from 10; P-in-c Compton Dundon from 13. *The Rectory, Vestry Road, Street BA16 0HZ* T: (01458) 442297 E: sharonannewalker@hotmail.com

WALKER, Mrs Sheila. b 45. Ex Univ MA 66 PGCE 66. SWMTC 12. **d** 14. NSM Whimple, Talaton and Clyst St Lawr *Ex* from 14; NSM Bradninch and Clyst Hydon from 14. *10 Franklea Close, Ottery St Mary EX11 1BQ* T: (01404) 813589 E: swalk2@btinternet.com

WALKER, Simon Glyn Nicholas. b 82. Trevelyan Coll Dur BA 03. Wycliffe Hall Ox BTh 11. **d** 11 **p** 12. C Hensingham *Carl* from 11. *The Vicarage, Oakfield Court, Whitehaven CA28 6TG* T: (01946) 63797 M: 07713-389980 E: simonwalker@hotmail.com

WALKER, Simon Patrick. b 71. Ch Ch Ox BA 93. Wycliffe Hall Ox BTh 94. **d** 97 **p** 98. C Abingdon *Ox* 97-01; PtO *Ches* 01-04; *Ox* 04-11; *B & W* from 11. *Address temp unknown* E: simon@humanecogroup.com

WALKER, Stanley Frederick. b 48. St Jo Coll Nottm. **d** 84 **p** 85. C Ellesmere Port *Ches* 84-89; V Seacombe 89-97; C Lache cum Saltney 97-03; TV Wrexham *St As* 03-09; C Rhyl w St Ann from 09. *93 Maes y Gog, Rhyl LL18 4QJ* M: 07802-960430 T: (01745) 369997 E: revstanwalker@aol.com

WALKER, Stephen Michael Maynard. b 62. St Jo Coll Dur BA 84. Trin Coll Bris 86. **d** 88 **p** 89. C Eastwood *S'well* 88-92; CF 92-02; C Marple All SS *Ches* 02-06; P-in-c Tewkesbury H Trin *Glouc* 06-10; V from 10. *Holy Trinity Vicarage, 49 Barton Street, Tewkesbury GL20 5PU* T: (01684) 293233

WALKER, Stephen Patrick. b 62. York Univ BSc 83 PGCE 84. St Jo Coll Nottm 87. **d** 90 **p** 91. C Hull St Jo Newland *York* 90-94; Min Grove Green LEP *Cant* 94-98; Children's Min Adv 96-98; TV Drypool *York* 98-99; TR 99-04; TR Binsey *Carl* 04-11; RD Derwent 10-11; P-in-c Theydon Bois and Theydon Garnon *Chelmsf* 11; V from 11. *The Vicarage, 2 Piercing Hill, Theydon Bois, Epping CM16 7JN* T: (01992) 814725 E: stephenwalker04@gmail.com

WALKER, Mrs Susan Joy. b 52. Univ of Wales (Lamp) BA 73 Hull Univ MA 91. Qu Coll Birm 75. **dss** 83 **d** 87 **p** 94. Kidderminster St Mary and All SS, Trimpley etc *Worc* 83-86; Keyingham w Ottringham, Halsham and Sunk Is *York* 86-87; Hon Par Dn 87-94; Hon C 94-98; Chapl Hull Coll of FE 89-98; Chapl N Lindsey Coll *Linc* 98-12; V Burstwick, Burton Pidsea etc *York* from 12; RD S Holderness from 14. *The Vicarage, Main Road, Thorngumbald, Hull HU12 9NA* T: (01964) 601381 E: susanwalkerfe@hotmail.co.uk

WALKER, The Ven Thomas Overington. b 33. Keble Coll Ox BA 58 MA 61. Oak Hill Th Coll 58. **d** 60 **p** 61. C Woking St Paul *Guildf* 60-62; C St Leonards St Leon *Chich* 62-64; Travelling Sec IVF 64-67; Succ Birm Cathl 67-70; V Harborne Heath 70-91; P-in-c Edgbaston St Germain 83-91; Hon Can Birm Cathl 80-91; RD Edgbaston 89-91; Adn Nottingham *S'well* 91-96; rtd 96; PtO *Heref* 07-08. *13 Buttinghill Drive, Cuckfield, Haywards Heath RH17 5GQ*

WALKER, Trevor John. b 51. Southn Univ BTh 80. Sarum & Wells Th Coll 75. **d** 78 **p** 79. C Standish *Blackb* 78-81; P-in-c N Somercotes *Linc* 81-82; P-in-c S Somercotes 81-82; V Somercotes 82-85; R Binbrook Gp from 85. *The Rectory, Louth Road, Binbrook, Lincoln LN8 6BJ* T: (01472) 398227 E: priest1@compuserve.com

WALKER, Valerie Anne. b 57. Leeds Poly BSc 80 Leeds Univ MHSc 92. TISEC 07. **d** 10 **p** 11. C Dunfermline and Alloa *St And* 10-12. *Address temp unknown* M: 07720-327766 E: revalerian@gmail.com

WALKER, Canon Walter Stanley. b 21. AKC 42. Cuddesdon Coll 42. **d** 44 **p** 45. C Southport All SS *Liv* 44-47; Miss to Seamen 47-48; C-in-c Kelsall CD *Ches* 48-53; V Birkenhead St Mary w St Paul 53-61; Chapl Barony Hosp Nantwich 61-66; R Wistaston *Ches* 61-66; R Bromborough 66-77; R Wallasey St Hilary 77-86; RD Wallasey 77-86; Hon Can Ches Cathl 80-86; rtd 86; PtO *Ches* from 86. *9 Chancery Place, Writtle, Chelmsford CM1 3DY*

WALKER-HILL, Richard John. b 51. WMMTC 06. **d** 09 **p** 10. C Oakengates and Wrockwardine Wood *Lich* 09-13; V Gravelly Hill *Birm* from 13; P-in-c Stockland Green from 13. *All Saints' Vicarage, Broomfield Road, Birmingham B23 7QA* T: 0121-373 0730 E: r.walkerhill@sky.com

WALKER-HUTCHINSON, Mrs Judith Anne. b 58. St Jo Coll Dur BA 07 CPFA 88. Cranmer Hall Dur 05. **d** 07 **p** 08. C Penhill *Ripon* 07-10; R Haddington *Edin* 10-11; rtd 11; PtO *Dur* from 11. *Westrill, Cotherstone, Barnard Castle DL12 9PF* T: (01833) 650396 M: 07977-507038 E: revjudith@outlook.com

WALKEY, Malcolm Gregory Taylor. b 44. Lon Univ. Kelham Th Coll 63. **d** 68 **p** 69. C Oadby *Leic* 68-72; TV Corby SS Pet and Andr w Gt and Lt Oakley 72-79; R Ashton w Hartwell 79-86; TR Halesworth w Linstead, Chediston, Holton etc *St E* 86-91; P-in-c Laxfield 93-01; rtd 01; PtO *St E* from 02. *4 Church View, Holton, Halesworth IP19 8PB* T: (01986) 872594

WALL, Colin. b 52. Hull Univ BEd 74 Humberside Coll of Educn BA 80. NEOC 02. **d** 05 **p** 06. NSM Hedon w Paull *York* 05-08; P-in-c Tuxford w Weston and Markham Clinton *S'well* 08-14; NSM Averham w Kelham from 14; NSM N and S Muskham from 14. *St Wilfrid's Vicarage, Marsh Lane, North Muskham, Newark NG23 6HG*

WALL, Canon David Oliver. b 39. TD JP. Bps' Coll Cheshunt 62. **d** 65 **p** 66. C Lt Ilford St Mich *Chelmsf* 65-68; CF 68-73; R Sudbourne w Orford *St E* 73-76; R Orford w Sudbourne and Chillesford w Butley 76-79; P-in-c Iken 76-79; R Drinkstone 79-82; R Rattlesden 79-82; R Chedburgh w Depden, Rede and Hawkedon 82-99; Sen Chapl ACF from 88; Chapl to Suffolk Fire Service *St E* 91-03; Hon Can St E Cathl 96-00; rtd 00; PtO *Ely* from 01. *45 Cross Penny Court, Cotton Lane, Bury St Edmunds IP33 1XY* T: (01284) 489180

WALL, Miss Elizabeth Anne. b 51. Birm Univ BDS 73. WMMTC 97. **d** 00 **p** 01. NSM Lich St Chad 00-14; NSM Alrewas from 14; NSM Wychnor from 14. *15 Gaia Lane, Lichfield WS13 7LW* M: 07711-557770 T: (01543) 254891 E: elizabeth@gaiacottage.wanadoo.co.uk

WALL, John Caswallen. b 60. York Univ BA 83 MA 85. St Steph Ho Ox BA 89. **d** 89 **p** 90. C Ifield *Chich* 89-94; C Brighton St Pet and St Nic w Chpl Royal 94-97; C Brighton St Pet w Chpl Royal 97-98; TV Newbury *Ox* 98-05; P-in-c Moulsecoomb *Chich* from 05. *St Andrew's Rectory, Hillside, Brighton BN2 4TA* T: (01273) 680680 E: jocaswall@hotmail.com

WALL, Márcia Zélia. b 59. NOC 04. **d** 07 **p** 08. C Oakenrod and Bamford *Man* 07-10; V Rhodes and Parkfield from 10; Borough Dean Rochdale from 12; Bp's Adv for Women's Min from 13; AD Heywood and Middleton from 15. *The Vicarage, 5 Wentworth Close, Middleton, Manchester M24 4BD* T: 0161-643 8701 M: 07823-332110 E: revdmarciawall@hotmail.co.uk

WALL, Matthew William. b 74. Westcott Ho Cam 12. **d** 14 **p** 15. C Stoke Newington St Mary *Lon* from 14. *Garden Flat, St Mary's Rectory, Stoke Newington Church Street, London N16 9ES* T: (020) 7254 7371 M: 07764-823266 E: mattwwall@gmail.com

WALL, Nicholas John. b 46. TD 01 MBE 02. Brasted Th Coll 69 Trin Coll Bris 71. **d** 73 **p** 74. C Morden *S'wark* 73-78; R Dunkeswell and Dunkeswell Abbey *Ex* 78-83; V Sheldon 78-83; P-in-c Upottery, Luppitt and Monkton 81-83; V Dunkeswell, Sheldon and Luppitt 83-03; V Dunkeswell, Luppitt, Sheldon and Upottery 03-11; rtd 11; CF(V) from 87. *Address temp unknown*

WALL, Mrs Pauline Ann. b 39. Bris Sch of Min 87. **dss** 85 **d** 87 **p** 94. Bris the Servant Stockwood 85-99; Hon Par Dn 87-94; Hon C 94-99; Chapl St Brendan's Sixth Form Coll 90-99; rtd 99; PtO *Bris* from 99. *41 Ladman Road, Bristol BS14 8QD* T: (01275) 833083

WALL, Richard David. b 78. Ch Ch Ox BA 99. St Steph Ho Ox 00. **d** 02 **p** 03. C Bocking St Mary *Chelmsf* 02-05; C Philadelphia St Clem USA from 05. *2013 Appletree Street, Philadelphia PA 19103-1409, USA* T: (001) (215) 563 1876 F: 563 7627 E: frrichardwall@s-clements.org *or* trrichardwall@yahoo.com

WALL, Robert. b 87. St Mellitus Coll 13. **d** 15. C Onslow Square and S Kensington St Aug *Lon* from 15. *Vicarage Flat, 117 Queen's Gate, London SW7 5LP* T: (020) 7726 4878 M: 07885-660886 E: rob.wall@htb.org

WALL, Robert William. b 52. Ex Coll Ox MA Ex Univ BPhil 77. Trin Coll Bris 80. **d** 83 **p** 84. C Blackb Sav 83-86; C Edgware *Lon* 86-89; C Barnsbury 89-90; TV 90-99; V Dalston St Mark w St Bart 99-07; Chapl St Geo Healthcare NHS Trust Lon from 07. *St George's Hospital, Blackshaw Road, London SW17 0QT* T: (020) 8725 3285 E: rob.wall@care4free.net

WALL, Timothy. b 87. Van Mildert Coll Dur MMath 09 St Jo Coll Dur BA 14. Cranmer Hall Dur 12. **d** 15. C Peterlee *Dur* from 15. *59 O'Neill Drive, Peterlee SR8 5UD* T: 0191-366 1545 M: 07805-744253 E: revtwall@gmail.com

WALLACE, Preb Alastair Robert. b 50. St Cath Coll Cam BA 71 MA 75 Lon Univ BD 75. Trin Coll Bris 72. **d** 75 **p** 76. C Ex St Leon w H Trin 75-79; Chapl Ridley Hall Cam 79-80; R Bath St Mich w St Paul *B & W* 83-96; RD Bath 90-96; Sub-Dean Wells 96-99; TR Ilminster and Distr 99-10; V Ilminster and Whitelackington 10-12; Hon Asst Dioc Missr 96-12; Preb Wells Cathl 96-12; rtd 12. *Houses Barton, Thurloxton, Taunton TA2 8RH* T: (01823) 412712 M: 07746-961191 E: alastair.wallace@btinternet.com

WALLACE, Mrs Ann. b 29. CITC 92. **d** 95 **p** 96. Aux Min Abbeyleix w Ballyroan etc *C & O* from 95. *Knapton, Abbeyleix, Portlaoise, Co Laois, Republic of Ireland* T: (00353) (57) 873 1010

WALLACE, Mrs Brenda Claire. b 52. Linc Th Coll 73 S'wark Ord Course 78. **dss** 80 **d** 87 **p** 94. Sutton at Home *Roch* 80-83; Borstal 83-89; Hon Par Dn 87-89; HM Pris Cookham Wood 83-89; Asst Chapl 87-89; NSM Stansted Mountfitchet *Chelmsf* 89-96; NSM Stansted Mountfitchet w Birchanger and Farnham 97; C Hutton 97-13; P-in-c Rettendon and Hullbridge from 13. *The Vicarage, 93 Ferry Road, Hullbridge, Hockley SS5 6EL* T: (01702) 233354
E: brenda.wallace93@btinternet.com

WALLACE, David Alexander Rippon. b 39. CEng MIET. Ox Min Course 94. **d** 96 **p** 97. NSM Haddenham w Cuddington, Kingsey etc *Ox* 96-97; NSM Worminghall w Ickford, Oakley and Shabbington 97-02; NSM Aylesbury Deanery 02-12; rtd 12. *11 Station Road, Haddenham, Aylesbury HP17 8AN*
T/F: (01844) 290670 E: revd@wallaces.org

WALLACE, Mrs Edwina Margaret. b 49. EMMTC 00. **d** 03 **p** 04. C Broughton Astley and Croft w Stoney Stanton *Leic* 03-07; C Sutton Coldfield St Chad *Birm* 07-11; P-in-c 11; V 11-14; rtd 14; PtO *Birm* from 14; *Leic* from 14. *The Hawthorns, Acresford Road, Donisthorpe, Swadlincote DE12 7PT*
M: 07766-714261 T: (01530) 274002
E: edwinawallace41@gmail.com

WALLACE, Godfrey Everingham. *See* EVERINGHAM, Georgina Wendy

WALLACE, Ian Malcolm. b 57. Southn Univ LLB 78 Solicitor 79. STETS 06. **d** 09 **p** 10. C Wisley w Pyrford *Guildf* 09-13; P-in-c Yate New Town *Bris* 13-14; TR Yate from 14. *The Rectory, 97 Canterbury Close, Yate, Bristol BS37 5TU*
T: (01454) 311483 M: 07799-076697
E: rector@yateparish.org.uk

WALLACE, James Marchant. **d** 11 **p** 12. C Waterford w Killea, Drumcannon and Dunhill *C & O* from 11. *The Rectory, Church Road, Tramore, Co Waterford, Republic of Ireland* T: (00353) (51) 391263 M: 87-272 1789 E: wallace1.jim@gmail.com

WALLACE, James Stephen. b 60. Plymouth Poly BSc 81 St Martin's Coll Lanc 90. Westcott Ho Cam 96. **d** 98 **p** 99. C Newport Pagnell w Lathbury and Moulsoe *Ox* 98-02; USPG Sri Lanka 02-08. *Address temp unknown*

WALLACE, Mark David. b 76. Worc Coll Ox BA 98 MA 01. Oak Hill Th Coll 05. **d** 08 **p** 09. C Trull w Angersleigh *B & W* 08-12; P-in-c Colchester St Pet and St Botolph *Chelmsf* from 12. *St Peter's Vicarage, Balkerne Close, Colchester CO1 1NZ*
T: (01206) 572641 M: 07772-615378
E: markdwallace@btinternet.com

WALLACE, Mark George. b 72. Qu Coll Cam BA 94. Oak Hill Th Coll BA 08. **d** 08 **p** 09. C Guildf Ch Ch w St Martha-on-the-Hill 08-12; V Lightwater from 12. *The Vicarage, 28 Broadway Road, Lightwater GU18 5SJ* T: (01276) 473477
E: mark@allsaintslightwater.org.uk

✠**WALLACE, The Rt Revd Martin William.** b 48. K Coll Lon BD 70 AKC 70. St Aug Coll Cant 70. **d** 71 **p** 72 **c** 03. C Attercliffe *Sheff* 71-74; C New Malden and Coombe *S'wark* 74-77; V Forest Gate St Mark *Chelmsf* 77-93; RD Newham 82-91; P-in-c Forest Gate Em w Upton Cross 85-89; Hon Can Chelmsf Cathl 89-03; P-in-c Forest Gate All SS 91-93; Dioc ACUPA Link Officer 91-97; P-in-c Bradwell on Sea 93-97; P-in-c St Lawrence 93-97; Ind Chapl Maldon and Dengie Deanery 93-97; Adn Colchester 97-03; Bp's Adv for Hosp Chapl 97-03; Suff Bp Selby *York* 03-13; rtd 13. *28 Alexandra Court, Bridlington YO15 2LB* T: (01262) 670265

WALLACE, Matt. b 75. Liv Univ BA 96. Trin Coll Bris BA 11. **d** 11 **p** 12. C Chase Terrace from 11; TV Chase Terrace and Boney Hay, St. John from 15. *3 Chapel Street, Chase Terrace WS7 1NL* M: 07855-960179 E: matt.wallace@o2.co.uk

WALLACE (née ALEXANDER), Mrs Nancy Joan. b 42. Roehampton Inst TCert 64 Ox Brookes Univ BA 97 PQCSW 97. SAOMC 95. **d** 98 **p** 99. NSM Worminghall w Ickford, Oakley and Shabbington *Ox* 98-02; NSM Aylesbury Deanery 02-12; rtd 12. *11 Station Road, Haddenham, Aylesbury HP17 8AN* T/F: (01844) 290670 E: revn@wallaces.org

WALLACE, Nicholas Robert. b 56. Trin Coll Bris 93. **d** 95 **p** 96. C Fishponds St Jo *Bris* 95-98; P-in-c Barton Hill St Luke w Ch Ch 98-99; P-in-c Barton Hill St Luke w Ch Ch and Moorfields 99-00; R Binstead *Portsm* 00-10; V Havenstreet St Pet 00-10; P Adelaide St Mary Australia 10-13; P Sorrento w Rye from 13. *The Vicarage, 3473 Point Nepean Road, Sorrento Vic 3943, Australia* E: nrwallace@hotmail.com

WALLACE, Richard Colin. b 39. Mert Coll Ox BA 61 MA 64. St Chad's Coll Dur 69. **d** 71 **p** 72. Tutor St Chad's Coll Dur 71-72; P-in-c Kimblesworth *Dur* 72-74; Chapl Bradf Univ 74-79; C Bingley All SS 79-80; TV 80-89; V Kelbrook *Bradf* 89-01; RD Skipton 00-05; rtd 06; PtO *Leeds* from 07. *15 Holme Park, Bentham, Lancaster LA2 7ND* T: (015242) 63136 E: richard.wallace@bradford.anglican.org

WALLACE, Richard Ernest. b 35. Ridley Coll Melbourne ThL 61 ACT 61. **d** 61 **p** 62. C Balwyn St Barn Australia 61-62; C S Yarra 62-64; C Bentleigh St Jo 64-65; I Northcote 65-66; C Ipswich St Fran *St E* 67-69; I Belgrave Australia 69-79; Dir Angl Renewal Min 79-82; I Blackburn St Jo 83-92; I Syndal St Jas 92-95; Sen Assoc P Glen Waverley 95-97; I Ringwood E H Trin 97-03; rtd 03. *3 Panorama Road, Kalorama Vic 3766, Australia* T: (0061) (3) 9728 4595 M: 408-596535
E: rwallace@melbpc.org.au

WALLACE, Robert. b 52. Sussex Univ BSc 73. Linc Th Coll 73. **d** 76 **p** 77. C Plaistow St Mary *Roch* 76-79; C Dartford H Trin 79-83; V Borstal 83-89; Chapl The Foord Almshouses 83-89; Chapl HM Pris Cookham Wood 83-89; P-in-c Farnham *Chelmsf* 89-96; V Stansted Mountfitchet 89-96; R Stansted Mountfitchet w Birchanger and Farnham 97; R Hutton from 97. *The Rectory, 175 Rayleigh Road, Hutton, Brentwood CM13 1LX* T: (01277) 215115 F: 263407
E: bob.huttonchurch@btinternet.com

WALLACE, Canon Susan Marilyn. b 67. Ch Ch Coll Cant BA(Ed) 90 Leeds Univ MA 06 Sheff Univ MA 15. NOC 03. **d** 06 **p** 07. NSM Acomb St Steph and St Aid *York* 06-10; NSM York St Mich-le-Belfrey 10; TV Leeds City *Ripon* 10-13; Can Res, Prec and Sacr Win Cathl from 14. *8 The Close, Winchester SO23 9LS* T: (01962) 857200 M: 07962-071621
E: sue.wallace@winchester-cathedral.org.uk

WALLBANK, Alison Patricia. b 59. **d** 09 **p** 10. OLM Whitworth w Facit *Man* 09-14; NSM Norden w Ashworth and Bamford 13-14; NSM Eggleston *Dur* from 14; NSM Middleton-in-Teesdale w Forest and Frith from 14. *1 Greta Place, Wesley Terrace, Middleton-in-Teesdale, Barnard Castle DL12 0SW* M: 07800-955791 E: alisonwallbank59@gmail.com

WALLER, Annalu. b 63. Cape Town Univ BSc 83 MSc 88 Dundee Univ PhD 92. TISEC 01. **d** 04 **p** 05. Hon C Dundee St Marg *Bre* from 04; Hon Chapl Dundee Univ from 07. *3 Invergowrie Drive, Dundee DD2 1RD* T: (01382) 644570 *or* 388223
E: awaller@dundee.ac.uk

WALLER, David James. b 58. Whitelands Coll Lon BA 85 K Coll Lon MA 95. Ripon Coll Cuddesdon 85. **d** 88 **p** 89. C Tettenhall Regis *Lich* 88-91; Chapl Greenwich Univ *S'wark* 92-97; P-in-c Yiewsley *Lon* 97-01; TR Plymstock and Hooe *Ex* 01-12; Chapl Palma de Mallorca *Eur* from 12. *Calle Nuñez de Balboa 6, 07014 Son Armadans, Palma de Mallorca, Spain* T: (0034) 971 737 279 E: davidwaller2000@btinternet.com

WALLER, Canon Derek James Keith. b 54. Em Coll Cam BA 75 PGCE 76. Trin Coll Bris 88. **d** 91 **p** 92. C Church Stretton *Heref* 91-95; R Appleby Gp *Leic* 95-04; P-in-c Rushden St Pet 04-07; V 08-14; RD Higham 11-14; Can Pet Cathl 13-14; CMS S Sudan from 14. *Address temp unknown*
E: derekwaller@btinternet.com

WALLER, Mrs Elizabeth Alison. b 49. Open Univ BA 89 Univ of Cen England in Birm MA 99 Wolfs Coll Cam PGCE 91. EAMTC 02. **d** 05 **p** 06. NSM Oundle w Ashton and Benefield w Glapthorn *Pet* 05-08; NSM Aldwincle, Clopton, Pilton, Stoke Doyle etc from 08. *Priory Cottage, 40 Church Street, Stilton, Peterborough PE7 3RF* T: (01733) 242412
E: eawaller@btinternet.com

WALLER, Ms Elizabeth Jean. b 58. Keswick Hall Coll BEd BTh. Linc Th Coll 84. **d** 87 **p** 94. Par Dn Mile End Old Town H Trin *Lon* 87-90; Manna Chr Cen 90-91; Chapl LSE *Lon* 91-96; Hon C Soho St Anne w St Thos and St Pet 91-96; Community Pastor CARA 96-00; NSM Notting Dale St Clem w St Mark and St Jas *Lon* 96-99; Chapl Ealing Hosp NHS Trust from 07. *52 Cromwell Road, Tunbridge Wells TN2 4UD*
E: lizawaller@hotmail.com

WALLER, Gordon Robert. b 50. Jes Coll Cam BA 72 MA 75. **d** 03 **p** 05. OLM Tooting All SS *S'wark* from 03. *131 Ribblesdale Road, London SW16 6SP* T: (020) 8769 6733
E: baldypevsner@yahoo.co.uk

WALLER, John. b 60. Man Univ BA 84 Liv Univ MA 07. St Jo Coll Nottm 85. **d** 87 **p** 88. C Chorlton-cum-Hardy St Clem *Man* 87-90; R Openshaw 90-95; Chapl Ancoats Hosp Man 93-95; TV Watling Valley *Ox* 95-96; TR 96-03; R Brickhills and Stoke Hammond from 03; AD Mursley 06-11. *The Rectory, 10 Pound Hill, Great Brickhill, Milton Keynes MK17 9AS* T: (01525) 261062 E: john.waller1@virgin.net

✠**WALLER, The Rt Revd John Stevens.** b 24. Peterho Cam BA 48 MA 53. Wells Th Coll 48. **d** 50 **p** 51 **c** 79. C Hillingdon St Jo *Lon* 50-52; C Twerton *B & W* 52-55; C-in-c Weston-super-Mare St Andr Bournville CD 55-59; V Weston-super-Mare St Andr Bournville 59-60; R Yarlington 60-63; Youth Chapl 60-63; Tr Officer C of E Youth Coun 63-67; V Frindsbury w Upnor *Roch* 67-72; P-in-c Strood St Fran 67-72; P-in-c Strood St Mary 67-72; P-in-c Strood St Nic 67-72; TR Strood 72-73; RD 67-73; R Harpenden St Nic *St Alb* 73-79; Suff Bp Stafford *Lich* 79-87; Asst Bp *B & W* 87-04; P-in-c Long Sutton w Long Load 87-88; TV Langport Area 88-89; rtd 89. *The College of St Barnabas, Blackberry Lane, Lingfield RH7 6NJ* T: (01342) 872818 E: wallers@collegeofstbarnabas.com

WALLER, Martha. d 10 **p** 11. NSM Raheny w Coolock *D & G* 10-13; NSM Dublin St Cath and St Jas w St Audoen from 13. *1 The Paddock, Ashdown, Dublin 7, Republic of Ireland* T: (00353) (1) 868 1655 M: 86-349 0571
E: martha.waller@ucd.ie

WALLER, Philip Thomas. b 56. Ex Coll Ox BA 78 MA 88 St Jo Coll Dur BA 87. Cranmer Hall Dur 85. **d** 88 **p** 89. C Enfield St Andr *Lon* 88-91; C Belper *Derby* 91-95; P-in-c Oakwood 95-05; P-in-c Long Eaton St Jo 05-10; V from 10; Asst Dir of Ords from 09. *St John's Vicarage, 59 Trowell Grove, Long Eaton, Nottingham NG10 4AY* T: 0115-973 4819
E: waller.family59@tiscali.com *or* philipstjohn@tiscali.co.uk

WALLEY, Peter Francis. b 60. Bris Univ BSc 82 CEng 89 MICE 89. Trin Coll Bris 96. **d** 98 **p** 99. C Ex St Jas 98-01; Asst Chapl Brussels *Eur* 01-05; Bp's Dom Chapl *Lich* 05-12; P-in-c Mickleover All SS *Derby* 12-14; P-in-c Mickleover St Jo 12-14; V Mickleover from 14; RD Derby S from 15. *All Saints' Vicarage, Etwall Road, Mickleover, Derby DE3 0DL* T: (01332) 513793 E: peterwalley@btinternet.com

WALLING, Mrs Carolyn. b 47. Rolle Coll CertEd 69. Episc Div Sch Cam Mass MDiv 87. **d** 86 **p** 87. Saudi Arabia 89; Par Dn Battersea St Mary *S'wark* 91-94; USA 94-96; C Lee Gd Shep w St Pet *S'wark* 96; rtd 07. *PO Box 947, General Post Office, Georgetown, 10820 Penang, Malaysia*

WALLINGTON, Martin John. b 59. SAOMC 95. **d** 98 **p** 99. NSM Chorleywood St Andr *St Alb* 98-03; P-in-c Wooburn Ox 03-08; V from 08. *Wooburn Vicarage, Windsor Hill, Wooburn Green, High Wycombe HP10 0EH* T: (01628) 521209

WALLINGTON, Paul. b 62. Birm Univ BCom 83 ACA 86. Trin Coll Bris BA 94. **d** 94 **p** 95. C Chorley St Laur *Blackb* 94-97; C Darwen St Pet w Hoddlesden 97-98; TV 98-00; rtd 00; PtO Man from 13. *551 Darwen Road, Dunscar, Bolton BL7 9RT* T: (01204) 308637 E: thewallingtons@hotmail.com

WALLIS, Anna Louise. b 73. Leic Univ BSc 95 PhD 99 Selw Coll Cam BA 05 MA 09. Westcott Ho Cam 03. **d** 06 **p** 07. C Huddersfield St Pet *Wakef* 06-09; Chapl Sheff Teaching Hosps NHS Foundn Trust 09-11; PtO *Sheff* 11-12. *23 Springwood Hall Gardens, Huddersfield HD1 4HA* T: (01484) 431810
E: anna.wallis121@gmail.com

WALLIS, Benjamin John. b 55. Wimbledon Sch of Art BA 79. Chich Th Coll 92. **d** 94 **p** 95. C Battersea Ch Ch and St Steph *S'wark* 94-98; C Wood Green St Mich w Bounds Green St Gabr etc *Lon* 98-03; V Barkingside St Geo *Chelmsf* from 03. *St George's Vicarage, Woodford Avenue, Ilford IG2 6XQ* T: (020) 8550 4149
E: pam@herdom.com

WALLIS, David Peter. b 72. Ripon Coll Cuddesdon BTh 03. **d** 03 **p** 04. C Eastbourne St Mary *Chich* 03-07; P-in-c Ditchling, Streat and Westmeston 07-08; R from 08. *St Margaret's Vicarage, 2 Charlton Gardens, Lewes Road, Ditchling, Hassocks BN6 8WA* T: (01273) 843165

WALLIS, Ian George. b 57. Sheff Univ BA 79 PhD 92 St Edm Ho Cam MLitt 87. Ridley Hall Cam 88. **d** 90 **p** 91. C Armthorpe *Sheff* 90-92; Chapl and Fell SS Coll Cam 92-95; Hon C Chesterton Gd Shep *Ely* 93-95; R Houghton le Spring *Dur* 95-07; AD Houghton 04-07; Tutor Aston Tr Scheme 93-97; Prin NOC 07-08; V Sheff St Mark Broomhill 09-14; rtd 14; PtO *Sheff* from 14. *1 Sike Close, Holmfirth HD9 1JD* M: 07717-417760 E: ian.wallis@sero.co.uk

WALLIS, John Anthony. b 36. St Pet Coll Ox BA 60 MA 65. Clifton Th Coll 60. **d** 62 **p** 63. C Blackpool St Mark *Blackb* 62-65; C Leeds St Geo *Ripon* 65-69; Korea 69-74; Nat Sec (Scotland) OMF 75-78; Home Dir OMF 78-89; Hon C Sevenoaks St Nic *Roch* 78-89; Chapl The Hague *Eur* 89-95; V Northwood Em *Lon* 95-01; rtd 01; PtO Nor from 03; *Ely* from 13. *Church Cottage, 61 Gayton Road, Grimston, King's Lynn PE32 1BG* T: (01485) 600336 E: johna.wallis@btinternet.com

WALLIS, Raymond Christopher. b 38. Moor Park Coll Farnham 62 Sarum Th Coll 63. **d** 66 **p** 67. C Allerton *Bradf* 66-68; C Langley Marish Ox 68-69; C Caister Nor 69-73; P-in-c E w W Bradenham 73-80; R Upwell St Pet and Outwell *Ely* 80-84; V Bishopstone *Chich* 84-97; rtd 97; PtO *Chich* from 97. *15 Llewelyn Lodge, Cooden Drive, Bexhill-on-Sea TN39 3DB* T: (01424) 220245

WALLMAN-GIRDLESTONE, Jane Elizabeth. b 61. Homerton Coll Cam BEd 83. St Steph Ho Ox 89 Sarum & Wells Th Coll BTh 92. **d** 93 **p** 94. C Woodbridge St Mary *St E* 93-96; V Ipswich St Thos 96-00; Dir Past Studies and Adv for Women's Min St Mich Coll Llandaff 00-02; Lect TISEC 03-07; Lect Qu Foundn Birm 04-05; LtO *Mor* from 06. *St Columba House, The Clattach, Alturlie Point, Allanfearn, Inverness IV2 7HZ* T: (01463) 230708 M: 07776-181824
E: janewallman@hotmail.co.uk

WALLS, Michael Peter. b 38. Cape Town Univ BA 57. Wells Th Coll 59. **d** 61 **p** 62. C Morecambe St Barn *Blackb* 61-64; C Birm St Paul 64-66; Ind Chapl 64-74; V Temple Balsall

66-74; Chapl Wroxall Abbey Sch 72-74; V Kings Heath *Birm* 74-76; Hon C Bordesley St Benedict 76-78; Sen Chapl Oakham Sch 78-83; P-in-c Leic St Sav 83-85; P-in-c Knossington and Cold Overton 85-87; P-in-c Owston and Withcote 85-87; V Tilton w Lowesby 85-87; P-in-c 87; V Whatborough Gp 87-90; Bp's Adv on Relns w People of Other Faiths 89-93; Hon Can Leic Cathl 89-93; V Leic St Mary 90-93; rtd 93; PtO Ban from 02. *Gwynt y Mor, 1A Bro Cymerau, Pwllheli LL53 5PY* T: (01758) 613495 E: michael.w@tinyworld.co.uk

WALMISLEY, Andrew John. b 55. Ex Univ BA 75 San Francisco State Univ MA 90. Ridley Hall Cam 76. **d** 78 **p** 79. C W Brompton St Mary w St Pet *Lon* 78-81; C Portola Valley Ch Ch USA 81-83; C San Francisco St Mary V 83-86; Chapl San Mateo St Matt 86-90; Chapl New York Trin Ch 90-93; R Redwood City St Pet 93-97; R Berkeley All So 97-07; Chapl Seabury Hall Coll Prep Sch Makawao from 07. *65 North Holokai Road, Haiku HI 96708, USA* T: (001) (808) 573 6848
E: frandreww@aol.com

WALMSLEY, Derek. b 57. Oak Hill Th Coll 89. **d** 91 **p** 92. C Bletchley Ox 91-95; C Utley *Bradf* 95-00; V Leeds from 00; P-in-c Keighley St Andr *Bradf* from 14. *St Mark's Vicarage, Green Head Road, Keighley BD20 6ED* T: (01535) 607003
E: derek.walmsley@bradford.anglican.org *or* dwalmsley9@aol.com

WALMSLEY, Jane. *See* LLOYD, Patricia Jane

WALMSLEY, John William. b 37. Hull Univ BA 71 MA 73 PhD 81. Wycliffe Hall Ox 71. **d** 72 **p** 73. C Clifton *York* 72-74; C Acomb St Steph and St Aid 74-76; P-in-c Newton upon Ouse 76-81; P-in-c Shipton w Overton 76-81; V York St Thos w St Maurice 81-89; V Barkingside St Laur *Chelmsf* 89-92; Dir Children in Distress 92-01; rtd 01. *966 Lomardy Street, Kingston ON K7M 8M7, Canada* T: (001) (613) 766 6058

WALMSLEY, Patricia Jane. *See* LLOYD, Patricia Jane

WALMSLEY-McLEOD, Paul Albert. b 56. St Cuth Soc Dur BA 82 Cam Univ CertEd 83. Westcott Ho Cam 85. **d** 87 **p** 88. C Gt Bookham *Guildf* 87-90; Asst Chapl St Chris Hospice Lon 90-93; Soc Care Team Member Phoenix Ho Fountain Project 93-95; C Catford (Southend) and Downham *S'wark* 95-96; TV 96-99; P-in-c Downham St Barn 00-02; R Friern Barnet St Jas *Lon* from 02; AD Cen Barnet from 10. *The Rectory, 147 Friern Barnet Lane, London N20 0NP* T: (020) 8445 7844
E: pawm_friernbarnet@hotmail.com

WALROND-SKINNER, Susan Mary. *See* PARFITT, Susan Mary
WALSALL, Archdeacon of. *See* WELLER, The Ven Susan Karen
WALSER (née SHIELS), Mrs Rosalinde Cameron. b 47. Edin Univ MA 68 Moray Ho Coll of Educn PGCE 69. NOC 92. **d** 95 **p** 97. NSM Scarborough St Mary w Ch Ch and H Apostles *York* 95-97; Chapl St Cath Hospice Scarborough 95-97; Chapl Scarborough Coll 95-97; P-in-c E Ayton *York* 97-06; rtd 06; PtO York from 07. *29 Sea Cliff Road, Scarborough YO11 2XU* T: (01723) 372382

WALSH, Mrs Alexandra Mary (Gussie). b 50. Wycliffe Hall Ox 06. **d** 08 **p** 09. C Penrith w Newton Reigny and Plumpton Wall *Carl* 08-12; C Buckingham Ox from 12. *The Rectory, Chapel Lane, Thornborough, Buckingham MK18 2DJ* T: (01280) 821616 E: gussiewalsh@hotmail.com *or* am@buckinghambenefice.org.uk

WALSH, Carys Ruth. b 62. Ex Univ BA 83 MPhil 89 Heythrop Coll Lon MA 00 PhD 11. STETS 10. **d** 13 **p** 14. C Chelsea St Luke and Ch Ch *Lon* from 13; Tutor St Mellitus Coll from 15. *2 Pembroke Road, London W8 6NT* M: 07931-750526
E: carys.walsh@me.com

WALSH, David Christopher. b 59. Warwick Univ BA 81 St Jo Coll Nottm BA 83. Ripon Coll Cuddesdon 00. **d** 02 **p** 03. C Greenwich St Alfege *S'wark* 02-06; C Kensington St Mary Abbots w Ch Ch and St Phil *Lon* from 06; AD Kensington from 11. *2 Pembroke Road, London W8 6NT* T: (020) 7603 4420 M: 07957-656643 E: vicar@specr.org

✠**WALSH, The Rt Revd Geoffrey David Jeremy. b** 29. Pemb Coll Cam BA 53 MA 58. Linc Th Coll 53. **d** 55 **p** 56 **c** 86. C Southgate Ch Ch *Lon* 55-58; SCM Sec Cam 58-61; C Cambridge Gt St Mary w St Mich *Ely* 58-61; V Moorfields *Bris* 61-66; R Marlborough *Sarum* 66-76; Can and Preb Sarum Cathl 73-76; Adn Ipswich *St E* 76-86; R Elmsett w Aldham 76-80; Suff Bp Tewkesbury *Glouc* 86-95; rtd 95; PtO *St E* from 95; Hon Asst Bp St E from 08. *6 Warren Lane, Martlesham Heath, Ipswich IP5 3SH* T: (01473) 620797

WALSH, Geoffrey Malcolm. b 46. Sarum & Wells Th Coll 82. **d** 84 **p** 85. C Wellington and Distr *B & W* 84-87; TV Axminster, Chardstock, Combe Pyne and Rousdon *Ex* 87-90; Chapl RN 90-94; R Huntspill *B & W* 94-11; rtd 11; PtO *Sarum* from 12; C Axminster, Chardstock, All Saints etc *Ex* from 14. *Thimbles, 70 Flax Meadow Lane, Axminster EX13 5FJ* T: (01297) 598361 E: geoffreywalsh@talktalk.net

WALSH, Gussie. *See* WALSH, Alexandra Mary

WALSH, John Alan. b 37. Chich Th Coll 63. **d** 66 **p** 67. C Wigan St Anne *Liv* 66-69; C Newport w Longford *Lich* 69-73; V Dunstall 73-82; V Rangemore 73-82; P-in-c Tatenhill 77-82; R Dunstall w Rangemore and Tatenhill 83; V Hartshill 83-03; rtd 03; PtO *Ches* from 04. *A9 Plumley Close, Vicars Cross, Chester CH3 5PD* T: (01244) 310936

WALSH, Neil-Allan. b 72. Cant Ch Ch Univ BA 03 Cape Town Univ DipEd 91. Westcott Ho Cam 06. **d** 08 **p** 09. C Lt Ilford St Mich *Chelmsf* 08-11; P-in-c Leytonstone St Marg w St Columba from 11; P-in-c Leytonstone H Trin and St Aug Harrow Green from 14; Black and Minority Ethnic Adv to Bp Barking from 14. *St Margaret's Vicarage, 15 Woodhouse Road, London E11 3NG* T: (020) 8519 0813 M: 07903-652874 E: neilallanwalsh@yahoo.com

WALSH, Nicholas Sean. b 83. Moorlands Coll BA 07 K Coll Lon MA 13. St Mellitus Coll 11. **d** 13 **p** 14. C Luton Lewsey St Hugh *St Alb* from 13. *247 Leagrave High Street, Luton LU4 0NA* M: 07774-516204 E: nswalsh@gmail.com

WALSH, Peter. b 64. Liv Univ BA 86 Nottm Univ BTh 90. Linc Th Coll 87. **d** 90 **p** 91. C Cantley *Sheff* 90-93; C Poulton-le-Fylde *Blackb* 93-95; V Blackpool St Steph 95-03; TR Ches 03-05; V Ches St Oswald and St Thos 05-11; Min Can Ches Cathl 04-05; V W Kirby St Andr from 11; Minl Development Review Officer 11-14. *St Andrew's Vicarage, 2 Lingdale Road, Wirral CH48 5DQ* T: 0151-632 4728 E: revpeterwalsh@btconnect.com

WALSH, Sarah Elaine. b 60. LLCM(TD) 90 CTABRSM 95. NEOC 04. **d** 07 **p** 10. NSM Waggoners *York* 07-08; NSM Crookes St Tim *Sheff* 09-11; NSM Walkley 11-12; Chapl HM Pris Nottm 12-13; Chapl HM Pris Stocken 12-13; Chapl HM Pris Lindholme from 13; Chapl HM Pris Moorland from 13. *HM Prison Moorland, Bawtry Road, Hatfield Woodhouse, Doncaster DN7 6BW* T: (01302) 523000 E: sarah.e.walsh@btinternet.com

WALSHAW, Mrs Caroline Elaine. b 59. SEITE 13. **d** 15. NSM Pembury *Roch* from 15. *42A Riding Lane, Hildenborough, Tonbridge TN11 9HZ* T: (01732) 832725 E: canrwalshaw@outlook.com

WALSHE, Marie Sylvia. b 54. RGN RCNT. **d** 99 **p** 00. NSM Kilkeel *D & D* 99-00; NSM Down H Trin w Hollymount 00-08; NSM Rathmullan w Tyrella 00-08; NSM Newcastle 08-13; NSM Gilnahirk from 13. *8 Castle View, Dundrum, Newcastle BT33 0SA* T: (028) 4375 1757 E: walshemarie@hotmail.com

WALT, Canon Trevor William. b 52. MBE 03. RMN 74 RNT 79. Ox NSM Course 83. **d** 86 **p** 87. NSM Crowthorne *Ox* 86-89; Chapl Asst Broadmoor Hosp Crowthorne 86-89; Chapl 89-10; Hon Can Ch Ch *Ox* 00-07; PtO *Chelmsf* from 10; Bp's Adv for Healing and Deliverance Min from 11; Chapl St Helena Hospice Colchester from 13. *1 Home Bridge Court, Hatfield Road, Witham CM8 1GJ* M: 07969-109587 E: twalt@sthelenahospice.org.uk

WALTER, Donald Alex. b 34. Ripon Hall Ox 57. **d** 60 **p** 61. C Ealing St Steph Castle Hill *Lon* 60-63; Jamaica 63-80; V Twickenham Common H Trin *Lon* 81-00; rtd 00; PtO *Lon* from 03. *Ebenezer, 23 Hawley Close, Hampton TW12 3XX* T: (020) 8941 5193 E: daw@maperche.co.uk

WALTER, Giles Robert. b 54. Cam Univ MA 76. Cranmer Hall Dur 78. **d** 82 **p** 83. C Finchley Ch Ch *Lon* 82-86; C Cambridge H Sepulchre w All SS *Ely* 86-92; C Cambridge H Sepulchre 92-93; P-in-c Tunbridge Wells St Jo *Roch* 93-95; V from 95. *St John's Vicarage, 1 Amherst Road, Tunbridge Wells TN4 9LG* T: (01892) 521183 *or* 540897

WALTER, Ian Edward. b 47. Edin Univ MA 69 Keble Coll Ox BA 71 MA 78. Cuddesdon Coll 71. **d** 73 **p** 74. C Greenock *Glas* 73-76; C Glas St Mary and Chapl Angl Students Glas 76-79; R Paisley St Barn 79-84; P-in-c Bolton St Phil *Man* 84-86; V 86-91; Dioc Ecum Officer 88-94; V Elton All SS 91-98; V Stalybridge 98-01; R Hawick *Edin* 01-08; rtd 08; Hon C Oban St Jo *Arg* from 08. *Balaclava, 56 Dalriach Road, Oban PA34 5JE* T: (01631) 564855 E: ian_walter@btinternet.com

WALTER, Michael. b 36. AKC 62. **d** 63 **p** 64. C Middlesbrough St Jo the Ev *York* 63-65; C Sherborne *Win* 65-68; C Bournemouth St Fran 68-69; Prec Newc Cathl 69-71; C Dur St Marg 72-74; P-in-c Deaf Hill cum Langdale 74-77; V Newington w Dairycoates *York* 77-88; PtO 88-92; C Feltham *Lon* 92-96; PtO 96-03; rtd 01. *15 Glanville Road, Bromley BR2 9LN* T: (020) 8313 3390

WALTER, Noël. b 41. St D Coll Lamp. **d** 66 **p** 67. C Mitcham Ascension *S'wark* 66-71; C Caterham 71-74; OCM 71-74; V Welling *S'wark* 74-82; C Warlingham w Chelsham and Farleigh 82-88; Chapl Warlingham Park Hosp Croydon 82-88; Chapl R Earlswood Hosp Redhill 88-90; Chapl Redhill Gen Hosp 88-91; Chapl E Surrey Hosp Redhill 88-96; Sen Chapl Gt Ormond Street Hosp for Children NHS Trust 96-06; rtd 06; PtO *Ex* 98-07; C Chagford, S Tawton, Drewsteignton etc 07-12. *Whiddon View, 13 Bretteville Close, Chagford, Newton Abbot TQ13 8DW* T: (01647) 432610

WALTER, Peter John. b 44. CEng MIGasE. Chich Th Coll 80. **d** 82 **p** 83. C Leominster *Heref* 82-85; P-in-c Brimfield 85-90; P-in-c Orleton 85-90; R Orleton w Brimfield 91-95; rtd 04. *Mews Cottage, 39 West Street, Leominster HR6 8EP* T: (01568) 614349

WALTER, Robin. b 37. Univ Coll Dur BA 63 MA 90 Linacre Coll Ox BA 65 MA 69. St Steph Ho Ox 63. **d** 66 **p** 68. C Peckham St Jo *S'wark* 66-69; Chapl Lon Univ 69-70; C Dur St Marg 70-74; R Burnmoor 74-79; Asst Master Barnard Castle Sch 79-97; NSM Barnard Castle Deanery 88-97; Hon C Whorlton *Dur* 82-83; Hon C Barnard Castle w Whorlton 83-88; P-in-c Redmarshall 97-01; R 01-03; P-in-c Bishopton w Gt Stainton 97-01; V 01-03; rtd 03; PtO *York* from 03; *Worc* from 04. *The Laurels, Worcester Road, Great Witley, Worcester WR6 6HR* T: (01299) 890190 E: rfw@myric.net

WALTERS, Christopher Rowland. b 47. Open Univ BA 78 Univ of Wales PGCE 94 MEd 95 Texas Wesleyan Univ PhD 02. **d** 02 **p** 10. Hd Master Mayflower Chr Sch Pontypool 90-05; OLM Abergavenny H Trin *Mon* 02-12; P-in-c Govilon w Llanfoist w Llanelen from 12; PtO *S & B* from 14. *The Rectory, Merthyr Road, Govilon, Abergavenny NP7 9PT* T: (01873) 831048 M: 07967-945320 E: church@chriswalters.co.uk

WALTERS, David Allan. b 48. Southn Univ MA 87 Bath Univ MEd 95. **d** 09 **p** 10. OLM Wylye and Till Valley *Sarum* 09-12; NSM Lower Wylye and Till Valley 12-14; NSM Salisbury Plain from 14. *Hillside, Chapel Lane, Shrewton, Salisbury SP3 4BX* T: (01980) 620038 E: david.a.walters@hotmail.com

WALTERS, David Michael Trenham. b 46. Open Univ BA 86. St D Coll Lamp. **d** 69 **p** 70. C Killay *S & B* 69-72; CF 72-89 and 91-01; Chapl Eagle Ho Prep Sch Crowthorne 89-91; Chapl R Memorial Chpl Sandhurst 97-01; P-in-c Llanrhnewydd *S & B* 01-05; V Llanrhidian w Llanyrnewydd 05-12; rtd 12; PtO *S & B* from 13. *Westwood Cottage, 65 Pennard Road, Pennard, Swansea SA3 2AD* T: (01792) 234307

WALTERS, David Trevor. b 37. Ex Coll Ox BA 58 MA 62. St Steph Ho Ox 62. **d** 64 **p** 65. C Cardiff St Mary *Llan* 64-69; C Brecon w Battle *S & B* 69-73; Min Can Brecon Cathl 69-73; V Llanddew and Talachddu 73-78; V Cefncoed and Capel Nantddu 78-80; V Cefn Coed and Capel Nantddu w Vaynor etc 80-87; V Talgarth and Llanelieu 87-04; rtd 04. *16 Dan-y-Bryn, Glasbury, Hereford HR3 5NH* T: (01497) 842966

WALTERS, Mrs Felicity Ann. b 56. WEMTC. **d** 01 **p** 02. C Glouc St Geo w Whaddon 01-05; C Matson 05-06; P-in-c Huntley and Longhope, Churcham and Bulley 06-11; P-in-c Hadfield *Derby* 11-14; V from 14; V Charlesworth and Gamesley from 14. *St Andrew's Vicarage, 122 Hadfield Road, Hadfield, Glossop SK13 2DR* T: (01457) 852431 E: walters@revfelicity.plus.com

WALTERS, Canon Francis Raymond. b 24. Ball Coll Ox BA 49 MA 54. Wycliffe Hall Ox 51. **d** 53 **p** 54. C Boulton *Derby* 53-56; Lect Qu Coll Birm 56-64; Succ Birm Cathl 56-58; C Harborne St Pet 58-64; V Leic St Nic 64-74; Chapl Leic Univ 64-74; R Appleby 74-77; Dioc Dir of Educn 77-89; Hon Can Leic Cathl 77-91; P-in-c Swithland 77-91; rtd 91; PtO *Nor* from 91. *2 Beeston Common, Sheringham NR26 8ES* T: (01263) 824414

WALTERS, Ian Robert. b 51. ACA 74 FCA 81. **d** 85 **p** 86. OLM Ingoldsby *Linc* 85-92; NSM Grantham St Anne New Somerby and Spitalgate 92-94; NSM Ingoldsby 94-06; NSM Ropsley 94-06; NSM Old Somerby 94-06; NSM Sapperton w Braceby 94-06; P-in-c Gosberton, Gosberton Clough and Quadring from 06. *The Vicarage, 6 Wargate Way, Gosberton, Spalding PE11 4NH* T/F: (01775) 840694 M: 07831-645683 E: ian@businessdevelopmentassociation.net

WALTERS, James Arthur. b 78. Selw Coll Cam BA 00 PhD 07. Westcott Ho Cam 03. **d** 07 **p** 08. C Hampstead St Jo *Lon* 07-10; Chapl LSE from 10; NSM Bloomsbury St Geo w Woburn Square Ch Ch from 11. *London School of Economics, Houghton Street, London WC2A 2AE* T: (020) 7955 7965 E: j.walters2@lse.ac.uk

WALTERS, Ms Jennifer Betty. b 56. Birm Univ BA 77. STETS. **d** 00 **p** 01. NSM Freemantle *Win* 00-07; NSM Southampton Thornhill St Chris 07-13; NSM Southampton St Mary Extra 13-14; NSM Woolston 13-14; rtd 14; PtO *Win* from 14. *41A Waterloo Road, Southampton SO15 3BD* T: (023) 8033 2613

WALTERS, Canon John Philip Hewitt. b 50. Coll of Resurr Mirfield 72. **d** 73 **p** 74. C Llangiwg *S & B* 73-76; Min Can Brecon Cathl 76-79; C Brecon w Battle 76-79; V Merthyr Cynog and Dyffryn Honddu etc 79-83; V Llandeilo Tal-y-bont 83-15; Hon Can Brecon Cathl 12-15; PtO *St D* 14-15; rtd 15. *12 Coles Close, Swansea SA1 2GD*

WALTERS, Linda. b 56. BSc PGCE. **d** 10 **p** 11. NSM Ilfracombe, Lee, Woolacombe, Bittadon etc *Ex* from 10. *9 South Burrow Road, Ilfracombe EX34 8JE* T: (01271) 866853

WALTERS, Canon Michael William. b 39. Dur Univ BSc 61. Clifton Th Coll 61. **d** 63 **p** 64. C Aldershot H Trin *Guildf* 63-66; C Upper Armley *Ripon* 66-69; NE Area Sec CPAS 69-75; V Hyde

St Geo *Ches* 75-82; V Knutsford St Jo and Toft 82-97; P-in-c Congleton St Pet 97-98; TR Congleton 98-05; rtd 05; Hon Can Ches Cathl 94-13; Hon C Davenham 05-13. *27 Alvanley Rise, Northwich CW9 8AY* T: (01606) 333126
E: michael@alvanleyrise.co.uk

WALTERS, Nicholas Humphrey. b 45. K Coll Lon BD 67 AKC 67. **d** 68 **p** 69. C Weston *Guildf* 68-71; Chapl and Lect NE Surrey Coll of Tech Ewell 71-77; Hon C Ewell *Guildf* 71-77; Warden Moor Park Coll Farnham 77-80; Tutor Surrey Univ *Guildf* from 80; Dir of Studies Guildf Inst from 82; Public Preacher *Guildf* 84-15. *9 Valley View, Godalming GU7 1RD* T: (01483) 415106 *or* 562142 E: n.walters@surrey.ac.uk

WALTERS, Peter. b 27. Leeds Univ BSc 48 Univ of Wales (Abth) MSc 52. Ripon Coll Cuddesdon 78. **d** 79 **p** 80. C Kingswood *Bris* 79-82; R Stanton St Quintin, Hullavington, Grittleton etc 82-88; rtd 88; PtO *Glouc* 88-97. *Holly Tree House, 12 Bethany Lane, West Cross, Swansea SA3 5TL* T: (01792) 405197

WALTERS, Raymond. *See* WALTERS, Francis Raymond

WALTERS, Mrs Sheila Ann Beatrice. b 37. Bris Univ DipEd 58. EMMTC 85. **d** 89 **p** 94. NSM Ashby-de-la-Zouch St Helen w Coleorton *Leic* 89-98; PtO 99-02; NSM Packington w Normanton-le-Heath 02-05; rtd 05; PtO *Sheff* from 06. *8 Kensington Park, Sheffield S10 4NJ* T: 0114-229 5497 E: churchmatters@sabwalters.co.uk

WALTERS, William Ivan. b 49. CBDTI 04. **d** 07 **p** 08. NSM Lea Blackb 07-14; rtd 14; PtO *Blackb* from 14. *9 Thornpark Drive, Lea, Preston PR2 1RE* T: (01772) 732573
E: ivanwalters@btinternet.com

WALTHEW, Mrs Nancy Jennifer. b 39. Leeds Inst of Educn CertEd 59. NOC 92. **d** 95 **p** 96. NSM Wilmslow *Ches* 95-02; PtO from 04. *44 Upper Culver Road, St Albans AL1 4EE*

WALTNER, Moise (Mike). b 75. ERMC 13. **d** 15. C Vienna *Eur* from 15. *Address temp unknown*

WALTON, Mrs Alison Claire. b 59. Homerton Coll Cam BEd 82. Lon Bible Coll Oak Hill Th Coll BA 90 MPhil 92. **d** 92 **p** 98. C Bedford Ch Ch *St Alb* 92-94; PtO *Ely* 94-95; *S'well* 95-98; NSM Lenton Abbey 98-99; Assoc Lect St Jo Coll Nottm 97-99; C Thorley *St Alb* 00-03; V Croxley Green St Oswald 03-07; Dir Ch Study and Practice Ridley Hall Cam from 07; Public Preacher *Ely* from 07. *Ridley Hall, Ridley Hall Road, Cambridge CB3 9HG* T: (01223) 746592 F: 746581 E: aw438@cam.ac.uk *or* ali.walton@cantab.net

WALTON, Ann Beverley. b 56. Huddersfield Poly BSc 78 Sheff Poly MPhil 84 Coll of Ripon & York St Jo MA 97. NOC 00. **d** 03 **p** 04. C Ecclesfield *Sheff* 03-06; R Adwick-le-Street w Skelbrooke from 06; P-in-c Owston from 14. *The Rectory, Village Street, Adwick-le-Street, Doncaster DN6 7AD* T: (01302) 723224 E: ann.walton@sheffield.anglican.org

WALTON, Brian. b 53. Sarum & Wells Th Coll 83. **d** 85 **p** 86. C Silksworth *Dur* 85-86; C Bishopwearmouth St Mich w St Hilda 86-88; Chapl RN 88-92; V Sugley *Newc* 92-95; Chapl Lemington Hosp 92-95; CF 95-13; Chapl Morden Coll Blackheath from 13; PtO *Roch* from 14. *Morden College, 19 St German's Place, London SE3 0PW* T: (020) 8463 8330

WALTON, Mrs Camilla Iris. b 56. STETS 97. **d** 00 **p** 01. C Lyndhurst and Emery Down and Minstead *Win* 00-04; V Boldre w S Baddesley 04-08; TV Beaconsfield *Ox* from 08; AD Amersham from 12. *The Parsonage, St Michael's Green, Beaconsfield HP9 2BN* T: (01494) 673464 F: 676694
E: camillawalton@googlemail.com

WALTON, Mrs Catherine. b 66. Lindisfarne Regional Tr Partnership. **d** 15. NSM Norton St Mary *Dur* from 15; NSM Norton St Mich from 15. *23 Wadham Grove, Darlington DL1 2GJ* T: (01325) 260274 M: 07581-043061
E: cathanshane@ntlworld.com

WALTON, David William. b 52. Open Univ BA 84 Leeds Univ BA 06 Alsager Coll of Educn CertEd 74. NOC 03. **d** 06 **p** 07. C Prenton *Ches* 06-08; V Baddiley and Wrenbury w Burleydam 08-12; rtd 12. *51 Haddon Close, Macclesfield SK11 7YG* E: rev.david.walton@btinternet.com

WALTON, Frank. b 34. **d** 04 **p** 05. OLM Woodhorn w Newbiggin *Newc* from 04. *6 New Queen Street, Newbiggin-by-the-Sea NE64 6AZ* T: (01670) 817568 E: notlaw@btopenworld.com

WALTON, The Ven Geoffrey Elmer. b 34. Dur Univ BA 59. Qu Coll Birm. **d** 61 **p** 62. C Warsop *S'well* 61-65; Dioc Youth Chapl 65-69; V Norwell 65-69; Recruitment Sec ACCM 69-75; V Weymouth H Trin *Sarum* 75-82; RD Weymouth 79-82; Can and Preb Sarum Cathl 81-00; Adn Dorset 82-00; P-in-c Witchampton and Hinton Parva, Long Crichel etc 82-93; P-in-c Vale of Allen 93-96; V Witchampton, Stanbridge and Long Crichel etc 96-00; rtd 00; PtO *Sarum* from 01. *Priory Cottage, 6 Hibberds Field, Cranborne, Wimborne BH21 5QL* T: (01725) 517167
E: geoffrey@waltoncranborne.freeserve.co.uk

WALTON, John Victor. b 45. Lon Univ BSc 67. Linc Th Coll 79. **d** 81 **p** 82. C Stevenage St Mary Shephall *St Alb* 81-85; TV

Bourne Valley *Sarum* 85-95; P-in-c Puddletown and Tolpuddle 95-02; R Puddletown, Tolpuddle and Milborne w Dewlish 02-04; rtd 04. *Serenity, Wootton Grove, Sherborne DT9 4DL* T: (01935) 814435 E: life@clara.co.uk

WALTON, Canon Kevin Anthony. b 64. St Chad's Coll Dur BA 87 Dur Univ PhD 99. Trin Coll Bris BA 91. **d** 92 **p** 93. C Stranton *Dur* 92-95; C Hartlepool H Trin 95-96; V Sunderland St Mary and St Pet 96-08; AD Wearmouth 05-08; Can and Chan St Alb *St Alb* from 08. *2 Sumpter Yard, St Albans AL1 1BY* T: (01727) 890242
E: canon@stalbanscathedral.org

WALTON, Luke. b 64. Leeds Univ LLB 87. Cranmer Hall Dur BA 94. **d** 97 **p** 98. C Didsbury St Jas and Em *Man* 97-02; C Clifton Ch Ch w Em *Bris* 02-06; Arts Development Officer Bible Soc from 06. *Bible Society, Stonehill Green, Westlea, Swindon SN5 7DG* T: (01793) 418100 M: 07799-414199 F: 418118

WALTON, Mrs Marjorie Sandra. b 46. WMMTC 97. **d** 00 **p** 01. NSM The Whitacres and Shustoke *Birm* 00-04; NSM Water Orton 04-06; NSM Lea Hall 06-11; rtd 11; PtO *Birm* from 11. *51 Station Road, Nether Whitacre, Coleshill, Birmingham B46 2JB* T: (01675) 464641

WALTON, Michael Roy. b 74. St Cuth Soc Dur BA 95. Oak Hill Th Coll BA 09. **d** 09 **p** 10. C W Kilburn St Luke w St Simon and St Jude *Lon* 09-12; R Chadwell *Chelmsf* from 12. *The Rectory, 10 Rigby Gardens, Grays RM16 4JJ* T: (01375) 842176 M: 07949-637377 E: mikewalton.online@gmail.com

WALTON, Reginald Arthur. b 40. St Jo Coll Nottm 80. **d** 81 **p** 82. C Woodthorpe *S'well* 81-84; P-in-c Nottingham St Andr 84-85; V 85-91; R Moreton *Ches* 91-01; P-in-c Whatton w Aslockton, Hawksworth, Scarrington etc *S'well* 01-05; V 05-07; rtd 07. *19 The Maltsters, Newark NG24 4RU* T: (01636) 659869 E: regwalton40@gmail.com

WALTON, Richard James. b 55. UMIST BSc 77 Sheff Univ MEd 84 Leeds Univ PhD 98 MA 10 CPhys MInstP. NOC 07. **d** 09 **p** 10. NSM Warmsworth *Sheff* 09-11; P-in-c Burghwallis and Campsall from 11; Bp's Adv for SSM from 14. *The Rectory, Village Street, Adwick-le-Street, Doncaster DN6 7AD* T: (01302) 723224 M: 07931-526333 E: r.j.walton@shu.ac.uk

WALTON, Stephen James. b 71. Mert Coll Ox BA 92 MA 97. Oak Hill Th Coll BA 01. **d** 02 **p** 03. C Thurnby w Stoughton *Leic* 02-07; R Marbury w Tushingham and Whitewell *Ches* 07-15; Chapl Düsseldorf *Eur* from 15. *Mulvany House, Rotterdamer Strasse 135, 40474 Düsseldorf, Germany* E: walton_stephen@hotmail.com

WALTON, Prof Stephen John. b 55. Birm Univ BSc 76 Fitzw Coll Cam BA 79 MA 82 Sheff Univ PhD 97. Ridley Hall Cam 77. **d** 83 **p** 84. C Bebington *Ches* 83-86; Voc and Min Adv CPAS 86-92; LtO *St Alb* 86-94; Public Preacher 00-04; Bp's Dom Chapl 94-95; Lect St Jo Coll Nottm 95-99; Lect Lon Sch of Th 99-03; Sen Lect 03-11; Prof NT 11-13; Hon Research Fell Tyndale Ho and Lect Div Cam Univ from 13; Prof NT and Research Fell St Mary's Univ Twickenham *Lon* from 13; Public Preacher *Ely* from 13. *8 Barrons Way, Comberton, Cambridge CB23 7EQ* T: (01223) 264198 E: steve.walton@cantab.net *or* steve.walton@smuc.ac.uk

WAMBUNYA, Timothy Livingstone (Amboko). b 66. Simon of Cyrene Th Inst 93 Oak Hill Th Coll BA 94. **d** 97 **p** 98. C Southall Green St Jo *Lon* 97-00; TV Tollington 00-07; Prin Carlile Coll Nairobi from 07. *Carlile College, Jogoo Road, PO Box 72584, Nairobi 00200, Kenya* T: (00254) (20) 550490 F: 550749 E: t.wamb@virgin.net *or* tim.wambunya@carlilecollege.org

WANDREY, Bryce. b 77. St Olaf Coll Minnesota BA 99. Concordia Th Sem Indiana MDiv 03 St Steph Ho Ox 07. **d** 08 **p** 09. C Highgate St Mich *Lon* from 08; C Highgate All SS 09-14; P-in-c from 14. *All Saints' Vicarage, 1B Church Road, London N6 4QH* E: wandreyb@yahoo.com

WANDSWORTH, Archdeacon of. *See* KIDDLE, Canon John

WANJIE, Lukas Macharia. b 50. Fitzw Coll Cam BA 79 MA 83 Birkbeck Coll Lon MSc 98. St Paul's Coll Limuru 72 Ridley Hall Cam 76. **d** 75 **p** 76. C Uthiru St Pet Kenya 75-76; C Mill End and Heronsgate w W Hyde *St Alb* 79; V Westlands St Mark Nairobi Kenya 80-84; Prin Trin Bible Coll Nairobi 85-91; C St Alb St Steph *St Alb* 91-94; PtO 94-95; Race Relations Adv Croydon *S'wark* 95-01; V Bermondsey St Kath w St Bart 01-12; rtd 13. *59 Manor Road, London Colney, St Albans AL2 1PP*

WANLISS, Hector. b 62. St Paul's Coll Grahamstown 85. **d** 88 **p** 90. S Africa 88-97; P-in-c Aylesham w Adisham *Cant* 97-99; CF 99-11. *Address temp unknown*

WANN, Canon Denis Francis. b 27. TCD BA 55 MA 77 Div Test 56. **d** 56 **p** 57. C Belfast St Donard *D & D* 56-58; BCMS Tanzania 58-72; Hon Can Moro from 72; C Lurgan Ch the Redeemer *D & D* 72-73; R Port Kembla Australia 73-78; R Albion Park 78-84; Adn Wollongong and Camden 82-84; R Turramurra 84-91; I Bailieborough w Knockbride, Shercock and Mullagh *K, E & A* 91-95; rtd 95; Hon C Wollongong Australia 96-01. *304 Woodlands, St Luke's Village, 4 Lindsay Evans Place, Dapto NSW 2530, Australia* T: (0061) (2) 4262 8545 E: dwann@telstra.easymail.com.au

WANSTALL, Noelle Margaret. *See* HALL, Noelle Margaret

WANT, Mrs Angela Patricia. b 47. Kent Univ BA 68. EAMTC 02. **d** 05 **p** 06. NSM Newport and Widdington *Chelmsf* 05-10; NSM Saffron Walden and Villages from 10. *3 Orchard Close, Newport, Saffron Walden CB11 3QT* T: (01799) 540051 E: angelawant@f2s.com

WANYOIKE, Julius Njuguna. b 70. Catholic Univ of E Africa BA 99. Bp Kariuki Bible Coll 91. **d** 93 **p** 93. Kenya 93-03; Provost Thika 02-03; PtO *Birm* 04-05; NSM Erdington from 05. *1 Abbotts Road, Birmingham B24 8HE* T: 0121-351 1245 E: wanyoikejrev@yahoo.com

WARBRICK, Canon Quentin David. b 66. Jes Coll Ox BA 88. Cranmer Hall Dur 89. **d** 92 **p** 93. C Birm St Martin w Bordesley St Andr 92-96; C Handsworth St Jas 96-00; V Packwood w Hockley Heath 00-10; AD Shirley 05-10; P-in-c Kings Heath 10-14; V from 14; Hon Can Birm Cathl from 14. *The Vicarage, 4 Vicarage Road, Kings Heath, Birmingham B14 7RA* T: 0121-444 0260 E: davidwarbrick@btinternet.com

WARBURTON, Andrew James. b 44. Oak Hill Th Coll 64. **d** 69 **p** 70. C New Milverton *Cov* 69-72; C Fulham St Matt *Lon* 72-76; C Chesham St Mary *Ox* 76-80; TV Gt Chesham 80-94; Chapl Paris St Mich *Eur* 94-97; Asst Chapl Amsterdam w Heiloo 97-99; rtd 99; PtO *Carl* from 11. *Burnbrae, Riccarton, Newcastleton TD9 0SN* T: (01387) 376293 M: 07962-622740 E: borderwarburton@yahoo.co.uk

WARD, Alan William. b 56. Trin Coll Bris 80. **d** 81 **p** 82. C New Ferry *Ches* 81-86; Dioc Youth Officer 86-91; C Charlesworth and Dinting Vale *Derby* 91-96; V Mickleover All SS 96-11; C Mickleover St Jo 06-11; R Wallasey St Hilary *Ches* from 11. *St Hilary's Rectory, Church Hill, Wallasey CH45 3NH* T: 0151-638 4771 E: alancaroline241@btinternet.com

WARD, Alfred John. b 37. Coll of Resurr Mirfield 93. **d** 93 **p** 94. C Hendon St Mary *Lon* 93-00; Chapl Convent of St Mary at the Cross Edgware 00-04; rtd 04; PtO *Cant* from 05. *60 Valley Road, Dover CT17 0QW* T: (01304) 824767

WARD, Alisoun Mary. *See* FRANCIS, Alisoun Mary

WARD (*née* WEIGHTMAN), Mrs Andrea Frances. b 66. Sheff Univ BA 87. Ridley Hall Cam 00. **d** 03 **p** 04. C Handforth *Ches* 03-07; V Blendon *Roch* from 07. *The Vicarage, 38 Bladindon Drive, Bexley DA5 3BS* T: (020) 8301 5387 M: 07983-851105 E: andreaward72@gmail.com

WARD, Andrew John. b 65. Cliff Th Coll 85 Trin Coll Bris BA 99. **d** 99 **p** 00. C Belper *Derby* 99-03; TV Walbrook Epiphany 03-11; TR from 11; RD Derby S 12-15. *St Augustine's Rectory, 155 Almond Street, Derby DE23 6LY* T: (01332) 766603 *or* 760846 E: andyward.parish@tiscali.co.uk

WARD, Canon Anthony Peter. b 46. Bris Univ BSc 67 Ox Univ DipEd 68. St Jo Coll Nottm. **d** 82 **p** 83. C Hellesdon *Nor* 82-85; P-in-c Nor St Aug w St Mary 85-91; P-in-c Norwich-over-the-Water Colegate St Geo 85-90; Norfolk Churches' Radio Officer 85-95; TV Norwich Over-the-Water 91-95; V Gorleston St Andr 95-11; RD Gt Yarmouth 98-02; Hon Can Nor Cathl 03-11; rtd 11. *20 The Butts, Belper DE56 1HX* T: (01773) 821639 E: revtw@btinternet.com

WARD, Arthur John. b 32. Lon Univ BD 57. St Aid Birkenhead 57. **d** 57 **p** 58. C Ecclesfield *Sheff* 57-60; C Fulwood 60-63; Tutor St Aid Birkenhead 63-66; R Denton St Lawr *Man* 66-74; CMS 74-82; TV Wolverhampton *Lich* 82-90; V Edgbaston SS Mary and Ambrose *Birm* 90-96; rtd 96; PtO *Heref* from 97. *Bramble Cottage, 6 Lower Forge, Eardington, Bridgnorth WV16 5LQ* T: (01746) 764758

WARD, Miss Beverley Jayne. b 61. Bolton Inst of Educn CertEd 97. St Steph Ho Ox 00. **d** 02 **p** 07. C Standish *Blackb* 02-07; C Thornton-le-Fylde 07-09; P-in-c Eccleston 09-12; V Cleveleys from 12. *The Vicarage, Rough Lea Road, Thornton-Cleveleys FY5 1DP* T: (01253) 852153 M: 07811-907274 E: rev.jayneward@gmail.com

WARD, Brett Ernest. b 62. Univ of Wales MTh 06. ACT 86. **d** 89 **p** 89. C E Maitland Australia 89; Asst P 89-91; Asst P Singleton 91-92; P-in-c Weston 92-97; C Forton *Portsm* 97-99; P-in-c 99-05; V 05-07; P-in-c Eltham H Trin *S'wark* 07-10; V from 10; AD Eltham and Mottingham from 13. *Holy Trinity Vicarage, 59 Southend Crescent, London SE9 2SD* T: (020) 8850 1246 *or* 8859 6274 E: fr.brett@ht-e.org.uk

WARD, Canon Calvin. b 34. Univ of Wales BA 57 DipEd 60 Fitzw Ho Cam BA 63 MA 67. Westcott Ho Cam 61. **d** 64 **p** 65. C Handsworth St Mich *Birm* 64-66; C Shaw Hill 66-69; V Windhill *Bradf* 69-76; V Esholt 76-81; V Oakworth 81-91; V Allerton 91-99; Hon Can Bradf Cathl 94-99; rtd 99; PtO *Leeds* from 99. *47 Wheatlands Drive, Bradford BD9 5JN* E: candmward@blueyonder.co.uk

WARD, Christopher John William. b 36. Bps' Coll Cheshunt 66 Qu Coll Birm 68. **d** 69 **p** 70. C Wednesbury St Bart *Lich* 69-73; CF 73-93; rtd 93; PtO *Sarum* from 93. *6 Meadow View, Blandford Forum DT11 7JB* T: (01258) 455140

WARD, Daran. b 65. Brunel Univ BSc 88. St Jo Coll Nottm 07. **d** 09 **p** 10. C Hartley Wintney, Elvetham, Winchfield etc *Win* 09-13; V Bramley *Sheff* from 13; P-in-c Thrybergh from 13. *The Vicarage, 88 Main Street, Bramley, Rotherham S66 2SQ* T: (01709) 290724 E: daran.ward@gmail.com

WARD, David. b 40. St Jo Coll Nottm 83. **d** 85 **p** 86. C Aspley *S'well* 85-89; V 89-04; rtd 04; PtO *S'well* from 06. *150 Robins Wood Road, Nottingham NG8 3LD* T: 0115-929 3231 M: 07971-092089

WARD, David Graham. b 51. CBDTI 03. **d** 06 **p** 07. OLM Higher Walton *Blackb* 06-07; NSM 07-10; P-in-c Brindle 10-11; R from 11. *Coppice Farm, Goose Foot Lane, Samlesbury, Preston PR5 0RQ* T: (01254) 852995 F: 851101 E: david@dbll.co.uk

WARD, Canon David Robert. b 51. Oak Hill Th Coll 74. **d** 77 **p** 78. C Kirkheaton *Wakef* 77-81; V Earl's Heaton 81-88; V Bradley *Leeds* from 88; P-in-c Fixby and Cowcliffe from 09; Hon Can Wakef Cathl from 02. *The Vicarage, 3 St Thomas Gardens, Huddersfield HD2 1SL* T: (01484) 427838 E: davidwardvic@tiscali.co.uk

WARD, Edward. *See* WARD, William Edward

WARD, Mrs Elisabeth. b 63. Trevelyan Coll Dur BA 85 Bath Spa Univ PGCE 99. Linc Sch of Th and Min 11. **d** 14 **p** 15. C Stamford St Geo w St Paul *Linc* from 14. *17 Turnpole Close, Stamford PE9 1DT* T: (01780) 480745 M: 07768-814698 E: liswardmail@googlemail.com

WARD, Elizabeth Joyce. *See* HOLMES, Elizabeth Joyce

WARD, The Very Revd Frances Elizabeth Fearn. b 59. St Andr Univ MTheol 83 Man Univ PhD 00 Bradf Univ MA 06 RGN 87. Westcott Ho Cam 87. **d** 89 **p** 94. Par Dn Westhoughton *Man* 89-93; Tutor Practical Th N Coll Man 93-98; Hon C Bury St Pet *Man* 93-98; C Unsworth 98-99; V Bury St Pet 99-05; C Leverhulme 05-06; Bp's Adv on Women in Min 02-04; Hon Can Man Cathl 04-06; Can Res Bradf Cathl 06-10; Dean St E from 10. *The Deanery, The Great Churchyard, Bury St Edmunds IP33 1RS* T: (01284) 748720 F: 768655 M: 07791-165774 E: fefward@gmail.com *or* dean@stedscathedral.org

WARD, Frank Wyatt. b 30. Oak Hill NSM Course 84. **d** 92 **p** 94. NSM Paddington St Pet *Lon* 92-09; NSM Paddington St Mary Magd and St Pet from 09. *82 Hill Rise, Greenford UB6 8PE* T: (020) 8575 5515

WARD, Garry William. b 67. Anglia Ruskin Univ MA 11 RGN 90 RM 92. Qu Coll Birm 01. **d** 03 **p** 04. C Wednesfield *Lich* 03-06; TV Wordsley *Worc* 06-11; V Claverley w Tuckhill *Heref* from 11. *The Vicarage, Lodge Park, Claverley, Wolverhampton WV5 7DP* T: (01746) 710304 E: garry@penfold.email

WARD, Geoffrey Edward. b 30. Linc Th Coll 62. **d** 64 **p** 65. C Oundle *Pet* 64-68; C Weston Favell 68-70; TV 70-72; R Cottingham w E Carlton 72-95; rtd 95; PtO *Pet* 95-04. *8 Chapman Close, Towcester NN12 7AQ* T: (01327) 354070

WARD, Prof Graham John. b 55. Fitzw Coll Cam BA 80 Selw Coll Cam MA 83. Westcott Ho Cam 87. **d** 90 **p** 91. C Bris St Mary Redcliffe w Temple etc 90-92; Chapl Ex Coll Ox 92-94; Dean Peterho Cam 95-99; Prof Contextual Th Man Univ 99-12; Regius Prof Div Ox Univ from 12; Can Res Ch Ch Ox from 12. *Christ Church, Oxford OX1 1DP* T: (01865) 276246 E: graham.ward@chch.ox.ac.uk

WARD, Helen Frances. b 48. EAMTC 02. **d** 04 **p** 05. NSM Gorleston St Andr *Nor* 04-11; rtd 11. *20 The Butts, Belper DE56 1HX* T: (01773) 821639 E: revhw@btinternet.com

WARD, Ian Stanley. b 62. K Coll Lon BD 83. Cranmer Hall Dur 84. **d** 86 **p** 87. C Moreton *Ches* 86-89; Chapl RAF from 89. *Chaplaincy Services (RAF), HQ Air Command, RAF High Wycombe HP14 4UE* T: (01494) 496800 F: 496343

WARD, Mrs Janice Ann. b 65. Univ of Wales (Lamp) BA 86. ERMC 05. **d** 08 **p** 09. C Haverhill w Withersfield *St E* 08-12; P-in-c Marown, Foxdale and Baldwin *S & M* 12-13; V from 13. *Marown Vicarage, Main Road, Crosby, Isle of Man IM4 4BH* T: (01624) 851378 M: 07624-406084 E: revjaniceward@manx.net

WARD, Jason David. b 71. Glas Univ BSc 93 PhD 98. Oak Hill Th Coll BA 06. **d** 06 **p** 07. C Cheadle Hulme St Andr *Ches* 06-09; C Harold Wood *Chelmsf* 09-13; V Chaddesden St Mary *Derby* from 13. *The Vicarage, 133 Chaddesden Lane, Chaddesden, Derby DE21 6LL* T: (01332) 280924 M: 07866-361054 E: jasethebass@gmail.com

WARD, Jayne. *See* WARD, Beverley Jayne

WARD, John. *See* WARD, Arthur John

WARD, John Frederick. b 55. St Mich Coll Llan 81. **d** 84 **p** 85. C Pembroke Dock *St D* 84-86; PV Llan Cathl 86-89; R St Brides Minor w Bettws 89-97; V Shard End *Birm* 97-04; V Twigworth, Down Hatherley, Norton, The Leigh etc *Glouc*

04-10; C Wotton-under-Edge w Ozleworth, N Nibley etc 10-12; C Charfield and Kingswood 10-11; C Charfield and Kingswood w Wickwar etc 11-12; V Quedgeley from 12. *The New Rectory, School Lane, Quedgeley, Gloucester GL2 4PN* T: (01452) 720411 M: 07967-636094
E: j.ward623@btinternet.com

WARD, Prof John Stephen Keith. b 38. Univ of Wales (Cardiff) BA 62 Linacre Coll Ox BLitt 68 DD 98 Trin Hall Cam MA 72 DD 99 FBA 01. Westcott Ho Cam 72. **d** 72 **p** 73. Lect Philosophy of Relig Lon Univ 71-75; Hon C Hampstead St Jo 72-75; Dean Trin Hall Cam 75-82; Prof Moral and Soc Th K Coll Lon 82-85; Prof Hist and Philosophy of Relig 85-91; Regius Prof Div Ox Univ 91-03; Can Res Ch Ch Ox 91-03; rtd 03. *Christ Church, Oxford OX1 1DP* T: (01865) 865513
E: keith.ward@chch.ox.ac.uk

WARD, Canon John Stewart. b 43. St Jo Coll Dur BA 66. Ripon Coll Cuddesdon 77. **d** 79 **p** 80. C High Harrogate Ch Ch *Ripon* 79-82; V Ireland Wood 82-86; Chapl Wells Cathl Sch 86-88; V Menston w Woodhead *Bradf* 88-95; R Bolton Abbey 95-06; RD Skipton 98-00; Hon Can Bradf Cathl 05-06; rtd 06. *33 Lamberton Shiels, Lamberton, Berwick-upon-Tweed TD15 1XB*

WARD, Jonathan James Hanslip. b 75. Southn Univ LLB 98 Anglia Ruskin Univ BA 07 Solicitor 02. Ridley Hall Cam 05. **d** 07 **p** 08. C Cheltenham St Mark *Glouc* 07-11; V W Wickham St Jo *S'wark* from 11. *The Rectory, 30 Coney Hill Road, West Wickham BR4 9BX* M: 07530-546474
E: jjhward@btinternet.com

WARD, Keith. *See* WARD, John Stephen Keith

WARD, Keith Raymond. b 37. Dur Univ BSc 60. Chich Th Coll 63. **d** 65 **p** 66. C Wallsend St Luke *Newc* 65-68; C Wooler 68-74; V Dinnington 74-81; V Bedlington 81-93; V Stannington 93-99; rtd 99; PtO *Newc* from 00. *2 Ethel's Close, Gloster Meadows, Amble, Morpeth NE65 0GD* T: (01665) 714357

WARD, Kevin. b 47. Edin Univ MA 69 Trin Coll Cam PhD 76. **d** 78 **p** 79. CMS 75-92; Uganda 76-90; Qu Coll Birm 91; PtO *Birm* 91; C Halifax *Wakef* 91-92; P-in-c Charlestown 92-95; NSM Headingley *Leeds* from 95; Lect Leeds Univ from 95. *8 North Grange Mews, Leeds LS6 2EW* T: 0113-278 7801
E: trskw@leeds.ac.uk

WARD, Lionel Owen. b 37. Univ of Wales (Cardiff) BA 58 Univ of Wales (Swansea) DipEd 59 MA 65 Lon Univ PhD 70. St Mich Coll Llan 83. **d** 85 **p** 86. NSM Swansea St Mary w H Trin *S & B* 85-89; P-in-c Swansea St Matt w Greenhill 89-00; TV Cen Swansea 00-01; Dioc Dir of Educn 97-01; RD Swansea 98-01; rtd 02; PtO *S'wark* from 10. *17 Gresham Court, 11 Pampisford Road, Purley CR8 2UU*
E: lionelward@hotmail.co.uk

WARD, Mrs Marjorie. b 38. Univ of Wales (Abth) BA 59 DipEd 60. NOC 83. **dss** 86 **d** 87 **p** 94. Keighley St Andr *Bradf* 86-88; Hon Par Dn 87-88; Hon Par Dn Oakworth 88-90; C Allerton 91-99; rtd 99; PtO *Leeds* from 99. *47 Wheatlands Drive, Bradford BD9 5JN* E: candmward@blueyonder.co.uk

WARD, Mark. b 62. Imp Coll Lon BScEng 84. Wycliffe Hall Ox BTh 93. **d** 93 **p** 94. C Parkham, Alwington, Buckland Brewer etc *Ex* 93-96; C S Molton w Nymet St George, High Bray etc 96-97; TV 97-05; TV Ottery St Mary, Alfington, W Hill, Tipton etc from 05. *The Vicarage, Newton Poppleford, Sidmouth EX10 0HB* T: (01395) 568390
E: revmarkward@btinternet.com

WARD, Matthew Alan James. b 69. Nottm Poly BSc 91. Ridley Hall Cam 94. **d** 97 **p** 98. C Birchwood *Linc* 97-00; Chapl Cov Univ 00-05; Chapl Leeds Univ from 05. *96 Becketts Park Drive, Leeds LS6 3PL* T: 0113-275 5692

WARD, Michael Henry. b 42. St Martin's Coll Lanc BA 02. **d** 03 **p** 04. NSM S Shore H Trin *Blackb* 03-06; NSM S Shore St Pet 06-10; PtO from 10. *509A Lytham Road, Blackpool FY4 1TE* T: (01253) 404204 E: mh.ward@btinternet.com

WARD, Michael Reginald. b 31. BNC Ox BA 54 MA 58. Tyndale Hall Bris 54. **d** 56 **p** 57. C Ealing St Mary *Lon* 56-59; C Morden *S'wark* 59-61; Area Sec (Midl and E Anglia) CCCS 61-66; V Chelsea St Jo *Lon* 66-73; P-in-c Chelsea St Andr 72-73; V Chelsea St Jo w St Andr 73-76; P-in-c Hawkesbury *Glouc* 76-80; P-in-c Alderley w Hillesley 79-80; P-in-c Bibury w Winson and Barnsley 80-85; V Barkby and Queniborough *Leic* 85-90; R Gunthorpe w Bale w Field Dalling, Saxlingham etc *Nor* 90-98; rtd 98; PtO *Heref* 98-08; *Glouc* 00-08. *4 Framland Drive, Melton Mowbray LE13 1HY* T: (01664) 500039

WARD (*née* MASSEY), Michelle Elaine (Shellie). Plymouth Univ BA 00. Trin Coll Bris BA 04. **d** 04 **p** 05. C Barrowby and Gt Gonerby *Linc* 04-09; P-in-c Saxonwell 09-12; P-in-c Claypole 11-12; P-in-c Broadway w Wickhamford *Worc* from 12. *The Vicarage, Church Street, Broadway WR12 7AE* M: 07876-645786 E: revdmichellem@aol.com

WARD, Nathan James. b 80. St Cuth Soc Dur BA 01 Leic Univ MSc 12. SEITE 11. **d** 14. NSM S Chatham H Trin *Roch* from 14. *19 Gladwyn Close, Gillingham ME8 9TQ* T: (01634) 230834 M: 07917-473586 E: wardnathan@me.com

WARD, Nigel Andrew. b 50. Peterho Cam BA 72 MA 76. Oak Hill NSM Course 89. **d** 92 **p** 93. NSM Frogmore *St Alb* from 92. *15 Park Street, St Albans AL2 2PE* T: (01727) 872667

WARD, Peter Macdonald. b 41. **d** 09 **p** 10. NSM Harrow Weald All SS *Lon* from 09. *129 Sylvia Avenue, Pinner HA5 4QL* T: (020) 8428 7887 M: 07733-001777
E: wardhatchend@hotmail.com

WARD, Peter Nicholas. b 59. Ban Ord Course 03. **d** 08 **p** 09. NSM Llanwnnog and Caersws w Carno *Ban* 08-11; NSM Bro Ddyfi Uchaf 11-14; NSM Bro Cyfeiliog a Mawddwy from 14. *Coed Cae, Clatter, Caersws SY17 5NW* T: (01686) 688034
E: peteandsand@btopenworld.com

WARD, Robert. b 60. Em Coll Cam BA 81 MA 85. Chich Th Coll. **d** 86 **p** 87. C Horfield H Trin *Bris* 86-90; C Stantonbury and Willen *Ox* 90; TV 90-96; V Knowle St Martin *Bris* 96-07; R Cradley w Mathon and Storridge *Heref* from 07; RD Ledbury from 13. *The Rectory, Cradley, Malvern WR13 5LQ* T: (01886) 880438 E: frrob@wardmail.fslife.co.uk

WARD, Robert Arthur Philip. b 53. Lon Univ BD 82 Open Univ BA 88. Qu Coll Birm 77. **d** 79 **p** 80. C Balsall Heath St Paul *Birm* 79-82; Chapl RAF 82-98; TR Blakenall Heath *Lich* 98-01; PtO 05-07; V Ravensthorpe and Thornhill Lees w Savile Town *Wakef* 07-13; P-in-c St Marychurch *Ex* from 13. *The Vicarage, Hampton Avenue, Torquay TQ1 3LA* T: (01803) 269258
E: father.robert@hotmail.co.uk

WARD, Robert Charles Irwin. b 48. Leic Univ LLB 70 Madras Bible Sem DD 01 Called to the Bar (Inner Temple) 72. Cranmer Hall Dur 78. **d** 80 **p** 81. C Byker St Mich w St Lawr *Newc* 80-85; PtO 86-07; NSM Newc St Andr and St Luke from 07; Dir Clarence Trust and NE Area Revival Min from 86; Asst Chapl HM Pris Frankland 91-95; rtd 13. *1 Hawthorn Villas, The Green, Wallsend NE28 7NT* T/F: 0191-234 3969 M: 07768-528181 E: rwarduk@mac.com

WARD, Canon Robin. b 66. Magd Coll Ox BA 87 MA 91 K Coll Lon PhD 03. St Steph Ho Ox 88. **d** 91 **p** 92. C Romford St Andr *Chelmsf* 91-94; C Willesden Green St Andr and St Fran *Lon* 94-96; V Sevenoaks St Jo *Roch* 96-06; Chapl Invicta Community Care NHS Trust 97-06; Hon Can Roch Cathl 04-06; Prin St Steph Ho Ox from 06. *St Stephen's House, 16 Marston Street, Oxford OX4 1JX* T: (01865) 613500
E: robin.ward@ssho.ox.ac.uk

WARD, Mrs Rosemary Clare. b 57. Westf Coll Lon BA 79 Liv Univ MA 80 MPhil 82. Trin Coll Bris BA 94. **d** 94 **p** 95. C Bris St Andr Hartcliffe 94-98; C Downend 98-02; P-in-c Broad Blunsdon 02-05; C Highworth w Sevenhampton and Inglesham etc 02-05; Dioc Lay Tr Adv 02-05; Leadership Development Adv CPAS 05-11; R Sawtry and Glatton *Ely* from 12. *The Rectory, Church Causeway, Sawtry, Huntingdon PE28 5TD* T: (01487) 830215 E: wardrosie@btinternet.com

WARD, Mrs Sandra Elizabeth. b 53. Lady Spencer Chu Coll of Educn TCert 75 Anglia Ruskin Univ MA 07. LCTP 08. **d** 13 **p** 14. NSM Orton and Tebay w Ravenstonedale etc *Carl* from 13; NSM Shap w Swindale and Bampton w Mardale from 13. *Two Bridges, 1 Frankland Park, Orton, Penrith CA10 3RP* T: (01539) 624125 M: 07946-633334

WARD, Mrs Sheena Mary. b 55. Newc Univ BA 76 PGCE 77. **d** 00 **p** 01. OLM Cramlington *Newc* from 00. *17 Yarmouth Drive, Cramlington NE23 1TL* T: (01670) 732211
E: sheena.ward@dsl.pipex.com

WARD, Simon William James. b 71. Dur Univ BA 94 Westmr Coll Ox PGCE 96. Ripon Coll Cuddesdon 98. **d** 00 **p** 01. C Aldershot St Mich *Guildf* 00-03; TV Sole Bay *St E* 03-09; Bp's Chapl *Nor* 09-14; P-in-c Earlham from 14. *The Vicarage, Bluebell Road, Norwich NR4 7LP* T: (01603) 501713
E: revdsimon@msn.com

WARD, Stanley. b 34. NEOC. **d** 84 **p** 85. NSM Jarrow *Dur* 84-90; P-in-c Thornley 90-99; rtd 99; PtO *Dur* from 00. *4 Church Walk, Thornley, Durham DH6 3EN* T/F: (01429) 821766

WARD, Stephen Philip. b 49. Sheff Univ BA 72. St Steph Ho Ox 77. **d** 79 **p** 80. C Narborough *Leic* 79-80; C Brentwood St Thos *Chelmsf* 81-82; PtO *Leic* 03-05; NSM Leic St Mary from 05. *56 Moor Lane, Loughborough LE11 1BA* T: (01509) 216945 E: casula@tiscali.co.uk

WARD, Mrs Susan Elizabeth. b 50. NOC 92. **d** 95 **p** 96. NSM Heyside *Man* 95-09; NSM Newhey from 09; NSM Belfield from 09; NSM Milnrow from 09. *45 Fold Green, Chadderton, Oldham OL9 9DX* T: 0161-620 2839

WARD, Timothy James. b 67. CCC Ox BA 90 MA 95 Edin Univ PhD 99. Oak Hill Th Coll BA 95. **d** 99 **p** 00. C Crowborough *Chich* 99-04; TV Hinckley H Trin *Leic* 04-10; R 10-13; Assoc Dir Cornhill Tr Course from 13; PtO *Roch* from 14. *7 Hayes Hill Road, Bromley BR2 7HH* T: (020) 8462 4870

WARD, Timothy John Conisbee. b 62. New Coll Ox BA 85 MA 02 PGCE 86. Wycliffe Hall Ox BA 91. **d** 92 **p** 93. C Dorking St Paul *Guildf* 92-96; C Herne Hill *S'wark* 96-02; V Walberton w Binsted *Chich* from 02. *St Mary's Vicarage, The Street, Walberton, Arundel BN18 0PQ* T: (01243) 551488 E: tjcward@uwclub.net

WARD, Timothy William. b 49. Open Univ BA 74 Birm Univ BPhil(Ed) 93. St Deiniol's Hawarden 78. **d** 79 **p** 80. NSM Handsworth St Mary Birm 79-95; PtO 95-05; NSM Gt Barr Lich from 95. *3 Dale Close, Birmingham B43 6AS* T: 0121-358 1880 *or* 358 2807 E: curate.greatbarr@btinternet.com

WARD, Preb William Edward. b 48. TD 04. FSAScot 71. AKC 71. **d** 72 **p** 73. C Heref St Martin 72-77; C Blakenall Heath Lich 77-78; TV 78-82; V Astley, Clive, Grinshill and Hadnall 82-91; R Edgmond w Kynnersley and Preston Wealdmoors from 91; P-in-c Tibberton w Bolas Magna and Waters Upton from 02; Chapl Harper Adams Univ Coll from 96; Preb Lich Cathl from 09; CF (TA) 87-05; CF (ACF) 05-10. *The Rectory, 37 High Street, Edgmond, Newport TF10 8JW* T: (01952) 820217 E: e.ward17@btinternet.com

WARD, William Francis. b 35. Ely Th Coll 61 Coll of Resurr Mirfield 64. **d** 64 **p** 65. C Byker St Ant Newc 64-67; C Glas St Marg 67-69; R Glas Ascension 69-73; Chapl RNR 72-74; Chapl RN 74-78; R Arbroath Bre 78-99; Hon Chapl Miss to Seafarers from 78; P-in-c Auchmithie Bre 79-90; rtd 99. *1 Denholm Gardens, Letham, Angus DD8 2XT* T: (01307) 818032 F: 818924 E: bykerbill@btinternet.com

WARD-SMITH, Richard. b 46. Ch Ch Coll Cant TCert 87 Ex Univ BTh 08. SWMTC 05. **d** 08 **p** 09. NSM Week St Mary Circle of Par Truro 08-10; NSM Kilkhampton w Morwenstow from 10. *11 Priestacott Park, Kilkhampton EX23 9TH* T: (01288) 321314 E: r.wardsmith@btinternet.com

WARDALE, Robert Christopher. b 46. Newc Univ BA 69. Coll of Resurr Mirfield 77. **d** 79 **p** 80. C Cockerton Dur 79-84; P-in-c Hedworth 84-87; V 87-92; V Darlington H Trin 92-06; rtd 06; PtO Dur from 12. *24 Beechcroft, Kenton Road, Newcastle upon Tyne NE3 4NB* T: 0191-285 5284 E: wardalerc@aol.com

WARDELL, Gareth Kevin. b 59. York Univ BA 81 MA 01. Ridley Hall Cam 03. **d** 05 **p** 06. C Selby Abbey York 05-08; C Kensington St Mary Abbots w Ch Ch and St Phil Lon 08-13; V Hampton All SS from 13. *All Saints' Vicarage, 40 The Avenue, Hampton TW12 3RS* T: (020) 8487 3823 E: wardellgareth@hotmail.com

WARDEN, John Michael. b 41. Univ Coll Lon BA 63 Trin Coll Ox BA 65 MA. NEOC 80. **d** 82 **p** 83. NSM Osmotherley w E Harlsey and Ingleby Arncliffe York 82-86; V Kirkdale 86-97; V Kirkdale w Harome, Nunnington and Pockley 98-07; rtd 07; PtO York from 07. *Laithwaite Cottage, Appleton Lane, Appleton-le-Street, Malton YO17 6TP* T: (01653) 699795

WARDEN, Richard James. b 57. Kent Univ BA 79 K Coll Lon MTh 86. Wycliffe Hall Ox 81. **d** 83 **p** 84. C Fulham St Mary N End Lon 83-85; CF 85-89; Chapl Wycombe Abbey Sch 89-01; Sen Chapl and Hd RS Wellington Coll Berks 01-04; P-in-c Finchampstead Ox 04-10; Chapl Mill Hill Sch Lon from 10. *Mill Hill School, The Ridgeway, London NW7 1QS* T: (020) 8959 1176 E: revrjw@hotmail.com

WARDLE, John Argyle. b 47. St Jo Coll Dur BA 71 ARCM 67 CertEd 73. **d** 73 **p** 74. C Mansfield SS Pet and Paul S'well 73-77; Chapl St Felix Sch Southwold 77-87; TV Haverhill w Withersfield, the Wrattings etc St E 87-90; V Choral S'well Minster 90-99; Bp's Adv on Healing 94-99; R Bridlington Priory York 99-08; RD Bridlington 03-08; rtd 08; PtO York from 12. *73 First Avenue, Bridlington YO15 2JW* T: (01262) 400127 E: jawardle27@btinternet.com

WARDLE, Robert. b 57. **d** 11 **p** 12. NSM Macclesfield Team Ches from 11. *38 Parkgate Road, Macclesfield SK11 7TA* T: (01625) 422541 E: robwardle@worthunlimited.co.uk

WARDMAN, Canon Carol Joy. b 56. Lon Univ BA 79 Man Univ MPhil 02. NOC 91. **d** 94 **p** 95. NSM Hebden Bridge Wakef 94-97; NSM Sowerby 97-10; Dioc Adv for Older People's Issues 08-11; NSM Halifax 10-11; Bps' Adv for Ch and Soc Ch in Wales from 11; Metrop Can Llan Cathl from 15. *Address temp unknown* E: carol.wardman@gmail.com *or* carolwardman@churchinwales.org.uk

WARE, Canon John Lawrence. b 37. Nottm Univ BA 59. Ridley Hall Cam 59. **d** 62 **p** 63. C Attercliffe Sheff 62-66; C Ranmoor 66-68; R Liddington and Soc and Ind Chapl Bris 68-74; Bp's Soc and Ind Adv and C-in-c Bris St Thos 74-79; V Kingswood 79-88; RD Bitton 85-87; P-in-c Broad Blunsdon 88-94; P-in-c Blunsdon St Andrew 88-94; R The Blunsdons 94-01; RD Cricklade 88-94; Hon Can Bris Cathl 76-01; rtd 01; PtO Bris from 01; Chapl HM Pris Bris 03-07. *26 Dongola Road, Bishopston, Bristol BS7 9HP* T: 0117-924 1304 E: jlwdongola@gmail.com

WARE, Ms Judith Marian. b 52. St Hugh's Coll Ox BA 74 MA 78 PGCE 75. CBDTI 00. **d** 02 **p** 03. NSM Windermere St Mary and Troutbeck Carl 02-05; C Thornes and Lupset Wakef 05-10; Chapl Wakef Cathl Sch 05-06; R Crumpsall Man from 10. *St Matthew's Rectory, 30 Cleveland Road, Manchester M8 4QU* T: 0161-740 0237 E: ware@judithware4.orangehome.co.uk

WARE, Stephen John. b 55. Univ of Wales (Lamp) BA 76. Ripon Coll Cuddesdon 77. **d** 79 **p** 80. C Lighthorne Cov 79-82; Chapl RAF 82-00; Command Chapl RAF 00-05; Selection Sec Min Division 05; V Bloxham w Milcombe and S Newington Ox 05-06; Warden of Readers Glouc 06-12; Asst Dioc Dir of Ords 06-14. *25 Beauchamp Meadow, Lydney GL15 5NS* T: (01594) 842299

WAREHAM, Mrs Caroline. b 32. Lightfoot Ho Dur 55. **dss** 80 **d** 87 **p** 94. Par Dn Stanwell Lon 87-88; C Epsom St Barn Guildf 88-95; C Aldershot St Mich 95-98; rtd 98; PtO Sarum from 00. *17 Homefield, Mere, Warminster BA12 6LT* T: (01747) 861716

WAREHAM, Mrs Sheila. b 36. CertEd 56. NOC 85. **d** 88 **p** 94. NSM Lostock Hall Blackb 88-90; NSM Allithwaite Carl 90-91; NSM Windermere RD 91-94; P-in-c Colton Carl 94-96; PtO 97-07. *Lyng Nook, Church Road, Allithwaite, Grange-over-Sands LA11 7RD* T: (015395) 35237

WARHAM, Mrs Jean. b 55. **d** 00 **p** 01. OLM Newcastle w Butterton Lich from 00. *166 High Street, Alsagers Bank, Stoke-on-Trent ST7 8BA* T: (01782) 721505

WARHURST (née HART), Mrs Jane Elizabeth. b 56. Sheff Univ BA 77. NOC 98. **d** 01 **p** 02. C Edge Hill St Cypr w St Mary Liv 01-06; V Toxteth St Bede w St Clem 06-14; V Irlam Man from 14; Dioc Ecum Officer from 14. *The Vicarage, Vicarage Road, Irlam, Manchester M44 6WA*

WARHURST, Richard. b 76. Univ Coll Chich BA 99. St Steph Ho Ox 00. **d** 02 **p** 03. C New Shoreham Chich 02-06; C Old Shoreham 02-06; R Chailey 06-10; Chapl Dorothy House Hospice Winsley 10-15; PtO B & W 11-15; R St Bartholomew Sarum from 15. *The Rectory, Semley, Shaftesbury SP7 9AU* T: (01747) 830174

WARING, Graham George Albert. b 37. ACII 62. Portsm Dioc Tr Course 86. **d** 87 **p** 02. Chapl Qu Alexandra Hosp Portsm 87-92; NSM Portsea All SS Portsm 92-94; NSM Widley w Wymering 94-95; NSM Wisbech St Aug Ely 95-98; Chapl King's Lynn and Wisbech Hosps NHS Trust 96-00; NSM Leverington Ely 98-00; NSM Southea w Murrow and Parson Drove 98-00; PtO from 00-02; NSM Scarborough St Sav w All SS 02-09; PtO from 09. *28 Newby Farm Road, Newby, Scarborough YO12 6UN* T: (01723) 353545 E: grachel.waring2@gmail.com

WARING, Jeffery Edwin. b 53. Trin Coll Bris 80. **d** 83 **p** 84. C Harpurhey Ch Ch Man 83-86; TV Eccles 86-92; P-in-c Hamworthy Sarum 92-04; P-in-c Red Post 04-13; rtd 13; Hon C Iwerne Valley Sarum from 14. *Glen View, Church Lane, Sutton Waldron, Blandford Forum DT11 8PB* E: jeffery@waring53.freeserve.co.uk

WARING, John Valentine. b 29. St Deiniol's Hawarden 65. **d** 67 **p** 68. C Bistre St As 67-71; C Blackpool St Thos Blackb 71-72; R Levenshulme St Pet Man 72-87; R Caerwys and Bodfari St As 87-94; rtd 94. *45 Glan y Morfa Court, Connah's Quay, Deeside CH5 4PL*

WARING, Mrs Margaret Ruth. b 44. Keele Univ CertEd 65. SWMTC 86. **d** 90 **p** 94. Par Dn Tavistock and Gulworthy Ex 90-94; C 94-96; TV Axminster, Chardstock, All Saints etc 96-04; rtd 04; PtO Ex from 04. *5 The Battens, Stockland, Honiton EX14 9DS* T: (01404) 881516

WARING, Rebecca Ann. b 69. **d** 13 **p** 14. NSM Stapleton Bris from 13; NSM Frenchay and Winterbourne Down from 13. *2 Castle Farm Road, Bristol BS15 3NJ* T: 0117-907 4266

WARING, Roger. b 32. CertEd 56 Open Univ BA 74 ACP 66. SWMTC 83. **d** 86 **p** 87. NSM Ex St Sidwell and St Matt 86-90; NSM Tavistock and Gulworthy 90-96; NSM Axminster, Chardstock, All Saints etc 96-99; PtO from 99. *5 The Battens, Stockland, Honiton EX14 9DS* T: (01404) 881516

WARKE, Alistair Samuel John. b 66. Ulster Univ BA 89. CITC BTh 92. **d** 92 **p** 93. C Arm St Mark 92-95; I Killyman 95-04; Hon V Choral Arm Cathl 95-04; Dioc C Clogh 11-14. *Address temp unknown* M: 07704-809265 E: awarke@btinternet.com

✠**WARKE, The Rt Revd Robert Alexander.** b 30. TCD BA 52 BD 60. **d** 53 **p** 54 **c** 88. C Newtownards D & D 53-56; C Dublin St Cath w St Victor D & G 56-58; C Dublin Rathfarnham 58-64; Min Can St Patr Cathl Dublin 59-64; I Dunlavin w Ballymore Eustace and Hollywood D & G 64-67; I Dublin Drumcondra w N Strand 67-71; I Dublin St Barn 67-71; I Dublin Zion Ch 71-88; Adn Dublin 80-88; Bp C, C & R 88-98; rtd 98. *6 Kerdiff Park, Monread Road, Naas, Co Kildare, Republic of Ireland* T: (00353) (45) 898144 E: rawarke@eircom.net

WARLAND, Peter William. b 35. K Coll Lon 56. **d** 60 **p** 61. C Pemberton St Jo Liv 60-64; C Warrington St Elphin 64-66; V Farnworth All SS Man 66-71; Chapl RN 71-92; QHC 88-92; Chapl Greenbank and Freedom Fields Hosps Ex 92-00; Chapl St Luke's Hospice Plymouth 94-00; rtd 00; PtO Ex from 00. *5 Evans Court, 6 Craigie Drive, Plymouth PL1 3TP* T: (01752) 663274

WARMAN, Canon John Richard. b 37. Pemb Coll Ox BA 61 MA. Ridley Hall Cam 61. **d** 63 **p** 64. C Huyton St Mich *Liv* 63-67; Asst Chapl Liv Univ 67-68; Chapl 68-74; P-in-c Holbrooke *Derby* 74-80; P-in-c Lt Eaton 74-80; R Sawley 80-96; RD Ilkeston 82-92; Hon Can Derby Cathl 91-02; V Allestree 96-02; rtd 02; PtO *Derby* from 02. *27 Swanmore Road, Littleover, Derby DE23 3SD* T: (01332) 510089
E: jpwarman1@btinternet.com

WARMAN, Miss Marion Alice. b 20. Newnham Coll Cam BA 43 MA 50. S'wark Ord Course 76. **dss** 79 **d** 87 **p** 94. Spring Grove St Mary *Lon* 79-87; Hon Par Dn 87-94; Hon C from 94; Chapl Asst W Middx Univ Hosp Isleworth 80-93; Chapl Volunteer Hounslow and Spelthorne NHS Trust 93-04; PtO *Lon* from 93. *43 Thornbury Road, Isleworth TW7 4LE* T: (020) 8560 5905

WARMAN, Philip Noel. b 64. Roehampton Inst BSc 85 PGCE 86. Ridley Hall Cam 99. **d** 01 **p** 02. C Burney Lane *Birm* 01-06; C Luton St Mary *St Alb* 06-09; V Brightside w Wincobank *Sheff* from 09. *The Vicarage, 24 Beacon Road, Sheffield S9 1AD* T: 0114-281 9360

WARNE, Miss Susan Annette. b 39. Man Univ BSc 61 Nottm Univ DipEd 62. **d** 00 **p** 01. OLM Yoxmere *St E* 00-09; PtO from 09. *Wynkyns, 22 Oakwood Park, Yoxford, Saxmundham IP17 3JU* T: (01728) 668410

WARNER, Alan Winston. b 51. Lon Univ BSc 73. Coll of Resurr Mirfield 73. **d** 76 **p** 77. C Willenhall St Anne *Lich* 76-78; C Baswich 78-81; V Wednesfield St Greg 81-87; Chapl Frimley Park Hosp 87-94; Chapl Frimley Park Hosp NHS Trust 94-04; Team Ldr Shrewsbury and Telford NHS Trust 04-10; Bp's Adv on Hosp Chapl *Lich* 06-10; rtd 10; PtO *Nor* from 11. *9 Beachmans Court, Wilson Road, Lowestoft NR33 0HZ* T: (01502) 218864 E: alan.warner@talktalk.net

WARNER, Canon Andrew Compton. b 35. Westcott Ho Cam BA 58 MA 62. Westcott Ho Cam 59. **d** 60 **p** 61. C Addlestone *Guildf* 60-64; C-in-c Ash Vale CD 64-71; V Hinchley Wood 71-80; R Gt Bookham 80-00; RD Leatherhead 88-93; Hon Can Guildf Cathl 99-00; rtd 00; PtO *Win* from 00. *5 Pearman Drive, Andover SP10 2SB* T: (01264) 391325
E: dandawarner@yahoo.co.uk

WARNER, Clifford Chorley. b 38. Hull Univ MA 88. EMMTC 76. **d** 79 **p** 80. NSM Swanwick and Pentrich *Derby* 79-88; NSM Allestree 88-98; PtO from 98. *3 Meadow Reach, Station Approach, Duffield, Belper DE56 4HT* T: (01332) 843389
E: cliffgwen@gmail.com

WARNER, David. b 80. Leic Univ BA 02 Sheff Univ BA 13. Coll of Resurr Mirfield 10. **d** 13 **p** 14. C Abbots Langley *St Alb* from 13. *40 Kindersley Way, Abbots Langley WD5 0DQ* M: 07961-558371 E: frdavidwarner@gmail.com

WARNER, David. b 40. AKC 63. **d** 64 **p** 65. C Castleford All SS *Wakef* 64-68; Warden Hollowford Tr and Conf Cen Sheff 68-72; R Wombwell *Sheff* 72-83; V Wortley w Thurgoland 83-95; RD Tankersley 88-93; V Worsbrough St Mary 95-00; P-in-c Bildeston w Wattisham *St E* 00-02; P-in-c Whatfield w Semer, Nedging and Naughton 00-02; R Bildeston w Wattisham and Lindsey, Whatfield etc 02-05; rtd 05; PtO *St E* from 05. *10 Magdalen Street, Eye IP23 7AJ* T: (01379) 870459 M: 07050-111478

WARNER, David Leonard John. b 24. Kelham Th Coll 47. **d** 51 **p** 52. C Mill Hill St Mich *Lon* 51-54; C Pimlico St Sav 54-56; S Africa 56-68; V Bournemouth H Epiphany *Win* 68-78; V Whitchurch w Tufton and Litchfield 78-89; RD Whitchurch /9-89; rtd 89; PtO *Win* from 89; Hon Chapl Win Cathl from 97. *9 Sparkford Close, Winchester SO22 4NH* T: (01962) 867343 E: david.warner@btinternet.com

WARNER, Dennis Vernon. b 46. Lon Univ BA 68 K Coll Lon BD 71. **d** 72 **p** 73. C W Bromwich All SS *Lich* 72-75; C Uttoxeter w Bramshall 75-79; NSM Stretton w Claymills from 79. *90 Beech Lane, Stretton, Burton-on-Trent DE13 0DU* T: (01283) 548058 E: densue@uku.co.uk

WARNER, Canon George Francis. b 36. Trin Coll Ox BA 60 MA 64 Qu Coll Cam BA 63. Westcott Ho Cam 61. **d** 63 **p** 64. C Birm St Geo 63-66; C Maidstone All SS w St Phil and H Trin *Cant* 66-69; Chapl Wellington Coll Berks 69-78; TR Coventry Caludon *Cov* 78-95; Hon Can Cov Cathl 85-02; RD Cov E 89-95; P-in-c Leamington Priors All SS 95-02; P-in-c Leamington Spa H Trin and Old Milverton 95-02; rtd 02; PtO *Cov* from 02. *Coll Leys Edge, Fant Hill, Upper Brailes, Banbury OX15 5AY* T: (01608) 685550
E: sandgwarner@btinternet.com

WARNER, John Philip. b 59. Keble Coll Ox BA 80 MA 84. St Steph Ho Ox 81. **d** 83 **p** 84. C Brighton Resurr *Chich* 83-87; C Paddington St Mary *Lon* 87-90; V Teddington St Mark and Hampton Wick 90-00; P-in-c Belgrade *Eur* 00-03; P-in-c St Magnus the Martyr w St Marg New Fish Street *Lon* 03-10; R from 10; P-in-c St Mary Abchurch 04-13; P-in-c St Clem Eastcheap w St Martin Orgar 08-11. *St Magnus the Martyr, Lower Thames Street, London EC3R 6DN* T: (020) 7626 4481 E: saintmagnus@bulldoghome.com

WARNER, Mrs Marjorie Anne. b 53. York Univ BA 74 York St Jo Univ MA 04. NEOC 06. **d** 09 **p** 10. NSM Masham and Healey *Leeds* from 09. *26 Larkhill Crescent, Ripon HG4 2HN* T: (01765) 606961 E: marjorie@26lhc.freeserve.co.uk

✠**WARNER, The Rt Revd Martin Clive.** b 58. St Chad's Coll Dur BA 80 MA 85 PhD 03. St Steph Ho Ox 82. **d** 84 **p** 85 **c** 10. C Plymouth St Pet *Ex* 84-88; TV Leic Resurr 88-93; Admin Shrine of Our Lady of Walsingham 93-02; P-in-c Hempton and Pudding Norton *Nor* 98-00; Hon Can Nor Cathl 00-02; C St Andr Holborn *Lon* 02-03; Can Res St Paul's Cathl 03-10; Suff Bp Whitby *York* 10-12; Bp Chich from 12; Master of Guardians Shrine of Our Lady of Walsingham from 06. *The Palace, Chichester PO19 1PY* T: (01243) 782161 F: 531322
E: bishop@chichester.anglican.org

WARNER, Canon Mary. b 52. Univ of Wales (Swansea) BSc 73 Aber Univ PhD 77. NEOC 90. **d** 93 **p** 94. C Bensham *Dur* 93-96; Asst Chapl Newcastle upon Tyne Hosps NHS Trust 96-98; Chapl Hartlepool and E Durham NHS Trust 98-99; Chapl N Tees and Hartlepool NHS Trust 99-04; Chapl City Hosps Sunderland NHS Foundn Trust from 04; Hon Can Dur Cathl from 10; PtO from 15. *The Chaplain's Office, Sunderland Royal Hospital, Kayll Road, Sunderland SR4 7TP* T: 0191-569 9180

WARNER, Canon Michael John William. b 41. Ex Univ MPhil 06. Sarum Th Coll 68. **d** 71 **p** 72. C Plympton St Mary *Ex* 71-75; V St Goran w Caerhays *Truro* 75-78; V Bishops Tawton *Ex* 78-79; V Newport 78-79; P-in-c *Truro* 79-83; V St Stythians w Perranarworthal and Gwennap 83-93; Sec Dioc Adv Cttee 93-01; P-in-c Budock 93-97; P-in-c Tregony w St Cuby and Cornelly 97-03; C Probus, Ladock and Grampound w Creed and St Erme 02-03; Hon Can Truro Cathl 98-03; rtd 03; PtO *Truro* from 03. *98 Porthpean Road, St Austell PL25 4PN* T: (01726) 64130
E: m.j.w.w@btinternet.com

WARNER, Nigel Bruce. b 51. St Jo Coll Cam BA 72 MA 76 ALCM 67. Wycliffe Hall Ox 75. **d** 77 **p** 78. C Luton St Mary *St Alb* 77-80; Prec Dur Cathl 80-84; R St John Lee *Newc* 84-91; V Lamesley *Dur* 91-98; V Bishopwearmouth St Nic 98-11; AD Wearmouth 99-05; V Heworth St Mary from 11. *Heworth Vicarage, High Heworth Lane, Gateshead NE10 0PB* T: 0191-469 2111 E: nigel.warner@durham.anglican.org

WARNER, Philip. See WARNER, John Philip

WARNER, Canon Robert William. b 32. TCD BA 54 MA 65 BD 65. TCD Div Sch Div Test 56. **d** 56 **p** 57. C Wythenshawe St Martin CD *Man* 56-60; R Hulme St Steph w St Mark 60-66; R Droylsden St Mary 66-76; R Stand 76-97; AD Radcliffe and Prestwich 85-96; Hon Can Man Cathl 87-97; rtd 97; PtO *Man* from 99. *28 Cow Lees, Westhoughton, Bolton BL5 3EG* T: (01942) 818821

WARNER, Terence. b 36. **d** 92 **p** 93. NSM Leek and Meerbrook *Lich* 92-98; NSM Odd Rode *Ches* 98-03; PtO *Lich* 03-15; NSM Brown Edge from 15. *36 Haig Road, Leek ST13 6BZ* T: (01538) 371988

WARNES, Brian Leslie Stephen. b 40. Natal Univ BSocSc 76. Kelham Th Coll 59. **d** 67 **p** 68. C Tonge Moor *Man* 67-71; S Africa 71-87; V Blean *Cant* 87-94; V Te Awamutu St Jo New Zealand 94-98; Chapl to Bp Christchurch 98-04; rtd 05. *57 Killarney Avenue, Torbay, North Shore City 0630, New Zealand* E: stephen.warnes@gmail.com

WARNES, David John. b 50. Jes Coll Cam BA 72 MA 76 PGCE 73. EAMTC 01. **d** 04 **p** 05. Chapl Ipswich Sch and NSM Ipswich St Mary-le-Tower *St E* 04-10; NSM Edin St Martin from 10. *7E Devon Place, Edinburgh EH12 5HJ* T: 0131-337 3574 M: 07732-654603 E: warnesdavid@googlemail.com

WARNES, Miss Marjorie. b 32. Leeds Inst of Educn CertEd 53. St Jo Coll Nottm 85. **d** 87 **p** 94. C Leamington Priors St Mary *Cov* 87-97; rtd 97; PtO *Cov* 97-05. *38 Ruston Avenue, Rustington, Littlehampton BN16 2AN* T: (01903) 778859

WARR, Timothy Gerald. b 59. Trin Coll Bris BA 86. **d** 88 **p** 89. C Yateley *Win* 88-91; C Chapel Allerton *Ripon* 91-93; V Wortley-de-Leeds 93-01; TR Borehamwood *St Alb* 01-05; TR Elstree and Borehamwood from 05. *The Rectory, 94 Shenley Road, Borehamwood WD6 1EB* T/F: (020) 8207 6603 T: 8905 1365 E: tim.warr@btinternet.com

WARREN, The Very Revd Alan Christopher. b 32. CCC Cam BA 56 MA 60. Ridley Hall Cam 56. **d** 57 **p** 58. C Cliftonville *Cant* 57-59; C Plymouth St Andr *Ex* 59-62; Chapl Kelly Coll Tavistock 62-64; V Leic H Apostles 64-72; Hon Can Cov Cathl 72-78; Dioc Missr 72-78; Provost Leic 78-92; rtd 92; PtO *Nor* from 92. *9 Queen's Drive, Hunstanton PE36 6EY* T: (01485) 534533

WARREN, Barbara. See CRUMP (formerly WARREN), Barbara
WARREN, Bunny. See WARREN, Gordon Lenham

✠**WARREN, The Rt Revd Cecil Allan.** b 24. Sydney Univ BA 51 Qu Coll Ox BA 56 MA 59. ACT ThL 52. **d** 50 **p** 51 **c** 65. Australia 50-83; Can Canberra and Goulbern 63-65; Asst Bp 65-72; Bp 72-83; Asst Bp Derby 83-89; TR Old Brampton and Loundsley Green 83-89; Hon Can Derby Cathl 83-89; r-d 89. *Symes Thorpe, 69 Stenner Street, Toowoomba Qld 4350, Australia*

WARREN, David Edward. b 39. S'wark Ord Course. **d** 87 **p** 88. NSM Mottingham St Andr w St Alban *S'wark* 87-05; rtd 05; PtO *S'wark* 07-14; *Cant* from 15. *20 Poets Walk, Walmer, Deal CT14 7QD* T: (01304) 721537

WARREN, Eric Anthony. b 28. MBE. Ex & Truro NSM Scheme. **d** 83 **p** 84. NSM Chudleigh *Ex* 83-88; PtO from 88. *Lower Radway House, Bishopsteignton, Teignmouth TQ14 9SS* T: (01626) 772135 *or* 779277

WARREN, Frederick Noel. b 30. TCD BA 52 MA 58 BD 66 QUB PhD 72. **d** 53 **p** 54. C Belfast St Matt *Conn* 53-56; C Belfast St Geo 56-59; I Castlewellan *D & D* 59-65; I Clonallon w Warrenpoint 65-69; I Newcastle 69-87; Can Belf Cathl 73-76; Preb Wicklow St Patr Cathl Dublin 76-88; I Dunfanaghy, Raymunterdoney and Tullaghbegley *D & R* 87-97; Preb Swords St Patr Cathl Dublin 89-97; rtd 97. *Runclevin, Dufanaghy, Letterkenny, Co Donegal, Republic of Ireland* T: (00353) (74) 913 6635

WARREN, Geoffrey. *See* WARREN, Robert Geoffrey

WARREN, Geoffrey Richard. b 44. Middx Poly MA 91 Middx Univ PhD 02. Bps' Coll Cheshunt 66 Qu Coll Birm 68. **d** 69 **p** 70. C Waltham Cross *St Alb* 69-73; C Radlett 73-78; C Tring 78-80; TV 80-95; V Watford St Andr 95-09; RD Watford 05-09; rtd 09. *41 Coombe Valley Road, Preston, Weymouth DT3 6NL* T: (01305) 832884 E: geoffwarren@btinternet.com

WARREN, Mrs Gillian. b 53. Sheff Univ BA 74 PGCE 75. WMMTC 89. **d** 92 **p** 94. Par Dn Tettenhall Regis *Lich* 92-94; C 94-95; TV Bilston 95-00; R Lich St Chad 00-02; V Wednesbury St Paul Wood Green 02-10; V Albrighton, Boningale and Donington 10-14; rtd 14. *Address temp unknown*

WARREN, Gordon Lenham (Bunny). b 45. Wycliffe Hall Ox 91. **d** 93 **p** 94. C Sunbury *Lon* 93-96; C Laleham 96-98; R Limehouse 98-13; Hon Chapl RN 08-13; rtd 13; PtO *Cant* from 14. *Hideaway Cottage, Avenue Road, Ramsgate CT11 8ES* T: (01843) 597299 E: gordonlwarren@aol.com

WARREN, Preb Henry Fiennes. b 21. Keble Coll Ox BA 42 MA 47. Cuddesdon Coll 42. **d** 48 **p** 49. C Weston-super-Mare St Jo *B & W* 48-53; R Exford 53-75; RD Wiveliscombe 65-73; Preb Wells Cathl 73-96; R W Monkton 75-86; rtd 86; PtO *B & W* from 86. *8 Beach Road West, Portishead, Bristol BS20 7HR* T: (01460) 57922

WARREN, James Randolph. b 54. St Paul's Coll Chelt CertEd 75 Bris Univ BEd 76 Birm Univ MEd 84. Ridley Hall Cam 90. **d** 92 **p** 93. C Boldmere *Birm* 92-95; V Torpoint *Truro* 95-01; Hon Chapl RN 98-01; V Shottery St Andr *Cov* from 01. *The Vicarage, Church Lane, Shottery, Stratford-upon-Avon CV37 9HQ* T: (01789) 293381 F: 296648

WARREN, Malcolm Clive. b 46. St D Coll Lamp. **d** 74 **p** 75. C Newport St Andr *Mon* 74-78; C Risca 78-79; V St Hilary Greenway 79-84; TV Grantham *Linc* 84-90; Ind Chapl Linc 87-90 and Worc 90-05; P-in-c Dudley St Aug Holly Hall *Worc* 95-96; PtO 96-97; TV Kidderminster St Mary and All SS w Trimpley etc 97-05; Ind Chapl *Bris* 05-10; TV Pontypool *Mon* from 10. *The Vicarage, Freeholdland Road, Pontnewynydd, Pontypool NP4 8LW* T: (01495) 741879 M: 07971-222739 E: malcolm.warren296@btinternet.com

WARREN, Martin John. b 59. Ch Coll Cam BA 81 MA 85. St Jo Coll Nottm LTh 85. **d** 86 **p** 87. C Littleover *Derby* 86-90; C Hermitage and Hampstead Norreys, Cold Ash etc *Ox* 90-91; TV 91-97; TV Hermitage 97-02; P-in-c Shebbear, Buckland Filleigh, Sheepwash etc *Ex* 02-15; TR from 15. *The Rectory, Shebbear, Beaworthy EX21 5RU* T: (01409) 281424

WARREN, Michael John. b 40. Kelham Th Coll 59. **d** 64 **p** 65. C Withington St Chris *Man* 64-67; C Worsley 67-69; C Witney *Ox* 69-72; V S Hinksey 72-80; Canada 80-99 and from 02; C Verwood *Sarum* 99-00; rtd 00. *1005-5th Avenue North, Lethbridge AB T1H 0MB, Canada*

WARREN, Michael Philip. b 62. Oak Hill Th Coll BA 91 MA 04. **d** 94 **p** 95. C Tunbridge Wells St Jo *Roch* 94-98; Assoc Min Heydon, Gt and Lt Chishill, Chrishall etc *Chelmsf* 98-04; V Tunbridge Wells St Pet *Roch* from 04. *St Peter's Vicarage, Bayhall Road, Tunbridge Wells TN2 4TP* T: (01892) 530384 E: stpetersmw@aol.com

WARREN, The Ven Norman Leonard. b 34. CCC Cam BA 58 MA 62. Ridley Hall Cam 58. **d** 60 **p** 61. C Bedworth *Cov* 60-63; V Leamington Priors St Paul 63-77; R Morden *S'wark* 77-88; TR 88-89; RD Merton 86-89; Adn Roch and Can Res Roch Cathl 89-00; rtd 00; PtO *Roch* 00-06; *Cov* from 08. *Cornerstone, 6 Hill View, Stratford-upon-Avon CV37 9AY* T: (01789) 414255

WARREN, Canon Paul Kenneth. b 41. Selw Coll Cam BA 63 MA 67. Cuddesdon Coll 64. **d** 67 **p** 68. C Lancaster St Mary *Blackb* 67-70; Chapl Lanc Univ 70-78; V Langho Billington 78-83; Bp's Dom Chapl and Chapl Whalley Abbey 83-88; R Standish 88-01; P-in-c Silverdale from 01; Hon Can Blackb Cathl from 91; RD Chorley 92-98; AD Tunstall 08-14. *The Vicarage, St John's Grove, Silverdale, Carnforth LA5 0RH* T: (01524) 701268

WARREN, Peter. b 40. Hull Univ MA 90 FCA 64. Oak Hill Th Coll 77. **d** 79 **p** 80. C Newcastle w Butterton *Lich* 79-82; TV Sutton St Jas and Wawne *York* 82-87; V Ledsham w Fairburn 87-95; R Ainderby Steeple w Yafforth and Kirby Wiske etc *Ripon* 95-03; rtd 03; PtO *York* from 04; *Sheff* from 08. *5 Bridge Farm, Pollington, Goole DN14 0BF* T: (01405) 862925 E: peter@rabbit22.plus.com

WARREN, Peter John. b 55. Worc Coll of Educn CertEd 76. Trin Coll Bris BA 86. **d** 86 **p** 87. C W Streatham St Jas *S'wark* 86-91; P-in-c Edin Clermiston Em 91-98; P-in-c Blackpool Ch Ch w All SS *Blackb* 98-03; V 03-09; Co-Pastor Internat Chr Fellowship Phnom Penh 09-13; Pastor from 13. *ICF, PO Box 98, Phnom Penh, Cambodia* T: (00855) 7788 6846 E: revpvwarren@googlemail.com

WARREN, Philip James. b 65. SS Paul & Mary Coll Cheltenham BA 87 Hughes Hall Cam PGCE 88 Kingston Univ MA 93. St Jo Coll Nottm MA 99. **d** 00 **p** 01. C Reigate St Mary *S'wark* 00-03; P-in-c Jersey Millbrook St Matt *Win* 03-06; V from 06; P-in-c Jersey St Lawr 03-06; R from 06. *The Rectory, La Route de l'Eglise, St Lawrence, Jersey JE3 1FF* T: (01534) 869013 E: philwarren@jerseymail.co.uk

WARREN, Robert. b 54. TCD BA 78 MA 81. CITC 76. **d** 78 **p** 79. C Limerick City *L & K* 78-81; Dioc Youth Adv (Limerick) 79-86; I Adare w Kilpeacon and Croom 81-88; Bp's Dom Chapl 81-95; Dioc Registrar (Limerick etc) 81-12; Dioc Registrar (Killaloe etc) 86-12; I Tralee w Kilmoyley, Ballymacelligott etc 88-12; Can Limerick, Killaloe and Clonfert Cathls 95-96; Chan 97-12; Asst Dioc Sec L & K 90-12; Adn Limerick, Ardfert and Aghadoe *L & K* 10-12; I Taney *D & G* from 12; Preb Taney St Patr Cathl Dublin 04-12; Preb Tipperkevin from 12. *Taney Rectory, 6 Stoney Road, Dundrum, Dublin 14, Republic of Ireland* T: (00353) (1) 298 4497 M: 87-252 1133 E: taney@dublin.anglican.org

WARREN, Robert Geoffrey. b 51. Trin Coll Bris 79. **d** 82 **p** 83. C Felixstowe SS Pet and Paul *St E* 82-86; V Gazeley w Dalham, Moulton and Kentford 86-90; P-in-c Ipswich St Clem w St Luke and H Trin 90-98; C Gt Finborough w Onehouse, Harleston, Buxhall etc 98-00; rtd 01; PtO *B & W* from 02. *5 Clarence House, 17 Clarence Road North, Weston-super-Mare BS23 4AS* T: (01934) 418916

WARREN, Robert Irving. b 38. Univ of BC BA 58 Ox Univ MA 73. Angl Th Coll (BC). **d** 61 **p** 63. C Lakes Miss Canada 61-66; R Hazelton 69-75; R New Westmr St Barn 75-89; R Northfield *Birm* 89-08; rtd 08; PtO *Birm* from 08; *Lich* from 13. *300 Lickey Road, Rednal, Birmingham B45 8RY* T: 0121-453 1572 E: riwarren@hotmail.com

WARREN, Robert James. b 58. McGill Univ Montreal BTh 82 Edin Univ MTh 11. Montreal Dioc Th Coll. **d** 84 **p** 85. C Victoria St Phil Canada 84-87; R Chibougamu Ch Ch 87-90; R Mascouche & P-in-c Montreal St Ignatius 90-92; R Westmount Ch of the Advent 92-99; Exec Dir Old Brewery Miss 99-03; Chapl Canadian Grenadier Guards 91-96; Chapl Miss to Seafarers 93-99; R Penicuik *Edin* 03-12; P-in-c W Linton 03-12. *Address temp unknown* M: 07963-910865 E: padre@btinternet.com

WARREN, Canon Robert Peter Resker. b 39. Jes Coll Cam BA 63 MA. ALCD 65. **d** 65 **p** 66. C Rusholme H Trin *Man* 65-68; C Bushbury *Lich* 68-71; TR Crookes St Thos *Sheff* 71-90 and 90-93; RD Hallam 78-83; Hon Can Sheff Cathl 82-93; Can Th Sheff Cathl 93-04; Nat Officer for Evang 93-04; Springboard Missr 98-04; rtd 04; PtO *Ripon* 03-10. *2 The Fairway, High Hauxley, Morpeth NE65 0JW* T: (01665) 714697 E: robert.warren@ukgateway.net

WARREN, William Frederick. b 55. Sarum & Wells Th Coll 83. **d** 86 **p** 87. C E Greenwich Ch Ch w St Andr and St Mich *S'wark* 86-91; C Richmond St Mary w St Matthias and St Jo 91-95; TV 96-97; V Putney St Marg 97-08; V S Croydon St Pet and St Aug from 08. *St Peter's Vicarage, 20 Haling Park Road, South Croydon CR2 6NE* T: (020) 8688 4715 E: wfwarren2003@yahoo.co.uk

WARREN, William John. b 86. Warwick Univ BA 08. Wycliffe Hall Ox BTh 13. **d** 13 **p** 14. C Heigham H Trin *Nor* from 13. *14 Trinity Street, Norwich NR2 2BQ* T: (01603) 443785 M: 07843-731598 E: curate@trinitynorwich.org

WARRENER, Mrs Kathleen Barbara. b 48. Coll of Resurr Mirfield 09. **d** 11. NSM Pontefract All SS *Leeds* from 11. *45 Northfield Drive, Pontefract WF8 2DJ* T: (01977) 600232 M: 07554-087728 E: babs@warrener4389.fsnet.co.uk

WARRICK, The Very Revd Mark. b 54. Aston Univ BSc 76 Nottm Univ BCombStuds 83. Linc Th Coll 80. **d** 83 **p** 84. C Grantham *Linc* 83-87; C Cirencester *Glouc* 87-91; V Over *Ely* 91-97; V Deeping St James *Linc* 97-09; P-in-c Stamford All SS w St Jo 09-13; V from 13; RD Aveland and Ness w Stamford 06-09 and 10-14; RD Stamford from 14; Dean Stamford from 11. *All Saints' Vicarage, Casterton Road, Stamford PE9 2YL* T: (01780) 756942
E: mark.warrick@stamfordallsaints.org.uk

WARRILLOW, Brian Ellis. b 39. Linc Th Coll 81. **d** 83 **p** 84. C Tunstall *Lich* 83-85; C Shrewsbury H Cross 86-87; P-in-c Tilstock 88; P-in-c Whixall 88; V Tilstock and Whixall 89-92; TV Hanley H Ev 92-94; rtd 94; PtO *Lich* 01-02; P-in-c Menton *Eur* 02-05; Hon C Wolstanton *Lich* 07-10; PtO from 14. *12 Sutton Avenue, Silverdale, Newcastle ST5 6TB* T: (01782) 700925 E: brian.warrillow@gmail.com

WARRILOW, Mrs Christine. b 42. Lanc Univ BA 86. NOC 86. **d** 89 **p** 94. C Netherton *Liv* 89-92; C Cantril Farm 92-94; V 94-96; V Hindley Green 96-02; rtd 02; PtO *Liv* 03-08; Hon C Stanley w Stoneycroft St Paul from 08. *10 Beacon View Drive, Upholland, Skelmersdale WN8 0HL*

WARRINGTON, Katherine Irene (Kay). b 44. Univ of Wales (Swansea) BSc 67 DipEd 68. St Mich Coll Llan 93. **d** 95. NSM Knighton and Norton *S & B* 95-98; NSM Llywel and Traeanglas w Llanulid 98-00; NSM Trallwng w Bettws Penpont w Aberyskir etc 00-04; Dioc Children's Officer from 96. *17 Ffordd Emlyn, Ystalyfera, Swansea SA9 2EW* T: (01639) 842874
E: kaywarrington@sky.com

WARRINGTON, Archdeacon of. *See* BRADLEY, The Ven Peter David Douglas

WARRINGTON, Suffragan Bishop of. *See* BLACKBURN, The Rt Revd Richard Finn

WARWICK, Gordon Melvin. b 31. NOC 79. **d** 80 **p** 81. NSM Darrington *Wakef* 80-87; TV Almondbury w Farnley Tyas 87-95; rtd 95; PtO *Newc* 95-09; Hon C Dumfries *Glas* from 11. *4 Glencaple Avenue, Dumfries DG1 4SJ* T: (01387) 731357
E: gordonwarwick1931@btinternet.com

WARWICK, Hugh Johnston. b 39. ARCM 63. SAOMC 97. **d** 00 **p** 01. NSM Rotherfield Peppard *Ox* 00-02; NSM Rotherfield Peppard and Kidmore End etc 02-08; rtd 08; PtO *Ox* from 08; *Pet* from 08. *Witan House, 38 Wheeler's Rise, Croughton, Brackley NN13 5ND* T: (01869) 819577 *or* 819596
E: hugh@pukekos.co.uk

WARWICK, Canon John Michael. b 37. Fitzw Ho Cam BA 58 MA 62. Ely Th Coll 58. **d** 60 **p** 61. C Towcester w Easton Neston *Pet* 60-63; C Leighton Buzzard *St Alb* 63-64; C Boston *Linc* 64-66; P-in-c Sutterton 66-72; V 72-74; V Sutton St Mary 74-84; V Bourne 84-02; Can and Preb Linc Cathl 89-02; RD Aveland and Ness w Stamford 93-00; Chapl Bourne Hosps Lincs 84-93; Chapl NW Anglia Healthcare NHS Trust 93-98; rtd 02. *24 Hurst Park Road, Twyford, Reading RG10 0EY* T: 0118-932 0649

WARWICK, Neil Michael. b 64. Nottm Univ BA 86. Ridley Hall Cam 03. **d** 05 **p** 06. C Towcester w Caldecote and Easton Neston etc *Pet* 05-09; V Earley St Nic *Ox* from 09. *St Nicolas' Vicarage, 53 Sutcliffe Avenue, Reading RG6 7JN* T: 0118-966 5060 E: revwarwick@btinternet.com *or* neil@stnicolas.org.uk

WARWICK, Archdeacon of. *See* RODHAM, The Ven Morris

WARWICK, Suffragan Bishop of. *See* STROYAN, The Rt Revd John Ronald Angus

WASEY, Kim Alexandra Clare. b 77. Man Univ BA 99 Birm Univ MPhil 03. Qu Coll Birm 00. **d** 02 **p** 03. C Rochdale *Man* 02-04; Chapl Man Univ 04-06; Chapl Man Metrop Univ 04-06; Chapl Salford Univ 06-09; Hon C Man Victoria Park from 09; Chapl Salford Univ from 12. *St Chrysostom's Rectory, 38 Park Range, Manchester M14 5HQ* T: 0161-224 6971 M: 07944-155772
E: kim.wasey@gmail.com

WASH, John Henry. b 46. CEng MIStructE 70. **d** 81 **p** 83. OLM Newington St Mary *S'wark* 81-04; PtO Cyprus and the Gulf from 05. *PO Box 60187, Paphos 8101, Cyprus* T: (00357) (26) 923860 E: wash@emailkissonerga.com

WASHBROOK, Mrs Mary. **d** 12 **p** 13. OLM Peak Forest and Dove Holes *Derby* from 12. *22 Alexander Road, Dove Holes, Buxton SK17 8BN* T: (01298) 815187 E: maryatdove@gmail.com

WASHFORD, Mrs Rhonwen Richarde Foster. b 50. RGN 99. ERMC 05. **d** 08 **p** 09. NSM Stalham, E Ruston, Brunstead, Sutton and Ingham Nor 08-11; NSM Thorpe St Andr 11-15; rtd 15; PtO *Nor* from 15. *60B The Close, Norwich NR1 4EH* T: (01603) 302800 E: rhonwenwashford@hotmail.com

WASHINGTON, Linda Jennifer. b 56. BA PGCE. **d** 07 **p** 08. NSM Woburn w Eversholt, Milton Bryan, Battlesden etc *St Alb* 07-14; Chapl Bedford Hosp NHS Trust 14-15; LtO *St Alb* from 14. *3 Avenue Mews, Flitwick, Bedford MK45 1BF* T: (01525) 714442

WASHINGTON, Nigel Leslie. b 50. St Paul's Coll Chelt BEd 73 Lon Univ MA 83. SAOMC 97. **d** 00 **p** 01. NSM Westoning w Tingrith *St Alb* 00-07; P-in-c 07-14; V from 14. *3 Avenue Mews, Flitwick, Bedford MK45 1BF* T: (01525) 714442
M: 07794-754986 E: nigelwash@hotmail.com

WASHINGTON, Canon Patrick Leonard. b 44. Nottm Univ BSc 66. St Steph Ho Ox 65. **d** 68 **p** 69. C Fleet *Guildf* 68-71; C Farnham 71-74; TV Staveley and Barrow Hill *Derby* 74-83; V Norbury St Phil *Cant* 83-84; V *S'wark* 85-10; RD Croydon N 90-99; Hon Can S'wark Cathl 01-10; rtd 10; PtO *Leic* from 10. *16 Saddington Road, Fleckney, Leicester LE8 8AW* T: 0116-240 3117

WASSALL, Canon Keith Leonard. b 45. Bede Coll Dur TCert 67. Chich Th Coll 68. **d** 71 **p** 72. C Upper Gornal *Lich* 71-74; C Codsall 74-75; TV Hanley All SS 75-79; Asst P Pembroke Bermuda 79-81; V Rickerscote *Lich* 81-92; P-in-c Coven 92-99; Asst Chapl HM Pris Featherstone 92-99; Can Res Bermuda 99-04; C Houghton le Spring *Dur* 04-06; C Eppleton and Hetton le Hole 04-06; C Lyons 04-06; C Millfield St Mark and Pallion St Luke 06-09; rtd 09; PtO *Dur* from 10. *28 Monteigne Drive, Bowburn, Durham DH6 5QB* T: 0191-377 8709
E: klwassall@tiscali.co.uk

WASTELL, Canon Eric Morse. b 33. St Mich Coll Llan. **d** 62 **p** 63. C Oystermouth *S & B* 62-65; C St Jo Cathl Antigua 65-66; R St Mary 66-73; R St Paul 73-74; Dioc Registrar 69-74; Hon Can Antigua 71-74; V Swansea St Gabr *S & B* 74-98; RD Clyne 88-96; Can Brecon Cathl from 90; rtd 98. *Stella Maris Care Home, Eaton Crescent, Swansea SA1 4QR* T: (01792) 473453

WASTIE, Canon David Vernon. b 37. Open Univ BA 84. Chich Th Coll 79. **d** 81 **p** 82. C Bitterne Park *Win* 81-83; TV Chambersbury *St Alb* 83-87; V Jersey St Luke *Win* 87-94; P-in-c Jersey St Jas 87-93; V 93-94; V Jersey St Luke w St Jas 94-95; V Southbourne St Kath 95-99; Hon Can Bukavu Congo from 94; rtd 02; PtO *Derby* 05-08; *Win* 09-13; C Bournemouth St Fran 13-14. *83 Model Village, Creswell, Worksop S80 4BN*
E: canonwastie@hotmail.com

WASWA, Martin Wanyama. b 63. St Steph Ho Ox. **d** 13. C Edmonton St Mary w St Jo *Lon* from 13; C Gt Cambridge Road St Jo and St Jas from 13. *St John and St James Vicarage, 113 Creighton Road, London N17 8JS*

WATCHORN, Canon Brian. b 39. Em Coll Cam BA 61 MA 65 Ex Coll Ox BA 62. Ripon Hall Ox 61. **d** 63 **p** 64. C Bolton St Pet *Man* 63-66; Chapl G&C Coll Cam 66-74; V Chesterton St Geo *Ely* 75-82; Fell Dean and Chapl Pemb Coll Cam 82-06; Hon Can Ely Cathl from 94; Chapter Can 00-10. *34 Petersfield Mansions, Petersfield, Cambridge CB1 1BB* T: (01223) 322378
E: bw214@pem.cam.ac.uk

WATERFIELD, Janet Lyn. b 60. Birm Univ BA 06. WMMTC 99. **d** 02 **p** 03. C Bilston *Lich* 02-07; TV 07-12; P-in-c Lich Ch Ch from 12; P-in-c Longdon from 12. *Christ Church Vicarage, 95 Christ Church Lane, Lichfield WS13 8AL* T: (01543) 410751
M: 07905-539111 E: janwaterfield@blueyonder.co.uk

WATERFORD, Dean of. *See* JANSSON, The Very Revd Maria Patricia

WATERHOUSE, Canon Peter. b 46. Linc Th Coll 68. **d** 70 **p** 71. C Consett *Dur* 70-73; C Heworth St Mary 73-76; V Stockton St Chad 76-83; V Lanchester 83-11; P-in-c Holmside 03-11; AD Lanchester 90-99; Hon Can Dur Cathl 03-11; rtd 11; PtO *Dur* from 11. *7 Dissington Place, Whickham, Newcastle upon Tyne NE16 5QX*

WATERMAN, Canon Albert Thomas. b 33. Roch Th Coll 61. **d** 64 **p** 65. C Dartford St Alb *Roch* 64-67; V Ilkeston St Jo *Derby* 67-75; V Mackworth St Fran 75-79; V Dartford St Alb *Roch* 79-98; RD Dartford 84-97; Hon Can Roch Cathl 96-98; rtd 98. *19 Beachfield Road, Bembridge PO35 5TN* T: (01983) 874286

WATERMAN, Mrs Jacqueline Mahalah. b 45. ALCM 71. Cant Sch of Min 82. **dss** 85 **d** 87 **p** 94. Wavertree H Trin *Liv* 85-90; Par Dn 87-90; Par Dn Anfield St Columba 90-94; C 94; TV Speke St Aid 94-97; P-in-c Walton St Jo 97-99; V 99-01; C Baildon *Bradf* 01-05; rtd 05; PtO *Leeds* from 05. *5 Lansdowne Close, Baildon, Shipley BD17 7LA* T: (01274) 468556

WATERS (née MUNRO-SMITH), Alison Jean. b 73. Regent's Park Coll Ox MA 94. Wycliffe Hall Ox 02. **d** 04 **p** 05. C Lostwithiel, St Winnow w St Nectan's Chpl etc *Truro* 04-08; C Shepperton and Littleton *Lon* 08-12; C Sonning *Ox* from 12. *6 Park View Drive South, Charvil, Reading RG10 9QX* T: 0118-934 3723 E: alisonmunrosmith@hotmail.com

WATERS, Arthur Brian. b 34. St Deiniol's Hawarden 71. **d** 73 **p** 74. C Bedwellty *Mon* 73-76; P-in-c Newport All SS 76-81; V Mynyddislwyn 81-91; C-in-c Maesglas and Duffryn 91-95; V 95-99; rtd 99. *3B Blaen-y-Pant Crescent, Blaen-y-Pant, Newport NP20 5QB* T: (01633) 855805

WATERS, Brenda Mary. b 51. Bp Otter Coll. **d** 99. NSM Whyke w Rumboldswhyke and Portfield *Chich* 99-04; NSM Chich Cathl from 05; Chapl St Wilfrid's Hospice Chich from 01. *69 Chatsworth Road, Chichester PO19 7YA* T: (01243) 839415
E: brenda.waters@stwh.co.uk

WATERS, Mrs Carolyn Anne. b 52. St Jo Coll Nottm BA 02. **d** 00 **p** 01. NSM Frodsham *Ches* 00-02; C Penhill *Bris* 02-06; P-in-c Stopham and Fittleworth *Chich* 06-09; rtd 09. *5 Leybourne Avenue, Newcastle upon Tyne NE12 7AP* M: 07789-430317 E: carolyn.anne.waters@googlemail.com

WATERS, Geoffrey John. b 64. UMIST BSc 85 Trin Coll Bris BA 99 Qu Coll Birm MA 08 St Hild Coll Dur PGCE 86. WMMTC 06. **d** 08 **p** 09. NSM Northampton St Giles *Pet* 08-13; P-in-c Shirehampton *Bris* 13-15; C Oldland from 15. *The Vicarage, 30 Church Road, Hanham, Bristol BS15 3AE* T: 0117-329 1404 E: geoffreyjwaters@btinternet.com

WATERS, Miss Jill Christine. b 43. CertEd 64. Cranmer Hall Dur 82. **dss** 82 **d** 87 **p** 94. New Milverton *Cov* 82-86; Draycott-le-Moors w Forsbrook *Lich* 86-96; Par Dn 87-94; C 94-96; P-in-c Mow Cop 96-10; rtd 10. *5 Moreland Croft, Minworth, Sutton Coldfield B76 1XZ* M: 07908-402143 E: jcw515@talktalk.net

WATERS, John Michael. b 30. Qu Coll Cam BA 53 MA 58. Ridley Hall Cam 53. **d** 55 **p** 56. C Southport Ch Ch *Liv* 55-57; C Farnworth 57-62; V Blackb H Trin 63-70; Sec Birm Coun Chr Chs 70-77; Chapl Birm Cathl 70-74; Dioc Ecum Officer 74-77; V Hednesford *Lich* 77-93; RD Rugeley 78-88; rtd 93; P-in-c Etton w Dalton Holme *York* 93-00; PtO from 00. *Blacksmith's Cottage, Middlewood Lane, Fylingthorpe, Whitby YO22 4UB* T: (01947) 880422

WATERS, John Sangster. b 48. CQSW 75. St Mich Coll Llan 67. **d** 13 **p** 13. NSM Caerwent w Dinham and Llanvair Discoed etc *Mon* 13-14; NSM Wentwood from 14. *Cae Golwg, Mynyddbach, Shirenewton, Chepstow NP16 6RT* T: (01291) 641449 M: 07836-585250 E: john@transientwaters.com

WATERS, Kenneth Robert. b 45. ERMC. **d** 10 **p** 11. NSM Grimshoe *Ely* from 10. *6 The Avenue, Brookville, Thetford IP26 4RF* T: (01366) 727220 E: ken.waters@btinternet.com

WATERS, Mark. b 51. Southn Univ BTh 85. Sarum & Wells Th Coll 79. **d** 82 **p** 83. C Clifton All SS w St Jo *Bris* 82-85; P-in-c Brislington St Anne 85-91; Dioc Soc Resp Officer *Sheff* 91-94; Community Org Citizen Organisation Foundn 94-00; NSM Rotherham *Sheff* 94-97; Hon C Gt Crosby St Faith and Waterloo Park St Mary *Liv* 97-00; NSM 05-09; TV Kirkby 00-04; Progr Manager Participation for Change Ch Action on Poverty 04-05; NSM Toxteth Park Ch Ch and St Mich w St Andr *Liv* 09-14; NSM St Luke in the City 12-14; TV from 14. *445 Aigburth Road, Liverpool L19 3PA* E: marko.waters@gmail.com

WATERS, Stephen. b 49. Chich Th Coll 83. **d** 85 **p** 86. C Baildon *Bradf* 85-87; C Altrincham St Geo *Ches* 87-89; TV Ellesmere Port 89-91; P-in-c Crewe St Jo 91-93; V Mossley 93-98; TV Congleton 98-99; P-in-c Alvanley 99-02; V Penhill *Bris* 02-05; rtd 05. *5 Leybourne Avenue, Newcastle upon Tyne NE12 7AP* M: 07796-694139 E: stephen@soulfriend.org.uk

WATERS, William Paul. b 52. Aston Tr Scheme 84 Chich Th Coll 86. **d** 88 **p** 89. C Tottenham St Paul *Lon* 88-91; C Stroud Green H Trin 91-95; TV Wickford and Runwell *Chelmsf* 95-98; Chapl Runwell Hosp Wickford 95-98; Chapl Qu Medical Cen Nottm Univ Hosp NHS Trust 98-10; C Ilkeston H Trin *Derby* 10-12; rtd 12; P-in-c Ilkeston St Jo *Derby* from 15. *22 Teesdale Court, Beeston, Nottingham NG9 5PJ* T: 0115-917 3429 E: paulwat04@gmail.com

WATERSON, Graham Peter. b 50. **d** 07 **p** 08. OLM Astley Bridge *Man* 07-10; NSM Thame *Ox* from 10. *The Rectory, 46 High Street, Tetsworth, Thames OX9 7AS* T: (01844) 281267 M: 07747-757657 E: peter-waterson@virginmedia.com

WATERSTONE, Albert Thomas. b 23. TCD BA 45 BD 67. CITC 46. **d** 46 **p** 47. C Kilkenny St Canice Cathl 46-50; P-in-c Borris-in-Ossory w Aghavoe 50-51; I 52-54; I Fiddown w Kilmacow 54-64; I Tullamore w Lynally and Rahan *M & K* 64-73; I Tullamore w Durrow, Newtownfertullagh, Rahan etc 73-90; Can Meath 81-90; rtd 90. *Lynally House, Mocklagh, Blue Ball, Tullamore, Co Offaly, Republic of Ireland* T/F: (00353) (57) 932 1367

WATERSTREET, Canon John Donald. b 34. Trin Hall Cam BA 58 MA 62. Lich Th Coll 58. **d** 60 **p** 61. C Blackheath *Birm* 60-64; C Aston SS Pet and Paul 64-67; R Sheldon 67-73; RD Coleshill 75-77; V Selly Oak St Mary 77-89; RD Edgbaston 84-89; Hon Can Birm Cathl 86-00; R The Whitacres and Shustoke 89-97; C Acocks Green 97-00; rtd 00; PtO *Birm* 00-12. *547 Fox Hollies Road, Hall Green, Birmingham B28 8RL* T: 0121-702 2080

WATERTON, Dawn. b 46. WMMTC 95. **d** 98 **p** 99. NSM Nuneaton St Nic *Cov* 98-07; NSM Chilvers Coton w Astley from 07. *65 Main Street, Higham on the Hill, Nuneaton CV13 6AH* T: (01455) 212861

WATES, John Norman. b 43. JP 82 OBE 14. BNC Ox MA 65 Solicitor 72 FRSA 00 Hon FRAM 09. **d** 02 **p** 03. OLM Chipstead *S'wark* 02-13; PtO from 13. *Elmore, High Road, Chipstead, Coulsdon CR5 3SB* T: (01737) 557550 F: 552918 E: john.wates@btinternet.com

WATHAN, Geraint David. b 75. Univ of Wales (Abth) BTh 01. St Mich Coll Llan. **d** 07 **p** 08. C Oystermouth *S & B* 07-09; C Sketty 09-11; P-in-c Gwastedyn from 11. *The Vicarage, Dark Lane, Rhayader LD6 5DA* T: (01597) 810223 M: 07789-254165 E: g_wathan@hotmail.com

WATHERSTON, Peter David. b 42. Lon Univ BSc 69 FCA 76. Ridley Hall Cam 75. **d** 77 **p** 78. C Barnsbury St Andr *Lon* 77-81; Chapl Mayflower Family Cen Canning Town *Chelmsf* 81-96; PtO from 96; Dir First Fruit Charity from 97; PtO *Dur* from 14. *2 The Clarence, Bishop Auckland DL14 7QY* T: (01388) 606357 M: 07913-694678 E: pwatherston@aol.com

WATKIN, David Glynne. b 52. Univ of Wales (Lamp) BA 74 PhD 78 Wolv Univ PGCE 87 MTS FRGS. **d** 02 **p** 03. OLM Wolverhampton St Matt *Lich* 02-09; OLM Bilston 09-12; Bp's Officer for OLM 07-11; V Heath Hayes from 12. *St John's Vicarage, 226 Hednesford Road, Heath Hayes, Cannock WS12 3DZ* T: (01543) 274104 M: 07810-412377 E: revglynne@hotmail.co.uk

WATKIN, David William. b 42. FCA 70. Qu Coll Birm 84. **d** 86 **p** 87. C Tunstall *Lich* 86-89; Camberwell Deanery Missr *S'wark* 89-95; V Trent Vale *Lich* 95-01; V Milton 01-10; rtd 10; PtO *Lich* from 10. *33 Station Grove, Stoke-on-Trent ST2 7EA* T: (01782) 253237 E: davidwwatkin@hotmail.com

WATKIN, Deborah Gail. b 58. Wolv Univ BEd 82. **d** 08 **p** 09. OLM Wolverhampton St Matt *Lich* 08-12; NSM Heath Hayes from 13. *St John's Vicarage, 226 Hednesford Road, Heath Hayes, Cannock WS12 3DZ* E: debbie_in_the_classroom@hotmail.co.uk

WATKIN, Paul Stephen George. b 75. Anglia Ruskin Univ BA 08. Westcott Ho Cam 06. **d** 08 **p** 09. C Harwich Peninsula *Chelmsf* 08-11; P-in-c Rivenhall 11-14; TV Witham and Villages from 14. *The Rectory, Western Lane, Silver End, Witham CM8 3SA* T: (01376) 583930 E: psgw100@aol.com

WATKIN, Prof Thomas Glyn. b 52. Pemb Coll Ox BA 74 MA 77 BCL 75 Barrister-at-Law (Middle Temple) 76. Llan Dioc Tr Scheme 89. **d** 92 **p** 94. NSM Roath St Martin *Llan* from 92. *49 Cyncoed Road, Penylan, Cardiff CF23 5SB* T: (029) 2049 5662

WATKIN, Adrian Raymond. b 57. St Andr Univ MA 80. Lon Bible Coll 82. **d** 07 **p** 08. Regional Manager (Asia) CMS from 00; LtO Amritsar India from 07; PtO *St E* 08-12; C Newmarket All SS 12-15; R N Hartismere from 15. *The Rectory, Oakley, Diss IP21 4BW* M: 07958-617665 E: adrianrwatkins@cms.org.uk *or* rectornorthhartismere@gmail.com

WATKINS, Mrs Andrea. b 71. ERMC. **d** 08 **p** 09. C Heyford w Stowe Nine Churches and Flore etc *Pet* 08-11; R Blisworth, Alderton, Grafton Regis etc from 11; Tr Co-ord for Lic Ev from 11. *The Rectory, 37 High Street, Blisworth, Northampton NN7 3BJ* T: (01604) 857619 E: andrealwatkins@hotmail.co.uk

WATKINS, Andrew Graeme Darroch. b 83. Chas Sturt Univ NSW BA 05. St Mellitus Coll BA 15. **d** 15. C E Twickenham St Steph *Lon* from 15. *82 Haliburton Road, Twickenham TW1 1PH* M: 07972-123946 E: awatkins83@gmail.com

WATKINS, Anthony John. b 42. St D Coll Lamp BA 64. St Steph Ho Ox 64. **d** 66 **p** 67. C E Dulwich St Jo *S'wark* 66-71; C Tewkesbury w Walton Cardiff *Glouc* 71-75; Prec and Chapl Choral Ches Cathl 75-81; V Brixworth w Holcot *Pet* 81-12; rtd 12. *20 Bromley College, London Road, Bromley BR1 1PE* T: (020) 8290 4700

WATKINS, Betty Anne. See MOCKFORD, Betty Anne

WATKINS, Charles Mark. b 57. Bradf Univ BTech 79. Westcott Ho Cam 06. **d** 08 **p** 09. C Almondbury w Farnley Tyas *Wakef* 08-11; TV Castleford *Leeds* from 11; C Smawthorpe *Wakef* 11-12. *St Michael's Vicarage, St Michael's Close, Castleford WF10 4ER* T: (01977) 511659 M: 07828-918678 E: wattycm@mac.com

WATKINS, Christopher. b 43. Sarum & Wells Th Coll 88. **d** 90 **p** 91. C Abergavenny St Mary w Llanwenarth Citra *Mon* 90-94; TV Cwmbran 94-96; TV Wordsley *Worc* 00-09; rtd 09; PtO *Mon* 09-15; P-in-c Newport All SS from 15. *287 Malpas Road, Newport NP20 6WA* T: (01633) 556583 E: chriswat1943@gmail.com

WATKINS, David James Hier. b 39. Trin Coll Carmarthen CertEd 60 Univ of Wales DipEd 67 BEd 76. St Mich Coll Llan. **d** 90 **p** 91. NSM Oystermouth *S & B* 90-09; Dioc Youth Chapl 91-09; Lect Gorseinon Coll 92-09; rtd 09; PtO *S & B* from 09. *10 Lambswell Close, Langland, Swansea SA3 4HJ* T: (01792) 369742

WATKINS (née ROBERTS), Mrs Gwyneth. b 35. Univ of Wales (Swansea) BA MEd. St Mich Coll Llan 90. **d** 91 **p** 97. C Llanbadarn Fawr w Capel Bangor and Goginan *St D* 91-94; P-in-c Maenordeifi and Capel Colman w Llanfihangel etc 94-97; R 97-98; rtd 98; PtO *Win* 09-15. *17 Carlinford, 26 Boscombe Cliff Road, Bournemouth BH5 1JW* T: (02102) 391076 E: gwynethwatkins1@hotmail.com

WATKINS, Mrs Hilary Odette. b 47. New Hall Cam MA 73. SAOMC 98. **d** 01 **p** 02. NSM Appleton and Besselsleigh *Ox* 01-04; C Aisholt, Enmore, Goathurst, Nether Stowey etc *B & W* 04-12; rtd 12; PtO *Ox* from 13. *3 Byron Close, Abingdon OX14 5PA* T: (01235) 535847 E: hilary.watkins1@tesco.net

WATKINS (née SMITH), Mrs Irene Victoria. b 45. SRN 66 SCM 69. **d** 03 **p** 04. OLM Lawton Moor *Man* 03-11; rtd 11; PtO *Man* from 11. *288 Wythenshawe Road, Manchester M23 9DA* T: 0161-998 4100 M: 07889-116856

WATKINS, John Graham. b 48. N Lon Poly CQSW 74. WEMTC 04. **d** 07 **p** 08. NSM Ledbury *Heref* from 07. *18 Pound Close, Tarrington, Hereford HR1 4AZ* T: (01432) 890595 E: john.watkins@cafcass.gov.uk

WATKINS, Jonathan. b 58. Padgate Coll of Educn BEd 79. Trin Coll Bris 90. **d** 92 **p** 93. C Wallington *S'wark* 92-97; C Hartley Wintney, Elvetham, Winchfield etc *Win* 97-99; Chapl Win Univ 99-08; P-in-c Stockbridge and Longstock and Leckford *Win* 10-12; R Test Valley from 12. *The Rectory, 11 Trafalgar Way, Stockbridge SO20 6ET* T: (01264) 810810

WATKINS, Michael Morris. b 32. MRCS 60 LRCP 60. St Jo Coll Nottm 77. **d** 81 **p** 81. C Hornchurch St Andr *Chelmsf* 81-84; P-in-c Snitterfield w Bearley *Cov* 84-90; V 90-92; rtd 93; PtO *Cov* from 93. *Glaslyn, Riverside, Tiddington Road, Stratford-upon-Avon CV37 7BD* T: (01789) 298085 E: michaelwatkins@talktalk.net

WATKINS, Canon Peter. b 51. Oak Hill Th Coll BA. **d** 82 **p** 83. C Whitnash *Cov* 82-86; V Wolston and Church Lawford 86-99; RD Rugby 94-99; V Finham 99-10; Hon Can Cov Cathl 04-10; rtd 11; PtO *Cov* from 11; AD Rugby from 13. *23 St Margaret's Avenue, Wolston, Coventry CV8 3LJ* T: (024) 7767 5779 E: pwatkins@talktalk.net

WATKINS, Peter Gordon. b 34. St Pet Coll Ox BA 57 MA 61. Wycliffe Hall Ox 58. **d** 59 **p** 60. C Wolverhampton St Geo *Lich* 59-60; C Burton St Chad 60-61; C Westmr St Jas *Lon* 61-63; USA 63-65; V Ealing Common St Matt *Lon* from 67. *St Matthew's Vicarage, 7 North Common Road, London W5 2QA* T: (020) 8567 3820 E: peterwatkins@amserve.com

WATKINS, Robert Henry. b 30. New Coll Ox BA 54 MA 60. Westcott Ho Cam 59. **d** 60 **p** 61. C Newc H Cross 60-63; C Morpeth 63-67; V Delaval 67-80; V Lanercost w Kirkcambeck and Walton *Carl* 80-90; rtd 90; PtO *Carl* from 90. *Lowpark, Loweswater, Cockermouth CA13 0RU* T: (01900) 85242

WATKINS, Susan Jane. *See* HEIGHT, Susan Jane

WATKINS, Canon William Hywel. b 36. St D Coll Lamp BA 58. Wycliffe Hall Ox 58. **d** 61 **p** 62. C Llanelli *St D* 61-68; V Llwynhendy 68-78; V Slebech and Uzmaston w Boulston 78-01; RD Daugleddau 87-01; Hon Can St D Cathl 91-93; Can St D Cathl 93-01; rtd 01. *Nant-yr-Arian, Llanbadarn Fawr, Aberystwyth SY23 3SZ* T/F: (01970) 623359

WATKINSON, Adam John McNicol. b 68. Keble Coll Ox BA 89 MA 93. St Martin's Coll Lanc PGCE 90. NOC 01. **d** 03 **p** 04. NSM Croston and Bretherton *Blackb* 03-05; Chapl Ormskirk Sch 02-03; Chapl Liv Coll 03-06; Chapl Repton Sch Derby from 06; PtO *Lich* from 14; *Carl* from 15. *4 Boot Hill, Repton, Derby DE65 6FT* T: (01283) 559284 E: ajw@repton.org.uk

WATKINSON, Mrs Denise. b 59. St Jo Coll Nottm 13. **d** 15. NSM Hyson Green and Forest Fields *S'well* from 15. *51 Oxclose Lane, Arnold, Nottingham NG5 6FW* M: 07806-385621 E: denise.watkinson1@sky.com

WATKINSON, Neil. b 64. Univ Coll Lon BSc 86. Oak Hill Th Coll BA 04. **d** 04 **p** 05. C Maidenhead St Andr and St Mary *Ox* 04-08; C Singapore St Andr Cathl from 08. *St George's Church, Minden Road, Singapore 248816, Republic of Singapore* T: (0065) 6473 2877 E: info@stgeorges.org.sg

WATKINSON, Ronald Frank. b 48. BA. EAMTC. **d** 04 **p** 05. NSM Paston *Pet* 04-10; P-in-c Pet St Paul from 10. *St Paul's Vicarage, 414 Lincoln Road, Peterborough PE1 2PA* T: (01733) 314117 E: revronkingdomyouth@btinternet.com

WATKINSON, Stephen Philip. b 75. York Univ BSc 96 DPhil 03 Edin Univ MSc 97. Oak Hill Th Coll BTh 09. **d** 09 **p** 10. C Blackb Redeemer 09-13; V Deeplish and Newbold *Man* from 13. *St Luke's Vicarage, 9 Deeplish Road, Rochdale OL11 1NY* M: 07793-143393 E: spwatkinson@talktalk.net

WATLING, His Honour Brian. b 35. QC 79. K Coll Lon LLB 56 Barrister 57. **d** 87 **p** 88. NSM Lavenham *St E* 87-90; NSM Nayland w Wiston 90-03; NSM Boxford, Edwardstone, Groton etc 03-07; PtO from 07. *5 High Street, Nayland, Colchester CO6 4JE*

WATLING, Sister Rosemary Dawn. b 32. Newnham Coll Cam BA 70 MA 73. Gilmore Course 70. **dss** 85 **d** 87 **p** 94. CSA 79-90; Paddington St Mary *Lon* 85-86; E Bris 86-87; Hon Par Dn 87; Par Dn Clifton H Trin, St Andr and St Pet 87-94; C 94-95; rtd 95; NSM Wraxall *B & W* 96-02; PtO 02-08. *The Garden House, St Monica Trust, Cote Lane, Bristol BS9 3UN* T: 0117-949 4000

WATMORE, Mrs Georgina Jane Ann. b 63. Univ Coll Ox BA 85 MA 92 Ox Brookes Univ BA 10. SNWTP 10. **d** 12 **p** 13. C Hale and Ashley *Ches* 12-15; R Tarporley from 15. *The Rectory, High Street, Tarporley CW6 0AG* M: 07926-654707 T: (01829) 732491 E: revgeorgina@me.com

WATSON, Adam Stewart. b 75. Southn Univ BA 99. St Jo Coll Nottm 08. **d** 10 **p** 11. C Alton *Win* 10-14; V Welton and Dunholme w Scothern *Linc* from 14. *The Vicarage, Holmes Lane, Dunholme, Lincoln LN2 3QT* E: watson_adam3@sky.com

WATSON, Alan. b 41. AKC 64. St Boniface Warminster. **d** 65 **p** 66. C Hendon St Ignatius *Dur* 65-68; C Sheff St Cecilia Parson Cross 68-70; C Harton Colliery *Dur* 70-72; TV 72-74; R Gorton Our Lady and St Thos *Man* 74-82; TR Swinton St Pet 82-87; TR Swinton and Pendlebury 87-89; R Rawmarsh w Parkgate *Sheff* 89-94; P-in-c Dunscroft St Edwin 96-99; V 99-09; rtd 10; PtO *Sheff* from 10; CMP from 98. *27 Gilbert Court, Duke Street, Sheffield S2 5QQ* T: 0114-273 7484 E: alan@alansatonb.wanadoo.co.uk

WATSON, Canon Alan. b 34. Lon Univ LLB 58. Linc Th Coll 58. **d** 60 **p** 61. C Spring Park *Cant* 60-63; C Sheerness H Trin w St Paul 63-68; R Allington 68-73; P-in-c Maidstone St Pet 73; R Allington and Maidstone St Pet 73-99; Hon Can Cant Cathl 85-99; RD Sutton 86-92; rtd 99; PtO *B & W* from 00; *Sarum* from 00. *68 Southgate Drive, Wincanton BA9 9ET* T: (01963) 34368 E: arw68@mypostoffice.co.uk

WATSON, Albert Victor. b 44. Ridley Hall Cam 85. **d** 87 **p** 88. C Hornchurch St Andr *Chelmsf* 87-94; P-in-c Tye Green w Netteswell 94-95; R 95-12; RD Harlow 99-04; rtd 12; Hon C Fyfield, Moreton w Bobbingworth etc *Chelmsf* from 12. *107 The Hoo, Harlow CM17 0HS* T: (01279) 453224 E: watson.albert73@gmail.com

✠**WATSON, The Rt Revd Andrew John.** b 61. CCC Cam BA 82 MA 90. Ridley Hall Cam 84. **d** 87 **p** 88 **c** 08. C Ipsley *Worc* 87-91; C Notting Hill St Jo and St Pet *Lon* 91-96; V E Twickenham St Steph 96-08; AD Hampton 03-08; Suff Bp Aston *Birm* 08-14; Bp Guildf from 14. *Willow Grange, Woking Road, Guildford GU4 7QS* T: (01483) 590500

WATSON, Andrew Murray. b 57. St Jo Coll Nottm BA 07. **d** 07 **p** 09. C Kennington St Jo w St Jas *S'wark* 07-09; C Sanderstead 09-12; TV Monkwearmouth *Dur* from 12. *12 Ormesby Road, Sunderland SR6 9HS* M: 07970-677241 E: rev.andrew@btinternet.com

WATSON, Anne-Marie Louise. *See* RENSHAW, Anne-Marie Louise

WATSON, Beverly Anne. b 64. K Coll Cam BA 86 MA 90 Surrey Univ MA 08 ALCM 83. STETS 05. **d** 08 **p** 09. C Spring Grove St Mary *Lon* 08; C Aston and Nechells *Birm* 08-12; TV Salter Street and Shirley 12-15; V Guildf All SS from 15. *Willow Grange, Woking Road, Guildford GU4 7QS,* or *The Vicarage, 18 Vicarage Gate, Guildford GU2 7QJ* M: 07547-416721 E: beverlyannewatson@btinternet.com

WATSON, Craig. b 60. Bath Univ BSc 82 CertEd 82 York St Jo Coll MA 04. NOC 00. **d** 03 **p** 04. NSM Thorpe Edge *Bradf* 03-04; NSM Halliwell St Pet *Man* from 04. *39 New Church Road, Bolton BL1 5QQ* T: (01204) 457559 E: craig@stpetersparish.info

WATSON, David. *See* WATSON, Leonard Alexander David

WATSON, David. **d** 12. NSM Honicknowle *Ex* 12-14; NSM Ernesettle, Whitleigh and Honicknowle from 14. *23 Norfolk Road, Plymouth PL3 6BS* T: (01752) 670207 E: david@compton-it.co.uk

WATSON, The Very Revd Derek Richard. b 38. Selw Coll Cam BA 61 MA 65. Cuddesdon Coll 62. **d** 64 **p** 65. C New Eltham All SS *S'wark* 64-66; Chapl Ch Coll Cam 66-70; Bp's Dom Chapl *S'wark* 70-73; V Surbiton St Mark 73-77; V Surbiton St Andr and St Mark 77-78; Can Res and Treas S'wark Cathl 78-82; Dioc Dir of Ords 78-82; P-in-c Chelsea St Luke *Lon* 82-85; R 85-87; P-in-c Chelsea Ch Ch 86-87; R Chelsea St Luke and Ch Ch 87-96; AD Chelsea 94-96; Dean Sarum 96-02; rtd 02. *29 The Precincts, Canterbury CT1 2EP* T: (01227) 865238

WATSON, Derek Stanley. b 54. NEOC 92. **d** 95 **p** 96. C W Acklam *York* 95-98; C-in-c Ingleby Barwick CD 98-00; V Ingleby Barwick 00-06; V Middlesbrough St Martin w St Cuth 06-11; rtd 12; PtO *Dur* from 14. *3 The Brother House, Greatham, Hartlepool TS25 2HS* T: (01429) 872848 E: derek@watson1954.freeserve.co.uk

WATSON, Mrs Diane Elsie. b 44. Ches Coll of HE MA 98. NOC 92. **d** 95 **p** 96. C Grange St Andr *Ches* 95-00; C Runcorn H Trin 96-00; R Thurstaston 00-07; rtd 07; C Oxton *Ches* 08-11; PtO from 11. *32 School Lane, Prenton CH43 7RQ* T: 0151-652 4288 E: de.watson@btinternet.com

WATSON, Mrs Emma Louise. b 69. Birm Univ BA 91 Leeds Metrop Univ BSc 97 RGN 95. St Jo Coll Nottm LTh 10. **d** 10 **p** 11. NSM Birkenhead Priory *Ches* 10-13; NSM Frankby w Greasby 13-14; P-in-c Tregony w St Cuby and Cornelly *Truro*

from 14. *Cuby House, Cuby Road, Tregony, Truro TR2 5TN*
M: 07854-719655 E: rev.emmalouise012@gmail.com

WATSON, Geoffrey. b 48. Liv Univ BEd 71. Linc Th Coll 81.
d 83 **p** 84. C Hartlepool St Luke *Dur* 83-87; P-in-c Shadforth
87-94; Soc Resp Officer 87-94; Dioc Rural Development Adv
90-94; V Staveley, Ings and Kentmere *Carl* 94-13; rtd 13.
15 Hawkins Way, Helston TR13 8FQ T: (01326) 619984
E: geof_watson@talktalk.net

WATSON, Mrs Gillian Edith. b 49. Cov Coll of Educn CertEd 70.
LCTP 06. **d** 09 **p** 10. NSM Standish *Blackb* 09-14; Chapl
Wrightington Wigan and Leigh NHS Trust 09-14; rtd 14.
Address temp unknown E: gillian.e.watson@gmail.com

WATSON, Canon Gordon Mark Stewart. b 67. Wolv Poly BA 90
DipEd. CITC BTh 95. **d** 95 **p** 96. C Ballymoney w Finvoy
and Rasharkin *Conn* 95-98; I Brackaville w Donaghendry and
Ballyclog *Arm* 98-01; I Killesher *K, E & A* 01-06; I Trory w
Killadeas *Clogh* from 06; Can Clogh Cathl from 14. *Trory
Rectory, Rossfad, Ballinamallard, Enniskillen BT94 2LS*
T/F: (028) 6638 8477 M: 07710-924660
E: trory@clogher.anglican.org *or*
revd.gmswatson@btinternet.com

WATSON, Graeme Campbell Hubert. b 35. Ch Ch Ox BA 58
BA 59 MA 61. Coll of Resurr Mirfield 59. **d** 61 **p** 62. C Edin
St Mary 61-63; C Carrington *S'well* 63-67; Tutor St Cyprian's
Coll Ngala Tanzania 67-69; Vice-Prin St Mark's Th Coll Dar es
Salaam 69-73; P-in-c Dar es Salaam St Alb 74-77; P-in-c
Kingston St Mary w Broomfield *B & W* 77-80; V 80-81;
R Kingston St Mary w Broomfield etc 81-95; P-in-c Feock *Truro*
95-00; Tutor SWMTC 95-00; rtd 00; PtO *Truro* 00-02; *Lon* from
02. *75 Winston Road, London N16 9LN* T: (020) 7249 8701
E: gchwatson@blueyonder.co.uk

WATSON, Hartley Roger. b 40. Lon Univ BD 91 MTh 94. K Coll
Lon. **d** 64 **p** 65. C Noel Park St Mark *Lon* 64-67; C Munster
Square St Mary Magd 67-68; C Stamford Hill St Jo 68-70;
Chapl RAF 70-76; R St Breoke *Truro* 76-84; P-in-c Egloshayle
82-84; R Wittering w Thornhaugh and Wansford *Pet* 84-00;
RD Barnack 98-00; R Brigstock w Stanion and Lowick and
Sudborough 00-07; rtd 07; Chapl Beauchamp Community
from 07. *The Chaplain's House, Newland, Malvern WR13 5AX*
T: (01684) 891529 *or* 562100

WATSON, Henry Stanley. b 36. **d** 72 **p** 74. NSM Bethnal Green
St Jas Less *Lon* 72-83 and 89-93; NSM Old Ford St Paul w
St Steph and St Mark 83-88; NSM Scarborough St Mary w
Ch Ch and H Apostles *York* 93-97; P-in-c Seamer 97-03;
rtd 03; Hon C Fauls *Lich* 03-08. *14 Oakfield Park, Much Wenlock
TF13 6HJ* T: (01952) 728794

WATSON, The Ven Ian Leslie Stewart. b 50. Wycliffe Hall
Ox 79. **d** 81 **p** 82. C Plymouth St Andr w St Paul and St Geo
Ex 81-85; TV Ipsley *Worc* 85-90; V Woodley St Jo the Ev *Ox*
90-92; TR Woodley 92-95; Chapl Amsterdam w Den Helder
and Heiloo *Eur* 95-01; Chief Exec ICS 01-07; Can Gib Cathl
02-07; Adn Cov 07-12; rtd 12. *Church View Barn, Atterby,
Market Rasen LN8 2BJ* M: 07714-214790 T: (01673) 818121
E: i.watson440@btinternet.com

WATSON, James Valentine John Giles. b 65. Newc Univ BA 87
Ox Univ BA 91 MA 97. Ripon Coll Cuddesdon 89. **d** 92 **p** 93.
C Newc St Geo 92-95; TV Daventry, Ashby St Ledgers,
Braunston etc *Pet* 95-00; V Woodplumpton *Blackb* 00-03;
TR Wheatley *Ox* 03-10; Chapl Old Buckenham Hall Sch
10-15; Chapl Maidwell Hall Sch from 15; C Maidwell w
Draughton, Lamport w Faxton *Pet* from 15. *The Rectory,
35 Main Street, Great Oxenden, Market Harborough LE16 8NE*
T: (01858) 461992 E: jvjgwatson1@gmail.com

WATSON, The Ven Jeffrey John Seagrief. b 39. Em Coll Cam
BA 61 MA 65. Clifton Th Coll 62. **d** 65 **p** 66. C Beckenham
Ch Ch *Roch* 65-69; C Southsea St Jude *Portsm* 69-71; V Win
Ch Ch 71-81; V Bitterne 81-93; RD Southampton 83-93;
Hon Can Win Cathl 91-93; Adn Win 93-04; Hon Can Ely
Cathl 93-04; rtd 04; PtO *Win* from 04. *7 Ferry Road, Hythe,
Southampton SO45 5GB* T: (023) 8084 1189
E: jjswatson@googlemail.com

WATSON, Mrs Joanna Margaret. b 57. All SS Cen for
Miss & Min. **d** 14 **p** 15. NSM Norden w Ashworth and
Bamford *Man* from 14. *21 Westfield Close, Rochdale OL11 5XB*
T: (01706) 524657 E: jo.m.watson@tiscali.co.uk

WATSON, John. b 34. AKC 59. **d** 60 **p** 61. C Stockton St Pet
Dur 60-64; C Darlington H Trin 64-66; V Swalwell
66-68; PtO 68-69; *Leic* 69-74; *Man* 74-76; rtd 96. *The
Flat, 194 Abington Avenue, Northampton NN1 4QA* T: (01604)
624300 E: john.moirawatson@virginmedia.com

WATSON, John Calum. b 69. Spurgeon's Coll BD 96. Trin Coll
Bris MA 03. **d** 03 **p** 04. C Richmond H Trin and Ch Ch *S'wark*
03-06; TV Deptford St Jo w H Trin and Ascension 06-08;
V Tupsley w Hampton Bishop *Heref* 08-14; V Dulwich St Barn
S'wark from 14. *38 Calton Avenue, London SE21 7DG*
E: john@allyu.org.uk

WATSON, John Lionel. b 39. G&C Coll Cam BA 61 MA 65.
Ridley Hall Cam 62. **d** 64 **p** 65. C Toxteth Park St Philemon w
St Silas *Liv* 64-69; C Morden *S'wark* 69-73; C Cambridge
St Phil *Ely* 73-74; Chapl Elstree Sch Woolhampton 74-77;
R Woolhampton w Midgham *Ox* 77-81; R Woolhampton w
Midgham and Beenham Valance 81-95; PtO *Win* 97-03; rtd 00.
Westfield House, Littleton Road, Crawley, Winchester SO21 2QD
T: (01962) 776892

WATSON, Jonathan Ramsay George. b 38. Oriel Coll Ox BA 61
MA 65 DipEd 62. Ridley Hall Cam 88. **d** 90 **p** 91. C Locks
Heath *Portsm* 90-94; V Erith St Paul *Roch* 94-01; rtd 01;
PtO *Chich* from 01. *14 Park Crescent, Midhurst GU29 9ED*
T: (01730) 816145 E: jrgwatson@netscapeonline.co.uk

WATSON, Ms Joyce. b 46. Ilkley Coll TCert 68. TISEC 06. **d** 09
p 10. NSM Iona *Arg* from 10. *Beannachd, Isle of Iona PA76 6SP*
T: (01681) 700525 E: joyce@iona76.plus.com

WATSON, Mrs Julie Ann. b 61. UWE BA 95 SS Coll Cam BTh 12.
Westcott Ho Cam 09. **d** 11 **p** 12. C Malvern Link w Cowleigh
Worc 11-14; TR Worc St Barn w Ch Ch from 14. *St Barnabas'
Rectory, Church Road, Worcester WR3 8NX* T: (01905) 23785
E: revjulieann@btinternet.com

WATSON, Julie Sandra. b 59. Liv Poly BSc 81 Teesside Poly
PhD 86. NEOC 99. **d** 02 **p** 03. NSM Redcar *York* 02-12; NSM
Selby Abbey from 12; Dean Self-Supporting Min from 09.
25 Fox Lane, Thorpe Willoughby, Selby YO8 9NA
T: (01757) 241935 E: j.s.watson@tees.ac.uk *or*
julie.watson@yorkdiocese.org

WATSON, Kenneth Roy. b 27. CEng 68 MIMechE 68.
EMMTC 83. **d** 86 **p** 87. NSM Ashby-de-la-Zouch St Helen w
Coleorton *Leic* 86-90; R Breedon cum Isley Walton and
Worthington 90-93; rtd 93; PtO *Leic* from 93; *Derby* from 93.
36 Chatsworth Court, Park View, Ashbourne DE6 1PF
T: (01335) 343929 E: rev.watson@homecall.co.uk

WATSON, Laurence Leslie. b 31. Keble Coll Ox BA 55 MA 59.
Ely Th Coll. **d** 57 **p** 58. C Solihull *Birm* 57-60; C Edgbaston
St Alb 60-62; V Smethwick St Steph *Birm* 62-67; V Billesley
Common 67-95; rtd 95; PtO *Cov* from 95; *Birm* 95-12.
10 Redwing Close, Bishopton, Stratford-upon-Avon CV37 9EX
T: (01789) 294569

WATSON, Canon Leonard Alexander David. b 37. Man Univ
BSc 59. Coll of Resurr Mirfield 62. **d** 64 **p** 65. C Rawmarsh w
Parkgate *Sheff* 64-68; C Empangeni S Africa 69-74; TV E
Runcorn w Halton *Ches* 74-79; TV Sanderstead All SS *S'wark*
79-86; TR Selsdon St Jo w St Fran 86-98; RD Croydon
Addington 90-95; P-in-c Horne and Outwood 98-02; Hon
Can S'wark Cathl 02-03; rtd 02; PtO *Win* 03-13. *49 Hilley Field
Lane, Fetcham, Leatherhead KT22 9UP*
E: dadiwatson@hotmail.com

WATSON, Linda. d 15. *Address temp unknown*

WATSON, Mark. *See* WATSON, Gordon Mark Stewart

WATSON, Mark Edward. b 68. Birm Univ BEng 91. St Jo Coll
Nottm 07. **d** 09 **p** 10. C Higher Bebington *Ches* 09-13; P-in-c
Frizinghall St Marg *Leeds* from 13; P-in-c Windhill from 13.
7 Red Beck Vale, Shipley BD18 3BN T: (01274) 986447
M: 07838-441568 E: lordsmyshepherd@yahoo.co.uk

WATSON, Michael Paul. b 58. Trin Coll Bris 91. **d** 93 **p** 94.
C Derby St Alkmund and St Werburgh 93-99; Lt Rock
St Andr USA 00-01; R Bridge Community Austin from 01.
10636 Floral Park Drive, Austin TX 78759-5104, USA
T: (001) (512) 527 8823
E: mike.bridgepoint@worldnet.att.net

WATSON, Nicholas Edgar. b 67. St Cath Coll Cam BA 88
MA 92. Wycliffe Hall Ox BA 91. **d** 92 **p** 93. C Benfieldside
Dur 92-95; C-in-c Stockton Green Vale H Trin CD 95; P-in-c
Stockton H Trin 96-00; Chapl Ian Ramsey Sch Stockton 95-00;
P-in-c Breadsall and Warden of Readers *Derby* 00-09; TR
Wednesfield *Lich* from 09; RD Wulfrun from 14. *The Rectory,
9 Vicarage Road, Wednesfield, Wolverhampton WV11 1SB*
T: (01902) 731462 E: newatson@btopenworld.com

WATSON, Prof Paul Frederick. b 44. MRCVS 69 RVC(Lon)
BSc 66 BVetMed 69 Sydney Univ PhD 73 Lon Univ DSc 95.
Oak Hill NSM Course 86. **d** 88 **p** 89. NSM Muswell Hill St Jas w
St Matt *Lon* 88-96; NSM Edmonton St Aldhelm 96-01;
PtO from 01; *St Alb* from 01. *50 New Road, Ware SG12 7BY*
T: (01920) 466941 E: pwatson@rvc.ac.uk

WATSON, Paul Robert. b 66. St Andr Univ MA 89 Glas Univ
BD 95 MTh 00. **d** 00 **p** 01. C Glas St Ninian 00-04; CMS Sri
Lanka 04-09; R Bieldside *Ab* from 09. *The Rectory, Baillieswells
Road, Bieldside, Aberdeen AB15 9AP* T: (01224) 861552
M: 07552-177690 E: paulrobertwatson@gmail.com *or*
paul@stdevenicks.org.uk

WATSON, Paul William. b 55. Huddersfield Poly BA. St Jo Coll
Nottm. **d** 86 **p** 87. C Meltham Mills *Wakef* 86-89; C Meltham
89-90; TV Borehamwood *St Alb* 90-96; V Oswaldtwistle
Immanuel and All SS *Blackb* 96-08; rtd 08. *214 Union Road,
Oswaldtwistle, Accrington BB5 3EG* T: (01254) 381441

WATSON, Peter David. b 69. St Andr Univ MA 92 Westmr Coll Ox PGCE 93. Cranmer Hall Dur 04. **d** 06 **p** 07. C Boston Spa and Thorp Arch w Walton *York* 06-10; R Brayton from 10. *The Rectory, Doncaster Road, Brayton, Selby YO8 9HE* T: (01757) 704707 E: pete.d.watson@outlook.com

WATSON, Philip. b 60. RGN 83. Qu Coll Birm 86. **d** 89 **p** 90. C Ordsall *S'well* 89-93; TV Benwell *Newc* 93-99; V Stocking Farm *Leic* 99-10; R Barwell w Potters Marston and Stapleton from 10. *The Rectory, 14 Church Lane, Barwell, Leicester LE9 8DG* T: (01455) 446993 E: frpwatson@aol.com

WATSON, Richard Francis. b 40. Yorks Min Course 08. **d** 09 **p** 10. NSM Ilkley All SS *Leeds* from 09. *23 St Helen's Way, Ilkley LS29 8NP* T: (01943) 430108

WATSON, Canon Richard Frederick. b 66. Avery Hill Coll BA 87. Trin Coll Bris 91. **d** 93 **p** 94. C Kempston Transfiguration *St Alb* 93-97; TV Dunstable 97-03; R E Barnet 03-11; RD Barnet 05-11; Can Res and Sub-Dean St Alb from 11. *Deanery Barn, Sumpter Yard, Holywell Hill, St Albans AL1 1BY* T: (01727) 890201 E: rf.watson@btopenworld.com *or* subdean@stalbanscathedral.org

WATSON, Richard Rydill. b 47. Sarum & Wells Th Coll 74. **d** 77 **p** 78. C Cayton w Eastfield *York* 77-80; C Howden 80-82; P-in-c Burton Pidsea and Humbleton w Elsternwick 82-83; V Dormanstown 83-87; V Cotehill and Cumwhinton *Carl* 87-89; Chapl Harrogate Distr and Gen Hosp 89-94; Chapl Harrogate Health Care NHS Trust 94-99; Asst Chapl Oldham NHS Trust 99-02; Asst Chapl Pennine Acute Hosps NHS Trust 02-07; Chapl 07-12; P-in-c Shaw *Man* 99-07; rtd 12; PtO *Man* from 13. *10 The Gabriels, Shaw, Oldham OL2 7HU*

WATSON, Robert Bewley. b 34. Bris Univ BA 59. Clifton Th Coll 56. **d** 61 **p** 62. C Bebington *Ches* 61-65; C Woking St Jo *Guildf* 65-68; V Knaphill 68-98; rtd 98; PtO *Guildf* from 98. *Endrise, 1 Wychelm Road, Lightwater GU18 5RT* T: (01276) 453822

WATSON, Roger. *See* WATSON, Hartley Roger

WATSON, The Ven Sheila Anne. b 53. St Andr Univ MA 75 MPhil 80. Edin Th Coll 79. **dss** 79 **d** 87 **p** 94. Bridge of Allan *St And* 79-80; Alloa 79-80; Monkseaton St Mary *Newc* 80-84; Adult Educn Officer *Lon* 84-87; Hon C Chelsea St Luke and Ch Ch 87-96; Selection Sec ABM 92-93; Sen Selection Sec 93-96; Adv on CME *Sarum* 97-02; Dir of Min 98-02; Can and Preb Sarum Cathl 00-02; Adn Buckingham *Ox* 02-07; Adn Cant and Can Res Cant Cathl from 07. *29 The Precincts, Canterbury CT1 2EP* T: (01227) 865238 E: archdeacon@canterbury-cathedral.org

WATSON, Stephanie Abigail. *See* MOYES, Stephanie Abigail

WATSON, Mrs Susan Judith. b 50. Birm Univ BA 72. Qu Coll Birm 09. **d** 12 **p** 13. C Cen Wolverhampton *Lich* from 12. *6 Newbridge Avenue, Wolverhampton WV6 0LW* T: (01902) 680689 M: 07932-175846 E: suewatson@telecomplus.org.uk *or* suewatson6@gmail.com

WATSON, Timothy Daniel. b 71. ERMC. **d** 11 **p** 12. C Liv Cathl 11-15; CME Officer *Chich* from 15. *30 Cambridge Road, Hove BN3 1DF* M: 07427-685651 E: tim.watson@chemin-neuf.org *or* tim.watson@chichester.anglican.org

WATSON, Timothy James. b 79. Coll of Ripon & York St Jo BA 01 Homerton Coll Cam PGCE 02 St Jo Coll Dur BA 10 MA 12. Cranmer Hall Dur 08. **d** 11 **p** 12. C Nantwich *Ches* 11-14; Pioneer Min from 14. *30 Oakhurst Drive, Crewe CW2 6UF* E: timothyjameswatson@hotmail.com

WATSON, Canon Timothy Patrick. b 38. ALCD 66. **d** 66 **p** 67. C Northwood Em *Lon* 66-70; TV High Wycombe *Ox* 70-76; Gen Sec ICS 76-82; R Bath Weston All SS w N Stoke *B & W* 82-93; R Bath Weston All SS w N Stoke and Langridge 93-94; TR Cheltenham St Mary, St Matt, St Paul and H Trin *Glouc* 94-03; rtd 03; PtO *Glouc* from 04; Can Kitgum from 05. *The Gateways, Farm Lane, Leckhampton, Cheltenham GL53 0NN* T: (01242) 514298 E: tigertimwatson@yahoo.co.uk

WATSON, William. b 36. Ripon Hall Ox 64. **d** 66 **p** 67. C Leamington Priors H Trin *Cov* 66-69; V Salford Priors 69-74; V Malin Bridge *Sheff* 74-79; Chapl Shrewsbury R Hosps 79-89; Chapl R Hallamshire Hosp Sheff 89-92; Chapl Cen Sheff Univ Hosps NHS Trust 92-93; P-in-c Alveley and Quatt *Heref* 93-96; Chapl N Gen Hosp NHS Trust Sheff 96-01; Chapl Weston Park Hosp Sheff 96-99; Chapl Cen Sheff Univ Hosps NHS Trust 99-01; rtd 96; PtO *Sheff* 01-07. *101 Larkfield Lane, Southport PR9 8NP* T: (01704) 226055

WATSON, William Henry Dunbar. b 31. Univ of W Ontario BA 60. **d** 58 **p** 60. C Westmr St Jas *Lon* 58-60; Canada 60-04; Asst Chapl and Prec Gibraltar Cathl 04-10; rtd 10. *1803-30 Hillsboro Avenue, Toronto ON M5R 1S7, Canada*

WATSON, William Lysander Rowan. b 26. TCD BA 47 MA 50 Clare Coll Cam MA 52 St Pet Hall Ox MA 57. **d** 49 **p** 50. C Chapelizod and Kilmainham *D & G* 49-51; Tutor Ridley Hall Cam 51-55; Chapl 55-57; Chapl St Pet Coll Ox 57-93; Fell and Tutor 59-93; Sen Tutor 77-81; Vice Master 83-85;

Lect Th Ox Univ 60-93; rtd 93. *Llandaff Barn, 11 Thames Street, Eynsham, Witney OX29 4HF* T: (01865) 464198 E: lysander.watson@ntlworld.com

WATSON WILLIAMS, Richard Hamilton Patrick. b 31. SS Coll Cam BA 57 MA 62. St Aug Coll Cant. **d** 59 **p** 60. C Dorking St Paul *Guildf* 59-63; C Portsea St Mary *Portsm* 63-66; V Culgaith *Carl* 66-71; V Kirkland 66-71; V Wigton 72-79; Warden Dioc Conf Ho Crawshawbooth *Man* 79-82; P-in-c Crawshawbooth 79-82; Master Lady Kath Leveson Hosp 82-98; P-in-c Temple Balsall *Birm* 82-84; V 84-98; rtd 98; PtO *Glouc* from 98. *16 Barton Mews, Barton Road, Tewkesbury GL20 5RP* T: (01684) 290509

WATT, John Cameron. b 67. Linc Sch of Th and Min 12. **d** 15. C Linc St Nic w St Jo Newport from 15. *24 Roselea Avenue, Welton, Lincoln LN2 3RT* E: cameron.watt@aol.com

WATT-WYNESS, Gordon. b 25. Cranmer Hall Dur 70. **d** 72 **p** 73. C Scarborough St Mary w Ch Ch, St Paul and St Thos *York* 72-76; R Rossington *Sheff* 76-90; rtd 90; PtO *York* 90-11. *Room 34, Manormead, Tilford Road, Hindhead GU26 6RA* T: (01428) 602500

WATTERS, Mrs Kay. b 44. SAOMC 98. **d** 01 **p** 02. OLM Prestwood and Gt Hampden *Ox* 01-07; Chapl to Bp Buckingham 04-07; rtd 07; PtO *Ox* from 07. *44 Akamantos, 8700 Drouseia, Paphos, Cyprus* T: (00357) (26) 332128 E: kay_watters@hotmail.com

WATTERSON, The Ven Susan Mary. b 50. S & M Dioc Inst 84. **d** 87 **p** 94. NSM Rushen *S & M* 87-89; Hon Par Dn Castletown 89-94; C 94-96; Dioc Youth Officer 87-91; Bp's Adv for Healing Min 91-94; Asst Chapl Bris Univ 96-99; Hon C Bris St Mich and St Paul 96-99; Project Leader Galway Chr Tr Inst 99-00; I Youghal Union *C, C & R* 00-03; Dir Ch's Min of Healing 03-07; P-in-c Killarney w Aghadoe and Muckross *L & K* 07-13; Can Limerick, Killaloe and Clonfert Cathls 10-13; I Tralee w Kilmoyley, Ballymacelligott etc from 13; Adn Limerick, Ardfert and Aghadoe from 14. *45 Liosdara, Oakpark, Tralee, Co Kerry, Republic of Ireland* M: 87-689 2025 T: (00353) (66) 712 2245 *or* 719 5416 E: tralee@ardfert.anglican.org

WATTLEY, Jeffery Richard. b 57. Univ of Wales (Abth) BSc(Econ) 79. Trin Coll Bris BA 92. **d** 92 **p** 93. C Reading Greyfriars *Ox* 92-96; V Wonersh *Guildf* 96-98; V Wonersh w Blackheath 98-06; V Egham from 06; RD Runnymede from 13. *Mauley Cottage, 13 Manorcrofts Road, Egham TW20 9LU* T: (01784) 432066 E: jeff@stjohnsegham.com

WATTS, Mrs Aline Patricia. b 57. St Jo Coll Nottm 02. **d** 04 **p** 05. C Lache cum Saltney *Ches* 04-08; P-in-c Leasowe from 08. *St Chad's Vicarage, 70 Castleway North, Wirral CH46 1RW* T: 0151-677 6889 E: alinewatts@tiscali.co.uk

WATTS (née DUCKWORTH), Mrs Angela Denise. b 58. RN 95 RM 98. Ripon Coll Cuddesdon 05. **d** 07 **p** 08. C Malvern H Trin and St Jas *Worc* 07-10; PtO Roch 10-11; *S'wark* 11-12; *Portsm* from 11; Win 12; Chapl St Mich Hospice Basingstoke 12-13; Chapl Hants Hosps NHS Foundn Trust from 13. *The Vicarage, 157 Main Road, Colden Common, Winchester SO21 1TL* T: (01962) 711216

WATTS, Canon Anthony George. b 46. K Coll Lon BD 69 AKC 69 Lon Univ CertEd 70. Sarum & Wells Th Coll 82. **d** 84 **p** 85. C Wimborne Minster and Holt *Sarum* 84-87; P-in-c Shilling Okeford 87-92; Chapl Croft Ho Sch Shillingstone 87-92; R W Parley *Sarum* 92-00; RD Wimborne 90-00; TR Cley Hill Warminster 00-06; Can and Preb Sarum Cathl 00-06; rtd 06; Chapl Warminster Sch 07-12. *12 Freesia Close, Warminster BA12 7RL* T: (01985) 847302 E: tony.watts@btinternet.com

WATTS, Anthony John. b 30. AKC 59. **d** 60 **p** 61. C Whitburn *Dur* 60-63; C Croxdale 63-65; V Warrington St Pet *Liv* 65-70; V Peel *Man* 70-78; P-in-c Bury St Mark 78-81; V Davyhulme Ch Ch 81-99; Chapl Trafford Gen Hosp 89-94; Chapl Trafford Healthcare NHS Trust 94-98; rtd 99; PtO *Ches* from 00; *Man* from 00. *11 Brackenfield Way, Winsford CW7 2UX* T: (01606) 590803

WATTS, Daniel John. b 70. Wycliffe Hall Ox 04. **d** 06 **p** 07. C Paddock Wood *Roch* 06-09; C Harrogate St Mark *Leeds* from 09. *2 Rossett Beck, Harrogate HG2 9NT* M: 07977-126438 E: daniel.watts11@btinternet.com

WATTS, David Henry. b 27. Ex Coll Ox BA 50 MA 55. Wells Th Coll 51. **d** 53 **p** 54. C Haslemere *Guildf* 53-55; C Chelmsf Cathl 55-58; Succ Chelmsf Cathl 55-58; V Chessington *Guildf* 58-62; Educn Officer Essex Educn Cttee 62-70; HMI of Schs 70-87; Hon C Wetherby *Ripon* 79-87; P-in-c Healaugh w Wighill, Bilbrough and Askham Richard *York* 87-89; Chapl HM Pris Askham Grange 87-96; rtd 89; PtO *York* from 98. *24 Grove Road, Boston Spa, Wetherby LS23 6AP* T: (01937) 842317

WATTS, Canon Frank Walter. b 30. St Boniface Warminster 53 K Coll Lon AKC 54. **d** 54 **p** 55. C Llandough w Leckwith *Llan* 54-56; C Llanishen and Lisvane 56-59; C Gt Marlow *Ox* 59-60;

R Black Bourton 60-63; V Carterton 60-63; C-in-c Brize Norton 61-63; V Brize Norton and Carterton 63-69; Australia from 69; Hon Can Perth from 78; rtd 95. *Villa 5, 178-180 Fern Road, Wilson WA 6107, Australia* T/F: (0061) (8) 9258 4532 M: 408-094991 E: frawawa@southwest.com.au

WATTS, Canon Fraser Norman. b 46. Magd Coll Ox BA 68 MA 74 K Coll Lon MSc 70 PhD 75 CPsychol 89 FBPsS 80. Westcott Ho Cam 88. **d** 90 **p** 91. NSM Harston w Hauxton *Ely* 90-95; P-in-c 91-95; Fell Qu Coll Cam 94-13; Lect Cam Univ 94-13; Chapl Cam St Edw *Ely* 95-13; Hon Can Ely Cathl 08-13; rtd 13. *19 Grantchester Road, Cambridge CB3 9ED*
T: (01223) 359223 F: 763003 E: fraser.watts@cantab.net

WATTS, Gordon Sidney Stewart. b 40. CITC 63. **d** 66 **p** 67. C Belfast St Steph *Conn* 66-69; CF 69-94; V Boldre w S Baddesley *Win* 94-96; P-in-c Warmfield *Wakef* 96-02; Sub Chapl HM Pris Wakef 97-02; Chapl Huggens Coll Northfleet 02-07; rtd 07; PtO *Ches* from 07. *8 Bramwell Avenue, Prenton CH43 0RH* T: 0151-200 0861 M: 07967-134101
E: gss.watts@ntlworld.com

WATTS, Graham Hadley Lundie. b 74. Man Metrop Univ BA 95. Ridley Hall Cam 98. **d** 02 **p** 03. C Camberley St Paul *Guildf* 02-06; C Northwood Em *Lon* 06-14; TV Gt Marlow w Marlow Bottom, Lt Marlow and Bisham *Ox* from 14. *165 Marlow Bottom, Marlow SL7 3PL* T: (01628) 473548 E: graham.watts7@ntlworld.com

WATTS, Ian Charles. b 63. Hull Univ BA 85. Linc Th Coll 86. **d** 88 **p** 89. C W Kirby St Bridget *Ches* 88-93; V High Lane 93-00; P-in-c Newton in Mottram 00-04; P-in-c Burnley St Cuth *Blackb* 04-11; Chapl The Peterborough Sch from 11. *The Peterborough School, Thorpe Road, Peterborough PE3 6AP*
T: (01733) 343357 E: chaplain@thepeterboroughschool.co.uk

WATTS, John Michael. d 04 **p** 10. OLM Ashtead *Guildf* from 04; Asst Chapl Guy's and St Thos' NHS Foundn Trust from 04. *31 Broadhurst, Ashtead KT21 1QB* T: (01372) 275134
E: j.m.watts@btinternet.com

WATTS, John Robert. b 39. Leeds Univ BSc 60 MSc 63 DipEd 63. Oak Hill Th Coll 88. **d** 90 **p** 91. C Partington and Carrington *Ches* 90-93; P-in-c Tintwistle 93-98; V Hollingworth w Tintwistle 98-04; RD Mottram 99-03; rtd 04; PtO *Ches* from 04. *16 Norley Drive, Vicars Cross, Chester CH3 5PG* T: (01244) 350439 E: revrobwatts@hotmail.co.uk

WATTS, John Stanley. b 28. LCP 62 Birm Univ DipEd 65 MEd 72 Nottm Univ MPhil 83. Qu Coll Birm 83. **d** 86 **p** 87. Lect Wolverhampton Poly 77-90; Hon C Dudley St Fran *Worc* 86-91; Lect Wolverhampton Univ 90-93; Hon C Sedgley St Mary *Worc* 91-98; PtO from 98. *5 Warren Drive, Sedgley, Dudley DY3 3RQ* T: (01902) 661265

WATTS, Jonathan Peter (Jonah). b 52. Lon Univ BA 74. Ripon Coll Cuddesdon 07. **d** 08 **p** 09. C Crayford *Roch* 08-11; V Twyford and Owslebury and Morestead etc *Win* from 11. *The Vicarage, 157 Main Road, Colden Common, Winchester SO21 1TL* T: (01962) 711216
E: jonah.watts1@btinternet.com

WATTS, Mrs Mary Kathleen. b 31. Lon Univ BA 86. Gilmore Ho 73. **dss** 77 **d** 87 **p** 94. Lower Streatham St Andr *S'wark* 77-88; C 87-88; C Streatham Immanuel w St Anselm 87-88; C Streatham Immanuel and St Andr 90-91; rtd 91; PtO *S'wark* 91-94 and from 05; Hon C Norbury St Oswald 94-05; PtO *Roch* from 10. *15 Bromley College, London Road, Bromley BR1 1PE* T: (020) 8290 6615

WATTS, Matthew David. b 79. Clare Coll Cam BA 01 MA 04 MSci 01 St Jo Coll Dur BA 05. Cranmer Hall Dur 03. **d** 06 **p** 07. C Comberton and Toft w Caldecote and Childerley *Ely* 06-09; V Burnside-Harewood New Zealand from 09. *40 Kendal Avenue, Burnside, Christchurch 8053, New Zealand* T: (0064) (3) 358 8174 E: vicar@burnside.org.nz

WATTS, Paul George. b 43. Nottm Univ BA 67. Wells Th Coll 67. **d** 69 **p** 70. C Sherwood *S'well* 69-74; Chapl Trent (Nottm) Poly 74-80; V Nottingham All SS 80-84; Public Preacher 84-06; rtd 06. *14 Tynd Grove, Nottingham NG3 5AD* T: 0115-960 9964 M: 07952-369066
E: wattses@yahoo.co.uk

WATTS, Sir Philip Beverley. b 45. KCMG 02. Leeds Univ BSc 66 MSc 69 Ox Brookes Univ BA 11 FInstP 80 FEI 90 FGS 98 FRGS 98. Ox Min Course 09. **d** 11 **p** 12. NSM Binfield *Ox* 11-13; P-in-c Waltham St Lawrence from 13. *Sunnyridge, Hill Farm Lane, Binfield, Bracknell RG42 5NR* T: (01344) 305965
E: philbwatts@gmail.com

WATTS (née SIMPER), Rachel Dawn. b 67. K Coll Lon BD 89. Westcott Ho Cam 90. **d** 92 **p** 94. Par Dn Clitheroe St Mary *Blackb* 92-94; C 94-95; C Nor St Pet Mancroft w St Jo Maddermarket 95-97; V Slyne w Hest *Blackb* 97-04; V Briercliffe 04-11; Women's Min Adv 00-11; Hon Can Blackb Cathl 10-11; R Uppingham w Ayston and Belton w Wardley *Pet* from 11; Asst Dir Ords from 14. *The Rectory, London Road, Uppingham, Oakham LE15 9TJ* T: (01572) 829956
E: rwatts789@btinternet.com

WATTS, Ms Rebecca Harriet. b 61. St Cath Coll Cam BA 83 MA. Wycliffe Hall Ox 87. **d** 90 **p** 94. C Goldsworth Park *Guildf* 90-94; Chapl Wadh Coll Ox 94-97; C Ox St Mary V w St Cross and St Pet 94-97; Chapl Somerville Coll Ox 97-98; PtO *Newc* 98-99 and from 02. *7 Westfield Avenue, Newcastle upon Tyne NE3 4YH* T: 0191-285 9840
E: rebecca.h.watts@blueyonder.co.uk

WATTS, Robert. *See* WATTS, John Robert

WATTS, Roger Edward. b 39. S'wark Ord Course 85. **d** 88 **p** 89. C Belmont *S'wark* 88-92; R Godstone 92-97; R Godstone and Blindley Heath 97-09; rtd 09; PtO *S'wark* from 09; Hon C Storrington *Chich* 09-15. *9 Longland Avenue, Storrington, Pulborough RH20 4HY* T: (01903) 740205
E: roger@watts39.wanadoo.co.uk

WATTS, Roger Mansfield. b 41. Univ of Wales (Cardiff) BSc 63 CEng 76 MIET 76. Chich Th Coll 89. **d** 91 **p** 92. C Chippenham St Andr w Tytherton Lucas *Bris* 91-93; C Henfield w Shermanbury and Woodmancote *Chich* 93-96; R Jedburgh *Edin* 96-99; R Wingerworth *Derby* 99-06; rtd 06; PtO *Llan* from 14. *99 Ffordd Maendy, Sarn, Bridgend CF32 9GF* T: (01656) 724928

WATTS, Ms Samantha Alison Lundie. b 70. Birm Univ BA 92 Cam Univ BA 01. Ridley Hall Cam 99. **d** 02 **p** 03. C Camberley St Paul *Guildf* 02-06; NSM Northwood Em *Lon* 06-14; TV Gt Marlow w Marlow Bottom, Lt Marlow and Bisham *Ox* from 14. *165 Marlow Bottom, Marlow SL7 3PL* T: (01628) 473548 E: samiwatts@btinternet.com

WATTS, Scott Antony. b 67. JP 08. FRMetS 99 MCMI 00 FRSA 12. EAMTC 00. **d** 03 **p** 04. NSM Brampton *Ely* 03-07; Chapl St Jo Hospice Moggerhanger 07-09; Lead Chapl Hinchingbrooke Health Care NHS Trust from 09. *Hinchingbrooke Health Care NHS Trust, Hinchingbrooke Hospital, Huntingdon PE29 6NT* T: (01480) 847474 M: 07701-039140
E: scott.watts@nhs.net

WATTS, Thomas Annesley. b 79. K Coll Cam BA 01 MA 05. Oak Hill Th Coll MTh 08. **d** 08 **p** 09. C Wharton *Ches* 08-12; C Gt Chesham *Ox* from 12. *230 Chartridge Lane, Chesham HP5 2SF* T: (01494) 786789 M: 07764-679210 E: tom@tomandsue.net

WATTS, Mrs Valerie Anne. b 44. UEA BEd 79. EAMTC 90. **d** 93 **p** 94. NSM N Walsham and Edingthorpe *Nor* 93-14; PtO from 15. *15 Millfield Road, North Walsham NR28 0EB* T: (01692) 405119 E: rev.valwatts@outlook.com

WATTS, William Henry Norbury. b 51. CertEd. St Jo Coll Nottm 87. **d** 89 **p** 90. C S Molton w Nymet St George, High Bray etc *Ex* 89-93; TV Swanage and Studland *Sarum* 93-10; P-in-c Basildon w Aldworth and Ashampstead *Ox* 10-14; V from 14; P-in-c Sulhamstead Abbots and Bannister w Ufton Nervet from 14; AD Bradfield from 11. *The Vicarage, Pangbourne Road, Upper Basildon, Reading RG8 8LS* T: (01491) 671714 E: revwillwatts@btinternet.com

WAUD, John David. b 31. NOC 82. **d** 85 **p** 86. C Cayton w Eastfield *York* 85-88; R Brandesburton 88-93; R Beeford w Frodingham and Foston 93-99; rtd 99; PtO *York* from 00. *21 Lowfield Road, Beverley HU17 9RF* T: (01482) 864726
E: jdw2@jdw2.karoo.co.uk

WAUDBY, Miss Christine. b 45. TCert 66. Trin Coll Bris. **d** 90 **p** 94. C Weston-super-Mare Ch Ch *B & W* 90-94; C Blackheath *Birm* 94-99; PtO 99-03; NSM Ipsley *Worc* 03-10; rtd 10; PtO *Heref* from 11. *2 Coppice Close, Withington, Hereford HR1 3PP*

WAUDE, Andrew Leslie. b 74. Leeds Univ BA 02. Coll of Resurr Mirfield 99. **d** 02 **p** 03. C Swinton and Pendlebury *Man* 02-05; C Lower Broughton Ascension 05-07; P-in-c Nottingham St Geo w St Jo *S'well* 07-12; P-in-c Sneinton St Cypr from 07. *The Vicarage, 19 Marston Road, Nottingham NG3 7AN* T: 0115-940 2868 M: 07708-004478
E: father.waude@googlemail.com

WAUGH, Ian William. b 52. Bede Coll Dur DipEd 74 BEd 75. NEOC 99. **d** 02 **p** 03. NSM Benfieldside *Dur* from 02. *36 Muirfield Close, Shotley Bridge, Consett DH8 5XE* T: (01207) 591923 M: 07808-412953
E: ian-barbara-waugh@lineone.net

WAUGH, Mrs Jane Leitch. b 38. CertEd 61 Toronto Univ MDiv 83. Trin Coll Toronto 80. **d** 84 **p** 94. Canada 84-87; Par Dn Dunnington *York* 88-90; PtO 90-93 and from 96; NSM York St Olave w St Giles 93-96; rtd 96. *c/o Messrs Langleys, Queens House, Micklegate, York YO1 6WG* T: (01904) 610886

WAUGH, Nigel John William. b 56. TCD BA 78 MA 81. CITC 76. **d** 79 **p** 80. C Ballymena w Ballyclug *Conn* 79-82; C Ballyholme *D & D* 82-84; I Bunclody w Kildavin *C & O* 84-85; I Bunclody w Kildavin, Clonegal and Kilrush 86-91 and I 91-98; Preb Ferns Cathl 88-91; Treas 91-96; Radio Officer (Cashel) 90-91; (Ferns) 92-98; Dioc Info Officer (Ferns) *C & O* 91-98; Prec Ferns Cathl 96-98; I Delgany *D & G* from 98. *The Rectory, 8 Elsinore, Delgany, Greystones, Co Wicklow, Republic of Ireland* T: (00353) (1) 287 4515 M: 86-102 8888
E: nigelwaugh@gmail.com

WAWERU, <u>Francis</u> John. b 55. CA Tr Coll Nairobi 82 Bp Kariuki Bible Coll 90. **d** 00 **p** 91. Kenya 90-98; V Uthip w Kikuyu 94-97; V Kamangu 97-98; PtO *Chelmsf* 01-03; *Bradf* 04-10; *Birm* from 10. *52 Gravelly Hill North, Erdington, Birmingham B23 6BB* T: 0121-686 0427 M: 07478-686101
E: fgwaweru@hotmail.com

WAXHAM, Derek Frank. b 33. Oak Hill Th Coll 76. **d** 79 **p** 80. NSM Old Ford St Paul w St Steph and St Mark *Lon* 79-89; NSM Bow w Bromley St Leon from 89. *39 Hewlett Road, London E3 5NA* T: (020) 8980 1748

WAY, Miss Alison Janet. b 61. York Univ BSc 83 FIBMS 86. St Mich Coll Llan 02. **d** 04 **p** 05. C Basingstoke *Win* 04-08; P-in-c Woodhill *Sarum* 08-10; R 10-14; NSM R Wootton Bassett and Lyneham w Bradenstoke 11-14; P-in-c S Nutfield w Outwood *S'wark* 14-15; V S Nutfield from 15; Officer for Lay Miss and Min Croydon Area from 14. *The Vicarage, 136 Mid Street, South Nutfield, Redhill RH1 5RP* T: (01737) 822211
E: revalisonway@gmail.com

WAY, Andrew Lindsay. b 43. Linc Th Coll 76. **d** 78 **p** 79. C Shenfield *Chelmsf* 78-82; C Waltham *Linc* 82-84; V New Waltham 84-89; R Duxford *Ely* 89-94; V Hinxton 89-94; V Ickleton 89-94; P-in-c Doddington w Benwick 94-97; P-in-c Wimblington 94-97; R Doddington w Benwick and Wimblington 97-98; R Eythorne and Elvington w Waldershare etc *Cant* 98-09; AD Dover 00-03; rtd 09; PtO *Cant* from 09. *The Vicarage, Thanet Road, Westgate-on-Sea CT8 8PB*
E: albeway@clara.net

WAY, Mrs Barbara Elizabeth. b 47. Open Univ BA 82 Hull Univ PGCE 86. Linc Th Coll IDC 78. **dss** 78 **d** 87 **p** 94. Shenfield *Chelmsf* 78-82; Adult Educn Adv *Linc* 82-85; Dioc Lay Min Adv 85; New Waltham 82-89; Min 87-89; Tetney 86-89; Min 87-89; NSM Duxford, Ickleton and Hinxton *Ely* 89-94; Dir Past Studies EAMTC 91-94; Min Pampisford 92-94; P-in-c Coates 94-95; TV Whittlesey, Pondersbridge and Coates 95-98; Local Min Adv *Cant* 98-02; Dioc Dir of Reader Selection and Tr 00-02; Dioc Adv in Women's Min 02-04; P-in-c Whitfield w Guston 02-10; Chapl E Kent Hosps NHS Trust 06-08; rtd 10; PtO *Cant* 10-13; C Westgate St Sav from 13. *The Vicarage, Thanet Road, Westgate-on-Sea CT8 8PB* E: belway@clara.co.uk

WAY, Colin George. b 31. St Cath Coll Cam BA 55 MA 59 Lon Inst of Educn PGCE 58. EAMTC. **d** 84 **p** 85. NSM Hempnall *Nor* 84-87; C Gaywood, Bawsey and Mintlyn 87-90; R Acle w Fishley and N Burlingham 90-96; RD Blofield 95-96; rtd 96; PtO *Nor* 96-97 and from 02; P-in-c Pulham Market, Pulham St Mary and Starston 97-99; Hon C Eaton 99-02. *347 Unthank Road, Norwich NR4 7QG* T: (01603) 458363
E: colin.way@ntlworld.com

WAY, David. b 54. Pemb Coll Ox MA DPhil St Jo Coll Dur BA. Cuddesdon Coll 83. **d** 85 **p** 86. C Chenies and Lt Chalfont *Ox* 85-87; C Chenies and Lt Chalfont, Latimer and Flaunden 87-88; Tutor and Dir Studies Sarum & Wells Th Coll 88-93; Selection Sec Min Division from 94; Sec Minl Educn Cttee from 94; Th Educn Sec Min Division from 99. *Ministry Division, Church House, Great Smith Street, London SW1P 3AZ* T: (020) 7898 1405 F: 7898 1421
E: david.way@churchofengland.org

WAY, David Charles. b 61. St Mich Coll Llan BTh 94. **d** 97 **p** 98. C Cardiff St Mary and St Steph w St Dyfrig etc *Llan* 97-02; V Aberaman and Abercwmboi w Cwmaman 02-15; P-in-c Plymouth St Pet and H Apostles *Ex* from 15. *St Peter's Vicarage, 23 Wyndham Square, Plymouth PL1 5EG* T: (01752) 240119
E: fr.dave@virgin.net

WAY, Lawrence William. b 32. St Mich Coll Llan 77. **d** 79 **p** 80. C Merthyr Dyfan *Llan* 79-82; V Abercynon 82-84; TV Cwmbran *Mon* 84-86; V Caerwent w Dinham and Llanfair Discoed etc 86-90; V Pontnewydd 90-93; rtd 93; PtO *Llan* from 03. *8 Ceredig Court, Llanyravon, Cwmbran NP44 8SA* T: (01633) 865309 F: 876830 E: frway.angelus@virgin.net

WAY, Michael David. b 57. K Coll Lon BD 78 AKC 78. St Steph Ho Ox 79. **d** 80 **p** 83. C Bideford *Ex* 80-81; Hon C Wembley Park St Aug *Lon* 81-84; C Kilburn St Aug w St Jo 84-89; V Earlsfield St Jo *S'wark* 89-92; Project Co-ord CARA 92-99; Consultant Cen Sch for Counselling and Therapy 99-00; Dir RADICLE *Lon* from 00. *14 St Peter's Gardens, London SE27 0PN* T: (020) 8670 3439 *or* 7932 1129

WEAKLEY, Susan Margaret. b 52. SEITE 05. **d** 08 **p** 09. NSM Merstham and Gatton *S'wark* 08-10; NSM Merstham, S Merstham and Gatton 10-13; NSM Reigate St Mark from 13. *81 Parkhurst Road, Horley RH6 8EX* T: (01293) 786693
M: 07887-888372

WEARING, Miss Julie Ann. b 65. Cov Poly BSc 89 St Jo Coll Dur BA 12. Cranmer Hall Dur 10. **d** 12 **p** 13. C Upton cum Chalvey *Ox* from 12. *21 Palmerston Avenue, Slough SL3 7PU* M: 07810-822405 E: julie.wearing@btinternet.com

WEARING, Malcolm Jamieson. b 72. Salford Univ BEng 94 PhD 00. All SS Cen for Miss & Min 11. **d** 14 **p** 15. OLM Farnworth, Kearsley and Stonecloough *Man* from 14. *16 Butterfield Road, Bolton BL5 1DU* T: (01204) 658334
E: malcolm@stjohnsfarnworth.co.uk

WEARMOUTH, Alan Wilfred. b 54. Bris Univ BEd 76. Glouc Sch of Min 85. **d** 88 **p** 89. NSM Coleford w Staunton *Glouc* 88-06; C Coleford, Staunton, Newland, Redbrook etc from 06. *Windhover, 2 Broadwell Bridge, Broadwell, Coleford GL16 7GA* T: (01594) 832660 M: 07811-118736
E: alanw22uk@yahoo.co.uk

WEARN, Simon Joseph. b 76. Pemb Coll Cam BA 00 MEng 00. Oak Hill Th Coll BA 09. **d** 09 **p** 10. C Gt Faringdon w Lt Coxwell *Ox* 09-13; R Hinckley H Trin *Leic* from 13. *Holy Trinity Vicarage, 1 Cleveland Road, Hinckley LE10 0AJ* M: 07980-910104 E: sjwearn@gmail.com

WEATHERHOGG, Susanne. *See* JUKES, Susanna

WEATHERILL, Stephen Robert. b 70. Roehampton Inst BA 98 Nottm Univ MA 00. St Jo Coll Nottm 98. **d** 00 **p** 02. C Bridlington Priory *York* 00-01; NSM Kendal St Thos *Carl* from 02. *31 Hallgarth Circle, Kendal LA9 5NW*
E: stephen@stkmail.org.uk

WEATHERLEY, Miss Mary Kathleen. b 36. SRN 57 SCM 59. SWMTC 78. **dss** 82 **d** 87 **p** 94. Littleham w Exmouth *Ex* 82-84; Heavitree w Ex St Paul 85-87; Hon Par Dn 87-88; Chapl Asst R Devon and Ex Hosp 85-93; LtO *Ex* 88-94; NSM Littleham w Exmouth from 98. *11 The Hollows, Exmouth EX8 1QT* T: (01395) 265528

WEATHERSTONE, Timothy Andrew Patrick. b 59. Bedf Coll Lon BSc 81 UEA MSc 82 Anglia Ruskin Univ BA 12. ERMC 05. **d** 08 **p** 09. C Bowthorpe *Nor* 08-11; C Shipdham w Bradenham 11-12; TV Barnham Broom and Upper Yare 11-15; TR from 15. *The Rectory, The Street, Reymerston, Norwich NR9 4AG* T: (01362) 858748 M: 07967-190976 *or* 858021
E: timweatherstone@mac.com *or* bb.office@btinternet.com

WEAVER, Alan William. b 63. Linc Th Coll 95. **d** 95 **p** 96. C Seaford w Sutton *Chich* 95-98; C Langney 98-01; P-in-c The Haven CD 02-05; P-in-c Jarvis Brook 05-07; V from 07. *St Michael's Vicarage, Crowborough Hill, Crowborough TN6 2HJ* T: (01892) 661565 E: angyalanweaver@waitrose.com

WEAVER, Angela Mary. *See* TOWNSHEND, Angela Mary

WEAVER, Brian John. b 34. Oak Hill Th Coll 82. **d** 84 **p** 85. C Nailsea H Trin *B & W* 84-88; R Nettlebed w Bix and Highmore *Ox* 88-98; rtd 98; Hon C Warfield *Ox* 99-05; PtO *Lich* from 06. *11A Leslie Road, Sutton Coldfield B74 3BS* T: 0121-580 8086 E: bri_jac@onetel.com

WEAVER, David Anthony. b 43. Hatf Coll Dur BSc 65. Lich Th Coll 68. **d** 71 **p** 72. C Walsall Wood *Lich* 71-75; C Much Wenlock w Bourton *Heref* 75-76; Canada 76-79 and 82; V Mow Cop *Lich* 79-82; P-in-c Burntwood 82-00; V 00-08; Chapl St Matt Hosp Burntwood 83-95; rtd 08. *Stone Gables, Ampney Crucis, Cirencester GL7 5RS* T: (01285) 851674

WEAVER, David Sidney George. b 46. Univ of Wales (Cardiff) BA 67 MA 71 Goldsmiths' Coll Lon MA 01 Lon Univ CertEd 76. SEITE 07. **d** 09 **p** 10. NSM Hove All SS *Chich* 09-12; P-in-c Haywards Heath St Rich from 12. *St Richard's Vicarage, Queens Road, Haywards Heath RH16 1EB* T: (01444) 413621
M: 07811-145656 E: frdavidweaver@gmail.com

WEAVER, Mrs Diane Beverley. b 57. LCTP 06. **d** 09 **p** 10. C Steeton *Bradf* 09-13; V Barnoldswick w Bracewell *Leeds* from 13. *131 Gisburn Road, Barnoldswick BB18 5JU* T: (01282) 812028 E: diane.weaver@bradford.anglican.org

WEAVER, Duncan Charles. b 60. Open Univ BA 99. St Jo Coll Nottm 92. **d** 94 **p** 95. C Watford *St Alb* 94-98; TV Bourne Valley *Sarum* 98-01; CF from 01. *c/o MOD Chaplains (Army)* F: 381824 T: (01264) 383430

WEAVER, Fiona Margaret. b 61. Westcott Ho Cam 99. **d** 00 **p** 01. C Islington St Jas w St Pet *Lon* 00-03; Asst Chapl Univ of N Lon 00-02; Asst Chapl Lon Metrop Univ 01-03; Chapl 03-05; Lead Chapl 05-11; Family and Youth Work Adv 12-13; P-in-c Purley St Swithun *S'wark* from 13; P-in-c Purley St Mark from 13. *The Vicarage, 2 Church Road, Purley CR8 3QQ* T: (020) 8668 0063 E: fionathegooner@gmail.com

WEAVER, Ian Douglas. b 65. Ridley Coll Melbourne BMin 96. **d** 96 **p** 96. C Essendone St Thos Australia 96; C E Frankston 97-98; TV Rushden St Mary w Newton Bromswold *Pet* 98-02; Dioc Youth Min Facilitator Melbourne Australia 03-05; P-in-c E Geelong from 05. *230 McKillop Street, East Geelong Vic 3219, Australia* T: (0061) (3) 5241 6895 *or* 5221 5353 F: 5222 5400 M: 409-604006 E: ianweaver@optusnet.com.au

WEAVER, Canon John. b 28. Ex Coll Ox BA 51 MA 55. St Steph Ho Ox 52. **d** 55 **p** 56. C Ex St Dav 55-58; S Africa from 58; Hon Can Mthatha from 81; Adn Midl S Africa 84-95; Hon Can Pietermaritzburg from 95. *PO Box 56, Underberg, 3257 South Africa* T: (0027) (33) 701 1124

WEAVER, Mrs Joyce Margaret. b 43. **d** 00 **p** 01. OLM Warrington St Ann *Liv* 00-13; rtd 13. *71 Orford Avenue, Warrington WA2 8PQ* T: (01925) 634993
E: joycearniew@aol.com

WEAVER, Martyn Graham. b 71. Salford Univ BEng 93. Cranmer Hall Dur 10. **d** 12 **p** 13. C Selby Abbey *York* from 12. *49 Woodville Terrace, Selby YO8 8AJ* T: (01904) 610491
E: martyn.weaver@tesco.net

WEAVER, Canon Michael Howard. b 39. Southn Univ MPhil 95 DipArch. Chich Th Coll 63. **d** 66 **p** 67. C Kidderminster St Jo *Worc* 66-69; Cathl Chapl and Dioc Architect Br Honduras 69-71; TV Droitwich *Worc* 71-76; V Arundel w Tortington and S Stoke *Chich* 76-96; P-in-c Clymping 84-87; RD Arundel and Bognor 88-93; Sub-Chapl HM Pris Ford 77-96; V Lymington *Win* 96-04; Chapl Southn Community Services NHS Trust 96-01; Chapl Southn City Primary Care Trust 01-04; rtd 04; Hon Can Enugu from 94; PtO *Win* 04-14; *Portsm* from 04; AD W Wight 10-12; PtO *Chich* from 14. *Tau Cottage, Crossbush, Arundel BN18 9PJ* T: (01903) 885087
E: junovicarage@hotmail.com

WEAVER, Canon William. b 40. Man Univ BA 63 BD 65. **d** 74 **p** 75. Lect Th Leeds Univ 67-91; Hon C Clifford *York* 82-86; Chapl K Edw Sch Birm 91-94; Provost Woodard Schs (Midl Division) 94-03; Hon Can Derby Cathl from 96; PtO from 96. *20 St Peter's Garth, Thorner, Leeds LS14 3EE* T: 0113-289 3689

WEBB, Alwyn Charles. b 62. Oak Hill Th Coll BA 95 K Coll Lon PGCE 96 MA 13. St Mellitus Coll 11. **d** 13 **p** 14. C Richmond H Trin and Ch Ch *S'wark* from 13. *23 Grena Road, Richmond TW9 1XU* T: (020) 8404 1112
E: alwynwebb87@hotmail.com

WEBB, Mrs Amy Lavinia. b 75. STETS 12. **d** 15. C Botley *Portsm* from 15; C Curdridge from 15; C Durley from 15. *78 Jenkyns Close, Botley, Southampton SO30 2UU* T: (01489) 790901
E: rev.amywebb@yahoo.co.uk

WEBB, Anthony John. b 24. Sarum & Wells Th Coll 79. **d** 81 **p** 82. C Yeovil *B & W* 81-84; P-in-c Cossington 84-87; P-in-c Woolavington 84-87; P-in-c Bawdrip 87; R Woolavington w Cossington and Bawdrip 87-91; rtd 91; PtO *B & W* from 91. *18 Channel Court, Burnham-on-Sea TA8 1NE* T: (01278) 787483

WEBB, Arthur Robert. b 33. Lanc Univ MA 82 FRSA LCP 67. Wells Th Coll 69. **d** 70 **p** 70. C W Drayton *Lon* 70-72; Hd Master St Jas Cathl Sch Bury St Edmunds 72-86; Min Can St E Cathl 72-87; Succ St E Cathl 81-87; P-in-c Seend and Bulkington *Sarum* 87-88; V 88-91; R Heytesbury and Sutton Veny 91-96; rtd 96; PtO *B & W* from 96; *Sarum* from 98; *Bris* from 00; P-in-c Las Palmas *Eur* 04-08. *27 Marlborough Buildings, Bath BA1 2LY* T: (01225) 484042

WEBB, Mrs Barbara Mary. b 39. Bedf Coll Lon BA 60 Cam Univ DipEd 61. Wycliffe Hall Ox 00. **d** 02 **p** 03. NSM Cumnor *Ox* 02-05; NSM Stanford in the Vale w Goosey and Hatford 05-09; P-in-c Shippon 09-10; rtd 10; PtO *Ox* 10-14; *Ches* from 14. *72A Station Road, Marple, Stockport SK6 6NY* T: 0161-221 2414
E: derry_barbara@msn.com

WEBB, Mrs Brenda Lynn. b 45. Stockwell Coll of Educn CertEd 66. EAMTC 97. **d** 00 **p** 01. NSM Saxmundham w Kelsale cum Carlton *St E* 00-10; Teacher Beacon Hill Sch 00-10; rtd 10; PtO *St E* from 12. *48 Pightle Close, Elmswell, Bury St Edmunds IP30 9EL* T: (01359) 242925

WEBB, Catharine Rosemary Wheatley. b 39. **d** 05 **p** 06. OLM Redhill St Matt *S'wark* from 05; PtO from 09. *6 Hurstleigh Drive, Redhill RH1 2AA* T/F: (01737) 769763
M: 07709-700602 E: webbcrw8@ntlworld.com

WEBB, Christopher Scott. b 70. Univ of Wales (Abth) BSc. Trin Coll Bris BA 96. **d** 96 **p** 97. C Dafen *St D* 96-98; C Cowbridge *Llan* 98-01; Officer for Renewal, Par Development and Local Ecum 01-04; V Llanfair Caereinion, Llanllugan and Manafon *St As* 04-07; President of Renovaré USA 07-12; V Lampeter *St D* 12-14; Dioc Spirituality Adv and Dep Warden Launde Abbey *Leic* from 14. *Launde Abbey, Launde Road, Launde, Leicester LE7 9XB* T: (01572) 717254

WEBB, Mrs Diane. b 45. **d** 93 **p** 94. OLM Stowmarket *St E* 93-05; OLM Haughley w Wetherden and Stowupland 05-10; Chapl W Suffolk Hosps NHS Trust from 10. *36 Wordsworth Road, Stowmarket IP14 1TT* T: (01449) 677880
E: revdiane.webb@btinternet.com

WEBB, Diane Silvia. Birm Univ BA 66 Dur Univ MA 93. NOC 82. **dss** 85 **d** 03 **p** 04. Wyther *Ripon* 85-86; PtO *York* 95-99; rtd 03; NSM Bow Common *Lon* 03-08; PtO *Cant* 08-09; NSM Selling w Throwley, Sheldwich w Badlesmere etc 09-13; PtO from 13. *13 Neames Forstal, Selling, Faversham ME13 9PP* T: (01227) 750144 E: diane@webb.lcbroadband.co.uk

WEBB, Dominic Mark. b 68. Oriel Coll Ox BA 91. Wycliffe Hall Ox BA 93. **d** 96 **p** 97. C Cradley *Worc* 96-99; C Leyton Ch Ch *Chelmsf* 99-02; P-in-c St Helier *S'wark* 02-06; Hon C Stratford St Paul and St Jas *Chelmsf* from 07. *32A Lister Road, London E11 3DS* T: (020) 8558 6354 E: webbdom@googlemail.com

WEBB, Mrs Eileen Marion. b 46. Bingley Coll of Educn CertEd. **d** 08 **p** 09. OLM Cheriton St Martin *Cant* 08-11; OLM

Cheriton All So w Newington 08-11; OLM Cheriton w Newington from 11. *4 Westfield Lane, Etchinghill, Folkestone CT18 8BZ* T: (01303) 864272 F: 864272 M: 07867-546929
E: bryleen@aol.com

WEBB, Frances Mary. See BATTIN, Frances Mary

WEBB, Mrs Gillian Anne. b 49. Whitelands Coll Lon CertEd 71 Heythrop Coll Lon MA 04. St Alb Minl Tr Scheme 83. **dss** 86 **d** 87 **p** 94. Kempston Transfiguration *St Alb* 86-96; NSM 87-96; NSM Kempston All SS 96-08; P-in-c Marston Morteyne w Lidlington from 08. *2 Hillson Close, Marston Moretaine, Bedford MK43 0QN* T: (01234) 767256
E: webbg@marston3.freeserve.co.uk

WEBB, Canon Gregory John. b 55. Man Univ LLB 77. Oak Hill Th Coll 89. **d** 91 **p** 92. C Bury St Edmunds St Geo *St E* 91-94; P-in-c Bury St Edmunds All SS 94-02; TR Bury St Edmunds All SS w St Jo and St Geo 02-08; RD Thingoe 01-08; P-in-c Sudbury and Chilton from 08; RD Sudbury from 13; Hon Can St E Cathl from 07. *The Rectory, Christopher Lane, Sudbury CO10 2AS* T: (01787) 372611
E: gregorywebb@btinternet.com

WEBB, Mrs Glenda Marjorie. b 61. Yorks Min Course 13. **d** 15. NSM Brayton *York* from 15. *Rockside, Springfield, Boston Spa, Wetherby LS23 6EB* T: (01937) 844859
E: glendamwebb@gmail.com

WEBB, Harold William. b 37. St Chad's Coll Dur BA 59. St Steph Ho Ox 59. **d** 61 **p** 62. C Plumstead St Nic *S'wark* 61-65; C De Aar S Africa 65; R Prieska 65-68; R Vryberg 68-70; Sacr Wakef Cathl 71-72; P-in-c Lane End *Ox* 72-76; V Lane End w Cadmore End 76-84; Chapl to the Deaf *Guildf* 84-96; V Roade and Ashton w Hartwell *Pet* 96-02; rtd 02; PtO *Chich* from 02. *16 Harrow Drive, West Wittering, Chichester PO20 8EJ* T: (01243) 673460

WEBB (née EDWARDS), Mrs Helen Glynne. b 57. SRN 79 RMN 81 Birkbeck Coll Lon MSc 94. Wycliffe Hall Ox 88. **d** 90 **p** 94. Par Dn Clapham St Jas *S'wark* 90-94; Chapl Asst Southmead Health Services NHS Trust 94-97; PtO *Bris* from 97. *13 The Green, Olveston, Bristol BS35 4DN* T/F: (01454) 615827

WEBB, Ian. b 77. UWE BA 00. Trin Coll Bris 12. **d** 14 **p** 15. C Dronfield w Holmesfield *Derby* from 14. *43 Firthwood Road, Coal Aston, Dronfield S18 3BW* M: 07795-030241
E: ian@webbhome.co.uk

WEBB, Mrs Janice Beryl. b 49. Dioc OLM tr scheme 05. **d** 08 **p** 09. NSM Stour Vale *Sarum* 08-11; NSM Barbourne *Worc* from 11. *5 Victoria Street, Worcester WR3 7BE* T: (01905) 28682
E: jan.dorset@gmail.com

WEBB, Jennifer Rose. b 48. Leeds Univ BA 70 Bedf Coll Lon CQSW 72. **d** 96 **p** 97. OLM Ham St Rich *S'wark* 96-05; NSM March St Mary *Ely* 05-14; P-in-c 14-15; NSM March St Pet 05-14; P-in-c 14-15. *3 Wherry Close, March PE15 9BX* T: (01354) 650855 E: revdjennywebb@btinternet.com

WEBB, John. See WEBB, William John

WEBB, John Christopher Richard. b 38. ACA 63 FCA 74. Wycliffe Hall Ox 64. **d** 67 **p** 68. C Hendon St Paul Mill Hill *Lon* 67-71; CF 71-93; R Bentworth and Shalden and Lasham *Win* 93-03; RD Alton 98-02; rtd 03; PtO *B & W* from 04. *Lower Farm Cottage, Church Street, Podimore, Yeovil BA22 8JE* T: (01935) 841465 E: john-cr.webb465@tiscali.co.uk

WEBB, Jonathan Paul. b 62. Bapt Th Coll Johannesburg BTh 98. **d** 02 **p** 03. NSM Linden S Africa 02-04; Asst P Bryanston 04-06; TV Bury St Edmunds All SS w St Jo and St Geo *St E* 07-10; V E Molesey *Guildf* 10-15; V Brighouse and Clifton *Wakef* from 15. *47 Bracken Road, Brighouse HD6 2HX*
E: revpaulwebb@gmail.com

WEBB, Kenneth Gordon. b 47. Lon Univ MB, BS 71. Trin Coll Bris BA 92. **d** 93 **p** 94. C Cheltenham St Mark *Glouc* 93-97; Banchang Ch Ch Thailand 97-02; P-in-c Duns *Edin* from 02. *The Rectory, Wellfield, Duns TD11 3EH* M: 07990-866918 T: (01361) 882209 E: kenwebb275@icloud.com

WEBB, Marjorie Valentine (Sister Elizabeth). b 31. Bedf Coll Lon Westmr Coll Ox MTh 98. **d** 88 **p** 94. CSF from 55; Revd Mother 71-86; Lic to Bp Heref 86-90; PtO *Lon* 88-90; LtO *Lich* 90-91; PtO *Cant* 95-00; *B & W* from 95; *Birm* 97-00; *Lich* from 00; *Lon* from 02; *Chelmsf* from 09. *The Vicarage, 11 St Mary's Road, London E13 9AE* T: (020) 8852 4019
E: elizabethcsf@franciscans.org.uk

WEBB, Martin George. b 46. SS Mark & Jo Coll Chelsea CertEd 68 Leeds Univ MEd 95. NOC 82. **d** 85 **p** 86. NSM Brotherton *Wakef* 85-87; PtO *York* 95-98; NSM Bethnal Green St Barn *Lon* 98-03; NSM Bromley by Bow All Hallows 03-08; P-in-c Selling w Throwley, Sheldwich w Badlesmere etc *Cant* 08-13; rtd 13; PtO *Cant* from 13. *13 Neames Forstal, Selling, Faversham ME13 9PP* T: (01227) 750144
E: martin@webb.lcbroadband.co.uk

WEBB, Michael David. b 59. K Coll Lon BD 82 PGCE 83. Ripon Coll Cuddesdon 88. **d** 90 **p** 91. C Broughton Astley *Leic* 90-93; C Hugglescote w Donington, Ellistown and Snibston 93-94; TV 94-98; R Castleford All SS and Whitwood *Wakef* 98-01;

P-in-c Glass Houghton 98-01; TR Castleford 02; rtd 02; PtO *S'well* from 06. *5A Northfield Road, Wetwang, Driffield YO25 9XY* E: michael@webbs-web.co.uk

WEBB, Canon Michael John. b 49. Linc Coll Ox BA 70 MA 74. Linc Th Coll 70. d 72 p 73. C Tring *St Alb* 72-75; C Chipping Barnet 75-78; C Chipping Barnet w Arkley 78-82; TV Cullercoats St Geo *Newc* 82-89; V Newc H Cross 89-97; Chapl MU 96-02; V Newc St Gabr 97-06; AD Newc E 97-04; V Alnwick 06-11; Hon Can Newc Cathl 02-11; rtd 11. *Underne, 24 Wordsworth Street, Keswick CA12 4BZ* T: (01768) 771180 E: michaeljwebb1@btinternet.com

WEBB, Nikola. *See* MARSHALL, Pauline Nikola

WEBB, Norma Fay. b 39. K Coll Dur BDS 62. d 04 p 05. OLM Thornhill and Whitley Lower *Wakef* 04-09; PtO *Leeds* from 10. *24 High Street, Thornhill, Dewsbury WF12 0PS* T: (01924) 463574 E: normafwebb@aol.com

WEBB, Paul. *See* WEBB, Jonathan Paul

WEBB, Peter Henry. b 55. Nottm Univ BA 77. St Steph Ho Ox 77. d 79 p 80. C Lancing w Coombes *Chich* 79-82; C The Hydneye CD 82-84; C-in-c 84-86; Chapl Sunderland Distr Gen Hosp 86-94; Chapl City Hosps Sunderland NHS Foundn Trust from 94. *The Chaplain's Office, Sunderland Royal General Hospital, Kayll Road, Sunderland SR4 7TP* T: 0191-565 6256 *or* 569 9180

WEBB, Richard. b 38. Oak Hill NSM Course 91. d 94 p 95. NSM Hanwell St Mary w St Chris *Lon* 94-04; rtd 04; PtO *Cant* from 05. *1 Haffenden Meadow, Charing, Ashford TN27 0JR* T: (01233) 714663

WEBB, Canon Richard Frederick. b 42. Cant Sch of Min. d 84 p 85. C Ipswich St Clem w H Trin *St E* 84-87; R Rougham and Beyton w Hessett 87-91; R Rougham, Beyton w Hessett and Rushbrooke 91-92; P-in-c Woodbridge St Jo 92-98; P-in-c Saxmundham 98-04; P-in-c Kelsale-cum-Carlton, Middleton, Theberton etc 02-04; R Saxmundham w Kelsale cum Carlton 04-10; RD Saxmundham 03-05; Hon Can St E Cathl 06-10; rtd 10; PtO *St E* from 10. *48 Pightle Close, Elmswell, Bury St Edmunds IP30 9EL* T: (01359) 242925 E: richard.webb380@btinternet.com

WEBB, Robert. *See* WEBB, Arthur Robert

WEBB, Rosemary. *See* WEBB, Catharine Rosemary Wheatley

WEBB, Rosemary. b 59. d 10 p 11. NSM Ascot Heath *Ox* 10-13; P-in-c Clewer St Andr from 13; R from 15; P-in-c New Windsor from 14. *St Andrew's Rectory, 16 Parsonage Lane, Windsor SL4 5EN* T: (01753) 852334 E: rosiewebb@btinternet.com

WEBB, Rowland James. b 33. Roch Th Coll 64. d 67 p 68. C Tavistock and Gulworthy *Ex* 67-70; Chapl RN 70-86; R Mundford w Lynford *Nor* 86-90; V Burnham *Chelmsf* 90-98; rtd 98; PtO *Chelmsf* from 98. *4 Pine Drive, Ingatestone CM4 9EF*

WEBB, Timothy Robert. b 57. Univ of Wales (Abth) BA 79 Univ of Wales (Ban) BTh 03 CQSW 89. d 03 p 04. C Machynlleth w Llanwrin and Penegoes *Ban* 03-06; C Deanery of Llyn and Eifionydd 07-14; R Bro Cymer from 14. *The Rectory, Pencefn Road, Dolgellau LL40 2YW* M: 07748-962193 E: tim-webb@tiscali.co.uk

WEBB, William John. b 43. Cuddesdon Coll 68. d 71 p 72. C Weston Favell *Pet* 71-73; C Newport w Longford *Lich* 74-77; C Baswich 77-79; P-in-c Stonnall and Wall 79-83; V Prees and Fauls 83-95; V St Martin's 95-06; rtd 06; PtO *Lich* from 09. *72 Market Street, Kingswinford DY6 9LH* T: (01384) 295856

WEBBER, Adam Andrew. b 79. St Chad's Coll Dur BA 00 St Mary's Coll Dur MA 01. Ridley Hall Cam 08. d 10 p 11. C Cowplain *Portsm* 10-13; Chapl RN from 13. *Royal Naval Chaplaincy Service, Mail Point 1.2, Leach Building, Whale Island, Portsmouth PO2 8BY* T: (023) 9262 5055 F: 9262 5134 E: adamwebber@live.co.uk

WEBBER, David Price. b 39. Chich Th Coll 90. d 91 p 92. NSM Shoreham Beach *Chich* 91-93; NSM Hove St Patr 93-96; Turks and Caicos Is from 96. *PO Box 24, Grand Turk, Turks and Caicos Islands*

WEBBER, The Very Revd Eric Michael. b 16. Lon Univ BD 54 Univ of Tasmania MEd 77 MHums 85. AKC 43. d 43 p 44. C Clapham H Spirit *S'wark* 43-47; C Wimbledon 47-50; R Eshowe S Africa 56-58; R Lapworth and Baddesley-Clinton 56-58; Dean Hobart 59-71; Sen Lect RS Tasmanian Coll Adv Educn Australia 71-81; rtd 94. *5B Kendrick Court, Dynnyrne Tas 7005, Australia* T: (0061) (3) 6223 6413

WEBBER, John Arthur. b 45. Keble Coll Ox BA 67 MA 71 Gen Th Sem NY STM 85. Cuddesdon Coll 70. d 71 p 72. C Penarth All SS *Llan* 71-74; USPG Bangladesh 85-91; USA 84-85; Asst P Stepney St Dunstan and All SS *Lon* 91-97; Bp's Adv Relns w People of Other Faiths 91-97; P-in-c Bethnal Green St Barn 97-00; Dir of Ords 00-04; TR Llantwit Major *Llan* 04-10; rtd 10; PtO *Llan* from 10. *2 Arundel Place, Cardiff CF11 8DP* T: (029) 2039 6400 M: 07745-874839 E: johnwebber342@btinternet.com

WEBBER, Lionel Frank. b 35. Kelham Th Coll St Mich Coll Llan. d 60 p 61. C Bolton Sav *Man* 60-63; C Aberavon *Llan* 63-65;

R Salford Stowell Memorial *Man* 65-69; V Aberavon H Trin *Llan* 69-74; TV Stantonbury *Ox* 74-76; TR Basildon St Martin w H Cross and Laindon *Chelmsf* 76-79; P-in-c Nevendon 77-79; RD Basildon 79-89; R Basildon St Martin w Nevendon 79-95; R Basildon St Martin 95-01; Hon Can Chelmsf Cathl 84-01; Chapl to The Queen 94-01; rtd 01. *12 Ramblers Way, Burnham-on-Crouch CM0 8LR* T: (01621) 785152

WEBBER, Lorna Violet. b 40. d 06 p 07. OLM Woodbridge St Jo and Bredfield *St E* 06-10; rtd 10; PtO *St E* from 10. *Deo Gratias, 43 Through Duncans, Woodbridge IP12 4EA* T: (01394) 384634 E: lorna@stjohnswoodbridge.org.uk

WEBBER, Canon Michael Champneys Wilfred. b 48. Man Univ BA 71 MA(Theol) 78. Cuddesdon Coll 73. d 75 p 76. C Caterham *S'wark* 75-79; P-in-c Kidbrooke St Jas 79-84; TV 84-85; V Earls Barton *Pet* 87-09; RD Wellingborough 00-06; P-in-c Daventry, Ashby St Ledgers, Braunston etc from 09; Can Pet Cathl from 04. *The Rectory, Golding Close, Daventry NN11 4FB* T: (01327) 876893 E: michaelc.webber@btinternet.com

WEBBER, Raymond John. b 40. Linc Th Coll 84. d 85 p 86. C Helston *Truro* 85; C Helston and Wendron 85-90; TV 90-93; R Kenton, Mamhead, Powderham, Cofton and Starcross *Ex* 93-03; rtd 03; PtO *Truro* from 03. *1 Seton Gardens, Camborne TR14 7JS* T: (01209) 711360

WEBBER, Thomas George Edward. b 63. LSE BSc 84. Trin Coll Bris. d 98 p 99. C Churchdown *Glouc* 98-02; TV Stoke Gifford *Bris* 02-12; V Weston super Mare Ch Ch and Em *B & W* from 12. *The Cedar, Montpelier, Weston-super-Mare BS23 2RQ* T: (01934) 709343 E: tomandchriswebber@tiscali.co.uk

WEBBER, Toby Roderic. b 75. St Jo Coll Dur BA 96. Wycliffe Hall Ox BA 01. d 02 p 03. C Chorley St Laur *Blackb* 02-06; P-in-c Bamber Bridge St Aid 06-12; P-in-c Walton-le-Dale St Leon w Samlesbury St Leon 11-12; Bp's Dom Chapl 12-15; V Altham w Clayton le Moors from 15. *The Vicarage, Church Street, Clayton le Moors, Accrington BB5 5HT*

WEBBLEY, Ms Rachel Catharine. b 75. Hatf Coll Dur BA 98. Qu Coll Birm BA 03. d 04 p 05. C Bicester w Bucknell, Caversfield and Launton *Ox* 04-07; TV Whitstable *Cant* from 07. *28A West Cliff, Whitstable CT5 1DN* T: (01227) 273329 E: rcwebbley@hotmail.com

WEBSTER, David Leslie Holbarow. b 37. SAOMC 00. d 02 p 03. NSM Hurst *Ox* 02-04; NSM Earley St Nic 04-07; PtO from 07. *515 Reading Road, Winnersh, Wokingham RG41 5HL* T: 0118-979 4568 F: 961 9575 E: dlhwebster@supanet.com

WEBSTER, David Robert. b 32. Selw Coll Cam BA 56 MA 60. Linc Th Coll 56. d 58 p 59. C Billingham St Cuth *Dur* 58-61; C Doncaster St Geo *Sheff* 61-64; Chapl Doncaster R Infirmary 61-64; V Lumley *Dur* 64-76; V Belmont 76-93; rtd 93; PtO *Dur* from 04. *25 Eldon Grove, Hartlepool TS26 9LY* T: (01429) 425915 E: david.webster50@ntlworld.com

WEBSTER, Dennis Eric. b 39. Fitzw Ho Cam BA 60 MA 64 Linacre Coll Ox MA 70 Lon Univ CertEd 61. Wycliffe Hall Ox 62. d 65 p 66. C Herne Bay Ch Ch *Cant* 65-68; C Tulse Hill H Trin *S'wark* 68-69; Missr Kenya 70-75; Chapl Pierrepont Sch Frensham 75-91; R Chiddingfold *Guildf* 91-02; rtd 02; PtO *Guildf* from 02. *Sylvan Cottage, 24 Longdown Road, Lower Bourne, Farnham GU10 3JL* T: (01252) 713919

WEBSTER, Derek Herbert. b 34. FRSA 82 Hull Univ BA 55 Lon Univ BD 55 Leic Univ MEd 68 PhD 73. Lambeth STh 67 Linc Th Coll 76. d 76 p 77. Lect Hull Univ from 72; Reader from 97; NSM Cleethorpes *Linc* from 76. *60 Queen's Parade, Cleethorpes DN35 0DG* T: (01472) 693786 E: dwebster@edrev.demon.co.uk

WEBSTER, Canon Diane Margaret. b 43. Oak Hill NSM Course 91. d 94 p 95. NSM Welwyn Garden City *St Alb* 94-99; P-in-c Burley Ville *Win* 99-10; RD Christchurch 03-10; Hon Can Win Cathl 08-10; rtd 10; PtO *Win* from 10. *Burwood, The Rise, Brockenhurst SO42 7SJ* T: (01590) 624927 E: diane.mwebster@tiscali.co.uk

WEBSTER, Geoffrey William. b 36. St Alb Minl Tr Scheme 77. d 80 p 81. NSM Harlington *St Alb* 80-82; C Belmont *Dur* 82-86; R Gateshead Fell 86-94; P-in-c Hamsterley 94-95; V Hamsterley and Witton-le-Wear 95-02; rtd 02; PtO *Dur* from 13. *38A Owton Manor Lane, Hartlepool TS25 3AE* T: (01429) 265798

✠**WEBSTER, The Rt Revd Glyn Hamilton.** b 51. SRN 73. Cranmer Hall Dur 74. d 77 p 78 c 13. C Huntington *York* 77-81; V York St Luke 81-92; Chapl York Distr Hosp 81-92; Sen Chapl York Health Services NHS Trust 92-99; Can and Preb York Minster 94-99; Can Res York Minster 99-13; RD City of York 97-04; Assoc Dioc Dir of Ords 05-10; Suff Bp Beverley (PEV) from 13; Hon Asst Bp Liv from 13; Hon Asst Bp Ches from 13; Hon Asst Bp Sheff from 14; Asst Bp Sheff from 14; Hon Asst Bp Man from 14. *Holy Trinity Rectory, Micklegate, York YO1 6LE* T: (01904) 628155 M: 07983-341323 E: office@seeofbeverley.org.uk

WEBSTER, James. *See* WEBSTER, Robin James Cook

WEBSTER, Prof John Bainbridge. b 55. Clare Coll Cam MA 81 PhD 82. **d** 83 **p** 84. Chapl and Dep Sen Tutor St Jo Coll Dur 83-86; Hon C Bearpark *Dur* 83-86; Assoc Prof Systematic Th Wycliffe Coll Toronto 86-93; Prof Systematic Th 93-95; Ramsay Armitage Prof Systematic Th 95-96; Lady Marg Prof Div and Can Res Ch Ch *Ox* 96-03; Prof Systematic Th Aber Univ *Ab* 03-13; Prof Div St Andr Univ *St And* from 13. *St Mary's College, University of St Andrews, St Andrews KY16 9JU* T: (01334) 462864 E: jbw5@st-andrews.ac.uk

WEBSTER, John Kelsey. b 62. SAOMC 00. **d** 03 **p** 04. NSM Woolhampton w Midgham and Beenham Valance *Ox* 03-06; P-in-c Tallangatta Australia from 06. *61 Queen Elizabeth Drive, Tallangatta Vic 3700, Australia* T/F: (0061) (2) 6071 2545 M: 44-849 9093 E: frjohnw@bigpond.com

WEBSTER, The Ven Martin Duncan. b 52. Nottm Univ BSc 74. Linc Th Coll 75. **d** 78 **p** 79. C Thundersley *Chelmsf* 78-81; C Canvey Is 81-82; TV 82-86; V Nazeing 86-99; RD Harlow 88-99; TR Waltham H Cross 99-09; Hon Can Chelmsf Cathl 00-09; Adn Harlow from 09. *Glebe House, Church Lane, Sheering, Bishop's Stortford CM22 7NR* T: (01279) 734524 F: 734426 E: a.harlow@chelmsford.anglican.org

WEBSTER, Mrs Monica. b 39. DipCOT 60. WMMTC 94. **d** 97 **p** 98. NSM Wolverton w Norton Lindsey and Langley *Cov* 97-01; Asst Chapl to the Deaf 97-01; NSM Stoneleigh w Ashow and Baginton 98-01; Chapl to the Deaf and Hard of Hearing *Carl* from 01; NSM Aldingham, Dendron, Rampside and Urswick 02-06; NSM Pennington and Lindal w Marton and Bardsea 02-06; rtd 06. *4 Chelsea Court, Milnthorpe LA7 7DJ* T: (015395) 64731

WEBSTER, Mrs Patricia Eileen. b 34. St Gabr Coll Lon TCert 54. Gilmore Ho 56. **d** 87 **p** 94. Par Dn Belmont *Dur* 87-93; rtd 93; PtO *Dur* from 04. *25 Eldon Grove, Hartlepool TS26 9LY* T: (01429) 425915 E: david.webster50@ntlworld.com

WEBSTER, Robin James Cook. b 62. Plymouth Poly BSc 86 Cranfield Inst of Tech MSc 87 Cranfield Univ PhD 06. St Jo Coll Nottm MTh 13. **d** 13 **p** 14. C Broxbourne w Wormley *St Alb* from 13. *11 Wharf Road, Broxbourne EN10 6HU* M: 07875-080949 E: jameswebster1@btinternet.com

WEBSTER, Rosamond Mary. *See* LATHAM, Rosamond Mary

WEBSTER, Sarah Vernoy. b 38. Univ of Georgia BSc 61. S'wark Ord Course 87. **d** 90 **p** 94. NSM Primrose Hill St Mary w Avenue Road St Paul *Lon* 90-01; Hon C Ann Arbor St Andr USA from 02. *4179 Eastgate Drive, Ann Arbor MI 48103, USA* T: (001) (734) 424 2750 E: revsalvalder@comcast.net

WEBSTER, Stephen Jeremy. b 71. Leic Univ BA 92 PGCE 93. Wycliffe Hall Ox 05. **d** 07 **p** 08. C Oundle w Ashton and Benefield w Glapthorn *Pet* 07-14; R from 14; RD Oundle from 13. *2 Herons Wood Close, Oundle, Peterborough PE8 4HW* T: (01832) 275631 E: stephen.webster@yahoo.co.uk

WEBSTER, Ms Susan Margaret. b 58. SRN 82 Worc Coll of Educn BA 89. WMMTC 91. **d** 94 **p** 95. C Worc SE 94-97; P-in-c Elmley Castle w Bricklehampton and Combertons 97-01; USA 01-10; NSM Walbury Beacon *Ox* from 14. *Enborne Rectory, Enborne, Newbury RG20 0HD* T: (01635) 32708 E: colontherapyonline@hotmail.com

WEDGBURY, John William. b 53. RMCS BSc 78. St Jo Coll Nottm 84. **d** 87 **p** 88. C Folkestone St Jo *Cant* 87-91; V Mangotsfield *Bris* 91-92; NSM Manselton *S & B* 00-02; P-in-c Caereithin 02-05; NSM Swansea St Thos and Kilvey 05-12; PtO from 12. *4 Ffynone Drive, Swansea SA1 6DD* T: (01792) 464194

WEDGE, Christopher Graham. b 67. LSE BSc(Econ) 89 Huddersfield Univ PGCE 94. NOC 00. **d** 06 **p** 07. C Castleford *Wakef* 06-09; Dep Chapl Manager United Lincs Hosps NHS Trust 09-11; C Boston *Linc* 11-12; TV 12-14; P-in-c Prestwich St Mary *Man* from 14. *The Rectory, Church Lane, Prestwich, Manchester M25 1AN* E: chrisshef@hotmail.com

WEDGEWOOD, Karsten Eric. b 77. **d** 12 **p** 13. C Davyhulme St Mary *Man* 12-13; C Farnworth, Kearsley and Stoneclough from 13. *St Stephen's Vicarage, Blair Street, Kearsley, Bolton BL4 8SP* M: 07525-831386 E: karstenwedgewood@gmail.com

WEDGEWORTH, Canon Michael John. b 40. MBE 10. Nottm Univ BSc 62. Wesley Ho Cam MA 66. **d** 93 **p** 94. In Methodist Ch 66-93; NSM Feniscowles *Blackb* 93-96; Sec DBF 95-05; Hon P Blackb Cathl from 95; LtO from 96; Hon Can Blackb Cathl 03-10. *Abbott House, 74 King Street, Whalley, Clitheroe BB7 9SN* T: (01254) 825694 E: mike.wedgeworth@blackburn.anglican.org.uk

WEDGWOOD GREENHOW, Stephen John Francis. b 57. Man Univ BA 82. Edin Th Coll MTh 84. **d** 84 **p** 85. C Wythenshawe Wm Temple Ch *Man* 84-87; USA from 87. *556 North George Washington Blvd, Yuba City CA 95993, USA* T: (001) (530) 822 0691

WEEDEN, Simon Andrew. b 55. York Univ BA 79. Wycliffe Hall Ox 88. **d** 90 **p** 91. C Gt Chesham *Ox* 90-94; P-in-c Haversham w Lt Linford, Tyringham w Filgrave 94-97; R Lamp 97-99; P-in-c Bramshott and Liphook *Portsm* 99-00; R 00-10; RD Petersfield 04-09; TR Whitton *Sarum* from 10. *The Rectory, Back Lane, Ramsbury, Marlborough SN8 2QH* T: (01672) 520235 E: simon@weeden.plus.com

WEEDING, Paul Stephen. b 62. Leic Poly BSc. Ripon Coll Cuddesdon 88. **d** 90 **p** 91. C Llanishen and Lisvane *Llan* 90-93; C Merthyr Tydfil Ch Ch 93-97; V Abercynon 97-03; Asst Chapl Qu Medical Cen Nottm Univ Hosp NHS Trust 03-10. *Address temp unknown*

WEEKES, David John. b 34. Magd Coll Cam BA 59 MA 68 Lon Univ PGCE 68 Aber Univ MTh 79 FSAScot. Clifton Th Coll 62. **d** 64 **p** 65. C Cheadle *Ches* 64-68; Chapl Ntare Sch Mbarara Uganda 69-73; PtO *St And* 73-74; Chapl and Hd of RE Fettes Coll Edin 74-94; Warden and Chapl Lee Abbey Internat Students' Club Kensington 94-01; rtd 01; PtO *Lon* 94-03. *Loaning Hill, Kilmany, Cupar KY15 4PT* T: (01382) 330183 M: 07855-761970 E: dw62@st-andrews.ac.uk

WEEKES, Robin Alasdair Rutley. b 73. Peterho Cam MA 94. Wycliffe Hall Ox BA 98 MA 98. **d** 99 **p** 00. C Wimbledon Em Ridgway Prop Chpl S'wark 99-03; Crosslinks India 03-10; Tutor Cornhill Tr Course 10-13; Min Wimbledon Em Ridgway Prop Chpl S'wark from 13. *Emmanuel Parsonage, 8 Sheep Walk Mews, London SW19 4QL* T: (020) 8946 4613 M: 07811-384350 E: robin.weekes@emmanuelwimbledon.org.uk

WEEKS, Ms Jane Anne. b 61. UEA BA 00. Aston Tr Scheme 95 EAMTC 97. **d** 00 **p** 01. C Hadleigh *St E* 00-02; C Hadleigh, Layham and Shelley 02-03; Chapl HM Pris Bullwood Hall 03-06; Chapl HM Pris Cookham Wood 06-08; PtO *Cant* 09-10; R Hever, Four Elms and Mark Beech *Roch* from 10. *The Rectory, Rectory Lane, Hever, Edenbridge TN8 7LH* T: (01732) 862249 E: revweeks@hotmail.com

WEEKS, Mrs Rachel Elizabeth. b 51. STETS 09. **d** 14. NSM Portsea N End St Mark *Portsm* from 14. *7 Kingfisher Court, Portsmouth PO3 5XE* T: (023) 9269 8969 M: 07878-299231 E: kimeweeks@gmail.com

WEEKS, Timothy Robert. b 47. SAOMC 03. **d** 08 **p** 09. NSM Royston *St Alb* 08-12; LtO from 12; Chapl Princess Alexandra Hosp NHS Trust from 08; PtO *Chelmsf* from 09. *6 Chantry Road, Bishop's Stortford CM23 2SF* T: (01279) 831404 *or* (01763) 243265 M: 07974-866016 E: angela.mweeks@ntlworld.com

WEETMAN, Mrs Dorothy. b 41. **d** 03 **p** 04. OLM Prudhoe *Newc* 03-09; rtd 09. *Station Gate East, Eltringham Road, Prudhoe NE42 6LA* T: (01661) 834538

WEETMAN, Canon John Charles. b 66. Qu Coll Ox BA 87 MA 92. Trin Coll Bris BA 91. **d** 91 **p** 92. C Hull St Jo Newland *York* 91-95; V Boosbeck w Moorsholm 95-02; V Redcar 02-11; RD Guisborough 99-11; V Selby Abbey from 11; Can and Preb York Minster from 05. *The Abbey Vicarage, 32A Leeds Road, Selby YO8 4HX* T: (01757) 705130 E: weetman217@btinternet.com

WEIGHTMAN, Andrea Frances. *See* WARD, Andrea Frances

WEIGHTMAN, David Courtenay. b 47. FRICS 88. **d** 04 **p** 05. OLM Oxted and Tandridge S'wark 04-14; OLM Oxted from 14. *13 Silkham Road, Oxted RH8 0NP* T: (01883) 715420 F: 717336 M: 07739-456947 E: david@survez.co.uk

WEIL, Thomas James. b 53. K Coll Lon BSc 74 PhD 79 AKC 74. S Tr Scheme 95. **d** 97 **p** 99. NSM Stoughton *Guildf* 97-03; PtO *Lon* 03-13; *Guildf* 04-15; NSM Worplesdon from 15. *17 Lyons Drive, Guildford GU2 9YP* T: (01483) 234535

WEIR, David Alexander. b 69. City Univ BSc 91 Fitzw Coll Cam BA 94 MA 99 Chich Univ BA 08. Westcott Ho Cam 92. **d** 95 **p** 97. C Locks Heath *Portsm* 95-96; C W Leigh 96-00; C Leigh Park and Warren Park 00-01; PtO 03-05; NSM Portsea St Mary 05-08; PtO *Truro* 08-09; P-in-c Exford, Exmoor, Hawkridge and Withypool *B & W* 09-12; P-in-c Exton and Winsford and Cutcombe w Luxborough 11-12; R Exmoor from 12; Warden of Readers Taunton Adnry from 14. *The Rectory, Exford, Minehead TA24 7LX* T: (01643) 831330 E: david.weir122@btinternet.com

WEIR, Graham Francis. b 52. GSM LASI. NOC 88. **d** 91 **p** 92. NSM High Crompton *Man* 91-92; NSM Heyside 92-94; Asst Chapl Bolton Hosps NHS Trust 94-96; Chapl 96-12; Dep Hd of Chapl 04-12; rtd 12; PtO *Man* from 13; Chapl OHP from 13. *St Hilda's Priory, Sneaton Castle, Whitby YO21 3QN* T: (01947) 602079

WEIR, John Michael Vavasour. b 48. K Coll Lon BD 72 AKC 72 MA 00. **d** 73 **p** 74. C Hatfield Hyde *St Alb* 73-76; C Watford St Mich 76-79; Asst Chapl Oslo St Edm *Eur* 80-81; V Bethnal Green St Pet w St Thos *Lon* 81-04; Chapl Qu Eliz Hosp for Children Lon 81-98; Chapl Team Ldr Toc H 01-10; Sen Chapl Dubai and Sharjah w N Emirates 04-10; rtd 10. *38 Belgrave Street, London E1 0NQ* T: (020) 7791 7957 E: jmvweir@gmail.com

WEIR, John William Moon. b 36. St Luke's Coll Ex CertEd 69 Ex Univ BEd 76. SWMTC 82. **d** 85 **p** 86. NSM Meavy, Sheepstor and Walkhampton Ex 85-87; NSM Yelverton, Meavy, Sheepstor and Walkhampton 87-05; Hd Master Princetown Primary Sch 86-94; Sub-Chapl HM Pris Dartmoor 86-94; PtO Ex from 05. *Goblin's Green, Dousland, Yelverton PL20 6ND* T: (01822) 852671

WEIR, Nicholas James. b 77. Pemb Coll Cam BA 98 MA 02 Green Coll Ox BM, BCh 01 MRCPsych 05. Oak Hill Th Coll MTh 11. **d** 11 **p** 12. C Eastrop *Win* 11-15; V Frogmore *St Alb* from 15. *The Vicarage, 39 Frogmore, St Albans AL2 2JU* T: (01256) 830028 E: nick.weir@stmarys-basingstoke.org.uk

WEIR, Ms Rachel Sian Shapland. b 66. Newnham Coll Cam BA 88 MA 91 Barrister 91. Ripon Coll Cuddesdon 04. **d** 07 **p** 08. Asst Nat Adv for Inter Faith Relns 07-08; NSM Wolvercote *Ox* 07-09; NSM Headington Quarry 09-11; Chapl Helen and Douglas Ho Ox 11-14; NSM Summertown *Ox* 12-14; Chapl Highgate Sch Lon from 14; PtO *Ox* from 14. *Highgate School, North Road, London N6 4AY* M: 07815-729565 T: (020) 8340 1524 E: rachelssweir@yahoo.co.uk

WEIR, William Daniel Niall. b 57. UEA BA 79. Ripon Coll Cuddesdon 80. **d** 83 **p** 84. C Chelsea St Luke *Lon* 83-87; PV Westmr Abbey 85-89; C Poplar *Lon* 87-88; TV 88-93; P-in-c Forest Gate Em w Upton Cross *Chelmsf* 93-97; V 97-99; Asst Chapl Southn Univ Hosps NHS Trust 99-00; Trust Chapl 00-03; R W Hackney *Lon* from 03. *The Rectory, 306 Amhurst Road, London N16 7UE* T: (020) 7254 3235 E: niall.weir@mac.com

WEISSERHORN, Julian Timothy David Moritz. *See* GADSBY, Julian Timothy David Moritz

WEITZMANN, Benjamin Edward Albert. b 80. Surrey Univ BSc 03. St Steph Ho Ox BTh 15. **d** 15. C Boxmoor St Jo *St Alb* from 15. *23 Beechfield Road, Hemel Hempstead HP1 1PP* M: 07887-484080 E: benjamin@weitzmann.co.uk

WELANDER, Canon David Charles St Vincent. b 25. FSA. Lon Coll of Div BD 47 ALCD 47. **d** 48 **p** 49. C Heigham H Trin *Nor* 48-51; Tutor Oak Hill Th Coll 51-52; Chapl and Tutor Lon Coll of Div 52-56; V Iver Ox 56-63; V Cheltenham Ch Ch *Glouc* 63-75; RD Cheltenham 73-75; Can Res Glouc Cathl 75-91; rtd 91; PtO *Glouc* 91-98; *Bris* from 91. *Willow Cottage, 1 Sandpits Lane, Sherston Magna, Malmesbury SN16 0NN* T: (01666) 840180

WELBOURN, David Anthony. b 41. K Coll Lon BD 63 AKC 63. St Boniface Warminster 63. **d** 64 **p** 65. C Stockton St Chad *Dur* 64-67; C S Westoe 69-74; Ind Chapl 69-80; *Nor* 80-90; Ind and Commerce Officer *Guildf* 90-06; rtd 06; PtO *Guildf* from 06. *3 Windgates, Guildford GU4 7DJ* T/F: (01483) 825541 E: welbourn@ntlworld.com

WELBY, Alexander. *See* WELBY, Richard Alexander Lyon

✠**WELBY, The Most Revd and Rt Hon Justin Portal.** b 56. PC 13. Trin Coll Cam BA 78 MA 90 St Jo Coll Dur BA 91 Hon FCT. Cranmer Hall Dur 89. **d** 92 **p** 93 **c** 11. C Chilvers Coton w Astley *Cov* 92-95; R Southam 95-02; V Ufton 96-02; Can Res Cov Cathl 02-07; Co-Dir Internat Min 02-05; Sub-Dean 05-07; P-in-c Cov H Trin 07; Dean Liv 07-11; Bp Dur 11-13; Abp Cant from 13. *Lambeth Palace, London SE1 7JU* T: (020) 7898 1200 E: contact@lambethpalace.org.uk

WELBY, Peter Edlin Brown. b 34. Open Univ BA 75. Cranmer Hall Dur 75. **d** 77 **p** 78. C Auckland St Andr and St Anne *Dur* 77-79; C S Westoe 79-81; V Tudhoe 81-93; R Croxdale and Tudhoe 93-99; rtd 99; PtO *Dur* from 04. *Blyth House, 9 Rhodes Terrace, Nevilles Cross, Durham DH1 4JW* T: 0191-384 8295

WELBY, Richard Alexander Lyon. b 58. St Jo Coll Nottm BTh 81 Leeds Univ MA 93. Ridley Hall Cam 83. **d** 84 **p** 85. C Stoke Bishop *Bris* 84-88; V Bowling St Steph *Bradf* 88-95; P-in-c Hatherleigh, Meeth, Exbourne and Jacobstowe Ex 95-05. *Address temp unknown* M: 07935-232058 E: alex.welby@virgin.net

WELCH, Amanda Jane. b 58. **d** 04 **p** 05. OLM Worplesdon *Guildf* from 04. *Glenlea, Liddington New Road, Guildford GU3 3AH* T: (01483) 233525 E: curate@worplesdonparish.com *or* revmandywelch@gmail.com

WELCH, David John. b 52. NTMTC 98. **d** 01 **p** 02. C Walthamstow *Chelmsf* 01-05; V Harlow St Mary and St Hugh w St Jo the Bapt from 05. *St Mary's Vicarage, 5 Staffords, Harlow CM17 0JR* T/F: (01279) 450633 E: davewelch@talktalkbusiness.net

WELCH, Gordon Joseph. b 47. Man Univ BSc 68 MSc 69 PhD 72. NOC 84. **d** 87 **p** 88. NSM Upton Ascension *Ches* 87-98; LtO 99-00; NSM Backford and Capenhurst 00-02; NSM Ellesmere Port from 02; RD Wirral S 06-11. *6 St James's Avenue, Upton, Chester CH2 1NH* T: (01244) 382196 M: 07890-993948 E: gordonwelch@btinternet.com

WELCH, Canon Grant Keith. b 40. AKC 63. **d** 64 **p** 65. C Nottingham St Mary *S'well* 64-68; V Cinderhill 68-73;

R Weston Favell *Pet* 73-88; Master St Jo Hosp Weston Favell 73-88; Can Pet Cathl 83-88; P-in-c Gt Houghton 84-85; C Loughton St Jo *Chelmsf* 89-92; TR 92-05; AD Epping Forest 00-04; rtd 05; PtO *B & W* from 05. *7 Hayes Lane, Compton Dundon, Somerton TA11 6PB* T: (01458) 272526 E: grantwelch@btinternet.com

WELCH, Ian Michael. b 59. Warwick Univ BA 81 Connecticut Univ MA 84. Ripon Coll Cuddesdon 00. **d** 02 **p** 03. C Lee St Aug *S'wark* 02-05; P-in-c Mottingham St Andr w St Alban 05-11; R from 11. *The Rectory, 233 Court Road, London SE9 4TQ* T: (020) 8851 1909 E: office@standrewschurch.freeserve.co.uk

WELCH, John Harry. b 52. Oak Hill Th Coll 85. **d** 87 **p** 88. C Parr *Liv* 87-90; V W Derby St Luke 90-00; V Eccleston Park 00-07; P-in-c St Helens St Matt Thatto Heath 06-07; TR Eccleston from 07. *St James's Vicarage, 159A St Helen's Road, Prescot L34 2QB* T: 0151-426 6421

WELCH, Pamela Jean. b 47. Girton Coll Cam MA 76 K Coll Lon BD 79 AKC 79 PhD 05. Qu Coll Birm 77. **dss** 80 **d** 87. Tottenham H Trin *Lon* 80-84; Asst Chapl Bryanston Sch 84-87; PtO *Chich* 87-94; C Mornington St Mary New Zealand from 02; rtd 07. *23 Byron Street, Mornington, Dunedin 9011, New Zealand* T/F: (0064) (3) 453 0052 E: welchfam@byronhurst.com

WELCH, Paul Baxter. b 47. Lanc Univ BEd 74 MA 75. St Alb Minl Tr Scheme 80. **d** 83 **p** 84. NSM Heath and Reach *St Alb* 83-84; Bp's Sch Adv *Win* 84-89; P-in-c Clungunford w Clunbury and Clunton, Bedstone etc *Heref* 89-93; V Wellingborough All SS *Pet* 93-01; R Pulborough *Chich* from 01; RD Storrington 04-11. *The Rectory, Hillcrest Park, Lower Street, Pulborough RH20 2AW* T: (01798) 875773 E: paulbwelch@live.co.uk

WELCH, Rebecca Anne. *See* JONES, Rebecca Anne

WELCH, Mrs Sally Ann. b 62. Pemb Coll Ox MA 88. SAOMC 96. **d** 99 **p** 00. NSM Abingdon *Ox* 99-01; P-in-c Kintbury w Avington 01-05; R Cherbury w Gainfield 05-09; C Ox St Giles and SS Phil and Jas w St Marg 09-15; V Charlbury w Shorthampton from 15; AD Chipping Norton from 15. *The Vicarage, Church Lane, Charlbury, Chipping Norton OX7 3PX* M: 07974-439630 E: sally.welch@19a.org.uk

WELCH, The Ven Stephan John. b 50. Hull Univ BA 74 Lon Univ MTh 98. Qu Coll Birm 74. **d** 77 **p** 78. C Waltham Cross *St Alb* 77-80; P-in-c Reculver *Cant* 80-86; P-in-c Herne Bay St Bart 82-86; V Reculver and Herne Bay St Bart 86-92; V Hurley and Stubbings *Ox* 92-00; P-in-c Hammersmith St Pet *Lon* 00-06; AD Hammersmith and Fulham 01-06; Adn Middx from 06. *98 Dukes Avenue, London W4 2AF* T: (020) 8742 8308 E: archdeacon.middlesex@london.anglican.org

WELDON, Nicholas Patrick. b 77. UWE BSc 99. Oak Hill Th Coll BA 07. **d** 07 **p** 08. C Moreton-in-Marsh w Batsford, Todenham etc *Glouc* 07-11; P-in-c N Tawton, Bondleigh, Sampford Courtenay etc *Ex* 11-13; TV Chagford, Gidleigh, Throwleigh etc from 13. *The Rectory, Essington Close, North Tawton EX20 2EX* T: (01837) 880183 M: 07970-984190 E: npweldon@gmail.com

WELDON, Robert Price. b 57. Cant Ch Ch Univ BA 12. SEITE 06. **d** 09 **p** 10. NSM Caterham *S'wark* 09-13; C G7 Benefice *Cant* from 13. *The Vicarage, Eastwell Lane, Westwell, Ashford TN25 4LQ* T: (01233) 712576 M: 07929-866879 E: revbob62@gmail.com

WELDON, William Ernest. b 41. TCD BA 62 MA 66. **d** 64 **p** 65. C Belfast Trin Coll Miss *Conn* 64-67; C Carnmoney 67-71; Chapl RN 71-96; QHC 93-96; Hon C Holbeton Ex 96-01; PtO from 01. *3 Garden Close, Holbeton, Plymouth PL8 1NQ* T: (01752) 830139 E: billanddinahweldon@btopenworld.com

WELFORD, Gillian Margaret. b 51. Westf Coll Lon BA 65. **d** 04 **p** 05. OLM Chiddingfold *Guildf* from 04. *15 Woodberry Close, Chiddingfold, Godalming GU8 4SF* T: (01428) 683620 E: gill@welford.myzen.co.uk

WELHAM, Mrs Clare. b 77. Univ Coll Dur BA 98 MA 00. WEMTC 09. **d** 12 **p** 13. C Stroud Team *Glouc* 12-14. *21 Clarence Drive, Harrogate HG1 2QE* M: 07570-798392 T: (01423) 537038 E: clarewelham77@gmail.com

WELHAM, Clive Richard. b 54. **d** 80 **p** 81. C Bellingham St Dunstan *S'wark* 80-84; Chapl Goldsmiths' Coll Lon 84-95; V Plumstead Ascension 95-10; P-in-c Plumstead St Mark and St Marg 07-10; V Plumstead Common from 10; AD Plumstead from 14. *The Vicarage, 42 Jago Close, London SE18 2TY* T: (020) 8854 3395

WELLER, David Christopher. b 60. UWIST BSc 83. St Jo Coll Nottm MA 96. **d** 96 **p** 97. C Wednesfield Heath *Lich* 96-99; TV Glascote and Stonydelph 99-05; Chapl Rio de Janeiro Ch Ch Brazil 05-11; P-in-c Pheasey *Lich* 11-12; Chapl HM Pris Oakwood from 12. *HM Prison Oakwood, 2 Oaks Drive, Featherstone, Wolverhampton WV10 7QD* T: (01902) 799700 M: 07890-691228 E: david.weller@uk.g4s.com

WELLER (née SPENCE), The Ven Susan Karen. b 65. Leeds Univ BSc 86 Liv Univ PhD 89. Wycliffe Hall Ox BA 95. **d** 96 **p** 97. C Caverswall and Weston Coyney w Dilhorne *Lich* 96-00; C Wilnecote 00-05; Dioc Adv for Women in Min 00-04; Brazil 05-11; PtO *Lich* 11-14; Adn Walsall from 15. *The Small Street Centre, 1A Small Steet, Walsall WS1 3PR*
E: archdeacon.walsall@lichfield.anglican.org

WELLINGTON, James Frederick. b 51. Leic Univ LLB 72 Fitzw Coll Cam BA 76. Ridley Hall Cam 74. **d** 77 **p** 78. C Mill Hill Jo Keble Ch *Lon* 77-80; C Wood Green St Mich w Bounds Green St Gabr etc 80-83; V Stocking Farm *Leic* 83-90; V Gt Glen, Stretton Magna and Wistow etc 90-98; Warden of Readers 91-97; RD Gartree II 96-98; TR Syston 98-07; RD Goscote 00-06; Hon Can Leic Cathl 94-07; R Keyworth and Stanton-on-the-Wolds and Bunny etc *S'well* from 07; AD E Bingham from 08. *The Rectory, Nottingham Road, Keyworth, Nottingham NG12 5FD* T: 0115-937 2017 E: jhcwelli@btinternet.com

WELLMAN, Mrs Karen Ann. b 62. BNC Ox BA 84. Ox Min Course 09. **d** 12 **p** 13. C Basingstoke *Win* 12-15; P-in-c Teddington St Mark and Hampton Wick *Lon* from 15. *The Vicarage, St Marks Road, Teddington TW11 9DE*

WELLS, Adrian Mosedale. b 61. SWMTC 96. **d** 99 **p** 00. NSM Kingskerswell w Coffinswell *Ex* 99-02; C Wolborough and Ogwell 02-13; TV Burrington, Chawleigh, Cheldon, Chulmleigh etc from 13. *The Vicarage, The Square, Witheridge, Tiverton EX16 8AE* E: amwells@talktalk.net

WELLS, Andrew Peter. b 54. **d** 15. NSM The Quinton *Birm* from 15. *89 Upper Meadow Road, Quinton, Birmingham B32 1NR Address temp unknown* T: 0121-689 0376
E: marchope@blueyonder.co.uk

WELLS, Andrew Stuart. b 48. St Jo Coll Dur BA 71 Man Metrop Univ PGCE 04. Cranmer Hall Dur. **d** 74 **p** 75. C Walmsley *Man* 74-77; C Failsworth H Family 77-79; R Openshaw 79-90; V Hindsford 90-98. *1 Henry Street, Haslington, Crewe CW1 5PS* T: (01270) 585303 E: andrewwells@hotmail.com

WELLS, Canon Anthony Martin Giffard. b 42. Open Univ BA 02. St Jo Coll Nottm 72. **d** 74 **p** 75. C Orpington Ch Ch *Roch* 74-78; P-in-c Odell *St Alb* 78-82; R 82-86; P-in-c Pavenham 78-82; V 82-86; RD Sharnbrook 81-86; R Angmering *Chich* 86-98; RD Arundel and Bognor 93-98; Chapl Paris St Mich *Eur* 98-06; Adn France 02-06; Can Gib Cathl 02-06; rtd 06; PtO *Eur* from 06; *Cov* from 08. *Shaunbrook House, Clark's Lane, Long Compton, Shipston-on-Stour CV36 5LB* T: (01608) 684337 E: anthonymgwells@btinternet.com

WELLS, Antony Ernest. b 36. Oak Hill Th Coll 58. **d** 61 **p** 62. C Bethnal Green St Jas Less *Lon* 61-64; SAMS Paraguay 64-69; V Kirkdale St Athanasius *Liv* 69-73; SAMS Argentina 73-75; V Warfield *Ox* 75-81; V Fairfield *Liv* 81-83; C Rainhill 83-85; TV Cheltenham St Mark *Glouc* 85-89; P-in-c Forest of Dean Ch Ch w English Bicknor 89-95; rtd 97; C Pinhoe and Broadclyst *Ex* 02-04. *4 Case Gardens, Seaton EX12 2AP* T: (01297) 20482

WELLS, Daniel Michael. b 74. Trin Coll Cam MA 95 Cam Inst of Educn PGCE 97. Wycliffe Hall Ox BTh 05. **d** 06 **p** 07. C Plymouth St Andr and Stonehouse *Ex* 06-09; C W Hampstead St Luke *Lon* 09-12; C Langham Place All So from 12. *241 Holcroft Court, Clipstone Street, London W1W 5DF* T: (020) 7637 9212 E: dan@wellsweb.org.uk

WELLS, David. *See* WELLS, William David Sandford

WELLS, David. b 63. Imp Coll Lon BSc 85 ARCS 85. EAMTC 97. **d** 00 **p** 01. C Sprowston w Beeston *Nor* 00-03; P-in-c Drayton w Felthorpe 03-05; R Drayton from 05. *The Rectory, 46 School Road, Drayton, Norwich NR8 6EF* T: (01603) 864749
E: david.wells@btinternet.com

WELLS, Mrs Gillian Lesley. b 50. Anglia Ruskin Univ BA 14. Nor Ord Course 07. **d** 10 **p** 11. OLM Reepham, Hackford w Whitwell, Kerdiston etc *Nor* 10-15; C Dereham and Distr from 15. *The Rectory, Church Close, Shipdham, Thetford IP25 7LX* T: (01362) 822404 M: 07597-306414
E: gilliewells1@btinternet.com

WELLS, Gillian Mary. *See* MANN, Gillian Mary

WELLS, Jeremy Stephen. b 47. Nottm Univ BA 69 UWE MSc 97. Chich Th Coll 72. **d** 73 **p** 74. C S Yardley St Mich *Birm* 73-76; C St Marychurch *Ex* 76-78; P-in-c Bridgwater H Trin *B & W* 78-82; P-in-c Brent Knoll 82-84; P-in-c E Brent w Lympsham 82-84; R Brent Knoll, E Brent and Lympsham 84-99; PtO *Chich* 99-07; rtd 07. *15A Victoria Close, Burgess Hill RH15 9QS* T: (01444) 244275

WELLS, Jo Bailey. b 65. CCC Cam BA 87 MA 90 Minnesota Univ MA 90 St Jo Coll Dur BA 92 PhD 97. Cranmer Hall Dur. **d** 95 **p** 96. Chapl Clare Coll Cam 95-98; Dean 98-01; PtO *Nor* 99-04; Tutor Ridley Hall Cam 01-05; Dir Angl Studies Duke Div Sch N Carolina USA 05-12; Abp's Chapl *Cant* from 13. *Lambeth Palace, London SE1 7JU* T: (020) 7898 1220

WELLS, John Rowse David. b 27. Kelham Th Coll 53. **d** 57 **p** 58. SSM from 57; LtO *S'well* 57-59; LtO Adelaide Australia 59-65;

Tutor St Mich Th Coll Crafers 61-65; C Teyateyaneng Lesotho 65-67; R Mantsonyane St Jas 67-77; Can SS Mary and Jas Cathl Maseru 77-96; Adn Cen Lesotho 85-95; PtO Melbourne Australia from 97. *St Michael's Priory, 75 Watsons Road, Diggers Rest Vic 3427, Australia* T: (0061) (3) 9740 1618 F: 9740 0007
E: ssm.melbourne@bigpond.com

WELLS, Judith Margaret. b 48. Whitelands Coll Lon CertEd 71. Trin Coll Bris 09. **d** 11 **p** 12. OLM Purton *Bris* from 11. *The Live and Let Live, 7 Upper Pavenhill, Purton, Swindon SN5 4DQ* T: (01793) 770627 M: 07760-400257
E: judith@judithwells.wanadoo.co.uk

WELLS, Leslie John. b 61. Univ of Wales (Ban) BTh 06. **d** 04 **p** 05. OLM St Helier *S'wark* 04-08; C Morden 08-10; TV from 10. *5 Willows Avenue, Morden SM4 5SG*
E: leswells80@hotmail.com

WELLS, Canon Lydia Margaret. b 50. St Aid Coll Dur BA 72 Sheff Univ MPhil 92 Leeds Univ MA 00. NOC 97. **d** 00 **p** 01. C Adwick-le-Street w Skelbrooke *Sheff* 00-03; V Doncaster Intake 03-09; V Sheff St Pet and St Oswald 09-14; AD Ecclesall 12-14; Hon Can Sheff Cathl 12-14; rtd 14; PtO *Sheff* from 14. *Apartment 1, 17 Bluecoat Rise, Sheffield S11 9DW*
M: 07977-740813 T: 0114-258 3097 E: lydwells@tesco.net

WELLS, Michael John. b 46. Univ Coll Ox BA 68 MA 73 Solicitor 74. S Dios Minl Tr Scheme 92. **d** 95 **p** 96. NSM Brighton St Pet w Chpl Royal *Chich* 95-98; Sen C 99-04; NSM Brighton St Bart 98-99; rtd 04; PtO *Chich* 04-10; P-in-c Brighton Annunciation from 10. *35 Park Crescent, Brighton BN2 3HB* T: (01273) 600735

WELLS, Canon Nicholas Anthony. b 60. Cranmer Hall Dur 88. **d** 91 **p** 92. C Accrington St Jo w Huncoat *Blackb* 91-94; C Douglas St Geo and St Barn *S & M* 94-95; C Douglas All SS and St Thos 95-97; V Onchan 97-03; V Netherton *Liv* 03-07; AD Bootle 05-07; P-in-c Maghull 07-09; TR Maghull and Melling from 09; AD Ormskirk from 10; Hon Can Liv Cathl from 05. *28B Willow Hey, Liverpool L31 3DL* T: 0151-286 2310
E: nick.the-vic@blueyonder.co.uk

WELLS, Canon Peter Robert. b 59. Wilson Carlile Coll 78 Sarum & Wells Th Coll 87. **d** 89 **p** 90. C Mortlake w E Sheen *S'wark* 89-93; Dir St Marylebone Healing and Counselling Cen 93-97; TV N Lambeth *S'wark* 97-00; Chapl Trin Hospice Lon 97-03; Chapl Brighton and Sussex Univ Hosps NHS Trust from 03; Can and Preb Chich Cathl from 10. *Royal Sussex County Hospital, Eastern Road, Brighton BN2 5BE* T: (01273) 696955 ext 7495 E: peter.wells@bsuh.nhs.uk

WELLS, Philip Anthony. b 83. UEA BA 04 Leeds Univ BA 07 MA 08. Coll of Resurr Mirfield 05. **d** 08 **p** 09. C Holt w High Kelling *Nor* 08-11; Bp's Dom Chapl *Wakef* 11-13; V Lamorbey H Trin *Roch* from 13. *The Vicarage, 1 Hurst Road, Sidcup DA15 9AE* T: (020) 8300 8231
E: vicar@holytrinitylamorbey.org

WELLS, Philip Anthony. b 57. BA MPhil. Coll of Resurr Mirfield. **d** 84 **p** 85. C Wylde Green *Birm* 84-87; Chapl and Succ Birm Cathl 87-91; Bp's Dom Chapl 91-97; V Polesworth from 97. *The Vicarage, 26 High Street, Polesworth, Tamworth B78 1DU* T: (01827) 892340 E: polesworthabbey@aol.com

WELLS, Richard John. b 46. St Mich Coll Llan 68 Cuddesdon Coll 70. **d** 71 **p** 72. C Kingston upon Hull St Alb *York* 71-75; C Addlestone *Guildf* 75-80; V Weston 80-88; V Milford and Chapl Milford Hosp Godalming 88-96; R Westbourne *Chich* 96-08; rtd 08. *39 Merryfield Crescent, Angmering, Littlehampton BN16 4DA* T: (01903) 776607

WELLS, Robert Crosby. b 28. St Jo Coll Dur BA 52. **d** 54 **p** 55. C S Shore H Trin *Blackb* 54-59; C-in-c Lea CD 59-69; V Ribby w Wrea 69-93; rtd 93; PtO *Blackb* from 93. *30 Fosbrooke House, 8 Clifton Drive, Lytham St Annes FY8 5RQ* T: (01253) 667052

WELLS, The Ven Roderick John. b 36. Dur Univ BA 63 Hull Univ MA 85. Cuddesdon Coll 63. **d** 65 **p** 66. C Lambeth St Mary the Less *S'wark* 65-66; C Kennington Cross St Anselm 66-68; P-in-c 68-71; R Skegness *Linc* 71-77; P-in-c Winthorpe 77; R Skegness and Winthorpe 77-78; TR Gt and Lt Coates w Bradley 78-89; RD Grimsby and Cleethorpes 83-89; Can and Preb Linc Cathl 86-01; Adn Stow 89-01; V Hackthorn w Cold Hanworth 89-93; P-in-c N w S Carlton 89-93; rtd 01; PtO *Linc* from 01; *Pet* from 01. *17 Ruddle Way, Langham, Oakham LE15 7NZ* T: (01572) 756532 E: venrjw@googlemail.com

WELLS, Mrs Sally Ursula. b 40. St Mark's Coll Canberra BTh 93 Ripon Coll Cuddesdon 96. **d** 97 **p** 98. Asst Chapl Vienna *Eur* 97-02; PtO 02-06; rtd 06; PtO *Sarum* from 11. *10 Park Street, Salisbury SP1 3AU* T: (01722) 322954
E: wellsfrance@gmail.com

WELLS, Canon Samuel Martin Bailey. b 65. Mert Coll Ox BA 87 MA 95 Edin Univ BD 91 Dur Univ PhD 96. Edin Th Coll 88. **d** 91 **p** 92. C Wallsend St Luke *Newc* 91-95; C Cherry Hinton St Andr *Ely* 95-97; C Teversham 95-97; P-in-c Earlham St Eliz *Nor* 97-03; RD Nor S 99-03; P-in-c Cambridge St Mark *Ely*

03-05; Can Th and Wiccamical Preb Chich Cathl from 04; Dean Duke Chpl Duke Univ N Carolina USA 05-12; V St Martin-in-the-Fields *Lon* from 12. *6 St Martin's Place, London WC2N 4JJ* T: (020) 7766 1107 E: sam.wells@smitf.org

WELLS, Terry Roy John. b 45. EAMTC 89. **d** 92 **p** 93. C Martlesham w Brightwell *St E* 92-95; R Higham, Holton St Mary, Raydon and Stratford 95-00; TV Walton and Trimley 00-07; rtd 07; PtO *Chelmsf* from 07; *St E* from 07. *Apartment 2, 1 The Maltings, The Quayside Maltings, High Street, Mistley, Manningtree CO11 1AL* T: (01206) 392957 E: terry.wells@tesco.net

WELLS, Canon William David Sandford. b 41. JP. Oriel Coll Ox BA 64 MA 66. Ridley Hall Cam 63. **d** 65 **p** 66. C Gt Malvern St Mary *Worc* 65-70; V Crowle 70-84; P-in-c Himbleton w Huddington 78-84; V E Bowbrook 84-89; Hon Can Worc Cathl 84-07; RD Droitwich 84-96; R Bowbrook S 89-07; rtd 07; PtO *Win* 08-14. *25 Greenmead Avenue, Everton, Lymington SO41 0UF* T: (01590) 642499 E: david.wells25@tiscali.co.uk

WELLS, Archdeacon of. *See* SULLIVAN, The Ven Nicola Ann

WELLS, Dean of. *See* CLARKE, The Very Revd John Martin

WELSBY, George Andrew. b 61. St Martin's Coll Lanc BA 82 Leeds Univ BA 98. Coll of Resurr Mirfield 96. **d** 98 **p** 99. C W Derby St Jo *Liv* 98-02; V Nuneaton St Mary *Cov* 02-07; PtO *Lich* 08-10; V Willenhall St Giles from 10; P-in-c Willenhall St Anne 10-14; V from 14; CMP from 06. *St Giles's Vicarage, Walsall Street, Willenhall WV13 2ER* T: (01902) 605722

WELSH, Colin. CITC. **d** 09 **p** 10. C Jordanstown *Conn* 09-12; I Castledawson *D & R* from 12. *The Rectory, 12 Station Road, Castledawson, Magherafelt BT45 8AZ* T: (028) 7946 8235 M: 07540-073475 E: colin.welsh@talktalk.net

WELSH, Jennifer Ann. b 48. Univ Coll Lon BA. **d** 81 **p** 98. NSM Newport St Matt *Mon* 81-85; NSM Risca 85-04; NSM Maindee Newport 04-09. *470 Caerleon Road, Newport NP19 7LW* T: (01633) 258287 E: mtrjen@btinternet.com

WELSH, Mrs Jennifer Lee. b 59. Calgary Univ BSc 81. Cam Episc Div Sch (USA) MDiv 87. **d** 87 **p** 88. C Calgary H Nativity Canada 87-89; Asst Chapl HM Pris Linc 89-94; Asst Chapl HM Pris Win 95-02; Chapl to Lutheran Students 03-08; PtO *Win* 95-02; *Lon* 03-08; Chapl Univ Coll 08-13; C St Pancras w St Jas and Ch Ch 08-13; C Kensington St Mary Abbots w Ch Ch and St Phil from 13. *Cottage 1, St Mary Abbots Vicarage, Vicarage Gate, London W8 4HW* T: (020) 7937 2364 E: jenniferwelsh@yahoo.co.uk

WELSH, Philip Peter. b 48. Keble Coll Ox BA 69 MA 73 Selw Coll Cam BA 72 MA 76. Westcott Ho Cam 71. **d** 73 **p** 74. C W Dulwich All SS and Em *S'wark* 73-76; C Surbiton St Andr and St Mark 76-79; Lect St Steph Coll Delhi India 79-81; V Malden St Jo *S'wark* 81-87; Min Officer *Linc* 87-94; TR Basingstoke *Win* 94-02; V Westmr St Steph w St Jo *Lon* 02-13; rtd 13. *Cottage 1, St Mary Abbots Vicarage, Vicarage Gate, London W8 4HW* T: (020) 7937 2364

WELSH, Robert Leslie. b 32. Sheff Univ BA 54. St Jo Coll Dur. **d** 58 **p** 59. C S Westoe *Dur* 58-62; C Darlington St Cuth 62-66; CF (TA) 64-67; V E Rainton *Dur* 66-85; R W Rainton 66-85; R Wolsingham and Thornley 85-97; rtd 97; PtO *Dur* from 97. *12 Lea Green, Wolsingham, Bishop Auckland DL13 3DU* T: (01388) 528529

WELSMAN, Derek Brian. b 65. Trin Coll Bris. **d** 99 **p** 00. C Ash *Guildf* 99-02; V Easebourne *Chich* 02-10; P-in-c Lurgashall, Lodsworth and Selham 08-10; V Easebourne, Lodsworth and Selham from 10; RD Midhurst from 10; Chapl K Edw VII Hosp Midhurst from 02. *Northgate, Dodsley Grove, Easebourne, Midhurst GU29 9BE* T: (01730) 812655 *or* 813341 E: derekwelsman@btinternet.com

WELTERS, Mrs Elizabeth Ann. b 49. Bris Univ BSc 70 Reading Univ PGCE 71. SAOMC 94. **d** 97 **p** 98. NSM Aylesbury *Ox* 97-03; NSM Schorne 03-10; rtd 10; PtO *Ox* from 11. *19 Scampton Close, Bicester OX26 4FF* T: (01869) 249481 E: lizwelters@yahoo.co.uk

WEMYSS, Canon Gary. b 52. Cranmer Hall Dur 79. **d** 80 **p** 81. C Blackb St Jas 80-83; C Padiham 83-86; V Stalmine 86-90; P-in-c Egton-cum-Newland and Lowick *Carl* 90-03; V Egton-cum-Newland and Lowick and Colton 03-14; RD Furness 04-10; Hon Can Carl Cathl 08-14; rtd 14. *5 Highfield Road, Sedbergh LA10 5DH* T: (015396) 22021 E: gwemyss@clara.co.uk

WENHAM, David. b 45. Pemb Coll Cam BA 67 MA Man Univ PhD 70. Ridley Hall Cam 81. **d** 84 **p** 85. Tutor Wycliffe Hall Ox 84-07; Dean 02-05; Vice-Prin 05-06; NSM Shelswell Ox 96-02; NSM Cumnor 03-07 and from 13; Tutor Trin Coll Bris from 07; Vice Prin 08-12. *66 Pinnocks Way, Oxford OX2 9DQ* T: (01865) 682984 E: todavidwenham@gmail.com

WENHAM, Michael Timothy. b 49. Pemb Coll Cam MA 75. Wycliffe Hall Ox. **d** 86 **p** 87. C Norbury *Ches* 86-89;

V Stanford in the Vale w Goosey and Hatford *Ox* 89-09; rtd 09; PtO *Ox* from 09. *19 Churchward Close, Grove, Wantage OX12 0QZ* T: (01235) 760094 M: 07719-715640 E: michaeltwenham@googlemail.com

WENHAM, Peter William. b 47. Pemb Coll Cam MA 73 MD 85 FRCS 76. St Jo Coll Nottm 98. **d** 01 **p** 02. NSM Wollaton Park *S'well* 01-06; NSM Nottingham W Deanery 06-07; P-in-c Edwalton *S'well* 07-12; rtd 12. *31 Sutton Passeys Crescent, Nottingham NG8 1BX* T: 0115-970 2481

✠**WENT, The Rt Revd John Stewart.** b 44. CCC Cam BA 66 MA 70. Oak Hill Th Coll 67. **d** 69 **p** 70 **c** 96. C Northwood Em *Lon* 69-75; V Margate H Trin *Cant* 75-83; Vice-Prin Wycliffe Hall Ox 83-89; Adn Surrey *Guildf* 89-96; Chmn Dioc Coun for Unity and Miss 90-96; Suff Bp Tewkesbury *Glouc* 96-13; Hon Can Glouc Cathl 96-13; rtd 13; Hon C Chenies and Lt Chalfont, Latimer and Flaunden *Ox* from 13; Hon Asst Bp Ox from 13. *The Rectory, Latimer, Chesham HP5 1UA* T: (01494) 765586

WENZEL, Andreas. b 81. St Steph Ho Ox MTh 14. **d** 14 **p** 15. C Horbury w Horbury Bridge *Leeds* from 14. *St Peter's Vicarage, Northgate, Horbury, Wakefield WF4 6AS* T: (01924) 283373 E: frandreas.wenzel@gmail.com

WENZEL, Peggy Sylvia. STh. Gilmore Ho. **d** 88 **p** 94. PtO *Sarum* 88-08. *Church Cottage, Church Street, Pewsey SN9 5DL* T: (01672) 563834

WERNER, Canon Donald Kilgour. b 39. Univ of Wales BA 61 Linacre Coll Ox BA 64 MA 67. Wycliffe Hall Ox 61. **d** 64 **p** 65. C Wrexham *St As* 64-69; Chapl Brasted Place Coll Westerham 69-73; Chapl Breis Univ 73-76; Hon C Clifton St Paul 73-76; Chapl Keele Univ *Lich* 77-79; P-in-c Keele 77-79; C York St Mich-le-Belfrey 79-83; Dir of Evang 79-83; R Holborn St Geo w H Trin and St Bart *Lon* 83-02; Hon Can Bujumbura from 99; Prof and Dean Th Light Univ Burundi from 03; Lic Preacher *Lon* 02-04; Dioc Discretion 02-04; Vice-Chan Burundi Chr Univ from 14. *The Old Rectory, Tedburn St Mary, Exeter EX6 6EN* E: donaldinburundi@hotmail.com

WERRELL, Ralph Sidney. b 29. Hull Univ PhD 02. Tyndale Hall Bris 54. **d** 56 **p** 57. C Penn Fields *Lich* 56-60; C Champion Hill St Sav *S'wark* 60-61; R Danby Wiske w Yafforth *Ripon* 61-65; P-in-c Hutton Bonville *York* 61-65; R Combs *St E* 65-75; V Bootle Ch Ch *Liv* 75-80; R Scole, Brockdish, Billingford, Thorpe Abbots etc *Nor* 80-83; R Southam w Stockton *Cov* 83-89; R Southam 89-94; rtd 95; PtO *Birm* 95-12; *Cov* from 95; *Lich* from 01. *Sameach, 2A Queens Road, Kenilworth CV8 1JQ* T/F: (01926) 858677

WERRETT, Olivia Margaret. b 50. Brighton Univ BA 08 Eastbourne Tr Coll FETC 82. **d** 03. NSM Bexhill St Pet *Chich* from 03. *127 Pebsham Lane, Bexhill-on-Sea TN40 2RP* T: (01424) 214144 E: owerrett@btinternet.com

WERWATH, Wolfgang Albert Richard Kurt. b 22. Ripon Hall Ox 54. **d** 56 **p** 57. C Hamer *Man* 56-58; C N Reddish 58-59; V Chadderton St Luke 59-67; V Whitfield *Derby* 67-75; V Bretby w Newton Solney 75-88; rtd 88; PtO *Derby* from 88; *S'well* from 90. *28 D'Ayncourt Walk, Farnsfield, Newark NG22 8DP* T: (01623) 882635

WESSON, Preb John Graham. b 38. St Pet Coll Ox BA 62 MA 68. Clifton Th Coll 63. **d** 65 **p** 66. C Southport Ch Ch w St Andr *Liv* 65-68; C Ox St Ebbe w St Pet 68-71; Chapl Poly Cen *Lon* 71-76; C-in-c Edin St Thos 76-82; Dir Past Studies Trin Coll Bris 82-86; R Birm St Martin w Bordesley St Andr 86-96; RD Birm City 88-95; Hon Can Birm Cathl 91-96; Dir Local Min Development *Lich* 96-98; Team Ldr Min Division 99-03; Team Ldr Bd of Min 99-03; C Lich St Mich w St Mary and Wall 96-03; Preb Lich Cathl 99-03; rtd 03. *11 Gordon Drive, Abingdon OX14 3SW* T: (01235) 526088

WESSON, William James. b 60. Lon Univ BA 82 Leeds Univ BA 07. Coll of Resurr Mirfield 05. **d** 07 **p** 08. C Moulsecoomb *Chich* 07-12; R Selsey 12-14. *Address temp unknown*

WEST, Alan David. b 61. Southn Univ BTh 92 Thames Valley Univ MA 97. Aston Tr Scheme 87 Sarum & Wells Th Coll 89. **d** 92 **p** 93. C S'wark St Geo the Martyr w St Jude 92-94; C S'wark St Geo w St Alphege and St Jude 95-96; V Boscoppa *Truro* 96-02; Chapl Mt Edgcumbe Hospice 02-05; Chapl R Cornwall Hosps Trust 05-10; Public Preacher *Truro* 10-12; Hon C St Blazey 12-14; Hon C Lanlivery 12-14; Hon C Luxulyan 12-14. *c/o Crockford, Church House, Great Smith Street, London SW1P 3AZ*

WEST, Andrew Victor. b 59. Wycliffe Hall Ox 87. **d** 90 **p** 91. C Leyland St Andr *Blackb* 90-94; C Blackpool St Jo 94-96; TV Bedworth *Cov* 96-98; Chapl Cheltenham and Glouc Coll of HE 98-01; Chapl Glos Univ 01-03; Chapl St Martin's Coll *Carl* 03-07; Chapl Cumbria Univ 07-10; C Carl St Jo 03-10; R Gateshead Fell *Dur* from 10; P-in-c Gateshead St Geo from 14. *The Rectory, 45 Shotley Gardens, Low Fell, Gateshead NE9 5DP* T: 0191-442 2463

WEST, Bernard Kenneth. b 31. Linc Th Coll. **d** 67 **p** 68. C E Ham St Geo *Chelmsf* 67-71; C Gt Bookham *Guildf* 71-73; R Esperance Australia 73-76; C Dalkeith 76-79; P-in-c Carine 80-82; R Carine w Duncraig 82-84; C Ravensthorpe 85-87; rtd 87. *9 Beaufort Street, Katanning WA 6317, Australia* T: (0061) (8) 9821 4571

WEST, Bryan Edward. b 39. Avery Hill Coll CertEd 69 BEd 80 Kent Univ MA 86. Cant Sch of Min 85. **d** 88 **p** 89. NSM Gravesend H Family w Ifield *Roch* 88-92; C Gravesend St Geo 92-95; NSM Hatcham Park All SS *S'wark* 95-98; NSM Stambridge and Ashingdon w S Fambridge *Chelmsf* 98-01; NSM Canvey Is 01-06; Chapl Southend Health Care NHS Trust 99-06; PtO *Chelmsf* 06-13. *4 Barton Court, Central Treviscoe, St Austell PL26 7PD* T: (01726) 823285 E: bryanwest@tiscali.co.uk

WEST, Miss Caroline Elisabeth. b 61. RGN 84. Wycliffe Hall Ox 93. **d** 95. NSM Eastrop *Win* from 95. *19 Beaulieu Court, Riverdene, Basingstoke RG21 4DQ* T: (01256) 350389 *or* 464249 E: caroline.west@stmarys-basingstoke.org.uk

WEST, Mrs Christine Cecily. TCD BA 60 MA 63 HDipEd 61. CITC 91. **d** 94 **p** 95. NSM Bray *D & G* 94-96; NSM Kilternan 96-99; LtO from 99. *55 Beech Park Road, Foxrock, Dublin 18, Republic of Ireland* T: (00353) (1) 289 6374 E: johncecily@eircom.net

WEST, David Marshall. b 48. St Jo Coll Dur BA 70. **d** 73 **p** 74. C Wylde Green *Birm* 73-76; C Wokingham St Paul *Ox* 76-79; V Hurst 79-88; V Maidenhead St Luke 88-95; C Whitley Ch Ch 95-99; P-in-c Reading Ch Ch 99-05; V 05-12; rtd 13. *The Old Tannery, Church Lane, Ledbury HR8 1DW* T: (01531) 636580 E: revdmwest@hotmail.com

WEST, Mrs Deirdre Ann. b 47. **d** 10 **p** 11. OLM Campsea Ashe w Marlesford, Parham and Hacheston *St E* 10-13; NSM 13-14; P-in-c from 14; OLM Brandeston w Kettleburgh and Easton 10-13; NSM 13-14; P-in-c from 14. *Smokey House, The Common, Turnstall, Woodbridge IP12 2JR* T: (01728) 688340 E: deirdre.west@btinternet.com

WEST, Derek Elvin. b 47. Hull Univ BA 69. Westcott Ho Cam 71. **d** 73 **p** 74. C Walthamstow St Pet *Chelmsf* 73-77; C Chingford SS Pet and Paul 77-80; TV W Slough *Ox* 80-88; Slough Community Chapl 88-95; TV Upton cum Chalvey 95-12; rtd 12; PtO *Lon* from 12. *35 Wallasey Crescent, Ickenham, Uxbridge UB10 8SA* M: 07957-158069 E: derekewest@gmail.com

WEST, Mrs Elizabeth Maxine. b 47. Liv Univ BA 69 Lon Inst of Educn PGCE 70 K Coll Lon BA 95 AKC. NTMTC. **d** 99 **p** 00. NSM Hornsey H Innocents *Lon* 99-00; NSM Highgate St Mich 00-03; C 03-11; rtd 12. *West Villa, Inderwick Road, London N8 9JU* T: (020) 8348 3042 E: maxineanddennis@hotmail.com

WEST, Canon Eric Robert Glenn. b 55. QUB BA 79 Man Univ DipEd 80. CITC BTh 92. **d** 92 **p** 93. C Enniskillen *Clogh* 92-95; I Lisbellaw 95-00; CF 00-03; I Annagh w Drumgoon, Ashfield etc *K, E & A* 03-06; I Derryvullen N w Castlearchdale *Clogh* 06-15; I Carnteel and Crilly *Arm* from 15; Can St Patr Cathl Dublin from 11. *St James's Rectory, 22 Carnteel Road, Aughnacloy BT69 6DU* M: 07969-332530 E: glenn.west55@hotmail.com

WEST, Mrs Heather June. b 55. SWMTC 12. **d** 15. NSM Three Rivers *Truro* from 15. *Lowarth Duw, 29 Liskeard Road, Callington PL17 7JD* T: (01579) 384130 E: pronter@btinternet.com

WEST, Henry Cyrano. b 28. K Coll Lon. **d** 51 **p** 52. C Braunstone *Leic* 51-53; C Wandsworth St Anne *S'wark* 53-55; C Raynes Park St Sav 55-58; CF 58-63; V Sculcoates *York* 63-71; P-in-c Kingston upon Hull St Jude w St Steph 67-71; LtO *Cov* 71-75; Man 75-87; Hon C Hulme Ascension 87-94; rtd 91; PtO *Man* 91-08. *6 King's Drive, Middleton, Manchester M24 4FB* T: 0161-643 4410

WEST, Jeffrey James. b 50. OBE 06. Worc Coll Ox BA 72 BPhil 74 MA 76 FSA 11 FRSA 01. Ripon Coll Cuddesdon 05. **d** 07 **p** 08. NSM Banbury *Ox* from 07; AD Deddington 12-15. *St Mary's Centre, Horse Fair, Banbury OX16 0AA* M: 07766-198484 E: curate@stmaryschurch-banbury.org.uk

WEST, Keith. *See* RYDER-WEST, Keith

WEST (formerly WINDIATE), Mrs Mary Elizabeth. b 49. Linc Th Coll 94. **d** 94 **p** 95. C Loughton St Jo *Chelmsf* 94-98; P-in-c Ashingdon w S Fambridge 98-01; P-in-c Stambridge 98-01; TV Canvey Is 01-07; P-in-c Greenstead w Colchester St Anne 07-08; TR 08-13; rtd 13. *4 Barton Court, Central Treviscoe, St Austell PL26 7PD* T: (01726) 823285 E: mothermary2@tiscali.co.uk

WEST, Maxine. *See* WEST, Elizabeth Maxine

WEST, Canon Michael Brian. b 39. Bris Univ BSc 60. Linc Th Coll 64. **d** 66 **p** 67. C Bp's Hatfield *St Alb* 66-69; Ind Chapl 69-81; Sen Ind Chapl 71-81; Hon Can St Alb 78-81; Sen Ind Chapl and Hon Can Sheff Cathl 81-01; Dir Open Forum for Economic Regeneration 02-04; rtd 04; PtO *Sheff*

from 02. *23 Walton Road, Sheffield S11 8RE* T: 0114-266 2188 E: mike.west23@tiscali.co.uk

WEST, The Ven Michael Frederick. b 50. Trin Coll Ox BA 72 MA 76 UEA PhD 96. Westcott Ho Cam 72. **d** 74 **p** 75. C Wolverhampton *Lich* 74-78; C Hanley H Ev 78-79; TV 79-82; Dioc Youth Officer *St E* 83-88; V Ipswich St Thos 88-95; Prin OLM Scheme 96-03; Hon Can St E Cathl 96-03; Can Res and Chan Linc Cathl 03-08; Dioc Dir Formation in Discipleship and Min 03-06; TR Wrexham *St As* 08-13; AD 08-13; Chan St As Cathl 11-13; Res Can Ban Cathl 13-14; Tr Adn from 14; CMD Officer from 13. *The Vicarage, Newgate Street, Y Felinheli LL56 4SQ* T: (01248) 671159 E: ministryarchdeacon@gmail.com

WEST, Michael John. b 33. Imp Coll Lon BScEng 54 ARSM 54 CEng 60 FIMMM 68 FREng 89 Hon FIMMM 96. S'wark Ord Course 85. **d** 88 **p** 89. NSM Caterham *S'wark* 88-98; PtO *Chich* from 97. *Minstrels, The Causeway, Horsham RH12 1HE* T: (01403) 263437 F: 249604 E: mwest.viabt@btinternet.com

WEST, Michael Oakley. b 31. Open Univ BA 97. Bris Bapt Coll 53 Wells Th Coll 62. **d** 63 **p** 64. C Swindon Ch Ch *Bris* 63-66; Libya 66-68; R Lydiard Millicent w Lydiard Tregoz *Bris* 68-75; V Breage w Germoe *Truro* 75-82; CMS 82-91; Chapl Tel Aviv 82-89; Chapl Shiplake Coll Henley 91-94; Asst Chapl Bryanston Sch 94-95; PtO *Eur* 95-97; rtd 96; PtO *Lon* 96-97; LtO Spokane USA from 97. *1932 East 25th Avenue, Spokane WA 99203, USA*

WEST, Paul John. b 66. Newc Univ Aus BA 87 DipEd 94. Westcott Ho Cam 04. **d** 06 **p** 07. C Albury Australia 06-08; C Dee Why 08-09; Asst P King Street 09-10; P-in-c Wisbech SS Pet and Paul *Ely* from 10. *The Vicarage, Love Lane, Wisbech PE13 1HP* T: (01945) 580375 M: 07584-897143 E: ppaulwest@hotmail.com or fatherpjfwest@gmail.com

WEST, Paul Leslie. b 57. OLM course 96. **d** 99 **p** 00. OLM Kinnerley w Melverley and Knockin w Maesbrook *Lich* from 99. *Braddan, Farm Hall, Kinnerley, Oswestry SY10 8EG* T: (01691) 682600

WEST, Penelope Ann. b 52. Chelt & Glouc Coll of HE MA 98 Univ of Wales (Lamp) MPhil 08 FIBMS 72. **d** 00 **p** 01. NSM Hartpury w Corse and Staunton *Glouc* 00-09; NSM Ashleworth, Corse, Hartpury, Hasfield etc 09-12. *Catsbury Cottage, Corsend Road, Hartpury GL19 3BP* T: (01425) 700314 E: revpennywest@gmail.com

WEST, Peter Harcourt. b 29. **d** 59 **p** 60. C Histon *Ely* 59-60; C Hampreston *Sarum* 60-61; C Braintree *Chelmsf* 61-63; PtO from 72; rtd 94. *Westgates, 139 Witham Road, Black Notley, Braintree CM77 8LR* T: (01376) 323048

WEST, Canon Philip William. b 48. Magd Coll Ox BA 70 MA 78. St Jo Coll Nottm BA 74. **d** 75 **p** 76. C Rushden w Newton Bromswold *Pet* 75-79; C Pitsmoor w Ellesmere *Sheff* 79-83; V Attercliffe 83-89; Ind Chapl 85-90; P-in-c Darnall 86-89; V Stannington 89-13; P-in-c Sheff St Bart 02-07; AD Hallam 96-02; Hon Can Sheff Cathl 01-13; rtd 13; PtO *Sheff* from 13. *Wesley House, Storrs Lane, Sheffield S6 6GY* E: philipwest@givemail.co.uk

WEST, Reginald Roy. b 28. St Deiniol's Hawarden 74. **d** 74 **p** 75. C Abergavenny St Mary w Llanwenarth Citra *Mon* 74-77; V Tredegar St Jas 77-96; rtd 96; LtO *Mon* from 96. *2 Croesonen Park, Abergavenny NP7 6PD* T: (01873) 857043

WEST, Roderic. *See* WEST, Thomas Roderic

WEST, Ruth. BSc BTh. **d** 09 **p** 10. C Waterford w Killea, Drumcannon and Dunhill *C & O* 09-12; I Inver w Mountcharles, Killaghtee and Killybegs *D & R* from 12. *The Rectory, Inver, Co Donegal, Republic of Ireland* T: (00353) (74) 973 6013 M: 87-625 9077 E: ruthjwest@hotmail.com

WEST, Stephen Peter. b 52. Liv Univ CertEd 74. Oak Hill Th Coll 87. **d** 89 **p** 90. C Gateacre *Liv* 89-92; V Liv All So Springwood 92-02; TV Teignmouth, Ideford w Luton, Ashcombe etc *Ex* from 02. *The Vicarage, 3 Moors Park, Bishopsteignton, Teignmouth TQ14 9RH* T/F: (01626) 775247 E: spmwest@btinternet.com

WEST, Mrs Suzanne Elizabeth. b 46. STETS 04. **d** 07 **p** 08. NSM Portsea St Geo *Portsm* 07-11; Asst to RD Gosport from 11. *64 Melville Road, Gosport PO12 4QX* T: (023) 9278 8782 E: melville64@ntlworld.com

WEST, The Ven Thomas Roderic. b 55. BTh 90. TCD Div Sch. **d** 86 **p** 87. C Dromore Cathl 86-89; I Carrowdore w Millisle 89-95; I Moira 95-12; I Seapatrick from 12; Can Dromore Cathl from 05; Chan Dromore Cathl 08-12; Adn Dromore from 11. *The Rectory, 63 Lurgan Road, Banbridge BT32 4LY* T: (028) 4062 2612 *or* 4062 2744 E: rodericwest@btinternet.com

WEST, Timothy Ralph. b 53. Bath Univ BSc 75. Ridley Hall Cam 82. **d** 85 **p** 86. C Mildenhall *St E* 85-88; TV Melbury *Sarum* 88-92; TR 92-98; TR Preston w Sutton Poyntz, Littlemoor etc from 98; RD Weymouth and Portland from 12. *The Rectory, Sutton Road, Preston, Weymouth DT3 6BX* T: (01305) 833142 M: 07000-785720 E: team.rector@hotmail.co.uk

WEST CUMBERLAND, Archdeacon of. *See* PRATT, The Ven Richard David

WEST HAM, Archdeacon of. *See* COCKETT, The Ven Elwin Wesley

WEST-LINDELL, Stein Erik. b 54. BA. Linc Th Coll 82. **d** 84 **p** 85. C Allington and Maidstone St Pet *Cant* 84-87; R Orlestone w Snave and Ruckinge w Warehorne 87-93; R Byfield w Boddington and Aston le Walls *Pet* 93-99; V Nor Lakenham St Alb and St Mark from 99. *2 Conesford Drive, Norwich NR1 2BB* T: (01603) 621843

WESTALL, Jonathan Mark. b 67. Nottm Univ BSc 88 K Coll Lon PGCE 93 St Jo Coll Dur BA 98. Cranmer Hall Dur 96. **d** 99 **p** 00. C St Helier *S'wark* 99-02; C Reading Greyfriars *Ox* 02-06; V E Acton St Dunstan w St Thos *Lon* from 06. *The Vicarage, 54 Perryn Road, London W3 7NA* T: (020) 8743 4117 E: jonwestall@btinternet.com

✠**WESTALL, The Rt Revd Michael Robert.** b 39. Qu Coll Cam BA 62 MA 66. Cuddesdon Coll 63 Harvard Div Sch 65. **d** 66 **p** 67 **c** 01. C Heref St Martin 66-70; Lect Bp's Coll Calcutta India 70-76; Vice Prin 76-79; Prin 79-83; Prin St Mark's Th Coll Dar-es-Salaam Tanzania 84-92; R Alfrick, Lulsley, Suckley, Leigh and Bransford *Worc* 93-00; Bp SW Tanganyika 01-06; rtd 06; P-in-c Torquay St Luke *Ex* 07-12; Hon Asst Bp Ex 07-12. *Oak House, Kingstone, Hereford HR2 9ET* T: (01981) 250259 E: michaelwestall39@gmail.com

WESTBROOK, Canon Colin David. b 36. Oriel Coll Ox BA 59. St Steph Ho Ox MA 63. **d** 61 **p** 62. C Roath St Martin *Llan* 61-66; C Roath 66-74; V Llantarnam *Mon* 74-79; V Newport St Jo Bapt 79-07; Hon Can St Woolos Cathl 88-91; Can St Woolos Cathl from 91; Warden of Ords 91-99. *St John's Vicarage, 62 Oakfield Road, Newport NP20 4LP* T: (01633) 265581

WESTBROOK (née REED), Mrs Ethel Patricia Ivy. b 42. Bris Univ CertEd 63. Cant Sch of Min 82. **dss** 84 **d** 87 **p** 94. Fawkham and Hartley *Roch* 84-85; Asst Dir of Educn 84-86; Cliffe at Hoo w Cooling 85-86; Corby SS Pet and Andr w Gt and Lt Oakley 86-90; Par Dn 87-90; Par Dn Roch 90-94; C Rainham 94-99; V Joydens Wood St Barn 99-05; Dioc Chapl MU 01-05; rtd 05; Hon C Banstead *Guildf* 05-11; PtO *Roch* from 05; *Cant* from 12. *5 Victoria Mews, Station Road, Westgate-on-Sea CT8 8RQ* T: (01843) 836022 E: patriciawipe@yahoo.co.uk

WESTBY, Martyn John. b 61. Leeds Univ BA 83. Trin Coll Bris 96. **d** 98 **p** 99. C Drypool *York* 98-01; P-in-c Cherry Burton 01-13; Chapl Bp Burton Coll York 01-13; Assoc Dioc Dir of Ords *York* 05-10; C Etton w Dalton Holme 11-13; TV Drypool from 13. *383 Southcoates Lane, Hull HU9 3UN* E: martynwestby@btinternet.com

WESTCOTT, James John. b 55. St Jo RC Sem Surrey 76. **d** 81 **p** 82. In RC Ch 81-93; C Westmr St Steph w St Jo *Lon* 93-96; P-in-c Haggerston St Chad 96-01; V from 01. *St Chad's Vicarage, Dunloe Street, London E2 8JR* T: (020) 7613 2229 E: chad@jameswestcott.co.uk

WESTERMANN-CHILDS, Miss Emma Jane. b 71. Univ of Wales (Ban) BA 93 Ox Univ MTh 99. Ripon Coll Cuddesdon 96. **d** 98 **p** 99. C Launceston *Truro* 98-01; P-in-c St Stephen in Brannel from 01. *The Rectory, 70 Rectory Road, St Stephen, St Austell PL26 7RL* T: (01726) 822236 E: emma.childs@btinternet.com

WESTERN, Canon Robert Geoffrey. b 37. Man Univ BSc 60. Qu Coll Birm. **d** 62 **p** 63. C Sedbergh *Bradf* 62-65; PV Linc Cathl 65-73; Hd Master Linc Cathl Sch 74-96; Can and Preb Linc Cathl 74-96; rtd 97; PtO *Carl* from 96. *2 Guldrey House, Guldrey Lane, Sedbergh LA10 5DS* T: (015396) 21426

WESTHAVER, George Derrick. b 68. St Mary's Univ Halifax NS BA 92. Wycliffe Coll Toronto MDiv 98. **d** 97 **p** 98. C Teversham and Cherry Hinton St Andr *Ely* 97-00; TV The Ramseys and Upwood 00-03; Chapl Linc Coll Ox 03-06; C Ox St Mich w St Martin and All SS 03-06; R Halifax St Geo Canada 07-13; Prin Pusey Ho from 13; Fell St Cross Coll Ox from 13. *Pusey House, St Giles, Oxford OX1 3LX* T: (01865) 278415 E: gwesthaver@gmail.com

WESTLAKE, Michael Paul. b 34. Ex Coll Ox BA 56 MA 64. Wells Th Coll 59. **d** 61 **p** 62. C Southmead *Bris* 61-67; V Eastville St Thos 67-74; V Eastville St Thos w St Anne 74-83; P-in-c Easton St Mark 79-83; V Marshfield w Cold Ashton and Tormarton etc 83-01; rtd 01; PtO *Birm* 03-14. *65 Duxford Road, Great Barr, Birmingham B42 2JD* T: 0121-358 7030

WESTLAND, Richard Theodore. b 27. **d** 87 **p** 88. OLM Freiston w Butterwick *Linc* 87-97; rtd 97; PtO *Linc* from 97. *76 Brand End Road, Butterwick, Boston PE22 0JD* T: (01205) 760572

WESTLEY, Stuart. b 24. Em Coll Cam BA 48 MA 52 Man Univ DASE 84. Wells Th Coll 49. **d** 50 **p** 51. C Prestwich St Marg *Man* 50-53; C Tonge w Alkrington 53-55; C-in-c Oldham St Ambrose 55-58; LtO *Blackb* 58-70; Chapl Arnold Sch Blackpool 58-66; Asst Chapl Denstone Coll Uttoxeter 70-73; Chapl Ermysted's Gr Sch Skipton 73-85; Hon C Blackpool

St Mich *Blackb* 75-77; PtO *Bradf* 77-78; LtO 78-85; C Padiham *Blackb* 85-89; rtd 89; PtO *Blackb* 89-11. *17 Fosbrooke House, Clifton Drive, Lytham St Annes FY8 5RQ* E: s.westley@amserve.net

WESTMACOTT, Rosemary Margaret. *See* FRANKLIN, Rosemary Margaret

WESTMINSTER, Archdeacon of. *See* TREMLETT, The Ven Andrew

WESTMINSTER, Dean of. *See* HALL, The Very Revd John Robert

WESTMORELAND, Diane Ruth. b 57. Man Univ BA 78 Dur Univ DThM 12. NEOC 95. **d** 98 **p** 99. NSM Tadcaster w Newton Kyme *York* 98-99; C 99-02; P-in-c Stamford Bridge Gp 02-08; P-in-c Amble *Newc* from 08. *The Vicarage, Straffen Court, Amble, Morpeth NE65 0HA* T: (01665) 714560 E: diane@dianewestmoreland.co.uk

WESTMORLAND AND FURNESS, Archdeacon of. *See* DRIVER, The Ven Penelope May

WESTNEY, Michael Edward William. b 29. Lich Th Coll 64. **d** 65 **p** 66. C Hughenden *Ox* 65-68; C Banbury 68-71; TV Trunch *Nor* 71-78; V Reading St Matt *Ox* 78-83; TV W Slough 83-88; TR 88-94; rtd 94; PtO *Ox* 97-00. *59 Portland Close, Burnham, Slough SL2 2LT* T: (01628) 660052

WESTON, Darlene Elisabeth. b 50. **d** 12 **p** 13. OLM Carr Dyke Gp *Linc* from 12. *Wilson House, 33 High Street, Walcott, Lincoln LN4 3SN* T: (01526) 861759

WESTON, Canon David Wilfrid Valentine. b 37. Lanc Univ PhD 93. **d** 67 **p** 68. OSB 60-84; LtO *Ox* 67-84; Prior Nashdom Abbey 71-74; Abbot 74-84; C Chorley St Pet *Blackb* 84-85; V Pilling 85-89; Bp's Dom Chapl *Carl* 89-94; Can Res Carl Cathl 94-05; Lib 95-05; Vice-Dean 05; rtd 05; PtO *Carl* from 06. *The Pond House, Ratten Row, Dalston, Carlisle CA5 7AY* T: (01228) 710673 E: helweston@gmail.com

WESTON, Gary James. b 72. Westmr Coll Ox BTh 95. Wycliffe Hall Ox 02. **d** 04 **p** 05. C Barrow St Paul *Carl* 04-08; C S Barrow 08-09; P-in-c Hinckley H Trin *Leic* 09-10; V Hinckley St Jo from 10; AD Sparkenhoe W from 15. *21 Windrush Drive, Hinckley LE10 0NY* T: (01455) 233552 E: gary.weston@ukonline.co.uk

WESTON, Ivan John. b 45. MBE 88. Chich Th Coll 71. **d** 74 **p** 75. C Harlow St Mary Magd *Chelmsf* 74-77; Chapl RAF 77-00; PtO *Nor* 93-95; *Ely* 00-11. *2 The Furlongs, Needingworth, St Ives PE27 4TX* T: (01480) 462107

WESTON, John Oglivy. b 30. St Pet Coll Ox BA 66 MA 70. Linc Th Coll 71. **d** 71 **p** 72. Lect Trent (Nottm) Poly 66-82; Hon C Long Clawson and Hose *Leic* 71-82; Hon C Bingham *S'well* 82-85; LtO 85-91; rtd 91; PtO *Heref* 91-12. *32 Cedar Avenue, Malvern WR14 2SG* T: (01684) 564888 E: johnweston@uwclub.net

WESTON, Mrs Judith. b 36. Open Univ BA 75 MSR 56. St Jo Coll Nottm 84. **dss** 85 **d** 87 **p** 94. Huddersfield H Trin *Wakef* 85-87; Par Dn 87-91; Par Dn Wakef St Andr and St Mary 91-94; C 94-95; Chapl Huddersfield NHS Trust 95-98; rtd 96; PtO *Leeds* from 98. *Overcroft, 8A Newland Road, Huddersfield HD5 0QT* T: (01484) 453591

WESTON, Neil. b 51. Jes Coll Ox BA 73 MA 78. Ridley Hall Cam 74. **d** 76 **p** 77. C Ealing St Mary *Lon* 76-80; P-in-c Pertenhall w Swineshead *St Alb* 80-89; P-in-c Dean w Yelden, Melchbourne and Shelton 80-89; R The Stodden Churches 89-91; R Newhaven *Chich* 91-98; P-in-c Radcliffe-on-Trent and Shelford etc *S'well* 98-04; R 04-05; V Radcliffe-on-Trent and Shelford 06-09; R Kington w Huntington, Old Radnor, Kinnerton etc *Heref* 09-14; rtd 14; PtO *Ox* from 14. *15 Longmead, Abingdon OX14 1JQ* T: (01235) 204147 E: neilweston@gmail.com

WESTON, Paul David Astley. b 57. Trin Hall Cam BA 80 MA 83 Westmr Coll Ox MPhil 92 K Coll Lon PhD 02. Wycliffe Hall Ox 83. **d** 85 **p** 86. C New Malden and Coombe *S'wark* 85-89; Lect Oak Hill Th Coll 89-97; Vice-Prin 97-00; Gen Sec UCCF 00-01; Assoc Lect Ridley Hall Cam 02-03; Tutor from 03; PtO *Ely* from 01. *Ridley Hall, Ridley Hall Road, Cambridge CB3 9HG* T: (01223) 746580 F: 746581 E: pdaw2@cam.ac.uk

WESTON, Phillip Richard. b 76. Bath Univ BSc 99 York Univ MSc 02. Wycliffe Hall Ox BA 09. **d** 10 **p** 11. C Aughton Ch Ch *Liv* 10-14; P-in-c Gidea Park *Chelmsf* from 14. *St Michael's Vicarage, Main Road, Romford RM2 5EL* T: (01708) 741084 M: 07939-129631 E: home@phweston.com

WESTON, Stephen John Astley. b 55. Aston Univ BSc 77. Ridley Hall Cam 78. **d** 81 **p** 82. C Gt Chesham *Ox* 81-85; C Southport Ch Ch *Liv* 85-87; P-in-c Gayhurst w Ravenstone, Stoke Goldington etc *Ox* 87-91; R 91-96; RD Newport 92-95; V Chipping Norton 96-01; TR 01-13; AD 02-07; Hon Can Ch Ch 06-13; P-in-c Ottery St Mary, Alfington, W Hill, Tipton etc *Ex* from 13. *The Vicar's House, The College, Ottery St Mary EX11 1DQ* T: (01404) 812979 E: revsweston@lineone.net

WESTON, Timothy Bernard Charles. b 48. **d** 03 **p** 04. OLM Watton w Carbrooke and Ovington *Nor* 03-07; OLM Ashill, Carbrooke, Ovington and Saham Toney 07-14; PtO from 14. *Sunset Barn, Morton Lane, Weston Longville, Norwich NR9 5JL* T: (01603) 879115 E: reverendweston@gmail.com

WESTON, Mrs Virginia Anne. b 58. UEA BSc 79. Wycliffe Hall Ox 84. **d** 87 **p** 02. Par Dn New Malden and Coombe *S'wark* 87-89; LtO *Lon* 89-01; Chapl to People at Work in Cam *Ely* 02-06. *65 Manor Place, Cambridge CB1 1LJ* T: (01223) 462279 E: virginiaweston@yahoo.co.uk

WESTWOOD, Canon John Richard. b 55. Clare Coll Cam BA 77 MA 81 Lambeth MA 98. Ripon Coll Cuddesdon 77. **d** 79 **p** 80. C Oakham w Hambleton and Egleton *Pet* 79-81; C Oakham, Hambleton, Egleton, Braunston and Brooke 81-83; V Gt w Lt Harrowden and Orlingbury 83-90; V Wellingborough St Andr 90-99; RD Wellingborough 92-97; R Irthlingborough 99-10; P-in-c Rothwell w Orton, Rushton w Glendon and Pipewell from 10; C Broughton w Loddington and Cransley etc from 10; Warden of Readers 95-05; Can Pet Cathl from 97. *The Vicarage, High Street, Rothwell, Kettering NN14 6BQ* T: (01536) 710268 E: revdjohn.westwood@tesco.net

WESTWOOD, Peter. b 38. Open Univ BA 76. AKC 65. **d** 65 **p** 66. C Acomb St Steph and St Aid *York* 65-68; Chapl HM Youth Cust Cen Onley 69-73; Chapl HM Pris Leic 73-77; Maidstone 77-81; Dur 81-87; Brixton 87-93; Wormwood Scrubs 93-98; PtO *S'wark* from 98; rtd 99. *St Stephen's Church, College Road, London SE21 7HN* T: (020) 8693 0082 E: westwood773@btinternet.com

WESTWOOD, Richard Andrew. b 64. Nottm Univ BSc 85 PGCE 86. St Jo Coll Nottm 02. **d** 04 **p** 05. C Gt Wyrley *Lich* from 04. *46 Gorsey Lane, Great Wyrley, Walsall WS6 6EX* T: (01922) 419161 E: westwood.richard@btinternet.com

WESTWOOD, Timothy. b 61. Wolv Poly MBA 91. WMMTC 95. **d** 98 **p** 99. NSM Sedgley St Mary *Worc* from 98. *85 High Park Crescent, Dudley DY3 1QY* T: (01902) 831078 E: twestwood@mac.com

WETHERALL, Canon Cecil Edward (Ted). b 29. St Jo Coll Dur 49. **d** 56 **p** 57. C Ipswich St Aug *St E* 56-59; R Hitcham 59-79; P-in-c Brettenham 61-63; P-in-c Kettlebaston 71-91; R Hitcham w Lt Finborough 79-91; P-in-c Preston 85-91; Hon Can *St E* Cathl 83-91; rtd 92; PtO *St E* 92-97; Asst Chapl Athens w Kifissia, Patras, Thessaloniki etc *Eur* 92-96. *Kastraki, Tolo, Nafplio, 210 56 Argolis, Greece*

WETHERALL, Mrs Joanne Elizabeth Julia. b 62. STETS 02. **d** 05 **p** 06. NSM Godalming *Guildf* 05-09; TV Tring *St Alb* 09-15; Dioc Children's and Families' Officer *Glouc* from 15. *Department of Mission and Ministry, 4 College Green, Gloucester GL1 2LR* E: joanne.wetherall@btinternet.com *or* jwetherall@glosdioc.org.uk

WETHERALL, Canon Nicholas Guy. b 52. Lon Univ BMus 73 Ox Univ CertEd 75. Chich Th Coll 82. **d** 84 **p** 85. C Cleobury Mortimer w Hopton Wafers *Heref* 84-87; TV Leominster 87-92; V Cuckfield *Chich* 92-14; RD 99-03; Can and Preb Chich Cathl 08-14; rtd 14. *4 Eden Place, Newlyn, Penzance TR18 5ET* T: (01736) 368887

WETHERELL, Ms Eileen Joyce. b 44. Westf Coll Lon BSc 66. S Dios Minl Tr Scheme 89. **d** 92 **p** 94. Par Dn Southampton Maybush St Pet *Win* 92-94; C 94-96; TV Totton 96-04; V Hythe 04-12; Dioc Adv for Women's Min 02-12; rtd 12; PtO *Win* from 12. *3 Creighton Road, Southampton SO15 4JF* T: (023) 8184 8598 E: ewetherell@tiscali.co.uk

WETHERELL, Philippa Clare. b 80. Univ of Wales (Cardiff) BSc 02. Trin Coll Bris BA 08. **d** 09 **p** 10. C W Derby St Mary and St Jas *Liv* 09-13; TV Kirkby from 13. *The Rectory, Old Hall Lane, Kirkby, Liverpool L32 5TH* M: 07770-892639 E: phillyfrog@yahoo.com

WEYMAN, Canon Richard Darrell George. b 46. Lon Univ BA Bris Univ PhD. Sarum & Wells Th Coll. **d** 84 **p** 85. C Sherborne w Castleton and Lillington *Sarum* 84-88; V Malden St Jo *S'wark* 88-92; P-in-c Marnhull *Sarum* 92-11; Dir Post Ord Tr 92-11; Can and Preb Sarum Cathl 99-11; Dioc Adv in Spiritual Direction 06-11; C Okeford and Hazelbury Bryan and the Hillside Par 08-11; rtd 11. *Millers Cottage, Angel Lane, Shaftesbury SP7 8DF* E: dweyman@btinternet.com

WEYMAN PACK-BERESFORD, John Derek Henry. b 31. Wells Th Coll 69. **d** 70 **p** 71. C Headley All SS *Guildf* 70-76; V Westcott 76-97; RD Dorking 84-89; rtd 97; PtO *Truro* from 99. *Kittiwake, Polurrian Cliff, Mullion, Helston TR12 7EW* T: (01326) 240457

WEYMONT, Martin Eric. b 48. St Jo Coll Dur BA 69 MA 74 Fitzw Coll Cam PGCE 73 Lon Inst of Educn PhD 89 Open Univ BSc 96. Westcott Ho Cam 71. **d** 73 **p** 74. C Blackheath *Birm* 73-76; Hon C Willesden St Matt *Lon* 76-77; Hon C Belmont 77-79; P-in-c W Twyford 79-85; NSM Cricklewood St Mich 85-88; Chapl St Pet Colleg Sch *Wolv* 88-91; Hon C Wolverhampton *Lich* 88-91; NSM Bickershaw *Liv* 91-97; P-in-c Mells w Buckland Dinham, Elm, Whatley etc *B & W* 97-15; rtd 15. *33 Ludlow Close, Warminster BA12 8BJ*

WHAITE, Richard Patrick. b 80. K Coll Lon MA 10. Ripon Coll Cuddesdon BA 14. **d** 14 **p** 15. C Fulham All SS *Lon* from 14. *All Saints' Fulham Parish Office, Pryors Bank, Bishops Park, London SW6 3LA* T: (020) 7371 7540 M: 07857-776247 E: curate@allsaints-fulham.org.uk

WHALE, David. b 81. Univ of Wales (Ban) BSc 02 Glos Univ PGCE 06. Wycliffe Hall Ox BTh 15. **d** 15. C Glouc St Cath from 15. *29 Windfall Way, Gloucester GL2 0RP* E: djmketos@gmail.com

WHALE, Desmond Victor. b 35. Bris Sch of Min 81. **d** 84 **p** 85. LtO *Bris* 84-88; C Parr *Liv* 88-91; R Winfarthing w Shelfanger w Burston w Gissing etc *Nor* 91-00; RD Redenhall 97-99; rtd 00; PtO *Nor* from 00; *Sarum* from 01. *18 St George's Court, Semington, Trowbridge BA14 6GA* M: 07887-717052 E: deswhale@talktalk.net

WHALE, Noel Raymond. b 41. Ox Univ 67. **d** 70 **p** 71. C Amersham *Ox* 70-73; C Geelong Australia 73-76; P-in-c Altona 76-79; I 79-85; I Ivanhoe 86-97; Prec and Min Can St Paul's Cathl 97-01; I Bundoora St Pet 01-11. *Unit 1, 33-35 Ligar Street, Sunbury VIC 3429, Australia* T: (0061) (3) 9740 3315 M: 41-219 6127 E: jonahnoel@hotmail.com

WHALE, Peter Richard. b 49. Auckland Univ MA 72 BSc 73 Down Coll Cam BA 74 MA 79 Otago Univ BD 78 Ex Univ PhD 90. St Jo Coll Auckland 75. **d** 77 **p** 78. C Takapuna New Zealand 77-80; Chapl K Coll Auckland 81-85; TV Saltash *Truro* 85-90; Jt Dir SW Minl Tr Course 86-90; Preb St Endellion *Truro* 89-90; Prin WMMTC 90-92; rtd 04. *6 Bluebell Walk, Coventry CV4 9XR* T: (024) 7646 4894 E: petegray@btinternet.com

WHALEY, Stephen John. b 57. York Univ BA 79. Cranmer Hall Dur BA 85. **d** 86 **p** 87. C Selby Abbey *York* 86-90; V Derringham Bank from 90; AD W Hull 98-00. *110 Calvert Road, Hull HU5 5DH* T: (01482) 352175

WHALLEY, Miss Alice Elizabeth. b 87. Univ Coll Lon BSc 09. St Steph Ho Ox BA 13. **d** 14. C Moulsecoomb *Chich* from 14. *43 Rushlake Road, Brighton BN1 9AE* T: (01273) 602812 M: 07745-809669 E: alice.whalley@me.com

WHALLEY, Anthony Allen. b 41. Linc Th Coll 77. **d** 79 **p** 80. C Upton cum Chalvey *Ox* 79-83; R Newton Longville w Stoke Hammond and Whaddon 83-96; R Winslow w Gt Horwood and Addington 99-06; rtd 06; PtO *Worc* from 09. *2 Charlock Road, Malvern WR14 3SR* T: (01684) 562897 E: tony.rosemary@btinternet.com

WHALLEY, Mrs Constance Mary. b 55. CBDTI 99. **d** 02 **p** 03. NSM Garstang St Helen and St Michaels-on-Wyre *Blackb* from 02. *Brierfield, Stoney Lane, Goosnargh, Preston PR3 2WH* T: (01995) 640652

WHALLEY, Edward Ryder Watson. b 31. G&C Coll Cam BA 54 MA 59. Westcott Ho Cam 55. **d** 57 **p** 58. C Ashton-on-Ribble St Andr *Blackb* 57-60; Chapl Magd Coll Cam 60-63; C Arnold *S'well* 63-67; rtd 96; PtO *Lon* from 03. *6 Cranleigh, 137-139 Ladbroke Road, London W11 3PX* T: (020) 7727 1985

WHALLEY, Eleanor Jean. b 72. **d** 14 **p** 15. C St Neots *Ely* from 14. *56 Stone Hill, St Neots PE19 6AA* E: eleanorjw@gmail.com

WHALLEY, George Peter. b 40. **d** 86 **p** 86. NSM Ellon *Ab* from 86; NSM Cruden Bay from 86. *128 Braehead Drive, Cruden Bay, Peterhead AB42 0NW* T: (01779) 812511 E: peter_whalley@btinternet.com

WHALLEY, Jonathan Peter Lambert. b 60. Wm Booth Memorial Coll 87. St Jo Coll Nottm BA 97. **d** 97 **p** 98. C Hattersley *Ches* 97-01; V The Marshland *Sheff* 01-09; P-in-c Wolsingham and Thornley *Dur* from 09; P-in-c Satley, Stanley and Tow Law from 09; CF(V) from 02. *The Rectory, 14 Rectory Lane, Wolsingham, Bishop Auckland DL13 3AJ* T: (01388) 527340

WHALLEY, Michael Thomas. b 30. AKC 55. **d** 56 **p** 57. C Nottingham All SS *S'well* 56-58; C Clifton St Fran 58-60; C Mansfield SS Pet and Paul 60; V N Wilford St Faith 60-66; Asst Chapl HM Pris Man 66-67; Chapl HM Youth Cust Cen Dover 67-69; LtO *Linc* 70-75; Chapl HM Pris Aylesbury 75-79; C Aylesbury *Ox* 79-83; P-in-c Bierton w Hulcott 83-89; TV Aylesbury 89-95; rtd 95; PtO *Linc* from 97. *17 Willowfield Avenue, Nettleham, Lincoln LN2 2TH* T: (01522) 595372

WHALLEY, Peter. *See* WHALLEY, George Peter

✣**WHALON, The Rt Revd Pierre Welté.** b 52. Boston Univ BMus 74 Duquesne Univ MMus 81. Virginia Th Sem MDiv 85. **d** 85 **p** 85 **c** 01. R N Versailles All So USA 85-91; R Philadelphia St Paul 91-93; R Fort Pierce St Andr 93-01; Bp in Charge Convocation of American Chs in Eur from 01; Hon Asst Bp Eur from 02. *23 avenue George V, 75008 Paris, France* T: (0033) 1 53 23 84 04 *or* T/F 1 47 20 02 23 E: bppwhalon@aol.com *or* cathedral@american.cathedral.com

WHARTON, Christopher Joseph. b 33. Keble Coll Ox BA 57 MA 61. **d** 79 **p** 80. NSM Harpenden St Nic *St Alb* 79-93; R Kimpton w Ayot St Lawrence 93-00; PtO from 00. *97 Overstone Road, Harpenden AL5 5PL* T: (01582) 761164

WHARTON, Ms Gillian Vera. b 66. TCD BTh 93 MPhil 99 HDipEd 02. CITC 90. **d** 93 **p** 94. C Glenageary *D & G* 93-96; PV Ch Ch Cathl Dublin from 96; Dioc Youth Officer 96-00; C Lucan w Leixlip 96-00; Chapl Rathdown Sch 00-04; I Dublin Booterstown *D & G* from 04; I Dublin Mt Merrion from 04. *The Rectory, Cross Avenue, Blackrock, Co Dublin, Republic of Ireland* T: (00353) (1) 288 7118 *or* 283 5873 M: 87-230 0767 E: booterstown@dublin.anglican.org *or* gillwharton@gmail.com

✠**WHARTON, The Rt Revd John Martin.** b 44. Van Mildert Coll Dur BA 69 Linacre Coll Ox BTh 71 MA 76. Ripon Hall Ox 69. **d** 72 **p** 73 **c** 92. C Birm St Pet 72-75; C Croydon St Jo *Cant* 76-77; Dir Past Studies Ripon Coll Cuddesdon 77-83; C Cuddesdon *Ox* 79-83; Sec to Bd of Min and Tr *Bradf* 83-92; Dir Post-Ord Tr 84-92; Hon Can Bradf Cathl 84-92; Can Res Bradf Cathl 92; Bp's Officer for Min and Tr 92; Area Bp Kingston *S'wark* 92-97; Bp Newc 97-14; rtd 14. *14 The College, Durham DH1 3EQ*

WHARTON, Canon Kate Elizabeth. b 78. Leeds Metrop Univ BSc 00. Wycliffe Hall Ox BTh 05. **d** 05 **p** 06. C W Derby St Luke *Liv* 05-09; P-in-c Everton St Geo from 09; AD Liv N from 13; Hon Can Liv Cathl from 13. *St George's Vicarage, 40 Northumberland Terrace, Liverpool L5 3QG* T: 0151-263 6005

WHARTON, Richard Malcolm. b 69. Univ of Cen England in Birm BA 91 PGCE 92. Ripon Coll Cuddesdon BTh 98. **d** 98 **p** 99. C Weoley Castle *Birm* 98-01; C Hall Green Ascension 01-04; P-in-c Hall Green St Mich 03-08; Chapl Univ Hosp Birm NHS Foundn Trust from 08. *15 Raglan Road, Birmingham B5 7RA* T: 0121-440 2196 E: richard.wharton@ubh.nhs.uk

WHARTON, Susan Jane. b 58. Leeds Univ BSc 79 Coll of Ripon & York St Jo MA 00. NOC 96. **d** 99 **p** 00. C Bingley All SS *Bradf* 99-03; P-in-c Weston w Denton 03-08; P-in-c Leathley w Farnley, Fewston and Blubberhouses 03-08; C Washburn and Mid-Wharfe 08-09; P-in-c 09-12; P-in-c Bethersden w High Halden and Woodchurch *Cant* from 12. *The Vicarage, Bull Lane, Bethersden, Ashford TN26 3HA* T: (01233) 820266 E: sue@whartons.org.uk

WHARTON, Thomas Geoffrey. b 72. Glas Univ BA 93. Westcott Ho Cam 03. **d** 05 **p** 06. C Linton in Craven and Burnsall w Rylstone *Bradf* 05-09; TV Knight's Enham and Smannell w Enham Alamein *Win* 09-13; P-in-c W End from 13. *The Vicarage, Elizabeth Close, West End, Southampton SO30 3LT* T: (023) 8047 2180 E: thomas.wharton@sky.com

WHATELEY, Stuart David. b 44. Ripon Hall Ox 71. **d** 73 **p** 74. C Chilvers Coton w Astley *Cov* 73-76; Chapl Miss to Seafarers from 76. *10 Merryman Garth, Hedon, Hull HU12 8NJ* T: (01482) 899166 M: 07802-281680 E: humber@mtsmail.org

WHATELEY, Thomas Roderick (Rod). b 52. St Jo Coll Nottm 94. **d** 96 **p** 97. C Willesborough *Cant* 96-99; P-in-c Cliftonville 99-03; R Orlestone w Snave and Ruckinge w Warehorne etc 03-13; R Saxon Shoreline from 13. *The Rectory, Cock Lane, Ham Street, Ashford TN26 2HU* T: (01233) 732274 E: rod.whateley@tiscali.co.uk

WHATLEY, Lionel Frederick. b 50. St Paul's Coll Grahamstown 77. **d** 79 **p** 80. C Vitenhage S Africa 79-80; R Newton Park 80-83; R Alexandria Plurality 83-84; R Waterberg 84-90; R Letaba 90-99; Adn NE 95-99; V Gen 97-99; R Ashington, Washington and Wiston w Buncton *Chich* 99-05; TV Langport Area *B & W* 05-07; TV Worthing Ch the King *Chich* 07-08; V Worthing H Trin w Ch Ch 08-11; P-in-c Highbrook and W Hoathly 11-12; V from 12. *The Vicarage, North Lane, West Hoathly, East Grinstead RH19 4QF* T: (01342) 810494 E: lionel.whatley@virginmedia.com

WHATLEY, Roger James. b 49. Chich Th Coll 94. **d** 96 **p** 04. NSM Newport St Thos and Newport St Jo *Portsm* 96-11; Chapl Is of Wight Fire and Rescue Service from 11. *Beechcroft, 46 Trafalgar Road, Newport PO30 1QG* T: (01983) 825938 E: whatleys138@btinternet.com

WHATMOUGH, Michael Anthony. b 50. ARCO 71 Ex Univ BA 72. Edin Th Coll BD 81. **d** 81 **p** 82. C Edin St Hilda and Edin St Fillan 81-84; C Salisbury St Thos and St Edm *Sarum* 84-86; R 86-93; RD Salisbury 90-93; V Bris St Mary Redcliffe w Temple etc 93-04; PtO *Lich* 08-10; C Cannock and Huntington 10-12; C Hatherton 10-12; P-in-c Headingley *Ripon* 12-14; TR *Leeds* from 14. *Headingley Vicarage, 16 Shire Oak Road, Leeds LS6 2DE* T: 0113-274 3238 M: 07711-335050 E: tony@whatmough.org.uk

WHATSON, Mark Edwin Chadwick. b 57. Southn Univ BSc 79 CEng 83 MIMechE 83. NOC 86. **d** 88 **p** 91. NSM Church Hulme *Ches* 88-91; NSM Goostrey 91-95; NSM Hardwicke, Quedgeley and Elmore w Longney *Glouc* 95-98; C Thornbury 98-01; Ind Chapl 99-01; R Freshwater *Portsm* from 01; R Yarmouth from 01. *1 The Nurseries, Freshwater PO40 9FG* T/F: (01983) 752010 E: mark.whatson@bigfoot.com

WHATTON, Joanna Nicola. See PAYNE, Joanna Nicola

WHAWELL, Arthur Michael. b 38. SRN 59. Sarum & Wells Th Coll 74. **d** 76 **p** 77. C Cottingham *York* 76-79; P-in-c Bessingby and Carnaby 79-84; V Birchencliffe *Wakef* 84-87; Chapl Huddersfield R Infirmary 84-87; V St Bart Less and Chapl St Barts Hosp Lon 87-95; P-in-c Wormingford, Mt Bures and Lt Horkesley *Chelmsf* 95-00; V 00-03; rtd 03; PtO *Pet* from 05. *Cherry Trees, Benefield Road, Upper Glapthorn, Peterborough PE8 5BQ* T: (01832) 272500 E: mwhawell@tiscali.co.uk

WHEALE, Alan Leon. b 43. Hull Univ MA 92 AKC 69. St Aug Coll Cant 69. **d** 70 **p** 71. C Tamworth *Lich* 70-73; C Cheddleton 73-75; V Garretts Green *Birm* 75-78; V Perry Beeches 78-83; V Winshill *Derby* 83-84; Deputation Appeals Org (E Midl) CECS 84-86; C Arnold *S'well* 86-88; V Daybrook 88-96; R Clifton Campville w Edingale and Harlaston *Lich* 96-06; P-in-c Thorpe Constantine 96-06; P-in-c Elford 97-06; rtd 06; PtO *Lich* 06-08; Hon C Tamworth 08-11; PtO 12-14; Hon C Rolleston from 14; Hon C Anslow from 14; Hon C Hanbury, Newborough, Rangemore and Tutbury from 14. *12 Bluebell Grove, Woodville, Swadlincote DE11 8FY* T: (01283) 221022 E: alan-wheale@supanet.com

WHEALE, Sarah Ruth. See BULLOCK, Sarah Ruth

WHEAT, Charles Donald Edmund. b 37. Nottm Univ BA 70 Sheff Univ MA 76. Kelham Th Coll 57. **d** 62 **p** 63. C Sheff Arbourthorne 62-67; LtO *S'well* 67-70; SSM from 69; Chapl St Martin's Coll Lanc 70-73; Prior SSM Priory Sheff 73-75; LtO *Sheff* 73-97; C Ranmoor 75-77; Asst Chapl Sheff Univ 75-77; Chapl 77-80; Prov SSM in England 81-91; Dir 82-89; LtO *Blackb* 81-88; V Middlesbrough All SS *York* 88-95; Roehampton Inst *S'wark* 96-97; Chapl OHP 97-98; Prior St Antony's Priory Dur 98-01; V Middlesbrough St Thos 01-03; rtd 03; Hon C S Bank *York* 03-07; PtO 07-11; *Ox* from 11. SSM *Priory, 1 Linford Lane, Willen, Milton Keynes MK15 9DL* E: ssmmbro@aol.com

WHEATLEY, Barbara Angela. b 46. **d** 13 **p** 14. NSM Bowbrook N *Worc* from 13; NSM Bowbrook S from 13. *Glen Cottage, 9 Mill Lane, Feckenham, Redditch B96 6HY* T: (01527) 892969 E: barbarawheatley@btinternet.com

WHEATLEY, David. b 44. **d** 02 **p** 03. OLM Castleford *Wakef* 02-09; Master Abp Holgate Hosp Hemsworth from 09. *The Master's Lodge, Robin Lane, Hemsworth, Pontefract WF9 4PP* T: (01977) 610434

WHEATLEY, David Maurice. b 69. Man Poly BA 91. Wycliffe Hall Ox 02. **d** 05 **p** 06. C Cheltenham St Mary, St Matt, St Paul and H Trin *Glouc* 05-07; C Cheltenham H Trin and St Paul 07-08; Chapl Headington Sch 10-11. *Address temp unknown* M: 07974-932071

WHEATLEY (née GRAHAM), Mrs Fiona Karen. b 57. Hull Univ BA 84 De Montfort Univ PGCE 94. SAOMC 03. **d** 06 **p** 07. C Stevenage St Hugh and St Jo *St Alb* 06-10; TV Bp's Hatfield, Lemsford and N Mymms 10-14; R Clothall, Rushden, Sandon, Wallington and Weston from 14. *The Vicarage, Payne End, Sandon, Buntingford SG9 0QU* T: (01763) 284189 E: fkwheatley@gmail.com

WHEATLEY, Gordon Howard. b 29. Trin Coll Cam MA 52. Lon Bible Coll. **d** 90 **p** 91. C Cockley Cley w Gooderstone *Nor* 90-94; C Didlington 90-94; C Gt and Lt Cressingham w Threxton 90-94; C Hilborough w Bodney 90-94; C Oxborough w Foulden and Caldecote 90-94; P-in-c Mundford w Lynford 94-98; P-in-c Ickburgh w Langford 94-98; P-in-c Cranwich 94-98; rtd 98; PtO *Nor* 98-10. *204 Baxter Village, 8 Robinsons Road, Frankston Vic 3199, Australia* T: (0061) (3) 5971 2569 E: revgordon@tiscali.co.uk

WHEATLEY, The Ven Ian James. b 62. Chich Th Coll BTh 94. **d** 94 **p** 95. C Braunton *Ex* 94-97; Chapl RN from 97; Prin Angl Chapl and Adn for the RN 12-14; Chapl of the Fleet and Adn for the RN from 14; Hon Can Portsm Cathl from 14; QHC from 14. *Royal Naval Chaplaincy Service, Mail Point 1-2, Leach Building, Whale Island, Portsmouth PO2 8BY* T: (023) 9262 5055 F: 9262 5134

WHEATLEY, Jane. See WHEATLEY, Sarah Jane

WHEATLEY, John. b 14. **d** 77 **p** 78. NSM Cambois *Newc* 77-87; rtd 87; PtO *Newc* from 87. *20 Cypress Gardens, Blyth NE24 2LP* T: (01670) 353353

WHEATLEY, Michael Robert Pearce. **d** 10 **p** 11. NSM Burry Port and Pwll *St D* 10-12; P-in-c from 12. *The Vicarage, 1 Cae Ffwrnes, Burry Port SA16 0FW* T: (01554) 832936

WHEATLEY, The Ven Paul Charles. b 38. St Jo Coll Dur BA 61. Linc Th Coll 61. **d** 63 **p** 64. C Bishopston *Bris* 63-68; Youth Chapl 68-73; V Swindon St Paul 73-77; TR Swindon Dorcan 77-79; R Ross *Heref* 79-81; P-in-c Brampton Abbotts 79-81; RD Ross and Archenfield 79-91; TR Ross w Brampton Abbotts, Bridstow and Peterstow 81-91; Preb Heref Cathl 87-91; Adn Sherborne *Sarum* 91-03; P-in-c W Stafford w Frome Billet 91-03; rtd 03; PtO *Heref* from 04. *The Farthings, Bridstow, Ross-on-Wye HR9 6QF* T: (01989) 566965 E: paulwheatley@buckcastle.plus.com

✠**WHEATLEY, The Rt Revd Peter William.** b 47. Qu Coll Ox BA 69 MA 73 Pemb Coll Cam BA 71 MA 75. Ripon Hall Ox 72. **d** 73 **p** 74 **c** 99. C Fulham All SS *Lon* 73-78; V St Pancras H Cross w St Jude and St Pet 78-82; P-in-c Hampstead All So 82-90; P-in-c Kilburn St Mary 82-90; P-in-c Kilburn St Mary w All So 90-95; V W Hampstead St Jas 82-95; Dir Post-Ord Tr 85-95; AD N Camden 88-93; Adn Hampstead 95-99; Area Bp Edmonton 99-14; rtd 15; Hon Asst Bp S'wark from 13. *47 Sedlescombe Road South, St Leonards-on-Sea TN38 0TB* T: (01424) 424814

WHEATLEY, Miss Sarah Jane. b 45. St Gabr Coll Lon Dip Teaching 67. St Alb Minl Tr Scheme 77. **d** 96 **p** 97. NSM Meppershall w Campton and Stondon *St Alb* 96-99; P-in-c Shillington 99-03; V Gravenhurst, Shillington and Stondon 03-12; rtd 12; PtO *St Alb* from 12. *16 Queen Street, Stotfold, Hitchin SG5 4NX* T: (01462) 731170
E: jane.wheatley5@btinternet.com

WHEATLEY PRICE, Canon John. b 31. Em Coll Cam BA 54 MA 58. Ridley Hall Cam 54. **d** 56 **p** 57. C Drypool St Andr and St Pet *York* 56-59; CMS 59-76; Uganda 60-74; Adn Soroti 72-74; Hon Can Soroti 78-97; Adn N Maseno Kenya 74-76; V Clevedon St Andr *B & W* 76-82; V Clevedon St Andr and Ch 82-87; Chapl Amsterdam *Eur* 87-92; P-in-c Cromford *Derby* 92-95; P-in-c Matlock Bath 92-95; V Matlock Bath and Cromford 95-96; rtd 96; PtO *Sarum* 96-01; *Birm* from 01. *2 Beausale Drive, Knowle, Solihull B93 0NS* T: (01564) 730067
E: john@wheatleyprice.co.uk

WHEATON, Canon Christopher. b 49. St Jo Coll Nottm BTh 80. **d** 80 **p** 81. C Hatcham St Jas *S'wark* 80-83; C Warlingham w Chelsham and Farleigh 83-87; V Carshalton Beeches 87-13; AD Sutton 03-13; Hon Can S'wark Cathl 07-13; rtd 13. *70 Gordon Road, West Bridgford, Nottingham NG2 5LS* T: 0115-982 7192 E: christopherwheaton@btinternet.com

WHEATON, Canon David Harry. b 30. St Jo Coll Ox BA 53 MA 56 Lon Univ BD 55. Oak Hill Th Coll 58. **d** 59 **p** 60. Tutor Oak Hill Th Coll 59-62; Prin 71-86; C Enfield Ch Ch Trent Park *Lon* 59-62; R Ludgershall *Ox* 62-66; V Onslow Square St Paul *Lon* 66-71; Chapl Brompton Hosp 69-71; Hon Can St Alb *St Alb* 76-96; V Ware Ch Ch 86-96; RD Hertford 88-91; rtd 96; Chapl to The Queen 90-00; PtO *Ox* 96-08; *St Alb* 96-10; *Sarum* from 09. *17 Riverside Road, Blandford Forum DT11 7ES* T: (01258) 489996

WHEATON, Patrick Edward. b 78. Ex Coll Ox BA 00. Trin Coll Bris BA 08. **d** 09 **p** 10. C Shill Valley and Broadshire *Ox* 09-13; C Cheltenham St Mary w St Matt and St Luke *Glouc* from 13. *38 College Road, Cheltenham GL53 7HX* M: 07974-986608
E: paddylouise@btinternet.com

WHEELDON, William Dennis. b 25. Leeds Univ BA 51. Coll of Resurr Mirfield 52. **d** 54 **p** 56. CR 55-76; Tutor Codrington Coll Barbados 59-63; Vice-Prin 63-66; Prin Coll of Resurr Mirfield 66-75; P-in-c New Whittington *Derby* 83-87; P-in-c Belper Ch Ch and Milford 87-90; rtd 90; PtO *Bradf* 90-04. *3 The Lodge, Newfield Drive, Menston, Ilkley LS29 6JQ*

WHEELER, Preb Alexander Quintin Henry (Alastair). b 51. Lon Univ BA 73 MBACP 07. St Jo Coll Nottm 74. **d** 77 **p** 78. C Kenilworth St Jo *Cov* 77-80; C Madeley *Heref* 80-83; P-in-c Draycott-le-Moors *Lich* 83-84; P-in-c Forsbrook 83-84; R Draycott-le-Moors w Forsbrook 84-91; V Nailsea Ch Ch *B & W* 91-96; R Nailsea Ch Ch w Tickenham 96-10; RD Portishead 95-01; V Wells St Cuth w Wookey Hole from 10; RD Shepton Mallet from 11; Preb Wells Cathl from 03. *3 Orchard Lea, Wells BA5 2LZ* T: (01749) 677810
E: aqhw@aol.com

WHEELER, Canon Andrew Charles. b 48. CCC Cam BA 69 MA 72 Makerere Univ Kampala MA 72 Leeds Univ PGCE 72. Trin Coll Bris BA 88. **d** 88 **p** 88. CMS from 76; C Whitton *Sarum* 88-89; C All SS Cathl Cairo Egypt 89-92; Co-ord for Th Educn Sudan 92-00; C All SS Cathl Nairobi Kenya 92-00; Abp's Sec for Angl Communion Affairs *Cant* 00-01; C Guildf St Sav from 02; Dioc World Miss Adv from 06. *8 Selbourne Road, Guildford GU4 7JP* T: (01483) 532310
E: andrew.wheeler@st-saviours.org.uk

WHEELER, Anthony. *See* WHEELER, Richard Anthony

WHEELER (née MILLAR), Mrs Christine. b 55. City of Lon Poly BSc 76 DipCOT 81. S Dios Minl Tr Scheme 84. **d** 87 **p** 94. NSM Kingston Buci *Chich* 87-89; Par Dn Merstham and Gatton *S'wark* 89-94; C 94-96; R Rockland St Mary w Hellington, Bramerton etc *Nor* 96-04; PtO from 04. *Mayland, Low Road, Strumpshaw, Norwich NR13 4HU* T: (01603) 713583
E: emailcw@btinternet.com

WHEELER, David Ian. b 49. Southn Univ BSc 70 PhD 78. NOC 87. **d** 90 **p** 91. C Blackpool St Jo *Blackb* 90-94; R Old Trafford St Jo *Man* 94-05; P-in-c Irlam 05-08; V 08-13; rtd 13. *22 Glamis Avenue, Northbourne, Bournemouth BH10 6DP* T: (01202) 577820

WHEELER, David James. b 49. Leeds Univ MA 95 CQSW 74. S Dios Minl Tr Scheme 87. **d** 90 **p** 91. C Hythe *Cant* 90-92; C Knaresborough *Ripon* 92-97; Asst Soc Resp Officer 94-97; P-in-c Gt and Lt Ouseburn w Marton cum Grafton etc 97-01; V 01-05; Jt AD Ripon 01-05; V Cobbold Road St Sav w St Mary *Lon* 05-12; rtd 12; PtO *St E* from 13. *24 Staithe Road, Bungay NR35 1ET* T: (01986) 892110
E: david.wheeler@phonecoop.coop

WHEELER, Sister Eileen Violet. b 28. TCert 48 Newnham Coll Cam MA 52. Chich Th Coll 85. **dss** 86 **d** 87 **p** 95. Bexhill St Pet *Chich* 86-95; Hon Par Dn 87-90; Par Dn 90-94; Hon C 94-95; rtd 94; Hon C Bexhill St Mark *Chich* 95-00; PtO 00-02; Hon C Horsham 02-08; Hon C St Leonards St Ethelburga and St Leon from 08. *17 Glebe Close, Bexhill-on-Sea TN39 3UY* T: (01424) 848150

WHEELER, Graham John. b 39. St Mich Coll Llan BD 78. **d** 66 **p** 67. C Roath St Martin *Llan* 66-71; C Cadoxton-juxta-Barry 71-75; PtO 75-79; C Highcliffe w Hinton Admiral *Win* 79-83; C Milton 83-90; P-in-c Bournemouth St Ambrose 90-06; rtd 06. *49 St Peters Court, St Peters Road, Bournemouth BH1 2JU* T: (01202) 764957

WHEELER, Mrs Helen Mary. b 38. Qu Coll Birm 04. **d** 06 **p** 07. NSM Smethwick Resurr *Birm* 06-12; rtd 12; PtO *Birm* from 12. *99 Brookfield Road, Birmingham B18 7JA* T: 0121-554 4721 M: 07804-450099 E: revhwheeler@hotmail.co.uk

WHEELER, James Albert. b 49. Sarum & Wells Th Coll 74. **d** 76 **p** 77. C Orpington All SS *Roch* 76-79; C Roch 79-81; C Bexley St Jo 81-84; V Penge Lane H Trin 84-93; P-in-c Tunbridge Wells St Luke 93-99; V 99-09; P-in-c Southborough St Thos 09-15; rtd 15. *19 Plover Close, Eastbourne BN23 7SB* T: (01323) 767533 E: j.wheeler@mybroadbandmail.com

WHEELER, John David. b 31. Selw Coll Cam BA 54 MA 58. Ely Th Coll 54. **d** 56 **p** 57. C Charlton St Luke w St Paul *S'wark* 56-60; C Northolt St Mary *Lon* 61-63; V Bush Hill Park St Mark 64-71; V Ealing St Pet Mt Park 71-74; V Truro St Paul 74-79; V Truro St Paul and St Clem 79-80; P-in-c Hammersmith St Sav *Lon* 80-83; V Cobbold Road St Sav w St Mary 83-96; rtd 96; PtO *Heref* 96-01; *Chich* 01-09. *63 Nelson Road, Twickenham TW2 7AR* T: (020) 8755 2018

WHEELER, Julian Aldous. b 48. Nottm Univ BTh 74. Kelham Th Coll 70. **d** 75 **p** 76. C Bideford *Ex* 75-79; LtO 79-86; Hon C Parkham, Alwington, Buckland Brewer etc 86-03. *Manorfield, Mount Raleigh Avenue, Bideford EX39 3NR* T: (01237) 477271
E: wheelerb58@btinternet.com

WHEELER, Leonie Marjorie. b 50. Univ of W Aus BA 75 St Ant Coll Ox DPhil 81. Qu Coll Birm 04. **d** 06 **p** 07. C Hadley and Wellington Ch Ch *Lich* 06-09; P-in-c Church Aston from 09; Chapl to the Deaf from 09. *St Andrew's Rectory, 7 Wallshead Way, Church Aston, Newport TF10 9JG* T: (01952) 810942

WHEELER, Preb Madeleine. b 42. Gilmore Course 76. **dss** 78 **d** 87 **p** 94. Ruislip Manor St Paul *Lon* 78-92; Par Dn 87-91; Team Dn 91-92; Chapl for Women's Min (Willesden Episc Area) 86-95; P-in-c N Greenford All Hallows *Lon* 94-00; Preb St Paul's Cathl 95-00; rtd 00; PtO *St Alb* from 00; *Lon* from 02. *178A Harefield Road, Uxbridge UB8 1PP* T: (01895) 257274
E: mm.wheeler@tiscali.co.uk

WHEELER, Nicholas Charles. b 50. LVO 09. Leic Univ BA 72. SEITE 00. **d** 03 **p** 04. NSM Blackheath St Jo *S'wark* 03-08; PtO 08-11; NSM Eltham H Trin from 11. *52 Oakways, London SE9 2PD* T: (020) 8859 7819

WHEELER, Nicholas Gordon Timothy. b 59. BCombStuds 84. Linc Th Coll. **d** 84 **p** 85. C Hendon St Alphage *Lon* 84-87; C Wood Green St Mich w Bounds Green St Gabr etc 87-89; TV 89-93; R Cranford 93-02; V Ruislip St Mary from 02. *St Mary's Vicarage, 9 The Fairway, Ruislip HA4 0SP* T: (020) 8845 3485 M: 07946-111968 E: nicholasgwheeler@aol.com

WHEELER, Canon Nicholas Paul. b 60. Ox Univ BA 86 MA 91. Wycliffe Hall Ox 83. **d** 87 **p** 88. C Wood Green St Mich w Bounds Green St Gabr etc *Lon* 87-91; Chapl to Bp Edmonton 91-96; P-in-c Somers Town 96-03; P-in-c Old St Pancras w Bedford New Town St Matt 96-03; P-in-c Camden Town St Mich w All SS and St Thos 96-03; P-in-c Camden Square St Paul 96-03; TR Old St Pancras 03-08; Brazil 08-15; R Upper Chelsea H Trin and St Sav *Lon* from 15. *97A Cadogan Lane, London SW1X 9DU* T: (020) 7730 7270
E: nicholaspaulwheeler@gmail.com

WHEELER, Richard Anthony (Tony). b 23. St Chad's Coll Dur BA 46 MA 48. **d** 48 **p** 49. C Kingswinford St Mary *Lich* 48-52; C Toxteth Park St Agnes *Liv* 52-54; V Upholland 54-64; R Dorchester H Trin w Frome Whitfield *Sarum* 64-73; TV Dorchester 73-87; rtd 87; PtO *Sarum* from 87. *30 Mountain Ash Road, Dorchester DT1 2PB* T: (01305) 264811
E: peewheet@cix.compulink.co.uk

WHEELER, Canon Richard Roy. b 44. K Coll Lon BD 72. St Aug Coll Cant. **d** 74 **p** 74. C Brixton St Matt *S'wark* 74-78; Dir

St Matt Meeting Place Brixton 78-79; Sec BCC Community Work Resource Unit 79-82; TV Southampton (City Cen) *Win* 83-88; TR 88-98; Hon Can Win Cathl 94-98; Soc Resp Adv *St Alb* 98-09; Can Res St Alb 01-09; rtd 09. *143 Well Hall Road, London SE9 6TS* T: (020) 8856 5271

WHEELER, Mrs Sally Ann Violet. b 59. Westmr Coll Ox BEd 81. SAOMC 94. **d** 97 **p** 98. NSM Chippenham St Paul w Hardenhuish etc *Bris* 97-01; C Gtr Corsham and Lacock 01-04; TV 04-12; P-in-c Marshfield w Cold Ashton and Tormarton etc from 12. *The Vicarage, Church Lane, Marshfield, Chippenham SN14 8NT* T: (01225) 892180 E: rjwheeler77@gmail.com

WHEELER-KILEY, Mrs Susan Elizabeth. b 47. **d** 06 **p** 07. NSM S Norwood St Mark *S'wark* from 06. *35 St Luke's Close, London SE25 4SX* T: (020) 8656 9923 M: 07890-780572 E: fs.kiley@btinternet.com

WHEELHOUSE, Brian Clifford Dunstan. b 69. St Steph Ho Ox BTh 93. **d** 96 **p** 97. C Brighton Resurr *Chich* 96-99; C Hangleton 99-00; PtO 00-01; C Kingstanding St Luke *Birm* 01-03; V Houghton Regis *St Alb* 03-13; P-in-c Eskdale, Irton, Muncaster and Waberthwaite *Carl* 13-14; PtO *Lich* from 15. *25 Lister Road, Stafford ST16 3NB* E: brianwheelhouse@hotmail.com

WHEELHOUSE, Paul Andrew. b 72. Bradf Univ BEd 95 Ox Brookes Univ MA 11 St Jo Coll Dur BATM 12. Cranmer Hall Dur 10. **d** 12 **p** 13. C Burley in Wharfedale *Leeds* from 12. *1 Grange Road, Burley in Wharfedale, Ilkley LS29 7NF* T: (01943) 864223 E: pawheelhouse@gmail.com

WHEELWRIGHT, Michael Harvey. b 39. Bps' Coll Cheshunt 64. **d** 67 **p** 68. C Glen Parva and S Wigston *Leic* 67-70; C Evington 70-74; V Leic St Eliz Nether Hall 74-79; Chapl Prudhoe Hosp Northd 79-99; PtO *Dur* from 79; *Newc* from 99; rtd 04. *6 Nunnykirk Close, Ovingham, Prudhoe NE42 6BP* T: (01661) 835749

WHELAN, Miss Patricia Jean. b 33. ACA 55 FCA 82. Dalton Ho Bris 58. **dss** 64 **d** 87 **p** 94. Stapleford *S'well* 62-69; Aylesbury *Ox* 69-75; Bushbury *Lich* 75-77; Patchway *Bris* 77-81; Trin Coll Bris 81-82; W Swindon LEP 82-86; High Wycombe *Ox* 86-87; Par Dn 87-91; Par Dn Ox St Ebbe w H Trin and St Pet 91-93; rtd 93. *81 Cogges Hill Road, Witney OX28 3XU* T: (01993) 779099

WHELAN, Peter Warwick Armstrong. b 34. Southn Univ BTh 80 Open Univ BA 80. Sarum Th Coll 69. **d** 71 **p** 72. C Salisbury St Mark *Sarum* 71-73; C Solihull *Birm* 73-77; TR Shirley 77-86; Chapl Whittington Hosp NHS Trust 86-99; Chapl Camden and Islington Community Health NHS Trust 86-98; PtO *Ex* from 98; rtd 99. *Olde Court Coach House, Higher Lincombe Road, Torquay TQ1 2EX* T: (01803) 212483

WHELAN, Raymond Keith. b 40. Cant Sch of Min 85. **d** 88 **p** 91. C Eastbourne St Andr *Chich* 88-93; C-in-c Parklands St Wilfrid CD 93-95; TV Church 95-00; V Chich St Wilfrid 00-01; rtd 04; PtO *Chich* from 04. *9 Ruislip Gardens, Aldwick, Bognor Regis PO21 4LB* T: (01243) 264865 E: wdiosc@aol.com

WHERLOCK, Mrs Evaline Prudence. b 50. WEMTC 98. **d** 01 **p** 02. NSM Bishopsworth and Bedminster Down *Bris* from 01. *63 Bridgwater Road, Bedminster Down, Bristol BS13 7AX* T: 0117-964 1035 M: 07899-932763 E: evawherlock@ukonline.co.uk

WHERRY, Anthony Michael. b 44. Nottm Univ BA 65. WMMTC 88. **d** 91 **p** 92. NSM Worc City St Paul and Old St Martin etc 91-95; NSM Worc E Deanery 95-02; NSM Worc SE from 02. *2 Redfern Avenue, Worcester WR5 1PZ* T: (01905) 358532 M: 07780-677942 E: tonywherry@btinternet.com

WHETTINGSTEEL, Raymond Edward. b 44. S Dios Minl Tr Scheme 79. **d** 82 **p** 83. NSM Sholing *Win* 82-84; C Southampton Maybush St Pet 84-89; R Hatherden w Tangley, Weyhill and Penton Mewsey 89-09; rtd 09; PtO *Win* from 11. *20 Clover Way, Hedge End, Southampton SO30 4RP* T: (01489) 787033 E: ray_whettingsteel@hotmail.com

WHETTLETON, Timothy John. b 53. Univ of Wales (Swansea) BA 74. St Mich Coll Llan 97. **d** 99 **p** 00. C Llansamlet *S & B* 99-01; P-in-c Gowerton 01-05. *8 Goetre Fawr Road, Killay, Swansea SA2 7QS* T: (01792) 206325

WHETTON, Nicholas John. b 56. Open Univ BA 94. St Jo Coll Nottm 83. **d** 86 **p** 87. C Hatfield *Sheff* 86-90; V Cornholme *Wakef* 90-96; P-in-c Livesey *Blackb* 96-99; V 99-03; P-in-c Ewood 96-97; Chapl HM Pris Hull from 03. *The Chaplain's Office, HM Prison, Hedon Road, Hull HU9 5LS* T: (01482) 282200

WHIFFIN, Mrs Vanessa Janet. b 68. Birm Univ BMus 89 ABSM 87. STETS 10. **d** 14 **p** 15. C Marshfield w Cold Ashton and Tormarton etc *Bris* from 14. *The Vicarage, 2 Coopers Meadow, Yatton Keynell, Chippenham SN14 7PZ* T: (01249) 783285 E: ness8@btinternet.com

✠**WHINNEY, The Rt Revd Michael Humphrey Dickens.** b 30. Pemb Coll Cam BA 55 MA 59. Gen Th Sem (NY) STM 90 Ridley Hall Cam 55. **d** 57 **p** 58 **c** 82. C Rainham *Chelmsf*

57-60; Hd Cam Univ Miss Bermondsey 60-67; Chapl 67-73; V Bermondsey St Jas w Ch Ch *S'wark* 67-73; Adn S'wark 73-82; Suff Bp Aston *Birm* 82-85; Bp S'well 85-88; Asst Bp Birm 88-95; Can Res Birm Cathl 92-95; rtd 96; Hon Asst Bp Birm from 96. *3 Moor Green Lane, Moseley, Birmingham B13 8NE* T/F: 0121-249 2856 E: michael.whinney@btinternet.com

WHINNEY, Nigel Patrick Maurice. b 43. Open Univ BA 91. SWMTC 95. **d** 97 **p** 98. NSM Ilminster and Distr *B & W* 97-08; Bp's Officer for Ord NSM (Taunton Adnry) 99-06; RD Crewkerne and Ilminster 01-07; rtd 08; PtO *B & W* 08-12; PtO Nelson New Zealand from 12. *376B Hardy Street, Nelson 7010, New Zealand* T: (0064) (354) 67765

WHINTON, William Francis Ivan. b 35. NOC 77. **d** 80 **p** 81. NSM Stockport St Mary *Ches* 80-82; NSM Disley 82-87; V Birtles 87-00; Dioc Officer for Disabled 89-00; rtd 00; Chapl for Deaf People *Ches* 00-04; PtO from 05; *Lich* from 09. *Allmeadows Cottage, Wincle, Macclesfield SK11 0QJ* T: (01260) 227278

WHIPP, Antony Douglas. b 46. Leeds Univ BSc 68 Lanc Univ PhD 04. Ripon Coll Cuddesdon 84. **d** 86 **p** 87. C Dalston *Carl* 86-89; V Holme Cultram St Mary 89-96; V Holme Cultram St Cuth 89-96; V Kells 96-00; V Hartlepool St Aid *Dur* 00-05; R Ebchester 05-13; V Medomsley 05-13; rtd 13; PtO *Dur* from 14. *34 Egglestone Drive, Consett DH8 7UB* T: (01207) 588407 E: tony.whipp@durham.anglican.org

WHIPP, Margaret Jane. b 55. LMH Ox BA 76 Sheff Univ MB, ChB 79 MRCP 82 FRCR 86 Hull Univ MA 99 Glas Univ PhD 08. NOC 87. **d** 90 **p** 94. NSM Wickersley *Sheff* 90-98; Tutor Cranmer Hall Dur 98-99; Dir Practical Th NEOC 00-04; Ecum Chapl Ox Brookes Univ 04-08; Lect Past Studies Ox Min Course 06-08; Dean of Studies Ripon Coll Cuddesdon 08-12; Chapl Ox Univ Hosps NHS Trust from 13. *2 All Saints Road, Oxford OX3 7AU* T: (01865) 765409 M: 07775-617129 E: margaretwhipp@btinternet.com

WHITAKER, Anthony. b 50. SS Mark & Jo Coll Chelsea CertEd 72 Middx Univ BA 02. NTMTC 99. **d** 02 **p** 03. C Blackmore and Stondon Massey *Chelmsf* 02-06; P-in-c St Keverne *Truro* 06-11; C Churt and Hindhead *Guildf* 11-15; rtd 15. *The Vicarage, Old Kiln Lane, Churt, Farnham GU10 2HX* T: (01428) 713368 M: 07905-013017 E: tony_whitaker@btinternet.com

WHITAKER, Benjamin. *See* WHITAKER, Michael Benjamin

WHITAKER, Irene Anne. b 57. **d** 01 **p** 02. OLM Parr *Liv* 01-06; TV Bootle from 06. *The Vicarage, Elm Road, Seaforth, Liverpool L21 1BH* T: 0151-920 2205 M: 07771-581886 E: irene369@blueyonder.co.uk

WHITAKER, Margaret Scott. b 45. Dioc OLM tr scheme 00 EAMTC 04. **d** 03 **p** 04. OLM Eaton *Nor* 03-05; C Sprowston w Beeston 05-07; C New Catton Ch Ch 07-11; R Horsford, Felthorpe and Hevingham from 11. *The Rectory, 1B Gordon Godfrey Way, Horsford, Norwich NR10 3SG* T: (01603) 710357 M: 07717-317900 E: mwhitaker1@btinternet.com

WHITAKER, Michael Benjamin. b 60. Nottm Univ BA 83. Sarum & Wells Th Coll 85. **d** 87 **p** 88. C Gt Grimsby St Mary and St Jas *Linc* 87-91; C Abingdon *Ox* 91-95; Chapl to the Deaf *Sarum* 95-00; Asst Chapl amongst Deaf People *Ox* from 00; Chapl HM Pris Grendon and Spring Hill from 07. *HM Prison Grendon, Grendon Underwood, Aylesbury HP18 0TL* T: (01865) 736100 E: whitaker@tribeandclan.freeserve.co.uk

WHITBY, Raymond Thomas. b 57. **d** 14 **p** 15. *52 Coroners Lane, Widnes WA8 9JB* T: 0151-423 6375 E: ramonw57@sky.com

WHITBY, Suffragan Bishop of. *See* FERGUSON, The Rt Revd Paul John

WHITCOMBE, William Ashley. b 78. UEA BA 01. St Steph Ho Ox BTh 04. **d** 04 **p** 05. C W Hendon St Jo *Lon* 04-08; Chapl HM Pris Wormwood Scrubs 08-11; Chapl Univ of the Arts *Lon* from 11; Hon C Highgate St Aug from 11; P in O from 12. *4 Silsoe House, 50 Park Village East, London NW1 7QH* M: 07866-472383 E: w.whitcombe@arts.ac.uk

WHITCROFT, Graham Frederick. b 42. Oak Hill Th Coll 64. **d** 66 **p** 67. C Cromer *Nor* 66-69; C Attercliffe *Sheff* 69-72; V Kimberworth Park 72-85; V Lepton *Wakef* 85-07; RD Kirkburton 98-05; rtd 07; PtO *Leeds* from 07. *18 Far Croft, Lepton, Huddersfield HD8 0LS* T: (01484) 609868 E: whitcroft@btopenworld.com

WHITE, Preb Alan. b 43. Ex Univ BA 65. Chich Th Coll 65. **d** 68 **p** 69. C Upper Clapton St Matt *Lon* 68-72; C Southgate Ch Ch 72-76; P-in-c Friern Barnet St Pet le Poer 76-79; V 79-85; TR Ex St Thos and Em 85-08; RD Christianity 99-03; Preb Ex Cathl 03-08; rtd 08. *Flat 3, 7 Courtenay Road, Newton Abbot TQ12 1HP* T: (01626) 332451 E: revalan.white@btopenworld.com

WHITE, Alan. b 18. Man Univ BSc 39 MSc 40 St Cath Soc Ox BA 42 MA 46 Leeds Univ MEd 52. Ripon Hall Ox 40. **d** 42 **p** 43. C Leic St Marg 42-45; Chapl and Asst Master Leeds Gr Sch 45-56; LtO *Worc* 56-89; Asst Master Bromsgrove

Sch 56-72; Chapl 72-83; rtd 83; P-in-c Tardebigge *Worc* 89-00; PtO from 00. *25 Leadbetter Drive, Bromsgrove B61 7JG* T: (01527) 877955

✠**WHITE, The Rt Revd Alison Mary.** b 56. St Aid Coll Dur BA 78 Leeds Univ MA 94. Cranmer Hall Dur 83. **dss** 86 **d** 87 **p** 94 **c** 15. NSM Chester le Street *Dur* 86-89; Dioc Adv in Local Miss 89-93; Hon Par Dn Birtley 89-93; Dir Past Studies Cranmer Hall Dur 93-98; Dir of Ords *Dur* 98-00; Springboard Missr 00-04; Adult Educn Officer *Pet* 05-10; Can Pet Cathl 09-10; Hon Can Th Sheff Cathl 10-15; P-in-c Riding Mill *Newc* 11-15; Adv for Spirituality and Spiritual Direction 11-15; Suff Bp Hull *York* from 15. *Hullen House, Woodfield Lane, Hessle HU13 0ES* T: (01482) 649019 F: 647449 E: alisonmarywhite@btinternet.com

WHITE, Canon Andrew Paul Bartholomew. b 64. MIOT 85 ABIST 85. Ridley Hall Cam 86. **d** 90 **p** 91. C Battersea Rise St Mark *S'wark* 90-93; P-in-c Balham Hill Ascension 93-97; V 97-98; Dir Internat Min and Can Res Cov Cathl 98-05; Chapl Iraq from 05; President Foundn for Relief and Reconciliation in the Middle E from 05. *The Croft, 66 Shepherds Way, Liphook GU30 7HH* T: (01428) 723939 or (00964) (7901) 265723 E: apbw2@cam.ac.uk

WHITE, Andrew Peter. b 65. Lon Univ BA 87. Sarum & Wells Th Coll BTh 94. **d** 94 **p** 95. C Croydon St Matt *S'wark* 94-96; C S Wimbledon H Trin and St Pet 96-98; TV Droitwich Spa *Worc* 98-05; RD Droitwich 02-04; P-in-c Hartlebury 05-07; Bps' Chapl 05-10; R Kirkley St Pet and St Jo *Nor* from 10. *Kirkley Rectory, Rectory Road, Lowestoft NR33 0ED* T: (01502) 502155

WHITE, Anne Margaret. b 55. Nottm Univ BEd 78. STETS 07. **d** 10 **p** 11. NSM Guernsey St Andr *Win* 10-13; P-in-c Aldbrough, Mappleton w Goxhill and Withernwick *York* from 13. *The Vicarage, Carlton Drive, Aldbrough, Hull HU11 4SF* T: (01964) 527230 M: 07911-712274 E: white.anne19@gmail.com

WHITE, Antony. See FELTHAM-WHITE, Antony James

WHITE, Camilla Elizabeth Zoë. b 56. Somerville Coll Ox BA 78 MA 83 Heythrop Coll Lon MA 06. Ripon Coll Cuddesdon 05. **d** 07 **p** 08. NSM Bramley and Grafham *Guildf* from 07. *Bramley Mill, Mill Lane, Bramley, Guildford GU5 0HW* T: (01483) 892645 E: camillawhite@waitrose.com

WHITE, Mrs Christine Margaret. b 46. Cov Coll of Educn CertEd 68 Kingston Univ BA 96. **d** 07 **p** 08. OLM Cuddington *Guildf* from 07. *5 Lady Hay, Worcester Park KT4 7LT* T: (020) 8337 1665 E: senwhite@talktalk.net

WHITE, Canon Christopher Norman Hessler. b 32. TD 76. St Cath Coll Cam BA 56 MA 60. Cuddesdon Coll 57. **d** 59 **p** 60. C Solihull *Birm* 59-62; C Leeds St Aid *Ripon* 62-65; CF (TA) 64-85; V Aysgarth *Ripon* 65-74; R Richmond 74-76; P-in-c Hudswell w Downholme and Marske 75-76; R Richmond w Hudswell 76-97; RD Richmond 75-80 and 93-97; Hon Can Ripon Cathl 89-97; Chapl St Fran Xavier Sch Richmond 89-97; rtd 97; PtO *Leeds* from 97. *Orchard House, Aske, Richmond DL10 5HN* T: (01748) 850968

WHITE, Colin Davidson. b 44. St And Dioc Tr Course 86. **d** 88 **p** 89. NSM Glenrothes *St And* 88-89; P-in-c 89-90; P-in-c Leven 90-92; R 92-95; V Grimethorpe *Wakef* 95-01; P-in-c Kellington w Whitley 01-02; TV Knottingley and Kellington w Whitley 02-10; rtd 10. *42 Glendale Avenue North, Belfast BT8 6LB* T: (028) 9029 6037 M: 07973-795560 E: col_the_rev@hotmail.co.uk

WHITE, Crispin Michael. b 42. Southn Univ MA 98 PhD 06 FRSA 94. Bps' Coll Cheshunt 62. **d** 65 **p** 66. C S Harrow St Paul *Lon* 65-67; C Mill Hill St Mich 67-68; I Labrador St Clem Canada 68-71; Toc H Padre (W Region) 71-75; (E Midl Region) 75-82; Ind Chapl *Portsm* 82-98; P-in-c Hatfield Broad Oak and Bush End *Chelmsf* 98-04; Ind Chapl 98-07; Harlow 98-04; Lon Thames Gateway 04-07; rtd 07. *6 Downlands, Firsdown Close, Worthing BN13 3BQ* T/F: (01903) 830785 M: 07962-057436 E: postmaster@crispinwhite.plus.com

WHITE, David. b 75. All Hallows Coll Dublin BA 09 Irish Sch of Ecum MPhil 10. St Jo Coll Nottm 10 CITC MTh 13. **d** 12 **p** 13. C Clonsast w Rathangan, Thomastown etc *M & K* 12-13; C Bandon Union *C, C & R* from 13. *3 The Pines, Kilbrittain Road, Bandon, Co Cork, Republic of Ireland* T: (00353) 23-884 4992 E: whitedk@eircom.net

WHITE, Canon David Christopher. b 51. Lon Univ LLB 73. St Jo Coll Nottm 86. **d** 88 **p** 89. C Bulwell St Mary *S'well* 88-92; V Nottingham All SS 92-98; TR Clarendon Park St Jo w Knighton St Mich *Leic* 98-05; R Emmaus Par Team 05-07; P-in-c Fosse 07-12; TR from 12; Bp's NSM Officer 02-08; Hon Can Leic Cathl from 08. *The Rectory, Upper Church Street, Syston, Leicester LE7 1HR* T: 0116-260 8276 E: davidwhite264@btinternet.com

WHITE, David John. b 26. Leeds Univ BA 53. Coll of Resurr Mirfield 53. **d** 55 **p** 56. C Brighton St Pet *Chich* 55-58; C Wednesbury St Jas *Lich* 58-60; C Bishops Hull St Jo *B & W*

60-61; R Morton *Derby* 61-62; In RC Ch 62-73; Lect Whitelands Coll Lon 73-75; R Tregony w St Cuby and Cornelly *Truro* 75-79; R Castle Bromwich SS Mary and Marg *Birm* 79-83; V Plymouth St Simon *Ex* 83-88; R Lapford, Nymet Rowland and Coldridge 88-93; RD Chulmleigh 93; rtd 93; PtO *Ex* 94-99. *The Belvedere, Peak Hill Road, Sidmouth EX10 0NW* T: (01395) 513365

WHITE, Canon David Paul. b 58. Oak Hill Th Coll. **d** 84 **p** 85. C Toxteth Park St Clem *Liv* 84-87; C Woodford Wells *Chelmsf* 87-89; C Woodside Park St Barn *Lon* 89-90; TV Canford Magna *Sarum* 90-93; V York St Mich-le-Belfrey 93-99; V St Austell *Truro* 99-10; Dioc Dir Miss 05-10; Hon Can Truro Cathl 05-10; V Chorleywood St Andr *St Alb* from 10. *St Andrew's Vicarage, 37 Quickley Lane, Chorleywood, Rickmansworth WD3 5AE* T: (01923) 332102 E: davidwhite305@yahoo.com

WHITE, David Peter. b 55. Anglia Ruskin Univ MA 07 AMICE 78. ERMC 09. **d** 12 **p** 13. NSM Felixstowe St Jo *St E* from 12. *The Vicarage, Church Lane, Trimley St Martin, Felixstowe IP11 0SW* T: (01394) 286388 M: 07932-003144 E: david.pwhite@talktalk.net

WHITE, Derek. b 35. MBE 97. **d** 84 **p** 85. C St Marylebone St Cypr *Lon* 84-96; Bp's Chapl for the Homeless 87-01; P-in-c St Mary le Strand w St Clem Danes 96-01; rtd 01; PtO *S'wark* from 04. *80 Coleraine Road, London SE3 7PE* T: (020) 8858 3622

WHITE, Mrs Doreen. b 51. RCN BSc 95. **d** 05 **p** 06. OLM Shelswell *Ox* 05-07; NSM Fawley *Win* 07-15; PtO *Ox* from 15. *32 Fortescue Drive, Chesterton, Bicester OX26 1UT* T: (01869) 572559 E: revdoreen@yahoo.co.uk

WHITE, Douglas Richard Leon. b 49. Linc Th Coll 81. **d** 83 **p** 84. C Warsop *S'well* 83-88; V Kirkby in Ashfield St Thos 88-93; Asst Chapl Qu Medical Cen Nottm Univ Hosp NHS Trust 93-98; Chapl Cen Notts Healthcare NHS Trust 98-01; Chapl Mansfield Distr Primary Care Trust 01-02; Chapl Geo Eliot Hosp NHS Trust Nuneaton 02-06; Chapl Mary Ann Evans Hospice 02-06; Chapl Compton Hospice 06-08; Chapl Marie Curie Hospice Solihull 08-11; Chapl Primrose Hospice Bromsgrove from 08; PtO *Birm* from 11; *Cov* from 06. *1 Glebe Avenue, Bedworth CV12 0DP* T: (024) 7636 0417 *or* (024) 0121-254 7800 E: rickwhite2@btinternet.com

WHITE, Duncan Ernest. b 45. **d** 07 **p** 08. OLM Tilehurst St Geo and Tilehurst St Mary *Ox* 07-11; PtO from 11. *41 Cambrian Way, Calcot, Reading RG31 7DD* T: 0118-380 0367 E: rev.duncan.white@gmail.com

WHITE, Eric James. b 46. **d** 01 **p** 02. OLM Pennington *Man* 01-11; C from 11. *18 Clifton Road, Leigh WN7 3LS* T: (01942) 678758 E: jackieanderic@penningtonchurch.com

✠**WHITE, The Rt Revd Francis.** b 49. Univ of Wales (Cardiff) BSc(Econ) 70. St Jo Coll Nottm. **d** 80 **p** 81 **c** 02. C Dur St Nic 80-84; C Chester le Street 84-87; Chapl Dur and Chester le Street Hosps 87-89; V Birtley *Dur* 89-97; RD Chester-le-Street 93-97; Adn Sunderland and Hon Can Dur Cathl 97-02; Can Pet Cathl from 02; Suff Bp Brixworth 02-10; Asst Bp Newc from 10. *Hullen House, Woodfield Lane, Hessle HU13 0ES* E: bishopfrank@newcastle.anglican.org

WHITE, Canon Gavin Donald. b 27. Toronto Univ BA 49 Trin Coll Toronto BD 61 Gen Th Sem NY STM 68 Lon Univ PhD 70. St Steph Ho Ox 51. **d** 53 **p** 54. C Quebec St Matt Canada 53-55; Chapl Dew Line 56-57; Miss Knob Lake 57-58; Miss Kideleko Zanzibar 59-62; Lect St Paul's Th Coll Limura Kenya 62-66; C Hampstead St Steph *Lon* 68-70; Lect Glas Univ 71-92; LtO *Glas* 71-90; rtd 92; Hon Can St Mary's Cathl from 92; Hon C St Andrews All SS *St And* from 94; PtO *Glas* from 09. *85D Market Street, St Andrews KY16 9NX* T: (01334) 477338 E: gavin.d.white@ukgateway.net

WHITE, Geoffrey Brian. b 54. Jes Coll Ox BA 76 MA 80. St Steph Ho Ox 76. **d** 79 **p** 80. C Huddersfield St Pet *Wakef* 79-82; C Flixton St Mich *Man* 82-84; TV Westhoughton 84-91; V Stevenage St Mary Shephall w Aston *St Alb* 91-06; RD Stevenage 01-06; R Norton *Sheff* from 06. *Norton Rectory, Norton Church Road, Norton, Sheffield S8 8JQ* T: 0114-274 5066 E: geoffreywhite_333@hotmail.com

WHITE, Canon Geoffrey Gordon. b 28. Selw Coll Cam BA 50 MA 54. Cuddesdon Coll 51. **d** 53 **p** 54. C Bradford-on-Avon H Trin *Sarum* 53-56; C Kennington St Jo *S'wark* 56-61; V Leeds St Wilfrid *Ripon* 61-63; Chapl K Coll Hosp Lon 63-66; V Aldwick *Chich* 66-76; V Brighton Gd Shep Preston 76-93; Can and Preb Chich Cathl 90-93; rtd 93; Hon C Stepney St Dunstan and All SS *Lon* 94-10. *7 Limetree Place, Great Bowden, Market Harborough LE16 7JE* T: (01858) 465186 E: jwhite.telford@virgin.net

WHITE, Gillian Margaret. b 57. Qu Eliz Coll Lon BSc 79 Sheff Univ MEd 96 PhD 02 Nottm Univ MA 07. EMMTC 05. **d** 07 **p** 08. NSM Derby St Paul 07-13; PtO 14-15; NSM Tideswell from 15. *The Vicarage, 6 Pursglove Drive, Tideswell, Buxton SK17 8PA* M: 07973-866848 T: (01298) 871317 E: g.m.white@tesco.net *or* gillianwhite1@me.com

WHITE, Graham John. b 76. Lon Bible Coll BTh 99 K Coll Lon MA 08. Ripon Coll Cuddesdon 13. **d** 15. C Tring *St Alb* from 15. *The Vicarage, Station Road, Aldbury, Tring HP23 5RS*
T: (01442) 828344   M: 07963-584458
E: grahamw@tringteamparish.org.uk

WHITE, Miss Hazel Susan. b 65. Nottm Univ BA 88 Birm Univ MPhil 11. Qu Coll Birm 05. **d** 07 **p** 08. C Woodfield *Leic* 07-12; C Moseley St Mary and St Anne *Birm* from 12. *15 Park Hill, Birmingham B13 8DU*   T: 0121-449 1071 *or* 449 2243
E: hazelwhite1@btinternet.com

WHITE, Hugh Richard Bevis. b 55. New Coll Ox BA 78 Ox Univ DPhil 85. S'wark Ord Course 93. **d** 96 **p** 97. NSM Westcote Barton w Steeple Barton, Duns Tew etc *Ox* 96-99; NSM Ox St Mary V w St Cross and St Pet 99-01; V Deddington w Barford, Clifton and Hempton 01-14; C Ironstone from 14. *28 Duns Tew, Bicester OX25 6JR*   T: (01869) 347889
E: vicarhugo@hotmail.com

WHITE, Ian Jeffrey. b 57. Leeds Univ BSc 80 PhD 86 BA 05 CChem 83 MRSC 83. Coll of Resurr Mirfield 03. **d** 05 **p** 06. C Stanningley St Thos *Ripon* 05-09; P-in-c Adel *Leeds* from 09; P-in-c Ireland Wood from 12; Dioc Environment Officer from 06. *The Rectory, 25 Church Lane, Adel, Leeds LS16 8DQ*
T: 0113-267 3676   E: rev.ianwhite@tesco.net

WHITE, Ian Terence. b 56. CertEd. Ripon Coll Cuddesdon 83. **d** 86 **p** 87. C Maidstone St Martin *Cant* 86-89; C Earley St Pet *Ox* 89-91; TV Schorne 91-96; V St Osyth *Chelmsf* 96-00; V The Suttons w Tydd *Linc* 00-04; rtd 04; PtO *Nor* from 06; *St E* from 10. *9 Haling Way, Thetford IP24 1EY*   T: (01842) 820180
E: revianwhite@aol.com

WHITE, James Holford. b 79. Trin Coll Bris 09. **d** 12 **p** 13. C Addiscombe St Mary Magd w St Martin *S'wark* from 12. *68 Elgin Road, Croydon CR0 6XA*   T: (020) 8654 3459
M: 07980-544443   E: whitejames79@gmail.com

WHITE, Miss Janice. b 49. Trin Coll Bris IDC 76. **d** 91 **p** 94. C Claygate *Guildf* 91-98; Assoc Min Stanford-le-Hope w Mucking *Chelmsf* 98-12; rtd 12; PtO *St E* from 12. *27 Canterbury Gardens, Hadleigh IP7 5BS*   T: (01473) 808835
E: wheeze4god@talktalk.net

WHITE, Jeremy Spencer. b 54. St Luke's Coll Ex BEd 78. Wycliffe Hall Ox 81. **d** 84 **p** 85. C S Molton w Nymet St George, High Bray etc *Ex* 84-87; TV 87-95; V Sway *Win* 95-00; P-in-c Uplyme w Axmouth *Ex* 00-03; R 03-09; RD Honiton 06-07; rtd 09. *Oakleigh, Woodbury Lane, Axminster EX13 5TL*   T: (01297) 32299   E: jeremy.white@onetel.net

WHITE, Jo. See WHITE, Julia Mary

WHITE, Canon John Austin. b 42. LVO 04. Hull Univ BA 64. Coll of Resurr Mirfield 64. **d** 66 **p** 67. C Leeds St Aid *Ripon* 66-69; Asst Chapl Leeds Univ 69-73; Chapl NOC 73-82; Can and Prec Windsor 82-12; rtd 12. *24 Camm Avenue, Windsor SL4 4NW*

WHITE, John Christopher. b 62. Keble Coll Ox BA 84 Ex Univ MA 98 PhD 10. Wycliffe Hall Ox BA 88. **d** 89 **p** 90. C Southway *Ex* 89-93; TV Plymouth Em, St Paul Efford and St Aug 93-99; Hon C Abbotskerswell 99-05; PtO *Birm* 05-10; TV Kings Norton 10-14; P-in-c Kingsbury from 14; P-in-c Baxterley w Hurley and Wood End and Merevale etc from 14. *The Vicarage, Church Lane, Kingsbury, Tamworth B78 2LR*
T: (01827) 874252   E: jwhite.harborne@live.co.uk

WHITE, John Cooper. b 58. LTCL 79 K Alfred's Coll Win BEd 82 Lon Univ MA 92 FRSA 94. St Steph Ho Ox 86. **d** 89 **p** 90. C Christchurch *Win* 89-93; P-in-c Bournemouth St Alb 93-94; V 94-00; P-in-c Southbourne St Kath 00-04; V from 04. *St Katharine's Vicarage, 7 Wollaston Road, Bournemouth BH6 4AR*   T: (01202) 423986   E: jcoopw@btconnect.com

WHITE, John Emlyn. See HARRIS-WHITE, John Emlyn

WHITE, Canon John Francis. b 47. Qu Coll Cam BA 69 MA 73. Cuddesdon Coll 72. **d** 72 **p** 73. Sacr Wakef Cathl 72-73; Prec 73-76; V Thurlstone *Wakef* 76-82; P-in-c Hoyland Swaine 81-82; V Chapelthorpe 82-06; RD Chevet 96-05; V Lindley 06-10; Hon Can Wakef Cathl 00-10; rtd 10. *16 Thorne End Road, Staincross, Barnsley S75 6NR*   T: (01226) 217440
E: john.white110@virginmedia.com

WHITE, John Malcolm. b 54. Aston Univ BSc 77. Trin Coll Bris BA 87. **d** 87 **p** 88. C Harborne Heath *Birm* 87-91; C S Harrow St Paul *Lon* 91-93; TV Roxeth 93-96; V Derby St Alkmund and St Werburgh 96-13; PtO *Sheff* from 13. *284 Springvale Road, Sheffield S10 1LJ*   T: 0114-263 1447
E: whitejm@globalnet.co.uk

WHITE, John McKelvey. b 57. QUB BA. **d** 82 **p** 83. C Clooney *D & R* 82-84; C Belfast H Trin *Conn* 84-86; I Kilcronaghan w Draperstown and Sixtowns *D & R* 86-94; I Ballybeen *D & D* 94-04; I Lurgan St Jo from 04. *St John's Rectory, Sloan Street, Lurgan, Craigavon BT66 8NT*   T: (028) 3832 2770

WHITE, Canon John Neville. b 41. Edin Univ MA 63. Cranmer Hall Dur. **d** 65 **p** 66. C Sedgefield *Dur* 65-68; C Stoke *Cov*

68-72; V Wrose *Bradf* 72-90; V Farsley 90-06; RD Calverley 93-98; Hon Can Bradf Cathl 96-06; rtd 06; PtO *Leeds* from 08. *34 Fourlands Drive, Bradford BD10 9SJ*   T: (01274) 415875

WHITE, John William. b 37. CEng 71 MIMechE 71. SAOMC 98. **d** 01 **p** 02. NSM Sandhurst *Ox* 01-10; PtO from 10. *21 Broom Acres, Sandhurst GU47 8PN*   T: (01344) 774349

WHITE (née REDMAN), Mrs Julia Elizabeth Hithersay. b 43. St Alb Minl Tr Scheme 87 SAOMC 99. **d** 99 **p** 00. NSM Harpenden St Jo *St Alb* 99-13; PtO from 13. *The Folly, 71 Station Road, Harpenden AL5 4RL*   T: (01582) 763869

WHITE, Julia Mary (Jo). b 52. Harris Coll CertEd 73 Man Univ BEd 85 MEd 87 PhD 92. NOC 00. **d** 03 **p** 04. C Ashbourne St Oswald w Mapleton *Derby* 03-07; R Wingerworth 07-13; R Thornton Dale w Allerston, Ebberston etc *York* from 13. *The Rectory, High Street, Thornton Dale, Pickering YO18 7QW*
T: (01751) 474244   E: jo@whiteshouse.plus.net

WHITE, Julian Edward Llewellyn. b 53. St D Coll Lamp BA 79 Bp Burgess Hall Lamp 73 Chich Th Coll 79. **d** 79 **p** 80. C Newport St Mark *Mon* 79-83; TV Llanmartin 83-86; R Llandogo and Tintern 86-90 and 91-98; P-in-c St Paul and St Thos St Kitts-Nevis 90-91; V Mathern and Mounton w St Pierre *Mon* 98-13; V Mathern from 13; AD Netherwent 05-13. *St Tewdric's Vicarage, Mathern, Chepstow NP16 6JA*
T: (01291) 622317

WHITE, Canon Justin Michael. b 70. Keble Coll Ox MEng 93 Warwick Univ MA 94 Trin Coll Cam BA 00. Westcott Ho Cam 98. **d** 01 **p** 02. C Chippenham St Andr w Tytherton Lucas *Bris* 01-04; Chapl SS Helen and Kath Sch Abingdon 04-06; Jun Chapl Win Coll 06-14; USA from 14. *1100 California Street, San Francisco, CA 94108, USA*   T: (001) (415) 749 6300   E: justin_white@mac.com

WHITE, Keith Robert. b 48. Open Univ BA 88. St Jo Coll Nottm 82. **d** 84 **p** 85. C Erith St Paul *Roch* 84-88; Chapl Salisbury Coll of Tech *Sarum* 88; PtO *Roch* 11-13; P-in-c Crockenhill All So from 13. *The Vicarage, Eynsford Road, Crockenhill, Swanley BR8 8JS*   T: (01322) 662157
E: keith.acts101@talktalk.net

WHITE, Kenneth Charles. b 26. Tyndale Hall Bris 48. **d** 54 **p** 56. Chapl Lotome Sch Karamoja Uganda 54-55; LtO Mombasa Kenya 55-57; C Morden *S'wark* 57-60; V Ramsey St Mary's w Ponds Bridge *Ely* 60-66; V Leyton Ch Ch *Chelmsf* 66-81; V Totland Bay *Portsm* 81-91; rtd 91; PtO *Llan* 91-07; *Lon* from 08. *286A Torbay Road, Harrow HA2 9QW*
T: (020) 8868 2431

WHITE, Malcolm Robert. b 46. Man Univ BSc 68. Cranmer Hall Dur 74. **d** 77 **p** 78. C Linthorpe *York* 77-81; C Sutton St Jas and Wawne 81-83; V Upper Holloway St Pet w St Jo *Lon* 83-95; TV Burnham w Dropmore, Hitcham and Taplow *Ox* 95-00; CMS Jordan 00-07; rtd 07; PtO *Ox* from 08. *Cherry Cottage, 1 Wymers Wood Road, Burnham, Slough SL1 8JQ*
T: (01628) 669085   E: whitesmv@gmail.com

WHITE, Marilyn Jeanne. b 32. Avery Hill Coll CertEd 69. WMMTC 85. **d** 88 **p** 94. NSM Westbury-on-Severn w Flaxley and Blaisdon *Glouc* 88-98; PtO *B & W* from 98. *7 Harbutts, Bathampton, Bath BA2 6TA*   T: (01225) 464450
E: ken4lyn@btinternet.com

WHITE (née DUNCOMBE), Mrs Maureen Barbara. b 42. Bris Univ BA 63 Ox Univ DipEd 64. Oak Hill Th Coll 87. **d** 89 **p** 00. NSM Wallington *S'wark* 89-91; PtO *Win* 99-00; NSM Totton 00-07; rtd 07; PtO *Win* from 07. *Address temp unknown*
M: 07786-908961   E: maureen@dhandmbwhite.plus.com

WHITE, Michael Godfrey. b 46. SAOMC 98. **d** 02 **p** 03. OLM Shelswell *Ox* 02-07; NSM Fawley *Win* 07-13; rtd 13; PtO *Win* 13-15; *Ox* from 15. *32 Fortescue Drive, Chesterton, Bicester OX26 1UT*   T: (01869) 572559   E: revmikewhite@yahoo.co.uk

WHITE, Nancy Kathleen. b 71. Roehampton Inst BA 96 PGCE 97 Leeds Univ MA 07. NOC 05. **d** 07 **p** 08. NSM Erringden *Wakef* 07-10; NSM Todmorden 10-13; NSM Todmorden w Cornholme and Walsden *Leeds* from 13. *774 Rochdale Road, Todmorden OL14 7UA*   T: (01706) 812007
E: nancy.white@3-c.coop

WHITE, Mrs Natalie Jane. b 65. Ridley Hall Cam 13. **d** 15. C Corby St Columba *Pet* from 15. *5 Hood Court, Corby NN17 2RH*
M: 07806-664495   T: (01536) 358269
E: revnatwhite@gmail.com

✠**WHITE, The Rt Revd Patrick George Hilliard.** Toronto Univ BA 67 DMin 93. Wycliffe Coll Toronto MDiv 77. **d** 77 **p** 78 **c** 09. Canada 77-97; Bermuda from 97; Bp Bermuda from 09. *Diocesan Office, PO Box HM 769, Hamilton HM CX, Bermuda*
T: (001) (441) 292 6987   F: 292 5421

WHITE, Paul John. b 68. JP 10. Middx Univ LLB 90 Bris Univ LLM 92 Solicitor 91. St Mellitus Coll BA 08. **d** 08 **p** 09. C Woodchurch *Cant* 08-12; V Hadlow *Roch* from 13. *The Vicarage, Maidstone Road, Hadlow, Tonbridge TN11 0DJ*
T: (01732) 850238   M: 07970-072757
E: pauljohnwhite@gmail.com

WHITE, Paul Matthew. b 73. Univ Coll Lon BSc 94 K Coll Lon PGCE 95. Oak Hill Th Coll BA 07. **d** 07 **p** 08. C Southborough St Pet w Ch Ch and St Matt etc *Roch* 07-11; C Ox St Andr from 11. *20 Haynes Road, Marston, Oxford OX3 0SF* T: (01865) 242788 M: 07790-697354 E: ppwhites@hotmail.com

✠**WHITE, The Rt Revd Paul Raymond.** b 49. St Mark's Coll Canberra BTh 86 Heythrop Coll Lon MTh 89. **d** 85 **p** 86 **c** 02. C N Goulburn Australia 85-87; P-in-c Reigate St Phil *S'wark* 87-89; R Queanbeyan Australia 89-92; V Redhill St Matt *S'wark* 92-97; V E Ivanhoe Australia 97-00; Dir Th Educn 00-07; Melbourne (W Region) 02-07; (S Region) from 07. *Anglican Centre, 209 Flinders Lane, Melbourne Vic 3000, Australia* T: (0061) (3) 9653 4214 F: 9653 4266 E: sthregbish@melbourne.anglican.com.au

WHITE, Peter Francis. b 27. St Edm Hall Ox BA 51 MA 55. Ridley Hall Cam 51. **d** 53 **p** 54. C Drypool St Columba *York* 53-56; V Dartford St Edm *Roch* 56-62; CF 62-78; R Barming *Roch* 78-89; rtd 89; PtO *Wakef* 89-98. *11 Brookes Barn, Rowsells Lane, Totnes TQ9 5AG* T: (01803) 862171

WHITE, Philip Craston. b 59. York Univ BA 81 Nottm Univ PGCE 84. Trin Coll Bris. **d** 99 **p** 00. C Countesthorpe w Foston *Leic* 99-03; C-in-c Hamilton CD 03-09; C Leic H Trin w St Jo 09-12; V Broughton *Ox* from 12. *24 King Edward Avenue, Aylesbury HP21 7JD* T: (01296) 484555 M: 07725-339236 E: phil@broughtonchurch.org

WHITE, Philip William. b 53. Bede Coll Dur CertEd 75 Coll of Ripon & York St Jo MA 01. St Jo Coll Nottm 89. **d** 91 **p** 92. C Clifton *York* 91-95; TV Heworth H Trin 95-01; P-in-c Scarborough St Jas w H Trin 01-15; Tr Officer E Riding 01-13; P-in-c Cayton w Eastfield 13-15; P-in-c Thurgarton w Hoveringham and Bleasby etc *S'well* from 15. *The Vicarage, Southwell Road, Thurgarton, Nottingham NG14 7GP* T: (01723) 583266 M: 07720-010066 E: phil_07@btinternet.com

WHITE, Mrs Philippa Judith. b 86. CCC Cam BA 08 MA 12. Ripon Coll Cuddesdon BA 13. **d** 14 **p** 15. C Linc St Jo from 14. *17 Gerald's Close, Lincoln LN2 4AL* M: 07474-958658 E: revdpjwhite@gmail.com

WHITE, Canon Phillip George. b 33. Univ of Wales (Lamp) BA 54. St Mich Coll Llan 54. **d** 56 **p** 57. C Tongwynlais Llan 56-58; C Mountain Ash 58-60; C Aberavon 60-62; Area Sec (Middx) CMS 62-64; V Treherbert *Llan* 64-75; P-in-c Treorchy 75-76; V Treherbert w Treorchy 76-77; V Pyle w Kenfig 77-99; RD Margam 86-99; Can Llan Cathl 91-99; rtd 99; PtO *Llan* from 99. *8 Heol Fair, Porthcawl CF36 5LA* T: (01656) 786297

WHITE, Canon Priscilla Audrey. b 62. St Hugh's Coll Ox BA 84 MA 88. Wycliffe Hall Ox 87. **d** 89 **p** 94. Par Dn Southway *Ex* 89-93; NSM Plymouth Em, St Paul Efford and St Aug 93-99; P-in-c Abbotskerswell 99-05; P-in-c Harborne St Faith and St Laur *Birm* 05-10; V from 10; AD Edgbaston from 10; Hon Can Birm Cathl from 15. *The Vicarage, Church Lane, Kingsbury, Tamworth B78 2LR* T: (01827) 874252 or 0121-427 2410 E: priscillawhite.harborne@btinternet.com

WHITE, Richard. See WHITE, Douglas Richard Leon

WHITE, Richard Alfred. b 49. CQSW. St Jo Coll Nottm. **d** 90 **p** 91. C Leic St Phil 90-95; C Old Dalby and Nether Broughton 95-98; R Ibstock w Heather 98-10; rtd 10; PtO *Leic* from 10. *3 Marston Way, Heather, Coalfield LE67 2RR* T: (01530) 260676 E: richard49white@googlemail.com

WHITE, Canon Richard Stanley. b 70. Trin Coll Bris BA 02. **d** 03 **p** 04. C Haydock St Mark *Liv* 03-06; Pioneer Min Dream Network 06-09; Can for Miss and Evang from 09. *3 Cathedral Close, Liverpool L1 7BR* T: 0151-702 7243 E: richard.white@liverpoolcathedral.org.uk

WHITE, Canon Robert Charles. b 61. Mansf Coll Ox BA 83. St Steph Ho Ox 83. **d** 85 **p** 86. C Forton *Portsm* 85-88; C Portsea N End St Mark 88-92; V Warren Park 92-00; P-in-c Leigh Park 94-96; V 96-00; RD Havant 98-00; V Portsea St Mary from 00; AD Portsm from 11; Hon Can Portsm Cathl from 97. *St Mary's Vicarage, Fratton Road, Portsmouth PO1 5PA* T: (023) 9282 2687 or 9282 2990 F: 9235 9320 E: revrcwhite@aol.com

WHITE, Robin Edward Bantry. b 47. TCD BA 70 BD 79. CITC 72. **d** 72 **p** 73. C Dublin Zion Ch *D & G* 72-76; Min Can St Patr Cathl Dublin 76-79; C Taney Ch Ch *D & G* 76-79; I Abbeystrewry Union *C, C & R* 79-89; I Douglas Union w Frankfield 89-02; I Moviddy Union 02-14; Can Cork Cathl 89-14; Can Ross Cathl 89-93; Adn Cork, Cloyne and Ross 93-14; Preb Castleknock St Patr Cathl Dublin 09-14; rtd 14. *Ardcairn, 26 Marble Court, Paulstown, Co Kilkenny, Republic of Ireland* M: 87-286 2178 T: (00353) (59) 972 6089 E: rebw@eircom.net or robinbantrywhite@gmail.com

WHITE, Roderick Harry. b 55. Trin Coll Bris BA 86. **d** 86 **p** 87. C Northampton St Giles *Pet* 86-89; C Godley cum Newton Green *Ches* 89-93; P-in-c 93-99; R Northiam *Chich* from 99. *The Rectory, 24 High Meadow, Northiam, Rye TN31 6GA* T: (01797) 253118 E: rod@rodwhite.freeuk.com

WHITE, Roger David. b 37. Univ of Wales (Cardiff) BTh 91. St Mich Coll Llan. **d** 66 **p** 67. C Mountain Ash *Llan* 66-71; C Port Talbot St Theodore 71-74; V Caerhun w Llangelynin w Llanbedr-y-Cennin *Ban* 74-85; R Llanbedrog w Llannor w Llanfihangel etc 85-88; V Llangeinor *Llan* 88-90; V Spittal w Trefgarn and Ambleston w St Dogwells *St D* 90-98; V Abergwili w Llanfihangel-uwch-Gwili etc 98-00; rtd 00. *Tir Na Nog, 18 Bryn Cir, Llanerchymedd LL71 8EG* T: (01248) 470159

WHITE, Roger Ian Scott. b 41. Leeds Univ BA 62 Culham Coll Ox PGCE 70. Coll of Resurr Mirfield 62. **d** 64 **p** 65. C Wotton-under-Edge *Glouc* 64-69; NSM Rugby St Andr *Cov* 71-80; W Germany 80-82; P-in-c Brinklow *Cov* 82-86; R 86-90; P-in-c Harborough Magna 82-86; R 86-90; P-in-c Monks Kirby w Pailton and Stretton-under-Fosse 82-86; V 86-90; Germany 90-92; V Lydgate w Friezland *Man* 92-01; Chapl Hamburg *Eur* 01-11; rtd 11. *Spannwisch 7, 22159 Hamburg, Germany* T: (0049) (40) 664316 E: roger.white@gmx.de

WHITE, Ronald Henry. b 36. Bris Univ BSc 58. SWMTC 82. **d** 85 **p** 86. C Ivybridge *Ex* 85-87; C Ivybridge w Harford 87-88; V Blackawton and Stoke Fleming 88-95; V Stoke Fleming, Blackawton and Strete 95-00; RD Woodleigh 95-99; rtd 00; PtO *Ex* from 02. *10 Hollingarth Way, Hemyock, Cullompton EX15 3XB* T: (01823) 681020

WHITE, Canon Roy Sidney. b 34. Sarum Th Coll 62. **d** 65 **p** 66. C Selsdon St Jo w St Fran *Cant* 65-68; C Ranmoor *Sheff* 68-72; V Croydon St Andr *Cant* 72-78; Dir Abp Coggan Tr Cen 78-85; Dir of Chr Stewardship *S'wark* 85-91; Hon Can S'wark Cathl 85-91; Can Res S'wark Cathl 91-99; Vice Provost S'wark 91-99; rtd 99; PtO *Cant* 00-09; *Chich* from 10. *52 Manton Court, Kings Road, Horsham RH13 5AE* T: (01403) 248036

WHITE, Mrs Sally Margaret. b 59. Univ of Wales (Cardiff) BTh 01. St Mich Coll Llan 99. **d** 01 **p** 02. C Berkeley w Wick, Breadstone, Newport, Stone etc *Glouc* 01-05; Co-ord Chapl HM Pris Bedf 05-09; Chapl HM Pris Jersey 09-12; Chapl Jersey Gp of Hosps 09-12. *Address withheld by request*

WHITE, Sandy Dulcie. b 44. **d** 98 **p** 99. OLM W Streatham St Jas *S'wark* 98-05; PtO *Wakef* 05-07; *Leeds* from 14; NSM Cornholme and Walsden *Wakef* 07-14. *774 Rochdale Road, Todmorden OL14 7UA* T: (01706) 812007

WHITE, Sheelagh Mary. See ASTON, Sheelagh Mary

WHITE, Simon Inigo Dexter. b 58. York Univ BA 80 Nottm Univ PGCE 81. St Jo Coll Nottm 87. **d** 90 **p** 91. C Chadkirk *Ches* 90-94; C Stockport St Geo 94; TV Stockport SW 94-99; Chapl Stockport Gr Sch 94-99; P-in-c W Hallam and Mapperley *Derby* 99-02; P-in-c Stanley 99-02; R W Hallam and Mapperley w Stanley 02-13; V Tideswell from 13. *The Vicarage, 6 Pursglove Drive, Tideswell, Buxton SK17 8PA* T: 0115-932 4695 or (01298) 871317 E: s.i.d.white@tesco.net or simon.white44@btinternet.com

WHITE, Simon James Hithersay. b 65. St Jo Coll Nottm 01. **d** 03 **p** 04. C Alnwick *Newc* 03-06; P-in-c Felton and Long-framlington w Brinkburn 06-13; Dioc Youth Officer from 06; R Morpeth from 13. *The Rectory, Cottingwood Lane, Morpeth NE61 1ED* T: (01670) 517716 E: rev.simonjhwhite@gmail.com

WHITE, Stephen Ross. b 58. Hull Univ BA 81 QUB PhD 94. Ripon Coll Cuddesdon BA 84. **d** 85 **p** 86. C Redcar *York* 85-88; P-in-c Gweedore, Carrickfin and Templecrone *D & R* 88-92; Bp's Dom Chapl 91-92; Dean Raphoe 92-02; I Raphoe w Raymochy and Clonleigh 93-01; Dean Killaloe and Clonfert *L & K* 02-12; Dean Raphoe 92-02; Chan St Patr Cathl Dublin 11-12; P-in-c Dunsfold and Hascombe *Guildf* from 12. *The Rectory, Church Green, Dunsfold, Godalming GU8 4LT* T: (01483) 200048 E: stephenwhite14@btinternet.com

WHITE, Mrs Susan Margaret. b 48. Univ of E Lon BA 84 Brunel Univ MBA 94 Anglia Poly Univ MA 04. EAMTC 01. **d** 04 **p** 05. C Harwich Peninsula *Chelmsf* 04-08; P-in-c Alkham w Capel le Ferne and Hougham *Cant* 08-12; P-in-c Eythorne and Elvington w Waldershare etc 12; P-in-c Whitfield w Guston 12; R Bewsborough from 13; AD Dover 11-15. *The Vicarage, Bewsbury Cross Lane, Whitfield, Dover CT16 3EZ* E: suewhite712@hotmail.com

WHITE, Sister Teresa Joan. b 36. Wellesley Coll (USA) BA 58 Harvard Univ STB 61 Lon Univ CertEd 74 Hon DD 86. **dss** 75 **d** 87 **p** 94. CSA from 72; Teacher Burlington-Danes Sch 74-76; Lect Inst of Chr Studies *Lon* 76-78; Gen Sec World Congress of Faiths 77-81; Lect Dioc Readers' Course *S'wark* 81-89; Asst Abp's Sec for Ecum Affairs 81-82; Ed Distinctive Diaconate News from 81; Ed DIAKONIA News 87-03; Ed Distinctive News of Women in Ministry from 94; LtO *Lon* 94-06; PtO from 06; Chapl Angl Communion Office from 04. *St Andrew's House, 16 Tavistock Crescent, London W11 1AP* T: (020) 7221 4604 E: teresajoan@btinternet.com

WHITE (née BUTLER), Mrs Valerie Joyce. b 58. EAMTC 99. **d** 02 **p** 03. NSM Southminster *Chelmsf* 02-06; Hon Chapl Miss to Seafarers Tilbury 05-06; C Bury St Edmunds All SS w St Jo and

St Geo *St E* 06-08; TV Walton and Trimley from 08. *The Vicarage, Church Lane, Trimley St Martin, Felixstowe IP11 0SW* T: (01394) 286388 E: valthevic@talktalk.net

WHITE, Canon Vernon Philip. b 53. Clare Coll Cam BA 75 MA 79 Oriel Coll Ox MLitt 80. Wycliffe Hall Ox. **d** 77 **p** 78. Tutor Wycliffe Hall Ox 77-83; Chapl and Lect Ex Univ 83-87; R Wotton and Holmbury St Mary *Guildf* 87-93; Dir of Ords 87-93; Can Res and Chan Linc Cathl 93-01; Prin STETS 01-11; Can Westmr Abbey from 11; Visiting Prof K Coll Lon from 11; Can Th Win Cathl from 06. *3 Little CLoisters, London SW1P 3PL* T: (020) 7654 4808 E: vernon.white@westminster-abbey.org

WHITE, William Frederick. b 30. St Jo Coll Nottm. **d** 02. NSM Hillingdon St Jo *Lon* 02-06; NSM Cowley 06-08; Asst Chapl Hillingdon Hosp NHS Trust 02-08; PtO *Lon* from 08. *31A Copperfield Avenue, Hillingdon, Uxbridge UB8 3NU* T: (01895) 236746 M: 07754-234233 E: billwhite2001@hotmail.com

WHITE, William John. b 54. BSc. Wycliffe Hall Ox. **d** 84 **p** 85. C Bowdon *Ches* 84-87; C Chadkirk 87-90; R Wistaston 90-07; RD Nantwich 98-01; TR Gd Shep TM *Carl* 07-13; R Greystoke w Penruddock, Mungrisdale etc from 13. *The Rectory, Greystoke, Penrith CA11 0TJ* T: (01768) 483293 E: revbillwhite@tiscali.co.uk

WHITE SPUNNER, Mrs Jessie Janet. b 37. SRN 59 SCM 61. CITC 91. **d** 94 **p** 95. NSM Shinrone w Aghancon etc *L & K* 94-10; rtd 10. *St Albans, Church Street, Birr, Co Offaly, Republic of Ireland* T: (00353) (57) 912 5637 M: 86-814 0213 E: janwspun@iol.ie

WHITEHALL, Adrian Leslie. b 53. Leeds Univ MB, ChB 76 Sheff Univ MMedSc 93 MRCGP 80. Ridley Hall Cam 04. **d** 06 **p** 07. C Todwick *Sheff* 06-09; Tanzania 10-11; PtO *Derby* from 12. *Meadow House, Ashbourne Road, Belper DE56 2DA* T: (01773) 826410 M: 07866-454148 E: adrian.whitehall@gmail.com

WHITEHEAD, Alexander. *See* WHITEHEAD, Matthew Alexander

WHITEHEAD, Andrew Paul. b 77. Lanc Univ BA 01 Cam Univ BTh 12. Westcott Ho Cam 10. **d** 12 **p** 13. C Clitheroe St Mary *Blackb* 12-15; C Cawston w Booton and Brandiston etc *Nor* from 15. *3 Abbot Walk, Clitheroe BB7 1JE* M: 07801-290649 E: a.p.whitehead@me.com

WHITEHEAD, Barry. b 30. Oriel Coll Ox BA 53 MA 62. St Steph Ho Ox 53. **d** 55 **p** 56. C Edgehill St Dunstan *Liv* 55-58; C Upholland 58-61; Ind Chapl 61-90; CF (TA) 64-78; V Aspull *Liv* 77-96; rtd 96; PtO *Blackb* from 96; *Liv* from 96. *5 Sedgely, Standish, Wigan WN6 0BZ* T: (01257) 427160

WHITEHEAD, Brian. b 36. Wycliffe Hall Ox. **d** 75 **p** 77. C Croydon St Aug *Cant* 75-78; C St Marychurch *Ex* 78-80; V Devonport St Mark Ford 80-87; V Castle Donington and Lockington cum Hemington *Leic* 87-98; Chapl Asmara St Geo Eritrea 98-99; Vice Provost All SS Cathl Cairo 99-00; Assoc P Abu Dhabi 00-01; rtd 01; PtO *Nor* 01-07. *1 Sarisbury Close, Bognor Regis PO22 8JN* T: (01243) 866549 E: britone@uk.packardbell.org

WHITEHEAD, Mrs Christine Sheila. b 63. BN MSc PGCE. STETS. **d** 14 **p** 15. NSM Chandler's Ford *Win* from 14. *96 Ashdown Road, Chandler's Ford, Eastleigh SO53 5QG* T: (023) 8026 0299 E: csw.pocf@gmail.com

WHITEHEAD, Christopher Martin Field. b 36. ALCD 62. **d** 62 **p** 63. C Higher Openshaw *Man* 62-63; C Halliwell St Pet 64-66; V Owlerton *Sheff* 66-75; V Hunmanby w Muston *York* 75-95; RD Scarborough 91-94; R Leconfield and Lund and Scorborough w Leconfield 95-01; rtd 01; PtO *York* from 01. *59 Cornelian Drive, Scarborough YO11 3AL* T: (01723) 377837 E: candjwhitehead59@gmail.com

WHITEHEAD, David. b 62. Newc Univ BSc 83 MSc 85 PhD 89. St Jo Coll Nottm BA 09. **d** 07 **p** 08. C Ambleside w Brathay *Carl* 07-10; TV Kirkby Lonsdale 10-14; P-in-c Windermere 14-15; Dioc Healing Adv 13-15; rtd 15. *Brandle Howe, Helm Road, Bowness-on-Windermere, Windermere LA23 3AA* T: (015394) 44393 E: davidcwhitehead@btopenworld.com

WHITEHEAD, Frederick Keith. b 35. K Coll Lon BD 58 AKC 58. St Boniface Warminster 58. **d** 59 **p** 60. C S Shore H Trin *Blackb* 59-63; C Whitfield *Derby* 63-66; LtO 66-93; V Glossop 93-98; Chapl Shire Hill Hosp Glossop 93-99; rtd 99; PtO *Derby* from 98; *Ches* from 10. *7 Badgers Way, Glossop SK13 6PP* T: (01457) 852717 E: f.whitehead1@hotmail.co.uk

WHITEHEAD, Gordon James. b 42. Culham Coll of Educn DipEd 64. Clifton Th Coll 66. **d** 73 **p** 74. C Romford Gd Shep *Chelmsf* 73; SAMS Santiago Chile 74-87; C Coleraine *Conn* 87-94; I Errigle Keerogue w Ballygawley and Killeshil *Arm* 94-02; I Bright w Ballee and Killough *D & D* 02-07; rtd 07. *75 Kensington Manor, Dollingstown, Craigavon BT66 7HR* T: (028) 3831 7989 E: whitehead105@btinternet.com

WHITEHEAD, Canon Hazel. b 54. K Coll Lon BD 76 AKC 76 Lambeth MA 97. Oak Hill Th Coll 93. **d** 94 **p** 95. Tutor Dioc Min Course *Guildf* 94-96; Prin 96-05; C Oatlands 95-04;

Dioc Dir Minl Tr from 05; Hon Can Guildf Cathl from 03. *The Rectory, The Spinning Walk, Shere, Guildford GU5 9HN* T: (01483) 202394 *or* 790307 E: hazel.whitehead@cofeguildford.org.uk

WHITEHEAD, Ian Richard. b 63. St Jo Coll Nottm BA 95. **d** 95 **p** 96. C Hillmorton *Cov* 95-97; C Whitnash 97-99; R Rolleston *Lich* from 99; V Anslow from 99; C Hanbury, Newborough, Rangemore and Tutbury from 14. *The Rectory, Church Road, Rolleston-on-Dove, Burton-on-Trent DE13 9BE* T: (01283) 810132 *or* 810151 E: revirwhite@aol.com

WHITEHEAD, Mrs Jennifer Jane. b 45. St Jo Coll York CertEd 67. **d** 98 **p** 99. OLM Winterton Gp *Linc* from 98. *11 Queen Street, Winterton, Scunthorpe DN15 9TR* T: (01724) 734027

WHITEHEAD, Mrs Joanne Louise. b 71. Hull Univ BA 92 PGCE 93 Nottm Univ MA 08. EMMTC 05. **d** 08 **p** 09. C Oakwood *Derby* 08-13; P-in-c Newhall from 13. *St John's Vicarage, Church Street, Newhall, Swadlincote DE11 0HY* T: (01283) 214685 E: jl.whitehead@btinternet.com

WHITEHEAD, John Stanley. b 38. Jes Coll Cam BA 63 MA 67 MPhil. Westcott Ho Cam 63. **d** 64 **p** 65. C Batley All SS *Wakef* 64-67; C Mitcham St Mark *S'wark* 67-70; C Frindsbury w Upnor *Roch* 70-72; TV Strood 72-75; R Halstead 75-82; V Betley and Keele 85-01; Asst Chapl Keele Univ 82-01; PtO *Ches* 02-09 and from 11; C Acton and Worleston, Church Minshull etc 10; PtO *Lich* from 09. *Paddock House, Longhill Lane, Hankelow, Crewe CW3 0JG* T: (01270) 812607 E: jbwhitehead@onetel.com

WHITEHEAD, Canon Matthew Alexander. b 44. Leeds Univ BA 65 Birm Univ MA 75 St Chad's Coll Dur DipEd 66 Newc Univ MPhil 03. Qu Coll Birm. **d** 69 **p** 70. C Bingley All SS *Bradf* 69-72; C Keele and Asst Chapl Keele Univ *Lich* 72-74; Bp's Dom Chapl *Dur* 74-80; V Escomb and Witton Park 74-80; V Birtley 80-89; RD Chester-le-Street 84-89; V Stockton St Pet 89-00; V The Trimdons 00-03; Dioc Warden of Readers 94-03; Hon Can Dur Cathl 96-03; P-in-c Stow Gp *Linc* 03-09; rtd 09; Dioc Warden of Readers *Linc* 03-11; Can and Preb Linc Cathl from 04; V Linc St Mary Magd w St Paul and St Mich from 14. *77 Yarborough Crescent, Lincoln LN1 3NE* M: 07518-746643 E: alex.whitehead@lincoln.anglican.org

WHITEHEAD, Canon Michael Hutton. b 33. St Chad's Coll Dur 54. **d** 58 **p** 59. CMP from 59; C Southwick St Columba *Dur* 58-64; V Hendon St Ignatius 64-70; P-in-c Sunderland 67-80; V Hendon 70-80; V Hendon and Sunderland 80-87; Hon Can Dur Cathl from 84; V Hartlepool St Aid 87-98; RD Hartlepool 91-95; rtd 98; PtO *Dur* from 98. *4 West Row, Greatham, Hartlepool TS25 2HW* T: (01429) 872922

WHITEHEAD, Canon Nicholas James. b 53. Univ of Wales (Ban) BTh 07 ACIB. Ridley Hall Cam 86. **d** 88 **p** 89. C Bourne *Guildf* 88-92; V Hersham 92-10; RD Emly 06-10; P-in-c Shere, Albury and Chilworth 10-14; R Shere w Albury etc 11-14; Hon Can Guildf Cathl from 12. *The Rectory, The Spinning Walk, Shere, Guildford GU5 9HN* T: (01483) 202394 M: 07946-389583 E: nick@nickhaze.demon.co.uk

WHITEHEAD, Paul Conrad. b 60. St Jo Coll Nottm LTh 92. **d** 92 **p** 93. C Mansfield Woodhouse *S'well* 92-96; C Carlton-in-the-Willows 96-02; C Colwick 96-02; CF (TA) from 96; NSM Trowell, Awsworth and Cossall *S'well* from 04. *84 Hillside Road, Beeston, Nottingham NG9 3AT* T: 0115-919 7030 M: 07973-727221 E: paulkirsten@ntlworld.com

WHITEHEAD, Philip. b 34. Kelham Th Coll 55. **d** 59 **p** 60. C Sugley *Newc* 59-62; C Alnwick St Paul 62-63; C Newc Sacrist 63-66; C Gosforth All SS 66-67; V Kenton Ascension 67-75; V Spittal 75-88; P-in-c Scremerston 81-88; V Cresswell and Lynemouth 88-96; PtO from 96; rtd 96. *13 Abbey Gate, Morpeth NE61 2XL* T: (01670) 514953

WHITEHEAD, Canon Robin Lawson. b 53. Bris Univ BA 76 Lon Univ MA 96. St Steph Ho Ox 77. **d** 80 **p** 81. C Cheshunt *St Alb* 80-83; C E Grinstead St Swithun *Chich* 83-85; V Friern Barnet St Pet le Poer *Lon* 85-92; R Friern Barnet St Jas 92-95; C Wood Green St Mich w Bounds Green St Gabr etc 96-97; TR *Leic* Resurr 97-04; V Boston *Linc* 04-05; TR 05-13; RD Holland E 09-10; RD Holland W 09-10; RD Holland 10-13; Can and Preb Linc Cathl 09-13; rtd 13; PtO *Cant* from 13; R Winchelsea and Icklesham *Chich* from 13. *The Rectory, St Thomas Street, Winchelsea TN36 4EB* E: robinwhitehead6@btinternet.com

WHITEHOUSE, Alan Edward. b 35. CEng 66. Glouc Sch of Min 89. **d** 92 **p** 93. NSM Evesham *Worc* 92-96; NSM Evesham w Norton and Lenchwick 96-02; rtd 02; PtO *Worc* from 03. *The Coppice, 56 Elm Road, Evesham WR11 3DW* T: (01386) 442427 M: 07789-081595 E: alan.coppice@tiscali.co.uk

WHITEHOUSE, David Garner. b 70. Sheff Univ BEng 91. EAMTC 03. **d** 05 **p** 06. C Cheadle *Ches* 05-10; P-in-c Southport SS Simon and Jude w All So *Liv* from 10. *The Vicarage, 72 Roe Lane, Southport PR9 7HT* E: davidgwhitehouse@googlemail.com

WHITEHOUSE, Nigel Andrew. b 57. St Mary's RC Sem Birm 75 Westcott Ho Cam 91. **d** 80 **p** 81. In RC Ch 81-87; C Whittlesey and Pondersbridge *Ely* 92-94; P-in-c Newton 94-98; R 98-03; P-in-c Gorefield 94-98; V 98-03; P-in-c Tydd St Giles 94-98; R 98-03; TR Whittlesey, Pondersbridge and Coates from 03; Hon Asst Dir of Ords 09-12; RD March from 09. *The Rectory, 9A St Mary's Street, Whittlesey, Peterborough PE7 1BG* T: (01733) 203676 E: nigel.whitehouse@hotmail.com

WHITEHOUSE, Canon Susan Clara. b 48. R Holloway Coll Lon BA 70. Westcott Ho Cam 87. **d** 89 **p** 94. Par Dn Farnley *Ripon* 89-93; Dioc Development Rep 92-03; C Bedale and Thornton Watlass w Thornton Steward 93-96; V Aysgarth and Bolton cum Redmire 96-06; R Penhill 06-13; Hon Can Ripon Cathl 02-13; AD Wensley 03-05; rtd 13. *157 The Murrays, Edinburgh EH17 8UN* E: suewhitehouse@carperby.fsnet.co.uk

WHITELEY, Canon Robert Louis. b 28. Leeds Univ BA 48. Coll of Resurr Mirfield 50. **d** 52 **p** 53. C Hollinwood *Man* 52-55; Br Honduras 56-61; V Illingworth *Wakef* 61-68; V Westgate Common 68-75; Can Res Wakef Cathl 75-80; Hon Can Wakef Cathl 80-93; V Almondbury 80-82; TR Almondbury w Farnley Tyas 82-92; RD Almondbury 81-93; rtd 93; PtO *Leeds* from 93; *Ox* 98-10; *Guildf* 10-13. *34 Elizabeth Court, Victoria Road, Wargrave, Reading RG10 8BP*

WHITELOCK, Mrs Susan Karen. b 62. STETS 98. **d** 01 **p** 06. NSM Portsea N End St Mark *Portsm* 01-06; NSM Portsea St Mary from 06. *404 Copnor Road, Portsmouth PO3 5EW* M: 07903-414029 E: sue.whitelock@ntlworld.com

WHITEMAN, Canon Cedric Henry. b 28. Lich Th Coll 59. **d** 61 **p** 62. C Abington *Pet* 61-64; V Kettering St Andr 64-79; RD Kettering 73-79; Can Pet Cathl 77-79; V Rotherham *Sheff* 79-87; RD 79-86; Hon Can Sheff Cathl 85-98; Bp's Dom Chapl 86-99; V Wentworth 87-91; rtd 91; PtO *Sheff* 99-12. *Oaklow, Shireoaks Road, Shireoaks, Worksop S81 8LX* T: (01909) 472253 E: cedric.whiteman@tiscali.co.uk

WHITEMAN, Christopher Henry Raymond. b 51. Portsm Poly BA 73 Worc Coll of Educn PGCE 74 Open Univ BSc 97. St Jo Coll Nottm MA 99. **d** 90 **p** 91. C Rockland St Mary w Hellington, Bramerton etc *Nor* 90-93; P-in-c Gillingham w Geldeston, Stockton, Ellingham etc 93-94; R 94-04; R Culworth w Sulgrave and Thorpe Mandeville etc *Pet* 04-11; rtd 11. *28 Penterry Park, Chepstow NP16 5AZ* E: chrwhiteman@aol.com

WHITEMAN, The Ven Rodney David Carter. b 40. Ely Th Coll 61. **d** 64 **p** 65. C Kings Heath *Birm* 64-70; V Rednal 70-79; V Erdington St Barn 79-89; RD Aston 81-86 and 88-89; Hon Can Birm Cathl 85-89; Adn Bodmin *Truro* 89-00; Adn Cornwall 00-05; P-in-c Cardynham and Helland 89-94; Hon Can Truro Cathl 89-05; rtd 06. *22 Treverbyn Gardens, Sandy Hill, St Austell PL25 3AW* T: (01726) 879043

WHITESIDE, Canon Peter George. b 30. St Cath Coll Cam BA 55 MA 61. Cuddesdon Coll 55. **d** 57 **p** 58. C Westmr St Steph w St Jo *Lon* 57-61; Chapl Clifton Coll Bris 61-70; Hd Master Linc Cathl Sch 71-73; Can and Preb Linc Cathl 72-73; Prin and Chapl Wadhurst C of E Gr Sch Australia 74-89; TV Brentford *Lon* 92-97; C Frankston St E Luke Australia 98-00; C Ormond 00-05; rtd 05. *52 Cove Road, Rustington, Littlehampton BN16 2QN* T: (01903) 786566 E: linda655@btinternet.com

WHITFIELD, Joy Verity. *See* CHAPMAN, Joy Verity

WHITFIELD, Leslie Turnbull. b 43. Cardiff Univ LLM 10 CEng 72 MIET 72 MCMI 74. St Jo Coll Nottm MA 00. **d** 00 **p** 01. C Bottesford w Ashby *Linc* 00-03; P-in-c Mablethorpe w Trusthorpe 03-07; Ind Chapl 07-08; rtd 08. *3 Burland Court, Washingborough, Lincoln LN4 1HL* T: (01522) 791195 M: 07913-247783 E: rev.les@tiscali.co.uk

WHITFIELD, Canon Trevor. b 48. Bedf Coll Lon BSc 71 Bris Univ PGCE 73 Fitzw Coll Cam BA 78 MA 88. Ridley Hall Cam 76. **d** 79 **p** 80. C Battersea St Pet and St Paul *S'wark* 79-82; Chapl Stockholm w Uppsala *Eur* 82-83; C-in-c Roundshaw St Paul CD *S'wark* 83-89; Asst Chapl R Victoria Infirmary Newc 89-92; Asst Chapl Berne w Neuchâtel *Eur* 92-95; Chapl Utrecht w Amersfoort, Harderwijk and Zwolle 95-02; Chapl Maisons-Laffitte 02-13; Can Gib Cathl 10-13; rtd 13. *Akkerstraat 1, 4116 Buren, The Netherlands* E: htcml@aol.com

WHITFIELD, William. b 47. Open Univ BA 80 Univ of Wales (Cardiff) LLM 95 FRSH 81. STETS 01. **d** 04 **p** 05. NSM Marchwood *Win* 04-08; NSM Millbrook 08-11; PtO from 11; *Portsm* from 13. *35 The Rowans, Marchwood, Southampton SO40 4YW* T: (023) 8086 0399 E: william.whitfield@btinternet.com

WHITFORD, Judith. *See* POLLINGER, Judith

WHITFORD (née FAULKNER), Mrs Margaret Evelyn. b 54. Goldsmiths' Coll Lon BEd 77. EAMTC 98. **d** 01 **p** 02. C Grays Thurrock *Chelmsf* 01-05; C Bradwell on Sea 05-08; C Bradwell on Sea and St Lawrence 08-11; C Brandon and Santon Downham w Elveden etc *St E* 11-15. *The Rectory, 7 Walton Way, Brandon IP27 0HP* E: mandlz@btinternet.com

WHITFORD, William Laurence. b 56. Open Univ BA 92. NOC 92. **d** 95 **p** 96. C Hindley All SS *Liv* 95-99; P-in-c E and W Tilbury and Linford *Chelmsf* 99-04; R 04-05; P-in-c Bradwell on Sea 05-08; R Bradwell on Sea and St Lawrence 08-11; R Brandon and Santon Downham w Elveden etc *St E* 11-15; rtd 15. *The Rectory, 7 Walton Way, Brandon IP27 0HP* E: mandlz@btinternet.com

WHITHAM, Ian Scott. b 66. Oak Hill Th Coll. **d** 01 **p** 02. C Yateley *Win* 01-03; C Yateley and Eversley 03-05; V W Ewell *Guildf* 05-15; P-in-c Hyde w Ellingham and Harbridge *Win* from 15. *The Vicarage, Frogham Hill, Stuckton, Fordingbridge SP6 2HH* M: 07403-061116 E: ianwhitham67@googlemail.com

WHITING, Graham James. b 58. Bris Univ BSc 81. Chich Th Coll 83. **d** 86 **p** 88. C Portslade St Nic and St Andr *Chich* 86-87; C W Tarring 87-91; C Seaford w Sutton 91-94; P-in-c Bournemouth St Clem *Win* 94-02; V Findon Valley *Chich* 02-14; P-in-c Hamble le Rice *Win* from 14. *The Vicarage, High Street, Hamble, Southampton SO31 4JF* T: (023) 8045 2148 E: grahamwhiting@yahoo.com

WHITING, Joseph Alfred. b 41. Oak Hill Th Coll 82. **d** 85 **p** 86. Hon C Sidcup St Andr *Roch* 85-88; C Southborough St Pet w Ch Ch and St Matt 88-92; C Aldridge *Lich* 92-97; TV Rye *Chich* 97-02; rtd 02; PtO *Roch* from 02. *238 Ralph Perring Court, Stone Park Avenue, Beckenham BR3 3LX* T: (020) 3583 3431 E: whitings71@tiscali.co.uk

WHITING, Stephen. b 60. Cranmer Hall Dur 06. **d** 08 **p** 09. C Scarborough St Mary w Ch Ch and H Apostles *York* 08-12; TV Leverhulme *Man* from 12. *St Chad's Vicarage, 9 Tonge Fold Road, Bolton BL2 6AW* T: (01204) 528159 M: 07789-950881 E: stevewhiting.1@btinternet.com

WHITLEY, Brian. b 58. Dundee Univ BA 97 Portsm Univ MA(Ed) 00 RMN 84 RGN 84. STETS BA 07. **d** 07 **p** 08. C Easthampstead *Ox* 07-10; P-in-c Woodplumpton *Blackb* 10-15; PtO from 15. *St Mark's Vicarage, Buncer Lane, Blackburn BB2 6SY* M: 07851-859296 T: (01254) 696359 E: bwhitley2@btinternet.com

WHITLEY, Eric Keir. b 47. Salford Univ BSc 68. Trin Coll Bris 77. **d** 79 **p** 80. C Nottingham St Ann w Em *S'well* 79-83; V Donisthorpe and Moira w Stretton-en-le-Field *Leic* 83-91; V Thorpe Acre w Dishley 91-00; V Loughb Gd Shep 00-15; rtd 15. *4 Lamport Close, Loughborough LE11 2TT*

WHITLEY, John William. b 46. TCD BA 68. Cranmer Hall Dur BA 71. **d** 71 **p** 72. C Belfast St Mary Magd *Conn* 71-73; C Toxteth St Philemon w St Gabr *Liv* 73-78; P-in-c Toxteth Park St Cleopas 78-88; TV Toxteth St Philemon w St Gabr and St Cleopas 89-95; P-in-c Litherland St Paul Hatton Hill 95-02; V from 02. *St Paul's Vicarage, Watling Avenue, Liverpool L21 9NU* T: 0151-928 2705 E: anthea.whitley@virgin.net

WHITLEY (née ALLISON), Rosemary Jean. b 45. LTCL 67. Trin Coll Bris 75 St Jo Coll Nottm 94. **d** 95 **p** 99. NSM Loughb Gd Shep *Leic* 95-98 and from 00; NSM Thorpe Acre w Dishley 98-00. *4 Lamport Close, Loughborough LE11 2TT*

WHITLOCK, Canon James Frederick. b 44. Ch Coll Cam BA 75 MA 78. Westcott Ho Cam 73. **d** 76 **p** 77. C Newquay *Truro* 76-79; P-in-c St Mawgan w St Ervan and St Eval 79-81; R 81; Bp's Dom Chapl 82-85; Dioc Dir of Ords 82-85; V Leagrave *St Alb* 85-89; TR Probus, Ladock and Grampound w Creed and St Erme *Truro* 89-95; V Penzance St Mary w St Paul 95-00; P-in-c Penzance St Jo 97-00; Hon Can Truro Cathl 98-00; rtd 00; PtO *Truro* from 00. *10 Barlandhu, Newlyn, Penzance TR18 5QT* T: (01736) 330474

WHITMARSH, Mrs Pauline. b 45. **d** 04 **p** 05. OLM Bramshaw and Landford w Plaitford *Sarum* 04-06; OLM Forest and Avon 06-14; rtd 14. *Dovera, North Lane, Nomansland, Salisbury SP5 2BU* T: (01794) 390534 E: paulinewhitmarsh@gmail.com

WHITMORE, Preb Benjamin Nicholas. b 66. Imp Coll Lon BEng 88. Cranmer Hall Dur 89. **d** 92 **p** 93. C Gt Wyrley *Lich* 92-95; C Hednesford 95-00; V Walsall Pleck and Bescot 00-07; Hon C Walsall and Walsall St Paul 05-07; V Penn from 07; Preb Lich Cathl from 13. *St Bartholomew's Vicarage, 68 Church Hill, Penn, Wolverhampton WV4 5JD* T: (01902) 341399 E: bennyjo@vicres.fsnet.co.uk

WHITMORE, Edward James. b 36. Lon Univ BD 66. Tyndale Hall Bris. **d** 68 **p** 69. Tanzania 68-76; LtO *Blackb* 77-09. *74 Greencroft, Penwortham, Preston PR1 9LB* T: (01772) 746522

WHITMORE, Stephen Andrew. b 53. Sheff Univ BSc 74. St Jo Coll Nottm 89. **d** 91 **p** 92. C Newbury *Ox* 91-95; TV High Wycombe from 95. *70 Marlow Road, High Wycombe HP11 1TH* T: (01494) 529586 E: banjovicar@hotmail.com

WHITNEY, Charles Edward. b 46. Goldsmiths' Coll Lon BA 71 TCert 72 ACP 75. WEMTC 01. **d** 04 **p** 05. NSM Tewkesbury w Walton Cardiff and Twyning *Glouc* from 04; NSM Deerhurst and Apperley w Forthampton etc from 10. *Sarn Hill Lodge, Bushley Green, Bushley, Tewkesbury GL20 6AD* T: (01684) 296764

WHITNEY, John Charles. b 59. St Jo Coll Dur BATM 11. Cranmer Hall Dur 09. **d** 11 **p** 12. C Kirkheaton *Leeds* from 11. *12 Greenfield Crescent, Grange Moor, Wakefield WF4 4WA* T: (01924) 849437

WHITTAKER, Canon Angela. b 68. Birm Univ BA 89 St Martin's Coll Lanc PGCE 91. NEOC 98. **d** 00 **p** 01. C Houghton le Spring *Dur* 00-04; TV Kirkby Lonsdale *Carl* 04-09; P-in-c Natland from 09; P-in-c Old Hutton and New Hutton from 09; RD Kendal from 12; Hon Can Carl Cathl from 14. *The Vicarage, Natland, Kendal LA9 7QQ* T: (01539) 560355 E: a-awhittaker.whittaker@tesco.co.uk

WHITTAKER, Brian Lawrence. b 39. Univ of Wales MTh 06. Clifton Th Coll 63. **d** 66 **p** 67. C Whitton and Thurleston w Akenham *St E* 66-69; C Normanton *Wakef* 69-74; P-in-c Castle Hall, Stalybridge and Dukinfield Ch Ch *Ches* 74-77; V Stalybridge H Trin and Ch Ch 77-83; TR Bucknall and Bagnall *Lich* 83-91; R Draycott-le-Moors w Forsbrook 91-05; rtd 05; PtO *Lich* from 05. *6 Rubens Way, Stoke-on-Trent ST3 7GQ* T: (01782) 397765 E: brianlesley.whittaker@tesco.net

WHITTAKER, Bryan. b 58. Southn Univ BTh 82. Chich Th Coll 82. **d** 84 **p** 85. C Whitleigh *Ex* 84-88; C Corringham *Chelmsf* 88-92; V Rush Green 92-94. *361 Dagenham Road, Romford RM7 0XX*

WHITTAKER, Derek. b 30. OBE 85. Liv Univ BEng 51 PhD 58 CEng 65. **d** 93 **p** 95. Zambia 93-96; NSM Broom Leys *Leic* 97-00; rtd 00; PtO *Leic* from 00. *44 St David's Crescent, Coalville LE67 4ST* T: (01530) 831071

WHITTAKER, Mrs Diane Claire. b 57. Newc Poly BA 79 Thames Poly BSc 87 Univ of Wales (Abth) MA 92. ERMC 06. **d** 08. C Welwyn *St Alb* 08-12; P-in-c Potterspury w Furtho and Yardley Gobion etc *Pet* from 12. *The Vicarage, 11 Church Lane, Potterspury, Towcester NN12 7PU* T: (01908) 542043 E: diane.whittaker7@btinternet.com

WHITTAKER, Edward Geoffrey. b 59. Birm Univ BSc 82 Avery Hill Coll PGCE 85 Dur Univ MA 95. Westcott Ho Cam 97. **d** 99 **p** 00. C Neston *Ches* 99-02; V Rocester and Croxden w Hollington *Lich* 02-10; P-in-c Uttoxeter Area 07-11; TR 11-15; P-in-c Upper Tean 13-14; RD Uttoxeter 04-11; P-in-c Shrawley, Witley, Astley and Abberley *Worc* from 15; P-in-c Teme Valley N from 15. *1 Chiltern Close, Great Witley WR6 6HL* M: 07791-484774 T: E: edward@orange.net

WHITTAKER, Garry. b 59. St Jo Coll Nottm 89. **d** 91 **p** 92. C Denton Ch Ch *Man* 91-95; P-in-c Waterhead 95-05; TR Bacup and Stacksteads 05-15; TV Fellside Team *Blackb* from 15. *The Vicarage, Church Lane, Bilsborrow, Preston PR3 0RL* T: (01995) 643245 E: braincapers59@aol.com

WHITTAKER, Helena Jane. b 69. Leic Univ BA 91 Open Univ MA 00. Qu Coll Birm 09. **d** 12 **p** 13. NSM Braunstone Park *Leic* from 12. *2 The Rills, Hinckley LE10 1NA* T: (01455) 698732 M: 07787-383282 E: hjwhittaker@tiscali.co.uk

WHITTAKER, Mrs Jennifer Margaret. b 43. Glas Univ MA 64. SAOMC 00. **d** 03 **p** 04. NSM Martley and Wichenford, Knightwick etc *Worc* 03-08; NSM Worcs W from 09. *The Key Barn, Half Key, Malvern WR14 1UP* T: (01886) 833897 E: jen.whittaker@tiscali.co.uk

WHITTAKER, Jeremy Paul. b 59. Ox Univ MA. Ripon Coll Cuddesdon 82. **d** 84 **p** 85. C Crowthorne *Ox* 84-87; C Westborough *Guildf* 87-88; TV 88-91; Chapl Pierrepont Sch Frensham 91-95; PtO *Guildf* from 95. *6 Springhaven Close, Guildford GU1 2JP*

WHITTAKER, John. b 69. Leic Univ BA 90 ACA 93. Ripon Coll Cuddesdon BTh 00. **d** 00 **p** 01. C Melton Mowbray *Leic* 00-03; P-in-c Barrow upon Soar w Walton le Wolds 03-11; P-in-c Wymeswold and Prestwold w Hoton 05-11; V Hinckley St Mary from 11. *2 The Rills, Hinckley LE10 1NA* T: (01455) 698732 E: johnhelena@tiscali.co.uk

WHITTAKER, Karl Paul. b 55. ATL. CITC BTh 95. **d** 95 **p** 96. C Killowen *D & R* 95-99; I Annaghmore *Arm* 99-04; P-in-c Sunbury St Mary Australia 04-05; I Errigal w Garvagh *D & R* from 05. *St Paul's Rectory, 58 Station Road, Garvagh, Coleraine BT51 5LA* T: (028) 2955 8226 E: revpaul07@btinternet.com

WHITTAKER, Canon Peter Harold. b 38. AKC 62. **d** 63 **p** 64. C Walton St Mary *Liv* 63-67; C Ross *Heref* 67-70; R Bridgnorth St Mary 70-78; P-in-c Oldbury 70-78; TR Bridgnorth, Tasley, Astley Abbotts and Oldbury 78-81; RD Bridgnorth 78-81; Preb Heref Cathl 80-81; V Leighton Buzzard w Eggington, Hockliffe etc *St Alb* 81-92; RD Dunstable 84-85; R Barton-le-Cley w Higham Gobion and Hexton 92-04; rtd 04; PtO *Lich* from 04. *12 Aldersley Way, Ruyton XI Towns, Shrewsbury SY4 1NE* T: (01939) 260059

WHITTAKER, Robert Andrew. b 49. Open Univ BA 75 Nottm Univ MA 83 DipEd. Linc Th Coll 85. **d** 87 **p** 88. C Mansfield Woodhouse *S'well* 87-90; V Norwell w Ossington, Cromwell and Caunton 90-95; Chapl Ranby Ho Sch Retford 95-03;

rtd 06; PtO *S'well* from 14. *23 Birchcroft Road, Retford DN22 7ZD* T: (01777) 470153

WHITTAKER, William Paul. See STAFFORD-WHITTAKER, William Paul

WHITTALL, The Very Revd Christopher Gordon. b 50. OAM 07. Macquarie Univ (NSW) BA 77 Sydney Univ MA 87 Gen Th Sem NY STM 88. St Jo Coll Morpeth BD 80. **d** 79 **p** 80. C Orange E Australia 79-80; C Blayney 80-83; R Bourke 83-87; Vice Prin St Jo Coll Morpeth 87-90; Dean Rockhampton 90-10; Chapl to Abp Wales *Llan* 10-11. *139 McCarthy Road, Maleny QLD 4552, Australia*

WHITTAM, Canon Kenneth Michael. b 26. Ball Coll Ox BA 50 MA 54. Cuddesdon Coll 50. **d** 52 **p** 53. C Adlington *Blackb* 52-55; C St Annes St Thos 55-58; R Halton w Aughton 58-62; R Colne St Bart 62-66; Chapl Highgate Sch Lon 66-75; V Shotwick *Ches* 75-89; Can Res Ches Cathl and Dioc Missr 75-85; Hon Can Ches Cathl 85-90; Clergy Study Officer 85-91; rtd 91; PtO *Ches* from 91. *22 Warwick Close, Little Neston, Neston CH64 0SR* T: 0151-336 8541

WHITTICK, Emma Louise. **d** 15. C Dafen and Felinfoel *St D* from 15. *25 Brynelli, Llanelli SA14 8PW* E: emma.whittick@googlemail.com

WHITTING, Dominic Peter. b 85. Cant Ch Ch Univ BA 07. Ripon Coll Cuddesdon 07. **d** 10 **p** 11. C St Breoke and Egloshayle *Truro* 10-14; V Crowan and Treslothan from 14. *Crowan Vicarage, 37 Trethannas Gardens, Praze, Camborne TR14 0LL* T: (01209) 831810 E: domwhitting@hotmail.com

WHITTINGHAM, Mrs Janet Irene. b 49. **d** 03 **p** 04. OLM Pendleton *Man* 03-09; OLM Salford All SS from 09; Chapl Salford R NHS Foundn Trust from 14. *24 Aylesbury Close, Salford M5 4FQ* T: 0161-736 5878

WHITTINGHAM, Peter. b 58. Sheff Univ BA 79 PGCE. St Jo Coll Nottm 88. **d** 90 **p** 91. C Northowram *Wakef* 90-93; C Airedale w Fryston 93-96; V Wrenthorpe 96-06; P-in-c Alverthorpe 02-06; V Attercliffe and Darnall *Sheff* 06-11; Chapl Shrewsbury Hosp from 11. *The Chaplain's House, Shrewsbury Hospital, Norfolk Road, Sheffield S2 2SU* T: 0114-275 9997 E: peter.whittingham@sheffield.anglican.org

WHITTINGHAM, Ronald Norman. b 43. Linc Coll Ox BA 65 MA 68. Coll of Resurr Mirfield 65. **d** 67 **p** 68. C Horninglow *Lich* 67-69; C Drayton in Hales 69-70; C Uttoxeter w Bramshall 71-75; P-in-c Burton St Paul 75-80; V Shareshill 80-83; V Silverdale and Knutton Heath 83-89; P-in-c Alsagers Bank 83-89; V Silverdale and Alsagers Bank 89-92; V Honley *Wakef* 92-99; TV Hugglescote w Donington, Ellistown and Snibston *Leic* 99-02; TV Leic Presentation 02-07; C Leic St Chad 02-07; rtd 07; PtO *Lich* from 08. *848 High Lane, Stoke-on-Trent ST6 6HG* T: (01782) 860466

WHITTINGTON, David John. b 45. OBE 01. Qu Coll Ox BA 67 MA 71. Coll of Resurr Mirfield 69. **d** 71 **p** 72. Chapl St Woolos Cathl 71-72; Chapl Qu Coll and C Ox St Mary V w St Cross and St Pet 72-76; V Stockton *Dur* 77-98; Hon Can Dur Cathl 93-98; Can Res and Dioc Dir of Educn 98-03; Nat Sch Development Officer Abps' Coun 03-08; rtd 08. *The Gatehouse Flat, Brancepeth Castle, Brancepeth, Durham DH7 8DE* M: 07702-036344 E: dj.whittington@btinternet.com

WHITTINGTON, Peter Graham. b 68. Ox Poly BA 90. Trin Coll Bris BA 95. **d** 95 **p** 96. C Gateacre *Liv* 95-99; V Huyton St Geo 99-05; V Orrell from 05. *St Luke's Vicarage, 10 Lodge Road, Orrell, Wigan WN5 7AT* T: (01695) 623410 E: whitts01@surfaid.org

WHITTINGTON, Richard Hugh. b 47. MBE 74. Sarum & Wells Th Coll. **d** 93 **p** 94. C Enfield St Jas *Lon* 93-96; P-in-c Ightham *Roch* 96-97; R 97-01; Chapl R Hosp Chelsea 01-13; PtO *Ox* from 14. *60 Walker Drive, Faringdon SN7 7FZ* M: 07979-360025 T: (01367) 243738 E: rhw47@btinternet.com

WHITTINGTON, Samuel Jack. b 80. Sheff Univ BA 02. Cranmer Hall Dur 13. **d** 15. C Gipsy Hill Ch Ch *S'wark* from 15. *38 College Green, London SE19 3PN* M: 07803-079001 E: samuelwhittington@yahoo.co.uk

WHITTINGTON, Mrs Sharon Ann. b 56. Leeds Univ BA 79 PGCE 80. NEOC. **d** 00 **p** 01. NSM The Street Par *York* 00-03; P-in-c York St Thos w St Maurice 03-05; NSM York St Olave w St Giles 03-09; NSM York St Helen w St Martin 04-09; PtO from 09; Chapl St Leon Hospice York from 11. *30 Marygate, York YO30 7BH* T: (01904) 627401 E: sa.whittington@btinternet.com

WHITTLE, Ian Christopher. b 60. Univ Coll Dur BA 81 Fitzw Coll Cam BA 88 MA 91. Ridley Hall Cam 85. **d** 88 **p** 89. C S Petherton w The Seavingtons *B & W* 88-91; Asst Chapl The Hague *Eur* 91-97; P-in-c Gayton Gp of Par *Nor* 97-99; R Gayton, Gayton Thorpe, E Walton, E Winch etc 99-10; RD Lynn 02-08; R Stiffkey and Bale from 10. *The Rectory, Langham, Holt NR25 7BX* T: (01328) 830246

WHITTLE, John William. b 46. Qu Mary Coll Lon BA 68. Sarum & Wells Th Coll 84. **d** 86 **p** 87. C Blandford Forum and Langton Long etc *Sarum* 86-88; NSM Pimperne, Stourpaine, Durweston and Bryanston from 02. *The Cottage, Queens Road, Blandford Forum DT11 7JZ* T: (01258) 454789
E: johnwwhittle@hotmail.com

WHITTLE, Canon Naomi Clare. b 54. Colchester Inst of Educn BA 75 Lon Univ PGCE 76 Middx Univ MA(Theol) 99 LGSM 77. SEITE 95. **d** 98 **p** 99. C Catford (Southend) and Downham *S'wark* 98-02; P-in-c Shooters Hill Ch Ch 02; V 02-10; Chapl Oxleas NHS Foundn Trust 06-10; V Stockwell St Andr and St Mich *S'wark* from 10; Hon Can S'wark Cathl from 15. *St Michael's Vicarage, 78 Stockwell Park Road, London SW9 0DA* T: (020) 7346 8650
E: n.whittle954@btinternet.com

WHITTLE, Robin Jeffrey. b 51. Bris Univ BA 72 Leic Univ CQSW 75. Sarum & Wells Th Coll 85. **d** 87 **p** 88. C Henbury *Bris* 87-91; V Capel *Guildf* 91-96; Chapl among Deaf People 96-09; PtO *S'wark* 97-99; *Roch* 97-99; P-in-c Walton-on-the-Hill *Guildf* 99-04; V Tattenham Corner 04-09; V Findon w Clapham and Patching *Chich* 09-13; rtd 13. *3 Hillside Road, Storrington, Pulborough RH20 3LZ* T: (01903) 740542
E: bobwhittle@btinternet.com

WHITTLE, Mrs Sheila Margaret. b 36. Glouc Th Course 83 NY Th Sem MA 88 Vancouver Sch of Th. **d** 90 **p** 90. R Bulkley Valley Canada 90-93; C Dunbar St Phil 93; P-in-c Maple Ridge St Jo the Divine 93-95; Lethbridge St Mary the Virgin 95-97; NSM Portsea N End St Mark *Portsm* 97-98; P-in-c Lezant w Lawhitton and S Petherwin w Trewen *Truro* 98-02; rtd 02; PtO *Glouc* from 03. *33 Graylag Crescent, Walton Cardiff, Tewkesbury GL20 7RR* T: (01684) 299981 E: sheila_whittle@onetel.com

WHITTLESEA, Grahame Stanley Jack Hammond. b 37. Kent Univ LLM 95. **d** 05 **p** 06. OLM Blean *Cant* 05-09; rtd 09; PtO *Cant* from 09; Retirement Officer (Cant Adnry) from 10. *4 Eastbridge Hospital, High Street, Canterbury CT1 2BD*
T: (01227) 472536 M: 07866-037774
E: gandawhittlesea@tiscali.co.uk

WHITTLEWORTH, Ann Marie. b 53. **d** 12 **p** 13. NSM Unsworth *Man* 12-14; NSM Hillock and Unsworth from 14; NSM Stand from 15. *10 North Avenue, Unsworth, Bury BL9 8AR*
T: 0161-796 1856 M: 07939-313253
E: awhittleworth@gmail.com

WHITTOCK (née MARBUS), Alida Janny. b 52. RGN 78. STETS 00. **d** 03 **p** 07. NSM Weymouth H Trin *Sarum* 03-09; NSM Abbotsbury, Portesham and Langton Herring 09-14; PtO from 14. *The Rectory, Church Lane, Portesham, Weymouth DT3 4HB* T: (01305) 871217 E: adamarbus@aol.com

WHITTOCK, Carol Jean. b 51. Goldsmiths' Coll Lon BA 74 Univ of Wales (Abth) PGCE 76. WEMTC 07. **d** 10 **p** 11. C Gt Hanwood and Longden and Annscroft etc *Heref* 10-14; C Churchstoke w Hyssington and Sarn from 14. *The Vicarage, Church Stoke, Montgomery SY15 6AF* T: (01588) 620693
E: carol@germandirect.co.uk

WHITTOCK, Preb Michael Graham. b 47. Hull Univ BA 69 Fitzw Coll Cam BA 71 MA 76. Westcott Ho Cam 69 Union Th Sem Virginia 71. **d** 72 **p** 73. C Kirkby *Liv* 72-76; C Prescot 76-79; R Methley w Mickletown *Ripon* 79-92; RD Whitkirk 88-92; V Morley St Pet w Churwell *Wakef* 92-01; R Gt Hanwood *Heref* 01-13; R Longden and Annscroft w Pulverbatch 01-13; R Gt Hanwood and Longden and Annscroft etc 13-14; RD Pontesbury 08-13; Preb Heref Cathl 10-14; rtd 14. *The Vicarage, Church Stoke, Montgomery SY15 6AF* T: (01588) 620693 E: mwhittock@germandirect.co.uk

WHITTON, Alysoun. b 55. St Steph Ho Ox 09. **d** 10 **p** 11. NSM Hampstead Em W End *Lon* 10-14; PtO *Cant* from 15. *5 St Christopher's Green, Broadstairs CT10 2SS*
M: 07985-020203 T: (01843) 579936
E: alysoun.whitton@gmail.com

WHITTY, Gordon William. b 35. WMMTC. **d** 82 **p** 83. NSM Willenhall St Giles *Lich* 82-84; NSM Coseley Ch Ch 84-85; C 85-87; TV Hanley H Ev 87-91; P-in-c Meir 91-98; P-in-c Hanbury w Newborough and Rangemore 98-99; V 99-03; rtd 03; PtO *Derby* from 04. *14 Cardrona Close, Oakwood, Derby DE21 2JN* T: (01332) 726320 E: gordonwhitty@vinweb.co.uk
or gordon.whitty@ntlworld.com

WHITTY, Harold George. b 41. TCD BA 64 MA 67. CITC Div Test 65. **d** 65 **p** 66. C Willowfield *D & D* 65-68; C Lisburn Ch Ch *Conn* 68-71; Bp's Dom Chapl 70-71; Asst Dir Exhibitions CMJ 71-72; C Enfield Ch Ch Trent Park *Lon* 72-75; TV Washfield, Stoodleigh, Withleigh etc *Ex* 75-83; R 83-84; TR 84-93; P-in-c Aylesbeare, Rockbeare, Farringdon etc 02-04; RD Tiverton 82-84; P-in-c Allithwaite *Carl* 93-97; TV Cartmel Peninsula 97-02; Local Min Officer 99-02; rtd 04. *The Old Pound, 1 Church Road, Silverton, Exeter EX5 4HS*
T: (01392) 860397 E: harold.whitty@btinternet.com

WHITWAM, Miss Diana Morgan. b 28. MCSP 54. **d** 93 **p** 94. OLM Stoke-next-Guildf 93-01; PtO from 02. *13 Abbots Hospital, High Street, Guildford GU1 3AJ* T: (01483) 565977
E: whitwamdm@talktalk.net

WHITWELL, Canon John Peter. b 36. Open Univ BA 07. Qu Coll Birm 62. **d** 65 **p** 66. C Stepney St Dunstan and All SS *Lon* 65-68; C Chingford SS Pet and Paul *Chelmsf* 68-71; V Walthamstow St Sav 71-78; P-in-c Lt Ilford St Mich 78-88; R 88-98; RD Newham 91-97; Hon Can Chelmsf Cathl 96-98; rtd 98; PtO *Ox* from 99. *152 Bath Road, Banbury OX16 0TT* T: (01295) 266243 E: jandawhitwell@aol.com

WHITWORTH, Benjamin Charles Battams. b 49. CCC Ox BA 71 MA 85. Linc Th Coll 83. **d** 85 **p** 86. C Swanborough *Sarum* 85-88; C Stanborough w Castleton and Lillington 88-91; V Milborne Port w Goathill *B & W* 91-98; rtd 98; PtO *B & W* from 00. *13 The Avenue, Taunton TA1 1EA* T: (01823) 272442
E: whitworth@talktalk.net

WHITWORTH, Canon Duncan. b 47. K Coll Lon BD 69 AKC 69. St Aug Coll Cant 69. **d** 70 **p** 71. C Tonge Moor *Man* 70-73; C Upper Norwood St Jo *Cant* 73-78; Asst Chapl Madrid *Eur* 78-82; Chapl Br Embassy Ankara 82-83; V Douglas St Matt *S & M* 84-12; RD Douglas 91-12; Can St German's Cathl 96-12; rtd 12. *24 Ballafurt Close, Port Erin, Isle of Man IM9 6HS* T: (01624) 837350

WHITWORTH, Canon Patrick John. b 51. Ch Ch Ox BA 72 MA 76. St Jo Coll Dur MA 78. **d** 76 **p** 77. C York St Mich-le-Belfrey 76-79; C Brompton H Trin w Onslow Square St Paul *Lon* 79-84; V Gipsy Hill Ch Ch *S'wark* 84-95; R Bath Weston All SS w N Stoke and Langridge *B & W* from 95; RD Bath 03-10; Hon Can Bauchi from 95; Preb Wells Cathl from 12. *The Vicarage, Weston, Bath BA1 4BU* T: (01225) 421159
E: pwhitworth@metronet.co.uk

WHITWORTH, Vincent Craig. b 80. Nottm Univ BA 01. St Jo Coll Nottm MTh 06. **d** 07 **p** 08. C Parr *Liv* 07-11; C Halliwell St Pet *Man* from 11; AD Bolton from 15. *St Paul's Vicarage, Vicarage Lane, Halliwell, Bolton BL1 8BP* T: (01204) 849079
M: 07759-920922 E: vincentwhitworth@hotmail.com

WHYBORN, Robert. b 42. NOC 87. **d** 90 **p** 91. NSM Milnrow *Man* 90-97; NSM Greenfield 97-03; NSM Saddleworth 03-05; rtd 05; PtO *Man* from 05. *4 Jackman Avenue, Heywood OL10 2NS* T: (01706) 369397 E: revrob8@aol.com

WHYBROW, Paul Andrew. b 59. St Paul's Coll Chelt BEd 80 Oak Hill Th Coll BA 90. Wycliffe Hall Ox 95. **d** 97 **p** 98. C Magor *Mon* 97-00; V Poughill *Truro* from 00. *The Vicarage, Poughill, Bude EX23 9ER* T: (01288) 355183
E: pa.whybrow59@icloud.com

WHYSALL, Canon Joan. b 42. Lady Mabel Coll CertEd 64 Nottm Univ MA 01. EMMTC 98. **d** 01 **p** 02. NSM Trowell, Awsworth and Cossall *S'well* 01-06; P-in-c Cinderhill 06-14; Hon Can S'well Minster 10-12; rtd 14. *55 Trowell Park Drive, Trowell, Nottingham NG9 3RA* T: 0115-939 6903
E: joan.whysall@btinternet.com

WHYTE, Alastair John. b 61. Coll of Ripon & York St Jo BA 83 Lanc Univ MA 95. Sarum & Wells Th Coll 83. **d** 85 **p** 86. C Chorley St Geo *Blackb* 85-88; C Poulton-le-Fylde 88-91; V Wesham 91-00; Chapl Blackpool, Wyre and Fylde Community NHS Trust 91-94 and 94-02; P-in-c Treales *Blackb* 98-00; V Garstang St Thos 00-02; AD Garstang 02; PtO *Man* from 10. *14 Waterbarn Lane, Bacup OL13 0NR*

WHYTE, Duncan Macmillan. b 25. St Jo Coll Dur BA 49 St Cath Soc Ox BA 51 MA 57. Wycliffe Hall Ox 49. **d** 51 **p** 53. C Garston St Jo 51-56; C St Leonards St Leon *Chich* 56-59; V Southsea St Simon *Portsm* 59-66; Gen Sec Lon City Miss 66-92; Hon C Blackheath St Jo *S'wark* 66-92; rtd 92; PtO *Sarum* from 92. *1 The Meadows, Salisbury SP1 2SS* T: (01722) 330528

WHYTE, Henry Lewis. b 38. ALCD 70 LTh 74. **d** 70 **p** 71. C Crawley *Chich* 70-74; V Bermondsey St Jas w Ch Ch *S'wark* 74-82; V Kingston Hill St Paul 82-94; V Blackheath Park St Mich 94-02; rtd 02; PtO *S'wark* from 03. *6 Horn Park Lane, London SE12 8UU* T: (020) 8318 9837
E: henry.whyte@hotmail.co.uk

WHYTE, Canon Robert Euan. b 44. St Pet Coll Ox BA 67. Cuddesdon Coll 67. **d** 69 **p** 70. C Blackheath Ascension *S'wark* 69-73; BCC 73-87; NSM Lewisham St Swithun *S'wark* 73-76; NSM Heston *Lon* 76-77; C Rusthall *Roch* 77-88; V 88-08; RD Tunbridge Wells 91-96; Hon Can Roch Cathl 00-08; rtd 08. *9 Thornhill Avenue, Belper DE56 1SH* T: (01773) 880531
E: whyterobert@hotmail.com

WHYTE, William Hadden. b 75. Wadh Coll Ox BA 97 MA 03 MSt 98 DPhil 02. SAOMC 03. **d** 06 **p** 07. NSM Kidlington w Hampton Poyle Ox from 06. *St John's College, Oxford OX1 3JP* T: (01865) 277138 F: 277300 E: william.whyte@sjc.ox.ac.uk

WIBBERLEY, Anthony Norman. b 36. K Coll Lon BSc 58 AKC 58. Sarum & Wells Th Coll 76. **d** 79 **p** 80. Hon C Tavistock and Gulworthy *Ex* 79-86; R Hoby cum Rotherby w Brooksby, Ragdale & Thru'ton *Leic* 86-90; V Ingol *Blackb*

90-96; PtO *Ely* 97-05; rtd 00. *13 Missleton Court, Cherry Hinton Road, Cambridge CB1 8BL*

WIBROE, Andrew Peter. b 56. K Coll Lon BD 83 AKC 83 Thames Poly PGCE 91. Ripon Coll Cuddesdon 83. **d** 86 **p** 87. C Purley St Mark *S'wark* 86-88; C Boyne Hill *Ox* 89-90; Hon C Milton next Gravesend Ch Ch *Roch* from 90. *32 Ayelands, New Ash Green, Longfield DA3 8JN* T: (01474) 879014
E: peter.wibroe@diocese-rochester.org *or* peterwibroe@aol.com

WICK, Canon Patricia Anne. b 54. Lon Bible Coll BA 80 Redcliffe Coll Glouc MA 12. Oak Hill Th Coll 84. **dss** 86 **d** 87 **p** 94. Halliwell St Luke *Man* 86-87; Par Dn 87-91; Par Dn Drypool *York* 91-94; C 94-95; TV 95-97; PtO 98-99; CMS Sudan 98-14; Canon Maridi from 09; PtO *York* 15; C Sutton St Mich from 15. *46 Arndale Way, Filey YO14 9EW*
M: 07527-523098 E: patricia@rcs-communication.com

WICKENS, Andrew Peter. b 63. St Jo Coll Dur BA 85 Magd Coll Cam MEd 97 PGCE 95 ARCM 84. Westcott Ho Cam 98. **d** 00 **p** 01. C Louth *Linc* 00-03; TV 03-07; Lect Boston 07-10; PV Linc Cathl 01-10; R Newton Heath *Man* from 11; P-in-c Moston St Chad and Moston St Jo 11-13. *All Saints' Rectory, 2 Culcheth Lane, Manchester M40 1LR* T: 0161-219 1807
E: andrew.wickens08@btinternet.com

WICKENS, Andrew St Lawrence John. b 63. Mert Coll Ox BA 85 Birm Univ MPhil 94 Dur Univ PGCE 86. Qu Coll Birm 89. **d** 92 **p** 93. C Birchfield *Birm* 92-96; TV PtO 96-97 and 00-01; Zambia 97-00; P-in-c St Mich Cathl Kitwe 99-00; Lect St Paul's United Th Coll Limuru Kenya 01-05; P-in-c Dudley St Jas *Worc* 05-09; TV Dudley from 09; Educn Chapl from 05; Hon Can Worc Cathl from 15. *St James's Vicarage, The Parade, Dudley DY1 3JA* T: (01384) 214487
E: awickens@cofe-worcester.org.uk

WICKENS, Laurence Paul. b 52. Selw Coll Cam BA 74 MA 78 Leeds Univ PhD 90 CEng 80 MIET 80 MIMechE 81 EurIng 90. EAMTC 02. **d** 06 **p** 07. NSM Cambridge St Barn *Ely* 06-08; NSM Meole Brace *Lich* 08-11; PtO *Cov* from 13. *31 Paddocks Close, Wolston, Coventry CV8 3GW* M: 07811-551583
T: (024) 7651 0305 E: laurence.wickens@gmail.com

WICKENS, Canon Moira. b 56. S Dios Minl Tr Scheme 91. **d** 94 **p** 08. NSM Ifield *Chich* 94-96; C Saltdean 96-03; C Ovingdean and Schs Liaison Officer 03-06; C Kingston Buci 06-08; P-in-c 08-10; Dioc Voc Adv 06-10; R New Fishbourne from 10; P-in-c Appledram from 10; Can and Preb Chich Cathl from 12. *The Rectory, 31 Caspian Close, Fishbourne, Chichester PO18 8AY* T: (01273) 783364

WICKERT, Keith Frederick. b 59. Birkbeck Coll Lon BSc 84. STETS 09. **d** 12 **p** 13. NSM Fareham H Trin *Portsm* from 12. *4 The Old Priory Mews, Victoria Road, Bishops Waltham, Southampton SO32 1NJ* T: (01489) 892977 M: 07717-312426
E: keithwickert@aol.com

WICKETT, Prof Reginald Ernest Yeatman. b 43. Toronto Univ BA 65 MEd 71 EdD 78 Em Coll Saskatoon Hon DCnL 96. Trin Coll Toronto 65. **d** 00 **p** 01. NSM Saskatoon All SS Canada 00-02; NSM St Jo Cathl from 02; PtO *Ely* from 12. *34 Thornton Court, Girton, Cambridge CB3 0NS* M: 07984-909693
E: reg.wickett@usask.ca *or* rw461@cam.ac.uk

WICKHAM, Mrs Jennifer Ruth. b 68. Univ of W Ontario BA 91. Cranmer Hall Dur BA 98. **d** 98 **p** 99. C Ponteland *Newc* 98-00; Assoc P Ottawa St Geo Canada from 01. *57A Tauvette Street, Ottawa ON K1B 3A2, Canada* T: (001) (613) 590 7921 *or* 235 1636 E: ajwickham@yahoo.com *or* revjw.stgeorge@cyberus.ca

WICKHAM, Lionel Ralph. b 32. St Cath Coll Cam BA 57 MA 61 PhD LRAM. Westcott Ho Cam 57. **d** 59 **p** 60. C Boston *Linc* 59-61; Tutor Cuddesdon Coll 61-63; V Cross Stone *Wakef* 63-67; Lect Th Southn Univ 67-78; Sen Lect 78-81; V Honley *Wakef* 81-87; Lect Cam Univ 87-00; NSM W Wratting *Ely* 89-00; NSM Weston Colville 89-00; rtd 00; PtO *Leeds* from 99. *19 Barrowstead, Skelmanthorpe, Huddersfield HD8 9UW*
T: (01484) 864185 E: lpatristic@aol.com

✠**WICKHAM, The Rt Revd Robert James.** b 72. Grey Coll Dur BA 94 K Coll Lon MA 12. Ridley Hall Cam 95. **d** 98 **p** 99 **c** 15. C Willesden St Mary *Lon* 98-01; C Somers Town 01-03; TV Old St Pancras 03-07; R St John-at-Hackney 07-15; AD Hackney 14-15; Area Bp Edmonton from 15. *The Rectory, 11 Clapton Square, London E5 8HP* T: (020) 8985 5374
E: rob.wickham@aol.com

WICKHAM, Timothy James. b 86. Oak Hill Th Coll 12. **d** 15. C Balderstone *Man* from 15. *32 Gilbrook Way, Rochdale OL16 4RT* M: 07555-919627
E: tjwickham1986@googlemail.com

WICKINGS, Luke Iden. b 59. Sheff Poly BA 81. Oak Hill Th Coll BA 90. **d** 90 **p** 91. C Fulham St Mary N End *Lon* 90-94; C Bletchley *Ox* 94-00; V W Norwood St Luke *S'wark* 00-07; Hon C New Malden and Coombe from 13. *12 Osborne Gardens, Thornton Heath CR7 8PA* T: (020) 8653 7767

WICKREMASINGHE, Rosemary Ethel. b 32. Reading Univ ATD 52 K Coll Lon BD 85 AKC 85. SAOMC 93. **d** 96 **p** 97. NSM Godrevy *Truro* 96-05; rtd 05; PtO *Truro* from 05. *10 Glebe Row, Phillack, Hayle TR27 5AJ* T: (01736) 757850

WICKS, Christopher Blair. b 59. Oak Hill Th Coll BA 88. **d** 88 **p** 89. C Edmonton All SS w St Mich *Lon* 88-92; C Southborough St Pet w Ch Ch and St Matt etc *Roch* 92-96; TV from 96. *72 Powder Mill Lane, Southborough, Tunbridge Wells TN4 9EJ* T: (01892) 529098
E: chris.wicks@diocese-rochester.org

WICKS, Susan Lynn. b 66. Trin Coll Bris 96. **d** 98 **p** 99. C Whitburn *Dur* 98-03; TV S Carl 03-12; V Harraby from 12. *St Elisabeth's Vicarage, Arnside Road, Carlisle CA1 3QA* T: (01228) 596427 E: sue.wicks@virgin.net

WICKSTEAD, Canon Gavin John. b 46. St Chad's Coll Dur BA 67. Linc Th Coll 82. **d** 84 **p** 85. C Louth *Linc* 84-87; P-in-c E Markham and Askham *S'well* 87-89; P-in-c Headon w Upton 87-89; P-in-c Grove 87-89; R E Markham w Askham, Headon w Upton and Grove 90-92; P-in-c Skegness and Winthorpe *Linc* 92-97; R 97-01; V Holbeach 01-11; RD Elloe E 05-07; Can and Preb Linc Cathl from 05; rtd 11. *1 Aspen Drive, Sleaford NG34 7GN* T: (01529) 410231
E: wickstead@btinternet.com

WIDDECOMBE, Roger James. b 70. Wycliffe Hall Ox 01. **d** 03 **p** 04. C Downend *Bris* 03-06; C Cheltenham St Mary, St Matt, St Paul and H Trin *Glouc* 06-07; TV Cheltenham H Trin and St Paul from 07. *85 Brunswick Street, Cheltenham GL50 4HA* T/F: (01242) 519520 E: roger@widde.com

WIDDESS, Jonathan Mark. b 73. Univ of Wales (Abth) BScEcon 95. Wycliffe Hall Ox 07. **d** 09 **p** 10. C Gabalfa *Llan* 09-13; P-in-c Bargoed and Deri w Brithdir from 13. *The Vicarage, Vicarage Lane, Bargoed CF81 8TR* T: (01443) 831069 M: 07595-996534 E: jwiddess@gmail.com

WIDDESS, Mrs Margaret Jennifer. b 48. Bedf Coll Lon BA 70 Clare Hall Cam PGCE 75 Lambeth MA 03. EAMTC 94. **d** 97 **p** 98. NSM Cambridge St Botolph *Ely* from 97. *69 Gwydir Street, Cambridge CB1 2LG* T: (01223) 313908
E: mjwiddess@btinternet.com

WIDDICOMBE, Peter John. b 52. Univ of Manitoba BA 74 St Cath Coll Ox MPhil 77 St Cross Coll Ox DPhil 90. Wycliffe Coll Toronto MDiv 81. **d** 81 **p** 82. Canada 81-84 and from 93; C Ox St Andr 84-86; Acting Chapl Trin Coll Ox 88; Linc Coll Ox 89; P-in-c Penn *Ox* 90-93. *1204-36 James Street South, Hamilton ON L8P 4W4, Canada*

WIDDOWS, David Charles Roland. b 52. Hertf Coll Ox BA 75 MA 79. St Jo Coll Nottm BA 77. **d** 79 **p** 80. C Blackley St Andr *Man* 79-83; P-in-c Rochdale Deeplish St Luke 83-84; V 84-92; TR Stoke Gifford *Bris* 92-06; Chapl Lee Abbey 06-10; P-in-c Wiveliscombe and the Hills *B & W* 10-11; R from 11. *The Rectory, South Street, Wiveliscombe, Taunton TA4 2LZ* M: 07890-758751

WIDDOWS, Edward John. b 45. Lon Coll of Div 66. **d** 70 **p** 71. C Formby St Pet *Liv* 70-72; C Uckfield, Isfield and Lt Horsted *Chich* 72-73; C Babbacombe *Ex* 73-76; V Sithney *Truro* 76-78; RD Kerrier 77-78; V Bude Haven 78-84; P-in-c Laneast w St Clether and Tresmere 84-85; P-in-c N Hill w Altarnon, Bolventor and Lewannick 84-85; P-in-c Boyton w N Tamerton 84-85; P-in-c N Petherwin 84-85; R Collingham w S Scarle and Besthorpe and Girton *S'well* 85-92; R Guernsey St Michel du Valle *Win* 92-99; R Compton and Otterbourne 99-02; rtd 02; PtO *Pet* from 02; *Leic* from 08. *Glebe Cottage, 4 Spring Back Way, Uppingham, Oakham LE15 9TT* T: (01572) 821980
E: ewiddows01@aol.com

WIDDOWS, Heather Susan. b 45. Open Univ BA 76. Moray Ord Course 91. **d** 96 **p** 97. NSM Kishorn *Mor* from 96; NSM Poolewe from 96. *2 Fasaich, Strath, Gairloch IV21 2DB* T: (01445) 712176 E: heather_widdows@yahoo.co.uk

WIDDOWS, Nicholas John. b 82. Ex Coll Ox MEng 05 CA 09. Trin Coll Bris 10. **d** 12 **p** 13. C Fowey *Truro* 12-14; C St Sampson 12-14; Chapl Jes Coll Cam from 14. *Jesus College, Cambridge CB5 8BL* M: 07789-680070 T: (01223) 330750 E: nickwiddows@hotmail.com

WIDDOWSON, Robert William. b 47. Linc Th Coll 83. **d** 85 **p** 86. C Syston *Leic* 85-88; R Husbands Bosworth w Mowsley and Knaptoft etc 88-93; R Asfordby 93-98; P-in-c Ab Kettleby Gp 93-98; P-in-c Old Dalby and Nether Broughton 95-98; P-in-c Charlton Musgrove, Cucklington and Stoke Trister *B & W* 98-03; P-in-c Ashwick w Oakhill and Binegar 03-12; Adv in Rural Affairs 03-12; rtd 12. *23 The Leaze, Radstock BA3 3YH* T: (01761) 439814 E: ruralrobert@fsmail.net

WIECK, Malcolm Rayment. b 44. Solicitor 70. **d** 08 **p** 09. OLM Bratton, Edington and Imber, Erlestoke etc *Sarum* 08-12; NSM 12-14; PtO from 14. *Sandy Lane Cottage, 12 Westbury Road, Edington, Westbury BA13 4QD* T: (01380) 830256 M: 07623-483986 E: malcolm.wieck@btinternet.com

WIEGMAN, Mrs Jacqueline Anne Cecilia. b 52. ERMC 10. **d** 13 **p** 14. NSM Longthorpe *Pet* from 13; NSM Pet H Spirit Bretton from 13; Sen Chapl HM Pris Peterborough from 13. *HM Prison Peterborough, Saville Road, Peterborough PE3 7PD* T: (01733) 217500 E: jackie.wiegman@sodexojusticeservices.com

WIFFEN, Richard Austin. b 58. St Pet Coll Ox BA 80. Trin Coll Bris BA 90. **d** 90 **p** 91. C Bowdon *Ches* 90-93; C Ellesmere Port 93-94; TV 94-02; Hon C 02-07. *Lime Tree Farm, Stanney Lane, Little Stanney, Chester CH2 4HT* T: 0151-355 1654

WIFFEN, Ronald. b 38. Glos Univ BA 99. SEITE 99. **d** 01 **p** 02. NSM Canvey Is *Chelmsf* 01-04; P-in-c Bowers Gifford w N Benfleet 04-06; NSM SW Gower *S & B* 06-08; P-in-c Southport St Luke *Liv* 08-09; rtd 09; PtO *Chelmsf* 09-11; P-in-c Mundford w Lynford *Nor* 11-15; P-in-c Ickburgh w Langford 11-15; P-in-c Cranwich 11-15; P-in-c W Tofts and Buckenham Parva 11-15. *Address temp unknown* M: 07855-733064 E: r.wiffen@btinternet.com

WIFFIN, Susan Elizabeth. *See* MACDONALD, Susan Elizabeth

WIGFIELD, Thomas Henry Paul. b 26. Edin Th Coll 46. **d** 49 **p** 50. C Seaham w Seaham Harbour *Dur* 49-52; C Dur St Marg 52-54; V Fatfield 54-63; Asst Dir Chs' TV Cen 63-79; PtO *Lon* 63-91; *St Alb* 66-91; Hd of Services Foundn for Chr Communication 79-84; Chs' Liaison Officer 84-91; rtd 91; PtO *Ox* from 91. *16 Fishers Field, Buckingham MK18 1SF* T: (01280) 817893

WIGGEN, Richard Martin. b 42. Open Univ BA 78 Hull Univ MA 86. Qu Coll Birm 64. **d** 67 **p** 68. C Penistone w Midhope *Wakef* 67-70; C Leeds St Pet *Ripon* 70-73; Asst Youth Chapl *Glouc* 73-76; Youth Officer *Liv* 76-80; V Kirkstall *Ripon* 80-90; V Meanwood 90-07; rtd 07. *19 Shadwell Lane, Leeds LS17 6DP* T: 0113-266 5241 E: wiggen@btopenworld.com

WIGGINS, Gillian Holt. b 33. Birm Univ MB, ChB 56. **d** 03 **p** 04. NSM Ascot Heath *Ox* 03-08; PtO 09-14. *Keren, 2 Kiln Lane, Winkfield, Windsor SL4 2DU* T: (01344) 884008 E: gilliwig@aol.com

WIGGINS, Karl Patrick. b 38. MRICS 64 FRICS 87. Trin Coll Bris BD 72. **d** 72 **p** 73. C Hildenborough *Roch* 72-76; Hon C Reading St Barn *Ox* 76-78; Hon C Chieveley w Winterbourne and Oare 78-80; Hon C Earley St Nic 80-83; Hon C Reading St Jo 83-88; Hon C Beech Hill, Grazeley and Spencers Wood 88-98; rtd 98; PtO *Ox* 99. *Willow Cottage, 37 New Road, Bradford-on-Avon BA15 1AP* T: (01225) 867007 E: kk-wiggins@msn.com

WIGGLESWORTH, Canon Mark. b 60. Clare Coll Cam BA 82 MA 96 St Jo Coll Dur MA 14. Cranmer Hall Dur 89. **d** 92 **p** 93. C Brinsworth w Catcliffe *Sheff* 92-93; C Brinsworth w Catcliffe and Treeton 93-95; C Goole 95-96; V Askern 96-11; AD Adwick 05-11; Dir Miss and Pioneer Min 11-14; Miss Development Adv Donaster Adnry from 14; Hon Can Sheff Cathl from 10. *The New Rectory, Grange Lane, Burghwallis, Doncaster DN6 9JL* T: (01302) 707815 M: 07818-416424 E: mark.dmpm@gmail.com

WIGGS, Robert James. b 50. Pemb Coll Cam BA 72 MA CertEd. Qu Coll Birm 78. **d** 80 **p** 81. C Stratford St Jo and Ch Ch w Forest Gate St Jas *Chelmsf* 80-83; C E Ham w Upton Park and Forest Gate 83-86; TV 86-91; TR Grays Thurrock 91-99; PtO from 99. *113 Moulsham Street, Chelmsford CM2 0JN* T: (01245) 359138 E: robwiggs@live.com

WIGHT, The Ven Dennis Marley. b 53. Southn Univ BTh 87. Sarum & Wells Th Coll 82. **d** 85 **p** 86. C Gillingham *Sarum* 85-87; Appeals Org CECS from 87; PtO *Birm* 89-90; V Coseley Ch Ch *Lich* 90-93; V *Worc* 93-94; R Stoke Prior, Wychbold and Upton Warren 94-02; RD Droitwich 96-99; V Dale and St Brides w Marloes *St D* 02-10; AD Roose 05-10; Dioc Warden Ords 09-11 and 12-14 and from 15; Bp's Chapl 10-14; Dir of Min from 10; Hon Can St D Cathl from 09; Adn St D from 13. *The Diocesan Office, Abergwili, Carmarthen SA31 2JG* T: (01267) 236145 M: 07827-909222 E: archdeacon.stdavids@churchinwales.org.uk

WIGHT (née JONES), Mrs Sian Hilary. b 54. CertEd 75 Birm Univ BEd 76 Southn Univ BTh 87. Sarum & Wells Th Coll 82. **dss** 85 **d** 87 **p** 94. Ex St Sidwell and St Matt 85-88; Par Dn 87-88; PtO *Lich* 89-90 and 93-96; Hon Par Dn Coseley Ch Ch 90-93; Hon Par Dn *Worc* 93-94; NSM Stoke Prior, Wychbold and Upton Warren 94-02; NSM Dale and St Brides w Marloes *St D* 02-05; P-in-c Herbrandston and Hasguard w St Ishmael's 05-08; P-in-c Herbrandston and Hasguard w St Ishmael's etc 08-10; P-in-c St Ishmael's w Llan-saint and Ferryside from 10. *The Vicarage, Water Street, Ferryside SA17 5RT* T: (01267) 267192 E: sianwight@btinternet.com

WIGHTMAN, David William Lyle. b 44. SNWTP. **d** 08 **p** 09. NSM Macclesfield Team *Ches* from 08. *The Old Vicarage, 12 Ryles Park Road, Macclesfield SK11 8AH* T: (01625) 266283 or 428443 E: david.wightman1@ntlworld.com

WIGHTMAN, William David. b 39. Birm Univ BA 61. Wells Th Coll 61. **d** 63 **p** 64. C Rotherham *Sheff* 63-67; C Castle Church *Lich* 67-70; V Buttershaw St Aid *Bradf* 70-76; V Cullingworth

76-83; R Peterhead *Ab* 83-91; R Strichen, Old Deer and Longside 90-91; Provost St Andr Cathl 91-02; R Aberdeen St Andr 91-02; P-in-c Aberdeen St Ninian 91-02; Hon Can Ch Ch Cathl Connecticut from 91; rtd 02; PtO *York* from 04. *66 Wold Road, Pocklington, York YO42 2QG* T: (01759) 301369 E: davidwightman@ntlworld.com

WIGLEY, Brian Arthur. b 31. Qu Coll Birm. **d** 82 **p** 83. C Houghton le Spring *Dur* 82-85; C Louth *Linc* 85-86; TV 86-89; Chapl City Hosp NHS Trust Birm 89-95; rtd 95; PtO *Ex* 95-09; *Leic* from 13. *11 Stuart Court, Kibworth, Leicester LE8 0LR* T: 0116-279 3682 E: p-bwigley@tiscali.co.uk

WIGLEY, Canon Harry Maxwell (Max). b 38. Oak Hill Th Coll 61. **d** 64 **p** 65. C Upton (Overchurch) *Ches* 64-67; C Gateacre *Liv* 67-69; C Chadderton Ch Ch *Man* 67; V Gt Horton *Bradf* 69-88; Hon Can Bradf Cathl 85-03; V Pudsey St Lawr and St Paul 88-96; V Yeadon St Jo 96-03; rtd 03; Hon Dioc Ev *Bradf* 04-10; PtO *Leeds* from 10. *20 Collier Lane, Baildon, Shipley BD17 5LN* T: (01274) 581988 E: max.wigley@bradford.anglican.org *or* maxwigley@aol.com

WIGLEY, Canon Jennifer. b 53. Bris Univ BA 74 Birm Univ MA 75 Ox Univ CertEd 76. Qu Coll Birm 86. **d** 87 **p** 97. C Llangollen w Trevor and Llantysilio *St As* 87-89; C Swansea St Jas *S & B* 89-94; NSM Aberystwyth *St D* 95-98; Tutor St Mich Coll Llan 98-00; C Sketty *S & B* 98-00; Chapl Univ of Wales (Swansea) 00-02; Dep Dir S Wales Ord Course from 02; TV Cen Cardiff *Llan* 03-06; R Radyr from 06; AD Llan from 10; Can Llan Cathl from 11. *The Rectory, 52 Heol Isaf, Radyr, Cardiff CF15 8DY* T: (029) 2084 2417 E: jennifer.wigley@ntlworld.com

WIGLEY, Mrs Trudie Anne. b 69. Somerville Coll Ox BA 91 MA 12 ACIB 94. Ripon Coll Cuddesdon 09. **d** 11 **p** 12. C Swindon Ch Ch *Bris* 11-14; P-in-c Swindon Dorcan from 14. *11 Merlin Way, Swindon SN3 5AN* T: (01793) 323769 M: 07505-652781 E: rev.trudie@wigley.org.uk

WIGMORE, John Anthony Kingsland. b 62. Oak Hill Th Coll 05. **d** 07 **p** 08. C Braintree *Chelmsf* 07-11; R Winklebury and Worting *Win* from 11. *The Rectory, Glebe Lane, Worting, Basingstoke RG23 8QA* T: (01256) 327305 E: rector@winkleburyandworting.org.uk

WIGMORE, Mrs Lisa Jayn. b 66. Trin Coll Bris 09. **d** 11 **p** 12. C Horfield H Trin *Bris* 11-15; Min Can Bris Cathl from 15. *52 Gladstone Street, Staple Hill, Bristol BS16 4RF* T: 0117-957 4297 M: 07799-883790 E: lisawigmore@blueyonder.co.uk

WIGNALL, Daniel Robert Phillip. b 65. Ox Poly BEd 88. St Jo Coll Nottm MA 98. **d** 98 **p** 99. C Fletchamstead *Cov* 98-01; C Abingdon *Ox* 01-07; V Shottermill *Guildf* from 07. *The Vicarage, Vicarage Lane, Haslemere GU27 1LQ* T: (01428) 645878 E: vicar@shottermillparish.org.uk

WIGNALL, Canon Paul Graham. b 49. Lanc Univ BA 72 Qu Coll Cam BA 74 MA 78. Westcott Ho Cam 72. **d** 74 **p** 75. C Chesterton Gd Shep *Ely* 74-76; Min Can Dur Cathl 76-79; Tutor Ripon Coll Cuddesdon 80-84; P-in-c Aston Rowant w Crowell *Ox* 81-83; C Shepherd's Bush St Steph w St Thos *Lon* 84-85; P-in-c St Just-in-Roseland and St Mawes *Truro* 99-01; C St Agnes and Mithian w Mount Hawke 01-06; Dir Tr and Development 01-05; Dir Min and Miss Resources 05-06; Hon Can Truro Cathl 05-06; rtd 06; IME Adv *Cov* 08-12; Hon C Aston Cantlow and Wilmcote w Billesley 08-11; Hon C Baginton w Bubbenhall and Ryton-on-Dunsmore 11-12; P-in-c Clun w Bettws-y-Crwyn and Newcastle *Heref* 12-14; P-in-c Clungunford w Clunbury and Clunton, Bedstone etc 12-14; P-in-c Hopesay 12-14; V Clun Valley 14; C Edstaston, Fauls, Prees, Tilstock and Whixall *Lich* from 14. *The Vicarage, Church Street, Prees, Whitchurch SY13 2EE* E: paul@box-tree.me.uk

WIGRAM, Andrew Oswald. b 39. Lon Univ BD 64. Bps' Coll Cheshunt 61. **d** 64 **p** 65. C Marton-in-Cleveland *York* 64-69; Kenya 69-82; Warden Trin Coll Nairobi 77-82; V Westcliff St Mich *Chelmsf* 82-95; RD Southend 89-94; R Cropwell Bishop w Colston Bassett, Granby etc *S'well* 95-05; rtd 05; PtO *Dur* from 05. *38 Pierremont Crescent, Darlington DL3 9PB* T: (01325) 371473 E: andrew.wigram@ntlworld.com

WIGRAM, John Michael. b 67. Ex Univ BSc 88. St Jo Coll Nottm MTh 04. **d** 05 **p** 06. C Hazlemere *Ox* 05-08; R Hambleden Valley 08-15; V Ripley *Derby* from 15. *26 Mount Pleasant, Ripley DE5 3DX* M: 07551-627761 E: revjohn@wigram.org.uk

WIGRAM (née CHAPMAN), Mrs Rachel Grace. b 67. Ex Univ BA 88. St Jo Coll Nottm 03. **d** 05 **p** 06. C Hazlemere *Ox* 05-08; PtO 08-14. *26 Mount Pleasant, Ripley DE5 3DX* M: 07986-732452 E: wigram@ntlworld.com

WIGRAM, Miss Ruth Margaret. b 41. CertEd 63. Cranmer Hall Dur 83. **dss** 84 **d** 87 **p** 94. Shipley St Paul and Frizinghall *Bradf* 84-90; Par Dn 87-90; Asst Dioc Dir of Ords 90-96; C Skipton H Trin 90-96; V Easby w Skeeby and Brompton on Swale etc *Ripon* 96-06; rtd 07; PtO *York* from 07. *Maythorn, 30 Ainderby Road, Northallerton DL7 8HD* T: (01609) 761852 E: ruthwigram@hotmail.co.uk

WIKELEY, Canon John Roger Ian. b 41. AKC 64. **d** 65 **p** 66. C Southport H Trin *Liv* 65-69; C Padgate 69-71; TV 71-73; R 73-74; TR 74-85; TR W Derby St Mary 85-98; V 98-06; P-in-c W Derby St Jas 04-06; AD W Derby 89-06; Hon Can Liv Cathl 94-06; rtd 06. *72 Carisbrooke Drive, Southport PR9 7JD* T: (01704) 225412 E: rogel4152@yahoo.co.uk

WIKNER, Richard Hugh. b 46. MSI. St Alb Minl Tr Scheme 79. **d** 94 **p** 95. NSM Lt Heath *St Alb* from 94. *Koinonia, 5 The Avenue, Potters Bar EN6 1EG* T: (01707) 650437 E: hughwikner@lineone.net

✠**WILBOURNE, The Rt Revd David Jeffrey.** b 55. Jes Coll Cam BA 78 MA 82. Westcott Ho Cam 79. **d** 81 **p** 82 **c** 09. C Stainton-in-Cleveland *York* 81-85; Chapl Asst Hemlington Hosp 81-85; R Monk Fryston and S Milford *York* 85-91; Abp's Dom Chapl 91-97; Dir of Ords 91-97; V Helmsley 97-09; P-in-c Upper Ryedale 09; Can and Preb York Minster 08-09; Asst Bp Llan from 09; Dir of Min from 10. *6 Llandaff Chase, Llandaff, Cardiff CF5 2NA* T: (029) 2056 2400 F: 2057 7129 E: asstbishop@churchinwales.org.uk

WILBRAHAM, Canon David. b 59. Oak Hill Th Coll BA 88. **d** 88 **p** 89. C Ince Ch Ch *Liv* 88-91; Min St Helens St Helen 91-93; PtO *Guildf* 96-99; NSM Hindhead 99-00; V 00-03; V Churt and Hindhead 03-07; Chapl Thames Valley Police *Ox* from 07; Hon Can Ch Ch from 11. *292 Thorney Leys, Witney OX28 5PB* T: (01993) 706656 M: 07779-262302 E: davidwilbraham@lineone.net

WILBY, Mrs Jean. b 38. Open Univ BA 82. Wycliffe Hall Ox 83. **dss** 85 **d** 87 **p** 94. Maidenhead St Andr and St Mary *Ox* 85-87; C 87; Team Dn Hermitage and Hampstead Norreys, Cold Ash etc 87-91; LtO 92-95; All SS Convent *Ox* 91-95; NSM Iffley *Ox* 94-95; C Denham 95-98; rtd 98; P-in-c Woolstone w Gotherington and Oxenton etc *Glouc* 98-06. *2 Somerset House, Knapp Road, Cheltenham GL50 3QQ* T: (01242) 584096

WILBY, Timothy David. b 59. Univ Coll Dur BA 80 MA 87 Open Univ BA 09 Man Univ MusM 12 ALCM 11. Ripon Coll Cuddesdon 81. **d** 83 **p** 84. C Standish *Blackb* 83-86; CF 86-89; V Chorley All SS *Blackb* 89-95; V Penwortham St Leon 95-00; TR Fellside Team 00-07; P-in-c Chorley St Geo 07-11; V from 11; P-in-c Charnock Richard 11-13; P-in-c Chorley St Pet from 15; AD Chorley from 11. *St George's Vicarage, Letchworth Place, Chorley PR7 2HJ* T: (01257) 263064 E: stgeorgeschorley@aol.com

WILBY, Canon Wendy Ann. b 49. St Hugh's Coll Ox BA 71 MA 93 Leeds Univ MA 01 ARCM 69 LRAM 72. NEOC. **d** 90 **p** 94. Par Dn Barwick in Elmet *Ripon* 90-93; C High Harrogate St Pet 93-94; P-in-c Birstwith 94-01; AD Harrogate 00-01; Chapl St Aid Sch Harrogate 94-01; V Halifax *Wakef* 01-07; RD 06-07; Can Res Bris Cathl 07-13; Dean Women's Min 11-13; rtd 13; PtO *Leeds* from 14. *Skelton Windmill, Ripon Road, Boroughbridge, York YO51 9DP* T: (01423) 323255 E: wilbywindmill@gmail.com

WILCOCK, Mrs Linda Jane. b 46. Nottm Univ TDip 67. **d** 09 **p** 10. OLM Melbury *Sarum* 09-12; TV from 12. *4 Beech Tree Close, Cattistock, Dorchester DT2 0JN* T: (01300) 321112 M: 07788-618412 E: linda.wilcock@virgin.net

WILCOCK, Michael Jarvis. b 32. Dur Univ BA 54. Tyndale Hall Bris 60. **d** 62 **p** 63. C Southport Ch Ch *Liv* 62-65; C St Marylebone All So w SS Pet and Jo *Lon* 65-69; V Maidstone St Faith *Cant* 69-77; Dir Past Studies Trin Coll Bris 77-82; V Dur St Nic 82-98; rtd 98; PtO *Chich* from 98. *1 Tudor Court, 51 Carlisle Road, Eastbourne BN21 4JR* T: (01323) 417170

WILCOCK, Paul Trevor. b 59. Bris Univ BA Leeds Univ MA 93. Trin Coll Bris 83. **d** 87 **p** 88. C Kirkheaton *Wakef* 87-90; Chapl Huddersfield Univ 90-92 and 92-93; Dir Student Services from 93; Chapl W Yorkshire Police from 02; NSM Huddersfield H Trin *Wakef* 92-09; NSM Bradley 09-14; PtO *York* from 13; *Leeds* from 14. *25 Mendip Avenue, Huddersfield HD3 3QG* T: (01484) 325232 E: paulwilcock@aol.com

WILCOCK, Terence Granville. b 50. Open Univ BA 82. EAMTC 99. **d** 02 **p** 03. NSM Oundle w Ashton and Benefield w Glapthorn *Pet* 02-04; NSM Crosscrake *Carl* 04-11; P-in-c 06-11; NSM Old Hutton and New Hutton 06-09; Asst Chapl Gtr Athens *Eur* 11-14; V Patterdale *Carl* from 14. *The Rectory, Patterdale, Penrith CA11 0NL* T: (017684) 82209 E: terryatash@aol.com

WILCOCKSON, The Ven Stephen Anthony. b 51. Nottm Univ BA 73 Ox Univ BA 75 MA 81. Wycliffe Hall Ox 73. **d** 76 **p** 77. C Pudsey St Lawr *Bradf* 76-78; C Wandsworth All SS *S'wark* 78-81; V Rock Ferry *Ches* 81-86; V Lache cum Saltney 86-95; V Howell Hill w Burgh Heath *Guildf* 95-09; RD Epsom 00-07; Par Development Officer *Ches* 09-12; Adn Doncaster *Sheff* from 12. *Fairview House, 14 Armthorpe Lane, Doncaster DN2 5LZ* T: (01302) 325787 *or* (01709) 309110 E: steve.wilcockson@sheffield.anglican.org

WILCOX, Anthony Gordon. b 41. ALCD 67. **d** 67 **p** 68. C Cheltenham Ch Ch *Glouc* 67-72; C Beccles St Mich *St E* 72-74; TV 74-81; V Ipswich All SS 81-06; rtd 06; PtO *St E* from 08. *58 Sproughton Court Mews, Sproughton, Ipswich IP8 3AJ* T: (01473) 461561

WILCOX, Brian Howard. b 46. Westcott Ho Cam 71. **d** 73 **p** 74. C Kettering SS Pet and Paul 73-78; V Eye 78-82; R Clipston w Naseby and Haselbech w Kelmarsh 82-90; V Hornsea w Atwick *York* 90-97; RD N Holderness 95-97; R Uckfield, Isfield and Lt Horsted *Chich* 97-11; rtd 11; PtO *Nor* from 12. *7 Bramble Way, Wymondham NR18 0UN* T: (01953) 605053 E: brian@wilcoxbh.plus.com

WILCOX, Canon Colin John. b 43. St Mich Coll Llan 84. **d** 86 **p** 87. C Newport St Andr *Mon* 86-88; C Llanmartin 88-90; TV 90-92; V Griffithstown 92-08; Hon Can St Woolos Cathl 07-08; rtd 08; PtO *Mon* from 08; *Llan* from 09. *2 Davies Place, Cardiff CF5 3AQ, or The Bungalow, Dingestow, Monmouth NP25 4DZ* T: (029) 2025 4294 *or* (01600) 740680

✠**WILCOX, The Rt Revd David Peter.** b 30. St Jo Coll Ox BA 52 MA 56. Linc Th Coll 52. **d** 54 **p** 55 **c** 86. C St Helier *S'wark* 54-56; C Ox St Mary V 56-59; Tutor Linc Th Coll 59-60; Chapl 60-61; Sub-Warden 61-63; India 64-70; R Gt w Lt Gransden *Ely* 70-72; Can Res Derby Cathl 72-77; Warden EMMTC 73-77; Prin Ripon Coll Cuddesdon 77-85; V Cuddesdon *Ox* 77-85; Suff Bp Dorking *Guildf* 86-95; rtd 95; Hon Asst Bp Chich from 95. *4 The Court, Hoo Gardens, Willingdon, Eastbourne BN20 9AX* T: (01323) 506108

WILCOX, David Thomas Richard. b 42. Down Coll Cam BA 63 Regent's Park Coll Ox BA 66. **d** 95 **p** 96. C Bris St Mary Redcliffe w Temple etc 95-97; TV Yate New Town 97-02; Hon C 02-06; rtd 02; PtO *B & W* from 06. *26 Lethbridge Road, Wells BA5 2FN* T: (01749) 673689 E: davidtrwilcox@hotmail.co.uk

WILCOX, Graham James. b 43. Qu Coll Ox BA 64 MA 75 Lon Univ BD 97 MTh 02. Ridley Hall Cam 64. **d** 66 **p** 67. C Edgbaston St Aug *Birm* 66-69; C Sheldon 69-72; Asst Chapl Wrekin Coll Telford 72-74; C Asterby w Goulceby *Linc* 74-77; R 77-81; R Benniworth w Market Stainton and Ranby 77-81; R Donington on Bain 77-81; R Stenigot 77-81; R Gayton le Wold w Biscathorpe 77-81; V Scamblesby w Cawkwell 77-81; R Asterby Gp 81-88; V Sutton le Marsh 88-90; R Sutton, Huttoft and Anderby 90-98; R Fyfield, Moreton w Bobbingworth etc *Chelmsf* 98-07; rtd 07; PtO *Cov* from 07. *7 Swallow Close, Stratford-upon-Avon CV37 6TT* T: (01789) 551759 E: g.wilcox4@ntlworld.com

WILCOX, Haydon Howard. b 56. Sarum & Wells Th Coll. **d** 82 **p** 83. C Fishponds St Jo *Bris* 82-85; TV Hucknall Torkard *S'well* 85-91; R Bilsthorpe 91-99; R Eakring 91-99; P-in-c Maplebeck 91-99; P-in-c Winkburn 91-99; P-in-c Aldershot St Mich *Guildf* 99-03; V 03; PtO 03-09; Chapl CSP from 07. *46 Barn Meadow Close, Church Crookham, Aldershot GU52 0YB* T/F: (01252) 621639 E: haydonwilcox@mac.com

WILCOX, Heather Yvonne. b 72. ERMC 05. **d** 08 **p** 09. C Pakefield *Nor* 08-11; R Stratton St Mary w Stratton St Michael etc from 11; P-in-c Bunwell, Carleton Rode, Tibenham, Gt Moulton etc from 14. *The Rectory, 8 Flowerpot Lane, Long Stratton, Norwich NR15 2TS* M: 07932-416233 E: rev.heather@btconnect.com

WILCOX, Canon Hugh Edwin. b 37. St Edm Hall Ox BA 62 MA 66. St Steph Ho Ox 62. **d** 64 **p** 65. C Colchester St Jas, All SS, St Nic and St Runwald *Chelmsf* 64-66; Hon C Clifton St Paul *Bris* 66-68; SCM 66-68; Sec Internat Dept BCC 68-76; Asst Gen Sec 74-76; V Ware St Mary *St Alb* 76-03; Hon Can St Alb 96-03; rtd 03; PtO *St Alb* from 03; *Ely* from 12. *The Briars, 1 Briary Lane, Royston SG8 9BX* T: (01763) 244212 E: hugh.wilcox@btinternet.com

WILCOX, Canon Jeffry Reed. b 40. MBE 05. K Coll Lon AKC 65 BA 78 Westmr Coll Ox MTh 97. **d** 66 **p** 67. C Ryhope *Dur* 66-69; C Cockerton 69-71; P-in-c Pallion 71-82; R Streatham St Leon *S'wark* 82-06; RD Streatham 92-00; Hon Can S'wark Cathl 05-06; rtd 06. *4 Lower Broad Street, Ludlow SY8 1PQ* T: (01584) 877199 E: jeffrywilcox@yahoo.co.uk

WILCOX, John Bower. b 28. AKC 55. **d** 58 **p** 59. C Orford St Marg *Liv* 58-60; C W Derby St Mary 60-63; Ind Chapl *Linc* 63-74; R Aisthorpe w W Thorpe and Scampton 63-74; R Brattleby 64-74; Ind Chapl *York* 74-89; P-in-c Middlesbrough St Cuth 89-93; Urban Development Officer 89-93; rtd 93; PtO *York* from 93. *5 Duncan Avenue, Redcar TS10 5BX* T: (01642) 489683

WILCOX, The Very Revd Peter Jonathan. b 61. St Jo Coll Dur BA 84 MA 91 St Jo Coll Ox DPhil 93. Ridley Hall Cam BA 86. **d** 87 **p** 88. C Preston on Tees *Dur* 87-90; NSM Ox St Giles and SS Phil and Jas w St Marg 90-93; TV Gateshead *Dur* 93-98; Dir Urban Miss Cen Cranmer Hall 93-98; P-in-c Walsall St Paul *Lich* 98-06; Hon C Walsall and Walsall Pleck and Bescot 05-06; Can Res Lich Cathl 06-12; Dean Liv from 12. *1 Cathedral Close, Liverpool L1 7BR* T: 0151-702 7202 E: pete.wilcox@liverpoolcathedral.org.uk

WILCOX, Stephen Charles Frederick. b 75. Qu Coll Ox BA 97 ACA 00. Oak Hill Th Coll 04. **d** 07 **p** 08. C Kirk Ella and Willerby *York* 07-11; V Anlaby St Pet from 11; V Anlaby

Common St Mark from 11. *The Vicarage, Church Street, Anlaby, Hull HU10 7DG* T: (01482) 653024 E: scfwilcox@yahoo.co.uk

WILD, Canon Alan James. b 46. **d** 97 **p** 98. OLM Walworth St Pet *S'wark* 97-07; NSM from 07; Hon Can S'wark Cathl from 15. *67 Liverpool Grove, London SE17 2HP* T: (020) 7708 1216

WILD, Hilda Jean. b 48. Linc Th Coll 95. **d** 95 **p** 96. C Newark *S'well* 95-99; V Earlsdon *Cov* 99-13; rtd 13; PtO *Man* from 13. *8 Littondale Close, Royton, Oldham OL2 6PN* T: 0161-652 3790

WILD, Roger Bedingham Barratt. b 40. Hull Univ MA 93. ALCD 64. **d** 65 **p** 65. C Shipley St Pet *Bradf* 65-68; C Pudsey St Lawr 68-71; P-in-c Rawthorpe *Wakef* 71-73; V 73-78; V Ripon H Trin 78-93; RD Ripon 86-93; OCM 80-91; R Barwick in Elmet *Ripon* 93-01; Asst Chapl Trin Th Coll Singapore 02-05; rtd 05; PtO *York* from 06. *Saddlers Cottage, 15 Chapel Street, Thirsk YO7 1LU* T: (01845) 524985 E: rbbwild@hotmail.com

WILDE, David Wilson. b 37. Lon Coll of Div ALCD 61 BD 62. **d** 62 **p** 63. C Kirkheaton *Wakef* 62-66; C Attenborough w Chilwell *S'well* 66-72; P-in-c Bestwood Park 72-83; R Kimberley 83-07; rtd 07. *2 Main Street, Kimberley, Nottingham NG16 2LL* T: 0115-938 5315 E: christwl@aol.co.uk

WILDEY, Canon Ian Edward. b 51. St Chad's Coll Dur BA 72. Coll of Resurr Mirfield 72. **d** 74 **p** 75. C Westgate Common *Wakef* 74-77; C Barnsley St Mary 77-81; V Ravensthorpe 81-95; R Barnsley St Mary 95-07; Dir Educn 96-98; *Leeds* from 07; Hon Can Wakef Cathl from 00. *29 Intake Lane, Barnsley S75 2HX* T: (01226) 291779 E: ian.wildey@sky.com

WILDING, Canon Anita *Pamela*. b 38. MBE 01. Blackpool and Fylde Coll of Further Tech TCert 61. CMS Tr Coll Chislehurst 65. **dss** 89 **d** 92 **p** 93. Chapl Kabare Girls' High Sch Kenya 92-04; Chapl St Andr Primary Boarding Sch Kabare 92-04; rtd 04; PtO *Blackb* from 04. *5 The Fairways, 35 The Esplanade, Knott End-on-Sea, Poulton-le-Fylde FY6 0AD* T: (01253) 810642 E: pamwilding@gofast.co.uk

WILDING, David. b 43. K Coll Lon BD 67 AKC 67. **d** 68 **p** 69. C Thornhill *Wakef* 68-70; C Halifax St Jo Bapt 70-72; V Scholes 72-79; V Lightcliffe 79-97; rtd 97; PtO *Leeds* from 97. *10 Stratton Park, Rastrick, Brighouse HD6 3SN* T: (01484) 387651

WILDING, Michael Paul. b 57. Chich Th Coll 82. **d** 85 **p** 86. C Treboeth *S & B* 85-87; C Llangiwg 87-88; V Defynnog w Rhydybriw and Llandeilo'r-fan 88-00; V Blaenwysg from 00; AD Brecon from 14. *Brynorsaf, Sennybridge, Brecon LD3 8RR* T: (01874) 638927

WILDING, Pamela. *See* WILDING, Anita Pamela

WILDS, The Ven Anthony Ronald. b 43. Hatf Coll Dur BA 64. Bps' Coll Cheshunt 64. **d** 66 **p** 67. C Newport Pagnell *Ox* 66-72; P-in-c Chipili Zambia 72-75; V Chandler's Ford *Win* 75-85; V Andover w Foxcott 85-97; RD Andover 89-94; Hon Can Win Cathl 91-97; TR Solihull *Birm* 97-01; Hon Can Birm Cathl 00-01; Adn Plymouth *Ex* 01-10; rtd 10. *9 rue du Commerce, 49490 Meigne-le-Vicomte, France* T: (0033) 2 41 82 24 52 E: tonywilds@gmail.com

WILES, Mrs Cathryn. b 51. BEd. **d** 04 **p** 05. NSM Wandsworth Common St Mary *S'wark* 04-11; Chapl SW Lon and St George's Mental Health NHS Trust 06-13; rtd 13; Hon C W Dulwich All SS *S'wark* from 14. *10 Waldeck Grove, London SE27 0BE* T: (020) 8761 4017 *or* 8682 6265 E: cathryn.wiles@ntlworld.com

WILES, Roger Kenneth. b 58. Witwatersrand Univ BA 80. St Paul's Coll Grahamstown 81. **d** 83 **p** 84. C Johannesburg St Gabr S Africa 83-84; C Belgravia St Jo 84-85; Chapl Jeppe Boys' High Sch 85-86; Chapl Witwatersrand Univ 86-93; R Edenvale Em 94-99; P-in-c Edin Clermiston Em 99-05; V Poulton Lancelyn H Trin *Ches* from 05. *6 Chorley Way, Wirral CH63 9LS* T: 0151-334 6780 *or* 334 9815

WILFORD (formerly GIBSON), Laura Mary. b 50. NOC 85. **d** 88 **p** 94. Par Dn Foley Park *Worc* 88-90; Par Dn Kidderminster St Jo and H Innocents 90-94; TV 94-96; P-in-c Mamble w Bayton, Rock w Heightington etc 96-99; TV Cartmel Peninsula *Carl* 99-01; Jt Dir of Ords 00-01; P-in-c Worminghall w Ickford, Oakley and Shabbington *Ox* 01-06; rtd 06. *5 Cookson Way, Brough with St Giles, Catterick Garrison DL9 4XG* T: (01748) 830017 E: lauramwilford@hotmail.co.uk

WILKES, Andrew Edward. b 63. Chich Univ BA 13. SEITE 07. **d** 10 **p** 11. NSM Whyke w Rumboldswhyke and Portfield *Chich* 10-11; NSM Chich St Wilfrid 11-15; R Selsey from 15. *The Rectory, 75 St Peter's Crescent, Selsey, Chichester PO20 0NA* M: 07799-558301 T: (01243) 601984 E: rector.selsey@gmail.com *or* drew2tssf@btopenworld.com

WILKES, Elizabeth Ann. *See* FRANKLIN, Elizabeth Ann

WILKES, Jonathan Peter. b 66. Leic Poly BA 88 K Coll Lon MA 00. Ripon Coll Cuddesdon BTh 96. **d** 96 **p** 97. C Hackney *Lon* 96-00; P-in-c Paddington St Pet 00-06; P-in-c Paddington St Mary Magd 04-06; P-in-c Kingston All SS w St Jo *S'wark* 06-07; TR 07-12; TR Kingston from 12. *All Saints'*

Vicarage, 15 Woodbines Avenue, Kingston upon Thames KT1 2AZ T: (020) 3132 8717 *or* 8546 5964

WILKES, Robert Anthony. b 48. Trin Coll Ox BA 70 MA 73. Wycliffe Hall Ox 71. **d** 74 **p** 75. C Netherton *Liv* 74-77; V 77-81; Bp's Dom Chapl 81-85; CMS Pakistan 85-86; Regional Sec Middle E and Pakistan 87-98; P-in-c Mossley Hill St Matt and St Jas *Liv* 98-05; TR Mossley Hill 05-06; Hon Can Liv Cathl 03-06; Dean Birm 06-09; P-in-c Ox St Mich w St Martin and All SS 09-13; V from 13. *St Frideswide's Vicarage, 23 Botley Road, Oxford OX2 0BL* T: (01865) 722724 E: revwilkes@btinternet.com

WILKIE, Mrs Donna Louise. b 81. Plymouth Univ BA 02 Leeds Univ MSc 04. Trin Coll Bris 12. **d** 15. C Clevedon St Andr and Ch Ch *B & W* from 15. *33 Ash Grove, Clevedon BS21 7JZ* M: 07789-771110 E: donnawilkie81@gmail.com

WILKIN, Kenneth. b 54. Open Univ BA 97. S'wark Ord Course 86 Wilson Carlile Coll. **d** 88 **p** 89. C Wolverhampton *Lich* 88-92; V W Bromwich St Andr w Ch Ch 92-98; Dep Chapl HM Pris Pentonville 98-00; Chapl HM Pris Holloway from 00. *HM Prison Holloway, 1 Parkhurst Road, London N7 0NU* T: (020) 7979 4561 E: kenneth.wilkin@hmps.gsi.gov.uk *or* kwilkin@aol.com

WILKIN, Paul John. b 56. Linc Th Coll 88. **d** 90 **p** 91. C Leavesden *St Alb* 90-93; C Jersey St Brelade *Win* 93-97; V Squirrels Heath *Chelmsf* 97-07; R Stansted Mountfitchet w Birchanger and Farnham from 07. *The Rectory, 5 St John's Road, Stansted CM24 8JP* T: (01279) 812203 E: paulwilkin@iname.com

WILKIN, Rose Josephine. *See* HUDSON-WILKIN, Rose Josephine

WILKINS, Graham Paul. b 82. York Univ MChem 05 Cam Univ BTh 12. Ridley Hall Cam 09. **d** 12 **p** 13. C N w S Wootton *Nor* from 12. *34 Castle Rising Road, South Wootton, King's Lynn PE30 3JB* T: (01553) 670868 E: revd.wilkins@gmail.com

WILKINS, Mrs Janice Joy. b 49. St D Coll Lamp 90. **d** 93 **p** 97. NSM Tredegar St Jas *Mon* 93-96; NSM Newbridge 96-97; C Mynyddislwyn 97-01; V Abercarn and Cwmcarn 01-06; AD Bedwellty 05-06; rtd 06. *10 Overdene, Pontllanfraith, Blackwood NP12 2JS* T: (01495) 225720

WILKINS, Michael Richard. b 71. W Sussex Inst of HE BA 92. Trin Coll Bris 07. **d** 09 **p** 10. C Bath Walcot *B & W* 09-13; V Huddersfield H Trin *Leeds* from 13. *2 Norfolk Close, Huddersfield HD1 5NJ* T: (01484) 513213 E: mike.wilkins1@btinternet.com

WILKINS, Nicki Anne. b 68. Indiana Univ BA 91 Yale Univ MDiv 03. **d** 05 **p** 07. NSM St Andrews St Andr *St And* 05-11; PtO from 11. *Address temp unknown* E: nwilkins@btinternet.com

WILKINS, Ralph Herbert. b 29. Lon Univ BD 61. St Aug Coll Cant 72. **d** 73 **p** 74. C Epsom Common Ch Ch *Guildf* 73-76; C Haslemere 77-79; P-in-c Market Lavington and Easterton *Sarum* 79-82; V 82-90; P-in-c Puddletown and Tolpuddle 90-94; P-in-c Milborne St Andrew w Dewlish 92-94; P-in-c Piddletrenthide w Plush, Alton Pancras etc 92-94; rtd 94; PtO *Ab* 94-01; *Heref* from 02. *The Mill, Marton, Welshpool SY21 8JY* T: (01938) 580566

WILKINS, Miss Susan Stafford. b 47. Dur Univ BA. Sarum Th Coll. **dss** 82 **d** 87 **p** 94. Redlynch and Morgan's Vale *Sarum* 82-88; Hon Par Dn 87-88; Hon Par Dn Bemerton 88-90; Par Dn Hilperton w Whaddon and Staverton etc 90-94; TV Worle *B & W* 94-99; P-in-c Hallwood *Ches* 99-04; V Hallwood Ecum Par 04-11; RD Frodsham 06-11; rtd 11. *84 Wallerscote Road, Weaverham, Northwich CW8 3LY* T: (01606) 246039 E: suewilkins@virginmedia.com

WILKINS, Vernon Gregory. b 53. Trin Coll Cam MA 74 Ox Univ BA 88. Wycliffe Hall Ox 86. **d** 89 **p** 90. C Boscombe St Jo *Win* 89-91; C Bursledon 91-94; V Ramsgate St Luke *Cant* 94-03; Dir Tr Bromley Chr Tr Cen Trust from 03; Hon C Bromley Ch Ch *Roch* from 03. *29 Heathfield Road, Bromley BR1 3RN* T: (020) 8464 5135 E: vernon@vgwilkins.freeserve.co.uk

WILKINSON, The Ven Adrian Mark. b 68. TCD BA 90 MA 94 BTh 94 NUI MA 00 HDipEd 91. CITC 91. **d** 94 **p** 95. C Douglas Union w Frankfield *C, C & R* 94-97; I Dunboyne Union *M & K* 97-02; Chapl NUI 97-02; Min Can St Patr Cathl Dublin 97-02; I Rathmolyon w Castlerickard, Rathcore and Agher *M & K* 01-02; I Douglas Union w Frankfield *C, C & R* from 02; Adn Cork, Cloyne and Ross from 14. *The Rectory, Carrigaline Road, Douglas, Cork, Republic of Ireland* T: (00353) (21) 489 1539 *or* 436 9578 M: 86-166 4805 E: archdeacon@cork.anglican.org

WILKINSON, Canon Alan Bassindale. b 31. St Cath Coll Cam BA 54 MA 58 PhD 59 DD 97. Coll of Resurr Mirfield 57. **d** 59 **p** 60. C Kilburn St Aug *Lon* 59-61; Chapl St Cath Coll Cam 61-67; V Barrow Gurney *B & W* 67-70; Asst Chapl and Lect St Matthias's Coll Bris 67-70; Prin Chich Th Coll 70-74; Can and Preb Chich Cathl 70-74; Warden Verulam Ho 74-75;

Dir of Aux Min Tr *St Alb* 74-75; Sen Lect Crewe and Alsager Coll of HE 75-78; Hon C Alsager St Mary *Ches* 76-78; Dioc Dir of Tr *Ripon* 78-84; P-in-c Thornthwaite w Thruscross and Darley 84-88; Hon Can Ripon Cathl 84-88; Tutor Open Univ 88-96; PtO *Portsm* from 88; Hon P Portsm Cathl 88-14; Hon Dioc Th 93-01; Hon Chapl Portsm Cathl 94-01; rtd 96; Visiting Lect Portsm Univ 98-05; Fell Geo Bell Inst Chich Univ from 96. *39 Henty Gardens, Chichester PO19 3DL* T: (01243) 839578

WILKINSON, Alice Margaret Marion. *See* BISHOP, Alice Margaret Marion

WILKINSON, Andrew Wilfrid. b 66. Nottm Univ BTh 96 Lanc Univ MA 99. Linc Th Coll 93. d 96 p 97. C Longridge *Blackb* 96-99; V Garstang St Helen and St Michaels-on-Wyre from 99; AD Garstang from 02; CF (TA) from 02. *The Vicarage, 6 Vicarage Lane, Churchtown, Preston PR3 0HW* T/F: (01995) 602294 E: awilkinson703@btinternet.com

WILKINSON, Carol Ann. b 54. Lon Univ BD 88 Man Univ PhD 95. CBDTI 04. d 06 p 07. NSM Poulton Carleton and Singleton *Blackb* 06-09; LtO from 09. *52 Lowick Drive, Poulton-le-Fylde FY6 8HB* T: (01253) 350700 M: 07894-830305

WILKINSON, Mrs Christine Margaret. b 52. Man Univ BA 74 Neville's Cross Coll of Educn Dur PGCE 75 Birm Univ MEd 78. d 04 p 05. OLM Eythorne and Elvington w Waldershare etc *Cant* 04-11; C Littlebourne and Ickham w Wickhambreaux etc from 11. *The Vicarage, Church Road, Littlebourne, Canterbury CT3 1UA* T: (01227) 721233 E: chriswilk.shep@virgin.net

WILKINSON, David Andrew. b 62. Edge Hill Coll of HE BA 83. Oak Hill Th Coll BA 85. d 88 p 89. C Upton (Overchurch) *Ches* 88-91; C Fulham St Matt *Lon* 91-94; V Duffield *Derby* 94-99; V Finchley St Paul and St Luke *Lon* 99-03. *Honeysuckle Cottage, 19 Church Street, Windermere LA23 1AQ* T: (015394) 43069

WILKINSON, David Edward Paul. b 36. Univ of Wales (Swansea) BSc 57. St Mich Coll Llan 57. d 59 p 60. C Brecon w Battle *S & B* 59-60; Min Can Brecon Cathl 60-66; R Llanelwedd w Llanfaredd, Cwmbach Llechryd etc 66-72; V Tycoch 72-74; Asst Master Churchmead Sch Datchet 75-82; TV Seacroft *Ripon* 82-01; rtd 01; Hon Min Can Ripon Cathl 01-07; Hon C Bishop Monkton and Burton Leonard 01-07; PtO *St As* from 07. *Lyngrove, New High Street, Ruabon, Wrexham LL14 6PW* T: (01978) 822725 M: 07909-961197 E: paulwilkinson36@googlemail.com

WILKINSON, Edward. b 55. Cranmer Hall Dur 86. d 88 p 89. C Bishopwearmouth St Nic *Dur* 88-92; P-in-c Newbottle 92-96; V from 96; AD Houghton 08-14. *The Vicarage, Front Street, Newbottle, Houghton le Spring DH4 4EP* T: 0191-584 3244

WILKINSON, Edwin. b 29. Oak Hill Th Coll 53. d 56 p 57. C Blackb Ch 56-58; C Cheltenham St Mark *Glouc* 58-61; V Tiverton St Geo *Ex* 61-66; V Rye Harbour *Chich* 66-73; V Camber and E Guldeford 73-79; V Westfield 79-87; V Bexhill St Steph 87-93; rtd 93; PtO *Chich* from 93. *51 Anderida Road, Eastbourne BN22 0PZ* T: (01323) 503083

WILKINSON, Mrs Elizabeth Mary. b 65. St Edm Hall Ox MA 91. NEOC 02. d 05 p 06. C Harlow Green and Lamesley *Dur* 05-09; P-in-c Burnmoor from 09; AD Houghton from 14. *The Rectory, 91 Old Durham Road, Gateshead NE8 4BS* T: 0191-477 3990

WILKINSON, Geoffrey. *See* WILKINSON, Roy Geoffrey

WILKINSON, Canon Guy Alexander. b 48. CBE 12. Magd Coll Cam BA 69. Ripon Coll Cuddesdon 85. d 87 p 88. C Coventry Caludon *Cov* 87-90; P-in-c Ockham w Hatchford *Guildf* 90-91; R 91-94; Bp's Dom Chapl 90-94; V Small Heath *Birm* 94-99; Adn Bradf 99-04; Abp's Sec for Inter Faith Relns 05-11; Nat Adv for Inter Faith Relns 05-11; V Fulham St Andr *Lon* from 12; AD Hammersmith and Fulham 12-15. *31 Lilyville Road, London SW6 5DP* T: (020) 7731 4771 M: 07515-327757 E: guy@gwilkinson.org.uk

WILKINSON, Miss Helen Mary. b 53. Homerton Coll Cam BEd 76. Trin Coll Bris d 04 p 05. C Newbury *Ox* 04-08; C Northwood Em *Lon* from 06. *54 Rofant Road, Northwood HA6 3BE* T: (01923) 829163 M: 07790-262631

WILKINSON, James Daniel. b 73. Westmr Coll Ox BTh 95 Reading Univ MA 07 MBACP 04. St Steph Ho Ox 97. d 99 p 00. C Wantage *Ox* 99-02; P-in-c S Hinksey 02-13; V from 13; Sec to Bp Ebbsfleet *Cant* 02-04. *The Vicarage, 33 Vicarage Road, Oxford OX1 4RD* T: (01865) 245879 E: frjwilkinson@gmail.com

WILKINSON, John Andrew. b 59. Pemb Coll Ox BA 83 MA 87 St Jo Coll Dur BA 86. Cranmer Hall Dur 84. d 87 p 88. C Broadheath *Ches* 87-91; TV Worthing Ch the King *Chich* 91-97; Chapl Chantilly *Eur* 97-06; Asst Chapl Fontainebleau 06-11; Chapl from 11; Can Malta Cathl from 10. *9 rue des Provenceaux, 77300 Fontainebleau, France* T: (0033) 1 60 71 86 55 E: chaplain@fontainebleauchurch.org

WILKINSON, John David. b 36. AKC 59. d 60 p 61. C Wythenshawe Wm Temple Ch CD *Man* 60-63; C Morley St Pet w Churwell *Wakef* 63-65; V Robert Town 65-75; V Battyeford 75-88; V Airedale w Fryston 88-98; P-in-c Cawthorne 98-04; rtd 04; PtO *Leeds* from 05; Retirement Officer (Pontefract Adnry) from 06. *29 Pontefract Road, Ferry Bridge, Knottingley WF11 8PN* T: (01977) 607250

WILKINSON, Canon John Donald. b 29. Mert Coll Ox BA 54 MA 56 Louvain Univ Belgium LTh 59 Lon Univ PhD 82 FSA 80. Gen Th Sem (NY) Hon STD 63 Cuddesdon Coll 54. d 56 p 57. C Stepney St Dunstan and All SS *Lon* 56-59; Jerusalem 61-63; Gen Ed USPG 63-69; Dean St Geo Coll Jerusalem 69-75; Can Jerusalem 73-75; P-in-c S Kensington H Trin w All SS *Lon* 75-78; Bp's Dir of Clergy Tr 75-79; Dir Br Sch of Archaeology Jerusalem 79-83; USA 83-91; NSM Kensington St Mary Abbots w St Geo *Lon* 91-94; rtd 94; Hon C St Marylebone St Cypr *Lon* 94-98; PtO 98-08. *7 Tenniel Close, London W2 3LE* T/F: (020) 7229 9205

WILKINSON, John Lawrence. b 43. Ch Coll Cam BA 65 MA 69 Birm Univ MLitt 91. Qu Coll Birm 67 Gen Th Sem (NY) STB 69. d 69 p 70. C Braunstone *Leic* 69-71; C Hodge Hill *Birm* 71-74; P-in-c Aston St Jas 75-84; Tutor Qu Coll Birm 85-95; Hon C Birm St Geo 86-95; V Kings Heath 95-08; Hon Can Birm Cathl 99-08; rtd 09; PtO *Birm* from 09. *203 Barclay Road, Smethwick B67 5LA* T: 0121-434 3526 E: jrwilkinson@dsl.pipex.com

WILKINSON, John Stoddart. b 47. CQSW 83. St D Coll Lamp. d 70 p 71. C Kells *Carl* 70-72; C Barrow St Geo w St Luke 72-74; PtO *Mon* 74-89; Sub-Chapl HM YOI Hewell Grange 89-90; Sub-Chapl HM Rem Cen Brockhill 89-90; rtd 02. *10 Fern Drive, Neyland, Milford Haven SA73 1RA* T: (01646) 601221

WILKINSON, Jonathan Charles. b 61. Leeds Univ BA 83. Wycliffe Hall Ox 85. d 87 p 88. C Plymouth St Andr w St Paul and St Geo *Ex* 87-90; C Oulton Broad *Nor* 90-93; V Hallwood *Ches* 93-99; TR Gateshead *Dur* from 99. *The Rectory, 91 Old Durham Road, Gateshead NE8 4BS* T: 0191-477 3990 E: wilkinson@clara.net

WILKINSON, Mrs Joyce Aileen. b 29. BSc(Econ) MA. d 99 p 00. NSM Bredon w Bredon's Norton *Worc* 99-04; rtd 04; PtO *Worc* from 04. *Foxgloves, Back Lane, Bredon, Tewkesbury GL20 7LH* T: (01684) 773389

WILKINSON, Canon Julia Mary. b 52. Cam Inst of Educn CertEd 73 Open Univ BA 85 Univ of Wales (Ban) BD 89. Linc Th Coll 92. d 92 p 94. Par Dn High Wycombe *Ox* 92-94; C 94-96; TV 96-01; Bp's Adv for Women in Ord Min 97-01; P-in-c St Merryn *Truro* 01-05; P-in-c St Issey w St Petroc Minor 01-05; R St Merryn and St Issey w St Petroc Minor from 06; Co Dioc Dir of Ords 01-12; Hon Can Truro Cathl from 06. *The Rectory, Glebe Crescent, St Issey, Wadebridge PL27 7HJ* T/F: (01841) 540314 E: canjulia@btinternet.com

WILKINSON, Canon Keith Howard. b 48. Hull Univ BA 70 FRSA 94 MCT 99. Westcott Ho Cam 74. d 76 p 77. C Pet St Jude 76-79; Chapl Eton Coll 79-84; PtO *Pet* 82-94; Chapl Malvern Coll 84-89; Hd Master Berkhamsted Sch Herts 89-96; LtO *St Alb* 89-96; Hd Master K Sch Cant 96-07; Hon Can Cant Cathl 96-07; Sen Chapl Eton Coll from 08. *3 Savile House, Eton College, Windsor SL4 0TD*

WILKINSON, The Ven Kenneth Samuel. b 31. TCD BA 60 MA 69. CITC 60. d 60 p 61. C Dublin St Michan w St Paul *D & G* 60-63; Min Can St Patr Cathl Dublin 62-67; C Dublin Ch Ch Leeson Park *D & G* 63-67; I Killegney *C & O* 67-70; I Enniscorthy w Clone, Clonmore, Monart etc 70-02; Preb Ferns Cathl 83-88; Adn Ferns 88-02; Dir of Ords (Ossory, Ferns and Leighlin) 94-02; rtd 02. *149 Hazelwood, Old Coach Road, Gorey, Co Wexford, Republic of Ireland* T: (00353) (53) 942 0784

WILKINSON, Margaret Anne. b 46. Lon Univ MB, BS 70 MSc 74 MRCPsych 77. SAOMC 95. d 98 p 99. NSM Heston *Lon* 98-06; Chapl HM YOI Feltham 01-06; NSM Penge Lane H Trin *Roch* from 07. *27 River Grove Park, Beckenham BR3 1HX* T: (020) 8650 2312 E: revdrwilkinson@tesco.net

WILKINSON, Miss Marlene Sandra. b 45. SRN 71. Trin Coll Bris IDC 78. dss 78 d 93 p 94. Wrose *Bradf* 78-82; Chapl St Luke's Hosp Bradf 78-82; Past Tutor Aston Tr Scheme 79-81; W Yorkshire CECS 82-84; Westgate Common *Wakef* 84-86; E Ardsley 86-92; Wakef St Jo 92-94; NSM 93-94; TV Barrow St Geo w St Luke *Carl* 94-00; TV Darwen St Pet w Hoddlesden *Blackb* 00-02; rtd 03; PtO *Leeds* from 10 and 12-14. *4 Hopefield Court, East Ardsley, Wakefield WF3 2LL* T: (01924) 872825

WILKINSON, Mrs Mary Frances. b 52. St As Minl Tr Course 99. d 03 p 04. NSM Shotton *St As* 03-05; NSM Llandrillo and Llandderfel 05-12; rtd 12. *8 Felin Goed, Llandrillo, Corwen LL21 0SJ* T: (01490) 440522

WILKINSON, Matthew John George. b 81. St Cuth Soc Dur BSc 02. St Mich Coll Llan BA 06. d 06 p 07. C Wrexham *St As*

06-11; PtO 11-12; C Minera w Coedpoeth and Bwlchgwyn 12-14; V Chirk from 14. *The Vicarage, Trevor Road, Chirk, Wrexham LL14 5HD* T: (01691) 778519
E: vicarofchirk@hotmail.com

WILKINSON, Michael Alan. b 27. Selw Coll Cam BA 51. Westcott Ho Cam 52. **d** 53 **p** 54. C Swindon Ch Ch *Bris* 53-57; C Knowle St Barn 57-59; C Eltham St Jo *S'wark* 59-65; C Sydenham St Bart 65-77; PtO *Ex* 77-84; P-in-c Yealmpton 84-91; P-in-c Brixton 87-91; V Yealmpton and Brixton 91-97; RD Ivybridge 91-93; rtd 97; PtO *Ex* from 97. *The Old Forge, Kingston, Kingsbridge TQ7 4PT* T: (01548) 810424

WILKINSON, Paul. *See* WILKINSON, David Edward Paul

WILKINSON, Paul. b 51. Sarum & Wells Th Coll 75. **d** 78 **p** 79. C Allerton *Bradf* 78-80; C Baildon 80-83; V Hengoed w Gobowen *Lich* 83-90; V Potterne w Worton and Marston *Sarum* 90-03; Chapl Roundway Hosp Devizes 92-03; P-in-c Leckhampton St Pet *Glouc* 03-09; P-in-c Cheltenham Em w St Steph 08-09; TR S Cheltenham 10-15; rtd 15. *Address temp unknown* E: pwilkinson@vicarage79.fsnet.co.uk

WILKINSON, Paul. b 69. **d** 11 **p** 12. OLM Fountain of Life *Nor* from 11. *10 Church Street, Ashill, Thetford IP25 7AW* T: (01760) 441443 E: paulwilkinson500@gmail.com

WILKINSON, Paul Martin. b 56. Brunel Univ BSc. Wycliffe Hall Ox 83. **d** 86 **p** 87. C Hinckley H Trin *Leic* 86-90; V Newbold on Avon *Cov* from 90. *The Vicarage, Main Street, Newbold, Rugby CV21 1HH* T: (01788) 543055 F: 542458
E: paulwilkinson54@btinternet.com

WILKINSON, Peter David Lloyd. b 67. Trin Coll Ox BA 89 MA 93. Ridley Hall Cam BA 94. **d** 95 **p** 96. C Brampton St Thos *Derby* 95-98; C Tunbridge Wells St Jo *Roch* 98-02; C Ox St Ebbe w H Trin and St Pet from 02. *10 Lincoln Road, Oxford OX1 4TB* T: (01865) 728885
E: pete@peteandjules.freeserve.co.uk

WILKINSON, Robert. *See* WILKINSON, Walter Edward Robert

WILKINSON, Robert Ian. b 43. MIMunE 73 MICE 84 CEng 73. Oak Hill NSM Course. **d** 88 **p** 89. NSM Hawkwell *Chelmsf* 88-89; NSM Thundersley 89-91; C New Thundersley 91-94; V Berechurch St Marg w St Mich 94-06; rtd 06; PtO *Leeds* from 07. *140 Keighley Road, Skipton BD23 2QT* T: (01756) 799748

WILKINSON, Robert John. b 66. Birkbeck Coll Lon BA 98 Fitzw Coll Cam BA 00 ACIB 90. Westcott Ho Cam 98. **d** 01 **p** 02. C Southgate Ch Ch *Lon* 01-04; TV Wood Green St Mich w Bounds Green St Gabr etc 04-11; V Tottenham St Paul from 11. *St Paul's Vicarage, 60 Park Lane, London N17 0JR* T: (020) 8808 7297 E: robert.wilkinson@london.anglican.org

WILKINSON, Robert Matthew. b 21. TCD BA 46. TCD Div Sch 47. **d** 47 **p** 48. C Limerick St Lawr w H Trin and St Jo *L & K* 47-49; C Arm St Mark 49-51; I Mullavilly 51-55; I Derryloran 55-73; Can Arm Cathl 67-73; I Ballymore 73-87; Treas Arm Cathl 73-75; Chan Arm Cathl 75-83; Prec Arm Cathl 83-87; rtd 87. *60 Coleraine Road, Portrush BT56 8HN* T: (028) 7082 2758

WILKINSON, Robert Samuel. b 52. Wycliffe Hall Ox 92. **d** 94 **p** 95. C Boughton Monchelsea *Cant* 94-96; C Parkwood CD 95-96; C Plymouth St Andr and Stonehouse *Ex* 96-01; P-in-c Whimple, Talaton and Clyst St Lawr 01-11; TV Cullompton, Willand, Uffculme, Kentisbeare etc 11-14; rtd 14. *60 Heavitree Road, Exeter EX1 2LQ*

WILKINSON, Rosamund. **d** 15. C Istanbul w Moda *Eur* from 15. *Address temp unknown*

WILKINSON, Roy Geoffrey. b 42. Open Univ BSc 93 Linc Univ MSc 99. Sarum Th Coll 67. **d** 70 **p** 71. C Belsize Park *Lon* 70-73; C Heston 73-75; C Hythe *Cant* 75-79; V Croydon Woodside *S'wark* 79-86; Asst Mental Health Chapl Skegness and Winthorpe *Linc* 96-97; Asst Chapl Linc Distr Healthcare NHS Trust 96-97; Chapl Lincs Partnership NHS Trust 97-05; rtd 05; Hon C Linc All SS from 06. *287 Monks Road, Lincoln LN2 5JZ* T: (01522) 522671 M: 07745-755614
E: sarah@comfort123.freeserve.co.uk

WILKINSON, Sharon Theresa. b 58. **d** 12 **p** 13. C Scotforth *Blackb* from 12. *6 Beechwood Gardens, Lancaster LA1 4PH*
E: fantine2001@aol.com

WILKINSON, Canon Simon Evelyn. b 49. Nottm Univ BA 74. Cuddesdon Coll 74. **d** 76 **p** 77. C Cheam *S'wark* 76-78; P-in-c Warlingham w Chelsham and Farleigh 78-83; Hd RS Radley Coll 83-89; R Bishop's Waltham and Upham *Portsm* 89-97; TR Shaston *Sarum* 97-03; P-in-c Amesbury 03-12; V 12-14; RD Stonehenge 03-10; Can and Preb Sarum Cathl 05-14; rtd 14. *5 Berkshire Road, Salisbury SP2 8NY*
E: s-wilkinson@sky.com

WILKINSON, Stephen. b 69. Brighton Poly BEng 91. Ridley Hall Cam 08. **d** 10 **p** 11. C Gtr Corsham and Lacock *Bris* 10-14; P-in-c Brinkworth w Dauntsey from 14; P-in-c Gt Somerford, Lt Somerford, Seagry, Corston etc from 14; P-in-c Garsdon, Lea and Cleverton and Charlton from 14. *The Rectory, Frog Lane, Great Somerford, Chippenham SN15 5JA* T: (01249) 723733 E: rector@woodbridgegroup.co.uk

WILKINSON, Stephen Graham. b 64. Leeds Univ BA 08. NOC 05. **d** 08 **p** 09. Chapl to Police and NSM Pennington *Man* 08-11; TV Cramlington *Newc* from 11. *St Nicholas' Vicarage, 1 Cateran Way, Cramlington NE23 6EX* T: (01670) 714271 E: revd.steve.wilkinson@googlemail.com

WILKINSON, Mrs Susan Ann. b 62. SEITE 10. **d** 14. NSM Lewes St Anne and St Mich and St Thos etc *Chich* from 14. *Upper Barn, The Lane, Westdean, Seaford BN25 4AL* T: (01323) 871243 M: 07713-097661 E: sueann_27@hotmail.com

WILKINSON, Walter Edward Robert. b 38. St Andr Univ MA 60. Lon Coll of Div BD 63 ALCD 63. **d** 63 **p** 64. C High Wycombe *Ox* 63-70; PV, Succ and Sacr Roch Cathl 70-73; P-in-c Asby w Ormside *Carl* 73-80; R Cherry Burton *York* 80-95; RD Beverley 88-94; P-in-c Grasmere *Carl* 95-03; rtd 03; PtO *Carl* from 03. *4 Heversham Gardens, Heversham, Milnthorpe LA7 7RA* T: (015395) 64044 E: bob@carliol.clara.co.uk

WILKS, Eric Percival. b 32. Wells Th Coll 67. **d** 68 **p** 69. C Fladbury w Throckmorton, Wyre Piddle and Moor *Worc* 68-70; PtO from 70. *4 Catherine Cottages, Droitwich Road, Hartlebury, Kidderminster DY10 4EL* T: (01299) 251580

WILKS, Ernest Howard. b 26. Oak Hill Th Coll 64. **d** 66 **p** 67. C Slough *Ox* 66-69; R Gressenhall w Longham and Bittering Parva *Nor* 69-77; Area Sec CMS St E and Nor 77-83; P-in-c Deopham w Hackford *Nor* 83-84; P-in-c Morley 83-84; P-in-c Wicklewood and Crownthorpe 83-84; R Morley w Deopham, Hackford, Wicklewood etc 84-88; CMS Nigeria 89-91; rtd 91; PtO *Nor* from 91. *23 Eckling Grange, Dereham NR20 3BB* T: (01362) 690485

WILL, Nicholas James. b 53. Birm Univ LLB 75. Qu Coll Birm 93. **d** 95 **p** 96. C Bridgnorth, Tasley, Astley Abbotts, etc *Heref* 95-00; R Raveningham Gp *Nor* from 00. *The Rectory, Church Road, Thurlton, Norwich NR14 6RN* T: (01508) 548648

WILLANS, Jonathan Michael Arthur. b 60. QUB BD. CITC 83. **d** 85 **p** 86. C Larne and Inver *Conn* 85-88; R Hawick *Edin* 88-91; P-in-c Brockham Green *S'wark* from 91; P-in-c Leigh from 91. *The Vicarage, Clayhill Road, Leigh, Reigate RH2 8PD* T/F: (01306) 611224

WILLANS, William Richard Gore. b 48. Qu Coll Ox BA 70 MA 74 Ox Univ PGCE 71. CITC 77. **d** 79 **p** 80. C Bonne Bay Canada 79-80; P-in-c Bonne Bay N 80-82; R 82-87; R Thunder Bay St Thos 87-98; I Craigs w Dunaghy and Killagan *Conn* from 98. *Craigs Rectory, 95 Hillmount Road, Cullybackey, Ballymena BT42 1NZ* T: (028) 2588 0248 *or* 2588 2225
E: willans@btinternet.com

WILLARD, John Fordham. b 38. K Coll Lon BD 62 AKC 62. **d** 63 **p** 64. C Balham Hill Ascension *S'wark* 63-67; C Leigh Park *Portsm* 67-73; C-in-c Leigh Park St Clare CD 73-75; R Bishop's Waltham 75-87; P-in-c Upham 78-79; R 79-87; V Dalston H Trin w St Phil *Lon* 87-97; P-in-c Haggerston All SS 90-97; P-in-c Fairford *Glouc* 97-98; V Fairford and Kempsford w Whelford 98-04; rtd 04; PtO *Glouc* from 05. *15 Highwood Avenue, Cheltenham GL53 0JJ* T: (01242) 530051

WILLCOCK, Canon Richard William. b 39. Hertf Coll Ox BA 62 MA 66. Ripon Hall Ox 62. **d** 64 **p** 65. C Ashton St Mich *Man* 64-68; Bp's Dom Chapl 68-72; V Charlestown 72-75; Chapl Casterton Sch Lancs 75-80; V Bamford *Man* 80-92; R Framlingham w Saxtead *St E* 92-04; RD Loes 95-97; Warden of Readers 98-03; Hon Can St E Cathl 00-04; rtd 04; PtO *Carl* from 05. *High Green Cottage, Sandford, Appleby-in-Westmorland CA16 6NR* T: (017683) 51021

WILLCOX, Canon Frederick John. b 29. Kelham Th Coll 49. **d** 54 **p** 55. C Tranmere St Paul *Ches* 54-56; Lt O *S'well* 57-61; Miss P St Patr Miss Bloemfontein S Africa 62-65; Dir 65-70; P-in-c Derby St Andr w St Osmund 70-74; V 74-80; V Netherton St Andr *Worc* 80-94; Hon Can Worc Cathl 91-94; rtd 94; PtO *Worc* 94-10. *22 Capel Court, The Burgage, Prestbury, Cheltenham GL52 3EL* T: (01242) 256373

WILLCOX (née THOMPSON), Mrs Pauline. b 44. EMMTC 81. **dss** 84 **d** 87 **p** 94. Derby St Aug 84-88; Par Dn 87-88; Par Dn Boulton 88-90; Par Dn Allestree 91-94; C 94-97; Sub-Chapl HM Pris Sudbury 92-94; P-in-c Hartington, Biggin and Earl Sterndale *Derby* 97-01; rtd 01; PtO *Derby* 01-06; Chapl HM Pris Jersey 06-09; PtO *Win* from 10. *9 Clos du Roncherez, Le Pont du Val, St Brelade, Jersey JE3 8FG* T: (01534) 745160
E: paulinewillcox@jerseymail.co.uk

WILLCOX, Ralph Arthur. b 32. Cranfield Inst of Tech MSc 80. St Alb Minl Tr Scheme 86. **d** 89 **p** 90. NSM Aspley Guise w Husborne Crawley and Ridgmont *St Alb* 89-92; Chapl HM Pris Bedf 92-99; Asst Chapl 99-02; LtO *St Alb* 92-03; rtd 02; PtO *St Alb* from 03. *5 Church Road, Woburn Sands, Milton Keynes MK17 8TE* T: (01908) 582510

WILLCOX, Richard John Michael. b 39. Birm Univ BSc 63 PhD 67. Qu Coll Birm 78. **d** 80 **p** 81. C Boldmere *Birm* 80-83; V Edgbaston SS Mary and Ambrose 83-89; V Evercreech w Chesterblade and Milton Clevedon *B & W* 89-97; Dioc Development Rep 90-01; V Bridgwater H Trin 97-01; rtd 01;

PtO *Heref* 05-13. *58 Forrester Green, Colerne, Chippenham SN14 8EA* E: rswil1cox@aol.com

WILLESDEN, Area Bishop of. *See* BROADBENT, The Rt Revd Peter Alan

WILLETT, Frank Edwin. b 45. Kelham Th Coll 64. **d** 68 **p** 69. C Oswestry H Trin *Lich* 68-71; C Bilston St Leon 71-74; USPG Zambia 75-80; V Curbar and Stoney Middleton *Derby* 80-88; Area Sec USPG Derby and Leic 88-91; V Chesterfield SS Aug *Derby* 91-98; Chapl Walton Hosp 91-98; Ind Chapl *Derby* 98-03; P-in-c Brampton St Mark 03-09; Hon P-in-c Loundsley Green 03-09; rtd 10; Hon C Boldre w S Baddesley *Win* 09-13; PtO from 13. *57 Fawn Gardens, New Milton BH25 5GJ* E: ff_willett@yahoo.co.uk

WILLETT, Canon Geoffrey Thomas. b 38. Dur Univ BA 59 MA 82. Cranmer Hall Dur. **d** 62 **p** 63. C Widnes St Paul *Liv* 62-65; C Harborne Heath *Birm* 65-68; V Wakef St Andr and St Mary 68-75; V Hinckley H Trin *Leic* 75-89; TR 89; RD Sparkenhoe II 84-87; RD Sparkenhoe W 87-89; P-in-c Markfield 89-90; R 90-99; P-in-c Thornton, Bagworth and Stanton 96-99; R Markfield, Thornton, Bagworth and Stanton etc 99-04; RD Sparkenhoe E 91-99; Hon Can Leic Cathl 87-04; rtd 04; PtO *Derby* from 04; *Leic* from 04; *Lich* from 10. *22 Clifton Way, Burton-on-Trent DE15 9DW* T: (01283) 548868 E: carolynwillett79@googlemail.com

WILLETT, Canon John Ivon. b 40. Ch Ch Ox BA 63 MA 65. Chich Th Coll 61. **d** 63 **p** 64. C Leic St Andr 63-66; C Bordesley St Alb *Birm* 66-72; Min Can, Prec and Sacr Pet Cathl 72-82; R Uppingham w Ayston and Wardley w Belton 82-99; Can Pet Cathl 97-99; V Cantley *Sheff* 99-12; AD Doncaster 04-10; rtd 12; PtO *Sheff* from 12. *16 Rosemary Close, Doncaster DN4 6BP* T: (01302) 370808

WILLETT, Stephen John. b 54. Ridley Hall Cam 88. **d** 90 **p** 91. C Chapeltown *Sheff* 90-94; V Hackenthorpe from 94; AD Attercliffe 07-13. *The Vicarage, 63 Sheffield Road, Sheffield S12 4LR* T: 0114-248 4486 E: stephenwillett63@gmail.com

WILLETTS, Ms Mary Elizabeth Willetts. b 33. St Hild Coll Dur BA 54 Hughes Hall Cam CertEd 55. Cranmer Hall Dur 02. **d** 02 **p** 03. NSM Stockton-on-the-Forest w Holtby and Warthill *York* 02-12; NSM Rural E York 12-13; rtd 13. *Walnut Cottage, Warthill, York YO19 5XL* T: (01904) 489874

WILLETTS, Simon Peter. b 75. St Jo Coll Nottm. **d** 10 **p** 11. C Leamington Priors St Paul *Cov* 10-14; C Virginia Water *Guildf* from 14. *Santana, Christchurch Road, Virginia Water GU25 4PT* E: simon@cc-vw.org

WILLETTS, Mrs Susan. b 60. EMMTC 05. **d** 08 **p** 09. C Burton All SS w Ch Ch *Lich* 08-11; TV Uttoxeter Area from 11. *5 Beech Close, Uttoxeter ST14 7PY*

WILLEY, Canon David Geoffrey. b 53. Imp Coll Lon BSc 74. Oak Hill Th Coll BA 86. **d** 86 **p** 87. C Cromer *Nor* 86-90; R High Halstow w All Hallows and Hoo St Mary *Roch* 90-94; R Gravesend St Geo 94-02; TR N Farnborough *Guildf* from 02; RD Aldershot 06-11; Hon Can Guildf Cathl from 13. *The Rectory, 66 Church Avenue, Farnborough GU14 7AP* T: (01252) 544754 E: rector@stpetersfarnborough.org.uk

WILLEY, Graham John. b 38. Moray Ord Course 91. **d** 93 **p** 94. NSM W Coast Jt Congregations *Mor* 93-99; NSM Stirling *St And* 99-03; rtd 03; Hon C Killin *St And* 04-13. *9 Victoria Terrace, Menstrie FK11 7EE* T: (01259) 761932 E: graham.john.willey@btinternet.com

WILLIAMS, Alan Ronald Norman. b 60. RMN 85. Linc Th Coll 95. **d** 95 **p** 96. C Malvern Link w Cowleigh *Worc* 95-99; TV 03-08; V Risca *Mon* 99-03; P-in-c Amblecote *Worc* from 08. *The Vicarage, 4 The Holloway, Amblecote, Stourbridge DY8 4DL* T: (01384) 394057 E: alan.r.williams@btinternet.com

WILLIAMS, Aled Jones. b a. Univ of Wales (Ban) BA 77. St Mich Coll Llan 77. **d** 79 **p** 80. C Conwy w Gyffin *Ban* 79-82; R Llanrug 82-86; R Machynlleth and Llanwrin 86-87; Member L'Arche Community 88-95; V Ynyscynhaearn w Penmorfa and Porthmadog *Ban* 95-01; V Porthmadog w Ynyscynhaearn and Dolbenmaen 01-09; rtd 10. *Frondeg, Gwaun Ganol, Criccieth LL52 0TB* T: (01766) 522175

WILLIAMS, Canon Aled Wyn. b 47. Univ of Wales (Abth) BA 69. St Mich Coll Llan 69. **d** 71 **p** 72. C Llanelli *St D* 71-73; P-in-c Capel Colman w Llanfihangel Penbedw etc 73-74; V 74-81; V Llanddewi Brefi w Llanbadarn Odwyn 81-84; V Llanddewi Brefi w Llanbadarn Odwyn, Cellan etc 84-01; V Lampeter and Llanddewibrefi Gp 01-06; TR Bro Teifi Sarn Helen 06-11; AD Lampeter and Ultra-Aeron 96-11; Can St D Cathl 97-11; rtd 11; PtO *St D* from 11. *Cwmawel, Llanllwni, Pencader SA39 9DR*

WILLIAMS, Miss Alison Lindsay. b 47. Univ of Wales (Abth) BA 69 PGCE 00. Wycliffe Hall Ox 00. **d** 00 **p** 01. C Stratton St Margaret w S Marston etc *Bris* 00-04; TV Chalke Valley *Sarum* 04-12; rtd 12. *5 Cherry Orchard, Highworth, Swindon SN6 7AU* T: (01793) 979110 E: alisonlwilliams@waitrose.com

WILLIAMS, Amanda Clare. *See* WILLIAMS-POTTER, Amanda Clare

WILLIAMS, Mrs Amanda Joy. b 61. Glos Univ BA 10. WEMTC 08. **d** 10 **p** 11. C Tupsley w Hampton Bishop *Heref* from 10. *Canal Cottage, Monkhide, Ledbury HR8 2TX* T: (01531) 670753 E: monkhide@btinternet.com

WILLIAMS, Andrea Caroll. b 46. Brighton Univ BA 05. Trin Coll Bris 06. **d** 07 **p** 08. NSM Ore St Helen and St Barn *Chich* 07-12; NSM Nettlebed w Bix, Highmoor, Pishill etc *Ox* from 12. *203 Greys Road, Henley-on-Thames RG9 1SP* T: (01491) 576954 M: 07806-463558 E: andrea.hastings@googlemail.com

WILLIAMS, Andrew Barrington. b 62. Ripon Coll Cuddesdon 96. **d** 98 **p** 99. C Oswaldtwistle Immanuel and All SS *Blackb* 98-01; C Whittle-le-Woods 01-02; P-in-c Hillock *Man* 02-08; P-in-c Unsworth 07-08; P-in-c Radcliffe St Andr 08-14; V Brinnington w Portwood *Ches* from 14. *St Luke's Vicarage, Brinnington Road, Stockport SK5 8BS* T: 0161-430 4164 M: 07565-483455 E: revandywilliams@me.com

WILLIAMS, Andrew David. b 67. Univ of Wales (Lamp) BA 91. Linc Th Coll 93. **d** 93 **p** 94. C Perry Street *Roch* 93-96; C Ealing St Pet Mt Park *Lon* 96-00; R Finchley St Mary 00-08; Warden of Readers Edmonton Area 05-08; R Applecross Australia 08-14; C Tottenham H Trin *Lon* from 14. *Address temp unknown* E: perth08@googlemail.com

WILLIAMS, Andrew Gibson. b 31. Edin Univ MA 57. Edin Th Coll 56. **d** 59 **p** 60. C Todmorden *Wakef* 59-61; C Clitheroe St Mary *Blackb* 61-63; V Burnley St Jas 63-65; CF (TA) 64-65; CF 65-71; R Winterslow *Sarum* 71-84; P-in-c Condover *Heref* 84-88; P-in-c Acton Burnell w Pitchford 84-88; P-in-c Frodesley 84-88; R Condover w Frodesley, Acton Burnell etc 88-90; R Whimple, Talaton and Clyst St Lawr *Ex* 90-94; rtd 94; PtO *Ex* 94-08. *Flat 7, Manormead, Tilford Road, Hindhead GU26 6RA* T: (01428) 601507

WILLIAMS, Andrew John. b 64. Univ Coll Lon BSc 85 Keele Univ PGCE 87 Lon Univ MSc 91. STETS 08. **d** 11 **p** 12. NSM Twickenham All Hallows *Lon* from 11; NSM Kingston *S'wark* from 14. *51 Moor Mead Road, Twickenham TW1 1JS* M: 07824-310311 E: andrew.williams.london@gmail.com

WILLIAMS, Andrew Joseph. b 55. St Jo Coll Nottm BTh 81. **d** 81 **p** 82. C Hollington St Leon *Chich* 81-84; C Sutton Coldfield H Trin *Birm* 84-87; PtO 87-01; Chapl Blue Coat Comp Sch Walsall 91-01; Chapl St Elphin's Sch Matlock 01-04; LtO *Derby* 01-06; Can Res Bradf Cathl 06-14; Duty Manager Foxhill Retreat and Conf Cen *Ches* from 14. *Chester Diocesan Conference Centre, Tarvin Road, Frodsham WA6 6XB* T: (01928) 733777 E: foxhill@chester.anglican.org

WILLIAMS, Andrew Thomas. b 66. Ex Univ LLB 88 Solicitor 90. Trin Coll Bris BA 00. **d** 00 **p** 01. C Whitchurch *Ex* 00-03; C Chorleywood St Andr *St Alb* 03-09; Pastor Greenwich Trin Ch USA from 09. *Trinity Church, 15 Sherwood Place, Greenwich CT 06830, USA* T: (001) (203) 618 0808 F: 618 0888 E: elena.w@virgin.net

WILLIAMS, Mrs Angela. b 50. Univ of Wales (Ban) BTh 05. **d** 05 **p** 06. Min Can Ban Cathl 05-09; V Llandegfan w Llandysilio 09-11; V Llandegfan w Llandysilio w Llansadwrn 11-14; V Bro Tysilio from 14; Dioc Children's Officer 05-11; Warden of Readers from 11. *The Vicarage, Mona Road, Menai Bridge LL59 5EA* T: (01248) 717265

WILLIAMS, Ann Joyce. *See* TEMPLEMAN, Ann Joyce

WILLIAMS, Anthea Elizabeth. b 50. Trevelyan Coll Dur BA 71 Kent Univ MA 97 Middx Univ MSc 00 Univ of E Lon PhD 10. Linc Th Coll 72. **dss** 79 **d** 87 **p** 94. Par Dn Maidstone St Martin *Cant* 87-91; Dn-in-c Rolvenden 91-94; P-in-c 94-04; P-in-c Sandhurst w Newenden 01-04; Chapl E Kent NHS and Soc Care Partnership Trust 91-04; Hon Chapl Kent Police *Cant* from 95; PtO from 04; *Chich* from 15. *2 Great Wigsell Cottages, Hastings Road, Bodiam, Robertsbridge TN32 5PU* M: 07956-704790 E: chaplain2sk@btinternet.com

WILLIAMS, Anthony. b 61. Ex Univ BA 83 Coll of SS Mark and Jo Plymouth MEd 04. SWMTC 09. **d** 11 **p** 12. NSM Elburton *Ex* from 11. *86 Ramsey Gardens, Manadon Park, Plymouth PL5 3UP* E: tonywilliams86@talktalk.net

WILLIAMS, Anthony David. b 38. LRCP 62 MRCS 62 MRCGP 68. S Dios Minl Tr Scheme 87. **d** 90 **p** 91. NSM Jersey St Pet *Win* 90-92; NSM Jersey St Helier from 92. *Beau Vallon Ouest, Mont de la Rosier, St Saviour, Jersey JE2 7HF* T: (01534) 863859 E: tonyw@jerseymail.co.uk

WILLIAMS, Capt Anthony James. b 57. **d** 08 **p** 09. NSM Bream *Glouc* 08-13; P-in-c Forest of Dean Ch Ch w English Bicknor 13-14; V from 14; Chapl HM Pris Glouc 12-13; Chapl HM Pris Eastwood Park from 13. *HM Prison Eastwood Park, Falfield, Wotton-under-Edge GL12 8DB* T: (01454) 382100 E: revtonyw@hotmail.com *or* anthony.williams@hmps.gsi.gov.uk

WILLIAMS, Anthony Michael. b 39. **d** 03 **p** 04. NSM Iver *Ox* 03-10; PtO 10-14. *Dyfi, The Folly, Longborough, Moreton-in-Marsh GL56 0QS*

WILLIAMS, The Very Revd Arfon. b 58. Univ of Wales (Abth) BD 83 Univ of Wales (Ban) MA 84. Wycliffe Hall Ox 83. **d** 84 **p** 85. C Carmarthen St Dav *St D* 84-86; TV Aberystwyth 86-88; V Glanogwen *Ban* 88-94; C Ewhurst and Dir Oast Ho Retreat Cen *Chich* 95-98; Asst to RD Rye 95-98; Co-ord for Adult Educn (E Sussex Area) *Chich* 97-98; I Jordanstown *Conn* 98-02; Adn Meirionnydd *Ban* 02-04; R Dolgellau w Llanfachreth and Brithdir etc 02-04; Dean Elphin and Ardagh *K, E & A* from 04; I Sligo w Knocknarea and Rosses Pt from 04. *The Deanery, Strandhill Road, Sligo, Republic of Ireland* T: (00353) (71) 915 7993
E: arvonwilliams@eircom.net

WILLIAMS, Barrie. b 33. Em Coll Cam BA 54 MA 58 Bris Univ MLitt 71. Lambeth STh 75 Ripon Hall Ox 62. **d** 63 **p** 64. C Penwortham St Mary *Blackb* 63-65; Hon C Salisbury St Martin *Sarum* 65-77; Chapl St Edw K and Martyr Cam *Ely* 77-84; Asst Chapl Trin Hall Cam 77-84; R Ashley w Weston by Welland and Sutton Bassett *Pet* 84-85; Asst Chapl St Hilda's Priory and Sch Whitby 85-97; rtd 98; PtO *York* from 98. *5 Grinkle Court, 9 Chubb Hill Road, Whitby YO21 1JU* T: (01947) 600766

WILLIAMS, Benjamin James. b 85. Pemb Coll Ox BA 06 Wolfs Coll Ox MSt 07. Ox Min Course 07. **d** 10 **p** 11. NSM Cowley St Jo Ox from 10; Chapl Wadh Coll Ox 12-15; PtO *Ox* from 15. *1 Magdalen Road, Oxford OX4 1RW* M: +07540-784156
E: hishtafel@hotmail.com

WILLIAMS, Brian. *See* WILLIAMS, Herbert Brian

WILLIAMS, Brian. b 48. WMMTC. **d** 83 **p** 84. NSM Lich St Chad 83-03; Asst Chapl Sandwell Health Care NHS Trust 98; Angl Chapl 98-99; Chapl Burton Hosps NHS Trust 99-03; Chapl R Bournemouth and Christchurch Hosps NHS Trust 03-14; rtd 14. *82 Walsall Road, Lichfield WS13 8AF*

WILLIAMS, Brian Frederick. b 35. Philippa Fawcett Coll CertEd 77 BEd 78. SEITE 98. **d** 01 **p** 02. NSM Folkestone St Mary and St Eanswythe *Cant* 01-10; NSM Folkestone St Mary, St Eanswythe and St Sav 09-11; PtO 11-12; C Alkham w Capel le Ferne and Hougham from 12. *The Vicarage, 20 Alexandra Road, Capel-le-Ferne, Folkestone CT18 7LD* T: (01303) 244119 E: brianwilliams@cheritonfolk.fsnet.co.uk

WILLIAMS, Canon Brian Luke. b 54. AKC 75. St Steph Ho Ox 76. **d** 77 **p** 78. C Kettering St Mary *Pet* 77-80; C Walsall St Gabr Fulbrook *Lich* 80-83; P-in-c Sneyd 83-85; V from 85; RD Stoke N 94-99; Preb Lich Cathl from 13; Can Ho Ghana from 14. *Sneyd Vicarage, Hamil Road, Stoke-on-Trent ST6 1AP* T/F: (01782) 825841

WILLIAMS, Brian Thomas. b 48. Linc Th Coll 89. **d** 91 **p** 92. C Liss *Portsm* 91-95; C Portsea N End St Mark 95-98; PtO 98; NSM Wymering 05-07; NSM Lee-on-the-Solent from 07. *56 Old Road, Gosport PO12 1RE*

WILLIAMS, Bryan George. b 37. **d** 01 **p** 02. OLM Fazeley *Lich* 01-05; rtd 05; PtO *Carl* from 06. *Lingmoor, 10 Laneside Road, Grange-over-Sands LA11 7BT* T: (015395) 33314

WILLIAMS, Ms Carol Jean Picknell. b 45. FCIPD 89. Ox NSM Course 86. **d** 89 **p** 94. NSM High Wycombe *Ox* 89-97; P-in-c Penn 97-01; rtd 01; PtO *Heref* from 02. *Châtelaine House, Kinsham, Presteigne LD8 2HP* T: (01544) 267067
E: caroljpwilliams@compuserve.com

WILLIAMS, Carole. *See* GARNER, Carole

WILLIAMS, Mrs Catherine Anne. b 65. Selw Coll Cam BA 87 MA 91. SEITE 98. **d** 00 **p** 01. C Chatham St Steph *Roch* 00-02; C Bishop's Cleeve *Glouc* 03-06; Dioc Voc Officer 06-10; Asst Dioc Dir of Ords 08-10; Selection Sec Min Division from 10; Nat Adv for Voc 11-15; Public Preacher *Glouc* from 11. *Ministry Division, Church House, Great Smith Street, London SW1P 3AZ* T: (020) 7898 1593 M: 07966-709577
E: catherine.williams@churchofengland.org

WILLIAMS, Ms Catherine Lois. b 51. Swansea Coll of Educn CertEd 74 Univ of Wales (Swansea) BEd 80. St Mich Coll Llan. **d** 00 **p** 01. C Gorseinon *S & B* 00-02; C Cen Swansea 03; TV 03-11; rtd 11; PtO *S & B* from 12; *Llan* from 13; *St D* from 14. *41 Ffordd y Glowyr, Godregraig, Swansea SA9 2BQ*

WILLIAMS (née BRERETON), Mrs Catherine Louise. b 69. St Aid Coll Dur BSc 90 Cranfield Univ MSc 92 Fitzw Coll Cam BTh 00. Ridley Hall Cam 97. **d** 00 **p** 01. C S Bank *York* 00-03; V Middlesbrough St Chad 03-09; TV Woughton *Ox* 09-14; Miss and Evang Officer *Glouc* from 14. *Church House, College Green, Gloucester GL1 2LY* T: (01452) 410022
E: cathi@woughton.org

✠**WILLIAMS, The Rt Revd Cecil Javed.** b 42. Punjab Univ MA(Ed) 67 Peshawar Univ MA 72. **d** 87 **p** 88 **c** 01. C Tarnab and St Jo Cathl Peshawar Pakistan 87-90; V St Jo Cathl Peshawar 90-01; Asst Bp Peshawar 01-02; C Potternewton *Ripon* 02-06; rtd 07; PtO *Bradf* 07-10. *48 Button Hill, Leeds LS7 3DA* T: 0113-262 1408 M: 07882-171040
E: cecilwilliams42@hotmail.com

WILLIAMS, Canon Cecil Peter. b 41. TCD BA 63 MA 67 Lon Univ BD 67 PhD 86 Bris Univ MLitt 77. Clifton Th Coll 64. **d** 67 **p** 68. C Maghull *Liv* 67-70; LtO *Bris* 70-91; Tutor Clifton Th Coll 70-72; Tutor Trin Coll Bris 72-91; Lib 73-81; Course Ldr 81-85; Vice-Prin 85-91; V Ecclesall *Sheff* 91-06; Hon Can Sheff Cathl 01-06; rtd 06; V Jersey Gouray St Martin *Win* 06-12; PtO *Ox* from 13. *Shalom, 23 Sandmartin Close, Buckingham MK18 1SD* T: (01280) 308394 M: 07801-353786
E: peter.williams@shalom23.co.uk

WILLIAMS, Mrs Christine Mary. b 51. City Univ BSc 72 Middx Univ BA 05. NTMTC 02. **d** 05 **p** 06. NSM Pitsea w Nevendon *Chelmsf* 05-08; TV Grays Thurrock from 08. *2 Foxleigh, Billericay CM12 9NS* T: (01277) 654370
E: christine.mwilliams@btopenworld.com

WILLIAMS, Christopher David. b 62. Spurgeon's Coll BD 99. St Jo Coll Nottm MA 06. **d** 06 **p** 07. C Haslemere and Grayswood *Guildf* 06-08; C Godalming 08-09; R Liss *Portsm* from 09. *The Rectory, 111 Station Road, Liss GU33 7AQ* M: 07803-135739 E: revchris@talktalk.net

WILLIAMS, Preb Clive Gregory. b 45. Trin Coll Bris 83. **d** 85 **p** 86. C Bedhampton *Portsm* 85-88; V Highley w Billingsley, Glazeley etc *Heref* 88-12; P-in-c Stottesdon w Farlow, Cleeton St Mary etc 08-10; RD Bridgnorth 96-05; Preb Heref Cathl 99-12; rtd 12; PtO *Portsm* from 13. *120 Hazleton Way, Waterlooville PO8 9DW* T: (023) 9259 5236

WILLIAMS, The Ven Colin Henry. b 52. Pemb Coll Ox BA 73 MA 78. St Steph Ho Ox BA 80. **d** 81 **p** 82. C Liv St Paul Stoneycroft 81-84; TV Walton St Mary 84-89; Chapl Walton Hosp *Liv* 86-89; Bp's Dom Chapl *Blackb* 89-94; Chapl Whalley Abbey 89-94; V Poulton-le-Fylde *Blackb* 94-99; Adn Lancaster 99-05; Gen Sec Conf of Eur Chs 05-10; Can Gib Cathl 07-10; TR Ludlow *Heref* from 10; Preb Heref Cathl from 14. *6 Summerfield, Ludlow SY8 2QA* T: (01584) 872143
E: colin_w@bluewin.ch

WILLIAMS, David. b 43. ACA 65 FCA. K Coll Lon AKC 69 BD 69. **d** 70 **p** 71. C Walkden Moor *Man* 70-72; C Deane 72-75; V Horwich St Cath 75-81; Hon C Chorley All SS *Blackb* 84-86; P-in-c Weeton 86-87; V Singleton w Weeton 87-97; C Lancaster St Mary w St John and St Anne 98-00; Chapl HM Pris Lanc Castle 98-00; rtd 00; PtO *Man* 02-08 and from 10. *153 Crompton Way, Bolton BL2 2SQ* T: (01524) 382362
E: goodfornowt@aol.com

WILLIAMS, David. b 49. BTh. **d** 88 **p** 89. C Lurgan etc w Ballymachugh, Kildrumferton etc *K, E & A* 88-91; I Kinsale Union *C, C & R* 91-14; Miss to Seafarers 91-14; Can Cork and Cloyne Cathls *C, C & R* 95-97; Treas Cork Cathl 97-14; Preb Tymothan St Patr Cathl Dublin 97-14; rtd 14. *Kilbeg Upper, Clonbur, Co Galway, Republic of Ireland*
E: dhw@gofree.indigo.ie

WILLIAMS, David Alun. b 65. St Thos Hosp Lon MB, BS 88 All Nations Chr Coll MA 98. Wycliffe Hall Ox BTh 94. **d** 94 **p** 95. C Ware Ch Ch *St Alb* 94-97; Crosslinks Kenya from 98; PtO *St Alb* 98-00. *PO Box 72584, Carlile College, Nairobi, Kenya* T: (00254) (2) 715561

WILLIAMS, David Frank. b 48. S Dios Minl Tr Scheme 91. **d** 94 **p** 95. NSM Romsey *Win* from 94. *24 Feltham Close, Romsey SO51 8PB* T: (01794) 524050 E: revdfw@talk21.com

WILLIAMS, David Gareth. b 58. Lon Univ BD 81. Ripon Coll Cuddesdon 82. **d** 84 **p** 85. C Chandler's Ford *Win* 84-88; C Alton St Lawr 88-90; R Crawley and Littleton and Sparsholt w Lainston 90-97; P-in-c Andover 97-09; TR Risborough Ox from 09. *The Rectory, Church Lane, Princes Risborough HP27 9AW* T: (01844) 344784
E: rector@stmarysrisborough.org.uk

WILLIAMS, David Gerald Powell. b 35. St Mich Coll Llan. **d** 62 **p** 63. C Canton St Jo *Llan* 62-64; Field Tr Officer Ch in Wales Prov Youth Coun 63-70; Prov Youth Chapl 65-70; V Treharris *Llan* 70-75; R Flemingston w Gileston and St Hilary 75-78; Warden of Ords 77-80; Dir Past Studies and Chapl St Mich Coll Llan 78-80; Sub-Warden 79-80; Dir Ch in Wales Publications and Communications 80-85; Prov Dir of Educn Ch in Wales 80-85; Dir of Miss Ch in Wales 85-87; Hon Can Llan Cathl 84-93; V Pendoylan w Welsh St Donats 87-93; R Llandudno *Ban* 93-95; Press Officer to Abp of Wales 93-00; rtd 00. *7 The Manor House, St Hilary, Cowbridge CF71 7DP*

WILLIAMS, Canon David Gordon. b 43. Selw Coll Cam BA 65 MA 69. Oak Hill Th Coll 66. **d** 68 **p** 69. C Maidstone St Luke *Cant* 68-71; C Rugby St Matt *Cov* 71-73; P-in-c Budbrooke 73-74; V 74-81; V Lenton *S'well* 81-87; TR Cheltenham St Mark *Glouc* 87-03; Hon Can Glouc Cathl 96-03; R Toodyay w Goomalling Australia 03-08; rtd 08; Miss Development P Avon Deanery 08-09; PtO *Derby* 09-11. *2 Butchers Row, High Street, Broadway WR12 7DP* T: (01386) 853849
M: 07766-837571 E: canondwilliams@westnet.com.au

✠**WILLIAMS, The Rt Revd David Grant.** b 61. Bris Univ BSocSc 83. Wycliffe Hall Ox 86. **d** 89 **p** 90 **c** 14. C Ecclesall *Sheff* 89-92; V Dore 92-02; RD Ecclesall 97-02; V Win Ch Ch 02-14; Hon Can Win Cathl 12-14; Suff Bp Basingstoke from 14. *Bishop's Lodge, Colden Lane, Old Alresford, Alresford SO24 9DY* M: 07889-547095

WILLIAMS, David Henry. b 33. Trin Coll Cam BA 56 MA 60 PhD 77. St D Coll Lamp 67. **d** 69 **p** 70. C Monmouth *Mon* 69-70; Chapl St Woolos Cathl 70-71; P-in-c Six Bells 71-76; Libya 76-79; P-in-c Crumlin *Mon* 79-80; R Llanddewi Skirrid w Llanvetherine etc 80-83; PtO 83-87; Guest Master Caldey Abbey 83-87; V Buttington and Pool Quay *St As* 87-95; Chapl Warsaw *Eur* 95-97; rtd 97; PtO *St D* from 14. *32 Cae Gwylan, Borth SY24 5LD* T: (01970) 871721
E: dhw.1933@ukonline.co.uk

WILLIAMS, Canon David Humphrey. b 23. Em Coll Cam BA 49 MA 54. St Steph Ho Ox 49. **d** 51 **p** 52. C Daybrook *S'well* 51-55; C-in-c Bilborough St Jo Bapt CD 55-62; V Bilborough St Jo 62-63; RD Bulwell 70-88; P-in-c Bestwood Park 71-78; R Hucknall Torkard 63-71; TR 71-88; Hon Can S'well Minster 75-88; rtd 88; PtO *S'well* from 88. *12 Wollaton Paddocks, Nottingham NG8 2ED* T: 0115-928 0639

WILLIAMS, David Ivan Ross. b 47. Imp Coll Lon BSc 70 Leic Univ MSc 72 ARCS 70 FBIS. STETS 00. **d** 03 **p** 04. NSM Havant *Portsm* 03-10; PtO *Ex* from 10. *11 Manor Gardens, Exbourne, Okehampton EX20 3RW* T: (01837) 851710 M: 07866-772025
E: david@dirw.demon.co.uk

WILLIAMS, David James. b 42. Chich Th Coll 67. **d** 70 **p** 71. C Charlton-by-Dover St Bart *Cant* 70-72; C Charlton-in-Dover 72-74; C Dorking w Ranmore *Guildf* 74-77; C Guildf H Trin w St Mary 77-78; P-in-c E Molesey St Paul 78-88; V Burpham 88-94; rtd 95. *1 Taleworth Close, Ashtead KT21 2PU*
T: (01372) 278056

WILLIAMS, David John. b 30. Open Univ BA 79. St D Coll Lamp 64. **d** 66 **p** 67. C Mold *St As* 66-69; C Llanrhos 69-71; R Llangynhafal and Llanbedr Dyffryn Clwyd 71-86; P-in-c Llanychan 77-85; P-in-c Llanbedr DC w Llangynhafal, Llanychan etc 86; RD Dyffryn Clwyd 86-95; R Ruthin w Llanrhydd 86-95; rtd 95; PtO *St As* from 09. *16 The Park, Ruthin LL15 1PW* T: (01824) 705746

WILLIAMS, David John. b 43. Wadh Coll Ox BA 64. St Jo Coll Nottm 73. **d** 75 **p** 76. C Newcastle w Butterton *Lich* 75-79; P-in-c Oulton 79-89; P-in-c Stone Ch Ch 84-89; V Stone Ch Ch and Oulton 89-96; P-in-c Ashley 96-04; P-in-c Mucklestone 96-04; R Ashley and Mucklestone 04-07; rtd 07. *23 Gravel Hill, Ludlow SY8 1QR* T: (01630) 672210
E: williamsjandm@btinternet.com

WILLIAMS, David John. b 52. NOC 92. **d** 95 **p** 96. C Gt Crosby St Luke *Liv* 95-99; V W Derby St Jas 99-04; Chapl R Liverpool Children's NHS Trust from 99. *Alder Hey Children's Hospital, Eaton Road, Liverpool L12 2AP* T: 0151-228 4811
E: revdw1999@hotmail.com

WILLIAMS, Canon David John. b 38. AKC 62. **d** 63 **p** 64. C Benchill *Man* 63-66; C Heywood St Jas 66-69; V Leesfield 69-73; Chapl TS Arethusa 73-74; TV Southend St Jo w St Mark, All SS w St Fran etc *Chelmsf* 74-80; V Horndon on the Hill 80-93; RD Thurrock 83-92; P-in-c Rochford 93-02; RD 96-02; P-in-c Sutton w Shopland 98-02; Hon Can Chelmsf Cathl 99-02; rtd 02; PtO *Leeds* from 02. *29 Stonebeck Avenue, Harrogate HG1 2BN* T: (01423) 522828

WILLIAMS, Canon David Leslie. b 35. ALCD 63. **d** 63 **p** 64. C Bexleyheath Ch Ch *Roch* 63-64; C Gt Faringdon w Lt Coxwell *Ox* 64-66; CMS Uganda 67-73; C Shortlands *Roch* 73-74; Fiji 74-77; V Bromley H Trin *Roch* 77-86; R Meopham w Nurstead 86-96; RD Cobham 86-96; Chapl Thames Gateway NHS Trust 96-01; Hon Can Roch Cathl 98-01; PtO from 02. *107 Ploughmans Way, Gillingham ME8 8LT* T: (01634) 372545
E: wendyanddavid@talktalk.net

WILLIAMS, David Michael. b 50. JP 86. Ex Univ BA 71 Lon Univ MA 77 FSA 81 FRSA 82. SEITE 05. **d** 08 **p** 09. NSM Redhill St Jo *S'wark* 08-10; NSM Redhill St Matt 10-11; P-in-c Gt Coxwell w Buscot, Coleshill etc *Ox* from 11. *The Vicarage, Great Coxwell, Faringdon SN7 7NG* T: (01367) 240665
E: davidwilliams24@btinternet.com

WILLIAMS, David Michael Rochfort. b 40. St Mich Coll Llan 62. **d** 65 **p** 66. C Pembroke Dock *St D* 65-68; Chapl Miss to Seamen and Ind Chapl 68-71; P-in-c Walwyn's Castle w Robeston W 68-70; R 70-71; Ind Chapl *Mon* 71-74; Hon Chapl St Woolos Cathl 71-74; V Blaenavon w Capel Newydd 74-77; Ind Chapl *St As* 77-88; V Whitford 81-87; V Ruabon 87-92; TR Cen Telford *Lich* 92-00; R Burton and Rosemarket *St D* 00-02; Chapl Miss to Seafarers Milford Haven 00-02; Southampton 02-05; rtd 05; PtO *Ox* from 05. *13 Sturt Road, Charlbury, Chipping Norton OX7 3SX* T: (01608) 811284

WILLIAMS, David Norman. b 54. Lanc Univ BSc 76 Leeds Univ BA 83. Coll of Resurr Mirfield 81. **d** 84 **p** 85. C Ireland Wood

Ripon 84-87; C Beeston 87-91; V Cross Roads cum Lees *Bradf* 91-99; V Skipton Ch Ch 99-07; P-in-c Carleton and Lothersdale 03-07; V Skipton Ch Ch w Carleton *Leeds* 07-15; rtd 15. *Shorley Croft, 8 Penrith Road, Keswick CA12 4HF*
E: dngc@hotmail.co.uk

WILLIAMS, David Paul. *See* HOWELL, David Paul

WILLIAMS, Canon David Roger. b 49. Open Univ BA. St D Coll Lamp. **d** 73 **p** 74. C Llansamlet *S & B* 73-76; C Oystermouth 76-79; V Aberedw w Llandeilo Graban and Llanbadarn etc 79-81; V Brynmawr 81-89; V Newport St Julian *Mon* 89-09; R Penarth and Llandough *Llan* 09-15; Hon Can St Woolos Cathl 09-15; rtd 15; PtO *Mon* from 15. *36 Priory Gardens, Usk NP15 1BB* E: fr.rogerwilliams@uwclub.net

WILLIAMS (formerly WRIGHT), Denise Ann. b 42. **d** 98. Par Dn Machen *Mon* 98-07; Par Dn Bedwas w Machen w Rudry 07-14; rtd 14; PtO *Mon* from 14. *16 Tollgate Close, Caerphilly CF83 3AY* T: (029) 2086 9792

WILLIAMS, Denise Laraine. b 50. Liv Univ TCert 71. NOC 00. **d** 03 **p** 04. C Padgate *Liv* 03-08; P-in-c Cinnamon Brow 08-13; TR Warrington E from 13. *The Vicarage, 1 Briers Close, Fearnhead, Warrington WA2 0DN* T: (01925) 823108

WILLIAMS, Derek. b 27. Man Univ BSc 49. St Deiniol's Hawarden 76. **d** 78 **p** 79. NSM Abergele *St As* 78-97; rtd 97; PtO *St As* 97-14. *48 Eldon Drive, Abergele LL22 7DA*
T: (01745) 833479

WILLIAMS, Derek Ivor. b 37. ACA 61 FCA 71. **d** 05 **p** 06. OLM Chollerton w Birtley and Thockrington *Newc* from 05. *Buteland House, Bellingham, Hexham NE48 2EX* T: (01434) 220389

WILLIAMS, Derek Lawrence. b 45. Tyndale Hall Bris 65. **d** 69 **p** 70. C Cant St Mary Bredin 69-71; Gen Sec Inter-Coll Chr Fellowship 71-75; LtO *St Alb* 78-84; *Bris* 85-92; PtO *Pet* 92-02; Par and Miss Co-ord Northampton St Giles 93-97; Dioc Millennium Officer 98-00; Dioc Communications Officer 00-05; *Eur* 02-05; Bp's Admin and Press Officer *Pet* 05-10; Hon C Brington w Whilton and Norton etc 02-08; LtO from 08; rtd 11; Dioc Media Adv *Pet* from 11; PtO from 12. *7 Montrose Close, Market Harborough LE16 9LJ*
T: (01858) 432709 M: 07770-981172
E: derek.williams@peterborough-diocese.org.uk

WILLIAMS, Derwyn Gavin. b 69. Trin Coll Cam BA 89 MA 93. Ripon Coll Cuddesdon. **d** 94 **p** 95. C Harpenden St Nic *St Alb* 94-97; Bp's Dom Chapl 97-00; R Sandy 00-13; RD Biggleswade 09-11; V Bishop's Stortford St Mich from 13. *St Michael's Vicarage, 8 Larkspur Close, Bishop's Stortford CM23 4LL*
T: (01279) 651415

WILLIAMS, Diana Mary. b 36. Bris Univ CertEd 56 Leeds Univ BSc 57. Oak Hill Th Coll 86. **d** 87 **p** 94. C S Mymms K Chas *St Alb* 87-95; V 95-98; R Sandon, Wallington and Rushden w Clothall 98-04; RD Buntingford 01-06; rtd 04; PtO *Ely* from 05. *7 Cockhall Close, Litlington, Royston SG8 0RB*
T: (01763) 853079 E: di.williams@btinternet.com

WILLIAMS, Ms Diane Patricia. b 53. MBE. Dur Univ CertEd 74 Lanc Univ MA 84. Cranmer Hall Dur 84. **dss** 86 **d** 87 **p** 94. Clubmoor *Liv* 86-90; Par Dn 87-90; Dioc Lay Tr Officer 90-96; Par Dn Everton St Geo 90-94; Assoc P 94-96; Chapl Lanc Univ *Blackb* 96-00; Chapl Edin Univ 00-11. *5 Roman Court, Pathhead EH37 5AH* T: (01875) 320981 M: 07779-922268
E: diwilliams.labyrinth@gmail.com

WILLIAMS, Diane Ruth. b 52. Hull Univ BA 80 Nottm Univ MA 94. Linc Th Coll 92. **d** 94 **p** 95. C Stokesley *York* 94-98; TV Louth *Linc* 98-06; Chapl Linc and Louth NHS Trust 98-01; Chapl United Lincs Hosps NHS Trust 01-06; P-in-c Needham Market w Badley *St E* from 06; RD Bosmere from 06. *10 Meadow View, Needham Market, Ipswich IP6 8RH* T: (01449) 720316 E: dnwil2@aol.com

WILLIAMS, Doiran George. b 26. Barrister-at-Law (Gray's Inn) 52. WMMTC 91. **d** 93 **p** 94. NSM Edvin Loach w Tedstone Delamere etc *Heref* 93-98; PtO from 98. *Howberry, Whitbourne, Worcester WR6 5RZ* T: (01886) 821189

WILLIAMS, Mrs Donna Ann. b 64. St Jo Coll Nottm BA 00. **d** 00 **p** 01. C Denton St Lawr *Man* 00-03; C Ashton Ch Ch 02-03; P-in-c Droylsden St Martin 03-10; P-in-c Hillock 10-14; P-in-c Unsworth 10-14; V Hillock and Unsworth from 14; C Stand from 15. *St George's Vicarage, Hollins Lane, Bury BL9 8JJ* T: 0161-796 8007 E: sweetpeawilliams@btinternet.com

WILLIAMS, Canon Dylan John. b 72. Univ of Wales (Ban) BTh 97. Ripon Coll Cuddesdon 97. **d** 99 **p** 00. C Holyhead *Ban* 99-01; C Dolgellau w Llanfachreth and Brithdir etc 01-02; P-in-c Amlwch 02-03; R 03-10; P-in-c Porthmadoc and Ynyscynhaearn and Dolbenmaen 10-11; P-in-c Bro Eifionydd 11-12; TR 12; V Bro'r Holl Saint from 12; AD Llyn and Eifionydd from 10; Asst Dir of Ords from 11; Can Ban Cathl from 12. *The Rectory, Y Maes, Criccieth LL52 0AG* T: (01766) 523743 E: canondylan@gmail.com

WILLIAMS, Edward Ffoulkes (Peter). b 34. ALA 65. Chich Th Coll 71. **d** 73 **p** 74. C Kidderminster St Geo *Worc* 73-78; TV Worc St Barn w Ch Ch 78-82; R Exhall w Wixford and V Temple Grafton w Binton *Cov* 82-00; rtd 00; PtO *Truro* from 00. *Penpons Cottage, Treviskey, Lanner, Redruth TR16 6AU* T: (01209) 820230

WILLIAMS, Prof Edward Sydney. b 23. FRCP FRCR K Coll Lon BSc PhD MB, BS MD AKC. Sarum & Wells Th Coll 84. **d** 87 **p** 88. NSM Bramley and Grafham *Guildf* 87-89; Hon C Shamley Green 89-94; PtO 94-05. *Little Hollies, The Close, Wonersh, Guildford GU5 0PA* T: (01483) 892591

WILLIAMS (née WITHERS), Eleanor Jane. b 61. Univ of Wales Coll of Medicine MB, BCh 85 Anglia Ruskin Univ MA 07 MRCGP 89. ERMC 04. **d** 07 **p** 08. NSM Milton *Ely* 07-11; V Burwell w Reach from 11. *The Vicarage, 22 Isaacson Road, Burwell, Cambridge CB25 0AF* T: (01638) 741262
E: vicar@stmarysburwell.org.uk

WILLIAMS, Canon Emlyn Cadwaladr. b 64. St Jo Coll Nottm 02. **d** 04 **p** 05. C Glanogwen w St Ann's w Llanllechid *Ban* 04-07; R Llanfihangel Ysgeifiog w Llangristiolus etc 07-12; R Seintiau Braint a Chefni 12-14; V Bro Cadwaladr from 15; AD Malltraeth from 13. *The Rectory, Holyhead Road, Gaerwen LL60 6HP* T: (01248) 421275 E: ecsaer@aol.com

WILLIAMS (née CALDERWOOD), Emma Louise. b 74. Derby Univ BSc 96 Univ of Wales (Cardiff) MTh 07. St Mich Coll Llan BTh 05. **d** 06 **p** 07. C Stanley w Stoneycroft St Paul *Liv* 06-11; V from 11. *28 Brookland Road West, Liverpool L13 3BQ* T: 0151-228 2426 E: revdem1411@btinternet.com

WILLIAMS, Eric Rees. b 30. Roch Th Coll 60 St Deiniol's Hawarden 71. **d** 72 **p** 73. C Llanelli *St D* 72-75; P-in-c Tregaron 75-76; V 76-82; RD Lampeter and Ultra-Aeron 82-87; V Tregaron w Ystrad Meurig and Strata Florida 82-87; V St Dogmael's w Moylgrove and Monington 87-98; rtd 98. *Ty Elli, 1 Heol Derw, Cardigan SA43 1NH* T: (01239) 612296

WILLIAMS, Evelyn Joyce. b 37. Cant Sch of Min 86. **d** 89 **p** 94. NSM Sittingbourne H Trin w Bobbing *Cant* 89-09; rtd 09; PtO *Cant* from 09. *32 Rock Road, Sittingbourne ME10 1JF* T: (01795) 470372

WILLIAMS, Frederick Errol. b 41. MBIM 80. Sarum & Wells Th Coll 86. **d** 88 **p** 89. C Milton *Win* 88-91; P-in-c Chilbolton cum Wherwell 91-94; R 94-06; RD Andover 99-06; rtd 06; TV S Cotswolds *Glouc* 10-14; PtO *Sarum* from 15. *Address temp unknown* E: errolsue69@btinternet.com

WILLIAMS, Gareth Wynn. *See* RAYNER-WILLIAMS, Gareth Wynn

WILLIAMS, Gavin John. b 61. Down Coll Cam BA 84 Wycliffe Hall Ox BA 88 Barrister-at-Law 85. **d** 89 **p** 90. C Muswell Hill St Jas w St Matt *Lon* 89-92; Asst Chapl Shrewsbury Sch 92-95; Chapl 95-02; Chapl Westmr Sch from 02; PV Westmr Abbey from 05. *Westminster School, Little Dean's Yard, London SW1P 3PF* T: (020) 7963 1128
E: gavin.williams@westminster.org.uk

WILLIAMS, George Maxwell Frazer. b 42. TCD BA 65 MA 69. Cuddesdon Coll 65. **d** 67 **p** 68. C Bolton St Jas w St Chrys *Bradf* 67-70; C Lich St Chad 70-73; V Shawbury 73-79; P-in-c Moreton Corbet 73-79; V Willenhall H Trin 79-86; TR 86-88; V Penn 88-07; Preb Lich Cathl 96-07; RD Trysull 02-06; rtd 07. *2 Highbury Close, Shrewsbury SY2 6SN* T: (01743) 362315

WILLIAMS, George Ola. b 55. Bradf Univ PhD 90 Waterloo Lutheran Univ MA 83. St Jo Coll Nottm MTh 95. **d** 96 **p** 97. C Enfield St Jas *Lon* 96-00; V Allerton *Leeds* from 00. *The Vicarage, Ley Top Lane, Allerton, Bradford BD15 7LT* T: (01274) 541948 E: george.williams@bradford.anglican.org

WILLIAMS, Canon Giles Peter. b 54. Lon Univ BA 77 MA 78. Trin Coll Bris 80. **d** 82 **p** 83. C Reading Greyfriars *Ox* 82-85; Rwanda Miss 85-90; Mid-Africa Miss (CMS) 90-94; Can Kigali Cathl Rwanda from 90; V Woking St Jo *Guildf* 95-10; RD Woking 08-10; Chapl Cannes *Eur* from 10. *Résidence Kent, 4 avenue Général Ferrié, 06400 Cannes, France* T: (0033) 4 93 94 54 61 F: 4 93 94 04 43
E: mail@holytrinitycannes.org

WILLIAMS, Gillian Jean Richeldis. b 47. St Mich Coll Llan. **d** 99 **p** 02. C Llanishen *Llan* 99-05; P-in-c Rhondda Fach Uchaf 05; rtd 06; P-in-c Llanishen w Trellech Grange and Llanfihangel etc *Mon* 13-14. *Faith House, 82 Kings Fee, Monmouth NP25 5BQ* T: (01600) 716696 E: revonthehill@btinternet.com

WILLIAMS, Glyn. b 54. K Coll Lon BD 77 AKC 77. Ripon Coll Cuddesdon 77. **d** 78 **p** 79. C Coppenhall *Ches* 78-81; C Northampton St Alb *Pet* 81-82; TV Birkenhead Priory *Ches* 82-85; Chapl RAF 85-90 and from 96; Dep Chapl HM Pris Wandsworth 90-91; Chapl HM Pris Elmley 91-95. *Chaplaincy Services (RAF), HQ Air Command, RAF High Wycombe HP14 4UE* T: (01494) 496800 F: 496343

WILLIAMS, Graham Parry. b 46. Bp Burgess Hall Lamp 67. **d** 70 **p** 71. C Ebbw Vale *Mon* 70-73; C Trevethin 73-74; V Nantyglo

74-76; Chapl RN 76-85; R Northlew w Ashbury *Ex* 85-87; R Bratton Clovelly w Germansweek 85-87; TV Pontypool *Mon* 88-90; C Skegness and Winthorpe *Linc* 90-91; V Sutton Bridge 91-94; P-in-c Witham Gp 94-97; P-in-c Ruskington 97-01; R 01-03; RD Lafford 02-03; P-in-c Ringstone in Aveland Gp 03-10; rtd 10. *7 Wilkie Drive, Folkingham, Sleaford NG34 0UE* T: (01529) 497632 E: frgraham@btinternet.com

WILLIAMS, Gwenllian. *See* GILES, Gwenllian

WILLIAMS, Gwilym Elfed. b 33. Univ of Wales (Lamp) BA 53. St Mich Coll Llan 53. **d** 56 **p** 57. C Llandudno *Ban* 56-59; C Aberdare *Llan* 59-63; C Penarth All SS 63-65; R Eglwysilan 65-70; V Mountain Ash 70-81; V Llanblethian w Cowbridge and Llandough etc 81-93; P-in-c St Hilary 87-91; V Lisvane 93-00; rtd 00; PtO *Glouc* 01-07. *55 Heol Llanishen Fach, Cardiff CF14 6LB* T: (029) 2062 3855

WILLIAMS, Harri Alan McClelland. b 85. Ball Coll Ox BA 07. St Mich Coll Llan BA 10. **d** 10 **p** 11. C Haverfordwest *St D* 10-13; V Milford Haven from 13. *The Nelms, 4 Pill Lane, Milford Haven SA73 2LB* T: (01646) 692476 M: 07891-473144
E: harri1985@gmail.com

WILLIAMS, Helena Maria Alija. *See* CERMAKOVA, Helena Maria Alija

WILLIAMS, Henry Gordon. b 33. JP 83. St Aid Birkenhead 57. **d** 60 **p** 61. C Radcliffe St Mary *Man* 60-63; Australia from 63; rtd 99. *36 Onslow Street, PO Box 259, Northampton WA 6535, Australia* T: (0061) (8) 9934 1259 F: 9934 1507
E: hgw@wn.com.au

WILLIAMS, Herbert Brian. b 18. BNC Ox BA 39 MA 48. Linc Th Coll 80. **d** 81 **p** 82. NSM Asterby Gp *Linc* 81-94; rtd 88; PtO *Linc* 94-97. *55 Upgate, Louth LN11 9HD* T: (01507) 608093

WILLIAMS, Hilary Susan. *See* PETTMAN, Hilary Susan

WILLIAMS, Howell Mark. b 56. Univ of Wales (Cardiff) BD 87. St Mich Coll Llan 84. **d** 87 **p** 88. C Swansea St Thos and Kilvey *S & B* 87-89; TV Aberystwyth *St D* 89-93; V Hirwaun *Llan* 93-99; V Swansea St Pet *S & B* 99-12; AD Penderi 05-12; V Swansea St Jas from 12; AD Swansea from 13. *The Vicarage, 1 Ffynone Drive, Swansea SA1 6DB* T: (01792) 470532
E: stjamesuplands1@googlemail.com

WILLIAMS, Hugh Marshall. b 38. Lon Univ MB, BS 62 Liv Univ MChOrth 71 K Coll Lon MA 10 FRCS 70. SAOMC 95. **d** 97 **p** 99. NSM Lt Compton w Chastleton, Cornwell etc *Ox* 97-01; NSM Chipping Norton 01-08; rtd 08; PtO *Ox* from 08; *Glouc* from 09; *Cov* from 09. *Wayside, Worcester Road, Salford, Chipping Norton OX7 5YJ* T: (01608) 646933
M: 07889-343456 E: hmwwayside@yahoo.co.uk

WILLIAMS, Canon Hugh Martin. b 45. AKC 73. St Aug Coll Cant 73. **d** 74 **p** 75. C Heston *Lon* 74-78; Chapl City Univ 78-84; PV Westmr Abbey 82-84; V Newquay *Truro* 84-93; V Christchurch *Win* 93-10; Hon Can Win Cathl 04-10; Preacher Charterhouse and Dep Master 10-14; V Cricket St Thomas *B & W* from 14. *14 Church Street, Crewkerne TA18 7HU* M: 07904-186414 T: (01460) 394814
E: hugh.m.williams@ukgateway.net

WILLIAMS, Ian Withers. b 43. Linc Th Coll 68. **d** 69 **p** 70. C Burney Lane *Birm* 69-72; C Cleobury Mortimer w Hopton Wafers *Heref* 72-75; V Knowbury 75-79; P-in-c Coreley w Doddington 75-79; V Lich Ch Ch 79-06; rtd 06; PtO *Heref* from 07; *Worc* from 07. *23 The Oaklands, Tenbury Wells WR15 8FB* T: (01584) 810528 M: 07711-260521
E: ian@theoaklands.com

WILLIAMS, Ifan. b 24. St D Coll Lamp 54. **d** 56 **p** 57. C Llangefni w Tregaean *Ban* 56-60; R Llanfachreth 60-67; Dioc Youth Officer 62-65; Area Sec (Merioneth) USPG 63-89; P-in-c Brithdir and Bryncoedifor *Ban* 65-67; R Ffestiniog w Blaenau Ffestiniog 67-89; RD Ardudwy 80-89; rtd 89; PtO *Ban* from 89. *Cil-y-Coed, 6 Stad Penrallt, Llanystumdwy, Criccieth LL52 0SR* T: (01766) 522978

WILLIAMS, Mrs Ikuko. b 58. Internat Chr Univ Tokyo BA 82 W Michigan Univ MA 83 Leeds Univ BA 07. NOC 04. **d** 07 **p** 08. NSM Burmantofts St Steph and St Agnes *Ripon* 07-10; NSM Leeds St Cypr Harehills 07-10; Chapl Leeds Teaching Hosps NHS Trust 10-12 and from 15. *97 Gledhow Lane, Leeds LS8 1NE* T: 0113-266 2385 E: ikuko.williams@ntlworld.com

WILLIAMS, James Llanfair Warren. b 48. St Mich Coll Llan 92. **d** 92 **p** 93. C Pembroke Dock *St D* 92-93; C Pembroke Dock w Cosheston w Nash and Upton 93-95; V Cwmaman 95-98; Chapl Costa Blanca *Eur* 98-00; V Meifod w Llangynyw w Pont Robert w Pont Dolanog *St As* 01-13; rtd 13; Hon C Yatton Moor *B & W* from 13. *Kingfisher Cottage, Back Lane, Kingston Seymour, Clevedon BS21 6XB* E: rev@jlwwilliams.plus.com

WILLIAMS, James Nicholas Owen. b 39. MBE. CEng. S'wark Ord Course. **d** 82 **p** 83. C Petersfield w Sheet *Portsm* 82-86; TV Droitwich Spa *Worc* 86-88; R Church Lench w Rous Lench and Abbots Morton 88-94; V Milton *B & W* 94-04; RD Locking 99-04; rtd 04; Dioc Ecum Officer *B & W* 04-08; Hon C Pill, Portbury and Easton-in-Gordano 04-09; PtO from 09.

151 Charlton Mead Drive, Brentry, Bristol BS10 6LP T: 0117-950 4152 M: 07808-772908 E: jnowil64@gmail.com

WILLIAMS, Janet Patricia. *See* FFRENCH, Janet Patricia

WILLIAMS, Canon Janet Patricia. b 61. Univ Coll Ox BA 83 MSt 85 K Alfred's Coll Win PhD 98. WEMTC 06. **d** 09 **p** 10. NSM Cirencester *Glouc* 09-12; Tutor WEMTC from 12; Dir Reader Tr from 12; Hon Can Glouc Cathl from 14. *April Cottage, 11 Hill View, Elkstone, Gloucester GL53 9PB* T: (01242) 870148 *or* (01452) 874969 M: 07989-707257 E: janet.williams@rcc.ac.uk

WILLIAMS, Jeff. b 62. Southn Univ BA MA MPhil Univ of Wales PGCE Surrey Univ BA. STETS 04. **d** 07 **p** 08. NSM Hedge End St Luke *Win* from 07; Dioc Dir of Educn from 14. *32 Goodlands Vale, Hedge End, Southampton SO30 4SL* T: (01489) 781448 E: jeff.w@ntlworld.com

WILLIAMS, Jeffrey. *See* WILLIAMS, Robert Jeffrey Hopkin

WILLIAMS, Jeffrey. b 52. Univ of Wales (Ban) BTh 06. Llan Ord Course 99. **d** 03 **p** 04. NSM Cardiff St Mary and St Steph w St Dyfrig etc *Llan* 03-07; Chapl Malta and Gozo *Eur* 07-13; P-in-c Chard Gd Shep Furnham *B & W* 13; V from 13. *The Vicarage, Furnham Road, Chard TA20 1AE* T: (01460) 419527 M: 07928-171187 E: fr.jeff@hotmail.com

WILLIAMS, Jennifer Ruth. b 66. St Hugh's Coll Ox BA 88 PGCE 89 Man Univ MA 00 PhD 11. Wycliffe Hall Ox 98 NOC 00. **d** 00 **p** 01. C Heatons *Man* 00-04; Hon C Burnage St Marg 04-05; Tutor Wycliffe Hall Ox from 05; NSM Wootton and Dry Sandford *Ox* from 11. *The Vicarage, Wootton Village, Boars Hill, Oxford OX1 5JL* T: (01865) 735661 M: 07784-304985 E: jenniwilliams@wycliffe.ox.ac.uk

WILLIAMS, John. *See* WILLIAMS, David John

WILLIAMS, John. b 82. St Chad's Coll Dur BA 04. Coll of Resurr Mirfield 05. **d** 07 **p** 08. C Upper Skerne *Dur* 07-10; C Liv Our Lady and St Nic 10-12; V Aintree St Giles w St Pet from 12. *St Giles's Vicarage, 132 Aintree Lane, Liverpool L10 8LE* T: 0151-476 5554

WILLIAMS, John Anthony. b 53. G&C Coll Cam BA 75 MA 79 St Jo Coll Dur BA 83 PhD 86. Cranmer Hall Dur 81. **d** 86 **p** 87. C Beverley Minster *York* 86-89; C Cloughton 89-90; P-in-c 90-93; Clergy Tr Officer E Riding 89-93; P-in-c Emley and Dioc Minl Tr Officer *Wakef* 93-98; Wakef Min Scheme 98-06; Co-ord for Local Min 02-06; Dean Wakef Min Scheme 06-08; Hon Can Wakef Cathl 08; Sen Lect York St Jo Univ from 08. *13 Marston Crescent, Acomb, York YO25 5DQ* T: (01904) 784476 E: j.a.williams23@btinternet.com

WILLIAMS, John Barrie. b 38. Univ of Wales (Cardiff) MSc 77 DipEd 80 PhD 91. St Mich Coll Llan 89. **d** 87 **p** 88. NSM Newcastle *Llan* 87-89; C Port Talbot St Theodore 89; PtO from 89. *Shorncliffe, 11 Priory Oak, Bridgend CF31 2HY* T: (01656) 660369

WILLIAMS, John Beattie. b 42. Univ of Wales BA 66. Cuddesdon Coll 67. **d** 69 **p** 69. C St Helier *S'wark* 69-70; C Yeovil H Trin *B & W* 70-76; Chapl to the Deaf *Sarum* 76-78; P-in-c Ebbesbourne Wake w Fifield Bavant and Alvediston 76-78; Chapl to the Deaf *B & W* 78-83; TV Fareham H Trin *Portsm* 83-94; R W Wittering and Birdham w Itchenor *Chich* 94-11; rtd 11; PtO *Chich* from 12. *28 Harrow Drive, West Wittering, Chichester PO20 8EJ* T: (01243) 670843 E: witteringjohn@hotmail.com

WILLIAMS, John David Anthony. b 55. Open Univ BA 98. St Steph Ho Ox 85. **d** 87 **p** 88. C Paignton St Jo *Ex* 87-90; C Heavitree w Ex St Paul 90-91; TV 91-01; P-in-c Exminster and Kenn 01-15; R Exminster, Kenn, Kenton w Mamhead, and Powderham from 15. *The Rectory, Milbury Lane, Exminster, Exeter EX6 8AD* T: (01392) 824283 E: john_williams55@btinternet.com

WILLIAMS, John Francis Meyler. b 34. St Jo Coll Cam BA 56 MA 60. Sarum & Wells Th Coll 79. **d** 81 **p** 82. C Hadleigh w Layham and Shelley *St E* 81-84; P-in-c Parham w Hacheston 84-87; P-in-c Campsey Ashe and Marlesford 84-87; R Campsea Ashe w Marlesford, Parham and Hacheston 87-95; P-in-c Kedington 95-97; rtd 97; Chapl St Kath Convent Parmoor 97-98; PtO *Ox* 01-05. *7 Capel Court, The Burgage, Prestbury, Cheltenham GL52 3EL* T: (01242) 577764 E: john.williams34@btinternet.com

WILLIAMS, John Frederick Arthur. b 26. Lon Univ BSc 50 Southn Univ PhD 53. Ridley Hall Cam 63. **d** 65 **p** 66. C Cambridge H Sepulchre w All SS *Ely* 65-66; P-in-c Cambridge St Mark 66-67; V Portswood Ch Ch *Win* 67-90; Assoc V 90-93; C Win Ch Ch 93-96; rtd 96; PtO *Win* from 96. *120 Bellemoor Road, Southampton SO15 7QY* T: (023) 8077 1482

WILLIAMS, John Gilbert. b 36. St Aid Birkenhead 64. **d** 67 **p** 68. C Bollington St Jo *Ches* 67-69; C Oxton 69-72; P-in-c Acton Beauchamp and Evesbatch w Stanford Bishop *Heref* 72-76; P-in-c Castle Frome 72-76; P-in-c Bishop's Frome 72-76; R Kingsland 76-83; P-in-c Eardisland 77-83; P-in-c Aymestrey

and Leinthall Earles w Wigmore etc 82-83; R Cradley w Mathon and Storridge 83-94; R Norton St Philip w Hemington, Hardington etc *B & W* 94-01; rtd 01; PtO *St D* from 02; *S & B* from 14. *Bronydd, 69 St Davids Park, Llanfaes, Brecon LD3 8EQ* T: (01874) 938196 E: cynwyl@tiscali.co.uk

WILLIAMS, Canon John Heard. b 35. Bris Univ BA 58. Clifton Th Coll 59. **d** 59 **p** 60. C Tunbridge Wells Ch Ch *Roch* 59-65; V Forest Gate St Sav *Chelmsf* 65-75; P-in-c W Ham St Matt 72-75; TR Forest Gate St Sav w W Ham St Matt 75-12; Hon Can Chelmsf Cathl 82-05; rtd 12. *10 Honeysuckle Close, Calne SN11 9US* E: jheardwilliams@yahoo.co.uk

WILLIAMS, John Keith. b 63. Ridley Hall Cam 95. **d** 97 **p** 98. C Potters Bar *St Alb* 97-99; C Bishop's Stortford St Mich 99-01; P-in-c Bishop's Stortford 01-08; TR Cheshunt from 08. *The Vicarage, Churchgate, Cheshunt, Waltham Cross EN8 9DY* T: (01992) 623121

WILLIAMS, Prof John Mark Gruffydd. b 52. St Pet Coll Ox BA 73 MSc 76 MA 77 DPhil 79 Ox Univ DSc FBPsS 84. EAMTC 86. **d** 89 **p** 90. NSM Girton *Ely* 89-91; PtO *Ban* 91-03; NSM Wheatley Ox 03-09; PtO from 09; Hon Can Ch From from 11. *Hollyfield Cottage, 17 Bell Lane, Wheatley, Oxford OX33 1XY* T: (01865) 422037 E: mark.williams@psychiatry.oxford.ac.uk

WILLIAMS, John Michael. b 44. CQSW 74 MBASW. St Deiniol's Hawarden 80. **d** 83 **p** 84. NSM Llanrhos *St As* 83-94; P-in-c Brynymaen w Trofarth 94-95; V 95-99; V Llanrhaeadr-yng-Nghinmeirch and Prion w Nantglyn 99-14; rtd 14; PtO *St As* from 14. *Monte Vista, Llanrhaeadr, Denbigh LL16 4HH*

WILLIAMS, Canon John Peter Philip. b 49. Open Univ BA 84. Chich Th Coll 71. **d** 72 **p** 73. C Abergele *St As* 72-77; R Henllan and Llannefydd 77-82; R Henllan and Llannefydd and Bylchau 82-11; AD Denbigh 98-09; Hon Can St As Cathl 01-11; rtd 11; PtO *St As* from 11. *72 Crud y Castell, Denbigh LL16 4PQ* T: (01745) 817319

WILLIAMS, John Roger. b 31. Bris Univ BA 55 Lon Univ BD 57. Tyndale Hall Bris 57. **d** 57 **p** 58. C Islington H Trin Cloudesley Square *Lon* 57-60; Travelling Sec IVF 60-64; V Selly Hill St Steph *Birm* 64-74; P-in-c Chilwell *S'well* 74-75; V 75-90; Dioc Tourism Officer 90-95; P-in-c Perlethorpe 90-95; P-in-c Norton Cuckney 90-95; rtd 95; PtO *Derby* 95-11; *S'well* from 11. *21 Chestnut Avenue, Nottingham NG3 6FU* T: 0115-962 2897 E: jrefw.chestnut@btinternet.com

WILLIAMS, Canon John Roger. b 37. Westmr Coll Ox MTh 97. Lich Th Coll 60. **d** 63 **p** 64. C Wem *Lich* 63-66; C Wolverhampton St Pet 66-69; R Pudleston w Hatf *Heref* 69-74; P-in-c Stoke Prior w Humber 69-74; P-in-c Docklow 69-74; V Fenton *Lich* 74-81; R Shipston-on-Stour w Honington and Idlicote *Cov* 81-92; RD Shipston 83-90; Hon Can Cov Cathl 90-00; R Lighthorne 92-00; V Chesterton 92-00; V Newbold Pacey w Moreton Morrell 92-00; P-in-c Denstone w Ellastone and Stanton *Lich* 00-05; Master St Jo Hosp Lich 05-11; rtd 11; PtO *Lich* from 11. *3 Curborough Road, Lichfield WS13 7NG* T: (01543) 419339

WILLIAMS, John Strettle. b 44. MBE 00. DipEd 73 BA 84. NOC 77. **d** 80 **p** 81. Chapl Cen Liv Coll of FE 80-85; Chapl City Coll Liv 85-09; NSM Liv St Paul Stoneycroft 80-83; NSM Liv Our Lady and St Nic 83-09; Chapl RNR 84-90; CF (TA) from 95; rtd 09. *28 Brook Street, Whiston, Prescot L35 5AP* T: 0151-426 9598

WILLIAMS, Jonathan Anthony. b 65. Wycliffe Hall Ox BTh 95. **d** 98 **p** 99. C Denton Ch Ch *Man* 98-02; R Burnage St Marg 02-05; Hon C Ox St Matt 09-11; P-in-c Wootton and Dry Sandford from 11. *The Vicarage, Wootton Village, Boars Hill, Oxford OX1 5JL* T: (01865) 735661 E: jon.williams@oxford.anglican.org

WILLIAMS, Jonathan Lane. b 59. Dorset Inst of HE 85. STETS 96. **d** 99 **p** 00. NSM Moordown *Win* from 99. *28 Queen Mary Avenue, Moordown, Bournemouth BH9 1TS* T/F: (01202) 531630 M: 07977-444186 E: jonathan.williams7@ntlworld.com

WILLIAMS, The Ven Jonathan Simon. b 60. Univ of Wales (Cardiff) BSc 81. Coll of Resurr Mirfield 83. **d** 86 **p** 87. C Gelligaer *Llan* 86-89; C Cwmbran *Mon* 89-90; TV 90-97; V Marshfield and Peterstone Wentloog etc 97-00; TR Bassaleg 00-12; AD 99-12; Adn Newport from 12; Can St Woolos Cathl from 07; Prec from 14. *The Archdeaconry, 93 Stow Hill, Newport NP20 4EA* T: (01633) 215206 E: archdeacon@newport.anglican.org *or* jonathanwilliams770@btinternet

WILLIAMS, Mrs Josephine. b 42. NOC 05. **d** 07 **p** 08. NSM Bootle Ch *Liv* from 07. *179 Worcester Road, Bootle L20 9AE* T: 0151-933 7729 F: 525 1995 E: josiewilliams1@aol.com

WILLIAMS, Ms Josephine Mary. b 47. Reading Univ BEd 78 Hatf Poly MEd 87. SAOMC 96. **d** 99 **p** 00. NSM Terriers *Ox* 99-02; Chapl HM YOI Aylesbury 02-09; rtd 09; PtO *Ox* 09-13; *Birm* from 13. *85 Newton Road, Knowle, Solihull B93 9HN* T: (01564) 898607 E: jo.williams58@gmail.com

WILLIAMS, Miss Josephine Sharne Emma. b 76. **d** 13 **p** 14. C Cen Wolverhampton *Lich* from 13. *1B Claremont Road, Wolverhampton WV3 0EA* M: 07977-142450 E: jsewilliams@gmail.com

WILLIAMS, Joyce. *See* WILLIAMS, Kathleen Joyce

WILLIAMS, Julian Thomas. b 65. Clare Coll Cam BA 87. Wycliffe Hall Ox BA 90. **d** 91 **p** 92. Min Can St D Cathl 91-94; C St D Cathl 91-94; V Cil-y-Cwm and Ystrad-ffin w Rhandirm-wyn etc 94-00; R Nursling and Rownhams *Win* from 00. *The Vicarage, 27 Horns Drove, Rownhams, Southampton SO16 8AH* T: (023) 8073 8293

WILLIAMS, Miss Juliet Susan Joyce. b 83. K Coll Lon BA 04 Anglia Ruskin Univ MA 14. Ridley Hall Cam 09. **d** 11 **p** 12. C St Agnes and Mount Hawke w Mithian *Truro* 11-14; P-in-c Boscoppa from 14. *St Luke's House, 5 Penhaligon Way, St Austell PL25 3AR* M: 07813-660961 T: (01726) 76282 E: emailjubean@gmail.com

WILLIAMS, Mrs Kathleen Joyce. b 47. Dur Univ TCert 71. St Jo Coll Nottm 03. **d** 05 **p** 06. C Exning St Martin w Landwade *St E* 05-08; V 08-12; rtd 12; Hon C Bath St Sav w Swainswick and Woolley *B & W* from 12. *St Mary's House, Upper Swainswick, Bath BA1 8BX* T: (01225) 851531 E: joyfulwilliams2004@virgin.co.uk

WILLIAMS, Keith. b 37. St Jo Coll Nottm 83. **d** 85 **p** 86. C Holbeck *Ripon* 85-88; R Swillington 88-95; V Batley All SS *Wakef* 95-01; P-in-c Purlwell 95-00; rtd 01; PtO *Leeds* from 01. *17 Kirkfield Drive, Colton, Leeds LS15 9DR* T: 0113-260 5852 M: 07709-027328 E: kwilliams000@btclick.com

WILLIAMS, Keith Douglas. b 41. EMMTC 86. **d** 89 **p** 90. NSM Netherfield *S'well* 89-07; NSM Colwick 89-07; NSM Gedling 95-07; Chapl Notts Healthcare NHS Trust 93-03; rtd 07; PtO *S'well* from 07. *36 Bramble Court, Carnarvon Grove, Gedling, Nottingham NG4 3HX* T: 0115-961 4850 E: keiwil@ntlworld.com

WILLIAMS, Keith Graham. b 38. Reading Univ MSc 70 MRICS 62. Cranmer Hall Dur. **d** 77 **p** 78. C Almondbury *Wakef* 77-81; C Chapelthorpe 81-82; V Ryhill 82-88; V E Ardsley 88-99; RD Wakef 96-99; rtd 03; PtO *Chich* from 03. *The Granary, 52-54 Belle Hill, Bexhill-on-Sea TN40 2AP* T: (01424) 734093

WILLIAMS, Kelvin George John. b 36. ALCD 62. **d** 62 **p** 63. C Bath Abbey w St Jas *B & W* 62-65; CF (TA) 64-65 and 70-79; Chapl R Nat Hosp for Rheumatic Diseases Bath 64-65; CF 65-68; C Clevedon St Andr *B & W* 68-70; V Ston Easton w Farrington Gurney 70-74; P-in-c Bradford 74-75; R Bradford w Oake, Hillfarrance and Heathfield 75-76; NSM Puriton and Pawlett 89-91; V 92-02; NSM Bridgwater Deanery 91-92; rtd 02; PtO *B & W* 03-04 and from 07; P-in-c Weston Zoyland w Chedzoy 04-07. *Highlands, Knowleyards Road, Middlezoy, Bridgwater TA7 0NY* T: (01823) 698413 E: kelvin@revwilliams.freeserve.co.uk

WILLIAMS (née HANNAH), Mrs Kimberley Victoria. b 75. Bp Grosseteste Coll BSc 98. Ripon Coll Cuddesdon BTh 01. **d** 01 **p** 02. C Machynlleth w Llanwrin and Penegoes *Ban* 01-02; C Twrcelyn Deanery 02-10; P-in-c Porthmadoc and Ynyscynhaearn and Dolbenmaen 10-11; TV Bro Eifionydd 11-12; TV Bro'r Holl Saint from 12. *The Rectory, Y Maes, Criccieth LL52 0AG* T: (01766) 523743

WILLIAMS, Lee Lawrence. b 75. St Steph Ho Ox 98. **d** 01 **p** 02. C Cowbridge *Llan* 01-04. *34 Queens Drive, Llantwit Fadre, Pontypridd CF83 2NT*

WILLIAMS, Mrs Linda Leonie Paula. b 56. UEA BA 79. SEITE 04. **d** 07 **p** 08. NSM Kenley *S'wark* 07-10; C Harpenden St Nic *St Alb* from 10. *10 Cross Way, Harpenden AL5 4RA* T: (01582) 713007 E: lindalpwilliams@hotmail.co.uk

WILLIAMS, Lloyd. b 43. Oak Hill Th Coll 71. **d** 74 **p** 75. C Laisterdyke *Bradf* 74-77; C Hoole Chee 77-80; V Rawthorpe *Wakef* 80-84; HM Pris Leeds 84-85; Chapl HM Pris Cardiff 85-88; Chapl HM Pris Aldington 88-95; R Aldington w Bonnington and Bilsington *Cant* 88-95; RD N Lympne 94-95; P-in-c Tuen Mun Hong Kong 95-99; V Clayton *Bradf* 99-03; rtd 03; PtO *York* 04-07; *Wakef* 07-14; *Blackb* from 14. *18 Fosbrooke House, 8 Clifton Drive, Lytham St Annes FY8 5RQ* T: (01253) 667011 M: 07866-604345 E: revlloydwilliams@gmail.com

WILLIAMS, Lois. *See* WILLIAMS, Catherine Lois

WILLIAMS, Mrs Louise Margaret. b 66. Lanc Univ BA 87. St Jo Coll Nottm 88. **d** 91 **p** 94. Par Dn W Ham *Chelmsf* 91-94; C Harold Hill St Geo 94-95; PtO 95-96; C Southend St Sav Westcliff 95-10; Chapl South Southend Health Care NHS Trust 97-10; R S Shoebury *Chelmsf* from 10. *The Rectory, 42 Church Road, Shoeburyness, Southend-on-Sea SS3 9EU* T: (01702) 292778 E: revlwilliams@aol.com

WILLIAMS, Marion. St Mellitus Coll 13. **d** 14 **p** 15. NSM Romford St Andr *Chelmsf* from 14; Chapl St Clare Hospice from 15. *18 Lansbury Avenue, Romford RM6 6SD* T: (020) 8559 7077 E: marionbubbs@aol.com

WILLIAMS, Marion Elizabeth. b 71. **d** 08 **p** 09. NSM Glouc St Cath 08-15; rtd 15. *6 Kingsholm Square, Gloucester GL1 2QJ* T: (01452) 538440 E: marion-williams@hotmail.co.uk

WILLIAMS, Mark. *See* WILLIAMS, Howell Mark

WILLIAMS, Mark. b 64. St Mich Coll Llan BTh 94. **d** 97 **p** 98. C Mountain Ash *Llan* 97; C Mountain Ash and Miskin 97-99; C Neath w Llantwit 99-01; C Neath 01-02; V Skewen 02-12; V Port Talbot St Theodore from 12. *St Theodore's Vicarage, Talbot Road, Port Talbot SA13 1LB* T: (01639) 883935

WILLIAMS, Mark. b 73. Pemb Coll Cam BA 94 MA 98 Ox Univ BA 98 MA 02. Ripon Coll Cuddesdon 95 Ven English Coll Rome 97. **d** 98 **p** 99. C Caerphilly *Llan* 98-00; V Walworth St Chris *S'wark* 00-10; Warden Pemb Coll Miss Walworth 00-10; P-in-c Kennington St Jo w St Jas 10; V from 10; Dioc Voc Adv from 02; Hon Canon Asante and Mampong Ghana from 15. *The Vicarage, 92 Vassall Road, London SW9 6JA* T: (020) 7735 9340 E: fr_mark@yahoo.com

WILLIAMS, Mark Andrew. b 71. STETS 11. **d** 14 **p** 15. C Portchester *Portsm* from 14. *24 Jute Close, Fareham PO16 8EZ* M: 07873-406558 E: williams_mark1@sky.com

WILLIAMS, Mark John. b 66. St Martin's Coll Lanc BA 88 PGCE 92 Heythrop Coll Lon MA 07. Cranmer Hall Dur 98. **d** 00 **p** 01. C Hockerill *St Alb* 00-03; TV Chipping Barnet 03-09; V Burnley St Matt w H Trin *Blackb* from 09. *St Matthew's Vicarage, Harriet Street, Burnley BB11 4JH* T: (01282) 424849 E: mark.john.williams@lineone.net

WILLIAMS, Mark Robert. b 62. Spurgeon's Coll Lon BA 83 Univ Coll of Swansea PGCE 84. Ripon Coll Cuddesdon 99. **d** 01 **p** 02. C Wellington and Distr *B & W* 01-05; V Belmont *S'wark* from 05; Ecum Adv Croydon Area from 13. *St John's Vicarage, Belmont Rise, Sutton SM2 6EA* T: (020) 8642 2363 E: blots@lineone.net

WILLIAMS, The Ven Martin Inffeld. b 37. SS Coll Cam BA 62 MA 92. Chich Th Coll 62. **d** 64 **p** 65. C Greenford H Cross *Lon* 64-70; Tutor Chich Th Coll 70-75; Vice-Prin 75-77; V Roath St German *Llan* 77-92; Adn Margam 92-01; Adn Morgannwg 02-04; Treas Llan Cathl 92-04; V Penydarren 92-04; rtd 04. *29 Blackfriars Court, Brecon LD3 8LJ* T: (01874) 622351

WILLIAMS, Martin Jonathan. b 63. Birm Univ BA 84. Trin Coll Bris 96. **d** 98 **p** 99. C Bisley and W End *Guildf* 98-01; C Gerrards Cross and Fulmer *Ox* 01-09; R from 09. *The Rectory, Oxford Road, Gerrards Cross SL9 7DJ* T: (01753) 883301 M: 07974-010703 E: martin.williams@saintjames.org.uk

WILLIAMS, Mary Edith. b 50. Darlington Tr Coll BEd 73. Cranmer Hall Dur 00. **d** 02 **p** 03. C Filey *York* 02-06; V 06-12; rtd 12; PtO *Leeds* from 13. *The Mill House, Parkgate Lane, Brompton on Swale, Richmond DL10 7HA* T: (01748) 811241 E: wilbaric@hotmail.com

WILLIAMS, Matthew David. b 79. Sussex Univ BSc 01. Wycliffe Hall Ox BTh 12. **d** 12 **p** 13. C Silverhill St Matt *Chich* from 12. *98 Sedlescombe Gardens, St Leonards-on-Sea TN38 0YW* M: 07986-097099 E: matthewdwilliams@live.co.uk

WILLIAMS, Mervyn Gwynne. b 66. WEMTC 97. **d** 06 **p** 07. NSM Stokesay *Heref* from 06; NSM Halford w Sibdon Carwood from 06; NSM Acton Scott from 06; PtO *Lich* from 08; Chapl Shrewsbury and Telford NHS Trust from 10. *Synolds Farm, All Stretton, Church Stretton SY6 6JP* T: (01694) 722093

WILLIAMS, Mervyn Rees. b 28. Univ of Wales (Swansea) BA 49 Lon Univ PGCE 54. St Deiniol's Hawarden 68. **d** 72 **p** 73. NSM Llangollen w Trevor and Llantysilio *St As* 72-94; rtd 94. *12 Wern Road, Llangollen LL20 8DU* T: (01978) 860369

WILLIAMS, Canon Meurig Llwyd. b 61. Univ of Wales (Abth) BA 83 PGCE 84 Univ of Wales (Cardiff) BD 90. Westcott Ho Cam 90. **d** 92 **p** 93. C Holyhead w Rhoscolyn w Llanfair-yn-Neubwll *Ban* 92-95; P-in-c Denio w Abererch 95-96; V 96-99; V Cardiff Dewi Sant *Llan* 99-05; Adn Ban 05-11; TR Bangor 06-11; TV 11; Bp's Commissary and Chapl *Eur* from 11; Can Malta Cathl from 11. *47 rue Capitaine Crespel, 1050 Brussels, Belgium* M: 07808-476270 T: (0032) (2) 213 7480 E: meurig.williams@churchofengland.org

WILLIAMS, Michael. *See* WILLIAMS, David Michael Rochford

WILLIAMS, Michael. b 70. St Jo Coll Nottm BA 98. **d** 98 **p** 99. C Shifnal *Lich* 98-01; TV Stafford 01-06; TR Penkridge 06-09; Asst Chapl Staffs Univ 09-12; Sen Chapl from 12. *D004, Beacon Building, Staffordshire University, Stafford ST18 0AD* T: (01782) 353382 M: 07887-655487 E: m.williams@staffs.ac.uk *or* revmickwilliams@btinternet.com

WILLIAMS, Michael Dermot Andrew. b 57. Ex Univ BA 86 Lon Univ MA 02. Ripon Coll Cuddesdon 90. **d** 92 **p** 93. NSM Christow, Ashton, Trusham and Bridford *Ex* 92-97; NSM Marston w Elsfield *Ox* 97-99; Chief Exec Radcliffe Infirmary NHS Trust 97-99; V Shipton-under-Wychwood w Milton, Fifield etc *Ox* 99-02; RD Chipping Norton 01-02; Exec Dir

Thames Valley HA 02-05; NSM Kennington *Ox* 04-05; Chief Exec Taunton and Somerset NHS Trust from 05; Hon C Topsham *Ex* 07-14; Hon C Wear 09-14; Hon C Topsham and Wear from 14. *3 Perriams, Old Ebford Lane, Ebford, Exeter EX3 0QB* T: (01392) 874087 E: williamsmda@btinternet.com

WILLIAMS, Michael John. b 31. St Edm Hall Ox BA 53 MA 57. Wells Th Coll 53. **d** 55 **p** 56. C Wood Green St Mich *Lon* 55-59; C Bedminster St Aldhelm *Bris* 59-62; C Witney *Ox* 62-65; C Thatcham 66-70; PtO *Ex* 70-81; C Rainhill *Liv* 81-86; Chapl Whiston Hosp 83-86; rtd 86; PtO *Ex* from 86. *1 Bramble Lane, Crediton EX17 1DA* T: (01363) 774005

WILLIAMS, Canon Michael Joseph. b 42. St Jo Coll Dur BA 68. Bernard Gilpin Soc Dur 63 Cranmer Hall Dur 64. **d** 70 **p** 71. C Toxteth Park St Philemon *Liv* 70-75; TV Toxteth St Philemon w St Gabr 75-78; Dir Past Studies St Jo Coll Dur 78-88; Prin NOC 89-99; Hon Can Liv Cathl 92-99; P-in-c Bolton St Pet *Man* 99-04; V 04-07; P-in-c Bolton St Phil 04-07; Hon Can Man Cathl 00-07; AD Bolton 02-05; rtd 07; PtO *Man* from 08. *51 Cotswold Drive, Horwich, Bolton BL6 7DE* T: (01204) 667162

WILLIAMS, Michael Robert John. b 41. Cranmer Hall Dur 67. **d** 70 **p** 71. C Middleton *Man* 70-73; C-in-c Blackley White Moss St Mark CD 73-79; R Blackley St Mark White Moss 79-86; R Gorton Em 86-96; R Gorton Em w St Jas 96-06; rtd 06; PtO *Man* from 06. *26 Hawthorn Avenue, Bury BL8 1DU* T: 0161-761 4712

WILLIAMS, Nia Catrin. b 69. Univ of Wales (Cardiff) BTh 96. St As Minl Tr Course 97. **d** 98 **p** 99. C Llanrhos *St As* 98-02; C Colwyn Bay 02-06; P-in-c Towyn and St George 06-08; V Glanogwen and Llanllechid w St Ann's and Pentir *Ban* 08-12; AD Ogwen 10-12; Can Missr Ban Cathl 12-15; CMD Officer 12-15; Dir of Ords 12-14; Dir of Voc *St As* from 15. *The Deanery, Upper Denbigh Road, St Asaph LL17 0RL* M: 07825-211978 E: niacatrin13@gmail.com

WILLIAMS, Nicholas Jolyon. b 68. Univ of Wales (Swansea) BA 89. Wycliffe Hall Ox BTh 96. **d** 96 **p** 97. C Ditton *Roch* 96-99; C N Farnborough *Guildf* 99-05; P-in-c Tongham 05-11; V Guildf Ch Ch w St Martha-on-the-Hill from 11. *Christ Church Vicarage, 25 Waterden Road, Guildford GU1 2AZ* T: (01483) 568870 E: nick@christchurchguildford.com

WILLIAMS, Nicholas Lindsey. b 62. Birkbeck Coll Lon BA 02 Kent Univ BA 09. SEITE 06. **d** 09 **p** 10. NSM Dartford H Trin *Roch* 09-11; P-in-c Darenth 11-14; P-in-c Horton Kirby and Sutton-at-Hone 13-14; V Darent Valley from 14. *Darenth Vicarage, Green Street Green Road, Lane End, Dartford DA2 7JR* E: nick.williams@rochester-diocese.org

WILLIAMS, Nick. *See* WILLIAMS, James Nicholas Owen

WILLIAMS, The Very Revd Nigel Howard. b 63. St Mich Coll Llan 93. **d** 95 **p** 96. C Denbigh and Nantglyn *St As* 95-97; P-in-c Llanrwst and Llanddoget and Capel Garmon 97-98; R 98-04; V Colwyn Bay 04-08; V Colwyn Bay w Brynymaen 08-11; AD Rhos 04-09; Dean and St As Cathl from 11; TR St As from 11. *The Deanery, Upper Denbigh Road, St Asaph LL17 0RL* T: (01745) 583597
E: nigelwilliams@churchinwales.org.uk

WILLIAMS, Norman Ernest. b 23. IEng FIEEE MIET. Llan Dioc Tr Scheme 78. **d** 82 **p** 83. NSM Llanblethian w Cowbridge and Llandough etc *Llan* 82-93; PtO *Llan* from 93. *The Poplars, Southgate, Cowbridge CF71 7BD* T: (01446) 772107
E: normanewilliams@compuserve.com

WILLIAMS, Norman Leigh. b 26. Open Univ BA 86 Trin Coll Carmarthen 83. **d** 85 **p** 86. NSM Loughor *S & B* 85-96; NSM Gower Adnry 87-96; rtd 96. *Gorwydd Villa, 13 The Woodlands, Gowerton, Swansea SA4 3DP* T: (01792) 874853

WILLIAMS, Olivia Hazel. b 55. Dun Laoghaire Inst CertEd 98 TCD BTh 01. CITC 98. **d** 01 **p** 02. C Greystones *D & G* 01-05; Abp's Dom Chapl 03-05; I Carlow w Urglin and Staplestown *C & O* from 05. *The Rectory, Green Road, Carlow, Republic of Ireland* T: (00353) (59) 913 2565
E: williams.olivia2@gmail.com *or* carlow@leighlin.anglican.org

WILLIAMS, Owen David. b 38. S'wark Ord Course 72. **d** 75 **p** 76. NSM Tatsfield *S'wark* 75-80; C Maidstone All SS w St Phil and H Trin *Cant* 80-81; C Maidstone All SS and St Phil w Tovil 81-82; V St Nicholas at Wade w Sarre and Chislet w Hoath 82-92; TV Bruton and Distr *B & W* 92-98; R Kirkby Fleetham w Langton on Swale and Scruton *Ripon* 98-03; rtd 03; P-in-c Walford and St John, Howle Hill etc *Heref* 03-08; Hon C Ross w Walford 08-10. *3 Claypatch Road, Wyesham, Monmouth NP25 3PN* T: (01600) 711518

WILLIAMS, Owen Leslie. b 80. Sussex Univ BSc 01 MSc Cam Univ BTh 13. Ridley Hall Cam 10. **d** 13 **p** 14. C Uppingham w Ayston and Belton w Wardley *Pet* from 13. *18 Siskin Road, Uppingham LE15 9UL* T: (01572) 495070
E: rev.o.l.williams@gmail.com

WILLIAMS, Canon Paul Andrew. b 62. Oak Hill Th Coll BA 91. **d** 91 **p** 92. C Ware Ch Ch *St Alb* 91-94; C Harold Wood

Chelmsf 94-99; C Langham Place All So *Lon* 99-06; V Fulwood *Sheff* from 06; Hon Can Sheff Cathl from 11. *The Vicarage, 2 Chorley Drive, Sheffield S10 3RR* T: 0114-230 1911
E: paulwilliams@fulwoodchurch.co.uk

✠**WILLIAMS, The Rt Revd Paul Gavin.** b 68. Grey Coll Dur BA 89. Wycliffe Hall Ox 90. **d** 92 **p** 93 **c** 09. C Muswell Hill St Jas w St Matt *Lon* 92-96; C Clifton Ch Ch w Em *Bris* 96-99; R Gerrards Cross and Fulmer *Ox* 99-09; Hon Can Ch Ch 07-09; Area Bp Kensington *Lon* 09-15; Bp S'well and Nottm from 15. *Bishop's Manor, Bishop's Drive, Southwell NG25 0JR* T: (01636) 812112 E: bishop@southwell.anglican.org

WILLIAMS, Canon Paul Rhys. b 58. St Andr Univ MTheol 82. Westcott Ho Cam 83. **d** 86 **p** 87. Asst Chapl Selw Coll Cam 86-87; C Chatham St Steph *Roch* 87-90; V Gillingham St Aug 90-95; Bp's Dom Chapl 95-03; Hon Can Roch Cathl 01-03; V Tewkesbury w Walton Cardiff and Twyning *Glouc* from 03; AD Tewkesbury and Winchcombe from 09; Hon Can Glouc Cathl from 06. *Abbey House, Church Street, Tewkesbury GL20 5SR* T: (01684) 293333 *or* 850959 F: 273113
E: vicar@tewkesburyabbey.org.uk

WILLIAMS, Paul Robert. b 66. Huddersfield Poly BA 88. Wycliffe Hall Ox. **d** 99 **p** 00. C Roxeth *Lon* 99-03; C Harlow St Mary and St Hugh w St Jo the Bapt *Chelmsf* 03-08; Eurasia Dir Radstock Min Mongolia from 09. *Radstock, 24 Elmfield Road, Doncaster DN1 2BA* T: (01302) 811319
E: paulwilliams@radstock.org

WILLIAMS, Mrs Pauline Mary. b 52. Univ of Wales (Cardiff) BD 96 Trin Coll Carmarthen PGCE 97. St Mich Coll Llan 00. **d** 02 **p** 03. C Coity w Nolton *Llan* 02-06; P-in-c Abercynon 06-11; V Baglan 11-13; Dioc Children's Officer 06-13; P-in-c Costa Almeria and Costa Calida *Eur* from 13. *Apartado 617, Mojácar Playa, 04638 Almeria, Spain* T: (0034) 950 478 432
E: williamspm89@hotmail.com

WILLIAMS, Canon Peris Llewelyn. b 39. Univ of Wales (Lamp) BA 59. Qu Coll Birm 59. **d** 62 **p** 63. C Upton Ascension *Ches* 62-65; C Davenham 65-68; C Grange St Andr 68-73; TV E Runcorn w Halton 73-74; V Backford 74-80; Youth Chapl 74-80; V Witton 80-86; V Hoylake 86-93; R Ches H Trin 93-02; Hon Can Ches Cathl 98-02; rtd 02; PtO *Ches* from 02; *Lon* from 02. *Padarn, 65 Long Lane, Chester CH2 2PG* T: (01244) 341305

WILLIAMS, Peter. *See* WILLIAMS, Cecil Peter

WILLIAMS, Peter. *See* WILLIAMS, Edward Ffoulkes

WILLIAMS, Peter Charles. b 50. SWMTC 98. **d** 01 **p** 02. OLM Landrake w St Erney and Botus Fleming *Truro* 01-15. *5 North Road, Landrake, Saltash PL12 5EL* T: (01752) 851260
E: peterfreda@5northroad.fsnet.co.uk

WILLIAMS, Peter Hurrell. b 34. Keble Coll Ox BA 58 MA 61. Tyndale Hall Bris 62. **d** 64 **p** 65. C Sparkbrook Ch Ch *Birm* 64-67; C Rushden St Pet 67-70; P-in-c Clapham Park All SS *S'wark* 70-78; R Stanford-le-Hope w Mucking *Chelmsf* 78-92; P-in-c St Oakley w Wix and Wrabness 96-97; R Gt Oakley w Wix and Wrabness 96-97; rtd 97; PtO *Chelmsf* from 01. *3 Hillcrest Close, Horndon-on-the-Hill, Stanford-le-Hope SS17 8LS* T: (01375) 643697

WILLIAMS, Canon Peter John. b 55. Southn Univ BTh 80. Chich Th Coll 76. **d** 80 **p** 81. C Chepstow *Mon* 80-84; C Morriston *S & B* 84-85; V Glantawe 85-88; R Reynoldston w Penrice and Llangennith 88-05; R Llangennith w Llanmadoc and Cheriton 05-14; Dioc Soc Resp Officer 88-14; Hon Can Brecon Cathl 01-14; Can Res Brecon Cathl 11-14; rtd 15; PtO *S & B* from 15. *10 Woodcote Green, Grovesend, Swansea SA4 8DR* T: (01792) 386391

WILLIAMS, Philip Allan. b 48. Bris Univ BSc 69 CertEd 74. Trin Coll Bris 86. **d** 88 **p** 89. C Heref St Pet w St Owen and St Jas 88-93; R Peterchurch w Vowchurch, Turnastone and Dorstone 93-96; P-in-c Holmer w Huntington 96-01; V 01-13; rtd 13. *128 Rugby Drive, Macclesfield SK10 2JF* T: (01625) 432037

WILLIAMS, Canon Philip Andrew. b 64. Sheff Univ BA 86. Cranmer Hall Dur 88. **d** 90 **p** 91. C Hillsborough and Wadsley Bridge *Sheff* 90-94; C Lenton Abbey S'well 94-96; P-in-c 96-02; C Wollaton Park 94-96; V Porchester from 02; AD Gedling from 05; Hon Can S'well Minster from 11. *St James's Vicarage, Marshall Hill Drive, Nottingham NG3 6FY* T: 0115-960 6185
E: phil.stjames@virgin.net

WILLIAMS, Philip James. b 52. St Chad's Coll Dur BA 73. Coll of Resurr Mirfield 74. **d** 76 **p** 77. C Stoke upon Trent *Lich* 76-80; TV 80; Chapl N Staffs Poly 80-84; TV Stoke-upon-Trent 80-84; R Shrewsbury St Giles w Sutton and Atcham 84-14; rtd 14. *Address temp unknown* E: flyingvic@btinternet.com

WILLIAMS, Philip Robert. b 78. St Mellitus Coll. **d** 13 **p** 14. C Onslow Square and S Kensington St Aug *Lon* 13-14; C Spitalfields Ch Ch w All SS from 14. *Flat D, 35 Buxton Street, London E1 5EH* M: 07815-146350
E: phil.williams@htb.org.uk

WILLIAMS, Mrs Rachel Mary. b 65. All SS Cen for Miss & Min 12. **d** 15. NSM Bolsover *Derby* from 15. *Manor*

Farm, 25 Dawgates Lane, Sutton-in-Ashfield NG17 3DA
T: (01623) 513048 E: keithandrachel@btinternet.com

WILLIAMS, Ray. b 23. Lon Univ DipEd 46. St Aid Birkenhead 56.
d 58 **p** 59. C Sparkhill St Jo *Birm* 58-60; Area Sec Chelmsf and
St Alb CMS 60-65; V Shenstone *Lich* 65-73; Asst P Blenheim
New Zealand 73-78; V Wakefield and Tapawera 78-83; P-in-c
Murchison 79-82; Asst P Nelson All SS 83-85; Asst P Havelock
and the Sounds 92-96. *8 Kivell Street, Ranui Heights, Porirua
6006, New Zealand* T: (0064) (4) 238 8911

WILLIAMS, Rhys. *See* WILLIAMS, Thomas Rhys

WILLIAMS, Richard Dennis. b 57. LTCL 79. Coll of Resurr
Mirfield 79. **d** 82 **p** 83. C Roath *Llan* 82-85; C Penarth w
Lavernock 85-88; V Abertillery *Mon* 88-95; V Tredunnoc and
Llantrisant w Llanhennock etc 95-00; V Llantrisant w
Llanhennock and Llanllowell 01; V Hay w Llanigon and
Capel-y-Ffin *S & B* from 01. *19 Gypsy Castle Lane, Hay-on-Wye,
Hereford HR3 1XX* T: (01497) 820448

WILLIAMS, Canon Richard Elwyn. b 57. Hull Univ BA 79. Coll
of Resurr Mirfield 79. **d** 81 **p** 82. C Altrincham St Geo *Ches*
81-84; C Stockport St Thos 84-85; C Stockport St Thos w St Pet
86; R Withington St Crispin *Man* 86-95; V Alveston *Cov* from
95; RD Fosse 99-07; Hon Can Cov Cathl from 06. *The Vicarage,
Wellesbourne Road, Alveston, Stratford-upon-Avon CV37 7QB*
T: (01789) 292777 E: rickvic@fsmail.net

WILLIAMS, Canon Richard Henry Lowe. b 31. Liv Univ BA 52.
K Coll (NS) BD 64 Ridley Hall Cam 54. **d** 56 **p** 57. C Drypool
St Andr and St Pet *York* 56-59; Canada 59-64; V Kirkdale
St Athanasius *Liv* 64-68; R Much Woolton 68-79; R Croft w
Southworth 79-89; Dioc Communications Officer 79-97;
Hon Can Liv Cathl 88-97; R Wavertree St Mary 89-97; rtd 97;
PtO *Liv* from 97. *16 Childwall Crescent, Liverpool L16 7PQ*
T: 0151-722 7962

WILLIAMS, Richard Huw. b 63. Bradf and Ilkley Coll BA 85.
St Jo Coll Nottm 86. **d** 89 **p** 90. C Forest Gate St Edm *Chelmsf*
89-90; C Plaistow 90-92; C Canning Town St Matthias 92-96;
V Southend St Sav Westcliff 96-10; RD Southend 05-10;
PtO 10-13; Chapl Havens Hospices 12-13; TV Chalke Valley
Sarum from 13. *The Vicarage, Nunton, Salisbury SP5 4HP*
T: (01722) 330628 M: 07833-940034
E: richard844williams@btinternet.com

WILLIAMS, Richard Lawrence. b 62. Warw Univ BSc 83
ACA 87. Wycliffe Hall Ox 95. **d** 97 **p** 98. C Wallington
S'wark 97-00; V Addiscombe St Mary Magd w St Martin 00-09;
P-in-c Cranbrook *Cant* 09-13; V 13-15; AD Weald 12-13.
The Vicarage, Waterloo Road, Cranbrook TN17 3JQ
T: (01580) 712150 E: revrwilliams@talktalk.net

WILLIAMS, Robert Jeffrey Hopkin. b 62. Univ of Wales (Abth)
BA 84 ALAM. Chich Th Coll BTh 90. **d** 90 **p** 91. C Eastbourne
St Mary *Chich* 90-94; R Upper St Leonards St Jo 94-02;
V Twickenham St Mary *Lon* from 02. *37 Arragon Road,
Twickenham TW1 3NG* T: (020) 8892 2318

WILLIAMS, The Ven Robert John. b 51. Cartrefle Coll of Educn
CertEd 72 Univ of Wales (Ban) BEd 73 MA 92. St Mich Coll
Llan BD 76. **d** 76 **p** 77. C Swansea St Mary and H Trin *S & B*
76-78; Chapl Univ of Wales (Swansea) 78-84; Children's Adv
81-88; Asst Dir of Educn 81-88; Bp's Chapl for Th Educn
83-88; R Reynoldston w Penrice and Llangennith 84-88;
R Denbigh and Nantglyn *St As* 88-94; V Sketty *S & B* 94-99;
Dir of Ords 94-99; P-in-c Port Eynon w Rhosili and Llanddewi
and Knelston 99-03; Can Brecon Cathl 95-00; Adn Gower
from 00. *35 Coedsaeson Crescent, Sketty, Swansea SA2 9DG*
T: (01792) 297817

WILLIAMS, Robert William. b 49. **d** 97 **p** 98. C W Derby
St Mary *Liv* 97-01; R Golborne 01-07; V Childwall St Dav from
07; V Stoneycroft All SS from 07. *St David's Vicarage, Rocky
Lane, Childwall, Liverpool L16 1JA* T: 0151-722 4549

WILLIAMS, Roger. *See* WILLIAMS, David Roger

WILLIAMS, Roger. *See* WILLIAMS, John Roger

WILLIAMS, Roger Anthony. b 54. Univ of Wales (Lamp) BA 76.
Bp Burgess Hall Lamp 72 Qu Coll Birm 76. **d** 78 **p** 79.
C Llanelli *St D* 78-82; V Monkton 82-86; Chapl to the Deaf
B & W 86-90; Chapl amongst Deaf People *Ox* from 90.
Denchworth House, Denchworth, Wantage OX12 0DX
T: AND MINICOM (01235) 868442 F: 867402
E: roger@williams24.freeserve.co.uk

WILLIAMS, Roger Stewart. b 54. Qu Coll Cam BA 75 MA 79.
Wycliffe Hall Ox BA 78 MA 82. **d** 79 **p** 80. C Hamstead St Paul
Birm 79-82; C Barking St Marg w St Patr *Chelmsf* 82-85;
V Mildmay Grove St Jude and St Paul *Lon* 85-95; P-in-c
Charles w Plymouth St Matthias *Ex* 95-09; Chapl Plymouth
Univ 95-09; TR Bloxwich *Lich* from 09. *Bloxwich Rectory,
3 Elmore Row, Walsall WS3 2HR* T: (01922) 476598
E: rswilliams@supanet.com

WILLIAMS, Roger Thomas. b 54. Man Univ BSc 76 Birm Univ
MSc 78 PhD 83 Pemb Coll Cam PGCE 92. Ridley Hall Cam 00.
d 02 **p** 03. C Cambridge St Martin *Ely* 02-05; V Cambridge

H Cross from 05. *Holy Cross Vicarage, 192 Peverel Road,
Cambridge CB5 8RL* T: (01223) 413343 M: 07751-601066
E: rogertw11@hotmail.com

WILLIAMS, Ronald Ernest Nathan. b 66. Univ of Sierra Leone
BSc 95. St Jo Coll Nottm MTh 05. **d** 05 **p** 06. C Cowplain
Portsm 05-09; V Rusthall *Roch* from 09. *The Vicarage, Bretland
Road, Rusthall, Tunbridge Wells TN4 8PB* T: (01892) 521357
M: 07796-655225 E: ronnierenw@hotmail.com

WILLIAMS, Ronald Hywel. b 35. St D Coll Lamp BA 62. **d** 63
p 64. C Machynlleth and Llanwrin *Ban* 63-66; C Llanaber w
Caerdeon 66-69; C Hawarden *St As* 69-73; R Llansantffraid
Glan Conwy and Eglwysbach 73-77; V Rhosllannerchrugog
77-88; R Cilcain and Nannerch and Rhydymwyn 88-92;
V Llanbadarn Fawr w Capel Bangor and Goginan *St D* 92-95;
V Llanbadarn Fawr 95-00; RD 94-00; rtd 00. *15 Maes y Garn,
Bow Street SY24 5DS* T: (01970) 820247

WILLIAMS (née TYDEMAN), Mrs Rosemary (Rose). b 47.
Roehampton Inst TCert 69. SAOMC 97. **d** 00 **p** 01. NSM
Walton H Trin *Ox* 00-03; NSM E and W Horndon w Lt
Warley and Childerditch *Chelmsf* 03-12; PtO *Ox*
from 12. *17 Wellington Avenue, Princes Risborough HP27 9HY*
T: (01844) 274225

WILLIAMS, Ms Rowan Clare. b 67. K Coll Cam BA 90 MA 93 Jes
Coll Cam BA 05 Clare Coll Cam PhD 14. Westcott Ho Cam 02.
d 05 **p** 06. C Leic Resurr 05-08; Chapl Univ Hosps Leic NHS
Trust 08-10; Chapl York Univ from 10. *St Lawrence's Vicarage,
11 Newland Park Close, York YO10 3HW* T: (01904) 415460
M: 07919-861912 E: rcw514@york.ac.uk

WILLIAMS, Canon Roy. b 28. Ely Th Coll 58. **d** 60 **p** 61.
C Daybrook *S'well* 60-63; V Bilborough St Jo 63-73; V Arnold
73-92; Hon Can S'well Minster 85-92; rtd 92; PtO *S'well*
from 92. *10 Maris Drive, Burton Joyce, Nottingham NG14 5AJ*
T: 0115-931 2030

WILLIAMS, Mrs Sandra Elizabeth. b 60. STETS 06. **d** 09 **p** 10.
C Wrockwardine Deanery *Lich* 09-13; NSM Appleshaw,
Kimpton, Thruxton, Fyfield etc *Win* from 13. *St Peter's
Vicarage, High Street, Shipton Bellinger, Tidworth SP9 7UF*
E: sandra.williams3@btinternet.com

WILLIAMS (née CROSLAND), Mrs Sarah Rosita. b 50. St Mary's
Coll Chelt CertEd 71 BEd 72. EAMTC 01. **d** 03 **p** 04.
C Warmley, Syston and Bitton *Bris* 03-06; Asst Chapl Tervuren
Eur 06-09; P-in-c Lydd *Cant* 09-13; R Brookland, Fairfield,
Brenzett w Snargate etc from 13. *All Saints' Rectory, Park Street,
Lydd, Romney Marsh TN29 9AY* T: (01797) 320345
E: revsarahwilliams@porfalas.plus.com

WILLIAMS, Canon Shamus Frank Charles. b 57. St Cath Coll
Cam BA 79 MA 83. Ripon Coll Cuddesdon 81. **d** 84 **p** 85.
C Swanage and Studland *Sarum* 84-87; C St Alb St Pet *St Alb*
87-90; TV Saffron Walden w Wendens Ambo and Littlebury
Chelmsf 90-95; R Shingay Gp *Ely* from 95; RD Shingay 97-13;
Hon Can Ely Cathl from 05. *18 High Street, Guilden Morden,
Royston SG8 0JP* T: (01763) 853067
E: shamuswilliams@waitrose.com

WILLIAMS, Mrs Sheena Jane. b 72. Aber Univ LLB 95 Win Univ
MA 11. STETS 07. **d** 10 **p** 11. C Swaythling *Win* 10-14;
C Chandler's Ford from 14. *45 Pantheon Road, Chandler's Ford,
Eastleigh SO53 2PD* T: (023) 8057 0459 M: 07787-155321
E: rev@williamspost.me.uk

WILLIAMS, Stephen Clark. b 47. Univ of Wales (Cardiff)
BSc(Econ) 69 Warw Univ MSc 70. Wycliffe Hall Ox 91. **d** 93
p 94. C High Wycombe *Ox* 93-96; C Walton H Trin 96-97;
TV 97-03; Acting TR 01-03; P-in-c E and W Horndon w
Lt Warley and Childerditch *Chelmsf* 03-12; Hon Chapl
05-12; rtd 12; PtO *Ox* from 12. *17 Wellington Avenue, Princes
Risborough HP27 9HY* T: (01844) 274225
E: stevecgs2003@yahoo.co.uk

WILLIAMS, Stephen Grant. b 51. K Coll Lon BD 73 AKC 73.
d 75 **p** 76. C Paddington Ch Ch *Lon* 75-78; C Paddington
St Jas 78-80; Chapl LSE 80-91; Chapl (Sen) Lon Univs 91-15;
rtd 15. *Address temp unknown*

WILLIAMS, Stephen James. b 52. Lon Univ BSc 73. Ridley Hall
Cam 73. **d** 78 **p** 79. C Waltham Abbey *Chelmsf* 78-82;
C Bedford St Paul *St Alb* 82-86; P-in-c Chalgrave 86-88;
V Harlington from 86. *The Vicarage, Church Road, Harlington,
Dunstable LU5 6LE* T: (01525) 872413
E: sjw@harlingtonchurch.org.uk or sjw@lutonsfc.ac.uk

WILLIAMS, The Very Revd Stephen John. b 49. Univ of NSW
BA 73 DipEd 73 Cam Univ BA 77 MA 81 Macquarie Univ
(NSW) MA 92. Ridley Hall Cam 75. **d** 78 **p** 79. Lect Th Bp
Tucker Coll Uganda 78; C Brompton H Trin w Onslow Square
St Paul *Lon* 79-82; C Shenton Park Australia 82-83; Chapl Blue
Mountains Gr Sch 84-90; R W Lindfield 91-01; Dean Armidale
from 02. *PO Box 749, Armidale NSW 2350, Australia* T: (0061)
(2) 6772 2269 F: 6772 0188 E: dean@northnet.com.au

WILLIAMS, Stephen Lionel. b 48. St Kath Coll Liv CertEd 73
Open Univ BA 77. NOC 93. **d** 96 **p** 97. NSM Hough Green

St Basil and All SS *Liv* 96-99; C Padgate 99-02; V Walton St Jo 02-13; rtd 13. *51 King Street, Liverpool L19 8EE* T: 0151-291 0214 E: frstephen320@hotmail.com

WILLIAMS, Canon Stephen Stuart. b 60. Magd Coll Ox BA 82 Dur Univ BA 88. Cranmer Hall Dur 86. **d** 89 **p** 90. C W Derby Gd Shep *Liv* 89-93; Relig Affairs Producer BBC Radio Merseyside 92-00; TV Liv Our Lady and St Nic w St Anne 93-01; P-in-c Prestwich St Gabr *Man* from 01; C Prestwich St Mary from 10; C Prestwich St Marg from 10; Bp's Dom Chapl 01-05; Interfaith Adv from 05; Hon Can Man Cathl from 10. *St Gabriel's Vicarage, 8 Bishops Road, Prestwich, Manchester M25 0HT* T: 0161-773 8839 or 792 2096 M: 07813-436170 E: saintgabriel@talktalk.net

WILLIAMS, Susan. b 50. Swansea Coll of Educn CertEd 72. Ban Ord Course 94. **d** 97 **p** 98. NSM Criccieth w Treflys *Ban* 97-00; P-in-c 00-01; P-in-c Criccieth and Treflys w Llanystumdwy etc 01-02; R 02-10; rtd 11; PtO *Ban* from 11. *Taleifion, High Street, Criccieth LL52 0RN* T: (01766) 523222 or (01248) 354999 F: 523183 E: rev.sue-williams@btopenworld.com

WILLIAMS, Mrs Susan Glynnis. b 41. Nottm Univ MA 00. EMMTC 05. **d** 06 **p** 07. NSM Graffoe Gp *Linc* from 06. *69 High Street, Navenby, Lincoln LN5 0ET* T: (01522) 810445

WILLIAMS, Ms Susan Jean. b 54. Ches Coll of HE MTh 00 Lanc Univ MA 02 PhD 09. NOC 95. **d** 98 **p** 99. C Prescot *Liv* 98-01; PtO *Blackb* 01-02; C Scotforth 02-05; P-in-c Chipping and Whitewell 05-09; Warden of Readers and Past Assts 09-13; Hon C Balderstone, Mellor and Samlesbury 11-13; V from 13; Hon C Salesbury and Langho Billington 11-13; Vice-Prin LCTP 05-13. *The Vicarage, Church Lane, Mellor, Blackburn BB2 7JL* T: (01254) 812154 E: williams.ammasue@gmail.com

WILLIAMS, Mrs Susan Merrilyn Marsh. b 62. Univ of Wales (Ban) BTh 05. Ban Ord Course 00. **d** 03 **p** 04. C Botwnnog w Bryncroes w Llangwnnadl w Penllech *Ban* 03-08; P-in-c Nefyn w Tudweiliog w Llandudwen w Edern 08-11; V 11-12; TV Sidmouth, Woolbrook, Salcombe Regis, Sidbury etc *Ex* from 12. *The Vicarage, Harcombe Lane, Sidford, Sidmouth EX10 9QN* T: (01395) 516036 E: susie.williams@sidvalley.org.uk

WILLIAMS, Suzan. b 71. WEMTC. **d** 11 **p** 12. C Church Stretton *Heref* from 11. *26 Churchill Road, Church Stretton SY6 6AE* T: (01694) 722588 M: 07921-825532 E: suzan.williams@strettonparish.org.uk

WILLIAMS, Terence. b 36. Univ of Wales (Abth) BSc 57 Univ of Wales (Cardiff) MA 67 Aston Univ PhD 71. Glouc Sch of Min 78. **d** 81 **p** 81. NSM Deerhurst, Apperley w Forthampton and Chaceley *Glouc* 81-87; NSM Tarrington w Stoke Edith, Aylton, Pixley etc *Heref* 87-88; P-in-c Upper and Lower Slaughter w Eyford and Naunton *Glouc* 88-91; P-in-c Redmarley D'Abitot, Bromesberrow w Pauntley etc 91-95; R 95-99; RD Forest N 95-99; rtd 99; PtO *Glouc* 99-02; P-in-c Hasfield w Tirley and Ashleworth 02-05. *Meadowside, Gloucester Road, Hartpury, Gloucester GL19 3BT* T: (01452) 700644

WILLIAMS, Terence James. b 76. St Jo Coll Dur BA 05. Cranmer Hall Dur 02. **d** 05 **p** 06. C Bolsover *Derby* 05-09; C Codnor 09-13; P-in-c Horsley and Denby and C Morley w Smalley and Horsley Woodhouse 11-13; P-in-c Loscoe 12-13; RD Heanor 11-13; PtO from 13; Dioc President Children's Soc from 14. *The Vicarage, Church Street, Horsley, Derby DE21 5BR* T: (01332) 880284 E: wterry774@aol.com

WILLIAMS, Terence John. b 36. Univ of Wales BSc 62. St Deiniol's Hawarden 85. **d** 86 **p** 87. C Llangyfelach *S & B* 86-88; C Morriston 88-89; V Llanwrtyd w Llanddulas in Tir Abad etc 89-91; V Llanedi w Tycroes and Saron *St D* 91-00; rtd 01. *Coedmawr, 50 Swansea Road, Penllergaer, Swansea SA4 9AQ* T: (01792) 892110

WILLIAMS, Thomas Bruce. b 41. Oak Hill Th Coll 74. **d** 76 **p** 77. C Liskeard w St Keyne and St Pinnock *Truro* 76-79; Min Bush Ch Aid Soc Paraburdoo Australia 79-80; C W Pilbara 79-81; R Wyndham and Kununarra 81-83; R Wyalkatchem w Dowerin and Koorda 83-87; R Tennan Creek 93-97; rtd 99; PtO Bendigo Australia from 99. *1 Thomas Street, Bendigo Vic 3550, Australia* T: (0061) (3) 5444 0485

WILLIAMS, Thomas Rhys. **d** 04 **p** 05. NSM Llandygai and Maes y Groes *Ban* 04-05; NSM Bangor 05-13; rtd 13; PtO *Ban* from 14. *Groeslon, Talybont, Bangor LL57 3YG* T: (01248) 372934

WILLIAMS, Timothy John. b 64. Kent Univ BA 86. St Mich Coll Llan BD 89. **d** 89 **p** 90. C Killay *S & B* 89-91; C Llwynderw 91-94; V Knighton and Norton 94-00; P-in-c Whitton and Pilleth and Cascob etc 99-00; V Killay from 00; Dioc Communications Officer from 10. *The Vicarage, 30 Goetre Fach Road, Killay, Swansea SA2 7SG* T: (01792) 204233 E: fr_tim_williams@ntlworld.com

WILLIAMS, Timothy John. b 54. BEd 83. Trin Coll Carmarthen. **d** 89 **p** 90. NSM Llansamlet *S & B* 89-97; P-in-c Bryngwyn and Newchurch and Llanbedr etc 97-01; V Aberedw w Llandeilo Graban and Llanbadarn etc 01-10; V Brecon St David w

Llanspyddid and Llanilltyd from 10. *Maes y Haf, Llanspyddid, Brecon LD3 8PB* T: (01874) 624774 E: timothy.williams462@btinternet.com

WILLIAMS, Mrs Tracey Lyn. b 62. Bris Univ BSc 83 MSc 85 PhD 88. Ripon Coll Cuddesdon 08. **d** 11 **p** 12. NSM Sunninghill and S Ascot *Ox* from 11. *14 Devon Chase, Warfield, Bracknell RG42 3JN* M: 07856-745434 E: tracey@ssaparish.org

✥**WILLIAMS, The Rt Revd Trevor Russell.** b 48. TCD BA 71. St Jo Coll Nottm BA 73. **d** 74 **p** 75 **c** 08. C Maidenhead St Andr and St Mary *Ox* 74-77; Asst Chapl QUB 78-80; Relig Broadcasting Producer BBC 81-88; I Newcastle *D & D* 88-93; Ldr Corrymeela Community 93-03; I Belfast H Trin and St Silas *Conn* 03-08; Preb Rathmichael St Patr Cathl Dublin 02-08; Bp L & K 08-14; rtd 14. *50 Murlough View, Dundrum, Newcastle BT33 0WE* T: (028) 4375 1838 E: bishoptrevor.williams@gmail.com

WILLIAMS, Canon Trevor Stanley Morlais. b 38. Jes Coll Ox BA 63 Univ of E Africa MA 67. Westcott Ho Cam BA 67. **d** 67 **p** 68. C Clifton St Paul *Bris* 67-70; Asst Chapl Bris Univ 67-70; Chapl and Fell Trin Coll Ox 70-05; Hon Can Ch Ch *Ox* 95-05; rtd 05. *13 Southmoore End, Oxford OX2 6RF* T: (01865) 553975 E: trevor.williams@trinity.ox.ac.uk

WILLIAMS, Valerie Jane. b 53. **d** 03 **p** 04. OLM Merstham and Gatton *S'wark* 03-10; OLM Merstham, S Merstham and Gatton from 10. *Merstham Lodge, Harps Oak Lane, Merstham, Redhill RH1 3AN* T: (01737) 644850 E: valwilliams@vwilliams99.freeserve.co.uk

WILLIAMS, Walter Haydn. b 31. Univ of Wales (Lamp) BA 53 Selw Coll Cam BA 55 MA 60. St Mich Coll Llan 55. **d** 56 **p** 57. C Denbigh *St As* 56-58; V Choral St As Cathl 58-61; C St As 58-61; R Llanfyllin 61-68; V Northop 68-73; V Mold 73-86; RD 79-86; Can St As Cathl 77-82; Prec 81-82; Preb and Chan 82-86; R Overton and Erbistock and Penley *St As* 86-94; Chmn Ch of Wales Liturg Cttee 86-94; rtd 94; PtO *St As* 09-14. *2 Park Lane, Craig y Don, Llandudno LL30 1PQ* T: (01492) 877294

WILLIAMS, Warren. *See* WILLIAMS, James Llanfair Warren

WILLIAMS, William David Brynmor. b 48. Open Univ BA 89. St D Coll Lamp 71. **d** 72 **p** 73. C Killay *S & B* 72-74; C Wokingham All SS *Ox* 74-75; CF 75-77; C Spilsby w Hundleby *Linc* 83-87; R Meppershall w Campton and Stondon *St Alb* 87-90; V Hemsby *Nor* 90-96; P-in-c Winterton w E and W Somerton and Horsey 94-96; rtd 96. *The Old School, 14 Weekley, Kettering NN16 9UW* T: (01536) 417612

WILLIAMS, William Garmon. b 42. Univ of Wales (Abth) BA 64. Linc Univ Sch of Th & Min Studies 04. **d** 09 **p** 10. OLM Spring Line Gp *Linc* from 09; Chapl Linc Distr Health Services and Hosps NHS Trust from 10. *16 The Green, Ingham, Lincoln LN1 2XT* T/F: (01522) 730365 M: 07811-347579 E: jennywilliams.bees@virgin.net

WILLIAMS-HUNTER, Ian Roy. b 44. Trin Coll Bris 71. **d** 73 **p** 74. C Redhill H Trin *S'wark* 73-75; C Deane *Man* 76-80; R Hartshorne *Derby* 80-02; P-in-c Bretby w Newton Solney 01-02; R Hartshorne and Bretby 02-11; rtd 11. *85 Hall Street, Church Gresley, Swadlincote DE11 9QT* T: (01283) 217866 *or* 224602 E: ianrwhunter@aol.com *or* ianrwhunter@sky.com

✥**WILLIAMS OF OYSTERMOUTH The Rt Revd and Rt Hon Lord (Rowan Douglas).** b 50. PC 02. Ch Coll Cam BA 71 MA 75 Wadh Coll Ox DPhil 75 DD 89 Erlangen Hon DrTheol 99 FBA 90 Hon FGCM 00. Coll of Resurr Mirfield 75. **d** 77 **p** 78 **c** 92. Tutor Westcott Ho Cam 77-80; Hon C Chesterton St Geo *Ely* 80-83; Lect Div Cam 80-86; Dean Clare Coll Cam 84-86; Can Th Leic Cathl 81-92; Lady Marg Prof Div Ox Univ 86-92; Can Res Ch Ch *Ox* 86-92; Bp Mon 92-02; Abp Wales 99-02; Abp Cant 02-12; Master Magd Coll Cam from 13; Hon Asst Bp Ely from 13; Hon Can Ely Cathl from 14. *Magdalene College, Cambridge CB3 0AG* T: (01223) 332100

WILLIAMS-POTTER, Mrs Amanda Clare. b 69. Univ of Wales (Ban) BD 90. Westcott Ho Cam 90. **d** 92 **p** 97. C Carmarthen St Dav *St D* 92-94; Chapl Trin Coll Carmarthen 94-99; V Llan-non *St D* 99-01; TV Cwm Gwendraeth 01-05; C Cynwil Elfed and Newchurch 05-06; C Cynwyl Elfed w Newchurch and Trelech a'r Betws 06-07; Bp's Chapl and Communications Officer 05-08. *3 Blende Road, Llandeilo SA19 6NE*

WILLIAMSON, Alfred Michael. b 28. Kelham Th Coll 53. **d** 58 **p** 59. C Nottingham St Geo w St Jo *S'well* 58-64; SSM 60-64; V Kenwyn St Geo *Truro* 64-73; V St Agnes 73-87; R Beverley w Brookton Australia 87-93; rtd 93. *19 Lakeview Crescent, Forster NSW 2428, Australia* T: (0061) (2) 6554 8702 E: coomba@tsn.cc

WILLIAMSON, Alister. *See* WILLIAMSON, Ivan Alister

WILLIAMSON, Andrew John. b 39. MRPharmS 62. St Alb Minl Tr Scheme 82. **d** 85 **p** 86. NSM Oxhey All SS *St Alb* 85-88; NSM Bricket Wood 88-97; NSM Campbeltown *Arg* 97-08;

LtO 08-13; PtO *Win* from 13. *6 Julius Close, Chandlers Ford SO53 2AB* M: 07970-708191 E: andrew.ajgsw@gmail.com

WILLIAMSON, Mrs Anne Campbell. b 57. **d** 04 **p** 05. NSM Blackheath St Jo *S'wark* 04-13; Co-ord Chapl Greenwich and Bexley Cottage Hospice 08-12; PtO *Roch* 10-14; USA from 13. *St John's Church, 101 Chapel Street, Portsmouth NI1 03801-3806, USA* T: (001) (603) 436 8283 E: annecwilliamson@aol.com

WILLIAMSON, Canon Anthony William. b 33. OBE 77 DL 98. Trin Coll Ox BA 56 MA 60. Cuddesdon Coll 56. **d** 60 **p** 61. Hon C Cowley St Jas *Ox* 60-79; TV 79-89; Dir of Educn (Schs) 89-00; Hon Can Ch Ch *Ox* 90-00; rtd 00. *9 The Goggs, Watlington OX49 5JX* T: (01491) 612143 E: tony_williamson@lineone.net

WILLIAMSON, Brian. *See* WILLIAMSON, John Brian Peter

WILLIAMSON, David Barry. b 56. St Jo Coll Nottm 80. **d** 83 **p** 84. C N Mymms *St Alb* 83-86; C Burley *Ripon* 86-92; Project Worker CECS 92-96; Youth and Children's Adv *B & W* 96-04; Dir Time For God 04-11; P-in-c Shepton Mallet w Doulting *B & W* 11-14. *34 Spencers Way, Harrogate HG1 3DN*

WILLIAMSON, Desmond Carl. b 63. QUB BSc 84 Westmr Coll Ox MTh 03. Trin Coll Bris 03. **d** 05 **p** 06. C Portishead *B & W* 05-10; V Tattenham Corner *Guildf* from 10. *St Mark's Vicarage, St Mark's Road, Epsom KT18 5RD* T: (01737) 353011 E: deswilliamson@tiscali.co.uk *or* minister@stmarkschurch.me.uk

WILLIAMSON, Gary. b 50. Surrey Univ BA 72 MA 92 MITI 01 MCIL 07. **d** 14 **p** 15. OLM Pirbright *Guildf* from 14. *Round Meadow, Aldershot Road, Pirbright, Woking GU24 0DQ* T: (01483) 236909 M: 07780-872897 E: revdgarywilliamson@yahoo.co.uk

WILLIAMSON, Henry Lyttle (Ray). b 47. Lon Bible Coll BA 02. **d** 95 **p** 96. P-in-c Edin St Marg 96-02; P-in-c Edin St Salvador 02-04; NSM Edin St Ninian 04-07. *6/5 St Triduana's Rest, Edinburgh EH7 6LN* T: 0131-652 0111 M: 07548-740250

WILLIAMSON, Ivan Alister. b 63. TCD BTh 90. CITC 87. **d** 90 **p** 91. C Lisburn St Paul *Conn* 90-95; C Roxbourne St Andr *Lon* 95-99; Lect QUB from 95; Bp's C Ematris w Rockcorry, Aghabog and Aughnamullan *Clogh* 99-01; I Errigle Keerogue w Ballygawley and Killeshil *Arm* 05-10. *Richmond Rectory, 24 Old Omagh Road, Ballygawley, Dungannon BT70 2AA* T: (028) 8556 7857 M: 07814-983746 E: revdalisterwilliamson@yahoo.co.uk

WILLIAMSON, Mrs Jennifer Irene. b 44. Glas Univ MA 66 Sunderland Poly Dip Teaching 79. NEOC 89. **d** 92 **p** 94. NSM Easby w Brompton on Swale and Bolton on Swale *Ripon* 92-95; P-in-c Gilling and Kirkby Ravensworth 95-05; rtd 05. *65 Whitefields Drive, Richmond DL10 7DL* T: (01748) 824365

WILLIAMSON, John Brian Peter. b 30. Selw Coll Cam PhD 55 CEng EurIng FIMechE FIEE FInstP FWeldI. WMMTC. **d** 84 **p** 87. NSM Malvern H Trin and St Jas *Worc* 84-94; PtO from 94. *Monkfield House, Newland, Malvern WR13 5BB* T: (01905) 830522 E: jbpwilliamson@iee.org

WILLIAMSON, Kathleen Lindsay. b 50. Leeds Univ Medical Sch MB, ChB 74 Liv Univ BSc 87. NOC 00. **d** 03 **p** 04. NSM Stretton and Appleton Thorn *Ches* 03-06; NSM Frodsham from 06. *37 Waterside Drive, Frodsham WA6 7NF* M: 07899-664068 E: kath@kathwilliamson.org.uk

WILLIAMSON, Mrs Mary Christine. b 46. Bulmershe Coll of HE BEd 79. SWMTC 05. **d** 09 **p** 10. NSM Launceston *Truro* from 09. *73 St John's Road, Launceston PL15 7DE* T: (01566) 778902 M: 07900-477181 E: mary878williamson@btinternet.com

WILLIAMSON, Michael. *See* WILLIAMSON, Alfred Michael

WILLIAMSON, Canon Michael John. b 39. ALCD 63. **d** 64 **p** 65. C Pennington *Man* 64-67; C Higher Openshaw 67-69; P-in-c Man St Jerome w Ardwick St Silas 69-72; C-in-c Holts CD 72-77; R Droylsden St Mary 77-04; Hon Can Man Cathl 97-04; rtd 04; PtO *Man* from 04. *49 Ennerdale Road, Astley, Tyldesley, Manchester M29 7AR* T: (01942) 870274

WILLIAMSON, Olwen Joan. b 43. **d** 03 **p** 04. OLM Mortlake w E Sheen *S'wark* 03-13; PtO from 13. *25 Christchurch Road, London SW14 7AB* T/F: (020) 8876 7183 E: olwenontour@hotmail.com

WILLIAMSON, Paul Nicholas. b 55. Univ of Otago BTh 79 Nottm Univ MPhil 93. St Jo Coll Auckland 80. **d** 80 **p** 81. C Andersons Bay New Zealand 80-82; V Winton-Otautau 82-86; C Selston *S'well* 86-88; V St Kilda New Zealand 88-90; Min Educator 88-92; V Milton-Tuapeka and Taieri 92-96; V Hataitai-Kilbirnie from 96; Nat Co-ord Angl Renewal Min 99-03; Ldr New Wine from 03. *94 Hamilton Road, Hataitai, Wellington 6021, New Zealand* T: (0064) (4) 971 2140 *or* 386 3042 F: 386 3041 E: leader@new-wine.net.nz

WILLIAMSON, Paul Stewart. b 48. K Coll Lon BD 71 AKC 71. **d** 72 **p** 73. C Deptford St Paul *S'wark* 72-75; Hon C Kennington St Jo 76-77; C Hoxton H Trin w St Mary *Lon* 78-83; C St Marylebone All SS 83-84; C Willesden St Mary 84-85; PtO 86-89; C Hanworth St Geo 89-92; P-in-c

from 92. *The Rectory, 7 Blakewood Close, Feltham TW13 7NL* T: (020) 8844 0457

WILLIAMSON, Ralph James. b 62. LSE BSc(Econ) 84. Ripon Coll Cuddesdon BA 89 MA 97 MTh 05. **d** 90 **p** 91. C Southgate St Andr *Lon* 90-93; TV Ross w Brampton Abbotts, Bridstow, Peterstow etc *Heref* 93-97; Chapl Ch Ch Ox 97-15; V Pimlico St Pet w Westmr Ch Ch *Lon* from 15. *1 St Peter's House, 119 Eaton Square, London SW1W 9AL* T: (020) 7235 4242 E: vicar@stpetereatonsquare.co.uk

WILLIAMSON, Ray. *See* WILLIAMSON, Henry Lyttle

WILLIAMSON, Robert Harvey (Robin). b 45. **d** 02 **p** 03. OLM Maidstone St Luke *Cant* 02-15; rtd 15. *Holly Bank, Bower Mount Road, Maidstone ME16 8AU* T: (01622) 682959 E: robin.helen@tesco.net

WILLIAMSON, Robert John. b 55. K Coll Lon BA 77. Coll of Resurr Mirfield 78. **d** 79 **p** 80. C Kirkby *Liv* 79-82; C Warrington St Elphin 82-84; P-in-c Burneside *Carl* 84-90; V Walney Is 90-00; V Darlington St Cuth *Dur* from 00. *The Vicarage, 26 Upsall Drive, Darlington DL3 8RB* T: (01325) 358911

✠**WILLIAMSON, The Rt Revd Robert Kerr (Roy).** b 32. Kingston Univ DEd 98. Oak Hill Th Coll 61. **d** 63 **p** 64 **c** 84. C Crowborough *Chich* 63-66; V Hyson Green *S'well* 66-72; V Nottingham St Ann w Em 72-76; V Bramcote 76-79; Adn Nottingham 78-84; Bp Bradf 84-91; Bp S'wark 91-98; rtd 98; Hon Asst Bp S'well and Nottm from 98. *30 Sidney Road, Beeston, Nottingham NG9 1AN* T/F: 0115-925 4901 E: roywilliamson@waitrose.com

WILLIAMSON, Robin. *See* WILLIAMSON, Robert Harvey

WILLIAMSON, Roger Brian. b 38. Imp Coll Lon BSc 59 MIET 61. St Steph Ho Ox 01. **d** 02 **p** 03. NSM Harting w Elsted and Treyford cum Didling *Chich* 02-05; P-in-c Stedham w Iping 05-15; rtd 15. *Hawthorn Cottage, North Lane, South Harting, Petersfield GU31 5PY* M: 07767-266031 E: rogerwilliamson1@btinternet.com

WILLIAMSON, Mrs Sheilagh Catherine. b 54. Dur Inst of Educn CertEd 76 St Martin's Coll Lanc MA 00. CBDTI 97. **d** 00 **p** 01. C Darlington St Hilda and St Columba *Dur* 00-03; P-in-c from 03; P-in-c Darlington St Jo from 13. *The Vicarage, 26 Upsall Drive, Darlington DL3 8RB* T: (01325) 358911

WILLIAMSON, Canon Thomas George. b 33. AKC 57. **d** 58 **p** 59. C Winshill *Derby* 58-61; C Hykeham *Linc* 61-64; V Brauncewell w Dunsby 64-78; R S w N Leasingham 64-78; RD Lafford 78-87; V Cranwell 78-80; R Leasingham 78-80; V Billinghay 80-87; V Gosberton 87-97; V Gosberton, Gosberton Clough and Quadring 97-98; Can and Preb Linc Cathl 94-98; rtd 98; PtO *Linc* 98-01. *10 Newton Way, Woolsthorpe, Grantham NG33 5NR* T: (01476) 861749 E: thomas.williamson1@btinternet.com

WILLIE, Canon Andrew Robert. b 43. Bris Univ BA 65 Fitzw Coll Cam BA 73 MA 77. Ridley Hall Cam 71. **d** 74 **p** 75. Chapl St Woolos Cathl 74-79; Chapl St Woolos Hosp Newport 75-79; V Newbridge *Mon* 79-85; V Mathern and Mounton w St Pierre 85-98; Post-Ord Tr Officer 85-98; V Newport St Mark 98-13; Warden of Readers 91-13; Can St Woolos Cathl 02-13; rtd 13; PtO *Mon* from 14. *6 Cordell Close, Llanfoist, Abergavenny NP7 9FE* T: (01873) 852063

WILLIN, Simon Wakefield. b 29. Magd Coll Cam BA 52 MA 55. Cuddesdon Coll 52. **d** 54 **p** 55. C Thornbury *Glouc* 54-57; C Tetbury w Beverston 57-60; R Siddington w Preston 60-64; C Kelburn St Mich New Zealand 65; V Takapau 65-70; LtO Waiapu 70-80; PtO *Ex* 90-92; Hon C Sidmouth, Woolbrook, Salcombe Regis, Sidbury etc 92-01; rtd 01; PtO *Ex* 01-08. *35B North End, Ditchling, Hassocks BN6 8TE*

WILLIS, Andrew Lyn. b 48. Univ of Wales (Lamp) BA 73. **d** 74 **p** 75. C Swansea St Mary w H Trin and St Mark *S & B* 74-81; V Glasbury and Llowes 81-83; Chapl RAF 83-03; Chapl Moray Hosps from 04; LtO *Mor* from 09. *Deanshaugh Croft, Mulben, Keith AB55 6YJ* T: (01542) 860240 E: andylwillis@hotmail.co.uk

WILLIS, Anthony Charles Sabine. b 53. Ex Coll Ox MA 82. ERMC 05. **d** 07 **p** 08. NSM Hatfield Hyde *St Alb* 07-10; PtO *Newc* 08-10. *Leazes House, Alston CA9 3NH* T: (01434) 382682 E: acswillis@gmail.com

WILLIS, Anthony David. b 40. Sarum & Wells Th Coll 87. **d** 89 **p** 90. C Ivybridge w Harford *Ex* 89-92; C Catherington and Clanfield *Portsm* 92-94; R Ellesborough, The Kimbles and Stoke Mandeville *Ox* 94-08; rtd 09; C Aylesbury *Ox* 09-12. *12 Fairford Leys Way, Aylesbury HP19 7FQ* T: (01296) 431934 E: revwillis@btinternet.com

WILLIS, Canon Anthony John. b 38. MBE 00. Univ of Wales (Lamp) BA 62. Qu Coll Birm. **d** 64 **p** 65. C Kidderminster St Jo *Worc* 64-68; C Dunstable *St Alb* 68-72; V Rubery *Birm* 72-80; R Salwarpe and Hindlip w Martin Hussingtree *Worc* 80-92; Chapl to Agric and Rural Life 85-03; Hon Can Worc Cathl

99-03; rtd 03; PtO *Worc* from 04. *1 Snowberry Avenue, Home Meadow, Worcester WR4 0JA* T: (01905) 723509 E: jwillis@cofe-worcester.org.uk

WILLIS, Christopher Charles Billopp. b 32. MCIPD. Bps' Coll Cheshunt 57. **d** 59 **p** 60. C Golders Green St Alb *Lon* 59-61; C N Harrow St Alb 61-64; V Shaw and Whitley *Sarum* 64-69; Ind Chapl *Ex* 69-77; C Swimbridge 70-77; LtO 77-92; Chapl W Buckland Sch Barnstaple 77-92; rtd 97; PtO *Ex* from 97. *Rose Cottage, Chittlehampton, Umberleigh EX37 9PU* T: (01769) 540289

WILLIS, David Anthony. b 81. Ripon Coll Cuddesdon BA 10. **d** 10 **p** 11. C Ifield *Chich* 10-13; V Midhurst from 13; R Woolbeding from 13. *The Vicarage, June Lane, Midhurst GU29 9EW* E: revdavewillis@live.co.uk

WILLIS, David George. b 45. Oak Hill Th Coll BA 79. **d** 79 **p** 80. C Wallington *S'wark* 79-84; V Ramsgate St Mark *Cant* 84-89; Hon C Woodnesborough w Worth and Staple 94-02; Hon C Eastry and Northbourne w Tilmanstone etc 02-06; PtO from 06. *33 Boystown Place, Eastry, Sandwich CT13 0DS* T: (01304) 611959 E: davidandjane@f2s.com

WILLIS, Geoffrey Stephen Murrell. b 58. Sussex Univ BA 80. Wycliffe Hall Ox 83. **d** 86 **p** 87. C Ashtead *Guildf* 86-89; Chapl Lee Abbey 89-94; R Dunsfold *Guildf* 94-01; R Dunsfold and Hascombe 01-06; PtO from 06. *The Barn, Stephens Orchard, Headley Road, Grayshott, Hindhead GU26 6DL* T: (01428) 609382 E: willisgeoffrey@mac.com

WILLIS, Guy Robin Fraser. b 86. Jes Coll Cam BA 08 MA 11. St Steph Ho Ox 12. **d** 15. C Holborn St Alb w Saffron Hill St Pet *Lon* from 15. *1 Leigh Place, London EC1N 7AB* M: 07989-798519 E: grfwillis@gmail.com

WILLIS, Hugh. b 39. Bris Univ BDS 63 MGDSRCSEng 82 FRSH 87. **d** 98 **p** 99. OLM Charminster and Stinsford *Sarum* 98-08; PtO from 09. *Glebe Farmhouse, West Hill, Charminster, Dorchester DT2 9RD* T/F: (01305) 262940 E: tournai@aol.com

WILLIS, Mrs Jane Elizabeth. b 59. Wycliffe Hall Ox 06. **d** 08 **p** 09. C Shrewsbury H Cross *Lich* 08-11; TV S Molton w Nymet St George, High Bray etc *Ex* 11-14; P-in-c Hurstpierpoint *Chich* from 14. *The Rectory, 21 Cuckfield Road, Hurstpierpoint, Hassocks BN6 9RP* T: (01903) 742888 E: revjanewillis@btinternet.com

WILLIS, Mrs Jennifer Anne. b 41. Bp Otter Coll TCert 63. **d** 11 **p** 12. OLM Wingerworth *Derby* from 11. *9 Pond Lane, Wingerworth, Chesterfield S42 6TW* T: (01246) 554430 E: jenn.willis@uwclub.net

WILLIS, John. *See* WILLIS, Anthony John

WILLIS, Joyce Muriel. b 42. Open Univ BA 86 CQSW 73. EAMTC 86. **d** 89 **p** 94. NSM Hadleigh *St E* 89-02; NSM Hadleigh, Layham and Shelley 02-07; rtd 07; PtO *St E* from 07. *26 Ramsey Road, Hadleigh, Ipswich IP7 6AN* T: (01473) 823165 E: willisjm@lineone.net

WILLIS, Maureen. **d** 15. C Branksome St Clem *Sarum* from 15. *Address temp unknown*

WILLIS, Mrs Patricia. b 50. RGN 85 Brunel Univ BSc 95 Ox Brookes Univ PGDE 98. SAOMC 96. **d** 99 **p** 00. C Warmley, Syston and Bitton *Bris* 99-03; V Hanham 03-10; rtd 10; PtO *Ox* from 10. *30 Tallis Lane, Reading RG30 3EB* M: 07731-331154 E: rev.pat.willis@blueyonder.co.uk

WILLIS, Paul. b 54. SAOMC 06 **d** 06 **p** 07. C High Wycombe *Ox* 06-10; TV 10-15; TV Loddon Reach from 15. *12 The Manor, Shinfield, Reading RG2 9DP* M: 07857-309018 T: 0118-988 3363 E: paulwillis54@btinternet.com

WILLIS, Peter Ambrose Duncan. b 34. Kelham Th Coll 55 Lich Th Coll 58. **d** 59 **p** 60. C Sevenoaks St Jo *Roch* 59-63; Trinidad and Tobago 63-68; P-in-c Diptford *Ex* 68-69; R 69-85; P-in-c N Huish 68-69; R 69-85; R Diptford, N Huish, Harberton and Harbertonford 85-96; rtd 96. *Sun Cottage, Church Street, Modbury, Ivybridge PL21 0QR* T: (01548) 830541

WILLIS, The Very Revd Robert Andrew. b 47. Warw Univ BA 68. Cuddesdon Coll 70. **d** 72 **p** 73. C Shrewsbury St Chad *Lich* 72-75; V Choral Sarum Cathl 75-78; TR Tisbury 78-87; RD Chalke 82-87; V Sherborne w Castleton and Lillington 87-92; Can and Preb Sarum Cathl 88-92; RD Sherborne 91-92; Chapl Cranborne Chase Sch 78-92; Dean Heref 92-01; P-in-c Heref St Jo 92-01; Dean Cant from 01. *The Deanery, The Precincts, Canterbury CT1 2EP* T: (01227) 865264 *or* 762862 E: dean@canterbury-cathedral.org

WILLIS, Mrs Rosemary Ann. b 39. **d** 93 **p** 96. OLM Fressingfield, Mendham, Metfield, Weybread etc *St E* 93-09; PtO from 09. *Priory House, Fressingfield, Eye IP21 5PH* T: (01379) 586254

WILLMINGTON, John Martin Vanderlure. b 45. St D Coll Lamp BA 69. St Steph Ho Ox 69. **d** 71 **p** 72. C Upper Teddington SS Pet and Paul *Lon* 71-75; C Kensington St Mary Abbots w St Geo 75-83; R Perivale 83-91; V Acton Green 91-14; rtd 14. *Flat 5, 42 Wellington Road, Hampton TW12 1JT* T: (020) 8241 3954

WILLMONT, Anthony Vernon. b 35. Lich Th Coll 62. **d** 63 **p** 64. C Yardley St Edburgha *Birm* 63-65; C Smethwick H Trin w St Alb 65-68; V Ropley w W Tisted *Win* 68-77; V Ipswich St Aug *St E* 77-84; R King's Worthy *Win* 84-90; R Headbourne Worthy 84-90; R Lapworth *Birm* 90-99; R Baddesley Clinton 90-99; P-in-c Thornton in Lonsdale w Burton in Lonsdale *Bradf* 99-02; rtd 02; PtO *Leeds* from 02. *9 Lowcroft, Butts Lane, Bentham, Lancaster LA2 2FD* T: (01524) 261655

WILLMOTT, Robert Owen Noel. b 41. Lich Th Coll 65. **d** 68 **p** 69. C Perry Hill St Geo *S'wark* 68-71; C Denham *Ox* 71-76; P-in-c Tingewick w Water Stratford 76-77; P-in-c Radclive 76-77; R Tingewick w Water Stratford, Radclive etc 77-89; R Wingrave w Rowsham, Aston Abbotts and Cublington 89-06; P-in-c Wing w Grove 04-06; rtd 06. *34 Portfield Way, Buckingham MK18 1BB* T: (01280) 813057

✥**WILLMOTT, The Rt Revd Trevor.** b 50. St Pet Coll Ox BA 71 MA 74. Westcott Ho Cam. **d** 74 **p** 75 **c** 02. C Norton *St Alb* 74-77; Asst Chapl Oslo w Bergen, Trondheim and Stavanger *Eur* 78-79; Chapl Naples w Sorrento, Capri and Bari 79-83; R Ecton *Pet* 83-89; Warden Ecton Ho 83-89; Dioc Dir of Ords and Dir Post-Ord Tr *Pet* 86-97; Can Res, Prec and Sacr Pet Cathl 89-97; Adn Dur and Can Res Dur Cathl 97-02; Suff Bp Basingstoke *Win* 02-09; Suff Bp Dover *Cant* from 10. *The Bishop's Office, Old Palace, Canterbury CT1 2EE* T: (01227) 459382 E: trevor.willmott@bishcant.org

WILLOUGHBY, Diane Joyce. b 56. Ex Univ BTh 12. SWMTC 07. **d** 10 **p** 11. C St Agnes and Mount Hawke w Mithian *Truro* from 10; C St Clement 12-15; V from 15. *Laurel Cottage, 1 Churchtown, Illogan, Redruth TR16 4SW* T: (01209) 843891 M: 07776-152759 E: illogan@hotmail.co.uk

WILLOUGHBY, Francis Edward John. b 38. St Jo Coll Nottm. **d** 83 **p** 84. C Tonbridge SS Pet and Paul *Roch* 83-87; V Sutton at Hone 87-02; P-in-c Horton Kirby 00-02; rtd 03; PtO *Chich* from 03. *23 Mountjoy, Battle TN33 0EQ* T: (01424) 775234

WILLOUGHBY, Canon Paul Moore. b 60. BA. **d** 86 **p** 87. C Dublin St Patr Cathl Gp 86-90; C Glenageary 90-92; I Dublin Booterstown 92-94; I Kilmocomogue *C, C & R* from 94; Can Cork and Ross Cathls from 00; Can St Patr Cathl Dublin from 14. *The Rectory, Durrus, Bantry, Co Cork, Republic of Ireland* T: (00353) (27) 61011 F: 61608 E: paul@durrusfete.ie

WILLOUGHBY, Mrs Serena Louise. b 72. Oak Hill Th Coll BA 96. **d** 96 **p** 97. C St Paul's Cray St Barn *Roch* 96-99; C Hildenborough 99-00; PtO 03-06; P-in-c Sevenoaks Weald 04-14; Chapl Ch Sch Richmond from 14. *Christ's School, Queens Road, Richmond TW10 6HW* M: 07786-076382 T: (020) 8940 6982 E: johnser@20judd.fsnet.co.uk

WILLOWS, David Keith. b 70. St Jo Coll Dur BA 90 K Coll Lon MA 94 PhD 99. Wycliffe Hall Ox. **d** 95 **p** 96. C Ox St Mary V w St Cross and St Pet 95-97; Asst Chapl Oxon Mental Healthcare NHS Trust 97-00; P-in-c St Martin Ludgate *Lon* 00-01; Research Dir Paternoster Cen from 00. *104C Camden Street, London NW1 0HY* T: (020) 7248 6233 E: david.willows@paternostercentre.com

WILLOWS, Michael John. b 35. Sarum & Wells Th Coll 70. **d** 72 **p** 73. C Pershore w Wick *Worc* 72-75; Ind Chapl 75-88; P-in-c Astley 75-81; P-in-c Hallow 81-85; V 85-88; V Wollaston 88-05; rtd 05; PtO *Worc* from 05; *Lich* from 12. *39 Hyperion Road, Stourton, Stourbridge DY7 6SD* T: (01384) 379794

WILLOX, Peter. b 63. Sunderland Poly BSc 85. Cranmer Hall Dur 86. **d** 89 **p** 90. C Bradley *Wakef* 89-92; C Utley *Bradf* 92-95; TV Bingley All SS 95-02; Chapl St Martin's Coll and C Ambleside w Brathay *Carl* 02-07; P-in-c Ben Rhydding *Bradf* 07-12; V Leeds from 12. *St John's Vicarage, 28 Wheatley Avenue, Ben Rhydding, Ilkley LS29 8PT* T: (01943) 607363 *or* 601430 E: peterwillox@yahoo.co.uk

WILLS, Andrea Jennifer. CITC. **d** 09 **p** 10. NSM Killala w Dunfeeny, Crossmolina, Kilmoremoy etc *T, K & A* 09-13; P-in-c Straid from 13. *Robin Hill, Foxford, Co Mayo, Republic of Ireland* T: (00353) (94) 925 6403 M: 86-261 7572 E: ajwills@iol.ie

WILLS, David. b 58. Oak Hill Th Coll 92. **d** 94 **p** 95. C Chadwell *Chelmsf* 94-99; P-in-c Darlaston St Lawr *Lich* 99-09; R 09-10; C Darlaston All SS 99-10; TR Bilston from 10. *The Vicarage, Dover Street, Bilston WV14 6AW* T: (01902) 491560

WILLS, Preb David Stuart Ralph. b 36. Chich Th Coll 64. **d** 66 **p** 67. C Bodmin *Truro* 66-70; V Bude Haven 70-78; TV Banbury *Ox* 78-83; Accredited Cllr from 81; V Launceston St Steph w St Thos *Truro* 83-88; P-in-c Kenwyn St Geo 88-93; V Truro St Geo and St Jo 93-96; Preb St Endellion 95-01; rtd 96. *Garden Cottage, Penwinnick Road, St Agnes TR5 0LA* T: (01872) 552033 F: 553121 M: 07773-402109 E: david.wills@cpt.cornwall.nhs.uk

WILLS, Edward Richard. b 64. STETS 07. **d** 10 **p** 11. NSM Wedmore w Theale and Blackford *B & W* 10-13; Chapl

RN from 13. *Royal Naval Chaplaincy Service, Mail Point 1.2, Leach Building, Whale Island, Portsmouth PO2 8BY* T: (023) 9262 5055 F: 9262 5134 M: 07971-511564
E: eddie@beonna.co.uk

WILLS, Canon Ian Leslie. b 49. Wycliffe Hall Ox 77. **d** 80 **p** 81. C Henbury *Bris* 80; C Gtr Corsham 80-83; C Whitchurch 83-86; Chapl HM Rem Cen Pucklechurch 86-96; P-in-c Pucklechurch and Abson w Dyrham *Bris* 86-87; V Pucklechurch and Abson 87-99; V Soundwell 99-15; Hon Can Bris Cathl 06-15; rtd 15. *39 The Laurels, Mangotsfield, Bristol BS16 9BT* T: 0117-239 0877 E: ianwills@icloud.com

WILLS, Morley. b 35. Ex w Truro NSM Scheme. **d** 80 **p** 81. NSM St Enoder *Truro* 80-82; NSM Kenwyn St Geo 82-85; NSM Truro St Paul and St Clem 85-88; P-in-c Crantock 89-05; rtd 05. *81 Vyvyan Drive, Quintrell Downs, Newquay TR8 4NF* T: (01637) 872648

WILLS, Nicholas Richard. b 71. Birm Univ BA 93. Cranmer Hall Dur. **d** 99 **p** 00. C Boldmere *Birm* 99-03; P-in-c Kettering St Andr *Pet* 03-11; V from 11. *St Andrew's Vicarage, Lindsay Street, Kettering NN16 8RG* T/F: (01536) 513858
E: nickandbecky@ntlworld.com

WILLSON, Andrew William. b 64. Oriel Coll Ox BA 85 Nottm Univ BTh 90 MA 98. Linc Th Coll 87. **d** 90 **p** 91. C Northampton St Mary *Pet* 90-93; C Cov E 93-96; PtO 96-01; Chapl Solihull Sixth Form Coll 98-01; Assoc Chapl Imp Coll *Lon* 01-03; Co-ord Chapl from 03; Assoc Chapl R Coll of Art 01-03; Co-ord Chapl from 03; Chapl (Sen) Lon Univs from 15. *1 Porchester Gardens, London W2 3LA* T: (020) 7229 6359
E: mary-andrew@clarkewillson.fsnet.co.uk

WILLSON, Mrs Patricia Rosemary. b 45. Trin Coll Bris 12. **d** 13 **p** 14. OLM Horfield St Greg *Bris* from 13. *12 Monks Park Avenue, Bristol BS7 0UE* T: 0117-979 2889 M: 07976-986694
E: pat.willson@yahoo.co.uk

WILLSON, Stephen Geoffrey. b 63. St Jo Coll Nottm BTh 90. **d** 90 **p** 91. C Newport St Andr *Mon* 90-92; C Risca 92-94; TV Cyncoed 94-96; Dioc Youth Chapl 94-99; Lay Past Asst 96-98; TV Cyncoed *Mon* 98-01; TR 01-11; R Welshpool, Castle Caereinion and Pool Quay *St As* 11-14; R Welshpool and Castle Caereinion from 14. *The Vicarage, Church Street, Welshpool SY21 7DP* T: (01938) 553164
E: revswillson@btinternet.com

WILLSON, Stuart Leslie. b 61. Nottm Univ BA 83. Sarum & Wells Th Coll 83. **d** 84 **p** 85. C Llandrindod w Cefnllys *S & B* 84-85; Chapl Angl Students Univ of Wales (Swansea) 85-88; C Llwynderw *S & B* 85-88; Ind Chapl Gatwick Airport *Chich* 88-95; Nene Coll of HE Northn 95-98; Dir Fundraising and Communication CUF from 98. *1D Northstead Cottage, Northstead Road, London SW2 3JN* T: (020) 8674 3146 E: stuart@willson.freeserve.co.uk

WILLSON-THOMAS, Chloe Ann Mary. *See* THOMAS, Chloe Ann Mary

WILMAN, Arthur Garth. b 37. EAMTC 84. **d** 87 **p** 88. NSM Swavesey *Ely* 87-90; NSM Fen Drayton w Conington 87-90; NSM Hardwick 90-98; NSM Toft w Caldecote and Childerley 90-98; PtO from 98. *27 Prentice Close, Longstanton, Cambridge CB24 3DY* T: (01954) 781400 E: wilman@ukonline.co.uk or awilman@btinternet.com

WILMAN, Mrs Dorothy Ann Jane. b 38. Reading Univ BSc 60. Westcott Ho Cam 89. **d** 90 **p** 94. NSM Toft w Caldecote and Childerley *Ely* 90-93; Dean's Asst Trin Hall Cam 92-98; Asst Chapl Cam St Edw *Ely* 93-98; P-in-c Hemingford Abbots 98-02; P-in-c Houghton w Wyton 98-02; rtd 02; PtO *Ely* from 02. *37 Prentice Close, Longstanton, Cambridge CB24 3DY* T: (01954) 781400 E: dorothywilman@ukonline.co.uk or dorothywilman@btinternet.com

WILMAN, Leslie Alan. b 37. Selw Coll Cam BA 61 MA 65. Ridley Hall Cam 61. **d** 63 **p** 64. C Skipton H Trin *Bradf* 63-67; C Guiseley 67-69; V Morton St Luke 69-79; R Swanton Morley w worthing *Nor* 79-82; P-in-c E Bilney w Beetley 79-82; P-in-c Hoe 80-82; R Swanton Morley w Beetley w E Bilney and Hoe 82-89 and 89-00; RD Brisley and Elmham 87-93; rtd 00; PtO *Nor* from 00. *7 Wallers Lane, Foulsham, Dereham NR20 5TN* T: (01328) 684109 E: lesliewilman@btinternet.com

WILMER, John Watts. b 26. Lich Th Coll 56. **d** 58 **p** 59. C Wolverhampton Ch Ch *Lich* 58-60; C Fenton 60-63; V Dresden 63-76; TV Sutton St Jas and Wawne *York* 76-80; R Bishop Wilton w Full Sutton 80; P-in-c Kirby Underdale w Bugthorpe 80; R Bishop Wilton w Full Sutton, Kirby Underdale etc 80-87; V York St Hilda 87-91; rtd 92; PtO *York* from 92. *27 Hunter's Way, York YO24 1JL* T: (01904) 709591

WILMOT, David Mark Baty. b 60. Liv Univ BA 82. Sarum & Wells Th Coll 84. **d** 87 **p** 88. C Penrith w Newton Reigny and Plumpton Wall *Carl* 87-91; C St Alb St Pet *St Alb* 91-93; Chapl City Coll St Alb 92-93; V Milton *Lich* 93-01; RD Leek 96-01; V Windermere St Mary and Troutbeck *Carl* from 01. *St Mary's Vicarage, Ambleside Road, Windermere LA23 1BA* T: (01539) 443032 E: vicar@stmaryswindermere.co.uk

WILMOT, Canon Jonathan Anthony de Burgh. b 48. St Jo Coll Nottm BTh 74. **d** 74 **p** 75. C Cambridge St Martin *Ely* 74-77; Chapl Chantilly *Eur* 77-82; Asst Chapl Paris St Mich 80-82; Chapl Versailles 82-87; V Blackheath St Jo *S'wark* 88-95; V Reading Greyfriars *Ox* 95-14; Hon Can Ch Ch 08-14; rtd 14. *7 Birkett Way, Chalfont St Giles HP8 4BH* E: jon.wilmot@gmail.com

WILMOT, Stuart Leslie. b 42. Oak Hill Th Coll 64. **d** 68 **p** 69. C Spitalfields Ch Ch w All SS *Lon* 68-71; C Islington St Mary 71-74; P-in-c Brixton St Paul *S'wark* 75-81; R Mursley w Swanbourne and Lt Horwood *Ox* 81-91; P-in-c Bermondsey St Jas w Ch Ch *S'wark* 91-96; V 96-99; V Bermondsey St Jas w Ch Ch and St Crispin 99-02; P-in-c Bermondsey St Anne 91-93; P-in-c Bermondsey St Anne and St Aug 93-96; V 96-02; RD Bermondsey 96-00; rtd 02. *Amberlea, College, East Chinnock, Yeovil BA22 9DY*

WILSHERE, Daile Marie. b 70. STETS 06. **d** 09 **p** 10. C Preston w Sutton Poyntz, Littlemoor etc *Sarum* 09-13; TV Savernake 13-15; R Saltford w Corston and Newton St Loe *B & W* from 15. *12 Beech Road, Saltford, Bristol BS31 3BE* T: (01225) 872275 M: 07810-551447 E: dailewilshere@live.co.uk

✠**WILSON, The Rt Revd Alan Thomas Lawrence.** b 55. St Jo Coll Cam BA 77 MA 81 Ball Coll Ox DPhil 89. Wycliffe Hall Ox 77. **d** 79 **p** 80 **c** 03. Hon C Eynsham *Ox* 79-81; C 81-82; C Caversham St Pet and Mapledurham etc 82-89; V Caversham St Jo 89-92; R Sandhurst 92-03; RD Sonning 98-03; Hon Can Ch Ch from 02; Area Bp Buckingham from 03. *Sheridan, Grimms Hill, Great Missenden HP16 9BG* T: (01494) 862173 F: 890508 M: 07525-655756
E: bishopbucks@oxford.anglican.org

WILSON, Canon Alfred Michael Sykes. b 32. Jes Coll Cam BA 56 MA 61. Ridley Hall Cam 56. **d** 58 **p** 59. C Fulwood *Sheff* 58-63; V Gt Horton *Bradf* 63-69; R Rushden w Newton Bromswold *Pet* 69-76; RD Higham 75-83; P-in-c Rushden St Pet 75-76; R Rushden w Newton Bromswold 77-83; Can Pet Cathl 77-83; R Preston and Ridlington w Wing and Pilton 83-97; RD Rutland 85-95; rtd 97; PtO *Nor* from 98. *Swallow Cottage, 2 Little Lane, Blakeney, Holt NR25 7NH* T: (01263) 740975

WILSON, Andrew. *See* WILSON, James Andrew Christopher

WILSON, Canon Andrew Alan. b 47. Nottm Univ BA 68. St Steph Ho Ox 68. **d** 71 **p** 72. C Streatham St Paul *S'wark* 71-75; TV Catford (Southend) and Downham 75-80; V Malden St Jas 80-89; Chapl Croydon Community Mental Health Unit 89-94; Chapl Bethlem and Maudsley NHS Trust Lon 94-99; Chapl S Lon and Maudsley NHS Foundn Trust 99-11; Mental Health Chapl (Croydon) 00-11; Hon Can S'wark Cathl 05-11; rtd 11; PtO *S'wark* from 11. *7 Roman Rise, London SE19 1JG* T: (020) 8761 0969
E: arwiljohn@btinternet.com

WILSON, Andrew Kenneth. b 62. Oak Hill Th Coll BA 91. **d** 91 **p** 92. C Springfield H Trin *Chelmsf* 91-96; V Sidcup Ch Ch *Roch* 96-10. *Release International, PO Box 54, Orpington BR5 9RT* T: (01689) 823491 F: 834647

WILSON, Andrew Marcus William. b 69. Ex Coll Ox BA 91 CCC Cam BA 93 K Coll Lon MA 99. Westcott Ho Cam 91. **d** 94 **p** 95. C Forest Gate Em w Upton Cross *Chelmsf* 94-97; TV Poplar *Lon* 99-09; R S Hackney St Jo w Ch from 09. *The Rectory, 9 Church Crescent, London E9 7DH* T: (020) 8985 5145 E: andrewmwwilson@tiscali.co.uk

WILSON, Andrew Martin. b 60. Bris Univ BSc 82 Univ Coll Chich BA 04. Trin Coll Bris 97. **d** 99 **p** 00. C Broadwater *Chich* 99-07; V Portsdown *Portsm* from 07; C Crookhorn from 13; C Purbrook from 13; Jt AD Havant from 14. *Portsdown Vicarage, 1A London Road, Widley, Waterlooville PO7 5AT* T: (023) 9237 5360 E: wilson@ntlworld.com or vicar@christchurchportsdown.org

WILSON, Antony Charles. b 69. Em Coll Cam MA 92 PGCE 92. Wycliffe Hall Ox 01. **d** 03 **p** 04. C Bath Walcot *B & W* 03-08; V Ipswich St Jo *St E* 08-12; CF from 12. *c/o MOD Chaplains (Army)* F: 381824 T: (01264) 383430
E: antony.wilson39@gmail.com

WILSON, Arthur Guy Ross. b 28. St Aid Birkenhead 58. **d** 59 **p** 60. C Bexley St Mary *Roch* 59-63; C Gravesend St Geo 63-66; C Belvedere All SS 66-70; V Brighton St Matthias *Chich* 70-77; V Bradf St Clem 77-84; LtO 84-87; C Baildon 87-88; V Skirwith, Ousby and Melmerby w Kirkland *Carl* 88-93; C Menston w Woodhead *Bradf* 93-96; Chapl High Royds Hosp Menston 93-96; rtd 96; PtO *Derby* 96-98; Hon C Tamworth *Lich* 98-03; PtO 04-14. *4 Damson Court, Rosy Cross, Tamworth B79 7NE* T: (01827) 767643

WILSON, Arthur Neville. *See* RUSDELL-WILSON, Arthur Neville

WILSON, Ashley Peter. b 58. Edin Univ BSc 81 BVM&S 83 St Jo Coll Dur BA 99. Cranmer Hall Dur 97. **p** 01. C Nunthorpe *York* 00-03; P-in-c Rounton w Welbury 03-08; Chapl St Chad's

Coll *Dur* from 08. *St Chad's College, 18 North Bailey, Durham DH1 3RH* T: 0191-334 3362 *or* 334 3358
E: ashley.wilson@dur.ac.uk

WILSON, Mrs Barbara Anne. b 38. Brighton Poly BEd 79. **d** 04. NSM Southwick *Chich* 04-11; NSM Kingston Buci 11-15; NSM Old Shoreham and Kingston Buci from 15. *10 Phoenix Crescent, Southwick, Brighton BN42 4HR* T: (01273) 269771
M: 07814-655121 E: barbara.a.wilson@btinternet.com

WILSON, Mrs Barbara Joyce. b 51. CBDTI 98. **d** 01 **p** 02. OLM Leyland St Jo *Blackb* 01-07; NSM from 07. *43 Hall Lane, Leyland PR25 3YD* T: (01772) 435340
E: barbara.j.wilson@btinternet.com

WILSON, Barry Frank. b 58. Man Metrop Univ BA 89 MPhil 96 MTh 99 Keele Univ PGCE 90. NOC 94. **d** 97 **p** 98. C Stone St Mich w Aston St Sav *Lich* 97-99; Chapl Abbots Bromley Sch 00-04; V Madeley and Betley *Lich* 04-13; R Nantwich *Ches* from 13. *The Rectory, Church Lane, Nantwich CW5 5RQ* T: (01270) 620668

WILSON, Barry Richard. b 46. WMMTC 88. **d** 91 **p** 92. NSM Leek and Meerbrook *Lich* 91-93; C Styvechale *Cov* 93-98; V Chesterton *Lich* 98-12; rtd 12; PtO *Lich* from 13. *9 Westwood Park Avenue, Leek ST13 8LR*
E: barry-hazel@breathemail.net

WILSON, Bernard Martin. b 40. St Jo Coll Cam BA 63 MA 68 Lon Univ CertEd 67. Ripon Hall Ox 72. **d** 73 **p** 74. C Bilton *Cov* 73-77; Dioc Development Officer *Birm* 78-83; Soc Resp Officer *Derby* 83-90; V Darley Abbey 83-90; Chapl Derbyshire R Infirmary 88-90; Educn Unit Dir Traidcraft Exchange 91; V Mickleover St Jo *Derby* 92-98; Adv to Bd of Miss and Soc Resp *Leic* 98-03; rtd 03; PtO *Leic* 03-06; *Lich* from 06; *Heref* from 14; *Lich* from 15. *2 Dargate Close, Shrewsbury SY3 9QE* T: (01743) 236300 E: bmartinwilson@gmail.com

WILSON (née HESLOP), Mrs Caroline Susan. b 62. St Cath Coll Cam BA 83 MA 87 ALCM 79. Ox Min Course 06. **d** 09 **p** 10. NSM Caversham St Andr *Ox* 09-11; PtO 11-12; *St Alb* 12-14; NSM St Alb St Sav from 14. *44 Carlisle Avenue, St Albans AL3 5LX* T: (01727) 859274 E: revd.carolinew@gmail.com

WILSON, Mrs Catherine Ann. b 61. Southn Univ BA 83 Leic Univ PGCE 84. SEITE 11. **d** 14 **p** 15. C Biddenden and Smarden *Cant* from 14. *The Rectory, The Street, Great Chart, Ashford TN23 3AY* M: 07511-625107
E: catherine.wilson@sbcofe.org

WILSON, Cecil Henry. b 40. CITC 67. **d** 69 **p** 70. C Lurgan St Jo *D & D* 69-72; Min Can Dromore Cathl 72-75; Youth Sec CMS Ireland 75-80; N Regional Sec 80-87; Gen Sec 87-07; Can Belf Cathl 00-07; rtd 07. *42 Magheraknock Road, Ballynahinch BT24 8TJ* T: (028) 9756 4300

WILSON, Charles Roy. b 30. Brasted Th Coll 56 St Aid Birkenhead 57. **d** 59 **p** 60. C Kirkdale St Paul N Shore *Liv* 59-62; C St Helens St Mark 62-66; V Wolverhampton St Matt *Lich* 66-74; V Ripley *Derby* 74-88; V Willington 88-95; V Findern 88-95; rtd 95; PtO *Derby* from 95. *Jubilate, 12 Oak Tree Close, Swanwick, Alfreton DE55 1FG* T: (01773) 541822

WILSON, Christella Helen. b 62. Yorks Min Course 08. **d** 11 **p** 12. C Pannal w Beckwithshaw *Leeds* 11-14; V Hampsthwaite and Killinghall and Birstwith from 14. *The Vicarage, Wreaks Road, Birstwith, Harrogate HG3 2NJ*
E: christella.wilson@yahoo.co.uk

WILSON (née BRAVERY), The Ven Christine Louise. b 58. STETS 94. **d** 97 **p** 98. C Henfield w Shermanbury and Woodmancote *Chich* 97-02; TV Hove 02-08; P-in-c Goring-by-Sea 08-10; Adn Chesterfield *Derby* from 10. *The Old Vicarage, Church Street, Baslow, Bakewell DE45 1RY* T: (01246) 583023 E: archchesterfield@derby.anglican.org

WILSON, Christopher Harry. b 59. Man Univ MusB 80 Ox Univ MTh 01. Wycliffe Hall Ox 88. **d** 91 **p** 92. C S Lafford *Linc* 91-95; P-in-c Billingborough 95-96; P-in-c Sempringham w Pointon and Birthorpe 95-96; P-in-c Horbling 95-96; P-in-c Billingborough Gp 95-96; V Wool 95-03; P-in-c Leamington Priors All SS *Cov* 03-15; V from 15; P-in-c Leamington Spa H Trin 03-15; V from 15. *Clive House, Kenilworth Road, Leamington Spa CV32 5TL* T: (01926) 424016
E: holy.trinity@btopenworld.com

WILSON, Mrs Claire Frances. b 43. Hull Univ BA 65. SWMTC 85. **d** 87 **p** 94. Par Dn Belsize Park *Lon* 87-94; C 94-97; C Chingford SS Pet and Paul *Chelmsf* 97-09; rtd 09; PtO *Lon* from 10. *Ground Floor Flat, 26 Frognal Lane, London NW3 7DT* T: (020) 7794 3801
E: revclairewilson@btinternet.com

WILSON, Colin Edward. b 63. Ripon Coll Cuddesdon BTh 94. **d** 94 **p** 95. C High Wycombe *Ox* 94-98; P-in-c Broadwell, Evenlode, Oddington and Adlestrop *Glouc* 98-00; P-in-c Westcote w Icomb and Bledington 98-00; R Broadwell, Evenlode, Oddington, Adlestrop etc 00-03; P-in-c Finchingfield and Cornish Hall End etc *Chelmsf* from 05. *The Vicarage, Bardfield Road, Finchingfield, Braintree CM7 4JR* T: (01371) 810309

WILSON, David. b 67. Univ of Northumbria at Newc BSc 94 St Jo Coll Dur BA 04. Cranmer Hall Dur 97. **d** 00 **p** 01. C Nantwich *Ches* 00-03; P-in-c Waverton 03-05; R Waverton w Aldford and Bruera 05-08; R St Andrews St Andr *St And* 08-12; Chapl Radley Coll from 12. *Radley College, Radley, Abingdon OX14 2HR* T: (01235) 543190 M: 07548-628695
E: d.w.wilson@radley.org.uk

WILSON, David Brian. b 47. QUB BA 68. CITC 71. **d** 71 **p** 72. C Ballyholme *D & D* 71-74; C Guildf Ch Ch 74-78; I Arvagh w Carrigallen, Gowna and Columbkille *K, E & A* 78-81; R Clogherny w Seskinore and Drumnakilly *Arm* 81-95; I Caledon w Brantry 95-11; rtd 11. *24 Ailsa Craig View, Grangemuir Road, Prestwick KA9 1GA*

WILSON, Preb David Gordon. b 40. Man Univ BSc 61 Clare Coll Cam BA 63 MA 68. Ridley Hall Cam 63. **d** 65 **p** 66. C Clapham Common St Barn *S'wark* 65-69; C Onslow Square St Paul *Lon* 69-73; V Leic H Apostles 73-84; V Spring Grove St Mary *Lon* 84-05; P-in-c Isleworth St Fran 90-05; Chapl Brunel Univ 90-02; AD Hounslow 97-02; Preb St Paul's Cathl 02-05; rtd 05; PtO *Portsm* from 05. *8 Clover Close, Locks Heath, Southampton SO31 6SQ* T/F: (01489) 571426
E: david.gwilson20@ntlworld.com

WILSON, David Mark. b 53. Lon Univ BSc 75. Wycliffe Hall Ox BA 77 MA 82. **d** 78 **p** 79. C Romford Gd Shep *Chelmsf* 78-81; C Cheadle Hulme St Andr *Ches* 81-85; V Huntington and Chapl Bp's Blue Coat C of E High Sch 85-95; V Birkenhead Ch Ch *Ches* 95-04; V Over St Jo 04-10; P-in-c W Coker w Hardington Mandeville, E Chinnock etc *B & W* 10-13; R Coker Ridge 13-15; rtd 15. *6 Helston Close, Portesham, Weymouth DT3 4EY* E: thevicar@fastmail.co.uk

WILSON, Deborah May. b 61. Man Univ BA 84 PhD 95 Lanc Univ PGCE 88. Cranmer Hall Dur 03. **d** 06 **p** 07. NSM Hartlepool St Luke *Dur* 06-15; Chapl St Pet Sch Cambridge New Zealand from 15. *St Peter's School, Private Bag 884, Cambridge 3450, New Zealand* T: (0064) (7) 827 9899
E: deborahwilson777@hotmail.co.uk

WILSON, Delyth Anne. **d** 15. NSM Cynwyl Gaeo w Llansawel and Talley etc *St D* from 15. *Y Felin, Abergorlech, Carmarthen SA32 7SN* T: (01558) 685764 E: delythawilson@gmail.com

WILSON, Derrick. b 33. Oak Hill Th Coll 69. **d** 71 **p** 72. C Lurgan Ch the Redeemer *D & D* 71-74; C Willowfield 74-75; I 83-88; I Knocknamuckley 75-83; I Tullylish 88-98; rtd 98. *Hollycroft, 6 Thornhill Crescent, Tandragee, Craigavon BT62 2NZ* T: (028) 3884 9900

WILSON, Mrs Dorothy Jean. b 35. St Mary's Coll Dur BA 57 DipEd 58 Newc Poly LLB 78. NEOC 86. **d** 88 **p** 96. NSM Dur St Giles 88-03; PtO *Newc* 88-96; Chapl Northumbria Univ 94-96; Chapl N Dur Healthcare NHS Trust 97-02; NSM Pittington, Shadforth and Sherburn *Dur* 03-05; rtd 05; PtO *Dur* from 05. *86 Gilesgate, Durham DH1 1HY* T: 0191-386 5016

WILSON, Edith Yvonne. b 43. St Martin's Coll Lanc MA 98. CBDTI 97. **d** 97 **p** 98. NSM Skerton St Chad *Blackb* 97-05; PtO from 05. *28 Roedean Avenue, Morecambe LA4 6SB* T: (01524) 417097 E: yvonne@ywilson7.freeserve.co.uk

WILSON, Miss Elizabeth Ann. b 76. Leic Univ BA 98 Southn Univ MA 01. St Jo Coll Nottm MTh 14. **d** 14 **p** 15. C Evington *Leic* from 14. *2 Westminster Road, Leicester LE2 2EG* M: 07510-797399 E: lizwilson738@gmail.com

WILSON, Canon Erik. b 51. Lanc Univ BA 72. Trin Coll Bris 83. **d** 85 **p** 86. C Linthorpe *York* 85-89; V Hull St Martin w Transfiguration 89-98; AD W Hull 96-98; V Linthorpe from 98; RD Middlesbrough 05-11; Can and Preb York Minster from 05. *St Barnabas' Vicarage, 8 The Crescent, Middlesbrough TS5 6SQ* T: (01642) 817306 E: erik.wilson@btinternet.com

WILSON, Frances Mary. b 61. Leeds Univ BA 98 MPhil 06. Westcott Ho Cam. **d** 00 **p** 01. C Rothwell *Ripon* 00-04; V Catterick 04-11; Initial Reader Tr Officer 04-11; P-in-c Balkwell *Newc* from 11. *St Peter's Vicarage, The Quadrant, North Shields NE29 7JA* E: franceswilson59@gmail.com

WILSON, Francis. b 34. ACP 67. Cuddesdon Coll 71. **d** 73 **p** 74. C Newc St Fran 73-79; V Wallsend St Jo 79-99; rtd 99; PtO *Newc* from 99. *65 Bede Close, Holystone, Newcastle upon Tyne NE12 9SP* T: 0191-270 0848

WILSON, Frederick John. b 25. Lon Univ BScEng 45. Oak Hill Th Coll 68. **d** 70 **p** 71. C Wandsworth All SS *S'wark* 70-75; P-in-c Garsdon w Lea and Cleverton *Bris* 75-84; P-in-c Charlton w Brokenborough and Hankerton 80-84; Chapl Barn Fellowship Whatcombe Ho 84-87; C Corby Epiphany w St Jo *Pet* 87-92; rtd 92; PtO *Linc* 93-02; *Pet* from 93; *Ely* from 05. *2 Thorseby Close, Peterborough PE3 9QS* T: (01733) 263386 E: fredrick.wilson1@ntlworld.com

WILSON, Geoffrey. See WILSON, Samuel Geoffrey

WILSON, Geoffrey. b 42. **d** 97 **p** 98. OLM Gunton St Pet *Nor* 97-08; NSM Lowestoft St Marg 08-12; rtd 12; PtO *Nor* from 13. *7 Monet Square, Gunton, Lowestoft NR32 4LZ* T: (01502) 564064 E: g.wilson570@btinternet.com

WILSON, Geoffrey Samuel Alan. b 46. TCD BA 69 QUB DipEd 70 TCD MA 72. CITC BTh 93. **d** 96 **p** 97. C Glendermott *D & R* 96-99; I Camus-juxta-Mourne 99-12; rtd 12. *42 Ferndale Park, Portstewart BT55 7JB* T: (028) 7083 3542 *or 3834 2969* M: 07803-554386 E: revgeoffwilson@comail.com

WILSON, George Thomas. b 47. CBDTI 97. **d** 00 **p** 01. NSM Barrow St Paul *Carl* 00-06; P-in-c Bootle, Corney, Whicham and Whitbeck 06-10; NSM Cartmel Peninsula from 10. *10 Fairfield, Flookburgh, Grange-over-Sands LA11 7NB* T: (01539) 559215 E: george860@btinternet.com

WILSON, Graham Whitelaw. b 46. Leeds Univ CertEd 77 Birm Univ MPhil 00 Derby Univ DMin 03. EMMTC. **d** 95 **p** 96. NSM Burbage w Aston Flamville *Leic* 95-97; C 97-01; C Fenn Lanes Gp 01-04; PtO from 04. *10 The Courtyard, Higham Lane, Stoke Golding, Nuneaton CV13 6EX* T: (01455) 213598 E: gwwilson@btinternet.com

WILSON, Canon Harold. b 29. St Jo Coll Ox BA 53 MA 57. Ridley Hall Cam 57. **d** 59 **p** 60. C Leamington Priors St Mary *Cov* 59-61; C Walsgrave on Sowe 61-64; V Potters Green 64-67; Chapl Barcelona *Eur* 67-73; V Bursledon *Win* 73-83; RD Eastleigh 75-83; V Yateley 83-94; RD Odiham 85-88; Hon Can Win Cathl 87-94; rtd 94; PtO *Win* from 94. *11 Hill Meadow, Overton, Basingstoke RG25 3JD* T: (01256) 771825

WILSON, Mrs Heather Clarissa. b 49. Hull Univ BA 71 Leic Univ PGCE 72 Anglia Poly Univ MA 05. EAMTC 01. **d** 03 **p** 04. NSM Duston *Pet* 03-15; TV 06-15; rtd 15; PtO *Pet* from 15. *12 Ardens Grove, Rothersthorpe, Northampton NN7 3JJ* M: 07702-033727 T: (01604) 830714 E: heather@wilson1214.freeserve.co.uk

WILSON, Mrs Hilary Anne. b 47. **d** 05 **p** 06. OLM Gt Chesham *Ox* 05-09; NSM from 09. *6 Greenway, Chesham HP5 2BL* T/F: (01494) 775564 E: hilaryaw6@aol.com

WILSON, Canon Ian Andrew. b 57. Nottm Univ BTh 89. Linc Th Coll 86. **d** 89 **p** 90. C Whitton and Thurleston w Akenham *St E* 89-93; P-in-c Elmsett w Aldham 93-02; R Elmsett w Aldham, Hintlesham, Chattisham etc 02; Chapl Woodbridge Sch from 03; Hon Can St E Cathl from 12. *12 Moorfield Road, Woodbridge IP12 4JN* T: (01394) 384573

WILSON, Mrs Irene Margaret. b 49. Leeds Univ BA 83 ALCM 69. Yorks Min Course 09. **d** 11 **p** 12. NSM Kingston upon Hull H Trin *York* from 11. *10 Westgate, North Cave, Brough HU15 2NJ* T: (01430) 470719 M: 07711-996519 E: irene@mulberryhouse.karoo.co.uk

WILSON, Canon James. b 65. St Steph Ho Ox. **d** 01 **p** 02. C Whitchurch *Bris* 01-03; C Horfield St Greg 03-05; P-in-c from 05; Hon Can Bris Cathl from 13. *St Gregory's Vicarage, Filton Road, Horfield, Bristol BS7 0PD* T: 0117-969 2839 E: revjameswilson@aol.com

WILSON, Canon James Andrew Christopher. b 48. Ex & Truro NSM Scheme. **d** 82 **p** 83. NSM Plymouth Crownhill Ascension *Ex* 82-83; NSM Yelverton 83-85; C Plymstock 85-87; R Lifton 87-92; R Kelly w Bradstone 87-92; V Broadwoodwidger 87-92; R Calstock *Truro* 92-13; RD E Wivelshire 00-11; P-in-c St Dominic, Landulph and St Mellion w Pillaton 12-13; rtd 14; Hon Can Truro Cathl from 04. *22 Riverside Mills, Launceston PL15 8GX* T: (01566) 774998 E: andrew.wilson@virgin.net

WILSON, James Kenneth. b 47. **d** 88 **p** 89. C Holyhead w Rhoscolyn w Llanfair-yn-Neubwll *Ban* 88-91; Chapl RAF 91-07; Mental Health Chapl Lincs Partnership NHS Foundn Trust 07-12; rtd 12; P-in-c Llaneugrad w Llanallgo and Penrhosllugwy etc *Ban* from 12. *29 Minffordd Estate, Benllech, Tyn-y-Gongl LL74 8QG* T: (01248) 852079 E: ken@kw22.co.uk *or padre.ken.wilson@gmail.com*

WILSON, James Lewis. b 39. TCD BA 62 HDipEd 63 MA 65 BD 71. TCD Div Sch Div Test 74. **d** 74 **p** 75. C Enniskillen *Clogh* 74-76; C Belfast St Matt *Conn* 76-79; I Killeshandra w Killegar *K, E & A* 79-81; I Derrylane 79-81; I Loughgilly w Clare *Arm* 81-10; rtd 10. *2 Tramway Drive, Bushmills BT57 8YS* T: (028) 2073 1353

WILSON, James Robert. b 36. CITC. **d** 66 **p** 67. C Ballywillan *Conn* 67-73; I Drummaul 73-79; I Drummaul w Duneane and Ballyscullion 79-01; Preb Conn Cathl 96; Treas Conn Cathl 96-98; Chan Conn Cathl 98-01; rtd 01. *90 Killycowan Road, Glarryford, Ballymena BT44 9HJ* T: (028) 2568 5737

WILSON, Jane Jennifer. b 43. Ch Ch Coll Cant TCert 65 Open Univ BA 84. Wycliffe Hall Ox 89. **d** 91 **p** 94. Par Dn Northwood Em *Lon* 91-94; C 94-98; TV Blythburgh w Reydon *St E* 98; TV Sole Bay 98-02; TR 02-07; RD Halesworth 01-07; Hon Can St E Cathl 05-07; P-in-c Offwell, Northleigh, Farway, Cotleigh etc *Ex* 07-11; rtd 11. *Hawthorns, 17 Ashleigh Park, Bampton, Tiverton EX16 9LF* T: (01398) 332135 E: janeoffwell@aol.com

WILSON, Mrs Janet Mary. b 44. Bedf Coll of Educn TCert 66 SRN 74. **d** 03 **p** 04. OLM S Croydon Em *S'wark* 03-10; PtO from 11. *Elmwood, 2 Weybourne Place, Sanderstead CR2 0RZ* T: (020) 8657 2195 E: revjanwilson@blueyonder.co.uk

WILSON, Janet Mary. b 54. SAOMC 02. **d** 05 **p** 06. C Oxhey All SS *St Alb* 05-09; TV Cheshunt from 09. *St Clement's House, 4 Haddestoke Gate, Cheshunt EN8 0XJ* T: (01992) 479882 E: janwilson@waitrose.com

WILSON, Jayaker. b 47. **d** 92 **p** 93. India 92-05; PtO *Chelmsf* from 05. *153 Northbrooks, Harlow CM19 4DQ* T: (01279) 412240

WILSON, Jeffery. b 59. **d** 06 **p** 07. OLM Kirton in Lindsey w Manton *Linc* from 06; OLM Grayingham from 06. *34 Richdale Avenue, Kirton Lindsey, Gainsborough DN21 4BL* T: (01652) 648687 E: jeff-wilson13@yahoo.co.uk

WILSON, John Anthony. b 34. Linc Th Coll. **d** 83 **p** 84. C Nunthorpe *York* 83-85; V Whorlton w Carlton and Faceby 85-94; V E Coatham 94-99; rtd 99; PtO *York* from 99; P-in-c Lower Swale 03-08; PtO *York* from 10. *29 Letch Hill Drive, Bourton-on-the-Water, Cheltenham GL54 2DQ* T: (01451) 820571 E: johnjean.wilson@virgin.net

WILSON, John Clifford. b 32. AKC 56. **d** 57 **p** 58. C Bordesley St Andr *Birm* 57-59; C Kings Norton 59-61; Somalia and Aden 61-63; V Lydbrook *Glouc* 64-67; TV Bow w Bromley St Leon *Lon* 69-73; P-in-c Stepney St Pet w St Benet 73-80; P-in-c Long Marton w Dufton and w Milburn *Carl* 80-81; R 81-87; V Annesley Our Lady and All SS *S'well* 87-95; V Annesley w Newstead 95-97; rtd 97; PtO *Heref* from 98. *Cwm Well Cottage, Upper Cwm, Little Dewchurch, Hereford HR2 6PS* T: (01432) 840559

WILSON, John Frederick. b 33. Qu Coll Birm 58. **d** 61 **p** 62. C Jarrow St Paul *Dur* 61-65; C Monkwearmouth All SS 65-68; Br Honduras 68-71; V Scunthorpe Resurr *Linc* 71-90; Chapl Divine Healing Miss Crowhurst 90-91; V Terrington St Clement *Ely* 91-99; rtd 99; PtO *Ely* from 99. *7 Oakleigh Crescent, Godmanchester, Huntingdon PE29 2JJ* T: (01480) 392791 E: john@jaywil.freeserve.co.uk

WILSON, Canon John Hamilton. b 29. St Chad's Coll Dur BA 53. Sarum Th Coll 53. **d** 55 **p** 56. C W End *Win* 55-59; C Fishponds St Mary *Bris* 59-64; V Bedminster St Fran 64-73; RD Bedminster 68-73; R Horfield H Trin 73-96; Hon Can Bris Cathl 77-96; rtd 96; PtO *Bris* from 96. *2 West Croft, Bristol BS9 4PQ* T/F: 0117-962 9204

WILSON, John Lake. b 34. Linc Th Coll 74. **d** 76 **p** 77. C N Lynn w St Marg and St Nic *Nor* 76-80; V Narborough w Narford 80-85; R Pentney St Mary Magd w W Bilney 80-85; V Lakenham St Mark 85-93; P-in-c Trowse 92-93; V Lakenham St Mark w Trowse 93-98; Chapl Whitlingham Hosp 93-98; rtd 98; PtO *Nor* from 98. *Slinmoor, Warham Road, Wells-next-the-Sea NR23 1NE* T: (01328) 711035 E: wslinmoor@aol.com

WILSON, Canon Judith Anne. b 48. Keele Univ BA 71 Leic Univ PGCE 72. S Dios Minl Tr Scheme 92. **d** 95 **p** 96. NSM Slaugham *Chich* 95-96; Sub Chapl HM Pris Wandsworth 95-96; Chapl HM Pris and YOI Hollesley Bay 96-01; Chapl HM Pris *Nor* 01-09; Chapl Gt Hosp *Nor* 09-15; P-in-c Nor St Helen 09-14; V 14-15; Bp's Adv for Women's Min 04-10; Hon Asst Dioc Dir of Ords 09-15; Hon Can Nor Cathl 07-15; rtd 15; PtO *Nor* from 15. *13 Hunters Lodge, Blofield, Norwich NR13 4LS* T: (01603) 211509 E: revjudithwilson@gmail.com

WILSON, Julian John. b 64. Collingwood Coll Dur BSc 85 Liv Univ BTh. NOC 01. **d** 04 **p** 05. C Uttoxeter Area *Lich* 04-07; Chapl Denstone Coll Uttoxeter 07-09; R Baschurch and Weston Lullingfield w Hordley *Lich* 09-15; World Development Officer (Salop) 11-15; RD Ellesmere 13-15; P-in-c Corfu *Eur* from 15. *c/o Holy Trinity Corfu, 21 L.Mavili Street, Corfu 49100* T: E: julesjwilson@gmail.com

WILSON, Mrs Kathleen. b 47. Bucks Coll of Educn BSc 90 Ox Brookes Univ MBA 93 RGN 69. **d** 03 **p** 04. OLM Iver *Ox* 03-10; P-in-c Colbury *Win* 10-13; Chapl Oakhaven Hospice Trust from 12. *The Vicarage, Deerleap Lane, Totton, Southampton SO40 7EH* T: (023) 8029 2132 M: 07770-944054

WILSON, Kenneth. b 59. Selw Coll Cam BA 82 MA 82 Birm Univ MPhil 95 MRICS 84. S'wark Ord Course 86. **d** 89 **p** 90. C Walthamstow St Pet *Chelmsf* 89-92; TV Wolverhampton *Lich* 92-97; PtO 00-08. *Address temp unknown*

WILSON, Ms Lauretta Joy. b 64. Bath Univ BSc 87 CertEd 87. SAOMC 02. **d** 05 **p** 06. C Boxmoor St Jo *St Alb* 05-08; TV Langelei from 08. *St Benedict's Vicarage, Peascroft Road, Hemel Hempstead HP3 8EP* T: (01442) 243934 E: ljwilson33@btinternet.com

WILSON, Louis. *See* WILSON, Philip Louis

WILSON, Mrs Maree Elizabeth. b 49. Ban Univ BTh 06 Anglia Ruskin Univ MA 12. ERMC 03. **d** 06 **p** 07. C Geneva *Eur* 06-10; Asst Chapl 10-11; TV Ludlow *Heref* 11-15; rtd 15. *Address temp unknown* E: revd_m_wilson@btinternet.com

WILSON, Marjorie Jayne. *See* SHIPTON, Marjorie Jayne

WILSON, Mark Anthony John. b 56. TCD BA 80. CITC 75. **d** 80 **p** 81. C Dublin Rathfarnham *D & G* 80-83; Bp's C Dublin Finglas 83-85; I Celbridge w Straffan and Newcastle-Lyons 85-88; CF 88-93; I Dundalk w Heynestown *Arm* 93-03; Chapl

Adelaide and Meath Hosp Dublin from 04. *7 Newlands Park, Clondalkin, Dublin 22, Republic of Ireland* M: 87-669 3215

WILSON, Mark Ashley John. b 87. Cranmer Hall Dur 12. **d** 15. C Kidsgrove *Lich* from 15. *26 Crown Bank, Talke, Stoke-on-Trent ST7 1PU* T: (01782) 788984
E: stthomascurate@btinternet.com

WILSON, Martin. *See* WILSON, Bernard Martin

WILSON, Canon Mavis Kirby. b 42. Ex Univ BA 64 Cam Univ CertEd 71. S Dios Minl Tr Scheme 82. **dss** 84 **d** 87 **p** 94. Chessington *Guildf* 84-85; Epsom St Martin 85-86; Epsom Common Ch Ch 86-87; C 87-96; Dioc Adv in Miss, Evang, and Par Development 90-02; R Frimley 02-13; Hon Can Guildf Cathl 94-13; rtd 13. *48 Byrefield Road, Guildford GU2 9UB*
T: (01483) 808097 E: maviswilson2@gmail.com

WILSON, Mervyn Raynold Alwyn. b 33. Qu Coll Cam BA 57 MA 61. Ripon Hall Ox 57. **d** 59 **p** 60. C Rubery *Birm* 59-62; C Kings Norton 62-63; V Hamstead St Bernard 63-69; R Bermondsey St Mary w St Olave, St Jo etc *S'wark* 69-78; R Bulwick, Blatherwycke w Harringworth and Laxton *Pet* 78-03; rtd 03; PtO *B & W* from 04. *The Red Post House, Fivehead, Taunton TA3 6PX* T: (01460) 281558
E: margaretwilson426@gmail.com

WILSON, The Very Revd Mervyn Robert. b 22. Bris Univ BA 51 Lon Univ BD 58. Tyndale Hall Bris 52. **d** 52 **p** 53. C Ballymacarrett St Patr *D & D* 52-56; C Donaghcloney 56-59; C Newtownards 59-61; I Ballyphilip w Ardquin 61-70; I Newry St Patr 70-92; Preb Dromore Cathl 83-85; Can Belf Cathl 85-89; Dean Dromore *D & D* 90-92; rtd 92. *31 Manor Drive, Lisburn BT28 1JH* T: (028) 9266 6361

WILSON, Michael. *See* WILSON, Alfred Michael Sykes

WILSON, Canon Michael. b 44. Liv Univ BA 66 Fitzw Coll Cam BA 68 MA 73 De Montfort Univ MBA 94. Westcott Ho Cam. **d** 69 **p** 70. C Worksop Priory *S'well* 69-71; C Gt Malvern St Mary *Worc* 71-75; V Leic St Anne 75-85; TR Leic Ascension 85-88; Hon Can Leic Cathl 85-88; Can Res and Treas Leic Cathl 88-09; rtd 09; PtO *Pet* from 09. *8 Wensum Close, Oakham LE15 6FU* T: (01572) 720853 E: mwilson@keme.co.uk

WILSON, Neil. b 61. Newc Univ BA 83. Ripon Coll Cuddesdon 85. **d** 88 **p** 89. C Wallsend St Luke *Newc* 88-91; C Monkseaton St Pet 91-93; V Earsdon and Backworth 93-04; P-in-c Newc St Jo 04-11; V Haltwhistle and Greenhead from 11. *The Vicarage, Edens Lawn, Haltwhistle NE49 0AB*
T: (01434) 320215 E: frneilwilson@btinternet.com

WILSON, Paul David. b 64. Cranmer Hall Dur 96. **d** 98 **p** 99. C Bramley and Ravenfield w Hooton Roberts etc *Sheff* 98-01; V Hatfield 01-13; AD Snaith and Hatfield 11-13; Hon Can Sheff Cathl 12-13; R Warrington St Elphin *Liv* from 13. *The Rectory, 129 Church Street, Warrington WA1 2TL* T: (01925) 635020 E: revpdwilson@aol.com

WILSON, Paul Thomas Wardley. b 43. AKC 67. St Aug Coll Cant. **d** 70 **p** 71. C Tokyngton St Mich *Lon* 70-74; Soc Community Worker Roch 74-81; PtO 81-90; Sen Adv Coun for Soc Resp Cant 83-88; Chief Exec Carr-Gomm Soc 88-10. *Address temp unknown*

WILSON, Peter Dennis. b 51. **d** 03 **p** 04. OLM Benwell *Newc* 03-15; OLM Benwell and Scotswood from 15. *34 Benwell Lane, Benwell, Newcastle upon Tyne NE15 6RR* T: 0191-273 2856

WILSON, Peter John. b 43. CertEd 76 BEd 84. Linc Th Coll. **d** 71 **p** 72. C Stretford St Matt *Man* 71-73; C Rugby St Andr *Cov* 73-76; TV Rugby 86-92; Hon C Bilton 76-79; Asst Dir of Educn *Blackb* 79-81; P-in-c Accrington St Paul 79-81; Dioc Officer for Stewardship *Carl* 92-02; P-in-c Dacre 95-02; Hon Can Carl Cathl 98-02; R Stone St Mich and St Wulfad w Aston St Sav *Lich* 02-05; rtd 05. *83 Salisbury Road, Stafford ST16 3SE*
E: ptr@wln1.fsnet.co.uk

WILSON, Peter Sheppard. b 39. TCD BA 61. CITC Div Test 62. **d** 62 **p** 63. C Killowen *D & R* 62-68; C Portadown St Columba *Arm* 68-70; I Convoy w Monellan and Donaghmore *D & R* 70-78; V Castletown *S & M* 78-83; R Kilmacolm and Bridge of Weir *Glas* 83-85; I Camus-juxta-Bann *D & R* 85-92; Bp's Dom Chapl 90-92; I Maguiresbridge w Derrybrusk *Clogh* 92-05; Chapl to Bp Clogh 98-00; Can Clogh Cathl 03-05; rtd 05. *25 Grogey Road, Fivemiletown BT75 0SQ* T: (028) 8952 1883

WILSON, Peter Stuart. b 45. Yorks Min Course 08. **d** 09 **p** 10. NSM Haworth *Leeds* 09-15; NSM Cross Roads cum Lees 09-15; NSM Haworth and Cross Roads cum Lees from 15. *25 Branshaw Grove, Keighley BD22 6NH* T: (01535) 674972
M: 07870-134272 E: peter@peterwilson25.wanadoo.co.uk

WILSON, Philip Louis. b 68. Bris Univ LLB 91. Oak Hill Th Coll BA 09. **d** 09 **p** 10. NSM Broadwell, Evenlode, Oddington, Adlestrop etc *Glouc* 09-12; R Denton w S Heighton and Tarring Neville *Chich* from 12. *The Rectory, 6 Heighton Road, Newhaven BN9 0RB* T: (01273) 514319 E: landjwilson@btinternet.com

WILSON, Rachel Claire. b 68. **d** 12 **p** 13. NSM Dartford St Edm *Roch* 12-14; C from 14. *62 Whitehill Road, Gravesend DA12 5PQ* T: (01474) 357006 M: 07817-206368
E: revdrachelwilson@gmail.com

WILSON, Mrs Rachel Elizabeth. b 56. Keswick Hall Coll BEd 79. NOC 00. **d** 03 **p** 04. NSM Slaidburn and Long Preston w Tosside *Bradf* 03-10; NSM Lower Wharfedale *Leeds* from 10; Min in Deaf Community from 14. *The Vicarage, Old Pool Bank, Pool in Wharfedale, Otley LS21 1EJ* T: 0113-284 3706
E: revrachel.wilson@googlemail.com

WILSON, Richard Graham. b 67. Bris Univ BSc 91 DipSW 93. Trin Coll Bris BA 01. **d** 01 **p** 02. C Wandsworth St Mich *S'wark* 01-05; TR Bath Twerton-on-Avon *B & W* from 05; RD Bath from 15. *The Rectory, Watery Lane, Bath BA2 1RL*
T: (01225) 421438 M: 07792-693062
E: richard@stmichaelstwerton.com

WILSON, Canon Robert Malcolm (Robin). b 35. St Andr Univ MA 59. ALCD 62. **d** 62 **p** 63. C Wallington *S'wark* 62-66; C Dur St Nic 66-70; V Colchester St Pet *Chelmsf* 70-01; RD Colchester 93-98; Hon Can Chelmsf Cathl 94-01; rtd 01; PtO *St E* from 01; *Chelmsf* from 01. *Hawthorns, Melton Road, Melton, Woodbridge IP12 1NH* T: (01394) 383514

WILSON, Robert Stoker. b 39. Dur Univ BSc 62. Oak Hill Th Coll 62. **d** 64 **p** 65. C High Elswick St Paul *Newc* 64-68; C Kirkheaton 68-70; Youth Chapl *Liv* 70-73; P-in-c S Shields St Steph *Dur* 73-78; R 78-83; Youth Chapl 73-77; P-in-c S Shields St Aid 81-83; V Greenside 83-94; Dioc Adv for IT 94-98; P-in-c Coniscliffe 98-04; Dioc Adv for IT 98-04; rtd 04; PtO *Dur* from 13. *9 Augusta Close, Darlington DL1 3HT*
M: 07808-911928 E: stoker.wilson@durham.anglican.org

WILSON, Mrs Rosamund Cynthia. b 54. Univ of Wales MSc 94 MCSP 75. Trin Coll Bris. **d** 01 **p** 02. NSM Stoke Bishop *Bris* 01-05; C Frenchay and Winterbourne Down 05-06; NSM Abbots Leigh w Leigh Woods 07-13. *10 Druid Stoke Avenue, Bristol BS9 1DD* T: 0117-968 7554 E: rosw@another.com

WILSON, Ross Robert. b 70. Bath Univ BSc 94. Trin Coll Bris MA 12. **d** 12 **p** 13. C Willowfield *D & D* 12-15; I Orangefield w Moneyreagh from 15. *The Rectory, 397A Castlereagh Road, Belfast BT5 6AB* M: 07564-232344 T: (028) 9070 4493
E: wilsons@gmx.us

WILSON, Roy. *See* WILSON, Charles Roy

WILSON, Samuel Geoffrey. b 62. CITC BTh 04. **d** 04 **p** 05. C Swanlinbar w Tomregan, Kinawley, Drumlane etc *K, E & A* 04-07; I Kildallon and Swanlinbar 07-09; I Lurgan Ch the Redeemer *D & D* from 09. *Shankill Rectory, 62 Bainbridge Road, Lurgan, Craigavon BT6 7HG* T: (028) 3832 3341
M: 07803-554386 E: revgeoffwilson@gmail.com

WILSON, Simon Anthony. b 67. Portsm Poly BA 88. Cranmer Hall Dur 96. **d** 99 **p** 00. NSM Barnham Broom *Nor* 99-00; NSM Barnham Broom and Upper Yare 00-02; NSM Hellesdon 02-03; Public Preacher 03; Chapl Norfolk Constabulary (Cen Area) 05-13; Chapl Norfolk Fire Service 05-13; Co-ord Dioc Forum for Soc and Community Concerns 06-13; Co Ecum Officer 10-13. *The Vicarage, Church Lane, Heacham, King's Lynn PE31 7HJ* T: (01485) 570697
E: simon.wilson@dioceseofnorwich.org

WILSON, Stephen Charles. b 51. Newc Univ BA 73 Cam Univ BA 78 MA 82. Westcott Ho Cam. **d** 79 **p** 80. C Fulham All SS *Lon* 79-82; C W Hampstead St Jas 82-85; P-in-c Alexandra Park St Sav 85-93; V Preston next Faversham, Goodnestone and Graveney *Cant* 93-14; V Preston-next-Faversham from 14; Hon Min Can Cant Cathl from 98; Asst Dir of Ords 07-10. *The Vicarage, Preston Lane, Faversham ME13 8LG* T: (01795) 536801 E: scwilson@coolblue.eclipse.co.uk

WILSON, Stephen Graham. b 70. Ridley Hall Cam 09. **d** 11 **p** 12. C Overton w Laverstoke and Freefolk *Win* 11-15; CF from 15. *c/o MOD Chaplains (Army)* M: 07968-272116
T: (01264) 383430 F: 381824
E: revstephenwilson@btinternet.com

WILSON, Canon Stephen John. b 45. Bradf Univ BTech 69. Trin Coll Bris 90. **d** 92 **p** 93. C Marple All SS *Ches* 92-96; P-in-c Moulton 96-01; Chapl Mid Cheshire Hosps Trust 96-99; V Hyde St Geo *Ches* 01-10; RD Mottram 03-08; Hon Can Ches Cathl 06-10; rtd 10; PtO *Ches* from 11. *18 Green Park, Weaverham, Northwich CW8 3EH* T: (01606) 851294
E: stephen.wilson888@btinternet.com

WILSON, Stoker. *See* WILSON, Robert Stoker

WILSON, Stuart Arnold. b 47. SWMTC 94. **d** 97 **p** 98. NSM Okehampton w Inwardleigh, Bratton Clovelly etc *Ex* 97-02; TV 02-09; rtd 10. *Red Spider Cottage, Bratton Clovelly, Okehampton EX20 4JD* T: (01837) 871248
E: s.wilson45@btinternet.com

WILSON, Susan Annette. b 60. Bath Univ BPharm 81 PhD 86 MRPharmS 82. Westcott Ho Cam 98. **d** 00 **p** 01. C Newc St Geo 00-03; Chapl Dame Allan's Schs Newc 02-03; TV Willington *Newc* 03-07; V Newc St Gabr 07-13; rtd 13. *2 Amberdale Avenue, Newcastle upon Tyne NE6 4UF*
E: wilsonsrh@btinternet.com

WILSON, Miss Susan Elizabeth. b 52. Lady Spencer Chu Coll of Educn BEd 75. WEMTC 96. **d** 99 **p** 00. NSM Saltford w

Corston and Newton St Loe *B & W* 99-06; P-in-c Heversham and Milnthorpe *Carl* from 06. *The Vicarage, Woodhouse Lane, Heversham, Milnthorpe LA7 7EW* T: (01539) 563125
E: revsuewilson@tiscali.co.uk

WILSON, Mrs Sylvia. b 57. Teesside Univ BA 96 Newc Univ MA 99. **d** 08 **p** 09. OLM Preston-on-Tees and Longnewton *Dur* 08-14; P-in-c Egglescliffe from 14. *7 Daltry Close, Yarm TS15 9XQ* T: (01642) 892254 M: 07886-852154
E: sylviawilson.stjohns@gmail.com

WILSON, Thomas D. b 58. Univ of W Ontario BA 80 MDiv 99 Drew Univ New Jersey DMin 10. **d** 01 **p** 01. R Blyth and Brussels Canada 01-07; Hon C Nice w Vence *Eur* 07-08; LtO Huron Canada 08-11; P-in-c Cambridge St Luke 11-12; R Paisley H Trin *Glas* from 12; R Paisley St Barn from 12. *The Rectory, 11 Tantallon Drive, Paisley PA2 9JT* T: (01505) 812359
E: tomdwilson@gmail.com

WILSON, Thomas Irven. b 30. TCD BA 51 Div Test 52 MA 58. **d** 53 **p** 54. C Ballymena *Conn* 53-56; Chapl RAF 56-85; Asst Chapl-in-Chief 73-85; QHC from 80; rtd 85. *Rathclaren House, Kilbrittain, Co Cork, Republic of Ireland* T: (00353) (23) 49689

WILSON, Thomas Kazimir. b 78. Ox Univ BA 01. Wycliffe Hall Ox BA 07. **d** 07 **p** 08. C Toxteth St Philemon w St Gabr and St Cleopas *Liv* 07-12; V Glouc St Jas and All SS and Ch Ch 12-15; Dir St Phil Cen *Leic* from 15. *St Philip's Centre, 2A Stoughton Drive North, Leicester LE5 5UB* T: 0116-273 3459
E: revtomwilson@gmail.com

WILSON, Canon Thomas Roderick. b 26. St Pet Hall Ox BA 50 MA 55. Sarum Th Coll 50. **d** 52 **p** 53. C Poulton-le-Sands *Blackb* 52-56; C Altham w Clayton le Moors 56-58; V Habergham Eaves H Trin 58-78; RD Burnley 70-78; Hon Can Blackb Cathl 75-89; V Bare 78-81; P-in-c Accrington St Jas 81-82; P-in-c Accrington St Paul 81-82; V Accrington St Jas w St Paul 82-89; rtd 89; PtO *Blackb* 89-11. *Fosbrooke House, 8 Clifton Drive, Lytham St Annes FY8 5RQ*

WILSON, Canon Timothy Charles. b 62. Oak Hill Th Coll BA 90. **d** 90 **p** 91. C Highley *Heref* 90-94; C Margate H Trin *Cant* 94-98; P-in-c Margate St Phil 98-02; V 02-03; V Gt Chart from 03; AD Ashford from 11; Hon Can Cant Cathl from 11. *The Rectory, The Street, Great Chart, Ashford TN23 3AY* T: (01233) 620371 E: tandcwilson@lineone.net

WILSON, Timothy John. b 58. St Pet Coll Ox MA 80. Trin Coll Bris 81. **d** 83 **p** 84. C Gt Horton *Bradf* 83-86; C Handforth *Ches* 86-90; V Halifax All SS *Wakef* 90-07; TR Southgate *Chich* from 07. *The Rectory, Forester Road, Crawley RH10 6EH* T: (01293) 523463 E: wilsons@domini.org

WILSON (née NICHOLSON), Mrs Veronica Mary. b 66. Nene Coll Northn BSc 88 Ches Coll of HE PGCE 90. Cranmer Hall Dur 96. **d** 99 **p** 00. C Barnham Broom *Nor* 99-00; C Barnham Broom and Upper Yare 00-02; C Hellesdon 02-06; V Foulsham, Guestwick, Stibbard, Themelthorpe etc 06-14; P-in-c Heacham from 14; C Snettisham w Ingoldisthorpe and Fring from 15; P-in-c Snettisham from 15. *The Vicarage, Church Lane, Heacham, King's Lynn PE31 7HJ* T: (01485) 570697
E: veronicandsimonwilson@btinternet.com

WILSON, Walter. b 33. Wm Temple Coll Rugby 55. **d** 59 **p** 60. C Sheff St Swithun 59-63; Ind Chapl 63-66; C Attercliffe 63-66; R Swallow w Cabourn *Linc* 66-72; Dioc Youth Officer *Heref* 72-77; Chapl Ipswich Sch 77-94; rtd 94; PtO *St E* 94-02. *Riverside Cottage, Mendlesham Green, Stowmarket IP14 5RF* T: (01449) 766198

WILSON, William Adam. b 53. Sheff Univ BA 74 St Jo Coll Dur BA 84. Cranmer Hall Dur 82. **d** 85 **p** 86. C S Croydon Em *S'wark* 85-89; C Wandsworth All SS 89-93; Chapl Fontainebleau *Eur* 93-00; V S Lambeth St Steph *S'wark* from 00. *The Vicarage, St Stephen's Terrace, London SW8 1DH* T: (020) 7564 1930 or 7735 8461 F: 7735 7171
E: vicar@ststephenssouthlambeth.org.uk

WILSON, William Gerard. b 42. St Chad's Coll Dur BA 65. **d** 67 **p** 68. C Hollinwood *Man* 67-71; V Oldham St Jas 71-79; R Birch w Fallowfield 79-93; V Paddington St Jas *Lon* 93-10; AD Westmr Paddington 97-06; rtd 10. *20 Portland Street, Brighton BN1 1RN* M: 07976-363480
E: synaxis52@hotmail.com

WILSON, William John. b 25. CEng MIET MRTvS. S Dios Minl Tr Scheme 79. **d** 82 **p** 83. NSM Weeke *Win* 82-88; NSM Win St Barn 89-95; Hon Chapl R Hants Co Hosp Win 89-95; rtd 95; PtO *Win* 95-04. *23 Buriton Road, Winchester SO22 6JE* T: (01962) 881904

WILSON, Yvonne. *See* WILSON, Edith Yvonne

WILSON-BARKER, Mrs Carol Amanda. b 64. Ex Univ BA 08. SWMTC 00. **d** 03 **p** 05. C Godrevy *Truro* 03-07; TV Hale w Badshot Lea *Guildf* 07-12; P-in-c Mere w W Knoyle and Maiden Bradley *Sarum* from 12. *The Vicarage, Angel Lane, Mere, Warminster BA12 6DH* T: (01747) 861859
E: carolw953@aol.com

WILSON-BROWN, Nigel Hugh. b 65. Goldsmiths' Coll Lon BSc 87. Wycliffe Hall Ox 95. **d** 97 **p** 98. C Wimbledon Em Ridgway Prop Chpl *S'wark* 97-00; Chapl K Sch Bruton from 00. *King's School, Plox, Bruton BA10 0ED* T: (01749) 814200 or 813326 E: chaplain@kingsbruton.somerset.sch.uk

WILTON, Mrs Carlyn Zena. b 54. R Holloway Coll Lon BA 75 Southn Univ PGCE 76. SWMTC 99. **d** 02 **p** 03. NSM Carbis Bay w Lelant *Truro* from 02. *Venton Elwyn, 61 Queensway, Hayle TR27 4NL* T: (01736) 752863 E: ventonelwyn@aol.com

WILTON, Canon Christopher. b 52. Lon Univ LLB 75 Solicitor 79. NEOC 97. **d** 00 **p** 01. NSM Sherburn in Elmet w Saxton *York* from 00; P-in-c 03-09; V from 09; P-in-c Aberford w Micklefield from 12; RD Selby from 06; Ghana from 14. *The Vicarage, 2 Sir John's Lane, Sherburn in Elmet, Leeds LS25 6BJ* T: (01977) 682122 or 732222 M: 07968-268622
E: frwilton@aol.com

WILTON, Canon Gary Ian. b 60. Bath Univ BSc 83 Trin Coll Bris MA 93 Nottm Univ EdD 05. Wycliffe Hall Ox 85. **d** 88 **p** 89. C Clevedon St Andr and Ch Ch *B & W* 88-92; Lect UWE Bris 92-93; TV Bath Twerton-on-Avon *B & W* 93-97; Dir Studies and Lect Wilson Carlile Coll of Evang 98-04; Assoc Prin 04-05; Sen Lect York St Jo Univ 05-08; Hd Postgraduate Progr 06-08; C of E Rep Eur Union 08-11; Abp Cant's Rep 11-13; Can Brussels Cathl 08-13; V Ecclesall *Sheff* from 13. *Ecclesall Vicarage, Ringinglow Road, Sheffield S11 7PQ* T: 0114-268 7574
E: vicar.parishoffice@ecclesall.parishchurch.org.uk

WILTON (née ADAMS), Mrs Gillian Linda. b 57. SRN 79 SCM 81. Trin Coll Bris 82. dss 85 **d** 87 **p** 94. Easton H Trin w St Gabr and St Lawr and St Jude *Bris* 85-91; Par Dn 87-91; Regional Adv (SW) CMJ 91-97; PtO *B & W* 92-93; NSM Bath Twerton-on-Avon 93-97; Chapl Sheff Children's Hosp NHS Trust 98-06; Chapl Team Ldr Sheff Children's NHS Foundn Trust 06-10; PtO *Eur* 08-10; Asst Chapl Tervuren 10-13; P-in-c Leuven 10-11; PtO *Sheff* 13-14; Chapl St Luke's Hospice Sheff from 14; Chapl Sheff Teaching Hosps NHS Foundn Trust from 14. *Ecclesall Vicarage, Ringinglow Road, Sheffield S11 7PQ* T: 0114-236 0084 E: gillian.wilton@hotmail.co.uk

WILTON, Glenn Warner Paul. b 33. Miami Univ Ohio BSc 55 Catholic Univ of America 69 Univ of Washington Seattle MSW 76. Pontifical Beda Coll Rome 66 Ch Div Sch of the Pacific (USA) 77. **d** 65 **p** 66. In RC Ch 65-72; NSM Seattle USA 77-81; Chapl Pastures Hosp Derby 82-88; Chapl St Martin's Hosp *Cant* 89-93; Chapl St Aug Hosp *Cant* 89-93; Chapl E Kent NHS and Soc Care Partnership Trust 93-03; rtd 03; PtO *Cant* from 03. *10 Lichfield Avenue, Canterbury CT1 3YA* T: (01227) 454230 E: gwpaulwilton@yahoo.co.uk

WILTS, Archdeacon of. *See* WORSLEY, The Ven Ruth Elizabeth

WILTSE, Joseph August Jean Paul. b 41. Leeds Univ BA 64. Coll of Resurr Mirfield 64. **d** 66 **p** 67. C Airedale w Fryston *Wakef* 66-70; Canada from 70. *6983 Richmond Street, Powell River BC V8A 1H7, Canada*

WILTSHIRE, Mrs Jennifer Mary. b 42. Trin Coll Bris 09. **d** 11 **p** 12. OLM Soundwell *Bris* from 11. *19 Yew Tree Drive, Bristol BS15 4UA* T: 0117-957 0435
E: jenny.wiltshire410@btinternet.com

WILTSHIRE, John Herbert Arthur. b 27. S'wark Ord Course 63. **d** 66 **p** 67. C Lee Gd Shep w St Pet *S'wark* 66-69; Min W Dulwich Em CD 69-79; R Coulsdon St Jo 79-93; rtd 93; PtO *Ches* from 93. *66 Meadow Lane, Willaston, Neston CH64 2TZ* T: 0151-327 6668

WILTSHIRE, Robert Michael. b 50. WMMTC. **d** 89 **p** 90. NSM Droitwich Spa *Worc* 89-93; Asst Chapl HM Pris Wormwood Scrubs 93-94; Chapl HM Pris Standford Hill 94-97; Chapl HM Pris Whitemoor 97-99; Asst Chapl Gen of Pris 99-06; Chapl HM Pris Shrewsbury 06-13; C Edstaston, Fauls, Prees, Tilstock and Whixall *Lich* 13-14; rtd 14; Hon C Hodnet *Lich* from 15. *Whitehayes, Whitchurch Road, Prees SY13 3JZ* E: rm_wiltshire@btinternet.com

WIMSETT, Paul. b 58. Univ of Wales (Abth) BSc(Econ) 79 Hull Univ MA 86. St Jo Coll Nottm 82. **d** 85 **p** 86. C Nuneaton St Nic *Cov* 85-89; C Loughborough Em *Leic* 89-92; TV Totnes, Bridgetown and Berry Pomeroy etc *Ex* 92-99; V Chudleigh w Chudleigh Knighton and Trusham from 99; RD Moreton from 05. *The Vicarage, Parade, Chudleigh, Newton Abbot TQ13 0JF* T: (01626) 853241 E: wimsett@tesco.net

WIMSHURST, Michael Alexander. b 33. St Jo Coll Ox BA 58. Westcott Ho Cam 59. **d** 60 **p** 61. C Lewisham St Mary *S'wark* 60-65; India 66-70; V Battersea St Pet *S'wark* 71-72; V Battersea St Pet and St Paul 72-97; rtd 97; PtO *Cant* from 98. *50 Broad Street, Canterbury CT1 2LS* T: (01227) 457889

WINBOLT-LEWIS, Martin John. b 46. Fitzw Coll Cam BA 69 MA 72. St Jo Coll Nottm. **d** 75 **p** 76. C Highbury Ch Ch *Lon* 75-78; C Nottingham St Nic *S'well* 79-82; R Carlton Colville *Nor* 82-83; R Carlton Colville w Mutford and Rushmere 83-88; V Burley *Ripon* 88-96; Asst Chapl Pinderfields and Pontefract Hosps NHS Trust 96-99; Chapl 99-00; Lead Chapl 00-02; Lead

Chapl Mid Yorks Hosps NHS Trust 02-05; Hd Chapl Services 05-10; rtd 11; PtO *Leeds* from 11. *Owl Pen, 2 Old Manor Farm, Church Hill, Bramhope, Leeds LS16 9BA* T: 0113-284 2274
E: winboltlewis@btinternet.com

WINCHESTER, Gordon Law. b 50. Trin Coll Bris. **d** 82 **p** 83. C Cheadle *Ches* 82-84; Asst Chapl Amsterdam *Eur* 84-88; C Hove Bp Hannington Memorial Ch *Chich* 88-96; V Wandsworth All SS *S'wark* 96-04; P-in-c Ewhurst *Chich* 04-05; R from 05; P-in-c Bodiam 04-05; V from 05. *The Rectory, Ewhurst Green, Robertsbridge TN32 5TB* T: (01580) 830268
E: gordon.winchester@btinternet.com

WINCHESTER, Paul. b 44. St Pet Coll Ox BA 66 MA 70 Weymouth Coll of Educn PGCE 73. Ridley Hall Cam 67. **d** 69 **p** 70. C Wednesfield Heath *Lich* 69-72; PtO *Sarum* 73-84; R Tushingham and Whitewell *Ches* 84-02; PtO *Ox* from 02. *12 The Pines, Faringdon SN7 8AU* T: (01367) 240725
E: paulwinchester@tiscali.co.uk

WINCHESTER, Paul Marc. b 53. Univ of Wales (Lamp) BA 80. St Mich Coll Llan 82. **d** 84 **p** 85. C Bedwellty *Mon* 84-86; C Chepstow 86-89; V Cwmcarn 89-93; V Fleur-de-Lis 93-98; R Bedwas and Rudry 98-05; P-in-c Llantilio Pertholey w Bettws Chpl etc 05-10; V Brynmawr *S & B* from 10. *14 Valley View, Brynmawr, Ebbw Vale NP23 4SN* T: (01495) 315324
E: paul.winchesterwinchester@btinternet.com

WINCHESTER, Archdeacon of. *See* HARLEY, The Ven Michael
WINCHESTER, Bishop of. *See* DAKIN, The Rt Revd Timothy John
WINCHESTER, Dean of. *See* ATWELL, The Very Revd James Edgar
WINDEBANK, Clive Leonard. b 41. New Coll Ox BA 62 MA 85. Ox NSM Course 75. **d** 78 **p** 79. Asst Chapl Ahmadi Kuwait 78-83; NSM Brompton H Trin w Onslow Square St Paul *Lon* 83-84; NSM Basildon w Aldworth and Ashampstead *Ox* 85-88; NSM Streatley w Moulsford 88-00; NSM Wallingford 00-03; Chapl Abu Dhabi St Andr UAE 03-09. *The Coombe House, The Coombe, Streatley, Reading RG8 9QL* T: (01491) 872174

WINDER, Cynthia Frances. *See* CLEMOW, Cynthia Frances
WINDIATE, Mary Elizabeth. *See* WEST, Mary Elizabeth
WINDLE, Mrs Catharine Elizabeth. b 72. Hatf Coll Dur BA 95 Homerton Coll Cam PGCE 96. St Jo Coll Nottm MTh 02. **d** 03 **p** 04. C Hucknall Torkard *S'well* 03-05; Hon C Hullavington, Norton and Stanton St Quintin *Bris* 05-06; P-in-c Bath Widcombe *B & W* 06-08; Hon C Malmesbury w Westport and Brokenborough *Bris* 09-13; Chapl SS Helen and Kath Sch Abingdon from 13; PtO *Ox* from 15. *Selwyn House, Pool Gastons Road, Malmesbury SN16 0DE* T: (01666) 826369
E: royandkatie@googlemail.com

WINDLE, Christopher Rodney. b 45. Univ of Wales (Lamp) BA 66. Qu Coll Birm. **d** 70 **p** 71. C Lache cum Saltney *Ches* 70-73; C Stockton Heath 73-76; P-in-c Bredbury St Barn 76-83; V 83-07; rtd 07; PtO *Ches* from 07. *6 Norbury Avenue, Marple, Stockport SK6 6NB* T: 0161-427 0375

WINDLE, Mrs Laurie Margaret. b 57. All SS Cen for Miss & Min. **d** 14 **p** 15. OLM Chorlton-cum-Hardy St Clem *Man* from 14. *239 Ryebank Road, Chorlton cum Hardy, Manchester M21 9LU* T: 0161-881 8313 M: 07914-380241
E: laurie-windle@hotmail.co.uk

WINDLEY, Caroline Judith. b 62. Trent Poly BA 84 Nottm Univ MA 97 CQSW 84. St Jo Coll Nottm MA 96. **d** 97 **p** 98. C Kidderminster St Geo *Worc* 97-01; P-in-c Quarry Bank 01-07; TV Brierley Hill 07-08; RD Kingswinford 04-08; Area Dir of Ord and Adv in Voc Development *Ox* from 08. *1 Cavalry Path, Aylesbury HP19 9RP* T: (01296) 432921 *or* (01865) 208283
E: caroline.windley@oxford.anglican.org

WINDON, Gary. b 62. N Staffs Poly BSc 85. Qu Coll Birm 98. **d** 00 **p** 01. C Penn *Lich* 00-04; TV Radcliffe *Man* 04-08; P-in-c Wrexham *St As* 08-13; Chapl Nightingale Ho Hospice 08-14. *Address temp unknown* E: gary@windon.co.uk *or* revgwindon@gmail.com

WINDRIDGE, Michael Harry. b 47. Sarum & Wells Th Coll 91. **d** 93 **p** 94. C Hempnall *Nor* 93-96; NSM Twickenham St Mary *Lon* 96-97; PtO *Nor* from 98. *Fritton Cottage, The Common, Fritton, Norwich NR15 2QS* T: (01508) 498577

WINDROSS, Preb Andrew. b 49. Univ of Wales (Ban) BA 71. Cuddesdon Coll 71. **d** 74 **p** 75. C Wakef St Jo 74-78; C Bromley All Hallows *Lon* 78-83; V De Beauvoir Town St Pet 83-02; AD Hackney 89-94; Bp's Officer for Ordained Min Stepney Area 02-11; Hon C S Hackney St Mich w Haggerston St Paul 02-11; Preb St Paul's Cathl 02-11; rtd 11. *Clare Cottage, Oulton, Norwich NR11 6NX* T: (01263) 587193
E: windrossandy@gmail.com

WINDROSS, Anthony Michael. b 50. CCC Cam BA 72 MA 75 Birm Univ PGCE 73. S Dios Minl Tr Scheme 90. **d** 93 **p** 94. NSM Eastbourne St Mary *Chich* 93-97; C E Grinstead St Swithun 97-99; V Sheringham *Nor* 99-08; V Hythe *Cant* 08-14; R Week St Mary Circle of Par *Truro* from 14. *The Rectory, The Glebe, Week St Mary, Holsworth EX22 6UY* T: (01288) 341600 M: 07771-148103 E: amw@windross.fsnet.co.uk

WINDSLOW, Kathryn Alison. b 62. Southn Univ BTh 83 K Coll Lon MPhil 01. Linc Th Coll 84. **dss** 86 **d** 87 **p** 94. Par Dn Littlehampton and Wick *Chich* 87-89; Dn-in-c Scotton w Northorpe *Linc* 89-94; P-in-c 94-97; Asst Local Min Officer 89-97; Local Min Officer and Prin OLM Course 97-02; R Graffoe Gp 02-14; Can and Preb Linc Cathl 09-14; Bp's Adv in Women's Min 08-14; R Storrington *Chich* from 14. *The Rectory, Rectory Road, Storrington, Pulborough RH20 4EF* T: (01903) 742888 E: kathryn.windslow@btinternet.com

WINDSOR, Graham. b 35. G&C Coll Cam BA 57 MA 64 PhD 67 Lon Univ BD 60. Clifton Th Coll 58 Trin Coll Bris 79. **d** 79 **p** 80. C Rainham *Chelmsf* 79-82; rtd 00. *Yanbian University, College of Science and Technology, Yanji, Jilin, China 133000* T: (0086) (43) 3291 2500 F: 3291 2510
E: graham_windsor@hotmail.com

WINDSOR, The Ven Julie Fiona. b 59. Ridley Hall Cam 98. **d** 00 **p** 01. C Chertsey *Guildf* 00-04; TV Papworth *Ely* 04-08; TR 08-14; Hon Can Ely Cathl 12-14; Adn Horsham *Chich* from 14. *20 Langley Lane, Ifield, Crawley RH11 0NA* E: fiona.windsor@btinternet.com

WINDSOR, Mark James. b 75. Bath Univ BSc 98. Wycliffe Hall Ox BTh 08. **d** 08 **p** 09. C Felsted and Lt Dunmow *Chelmsf* 08-12; Par Missr Harwich Peninsula 12-13; TV Vale of Pewsey *Sarum* from 13. *The Vicarage, Wilcot, Pewsey SN9 5NS* T: (01672) 564265 M: 07544-718191
E: markwindsor923@btinternet.com

WINDSOR, Dean of. *See* CONNER, The Rt Revd David John
WINFIELD, Canon Flora Jane Louise. b 64. Univ of Wales (Lamp) BA 85 Virginia Th Sem DD 10 FRSA 98. Ripon Coll Cuddesdon 87. **d** 89 **p** 94. Par Dn Stantonbury and Willen *Ox* 89-92; Co Ecum Officer *Glouc* 92-94; Chapl Mansf Coll *Ox* 94-97; Local Unity Sec Coun for Chr Unity 97-02; CF (TA) from 97; Can Res Win Cathl 02-05; Asst Sec Gen World Conf of Relig for Peace 05-06; Special Adv from 06; Sec Internat Affairs CTBI 06-09; Abp's Sec for Angl Relns *Cant* 07-14; P-in-c St Mary at Hill w St Andr Hubbard etc *Lon* 08-14; Angl Communion Rep UN Institutions Geneva from 14. *Anglican Consultative Council, 16 Tavistock Crescent, London W11 1AP* E: flora.winfield@anglicancommunion.org

WINFIELD, Miss June Mary. b 29. Gilmore Ho 57. **dss** 66 **d** 87 **p** 94. Is of Dogs Ch Ch and St Jo w St Luke *Lon* 66-68; Bracknell *Ox* 68-74; Dean of Women's Min 74-80; St Marylebone w H Trin *Lon* 80-82; Ind Chapl 82-89; rtd 89; NSM Ealing St Steph Castle Hill *Lon* 89-97; Asst Dioc Dir Ords Willesden Area 94-97; PtO *Lon* 97-02. *25 Trinity Road, Marlow SL7 3AN* T: (01628) 484317

WINFIELD, Russell James. b 79. Sheff Hallam Univ BA 00 Down Coll Cam BTh 12. St Mellitus Coll MA 14. **d** 14 **p** 15. C Brentford *Lon* from 14. *34 Brook Road South, Brentford TW8 0NN* M: 07805-160853 E: russjw@outlook.com

WINFREY, Rebecca Anne. b 66. Newnham Coll Cam BA 88 MB, BCh 90 Anglia Ruskin Univ MA 14. ERMC 10. **d** 13 **p** 14. C Barnack w Ufford and Bainton *Pet* 13-14; C The Ortons *Ely* from 14. *Manor Farm House, Manor Farm Lane, Castor, Peterborough PE5 7BW*

WING, Mrs Julie. b 62. Teesside Univ BSc 99. NEOC 02. **d** 05 **p** 06. C Sunderland St Chad *Dur* 05-09; TV Gt Aycliffe 09-14; R Usworth from 14. *Usworth Rectory, 14 Prestwick Close, Washington NE37 2LP* M: 07812-589653
E: julie_wing_1@hotmail.com

WING, Miss Myra Susan. b 45. Cranmer Hall Dur 92. **d** 94 **p** 95. C Appledore w Brookland, Fairfield, Brenzett etc *Cant* 94-98; Hon C Wittersham w Stone and Ebony 95-98; V Grayshott *Guildf* 98-08; rtd 08; PtO *Cant* from 09. *142 Minster Road, Westgate-on-Sea CT8 8DQ* T: (01843) 836430
E: susan@wing63.fsnet.co.uk

WINGATE, Canon Andrew David Carlile. b 44. Worc Coll Ox BA 66 MA 71 MPhil 68 Birm Univ PhD 95. Linc Th Coll 70. **d** 72 **p** 73. C Halesowen *Worc* 72-75; Lect Tamilnadu Th Sem India 76-82; Prin WMMTC 82-90; Prin United Coll of Ascension Selly Oak 90-00; Hon Can Birm Cathl 97-00; Dir Min and Tr *Leic* 00-03; Dir Interfaith Relns and Co-ord Lay Tr 03-10; rtd 10; Can Th Leic Cathl from 00; Chapl to The Queen 07-14. *23 Roundhill Road, Leicester LE5 5RJ* T: 0116-221 6146 M: 07808-586259 E: andrewwingate5@gmail.com

WINGFIELD, Christopher Laurence. b 57. Westmr Coll Ox BTh 99. Ripon Coll Cuddesdon 93. **d** 95 **p** 96. C Hadleigh *St E* 95-99; P-in-c Melton 99-00; R 00-01; R Sproughton w Burstall, Copdock w Washbrook etc 01-09; RD Samford 06-09; P-in-c Bromsgrove St Jo *Worc* 09-12; TR Bromsgrove 12-14; R Harton *York* from 14. *The Vicarage, Sand Hutton, York YO41 1LB* T: (01904) 468418 E: chris.wingfield@btinternet.com

WINGFIELD DIGBY, Canon Andrew Richard. b 50. Keble Coll Ox BA 72. Wycliffe Hall Ox 74. **d** 77 **p** 78. C Cockfosters Ch Ch CD *Lon* 77-80; C Hadley Wood St Paul Prop Chpl

80-84; Dir Chrs in Sport 84-02; V Ox St Andr from 02; Six Preacher Cant Cathl 97-07; Hon Can Ch Ch *Ox* from 13. *St Andrew's Vicarage, 46 Charlbury Road, Oxford OX2 6UX* T: (01865) 310370 *or* T/F: 311212 M: 07768-611232 E: andrew.wingfield.digby@standrewsoxford.org

WINKETT, Miss Lucy Clare. b 68. Selw Coll Cam BA 90 MA 94 ARCM 92. Qu Coll Birm BD 94. **d** 95 **p** 96. C Lt Ilford St Mich *Chelmsf* 95-97; Min Can and Chapl St Paul's Cathl 97-03; Can Res and Prec 03-10; R Westmr St Jas from 10. *St James's Rectory, 197 Piccadilly, London W1 9LL* T: (020) 7734 4511 *or* 7292 4860. E: rector@st-james-piccadilly.org

WINKS, Paul David. b 45. Ex Univ BA 67. Cuddesdon Coll 68. **d** 70 **p** 71. C Rickerscote *Lich* 70-73; Chapl RAF 73-75; C Yate *Bris* 76-77; TV Yate New Town 77-83; P-in-c Leigh upon Mendip w Stoke St Michael *B & W* 83-84; V 84-10; rtd 10; PtO *B & W* from 10. *21 Alfords Ridge, Coleford, Radstock BA3 5YJ* T: (01373) 812787

WINN, Alan John. b 42. FRSA 73. **d** 01 **p** 02. OLM Ringwould w Kingsdown *Cant* 01-04; OLM Ringwould w Kingsdown and Ripple etc 05-12; rtd 12; PtO *Cant* from 12. *Chilterns, Back Street, Ringwould, Deal CT14 8HL* T: (01304) 361030 E: revjohnwinn@aol.com

WINN, Mrs Jean Elizabeth. b 58. Man Univ BSc 80. Wycliffe Hall Ox 85. **d** 88 **p** 98. C W Derby St Luke *Liv* 88-89; PtO 89-98; NSM Seaforth 98-02; NSM Anfield St Marg from 02. *St Margaret's Vicarage, Rocky Lane, Liverpool L6 4BA* T: 0151-263 3118

WINN, Paul William James. b 44. Liv Univ BSc 66. EMMTC 86. **d** 89 **p** 90. NSM Spalding St Paul *Linc* 89-98; PtO 98-00; P-in-c Cowbit 00-01; V 01-07; rtd 07. *6 Hawthorn Chase, Moulton, Spalding PE12 6GA* T: (01406) 373662 E: paulwinn80@hotmail.com

WINN, Peter Anthony. b 60. Worc Coll Ox BA 82 MA 86. Wycliffe Hall Ox 83. **d** 86 **p** 87. C W Derby Gd Shep *Liv* 86-89; V Seaforth 89-02; P-in-c Anfield St Marg 02-09; V from 09. *St Margaret's Vicarage, Rocky Lane, Liverpool L6 4BA* T: 0151-263 3118

WINN, Simon Reynolds. b 66. Bris Univ BA 88. Trin Coll Bris 96. **d** 98 **p** 99. C Portswood Ch Ch *Win* 98-02; V Northolt St Jos *Lon* 02-10; Dir of Ords Willesden Area 07-10; V Hataitai-Kilbirnie New Zealand from 10. *94 Hamilton Road, Hataitai, Wellington 6021, New Zealand* T: (0064) (4) 971 2140 *or* 971 2142 E: simonwinn66@yahoo.co.uk *or* vicar@allsaints.org.nz

WINNARD, Jack. b 30. Oak Hill Th Coll 79. **d** 81 **p** 82. C Skelmersdale St Paul *Liv* 81-84; C Goose Green 84-85; V Wigan St Barn Marsh Green 85-98; rtd 99; PtO *Liv* from 00. *Maranatha, 11 Beech Walk, Winstanley, Wigan WN3 6DH* T: (01942) 222339

WINNEY, Mrs Samantha Jane. b 71. St Mellitus Coll BA 10. **d** 10 **p** 11. NSM Harwich Peninsula *Chelmsf* 10-12; PtO from 13. *Wisteria, Mill Lane, Bradfield, Manningtree CO11 2UT* T: (01255) 870618 M: 07903-522955 E: rev.samantha@googlemail.com

WINNINGTON-INGRAM, David Robert. b 59. Hertf Coll Ox BA 82 MA 85 K Coll Cam BA 89. Westcott Ho Cam 87. **d** 90 **p** 91. C Bishop's Cleeve *Glouc* 90-94; TV Colyton, Southleigh, Offwell, Widworthy etc *Ex* 94-00; V S Brent and Rattery from 00. *The Vicarage, Firswood, South Brent TQ10 9AN* T: (01364) 649070 *or* 72774 E: wis100acre.wood@virgin.net

WINROW, Terence. b 60. **d** 12 **p** 13. NSM Newbury *Ox* 12-15; NSM Newbury St Geo and St Jo from 15. *Pineridge, 244A Andover Road, Newbury RG14 6PT*

WINSBURY, Leigh Darren. b 67. St Jo Coll Nottm 13. **d** 15. C. Bideford, Northam, Westward Ho!, Appledore etc *Ex* from 15. *The Vicarage, Mines Road, Bideford EX39 4BZ* E: lwinsbury@googlemail.com

WINSLADE, Richard Clive. b 69. Aston Tr Scheme 91 Linc Th Coll BTh 93. **d** 96 **p** 97. C Waltham Cross *St Alb* 96-99; C Leavesden 99-03; R Maulden 03-13; V Gravenhurst, Shillington and Stondon from 13. *All Saints' Vicarage, Vicarage Close, Shillington, Hitchin SG5 3LS* T: (01462) 713797 E: richardrev@btinternet.com

WINSPER, Arthur William (Brother Benedict). b 46. Ox Brookes Univ BA 10. Glas NSM Course 89. **d** 91 **p** 92. SSF from 70; NSM Barrowfield *Glas* 91-96; P-in-c St Aug Miss Penhalonga Zimbabwe 96-98; PtO *Worc* 98-08; *Sheff* 09-12; *Chelmsf* from 13. *St Matthias' Vicarage, 45 Mafeking Road, London E16 4NS*

✠**WINSTANLEY, The Rt Revd Alan Leslie.** b 49. Nottm Univ BTh 72. St Jo Coll Nottm 68 ALCD 72. **d** 72 **p** 73 **c** 88. C Livesey *Blackb* 72-75; C Gt Sankey *Liv* 75-77; P-in-c Penketh 75-77; V 78-81; SAMS 81-93; Bp Bolivia and Peru 88-93; V Eastham *Ches* 94-03; Hon Asst Bp Ches 94-03; V Whittle-le-Woods *Blackb* 03-12; Hon Asst Bp Blackb 03-12; TV Shirwell, Loxhore, Kentisbury, Arlington, etc *Ex* 12-14; Hon Asst Bp Ex 12-14; rtd 14. *51 Warrington Road, Penketh, Warrington*

WA5 2BW T: (01925) 722250 E: alanlwinstanley@gmail.com

WINSTANLEY, John Graham. b 47. K Coll Lon 67. **d** 71 **p** 72. C Wandsworth St Paul *S'wark* 71-74; Chapl Salford Univ *Man* 75-79; R Kersal Moor 79-87. *14 Lyndhurst Avenue, Prestwich, Manchester M25 0GF* T: 0161-740 2715 F: 720 6916 E: john@blots.co.uk

WINSTONE, Canon Peter John. b 30. Jes Coll Ox BA 52 MA 56. Ridley Hall Cam 53. **d** 55 **p** 56. C Bitterne Win 55-58; C Keighley *Bradf* 58-60; PC Fairweather Green 60-67; V Clapham 67-84; R Leathley w Farnley, Fewston and Blubberhouses 84-95; Hon Can Bradf Cathl 89-95; rtd 95; PtO *Worc* from 95. *7 Kingfisher Close, Worcester WR5 3RY* T: (01905) 763114

WINTER, Andrew Christopher. b 73. Dur Univ BSc 95 PGCE 96. **d** 03 **p** 04. C Mosman St Clem Australia 03-05; NSM Hinckley H Trin *Leic* 06-10; Chapl Ipswich Sch 10-15; Chapl Reed's Sch Cobham from 15. *Reeds' School, Sandy Lane, Cobham KT11 2ES* T: (01932) 869044

WINTER, Anthony Cathcart. b 28. FCA. Ridley Hall Cam 54. **d** 56 **p** 57. C Childwall St Dav *Liv* 56-58; C Hackney St Jo *Lon* 58-63; V Newmarket All SS *St E* 63-73; LtO 74-81; PtO *Lon* 78-81 and 97-99; Hon C St Andr-by-the-Wardrobe w St Ann, Blackfriars 81-86; Hon C Smithfield St Bart Gt 86-95; Chapl S'wark Cathl from 99; PtO from 99. *25 Bowater House, Golden Lane Estate, London EC1Y 0RJ* T: (020) 7490 5765 F: 7490 1064 E: a.c.winter@btinternet.com

WINTER, Canon David Brian. b 29. K Coll Lon BA 53 CertEd 54. Oak Hill NSM Course. **d** 87 **p** 88. NSM Finchley St Paul and St Luke *Lon* 87-89; Hd Relig Broadcasting BBC 87-89; Bp's Officer for Evang *Ox* 89-95; P-in-c Ducklington 89-95; Hon Can Ch Ch 95; rtd 95; Hon C Hermitage *Ox* 95-00; Hon C Dorchester 02-05; PtO 00-02 and from 06. *51 Nideggen Close, Thatcham RG19 4HS* T: (01635) 873639 E: david_winter1@btinternet.com

WINTER, Canon Dennis Graham St Leger. b 33. K Coll Lon BSc 54 AKC 54. Tyndale Hall Bris BD 62. **d** 61 **p** 62. C Pennycross *Ex* 61-64; C Maidstone St Faith *Cant* 64-66; V Paddock Wood *Roch* 66-99; RD Tonbridge 89-95; RD Paddock Wood 95-99; Hon Can Roch Cathl 90-99; rtd 99; PtO *Newc* from 00. *4 Oaky Balks, Alnwick NE66 2QE* T: (01665) 602658

WINTER, Mrs Fiona Helen. b 64. Sheff Univ BSc 87. NEOC 97. **d** 00. NSM Gt Ayton w Easby and Newton-in-Cleveland *York* 00-02. *9 The Acres, Stokesley, Middlesbrough TS9 5QA* T: (01642) 713146

WINTER, Mrs Jane Marion. b 62. Avery Hill Coll BEd 84 York St Jo Coll MA 09. Ripon Coll Cuddesdon 12. **d** 14. C Orpington St Andr *Roch* 14-15; C Cray Valley from 15. *39 Chelsfield Road, Orpington BR5 4DS* T: (01689) 817250 M: 07734-962140 E: jane.winter@gmail.com

WINTER, Jonathan Gay. b 37. Lon Inst of Educn DipEd 84. AKC 64. **d** 65 **p** 66. C W Dulwich All SS and Em *S'wark* 65-69; Asst Master Kidbrooke Sch 69-77; Norwood Sch 77-80; Dep Hd Lewisham Sch 80-89; Hon C Dulwich St Barn *S'wark* 90-08; Chapl Dulwich Coll 95-98; Cllr from 98; Dean of MSE (Woolwich) 00-04; PtO *S'wark* 08-11. *18 Garden Walk, Maidstone ME15 8GA* M: 07811-529503 E: jonathanwinter@btinternet.com

WINTER, Mrs Mary Elizabeth. b 56. Man Univ BEd 78 Leeds Univ AdDipEd 85. Yorks Min Course 08. **d** 11 **p** 12. C Skipton Ch Ch w Carleton *Leeds* 11-15; C Skipton H Trin 11-15; P-in-c Thorpe Edge *Bradf* from 15. *The Vicarage, Northwood Crescent, Bradford BD10 9HX* M: 07813-687680 T: (01274) 614898 E: mary.winter@hotmail.co.uk

WINTER, Nichola Jane. b 58. Trevelyan Coll Dur BA 79. **d** 02 **p** 03. OLM Aldeburgh w Hazlewood *St E* 02-13; NSM from 13; Chapl Suffolk Coastal Primary Care Trust from 06. *Threeways, Donkey Lane, Friston, Saxmundham IP17 1PL* T: (01728) 688979 E: njwinter@clara.co.uk

WINTER, Rebecca Anne. *See* BEVAN, Rebecca Anne

WINTER, Stephen Christopher. b 55. Southn Univ BA 76. Trin Coll Bris 85. **d** 88 **p** 89. C Birm St Luke 88-92; TV Kings Norton 92-98; Ind Chapl *Worc* 98-04; Asst Dir Development (Discipleship) 04-11; C Finstall 04-11; rtd 11. *2 Canal Cottages, Hanbury Wharf, Hanbury Road, Droitwich WR9 7DU* E: mail@stephenwinter.net

WINTER, Thomas Andrew. b 24. Wadh Coll Ox BA 51 MA 63. Ely Th Coll 51. **d** 53 **p** 54. C Horninglow *Lich* 53-56; S Africa 56-83; R Woodston *Ely* 83-90; rtd 90; PtO *Ely* 90-97; *Chich* from 90. *6 The Close, Shoreham-by-Sea BN43 5AH* T: (01273) 452606

WINTERBOTTOM, Canon Ian Edmund. b 42. St Andr Univ MA 66. Linc Th Coll 66. **d** 68 **p** 69. C Blackb St Steph 68-71; C Wingerworth *Derby* 71-73; P-in-c Brimington 73-77; R 77-89; RD Bolsover and Staveley 86-93; R Pleasley 89-94; P-in-c Shirebrook 92-94; TR E Scarsdale 94-00; Hon Can Derby Cathl 95-08; Prin Ind Chapl 00-08; rtd 08. *17 Coach Way, Willington, Derby DE65 6ES* T: (01283) 704322
E: ianwinterbottom@aol.com

WINTERBURN, Derek Neil. b 60. Bris Univ BSc 82 Ox Univ BA 85. Wycliffe Hall Ox 83. **d** 86 **p** 87. C Mildmay Grove St Jude and St Paul *Lon* 86-89; C Hackney Marsh 89-91; TV 91-96; V Hampton St Mary from 96; AD Hampton 08-14. *St Mary's Vicarage, Church Street, Hampton TW12 2EB* T: (020) 8979 3071 F: 8941 7221 E: stmary@bigfoot.com *or* vicar@winterburn.me.uk

WINTGENS, Peter Brendon. b 47. Surrey Univ BSc 70 Cant Ch Ch Univ BA 12. SEITE 06. **d** 09 **p** 10. NSM Battersea St Mary *S'wark* from 09. *5 Beechmore Road, London SW11 4ET* T: (020) 7720 9708 E: wintgens@btinternet.com

WINTLE, Anthony Robert. b 44. K Coll Lon 64. St Mich Coll Llan. **d** 68 **p** 69. C Llandaff N *Llan* 68-70; C Baglan 70-75; V Treharris 75-85; V Treharris w Bedlinog 86-90; R St Fagans and Michaelston-super-Ely 90-13; rtd 13; PtO *St D* from 13. *Porth y Castell, Market Street, Newport SA42 0PH* T: (01239) 820414

WINTLE, David Robert. b 56. Open Univ BA 84. Qu Coll Birm 93. **d** 95 **p** 96. C Cov St Mary 95-00; P-in-c Baginton w Bubbenhall and Ryton-on-Dunsmore 00-05; V from 05. *The Vicarage, Church Road, Ryton on Dunsmore, Coventry CV8 3ET* T: (024) 7630 1283 E: david@wintled.fsnet.co.uk

WINTLE, Graham. b 52. Bris Univ BSc 73. Oak Hill Th Coll BA 86. **d** 86 **p** 87. C Southgate *Chich* 86-89; C New Malden and Coombe *S'wark* 89-92; V Surbiton Hill Ch Ch 92-06; R Willoughby Australia from 06. *211 Mowbray Road, Willoughby NSW 2068, Australia* T: (0061) (2) 9411 2172 E: graham.wintle@gmail.com

WINTLE, Canon Ruth Elizabeth. b 31. Westf Coll Lon BA 53 St Hugh's Coll Ox BA 67 MA 74. St Mich Ho Ox 63. **dss** 72 **d** 87 **p** 94. Tutor St Jo Coll Dur 72-74; Selection Sec ACCM 74-83; St Jo in Bedwardine *Worc* 83-87; Par Dn 87-94; Dir of Ords 84-92; Hon Can Worc Cathl 87-97; rtd 95; Bp's Adv on Women's Min *Worc* 95-97; PtO from 98. *6 Coronation Avenue, Rushwick, Worcester WR2 5TF* T: (01905) 427109 E: ruth.wintle@btinternet.com

WINTLE, Thomas Gerrard. b 82. Stirling Univ BA 09. St Steph Ho Ox BTh 15 Nottm Univ MA 11. **d** 15. C Nuneaton St Mary *Cov* from 15. *The Vicarage, Cedar Road, Nuneaton CV10 9DL* M: 07812-377004 E: t.g.b.wintle@gmail.com

✠**WINTON, The Rt Revd Alan Peter.** b 58. Sheff Univ BA 83 PhD 87. Linc Th Coll 91. **d** 91 **p** 92 **c** 09. C Southgate Ch Ch *Lon* 91-95; P-in-c St Paul's Walden and Dioc CME Officer *St Alb* 95-99; R Welwyn w Ayot St Peter 99-05; TR Welwyn 05-09; Hon Can St Alb 07-09; Suff Bp Thetford *Nor* from 09. *The Red House, 53 Norwich Road, Stoke Holy Cross, Norwich NR14 8AB* T: (01508) 491014 F: 538371 E: bishop.thetford@norwich.anglican.org

WINTON, Ms Philippa Mary. b 56. Nottm Univ BA 78. Trin Coll Bris 79. **dss** 83 **d** 87 **p** 94. Sheff St Jo 83-86; Sheff Gillcar St Silas 86-87; Chapl Asst R Hallamshire Hosp Sheff 87; Hon Par Dn Linc St Faith and St Martin w St Pet 90-92; Chapl Asst W Middx Univ Hosp Isleworth 92-93; PtO *Lon* 93-95; *St Alb* 95-09. *The Red House, 53 Norwich Road, Stoke Holy Cross, Norwich NR14 8AB* T: (01508) 492105

WINTON, Stanley Wootton. b 30. Sarum & Wells Th Coll 70. **d** 72 **p** 73. C Birkenhead St Jas w St Bede *Ches* 72-75; V 75-79; TR Ellesmere Port 79-88; Chapl Ellesmere Port and Manor Hosps 79-95; R Delamere *Ches* 88-95; rtd 95; PtO *Ches* from 95. *26 Wimborne Avenue, Thingwall, Wirral CH61 7UL* T: 0151-648 0176

WINTOUR, Mrs Anne Elizabeth. b 52. **d** 03 **p** 04. OLM Melksham *Sarum* 03-12; OLM Atworth w Shaw and Whitley 07-12; OLM Broughton Gifford, Gt Chalfield and Holt 07-12; PtO from 12; Asst Dioc Dir of Ords from 13; NSM Rowde and Bromham from 14. *Weavers House, 264 Sandridge Lane, Bromham, Chippenham SN15 2JW* T: (01380) 850880 E: anniewintour@btinternet.com

WINWARD, Stuart James. b 36. Open Univ BA 85. Lich Th Coll 65. **d** 68 **p** 69. C Lytham St Cuth *Blackb* 68-71; C Padiham 71-73; V Musbury 73-84; R Old Trafford St Hilda *Man* 84-89; V Davyhulme St Mary 89-98; rtd 98; PtO *Ches* 99-12. *190 Causeway Road, Bushmills BT57 8SY*

WIPPELL, David Stanley. b 46. Univ of Qld BSc 67 Selw Coll Cam BA 77 MA. Westcott Ho Cam 76. **d** 78 **p** 79. C Wolvercote w Summertown *Ox* 78-80; Asst Chapl St Edw Sch Ox 78-00; Chapl 00-06; Housemaster 85-97; Chapl

St Hugh's Coll Ox 80-85; NSM Ray Valley *Ox* 06-15; PtO from 15. *Rivermead, 1A Mill Street, Islip, Kidlington OX5 2TG* T: (01865) 849497 M: 07970-024316
E: davidwippell1@gmail.com

WISE, David Reginald. b 46. Glas Univ BSc 68 QUB PhD 74 LRAM 67. Edin Th Coll 72. **d** 74 **p** 75. Chapl St Andr Cathl 74-75; C Ayr *Glas* 75-78; R Airdrie 78-81; P-in-c Gartcosh 78-81; P-in-c Leic St Nic 81-82; Chapl Leic Univ 81-89; TV Leic H Spirit 82-89; Chapl St Hilda's Priory and Sch Whitby 89-96; TV Louth *Linc* 96-98; V Mexborough *Sheff* from 98. *The Vicarage, Church Street, Mexborough S64 0ER* T: (01709) 582321

WISE, Jacqueline Joy. b 65. Yorks Min Course. **d** 09 **p** 10. C Crewe All SS and St Paul w St Pet *Ches* 09-11; C Heswall from 11. *15 Castle Drive, Heswall, Wirral CH60 4RJ* T: 0151-342 4841 E: jacky.wise@ymail.com

WISE, Canon Pamela Margaret. b 51. CertEd 73 BA 79. Ripon Coll Cuddesdon 89. **d** 91 **p** 94. Par Dn Tokyngton St Mich *Lon* 91-94; C N Greenford All Hallows 94; C Bedford All SS *St Alb* 94-97; TV Hitchin 97-03; V Oxhey All SS from 03; Hon Can St Alb from 09. *All Saints' Vicarage, Gosforth Lane, Watford WD19 7AX* T: (020) 8421 5949 E: pamela.wise@gmail.com

WISE, Richard Edmund. b 67. Clare Coll Cam BA 88 MusB 89 LRAM 91. Cranmer Hall Dur 01. **d** 03 **p** 04. C Stanmore *Win* 03-07; P-in-c Bishopstoke 07-09; R from 09. *The Rectory, 10 Stoke Park Road, Eastleigh SO50 6DA* T: (023) 8061 2192 E: rwise@talktalk.net

WISE, Susan Jacqueline. St Mellitus Coll 14. **d** 15. NSM Wickford and Runwell *Chelmsf* from 15. *6 Tamarisk, Benfleet SS7 5PW*

WISEMAN, Canon David John. b 51. Lon Univ BD 80 Derby Univ MA 99. Cranmer Hall Dur 77. **d** 80 **p** 81. C Bilston *Lich* 80-84; P-in-c W Bromwich St Phil 84-86; V 86-89; P-in-c Cheetham St Mark *Man* 89-94; Dioc Community Relns Officer 89-96; P-in-c Ashton H Trin 94-99; TR Ashton 00-03; Chapl Tameside Coll 94-03; Soc Resp Adv *Pet* 03-07; P-in-c Northampton Ch Ch from 07; AD Gtr Northn from 07; Can Pet Cathl from 09. *Christ Church Vicarage, 3 Christ Church Road, Northampton NN1 5LL* T: (01604) 633254 E: david@wiseman50.freeserve.co.uk

WISEMAN, John. b 56. Sarum & Wells Th Coll 80. **d** 83 **p** 84. C Swinton St Pet *Man* 83-87; C Swinton and Pendlebury 87-88; TV Atherton 88-93; V Bedford Leigh 93-02; V Lt Lever from 02. *The Vicarage, Market Street, Little Lever, Bolton BL3 1HH* T: (01204) 700936

WISEMAN, Sister Julie. b 53. ERMC 05. **d** 08 **p** 09. NSM Roughton and Felbrigg, Metton, Sustead etc *Nor* 08-10; Public Preacher from 10. *32B Beeston Common, Sheringham NR26 8ES* T: (01263) 825623 E: juliessl@btinternet.com

WISHART, Michael Leslie. b 45. St Mich Coll Llan 70. **d** 73 **p** 74. C Llangyfelach *S & B* 73-76; Chapl RN 76-80 and 85-96; V Beguildy and Heyope *S & B* 80-84; V Gowerton 84-85; Chapl RNR 80-85; R Dowlais *Llan* 97-04; R Bishops Lydeard w Bagborough and Cothelstone *B & W* 04-11; P-in-c Lydeard St Lawrence and Combe Florey 10-11; rtd 11; PtO *Llan* from 11. *Hollands Cottage, Higher End, St Athan, Barry CF62 4LW* T: (01446) 751600 E: michael.wishart@btopenworld.com

WISKEN, Canon Brian Leonard. b 34. Dur Univ BA 58. Linc Th Coll 58. **d** 60 **p** 61. C Lobley Hill *Dur* 60-63; C Ipswich All Hallows *St E* 63-65; P-in-c Scunthorpe All SS *Linc* 65-69; V 69-71; Dioc Stewardship Adv 70-75; R Panton w Wragby 71-75; V Langton by Wragby 71-75; R Cleethorpes 75-77; TR 77-89; V Linc St Nic w St Jo Newport 89-99; Can and Preb Linc Cathl 88-00; rtd 99; PtO *Nor* from 99; *St E* from 99. *49 Gainsborough Drive, Lowestoft NR32 4NJ* T: (01502) 512378 E: b.wisken@btinternet.com

WISKEN, Robert Daniel. b 30. ACT. **d** 60 **p** 60. C N Rockhampton St Barn Australia 60; V N Rockhampton St Matt 61-63; V Winton *Man* 63-65; R Luddington w Hemington and Thurning *Pet* 65-69; P-in-c Clopton *St E* 66-69; V Ipswich All SS 69-73; V Sompting *Chich* 74-78; Org Sec (SW England) CECS 78-80; R Edmundbyers w Muggleswick *Dur* 80-83; R Wexham *Ox* 83-86; Australia from 86; rtd 95. *11-64 Riverwalk Avenue, Robina QLD 4226, Australia* E: randjwisken@bigpond.com

WITCHELL, David William. b 47. St Jo Coll Nottm BTh 75. **d** 75 **p** 76. C Northampton St Mary *Pet* 75-78; C Oakham w Hambleton and Egleton 78-81; C Oakham, Hambleton, Egleton, Braunston and Brooke 81-82; V Weedon Bec w Everdon 82-90; V Wellingborough St Barn 90-00; RD Wellingborough 98-00; P-in-c Paignton St Paul Preston *Ex* 00-02; V Paignton Ch Ch and Preston St Paul from 03; RD Torbay 03-09. *St Paul's Vicarage, Locarno Avenue, Paignton TQ3 2DH* T: (01803) 522872

WITCHELL, Derek William Frederick. b 49. SAOMC 00. **d** 03 **p** 04. C Bloxham w Milcombe and S Newington *Ox* 03-06; P-in-c Wing w Grove 06-12; P-in-c Wingrave w Rowsham,

Aston Abbotts and Cublington 06-12; P-in-c Cheddington w Mentmore 08-12; TV Cottesloe 12-13; rtd 13; PtO *Ox* from 13. *11 Hunt Road, Thame OX9 3LG* T: (01844) 215798 M: 07847-167507 E: witchell@psaconnect.net

WITCHER, Ian. b 49. CertEd 93 Lon Inst of Educn Lic 97. d 97 p 98. OLM Shaston *Sarum* 97-08. *7 Old Boundary Road, Shaftesbury SP7 8ND* T: (01747) 854878

WITCOMBE, The Very Revd John Julian. b 59. Cam Univ MA 84 Nottm Univ MPhil 91. St Jo Coll Nottm BA 83. d 84 p 85. C Birtley *Dur* 84-87; C Chilwell *S'well* 87-91; V Lodge Moor St Luke *Sheff* 91-95; TR Uxbridge *Lon* 95-98; Dean St Jo Coll Nottm 98-05; Officer for Min *Glouc* 05-10; Hon Can Glouc Cathl 09-10; Can Res Glouc Cathl 10-13; Dir Discipleship and Min 10-13; Dean Cov from 13. *8 Priory Row, Coventry CV1 5EX* T: (024) 7652 1391

WITCOMBE, Michael David. b 53. Univ of Wales (Lamp) BA 76. Qu Coll Birm 76. d 78 p 79. C Neath w Llantwit *Llan* 78-80; C Whitchurch 80-83; V Newcastle 83-02; P-in-c Ewenny 84-86; V Llanishen from 02. *The Vicarage, 2 The Rise, Llanishen, Cardiff CF14 0RA* T: (029) 2075 2545

WITCOMBE, Ricarda Jane. b 64. Ch Coll Cam BA 86 MA 90. St Jo Coll Nottm MA(TS) 99. d 01 p 02. C Wilford *S'well* 01-05; P-in-c Glouc St Paul 05-09; V Glouc St Paul and St Steph 09-13; PtO 13-14; Chapl Team Ldr Geo Eliot Hosp NHS Trust Nuneaton from 14. *The Chaplaincy, George Eliot Hospital, College Street, Nuneaton CV10 7DJ* T: (024) 7686 5281 E: ricarda@ricarda.fsnet.co.uk *or* ricarda.witcombe@geh.nhs.uk

WITCOMBE, Simon Christopher. b 61. Dundee Univ MA 83 PGCE 84 St Jo Coll Dur BA 90. Cranmer Hall Dur 88. d 91 p 92. C Earlham St Anne *Nor* 91-95; Assoc P Skegness and Winthorpe *Linc* 95-98; Gen Preacher 95-98; R Woodhall Spa Gp 98-07; V Codsall *Lich* from 07; P-in-c Bilbrook and Coven 13-14; RD Penkridge from 11. *The Vicarage, 48 Church Road, Codsall, Wolverhampton WV8 1EH* T: (01902) 842168 E: simonwitcombe50@gmail.com

WITHERIDGE, John Stephen. b 53. Kent Univ BA 76 Ch Coll Cam BA 78 MA 82 FRSA 98. Ridley Hall Cam 78. d 79 p 80. C Luton St Mary *St Alb* 79-82; Asst Chapl Marlborough Coll 82-84; Abp's Chapl *Cant* 84-87; Conduct Eton Coll 87-96; Hd Charterhouse Sch Godalming 96-14; PtO *Guildf* 96-09; rtd 14; PtO *Ox* from 14. *Address withheld by request* T: (01608) 810383 E: john.witheridge@outlook.com

WITHERS, Mrs Christine Mary. b 37. ALA 60. Gilmore Ho. dss 81 d 87 p 94. Chorleywood Ch Ch *St Alb* 81-86; Darley *Derby* 86-92; C 87-92; Chapl HM Pris Drake Hall 92-95; P-in-c Standon and Cotes Heath *Lich* 96-98; PtO *Heref* from 98. *2 Ash Meadow, Westbury, Shrewsbury SY5 9QJ* T: (01743) 885038

WITHERS, Eleanor Jane. See WILLIAMS, Eleanor Jane

WITHERS, Geoffrey Edward. b 68. QUB BSc 90 TCD BTh 93. CITC 90. d 93 p 94. C Ballymena w Ballyclug *Conn* 93-97; I Monkstown 97-01; Chapl RAF from 01. *Chaplaincy Services (RAF), HQ Air Command, RAF High Wycombe HP14 4UE* T: (01494) 496800 F: 496343 E: stchap.dgcs@ptc.raf.mod.uk *or* gwithers@vodafonc.net

WITHERS, Miss Gillian. b 58. Stranmillis Coll BEd 80. St Jo Coll Nottm 94. d 97 p 98. NSM Mossley *Conn* 97-03; C Bangor St Comgall *D & D* 03-05; V Knock 05-08; I Grey Abbey w Kircubbin from 08. *4 Rectory Wood, Portaferry, Newtownards BT22 1LJ* T: (028) 4272 9307 E: vicarofdibley@hotmail.com

WITHERS, John Geoffrey. b 39. St Jo Coll Dur BA 61 Birm Univ CertEd 63 CQSW 72. SWMTC 84. d 87 p 88. NSM Drewsteignton *Ex* 87-01; P-in-c 99-01; P-in-c Hittisleigh and Spreyton 99-01; P-in-c Chagford, Drewsteignton, Hittisleigh etc 01; C 01-07; Sub Chapl HM Pris Ex 96-07; PtO *Ex* from 07. *Lane's End, Broadwoodwidger, Lifton PL16 0JH* T: (01566) 780544

WITHERS, Michael. b 41. TCD BA 66 Edin Univ BD 70 QUB MTh 83 Birm Univ PGCE 67. Union Th Sem (NY) STM 71. d 71 p 73. C Seagoe *D & D* 71-77; C Seapatrick 77-80; I Belfast St Chris 80-89; I Movilla 89-96; rtd 96. *5 Pembridge Mews, Belfast BT5 6HA* T: (028) 9047 1037

WITHEY, Michael John. b 45. Open Univ BA 80 Ox Univ MTh 98 SRN 66. Oak Hill Th Coll 71. d 74 p 75. C St Alb St Paul *St Alb* 74-76; C Luton St Mary 77; C Luton St Fran 77-80; V Woodside w E Hyde 80-87; CF (TA) 83-87; Dioc Stewardship Adv *Ox* 87-89; Chapl HM YOI Onley 89-91; V Hengoed w Gobowen *Lich* 91-95; Chapl Robert Jones and Agnes Hunt Orthopaedic Hosp 91-95; P-in-c Chasetown *Lich* 95-00; V 00-02; V Stroud H Trin *Glouc* 02-13; Chapl Cotswold and Vale Primary Care Trust 02-06; Chapl Glos Primary Care Trust 06-11; Chapl Glos Partnership Trust 02-11; rtd 13. *24 Cwrt Deri, Cwmann, Lampeter SA48 8EJ* E: meic.clydogau@media-maker.com

WITHINGTON, Canon Brian James. b 54. Leic Univ MSc 01 CQSW 76. EAMTC 94. d 97 p 98. NSM Pet St Jo 97-04; P-in-c

Broughton w Loddington and Cransley etc 04-10; C from 10; RD Kettering from 07; Bp's Adv for Pioneer Min 10-13; Asst Dir Ords from 14; Can Pet Cathl from 13. *The Rectory, Gate Lane, Broughton, Kettering NN14 1ND* T/F: (01536) 791373 E: revdbrian@uwclub.net

WITHINGTON, George Kenneth. b 37. Birm Univ BA 59. Wells Th Coll 59. d 61 p 62. C Hartcliffe St Andr CD *Bris* 61-65; V Swindon St Jo 65-73; V Cricklade w Latton 73-97; RD Cricklade 94-97; rtd 97; PtO *Heref* from 97; *Worc* from 97. *19 Oak Drive, Colwall, Malvern WR13 6RA* T: (01684) 540590 E: kandjw@btinternet.com

WITHINGTON, Canon Keith. b 32. Univ of Wales (Lamp) BA 55. Qu Coll Birm 55. d 57 p 58. C Bournville *Birm* 57-61; V 61-00; RD Moseley 81-91; Hon Can Birm Cathl 83-00; rtd 00; PtO *Birm* from 00; *Worc* from 00. *44 Dugard Way, Droitwich WR9 8UX* T: (01905) 795847 E: keithkw1000@aol.com

WITHINGTON, Paul Martin. b 60. Kent Univ BSc 86. Trin Coll Bris 01. d 03 p 04. C Elworth and Warmingham *Ches* 03-06; TV Congleton from 06. *The Vicarage, 14 Chapel Street, Congleton CW12 4AB* T: (01260) 278288 E: pgrawith@dialstart.net

WITHNELL, Roderick David. b 55. EMMTC 86 Ridley Hall Cam 89. d 90 p 91. C Shenfield *Chelmsf* 90-94; C Woodleigh and Loddiswell *Ex* 94-95; TV Modbury, Bigbury, Ringmore w Kingston etc 95-00; Canada 00-01; TR Burrington, Chawleigh, Cheldon, Chulmleigh etc *Ex* from 01. *The Rectory, Church Lane, Chulmleigh EX18 7BY* T: (01769) 580537

WITHY, John Daniel Forster. b 38. ALCD 64. d 64 p 65. C Belfast St Aid *Conn* 64-68; Dir Chr Conf Cen Sion Mills from 68. *Zion House, 120 Melmont Road, Strabane BT82 9ET* T: (028) 8165 8672

WITT, Canon Bryan Douglas. b 52. St Mich Coll Llan BD 84. d 84 p 85. C Betws w Ammanford *St D* 84-87; V Llanllwni 87-91; V Llangennech and Hendy 91-04; V St Clears w Llangynin and Llanddowror etc 04-15; AD St Clears 13-14; P-in-c Llanarthne and Llanddarog from 15; Hon Can St D Cathl 11-13; Can Cursal from 13. *The New Vicarage, Llanddarog, Carmarthen SA32 8PA* E: heather.witt@virgin.net

WITT, Caroline Elizabeth. See SACKLEY, Caroline Elizabeth

WITTER, Mrs Tania Judy Ingram. b 37. Girton Coll Cam BA 58 MA 63. Oak Hill Th Coll 94. d 95 p 96. NSM Highbury Ch Ch w St Jo and St Sav *Lon* 95-03 and from 14; PtO 03-13; *Eur* from 03. *26 Viewpoint Apartments, 30-32 Highbury Grove, London N5 2DL* T: (020) 7226 6908 E: tania.witter@btinternet.com

WITTS, Donald Roger. b 47. Cranmer Hall Dur 86. d 88 p 89. C Leyland St Ambrose *Blackb* 88-90; C Staines St Mary and St Pet *Lon* 90-93; Ind Missr *Man* 93-95; Dioc Communications Officer *Cant* 95-00; P-in-c Blean 95-01; P-in-c Birchington w Acol and Minnis Bay 01-03; V from 03. *All Saints' Vicarage, 15 Minnis Road, Birchington CT7 9SE* T: (01843) 841117 E: don.witts@btopenworld.com

WITTS, Graham Robert. b 53. Newc Univ BEd Bris Univ MA 01. Linc Th Coll 79. d 82 p 83. C Horncastle w Low Toynton *Linc* 82-85; TV Gt Grimsby St Mary and St Jas 85-89; TR Yelverton, Meavy, Sheepstor and Walkhampton *Ex* 89-93; C Glastonbury w Meare *B & W* 93-03; RD Glastonbury 00-03; V Burnham from 03; Warden of Readers Wells Adnry from 10. *The Vicarage, Rectory Road, Burnham-on-Sea TA8 2BZ* T: (01278) 782991 E: thewittsonweb@hotmail.com

WOADDEN, Christopher Martyn. b 56. St Jo Coll Nottm LTh. d 87 p 88. C Mickleover All SS *Derby* 87-90; C Wirksworth w Alderwasley, Carsington etc 90-92; C Wirksworth 92; TV Gt and Lt Coates w Bradley *Linc* 92-98; V Holton-le-Clay and Tetney 98-07; V Holton-le-Clay, Tetney and N Cotes from 07. *The Vicarage, Church Walk, Holton-le-Clay, Grimsby DN36 5AN* T: (01472) 824082

WOAN, Miss Susan Ann. b 52. Univ of Wales (Abth) BSc 72 Lon Univ PGCE 73 Ch Ch Coll Cant MA 91 Rob Coll Cam BA 95. Ridley Hall Cam 93. d 96 p 97. C Histon *Ely* 96-97; C Radipole and Melcombe Regis *Sarum* 97-00; Chapl Bournemouth and Poole Coll of FE *Win* 00-04; Hon C Bournemouth St Jo w St Mich 00-04; Vice-Prin Dioc Min Course *Nor* 04-06; Prin Dioc Min Course 07-13; Vice-Prin ERMC 07-10; rtd 13; PtO *Cant* from 14. *Red Sails, 3 Old Farm Road, Birchington CT7 9PH* T: (01843) 843336 E: suewoan1@gmail.com

WODEHOUSE, Armine Boyle. b 24. Oak Hill Th Coll 83. d 86 p 86. NSM Gt Parndon *Chelmsf* 86-92; PtO *Eur* 89-92; Chapl Menton 92-99; rtd 99; PtO *Eur* from 02. *Flat 12, 105 Onslow Square, London SW7 3LU* T: (020) 7584 4845

WODEHOUSE, Carol Lylie. See KIMBERLEY, Countess of

WODEMAN, Cyril Peter Guy. b 28. Qu Coll Cam BA 50 MA 55 ARCO 54 LRAM 58 ARCM 58. Cranmer Hall Dur 72. d 73 p 74. C Penwortham St Mary *Blackb* 73-77; V Burnley St Steph 77-85; V Hornby w Claughton 85-93; rtd 93; PtO *Blackb* from 93; *Carl* from 93. *5 Harling Bank, Kirkby Lonsdale, Carnforth LA6 2DJ* T: (015242) 72474

WOFFENDEN (née HANCOCK), Mrs Dorothy Myfanwy. b 41. NOC 01. **d** 03 **p** 04. NSM Brinnington w Portwood *Ches* 03-05; C Waverton w Aldford and Bruera 05-09. *8 Churchill Crescent, Marple, Stockport SK6 6HJ* T: 0161-427 6839 E: dwoffenden@talktalk.net

WOGAN, Adam Charles. b 87. Hull Univ BA 12. St Steph Ho Ox BTh 15. **d** 15. C Scarborough St Martin *York* from 15. *St Michael's House, 136 Filey Road, Scarborough YO11 3AA* M: 07768-195363 E: adamwogan@hotmail.co.uk

WOLF, Darren John. b 66. **d** 14 **p** 15. C Spitalfields Ch Ch w All SS *Lon* from 14. *133 Woodseer Street, London E1 5HG* M: 07545-202084 E: darren.wolf@gmail.com

WOLFE, Canon Michael Matheson. b 29. Pemb Coll Ox BA 49 MA 53. Cuddesdon Coll 51. **d** 53 **p** 54. C Moorfields *Bris* 53-57; P-in-c Fochabers *Mor* 57-58; Sub-Warden Aberlour Orphanage 58-59; V Southport St Paul *Liv* 59-65; V Upholland 65-73; TR 73-82; RD Ormskirk 78-82; RD Ormskirk and Hon Can Liv Cathl 78-82; Can Res Liv Cathl 82-96; Merseyside Ecum Officer 82-89; AD Toxteth and Wavertree 89-96; rtd 96; PtO *Liv* from 97; Hon Chapl Liv Cathl from 97. *23 Hunters Lane, Liverpool L15 8HL* T: 0151-733 1541

WOLFENDEN, Peter Graham. b 40. St Pet Coll Ox BA 63 MA 66. Linc Th Coll 62. **d** 64 **p** 65. C Adlington *Blackb* 64-66; Asst Master Barton Peveril Gr Sch 66-69; Chapl Bp Wordsworth Sch Salisbury 69-72; Hon C Bishopstoke *Win* 66-72; Hon C Ponteland *Newc* 72-02; Hd Master Richard Coates Middle Sch Ponteland 78-01; Chapl Malta and Gozo *Eur* 02-07; Chapl Málaga 07-10; P-in-c Ovingdean *Chich* from 10. *St Wulfran's Rectory, 21 Ainsworth Avenue, Ovingdean, Brighton BN2 7BG* E: anglican@onvol.net

WOLLEY, John. b 44. BSc. **d** 85 **p** 86. Hon C Croydon St Aug *S'wark* 85-89; PtO *Linc* 89-01. *7 Royal Oak Court, Upgate, Louth LN11 9JA* T: (01507) 601614

WOLLEY, Richard. b 33. CCC Ox BA 56 MA 58. S Dios Minl Tr Scheme 82. **d** 85 **p** 86. NSM Brighton Resurr *Chich* 85-88; C 88-89; C Brighton St Geo w St Anne and St Mark 89-91; R Buxted and Hadlow Down 91-98; rtd 98; PtO *Chich* from 98; RD Uckfield 04-06. *18 Millington Court, Mill Lane, Uckfield TN22 5AZ* T: (01825) 761042 E: elwandrw@tiscali.co.uk

WOLSTENCROFT, The Ven Alan. b 37. Cuddesdon Coll. **d** 69 **p** 70. C Halliwell St Thos *Man* 69-71; C Stand 71-73; V Wythenshawe St Martin 73-80; AD Withington 78-91; Chapl Wythenshawe Hosp Man 80-89; V Baguley *Man* 80-91; V Bolton St Pet 91-98; Hon Can Man Cathl 86-98; Can Res Man Cathl 98-04; Adn Man 98-04; rtd 04; PtO *Man* from 04; Rtd Clergy and Widows Officer from 04. *The Bakehouse, 1 Latham Row, Horwich, Bolton BL6 6QZ* T: (01204) 469985 E: wolstencroftalan@gmail.com

WOLTON, Adrian Kevin. b 78. **d** 14 **p** 15. C Weston-super-Mare St Paul *B & W* from 14. *15 Clarence Road North, Weston-super-Mare BS23 4AT* M: 07811-197627 E: ady@thewoltons.co.uk

WOLTON, Andrew John. b 54. Cranfield Univ MDA 00. St Jo Coll Nottm BA 08. **d** 08 **p** 09. C Bures w Assington and Lt Cornard *St E* 08-11; R Saxmundham w Kelsale cum Carlton from 11. *The Rectory, Manor Gardens, Saxmundham IP17 1ET* T: (01728) 602687 M: 07769-946364 E: andywolton@btinternet.com

WOLTON, Peter. b 47. **d** 14 **p** 15. C Holland Park *Lon* from 14. *Address temp unknown*

WOLVERHAMPTON, Area Bishop of. *See* GREGORY, The Rt Revd Clive Malcolm

WOLVERSON, Marc Ali Morad. b 68. Univ of Kansas BA 91. Ripon Coll Cuddesdon 93. **d** 96 **p** 97. C Nantwich *Ches* 96-99; C Baton Rouge St Luke USA 99-00; C Bramhall *Ches* 00-04; V High Lane 04-09; P-in-c Douglas All SS *S & M* 09-13; AD Douglas 12; P-in-c Leyland St Jas *Blackb* from 13. *St James's Vicarage, 201 Slater Lane, Leyland PR26 7SH* T: (01772) 421034 E: revmarc@mcb.net

WOMACK, Michael John. b 62. Anglia Ruskin Univ MA 07. Westcott Ho Cam 08. **d** 10 **p** 11. C Framlingham w Saxtead *St E* 10-13; R Athelington, Denham, Horham, Hoxne etc from 13. *St Andrew's House, Vicarage Road, Wingfield, Diss IP21 5RB* T: (01379) 388889 E: hoxnebenefice@gmail.com

WOMERSLEY, Sally Ann. b 61. Westcott Ho Cam 06. **d** 08 **p** 09. C Charing w Charing Heath and Lt Chart *Cant* 08-11; Chapl Cant Ch Ch Univ 11-14; TV N Hinckford *Chelmsf* from 14. *The Vicarage, Gages Road, Belchamp St Paul, Sudbury CO10 7BT* T: (01787) 277850 E: sallywomersley@yahoo.co.uk

WONG (née RUNDLE), Hilary. b 66. St Hugh's Coll Ox BA 88 Cheltenham & Glouc Coll of HE PGCE 90. Trin Coll Bris 01. **d** 03 **p** 04. C Chipping Sodbury and Old Sodbury *Glouc* 03-07; P-in-c St Helier *S'wark* 07-11; V from 11. *St Peter's Vicarage,*

193 Bishopsford Road, Morden SM4 6BH T: (020) 8685 9878 E: hilary193wong@hotmail.co.uk

WOO, Arthur Cheumin. b 66. Qu Univ Kingston Ontario BSc 89 MEng 91. St Jo Coll Nottm MTh 08. **d** 08 **p** 09. C Highworth w Sevenhampton and Inglesham etc *Bris* 08-12; V Cheylesmore *Cov* from 12. *Christ Church Vicarage, 11 Frankpledge Road, Coventry CV3 5GT* T: (024) 7650 2770 E: arthur@2woos.co.uk

WOOD, Alastair Paul. b 59. Ox Min Course 06. **d** 09 **p** 10. C Headington Quarry *Ox* 09-13; V Hadley and Wellington Ch Ch *Lich* from 13. *The Vicarage, 1 Church Walk, Wellington, Telford TF1 1RW* T: (01952) 261010 M: 07948-989153 E: narniacurate09@btinternet.com

WOOD, Alexander James. b 84. St Mellitus Coll. **d** 13 **p** 14. C Brighton St Pet *Chich* from 13. *2 Windlesham Road, Brighton BN1 3AG* M: 07731-465151 E: alex@stpetersbrighton.org

WOOD, Mrs Alison Jaye (Alice). b 54. La Sainte Union Coll BEd 79. STETS 09. **d** 12 **p** 13. NSM Farlington *Portsm* from 12. *The Brackens, Drift Road, Whitehill, Borden GU35 9EA* T: (01420) 472656 M: 07808-276964 E: woodcrew@tiscali.co.uk

WOOD, Mrs Ann Rene. b 49. St Deiniol's Hawarden 87. **d** 90 **p** 94. Par Dn Bamber Bridge St Aid *Blackb* 90-93; C W Burnley All SS 93-95; V Marton Moss 95-00; Hon Can Blackb Cathl 98-00; R Whiston *Sheff* 00-07; V Kimberworth 07-11; AD Rotherham 04-08; P-in-c Kimberworth Park 10-11; C Rawmarsh w Parkgate 10-11; C Greasbrough 10-11; rtd 11; PtO *Blackb* 11-14; AD Kirkham 14-15; P-in-c Lytham St Jo from 15. *St John's Vicarage, East Beach, Lytham St Annes FY8 5EX* T: E: ann.wood6@btopenworld.com

WOOD (née BLACKBURN), Mrs Anne Dorothy. b 54. Keele Univ BA 76 Bradf Univ MSc 90. NOC 95. **d** 98 **p** 99. NSM Batley St Thos *Wakef* 98-00; Jt P-in-c Morley St Paul 01-02; C Bruntcliffe 01-02; C Morley 02-03; TV 03-07; TV Oakenshaw, Wyke and Low Moor *Bradf* 07-10; Chapl Wakefield Hospice from 11. *24 Heaton Avenue, Dewsbury WF12 8AQ* T: (01924) 456282 M: 07929-452439 E: anne.d.wood@talk21.com

WOOD, Preb Anthony James. b 38. Kelham Th Coll 58. **d** 63 **p** 64. C Shrewsbury St Alkmund *Lich* 63; C Harlescott 63-66; C Porthill 66-70; P-in-c Priorslee 70-76; Chapl Telford Town Cen 73-76; V Barton-under-Needwood *Lich* 76-97; V Barton under Needwood w Dunstall 97-09; V Barton under Needwood w Dunstall and Tatenhill 09-10; RD Tutbury 02-10; Preb Lich Cathl 08-09; rtd 10; PtO *Lich* 11-14; *Leic* from 14. *2 Shipley Close, Branston, Burton-on-Trent DE14 3HB* T: (01283) 516772 E: tonywood@preb.co.uk

WOOD, Audrey Elizabeth. *See* COUPER, Audrey Elizabeth

WOOD, Barbara Ann. b 59. St Mich Coll Llan 00. **d** 02 **p** 03. C Glan Ely *Llan* 02-05; P-in-c Llanharan w Peterston-super-Montem from 05. *The Vicarage, Brynna Road, Brynna, Pontyclun CF72 9QE* T: (01443) 226837 E: babswood01@hotmail.com

WOOD, Barry. b 56. Open Univ BA 87 Sheff Univ MMin 01 CQSW 81. St Steph Ho Ox 87. **d** 89 **p** 90. C Tranmere St Paul w St Luke *Ches* 89-92; TV *Ches* 92-94; P-in-c S Tawton and Belstone *Ex* 94-00; R 00-02; RD Okehampton 98-02; TR Wylye and Till Valley *Sarum* 02-03; rtd 03; PtO *Ex* 03-05; *Truro* 05-07; Hon C Chaffcombe, Cricket Malherbie etc *B & W* 07-09; Hon C Blackdown 09-11. *5 Case Gardens, Seaton EX12 2AP*

WOOD, Beresford Donald Richard. b 32. Leeds Univ BA 58. Cant Sch of Min 91. **d** 94 **p** 95. Chapl St Mary's Sch Westbrook from 94; NSM Folkestone St Mary and St Eanswythe *Cant* 94-02; PtO from 02. *St Katherine's Cottage, Pound Lane, Elham, Canterbury CT4 6TS* T: (01303) 840817

WOOD, Canon Beryl Jean. b 54. Linc Th Coll 85. **d** 87 **p** 94. C Gaywood, Bawsey and Mintlyn *Nor* 87-92; Asst Chapl Univ Hosp Nottm 93-95; R Shipdham w Bradenham *Nor* 95-06; RD Dereham in Mitford 00-04; Dep Warden Launde Abbey *Leic* 06-09; TR Gaywood *Nor* 10-15; Hon Can Nor Cathl 05-06 and 13-15; rtd 15. *Address temp unknown* E: beryljwood@yahoo.com

WOOD, Mrs Brenda. b 46. Eliz Gaskell Coll Man TCert 67 Leeds Metrop Univ BEd 94 Leeds Univ MA 04. NOC 00. **d** 03 **p** 04. NSM Kirkstall *Ripon* 03-11; rtd 11. *18 Wentworth Crescent, Leeds LS17 7TW* T: 0113-226 7991 E: bwood@ntlworld.com

WOOD, Canon Brian Frederick. b 31. Leeds Univ BA 52. Coll of Resurr Mirfield 55. **d** 57 **p** 58. C Wigan St Anne *Liv* 57-60; C Elland *Wakef* 60-63; V Carlinghow 63-73; V Drighlington 73-94; RD Birstall 83-92; Hon Can Wakef Cathl 89-94; rtd 94; PtO *Wakef* 94-14; Leeds from 14. *10 Grove Road, Menston, Ilkley LS29 6JD* T: (01943) 872820

WOOD, Brian Richard. b 49. Sheff Univ BA 70 MCMI 78 RIBA 85 MRICS 00 FCIOB 00. Ox Min Course 04. **d** 07 **p** 08. NSM Blenheim *Ox* 07-12; NSM Akeman from 12. *The Vicarage, Alchester Road, Chesterton, Bicester OX26 1UW* T: (01869) 369815 E: revbrianwood@gmail.com

WOOD, Mrs Bryony Ann. b 59. St Jo Coll Nottm BA 10. **d** 10 **p** 11. C Derby St Pet and Ch Ch w H Trin 10-11; C Ashbourne St Oswald w Mapleton 11-12; C Hadfield 12-14; V Whatton w Aslockton, Hawksworth, Scarrington etc S'well from 14. *The Vicarage, Main Street, Aslockton, Nottingham NG13 9AL* M: 07967-113028 E: bryony.wood@yahoo.co.uk

WOOD, Ms Carolyn Marie Therese. b 57. Sussex Univ BA 91. St Mich Coll Llan 02. **d** 04 **p** 05. C Monkton St D 04-07; PtO 08-10; NSM Cydweli Deanery 10-14; P-in-c Carew and Cosheston and Nash and Redberth St D from 14. *9 Sageston Fields, Sageston, Tenby SA70 8TQ* T: (01646) 651970 E: vicartubbs@gmail.com

WOOD, Sister Catherine Rosemary. b 54. Melbourne Coll of Div 82 St Jo Coll Auckland 83. **d** 83 **p** 84. C Howick New Zealand 83-87; C Auckland St Paul 88; P-in-c Mangere E 89-90; Co-ord Environmental Educn 90-95; N Fieldworker Chr World Service 96-01; Hon C Glen Eden 90-97; NSM Auckland Cathl 98-01; PtO S'wark 01-02; P-in-c Tatsfield 02-08; C Limpsfield and Titsey 02-03; Min Limpsfield Chart St Andr CD 03-08; PtO 08-11; Chapl HM Pris Latchmere Ho 09-11; Chapl HM Pris Wormwood Scrubs 12-14; PtO Lon from 13; S'wark from 13. *St Michael's Convent, 56 Ham Common, Richmond TW10 7JH* M: 07960-088873 T: (020) 8940 8711 E: silentmiaow@yahoo.co.uk

WOOD, Christine Denise. b 48. EMMTC. **d** 05 **p** 06. NSM Clifton S'well 05-07; Asst Chapl Notts Healthcare NHS Trust 07-10; Lead Chapl St Andr Healthcare from 10; NSM Morton and Stonebroom w Shirland Derby from 09. *St Andrew's Healthcare, Sherwood Avenue, Sherwood Oaks Business Park, Mansfield NG18 4GW* T: (01623) 665280 E: cdjoakwood8@btinternet.com

WOOD, Christopher David. b 60. Worc Coll Ox BA 83 Leeds Univ MA 06. Coll of Resurr Mirfield 04. **d** 06 **p** 07. C King's Lynn St Marg w St Nic Nor 06-09; R Hunstanton St Mary w Ringstead Parva etc 09-14; R Nor St Jo w St Julian from 14. *The Rectory, 8 Kilderkin Way, Norwich NR1 1RD* T: (01603) 626104 E: christopherd1760@hotmail.co.uk

WOOD, Christopher William. b 44. Rhodes Univ BA 66 UNISA BTh 82. St Bede's Coll Umtata 79. **d** 80 **p** 82. S Africa 80-87; C Houghton Regis St Alb 87-00; C Milton Portsm 00-03; PtO Lich from 04. *27 Penton Walk, Stoke-on-Trent ST3 3DG* T: (01782) 311779

WOOD, Mrs Claire. b 63. SAOMC 03. **d** 06 **p** 07. C Buckingham Ox 06-09; R Olney from 09; AD Newport from 15. *Olney Rectory, 9 Orchard Rise, Olney MK46 5HB* T: (01234) 713308 M: 07896-696842 E: revclairewood@gmail.com

WOOD, Clive Marcus. b 52. Bradf Univ BSc 75. SEITE BA 14. **d** 14. NSM Belvedere All SS Roch from 14. *15 Denver Road, Dartford DA1 3LA* T: (01322) 270942 M: 07982-392809 E: clivemwood@yahoo.co.uk

WOOD, Canon Colin Arthur. b 41. S'wark Ord Course 86. **d** 89 **p** 90. C Tadworth S'wark 89-93; TV Morden 93-06; Hon Can S'wark Cathl 05-06; rtd 06. *44 Leonora Drive, Bognor Regis PO21 3NH* T: (01243) 264192 E: colinwood685@btinternet.com

WOOD, David Christopher. b 52. Oak Hill Th Coll 89. **d** 91 **p** 92. C Kendal St Thos Carl 91-95; P-in-c Asby, Bolton and Crosby Ravensworth 95-05; P-in-c Barton, Pooley Bridge and Martindale 05-13; V Barton, Pooley Bridge, Martindale etc from 13. *The Vicarage, Pooley Bridge, Penrith CA10 2LT* T: (01768) 486220 E: revdavidcwood@hotmail.com

WOOD, David John. b 48. Newc Univ BSc 70 PGCE 71 Open Univ MA 91. **d** 01 **p** 02. OLM Bedlington Newc 01-07; OLM Shotley 07-15; NSM from 15. *St John's Vicarage, Snod's Edge, Shotley Bridge, Consett DH8 9TL* T: (01207) 255665 E: davwd50@hotmail.com

WOOD, David Michael. b 39. Chich Th Coll. **d** 82 **p** 83. C Epping St Jo Chelmsf 82-85; C Totton Win 85-88; V Southway Ex 88-97; P-in-c Black Torrington, Bradford w Cookbury etc 97-01; R 01-04; rtd 04; PtO Portsm from 04. *47 Queens Crescent, Stubbington, Fareham PO14 2QG*

WOOD, Dennis William. b 28. Qu Mary Coll Lon BSc 53 Glas Univ PhD 57. NEOC 82. **d** 85 **p** 85. NSM Stanhope Dur 85-86; NSM Stanhope w Frosterley 86-94; NSM Eastgate w Rookhope 86-94; NSM Melrose Edin from 94. *Gordonlee, Ormiston Terrace, Melrose TD6 9SP* T: (01896) 823835

WOOD, Donald. b 40. **d** 95 **p** 96. NSM Caldicot Mon 95-99; P-in-c Llangwm Uchaf and Llangwm Isaf w Gwernesney etc 99-06; LtO from 06. *13 Deepweir, Caldicot NP26 5JG* T: (01291) 425214

WOOD, Elaine Mary. See RICHARDSON, Elaine Mary

WOOD, Elizabeth Jane. See SCOTT, Elizabeth Jane

WOOD, Elizabeth Lucy. b 35. WMMTC 89. **d** 92 **p** 94. NSM Wellingborough St Mark Pet 92-95; P-in-c Stanwick w Hargrave 95-00; PtO 00-13; Chapl to Retired Clergy and Clergy Widows' Officer 08-12. *21 Meadow Way,*

Irthlingborough, Wellingborough NN9 5RS T: (01933) 652319 E: elizwood@tiscali.co.uk

WOOD, Geoffrey. b 33. Tyndale Hall Bris 56. **d** 61 **p** 62. C Tranmere St Cath Ches 61-64; C Newburn Newc 64-68; R Gt Smeaton w Appleton upon Wiske Ripon 69-79; P-in-c Cowton w Birkby 73-79; P-in-c Danby Wiske w Yafforth and Hutton Bonville 76-79; R Gt Smeaton w Appleton Wiske and Birkby etc 79-89; R Fressingfield, Mendham, Metfield, Weybread etc St E 92-98; rtd 98; PtO Dur 98-04; LtO Edin 08-10. *15 Greencroft Close, Darlington DL3 8HW* T: (01325) 380309

WOOD, Geoffrey James. b 47. NOC 88. **d** 91 **p** 92. C Stainton-in-Cleveland York 91-94; V Middlesbrough St Oswald 94-99; V Eskdaleside w Ugglebarnby and Sneaton 99-06; rtd 06; PtO York from 06. *22 Hedley Street, Guisborough TS14 6EG* T: (01287) 619286 E: frgeoff@btinternet.com

WOOD, George Albert. b 22. St Paul's Coll Grahamstown. **d** 54 **p** 55. C Hillcrest S Africa 54-57; C W Suburbs Pretoria 57-60; C Cheam S'wark 60-63; R Eshowe S Africa 63-69; Can Zululand 68-73; Dean Eshowe 70-73; R Port Elizabeth Ch the K 74-77; Area Sec United Soc Chich from 78; TV Little-hampton and Wick Chich 86-88; rtd 88; PtO Chich from 88. *3 Orchard Gardens, Rustington, Littlehampton BN16 3HN* T: (01903) 787746

WOOD, Heather Dawn. See ATKINSON, Heather Dawn

WOOD, Miss Helen Ruth. b 54. Bedf Coll Lon BA 75. Glouc Sch of Min 87. **d** 91 **p** 94. NSM Up Hatherley Glouc 91-94; NSM Cheltenham Em w St Steph 94-09; NSM S Cheltenham from 10; Asst Chapl Cheltenham Ladies' Coll from 91. *9 Stonefield Manor Park, Sandy Lane, Charlton Kings, Cheltenham GL53 9DJ* T: (01242) 242793 E: woodh@cheltladiescollege.org

WOOD, Henry. b 70. SNWTP. **d** 13 **p** 14. NSM St Helens Town Cen Liv from 13. *12 Clipsley Crescent, Haydock, St Helens WA11 0UH* T: (01744) 454671 E: a1harry.wood@gmail.com

WOOD, Jane. b 52. Ripon Coll Cuddesdon. **d** 08 **p** 09. C Kirby Muxloe Leic 08-11; Chapl for People affected by HIV from 11; Chapl Univ Hosps Leic NHS Trust from 13. *72 Fleckney Road, Kibworth, Leicester LE8 0HG* T: 0116-279 1133 E: janewood72@googlemail.com

WOOD, Mrs Jennifer Sarah. b 40. Sarum Dioc Tr Coll CertEd 60. Oak Hill Th Coll 92. **d** 94 **p** 95. C St Illogan Truro 94-98; R Heanton Punchardon w Marwood Ex 98-10; C Ilfracombe SS Phil and Jas w W Down 09-10; rtd 10. *32 Stallards, Braunton EX33 1BP* T: (01271) 812730

WOOD, John. b 37. LNSM course 75. **d** 77 **p** 79. NSM Haddington Edin from 77. *7 Herdmanflatt, Haddington EH41 3LN* T: (01620) 822838

WOOD, John Anthony Scriven. b 48. Leeds Univ BSc 70. St Jo Coll Nottm 76. **d** 79 **p** 80. C Colwich Lich 79-82; C W Bridgford S'well 82-90; V Gamston and Bridgford 90-95; Chapl Kings Mill Cen NHS Trust 95-01; Chapl Sherwood Forest Hosps NHS Trust 01-13; rtd 13; NSM Morton and Stonebroom w Shirland Derby from 08. *The Old Post Office, 8 Main Road, Higham, Alfreton DE55 6EF* T: (01773) 833152

WOOD, John Arthur. b 23. Roch Th Coll 68. **d** 70 **p** 71. C Wetherby Ripon 70-71; P-in-c Sheff Arbourthorne 71-75; TV Sheff Manor 75-81; R Rodney Stoke w Draycott B & W 81-88; rtd 88; PtO Sheff from 88. *36 The Glen, Sheffield S10 3FN* T: 0114-266 5173

WOOD, John Maurice. b 58. MBE 14. Qu Coll Cam BA 80 MA 83. Wycliffe Hall Ox BA 87. **d** 87 **p** 88. C Northwood Em Lon 87-91; C Muswell Hill St Jas w St Matt 91-94; P-in-c S Tottenham St Ann 94-01; V from 01. *St Ann's Vicarage, South Grove, London N15 5QG* T/F: (020) 8800 3506 M: 07771-867359 E: johnwood@st-anns.fsnet.co.uk

WOOD, Canon John Samuel. b 47. Lanchester Poly Cov BSc 69 Sheff Univ DipEd. Westcott Ho Cam 72. **d** 81 **p** 82. NSM Haverhill St E 81-82; NSM Haverhill w Withersfield, the Wrattings etc 82-83; C Whitton and Thurleston w Akenham 83-86; P-in-c Walsham le Willows 86-88; P-in-c Finningham w Westhorpe 86-88; R Walsham le Willows and Finningham w Westhorpe 88-94; Min Can St E Cathl 89-94; TR Whitstable Cant 94-02; Chapl E Kent Community NHS Trust 94-02; Hon Min Can Cant Cathl 96-02; TR Swanage and Studland Sarum from 02; RD Purbeck 07-15; Can and Preb Sarum Cathl from 12. *The Rectory, 12 Church Hill, Swanage BH19 1HU* T: (01929) 422916 F: 422291 E: john.s.wood@btinternet.com

WOOD, Kathleen. b 46. EMMTC 04. **d** 06 **p** 07. NSM Newhall Derby 06-09; NSM Etwall w Egginton 09-10; P-in-c Stapenhill Immanuel 10-14; rtd 14; PtO Derby from 14; Lich from 14. *28 Eastfield Road, Midway, Swadlincote DE11 0DG* T: (01283) 212490 M: 07401-292180 E: rkw28@btinternet.com

WOOD, Keith. b 49. St Steph Ho Ox 76. **d** 78 **p** 79. C Bognor Chich 78-81; C Hangleton 81-83; R W Blatchington 83-87;

V W Worthing St Jo 87-96; R Winchelsea and Icklesham 96-00; rtd 00. *The Bungalow, Lower Locrenton, St Keyne, Liskeard PL14 4RN*

WOOD, Canon Keith Ernest. b 33. Qu Coll Ox BA 55 BCL 56 MA 70. Wycliffe Hall Ox 56. **d** 58 **p** 59. C Barking St Marg *Chelmsf* 58-61; Min Basildon St Andr ED 61-70; V Brampton Bierlow *Sheff* 70-82; R Grasmere *Carl* 82-94; RD Windermere 89-94; Hon Can Carl Cathl 91-94 and 98-01; Bp's Dom Chapl 94-01; rtd 01; PtO *Carl* from 01. *The Old Tower, Brackenburgh, Calthwaite CA11 9PW* T: (01768) 894273

WOOD, Mrs Lorna. b 43. EAMTC 85. **d** 88 **p** 94. NSM Sprowston *Nor* 88-90; NSM Sprowston w Beeston 90-95; P-in-c Nor St Helen 95-01; Chapl Gt Hosp Nor 95-99; NSM Coltishall w Gt Hautbois and Horstead *Nor* 01-04; PtO 04-07 and from 10; NSM Thorpe St Andr 07-10. *39 Inman Road, Sprowston, Norwich NR7 8JT* T: (01603) 400150
E: robert.wood68@btinternet.com

WOOD (née DROBIG), Mrs Marion. b 76. Hannover Univ MA 01 Pemb Coll Ox DPhil 05. ERMC 04. **d** 06 **p** 07. C Newmarket All SS *St E* 06-09; R Shaw cum Donnington *Ox* from 09. *The Rectory, Well Meadow, Shaw, Newbury RG14 2DS* T: (01635) 600532 M: 07979-534948
E: mariondrobig@hotmail.com

WOOD, Mark Robert. b 68. Trin Coll Ox BA 89 ALCM 83 ARCO 89. STETS 02. **d** 05 **p** 06. C Mere w W Knoyle and Maiden Bradley *Sarum* 05-08; P-in-c W Netherhampton and Fuggleston 08-13; R from 13; RD Chalke from 15. *The Rectory, 27A West Street, Wilton, Salisbury SP2 0DL* M: 07770-305990 T: (01722) 744755
E: mands@thewoods2006.orangehome.co.uk

WOOD, Martin. *See* WOOD, Nicholas Martin

WOOD, Martin Robert. b 65. Birm Univ BSc 86. Trin Coll Bris 98. **d** 00 **p** 01. C Wells St Cuth w Wookey Hole *B & W* 00-03; C Shepton Mallet w Doulting 03-07; P-in-c Tedburn St Mary, Whitestone, Oldridge etc *Ex* 07-10; V Tedburn St Mary, Cheriton Bishop, Whitestone etc from 10. *The Rectory, Church Lane, Cheriton Bishop, Exeter EX6 6HY* T: (01647) 24119 E: revwood@btinternet.com

WOOD, Michael Edmund. b 46. Dur Univ BA 67 PGCE 68. Coll of Resurr Mirfield 94. **d** 96 **p** 97. NSM Battyeford *Leeds* from 96; Asst Chapl Kirkwood Hospice Huddersfield 96-97; Chapl from 97. *9 Dorchester Road, Huddersfield HD2 2JZ* T: (01484) 536496 E: revmike@kirkwoodhospice.co.uk

WOOD, Michael Frank. b 55. Nottm Univ BCombStuds. Linc Th Coll. **d** 84 **p** 85. C Marton *Blackb* 84-88; TV Ribbleton 88-93; V Blackpool St Mary 93-00; P-in-c S Shore St Pet 98-00; RD Blackpool 96-00; TR Brighouse and Clifton *Wakef* 00-08; RD Brighouse and Elland 06-08; TR Castleford *Leeds* from 08; P-in-c Smawthorpe *Wakef* 11-12. *The Rectory, 15 Barnes Road, Castleford WF10 5AA* T: (01977) 518127
E: frmw@hotmail.co.uk

WOOD, Mrs Michaela. b 67. **d** 01 **p** 02. NSM Sunbury *Lon* 01-04; NSM Whitton St Aug 04-06; NSM Aylesbury *Ox* 06-13; NSM Salfords *S'wark* from 13. *The Vicarage, Honeycrock Lane, Redhill RH1 5DF* T: (01737) 762784
E: michaelawood@aol.com

WOOD, Canon Nicholas Martin. b 51. Univ of Wales (Lamp) MTh 09. AKC 74. **d** 75 **p** 76. C E Ham w Upton Park and Forest Gate *Chelmsf* 75-78; C Leyton St Luke 78-81; V Rush Green 81-91; Chapl Barking Tech Coll 81-91; TR Elland *Wakef* 91-05; RD Brighouse and Elland 96-05; Hon Can Wakef Cathl 00-05; Par Development Adv (Bradwell Area) *Chelmsf* 05-12; Miss and Min Adv (Bradwell Area) from 12; Chapl to Bp Bradwell 11-12; Hon C Basildon St Martin from 11; Hon Can Chelmsf Cathl from 08. *101 London Road, Bowers Gifford, Basildon SS13 2DU* T: (01268) 552219
E: mwood@chelmsford.anglican.org

WOOD, Paul Dominic. b 52. Tas Coll of Ad Educn DipEd 80. Ridley Coll Melbourne BTh 87. **d** 87 **p** 88. C Newton St Jas Australia 87-89; C Launceston St Jo 89-91; TV Ifield *Chich* 92-95; P-in-c Lancefield w Romsey Australia 96-97; I 97-00; R Mansfield 01-05. *38 Pine Street, Reservoir VIC 3073, Australia* T/F: (0061) (3) 9478 0841 E: qwoodies@bigpond.com

WOOD, Philip James. b 48. Bris Univ BSc 69 Westmr Coll Ox MTh 93. Oak Hill Th Coll 71. **d** 74 **p** 75. C Islington St Mary *Lon* 74-77; C Stapenhill w Cauldwell *Derby* 77-80; V Walthamstow St Luke *Chelmsf* 80-94; AD Waltham Forest 89-94; Can Chelmsf Cathl 93-94; NSM Hackney Wick St Mary of Eton w St Aug *Lon* 01-02; TV Becontree W *Chelmsf* 02-07; V Becontree St Thos from 07. *St Thomas's Vicarage, 187 Burnside Road, Dagenham RM8 2JN* T: (020) 8590 6190 E: philipwoodstb@googlemail.com

WOOD, Philip Norman. b 52. EMMTC 97. **d** 00 **p** 01. NSM Pleasley Hill *S'well* 00-04; NSM Mansfield St Aug 00-04; NSM Ladybrook 00-04; TV Newton Flotman, Swainsthorpe, Tasburgh, etc *Nor* 04-08; R Bacton, Happisburgh, Hempstead

w Eccles etc 08-13; rtd 13. *38 Middlegate Road, Frampton, Boston PE20 1BX* M: 07961-524495 E: philyvonne@hotmail.com

WOOD, Ms Rachel Astrid. b 71. Birm Univ BA 92 MA 99. Qu Coll Birm BD 98. **d** 99 **p** 00. C Attercliffe, Darnall and Tinsley *Sheff* 99-01; C Roundhay St Edm *Ripon* 01-04; Local Min Development Officer *Newc* from 12. *St Hilda's Vicarage, Preston Gate, North Shields NE29 9QB* T: 0191-257 3901 M: 07591-280905 E: r.wood@newcastle.anglican.org

WOOD, Raymond John Lee. b 28. ACII 55 ACIArb. Linc Th Coll 66. **d** 68 **p** 69. C Beaconsfield *Ox* 68-72; CF 70-72; V Wath-upon-Dearne w Adwick-upon-Dearne *Sheff* 72-77; R St Tudy w Michaelstow *Truro* 77-86; P-in-c St Mabyn 82-86; R St Tudy w St Mabyn and Michaelstow 86-95; Chapl Bodmin Fire Brigade from 91; rtd 95; PtO *Truro* from 96. *1 Wesley Chapel, Harewood Road, Calstock PL18 9QN* T: (01822) 835918 E: rlwood@tesco.net

WOOD, Richard. *See* WOOD, Beresford Donald Richard

WOOD, Richard James. b 71. Oak Hill Th Coll BA 07. **d** 08 **p** 09. C Dagenham *Chelmsf* 08-09; C Leyton Ch Ch 09-12; P-in-c Aberporth w Blaenporth w Betws Ifan *St D* 12-14. *6 Dolydd Terrace, Tanygrisiau, Blaenau Ffestiniog LL41 3TN* M: 07947-137586 E: woodyis@mac.com

WOOD, Richard Stanton. b 79. Univ of Wales (Abth) BSc 02 Univ of Wales (Cardiff) BA 08. **d** 08 **p** 09. C Henfynyw w Aberaeron and Llanddewi Aberarth etc *St D* 08-11; TV Llanelli 11-13; V Bro Madryn *Ban* from 13. *3 Llys Madryn, Morfa Nefyn, Pwllheli LL53 6EX* T: (01758) 720707 M: 07855-817740 E: revdrich@gmail.com

WOOD, Roger Graham. b 49. K Coll Lon BD. Chich Th Coll 74. **d** 76 **p** 77. C Skipton H Trin *Bradf* 76-79; Dioc Youth Chapl 79-87; V Queensbury 87-96; P-in-c Langcliffe w Stainforth and Horton 96-01; V 01-13; R Bolton by Bowland w Grindleton 13-14; RD Bowland 08-14; R Bolton by Bowland w Grindleton *Blackb* from 14. *The Rectory, Sawley Road, Grindleton, Clitheroe BB7 4QS* E: rgwood49@gmail.com

WOOD, Roger William. b 43. Leeds Univ BA 65 MA 67 Fitzw Coll Cam BA 69 MA 75. Westcott Ho Cam 67. **d** 70 **p** 71. C Bishop's Stortford St Mich *St Alb* 70-74; C Sundon w Streatley 75-79; V Streatley 80-09; rtd 09. *8 Ramsey Road, Barton-le-Clay, Bedford MK45 4PE* T: (01582) 883277

WOOD, Ronald Ernest. b 49. Sarum & Wells Th Coll 79. **d** 81 **p** 82. C Weston-super-Mare Cen Par *B & W* 81-84; C Forest of Dean Ch Ch w English Bicknor *Glouc* 84-88; R Sixpenny Handley w Gussage St Andrew etc *Sarum* 88-05; P-in-c Seale, Puttenham and Wanborough *Guildf* 05-10; rtd 10; Hon C Camelot Par *B & W* from 10. *Fourposts, Long Street, Galhampton, Yeovil BA22 7AZ* T: (01963) 441192

WOOD, Sarah. *See* WOOD, Jennifer Sarah

WOOD, Shane Grant Lindsay. b 60. Southn Univ BTh 91. St Steph Ho Ox 95. **d** 97 **p** 98. C Parkstone St Pet w Branksea and St Osmund *Sarum* 97-00; V Teddington SS Pet and Paul and Fulwell *Lon* 00-06; TR Aylesbury *Ox* 06-13; V Salfords *S'wark* from 13; Bp's Adv for Min Development from 13. *The Vicarage, Honeycrock Lane, Redhill RH1 5DF* T: (01737) 762784 E: shaneglwood@aol.com

WOOD, Stanley Charles. b 26. Glouc Th Course 80. **d** 83 **p** 84. NSM Lower Cam w Coaley *Glouc* 83-87; P-in-c Shipton Moyne w Westonbirt and Lasborough 87-91; rtd 92; PtO *Glouc* 92-05. *Henlow Court, Henlow Drive, Dursley GL11 4BE* T: (01453) 542850

WOOD, Stella Margaret. b 70. Trin Coll Ox BA 91 MA DPhil 95. STETS 95. **d** 97 **p** 98. NSM Mere w W Knoyle and Maiden Bradley *Sarum* 97-08; Chapl Sherborne Sch for Girls 00-08; Teacher 08-14; Lic to RD Sarum 08-11; Co-ord for Learning and Discipleship *Sarum* 11-14; Chapl Godolphin Sch from 14; NSM Wilton w Netherhampton and Fugglestone *Sarum* from 14. *The Rectory, 27A West Street, Wilton, Salisbury SP2 0DL* T: (01722) 742571 E: stella.wood@salisbury.anglican.org

WOOD, Steven Paul. b 54. Fitzw Coll Cam MA 75. ERMC. **d** 07 **p** 08. NSM Hitchin *St Alb* 07-10; P-in-c Streatley from 10. *Tythe Farm House, Streatley Road, Sundon, Luton LU3 3PH* T: (01525) 876197 M: 07704-922984
E: steve.wood@stmargaret-streatley.org.uk

WOOD, Stuart Hughes. b 32. ACIB 64. Guildf Dioc Min Course 93. **d** 95 **p** 96. OLM Camberley St Martin Old Dean *Guildf* 95-02; OLM Camberley St Paul 99-02; OLM Camberley St Mich Yorktown 99-02; rtd 02; PtO *Guildf* 02-05. *42 Roundway, Camberley GU15 1NS* T: (01276) 22115
E: stuart.wood1@tesco.net

WOOD, Susan Joyce. b 52. Sheff City Coll of Educn CertEd 74. **d** 09 **p** 10. OLM Ramsbottom and Edenfield *Man* 09-14. *243 Whittingham Drive, Ramsbottom, Bury BL0 9NY* T: (01706) 825464 E: woodsuej@btinternet.com

WOOD, Susan Pauline. b 47. Maria Grey Coll Lon TCert 68. STETS 07. **d** 10 **p** 11. NSM Staines *Lon* from 10. *60 St Nicholas Drive, Shepperton TW17 9LD* T: (01932) 228712
E: sue_p.wood@yahoo.co.uk

WOOD, Sylvia Marian. See CHAPMAN, Sylvia Marian

WOOD, Timothy Robert. b 55. **d** 02 **p** 03. OLM Maidstone St Paul *Cant* 02-06; NSM Hayling Is St Andr and N Hayling St Pet *Portsm* 08-12; NSM Purbrook from 12. *9 Ward Court, 65 Seafront, Hayling Island PO11 0AL* T: (023) 9246 1575 E: jane_wood@lineone.net

WOOD, Valerie Rosemary. See SMITH, Valerie Rosemary

✠**WOOD, The Rt Revd Wilfred Denniston.** b 36. KA 00. Gen Th Sem NY Hon DD 86 Open Univ Hon DUniv 00 Univ of W Indies Hon LLD 02 FRSA 93. Codrington Coll Barbados 57. **d** 61 **p** 62 **c** 85. C Hammersmith St Steph *Lon* 62-63; C Shepherd's Bush St Steph w St Thos 63-74; Bp's Chapl for Community Relns 67-74; V Catford St Laur *S'wark* 74-82; Hon Can S'wark Cathl 77-82; RD E Lewisham 77-82; Borough Dean S'wark 82-85; Adn S'wark 82-85; Suff Bp Croydon 85-91; Area Bp Croydon 91-02; rtd 02. *69 Pegwell Gardens, Christ Church, Barbados* T: (001) (246) 420 1822 F: 420 3426 E: wilfredwoodbarbados@caribsurf.com

WOOD-ROBINSON, David Michael. b 28. Glas Univ BSc 50 Lon Univ BD 54. **d** 57 **p** 57. C Erith St Jo *Roch* 57-58; CMS Japan 58-71; R Holton and Waterperry *Ox* 71-88; RD Aston and Cuddesdon 88-92; R Holton and Waterperry w Albury and Waterstock 88-94; Chapl Ox Brookes Univ 90-94; rtd 94. *16 Pound Meadow, Ledbury HR8 2EU* T: (01531) 632347

WOOD-ROE (née BRYANT), Mrs Sarah Elizabeth. b 82. Grey Coll Dur BA 05 Wolfs Coll Cam MPhil 07. Westcott Ho Cam 06. **d** 08 **p** 09. C Branksome St Aldhelm *Sarum* 08-11; Chapl St Jo Sch Leatherhead from 11. *St John's School, Epsom Road, Leatherhead KT22 8SP* T: (01372) 373000 E: swood-roe@stjohns.surrey.sch.uk

WOODALL, Ms Bridget Ann. b 65. CQSW 92. St Jo Coll Nottm 11. **d** 13 **p** 14. C Brierley Hill *Worc* from 13. *9 Bickon Drive, Quarry Bank, Brierley Hill DY5 2JF* M: 07952-159416 E: bridget.woodall65@gmail.com

WOODALL, David Paul. b 59. Ches Coll of HE BTh 03. NOC 00. **d** 03 **p** 04. C Darwen St Pet w Hoddlesden St Paul *Blackb* 03-06; TV Bacup and Stacksteads *Man* 06-12; P-in-c Norden w Ashworth 12-13; C Oakenrod and Bamford 12-13; V Norden w Ashworth and Bamford from 13. *The Vicarage, 389 Bury and Rochdale Old Road, Heywood OL10 4AT* T: (01706) 369610

WOODALL, Johanna Karin (Hanna). b 62. Leic Univ BA 84 PGCE 87. Trin Coll Bris BA 06. **d** 06 **p** 07. C Winchcombe *Glouc* 06-09; Hon C Churchdown St Jo and Innsworth 10; NSM Badgeworth, Shurdington and Witcombe w Bentham 10-12; Asst Chapl Myton Hamlet Hospice 10-12; V Foleshill St Paul *Cov* from 13. *St Paul's Vicaraage, 13 St Paul's Road, Coventry CV6 5DE* T: (024) 7668 1332 E: hanna_woodall@yahoo.co.uk

WOODALL, Mrs Lynda Edith Maria. b 53. Leeds Univ BA 07. NOC 04. **d** 07 **p** 08. C Goodshaw and Crawshawbooth *Man* 07-10; V Whitworth w Facit from 10; AD Rossendale from 15. *St John's Vicarage, Stud Brow, Facit, Rochdale OL12 8LU* T: (01706) 878293 E: lyn.woodall@googlemail.com

WOODALL, Reginald Homer. b 38. St Mich Coll Llan 59. **d** 61 **p** 62. C Newtown w Llanllwchaiarn w Aberhafesp *St As* 61-65; C Rhosddu 65-66; C Hawarden 66-70; CF 70-74; C Thornton Heath St Jude *Cant* 74-77; TV Cannock *Lich* 77-79; TV Basildon St Martin w H Cross and Laindon etc *Chelmsf* 79-84; P-in-c Canning Town St Cedd 84-93; rtd 93. *64 Stephens Road, London E15 3JL*

WOODALL, Ms Rosemary Helen. b 80. Newc Univ BSc 01. Ripon Coll Cuddesdon BA 09. **d** 10 **p** 11. C Glouc City and Hempsted 10-13; P-in-c Bisley, Chalford, France Lynch, and Oakridge 13-15; P-in-c Bussage 14-15; V Bisley, Chalford, France Lynch, and Oakridge and Bussage w Eastcombe from 15. *The Vicarage, Cheltenham Road, Bisley, Stroud GL6 7BJ* T: (01452) 771084 M: 07816-420788 E: rosiewoodall@hotmail.co.uk

WOODASON, Antony Norman. b 37. MCIPD 96. SWMTC 02. **d** 04 **p** 05. NSM Bovey Tracey St Jo w Heathfield *Ex* 04-06; C Shaldon, Stokeinteignhead, Combeinteignhead etc 06-13. *22 Millwood, New Park, Bovey Tracey, Newton Abbot TQ13 9JW* T: (01626) 832033 E: woodason@nosadowe.fsnet.co.uk

WOODBRIDGE, Trevor Geoffrey. b 31. Lon Univ BSc 52. ALCD 57. **d** 58 **p** 59. C Bitterne *Win* 58-61; C Ilkeston St Mary *Derby* 61-65; Area Sec CMS Ex and Truro 65-81; SW Regional Sec 70-81; TV Clyst St George, Aylesbeare, Clyst Honiton etc *Ex* 82-84; V Aylesbeare, Rockbeare, Farringdon etc 85-95; rtd 95; PtO *Ex* 95-09. *17 Lowfield Crescent, Silsden, Keighley BD20 0QE* T: (01535) 658216

WOODCOCK, Anne Caroline. b 63. Man Metrop Univ BA 97 Man Univ MA 07 RGN. SNWTP 08. **d** 10 **p** 11. C Newton in Mottram *Ches* 10-11; C Newton w Flowery Field 11-13; V from 13. *St Mary's Vicarage, 39 Bradley Green Road, Hyde SK14 4NA* M: 07960-114969 E: annie.woodcock@virginmedia.com

WOODCOCK, Canon Carolyn. b 47. NOC BTh 98. **d** 98 **p** 99. NSM Laneside *Blackb* 98-00; Chapl HM Pris Lanc Castle 00-10; Hon Can Blackb Cathl 08-10; rtd 10; PtO *Blackb* from 10. *Address withheld by request*

WOODCOCK, Edward Marsden. b 47. Hull Univ MSc 01 Leeds Univ BA 03. Coll of Resurr Mirfield 01. **d** 03 **p** 04. C Wrenthorpe *Wakef* 03-06; C Alverthorpe 03-06; P-in-c Ferrybridge *Leeds* from 06; P-in-c Brotherton from 06. *St Andrew's Vicarage, 5 Pontefract Road, Ferrybridge, Knottingley WF11 8PN* T: (01977) 672772 E: edward@thewoodcocks.plus.com

WOODCOCK, John Charles Gerard. b 31. Kelham Th Coll 52. **d** 56 **p** 57. SSM 56-88; S Africa 56-62 and 76-83; Lesotho 62-76; Chapl Bede Ho Staplehurst 83-87; C Auckland St Andr and St Anne *Dur* 87-88. *3 Helena Terrace, Cockton Hill, Bishop Auckland DL14 6BP* T: (01388) 604956

WOODCOCK, Matthew Ross. b 75. Portsm Univ BA 97. Cranmer Hall Dur 09. **d** 11 **p** 12. C Kingston upon Hull H Trin *York* from 11. *1 Ha'penny Bridge Way, Hull HU9 1HD* T: (01482) 214192 M: 07852-340616 E: mattwoodcock630@gmail.com

WOODCOCK, Michael David. b 67. Avery Hill Coll BEd 91. Wycliffe Hall Ox BTh 96. **d** 96 **p** 97. C Orpington Ch Ch *Roch* 96-99; R Knockholt w Halstead 99-06; P-in-c Crosthwaite Kendal *Carl* from 06; P-in-c Cartmel Fell from 06; P-in-c Winster from 06; P-in-c Witherslack from 06. *The Vicarage, Crosthwaite, Kendal LA8 8HX* T: (015395) 68276 E: mich@elwoodcock.com

WOODCOCK, Michael Paul. b 71. Univ of Greenwich BA 93. St Jo Coll Nottm MA 98. **d** 99 **p** 00. C Brinsley w Underwood *S'well* 99-02; C New Malden and Coombe *S'wark* 02-07; C Ambleside w Brathay *Carl* 07-10; TV Loughrigg 10; Chapl Cumbria Univ 07-10; P-in-c Dromana Australia from 10. *12 Verdon Street, PO Box 99, Dromana VIC 3936, Australia* T: (0061) (3) 5987 2856 E: paul-woodcock@sky.com *or* stmarksdromana@bigpond.com

WOODCOCK, Mrs Michelle Lisa. b 74. Dartington Coll of Art BA 96 Cant Ch Ch Univ PGCE 98. LCTP 08. **d** 10 **p** 11. NSM Kendal St Thos *Carl* from 10; NSM Crook from 10; NSM Crosthwaite, Cartmel Fell, Winster and Witherslack 10-15; TV Cartmel Peninsula from 15; NSM Helsington from 10; NSM Underbarrow from 10. *The Vicarage, Crosthwaite, Kendal LA8 8HX* T: (015395) 68276 E: michellewoodcock74@hotmail.com

WOODCOCK, Nicholas Ethelbert. b 46. FRSA 90. Cant Sch of Min 80. **d** 90 **p** 91. Chief Exec and Co Sec Keston Coll Kent 89-92; NSM Clerkenwell H Redeemer w St Phil *Lon* 90-92; NSM Clerkenwell H Redeemer and St Mark 92-93; Chapl RN 93-01; Min Can, Prec and Sacr Ely Cathl 01-03; R Lavenham w Preston *St E* 03-09; Min Can St E Cathl 03-09; Chapl Morden Coll Blackheath 09-13; rtd 13. *Address withheld by request*

WOODE, Mrs Elizabeth. b 43. **d** 06 **p** 07. NSM Middlewich w Byley *Ches* from 06. *6 The Grange, Hartford, Northwich CW8 1QH* T: (01606) 75030 E: tonylizwoode@hotmail.com

WOODERSON, Mrs Marguerite Ann. b 44. RGN SCM. Qu Coll Birm 86. **d** 89 **p** 94. Par Dn Stoneydelph St Martin CD *Lich* 89-90; Par Dn Glascote and Stonydelph 90-91; Par Dn Chasetown 91-94; C 94; C-in-c Chase Terrace St Jo Distr Ch 92-94; Chapl Naas Gen Hosp 94-98; I Celbridge w Straffan and Newcastle-Lyons *D & G* 98-06. *Lazena, Rosses Point, Co Sligo, Republic of Ireland* T: (00353) (71) 911 7852 E: annwooderson@gmail.com

WOODERSON, Michael George. b 39. Southn Univ BA 61. Lon Coll of Div BD 69. **d** 69 **p** 70. C Morden *S'wark* 69-73; C Aldridge *Lich* 73-81; V Chasetown and P-in-c Hammerwich 91-94; RD Lich 86-94; Preb Lich Cathl 89-94; I Naas w Kill and Rathmore *M & K* 94-06; rtd 06. *Lazena, Rosses Point, Co Sligo, Republic of Ireland* T: (00353) (71) 911 7852 M: 86-336 8503 E: michaelwooderson@icloud.com

WOODFIELD, Benjamin Robert. b 81. St Jo Coll Nottm. **d** 14 **p** 15. C Astley Bridge *Man* from 14. *24 Mackenzie Street, Bolton BL1 6QW* M: 07800-746918 E: revbenwoodfield@gmail.com

WOODGATE, Mrs Elizabeth Mary. b 66. W Sussex Inst of HE BEd 87. St Jo Coll Nottm MTh 02. **d** 02 **p** 04. C Crofton *Portsm* 02-03; C Lee-on-the-Solent 03-05; C Rowner and Bridgemary 05-07; NSM Kuwait 07-10; PtO *Portsm* 11-15; V Ringmer *Chich* from 15. *The Vicarage, Vicarage Way, Ringmer, Lewes BN8 5LA* T: (01273) 812243 E: revdbethwoodgate@outlook.com

WOODGATES, Mrs Margaret. b 47. St D Coll Lamp BA 67. WMMTC 00. **d** 03 **p** 04. NSM Redditch, The Ridge *Worc* 03-05; NSM Redditch Ch the K 05-06; NSM Finstall 06-11; PtO from 12. *18 Warwick Hall Gardens, Bromsgrove B60 2AU* T: (01527) 577785 E: margaret.woody@talktalk.net

WOODGER, John McRae. b 36. Univ of Wales MTh 08. Tyndale Hall Bris 60. **d** 63 **p** 64. C Heref St Pet w St Owen 63-66; C Macclesfield St Mich *Ches* 66-69; V Llangarron w Llangrove *Heref* 69-74; P-in-c Garway 70-74; R Church Stretton 74-84; Preb Heref Cathl 82-84; V Watford *St Alb* 84-01; rtd 01; PtO *Heref* from 01. *39 Bronte Drive, Ledbury HR8 2FZ* T: (01531) 636745 E: woodger@talktalk.net

WOODGER, John Page. b 30. Master Mariner 56. St Aid Birkenhead 56. **d** 59 **p** 60. C Kimberworth *Sheff* 59-62; Chapl HM Borstal Pollington 62-70; C Goole *Sheff* 62-63; V Balne 63-70; C Halesowen *Worc* 70-74; V Cookley 74-81; TV Droitwich 81-85; TV Bedminster *Bris* 85-93; rtd 93; PtO *Bris* 93-97; *Worc* from 98. *1 Barbel Crescent, Worcester WR5 3QU* T: (01905) 769065 E: john.woodger@cmail.co.uk

WOODGER, Richard William. b 50. Sarum & Wells Th Coll 76. **d** 79 **p** 80. C Chessington *Guildf* 79-82; C Frimley and Frimley Green 82-85; V N Holmwood 85-90; TR Headley All SS 90-98; TR Penrith w Newton Reigny and Plumpton Wall *Carl* 98-05; P-in-c Northleach w Hampnett and Farmington etc *Glouc* 05-13; C Sherborne, Windrush, the Barringtons etc 08-13; AD Northleach 09-10; rtd 13; PtO *Lon* from 14. *6 Sylvia Avenue, Pinner HA5 4QE* E: dickwoodger@yahoo.co.uk

WOODHALL, Neil Baxter. b 53. Yorks Min Course 13. **d** 15. NSM Selby Abbey *York* from 15. *6 Priory Park Grove, Monk Fryston, Leeds LS25 5EU* T: (01977) 682091 E: nbwoodhall@btinternet.com

WOODHALL, Peter. b 32. Edin Th Coll 57. **d** 60 **p** 61. C Carl St Barn 60-63; Hon Chapl Estoril *Eur* 63-65; Chapl RN 66-82; TR Is of Scilly *Truro* 82-90; V Mithian w Mount Hawke 90-95; rtd 97. *17 Emu Close, Heath and Reach, Leighton Buzzard LU7 0AT*

WOODHAM, Richard Medley Swift. b 43. Master Mariner 70. S'wark Ord Course 71. **d** 73 **p** 74. C Gravesend St Aid *Roch* 73-75; C Chessington *Guildf* 75-78; Warden Dioc Conf Ho Horstead *Nor* 78-87; R Horstead 78-87; Youth Chapl 78-88; V Nor St Mary Magd w St Jas 87-91; R Norwich Over-the-Water 91-98; P-in-c Lakenham St Jo 98-99; V Nor Lakenham St Jo and All SS and Tuckswood 99-06; RD Nor E 02-06; rtd 06; PtO *Nor* from 06. *40 Anchor Street, Coltishall, Norwich NR12 7AQ* T: (01603) 736411 E: richardmwoodham@gmail.com

WOODHAMS, Raymond John. b 40. Garnett Coll Lon CertEd 68 IEng. STETS 98. **d** 01 **p** 02. NSM E Blatchington *Chich* 01-08; NSM E Blatchington and Bishopstone from 08. *Address temp unknown* E: raymondj.woodhams@virgin.net

WOODHAMS, Roy Owen. b 57. ARCM 76 GRSM 78 Lon Inst of Educn TCert 79. Ripon Coll Cuddesdon 91. **d** 93 **p** 94. C Deal St Leon and St Rich and Sholden *Cant* 93-97; P-in-c Cherbury *Ox* 97-02; P-in-c Gainfield 99-02; R Cherbury w Gainfield 02-04; AD Vale of White Horse 01-04; V Fleet *Guildf* 04-13; R Cranleigh from 13. *The Rectory, 15 High Street, Cranleigh GU6 8AS* T: (01483) 800655 E: roy.woodhams@gmail.com

WOODHAMS, Mrs Sophie Harriet. b 27. Cranmer Hall Dur 66. **dss** 80 **d** 87. Raveningham *Nor* 80-81; Henleaze *Bris* 81-87; rtd 87. *22 Manormead, Tilford, Hindhead GU26 6RA* T: (01428) 602500

WOODHEAD, Mrs Bernice. b 45. **d** 01 **p** 02. OLM Calderbrook and Shore *Man* 01-13; OLM Littleborough 13-15; PtO from 15. *2 Mount Avenue, Littleborough OL15 9JP* T: (01706) 379517

WOODHEAD, Miss Helen Mary. b 45. Bedf Coll Lon BA 57. Westcott Ho Cam 86. **d** 87 **p** 94. Par Dn Daventry *Pet* 87-90; Asst Dioc Dir of Ords *Guildf* 90-00; C Godalming 90-95; C Worplesdon 95-00; rtd 00; PtO *Lich* from 00. *12 Barley Croft, Whittington, Lichfield WS14 9LY* T: (01543) 432345

WOODHEAD, Canon Michael. b 51. St Jo Coll Nottm 88. **d** 90 **p** 91. C Stannington *Sheff* 90-93; V Deepcar 93-01; TV Crookes St Thos 01-05; TR from 05; Hon Can Sheff Cathl from 11. *St Thomas Church, Nairn Street, Sheffield S10 1UL* T: 0114-267 1090 E: mick.woodhead@sheffield.anglican.org

WOODHEAD, Mrs Sandra Buchanan. b 42. Man Poly BA 82 Man Univ BD 85. St Deiniol's Hawarden. **dss** 86 **d** 87 **p** 94. High Lane *Ches* 86-90; Hon Par Dn 87-90; C Brinnington w Portwood 91-94; V 94-00; R Withington St Paul *Man* 00-09; rtd 09; PtO *Ches* 09-14; Hon C Stockport St Geo from 14. *Woodbank, Light Alders Lane, Disley, Stockport SK12 2LW* T: (01663) 765708 E: deniswoodhead@btinternet.com

WOODHOUSE, Canon Alison Ruth. b 43. Bedf Coll of Educn CertEd 64. Dalton Ho Bris 68. **dss** 79 **d** 87 **p** 94. Par Dn Burscough Bridge *Liv* 87-94; C 94-95; V Formby St Luke 95-07; AD Sefton 00-05; Hon Can Liv Cathl 02-07; rtd 07; Chapl to The Queen 06-13. *16 Fountains Way, Liverpool L37 4HE* T: (01704) 877423

WOODHOUSE, The Ven Andrew Henry. b 23. DSC 45. Qu Coll Ox BA 48 MA 49. Linc Th Coll 48. **d** 50 **p** 51. C Poplar All SS w St Frideswide *Lon* 50-56; V W Drayton 56-70; RD Hillingdon 67-70; Adn Ludlow *Heref* 70-82; R Wistanstow 70-82; P-in-c Acton Scott 70-73; Can Res Heref Cathl 82-91; Treas Heref Cathl 82-85; Adn Heref 82-91; rtd 91; PtO *Guildf* 91-15. *Orchard Cottage, Bracken Close, Woking GU22 7HD* T: (01483) 760671

WOODHOUSE, The Ven Charles David Stewart. b 34. Kelham Th Coll 55. **d** 59 **p** 60. C Leeds Halton St Wilfrid *Ripon* 59-63; Youth Chapl *Liv* 63-66; Bermuda 66-69; Asst Gen Sec CEMS 69-70; Gen Sec 70-76; Bp's Dom Chapl *Ex* 76-81; R Ideford, Luton and Ashcombe 76-81; V Hindley St Pet *Liv* 81-92; Adn Warrington 81-01; Hon Can Liv Cathl 83-01; rtd 01; PtO *Liv* from 03. *9 Rob Lane, Newton-le-Willows WA12 0DR*

WOODHOUSE, David Edwin. b 45. Lon Univ BSc 68. Cuddesdon Coll 68. **d** 71 **p** 72. C E Dulwich St Jo *S'wark* 71-74; LtO 74-77; PtO *Bris* 77-79; LtO 79-98; rtd 10. *Kingsbury Hall, The Green, Calne SN11 8DG* T: (01249) 821521 F: 817246 E: kingsburyhallcd@aol.com

WOODHOUSE, David Maurice. b 40. Lon Univ BA 62. Clifton Th Coll 63. **d** 65 **p** 66. C Wellington w Eyton *Lich* 65-68; C Meole Brace 68-71; V Colwich 71-82; P-in-c Gt Haywood 78-82; R Clitheroe St Jas *Blackb* 82-88; Ellel Grange Chr Healing Cen 88-91; V The Lye and Stambermill *Worc* 91-99; Chapl Acorn Chr Foundn 99-02; Dioc Healing Adv *Guildf* 00-02; rtd 02; PtO *Blackb* from 04. *1 Lilac Avenue, Penwortham, Preston PR1 9PB* T: (01772) 742088 E: david.woodhouse@classicfm.net

WOODHOUSE, Canon Keith Ian. b 33. K Coll Lon 54. **d** 58 **p** 59. C Stockton St Chad CD *Dur* 58-61; C Man St Aid 61-64; V Peterlee *Dur* 64-99; AD Easington 72-98; Hon Can Dur Cathl 79-99; rtd 99; Dioc Pensions and Widows Officer *Dur* from 00; PtO from 04. *85 Baulkham Hills, Penshaw, Houghton le Spring DH4 7RZ* T/F: 0191-584 3977 E: keithianwoodhouse@excite.com

WOODHOUSE, Canon Patrick Henry Forbes. b 47. Ch Ch Ox BA 69 MA 81. St Jo Coll Nottm 69 Lon Coll of Div ALCD 71 LTh 71. **d** 72 **p** 73. C Birm St Martin 72-74; C Whitchurch *Bris* 75-76; C Harpenden St Nic *St Alb* 76-80; Tanzania 80-81; Soc Resp Officer *Carl* 81-85; P-in-c Dean 81-85; Dir Soc Resp *Win* 85-90; V Chippenham St Andr w Tytherton Lucas *Bris* 90-00; Can Res and Prec Wells Cathl 00-12; rtd 12. *Woodside, Rimpton, Yeovil BA22 8AF* T: (01935) 850915 M: 07812-395912 E: pwoodhouse09@gmail.com

WOODHOUSE, Canon Thomas Mark Bews. b 66. Chelt & Glouc Coll of HE BA 98 Glos Univ MA 05 FRSA 05. Aston Tr Scheme 90 Westcott Ho Cam 92. **d** 95 **p** 96. C Cainscross w Selsley *Glouc* 95-98; V Hardwicke and Elmore w Longney 98-05; P-in-c Wootton Bassett *Sarum* 05-10; V Wootton Bassett 10-14; P-in-c Lyneham w Bradenstoke 11-14; NSM Woodhill 11-14; RD Calne 06-14; TR Dorchester and the Winterbournes from 14; Can and Preb Sarum Cathl from 09; TR Dorchester and the Winterbournes from 14. *The Rectory, 17A Edward Road, Dorchester DT1 2HL* T: (01305) 267944

WOODING, Alison. b 67. Yorks Min Course 05. **d** 10 **p** 11. C Ranmoor *Sheff* 10-15; P-in-c Kimberworth and Kimberworth Park from 15; C Rawmarsh w Parkgate from 15; C Greasbrough from 15. *49 Admirals Crest, Scholes, Rotherham S61 2SW* M: 07891-064370 E: alison.wooding@sheffield.anglican.org

WOODING JONES, Andrew David. b 61. Hull Univ MBA 01. Oak Hill Th Coll BA 91. **d** 91 **p** 92. C Welling *Roch* 91-95; TV Crookes St Thos *Sheff* 95-00; Resident Dir Ashburnham Trust 00-12; NSM Ashburnham w Penhurst *Chich* 01-12; Dir World Prayer Cen Birm 12-14; PtO *Roch* from 14; *Chich* from 15. *Lytlewood, Riding Lane, Hildenborough, Tonbridge TN11 9LR* E: andrew@woodingjones.net

WOODLEY, David James. b 38. K Coll Lon BD 61 AKC 61 Open Univ BA 98. **d** 62 **p** 63. C Lancing St Jas *Chich* 62-64; C St Alb St Pet *St Alb* 64-67; Malaysia 67-70; LtO *Linc* 71-72; V Westoning w Tingrith *St Alb* 72-77; Asst Chapl HM Pris Wormwood Scrubs 77-78; Chapl HM Pris Cardiff 78-84; Chapl HM Rem Cen Risley 84-92; Chapl HM Pris Styal 92-98; rtd 98; PtO *Ches* from 98. *18 Longcroft Road, Yeovil BA21 4RR* T: (01935) 474072

WOODLEY, Canon John Francis Chapman. b 33. Univ of Wales (Lamp) BA 58. Edin Th Coll 58. **d** 60 **p** 61. C Edin All SS 60-65; Chapl St Andr Cathl 65-67; Prec 67-71; R Glas St Oswald 71-77; P-in-c Cumbernauld 77-93; Can St Mary's Cathl 82-99; CSG from 82; R Dalbeattie *Glas* 93-99; rtd 99; Hon Can St Mary's Cathl from 99; Dioc Supernumerary 99-03; LtO from 03. *3 Highburgh Drive, Rutherglen, Glasgow G73 3RR* T: 0141-647 3118 E: jfcwoodley@talk21.com

WOODLEY, Priscilla Elizabeth. *See* SLUSAR, Priscilla Elizabeth

WOODLEY, The Ven Ronald John. b 25. Bps' Coll Cheshunt 50. **d** 53 **p** 54. C Middlesbrough St Martin *York* 53-58; C Whitby 58-61; C-in-c Middlesbrough Berwick Hills CD 61-66; V Middlesbrough Ascension 66-71; R Stokesley 71-85; RD

77-85; Can and Preb York Minster 82-00; Adn Cleveland 85-91; rtd 91; PtO *Leeds* from 91; *York* from 00. *The Old Joiner's Cottage, Cross Lane, Ingleby Arncliffe, Northallerton DL6 3ND* T: (01609) 882983

WOODLEY, Simon Andrew. b 66. Liv Univ BA 88 Univ of Cen England in Birm 96. Ridley Hall Cam BTh 00. **d** 00 **p** 01. C Birm St Martin w Bordesley St Andr 00-04; TR Bemerton *Sarum* from 04. *St Michael's Rectory, St Michael's Road, Salisbury SP2 9EQ* T: (01722) 333750 E: revwoodley@yahoo.co.uk

WOODMAN, Brian Baldwin. b 35. Leeds Univ BA 57 PhD 73. NOC 84. **d** 87 **p** 88. C Guiseley w Esholt *Bradf* 87-90; TV Bingley All SS 90-94; P-in-c St Merryn *Truro* 94-00; rtd 00; PtO *Truro* from 00. *1 Sarahs Close, Padstow PL28 8BJ* T: (01841) 532973

WOODMAN, Christopher James. b 65. Chich Th Coll BTh 93. **d** 93 **p** 94. C Leigh-on-Sea St Marg *Chelmsf* 93-97; TV Canvey Is 97-00; TV Moulsecoomb *Chich* 00-03; C Brighton St Matthias 03-06; TV Brighton Resurr 06-09; V Brighton St Luke Queen's Park 09-10; P-in-c Fareham SS Pet and Paul *Portsm* 10-12; rtd 12; PtO *Ely* from 12. *Shama, Little Lane, Stoke Ferry, King's Lynn PE33 9SS* T: (01366) 500284 E: cjw@btinternet.com

WOODMAN, Oliver Nigel. b 47. FCIPD. Sarum Th Coll 67. **d** 70 **p** 82. C Stepney St Dunstan and All SS *Lon* 70-71; NSM Ovingdean w Rottingdean and Woodingdean *Chich* 81-87; NSM Eastbourne St Sav and St Pet 88-93; Asst to RD Eastbourne 93-98; NSM Eastbourne St Sav and St Pet 98-01; PtO *Win* 02-10; Hon Chapl Win and Eastleigh Healthcare NHS Trust 09-10; PtO *Lich* 10-15. *25A Wissage Lane, Lichfield WS13 6DF* T: (01543) 256655 E: ojwoodman56@googlemail.com

WOODMAN, The Ven Peter Wilfred. b 36. Univ of Wales (Lamp) BA 58. Wycliffe Hall Ox 58. **d** 60 **p** 61. C New Tredegar *Mon* 60-61; C Newport St Paul 61-64; C Llanfrechfa All SS 64-66; Abp of Wales's Messenger 66-67; V Llantilio Pertholey w Bettws Chpl etc *Mon* 67-74; V Bassaleg 74-90; Can St Woolos Cathl 84-01; V Caerwent w Dinham and Llanfair Discoed etc 90-96; Adn Mon 93-01; R Mamhilad and Llanfihangel Pontymoile 96-01; rtd 01. *Glaslyn, 40 Longhouse Barn, Penperlleni, Pontypool NP4 0BD* T: (01873) 881322

WOODMANSEY, Michael Balfour. b 55. Leic Univ BSc. Ridley Hall Cam. **d** 83 **p** 84. C St Paul's Cray St Barn *Roch* 83-89; C S Shoebury *Chelmsf* 89-93; R Stifford 93-01; TR Heworth H Trin *York* 01-07; R Heworth H Trin and St Wulstan from 07. *Heworth Rectory, Melrosegate, York YO31 0RP* T/F: (01904) 422958 E: vicar@holytrinitystwulstan.org.uk

WOODMORE, Mrs Dilys Mary. b 44. SAOMC 98. **d** 01 **p** 02. NSM Dedworth *Ox* 01-04; NSM Burchetts Green 04-14; rtd 14; PtO *Ox* from 14. *59 Terrington Hill, Marlow SL7 2RE* T: (01628) 486274

WOODROFFE, Ian Gordon. b 46. Edin Th Coll 69. **d** 72 **p** 73. C Soham *Ely* 72-75; P-in-c Swaffham Bulbeck 75-80; Youth Chapl 75-80; V Cambridge St Jas 80-87; Chapl Mayday Univ Hosp Thornton Heath 87-94; Chapl Mayday Healthcare NHS Trust Thornton Heath 94-97; Staff Cllr Epsom and St Helier NHS Trust 97-02. *4 Station Road, Swaffham Bulbeck, Cambridge CB25 0NW* T: (01223) 811255 E: ian@goldtraining.co.uk

WOODROW, Miss Alinda Victoria. b 60. Newnham Coll Cam BA 82 MA 86. Ripon Coll Cuddesdon 04. **d** 06 **p** 07. C Attleborough w Besthorpe *Nor* 06-08; C Sprowston w Beeston 08-12; PtO 12-15; Chapl Norfolk and Nor Univ Hosp NHS Trust from 15. *61 Sparhawk Road, Norwich NR7 8BS* T: (01603) 927523 E: alindawoodrow316@gmail.com

WOODROW, Mark Jason. b 72. MInstLM 10. Ripon Coll Cuddesdon 11. **d** 13 **p** 14. C Lavenham w Preston *St E* from 13. *7 Weavers Close, Lavenham, Sudbury CO10 9QN* T: (01787) 247959 M: 07890-871271 E: revdmarkwoodrow@gmail.com

WOODRUFF, Mrs Celia Mary. b 42 **p** 15. NSM Vale and Cotswold Edge *Glouc* from 14. *West End Farm, Main Street, Sedgeberrow, Evesham WR11 7WA* T: (01386) 881033 E: ronaldandcelia@btinternet.com

WOODS, The Very Revd Alan Geoffrey. b 42. TD 93. ACCA 65 FCCA 80. Sarum Th Coll 67. **d** 70 **p** 71. C Bedminster St Fran *Bris* 70-73; Youth Chapl 73-76; Warden Legge Ho Res Youth Cen 73-76; P-in-c Neston *Bris* 76-79; TV Gtr Corsham 79-81; CF (TA) 80-94; P-in-c Charminster *Sarum* 81-83; V Charminster and Stinsford 83-90; RD Dorchester 85-90; Chapl Dorchester Hosps 86-87; V Calne and Blackland *Sarum* 90-96; RD Calne 90-96; Chapl St Mary's Sch Calne 90-96; Can and Preb Sarum Cathl 92-96; Sen Chapl Malta and Gozo *Eur* 96-03; Chan Malta Cathl 96-03; Dean Gib 03-08; V Gen to Bp Eur 03-05; Adn Gib 05-08; P-in-c Málaga 06-07; rtd 08; PtO *Sarum* from 08; *Eur* from 08; Dioc Retirement Officer *Sarum* from 10. *6 Maumbury Square, Weymouth Avenue, Dorchester DT1 1TY* T: (01305) 264877 E: abwoods@tiscali.co.uk

WOODS, Charles William. b 31. Lich Th Coll 55. **d** 58 **p** 59. C Hednesford 58-62; V Wilnecote 62-67; V Basford 67-76; V Chasetown 76-81; P-in-c Donington 81-83; V 83-96; V Boningale 83-96; RD Shifnal 84-89; rtd 96; PtO *Lich* from 96. *17 Campion Drive, Donnington Wood, Telford TF2 7RH* T: (01952) 677134

WOODS, Christopher Guy Alistair. b 35. Dur Univ BA 60. Clifton Th Coll 60. **d** 62 **p** 63. C Rainham *Chelmsf* 62-65; C Edin St Thos 65-69; Sec Spanish and Portuguese Ch Aid Soc 69-79; C Willesborough w Hinxhill *Cant* 74-80; P-in-c Murston w Bapchild and Tonge 80-87; R 87-90; R Gt Horkesley *Chelmsf* 90-98; RD Dedham and Tey 91-98; rtd 98; P-in-c Tenerife Sur *Eur* 99-00; PtO *Chelmsf* from 00. *Bluebonnet, Mill Lane, Bradfield, Manningtree CO11 2UT* T: (01255) 870411

WOODS, Christopher Morrison. b 77. St Andr Univ MA 00 TCD BTh 04. CITC 01. **d** 04 **p** 05. C Dundela St Mark *D & D* 04-07; Chapl Ch Coll Cam 07-10; Sec C of E Liturg Commn and Nat Worship Development Officer Abps' Coun 11-13; Tutor Westcott Ho Cam 12-13; PV St Jo Coll Cam 12-13; P-in-c Hoxton St Anne w St Columba *Lon* 13-15; V from 15; Educator in Adult Learning and Development Stepney Area from 13. *St Anne's Vicarage, 37 Hemsworth Street, London N1 5LF* T: (020) 7033 3446 *or* 7729 1243 E: christopher.woods@london.anglican.org

WOODS, David Arthur. b 28. Bris Univ BA 52. Tyndale Hall Bris 48. **d** 53 **p** 54. C Camborne *Truro* 53-56; C Bromley Ch Ch *Roch* 56-58; V Tewkesbury H Trin *Glouc* 58-66; V Stapleford S'well 66-70; Hon Chapl Miss to Seamen 70-93; V Fowey *Truro* 70-93; RD St Austell 80-88; rtd 93; PtO *Truro* from 93. *Linden, 7 Richmond Road, Pelynt, Looe PL13 2NH* T: (01503) 220374

WOODS, David Benjamin. b 42. Linc Th Coll 88. **d** 90 **p** 91. C Louth *Linc* 90-93; P-in-c Ingoldmells w Addlethorpe 93-97; R 97-01; P-in-c Sutton Bridge 01-08; rtd 08; Hon C Digby Gp *Linc* from 08. *10 Mayflower Drive, Heckington, Sleaford NG34 9UX* M: 07840-544384 E: woods_david4@sky.com

WOODS, David Edward. b 36. City Univ FBCO 61 FSMC 61. SWMTC 83 S Dios Minl Tr Scheme 94. **d** 95 **p** 96. NSM Bemerton *Sarum* 95-98; NSM Salisbury St Martin 98-00; NSM Laverstock 98-00; NSM Salisbury St Martin and Laverstock 00-05; PtO *Truro* from 05. *8 Tower Meadows, St Buryan, Penzance TR19 6AJ* T: (01736) 811253

WOODS, Edward Christopher John. b 44. NUI BA 67. CITC 66. **d** 67 **p** 68. C Drumglass *Arm* 67-70; C Belfast St Mark *Conn* 70-73; I Kilcolman *L & K* 73-78; I Portarlington w Cloneyhurke and Lea *M & K* 78-84; Chan Kildare Cathl 81-84; I Killiney Ballybrack *D & G* 85-92; I Dublin Rathfarnham 93-14; Dir of Ords (Dub) 98-14; Internship Co-ord CITC 10-14; rtd 14. *St Peter's Vicarage, Cricket Path, Formby, Liverpool L37 7DP* T: (01704) 873369 E: tedwoods@eircom.net

WOODS, Canon Eric John. b 51. DL 12. Magd Coll Ox BA 72 MA 77 Trin Coll Cam BA 77 MA 83 FRSA 94. Westcott Ho Cam 75. **d** 78 **p** 79. C Bris St Mary Redcliffe w Temple etc 78-81; Hon C Clifton St Paul 81-83; Asst Chapl Bris Univ 81-83; V Wroughton 83-93; RD 88-93; V Sherborne w Castleton, Lillington and Longburton *Sarum* from 93; Chapl Sherborne Sch for Girls 93-99; RD Sherborne *Sarum* 96-04; Can and Preb Sarum Cathl from 98; Chapl Dorset Community NHS Trust 93-00; Chapl SW Dorset Primary Care Trust from 01; Chapl St Antony's Leweston Sch Sherborne from 03. *The Vicarage, Abbey Close, Sherborne DT9 3LQ* T: (01935) 812452 F: 812206 E: vicar@sherborneabbey.com

WOODS, Frederick James. b 45. Southn Univ BA 66 MPhil 74 Fitzw Coll Cam BA 76 MA 79. Ridley Hall Cam 74. **d** 77 **p** 78. C Stratford-on-Avon w Bishopton *Cov* 77-81; V Warminster Ch Ch *Sarum* 81-96; RD Heytesbury 91-96; TR Woodley *Ox* 96-01; V Colchester St Pet and St Botolph *Chelmsf* 01-11; rtd 11. *36 Church Road, Otley, Ipswich IP6 9NP* T: (01473) 890786 E: fredjwoods@hotmail.com

WOODS, Geoffrey Edward. b 49. Lon Univ BD 70 K Coll Lon MA 94. Tyndale Hall Bris 67. **d** 73 **p** 74. C Gipsy Hill Ch Ch *S'wark* 73-76; C Uphill *B & W* 76-79; R Swainswick w Langridge and Woolley 79-84; PtO *Bris* 84-96; NSM Colerne w N Wraxall 96-12; NSM By Brook 06-11; NSM Box w Hazlebury and Ditteridge 11-12; rtd 14. *22 Watergates, Colerne, Chippenham SN14 8DR* T: (01225) 743675

WOODS, John. **d** 12 **p** 13. C Sligo w Knocknarea and Rosses Pt *K, E & A* 12-13; Bp's C Kildallon and Swanlinbar from 13. *The Rectory, Church Road, Swanlinbar, Co Cavan, Republic of Ireland* T: (00353) (49) 4338204 M: 87-607 7392 E: johnjameswoods@yahoo.co.uk

WOODS, Joseph Richard Vernon. b 31. Solicitor 57. Cuddesdon Coll 58. **d** 60 **p** 61. C Newc St Gabr 60-63; Trinidad and Tobago 63-67; Chapl Long Grove Hosp Epsom 67-76; P-in-c Ewell St Fran *Guildf* 76-79; V 79-87; V Englefield Green 87-96; rtd 96; PtO *Win* 97-03. *8 Wren Close, Christchurch BH23 4BD* T: (01425) 270799 E: trendi2@btinternet.com

WOODS, Michael. b 57. Ripon Coll Cuddesdon 99. **d** 01 **p** 02. C Bamber Bridge St Aid *Blackb* 01-06; P-in-c Rishton 06-11; V from 11; AD Whalley from 11. *The Vicarage, Somerset Road, Rishton, Blackburn BB1 4BP* T: (01254) 886191
E: mwoods4@supanet.com

WOODS, Canon Michael Spencer. b 44. K Coll Lon BD 66 AKC 66 Sheff Univ MMinTheol 99. **d** 67 **p** 68. C Sprowston *Nor* 67-70; Malaysia 70-74; TV Hempnall *Nor* 74-79; TV Halesworth w Linstead, Chediston, Holton etc *St E* 79-85; TR Braunstone *Leic* 85-92; RD Sparkenhoe E 89-91; TR Gt Yarmouth *Nor* 92-09; Hon Can Nor Cathl 96-09; rtd 09. *4 Old Church Close, Caistor St Edmund, Norwich NR14 8QX*
T: (01508) 493650 E: michael.woods@rjt.co.uk

WOODS, Canon Norman Harman. b 35. K Coll Lon BD 62 AKC 62. **d** 63 **p** 64. C Poplar All SS w St Frideswide *Lon* 63-68; C-in-c W Leigh CD *Portsm* 68-76; V Hythe *Cant* 76-01; RD Elham 83-89; Hon Can Cant Cathl 90-01; rtd 01; PtO *Cant* from 01. *36 Abbey Gardens, Canterbury CT2 7EU*
T: (01227) 470957 E: normanwoods@v21.me.net

WOODS, Richard. *See* WOODS, Joseph Richard Vernon

WOODS, Richard Thomas Evelyn Brownrigg. b 51. St Steph Ho Ox 83. **d** 85 **p** 86. C Southgate Ch Ch *Lon* 85-88; C Northampton All SS w St Kath *Pet* 88-89; V Maybridge *Chich* 89-99; V E Dean 99-05; R Singleton 99-05; V W Dean 99-05; R E Dean, Singleton, and W Dean 05-13; rtd 13. *12 Whittington Terrace, Cox Hill, Shepherdswell, Dover CT15 7NH*
T: (01304) 268013 M: 07717-473774 E: rwoods@onetel.com

WOODS, Roger Andrew. b 60. Southn Univ BSc 81. Oak Hill Th Coll BA 01. **d** 98 **p** 99. C Audley *Lich* 98-02; TV Leek and Meerbrook 02-15; V Kings Heath *Pet* from 15; Dioc Urban Support Officer from 15. *The Vicarage, The Bartons Close, Northampton NN5 7HQ*

WOODS, Stephanie Ruth. b 64. Westhill Coll Birm BEd 92 TCD MTh 12. **d** 11 **p** 12. C Drung w Castleterra, Larah and Lavey etc *K, E & A* 12-15; I Lisbellaw *Clogh* from 15. *The Rectory, Drummeer Road, Faughard, Lisbellaw, Enniskillen BT94 5ES*
M: 07759-949932 M: (00353) 86-160 1318
E: alldonkeysneedshelter@yahoo.ie

WOODS, Tanya Joy. b 73. CITC 99. **d** 02 **p** 03. NSM Killesher *K, E & A* 02-11; NSM Annagh w Drumaloor, Cloverhill and Drumlane 11-13; C from 13. *Cornacrea, Cavan Town, Republic of Ireland* T: (00353) (49) 433 2188 *or* (42) 966 9229
M: 86-060 2450 F: 966 9119 E: revtanyawoods@hotmail.com

WOODS, Theodore Frank Spreull. b 37. Lam Univ BA 58 DipEd 80. Wells Th Coll 60. **d** 62 **p** 63. C Stocking Farm CD *Leic* 62-67; Papua New Guinea 67-77; V Knighton St Jo *Leic* 77-80; Chapl Angl Ch Gr Sch Brisbane Australia 80-88; Chapl Hillbrook Angl Sch 89-06; rtd 06. *44 Merle Street, Carina QLD 4152, Australia* T: (0061) (7) 3398 4437 M: 40-961 6150
E: tandlwoods@bigpond.com

WOODS, Timothy James. b 52. Poly Cen Lon BA 78 MSc 79 Ex Univ MA 96 ACIB 75. Qu Coll Birm 81. **d** 83 **p** 84. C Brierley Hill *Lich* 83-86; C Stoneydelph St Martin CD 86-88; World Development Officer 86-88; Chr Aid Area Sec (SE Lon) 88-91; V Estover *Ex* 91-97; TR Brixham w Churston Ferrers and Kingswear 97-00; Dir Bd of Ch and Soc *Sarum* 00-05; RD Salisbury 05-07; Advocacy and Middle E Desk Officer USPG 05-08; Regional Co-ord Wales and W of England 10; In Methodist Ch 08-09; LtO *Ex* 10-12; Miss Enabler Devonport St Aubyn and Plymouth Waterfront from 13. *St Aubyn's Church, c/o Devonport Library, 16 Chapel Street, Devonport, Plymouth PL1 4DP* T: (01752) 568720
E: timber.woods@tiscali.co.uk

WOODS, William. *See* WOODS, Charles William

WOODSFORD, Canon Andrew Norman. b 43. Nottm Univ BA 65. Ridley Hall Cam 65. **d** 67 **p** 68. C Radcliffe-on-Trent *S'well* 67-70; P-in-c Ladybrook 70-73; P-in-c Barton in Fabis 73-81; P-in-c Thrumpton 73-81; R Gamston w Eaton and W Drayton 81-88; Chapl Bramcote Sch Notts 81-93; Warden of Readers *S'well* 88-08; Hon Can *S'well* Minster 93-08; RD Retford 93-00; rtd 08. *3 Clinton Rise, Gamston, Retford DN22 0QJ* T: (01777) 838706 E: woodsford@msn.com

WOODSFORD, Martyn Paul. b 64. Oak Hill Th Coll 01. **d** 03 **p** 04. C Southover *Chich* 03-07; P-in-c S Malling 07-09; R Adelaide St Luke Australia from 09. *17 Whitmore Square, Adelaide SA 5000, Australia* E: revwoody@macdream.net

WOODWARD, Andrew John. b 59. ACIB 85. SEITE 96. **d** 99 **p** 00. NSM Weybridge *Guildf* 99-03; NSM St Botolph Aldgate w H Trin Minories *Lon* 03-07; PtO *Guildf* 03-07; P-in-c Kemp Town St Mary *Chich* from 07; RD Brighton from 15. *10 Chesham Street, Brighton BN2 1NA* T: (01273) 698601
M: 07434-605749 E: thewoodys1@tiscali.co.uk *or* ruraldeanbrighton@gmail.com

WOODWARD, Anthony John. b 50. Salford Univ BSc 78. St Jo Coll Nottm 79. **d** 81 **p** 82. C Deane *Man* 81-84; CF 84-87; R Norris Bank *Man* 87-90; V Lostock St Thos and St Jo 90-96;

PtO 96-01; C Halliwell 01-02; TV 02-04; P-in-c Chard and Distr *B & W* 04-06; V Chard St Mary 06-09; P-in-c Combe St Nicholas w Wambrook and Whitestaunton 08-09; rtd 09; PtO *Man* from 14; C W Monkton w Kingston St Mary, Broomfield etc *B & W* from 15. *The Vicarage, Kingston St Mary, Taunton TA2 8HW* M: 07827-917209
E: tonyjohn1950@gmail.com

WOODWARD, Arthur Robert Harry (Bob). b 28. **d** 76 **p** 77. Rhodesia 76-80; Zimbabwe 80-87; Adn E Harare 82-87; R Wymington w Podington *St Alb* 87-97; RD Sharnbrook 89-97; rtd 97; PtO *Portsm* from 97. *9 Briarfield Gardens, Horndean, Waterlooville PO8 9HX* T: (023) 9259 6983
E: woodward@bushinternet.com

WOODWARD, Clive Ian. b 49. City of Lon Poly BSc 84. STETS 01. **d** 04 **p** 05. NSM Willingdon *Chich* 04-06 and from 12; Chapl E Sussex Hosps NHS Trust 06-12. *61 Rowan Avenue, Eastbourne BN22 0RX* T: (01323) 509891
E: clive.woodward@tiscali.com

WOODWARD, Dennis Andrew. b 82. Maastricht Hotel Management Sch BBA 06. Ridley Hall Cam 12. **d** 15. C Beckenham Ch Ch *Roch* from 15. *25 Rectory Road, Beckenham BR3 1HL* M: 07772-035525
E: revdenniswoodward@gmail.com

WOODWARD, Canon Ian. b 44. OLM course 96. **d** 97 **p** 98. OLM Queen Thorne *Sarum* 97-99; Adv to Bd of Ch and Soc 97-00; NSM Wilton w Netherhampton and Fugglestone *Sarum* 00-02; R Bere Regis and Affpuddle w Turnerspuddle 02-14; Can and Preb Sarum Cathl 07-14; rtd 14; V of Close Sarum Cathl from 14. *68A The Close, Salisbury SP1 2EN*
M: 07973-318866 T: (01722) 555192
E: revianw@btinternet.com *or* voc@salcath.co.uk

WOODWARD, Canon James Welford. b 61. K Coll Lon BD 82 AKC 82 Lambeth STh 85 Birm Univ MPhil 91 Open Univ PhD 99 FRSA 07. Westcott Ho Cam 83. **d** 85 **p** 86. C Consett *Dur* 85-87; Bp's Dom Chapl *Ox* 87-90; Chapl Qu Eliz Hosp Birm 90-96; Distr Chapl Co-ord S Birm HA 90-96; Chapl Manager Univ Hosp Birm NHS Trust 92-96; P-in-c Middleton *Birm* 96-98; P-in-c Wishaw 96-98; Bp's Adv on Health and Soc Care 96-09; V Temple Balsall 98-09; Master Foundn and Hosp of Lady Katherine Leveson 98-09; Dir Leveson Cen for the Study of Ageing, Spirituality and Soc Policy 00-09; Can Windsor 09-15; Prin Sarum Coll from 15. *Address temp unknown* T: 01722 424801 Email jww@sarum.ac.uk

WOODWARD, Canon John Clive. b 35. Univ of Wales (Lamp) BA 56. St Jo Coll Dur 56. **d** 58 **p** 59. C Risca *Mon* 58-63; C Chepstow 63-66; V Ynysddu 66-74; V Newport Ch Ch 74-84; Can St Woolos Cathl 82-00; TR Cyncoed 84-00; rtd 00. *17 Carisbrooke Way, Cyncoed, Cardiff CF23 9HS*
T: (029) 2048 4448

WOODWARD, Mrs Margaret Ruth. b 59. EMMTC 04. **d** 08 **p** 09. NSM Flintham *S'well* 08-14; NSM Car Colston w Screveton 08-14; NSM Hickling w Kinoulton and Broughton Sulney from 14. *The Rectory, 41 Main Street, Kinoulton, Nottingham NG12 3EN* T: (01949) 81183
E: maggie.woodward@ntlworld.com

WOODWARD, Mark Christian. b 73. Univ of Wales (Lamp) BA 95 Trin Coll Carmarthen PGCE 97. Trin Coll Bris MA 02. **d** 02 **p** 03. C Egham *Guildf* 02-06; R Stoke-next-Guildf from 06; Chapl Guildf Coll of FE and HE from 06. *8 Broadway Close, Guildford GU1 2LW* T: (01483) 559886 M: 07949-630031
E: mark@stjohnstoke.com

WOODWARD, Matthew Thomas. b 75. Brunel Univ BA 97 K Coll Lon MA 99 Anglia Poly Univ MA 05. Westcott Ho Cam 99. **d** 01 **p** 02. C Hampstead St Jo *Lon* 01-05; P-in-c Pimlico St Saviour 05-10; R San Mateo Transfiguration USA from 10. *3900 Alameda de las Pulgas, San Mateo CA 94403-4110, USA* T: (001) (650) 341 8206 E: matthewwoodward@mac.com

WOODWARD, Merriel Frances. b 55. Brighton Univ BA 08 RGN 81. Ripon Coll Cuddesdon 10. **d** 11 **p** 12. NSM Langney *Chich* from 11. *61 Rowan Avenue, Eastbourne BN22 0RX*
T: (01323) 509891

WOODWARD (née HIGGINS), Natasha Caroline. b 76. Clare Coll Cam BA 98 MA 02. Westcott Ho Cam 03. **d** 06 **p** 07. C Crayford *Roch* 06-07; C Orpington All SS 08-10; C Chingford SS Pet and Paul *Chelmsf* 10-13; V Kingsbury H Innocents *Lon* from 13; Lic Lay Min Tr Officer Willesden Area from 15. *Kingsbury Vicarage, 54 Roe Green, London NW9 0PJ*
T: (020) 8204 7531 E: natasha.c.woodward@gmail.com

WOODWARD, Canon Peter Cavell. b 36. St Cath Coll Cam BA 58 MA 62. Bps' Coll Cheshunt 58. **d** 60 **p** 61. C Chingford St Anne *Chelmsf* 60-63; Madagascar 63-75; V Weedon Bec *Pet* 75-76; P-in-c Everdon w Farthingstone 75-76; V Weedon Bec w Everdon 76-81; RD Daventry 79-81; Can Pet Cathl 81-02; V Brackley Pet w St Jas 81-02; Chapl Brackley Cottage Hosp 81-02; RD Brackley *Pet* 82-88; rtd 02; PtO *Pet* from 02; Chapl to Retired Clergy and Clergy Widows' Officer from 08.

7 Glastonbury Road, Northampton NN4 8BB T: (01604) 660679 E: peterandmary@oddbod.org.uk

WOODWARD, Robert. *See* WOODWARD, Arthur Robert Harry

WOODWARD, Roger David. b 38. WMMTC 87. **d** 90 **p** 91. C Castle Bromwich SS Mary and Marg *Birm* 90-93; C Kingstanding St Luke 93-04; C Kingstanding St Mark 93-04; rtd 04; Hon C Kingstanding St Mark *Birm* 04-07. *10 Baldwin Road, Bewdley DY12 2BP* T: (01299) 401119 E: lorrainewoodward@yahoo.com

WOODWELL, Sister Anita Marie. b 42. Nottm Univ BA 74 CertEd 80. St Deiniol's Hawarden 85. **dss** 86 **d** 87 **p** 05. Mottram in Longdendale w Woodhead *Ches* 86-89; Par Dn 87-89; Team Dn Birkenhead Priory 89; PtO *Ban* from 01; *St D* from 04; P-in-c Llanfrechfa and Llanddewi Fach w Llandegfeth *Mon* 05-09; Dioc Adv on Spirituality 09-13; PtO from 13. *1 White Houses, Pentwyn, Abersychan, Pontypool NP4 7SY* T: (01495) 753195 E: awoodwell@yahoo.com

WOOFF, Ms Erica Mielle. b 67. City Univ BSc 90 Lon Inst of Educn MA 95 Heythrop Coll Lon MA 05. SEITE 02. **d** 05 **p** 06. C Sydenham St Bart *S'wark* 05-08; P-in-c Charlton 08-09; R from 09. *St Thomas House, Maryon Road, London SE7 8DJ* T: (020) 8855 1718 E: ericauk@aol.com

WOOKEY, Canon Frances Anne. b 52. ACII 73. WEMTC 94. **d** 97 **p** 98. C Glouc St Jas and All SS 97-01; V Hanley Castle, Hanley Swan and Welland *Worc* 01-15; P-in-c Upton-on-Severn, Ripple, Earls Croome etc 11-15; RD Upton 05-11; Hon Can Worc Cathl 07-15; rtd 15. *51 Marlstone Road, Norman Hill, Dursley GL11 5SA* T: (01453) 519099 E: fawookey@gmail.com

WOOKEY, Stephen Mark. b 54. Em Coll Cam BA 76 MA 80. Wycliffe Hall Ox 77. **d** 80 **p** 81. C Enfield Ch Ch Trent Park *Lon* 80-84; Asst Chapl Paris St Mich *Eur* 84-87; C Langham Place All So *Lon* 87-96; R Moreton-in-Marsh w Batsford, Todenham etc *Glouc* from 96; RD Stow 99-04. *The Rectory, Bourton Road, Moreton-in-Marsh GL56 0BG* T: (01608) 652680 E: stevewookey@mac.com

WOOLCOCK, Christine Ann. *See* FROUDE, Christine Ann

WOOLCOCK, John. b 47. Open Univ BA 82 BA 86. Wm Temple Coll Rugby 69 Sarum & Wells Th Coll 70. **d** 72 **p** 73. C Kells *Carl* 72-76; C Barrow St Matt 76-78; R Distington 78-86; V Staveley w Kentmere 86-93; Soc Resp Officer 89-93; Hon Can Carl Cathl 91-93; TR Egremont and Haile 93-08; P-in-c Seascale and Drigg 08-13; RD Calder 07-12; rtd 13. *6 Highfields, Whitehaven CA28 6TS* E: john.woolcock@btinternet.com

WOOLCOCK, Mrs Olwen Sylvia. b 57. Birm Univ BA 78. WEMTC 02. **d** 05 **p** 06. C Claines St Jo *Worc* 05-08; TR Hugglescote w Donington, Ellistown and Snibston *Leic* from 08. *The Rectory, 12 Grange Road, Hugglescote, Coalville LE67 2BQ* T: (01530) 839368 E: olwen@woolcock.org

WOOLDRIDGE, Derek Robert. b 33. Nottm Univ BA 57. Oak Hill Th Coll. **d** 59 **p** 60. C Chesterfield H Trin *Derby* 59-63; C Heworth w Peasholme St Cuth *York* 63-70; R York St Paul 70-00; rtd 01; PtO *York* from 01. *80 Grantham Drive, York YO26 4TZ* T: (01904) 798393 E: drw80@btinternet.com

WOOLF, Ms Elizabeth Louise. b 73. Qu Coll Cam BA 95 MA 99. Wycliffe Hall Ox BA 05. **d** 06 **p** 07. C Holborn St Geo w H Trin and St Bart *Lon* 06-08; C Hammersmith St Paul 08-09; C Leamington Priors St Paul *Cov* from 09. *40 Leicester Street, Leamington Spa CV32 4TE* E: lizzy@stpl.org.uk

WOOLHOUSE, Kenneth. b 38. BNC Ox BA 61 MA 65. Cuddesdon Coll 61. **d** 64 **p** 65. C Old Brumby *Linc* 64-67; Pastor Michaelshoven Soc Work Village W Germany 67-68; Chapl Cov Cathl 68-75; C-in-c Hammersmith SS Mich and Geo White City Estate CD *Lon* 75-81; Dir Past Studies Chich Th Coll 81-86; P-in-c Birdham w W Itchenor *Chich* 81-86; Chapl W Sussex Inst of HE 86-95; TV N Lambeth *S'wark* 95-01; rtd 01; PtO *S'wark* from 01. *15 Tavistock Tower, Russell Place, London SE16 7PQ* T: (020) 7237 8147

WOOLLARD, David John. b 39. Leic Univ BSc 62. Trin Coll Bris 86. **d** 88 **p** 89. C Clifton *York* 88-91; C York St Luke 91-94; V Selby St Jas 94-07; V Wistow 94-96; rtd 07; PtO *York* from 07. *6 Town Street, Settrington, Malton YO17 8NR* T: (01944) 768665 E: dwoollard@yahoo.co.uk

WOOLLASTON, Brian. b 53. CertEd 76. St Paul's Coll Grahamstown 81. **d** 83 **p** 84. C Kington w Huntington, Old Radnor, Kinnerton etc *Heref* 88-89; C Tupsley 89-91; V Newbridge-on-Wye and Llanfihangel Brynpabuan etc *S & B* 91-98; CF 98-03; V Whiteshill and Randwick *Glouc* 03-14; TV Stroud Team from 14. *The Vicarage, 98 Farmhill Lane, Stroud GL5 4DD* T: (01453) 764757

WOOLLCOMBE (née DEARMER), Mrs Juliet. b 38. St Mary's Coll Dur BA 60 Hughes Hall Cam DipEd 61. Gilmore Course 74. **dss** 77 **d** 87 **p** 94. St Marylebone Ch Ch *Lon* 77-80; Dean of Women's Min (Lon Area) 87-89; Dn-in-c Upton Snodsbury and Broughton Hackett etc *Worc* 89-94; NSM

Pershore w Pinvin, Wick and Birlingham 94-98; rtd 98; PtO *Worc* 98-10; *Cant* from 11. *36 Sturry Court Mews, Sturry Hill, Sturry, Canterbury CT2 0ND* T: (01227) 710346 E: juliet.woollcombe1238@btinternet.com

WOOLMER, Preb John Shirley Thursby. b 42. Wadh Coll Ox BA 63 MA 69. St Jo Coll Nottm 70. **d** 71 **p** 72. Asst Chapl Win Coll 72-75; C Ox St Aldate w H Trin 75-82; R Shepton Mallet w Doulting *B & W* 82-02; Chapl Bath and West Community NHS Trust 97-01; Preb Wells Cathl 00-02; NSM Leic H Trin w St Jo 02-07; Par Evang 02-07; Springboard Missr 02-04; rtd 07. *Fig Tree Cottage, Roecliffe Road, Cropston, Leicester LE7 7HQ* T: 0116-235 5237

WOOLMER, Kelvin Frederick. b 55. EAMTC 98. **d** 01 **p** 02. NSM Squirrels Heath *Chelmsf* 01-05; NSM Harold Hill St Paul 05-06; P-in-c Stratford New Town St Paul 06-12; Ind Chapl 06-12; TV Waltham H Cross from 12; Chapl Lon City Airport from 12. *St Lawrence House, 46 Mallion Court, Waltham Abbey EN9 3EQ* T: (01992) 767916 E: kelvin.fwoolmer@yahoo.co.uk

WOOLNOUGH, Murray Robert. Wycliffe Hall Ox 07. **d** 09 **p** 10. C Newbury *Ox* 09-11; P-in-c Woy Woy Australia from 11. *151 Blackwell Road, Woy Woy NSW 2256, Australia* E: mrwoolnough@gmail.com

WOOLVEN, Mrs Catherine Merris. b 60. Trin Coll Bris 07. **d** 09 **p** 10. Chapl Lee Abbey 09-10; C Kilmington, Stockland, Dalwood, Yarcombe etc *Ex* 10-14; P-in-c Uplyme w Axmouth from 14. *The Rectory, Rhode Lane, Uplyme, Lyme Regis DT7 3TX* T: (01297) 444581 M: 07754-582395 E: katewoolven@hotmail.co.uk

WOOLVEN, Ronald. b 36. Oak Hill Th Coll 60. **d** 63 **p** 64. C Romford Gd Shep *Chelmsf* 63-68; C Widford 68-73; P-in-c Barling w Lt Wakering 73-84; V 84-05; rtd 05; PtO *Chelmsf* from 05. *119 Ness Road, Shoeburyness, Southend-on-Sea SS3 9ES* T: (01702) 294436 E: r.woolven@btopenworld.com

WOOLVERIDGE, Gordon Hubert. b 27. CCC Cam BA 51 MA 55 Barrister-at-Law 52. S Dios Minl Tr Scheme 81. **d** 84 **p** 85. NSM St Edm the King w St Nic Acons etc *Lon* 84-85; NSM Chich St Paul and St Pet 85-88; P-in-c Greatham w Empshott and Hawkley w Prior's Dean *Portsm* 88-92; rtd 92; PtO *Sarum* from 93. *21 Back Lane, Cerne Abbas, Dorchester DT2 7JW* T: (01300) 341020

WOOLWAY, Joanne. *See* GRENFELL, Joanne Woolway

WOOLWICH, Area Bishop of. *See* IPGRAVE, The Rt Revd Michael Geoffrey

WOON, Canon Edward Charles. b 43. SWMTC 94. **d** 96 **p** 97. OLM Tuckingmill *Truro* 96-02; P-in-c 02-11; TV Redruth w Lanner and Treleigh 04-13; Hon Can Truro Cathl 09-13; rtd 13. *31 Trevelthan Road, Redruth TR16 4DX* T: (01209) 212191 M: 07974-431863 E: eddie.woon@btopenworld.com

WOOSTER, Patrick Charles Francis. b 38. Qu Coll Birm 63. **d** 65 **p** 66. C Chippenham St Andr w Tytherton Lucas *Bris* 65-70; C Cockington *Ex* 70-72; V Stone w Woodford *Glouc* 72-73; P-in-c Hill 72-73; V Stone w Woodford and Hill 73-99; rtd 99; PtO *Worc* from 99. *20 Hylton Road, Hampton, Evesham WR11 2QB* T: (01386) 45907

WOOSTER, Mrs Ruth Mary. b 45. SAOMC 95. **d** 98 **p** 99. OLM High Wycombe *Ox* from 98. *2 Beechwood View, Wycombe Road, Saunderton, High Wycombe HP14 4HR* E: ruth@woosies.freeserve.co.uk

WOOTTON, Philip Charles. b 63. Hatf Coll Dur BA 85 Dur Inst of Educn PGCE 86. Cranmer Hall Dur 98. **d** 00 **p** 01. C Meopham w Nurstead *Roch* 00-04; TV S Chatham H Trin 04-12; TR Tettenhall Wood and Perton *Lich* from 12. *Tettenhall Wood Rectory, 7 Broxwood Park, Wolverhampton WV6 8LZ* T: (01902) 751116 E: philwootton@supanet.com

WORCESTER, Archdeacon of. *See* JONES, The Ven Robert George

WORCESTER, Bishop of. *See* INGE, The Rt Revd John Geoffrey

WORCESTER, Dean of. *See* ATKINSON, The Very Revd Peter Gordon

WORDSWORTH, Jeremy Nathaniel. b 30. Clare Coll Cam BA 54 MA 58. Ridley Hall Cam 54. **d** 56 **p** 57. C Gt Baddow *Chelmsf* 56-59; Chapl Felsted Sch 59-63; Chapl Sherborne Sch 63-71; PV and Succ S'wark Cathl 71-73; P-in-c Stone *Worc* 73-77; V Malvern St Andr 77-82; V Combe Down w Monkton Combe and S Stoke *B & W* 82-95; rtd 95; PtO *B & W* from 05. *4 The Glebe, Hinton Charterhouse, Bath BA2 7SB* T: (01225) 722520 E: hintonwords@btinternet.com

WORDSWORTH, Paul. b 42. Birm Univ BA 64. Wells Th Coll 64. **d** 66 **p** 67. C Anlaby St Pet *York* 66-71; C Marfleet 71-72; TV 72-77; V Sowerby 77-90; P-in-c Sessay 77-90; V York St Thos w St Maurice 90-01; Local Community Miss Project Ldr 90-96; Abp's Miss Adv 96-00; Miss Strategy Development Officer 01-07; Abp's Officer for Miss and Evang 01-07; rtd 07; PtO *York* from 07. *10 Burniston Grove, York YO10 3RP* T: (01904) 426891 M: 07711-371046 E: paul.wordsworth@homecall.co.uk

WORGAN, Maurice William. b 40. Ely Th Coll 62 Sarum Th Coll 64. **d** 65 **p** 66. C Cranbrook *Cant* 65-69; C Maidstone St Martin 69-72; R Lyminge w Paddlesworth 72-73; P-in-c Stanford w Postling and Radegund 72-73; R Lyminge w Paddlesworth, Stanford w Postling etc 73-88; V Cant St Dunstan w H Cross 88-09; rtd 09; PtO *Cant* 09-12. *Old Trees, 13 Weatherall Close, Dunkirk, Faversham ME13 9UL* T: (01227) 363339 E: maurice@maurice-worgan.co.uk

WORKMAN, Aileen. d 15. NSM Spalding St Mary and St Nic *Linc* from 15; NSM Spalding St Paul from 15. *Address temp unknown*

WORKMAN, John Lewis. b 26. St Deiniol's Hawarden 82. **d** 83 **p** 84. C Brecon St Mary and Battle w Llanddew *S & B* 83-86; Min Can Brecon Cathl 83-86; P-in-c Swansea St Luke 86-87; V 87-95; rtd 95. *12 Grove House, Clyne Close, Mayals, Swansea SA3 5HL* T: (01792) 405674

WORKMAN, Michael. b 49. Univ Coll Lon BSc 70 Reading Univ PhD 75. WEMTC 03. **d** 06 **p** 07. NSM Cheltenham St Mary w St Matt *Glouc* 06-12; NSM Cheltenham St Mary w St Matt and St Luke from 12. *Owls Barn, Badgeworth Lane, Badgeworth, Cheltenham GL51 4UH* T: (01242) 863360 M: 07762-545098 E: mikew@stmstm.org.uk

WORLEDGE, Paul Robert. b 70. Hertf Coll Ox BA 91 Lon Inst of Educn PGCE 92. Oak Hill Th Coll BA 00. **d** 00 **p** 01. C Boscombe St Jo *Win* 00-04; V Ramsgate St Luke *Cant* from 04; P-in-c Westgate St Sav from 13; AD Thanet from 09. *St Luke's Vicarage, St Luke's Avenue, Ramsgate CT11 7JX* T: (01843) 592562 E: worledge@bigfoot.com

WORLEY, William. b 37. TD 89. Cranmer Hall Dur 69. **d** 72 **p** 73. C Consett *Dur* 72-76; V Seaton Carew 76-03; CF (TA) from 77; rtd 03; PtO *Dur* from 03. *5 Peakston Close, Hartlepool TS26 0PN*

WORMALD, Roy Henry. b 42. Chich Th Coll 64. **d** 67 **p** 68. C Walthamstow St Mich *Chelmsf* 67-69; C Cov St Thos 69-72; C Cov St Jo 69-72; C Wood Green St Mich *Lon* 72-77; P-in-c Hanwell St Mellitus 77-80; V Hanwell St Mellitus w St Mark 80-95; C Hillingdon St Jo 95-99; R Kirkley St Pet and St Jo *Nor* 99-09; rtd 09; PtO *Nor* from 09; *St E* from 11. *12 Coppleston Close, Worlingham, Beccles NR34 7SF* T: (01502) 713331

WORN, Nigel John. b 56. Sarum & Wells Th Coll. **d** 84 **p** 85. C Walworth St Jo *S'wark* 84-88; Succ S'wark Cathl 88-92; V Mitcham Ascension 92-01; RD Merton 97; V Kew from 01. *The Vicarage, 278 Kew Road, Kew, Richmond TW9 3EE* T: (020) 8940 4616 E: nigel.worn@gmail.com

WORRALL, Frederick Rowland. b 27. **d** 86 **p** 87. NSM Chellaston *Derby* 86-93; NSM Barrow-on-Trent w Twyford and Swarkestone 94-97; PtO from 97. *37 St Peter's Road, Chellaston, Derby DE73 6UU* T: (01332) 701890

WORRALL, Peter Henry. b 62. CA Tr Coll 85 WMMTC 93. **d** 95 **p** 96. C Bromsgrove St Jo *Worc* 95-99; P-in-c Hartlebury 99-04; Par Support Officer CA 06-07; TV Redditch H Trin *Worc* 07-12. *Address temp unknown*

WORRALL, Suzanne. See SHERIFF, Suzanne

WORSDALE, Barry. b 58. **d** 10 **p** 11. NSM Elloughton and Brough w Brantingham *York* 10-13; P-in-c N Cave w Cliffe from 13; P-in-c Hotham from 13; Chapl HM Pris Wolds from 11. *The Vicarage, Church Lane, North Cave, Brough HU15 2GJ* T: (01430) 470716 E: bworsdale@hotmail.co.uk

WORSDALL, John Robin. b 33. Dur Univ BA 57. Linc Th Coll 62. **d** 63 **p** 64. C Manthorpe w Londonthorpe *Linc* 63-66; C Folkingham w Laughton 66-68; V New Bolingbroke w Carrington 68-74; P-in-c S Somercotes 74-80; V N Somercotes 74-80; P-in-c Stickney 80-82; P-in-c E Ville w Mid Ville 80-82; P-in-c Stickford 80-82; R Stickney Gp 82-98; rtd 98. *2 Streathers Court, Raunds, Wellingborough NN9 6DR* T: (01933) 460078

WORSFOLD, Ms Caroline Jayne. b 61. St Steph Ho Ox. **d** 88 **p** 94. Chapl Asst Leic R Infirmary 88-90; C Sunderland Pennywell St Thos *Dur* 90-91; Sunderland HA Chapl 90-94; Chapl Priority Healthcare Wearside NHS Trust 94-06; Chapl Northumberland, Tyne and Wear NHS Foundn Trust from 06. *The Barton Centre, Cherry Knowle Hospital, Ryhope, Sunderland SR2 0NB* T: 0191-522 7347 or 565 6256 ext 43370 E: caroline.worsfold@stw.nhs.uk

WORSFOLD, Richard Vernon. b 64. Ex Univ LLB 86. Cranmer Hall Dur BA 94. **d** 95 **p** 96. C Countesthorpe w Foston *Leic* 95-99; TV Bradgate Team 99-01; TR 01-09; V Leic Martyrs from 09; AD City of Leic from 14. *49 Westcotes Drive, Leicester LE3 0QT* T: 0116-223 2632 E: rworsfold@virginmedia.com

WORSLEY, Christine Anne. b 52. Hull Univ BA 73 Bris Univ CertEd 74 Birm Univ MPhil 94. WMMTC 82. **dss** 84 **d** 87 **p** 94. Smethwick St Mary *Birm* 84-87; Par Dn Smethwick H Trin w St Alb 87-89; Par Dn Coventry Caludon *Cov* 89-91; Chapl Myton Hamlet Hospice 91-95; Tutor WMMTC 95-04; MinI and Adult Learning Officer *Ely* 05-13; Hon Can Ely Cathl 12-13; Kingdom People Development Officer *Worc* from 13. *The Rectory, 22 Parkwood, Elmley Castle, Pershore WR10 3HT* T: (01386) 710394

WORSLEY, Howard John. b 61. Man Univ BA 83 Leeds Univ PGCE 85 Birm Univ PhD 00. St Jo Coll Nottm MTh 93. **d** 93 **p** 94. C Huthwaite *S'well* 93-96; V Radford St Pet 96-01; Dir Studies St Jo Coll Nottm 02-04; Dir of Educn *S'well* 04-10; *Lon* 10-11; Chapl Lon S Bank Univ *S'wark* 11-12; PtO from 12. *Southbroom House, London Road, Devizes SN10 1LT* M: 07528-565600 E: h.j.worsley@aol.com

WORSLEY, Malcolm. b 37. Carl Dioc Tr Inst 94. **d** 96 **p** 97. NSM Hawes Side *Blackb* 96-98 and 01-04; NSM Lt Thornton 98-01; rtd 04; PtO *Blackb* from 04. *14 Winslow Avenue, Carleton, Poulton-le-Fylde FY6 7PQ* T: (01253) 882208 or 621859 F: 751156 E: m_worsley@dial.pipex.com

WORSLEY, Richard John. b 52. Qu Coll Cam BA 74 MA 78 Univ of Wales CertEd 76 Birm Univ MPhil 91 Warwick Univ MA 96. Qu Coll Birm 77. **d** 80 **p** 81. C Styvechale *Cov* 80-84; V Smethwick H Trin w St Alb *Birm* 84-89; TV Coventry Caludon *Cov* 89-96; Hon C Binley 96-05; PtO *Ely* 05-08; Hon C Soham and Wicken 08-13; P-in-c Elmley Castle w Bricklehampton and Combertons *Worc* from 13; P-in-c Overbury w Teddington, Alstone etc from 13. *The Rectory, 22 Parkwood, Elmley Castle, Pershore WR10 3HT* T: (01386) 710394 M: 07854-543218 E: richardjworsley@btinternet.com

WORSLEY, The Ven Ruth Elizabeth. b 62. **d** 96 **p** 97. C Basford w Hyson Green *S'well* 96-98; C Hyson Green and Forest Fields 98-01; P-in-c 01-08; AD Nottm N 06-08; P-in-c Sneinton St Chris w St Phil 08-10; Dean of Women's Min 07-10; Hon Can S'well Minster 07-10; Par Development Officer Woolwich Area *S'wark* 10-13; Adn Wilts *Sarum* from 13; Chapl to The Queen from 09. *Southbroom House, London Road, Devizes SN10 1LT* T: (01722) 438662 M: 07917-693285 E: adwilts@salisbury.anglican.org or ruthworsley@aol.com

WORSLEY, Thomas Robert. b 54. Sunderland Univ CertEd 00. Lindisfarne Regional Tr Partnership 10. **d** 12 **p** 13. NSM Felling *Dur* from 12. *Bretton Law, Nursery Lane, Gateshead NE10 9TH* M: 07757-949836 E: tom.worsley@blueyonder.co.uk

WORSNIP, Harry. b 29. St Alb MinI Tr Scheme 89. **d** 92 **p** 93. NSM Arlesey w Astwick *St Alb* 92-96; NSM Goldington 96-99; PtO from 00. *28 Milburn Road, Bedford MK41 0NZ* T: (01234) 266422

WORSSAM, Brother Nicholas Alan. b 65. Selw Coll Cam BA 87 MA 91. Qu Coll Birm MA 04. **d** 06 **p** 07. SSF from 99. *Glasshampton Monastery, Shrawley, Worcester WR6 6TQ* T: (01299) 896345 F: 896083 E: nicholasalanssf@btconnect.com

WORSSAM, Richard Mark. b 61. St Jo Coll Dur BA 83 Selw Coll Cam BA 92 Heythrop Coll Lon MA 06 K Coll Lon MSc 09. Ridley Hall Cam 90. **d** 93 **p** 94. C Green Street Green and Pratts Bottom *Roch* 93-97; R Fawkham and Hartley 97-08; V Otford from 08. *The Vicarage, The Green, Otford, Sevenoaks TN14 5PD* T: (01959) 525417 or 523185 E: richard.worssam@tiscali.co.uk

WORT, Gavin. b 78. K Alfred's Coll Win BTh 99 St Jo Coll Dur MA 10. Westcott Ho Cam 00. **d** 02 **p** 03. C Eastleigh *Win* 02-06; Chapl Northumbria Univ *Newc* 06-11; V Newc H Cross from 11. *Holy Cross Vicarage, 16 Whittington Grove, Newcastle upon Tyne NE5 2QP* T: 0191-274 5580 E: g.wort@btopenworld.com

WORTHEN, Canon Jeremy Frederick. b 65. Rob Coll Cam BA 86 MPhil 88 Toronto Univ PhD 92. Ripon Coll Cuddesdon 92. **d** 94 **p** 95. C Bromley SS Pet and Paul *Roch* 94-97; Tutor SEITE 97-05; Prin 05-13; Sec Ecum Relns and Th Coun for Chr Unity from 14; Wiccamical Preb Chich Cathl from 09; Hon Can Cant Cathl from 11. *Council for Christian Unity, Church House, Great Smith Street, London SW1P 3AZ* T: (020) 7898 1488 E: jeremy.worthen@churchofengland.org

WORTHINGTON, Mark. b 55. Solicitor 80 Leeds Poly BA 77. Cranmer Hall Dur 93. **d** 93 **p** 94. C Monkwearmouth St Andr *Dur* 93-96; C Chester le Street 96-00; V Harlow Green and Lamesley from 00. *The Vicarage, Lamesley, Gateshead NE11 0EU* T: 0191-487 6490 E: mark.worthington@durham.anglican.org

WORTLEY, Prof John Trevor. b 34. Dur Univ BA 57 MA 60 DD 86 Lon Univ PhD 69 FRHistS. Edin Th Coll 57. **d** 59 **p** 60. C Huddersfield St Jo *Wakef* 59-64; Canada from 64; Prof Medieval Hist Manitoba Univ 69-02; Visiting Prof Sorbonne Univ 99; rtd 02. *298 Yale Avenue, Winnipeg MB R3M 0M1, Canada or Manitoba University, Winnipeg MB R3T 2N2, Canada* T: (001) (204) 284 7554 E: wortley@cc.umanitoba.ca

WORTLEY, Mrs Lyn Sharon. b 59. Open Univ BA 94 Coll of Ripon & York St Jo MA 98. NOC 95. **d** 98 **p** 99. C Greasbrough *Sheff* 98-01; P-in-c Bramley and Ravenfield w Hooton Roberts etc 01-04; V Bramley 04-12; P-in-c Greasbrough from 12; C Kimberworth and Kimberworth Park from 12; C Rawmarsh w Parkgate from 12; AD Rotherham from 14. *The Vicarage, 16 Church Street, Greasbrough, Rotherham S61 4DX* T: (01709) 279192 E: lyn.wortley@gmail.com

WORTON, David Reginald Paschal. b 56. St Steph Ho Ox 88. **d** 90 **p** 90. SSF 77-11; NSM Anfield St Columba *Liv* 90-92; Asst P Harare Cathl Zimbabwe 92-93; Asst P St Aug Miss Penhalonga 93-94; LtO *Newc* 94-08; Guardian Alnmouth Friary 01-08; Asst P Shrine of Our Lady of Walsingham 08-11; TV Old St Pancras *Lon* from 12. *St Mary's House, Eversholt Street, London NW1 1BN* T: (020) 7387 7301
E: fr.paschal@posp.co.uk

WOSTENHOLM, David Kenneth. b 56. Edin Univ BSc 77 MB, ChB 80 Southn Univ BTh 88. Chich Th Coll 82. **d** 85 **p** 86. C Leytonstone St Marg w St Columba *Chelmsf* 85-90; V Brighton Annunciation *Chich* 90-01; TR Hove 01-07; RD 03-05; P-in-c Glas St Matt from 07. *104 Erradale Street, Glasgow G22 6PT* T: 0141-336 7480 *or* 347 1726 M: 07908-537085
E: stmatthews@btclick.com *or*
david.wostenholm@hotmail.co.uk

WOTHERSPOON, David Colin. b 36. Portsm Coll of Tech CEng 65 MIMechE 65. Cranmer Hall *Dur* 76. **d** 78 **p** 79. C Blackb St Gabr 78-81; V Witton 81-90; Chapl Berne w Neuchâtel *Eur* 90-01; rtd 01; PtO *Blackb* from 01. *24 Copperfield Close, Clitheroe BB7 1ER*

WOTTON, David Ashley. b 44. Chich Th Coll 71. **d** 74 **p** 75. C Allington and Maidstone St Pet *Cant* 74-77; C Ham St Andr *S'wark* 78-79; Chapl HM Rem Cen Latchmere Ho 78-79; C Tattenham Corner and Burgh Heath *Guildf* 85-88; P-in-c E Molesey St Mary 88-93; R Headley w Box Hill 93-06; OCM 93-06; rtd 06. *Lion House, 6 Copper Beeches, St Leonards-on-Sea TN37 7RR* T: (01424) 757122

WRAGG, Christopher William. b 60. SEITE 97. **d** 00 **p** 01. C Gt Warley Ch Ch *Chelmsf* 00-01; C Warley Ch Ch and Gt Warley St Mary 01-04; TV Buckhurst Hill 04-08; V Squirrels Heath from 08. *30 Wakerfield Close, Hornchurch RM11 2TH*
T: (020) 8504 6698 M: 07714-507147
E: vicarchris@btinternet.com

WRAGG, Peter Robert. b 46. Lon Univ BSc 68. Sarum & Wells Th Coll 71. **d** 74 **p** 75. C Feltham *Lon* 74-79; TV Hackney 79-85; P-in-c Isleworth St Mary 85-94; V Feltham 94-12; rtd 12. *3 Woodland Avenue, Eastbourne BN22 0HD*
T: (01323) 507338 E: peter.wragg@tesco.net

WRAIGHT, John Radford. b 58. St Chad's Coll Dur BA 62. **d** 64 **p** 65. C Shildon *Dur* 64-67; C Newton Aycliffe 67-70; C Darlington St Jo 70-75; P-in-c Livingston LEP *Edin* 75-80; TV Carl H Trin and St Barn 80-85; P-in-c Lindale w Field Broughton 85-95; R Middleton Tyas w Croft and Eryholme *Ripon* 95-03; rtd 03; PtO *Dur* from 04. *14 Colorado Grove, Darlington DL1 2YW* T: (01325) 354613
E: j.r.wraight@amserve.net

WRAKE, John. b 28. RMA. Clifton Th Coll 56. **d** 59 **p** 60. C Gt Baddow *Chelmsf* 59-62; CF 62-66; V Tilton w Lowesby *Leic* 66-73; R Maresfield *Chich* 73-79; rtd 93. *Parkfield, Batts Ridge Road, Maresfield, Uckfield TN22 2HJ* T: (01825) 762727

WRAPSON, Donald. b 36. St Aid Birkenhead 60. **d** 65 **p** 66. C Bacup St Sav *Man* 65-68; C Wolverhampton St Matt *Lich* 68-72; C Normanton *Derby* 72-78; V Dordon *Birm* 78-82; Chapl Birm Accident Hosp 82-92; Chapl Selly Oak Hosp Birm 82-92; Chapl Trauma Unit Birm Gen Hosp 92-95; Chapl S Birm Community Health NHS Trust 95-01; rtd 01; PtO *Birm* 01-14; *Worc* from 03. *7 Glebe Road, Avelchurch, Birmingham B48 7PS* T: 0121-445 6568 E: donaldwrapson@tiscali.co.uk

WRATTEN, Martyn Stephen. b 34. AKC 58 St Boniface Warminster 58. **d** 59 **p** 60. C Wandsworth Common St Mary *S'wark* 59-62; C Putney St Mary 62-65; C Pembury *Roch* 65-70; R Stone 70-76; Chapl Joyce Green Hosp Dartford 70-73; Stone Ho Hosp Kent 73-76; Hillcrest Hosp and Netherne Hosp Coulsdon 76-87; Hon C Netherne St Luke CD *S'wark* 76-87; V Gt Doddington *Pet* 87-88; V Gt Doddington and Wilby 88-95; Hon C N Petherton w Northmoor Green *B & W* 95-96; rtd 96; PtO *B & W* from 96. *1 Baymead Close, North Petherton, Bridgwater TA6 6QZ* T: (01278) 662873
E: martyn.wratten@btinternet.com

WRATTEN, Sonya Helen Joan. b 77. Liv Jo Moores Univ BA 00. St Mich Coll Llan 07. **d** 10 **p** 11. C Leic St Phil 10-14; P-in-c Bedford All SS *St Alb* from 14. *All Saints' Vicarage, 1 Cutcliffe Place, Bedford MK40 4DF* M: 07948-714922
E: son.the.rev@me.com

✠**WRAW, The Rt Revd John Michael.** b 59. Linc Coll Ox BA 81 Fitzw Ho Cam BA 84. Ridley Hall Cam 82. **d** 85 **p** 86 **c** 12. C Bromyard *Heref* 85-88; TV Sheff Manor 88-92; V Clifton St Jas 92-01; P-in-c Wickersley 01-04; AD Rotherham 98-04; Hon Can Sheff Cathl 01-04; Adn Wilts *Sarum* 04-12; Area Bp Bradwell *Chelmsf* from 12. *Bishop's House, Orsett Road, Horndon-on-the-Hill, Stanford-le-Hope SS17 8NS* T: (01375) 673806

WRAY, Christopher. b 48. Hull Univ BA 70. Cuddesdon Coll 70. **d** 73 **p** 74. C Brighouse *Wakef* 73-76; C Almondbury 76-78; C Tong *Bradf* 78-80; V Ingleton w Chapel le Dale 80-86; R Brompton Regis w Upton and Skilgate *B & W* 86-91; V Yoxford and Peasenhall w Sibton *St E* 91-94; PtO *Carl* 94-97; R Brough w Stainmore, Musgrave and Warcop 97-02; R Walkingham Hill *Ripon* 02-07; V Ripponden and Barkisland w W Scammonden *Wakef* 07-13; rtd 13. *3 Stonelea, Barkisland, Halifax HX4 0HD* T: (01422) 825208

WRAY, Christopher Brownlow. b 46. Open Univ BA 91. Oak Hill Th Coll 86. **d** 88 **p** 89. C Quidenham *Nor* 88-91; TV Chippenham St Paul w Hardenhuish etc *Bris* 91-97; P-in-c Chipping Sodbury and Old Sodbury *Glouc* 97-09; P-in-c Horton and Lt Sodbury 04-09; rtd 09; Hon C Hardington Vale *B & W* 11-12. *52 Linden Park, Shaftesbury SP7 8RN*
T: (01747) 851961 E: wrays1@directsave.net

WRAY, Kenneth Martin. b 43. Linc Th Coll 72. **d** 75 **p** 76. C Shipley St Paul *Bradf* 75-79; V Edlington *Sheff* 79-85; V Nether Hoyland St Pet 85-97; V Up Hatherley *Glouc* 97-04; rtd 07. *5 Benall Avenue, Cheltenham GL51 6AF* T: (01242) 236966 E: kmartinw026@btinternet.com

WRAY, Martin John. b 51. St Steph Ho Ox 86. **d** 88 **p** 89. C E Boldon *Dur* 88-90; C Seaham w Seaham Harbour 90-92; P-in-c Chopwell 92-95; V Shildon 98-00; C Croxdale and Tudhoe 00-04; P-in-c 04-06; C Spennymoor, Whitworth and Merrington 04-06; V Horsley Hill St Lawr 06-11; rtd 11. *68 Bainbridge Avenue, South Shields NE34 9QY*
E: m.wray@sky.com

WRAY, Michael. b 49. Univ of Wales (Cardiff) BSc(Econ) 77 Keele Univ PGCE 78 RGN 87. Ripon Coll Cuddesdon 80. **d** 82 **p** 83. C Blackpool St Steph *Blackb* 82-83; C Torrisholme 83-84; NSM Headington Quarry *Ox* 93-95; C Kennington *Cant* 95-99; CF (TA) 95-99; P-in-c Isham w Pytchley *Pet* 99-04; Chapl Rockingham Forest NHS Trust 99-01; Chapl Northants Healthcare NHS Trust 01-04; R Potterspury w Furtho and Yardley Gobion etc *Pet* 04-11; rtd 11. *19 Cosgrove Road, Old Stratford, Milton Keynes MK19 6AG* T: (01908) 566824
E: revwray@btinternet.com

WRAYFORD, Geoffrey John. b 38. Ex Coll Ox BA 61 MA 65. Linc Th Coll 61. **d** 63 **p** 64. C Cirencester *Glouc* 63-69; V 70-74; Chapl Chelmsf Cathl 69-74; V Canvey Is 74-76; TR 76-80; P-in-c Woodlands *B & W* 80-88; V 89-92; P-in-c Frome St Jo 80-88; P-in-c Frome Ch Ch 80-85; P-in-c Frome St Mary 85-88; V Frome St Jo and St Mary 89-92; V Minehead 92-03; Chapl Taunton and Somerset NHS Trust 92-03; rtd 03; PtO *B & W* from 02. *Little Garth, Longmeadow Road, Lympstone, Exmouth EX8 5LF* T: (01395) 267838
E: geoffjanw@googlemail.com

WREN, Ann. *See* WREN, Kathleen Ann

WREN, Christopher John. b 54. Dur Univ BEd 76 MA 85. St Steph Ho Ox 77. **d** 79 **p** 80. C Stockton St Pet *Dur* 79-82; C Newton Aycliffe 82-85; V Gateshead St Chad Bensham 85-91; TR Bensham 91-98; V Marton *Blackb* from 98. *St Paul's Vicarage, 55 Vicarage Lane, Marton, Blackpool FY4 4EF* T: (01253) 762679 *or* 692047 M: 07957-323184
E: wthenest@aol.com *or* wrenpaul1@aol.com

WREN, Douglas Peter. b 59. Lanc Univ BA 82. Trin Coll Bris BA 88. **d** 88 **p** 89. C Nantwich *Ches* 88-91; C Chatham St Phil and St Jas *Roch* 91-94; R Kingsdown 94-02; R Speldhurst w Groombridge and Ashurst from 02. *The Rectory, Southfields, Speldhurst, Tunbridge Wells TN3 0PD* T: (01892) 862821
E: douglas.wren@diocese-rochester.org

WREN, John Aubrey. b 46. St Chad's Coll Dur BA 69 Sussex Univ MA 92. Cuddesdon Coll 72. **d** 74 **p** 75. C Fenny Stratford and Water Eaton *Ox* 74-77; TV Brighton Resurr *Chich* 77-84; V Eastbourne St Andr 84-92; V Hove St Barn and St Agnes 92-96. *24 Marlborough Road, Lowestoft NR32 3BU*
T: (01502) 530243

WREN, Mrs Kathleen Ann. b 50. St Steph Ho Ox 83. **dss** 85 **d** 87. Gateshead St Cuth w St Paul *Dur* 85-86; Gateshead St Chad Bensham 86-91; Par Dn 87-91; Adv for Women's Min 90-98; Par Dn Bensham 91-94; C 94-98; Hon Can Dur Cathl 93-98; C Marton *Blackb* from 98. *St Paul's Vicarage, 55 Vicarage Lane, Marton, Blackpool FY4 4EF* T: (01253) 762679 F: 318791
E: wthenest@aol.com

WREN, Comdr Richard. b 35. S Dios Minl Tr Scheme 88. **d** 90 **p** 91. NSM Tisbury *Sarum* 90-01; TV 95-01; TV Nadder Valley *Sarum* 01-05; rtd 05; PtO *Sarum* from 06. *Gaston House, Tisbury, Salisbury SP3 6LG* T: (01747) 870674
E: twowrens@cuffslane.plus.com

WRENN, Peter Henry. b 34. Lon Univ BA 56. Qu Coll Birm 58. **d** 60 **p** 61. V Dronfield *Derby* 60-64; C Hessle *York* 64-65; V Loscoe *Derby* 65-70; Asst Chapl Solihull Sch 71-77; Chapl 77-97; rtd 97; PtO *Birm* 97-12. *63 Shakespeare Drive, Shirley, Solihull B90 2AN* T: 0121-744 3941

WREXHAM, Archdeacon of. See GRIFFITHS, The Ven Robert Herbert

WRIGHT, Alan James. b 38. Chich Th Coll 63. **d** 66 **p** 67. C Edgehill St Dunstan Liv 66-69; Swaziland 69-71; P-in-c Seaforth Liv 71-76; V Taunton All SS B & W 76-95; rtd 99. Bethel, Langford Lane, Norton Fitzwarren, Taunton TA2 6NZ T: (01823) 326558

WRIGHT, Alan Richard. b 31. **d** 96 **p** 97. OLM Quidenham Gp Nor 96-04; PtO from 04. Upgate Farm, Carleton Rode, Norwich NR16 1NJ T: (01953) 860300

WRIGHT, Alan William. b 44. Hull Univ BA 66 Bris Univ PGCE 67 AMusTCL 71. **d** 95 **p** 96. OLM Barton upon Humber Linc from 95. 1 Birchdale, Barton-upon-Humber DN18 5ED T: (01652) 632364 E: wrightherewrightnow@hotmail.com

WRIGHT, Alfred John. b 22. Wycliffe Hall Ox 66. **d** 66 **p** 67. C Newbury St Jo Ox 66-71; V E Challow 71-91; Chapl Community of St Mary V Wantage 75-89; rtd 91; PtO Ox 92-09. Polperro, Hampstead Norreys Road, Hermitage, Thatcham RG18 9RS T: (01635) 202889 E: sheba@eggconnect.net

WRIGHT, Andrew David Gibson. b 58. St Andr Univ MTheol 81. Ridley Hall Cam. **d** 83 **p** 84. C W Derby Gd Shep Liv 83-86; C Carl H Trin and St Barn 86-88; V Wigan St Jas w St Thos Liv 88-91; Chapl St Edw Sch Ox 91-97 and 06-07; Ho Master 97-07; Miss Chapl R Nat Miss to Deep Sea Fishermen 07-13; Sec Gen Miss to Seafarers from 13; PtO Ox from 15. 34 Mill Street, Oxford OX2 0AJ T: (020) 7246 2934 M: 07876-824414 E: andrew.wright@missiontoseafarers.org

WRIGHT, Anna Chang. b 55. Univ of San Carlos Cebu City BA 74 Univ of Philippines MA 78 Ban Univ BTh 07. **d** 02 **p** 03. OLM Blyth Valley St E 02-13; NSM 13-14; PtO from 14. Rose End, Back Road, Wenhaston, Halesworth IP19 9DY T: (01502) 478411 E: wrightsphere@googlemail.com

WRIGHT, Anne. See WRIGHT, Jacqueline Anne

WRIGHT, Anthony. See WRIGHT, Derek Anthony

WRIGHT, Canon Anthony John. b 47. Ex Univ MA 98 ACA 70 FCA 77. Ripon Coll Cuddesdon 86. **d** 88 **p** 89. C Kidderminster St Mary and All SS w Trimpley etc Worc 88-91; P-in-c Offenham and Bretforton 91-96; R Backwell w Chelvey and Brockley B & W 96-02; RD Portishead 01-02; P-in-c Tetbury w Beverston Glouc 02-03; R 03-06; R Tetbury, Beverston, Long Newnton etc 07-13; Hon Can Glouc Cathl 11-13; rtd 13. Fair Field House, 1 Bromwich Road, Worcester WR2 4AD T: (01905) 339661 E: fairfieldwright@gmail.com

WRIGHT, Canon Anthony Robert. b 49. LVO 10. Lanchester Poly Cov BA 70. St Steph Ho Ox 70. **d** 73 **p** 74. C Amersham on the Hill Ox 73-76; C Reading St Giles 76-78; P-in-c Prestwood 78-84; P-in-c Wantage 84-87; V 87-92; RD 84-92; P-in-c W w E Hanney 88-91; V Portsea St Mary Portsm 92-98; Hon Can Portsm Cathl 96-98; R Westmr St Marg and Chapl to Speaker of Ho of Commons 98-10; Can Westmr Abbey 98-10; Sub Dean Westmr 05-10; Adn Westmr 09-10; rtd 10; PtO Ox from 11. The Malt House, 37 West End, Witney OX28 1NJ T: (01993) 774160 E: priestpainter@gmail.com

WRIGHT, Canon Barry Owen. b 38. S'wark Ord Course 66. **d** 69 **p** 70. C Plumstead Ascension S'wark 69-74; Hon C Welling 74-89; Hon Can S'wark Cathl 79-89; Sen Chapl W Midl Police Birm 89-93; Sen Chapl Metrop Police Lon 93-09; V Mill Hill St Mich 02-10; rtd 10; PtO Roch from 10. 54 Elmbourne Drive, Belvedere DA17 6JF T: (01322) 463564 E: bwrg8@aol.com

WRIGHT, Caroline. b 60. **d** 09 **p** 10. NSM Pontesbury I and II Heref from 09. 1 Higher Netley, Netley, Dorrington, Shrewsbury SY5 7SY T: (01743) 718790 E: info@carosbandb.co.uk

WRIGHT, Catherine Jane. b 62. Bris Univ BA 84 MA 92 PhD 00 Selw Coll Cam BA 96. Ridley Hall Cam 94. **d** 97 **p** 98. C Highworth w Sevenhampton and Inglesham etc Bris 97-00; PtO Ex 00-01; NSM Stoke St Gregory w Burrowbridge and Lyng B & W 01-05; Dioc Voc Adv 02-10; Dir of Voc 10-14; Assoc Dir of Ords 02-14; Dean of Women Clergy and Preb Wells Cathl 05-14; Dir IME 4-7 10-14; Tutor Ridley Hall Cam from 14. Ridley Hall, Ridley Hall Road, Cambridge CB3 9HG T: (01223) 746580 E: cjw28@cam.ac.uk

WRIGHT, Charles Kenneth. b 38. CEng 73 MIMechE 73 MBIM 91. Sarum & Wells Th Coll 91. **d** 93 **p** 94. C Bridgwater St Mary, Chilton Trinity and Durleigh B & W 93-96; Chapl Workington Carl 96-03; C Camerton, Seaton and W Seaton 96-03; Chapl W Cumbria Health Care NHS Trust 96-01; Chapl N Cumbria Acute Hosps NHS Trust 01-03; rtd 03; PtO Carl from 03. Naemair, 72 Ruskin Close, High Harrington, Workington CA14 4LS T: (01946) 833536

WRIGHT, Canon Clifford Nelson. b 35. K Coll Lon BD 59 AKC 59. **d** 60 **p** 61. C Stevenage St Alb 60-67; V Camberwell St Luke S'wark 67-81; RD Camberwell 75-80; Hon Can S'wark Cathl 79-80; TR Basingstoke Win 81-93; RD 84-93; Hon Can Win Cathl 89-00; R Win St Matt 93-00; rtd 00; PtO Win

WRIGHT, David Evan Cross. b 35. K Coll Lon BD 64 AKC 64. **d** 65 **p** 66. C Morpeth Newc 65-69; C Benwell St Jas 69-70; C Bushey St Alb 70-74; V High Wych 74-77; R High Wych and Gilston w Eastwick 77-80; V St Alb St Mary Marshalswick 80-89; P-in-c Sandridge 87-89; R Lenham w Boughton Malherbe Cant 89-00; rtd 00; P-in-c Fuengirola St Andr Eur 01-06; PtO Chich 01-06. 536 Urban, Cerros del Aguila, 29649 Mijas (Málaga), Spain

WRIGHT, David Henry. b 23. Keble Coll Ox BA 48. St Steph Ho Ox 52. **d** 54 **p** 55. C Penton Street St Silas w All SS Lon 54-57; V Barnsbury St Clem 57-66; V Wandsworth St Anne S'wark 66-73; P-in-c Stanley St And 73-75; R Dunkeld 73-92; R Strathtay 75-92; rtd 92; Hon C Aberdeen St Marg Ab from 00. 28 Midstocket Mews, Aberdeen AB15 5FG T: (01224) 636554

WRIGHT, Preb David William. b 63. Liv Univ LLB 85 Fitzw Coll Cam BA 92 Cam Univ MA 96 Univ of Wales (Cardiff) LLM 99 Barrister 86. Westcott Ho Cam 90. **d** 93 **p** 94. C Chorlton-cum-Hardy St Clem Man 93-97; P-in-c Donnington Wood Lich 97-99; V 99-09; TR Cen Wolverhampton from 09; AD Wolverhampton from 11; Preb Lich Cathl from 15. The Rectory, 42 Park Road East, Wolverhampton WV1 4QA T: (01902) 423388 M: 07977-543735 E: david.wright@lichfield.anglican.org

WRIGHT, Denise Ann. See WILLIAMS, Denise Ann

WRIGHT, Derek Anthony. b 35. ACP 66 Lon Univ CertEd 57. Cranmer Hall Dur 80. **d** 81 **p** 82. C Auckland St Andr and St Anne Dur 81-83; V Cornforth 83-87; P-in-c Thornley 87-88; R Gt and Lt Glemham, Blaxhall etc St E 88-90; V Evenwood Dur 90-93; P-in-c Satley and Tow Law 93-95; V 95-99; rtd 99; PtO Dur from 00. 39 Hilltop Road, Bearpark, Durham DH7 7TA

WRIGHT, Dominic Edwyn. b 76. Qu Coll Birm. **d** 13 **p** 14. C Birm St Martin w Bordesley St Andr from 13. 93 Gillott Road, Birmingham B16 0EU T: 0121-454 4607 M: 07871-814261 E: dominicwright1@gmail.com or dom@bullring.org

WRIGHT, Edward Maurice Alexanderson. b 54. Wycliffe Hall Ox. **d** 88 **p** 91. C Maidstone St Luke Cant 88-93; R Cliffe at Hoo w Cooling Roch 93-15; R Wrotham from 15. The Rectory, Borough Green Road, Wrotham, Sevenoaks TN15 7RA T: (01732) 882211 E: edward.wright@diocese-rochester.org

WRIGHT, Edward Michael. b 37. St Cath Soc Ox BA 61 MA 65. Cuddesdon Coll. **d** 64 **p** 65. C Willesden St Andr Lon 64-68; Bahamas 68-71; V Lewisham St Steph and St Mark S'wark 72-80; V Ox St Barn and St Paul 80-07; rtd 07; PtO Ox from 08. 9 Binswood Avenue, Headington, Oxford OX3 8NY E: emichaelwright@ntlworld.com

WRIGHT, Frank Albert. b 51. Portsm Univ MA 02. Sarum & Wells Th Coll 80. **d** 83 **p** 84. C Buckingham Ox 83-86; C Newport Pagnell w Lathbury and Moulsoe 86-89; TV W Slough 89-95; TR 95-99; TR Fareham H Trin Portsm 99-09; Dioc Interfaith Adv 01-06; R Westbourne Chich from 09. The Rectory, Westbourne Road, Westbourne, Emsworth PO10 8UL T: (01243) 372867 E: westrecwbourne@tiscali.co.uk

WRIGHT, Frederic Ian. b 64. City Univ BSc 85. Wycliffe Hall Ox BTh 94. **d** 94 **p** 95. C Carl St Jo 94-98; C Bassenthwaite, Isel and Setmurthy 98-00; C Binsey 00-02; TV 02-07. Aden House, The Square, Allonby, Maryport CA15 6QA T: (01900) 881095

WRIGHT, Graham. b 50. Oak Hill Th Coll 73. **d** 76 **p** 77. C Northampton St Giles Pet 76-79; C Man Resurr 79-82; V Barkingside St Laur Chelmsf 82-88; Chapl K Geo V Hosp Ilford 82-88; P-in-c Yoxford and Chapl Suffolk Constabulary St E 88-90; PtO Linc 03-05; Lic Preacher 05-07; R Rockingham w Safety Bay Australia 07-09; Chapl Hakea, Bandyup and Wooroloo Pris 09-11; Chapl Casuarina Pris from 11. 8/178 Kent Street, Rockingham WA 6168, Australia M: 40-747 0013 E: therockingrev@bigpond.com

WRIGHT, Graham John Aston. b 57. Moorlands Th Coll 77 Wycliffe Hall Ox 05. **d** 06 **p** 07. NSM Marston w Elsfield Ox 06-08; Asst Chapl St Edw Sch Ox 06-08; Chapl Queenswood Sch Herts 09-12; Chapl Qu Mary's Sch Baldersby Park from 13. Queen Mary's School, Baldersby Park, Topcliffe, Thirsk YO7 3BZ T: (01845) 575000

WRIGHT, Gwynne Ann. b 49. Marymount Coll California BA 71 Keller Graduate Sch of Management Illinois MA 98. Seabury-Western Th Sem MDiv 04. **d** 04 **p** 04. C Arlington Heights USA 04-06; P-in-c W Dundee 06-08; P-in-c Dekalb 08-10; R Northfield St Jas 10-14; PtO York from 14. 43 Rawcliffe Croft, York YO30 5US T: (01904) 635095 M: 07710-496594 E: gwynne.wright@me.com

WRIGHT, Mrs Heather Margaret. b 47. EAMTC 93. **d** 96 **p** 97. NSM Heigham St Thos Nor 96-99; Hon Asst Dioc Chapl among deaf and deaf-blind people from 99; NSM Sprowston w Beeston from 03. 133 Moore Avenue, Norwich NR6 7LQ T: (01603) 301329 F: and minicom as telephone E: heatherwright404@btinternet.com

WRIGHT, Mrs Hilary. b 55. d 08. OLM Parkstone St Pet and St Osmund w Branksea *Sarum* 08-12; NSM from 12. *18 Springfield Crescent, Poole BH14 0LL* T: (01202) 747369
E: hilary.wright@ntlworld.com

WRIGHT, Howard John Douglas. b 64. BA 85. Trin Coll Bris BA 94. d 96 p 97. C Ipswich St Matt *St E* 96-00; V Four Marks *Win* from 00; RD Alton from 09. *The Vicarage, 22 Lymington Bottom, Four Marks, Alton GU34 5AA* T: (01420) 563344
E: howardwright.cogs@gmail.com

WRIGHT, Hugh Edward. b 57. BNC Ox BA 79 MA 87 Ex Univ CertEd 81. Sarum & Wells Th Coll 85. d 87 p 88. C Hobs Moat *Birm* 87-90; C W Drayton *Lon* 90-92; V Oakfield St Jo *Portsm* 92-13; RD E Wight 00-05; V Ventnor H Trin from 13; V Ventnor St Cath from 13; R Bonchurch from 13. *The Vicarage, Maples Drive, Ventnor PO38 1NR* T: (01983) 853729
E: hugh.wright1957@btinternet.com

WRIGHT, Ian. *See* WRIGHT, Frederic Ian

WRIGHT, Ian. b 65. Coll of Resurr Mirfield 97. d 99 p 00. C S Lafford *Linc* 99-01; C Hawley H Trin *Guildf* 01-03; Chapl Bonn w Cologne *Eur* 03-06; P-in-c Armley w New Wortley *Leeds* 06-15; P-in-c Leeds Richmond Hill 12-15; V Eyres Monsell *Leic* from 15. *St Hugh's Vicarage, 51 Pasley Road, Leicester LE2 9BU*

WRIGHT, Miss Jacqueline Anne. b 39. Dalton Ho Bris 67. dss 76 d 87 p 94. BCMS Uganda 71-77; N Area Sec BCMS 78-88; Pudsey St Lawr and St Paul *Bradf* 82-88; Hon Par Dn 87-88; Par Dn Kingston upon Hull H Trin 88-93; Hd of Min amongst Women CPAS 93-02; CPAS Consultant (W Midl) 96-02; Regional Consultant (Midl) 99-02; PtO *Cov* 93-04; *Birm* 96-02; *Worc* 96-02; *Leic* 99-02; rtd 02; PtO *York* from 04. *Oxenby, Whitby Road, Pickering YO18 7HL* T: (01751) 472689
E: jacqw@talktalk.net

WRIGHT, Mrs Jane. b 62. ERMC 12. d 15. NSM Monks Eleigh w Chelsworth and Brent Eleigh etc *St E* from 15. *32 Priory Road, Sudbury CO10 1LB* T: (01787) 372080
E: janeandalanwright@talktalk.net

WRIGHT, Mrs Jean. b 41. Man Univ BA 63 CertEd 64. Carl Dioc Tr Inst 88. d 91 p 94. NSM Kirkby Stephen w Mallerstang etc *Carl* from 91. *Mains View, Crosby Garrett, Kirkby Stephen CA17 4PR* T: (01768) 371457

WRIGHT, John. *See* WRIGHT, Nicholas John

WRIGHT, John. *See* WRIGHT, Alfred John

WRIGHT, John. *See* WRIGHT, Anthony John

WRIGHT, John Douglas. b 42. Birm Univ BSc 64 CertEd 66. St Steph Ho Ox 69. d 69 p 70. C Swanley St Mary *Roch* 69-74; C Stockwell Green St Andr *S'wark* 74-79; V Leigh St Jo *Man* 79-82; P-in-c Whitehawk *Chich* 82-11; V 11-13; rtd 13. *The Wedge, Spencer Road, Eastbourne BN21 4PB* T: (01323) 723584
M: 07944-419007 E: jonda9@mail.com

WRIGHT, Canon John Harold. b 36. Dur Univ BA 58 Ch Ch Coll Cant MA 96 ATCL. Ely Th Coll 58. d 61 p 62. C Boston *Linc* 61-64; C Willesborough w Hinxhill *Cant* 64-68; V Westwell 68-75; R Eastwell w Boughton Aluph 68-75; V Rolvenden 75-84; R Cheriton St Martin 84-01; Hon Can Cant Cathl 97-01; rtd 01; PtO *Cant* from 01. *1 Cliff Road, Hythe CT21 5XA* T: (01303) 265303

WRIGHT, Jonathan James Gerald. b 67. Oak Hill Th Coll. d 10 p 11. C Horncastle Gp *Linc* 10-14; R Hedon, Paull, Sproatley and Preston *York* from 14. *The Rectory, 68 Staithes Road, Preston, Hull HU12 8TB*

WRIGHT, Jonathon Stuart. b 84. St Steph Ho Ox 12. d 15. C Whitchurch *Llan* from 15. *16 St John's Crescent, Whitchurch, Cardiff CF14 7AF* T: (029) 2061 9385
E: curate@beneficeofwhitchurch.org.uk

WRIGHT, Judith Mary. b 44. Ex Univ MSc 98 BA 10 SRN 10 SCM 10. SWMTC 04. d 07 p 08. NSM Silverton, Butterleigh, Bickleigh and Cadeleigh *Ex* 07-11; C Bradninch and Clyst Hydon from 11; C Broadhembury, Payhembury and Plymtree from 11. *4 Hele Square, Hele, Exeter EX5 4PN* T: (01392) 882019 E: d.j.wright@btinternet.com

WRIGHT, Miss Julia Mary. b 64. Reading Univ BA 88. Trin Coll Bris 96. d 98 p 99. C Woodley *Ox* 98-03; TV Aylesbury 03-05; C Bernwode 05-07; Chapl Burrswood Chr Hosp from 08. *The Chaplaincy, Burrswood, Groombridge, Tunbridge Wells TN3 9PY* T: (01892) 863637 F: 863623

WRIGHT, Ken. *See* WRIGHT, Charles Kenneth

WRIGHT, Canon Kenyon Edward. b 32. CBE 99. Glas Univ MA 53 Fitzw Coll Cam BA 55 Serampore Coll MTh 61 Edin Univ DLitt 00. Wesley Ho Cam 53. d 71 p 71. In Meth Ch India 57-71; Dir Urban Min Cov Cathl 71-81; Dir of Internat Min and Can Res 72-81; Public Preacher *Cov* 72-74; Gen Sec Scottish Chs Coun 81-90; Dir Scottish Chs Ho Dunblane 81-90; Dir Kairos Trust 90-92; Hon C Glas H Cross 91-92; rtd 92; P-in-c Glencarse *Bre* 94-00. *1 Churchill Close, Ettington, Stratford-upon-Avon CV37 7SP* T/F: (01789) 740356
M: 07801-849941 E: kenyonwright@aol.com

WRIGHT, Kevin John. b 54. Southn Univ BSc 75 PGCE 76. Ox Min Course 06. d 10 p 11. C Radley and Sunningwell *Ox* 10-13; C Kennington 10-13; R Woolavington w Cossington and Bawdrip *B & W* from 13. *The Rectory, 7 Vicarage Road, Woolavington, Bridgwater TA7 8DX* T: (01278) 686440
M: 07808-171884 E: kjwright2010@talktalk.net

WRIGHT, Mrs Kim Beatrice Elizabeth. b 66. STETS 07. d 10 p 11. NSM Walton-on-Thames *Guildf* 10-12; NSM Oxshott 12-14. *Address withheld by request* M: 07941-947866
E: kbewright@live.co.uk

WRIGHT, Lawrence Charles. b 57. Hull Univ MA 94. EMMTC 93. d 96 p 96. C Heathridge and Joondalup Australia 96-98; C Penzance St Jo *Truro* 98-02; TV Penzance St Mary w St Paul and St Jo 02-04; Chapl Yarlswood Immigration and Detention Cen 04-06; Chapl W Lon YMCA 06-07; SSF 07-09; R Birm St Geo from 09; P-in-c Lozells St Paul and St Silas from 14. *St George's Rectory, 100 Bridge Street West, Birmingham B19 2YX* T: 0121-359 2000 E: stgeorge100@live.co.uk

WRIGHT, Leslie Vandernoll. b 24. Trin Hall Cam MA 50. Ridley Hall Cam 49. d 51 p 52. C Aldershot H Trin *Guildf* 51-53; C Cambridge H Trin *Ely* 53-57; V Marston *Ox* 57-59; Asst Master Castle Ct Sch Parkstone 59-61; Asst Chapl Stowe Sch 61-64; Hd Master St Mich Prep Sch Five Oaks Jersey 64-66; Chapl Windlesham Ho Sch Sussex 66-68; Chapl Vevey *Eur* 68-73; Hd St Geo Sch Clarens 73-89; rtd 89; Chapl Lugano *Eur* 89-92. *18 avenue Schubert, Domaine Château Tournon, 83440 Montauroux, France* T: (0033) 4 94 47 62 43
E: leslie.wright@orange.fr

WRIGHT, Mrs Lorraine. d 14 p 15. OLM Addlestone *Guildf* from 14. *47 Springfields Close, Chertsey KT16 8JT*
T: (01932) 568573

WRIGHT, Mrs Louisa Mary (Lisa). b 33. S'wark Ord Course. d 87 p 94. NSM Streatham Hill St Marg *S'wark* 87-95; Hon C Streatham St Leon 95-02; rtd 02; PtO *S'wark* from 02. *19 Hillside Road, London SW2 3HL* T: (020) 8671 8037
E: lisaw@phonecoop.coop

WRIGHT, Mrs Marion Jane. b 47. Whitelands Coll Lon CertEd 69. Cranmer Hall Dur 73. d 00 p 02. NSM Scalby *York* 00-15; NSM Cloughton and Burniston 14-15; NSM Ravenscar and Staintondale 14-15. *3 East Park Road, Scalby, Scarborough YO13 0PZ* T: (01723) 350208
E: marianne.forsyth@hotmail.co.uk

WRIGHT, Martin. b 48. Avery Hill Coll BEd 81 K Alfred's Coll Win CertEd 69 LRAM 76. SAOMC 95. d 98 p 99. NSM St Alb St Mary Marshalswick *St Alb* 98-01; C St Alb St Pet 02-05; V Reigate St Mark *S'wark* 05-13; rtd 13. *18 Brocks Drive, Fairlands, Guildford GU3 3NE* M: 07774-923550

WRIGHT, Canon Martin Neave. b 37. AKC 61. St Boniface Warminster. d 62 p 63. C Corby St Columba *Pet* 62-65; Ind Chapl 65-71; Nigeria 71-75; P-in-c Honiley *Cov* 75-84; P-in-c Wroxall 75-84; Ind Chapl 75-84; Soc Resp Officer 84-96; Hon Can Cov Cathl 95-96; Bp's Chapl and Past Asst *B & W* 96-02; Preb Wells Cathl 96-02; Sub-Dean Wells 00-02; rtd 02; PtO *Cov* from 02. *2 Honiwell Close, Harbury, Leamington Spa CV33 9LY* T: (01926) 613699
E: martinwright@honeypot100.fsnet.co.uk

WRIGHT, Michael. *See* WRIGHT, Edward Michael

WRIGHT, Canon Michael. b 30. St Chad's Coll Dur BA 55 De Montfort Univ MPhil 04. d 56 p 57. C New Cleethorpes *Linc* 56-59; C Skegness 59-62; V Louth St Mich 62-73; R Stewton 62-73; R Warmsworth *Sheff* 73-86; Warden Dioc Readers' Assn 81-86; Hon Can Sheff Cathl 82-95; V Wath-upon-Dearne w Adwick-upon-Dearne 86-94; V Wath-upon-Dearne 94-95; RD Wath 92-95; rtd 95; PtO *Linc* from 95. *17 Ashfield Road, Sleaford NG34 7DZ* T: (01529) 415698

WRIGHT, Michael Christopher. b 44. Leeds Univ BA 65 CertEd 67 MSc 75 Sheff Univ PhD 02 FRSA 95. Wells Th Coll 65. d 67 p 68. C Dormanstown *York* 67-69; PtO *Linc* 69-88; *Sheff* 71-95; Hd Master Eastmoor High Sch Wakef 84-87; Hd Master Carleton High Sch Pontefract 87-95; C-in-c St Edm Anchorage Lane CD *Sheff* 95-96; Chapl Doncaster R Infirmary and Montagu Hosp NHS Trust 95-01; Research Fell Sheff Univ 01-03; Sen Research Fell Lanc Univ *Blackb* from 03; Hon C Gt Snaith *Sheff* 01-07; PtO *Leeds* from 01; *Eur* from 06; *Sheff* from 07. *Orchard End, Finkle Street, Hensall, Goole DN14 0QY* T: (01977) 661900 *or* (01524) 593152
E: mc.wright@btinternet.com *or* m.c.wright@lancaster.ac.uk

WRIGHT, Michael George. b 52. WEMTC 01. d 04 p 05. NSM Woodchester and Brimscombe *Glouc* from 04. *The Trumpet, West End, Minchinhampton, Stroud GL6 9JA* T: (01453) 883027
M: 07974-303527 E: thetrumpet.antiques@virgin.net

WRIGHT, Michael John. b 38. Dur Univ MA 91. Chich Th Coll 59. d 62 p 63. C Yate *Glouc* 62-65; C Kirby Moorside w Gillamoor *York* 65-68; V 68-72; V Bransdale cum Farndale 68-72; V Kirkbymoorside w Gillamoor, Farndale etc 72-73;

Dioc Communications Officer 72-74; V Ormesby 74-80; P-in-c Middlesbrough St Cuth 81-88; PtO 88-99; NSM W Acklam 91-97; Chapl Butterwick Hospice Stockton-on-Tees 97-99; Chapl S Dur Hospice Bp Auckland 97-99; rtd 03. *25 Thornfield Road, Middlesbrough TS5 5DD* T: (01642) 816247
E: mjw@careatwork.fsnet.co.uk

WRIGHT, Nicholas John. b 65. Liv Univ BA 87. Wycliffe Hall Ox 89. **d** 92 **p** 93. C Burley *Ripon* 92-95; C Brightside w Wincobank *Sheff* 95-97; TV Sheff Manor 97-03; PtO from 03. *22 Norfolk Road, Sheffield S2 2SX*

WRIGHT, Canon Nicholas Mark. b 59. Loughb Univ BSc 80. Qu Coll Birm 82. **d** 85 **p** 86. C Coney Hill *Glouc* 85-89; C Rotherham *Sheff* 89-91; TV Worc SE 91-98; R Inkberrow w Cookhill and Kington w Dormston 98-15; Hon Can Worc Cathl 11-15; rtd 15; Asst P Evesham Deanery *Worc* from 15. *6 Alder Grove, Evesham WR11 1XP* T: (01386) 443310
E: ncbjmswright@btinternet.com

✠**WRIGHT, The Rt Revd Prof Nicholas Thomas.** b 48. Ex Coll Ox BA 71 MA 75 DPhil 81 DD 00. Wycliffe Hall Ox BA 73. **d** 75 **p** 76 **c** 03. Fell Mert Coll Ox 75-78; Chapl 76-78; Chapl and Fell Down Coll Cam 78-81; Asst Prof NT Studies McGill Univ Montreal 81-86; Chapl and Fell Worc Coll Ox and Univ Lect Th 86-93; Dean Lich 93-99; Can Th Cov Cathl 92-99; Lector Theologiae and Can Westmr Abbey 00-03; Bp Dur 03-10; Chair NT and Early Christianity St Andr Univ *St And* from 10. *St Mary's College, South Street, St Andrews KY16 9JU*
E: ntw2@st-andrews.ac.uk

WRIGHT, Nigel Christopher James. b 67. Leeds Univ BA 07 MA 13 FCCA 99. NOC 04. **d** 07 **p** 08. NSM Utley *Bradf* 07-10; NSM Oxenhope 10-13; P-in-c *Leeds* from 13. *The Vicarage, 20 Gledhow Drive, Oxenhope, Keighley BD22 9SA* T: (01535) 642529 M: 07970-751670
E: nigel.wright@bradford.anglican.org

WRIGHT, Ms Pamela Anne. b 45. Open Univ BSc 00. St As Minl Tr Course 01. **d** 03 **p** 10. NSM Llanrhos *St As* 03-09; NSM Rhos-Cystennin 09-11; rtd 11; PtO *St As* from 11; *Ban* from 15. *Brackenrigg, Bryn Pydew Road, Bryn Pydew, Llandudno Junction LL31 9JH* T: (01492) 541552 F: 541652 M: 07850-180420
E: pamscot45@aol.com

WRIGHT, Miss Pamela Jean. b 38. ALA 63. NTMTC 02. **d** 03 **p** 04. NSM Harrow Trin St Mich *Lon* 03-05; NSM Harrow Weald St Mich 05-12; PtO from 12. *14 Broadlawns Court, Harrow HA3 7HN* T: (020) 8954 9821
E: pamela.jwright@btinternet.com

WRIGHT, Ms Patricia. b 46. MBE 02. SRN 68. S'wark Ord Course 80. **dss** 85 **d** 89. Asst Chapl R Lon Hosp (Mile End) 83-85; Bethnal Green St Matt w St Jas the Gt *Lon* 85-88; Hon C St Botolph Aldgate w H Trin Minories 89-05; Cathl Dn and Dioc HIV/AIDS Co-ord Swaziland 00-04; Hon C St Geo-in-the-East St Mary *Lon* 06-14; PtO *Cant* from 15. *62 College Road, Deal CT14 6BS* T: (01304) 239031
E: patw@patthedeacon.com

WRIGHT, Mrs Patricia Yvonne. b 51. **d** 10 **p** 11. OLM Bramford *St E* 10-13; NSM from 13; OLM Gt and Lt Blakenham w Baylham and Nettlestead 10-13; NSM from 13. *Hildern, Whitton Leyer, Bramford IP8 4BD* T: (01473) 464748

WRIGHT, The Ven Paul. b 54. K Coll Lon BD 78 AKC 78 Heythrop Coll Lon MTh 90 Univ of Wales (Lamp) DMin 09. Ripon Coll Cuddesdon 78. **d** 79 **p** 80. C Beckenham St Geo *Roch* 79-83; Chapl Ch Sch Richmond 83-84; C Richmond St Mary w St Matthias and St Jo *S'wark* 83-85; V Gillingham St Aug *Roch* 85-90; R Crayford 90-99; RD Erith 93-97; V Sidcup St Jo 99-03; Adn Bromley and Bexley from 03; Bp's Adv for Inter-Faith Concerns 11-15; P-in-c Bromley Common St Luke 12-15; Hon Can Roch Cathl from 98. *The Archdeaconry, The Glebe, Chislehurst BR7 5PX* T/F: (020) 8467 8743 M: 07985-902601
E: archdeacon.bromley@rochester.anglican.org

WRIGHT, Canon Paul Stephen. b 66. Cen Lancs Univ BA 88 Liv Univ MA 96 Univ of Wales (Cardiff) MTh 11. Westcott Ho Cam 90. **d** 93 **p** 94. C Upholland *Liv* 93-96; CF 96-08; Sen CF 08-14; Chapl Guards Chpl Lon 08-10; Chapl R Memorial Chpl Sandhurst 12-14; Dom Chapl to The Queen from 14 and from 15; Can Chpls R from 15. *The Chapel Royal, St James's, London SW1A 1BA* T: (020) 7024 5576
E: paul.wright@royal.gsx.gov.uk

WRIGHT, Canon Peter. b 35. K Coll Lon AKC 61 Hull Univ MA 86. St Boniface Warminster 61. **d** 62 **p** 63. C Goole *Sheff* 62-67; V Norton Woodseats St Chad 67-80; R Aston cum Aughton 80-84; P-in-c Ulley 80-84; Chapl Rotherham Priority Health Services NHS Trust 80-84; R Aston cum Aughton and Ulley *Sheff* 84-93; TR Aston cum Aughton w Swallownest, Todwick etc 93-00; RD Laughton 85-93; Chapter Clerk and Hon Can Sheff Cathl 92-00; rtd 00; PtO *Sheff* from 01; Chapl to Rtd Clergy and Clergy Widows Officer from 09.

40 Chancet Wood Drive, Sheffield S8 7TR T/F: 0114-274 7218
E: allsaints.apw@talk21.com

WRIGHT, Peter Geoffrey. b 60. Ex Univ BSc 81 FCIM 09. Ox Min Course 09. **d** 12 **p** 13. NSM Bicester w Bucknell, Caversfield and Launton *Ox* from 12. *18 Dickens Close, Bicester OX26 2NG* T: (01869) 250222 M: 07966-531921
E: revpeterwright@gmail.com

WRIGHT, Peter Reginald. b 34. St Chad's Coll Dur BA 60. Linc Th Coll 60. **d** 62 **p** 63. C Lt Ilford St Mich *Chelmsf* 62-65; C Billingham St Aid *Dur* 65-68; TV 68-71; TR 71-76; Chapl Portsm Poly 76-87; Sec Chapls in HE Gen Syn Bd of Educn 88-95; rtd 95; PtO *Portsm* 95-10. *6 Garden Lane, Southsea PO5 3DP* T: (023) 9273 6651

WRIGHT, Philip. b 32. G&C Coll Cam BA 53 MA 57. Wells Th Coll 56. **d** 57 **p** 58. C Barnard Castle *Dur* 57-60; C Heworth St Mary 60-64; V Tow Law 64-70; V Tanfield 70-78; V Gateshead Ch Ch 78-02; rtd 02; PtO *Dur* from 02. *Meldon, High Heworth Lane, Gateshead NE10 0PB* T: 0191-469 2161

WRIGHT, Philip John. b 69. Anglia Ruskin Univ MA 11. St Mellitus Coll BA 14. **d** 14 **p** 15. Chapl Barking Havering and Redbridge Hosps NHS Trust from 08; NSM Cranham Park *Chelmsf* from 14. *57 Heron Way, Upminster RM14 1EW* M: 07976-378042 E: philwright69@gmail.com

WRIGHT, Phillip. b 35. Kelham Th Coll 57 St Aid Birkenhead 59. **d** 61 **p** 62. C Goldthorpe *Sheff* 61-65; V Doncaster St Jude 65-71; V Kettering All SS *Pet* 71-82; V S Kirkby *Wakef* 82-94; rtd 98. *2 The Grove, Wickersley, Rotherham S66 2BP* T: (01709) 543922 E: thegrove@onetel.com

WRIGHT, Robert. *See* WRIGHT, Anthony Robert

WRIGHT, Robert James. b 74. St Chad's Coll Dur BA 96 K Coll Lon MA 98. St Steph Ho Ox 00. **d** 02 **p** 04. C Ilfracombe, Lee, Woolacombe, Bittadon etc *Ex* 02-05; PtO *S'wark* 11-14; P-in-c Mitcham St Olave from 14. *20 Hatton Gardens, Mitcham CR4 4LG* T: (020) 8648 5846 E: robwri99@gmail.com

WRIGHT, Robert John. b 47. St Jo Coll Dur BA 70. SEITE 00. **d** 03 **p** 04. NSM Notting Hill St Jo *Lon* 03-06; NSM Notting Hill St Pet 03-06; NSM N Hammersmith St Kath 06-08; NSM Cheddington w Mentmore *Ox* 08-12; TV Cottesloe 12-13. *Tattlers, Castle Street, Wingrave, Aylesbury HP22 4PT* T: (01296) 680348 M: 07988-978419 E: robert@robert-wright.com

WRIGHT (née PRECIOUS), Sally Joanne. b 75. Hatf Coll Dur BA 97 Anglia Poly Univ MA 03. Westcott Ho Cam 00. **d** 02 **p** 03. C Chich St Paul and Westhampnett 02-05; PtO *S'wark* 05-06; Hon C Peckham St Jo w St Andr 06-09; Chapl Guildhall Sch of Music and Drama *Lon* 06-09; Hon C Witney *Ox* from 09. *The Rectory, 13 Station Lane, Witney OX28 4BB* T: (01993) 704441 E: sally-wright@btconnect.com

WRIGHT, Samuel. *See* WRIGHT, William Samuel

WRIGHT, Simon Andrew. b 63. Clare Coll Cam BA 84 MA 88 Lon Univ MB, BS 87. SNWTP 10. **d** 12 **p** 13. OLM Davyhulme St Mary *Man* from 12. *12 Davyhulme Road, Urmston, Manchester M41 7DS* T: 0161-746 8758 M: 07759-814499
E: sueandsimonwright@hotmail.co.uk

WRIGHT, Canon Simon Christopher. b 44. AKC 67. **d** 68 **p** 69. C Bitterne Park *Win* 68-72; C Kirkby *Liv* 72-74; V Wigan St Anne 74-79; Abp's Dom Chapl and Dioc Dir of Ords *York* 79-84; V W Acklam 84-00; RD Middlesbrough 87-98; Can and Preb York Minster 94-00; V Dartmouth and Dittisham *Ex* 00-10; rtd 10; PtO *York* from 10. *48 Langton Road, Norton, Malton YO17 9AD* T: (01653) 698106
E: scwright44@btinternet.com

WRIGHT, Stephen Irwin. b 58. Ex Coll Ox BA 80 MA 84 Selw Coll Cam BA 85 MA 90 Lanc Univ MA 92 St Jo Coll Dur PhD 97. Ridley Hall Cam 83. **d** 86 **p** 87. C Newbarns w Hawcoat *Carl* 86-94; C Burton and Holme 90-94; NSM Esh *Dur* 94-97; NSM Hamsteels 94-97; C Consett 97-98; Dir Coll of Preachers 98-06; Tutor Spurgeon's Coll from 06; PtO *S'wark* from 99. *Spurgeon's College, 189 South Norwood Hill, London SE25 6DJ* T: (020) 8653 0850 F: 8711 0959 T: (020) 8768 0878 ext 233 E: s.wright@spurgeons.ac.uk

WRIGHT, Canon Stephen Mark. b 60. Keele Univ BA 83. Trin Coll Bris 86. **d** 89 **p** 90. C Thorne *Sheff* 89-92; CMS 92-05; Nigeria 93-98; Hon Can Asaba from 98; Chapl Ahmadi St Paul Kuwait 99-03; Chapl Dubai and Sharjah w N Emirates 03-14; P-in-c Quidenham Gp *Nor* from 15. *The Rectory, Church Hill, Banham, Norwich NR16 2HN*
E: canonstevewright@gmail.com

WRIGHT, Stewart. *See* WRIGHT, William Charles Stewart

WRIGHT, Stuart Kendle. b 73. **d** 08 **p** 09. C Tollington *Lon* 08-14; P-in-c Hounslow H Trin w St Paul and St Mary 14-15; P-in-c Hounslow H Trin from 15. *14 Lampton Park Road, Hounslow TW3 4HS* M: 07867-888999
E: vegetablestu@blueyonder.co.uk

WRIGHT, Thomas. *See* WRIGHT, Nicholas Thomas

WRIGHT, Timothy. b 63. NUU BSc 85. Cranmer Hall Dur 86. **d** 89 **p** 90. C Bramcote *S'well* 89-93; I Glenavy w Tunny and Crumlin *Conn* 93-98; Chapl RAF from 98; Dep Chapl-in-Chief from 13. *Chaplaincy Services (RAF), HQ Air Command, RAF High Wycombe HP14 4UE* T: (01494) 496800 F: 496343

WRIGHT, Timothy John. b 54. Nottm Univ BA 76. Ripon Coll Cuddesdon 90. **d** 92 **p** 93. C Dawlish *Ex* 92-95; TV Teignmouth, Ideford w Luton, Ashcombe etc 95-01; Chapl Wycombe Abbey Sch 01-08; NSM Wycombe Deanery 08-09; P-in-c Petworth *Chich* 09-15; P-in-c Egdean 09-15; rtd 15. *The Red House, Lower Street, Fittleworth, Pulborough RH20 1EJ*

WRIGHT, Timothy John. b 41. K Coll Lon BD 63 AKC 63. **d** 64 **p** 65. C Highfield *Ox* 64-68; Asst Chapl Worksop Coll Notts 68-71; Chapl Malvern Coll 71-77; Ho Master 77-86; Hd Master Jo Lyon Sch Harrow 86-01; rtd 01; PtO *Worc* from 09. *Beech House, Colwall Green, Malvern WR13 6DX* T: (01684) 541102

WRIGHT, Timothy Stanley. b 63. Derby Coll of Educn BEd 86. Cranmer Hall Dur 89. **d** 92 **p** 93. C Eccleshill *Bradf* 92-96; TV Southend *Chelmsf* 96-00; V Boulton *Derby* 00-13; Chapl HM YOI Glen Parva from 13; PtO *Derby* from 13. *HM Young Offender Institution, Glen Parva, 10 Tigers Road, Wigston LE18 4TN* T: 0116-228 4100 E: revboulton@tiscali.co.uk *or* timwright2005@talktalk.net

WRIGHT, Toby Christopher. b 75. New Coll Ox BA 98 MA 01 Leeds Univ MA 01. Coll of Resurr Mirfield 99. **d** 01 **p** 02. C Petersfield *Portsm* 01-04; P-in-c Peckham St Jo w St Andr *S'wark* 04-06; V 06-09; AD Camberwell 06-09; TR Witney *Ox* from 09; AD from 13. *The Rectory, 13 Station Lane, Witney OX28 4BB* T: (01993) 704441 E: toby-wright@btconnect.com

WRIGHT, Mrs Vyvienne Mary. b 35. S Dios Minl Tr Scheme 80. **dss** 83 **d** 87 **p** 94. Martock w Ash *B & W* 83-00; Hon C 87-00; PtO from 00. *36 Church Close, Martock TA12 6DS* T: (01935) 823292 M: 07931-686362

WRIGHT, Canon William Charles Stewart. b 53. Ulster Poly BSc 81. CITC BTh 95. **d** 95 **p** 96. C Ballyholme *D & D* 95-98; I Conwal Union w Gartan *D & R* from 98; Can Raphoe Cathl from 10. *Conwal Rectory, New Line Road, Letterkenny, Co Donegal, Republic of Ireland* T: (00353) (74) 912 2573 E: stewartwright@live.ie

WRIGHT, Canon William Samuel. b 59. TCD BTh 89 MA 90. **d** 87 **p** 88. C Belfast St Aid *Conn* 87-91; Sec Dioc Bd of Miss 90-91; I Cleenish w Mullaghdun *Clogh* 91-99; I Lisburn Ch Ch Cathl from 99; Can and Preb Conn Cathl from 01; Prec from 12. *Cathedral Rectory, 11D Magheralave, Lisburn BT28 3BE* T: (028) 9209 0260 E: sam.wright@lisburncathedral.org

WRIGHTSON, Bernard. b 25. CertEd 50 ACP 65. Linc Th Coll 83. **d** 83 **p** 84. NSM Alford w Rigsby *Linc* 83-86; PtO 86-89; NSM Mablethorpe w Trusthorpe 89-94; PtO 94-04. *Pipits Acre, 64 Church Lane, Mablethorpe LN12 2NU* T: (01507) 472394

WRIGLEY, George Garnett. b 50. St Cath Coll Cam BA 71 Loughb Coll of Educn PGCE 72. NTMTC 02. **d** 04 **p** 05. NSM Hounslow H Trin w St Paul and St Mary *Lon* 04-08; P-in-c Langdale *Carl* 08-10; TV Loughrigg from 10. *The Vicarage, Chapel Stile, Ambleside LA22 9JG* T: (015394) 37267 E: georgewrig@hotmail.com

WRISDALE, Jean May. b 40. **d** 90 **p** 94. NSM Fotherby *Linc* 90-14. *The Meadows, Livesey Road, Ludborough, Grimsby DN36 5SQ* T: (01472) 840474

WROE, Mark. b 69. Surrey Univ BA 92. Ridley Hall Cam 94. **d** 96 **p** 97. C Chilvers Coton w Astley *Cov* 96-00; P-in-c Heworth St Alb *Dur* 00-03; V Windy Nook St Alb 03-07; V Jesmond H Trin *Newc* from 07; P-in-c Newc St Barn and St Jude from 07. *13 Glastonbury Grove, Newcastle upon Tyne NE2 2HA* T: 0191-240 1017 E: mark@htj.org.uk

WROE, Martin Daniel Edward. b 61. NTMTC. **d** 04 **p** 05. NSM Covent Garden St Paul *Lon* 04-07; NSM W Holloway St Luke from 07. *45 Penn Road, London N7 9RE* T: (020) 7607 6086 E: martinwroe@blueyonder.co.uk

WUTSCHER, Christoph Johannes. b 79. Ban Univ MA 12. Westcott Ho Cam 10. **d** 13 **p** 14. C Wanstead St Mary w Ch Ch *Chelmsf* 13. *13 Wanstead Place, London E11 2SW* M: 07583-270533 E: christoph.wutscher@phaidon.org

WUYTS, Fabian René Marc. b 73. ISFSC BA 96. Tyndale Th Sem Amsterdam MA 99 Evang Th Faculty Leuven MTh 08. **d** 14 **p** 15. C Whitstable *Cant* from 14. *St Andrew's Vicarage, 38A Saddleton Road, Whitstable CT5 4JH* M: 07547-195760 E: fabian.wuyts@gmail.com

WYARD, Peter Joseph. b 54. Pemb Coll Cam MA 76 Sussex Univ MSc 80 Brunel Univ MSc 88 Anglia Ruskin Univ MA 07. EAMTC 99. **d** 02 **p** 03. C Framlingham w Saxtead *St E* 02-05; P-in-c Riverside *Ox* 05-08; V Colnbrook and Datchet from 08. *St Mary's Vicarage, London Road, Datchet, Slough SL3 9JW* T: (01753) 580467 E: peter.wyard@btinternet.com

WYATT, Colin. b 27. Ex Coll Ox BA 54 MA 55 Lon Univ BD 62. Tyndale Hall Bris 60. **d** 63 **p** 64. C Radipole *Sarum* 63-66;

C Southborough St Pet *Roch* 66-67; V Tetsworth *Ox* 67-72; Lect Bible Tr Inst Glas 72-74; R Hurworth *Dur* 74-79; P-in-c Dinsdale w Sockburn 74-76; R 76-79; R Sadberge 79-84; R Bacton w Wyverstone and Cotton *St E* 84-92; rtd 92; PtO *Leeds* from 92. *20 Harrogate Road, Ripon HG4 1SR* T: (01765) 606810

WYATT, Canon David Stanley Chadwick. b 36. Fitzw Ho Cam BA 59 MA 71. Ely Th Coll 59. **d** 61 **p** 62. C Rochdale *Man* 61-63; Bp's Dom Chapl 63-68; R Salford St Paul w Ch Ch from 68; P-in-c Salford Ordsall St Clem 91-96; P-in-c Lower Broughton Ascension from 05; AD Salford 97; Hon Can Man Cathl from 82. *St Paul's Church House, Broadwalk, Salford M6 5FX* T: 0161-736 8868

WYATT, Peter Charles. b 62. Bris Univ BSc 85 CEng MIEE 92. St Jo Coll Nottm 05. **d** 07 **p** 08. C Becontree St Thos *Chelmsf* 07-11; Min Selsdon St Fran CD *S'wark* from 11. *St Francis' Vicarage, 146 Tedder Road, Croydon CR2 8AH* T: (020) 8657 7864 E: peter.michelle@gmail.com

WYATT, Peter John. b 38. Kelham Th Coll 58. **d** 64 **p** 65. C N Stoneham *Win* 64-68; C Brixham *Ex* 68-69; Dominica 69-75; Zambia 76-78; P-in-c Ettington *Cov* 78-79; V Butlers Marston and the Pillertons w Ettington 79-86; V Codnor and Loscoe *Derby* 86-91; Chapl for Deaf People 91-03; rtd 03; PtO *Heref* from 04; *St As* from 09. *16 Cae Melyn, Tregynon, Newtown SY16 3EF* T: (01686) 650368

WYATT, Richard Norman. b 21. LVCM. **d** 84 **p** 85. C Puttenham and Wanborough *Guildf* 84-90; PtO *Chich* 91-93 and from 97; P-in-c Stedham w Iping 93-97; rtd 97; RD Midhurst *Chich* 98-99. *Trenethick, June Lane, Midhurst GU29 9EL* T: (01730) 813447 E: norman.wyatt@homecall.co.uk

WYATT, Royston Dennis. b 36. FRICS 67. Sarum & Wells Th Coll 74. **d** 77 **p** 78. NSM Canford Magna *Sarum* 77-82; V Abbotsbury, Portesham and Langton Herring 82-88; Dioc Missr *Linc* 88-95; R Welford w Weston *Glouc* 95-05; RD Campden 96-01; rtd 05; PtO *B & W* from 06. *78 Lower Meadow, Ilminster TA19 9DP* T: (01460) 53996 E: revrdw@gmail.com

WYATT (née OWEN), Canon Susan Elizabeth. b 53. Bris Univ BSc 75 Bath Univ PGCE 78. EAMTC 97. **d** 00 **p** 01. Asst Dioc Adv in Miss and Evang *Ely* from 00; C Over 00-06; C Long Stanton w St Mich 02-06; V Cherry Hinton St Jo from 06; Hon Can Ely Cathl from 10. *St John's Vicarage, 9 Luard Road, Cambridge CB2 8PJ* T: (01223) 247451 *or* 241316 M: 07713-241261 E: sue.wyatt1@ntlworld.com *or* sue.wyatt@ely.anglican.org

WYATT, Trevor. b 60. Keele Univ BSc 81. SEITE 97. **d** 00 **p** 01. NSM Wilmington *Roch* 00-14; V Bexleyheath Ch Ch from 14. *The Vicarage, 57 Townley Road, Bexleyheath DA6 7HY* T: (020) 8301 5086 M: 07860-306746 E: trevor.wyatt@diocese-rochester.org *or* trevor.wyatt@bt.com

WYBER, Richard John. b 47. G&C Coll Cam BA 69 MA 72 FCA 73. SEITE 03. **d** 06 **p** 07. NSM Wanstead St Mary w Ch Ch *Chelmsf* from 06. *7 Mornington Close, Woodford Green IG8 0TT* T: (020) 8504 2447

WYBREW, Canon Hugh Malcolm. b 34. Qu Coll Ox BA 58 MA. Linc Th Coll 59. **d** 60 **p** 61. C E Dulwich St Jo *S'wark* 60-64; Tutor St Steph Ho Ox 65-71; Chapl Bucharest *Eur* 71-73; V Pinner *Lon* 73-83; Sec Fellowship of SS Alb and Sergius 84-86; Dean Jerusalem 86-89; Hon Can Gib Cathl 89-04; V Ox St Mary Magd 89-04; Hon Can Ch Ch 01-04; rtd 04. *96 Warwick Street, Oxford OX4 1SY* T: (01865) 241355 E: hugh.wybrew@queens.ox.ac.uk

WYER, Mrs Janet Beatrice. b 58. UEA BA 00. ERMC 04. **d** 07 **p** 08. C Loddon, Sisland, Chedgrave, Hardley and Langley *Nor* 07-10; C Nor St Pet Mancroft w St Jo Maddermarket 10-15; R Kessingland, Gisleham and Rushmere from 15. *1 Wash Lane, Kessingland, Lowestoft NR33 7QZ* M: 07990-576118 E: wyer@supanet.com

WYER, Keith George. b 45. St Paul's Coll Chelt CertEd 66 K Coll Lon BD 71 AKC 71. St Aug Coll Cant 71. **d** 72 **p** 73. C Moseley St Mary *Birm* 72-76; Chapl RNR 73-92; C Walsall *Lich* 76-77; Min Walsall St Martin 77-79; Chapl Colston's Sch Bris 79-86; Chapl Kelly Coll Tavistock 86-92; R Combe Martin and Berrynarbor *Ex* 92-95; TR Combe Martin, Berrynarbor, Lynton, Brendon etc 96-10; RD Shirwell 95-01; rtd 10. *Highlands, 6 Holland Park Avenue, Combe Martin, Ilfracombe EX34 0HL* E: keith@wyer.org

WYKES, Canon Peter. b 44. Lon Univ MB, BS 68. Ban & St As Minl Tr Course 97. **d** 00 **p** 01. NSM Trefnant w Tremeirchion *St As* 00-01; NSM Cefn w Trefnant w Tremeirchion 01-14; Hon Can St As Cathl 12-14; rtd 14; PtO *St As* from 14. *2 Llys y Tywysog, Tremeirchion, St Asaph LL17 0UL* T: (01745) 710363

WYLAM, John. b 43. AKC 66 FE TCert 75. **d** 67 **p** 68. C Derby St Bart 67-70; SSF 70-73; C Seaton Hirst *Newc* 74-77; V Byker St Silas 77-83; V Alwinton w Holystone and Alnham 83-98; V Chollerton w Birtley and Thockrington 98-09; rtd 09. *Nether House, Garleigh Road, Rothbury, Morpeth NE65 7RG* T: (01669) 622805 E: johnwylam@btopenworld.com

WYLD, Kevin Andrew. b 58. St Cath Coll Ox BA 79 MA 85 Univ Coll Dur MSc 83 Edin Univ BD 85. Edin Th Coll 82. **d** 85 **p** 86. C Winlaton *Dur* 85-87; C Houghton le Spring 87-90; V Medomsley 90-95; V High Spen and Rowlands Gill 95-00; R Winter Park St Rich USA 00-04. *15 Hullock Road, Newton Aycliffe DL5 4LT* T: (01325) 312286 E: kevinwyld@gmail.com

WYLD, Richard Michael. b 81. Surrey Univ BMus 04 St Jo Coll Dur BA 09 MA 10 PhD 14. Cranmer Hall Dur 06. **d** 13 **p** 14. C Sherborne w Castleton, Lillington and Longburton *Sarum* from 13. *32 Abbots Way, Sherborne DT9 6DT* T: (01935) 389962 M: 07971-876699 E: rickwyld4@hotmail.com

WYLD (née CHAPMAN), Mrs Ruth Elizabeth. b 84. St Jo Coll Dur MA 13. Cranmer Hall Dur 10. **d** 13 **p** 14. C Queen Thorne *Sarum* from 13. *32 Abbots Way, Sherborne DT9 6DT* T: (01935) 389962 M: 07739-161120 E: revruthwyld@gmail.com

WYLES, Mrs Kate Elizabeth. b 66. Bournemouth Univ BA 89 Win Univ BA 11. STETS 07. **d** 11 **p** 12. C Godalming *Guildf* 11-13; C Stoke-next-Guildf 13-15; V Goldsworth Park from 15. *St Andrew's Vicarage, 8 Cardingham, Woking GU21 3LN* T: (01483) 764523 E: jkwyles@hotmail.co.uk

WYLIE, Alan. b 47. Is of Man Tr Inst S&M. **d** 92 **p** 93. NSM Douglas St Geo *S & M* 92-97; NSM Challoch *Glas* 97-00; P-in-c Motherwell from 00; P-in-c Wishaw from 00. *The Rectory, 14 Crawford Street, Motherwell ML1 3AD* T: (01698) 249441 E: alan.rev@hotmail.com

WYLIE, Clive George. b 64. QUB BSc 86 TCD BTh 90 MA 93. CITC 87. **d** 90 **p** 91. C Drumglass w Moygashel *Arm* 90-93; I Tynan, Aghavilly and Middletown 93-98; Hon V Choral Arm Cathl 93-98; Team P Glas E End 98-03; TR 03-08; Miss 21 Co-ord 98-03; PtO *Nor* 09-12; R N and S Creake w Waterden, Syderstone etc from 12. *The Rectory, 18 Front Street, South Creake, Fakenham NR21 9PE* T: (01328) 823293 M: 07970-875052 E: frclive.wylie@gmail.com

WYLIE, David Victor. b 61. ACA 86 LSE BSc(Econ) 82 Leeds Univ BA 91. Coll of Resurr Mirfield 89. **d** 92 **p** 93. C Kilburn St Aug w St Jo *Lon* 92-95; C Heston 95-98; Chapl RN from 98. *Royal Naval Chaplaincy Service, Mail Point 1-2, Leach Building, Whale Island, Portsmouth PO2 8BY* T: (023) 9262 5055 F: 9262 5134

WYLIE, Kenneth Andrew. b 66. St Mellitus Coll BA 14. **d** 14 **p** 15. C Hornchurch St Andr *Chelmsf* from 14. *49 Burnway, Hornchurch RM11 3SN* E: ken847@btinternet.com

WYLIE-SMITH, Ms Megan Judith. b 52. S'wark Ord Course 88. **d** 91 **p** 94. C Greenstead *Chelmsf* 91-94; C W Ham 94-97; TV Becontree S 97-01; rtd 01; PtO *Chelmsf* from 01. *6 Manor Court Lodge, 175 High Road, London E18 2PD* E: megan@wylie-smith.freeserve.co.uk

WYNBURNE, Canon John Paterson Barry. b 48. St Jo Coll Dur BA 70. Wycliffe Coll Toronto MDiv 72 Ridley Hall Cam 72. **d** 73 **p** 74. C gt Stanmore *Lon* 73-76; Chapl Bucharest w Sofia *Eur* 76-77; C Dorking w Ranmore *Guildf* 77-80; V Send 80-88; V York Town St Mich 88-93; V Camberley St Mich Yorktown 93-95; TR Beaconsfield *Ox* 95-09; AD Amersham 04-09; V Long Crendon w Chearsley and Nether Winchendon 09-15; Hon Can Ch Ch 11-15; rtd 15. *66 Windmill Street, Brill, Aylesbury HP18 9TG* E: revwynburne@btinternet.com

WYNFORD-HARRIS, Robert William. b 61. Anglia Ruskin Univ BA 10 MA 14 LGSM 90. Ridley Hall Cam 06. **d** 08 **p** 09. C Sawbridgeworth *St Alb* 08-11; C Thorley 11-14; P-in-c St Helens *Portsm* from 14; P-in-c Sea View from 14. *The Vicarage, Eddington Road, Seaview PO34 5EF* T: (01983) 567494 M: 07722-068018 E: wynhar@hotmail.com

WYNN, Edward Laurence. b 65. MBE 11. Leeds Metrop Univ BSc 96 Leeds Univ MA 02 RGN 88. NOC 98. **d** 01 **p** 02. C Emley *Wakef* 01-04; C Flockton cum Denby Grange 01-04; Chapl RAF 04-12; Chapl Wolv Univ *Lich* from 12; Chapl Birm Women's NHS Foundn Trust from 12; Chapl RAuxAF from 12; PtO *Birm* from 12. *The Chaplaincy Centre, City Campus North, Molineux Street, Wolverhampton WV1 1DT* T: (01902) 322904 E: eddie.wynn@wlv.ac.uk

WYNN, Richard David. b 44. Univ Coll of Rhodesia & Nyasaland Inst of Educn TCert 65. St Paul's Coll Grahamstown 86. **d** 88 **p** 89. C Kirby-Hilton Ascension S Africa 88-91; R Ixopo St Jo 91-99; R Richmond-cum-Byrne St Mary 99-02; P-in-c Cinderford St Steph w Littledean *Glouc* 02-10; P-in-c Cinderford St Jo 06-10; P-in-c Stopham and

Fittleworth *Chich* 10-13; rtd 14. *11 Long Avenue, Bexhill-on-Sea TN40 2SJ* T: (01424) 223691

WYNN (née ARMSTRONG), Rosemary. b 40. **d** 06. OLM Sturminster Newton, Hinton St Mary and Lydlinch *Sarum* 06-14; PtO from 14. *2 Mounters Close, Marnhull, Sturminster Newton DT10 1NT* T: (01258) 820806 E: rw@sturminster.orangehome.co.uk

WYNNE, Preb Alan John. b 46. St Luke's Coll Ex CertEd 71. St Steph Ho Ox BA 71 MA 75. **d** 71 **p** 72. C Watford St Pet *St Alb* 71-74; Chapl Liddon Ho Lon 74-75; Chapl Abp Tenison's Sch Kennington 75-86; Hon C St Marylebone Annunciation Bryanston Street *Lon* 81-86; V Hoxton St Anne w St Columba 86-94; TR Poplar 94-14; Preb St Paul's Cathl 01-14; AD Tower Hamlets 01-06; rtd 14. *194 Long Lane, London SE1 4PZ* E: alanjwynne@tiscali.co.uk

WYNNE (née GORTON), Mrs Angela Deborah. b 60. Leeds Univ BSc 82 CSci 04. CBDTI 04. **d** 07 **p** 08. NSM Penwortham St Mary *Blackb* 07-11; NSM Charnock Richard from 11; NSM Eccleston from 13. *11 Freeman's Lane, Charnock Richard, Chorley PR7 5ER* T: (01257) 791760 E: adwynne@yahoo.co.uk

WYNNE, The Very Revd Frederick John Gordon. b 44. Chu Coll Cam BA 66 MA 70. CITC 81. **d** 84 **p** 85. C Dublin St Patr Cathl Gp 84-86; C Romsey *Win* 86-89; R Broughton, Bossington, Houghton and Mottisfont 89-97; I Dunleckney w Nurney, Lorum and Kiltennel *C & O* 97-08; I Leighlin w Grange Sylvae, Shankill etc 08-10; Chan Ossory Cathl 00-10; Chan Leighlin Cathl 00-04; Dean Leighlin 04-10; rtd 10; PtO *Win* from 13. *12 Avenue Road, Lymington SO41 9GJ* T: (01590) 672082

WYNNE, Preb Geoffrey. b 41. K Coll Lon BD 64 AKC 64 Lon Univ BSc(Soc) 75 Heythrop Coll Lon MTh 86. **d** 66 **p** 67. C Wolverhampton St Pet *Lich* 66-70; Chapl Wolv Poly 66-79; Sen Chapl 79-92; Sen Chapl Wolv Univ 92-10; Dir of Ords 76-83; Preb Lich Cathl 83-10; AD Wolverhampton 03-10; Bp's Adv for Univ and HE Chapl 04-10; rtd 10; PtO *Lich* from 12. *West House, Haywood Drive, Wolverhampton WV6 8RF* T: (01902) 219196 E: g.wynne@wlv.ac.uk

WYNNE, Ian Charles. b 53. Bris Univ MB, ChB 76 FRCGP 06. SNWTP 09. **d** 11 **p** 12. NSM Haydock St Jas *Liv* from 11. *123 Ashton Road, Newton-le-Willows WA12 0AH* M: 07885-823786 E: ian_cw@hotmail.com

WYNNE, Jago Robert Owen. b 76. Magd Coll Cam BA 98 MA 01. Wycliffe Hall Ox 08. **d** 10 **p** 11. C Onslow Square and S Kensington St Aug *Lon* 10-12; C Clapham H Trin and St Pet S'wark from 12. *68 North Street, London SW4 0HE* M: 07979-606720 E: jago.wynne@ymail.com

WYNNE, Jean. **d** 02 **p** 03. NSM Mullingar, Portnashangan, Moyliscar, Kilbixy etc *M & K* 02-10; LtO from 10. *3 Doctor's Court, Rathangan, Co Kildare, Republic of Ireland* T: (00353) (45) 524057 M: 86-356 4590

WYNNE, Mrs Teresa Anne Jane. b 58. Anglia Poly Univ BEd 94 Middx Univ BA 07. NTMTC 04. **d** 07 **p** 08. C Takeley w Lt Canfield *Chelmsf* 07-10; P-in-c Lexden from 10. *The Rectory, 2 Wroxham Close, Colchester CO3 3RQ* T: (01206) 575966 E: revteresawynne@gmail.com

WYNNE-GREEN, Roy Rowland. b 36. Chich Th Coll 67. **d** 70 **p** 71. C Fleetwood St Pet *Blackb* 70-73; C Cen Torquay *Ex* 73-75; Chapl SW Hosp Lon 75-85; Asst Chapl St Thos Hosp 75-85; Chapl R Surrey Co Hosp Guildf 85-94; Chapl R Surrey Co Hosp NHS Trust 94-01; Chapl Heathlands Mental Health Trust Surrey 94-98; Chapl Surrey Hants Borders NHS Trust 98-01; rtd 01; PtO *Guildf* from 02. *St Benedict's House, 6 Lawn Road, Guildford GU2 5DE* T: (01483) 574582

WYNNE-JONES, Nicholas Winder. b 45. Jes Coll Ox BA 67 MA 72 Selw Coll Cam 71. Oak Hill Th Coll 69. **d** 72 **p** 73. C St Marylebone All So w SS Pet and Jo *Lon* 72-75; Chapl Stowe Sch 75-83; V Gt Clacton *Chelmsf* 83-95; V Beckenham Ch Ch *Roch* 95-13; RD Beckenham 00-05; rtd 13; Hon C Theale and Englefield *Ox* from 13. *St Mark's House, Englefield, Reading RG7 5EP* E: mail@wynne-jones.org.uk

WYNTER, Peter John Pallant. b 78. Rolle Coll BEd 01. Ridley Hall Cam 12. **d** 14 **p** 15. C Onslow Square and S Kensington St Aug *Lon* from 14. *68 Pulborough Road, London SW18 5UJ* M: 07833-088038 E: pete@onelifeonline.org.uk

Y

YABBACOME, David Wallace. b 55. Bp Otter Coll BEd. Linc Th Coll. **d** 83 **p** 84. C Egham Hythe *Guildf* 83-86; C Cen Telford *Lich* 86-87; TV 87-92; R Cheadle w Freehay 92-00; V Linc St Nic w St Jo Newport 00-13; V E Trent *S'well* 13-15; rtd 15. *Address temp unknown* M: 07779-557541
E: revyabb@gmail.com

YABSLEY, Mrs Janet. b 42. St Alb Minl Tr Scheme 81. **dss** 84 **d** 87 **p** 94. Luton St Andr *St Alb* 84-87; NSM Luton St Aug Limbury 87-00; NSM Luton All SS w St Pet 00-06; PtO from 06. *11 Dale Road, Dunstable LU5 4PY* T: (01582) 661480

YACOMENI, Peter Frederick. b 34. Worc Coll Ox BA 58 MA 61. Wycliffe Hall Ox 58. **d** 60 **p** 61. C New Malden and Coombe *S'wark* 60-64; C Bethnal Green St Jas Less *Lon* 64-68; V Barton Hill St Luke w Ch Ch *Bris* 68-75; V Bishopsworth 75-86; RD Bedminster 84-86; P-in-c Wick w Doynton 86-87; V Wick w Doynton and Dyrham 87-98; RD Bitton 95-98; rtd 98; Chapl Wilts and Swindon Healthcare NHS Trust from 98; PtO *Bris* from 98. *15 Orwell Close, Malmesbury SN16 9UB*
T: (01666) 826628

YACOMENI, Thomas Peter Bruce. b 71. Ex Univ BEng 94. Trin Coll Bris BA 09. **d** 09 **p** 10. C Weston-super-Mare St Paul B & W 09-13; Pioneer Min from 13. *78 Bransby Way, Weston-super-Mare BS24 7BW* M: 07786-806640
E: tom.yacomeni@googlemail.com

YALLOP, John. b 47. Oak Hill Th Coll BA 79. **d** 79 **p** 80. C Brinsworth w Catcliffe *Sheff* 79-81; C Heeley 81-83; C Pitsmoor Ch Ch 83-86; V Ellesmere St Pet 86-88; C Worksop St Jo *S'well* 90-94; P-in-c Cliftonville *Cant* 94-99. *152 Addison Street, Blackburn BB2 1HN*

YAM, David Tong Kho. See HAOKIP, David Tongkhoyam

YANDELL, Caroline Jane. b 63. St Hugh's Coll Ox BA 85 MA 92 Bris Univ MB, ChB 97 LSHTM MSc 05 Bris Univ PhD 07 Wolfs Coll Cam BTh 08 St Jo Coll Cam MPhil 09 MRCGP 01. Ridley Hall Cam 06. **d** 09 **p** 10. C Henleaze *Bris* 09-13; P-in-c Bassingbourn *Ely* 13-15; V from 15; P-in-c Whaddon 13-15; V from 15. *The Vicarage, 21 North End, Bassingbourn, Royston SG8 5NZ* T: (01763) 244836
E: caroline.yandell@cantab.net

YANGON, Bishop of. See SAN SI HTAY, Samuel

YAP, Thomas Fook Piau. b 75. Leeds Univ BA 98 MA 99. St Jo Coll Nottm MTh 02. **d** 03 **p** 04. C Starbeck *Ripon* 03-07; Chapl Essex Univ *Chelmsf* 07-12; Chapl S Lon and Maudsley NHS Foundn Trust 12-15; PtO *S'wark* from 15. *Address temp unknown* E: revthomas@hotmail.co.uk

YARRIEN (nee FRYER), Cora Lynette. b 74. Man Univ BSc 95 Warwick Univ MSc 97 BA 01. Cranmer Hall Dur 12. **d** 14 **p** 15. C Epperstone, Gonalston, Oxton and Woodborough *S'well* from 14. *131B Main Street, Woodborough, Nottingham NG14 6DD* M: 07885-635374 E: cora.fryer@googlemail.com

YATES, Andrew Martin. b 55. St Chad's Coll Dur BA 77. Linc Th Coll 78. **d** 80 **p** 81. C Brightside St Thos and St Marg *Sheff* 80-83; TV Haverhill w Withersfield, the Wrattings etc *St E* 84-90; Ind Chapl 84-90; R Aylesham w Adisham *Cant* 90-96; P-in-c Dudley St Aug Holly Hall *Worc* 96-03; Chapl Merry Hill Shopping Cen 96-03; Dioc Soc Resp Officer *Truro* from 03; P-in-c Tresillian and Lamorran w Merther 03-12; P-in-c St Michael Penkevil 03-12; P-in-c Paul from 12; C Newlyn St Pet from 12; C Penzance St Mary w St Paul and St Jo from 12. *Hanover House, 6A Kings Road, Penzance TR18 4LG* T: (01736) 367863 E: andrew.yates@truro.anglican.org

YATES, Canon Anthony Hugh. b 39. Univ of Wales BA 62. Wycliffe Hall Ox 62. **d** 65 **p** 66. C Withington St Crispin *Man* 65-68; C Sheff St Cecilia Parson Cross 68-73; V Middlesbrough St Thos *York* 73-82; V Fenton *Lich* 82-95; V Kilburn St Aug w St Jo *Lon* 95-11; rtd 11; CMP from 69; Hon Can Koforidua from 07. *8 Bishop Street, London N1 8PH* T: (020) 7704 6275 M: 07947-646377 E: fatheryates@btinternet.com

YATES, Mrs Esther Christine. b 46. Moray Ho Coll of Educn DipEd 67 Cartrefle Coll of Educn BEd 80. St As Minl Tr Course 02. **d** 05 **p** 06. NSM Newtown w Llanllwchaiarn w Aberhafesp *St As* 05-07; NSM Llanllwchaiarn and Newtown w Aberhafesp 07-10; NSM Berriew from 10. *Gwawr-y-Grug, 7 Mill Fields, Milford, Newtown SY16 3JP* T: (01686) 625559

YATES, Francis Edmund. b 49. Ox Univ BEd 72 Sheff Univ MEd 88. Linc Th Coll 95. **d** 95 **p** 96. C Chesterfield St Mary and All SS *Derby* 95-98; P-in-c Newlyn St Newlyn *Truro* 98-03; Dioc Adv for Schs and RE 98-03; P-in-c Tideswell *Derby*

03-11; V 11-12; C Wormhill, Peak Forest w Peak Dale and Dove Holes 07-11; rtd 12. *Address temp unknown*
E: fryates@msn.com

YATES, Herbert. See YATES, William Herbert

YATES, Jennifer Clare. See TOTNEY, Jennifer Clare

YATES, Miss Joanna Mary. b 49. St Anne's Coll Ox BA 71 MA 74 K Coll Lon PGCE 72. S'wark Ord Course 89. **d** 91 **p** 94. Promotions and Publications Officer Nat Soc 85-95; Chapl Ch Ho Westmr 91-95; C Regent's Park St Mark *Lon* 91-95; C Finchley St Mary 95-01; TV Leeds City *Ripon* 01-09; rtd 09; PtO *Lon* from 10. *8 Frith Court, London NW7 1JP* T: (020) 8349 1076 M: 07961-654430
E: revjoannayates325@btinternet.com

YATES, Keith Leonard. b 36. K Coll Lon BD AKC 61 Nottm Univ MPhil 79. Wells Th Coll. **d** 69 **p** 70. C Luton Ch Ch *St Alb* 69-73; Hon C Luton St Andr 73-76; R Grimoldby w Manby *Linc* 76-80; P-in-c Yarburgh 76-78; R 78-80; P-in-c Alvingham w N and S Cockerington 76-78; V 78-80; P-in-c Gt w Lt Carlton 77-78; R 78-80; Lect Sarum & Wells Th Coll 80-87; R Upper Chelsea H Trin *Lon* 87-96; rtd 96; PtO *Sarum* from 97. *50 Culverhayes, Beaminster DT8 3DG* T: (01308) 863409

YATES, Lindsay Anne. b 69. Selw Coll Cam BA 91 MA 95 Univ of Wales (Lamp) MTh 10 Barrister 92. Ripon Coll Cuddesdon BTh 99. **d** 99 **p** 00. C Bampton w Clanfield *Ox* 99-02; Chapl Pemb Coll Cam 02-06; Chapl Westcott Ho Cam 07-14; NSM Winchmore Hill St Paul *Lon* from 14; Tutor St Mellitus Coll from 14. *St Paul's Vicarage, Church Hill, London N21 1JA* T: (020) 8886 3545 E: lindsay.yates@stmellitus.ac.uk

YATES, Margaret Helen. b 51. **d** 10 **p** 11. NSM Walbury Beacon *Ox* 10-14; NSM Newbury St Nic and Speen from 15. *5 Halfway Cottages, Bath Road, Newbury RG20 8NG* T: (01488) 658092
E: m.h.yates@reading.ac.uk

YATES, Michael Anthony. b 48. Oak Hill Th Coll. **d** 82 **p** 83. C Hebburn St Jo *Dur* 82-85; C Sheldon *Birm* 85-87; V Lea Hall 87-92; TV Old Brampton and Loundsley Green *Derby* 92-98; V Loundsley Green 98-01; V Riddings and Ironville 01-07; P-in-c Seale and Lullington w Coton in the Elms 07-11; R from 11; C Walton-on-Trent w Croxall, Rosliston etc from 13. *The Rectory, 24 Church Street, Nethersеal, Swadlincote DE12 8DF* T: (01283) 760485 E: mikeanbike@tiscali.co.uk

YATES, Michael Peter. b 47. JP 91. Leeds Univ BA 69 MA 70 MPhil 85 Potchefstroom Univ PhD 03. Coll of Resurr Mirfield 69. **d** 71 **p** 72. C Crewe St Andr *Ches* 71-76; V Wheelock 76-79; Chapl Rainhill Hosp *Liv* 79-89; Chapl Barnsley Distr Gen Hosp 89-94; Chapl Barnsley Distr Gen Hosp NHS Trust 94-11; Chapl Barnsley Hosp NHS Foundn Trust 05-11; rtd 11. *40 Rainton Grove, Barnsley S75 2QZ* E: mpyates@hotmail.com

YATES, Paul David. b 47. Sussex Univ BA 73 DPhil 80. Sarum & Wells Th Coll 88. **d** 91 **p** 92. NSM Lewes All SS, St Anne, St Mich and St Thos *Chich* 91-00; NSM Lewes St Mich and St Thos at Cliffe w All SS 00-10; NSM Lewes St Anne and St Mich and St Thos etc from 10. *17 St Swithun's Terrace, Lewes BN7 1UJ* T: (01273) 473463

YATES, Peter Francis. b 47. Sheff Univ BA 69. Kelham Th Coll 69 NW Ord Course 73. **d** 74 **p** 75. C Mexborough *Sheff* 74-78; C Sevenoaks St Jo *Roch* 78-81; CSWG from 81; LtO *Chich* from 85. *The Monastery, Crawley Down, Crawley RH10 4LH* T: (01342) 712074 E: father.peter@cswg.org.uk

YATES, Raymond Paul. b 55. Oak Hill Th Coll BA 88. **d** 88 **p** 89. C Bootle St Mary w St Paul *Liv* 88-91; C Drypool *York* 91-92; TV 92-97; C Orpington All SS *Roch* 97-00; R Beeford w Frodingham and Foston *York* 00-06; RD N Holderness 02-06; Chapl HM Pris Hull 01-02; P-in-c Quinton Road W St Boniface *Birm* 06-09; V from 09. *The Vicarage, Quinton Road West, Birmingham B32 2QD* T: 0121-427 8551 *or* 426 3166
E: raymondyates@btinternet.com

YATES, Ricky. See YATES, Warwick John

YATES, Canon Roger Alan. b 47. Trin Coll Cam BA 68 MA 72 MB, BChir 71 Bris Univ PhD 75 MRCP 77 FFPM 93. NOC 84. **d** 87 **p** 88. NSM Wilmslow *Ches* from 87; Bp's Officer for NSM from 93; Hon Can Ches Cathl from 99; RD Knutsford 06-13. *3 Racecourse Park, Wilmslow SK9 5LU* T: (01625) 520246
E: raycandoc@yahoo.co.uk

YATES, Mrs Rosamund. b 63. Rob Coll Cam BA 84 MA 88. Oak Hill Th Coll BA 93. **d** 93. C Holloway St Mary Magd *Lon* 93-95; NSM Tervuren w Liège *Eur* 95-97; NSM W Ealing St Jo w St Jas *Lon* 01-05; PtO *Eur* 05-08; NSM E Acton St Dunstan w

St Thos *Lon* from 08. *14 Rosemount Road, London W3 9LR* T: (020) 8993 6614 E: rosyates@tiscali.co.uk

YATES, Mrs Sian. b 57. Univ of Wales (Ban) Westmr Coll Ox MTh 91. Linc Th Coll 78. **d** 80 **p** 94. C Risca *Mon* 80-83; Chapl Ch Hosp Horsham 83-85; Team Dn Haverhill w Withersfield, the Wrattings etc *St E* 85-90; Dioc Youth Chapl *Cant* 90-93; Assoc Min Cant St Martin and St Paul 93-96; Educn Chapl *Worc* 96-03; P-in-c Dudley St Jas 96-03; P-in-c Dudley St Barn 01-02; P-in-c Tregony w St Cuby and Cornelly *Truro* 03-12; Dioc Adv in RE 03-10; TR Penzance St Mary w St Paul and St Jo from 12; C Newlyn St Pet from 12; C Paul from 12. *Hanover House, 6A Kings Road, Penzance TR18 4LG* T: (01736) 367863 E: yates252@btinternet.com

YATES, Canon Timothy Edward. b 35. Magd Coll Cam BA 59 MA 62 Uppsala Univ DTh 78. Ridley Hall Cam 58. **d** 60 **p** 61. C Tonbridge SS Pet and Paul *Roch* 60-63; Tutor St Jo Coll Dur 63-71; Warden Cranmer Hall Dur 71-79; P-in-c Darley w S Darley *Derby* 79-82; R Darley 82-90; Dioc Dir of Ords 85-95; Hon Can Derby Cathl 89-00; C Ashford w Sheldon and Longstone 90-00; rtd 00; Perm to Offic 01; Hon Fell St Jo Coll Dur from 04. *Holly House, South Church Street, Bakewell DE45 1FD* T: (01629) 812686

YATES, Timothy John Sturgis. b 56. Bradf Univ BTech 83 Univ Coll Lon PhD 86. ERMC 05. **d** 07 **p** 08. NSM Gt Chesham *Ox* from 07. *16 Chapmans Crescent, Chesham HP5 2QU* T: (01494) 772914 M: 07802-155072 E: timyates3@btinternet.com

YATES, Warwick John (Ricky). b 52. Univ of Wales (Lamp) BA 78. Wycliffe Hall Ox 87. **d** 89 **p** 90. C Hoddesdon *St Alb* 89-93; R Finmere w Mixbury, Cottisford, Hardwick etc *Ox* 93-95; R Shelswell 95-08; P-in-c Prague *Eur* from 08. *Pat'anka 2614/11B, Flat 7, 160 00 Praha 6 - Dejvice, Czech Republic* T: (00420) (2) 3331 0266 E: chaplain@anglican.cz

YATES, William Herbert. b 35. Man Univ BA 59. Chich Th Coll 60. **d** 61 **p** 62. C Blackpool St Steph *Blackb* 61-65; C Wednesbury St Jo *Lich* 65-69; V Porthill 69-78; R Norton in the Moors 78-84; R Church Aston 84-00; rtd 00; PtO *Lich* from 01. *83 Stallington Road, Blythe Bridge, Stoke-on-Trent ST11 9PD* T: (01782) 397182

YATES, Mrs Yvonne Louise. b 52. NEOC 01. **d** 04 **p** 05. NSM Kirkbymoorside w Gillamoor, Farndale etc *York* 04-07; Chapl Oakhill Secure Tr Cen 07-08; Co-ord Chapl HM Pris Kirklevington Grange 08-11; TV Combe Martin, Berrynarbor, Lynton, Brendon etc *Ex* 11-14; Chapl HM Pris Styal from 14. *HM Prison, Styal Road, Styal, Wilmslow SK9 4HR* T: (01625) 553000 E: ylyates@btinternet.com

YEADON, Mrs Penelope Susan. b 60. NEOC 03. **d** 06 **p** 07. NSM Penhill *Leeds* from 06. *Dale Cottage, Aysgarth, Leyburn DL8 3AB* T: (01969) 663505

YEADON, Ms Victoria Jane. b 69. Univ Coll Lon BSc 91 MSc 92 Anglia Ruskin Univ BA 09. Ridley Hall Cam 07. **d** 09 **p** 10. C Deptford St Nic and St Luke *S'wark* 09-12; TV Thamesmead from 12. *5 Finchdale Road, London SE2 9PG* M: 07952-292113

YEAGER, Robert Timothy. b 50. Univ of Iowa BA 72 JD 77. **d** 10 **p** 11. USA 10-14; TV E Greenwich *S'wark* from 14. *Address temp unknown* E: rtyeager@gmail.com

YEARWOOD, Jean Cornilia. b 43. Heythrop Coll Lon MA 05 RGN 74 RM 76. **d** 07 **p** 08. NSM Croydon Woodside *S'wark* 07-14; PtO from 14. *59 Bradley Road, London SE19 3NT* T: (020) 8771 7743 M: 07913-005545 E: j.yearwood@btopenworld.com

YEATES, James Paul. b 81. St Mellitus Coll. **d** 13 **p** 14. C Highgate St Mich *Lon* from 13. *17 Bisham Gardens, London N6 6DJ* T: (020) 8144 3056 M: 07968-533298 E: jpyeates@gmail.com

YEATS, Charles. b 56. Natal Univ BCom 77 Witwatersrand Univ MBA 79 Ball Coll Ox MA 85 K Coll Lon MTh 90 Dur Univ PhD 99. Wycliffe Hall Ox 85. **d** 87 **p** 88. C Islington St Mary *Lon* 87-90; Research Fell Whitefield Inst Ox 90-92; Chapl and Fell Univ Coll Dur 92-00; PtO *Dur* 00-08. *58 Archery Rise, Durham DH1 4LA* T: 0191-384 0606

YELDHAM, Anthony Paul Richard. *See* KYRIAKIDES-YELDHAM, Anthony Paul Richard

YELDHAM, Denise Linda. b 51. Leeds Univ BSc 72 MB, ChB 75 Univ of Wales (Lamp) MA 08 MRCPsych 80. Westcott Ho Cam 06. **d** 08 **p** 09. C Plymstock and Hooe *Ex* 08-11; C Westmr St Steph w St Jo *Lon* 11-14; P-in-c Margate All SS *Cant* from 14; P-in-c Margate St Jo from 14. *The Vicarage, 24 St Peter's Road, Margate CT9 1TH* M: 07814-193632 E: denise.yeldham@gmail.com

YELLAND, Jeffrey Charles. b 46. CEng MIStructE 72. STETS 98. **d** 01 **p** 02. NSM Effingham w Lt Bookham *Guildf* 01-04; NSM Dorking St Paul from 04. *32 Hookfield, Epsom KT19 8JG* T/F: (01372) 807096 M: 07918-030513 E: jeff@stpaulsdorking.org.uk

YENDALL, John Edward Thomas. b 52. St Jo Coll Dur BA 88. Cranmer Hall Dur 84. **d** 88 **p** 89. C Bangor *Ban* 88-90; C

Botwnnog 90-91; R Trefdraeth w Aberffraw etc 91-01; RD Malltraeth 97-01; V Llanwddyn and Llanfihangel-yng-Nghwynfa etc *St As* 01-07; V Llanrhaeadr ym Mochnant etc 07-11; P-in-c Llansantffraid Glyn Ceirog and Llanarmon etc from 11. *The New Vicarage, High Street, Glyn Ceiriog, Llangollen LL20 7EH* T: (01691) 718425

✠**YEOMAN, The Rt Revd David.** b 44. St Mich Coll Llan 66. **d** 70 **p** 71 **c** 04. C Cardiff St Jo *Llan* 70-72; C Caerphilly 72-76; V Ystrad Rhondda w Ynyscynon 76-81; V Mountain Ash 81-96; R Coity w Nolton 96-04; Can Llan Cathl 00-09; Asst Bp Llan 04-09; Adn Morgannwg 04-06; rtd 09. *4 Llety Gwyn, Bridgend CF31 1RG* T: (01656) 649919 M: 07971-926631

YEOMAN, Douglas. b 35. ACII 63. **d** 77 **p** 78. NSM Edin St Martin 77-96; NSM Wester Hailes St Luke 79-90; Chapl Edinburgh Healthcare NHS Trust 95-99; Chapl Lothian Primary Healthcare NHS Trust 98-06; NSM Edin St Cuth 96-06; LtO from 06. *6 Craiglockhart Crescent, Edinburgh EH14 1EY* T: 0131-443 5449 E: douglas.yeoman@btinternet.com

YEOMAN, Miss Ruth Jane. b 60. Sheff Univ BSc 82 MSc 85 Dur Univ PGCE 83. Ripon Coll Cuddesdon BA 90 MA 94. **d** 91 **p** 94. C Coleshill *Birm* 91-95; C Hodge Hill 95-01; Bp's Adv for Children's Work 95-01; L'Arche Lambeth Community 01-03; PtO *S'wark* 01-03; *Birm* 03; V Menston w Woodhead *Leeds* from 03. *The Vicarage, 12 Fairfax Gardens, Menston, Ilkley LS29 6ET* T: (01943) 877739 *or* 872433 M: 07752-912646 E: vicar@stjohnmenston.org.uk *or* ruthjyeoman@hotmail.com

YEOMANS, Robert John. b 44. AKC 66. **d** 67 **p** 68. C Pontesbury I and II *Heref* 67-70; Asst Youth Officer *St Alb* 70-72; Project Officer (Dio St Alb) Gen Syn Bd of Educn 73-77; V Is of Dogs Ch Ch and St Jo w St Luke *Lon* 77-87; V Waterloo St Jo w St Andr *S'wark* 87-93; Chapl United Bris Healthcare NHS Trust 93-02; Chapl Ex Hospiscare 02-06; rtd 06; PtO *Truro* from 02. *The White Barn, Maxworthy, Launceston PL15 8LY* T: (01566) 781570 E: robyeomans30@gmail.com

YERBURGH, Canon David Savile. b 34. Magd Coll Cam BA 57 MA 61. Wells Th Coll 57. **d** 59 **p** 60. C Cirencester *Glouc* 59-63; C Bitterne Park *Win* 63-67; V Churchdown St Jo *Glouc* 67-74; RD Glouc N 73-74; V Charlton Kings St Mary 74-85; R Minchinhampton 85-95; Hon Can Glouc Cathl 86-95; rtd 95; PtO *Sarum* from 95. *2 Mill Race Close, Mill Road, Salisbury SP2 7RX* T: (01722) 320064 E: d.yerburgh@btinternet.com

YERBURGH, Peter Charles. b 31. Magd Coll Cam BA 53 MA 57. Wells Th Coll 53. **d** 55 **p** 56. C Southbroom *Sarum* 55-58; Chapl Wells Cathl Sch 58-71; Chapl Durlston Court Sch 71-91; rtd 91. *2 Mill Race Close, Mill Road, Salisbury SP2 7RX* T: (01722) 327796

YERBURY, Gregory Howard. b 67. Trin Coll Bris BA 93. St Jo Coll Nottm 94. **d** 96 **p** 97. C Crofton *Portsm* 96-00; P-in-c Bolton St Jo *Man* 00-06; P-in-c Bolton Breightmet St Jas 05-06; TR Leverhulme 06-11; TR Penkridge *Lich* from 11. *The Rectory, New Road, Penkridge, Stafford ST19 5DN* T: (01785) 714344 E: rector@stmichaelspenkridge.co.uk

YESUDAS, Alex. b 71. **d** 01 **p** 01. India 01-14; PtO *Birm* from 14. *Queen's College, Somerset Road, Edgbaston, Birmingham B15 2QH* M: 07904-459051 E: alex_yesudas@yahoo.co.in

YETMAN, Miss Sarah Elizabeth. b 85. St Mary's Coll Dur BA 09 Cam Univ BTh 13. Ridley Hall Cam 10. **d** 13 **p** 14. C Yateley *Win* from 13. *St Barnabas House, Green Lane, Frogmore, Camberley GU17 0NU* E: sarah.yetman@googlemail.com

YEWDALL, Mrs Mary Doreen. b 23. Nottm Univ DipEd 71 BTh 85. EMMTC 76. **dss** 79 **d** 87 **p** 94. Kirkby in Ashfield St Thos *S'well* 79-81; Daybrook 81-87; Par Dn 87-89; rtd 89; Hon Par Dn Bilsthorpe *S'well* 89-91; Hon Par Dn Eakring 89-91; Hon Par Dn Winkburn 89-91; Hon Par Dn Maplebeck 89-91; NSM Norton juxta Malton *York* 92-95; NSM Whitwell w Crambe, Flaxton, Foston etc 95-98; PtO from 98. *17 Dulverton Hall, Esplanade, Scarborough YO11 2AR* T: (01723) 340130

YIEND, Paul Martin. b 57. UEA BA 80. St Jo Coll Nottm MA 96. **d** 92 **p** 94. C Bushbury *Lich* 92-95; Asst Chapl Brussels *Eur* 99-00; P-in-c Charleroi 00-03; P-in-c Liège from 00. *rue Basse des Canes 11, 5300 Andenne, Belgium* T/F: (0032) (85) 844482 E: paul.yiend@skynet.be

YILDIRIM, Engin. **d** 07 **p** 08. C Istanbul *Eur* from 07. *Swedish Chapel of Istanbul, Seraskerci Çikmazi, No 9, Beyoglu, Istanbul, Turkey* E: beyogluanglican@yahoo.com

YONG, Sok Han. b 61. Ox Brookes Univ MA 14. Malaysia Th Sem BTheol 86. **d** 10 **p** 11. NSM Ox St Aldate 10-11; NSM Abingdon 11-14; NSM St Andr Hong Kong from 14. *138 Nathan Road, Kowloon, Hong Kong* T: (00852) 2367 1478 E: info@standrews.org.hk

YONGE, James Mohun (Brother Amos). b 47. Keele Univ BA 71. WMMTC 91. **d** 94 **p** 95. SSF from 76; PtO *Worc* from

09. *Glasshampton Monastery, Shrawley, Worcester WR6 6TQ* F: 896083 T: (01299) 896345 E: amosssf@franciscans.org.uk

YORK, Mrs Elizabeth Joy. b 70. St Jo Coll Nottm 13. **d** 15. C Barrow upon Soar w Walton le Wolds *Leic* from 15; C Wymeswold and Prestwold w Hoton from 15. *Address temp unknown*

YORK, Canon Humphrey Bowmar. b 28. St Chad's Coll Dur BA 54 Univ of Wales (Lamp) MA 04. **d** 55 **p** 56. C Beamish *Dur* 55-57; C Tettenhall Regis *Lich* 57-62; P-in-c Lansallos w Pelynt *Truro* 62-63; R Lanreath 62-67; V Pelynt 63-67; P-in-c Lanlivery 67-74; P-in-c Luxulyan 67-74; P-in-c Lanlivery w Luxulyan 74-83; RD Bodmin 76-82; R Antony w Sheviock 83-93; Hon Can Truro Cathl 90-93; rtd 93; PtO *Truro* from 93; *Sarum* from 93. *8 Huntingdon Street, Bradford-on-Avon BA15 1RF* E: canonhumphrey@tinyworld.co.uk

YORK, Mrs Paula. b 67. **d** 12 **p** 13. C Earls Barton *Pet* 12-15; R Yardley Hastings, Denton and Grendon etc from 15. *14 The Leys, Denton, Northampton NN7 1DH* E: revpaula@gmx.com

YORK, Archbishop of. *See* SENTAMU, The Most Revd and Rt Hon John Tucker Mugabi

YORK, Archdeacon of. *See* BULLOCK, The Ven Sarah Ruth

YORK, Dean of. *See* FAULL, The Very Revd Vivienne Frances

YORKE, John Andrew. b 47. Cranmer Hall Dur 70. **d** 73 **p** 74. C Spitalfields Ch Ch w All SS *Lon* 73-78; R Tuktoyaktuk Canada 78-88; R Fort McPherson 89-92; V Totland Bay *Portsm* 92-12; V Thorley 95-12; rtd 12; PtO *Portsm* from 12; *Sarum* from 15. *7 Broadmead, Trowbridge BA14 9BX* T: (01225) 680529 E: andyyorke.iow@tiscali.co.uk

YORKE, The Very Revd Michael Leslie. b 39. Magd Coll Cam BA 62 MA 66. Cuddesdon Coll 62. **d** 64 **p** 65. C Croydon St Jo *Cant* 64-68; Succ Chelmsf Cathl 68-69; Prec and Chapl 69-73; Dep Dir Cathl Cen for Research and Tr 72-74; P-in-c Ashdon w Hadstock 74-76; R 76-78; Can Res Chelmsf Cathl 78-88; Vice-Provost 84-88; P-in-c N Lynn w St Marg and St Nic *Nor* 88-92; P-in-c King's Lynn St Marg w St Nic 92-94; Chmn Dioc Adv Bd for Min 90-94; Hon Can Nor Cathl 93-94; Provost Portsm 94-99; Dean *Lich* 99-04; rtd 04; PtO *Nor* from 04. *The Old Chapel, 34 West Street, North Creake, Fakenham NR21 9LQ* T: (01328) 738833 E: michaellyorke@aol.com

YORKSTONE, Peter. b 48. Loughb Univ BTech 72. Oak Hill Th Coll 79. **d** 81 **p** 82. C Blackpool St Thos *Blackb* 81-85; V Copp 85-00; P-in-c Giggleswick and Rathmell w Wigglesworth *Bradf* 00-07; V Kettlewell w Conistone, Hubberholme etc *Leeds* 07-14; rtd 14. *24 St Laurence Way, Stanwick, Wellingborough NN9 6QS* E: peter@pyorkstone.freeserve.co.uk

YOUATT, Jennifer Alison. *See* MONTGOMERY, Jennifer Alison

YOUDE, Paul Crosland. b 47. Birm Univ LLB 68. WEMTC 93. **d** 96 **p** 97. NSM Cheltenham St Luke and St Jo *Glouc* 96-99; C Cirencester 99-03; P-in-c Lydney 03-09; P-in-c Woolaston w Alvington and Aylburton 07-09; rtd 09; Hon C Kemble, Poole Keynes, Somerford Keynes etc *Glouc* 09-13. *107 Painswick Road, Cheltenham GL50 2EX* T: (01242) 463174 E: paul.youde@btinternet.com

YOUELL, Mrs Deborah Mary. b 57. STETS 01. **d** 04 **p** 14. NSM Cowplain *Portsm* 04-08; NSM Crookhorn from 08. *42 The Yews, Horndean, Waterlooville PO8 0BH* T: (023) 9279 9946 E: deborah.youell@ntlworld.com

YOUENS, Edward. *See* MONTAGUE-YOUENS, Hubert Edward

YOUINGS, Arthur. b 65. Ex Univ BSc 86 Bath Univ PhD 90. Wycliffe Hall Ox 93. **d** 96 **p** 97. C Dorking St Paul *Guildf* 96-99; C S Croydon Em *S'wark* 99-03; R Trull w Angersleigh *B & W* from 03; RD Taunton from 15. *The Rectory, Wild Oak Lane, Trull, Taunton TA3 7JT* T: (01823) 253518

YOULD, Guy Martin. b 37. Keble Coll Ox BA 61 MA 65 Magd Coll Ox BD 68 Hull Univ PhD 80 Lambeth STh 75 FSAScot 75. St Steph Ho Ox 61. **d** 63 **p** 64. C Middlesbrough St Jo the Ev *York* 63-65; Chapl Magd Coll and C Cowley St Jo *Ox* 65-68; Asst Chapl Radley Coll 68-71; C W Kirby St Bridget *Ches* 71-74; Chapl Loretto Sch Musselburgh 74; V Liscard St Mary w St Columba *Ches* 74-78; St Barn Coll Belair Australia 78-80; C Doncaster St Leon and St Jude *Sheff* 80-81; V Brodsworth w Hooton Pagnell, Frickley etc 81-87; Chapl St Mary's Sch Wantage 87-93; R Chapel Chorlton, Maer and Whitmore *Lich* 93-98; P-in-c Altarnon w Bolventor, Laneast and St Clether *Truro* 98-02; P-in-c Lezant w Lawhitton and S Petherwin w Trewen 98-02; rtd 03; C Gt and Lt Torrington and Frithelstock *Ex* 03-05; P-in-c Bishopstone *Chich* 05-13. *Chalcot, Alfriston Road, Seaford BN25 3JJ* T: (01323) 890208

YOUNG, Adam Charles. b 89. Wycliffe Hall Ox BA 10 MTh 12. **d** 12 **p** 13. C Saltburn-by-the-Sea *York* from 12. *4 Oxford Street, Saltburn-by-the-Sea TS12 1LG* M: 07708-477608 E: alpha-to-omega@hotmail.com

YOUNG, Andrew Charles. b 54. FIBMS 83. NOC 98. **d** 01 **p** 02. C Heywood *Man* 01-05; TV Eccles from 05; AD from 13. *St Paul's Vicarage, Egerton Road, Eccles, Manchester M30 9LR* T: 0161-789 2420 E: andrew.young66@ntlworld.com

YOUNG, Andrew John. b 50. St Jo Coll Dur BA 73. Westcott Ho Cam 73. **d** 75 **p** 89. C Nailsworth *Glouc* 75-76; NSM Yeovil w Kingston Pitney *B & W* 89-93; NSM Tintinhull w Chilthorne Domer, Yeovil Marsh etc from 93. *15 Cook Avenue, Chard TA20 2JR* T: (01460) 62182

YOUNG, Miss Anne Patricia. b 44. Cov Coll of Educn CertEd 66 Leeds Univ BEd 76 Sheff Univ MEd 82 Liv Univ BTh 05. NOC 01. **d** 05 **p** 06. NSM Middlestown *Wakef* 05-10; NSM Emley *Leeds* from 11; NSM Flockton cum Denby Grange from 11. *58 The Crofts, Emley, Huddersfield HD8 9RU* T/F: (01924) 840738 M: 07906-835309 E: anne@ayoung94.fsbusiness.co.uk

YOUNG, Arthur. b 65. Belf Bible Coll BTh 92. CITC 99. **d** 01 **p** 02. C Donaghadee *D & D* 01-04; I Tullylish 04-13; I Kill *D & G* from 13. *The Rectory, Kill Lane, Deansgrange, Blackrock, Co Dublin, Republic of Ireland* T: (00353) (1) 280 1721 *or* 289 6442 M: 86-055 7698 E: rectory@kotg.ie

YOUNG, Canon Brian Thomas. b 42. Linc Th Coll 67. **d** 70 **p** 71. C Monkseaton St Mary *Newc* 70-73; C Berwick H Trin 73-77; P-in-c Gt Broughton *Carl* 77-80; V Gt Broughton and Broughton Moor 80-83; V Chorley *Ches* 83-90; V Alderley Edge 90-07; RD Knutsford 96-06; Hon Can Ches Cathl 97-07; rtd 07. *6 St Denys Avenue, Sleaford NG34 8AR* T: (01529) 306332 E: byoung@alderley.fsworld.co.uk

YOUNG, Canon Charles John. b 24. Open Univ BA 98. Qu Coll Birm 52. **d** 55 **p** 56. C Dudley St Thos and St Luke *Worc* 55-58; C Beeston *S'well* 58-61; V Lady Bay 61-66; R Kirkby in Ashfield 66-75; V Balderton 75-92; RD Newark 82-90; Hon Can S'well Minster 84-92; rtd 92; Bp's Chapl for Rtd Clergy *S'well* 92-04; PtO from 04. *9 The Paddocks, Newark NG24 1SS* T: (01636) 613445

YOUNG, Christopher Terence. b 53. Cape Town Univ BA 76 UNISA BTh 80. St Bede's Coll Umtata 79. **d** 80 **p** 81. S Africa 80-86 and from 88; C Rainham *Chelmsf* 86-88. *Riversong Cottage, 11 Church Street, Villiersdorp, 6848 South Africa* T/F: (0027) (28) 840 0841 M: 82-377 8401

✠**YOUNG, The Rt Revd Clive.** b 48. St Jo Coll Dur BA 70. Ridley Hall Cam 70. **d** 72 **p** 73 **c** 99. C Neasden cum Kingsbury St Cath *Lon* 72-75; C Hammersmith St Paul 75-79; P-in-c Old Ford St Paul w St Steph 79-82; V Old Ford St Paul w St Steph and St Mark 82-92; AD Tower Hamlets 88-92; Adn Hackney 92-99; V St Andr Holborn 92-99; Suff Bp Dunwich *St E* 99-13; rtd 13; Hon Asst Bp Heref from 13. *The Sycamores, Ewyas Harold, Hereford HR2 0JD* E: clive@2youngs.co.uk

YOUNG, Daniel George Harding. b 52. New Coll Ox BA 73 MA 83 Westmr Coll Ox PGCE 74. Cranmer Hall Dur 77. **d** 80 **p** 81. C Bushbury *Lich* 80-83; Chapl Dean Close Sch Cheltenham 83-99; Titus Trust 99-10; PtO *Win* 01-10; C Knutsford St Jo and Toft *Ches* from 10. *35 Beggarmans Lane, Knutsford WA16 9BA* T: (01565) 228216 M: 07974-945651 E: dan-young@tiscali.co.uk

YOUNG, David. b 37. STh 79 Open Univ PhD 89. Ely Th Coll 61 Linc Th Coll 64. **d** 67 **p** 68. C Crofton *Wakef* 67-68; C Heckmondwike 68-71; V Stainland 71-76; R Patrington w Winestead *York* 76-80; Chapl Winestead Hosp 76-80; Gen Preacher *Linc* from 80; Chapl St Jo Hosp Linc 80-90; Chapl N Lincs Mental Health Unit 90-93; Chapl Linc Distr Healthcare NHS Trust 93-97; Dep Chapl 98-04; rtd 04. *Westview, Aisthorpe, Lincoln LN1 2SG* T: (01522) 730912

YOUNG, David Charles. b 54. Open Univ BA 95 PGCE 97 CQSW 82. SEITE 03. **d** 06 **p** 07. NSM Haywards Heath St Wilfrid *Chich* from 06. *4 Ashurst Place, Heath Road, Haywards Heath RH16 3EJ* T: (01444) 416074 M: 07921-144480 E: youngshouse1@yahoo.co.uk

YOUNG, David John. b 43. Nottm Univ BA 64 MPhil 89 Lambeth STh 87. Coll of Resurr Mirfield 64. **d** 66 **p** 67. C Warsop *S'well* 66-68; C Harworth 68-71; P-in-c Hackenthorpe Ch Ch *Derby* 71-72; TV Frecheville and Hackenthorpe 73-75; V Chaddesden St Phil 75-83; R Narborough and Huncote *Leic* 83-89; RD Guthlaxton I 87-90; Chapl Leic Univ 90-95; V Eyres Monsell 95-98; PtO 98-99; rtd 03. *57 Castle Fields, Leicester LE4 1AN* T: 0116-236 5634

YOUNG, David Lun Ming. b 81. Leeds Univ BA 02 St Jo Coll Dur BA 09. Cranmer Hall Dur 07. **d** 10 **p** 11. C Upper Armley *Ripon* 10-14; TV Moor Allerton and Shadwell *Leeds* from 14. *The Vicarage, 2 Church Farm Garth, Leeds LS17 8HD* M: 07736-678558 E: revdaveyoung@gmail.com

YOUNG, Derek John. b 42. St D Coll Lamp. **d** 73 **p** 74. C Griffithstown *Mon* 73-76; C Ebbw Vale 76-77; V Penmaen 77-81; V Penmaen and Crumlin 81-87; Chapl Oakdale Hosp Gwent 83-87; V New Tredegar *Mon* 87-99; V Llanfihangel Crucorney w Oldcastle etc 99-11; P-in-c from 12. *The Vicarage, Llanfihangel Crucorney, Abergavenny NP7 8DH* T: (01873) 890349

YOUNG, Mrs Diana Joan. b 56. St Hilda's Coll Ox BA 78 MA 82. Ripon Coll Cuddesdon 11. **d** 13 **p** 14. C Hampstead St Jo *Lon*

from 13. *122 Woodgrange Avenue, London N12 0PS*   T: (020) 7794 5808 E: diana.young@hampsteadparishchurch.org.uk

YOUNG, Emma. b 89. Trin Coll Ox BA 10 Aber Univ MTh 12. Ripon Coll Cuddesdon MTh 14. **d** 14 **p** 15. C Luton St Aug Limbury *St Alb* from 14. *25 Milburn Close, Luton LU3 4EH* T: (01582) 947145 M: 07593-652689
E: revd.emma.young@hotmail.co.uk

YOUNG, George William. b 31. Lon Coll of Div ALCD 55. **d** 56 **p** 57. C Everton Em *Liv* 56-58; C Halliwell St Pet *Man* 58-61; V Newburn *Newc* 61-67; P-in-c Tyler's Green *Ox* 67-69; V 69-80; LtO 80-84; Area Sec (W England) SAMS 80-84; Hon C Purley Ch Ch *S'wark* 84-87; V Beckenham St Jo *Roch* 87-92; rtd 92; PtO *S'wark* from 92. *9 Shortacres, High Street, Nutfield, Redhill RH1 4HJ* T: (01737) 822363
E: theyoungs88@yahoo.com

YOUNG, Mrs Hilary Antoinette Francesca. b 57. **d** 01 **p** 02. NSM Thorne *Sheff* 03-05; V Wigan St Jas w St Thos *Liv* 05-12; P-in-c Settle *Leeds* from 12; P-in-c Giggleswick and Rathmell w Wigglesworth from 12. *The Vicarage, 2 Townhead Way, Settle BD24 9RG* T: (01729) 824191
E: h.young009@btinternet.com

YOUNG, Hyacinth Loretta. b 49. NTMTC 95. **d** 98 **p** 99. NSM Harlesden All So *Lon* 98-00; TV Wembley Park 00-12; V Tokyngton St Mich from 12. *The Vicarage, St Michael's Avenue, Wembley HA9 6SL* T: (020) 8902 3290
E: hyacinth512@aol.com

YOUNG, Iain Clavering. b 56. Newc Poly BA 79. Coll of Resurr Mirfield 80. **d** 83 **p** 84. C Wallsend St Luke *Newc* 83-86; C Horton 86-87; V 87-92; V Friern Barnet St Pet le Poer *Lon* 92-95; C Holborn St Alb w Saffron Hill St Pet 96-97; P-in-c Hoxton H Trin w St Mary 97-02; V 02-09; Chapl Moorfields Eye Hosp NHS Trust 97-03; P-in-c Lavender Hill Ascension etc *S'wark* 09-12; V from 12. *The Clergy House, Pountney Road, London SW11 5TU* T: (020) 7228 5340
E: iain.young@ifightpoverty.com

YOUNG, James Andrew. b 80. St Jo Coll Nottm. **d** 14 **p** 15. C Horsham *Chich* from 14. *18 Queensway, Horsham RH13 5AY* M: 07903-813077 E: jimmy@christianjimmy.com

YOUNG, Mrs Janette. b 57. All SS Cen for Miss & Min. **d** 14 **p** 15. NSM Heatons *Man* from 14. *51 Sherwood Road, Denton, Manchester M34 2QE* T: 0161-336 3667
E: j.young583@btinternet.com

YOUNG, Jeremy Michael. b 54. Ch Coll Cam BA 76 MA 80 Lon Univ MTh 94. Coll of Resurr Mirfield 78. **d** 80 **p** 81. C Whitworth w Spennymoor *Dur* 80-83; C Boxmoor St Jo *St Alb* 83-86; V Croxley Green St Oswald 86-94; Dir Past Studies CITC 94-99; LtO *D & G* 99-03; PtO *B & W* from 06. *Westerley House, Tellisford, Bath BA2 7RL* T: (01373) 830920
E: jeremy_young@mac.com

YOUNG, John. *See* YOUNG, David John

YOUNG, Canon John David. b 37. Lon Univ BD 65 Sussex Univ MA 77. Clifton Th Coll 62. **d** 65 **p** 66. C Plymouth St Jude *Ex* 65-68; Hd of RE Northgate Sch Ipswich 68-71; Chapl and Sen Lect Bp Otter Coll Chich 71-81; Chapl and Sen Lect W Sussex Inst of HE 77-81; Chapl and Sen Lect York St Jo Coll 81-87; C York St Paul 87-88; Dioc Ev 88-02; Can and Preb York Minster 92-03; Miss Strategy Development Officer 00-02; rtd 02; LtO *York* 02-10; PtO from 10. *72 Middlethorpe Grove, York YO24 1JY* T: (01904) 704195
E: john.young@yorkcourses.co.uk

YOUNG, John Kenneth. Edin Th Coll 62. **d** 64 **p** 65. C Gosforth All SS *Newc* 64-67; C Newc St Gabr 67-69; R Bowers Gifford *Chelmsf* 69-72; R Bowers Gifford w N Benfleet 72-75; P-in-c Kirkwhelpington *Newc* 75-79; P-in-c Kirkharle 77-79; P-in-c Kirkheaton 75-79; P-in-c Cambo 77-79; V Kirkwhelpington, Kirkharle, Kirkheaton and Cambo 79-82; V Gosforth St Nic 82-92; V Healey and Slaley 92-97; rtd 97; PtO *Newc* from 97. *1 Raynes Close, Morpeth NE61 2XX* T: (01670) 515191

YOUNG, John Robert. b 43. SSM 63. **d** 68 **p** 69. C Ch Ch Cathl Darwin Australia 68-70; C Murrumbeena 70-72; C Stocking Farm *Leic* 72-74; P-in-c W Reservoir Australia 75-78; I Montmorency 78-85; I E Burwood 85-96; R Warracknabeal 96-00; R Port Fairy 00-05; R Yea from 05. *St Luke's Rectory, Pellisier Street, PO Box 60, Yea Vic 3717, Australia* T: (0061) (3) 5797 2281 F: 5797 2082

YOUNG, Canon Jonathan Frederick. b 25. Univ of Wales (Lamp) BA 51 Birm Univ MA 81. St Mich Coll Llan 51. **d** 53 **p** 54. C Roath St Martin *Llan* 53-59; LtO *Ov* 59-74; SSJE 62-71; Bp's Chapl for Community Relns Birm 71-74; Chapl Coun for Soc Resp 74-85; Hon Can Birm Cathl 84-85; USA from 85; rtd 90. *204 Linden Ponds Way, Apt WC418, Hingham MA 02043, USA* T: (001) (781) 749 7077
E: youngmj@aol.com

YOUNG, Canon Jonathan Priestland. b 44. AKC 68. **d** 69 **p** 70. C Clapham H Trin *S'wark* 69-73; C Mitcham St Mark 73-74;

V Godmanchester *Ely* 74-82; P-in-c Cambridge St Giles w St Pet 82; P-in-c Chesterton St Luke 82; TR Cambridge Ascension 82-01; Chapl St Jo Coll Sch Cam 88-93; P-in-c Ellington *Ely* 01-02; P-in-c Grafham 01-02; P-in-c Easton 01-02; P-in-c Spaldwick w Barham and Woolley 01-02; R E Leightonstone 02-14; P-in-c Alconbury cum Weston 04-11; P-in-c Buckworth 04-11; P-in-c Hamerton 09-11; P-in-c Winwick 09-11; P-in-c Gt w Lt Gidding and Steeple Gidding 09-11; RD Leightonstone 02-04; Hon Can Ely Cathl 01-14; rtd 14; PtO *Ely* from 14. *Charis House, 15 The Causeway, Godmanchester, Huntingdon PE29 2HA* T: (01480) 453350
E: jonathan.young@ely.anglican.org

YOUNG, Joshua Mark. b 87. Nottm Univ BA 10. Ripon Coll Cuddesdon MTh 13. **d** 13 **p** 14. C Welwyn Garden City *St Alb* from 13. *25 Milburn Close, Luton LU3 4EH* M: 07957-978184 T: (01582) 947145
E: revdjoshyoung@hotmail.co.uk

YOUNG, Karen Georgina. b 58. Cranmer Hall Dur. **d** 13 **p** 14. C Chich St Paul and Westhampnett from 13. *37 Somerstown, Chichester PO19 6AL* M: 07836-254320
E: karenyoung58@gmail.com

YOUNG, Karen Heather. b 66. Nottm Univ BA 01. Westcott Ho Cam 02. **d** 05 **p** 07. C Airedale w Fryston *Wakef* 05-06; Hon C Ravenshead *S'well* 07-09; Mental Health Chapl Notts Healthcare NHS Trust 08-09; NSM Shill Valley and Broadshire *Ox* from 14. *The Vicarage, Filkins, Lechlade GL7 3JQ*

YOUNG, Kathleen Margaret. *See* BROWN, Kathleen Margaret

YOUNG, Kenneth. *See* YOUNG, John Kenneth

YOUNG, Leonard Thomas. b 55. Ches Coll of HE BTh 04 Leeds Univ MA 06. Coll of Resurr Mirfield 04. **d** 06 **p** 07. C Failsworth H Family *Man* 06-09; P-in-c Man Clayton St Cross w St Paul 09-15; R from 15. *St Cross Rectory, 54 Clayton Hall Road, Manchester M11 4WH* T: 0161-223 0766
E: frleonardyoung@aol.com

YOUNG, Mandy Elizabeth. b 58. Leeds Univ BA 91 PhD 94. SEITE 11. **d** 14. C Snodland All SS w Ch Ch *Roch* from 14. *20 Lewis Mews, Snodland ME6 5LN* T: (01634) 249446 M: 07551-993619 E: mandyyoung612@outlook.com

YOUNG, Margaret Dorothy. *See* COOLING, Margaret Dorothy

YOUNG, Mrs Margaret Elizabeth. b 66. Open Univ BSc 00. All SS Cen for Miss & Min 07. **d** 10 **p** 11. C Wythenshawe *Man* 10-13; TV 13-15; V Easingwold w Raskelf *York* from 15. *The Vicarage, Church Hill, Easingwold, York YO61 3JT* T: (01347) 821394 E: margareteyoung@btopenworld.com

YOUNG, Mrs Margaret Rose. SNWTP. **d** 14 **p** 15. NSM Royton St Anne *Man* from 14. *24 Haymaker Rise, Wardle, Rochdale OL12 9LA* T: (01706) 376309 E: margaretathome@aol.com

YOUNG, Mark Gilbert Campbell. b 60. Mert Coll Ox BA 88. Wycliffe Hall Ox 86. **d** 91 **p** 92. C Holborn St Geo w H Trin and St Bart *Lon* 91-95; C St Pancras w St Jas and Ch Ch 95-99; V W Hampstead Trin 99-06; P-in-c W Hampstead St Cuth 01-06; Hon C Smithfield St Bart Gt 09-15; Hon C St Bart Less 12-15; Hon C Smithfield Gt St Bart from 15. *Parish Office, 6 Kinghorn Street, London EC1A 7HW* T: (020) 7606 5171
E: pastor@greatstbarts.com

YOUNG, Martin Edward. b 20. Oriel Coll Ox BA 41 MA 45. Cuddesdon Coll 41. **d** 43 **p** 44. C Newbury *Ox* 43-45; C Wymondham *Nor* 45-49; C Gt Berkhamsted *St Alb* 49-51; V Littlemore *Ox* 51-64; R Wootton w Quinton *Pet* 64-72; R Wootton w Quinton and Preston Deanery 72-78; V Welford w Sibbertoft 78-82; V Welford w Sibbertoft and Marston Trussell 82-88; rtd 88; PtO *Pet* 88-98. *2 Knutsford Lane, Long Buckby, Northampton NN6 7RL* T: (01327) 843929

YOUNG, Martin John. b 72. Univ Coll Lon BSc 93. Oak Hill Th Coll BA 01. **d** 01 **p** 02. C Heigham H Trin *Nor* 01-05; P-in-c Nor St Andr from 05. *24 Carnoustie, Norwich NR4 6AY* T: (01603) 498821 E: martin@standrewsnorwich.org *or* mjy@ntlworld.com

YOUNG, Mrs Maureen. b 47. SEITE 02. **d** 04 **p** 12. NSM Roughey *Chich* 04-11; NSM Rusper w Colgate 11-13; NSM Bishop's Lydeard w Lydeard St Lawrence etc *B & W* from 13. *The Rectory, Lydeard St Lawrence, Taunton TA4 3SF*
E: revdmaureen12@hotmail.co.uk

YOUNG, Maurice. *See* YOUNG, William Maurice

YOUNG, Max Jonathan. b 44. **d** 06 **p** 07. NSM Filey *York* 06-10; PtO *Ox* from 10. *8 Eastfield Court, Church Street, Faringdon SN7 8SL* T: (01367) 243120 E: max1234@btinternet.com

YOUNG, Michael. b 44. STETS 08. **d** 11 **p** 12. NSM Wareham *Sarum* from 11. *5 Tuckers Mill Close, Wareham BH20 5BS* T: (01929) 554207 E: myng220@btopenworld.com

YOUNG, Norman Keith. b 35. EAMTC 85. **d** 87 **p** 88. C Burwell *Ely* 87-91; V Swaffham Bulbeck and Swaffham Prior w Reach 91-92; V Barnby Dun *Sheff* 92-05; Ind Chapl 92-05; AD Doncaster 98-04; rtd 05; P-in-c Aspull St Eliz *Liv* 05-06; Hon C Haigh and Aspull 06-12; PtO *Leeds* from 12. *The Vicarage, 2 Townhead Way, Settle BD24 9RG* T: (01729) 824191
E: norman@youngvic.u-net.com

YOUNG, Philip Anderson. b 53. St Jo Coll Dur BA 75 Fitzw Coll Cam BA 78 MA 89. Ridley Hall Cam 75. **d** 78 **p** 79. C Surbiton St Andr and St Mark *S'wark* 78-80; NSM Aylsham *Nor* 04-05; C Bressingham w N and S Lopham and Fersfield 05-07; C Roydon St Remigius 05-07; V Heigham St Thos 07-12; Dioc Environmental Officer from 12. *Cambridge House, South Hill, Felixstowe IP11 2AA* M: 07527-574982 T: (01394) 809069 E: philipyoung@btinternet.com

YOUNG, Rachel Elizabeth. b 61. Man Univ MusB 82 Leeds Univ MA 09 Lon Inst of Educn PGCE 84. NOC 06. **d** 09 **p** 10. NSM Beverley Minster *York* 09-15; P-in-c Bishop Burton from 15; P-in-c Rowley w Skidby from 15; P-in-c Walkington from 15. *Address temp unknown* E: rachel.e.young@tesco.net

YOUNG, Richard Christian. b 65. Southn Univ LLB 87 Solicitor 91. St Jo Coll Nottm 02. **d** 04 **p** 05. C Alperton *Lon* 04-07; V Yiewsley from 07. *St Matthew's Vicarage, 93 High Street, Yiewsley, West Drayton UB7 7QH* T: (01895) 442093 M: 07886-782473 E: richard.youngsofyiewsley@gmail.com

YOUNG, Richard Michael. b 63. **d** 96 **p** 97. NSM Brunswick *Man* from 96. *2 Birch Grove, Rusholme, Manchester M14 5JY* T: 0161-225 0884 M: 07778-817784 E: richard_young@3igroup.com

YOUNG, Robert William. b 47. MRTPI 73. Cranmer Hall Dur 10. **d** 11 **p** 12. NSM Owlerton *Sheff* 11-12; P-in-c Wadsley 12-14; PtO 14-15; NSM Owlerton from 15. *101 Carr Road, Sheffield S6 2WY* T: 0114-231 3036 E: robwyoung101@gmail.com

YOUNG, Ruth. *See* YOUNG, Vivienne Ruth

YOUNG, Simon Robert. b 72. Trevelyan Coll Dur BSc 94 Fitzw Coll Cam BA 98. Westcott Ho Cam BA 98 CTM 99. **d** 99 **p** 15. C Plaistow St Mary *Roch* 99-00; C Kingsnorth and Shadoxhurst *Cant* 14-15; C Faversham from 15; C The Brents and Davington from 15. *19 Nobel Court, Faversham ME13 7SD* E: simonryoung@aol.com

YOUNG, Stephen. b 33. St Edm Hall Ox MA 61. St Jo Coll Nottm 75 ALCD 77. **d** 77 **p** 78. C Crofton *Portsm* 77-81; C Rainham *Chelmsf* 81-87; V Ramsgate Ch Ch *Cant* 87-98; rtd 98; PtO *Cant* 98-14. *9 Egerton Drive, Cliftonville, Margate CT9 9YE* T: (01843) 223071

YOUNG, Stephen Edward. b 52. K Coll Lon BD 73 AKC 73 Open Univ PhD 04 Ch Ch Coll Cant CertEd 74. **d** 75 **p** 76. C Walton St Mary *Liv* 75-79; C St Marylebone All SS *Lon* 83; C Pimlico St Gabr 83-85; Chapl Whitelands Coll of HE *S'wark* 85-88; Asst Chapl St Paul's Sch Barnes 88-91; Chapl 91-02; Chapl Dulwich Coll 02-11; Hon C Pimlico St Mary Bourne Street *Lon* 94-11; C Wilton Place St Paul 11-13; P-in-c Deal St Andr *Cant* from 13; P in O 91-11; Dep P in O from 11. *St Andrew's Rectory, St Andrew's Road, Deal CT14 6AS* M: 07847-289199

YOUNG, Steven Peter. b 81. Lon Inst BA 02 Leeds Univ BA 07 MA 08. Coll of Resurr Mirfield 05. **d** 08 **p** 09. C W Hendon

St Jo *Lon* 08-11; P-in-c Mill Hill St Mich from 11; C Mill Hill Jo Keble Ch from 11. *St Michael's Vicarage, 9 Flower Lane, London NW7 2JA* T: (020) 8959 1857 M: 07590-636912 E: steven_young81@hotmail.com

YOUNG, Stuart Kincaid. b 59. **d** 95 **p** 96. C Letchworth St Paul w Willian *St Alb* 95-00; V Pucklechurch and Abson *Bris* from 00. *The Vicarage, Westerleigh Road, Pucklechurch, Bristol BS16 9RD* T: 0117-937 2260 E: vicar@pucklechurchandabson.org.uk

YOUNG (*née* SMITH), Mrs Vivienne Ruth. b 57. St Jo Coll Dur BA 79. NOC 95. **d** 00 **p** 01. C Heckmondwike *Wakef* 00-03; TV Dewsbury 03-06; Community Miss Adv Livability from 06; PtO *Dur* from 15. *Livability, 50 Scrutton Street, London EC2A 4XQ* M: 07443-547906 E: ruth61157@gmail.com

YOUNG, William Maurice. b 32. St Jo Coll Nottm 80. **d** 81 **p** 82. C Harlescott *Lich* 81-84; V Hadley 84-94; rtd 94; PtO *Heref* from 94. *Old Chapel School, Newport Street, Clun, Craven Arms SY7 8JZ* T: (01588) 640846

YOUNGER, Jeremy Andrew. b 46. Nottm Univ BA 68 Bris Univ MA 71. Wells Th Coll 68. **d** 70 **p** 71. C Basingstoke *Win* 70-74; C Harpenden St Nic *St Alb* 74-76; Dir Communications 77-81; Chapl Sarum & Wells Th Coll 77-81; V Clifton All SS w St Jo *Bris* 81-84; Relig Affairs Producer BBC Radio Nottm *S'well* 84-86; C Bow w Bromley St Leon *Lon* 86-88; Projects and Min Manager Westmr St Jas 89-93; Hon C St Marylebone All SS 89-93; New Zealand from 93. *1/102 Valley Road, Mount Eden, Auckland 1024, New Zealand* T: (0064) (9) 630 7867 E: jeremyyounger@clear.net.nz

YOUNGMAN, Christopher Anthony. b 65. Warwick Univ BSc 87. St Jo Coll Nottm 10. **d** 12 **p** 13. C Radcliffe-on-Trent and Shelford *S'well* 12-15; V Whitefriars Rushden *Pet* from 15. *18 Wymington Park, Rushden NN10 9JP* M: 07504-307418 E: chris.youngman@ntlworld.com

YOUNGS, Denise. b 60. WMMTC. **d** 09 **p** 10. NSM Lich St Mich w St Mary and Wall from 09. *10 Tame Avenue, Burntwood WS7 9JQ* T: (01543) 672646

YOUNGS-DUNNETT, Elizabeth Nigella. b 43. **d** 05 **p** 06. OLM Alde River *St E* 05-13; NSM 13; rtd 13; PtO *St E* from 14. *The Cottage, Ship Corner, Blaxhall, Woodbridge IP12 2DY* T: (01728) 688660 E: nigellaatblaxhall@btinternet.com

YOUNGSON, David Thoms. b 38. Cuddesdon Coll 71. **d** 73 **p** 74. C Norton St Mary *Dur* 73-76; C Hartlepool St Paul 76-79; P-in-c Stockton St Jo CD 79-84; V Stockton St Jo 84-86; V Owton Manor 86-90; rtd 90; PtO *Dur* 90-99. *35 Buxton Gardens, Billingham TS22 5AJ*

YULE, John David. b 49. G&C Coll Cam BA 70 MA 74 PhD 76. Westcott Ho Cam 79. **d** 81 **p** 82. C Cherry Hinton St Andr *Ely* 81-84; C Almondbury w Farnley Tyas *Wakef* 84-87; V Swavesey *Ely* 87-95; V Fen Drayton w Conington 87-95; R Fen Drayton w Conington and Lolworth etc 95-15; rtd 15. *Address temp unknown*

Z

ZAIDI-CROSSE, Philip Kenneth. b 63. **d** 05 **p** 06. NSM Erdington *Birm* 05-12. *Address temp unknown*

ZAIR, Richard George. b 52. Newc Univ BSc 74. Trin Coll Bris 75 Cranmer Hall Dur 79. **d** 80 **p** 81. C Bishopsworth *Bris* 80-83; C New Malden and Coombe *S'wark* 83-91; Dir of Evang CPAS 91-99; Regional Dir 99-09; P-in-c Marcham w Garford *Ox* 09-14; P-in-c Shippon 11-14; AD Abingdon from 13; V Marcham w Garford and Shippon from 14. *41 North Street, Marcham, Abingdon OX13 6NQ* T: (01865) 391319 M: 07411-234710 E: r_zair@yahoo.co.uk

ZAMMIT, Mark Timothy Paul. b 60. Ox Brookes Univ MA 07. Aston Tr Scheme 90 Sarum & Wells Th Coll 94. **d** 94 **p** 95. C Bitterne Park *Win* 94-98; TV Shaston *Sarum* 98-03; TR 03-08; RD Blackmore Vale 01-08; Chapl Port Regis Sch 99-08; P-in-c Durrington *Sarum* 08-11; C Avon Valley 08-11; TR Avon River 11-15; RD Stonehenge 10-15; TR Almondbury w Farnley Tyas *Leeds* from 15. *The Rectory, 2 Westgate, Almondbury, Huddersfield HD5 8XE* M: 07733-077957 T: (01484) 302914 E: zammitparish@yahoo.co.uk

ZANDSTRA-HOUGH, Wendy Lorraine. *See* HOUGH, Wendy Lorraine

ZANKER, Mrs Diana. b 39. Leeds Univ BA 01 Edge Hill Coll of HE TCert 59. NOC 04. **d** 05 **p** 06. NSM Leeds St Aid *Ripon* 05-11; NSM Leeds All So and St Aid from 11. *10 Mount Gardens, Leeds LS17 7QN* T: 0113-267 5893 E: revdiana@staidan-leeds.org.uk

ZAPHIRIOU, Paul Victor. b 49. Hamilton Coll (NY) BA 73 INSEAD MBA 74. Wycliffe Hall Ox 00. **d** 02 **p** 03. C Holborn St Geo w H Trin and St Bart *Lon* 02-06; V Holloway St Mary Magd from 06; Bp's Adv for Corporate Soc Resp from 05. *108 Liverpool Road, London N1 0RE* T: (020) 7226 0854 M: 07899-796409 E: paul.zaphiriou@n7parish.net

ZAREK, Jennifer Hilary. b 51. Newnham Coll Cam BA 72 MA 76 Southn Univ MSc 73 PhD 78 Ox Univ BTh 98 Garnett Coll Lon CertEd 83. St Steph Ho Ox 95. **d** 97 **p** 98. C Caterham *S'wark* 97-00; V Hutton Cranswick w Skerne, Watton and Beswick *York* 00-05; rtd 05; PtO *York* from 06. *Horsedale House, Silver Street, Huggate, York YO42 1YB* T: (01377) 288525 E: jzarek@btinternet.com

ZASS-OGILVIE, Ian David. b 38. MRICS 72 FRICS 80. AKC 65 St Boniface Warminster 65. **d** 66 **p** 67. C Washington *Dur* 66-70; Bp's Soc and Ind Adv for N Dur 70-73; Hon C Newc St Jo 73-75; V Tynemouth St Jo 75-78; Hon C St Marylebone St Mary *Lon* 78-81; V Bromley St Jo *Roch* 81-84; R Keith, Huntly and Aberchirder *Mor* 84-88; R Edin St Pet 88-00; Dir Churches' Regional Commn in the NE Newc and *Dur* 00-05; rtd 05; Chapl PtO *Ab* from 05; *Dur* from 05; Tutor St Chad's Coll from 06. *12 St Giles Close, Gilesgate, Durham DH1 1XH* T: 0191-383 0887 E: ianzassogilvie@tiscali.co.uk

ZEAL, Stanley Allan. b 33. Leeds Univ BA 55. Coll of Resurr Mirfield. **d** 57 **p** 58. C Perry Hill St Geo *S'wark* 57-61;

C Cobham *Guildf* 61-64; R Ash and V Ash Vale 64-69; V Aldershot St Mich 69-98; Chapl Northfield Hosp Aldershot 69-98; rtd 98; PtO *Llan* from 99. *4 Spencers Row, Cardiff CF5 2EP* T: (029) 2056 0778

ZIETSMAN, Sheila. d 90 **p** 91. C Geashill w Killeigh and Ballycommon *M & K* 90-91; C Mullingar, Portnashangan, Moyliscar, Kilbixy etc 91-96; Chapl Wilson's Hosp Sch Multyfarnham 91-96; Chapl E Glendalough Sch from 96. *East Glendalough School, Station Road, Wicklow, Republic of Ireland* T: (00353) (404) 69608 F: 68180

ZIHNI, Andrew Stephen. b 77. Mert Coll Ox BA 99 MA 06. St Steph Ho Ox BA 01. **d** 02 **p** 03. C Goldthorpe w Hickleton *Sheff* 02-06; Min Can Windsor 06-14; Chapl St Geo Sch Windsor 06-14; Asst Dioc Dir of Ords *S'wark* from 14. *Trinity House, 4 Chapel Court, London SE1 1HW* T: (020) 7939 9400 F: 7939 9468 E: frazihni4277@aol.com

ZIMMERMAN, Douglas Lee. b 69. Rhodes Coll Memphis BA 91. Virginia Th Sem MDiv 98. **d** 98. USA 98-14; TR Aylesbury *Ox* from 14. *St Mary's Vicarage, Parsons Fee, Aylesbury HP20 2QZ* M: 07939-106600 E: frdougz@gmail.com

ZIPFEL, Marilyn Ellen. b 48. Open Univ BA 94 MA 98 Goldsmiths' Coll Lon TCert 70 LTCL 97. Dioc OLM tr scheme 01. **d** 03 **p** 04. OLM Oulton Broad *Nor* from 03; Chapl Jas Paget Healthcare NHS Trust from 11. *James Paget Hospital, Lowestoft Road, Gorleston, Great Yarmouth NR31 6LA* T: (01493) 452408 M: 07818-093133 E: marilyn.zipfel@jpaget.nhs.uk

ZIPPERLEN, John Marcus. b 71. **d** 13 **p** 14. C Haverfordwest *St D* from 13. *St Thomas House, 3 Scarrowscant Lane, Haverfordwest SA61 1EP* T: (01437) 768365 E: marcus@zipperlen.com

ZORAB, Mark Elston. b 53. FRICS 77. Mon Dioc Tr Scheme 92. **d** 94. NSM Itton and St Arvans w Penterry and Kilgwrrwg w Devauden *Mon* from 94. *Oak Cottage, Itton Road, Chepstow NP16 6BQ* T: (01291) 626222 *or* 672138 E: fr.mark@elstons.co.uk

ZOTOV, Mrs Carolyn Ann. b 47. Lady Mabel Coll CertEd 68 Open Univ BA 78. EMMTC 91. **d** 92 **p** 94. NSM Hykeham *Linc* 92-94; NSM Aisthorpe w Scampton w Thorpe le Fallows etc 94; C Ingham w Cammeringham w Fillingham 94-97; C Linc Minster Gp 97-01; rtd 01; Assoc P Nettleham *Linc* from 01. *Greenleaves, 1 The Drive, Church Lane, Lincoln LN2 1QR* T: (01522) 525435 E: caz@greenleaves.fsnet.co.uk

ZUCCA, Peter Rennie. b 43. **d** 96 **p** 97. NSM Spotland *Man* 96-99; NSM Bamford 99-05; NSM Rochdale St Geo w St Alb 99-05; NSM Oakenrod and Bamford 05-13; rtd 13. *19 Judith Street, Rochdale OL12 7HS* T: (01706) 675830 *or* 346003

ZVIMBA, Josephat. b 60. SEITE. **d** 04 **p** 05. C W Norwood St Luke *S'wark* 04-07; V Dalston St Mark w St Bart *Lon* from 07. *St Mark's Vicarage, Sandringham Road, London E8 2LL* T: (020) 7241 1771 E: janjosh@talktalk.net

ZWALF, Canon Willem Anthony Louis (Wim). b 46. AKC 68. **d** 71 **p** 72. C Fulham St Etheldreda w St Clem *Lon* 71-74; Chapl City Univ 74-78; R Coalbrookdale, Iron-Bridge and Lt Wenlock *Heref* 78-90; V Wisbech SS Pet and Paul *Ely* 90-08; P-in-c Wisbech St Aug 03-04; C 04-08; RD Wisbech Lynn Marshland 02-08; Hon Can Ely Cathl 07-08; rtd 09; PtO *Pet* from 12. *1 The Dell, Oakham LE15 6JG* T: (01572) 770082 E: wimzwalf@aol.com

ZYCH, Berkeley James. b 83. SS Coll Cam BA 05 MSci 05 MA 08 PhD 09 Fitzw Coll Cam BA 12. Westcott Ho Cam 10. **d** 13 **p** 14. C Grimshoe *Ely* from 13. *19 Wilton Road, Feltwell, Thetford IP26 4AY* T: (01842) 827209 E: b.j.zych.01@cantab.net *or* berkeley@grimshoebenefice.com

DEACONESSES

BRIERLY, Margaret Ann. b 32. Dalton Ho Bris 54. **dss** 85. Wreningham *Nor* 85-86; Tetsworth, Adwell w S Weston, Lewknor etc *Ox* 86-95; rtd 95; PtO *Blackb* 03-15. *13 Pinewood Avenue, Brookhouse, Lancaster LA2 9NU*

BUTLER, Miss Ann. b 41. St Mich Ho Ox 67 Dalton Ho Bris IDC 69. **dss** 82. Bucknall and Bagnall *Lich* 82-87; Leyton St Mary w St Edw *Chelmsf* 89-96; Leyton St Mary w St Edw and St Luke 96-02; rtd 02; PtO *Lich* from 10. *40 Lichfield Street, Stone ST15 8NB* T: (01785) 818160

CARTER, Miss Crystal Dawn. b 49. SRN 77 RSCN 77. Trin Coll Bris 79. **dss** 82. Hengrove *Bris* 82-86; Dagenham *Chelmsf* 86-88; PtO 88-14. *35 Station Road, Rugeley WS15 2HE* M: 07762-849403

CHERRETT, Diana. *See* EVANS, Diana

COOPER, Janet Pamela. b 46. Glos Coll of Educn TCert 67 Ox Poly CETD 79. Trin Coll Bris. **dss** 83. Patchway *Bris* 83-88; PtO *Glouc* 90-96. *Ephraim Cottage, Kington Mead Farm, Kington Road, Thornbury, Bristol BS35 1PQ* T: (01454) 415280 E: jan.ephraimcottage@uhu.co.uk

DEE, Mary. b 21. St Chris Coll Blackheath 55. **dss** 64. Shottermill *Guildf* 63-66; Bishop's Waltham *Portsm* 66-72; Cumnor *Ox* 75-81; rtd 81. *49 Kingsley Avenue, 21 Coronation Avenue, Bournemouth BH9 1TB* T: (01202) 533662

ESSAM, Susan Catherine. b 46. Southn Univ BA 67 CertEd 68. Linc Th Coll. **dss** 80. Pershore w Pinvin, Wick and Birlingham *Worc* 78-82; CMS Nigeria from 83. *Bishopscourt, PO Box 6283, Jos 930001, Plateau State, Nigeria* T: (00234) (806) 876 9443 E: susanessam@aol.com

EVANS, Mrs Diana. b 59. Somerville Coll Ox BA 81 MA 85 Warwick Univ CertEd 96. St Steph Ho Ox 81. **dss** 84. Sherborne w Castleton and Lillington *Sarum* 84-88; Northampton St Paul *Pet* 93-98; Sec Dioc Adv Cttee 94-08; Hd Places of Worship Policy English Heritage from 08; LtO *Pet* 98-10. *21 Beaumont Street, London W1G 6DQ* T: (020) 7935 8965

GOUGH, Janet Ainley. b 46. SRN 67 RSCN 68 SCM 70. Dalton Ho Bris 70. **dss** 76. Leic H Apostles 73-80; Kansas City All SS USA 80-81; PtO *Leic* 81-96 and from 05. *410 Hinckley Road, Leicester LE3 0WA* T: 0116-285 4284 E: jangough@hotmail.com

HAMILTON, Miss Pamela Moorhead. b 43. SRN 64 SCM 66. Trin Coll Bris 75. **dss** 77. Derby St Pet and Ch Ch w H Trin 77-84; Bedworth *Cov* from 85; PtO from 13. *10 William Street, Bedworth, Nuneaton CV12 9DS* T: (024) 7649 1608 E: allsaints_bedworth@lineone.net

HARRIS, Audrey Margaret. *See* STOKES, Audrey Margaret

HARRISON, Mrs Ann. b 55. Ex Univ BSc 77. Linc Th Coll 79. **dss** 82. Acomb H Redeemer *York* 82-83; LtO *Wakef* 83-91. *24 The Manor Beeches, Dunnington, York YO19 5PX*

HEWITT, Miss Joyce Evelyn. b 30. SRN 51 SCM 55. St Mich Ho Ox IDC 61. **dss** 67. Spitalfields Ch Ch w All SS *Lon* 67-70; CMJ 71-73; Canonbury St Steph *Lon* 73-75; Chorleywood RNIB Coll for Blind Girls 75-80; rtd 90. *38 Ashridge Court, Station Road, Newbury RG14 7LL* T: (01635) 47829

HIDER, Ms Margaret Joyce Barbara. b 25. St Mich Ho Ox 52. **dss** 77. Bris H Cross Inns Court 77-84; Uphill *B & W* 84-89; rtd 89; PtO *B & W* 89-05. *15 Stuart Court, High Street, Kibworth, Leicester LE8 0LR* T: 0116-279 6885

HINDE, Miss Mavis Mary. b 29. Lightfoot Ho Dur. **dss** 65. Hitchin St Mary *St Alb* 65-68; Ensbury *Sarum* 69-70; Portsea St Alb *Portsm* 70-76; Houghton Regis *St Alb* 77-85; Eaton Socon 85-94; rtd 94; PtO *Ely* from 94. *8 Burnt Close, Eynesbury, St Neots PE19 2LZ* T: (01480) 218219 E: mavishinde@virginmedia.com

HORNBY-NORTHCOTE, Mrs Vivien Sheena. b 42. Birkbeck Coll Lon BA 91 Warwick Univ MA 96. Gilmore Course 74. **dss** 79. Mitcham St Olave *S'wark* 79-81; St Dunstan in the West *Lon* 82-86; St Marg Lothbury and St Steph Coleman Street etc 86; rtd 98. *3 Priory Mews, Sidney Street, Cheltenham GL52 6DJ* T: (01242) 525659

MacCORMACK, Mrs June Elizabeth. b 45. Ab Dioc Tr Course 82 St Jo Coll Nottm 85. **dss** 86. Bieldside *Ab* from 86. *5 Overton Park, Dyce, Aberdeen AB21 7FT* T: (01224) 722691 E: june@maccormack.co.uk

NORTHCOTE, Vivien. *See* HORNBY-NORTHCOTE, Vivien Sheena

OBEE, Sister Monica May. b 37. **dss** 82. Radford *Cov* 82-97; rtd 97. *23 Rowland Hill Almshouses, Feltham Hill Road, Ashford TW15 2DS*

OLIVER, Miss Kathleen Joyce. b 44. Man Univ BA 65. NOC 80. **dss** 83. Littleborough *Man* from 83. *Littleborough Christian Centre, 43 Todmorden Road, Littleborough OL15 9EA* T: (01706) 376477 F: 375520

OLPHIN, Miss Maureen Rose. b 30. Lon Univ BSc Sheff Univ DipEd. **dss** 84. Sheff StBarn and St Mary 84-90; rtd 90. *c/o G Johnson Esq, Mayfields, 1A Bishopton Lane, Ripon HG4 2QN* T: (01765) 607956

PIERSON, Mrs Valerie Susan. b 44. TCert 65. Trin Coll Bris 76. **dss** 79. Fulham St Matt *Lon* from 79. *48 Peterborough Road, London SW6 3EB* T: (020) 7731 6544 F: 7731 1858 E: sue@lancepierson.org

PRICE, Mrs Patricia Kate Lunn. *See* SCHMIEGELOW, Patricia Kate Lunn

RAINEY, Miss Irene May. b 14. RSCN 36 SCM 38. Gilmore Ho 69. **dss** 72. Filton *Bris* 70-74; Crowthorne *Ox* 74-79; rtd 79; PtO *Ely* 80-03. *12 Stevens Close, Cottenham, Cambridge CB24 8TT* T: (01954) 251634

SAMPSON, Miss Hazel. b 35. Lightfoot Ho Dur 58. **dss** 64. Fenton *Lich* 64-67; Gt Wyrley 67-69; Asst Chapl Manor Hosp Walsall 69-76; Lich St Mary w St Mich 76-95; rtd 95; PtO *Lich* 95-03. *107 Walsall Road, Lichfield WS13 8DD* T: (01543) 419664

SCHMIEGELOW, Patricia Kate Lunn. b 37. St Mich Ho Ox IDC 65. **dss** 86. The Hague *Eur* 86-89; PtO *Glouc* from 90; Gen Sec ICS 92-97; rtd 97. *61 Coln St Aldwyns, Cirencester GL7 5AJ* T/F: (01285) 750218

SKINNER, Mrs Elizabeth Alice. b 53. **dss** 82. Bourne *Guildf* 82-84. *145A Victoria Grove, Bridport DT6 3AG*

SPROSON, Doreen. b 31. St Mich Ho Ox IDC 58. **dss** 70. Wandsworth St Mich *S'wark* 68-71; Women's Sec CMS 71-74; Goole *Sheff* 74-76; Kirby Muxloe *Leic* 76-77; PtO *S'wark* 85-97; rtd 91. *20 Huggens' College, College Road, Northfleet, Gravesend DA11 9LL* T: (01474) 325262

STOKES, Audrey Margaret. b 39. Dalton Ho Bris 68. **dss** 82. Collier Row St Jas *Chelmsf* 82-85; Woking St Mary *Guildf* 85-95; rtd 95. *1 Greet Park Close, Southwell NG25 0EE*

SYMES, Miss Annabel. b 41. AIMLS 68. S Dios MinI Tr Scheme 79. **dss** 85. Chapl Asst Salisbury NHS Foundn Trust from 85; Barford St Martin, Dinton, Baverstock etc *Sarum* 89-01; Nadder Valley from 01. *7 Shaftesbury Road, Barford St Martin, Salisbury SP3 4BL* T: (01722) 744110

TAYLOR, Muriel. b 28. CA Tr Coll 48. **dss** 76. Gateshead Fell *Dur* 76-86; Gateshead Harlow Green 86-88; rtd 88. *22 Church Road, West Kirby, Wirral CH48 0RW*

THUMWOOD, Janet Elizabeth. b 30. STh 60. Trin Coll Toronto 58. **dss** 62. Canada 62-63; Mile End Old Town H Trin *Lon* 63-65; CSF 66-77; rtd 90. *24 Ramsay Hall, 11-13 Byron Road, Worthing BN11 3HN* T: (01903) 203586

TIER, Annabel. *See* SYMES, Annabel

WEBB, Sybil Janet. b 20. SRN 42 Wheaton Coll Illinois BA 07 SCM 43 MDiv 94 Spurgeon's Coll BD 94. Gilmore Course 69 Yorks Min Course Lindisfarne Regional Tr Partnership 13. **dss** 77. Worthing St Geo *Chich* 77-80; rtd 80; PtO *Chich* from 80. *Ringstead, 12 Roedean Road, Worthing BN11 2BP*

WRIGHT, Edith Mary. b 22. St Hugh's Coll Ox MA 46 DipEd 46. Gilmore Ho STh 58. **dss** 61. St Marylebone St Mary *Lon* 58-71; Lect Linc Th Coll 71-73; Oatlands *Guildf* 73-76; Roehampton H Trin *S'wark* 76-82; rtd 82. *26 Hazelwood Close, Harrow HA2 6HD* T: (020) 8863 7320

WRIGHT, Gloria Mary. b 40. **dss** 83. Smethwick St Matt w St Chad *Birm* 83-84; Tottenham H Trin *Lon* 84-86. *5 The Pastures, Anstey, Leicester LE7 7QR*

DIOCESAN, AREA, SUFFRAGAN AND ASSISTANT BISHOPS AND PROVINCIAL EPISCOPAL VISITORS IN ENGLAND, WALES, SCOTLAND AND IRELAND

BATH AND WELLS
Bishop of Bath and Wells — P HANCOCK
Honorary Assistant Bishops — B ROGERSON
G H CASSIDY
J F PERRY
P E BARBER
R F SAINSBURY
R H M THIRD
W M D PERSSON
Suffragan Bishop of Taunton — R E WORSLEY

BIRMINGHAM
Bishop of Birmingham — D A URQUHART
Honorary Assistant Bishops — I K MOTTAHEDEH
M H D WHINNEY
M SANTER
M W SINCLAIR
Suffragan Bishop of Aston — A E HOLLINGHURST

BLACKBURN
Bishop of Blackburn — J T HENDERSON
Honorary Assistant Bishops — C G ASHTON
D M HOPE OF THORNES
Suffragan Bishop of Burnley — P J NORTH
Suffragan Bishop of Lancaster — G S PEARSON

BRISTOL
Bishop of Bristol — M A HILL
Honorary Assistant Bishops — J M GOODALL
P J FIRTH
P ST G VAUGHAN
Suffragan Bishop of Swindon — L S RAYFIELD

CANTERBURY
Archbishop of Canterbury, Primate of All England and Metropolitan — J P WELBY
Honorary Assistant Bishops — A M A TURNBULL
J R A LLEWELLIN
M F GEAR
Suffragan Bishop of Dover — T WILLMOTT
Suffragan Bishop of Maidstone — R C H THOMAS
Suffragan Bishop of Ebbsfleet (Provincial Episcopal Visitor) — J M GOODALL
Suffragan Bishop of Richborough (Provincial Episcopal Visitor) — N BANKS

CARLISLE
Bishop of Carlisle — J W S NEWCOME
Honorary Assistant Bishops — A A K GRAHAM
G H THOMPSON
G L HACKER
I M GRIGGS
J H RICHARDSON
R C A HENDERSON
R M HARDY
Suffragan Bishop of Penrith — R J FREEMAN

CHELMSFORD
Bishop of Chelmsford — S G COTTRELL
Honorary Assistant Bishops — C D BOND
J M BALL
M T S MWAMBA
Area Bishop of Barking — P HILL
Area Bishop of Bradwell — J M WRAW
Area Bishop of Colchester — R A B MORRIS

CHESTER
Bishop of Chester — P R FORSTER
Honorary Assistant Bishops — C F BAZLEY
G G DOW
G H WEBSTER
G M TURNER
J D HAYDEN
W A PWAISIHO
Suffragan Bishop of Birkenhead — G K SINCLAIR
Suffragan Bishop of Stockport — E J H LANE

CHICHESTER
Bishop of Chichester — M C WARNER

Honorary Assistant Bishops — A D CHESTERS
C H MORGAN
D G ROWELL
D P WILCOX
K L BARHAM
L A GREEN
M E ADIE
M E MARSHALL
M L LANGRISH
M R J MANKTELOW
N S READE
Area Bishop of Horsham — M C R SOWERBY
Area Bishop of Lewes — R C JACKSON

COVENTRY
Bishop of Coventry — C J COCKSWORTH
Honorary Assistant Bishops — D R J EVANS
J M GOODALL
Suffragan Bishop of Warwick — J R A STROYAN

DERBY
Bishop of Derby — A L J REDFERN
Honorary Assistant Bishops — J NICHOLLS
R M C BEAK
R N INWOOD
Suffragan Bishop of Repton — *Vacant*

DURHAM
Bishop of Durham — P R BUTLER
Honorary Assistant Bishops — D S STANCLIFFE
J L PRITCHARD
Suffragan Bishop of Jarrow — M W BRYANT

ELY
Bishop of Ely — S D CONWAY
Honorary Assistant Bishops — G P KNOWLES
J B TAYLOR
J R FLACK
M A SEELEY
N BANKS
P S DAWES
R D WILLIAMS OF OYSTERMOUTH
S BARRINGTON-WARD
Suffragan Bishop of Huntingdon — D THOMSON

EXETER
Bishop of Exeter — R R ATWELL
Honorary Assistant Bishops — A M SHAW
G W E C ASHBY
J M GOODALL
R S HAWKINS
Suffragan Bishop of Crediton — S E MULLALLY
Suffragan Bishop of Plymouth — N H P MCKINNEL

GLOUCESTER
Bishop of Gloucester — R TREWEEK
Honorary Assistant Bishops — A M PRIDDIS
C J HILL
D W M JENNINGS
J R G NEALE
P B HARRIS
P J FIRTH
R J S EVENS
Suffragan Bishop of Tewkesbury — M J SNOW

GUILDFORD
Bishop of Guildford — A J WATSON
Honorary Assistant Bishops — C W HERBERT
M A BAUGHEN
N BANKS
Suffragan Bishop of Dorking — *Vacant*

HEREFORD
Bishop of Hereford — R M C FRITH
Honorary Assistant Bishop — C YOUNG
Suffragan Bishop of Ludlow — A J MAGOWAN

LEEDS (West Yorkshire and the Dales)
Bishop of Leeds	N BAINES
Suffragan Bishop of Bradford	T M HOWARTH
Suffragan Bishop of Huddersfield	J R GIBBS
Suffragan Bishop of Richmond	P J SLATER
Suffragan Bishop of Ripon	J H BELL
Suffragan Bishop of Wakefield	A W ROBINSON

LEICESTER
Bishop of Leicester	*Vacant*
Assistant Bishop	C J BOYLE

LICHFIELD
Bishop of Lichfield	*Vacant*
Honorary Assistant Bishops	D E BENTLEY
	I K MOTTAHEDEH
	J M GOODALL
Area Bishop of Shrewsbury	M J RYLANDS
Area Bishop of Stafford	G P ANNAS
Area Bishop of Wolverhampton	C M GREGORY

LINCOLN
Bishop of Lincoln	C LOWSON
Honorary Assistant Bishops	D D J ROSSDALE
	D G SNELGROVE
	D TUSTIN
	T W ELLIS
Suffragan Bishop of Grantham	N A CHAMBERLAIN
Suffragan Bishop of Grimsby	D E COURT

LIVERPOOL
Bishop of Liverpool	P BAYES
Honorary Assistant Bishops	C G ASHTON
	G H WEBSTER
	I C STUART
	S R LOWE
Suffragan Bishop of Warrington	R F BLACKBURN

LONDON
Bishop of London	R J C CHARTRES
Honorary Assistant Bishops	E HOLLAND
	M J COLCLOUGH
	S G PLATTEN
Area Bishop of Edmonton	R J WICKHAM
Suffragan Bishop of Fulham	J M R BAKER
Suffragan Bishop of Islington	*Vacant*
Area Bishop of Kensington	G S TOMLIN
Area Bishop of Stepney	A NEWMAN
Area Bishop of Willesden	P A BROADBENT

MANCHESTER
Bishop of Manchester	D S WALKER
Honorary Assistant Bishops	G G DOW
	G H WEBSTER
	J NICHOLLS
	R W N HOARE
Suffragan Bishop of Bolton	C P EDMONDSON
Suffragan Bishop of Hulme	*Vacant*
Suffragan Bishop of Middleton	M DAVIES

NEWCASTLE
Bishop of Newcastle	C E HARDMAN
Assistant Bishops	F WHITE
	J H RICHARDSON
	J R PACKER
	S G PLATTEN

NORWICH
Bishop of Norwich	G R JAMES
Honorary Assistant Bishops	A C FOOTTIT
	D K GILLETT
	D LEAKE
	J W SALT
	L G URWIN
	M J MENIN
	N BANKS
	P J FOX
	R GARRARD
	C J MEYRICK
	A P WINTON
Suffragan Bishop of Lynn	C J MEYRICK
Suffragan Bishop of Thetford	A P WINTON

OXFORD
Bishop of Oxford	*Vacant*
Honorary Assistant Bishops	A J RUSSELL
	A R M GORDON
	D W M JENNINGS
	F H A RICHMOND
	H I J SOUTHERN
	H W SCRIVEN
	J H GARTON
	J M GOODALL
	J N JOHNSON
	J S WENT
	K A ARNOLD
	P J NOTT
	W J D DOWN
Area Bishop of Buckingham	A T L WILSON
Area Bishop of Dorchester	C W FLETCHER
Area Bishop of Reading	A J PROUD

PETERBOROUGH
Bishop of Peterborough	D S ALLISTER
Honorary Assistant Bishop	J R FLACK
Suffragan Bishop of Brixworth	J E HOLBROOK

PORTSMOUTH
Bishop of Portsmouth	C R J FOSTER
Honorary Assistant Bishops	D G ROWELL
	J W HIND
	T J BAVIN

ROCHESTER
Bishop of Rochester	J H LANGSTAFF
Honorary Assistant Bishop	M F GEAR
Suffragan Bishop of Tonbridge	*Vacant*

ST ALBANS
Bishop of St Albans	A G C SMITH
Honorary Assistant Bishops	N BANKS
	R J N SMITH
	S S VENNER
Suffragan Bishop of Bedford	R W B ATKINSON
Suffragan Bishop of Hertford	N M R BEASLEY

ST EDMUNDSBURY AND IPSWICH
Bishop of St Edmundsbury and Ipswich	M A SEELEY
Honorary Assistant Bishops	G D J WALSH
	G H REID
	G P KNOWLES
	J A K MILLAR
	J WAINE
	N BANKS
Suffragan Bishop of Dunwich	*Vacant*

SALISBURY
Bishop of Salisbury	N R HOLTAM
Honorary Assistant Bishops	D M HALLATT
	J D G KIRKHAM
	J K CAVELL
Area Bishop of Ramsbury	E F CONDRY
Area Bishop of Sherborne	*Vacant*

SHEFFIELD
Bishop of Sheffield	S J L CROFT
Honorary Assistant Bishops	D C HAWTIN
	G H WEBSTER
	T W ELLIS
Suffragan Bishop of Doncaster	P BURROWS

SODOR AND MAN
Bishop of Sodor and Man	R M E PATERSON

SOUTHWARK
Bishop of Southwark	C T J CHESSUN
Honorary Assistant Bishops	D J ATKINSON
	G R KINGS
	M D DOE
	P S M SELBY
	P W WHEATLEY
	R D HARRIES OF PENTREGARTH
	S G PLATTEN
	W N STOCK
Area Bishop of Croydon	J D CLARK
Area Bishop of Kingston-upon-Thames	R I CHEETHAM
Area Bishop of Woolwich	M G IPGRAVE

SOUTHWELL AND NOTTINGHAM
Bishop of Southwell and Nottingham	P G WILLIAMS
Honorary Assistant Bishops	J T FINNEY
	M W JARRETT
	R J MILNER
	R K WILLIAMSON
Suffragan Bishop of Sherwood	A PORTER

TRURO
Bishop of Truro — T M THORNTON
Suffragan Bishop of St Germans — C D GOLDSMITH

WINCHESTER
Bishop of Winchester — T J DAKIN
Honorary Assistant Bishops — C W HERBERT
H W SCRIVEN
J A ELLISON
J DENNIS
T J BAVIN
Suffragan Bishop of Basingstoke — D G WILLIAMS
Suffragan Bishop of Southampton — J H FROST

WORCESTER
Bishop of Worcester — J G INGE
Honorary Assistant Bishops — C J MAYFIELD
H V TAYLOR
J M GOODALL
J RUHUMULIZA
M SANTER
Suffragan Bishop of Dudley — G B USHER

YORK
Archbishop of York, Primate of England and Metropolitan — J T M SENTAMU
Honorary Assistant Bishops — C C BARKER
D G GALLIFORD
D J SMITH

Suffragan Bishop of Hull — A M WHITE
Suffragan Bishop of Selby — J B THOMSON
Suffragan Bishop of Whitby — P J FERGUSON
Suffragan Bishop of Beverley (Provincial Episcopal Visitor) — G H WEBSTER

GIBRALTAR IN EUROPE
Bishop of Gibraltar in Europe — R N INNES
Honorary Assistant Bishops — A M A TURNBULL
D J SMITH
D S STANCLIFFE
E HOLLAND
F L SOARES
F-R MULLER
J B TAYLOR
J G VOBBE
J R FLACK
M J COLCLOUGH
M R J MANKTELOW
N S READE
P B HARRIS
P W WHALON
R GARRARD
S S VENNER
Suffragan Bishop in Europe — D HAMID

G BATES
J S JONES
M HENSHALL
R G G FOLEY

CHURCH IN WALES

ST ASAPH
Bishop of St Asaph — G K CAMERON

BANGOR
Bishop of Bangor — A T G JOHN

ST DAVIDS
Bishop of St Davids — J W EVANS

LLANDAFF
Bishop of Llandaff — B C MORGAN
Assistant Bishop — D J WILBOURNE

MONMOUTH
Bishop of Monmouth — R E PAIN

SWANSEA AND BRECON
Bishop of Swansea and Brecon — J D E DAVIES
Honorary Assistant Bishops — E W M WALKER
LORD CAREY OF CLIFTON
J K OLIVER

SCOTTISH EPISCOPAL CHURCH

ABERDEEN AND ORKNEY
Bishop of Aberdeen and Orkney — R A GILLIES

ARGYLL AND THE ISLES
Bishop of Argyll and The Isles — K PEARSON

BRECHIN
Bishop of Brechin — N PEYTON

EDINBURGH
Bishop of Edinburgh — J A ARMES

GLASGOW AND GALLOWAY
Bishop of Glasgow and Galloway — G D DUNCAN
Honorary Assistant Bishop — J M TAYLOR

MORAY, ROSS AND CAITHNESS
Bishop of Moray, Ross and Caithness — M J STRANGE

ST ANDREWS, DUNKELD AND DUNBLANE
Bishop of St Andrews, Dunkeld and Dunblane — D R CHILLINGWORTH

CHURCH OF IRELAND

ARMAGH
Archbishop of Armagh and Primate of All Ireland and Metropolitan — R L CLARKE

CASHEL AND OSSORY
Bishop of Cashel and Ossory — M A J BURROWS

CLOGHER
Bishop of Clogher — F J MCDOWELL

CONNOR
Bishop of Connor — A F ABERNETHY

CORK, CLOYNE AND ROSS
Bishop of Cork, Cloyne and Ross — W P COLTON

DERRY AND RAPHOE
Bishop of Derry and Raphoe — K R GOOD

DOWN AND DROMORE
Bishop of Down and Dromore — H C MILLER

DUBLIN AND GLENDALOUGH
Archbishop of Dublin, Bishop of Glendalough, Primate of Ireland and Metropolitan — M G ST A JACKSON

KILMORE, ELPHIN AND ARDAGH
Bishop of Kilmore, Elphin and Ardagh — S F GLENFIELD

LIMERICK AND KILLALOE
Bishop of Limerick and Killaloe — K A KEARON

MEATH AND KILDARE
Bishop of Meath and Kildare — P L STOREY

TUAM, KILLALA AND ACHONRY
Bishop of Tuam, Killala and Achonry — P W ROOKE

BISHOPS IN THE HOUSE OF LORDS

The Archbishops of Canterbury and York, and the Bishops of London, Durham and Winchester always have seats in the House of Lords. Twenty-one of the remaining Diocesan Bishops also sit in the Upper House. In general those places are filled on the basis of seniority in office as a Diocesan Bishop, any vacant place being filled by the Diocesan Bishop who has been longest in office without sitting in the House of Lords. However, for a transitional period of ten years from 2015, if there is a female Diocesan Bishop in office when a vacancy arises, she (or the most senior female Diocesan Bishop, if more than one are in office) will take up the place. Translation of a Bishop from one See to another does not affect his or her right to sit in the House of Lords.

The Bishop of Sodor and Man and the Bishop of Gibraltar in Europe are not eligible to sit in the House of Lords, but the former has a seat in the Upper House of the Tynwald, Isle of Man.

ARCHBISHOPS

	Enthroned	Entered House of Lords
CANTERBURY	2011	2012
YORK	2005	2006

BISHOPS SITTING IN THE HOUSE OF LORDS
(as at 1 December 2015)

	Became Diocesan Bishop	Entered House of Lords
LONDON	1995	1996
DURHAM	2009	2014
WINCHESTER	2011	2012
CHESTER	1996	2001
NORWICH	1999	2004
BRISTOL	2003	2009
DERBY	2005	2010
BIRMINGHAM	2006	2010
WORCESTER	2007	2012
COVENTRY	2008	2013
TRURO	2008	2013
SHEFFIELD	2009	2013
ST ALBANS	2009	2013
CARLISLE	2009	2013
PETERBOROUGH	2010	2014
PORTSMOUTH	2010	2014
CHELMSFORD	2010	2014
ROCHESTER	2010	2014
ELY	2010	2014
SOUTHWARK	2011	2014
LEEDS	2011	2015
SALISBURY	2011	2015
GLOUCESTER	2015	2015
NEWCASTLE	2015	*awaiting introduction*

BISHOPS AWAITING SEATS IN THE HOUSE OF LORDS
(in order of seniority)

	Became Diocesan Bishop
LINCOLN	2011
CHICHESTER	2012
BLACKBURN	2013
MANCHESTER	2013
BATH AND WELLS	2014
EXETER	2014
LIVERPOOL	2014
HEREFORD	2014
GUILDFORD	2014
ST EDMUNDSBURY & IPSWICH	2015
SOUTHWELL & NOTTINGHAM	2015

HISTORICAL SUCCESSION OF ARCHBISHOPS AND BISHOPS

In a number of dioceses, especially for the mediaeval period, the dating of some episcopal appointments is not known for certain. For ease of reference, the date of consecration is given when known, or, in the case of more modern appointments, the date of confirmation of election. More information on the dates of individual bishops can be found in the Royal Historical Society's *Handbook of British Chronology*.

ENGLAND

PROVINCE OF CANTERBURY

Canterbury

Description of arms. Azure, an archiepiscopal cross in pale or surmounted by a pall proper charged with four crosses patée fitchée sable.

597	Augustine
604	Laurentius
619	Mellitus
624	Justus
627	Honorius
655	Deusdedit
668	Theodorus
693	Berhtwald
731	Tatwine
735	Nothelm
740	Cuthbert
761	Bregowine
765	Jaenberht
793	Æthelheard
805	Wulfred
832	Feologild
833	Ceolnoth
870	Æthelred
890	Plegmund
914	Æthelhelm
923	Wulfhelm
942	Oda
959	Ælfsige
959	Byrhthelm
960	Dunstan
c.988	Athelgar
990	Sigeric Serio
995	Ælfric
1005	Ælfheah
1013	Lyfing [Ælfstan]
1020	Æthelnoth
1038	Eadsige
1051	Robert of Jumièges
1052	Stigand
1070	Lanfranc
1093	Anselm
1114	Ralph d'Escures
1123	William de Corbeil
1139	Theobald of Bec
1162	Thomas Becket
1174	Richard [of Dover]
1184	Baldwin
1193	Hubert Walter
1207	Stephen Langton

1229	Richard le Grant
1234	Edmund Rich
1245	Boniface of Savoy
1273	Robert Kilwardby
1279	John Pecham
1294	Robert Winchelsey
1313	Walter Reynolds
1328	Simon Mepham
1333	John Stratford
1349	Thomas Bradwardine
1349	Simon Islip
1366	Simon Langham
1368	William Whittlesey
1375	Simon Sudbury
1381	William Courtenay
1396	Thomas Arundel[1]
1398	Roger Walden
1414	Henry Chichele
1443	John Stafford
1452	John Kempe
1454	Thomas Bourgchier
1486	John Morton
1501	Henry Deane
1503	William Warham
1533	Thomas Cranmer
1556	Reginald Pole
1559	Matthew Parker
1576	Edmund Grindal
1583	John Whitgift
1604	Richard Bancroft
1611	George Abbot
1633	William Laud
1660	William Juxon
1663	Gilbert Sheldon
1678	William Sancroft
1691	John Tillotson
1695	Thomas Tenison
1716	William Wake
1737	John Potter
1747	Thomas Herring
1757	Matthew Hutton
1758	Thomas Secker
1768	Frederick Cornwallis
1783	John Moore
1805	Charles Manners Sutton
1828	William Howley
1848	John Bird Sumner
1862	Charles Thomas Longley
1868	Archibald Campbell Tait
1883	Edward White Benson
1896	Frederick Temple
1903	Randall Thomas Davidson
1928	Cosmo Gordon Lang
1942	William Temple
1945	Geoffrey Francis Fisher
1961	Arthur Michael Ramsey
1974	Frederick Donald Coggan
1980	Robert Alexander Kennedy Runcie
1991	George Leonard Carey
2002	Rowan Douglas Williams
2013	Justin Portal Welby

London

Description of arms. Gules, two swords in saltire argent hilts and pommels or.

	Theanus
	Eluanus
	Cadar
	Obinus
	Conanus
	Palladius
	Stephanus
	Iltutus
	Theodwinus
	Theodredus
	Hilarius
314	Restitutus
	Guitelinus
	Fastidius
	Vodinus
	Theonus
c.604	Mellitus
664	Cedd[2]
666	Wini
675	Eorcenwald
693	Waldhere
716	Ingwald
745	Ecgwulf
772	Wigheah
782	Eadbeorht
789	Eadgar
793	Coenwalh
796	Eadbald
798	Heathoberht
803	Osmund
c.811	Æthelnoth
824	Ceolberht
862	Deorwulf
898	Swithwulf
898	Heahstan
900	Wulfsige
c.926	Æthelweard
926	Leofstan
926	Theodred
—	Wulfstan I
953	Brihthelm
959	Dunstan
964	Ælfstan
996	Wulfstan II
1004	Ælfhun
1014	Ælfwig

---

[1] On 19 October 1399 Boniface IX annulled Arundel's translation to St Andrews and confirmed him in the See of Canterbury.
[2] See vacant for a term of years.

1035 Ælfweard
1044 Robert of Jumièges
1051 William
1075 Hugh of Orival
1086 Maurice
1108 Richard de Belmeis
1128 Gilbert [the Universal]
1141 Robert de Sigillo
1152 Richard de Belmeis II
1163 Gilbert Foliot
1189 Richard Fitz Neal
1199 William of Ste-Mere-Eglise
1221 Eustace de Fauconberg
1229 Roger Niger
1244 Fulk Basset
1260 Henry Wingham
1263 Henry of Sandwich
1274 John Chishull
1280 Richard Gravesend
1306 Ralph Baldock
1313 Gilbert Segrave
1317 Richard Newport
1319 Stephen Gravesend
1338 Richard Bintworth
1340 Ralph Stratford
1355 Michael Northburgh
1362 Simon Sudbury
1375 William Courtenay
1382 Robert Braybrooke
1404 Roger Walden
1406 Nicholas Bubwith
1407 Richard Clifford
1421 John Kempe
1426 William Gray
1431 Robert Fitz-Hugh
1436 Robert Gilbert
1450 Thomas Kempe
1489 Richard Hill
1496 Thomas Savage
1502 William Warham
1504 William Barons [Barnes]
1506 Richard Fitz-James
1522 Cuthbert Tunstall [Tonstall]
1530 John Stokesley
1540 Edmund Bonner
1550 Nicholas Ridley
1553 Edmund Bonner (restored)
1559 Edmund Grindal
1570 Edwin Sandys
1577 John Aylmer
1595 Richard Fletcher
1597 Richard Bancroft
1604 Richard Vaughan
1607 Thomas Ravis
1610 George Abbot
1611 John King
1621 George Monteigne [Mountain]
1628 William Laud
1633 William Juxon
1660 Gilbert Sheldon
1663 Humfrey Henchman
1676 Henry Compton
1714 John Robinson
1723 Edmund Gibson
1748 Thomas Sherlock
1761 Thomas Hayter
1762 Richard Osbaldeston
1764 Richard Terrick
1778 Robert Lowth
1787 Beilby Porteus
1809 John Randolph
1813 William Howley
1828 Charles James Blomfield
1856 Archibald Campbell Tait
1869 John Jackson
1885 Frederick Temple
1897 Mandell Creighton
1901 Arthur Foley Winnington-
      Ingram
1939 Geoffrey Francis Fisher
1945 John William Charles Wand

1956 Henry Colville Montgomery
      Campbell
1961 Robert Wright Stopford
1973 Gerald Alexander Ellison
1981 Graham Douglas Leonard
1991 David Michael Hope
1995 Richard John Carew Chartres

Westminster[1]

1540 Thomas Thirlby

Winchester

Description of arms. Gules, two keys endorsed and conjoined at the bows in bend, the upper or, the lower argent, between which a sword in bend sinister of the third, hilt and pommel gold.

BISHOPS OF THE WEST SAXONS

634 Birinus
650 Ægilberht

BISHOPS OF WINCHESTER

660 Wine
670 Leutherius
676 Haedde
705 Daniel
744 Hunfrith
756 Cyneheard
778 Æthelheard
778 Ecbald
785 Dudd
c.785 Cyneberht
803 Eahlmund
814 Wigthegn
825 Herefrith[2]
838 Eadmund
c.838 Eadhun
839 Helmstan
852 Swithhun
867 Ealhferth
877 Tunberht
879 Denewulf
909 Frithestan
931 Byrnstan
934 Ælfheah I
951 Ælfsige I
960 Brihthelm
963 Æthelwold I
984 Ælfheah II
1006 Cenwulf
1006 Æthelwold II
c.1014 Ælfsige II
1032 Ælfwine
1043 Stigand
      Ælfsige III?
1070 Walkelin
1107 William Giffard
1129 Henry of Blois
1174 Richard of Ilchester (Toclyve)
1189 Godfrey de Lucy
1205 Peter des Roches
1244 Will. de Raleigh
1260 Aymer de Valance [of Lusignan]
1262 John Gervaise

1268 Nicholas of Ely
1282 John of Pontoise
1305 Henry Merewell [or Woodlock]
1316 John Sandale
1320 Rigaud of Assier
1323 John Stratford
1333 Adam Orleton
1346 William Edendon [Edington]
1367 William of Wykeham
1404 Henry Beaufort
1447 William of Waynflete
1487 Peter Courtenay
1493 Thomas Langton
1501 Richard Fox
1529 Thomas Wolsey
1531 Stephen Gardiner (deposed)
1551 John Ponet [Poynet]
1553 Stephen Gardiner (restored)
1556 John White (deposed)
1561 Robert Horne
1580 John Watson
1584 Thomas Cowper [Cooper]
1595 William Wickham [Wykeham]
1596 William Day
1597 Thomas Bilson
1616 James Montague
1619 Lancelot Andrewes
1628 Richard Neile
1632 Walter Curll
1660 Brian Duppa
1662 George Morley
1684 Peter Mews
1707 Jonathan Trelawney
1721 Charles Trimnell
1723 Richard Willis
1734 Benjamin Hoadly
1761 John Thomas
1781 Brownlow North
1820 George Pretyman Tomline
1827 Charles Richard Sumner
1869 Samuel Wilberforce
1873 Edward Harold Browne
1891 Anthony Wilson Thorold
1895 Randall Thomas Davidson
1903 Herbert Edward Ryle
1911 Edward Stuart Talbot
1923 Frank Theodore Woods
1932 Cyril Forster Garbett
1942 Mervyn George Haigh
1952 Alwyn Terrell Petre Williams
1961 Sherard Falkner Allison
1975 John Vernon Taylor
1985 Colin Clement Walter James
1995 Michael Charles Scott-Joynt
2011 Timothy John Dakin

Bath and Wells

Description of arms. Azure, a saltire per saltire quarterly counterchanged or and argent.

BISHOPS OF WELLS

909 Athelm
925 Wulfhelm I
928 Ælfheah
938 Wulfhelm II
956 Byrhthelm

---

[1] Indicates a diocese no longer extant, or united with another diocese.
[2] Never signed without Wigthegn.

974 Cyneweard
979 Sigegar
997 Ælfwine
999 Lyfing
1013 Æthelwine (ejected)
1013 Beorhtwine (deposed)
    Æthelwine (restored)
    Beorhtwine (restored)
1024 Brihtwig [also Merehwit]
1033 Duduc
1061 Gisa
1088 John of Tours [de Villula]

BISHOPS OF BATH

1090 John of Tours [de Villula]
1123 Godfrey
1136 Robert
1174 Reg. Fitz Jocelin
1192 Savaric FitzGeldewin

BATH AND GLASTONBURY

1206 Jocelin of Wells

BATH AND WELLS

1244 Roger of Salisbury
1248 William Bitton I
1265 Walter Giffard
1267 William Bitton II
1275 Robert Burnell
1293 William of March
1302 Walter Hasleshaw
1309 John Droxford
1329 Ralph of Shrewsbury
1364 John Barnet
1367 John Harewell
1386 Walter Skirlaw
1388 Ralph Erghum
1401 Henry Bowet
1407 Nicholas Bubwith
1425 John Stafford
1443 Thomas Beckington
1466 Robert Stillington
1492 Richard Fox
1495 Oliver King
1504 Adriano de Castello [di
    Corneto]
1518 Thomas Wolsey
1523 John Clerk
1541 William Knight
1548 William Barlow
1554 Gilbert Bourne
1560 Gilbert Berkeley
1584 Thomas Godwin
1593 John Still
1608 James Montague
1616 Arthur Lake
1626 William Laud
1628 Leonard Mawe
1629 Walter Curll
1632 William Piers
1670 Robert Creighton
1673 Peter Mews
1685 Thomas Ken (deposed)
1691 Richard Kidder
1704 George Hooper
1727 John Wynne
1743 Edward Willes
1774 Charles Moss
1802 Richard Beadon
1824 George Henry Law
1845 Richard Bagot
1854 Robert John Eden, Lord
    Auckland
1869 Arthur Charles Hervey
1894 George Wyndham Kennion
1921 St John Basil Wynne Wilson
1937 Francis Underhill
1943 John William Charles Wand
1946 Harold William Bradfield
1960 Edward Barry Henderson
1975 John Monier Bickersteth
1987 George Leonard Carey
1991 James Lawton Thompson
2002 Peter Bryan Price
2014 Peter Hancock

Birmingham

Description of arms. Per pale indented or and gules, five roundels, two, two, and one, and in chief two crosses patée all counterchanged.

1905 Charles Gore
1911 Henry Russell Wakefield
1924 Ernest William Barnes
1953 John Leonard Wilson
1969 Laurence Ambrose Brown
1978 Hugh William Montefiore
1987 Mark Santer
2002 John Mugabi Sentamu
2006 David Andrew Urquhart

Bristol

Description of arms. Sable, three ducal coronets in pale or.

1542 Paul Bush
1554 John Holyman
1562 Richard Cheyney
1581 John Bullingham (held
    Gloucester and Bristol
    1586–9)
1589 Richard Fletcher
    [See vacant for ten
    years]
1603 John Thornborough
1617 Nicholas Felton
1619 Rowland Searchfield
1623 Robert Wright
1633 George Coke
1637 Robert Skinner
1642 Thomas Westfield
1644 Thomas Howell
1661 Gilbert Ironside
1672 Guy Carleton
1679 William Gulston
1684 John Lake
1685 Jonathan Trelawney
1689 Gilbert Ironside
1691 John Hall
1710 John Robinson
1714 George Smalridge
1719 Hugh Boulter
1724 William Bradshaw
1733 Charles Cecil
1735 Thomas Secker
1737 Thomas Gooch
1738 Joseph Butler
1750 John Conybeare
1756 John Hume
1758 Philip Yonge
1761 Thomas Newton
1782 Lewis Bagot
1783 Christopher Wilson
1792 Spencer Madan
1794 Henry Reginald Courtenay

1797 Ffolliott Herbert Walker
    Cornewall
1803 George Pelham
1807 John Luxmoore
1808 William Lort Mansel
1820 John Kaye
1827 Robert Gray
1834 Joseph Allen
[1836 to 1897 united with Gloucester]
1897 George Forrest Browne
1914 George Nickson
1933 Clifford Salisbury Woodward
1946 Frederick Arthur Cockin
1959 Oliver Stratford Tomkins
1976 Ernest John Tinsley
1985 Barry Rogerson
2003 Michael Arthur Hill

Chelmsford

Description of arms. Or, on a saltire gules a pastoral staff of the first and a sword argent, hilt and pommel gold.

1914 John Edwin Watts-Ditchfield
1923 Frederic Sumpter Guy Warman
1929 Henry Albert Wilson
1951 Sherard Falkner Allison
1962 John Gerhard Tiarks
1971 Albert John Trillo
1986 John Waine
1996 John Freeman Perry
2003 John Warren Gladwin
2010 Stephen Geoffrey Cottrell

Chichester

Description of arms. Azure, our blessed Lord in judgement seated in His throne, His dexter hand upraised or, His sinister hand holding an open book proper, and issuant from His mouth a two-edged sword point to the sinister gules.

BISHOPS OF SELSEY

681 Wilfrid
716 Eadberht
731 Eolla
733 Sigga [Sigeferth]
765 Aaluberht
c.765 Oswald [Osa]
780 Gislhere
786 Tota
c.789 Wihthun
c.811 Æthelwulf
824 Cynered
845 Guthheard
900 Wighelm
909 Beornheah
931 Wulfhun
943 Ælfred
955 Daniel

956	Brihthelm
963	Eadhelm
980	Æthelgar
990	Ordbriht
1009	Ælfmaer
1032	Æthelric I
1039	Grimketel
1047	Heca
1058	Æthelric II
1070	Stigand

BISHOPS OF CHICHESTER

1075	Stigand
1088	Godfrey
1091	Ralph Luffa
1125	Seffrid I [d'Escures Pelochin]
1147	Hilary
1174	John Greenford
1180	Seffrid II
1204	Simon FitzRobert
1215	Richard Poore
1218	Ranulf of Wareham
1224	Ralph Nevill
1245	Richard Wich
1254	John Climping
1262	Stephen Bersted [or Pagham]
1288	Gilbert de St Leoford
1305	John Langton
1337	Robert Stratford
1362	William Lenn
1369	William Reade
1386	Thomas Rushock
1390	Richard Mitford
1396	Robert Waldby
1397	Robert Reade
1417	Stephen Patrington
1418	Henry de la Ware
1421	John Kempe
1421	Thomas Polton
1426	John Rickingale
1431	Simon Sydenham
1438	Richard Praty
1446	Adam de Moleyns
1450	Reginald Pecock
1459	John Arundel
1478	Edward Story
1504	Richard Fitz-James
1508	Robert Sherburne
1536	Richard Sampson
1543	George Day (deposed)
1552	John Scory
1553	George Day (restored)
1557	John Christopherson
1559	William Barlow
1570	Richard Curtis
1586	Thomas Bickley
1596	Anthony Watson
1605	Lancelot Andrewes
1609	Samuel Harsnett
1619	George Carleton
1628	Richard Montague
1638	Brian Duppa
1642	Henry King
1670	Peter Gunning
1675	Ralph Brideoake
1679	Guy Carleton
1685	John Lake
1689	Simon Patrick
1691	Robert Grove
1696	John Williams
1709	Thomas Manningham
1722	Thomas Bowers
1724	Edward Waddington
1731	Francis Hare
1740	Matthias Mawson
1754	William Ashburnham
1798	John Buckner
1824	Robert James Carr
1831	Edward Maltby
1836	William Otter
1840	Philip Nicholas Shuttleworth
1842	Ashurst Turner Gilbert

1870	Richard Durnford
1896	Ernest Roland Wilberforce
1908	Charles John Ridgeway
1919	Winfrid Oldfield Burrows
1929	George Kennedy Allen Bell
1958	Roger Plumpton Wilson
1974	Eric Waldram Kemp
2001	John William Hind
2012	Martin Clive Warner

Coventry

Description of arms. Gules, within a bordure argent charged with eight torteaux, a cross potent quadrate of the second.

1918	Huyshe Wolcott Yeatman-Biggs
1922	Charles Lisle Carr
1931	Mervyn George Haigh
1943	Neville Vincent Gorton
1956	Cuthbert Killick Norman Bardsley
1976	John Gibbs
1985	Simon Barrington-Ward
1998	Colin James Bennetts
2008	Christopher John Cocksworth

Derby

Description of arms. Purpure, a cross of St Chad argent beneath three fountains in chief.

1927	Edmund Courtenay Pearce
1936	Alfred Edward John Rawlinson
1959	Geoffrey Francis Allen
1969	Cyril William Johnston Bowles
1988	Peter Spencer Dawes
1995	Jonathan Sansbury Bailey
2005	Alastair Llewellyn John Redfern

Dorchester[1]

634	Birinus
650	Agilbert
c.660	Ætla
c.888	Ahlheard

Ely

Arms of Ely.

Description of arms. Gules, three ducal coronets or.

1109	Hervey
1133	Nigel
1174	Geoffrey Ridel
1189	William Longchamp
1198	Eustace
1220	John of Fountains
1225	Geoffrey de Burgo
1229	Hugh of Northwold
1255	William of Kilkenny
1258	Hugh of Balsham
1286	John of Kirkby
1290	William of Louth
1299	Ralph Walpole
1303	Robert Orford
1310	John Ketton
1316	John Hotham
1337	Simon Montacute
1345	Thomas de Lisle
1362	Simon Langham
1367	John Barnet
1374	Thomas Arundel
1388	John Fordham
1426	Philip Morgan
1438	Lewis of Luxembourg
1444	Thomas Bourgchier
1454	William Grey
1479	John Morton
1486	John Alcock
1501	Richard Redman
1506	James Stanley
1515	Nicholas West
1534	Thomas Goodrich
1555	Thomas Thirlby
1559	Richard Cox
1600	Martin Heton
1609	Lancelot Andrewes
1619	Nicolas Felton
1628	John Buckeridge
1631	Francis White
1638	Matthew Wren
1667	Benjamin Laney
1675	Peter Gunning
1684	Francis Turner
1691	Simon Patrick
1707	John Moore
1714	William Fleetwood
1723	Thomas Greene
1738	Robert Butts
1748	Thomas Gooch
1754	Matthias Mawson
1771	Edmund Keene
1781	James Yorke
1808	Thomas Dampier
1812	Bowyer Edward Sparke
1836	Joseph Allen
1845	Thomas Turton
1864	Edward Harold Browne
1873	James Russell Woodford
1886	Alwyne Frederick Compton
1905	Frederick Henry Chase
1924	Leonard Jauncey White-Thomson
1934	Bernard Oliver Francis Heywood
1941	Harold Edward Wynn
1957	Noel Baring Hudson

---

[1] Originally a West Saxon, after Ahlheard's time a Mercian, bishopric. See transferred to Lincoln 1077.

1964 Edward James Keymer Roberts
1977 Peter Knight Walker
1990 Stephen Whitefield Sykes
2000 Anthony John Russell
2010 Stephen David Conway

Exeter

Description of arms. Gules, a sword
erect in pale argent hilt or surmounted
by two keys addorsed in saltire gold.

BISHOPS OF CORNWALL

870 Kenstec
893 Asser
931 Conan
950 Æthelge[ard]
c.955 Daniel
963 Wulfsige Comoere
990 Ealdred
1009 Æthelsige
1018 Buruhwold
1027 Lyfing, Bishop of Crediton,
    Cornwall and Worcester
1046 Leofric, Bishop of Crediton and
    Cornwall
[See transferred to Exeter 1050]

BISHOPS OF CREDITON

909 Eadwulf
934 Æthelgar
953 Ælfwold I
973 Sideman
979 Ælfric
987 Ælfwold II
1008 Ælfwold III
1015 Eadnoth
1027 Lyfing
1046 Leofric[1]

BISHOPS OF EXETER

1050 Leofric
1072 Osbern Fitz-Osbern
1107 Will. Warelwast
1138 Robert Warelwast
1155 Robert II of Chichester
1161 Bartholomew
1186 John the Chanter
1194 Henry Marshall
1214 Simon of Apulia
1224 William Brewer
1245 Richard Blund
1258 Walter Bronescombe
1280 Peter Quinel [Wyvill]
1292 Thomas Bitton
1308 Walter Stapeldon
1327 James Berkeley
1328 John Grandisson
1370 Thomas Brantingham
1395 Edmund Stafford
1419 John Catterick
1420 Edmund Lacy
1458 George Nevill
1465 John Booth
1478 Peter Courtenay
1487 Richard Fox
1493 Oliver King

1496 Richard Redman
1502 John Arundel
1505 Hugh Oldham
1519 John Veysey (resigned)
1551 Miles Coverdale
1553 John Veysey (restored)
1555 James Turberville
1560 William Alley [or Allei]
1571 William Bradbridge
1579 John Woolton
1595 Gervase Babington
1598 William Cotton
1621 Valentine Carey
1627 Joseph Hall
1642 Ralph Brownrigg
1660 John Gauden
1662 Seth Ward
1667 Anthony Sparrow
1676 Thomas Lamplugh
1689 Jonathan Trelawney
1708 Offspring Blackall
1717 Lancelot Blackburn
1724 Stephen Weston
1742 Nicholas Claget
1747 George Lavington
1762 Frederick Keppel
1778 John Ross
1792 William Buller
1797 Henry Reginald Courtenay
1803 John Fisher
1807 George Pelham
1820 William Carey
1830 Christopher Bethell
1831 Henry Phillpotts
1869 Frederick Temple
1885 Edward Henry Bickersteth
1901 Herbert Edward Ryle
1903 Archibald Robertson
1916 Rupert Ernest William
    Gascoyne Cecil
1936 Charles Edward Curzon
1949 Robert Cecil Mortimer
1973 Eric Arthur John Mercer
1985 Geoffrey Hewlett Thompson
1999 Michael Laurence Langrish
2014 Robert Ronald Atwell

Gibraltar in Europe

Description of arms. Argent, in base
rising out of the waves of the sea a
rock proper, thereon a lion guardant
or supporting a passion cross erect
gules, on a chief engrailed of the last
a crosier in bend dexter and a key in
bend sinister or surmounted by a
Maltese cross argent fimbriated gold.

BISHOPS OF GIBRALTAR

1842 George Tomlinson
1863 Walter John Trower
1868 Charles Amyand Harris
1874 Charles Waldegrave Sandford
1904 William Edward Collins
1911 Henry Joseph Corbett Knight
1921 John Harold Greig
1927 Frederick Cyril Nugent Hicks
1933 Harold Jocelyn Buxton

1947 Cecil Douglas Horsley
1953 Frederick William Thomas
    Craske
1960 Stanley Albert Hallam Eley
1970 John Richard Satterthwaite[2]

BISHOPS OF GIBRALTAR IN EUROPE

1980 John Richard Satterthwaite
1993 John William Hind
2001 Douglas Geoffrey Rowell
2014 Robert Neil Innes

Gloucester

Description of arms. Azure, two keys
addorsed in saltire the wards upwards
or.

1541 John Wakeman *alias* Wiche
1551 John Hooper
1554 James Brooks
1562 Richard Cheyney[3]
1581 John Bullingham[4]
1598 Godfrey Goldsborough
1605 Thomas Ravis
1607 Henry Parry
1611 Giles Thompson
1612 Miles Smith
1625 Godfrey Goodman
1661 William Nicolson
1672 John Pritchett
1681 Robert Frampton
1691 Edward Fowler
1715 Richard Willis
1721 Joseph Wilcocks
1731 Elias Sydall
1735 Martin Benson
1752 James Johnson
1760 William Warburton
1779 James Yorke
1781 Samuel Hallifax
1789 Richard Beadon
1802 George Isaac Huntingford
1815 Henry Ryder
1824 Christopher Bethell
1830 James Henry Monk
[1836 to 1897, united with Bristol]

BISHOPS OF GLOUCESTER AND
BRISTOL

1836 James Henry Monk
1856 Charles Baring
1861 William Thomson
1863 Charles John Ellicott[5]

BISHOPS OF GLOUCESTER

1897 Charles John Ellicott
1905 Edgar Charles Sumner Gibson
1923 Arthur Cayley Headlam
1946 Clifford Salisbury Woodward
1954 Wilfred Marcus Askwith
1962 Basil Tudor Guy
1975 John Yates
1992 Peter John Ball
1993 David Edward Bentley
2004 Michael Francis Perham
2015 Rachel Treweek

---

[1] Removed See from Crediton.
[4] Held Gloucester and Bristol 1581-9.

[2] Bishop of Fulham and Gibraltar from 1970 to 1980.
[5] Gloucester only from 1897.

[3] Also Bishop of Bristol.

Guildford

Description of arms. Gules, two keys conjoined wards outwards in bend, the uppermost or, the other argent, interposed between them in bend sinister a sword of the third, hilt and pommel gold, all within a bordure azure charged with ten wool-packs argent.

1927 John Harold Greig
1934 John Victor Macmillan
1949 Henry Colville Montgomery
   Campbell
1956 Ivor Stanley Watkins
1961 George Edmund Reindorp
1973 David Alan Brown
1983 Michael Edgar Adie
1994 John Warren Gladwin
2004 Christopher John Hill
2014 Andrew John Watson

Hereford

Description of arms. Gules, three leopards' faces jessant-de-lis reversed or.

676 Putta
688 Tyrhtel
710 Torhthere
c.731 Wahistod
736 Cuthberht
741 Podda
c.758 Acca
c.770 Headda
777 Aldberht
786 Esne
c.788 Ceolmund
c.798 Utel
801 Wulfheard
824 Beonna
c.832 Eadwulf
c.839 Cuthwulf
866 Mucel
c.866 Deorlaf
888 Cynemund
890 EadBar
c.931 Tidhelm
940 Wulfhelm
c.940 Ælfric
971 Æthelwulf
1016 Æthelstan
1056 Leofgar
1056 Ealdred, Bishop of Hereford and
   Worcester

1060 Walter
1079 Robert Losinga
1096 Gerard
1107 Reinhelm
1115 Geoffrey de Clive
1121 Richard de Capella
1131 Robert de Bethune
1148 Gilbert Foliot
1163 Robert of Melun
1174 Robert Foliot
1186 William de Vere
1200 Giles de Braose
1216 Hugh of Mapenore
1219 Hugh Foliot
1234 Ralph Maidstone
1240 Peter d'Aigueblanche
1269 John Breton
1275 Thomas Cantilupe
1283 Richard Swinfeld
1317 Adam Orleton
1327 Thomas Chariton
1344 John Trilleck
1361 Lewis Charleton
1370 William Courtenay
1375 John Gilbert
1389 John Trefnant
1404 Robert Mascall
1417 Edmund Lacy
1420 Thomas Polton
1422 Thomas Spofford
1449 Richard Beauchamp
1451 Reginald Boulers
1453 John Stanbury
1474 Thomas Milling
1492 Edmund Audley
1502 Adriano de Castello [di
   Corneto]
1504 Richard Mayeu
1516 Charles Booth
1535 Edward Fox
1539 John Skip
1553 John Harley
1554 Robert Parfew or Wharton
1559 John Scory
1586 Herbert Westfaling
1603 Robert Bennett
1617 Francis Godwin
1634 Augustine Lindsell
1635 Matthew Wren
1635 Theophilus Field
1636 George Coke
1661 Nicolas Monk
1662 Herbert Croft
1691 Gilbert Ironside
1701 Humphrey Humphries
1713 Philip Bisse
1721 Benjamin Hoadly
1724 Henry Egerton
1746 James Beauclerk
1787 John Harley
1788 John Butler
1803 Ffolliott Herbert Walker
   Cornewall
1808 John Luxmoore
1815 George Isaac Huntingford
1832 Edward Grey
1837 Thomas Musgrave
1848 Renn Dickson Hampden
1868 James Atlay
1895 John Percival
1918 Herbert Hensley Henson
1920 Martin Linton Smith
1931 Charles Lisle Carr
1941 Richard Godfrey Parsons
1949 Tom Longworth
1961 Mark Allin Hodson
1974 John Richard Gordon Eastaugh
1990 John Keith Oliver
2004 Anthony Martin Priddis
2014 Richard Michael Cokayne Frith

Leicester

see also under Lincoln

Description of arms. Gules, a pierced cinquefoil ermine, in chief a lion passant guardant grasping in the dexter forepaw a cross crosslet fitchée or.

NEW FOUNDATION

1927 Cyril Charles Bowman Bardsley
1940 Guy Vernon Smith
1953 Ronald Ralph Williams
1979 Cecil Richard Rutt
1991 Thomas Frederick Butler
1999 Timothy John Stevens

Lichfield

Description of arms. Per pale gules and argent, a cross potent quadrate in the centre per pale argent and or between four crosses patée those to the dexter argent and those to the sinister gold.

BISHOPS OF MERCIA

656 Diuma[1]
658 Ceollach
659 Trumhere
662 Jaruman

BISHOPS OF LICHFIELD

669 Chad[2]
672 Winfrith
676 Seaxwulf
691 Headda[3]
731 Aldwine
737 Hwita
757 Hemele
765 Cuthfrith
769 Berhthun
779 Hygeberht[4]
801 Aldwulf
816 Herewine
818 Æthelwald
830 Hunberht
836 Cyneferth
845 Tunberht
869 Eadberht
883 Wulfred
900 Wigmund or Wilferth
915 Ælfwine
941 Wulfgar
949 Cynesige

[1] Archbishop of the Mercians, the Lindisfari, and the Middle Angles.
[2] Bishop of the Mercians and the Lindisfari.
[3] Bishop of Lichfield and Leicester.
[4] Archbishop of Lichfield after 787.

964 Wynsige
975 Ælfheah
1004 Godwine
1020 Leofgar
1026 Brihtmaer
1039 Wulfsige
1053 Leofwine
1072 Peter

BISHOPS OF LICHFIELD, CHESTER AND COVENTRY[1]

1075 Peter
1086 Robert de Limesey
1121 Robert Peche
1129 Roger de Clinton
1149 Walter Durdent
1161 Richard Peche
1183 Gerard La Pucelle
1188 Hugh Nonant
1198 Geoffrey Muschamp
1215 William Cornhill
1224 Alex. Stavensby
1240 Hugh Pattishall
1246 Roger Weseham
1258 Roger Longespee
1296 Walter Langton
1322 Roger Northburgh
1360 Robert Stretton
1386 Walter Skirlaw
1386 Richard le Scrope
1398 John Burghill
1415 John Catterick
1420 William Heyworth
1447 William Booth
1452 Nicholas Close
1453 Reginald Boulers
1459 John Hales
1493 William Smith
1496 John Arundel
1503 Geoffrey Blyth
1534 Rowland Lee
1541 [Chester formed as a bishopric]
1543 Richard Sampson
1554 Ralph Baynes
1560 Thomas Bentham
1580 William Overton
1609 George Abbot
1610 Richard Neile
1614 John Overall
1619 Thomas Morton
1632 Robert Wright
1644 Accepted Frewen
1661 John Hackett
1671 Thomas Wood
1692 William Lloyd
1699 John Hough
1717 Edward Chandler
1731 Richard Smalbroke
1750 Fred. Cornwallis
1768 John Egerton
1771 Brownlow North
1775 Richard Hurd
1781 James Cornwallis [4th Earl Cornwallis]
1824 Henry Ryder
1836 [Coventry transferred to Worcester diocese]
1836 Samuel Butler
1840 James Bowstead
1843 John Lonsdale
1868 George Augustus Selwyn
1878 William Dalrymple Maclagan
1891 Augustus Legge
1913 John Augustine Kempthorne
1937 Edward Sydney Woods
1953 Arthur Stretton Reeve
1975 Kenneth John Fraser Skelton

1984 Keith Norman Sutton
2003 Jonathan Michael Gledhill

Lincoln

Description of arms. Gules, two lions passant guardant or, on a chief azure, the Virgin ducally crowned sitting on a throne issuant from the chief, on her dexter arm the infant Jesus, and in her sinister hand a sceptre all gold.

BISHOPS OF LINDSEY

634 Birinus
650 Agilbert
660 Aetlai
678 Eadhaed
680 Æthelwine
693 (?)Edgar
731 (?)Cyneberht
733 Alwig
750 Aldwulf
767 Ceolwulf
796 Eadwulf
839 Beorhtred
869 Burgheard
933 Ælfred
953 Leofwine
996 Sigefrith

BISHOPS OF LEICESTER

664 Wilfrid, translated from York
679 Cuthwine
691 Headda[2] (founder of Lichfield Cathedral 705–37)
727 Aldwine
737 Torhthelm
764 Eadberht
785 Unwona
803 Wernberht
816 Raethhun
840 Ealdred
844 Ceolred
874 [See of Leicester removed to Dorchester]

BISHOPS OF DORCHESTER

(after it became a Mercian See)
c.888 Ahlheard
900 Wigmund or Wilferth
909 Cenwulf
925 Wynsige
c.951 Osketel
953 Leofwine
975 Ælfnoth
979 Æscwig
1002 Ælftheln
1006 Eadnoth I
1016 Æthelric
1034 Eadnoth II
1049 Ulf
1053 Wulfwig
1067 Remigius

BISHOPS OF LINCOLN

1072 Remigius
1094 Robert Bloett
1123 Alexander
1148 Robert de Chesney
1183 Walter de Coutances
1186 Hugh of Avalon
1203 William of Blois
1209 Hugh of Wells
1235 Robert Grosseteste
1254 Henry Lexington [Sutton]
1258 Richard Gravesend
1280 Oliver Sutton [Lexington]
1300 John Dalderby
1320 Henry Burghersh
1342 Thomas Bek
1347 John Gynewell
1363 John Bokyngham [Buckingham]
1398 Henry Beaufort
1405 Philip Repingdon
1420 Richard Fleming
1431 William Gray
1436 William Alnwick
1450 Marmaduke Lumley
1452 John Chedworth
1472 Thomas Rotherham [Scott]
1480 John Russell
1495 William Smith
1514 Thomas Wolsey
1514 William Atwater
1521 John Longland
1547 Henry Holbeach [Rands]
1552 John Taylor
1554 John White
1557 Thomas Watson
1560 Nicholas Bullingham
1571 Thomas Cooper
1584 William Wickham
1595 William Chaderton
1608 William Barlow
1614 Richard Neile
1617 George Monteigne [Mountain]
1621 John Williams
1642 Thomas Winniffe
1660 Robt. Sanderson
1663 Benjamin Laney
1667 William Fuller
1675 Thomas Barlow
1692 Thomas Tenison
1695 James Gardiner
1705 William Wake
1716 Edmund Gibson
1723 Richard Reynolds
1744 John Thomas
1761 John Green
1779 Thomas Thurlow
1787 George Pretyman [Pretyman Tomline after June 1803]
1820 George Pelham
1827 John Kaye
1853 John Jackson
1869 Christopher Wordsworth
1885 Edward King
1910 Edward Lee Hicks
1920 William Shuckburgh Swayne
1933 Frederick Cyril Nugent Hicks
1942 Henry Aylmer Skelton
1946 Leslie Owen
1947 Maurice Henry Harland
1956 Kenneth Riches
1975 Simon Wilton Phipps
1987 Robert Maynard Hardy
2001 John Charles Saxbee
2011 Christopher Lowson

---

[1] 1102 Robert de Limesey, Bishop of Lichfield, moved the See to Coventry. Succeeding bishops are usually termed *of Coventry* until 1228. Then *Coventry and Lichfield* was the habitual title until the Reformation. *Chester* was used by some 12th-century bishops, and popularly afterwards. After the Reformation *Lichfield and Coventry* was used until 1846.
[2] Bishop of Leicester and Lichfield.

Norwich

Description of arms. Azure, three labelled mitres or.

BISHOPS OF DUNWICH

631	Felix
648	Thomas
c.653	Berhtgils [Boniface]
c.670	Bisi
c.673	Æcce
693	Alric (?)
716	Eardred
731	Aldbeorht I
747	Æscwulf
747	Eardwulf
775	Cuthwine
775	Aldbeorht II
781	Ecglaf
781	Heardred
793	Ælfhun
798	Tidferth
824	Waermund[1]
825	Wilred
836	Husa
870	Æthelwold

BISHOPS OF ELMHAM

673	Beaduwine
706	Nothberht
c.731	Heathulac
736	Æthelfrith
758	Eanfrith
c.781	Æthelwulf
c.785	Alhheard
814	Sibba
824	Hunferth
824	Hunbeorht
836	Cunda[2]
c.933	Ælfred[3]
c.945	Æthelweald
956	Eadwulf
970	Ælfric I
974	Theodred I
982	Theodred II
997	Æthelstan
1001	Ælfgar
1021	Ælfwine
1038	Ælfric II
1039	Ælfric III
1043	Stigand[4]
1043	Grimketel[5]
1044	Stigand (restored)
1047	Æthelmaer

BISHOPS OF THETFORD

1070	Herfast
1086	William de Beaufai
1091	Herbert Losinga

BISHOPS OF NORWICH

1091	Herbert Losinga
1121	Everard of Montgomery
1146	William de Turbe
1175	John of Oxford
1200	John de Gray
1222	Pandulf Masca

1226	Thomas Blundeville
1239	William Raleigh
1245	Walter Suffield or Calthorp
1258	Simon Walton
1266	Roger Skerning
1278	William Middleton
1289	Ralph Walpole
1299	John Salmon
1325	[Robert de Baldock]
1325	William Ayermine
1337	Anthony Bek
1344	William of Norwich [Bateman]
1356	Thomas Percy
1370	Henry Spencer [Dispenser]
1407	Alexander Tottington
1413	Richard Courtenay
1416	John Wakeryng
1426	William Ainwick
1436	Thomas Brown
1446	Walter Lyhert [le Hart]
1472	James Goldwell
1499	Thomas Jane
1501	Richard Nykke
1536	William Reppes [Rugge]
1550	Thomas Thirlby
1554	John Hopton
1560	John Parkhurst
1575	Edmund Freke
1585	Edmund Scambler
1595	William Redman
1603	John Jegon
1618	John Overall
1619	Samuel Harsnett
1629	Francis White
1632	Richard Corbet
1635	Matthew Wren
1638	Richard Montagu
1641	Joseph Hall
1661	Edward Reynolds
1676	Antony Sparrow
1685	William Lloyd
1691	John Moore
1708	Charles Trimnell
1721	Thomas Green
1723	John Leng
1727	William Baker
1733	Robert Butts
1738	Thomas Gooch
1748	Samuel Lisle
1749	Thomas Hayter
1761	Philip Yonge
1783	Lewis Bagot
1790	George Horne
1792	Charles Manners Sutton
1805	Henry Bathurst
1837	Edward Stanley
1849	Samuel Hinds
1857	John Thomas Pelham
1893	John Sheepshanks
1910	Bertram Pollock
1942	Percy Mark Herbert
1959	William Launcelot Scott Fleming
1971	Maurice Arthur Ponsonby Wood
1985	Peter John Nott
1999	Graham Richard James

Oxford

Description of arms. Sable, a fess argent, in chief three demi-ladies couped at the waist heads affrontée proper crowned or arrayed and veiled of the second, in base an ox of the last, horned and hoofed gold, passing a ford barry wavy of six azure and argent.

1542	Robert King[6]
1558	[Thomas Goldwell]
1567	Hugh Curen [Curwen]
1589	John Underhill
1604	John Bridges
1619	John Howson
1628	Richard Corbet
1632	John Bancroft
1641	Robert Skinner
1663	William Paul
1665	Walter Blandford
1671	Nathaniel Crewe [Lord Crewe]
1674	Henry Compton
1676	John Fell
1686	Samuel Parker
1688	Timothy Hall
1690	John Hough
1699	William Talbot
1715	John Potter
1737	Thomas Secker
1758	John Hume
1766	Robert Lowth
1777	John Butler
1788	Edward Smallwell
1799	John Randolph
1807	Charles Moss
1812	William Jackson
1816	Edward Legge
1827	Charles Lloyd
1829	Richard Bagot
1845	Samuel Wilberforce
1870	John Fielder Mackarness
1889	William Stubbs
1901	Francis Paget
1911	Charles Gore
1919	Hubert Murray Burge
1925	Thomas Banks Strong
1937	Kenneth Escott Kirk
1955	Harry James Carpenter
1971	Kenneth John Woollcombe
1978	Patrick Campbell Rodger
1987	Richard Douglas Harries
2007	John Lawrence Pritchard

---

[1] Bishop of Dunwich or Elmham.
[2] Bishop of Elmham or Dunwich.
[3] Bishop of Elmham or Lindsey.
[4] Deposed before consecration.
[5] Bishop of Selsey and Elmham.
[6] Bishop Rheon. *in partibus.* Of Oseney 1542-5. See transferred to Oxford 1545.

1023

Peterborough

Description of arms. Gules, two keys in saltire the wards upwards between four cross crosslets fitchée or.

1541 John Chamber
1557 David Pole
1561 Edmund Scambler
1585 Richard Howland
1601 Thomas Dove
1630 William Piers
1633 Augustine Lindsell
1634 Francis Dee
1639 John Towers
1660 Benjamin Laney
1663 Joseph Henshaw
1679 William Lloyd
1685 Thomas White
1691 Richard Cumberland
1718 White Kennett
1729 Robert Clavering
1747 John Thomas
1757 Richard Terrick
1764 Robert Lambe
1769 John Hinchliffe
1794 Spencer Madan
1813 John Parsons
1819 Herbert Marsh
1839 George Davys
1864 Francis Jeune
1868 William Connor Magee
1891 Mandell Creighton
1897 Edward Carr Glyn
1916 Frank Theodore Woods
1924 Cyril Charles Bowman
        Bardsley
1927 Claude Martin Blagden
1949 Spencer Stottisbury Gwatkin
        Leeson
1956 Robert Wright Stopford
1961 Cyril Eastaugh
1972 Douglas Russell Feaver
1984 William John Westwood
1996 Ian Patrick Martyn Cundy
2010 Donald Spargo Allister

Portsmouth

Description of arms. Per fess or and gules, in chief upon waves of the sea proper a lymphad sable, and in base two keys conjoined wards outwards in bend, the uppermost or, the other argent, interposed between them in bend sinister a sword also argent, hilt and pommel gold.

1927 Ernest Neville Lovett
1936 Frank Partridge
1942 William Louis Anderson

1949 William Launcelot Scott
        Fleming
1960 John Henry Lawrence Phillips
1975 Archibald Ronald McDonald
        Gordon
1985 Timothy John Bavin
1995 Kenneth William Stevenson
2010 Christopher Richard James
        Foster

Rochester

Description of arms. Argent, on a saltire gules an escallop or.

604 Justus
624 Romanus
633 Paulinus
644 Ithamar
664 Damianus
669 Putta
676 Cwichelm
678 Gebmund
716 Tobias
727 Aldwulf
741 Dunn
747 Eardwulf
772 Diora
785 Waermund I
805 Beornmod
844 Tatnoth
868 Badenoth
868 Waermund II
868 Cuthwulf
880 Swithwulf
900 Ceolmund
c.926 Cyneferth
c.934 Burhric
949 Beorhtsige
955 [Daniel?] Rochester or
        Selsey
964 Ælfstan
995 Godwine I
1046 Godwine II
1058 Siward
1076 Arnost
1077 Gundulf
1108 Ralph d'Escures
1115 Ernulf
1125 John
1137 John II
1142 Ascelin
1148 Walter
1182 Waleran
1185 Gilbert Glanvill
1215 Benedict of Sausetun
        [Sawston]
1227 Henry Sandford
1238 Richard Wendene
1251 Lawrence of St Martin
1274 Walter Merton
1278 John Bradfield
1283 Thomas Ingoldsthorpe
1292 Thomas of Wouldham
1319 Hamo Hethe
1353 John Sheppey
1362 William of Whittlesey
1364 Thomas Trilleck
1373 Thomas Brinton
1389 William Bottlesham
        [Bottisham]
1400 John Bottlesham
1404 Richard Young

1419 John Kempe
1422 John Langdon
1435 Thomas Brouns
1437 William Wells
1444 John Low
1468 Thomas Rotherham [otherwise
        Scott]
1472 John Alcock
1476 John Russell
1480 Edmund Audley
1493 Thomas Savage
1497 Richard Fitz-James
1504 John Fisher
1535 John Hilsey [Hildesleigh]
1540 Nicolas Heath
1544 Henry Holbeach
1547 Nicholas Ridley
1550 John Ponet [Poynet]
1551 John Scory
1554 Maurice Griffith
1560 Edmund Gheast [Guest]
1572 Edmund Freke
1576 John Piers
1578 John Young
1605 William Barlow
1608 Richard Neile
1611 John Buckeridge
1628 Walter Curil
1630 John Bowle
1638 John Warner
1666 John Dolben
1683 Francis Turner
1684 Thomas Sprat
1713 Francis Atterbury
1723 Samuel Bradford
1731 Joseph Wilcocks
1756 Zachary Pearce
1774 John Thomas
1793 Samuel Horsley
1802 Thomas Dampier
1809 Walker King
1827 Hugh Percy
1827 George Murray
1860 Joseph Cotton Wigram
1867 Thomas Legh Claughton
1877 Anthony Wilson Thorold
1891 Randall Thomas Davidson
1895 Edward Stuart Talbot
1905 John Reginald Harmer
1930 Martin Linton Smith
1940 Christopher Maude Chavasse
1961 Richard David Say
1988 Anthony Michael Arnold
        Turnbull
1994 Michael James Nazir-Ali
2010 James Henry Langstaff

St Albans

Description of arms. Azure, a saltire or, overall a sword erect in pale proper, hilt and pommel gold, in chief a celestial crown of the same.

1877 Thomas Legh Claughton
1890 John Wogan Festing
1903 Edgar Jacob
1920 Michael Bolton Furse
1944 Philip Henry Loyd
1950 Edward Michael Gresford Jones
1970 Robert Alexander Kennedy
        Runcie

1980 John Bernard Taylor
1995 Christopher William Herbert
2009 Alan Gregory Clayton Smith

St Edmundsbury and Ipswich

Description of arms. Per pale gules and azure, between three ducal coronets a demi-lion passant guardant conjoined to the demi-hulk of an ancient ship or.

1914 Henry Bernard Hodgson
1921 Albert Augustus David
1923 Walter Godfrey Whittingham
1940 Richard Brook
1954 Arthur Harold Morris
1966 Leslie Wilfrid Brown
1978 John Waine
1986 John Dennis
1997 John Hubert Richard Lewis
2007 William Nigel Stock
2015 Martin Alan Seeley

Salisbury

Description of arms. Azure, our Lady crowned, holding in her dexter arm the infant Jesus, and in her sinister arm a sceptre all or, round both the heads circles of glory gold.

BISHOPS OF SHERBORNE

705 Ealdhelm
709 Forthhere
736 Hereweald
774 Æthelmod
793 Denefrith
801 Wigberht
825 Ealhstan
868 Heahmund
877 Æthelheah
889 Wulfsige I
900 Asser
c.909 Æthelweard
c.909 Waerstan
925 Æthelbald
925 Sigehelm
934 Ælfred
943 Wulfsige II
958 Ælfwold I
979 Æthelsige I
992 Wulfsige III
1002 Æthelric

1012 Æthelsige II
1017 Brihtwine I
1017 Ælfmaer
1023 Brihtwine II
1045 Ælfwold II
1058 Hereman, Bishop of Ramsbury

BISHOPS OF RAMSBURY

909 Æthelstan
927 Oda
949 Ælfric I
951 Osulf
970 Ælfstan
981 Wulfgar
986 Sigeric
993 Ælfric II
1005 Brihtwold
1045 Hereman[1]

BISHOPS OF SALISBURY

1078 Osmund Osmer
1107 Roger
1142 Jocelin de Bohun
1189 Hubert Walter
1194 Herbert Poore
1217 Richard Poore
1229 Robert Bingham
1247 William of York
1257 Giles of Bridport
1263 Walter de la Wyle
1274 Robert Wickhampton
1284 Walter Scammel
1287 Henry Brandeston
1289 William de la Corner
1292 Nicholas Longespee
1297 Simon of Ghent
1315 Roger de Mortival
1330 Robert Wyville
1375 Ralph Erghum
1388 John Waltham
1395 Richard Mitford
1407 Nicholas Bubwith
1407 Robert Hallum
1417 John Chaundler
1427 Robert Nevill
1438 William Aiscough
1450 Richard Beauchamp
1482 Lionel Woodville
1485 Thomas Langton
1494 John Blythe
1500 Henry Deane
1502 Edmund Audley
1525 Lorenzo Campeggio
1535 Nicholas Shaxton
1539 John Salcot [Capon]
1560 John Jewell
1571 Edmund Gheast [Guest]
1577 John Piers
1591 John Coldwell
1598 Henry Cotton
1615 Robert Abbot
1618 Martin Fotherby
1620 Robert Townson [Toulson]
1621 John Davenant
1641 Brian Duppa
1660 Humfrey Henchman
1663 John Earle
1665 Alexander Hyde
1667 Seth Ward
1689 Gilbert Burnet
1715 William Talbot
1721 Richard Wilis
1723 Benjamin Hoadly
1734 Thomas Sherlock
1748 John Gilbert
1757 John Thomas
1761 Robert Hay Drummond
1761 John Thomas
1766 John Hume
1782 Shute Barrington

1791 John Douglas
1807 John Fisher
1825 Thomas Burgess
1837 Edward Denison
1854 Walter Kerr Hamilton
1869 George Moberly
1885 John Wordsworth
1911 Frederic Edward Ridgeway
1921 St Clair George Alfred Donaldson
1936 Ernest Neville Lovett
1946 Geoffrey Charles Lester Lunt
1949 William Louis Anderson
1963 Joseph Edward Fison
1973 George Edmund Reindorp
1982 John Austin Baker
1993 David Staffurth Stancliffe
2011 Nicholas Roderick Holtam

Southwark

Description of arms. Argent, eleven fusils in cross conjoined, seven in pale fesswise, four in fess palewise, in the dexter chief a mitre all gules.

1905 Edward Stuart Talbot
1911 Hubert Murray Burge
1919 Cyril Forster Garbett
1932 Richard Godfrey Parsons
1942 Bertram Fitzgerald Simpson
1959 Arthur Mervyn Stockwood
1980 Ronald Oliver Bowlby
1991 Robert Kerr Williamson
1998 Thomas Frederick Butler
2011 Christopher Thomas James Chessun

Truro

Description of arms. Argent, on a saltire gules a sword and key or and in base a fleur-de-lis sable all within a bordure of the last charged with fifteen besants.

1877 Edward White Benson
1883 George Howard Wilkinson
1891 John Gott
1906 Charles William Stubbs
1912 Winfrid Oldfield Burrows
1919 Frederic Sumpter Guy Warman
1923 Walter Howard Frere
1935 Joseph Wellington Hunkin
1951 Edmund Robert Morgan

---

[1] Ramsbury was added to Sherbourne in 1058 when Hereman became Bishop of Sherbourne. The See was moved to Salisbury in 1078.

1960 John Maurice Key
1973 Graham Douglas Leonard
1981 Peter Mumford
1990 Michael Thomas Ball
1997 William Ind
2008 Timothy Martin Thornton

Worcester

Description of arms. Argent, ten torteaux, four, three, two, and one.

680 Bosel
691 Offtor
693 Ecgwine
718 Wilfrid I
745 Milred
775 Waermund
777 Tilhere
781 Heathured
798 Deneberht
822 Heahberht
845 Alhhun
873 Waerferth
915 Æthelhun
922 Wilferth II
929 Cenwald
957 Dunstan
961 Oswald
992 Ealdwulf
1002 Wulfstan I
1016 Leofsige
1027 Lyfing
1033 Brihtheah
1040 Æltric Puttoc, Bishop of
     York and Worcester
1041 Lyfing (restored)
1046 Ealdred Bishop of Hereford
     and Worcester 1056–60

1062 Wulfstan II
1096 Samson
1115 Theulf
1125 Simon
1151 John of Pagham
1158 Aldred
1164 Roger of Gloucester
1180 Baldwin
1186 William of Northolt
1191 Robert Fitz Ralph
1193 Henry de Sully
1196 John of Coutances
1200 Mauger
1214 Walter de Gray
1216 Silvester of Evesham
1218 William of Blois
1237 Walter Cantilupe
1266 Nicolas of Ely
1268 Godfrey Giffard
1302 William Gainsborough
1308 Walter Reynolds
1313 Walter Maidstone
1317 Thomas Cobham
1327 Adam Orleton
1334 Simon Montacute
1337 Thomas Hempnall
1339 Wulstan Bransford
1350 John Thoresby
1353 Reginald Brian
1362 John Barnet
1364 William of Whittlesey
1369 William Lenn
1375 Henry Wakefield
1396 Robert Tideman of
     Winchcomb
1401 Richard Clifford
1407 Thomas Peverel
1419 Philip Morgan
1426 Thomas Polton
1435 Thomas Bourgchier
1444 John Carpenter
1476 John Alcock
1487 Robert Morton
1497 Giovanni de' Gigli
1499 Silvestro de' Gigli
1521 Julius de Medici Guilio de
     Medici (administrator)
1523 Geronimo Ghinucci
1535 Hugh Latimer
1539 John Bell
1544 Nicholas Heath
     (deposed)

1552 John Hooper
1554 Nicholas Heath
     (restored)
1555 Richard Pates
1559 Edwin Sandys
1571 Nicholas Bullingham
1577 John Whitgift
1584 Edmund Freke
1593 Richard Fletcher
1596 Thomas Bilson
1597 Gervase Babington
1610 Henry Parry
1617 John Thornborough
1641 John Prideaux
1660 George Morley
1662 John Gauden
1662 John Earle
1663 Robert Skinner
1671 Walter Blandford
1675 James Fleetwood
1683 William Thomas
1689 Edward Stillingfleet
1699 William Lloyd
1717 John Hough
1743 Isaac Maddox
1759 James Johnson
1774 Brownlow North
1781 Richard Hurd
1808 Ffolliott Herbert Walker
     Cornewall
1831 Robert James Carr
1841 Henry Pepys
1861 Henry Philpott
1891 John James Stewart
     Perowne
1902 Charles Gore
1905 Huyshe Wolcott
     Yeatman-Biggs
1919 Ernest Harold Pearce
1931 Arthur William Thomson
     Perowne
1941 William Wilson Cash
1956 Lewis Mervyn
     Charles-Edwards
1971 Robert Wylmer Woods
1982 Philip Harold Ernest
     Goodrich
1997 Peter Stephen Maurice
     Selby
2007 John Geoffrey Inge

PROVINCE OF YORK

York

Description of arms. Gules, two keys in saltire argent, in chief a regal crown proper.

BISHOPS

314 Eborius
625 Paulinus [Vacancy
     633–64]

664 Cedda
664 Wilfrid I
678 Bosa (retired)
686 Bosa (restored)
691 Wilfrith (restored)
706 John of Beverley
718 Wilfrid II

ARCHBISHOPS

734 Egberht
767 Æthelberht
780 Eanbald I
796 Eanbald II
808 Wulfsige
837 Wigmund
854 Wulfhere
900 Æthelbald
c.928 Hrothweard
931 Wulfstan I
956 Osketel
971 Oswald

971 Edwald
992 Ealdwulf [1]
1003 Wulfstan II
1023 Ælfric Puttoc
1041 Æthelric
1051 Cynesige
1061 Ealdred
1070 Thomas I of Bayeux
1100 Gerard
1109 Thomas II
1119 Thurstan
1143 William Fitzherbert
1147 Henry Murdac
1153 William Fitzherbert
     (restored)
1154 Roger of Pont l'Eveque
1191 Geoffrey Plantagenet
1215 Walter de Gray
1256 Sewal de Bovill
1258 Godfrey Ludham
     [Kineton]

[1] Ealdwulf and Wulfstan II held the Sees of York and Worcester together, Ælfric Puttoc held both 1040-41 and Ealdred 1060-61.

1266 Walter Giffard
1279 William Wickwane
1286 John Romanus [le Romeyn]
1298 Henry Newark
1300 Thomas Corbridge
1306 William Greenfield
1317 William Melton
1342 William de la Zouche
1352 John Thoresby
1374 Alexander Neville
1388 Thomas Arundel
1396 Robert Waldby
1398 Richard le Scrope
1407 Henry Bowet
1426 John Kempe
1452 William Booth
1464 George Nevill
1476 Lawrence Booth
1480 Thomas Rotherham
          [Scott]
1501 Thomas Savage
1508 Christopher Bainbridge
1514 Thomas Wolsey
1531 Edward Lee
1545 Robert Holgate
1555 Nicholas Heath
1561 Thomas Young
1570 Edmund Grindal
1577 Edwin Sandys
1589 John Piers
1595 Matthew Hutton
1606 Tobias Matthew
1628 George Monteigne
          [Mountain]
1629 Samuel Harsnett
1632 Richard Neile
1641 John Williams
1660 Accepted Frewen
1664 Richard Sterne
1683 John Dolben
1688 Thomas Lamplugh
1691 John Sharp
1714 William Dawes
1724 Lancelot Blackburn
1743 Thomas Herring
1747 Matthew Hutton
1757 John Gilben
1761 Roben Hay Drummond
1777 William Markham
1808 Edward Venables Vernon
          Harcourt
1847 Thomas Musgrave
1860 Charles Thomas Longley
1863 William Thomson
1891 William Connor Magee
1891 William Dalrymple
          Maclagan
1909 Cosmo Gordon Lang
1929 William Temple
1942 Cyril Forster Garbett
1956 Arthur Michael Ramsey
1961 Frederick Donald Coggan
1975 Stuart Yarworth Blanch
1983 John Stapylton Habgood
1995 David Michael Hope
2005 John Tucker Mugabi
          Sentamu

Durham

Description of arms. Azure, a cross or
between four lions rampant argent.

BISHOPS OF LINDISFARNE[1]

635 Aidan
651 Finan
661 Colman
664 Tuda [Complications involving
          Wilfrid and Chad]
681 Eata
685 Cuthberht [Vacancy during
          which Wilfrid administered
          the See]
688 Eadberht
698 Eadfenh
731 Æthelweald
740 Cynewulf
781 Higbald
803 Ecgberht
821 Heathwred
830 Ecgred
845 Eanberht
854 Eardwulf

BISHOPS OF HEXHAM

664 Wilfrith
678 Eata
681 Tunberht
684 Cuthbert
685 Eata (restored)
687 John of Beverley
709 Acca
734 Frithoberht
767 Ahimund
781 Tilberht
789 Æthelberht
797 Heardred
800 Eanberht
813 Tidferth

BISHOPS OF
CHESTER-LE-STREET[2]

899 Eardwulf
899 Cutheard
915 Tilred
925 Wigred
944 Uhtred
944 Seaxhelm
944 Ealdred
968 Ælfsige
990 Aldhun

BISHOPS OF DURHAM

990 Aldhun d. 1018 [See vacant
          1018–1020]
1020 Edmund
c.1040 Eadred
1041 Æthelric
1056 Æthelwine
1071 Walcher
1081 William of Saint Calais
1099 Ralph [Ranulf] Flambard
1133 Geoffrey Rufus
1143 William of Sainte-Barbe
1153 Hugh of le Puiset
1197 Philip of Poitiers
1217 Richard Marsh

1228 Richard Poore
1241 Nicholas Farnham
1249 Walter Kirkham
1261 Robert Stichill
1274 Robert of Holy Island
1284 Anthony Bek
1311 Richard Kellaw
1318 Lewis de Beaumont
1333 Richard of Bury
1345 Thomas Hatfield
1382 John Fordham
1388 Walter Skirlaw
1406 Thomas Langley
1438 Robert Nevill
1457 Lawrence Booth
1476 William Dudley
1485 John Shirwood
1494 Richard Fox
1502 William Senhouse
          [Sever]
1507 Christopher Bainbridge
1509 Thomas Ruthall
1523 Thomas Wolsey
1530 Cuthbert Tunstall
1561 James Pilkington
1577 Richard Barnes
1589 Matthew Hutton
1595 Tobias Matthew
1606 William James
1617 Richard Neile
1628 George Monteigne
          [Mountain]
1628 John Howson
1632 Thomas Morton
1660 John Cosin
1674 Nathaniel Crew
          [Lord Crew]
1721 William Talbot
1730 Edward Chandler
1750 Joseph Butler
1752 Richard Trevor
1771 John Egerton
1787 Thomas Thurlow
1791 Shute Barrington
1826 William Van Mildert
1836 Edward Maltby
1856 Charles Thomas Longley
1860 Henry Montagu Villiers
1861 Charles Baring
1879 Joseph Barber Lightfoot
1890 Brooke Foss Westcott
1901 Handley Carr Glyn Moule
1920 Herbert Hensley Henson
1939 Alwyn Terrell Petre
          Williams
1952 Arthur Michael Ramsey
1956 Maurice Henry Harland
1966 Ian Thomas Ramsey
1973 John Stapylton Habgood
1984 David Edward Jenkins
1994 Anthony Michael Arnold
          Turnbull
2003 Nicholas Thomas Wright
2011 Justin Portal Welby
2014 Paul Roger Butler

---

[1] See transferred to Chester-le-Street 883.   [2] See transferred to Durham 995.

Blackburn

Description of arms. Per fess gules and or, in chief two keys in saltire wards downwards argent, in base a rose of the first barbed and seeded proper.

1926 Percy Mark Herbert
1942 Wilfred Marcus Askwith
1954 Walter Hubert Baddeley
1960 Charles Robert Claxton
1972 Robert Arnold Schürhoff
      Martineau
1982 David Stewart Cross
1989 Alan David Chesters
2004 Nicholas Stewart Reade
2013 Julian Tudor Henderson

Bradford

Description of arms. Azure, two keys in saltire or, in chief a woolpack proper corded gold.

1920 Arthur William Thomson
      Perowne
1931 Alfred Walter Frank
      Blunt
1956 Frederick Donald
      Coggan
1961 Clement George
      St Michael Parker
1972 Ross Sydney Hook
1981 Geoffrey John Paul
1984 Robert Kerr Williamson
1992 David James Smith
2002 David Charles James
2011 Nicholas Baines
2014 Dissolved upon the creation of
      the new Diocese of Leeds
      (q.v.).

Carlisle

Description of arms. Argent, on a cross sable a labelled mitre or.

1133 Æthelwulf
1203 Bernard
1219 Hugh of Beaulieu
1224 Walter Mauclerc
1247 Silvester Everdon
1255 Thomas Vipont
1258 Robert de Chause
1280 Ralph Ireton
1292 John of Halton
1325 John Ross
1332 John Kirkby
1353 Gilbert Welton
1363 Thomas Appleby
1396 Robert Reade
1397 Thomas Merks
1400 William Strickland
1420 Roger Whelpdale
1424 William Barrow
1430 Marmaduke Lumley
1450 Nicholas Close
1452 William Percy
1462 John Kingscote
1464 Richard le Scrope
1468 Edward Story
1478 Richard Bell
1496 William Senhouse
      [Sever]
1504 Roger Layburne
1508 John Penny
1521 John Kite
1537 Robert Aldrich
1556 Owen Oglethorpe
1561 John Best
1570 Richard Barnes
1577 John May
1598 Henry Robinson
1616 Robert Snowden
1621 Richard Milbourne
1624 Richard Senhouse
1626 Francis White
1629 Barnabas Potter
1642 James Ussher
1660 Richard Sterne
1664 Edward Rainbowe
1684 Thomas Smith
1702 William Nicolson
1718 Samuel Bradford
1723 John Waugh
1735 George Fleming
1747 Richard Osbaldeston
1762 Charles Lyttleton
1769 Edmund Law
1787 John Douglas
1791 Edward Venables Vernon
      [Harcourt]
1808 Samuel Goodenough
1827 Hugh Percy
1856 Henry Montagu Villiers
1860 Samuel Waldegrave
1869 Harvey Goodwin
1892 John Wareing Bardsley
1905 John William Diggle
1920 Henry Herbert Williams
1946 Thomas Bloomer
1966 Sydney Cyril Bulley
1972 Henry David Halsey
1989 Ian Harland
2000 Geoffrey Graham Dow
2009 James William Scobie
      Newcome

Chester

Description of arms. Gules, three labelled mitres or.

1541 John Bird
1554 George Cotes
1556 Cuthbert Scott
1561 William Downham
1579 William Chaderton
1595 Hugh Bellott
1597 Richard Vaughan
1604 George Lloyd
1616 Thomas Morton
1619 John Bridgeman
1660 Brian Walton
1662 Henry Ferne
1662 George Hall
1668 John Wilkins
1673 John Pearson
1686 Thomas Cartwright
1689 Nicolas Stratford
1708 William Dawes
1714 Francis Gastrell
1726 Samuel Peploe
1752 Edmund Keene
1771 William Markham
1777 Beilby Porteus
1788 William Cleaver
1800 Henry William Majendie
1810 Bowyer Edward Sparke
1812 George Henry Law
1824 Charles James Blomfield
1828 John Bird Sumner
1848 John Graham
1865 William Jacobson
1884 William Stubbs
1889 Francis John Jayne
1919 Henry Luke Paget
1932 Geoffrey Francis Fisher
1939 Douglas Henry Crick
1955 Gerald Alexander Ellison
1974 Hubert Victor Whitsey
1982 Michael Alfred Baughen
1996 Peter Robert Forster

Leeds (West Yorkshire and the Dales)

Description of arms. Azure a cross formy throughout the limbs in pale taking the form of a Greek rho or, in the first quarter a rose argent barbed and seeded proper.

2014 Nicholas Baines

Liverpool

Description of arms. Argent, an eagle with wings expanded sable, holding in its dexter claw an ancient inkhorn proper, around its head a nimbus or, a chief paly azure and gules, the dexter charged with an open book or, inscribed with the words 'Thy Word is Truth', the sinister charged with a lymphad gold.

1880 John Charles Ryle
1900 Francis James Chavasse
1923 Albert Augustus David
1944 Clifford Arthur Martin
1966 Stuart Yarworth Blanch
1975 David Stuart Sheppard
1998 James Stuart Jones
2014 Paul Bayes

Manchester

Description of arms. Or, on a pale engrailed gules three mitres of the first, on a canton of the second three bendlets enhanced gold.

1848 James Prince Lee
1870 James Fraser
1886 James Moorhouse
1903 Edmund Arbuthnott Knox
1921 William Temple
1929 Frederic Sumpter Guy Warman
1947 William Derrick Lindsay Greer
1970 Patrick Campbell Rodger
1979 Stanley Eric Francis Booth-
     Clibborn
1993 Christopher John Mayfield
2002 Nigel Simeon McCulloch
2013 David Stuart Walker

Newcastle

Description of arms. Gules, a cross between four lions rampant or, on a chief gold three triple-towered castles of the first.

1882 Ernest Roland Wilberforce
1896 Edgar Jacob
1903 Arthur Thomas Lloyd
1907 Norman Dumenil John Straton
1915 Herbert Louis Wild
1927 Harold Ernest Bilbrough
1941 Noel Baring Hudson
1957 Hugh Edward Ashdown
1973 Ronald Oliver Bowlby
1981 Andrew Alexander Kenny
     Graham
1997 John Martin Wharton

Ripon and Leeds
(Ripon until 1999)

Description of arms. Argent, on a saltire gules two keys wards upwards or, on a chief of the second a Holy Lamb proper.

*c.*678 Eadheath

NEW FOUNDATION

1836 Charles Thomas Longley
1857 Robert Bickersteth
1884 William Boyd Carpenter
1912 Thomas Wortley Drury
1920 Thomas Banks Strong
1926 Edward Arthur Burroughs
1935 Geoffrey Charles Lester Lunt
1946 George Armitage Chase
1959 John Richard Humpidge
     Moorman
1975 Stuart Hetley Price
1977 David Nigel de Lorentz Young
2000 John Richard Packer
2014 Dissolved upon the creation
     of the new Diocese of Leeds
     (q.v.)

Sheffield

Description of arms. Azure, a crosier in pale ensigned by a fleur-de-lis vert, between in fess a key surmounted by a sword in saltire to the dexter, and to the sinister eight arrows interlaced and banded saltirewise, all or.

1914 Leonard Hedley Burrows
1939 Leslie Stannard Hunter
1962 Francis John Taylor
1971 William Gordon Fallows
1980 David Ramsay Lunn
1997 John Nicholls
2009 Steven John Lindsey Croft

Sodor and Man[1]

Description of arms. Argent, upon a pedestal between two coronetted pillars the Virgin Mary with arms extended, in her dexter hand a church proper and in base upon an escutcheon, surmounted by a mitre, the arms of Man – viz. gules, three legs in armour conjoined at the thigh and flexed at the knee.

447 Germanus
    Conindrius
    Romulus
    Machutus
    Conanus
    Contentus
    Baldus
    Malchus
    Torkinus
    Brendanus
[Before 1080 Roolwer]
    William
    Hamond
1113 Wimund
1151 John
1160 Gamaliel
    Ragnald
    Christian of Argyle
    Michael
1203 Nicholas de Meaux
    Nicholas II
1217 Reginald
1226 John
1229 Simon of Argyle
1252 Richard
1275 Mark of Galloway
1305 Alan
1321 Gilbert Maclelan
1329 Bernard de Linton
1334 Thomas

[1] Included in the province of York by Act of Parliament 1542. Prior to Richard Oldham there is some uncertainty as to several names and dates. From 1425 to 1553 there was an English and Scottish succession. It is not easy to say which claimant was Bishop either *de jure* or *de facto*.

1348 William Russell
1387 John Donegan
1387 Michael
1392 John Sproten
1402 Conrad
1402 Theodore Bloc
1429 Richard Messing Andrew
1435 John Seyre
1455 Thomas Burton
1458 Thomas Kirklam
1472 Angus
1478 Richard Oldham
1487 Hugh Blackleach
1513 Hugh Hesketh
1523 John Howden
1546 Henry Man
1556 Thomas Stanley
1570 John Salisbury
1576 John Meyrick
1600 George Lloyd
1605 John Philips
1634 William Forster
1635 Richard Parr
1661 Samuel Rutter
1663 Isaac Barrow
1671 Henry Bridgman
1683 John Lake
1685 Baptist Levinz
1698 Thomas Wilson
1755 Mark Hildesley
1773 Richard Richmond
1780 George Mason
1784 Claudius Crigan
1814 George Murray
1828 William Ward
1838 James Bowstead
1840 Henry Pepys
1841 Thomas Vowler Short
1847 Walter Augustus Shirley
1847 Robert John Eden
1854 Horatio Powys
1877 Rowley Hill
1887 John Wareing Bardsley
1892 Norman Dumenil John Straton

1907 Thomas Wortley Drury
1912 James Denton Thompson
1925 Charles Leonard Thornton-
      Duesbery
1928 William Stanton Jones
1943 John Ralph Strickland Taylor
1954 Benjamin Pollard
1966 George Eric Gordon
1974 Vernon Sampson Nicholls
1983 Arthur Henry Attwell
1989 Noël Debroy Jones
2003 Graeme Paul Knowles
2008 Robert Mar Erskine Paterson

Southwell and Nottingham
(Southwell until 2005)

Description of arms. Sable, three
fountains proper, on a chief or a pale
azure, charged with a representation of
the Virgin Mary seated bearing the
Infant Christ or between a stag lodged
proper and two staves raguly crossed
vert.

1884 George Ridding
1904 Edwyn Hoskyns
1926 Bernard Oliver Francis
      Heywood
1928 Henry Mosley

1941 Frank Russell Barry
1964 Gordon David Savage
1970 John Denis Wakeling
1985 Michael Humphrey Dickens
      Whinney
1988 Patrick Burnet Harris
1999 George Henry Cassidy
2009 Paul Roger Butler
2015 Paul Gavin Williams

Wakefield

Description of arms. Or, a fleur-de-lis
azure, on a chief of the last three
celestial crowns gold.

1888 William Walsham How
1897 George Rodney Eden
1928 James Buchanan Seaton
1938 Campbell Richard Hone
1946 Henry McGowan
1949 Roger Plumpton Wilson
1958 John Alexander Ramsbotham
1968 Eric Treacy
1977 Colin Clement Walter James
1985 David Michael Hope
1992 Nigel Simeon McCulloch
2003 Stephen George Platten
2014 Dissolved upon the creation
      of the new Diocese of Leeds
      (q.v.)

BISHOPS SUFFRAGAN IN ENGLAND

Aston (Birmingham)

1954 Clement George St Michael
      Parker
1962 David Brownfield Porter
1972 Mark Green
1982 Michael Humphrey Dickens
      Whinney
1985 Colin Ogilvie Buchanan
1989–92 *no appointment*
1992 John Michael Austin
2005–2008 *no appointment*
2008 Andrew John Watson
2015 Anne Elizabeth Hollinghurst

Barking (Chelmsford)

[in St Albans diocese to 1914]

1901 Thomas Stevens
1919 James Theodore Inskip
1948 Hugh Rowlands Gough
1959 William Frank Percival
      Chadwick
1975 Albert James Adams
1983 James William Roxburgh
1991 Roger Frederick Sainsbury
2002 David John Leader Hawkins
2014 Peter Hill

Barrow-in-Furness (Carlisle)

1889 Henry Ware
1909 Campbell West-Watson

1926 Henry Sidney Pelham
1944 *in abeyance*

Basingstoke (Winchester)

1973 Colin Clement Walter James
1977 Michael Richard John
      Manktelow
1994 Douglas Geoffrey Rowell
2002 Trevor Willmott
2010 Peter Hancock
2014 David Grant Williams

Bedford (St Albans)

1537 John Hodgkins[1]
1560–1879 *in abeyance*
1879 William Walsham How[2]
1888 Robert Claudius Billing[3]
1898–1935 *in abeyance*
1935 James Lumsden Barkway
1939 Aylmer Skelton
1948 Claude Thomas Thellusson
      Wood
1953 Angus Campbell MacInnes
1957 Basil Tudor Guy
1963 Albert John Trillo
1968 John Tyrrell Holmes Hare
1977 Andrew Alexander Kenny
      Graham
1981 David John Farmbrough
1994 John Henry Richardson
2003 Richard Neil Inwood

2012 Richard William Bryant
      Atkinson

Berwick (Durham)

1536 Thomas Sparke
1572 *in abeyance*

Beverley (York)

1889 Robert Jarratt Crosthwaite
1923–94 *in abeyance*
1994 John Scott Gaisford
2000 Martyn William Jarrett
2013 Glyn Hamilton Webster

Birkenhead (Chester)

1965 Eric Arthur John Mercer
1974 Ronald Brown
1993 Michael Laurence Langrish
2000 David Andrew Urquhart
2007 Gordon Keith Sinclair

Bolton (Manchester)

1984 David George Galliford
1991 David Bonser
1999 David Keith Gillett
2008 Christopher Paul Edmondson

Bradford (Leeds)

2014 Toby Matthew Howarth

[1] Appointed for the diocese of London.   [2] Appointed for the diocese of London.
[3] Appointed for the diocese of London, and retained title after resigning his suffragan duties in 1895.

Bradwell (Chelmsford)

1968　William Neville Welch
1973　John Gibbs
1976　Charles Derek Bond
1993　Laurence Alexander Green
2011　John Michael Wraw

Bristol (Worcester)

1538　Henry Holbeach [Rands]
1542　*became diocesan see*

Brixworth (Peterborough)

1989　Paul Everard Barber
2002　Francis White
2011　John Edward Holbrook

Buckingham (Oxford)

1914　Edward Domett Shaw
1921　Philip Herbert Eliot
1944　Robert Milton Hay
1960　Gordon David Savage
1964　George Christopher Cutts
　　　Pepys
1974　Simon Hedley Burrows
1994　Colin James Bennetts
1998　Michael Arthur Hill
2003　Alan Thomas Lawrence
　　　Wilson

Burnley (Blackburn)

[in Manchester diocese to 1926]

1901　Edwyn Hoskyns
1905　Alfred Pearson
1909　Henry Henn
1931　Edgar Priestley Swain
1950　Charles Keith Kipling Prosser
1955　George Edward Holderness
1970　Richard Charles Challinor
　　　Watson
1988　Ronald James Milner
1994　Martyn William Jarrett
2000　John William Goddard
2015　Philip John North

Colchester (Chelmsford)

[in London diocese to 1845
in Rochester diocese to 1877
in St Albans diocese 1877–1914]

1536　William More
1541–91　*in abeyance*
1592　John Sterne
1608–1882　*in abeyance*
1882　Alfred Blomfield
1894　Henry Frank Johnson
1909　Robert Henry Whitcombe
1922　Thomas Alfred Chapman
1933　Charles Henry Ridsdale
1946　Frederick Dudley Vaughan
　　　Narborough
1966　Roderic Norman Coote
1988　Michael Edwin Vickers
1995　Edward Holland
2001　Christopher Heudebourck
　　　Morgan
2014　Roger Anthony Brett Morris

Coventry (Worcester)

see also under Lichfield

1891　Henry Bond Bowlby
1894　Edmund Arbuthnott Knox
1903–18　*no appointment*
1918　*became diocesan see*

Crediton (Exeter)

1897　Robert Edward Trefusis
1930　William Frederick Surtees
1954　Wilfred Arthur Edmund Westall
1974　Philip John Pasterfield
1984　Peter Everard Coleman
1996　Richard Stephen Hawkins
2004　Robert John Scott Evens
2012　Nicholas Howard Paul
　　　McKinnel
2015　Sarah Elisabeth Mullally

Croydon (Southwark)

(in Canterbury diocese to 1985)

1904　Henry Horace Pereira
1924–30　*no appointment*
1930　Edward Sydney Woods
1937　William Louis Anderson
1942　Maurice Henry Harland
1947　Cuthbert Killick Norman
　　　Bardsley
1957　John Taylor Hughes
1977　Geoffrey Stuart Snell
1985　Wilfred Denniston Wood
2003　Nicholas Baines
2012　Jonathan Dunnett Clark

Derby (Southwell)

1889　Edward Ash Were
1909　Charles Thomas Abraham
1927　*became diocesan see*

Doncaster (Sheffield)

1972　Stuart Hetley Price
1976　David Stewart Cross
1982　William Michael Dermot
　　　Persson
1993　Michael Frederick Gear
2000　Cyril Guy Ashton
2012　Peter Burrows

Dorchester (Oxford)

see also under Dorchester (*diocesan
　　　see) and* Lincoln

1939　Gerald Burton Allen
1952　Kenneth Riches
1957　David Goodwin Loveday
1972　Peter Knight Walker
1979　Conrad John Eustace Meyer
1988　Anthony John Russell
2000　Colin William Fletcher

Dorking (Guildford)

[in Winchester diocese to 1927]

1905　Cecil Henry Boutflower
1909–68　*in abeyance*
1968　Kenneth Dawson Evans
1986　David Peter Wilcox
1996　Ian James Brackley

Dover (Canterbury)

1537　Richard Yngworth
1545　Richard Thornden
1557–69　*no appointment*
1569　Richard Rogers
1597–1870　*in abeyance*
1870　Edward Parry
1890　George Rodney Eden
1898　William Walsh
1916　Harold Ernest Bilbrough
1927　John Victor Macmillan
1935　Alfred Careywollaston Rose
1957　Lewis Evan Meredith

1964　Anthony Paul Tremlett
1980　Richard Henry McPhail Third
1992　John Richard Allan Llewellin
1999　Stephen Squires Venner
2010　Trevor Willmott

Dudley (Worcester)

1974　Michael Ashley Mann
1977　Anthony Charles Dumper
1993　Rupert William Noel Hoare
2000　David Stuart Walker
2014　Graham Barham Usher

Dunwich (St Edmundsbury and Ipswich)

see also under Norwich

1934　Maxwell Homfray Maxwell-
　　　Gumbleton
1945　Clement Mallory Ricketts
1955　Thomas Herbert Cashmore
1967　David Rokeby Maddock
1977　William Johnston
1980　Eric Nash Devenport
1992　Jonathan Sansbury Bailey
1995　Timothy John Stevens
1999　Clive Young

Ebbsfleet (Canterbury)

1994　John Richards
1998　Michael Alan Houghton
2000　Andrew Burnham
2011　Jonathan Mark Richard Baker
2013　Jonathan Michael Goodall

Edmonton (London)

1970　Alan Francis Bright Rogers
1975　William John Westwood
1985　Brian John Masters
1999　Peter William Wheatley
2015　Robert James Wickham

Europe (Europe)

1980　Ambrose Walter Marcus Weekes
1986　Edward Holland
1995　Henry William Scriven
2002　David Hamid

Fulham (London)[1]

1926　Basil Staunton Batty
1947　William Marshall Selwyn
1949　George Ernest Ingle
1955　Robert Wright Stopford
1957　Roderic Norman Coote
1966　Alan Francis Bright Rogers
1970　John Richard Satterthwaite[2]
1980–1982　*no appointment*
1982　Brian John Masters
1985　Charles John Klyberg
1996　John Charles Broadhurst
2013　Jonathan Mark Richard Baker

Grantham (Lincoln)

1905　Welbore MacCarthy
1920　John Edward Hine
1930　Ernest Morell Blackie
1935　Arthur Ivan Greaves
1937　Algernon Augustus Markham
1949　Anthony Otter
1965　Ross Sydney Hook
1972　Dennis Gascoyne Hawker
1987　William Ind
1997　Alastair Lewellyn John Redfern
2006　Timothy William Ellis

---

[1]　From 1926 to 1980 exercised the Bishop of London's extra-diocesan jurisdiction over chaplaincies in Northern and Central Europe. Since 1996 has assisted the Diocesan Bishop in all matters not delegated to the Areas, and in pastoral care of parishes operating under the London Plan.
[2]　Bishop of Fulham and Gibraltar.

Grimsby (Lincoln)

1935 Ernest Morell Blackie
1937 Anhur Ivan Greaves
1958 Kenneth Healey
1966 Gerald Fitzmaurice Colin
1979 David Tustin
2000 David Douglas James Rossdale
2014 David Eric Court

Guildford (Winchester)

1874 John Sutton Utterton
1888 George Henry Sumner
1909 John Hugh Granville Randolph
1927 *became diocesan see*

Hertford (St Albans)

1968 Albert John Trillo
1971 Hubert Victor Whitsey
1974 Peter Mumford
1982 Kenneth Harold Pillar
1990 Robin Jonathan Norman Smith
2001 Christopher Richard James
      Foster
2010 Paul Bayes
2015 Noel Michael Roy Beasley

Horsham (Chichester)

1968 Simon Wilton Phipps
1975 Ivor Colin Docker
1991 John William Hind
1993 Lindsay Goodall Urwin
2009 Mark Crispin Rake Sowerby

Huddersfield (Leeds)

2014 Jonathan Robert Gibbs

Hull (York)

1538 Robert Sylvester (Pursglove)
1579–1891 *in abeyance*
1891 Richard Frederick Lefevre Blunt
1910 John Augustus Kempthome
1913 Francis Gurdon
1929–31 *no appointment*
1931 Bemard Oliver Francis
      Heywood
1934 Henry Townsend Vodden
1957 George Frednck Townley
1965 Hubert Laurence Higgs
1977 Geoffrey John Paul
1981 Donald George Snelgrove
1994 James Stuart Jones
1998 Richard Michael Cockayne
      Frith
2014 Alison Mary White

Hulme (Manchester)

1924 John Charles Hill
1930 Thomas Sherwood Jones
1945 Hugh Leycester Homby
1953 Kenneth Venner Ramsey
1975 David George Galliford
1984 Colin John Fraser Scott
1999 Stephen Richard Lowe

Huntingdon (Ely)

1966 Robert Arnold Schürhoff
      Martineau
1972 Eric St Quintin Wall
1980 William Gordon Roe
1997 John Robert Flack
2003 John Geoffrey Inge
2008 David Thomson

Ipswich (Norwich)

1536 Thomas Manning[1]
?–1899 *in abeyance*[2]
1899 George Carnac Fisher
1906 Henry Luke Paget
1909 *no appointment*
1914 *became diocesan see with*
      St Edmundsbury

Islington (London)

1898 Charles Henry Turner
1923–2015 *in abeyance*
2015 Richard Charles Thorpe

Jarrow (Durham)

1906 George Nickson
1914 John Nathaniel Quirk
1924 Samuel Kirshbaum Knight
1932 James Geoffrey Gordon
1939 Leslie Owen
1944 David Colin Dunlop
1950 John Alexander Ramsbotham
1958 Mervyn Armstrong
1965 Alexander Kenneth Hamilton
1980 Michael Thomas Ball
1990 Alan Smithson
2002 John Lawrence Pritchard
2007 Mark Watts Bryant

Kensington (London)

1901 Frederic Edward Ridgeway
1911 John Primatt Maud
1932 Bertram Fitzgerald Simpson
1942 Henry Colville Montgomery
      Campbell
1949 Cyril Eastaugh
1962 Edward James Keymer Roberts
1964 Ronald Cedric Osbourne
      Goodchild
1981 Mark Santer
1987 John George Hughes
1994–96 *no appointment*
1996 Michael John Colclough
2009 Paul Gavin Williams
2015 Graham Stuart Tomlin

Kingston-upon-Thames

(Southwark)

1905 Cecil Hook
1915 Samuel Mumford Taylor
1922 Percy Mark Herbert
1927 Frederick Ochterlony Taylor
      Hawkes
1952 William Percy Gilpin
1970 Hugh William Montefiore
1978 Keith Norman Sutton
1984 Peter Stephen Maurice Selby
1992 John Martin Wharton
1997 Peter Bryan Price
2002 Richard Ian Cheetham

Knaresborough (Ripon)

1905 Lucius Frederick Moses
      Bottomley Smith
1934 Paul Fulcrand Dalacour de
      Labilliere
1938 John Norman Bateman-
      Champain
1948 Henry Handley Vully de
      Candole
1965 John Howard Cruse
1972 Ralph Emmerson
1979 John Dennis
1986 Malcolm James Menin

1997 Frank Valentine Weston
2004 James Harold Bell
2014 *renamed* Ripon

Lancaster (Blackburn)

1936 Benjamin Pollard
1955 Anthony Leigh Egerton
      Hoskyns-Abrahall
1975 Dennis Fountain Page
1985 Ian Harland
1990 John Nicholls
1998 Geoffrey Stephen Pedley
2006 Geoffrey Seagrave Pearson

Leicester (Peterborough)

see also under Lichfield *and* Lincoln

1888 Francis Henry Thicknesse
1903 Lewis Clayton
1913 Norman MacLeod Lang
1927 *became diocesan see*

Lewes (Chichester)

1909 Leonard Hedley Burrows
1914 Herbert Edward Jones
1920 Henry Kemble Southwell
1926 Thomas William Cook
1929 William Champion Streatfield
1929 Hugh Maudsley Hordern
1946 Geoffrey Hodgson Warde
1959 James Herbert Lloyd Morrell
1977 Peter John Ball
1992 Ian Patrick Martyn Cundy
1997 Wallace Parke Benn
2014 Richard Charles Jackson

Ludlow (Hereford)

1981 Stanley Mark Wood
1987 Ian Macdonald Griggs
1994 John Charles Saxbee
2002 Michael Wrenford Hooper
2009 Alistair James Magowan

Lynn (Norwich)

1963 William Somers Llewellyn
1972 William Aubrey Aitken
1986 David Edward Bentley
1994 David John Conner
1999 Anthony Charles Foottit
2004 James Henry Langstaff
2011 Cyril Jonathan Meyrick

Maidstone (Canterbury)

1944 Leslie Owen
1946–56 *no appointment*
1956 Stanley Woodley Betts
1966–69 *no appointment*
1969 Geoffrey Lewis Tiarks
1976 Richard Henry McPhail Third
1980 Robert Maynard Hardy
1987 David James Smith
1992 Gavin Hunter Reid
2001 Graham Alan Cray
2009–2015 *no appointment*
2015 Roderick Charles Howell
      Thomas

Malmesbury (Bristol)

1927 Ronald Erskine Ramsay
1946 Ivor Stanley Watkins
1956 Edward James Keymer Roberts
1962 Clifford Leofric Purdy Bishop
1973 Frederick Stephen Temple
1983 Peter James Firth
1994 *renamed* Swindon

---

[1] Manning does not appear to have acted as a suffragan bishop in the diocese of Norwich.   [2] The date of Manning's death is not known.

Marlborough

1537 Thomas Morley (Bickley)[1]
c1561–1888 in abeyance
1888 Alfred Earle[2]
1919 in abeyance

Middleton (Manchester)

1927 Richard Godfrey Parsons
1932 Cecil Wilfred Wilson
1938 Arthur Fawssett Alston
1943 Edward Worsfold Mowll
1952 Frank Woods
1958 Robert Nelson
1959 Edward Ralph Wickham
1982 Donald Alexander Tytler
1994 Stephen Squires Venner
1999 Michael Augustine Owen Lewis
2008 Mark Davies

Nottingham (Lincoln)

[in York diocese to 1837]

1567 Richard Barnes
1570–1870 in abeyance
1870 Henry Mackenzie
1877 Edward Trollope
1893 in abeyance

Penrith (Carlisle)

see also under Richmond

1537 John Bird[3]
1539–1888 in abeyance
1888 John James Pulleine[4]
1939 Grandage Edwards Powell
1944 Herbert Victor Turner
1959 Sydney Cyril Bulley
1967 Reginald Foskett
1970 William Edward Augustus Pugh
1979 George Lanyon Hacker
1994 Richard Garrard
2002 James William Scobie Newcome
2011 Robert John Freeman

Plymouth (Exeter)

1923 John Howard Bertram
     Masterman
1934 Francis Whitfield Daukes
1950 Norman Harry Clarke
1962 Wilfred Guy Sanderson
1972 Richard Fox Cartwright
1982 Kenneth Albert Newing
1988 Richard Stephen Hawkins
1996 John Henry Garton
2005 John Frank Ford
2015 Nicholas Howard Paul
     McKinnel

Pontefract (Wakefield)

1931 Campbell Richard Hone
1939 Tom Longworth
1949 Arthur Harold Morris
1954 George William Clarkson
1961 Eric Treacy
1968 William Gordon Fallows
1971 Thomas Richard Hare
1993 John Thornley Finney
1998 David Charles James
2002 Anthony William Robinson
2014 renamed Wakefield

Ramsbury (Salisbury)

see also under Salisbury

1974 John Robert Geoffrey Neale
1989 Peter St George Vaughan
1999 Peter Fearnley Hullah

Reading (Oxford)

1889 James Leslie Randall
1909–42 in abeyance
1942 Arthur Groom Parham
1954 Eric Henry Knell
1972 Eric Wild
1982 Ronald Graham Gregory Foley
1989 John Frank Ewan Bone
1997 Edward William Murray Walker
2004 Stephen Geoffrey Cottrell
2011 Andrew John Proud

Repton (Derby)

1965 William Warren Hunt
1977 Stephen Edmund Verney
1986 Francis Henry Arthur
     Richmond
1999 David Christopher Hawtin
2007 Humphrey Ivo John Southern

Richborough (Canterbury)

1995 Edwin Ronald Barnes
2002 Keith Newton
2011 Norman Banks

Richmond (Leeds)

1889 John James Pulleine[5]
1913 Francis Charles Kilner
1921–2015 in abeyance
2015 Paul John Slater

Ripon (Leeds)

formerly Knaresborough

2004 James Harold Bell

St Germans (Truro)

1905 John Rundle Cornish
1918–74 in abeyance
1974 Cecil Richard Rutt
1979 Reginald Lindsay Fisher
1985 John Richard Allan Llewellin
1993 Graham Richard James
2000 Royden Screech
2013 Christopher David Goldsmith

Selby (York)

1939 Henry St John Stirling
     Woollcombe
1941 Carey Frederick Knyvett
1962 Douglas Noel Sargent
1972 Morris Henry St John Maddocks
1983 Clifford Conder Barker
1991 Humphrey Vincent Taylor
2003 Martin William Wallace
2014 John Bromilow Thomson

Shaftesbury (Salisbury)

[in Bristol diocese 1542–1836]

1539 John Bradley
? in abeyance[6]

Sheffield (York)

1901 John Nathaniel Quirk
1914 became diocesan see

Sherborne (Salisbury)

1925 Robert Crowther Abbott
1928 Gerald Burton Allen

Marlborough

1537 Thomas Morley (Bickley)[1]

2006 Stephen David Conway
2012 Edward Francis Condry

1936 Harold Nickinson Rodgers
1947 John Maurice Key
1960 Victor Joseph Pike
1976 John Dudley Galtrey Kirkham
2001 Timothy Martin Thornton
2009 Graham Ralph Kings

Sherwood (Southwell)

1965 Kenneth George Thompson
1975 Harold Richard Darby
1989 Alan Wyndham Morgan
2006 Anthony Porter

Shrewsbury (Lichfield)

1537 Lewis Thomas[7]
1561–1888 in abeyance
1888 Sir Lovelace Tomlinson Stamer
1905–40 in abeyance
1940 Eric Knightley Chetwode
     Hamilton
1944 Robert Leighton Hodson
1959 William Alonzo Parker
1970 Francis William Cocks
1980 Leslie Lloyd Rees
1987 John Dudley Davies
1994 David Marrison Hallatt
2001 Alan Gregory Clayton Smith
2009 Mark James Rylands

Southampton (Winchester)

1895 William Awdry
1896 George Carnac Fisher
1898 The Hon Arthur Temple
     Lyttelton
1903 James Macarthur
1921 Cecil Henry Boutflower
1933 Arthur Baillie Lumsdaine
     Karney
1943 Edmund Robert Morgan
1951 Kenneth Edward Norman
     Lamplugh
1972 John Kingsmill Cavell
1984 Edward David Cartwright
1989 John Freeman Perry
1996 Jonathan Michael Gledhill
2004 Paul Roger Butler
2010 Jonathan Hugh Frost

Southwark (Rochester)

1891 Huyshe Wolcott Yeatman-Biggs
1905 became diocesan see

Stafford (Lichfield)

1909 Edward Ash Were
1915 Lionel Payne Crawfurd
1934 Douglas Henry Crick
1938 Lemprière Durell Hammond
1958 Richard George Clitherow
1975 John Waine
1979 John Stevens Waller
1987 Michael Charles Scott-Joynt
1996 Christopher John Hill
2005 Alfred Gordon Mursell
2010 Geoffrey Peter Annas

Stepney (London)

1895 George Forrest Browne
1897 Arthur Foley Winnington-
     Ingram
1901 Cosmo Gordon Lang
1909 Henry Luke Paget
1919 Henry Mosley
1928 Charles Edward Curzon
1936 Robert Hamilton Moberly
1952 Joost de Blank

---

[1] Appointed for the diocese of London.   [2] Appointed for the diocese of London, but retained the title while Dean of Exeter 1900-18.
[3] Appointed for the diocese of Lichfield.   [4] Appointed for the diocese of Ripon.
[5] His suffragan title was changed from Penrith to Richmond by Royal Warrant.
[6] The date of Bradley's death is not known.   [7] Not appointed for Lichfield, but probably for Llandaff.

1957 Francis Evered Lunt
1968 Ernest Urban Trevor
      Huddleston
1978 James Lawton Thompson
1992 Richard John Carew Chartres
1996 John Mugabi Sentamu
2003 Stephen John Oliver
2011 Adrian Newman

Stockport (Chester)

1949 Frank Jackson Okell
1951 David Henry Saunders
      Saunders-Davies
1965 Rupert Gordon Strutt
1984 Frank Pilkington Sargeant
1994 Geoffrey Martin Turner
2000 William Nigel Stock
2008 Robert Ronald Atwell
2015 Elizabeth Jane Holden Lane

Swindon (Bristol)

formerly Malmesbury

1994 Michael David Doe
2005 Lee Stephen Rayfield

Taunton (Bath and Wells)

1538 William Finch
1559–1911 *in abeyance*
1911 Charles Fane de Salis
1931 George Arthur Hollis
1945 Harry Thomas
1955 Mark Allin Hodson
1962 Francis Horner West
1977 Peter John Nott
1986 Nigel Simeon McCulloch
1992 John Hubert Richard Lewis
1997 William Allen Stewart
1998 Andrew John Radford
2006 Peter David Maurice
2015 Ruth Elizabeth Worsley

Tewkesbury (Gloucester)

1938 Augustine John Hodson
1955 Edward Barry Henderson
1960 Forbes Trevor Horan
1973 Thomas Carlyle Joseph Robert
      Hamish Deakin
1986 Geoffrey David Jeremy Walsh
1996 John Stewart Went
2013 Martyn James Snow

Thetford (Norwich)

see also under Norwich

1536 John Salisbury
1570–1894 *in abeyance*
1894 Arthur Thomas Lloyd
1903 John Philips Alcott Bowers
1926–45 *no appointment*
1945 John Walker Woodhouse
1953 Manin Patrick Grainge Leonard
1963 Eric William Bradley Cordingly
1977 Hugh Charles Blackburne
1981 Timothy Dudley-Smith
1992 Hugo Ferdinand de Waal
2001 David John Atkinson
2009 Alan Peter Winton

Tonbridge (Rochester)

1959 Russell Berridge White
1968 Henry David Halsey
1973 Philip Harold Ernest Goodrich
1982 David Henry Bartleet
1993 Brian Arthur Smith
2002 Brian Colin Castle

Wakefield (Leeds)

formerly Pontefract

2014 Anthony William Robinson

Warrington (Liverpool)

1918 Martin Linton Smith
1920 Edwin Hone Kempson
1927 Herbert Gresford Jones
1946 Charles Robert Claxton
1960 Laurence Ambrose Brown
1970 John Monier Bickersteth
1976 Michael Henshall
1996 John Richard Packer
2000 David Wilfred Michael Jennings
2009 Richard Finn Blackburn

Warwick (Coventry)

1980 Keith Appleby Arnold
1990 Clive Handford
1996 Anthony Martin Priddis
2005 John Ronald Angus Stroyan

Whalley (Blackburn)

[in Manchester diocese to 1926]

1909 Atherton Gwillym Rawstorne
1936 *in abeyance*

Whitby (York)

1923 Harry St John Stirling
      Woollcombe
1939 Harold Evelyn Hubbard
1947 Walter Hubert Baddeley
1954 Philip William Wheeldon
1961 George D'Oyly Snow
1972 John Yates
1976 Clifford Conder Barker
1983 Gordon Bates
1999 Robert Sidney Ladds
2010 Martin Clive Warner
2014 Paul John Ferguson

Willesden (London)

1911 William Willcox Perrin
1929 Guy Vernon Smith
1940 Henry Colville Montgomery
      Campbell
1942 Edward Michael Gresford
      Jones
1950 Gerald Alexander Ellison
1955 George Ernest Ingle
1964 Graham Douglas Leonard
1974 Geoffrey Hewlett Thompson
1985 Thomas Frederick Butler
1992 Geoffrey Graham Dow
2001 Peter Alan Broadbent

Wolverhampton (Lichfield)

1979 Barry Rogerson
1985 Christopher John Mayfield
1994 Michael Gay Bourke
2007 Clive Malcolm Gregory

Woolwich (Southwark)

1905 John Cox Leeke
1918 William Woodcock Hough
1932 Arthur Llewellyn Preston
1936 Leslie Hamilton Lang
1947 Robert William Stannard
1959 John Arthur Thomas
      Robinson
1969 David Stuart Sheppard
1975 Michael Eric Marshall
1984 Albert Peter Hall
1996 Colin Ogilvie Buchanan
2005 Christopher Thomas James
      Chessun
2012 Michael Geoffrey Ipgrave

WALES

Archbishops of Wales

1920 Alfred George Edwards
      (St Asaph 1889–1934)
1934 Charles Alfred Howell Green
      (Bangor 1928–44)
1944 David Lewis Prosser (St Davids
      1927–50)
1949 John Morgan (Llandaff
      1939–57)
1957 Alfred Edwin Morris
      (Monmouth 1945–67)
1968 William Glyn Hughes Simon
      (Llandaff 1957–71)
1971 Gwilym Owen Williams
      (Bangor 1957–82)
1983 Derrick Greenslade Childs
      (Monmouth 1972–87)
1987 George Noakes (St Davids
      1982–91)
1991 Alwyn Rice Jones (St Asaph
      1982–99)
1999 Rowan Douglas Williams
      (Monmouth 1992–2002)

2003 Barry Cennydd Morgan
      (Llandaff 1999–)

Bangor[1]

Description of arms. Gules, a bend or
guttée de poix between two mullets
pierced argent.

*c.*550 Deiniol [Daniel]
*c.*775 Elfod [Elbodugen]
1092 Herve
[*Vacancy* 1109–20]
1120 David the Scot
1140 Maurice (Meurig)
[*Vacancy* 1161–77]
1177 Guy Rufus [Gwion Goch]
[*Vacancy c*1190–95]
1195 Alan [Alban]
1197 Robert of Shrewsbury
[*Vacancy* 1212–15]
1215 Cadwgan
1237 Richard
1267 Anian [or Einion]
1307 Gruflydd ab Iowerth
1309 Anian [Einion] Sais
1328 Matthew de Englefield
1357 Thomas de Ringstead
1366 Gervase de Castro
1371 Hywel ap Gronwy
1372 John Gilbert
1376 John Swaffham
1400 Richard Young
[*Vacancy c*1404–8]
1408 Benedict Nicolls
1418 William Barrow

[1] Very few of the names of the Celtic bishops have been preserved.

1425 John Cliderow
1436 Thomas Cheriton
1448 John Stanbury
1453 James Blakedon
1465 Richard Edenham
1495 Henry Dean
1500 Thomas Pigot
1505 Thomas Penny
1509 Thomas Skevington
1534 John Salcot [or Capon]
1539 John Bird
1542 Arthur Bulkeley
1555 William Glynn
1559 Rowland Meyrick
1566 Nicholas Robinson
1586 Hugh Bellot
1596 Richard Vaughan
1598 Henry Rowlands
1616 Lewis Bayly
1632 David Dolben
1634 Edmund Griffith
1637 William Roberts
1666 Robert Morgan
1673 Humphrey Lloyd
1689 Humphrey Humphreys
1702 John Evans
1716 Benjamin Hoadley
1721 Richard Reynolds
1723 William Baker
1728 Thomas Sherlock
1734 Charles Cecil
1738 Thomas Herring
1743 Matthew Hutton
1748 Zachary Pearce
1756 John Egerton
1769 John Ewer
1775 John Moore
1783 John Warren
1800 William Cleaver
1807 John Randolph
1809 Henry William Majendie
1830 Christopher Bethell
1859 James Colquhoun Campbell
1890 Daniel Lewis Lloyd
1899 Watkin Herbert Williams
1925 Daniel Davies
1928 Charles Alfred Howell Green
    (Archbishop of Wales 1934)
1944 David Edwardes Davies
1949 John Charles Jones
1957 Gwilym Owen Williams
    (Archbishop of Wales 1971)
1982 John Cledan Mears
1993 Barry Cennydd Morgan
1999 Francis James Saunders Davies
2004 Phillip Anthony Crockett
2008 Andrew Thomas Griffith John

Llandaff[1]

Description of arms. Sable, two pastoral
staves endorsed in saltire, the dexter or,
the sinister argent. On a chief azure
three labelled mitres or.

*c.*550 Teiliau
*c.*872 Cyfeiliag
*c.*880 Libiau
*c.*940 Marchlwys
 982 Gwyzan

*c.*995 Bledri
1027 Joseph
1056 Herewald
1107 Urban
[*Vacancy of six years*]
1140 Uchtryd
1148 Nicolas ap Gwrgant
[*Vacancy of two years*]
1186 William Saltmarsh
1193 Henry of Abergavenny
1219 William of Goldcliff
1230 Elias of Radnor
1245 William de Burgh
1254 John de Ware
1257 William of Radnor
1266 Willam de Breuse [or Brus]
1297 John of Monmouth
1323 John of Eaglescliffe
1344 John Paschal
1361 Roger Cradock
1383 Thomas Rushook
1386 William Bottesham
1389 Edmund Bromfield
1393 Tideman de Winchcomb
1395 Andrew Barret
1396 John Burghill
1398 Thomas Peverel
1408 John de la Zouch [Fulford]
1425 John Wells
1441 Nicholas Ashby
1458 John Hunden
1476 John Smith
1478 John Marshall
1496 John Ingleby
1500 Miles Salley
1517 George de Athequa
1537 Robert Holdgate [or Holgate]
1545 Anthony Kitchin
1567 Hugh Jones
1575 William Blethin
1591 Gervase Babington
1595 William Morgan
1601 Francis Godwin
1618 George Carleton
1619 Theophilus Field
1627 William Murray
1640 Morgan Owen
1660 Hugh Lloyd
1667 Francis Davies
1675 William Lloyd
1679 William Beaw
1706 John Tyler
1725 Robert Clavering
1729 John Harris
1739 Matthias Mawson
1740 John Gilbert
1749 Edward Cressett
1755 Richard Newcome
1761 John Ewer
1769 Jonathan Shipley
1769 Shute Barrington
1782 Richard Watson
1816 Herbert Marsh
1819 William Van Mildert
1826 Charles Richard Sumner
1828 Edward Copleston
1849 Alfred Ollivant
1883 Richard Lewis
1905 Joshua Pritchard Hughes
1931 Timothy Rees
1939 John Morgan (Archbishop
    of Wales 1949)
1957 William Glyn Hughes Simon
    (Archbishop of Wales
    1968)
1971 Eryl Stephen Thomas
1975 John Richard Worthington
    Poole-Hughes
1985 Roy Thomas Davies
1999 Barry Cennydd Morgan
    (Archbishop of Wales 2003)

Monmouth

Description of arms. Per pale azure and
sable, two crosiers in satire or between
in chief a besant charged with a lion
passant guardant gules, in fess two
fleurs-de-lis and in base a fleur-de-lis all
of the third.

1921 Charles Alfred Howell Green
1928 Gilbert Cunningham Joyce
1940 Alfred Edwin Monahan
1945 Alfred Edwin Morris
    (Archbishop of Wales 1957)
1968 Eryl Stephen Thomas
1972 Derrick Greenslade Childs
    (Archbishop of Wales 1983)
1986 Royston Clifford Wright
1992 Rowan Douglas Williams
    (Archbishop of Wales 1999)
2003 Edward William Murray Walker
2013 Richard Edward Pain

St Asaph[2]

Description of arms. Sable, two keys
endorsed in saltire the wards upwards
argent.

*c.*560 Kentigern
*c.*573 Asaph
1143 Gilbert
1152 Geoffrey of Monmouth
1154 Richard
1160 Godfrey
1175 Adam
1183 John I
1186 Reiner
1225 Abraham
1235 Hugh
1242 Hywel Ab Ednyfed
1249 Anian I [or Einion]
1267 John II
1268 Anian II
1293 Llywelyn de Bromfield
1315 Dafydd ap Bleddyn
1346 John Trevor I
1357 Llywelyn ap Madoc ab Ellis
1377 William de Spridlington
1382 Lawrence Child
1390 Alexander Bache
1395 John Trevor II
1411 Robert de Lancaster
1433 John Lowe
1444 Reginald Pecock
1451 Thomas Bird *alias* Knight
1471 Richard Redman
1496 Michael Deacon

---

[1] The traditional list of bishops of the Celtic Church has little historical foundation. But the names of the following, prior to Urban, may be regarded as fairly trustworthy, though the dates are very uncertain.
[2] Prior to the Norman period there is considerable uncertainty as to names and dates.

1500 Dafydd ab Iorwerth
1504 Dafydd ab Owain
1513 Edmund Birkhead
1518 Henry Standish
1536 Robert Warton [or Parfew]
1555 Thomas Goldwell
1560 Richard Davies
1561 Thomas Davies
1573 William Hughes
1601 William Morgan
1604 Richard Parry
1624 John Hanmer
1629 John Owen
1660 George Griffith
1667 Henry Glemham
1670 Isaac Barrow
1680 William Lloyd
1692 Edward Jones
1703 George Hooper
1704 William Beveridge
1708 Will. Fleetwood
1715 John Wynne
1727 Francis Hare
1732 Thomas Tanner
1736 Isaac Maddox
1744 Samuel Lisle
1748 Robert Hay Drummond
1761 Richard Newcome
1769 Jonathan Shipley
1789 Samuel Hallifax
1790 Lewis Bagot
1802 Samuel Horsley
1806 William Cleaver
1815 John Luxmore
1830 William Carey
1846 Thomas Vowler Short
1870 Joshua Hughes
1889 Alfred George Edwards
     (Archbishop of Wales 1920)
1934 William Thomas Havard
1950 David Daniel Bartlett
1971 Harold John Charles
1982 Alwyn Rice Jones (Archbishop
     of Wales 1991)
1999 John Stewart Davies
2009 Gregory Kenneth Cameron

St Davids[1]

Description of arms. Sable, on a cross or
five cinquefoils of the first.

c.601 David
c.606 Cynog
 831 Sadyrnfyw
     Meurig

c.840 Novis
     ?Idwal
c.906 Asser
     Llunwerth
 944 Eneuris
c.961 Rhydderch
c.999 Morgeneu
1023 Morgeneu
1023 Erwyn
1039 Tramerin
1061 Joseph
1061 Bleddud
1072 Sulien
1078 Abraham
1080 Sulien
1085 Wilfrid
1115 Bernard
1148 David Fitz-Gerald
1176 Peter de Leia
1203 Geoffrey de Henlaw
1215 Gervase [Iorwerth]
1231 Anselm le Gras
1248 Thomas le Waleys
1256 Richard de Carew
1280 Thomas Bek
1296 David Martin
1328 Henry Gower
1347 John Thoresby
1350 Reginald Brian
1352 Thomas Fastolf
1362 Adam Houghton
1389 John Gilbert
1397 Guy de Mohne
1408 Henry Chichele
1414 John Catterick
1415 Stephen Patrington
1418 Benedict Nichols
1434 Thomas Rodburn
     [Rudborne]
1442 William Lindwood
1447 John Langton
1447 John de la Bere
1460 Robert Tully
1482 Richard Martin
1483 Thomas Langton
1485 Hugh Pavy
1496 John Morgan [Young]
1505 Robert Sherborn
1509 Edward Vaughan
1523 Richard Rawlins
1536 William Barlow
1548 Robert Ferrar
1554 Henry Morgan
1560 Thomas Young
1561 Richard Davies
1582 Marmaduke Middleton
1594 Anthony Rudd
1615 Richard Milbourne
1621 William Laud
1627 Theophilus Field
1636 Roger Mainwaring
1660 William Lucy
1678 William Thomas
1683 Laurence Womock
1686 John Lloyd
1687 Thomas Watson
[*Vacancy* 1699–1705]
1705 George Bull

1710 Philip Bisse
1713 Adam Ottley
1724 Richard Smallbrooke
1731 Elias Sydall
1732 Nicholas Claggett
1743 Edward Willes
1744 Richard Trevor
1753 Anthony Ellis
1761 Samuel Squire
1766 Robert Lowth
1766 Charles Moss
1774 James Yorke
1779 John Warren
1783 Edward Smallwell
1788 Samuel Horsley
1794 William Stewart
1801 George Murray
1803 Thomas Burgess
1825 John Banks Jenkinson
1840 Connop Thirlwall
1874 William Basil Tickell Jones
1897 John Owen
1927 David Lewis Prosser
     (Archbishop of Wales 1944)
1950 William Thomas Havard
1956 John Richards Richards
1971 Eric Matthias Roberts
1982 George Noakes (Archbishop of
     Wales 1987)
1991 John Ivor Rees
1996 David Huw Jones
2002 Carl Norman Cooper
2008 John Wyn Evans

Swansea and Brecon

Description of arms. Per fess azure and or,
in chief surmounting a catherine wheel
issuant an eagle rising regardant of the
second and in base a fleur-de-lis of the
first.

1923 Edward Latham Bevan
1934 John Morgan
1939 Edward William Williamson
1953 William Glyn Hughes Simon
1958 John James Absalom Thomas
1976 Benjamin Noel Young Vaughan
1988 Dewi Morris Bridges
1999 Anthony Edward Pierce
2008 John David Edward Davies

Provincial Assistant Bishop

1996–2008 David Thomas

---

[1] The following names occur in early records though the dates given cannot always be reconciled.

SCOTLAND

Sources: Bp Dowden's *The Bishops of Scotland* (Glasgow 1912), for all the sees up to the Reformation, and for Aberdeen and Moray to the present time.

For bishops after the Reformation (and for a few of the earliest ones before Queen Margaret) – Grub, *Ecclesiastical History of Scotland* (Edinburgh 1861, 4 Vols.) and Bp Keith and Bp Russel, *Scottish Bishops* (2nd ed. Edinburgh 1824).

Scottish episcopal elections became subject immediately to Roman confirmation in 1192. The subordination of the Scottish Church to York became less direct in 1165, and its independence was recognized in a bill of Celestine III in 1192. St Andrews was raised to metropolitan rank on 17 August 1472 and the Archbishop became primate of all Scotland with the same legative rights as the Archbishop of Canterbury on 27 March 1487.

The dates in the margin are those of the consecration or translation to the particular see of the bishops named; or in the case of bishops elect, who are not known to have been consecrated, they are those of the election; or in the case of titular bishops, of the date of their appointment.

The date of the death has been given where there was a long interregnum, or where there is dislocation (as at the Reformation and at the Revolution), or for some special reason to make the history intelligible.

The extra information in the list of College Bishops is given for the reason just stated.

St Andrews

St Andrews, Dunkeld and Dunblane

Description of arms. Quarterly, 1st azure, a saltire argent (for the See of St Andrews); 2nd per fess sable and vert, an open book proper in base, fore-edges and binding or, a dove argent, her wings displayed in chief perching thereon and holding in her beak a spray of olive of the second (for the See of Dunkeld); 3rd chevronny or and gules, a saltire engrailed azure, charged at the fess point with a crescent inverted argent (for the See of Dunblane); 4th azure, a saltire argent supported in front of and by St Andrew enhaloed or and vested pupure with mantle vert, and in base a crescent inverted of the second (for the See of St Andrews).

906 Cellach I
915(?) Fothad I
955 Malisius I
963 Maelbridge
970 Cellach II
996(?) Malasius II
(?) Malmore
1025 Alwyn
1028 Maelduin
1055 Tuthald or Tuadal
1059 Fothad II
1077 ⎱ Gregory (elect)
to ⎰ Catharas (elect)
1107 ⎰ Edmarus (elect)
 ⎱ Godricus (elect)
1109 Turgot
1120 Eadmer (elect)
1127 Robert
1159 Waldeve (elect)
1160 Ernald
1165 Richard
1178 Hugh
1180 John the Scot
1198 Roger de Beaumon
1202 William Malveisin
1238 Geoffrey (elect)
1240 David de Bernham
1253 Robert de Stuteville (elect)
1254 Abel de Golin
1255 Gamelin
1273 William Wischard
1280 William Fraser

1298 William de Lamberton
1328 James Bennet
1342 William de Laundels
1385 Stephen de Pay (elect)
1386(?) Walter Trayl
1388 Alexander de Neville
1398 Thomas de Arundel
1401 Thomas Stewart (elect)
1402 Walter de Danielston (elect)
1403(?) Gilbert Greenlaw
1403 Henry Wardlaw
1408 John Trevor
1440 James Kennedy

ARCHBISHOPS

1465 Patrick Graham
1478 William Scheves
1497 James Stewart (elect)
1504 Alexander Stewart (elect)
1513 John Hepburn (elect)
1513 Innocenzo Cibo (elect)
1514 Andrew Forman
1522 James Betoun
1538 David Betoun [coadjutor]
1547 John Hamilton
1551 Gavin Hamilton [coadjutor] died 1571
1572 John Douglas (titular)
1576 Patrick Adamson (titular) died 1592
1611 George Gladstanes
1615 John Spottiswoode, died 1639
1661 James Sharp
1679 Alexander Burnet
1684 Arthur Rose, died 1704

BISHOPS OF FIFE

[1704–26 See vacant]
1726 James Rose
1733 Robert Keith
1743 Robert White
1761 Henry Edgar

BISHOPS OF ST ANDREWS

1842 Patrick Torry
1853 Charles Wordsworth
1893 George Howard Wilkinson
1908 Charles Edward Plumb
1931 Edward Thomas Scott Reid
1938 James Lumsden Barkway
1949 Arnold Brian Burrowes
1955 John William Alexander Howe
1969 Michael Geoffrey Hare Duke
1995 Michael Harry George Henley
2005 David Robert Chillingworth

†Dunkeld

849(?) Tuathal
865(?) Flaithbertach
1114 Cormac

1147 Gregory
1170 Richard I
1178 Walter de Bidun (elect)
1183(?) John I, the Scot
1203 Richard II, de Prebenda
1212(?) John II, de Leycester
1214(?) Hugh de Sigillo
1229 Matthew Scot (elect)
1229 Gilbert
1236(?) Geoffrey de Liberatione
1252 Richard III, of Inverkeithing
1273(?) Robert de Stuteville
1283(?) Hugh de Strivelin [Stirling] (elect)
1283 William
1288 Matthew de Crambeth
1309 John de Leek (elect)
1312 William Sinclair
1337 Malcolm de Innerpeffray (elect)
1344 Richard de Pilmor
1347 Robert de Den (elect)
1347(?) Duncan de Strathearn
1355 John Luce
1370 John de Carrick (elect)
1371(?) Michael de Monymusk
1377(?) Andrew Umfray (elect)
1379 John de Peblys [? of Peebles]
1379 Robert de Derling
1390(?) Nicholas Duffield
1391 Robert Sinclair
1398(?) Robert de Cardeny
1430 William Gunwardby
1437 Donald MacNaughton (elect)
1438 James Kennedy
1440(?) Thomas Livingston
1440 Alexander de Lawedre [Lauder] (elect)
1442 James de Brois [Brewhous]
1447 William Turnbull (elect)
1448 John Ralston
1452(?) Thomas Lauder
1476 James Livingston
1483 Alexander Inglis (elect)
1484 George Brown
1515 Andrew Stewart (elect)
1516 Gavin Douglas
1524 Robert Cockburn
1526(?) George Crichton
1546 John Hamilton
1552 Robert Crichton
1572 James Paton (titular)
1585 Peter Rollock (titular)
1607 James Nicolson (titular)
1611(?) Alexander Lindsay (deposed 1638)
1662 George Haliburton
1665 Henry Guthrie
1677 William Lindsay
1679 Andrew Bruce
1686 John Hamilton
1717 Thomas Rattray
1743 John Alexander
1776(?) Charles Rose
1792 Jonathan Watson

† Indicates a diocese no longer extant, or united with another diocese.

1808 Patrick Torry
1842 Held with St Andrews

†Dunblane

1162 Laurence
*c.*1180 Symon
1196 W[illelmus]
1198 Jonathan
1215 Abraham
1225 Ralph (elect)
1227 Osbert
1233 Clement
1259 Robert de Prebenda
1284 William I
1296 Alpin
1301 Nicholas
1307 Nicholas de Balmyle
1318(?) Roger de Balnebrich (elect)
1322 Maurice
*c.*1347 William II
*c.*1361 Walter de Coventre
*c.*1372 Andrew
*c.*1380 Dougal
1403(?) Finlay or Dermoch
1419 William Stephen
1430 Michael Ochiltree
1447(?) Robert Lauder
1468 John Hepburn
1487 James Chisolm
1527 William Chisolm I
1561 William Chisolm II [coadjutor]
1575 Andrew Graham (titular)
1611 George Graham
1616 Adam Bellenden
1636 James Wedderburn
1661 Robert Leighton
1673 James Ramsay
1684 Robert Douglas
[1716–31 See vacant]
1731 John Gillan
1735 Robert White
1744 Thomas Ogilvie (elect)
1774 Charles Rose, died 1791
1776 Held with Dunkeld

Edinburgh

Description of arms. Azure, a saltire and, in chief, a labelled mitre argent.

1634 William Forbes
1634 David Lindsay
1662 George Wishart
1672 Alexander Young
1679 John Paterson
1687 Alexander Rose
1720 John Fullarton
1727 Arthur Millar
1727 Andrew Lumsden
1733 David Freebairn
[1739–76 See vacant]
1776 William Falconer
1787 William Abernethy Drummond
1806 Daniel Sandford
1830 James Walker
1841 Charles Hughes Terrot
1872 Henry Cotterill
1886 John Dowden
1910 George Henry Somerset
         Walpole
1929 Harry Seymour Reid
1939 Ernest Denny Logie Danson

1947 Kenneth Charles Harman
         Warner
1961 Kenneth Moir Carey
1975 Alastair Iain Macdonald
         Haggart
1986 Richard Frederick Holloway
2001 Brian Arthur Smith
2012 John Andrew Armes

Aberdeen

Aberdeen and Orkney

Description of arms. Azure, parted per pale: dexter, a chevron round embattled on its upper edge between a fleur-de-lis argent ensigned of an open crown or in dexter chief, and in base a bishop proper, attired of the second, mitred and holding in his sinister hand a pastoral staff of the third, his dexter hand raised in benediction over three children gules issuant from a cauldron of the third; sinister, an open boat or, an anchor argent pendant from its prow, issuant therefrom a saint proper, attired of the third, enhaloed and holding in his sinister hand a pastoral staff of the second; over all and issuant from the chief a sunburst or, the central ray projected along the palar line to the base.

BISHOPS AT MURTHLAC

(?) Beyn [Beanus]
(?) Donort
(?) Cormac

BISHOPS AT ABERDEEN

1132 Nechtan
*c.*1150 Edward
*c.*1172 Matthew
*c.*1201 John
*c.*1208 Adam de Kalder
1228 Matthew Scot (elect)
1230 Gilbert de Strivelyn
1240 Radulf de Lamley
1247 Peter de Ramsey
1258 Richard de Pottun
1272 Hugh de Bennum
1282 Henry le Chene
1329 Walter Herok (elect)
1329 Alexander I, de Kyninmund
1344 William de Deyn
1351 John de Rate
1356 Alexander II, de Kyninmund
1380 Adam de Tynyngham
1391 Gilbert de Grenlaw
1422 Henry de Lychton [Leighton]
*c.*1441 Ingram de Lindsay
1458 Thomas Spens
1480 Robert Blackadder (elect)
1488 William Elphinstone
1515 Robert Forman (elect)
1516 Alexander Gordon
1519 Gavin Dunbar
1529 George Learmonth [coadjutor]
1533 William Stewart
1547 William Gordon
1577 David Cunningham (elect)
1611 Peter Blackburn
1616 Alexander Forbes

1618 Patrick Forbes of Corse
1635 Adam Bellenden [Bannatyne]
1662 David Mitchell
1663 Alexander Burnet
1664 Patrick Scougal
1682 George Halyburton
[1715–21 See vacant]
1721 Archibald Campbell
1724 James Gadderar
1733 William Dunbar
1746 Andrew Gerard
1768 Robert Kilgour
1786 John Skinner
1816 William Skinner
1857 Thomas George Spink Suther
1883 Arthur Gascoigne Douglas
1906 Rowland Ellis
1912 Anthony Mitchell
1917 Frederic Llewellyn Deane
1943 Herbert William Hall
1956 Edward Frederick Easson
1973 Ian Forbes Begg
1978 Frederick Charles Darwent
1992 Andrew Bruce Cameron
2007 Robert Arthur Gillies

†Orkney

1035 Henry
1050 Turolf
1072 John I
1072 Adalbert
1073 Radulf
1102 William I, 'the Old'
1108 Roger
1114 Radulf Novell
1168(?) William II
1188(?) Bjarni
1224 Jofreyrr
1248 Henry I
1270 Peter
1286 Dolgfinn
1310 William III
*c.*1369 William IV
*c.*1384 Robert Sinclair
1384(?) John
1394 Henry II
1396(?) John Pak
1407 Alexander Vaus (elect)
1415 William Stephenson
1420 Thomas Tulloch
1461 William Tulloch
1477 Andrew Painter
1500 Edward Stewart
1524 John Benston [coadjutor]
1526(?) Robert Maxwell
1541 Robert Reid
1559 Adam Bothwell
1611 James Law
1615 George Graham
1639 Robert Barron (elect)
1661 Thomas Sydserf
1664 Andrew Honeyman
1677 Murdo Mackenzie
1688 Andrew Bruce, See afterwards
         administered with Caithness
1857 Held with Aberdeen

Brechin

Description of arms. Or, three piles in point purpure.

1153(?) Samson
1178 Turpin
1202 Radulf
1215 Hugh
1218 Gregory
1246 Albin
1269(?) William de Crachin (elect)
1275 William Comyn
1296 Nicholas
1298 John de Kyninmund
1328 Adam de Moravia
1350 Philip Wilde
1351 Patrick de Locrys [Leuchars]
1383 Stephen de Cellario
1411 Walter Forrester
1426 John de Crannach
1455 George Schoriswood
1464 Patrick Graham
1465 John Balfour
1489 William Meldrum
1523 John Hepburn
1557 Donald Campbell (elect)
1565(?) John Sinclair (elect)
1566 Alexander Campbell (titular)
1610 Andrew Lamb
1619 David Lindsay
1634 Thomas Sydserf
1635 Walter Whitford
1662 David Strachan
1672 Robert Laurie
1678 George Haliburton
1682 Robert Douglas
1684 Alexander Cairncross
1684 James Drummond
1695–1709 Held with Edinburgh
1709 John Falconar
1724 Robert Norrie
1726 John Ochterlonie
1742 James Rait
1778 George Innes
1787 William Abernethy Drummond
1788 John Strachan
1810 George Gleig
1840 David Moir
1847 Alexander Penrose Forbes
1876 Hugh Willoughby Jermyn
1904 Walter John Forbes Robberds
1935 Kenneth Donald Mackenzie
1944 Eric Graham
1959 John Chappell Sprott
1975 Lawrence Edward Luscombe
1990 Robert Taylor Halliday
1997 Neville Chamberlain
2005 John Ambrose Cyril Mantle
2011 Nigel Peyton

Moray

Moray, Ross and Caithness

Description of arms. Party per fess and in chief per pale: 1 or, two lions combatant gules, pulling at a cushion of the last issuant from a crescent azure, on a chief wavy of the third three mullets argent (for the See of Moray); 2 argent, a bishop standing in the sinister vested purpure, mitred and holding in his sinister hand a crosier or and pointing with the dexter hand to a saint affontée, his hands clasped on this breast proper, habited gules, above his head a halo of the third (for the See of Ross); 3 azure, issuant from an antique boat or, a demi-bishop proper vested argent, his mitre and pastoral staff in hand sinister of the second, accompanied by two demi-angels, one in the dexter and the other in the sinister chief holding open books proper, their wings addorsed, also of the second (for the See of Caithness).

1114 Gregory
1153(?) William
1164 Felix
1172 Simon de Tonei
1187 Richard de Lincoln
1203 Brice de Douglas
1224(?) Andrew de Moravia
1244(?) Simon
1251 Radulf de Leycester (elect)
1253 Archibald
1299 David de Moravia
1326 John de Pilmor
1363 Alexander Bur
1397 William de Spyny
1407 John de Innes
1415 Henry Leighton
1422 Columba de Dunbar
1437 John de Winchester
1460(?) James Stewart
1463 David Stewart
1477 William de Tulloch
1487 Andrew Stewart
1501(?) Andrew Forman
1516(?) James Hepburn
1525 Robert Shaw
1532(?) Alexander Stewart
1538(?) Patrick Hepburn
1574 George Douglas
1611 Alexander Douglas
1623 John Guthrie
1662 Murdo Mackenzie
1677 James Aitken
1680 Colin Falconer
1687 Alexander Rose
1688 William Hay
1707 Held with Edinburgh
1725 Held with Aberdeen
1727 William Dunbar
1737 George Hay (elect)
1742 William Falconar
1777 Arthur Petrie
1787 Andrew Macfarlane
1798 Alexander Jolly
1838 Held with Ross
1851 Robert Eden
1886 James Butler Knill Kelly
1904 Arthur John Maclean
1943 Piers Holt Wilson
1953 Duncan Macinnes

1970 George Minshull Sessford
1994 Gregor Macgregor
1999 John Michael Crook
2007 Mark Jeremy Strange

†Ross

1131(?) Macbeth
1150(?) Simon
1161 Gregory
1195 Reginald
1213 Andrew de Moravia (elect)
1215(?) Robert I
1250 Robert II
1272 Matthew
1275(?) Robert II de Fyvin
1295(?) Adam de Derlingtun (elect)
1297(?) Thomas de Dundee
1325 Roger
1351 Alexander Stewart
1372 Alexander de Kylwos
1398(?) Alexander de Waghorn
1418 Thomas Lyell (elect)
Griffin Yonge (elect)
1420 John Bulloch
1441(?) Andrew de Munro (elect)
1441(?) Thomas Tulloch
1464(?) Henry Cockburn
1478 John Wodman
1481 William Elphinstone (elect)
1483 Thomas Hay
1492 John Guthrie
1498 John Frisel [Fraser]
c.1507 Robert Cockburn
1525 James Hay
c.1539 Robert Cairncross
1552 David Painter
1561(?) Henry Sinclair
1566 John Lesley
1575 Alexander Hepburn
1611 David Lindsay
1613 Patrick Lindsay
1633 John Maxwell
1662 John Paterson
1679 Alexander Young
1684 James Ramsay
1696 See vacant or held with
Caithness until 1727
1727 Held with Moray
1742 Held with Caithness
1762 Robert Forbes
1777 Held with Moray
1819 David Low
1851 Held with Moray

†Caithness

c.1146 Andrew
c.1187 John
1214 Adam
1223(?) Gilbert de Moravia
1250(?) William
1263 Walter de Baltrodin
1273(?) Nicholas (elect)
1275 Archibald Herok
1278 Richard (elect)
1279(?) Hervey de Dundee (elect)
1282 Alan de St Edmund
1295 John or James (elect)
1296 Adam de Derlingtun
1297 Andrew
1306 Fercard Belegaumbe
1328(?) David
1341 Alan de Moravia
1343 Thomas de Fingask
1370 Malcolm de Dumbrek
1381 Alexander Man
1414 Alexander Vaus
1425 John de Crannach
1428 Robert Strabrok
1446 John Innes
1448 William Mudy

1478(?) Prospero Camogli de Medici
1484(?) John Sinclair (elect)
1502 Andrew Stewart I
1517(?) Andrew Stewart II
1542 Robert Stewart (elect)
1600 George Gledstanes (elect)
1611 Alexander Forbes
1616 John Abernethy
1662 Patrick Forbes
1680 Andrew Wood
[1695 See vacant]
1731 Robert Keith
1741 Wm. Falconas
1762 Held with Ross
[1742 See Vacant]
1777 Held with Moray

Glasgow

Glasgow and Galloway

Description of arms. Party per pale:
dexter, vert, a fess wavy argent charged
with a bar wavy azure between a
representation of St Mungo issuant
from the fess proper, habited or, his
dexter hand raised in benediction and
in his sinister hand a Celtic cross of the
same in chief, in nombril point a
salmon proper and in base an annulet
of the fourth; sinister, argent a
representation of St Ninian standing
full-faced proper, clothed in a pontifical
robe purpure, on his head a mitre and
in his dexter hand a crosier or.

550(?) Kentigern or Mungo (no record
        of his successors)
1114(?) (Michael)
1118(?) John
1147 Herbert
1164 Ingram
1175 Jocelin
1199 Hugh de Roxburgh (elect)
1200 William Malveisin
1202 Florence (elect)
1208 Walter de St Albans
1233 William de Bondington
1259 Nicholas de Moffat (elect)
1259 John de Cheam
1268 Nicholas de Moffat (elect)
1271 William Wischard (elect)
1273 Robert Wischard
1317 Stephen de Donydouer (elect)
1318 John de Eglescliffe
1323 John de Lindsay
1337 John Wischard
1339 William Rae
1367 Walter Wardlaw
1388 Matthew de Glendonwyn
1391 John Framisden (titular)
1408 William Lauder
1427 John Cameron
1447 James de Brois [Brewhouse]
1448 William Turnbull
1456 Andrew de Durrisdeer
1475 John Laing
1483 George Carmichael (elect)

ARCHBISHOPS

1483 Robert Blackadder (Archbishop
        9 Jan 1492)
1509 James Betoun I
1525 Gavin Dunbar
1551 Alexander Gordon
1552 James Betoun II (restored 1587)
1571 John Porterfield (titular)
1573 James Boyd (titular)
1581 Robert Montgomery (titular)
1585 William Erskine (titular)
1610 John Spottiswoode
1615 James Law
1633 Patrick Lindsay
1661 Andrew Fairfoul
1664 Alexander Burnet (restored
        1674)
1671 Robert Leighton, died 1684
        (resigned 1674)
1679 Arthur Rose
1684 Alexander Cairncross, died
        1701
1687 John Paterson,[1] died 1708
[1708 Vacant]

BISHOPS
1731 Alexander Duncan, died 1733
[1733 Vacant]
1787 Held with Edinburgh
1805 William Abernethy Drummond
1809–37 Held with Edinburgh
1837 Michael Russell
1848 Walter John Trower
1859 William Scott Wilson
1888 William Thomas Harrison
1904 Archibald Ean Campbell
1921 Edward Thomas Scott Reid
1931 John Russell Darbyshire
1938 John Charles Halland How
1952 Francis Hamilton Moncreiff
1974 Frederick Goldie
1981 Derek Alec Rawcliffe
1991 John Mitchell Taylor
1998 Idris Jones
2010 Gregor Duthrie Duncan

†Galloway or Candida Casa
or Whithorn[2]

      Ninian, died 432(?)
(?) Octa
681 Trumwine
731 Penthelm, died 735(?)
735 Frithowald, died 764
763 Pehtwine, died 776
777 Ethelbert
791 Beadwulf
1140 Gilla-Aldan
1154 Christian
1189 John
1214 Walter
1235 Odo Ydonc (elect)
1235 Gilbert
1255 Henry
1294 Thomas de Kircudbright [de
        Daltoun]
1327 Simon de Wedale
1355 Michael Malconhalgh
1359(?) Thomas Macdowell (elect)
1359 Thomas
1364 Adam de Lanark
(?) David Douglas, died 1373
(?) James Carron (resigned 1373)
1378 Ingram de Kethnis (elect)
1379 Oswald
1380 Thomas de Rossy
(?) Francis Ramsay, died 1402

1406 Elisaeus Adougan
1414(?) Gilbert Cavan (elect)
1415 Thomas de Butil
1422 Alexander Vaus
1451 Thomas Spens
1457(?) Thomas Vaus (elect)
1459 Ninian Spot
1482(?) George Vaus
1508(?) James Betoun (elect)
1509(?) David Arnot
1526 Henry Wemyss
1541(?) Andrew Dury
1559(?) Alexander Gordon
1610 Gavin Hamilton
1612(?) William Couper
1619 Andrew Lamb
1635 Thomas Sydserf
1661 James Hamilton
1675 John Paterson
1679 Arthur Rose
1680 James Aitken
1688 John Gordon, died 1726
1697 Held with Edinburgh
1837 Held with Glasgow

Argyll or Lismore

Argyll and The Isles

Description of arms. Azure, two crosiers
in saltire and in chief a mitre or.

1193 Harald
1240 William
1253 Alan
1268 Laurence de Erganis
1300 Andrew
1342 Angusde Ergadia (elect)
1344 Martinde Ergaill
1387 John Dugaldi
1397(?) Bean Johannis
1420(?) Finlay de Albany
1428 George Lauder
1476 Robert Colquhoun
1504 David Hamilton
1532 Robert Montgomery
1539(?) William Cunningham
        (elect)
1553(?) James Hamilton (elect)
1580 Neil Campbell (titular)
1611 John Campbell (titular)
1613 Andrew Boyd
1637 James Fairlie
1662 David Fletcher
1665 John Young (elect)
1666 William Scroggie
1675 Arthur Rose
1679 Colin Falconer
1680 Hector Maclean
1688 Alexander Monro (elect)
Held with Ross
1847 Alexander Ewing
1874 George Mackarness
1883 James Robert Alexander
        Chinnery-Haldane
1907 Kenneth Mackenzie
1942 Thomas Hannay
1963 Richard Knyvet Wimbush

---

[1] After the deposition of John Paterson at the Revolution the See ceased to be Archiepiscopal.
[2] The traditional founder of the See is St Ninian, but nothing authentic is known of the bishops prior to the accession of Gilla-Aldan between 1133 and 1140.

1977 George Kennedy Buchanan
     Henderson
1993 Douglas MacLean Cameron
2004 Alexander Martin Shaw
2011 Kevin Pearson

†The Isles

900 Patrick
1080 Roolwer
1080 William
1095 Hamundr
1138 Wimund
1152 John I
1152(?) Ragnald
1154 Gamaliel
1170 Christian
1194 Michael
1210 Nicholas I
1219 Nicholas II of Meaux
1226(?) Reginald
1226 Simon
1249 Laurence (elect)
1253 Richard
1275 Gilbert (elect)
1275 Mark
1305 Alan
1324 Gilbert Maclelan
1328 Bernard de Linton
1331 Thomas de Rossy
1349 William Russell
1374 John Donkan
1387 Michael
1392 John Sproten (Man) (titular)
1402(?) Conrad (Man) (titular)
1402(?) Theodore Bloc (Man)
     (titular)
1410 Richard Messing (Man)
1422 Michael Anchire
1425(?) John Burgherlinus (Man)
1428 Angus I
1441(?) John Hectoris [McCachane]
     Macgilleon
1472 Angus II
1487 John Campbell
1511 George Hepburn
1514 John Campbell (elect)
1530(?) Ferchar MacEachan (elect)
1550(?) Roderick Maclean
1553(?) Alexander Gordon
1567 John Carswell (titular)
1573 John Campbell
1605 Andrew Knox
1619 Thomas Knox
1628 John Leslie
1634 Neil Campbell
1662 Robert Wallace

1677 Andrew Wood
1680 Archibald Graham [or
     McIlvernock]
     Held with Orkney and
     Caithness
1819 Held with Argyll

College Bishops, Consecrated without Sees

1705 John Sage, died 1711
1705 John Fullarton (Edinburgh
     1720), died 1727
1709 Henry Christie, died 1718
1709 John Falconar (Fife 1720), died
     1723
1711 Archibald Campbell (Aberdeen
     1721), died 1744
1712 James Gadderar (Aberdeen
     1725, Moray 1725), died
     1733
1718 Arthur Millar (Edinburgh 1727),
     died 1727
1718 William Irvine, died 1725
1722 Andrew Cant, died 1730
1722 David Freebairn (Edinburgh
     1733)
1726 John Ochterlonie (Brechin
     1731), died 1742
1726 James Ross (Fife 1731), died
     1733
1727 John Gillan (Dunblane 1731),
     died 1735
1727 David Ranken, died 1728

Bishops who have held the Office of Primus

1704 Alexander Rose (Edinburgh
     1704–20)
1720 John Fullarton (Edinburgh
     1720–27)
1727 Arthur Millar (Edinburgh
     1727)
1727 Andrew Lumsden (Edinburgh
     1727–33)
1731 David Freebairn (Edinburgh
     1733–39)
1738 Thomas Rattray (Dunkeld
     1727–43)
1743 Robert Keith (Caithness 1731–
     41)
1757 Robert White (Dunblane 1735–
     43, St Andrews 1743–61)

1762 William Falconar (Orkney and
     Caithness 1741–62)
1782 Robert Kilgour (Aberdeen 1768–
     86)
1788 John Skinner (Aberdeen 1786–
     1816)
1816 George Gleig (Brechin 1810–40)
1837 James Walker (Edinburgh 1880–
     41)
1841 William Skinner (Aberdeen
     1816–57)
1857 Charles Hughes Terrot
     (Edinburgh 1841–72)
1862 Robert Eden (Moray, Ross, and
     Caithness 1851–86)
1886 Hugh Willoughby Jermyn
     (Brechin 1875–1903)
1901 James Butler Knill Kelly (Moray,
     Ross, and Caithness 1886–
     1904)
1904 George Howard Wilkinson (St
     Andrews, Dunkeld, and
     Dunblane 1893–1907)
1908 Walter John Forbes Robberds
     (Brechin 1904–34)
1935 Arthur John Maclean (Moray,
     Ross, and Caithness
     1904–43)
1943 Ernest Denny Logie Danson
     (Edinburgh 1939–46)
1946 John Charles Halland How
     (Glasgow and Galloway
     1938–52)
1952 Thomas Hannay (Argyll and
     The Isles 1942–62)
1962 Francis Hamilton Moncreiff
     (Glasgow and Galloway
     1952–74)
1974 Richard Knyvet Wimbush
     (Argyll and The Isles
     1963–77)
1977 Alastair Iain Macdonald
     Haggart (Edinburgh
     1975–85)
1985 Lawrence Edward Luscombe
     (Brechin 1975–90)
1990 George Kennedy Buchanan
     Henderson (Argyll and
     The Isles 1977–92)
1992 Richard Frederick Holloway
     (Edinburgh 1986–2000)
2000 Andrew Bruce Cameron
     (Aberdeen 1992–2006)
2006 Idris Jones (Glasgow and
     Galloway 1998–2009)
2009 David Robert Chillingworth
     (St Andrews, Dunkeld, and
     Dunblane 2005–)

IRELAND

PROVINCE OF ARMAGH

†Achonry

BISHOPS

c.558 Cathfuidh
1152 Mael Ruanaid ua Ruadain
1159 Gille na Naehm O Ruadain
     [Gelasius]
1208 Clemens O Sniadaig
1220 Connmach O Torpaig
     [Carus]
1226 Gilla Isu O Cleirig [Gelasius]
1237 Tomas O Ruadhan

1238 Oengus O Clumain [Elias]
1251 Tomas O Maicin
1266 Tomas O Miadachain
     [Dionysus]
1286 Benedict O Bracain
1312 David of Kilheny
1348 David II
1348 Nicol Alias Muircheartach O
     hEadhra
1374 William Andrew
1385 Simon
c.1390 Tomas mac Muirgheasa
     MacDonn-chadha

1401 Brian mac Seaain O hEadhra
1410 Maghnus O h Eadhra
1424 Donatus
1424 Richard Belmer
1436 Tadhg O Dalaigh
1442 James Blakedon
1449 Cornelius O Mochain
1463 Brian O hEasdhra
     [Benedictus]
1470 Nicholas Forden
1475 Robert Wellys
1484 Thomas fitzRichard
1484 Tomas O Conghalain

† Indicates a diocese no longer extant, or united with another diocese.

1489 John Bustamente
1492 Thomas Ford
1508 Eugenius O Flannagain
1522 Cormac O Snighe
1547 Thomas O Fihilly
1562 Eugene O'Harte
1613 Miler Magrath (with Cashel)
         United to Killala 1622

†Annadown

BISHOPS

1189 Conn ua Mellaig [Concors]
1202 Murchad ua Flaithbertaig
1242 Tomas O Mellaig
1251 Conchobar [Concors]
1283 John de Ufford
1308 Gilbert O Tigernaig
1323 Jacobus O Cethernaig
1326 Robert Petit
1328 Albertus
1329 Tomas O Mellaig
1359 Dionysius
1393 Johannes
1394 Henry Trillow
1402 John Bryt
1408 John Wynn
1421 John Boner [Camere]
1425 Seean Mac Braddaigh
1428 Seamus O Lonnghargain
1431 Donatus O Madagain
1446 Thomas Salscot
1450 Redmund Bermingham
1458 Thomas Barrett
1496 Francis Brunand
1540 John Moore
United to Tuam c.1555

†Ardagh

454 Mel
c.670 Erard
874 Faelghus
         Cele 1048
1152 Mac Raith ua Morain
1172 Gilla Crist O hEothaig
         [Christianus]
         O'Tirlenain 1187
         ua hEislinnen
         Annud O Muiredaig 1216
1217 Robert
1224 M.
1228 Loseph mac Teichthechain
1229 Mac Raith Mac Serraig
1232 Gilla Isu mac in Scelaige O
         Tormaid [Gelasius]
1232 Iocelinus
1238 Brendan Mac Teichthechain
1256 Milo of Dunstable
1290 Matha O'h-Eothaig [Mattheus]
1323 Robert Wirsop (did not get
         possession)
1324 Mac Eoaighseoan
1347 Eoghan O Ferghail
         [Audovenus]
1368 William Mac Carmaic
1373 Cairbre O'Ferghail [Charles]
1373 John Aubrey
1392 Henry Nony (did not get
         possession)
1396 Comedinus Mac Bradaigh
         [Gilbert]
1400 Adam Leyns
1419 Conchobar O'Ferghail
         [Cornelius]
1425 Risdeard O'Ferghail
[1444 O'Murtry, not consecrated
         resigned]
1445 Cormac Mac Shamhradhain
1462 Seaan O'Ferghail
1467 Donatus O'Ferghail
1482 William O'Ferghail
1517 Ruaidri O'Maoileoin

1517 Rory O'Mallone [Roger O
         Melleine]
1541 Richard O'Ferrall
1553 Patrick MacMahon
[1572 John Garvey, not consecrated]
1583 Lysach O'Ferrall
1604 Robert Draper
1613 Thomas Moigne
1679 William Bedell
1633 John Richardson
1661 Robert Maxwell
1673 Francis Marsh
1682 William Sheridan
1692 Ulysses Burgh
1604–33, 1661–92 and 1692–1751
         Held by the Bishops of
         Kilmore
1751–1839 Held by the Archbishops
         of Tuam
United to Kilmore 1839

Armagh

Description of arms. Azure, an
archiepiscopal staff in pale argent
ensigned with a cross pattée or,
surmounted by a pall argent fimbriated
and fringed or, charged with four
crosses pattées-fitchées sable.

BISHOPS

444 Patrick
         Benignus 467
         Jarlath 481
         Cormac 497
         Dubthach 513
         Ailill I 526
         Ailill II 536
         David O'Faranan 551
         Carlaen 588
         MacLaisre 623
–640 Thomian MacRonan
         Segeni 688
         Suibhne 730
–732 Congusa
         Affinth 794
–811 Nundha
–818 Artri
835 Forannan
         Mael Patraic I 862
         Fethgna 875
         Cathasach MacRobartach 883
         Mochta 893
900 Maelaithghin
         Cellach
         Mael Ciarain 915
         Joseph 936
         Mael Patraic II 936
         Cathasach MacDolgen 966
         Maelmiure 994
         Airindach 1000
         Maeltuile 1032
1032 Hugh O'Ferris
         Mael Patraic III 1096
1099 Caincomrac O'Boyle

ARCHBISHOPS

1105 Cellach mac Aeda meic Mael Isu
         [Celsus]
1132 Mael maedoc Ua Morgair
         [Malachais]
1137 Gilla Meic Liac mac Diarmata
         meic Ruaidri [Gelasius]

1174 Conchobar O Conchaille
         [Concors]
1175 Gille in Coimhedh O Caran
         [Gilbertus]
1180 Tomaltach O Conchobair
         [Thomas]
1184 Mael Isu Ua Cerbaill [Malachias]
1202 Echdonn mac Gilla Uidir
         [Eugenius]
1217 Lucas Neterville
1227 Donatus O Fidabra
1240 Albert Suebeer of Cologne
1247 Reginald
1258 Abraham O'Conallain
1261 Mael Patraic O Scannail
1270 Nicol Mac Mael Isu
1303 Michael MacLochlainn (not
         confirmed)
1304 Dionysius (not confirmed)
1306 John Taaffe
1307 Walter Jorz
1311 Roland Jorz
1324 Stephen Segrave
1334 David Mag Oireachtaigh
1347 Richard FitzRalph
1362 Milo Sweetman
1383 John Colton
1404 Nicholas Fleming
1418 John Swayne
1439 John Prene
1444 John Mey
1457 John Bole [Bull]
1471 John Foxhalls or Foxholes
1475 Edmund Connesburgh
1480 Ottaviano Spinelli [de Palatio]
1513 John Kite
1521 George Cromer
1543 George Dowdall
1552 Hugh Goodacre
1553 George Dowdall (again)
[1560 Donat MacTeague, not
         recognized by the Crown,
         1562]
1563 Adam Loftus
1568 Thomas Lancaster
1584 John Long
1589 John Garvey
1595 Henry Ussher
1613 Christopher Hampton
1625 James Ussher
[Interregnum 1656–61]
1661 John Bramhall
1663 James Margetson
1679 Michael Boyle
1703 Narcissus Marsh
1714 Thomas Lindsay
1724 Hugh Boulter
1742 John Hoadly
1747 George Stone
1765 Richard Robinson [afterwards
         Baron Rokeby]
1795 William Newcome
1800 William Stuart
1822 John George Beresford
United to Clogher 1850–86
1862 Marcus Gervais Beresford
1886 Robert Bentknox
1893 Robert Samuel Gregg
1896 William Alexander
1911 John Baptist Crozier
1920 Charles Frederick D'Arcy
1938 John Godfrey FitzMaurice Day
1939 John Allen Fitzgerald Gregg
1959 James McCann
1969 George Otto Simms
1980 John Ward Armstrong
1986 Robert Henry Alexander Eames
2007 Alan Edwin Thomas Harper
2012 Richard Lionel Clarke

Clogher

Description of arms. Azure, a bishop seated in full pontificals proper, in the act of benediction, and holding his pastoral staff in the left hand.

c.493 MacCarthinn or Ferdachrioch
    Ailill 869
1135 Cinaeth O Baigill
1135 Gilla Crist O Morgair
    [Christianus] (moved his see
    to Louth)

BISHOPS OF LOUTH

1135 Gilla Crist O Morgair
    [Christianus]
1138 Aed O Ceallaide [Edanus]
1178 Mael Isu O Cerbaill [Malachias]
1187 Gilla Crist O Mucaran
    [Christinus]
1194 Mael Isu Ua Mael Chiarain
1197 Gilla Tigernaig Mac Gilla
    Ronain [Thomas]

BISHOPS OF CLOGHER

1218 Donatus O Fidabra
1228 Nehemias
1245 David O Bracain
1268 Michael Mac an tSair
1287 Matthew Mac Cathasaigh I
–1310 Henricus
1316 Gelasius O Banain
1320 Nicholas Mac Cathasaigh
1356 Brian Mac Cathmaoil [Bernard]
1362 Matthew Mac Cathasaigh II
  — Aodh O hEothaigh [*alias* O
    Neill]
1373 John O Corcrain [Wurzburg]
1390 Art Mac Cathmhail
1433 Piaras Mag Uidhir [Petrus]
1450 Rossa mac Tomais Oig Mag
    Uidhir [Rogerius]
1475 Florence Woolley
[1484 Niall mac Seamuis Mac
    Mathghamna]
1484 John Edmund de Courci
1494 Seamus Mac Pilip Mac
    Mathghamna
1500 Andreas
1502 Nehemias O Cluainin
1504 Giolla Padraig O Conalaigh
    [Patrick]
1505 Eoghan Mac Cathmhail
    [Eugenius]
1517 Padraig O Cuilin
1535 Aodh O Cearbhalain [Odo]
1517 Patrick O'Cullen
1535 Hugh O'Carolan
1570 Miler Magrath
1605 George Montgomery
1621 James Spottiswood
1645 Henry Jones
1661 John Leslie
1671 Robert Leslie
1672 Roger Boyle
1691 Richard Tennison
1697 St George Ashe
1717 John Stearne
1745 Robert Clayton
1758 John Garnett
1782 John Hotham
1796 William Foster
1797 John Porter

1819 John George Beresford
1820 Percy Jocelyn
1822 Robert Ponsonby Tottenham
    Luftus
United to Armagh 1850–86
1886 Charles Maurice Stack
1903 Charles Frederick D'Arcy
1908 Maurice Day
1923 James MacManaway
1944 Richard Tyner
1958 Alan Alexander Buchanan
1970 Richard Patrick Crosland
    Hanson
1973 Robert William Heavener
1980 Gordon McMullan
1986 Brian Desmond Anthony
    Hannon
2002 Michael Geoffrey St Aubyn
    Jackson
2011 Francis John McDowell

Connor

Description of arms. Azure, a lamb passant supporting with the dexter foreleg a staff proper flying therefrom a pennant argent charged with a saltire gules between three cross crosslets or; on a chief of the last two crosiers in saltire of the first.

506 Oengus MacNessa 514
    Lughadh 543
640 Dimma Dubh [the Black]
    Duchonna the Pious 725
    Cunnen or Cuinden 1038
    Flann O'Sculu 1117
1124 Mael Maedoc Ua Morgair
    [Malachias]
–1152 MaelPatraic O'Banain
1172 Nehemias
1178 Reginaldus
1226 Eustacius
1242 Adam
1245 Isaac de Newcastle-on-Tyne
1258 William de Portroyal
1261 William de Hay [or la Haye]
1263 Robert de Flanders
1275 Peter de Dunach
1293 Johannes
1320 Richard
1321 James de Couplith
1323 John de Eglecliff
1323 Robert Wirsop
1324 Jacabus O Cethernaig
1353 William Mercier
1374 Paulus
1389 Johannes
[1420 Seaan O Luachrain, not
    consecrated]
1423 Eoghan O'Domhnaill
1429 Domhnall O'Meraich
1431 John Fossade [Festade]
1459 Patricius
1459 Simon Elvington
United to Down 1441
1945 Charles King Irwin
1956 Robert Cyril Hamilton Glover
    Elliott
1969 Arthur Hamilton Butler
1981 William John McCappin
1987 Samuel Greenfield Poyntz
1995 James Edward Moore

2002 Alan Edwin Thomas Harper
2007 Alan Francis Abernethy

Derry

Derry and Raphoe

Description of arms. Party per pale: dexter gules, two swords in saltire proper, and on a chief azure a harp or stringed argent (for the See of Derry); sinister ermine, a chief per pale azure and or, the first charged with a sun in splendour of the last, the second with a cross pattée gules (for the See of Raphoe).

    Caencomhrac 927
–937 Finachta MacKellach
–949 Mael Finnen

BISHOPS OF MAGHERA

(Where the See was in the twelfth
and the thirteenth centuries)
1107 Mael Coluim O Brolchain
  — Mael Brigte O Brolchain
1152 O Gormgaile Muiredach O
    Cobthaig [Mauricius]
1173 Amhlaim O Muirethaig
1185 Fogartach O Cerballain
    [Florentius]
c.1230 Gilla in Coimhded O Cerballain
    [Germanus]
c.1280 Fogartach O Cerballain II
    [Florentius]

BISHOPS OF DERRY

(Where the See was resettled)
1295 Enri Mac Airechtaig [O'Reghly]
    [of Ardagh]
1297 Gofraid MacLochlainn
    [Godfrey]
1316 Aed O Neill [Odo]
1319 Michael Mac Lochlainn
    [Maurice]
1349 Simon
1391 Johannes
1391 John Dongan
1394 Seoan O Mochain
1398 Aodh [Hugo]
1401 Seoan O Flannabhra
1415 Domhnall Mac Cathmhail
1419 Domhnall O Mearaich
1429 Eoghan O Domhnaill
    [Eugenius]

1433 John Oguguin
[1456 John Bole, appointment not
completed, translated to
Armagh]
1458 Bartholomew O Flannagain
c.1464 Johannes
1467 Nicholas Weston
1485 Domhnall O Fallamhain
1501 Seamus mac Pilip Mac
Mathghamna [MacMahon]
1520 Ruaidhri O Domhnaill
1520 Rory O'Donnell
1554 Eugene O'Doherty
1568 F. [doubtful authority]
1569 Redmond O'Gallagher
[1603 Denis Campbell, not
consecrated]
1605 George Montgomery
1610 Brutus Babington
[1611 Christopher Hampton,
consecrated]
1613 John Tanner
1617 George Downham
1634 John Bramhall
1661 George Wild
1666 Robert Mossom
1680 Michael Ward
1681 Ezekiel Hopkins
1691 William King
1703 Charles Hickman
1714 John Hartstonge
1717 St George Ashe
1718 William Nicolson
1727 Henry Downes
1735 Thomas Rundle
1743 Carew Reynell
1745 George Stone
1747 William Barnard
1768 Frederick Augustus Hervey
[afterwards Earl of Bristol]
1803 William Knox
1831 Richard Ponsonby
Raphoe united to Derry from 1834
1853 William Higgin
1867 William Alexander
1896 George Alexander Chadwick
(resigned)
1916 Joseph Irvine Peacocke
1945 Robert M'Neil Boyd
1958 Charles John Tyndall
1970 Cuthbert Irvine Peacocke
1975 Robert Henry Alexander Eames
1980 James Mehaffey
2002 Kenneth Raymond Good

Down

Down and Dromore

Description of arms. Quarterly, 1 and 4
azure, two keys endorsed in saltire the
wards in chief or, surmounted in the
fess point by a lamb passant proper (for
the See of Down); 2 and 3 Argent, two
keys endorsed in saltire the wards in
chief gules, surmounted by an open
book in fess proper between two crosses
pattées-fitchées in pale sable (for the See
of Dromore).

Fergus 584
Suibhne 825
Graithene 956
Finghin 964

Flaithbertach 1043
MaelKevin 1086
— Mael Muire 1117
Oengus Ua Gormain 1123
— [Anonymous]
c.1124 Mael Maedoc O Morgair
[Malachias]
1152 Mael Isu mac in Chleirig Chuirr
[Malachias]
1175 Gilla Domangairt Mac Cormaic
c.1176 Echmilid [Malachias]
c.1202 Radulfus
1224 Thomas
1251 Randulphus
1258 Reginaldus
1265 Thomas Lydel
1277 Nicholas le Blund
1305 Thomas Ketel
1314 Thomas Bright
1328 John of Baliconingham
1329 Ralph of Kilmessan
1353 Richard Calf I
1365 Robert of Aketon
1367 William White
1369 Richard Calf [II]
1386 John Ross
1394 John Dongan
1413 John Cely [or Sely]
1445 Ralph Alderle

BISHOPS OF DOWN AND CONNOR

1441 John Fossard
1447 Thomas Pollard
1451 Richard Wolsey
1456 Thomas Knight
1469 Tadhg O Muirgheasa
[Thaddaeus]
1489 Tiberio Ugolino
1520 Robert Blyth
1542 Eugene Magennis
1565 James MacCawell
1569 John Merriman
1572 Hugh Allen
1593 Edward Edgeworth
1596 John Charden
1602 Roben Humpston
1607 John Todd (resigned)
1612 James Dundas
1613 Robert Echlin
1635 Henry Leslie
1661 Jeremy Taylor
1667 Roger Boyle
1672 Thomas Hacket
1694 Samuel Foley
1695 Edward Walkington
1699 Edward Smyth
1721 Francis Hutchinson
1739 Carew Reynell
1743 John Ryder
1752 John Whitcombe
1752 Robert Downes
1753 Arthur Smyth
1765 James Traill
1784 William Dickson
1804 Nathaniel Alexander
1823 Richard Mant

BISHOPS OF DOWN, CONNOR AND
DROMORE

1849 Robert Bent Knox
1886 William Reeves
1892 Thomas James Welland
1907 John Baptist Crozier
1911 Charles Frederick D'Arcy
1919 Charles Thornton Primrose
Grierson
1934 John Frederick McNeice
1942 Charles King Irwin

BISHOPS OF DOWN AND DROMORE

1945 William Shaw Kerr
1955 Frederick Julian Mitchell
1970 George Alderson Quin
1980 Robert Henry Alexander Eames

1986 Gordon McMullan
1997 Harold Creeth Miller

†Dromore

Mael Brighde 974
Riagan 1101
1197 Ua Ruanada
1227 Geraldus
1245 Andreas
1284 Tigernach I
1290 Gervasius
— Tigernach II
1309 Florentius Mac Donnocain
1351 Anonymous
1366 Milo
1369 Christophorus Cornelius
1382
1382 John O'Lannoy
1398 Thomas Orwell
1400 John Waltham
1402 Roger Appleby
1408 Richard Payl
1410 Marcus
1411 John Chourles
1414 Seaan O Ruanadha
1419 Nicholas Wartre
1429 Thomas Rackelf
1431 William
1431 David Chirbury
1450 Thomas Scrope [Bradley]
1450 Thomas Radcliff
1456 Donatus O h-Anluain
[Ohendua]
1457 Richard Messing
1463 William Egremond
— Aonghus [Aeneas] 1476
1476 Robert Kirke
1480 Yvo Guillen
1483 George Braua
1511 Tadhg O Raghallaigh
[Thaddeus]
1536 Quintin O Quigley [Cogley]
1539 Roger McHugh
1540 Arthur Magennis
1607 John Todd
[1613 John Tanner, not consecrated]
1613 Theophilus Buckworth
1661 Robert Leslie
1661 Jeremy Taylor (administered
the diocese)
1667 George Rust
1671 Essex Digby
1683 Capel Wiseman
1695 Tobias Pullein
1713 John Stearne
1717 Ralph Lambert
1727 Charles Cobbe
1732 Henry Maule
1744 Thomas Fletcher
1745 Jemmett Browne
1745 George Marlay
1763 John Oswald
1763 Edward Young
1765 Henry Maxwell
1766 William Newcome
1775 James Hawkins
1780 William de la Poer Beresford
1782 Thomas Percy
1811 George Hall
1812 John Leslie
1819 James Saurin
United to Down since 1842

†Elphin

Domnall mac Flannacain Ua
Dubhthaig 1136
Muiredach O Dubhthaig 1150
1152 Mael Isu O Connachtain
Flannacan O Dubhthaig 1168
c.1177 Tomaltach mac Aeda Ua
Conchobhair [Thomas]

*c.*1180 Florint Ua Riacain Ui
      Maelrvanaid
1206 Ardgar O Conchobhair
1226 Dionysius O Mordha
*c.*1230 Alanus
1231 Donnchad mac Fingein O
      Conchobhair [Dionysius
      Donatus]
1245 Eoin O Mugroin
1247 Tomaltach macToirrdelbaig
      O Conchobhair [Thomas]
1260 Mael Sechlainn O Conchobhair
      [Milo]
1262 Tomas mac Fergail mac
      Diarmata
1266 Muiris O Conchobhair
[1285 Amiaim O Tommaltaig, not
      consecrated]
1285 Gilla Isu mac in Liathana O
      Conchobhair
1297 Maelsechlainn mac Briain
      [Malachias]
1303 Donnchad O Flannacain,
      [Donatus]
1307 Cathal O Conchobhair
1310 Mael Sechlainn Mac Aedha
1313 Lurint O Lachtnain
      [Laurence]
1326 Sean O Finnachta
1355 Carolus
1357 Gregory O Mochain
1372 Thomas Barrett
1383 Seoan O Mochain
1407 Seaan O Grada
1405 Gerald Caneton
1412 Thomas Colby
1418 Robert Fosten
1421 Edmund Barrett
1427 Johannes
1429 Laurence O Beolain
1429 William O hEidighean
1448 Conchobhar O Maolalaidh
1458 Nicholas O Flanagan
1487 Hugo Arward
1492 Rlocard mac Briain O gCuanach
1499 George Brana
1501 Cornelius O Flannagain
1508 Christopher Fisher
1525 John Maxey
1539 William Maginn 1541(?)
1539 Gabriel de Sancto Serio
1541 Conach or Con O'Negall or
      O'Shyagall
1552 Roland Burke [de Burgo]
1582 Thomas Chester
1583 John Lynch
1611 Edward King
1639 Henry Tilson
1661 John Parker
1667 John Hodson
1691 Simon Digby
1720 Henry Downes
1724 Theophilus Bolton
1730 Robert Howard
1740 Edward Synge
1762 William Gore
1772 Jemmett Browne
1775 Charles Dodgson
1795 John Law
1810 Power le Poer Trench
1819 John Leslie 1854
United to Kilmore and Ardagh on
the death of Bishop Beresford in
1841, when Bishop Leslie became
Bishop of the united dioceses.

†Killala

Muiredach
Kellach
O Maolfogmair I 1137
O Maolfogmair II 1151
Imar O Ruaidhin 1176
1179 O Maolfogmair III
1199 Domnall Ua Becdha

1207 Cormac O'Tarpy
      O'Kelly 1214
1226 Aengus O Maolfogmair [Elias]
      Gille Cellaig O Ruaidhin
1253 Seoan O Laidlg
1281 Donnchad O Flaithbertaig
      [Donatus]
1307 John Tankard
      Sean O Flaithim 1343
1344 James Bermingham
1347 William O DusucBhda
1351 Robert Elyot
1381 Thomas Lodowys
1383 Conchobar O Coineoil
      [Cornelius]
1390 Thomas Horwell [Orwell]
1400 Thomas Barrett
1403 Muircheartach Cleirach mac
      Donnchadha O DusucBhda
      Connor O'Connell 1423
1427 Fergal Mac Martain
1431 Thaddaeus Mac Creagh
1432 Brian O Coneoil
1447 Robert Barrett
1452 Ruaidhri Bairead [Barrett]
1453 Thomas
1459 Richard Viel
      Miler O'Connell
1461 Donatus O Conchobhair
1470 Tomas Bairead [Barrett]
1487 John de Tuderto [Seaan O
      Caissin]
1500 Thomas Clerke
1508 Malachias O Clumhain
1513 Risdeard Bairead
1545 Redmond O'Gallagher
1570 Donat O'Gallagher
1580 John O'Casey
1592 Owen O'Conor
1613 Miler Magrath
Achonry united to Killala 1622
1623 Archibald Hamilton
1630 Archibald Adair (deposed, but
      subsequently restored)
164? John Maxwell
1661 Henry Hall
1664 Thomas Bayly
1671 Thomas Otway
1680 John Smith
1681 William Smyth
1682 Richard Tennison
1691 William Lloyd
1717 Henry Downes
1720 Charles Cobbe
1727 Robert Howard
1730 Robert Clayton
173? Mordecai Cary
175? Richard Robinson [afterwards
      Baron Rokeby]
1759 Samuel Hutchinson
1781 William Cecil Pery
1784 William Preston
1787 John Law
1795 John Porter
1798 Joseph Stock
1810 James Verschoyle
United to Tuam since 1834

Kilmore

Kilmore, Elphin and Ardagh

Description of arms. Argent, on a cross
azure a pastoral staff enfiling a mitre, all
or (for the See of Kilmore). Sable, two
pastoral staves in saltire or, in base a
lamb couchant, argent (for the See of
Elphin). Or, a cross gules between four
trefoils slipped vert, on a chief sable, a
key erect of the first (for the See of
Ardagh).

— Aed Ua Finn 1136
— Muirchenach Ua
      Maelmoeherge 1149
1152 Tuathal Ua Connachtaig
      [Thadeus]
1202 Mi Ua Dobailen
— Flann O Connachtaig
      [Florentius] 1231
1237 Congalach Mac Idneoil
1251 Simon O Ruairc
1286 Mauricius
— Matha Mac Duibne 1314
1320 Padraig O Cridecain
— Conchobhar Mac Conshnamha
      [Ford] 1355
1356 Richard O Raghilligh
1373 Johannes
1388 Thomas Rushook
1392 Sean O Raghilligh I [John]
1398 Nicol Mac Bradaigh
1401 Sean O'Raghilligh II
1407 John Stokes
1409 David O'Fairchellaigh
1422 Domhnall O Gabhann
1445 Aindrias Mac Bradaigh
1455 Fear Sithe Mag Dhuibhne
1465 Sean O Raghilligh II
1476 Cormac Mag Shamhradhain
1480 Tomas MacBradaigh
1512 Diarmaid O Raghilligh
1530 Edmund Nugent
1540 Sean Mac Bradaigh
1585 John Garvey
1604 Robert Draper
1613 Thomas Moigne
1629 William Bedell
1643 Robert Maxwell
1673 Francis Marsh
1682 William Sheridan
1693 William Smyth
1699 Edward Wetenhall
1715 Timothy Godwin
1727 Josiah Hott
1742 Joseph Story
1757 John Cradock
1772 Denison Cumberland
1775 George Lewis Jones
1790 William Foster
1796 Charles Broderick
1802 George de la Poer Beresford
Ardagh united to Kilmore 1839
Elphin united to Kilmore 1841
1841 John Leslie
1854 Marcus Gervais Beresford
1862 Hamilton Verschoyle
1870 Charles Leslie
1870 Thomas Carson
1874 John Richard Darley
1884 Samuel Shone
1897 Alfred George Elliott
1915 William Richard Moore

1930 Arthur William Barton
1939 Albert Edward Hughes
1950 Frederick Julian Mitchell
1956 Charles John Tyndall
1959 Edward Francis Butler Moore
1981 William Gilbert Wilson
1993 Michael Hugh Gunton Mayes
2001 Kenneth Harbert Clarke
2013 Samuel Ferran Glenfield

†Mayo

Gerald 732
Muiredach [or Murray]
Mcinracht 732
Aidan 773
1172 Gilla Isu Ua Mailin
Cele O Dubhthaig 1210
1210 ?Patricius
1428 William Prendergast
1430 Nicholas 'Wogmay'
1439 Odo O h-Uiginn
1432 Martin Campania
1457 Simon de Duren
1493 John Bel
1541 Eugenius Macan Brehon
United to Tuam 1559

†Raphoe

Sean O Gairedain
Donell O Garvan
Felemy O Syda
Oengus O'Lappin 959
1150 Muiredhach O'Cofley
1156 Gille in Coimhded Ua Carain
[Gilbertus]
— Anonymous
1204 Mael Isu Ua Doirig
— Anonymous
1253 Mael Padraig O Scannail
[Patricius]
1263 John de Alneto
1265 Cairpre O Scuapa
1275 Fergal O Firghil [Florentius]
1306 Enri Mac-in-Chrossain
[Henricus]
1319 Tomas Mac Carmaic Ui
Domhnaill
1363 Padraig Mac Maonghail
1367 Conchobar Mac Carmaic Ui
Domhnaill [Cornelius]
1397 Seoan MacMenmain
1400 Eoin MacCarmaic [Johannes]
–1413 Anthony
–1414 Robert Rubire
1416 John McCormic
1420 Lochlainn O Gallchobhair I
[Laurentius]
1440 Cornelius Mac Giolla Brighde
1443 Lochlainn O Gallchobhair II
[Laurentius]
1479 John de Rogeriis
1482 Meanma Mac Carmail
[Menclaus Mac Carmacain]
1514 Conn O Cathain [Cornelius]
1534 Eamonn O Gallchobhair
1547 Arthur o'Gallagher

1563 Donnell Magonigle [or
McCongail]
[1603 Denis Campbell, not
consecrated]
1605 George Montgomery
1611 Andrew Knox
1633 John Leslie
1661 Robert Leslie
1671 Ezekiel Hopkins
1682 William Smyth
1693 Alexander Cairncross
1701 Robert Huntington
1702 John Pooley
1713 Thomas Lindsay
1714 Edward Synge
1716 Nicholas Forster
1744 William Barnard
1747 Philip Twysden
1753 Robert Downes
1763 John Oswald
1780 James Hawkins
1807 John George Beresford
1819 William Magee
1822 William Bissett
United to Derry since 1834

Tuam

Tuam, Killala and Achonry

Description of arms. Azure beneath a
triple architectural canopy three figures,
in the centre the Blessed Virgin Mary
holding in her arms the Holy Child,
between, on the dexter the figure of a
bishop (St Jarlath) in pontificalibus and
in the act of benediction, and, on the
sinister St John supporting with his left
arm a lamb argent, each in proper
vestments or, the hands, feet, and faces
proper.

BISHOPS

Murrough O'Nioc 1032
Hugh O'Hessian 1085
Cathusach Ua Conaill 1117
O Clerig 1137
Muiredach Ua Dubhthaig 1150

ARCHBISHOPS

1152 Aed Ua h-Oisin [Edanus]
1167 Cadhla Ua Dubhthaig
[Catholicus]
1202 Felix Ua Ruanada
1236 Mael Muire O Lachtain
[Marianus]

1250 Flann Mac Flainn [Florentius]
[1256 James O'Laghtnan, not
confirmed or consecrated]
1257 Walter de Salerno
1258 Tomaltach O Conchobair
[Thomas]
1286 Stephen de Fulbourn
1289 William de Bermingham
1312 Mael Sechlainn Mac Aeda
1348 Tomas MacCerbhaill
[MacCarwill]
1364 Eoin O Grada
1372 Gregory O Mochain I
1384 Gregory O Mochain II
1387 William O Cormacain
1393 Muirchertach mac Pilb O
Cellaigh
1410 John Babingle
1411 Cornelius
1430 John Bermingham [Winfield]
1438 Tomas mac Muirchearthaigh O
Cellaigh
1441 John de Burgo
1452 Donatus O Muiredaigh
1485 William Seoighe [Joyce]
1503 Philip Pinson
1506 Muiris O Fithcheallaigh
1514 Tomas O Maolalaidh
1537 Christopher Bodkin
1573 William O'Mullally [or Lealy]
Annadown united to Tuam c.1555
Mayo united to Tuam 1559
1595 Nehemiah Donnellan
1609 William O'Donnell [or
Daniel]
1629 Randolph or Ralph Barlow
1638 Richard Boyle
1645 John Maxwell
1661 Samuel Pullen
1667 John Parker
1679 John Vesey
1716 Edward Synge
1742 Josiah Hort
1752 John Ryder
1775 Jemmett Browne
1782 Joseph Dean Bourke [afterwards
Earl of Mayo]
1794 William Beresford [afterwards
Baron Decies]
1819 Power le Poer Trench
Killala united to Tuam from 1834

BISHOPS

1839 Thomas Plunket [afterwards
Baron Plunket]
1867 Charles Brodrick Bernard
1890 James O'Sullivan
1913 Benjamin John Plunket
1920 Arthur Edwin Ross
1923 John Ort
1928 John Mason Harden
1932 William Hardy Holmes
1939 John Winthrop Crozier
1958 Arthur Hamilton Butler
1970 John Coote Duggan
1986 John Robert Winder Neill
1998 Richard Crosbie Aitken
Henderson
2011 Patrick William Rooke

PROVINCE OF DUBLIN

†Ardfert

BISHOPS

Anmchad O h-Anmchada 1117
1152 Mael Brenain Ua Ronain
Gilla Mac Aiblen O'Anmehadha 1166
Domnall O Connairche 1193
1200 David Ua Duibdithrib
Anonymous 1217
1218 John
1218 Gilbertus
1237 Brendan
1253 Christianus
1257 Philippus
1265 Johannes
1286 Nicolaus
1288 Nicol O Samradain
1336 Ailin O hEichthighirn
1331 Edmund of Caermaerthen
1348 John de Valle
1372 Cornelius O Tigernach
1380 William Bull
1411 Nicholas FitzMaurice
1404 Nicholas Ball
1405 Tomas O Ceallaigh
1409 John Attilburgh [Artilburch]
1450 Maurice Stack
1452 Maurice O Conchobhair
1461 John Stack
1461 John Pigge
1473 Philip Stack
1495 John FitzGerald
[See vacant in 1534]
1536 James FitzMaurice
1588 Nicholas Kenan
1600 John Crosbie
1622 John Steere
1628 William Steere
1641 Thomas Fulwar
United to Limerick 1661

†Ardmore

1153 Eugenius
Incorporated with Lismore 1192

Cashel

*Cashel, Waterford, Lismore, Ossory,
Ferns and Leighlin*

Description of arms. Gules, two keys
addorsed in saltire the wards in
chief, or.

BISHOPS

Cormac MacCuillenan 908
Donnell O'Heney 1096 *or*
1098

ARCHBISHOPS

*c.*1111 Mael los Ua h-Ainmire
Mael losa Ua Fogludha
[Mauricius] 1131
Domnall Ua Conaing 1137
Gilla Naomh O'Marty 1149

−1152 Donat O'Lonergan I
−*c.*1160 M.
1172 Domnall O h-Ualla-chain [Donatus]
1186 Muirghes O h-Enna [Matheus]
*c.*1208 Donnchad Ua Longargain I [Donatus]
1216 Donnchad Ua Longargain II [Donatus]
1224 Mairin O Briain [Marianus]
1238 David mac Ceallaig [O'Kelly]
1254 David Mac Cearbaill [Mac Carwill]
1290 Stiamna O Bracain
1303 Maurice Mac Cearbaill
1317 William FitzJohn
1327 Seoan Mac Cerbaill
1329 Walter le Rede
1332 Eoin O Grada
1346 Radulphus O Cellaigh [Kelly]
1362 George Roche [de Rupe]
1365 Tomas Mac Cearbhaill
1374 Philip of Torrington
1382 Michael
1384 Peter Hackett
1406 Richard O Hedian
1442 John Cantwell I
1452 John Cantwell II
1484 David Creagh
1504 Maurice FitzGerald
1525 Edmund Butler
1553 Roland Baron or FitzGerald
1567 James MacCawell
Emly united to Cashel 1569
1571 Miler Magrath (Bishop of Cashel and Waterford from 1582)
1623 Malcolm Hamilton
1630 Archibald Hamilton
1661 Thomas Fulwar
1667 Thomas Price
[See vacant 1685–91]
1691 Narcissus Marsh
1694 William Palliser
[1727 William Nicolson, not enthroned]
1727 Timothy Goodwin
1730 Theophilus Bolton
1744 Arthur Price
1752 John Whitcombe
1754 Michael Cox
1779 Charles Agar
1801 Charles Brodrick
1822 Richard Laurence
Waterford and Lismore united to Cashel from 1833; on the death of Abp Laurence in 1838 the province was united to Dublin and the see ceased to be an Archbishopric

BISHOPS

1839 Stephen Creagh Sandes
1843 Robert Daly
1872 Maurice FitzGerald Day
1900 Henry Stewart O'Hara
1919 Robert Miller
1931 John Frederick McNeice
1935 Thomas Arnold Harvey
1958 William Cecil De Pauley
1968 John Ward Armstrong
Ossory united to Cashel 1977
1980 Noel Vincent Willoughby
1997 John Robert Winder Neill
2003 Peter Francis Barrett
2006 Michael Andrew James Burrows

†Clonfert

Moena, or Moynean, or Moeinend 572
Cummin the Tall 662
Ceannfaeladh 807
Laithbheartach 822
Ruthnel or Ruthme 826
Cormac MacEdain 922
Ciaran O'Gabbla 953
Cathal 963
Eochu 1031
O'Corcoran 1095
Muiredach Ua h-Enlainge 1117
Gille Patraic Ua Ailcinned 1149
*c.*1152 Petrus Ua Mordha
1172 Mail Isu mac in Baird
1179 Celechair Ua h-Armedaig
Muirchertach Ua'Maeluidir 1187
Domnall Ua Finn 1195
Muirchertach Ua Carmacain 1204
1205 Mael Brigte Ua hErurain
1224 Cormac O Luimlin [Carus]
1248 Thomas
1259 Tomas mac Domnaill Moire O Cellaig
1266 Johannes de Alatre
1296 Robert
*c.*1302 John
1308 Gregorius O Brocaig
1320 Robert Le Petit
1322 Seoan O Leaain
1347 Tomas mac Gilbert O Cellaigh I
1378 Muircheartach mac Pilib O Cellaigh [Maurice]
1393 William O Cormacain
1398 David Corre
1398 Enri O Conmaigh
1405 Tomasi O Cellaigh II
1410 Cobhthach O Madagain
1438 Seaan O hEidin
1441 John White
1447 Conchobhar O Maolalaidh
1448 Cornelius O Cuinnlis
1463 Matthaeus Mag Raith
1508 David de Burgo
1509 Dionysius O'Mordha
1534 Roland de Burgo
1536 Richard Nangle
1580 Hugh
1582 Stephen Kirwan
1602 Roland Lynch
1627 Robert Dawson
1644 William Baily
1665 Edward Wolley
1691 William FitzGerald
1722 Theophilus Bolton
1724 Arthur Price
1730 Edward Synye
1732 Mordecai Cary
1716 John Whitcombe
1752 Arthur Smyth
1753 William Carmichael
1758 William Gote
1762 John Oswald
1763 Denison Cumberland
1772 Walter Cope
1782 John Law
1787 Richard Marlay
1795 Charles Broderick
1796 Hugh Hamilton
1798 Matthew Young
1801 George de la l'oer Beresford
1802 Nathaniel Alexander
1804 Christopher Butson
United to Killaloe since 1834

†Clonmacnoise

–663	Baitan O'Cormac
–839	Joseph [of Rossmore]
	Maclodhar 890
	Cairbre Crom 904
	Loingsech 919
–940	Donough I
–953	Donough II
–966	Cormae O Cillin
	Maenach 971
	Conaing O'Cosgraigh 998
	Male Poil 1001
	Flaithbertach 1038
	Celechar 1067
	O'Mallaen 1093
	Christian Aherne 1104
?1111	Domnall mac Flannacain Ua Dubthaig
1152	Muirchertach Ua Maeluidir
	Cathal Ua Maeileoin 1207
c.1207	Muirchertach Ua Muiricen
1214	Aed O Maeileoin I
1227	Aed O Maeileoin II [Elias]
1236	Thomas Fitzpatrick
1252	Tomas O Cuinn
1280	Anonymous
1282	Gilbert (not consecrated)
1290	William O Dubhthaig
1298	William O Finnein
1303	Domnall O Braein
1324	Lughaid O Dalaigh
1337	Henricus
1349	Simon
1369	Richard [Braybroke]
1371	Hugo
1388	Philippus O Maoil
1389	Milo Corr
1397	O'Gallagher
1397	Philip Nangle
1423	David Prendergast
1426	Cormac Mac Cochlain [Cornelius]
1444	Sean O Dalaigh
1449	Thomas
1458	Robertus
1458	William
1459	John
1487	Walter Blake
1509	Tomas O Maolalaidh
1516	Quintin O h-Uiginn
1539	Richard O'Hogan
1539	Florence Kirwan
1556	Peter Wall [Wale]
	United to Meath 1569

†Cloyne

	Reachtaidh 887
1148	Gilla na Naem O Muirchertaig [Nehemias]
	Ua Dubcroin 1159
	Ua Flannacain 1167
1177	Matthaeus Ua Mongaig
1201	Laurence Ua Suilleabain
1205	C.
1281	Luke
c.1224	Florence
1226	Daniel
1237	David mac Cellaig [O'Kelly]
1240	Ailinn O Suilleabain
1247	Daniel
1265	Reginaldus
1275	Alan O Longain
1284	Nicholas of Effingham
1323	Maurice O Solchain
1333	John Brid
1351	John Whitekot
1363	John Swaffham
1376	Richard Wye
1394	Gerard Caneton
1413	Adam Payn
	United to Cork 1418–1638
1638	George Synge
1661–78	Held by the Bishops of Cork

1679	Patrick Sheridan
1683	Edward Jones
1693	William Palliser
1694	Tobias Pullein
1695	St George Ashe
1697	John Pooley
1702	Charles Crow
1726	Henry Maule
1732	Edward Synge
1734	George Berkeley
1753	James Stopford
1759	Robert Johnson
1767	Frederick Augustus Hervery
1768	Charles Agar
1780	George Chinnery
1781	Richard Woodward
1794	William Bennett
1820	Charles Mongan Warhurton
1826	John Brinkley
	United to Cork on the death of Bp Brinkley in 1835

Cork

Cork, Cloyne and Ross

Description of arms. Argent, on a plain cross, the ends pattée, gules, a pastoral staff, surmounted on a mitre, or (for the See of Cork). Azure, a mitre proper labelled or, between three crosses pattées-fitchées argent (for the See of Cloyne). No arms are borne for the See of Ross.

	Donnell 876
	Soer Bhreatach 892
	DusucBhdhurn O'Stefam 959
	Cathmogh 969
	Mugron O'Mutan 1057
1138	Gregory
?	Ua Menngorain 1147
1148	Gilla Aedha Ua Maigin
1174	[Gregorius] O h-Aedha [O Hea]
c.1182	Reginaldus I
1187	Aicher
1192	Murchad Ua h-Aedha
	Anonymous 1214
1215	Mairin Ua Briain [Marianus]
1225	Gilbertus
1248	Laurentius
1265	William of Jerpoint
1267	Reginaldus
1277	Robert Mac Donnchada
1302	Seoan Mac Cearbaill [Mac Carwill]
1321	Philip of Slane
1327	Walter le Rede
1330	John of Ballyconingham
1347	John Roche
1359	Gerald de Barri
1396	Roger Ellesmere
1406	Richard Kynmoure
1409	Patrick Fox
1409	Milo fitzJohn
1425	John Paston
1418	Adam Payn
1429	Jordan Purcell
1463	Gerald FitzGerald
1472	William Roche (Coadjutor)
1490	Tadhg Mac Carthaigh
1499	John FitzEdmund FitzGerald
1499	Patrick Cant
1523	John Benet

1536	Dominic Tyrre [Tirrey]
1562	Roger Skiddy
1570	Richard Dyxon
1572	Matthew Sheyn
	Ross united to Cork 1583
1583	William Lyon
1618	John Boyle
1620	Richard Boyle
1638	William Chappell
1661	Michael Boyle
1663	Edward Synge
1679	Edward Wetenhall
1699	Dive Downes
1710	Peter Browne
1735	Robert Clayton
1745	Jemmett Browne
1772	Isaac Mann
1789	Euseby Cleaver
1789	William Foster
1790	William Bennet
1794	Thomas Stopford
1805	John George Beresford
1807	Thomas St Laurence
1831	Samuel Kyle
	Cloyne united to Cork from 1835
1848	James Wilson
1857	William FitzGerald
1862	John Gregg
1878	Robert Samuel Gregg
1894	William Edward Meade
1912	Charles Benjamin Dowse
1933	William Edward Flewett
1938	Robert Thomas Hearn
1952	George Otto Sims
1957	Richard Gordon Perdue
1978	Samuel Greenfield Poyntz
1988	Robert Alexander Warke
1999	William Paul Colton

Dublin

Dublin and Glendalough

Description of arms. Azure, an episcopal staff argent, ensigned with a cross pattée or, surmounted by a pallium of the second edged and fringed or, charged with five crosses formée fitchée, sable.

BISHOPS

	Sinhail 790
c.1028	Dunan [Donatus]
1074	Gilla Patraic
1085	Donngus
1096	Samuel Ua'h-Aingliu

ARCHBISHOPS

1121	Grene [Gregorius]
1162	Lorcan Ua'Tuathail [Laurentius]
1182	John Cumin
1213	Henry de Loundres
	Glendalough united to Dublin
1230	Luke
125?	Fulk de Sandford
1279	John de Derlington
1286	John de Sandford
1295	Thomas de Chadworth
1296	William de Hotham
1299	Richard de Ferings
[1307	Richard de Havering, not consecrated]
1311	John de Leche

1317 Alexander de Bicknor
1349 John de St Paul
1363 Thomas Minot
1376 Robert de Wikeford
1391 Robert Waldeby
1396 Richard Northalis
1397 Thomas Cranley
1418 Richard Talbot
1451 Michael Tregury
1472 John Walton
1484 Walter Fitzsimons
1512 William Rokeby
1521 Hugh Inge
1529 John Alan
1535 George Browne
1555 Hugh Curwin
1567 Adam Loftus
1605 Thomas Jones
1619 Lancelot Bulkeley
1661 James Margetson
1663 Michael Boyle
1679 John Parker
1682 Francis Marsh
1694 Narcissus Marsh
1703 William King
1730 John Hoadly
1743 Charles Cobbe
1765 William Carmichael
1766 Arthur Smyth
1772 John Cradock
1779 Robert Fowler
1801 Charles Agar [Earl of
       Normanton]
1809 Euseby Cleaver
1820 John George Beresford
1822 William Magee
1831 Richard Whately
Kildare united to Dublin 1846
1864 Richard Chenevix Trench
       (resigned)
1885 William Conyngham [Lord
       Plunket]
1897 Joseph Ferguson Peacocke
1915 John Henry Bernard
1919 Charles Frederick D'Arcy
1920 John Allen Fitzgerald Gregg
1939 Arthur William Barton
1956 George Otto Simms
1969 Alan Alexander Buchanan
1977 Henry Robert McAdoo
1985 Donald Arthur Richard Caird
1996 Walton Newcome Francis
       Empey
2002 John Robert Winder Neill
2011 Michael Geoffrey St Aubyn
       Jackson

†Emly

Raidghil 881
Ua Ruaich 953
Faelan 980
MaelFinan 1030
Diarmait Ua Flainnchua 1114
1152 Gilla in Choimhded Ua h-
       Ardmhail Mael Isu Ua
       Laigenain 1163
1172 Ua Meic Stia
1177 Charles O'Buacalla
1177 Isaac O'Hamery
1192 Ragnall Ua Flainnchua
1205 M.
1209 William
1212 Henry
1227 John Collingham
1238 Daniel
1238 Christianus
1251 Gilbert O'Doverty
1266 Florence or Laurence O'hAirt
1272 Matthew MacGormain
1275 David O Cossaig
1286 William de Clifford
1306 Thomas Cantock [Quantock]
1309 William Roughead

1335 Richard le Walleys
1353 John Esmond
1363 David Penlyn [Foynlyn]
1363 William
1405 Nicholas Ball
1421 John Rishberry
1422 Robert Windell
1428 Thomas de Burgo
1428 Robert Portland
1445 Cornelius O Cuinnlis
1444 Robert
1448 Cornelius O Maolalaidh
1449 William O Hetigan
1476 Pilib O Cathail
1494 Donatus Mac Briain
1498 Cinneidigh Mac Briain
1507 Tomas O hUrthaille
1543 Angus O'Hernan
1551 Raymond de Burgo
United to Cashel 1569
Transferred to Limerick 1976

†Ferns

–598 Edan [or Maedoc or Hugh]
       Maeldogair 676
       Coman 678
       Diratus 693
       Cillenius 715
       Cairbre O'Kearney 1095
       Ceallach Ua Colmain 1117
       Mael Eoin Ua Dunacain 1125
       Ua Cattain 1135
1178 Loseph Ua h-Aeda
1186 Ailbe Ua Maelmuaid [Albinus]
1224 John of St John
1254 Geoffrey of St John
1258 Hugh of Lamport
1283 Richard of Northampton
1304 Simon of Evesham
1305 Robert Walrand
1312 Adam of Northampton
1347 Hugh de Saltu [of Leixlip]
1347 Geoffrey Grandfeld
1349 John Esmond
1350 William Charnells
1363 Thomas Dene
1400 Patrick Barret
1418 Robert Whittey
1453 Tadhg O Beirn
1457 John Purcell I
1479 Laurence Nevill
1505 Edmund Comerford
1510 Nicholas Comyn
1519 John Purcell II
1539 Alexander Devereux
1566 John Devereux
1582 Hugh Allen
Leighlin united to Ferns 1597
1600 Robert Grave
1601 Nicholas Stafford
1605 Thomas Ram
1635 George Andrews
1661 Robert Price
1667 Richard Boyle
1683 Narcissus Marsh
1691 Bartholomew Vigors
1722 Josiah Hort
1727 John Hoadly
1730 Arthur Price
1734 Edward Synge
1740 George Stone
1743 William Cottrell
1744 Robert Downes
1752 John Garnet
1758 William Carmichael
1758 Thomas Salmon
1759 Richard Robinson
1761 Charles Jackson
1765 Edward Young
1772 Joseph Deane Bourke
1782 Walter Cope
1787 William Preston
1789 Euseby Cleaver
1809 Percy Jocelyn

1820 Robert Ponsonby Tottenham
       Loftus
1822 Thomas Elrington
United to Ossory 1835

†Glendalough

Dairchell 678
Eterscel 814
Dungal 904
Cormac 927
Nuadha 920 [or Neva]
Gilda Na Naomh c.1080
Cormac O'Mail 1101
Aed Ua Modain 1126
1140 Anonymous
1152 Gilla na Naem
1157 Cinaed O Ronain [Celestinus]
1176 Maelcallann Ua Cleirchen
       [Malchus]
1186 Macrobius
1192 William Piro
1214 Robert de Bedford
United to Dublin
After the union with Dublin some
rival bishops appear.
c.1216 Bricheus
1468 John
1475 Michael
1481 Denis White John 1494
1494 Ivo Ruffi
1495 John
1500 Francis Fitzjohn of Corduba

†Iniscattery (Scattery Island)

861 Aidan
959 Cinaeda O'Chommind
973 Scandlam O'Lenz
       O'Bruil 1069
       O'Bruil II 1081
       Dermot O Lennain 1119
       Aed Ua Bechain I 1188
       Cearbhal Ua'h-Enna [Carolus]
       1193
1360 Tomas Mac Mathghamhna
1392 John Donkan
1414 Richard Belmer
       Dionysius 1447
1447 John Grene
Incorporated with Limerick

†Kells

Mael Finnen 968
c.1152 Tuathal Ua Connachtarg
1185 Anonymous
1202 M. Ua Dobailen
Incorporated with Meath

†Kildare

Conlaedh 520
Hugh [or Hed] the Black 639
Maeldoborcon 709
Eutigern 762
Lomthiull 787
Snedbran 787
Tuatchar 834
Orthanach 840
Aedgene Britt 864
Macnghal 870
Lachtnan 875
Suibhne 881
Scannal 885
Lergus 888
Mael Findan 950
Annchadh 981
Murrough McFlan 986
1030 MaelMartain
       MaelBrighde 1042
       Finn 1085

MaelBrighde O Brolchan 1097
Hugh [Heremon] 1100
Ferdomnach 1101
Cormac O Cathassaig 1146
Ua Duibhin 1148
1152 Finn mac Mael Muire Mac
    Cianain
    Fin mac Gussain Ua Gormain
1161 Malachias Ua Brain
1177 Nehemias
1206 Cornelius Mac Fealain
1223 Ralph of Bristol
1233 John of Taunton
1258 Simon of Kilkenny
1280 Nicholas Cusack
1300 Walter Calf [de Veel]
1333 Richard Houlot
1352 Thomas Giffard
1366 Robert of Aketon [Acton]
1404 John Madock
1431 William fitzEdward
1449 Geoffrey Hereford
1456 John Bole [Bull]
1464 Richard Lang
1474 David Cone
1475 James Wall
    William Barret
1480 Edward Lane
1526 Thomas Dillon
1529 Walter Wellesley
1540 William Miagh
1550 Thomas Lancaster
1555 Thomas Leverous
1560 Alexander Craik
1564 Robert Daly
1583 Daniel Neylan
1604 William Pilsworth
1636 Robert Ussher
1644 William Golborne
1661 Thomas Price
1667 Ambrose Jones
1679 Anthony Dopping
1682 William Moreton
1705 Welbore Ellis
1731 Charles Cobbe
1743 George Stone
1745 Thomas Fletcher
1761 Richard Robinson
1765 Charles Jackson
1790 George Lewis Jones
1804 Charles Lindsay
United to Dublin after the death of Bp
    Lindsay in 1846
1976 Separated from Dublin and
    united to Meath

†Kilfenora

1172 Anonymous
1205 F.
1224 Johannes
1254 Christianus
    Anonymous 1264
1266 Mauricius
1273 Florentius O Tigernaig
1281 Congalach [O Lochlainn]
1291 G.
1299 Simon O Cuirrin
1303 Maurice O Briain
1323 Risdeard O Lochlainn
c.1355 Dionysius
1372 Henricus
    Cornelius
1390 Patricius
1421 Feidhlimidh mac
    Mathghamhna O Lochlainn
    [Florentius]
1433 Fearghal
1434 Dionysius O Connmhaigh
1447 John Greni
1476 [? Denis] O Tombaigh
1491 Muircheartach mac Murchadha
    O Briain [Mauricius]
1514 Maurice O'Kelly
1541 John O'Neylan

−1585 Daniel, bishop-elect
1606 Bernard Adams [with Limerick
    q.v.]
1617 John Steere
1622 William Murray
[1628 Richard Betts, not consecrated]
1630 James Heygate
1638 Robert Sibthorp
1661–1741 Held by the Archbishops
    of Tuam
1742–52 Held by the Bishop of
    Clonfert
United to Killaloe 1752

†Killaloe

BISHOPS

    O'Gerruidher 1054
    Domnall Ua hEnna 1098
    Mael Muire O Dunain 1117
    Domnall Ua Conaing 1131
    Domnall Ua Longargain 1137
    Tadg Ua Longargain 1161
    Donnchad mac Diarmata Ua
    Briain 1164
1179 Constantin mac Toirrdelbaig Ua
    Briain
1194 Diarmait Ua Conaing
1201 Conchobhar Ua h-Enna
    [Cornelius]
1217 Robert Travers
1221 Domnall Ua h-Enna [Donatus]
1231 Domnall O Cenneitig [Donatus]
1253 Isoc O Cormacain [Isaac]
1268 Mathgamain O h-Ocain [O
    Hogan]
1281 Maurice O h-Ocain
1299 David Mac Mathghamna [Mac
    Mahon]
1317 Tomas O Cormacain I
1323 Brian O Cosgraig
1326 David Mac Briain [David of
    Emly]
?1326 Natus O Heime
1343 Tomas O h-Ogain
1355 Tomas O Cormacain II
1389 Mathghamain Mag Raith
1400 Donatus Mag Raith
1409 Robert Mulfield
1418 Eugenius O Faolain
1423 Thadeus Mag Raith I
1429 Seamus O Lonnghargain
1443 Donnchadh mac
    Toirdhealbhaigh O Briain
1460 Thadeus Mag Raith II
1463 Matthaeus O Griobhtha
1483 Toirdhealbhach mac
    Mathghamhna O Briain
    [Theodoricus]
1523 Thadeus
1526 Seamus O Cuirrin
1546 Cornelius O Dea
1554 Turlough [or Terence] O'Brien II
1570 Maurice [or Murtagh] O'Brien-
    Arra
1613 John Rider
1633 Lewis Jones
1647 Edward Parry
1661 Edward Worth
1669 Daniel Wytter
1675 John Roan
1693 Henry Ryder
1696 Thomas Lindsay
1713 Thomas Vesey
1714 Nicholas Forster
1716 Charles Carr
1740 Joseph Story
1742 John Ryder
1743 Jemmet Browne
1745 Richard Chenevix
1746 Nicholas Synge
Kilfenora united to Killaloe 1752
1771 Robert Fowler
1779 George Chinnery

1780 Thomas Barnard
1794 William Knox
1803 Charles Dalrymple Lindsay
1804 Nathaniel Alexander
1804 Robert Ponsonby Tottenham
    Loftus
1820 Richard Mant
1823 Alexander Arbuthnot
1828 Richard Ponsonby
1831 Edmund Knox [with Clonfert]
Clonfert united to Killaloe 1834
Kilmacduagh united to Killaloe 1834
1834 Christopher Butson
1836 Stephen Crengh Sandes
1839 Ludlow Tonson [afterwards
    Baron Riversdale]
1862 William FitzGerald
1884 William Bennet Chester
1893 Frederick Richards Wynne
1897 Mervyn Archdall
1912 Charles Benjamin Dowse
1913 Thomas Sterling Berry
    (resigned)
1924 Henry Edmund Patton
1943 Robert M'Neil Boyd
1945 Hedley Webster
1953 Richard Gordon Perdue
1957 Henry Arthur Stanistreet
1972 Edwin Owen
1976 United to Limerick

†Kilmacduagh

 ? Ua Cleirig 1137
    Imar Ua Ruaidin 1176
    Rugnad O'Rowan 1178
1179 Mac Gilla Cellaig Ua Ruaidin
1206 Ua Cellaig
    Mael Muire O Connmaig 1224
1227 Aed [Odo]
    Conchobhar O Muiredaig 1247
1248 Gilla Cellaig O Ruaidin
    [Gilbertus]
1249 David yFredrakern
1254 Mauricius O Leaain
1284 David O Setachain
1290 Luirint O Lachtnain
    [Laurentius]
1307 Lucas
1326 Johannes
1360 Nicol O Leaain
1394 Gregory O Leaain
1405 Enri O Connmhaigh
1409 Dionysius
1409 Eugene O Faolain
1418 Diarmaid O Donnchadha
1419 Nicol O Duibhghiolla
1419 Seaan O Connmhaigh
1441 Dionysius O Donnchadha
1479 Cornelius O Mullony
1503 Matthaeus O Briain
1533 Christopher Bodkin
1573 Stephen O'Kirwan
[1584 Thomas Burke, not
    consecrated]
1587 Roland Lynch
1627–1836 Held in commendam by
    the Bishops of Clonfert
United to Killaloe since 1834

†Leighlin

−633 Laserian or Molaise
−865 Mainchin
−940 Conella McDonegan Daniel 969
    Cleitic O'Muinic 1050
c.1096 Ferdomnac
    Mael Eoin Ua Dunacain 1125
    Sluaigedach Ua Cathain 1145
1152 Dungal O Caellaide
1192 Johannes
1197 Johannes
1202 Herlewin
1217 Richard [Fleming]

1228 William le Chauniver
1252 Thomas
1275 Nicholas Chever
1309 Maurice de Blanchville
1321 Meiler le Poer
1344 Radulphus O Ceallaigh
1349 Thomas of Brakenberg
1360 Johannes
1362 William (not consecrated)
1363 John Young
1371 Philip FitzPeter
1385 John Griffin
1398 Thomas Peverell
1400 Richard Bocomb
1419 John Mulgan
1432 Thomas Fleming
— Diarmaid 1464
1464 Milo Roche
1490 Nicholas Magwyr
1513 Thomas Halsey
1524 Mauricius O Deoradhain
1527 Matthew Sanders
1550 Robert Travers
1555 Thomas O'Fihelly
1567 Donnell or Daniel Cavanagh
1589 Richard Meredith
United to Ferns since 1597 on the
    death of Bp Meredith

Limerick

Limerick, Ardfert, Aghadoe, Killaloe,
Kilfenora, Clonfert, Kilmacduagh and
Emly

Description of arms. Azure two keys
addorsed in saltire the wards upwards;
in the dexter chief a crosier paleways, in
the sinister a mitre, all or.

–1106 Gilli alias Gilla Espaic
1140 Patricius
1150 Erolb [? = Harold]
1152 Torgesius
1179 Brictius
1203 Donnchad Ua'Briain [Donatus]
1207 Geoffrey
–1215 Edmund
1223 Hubert de Burgo
1252 Robert de Emly or Neil
1273 Gerald [or Miles] de Mareshall
1302 Robert de Dundonald
1312 Eustace de Aqua or de l'Eau
1336 Maurice de Rochfort
1354 Stephen Lawless
1360 Stephen Wall [de Valle]
1369 Peter Curragh
1399 Bernardus O Conchobhair
1400 Conchobhar O Deadhaidh
1426 John Mothel (resigned)
Iniscattery incorporated with
    Limerick
1456 Thomas Leger
1458 William Russel, *alias* Creagh
1463 Thomas Arthur
[1486 Richard Stakpoll, not
    consecrated]
1486 John Dunowe
1489 John O'Phelan [Folan]
1524 Sean O Cuinn
1551 William Casey
1557 Hugh de Lacey or Lees
    (deposed)

1571 William Casey
1594 John Thornburgh
1604 Bernard Adams
1626 Francis Gough
1634 George Webb
1643 Robert Sibthorp
Ardfert united to Limerick 1661
1661 Edward Synge
1664 William Fuller
1667 Francis Marsh
1673 John Vesey
1679 Simon Digby
1692 Nathaniel Wilson
1695 Thomas Smyth
1725 William Burscough
1755 James Leslie
1771 James Averill
1772 William Gore
1784 William Cecil Pery
1794 Thomas Barnard
1806 Charles Morgan Warburton
1820 Thomas Elrington
1823 John Jebb
1834 Edmund Knox
1849 William Higgin
1854 Henry Griffin
1866 Charles Graves
1899 Thomas Bunbury
1907 Raymond D'Audemra Orpen
1921 Harry Vere White
1934 Charles King Irwin
1942 Evelyn Charles Hodges
1961 Robert Wyse Jackson
1970 Donald Arthur Richard Caird
Killaloe united to Limerick 1976
Emly transferred to Limerick 1976
1976 Edwin Owen
1981 Walton Newcome Francis
    Empey
1985 Edward Flewett Darling
2000 Michael Hugh Gunton Mayes
2008 Trevor Russell Williams
2015 Kenneth Arthur Kearon

†Lismore

Ronan 764
Cormac MacCuillenan 918
–999 Cinneda O'Chonmind
Niall mac Meic Aedacain 1113
Ua Daightig 1119
1121 Mael Isu Ua h-Ainmere
Mael Muire Ua Loingsig 1150
1151 Gilla Crist Ua Connairche
    [Christianus]
1179 Felix
Ardmore incorporated with Lismore
    1192
1203 Malachias, O'Heda or O'Danus
1216 Thomas
1219 Robert of Bedford
1228 Griffin Christopher
1248 Ailinn O Suilleabain
1253 Thomas
1270 John Roche
1280 Richard Corre
1309 William Fleming
1310 R.
1322 John Leynagh
1356 Roger Cradock, provision
    annulled
1358 Thomas le Reve
United to Waterford 1363

Meath

Meath and Kildare

Description of arms. Sable three mitres
argent, two, and one.

BISHOPS OF THE SEE OF CLONARD

Senach 588
–640 Colman 654
DusucBhduin O'Phelan 718
Tole 738
–778 Fulartach 779
Clothcu 796
Clemens 826
Cormac MacSuibhne
Cumsuth 858
Suarlech 870
Ruman MacCathasaid 922
Colman MacAililid 926
Tuathal O'Dubhamaigh 1028

BISHOPS OF MEATH

1096 Mael Muire Ua Dunain
1128 Eochaid O Cellaig
1151 Etru Ua Miadacain [Eleuzerius]
1177 Echtigern mac Mael Chiarain
    [Eugenius]
1192 Simon Rochfort
(The See was transferred from Clonard
    to Newtown near Trim, 1202)
Kells incorporated with Meath
1224 Donan De [Deodatus] (not
    consecrated)
1227 Ralph Petit
1231 Richard de la Corner
1253 Geoffrey Cusack
1255 Hugo de Taghmon
1283 Walter de Fulburn
1287 Thomas St Leger
1322 Seoan Mac Cerbaill [John
    MacCarwill]
1327 William de Paul
1350 William St Leger
1353 Nicholas [Allen]
1369 Stephen de Valle [Wall]
1380 William Andrew
1385 Alexander Petit [or de Balscot]
1401 Robert Montayne
1412 Edward Dantesey
[1430 Thomas Scurlog, apparently not
    consecrated]
1430 William Hadsor
1435 William Silk
1450 Edmund Ouldhall
1460 William Shirwood
1483 John Payne
1507 William Rokeby
1512 Hugh Inge
1523 Richard Wilson
1529 Edward Staples
1554 William Walsh
1563 Hugh Brady
Clonmacnoise united to Meath 1569
1584 Thomas Jones
1605 Roger Dod
1612 George Montgomery
1621 James Usher
1625 Anthony Martin
[Interregnum 1650–61]
1661 Henry Leslie
1661 Henry Jones
1682 Anthony Dopping
1697 Richard Tennison

1705 William Moreton
1716 John Evans
1724 Henry Downes
1727 Ralph Lambert
1732 Welbore Ellis
1734 Arthur Price
1744 Henry Maule
1758 William Carmichael
1765 Richard Pococke
1765 Arthur Smyth
1766 Henry Maxwell
1798 Thomas Lewis O'Beirne
1823 Nathaniel Alexander
1840 Charles Dickinson
1842 Edward Stopford
1850 Thomas Stewart Townsend
1852 James Henderson Singer
1866 Samuel Butcher
1876 William Conyngham [Lord
     Plunket]
1885 Charles Parsons Reichel
1894 Joseph Ferguson Peacocke
1897 James Bennett Keene
1919 Benjamin John Plunket
1926 Thomas Gibson George Collins
1927 John Orr
1938 William Hardy Holmes
1945 James McCann
1959 Robert Bonsall Pike
Kildare united to Meath 1976
1976 Donald Arthur Richard Caird
1985 Walton Newcome Francis
     Empey
1996 Richard Lionel Clarke
2013 Patricia Louise Storey

†Ossory

Dermot 973
1152 Domnall Ua Fogartaig
1180 Felix Ua Duib Slaine
1202 Hugo de Rous [Hugo Rufus]
1220 Peter Mauveisin
1231 William of Kilkenny
1233 Walter de Brackley
1245 Geoffrey de Turville
1251 Hugh de Mapilton
1260 Geoffrey St Leger
1287 Roger of Wexford
1289 Michael d'Exeter
1303 William FitzJohn
1317 Richard Ledred
1361 John de Tatenhale
1366 William
  — John of Oxford
1371 Alexander Petit [de Balscot]
1387 Richard Northalis
1396 Thomas Peverell
1399 John Waltham
1400 John Griffin
1400 John
1401 Roger Appleby
1402 John Waltham
1407 Thomas Snell
1417 Patrick Foxe
1421 Dionysius O Deadhaidh
1427 Thomas Barry
1460 David Hacket
1479 Seaan O hEidigheain
1487 Oliver Cantwell
1528 Milo Baron [or FitzGerald]
1553 John Bale
1554 John Tonory
1567 Christopher Gaffney
1577 Nicholas Walsh
1586 John Horsfall
1610 Richard Deane
1613 Jonas Wheeler

1641 Griffith Williams
1672 John Parry
1678 Benjamin Parry
1678 Michael Ward
1680 Thomas Otway
1693 John Hartstonge
1714 Thomas Vesey
1731 Edward Tennison
1736 Charles Este
1741 Anthony Dopping
1743 Michael Cox
1754 Edward Maurice
1755 Richard Pococke
1765 Charles Dodgson
1775 William Newcome
1779 John Hotham
1782 William Heresford
1795 Thomas Lewis O'Beirne
1799 Hugh Hamilton
1806 John Kearney
1813 Robert Fowler
Ferns united to Ossory 1835
1842 James Thomas O'Brien
1874 Robert Samuel Gregg
1878 William Pakenham Walsh
1897 John Baptist Crozier
1907 Charles Frederick D'Arcy
1911 John Henry Bernard
1915 John Allen Fitzgerald Gregg
1920 John Godfrey FitzMaurice Day
1938 Ford Tichbourne
1940 John Percy Phair
1962 Henry Robert McAdoo
United to Cashel 1977

†Ross

Nechtan MacNechtain 1160
Isaac O'Cowen 1161
O'Carroll 1168
1177 Benedictus
1192 Mauricius
1198 Daniel
1224 Fineen O Clothna [Florentius]
c.1250 Malachy
1254 Mauricius
1269 Walter O Mithigein
1275 Peter O h-Uallachain [?
     Patrick]
1291 Laurentius
1310 Matthaeus O Finn
1331 Laurentius O h-Uallachain
1336 Dionysius
1379 Bernard O Conchobhair
1399 Peter Curragh
1400 Thadeus O Ceallaigh
1401 Mac Raith O hEidirsgeoil
     [Macrobius]
1402 Stephen Brown
1403 Matthew
1418 Walter Formay
1424 John Bloxworth
1426 Conchobhar Mac Fhaolchadha
     [Cornelius]
     Maurice Brown 1431
1431 Walter of Leicester
1434 Richard Clerk
1448 Domhnall O Donnobhain John
     1460
1460 Robert Colynson
–1464 Thomas
1464 John Hornse alias Skipton
1473 Aodh O hEidirsgeoil [Odo]
1482 Tadhg Mac Carthaigh
1494 John Edmund Courci
1517 Seaan O Muirthile

1519 Tadgh O Raghallaigh
     [Thaddeus]
1523 Bonaventura
1526 Diarmaid Mac Carthaigh
1544 Dermot McDonnell
1551 John
1554 Maurice O'Fihelly
1559 Maurice O'Hea
1561 Thomas O'Herlihy
1582 William Lyon [with Cork and
     Cloyne after 1581]
United to Cork 1583

†Waterford

1096 Mael lus Ua h-Ainmere
1152 Toistius
1175 Augustinus Ua Selbaig
     Anonymous 1199
1200 Robert I
1204 David the Welshman
1210 Robert II [Breathnach]
1223 William Wace
1227 Walter
1232 Stephen
1250 Henry
1252 Philip
1255 Walter de Southwell
1274 Stephen de Fulbourn
1286 Walter de Fulbourn
1308 Matthew
1323 Nicholas Welifed
1338 Richard Francis
1349 Robert Elyot
1350 Roger Cradock
Lismore united to Waterford 1363
1363 Thomas le Reve
1394 Robert Read
1396 Thomas Sparklord
1397 John Deping
1400 Thomas Snell
1407 Roger of Appleby (see under
     Ossory)
1409 John Geese
1414 Thomas Colby
1421 John Geese
1426 Richard Cantwell
1446 Robert Poer
1473 Richard Martin
1475 John Bulcomb
1480 Nicol O hAonghusa
1483 Thomas Purcell
1519 Nicholas Comyn
1551 Patrick Walsh
1579 Marmaduke Middleton
1582 Miler Magrath (Bishop
     of Cashel and
     Waterford)
1589 Thomas Wetherhead [or
     Walley]
1592 Miler Magrath
1608 John Lancaster
1619 Michael Boyle
1636 John Atherton
1641 Archibald Adair
1661 George Baker
1666 Hugh Gore
1691 Nathaniel Foy
1708 Thomas Mills
1740 Charles Este
1746 Richard Chenevix
1779 William Newcome
1795 Richard Marlay
1802 Power le Poer Trench
1810 Joseph Stock
1813 Richard Bourke
United to Cashel under Church
     Temporalities Act 1833

CATHEDRALS

CHURCH OF ENGLAND

(BATH AND) WELLS (St Andrew)   Dean J M CLARKE,
 Can Res A FEATHERSTONE, THE VEN N A SULLIVAN,
 G M DODDS, N L JEPSON-BIDDLE
BIRMINGHAM (St Philip)   Dean C OGLE, Can Res N A HAND,
 J E CHAPMAN
BLACKBURN (St Mary)   Dean C J ARMSTRONG,
 Can Res A D HINDLEY, S I PENFOLD, I G STOCKTON
BRADFORD (St Peter)   Dean J J LEPINE, Can Res S J C CORLEY,
 M R COUTTS, C C M THATCHER
BRISTOL (Holy Trinity)   Dean D M HOYLE, Can Res R D BULL,
 N V STANLEY, D C CHEDZEY
CANTERBURY (Christ)   Dean R A WILLIS,
 Can Res D C EDWARDS, C P IRVINE, N PAPADOPULOS,
 THE VEN S A WATSON, Prec M J RUSHTON
CARLISLE (Holy Trinity)   Dean M C BOYLING,
 Can Res J E KEARTON, M A MANLEY, THE VEN K T ROBERTS
CHELMSFORD (St Mary, St Peter and St Cedd)
 Dean N J HENSHALL, Can Res E J CARTER, S J POTHEN,
 I R MOODY
CHESTER (Christ and Blessed Virgin Mary)
 Dean G F McPHATE, Vice-Dean P HOWELL-JONES,
 Can Res R J BROOKE, J N N C DUSSEK
CHICHESTER (Holy Trinity)   Dean S J WAINE,
 Can Res N T SCHOFIELD, A W N S CANE
COVENTRY (St Michael)   Dean J J WITCOMBE,
 Can Res D A STONE, K C FLEMING, S L FIELDING, S A ST L HILLS
DERBY (All Saints)   Dean J H DAVIES, Can Res S J TAYLOR,
 C A R MOORSOM, E J THOMSON Chapl A P DICKENS
DURHAM (Christ and Blessed Virgin Mary)
 Dean M SADGROVE, Can Res D J KENNEDY, R BROWN,
 THE VEN I JAGGER, S R JELLEY
ELY (Holy Trinity)   Dean M P J BONNEY,
 Can Res A L HARGRAVE, J R GARRARD, V L JOHNSON,
 Chapter Can H D SHILSON-THOMAS
EXETER (St Peter)   Dean J L DRAPER, Can Res C F TURNER,
 I C MORTER, A E NORMAN-WALKER, J F SEARLE, V A THURTELL
GLOUCESTER (St Peter and Holy Trinity)   Dean S D LAKE,
 Can Res N C HEAVISIDES, C S M THOMSON,
 THE VEN J A SEARLE, N M ARTHY, A J BRADDOCK,
 Min Can J P HOSKINS
GUILDFORD (Holy Spirit)   Dean D L GWILLIAMS,
 Sub-Dean N J THISTLETHWAITE, Can Res THE VEN S A BEAKE,
 A S BISHOP, J A GITTOES
HEREFORD (Blessed Virgin Mary and St Ethelbert)
 Dean M E TAVINOR, Can Res A PIPER, C PULLIN,
 Min Can P A ROW
LEICESTER (St Martin)   Dean D R M MONTEITH,
 Can Res J ARENS, R A FAIRHURST,
LICHFIELD (Blessed Virgin Mary and St Chad)
 Dean A J DORBER, Vice Dean A M MOORE,
 Can Res A M STEAD, P L HOLLIDAY, P S HAWKINS
LINCOLN (Blessed Virgin Mary)   Dean P J W BUCKLER,
 Can Res G J KIRK, M D HOCKNULL, J A PATRICK,
 PV S-A McDOUGALL, I G SILK
LIVERPOOL (Christ)   Dean P J WILCOX, Can Res M C DAVIES,
 C DOWDLE, R S WHITE, P D RATTIGAN
LONDON (St Paul)   Dean D J ISON, Can Res M D OAKLEY,
 M H J HAMPEL, P A BOARDMAN, P D HILLAS,
 Min Can J H MILNE, R J MORTON
MANCHESTER (St Mary, St Denys and St George)
 Dean R M GOVENDER, Sub Dean P N BARRATT,
 Can Res THE VEN M D ASHCROFT, D A HOLGATE,
 Chapl A M RHODES, P G BELLAMY-KNIGHTS
NEWCASTLE (St Nicholas)   Dean C C DALLISTON,
 Can Res THE VEN G V MILLER, S C HARVEY, J R SINCLAIR

NORWICH (Holy Trinity)   Dean J B HEDGES,
 Vice-Dean J M HASELOCK, Can Res P M DOLL,
 A W BRYANT
OXFORD (Christ Church)   Dean M W PERCY,
 Sub Dean E J NEWEY, Can Res N J BIGGAR, A C W TILBY,
 G J WARD, Prec J W S PATON
PETERBOROUGH (St Peter, St Paul and St Andrew)
 Dean C W TAYLOR, Can Res J W BAKER, R B RUDDOCK,
 I C BLACK, T M ALBAN JONES
PORTSMOUTH (St Thomas of Canterbury)
 Dean D C BRINDLEY, Can Res A C RUSTELL, N R RALPH,
 P P LEONARD
RIPON (St Peter and St Wilfrid)   Dean J DOBSON,
 Can Res R E HIND, P GREENWELL, E J SEWELL,
 Chapl G M RIDER
ROCHESTER (Christ and Blessed Virgin
 Mary)   Dean vacant, Can Res P J HESKETH, N H THOMPSON,
 THE VEN S D BURTON-JONES, J KERR
ST ALBANS (St Alban)   Dean J P H JOHN,
 Sub-Dean R F WATSON, Can Res K A WALTON, T M BULL,
 Min Can S J JONES
ST EDMUNDSBURY (St James)   Dean F E F WARD,
 Sub-Dean M J VERNON, Can Res P C BANKS,
 Chapl D CRAWLEY
SALISBURY (Blessed Virgin Mary)   Dean J OSBORNE,
 Can Res E C PROBERT, T E CLAMMER
SHEFFIELD (St Peter and St Paul)   Dean P E BRADLEY,
 Can Res C M BURKE, K FARROW, Min Can I MAHER
SODOR AND MAN (St German)   Dean N P GODFREY,
 Can I BRADY, J F P GOMES, M A BURROW,
 Min Can I C FAULDS
SOUTHWARK (St Saviour and St Mary Overie)
 Dean A P NUNN, Vice Dean M G RAWSON,
 Can Res G M MYERS, S J HANCE, L K ROBERTS, A K FORD,
 Succ S F STAVROU
SOUTHWELL (Blessed Virgin Mary) Dean vacant,
 Can Res J D JONES, N J COATES, PV A G MILBANK
TRURO (St Mary)   Dean R C BUSH, Can Res P R GAY,
 L M BARLEY, A G BASHFORTH
WAKEFIELD (All Saints)   Dean J D F GREENER,
 Sub Dean A S MACPHERSON Can Res A W ROBINSON,
 J A LAWSON, A M HOFBAUER, PV J M LAWON
WINCHESTER (Holy Trinity, St Peter, St Paul and
 St Swithun)   Dean J E ATWELL, Vice-Dean R G A RIEM,
 Can Res S M WALLACE, M P C COLLINSON
WORCESTER (Christ and Blessed Virgin Mary)
 Dean P G ATKINSON, Can Res A L PETTERSEN, G A BYRNE,
 M W BRIERLEY, Min Can M R DORSETT, C M MANSHIP,
 E A SHIPP
YORK (St Peter)   Dean V F FAULL, Can Res P J MOGER,
 THE VEN R M C SEED, C P COLLINGWOOD, M D SMITH,
 THE VEN D J BUTTERFIELD

Collegiate Churches

WESTMINSTER ABBEY
ST GEORGE'S CHAPEL, WINDSOR
See Royal Peculiars, p. 1055.

Diocese in Europe

GIBRALTAR (Holy Trinity)   Dean J A B PADDOCK
MALTA Valletta (St Paul) Pro-Cathedral   Chan S H GODFREY
BRUSSELS (Holy Trinity) Pro-Cathedral   Chan P D VROLIJK

CHURCH IN WALES

ST ASAPH (St Asaph)   Dean N H WILLIAMS
BANGOR (St Deiniol)   Dean vacant
ST DAVIDS (St David and St Andrew)   Dean D J R LEAN
LLANDAFF (St Peter and St Paul)   Dean G H CAPON

MONMOUTH Newport (St Woolos)   Dean L TONGE
(SWANSEA AND) BRECON (St John the Evangelist)
 Dean A P SHACKERLEY

SCOTTISH EPISCOPAL CHURCH

For the members of the chapter the *Scottish Episcopal Church Directory* should be consulted.

Aberdeen and Orkney
ABERDEEN (St Andrew) **Provost** *vacant*

Argyll and The Isles
OBAN (St John) **Provost** N McNELLY
CUMBRAE (Holy Spirit) Cathedral of The Isles
Provost K PEARSON *Bishop of Argyll and The Isles*

Brechin
DUNDEE (St Paul) **Provost** J R AULD

Edinburgh
EDINBURGH (St Mary) **Provost** G J T FORBES,
Vice Provost J M McLUCKIE

Glasgow and Galloway
GLASGOW (St Mary) Provost K HOLDSWORTH,
Vice Provost C L BLAKEY

Moray, Ross and Caithness
INVERNESS (St Andrew) **Provost** M J STRANGE *Bishop of Moray, Ross and Caithness*

St Andrews, Dunkeld and Dunblane
PERTH (St Ninian) **Provost** H B FARQUHARSON

CHURCH OF IRELAND

Most cathedrals are parish churches, and the dean is usually, but not always, the incumbent. For the members of the chapter the *Church of Ireland Directory* should be consulted. The name of the dean is given, together with those of other clergy holding full-time appointments.

NATIONAL CATHEDRAL OF ST PATRICK, Dublin **Dean** V G STACEY, **Dean's V** C W MULLEN

CATHEDRAL OF ST ANNE, Belfast Dean J O MANN
(St Anne's is a cathedral of the dioceses of Down and Dromore and of Connor)

Province of Armagh

Armagh
ARMAGH (St Patrick) G J O DUNSTAN

Clogher
CLOGHER (St Macartan) K R J HALL
ENNISKILLEN (St Macartin) K R J HALL

Derry and Raphoe
DERRY (St Columb) W W MORTON
RAPHOE (St Eunan) K A L BARRETT

Down and Dromore
DOWN (Holy and Undivided Trinity) T H HULL
DROMORE (Christ the Redeemer) B T KERR

Connor
LISBURN (Christ) *(Dean of Connor)* J F A BOND, **I** W S WRIGHT

Kilmore, Elphin and Ardagh
KILMORE (St Fethlimidh) N N CROSSEY
SLIGO (St Mary and St John the Baptist) A WILLIAMS

Tuam, Killala and Achonry
TUAM (St Mary) A J GRIMASON, **Provost** M S RYAN
KILLALA (St Patrick) A J GRIMASON

Province of Dublin

Dublin and Glendalough
DUBLIN (Holy Trinity) Christ Church D P M DUNNE

Meath and Kildare
TRIM (St Patrick) P D BOGLE *Dean of Clonmacnoise*
KILDARE (St Brigid) *vacant*

Cashel and Ossory
CASHEL (St John the Baptist) G G FIELD
WATERFORD (Blessed Trinity) Christ Church M P JANSSON
LISMORE (St Carthage) P R DRAPER
KILKENNY (St Canice) K M POULTON *Dean of Ossory*
LEIGHLIN (St Laserian) T W GORDON
FERNS (St Edan) P G MOONEY

Cork, Cloyne and Ross
CORK (St Fin Barre) N K DUNNE
CLOYNE (St Colman) A G MARLEY
ROSS (St Fachtna) C L PETERS

Limerick and Killaloe
LIMERICK (St Mary) S A PRAGNELL
KILLALOE (St Flannan) G A PAULSEN

ROYAL PECULIARS, CLERGY OF THE QUEEN'S HOUSEHOLD, ETC.

Royal Peculiars

Description of arms. Azure the reputed arms of Edward the Confessor, viz. a cross patonce between five martlets or, on a chief of the same, between two double roses of Lancaster and York, barbed and seeded proper, a pale charged with the Royal arms (viz. Quarterly of France and England).

Collegiate Church of St Peter in Westminster (Westminster Abbey)
Dean J R HALL, **Can** J E M SINCLAIR, D J STANTON, A TREMLETT, V P WHITE, **Min Can** C B STOLTZ, M R BIRCH, P I ARBUTHNOT, **PV** P A BAGOTT, A R BODDY, P A E CHESTER, C M CHIVERS, B D FENTON, R C GODSALL, A G GYLE, S E ARCHER, R J HUDSON-WILKIN, L J JØRGENSEN, P MCGEARY, A MOUGHTIN-MUMBY, J L OSBORNE, F L STEWART-DARLING, V A STOCK, G D SWINTON, J WHITE, G J WILLIAMS

Description of arms. The arms of the Order of the Garter, viz. Argent, a St George's Cross gules. The shield is encircled by the blue Garter with its motto.

Queen's Free Chapel of St George Windsor Castle (St George's Chapel)
Dean THE RT REVD D J CONNER, **Can** H E FINLAY, M G POLL, **Min Can** O Y F LEE

The Queen's Household

Royal Almonry

High Almoner THE RT REVD J G INGE (Bishop of Worcester)
Sub-Almoner P S WRIGHT

The College of Chaplains

Clerk of the Closet THE RT REVD J W S NEWCOME (Bishop of Carlisle)
Deputy Clerk of the Closet P S WRIGHT

Chaplains to The Queen

C P ANDREWS	J M HASELOCK	G MOFFAT
G R P ASHENDEN	R A J HILL	D NICHOLSON
P D L AVIS	P L HOLLIDAY	W A NOBLETT
H W BEARN	R J HUDSON-WILKIN	H PALMER
M E BIDE	G I KOVOOR	S C PALMER
J V BYRNE	J LEE	G P RAVALDE
G M CALVER	E J LEWIS	J REES
A CLITHEROW	P LOCKETT	J B V RIVIERE
R T COOPER	E MASON	R B RUDDOCK
I A DAVENPORT	K S MCCORMACK	A M SHEPHERD
A R EASTER	P MILLER	N J THISTLETHWAITE
K B GARLICK		

Extra Chaplains to The Queen

A D CAESAR	A HOWE	J P ROBSON

Chapels Royal

Dean of the Chapels Royal THE BISHOP OF LONDON
Sub-Dean of the Chapels Royal P S WRIGHT
Priests in Ordinary R D E BOLTON, W A WHITCOMBE
Deputy Priests in Ordinary R J HALL, A HOWE, M D OAKLEY, S E YOUNG
Domestic Chaplain, Buckingham Palace P S WRIGHT
Domestic Chaplain, Windsor Castle THE DEAN OF WINDSOR
Domestic Chaplain, Sandringham J B V RIVIERE
Chaplain, Royal Chapel, Windsor Great Park M G POLL
Chaplain, Hampton Court Palace A HOWE
Chaplain, HM Tower of London R J HALL

The Queen's Chapel of the Savoy

Chaplain P J GALLOWAY

Royal Memorial Chapel, Sandhurst

Chaplain M PARKER

Royal Foundation of St Katharine in Ratcliffe

Master C W M AITKEN

DIOCESAN OFFICES

CHURCH OF ENGLAND

BATH AND WELLS Diocesan Office, The Old Deanery, Wells BA5 2UG
T: (01749) 670777 F: 674240 E: general@bathwells.anglican.org
W: www.bathwells.anglican.org

BIRMINGHAM Diocesan Office, 1 Colmore Row, Birmingham B3 2BJ
T: 0121–426 0400 F: 428 1114 E: reception@birmingham.anglican.org
W: www.birmingham.anglican.org

BLACKBURN Church House, Cathedral Close, Blackburn BB1 5AA
T: (01254) 503070 F: 667309 E: diocese@blackburn.anglican.org
W: www.blackburn.anglican.org

BRISTOL 1st Floor, Hillside House, Unit 1500 Bristol Parkway North, Newbrick Road, Stoke Gifford, Bristol BS34 8YU
T: 0117–906 0100 F: 925 0460
W: www.bristol.anglican.org

CANTERBURY Diocesan House, Lady Wootton's Green, Canterbury CT1 1NQ
T: (01227) 459401 F: 450964 E: reception@diocant.org
W: www.canterburydiocese.org

CARLISLE Church House, West Walls, Carlisle CA3 8UE
T: (01228) 522573 F: 815400 E: enquiries@carlislediocese.org.uk
W: www.carlislediocese.org.uk

CHELMSFORD Diocesan Office, 53 New Street, Chelmsford CM1 1AT
T: (01245) 294400 F: 294477 E: reception@chelmsford.anglican.org
W: www.chelmsford.anglican.org

CHESTER Church House, 5500 Daresbury Park, Daresbury, Warrington WA4 4GE
T: (01928) 718834 F: 620456 E: churchhouse@chester.anglican.org
W: www.chester.anglican.org

CHICHESTER Diocesan Church House, 211 New Church Road, Hove BN3 4ED
T: (01273) 421021 F: 421041 E: enquiry@chichester.anglican.org
W: www.chichester.anglican.org

COVENTRY Cathedral and Diocesan Offices, 1 Hill Top, Coventry CV1 5AB
T: (024) 7652 1200 F: 7652 1330 E: simon.lloyd@covcofe.org
W: www.dioceseofcoventry.org

DERBY Derby Church House, Full Street, Derby DE1 3DR
T: (01332) 388650 F: 292969 E: enquiries@derby.anglican.org
W: www.derby.anglican.org

DURHAM Cuthbert House, Stonebridge, Durham DH1 3RY
T: (01388) 604515 F: 603695 E: diocesan.office@durham.anglican.org
W: www.durham.anglican.org

ELY Diocesan Office, Bishop Woodford House, Barton Road, Ely CB7 4DX
T: (01353) 652701 F: 652745 E: office@ely.anglican.org
W: www.ely.anglican.org

EUROPE Diocesan Office, 14 Tufton Street, London SW1P 3QZ
T: (020) 7898 1155 F: 7898 1166 E: bron.panter@churchofengland.org
W: www.europe.anglican.org

EXETER The Old Deanery, The Cloisters, Exeter EX1 1HS
T: (01392) 272686 F: 499594 E: admin@exeter.anglican.org
W: www.exeter.anglican.org

GLOUCESTER Church House, College Green, Gloucester GL1 2LY
T: (01452) 410022 F: 308324 E: church.house@glosdioc.org.uk
W: www.gloucester.anglican.org

GUILDFORD Diocesan House, Quarry Street, Guildford GU1 3XG
T: (01483) 790300 F: 790333 E: guildford.info@cofeguildford.org.uk
W: www.guildford.anglican.org

HEREFORD Diocesan Office, The Palace, Hereford HR4 9BL
T: (01432) 373300 F: 352952 E: diooffice@hereford.anglican.org
W: www.hereford.anglican.org

LEEDS	Diocesan Office, St Mary's Street, Leeds LS9 7DP T: 0113–200 0540 F: 249 1129 E: reception.leeds@westyorkshiredales.anglican.org W: www.westyorkshiredales.anglican.org
LEICESTER	St Martin's House, 7 Peacock Lane Leicester LE1 5PZ T: 0116–261 5200 F: 261 5220 E: leicesterreception@stmartinshouse.com W: www.leicester.anglican.org
LICHFIELD	St Mary's House, The Close, Lichfield WS13 7LD T: (01543) 306030 F: 306039 E: info@lichfield.anglican.org W: www.lichfield.anglican.org
LINCOLN	Diocesan Office, Edward King House, Minster Yard, Lincoln LN2 1PU T: (01522) 504050 E: reception@lincoln.anglican.org W: www.lincoln.anglican.org
LIVERPOOL	St James's House, 20 St James Road, Liverpool L1 7BY T: 0151–709 9722 F: 709 2885 E: enquiries@liverpool.anglican.org W: www.liverpool.anglican.org
LONDON	Diocesan House, 36 Causton Street, London SW1P 4AU T: (020) 7932 1100 F: 7932 1112 E: reception@london.anglican.org W: www.london.anglican.org
MANCHESTER	Diocesan Church House, 90 Deansgate, Manchester M3 2GH T: 0161–828 1400 F: 828 1480 E: manchesterdbf@manchester.anglican.org W: www.manchester.anglican.org
NEWCASTLE	Church House, St John's Terrace, North Shields NE29 6HS T: 0191–270 4100 F: 270 4101 E: info@newcastle.anglican.org W: www.newcastle.anglican.org
NORWICH	Diocesan House, 109 Dereham Road, Easton, Norwich NR9 5ES T: (01603) 880853 F: 881083 E: diocesan.house@dioceseofnorwich.org W: www.norwich.anglican.org
OXFORD	Diocesan Church House, North Hinksey Lane, Botley, Oxford OX2 0NB T: (01865) 208200 F: 790470 E: reception@oxford.anglican.org W: www.oxford.anglican.org
PETERBOROUGH	The Palace, Peterborough PE1 1YB T: (01733) 887000 F: 555271 E: office@peterborough-diocese.org.uk W: www.peterborough-diocese.org.uk
PORTSMOUTH	First Floor, Peninsular House, Wharf Road, Portsmouth PO2 8HB T: (023) 9289 9650 F: 9289 9651 E: admin@portsmouth.anglican.org W: www.portsmouth.anglican.org
ROCHESTER	St Nicholas Church, Boley Hill, Rochester ME1 1SL T: (01634) 560000 F: 408942 E: enquiries@rochester.anglican.org W: www.rochester.anglican.org
ST ALBANS	Holywell Lodge, 41 Holywell Hill, St Albans AL1 1HE T: (01727) 854532 F: 844469 E: mail@stalbans.anglican.org W: www.stalbans.anglican.org
ST EDMUNDSBURY AND IPSWICH	St Nicholas Centre, 4 Cutler Street, Ipswich IP1 1UQ T: (01473) 298500 F: 298501 E: dbf@cofesuffolk.org W: www.stedmundsbury.anglican.org
SALISBURY	Church House, Crane Street, Salisbury SP1 2QB T: (01722) 411922 F: 411990 E: enquiries@salisbury.anglican.org W: www.salisbury.anglican.org
SHEFFIELD	Diocesan Church House, 95–99 Effingham Street, Rotherham S65 1BL T: (01709) 309100 F: 512550 E: reception@sheffield.anglican.org W: www.sheffield.anglican.org
SODOR AND MAN	Thie yn Aspick, 4 The Falls, Tromode Road, Douglas, Isle of Man IM4 4PZ T: (01624) 622108 E: secretary@sodorandman.im W: www.sodorman.anglican.org
SOUTHWARK	Trinity House, 4 Chapel Court, Borough High Street, London SE1 1HW T: (020) 7939 9400 F: 7939 9468 E: trinity@southwark.anglican.org W: www.southwark.anglican.org
SOUTHWELL AND NOTTINGHAM	Jubilee House, 8 Westgate, Southwell NG25 0JH T: (01636) 814331 F: 815084 E: mail@southwell.anglican.org W: www.southwell.anglican.org

TRURO Church House, Woodlands Court, Truro Business Park, Threemilestone, Truro TR4 9NH
T: (01872) 274351 F: 222510 E: info@truro.anglican.org
W: www.truro.anglican.org

WEST YORKSHIRE *See* LEEDS
AND THE DALES

WINCHESTER The Diocesan Office, Old Alresford Place, Old Alresford, Alresford SO24 9DH
T: (01962) 737300 F: 7373585 E: reception@winchester.anglican.org
W: www. winchester.anglican.org

WORCESTER The Old Palace, Deansway, Worcester WR1 2JE
T: (01905) 20537 F: 612302 E: generalinfo@cofe-worcester.org.uk
W: www.cofe-worcester.org.uk

YORK Diocesan House, Aviator Court, Clifton Moor, York YO30 4WJ
T: (01904) 699500 F: 699501 E: office@yorkdiocese.org
W: www.dioceseofyork.org.uk

CHURCH IN WALES

BANGOR Diocesan Office, Cathedral Close, Bangor LL57 1RL
T: (01248) 354999 F: 353882 E: bangor@churchinwales.org.uk
W: http://bangor.churchinwales.org.uk/

LLANDAFF Diocesan Office, The Court, Coychurch, Bridgend CF35 5EH
T: (01656) 868868 F: 868869 E: rowenasmall@churchinwales.org.uk
W: http://llandaff.churchinwales.org.uk/

MONMOUTH Diocesan Office, 64 Caerau Road, Newport NP20 4HJ
T: (01633) 267490 F: 265586
W: http://monmouth.churchinwales.org.uk/

ST ASAPH Diocesan Office, High Street, St Asaph LL17 0RD
T: (01745) 582245 F: 530078
W: http://stasaph.churchinwales.org.uk/

ST DAVIDS Diocesan Office, Abergwili, Carmarthen SA31 2JG
T: (01267) 236145 F: 223046 E: diocese.stdavids@churchinwales.org.uk
W: http://stdavids.churchinwales.org.uk/

SWANSEA AND Diocesan Centre, Cathedral Close, Brecon LD3 9DP
BRECON T: (01874) 623716 F: 623716 E: diocese.swanbrec@churchinwales.org.uk
W: http://swanseaandbrecon.churchinwales.org.uk/

SCOTTISH EPISCOPAL CHURCH

ABERDEEN AND Diocesan Office, St Clement's Church House, Mastrick Drive, Aberdeen AB16 6UF
ORKNEY T: (01224) 662247 F: 662168 E: office@aberdeen.anglican.org
W: www.aberdeen.anglican.org

ARGYLL AND THE St Moluag's Diocesan Centre, Croft Avenue, Oban PA34 5JJ
ISLES T: (01631) 570870 F: 570411 E: office@argyll.anglican.org
W: www.argyll.anglican.org

BRECHIN Diocesan Office, 14 Prospect III, Gemini Crescent, Technology Park, Dundee DD2 1SW
T: (01382) 562244 E: office@brechin.anglican.org
W: www.thedioceseofbrechin.org

EDINBURGH Diocesan Centre, 21A Grosvenor Crescent, Edinburgh EH12 5EL
T: 0131–538 7033 F: 538 7088 E: office@edinburgh.anglican.org
W: www.edinburgh.anglican.org

GLASGOW AND Diocesan Office, 5 St Vincent Place, Glasgow G1 2DH
GALLOWAY T: 0141–221 5720 F: 221 7014 E: office@glasgow.anglican.org
W: www.glasgow.anglican.org

MORAY, ROSS Diocesan Office, 9–11 Kenneth Street, Inverness IV3 5NR
AND CAITHNESS T: (01463) 237503 E: office@moray.anglican.org
W: www.moray.anglican.org

ST ANDREWS, Perth Diocesan Centre, 28A Balhousie Street, Perth PH1 5HJ
DUNKELD AND T: (01738) 443173 F: 443174 E: office@standrews.anglican.org
DUNBLANE W: www.standrews.anglican.org

CHURCH OF IRELAND

PROVINCE OF ARMAGH

ARMAGH
Church House, 46 Abbey Street, Armagh BT61 7DZ
T: (028) 3752 2858   F: 3751 0596   E: office@armagh.anglican.org
W: armagh.anglican.org

CLOGHER
Diocesan Office, St Macartin's Cathedral Hall, Hall's Lane, Enniskillen BT74 7DR
T: and   F: (028) 6634 7879   E: secretary@clogher.anglican.org
W: www.clogher.anglican.org

CONNOR
Diocesan Office, Church of Ireland House, 61–67 Donegall Street, Belfast BT1 2QH
T: (028) 9082 8830   F: 9032 1635   E: office@diocoff-belfast.org
W: www.connor.anglican.org

DERRY AND
RAPHOE
Diocesan Office, 24 London Street, Londonderry BT48 6RQ
T: (028) 7126 2440   F: 7137 2100   E: office.derry@btconnect.com
W: www.derry.anglican.org

DOWN AND
DROMORE
Diocesan Office, Church of Ireland House, 61–67 Donegall Street, Belfast BT1 2QH
T: (028) 9082 8830   F: 9032 1635   E: office@diocoff-belfast.org
W: www.down.anglican.org

KILMORE
Kilmore Diocesan Office, The Rectory, Cootehill, Co Cavan, Republic of Ireland
T: (00353) (49) 555 9954   F: 555 9957   E: office@kilmore.anglican.org
W: www.kilmore.anglican.org

ELPHIN AND
ARDAGH
The Moffatt Building, The Diamond, Raphoe, Co Donegal, Republic of Ireland
T: (00353) (89) 459 3219   E: diosecea@eirom.net

TUAM, KILLALA
AND ACHONRY
Stonehall House, Ballisodare, Co Sligo, Republic of Ireland
T: (00353) (71) 916 7280   E: heathersherlock7@gmail.com
W: www.tuam.anglican.org

PROVINCE OF DUBLIN

CASHEL AND
OSSORY
Diocesan Office, The Palace Coach House, Church Lane, Kilkenny, Republic of Ireland
T: (00353) (56) 776 1910   F: 51813   E: info@office.cashel.anglican.org
W: www.cashel.anglican.org

CORK, CLOYNE
AND ROSS
Diocesan Office, St Nicholas' House, 14 Cove Street, Cork, Republic of Ireland
T: (00353) (21) 500 5080   F: 432 0960   E: secretary@cork.anglican.org
W: www.cork.anglican.org

DUBLIN AND
GLENDALOUGH
Diocesan Office, Church of Ireland House, Church Avenue, Rathimines, Dublin 6,
Republic of Ireland
T: (00353) (1) 496 6981   F: 497 2865   E: admin@dublin.anglican.org
W: www.dublin.anglican.org

LIMERICK AND
KILLALOE
St John's Rectory, Ashe Street, Tralee, Co Kerry, Republic of Ireland
T: (00353) (66) 712 2245   F: 712 9004   E: secretary@limerick.anglican.org
W: www.limerick.anglican.org

MEATH AND
KILDARE
Meath and Kildare Diocesan Centre, Moyglare, Maynooth, Co Kildare, Republic
of Ireland
T: (00353) (1) 629 2163   E: secretary@meath.anglican.org
W: www.meath.anglican.org

ARCHDEACONRIES, DEANERIES AND RURAL/AREA DEANS OF THE CHURCH OF ENGLAND AND THE CHURCH IN WALES

CHURCH OF ENGLAND

BATH AND WELLS

ARCHDEACONRY OF WELLS

1. AXBRIDGE   S M J CROSSMAN
2. BRUTON AND CARY   R A HOSKINS
3. FROME   C ALSBURY
4. GLASTONBURY JURISDICTION   D J L MACGEOCH
5. IVELCHESTER   B S FAULKNER
6. YEOVIL   A PERRIS
7. SHEPTON MALLET   A Q H WHEELER

ARCHDEACONRY OF BATH

8. BATH   R G WILSON
9. CHEW MAGNA   J L CHAMBERLAIN
10. LOCKING   R J TAYLOR
11. MIDSOMER NORTON   C D NORTH
12. PORTISHEAD   N A HECTOR

ARCHDEACONRY OF TAUNTON

13. SEDGEMOOR   C D KEYS
14. CREWKERNE   J R MORRIS
15. EXMOOR   S STUCKES
16. ILMINSTER   S TUCKER
17. QUANTOCK   J G ROSE
18. TAUNTON   A YOUINGS
19. TONE   H E ALLEN

BIRMINGHAM

ARCHDEACONRY OF BIRMINGHAM

1. CENTRAL BIRMINGHAM   I HARPER
2. EDGBASTON   P A WHITE
3. HANDSWORTH   P CALVERT
4. KINGS NORTON   M F SIBANDA
5. MOSELEY   C A GRYLLS
6. SHIRLEY   T D HILL-BROWN
7. WARLEY   I R SHELTON

ARCHDEACONRY OF ASTON

8. ASTON   N M A TRAYNOR
9. COLESHILL   S C CARTER
10. POLESWORTH   A SIMMONS
11. SOLIHULL   D C J BALLARD
12. SUTTON COLDFIELD   D A LEAHY
13. YARDLEY AND BORDESLEY   A T BULLOCK

BLACKBURN

ARCHDEACONRY OF BLACKBURN

1. ACCRINGTON   J S HOLLAND
2. BLACKBURN AND DARWEN   A RAYNES
3. BURNLEY   M A JONES
4. CHORLEY   T D WILBY
5. LEYLAND   A MCHAFFIE
6. PENDLE   E A SAVILLE
7. WHALLEY   M WOODS

ARCHDEACONRY OF LANCASTER

8. BLACKPOOL   S J COX
9. GARSTANG   A W WILKINSON
10. KIRKHAM   R W BUNDAY
11. LANCASTER AND MORECAMBE   M R PEATMAN
12. POULTON   M P KEIGHLEY
13. PRESTON   B R MCCONKEY
14. TUNSTALL   D M PORTER

BRISTOL

ARCHDEACONRY OF BRISTOL

1. BRISTOL SOUTH   D G OWEN
2. BRISTOL WEST   C M PILGRIM
3. CITY DEANERY   R P SYMMONS

ARCHDEACONRY OF MALMESBURY

4. CHIPPENHAM   S A V WHEELER
5. KINGSWOOD AND SOUTH GLOUCESTERSHIRE   S JONES
6. NORTH WILTSHIRE   N J ARCHER
7. SWINDON   S M STEVENETTE

CANTERBURY

ARCHDEACONRY OF CANTERBURY

1. EAST BRIDGE   S J A HARDY
2. WEST BRIDGE   P R RATCLIFF
3. CANTERBURY   B J DE LA T DE BERRY
4. RECULVER   E M RICHARDSON
5. THANET   P R WORLEDGE

ARCHDEACONRY OF ASHFORD

6. ASHFORD   T C WILSON
7. DOVER   J A P WALKER
8. ELHAM   D J ADLINGTON
9. SANDWICH   S W COOPER
10. ROMNEY AND TENTERDEN   L J HAMMOND

ARCHDEACONRY OF MAIDSTONE

11. WEALD   A A DUGUID
12. MAIDSTONE   A W SEWELL
13. NORTH DOWNS   S P HUGHES
14. OSPRINGE   S H LILLICRAP
15. SITTINGBOURNE   M J RESCH

CARLISLE

ARCHDEACONRY OF CARLISLE

1. APPLEBY   S J FYFE
2. BRAMPTON   K T ROBERTS
3. CARLISLE   M A MANLEY
4. PENRITH   D G SARGENT

ARCHDEACONRY OF WEST CUMBERLAND

5. CALDER   A J BANKS
6. DERWENT   W E SANDERS
7. SOLWAY   B ROWE

ARCHDEACONRY OF WESTMORLAND AND FURNESS

8. BARROW   G M CREGEEN
9. FURNESS   A C BING
10. KENDAL   A WHITTAKER
11. WINDERMERE   J J RICHARDS

CHELMSFORD

ARCHDEACONRY OF BARKING (BISHOP OF BARKING)

1. BARKING AND DAGENHAM   E J FLEMING
2. HAVERING   D H HAGUE

ARCHDEACONRY OF HARLOW (BISHOP OF BARKING)

3. EPPING FOREST AND ONGAR   J M SMITH
4. HARLOW   M J HARRIS

ARCHDEACONRY OF WEST HAM
(BISHOP OF BARKING)

5. NEWHAM   J S FRASER
6. REDBRIDGE   M SEGAL
7. WALTHAM FOREST   A W M SUMMERS

ARCHDEACONRY OF CHELMSFORD
(BISHOP OF BRADWELL)

8. BRENTWOOD   P S HAMILTON
9. CHELMSFORD NORTH   T W PAGE
10. CHELMSFORD SOUTH   A T GRIFFITHS
11. MALDON AND DENGIE   S E MANLEY

ARCHDEACONRY OF SOUTHEND
(BISHOP OF BRADWELL)

12. BASILDON   M A SHAW
13. HADLEIGH   D ST C TUDOR
14. ROCHFORD   R W JORDAN
15. SOUTHEND-ON-SEA   J COLLIS
16. THURROCK   D BARLOW

ARCHDEACONRY OF STANSTED
(BISHOP OF COLCHESTER)

17. BRAINTREE   E J BENDREY
18. DUNMOW AND STANSTED   C M HAWKES
19. HINCKFORD   J D LOWE
20. SAFFRON WALDEN   D R TOMLINSON

ARCHDEACONRY OF COLCHESTER
(BISHOP OF COLCHESTER)

21. COLCHESTER   P R NORRINGTON
22. HARWICH   G D A THORBURN
23. ST OSYTH   G D A THORBURN
24. WITHAM   G B T BAYLISS

CHESTER

ARCHDEACONRY OF CHESTER

1. BIRKENHEAD   D J AYLING
2. CHESTER   P C O DAWSON
3. FRODSHAM   P RUGEN
4. GREAT BUDWORTH   A G BROWN
5. MALPAS   I A DAVENPORT
6. MIDDLEWICH   S M DREW
7. WALLASEY   G J COUSINS
8. WIRRAL NORTH   P M FROGGATT
9. WIRRAL SOUTH   E A GLOVER

ARCHDEACONRY OF MACCLESFIELD

10. BOWDON   J R HEATON
11. CONGLETON   D J PAGE
12. KNUTSFORD   P J PARRY
13. MACCLESFIELD   V W HYDON
14. MOTTRAM   A C COX
15. NANTWICH   H F CHANTRY
16. CHADKIRK   J E PARKER
17. CHEADLE   R I MCLAREN
18. STOCKPORT   D V COOKSON

CHICHESTER

ARCHDEACONRY OF CHICHESTER

1. ARUNDEL AND BOGNOR   M J STANDEN
2. CHICHESTER   J A T RUSSELL
3. WESTBOURNE   M J LANE
4. WORTHING   C G H KASSELL

ARCHDEACONRY OF HORSHAM

5. CUCKFIELD   G D SIMMONS
6. EAST GRINSTEAD   Vacant
7. HORSHAM   G S BRIDGEWATER
8. HURST   K M O'BRIEN
9. MIDHURST   D B WELSMAN
10. PETWORTH   D A TWINLEY
11. STORRINGTON   D M BEAL

ARCHDEACONRY OF HASTINGS

12. BATTLE AND BEXHILL   J J FRAIS
13. DALLINGTON   M A LLOYD
14. EASTBOURNE   J T GUNN

15. HASTINGS   M S COE
16. ROTHERFIELD   J M PACKMAN
17. RYE   D R FROST
18. UCKFIELD   Vacant

ARCHDEACONRY OF BRIGHTON AND LEWES

19. BRIGHTON   A J WOODWARD
20. HOVE   T S STRATFORD
21. LEWES AND SEAFORD   G M DAW

COVENTRY

ARCHDEACONRY OF COVENTRY

1. COVENTRY EAST   C D HOGGER
2. COVENTRY NORTH   R N TREW
3. COVENTRY SOUTH   S R BURCH
4. KENILWORTH   M Q BRATTON
5. NUNEATON   R W HARE
6. RUGBY   P WATKINS

ARCHDEACONRY OF WARWICK

7. ALCESTER   D SILVESTER
8. FOSSE   C E MIER
9. SHIPSTON   J TUCKER
10. SOUTHAM   C R GROOCOCK
11. WARWICK AND LEAMINGTON   C GALE

DERBY

ARCHDEACONRY OF CHESTERFIELD

1. ALFRETON   P D BROOKS
2. BAKEWELL AND EYAM   C G PEARSON
3. BOLSOVER AND STAVELEY   H GUEST
4. BUXTON   C G PEARSON
5. CHESTERFIELD   K E HAMBLIN
6. GLOSSOP   C G PEARSON
7. WIRKSWORTH   D C TRUBY

ARCHDEACONRY OF DERBY

8. ASHBOURNE   A B LARKIN
9. DERBY NORTH   J F HOLLYWELL
10. DERBY SOUTH   P F WALLEY
11. DUFFIELD   J M PAGE
12. HEANOR   K PADLEY
13. EREWASH   P J DAVEY
14. LONGFORD   A G MURPHIE
15. MELBOURNE   A LUKE
16. REPTON   G P RUTTER

DURHAM

ARCHDEACONRY OF DURHAM

1. DURHAM   R W LAWRANCE
2. EASINGTON   M J VOLLAND
3. HARTLEPOOL   J BURBURY
4. LANCHESTER   H MURRAY
5. SEDGEFIELD   Vacant

ARCHDEACONRY OF AUCKLAND

6. AUCKLAND   N P VINE
7. BARNARD CASTLE   A J HARDING
8. DARLINGTON   L E GOUGH
9. STANHOPE   V T FENTON
10. STOCKTON   D M BROOKE

ARCHDEACONRY OF SUNDERLAND

11. CHESTER-LE-STREET   D C GLOVER
12. GATESHEAD   Vacant
13. GATESHEAD WEST   Vacant
14. HOUGHTON LE SPRING   E M WILKINSON
15. JARROW   R O DICK
16. WEARMOUTH   S J BAMBER

ELY

ARCHDEACONRY OF CAMBRIDGE

1. BOURN   M P M BOOKER
2. CAMBRIDGE NORTH   D J MAHER
3. CAMBRIDGE SOUTH   D H JONES
4. FORDHAM AND QUY   M G BANYARD

5. GRANTA   J M NORRIS
6. NORTH STOWE   N J BLANDFORD-BAKER
7. SHINGAY   *Vacant*

ARCHDEACONRY OF HUNTINGDON AND WISBECH

8. ELY   J H ROBSON
9. FINCHAM AND FELTWELL   B L BURTON
10. HUNTINGDON   E B ATLING
11. MARCH   N A WHITEHOUSE
12. ST IVES   F J KILNER
13. ST NEOTS   A S REED
14. WISBECH LYNN MARSHLAND   M L BRADBURY
15. YAXLEY   D C R MCFADYEN

EXETER

ARCHDEACONRY OF EXETER

1. AYLESBEARE   J B B HUTCHINGS
2. CADBURY   *Vacant*
3. CHRISTIANITY   S L BESSENT
4. HONITON   J C TREW
5. KENN   G K MAYER
6. OTTERY   C E EDMONDS
7. TIVERTON AND CULLOMPTON   R J GORDON

ARCHDEACONRY OF TOTNES

8. MORETON   P WIMSETT
9. NEWTON ABBOT AND IPPLEPEN   *Vacant*
10. OKEHAMPTON   R P HANSFORD
11. TORBAY   *Vacant*
12. TOTNES   *Vacant*
13. WOODLEIGH   D A FRENCH

ARCHDEACONRY OF BARNSTAPLE

14. BARNSTAPLE   G A B KING-SMITH
15. HARTLAND   *Vacant*
16. HOLSWORTHY   C W PENN
17. SHIRWELL   *Vacant*
18. SOUTH MOLTON   *Vacant*
19. TORRINGTON   *Vacant*

ARCHDEACONRY OF PLYMOUTH

20. IVYBRIDGE   *Vacant*
21. PLYMOUTH CITY   K F FREEMAN
22. TAVISTOCK   *Vacant*

GLOUCESTER

ARCHDEACONRY OF GLOUCESTER

1. FOREST SOUTH   P A BRUNT
2. GLOUCESTER CITY   J D FAULL
3. SEVERN VALE   R J A MITCHELL
4. STROUD   M S KING
5. WOTTON   D J RUSSELL

ARCHDEACONRY OF CHELTENHAM

6. CHELTENHAM   T F L GRIFFITHS
7. CIRENCESTER   H N GILBERT
8. NORTH COTSWOLD   K R SCOTT
9. TEWKESBURY AND WINCHCOMBE   P R WILLIAMS

GUILDFORD

ARCHDEACONRY OF SURREY

1. ALDERSHOT   G P H NEWTON
2. CRANLEIGH   D M SELLIN
3. FARNHAM   A E GELL
4. GODALMING   C G POTTER
5. GUILDFORD   F SCAMMELL
6. SURREY HEATH   R J PECK

ARCHDEACONRY OF DORKING

7. DORKING   A C JONAS
8. EMLY   P J J PLYMING
9. EPSOM   D C WILLIAMSON
10. LEATHERHEAD   E R JENKINS
11. RUNNYMEDE   J R WATTLEY
12. WOKING   C J BLAIR

HEREFORD

ARCHDEACONRY OF HEREFORD

1. ABBEYDORE   N G LOWTON
2. BROMYARD   *Vacant*
3. HEREFORD   P TOWNER
4. KINGTON AND WEOBLEY   S HOLLINGHURST
5. LEDBURY   R WARD
6. LEOMINSTER   M J KNEEN
7. ROSS AND ARCHENFIELD   M JOHNSON

ARCHDEACONRY OF LUDLOW

8. BRIDGNORTH   J H STOKES
9. CLUN FOREST   N F M MORRIS
10. CONDOVER   R H O HILL
11. LUDLOW   *Vacant*
12. PONTESBURY   M A JONES
13. TELFORD SEVERN GORGE   I S NAYLOR

LEEDS (West Yorkshire and the Dales)

ARCHDEACONRY OF BRADFORD

1. AIREDALE   G S HODGSON
2. BOWLING AND HORTON   V POLLARD
3. BRADFORD NORTH   P Q TUDGE
4. ILKLEY   P C GRAY
5. KEIGHLEY   S A GRIFFITHS

ARCHDEACONRY OF HALIFAX

6. ALMONDBURY   R J STEEL
7. BIRSTALL   P J KNIGHT
8. BRIGHOUSE AND ELLAND   D BURROWS
9. CALDER VALLEY   O R PAGE
10. DEWSBURY   K PARTINGTON
11. HALIFAX   J S BRADBERRY
12. HUDDERSFIELD   *Vacant*
13. KIRKBURTON   J R JONES

ARCHDEACONRY OF LEEDS

14. ALLERTON   *Vacant*
15. ARMLEY   A SEN
16. HEADINGLEY   R J DIMERY
17. WHITKIRK   M P BENWELL

ARCHDEACONRY OF PONTEFRACT

18. BARNSLEY   S P RACE
19. PONTEFRACT   R G COOPER
20. WAKEFIELD   S P KELLY

ARCHDEACONRY OF RICHMOND AND CRAVEN

21. BOWLAND   I F GREENHALGH
22. EWECROSS   I F GREENHALGH
23. HARROGATE   B A GIBLIN
24. RICHMOND   J M RICHARDS
25. RIPON   *Vacant*
26. SKIPTON   P A TURNER
27. WENSLEY   C M A HEPPER

LEICESTER

ARCHDEACONRY OF LEICESTER

1. CITY OF LEICESTER   R V WORSFOLD
2. FRAMLAND (Melton)   M W R COVINGTON
3. GARTREE FIRST DEANERY (Harborough)   R H G BRAND
4. GARTREE SECOND DEANERY (Wigston)   R H G BRAND
5. GOSCOTE   R M GLADSTONE

ARCHDEACONRY OF LOUGHBOROUGH

6. AKELEY EAST (Loughborough)   T E EDMONDS
7. GUTHLAXTON   *Vacant*
8. NORTH WEST LEICESTERSHIRE   V M ELPHICK
9. SPARKENHOE EAST   P G HOOPER
10. SPARKENHOE WEST   G J WESTON

LICHFIELD

ARCHDEACONRY OF LICHFIELD

1. LICHFIELD   M M MATTOCKS
2. PENKRIDGE   S C WITCOMBE
3. RUGELEY   S C DAVIS
4. TAMWORTH   D A DYSON

ARCHDEACONRY OF STOKE-ON-TRENT

5. ALSTONFIELD   J O FORRESTER
6. CHEADLE   S E GOODWIN
7. ECCLESHALL   N A CLEMAS
8. LEEK   M S J CANNAM
9. NEWCASTLE   T B BLOOR
10. STAFFORD   P S DANIEL
11. STOKE NORTH   W E SLATER
12. STOKE   N W R EVANS
13. STONE   P D DAKIN
14. TUTBURY   M R FREEMAN
15. UTTOXETER   B S P LEATHERS

ARCHDEACONRY OF SALOP

16. EDGMOND AND SHIFNAL   K HODSON
17. ELLESMERE   K E DAVIES
18. HODNET   M P TANNER
19. OSWESTRY   A R BAILEY
20. SHREWSBURY   M H SALMON
21. TELFORD   A P L SMITH
22. WEM AND WHITCHURCH   A J B CLAYTON
23. WROCKWARDINE   D F CHANTREY

ARCHDEACONRY OF WALSALL

24. TRYSULL   M P HOBBS
25. WALSALL   M C RUTTER
26. WEDNESBURY   A J GWILLIM
27. WEST BROMWICH   M J CLARIDGE
28. WOLVERHAMPTON   D W WRIGHT
29. WULFRUN   N E WATSON

LINCOLN

ARCHDEACONRY OF STOW AND LINDSEY

1. AXHOLME, ISLE OF   J W THACKER
2. CORRINGHAM   P WAIN
3. GRIMSBY AND CLEETHORPES   A P DODD
4. HAVERSTOE   *Vacant*
5. LAWRES   R H CROSSLAND
6. MANLAKE   J W THACKER
7. WEST WOLD   I ROBINSON
8. YARBOROUGH   D P ROWETT

ARCHDEACONRY OF LINCOLN

9. BOLINGBROKE   P F COATES
10. CALCEWAITHE AND CANDLESHOE   T STEELE
11. CHRISTIANITY   D J OSBOURNE
12. GRAFFOE   R G BILLINGHURST
13. HORNCASTLE   M N HOLDEN
14. LAFFORD   C PENNOCK
15. LOUTHESK   S A ALLISON

ARCHDEACONRY OF BOSTON

16. STAMFORD   M WARRICK
17. BELTISLOE   C J ATKINSON
18. ELLOE EAST   R J SEAL
19. ELLOE WEST   P BRENT
20. GRANTHAM   C P BOLAND
21. HOLLAND   *Vacant*
22. LOVEDEN   S P BARRON

LIVERPOOL

ARCHDEACONRY OF LIVERPOOL

1. BOOTLE   R J DRIVER
2. HUYTON   J A TAYLOR
3. LIVERPOOL NORTH   H CORBETT
4. LIVERPOOL SOUTH   R HARVEY
5. SEFTON   *Vacant*
6. TOXTETH AND WAVERTREE   G C ELSMORE
7. WALTON   E F LOUDON
8. WEST DERBY   S MCGANITY

ARCHDEACONRY OF WARRINGTON

9. NORTH MEOLS   P C GREEN
10. ST HELENS   D D EASTWOOD
11. ORMSKIRK   N A WELLS
12. WARRINGTON   S W BOYD
13. WIDNES   J M COLLIER
14. WIGAN   M J SHERWIN
15. WINWICK   J M MATTHEWS

LONDON

ARCHDEACONRY OF LONDON

1. THE CITY   O C M ROSS

ARCHDEACONRY OF CHARING CROSS

2. WESTMINSTER PADDINGTON   J R ALLCOCK
3. WESTMINSTER ST MARGARET   P A E CHESTER
4. WESTMINSTER ST MARYLEBONE   L A MOSES

ARCHDEACONRY OF HACKNEY
(STEPNEY AREA)

5. HACKNEY   *Vacant*
6. ISLINGTON   J D BREWSTER
7. TOWER HAMLETS   A RIDER

ARCHDEACONRY OF MIDDLESEX
(KENSINGTON AREA)

8. CHELSEA   D P E REINDORP
9. HAMMERSMITH AND FULHAM   T J STILWELL
10. HAMPTON   J B MOFFATT
11. HOUNSLOW   R S FRANK
12. KENSINGTON   D C WALSH
13. SPELTHORNE   A SAVILLE

ARCHDEACONRY OF HAMPSTEAD
(EDMONTON AREA)

14. BARNET, CENTRAL   P A WALMSLEY-MCLEOD
15. BARNET, WEST   *Vacant*
16. CAMDEN, NORTH (Hampstead)   S R TUCKER
17. CAMDEN, SOUTH (Holborn and St Pancras)
   A J B MELDRUM
18. ENFIELD   R D JAMES
19. HARINGEY, EAST   O A FAGBEMI
20. HARINGEY, WEST   P H SUDELL

ARCHDEACONRY OF NORTHOLT
(WILLESDEN AREA)

21. BRENT   G P NOYCE
22. EALING   C RAMSAY
23. HARROW   P R BARNES
24. HILLINGDON   D P BANISTER

MANCHESTER

ARCHDEACONRY OF MANCHESTER

1. ARDWICK   R CASSIDY
2. HEATON   M H MAXWELL
3. HULME   K FLOOD
4. MANCHESTER, NORTH   M J P MCGURK
5. STRETFORD   A H CLEPHANE
6. WITHINGTON   S M EDWARDS

ARCHDEACONRY OF BOLTON

7. BOLTON   V C WHITWORTH
8. BURY   G F JOYCE
9. DEANE   T P CLARK
10. RADCLIFFE AND PRESTWICH   A J HARDY
11. ROSSENDALE   L E M WOODALL
12. WALMSLEY   H MOLLOY

ARCHDEACONRY OF ROCHDALE

13. ASHTON-UNDER-LYNE   R FARNWORTH
14. HEYWOOD AND MIDDLETON   M Z WALL
15. OLDHAM EAST   G HOLLOWOOD
16. OLDHAM WEST   D R PENNY
17. ROCHDALE   J M COLEMAN

ARCHDEACONRY OF SALFORD

18. ECCLES   A C YOUNG
19. LEIGH   *Vacant*
20. SALFORD   L K BATTYE

NEWCASTLE

ARCHDEACONRY OF NORTHUMBERLAND

1. BEDLINGTON   P G J HUGHES
2. NEWCASTLE CENTRAL   *Vacant*
3. NEWCASTLE EAST   M P LEE
4. NEWCASTLE WEST   N P DARBY
5. TYNEMOUTH   F M WILSON

ARCHDEACONRY OF LINDISFARNE

6. ALNWICK   *Vacant*
7. BAMBURGH AND GLENDALE   B C HURST
8. BELLINGHAM   S M RAMSARAN
9. CORBRIDGE   D B HEWLETT
10. HEXHAM   J W RUSSELL
11. MORPETH   J C PARK
12. NORHAM   G R KELSEY

NORWICH

ARCHDEACONRY OF NORWICH

1. NORWICH EAST   D T THORNTON
2. NORWICH NORTH   P D MACKAY
3. NORWICH SOUTH   A M STRANGE

ARCHDEACONRY OF NORFOLK

4. BLOFIELD   N J H GARRARD
5. DEPWADE   M M KINGSTON
6. GREAT YARMOUTH   C L TERRY
7. HUMBLEYARD   C J DAVIES
8. LODDON   R H PARSONAGE
9. LOTHINGLAND   J S BISHOP
10. REDENHALL   N O TUFFNELL
11. THETFORD AND ROCKLAND   M C JACKSON
12. ST BENET AT WAXHAM AND TUNSTEAD   S P LAWRENCE

ARCHDEACONRY OF LYNN

13. BRECKLAND   S R NAIRN
14. BRISLEY AND ELMHAM   *Vacant*
15. BURNHAM AND WALSINGHAM   P B FOREMAN
16. HEACHAM AND RISING   J B V RIVIERE
17. DEREHAM IN MITFORD   A F AUBREY-JONES
18. HOLT   J G SYKES
19. INGWORTH   A M BEANE
20. LYNN   J A NASH
21. REPPS   C J HEYCOCKS
22. SPARHAM   T C P DEAN

OXFORD

ARCHDEACONRY OF OXFORD

1. COWLEY   T J STEAD
2. OXFORD   W R DONALDSON

ARCHDEACONRY OF BERKSHIRE
(BISHOP OF READING)

3. BRACKNELL   H D UFFINDELL
4. BRADFIELD   W H N WATTS
5. MAIDENHEAD AND WINDSOR   M K BIRD
6. NEWBURY   M D BENNET
7. READING   S J PULLIN
8. SONNING   J F RAMSBOTTOM

ARCHDEACONRY OF BUCKINGHAM

9. AMERSHAM   C I WALTON
10. AYLESBURY   A K E BLYTH
11. BUCKINGHAM   R M BUNDOCK
12. BURNHAM AND SLOUGH   R J COSH
13. CLAYDON   D J MEAKIN
14. MILTON KEYNES   T NORWOOD
15. MURSLEY   *Vacant*
16. NEWPORT   C WOOD
17. WENDOVER   M C DEARNLEY
18. WYCOMBE   S N CRONK

ARCHDEACONRY OF DORCHESTER

19. ABINGDON   R G ZAIR
20. ASTON AND CUDDESDON   A W GARRATT
21. BICESTER AND ISLIP   S R GRIFFITHS
22. CHIPPING NORTON   S A WELCH
23. DEDDINGTON   H A CAMPBELL
24. HENLEY   K G DAVIES
25. VALE OF WHITE HORSE   C J DRAPER
26. WALLINGFORD   J P ST JOHN NICOLLE
27. WANTAGE   J P ST JOHN NICOLLE
28. WITNEY   T C WRIGHT
29. WOODSTOCK   D S TYLER

PETERBOROUGH

ARCHDEACONRY OF NORTHAMPTON

1. BRACKLEY   S P DOMMETT
2. BRIXWORTH   S TROTT
3. DAVENTRY   S R D BROWN
4. NORTHAMPTON, GREATER   D J WISEMAN
5. TOWCESTER   P D MCLEOD
6. WELLINGBOROUGH   M J HAYES

ARCHDEACONRY OF OAKHAM

7. CORBY   I A PULLINGER
8. HIGHAM   S K PRIOR
9. KETTERING   B J WITHINGTON
10. OUNDLE   S J WEBSTER
11. PETERBOROUGH   I C BLACK
12. RUTLAND   L T FRANCIS-DEHQANI

PORTSMOUTH

ARCHDEACONRY OF THE MEON

1. BISHOP'S WALTHAM   G R MENSINGH
2. FAREHAM   S ALLMAN
3. GOSPORT   *Vacant*
4. PETERSFIELD   W P M HUGHES

ARCHDEACONRY OF PORTSDOWN

5. HAVANT   K B GREEN
6. PORTSMOUTH   R C WHITE

ARCHDEACONRY OF ISLE OF WIGHT

7. WIGHT, EAST   *Vacant*
8. WIGHT, WEST   *Vacant*

ROCHESTER

ARCHDEACONRY OF ROCHESTER

1. COBHAM   H P C BROADBENT
2. DARTFORD   *Vacant*
3. GILLINGHAM   A RICHARDSON
4. GRAVESEND   S C BREWER
5. ROCHESTER   P FOREMAN
6. STROOD   D W GREEN

ARCHDEACONRY OF TONBRIDGE

7. MALLING   M A J BUCHAN
8. PADDOCK WOOD   *Vacant*
9. SEVENOAKS   M R GRIFFIN
10. SHOREHAM   *Vacant*
11. TONBRIDGE   M E BROWN
12. TUNBRIDGE WELLS   B S SENIOR

ARCHDEACONRY OF BROMLEY AND BEXLEY

13. BECKENHAM   R M HINTON
14. BROMLEY   A KEELER
15. ERITH   J A CONALTY
16. ORPINGTON   J TRANTER
17. SIDCUP   C A TERRY

ST ALBANS

ARCHDEACONRY OF ST ALBANS

1. BERKHAMSTED   J A GORDON
2. HEMEL HEMPSTEAD   E M HOOD
3. HITCHIN   M A H RODEN
4. RICKMANSWORTH   D J SNOWBALL
5. ST ALBANS   M A SLATER
6. WATFORD   D J MIDDLEBROOK
7. WHEATHAMPSTEAD   W J M GIBBS

ARCHDEACONRY OF BEDFORD

8. AMPTHILL AND SHEFFORD   L KLIMAS
9. BEDFORD   R C HIBBERT
10. BIGGLESWADE   L C DEW
11. DUNSTABLE   B J MINTON
12. LUTON   J MACKENZIE
13. SHARNBROOK   S J LILEY

ARCHDEACONRY OF HERTFORD

14. BARNET   M J BURNS
15. BISHOP'S STORTFORD   A J GILES

16. BUNTINGFORD   R M MORGAN
17. CHESHUNT   R S PHILLIPS
18. WELWYN HATFIELD   R E PYKE
19. HERTFORD AND WARE   J M H LOVERIDGE
20. STEVENAGE   T E HORLOCK

ST EDMUNDSBURY AND IPSWICH

ARCHDEACONRY OF IPSWICH

1. BOSMERE   D R WILLIAMS
2. COLNEYS   A S DOTCHIN
3. HADLEIGH   M C THROWER
4. IPSWICH   C A G JENKIN
5. SAMFORD   L OOSTERHOF
6. STOWMARKET   B B BILSTON
7. WOODBRIDGE   H C SANDERS

ARCHDEACONRY OF SUDBURY

8. CLARE   C A COLLINS
9. IXWORTH   D H MESSER
10. LAVENHAM   S G F EARL
11. MILDENHALL   S J MITCHELL
12. SUDBURY   G J WEBB
13. THINGOE   M N HAWORTH

ARCHDEACONRY OF SUFFOLK

14. HARTISMERE   S A LOXTON
15. HOXNE   S A LOXTON
16. LOES   M SANDERS
17. SAXMUNDHAM   C H REDGRAVE
18. WAVENEY AND BLYTH   S J PITCHER

SALISBURY

ARCHDEACONRY OF SHERBORNE

1. DORCHESTER   P J SMITH
2. LYME BAY   J DELANEY
3. SHERBORNE   V J ENEVER
4. WEYMOUTH AND PORTLAND   T R WEST

ARCHDEACONRY OF DORSET

5. BLACKMORE VALE   D R R SEYMOUR
6. MILTON AND BLANDFORD   J H SIMMONS
7. POOLE   J H T DE GARIS
8. PURBECK   R C FLOATE
9. WIMBORNE   C M TEBBUTT

ARCHDEACONRY OF SARUM

10. ALDERBURY   D G BACON
11. CHALKE   M R WOOD
12. HEYTESBURY   P A REID
13. SALISBURY   P F D TAYLOR
14. STONEHENGE   E J RANCE

ARCHDEACONRY OF WILTS

15. BRADFORD   S F DEACON
16. CALNE   V E BURROWS
17. DEVIZES   P RICHARDSON
18. MARLBOROUGH   A G STUDDERT-KENNEDY
19. PEWSEY   G E R OSBORNE

SHEFFIELD

ARCHDEACONRY OF SHEFFIELD AND ROTHERHAM

1. ATTERCLIFFE   D W FRY
2. ECCLESALL   T K HOLE
3. ECCLESFIELD   A T ISAACSON
4. HALLAM   P J BATCHFORD
5. LAUGHTON   M CAUNT
6. ROTHERHAM   L S WORTLEY

ARCHDEACONRY OF DONCASTER

7. ADWICK-LE-STREET   B A J BARRACLOUGH
8. DONCASTER   J M FODEN
9. DONCASTER, WEST   N M REDEYOFF
10. SNAITH AND HATFIELD   E A TURNER-LOISEL
11. TANKERSLEY   K J E HALE
12. WATH   A R BREWERTON

SOUTHWARK

ARCHDEACONRY OF LEWISHAM AND GREENWICH
(BISHOP OF WOOLWICH)

1. CHARLTON   K W HITCH
2. DEPTFORD   P D BUTLER
3. ELTHAM AND MOTTINGHAM   B E WARD
4. LEWISHAM, EAST   J L KUSTNER
5. LEWISHAM, WEST   M J KINGSTON
6. PLUMSTEAD   C R WELHAM

ARCHDEACONRY OF SOUTHWARK
(BISHOP OF WOOLWICH)

7. BERMONDSEY   M R NICHOLLS
8. CAMBERWELL   *Vacant*
9. DULWICH   *Vacant*
10. SOUTHWARK AND NEWINGTON
    A D P MOUGHTIN-MUMBY

ARCHDEACONRY OF LAMBETH
(BISHOP OF KINGSTON)

11. LAMBETH NORTH   D L MATTHEWS
12. LAMBETH SOUTH   D J STEPHENSON
13. MERTON   R P LANE

ARCHDEACONRY OF WANDSWORTH (BISHOP OF KINGSTON)

14. BATTERSEA   G N OWEN
15. KINGSTON   S C COUPLAND
16. RICHMOND AND BARNES   T H PATTERSON
17. TOOTING   W ROEST
18. WANDSWORTH   G S PRIOR

ARCHDEACONRY OF CROYDON

19. CROYDON ADDINGTON   J J E ROWLEY
20. CROYDON CENTRAL   T A MAPSTONE
21. CROYDON NORTH   L S A MARSH
22. CROYDON SOUTH   C F SPURWAY
23. SUTTON   D N MILLER

ARCHDEACONRY OF REIGATE
(BISHOP OF CROYDON)

24. CATERHAM   D J SWAN
25. GODSTONE   P MOSELING
26. REIGATE   A T CUNNINGTON

SOUTHWELL AND NOTTINGHAM

ARCHDEACONRY OF NEWARK

1. BASSETLAW AND BAWTRY   S A CASH
2. MANSFIELD   A FLETCHER
3. NEWARK AND SOUTHWELL   W D MILNER
4. NEWSTEAD   R KELLETT

ARCHDEACONRY OF NOTTINGHAM

5. EAST BINGHAM   J F WELLINGTON
6. WEST BINGHAM   J W BENTHAM
7. GEDLING   P A WILLIAMS
8. NOTTINGHAM NORTH   E SNOWDEN
9. NOTTINGHAM SOUTH   K S F ROOMS

TRURO

ARCHDEACONRY OF CORNWALL

1. ST AUSTELL   M L BARRETT
2. CARNMARTH NORTH   O STEVENS
3. CARNMARTH SOUTH   G K BENNETT
4. KERRIER   L A WALKER
5. PENWITH   D J STEVENS
6. POWDER   K J BOULLIER
7. PYDAR   H L SAMSON

ARCHDEACONRY OF BODMIN

8. STRATTON   R S THEWSEY
9. TRIGG MAJOR   D J M JASPER
10. TRIGG MINOR AND BODMIN   D J ELKINGTON
11. WIVELSHIRE, EAST   M E GOODLAND
12. WIVELSHIRE, WEST   P P C SHARP
    WEST YORKSHIRE AND THE DALES   *see* LEEDS

WEST YORKSHIRE AND THE DALES

see LEEDS

WINCHESTER

ARCHDEACONRY OF WINCHESTER

1. ALRESFORD   P H N COLLINS
2. ALTON   H J D WRIGHT
3. ANDOVER   J P HARKIN
4. BASINGSTOKE   R J ST C HARLOW
5. ODIHAM   P W DYSON
6. WHITCHURCH   K J INGLIS
7. WINCHESTER   P A KENNEDY

ARCHDEACONRY OF BOURNEMOUTH

8. BOURNEMOUTH   A L MCPHERSON
9. CHRISTCHURCH   G J PHILBRICK
10. EASTLEIGH   P A VARGESON
11. LYNDHURST   P B C SALISBURY
12. ROMSEY   T C K SLEDGE
13. SOUTHAMPTON   J J BAKKER

THE CHANNEL ISLANDS

14. GUERNSEY   *Vacant*
15. JERSEY   R F KEY

WORCESTER

ARCHDEACONRY OF WORCESTER

1. EVESHAM   *Vacant*
2. MALVERN   P J KNIGHT
3. MARTLEY AND WORCESTER WEST   D R SHERWIN
4. PERSHORE   S K RENSHAW
5. UPTON   C A MOSS
6. WORCESTER EAST   K A BOYCE

ARCHDEACONRY OF DUDLEY

7. BROMSGROVE   G E P NATHANIEL
8. DROITWICH   *Vacant*
9. DUDLEY   D MELVILLE
10. KINGSWINFORD   *Vacant*
11. KIDDERMINSTER   H A BURTON
12. STOURBRIDGE   P G HARRISON
13. STOURPORT   M TURNER

YORK

ARCHDEACONRY OF YORK (BISHOP OF SELBY)

1. AINSTY, NEW   C I COATES
2. DERWENT   A CLEMENTS
3. EASINGWOLD   E C HASSALL
4. SELBY   C WILTON
5. SOUTH WOLD   A F WAKEFIELD
6. SOUTHERN RYEDALE   R A HIRST
7. YORK, CITY OF   T MCDONOUGH

ARCHDEACONRY OF EAST RIDING
(BISHOP OF HULL)

8. BEVERLEY   J J FLETCHER
9. BRIDLINGTON   G J OWEN
10. HARTHILL   D E FLETCHER
11. HOLDERNESS, NORTH   J E GRAINGER-SMITH
12. HOLDERNESS, SOUTH   S J WALKER
13. HOWDEN   M J PROCTOR
14. HULL   T M H BOYNS
15. SCARBOROUGH   D C PYNN

ARCHDEACONRY OF CLEVELAND
(BISHOP OF WHITBY)

16. GUISBOROUGH   R E HARRISON
17. MIDDLESBROUGH   D P BLACK
18. MOWBRAY   I D HOUGHTON
19. NORTHERN RYEDALE   T J ROBINSON
20. STOKESLEY   W J FORD
21. WHITBY   B J PYKE

CHURCH IN WALES

ST ASAPH

ARCHDEACONRY OF ST ASAPH

1. ST ASAPH   C I DAY
2. DENBIGH   C E MANSLEY
3. DYFFRYN CLWYD   P V F CHEW
4. HOLYWELL   A W COLEMAN
5. LLANRWST AND RHOS   N W CARTER

ARCHDEACONRY OF MONTGOMERY

6. CEDEWAIN   N W MORRIS

ARCHDEACONRY OF MONTGOMERY

7. MATHRAFAL
8. POOL   T E BENNETT

ARCHDEACONRY OF WREXHAM

9. ALYN   J P HARRIS
10. DEE VALLEY   S M HUYTON
11. HAWARDEN   M J BATCHELOR
12. MOLD   A W A COPPING
13. PENLLYN AND EDEIRNION   M K SNELLGROVE
14. WREXHAM   *Vacant*

BANGOR

ARCHDEACONRY OF BANGOR

1. ARFON   R W TOWNSEND
2. ARCHLLECHWEDD   J E NICE
3. LLIFON AND TALYBOLION   C A LLEWELLYN
4. MALLTRAETH   E C WILLIAMS
5. OGWEN   *Vacant*
6. TINDAETHWY   R G R SMITH
7. TWRCELYN   *Vacant*

ARCHDEACONRY OF MEIRIONNYDD

8. ARDUDWY   K G HORSWELL
9. ARWYSTLI   H A CHIPLIN
10. CYFEILIOG AND MAWDDWY   R P BARNES
11. LLYN AND EIFIONYDD   D J WILLIAMS
12. YSTUMANER   N D ADAMS

ST DAVIDS

ARCHDEACONRY OF ST DAVIDS

1. DAUGLEDDAU   N CALE
2. DEWISLAND AND FISHGUARD   C C BROWN
3. PEMBROKE   A J DAVIES
4. ROOSE   A M CHADWICK

ARCHDEACONRY OF CARDIGAN

5. CEMAIS AND SUB-AERON   J S BENNETT
6. EMLYN   D J L ROBERTS
7. GLYN AERON   C L BOLTON
8. LAMPETER AND ULTRA-AERON   P W DAVIES
9. LLANBADARN FAWR   P O JONES

ARCHDEACONRY OF CARMARTHEN

10. CARMARTHEN   L L RICHARDSON
11. CYDWELI   D G DAVIES
12. DYFFRYN AMAN   *Vacant*
13. LLANDEILO   I H AVESON
14. LLANDOVERY   I H AVESON
15. ST CLEARS   *Vacant*

LLANDAFF

ARCHDEACONRY OF LLANDAFF

1. CARDIFF   R M CAPPER
2. LLANDAFF   J WIGLEY
3. PENARTH AND BARRY   P A COX

ARCHDEACONRY OF MARGAM

4. BRIDGEND   *Vacant*
5. MARGAM   P R MASSON
6. NEATH   *Vacant*
7. VALE OF GLAMORGAN   M J DAVIES

ARCHDEACONRY OF MORGANNWG

8. CYNON VALLEY   M K JONES
9. MERTHYR TYDFIL AND CAERPHILLY   S P KIRK
10. PONTYPRIDD   M D GABLE
11. RHONDDA   H H ENGLAND-SIMON

MONMOUTH

ARCHDEACONRY OF MONMOUTH

1. ABERGAVENNY   M SOADY
2. MONMOUTH   D J MCGLADDERY
3. NETHERWENT   J D HARRIS
4. RAGLAN-USK   T G CLEMENT

ARCHDEACONRY OF NEWPORT

5. BASSALEG   C M LAWSON-JONES
6. BEDWELLTY   M OWEN
7. NEWPORT   D NEALE
8. PONTYPOOL   M J PHILLIPS

SWANSEA AND BRECON

ARCHDEACONRY OF BRECON

1. BRECON   M P WILDING
2. BUILTH   *Vacant*
3. CRICKHOWELL   B LETSON
4. HAY   R T EDWARDS
5. MAELIENYDD   M T BEATON

ARCHDEACONRY OF GOWER

6. CLYNE   P J GWYNN
7. CWMTAWE   H M LERVY
8. GOWER   *Vacant*
9. LLWCHWR   M L COX
10. PENDERI   J B DAVIES
11. SWANSEA   H M WILLIAMS

ENGLISH BENEFICES AND CHURCHES

An index of benefices, conventional districts, local ecumenical projects, and proprietary chapels (shown in bold type), together with entries for churches and other licensed places of worship listed on the Parish Index of the Central Board of Finance. Where the church name is the same as that of the benefice (or as that of the place whose name forms the beginning of the benefice name), the church entry is omitted. Church dedications are indicated in brackets.

The benefice entry gives the full legal name, followed by the diocese, its deanery number (p. 1039), the patron(s), and the name(s) and appointment(s) of clergy serving there. The following are the main abbreviations used; for others see the full list of abbreviations.

C	Curate	OLM	Ordained Local Minister
C-in-c	Curate-in-charge	P	Patron(s)
Dn-in-c	Deacon-in-charge	P-in-c	Priest-in-charge
Dss	Deaconess	Par Dn	Parish Deacon
Hon C	Honorary Curate	R	Rector
Hon Par Dn	Honorary Parish Deacon	TM	Team Minister
I	Incumbent (includes Rector or Vicar)	TR	Team Rector
Min	Minister	TV	Team Vicar
NSM	Non-stipendiary Minister	V	Vicar

Listed below are the elements in place names which are not normally treated as substantive in the index:

CENTRAL	HIGHER	MUCH	OVER
EAST	LITTLE	NETHER	SOUTH
GREAT	LOW	NEW	THE
GREATER	LOWER	NORTH	UPPER
HIGH	MIDDLE	OLD	WEST

Thus WEST WIMBLEDON (Christ Church) appears as **WIMBLEDON, WEST (Christ Church)** and CENTRAL TELFORD as **TELFORD, CENTRAL**. The only exception occurs where the second element of the place name is a common noun thus, NEW LANE remains as **NEW LANE**, and WEST TOWN as **WEST TOWN**.

4SAINTS TEAM (Huyton Deanery) *Liv 2*   P *Patr Bd*
TR A D STOTT   TV J VAN DEN BERG-OWENS, N H LEA-WILSON
NSM G D THOMSON, P COWLEY
A 20 Benefice, The *Cant 6*   P *Abp*   V R L LE ROSSIGNOL
C I G CAMPBELL
AB KETTLEBY (St James) and Holwell w Asfordby *Leic 2*
P *DBP, MMCET and V Rothley (jt)*   R *vacant*
ABBAS and Templecombe, Henstridge and Horsington
B & W 2   P *Bp and Ch Trust Fund Trust*   R P HALLETT
ABBERLEY (St Mary)   *see* Shrawley, Witley, Astley and Abberley
Worc
ABBERLEY (St Michael) *as above*
ABBERTON (St Andrew)   *see* Fingringhoe w E Donyland and
Abberton *etc Chelmsf*
**ABBERTON (St Edburga), The Flyfords, Naunton Beauchamp
and Bishampton w Throckmorton** *Worc 4*   P *Bp and
Croome Estate Trustees (1 turn), and Ld Chan (1 turn)*
R *vacant*
ABBESS RODING (St Edmund King and Martyr)   *see* S Rodings
Chelmsf
ABBEY HULTON (St John)   *see* Bucknall *Lich*
ABBEY WOOD (St Michael and All Angels) *S'wark 6*   P *Bp*
V D A SHERRATT
ABBEY WOOD (William Temple)   *see* Thamesmead *S'wark*
ABBEYDALE (St John the Evangelist) and Millhouses *Sheff 2*
P *Bp and Trustees (jt)*   V P A INGRAM
ABBEYDORE (St Mary)   *see* Ewyas Harold w Dulas,
Kenderchurch *etc Heref*
ABBEYLANDS Team Ministry *Leeds 16*   P *Patr Bd*
TR N C SINCLAIR   TV J SMITH   C S L BROWN,
S M KAYE
**ABBOTS BROMLEY (St Nicholas), Blithfield, Colton,
Colwich and Great Haywood** *Lich 3*   P *Bp and D&C (jt)*
R S C DAVIS   C S C TORR   NSM L J FARRINGTON,
M A DAVYS   OLM P A MERRIOTT
ABBOTS LANGLEY (St Lawrence) *St Alb 6*   P *Bp*
C D WARNER
ABBOTS LEIGH (Holy Trinity) w Leigh Woods *Bris 2*   P *Bp*
V S H E JONES
ABBOTS MORTON (St Peter)   *see* Church Lench w Rous Lench
and Abbots Morton *etc Worc*
ABBOTS RIPTON (St Andrew)   *see* Huntingdon St Barn and the
Riptons *Ely*
ABBOTSBURY (St Mary)   *see* Highweek *Ex*
ABBOTSBURY (St Nicholas), Portesham and Langton Herring
Sarum 4   P *The Hon C A Townshend and Bp (alt)*
P-in-c J C BRADING   NSM M PREUSS-HIGHAM
ABBOTSHAM (St Helen) *Ex 15*   P *PCC*   V *vacant*
ABBOTSKERSWELL (Blessed Virgin Mary) *Ex 9*   P *Ld Chan*
P-in-c J F LEONARD   C G STILL

ABBOTSLEY (St Margaret)   *see* Gt Gransden and Abbotsley and
Lt Gransden *etc Ely*
ABBOTSWOOD (St Nicholas Family Centre)   *see* Yate *Bris*
**ABBOTTS ANN (St Mary) and Upper Clatford and Goodworth
Clatford** *Win 3*   P *Exors T P de Paravicini Esq and Bp (jt)*
R *vacant*
ABDON (St Margaret) *Heref 11*   P *Bp*   R *vacant*
ABENHALL (St Michael) w Mitcheldean *Glouc 3*   P *DBP*
P-in-c D A GILL   C C STERRY
ABERFORD (St Ricarius) w Micklefield *York 4*   P *Abp and Oriel
Coll Ox (jt)*   P-in-c C WILTON   C M J OTTER
NSM D T HAYES
ABINGDON, NORTH (Christ Church) *Ox 19*   P *Bp*
V T C DAVIS   C J K PATEL, K O DUNNETT   NSM S M STEER
**ABINGDON-ON-THAMES (St Helen) (St Michael and All
Angels) (St Nicolas)** *Ox 19*   P *Patr Bd*   TR E C MILLER
TV P A SMITH   NSM J BAUN, J R BAUN
**ABINGER (St James) and Coldharbour and Wotton and
Holmbury St Mary** *Guildf 7*   P *Bp, Ch Patr Trust, and J P M H
Evelyn Esq (jt)*   R A N BERRY
ABINGTON (St Peter and St Paul) *Pet 4*   P *Bp*   R P J BALL
ABINGTON PIGOTTS (St Michael and All Angels)   *see* Shingay
Gp *Ely*
ABINGTON, GREAT (St Mary the Virgin) w LITTLE (St Mary)
Ely 5   P *MMCET*   P-in-c J M NORRIS   Hon C J M FELLOWS
NSM K R BISHOP
ABRAM (St John) *Liv 14*   P *R Wigan*   P-in-c A E STEIN
ABRIDGE (Holy Trinity)   *see* Lambourne w Abridge and
Stapleford Abbotts *Chelmsf*
ABSON (St James the Great)   *see* Pucklechurch and Abson *Bris*
ABTHORPE (St John the Baptist)   *see* Silverstone and Abthorpe
w Slapton *etc Pet*
ACASTER MALBIS (Holy Trinity) *York 1*   P *R A G Raimes Esq*
V C I COATES   NSM P J MACNAUGHTON
ACASTER SELBY (St John)   *see* Appleton Roebuck w Acaster
Selby *York*
ACCRINGTON (St Andrew) (St Mary Magdalen) (St Peter)
Blackb 1   P *Bp and DBP (jt)*   V L W CARSON-FEATHAM
C T F MURNANE
ACCRINGTON (St James) (St Paul) *Blackb 1*   P *Bp and DBP (jt)*
V I P ENTICOTT   NSM D J BACON
ACCRINGTON (St John) w Huncoat St Augustine *Blackb 1*
P *Bp and V Accrington St Jas w St Paul (jt)*   V *vacant*
ACCRINGTON Christ Church *Blackb 1*   P *Bp and V S Shore H
Trin (jt)*   P-in-c M F J ALLEN
ACKLAM (St John the Baptist)   *see* W Buckrose *York*
ACKLAM, WEST (St Mary) *York 17*   P *Trustees*   V *vacant*
ACKLETON (Mission Room)   *see* Worfield *Heref*
ACKLINGTON (St John the Divine)   *see* Warkworth and
Acklington *Newc*

ACKWORTH (All Saints) (St Cuthbert) *Leeds 19* **P** *Duchy of Lanc* **R** P HARTLEY **NSM** P A FOX

ACLE (St Edmund) and Bure to Yare *Nor 4* **P** *Bp, Ch Soc Trust, Personal Reps K M Mills Esq, and DBP (jt)* **R** M GREENLAND **Hon C** L G ALLIES

ACOCKS GREEN (St Mary) *Birm 13* **P** *Trustees* **V** A T BULLOCK

ACOL (St Mildred) *see* Birchington w Acol and Minnis Bay *Cant*

ACOMB (Holy Redeemer) *York 7* **P** *The Crown* **V** M A HAND

ACOMB (St Stephen and St Aidan) *York 7* **P** *Trustees* **C** E J LUNN

ACOMB MOOR (James the Deacon) *York 7* **P** *Abp* **V** *vacant*

ACRISE (St Martin)

ACTON (All Saints) w Great Waldingfield *St E 12* **P** *Bp* **P-in-c** C M HALLETT

ACTON (St Mary) *Lon 22* **P** *Bp* **R** N G JONES **NSM** M J SPREDBURY

ACTON (St Mary) and Worleston, Church Minshull and Wettenhall *Ches 15* **P** *Bp, V Over St Chad, and R C Roundell Esq (jt)* **V** S A LAWSON

ACTON BEAUCHAMP (St Giles) *see* Frome Valley *Heref*

ACTON BURNELL (St Mary) *see* Condover w Frodesley, Acton Burnell etc *Heref*

ACTON GREEN (St Peter) (All Saints) *Lon 22* **P** *Bp* **P-in-c** K J MORRIS

ACTON ROUND (St Mary) *Heref 8* **P** *DBP* **Hon C** H J PATTERSON

ACTON SCOTT (St Margaret) *Heref 10* **P** *DBP* **P-in-c** T E JESSIMAN **NSM** M G WILLIAMS

ACTON TRUSSELL (St James) *see* Penkridge *Lich*

ACTON TURVILLE (St Mary) *see* Boxwell, Leighterton, Didmarton, Oldbury etc *Glouc*

ACTON, EAST (St Dunstan w St Thomas) *Lon 22* **P** *Bp* **V** J M WESTALL **NSM** R YATES

ACTON, NORTH (St Gabriel) *Lon 22* **P** *Bp* **V** T J N L'ESTRANGE

ACTON, WEST (St Martin) *Lon 22* **P** *Bp* **V** N P HENDERSON

ADBASTON (St Michael and All Angels), High Offley, Knightley, Norbury, Woodseaves, Gnosall and Moreton *Lich 7* **P** *Bp* **NSM** K M HAMMOND

ADDERBURY (St Mary) w Milton *Ox 23* **P** *New Coll Ox* **V** S W FLETCHER

ADDERLEY (St Peter), Ash, Calverhall, Ightfield and Moreton Say *Lich 18* **P** *C Corbet Esq, Sir Algernon Heber-Percy KCVO, T C Heywood-Lonsdale Esq, and R Whitchurch (jt)* **R** M L E LAST

ADDINGHAM (St Michael) *see* Cross Fell Gp *Carl*

ADDINGHAM (St Peter) *Leeds 4* **P** *J R Thompson-Ashby Esq* **R** J PERRETT **Hon C** P A SUMMERS **NSM** AJ HOWORTH, B CLARKE

ADDINGTON (St Margaret) *see* Birling, Addington, Ryarsh and Trottiscliffe *Roch*

ADDINGTON (St Mary) *S'wark 19* **P** *Abp* **NSM** B C GENTILELLA

ADDINGTON (St Mary) *see* Winslow w Gt Horwood and Addington *Ox*

ADDINGTON, GREAT (All Saints) *see* Irthlingborough, Gt Addington, Lt Addington etc *Pet*

ADDINGTON, LITTLE (St Mary the Virgin) *as above*

ADDINGTON, NEW (St Edward) *S'wark 19* **P** *Bp* **P-in-c** J B EASTON-CROUCH

ADDISCOMBE (St Mary Magdalene) *S'wark 20* **P** *Trustees* **V** A S JOHNSON

ADDISCOMBE (St Mildred) *S'wark 20* **P** *Bp* **V** R C HAGON **NSM** S SCHLOSS

ADDLESTONE (St Augustine) (St Paul) *Guildf 11* **P** *Bp* **V** B H BEECROFT **C** C M BEECROFT **OLM** L WRIGHT

ADDLETHORPE (St Nicholas) *see* Skegness Gp *Linc*

ADEL (St John the Baptist) *Leeds 16* **P** *Brig R G Lewthwaite, D R Lewthwaite Esq, and J V Lewthwaite Esq (jt)* **P-in-c** I J WHITE **NSM** I H JOHNSTON

ADEYFIELD (St Barnabas) *see* Hemel Hempstead *St Alb*

ADISHAM (Holy Innocents) *see* Aylesham w Adisham and Nonington *Cant*

ADLESTROP (St Mary Magdalene) *see* Broadwell, Evenlode, Oddington, Adlestrop etc *Glouc*

ADLINGFLEET (All Saints) *see* The Marshland *Sheff*

ADLINGTON (St John's Mission Church) *see* Prestbury *Ches*

ADLINGTON (St Paul) *Blackb 4* **P** *V D A ARNOLD*

ADSTOCK (St Cecilia) *see* Lenborough *Ox*

ADSTONE (All Saints) *see* Lambfold *Pet*

ADSWOOD (St Gabriel's Mission Church) *see* Stockport St Geo *Ches*

ADVENT (St Adwena) *see* Lanteglos by Camelford w Advent *Truro*

ADWELL (St Mary) *see* Thame *Ox*

ADWICK-LE-STREET (St Laurence) w Skelbrooke *Sheff 7* **P** *Mrs P N Fullerton and Bp (alt)* **R** A B WALTON

ADWICK-UPON-DEARNE (St John the Baptist) *see* Barnburgh w Melton on the Hill etc *Sheff*

AFFPUDDLE (St Laurence) *see* Bere Regis and Affpuddle w Turnerspuddle *Sarum*

AIGBURTH (St Anne) *Liv 4* **P** *Trustees* **V** I R GREENWOOD

AIKTON (St Andrew) *see* Barony of Burgh *Carl*

AINDERBY STEEPLE (St Helen) *see* Lower Swale *Leeds*

AINSDALE (St John) *Liv 9* **P** *R Walton, Bp, and Adn (jt)* **V** G J BIRCH

AINSTABLE (St Michael and All Angels) *see* Inglewood Gp *Carl*

AINSTY, NORTH *York 1* **P** *MMCET, Col E C York, Abp, and A G Wailes-Fairbairn Esq (jt)* **V** M R SHAW

AINSTY, RURAL *York 1* **P** *Abp (3 turns), D&C (1 turn)* **V** *vacant*

AINSWORTH (Christ Church) *Man 10* **P** *Bp* **P-in-c** D F THOMSON **OLM** E V LARKIN

AINTREE (St Giles) w St Peter *Liv 7* **P** *Bp* **V** J WILLIAMS

AIREDALE (Holy Cross) w Fryston *Leeds 19* **P** *Bp* **V** T A IBBOTSON

AIRMYN (St David), Hook and Rawcliffe *Sheff 10* **P** *Bp and Ch Soc Trust (jt)* **V** P J BALL

AISHOLT (All Saints), Enmore, Goathurst, Nether Stowey, Over Stowey and Spaxton w Charlynch *B & W 17* **P** *Bp, D&C Windsor, MMCET, and Ch Trust Fund Trust (jt)* **R** C E M KINGDON **NSM** M JONES

AISLABY (St Margaret) *see* Lower Esk *York*

AISTHORPE (St Peter) *see* Spring Line Gp *Linc*

AKELEY (St James) *see* N Buckingham *Ox*

AKEMAN *Ox 21* **P** *New Coll and Ch Ch (1 turn), Qu Coll, St Jo Coll, and Period and Country Houses Ltd (1 turn)* **R** J M HEMMINGS **NSM** B R WOOD

ALBERBURY (St Michael and All Angels) *see* Ford, Gt Wollaston and Alberbury w Cardeston *Heref*

ALBOURNE (St Bartholomew) w Sayers Common and Twineham *Chich 8* **P** *Bp (2 turns), Ex Coll Ox (1 turn)* **R** *vacant*

ALBRIGHTON (St John the Baptist) *see* Leaton and Albrighton w Battlefield *Lich*

ALBRIGHTON (St Mary Magdalene), Boningale and Donington *Lich 16* **P** *Haberdashers' Co and MMCET (jt)* **V** M R WADE

ALBURGH (All Saints) *see* Ditchingham, Hedenham, Broome, Earsham etc *Nor*

ALBURY (St Helen) w Tiddington, Holton, Waterperry, Waterstock and Wheatley *Ox 20* **P** *Bp and DBP (jt)* **V** N A R HAWKES **Hon C** M P GRANTHAM **NSM** J EDMONDS-SEAL, L M GARDNER

ALBURY (St Mary), Braughing, Furneux Pelham, Lt Hadham, Much Hadham and Stocking Pelham *St Alb 15* **P** *Patr Bd* **TR** G D TULK **TV** J A GAWTHROPE

ALBURY (St Peter and St Paul) *see* Shere, Albury and Chilworth *Guildf*

ALBY (St Ethelbert) *see* Erpingham w Calthorpe, Ingworth, Aldborough etc *Nor*

ALCESTER MINSTER (St Nicholas) *Cov 7* **P** *Bp and Marquess of Hertford (jt)* **R** A M GUTHRIE

ALCISTON (not known) *see* Arlington, Berwick, Selmeston w Alciston etc *Chich*

ALCOMBE (St Michael the Archangel) *B & W 15* **P** *Bp* **V** S STUCKES

ALCONBURY (St Peter and St Paul) *see* N Leightonstone *Ely*

ALDBOROUGH (St Andrew) w Boroughbridge and Roecliffe *Leeds 25* **P** *D&C York and Bp (alt)* **V** *vacant*

ALDBOROUGH (St Mary) *see* Erpingham w Calthorpe, Ingworth, Aldborough etc *Nor*

ALDBOROUGH HATCH (St Peter) *Chelmsf 6* **P** *The Crown* **P-in-c** K P B LOVESEY

ALDBOURNE (St Michael) *see* Whitton *Sarum*

ALDBROUGH (St Bartholomew) and Mappleton w Goxhill and Withernwick *York 11* **P** *Ld Chan, Abp, and Adn E Riding (by turn)* **P-in-c** A M WHITE

ALDBROUGH (St Paul) *see* Forcett and Aldbrough and Melsonby *Leeds*

ALDBURY (St John the Baptist) *see* Tring *St Alb*

ALDE RIVER Benefice, The *St E 17* **P** *Earl of Guilford, Major P W Hope-Cobbold, DBP, CPAS, Miss S F R Heycock-Hollond, and Exors Mrs A C V Wentworth (jt)* **R** M E REYNOLDS

ALDE, UPPER *St E 16* **P** *R C Rous Esq, DBP, and CPAS (jt)* **R** J P T OLANCZUK

ALDEBURGH (St Peter and St Paul) w Hazlewood *St E 17* **P** *Mrs A C V Wentworth* **P-in-c** P M LOWTHER **NSM** N J WINTER

ALDEBY (St Mary) *see* Raveningham Gp *Nor*

ALDENHAM (St John the Baptist), Radlett and Shenley
St Alb 5   **P** *Patr Bd*   **TR** J IQBAL   **TV** D M MCCARTHY,
R A FLETCHER   **C** H S E KING   **NSM** D D PRICE
ALDERBROOK (St Richard)   *see* Crowborough *Chich*
ALDERBURY (St Mary the Virgin)   *see* Clarendon *Sarum*
ALDERCAR (St John)   *see* Langley Mill and Aldercar *Derby*
ALDERFORD (St John the Baptist)   *see* Wensum Benefice *Nor*
ALDERHOLT (St James) *Sarum 9*   **P** *DBP*   **V** P J MARTIN
OLM D A DENNIS
ALDERLEY (St Kenelm)   *see* Tyndale *Glouc*
ALDERLEY (St Mary) w Birtles *Ches 12*   **P** *Trustees and Bp (alt)*
R vacant
ALDERLEY EDGE (St Philip) *Ches 12*   **P** *Trustees*   **V** P J PARRY
NSM L C A ALEXANDER
ALDERMASTON (St Mary the Virgin) and Woolhampton *Ox 4*
P *Bp, Keble Coll Ox, CPAS, Lady Dugdale, Worc Coll Ox, and DBP*
(jt)   **R** R A BEVAN   **C** J M MACDONALD
NSM P F M BHUTTA
ALDERMINSTER (St Mary and Holy Cross)   *see* Stourdene Gp
Cov
ALDERNEY (St Anne) *Win 14*   **P** *The Crown*   **V** S M MASTERS
ALDERSBROOK (St Gabriel) *Chelmsf 6*   **P** *DBP*
V M J HAWKES   **NSM** C J SMALING, M A KENNY
ALDERSHOT (Holy Trinity) *Guildf 1*   **P** *CPAS*
V G P H NEWTON   **NSM** C J B KELLAGHER
ALDERSHOT (St Augustine) *Guildf 1*   **P** *Bp*   **V** K M HODGES
ALDERSHOT (St Michael the Archangel) (Ascension) *Guildf 1*
P *Bp*   **V** J A MARTIN   **C** T S MOORE
ALDERSLEY (Christ the King)   *see* Tettenhall Regis *Lich*
ALDERTON (St Andrew)   *see* Wilford Peninsula *St E*
ALDERTON (St Giles)   *see* Sherston Magna, Easton Grey,
Luckington etc *Bris*
ALDERTON (St Margaret of Antioch)   *see* Winchcombe *Glouc*
ALDERTON (St Margaret)   *see* Blisworth, Alderton, Grafton
Regis etc *Pet*
ALDERWASLEY (All Saints)   *see* Wirksworth *Derby*
ALDFIELD (St Lawrence)   *see* Fountains Gp *Leeds*
ALDFORD (St John the Baptist)   *see* Waverton w Aldford and
Bruera *Ches*
ALDHAM (St Margaret and St Catherine)   *see* Marks Tey and
Aldham *Chelmsf*
ALDHAM (St Mary)   *see* Elmsett w Aldham, Hintlesham,
Chattisham etc *St E*
**ALDINGBOURNE (St Mary the Virgin), Barnham and
Eastergate** *Chich 1*   **P** *Bp and D&C (jt)*   **R** M POWELL
NSM A R BRANT, S M HIGGINS
**ALDINGHAM (St Cuthbert) and Dendron and Rampside and
Urswick** *Carl 9*   **P** *Prime Min (1 turn), V Dalton-in-Furness and
Resident Landowners of Urswick (1 turn)*
P-in-c A M ARMSTRONG
ALDINGTON (St Martin)   *see* Saxon Shoreline *Cant*
ALDRIDGE (St Mary the Virgin) (St Thomas) *Lich 25*
P *MMCET*   **R** J E COYNE   **C** C J HASSELL, M P CASTLETON
OLM J E BAKEWELL, S E QUIBELL
ALDRINGHAM (St Andrew)   *see* Whinlands *St E*
ALDRINGTON (St Leonard) *Chich 20*   **P** *Bp*   **R** S J TERRY
ALDSWORTH (St Bartholomew)   *see* Sherborne, Windrush, the
Barringtons etc *Glouc*
ALDWARK (St Stephen)   *see* Alne *York*
ALDWICK (St Richard) *Chich 1*   **P** *Bp*   **V** L C J NAGEL
**ALDWINCLE (St Peter), Clopton, Pilton, Stoke Doyle, Thorpe
Achurch, Titchmarsh and Wadenhoe** *Pet 10*   **P** *G C Capron
Esq, Wadenhoe Trust, Soc Merchant Venturers Bris, and DBP (jt)*
R J B MYNORS   **NSM** C H BRAZIER, E A WALLER
ALDWORTH (St Mary the Virgin)   *see* Basildon w Aldworth and
Ashampstead *Ox*
ALEXANDRA PARK (St Andrew) *Lon 20*   **P** *Bp*   **V** A F PYBUS
ALFINGTON (St James and St Anne)   *see* Ottery St Mary,
Alfington, W Hill, Tipton etc *Ex*
ALFOLD (St Nicholas) and Loxwood *Guildf 2*   **P** *Bp and
CPAS (jt)*   **R** vacant
ALFORD (All Saints)   *see* Six Pilgrims *B & W*
ALFORD (St Wilfrid) w Rigsby *Linc 10*   **P** *Bp*
P-in-c R M LATHAM   **NSM** J M MORTON
OLM R D BARRETT
ALFRED JEWEL *B & W 13*   **P** *D&C Windsor (4 turns), Bp (2
turns), Sir Benjamin Slade Bt (1 turn)*   **R** J HASLAM
C E O KING, P DENISON   **NSM** M H HASLAM
ALFRETON (St Martin) *Derby 1*   **P** *Bp*
P-in-c F J C MERCURIO
ALFRICK (St Mary Magdalene)   *see* Worcs W *Worc*
**ALFRISTON (St Andrew) w Lullington, Litlington, West Dean
and Folkington** *Chich 21*   **P** *Ld Chan (3 turns), Duke of
Devonshire, R A Brown Esq, and Mrs S J Harcourt-Smith (1 turn
each)*   **R** D J MERCERON
ALGARKIRK (St Peter and St Paul)   *see* Kirton in Holland w
Algarkirk and Fosdyke *Linc*

ALHAMPTON (Mission Church)   *see* Fosse Trinity *B & W*
ALKBOROUGH (St John the Baptist) *Linc 6*   **P** *Bp*
V A F PLEDGER
ALKERTON (St Michael and All Angels)   *see* Ironstone *Ox*
ALKHAM (St Anthony) w Capel le Ferne and Hougham *Cant 7*
P *Abp*   **C** B F WILLIAMS
ALKMONTON (St John)   *see* S Dales *Derby*
ALL CANNINGS (All Saints)   *see* The Cannings and Redhorn
Sarum
ALL STRETTON (St Michael and All Angels)   *see* Church Stretton
Heref
ALLENDALE (St Cuthbert) w Whitfield *Newc 10*   **P** *Viscount
Allendale and J C Blackett-Ord Esq (alt)*   **R** J W RUSSELL
ALLENS CROSS (St Bartholomew) *Birm 4*   **P** *Bp*
P-in-c P A FLEMING
ALLENSMORE (St Andrew)   *see* Cagebrook *Heref*
ALLENTON (St Edmund) and Shelton Lock *Derby 15*   **P** *Bp*
P-in-c T E MORRIS
ALLER (St Andrew)   *see* Langport Area *B & W*
ALLERSTON (St John)   *see* Thornton Dale w Allerston,
Ebberston etc *York*
ALLERTON (All Hallows)   *see* Mossley Hill *Liv*
ALLERTON (not known)   *see* Mark w Allerton *B & W*
ALLERTON (St Peter) (St Francis of Assisi) *Leeds 1*   **P** *Bp*
V G O WILLIAMS
ALLERTON BYWATER (St Mary)   *see* Kippax w Allerton Bywater
Leeds
ALLESLEY (All Saints) *Cov 2*   **P** *J R W Thomson-Bree Esq*
R R N TREW
ALLESLEY PARK (St Christopher) and Whoberley *Cov 3*   **P** *Bp*
V A MARCH   **C** J LANGLANDS   **NSM** P A STOTE
**ALLESTREE (St Edmund King and Martyr) and Darley Abbey
St Matthew** *Derby 11*   **P** *Bp and DBP (jt)*   **V** vacant
ALLESTREE (St Nicholas) *Derby 11*   **P** *Bp*   **V** W F BATES
NSM J M NEEDLE
ALLINGTON (St Nicholas) and Maidstone St Peter *Cant 12*
P *Abp*   **P-in-c** C P LAVENDER
ALLINGTON (St Swithin)   *see* Bridport *Sarum*
ALLINGTON, EAST (St Andrew)   *see* Modbury, Bigbury,
Ringmore etc *Ex*
ALLINGTON, WEST (Holy Trinity)   *see* Saxonwell *Linc*
ALLITHWAITE (St Mary)   *see* Cartmel Peninsula *Carl*
ALLONBY (Christ Church), Cross Canonby and Dearham
Carl 7   **P** *TR Solway Plain, D&C, and Bp (jt)*   **V** M E DAY
C J A BATE
ALMELEY (St Mary)   *see* Eardisley w Bollingham, Willersley,
Brilley etc *Heref*
ALMER (St Mary)   *see* Red Post *Sarum*
**ALMONDBURY (St Michael and St Helen) (St Mary) (All
Hallows) w Farnley Tyas** *Leeds 6*   **P** *DBP*   **TR** M T P ZAMMIT
ALMONDSBURY (St Mary the Virgin) and Olveston *Bris 2*
P *Bp and D&C (jt)*   **V** P W ROWE   **Hon C** D R F BAIN
OLM A LLOYD, D H BONE, P A VAN ROSSUM
ALNE (St Mary) *York 3*   **P** *CPAS and MMCET (alt)*
P-in-c C J PARK   **NSM** C C GITTENS, R WADSWORTH
ALNE, GREAT (St Mary Magdalene)   *see* Alcester Minster *Cov*
ALNHAM (St Michael and All Angels)   *see* Upper Coquetdale
Newc
ALNMOUTH (St John the Baptist)   *see* Lesbury w Alnmouth
Newc
ALNWICK (St Michael and St Paul) *Newc 6*   **P** *Duke of
Northumberland*   **V** P M SCOTT   **C** J M MYLES
ALPERTON (St James) *Lon 21*   **P** *CPAS*   **V** A I TAYLOR
C A MORE, S G TAYLOR
ALPHAMSTONE (not known)   *see* N Hinckford *Chelmsf*
ALPHETON (St Peter and St Paul)   *see* Chadbrook *St E*
**ALPHINGTON (St Michael and All Angels), Shillingford
St George and Ide** *Ex 3*   **P** *DBP, D&C, and Mrs J M
Michelmore (jt)*   **R** S L BESSENT   **C** M A NIGHTINGALE
ALRESFORD (St Andrew) and Frating w Thorrington
Chelmsf 23   **P** *Bp*   **V** P C M SCOTT   **OLM** P J HART
ALRESFORD, NEW (St John the Baptist)   *see* Arle Valley *Win*
ALRESFORD, OLD (St Mary) *as above*
ALREWAS (All Saints) *Lich 1*   **P** *Bp*   **V** J W ALLAN
NSM E A WALL
ALSAGER (Christ Church) *Ches 11*   **P** *Bp*   **V** T S MAY
ALSAGER (St Mary Magdalene) (St Patrick's Mission Church)
Ches 11   **P** *Bp*   **P-in-c** J E SHEPHERD
ALSAGERS BANK (St John), Audley and Talke *Lich 9*
P *Patr Bd*   **C** G K CHELASHAW
ALSOP-EN-LE-DALE (St Michael and All Angels)   *see* Fenny
Bentley, Thorpe, Tissington, Parwich etc *Derby*
ALSTON MOOR (St Augustine) *Newc 10*   **P** *Bp*
R M C V NASH-WILLIAMS
ALSTONE (St Margaret)   *see* Overbury w Teddington, Alstone
etc *Worc*

ALSTONFIELD (St Peter), Butterton, Ilam, Warslow w Elkstone and Wetton *Lich 5* **P** *Bp, DBP, V Mayfield, and Sir Peter Walker-Okeover Bt (jt)* **V** A C BALLARD

ALTARNON (St Nonna) *see* Moorland Gp *Truro*

ALTCAR (St Michael and All Angels) *see* Formby H Trin and Altcar *Liv*

ALTHAM (St James) w Clayton le Moors *Blackb 1* **P** *DBP and Trustees (alt)* **V** T R WEBBER

ALTHORNE (St Andrew) and Latchingdon w North Fambridge *Chelmsf 11* **P** *Abp and Ld Chan (alt)* **V** S E MANLEY **C** B C R JOHNSON

ALTHORPE (St Oswald) *see* Belton Gp *Linc*

ALTOFTS (St Mary Magdalene) *Leeds 20* **P** *Meynall Ingram Trustees* **V** *vacant*

ALTON (St Peter) w Bradley-le-Moors and Denstone w Ellastone and Stanton and Mayfield *Lich 15* **P** *Earl of Shrewsbury and Waterford, DBP, Personal Reps Col Sir Walter Bromley-Davenport, Bp, and Ch Soc Trust (jt)* **V** B S P LEATHERS **C** J RICHARDSON, R P OWEN

ALTON BARNES (St Mary the Virgin) *see* Vale of Pewsey *Sarum*

ALTON PANCRAS (St Pancras) *see* Piddle Valley, Hilton, Cheselbourne etc *Sarum*

ALTON Resurrection (All Saints) (St Lawrence) *Win 2* **P** *Bp and D&C (jt)* **V** A M MICKLEFIELD **C** D J HINKS

ALTRINCHAM (St George) *Ches 10* **P** *V Bowdon* **V** E J BETTS **NSM** D R LAW

ALTRINCHAM (St John the Evangelist) *Ches 10* **P** *Bp* **P-in-c** E J BETTS

ALVANLEY (St John the Evangelist) *Ches 3* **P** *Bp* **V** R J SAMUELS

ALVASTON (St Michael and All Angels) *Derby 15* **P** *PCC* **NSM** I P MUNRO

ALVECHURCH (St Lawrence) *Worc 7* **P** *Bp* **P-in-c** R D BUBBERS

ALVEDISTON (St Mary) *see* Chalke Valley *Sarum*

ALVELEY (St Mary the Virgin) and Quatt *Heref 8* **P** J W H *Thompson Esq and Lady Labouchere (jt)* **NSM** R M SIMS

ALVERDISCOTT (All Saints) *see* Newton Tracey, Horwood, Alverdiscott etc *Ex*

ALVERSTOKE (St Faith) (St Francis) (St Mary) *Portsm 3* **P** *Bp* **P-in-c** A P NORRIS **C** C E RICHARDSON

ALVERTHORPE (St Paul) *Leeds 20* **P** *Bp* **P-in-c** G A SYKES **NSM** K KIDD

ALVESCOT (St Peter) *see* Shill Valley and Broadshire *Ox*

ALVESTON (St Helen) and Littleton-on-Severn w Elberton *Bris 2* **P** *Bp and D&C (jt)* **V** *vacant*

ALVESTON (St James) *Cov 8* **P** *R Hampton Lucy w Charlecote and Loxley* **V** R E WILLIAMS

ALVINGHAM (St Adelwold) *see* Mid Marsh Gp *Linc*

ALVINGTON (St Andrew) *see* Woolaston w Alvington and Aylburton *Glouc*

ALVINGTON, WEST (All Saints) *see* Kingsbridge, Dodbrooke, and W Alvington *Ex*

ALWALTON (St Andrew) and Chesterton *Ely 15* **P** *Bp and Sir Philip Naylor-Leyland Bt (jt)* **V** M J INGHAM

ALWINGTON (St Andrew) *see* Parkham, Alwington, Buckland Brewer etc *Ex*

ALWINTON (St Michael and All Angels) *see* Upper Coquetdale *Newc*

ALWOODLEY (St Barnabas) *see* Moor Allerton and Shadwell *Leeds*

AMBERGATE (St Anne) and Heage *Derby 11* **P** *V Duffield and Exors M A T Johnson Esq* **P-in-c** V M HART

AMBERLEY (Holy Trinity) *see* Minchinhampton w Box and Amberley *Glouc*

AMBERLEY (no dedication) *see* Maund Gp *Heref*

AMBERLEY (St Michael) w North Stoke and Parham, Wiggonholt and Greatham *Chich 11* **P** *Bp and Parham Estate Trustees (jt)* **V** A M PATTENDEN

AMBLE (St Cuthbert) *Newc 6* **P** *Bp* **P-in-c** D R WESTMORELAND

AMBLECOTE (Holy Trinity) *Worc 12* **P** *Bp* **P-in-c** A R N WILLIAMS

AMBLESIDE (St Mary) *see* Loughrigg *Carl*

AMBROSDEN (St Mary the Virgin) *see* Ray Valley *Ox*

AMCOTTS (St Mark) *see* Belton Gp *Linc*

AMERSHAM (St Mary the Virgin) *Ox 9* **P** *Capt F Tyrwhitt Drake* **R** T J L HARPER **OLM** T J W BARNARD

AMERSHAM ON THE HILL (St Michael and All Angels) *Ox 9* **P** *Bp* **NSM** P R BINNS **OLM** S ROBERTS

AMESBURY (St Mary and St Melor) *Sarum 14* **P** *D&C Windsor* **P-in-c** D A'COURT **NSM** J M NAISH, P M POWELL

AMINGTON (St Editha) *Birm 10* **P** *Bp* **V** *vacant*

AMOTHERBY (St Helen) *see* The Street Par *York*

AMPFIELD (St Mark), Chilworth and N Baddesley *Win 12* **P** *Mrs P M A T Chamberlayne-MacDonald* **NSM** C G STRIDE, H L HEALEY, V J LAWRENCE

AMPLEFORTH (St Hilda) w Oswaldkirk, Gilling East and Stonegrave *York 19* **P** *Abp and Trin Coll Cam (jt) and Prime Min (by turn)* **V** S F BOND

AMPNEY (St Mary) *see* S Cotswolds *Glouc*

AMPNEY (St Peter) *as above*

AMPNEY CRUCIS (Holy Rood) *as above*

AMPORT (St Mary) *see* Portway and Danebury *Win*

AMPTHILL (St Andrew) w Millbrook and Steppingley *St Alb 8* **P** *Ld Chan* **R** M J TRODDEN

AMPTON (St Peter) *see* Blackbourne *St E*

AMWELL, GREAT (St John the Baptist) w St Margaret's and Stanstead Abbots *St Alb 19* **P** *Bp, Peache Trustees, and Haileybury Coll (jt)* **V** E A DONALDSON

AMWELL, LITTLE (Holy Trinity) *see* Hertford *St Alb*

ANCASTER (St Martin) *see* Ancaster Wilsford Gp *Linc*

ANCASTER WILSFORD Group, The *Linc 22* **P** *Bp (2 turns), DBP (1 turn), and Mrs G V Hoare (1 turn)* **R** *vacant*

ANCHORSHOLME (All Saints) *Blackb 8* **P** *Bp, V Bispham, and Ch Soc Trust (jt)* **V** S M DNISTRIANSKYJ **C** S I HASKETT

ANCROFT (St Anne) *see* Lowick and Kyloe w Ancroft *Newc*

ANDERBY (St Andrew) *see* Sutton, Huttoft and Anderby *Linc*

ANDOVER (St Mary) *Win 3* **P** *St Mary's Coll Win* **V** J P HARKIN **C** L DAVIES

ANDOVER (St Thomas) *see* Pastrow *Win*

ANDOVER, WEST (St Michael and All Angels) *see* Portway and Danebury *Win*

ANDREAS (St Andrew) (St Jude), Ballaugh, Jurby and Sulby *S & M* **P** *The Crown* **R** C D ROGERS

ANERLEY (Christ Church) (St Paul) *Roch 13* **P** *Patr Bd* **TR** M D FITTER

ANFIELD (St Columba) *Liv 7* **P** *Bp* **V** R S BRIDSON **C** D T HOWARD **NSM** K L MILLER

ANFIELD (St Margaret) *Liv 3* **P** *Bp* **V** P A WINN **NSM** J E WINN

ANGELL TOWN (St John the Evangelist) *S'wark 11* **P** *Bp* **V** M R MALLETT **NSM** P J MILLIGAN

ANGERSLEIGH (St Michael) *see* Trull w Angersleigh *B & W*

ANGLESEY Group, The *Ely 4* **P** *Trin Coll Cam, D&C, and Bp (jt)* **V** S J GILES

ANGMERING (St Margaret) *Chich 1* **P** J F P *Somerset Esq and Ch Patr Trust (jt)* **R** M J STANDEN **C** B J REDDING, T I ROBSON **NSM** P S GILES

ANLABY (St Peter) *York 14* **P** *Trustees* **V** S C F WILCOX **C** J A TELFORD

ANLABY COMMON (St Mark) *Hull York 14* **P** *Abp* **V** S C F WILCOX **C** J A TELFORD

ANNESLEY (Our Lady and All Saints) w Newstead and Kirkby Woodhouse *S'well 4* **P** *Bp and Exors Major R P Chaworth-Musters (jt)* **V** *vacant*

ANNFIELD PLAIN (St Aidan) *see* Collierley w Annfield Plain *Dur*

ANNSCROFT (Christ Church) *see* Gt Hanwood and Longden and Annscroft etc *Heref*

ANSFORD (St Andrew) *see* Castle Cary w Ansford *B & W*

ANSLEY (St Lawrence) and Arley *Cov 5* **P** *Ch Patr Trust, N W H Sylvester Esq, and A C D'O Ransom Esq (jt)* **R** P B ALLAN

ANSLOW (Holy Trinity) *Lich 14* **P** *MMCET* **V** I R WHITEHEAD **C** L REES **Hon C** A L WHEALE

ANSTEY (St George) *see* Hormead, Wyddial, Anstey, Brent Pelham etc *St Alb*

ANSTEY (St Mary) and Thurcaston w Cropston *Leic 9* **P** *Bp and Em Coll Cam (jt)* **R** D S MCDONOUGH

ANSTEY, EAST (St Michael) *see* Bishopsnympton, Rose Ash, Mariansleigh etc *Ex*

ANSTEY, WEST (St Petrock) *as above*

ANSTON (St James) *Sheff 5* **P** *Bp* **V** M CAUNT **NSM** B A CUSHING

ANSTY (St James) *see* Nadder Valley *Sarum*

ANSTY (St James) and Shilton *Cov 2* **P** *Ld Chan* **P-in-c** A D COLEMAN **NSM** N W STEVENS

ANTINGHAM (St Mary) *see* Poppyland *Nor*

ANTONY (St James the Great) w Sheviock and Torpoint *Truro 11* **P** *Bp and Sir John Carew Pole Bt (alt)* **V** L PARKER **C** C MCILROY

ANTROBUS (St Mark) *Ches 4* **P** *V Gt Budworth* **P-in-c** A G BROWN **NSM** S R COLLINGRIDGE

ANWICK (St Edith) *see* N Lafford Gp *Linc*

APEDALE Group, The *Heref 10* **P** *DBP, Mrs R Bell, Bp Birm, and S Pennington Esq (by turn)* **R** N T CLEATON **NSM** J M BELLAMY **OLM** V CLEMENTS

APETHORPE (St Leonard) *see* Nassington, Apethorpe, Thornhaugh etc *Pet*

APLEY (St Andrew) *see* Bardney *Linc*

APPERLEY (Holy Trinity) *see* Deerhurst and Apperley w Forthampton etc *Glouc*

APPLEBY (St Bartholomew) *see* Winterton Gp *Linc*

APPLEBY (St Lawrence)   *see* Heart of Eden *Carl*

APPLEBY MAGNA (St Michael and All Angels)   *see* Woodfield *Leic*

APPLEDORE (St Mary)   *see* Bideford, Northam, Westward Ho!, Appledore etc *Ex*

APPLEDORE (St Peter and St Paul)   *see* Rother and Oxney *Cant*

APPLEDRAM (St Mary the Virgin) *Chich 2*   **P** *D&C*   **P-in-c** M WICKENS

APPLEFORD (St Peter and St Paul)   *see* Sutton Courtenay w Appleford *Ox*

APPLESHAW (St Peter) Kimpton, Thruxton, Fyfield and Shipton Bellinger *Win 3*   **P** *Bp (1 turn), and Bp, D&C, and M H Routh Esq (1 turn)*   **R** I J TOMLINSON   **NSM** S E WILLIAMS

APPLETHWAITE (St Mary)   *see* Windermere St Mary and Troutbeck *Carl*

APPLETON (All Saints)   *see* The Street Par *York*

APPLETON (St Laurence) *Ox 19*   **P** *Magd Coll Ox*   **P-in-c** L L SAPWELL

APPLETON (St Mary Magdalene)   *see* Stockton Heath *Ches*

APPLETON ROEBUCK (All Saints) w Acaster Selby *York 1*   **P** *Abp*   **V** C I COATES   **NSM** P J MACNAUGHTON

APPLETON THORN (St Cross)   *see* Stretton and Appleton Thorn *Ches*

APPLETON WISKE (St Mary)   *see* E Richmond *Leeds*

APPLETON-LE-MOORS (Christ Church)   *see* Lastingham w Appleton-le-Moors, Rosedale etc *York*

APPLETREEWICK (St John the Baptist)   *see* Burnsall w Rylstone *Leeds*

APPLEY BRIDGE (All Saints) and Parbold *Blackb 4*   **P** *Bp*   **V** S A GLYNN   **C** A J P GOODWIN-HUDSON   **NSM** J R MOUNTAIN

ARBORFIELD (St Bartholomew) w Barkham *Ox 8*   **P** *DBP*   **R** E P BICKERSTETH   **C** B R THORNDIKE, J P BIDGOOD, M G HUDDLESTON

ARBORY (St Columba) and Castletown *S & M*   **P** *The Crown and Bp (alt)*   **V** J F P GOMES   **NSM** C L BARRY

ARBOURTHORNE (St Paul) and Norfolk Park *Sheff 1*   **P** *Bp and V Sheffield (jt)*   **V** J T HODGES

ARDELEY (St Lawrence), Benington, Cottered w Throcking and Walkern *St Alb 16*   **P** *K Coll Cam, D&C St Paul's, and Bp (jt)*   **R** M J LEVERTON

ARDEN MARCHES *Cov 7*   **P** *Ld Chan, Mrs J M Pinney, and Bp (by turn)*   **R** D SILVESTER   **C** B C GREEN, N S DUNLOP   **NSM** A W SHEARN

ARDEN VALLEY *Cov 7*   **P** *Bp and V Wootton Wawen (jt)*   **R** R LIVINGSTON

ARDINGLY (St Peter) *Chich 5*   **P** *MMCET*   **R** J H CRUTCHLEY   **NSM** S L UPCHURCH

ARDINGTON (Holy Trinity)   *see* Wantage Downs *Ox*

ARDLEIGH (St Mary the Virgin) and Bromleys, The *Chelmsf 22*   **P** *Ld Chan (2 turns), CR (1 turn), Wadh Coll Ox (1 turn)*   **R** *vacant*

ARDLEY (St Mary)   *see* Cherwell Valley *Ox*

ARDSLEY (Christ Church) *Sheff 12*   **P** *R Darfield*   **V** F M KOUBLE

ARDSLEY, EAST (St Gabriel) (St Michael) *Leeds 15*   **P** E C S J G Brudenell Esq   **V** G COGGINS

ARDSLEY, WEST (St Mary) *Leeds 15*   **P** E C S J G Brudenell Esq   **V** *vacant*

ARELEY KINGS (St Bartholomew) *Worc 13*   **P** *R Martley*   **R** M TURNER   **NSM** J M CALAM

ARICONIUM : Aston Ingham, Hope Mansel, Linton, The Lea, Upton Bishop and Weston-under-Penyard *Heref 7*   **P** *Bp (3 turns), St Jo Coll Ox (2 turns), Exors Preb H L Whatley (1 turn)*   **R** N S PATTERSON

ARKENDALE (St Bartholomew)   *see* Walkingham Hill *Leeds*

ARKENGARTHDALE (St Mary)   *see* Swaledale *Leeds*

ARKESDEN (St Mary the Virgin)   *see* Clavering w Langley, Arkesden etc *Chelmsf*

ARKHOLME (St John the Baptist)   *see* Hornby w Claughton and Whittington etc *Blackb*

ARKLEY (St Peter)   *see* Chipping Barnet *St Alb*

ARKSEY (All Saints)   *see* New Bentley w Arksey *Sheff*

ARLE VALLEY Benefice, The *Win 1*   **P** *Bp*   **R** P H N COLLINS

ARLECDON (St Michael)   *see* Crosslacon *Carl*

ARLESEY (St Andrew) (St Peter) w Astwick *St Alb 8*   **P** *DBP*   **P-in-c** G M BOULT

ARLEY (St Michael)   *see* Ansley and Arley *Cov*

ARLEY (St Wilfred) *as above*

ARLEY, UPPER (St Peter)   *see* Kidderminster Ismere *Worc*

ARLINGHAM (St Mary the Virgin)   *see* Frampton on Severn, Arlingham, Saul etc *Glouc*

ARLINGTON (St James)   *see* Shirwell, Loxhore, Kentisbury, Arlington, etc *Ex*

ARLINGTON (St Pancras), Berwick, Selmeston w Alciston and Wilmington *Chich 21*   **P** *Bp Lon, D&C, Miss I M Newson, and Mrs R Fitzherbert (jt)*   **R** P M BLEE   **Hon C** F J FOX-WILSON

ARMATHWAITE (Christ and St Mary)   *see* Inglewood Gp *Carl*

ARMINGHALL (St Mary)   *see* Stoke H Cross w Dunston, Arminghall etc *Nor*

ARMITAGE (St John the Baptist) *Lich 3*   **P** *Bp*   **R** D R H THOMAS

ARMITAGE BRIDGE (St Paul)   *see* Em TM *Leeds*

ARMLEY (St Bartholomew) w New Wortley *Leeds 15*   **P** *Bp, DBP, and Hyndman Trustees (jt)*   **V** *vacant*

ARMLEY HEIGHTS (Church of the Ascension)   *see* Upper Armley *Leeds*

ARMLEY, UPPER (Christ Church) *Leeds 15*   **P** *Ch Patr Trust*   **V** A SEN

ARMTHORPE (St Leonard and St Mary) *Sheff 8*   **P** *Bp*   **R** J M FODEN

ARNCLIFFE (St Oswald)   *see* Kettlewell w Conistone, Hubberholme etc *Leeds*

ARNE (St Nicholas)   *see* Wareham *Sarum*

ARNESBY (St Peter)   *see* Hexagon *Leic*

ARNOLD (Emmanuel)   *see* Bestwood Em w St Mark *S'well*

ARNOLD (St Mary) *S'well 7*   **P** *Bp*   **NSM** S J HUSTWAYTE

ARNSIDE (St James) *Carl 10*   **P** *Bp*   **P-in-c** D P COOPER

ARRETON (St George) *Portsm 7*   **P** *Bp*   **V** J F O'SHAUGHNESSY

ARRINGTON (St Nicholas)   *see* Orwell Gp *Ely*

ARROW (Holy Trinity)   *see* Alcester Minster *Cov*

ARTHINGWORTH (St Andrew) and Harrington w Oxendon and East Farndon *Pet 2*   **P** *St Jo Coll Ox (2 turns), Nugee Foundn (2 turns), and Bp (1 turn)*   **P-in-c** M Y GARBUTT

ARTHURET (St Michael and All Angels) w Kirkandrews-on-Esk and Nicholforest *Carl 2*   **P** *Sir James Graham Bt (2 turns), Bp (1 turn)*   **R** R TAGUE

ARUNDEL (St Nicholas) w Tortington and South Stoke *Chich 1*   **P** *Bp (2 turns), Duke of Norfolk (1 turn)*   **V** *vacant*

ASBY (St Peter)   *see* Heart of Eden *Carl*

ASCENSION Team Ministry, The *Leic 1*   **P** *Patr Bd*   **TR** *vacant*

ASCOT HEATH (All Saints) *Ox 3*   **P** *Bp*   **R** D D HANNAH   **C** P E GILDAY

ASCOT, SOUTH (All Souls)   *see* Sunninghill and S Ascot *Ox*

ASCOTT UNDER WYCHWOOD (Holy Trinity)   *see* Chase *Ox*

ASFORDBY (All Saints)   *see* Ab Kettleby and Holwell w Asfordby *Leic*

ASGARBY (St Andrew)   *see* Heckington and Helpringham Gp *Linc*

ASH (Christ Church)   *see* Adderley, Ash, Calverhall, Ightfield etc *Lich*

ASH (Holy Trinity)   *see* Martock w Kingsbury Episcopi and Ash *B & W*

ASH (St Nicholas)   *see* Canonry *Cant*

ASH (St Peter and St Paul) *Roch 1*   **P** *J R A B Scott Esq*   **P-in-c** R OATES   **NSM** E M ROBERTSON

ASH (St Peter) *Guildf 1*   **P** *Win Coll*   **R** K R M BRISTOW

ASH (Thomas Chapel)   *see* Sampford Peverell, Uplowman, Holcombe Rogus etc *Ex*

ASH PRIORS (Holy Trinity)   *see* Milverton w Halse, Fitzhead and Ash Priors *B & W*

ASH VALE (St Mary) *Guildf 1*   **P** *Bp*   **V** N J LAMBERT

ASHAMPSTEAD (St Clement)   *see* Basildon w Aldworth and Ashampstead *Ox*

ASHBOCKING (All Saints)   *see* Carlford *St E*

ASHBOURNE (St John the Baptist) *Derby 8*   **P** *Wright Trustees*   **P-in-c** G P POND   **C** C E MCDONALD   **NSM** P A SHORT

ASHBOURNE (St Oswald) w Mapleton *Derby 8*   **P** *Bp*   **V** G P POND   **C** C E MCDONALD   **NSM** P A SHORT

ASHBRITTLE (St John the Baptist)   *see* Wellington and Distr *B & W*

ASHBURNHAM (St Peter) w Penhurst *Chich 12*   **P** *Ashburnham Chr Trust*   **P-in-c** P S MCVEAGH   **NSM** J H SYKES

ASHBURTON (St Andrew), Bickington, Buckland in the Moor, Holne, Huccaby, Leusdon, Princetown, Postbridge, and Widecombe-in-the-Moor *Ex 8*   **P** *Duchy of Cornwall (1 turn), Patr Bd (1 turn)*   **P-in-c** D C SHERWOOD   **TV** G E C FENTON

ASHBURY (St Mary the Virgin)   *see* Shrivenham and Ashbury *Ox*

ASHBY (St Mary)   *see* Somerleyton, Ashby, Fritton, Herringfleet etc *Nor*

ASHBY (St Mary)   *see* Thurton *Nor*

ASHBY (St Paul)   *see* Bottesford w Ashby *Linc*

ASHBY CUM FENBY (St Peter)   *see* Waltham Gp *Linc*

ASHBY DE LA LAUNDE (St Hybald)   *see* Digby Gp *Linc*

ASHBY FOLVILLE (St Mary)   *see* S Croxton Gp *Leic*

ASHBY MAGNA (St Mary)   *see* Willoughby Waterleys, Peatling Magna etc *Leic*

ASHBY PARVA (St Peter)   *see* Upper Soar *Leic*

ASHBY PUERORUM (St Andrew)   *see* Horncastle Gp *Linc*
ASHBY ST LEDGERS (St Mary)   *see* Daventry, Ashby St Ledgers, Braunston etc *Pet*
ASHBY, WEST (All Saints)   *see* Hemingby Gp *Linc*
ASHBY-BY-PARTNEY (St Helen)   *see* Bolingbroke Deanery *Linc*
ASHBY-DE-LA-ZOUCH (Holy Trinity) (St Helen) and Breedon on the Hill *Leic 8*   **P** *Patr Bd*   **TV** M E GREGORY, T L PHILLIPS   **NSM** A E ADSHEAD, J W A DAWSON
ASHCHURCH (St Nicholas) and Kemerton *Glouc 9*   **P** *DBP and K Storey Esq (jt)*   **P-in-c** S GRINDROD
ASHCOMBE (St Nectan)   *see* Teignmouth, Ideford w Luton, Ashcombe etc *Ex*
ASHCOTT (All Saints)   *see* Polden Wheel *B & W*
ASHDON (All Saints)   *see* Saffron Walden and Villages *Chelmsf*
ASHE (Holy Trinity and St Andrew)   *see* N Waltham and Steventon, Ashe and Deane *Win*
ASHEN (St Augustine)   *see* Two Rivers *Chelmsf*
ASHENDON (St Mary)   *see* Bernwode *Ox*
ASHFIELD CUM THORPE (St Mary)   *see* Mid Loes *St E*
ASHFIELD, GREAT (All Saints)   *see* Badwell and Walsham *St E*
ASHFORD (St Hilda) *Lon 13*   **P** *Bp*   **V** C A ROGERS
ASHFORD (St Mary the Virgin) *Cant 6*   **P** *Abp*   **V** *vacant*
ASHFORD (St Matthew) *Lon 13*   **P** *Ld Chan*   **P-in-c** S J KING
ASHFORD (St Peter)   *see* Barnstaple *Ex*
ASHFORD BOWDLER (St Andrew)   *see* Ludlow *Heref*
ASHFORD CARBONELL (St Mary) *as above*
ASHFORD HILL (St Paul)   *see* Kingsclere and Ashford Hill w Headley *Win*
ASHFORD IN THE WATER (Holy Trinity)   *see* Bakewell, Ashford w Sheldon and Rowsley *Derby*
ASHFORD, SOUTH (Christ Church) *Cant 6*   **P** *Abp*   **P-in-c** A M HIRST
ASHFORD, SOUTH (St Francis of Assisi) *Cant 6*   **P** *Abp*   **P-in-c** A M HIRST
ASHILL (Blessed Virgin Mary)   *see* Isle Valley *B & W*
ASHILL (St Nicholas), Carbrooke, Ovington and Saham Toney *Nor 13*   **P** *Bp, New Coll Ox, Cam Univ, and SMF (jt)*   **V** J E ATKINS
ASHILL (St Stephen)   *see* Willand, Uffculme, Kentisbeare etc *Ex*
ASHINGDON (St Andrew) w South Fambridge, Canewdon and Paglesham *Chelmsf 14*   **P** *D&C Westmr, Hyndman Trustees, and CCC Cam (jt)*   **R** T F CLAY
ASHINGTON (Holy Sepulchre) *Newc 11*   **P** *Bp*   **NSM** L BEADLE
ASHINGTON (St Peter and St Paul), Washington and Wiston w Buncton *Chich 11*   **P** *Bp and R H Goring Esq (alt)*   **R** J A DI CASTIGLIONE
ASHINGTON (St Vincent)   *see* Chilton Cantelo, Ashington, Mudford, Rimpton etc *B & W*
ASHLEWORTH (St Bartholomew), Corse, Hartpury, Hasfield, Maisemore, Staunton and Tirley *Glouc 3*   **P** *Bp and W G F Meath-Baker Esq (1 turn), Ld Chan (1 turn), Bp (1 turn), and Bp and DBP (1 turn)*   **R** J LONGUET-HIGGINS
ASHLEY (St Elizabeth)   *see* Hale and Ashley *Ches*
ASHLEY (St James), Crudwell, Hankerton and Oaksey *Bris 6*   **P** *Bp and Personal Reps W A Sole (3 turns), Duchy of Lancaster (1 turn)*   **P-in-c** P J DANIELS   **OLM** S J WYMAN
ASHLEY (St John the Baptist) and Mucklestone and Broughton and Croxton *Lich 7*   **P** *Bp, Meynell Ch Trustees, Mrs F F Friend, and T A J Hall Esq (jt)*   **R** J P EADES   **C** D HEMING
ASHLEY (St Mary the Virgin)   *see* Stoke Albany w Wilbarston and Ashley etc *Pet*
ASHLEY (St Mary) w Silverley *Ely 4*   **P** *Bp and DBP (alt)*   **R** *vacant*
ASHLEY (St Peter and St Paul)   *see* Test Valley *Win*
ASHLEY (St Peter)   *see* Milton *Win*
ASHLEY GREEN (St John the Evangelist)   *see* Gt Chesham *Ox*
ASHMANHAUGH (St Swithin), Barton Turf, Beeston St Laurence, Horning, Irstead and Neatishead *Nor 12*   **P** *Bp and Sir Ronald Preston Bt (jt)*   **OLM** R R HUME
ASHMANSWORTH (St James)   *see* NW Hants *Win*
ASHMORE (St Nicholas)   *see* Iwerne Valley *Sarum*
ASHMORE PARK (St Alban)   *see* Wednesfield *Lich*
ASHOVER (All Saints) and Brackenfield w Wessington *Derby 5*   **P** *Exors Revd J J C Nodder, Duke of Devonshire, V Crich and S Wingfield, and DBF (jt)*   **R** R G LAWRENCE
ASHOW (Assumption of Our Lady)   *see* Stoneleigh w Ashow *Cov*
ASHPERTON (St Bartholomew)   *see* Ledbury *Heref*
ASHPRINGTON (St David)   *see* Totnes w Bridgetown, Berry Pomeroy etc *Ex*
ASHREIGNEY (St James) *Ex 19*   **P** *DBP*   **R** P J NORMAN
ASHTEAD (St George) (St Giles) *Guildf 10*   **P** *Bp*   **R** J R JONES   **C** J R L PRIOR, S R BUTLER

ASHTON (Annunciation)   *see* W Kerrier *Truro*
ASHTON (St John the Baptist)   *see* Christow, Ashton, Bridford, Dunchideock etc *Ex*
ASHTON (St Michael and All Angels)   *see* Salcey *Pet*
ASHTON GATE (St Francis)   *see* Bedminster *Bris*
ASHTON HAYES (St John the Evangelist) *Ches 2*   **P** *Keble Coll Ox*   **V** D A LAMB
ASHTON KEYNES (Holy Cross), Leigh and Minety *Bris 6*   **P** *Bp*   **NSM** S E DANBY
ASHTON UNDER HILL (St Barbara)   *see* Overbury w Teddington, Alstone etc *Worc*
ASHTON, WEST (St John)   *see* Trowbridge St Thos and W Ashton *Sarum*
ASHTON-IN-MAKERFIELD (Holy Trinity) *Liv 14*   **P** *Bp*   **R** *vacant*
ASHTON-IN-MAKERFIELD (St Thomas) *Liv 14*   **P** *R Ashton-in-Makerfield H Trin*   **V** J P THOMAS   **C** H T COFFEY   **OLM** I SCHAFER
ASHTON-ON-RIBBLE (St Andrew)   *see* W Preston *Blackb*
ASHTON-ON-RIBBLE (St Michael and All Angels) *as above*
ASHTON-UNDER-LYNE (Christ Church) *Man 13*   **P** *Bp*   **OLM** A A HILLS
ASHTON-UNDER-LYNE Good Shepherd (Holy Trinity) (St James) (St Michael and All Angels) (St Gabriel) (St Peter) *Man 13*   **P** *Patr Bd*   **TR** R FARNWORTH   **TV** R D BATTERSHELL   **C** G E C REEVES, R W A REECE   **NSM** R FOX
ASHTON-UPON-MERSEY (St Martin) *Ches 10*   **P** *SMF*   **P-in-c** S CONLON
ASHTON-UPON-MERSEY (St Mary Magdalene) *Ches 10*   **P** *Trustees*   **V** S B RANKIN   **C** J BEAUMONT, J F C NEAL
ASHURST (St James) *Chich 11*   **P** *Bp*   **R** N C ROBERTS   **NSM** R W TOOVEY
ASHURST (St Martin of Tours)   *see* Speldhurst w Groombridge and Ashurst *Roch*
ASHURST WOOD (St Dunstan)   *see* Forest Row *Chich*
ASHWATER (St Peter ad Vincula), Halwill, Beaworthy, Clawton and Tetcott w Luffincott *Ex 16*   **P** *Ld Chan (1 turn), Ms C A Friswell, Lt Col Sir John Molesworth St Aubyn Bt, and Bp (jt) (2 turns)*   **R** J E LUCAS
ASHWELL (St Mary the Virgin) w Hinxworth and Newnham *St Alb 16*   **P** *Bp, N J A Farr Esq, and T D Smyth Esq (jt) (1 turn), Bp (3 turns)*   **R** R A EVENS
ASHWELL (St Mary)   *see* Oakham, Ashwell, Braunston, Brooke, Egleton etc *Pet*
ASHWELLTHORPE (All Saints)   *see* Upper Tas Valley *Nor*
ASHWICK (St James) w Oakhill and Binegar *B & W 7*   **P** *Bp*   **P-in-c** R A PRIESTLEY   **C** M L PRIESTLEY
ASHWICKEN (All Saints) w Leziate, Bawsey and Mintlyn, Congham, E Walton, Gayton, Gayton Thorpe, Gt Massingham, Grimston, Harpley, Lt Massingham and Roydon *Nor 20*   **P** *Patr Bd*   **TR** J M HOLMES   **TV** J M POLLARD
ASHWORTH (St James)   *see* Norden w Ashworth and Bamford *Man*
ASKAM (Church Centre)   *see* Dalton-in-Furness and Ireleth-with-Askam *Carl*
ASKAM (St Peter) *as above*
ASKERN (St Peter) *Sheff 7*   **P** *Bp*   **V** D J FRANKLIN
ASKERSWELL (St Michael), Loders, Powerstock and Symondsbury *Sarum 2*   **P** *Bp, D&C, and Lady Laskey (3 turns), Ld Chan (1 turn)*   **R** J DELANEY
ASKHAM (St Nicholas)   *see* Retford Area *S'well*
ASKHAM (St Peter)   *see* Lowther and Askham and Clifton and Brougham *Carl*
ASKHAM BRYAN (St Nicholas) *York 1*   **P** *Abp*   **V** G R MUMFORD
ASKHAM RICHARD (St Mary)   *see* N Ainsty *York*
ASKRIGG (St Oswald)   *see* Upper Wensleydale *Leeds*
ASLACKBY (St James)   *see* Billingborough Gp *Linc*
ASLACTON (St Michael)   *see* Bunwell, Carleton Rode, Tibenham, Gt Moulton etc *Nor*
ASLOCKTON (St Thomas)   *see* Whatton w Aslockton, Hawksworth, Scarrington etc *S'well*
ASPALL (St Mary of Grace)   *see* Debenham and Helmingham *St E*
ASPATRIA (St Kentigern) w Hayton and Gilcrux *Carl 7*   **P** *Bp*   **P-in-c** T D HERBERT   **Hon C** D R KING   **NSM** C J KENNEDY
ASPENDEN (St Mary), Buntingford and Westmill *St Alb 16*   **P** *CPAS, MCET, and K Coll Lon (jt)*   **R** I R HILL
ASPLEY (St Margaret) *S'well 8*   **P** *Trustees*   **V** J G HUTCHINSON   **NSM** W J BRADLEY
ASPLEY GUISE (St Botolph) w Husborne Crawley and Ridgmont *St Alb 8*   **P** *Ld Chan (1 turn), Trustees Bedf Estates (1 turn), and Bp (2 turns)*   **R** G BRADSHAW

ASPULL (St Elizabeth) *see* Wigan All SS *Liv*
ASSINGTON (St Edmund) *see* Bures w Assington and Lt Cornard *St E*
ASTBURY (St Mary) and Smallwood *Ches 11* P *Sir Richard Baker Wilbraham Bt* R J C CUTTELL
ASTERBY Group, The *Linc 13* P *Bp, DBP, C N A f Heneage Esq, and F Smith Esq (jt)* R P J FRASER
ASTHALL (St Nicholas) *see* Burford w Fulbrook, Taynton, Asthall etc *Ox*
ASTLEY (St Mary the Virgin) *see* Chilvers Coton w Astley *Cov*
ASTLEY (St Mary), Clive, Grinshill and Hadnall *Lich 22* P D R B Thompson Esq P-in-c R R HAARHOFF
ASTLEY (St Peter) *see* Shrawley, Witley, Astley and Abberley *Worc*
ASTLEY (St Stephen), Tyldesley and Mosley Common *Man 19* P *DBP and V Leigh* TV J J HARTLEY NSM J HARNEY OLM A J DAND
ASTLEY ABBOTTS (St Calixtus) *see* Bridgnorth, Tasley, Astley Abbotts, etc *Heref*
ASTLEY BRIDGE (St Paul) *Man 12* P *The Crown* V N J MCKEE C B R WOODFIELD
ASTON (St Giles) *see* Wigmore Abbey *Heref*
ASTON (St James) (St Peter and St Paul) and Nechells *Birm 8* P *Patr Bd* V A J JOLLEY C R A JONES NSM G S KAYLA, M E HARMON
ASTON (St Mary) *see* Woore and Norton in Hales *Lich*
ASTON (St Mary) *see* Stevenage St Mary Shephall w Aston *St Alb*
ASTON (St Peter) *see* Aston by Sutton, Lt Leigh and Lower Whitley *Ches*
ASTON (St Saviour) *see* Stone St Mich and St Wulfad w Aston *St Sav Lich*
ASTON ABBOTS (St James the Great) *see* Cottesloe *Ox*
ASTON BOTTERELL (St Michael and All Angels) *see* Ditton Priors w Neenton, Burwarton etc *Heref*
ASTON BY SUTTON (St Peter), Little Leigh and Lower Whitley *Ches 4* P *Bp, V Gt Budworth, Lord Daresbury, and B H Talbot Esq (jt)* V C M Y JONES
ASTON CANTLOW (St John the Baptist) and Wilmcote w Billesley *Cov 7* P *SMF* P-in-c R LIVINGSTON Hon C P R BROWN
ASTON CLINTON (St Michael and All Angels) w Buckland and Drayton Beauchamp *Ox 17* P *Bp, A R Pegg Esq, and Jes Coll Ox (jt)* R E J MOXLEY C S BOTTOMER
ASTON CUM AUGHTON (All Saints) w Swallownest and Ulley *Sheff 5* P *Bp* C S M COLVER
ASTON EYRE (not known) *see* Morville w Aston Eyre *Heref*
ASTON FLAMVILLE (St Peter) *see* Burbage w Aston Flamville *Leic*
ASTON INGHAM (St John the Baptist) *see* Ariconium *Heref*
ASTON ON TRENT (All Saints), Elvaston, Weston on Trent and Shardlow, Barrow upon Trent with Twyford and Swarkestone *Derby 15* P *Bp, Earl of Harrington, and Repton Sch (jt)* R A LUKE NSM P HYGATE
ASTON ROWANT (St Peter and St Paul) *see* Chinnor, Sydenham, Aston Rowant and Crowell *Ox*
ASTON SANDFORD (St Michael and All Angels) *see* Haddenham w Cuddington, Kingsey etc *Ox*
ASTON SOMERVILLE (St Mary) *see* Winchcombe *Glouc*
ASTON TIRROLD (St Michael) *see* The Churn *Ox*
ASTON UPTHORPE (All Saints) *as above*
ASTON, LITTLE (St Peter) *Lich 1* P *Patr Bd* V P MOON C A C J GOMPERTZ
ASTON, NORTH (St Mary the Virgin) *see* Steeple Aston w N Aston and Tackley *Ox*
ASTON-LE-WALLS (St Leonard), Byfield, Boddington, Eydon and Woodford Halse *Pet 1* P *Bp, CCC Ox, and Em Coll Cam (2 turns), Ld Chan (1 turn)* R S CROSS NSM G D MOORE
ASTON-SUB-EDGE (St Andrew) *see* Vale and Cotswold Edge *Glouc*
ASTWELL Group of Parishes, The *Pet 1* P *Bp, Worc Coll Ox, Ox Univ, Mert Coll Ox, DBP, and Jes Coll Ox (jt)* R C J PETERS
ASTWICK (St Guthlac) *see* Arlesey w Astwick *St Alb*
ASTWOOD BANK (St Matthias and St George) *see* Redditch Ch the K *Worc*
ASWARBY (St Denys) *see* S Lafford *Linc*
ASWARDBY (St Helen) *see* Bolingbroke Deanery *Linc*
ATCHAM (St Eata) *see* Shrewsbury St Giles w Sutton and Atcham *Lich*
ATHELINGTON (St Peter), Denham, Horham, Hoxne, Redlingfield, Syleham and Wingfield *St E 15* P *Bp, DBP, Lt Comdr G C Marshall, and H F Soden Esq (jt)* R M J WOMACK
ATHELNEY Benefice, The *B & W 13* P *D&C* V P A STAPLE
ATHERINGTON (St Mary) *see* Newton Tracey, Horwood, Alverdiscott etc *Ex*

ATHERSLEY (St Helen) and Carlton *Leeds 18* P *DBP and Bp (jt)* V R H MARSHALL
ATHERSTONE (St Mary) *Cov 5* P V *Mancetter* V *vacant*
ATHERTON (St John the Baptist) (St George) (St Philip) and Hindsford w Howe Bridge *Man 19* P *DBP* TV R W SINCLAIR OLM D SIVILL, K E SLAYEN
ATLOW (St Philip and St James) *see* Hulland, Atlow, Kniveton, Bradley and Hognaston *Derby*
ATTENBOROUGH (St Mary the Virgin) *S'well 9* P *CPAS* V J P SMITHURST
ATTERCLIFFE (St Alban) and Darnall *Sheff 1* P *Bp, Dean Sheff, and Sheff Ch Burgesses Trust (jt)* V *vacant*
ATTLEBOROUGH (Assumption of the Blessed Virgin Mary) w Besthorpe *Nor 11* P *CR and Mrs S P J Scully (jt)* R M C JACKSON C R O STANTON
ATTLEBOROUGH (Holy Trinity) *Cov 5* P V *Nuneaton* V C JONES
ATTLEBRIDGE (St Andrew) *see* Wensum Benefice *Nor*
ATWICK (St Lawrence) *see* Hornsea w Atwick *York*
ATWORTH (St Michael and All Angels) w Shaw and Whitley *Sarum 15* P *D&C Bris and R Melksham (alt)* V S M HOAD C A E EVANS NSM R E GILLINGS
AUBOURN (St Peter) *see* Bassingham Gp *Linc*
AUCKLAND (St Andrew) *see* Bishop Auckland *Dur*
AUCKLAND (St Anne) *as above*
AUCKLAND (St Helen) *Dur 6* P *Bp* V R I MCTEER
AUCKLEY (St Saviour) *see* Finningley w Auckley *Sheff*
AUDENSHAW (St Hilda) *Man 13* P *Bp* V J H KERSHAW
AUDENSHAW (St Stephen) *Man 13* P *Bp* V P R DIXON C A S MITCHELL, E M POPE, M HOWARTH
AUDLEM (St James) *see* Wybunbury and Audlem w Doddington *Ches*
AUDLEY (St James the Great) *see* Alsagers Bank, Audley and Talke *Lich*
AUGHTON (All Saints) *see* Bubwith w Skipwith *York*
AUGHTON (Christ Church) *Liv 11* P *R Aughton St Mich* V R MOUGHTIN C S H O'DONOGHUE
AUGHTON (St Michael) and Bickerstaffe *Liv 11* P *Bp and Earl of Derby (jt)* R A A HOUSLEY Hon C M P ADAMS
AUGHTON (St Saviour) *see* Slyne w Hest and Halton w Aughton *Blackb*
AULT HUCKNALL (St John the Baptist) and Scarcliffe *Derby 3* P *Bp and Duke of Devonshire (alt)* V *vacant*
AUNSBY (St Thomas of Canterbury) *see* S Lafford *Linc*
AUST (not known) *see* Almondsbury and Olveston *Bris*
AUSTERFIELD (St Helen) *see* Bawtry w Austerfield, Misson, Everton and Mattersey *S'well*
AUSTREY (St Nicholas) *see* N Warks *Birm*
AUSTWICK (Epiphany) *see* Clapham-with-Keasden and Austwick *Leeds*
AVEBURY (St James) *see* Upper Kennet *Sarum*
AVENING (Holy Cross) w Cherington *Glouc 7* P *E A Tarlton Esq (1 turn), D&C (2 turns)* R V J HUGHES
AVERHAM (St Michael and All Angels) w Kelham *S'well 3* P *DBP* NSM C WALL
AVETON GIFFORD (St Andrew) *see* Modbury, Bigbury, Ringmore etc *Ex*
AVINGTON (St Mary) *see* Itchen Valley *Win*
AVON DASSETT w Farnborough and Fenny Compton *Cov 8* P *G V L Holbech Esq and Mrs A D Seyfried (jt), CCC Ox, and Bp (alt)* P-in-c M G CADWALLADER
AVON RIVER Team *Sarum 14* P *Patr Bd* TV G A HUNT NSM R A BUSSEY OLM T DRAYCOTT
AVONMOUTH (St Andrew) *see* Lawrence Weston and Avonmouth *Bris*
AVONWICK (St James' Chapel) *see* Diptford, N Huish, Harberton, Harbertonford etc *Ex*
AWBRIDGE (All Saints) *see* Michelmersh and Awbridge and Braishfield etc *Win*
AWLISCOMBE (St Michael and All Angels) *see* Honiton, Gittisham, Combe Raleigh, Monkton etc *Ex*
AWRE (St Andrew) *see* Newnham w Awre and Blakeney *Glouc*
AWSWORTH (St Peter) *see* Trowell, Awsworth and Cossall *S'well*
AXBRIDGE (St John the Baptist) w Shipham and Rowberrow *B & W 1* P *Bp and D&C (alt)* R T D HAWKINGS
AXFORD (St Michael) *see* Whitton *Sarum*
AXMINSTER (St Mary), Chardstock, All Saints, Combpyne w Rousdon and Membury *Ex 4* P *Bp* TR J W STREETING C G M WALSH
AXMOUTH (St Michael) *see* Uplyme w Axmouth *Ex*
AYCLIFFE (Church Centre) *see* Dover Town *Cant*
AYCLIFFE, GREAT (St Andrew) (St Clare) *Dur 5* P *Patr Bd* TR C W PEARSON TV E A BLAND C D J LOUGHRAN
AYLBURTON (St Mary) *see* Woolaston w Alvington and Aylburton *Glouc*

AYLESBEARE (Blessed Virgin Mary), Clyst St George, Clyst St Mary, Farringdon, Woodbury w Exton, and Woodbury Salterton *Ex 1* **P** *Bp, D&C, Lord Wraxall, and Mrs S Radcliffe (jt)* **V** K P SPRAY **C** C S T CANT
AYLESBURY (St Mary the Virgin) *Ox 10* **P** *Bp and Patr Bd (jt)* **TR** D L ZIMMERMAN **TV** G E LANE
AYLESBURY (St Mary the Virgin) *see Aylesbury Ox*
AYLESBY (St Lawrence) *see Wolds Gateway Group Linc*
AYLESFORD (St Peter and St Paul) *Roch 7* **P** *D&C* **V** C J VAN STRAATEN
AYLESHAM (St Peter) w Adisham and Nonington *Cant 1* **P** *Abp and Lord Fitzwalter (jt)* **C** M D TERRY
AYLESTONE (St Andrew) w St James *Leic 1* **P** *Bp* **R** *vacant*
AYLMERTON (St John the Baptist), Runton, Beeston Regis, Gresham *Nor 21* **P** *Bp and Guild of All So (2 turns), Duchy of Lanc (1 turn)* **R** D N HEAD
AYLSHAM (St Michael) *Nor 19* **P** *D&C Cant* **P-in-c** A M BEANE
AYLTON (not known) *see Ledbury Heref*
AYMESTREY (St John the Baptist and St Alkmund) *see Kingsland w Eardisland, Aymestrey etc Heref*
AYNHO (St Michael) and Croughton w Evenley and Farthinghoe and Hinton-in-the-Hedges w Steane *Pet 1* **P** *Bp (2 turns), Mrs E A J Cartwright-Hignett (1 turn), Magd Coll Ox (1 turn), and Ld Chan (1 turn)* **R** S P DOMMETT **C** S MATHEW
AYOT ST LAWRENCE (St Lawrence) *see Kimpton w Ayot St Lawrence St Alb*
AYOT ST PETER (St Peter) *see Welwyn St Alb*
AYSGARTH (St Andrew) *see Penhill Leeds*
AYTHORPE RODING (St Mary) *see Gt Canfield w High Roding and Aythorpe Roding Chelmsf*
AYTON, EAST (St John the Baptist) *see Seamer w East Ayton York*
AYTON, GREAT (All Saints) (Christ Church) w Easby and Newton under Roseberry *York 20* **P** *Abp* **V** P H PEVERELL **NSM** G S JAQUES, J C DEAN
BABBACOMBE (All Saints) *Ex 11* **P** *V St Marychurch* **P-in-c** P E JONES
BABCARY (Holy Cross) *see Six Pilgrims B & W*
BABRAHAM (St Peter) *Ely 5* **P** *H R T Adeane Esq* **P-in-c** A C PARTRIDGE
BABWORTH (All Saints) *see Retford Area S'well*
BACKFORD (St Oswald) and Capenhurst *Ches 9* **P** *Bp* **R** S M SOUTHGATE
BACKWELL (St Andrew) w Chelvey and Brockley *B & W 12* **P** *DBP* **R** M R CAMPBELL
BACKWORTH (St John) *see Earsdon and Backworth Newc*
BACONSTHORPE (St Mary) *see Barningham w Matlaske w Baconsthorpe etc Nor*
BACTON (St Andrew), Happisburgh, Hempstead w Eccles and Lessingham, Ridlington, Sea Palling w Waxham, Walcott, and Witton *Nor 12* **P** *Bp, Earl of Kimberley, K Coll Cam, and Sir Edward Evans-Lombe (jt)* **R** C H DOBSON
BACTON (St Faith) *see Ewyas Harold w Dulas, Kenderchurch etc Heref*
BACTON (St Mary the Virgin) w Wyverstone, Cotton and Old Newton, and Wickham Skeith *St E 6* **P** *Patr Bd (2 turns), Ld Chan (1 turn)* **R** *vacant*
BACUP Christ Church and Stacksteads *Man 11* **P** *Patr Bd* **TV** D BRAE **OLM** D ALLEN
BADBY (St Mary) w Newnham and Charwelton w Fawsley and Preston Capes *Pet 3* **P** *Bp* **R** S A FAULKNER
BADDESLEY CLINTON (St Michael) *Birm 6* **P** *T W Ferrers-Walker Esq* **R** P H GERARD
BADDESLEY ENSOR (St Nicholas) w Grendon *Birm 10* **P** *Bp, V Polesworth, and PCC (jt)* **V** R E CHAMBERLAIN
BADDESLEY, NORTH (All Saints' Mission Church) *see Ampfield, Chilworth and N Baddesley Win*
BADDESLEY, NORTH (St John the Baptist) *as above*
BADDESLEY, SOUTH (St Mary the Virgin) *see Boldre w S Baddesley Win*
BADDILEY (St Michael) and Wrenbury w Burleydam *Ches 15* **P** *V Acton and Bp (alt)* **P-in-c** A J FULFORD
BADDOW, GREAT (Meadgate Church Centre) (St Mary the Virgin) (St Paul) *Chelmsf 10* **P** *Patr Bd* **TR** D P RITCHIE **TV** P J W SHELDRAKE, T W BALL **C** R HAMBORG, K E DE BOURCIER **Hon C** R C MATTHEWS **OLM** S FINCH
BADDOW, LITTLE (St Mary the Virgin) *Chelmsf 10* **P** *Bp* **C** G R HAMBORG
BADGER (St Giles) *see Beckbury, Badger, Kemberton, Ryton, Stockton etc Lich*
BADGEWORTH (Holy Trinity), Shurdington and Witcombe w Bentham *Glouc 3* **P** *Bp and F D Hicks Beach Esq (jt)* **R** R J A MITCHELL **C** S A DANGERFIELD **NSM** A E JONES
BADGWORTH (St Congar) *see Crook Peak B & W*

BADLESMERE (St Leonard) *see Downsfoot Cant*
BADMINTON (St Michael and All Angels) *see Boxwell, Leighterton, Didmarton, Oldbury etc Glouc*
BADMINTON, LITTLE (St Michael and All Angels) *as above*
BADSEY (St James) w Aldington and Offenham and Bretforton *Worc 1* **P** *Bp and Ch Ch Ox (jt)* **V** *vacant*
BADSHOT LEA (St George) and Hale *Guildf 3* **P** *Bp* **R** L J CRAWLEY **NSM** A J CRAWLEY
BADSWORTH (St Mary the Virgin) *Leeds 19* **P** *DBP* **P-in-c** S J HOTCHEN
BADWELL (St Mary) and Walsham *St E 9* **P** *Bp, DBP, R M Martineau Esq, and Soc of the Faith (jt)* **C** K A VALENTINE
BAG ENDERBY (St Margaret) *see S Ormsby Gp Linc*
BAGBOROUGH (St Pancras) *see Bishop's Lydeard w Lydeard St Lawrence etc B & W*
BAGBY (St Mary) *see Thirkleby w Kilburn and Bagby York*
BAGENDON (St Margaret) *see Churn Valley Glouc*
BAGINTON (St John the Baptist) w Bubbenhall and Ryton-on-Dunsmore *Cov 6* **P** *D&C (2 turns), Bp (1 turn), Lord Leigh and Bp (1 turn)* **V** D R WINTLE
BAGNALL (St Chad) w Endon *Lich 8* **P** *R Leek and Meerbrook and A D Owen Esq (jt)* **V** A J BETTS
BAGSHOT (Good Shepherd) *see Savernake Sarum*
BAGSHOT (St Anne) *Guildf 6* **P** *Ld Chan* **V** A SISTIG
BAGULEY (St John the Divine) Brooklands *Man 6* **P** *Bp and A W Hargreaves Esq (jt)* **V** *vacant*
BAILDON (St John the Evangelist) (St Hugh Mission Church) (St James) *Leeds 1* **P** *J P Baxter Esq* **NSM** C V SKELTON, S KENNEDY
BAIN VALLEY Group, The *Linc 13* **P** *Baroness Willoughby de Eresby, T J Spurrier Esq, and DBP (1 turn), Ld Chan (1 turn)* **NSM** R E DONE **OLM** M DONE
BAINTON (St Andrew) *see Woldsburn York*
BAINTON (St Mary) *see Barnack w Ufford and Bainton Pet*
BAKEWELL (All Saints), Ashford in the Water w Sheldon and Rowsley *Derby 2* **P** *Bp, D&C, and Duke of Rutland (jt)* **V** A P KAUNHOVEN **C** A B SIMPSON, P L DAVIS
BALBY (St John the Evangelist) *Sheff 9* **P** *Bp* **P-in-c** A PRICE
BALCOMBE (St Mary) *Chich 5* **P** *P A D Secretan Esq* **P-in-c** D J BURTON
BALDERSBY (St James) *see Topcliffe, Baldersby w Dishforth, Dalton etc York*
BALDERSTONE (St Leonard), Mellor and Samlesbury *Blackb 7* **P** *V Blackb St Mary and St Paul* **V** S J WILLIAMS
BALDERSTONE (St Mary) *Man 17* **P** *Trustees* **V** A FORD **C** T J WICKHAM
BALDERTON (St Giles) and Barnby-in-the-Willows *S'well 3* **P** *Bp and Ld Chan (alt)* **V** *vacant*
BALDOCK (St Mary the Virgin) w Bygrave *St Alb 16* **P** *Bp and Marquess of Salisbury (jt)* **R** A P HOLFORD
BALDWIN (St Luke) *see Marown, Foxdale and Baldwin S & M*
BALE (All Saints) *see Stiffkey and Bale Nor*
BALHAM (St Mary and St John the Divine) *S'wark 17* **P** *Bp and Keble Coll Ox (jt)* **V** W ROEST **NSM** I S FAULKNER **OLM** R E SERBUTT
BALHAM HILL (Ascension) *S'wark 17* **P** *Bp* **V** M T GIBBS **C** A L WILLIAMS
BALKWELL (St Peter) *Newc 5* **P** *Bp* **P-in-c** F M WILSON **NSM** A M MCGIVERN
BALLAM (St Matthew) *see Ribby cum Wrea and Weeton Blackb*
BALLAUGH (St Mary Old Church) *see Andreas, Ballaugh, Jurby and Sulby S & M*
BALLAUGH (St Mary) *as above*
BALLINGER (St Mary Mission Hall) *see Gt Missenden w Ballinger and Lt Hampden Ox*
BALSALL COMMON (St Peter) *Birm 11* **P** *Bp* **V** P W THOMAS
BALSALL HEATH (St Barnabas) *see Sparkbrook St Agatha w Balsall Heath St Barn Birm*
BALSALL HEATH (St Paul) and Edgbaston *Birm 5* **P** *Bp and Sir Euan Anstruther-Gough-Calthorpe Bt (jt)* **V** C A GRYLLS **C** D M COLLINS
BALSCOTE (St Mary Magdalene) *see Ironstone Ox*
BALSHAM (Holy Trinity), Weston Colville, West Wickham and West Wratting *Ely 5* **P** *Bp, D&C, and Charterhouse (jt)* **P-in-c** J M NORRIS **Hon C** J M FELLOWS **NSM** K R BISHOP
BALTERLEY (All Saints' Memorial Church) *see Barthomley Ches*
BALTONSBOROUGH (St Dunstan) w Butleigh, West Bradley and West Pennard *B & W 4* **P** *Bp* **P-in-c** J A JEFFERY
BAMBER BRIDGE (St Aidan) *Blackb 5* **P** *Bp* **P-in-c** S JOHNSON **NSM** N J PROCTER
BAMBER BRIDGE (St Saviour) *Blackb 5* **P** *V Blackb* **V** G HALSALL
BAMBURGH (St Aidan) *Newc 7* **P** *Exors Lady Armstrong* **V** B C HURST

BAMFORD (St John the Baptist) *see* Hathersage w Bamford and Derwent and Grindleford *Derby*

BAMFORD (St Michael) *see* Norden w Ashworth and Bamford *Man*

BAMPTON (Holy Trinity) (St James) (St Mary) w Clanfield *Ox 28* **P** *Bp, DBP, St Jo Coll Ox, D&C Ex, and B Babington-Smith Esq (jt)* **V** D J LLOYD

BAMPTON (St Michael and All Angels), Morebath, Clayhanger, Petton and Huntsham *Ex 7* **P** *Bp, DBP, and D&C (jt)* **V** K D N CHANDRA

BAMPTON (St Patrick) *see* Shap w Swindale and Bampton w Mardale *Carl*

BAMPTON ASTON (St James) *see* Bampton w Clanfield *Ox*

BAMPTON LEW (Holy Trinity) *as above*

BAMPTON PROPER (St Mary) *as above*

BANBURY (St Francis) *Ox 23* **P** *Bp* **V** C T GAYNOR **C** J P GOODMAN

BANBURY (St Hugh) *Ox 23* **P** *Bp* **P-in-c** A E SMITH

BANBURY (St Leonard) *Ox 23* **P** *Bp* **V** E S BURCHELL

BANBURY (St Mary) *Ox 23* **P** *Bp* **R** L J GREEN **C** B J SHIN **NSM** J J WEST

BANBURY (St Paul) *Ox 23* **P** *Bp* **C** R V J POWER

BANHAM (St Mary) *see* Quidenham Gp *Nor*

BANKFOOT (St Matthew) and Bowling St Stephen *Leeds 2* **P** *Bp and CPAS (jt)* **V** J W HINTON **C** A S TREASURE

BANNINGHAM (St Botolph) *see* King's Beck *Nor*

BANSFIELD *St E 8* **P** *DBP, Mrs G S M Slater, and Ld Chan (by turn)* **R** D B SINGLETON

BANSTEAD (All Saints) *Guildf 9* **P** *Bp* **V** M PALLIS **C** A S MACVEAN **NSM** V TURNER

BANWELL (St Andrew) *B & W 10* **P** *D&C Bris* **C** J E S BILLETT **NSM** J M H SIMS

BAPCHILD (St Laurence) *see* Murston w Bapchild and Tonge *Cant*

BAR HILL (not known) *Ely 6* **P** *Bp* **V** *vacant*

BARBON (St Bartholomew) *see* Kirkby Lonsdale *Carl*

BARBOURNE (St Stephen) *Worc 6* **P** *Bp* **V** S W CURRIE **C** A G TODD **NSM** G D MORPHY, J B WEBB

BARBY (St Mary) w Kilsby *Pet 3* **P** *Bp* **R** *vacant*

BARCHESTON (St Martin) *see* S Warks Seven Gp *Cov*

BARCOMBE (St Francis) (St Mary the Virgin) *Chich 21* **P** *Ld Chan* **R** J W HOLLINGSWORTH **C** P K MUNDY

BARDFIELD, GREAT (St Mary the Virgin) and LITTLE (St Katherine) *Chelmsf 18* **P** *Ch Union Trust* **P-in-c** R W F BEAKEN

BARDNEY (St Lawrence) *Linc 13* **P** *DBP (1 turn), Bp (2 turns), and St Jo Coll Cam (1 turn)* **R** D W BARTLETT **NSM** H E JEFFERY

BARDON HILL (St Peter) *see* Coalville w Bardon Hill and Ravenstone *Leic*

BARDSEA (Holy Trinity) *see* Pennington and Lindal w Marton and Bardsea *Carl*

BARDSEY (All Hallows) *Leeds 14* **P** *G L Fox Esq* **P-in-c** C M SEDGEWICK

BARDSLEY (Holy Trinity) *Man 16* **P** *Wm Hulme Trustees* **V** A D GRANT **OLM** E M LOWE

BARDWELL (St Peter and St Paul) *see* Blackbourne *St E*

BARE (St Christopher) *Blackb 11* **P** *Bp* **V** D L HEAP

BARFORD (St Botolph) *see* Barnham Broom and Upper Yare *Nor*

BARFORD (St John) *see* Deddington w Barford, Clifton and Hempton *Ox*

BARFORD (St Martin) *see* Nadder Valley *Sarum*

BARFORD (St Michael) *see* Deddington w Barford, Clifton and Hempton *Ox*

BARFORD (St Peter) w Wasperton and Sherbourne *Cov 8* **P** *Major J M Mills, R Hampton Lucy, and Lady Jeryl Smith-Ryland (jt)* **P-in-c** D C JESSETT

BARFORD, GREAT (All Saints) *see* Riversmeet *St Alb*

BARFREYSTONE (St Nicholas) *see* Bewsborough *Cant*

BARHAM (St Giles) *see* E Leightonstone *Ely*

BARHAM (St John the Baptist) *see* Barham Downs *Cant*

BARHAM (St Mary) *see* Claydon and Barham *St E*

BARHAM DOWNS *Cant 1* **P** *Abp* **P-in-c** S J A HARDY **NSM** L A HARDY

BARHOLME (St Martin) *see* Uffington Gp *Linc*

BARKBY (St Mary) *see* Fosse *Leic*

BARKESTONE (St Peter and St Paul) *see* Vale of Belvoir *Leic*

BARKHAM (St James) *see* Arborfield w Barkham *Ox*

BARKING (St Erkenwald) *Chelmsf 1* **P** *Bp* **V** *vacant*

BARKING (St Margaret) (St Patrick) (Christ Church) *Chelmsf 1* **P** *Patr Bd* **TR** M T S MWAMBA **TV** C CHAMBERS, G P DOWLING **NSM** E JOHN

BARKING (St Mary) *see* Ringshall w Battisford, Barking w Darmsden etc *St E*

BARKINGSIDE (Holy Trinity) *Chelmsf 6* **P** *V Gt Ilford* **P-in-c** S W BATTEN **NSM** M FLINTOFT-CHAPMAN **OLM** R POTTEN

BARKINGSIDE (St Cedd) *Chelmsf 6* **P** *Bp* **V** *vacant*

BARKINGSIDE (St Francis of Assisi) *Chelmsf 6* **P** *Bp* **P-in-c** S W BATTEN **C** M L BRADLEY **NSM** M L BRADLEY

BARKINGSIDE (St George) *Chelmsf 6* **P** *Bp* **V** B J WALLIS

BARKINGSIDE (St Laurence) *Chelmsf 6* **P** *Bp* **P-in-c** C M BURROWS **OLM** H MUSKER

BARKISLAND (Christ Church) w West Scammonden *Leeds 11* **P** *V Halifax* **V** C J BALL **NSM** C A HIRST

BARKSTON (St Nicholas) and Hough Group, The *Linc 22* **P** *Sir Oliver Thorold Bt, J R Thorold Esq, Lord Brownlow, and Sir Lyonel Tollemache Bt (by turn)* **C** L E M HALL **NSM** S J HADLEY

BARKSTON ASH (Holy Trinity) *see* Sherburn in Elmet w Saxton *York*

BARKWAY (St Mary Magdalene), Reed and Buckland w Barley *St Alb 16* **P** *The Crown and DBP (alt)* **NSM** S O FALASCHI-RAY

BARKWITH Group, The *Linc 7* **P** *D&C, J N Heneage Esq, K Coll Lon, and DBP (by turn)* **R** *vacant*

BARKWITH, EAST (St Mary) *see* Barkwith Gp *Linc*

BARLASTON (St John the Baptist) *Lich 13* **P** *Countess of Sutherland* **P-in-c** H M BARTON **C** C M CASE

BARLAVINGTON (St Mary), Burton w Coates and Sutton w Bignor *Chich 10* **P** *Lord Egremont and Miss J B Courtauld (jt)* **P-in-c** J F H GREEN

BARLBOROUGH (St James) and Clowne *Derby 3* **P** *Ld Chan and Mrs A Hayward (alt)* **R** S T SHORT

BARLBY (All Saints) *see* Riccall, Barlby and Hemingbrough *York*

BARLESTONE (St Giles) *see* Newbold de Verdun, Barlestone and Kirkby Mallory *Leic*

BARLEY (St Margaret of Antioch) *see* Barkway, Reed and Buckland w Barley *St Alb*

BARLEY HILL *see* Thame *Ox*

BARLING (All Saints) w Little Wakering *Chelmsf 14* **P** *D&C St Paul's and Bp (alt)* **P-in-c** A J HURD

BARLING MAGNA (All Saints) *see* Barling w Lt Wakering *Chelmsf*

BARLINGS (St Edward) *Linc 5* **P** *DBP* **V** D P GREEN **C** C W HEWITT

BARLOW MOOR (Emmanuel) *see* Didsbury St Jas and Em *Man*

BARLOW, GREAT (St Lawrence) *see* Old Brampton and Great Barlow *Derby*

BARMBY MOOR Group, The (St Catherine) *York 5* **P** *Abp (1 turn), Abp and Trustees Duke of Norfolk's Settlement Everingham Fund (2 turns)* **V** J F HARDY

BARMING (St Margaret of Antioch) w West Barming *Roch 7* **P** *Ld Chan* **R** W W NORTH

BARMING HEATH (St Andrew) *Cant 12* **P** *Abp* **P-in-c** C P LAVENDER

BARMSTON (All Saints) *see* Skipsea and Barmston w Fraisthorpe *York*

BARNACK (St John the Baptist) w Ufford and Bainton *Pet 11* **P** *Bp and St Jo Coll Cam (alt)* **P-in-c** D C MAYLOR

BARNACRE (All Saints) *see* Scorton and Barnacre and Calder Vale *Blackb*

BARNARD CASTLE (St Mary) w Whorlton *Dur 7* **P** *Trin Coll Cam* **V** A J HARDING

BARNARDISTON (All Saints) *see* Stourhead *St E*

BARNBURGH (St Peter) w Melton on the Hill and Aldwick-upon-Dearne *Sheff 12* **P** *Ld Chan (2 turns), Bp (1 turn)* **P-in-c** A C GRIFFITHS

BARNBY (St John the Baptist) *see* Worlingham w Barnby and N Cove *St E*

BARNBY DUN (St Peter and St Paul) *Sheff 8* **P** *Bp* **P-in-c** D D SIRCAR

BARNBY IN THE WILLOWS (All Saints) *see* Balderton and Barnby-in-the-Willows *S'well*

BARNEHURST (St Martin) *Roch 15* **P** *Bp* **V** G J BOWEN

BARNES Team Ministry, The (St Mary) (Holy Trinity) (St Michael and All Angels) *S'wark 16* **P** *Patr Bd* **TR** R M SEWELL **TV** D M R COOKE **C** A G RYLETT, A L LYNES

BARNET (Christ Church) *see* S Mimms Ch Ch *Lon*

BARNET (St John the Baptist) *see* Chipping Barnet *St Alb*

BARNET (St Stephen) *as above*

BARNET VALE (St Mark) *as above*

BARNET, EAST (St Mary the Virgin) *St Alb 14* **P** *The Crown* **R** J E A MUSTARD **C** S C KORN

BARNET, NEW (St James) *St Alb 14* **P** *Ch Patr Trust* **V** B UNWIN

BARNETBY LE WOLD (St Barnabas) *see* N Wolds Gp *Linc*

BARNEY (St Mary), Hindringham, Thursford, Great Snoring, Little Snoring and Kettlestone and Pensthorpe *Nor* 15
   P *D&C (1 turn), DBP and Lord Hastings (1 turn), St Jo Coll Cam (1 turn)*   R J MUGGLETON
BARNHAM (St Gregory)   *see Blackbourne St E*
BARNHAM (St Mary)   *see Aldingbourne, Barnham and Eastergate Chich*
BARNHAM BROOM (St Peter and St Paul) and Upper Yare *Nor* 17   P *Patr Bd*   TR T A P WEATHERSTONE
   OLM R A JACKSON
BARNINGHAM (St Andrew)   *see Stanton, Hopton, Market Weston, Barningham etc St E*
BARNINGHAM (St Mary the Virgin) w Matlaske w Baconsthorpe w Plumstead w Hempstead *Nor* 18   P *Duchy of Lanc (1 turn), Lady Mott-Radclyffe, CPAS, and D&C (jt) (1 turn)*   P-in-c M J HARRISON   Hon C B T FAULKNER
BARNINGHAM (St Michael and All Angels) w Hutton Magna and Wycliffe *Leeds* 24   P *Bp and V Gilling and Kirkby Ravensworth (jt)*   P-in-c A P KIRBY
BARNINGHAM WINTER (St Mary the Virgin)   *see Barningham w Matlaske w Baconsthorpe etc Nor*
BARNINGHAM, LITTLE (St Andrew), Blickling, Edgefield, Itteringham w Mannington, Oulton w Irmingland, Saxthorpe w Corpusty and Wickmere w Wolterton *Nor* 19
   P *Bp, Lord Walpole, SMF, MMCET (2 turns), and Pemb Coll Cam (1 turn)*   P-in-c M J HARRISON   Hon C B T FAULKNER
BARNOLDBY LE BECK (St Helen)   *see Waltham Gp Linc*
BARNOLDSWICK (Holy Trinity) (St Mary le Gill) w Bracewell *Leeds* 26   P *Bp*   V D B WEAVER   Hon C H C GREENWOOD
BARNSBURY (St Andrew) *Lon* 6   P *Patr Bd*
   TR M W LEARMOUTH   TV D E FELL   C J S SWIFT, M FLETCHER
BARNSLEY (St Edward the Confessor) *Leeds* 18   P *Bp*
   P-in-c M S POSKITT
BARNSLEY (St George's Parish Church Centre) *Leeds* 18
   P *Bp*   V D P J MUNBY
BARNSLEY (St Mary) *Leeds* 18   P *Bp*   R vacant
BARNSLEY (St Mary)   *see S Cotswolds Glouc*
BARNSLEY (St Paul) Old Town   *see Barnsley St Mary Leeds*
BARNSLEY (St Peter and St John the Baptist) *Leeds* 18   P *Bp*
   P-in-c P CARTWRIGHT
BARNSTAPLE (St Peter and St Mary Magdalene) (Holy Trinity) *Ex* 14   P *Patr Bd (4 turns), Ld Chan (1 turn)*
   TV G CHAVE-COX, N B DILKES   C A DODWELL, D M FLETCHER, S G MAY   NSM M SANDERS, S A PATERSON
BARNSTON (Christ Church) *Ches* 8   P *Bp*   V P M FROGGATT
   C I G URQUHART, J DURBIN
BARNSTON (St Andrew)   *see Gt Dunmow and Barnston Chelmsf*
BARNSTONE (St Mary Mission Room)   *see Cropwell Bishop w Colston Bassett, Granby etc S'well*
BARNT GREEN (St Andrew)   *see Cofton Hackett w Barnt Green Birm*
BARNTON (Christ Church) *Ches* 4   P *Bp*   V P NEWMAN
BARNWELL (All Saints) (St Andrew), Hemington, Luddington in the Brook, Lutton, Polebrook and Thurning *Pet* 10
   P *Bp, MMCET, Em Coll Cam, DBP, and Sir Philip Naylor-Leyland Bt (jt)*   R C R IEVINS
BARNWOOD (St Lawrence) *Glouc* 2   P *D&C*
   P-in-c A MORRIS   C S P COOKE   NSM A D HAYMAN
BARONY OF BURGH, The (St Michael)   P *Patr Bd*
   P-in-c T A BODDAM-WHETHAM
BARR, GREAT (St Margaret) *Lich* 25   P *M D S Farnham*
   V M C RUTTER   NSM T W WARD
BARRINGTON (All Saints)   *see Orwell Gp Ely*
BARRINGTON (Blessed Virgin Mary)   *see Winsmoor B & W*
BARRINGTON, GREAT (St Mary)   *see Sherborne, Windrush, the Barringtons etc Glouc*
BARRINGTON, LITTLE (St Peter) *as above*
BARROW (All Saints) *St E* 13   P *Ld Chan (1 turn), Mrs E C Gordon-Lennox, the Russell-Cooke Trust Co and Bp (1 turn), and St Jo Coll Cam (1 turn)*   V B L K SHERLOCK
BARROW (St Bartholomew) *Ches* 2   P *D Okell Esq*
   R A J STINSON
BARROW (St Giles)   *see Broseley w Benthall, Jackfield, Linley etc Heref*
BARROW and Goxhill *Linc* 8   P *Ld Chan*   V J C GIRTCHEN
   OLM M A HUTSON
BARROW GURNEY (The Blessed Virgin Mary and St Edward King an d Martyr)   *see Long Ashton w Barrow Gurney and Flax Bourton B & W*
BARROW HILL (St Andrew)   *see Staveley and Barrow Hill Derby*
BARROW IN FURNESS (St Paul) *Carl* 8   P *Simeon's Trustees*
   R D H PRICE   NSM E A BATES
BARROW UPON SOAR (Holy Trinity) w Walton le Wolds *Leic* 6
   P *St Jo Coll Cam and DBP (jt)*   P-in-c R M PADDISON
   C E J YORK   NSM S J RICHARDSON

BARROW, NORTH (St Nicholas)   *see Six Pilgrims B & W*
BARROW, NORTH Team Ministry, The (St Matthew) (St James the Great) *Carl* 8   P *Patr Bd*   TV J D HODGKINSON
BARROW, SOUTH (St Peter)   *see Six Pilgrims B & W*
BARROW, SOUTH Team Ministry, The *Carl* 8   P *Bp*
   TR G M CREGEEN   TV J E NORTHEY   C M HORNBY, R P HAM
BARROWBY (All Saints) and Great Gonerby *Linc* 20   P *R Grantham, and Duke of Devonshire (by turn)*   R P HOPKINS
BARROWDEN (St Peter) and Wakerley w South Luffenham and Morcott w Duddington and Tixover *Pet* 12   P *Burghley Ho Preservation Trust, P W Rowley Esq, and Bp (3 turns), Ball Coll Ox (1 turn)*   R vacant
BARROWFORD (St Thomas) and Newchurch-in-Pendle *Blackb* 6   P *Ld Chan and trustees (alt)*   V J M HALLOWS
BARROW-IN-FURNESS (St Aidan)   *see S Barrow Carl*
BARROW-IN-FURNESS (St George) *as above*
BARROW-IN-FURNESS (St John the Evangelist) *Carl* 8   P *DBP*
   V vacant
BARROW-IN-FURNESS (St Mark) *Carl* 8   P *Bp*   V I K HOOK
BARROW-IN-FURNESS (St Mary the Virgin)   *see Walney Is Carl*
BARROW-ON-HUMBER (Holy Trinity)   *see Barrow and Goxhill Linc*
BARROW-ON-TRENT (St Wilfrid)   *see Aston on Trent, Elvaston, Weston on Trent etc Derby*
BARSHAM (Holy Trinity)   *see Bungay St E*
BARSHAM, EAST (All Saints)   *see Walsingham, Houghton and Barsham Nor*
BARSHAM, NORTH (All Saints) *as above*
BARSHAM, WEST (The Assumption of the Blessed Virgin Mary) *as above*
BARSTON (St Swithin) *Birm* 11   P *MMCET*
   P-in-c D C J BALLARD
BARTESTREE CROSS Group of Parishes *Heref* 3   P *D&C (3 turns), Bp (1 turn), Personal Reps A T Foley (1 turn)*
   R J A DAVIES   C P M ROBERTS
BARTHOMLEY (St Bertoline) *Ches* 11   P *Lord O'Neill*
   P-in-c D C SPEEDY   Hon C A M SPEEDY
BARTLEY GREEN (St Michael and All Angels) *Birm* 2   P *Bp*
   V R I ATKINSON
BARTON (St Cuthbert w St Mary)   *see E Richmond Leeds*
BARTON (St Lawrence)   *see Fellside Team Blackb*
BARTON (St Mark's Chapel) w Peel Green (St Michael and All Angels) (St Catherine) *Man* 18   P *Bp and TR Eccles*
   P-in-c I A HALL
BARTON (St Martin)   *see Torquay St Martin Barton Ex*
BARTON (St Michael), Pooley Bridge, Martindale and Watermillock *Carl* 4   P *Bp and Earl of Lonsdale (jt)*
   V D C WOOD
BARTON (St Paul) *Portsm* 8   P *R Whippingham*   V vacant
BARTON (St Peter)   *see Lordsbridge Ely*
BARTON BENDISH (St Andrew) w Beachamwell and Shingham *Ely* 9   P *Bp and DBP (alt)*   P-in-c B L BURTON
BARTON HARTSHORN (St James)   *see The Claydons and Swan Ox*
BARTON HILL (St Luke w Ch Ch) and Moorfields St Matthew *Bris* 3   P *Bp, CPAS, and V Bris St Phil and St Jacob w Em (jt)*
   P-in-c J M GAINSBOROUGH   OLM W D GARDINER
BARTON IN FABIS (St George) *S'well* 6   P *Ld Chan*
   P-in-c R I COLEMAN
BARTON MILLS (St Mary)   *see Mildenhall St E*
BARTON SEAGRAVE (St Botolph) w Warkton *Pet* 9   P *Ch Soc Trust (2 turns), Duke of Buccleuch (1 turn)*   R M W LUCAS
   C A J CLARK, N C ADAMS
BARTON ST DAVID (St David)   *see Wheathill Priory Gp B & W*
BARTON STACEY (All Saints)   *see Lower Dever Win*
BARTON TURF (St Michael)   *see Ashmanhaugh, Barton Turf etc Nor*
BARTON UNDER NEEDWOOD (St James) w Dunstall and Tatenhill *Lich* 14   P *Bp and Sir Rupert Hardy Bt (jt)*
   V A R RIDLEY
BARTON UPON HUMBER (St Mary) *Linc* 8   P *Bp*
   V D P ROWETT   NSM A E BROWN   OLM A W WRIGHT
BARTON, GREAT (Holy Innocents) and Thurston *St E* 13
   P *Bp and Sir Michael Bunbury Bt (jt)*   V vacant
BARTON-LE-CLEY (St Nicholas) w Higham Gobion and Hexton *St Alb* 8   P *The Crown (3 turns), Mrs F A A Cooper (1 turn)*   R A P JOHNSON
BARTON-LE-STREET (St Michael)   *see The Street Par York*
BARTON-ON-THE-HEATH (St Lawrence)   *see S Warks Seven Gp Cov*
BARWELL (St Mary) w Potters Marston and Stapleton *Leic* 10
   P R J W Titley Esq   R P WATSON
BARWICK (St Mary Magdalene)   *see Yeovil H Trin w Barwick B & W*
BARWICK IN ELMET (All Saints) *Leeds* 17   P *Duchy of Lanc*
   P-in-c A J NICHOLSON

BASCHURCH (All Saints) and Weston Lullingfield w Hordley
Lich 17 **P** *Ch Patr Trust and Bp (jt)* **NSM** D M COATSWORTH
BASEGREEN (St Peter) *see Gleadless Sheff*
BASFORD (St Leodegarius) (St Aidan) *S'well 8* **P** *Bp*
V R SHAW
BASFORD (St Mark) *Lich 9* **P** *Bp* **P-in-c** T B BLOOR
NSM F P DUNN
BASHLEY (St John) *see Milton Win*
BASILDON (St Andrew) (Holy Cross) *Chelmsf 12* **P** *Bp*
TV M A SHAW **C** A G SMITH
BASILDON (St Martin of Tours) *Chelmsf 12* **P** *Bp*
R E E MCCAFFERTY **Hon C** N M WOOD
BASILDON (St Stephen) w Aldworth and Ashampstead *Ox 4*
P *St Jo Coll Cam, Simeon's Trustees, and DBF (by turn)*
V W H N WATTS
BASING, OLD (St Mary) and Lychpit *Win 4* **P** *Magd Coll Ox*
V A R F BATTEY **NSM** R F HARTLAND, S J LLOYD
BASINGSTOKE (All Saints) (St Michael) *Win 4* **P** *Patr Bd*
TR J M STOKER **TV** A BENNETT, E L GRIFFITHS,
R E RUTHERFORD **NSM** P PALMER
BASINGSTOKE (St Gabriel) *see Popley w Limes Park and*
Rooksdown Win
BASINGSTOKE Brighton Hill (Christ the King) *see Basingstoke*
Win
BASINGSTOKE Popley (Bethlehem Chapel) *as above*
BASINGSTOKE South Ham (St Peter) *as above*
BASLOW (St Anne) and Eyam *Derby 2* **P** *Duke of Devonshire*
and Earl Temple (jt) **R** M V GILBERT
BASSETT (St Michael and All Angels) *see N Stoneham and*
Bassett Win
BASSINGBOURN (St Peter and St Paul) *Ely 7* **P** *D&C Westmr*
V C J YANDELL
BASSINGHAM Group, The (St Michael and All Angels) *Linc 12*
P *Lady Jean Nevile, CCC Ox, Lord Middleton, Bp, and W R S*
Brown Esq (jt) **C** A J JACKSON-PARR
BASSINGTHORPE (St Thomas à Becket) *see N Beltisloe Gp*
Linc
BASTON (St John the Baptist) *see Ness Gp Linc*
BASWICH or Berkswich (Holy Trinity) *Lich 10* **P** *Bp*
V P A GRAYSMITH **NSM** E J BISHOP, K A SHAW
BATCOMBE (Blessed Virgin Mary) *see Bruton and Distr B & W*
BATCOMBE (St Mary) *see Three Valleys Sarum*
BATH (St Barnabas) w Englishcombe *B & W 8* **P** *Bp*
P-in-c C A SOURBUT
BATH (St Bartholomew) *B & W 8* **P** *Simeon's Trustees*
V I R LEWIS **C** M T FARRIER
BATH (St Luke) *B & W 8* **P** *Simeon's Trustees*
P-in-c M D H FRANKUM
BATH (St Mary Magdalene) Holloway, Extra-parochial
Chapelry *B & W 10* D J PROTHERO
BATH (St Michael w St Paul) *B & W 8* **P** *CPAS*
NSM K U MADDEN
BATH (St Saviour) w Swainswick and Woolley *B & W 8*
P *Ch Patr Trust and Or Coll Ox (jt)* **R** M J NORMAN
Hon C K J WILLIAMS
BATH (St Stephen) *see Charlcombe w Bath St Steph B & W*
BATH ABBEY (St Peter and St Paul) w St James *B & W 8*
P *Simeon's Trustees* **R** T E MASON **C** C E ROBSON,
J M HOFFMANN, S P GIRLING **NSM** E M LEE-BARBER
BATH Bathwick (St John the Baptist) (Blessed Virgin Mary)
B & W 8 **P** *Bp* **P-in-c** P R H EDWARDS
BATH Odd Down (St Philip and St James) w Combe
Hay *B & W 8* **P** *Simeon's Trustees* **V** A BAIN
NSM M JOYCE
BATH Twerton-on-Avon (Ascension) (St Michael) *B & W 8*
P *Patr Bd* **TR** R G WILSON **TV** R J PIMM
C C M VAUGHAN
BATH Walcot (St Andrew) (St Swithin) *B & W 8* **P** *Simeon's*
Trustees **R** S G HOLLAND **C** E SMITH
BATH Weston (All Saints) w North Stoke and Langridge *B &*
W 8 **P** *Ld Chan* **R** P J WHITWORTH **C** S P FLINT
NSM J N RAWLINSON
BATH Weston (St John the Evangelist) (Emmanuel) w Kelston
B & W 8 **P** *Ld Chan* **R** C R GARRETT
BATH Widcombe (St Matthew) (St Thomas à Becket) *B & W 8*
P *Simeon's Trustees* **P-in-c** T S BUCKLEY
BATHAMPTON (St Nicholas) w Claverton *B & W 8* **P** *D&C*
Bris and Personal Reps R L D Skrine Esq (jt) **R** J P FRITH
BATHEALTON (St Bartholomew) *see Wellington and Distr*
B & W
BATHEASTON (St John the Baptist) (St Catherine) *B & W 8*
P *Ch Ch Ox* **P-in-c** I RATHBONE
BATHFORD (St Swithun) *B & W 8* **P** *D&C Bris*
P-in-c J E BURGESS **NSM** C A R BURGESS
BATHWICK (Blessed Virgin Mary) *see Bath Bathwick B & W*
BATHWICK (St John the Baptist) *as above*

BATLEY (All Saints) and Purlwell *Leeds 10* **P** E C S J G
Brudenell Esq, Trustees D Stubley Esq, and Bp (jt)
P-in-c M NAYLOR **NSM** V KEATING **OLM** B R ASQUITH
BATLEY (St Thomas) *Leeds 10* **P** *V Batley* **V** *vacant*
BATLEY CARR (Holy Trinity) *see Dewsbury Leeds*
BATSFORD (St Mary) *see Moreton-in-Marsh w Batsford,*
Todenham etc Glouc
BATTERSEA (Christ Church and St Stephen) *S'wark 14* **P** *Bp*
and V Battersea St Mary (alt) **V** G N OWEN
BATTERSEA (St George) *see Battersea Fields S'wark*
BATTERSEA (St Luke) *S'wark 14* **P** *Bp* **V** E A MORSE
BATTERSEA (St Mary) *S'wark 14* **P** *Earl Spencer* **V** S BUTLER
C P L KRINKS **NSM** P B WINTGENS
BATTERSEA (St Michael) Wandsworth Common *S'wark 14*
P *V Battersea St Mary* **P-in-c** P A KURK
BATTERSEA (St Peter) (St Paul) *S'wark 14* **P** *V Battersea*
St Mary **P-in-c** R P MALONE **C** K E SMITH
BATTERSEA FIELDS (St Saviour) (All Saints) (St George)
S'wark 14 **P** *Bp, CPAS, and Ch Patr Trust (jt)* **V** G M VEVERS
C S A A ANAND
BATTERSEA PARK (All Saints) *see Battersea Fields S'wark*
BATTERSEA PARK (St Saviour) *as above*
BATTERSEA RISE (St Mark) *S'wark 14* **P** *V Battersea St Mary*
V P J S PERKIN
BATTISFORD (St Mary) *see Ringshall w Battisford, Barking w*
Darmsden etc St E
BATTLE (Church of the Ascension) (St Mary the Virgin)
Chich 12 **P** *The Crown* **V** J J W EDMONDSON
BATTLE HILL (Good Shepherd) *see Willington Newc*
BATTLESDEN (St Peter and All Saints) *see Woburn w Eversholt,*
Milton Bryan, Battlesden etc St Alb
BATTYEFORD (Christ the King) *Leeds 10* **P** *V Mirfield*
V M A MCLEAN **NSM** M E WOOD
BAUGHURST (St Stephen) and Ramsdell and Wolverton w
Ewhurst and Hannington *Win 4* **P** *Ld Chan, Duke of*
Wellington, and Bp (by turn) **R** D BARLOW
BAULKING (St Nicholas) *see Uffington, Shellingford,*
Woolstone and Baulking Ox
BAUMBER (St Swithin) *see Hemingby Gp Linc*
BAUNTON (St Mary Magdalene) *see Churn Valley Glouc*
BAVERSTOCK (St Editha) *see Nadder Valley Sarum*
BAWBURGH (St Mary and St Walstan) *see Easton, Colton,*
Marlingford and Bawburgh Nor
BAWDESWELL (All Saints) *see Lyng, Sparham, Elsing, Bylaugh,*
Bawdeswell etc Nor
BAWDRIP (St Michael and All Angels) *see Woolavington w*
Cossington and Bawdrip B & W
BAWDSEY (St Mary) *see Wilford Peninsula St E*
BAWTRY (St Nicholas) w Austerfield, Misson, Everton and
Mattersey *S'well 1* **P** *Bp and Ld Chan (alt)*
V J E T STRICKLAND **C** P A SAVAGE
BAXENDEN (St John) *Blackb 1* **P** *Bp* **V** T A DONAGHEY
BAXTERLEY (not known) w Hurley and Wood End and
Merevale w Bentley *Birm 10* **P** *Ld Chan (1 turn), Bp and*
Sir William Dugdale Bt (1 turn) **P-in-c** J C WHITE
BAYDON (St Nicholas) *see Whitton Sarum*
BAYFORD (Mission Room) *see Charlton Musgrove,*
Cucklington and Stoke Trister B & W
BAYFORD (St Mary) *see Lt Berkhamsted and Bayford,*
Essendon etc St Alb
BAYLHAM (St Peter) *see Gt and Lt Blakenham w Baylham and*
Nettlestead St E
BAYSTON HILL (Christ Church) *Lich 20* **P** *V Shrewsbury H Trin*
w St Julian **V** T M LOMAX **C** U F PENCAVEL
NSM K J LOMAX
BAYSWATER (St Matthew) *Lon 2* **P** *Exors Dame Jewell Magnus-*
Allcroft **V** J R ALLCOCK **C** W P H COLERIDGE
NSM M J LEE
BAYTON (St Bartholomew) *see Mamble w Bayton, Rock w*
Heightington etc Worc
BEACHAMPTON (Assumption of the Blessed Virgin Mary)
see Buckingham Ox
BEACHAMWELL (St Mary) *see Barton Bendish w Beachamwell*
and Shingham Ely
BEACON Team Ministry, The *Carl 10* **P** *Patr Bd*
TR N L DAVIES **C** R A LATHAM **Hon C** C V TAYLOR
OLM J F RADLEY **Hon Par Dn** J L TYRER
BEACON, The *York 10* **P** *Ld Chan (2 turns), Sir Charles Legard*
Bt (1 turn) **P-in-c** J H ANDERSON
BEACONSFIELD (St Mary and All Saints) (St Michael and All
Angels) *Ox 9* **P** *Patr Bd* **TR** J P BROOKS **TV** C I WALTON,
N J K TEGALLY **C** K V BEER **NSM** C E CROISDALE-APPLEBY,
C E L SMITH
BEADLAM (St Hilda) *see Kirkdale w Harome, Nunnington and*
Pockley York

BEADNELL (St Ebba) *Newc 7* **P** *Newc Dioc Soc* **V** J R GLOVER

BEAFORD (All Saints) *see* Newton Tracey, Horwood, Alverdiscott etc *Ex*

BEALINGS, GREAT (St Mary) and LITTLE (All Saints) w Playford and Culpho *St E 7* **P** *Lord Cranworth (1 turn), Bp (3 turns)* **P-in-c** C J COOK **NSM** P J MERRY

BEAMINSTER AREA (St Mary of the Annunciation) *Sarum 2* **P** *Patr Bd* **TR** D F B BALDWIN **TV** J B NEARY **C** D E INGLES **Hon C** E B SAVIGEAR

BEAMISH (St Andrew) *see* Stanley and S Moor *Dur*

BEARLEY (St Mary the Virgin) *see* Arden Valley *Cov*

BEARPARK (St Edmund) *see* Dur N *Dur*

BEARSTED (Holy Cross) w Thurnham *Cant 13* **P** *Abp* **V** J CORBYN **C** A E PINNEGAR

BEARWOOD (St Catherine) *see* Winnersh *Ox*

BEARWOOD (St Mary the Virgin) *Birm 7* **P** *V Smethwick* **V** A H PERRY

BEAUCHAMP RODING (St Botolph) *see* S Rodings *Chelmsf*

BEAUDESERT (St Nicholas) and Henley-in-Arden w Ullenhall *Cov 7* **P** *MMCET, Bp, and High Bailiff of Henley-in-Arden (jt)* **R** J F GANJAVI

BEAULIEU (Blessed Virgin and Holy Child) and Exbury and East Boldre *Win 11* **P** *Bp and Lord Montagu of Beaulieu (jt)* **P-in-c** J C WHITE

BEAUMONT CUM MOZE (St Leonard and St Mary) *see* Tendring and Lt Bentley w Beaumont cum Moze *Chelmsf*

BEAUMONT LEYS (Christ the King) *see* Stocking Farm and Beaumont Leys *Leic*

BEAUWORTH (St James) *see* Upper Itchen *Win*

BEAWORTHY (St Alban) *see* Ashwater, Halwill, Beaworthy, Clawton etc *Ex*

BEBINGTON (St Andrew) *Ches 8* **P** *M C Saunders-Griffiths Esq* **R** D A VESTERGAARD **C** A M RODGERS, D G B NEWSTEAD

BEBINGTON, HIGHER (Christ Church) *Ches 8* **P** *Bp* **V** M G LOACH

BECCLES (St Michael the Archangel) (St Luke's Church Centre) *St E 18* **P** *Simeon's Trustees* **NSM** P H O MILLER

BECK ROW (St John) *see* Mildenhall *St E*

BECKBURY (St Milburga), Badger, Kemberton, Ryton, Stockton and Sutton Maddock *Lich 16* **P** *Lord Hamilton of Dalzell, Or Coll Ox, and MMCET (2 turns), Ld Chan (1 turn)* **R** K HODSON

BECKENHAM (Christ Church) *Roch 13* **P** *Ch Trust Fund Trust* **V** R M HINTON **C** D A WOODWARD **Hon C** J T ANSCOMBE

BECKENHAM (Holy Trinity) *see* Penge Lane H Trin *Roch*

BECKENHAM (St Barnabas) *Roch 13* **P** *Keble Coll Ox* **P-in-c** T J HIDE

BECKENHAM (St George) *Roch 13* **P** *Bp* **C** T J KELSEY

BECKENHAM (St James) Elmers End *Roch 13* **P** *Bp* **V** L C CARBERRY

BECKENHAM (St John the Baptist) Eden Park *Roch 13* **P** *Ch Trust Fund Trust, Bp and Adn Bromley (jt)* **V** E A LANDER **C** S A SMITH

BECKENHAM (St Michael and All Angels) w St Augustine *Roch 13* **P** *SMF and Bp (jt)* **P-in-c** L C CARBERRY

BECKENHAM, NEW (St Paul) *Roch 13* **P** *Bp* **V** V C SHORT **Hon C** N E BAINES

BECKERMET (St Bridget) (St Bridget Old Church) (St John) w Ponsonby *Carl 5* **P** *Bp, Adn W Cumberland, P Stanley Esq, and PCCs of Beckermet St Jo and St Bridget (jt)* **V** J G RILEY **NSM** L A RILEY

BECKFORD (St John the Baptist) *see* Overbury w Teddington, Alstone etc *Worc*

BECKHAM, WEST (St Helen and All Saints) *see* Weybourne Gp *Nor*

BECKINGHAM (All Saints) *see* Brant Broughton and Beckingham *Linc*

BECKINGHAM (All Saints), Walkeringham, Misterton, W Stockwith, Clayworth and Gringley-on-the-Hill *S'well 1* **P** *D&C York (3 turns), Ld Chanc (1 turn), Bp (1 turn)* **V** J D HENSON

BECKINGTON (St George) w Standerwick, Berkley, Rodden, Lullington and Orchardleigh *B & W 3* **P** *Bp (3 turns), Ch Soc Trust (1 turn), and Exors A Duckworth Esq* **R** A W G CHALKLEY

BECKLEY (All Saints) *see* Brede w Udimore and Beckley and Peasmarsh *Chich*

BECKLEY (Assumption of the Blessed Virgin Mary), Forest Hill, Horton-cum-Studley and Stanton St John *Ox 20* **P** *Linc Coll Ox and New Coll Ox (jt)* **V** A J D PRITCHARD-KEENS **C** D C BENDOR-SAMUEL **NSM** J C H M LEE

BECKTON (St Mark) *Chelmsf 5* **P** *Bp* **V** *vacant*

BECKWITHSHAW (St Michael and All Angels) *see* Pannal w Beckwithshaw *Leeds*

BECONTREE (St Cedd) *Chelmsf 1* **P** *Bp* **V** A F RABLEN **OLM** R A DOWLEY

BECONTREE (St Elisabeth) *Chelmsf 1* **P** *Bp* **V** S J HANNA

BECONTREE (St George) *Chelmsf 1* **P** *Bp* **V** S L SMALLWOOD

BECONTREE (St Mary) *Chelmsf 1* **P** *CPAS* **V** E J FLEMING **C** S O LEWIS

BECONTREE (St Thomas) *Chelmsf 1* **P** *Bp* **OLM** C A NEWNHAM

BECONTREE SOUTH (St Alban) (St John the Divine) (St Martin) *Chelmsf 1* **P** *Patr Bd* **TR** P J SAYER **C** M F J BLAKELY, Y A GOOLJARY **OLM** R P C DESCOMBES

BEDALE (St Gregory) and Leeming and Thornton Watlass *Leeds 27* **P** *Bp, Sir Henry Beresford-Peirse Bt, R Kirklington w Burneston and Wath and Pickhill, and D S Dodsworth Esq (jt)* **R** I M ROBINSON **NSM** L A ROBINSON

BEDDINGHAM (St Andrew) *see* Glynde, W Firle and Beddingham *Chich*

BEDDINGTON (St Mary) *S'wark 23* **P** *D&C* **R** A R FENBY

BEDDINGTON, SOUTH (St Michael and All Angels) and Roundshaw *S'wark 23* **P** *Bp* **V** A M A GBEBIKAN **C** M H ONUIGBO **NSM** S L BILLIN

BEDFONT, EAST (St Mary the Virgin) *Lon 11* **P** *Ld Chan* **V** P J SMITH

BEDFORD (All Saints) *St Alb 9* **P** *Bp* **P-in-c** S H J WRATTEN

BEDFORD (Christ Church) *St Alb 9* **P** *Bp* **V** R C HIBBERT **C** P R BOULTER

BEDFORD (St Andrew) *St Alb 9* **P** *Ld Chan* **V** J S REVELEY **C** A C GAINES

BEDFORD (St John the Baptist) (St Leonard) *St Alb 9* **P** *MMCET* **R** N COOPER

BEDFORD (St Mark) *St Alb 9* **P** *Bp* **V** C ROYDEN **NSM** G R CAPPLEMAN

BEDFORD (St Martin) *St Alb 9* **P** *Bp* **V** *vacant*

BEDFORD (St Michael and All Angels) *see* Elstow *St Alb*

BEDFORD (St Paul) *St Alb 9* **P** *Bp* **V** K I GOSS **C** P N W BRYSON

BEDFORD (St Peter de Merton) w St Cuthbert *St Alb 9* **P** *Ld Chan* **R** M L FUDGER

BEDFORD LEIGH (St Thomas) (All Saints' Mission) *Man 19* **P** *V Leigh St Mary* **V** R DIXON

BEDFORD PARK (St Michael and All Angels) *Lon 11* **P** *Bp* **V** K J MORRIS **C** F PESCE **NSM** G MORGAN

BEDGROVE (Holy Spirit) *Ox 10* **P** *DBP* **V** M G KUHRT

BEDHAMPTON (St Nicholas's Mission Church) (St Thomas) *Portsm 5* **P** *Bp* **R** D J PROUD

BEDINGFIELD (St Mary) *see* Eye *St E*

BEDINGHAM (St Andrew) *see* Hempnall *Nor*

BEDLINGTON (St Cuthbert) *Newc 1* **P** *D&C Dur* **V** J F TWOMEY **C** I J HENNEBRY **NSM** E A M G BROWN

BEDMINSTER (St Aldhelm) (St Paul) *Bris 1* **P** *Bp* **P-in-c** A J DOARKS **C** H L JOHNSON, N J HAY

BEDMINSTER (St Michael and All Angels) *Bris 1* **P** *Bp* **V** D S MOSS

BEDMINSTER DOWN (St Oswald) *see* Bishopsworth and Bedminster Down *Bris*

BEDMOND (Ascension) *see* Abbots Langley *St Alb*

BEDNALL (All Saints) *see* Penkridge *Lich*

BEDSTONE (St Mary) *see* Middle Marches *Heref*

BEDWORTH (All Saints) *Cov 5* **P** *Patr Bd* **TR** R W HARE **TV** M J HAMMOND **Dss** P M HAMILTON

BEDWYN, GREAT (St Mary) *see* Savernake *Sarum*

BEDWYN, LITTLE (St Michael) *as above*

BEECH (St Peter) *see* Alton *Win*

BEECH HILL (St Mary the Virgin) *see* Loddon Reach *Ox*

BEECH, HIGH (Holy Innocents) *see* Waltham H Cross *Chelmsf*

BEECHDALE ESTATE (St Chad) *see* Blakenall Heath *Lich*

BEECHINGSTOKE (St Stephen) *see* Vale of Pewsey *Sarum*

BEEDING (St Peter) and Bramber w Botolphs *Chich 11* **P** *Bp* **R** J W A CHALLIS **NSM** S Y GARDNER

BEEDING, LOWER (Holy Trinity) (St John the Evangelist) *Chich 7* **P** *Bp* **V** M J BETSON

BEEDON (St Nicholas) *see* E Downland *Ox*

BEEFORD (St Leonard) w Frodingham and Foston *York 11* **P** *Abp and Ch Soc Trust (jt)* **R** J E GRAINGER-SMITH

BEELEY (St Anne) and Edensor *Derby 2* **P** *Duke of Devonshire* **V** D PERKINS

BEELSBY (St Andrew) *see* Wolds Gateway Group *Linc*

BEENHAM VALENCE (St Mary) *see* Aldermaston and Woolhampton *Ox*

BEER (St Michael) *see* Seaton and Beer *Ex*

BEER HACKETT (St Michael) *see* Three Valleys *Sarum*

BEERCROCOMBE (St James) *see* Beercrocombe w Curry Mallet, Hatch Beauchamp etc *B & W*

BEERCROCOMBE (St James) w Curry Mallet, Hatch Beauchamp, Orchard Portman, Staple Fitzpaine, Stoke St Mary w Thurlbear and West Hatch *B & W 16* **P** *Bp, Ch Trust Fund Trust, and D&C (4 turns), Duchy of Cornwall (1 turn)* **R** P A REYNOLDS **C** M L GODIN **NSM** C R AGER

BEESANDS (St Andrew)   *see* Stokenham, Slapton, Charleton w
Buckland etc *Ex*
BEESBY (St Andrew)   *see* Saleby w Beesby and Maltby *Linc*
BEESTON (St John the Baptist) *S'well 9*   **P** *Duke of Devonshire*
V W R PLIMMER   **NSM** R C W WIGGINS
BEESTON (St Lawrence)   *see* Ashmanhaugh, Barton Turf etc
Nor
BEESTON (St Mary the Virgin) *Leeds 15*   **P** *Patr Bd*
P-in-c L C PEARSON   **NSM** J H TURNER
BEESTON NEXT MILEHAM (St Mary the Virgin)   *see* Litcham w
Kempston, E and W Lexham, Mileham etc *Nor*
BEESTON REGIS (All Saints)   *see* Aylmerton, Runton, Beeston
Regis and Gresham *Nor*
BEETHAM (St Michael and All Angels) *Carl 10*   **P** *Bp*
P-in-c L LONSDALE
BEETLEY (St Mary)   *see* Dereham and Distr *Nor*
BEGBROKE (St Michael)   *see* Blenheim *Ox*
BEIGHTON (All Saints)   *see* Acle and Bure to Yare *Nor*
BEIGHTON (St Mary the Virgin) *Sheff 1*   **P** *Bp*
P-in-c M H E HEALEY
BEKESBOURNE (St Peter)   *see* Bridge *Cant*
BELAUGH (St Peter)   *see* Wroxham w Hoveton and Belaugh
Nor
BELBROUGHTON (Holy Trinity) w Fairfield and Clent *Worc 12*
P *Ld Chan and St Jo Coll Ox (alt)*   **Hon C** P G HARRISON,
R J C NEWTON
BELCHALWELL (St Aldheim)   *see* Hazelbury Bryan and the
Hillside Par *Sarum*
BELCHAMP (St Paul and St Andrew)   *see* N Hinckford *Chelmsf*
BELCHAMP OTTEN (St Ethelbert and All Saints) *as above*
BELCHAMP WALTER (St Mary the Virgin) *as above*
BELCHFORD (St Peter and St Paul)   *see* Hemingby Gp *Linc*
BELFIELD (St Ann) *Man 17*   **P** *Bp*   **P-in-c** G W LINDLEY
NSM S E WARD
BELFORD (St Mary) and Lucker *Newc 7*   **P** *V Bamburgh and
Beadnell and Bp (alt)*   **V** J J BECKWITH
BELLE GREEN (Mission)   *see* Wigan All SS *Liv*
BELLE ISLE (St John and St Barnabas)   *see* Leeds Belle Is St Jo and
St Barn *Leeds*
BELLEAU (St John the Baptist)   *see* Legbourne and Wold Marsh
Linc
BELLERBY (St John)   *see* Leyburn w Bellerby *Leeds*
BELLINGDON (St John the Evangelist)   *see* Gt Chesham *Ox*
BELLINGHAM (St Cuthbert)   *see* N Tyne and Redesdale *Newc*
BELLINGHAM (St Dunstan) *S'wark 4*   **P** *Bp*   **P-in-c** T B SINGH
NSM D L RILEY
BELMONT (St Anselm) *Lon 23*   **P** *Bp*   **V** C M A ROBINSON
NSM R Y KHAN
BELMONT (St John) *S'wark 23*   **P** *R Cheam*   **V** M R WILLIAMS
BELMONT (St Mary Magdalene) and Pittington *Dur 1*
P *Prime Min and D&C (alt)*   **V** M THRELFALL-HOLMES
BELMONT (St Peter)   *see* Turton Moorland *Man*
BELPER (Christ Church) w Turnditch *Derby 11*   **P** *Bp*
V J M PAGE   **C** I N L BLACK   **NSM** A M V ROOME
BELPER (St Peter) *Derby 11*   **P** *V Duffield*   **V** A M STRATTON
C A J BAGULEY   **NSM** A TOMPKINS
BELSIZE PARK (St Peter) *Lon 16*   **P** *D&C Westmr*
P-in-c P S NICHOLSON   **NSM** M W SPEEKS
BELSTEAD (St Mary the Virgin)   *see* Sproughton w Burstall,
Copdock w Washbrook etc *St E*
BELSTONE (St Mary)   *see* Okehampton, Inwardleigh, Belstone,
Sourton etc *Ex*
BELTINGHAM (St Cuthbert)   *see* Haydon Bridge and
Beltingham w Henshaw *Newc*
BELTISLOE, NORTH Group *Linc 17*   **P** *Ch Coll Cam, Sir Lyonel
Tollemache Bt, D&C, Bp, DBP, Sir Richard Welby Bt, and Baroness
Willoughby de Eresby (jt)*   **R** M C DOYLE   **OLM** W KING
BELTON (All Saints) and Burgh Castle *Nor 6*   **P** *Bp and Ld
Chan (alt)*   **R** R J BUNN
BELTON (St John the Baptist)   *see* Kegworth, Hathern, Long
Whatton, Diseworth etc *Leic*
BELTON (St Peter and St Paul)   *see* Barkston and Hough Gp
Linc
BELTON (St Peter)   *see* Uppingham w Ayston and Belton w
Wardley *Pet*
BELTON Group, The (All Saints) *Linc 1*   **P** *Bp and Prime Min
(alt)*   **V** *vacant*
BELVEDERE (All Saints) *Roch 15*   **P** *DBP*   **V** W J EDWARDS
NSM C M WOOD
BELVEDERE (St Augustine) *Roch 15*   **P** *Bp*   **V** C W JONES
BEMBRIDGE (Holy Trinity) (St Luke's Mission Church)
Portsm 7   **P** *V Brading*   **NSM** L M BUSHELL
**BEMERTON (St Andrew) (St John the Evangelist) (St Michael
and All Angels)** *Sarum 13*   **P** *Prime Min (2 turns) and
Bp (1 turn)*   **TR** S A WOODLEY   **C** A C BRIDEWELL
NSM S J DREWETT

BEMPTON (St Michael) w Flamborough, Reighton w Speeton
York 9   **P** *Patr Bd*   **P-in-c** A PATTERSON
BEN RHYDDING (St John the Evangelist) *Leeds 4*   **P** *V Ilkey*
V P WILLOX   **NSM** J H COPSEY
BENCHILL (St Luke the Physician)   *see* Wythenshawe *Man*
BENEFIELD (St Mary the Virgin)   *see* Oundle w Ashton and
Benefield w Glapthorn *Pet*
BENENDEN (St George and St Margaret) and Sandhurst
Cant 10   **P** *Abp*   **V** D J COMMANDER
BENFIELDSIDE (St Cuthbert) *Dur 4*   **P** *Bp*   **V** M JACKSON
NSM I W WAUGH
BENFLEET, SOUTH (St Mary the Virgin) *Chelmsf 13*   **P** *D&C
Westmr*   **V** L S DRAKE
BENGEO (Holy Trinity)   *see* Hertford *St Alb*
BENGEO (St Leonard) *as above*
BENGEWORTH (St Peter) *Worc 1*   **P** *Bp*
P-in-c M J G BINNEY
BENHALL (St Mary)   *see* Alde River *St E*
BENHILTON (All Saints) *S'wark 23*   **P** *Bp*   **V** P J HARNDEN
BENINGTON (St Peter)   *see* Ardeley, Benington, Cottered w
Throcking etc *St Alb*
BENNIWORTH (St Julian)   *see* Asterby Gp *Linc*
BENSHAM AND TEAMS (St Chad) *Dur 12*   **P** *Bp*
V M M GILLEY
BENSON (St Helen) *Ox 20*   **P** *Ch Ch Ox*   **V** *vacant*
**BENTHAM (St John the Baptist), Burton-in-Lonsdale,
Chapel-leDale, Ingleton and Thornton-in-Lonsdale** *Leeds 22*
P *Bp*   **TV** C H ELLIS
BENTILEE (St Stephen)   *see* Bucknall *Lich*
BENTLEY (Emmanuel) and Willenhall Holy Trinity *Lich 29*
P *Patr Bd*   **TR** J D DEAKIN   **TV** S L HOUGH
BENTLEY (St Mary)   *see* Sproughton w Burstall, Copdock w
Washbrook etc *St E*
BENTLEY (St Mary), Binsted and Froyle *Win 2*   **P** *D&C,
Adn Surrey, and Guild of All So (jt)*   **R** Y DUBREUIL
BENTLEY (St Peter) *Sheff 7*   **P** *Bp*   **V** D N BERRY
BENTLEY COMMON (St Paul), Kelvedon Hatch and Navestock
Chelmsf 8   **P** *Bp*   **R** M N JAMES   **Hon C** A V COLEMAN
NSM A V COLEMAN
BENTLEY HEATH (St James)   *see* Dorridge *Birm*
BENTLEY, GREAT (St Mary the Virgin)   *see* St Osyth and Great
Bentley *Chelmsf*
BENTLEY, LITTLE (St Mary)   *see* Tendring and Lt Bentley w
Beaumont cum Moze *Chelmsf*
BENTLEY, LOWER (St Mary)
BENTLEY, NEW (St Philip and St James) w Arksey *Sheff 7*
P *Bp and DBP (jt)*   **V** S P DICKINSON
BENTWORTH (St Mary), Lasham, Medstead and Shalden
Win 2   **P** *J L Jervoise Esq and Ld Chan (alt)*   **R** B R G FLENLEY
**BENWELL (St James) (St John) (Venerable Bede) and
Scotswood Team, The** *Newc 4*   **P** *Bp*   **C** A J HARDING
OLM P D WILSON
BEOLEY (St Leonard)   *see* Redditch H Trin *Worc*
BEOLEY Church Hill (St Andrew's Church Centre) *as above*
BEPTON (St Mary)   *see* Cocking w W Lavington, Bepton and
Heyshott *Chich*
BERDEN (St Nicholas)   *see* Clavering w Langley, Arkesden etc
Chelmsf
BERE ALSTON (Holy Trinity)   *see* Bere Ferrers *Ex*
BERE FERRERS (St Andrew) *Ex 22*   **P** *DBP*   **R** N C LAW
C A P BARTON
**BERE REGIS (St John the Baptist) and Affpuddle w
Turnerspuddle** *Sarum 8*   **P** *Ball Coll Ox (2 turns), Bp (1 turn)*
R *vacant*
BERECHURCH (St Margaret w St Michael) *Chelmsf 21*   **P** *Bp*
V A I FORDYCE   **C** , C E MARTIN
BERGH APTON (St Peter and St Paul)   *see* Thurton *Nor*
BERGHOLT, EAST (St Mary the Virgin) and Brantham *St E 5*
P *Em Coll Cam*   **R** S VAN DER TOORN   **C** M K LING
NSM R J NEEDLE
BERGHOLT, WEST (St Mary the Virgin) and Great Horkesley
Chelmsf 21   **P** *Bp and Ball Coll Ox (alt)*   **P-in-c** A J ELMES
BERINSFIELD (St Mary and St Berin)   *see* Dorchester *Ox*
**BERKELEY (St Mary the Virgin) w Wick, Breadstone,
Newport, Stone, Woodford and Hill** *Glouc 5*   **P** *Bp,
Berkeley Will Trustees, and Mrs J D Jenner-Fust (jt)*   **V** R J AVERY
NSM R P CHIDLAW
**BERKHAMSTED, GREAT (All Saints) (St Peter), Great
Gaddesden, Little Gaddesden, Nettleden and Potten End**
St Alb 1   **P** *Patr Bd*   **TR** T W PILKINGTON   **TV** J B RUSSELL,
P J NASH   **C** T R PLANT   **NSM** L GEOGHEGAN
**BERKHAMSTED, LITTLE (St Andrew) and Bayford, Essendon
and Ponsbourne** *St Alb 19*   **P** *Marquess of Salisbury (2 turns),
CPAS (1 turn), and Bp (1 turn)*   **R** P M HIGHAM
BERKHAMSYTCH (St Mary and St John)   *see* Ipstones w
Berkhamsytch and Onecote w Bradnop *Lich*

BERKLEY (Blessed Virgin Mary)   *see* Beckington w Standerwick, Berkley, Rodden etc *B & W*

BERKSWELL (St John the Baptist) *Cov 4*   **P** *Trustees* Col C J H Wheatley   **R** M Q BRATTON

BERMONDSEY (St James w Christ Church) (St Anne) *S'wark 7*   **P** *Bp, R Bermondsey St Mary, and F W Smith Esq (3 turns), Prime Min (1 turn)*   **V** G J JENKINS   **C** J S DOWNEY

BERMONDSEY (St Katharine) w St Bartholomew *S'wark 7*   **P** *Bp and R Rotherhithe St Mary w All SS (jt)*   **P-in-c** M R NICHOLLS   **NSM** E J F GBONDA

BERMONDSEY (St Mary Magdalen w St Olave, St John and St Luke) *S'wark 7*   **P** *Ch Patr Soc (2 turns), Ld Chan (1 turn), and Bp (1 turn)*   **R** C D MOORE

BERNWODE *Ox 10*   **P** *Bp, CPAS, Earl Temple of Stowe, and Sir Henry Aubrey-Fletcher Bt (jt)*   **R** P E SLUSAR   **C** J EDMANS, V I D F PLUMB

BERRICK SALOME (St Helen)   *see* Chalgrove w Berrick Salome *Ox*

BERRINGTON (All Saints)   *see* Wenlock *Heref*

BERROW (Blessed Virgin Mary) and Breane *B & W 1*   **P** *Adn Wells*   **R** *vacant*

BERROW (St Faith) w Pendock, Eldersfield, Hollybush and Birtsmorton *Worc 5*   **P** *Bp, D&C, and Exors Sir Berwick Lechmere Bt (jt)*   **R** J M JAMES   **NSM** A E L ELSTON, F B KINGS

BERRY POMEROY (St Mary)   *see* Totnes w Bridgetown, Berry Pomeroy etc *Ex*

BERRYNARBOR (St Peter)   *see* Combe Martin, Berrynarbor, Lynton, Brendon etc *Ex*

BERSTED, NORTH (Holy Cross) *Chich 1*   **P** *Abp* **P-in-c** G A CLARKE

BERSTED, SOUTH (St Mary Magdalene) w NORTH *Chich 1*   **P** *Abp*   **V** T M CROOK

BERWICK (Holy Trinity) (St Mary) *Newc 12*   **P** *Bp (2 turns), D&C Dur (1 turn)*   **V** D F HANDLEY

BERWICK (St John)   *see* Chalke Valley *Sarum*

BERWICK (St Michael and All Angels)   *see* Arlington, Berwick, Selmeston w Alciston etc *Chich*

BERWICK ST JAMES (St James)   *see* Lower Wylye and Till Valley *Sarum*

BESFORD (St Peter's Chapelry)   *see* Defford w Besford *Worc*

BESSACARR, WEST (St Francis of Assisi) *Sheff 8*   **P** *Bp* **V** R A HEARD   **C** A J PRIESTLEY

BESSELSLEIGH (St Lawrence) *Ox 19*   **P** *Ox Ch Trust* **P-in-c** L L SAPWELL

BESSINGBY (St Magnus) (St Mark) *York 9*   **P** *Patr Bd* **V** J G COUPER

BESSINGHAM (St Mary)   *see* Roughton and Felbrigg, Metton, Sustead etc *Nor*

BESTHORPE (All Saints)   *see* Attleborough w Besthorpe *Nor*

BESTHORPE (Holy Trinity)   *see* E Trent *S'well*

BESTWOOD (Emmanuel) (St Mark) *S'well 8*   **P** *Bp and Ch Patr Trust (jt)*   **V** E SNOWDEN   **C** C LITTLE

BESTWOOD (St Matthew on the Hill) (St Philip) *S'well 8* **P** *Bp and Ch Patr Trust (jt)*   **V** E A MORRIS

BESTWOOD PARK (no dedication) w Rise Park *S'well 8* **P** *Bp and Ch Patr Trust (jt)*   **Hon C** N J ROOMS

BESWICK (St Margaret)   *see* Hutton Cranswick w Skerne, Watton and Beswick *York*

BETCHWORTH (St Michael and All Angels) and Buckland *S'wark 26*   **P** *D&C Windsor and All So Coll Ox (jt)* **R** C A COSLETT

BETHERSDEN (St Margaret) w High Halden and Woodchurch *Cant 10*   **P** *Abp*   **P-in-c** S J WHARTON   **C** C R T DENYER

BETHESDA (Shared Church)   *see* Hallwood Ecum Par *Ches*

BETHNAL GREEN (St Barnabas) *Lon 7*   **P** *D&C Cant* **V** B C RALPH   **NSM** S M LEE

BETHNAL GREEN (St James the Less) *Lon 7*   **P** *CPAS* **V** C D NEWMAN-DAY

BETHNAL GREEN (St John)   *see* St Jo on Bethnal Green *Lon*

BETHNAL GREEN (St Matthew w St James the Great) *Lon 7* **P** *Bp*   **R** K J SCULLY   **NSM** J E BLACKBURN

BETHNAL GREEN (St Peter) (St Thomas) *Lon 7*   **P** *City Corp* **V** A ATKINSON

BETLEY (St Margaret) *Lich 9*   **P** *DBP*   **V** P T CHANTRY **NSM** G A BAILEY

BETTISCOMBE (St Stephen)   *see* Golden Cap Team *Sarum*

BETTON STRANGE (St Margaret)   *see* Wenlock *Heref*

BETTWS-Y-CRWYN (St Mary)   *see* Clun Valley *Heref*

BEVERLEY (St Mary) *York 8*   **P** *Abp*   **V** R A LUMLEY **NSM** A R DOOLAN

BEVERLEY (St Nicholas) *York 8*   **P** *Abp*   **V** R J WALKER **C** S L BRAY

BEVERLEY MINSTER (St John and St Martin) *York 8* **P** *Simeon's Trustees*   **V** J J FLETCHER   **C** G W ATHA   **Hon C** V D CLARKE

BEVERSTON (St Mary the Virgin)   *see* Tetbury, Beverston, Long Newnton etc *Glouc*

BEWBUSH (Community Centre)   *see* Ifield *Chich*

BEWCASTLE (St Cuthbert), Stapleton and Kirklinton w Hethersgill *Carl 2*   **P** *Bp, D&C, and DBP (jt)* **R** P A GREENHALGH   **NSM** R P C BROWN

BEWDLEY (St Anne)   *see* Ribbesford w Bewdley and Dowles and Wribbenhall *Worc*

BEWERLEY GRANGE (Chapel)   *see* Upper Nidderdale *Leeds*

BEWHOLME (St John the Baptist)   *see* Sigglesthorne w Nunkeeling and Bewholme *York*

BEWICK, OLD (Holy Trinity)   *see* Glendale Gp *Newc*

BEWSBOROUGH *Cant 7*   **P** *Abp, D&C, St Jo Coll Ox, and Earl of Guilford (jt)*   **R** S M WHITE   **C** V M ASHMAN **NSM** S J CAROLAN-EVANS

BEXHILL (All Saints)   *see* Sidley *Chich*

BEXHILL (St Augustine) *Chich 12*   **P** *Bp*   **V** R COATES **Hon C** P A FROSTICK

BEXHILL (St Barnabas) *Chich 12*   **P** *Bp*   **V** *vacant*

BEXHILL (St Mark) *Chich 12*   **P** *Bp*   **R** J J FRAIS

BEXHILL (St Peter) (St Michael) (Good Shepherd) (St Andrew) *Chich 12*   **P** *Bp*   **TR** D S REYNISH **TV** S D HUGGINS   **NSM** O M WERRETT

BEXHILL (St Stephen) *Chich 12*   **P** *Bp*   **V** T J VOLTZENLOGEL

BEXLEY (St John the Evangelist) (St Mary) *Roch 17*   **P** *Prime Min and Patr Bd (alt)*   **TR** S I LAMB   **TV** A C LETSCHKA **C** J E BOWEN

BEXLEYHEATH (Christ Church) *Roch 15*   **P** *Bp*   **V** T WYATT **NSM** S E TWYNAM

BEXLEYHEATH (St Peter) *Roch 15*   **P** *Bp*   **V** J R CHARLES

BEXWELL (St Mary)   *see* Denver and Ryston w Roxham and W Dereham etc *Ely*

BEYTON (All Saints)   *see* Rougham, Beyton w Hessett and Rushbrooke *St E*

BIBURY (St Mary)   *see* S Cotswolds *Glouc*

BICESTER (St Edburg) w Bucknell, Caversfield and Launton *Ox 21*   **P** *Patr Bd*   **TR** V BREED   **TV** I R BISCOE, R C MATHEW   **C** E J BISCOE   **NSM** P G HILL, P G WRIGHT, R B ATKINS   **OLM** C HILL

BICKENHILL (St Peter)   *see* Hampton-in-Arden w Bickenhill *Birm*

BICKER (St Swithin)   *see* Haven Gp *Linc*

BICKERSHAW (St James and St Elizabeth) *Liv 14*   **P** *Bp* **P-in-c** A E STEIN

BICKERSTAFFE (Holy Trinity)   *see* Aughton St Mich and Bickerstaffe *Liv*

BICKERTON (Holy Trinity)   *see* Malpas and Threapwood and Bickerton *Ches*

BICKINGTON (St Andrew)   *see* Fremington, Instow and Westleigh *Ex*

BICKINGTON (St Mary the Virgin)   *see* Ashburton, Bickington, Buckland in the Moor etc *Ex*

BICKINGTON, HIGH (St Mary)   *see* Newton Tracey, Horwood, Alverdiscott etc *Ex*

BICKLEIGH (St Mary)   *see* Silverton, Butterleigh, Bickleigh and Cadeleigh *Ex*

BICKLEIGH Roborough (St Mary the Virgin) and Shaugh Prior *Ex 21*   **P** *Patr Bd*   **P-in-c** S P RUNDELL **C** C J ROUTLEDGE   **NSM** D K COLEMAN, M J FAIRALL

BICKLEY (St George) *Roch 14*   **P** *SMF*   **V** R J NORMAN

BICKLEY (St Wenefrede) *Ches 5*   **P** *Marquess of Cholmondeley* **P-in-c** R J DIGGLE

BICKNACRE (St Andrew)   *see* Woodham Ferrers and Bicknacre *Chelmsf*

BICKNOLLER (St George)   *see* Quantock Towers *B & W*

BICKNOR (St James)   *see* Tunstall and Bredgar *Cant*

BICTON (Holy Trinity), Montford w Shrawardine and Fitz *Lich 20*   **P** *Earl of Powis, N E E Stephens Esq, and J G O Wingfield Esq (jt)*   **P-in-c** M TOOP   **Hon C** R M PARSONS

BICTON (St Mary)   *see* Budleigh Salterton, E Budleigh w Bicton etc *Ex*

BIDBOROUGH (St Lawrence)   *see* Southborough St Pet w Ch Ch and St Matt etc *Roch*

BIDDENDEN (All Saints) and Smarden *Cant 10*   **P** *Abp* **P-in-c** A BIENFAIT   **C** C A WILSON

BIDDENHAM (St James) *St Alb 9*   **P** *Bp*   **V** S L HUCKLE

BIDDESTONE (St Nicholas)   *see* By Brook *Bris*

BIDDISHAM (St John the Baptist)   *see* Crook Peak *B & W*

BIDDLESDEN (St Margaret)   *see* W Buckingham *Ox*

BIDDULPH (St Lawrence) *Lich 8*   **P** *MMCET*   **C** T H RAAFF **OLM** L J CLOWES

BIDDULPH MOOR (Christ Church) and Knypersley *Lich 8* **P** *Ch Patr Trust and MMCET (jt)*   **R** D A FRASER

BIDEFORD (St Mary) (St Peter East the Water), Northam, Westward Ho!, Appledore, Weare Giffard, Littleham, Landcross and Monkleigh *Ex 15*   **P** *Patr Bd* **P-in-c** C P ROSE-CASEMORE   **TV** D J CARRINGTON, G A SMITH, I J LOVETT   **NSM** A GLOVER, M M E BRAY, S C HUNT, S E JUNIPER

BIDFORD-ON-AVON (St Laurence)   *see* Heart of England *Cov*
BIDSTON (St Oswald) *Ches 1*   **P** *Bp*   **V** R E IVESON
BIELBY (St Giles)   *see* Holme and Seaton Ross Gp *York*
BIERLEY (St John the Evangelist) *Leeds 2*   **P** *DBP*
  V *vacant*
BIERLEY, EAST (St Luke)   *see* Birkenshaw w Hunsworth *Leeds*
BIERTON (St James the Great) and Hulcott *Ox 10*   **P** *Bp and*
  D&C Linc (jt)   **V** C M ACKFORD
BIGBURY (St Lawrence)   *see* Modbury, Bigbury, Ringmore
  etc *Ex*
BIGBY (All Saints)   *see* N Wolds Gp *Linc*
BIGGIN (St Thomas)   *see* Taddington, Chelmorton and
  Monyash etc *Derby*
BIGGIN HILL (St Mark) *Roch 14*   **P** *Bp*   **V** *vacant*
BIGGLESWADE (St Andrew) *St Alb 10*   **P** *Bp*   **V** G C SCOTT
  C R E B PENNANT
BIGHTON (All Saints)   *see* Arle Valley *Win*
BIGNOR (Holy Cross)   *see* Barlavington, Burton w Coates,
  Sutton and Bignor *Chich*
BIGRIGG (St John)   *see* Egremont and Haile *Carl*
BILBOROUGH (St John) (St Martin) and Strelley *S'well 8*
  P *SMF and Bp (jt)*   **R** A J CARTWRIGHT   **C** D C CORCORAN
  NSM G M HALL
BILBROOK (Holy Cross)   *see* Tettenhall Regis *Lich*
BILBROUGH (St James)   *see* N Ainsty *York*
BILDESTON (St Mary Magdalene) w Wattisham and Lindsey,
  Whatfield w Semer, Nedging and Naughton *St E 3*
  P *Abp, Bp, CPAS, Jes Coll Cam, and Reformation Ch Trust (jt)*
  Hon C E A LAW
BILHAM *Sheff 12*   **P** *Bp, Major W Warde-Aldam, W G A Warde-*
  Norbury Esq, and Mrs S Grant-Dalton (jt)   **V** *vacant*
BILLERICAY (Christ Church) (Emmanuel) (St John the Divine)
  (St Mary Magdalen) and Little Burstead *Chelmsf 12*
  P *Bp*   **TR** P A CARR   **TV** P A GAMBLING   **OLM** M J FOWLER
BILLESDON (St John the Baptist)   *see* Coplow *Leic*
BILLESLEY COMMON (Holy Cross) *Birm 5*   **P** *Bp*
  V P OGILVIE
BILLING, GREAT (St Andrew) w LITTLE (All Saints) *Pet 4*
  P *BNC Ox and Bp (alt)*   **R** S R PALMER
  C L M LAVARELLO-SMITH   **Hon C** D LUNN
  NSM D SPENCELEY
BILLINGBOROUGH Group, The (St Andrew) *Linc 14*
  P *Prime Min (2 turns), Bp and St Jo Coll Dur (1 turn)*
  P-in-c A K E SORENSEN   **OLM** A L STEELE, J G SPREADBURY
BILLINGE (St Aidan) *Liv 14*   **P** R *Wigan*   **V** A OVEREND
BILLINGFORD (St Leonard)   *see* Redenhall w Scole *Nor*
BILLINGFORD (St Peter)   *see* N Elmham, Billingford, Bintree,
  Guist etc *Nor*
BILLINGHAM (St Aidan) (St Cuthbert) (St Luke) (St Mary
  Magdalene) *Dur 10*   **P** *Patr Bd*   **TR** L J MCWILLIAMS
  TV R B RADLEY, W E BRAVINER
BILLINGHAY (St Michael)   *see* Carr Dyke Gp *Linc*
BILLINGSHURST (St Mary the Virgin) *Chich 7*   **P** *Bp*
  V B J PRITCHARD
BILLINGTON (St Michael and All Angels)   *see* Ouzel Valley
  St Alb
BILLOCKBY (All Saints)   *see* S Trin Broads *Nor*
BILLY MILL (St Aidan) *Newc 5*   **P** *Bp*   **V** P S BAGSHAW
BILNEY, EAST (St Mary)   *see* Dereham and Distr *Nor*
BILSBORROW (St Hilda)   *see* Fellside Team *Blackb*
BILSBY (Holy Trinity) w Farlesthorpe *Linc 10*   **P** *Bp*
  NSM J M MORTON   **OLM** R D BARRETT
BILSDALE MIDCABLE (St John)   *see* Upper Ryedale *York*
BILSDALE PRIORY (St Hilda)   *see* Ingleby Greenhow, Bilsdale
  Priory etc *York*
BILSINGTON (St Peter and St Paul)   *see* Saxon Shoreline *Cant*
BILSON (Mission Church)   *see* Cinderford w Littledean *Glouc*
BILSTHORPE (St Margaret) *S'well 3*   **P** *DBP*
  NSM M A GROVES
BILSTON (St Leonard) (St Chad) (St Mary the Virgin) *Lich 28*
  P *Patr Bd*   **TR** D WILLS   **TV** M S HATHORNE
  OLM C E DAVIES
BILTON (St John the Evangelist) and St Luke *Leeds 23*   **P** *Bp*
  TR *vacant*
BILTON (St Mark) *Cov 6*   **P** N M Assheton Esq
  R T D COCKELL   **NSM** M J SHARPE
BILTON IN HOLDERNESS (St Peter) *York 12*   **P** *Abp*
  V *vacant*
BILTON, NEW (St Matthew and St Oswald)   *see* Rugby W *Cov*
BILTON-IN-AINSTY (St Helen)   *see* Rural Ainsty *York*
BINBROOK Group, The (St Mary) *Linc 4*   **P** *Ld Chan, DBP and*
  G F Sleight Esq (alt)   **R** T J WALKER
BINCOMBE (Holy Trinity) w Broadwey, Upwey and Buckland
  Ripers *Sarum 4*   **P** *G&C Coll Cam (2 turns), Miss M B F*
  Frampton (1 turn), and Bp (1 turn)   **R** R A C SIMMONS
  NSM B E J ELLIS

BINEGAR (Holy Trinity)   *see* Ashwick w Oakhill and Binegar
  B & W
BINFIELD (All Saints) (St Mark) *Ox 3*   **P** *Ld Chan*
  R L A J TAYLOR   **NSM** N RICHARDS   **OLM** N RICHARDS
BINGFIELD (St Mary)   *see* St Oswald in Lee w Bingfield *Newc*
BINGHAM (St Mary and All Saints) *S'well 5*   **P** *The Crown*
  R D L HARPER
BINGLEY (All Saints) *Leeds 1*   **P** *Bp*   **V** B A MASON
BINGLEY (Holy Trinity) *Leeds 1*   **P** *Bp*   **V** A J CLARKE
BINHAM (St Mary)   *see* Stiffkey and Bale *Nor*
BINLEY (St Bartholomew) *Cov 1*   **P** *Bp*   **V** J P TAYLOR
BINSEY (St Margaret)   *see* Osney *Ox*
BINSEY Team Ministry *Carl 6*   **P** *Patr Bd*   **TR** P A ROGERS
  TV P M F STREATFEILD   **C** L A LUNN
  NSM C C FRYER-SPEDDING
BINSTEAD (Holy Cross) *Portsm 7*   **P** *Bp*   **NSM** V J HARDS
BINSTED (Holy Cross)   *see* Bentley, Binsted and Froyle *Win*
BINSTED (St Mary)   *see* Walberton w Binsted *Chich*
BINTON (St Peter)   *see* Heart of England *Cov*
BINTREE (St Swithin)   *see* N Elmham, Billingford, Bintree,
  Guist etc *Nor*
BIRCH (St James) w Fallowfield *Man 3*   **P** *Bp*
  R H D Y MATTHEWS
BIRCHANGER (St Mary the Virgin)   *see* Stansted Mountfitchet w
  Birchanger and Farnham *Chelmsf*
BIRCHENCLIFFE (St Philip the Apostle)   *see* Birkby and
  Birchencliffe *Leeds*
BIRCHES HEAD (St Matthew)   *see* Hanley H Ev *Lich*
BIRCHFIELD (Holy Trinity) *Birm 3*   **P** *Bp*   **V** E I PITTS
BIRCHILLS, THE (St Andrew)   *see* Walsall St Andr *Lich*
BIRCHIN COPPICE (St Peter)   *see* Kidderminster St Jo and
  H Innocents *Worc*
BIRCHINGTON (All Saints) w Acol and Minnis Bay *Cant 5*
  P *Abp*   **V** D R WITTS
BIRCH-IN-RUSHOLME (St Agnes) w Longsight St John w
  St Cyprian *Man 1*   **P** *Prime Min and Bp (alt)*
  P-in-c E O ADOYO
BIRCHMOOR (St John)   *see* Polesworth *Birm*
BIRCHOVER (St Michael)   *see* Youlgreave, Middleton, Stanton-
  in-Peak etc *Derby*
BIRCHWOOD (Mission Church)   *see* Blackdown *B & W*
BIRCHWOOD (St Luke) *Linc 11*   **P** *Bp*   **V** L M HARRIS
BIRCHWOOD (Transfiguration)   *see* Warrington E *Liv*
BIRCLE (St John the Baptist) *Man 8*   **P** R *Middleton St Leon*
  P-in-c G F JOYCE
BIRDBROOK (St Augustine)   *see* Two Rivers *Chelmsf*
BIRDHAM (St James)   *see* W Wittering and Birdham w Itchenor
  Chich
BIRDINGBURY (St Leonards)   *see* Draycote Gp *Cov*
BIRDLIP (St Mary in Hamlet)   *see* Brimpsfield w Birdlip, Syde,
  Daglingworth etc *Glouc*
BIRDSALL (St Mary)   *see* W Buckrose *York*
BIRKBY (St Cuthbert) Huddersfield and Birchencliffe *Leeds 12*
  P *V Lindley and Bp (jt)*   **V** M RAILTON-CROWDER
  C S L FARRIMOND   **NSM** M FOSSEY   **OLM** J SARGENT
BIRKBY (St John the Evangelist) Huddersfield and
  Woodhouse *Leeds 12*   **P** *Bp and DBP (jt)*
  P-in-c D J CARPENTER   **C** S PERVEZ
BIRKBY (St Peter)   *see* E Richmond *Leeds*
BIRKDALE (St James) *Liv 9*   **P** *Trustees*   **P-in-c** I G MAINEY
BIRKDALE (St John) *Liv 9*   **P** *Trustees*   **P-in-c** J P LEFFLER
BIRKDALE (St Peter) *Liv 9*   **P** *Trustees*   **P-in-c** I G MAINEY
  C D L COLLIER   **OLM** E LOXHAM
BIRKENHEAD (Christ Church) *Ches 1*   **P** *Bp*
  P-in-c K L FREEMAN
BIRKENHEAD (St James) w St Bede *Ches 1*   **P** *Trustees*
  V S M MANSFIELD
BIRKENHEAD PRIORY (Christ the King) *Ches 1*   **P** *Patr Bd*
  R D J AYLING
BIRKENSHAW (St Paul) w Hunsworth *Leeds 7*   **P** *V Birstall*
  V A D WALKER   **NSM** C WALKER, D S ANDREW
  OLM R DAVIDSON
BIRKIN (St Mary)   *see* Haddlesey w Hambleton and Birkin
  York
BIRLEY (St Peter)   *see* Canon Pyon w King's Pyon, Birley and
  Wellington *Heref*
BIRLING (All Saints), Addington, Ryarsh and Trottiscliffe
  Roch 7   **P** *Bp*   **R** L K SHUKER
BIRLING, LOWER (Christ Church)   *see* Snodland All SS w
  Ch Ch *Roch*
BIRLINGHAM (St James the Great)   *see* Pershore w Pinvin,
  Wick and Birlingham *Worc*
BIRMINGHAM (Bishop Latimer w All Saints) *Birm 3*
  P *St Martin's Trustees*   **P-in-c** J R A SAMPSON
BIRMINGHAM (St George w St Michael)   *see* Edgbaston St Geo
  Birm

BIRMINGHAM (St George) *Birm 1*　**P** *St Martin's Trustees*
R L C WRIGHT　**C** N BOUMENJEL
BIRMINGHAM (St John the Evangelist)　*see* Ladywood St Jo and
St Pet *Birm*
BIRMINGHAM (St Luke) *Birm 1*　**P** *Trustees*
P-in-c T D L HUGHES　**C** A J HOWETT
BIRMINGHAM (St Martin-in-the-Bull-Ring) w Bordesley
St Andrew *Birm 1*　**P** *St Martin's Trustees*　**R** S W JONES
C D E WRIGHT　**NSM** E BLAIR-CHAPPELL
BIRMINGHAM (St Paul) *Birm 1*　**P** *St Martin's Trustees*
V M R GILBERT
BIRSTALL (St James the Great) and Wanlip *Leic 5*　**P** *Bp and*
C A Palmer-Tomkinson Esq (jt)　**V** V J JUPP
NSM A D CROSBY
BIRSTALL (St Peter) *Leeds 7*　**P** *Bp*　**V** P J KNIGHT
BIRSTWITH (St James)　*see* Hampsthwaite and Killinghall and
Birstwith *Leeds*
BIRTLES (St Catherine)　*see* Alderley w Birtles *Ches*
BIRTLEY (St Giles)　*see* Chollerton w Birtley and Thockrington
Newc
BIRTLEY (St John the Evangelist) *Dur 11*　**P** *R Chester le Street*
V E G LLOYD　**Hon C** B M C BROGGIO
BIRTSMORTON (St Peter and St Paul)　*see* Berrow w Pendock,
Eldersfield, Hollybush etc *Worc*
BISBROOKE (St John the Baptist)　*see* Lyddington, Bisbrooke,
Caldecott, Glaston etc *Pet*
BISCATHORPE (St Helen)　*see* Asterby Gp *Linc*
BISCOT (Holy Trinity) *St Alb 12*　**P** *Bp*　**V** T B SINGH
BISHAM (All Saints)　*see* Gt Marlow w Marlow Bottom, Lt
Marlow and Bisham *Ox*
BISHAMPTON (St James)　*see* Abberton, The Flyfords, Naunton
Beauchamp etc *Worc*
BISHOP AUCKLAND (St Andrew) (St Anne) *Dur 6*　**P** *Prime*
Min and Bp (alt)　**V** N P VINE
BISHOP AUCKLAND Woodhouse Close Area of Ecumenical
Experiment (Conventional District) *Dur 10*　**C-in-c** S S GILL
BISHOP BURTON (All Saints) *York 8*　**P** *Abp*
P-in-c R E YOUNG
BISHOP CAUNDLE (not known)　*see* Three Valleys *Sarum*
BISHOP MIDDLEHAM (St Michael)　*see* Upper Skerne *Dur*
BISHOP NORTON (St Peter), Waddingham and Snitterby
Linc 8　**P** *Bp and The Crown (alt)*　**P-in-c** K E COLWELL
BISHOP SUTTON (Holy Trinity)　*see* Clutton w Cameley,
Bishop Sutton and Stowey *B & W*
BISHOP THORNTON (St John the Evangelist), Burnt Yates,
Markington, Ripley and South Stainley *Leeds 25*
P *Sir Thomas Ingilby Bt*　**R** P R HARFORD
BISHOP WILTON (St Edith)　*see* Garrowby Hill *York*
BISHOPHILL JUNIOR (St Mary)　*see* York St Clem w St Mary
Bishophill *York*
BISHOPHILL SENIOR (St Clement w St Mary) *as above*
BISHOP'S CANNINGS (St Mary the Virgin)　*see* The Cannings
and Redhorn *Sarum*
BISHOP'S CASTLE (St John the Baptist) w Mainstone,
Lydbury North and Edgton *Heref 9*　**P** *Earl of Powis (3 turns),*
Ld Chan (1 turn), and Mrs R E Bell (1 turn)
P-in-c S A C FOUNTAIN　**C** S L HARE
BISHOP'S CLEEVE (St Michael and All Angels) and Woolstone
w Gotherington and Oxenton *Glouc 9*　**P** *Patr Bd*
TR M ALLEN　**TV** R F REAKES
BISHOP'S FROME (St Mary the Virgin)　*see* Frome Valley *Heref*
BISHOP'S HATFIELD (St Etheldreda) (St Luke) (St John)
(St Michael and All Angels), Lemsford and North Mymms
St Alb 18　**P** *Patr Bd*　**TR** R E PYKE　**TV** A J DUNCAN,
J BOOTHBY　**NSM** S M STILWELL
BISHOPS HULL (St Peter and St Paul) *B & W 18*
P *Adn Taunton*　**V** P J HUGHES
BISHOP'S ITCHINGTON (St Michael) *Cov 10*　**P** *Bp*
P-in-c M C GREEN　**C** V J BISIKER
BISHOP'S LAVINGTON (All Saints)　*see* The Lavingtons,
Cheverells, and Easterton *Sarum*
BISHOP'S LYDEARD (Blessed Virgin Mary) w Lydeard
St Lawrence, Bagborough, Combe Florey and Cothelstone
B & W 19　**P** *Bp, D&C, W H J Hancock Esq, and Mrs P M G*
Mitford (jt)　**R** M J TREGENZA　**NSM** M YOUNG
BISHOP'S STORTFORD (Holy Trinity) *St Alb 15*　**P** *Bp*
V M K BROWN
BISHOP'S STORTFORD (St Michael) *St Alb 15*　**P** *Bp*
V D G WILLIAMS　**C** E L DAVIS
BISHOP'S SUTTON (St Nicholas) and Ropley and West Tisted
Win 1　**P** *Peache Trustees*　**R** *vacant*
BISHOP'S TACHBROOK (St Chad) *Cov 11*　**P** *Bp*
P-in-c E SCRIVENS
BISHOPS TAWTON (St John the Baptist)　*see* Barnstaple *Ex*
BISHOP'S WALTHAM (St Peter) *Portsm 1*　**P** *Bp*　**R** J C HUNT
NSM J BELOE

BISHOPS WOOD (St John the Evangelist) *Lich 2*　**P** *V Brewood*
NSM M J COULTER
BISHOP'S WOOD (St Mary)　*see* Hartlebury *Worc*
BISHOPSBOURNE (St Mary)　*see* Barham Downs *Cant*
BISHOPSNYMPTON (St Mary the Virgin), Rose Ash,
Mariansleigh, Molland, Knowstone, East Anstey and West
Anstey *Ex 18*　**P** *DBP*　**C** D P BAKER
BISHOPSTEIGNTON (St John the Baptist)　*see* Teignmouth,
Ideford w Luton, Ashcombe etc *Ex*
BISHOPSTOKE (St Mary) (St Paul) *Win 10*　**P** *Bp*　**R** R E WISE
BISHOPSTON (Church of the Good Shepherd)　*see* Bishopston
and St Andrews *Bris*
BISHOPSTON (St Michael and All Angels) *as above*
BISHOPSTON (St Michael and All Angels) (Church of the
Good Shepherd) and St Andrews *Bris 3*　**P** *Patr Bd*
P-in-c J C W STEVENSON　**TV** W P MASSEY
NSM B J PULLAN, M J SALMON, V LEE
BISHOPSTONE (St Lawrence)　*see* Credenhill w Brinsop and
Wormsley etc *Heref*
BISHOPSTONE (St Mary the Virgin)　*see* Lyddington and
Wanborough and Bishopstone etc *Bris*
BISHOPSTONE (St Andrew)　*see* E Blatchington and
Bishopstone *Chich*
BISHOPSTONE (St John the Baptist)　*see* Chalke Valley
Sarum
BISHOPSTROW (St Aldhelm) and Boreham *Sarum 12*
P *DBP*　**R** D R A BRETT
BISHOPSWOOD (All Saints)　*see* Wye Reaches Gp *Heref*
BISHOPSWORTH (St Peter) and Bedminster Down *Bris 1*
P *Bp*　**TR** T R J GODDEN　**NSM** E P WHERLOCK, R A LANE
BISHOPTHORPE (St Andrew) *York 1*　**P** *Abp*　**V** C I COATES
NSM P J MACNAUGHTON
BISHOPTON (St Peter)　*see* Stockton Country Par *Dur*
BISHOPWEARMOUTH (Good Shepherd) *Dur 1*　**P** *Bp*
P-in-c B SKELTON　**NSM** D RAINE
BISHOPWEARMOUTH (St Gabriel) *Dur 1*　**P** *V Sunderland*
NSM J P TALBOT
BISHOPWEARMOUTH (St Luke Pallion)　*see* Millfield St Mark
and Pallion St Luke *Dur*
BISHOPWEARMOUTH (St Mary)　*see* Millfield St Mary *Dur*
BISHOPWEARMOUTH (St Nicholas) (Christ Church) *Dur 1*
P *Bp*　**V** S CLARK　**NSM** S V E NDALISO
BISLEY (All Saints), Chalford, France Lynch, and Oakridge
and Bussage w Eastcombe *Glouc 4*　**P** *Ld Chan (1 turn),*
Bp and Adn (1 turn)　**V** R H WOODALL　**Hon C** M D CLARK
NSM S J JARVIS
BISLEY (St John the Baptist) and West End (Holy Trinity)
Guildf 6　**P** *Bp*　**R** A J ARMITT　**NSM** D H ROBINSON
BISPHAM (All Hallows) *Blackb 8*　**P** *Ch Soc Trust*　**R** S J COX
C D E PLATT　**Emer** N R BRALESFORD
BISTERNE (St Paul)　*see* Ringwood *Win*
BITCHFIELD (St Mary Magdalene)　*see* N Beltisloe Gp *Linc*
BITTADON (St Peter)　*see* Ilfracombe, Lee, Woolacombe,
Bittadon etc *Ex*
BITTERING PARVA (St Peter and St Paul)　*see* Gressenhall w
Longham w Wendling etc *Nor*
BITTERLEY (St Mary)　*see* Ludlow *Heref*
BITTERNE (Holy Saviour) *Win 13*　**P** *Bp*
P-in-c A M M PARKER
BITTERNE PARK (All Hallows) (Ascension) *Win 13*　**P** *Bp*
P-in-c A SMITH
BITTESWELL (St Mary)　*see* Lutterworth w Cotesbach and
Bitteswell *Leic*
BITTON (St Mary)　*see* Warmley, Syston and Bitton *Bris*
BIX (St James)　*see* Nettlebed w Bix, Highmoor, Pishill etc *Ox*
BIXLEY (St Wandregesilus)　*see* Poringland *Nor*
BLABY (All Saints) *Leic 7*　**P** *Bp*　**P-in-c** J G GIBBINS
BLACK BOURTON (St Mary the Virgin)　*see* Shill Valley and
Broadshire *Ox*
BLACK NOTLEY (St Peter and St Paul) *Chelmsf 17*　**P** *St Jo Coll*
Cam　**R** E J BENDREY　**C** O C MAXFIELD-COOTE
BLACK TORRINGTON (St Mary), Bradford w Cookbury,
Thornbury and Highampton *Ex 16*　**P** *DBP*
R K M ROBERTS
BLACKAWTON (St Michael)　*see* Stoke Fleming, Blackawton
and Strete *Ex*
BLACKBIRD LEYS (Holy Family) *Ox 1*　**P** *Bp*　**V** H R CARTER
BLACKBOURNE *St E 9*　**P** *Patr Bd*　**TR** P R GARBETT
NSM A J REDMAN
BLACKBROOK (St Paul)　*see* Parr *Liv*
BLACKBURN (Christ Church w St Matthew) *Blackb 2*　**P** *Bp*
V A RAYNES　**C** P A BYE
BLACKBURN (Holy Trinity Worship Centre)　*see* N and E *Blackb*
Blackb
BLACKBURN (St Aidan) (St Luke) St Mark and St Philip
Blackb 2　**P** *Bp and V Blackb (jt)*　**V** C E BROOKS

BLACKBURN (St Barnabas) *Blackb 2*   **P** *Bp*
V J P MILTON-THOMPSON
BLACKBURN (St Gabriel) *Blackb 2*   **P** *Bp*   **V** S P CORBETT
BLACKBURN (St Jude)   *see* N and E Blackb *Blackb*
BLACKBURN (St Luke)   *see* Blackb St Aid, St Luke, St Mark and St Phil *Blackb*
BLACKBURN (St Michael and All Angels)   *see* N and E Blackb *Blackb*
BLACKBURN (St Silas) *Blackb 2*   **P** *Trustees*   **V** *vacant*
BLACKBURN (St Stephen) (St James) *Blackb 2*   **P** *Bp, DBP, and Exors the Ven C W D Carroll (jt)*   **V** A A JOHN
BLACKBURN The Redeemer (St Bartholomew) (The Saviour) *Blackb 2*   **P** *Bp and CPAS (jt)*   **V** R A H MARSHALL
BLACKBURN, NORTH and EAST (St Jude) (St Michael and All Angels) (Holy Trinity Worship Centre) *Blackb 2*   **P** *V Blackb, J Whittaker Esq, and Mrs V Edge (jt)*   **V** L M DANIELS
BLACKDOWN (Holy Trinity)   *see* Beaminster Area *Sarum*
BLACKDOWN Benefice, The *B & W 16*   **P** *DBP (4 turns), Pitminster PCC and Corfe PCC (1 turn)*   **R** J A FALLON
NSM D G AGER
BLACKFEN (Good Shepherd)   *see* Lamorbey H Redeemer *Roch*
BLACKFORD (Holy Trinity)   *see* Wedmore w Theale and Blackford *B & W*
BLACKFORD (St John the Baptist)   *see* Rockcliffe and Blackford *Carl*
BLACKFORD (St Michael)   *see* Camelot Par *B & W*
BLACKFORDBY (St Margaret) and Woodville *Leic 8*   **P** *Bp*
V T S G VALE
BLACKHALL (St Andrew), Castle Eden and Monkhesleden *Dur 2*   **P** *Bp*   **P-in-c** A M RICHARDSON
BLACKHAM (All Saints)   *see* Withyham St Mich *Chich*
BLACKHEATH (All Saints) *S'wark 4*   **P** *V Lewisham St Mary*
V N W S CRANFIELD   **C** T W CHATTERTON
BLACKHEATH (St John the Evangelist) *S'wark 1*   **P** *CPAS*
V E F A L SCRASE-FIELD   **C** H O APARANGA
NSM A M BESWETHERICK
BLACKHEATH (St Martin)   *see* Wonersh w Blackheath *Guildf*
BLACKHEATH (St Paul) *Birm 7*   **P** *Bp*   **V** M J SERMON
C K L EVANS   **NSM** C G CHRISTENSEN
BLACKHEATH PARK (St Michael and All Angels) *S'wark 1*
P *Bp*   **V** A R CHRISTIE   **C** E A FRANKLIN   **NSM** A SCOTT
BLACKLAND (St Peter)   *see* Marden Vale *Sarum*
BLACKLANDS Hastings (Christchurch and St Andrew)
Chich 15   **P** *Ch Patr Trust*   **P-in-c** C M HILL
BLACKLEY (Holy Trinity) *Man 4*   **P** *Bp*   **R** P A STAMP
BLACKLEY (St Andrew) *Man 4*   **P** *Bp*   **P-in-c** I C FELLOWS
BLACKLEY (St Paul) *Man 4*   **P** *Bp*   **P-in-c** E M ROBERTS
C H CORCORAN   **NSM** H TOMLINSON
BLACKLEY (St Peter) *Man 4*   **P** *D&C*   **P-in-c** E M ROBERTS
C H CORCORAN
BLACKMOOR (St Matthew) and Whitehill *Portsm 4*   **P** *Earl of Selborne*   **P-in-c** D J CLARKE
BLACKMORE (St Laurence) and Stondon Massey *Chelmsf 3*
P *Bp*   **V** *vacant*
BLACKPOOL (Christ Church w All Saints) (St Andrew)
Blackb 8   **P** *Bp and Trustees (jt)*   **V** A BYROM
BLACKPOOL (Holy Cross) South Shore *Blackb 8*   **P** *Bp*
V P ENNION
BLACKPOOL (Holy Trinity)   *see* S Shore H Trin *Blackb*
BLACKPOOL (St John) *Blackb 8*   **P** *Trustees*   **V** D CONNOLLY
C L M TOMKINSON
BLACKPOOL (St Mark)   *see* Layton and Staining *Blackb*
BLACKPOOL (St Mary) South Shore *Blackb 8*   **P** *Bp*
V P ENNION
BLACKPOOL (St Michael and All Angels)   *see* Layton and Staining *Blackb*
BLACKPOOL (St Paul's Worship Centre) *Blackb 8*   **P** *Trustees*
P-in-c D A PREST
BLACKPOOL (St Peter)   *see* S Shore St Pet *Blackb*
BLACKPOOL (St Stephen on the Cliffs) *Blackb 8*   **P** *Bp, R Bispham All Hallows, and Ch Wardens (jt)*   **V** A G SAGE
BLACKPOOL (St Thomas) *Blackb 8*   **P** *CPAS*
V R F T MURPHY
BLACKPOOL (St Wilfrid) Mereside *Blackb 8*   **P** *Bp*
V *vacant*
BLACKROD (St Catherine) (Scot Lane School) *Man 9*   **P** *V Bolton-le-Moors St Pet*   **C** M C BEHREND, S FLETCHER
OLM T LITHERLAND
BLACKTOFT (Holy Trinity)   *see* Howden *York*
BLACKWELL (All Saints) and Salutation *Dur 8*   **P** *Bp*
V D J RAILTON
BLACKWELL (St Catherine)   *see* The Lickey *Birm*
BLACKWELL (St Werburgh) w Tibshelf *Derby 1*   **P** *Bp and MMCET (jt)*   **V** G MANLEY   **OLM** D HESKETH
BLADON (St Martin)   *see* Blenheim *Ox*

BLAGDON (St Andrew) w Compton Martin and Ubley *B & W 9*   **P** *Bp and Sir John Wills Bt (jt)*
R J L CHAMBERLAIN
BLAGREAVES (St Andrew) *Derby 10*   **P** *Bp, Churchwardens, and CPAS (jt)*   **V** P G BYSOUTH
BLAISDON (St Michael and All Angels)   *see* Westbury-on-Severn w Flaxley, Blaisdon etc *Glouc*
BLAKEDOWN (St James the Great)   *see* Churchill-in-Halfshire w Blakedown and Broome *Worc*
BLAKEMERE (St Leonard)   *see* Cusop w Blakemere, Bredwardine w Brobury etc *Heref*
BLAKENALL HEATH (Christ Church) *Lich 25*   **P** *Patr Bd*
C M J DANKS   **NSM** J P PHILLIPS
BLAKENEY (All Saints)   *see* Newnham w Awre and Blakeney *Glouc*
BLAKENEY (St Nicholas w St Mary and St Thomas) w Cley, Wiveton, Glandford and Letheringsett *Nor 18*   **P** *Bp and Keble Coll Ox (jt)*   **R** E A DADY
BLAKENHAM, GREAT (St Mary) and LITTLE (St Mary) w Baylham and Nettlestead *St E 1*   **P** *Bp and MMCET (jt)*
C J FENNELL   **NSM** P Y WRIGHT
BLAKESLEY (St Mary)   *see* Lambfold *Pet*
BLANCHLAND (St Mary's Abbey) w Hunstanworth and Edmundbyers and Muggleswick *Newc 9*   **P** *D E Scott-Harden Esq, Lord Crewe's Trustees and D&C (alt)*
R H SAVAGE
BLANDFORD FORUM (St Peter and St Paul) and Langton Long *Sarum 6*   **P** *Bp*   **R** J P TRIFFITT
BLANDFORD ST MARY (St Mary)   *see* Spetisbury w Charlton Marshall etc *Sarum*
BLANKNEY (St Oswald)   *see* Metheringham w Blankney and Dunston *Linc*
BLASTON (St Giles)   *see* Six Saints circa Holt *Leic*
BLATCHINGTON, EAST (St John the Evangelist) (St Peter) and Bishopstone *Chich 21*   **P** *Bp and Bp Lon (alt)*   **R** A D MAYES
Hon C T C SMYTH   **NSM** R J WOODHAMS
BLATCHINGTON, WEST (St Peter) *Chich 20*   **P** *Bp*
R D B SMITH
BLAXHALL (St Peter)   *see* Alde River *St E*
BLAYDON (St Cuthbert) and Swalwell *Dur 13*   **P** *Bp*
R A THORP   **NSM** B HOWELL, H M THORP, J ROBINSON, L GARDNER
BLEADON (St Peter and St Paul) *B & W 10*   **P** *Guild of All So*
P-in-c T J ERRIDGE
BLEAN (St Cosmus and St Damian) *Cant 3*   **P** *Master of Eastbridge Hosp*   **P-in-c** S C E LAIRD   **C** C R PINCHBECK
BLEASBY (St Mary)   *see* Thurgarton w Hoveringham and Bleasby etc *S'well*
BLEASDALE (St Eadmor)   *see* Fellside Team *Blackb*
BLEATARN (Chapel of Ease)   *see* Brough w Stainmore, Musgrave and Warcop *Carl*
BLEDINGTON (St Leonard)   *see* Broadwell, Evenlode, Oddington, Adlestrop etc *Glouc*
BLEDLOW (Holy Trinity)   *see* Risborough *Ox*
BLEDLOW RIDGE (St Paul)   *see* W Wycombe w Bledlow Ridge, Bradenham and Radnage *Ox*
BLENDON (St James the Great) *Roch 17*   **P** *The Crown*
V A F WARD   **NSM** P A PERCIVAL
BLENDWORTH (Holy Trinity) w Chalton w Idsworth *Portsm 5*
P *Bp*   **P-in-c** R A DONALD
BLENHEIM *Ox 29*   **P** *Patr Bd*   **TR** A M DAFFERN
TV N J JARVIS   **C** A H VENNING   **NSM** S C HENSON
BLETCHINGDON (St Giles)   *see* Akeman *Ox*
BLETCHINGLEY (St Mary) and Nutfield *S'wark 25*   **P** *Em Coll Cam and Jes Coll Ox (jt)*   **R** P MOSELING
NSM P J SHERRINGTON
BLETCHLEY (St Mary) (St John's District Church) *Ox 14*
P *DBP*   **R** D R MCDOUGALL   **C** C BUTT   **Emer** C BUTT
BLETSOE (St Mary)   *see* Riseley w Bletsoe *St Alb*
BLEWBURY (St Michael and All Angels)   *see* The Churn *Ox*
BLICKLING (St Andrew)   *see* Lt Barningham, Blickling, Edgefield etc *Nor*
BLIDWORTH (St Mary of the Purification) w Rainworth
S'well 2   **P** *DBP and Ld Chan (alt)*   **V** H ROBINSON
BLIDWORTH, NEW (St Andrew)   *see* Blidworth w Rainworth *S'well*
BLINDLEY HEATH (St John the Evangelist)   *see* Godstone and Blindley Heath *S'wark*
BLISLAND (St Protus and St Hyacinth) w Temple, St Breward and Helland *Truro 10*   **P** *SMF, D&C, and MMCET (jt)*
R S L BRYAN
BLISWORTH (St John the Baptist), Alderton, Grafton Regis, Milton Malsor and Stoke Bruerne w Shutlanger *Pet 5*
P *Bp, MMCET and Hyndman Trustees (2 turns), Ld Chan (1 turn)*
R A L WATKINS   **C** S T COOPER
BLITHFIELD (St Leonard)   *see* Abbots Bromley, Blithfield, Colton, Colwich etc *Lich*

BLO' NORTON (St Andrew)　*see* Guiltcross *Nor*

BLOCKLEY (St Peter and St Paul)　*see* Vale and Cotswold Edge *Glouc*

BLOFIELD (St Andrew and St Peter) *Nor 4*　**P** *G&C Coll Cam and Ch Soc Trust (jt)*　**R** K M BILLSON

BLOOMSBURY (St George) w Woburn Square (Christ Church) *Lon 17*　**P** *Ld Chan*　**R** D T PEEBLES　**NSM** J A WALTERS

BLORE RAY (St Bartholomew)　*see* Calton, Cauldon, Grindon, Waterfall etc *Lich*

BLOXHAM (Our Lady of Bloxham) w Milcombe and South Newington *Ox 23*　**P** *Ex Coll Ox and Eton Coll (jt)*　**V** *vacant*

BLOXHOLME (St Mary)　*see* Digby Gp *Linc*

BLOXWICH (All Saints) (Holy Ascension) *Lich 25*　**P** *Patr Bd*　**TR** R S WILLIAMS　**TV** C J TURNER　**OLM** P A NESBITT

BLOXWORTH (St Andrew)　*see* Red Post *Sarum*

BLUBBERHOUSES (St Andrew)　*see* Washburn and Mid-Wharfe *Leeds*

BLUE BELL HILL (St Alban)　*see* S Chatham H Trin *Roch*

BLUNDELLSANDS (St Michael) *Liv 5*　**P** *Trustees*　**V** *vacant*

BLUNDELLSANDS (St Nicholas) *Liv 5*　**P** *Trustees*　**V** *vacant*

BLUNDESTON (St Mary)　*see* Somerleyton, Ashby, Fritton, Herringfleet etc *Nor*

BLUNHAM (St Edmund King and Martyr and St James)　*see* Riversmeet *St Alb*

BLUNSDON (St Andrew)　*see* N Swindon St Andr *Bris*

BLUNTISHAM (St Mary) cum Earith w Colne and Holywell cum Needingworth *Ely 12*　**P** *Ch Ch Ox and Bp (jt)*　**V** S M ANTHONY　**C** J J CHAMBERLIN

BLURTON (St Alban)　*see* Blurton and Dresden *Lich*

BLURTON (St Bartholomew) (St Alban) and Dresden *Lich 12*　**P** *Bp*　**V** P J MOCKFORD　**C** M A EVANS　**OLM** L J WALKER

BLYBOROUGH (St Alkmund)　*see* Trentcliffe Gp *Linc*

BLYFORD (All Saints)　*see* Blyth Valley *St E*

BLYMHILL (St Mary)　*see* Watershed *Lich*

BLYTH (St Cuthbert) *Newc 1*　**P** *Bp*　**V** S MCMAHON

BLYTH (St Mary and St Martin) and Scrooby w Ranskill *S'well 1*　**P** *Bp and Trin Coll Cam (jt)*　**V** K BOTTLEY

BLYTH (St Mary) *Newc 1*　**P** *Bp*　**V** A J ELDER　**NSM** J R SWINHOE

BLYTH VALLEY Team Ministry, The *St E 18*　**P** *Patr Bd*　**TR** E L RENNARD　**TV** E M CANNON, J L BUNDAY

BLYTHBURGH (Holy Trinity)　*see* Sole Bay *St E*

BLYTON (St Martin)　*see* Trentcliffe Gp *Linc*

BOARHUNT (St Nicholas)　*see* Southwick w Boarhunt *Portsm*

BOARSTALL (St James)　*see* Bernwode *Ox*

BOBBING (St Bartholomew)　*see* Sittingbourne w Bobbing *Cant*

BOBBINGTON (Holy Cross)　*see* Smestow Vale *Lich*

BOBBINGWORTH (St Germain)　*see* Fyfield, Moreton w Bobbingworth etc *Chelmsf*

BOCKING (St Mary) *Chelmsf 17*　**P** *Abp Cant*　**P-in-c** R A M REID

BOCKING (St Peter) *Chelmsf 17*　**P** *Abp Cant*　**P-in-c** T BARNES　**NSM** I R BENDREY

BOCONNOC (not known)　*see* Lostwithiel, St Winnow w St Nectan's Chpl etc *Truro*

BODDINGTON (St John the Baptist)　*see* Aston-le-Walls, Byfield, Boddington, Eydon etc *Pet*

BODDINGTON (St Mary Magdalene)　*see* Twigworth, Down Hatherley, Norton, The Leigh etc *Glouc*

BODENHAM (St Michael and All Angels)　*see* Maund Gp *Heref*

BODHAM (All Saints)　*see* Weybourne Gp *Nor*

BODIAM (St Giles) *Chich 17*　**P** *All So Coll Ox*　**V** G L WINCHESTER

BODICOTE (St John the Baptist) *Ox 23*　**P** *New Coll Ox*　**V** S E HARPER　**OLM** B C GARDNER

BODINNICK (St John)　*see* Lanteglos by Fowey *Truro*

BODLE STREET GREEN (St John the Evangelist)　*see* Warbleton, Bodle Street Green and Dallington *Chich*

BODMIN (St Petroc) (St Lawrence w St Leonard) w Lanhydrock and Lanivet *Truro 10*　**P** *DBP*　**C** D A GRIGG, D J ELKINGTON　**NSM** C F CLEMOW, E J MUNDAY, S I BAWDEN

BODNEY (St Mary)　*see* Hilborough w Bodney *Nor*

BOGNOR (St Wilfrid) *Chich 1*　**P** *Abp*　**V** A J WADSWORTH

BOLAM (St Andrew)　*see* Heighington and Darlington St Matt and St Luke *Dur*

BOLAM (St Andrew) w Whalton and Hartburn w Meldon *Newc 11*　**P** *Ld Chan (2 turns), J I K Walker Esq (1 turn), and D&C Dur (1 turn)*　**R** M A G BRYCE　**NSM** F J SAMPLE

BOLAS MAGNA (St John the Baptist)　*see* Tibberton w Bolas Magna and Waters Upton *Lich*

BOLDMERE (St Michael) *Birm 12*　**P** *Birm Dioc Trustees*　**V** R G BIRCHALL　**NSM** E C M SYKES

BOLDONS, The (St George) (St Nicholas) *Dur 15*　**P** *Bp (2 turns), Prime Min (1 turn)*　**R** R O DICK　**C** J S BAIN, R L TOBIN　**Hon C** D M DUKE　**NSM** O N NWOGU

BOLDRE (St John the Baptist) w South Baddesley *Win 11*　**P** *Bp and Lord Teynham (jt)*　**V** N R SMART　**Hon C** A D I NEAUM

BOLDRE, EAST (St Paul)　*see* Beaulieu and Exbury and E Boldre *Win*

BOLE (St Martin)　*see* Retford Area *S'well*

BOLINGBROKE Deanery (St Peter and St Paul) *Linc 9*　**P** *Patr Bd*　**TR** P F COATES　**TV** F A JEFFRIES　**C** M T FAULKNER　**OLM** J COATES

BOLLINGHAM (St Silas)　*see* Eardisley w Bollingham, Willersley, Brilley etc *Heref*

BOLLINGTON (Holy Trinity)　*see* Rostherne w Bollington *Ches*

BOLLINGTON (St Oswald) (Holy Trinity) *Ches 13*　**P** *V Prestbury*　**V** V W HYDON　**NSM** M F FOX

BOLNEY (St Mary Magdalene) *Chich 5*　**P** *K Coll Lon*　**P-in-c** K D LITTLEJOHN　**NSM** M MILLS

BOLNHURST (St Dunstan) w Keysoe *St Alb 13*　**P** *Bp*　**V** *vacant*

BOLSOVER (St Mary and St Laurence) *Derby 3*　**P** *Bp*　**V** R C GOULDTHORPE　**NSM** R M WILLIAMS

BOLSTERSTONE (St Mary) *Sheff 3*　**P** *R B Rimington-Wilson Esq*　**P-in-c** H R ISAACSON

BOLTBY (Holy Trinity)　*see* Felixkirk w Boltby *York*

BOLTON (All Saints) *Carl 1*　**P** *V Morland w Thrimby etc*　**P-in-c** S J FYFE

BOLTON (St Chad)　*see* Leverhulme *Man*

BOLTON (St James w St Chrysostom) *Leeds 3*　**P** *Bp*　**V** S D LEES　**Hon C** P B STOODLEY

BOLTON ABBEY (St Mary and St Cuthbert) *Leeds 26*　**P** *Duke of Devonshire*　**R** S C COWLING　**C** J M F CAIN

BOLTON BY BOWLAND (St Peter and St Paul) w Grindleton *Blackb 7*　**P** *Bp and V Hurst Green and Mitton*　**R** R G WOOD

BOLTON Chapel (unknown)　*see* Whittingham and Edlingham w Bolton Chapel *Newc*

BOLTON LE MOORS (St Bede) *Man 9*　**P** *Bp*　**OLM** M W BRISTOW

BOLTON ON SWALE (St Mary)　*see* Easby w Skeeby and Brompton on Swale etc *Leeds*

BOLTON PERCY (All Saints) *York 1*　**P** *Abp*　**R** G R MUMFORD

BOLTON, WEST (Emmanuel) (St Luke) (St Matthew w St Barnabas) (St Paul) (St Thomas the Apostle) *Man 7*　**P** *Patr Bd*　**TR** A S CORNES　**TV** D R PETCH, F ADMAN　**C** C E THRELFALL

BOLTON-LE-MOORS (St Peter) (St Philip) *Man 7*　**P** *Bp*　**V** M THOMPSON　**C** M E SLACK　**NSM** B S GASKELL, K G C NEWPORT

BOLTON-LE-SANDS (Holy Trinity) *Blackb 14*　**P** *Bp*　**V** N E GOODRICH

BOLTONS, THE　*see* W Brompton St Mary w St Peter and St Jude *Lon*

BOLTON-UPON-DEARNE (St Andrew the Apostle) *Sheff 12*　**P** *Meynall Ch Trust*　**V** *vacant*

BOLVENTOR (Holy Trinity)　*see* Moorland Gp *Truro*

BOMERE HEATH (Mission Room)　*see* Leaton and Albrighton w Battlefield *Lich*

BONBY (St Andrew) *Linc 8*　**P** *DBP*　**V** G O MITCHELL

BONCHURCH (St Boniface) (St Boniface Old Church) *Portsm 7*　**P** *Ch Patr Trust*　**R** H E WRIGHT

BONDLEIGH (St James the Apostle)　*see* Chagford, Gidleigh, Throwleigh etc *Ex*

BONINGALE (St Chad)　*see* Albrighton, Boningale and Donington *Lich*

BONNINGTON (St Rumwold)　*see* Saxon Shoreline *Cant*

BONSALL (St James the Apostle)　*see* Wirksworth *Derby*

BOOKER (Christ the Servant King)　*see* High Wycombe *Ox*

BOOKHAM, GREAT (St Nicolas) *Guildf 10*　**P** *Bp*　**R** A D JENKINS　**C** D SIGSWORTH　**OLM** B J MCDONALD

BOOKHAM, LITTLE (All Saints)　*see* Effingham w Lt Bookham *Guildf*

BOOSBECK (St Aidan) and Lingdale *York 16*　**P** *Abp*　**V** V E M-B HAYNES

BOOTHBY GRAFFOE (St Andrew)　*see* Graffoe Gp *Linc*

BOOTHBY PAGNELL (St Andrew)　*see* N Beltisloe Gp *Linc*

BOOTHSTOWN (St Andrew's Church Institute)　*see* Worsley *Man*

BOOTLE (Christ Church) *Liv 1*　**P** *Bp*　**V** T RICH　**NSM** J WILLIAMS

BOOTLE (St Andrew) (St Leonard) (St Mary w St Paul) (St Matthew) (St Thomas) *Liv 1*　**P** *Patr Bd*　**TR** R J DRIVER　**TV** I A WHITAKER

BOOTLE (St Michael and All Angels), Corney, Whicham and Whitbeck *Carl 5*　**P** *Earl of Lonsdale*　**R** *vacant*

BORASTON (not known)　*see* Tenbury *Heref*

BORDEN (St Peter and St Paul) *Cant 15*   P *SMF*
V J H G LEWIS
BORDESLEY (St Alban the Martyr and St Patrick)   *see* Highgate *Birm*
BORDESLEY (St Benedict) *Birm 13*   P *Keble Coll Ox*
V *vacant*
BORDESLEY GREEN (St Paul)   *see* Ward End w Bordesley Green *Birm*
BORDON (St Mark) *Guildf 3*   P *Bp*   V D J SCOTT-BROMLEY
NSM W N MALLAS
BOREHAM (St Andrew) *Chelmsf 10*   P *Bp*
P-in-c L P BATSON   NSM S E HOWLETT
BOREHAM (St John the Evangelist)   *see* Bishopstrow and Boreham *Sarum*
BOREHAMWOOD (All Saints)   *see* Elstree and Borehamwood *St Alb*
BOREHAMWOOD (Holy Cross) *as above*
BOREHAMWOOD (St Michael and All Angels) *as above*
BORLEY (not known)   *see* N Hinckford *Chelmsf*
BOROUGH GREEN (Good Shepherd) *Roch 10*   P *Bp*
V A J POWELL
BOROUGHBRIDGE (St James)   *see* Aldborough w Boroughbridge and Roecliffe *Leeds*
BORROWASH (St Stephen's Chapel)   *see* Ockbrook *Derby*
BORROWDALE (St Andrew)   *see* Upper Derwent *Carl*
BORSTAL (St Matthew) *Roch 5*   P V Rochester St Marg
V A Y BENNETT
BORWICK (St Mary)   *see* Warton St Oswald w Yealand Conyers *Blackb*
BOSBURY (Holy Trinity)   *see* Ledbury *Heref*
BOSCASTLE and Tintagel Group, The *Truro 8*   P *DBP and D&C Windsor (jt)*   R R S THEWSEY   C P J BEYNON
NSM M PARSONS
BOSCOMBE (St Andrew) *Win 8*   P *Bp*   P-in-c N J HOULTON
NSM J HOULTON
BOSCOMBE (St Andrew)   *see* Bourne Valley *Sarum*
BOSCOMBE (St Clement)   *see* Bournemouth St Clem *Win*
BOSCOMBE (St John the Evangelist) *Win 8*   P *Peache Trustees*
V R P KHAKHRIA
BOSCOPPA *Truro 1*   P *Prime Min*   P-in-c J S J WILLIAMS
BOSHAM (Holy Trinity) *Chich 3*   P *Bp*   V M J LANE
BOSLEY (St Mary the Virgin)   *see* Sutton, Wincle, Wildboarclough and Bosley *Ches*
BOSSALL (St Botolph)   *see* Harton *York*
BOSSINGTON (St James)   *see* Broughton, Bossington, Houghton and Mottisfont *Win*
BOSTALL HEATH (St Andrew) *Roch 15*   P *DBP*
V S SHAHZAD
BOSTON (St Botolph) (St Christopher) *Linc 21*   P *Bp*
TR A C BUXTON   C S R HOLT
BOSTON SPA (St Mary)   *see* Bramham *York*
BOSWORTH (St Peter) and Sheepy Group *Leic 10*   P *Patr Bd (2 turns), Ld Chan (1 turn)*   TV J G HARGREAVES
BOTCHERBY (St Andrew)   *see* Carl St Aid and Ch Ch *Carl*
BOTESDALE (St Botolph)   *see* Redgrave cum Botesdale w Rickinghall *St E*
BOTHAL (St Andrew) and Pegswood w Longhirst *Newc 11*
P *Bp*   R J C PARK
BOTHAMSALL (Our Lady and St Peter)   *see* Retford Area *S'well*
BOTHENHAMPTON (Holy Trinity)   *see* Bridport *Sarum*
BOTLEY (All Saints) *Portsm 1*   P *Bp*   R G R MENSINGH
C A L WEBB
BOTLEY (St Peter and St Paul)   *see* Osney *Ox*
BOTLEYS AND LYNE (Holy Trinity)   *see* Chertsey, Lyne and Longcross *Guildf*
BOTTESFORD (St Mary the Virgin)   *see* Vale of Belvoir *Leic*
BOTTESFORD (St Peter) w Ashby *Linc 6*   P *Patr Bd*
P-in-c T R ASTIN
BOTTISHAM (Holy Trinity)   *see* Anglesey Gp *Ely*
BOTUS FLEMING (St Mary)   *see* Landrake w St Erney and Botus Fleming *Truro*
BOUGHTON (All Saints) *Ely 9*   P *Bp*   P-in-c B L BURTON
BOUGHTON (St John the Baptist)   *see* Pitsford w Boughton *Pet*
BOUGHTON (St Matthew)   *see* Ollerton w Boughton *S'well*
BOUGHTON ALUPH (All Saints)   *see* Wye *Cant*
BOUGHTON MALHERBE (St Nicholas)   *see* Len Valley *Cant*
BOUGHTON MONCHELSEA (St Augustine) (St Peter) *Cant 13*
P *Abp*   V P J F GOODEY
BOUGHTON UNDER BLEAN (St Barnabas) (St Peter and St Paul) w Dunkirk and Hernhill *Cant 14*   P *Abp*
P-in-c J BURROWS   C P J STUBBINGS
BOULGE (St Michael)   *see* Carlford *St E*
BOULTHAM (Holy Cross) (St Helen) *Linc 11*   P *DBP*
R D J OSBOURNE   C M J GODBOLD
BOULTON (St Mary the Virgin) *Derby 15*   P *Bp*
V N P GURNEY

BOURN (St Helena and St Mary)   *see* Papworth *Ely*
BOURNE (St Peter and St Paul) *Linc 17*   P *DBP*
V C J ATKINSON   C S F CLEATON   OLM P W R LISTER
BOURNE END (St John)   *see* Sunnyside w Bourne End *St Alb*
BOURNE END (St Mark)   *see* Hedsor and Bourne End *Ox*
BOURNE VALLEY *Sarum 10*   P *Patr Bd*   P-in-c P A OSTLI-EAST
C P F D TAYLOR   Hon C P A JOYCE   NSM D M COATES
BOURNE, LOWER (St Martin)   *see* The Bourne and Tilford *Guildf*
BOURNE, The (St Thomas) and Tilford *Guildf 3*   P *Bp and Adn Surrey (alt)*   V K E HUTCHINSON   Hon C H M HUMPHREY   NSM E J COLLINS, E M LANE
BOURNEMOUTH (Holy Epiphany) *Win 8*   P *Bp*
NSM D S THOMPSON
BOURNEMOUTH (St Alban) *Win 8*   P *Bp*   V *vacant*
BOURNEMOUTH (St Ambrose) *Win 8*   P *Bp*
P-in-c A F PEARCE
BOURNEMOUTH (St Andrew) Bennett Road *Win 8*
P *Trustees*   V G M ROBERTS   Hon C J W DAVIES
BOURNEMOUTH (St Barnabas) Queen's Park   *see* Holdenhurst and Iford *Win*
BOURNEMOUTH (St Christopher)   *see* Southbourne St Chris *Win*
BOURNEMOUTH (St Clement) *Win 8*   P *DBP*
P-in-c M R POWIS
BOURNEMOUTH (St Francis) *Win 8*   P *CR*
NSM A F PEARCE
BOURNEMOUTH (St John the Baptist)   *see* Moordown *Win*
BOURNEMOUTH (St John) (St Michael and All Angels) *Win 8*
P *Bp and S R Willcox Esq (jt)*   P-in-c R D BALDOCK
BOURNEMOUTH (St Luke) *Win 8*   P *Bp*   V *vacant*
BOURNEMOUTH Town Centre (St Augustin) (St Peter) (St Stephen) w St Swithun and Holy Trinity *Win 8*   P *Patr Bd*   TR I A TERRY   C T J MATTHEWS   Emer H G JAMES
BOURNVILLE (St Andrew)   *see* Weston-super-Mare St Andr Bournville *B & W*
BOURNVILLE (St Francis) *Birm 5*   P *Bp*   V P G BABINGTON
BOURTON (Holy Trinity)   *see* Wenlock *Heref*
BOURTON (St George)   *see* Upper Stour *Sarum*
BOURTON (St James)   *see* Shrivenham and Ashbury *Ox*
BOURTON (St Peter)   *see* Draycote Gp *Cov*
BOURTON ON THE HILL (St Lawrence)   *see* Vale and Cotswold Edge *Glouc*
BOURTON, GREAT (All Saints)   *see* Shires' Edge *Ox*
BOURTON-ON-THE-WATER (St Lawrence) w Clapton and The Rissingtons *Glouc 8*   P *Wadh Coll Ox, DBP and C T R Wingfield Esq, and Ld Chan (by turn)*   R R C ROSBOROUGH   C M L PORTER-BABBAGE   NSM C C ETHERTON
BOVEY TRACEY (St John the Evangelist) w Heathfield *Ex 8*
P *Guild of All So*   V G J STANTON
BOVEY TRACEY (St Peter and St Paul and St Thomas of Canterbury) w Hennock *Ex 8*   P *Prime Min (2 turns), MMCET (1 turn)*   V W G HAMILTON   C C C MURPHY
Hon C R H TOTTERDELL
BOVEY, NORTH (St John the Baptist)   *see* Moretonhampstead, Manaton, N Bovey and Lustleigh *Ex*
BOVINGDON (St Lawrence) *St Alb 4*   P *Ch Soc Trust*
V C E BURCH
BOW (All Hallows)   *see* Bromley by Bow All Hallows *Lon*
BOW (St Bartholomew) w Broad Nymet *Ex 2*   P *DBP*
R *vacant*
BOW (St Mary) and Holy Trinity w Bromley St Leonard *Lon 7*
P *Bp and Grocers' Co (jt)*   R D FRAZER   NSM D F WAXHAM, W A O'REILLY
BOW BRICKHILL (All Saints)   *see* Brickhills and Stoke Hammond *Ox*
BOW COMMON (St Paul) *Lon 7*   P *Bp*   V B G HEGARTY
BOWBROOK NORTH : Feckenham and Hanbury and Stock and Bradley *Worc 8*   P *Bp and D&C (jt)*   P-in-c A D MORRIS
NSM B A WHEATLEY, V W BEYNON
BOWBROOK SOUTH : Crowle w Bredicot and Hadzor w Oddingley and Tibberton and Himbleton and Huddington *Worc 8*   P *Bp, D&C, R J G Berkeley Esq, and J F Bennett Esq (jt)*
P-in-c A D MORRIS   NSM B A WHEATLEY, V W BEYNON
BOWBURN (Christ the King)   *see* Cassop cum Quarrington *Dur*
BOWDEN HILL (St Anne)   *see* Gtr Corsham and Lacock *Bris*
BOWDEN, GREAT (St Peter and St Paul)   *see* Market Harborough and The Transfiguration etc *Leic*
BOWDEN, LITTLE (St Hugh) *as above*
BOWDEN, LITTLE (St Nicholas) *as above*
BOWDON (St Luke) (St Mary the Virgin) *Ches 10*   P *Bp*
V R M H PREECE   C M R OWEN   NSM P POTTER
BOWERCHALKE (Holy Trinity)   *see* Chalke Valley *Sarum*
BOWERS GIFFORD (St John) (St Margaret) w North Benfleet *Chelmsf 12*   P *Em Coll Cam and Brig R H C Bryhers CBE (alt)*
P-in-c D A O IBIAYO

BOWES (St Giles)　　*see* Startforth and Bowes and Rokeby w Brignall *Leeds*

BOWES PARK (St Michael-at-Bowes)　　*see* Wood Green St Mich w Bounds Green St Gabr etc *Lon*

BOWLING (St John) *Leeds 2*　　P *V Bradford*　　V H K ASTIN　　NSM C BARNES

BOWLING (St Stephen)　　*see* Bankfoot and Bowling St Steph *Leeds*

BOWNESS-ON-SOLWAY (St Michael), Kirkbride and Newton Arlosh *Carl 3*　　P Earl of Lonsdale (2 turns), V Holme Cultram (1 turn)　　R R P BLACKETT

BOWTHORPE (St Michael) *Nor 3*　　P Bp and CPAS (jt)　　V *vacant*

BOX (St Barnabas)　　*see* Minchinhampton w Box and Amberley *Glouc*

BOX (St Thomas à Becket) w Hazlebury and Ditteridge *Bris 4*　　P Bp　　P-in-c J M ANDERSON-MACKENZIE　　NSM A M E KEMP　　OLM C M SOUTHGATE

BOX HILL (St Andrew)　　*see* Headley w Box Hill *Guildf*

BOXFORD (St Andrew)　　*see* E Downland *Ox*

BOXFORD (St Mary), Edwardstone, Groton, Little Waldingfield and Newton *St E 12*　　P DBP and The Hon Thomas Lindsay (1 turn), Ld Chan (2 turns), Peterho Cam (1 turn)　　P-in-c J SWEETMAN

BOXGROVE (St Mary and St Blaise) *Chich 2*　　P Duke of Richmond and Gordon　　P-in-c I M FORRESTER

BOXLEY (St Mary the Virgin and All Saints) w Detling *Cant 13*　　P Abp　　NSM E A ATTAWAY

BOXMOOR (St John the Evangelist) *St Alb 2*　　P Bp　　V M D MACEY　　C B E A WEITZMANN

BOXTED (Holy Trinity)　　*see* Glemsford, Hartest w Boxted, Somerton etc *St E*

BOXTED (St Peter)　　*see* Langham w Boxted *Chelmsf*

BOXWELL (St Mary the Virgin), Leighterton, Didmarton, Oldbury-on-the-Hill, Sopworth, Badminton w Little Badminton, Acton Turville, Hawkesbury, Westonbirt and Lasborough *Glouc 5*　　P Duke of Beaufort, J A Hutley Esq, and Westonbirt Sch (jt)　　P-in-c R W B THOMSON　　NSM A F THORESEN, E M NICHOLS, H K NICHOLS

BOXWORTH (St Peter)　　*see* Papworth *Ely*

BOYATT WOOD (St Peter) *Win 10*　　P Bp　　P-in-c I S MCFARLANE

BOYLESTONE (St John the Baptist), Church Broughton, Dalbury, Longford, Long Lane, Radbourne, Sutton on the Hill and Trusley *Derby 14*　　P Patr Bd　　R P M BISHOP　　NSM J M LEGH

BOYNE HILL (All Saints) *Ox 5*　　P Bp　　V J M HARRIS　　NSM N D BRYSON

BOYNTON (St Andrew)　　*see* Rudston w Boynton, Carnaby and Kilham *York*

BOYTHORPE (St Francis)　　*see* Chesterfield SS Aug *Derby*

BOYTON (Holy Name), North Tamerton, Werrington, St Giles-in-the-Heath and Virginstow *Truro 9*　　P Duchy of Cornwall, MMCET, Ld Chan, and R Williams Esq (by turn)　　R K WAKEFIELD

BOYTON (St Andrew)　　*see* Wilford Peninsula *St E*

BOYTON (St Mary the Virgin)　　*see* Upper Wylye Valley *Sarum*

BOZEAT (St Mary)　　*see* Wollaston w Strixton and Bozeat etc *Pet*

BRABOURNE (St Mary the Blessed Virgin)　　*see* A20 Benefice *Cant*

BRACEBOROUGH (St Margaret)　　*see* Uffington Gp *Linc*

BRACEBRIDGE (All Saints) *Linc 11*　　P Mrs B M Ellison-Lendrum　　V *vacant*

BRACEBRIDGE HEATH (St John the Evangelist) *Linc 11*　　P Bp　　V *vacant*

BRACEBY (St Margaret)　　*see* N Beltisloe Gp *Linc*

BRACEWELL (St Michael)　　*see* Barnoldswick w Bracewell *Leeds*

BRACKENFIELD (Holy Trinity)　　*see* Ashover and Brackenfield w Wessington *Derby*

BRACKLEY (St Peter w St James) *Pet 1*　　P Bp　　V N J GANDY　　C J A MCDONALD

BRACKNELL (Holy Trinity) *Ox 3*　　P Bp　　P-in-c H D UFFINDELL　　TV L P P JESUDASON　　C A BRADFORD, J D BARLOW　　Hon C M G CLARKE

BRACON ASH (St Nicholas)　　*see* Mulbarton w Bracon Ash, Hethel and Flordon *Nor*

BRADBOURNE (All Saints)　　*see* Wirksworth *Derby*

BRADDAN (St Brendan) *S & M*　　P Bp　　V D M H RICHARDS

BRADDEN (St Michael)　　*see* Towcester w Caldecote and Easton Neston etc *Pet*

BRADELEY (St Mary and All Saints), Church Eaton, Derrington and Haughton *Lich 10*　　P Bp and Mrs M N Nutt (jt)　　R S M SYMONS

BRADENHAM (St Botolph)　　*see* W Wycombe w Bledlow Ridge, Bradenham and Radnage *Ox*

BRADENHAM, WEST (St Andrew)　　*see* Dereham and Distr *Nor*

BRADENSTOKE (St Mary)　　*see* Lyneham w Bradenstoke *Sarum*

BRADFIELD (St Andrew) and Stanford Dingley *Ox 4*　　P Ch Soc Trust　　L E BLISS

BRADFIELD (St Giles)　　*see* Trunch Group *Nor*

BRADFIELD (St Lawrence)　　*see* Mistley w Manningtree and Bradfield *Chelmsf*

BRADFIELD (St Nicholas) *Sheff 3*　　P V Ecclesfield　　R A T ISAACSON

BRADFIELD COMBUST (All Saints)　　*see* St Edm Way *St E*

BRADFIELD ST CLARE (St Clare), Bradfield St George w Little Whelnetham, Cockfield, Felsham and Gedding *St E 10*　　P St Jo Coll Cam (1 turn), Bp and Lt Col J G Aldous (1 turn)　　R S J POTTER　　C C N MELVILLE

BRADFIELD ST GEORGE (St George)　　*see* Bradfield St Clare, Bradfield St George etc *St E*

BRADFORD (All Saints)　　*see* Black Torrington, Bradford w Cookbury etc *Ex*

BRADFORD (St Augustine) Undercliffe *Leeds 3*　　P V Bradf　　P-in-c D BARTON　　C T A MILNE　　NSM A CHALLENGER

BRADFORD (St Clement) *Leeds 3*　　P Bp (2 turns) and Trustees (1 turn)　　P-in-c D BARTON　　C T A MILNE　　NSM A CHALLENGER

BRADFORD (St Martin)　　*see* Heaton St Martin *Leeds*

BRADFORD (St Oswald)　　*see* Lt Horton *Leeds*

BRADFORD (St Saviour)　　*see* Fairweather Green *Leeds*

BRADFORD (St Stephen)　　*see* Bankfoot and Bowling St Steph *Leeds*

BRADFORD (St Wilfrid) (St Columba w St Andrew) *Leeds 2*　　P Bp　　V P M BILTON

BRADFORD ABBAS (St Mary the Virgin)　　*see* Three Valleys *Sarum*

BRADFORD ON AVON (Holy Trinity), Westwood and Wingfield *Sarum 15*　　P Bp, D&C Sarum, D&C Bris, and CPAS (jt)　　R J M ABECASSIS　　NSM A M GREEN

BRADFORD ON AVON, NORTH (Christ Church) and Villages *Sarum 15*　　P D&C Bris (2 turns), Bp (1 turn), V Bradf H Trin (1 turn)　　R A B KEATING　　NSM A K CHARNLEY, B F CHAPMAN

BRADFORD ON TONE (St Giles)　　*see* Wellington and Distr *B & W*

BRADFORD PEVERELL (Church of the Assumption), Stratton, Frampton and Sydling St Nicholas *Sarum 1*　　P Win Coll and Bp (alt)　　P-in-c P J SMITH　　Hon C A J K MACKENZIE

BRADING (St Mary the Virgin) w Yaverland *Portsm 7*　　P Bp and Trin Coll Cam (jt)　　P-in-c D L DENNIS

BRADLEY (All Saints)　　*see* Hulland, Atlow, Kniveton, Bradley and Hognaston *Derby*

BRADLEY (All Saints)　　*see* Farleigh, Candover and Wield *Win*

BRADLEY (St George)　　*see* Gt and Lt Coates w Bradley *Linc*

BRADLEY (St John the Baptist)　　*see* Bowbrook N *Worc*

BRADLEY (St Martin) *Lich 28*　　P Baldwin Pugh Trustees　　V R T M J DUCKETT

BRADLEY (St Mary)　　*see* Cononley w Bradley *Leeds*

BRADLEY (St Thomas) *Leeds 12*　　P Bp　　V D R WARD

BRADLEY STOKE (Christ the King)　　*see* Stoke Gifford *Bris*

BRADLEY STOKE NORTH (Holy Trinity) Conventional District *Bris 5*　　C C S BEAUMONT

BRADLEY, GREAT (St Mary the Virgin)　　*see* Stourhead *St E*

BRADLEY, LITTLE (All Saints) *as above*

BRADLEY, NORTH (St Nicholas), Southwick, Heywood and Steeple Ashton *Sarum 15*　　P Win Coll and Magd Coll Cam (jt)　　V J R PARKER　　OLM L J DOVE

BRADLEY, WEST (not known)　　*see* Baltonsborough w Butleigh, W Bradley etc *B & W*

BRADLEY-LE-MOORS (St Leonard)　　*see* Alton w Bradley-le-Moors and Denstone etc *Lich*

BRADMORE (Mission Room)　　*see* Keyworth and Stanton-on-the-Wolds and Bunny etc *S'well*

BRADNINCH (St Disen) and Clyst Hydon *Ex 7*　　P D&C and D&C Windsor (jt)　　C C E MARTIN, J M WRIGHT　　NSM S WALKER

BRADNOP (Mission Church)　　*see* Ipstones w Berkhamsytch and Onecote w Bradnop *Lich*

BRADOC (Blessed Virgin Mary)　　*see* Lanreath, Pelynt and Bradoc *Truro*

BRADPOLE (Holy Trinity)　　*see* Bridport *Sarum*

BRADSHAW (St John the Evangelist) and Holmfield *Leeds 11*　　P Bp　　V K A SHOESMITH

BRADSHAW (St Maxentius)　　*see* Turton Moorland *Man*

BRADWELL (Holy Trinity)　　*see* Cressing w Stisted and Bradwell etc *Chelmsf*

BRADWELL (St Barnabas)　　*see* Hope, Castleton and Bradwell *Derby*

BRADWELL (St Barnabas) and Porthill *Lich 9* **P** *Bp*
V C S B ROUTLEDGE

BRADWELL (St Lawrence and Methodist United)
see Stantonbury and Willen *Ox*

BRADWELL (St Nicholas) *Nor 6* **P** *Bp* **R** C G TINKER
NSM C M UPTON, S D UPTON

BRADWELL ON SEA (St Thomas) (St Peter-on-the-Wall) and
St Lawrence *Chelmsf 11* **P** *Bp* **NSM** B M H MAIN

BRADWELL, NEW (St James) *see* Stantonbury and Willen *Ox*

BRADWORTHY (St John the Baptist), Sutcombe, Putford,
Abbots Bickington and Bulkworthy *Ex 16* **P** *Prime Min and
Bp (alt)* **R** R A FREEMAN

BRAFFERTON (St Peter) w Pilmoor, Myton-on-Swale and
Thormanby *York 3* **P** *Abp and Prof Sir Anthony Milnes Coates
Bt (jt)* **P-in-c** C J PARK **NSM** C C GITTENS

BRAFIELD ON THE GREEN (St Laurence) *see* Cogenhoe and
Gt and Lt Houghton w Brafield *Pet*

BRAILES (St George) *Cov 9* **P** *D&C* **V** N J MORGAN
NSM J W ROLFE

BRAILSFORD (All Saints) w Shirley, Osmaston w Edlaston
and Yeaveley *Derby 8* **P** *Bp, Earl Ferrers, and Sir Peter
Walker-Okeover Bt (by turn)* **R** P M TAYLOR **C** D A GLEN,
F J CROCKER

BRAINTREE (St Michael) *Chelmsf 17* **P** *Ch Trust Fund Trust*
V C O MASON

BRAINTREE (St Paul) *Chelmsf 17* **P** *Ch Trust Fund Trust*
P-in-c S L HAYWARD

BRAISHFIELD (All Saints) *see* Michelmersh and Awbridge and
Braishfield etc *Win*

BRAITHWAITE (St Herbert) *see* Upper Derwent *Carl*

BRAITHWELL (St James) *see* Ravenfield, Hooton Roberts and
Braithwell *Sheff*

BRAMBER (St Nicholas) *see* Beeding and Bramber w Botolphs
Chich

BRAMBLETON (not known) *see* The Bourne and Tilford *Guildf*

BRAMCOTE (St Michael and All Angels) *S'well 9* **P** *CPAS*
V P F REYNOLDS

BRAMDEAN (St Simon and St Jude) *see* Upper Itchen *Win*

BRAMDEAN COMMON (Church in the Wood) *as above*

BRAMERTON (St Peter) *see* Rockland St Mary w Hellington,
Bramerton etc *Nor*

BRAMFIELD (St Andrew) *see* Blyth Valley *St E*

BRAMFIELD (St Andrew), Stapleford, Waterford and Watton-
at-Stone *St Alb 19* **P** R M A Smith Esq (3 turns), Grocers' Co
(1 turn)* **P-in-c** J GRAY

BRAMFORD (St Mary the Virgin) *St E 1* **P** *D&C Cant*
P-in-c J M SEGGAR **C** J FENNELL **NSM** P Y WRIGHT

BRAMHALL (St Michael and All Angels) (Hall Chapel) *Ches 17*
P *Trustees* **V** S R MARSH

BRAMHAM (All Saints) *York 1* **P** *Ch Ch Ox, G F Lane Fox Esq,
and Lady Elizabeth Hastings Estate Charity (jt)* **V** P E BRISTOW
C J C D BROWN **NSM** P M ANSLOW

BRAMHOPE (St Giles) *Leeds 16* **P** *Trustees* **P-in-c** J L SMITH

BRAMLEY (Holy Trinity) and Grafham *Guildf 2* **P** *Ld Chan*
NSM C E Z WHITE

BRAMLEY (St Francis) *Sheff 6* **P** *Bp and Sir Philip Naylor-
Leyland Bt (jt)* **V** D WARD

BRAMLEY (St James) *see* Sherfield-on-Loddon and Stratfield
Saye etc *Win*

BRAMLEY (St Peter) *Leeds 15* **P** *DBP* **P-in-c** P A CRABB

BRAMPFORD SPEKE (St Peter), Cadbury, Newton St Cyres,
Poltimore, Rewe, Stoke Canon, Thorverton and Upton
Pyne *Ex 2* **P** *Bp, Earl of Iddesleigh, DBP, D&C (1 turn), Ld
Chan (1 turn)* **NSM** S SHEPPARD

BRAMPTON (St Mark) *Derby 5* **P** *Bp* **V** *vacant*

BRAMPTON (St Martin) *see* Eden, Gelt and Irthing *Carl*

BRAMPTON (St Mary Magdalene) *Ely 10* **P** *Bp*
P-in-c J V TAYLOR

BRAMPTON (St Michael) *Heref 7* **P** *Bp (7 turns), D&C
(2 turns), Exors Brig A F L Clive (1 turn)* **V** *vacant*

BRAMPTON (St Peter) *see* Bure Valley *Nor*

BRAMPTON (St Thomas the Martyr) *Derby 5* **P** *Bp*
R M J BARNES **C** B D GRIFFITHS, M R BROOMHEAD **Hon**
C W F BAZELY

BRAMPTON ASH (St Mary) *see* Desborough, Brampton Ash,
Dingley and Braybrooke *Pet*

BRAMPTON BIERLOW (Christ Church) *Sheff 12* **P** *V Wath-
upon-Dearne* **V** C A LACEY

BRAMPTON BRYAN (St Barnabas) *see* Wigmore Abbey *Heref*

BRAMPTON, OLD (St Peter and St Paul) (Cutthorpe Institute)
and Great Barlow *Derby 5* **P** *Bp and TR Staveley and Barrow
Hill (jt)* **R** P J GREEN

BRAMSHALL (St Laurence) *see* Uttoxeter Area *Lich*

BRAMSHAW (St Peter) *see* Forest and Avon *Sarum*

BRAMSHILL (Mission Church) *see* Darby Green and Eversley
Win

BRAMSHOTT (St Mary the Virgin) and Liphook *Portsm 4*
P *Qu Coll Ox* **P-in-c** V W INGLIS-JONES

BRANCASTER (St Mary the Virgin) *see* Hunstanton St Mary w
Ringstead Parva etc *Nor*

BRANCEPETH (St Brandon) *Dur 1* **P** *Bp*
P-in-c R L SIMPSON **NSM** A C HOBBS

BRANDESBURTON (St Mary) and Leven *York 11* **P** *St Jo Coll
Cam and Simeon's Trustees (jt)* **V** J E GRAINGER-SMITH

BRANDESTON (All Saints) w Kettleburgh and Easton *St E 16*
P *J Austin Esq, Capt J L Round-Turner, and MMCET (jt)*
P-in-c D A WEST

BRANDLESHOLME (St Francis House Chapel) *see* Kirklees
Valley *Man*

BRANDON (Chapel) *see* Barkston and Hough Gp *Linc*

BRANDON (St John the Evangelist) and Ushaw Moor *Dur 1*
P *R Brancepeth* **P-in-c** C R PETERS

BRANDON (St Peter) and Santon Downham w Elveden and
Lakenheath *St E 11* **P** *Ld Chan (1 turn), Bp, M F Carter Esq,
Earl of Iveagh, and D&C Ely (2 turns)* **R** W L WHITFORD
C M E WHITFORD **NSM** P W TAMS

BRANDON PARVA (All Saints) *see* Barnham Broom and Upper
Yare *Nor*

BRANDSBY (All Saints) *see* Crayke w Brandsby and Yearsley
York

BRANDWOOD (St Bede) *Birm 5* **P** *Bp* **V** A M DELMEGE
NSM R J REYNOLDS

BRANKSEA ISLAND (St Mary) *see* Parkstone St Pet and
St Osmund w Branksea *Sarum*

BRANKSOME (St Aldhelm) (St Francis) *Sarum 7* **P** *Bp*
NSM J P T G SMITH

BRANKSOME (St Clement) (St Barnabas) *Sarum 8*
P *MMCET* **V** J G V FOSTER **C** L J BOWERMAN, M WILLIS

BRANKSOME PARK (All Saints) *Sarum 7* **P** *MMCET*
V C R BOYLE

BRANSCOMBE (St Winifred) *see* Colyton, Musbury,
Southleigh and Branscombe *Ex*

BRANSDALE (St Nicholas) *see* Kirkbymoorside w Gillamoor,
Farndale etc *York*

BRANSFORD (St John the Baptist) *see* Worcs W *Worc*

BRANSGORE (St Mary the Virgin) and Hinton Admiral *Win 9*
P *Sir George Meyrick Bt and Exors P W Jesson (jt)*
P-in-c B C SARGENT

BRANSHOLME (St John the Evangelist) *York 14* **P** *Abp*
V M A MARTINSON

BRANSTON (All Saints) w Nocton and Potterhanworth
Linc 12 **P** *Stowe Sch (2 turns), Ld Chan (1 turn), and Nocton
Ltd (1 turn)* **C** J S PARKIN

BRANSTON (St Saviour) *Lich 14* **P** *Simeon's Trustees*
V M K ELLOR

BRANSTON BY BELVOIR (St Guthlac) *see* High Framland Par
Leic

BRANT BROUGHTON (St Helen) and Beckingham *Linc 22*
P *Bp and Sir Richard Sutton Bt (alt)* **R** A S J HEALY

BRANTHAM (St Michael and All Angels) *see* E Bergholt and
Brantham *St E*

BRANTINGHAM (All Saints) *see* Elloughton and Brough w
Brantingham *York*

BRANXTON (St Paul) *Newc 12* **P** *Abp* **P-in-c** G R KELSEY

BRASSINGTON (St James) *see* Wirksworth *Derby*

BRASTED (St Martin) *Roch 9* **P** *Abp* **R** L A GREEN

BRATHAY (Holy Trinity) *see* Loughrigg *Carl*

BRATOFT (St Peter and St Paul) *see* Burgh Gp *Linc*

BRATTLEBY (St Cuthbert) *see* Spring Line Gp *Linc*

BRATTON (St James the Great) (Oratory), Edington and
Imber, Erlestoke and Coulston *Sarum 17* **P** *Bp and V
Westbury (jt)* **R** M JONES

BRATTON CLOVELLY (St Mary the Virgin) *see* Okehampton,
Inwardleigh, Belstone, Sourton etc *Ex*

BRATTON FLEMING (St Peter) *see* Shirwell, Loxhore,
Kentisbury, Arlington, etc *Ex*

BRATTON ST MAUR (St Nicholas) *see* Camelot Par *B & W*

BRAUGHING (St Mary the Virgin) *see* Albury, Braughing,
Furneux Pelham, Lt Hadham etc *St Alb*

BRAUNSTON (All Saints) *see* Daventry, Ashby St Ledgers,
Braunston etc *Pet*

BRAUNSTON (All Saints) *see* Oakham, Ashwell, Braunston,
Brooke, Egleton etc *Pet*

BRAUNSTONE PARK (St Peter) *Leic 1* **P** *Bp* **V** *vacant*

BRAUNSTONE TOWN (St Crispin) w Thorpe Astley *Leic 9*
P *Bp* **P-in-c** A C DEEGAN

BRAUNTON (St Brannock) *Ex 14* **P** *Bp* **P-in-c** A THORNE
Hon C L A BUTTLE **NSM** J S LOVEDAY

BRAXTED, GREAT (All Saints) *see* Thurstable and Winstree
Chelmsf

BRAXTED, LITTLE (St Nicholas) *see* Wickham Bishops w
Lt Braxted *Chelmsf*

BRAY (St Michael) and Braywood *Ox 5* **P** *Bp*
V R M COWLES

BRAY, HIGH (All Saints) *see* S Molton w Nymet St George,
High Bray etc *Ex*

BRAYBROOKE (All Saints) *see* Desborough, Brampton Ash,
Dingley and Braybrooke *Pet*

BRAYDESTON (St Michael) *see* Brundall w Braydeston and
Postwick *Nor*

BRAYTON (St Wilfrid) *York 4* **P** *Abp* **R** P D WATSON
NSM G M WEBB, R D BATTERSBY

BREADSALL (All Saints) *Derby 9* **P** *Miss A I M Harpur-Crewe*
P-in-c A J MADDOCKS

BREAGE (St Breaca) *see* W Kerrier *Truro*

BREAM (St James) *Glouc 1* **P** *Bp* **V** C W MACLAY

BREAMORE (St Mary) *see* Fordingbridge and Breamore and
Hale etc *Win*

BREAN (St Bridget) *see* Berrow and Breane *B & W*

BREARTON (St John the Baptist) *see* Knaresborough *Leeds*

BREASTON (St Michael) *see* Wilne and Draycott w Breaston
Derby

BRECKLES (St Margaret) *see* Caston, Griston, Merton,
Thompson etc *Nor*

BREDBURY (St Barnabas) *Ches 16* **P** *V Bredbury St Mark*
V *vacant*

BREDBURY (St Mark) *Ches 16* **P** *Bp* **P-in-c** A D BULL
C K E HANDLEY

BREDE (St George) *see* Brede w Udimore and Beckley and
Peasmarsh *Chich*

BREDE (St George) w Udimore and Beckley and Peasmarsh
Chich 17 **P** *Bp, SS Coll Cam, Univ Coll Ox, and Dr P M J Crook*
(jt) **R** M N HARPER **NSM** J D BURGESS

BREDENBURY (St Andrew) *Heref 2* **P** *DBP, V Bromyard, and*
J H Barneby Esq (jt) **R** E S SIDWELL

BREDFIELD (St Andrew) *see* Woodbridge St Jo and Bredfield
St E

BREDGAR (St John the Baptist) *see* Tunstall and Bredgar *Cant*

BREDHURST (St Peter) *see* S Gillingham *Roch*

BREDICOT (St James the Less) *see* Bowbrook S *Worc*

BREDON (St Giles) w Bredon's Norton *Worc 4* **P** *Bp*
R M T C BAYNES

BREDON'S NORTON (not known) *see* Bredon w Bredon's
Norton *Worc*

BREDWARDINE (St Andrew) *see* Cusop w Blakemere,
Bredwardine w Brobury etc *Heref*

BREDY, LITTLE (St Michael and All Angels) *see* Bride Valley
Sarum

BREEDON-ON-THE-HILL (St Mary and St Hardulph) *see* Ashby-
de-la-Zouch and Breedon on the Hill *Leic*

BREIGHTMET (St James) *see* Leverhulme *Man*

BREIGHTMET Top o' th' Moss (St John the Evangelist) *as above*

BREINTON (St Michael) *see* W Heref *Heref*

BREMHILL (St Martin) *see* Marden Vale *Sarum*

BRENCHLEY (All Saints) *Roch 8* **P** *D&C Cant* **V** R C PAGET

BRENT ELEIGH (St Mary) *see* Monks Eleigh w Chelsworth and
Brent Eleigh etc *St E*

BRENT KNOLL (St Michael) and East Brent and Lympsham
B & W 1 **P** *Adn Wells (1 turn), Bp (2 turns)*
P-in-c S W LEWIS

BRENT PELHAM (St Mary the Virgin) *see* Hormead, Wyddial,
Anstey, Brent Pelham etc *St Alb*

BRENT TOR (Christ Church) *see* Tavistock, Gulworthy and
Brent Tor *Ex*

BRENT TOR (St Michael) *as above*

BRENT, EAST (The Blessed Virgin Mary) *see* Brent Knoll, E Brent
and Lympsham *B & W*

BRENT, SOUTH (St Petroc) and Rattery *Ex 12* **P** *Bp and Sir*
Rivers Carew Bt (jt) **V** D R WINNINGTON-INGRAM

BRENTFORD (St Paul w St Lawrence and St George) (St Faith)
Lon 11 **P** *Bp* **TR** D J SIMPSON
TV O A DOUGLAS-PENNANT **C** O D PENNANT, R J WINFIELD

BRENTS and Davington, The *Cant 14* **P** *Abp*
P-in-c S D ROWLANDS **C** S R YOUNG, T J BATESON

BRENTWOOD (St George the Martyr) *Chelmsf 8* **P** *DBP*
V G F JENKINS

BRENTWOOD (St Thomas) *Chelmsf 8* **P** *DBP*
V C E HEWITT

BRENZETT (St Eanswith) *see* Brookland, Fairfield, Brenzett w
Snargate etc *Cant*

BRERETON (St Michael) and Rugeley *Lich 3* **P** *Patr Bd*
TV G L HOLDING **OLM** B D TABERNOR

BRERETON (St Oswald) *Ches 11* **P** *DBP* **V** R H MOSLEY

BRESSINGHAM (St John the Baptist) *see* Diss *Nor*

BRETBY (St Wystan) *see* Hartshorne and Bretby *Derby*

BRETFORTON (St Leonard) *see* Badsey w Aldington and
Offenham and Bretforton *Worc*

BRETHERTON (St John the Baptist) *see* Croston, Bretherton
and Mawdesley w Bispham *Blackb*

BRETTENHAM (St Andrew) *see* E w W Harling, Bridgham w
Roudham, Larling etc *Nor*

BRETTENHAM (St Mary) *see* Rattlesden w Thorpe Morieux,
Brettenham etc *St E*

BRETTON (Holy Spirit) *see* Pet H Spirit Bretton *Pet*

BREWHAM, SOUTH (St John the Baptist) *see* Bruton and Distr
B & W

BREWOOD (St Mary and St Chad) *Lich 2* **P** *Bp*
NSM M J COULTER

BRICETT, GREAT (St Mary and St Lawrence) *see* Ringshall w
Battisford, Barking w Darmsden etc *St E*

BRICKENDON (Holy Cross and St Alban) *see* Lt Berkhamsted
and Bayford, Essendon etc *St Alb*

BRICKET WOOD (St Luke) *St Alb 5* **P** *CPAS* **V** M RAJKOVIC

BRICKHILL, GREAT (St Mary) *see* Brickhills and Stoke
Hammond *Ox*

BRICKHILL, LITTLE (St Mary Magdalene) *as above*

BRICKHILL, NORTH (St Mark) *see* Bedf St Mark *St Alb*

BRICKHILLS and Stoke Hammond, The *Ox 15* **P** *Bp,*
Major Sir Philip Pauncefort-Duncombe Bt, St Edw Sch Ox,
and Cam Univ (jt) **R** J WALLER

BRICKLEHAMPTON (St Michael) *see* Elmley Castle w
Bricklehampton and Combertons *Worc*

BRIDE (St Bridget), Lezayre and North Ramsey *S & M* **P** *The*
Crown **R** B G EVANS-SMITH

BRIDE VALLEY *Sarum 2* **P** *Sir Robert Williams Bt and G A L-F*
Pitt-Rivers Esq (jt) **R** S R BATTY **NSM** R R ROGERS
OLM S LINFORD

BRIDEKIRK (St Bridget) *see* Cockermouth Area *Carl*

BRIDESTOWE (St Bridget) *see* Okehampton, Inwardleigh,
Belstone, Sourton etc *Ex*

BRIDFORD (St Thomas à Becket) *see* Christow, Ashton,
Bridford, Dunchideock etc *Ex*

BRIDGE (St Peter) *Cant 1* **P** *Abp and St Jo Coll Ox (jt)*
P-in-c J W LLOYD

BRIDGE Parishes, The *Sarum 9* **P** *Eton Coll and Nat Trust (alt)*
P-in-c A J H EDWARDS

BRIDGE SOLLARS (St Andrew) *see* Credenhill w Brinsop and
Wormsley etc *Heref*

BRIDGEMARY (St Matthew) *Portsm 3* **P** *Bp*
P-in-c K I MITCHELL

BRIDGFORD, EAST (St Peter) and Kneeton *S'well 5*
P *Magd Coll Ox (2 turns), C G Neale Esq (1 turn)*
P-in-c O J LEARMONT

BRIDGFORD, WEST (St Giles) (St Luke) *S'well 6*
P *Waddington Trustees* **R** L J PROUDLOVE

BRIDGHAM (St Mary) *see* E w W Harling, Bridgham w
Roudham, Larling etc *Nor*

BRIDGNORTH (St Mary Magdalene) (St Leonard) (St James),
Tasley, Astley Abbotts, Oldbury and Quatford *Heref 8*
P *DBP (3 turns) and Ld Chan (1 turn)* **TR** S H CAWDELL
TV E P ANGELL **C** L M HILL **OLM** M A BROOKS

BRIDGWATER (Holy Trinity) and Durleigh St Hugh *B & W 13*
P *Bp (2 turns) and Ld Chan (1 turn)* **V** W H H LANE
C H S J ALDERSON

BRIDGWATER (St Francis of Assisi) *B & W 13* **P** *Bp*
V B D JOY

BRIDGWATER (St John the Baptist) *B & W 13* **P** *Bp*
P-in-c E J SPARROW

BRIDGWATER (St Mary) and Chilton Trinity *B & W 13* **P** *Ld*
Chan **V** P A OLLIVE

BRIDLINGTON (Emmanuel) *York 9* **P** *Trustees* **V** *vacant*

BRIDLINGTON (Holy Trinity) and Sewerby w Marton *York 9*
P *Abp* **V** D J MATHER

BRIDLINGTON (St Mary's Priory Church) *York 9* **P** *Simeon's*
Trustees **R** M R POLLARD **NSM** C A STRAND

BRIDLINGTON QUAY (Christ Church) *York 9* **P** *R Bridlington*
Priory **V** J G COUPER

BRIDPORT (St Mary) *Sarum 2* **P** *Patr Bd (2 turns) and Ld Chan*
(1 turn) **TR** A EVANS **TV** P J M STONE **NSM** A M AYLING
OLM J E MOORE

BRIDSTOW (St Bridget) *see* Brampton *Heref*

BRIERCLIFFE (St James) *Blackb 3* **P** *Hulme Trustees*
V G A C P SAWYER

BRIERFIELD (St Luke) *Blackb 6* **P** *Bp* **V** S A ADESANYA

BRIERLEY HILL (St Michael) (St Paul) *Worc 10* **P** *Ld Chan (2*
turns), Patr Bd (1 turn) **TR** D J HOSKIN **C** B A WOODALL
NSM B I PRITCHETT

BRIGG (St John the Evangelist), Wrawby and Cadney cum
Howsham *Linc 8* **P** *Bp* **V** G O MITCHELL

BRIGHAM (St Bridget), Great Broughton and Broughton
Moor *Carl 7* **P** *Bp and Earl of Lonsdale (jt)*
C S SARVANANTHAN

BRIGHOUSE (St Chad) *see* Lightcliffe and Hove Edge *Leeds*

BRIGHOUSE (St Martin) and Clifton *Leeds 8* **P** *Bp*
V *vacant*

BRIGHSTONE (St Mary the Virgin) and Brooke w Mottistone
Portsm 8 **P** *Bp (2 turns), D&C St Paul's (1 turn)*
P-in-c H L O'SULLIVAN

BRIGHTLING (St Thomas of Canterbury), Mountfield and
Netherfield *Chich 13* **P** *Bp, Adn Lewes and Hastings,
H C Grissell Esq, Mrs A Egerton, and Mrs L A Fraser (jt)*
P-in-c A-M CROSSE

BRIGHTLINGSEA (All Saints) (St James) *Chelmsf 23* **P** *Ld
Chan* **P-in-c** A M HOWSON

BRIGHTON (Annunciation) *Chich 19* **P** *Wagner Trustees*
P-in-c M J WELLS

BRIGHTON (Chapel Royal) *Chich 19* **P** *Bp* **P-in-c** D J BIGGS

BRIGHTON (Good Shepherd) Preston *Chich 19* **P** *Bp*
P-in-c F P A MASCARENHAS **Hon C** C E JAMES
NSM H RAWLINGS

BRIGHTON (St Bartholomew) *Chich 19* **P** *Wagner Trustees*
P-in-c D C CLUES

BRIGHTON (St Cuthman) *see* Whitehawk *Chich*

BRIGHTON (St George w St Anne and St Mark) *Chich 19*
P *Bp and V Brighton (jt)* **V** A H MANSON-BRAILSFORD

BRIGHTON (St John) *see* Preston St Jo w Brighton St Aug and
St Sav *Chich*

BRIGHTON (St Luke) Queen's Park *Chich 19* **P** *Bp*
C J NEWSON

BRIGHTON (St Martin) w St Wilfrid and St Alban *Chich 19*
P *SMF* **V** T G BUXTON **C** M T A RICHARDS

BRIGHTON (St Mary the Virgin) *see* Kemp Town St Mary *Chich*

BRIGHTON (St Matthias) *Chich 19* **P** *V Preston* **V** *vacant*

BRIGHTON (St Michael and All Angels) (St Paul) *Chich 19*
P *SMF* **NSM** A S WALKER, J N BALDRY

BRIGHTON (St Nicholas) *Chich 19* **P** *Bp* **V** R CHAVNER

BRIGHTON (St Peter) *Chich 19* **P** *Bp and V Brompton H Trin
(jt)* **V** R M COATES **C** A J WOOD, J P GUMBEL, T J HOLBIRD

BRIGHTON, NEW (St James) (Emmanuel) *Ches 7* **P** *Bp*
V F R CAIN

BRIGHTSIDE (St Thomas and St Margaret) w Wincobank
Sheff 3 **P** *The Crown and Sheff Ch Burgesses (alt)*
V P N WARMAN

BRIGHTWALTON (All Saints) *see* W Downland *Ox*

BRIGHTWELL (St Agatha) *see* Wallingford *Ox*

BRIGHTWELL (St John the Baptist) *see* Martlesham w
Brightwell *St E*

BRIGHTWELL BALDWIN (St Bartholomew) *see* Ewelme,
Brightwell Baldwin, Cuxham w Easington *Ox*

BRIGNALL (St Mary) *see* Startforth and Bowes and Rokeby w
Brignall *Leeds*

BRIGSLEY (St Helen) *see* Waltham Gp *Linc*

BRIGSTOCK (St Andrew) w Stanion and Lowick and
Sudborough *Pet 7* **P** *Bp (2 turns), L G Stopford Sackville Esq
(1 turn)* **P-in-c** C G SIMPSON **Hon C** J M BOWERS

BRILL (All Saints) *see* Bernwode *Ox*

BRILLEY (St Mary) *see* Eardisley w Bollingham, Willersley,
Brilley etc *Heref*

BRIMFIELD (St Michael) *see* Leominster *Heref*

BRIMINGTON (St Michael) *Derby 3* **P** *V Chesterfield*
R D B COOKE

BRIMPSFIELD (St Michael) w Birdlip, Syde, Daglingworth,
The Duntisbournes, Winstone, Miserden and Edgeworth
Glouc 7 **P** *Ld Chan (1 turn), Bp, DBP, Major M N T H Wills and
CCC Ox (1 turn)* **R** V J BEXON **NSM** R H GEORGE

BRIMPTON (St Peter) *see* Aldermaston and Woolhampton *Ox*

BRIMSCOMBE (Holy Trinity) *see* Woodchester and
Brimscombe *Glouc*

BRINDLE (St James) *Blackb 4* **P** *Trustees* **R** D G WARD

BRINGHURST (St Nicholas) *see* Six Saints circa Holt *Leic*

BRINGTON (All Saints) *see* W Leightonstone *Ely*

BRINGTON (St Mary w St John) w Whilton and Norton and
Church Brampton w Chapel Brampton and Harlestone and
East Haddon and Holdenby *Pet 2* **P** *Patr Bd (5 turns), Prime
Min (1 turn)* **R** S J KIPLING

BRININGHAM (St Maurice) *see* Brinton, Briningham,
Hunworth, Stody etc *Nor*

BRINKBURN (St Peter and St Paul) *see* Longframlington w
Brinkburn *Newc*

BRINKHILL (St Philip) *see* S Ormsby Gp *Linc*

BRINKLEY (St Mary) *see* Raddesley Gp *Ely*

BRINKLOW (St John the Baptist) *see* Revel Gp *Cov*

BRINKWORTH (St Michael and All Angels) w Dauntsey *Bris 6*
P *Bp* **P-in-c** S WILKINSON

BRINNINGTON (St Luke) w Portwood St Paul *Ches 18* **P** *Bp*
V A B WILLIAMS

BRINSCALL (St Luke) *see* Heapey and Withnell *Blackb*

BRINSLEY (St James the Great) w Underwood *S'well 4* **P** *Bp*
P-in-c D A STEVENSON **C** A K ALLS

BRINSOP (St George) *see* Credenhill w Brinsop and Wormsley
etc *Heref*

BRINSWORTH (St Andrew) *see* Rivers Team *Sheff*

BRINTON (St Andrew), Briningham, Hunworth, Stody,
Swanton Novers and Thornage *Nor 18* **P** *J S Howlett Esq,
Lord Hastings, and DBP (by turn)* **P-in-c** B W TOMLINSON

BRISLEY (St Bartholomew) *see* Upper Wensum Village
Gp *Nor*

BRISLINGTON (St Anne) *Bris 1* **P** *Bp* **P-in-c** I L GARRETT

BRISLINGTON (St Christopher) *Bris 1* **P** *Simeon's Trustees*
P-in-c A W E SCHUMAN **OLM** P A HUNTER

BRISLINGTON (St Cuthbert) *Bris 1* **P** *Bp*
P-in-c I L GARRETT

BRISLINGTON (St Luke) *Bris 1* **P** *Bp* **V** D M DEWES

BRISTOL (Christ Church) w St Ewen, All SS and St George
Bris 3 **P** *J E Heal Esq* **R** *vacant*

BRISTOL (Christ the Servant) Stockwood *Bris 1* **P** *Bp*
V D G OWEN

BRISTOL (St Andrew w St Bartholomew) *see* Bishopston and
St Andrews *Bris*

BRISTOL (St Andrew) Hartcliffe *Bris 1* **P** *Bp*
P-in-c D A J MADDOX

BRISTOL (St Mary the Virgin) Redcliffe w Temple and
Bedminster St John the Baptist *Bris 1* **P** *Bp*
V D F TYNDALL **C** K M CAMPION-SPALL

BRISTOL (St Matthew and St Nathanael) (St Katharine) *Bris 3*
P *Bp and CPAS (jt)* **V** M J R NELSON **OLM** A J HULL,
J M CAITHNESS

BRISTOL (St Philip and St Jacob w Emmanuel) *Bris 3*
P *Trustees* **V** T J SILK **C** J HEYWARD

BRISTOL (St Stephen) w St James and St John the Baptist w
St Michael and St George *Bris 3* **P** *Ld Chan (1 turn), Bp,
Bris Ch Trustees, and D&C (2 turns)* **P-in-c** L BARNES
NSM R CROFT **OLM** F M HOUGHTON, J D A BROOKE-TAYLOR

BRISTOL Lockleaze (St Mary Magdalene w St Francis) *Bris 3*
P *Bp* **V** *vacant*

BRISTOL St Aidan w St George *Bris 3* **P** *Bp and SMF*
P-in-c R J LING **C** M K MARTIN **OLM** N G CALLEN,
T M DENLEY

BRISTOL St Paul's (St Agnes) *Bris 3* **P** *Ld Chan and Patr Bd
(alt)* **TR** *vacant*

BRISTOL, EAST (St Aidan) *see* Bristol St Aid w St Geo *Bris*

BRISTOL, EAST (St Ambrose) (St Leonard) *Bris 3* **P** *Bp*
V R D JAMES

BRISTON (All Saints), Burgh Parva, Hindolveston and Melton
Constable *Nor 18* **P** *Bp, Lord Hastings, and D&C (jt)*
P-in-c J G SYKES

BRITFORD (St Peter) *see* Chalke Valley *Sarum*

BRITWELL SALOME (St Nicholas) *see* Icknield *Ox*

BRITWELL St George *Ox 12* **P** *Eton Coll* **V** N MCCATHIE

BRIXHAM (St Mary) (All Saints) w Churston Ferrers and
Kingswear *Ex 11* **P** *The Crown* **TR** I H BLYDE
TV J C N GAY

BRIXTON (St Mary) *see* Yealmpton and Brixton *Ex*

BRIXTON (St Matthew) (St Jude) *S'wark 11* **P** *Abp and Ch Soc
Trust (jt)* **V** S M SICHEL **NSM** A HOLE

BRIXTON (St Paul) (St Saviour) *S'wark 11* **P** *Ch Soc Trust*
V B GOODYEAR **C** T-A L EWINS

BRIXTON DEVERILL (St Michael) *see* Cley Hill Villages *Sarum*

BRIXTON ROAD (Christ Church) *S'wark 11* **P** *CPAS*
V T J JEFFREYS

BRIXTON, NORTH (Christ Church) *see* Brixton Road Ch Ch
S'wark

BRIXWORTH (All Saints) w Holcot *Pet 2* **P** *Bp*
P-in-c C A M THOMAS

BRIZE NORTON (St Britius) and Carterton *Ox 28* **P** *Patr Bd*
TR W G BLAKEY **TV** J T MADDERN

BROAD BLUNSDON (St Leonard) *Bris 7* **P** *Bp*
P-in-c G D SOWDEN **C** D R CAPORN **NSM** T M DAY

BROAD BLUNSDON (St Leonard) *see* Broad Blunsdon *Bris*

BROAD CAMPDEN (St Michael and All Angels) *see* Vale and
Cotswold Edge *Glouc*

BROAD HINTON (St Peter ad Vincula) *see* Upper Kennet
Sarum

BROAD OAK (St George) *see* Heathfield *Chich*

BROAD TOWN (Christ Church) *see* Woodhill *Sarum*

BROADBOTTOM (St Mary Magdalene) *see* Mottram in
Longdendale *Ches*

BROADBRIDGE HEATH (St John) *see* Horsham *Chich*

BROADCHALKE (All Saints) *see* Chalke Valley *Sarum*

BROADCLYST (St John the Baptist), Clyst Honiton, Pinhoe,
Rockbeare and Sowton *Ex 1* **P** *Patr Bd* **TR** M J PARTRIDGE
C S J DYSON

BROADFIELD (Christ the Lord) *see* Southgate *Chich*

BROADHEATH (Christ Church) *see* Worc St Clem and Lower
Broadheath *Worc*

BROADHEATH (St Alban) *Ches 10* **P** *Bp* **V** H SCARISBRICK
NSM L REDFERN

BROADHEMBURY (St Andrew the Apostle and Martyr), Payhembury and Plymtree *Ex 6* **P** *W Drewe Esq, Ex Coll Ox, and Or Coll Ox (by turn)* **C** C E EDMONDS, J M WRIGHT, R G PECKHAM

BROADHEMPSTON (St Peter and St Paul) *see* Ipplepen w Torbryan, Denbury and Broadhempston w Woodland *Ex*

BROADMAYNE (St Martin) *see* Watercombe *Sarum*

BROADOAK (St Paul) *see* Askerswell, Loders, Powerstock and Symondsbury *Sarum*

BROADSIDE *Nor 4* **P** *Bp, Qu Coll Cam, and J Cator Esq (jt)* **R** N J H GARRARD **OLM** E H GARRARD

BROADSTAIRS (Holy Trinity) *Cant 5* **P** *V St Peter-in-Thanet* **NSM** C S ARNOLD, S C THOMAS

BROADSTONE (not known) *see* Diddlebury w Munslow, Holdgate and Tugford *Heref*

BROADSTONE (St John the Baptist) *Sarum 7* **P** *Bp* **V** N J C LLOYD **C** L S CARTER

BROADWAS (St Mary Magdalene) *see* Worcs W *Worc*

BROADWATER (Queen Street Church Centre) *see* Broadwater *Chich*

BROADWATER (St Mary) (St Stephen) (Queen Street Church Centre) *Chich 4* **P** *Patr Bd* **TR** P E IRWIN-CLARK **TV** G R NEAL, W M TSANG **C** S P COLLIER

BROADWATERS (St Oswald) *see* Kidderminster Ismere *Worc*

BROADWAY (St Aldhem and St Eadburga) *see* Isle Valley *B & W*

BROADWAY (St Eadburgha) (St Michael and All Angels) w Wickhamford *Worc 1* **P** *Peache Trustees and Ch Ch Ox (jt)* **P-in-c** M E WARD

BROADWELL (Good Shepherd) *see* Coleford, Staunton, Newland, Redbrook etc *Glouc*

BROADWELL (St Paul), Evenlode, Oddington, Adlestrop and Westcote w Icomb and Bledington *Glouc 8* **P** *Bp, Ch Soc Trust, Lord Leigh and DBP (1 turn), and Ch Ch Ox and D&C Worc (1 turn)* **R** R J RENDALL **C** N J CHARLES

BROADWELL (St Peter and St Paul) *see* Shill Valley and Broadshire *Ox*

BROADWEY (St Nicholas) *see* Bincombe w Broadwey, Upwey and Buckland Ripers *Sarum*

BROADWINDSOR (St John the Baptist) *see* Beaminster Area *Sarum*

BROADWOODKELLY (All Saints) *Ex 19* **P** *DBP* **R** P J NORMAN

BROADWOODWIDGER (St Nicholas) *see* Lifton, Broadwoodwidger, Stowford etc *Ex*

BROCKDISH (St Peter and St Paul) *see* Redenhall w Scole *Nor*

BROCKENHURST (St Nicholas) (St Saviour) *Win 11* **P** E J F *Morant Esq* **V** N R SMART **Hon C** R DROWN

BROCKHALL (St Peter and St Paul) *see* Heyford w Stowe Nine Churches and Flore etc *Pet*

BROCKHAM GREEN (Christ Church) *S'wark 26* **P** *Hon R P Hamilton* **P-in-c** J M A WILLANS

BROCKHAMPTON (All Saints) *see* Fownhope w Mordiford, Brockhampton etc *Heref*

BROCKHAMPTON (Chapel) *see* Bromyard and Stoke Lacy *Heref*

BROCKHOLES (St George) *see* Honley *Leeds*

BROCKLESBY PARK (All Saints) *Linc 8* **P** *Earl of Yarborough* **V** *vacant*

BROCKLEY (St Andrew) *see* Horringer *St E*

BROCKLEY (St Peter) *S'wark 2* **P** *Bp* **V** C M E G TOURNAY

BROCKLEY HILL (St Saviour) *S'wark 5* **P** *V Forest Hill Ch Ch* **V** A S PEBERDY

BROCKWORTH (St George) *Glouc 3* **P** *DBP* **V** J WALDEN **C** S W NEWNES

BROCTON (All Saints) *see* Baswich *Lich*

BRODSWORTH (St Michael and All Angels) *see* Bilham *Sheff*

BROKENBOROUGH (St John the Baptist) *see* Malmesbury w Westport and Brokenborough *Bris*

BROKERS WOOD (All Saints) *see* White Horse *Sarum*

BROMBOROUGH (St Barnabas) *Ches 9* **P** *D&C* **R** J S GILLIES **NSM** J E BISSON

BROME (St Mary) *see* N Hartismere *St E*

BROMESWELL (St Edmund) *see* Wilford Peninsula *St E*

BROMFIELD (St Mary the Virgin) *see* Ludlow *Heref*

BROMFIELD (St Mungo) *see* Solway Plain *Carl*

BROMHAM (St Nicholas) *see* Rowde and Bromham *Sarum*

BROMHAM (St Owen) w Oakley and Stagsden *St Alb 13* **P** *Bp* **P-in-c** L BOND **NSM** P A VENNELLS

BROMLEY (Christ Church) *Roch 14* **P** *CPAS* **V** I J BROOMFIELD **C** D A HOWARTH, D M LLOYD **Hon C** V G WILKINS

BROMLEY (St Andrew) *Roch 14* **P** *Bp* **NSM** E J DAVIS

BROMLEY (St John the Evangelist) *Roch 14* **P** *Bp* **V** A D MCCLELLAN

BROMLEY (St Mark) *Roch 14* **P** *V Bromley SS Pet & Paul* **V** S C VARNEY

BROMLEY (St Mary) *see* Plaistow St Mary *Roch*

BROMLEY (St Peter and St Paul) *Roch 14* **P** *Bp* **V** A J JABLONSKI **C** A P JABLONSKI

BROMLEY BY BOW (All Hallows) *Lon 7* **P** *Bp and Grocers' Co (jt)* **R** C I ROGERS **NSM** R M ROGERS

BROMLEY COMMON (Holy Trinity) *Roch 14* **P** *The Crown* **V** R BRISTOW **NSM** G E COLLETT

BROMLEY COMMON (St Augustine) *Roch 14* **P** *Bp* **V** K C BARNES **C** A D HOBBS

BROMLEY COMMON (St Luke) *Roch 14* **P** *Bp* **P-in-c** G E COLLETT

BROMLEY CROSS (St Andrew's Mission Church) *see* Turton Moorland *Man*

BROMLEY, GREAT (St George) *see* Ardleigh and The Bromleys *Chelmsf*

BROMLEY, LITTLE (St Mary the Virgin) *as above*

BROMPTON (St Thomas) w Deighton *York 18* **P** *D&C Dur* **V** J M E COOPER **NSM** M J KING

BROMPTON ON SWALE (St Paul) *see* Easby w Skeeby and Brompton on Swale etc *Leeds*

BROMPTON RALPH (The Blessed Virgin Mary) *see* Wiveliscombe and the Hills *B & W*

BROMPTON REGIS (Blessed Virgin Mary) *see* Dulverton w Brushford, Brompton Regis etc *B & W*

BROMPTON, NEW (St Luke) *Roch 3* **P** *Bp* **P-in-c** P MATTHIAS

BROMPTON, WEST (St Jude) (St Mary) St Peter *Lon 8* **P** *Bp and Sir Laurence Magnus Bt (jt)* **V** S E HARTLEY

BROMPTON-BY-SAWDON (All Saints) *see* Upper Derwent *York*

BROMSBERROW (St Mary the Virgin) *see* Redmarley D'Abitot, Bromesberrow, Pauntley etc *Glouc*

BROMSGROVE (All Saints) (St John the Baptist) *Worc 7* **P** *Patr Bd* **TR** C A HOLZAPFEL **TV** B A ROBERTSON, R A KHAN **C** C J SALEH

BROMWICH, WEST (All Saints) (St Mary Magdalene) *Lich 27* **P** *Bp* **V** *vacant*

BROMWICH, WEST (Good Shepherd w St John) *Lich 27* **P** *Bp* **V** K S NJENGA

BROMWICH, WEST (Holy Trinity) *Lich 27* **P** *Peache Trustees* **V** J N ROBBIE

BROMWICH, WEST (St Andrew) (Christ Church) *Lich 27* **P** *Bp and V W Bromwich All SS (jt)* **V** M J CLARIDGE

BROMWICH, WEST (St Francis of Assisi) *Lich 27* **P** *Bp* **V** R A FARRELL **OLM** G HARTILL

BROMWICH, WEST (St James) (St Paul) *Lich 27* **P** *Bp and V Tipton St Martin and St Paul* **V** D HART

BROMWICH, WEST (St Peter) *Lich 27* **P** *Bp* **V** L A COX

BROMWICH, WEST (St Philip) *Lich 27* **P** *Bp* **P-in-c** P O DANIEL

BROMYARD (St Peter) and Stoke Lacy *Heref 2* **P** *Bp (4 turns), Exors P H G Morgan Esq (1 turn)* **V** C R EVANS **NSM** C A STOKES, D B HYETT

BRONDESBURY (Christ Church) (St Laurence) *Lon 21* **P** *Ld Chan* **R** S M FRANCE

BRONDESBURY St Anne w Kilburn (Holy Trinity) *Lon 21* **P** *Bp and Ch Patr Soc (alt)* **V** C E CARGILL **NSM** L C F HILLEL

BROOKE (St Mary the Virgin) *see* Brighstone and Brooke w Mottistone *Portsm*

BROOKE (St Peter) *see* Oakham, Ashwell, Braunston, Brooke, Egleton etc *Pet*

BROOKE (St Peter), Kirstead, Mundham w Seething and Thwaite *Nor 5* **P** *G&C Coll Cam, Gt Hosp and Countess Ferrers, and Ld Chan (by turn)* **R** *vacant*

BROOKFIELD (St Anne), Highgate Rise *Lon 17* **P** *Bp* **V** A J B MELDRUM

BROOKFIELD (St Margaret) *York 20* **P** *Abp* **V** V G HATTON **NSM** W A DEWING

BROOKFIELD (St Mary) *Lon 17* **P** *Bp* **V** C G POPE

BROOKHOUSE (St Paul) *see* Caton w Littledale *Blackb*

BROOKLAND (St Augustine), Fairfield, Brenzett w Snargate and Lydd *Cant 10* **P** *Abp* **R** S R WILLIAMS **NSM** S J BODY

BROOKSBY (St Michael and All Angels) *see* Upper Wreake *Leic*

BROOKWOOD (St Saviour) *see* Knaphill w Brookwood *Guildf*

BROOM (St Matthew) *see* Heart of England *Cov*

BROOM LEYS (St David) *Leic 8* **P** *Bp* **P-in-c** A C RHOADES **C** N T GRIFFITHS **NSM** R M PASSEY

BROOME (St Michael) *see* Ditchingham, Hedenham, Broome, Earsham etc *Nor*

BROOME (St Peter) *see* Churchill-in-Halfshire w Blakedown and Broome *Worc*

BROOMFIELD (St Margaret) *see* Hollingbourne and Hucking w Leeds and Broomfield *Cant*

BROOMFIELD (St Mary and All Saints) *see* W Monkton w Kingston St Mary, Broomfield etc *B & W*

BROOMFIELD (St Mary w St Leonard) *Chelmsf 9*   **P** *Bp*
V C A TIBBOTT   **NSM** R A HARVEY

BROOMFLEET (St Mary)   *see* S Cave and Ellerker w Broomfleet
York

BROOMHILL (St Mark)   *see* Sheff St Mark Broomhill *Sheff*

BROSELEY (All Saints)   *see* Broseley w Benthall, Jackfield, Linley
etc *Heref*

**BROSELEY (All Saints) w Benthall, Jackfield, Linley, Willey and
Barrow** *Heref 13*   **P** *Patr Bd*   **R** S BEVERLY

**BROTHERTOFT Group, The (Christ Church) (St Gilbert of
Sempringham)** *Linc 21*   **P** *Bp (2 turns), V Algarkirk (1 turn)*
V R E TAYLOR   **OLM** M L HOULDERSHAW

BROTHERTON (St Edward the Confessor) *Leeds 19*   **P** *D&C*
York   **P-in-c** E M WOODCOCK   **NSM** S HULME

BROTTON PARVA (St Margaret) *York 16*   **P** *Abp*
R J P RHODES

BROUGH (All Saints)   *see* Elloughton and Brough w
Brantingham *York*

BROUGH (St Michael) w Stainmore, Musgrave and Warcop
Carl 1   **P** *Bp (2 turns) and Lord Hothfield (1 turn)*   **R** *vacant*

BROUGHAM (St Wilfrid Chapel)   *see* Lowther and Askham and
Clifton and Brougham *Carl*

BROUGHTON (All Saints)   *see* Warboys w Broughton and Bury
w Wistow *Ely*

BROUGHTON (All Saints), Marton and Thornton *Leeds 26*
P *Ch Ch Ox and Exors Dame Harriet Nelson (jt)*   **R** N A TURNER
C P A TURNER

BROUGHTON (no church) *Ox 10*   **P** *Ch Patr Trust*
V P C WHITE

**BROUGHTON (St Andrew) w Loddington and Cransley and
Thorpe Malsor** *Pet 9*   **P** *Ld Chan (1 turn), Bp (2 turns), and
Keble Coll Ox (1 turn)*   **C** B J WITHINGTON, J R WESTWOOD,
N HOBBS

**BROUGHTON (St James) (St Clement and St Matthias)
St John the Baptist** *Man 20*   **P** *Patr Bd*   **TR** G KENNEDY
NSM G TURNER   **OLM** J S CORRIE

BROUGHTON (St John the Baptist) *Blackb 13*   **P** *Trustees*
V S BALDWIN   **C** C P WALKER   **OLM** P F TAYLOR

**BROUGHTON (St Mary Magdalene) (Holy Innocents) and
Duddon** *Carl 9*   **P** *V Millom, Lt Col D A S Pennefather, and
Ch Patr Trust (by turn)*   **P-in-c** N A THORNLEY

BROUGHTON (St Mary the Virgin)   *see* Wykeham *Ox*

BROUGHTON (St Mary) *Lich 22*   **P** *D R B Thompson Esq*
P-in-c A J B CLAYTON   **OLM** A EVANS

BROUGHTON (St Mary) *Linc 8*   **P** *MMCET*   **P-in-c** D J EAMES

**BROUGHTON (St Mary) w Bossington and Houghton
and Mottisfont** *Win 12*   **P** *Ld Chan (1 turn), Mr and Mrs
R G L Pugh, A Humbert Esq and Miss R A Humbert (jt) (2 turns)*
R R A CORNE   **C** G M NOBES

BROUGHTON (St Peter)   *see* Ashley and Mucklestone and
Broughton and Croxton *Lich*

BROUGHTON ASTLEY (St Mary) and Croft w Stoney Stanton
Leic 7   **P** *Patr Bd*   **TR** S J CONSTABLE   **C** A A COSLETT

**BROUGHTON GIFFORD (St Mary the Virgin), Great Chalfield
and Holt St Katharine** *Sarum 15*   **P** *D&C Bris (3 turns), Ld
Chan (2 turns), and R C Floyd Esq (1 turn)*   **R** A E EVANS
NSM R MECREDY

BROUGHTON HACKETT (St Leonard)   *see* Peopleton and
White Ladies Aston w Churchill etc *Worc*

BROUGHTON IN FURNESS (St Mary Magdalene)
see Broughton and Duddon *Carl*

BROUGHTON MILLS (Holy Innocents) *as above*

BROUGHTON MOOR (St Columba)   *see* Brigham, Gt
Broughton and Broughton Moor *Carl*

BROUGHTON POGGS (St Peter)   *see* Shill Valley and
Broadshire *Ox*

BROUGHTON, GREAT (Christ Church)   *see* Brigham, Gt
Broughton and Broughton Moor *Carl*

BROUGHTON, LOWER (Ascension) *Man 20*   **P** *Trustees*
P-in-c D S C WYATT

BROUGHTON, NETHER (St Mary the Virgin)   *see* Old Dalby,
Nether Broughton, Saxelbye etc *Leic*

BROUGHTON, UPPER (St Luke)   *see* Hickling w Kinoulton and
Broughton Sulney *S'well*

BROWN CANDOVER (St Peter)   *see* Farleigh, Candover and
Wield *Win*

BROWN EDGE (St Anne) *Lich 8*   **P** *Bp*   **P-in-c** A J BETTS
NSM T WARNER

BROWNHILL (St Saviour) *Leeds 7*   **P** *V Batley*
V L A MATTACKS

BROWNSOVER (Christ Church)   *see* Clifton w Newton and
Brownsover *Cov*

BROWNSWOOD PARK (St John the Evangelist) *Lon 5*   **P** *City
Corp*   **V** D P SANDHAM   **NSM** J C GAU

BROXBOURNE (St Augustine) w Wormley *St Alb 17*   **P** *Bp
and Peache Trustees (jt)*   **R** C E C HUDSON   **C** R J C WEBSTER

**BROXTED (St Mary the Virgin) w Chickney and Tilty and
Great and Little Easton** *Chelmsf 18*   **P** *Mrs F Spurrier
(2 turns), DBP (1 turn), and MMCET (1 turn)*
P-in-c I E CRAWFORD

BROXTOWE (St Martha) *S'well 8*   **P** *Bp*   **V** J M KIRKHAM
C D C CORCORAN

BRUERA (St Mary)   *see* Waverton w Aldford and Bruera *Ches*

BRUISYARD (St Peter)   *see* Upper Alde *St E*

BRUMBY (St Hugh) (All Saints) *Linc 6*   **P** *Bp*
TR C A B MARTIN   **NSM** J A CLARK   **OLM** A K PEAT

BRUNDALL (St Lawrence) w Braydeston and Postwick *Nor 4*
P *Bp and MMCET (jt)*   **R** P-J B LEECH

BRUNDISH (St Lawrence)   *see* Four Rivers *St E*

BRUNSTEAD (St Peter)   *see* Stalham, E Ruston, Brunstead,
Sutton and Ingham *Nor*

BRUNSWICK (Christ Church) *Man 3*   **P** *Ch Soc Trust*
R S J T GATENBY   **C** M P CORCORAN   **NSM** R M YOUNG

BRUNSWICK (St Cuthbert)   *see* Ch the King *Newc*

BRUNTCLIFFE (St Andrew)   *see* Morley *Leeds*

BRUNTINGTHORPE (St Mary)   *see* Hexagon *Leic*

BRUNTON PARK (St Aidan)   *see* Ch the King *Newc*

BRUSHFORD (St Mary the Virgin) *Ex 19*   **P** *D&C*
V P J NORMAN

BRUSHFORD (St Nicholas)   *see* Dulverton w Brushford,
Brompton Regis etc *B & W*

BRUTON (St Mary the Virgin) and District *B & W 2*   **P** *Patr Bd*
P-in-c J M BAILEY   **C** R C LUNN   **Hon C** M D ELLIS

BRYANSTON SQUARE (St Mary) w St Marylebone (St Mark)
Lon 4   **P** *The Crown*   **R** J P T PETERS   **C** B M JONES,
E B W FLINT   **NSM** B J KISSELL

BRYANSTON STREET (Annunciation)   *see* St Marylebone
Annunciation Bryanston Street *Lon*

BRYHER (All Saints)   *see* Is of Scilly *Truro*

BRYMPTON (St Andrew)   *see* Odcombe, Brympton, Lufton and
Montacute *B & W*

BRYN (St Peter) *Liv 14*   **P** *Bp*   **V** S GASSON

BUBBENHALL (St Giles)   *see* Baginton w Bubbenhall and
Ryton-on-Dunsmore *Cov*

BUBWITH (All Saints) w Skipwith *York 2*   **P** *Abp and D&C, and
Ld Chan (alt)*   **P-in-c** R M KIRKMAN   **Hon C** K J GARDINER

BUCKDEN (St Mary) w the Offords *Ely 13*   **P** *Bp and Ld Chan
(alt)*   **P-in-c** J W SALT

BUCKENHAM, NEW (St Martin)   *see* Quidenham Gp *Nor*

BUCKENHAM, OLD (All Saints) *as above*

BUCKERELL (St Mary and St Giles)   *see* Honiton, Gittisham,
Combe Raleigh, Monkton etc *Ex*

BUCKFAST SANCTUARY (not known)   *see* Staverton w
Landscove, Littlehempston, Buckfastleigh and Dean Prior *Ex*

BUCKFASTLEIGH (Holy Trinity) *as above*

BUCKFASTLEIGH (St Luke's Mission) *as above*

BUCKHORN WESTON (St John the Baptist)   *see* Stour Vale
Sarum

**BUCKHURST HILL (St Elisabeth) (St John the Baptist)
(St Stephen)** *Chelmsf 3*   **P** *Patr Bd*   **TR** I D FARLEY
C S GUINNESS

BUCKINGHAM (St Peter and St Paul) *Ox 11*   **P** *Bp, Adn
Buckm, Mrs S A J Doulton, G&C Coll Cam, New Coll Ox, and
Exors R J Dalziel Smith Esq (jt)*   **R** W O C PEARSON-GEE
C A M WALSH, R E RUGG   **NSM** J K ING

BUCKINGHAM, NORTH *Ox 11*   **P** *Ch Soc Trust, Mrs J M
Williams, and D J Robarts Esq (by turn)*   **R** J A TALING

BUCKINGHAM, WEST *Ox 11*   **P** *Bp, D&C Westmr, G Purefoy
Esq, and R L Randall Esq (1 turn), New Coll Ox (1 turn), and
DBP (1 turn)*   **R** E A SIMPSON

BUCKLAND (All Saints)   *see* Aston Clinton w Buckland and
Drayton Beauchamp *Ox*

BUCKLAND (St Mary the Virgin)   *see* Cherbury w Gainfield *Ox*

BUCKLAND (St Mary the Virgin)   *see* Betchworth and Buckland
S'wark

BUCKLAND (St Michael)   *see* Winchcombe *Glouc*

BUCKLAND BREWER (St Mary and St Benedict)   *see* Parkham,
Alwington, Buckland Brewer etc *Ex*

BUCKLAND DINHAM (St Michael and All Angels)   *see* Mells w
Buckland Dinham, Elm, Whatley etc *B & W*

BUCKLAND FILLEIGH (St Mary and Holy Trinity)   *see* Shebbear,
Buckland Filleigh, Sheepwash etc *Ex*

BUCKLAND IN THE MOOR (St Peter)   *see* Ashburton,
Bickington, Buckland in the Moor etc *Ex*

BUCKLAND MONACHORUM (St Andrew) *Ex 22*   **P** *Bp*
V G M COTTER

**BUCKLAND NEWTON (Holy Rood), Cerne Abbas,
Godmanstone and Minterne Magna** *Sarum 1*   **P** *Adn
Sherborne, Lord Digby, D H C Batten Esq, H E Gallia Esq, and
Col J L Yeatman (jt)*   **V** J T L STILL

BUCKLAND RIPERS (St Nicholas)   *see* Bincombe w Broadwey,
Upwey and Buckland Ripers *Sarum*

BUCKLAND ST MARY (Blessed Virgin Mary)   *see* Blackdown *B & W*

BUCKLAND TOUT SAINTS (St Peter)   *see* Stokenham, Slapton, Charleton w Buckland etc *Ex*

BUCKLAND VALLEY (St Nicholas)   *see* Dover Town *Cant*

BUCKLAND, EAST (St Michael)   *see* S Molton w Nymet St George, High Bray etc *Ex*

BUCKLAND, WEST (Blessed Virgin Mary)   *see* Wellington and Distr *B & W*

BUCKLAND, WEST (St Peter)   *see* Swimbridge w W Buckland and Landkey *Ex*

BUCKLAND-IN-DOVER (St Andrew)   *see* Dover Town *Cant*

BUCKLEBURY (St Mary) w Marlston *Ox 4*   **P** *C J Pratt Esq* **P-in-c** J T D M GADSBY   **NSM** L E BLISS

BUCKLEBURY, UPPER (All Saints)   *see* Bucklebury w Marlston *Ox*

BUCKLERS HARD (St Mary)   *see* Beaulieu and Exbury and E Boldre *Win*

BUCKLESHAM (St Mary)   *see* Nacton and Levington w Bucklesham etc *St E*

BUCKMINSTER (St John the Baptist)   *see* S Framland *Leic*

BUCKNALL (St Margaret)   *see* Woodhall Spa Gp *Linc*

BUCKNALL Team Ministry, The (St Mary the Virgin) *Lich 12* **P** *Patr Bd*   **TR** N W R EVANS   **TV** D STREET, M N STEPHENS **OLM** J MARSHALL

BUCKNELL (St Mary)   *see* Middle Marches *Heref*

BUCKNELL (St Peter)   *see* Bicester w Bucknell, Caversfield and Launton *Ox*

BUCKROSE CARRS *York 6*   **P** *Prime Min, H J N Cholmley Esq, Sir Philip Naylor-Leyland Bt, and D&C (by turn)* **R** J T KINSELLA

BUCKROSE, WEST *York 6*   **P** *Ld Chan (1 turn), Lord Middleton and Abp (3 turns)*   **R** *vacant*

BUCKS MILLS (St Anne)   *see* Parkham, Alwington, Buckland Brewer etc *Ex*

BUCKWORTH (All Saints)   *see* N Leightonstone *Ely*

BUDBROOKE (St Michael) *Cov 11*   **P** *MMCET* **V** D A BROWN   **OLM** M LODGE

BUDE HAVEN (St Michael and All Angels) and Marhamchurch *Truro 8*   **P** *Bp and PCC (jt)* **P-in-c** D K BARNES   **C** A J HARDY

BUDLEIGH SALTERTON (St Peter), East Budleigh w Bicton, and Otterton *Ex 1*   **P** *Lord Clinton*   **V** E A CHARLTON **C** P F HARTOPP   **NSM** A DENNY

BUDLEIGH, EAST (All Saints)   *see* Budleigh Salterton, E Budleigh w Bicton etc *Ex*

BUDOCK (St Budock) *Truro 3*   **P** *Bp*   **V** G K BENNETT

BUDWORTH, GREAT (St Mary and All Saints) *Ches 4* **P** *Ch Ch Ox*   **V** A G BROWN

BUDWORTH, LITTLE (St Peter)   *see* Whitegate w Lt Budworth *Ches*

BUGBROOKE (St Michael and All Angels), Harpole, Kislingbury and Rothersthorpe *Pet 3*   **P** *Bp, Exors E W Harrison, DBP, and Sir Philip Naylor-Leyland Bt (jt)* **R** S R J FRENCH

BUGLAWTON (St John the Evangelist)   *see* Congleton *Ches*

BUGTHORPE (St Andrew)   *see* Garrowby Hill *York*

BUILDWAS (Holy Trinity)   *see* Wrockwardine Deanery *Lich*

BULCOTE (Holy Trinity)   *see* Burton Joyce w Bulcote and Stoke Bardolph *S'well*

BULFORD (St Leonard)   *see* Avon River *Sarum*

BULKINGTON (Christ Church)   *see* Seend, Bulkington and Poulshot *Sarum*

BULKINGTON (St James) *Cov 5*   **P** *Ld Chan* **P-in-c** P J MESSAM   **NSM** E JONES

BULLEY (St Michael and All Angels)   *see* Huntley and Longhope, Churcham and Bulley *Glouc*

BULLINGHOPE, UPPER (St Peter)   *see* Heref S Wye *Heref*

BULLINGTON (St Michael and All Angels)   *see* Lower Dever *Win*

BULMER (St Andrew)   *see* N Hinckford *Chelmsf*

BULMER (St Martin)   *see* Howardian Gp *York*

BULPHAN (St Mary the Virgin)   *see* Orsett and Bulphan and Horndon on the Hill *Chelmsf*

BULWELL (St John the Divine) *S'well 8*   **P** *Bp*   **V** D GRAY **NSM** R C STEPHENS

BULWELL (St Mary the Virgin and All Souls) *S'well 8*   **P** *Bp* **R** *vacant*

BULWICK (St Nicholas)   *see* King's Cliffe, Bulwick and Blatherwycke etc *Pet*

BUNBURY (St Boniface) and Tilstone Fearnall *Ches 5* **P** *Haberdashers' Co*   **C** V T D M HAYWARD   **C** V G GREEN

BUNCTON (All Saints)   *see* Ashington, Washington and Wiston w Buncton *Chich*

BUNGAY (Holy Trinity) *St E 18*   **P** *DBP, Mrs B I T Suckling, and CPAS (jt)*   **V** I B BYRNE   **C** R H P THORNBURGH **NSM** J E A MILLER

BUNGAY (Holy Trinity)   *see* Bungay *St E*

BUNNY (St Mary the Virgin)   *see* Keyworth and Stanton-on-the-Wolds and Bunny etc *S'well*

BUNTINGFORD (St Peter)   *see* Aspenden, Buntingford and Westmill *St Alb*

BUNWELL (St Michael and All Angels), Carleton Rode, Tibenham, Great Moulton and Aslacton *Nor 5*   **P** *Bp and DBP (alt)*   **P-in-c** H Y WILCOX   **C** J Y MADINDA

BURBAGE (All Saints)   *see* Savernake *Sarum*

BURBAGE (Christ Church)   *see* Buxton w Burbage and King Sterndale *Derby*

BURBAGE (St Catherine) w Aston Flamville *Leic 10*   **P** *Ball Coll Ox*   **R** A D HALL   **NSM** D MCLEAN

BURCHETTS GREEN *Ox 5*   **P** *DBP and Bp (jt)*   **V** K B NICHOLLS **NSM** T M MOLYNEUX

BURE VALLEY Benefice, The *Nor 19*   **P** *Bp, Mercers' Co, and J M Roberts Esq (jt)*   **P-in-c** F B CAPIE   **C** D A COUSINS

BURES (St Mary the Virgin) w Assington and Lt Cornard *St E 12*   **P** *DBP and Bp (jt)*   **V** S R MORLEY **NSM** J L GOYMOUR, M J CANTACUZENE, P J BOX

BURFORD (St John the Baptist) w Fulbrook, Taynton, Asthall, Swinbrook and Widford *Ox 28*   **P** *Bp and Capt D Mackinnon (jt)*   **V** R M COOMBS   **C** R J D WAINWRIGHT **OLM** C REAVLEY

BURFORD (St Mary)   *see* Tenbury *Heref*

BURGATE (St Mary)   *see* N Hartismere *St E*

BURGESS HILL (St Andrew) *Chich 8*   **P** *Bp*   **C** C A SMITH

BURGESS HILL (St Edward) *Chich 8*   **P** *Bp Chich, Bp Horsham, and R Clayton w Keymer (jt)*   **V** D M BRADSHAW **NSM** S S MACCARTHY

BURGESS HILL (St John the Evangelist) *Chich 8*   **P** *Bp Chich, Bp Horsham, and R Clayton w Keymer (jt)*   **V** K M O'BRIEN

BURGH (St Botolph)   *see* Carlford *St E*

BURGH (St Margaret and St Mary)   *see* S Trin Broads *Nor*

BURGH (St Peter)   *see* Raveningham Gp *Nor*

BURGH CASTLE (St Peter and St Paul)   *see* Belton and Burgh Castle *Nor*

BURGH Group, The *Linc 10*   **P** *Bp (2 turns), H J Montgomery-Massingberd Esq (1 turn), SMF (1 turn)*   **R** T STEELE

BURGH HEATH (St Mary the Virgin)   *see* Howell Hill w Burgh Heath *Guildf*

BURGH LE MARSH (St Peter and St Paul)   *see* Burgh Gp *Linc*

BURGH PARVA (St Mary)   *see* Briston, Burgh Parva, Hindolveston etc *Nor*

BURGH-BY-SANDS (St Michael)   *see* Barony of Burgh *Carl*

BURGHCLERE (Ascension) (All Saints) w Newtown and Ecchinswell w Sydmonton *Win 6*   **P** *Earl of Carnarvon* **R** D G BARTHOLOMEW

BURGHFIELD (St Mary the Virgin) *Ox 4*   **P** *Earl of Shrewsbury* **R** G J LOVELL   **C** A F K JONES

BURGHILL (St Mary the Virgin) *Heref 3*   **P** *DBP* **P-in-c** P A LITTLEWOOD   **NSM** E S V VERWEY

BURGH-NEXT-AYLSHAM (St Mary)   *see* Bure Valley *Nor*

BURGH-ON-BAIN (St Helen)   *see* Asterby Gp *Linc*

BURGHWALLIS (St Helen) and Campsall *Sheff 7*   **P** *Bp (2 turns), Mrs E H I Ellison-Anne (1 turn)*   **P-in-c** R J WALTON

BURHAM (Methodist Church) and Wouldham *Roch 5* **P** *Bp and Ld Chan (alt)*   **P-in-c** M J HAYES

BURITON (St Mary the Virgin) *Portsm 4*   **P** *Bp* **R** W P M HUGHES   **NSM** J M BEE

BURLESCOMBE (St Mary)   *see* Sampford Peverell, Uplowman, Holcombe Rogus etc *Ex*

BURLEY (St Matthias) *Leeds 16*   **P** *G M Bedford Esq, J C Yeadon Esq, E Beety Esq, Mrs M E Dunham, and Mrs L M Rawse (jt)* **P-in-c** K TROUT   **NSM** M PLANT

BURLEY IN WHARFEDALE (St Mary the Virgin) *Leeds 4* **P** *Bp*   **C** P A WHEELHOUSE

BURLEY VILLE (St John the Baptist) *Win 9*   **P** *V Ringwood* **P-in-c** E A M GAMMON

BURLEYDAM (St Mary and St Michael)   *see* Baddiley and Wrenbury w Burleydam *Ches*

BURLINGHAM (St Andrew)   *see* Blofield *Nor*

BURLINGHAM (St Edmund King and Martyr) w Lingwood, Strumpshaw w Hassingham and Buckenham *Nor 4* **P** *Ch Soc Trust, MMCET, and Bp (jt)*   **R** D K WAKEFIELD

BURLTON (St Anne)   *see* Loppington w Newtown *Lich*

BURMANTOFTS (St Stephen and St Agnes) *Leeds 14* **P** *Ch Trust Fund Trust*   **P-in-c** A S KASIBANTE

BURMARSH (All Saints)   *see* Romney Marsh *Cant*

BURMINGTON (St Nicholas and St Barnabas)   *see* S Warks Seven Gp *Cov*

BURNAGE (St Margaret) *Man 2*   **P** *Bp*   **R** I D THOMPSON

BURNAGE (St Nicholas) *Man 6*   **P** *Trustees*   **P-in-c** R MANN **NSM** A J SIMPSON

BURNBY (St Giles)   *see* Londesborough Wold *York*

BURNESIDE (St Oswald)   *see* Beacon *Carl*

BURNESTON (St Lambert)   *see* Kirklington w Burneston and Wath and Pickhill *Leeds*

BURNETT (St Michael)   *see* Keynsham *B & W*

BURNEY LANE (Christ Church)   *see* Ward End w Bordesley Green *Birm*

BURNHAM (St Andrew) *B & W 1*   **P** *D&C*   **V** G R WITTS   **NSM** S A ELDERGILL

BURNHAM (St Mary the Virgin) *Chelmsf 11*   **P** *N D Beckett Esq and Walsingham Coll Trust (jt)*   **V** M R NORTH

BURNHAM (St Peter) *Ox 12*   **P** *Eton Coll*   **V** W S JACKSON

BURNHAM DEEPDALE (St Mary)   *see* Hunstanton St Mary w Ringstead Parva etc *Nor*

BURNHAM NORTON (St Margaret)   *see* Burnham Gp of Par *Nor*

BURNHAM OVERY (St Clement) *as above*

BURNHAM THORPE (All Saints) *as above*

BURNHAM ULPH (All Saints) *as above*

BURNHAM WESTGATE (St Mary), Burnham Norton, Burnham Overy, Burnham Thorpe, and Burnham Sutton w Ulph (The Burnham Group of Parishes) *Nor 15*   **P** *Ch Coll Cam (1 turn), Ld Chan (2 turns), and DBP (1 turn)*   **R** G E D HITCHINS

BURNHAM-ON-CROUCH (St Mary the Virgin)   *see* Burnham *Chelmsf*

BURNHAM-ON-SEA (St Andrew)   *see* Burnham *B & W*

BURNLEY (St Andrew) w St Margaret and Burnley St James *Blackb 3*   **P** *Prime Min and R Burnley St Pet (alt)*   **V** P R HAPGOOD-STRICKLAND

BURNLEY (St Catherine) (St Alban) and St Paul *Blackb 3*   **P** *R Burnley*   **V** R T D PARKER

BURNLEY (St Cuthbert) *Blackb 3*   **P** *R Burnley*   **V** S A ADESANYA

BURNLEY (St Mark) *Blackb 3*   **P** *Bp*   **P-in-c** P R HAPGOOD-STRICKLAND

BURNLEY (St Matthew the Apostle) Habergham Eaves w Holy Trinity *Blackb 3*   **P** *R Burnley*   **V** M J WILLIAMS   **C** A D J FROST

BURNLEY (St Peter) (St Stephen) *Blackb 3*   **P** *Bp and DBP (jt)*   **R** P N A SENIOR

BURNLEY, WEST (All Saints) *Blackb 3*   **P** *Bp and R Burnley (jt)*   **V** C W HILL

BURNMOOR (St Barnabas) *Dur 14*   **P** *Lord Lambton*   **P-in-c** E M WILKINSON

BURNOPFIELD (St James)   *see* Tanfield w Burnopfield and Dipton *Dur*

BURNSALL (St Wilfrid) w Rylstone *Leeds 26*   **P** *Exors Earl of Craven and CPAS (jt)*   **P-in-c** D MACHA   **C** F JENKINS

BURNT YATES (St Andrew)   *see* Bishop Thornton, Burnt Yates, Markington etc *Leeds*

BURNTWOOD (Christ Church), Chase Terrace, Chasetown and Hammerwich *Lich 1*   **P** *Patr Bd*   **TR** M M MATTOCKS   **TV** M WALLACE   **NSM** L HOOD   **OLM** D T BROOK

BURPHAM (Holy Spirit) (St Luke) Guildford *Guildf 5*   **P** *Bp*   **V** J A LEVASIER   **C** J M LEVASIER   **NSM** J C L RUNNACLES

BURPHAM (St Mary the Virgin) *Chich 1*   **P** *D&C*   **P-in-c** M M SLATTERY

BURRADON (Good Shepherd)   *see* Weetslade *Newc*

BURRILL (Mission Church)   *see* Bedale and Leeming and Thornton Watlass *Leeds*

BURRINGTON (Holy Trinity)   *see* Wrington w Butcombe and Burrington *B & W*

BURRINGTON (Holy Trinity), Chawleigh, Cheldon, Chulmleigh, Meshaw, Romansleigh, Thelbridge, Wembworthy w Eggesford, Witheridge w Creacombe, East Worlington and West Worlington *Ex 18*   **P** *Patr Bd*   **TV** A M WELLS

BURRINGTON (St George)   *see* Wigmore Abbey *Heref*

BURROUGH GREEN (St Augustine of Canterbury)   *see* Raddesley Gp *Ely*

BURROUGH HILL Parishes, The: Burrough on the Hill, Great Dalby, Little Dalby, Pickwell and Somerby *Leic 2*   **P** *Bp, DBP, and Mrs M Burdett Fisher (jt)*   **V** *vacant*

BURROUGH ON THE HILL (St Mary the Virgin)   *see* Burrough Hill Pars *Leic*

BURROWBRIDGE (St Michael)   *see* Athelney *B & W*

BURRSVILLE (St Mark)   *see* Gt Clacton *Chelmsf*

BURSCOUGH BRIDGE (St John) (St Andrew) (St Cyprian) *Liv 11*   **P** *V Ormskirk*   **C** I R JONES

BURSDON MOOR (St Martin)   *see* Parkham, Alwington, Buckland Brewer etc *Ex*

BURSEA (Chapel)   *see* Holme and Seaton Ross Gp *York*

BURSLEDON (St Leonard) *Win 10*   **P** *Bp*   **V** P A VARGESON   **C** C E CHALLIS, R W SANDAY

BURSLEDON Pilands Wood (St Paul)   *see* Bursledon *Win*

BURSLEM (St John the Baptist) (St Paul) *Lich 11*   **P** *Bp and MMCET (jt)*   **R** D L MCINDOE

BURSLEM (St Werburgh) *Lich 11*   **P** *Bp*   **V** K L ROUND

BURSTALL (St Mary the Virgin)   *see* Sproughton w Burstall, Copdock w Washbrook etc *St E*

BURSTEAD, GREAT (St Mary Magdalene) w Ramsden Crays *Chelmsf 12*   **P** *Bp*   **P-in-c** M A HALL

BURSTEAD, LITTLE (St Mary)   *see* Billericay and Lt Burstead *Chelmsf*

BURSTOCK (St Andrew)   *see* Beaminster Area *Sarum*

BURSTON (St Mary)   *see* Winfarthing w Shelfanger w Burston w Gissing etc *Nor*

BURSTON (St Rufin)   *see* Mid Trent *Lich*

BURSTOW (St Bartholomew)   *see* The Windmill *S'wark*

BURSTWICK (All Saints), Burton Pidsea, Humbleton w Elsternwick, Halsham, and Thorngumbald *York 12*   **P** *Abp (2 turns), Ld Chan (1 turn), D&C (1 turn)*   **V** S J WALKER

BURTLE (St Philip and St James)   *see* Polden Wheel *B & W*

BURTON (All Saints) w Christ Church *Lich 14*   **P** *CPAS and Ch Soc Trust (jt)*   **P-in-c** M K ELLOR   **C** S R LORD

BURTON (St Aidan) (St Paul) *Lich 14*   **P** *Bp and Lord Burton (jt)*   **V** W S MONKHOUSE   **NSM** P J ORTON

BURTON (St James) and Holme *Carl 10*   **P** *Simeon's Trustees*   **P-in-c** G J BURROWS

BURTON (St Luke) and Sopley *Win 9*   **P** *Bp and D&C Cant (alt)*   **V** *vacant*

BURTON (St Nicholas) and Shotwick *Ches 9*   **P** *D&C (1 turn) and St Jo Hosp Lich (2 turns)*   **V** C M HELM   **NSM** M R J TURNER

BURTON (St Richard)   *see* Barlavington, Burton w Coates, Sutton and Bignor *Chich*

BURTON AGNES (St Martin)   *see* The Beacon *York*

BURTON BRADSTOCK (St Mary)   *see* Bride Valley *Sarum*

BURTON BY LINCOLN (St Vincent)   *see* Spring Line Gp *Linc*

BURTON COGGLES (St Thomas à Becket)   *see* N Beltisloe Gp *Linc*

BURTON DASSETT (All Saints) *Cov 8*   **P** *Bp*   **P-in-c** M G CADWALLADER

BURTON FLEMING (St Cuthbert) w Fordon, Grindale and Wold Newton *York 9*   **P** *Abp and MMCET (jt)*   **P-in-c** G J OWEN   **NSM** B E HODGSON, J A TROWSDALE

BURTON HASTINGS (St Botolph)   *see* Wolvey w Burton Hastings, Copston Magna etc *Cov*

BURTON JOYCE (St Helen) w Bulcote and Stoke Bardolph *S'well 7*   **P** *MMCET*   **V** G R HARPER

BURTON LATIMER (St Mary the Virgin) *Pet 9*   **P** *Bp*   **R** J SAFFORD

BURTON LAZARS (St James)   *see* Melton Mowbray *Leic*

BURTON OVERY (St Andrew)   *see* Glen Magna cum Stretton Magna etc *Leic*

BURTON PEDWARDINE (St Andrew and the Blessed Virgin Mary and St Nicholas)   *see* Heckington and Helpringham Gp *Linc*

BURTON PIDSEA (St Peter)   *see* Burstwick, Burton Pidsea etc *York*

BURTON UPON STATHER (St Andrew)   *see* Flixborough w Burton upon Stather *Linc*

BURTON w COATES (St Agatha)   *see* Barlavington, Burton w Coates, Sutton and Bignor *Chich*

BURTON-IN-LONSDALE (All Saints)   *see* Bentham, Burton-in-Lonsdale, Chapel-le-Dale etc *Leeds*

BURTON-ON-TRENT (All Saints)   *see* Burton All SS w Ch Ch *Lich*

BURTON-ON-TRENT (St Aidan)   *see* Burton St Aid and St Paul *Lich*

BURTON-ON-TRENT (St Chad) *Lich 14*   **P** *Bp*   **P-in-c** G J CROSSLEY   **C** N J F GREY

BURTON-ON-TRENT (St Modwen)   *see* Burton St Modwen *Lich*

BURTON-ON-TRENT (St Paul)   *see* Burton St Aid and St Paul *Lich*

BURTON-UPON-TRENT (St Modwen) *Lich 14*   **P** *Bp*   **V** W S MONKHOUSE

BURTONWOOD (St Michael) *Liv 15*   **P** *R Warrington*   **V** J L STEVENTON   **Hon C** A LITTON

BURWARDSLEY (St John)   *see* Tattenhall w Burwardsley and Handley *Ches*

BURWASH (St Bartholomew) *Chich 12*   **P** *BNC Ox*   **P-in-c** S A EPPS

BURWASH WEALD (St Philip) *Chich 13*   **P** *Bp*   **V** *vacant*

BURWELL (St Andrew) (St Mary) w Reach *Ely 4*   **P** *DBP*   **V** E J WILLIAMS

BURY (Christ Church)   *see* Walmersley Road, Bury *Man*

BURY (Holy Cross)   *see* Warboys w Broughton and Bury w Wistow *Ely*

BURY (St John the Evangelist) w Houghton and Coldwaltham and Hardham *Chich 10*   **P** *Pemb Coll Ox, D&C, and Col Sir Brian Barttelot Bt (jt)*   **V** D A TWINLEY

BURY (St John w St Mark)   *see* Walmersley Road, Bury *Man*

BURY (St Mary the Virgin) *Man 8* **P** *Earl of Derby*
R J C FINDON **C** D F THOMSON, G F JOYCE
NSM R C FINDLOW
BURY ST EDMUNDS (All Saints) (St John the Evangelist) (St George) *St E 13* **P** *Patr Bd* **TR** M N HAWORTH
Hon C T L JONES **NSM** J C MANN
BURY ST EDMUNDS (Cathedral of St James) District *St E 13*
V *vacant*
BURY ST EDMUNDS (Christ Church) Moreton Hall *St E 13*
P *Bp, V Bury St Edm St Jas, and V Bury St Edm St Mary (jt)*
V J L ALDERTON-FORD **NSM** D CARPENTER
BURY ST EDMUNDS (St Mary) (St Peter's District Church)
St E 13 **P** *Hyndman Trustees* **V** M D ROGERS
C L R SMITH, N E ALEXANDER **NSM** D T CROFTS
BURY St Paul *Man 8* **P** *Trustees* **V** *vacant*
BURY, NEW (St Catherine) (St George) (St James) w Great Lever *Man 7* **P** *Bp* **TR** R J HORROCKS
TV J GREENHALGH **C** S L FLETCHER **OLM** J NICHOLLS, N A COWELL
BURY, ROCH VALLEY (Christ the King) (St Peter) *Man 8*
P *Patr Bd* **V** G F JOYCE **NSM** J L LYSSEJKO
BURYTHORPE (All Saints) *see* W Buckrose *York*
BUSBRIDGE (St John the Baptist) and Hambledon *Guildf 4*
P *Patr Bd* **R** S D K TAYLOR **C** C S MCBRIDE, J C R GIBSON
NSM C A SOH, M P W SPENCER **OLM** A SPENCER, D W JENKINS
BUSCOT (St Mary) *see* Gt Coxwell w Buscot, Coleshill etc *Ox*
BUSH END (St John the Evangelist) *see* Hatfield Broad Oak and Bush End *Chelmsf*
BUSH HILL PARK (St Mark) *Lon 18* **P** *Bp* **V** P C ATHERTON
NSM S E HEARD
BUSH HILL PARK (St Stephen) *Lon 18* **P** *V Edmonton All SS*
P-in-c P C ATHERTON **NSM** S E HEARD
BUSHBURY (St Mary) *Lich 29* **P** *Patr Bd* **TV** G R SMITH, I R M POOLE
BUSHEY (Holy Trinity) (St James) (St Paul) *St Alb 6* **P** *Bp*
R N G KELLEY **C** A F UNDERWOOD, D E POULTNEY, G W ADAMSON **NSM** M P L KINGSLEY
BUSHEY HEATH (St Peter) *St Alb 6* **P** *Bp* **V** A J BURTON
BUSHLEY (St Peter) *see* Longdon, Castlemorton, Bushley, Queenhill etc *Worc*
BUSHMEAD (Christ Church) *St Alb 12* **P** *Bp* **V** *vacant*
BUSSAGE (St Michael and All Angels) *see* Bisley, Chalford, France Lynch, and Oakridge and Bussage w Eastcombe *Glouc*
BUTCOMBE (St Michael and All Angels) *see* Wrington w Butcombe and Burrington *B & W*
BUTLEIGH (St Leonard) *see* Baltonsborough w Butleigh, W Bradley etc *B & W*
BUTLERS MARSTON (St Peter and St Paul) *see* Stourdene Gp *Cov*
BUTLEY (St John the Baptist) *see* Wilford Peninsula *St E*
BUTTERCRAMBE (St John the Evangelist) *see* Harton *York*
BUTTERMERE (St James the Great) *see* Savernake *Sarum*
BUTTERMERE (St James) *see* Lorton and Loweswater w Buttermere *Carl*
BUTTERSHAW (St Aidan) *see* Shelf w Buttershaw St Aid *Leeds*
BUTTERTON (St Bartholomew) *see* Alstonfield, Butterton, Ilam etc *Lich*
BUTTERTON (St Thomas) *see* Newcastle w Butterton *Lich*
BUTTERWICK (St Andrew) *see* Freiston, Butterwick w Bennington, and Leverton *Linc*
BUTTERWICK (St Nicholas) *see* Langtoft w Foxholes, Butterwick, Cottam etc *York*
BUTTERWICK, EAST (St Andrew) *see* Messingham *Linc*
BUTTERWICK, WEST (St Mary the Virgin) *see* Epworth Gp *Linc*
BUTTSBURY (St Mary) *see* Margaretting w Mountnessing and Buttsbury *Chelmsf*
BUXHALL (St Mary) *see* Gt Finborough w Onehouse, Harleston, Buxhall etc *St E*
BUXTED (St Margaret the Queen) (St Mary) and Hadlow Down *Chich 18* **P** *Abp, Bp, and Wagner Trustees (jt)*
NSM D J BLACKDEN
BUXTON (St Andrew) *see* Bure Valley *Nor*
BUXTON (St Anne) (St John the Baptist) (St Mary the Virgin) w Burbage and King Sterndale *Derby 4* **P** *Patr Bd*
TR J F HUDGHTON **TV** K COCKING **NSM** M M SLYFIELD
BUXTON (Trinity Chapel) Proprietary Chapel *Derby 4*
C-in-c R MARSDEN **C** P D HANCOCK, P J SELBY
BUXWORTH (St James) *see* Hayfield and Chinley w Buxworth *Derby*
BY BROOK *Bris 4* **P** *Patr Bd* **P-in-c** J M PHILPOTT
NSM S R EVANS **OLM** G E PARKIN
BYERS GREEN (St Peter) *Dur 6* **P** *Bp* **P-in-c** C A FRISWELL
BYFIELD (Holy Cross) *see* Aston-le-Walls, Byfield, Boddington, Eydon etc *Pet*

BYFLEET (St Mary) *Guildf 12* **P** *Ld Chan* **R** J H MCCABE
Hon C P M S ROSS-MCCABE
BYFLEET, WEST (St John) *Guildf 12* **P** *Bp*
P-in-c C P HOLLINGSHURST
BYFORD (St John the Baptist) *see* Letton w Staunton, Byford, Mansel Gamage etc *Heref*
BYGRAVE (St Margaret of Antioch) *see* Baldock w Bygrave *St Alb*
BYKER (St Anthony) *Newc 3* **P** *Bp* **P-in-c** S E HERBERT
BYKER (St Martin) Newcastle upon Tyne *Newc 3* **P** *Bp*
P-in-c S E HERBERT **C** C M NOPPEN
BYKER (St Michael w St Lawrence) *Newc 3* **P** *Bp*
P-in-c P J A MEDLEY, S E HERBERT **C** C M NOPPEN
BYKER (St Silas) *Newc 3* **P** *Bp* **P-in-c** D MACNAUGHTON
NSM A F TAYLOR
BYKER St Mark and Walkergate (St Oswald) *Newc 3* **P** *Bp and Ch Trust Fund Trust (jt)* **V** K MOULDER
BYLAND, OLD (All Saints) *see* Upper Ryedale *York*
BYLAUGH (St Mary) *see* Lyng, Sparham, Elsing, Bylaugh, Bawdeswell etc *Nor*
BYLEY CUM LEES (St John the Evangelist) *see* Middlewich w Byley *Ches*
BYRNESS (St Francis) *see* N Tyne and Redesdale *Newc*
BYTHAM, LITTLE (St Medardus) *see* Castle Bytham w Creeton *Linc*
BYTHORN (St Lawrence) *see* W Leightonstone *Ely*
BYTON (St Mary) *see* Pembridge w Moor Court, Shobdon, Staunton etc *Heref*
BYWELL (St Peter) and Mickley *Newc 9* **P** *Bp and Adn Lindisfarne (jt)* **V** W RIGBY
BYWORTH (St Francis) *see* Farnham *Guildf*
CABLE STREET (St Mary) *see* St Geo-in-the-East St Mary *Lon*
CABOURNE (St Nicholas) *see* Swallow *Linc*
CADBURY (St Michael and All Angels) *see* Brampford Speke, Cadbury, Newton St Cyres etc *Ex*
CADBURY, NORTH (St Michael the Archangel) *see* Camelot Par *B & W*
CADBURY, SOUTH (St Thomas à Becket) *as above*
CADDINGTON (All Saints) *St Alb 12* **P** *D&C St Paul's*
P-in-c R P O'NEILL **NSM** S SMITH
CADEBY (All Saints) *see* Bosworth and Sheepy Gp *Leic*
CADELEIGH (St Bartholomew) *see* Silverton, Butterleigh, Bickleigh and Cadeleigh *Ex*
CADGWITH (St Mary) *see* St Ruan w St Grade and Landewednack *Truro*
CADISHEAD (St Mary the Virgin) *Man 18* **P** *Bp* **V** A E KAY
OLM J DODD
CADMORE END (St Mary le Moor) *see* Lane End w Cadmore End *Ox*
CADNEY (All Saints) *see* Brigg, Wrawby and Cadney cum Howsham *Linc*
CADOGAN SQUARE (St Simon Zelotes) *see* Upper Chelsea St Simon *Lon*
CAERHAYS (St Michael) *see* St Goran w Caerhays *Truro*
CAGE GREEN (St Philip) *see* Tonbridge SS Pet and Paul *Roch*
CAGEBROOK Parishes *Heref 1* **P** *Bp (2 turns), Prime Min (1 turn)* **R** H J MORGAN **NSM** E A HITCHINER
CAINSCROSS (St Matthew) *see* Stroud Team *Glouc*
CAISTER NEXT YARMOUTH (Holy Trinity) (St Edmund) *Nor 6*
P SMF **R** T C THOMPSON
CAISTOR Group, The (St Peter and St Paul) *Linc 7* **P** *Bp and D&C (jt)* **V** I ROBINSON **Hon C** S W ANDREW
NSM J MCMANN
CAISTOR ST EDMUND (St Edmund) *see* Stoke H Cross w Dunston, Arminghall etc *Nor*
CALBOURNE (All Saints) w Newtown *Portsm 8* **P** *Bp*
V D J BEVINGTON
CALCOT (St Birinus) *see* Tilehurst St Cath and Calcot *Ox*
CALDBECK (St Mungo) (Fellside), Castle Sowerby and Sebergham *Carl 3* **P** *Bp and D&C (alt)*
P-in-c N L ROBINSON **Hon C** M L RICHES
CALDECOTE (All Saints), Northill and Old Warden *St Alb 10*
P *Grocers' Co (2 turns), R O Shuttleworth Remembrance Trust (1 turn)* **V** F COLEMAN **NSM** J S HUMPHRIES
CALDECOTE (St Michael and All Angels) *see* Lordsbridge *Ely*
CALDECOTE (St Theobald and St Chad) *see* Weddington and Caldecote *Cov*
CALDECOTT (St John the Evangelist) *see* Lyddington, Bisbrooke, Caldecott, Glaston etc *Pet*
CALDER GROVE (St John the Divine) *see* Chapelthorpe *Leeds*
CALDER VALE (Mission) *see* Scorton and Barnacre and Calder Vale *Blackb*
CALDER VALE (St John the Evangelist) *as above*
CALDERBROOK (St James the Great) *see* Littleborough *Man*
CALDMORE (St Michael and All Angels) w All Saints Palfrey *Lich 25* **P** *Bp* **V** *vacant*

CALDWELL (Chapel)   see Forcett and Aldbrough and Melsonby *Leeds*
CALDWELL (St Giles)   see Stapenhill w Cauldwell *Derby*
CALDY (Church of the Resurrection and All Saints)   see W Kirby St Bridget *Ches*
CALEDONIAN ROAD (All Saints Hall)   see Barnsbury *Lon*
CALIFORNIA (St Mary and St John)   see Finchampstead and California *Ox*
CALLINGTON (St Mary)   see S Hill w Callington *Truro*
CALLOW END (St James)   see Powick and Guarlford and Madresfield w Newland *Worc*
CALMORE (St Anne)   see Totton *Win*
CALNE (Holy Trinity)   see Marden Vale *Sarum*
CALNE (St Mary the Virgin)   as above
CALOW (St Peter) and Sutton cum Duckmanton *Derby 3*
  P *Bp and V Chesterfield (jt)*   **R** K H BALL
CALSHOT (St George)   see Fawley *Win*
CALSTOCK (St Andrew) *Truro 11*   **P** *Duchy of Cornwall*
  P-in-c C M PAINTER
CALSTONE WELLINGTON (St Mary the Virgin)   see Oldbury *Sarum*
CALTHORPE (Our Lady w St Margaret)   see Erpingham w Calthorpe, Ingworth, Aldborough etc *Nor*
CALTHWAITE (All Saints)   see Inglewood Gp *Carl*
CALTON (St Mary the Virgin), Cauldon, Grindon, Waterfall and Blore Ray w Okeover *Lich 5*   **P** *Bp and Sir Peter Walker-Okeover Bt (jt)*   **R** vacant
CALVELEY CHURCH (not known)   see Bunbury and Tilstone Fearnall *Ches*
CALVERHALL or CORRA (Holy Trinity)   see Adderley, Ash, Calverhall, Ightfield etc *Lich*
CALVERLEIGH (St Mary the Virgin)   see Washfield, Stoodleigh, Withleigh etc *Ex*
CALVERLEY (St Wilfrid) *Leeds 15*   **P** *Bp*   **V** P R ARNOLD
CALVERTON (All Saints)   see Stony Stratford w Calverton *Ox*
CALVERTON (St Wilfrid) *S'well 3*   **P** *Bp*   **V** P HEMSTOCK
  NSM M N TAYLOR
CAM (St George) w Stinchcombe *Glouc 5*   **P** *Bp*
  V J M MCKENZIE   **NSM** S C A ACLAND
CAM VALE *B & W 2*   **P** *Bp and DBP (2 turns), CPAS, MMCET and Revd G Bennett (1 turn)*   **R** J DAVIES
  NSM R A HOSKINS
CAM, LOWER (St Bartholomew) w Coaley *Glouc 5*   **P** *Bp*
  V S K GREATOREX
CAMBER (St Thomas)   see Rye *Chich*
CAMBERLEY (St Martin) Old Dean *Guildf 6*   **P** *Bp*
  V R J PECK
CAMBERLEY (St Mary) *Guildf 6*   **P** *Bp*   **V** A J KNOWLES
  OLM R WALKER
CAMBERLEY (St Michael) Yorktown *Guildf 6*   **P** *Bp*
  V B NICOLE   **NSM** A MITCHELL   **OLM** K M MURRAY
CAMBERLEY (St Paul) (St Mary) *Guildf 6*   **P** *Bp*   **C** R W GANT
  OLM C V ISHERWOOD
CAMBERLEY HEATHERSIDE (Community Centre) *Guildf 6*
  P *Bp*   **P-in-c** L J W BAIN
CAMBERWELL (Christ Church) *S'wark 8*   **P** *MMCET*
  V H R BALFOUR   **Hon C** J A NICKOLS
CAMBERWELL (St George) *S'wark 8*   **P** *Bp and Trin Coll Cam (jt)*   **V** N J ELDER   **OLM** M JOHN
CAMBERWELL (St Giles) (St Matthew) *S'wark 8*   **P** *Bp*
  V N P GEORGE   **NSM** S NJOKA
CAMBERWELL (St Luke) *S'wark 8*   **P** *Bp*   **P-in-c** I J MOBSBY
CAMBERWELL (St Michael and All Angels w All Souls w Emmanuel) *S'wark 10*   **P** *DBP*   **P-in-c** J G A ROBERTS
  NSM D SWABY
CAMBERWELL (St Philip) and St Mark *S'wark 7*   **P** *The Crown*
  P-in-c A J M MACHAM   **C** M D VYVYAN
CAMBO (Holy Trinity)   see Kirkwhelpington, Kirkharle, Kirkheaton and Cambo *Newc*
CAMBOIS St Peter (St Andrew's Mission Church) and Sleekburn *Newc 1*   **P** *D&C*   **P-in-c** J F TWOMEY
CAMBORNE (St Martin and St Meriadoc) and Tuckingmill *Truro 2*   **P** *Bp and Ch Soc Trust (jt)*   **R** O STEVENS
  NSM N J POTTER
CAMBOURNE *Ely 1*   **P** *Bp*   **P-in-c** M J H TRICK
CAMBRIDGE (Christ Church)   see Cambridge St Andr Less *Ely*
CAMBRIDGE (Good Shepherd)   see Chesterton Gd Shep *Ely*
CAMBRIDGE (Holy Cross) *Ely 2*   **P** *Bp*   **V** R T WILLIAMS
CAMBRIDGE (Holy Sepulchre) (St Andrew the Great) *Ely 2*
  P PCC   **V** A D M PAINE   **C** J C D NEWCOMBE, N J BUTTERY,
  R J L ALLDRITT
CAMBRIDGE (Holy Trinity) *Ely 3*   **P** *D&C and Peache Trustees (jt)*   **V** R A CHARKHAM   **C** J D IRVINE, O W Y BENYON
  NSM C M MEAKIN
CAMBRIDGE (St Andrew the Great)   see Cambridge H Sepulchre *Ely*

CAMBRIDGE (St Andrew the Less) (Christ Church) *Ely 2*
  P *Ch Trust Fund Trust*   **V** S N MIDGLEY   **C** J D TUCKWELL,
  R A H EVANS   **NSM** P D MYERS
CAMBRIDGE (St Augustine of Canterbury)   see Cambridge Ascension *Ely*
CAMBRIDGE (St Barnabas) *Ely 3*   **P** *V Cam St Paul*
  V A F MACLAURIN   **C** A J TAYLOR, T J FINNEMORE
CAMBRIDGE (St Benedict) *Ely 3*   **P** *CCC Cam*
  V A R MATTHEWS   **NSM** R M NICHOLLS
CAMBRIDGE (St Botolph) *Ely 3*   **P** *Qu Coll Cam*
  P-in-c W HORBURY   **NSM** M J WIDDESS
CAMBRIDGE (St Clement) *Ely 2*   **P** *Jes Coll Cam*
  P-in-c N I MOIR   **NSM** S G ANDERSON
CAMBRIDGE (St Edward King and Martyr) Proprietary Chapel *Ely 3*   A E F C N AAAGÜBLER
CAMBRIDGE (St Giles)   see Cambridge Ascension *Ely*
CAMBRIDGE (St James) *Ely 3*   **P** *Bp*   **NSM** D P FORD,
  S J PLANT
CAMBRIDGE (St Luke the Evangelist)   see Cambridge Ascension *Ely*
CAMBRIDGE (St Mark) *Ely 3*   **P** *DBP*   **Hon C** M M G ROBERTS   **NSM** M SCARLATA
CAMBRIDGE (St Martin) (St Thomas) *Ely 3*   **P** *V Cam St Paul*
  C P A PRESTON
CAMBRIDGE (St Mary the Great) w St Michael *Ely 2*   **P** *Trin Coll Cam*   **V** J R E BINNS   **C** P J HAYLER
CAMBRIDGE (St Mary the Less) *Ely 3*   **P** *Peterho Cam*
  V R M MACKLEY   **NSM** M A BISHOP, M J KRAMER
CAMBRIDGE (St Matthew) *Ely 2*   **P** *V Cam St Andr the Less*
  P-in-c F L PRICE   **C** A R THOMAS
CAMBRIDGE (St Paul) *Ely 3*   **P** *Ch Trust Fund Trust*
  V M S BECKETT   **C** J G CANESSA
CAMBRIDGE (St Philip) (St Stephen) *Ely 3*   **P** *Ch Trust Fund Trust*   **V** S TAYLOR   **C** S J BUTLER
CAMBRIDGE (St Thomas)   see Cambridge St Martin *Ely*
CAMBRIDGE Ascension (St Giles) (St Luke the Evangelist) (St Augustine of Canterbury) (All Souls Chapel) *Ely 2*
  P *Bp*   **TR** P A KING   **TV** J C BUNKER   **C** G J W DUMBRECK
  NSM A C RIGELSFORD
CAMDEN TOWN (St Michael)   see Old St Pancras *Lon*
CAMEL, WEST (All Saints)   see Cam Vale *B & W*
CAMELFORD (St Julitta)   see Lanteglos by Camelford w Advent *Truro*
CAMELFORD (St Thomas of Canterbury)   as above
CAMELOT Parishes, The *B & W 2*   **P** *Patr Bd*
  R T G RAE SMITH   **Hon C** R E WOOD   **NSM** A L PARRIS
CAMELSDALE (St Paul)   see Lynchmere and Camelsdale *Chich*
CAMERTON (St Peter)   see Timsbury w Priston, Camerton and Dunkerton *B & W*
CAMERTON (St Peter), Seaton and West Seaton *Carl 7*
  P *D&C and Ch Trust Fund Trust (jt)*   **V** I GRAINGER
  NSM I FEARON
CAMMERINGHAM (St Michael)   see Spring Line Gp *Linc*
CAMP HILL (St Mary and St John) *Cov 5*   **P** *Bp*   **V** vacant
CAMPSALL (St Mary Magdalene)   see Burghwallis and Campsall *Sheff*
CAMPSEA ASHE (St John the Baptist) w Marlesford, Parham and Hacheston *St E 16*   **P** *Prime Min, Ch Soc Trust, and J S Schreiber Esq (by turn)*   **P-in-c** D A WEST
CAMPTON (All Saints), Clophill and Haynes *St Alb 8*   **P** *Bp and Ball Coll Ox (alt)*   **R** D HENLEY
CANALSIDE Benefice, The *Sarum 15*   **P** *Viscount Long, Magd Coll Cam, and R Trowbridge St Jas and Keevil (by turn)*
  R S A BALL
CANDLESBY (St Benedict)   see Bolingbroke Deanery *Linc*
CANEWDON (St Nicholas)   see Ashingdon w S Fambridge, Canewdon and Paglesham *Chelmsf*
CANFIELD, GREAT (St Mary) w High Roding and Aythorpe Roding *Chelmsf 18*   **P** *A Sainthill Esq, Ch Soc Trust, and Bp (by turn)*   **P-in-c** J D GANNON
CANFIELD, LITTLE (All Saints)   see Takeley w Lt Canfield *Chelmsf*
CANFORD CLIFFS (Transfiguration) and Sandbanks *Sarum 7*
  P *Bp*   **V** A D O'BRIEN
CANFORD HEATH (St Paul)   see N Poole Ecum Team *Sarum*
CANFORD MAGNA (no dedication) (Bearwood) (The Lantern) *Sarum 9*   **P** *Patr Bd*   **TR** C M TEBBUTT
  TV A M RIMMER, G BOLAND   **C** S H PARTRIDGE
  NSM A P HANSON, H WALDSAX, S E TEBBUTT
CANLEY (St Stephen) *Cov 3*   **P** *Bp*   **P-in-c** D G HAMMOND
  NSM A M HOWARTH, C R HOWARTH
CANNINGS and REDHORN, The *Sarum 17*   **P** *Patr Bd*
  TR W D LANG   **Hon C** E C BROWN
  NSM E P LORT-PHILLIPS, S G ASCOUGH
CANNINGTON (Blessed Virgin Mary), Otterhampton, Combwich and Stockland *B & W 17*   **P** *Bp*   **R** vacant

CANNOCK (St Luke) and Huntington *Lich 3*　**P** *Bp and D&C (jt)*　**V** P O HART　**C** A E MANN　**NSM** S P REYNOLDS

CANON FROME (St James)　*see Ledbury Heref*

CANON PYON (St Lawrence) w King's Pyon, Birley and Wellington *Heref 6*　**P** *Bp, Ch Union, and D&C (jt)*　**V** M C CLUETT

CANONBURY (St Stephen) *Lon 6*　**P** *V Islington St Mary*　**V** J N BEAUCHAMP　**NSM** M E EVANS

CANONRY Benefice, The *Cant 1*　**P** *Abp, D&C, and Lord Fitzwalter*　**V** D I MOULDEN

CANTERBURY (All Saints) *Cant 3*　**P** *Abp*　**P-in-c** N M HALL　**C** P GREIG

CANTERBURY (St Dunstan w Holy Cross) *Cant 3*　**P** *Abp*　**P-in-c** M F BALL　**NSM** K C GOODMAN

CANTERBURY (St Martin) (St Paul) *Cant 3*　**P** *Abp*　**R** N M HALL　**C** J S RICHARDS

CANTERBURY (St Mary Bredin) *Cant 3*　**P** *Simeon's Trustees*　**V** B J DE LA T DE BERRY　**C** C A HUNT

CANTERBURY (St Peter w St Alphege) (St Mildred) and St Margaret w St Mary de Castro *Cant 3*　**P** *The Crown*　**P-in-c** M F BALL

CANTERBURY (St Stephen)　*see Hackington Cant*

CANTLEY (St Margaret)　*see Acle and Bure to Yare Nor*

CANTLEY (St Wilfrid) *Sheff 8*　**P** *Guild of All So*　**V** A HOWARD　**C** E J S MORRISON

CANTLEY, NEW (St Hugh of Lincoln) (Holy Trinity) *Sheff 8*　**P** *Guild of All So and SMF (jt)*　**V** W J STOKOE

CANVEY ISLAND (St Anne) (St Katherine's Worship Centre) (St Nicholas) *Chelmsf 13*　**P** *Bp and Patr Bd (jt)*　**TR** D S C TUDOR　**TV** M G WALFORD, P A MALLINSON　**NSM** J M BARHAM　**OLM** L A MCGLYNN

CANWELL (St Mary, St Giles and All Saints) *Lich 4*　**P** *Bp*　**V** J R IDDON　**NSM** R G DAVIES

CANWICK (All Saints)　*see Washingborough w Heighington and Canwick Linc*

CAPEL (St John the Baptist)　*see Surrey Weald Guildf*

CAPEL LE FERNE (St Radigund)　*see Alkham w Capel le Ferne and Hougham Cant*

CAPEL ST MARY (St Mary) w Little Wenham and Great Wenham *St E 5*　**P** *Bp and SMF (jt)*　**P-in-c** J G PENDORF

CAPENHURST (Holy Trinity)　*see Backford and Capenhurst Ches*

CAPESTHORNE (Holy Trinity)　*see Marton, Siddington w Capesthorne, and Eaton etc Ches*

CAR COLSTON (St Mary) w Screveton *S'well 5*　**P** H S Blagg Esq　**P-in-c** O J LEARMONT

CARBIS BAY (St Anta and All Saints) w Lelant (St Uny) *Truro 5*　**P** *Bp*　**P-in-c** S E HOSKING　**NSM** C Z WILTON

CARBROOKE (St Peter and St Paul)　*see Watton Nor*

CARBURTON (St Giles)　*see Worksop Priory S'well*

CARDESTON (St Michael)　*see Ford, Gt Wollaston and Alberbury w Cardeston Heref*

CARDINGTON (St Mary)　*see Elstow St Alb*

CARDYNHAM (St Meubred)　*see St Neot and Warleggan w Cardynham Truro*

CAREBY (St Stephen)　*see Castle Bytham w Creeton Linc*

CARHAM (St Cuthbert)　*see Cornhill w Carham Newc*

CARHAMPTON (St John the Baptist)　*see Dunster, Carhampton, Withycombe w Rodhuish etc B & W*

CARHARRACK (St Piran's Mission Church)　*see Chacewater w St Day and Carharrack Truro*

CARISBROOKE (St Mary the Virgin) *Portsm 8*　**P** *Qu Coll Ox*　**V** M C BAGG

CARISBROOKE St Nicholas in the Castle *Portsm 8*　**P** *Qu Coll Ox*　**V** M C BAGG

CARLBY (St Stephen)　*see Ryhall w Essendine and Carlby Pet*

CARLETON (St Mary the Virgin)　*see Skipton Ch Ch w Carleton Leeds*

CARLETON (St Michael) and E Hardwick *Leeds 19*　**P** *V Pontefract and Cawood Trustees (jt)*　**V** S A STACEY

CARLETON (St Peter)　*see Rockland St Mary w Hellington, Bramerton etc Nor*

CARLETON IN CRAVEN　*see Skipton Ch Ch w Carleton Leeds*

CARLETON RODE (All Saints)　*see Bunwell, Carleton Rode, Tibenham, Gt Moulton etc Nor*

CARLETON, EAST (St Mary)　*see Swardeston w E Carleton, Intwood, Keswick etc Nor*

CARLFORD *St E 7*　**P** *Ld Chan (1 turn), Bp and DBP (2 turns)*　**R** H C SANDERS　**NSM** J D HALL, W E GOURLAY　**OLM** C G L A T BEAUMONT

CARLIN HOW (St Helen)　*see Loftus and Carlin How w Skinningrove York*

CARLINGHOW (St John the Evangelist)　*see Staincliffe and Carlinghow Leeds*

CARLISLE (Holy Trinity) (St Barnabas) *Carl 3*　**P** *Patr Bd*　**P-in-c** E M C HANCOCK　**NSM** I JOHNSTON

CARLISLE (St Aidan) and Christ Church *Carl 3*　**P** *Bp*　**P-in-c** K TEASDALE

CARLISLE (St Cuthbert) *Carl 3*　**P** *D&C*　**V** K TEASDALE

CARLISLE (St Herbert) w St Stephen *Carl 3*　**P** *Bp*　**V** A JONES

CARLISLE (St James)　*see Denton Holme Carl*

CARLISLE (St John the Evangelist) *Carl 3*　**P** *CPAS*　**V** S DONALD

CARLISLE (St Luke) Morton *Carl 3*　**P** *Bp*　**P-in-c** P MAGINN　**C** G A J POTTER

CARLISLE (St Michael)　*see Stanwix Carl*

CARLISLE Belah (St Mark) *as above*

CARLTON (St Aidan)　*see Helmsley York*

CARLTON (St Andrew)　*see Nailstone and Carlton w Shackerstone Leic*

CARLTON (St Botolph)　*see Whorlton w Carlton and Faceby York*

CARLTON (St John the Baptist) *S'well 7*　**P** *Bp*　**P-in-c** A H DIGMAN

CARLTON (St John the Evangelist)　*see Athersley and Carlton Leeds*

CARLTON (St Mary)　*see Harrold and Carlton w Chellington St Alb*

CARLTON (St Peter)　*see Raddesley Gp Ely*

CARLTON (St Peter)　*see Saxmundham w Kelsale cum Carlton St E*

CARLTON BY SNAITH (St Mary) and Drax *York 4*　**P** *Abp and Ch Trust Fund Trust (jt)*　**V** *vacant*

CARLTON COLVILLE (St Peter) and Mutford *Nor 9*　**P** *Simeon's Trustees and G&C Coll Cam (jt)*　**V** J S BISHOP　**C** M A CAPRON

CARLTON CURLIEU (St Mary the Virgin)　*see Glen Magna cum Stretton Magna etc Leic*

CARLTON FOREHOE (St Mary)　*see Barnham Broom and Upper Yare Nor*

CARLTON HUSTHWAITE (St Mary)　*see Coxwold and Husthwaite York*

CARLTON MINIOTT (St Lawrence)　*see Thirsk York*

CARLTON SCROOP (St Nicholas)　*see Caythorpe Linc*

CARLTON, EAST (St Peter)　*see Gretton w Rockingham and Cottingham w E Carlton Pet*

CARLTON, GREAT (St John the Baptist)　*see Mid Marsh Gp Linc*

CARLTON, NORTH (St Luke)　*see Spring Line Gp Linc*

CARLTON, SOUTH (St John the Baptist) *as above*

CARLTON-IN-LINDRICK (St John the Evangelist) and Langold w Oldcotes *S'well 1*　**P** *Bp and Ld Chan (alt)*　**R** J L BLATHERWICK

CARLTON-IN-THE-WILLOWS (St Paul) *S'well 7*　**P** *MMCET*　**R** B HALL　**NSM** S MURPHY

CARLTON-LE-MOORLAND (St Mary)　*see Bassingham Gp Linc*

CARLTON-ON-TRENT (St Mary)　*see Norwell w Ossington, Cromwell etc S'well*

CARNABY (St John the Baptist)　*see Rudston w Boynton, Carnaby and Kilham York*

CARNFORTH (Christ Church) *Blackb 14*　**P** *Bp*　**V** S L JONES

CARNFORTH (Holy Trinity)　*see Bolton-le-Sands Blackb*

CARR CLOUGH (St Andrew)　*see Kersal Moor Man*

CARR DYKE GROUP, The *Linc 14*　**P** *Sir Philip Naylor-Leyland Bt and Ld Chan (alt)*　**V** M M ROSE　**OLM** D E WESTON

CARR MILL (St David) *Liv 10*　**P** *V St Helens St Mark and Bp (jt)*　**V** S L DAVIES

CARRINGTON (St John the Evangelist) *S'well 9*　**P** *Bp*　**V** J W B TOMLINSON

CARRINGTON (St Paul)　*see Sibsey w Frithville Linc*

CARSHALTON (All Saints) *S'wark 23*　**P** *Bp*　**R** J C THEWLIS　**NSM** D R BILLIN

CARSHALTON BEECHES (Good Shepherd) *S'wark 23*　**P** *Bp*　**V** W M PIDGEON

CARSINGTON (St Margaret)　*see Wirksworth Derby*

CARTERTON (St John the Evangelist)　*see Brize Norton and Carterton Ox*

CARTMEL FELL (St Anthony) *Carl 10*　**P** *Bp*　**P-in-c** M D WOODCOCK

CARTMEL PENINSULA Team Ministry, The (St Mary and St Michael) *Carl 11*　**P** *Patr Bd*　**TR** N J ASH　**TV** M L WOODCOCK, N E DEVENISH　**C** A B NORMAN　**NSM** G T WILSON

CASSINGTON (St Peter)　*see Eynsham and Cassington Ox*

CASSOP CUM QUARRINTON *Dur 5*　**P** *Bp*　**P-in-c** J LIVESLEY

CASTERTON (Holy Trinity)　*see Kirkby Lonsdale Carl*

CASTERTON, GREAT (St Peter and St Paul) and LITTLE (All Saints) w Pickworth and Tickencote *Pet 12*　**P** *Burghley Ho Preservation Trust (2 turns), Lord Chesham (1 turn), and Bp (1 turn)*　**P-in-c** J M SAUNDERS

CASTLE ACRE (St James)　*see Nar Valley Nor*

CASTLE ASHBY (St Mary Magdalene)   *see* Yardley Hastings, Denton and Grendon etc *Pet*

CASTLE BOLTON (St Oswald)   *see* Penhill *Leeds*

CASTLE BROMWICH (St Clement) Birm 9   **P** *Bp*
V S C CARTER

CASTLE BROMWICH (St Mary and St Margaret) Birm 9
P *Earl of Bradf*   **R** G A DOUGLAS

CASTLE BYTHAM (St James) w Creeton Linc 17   **P** *D&C, Bp, Ld Chan, and DBP (by turn)*   **R** *vacant*

CASTLE CARROCK (St Peter)   *see* Eden, Gelt and Irthing *Carl*

CASTLE CARY (All Saints) w Ansford B & W 2   **P** *Bp*
P-in-c E A MORTIMER

CASTLE CHURCH (St Mary) Lich 10   **P** *Bp*
V P J SOWERBUTTS   **C** P J MULLINS   **NSM** C V SYKES

CASTLE COMBE (St Andrew)   *see* By Brook *Bris*

CASTLE DONINGTON (St Edward the King and Martyr) and Lockington cum Hemington Leic 6   **P** *Lady Gretton and C H C Coaker Esq (jt)*   **V** A Q MICKLETHWAITE
NSM M J BENNETT

CASTLE EATON (St Mary the Virgin)   *see* S Cotswolds *Glouc*

CASTLE EDEN (St James)   *see* Blackhall, Castle Eden and Monkhesleden *Dur*

CASTLE FROME (St Michael)   *see* Frome Valley *Heref*

CASTLE HEDINGHAM (St Nicholas)   *see* Sible Hedingham w Castle Hedingham *Chelmsf*

CASTLE HILL (St Philip)   *see* Hindley All SS *Liv*

CASTLE NORTHWICH (Holy Trinity)   *see* Northwich St Luke and H Trin *Ches*

CASTLE RISING (St Lawrence) Nor 16   **P** *G Howard Esq*
R J B V RIVIERE

CASTLE SOWERBY (St Kentigern)   *see* Caldbeck, Castle Sowerby and Sebergham *Carl*

CASTLE VALE (St Cuthbert of Lindisfarne) w Minworth
Birm 12   **P** *Bp*   **V** J B A COPE

CASTLE VIEW ESTATE (St Francis)   *see* Langley Marish *Ox*

CASTLECROFT (The Good Shepherd)   *see* Tettenhall Wood and Perton *Lich*

CASTLEFIELDS (All Saints and St Michael)   *see* Shrewsbury All SS w St Mich *Lich*

CASTLEFORD Team Parish (All Saints) (St Michael and All Angels) Leeds 19   **P** *Duchy of Lanc and Bp (alt)*
TR M F WOOD   **TV** C M WATKINS   **C** K A N GREAVES

CASTLEMORTON (St Gregory)   *see* Longdon, Castlemorton, Bushley, Queenhill etc *Worc*

CASTLESIDE (St John the Evangelist) Dur 4   **P** *Bp*
P-in-c M JACKSON

CASTLETHORPE (St Simon and St Jude)   *see* Hanslope w Castlethorpe *Ox*

CASTLETON (St Edmund)   *see* Hope, Castleton and Bradwell *Derby*

CASTLETON (St Mary Magdalene)   *see* Sherborne w Castleton, Lillington and Longburton *Sarum*

CASTLETON (St Michael and St George)   *see* Danby w Castleton and Commondale *York*

CASTLETON MOOR (St Martin) Man 14   **P** *Bp*
P-in-c F C GUITE

CASTON (St Cross), Griston, Merton, Thompson, Stow Bedon, Breckles and Great Hockham Nor 13   **P** *Bp and DBP (jt)*   **R** R W NICHOLS

CASTOR (St Kyneburgha) w Upton and Stibbington and Water Newton, Marholm and Sutton Pet 11
P *Mrs V S V Gunnery, Sir Philip Naylor-Leyland Bt, and Keble Coll Ox (jt)*   **NSM** R HEMINGRAY

CATCLIFFE (St Mary)   *see* Rivers Team *Sheff*

CATCOTT (St Peter)   *see* Polden Wheel *B & W*

CATERHAM (St Mary the Virgin) (St Laurence) (St Paul) (St John the Evangelist) S'wark 24   **P** *Bp*   **TR** D J SWAN
TV C L DOWLAND-PILLINGER, J GARTON, T GOODE
NSM A-M GARTON, F M LONG, S J ELLISON

CATESBY (St Mary)   *see* Daventry, Ashby St Ledgers, Braunston etc *Pet*

CATFIELD (All Saints)   *see* Ludham, Potter Heigham, Hickling and Catfield *Nor*

CATFORD (St Andrew) S'wark 4   **P** *Bp*   **V** L T MCKENNA

CATFORD (St John) Southend and Downham S'wark 4   **P** *Bp*
TV P G JORDAN, S D LECK   **C** S J DENNIS   **NSM** C F NESTOR

CATFORD (St Laurence) S'wark 4   **P** *Bp*   **V** C F PICKSTONE
C H F ADAN-FERNANDEZ   **OLM** I J FARQUHAR

CATHERINGTON (All Saints) and Clanfield Portsm 5   **P** *Bp*
V G B HILL   **NSM** A M GOTHARD

CATHERSTON LEWESTON (St Mary)   *see* Golden Cap Team *Sarum*

CATON (St Paul) w Littledale Blackb 14   **P** *V Lanc*
P-in-c G A POLLITT

CATSFIELD (St Laurence) and Crowhurst Chich 12   **P** *Bp and J P Papillon (alt)*   **R** M A BRYDON

CATSHILL (Christ Church)   *see* Bromsgrove *Worc*

CATTERICK (St Anne) Leeds 24   **P** *Bp*   **V** L M SOUTHERN

CATTHORPE (St Thomas)   *see* Gilmorton, Peatling Parva, Kimcote etc *Leic*

CATTISTOCK (St Peter and St Paul)   *see* Melbury *Sarum*

CATTON (All Saints)   *see* Stamford Bridge Gp *York*

CATTON, NEW (Christ Church) Nor 2   **P** *Bp*
V K G CROCKER

CATTON, NEW (St Luke) w St Augustine Nor 2   **P** *Bp, D&C, and CPAS (jt)*   **V** *vacant*

CATTON, OLD (St Margaret) Nor 2   **P** *D&C*
V A D PARSONS

CATWICK (St Michael)   *see* Skirlaugh, Catwick, Long Riston, Rise, Swine w Ellerby *York*

CATWORTH, GREAT (St Leonard)   *see* W Leightonstone *Ely*

CAULDON (St Mary and St Laurence)   *see* Calton, Cauldon, Grindon, Waterfall etc *Lich*

CAUNDLE MARSH (St Peter and St Paul)   *see* Three Valleys *Sarum*

CAUNTON (St Andrew)   *see* Norwell w Ossington, Cromwell etc *S'well*

CAUSEWAY HEAD (St Paul)   *see* Solway Plain *Carl*

CAUTLEY (St Mark)   *see* Sedbergh, Cautley and Garsdale *Carl*

CAVENDISH (St Mary)   *see* Stour Valley *St E*

CAVENHAM (St Andrew)   *see* Mildenhall *St E*

CAVERSFIELD (St Laurence)   *see* Bicester w Bucknell, Caversfield and Launton *Ox*

CAVERSHAM (Park Church)   *see* Emmer Green w Caversham Park *Ox*

CAVERSHAM (St Andrew) Ox 7   **P** *Bp*   **V** N D JONES

CAVERSHAM (St John the Baptist)   *see* Caversham Thameside and Mapledurham *Ox*

CAVERSHAM (St Peter)   *as above*

CAVERSHAM HEIGHTS (St Andrew)   *see* Caversham St Andr *Ox*

CAVERSHAM THAMESIDE (St Peter) (St John the Baptist) and Mapledurham Ox 7   **P** *Ch Ch Ox, Eton Coll, and Bp (jt)*
R M K J SMITH   **NSM** R A ROSS   **OLM** A M PYKE

CAVERSWALL (St Peter) and Weston Coyney w Dilhorne
Lich 6   **P** *D&C*   **V** S J OSBOURNE   **C** L P LUCKING

CAWOOD (All Saints) w Ryther and Wistow York 4   **P** *Abp and Ld Chan (alt)*   **R** I M W ELLERY

CAWSAND (St Andrew's Mission Church)   *see* Maker w Rame *Truro*

CAWSTON (St Agnes) w Booton and Brandiston, Haveringland and Heydon Nor 19   **P** *Pemb Coll Cam (3 turns), DBP (1 turn)*   **P-in-c** A M BEANE

CAWTHORNE (All Saints) Leeds 18   **P** *S W Fraser Esq*
P-in-c J M MACGILLIVRAY

CAXTON (St Andrew)   *see* Papworth *Ely*

CAYNHAM (St Mary)   *see* Ludlow *Heref*

CAYTHORPE (St Aidan)   *see* Lowdham w Caythorpe, and Gunthorpe *S'well*

CAYTHORPE (St Vincent) Linc 22   **P** *Bp, J F Fane Esq, and S J Packe-Drury-Lowe Esq (by turn)*   **P-in-c** A S J HEALY

CAYTON (St John the Baptist) w Eastfield York 15   **P** *Abp*
P-in-c P W WHITE   **C** M JOBLING, S FOSTER

CENTRAL   *see under substantive place names*

CERNE ABBAS (St Mary)   *see* Buckland Newton, Cerne Abbas, Godmanstone etc *Sarum*

CERNEY WICK (Holy Trinity)   *see* S Cerney w Cerney Wick, Siddington and Preston *Glouc*

CERNEY, NORTH (All Saints)   *see* Churn Valley *Glouc*

CERNEY, SOUTH (All Hallows) w Cerney Wick, Siddington and Preston Glouc 7   **P** *Bp and Mrs P Chester-Master (1 turn), Ld Chan (1 turn)*   **V** D BOWERS   **NSM** A M AUSTIN

CHACELEY (St John the Baptist)   *see* Deerhurst and Apperley w Forthampton etc *Glouc*

CHACEWATER (St Paul) w St Day and Carharrack Truro 2
P *D&C and R Kenwyn w St Allen (jt)*   **P-in-c** S A BONE
C D J F JONES   **NSM** A L BUTCHER, E M SHEARD,
S J C FLETCHER

CHACOMBE (St Peter and St Paul)   *see* Chenderit *Pet*

CHADBROOK St E 12   **P** *Bp and DBP (jt)*   **R** M C O LAWSON

CHADDERTON (Christ Church) (St Saviour) Man 16
P *Trustees*   **V** J G SIMMONS   **C** D J HANSON
NSM R D BREWIS

CHADDERTON (St Mark) Man 16   **P** *The Crown*   **V** *vacant*

CHADDERTON (St Matthew) St Luke Man 16   **P** *Bp and Prime Min (alt)*   **V** D R PENNY   **C** D S A SANDERCOCK

CHADDERTON Emmanuel (St George) Man 16   **P** *Trustees*
V E D H LEAF

CHADDESDEN (St Mary) Derby 9   **P** *MMCET*   **V** J D WARD

CHADDESDEN (St Philip) w Derby St Mark Derby 9   **P** *Bp*
V R J SHRISUNDER   **Hon C** M R FUTERS

CHADDESLEY CORBETT (St Cassian)   *see* Kidderminster E *Worc*

CHADDLEWORTH (St Andrew)   *see* W Downland *Ox*

CHADLINGTON (St Nicholas)   *see* Chase *Ox*

CHADSMOOR (St Aidan) (St Chad) *Lich 3* **P** *Bp and D&C (jt)*
V J NASH
CHADWELL (Emmanuel) (St Mary) *Chelmsf 16* **P** *Ch Soc Trust* **R** M R WALTON
CHADWELL HEATH (St Chad) *Chelmsf 1* **P** *Vs Dagenham and Ilford (alt)* **V** M J COURT **NSM** C J HARDING
CHAFFCOMBE (St Michael and All Angels), Cricket Malherbie w Knowle St Giles, Tatworth, Thorncombe and Winsham *B & W 16* **P** *Bp and C G S Eyre Esq (jt)* **V** T F PRICE **Hon C** J EVANS **NSM** J ABBOTT
CHAGFORD (St Michael), Gidleigh, Throwleigh, Drewsteignton, South Tawton, Spreyton, Hittisleigh, North Tawton, Bondleigh, Honeychurch and Sampford Courtenay *Ex 10* **P** *Patr Bd* **TR** P S SEATON-BURN **TV** N P WELDON **C** C K GRASSKE **NSM** H M EVERY, R I BULLWORTHY
CHAILEY (St Peter) *Chich 18* **P** *J P B Tillard Esq* **P-in-c** J M MILLER-MASKELL
CHALBURY (All Saints) *see* Horton, Chalbury, Hinton Martel and Holt St Jas *Sarum*
CHALDON (St Peter and St Paul) *see* Caterham *S'wark*
CHALDON HERRING (St Nicholas) *see* The Lulworths, Winfrith Newburgh and Chaldon *Sarum*
CHALE (St Andrew) *Portsm 8* **P** *Keble Coll Ox* **P-in-c** N J PORTER
CHALFIELD, GREAT (All Saints) *see* Broughton Gifford, Gt Chalfield and Holt *Sarum*
CHALFONT ST GILES (St Giles), Seer Green and Jordans *Ox 9* **P** *Bp* **R** I D BROWN **C** J M TEBBOTH **NSM** C M MESSERVY, M T BLEAKLEY
CHALFONT ST PETER (St Peter) *Ox 9* **P** *St Jo Coll Ox* **R** C H OVERTON **C** B M TOPHAM **OLM** W GRAHAM
CHALFONT, LITTLE (St George) *see* Chenies and Lt Chalfont, Latimer and Flaunden *Ox*
CHALFORD (Christ Church) *see* Bisley, Chalford, France Lynch, and Oakridge and Bussage w Eastcombe *Glouc*
CHALGRAVE (All Saints) *see* Toddington and Chalgrave *St Alb*
CHALGROVE (St Mary) w Berrick Salome *Ox 20* **P** *Ch Ch Ox* **V** I G H COHEN
CHALK (St Mary) *Roch 4* **P** *R Milton* **V** N I BOURNE **C** C R H KILGOUR
CHALKE VALLEY (Team Ministry) *Sarum 11* **P** *Bp, DBP, and K Coll Cam (by turn)* **TR** C BLUNDELL **TV** J A TAYLOR, R H WILLIAMS
CHALLACOMBE (Holy Trinity) *see* Shirwell, Loxhore, Kentisbury, Arlington, etc *Ex*
CHALLOCK (St Cosmas and St Damian) *see* King's Wood *Cant*
CHALLOW, EAST (St Nicolas) *see* Vale *Ox*
CHALLOW, WEST (St Laurence) *see* Ridgeway *Ox*
CHALTON (St Michael and All Angels) *see* Blendworth w Chalton w Idsworth *Portsm*
CHALVEY (St Peter) *see* Upton cum Chalvey *Ox*
CHALVINGTON (St Bartholomew) *see* Laughton w Ripe and Chalvington *Chich*
CHANDLER'S FORD (St Boniface) (St Martin in the Wood) *Win 10* **P** *Bp* **V** I N BIRD **C** S J WILLIAMS **NSM** C S WHITEHEAD
CHANTRY (Holy Trinity) *see* Mells w Buckland Dinham, Elm, Whatley etc *B & W*
CHAPEL ALLERTON (St Matthew) *Leeds 14* **P** *V Leeds St Pet* **V** D M ROBINSON **NSM** S RUSHOLME
CHAPEL CHORLTON (St Laurence), Maer and Whitmore *Lich 7* **P** *Bp and G Cavenagh-Mainwaring Esq (jt)* **R** N A CLEMAS
CHAPEL GREEN (St Oswald) *see* Lt Horton *Leeds*
CHAPEL HOUSE (Holy Nativity) *Newc 4* **P** *Bp* **V** J STEPHENSON **OLM** D P MARR
CHAPEL LAWN (St Mary) *see* Middle Marches *Heref*
CHAPEL PLAISTER (not known) *see* Box w Hazlebury and Ditteridge *Bris*
CHAPEL ST LEONARDS (St Leonard) w Hogsthorpe *Linc 10* **P** *V Willoughby St Helen* **P-in-c** T R BARDELL
CHAPEL-EN-LE-FRITH (St Thomas à Becket) *Derby 4* **P** *PCC* **P-in-c** C G PEARSON **NSM** D H MUNDY
CHAPEL-LE-DALE (St Leonard) *see* Bentham, Burton-in-Lonsdale, Chapel-le-Dale etc *Leeds*
CHAPELTHORPE (St James) *Leeds 20* **P** *V Sandal* **V** I M GASKELL
CHAPELTOWN (St John the Baptist) *Sheff 3* **P** *Bp* **V** R A STORDY **C** R BRIDGEWATER
CHAPMANSLADE (St Philip and St James) *see* Cley Hill Villages *Sarum*
CHAPPEL (St Barnabas) *see* Gt and Lt Tey w Wakes Colne and Chappel *Chelmsf*

CHARD (Blessed Virgin Mary) w Combe St Nicholas, Wambrook and Whitestaunton *B & W 16* **P** *Bp and T V D Eames Esq (jt)* **R** S TUCKER **C** G A VYE
CHARD (Good Shepherd) Furnham *B & W 14* **P** *Bp* **V** J WILLIAMS
CHARDSTOCK (All Saints) *see* Axminster, Chardstock, All Saints etc *Ex*
CHARDSTOCK (St Andrew) *as above*
CHARFIELD (St John) and Kingswood w Wickwar, Rangeworthy and Hillesley *Glouc 5* **P** *Bp, DBP, R W Neeld Esq, and Earl of Ducie (jt)* **R** D J RUSSELL **Hon C** C D MASON **NSM** P T FEWINGS
CHARFORD (St Andrew) *see* Bromsgrove *Worc*
CHARING (St Peter and St Paul) *see* G7 Benefice *Cant*
CHARING HEATH (Holy Trinity) *as above*
CHARLBURY (St Mary the Virgin) w Shorthampton *Ox 22* **P** *St Jo Coll Ox* **V** S A WELCH **NSM** J W FIELDEN
CHARLCOMBE (Blessed Virgin Mary) w Bath (St Stephen) *B & W 8* **P** *DBP and Simeon's Trustees (jt)* **P-in-c** P A HAWTHORN **NSM** D J POW
CHARLECOTE (St Leonard) *see* Hampton Lucy w Charlecote and Loxley *Cov*
CHARLES (St John the Baptist) *see* S Molton w Nymet St George, High Bray etc *Ex*
CHARLES w Plymouth St Matthias *Ex 21* **P** *Ch Patr Trust* **P-in-c** P R BRYCE
CHARLESTOWN (St George) *see* Salford All SS *Man*
CHARLESTOWN (St Paul) *Truro 1* **P** *The Crown* **P-in-c** P A SPREADBRIDGE
CHARLESTOWN (St Thomas the Apostle) *see* Southowram and Claremount *Leeds*
CHARLESWORTH (St John the Evangelist) and Gamesley *Derby 6* **P** *Prime Min* **V** F A WALTERS
CHARLETON (St Mary) *see* Stokenham, Slapton, Charleton w Buckland etc *Ex*
CHARLTON (All Saints) *see* Chalke Valley *Sarum*
CHARLTON (Holy Trinity) *see* Wantage *Ox*
CHARLTON (St John the Baptist) *see* Garsdon, Lea and Cleverton and Charlton *Bris*
CHARLTON (St John the Baptist) *see* St Bartholomew *Sarum*
CHARLTON (St John) *see* Fladbury, Hill and Moor, Wyre Piddle etc *Worc*
CHARLTON (St Luke w Holy Trinity) (St Richard) (St Thomas) *S'wark 1* **P** *Bp and Viscount Gough (jt)* **R** E M WOOFF **C** J DANIELS-WHITE **OLM** B J SPONG, E A NEWMAN
CHARLTON (St Peter and St Paul) *see* Dover Town *Cant*
CHARLTON (St Peter) *see* Vale of Pewsey *Sarum*
CHARLTON ABBOTS (St Martin) *see* Sevenhampton w Charlton Abbots, Hawling etc *Glouc*
CHARLTON ADAM (St Peter and St Paul) *see* Somerton w Compton Dundon, the Charltons etc *B & W*
CHARLTON HORETHORNE (St Peter and St Paul) *see* Milborne Port w Goathill etc *B & W*
CHARLTON KINGS (Holy Apostles) *Glouc 6* **P** *R Cheltenham* **V** R J PATERSON **C** R M BELL
CHARLTON KINGS (St Mary) *Glouc 6* **P** *Bp* **V** M GARLAND
CHARLTON MACKRELL (St Mary the Virgin) *see* Somerton w Compton Dundon, the Charltons etc *B & W*
CHARLTON MARSHALL (St Mary the Virgin) *see* Spetisbury w Charlton Marshall etc *Sarum*
CHARLTON MUSGROVE (St John) (St Stephen), Cucklington and Stoke Trister *B & W 2* **P** *Bp* **R** *vacant*
CHARLTON ON OTMOOR (St Mary) *see* Ray Valley *Ox*
CHARLTON, SOUTH (St James) *see* Glendale Gp *Newc*
CHARLWOOD (St Nicholas) *S'wark 26* **P** *DBP* **R** *vacant*
CHARMINSTER (St Mary the Virgin) and Stinsford *Sarum 1* **P** *The Hon C A Townshend and Bp (alt)* **V** P J SMITH **Hon C** A J K MACKENZIE, C L MCCLELLAND **NSM** P A C KENNEDY, R P VAN DER HART
CHARMOUTH (St Andrew) *see* Golden Cap Team *Sarum*
CHARNEY BASSETT (St Peter) *see* Cherbury w Gainfield *Ox*
CHARNOCK RICHARD (Christ Church) *Blackb 4* **P** *DBF* **P-in-c** A J BROWN **NSM** A D WYNNE
CHARSFIELD W DEBACH (St Peter) *see* Mid Loes *St E*
CHART SUTTON (St Michael) *see* Headcorn and The Suttons *Cant*
CHART, GREAT (St Mary) *Cant 6* **P** *Abp* **P-in-c** T C WILSON
CHART, LITTLE (St Mary) *see* G7 Benefice *Cant*
CHARTERHOUSE-ON-MENDIP (St Hugh) *see* Blagdon w Compton Martin and Ubley *B & W*
CHARTHAM (St Mary) and Upper Hardres w Stelling *Cant 2* **P** *Abp and Trustees Lord Tomlin (jt)* **V** P A BROWN **C** L R ROGERS
CHARWELTON (Holy Trinity) *see* Badby w Newham and Charwelton w Fawsley etc *Pet*
CHASE *Ox 22* **P** *Bp and D&C Ch Ch (jt)* **R** M E J ABREY **NSM** M R NEEDHAM

CHASE *Sarum 6*   **P** *Bp, Adn Dorset, Ch Soc Trust, Pemb Coll Cam, Univ Coll Ox, J P C Bourke Esq (4 turns), Ld Chan (1 turn)*   **R** M J FOSTER   **C** M R B DURRANT   **Hon C** W H G JOHNSTONE

CHASETOWN (St Anne)   *see* Burntwood, Chase Terrace etc *Lich*

CHASETOWN (St John) *as above*

CHASTLETON (St Mary the Virgin)   *see* Chipping Norton *Ox*

CHATBURN (Christ Church) and Downham *Blackb 7*   **P** *Hulme Trustees and Lord Clitheroe (jt)*   **P-in-c** A W FROUD

CHATHAM (St Mary and St John) *Roch 5*   **P** *D&C*   **P-in-c** P FOREMAN   **C** M S M DAHL

CHATHAM (St Paul w All Saints) *Roch 5*   **P** *Bp*   **V** K M JOHNSON   **C** M S M DAHL

CHATHAM (St Philip and St James) *Roch 5*   **P** *Ch Soc Trust*   **V** M L J SAUNDERS   **NSM** S C SPENCER

CHATHAM (St Stephen) *Roch 5*   **P** *Bp*   **P-in-c** B J LINNEY

CHATHAM, SOUTH Holy Trinity (St William) (St Alban) (St David) *Roch 5*   **P** *Bp*   **TR** E CRANMER   **TV** D A KICHENSIDE   **NSM** N J WARD

CHATTERIS (St Peter and St Paul) *Ely 11*   **P** *G&C Coll Cam*   **V** W L THOMSON   **Hon C** J M THOMSON

CHATTISHAM (All Saints and St Margaret)   *see* Elmsett w Aldham, Hintlesham, Chattisham etc *St E*

CHATTON (Holy Cross)   *see* Glendale Gp *Newc*

CHAVEY DOWN (St Martin)   *see* Winkfield and Cranbourne *Ox*

CHAWLEIGH (St James)   *see* Burrington, Chawleigh, Cheldon, Chulmleigh etc *Ex*

CHAWTON (St Nicholas)   *see* Northanger *Win*

CHEADLE (All Hallows) (St Philip's Mission Church) *Ches 17*   **P** *R Cheadle*   **V** P J CUMMING   **NSM** S MAYO

CHEADLE (St Cuthbert) (St Mary) *Ches 17*   **P** *Ch Soc Trust*   **R** R S MUNRO   **C** J E M NEWMAN, S J DONOHOE   **Hon C** M A LOWE   **NSM** N C HALL

CHEADLE (St Giles) w Freehay *Lich 6*   **P** *DBP*   **R** J R ROSIE

CHEADLE HULME (All Saints) *Ches 17*   **P** *Bp*   **V** J A BACON   **C** D A PARKER, R A GIBBS

CHEADLE HULME (St Andrew) *Ches 17*   **P** *R Cheadle*   **V** D W GUEST   **C** A J BARNSHAW

CHEAM (St Dunstan) (St Alban the Martyr) (St Oswald) *S'wark 23*   **P** *Patr Bd*   **TR** D N MILLER   **TV** L R DENNY   **OLM** D W F BRICE

CHEARSLEY (St Nicholas)   *see* Long Crendon w Chearsley and Nether Winchendon *Ox*

CHEBSEY (All Saints), Creswell, Ellenhall, Ranton and Seighford *Lich 7*   **P** *D&C, Qu Eliz Grant Trustees, Trustees Earl of Lich, and J Eld Esq (jt)*   **V** *vacant*

CHECKENDON (St Peter and St Paul)   *see* Langtree *Ox*

CHECKLEY (Mission Room)   *see* Fownhope w Mordiford, Brockhampton etc *Heref*

CHECKLEY (St Mary and All Saints)   *see* Uttoxeter Area *Lich*

CHEDBURGH (All Saints)   *see* Chevington w Hargrave, Chedburgh w Depden etc *St E*

CHEDDAR (St Andrew), Draycott and Rodney Stoke *B & W 1*   **P** *Bp and D&C (jt)*   **R** *vacant*

CHEDDINGTON (St Giles)   *see* Cottesloe *Ox*

CHEDDLETON (St Edward the Confessor), Horton, Longsdon and Rushton Spencer *Lich 8*   **P** *Bp and R Leek and Meerbrook (jt)*   **V** A S G PIKE   **OLM** D M OLIVER

CHEDDON FITZPAINE (The Blessed Virgin Mary)   *see* W Monkton w Kingston St Mary, Broomfield etc *B & W*

CHEDGRAVE (All Saints)   *see* Loddon, Sisland, Chedgrave, Hardley and Langley *Nor*

CHEDISTON (St Mary)   *see* Blyth Valley *St E*

CHEDWORTH (St Andrew), Yanworth and Stowell, Coln Rogers and Coln St Denys *Glouc 8*   **P** *Ld Chan (2 turns), Qu Coll Ox (1 turn)*   **P-in-c** S J GOUNDREY-SMITH

CHEDZOY (The Blessed Virgin Mary)   *see* Weston Zoyland w Chedzoy *B & W*

CHEETHAM (St Mark) and Lower Crumpsall *Man 4*   **P** *Patr Bd*   **V** J M A PARTRIDGE

CHELBOROUGH, EAST (St James)   *see* Melbury *Sarum*

CHELBOROUGH, WEST (St Andrew) *as above*

CHELDON (St Mary)   *see* Burrington, Chawleigh, Cheldon, Chulmleigh etc *Ex*

CHELFORD (St John the Evangelist) and Lower Withington w Marthall *Ches 12*   **P** *DBP*   **V** G V TETZLAFF

CHELL (St Michael) *Lich 11*   **P** *Ch Patr Trust and V Newchapel St Jas (jt)*   **OLM** J CRANE

CHELL HEATH (Saviour)   *see* Chell *Lich*

CHELLASTON (St Peter) *Derby 15*   **P** *Bp*   **V** J FACEY

CHELLS (St Hugh and St John)   *see* Stevenage St Hugh and St Jo *St Alb*

CHELMONDISTON (St Andrew)   *see* Shoreline *St E*

CHELMORTON AND FLAGG (St John the Baptist)   *see* Taddington, Chelmorton and Monyash etc *Derby*

CHELMSFORD (Ascension) (All Saints) (St Michael's Church Centre) *Chelmsf 9*   **P** *Bp*   **V** T W PAGE   **C** L P ROGERS

CHELMSFORD (St Andrew) *Chelmsf 9*   **P** *Bp*   **V** P H GREENLAND

CHELMSLEY WOOD (St Andrew) *Birm 9*   **P** *Bp*   **R** *vacant*

CHELSEA (All Saints) (Old Church) *Lon 8*   **P** *R Chelsea St Luke and Earl Cadogan (jt)*   **V** D P E REINDORP

CHELSEA (St John w St Andrew) (St John) *Lon 8*   **P** *CPAS and Lon Coll of Div (jt)*   **V** P R DAWSON   **C** H S ASHTON   **NSM** A MASON

CHELSEA (St Luke) (Christ Church) *Lon 8*   **P** *Earl Cadogan*   **R** B LEATHARD   **C** C R WALSH, E R DINWIDDY SMITH

CHELSEA, UPPER (Holy Trinity) (St Saviour) *Lon 8[*J*R* G RAINFORD   **P** *Earl Cadogan*   **R** N P WHEELER   **Hon C** N NASSAR

CHELSEA, UPPER (St Simon Zelotes) *Lon 8*   **P** *Hyndman's Trustees (jt)*   **V** M R J NEVILLE

CHELSFIELD (St Martin of Tours) *Roch 16*   **P** *All So Coll Ox*   **R** J TRANTER

CHELSHAM (St Christopher)   *see* Warlingham w Chelsham and Farleigh *S'wark*

CHELSHAM (St Leonard) *as above*

CHELSTON (St Peter)   *see* Cockington *Ex*

CHELSWORTH (All Saints)   *see* Monks Eleigh w Chelsworth and Brent Eleigh etc *St E*

CHELTENHAM (All Saints)   *see* N Cheltenham *Glouc*

CHELTENHAM (Christ Church) *Glouc 6*   **P** *Simeon's Trustees*   **V** T J E MAYFIELD   **C** M D SMITH

CHELTENHAM (Emmanuel)   *see* S Cheltenham *Glouc*

CHELTENHAM (Holy Trinity) (St Paul) *Glouc 6*   **P** *Patr Bd*   **TR** M R BAILEY   **TV** R J WIDDECOMBE, T R GREW   **Hon C** A S COLLISHAW   **NSM** G L DICKINSON

CHELTENHAM (St Luke) (St Mary) (St Matthew) *Glouc 6*   **P** *Simeon's Trustees*   **R** T F L GRIFFITHS   **C** A J HALL, D A DE J GRIFFITHS, P E WHEATON   **NSM** C L DYSON, D A DE J GRIFFITHS, M WORKMAN, S E KNIGHT

CHELTENHAM (St Mark) (St Barnabas) (St Aidan) (Emmanuel) *Glouc 6*   **P** *Patr Bd*   **TR** S A BOWEN   **TV** P D SMITH, R E CROFTON   **C** R GREENHALGH   **NSM** A P HOLDERNESS

CHELTENHAM (St Michael) *Glouc 6*   **P** *Bp*   **P-in-c** R J PATERSON   **C** J H WHITE

CHELTENHAM (St Stephen)   *see* S Cheltenham *Glouc*

CHELTENHAM Benefice, The NORTH *Glouc 6*   **P** *Patr Bd*   **TR** D R SMITH   **TV** S W ELDRIDGE   **C** E PALIN   **NSM** A E SMITH, A J SWINBANK, M J FRENCH

CHELTENHAM, SOUTH *Glouc 6*   **P** *Patr Bd*   **TV** K L SHILL, N D DAVIES   **C** E E MITCHELL, N M BURFITT   **NSM** B K C DUNLOP, H R WOOD

CHELVESTON (St John the Baptist)   *see* Higham Ferrers w Chelveston *Pet*

CHELVEY (St Bridget)   *see* Backwell w Chelvey and Brockley *B & W*

CHELWOOD (St Leonard)   *see* Publow w Pensford, Compton Dando and Chelwood *B & W*

CHELWOOD GATE (not known)   *see* Danehill *Chich*

CHENDERIT *Pet 1*   **P** *Bp and BNC Ox (2 turns), Ld Chan (1 turn)*   **R** C D JEFFERSON

CHENIES (St Michael) and Little Chalfont, Latimer and Flaunden *Ox 9*   **P** *Bedford Estates Trustees and Lord Chesham (jt)*   **R** D G ALLSOP   **Hon C** J S WENT   **NSM** R F BOUGHTON

CHEQUERFIELD (St Mary)   *see* Pontefract St Giles *Leeds*

CHERBURY w Gainfield *Ox 25*   **P** *Bp, DBP, Jes Coll, Oriel Coll, and Worc Coll Ox (jt)*   **R** T I TRACEY-MACLEOD

CHERHILL (St James the Great)   *see* Oldbury *Sarum*

CHERINGTON (St John the Baptist)   *see* S Warks Seven Gp *Cov*

CHERINGTON (St Nicholas)   *see* Avening w Cherington *Glouc*

CHERITON (St Martin) w Newington Benefice, The *Cant 8*   **P** *Abp*   **OLM** E M WEBB

CHERITON (St Michael and All Angels)   *see* Upper Itchen *Win*

CHERITON BISHOP (St Mary)   *see* Tedburn St Mary, Cheriton Bishop, Whitestone etc *Ex*

CHERITON FITZPAINE (St Matthew)   *see* N Creedy *Ex*

CHERITON STREET (All Souls)   *see* Cheriton w Newington *Cant*

CHERITON, NORTH (St John the Baptist)   *see* Camelot Par *B & W*

CHERRY BURTON (St Michael) *York 8*   **P** *E D F Burton*   **R** R F PARKINSON

CHERRY HINTON (St Andrew) *Ely 3*   **P** *Peterho Cam*   **V** *vacant*

CHERRY HINTON (St John the Evangelist) *Ely 3*   **P** *Bp*   **V** S E WYATT   **C** P J SHAKESHAFT   **Hon C** P S HESLAM

CHERRY WILLINGHAM (St Peter and St Paul)   *see* S Lawres Gp *Linc*

CHERTSEY (St Peter w All Saints), Lyne and Longcross
Guildf 11 **P** *Bp and Haberdashers' Co (jt)* **V** T J HILLIER
C E K SHIPTON, L W GAMLEN

CHERWELL VALLEY *Ox 21* **P** *Patr Bd* **TR** S R GRIFFITHS
TV G D G PRICE

CHESELBORNE (St Martin) *see* Piddle Valley, Hilton,
Cheselbourne etc *Sarum*

CHESHAM BOIS (St Leonard) *Ox 9* **P** *Peache Trustees*
R L S CLOW **NSM** C CLARE

**CHESHAM, GREAT (Christ Church) (Emmanuel) (St Mary the
Virgin)** *Ox 9* **P** *Patr Bd* **TR** S J L CANSDALE
TV J M SHEPHERD, S I A LIYANAGE **C** S BAILY, T A WATTS
NSM H A WILSON, T J S YATES

CHESHUNT (St Mary the Virgin) *St Alb 17* **P** *Patr Bd*
TR J K WILLIAMS **TV** C J SELBY, J E DICKER, J M WILSON
NSM A LYNAS

CHESSINGTON (St Mary the Virgin) *Guildf 9* **P** *Mert Coll Ox*
V S EDWARDS

CHESTER (Christ Church) *Ches 2* **P** *Bp and Simeon's Trustees
(jt)* **V** G L SHAW **NSM** G JONES, R J KEMP

CHESTER (Holy Trinity without the Walls) *Ches 2* **P** *Bp*
R C P UPTON **C** C P BURKETT, D J COWIE

CHESTER (St John the Baptist) *Ches 2* **P** *Duke of Westminster*
V D N CHESTERS

CHESTER (St Mary on the Hill) *Ches 2* **P** *Duke of Westmr*
R P C O DAWSON

CHESTER (St Paul) *Ches 2* **P** *R Ches* **V** S T PENDLEBURY
C C J S BLUNT

CHESTER (St Peter) *Ches 2* **P** *Bp* **V** *vacant*

CHESTER GREEN (St Paul) *see* Derby St Paul *Derby*

CHESTER LE STREET (St Mary and St Cuthbert) *Dur 11*
P *St Jo Coll Dur* **TR** J TULLY **C** D C CHRISTIAN,
J A ASHURST **NSM** D M LINDLEY

CHESTER SQUARE (St Michael) (St Philip) *Lon 3* **P** *Duke of
Westmr* **V** C C MARNHAM **C** J C G ASH, T D MULLINS

CHESTER St Oswald (St Thomas of Canterbury) *Ches 2*
P *D&C* **V** R J E CLACK

CHESTERBLADE (The Blessed Virgin Mary) *see* Evercreech w
Chesterblade and Milton Clevedon *B & W*

CHESTERFIELD (Holy Trinity) (Christ Church) *Derby 5*
P *CPAS* **R** D J HORSFALL **C** M R BROOMHEAD

**CHESTERFIELD (St Augustine of Hippo and St Augustine of
Canterbury)** *Derby 5* **P** *Bp* **C** M R BROOMHEAD
NSM H J MOORE

CHESTERFIELD (St Mary and All Saints) *Derby 5* **P** *Bp*
V P F COLEMAN **C** M R BROOMHEAD

CHESTERFORD, GREAT (All Saints) *see* Saffron Walden and
Villages *Chelmsf*

CHESTERFORD, LITTLE (St Mary the Virgin) *as above*

CHESTERTON (Good Shepherd) *Ely 2* **P** *Bp* **V** D J MAHER
C C A LOWE, R E BLANCHFLOWER **NSM** J A GRETTON-DANN

CHESTERTON (Holy Trinity) (St Chad) *Lich 9* **P** *Prime Min*
V S R BOXALL **NSM** S SIDEBOTTOM

CHESTERTON (St Andrew) *Ely 2* **P** *Trin Coll Cam*
V N I MOIR **C** H M ORR **NSM** A J COLES,
D H PEYTON JONES

CHESTERTON (St George) *Ely 2* **P** *Bp* **V** R H ADAMS
NSM L B TAYLOR

CHESTERTON (St Giles) *Cov 8* **P** *Lady Willoughby de Broke*
V J D PARKER

CHESTERTON (St Lawrence) *see* Cirencester *Glouc*

CHESTERTON (St Michael) *see* Alwalton and Chesterton *Ely*

CHESTERTON, GREAT (St Mary) *see* Akeman *Ox*

**CHESWARDINE (St Swithun), Childs Ercall, Hales, Hinstock,
Sambrook and Stoke on Tern** *Lich 18* **P** *Patr Bd*
TR D A ACKROYD **C** D J STORK BANKS **NSM** C SIMPSON

CHETNOLE (St Peter) *see* Three Valleys *Sarum*

CHETTISHAM (St Michael and All Angels) *see* Ely *Ely*

CHETTLE (St Mary) *see* Chase *Sarum*

CHETWODE (St Mary and St Nicholas) *see* The Claydons and
Swan *Ox*

CHETWYND (St Michael and All Angels) *see* Newport w
Longford, and Chetwynd *Lich*

CHEVELEY (St Mary) *Ely 4* **P** *DBP and Mrs D A Bowlby (alt)*
P-in-c P L TAIT

CHEVENING (St Botolph) *Roch 9* **P** *Abp* **R** C J SMITH
NSM S L SUTHERLAND

CHEVERELL, GREAT (St Peter) *see* The Lavingtons, Cheverells,
and Easterton *Sarum*

CHEVERELL, LITTLE (St Peter) *as above*

**CHEVINGTON (All Saints) w Hargrave, Chedburgh w
Depden, Rede and Hawkedon** *St E 8* **P** *Guild of All So
(1 turn), Ld Chan (2 turns), Bp and DBP (1 turn)*
P-in-c C A COLLINS

CHEVINGTON (St John the Divine) *Newc 6* **P** *Bp*
P-in-c S J REILLY **NSM** C C ASKEW

CHEVITHORNE (St Thomas) *see* Tiverton St Pet and
Chevithorne w Cove *Ex*

**CHEW MAGNA (St Andrew) w Dundry, Norton Malreward
and Stanton Drew** *B & W 9* **P** *Bp and Adn (jt)*
R C R M ROBERTS **NSM** S E LOVERN

CHEW STOKE (St Andrew) w Nempnett Thrubwell *B & W 9*
P *Bp and SMF (jt)* **P-in-c** C R M ROBERTS **NSM** V L BARLEY

CHEWTON (Mission Church) *see* Keynsham *B & W*

**CHEWTON MENDIP (St Mary Magdalene) w Ston Easton,
Litton and Emborough** *B & W 7* **P** *Earl Waldegrave (2 turns),
Bp (1 turn)* **P-in-c** T C OSMOND **NSM** C M COWLIN,
H J LATTY

CHEYLESMORE (Christ Church) *Cov 3* **P** *Ch Trust Fund Trust*
V A C WOO **C** J C HILL

CHICHELEY (St Laurence) *see* Sherington w Chicheley, N
Crawley, Astwood etc *Ox*

CHICHESTER (St Pancras and St John) *Chich 2* **P** *Simeon's
Trustees (2 turns), St Jo Chpl Trustees (1 turn)* **R** M J T PAYNE
C C J STYLES, I E SMALE

**CHICHESTER (St Paul) (Immanuel) and Westhampnett
St Peter** *Chich 2* **P** *Bp and D&C (jt)* **R** S P HOLLAND
C K G YOUNG **NSM** S T FLASHMAN

CHICHESTER (St Wilfrid) *Chich 2* **P** *Bp* **V** *vacant*

CHICKERELL (St Mary) w Fleet *Sarum 4* **P** *Bp*
R J C BRADING

CHICKLADE (All Saints) *see* Nadder Valley *Sarum*

CHIDDINGFOLD (St Mary) *Guildf 4* **P** *Ld Chan*
R S A BROUGH **NSM** S A BELL **OLM** G M WELFORD

CHIDDINGLY (not known) w East Hoathly *Chich 18* **P** *Bp*
R P A HODGINS

CHIDDINGSTONE (St Mary) w Chiddingstone Causeway
Roch 11 **P** *Abp and Bp (jt)* **R** S M BEAUMONT

CHIDDINGSTONE CAUSEWAY (St Luke) *see* Chiddingstone w
Chiddingstone Causeway *Roch*

CHIDEOCK (St Giles) *see* Golden Cap Team *Sarum*

CHIDHAM (St Mary) *Chich 3* **P** *Bp* **V** P MATTHEWS

CHIEVELEY (St Mary the Virgin) *see* E Downland *Ox*

CHIGNAL SMEALEY (St Nicholas) *see* The Chignals w
Mashbury *Chelmsf*

CHIGNALS w Mashbury, The *Chelmsf 9* **P** *CPAS (2 turns),
Bp (1 turn)* **P-in-c** C J BROWN **OLM** R F BRAISBY, S SYKES

CHIGWELL (St Mary) (St Winifred) and Chigwell Row
Chelmsf 3 **P** *The Crown and Patr Bd (alt)* **TV** B W KING
C S M GUEST **NSM** N A TAYLOR

CHIGWELL ROW (All Saints) *see* Chigwell and Chigwell Row
Chelmsf

CHILBOLTON (St Mary) *see* The Downs *Win*

CHILCOMB (St Andrew) *see* E Win *Win*

CHILCOMBE (not known) *see* Bride Valley *Sarum*

**CHILCOMPTON (St John the Baptist) w Downside and
Stratton on the Fosse** *B & W 11* **P** *Bp, MMCET, and V
Midsomer Norton (jt)* **P-in-c** C D NORTH

CHILCOTE (St Matthew's Chapel) *see* Mease Valley *Lich*

CHILDE OKEFORD (St Nicholas) *see* Okeford *Sarum*

CHILDERDITCH (All Saints and St Faith) *see* E and W Horndon
w Lt Warley and Childerditch *Chelmsf*

CHILDREY (St Mary the Virgin) *see* Ridgeway *Ox*

CHILDS ERCALL (St Michael and All Angels) *see* Cheswardine,
Childs Ercall, Hales, Hinstock etc *Lich*

CHILDS HILL (All Saints) *see* Hendon All SS Childs Hill *Lon*

CHILDSWYCKHAM (St Mary the Virgin) *see* Winchcombe
Glouc

CHILDWALL (All Saints) *Liv 4* **P** *Bp* **V** G J RENISON
OLM S J GILLIES

CHILDWALL (St David) *Liv 4* **P** *Bp* **V** R W WILLIAMS
NSM S-A MASON

CHILDWALL VALLEY (St Mark) *see* Gateacre *Liv*

CHILDWICK (St Mary) *see* St Alb St Mich *St Alb*

CHILFROME (Holy Trinity) *see* Melbury *Sarum*

CHILHAM (St Mary) *see* King's Wood *Cant*

CHILLENDEN (All Saints) *see* Canonry *Cant*

CHILLESFORD (St Peter) *see* Wilford Peninsula *St E*

CHILLINGHAM (St Peter) *see* Glendale Gp *Newc*

CHILLINGTON (St James) *see* Winsmoor *B & W*

CHILMARK (St Margaret of Antioch) *see* Nadder Valley *Sarum*

CHILTHORNE DOMER (Blessed Virgin Mary) *see* Tintinhull w
Chilthorne Domer, Yeovil Marsh etc *B & W*

CHILTINGTON, EAST (not known) *see* Plumpton w E
Chiltington cum Novington *Chich*

CHILTINGTON, WEST (St Mary) *Chich 11* **P** *Bp* **R** D M BEAL

CHILTON (All Saints) *see* Harwell w Chilton *Ox*

CHILTON (St Aidan) *Dur 5* **P** *Bp* **P-in-c** D J BELL

CHILTON (St Mary) *see* Bernwode *Ox*

**CHILTON CANTELO (St James) w Ashington, Mudford,
Rimpton and Marston Magna** *B & W 6* **P** *DBP and D&C,
D&C Bris, and Bp Lon (by turn)* **R** B STANTON

CHILTON FOLIAT (St Mary) *see* Whitton *Sarum*
CHILTON MOOR (St Andrew) *Dur 14* **P** *Bp*
P-in-c D NEWTON
CHILTON POLDEN (St Edward) *see* Polden Wheel *B & W*
CHILTON TRINITY (Holy Trinity) *see* Bridgwater St Mary and
Chilton Trinity *B & W*
CHILVERS COTON (All Saints) w Astley *Cov 5* **P** *Viscount
Daventry* **V** F P SELDON **C** S MEDLEY
NSM D WATERTON, J FRYER
CHILWELL (Christ Church) *S'well 9* **P** *CPAS* **V** A R HOWE
C L P B O'BOYLE **Hon C** A DE C LADD, N M LADD
CHILWORTH (St Denys) *see* Ampfield, Chilworth and N
Baddesley *Win*
CHILWORTH (St Thomas) *see* Shere, Albury and Chilworth
Guildf
CHINEHAM (Christ Church) *Win 4* **P** *Bp* **V** I R BENTLEY
NSM G C RANDALL
CHINESE CONGREGATION *see* St Martin-in-the-Fields *Lon*
CHINGFORD (All Saints) (St Peter and St Paul) *Chelmsf 7*
P *Bp* **R** A P C TRENIER **Hon C** S H SPEERS
OLM T P ROLLINGS
CHINGFORD (St Anne) *Chelmsf 7* **P** *Bp* **V** J R BULLOCK
OLM M L SCOTCHMER
CHINGFORD (St Edmund) *Chelmsf 7* **P** *Bp*
V L A GOLDSMITH
CHINLEY (St Mary) *see* Hayfield and Chinley w Buxworth
Derby
CHINNOCK, EAST (Blessed Virgin Mary) *see* Coker Ridge
B & W
CHINNOCK, MIDDLE (St Margaret) *see* Norton sub Hamdon,
W Chinnock, Chiselborough etc *B & W*
CHINNOCK, WEST (Blessed Virgin Mary) *as above*
**CHINNOR (St Andrew), Sydenham, Aston Rowant and
Crowell** *Ox 20* **P** *Bp, DBP, and Peache Trustees (jt)*
R K W CAMPBELL, M R C THORNE **OLM** S Q HUTTON
CHIPPENHAM (St Andrew) w Tytherton Lucas *Bris 4*
P *Ch Ch Ox* **V** R C H KEY
CHIPPENHAM (St Margaret) *see* Three Rivers Gp *Ely*
CHIPPENHAM (St Paul) w Hardenhuish and Langley Burrell
Bris 4 **P** *Patr Bd* **P-in-c** S D DUNN **OLM** D J KILMISTER
CHIPPENHAM (St Peter) *Bris 4* **P** *Bp* **P-in-c** A M GUBBINS
CHIPPERFIELD (St Paul) *see* Sarratt and Chipperfield *St Alb*
CHIPPING (St Bartholomew) and Whitewell (St Michael)
Blackb 7 **P** *Bp and Hulme Trustees (jt)* **V** *vacant*
**CHIPPING BARNET (St John the Baptist) (St Mark)
(St Stephen)** *St Alb 14* **P** *Prime Min (2 turns) and Bp (1 turn)*
TR S C FERRIS **TV** T D CHAPMAN
CHIPPING CAMPDEN (St James) *see* Vale and Cotswold Edge
Glouc
CHIPPING NORTON (St Mary the Virgin) *Ox 22* **P** *Patr Bd*
TR J E KENNEDY **TV** D W SALTER **C** J P JONES,
M G SIMPSON **NSM** S BLAKE
CHIPPING ONGAR (St Martin) w Shelley *Chelmsf 3* **P** *Guild
of All So and Keble Coll Ox* **P-in-c** N R TAYLOR
C S E BRAZIER-GIBBS
CHIPPING SODBURY (St John the Baptist) *see* Sodbury Vale
Glouc
CHIPPING WARDEN (St Peter and St Paul) *see* Culworth w
Sulgrave and Thorpe Mandeville etc *Pet*
CHIPSTABLE (All Saints) *see* Wiveliscombe and the Hills *B & W*
CHIPSTEAD (Good Shepherd) *see* Chevening *Roch*
CHIPSTEAD (St Margaret of Antioch) *S'wark 26* **P** *Abp*
R P M JACKSON
**CHIRBURY (St Michael), Marton, Middleton and Trelystan w
Leighton** *Heref 12* **P** *Bp (3 turns), N E E Stephens Esq (1 turn)*
V R N LEACH
CHIRTON (St John the Baptist) *see* The Cannings and Redhorn
Sarum
CHISELBOROUGH (St Peter and St Paul) *see* Norton sub
Hamdon, W Chinnock, Chiselborough etc *B & W*
CHISHILL, GREAT (St Swithun) *see* Icknield Way Villages
Chelmsf
CHISHILL, LITTLE (St Nicholas) *as above*
CHISLEDON (Holy Cross) *see* Ridgeway *Sarum*
CHISLEHURST (Annunciation) *Roch 14* **P** *Keble Coll*
V P A FARTHING
CHISLEHURST (Christ Church) *Roch 14* **P** *CPAS*
V D G S JOHNSTON
CHISLEHURST (St Nicholas) *Roch 14* **P** *Bp* **R** A A MUSTOE
C J DURRANS **NSM** J B HURN
CHISLET (St Mary the Virgin) *see* Wantsum Gp *Cant*
CHISWICK (St Michael and All Angels) *see* Bedford Park *Lon*
CHISWICK (St Michael) *Lon 11* **P** *V St Martin-in-the-Fields*
V M A OBORNE
CHISWICK (St Nicholas w St Mary Magdalene) *Lon 11*
P *D&C St Paul's* **V** S F BRANDES **C** A V J DOWNES

CHISWICK (St Paul) Grove Park *Lon 11* **P** *V Chiswick*
V M C RILEY
CHITHURST (St Mary) *see* Rogate w Terwick and Trotton w
Chithurst *Chich*
CHITTERNE (All Saints and St Mary) *see* Salisbury Plain *Sarum*
CHITTLEHAMHOLT (St John) *see* S Molton w Nymet St George,
High Bray etc *Ex*
CHITTLEHAMPTON (St Hieritha) *as above*
CHITTS HILL (St Cuthbert) *Lon 19* **P** *CPAS*
P-in-c M JONES PARRY, P H SUDELL
CHIVELSTONE (St Sylvester) *see* Stokenham, Slapton,
Charleton w Buckland etc *Ex*
CHOBHAM (St Lawrence) w Valley End *Guildf 6* **P** *Bp and
Brig R W Acworth (alt)* **V** C D BESSANT **OLM** C J BEDFORD
CHOLDERTON (St Nicholas) *see* Bourne Valley *Sarum*
CHOLESBURY (St Lawrence) *see* Hawridge w Cholesbury and
St Leonard *Ox*
CHOLLERTON w Birtley and Thockrington *Newc 8*
P *Mrs P I Enderby (2 turns), Newc Dioc Soc (1 turn)* **V** M J SLADE
OLM D I WILLIAMS
CHOLSEY (St Mary) and Moulsford *Ox 26* **P** *Ld Chan and Bp
(alt)* **V** A M PETIT **NSM** D A J LEE-PHILPOT
OLM V M L GIBBONS
CHOPPARDS (Mission Room) *see* Upper Holme Valley *Leeds*
CHOPPINGTON (St Paul the Apostle) *Newc 1* **P** *D&C*
V T MOAT
CHOPWELL (St John the Evangelist) *Dur 13* **P** *Bp*
P-in-c P R MURRAY
CHORLEY (All Saints) *Blackb 4* **P** *Bp* **V** E N STRASZAK
CHORLEY (St George) *Blackb 4* **P** *R Chorley* **V** T D WILBY
NSM C L MARTLEW
CHORLEY (St James) *Blackb 4* **P** *R Chorley* **V** D K PHILLIPS
CHORLEY (St Laurence) *Blackb 4* **P** *Bp* **R** M B COX
Hon C T H STOKES
CHORLEY (St Peter) *Blackb 4* **P** *R Chorley* **P-in-c** T D WILBY
C P H SMITH
CHORLEY (St Philip) *see* Alderley Edge *Ches*
CHORLEYWOOD (Christ Church) *St Alb 4* **P** *CPAS*
V D M HALL **C** D K SHORT
CHORLEYWOOD (St Andrew) *St Alb 4* **P** *Bp* **V** D P WHITE
CHORLTON-CUM-HARDY (St Clement) (St Barnabas) *Man 3*
P *D&C* **R** K FLOOD **OLM** J KING, L M WINDLE
CHORLTON-CUM-HARDY (St Werburgh) *Man 3* **P** *Bp*
P-in-c F SHER
CHRISHALL (Holy Trinity) *see* Icknield Way Villages *Chelmsf*
CHRIST THE KING in the Diocese of Newcastle *Newc 2* **P** *Patr
Bd* **TR** M A C DALLISTON **TV** G M SHORT, M A EDWARDS
C P D DOBSON
CHRISTCHURCH (Christ Church) and Manea and Welney
Ely 11 **P** *Bp and R T Townley Esq (jt)* **R** *vacant*
CHRISTCHURCH (Holy Trinity) *Win 9* **P** *Bp*
P-in-c C STEWART **NSM** A M NEWTON, A M SMITH,
R B PARTRIDGE
CHRISTCHURCH Stourvale (St George) *see* Christchurch *Win*
CHRISTIAN MALFORD (All Saints) *see* Draycot *Bris*
CHRISTLETON (St James) *Ches 2* **P** *Bp* **R** M COWAN
CHRISTON (Blessed Virgin Mary) *see* Crook Peak *B & W*
**CHRISTOW (St James), Ashton, Bridford, Dunchideock,
Dunsford and Doddiscombsleigh** *Ex 5* **P** *Bp, MMCET, SMF,
Mrs J M Michelmore, Viscount Exmouth, and F C Fulford Esq (jt)*
V G K MAYER
**CHUDLEIGH (St Mary and St Martin) w Chudleigh Knighton
and Trusham** *Ex 8* **P** *Patr Bd* **V** P WIMSETT
NSM M J FLETCHER
CHUDLEIGH KNIGHTON (St Paul) *see* Chudleigh w Chudleigh
Knighton and Trusham *Ex*
CHULMLEIGH (St Mary Magdalene) *see* Burrington,
Chawleigh, Cheldon, Chulmleigh etc *Ex*
CHURCH ASTON (St Andrew) *Lich 16* **P** *R Edgmond*
P-in-c L M WHEELER
CHURCH BRAMPTON (St Botolph) *see* Brington w Whilton
and Norton etc *Pet*
CHURCH BROUGHTON (St Michael) *see* Boylestone, Church
Broughton, Dalbury, etc *Derby*
CHURCH EATON (St Editha) *see* Bradeley, Church Eaton,
Derrington and Haughton *Lich*
CHURCH HONEYBOURNE (St Ecgwyn) *see* Vale and Cotswold
Edge *Glouc*
CHURCH HULME (St Luke) *Ches 11* **P** *V Sandbach*
V P MASON
CHURCH KIRK (St James) *Blackb 1* **P** *Hulme Trustees*
R *vacant*
CHURCH KNOWLE (St Peter) *see* Corfe Castle, Church
Knowle, Kimmeridge etc *Sarum*
CHURCH LANGLEY (Church and Community Centre)
Chelmsf 4 **P** *V Harlow* **V** A L KOSLA **Hon C** C A KOSLA

CHURCH LANGTON (St Peter)   *see* The Langtons and Shangton *Leic*

CHURCH LAWFORD (St Peter)   *see* Wolston and Church Lawford *Cov*

CHURCH LAWTON (All Saints) *Ches 11*   **P** *J Lawton Esq*   **R** *vacant*

CHURCH LENCH (All Saints) w Rous Lench and Abbots Morton and Harvington *Worc 1*   **P** *Bp and D&C (jt)*   **R** R J G THORNILEY   **NSM** F M BATTIN

CHURCH MINSHULL (St Bartholomew)   *see* Acton and Worleston, Church Minshull etc *Ches*

CHURCH OAKLEY (St Leonard)   *see* Oakley w Wootton St Lawrence *Win*

CHURCH PREEN (St John the Baptist)   *see* Wenlock *Heref*

CHURCH STRETTON (St Laurence) *Heref 10*   **P** *Ch Patr Trust*   **R** R H O HILL   **C** S WILLIAMS   **Hon C** V R MORRIS   **NSM** A J HUGHES, M L MAGOWAN

CHURCHAM (St Andrew)   *see* Huntley and Longhope, Churcham and Bulley *Glouc*

CHURCHDOWN (St Andrew) (St Bartholomew) *Glouc 3*   **P** *D&C*   **V** J G PERKIN   **C** B J LILLIE   **NSM** C M INGRAM

CHURCHDOWN (St John the Evangelist) and Innsworth *Glouc 3*   **P** *Bp*   **V** J D HYDE   **NSM** P J DONALD

CHURCHILL (All Saints)   *see* Chipping Norton *Ox*

CHURCHILL (St John the Baptist) and Langford *B & W 10*   **P** *D&C Bris*   **P-in-c** K M SAX

CHURCHILL-IN-HALFSHIRE (St James) w Blakedown and Broome *Worc 12*   **P** *Exors Viscount Cobham and N A Bourne Esq (jt)*   **P-in-c** P G HARRISON

CHURCHOVER (Holy Trinity)   *see* Revel Gp *Cov*

CHURCHSTANTON (St Peter and St Paul)   *see* Blackdown *B & W*

CHURCHSTOKE (St Nicholas) w Hyssington and Sarn *Heref 9*   **P** *The Crown (1 turn), Earl of Powis (2 turns)*   **P-in-c** S A C FOUNTAIN   **C** C J WHITTOCK   **NSM** I R BALL   **Emer** N F M MORRIS

CHURCHSTOW (St Mary)   *see* Thurlestone, S Milton, Churchstow etc *Ex*

CHURCHTOWN (St Helen)   *see* Garstang St Helen and St Michaels-on-Wyre *Blackb*

CHURN VALLEY Benefice, The *Glouc 7*   **P** *Jes Coll Ox, Univ Coll Ox, Mrs P Chester-Master, Sir H Elwes, Mrs S Pearce, Major M Wills (2 turns), Ld Chan (1 turn)*   **R** W G HEATHCOTE   **NSM** A CHAMPION, C R POOLEY

CHURN, THE (Aston Tirrold w Aston Upthorpe, Blewbury, Hagbourne, North Moreton, South Moreton, and Upton) *Ox 26*   **P** *Bp and Magd Coll Ox (1 turn), Adn Berks and Hertf Coll Ox (1 turn)*   **R** J P ST JOHN NICOLLE   **Hon C** J P H CLARKE   **OLM** L G N BUTLER

CHURSTON FERRERS (St Mary the Vigin)   *see* Brixham w Churston Ferrers and Kingswear *Ex*

CHURT (St John the Evangelist) and Hindhead *Guildf 3*   **P** *Adn Surrey*   **V** R T BODLE   **C** A WHITAKER

CHURWELL (All Saints)   *see* Morley *Leeds*

CHUTE (St Nicholas)   *see* Savernake *Sarum*

CINDERFORD (St John the Evangelist) (St Stephen) w Littledean *Glouc 1*   **P** *Prime Min and Ch Patr Trust (alt)*   **V** M J BARNSLEY

CINDERHILL (Christ Church) *S'well 8*   **P** *Bp*   **V** P J THOMAS

CINNAMON BROW (Resurrection)   *see* Warrington E *Liv*

CIPPENHAM (St Andrew) *Ox 12*   **P** *Eton Coll*   **V** J M MINKKINEN

CIRENCESTER (St John the Baptist) *Glouc 7*   **P** *Bp*   **V** L W DOOLAN   **C** G B GRADY, H N GILBERT, K R RICHARDSON   **Hon C** M J BETTIS   **NSM** P A LIGHT

CLACTON, GREAT (St John the Baptist) *Chelmsf 23*   **P** *Ch Patr Trust*   **V** G D A THORBURN   **C** P D SACRE, T M MULRYNE

CLACTON, LITTLE (St James)   *see* Weeley and Lt Clacton *Chelmsf*

CLACTON-ON-SEA (St Christopher) (St James) *Chelmsf 23*   **P** *Bp*   **V** P D C KANE

CLACTON-ON-SEA (St Paul) *Chelmsf 23*   **P** *Ch Patr Trust*   **P-in-c** P C POOLEY

CLAINES (St George w St Mary Magdalene)   *see* Worc St Geo w St Mary Magd *Worc*

CLAINES (St John the Baptist) *Worc 6*   **P** *Bp*   **P-in-c** J C MUSSON   **NSM** D P DAVIES

CLANDON, EAST (St Thomas of Canterbury) and WEST (St Peter and St Paul) *Guildf 5*   **P** *Earl of Onslow and Bp (alt)*   **R** B C R PERKINS

CLANFIELD (St James)   *see* Catherington and Clanfield *Portsm*

CLANFIELD (St Stephen)   *see* Bampton w Clanfield *Ox*

CLANNABOROUGH (St Petrock)   *see* N Creedy *Ex*

CLAPHAM (Christ Church) (St John the Evangelist) *S'wark 11*   **P** *Bp*   **V** P J ROSE-CASEMORE

CLAPHAM (Holy Spirit) *S'wark 11*   **P** *Bp*   **V** R A BURGE-THOMAS

CLAPHAM (Holy Trinity) *S'wark 11*   **P** *DBP*   **C** J R O WYNNE   **NSM** C A CLARKE

CLAPHAM (St James) *S'wark 12*   **P** *CPAS*   **P-in-c** N K GUNASEKERA   **Hon C** J MARSHALL

CLAPHAM (St Mary the Virgin)   *see* Findon w Clapham and Patching *Chich*

CLAPHAM (St Paul) *S'wark 11*   **P** *Bp*   **V** D L MATTHEWS

CLAPHAM (St Peter) *S'wark 11*   **P** *Bp*   **V** *vacant*

CLAPHAM (St Thomas of Canterbury) *St Alb 13*   **P** *MMCET*   **V** S J LILEY

CLAPHAM COMMON (St Barnabas) *S'wark 14*   **P** *Ch Trust Fund Trust*   **V** R G TAYLOR   **NSM** A F P COCKING

CLAPHAM PARK (All Saints) *S'wark 12*   **P** *CPAS*   **V** *vacant*

CLAPHAM PARK (St Stephen)   *see* Telford Park *S'wark*

CLAPHAM-WITH-KEASDEN (St James) and Austwick *Leeds 22*   **P** *Bp*   **V** I F GREENHALGH

CLAPTON (St James) *Lon 5*   **P** *Bp*   **V** R BROWN

CLAPTON (St James)   *see* Bourton-on-the-Water w Clapton etc *Glouc*

CLAPTON, UPPER (St Matthew) *Lon 5*   **P** *D&C Cant*   **P-in-c** W G CAMPBELL-TAYLOR   **NSM** S PADDOCK

CLARBOROUGH (St John the Baptist)   *see* Retford Area *S'well*

CLARE (St Peter and St Paul)   *see* Stour Valley *St E*

CLAREMOUNT (St Thomas the Apostle)   *see* Southowram and Claremount *Leeds*

CLARENCE GATE GARDENS (St Cyprian)   *see* St Marylebone St Cypr *Lon*

CLARENDON (Team Ministry) *Sarum 11*   **P** *Patr Bd*   **TR** N H S BERSWEDEN   **C** A C A THOMASSON-ROSINGH, S E WOOD-ROE   **Hon C** I M COWLEY   **NSM** F J DUNLOP

CLARENDON PARK (St John the Baptist)   *see* Emmaus Par Team *Leic*

CLATFORD, UPPER (All Saints)   *see* Abbotts Ann and Upper and Goodworth Clatford *Win*

CLATWORTHY (St Mary Magdalene)   *see* Wiveliscombe and the Hills *B & W*

CLAUGHTON VILLAGE (St Bede)   *see* Birkenhead St Jas w St Bede *Ches*

CLAVERDON (St Michael and All Angels) w Preston Bagot *Cov 7*   **P** *Bp*   **NSM** P A HANSON

CLAVERHAM (St Barnabas)   *see* Yatton Moor *B & W*

CLAVERING (St Mary and St Clement) w Langley, Arkesden, Wicken Bonhunt, Manuden and Berden *Chelmsf 21*   **P** *Ch Hosp and Keble Coll Ox (jt)*   **V** M A DAVIS

CLAVERLEY (All Saints) w Tuckhill *Heref 8*   **P** *Bp and E M A Thompson Esq (jt)*   **V** G W WARD

CLAVERTON (Blessed Virgin Mary)   *see* Bathampton w Claverton *B & W*

CLAWTON (St Leonard)   *see* Ashwater, Halwill, Beaworthy, Clawton etc *Ex*

CLAXBY (St Mary)   *see* Walesby *Linc*

CLAXTON (St Andrew)   *see* Rockland St Mary w Hellington, Bramerton etc *Nor*

CLAY CROSS (St Bartholomew)   *see* N Wingfield, Clay Cross and Pilsley *Derby*

CLAY HILL (St John the Baptist) (St Luke) *Lon 18*   **P** *V Enfield St Andr and Bp (jt)*   **V** R E M DOWLER

CLAYBROOKE (St Peter)   *see* Upper Soar *Leic*

CLAYDON (St James the Great)   *see* Shires' Edge *Ox*

CLAYDON and Barham *St E 1*   **P** *G R Drury Esq*   **NSM** J V ABLETT

CLAYDONS, The (St Mary) (All Saints) and Swan *Ox 13*   **P** *Patr Bd*   **TR** D A HISCOCK   **TV** W M CALLAN   **NSM** A MANN

CLAYGATE (Holy Trinity) *Guildf 8*   **P** *Ch Patr Trust*   **V** P J J PLYMING   **C** M J BARTON   **NSM** L M MORGAN, M R HARLE

CLAYHANGER (St Peter)   *see* Bampton, Morebath, Clayhanger, Petton etc *Ex*

CLAYHIDON (St Andrew)   *see* Hemyock w Culm Davy, Clayhidon and Culmstock *Ex*

CLAYPOLE (St Peter) *Linc 22*   **P** *DBP (2 turns), J R Thorold Esq (1 turn)*   **R** S P BARRON

CLAYTON (St Cross w St Paul)   *see* Man Clayton St Cross w St Paul *Man*

CLAYTON (St James the Great) *Lich 9*   **P** *Bp*   **V** N M EDWARDS   **NSM** S S GREENSMITH

CLAYTON (St John the Baptist) *Leeds 2*   **P** *V Bradf*   **V** V POLLARD

CLAYTON (St John the Baptist) w Keymer *Chich 8*   **P** *BNC Ox*   **R** C J POWELL   **NSM** T E CAMERON

CLAYTON BROOK (Community Church)   *see* Whittle-le-Woods *Blackb*

CLAYTON LE MOORS (All Saints)   *see* Altham w Clayton le Moors *Blackb*

CLAYTON WEST w HIGH HOYLAND (All Saints)   *see* High Hoyland, Scissett and Clayton W *Leeds*

CLAYWORTH (St Peter)   *see* Beckingham, Walkeringham, Misterton, W Stockwith, Clayworth and Gringley-on-the-Hill *S'well*

CLEADON (All Saints) *Dur 15*   **P** R *Whitburn*
P-in-c V J CUTHBERT

CLEADON PARK (St Mark and St Cuthbert) *Dur 15*   **P** *Bp*
V *vacant*

CLEARWELL (St Peter)   *see* Coleford, Staunton, Newland, Redbrook etc *Glouc*

CLEASBY (St Peter)   *see* E Richmond *Leeds*

CLEATOR (St Leonard)   *see* Crosslacon *Carl*

CLEATOR MOOR (St John) *as above*

CLECKHEATON (St John the Evangelist)   *see* Cleckheaton *Leeds*

CLECKHEATON (St Luke) *as above*

CLECKHEATON (St Luke) (St John the Evangelist) (Whitechapel) *Leeds 7*   **P** *Bp* and V *Birstall (jt)*
V B H G JAMES   **NSM** J C PARKES, R M CAVE

CLECKHEATON (Whitechapel)   *see* Cleckheaton *Leeds*

CLEDFORD (Mission Room)   *see* Middlewich w Byley *Ches*

CLEE HILL (St Peter)   *see* Tenbury *Heref*

CLEE ST MARGARET (St Margaret)   *see* Ludlow *Heref*

CLEE, NEW (St John the Evangelist) (St Stephen) *Linc 3*
P *Bp*   **NSM** A P TAPPIN   **OLM** K S JONES

CLEE, OLD (Holy Trinity and St Mary the Virgin) *Linc 3*
P *Bp*   **P-in-c** R G HOLDEN

CLEETHORPE (Christ Church)   *see* Clee *Linc*

CLEETHORPES (St Peter) *Linc 3*   **P** *Bp*   **R** P HUNTER
NSM D H WEBSTER

CLEETHORPES St Aidan *Linc 3*   **P** *Bp*   **P-in-c** R G HOLDEN

CLEETON (St Mary)   *see* Stottesdon w Farlow, Cleeton St Mary etc *Heref*

CLEEVE (Holy Trinity)   *see* Yatton Moor *B & W*

CLEEVE PRIOR (St Andrew) and The Littletons *Worc 1*
P *D&C and Ch Ch Ox (alt)*   **V** *vacant*

CLEEVE, OLD (St Andrew), Leighland and Treborough *B & W 15*   **P** *Selw Coll Cam (2 turns), Personal Reps G R Wolseley Esq (1 turn)*   **R** K J CROSS

CLEHONGER (All Saints)   *see* Cagebrook *Heref*

CLENCHWARTON (St Margaret) and West Lynn *Ely 14*
P *DBP*   **R** A J DAVEY

CLENT (St Leonard)   *see* Belbroughton w Fairfield and Clent *Worc*

CLEOBURY MORTIMER (St Mary the Virgin) w Hopton Wafers, Neen Sollars and Milson, Neen Savage w Kinlet and Doddington *Heref 11*   **P** *Patr Bd (2 turns), Ld Chan (1 turn)*
R W A BUCK   **C** R D MUTTER   **NSM** J T PARKER

CLEOBURY NORTH (St Peter and St Paul)   *see* Ditton Priors w Neenton, Burwarton etc *Heref*

CLERKENWELL (Our Most Holy Redeemer) *Lon 6*   **P** *Trustees*
V C P TRUNDLE   **NSM** A S MCGREGOR, P J BERNHARD

CLERKENWELL (St James and St John) (St Peter) *Lon 6*   **P** *Ch Patr Trust and PCC (jt)*   **V** A J BAUGHEN

CLERKENWELL (St Mark) *Lon 6*   **P** *City Corp*   **V** C P TRUNDLE
C A O J PYMBLE, J G HOBSON

CLEVEDON (St Andrew) (Christ Church) (St Peter) *B & W 12*
P *Simeon's Trustees (1 turn), Ld Chan (2 turns)*
P-in-c T R CRANSHAW   **C** C J JENNINGS, D L WILKIE

CLEVEDON (St John the Evangelist) *B & W 12*   **P** *SMF*
V *vacant*

CLEVEDON, EAST (All Saints) w Clapton in Gordano, Walton Clevedon, Walton in Gordano and Weston in Gordano *B & W 12*   **P** *Bp and SMF (jt)*   **R** N A HECTOR   **Hon**
C A I COOK   **NSM** J A ROBINSON

CLEVELEYS (St Andrew) *Blackb 12*   **P** *Trustees*   **V** B J WARD

CLEWER (St Andrew) *Ox 5*   **P** *Eton Coll*   **R** R WEBB
P-in-c R WEBB

CLEWER (St Stephen)   *see* New Windsor *Ox*

CLEY (St Margaret)   *see* Blakeney w Cley, Wiveton, Glandford etc *Nor*

CLEY HILL Villages, The *Sarum 12*   **P** *Bp and DBP (jt)*
P-in-c P A REID   **NSM** D J BRITTEN

CLIBURN (St Cuthbert)   *see* Morland, Thrimby, Gt Strickland and Cliburn *Carl*

CLIDDESDEN (St Leonard)   *see* Farleigh, Candover and Wield *Win*

CLIFFE (St Andrew)   *see* Riccall, Barlby and Hemingbrough *York*

CLIFFE AT HOO (St Helen) w Cooling *Roch 6*   **P** *D&C*
NSM J E WRIGHT

CLIFFE, SOUTH (St John)   *see* N Cave w Cliffe *York*

CLIFFORD (St Luke) *York 1*   **P** *G Lane-Fox Esq*
P-in-c K F A GABBADON

CLIFFORD (St Mary the Virgin)   *see* Cusop w Blakemere, Bredwardine w Brobury etc *Heref*

CLIFFORD CHAMBERS (St Helen)   *see* Stratford-upon-Avon, Luddington etc *Cov*

CLIFFORDS MESNE (St Peter)   *see* Newent and Gorsley w Cliffords Mesne *Glouc*

CLIFFSEND (St Mary the Virgin)   *see* St Laur in Thanet *Cant*

CLIFTON (All Saints w St John) *Bris 2*   **P** *Bp*   **V** C E SUTTON
NSM R DURBIN

CLIFTON (All Saints) and Southill *St Alb 8*   **P** *Bp and C E S Whitbread Esq (jt)*   **R** A M HINDLE   **NSM** C T TOPLEY

CLIFTON (Christ Church w Emmanuel) *Bris 2*   **P** *Simeon's Trustees*   **V** P J LANGHAM   **C** J N WALFORD, T J MEATHREL
NSM E C BEBB, L W CARR   **OLM** J LEE

CLIFTON (Holy Trinity) *Derby 8*   **P** *Mrs M F Stanton, T W Clowes Esq, and V Ashbourne (by turn)*   **P-in-c** G P POND
C C E MCDONALD   **NSM** P A SHORT

CLIFTON (Holy Trinity) (St Francis) (St Mary the Virgin) *S'well 6*   **P** *DBP*   **TV** A V NOBLE   **C** M ORR, R H DAVEY

CLIFTON (Holy Trinity, St Andrew the Less and St Peter) *Bris 3*
P *Simeon's Trustees*   **P-in-c** L BARNES   **NSM** R CROFT
OLM F M HOUGHTON, J D A BROOKE-TAYLOR

CLIFTON (Mission Church)   *see* Conisbrough *Sheff*

CLIFTON (St Anne) (St Thomas) *Man 18*   **P** *Bp*
V C D BOLSTER   **NSM** A P GORDON

CLIFTON (St Cuthbert)   *see* Lowther and Askham and Clifton and Brougham *Carl*

CLIFTON (St George)   *see* E Trent *S'well*

CLIFTON (St James) *Sheff 6*   **P** *Bp*   **V** A L THOMPSON
C P D MELLARS

CLIFTON (St John the Evangelist)   *see* Lund *Blackb*

CLIFTON (St John the Evangelist)   *see* Brighouse and Clifton *Leeds*

CLIFTON (St Luke), Dean and Mosser *Carl 6*   **P** *Patr Bd*
P-in-c S SARVANANTHAN

CLIFTON (St Paul)   *see* Cotham St Sav w St Mary and Clifton St Paul *Bris*

CLIFTON (St Philip and St James) *York 7*   **P** *Trustees*
V D O CASSWELL   **C** P M HALLSWORTH

CLIFTON CAMPVILLE (St Andrew)   *see* Mease Valley *Lich*

CLIFTON HAMPDEN (St Michael and All Angels)
see Dorchester *Ox*

CLIFTON REYNES (St Mary the Virgin)   *see* Lavendon w Cold Brayfield, Clifton Reynes etc *Ox*

CLIFTON UPON DUNSMORE (St Mary) w Newton and Brownsover *Cov 6*   **P** *Bp and H A F W Boughton-Leigh Esq (jt)*
V T A DAVIS   **OLM** D J BUSSEY

CLIFTON-ON-TEME (St Kenelm)   *see* Worcs W *Worc*

CLIFTONVILLE (St Paul) *Cant 5*   **P** *Ch Patr Trust*
V P L S ELLISDON   **NSM** N H B RATCLIFFE

CLIPPESBY (St Peter)   *see* Martham and Repps w Bastwick, Thurne etc *Nor*

CLIPSHAM (St Mary)   *see* Cottesmore and Burley, Clipsham, Exton etc *Pet*

CLIPSTON (All Saints) w Naseby and Haselbech w Kelmarsh *Pet 2*   **P** *Ch Coll Cam, DBP, Mrs M F Harris, Exors Miss C V Lancaster (by turn)*   **P-in-c** A M HUGHES

CLIPSTONE (All Saints) *S'well 2*   **P** *Bp*   **P-in-c** A N EVANS
C E L HOLLIDAY   **NSM** H M ENGLISH

CLITHEROE (St James) *Blackb 7*   **P** *Trustees*
R M W L PICKETT   **C** A S GRAY

CLITHEROE (St Mary Magdalene) *Blackb 7*   **P** *J R Peel Esq*
V A W FROUD   **C** A P WHITEHEAD

CLITHEROE (St Paul) Low Moor *Blackb 7*   **P** *Bp*
P-in-c M W L PICKETT

CLIVE (All Saints)   *see* Astley, Clive, Grinshill and Hadnall *Lich*

CLODOCK (St Clydog) and Longtown w Craswall, Llanveynoe, St Margaret's, Michaelchurch Escley and Newton *Heref 1*   **P** *DBP (2 turns), MMCET (1 turn)*
V N G LOWTON

CLOFORD (St Mary)   *see* Nunney and Witham Friary, Marston Bigot etc *B & W*

CLOPHILL (St Mary the Virgin)   *see* Campton, Clophill and Haynes *St Alb*

CLOPTON (St Mary)   *see* Carlford *St E*

CLOPTON (St Peter)   *see* Aldwincle, Clopton, Pilton, Stoke Doyle etc *Pet*

CLOSWORTH (All Saints)   *see* Coker Ridge *B & W*

CLOTHALL (St Mary the Virgin), Rushden, Sandon, Wallington and Weston *St Alb 16*   **P** *Duchy of Lanc (1 turn), Bp, Marquess of Salisbury, and J A Cherry (4 turns)*
R F K WHEATLEY   **C** M FANE DE SALIS

CLOUGHTON (St Mary) and Burniston *York 15*   **P** *Abp*
V M J LEIGH   **NSM** D C PYNN, D MACIVER

CLOVELLY (All Saints)   *see* Parkham, Alwington, Buckland Brewer etc *Ex*

CLOVELLY (St Peter) *as above*

CLOWNE (St John the Baptist)   *see* Barlborough and Clowne *Derby*

CLOWS TOP (Mission Room)   *see* Mamble w Bayton, Rock w Heightington etc *Worc*

CLUBMOOR (St Andrew) *Liv 8*   **P** *Bp*   **V** S MCGANITY   **C** D M OWENS   **OLM** S J JAMIESON

CLUMBER PARK (St Mary the Virgin)   *see* Worksop Priory *S'well*

CLUN (St George)   *see* Clun Valley *Heref*

CLUN VALLEY Benefice, The *Heref 9*   **P** *Earl of Powis (5 turns), Earl of Powis and Mrs R E Bell (1 turn)*   **V** *vacant*

CLUNBURY (St Swithin)   *see* Clun Valley *Heref*

CLUNGUNFORD (St Cuthbert)   *see* Middle Marches *Heref*

CLUNTON (St Mary)   *see* Clun Valley *Heref*

CLUTTON (St Augustine of Hippo) w Cameley, Bishop Sutton and Stowey *B & W 9*   **P** *Bp, DBP, and Exors J P Hippisley Esq (jt)*   **R** M CREGAN

CLYFFE PYPARD (St Peter)   *see* Woodhill *Sarum*

CLYMPING (St Mary the Virgin) and Yapton w Ford *Chich 1*   **P** *Bp (2 turns), Ld Chan (1 turn)*   **R** R H HAYES   **NSM** P G SWADLING

CLYST HONITON (St Michael and All Angels)   *see* Broadclyst, Clyst Honiton, Pinhoe, Rockbeare etc *Ex*

CLYST HYDON (St Andrew)   *see* Bradninch and Clyst Hydon *Ex*

CLYST ST GEORGE (St George)   *see* Aylesbeare, Clyst St George, Clyst St Mary etc *Ex*

CLYST ST LAWRENCE (St Lawrence)   *see* Whimple, Talaton and Clyst St Lawr *Ex*

CLYST ST MARY (St Mary)   *see* Aylesbeare, Clyst St George, Clyst St Mary etc *Ex*

COALBROOKDALE (Holy Trinity), Iron-Bridge and Little Wenlock *Heref 13*   **P** *Bp, Lord Forester, V Madeley, and V Much Wenlock (jt)*   **P-in-c** I S NAYLOR   **NSM** J M EDWARDS, P M JORDAN

COALEY (St Bartholomew)   *see* Lower Cam w Coaley *Glouc*

COALPIT HEATH (St Saviour) *Bris 5*   **P** *Bp*   **V** C P LUNT

COALVILLE (Christ Church) w Bardon Hill and Ravenstone *Leic 8*   **P** *Simeon's Trustees and R Hugglescote (2 turns), Ld Chan (1 turn)*   **V** M J T JOSS

COATES (Holy Trinity)   *see* Whittlesey, Pondersbridge and Coates *Ely*

COATES (St Edith)   *see* Stow Gp *Linc*

COATES (St Matthew)   *see* Kemble, Poole Keynes, Somerford Keynes etc *Glouc*

COATES, GREAT (St Nicholas) and LITTLE (Bishop Edward King Church) (St Michael) w Bradley *Linc 3*   **P** *Patr Bd*   **TR** P M MULLINS   **TV** D M MCCORMICK   **C** J A BARROW   **Hon C** A I MCCORMICK

COATES, NORTH (St Nicholas)   *see* Holton-le-Clay, Tetney and N Cotes *Linc*

COATHAM (Christ Church) and Dormanstown *York 16*   **P** *Trustees*   **V** R M HAUGHTY

COBBOLD ROAD (St Saviour) w St Mary *Lon 9*   **P** *Bp*   **P-in-c** C J B LEE   **NSM** P P Y MULLINGS

COBERLEY (St Giles)   *see* Churn Valley *Glouc*

COBHAM (St Andrew) (St John the Divine) and Stoke D'Abernon *Guildf 10*   **P** D C H Combe Esq and K Coll Cam (jt)   **R** E R JENKINS   **C** F O OLOKOSE, R G HILLIARD   **NSM** C HOLLINGTON   **OLM** R PITTARIDES

COBHAM (St Mary Magdalene) w Luddesdowne and Dode *Roch 1*   **P** *Earl of Darnley and CPAS (alt)*   **P-in-c** A J WALKER

COBHAM Sole Street (St Mary's Church Room)   *see* Cobham w Luddesdowne and Dode *Roch*

COBRIDGE (Christ Church)   *see* Hanley H Ev *Lich*

COCKAYNE HATLEY (St John the Baptist)   *see* Potton w Sutton and Cockayne Hatley *St Alb*

COCKERHAM (St Michael) w Winmarleigh St Luke and Glasson Christ Church *Blackb 11*   **P** *Bp (2 turns), Trustees (1 turn)*   **V** G LEWIS

COCKERINGTON, SOUTH (St Leonard)   *see* Mid Marsh Gp *Linc*

COCKERMOUTH AREA Team, The (All Saints) (Christ Church) *Carl 6*   **P** *Patr Bd*   **TR** G J BUTLAND   **TV** A D THOMPSON

COCKERNHOE (St Hugh)   *see* Luton St Fran *St Alb*

COCKERTON (St Mary) *Dur 8*   **P** *Bp*   **V** D J BAGE   **C** K G MCNEIL

COCKFIELD (St Mary) *Dur 7*   **P** *Bp*   **C** C A GIBBS

COCKFIELD (St Peter)   *see* Bradfield St Clare, Bradfield St George etc *St E*

COCKFOSTERS (Christ Church) Trent Park   *see* Enfield Ch Ch Trent Park *Lon*

COCKING (not known) w West Lavington, Bepton and Heyshott *Chich 3*   **P** *Ld Chan, and Bp, Cowdray Trust and Rathbone Trust (alt)*   **R** L M ROBERTSON

COCKINGTON (St George and St Mary) (St Matthew) *Ex 11*   **P** *Bp*   **NSM** P D EVANS

COCKLEY CLEY (All Saints) w Gooderstone *Nor 13*   **P** *Bp*   **P-in-c** C P SHERLOCK

COCKSHUTT (St Simon and St Jude)   *see* Petton w Cockshutt, Welshampton and Lyneal etc *Lich*

COCKYARD (Church Hall)   *see* Chapel-en-le-Frith *Derby*

CODDENHAM (St Mary) w Gosbeck and Hemingstone w Henley *St E 1*   **P** *Pemb Coll Cam (2 turns), Lord de Saumarez (1 turn)*   **P-in-c** P J PAYNE   **NSM** C B AUSTIN, H NORRIS

CODDINGTON (All Saints)   *see* Colwall w Upper Colwall and Coddington *Heref*

CODDINGTON (All Saints)   *see* Newark w Coddington *S'well*

CODDINGTON (St Mary)   *see* Farndon and Coddington *Ches*

CODFORD (St Mary)   *see* Upper Wylye Valley *Sarum*

CODFORD (St Peter) *as above*

CODICOTE (St Giles) *St Alb 18*   **P** *Abp*   **V** *vacant*

CODNOR (St James) *Derby 12*   **P** *The Crown*   **P-in-c** A TAYLOR-COOK   **OLM** C C HOLDEN, M D JONES

CODSALL (St Nicholas) *Lich 2*   **P** *Bp and Lady Wrottesley (jt)*   **V** S C WITCOMBE   **C** E A ENGLAND   **NSM** M A O FOX   **OLM** C J LINTERN

CODSALL WOOD (St Peter)   *see* Codsall *Lich*

COFFINSWELL (St Bartholomew)   *see* Kingskerswell w Coffinswell *Ex*

COFTON (St Mary)   *see* Dawlish, Cofton and Starcross *Ex*

COFTON HACKETT (St Michael) w Barnt Green *Birm 4*   **P** *Bp*   **V** R S FIELDSON

COGENHOE (St Peter) and Great Houghton and Little Houghton w Brafield on the Green *Pet 6*   **P** C G V Davidge Esq, Mrs A C Usher, Magd Coll Ox, and DBP (jt)   **R** E G SMITH

COGGES (St Mary) and South Leigh *Ox 28*   **P** *Bp and Payne Trustees (jt)*   **V** S T KIRBY   **C** M I G DIXON   **NSM** N K PIKE

COGGESHALL (St Peter ad Vincula) w Markshall *Chelmsf 17*   **P** *Bp (2 turns), SMF (1 turn)*   **P-in-c** C M DAVEY   **NSM** K M KING, N F TOZER

COGGESHALL, LITTLE (St Nicholas)   *see* Coggeshall w Markshall *Chelmsf*

COKER RIDGE, The *B & W 6*   **P** *D&C Ex, MMCET, Ox Chs Trust, and DBP (jt)*   **R** *vacant*

COKER, EAST (St Michael and All Angels)   *see* Coker Ridge *B & W*

COKER, WEST (St Martin of Tours) *as above*

COLATON RALEIGH (St John the Baptist)   *see* Ottery St Mary, Alfington, W Hill, Tipton etc *Ex*

COLBURN (St Cuthbert)   *see* Hipswell *Leeds*

COLBURY (Christ Church) *Win 11*   **P** *Bp*   **P-in-c** P R HOLLEY

COLBY (St Giles)   *see* King's Beck *Nor*

COLCHESTER (Christ Church w St Mary at the Walls) *Chelmsf 21*   **P** *Bp*   **R** P R NORRINGTON

COLCHESTER (St Anne)   *see* Greenstead w Colchester St Anne *Chelmsf*

COLCHESTER (St Barnabas) Old Heath *Chelmsf 21*   **P** *Bp*   **V** R E TILLBROOK

COLCHESTER (St James) and St Paul w All Saints, St Nicholas and St Runwald *Chelmsf 21*   **P** *Bp*   **R** P S WALKER

COLCHESTER (St John the Evangelist) *Chelmsf 21*   **P** *Adn Colchester*   **P-in-c** A J SACHS   **C** H PATTON   **Hon C** P H ADAMS

COLCHESTER (St Luke) *Chelmsf 21*   **P** *Adn Colchester*   **V** J A NOLES   **NSM** S G NOLES

COLCHESTER (St Michael) Myland *Chelmsf 21*   **P** *Ball Coll Ox*   **P-in-c** R G GIBBS   **NSM** J CHANDLER

COLCHESTER (St Peter) (St Botolph) *Chelmsf 21*   **P** *Bp and Simeon's Trustees (jt)*   **P-in-c** M D WALLACE   **C** A R F B GAGE

COLCHESTER (St Stephen)   *see* Colchester, New Town and The Hythe *Chelmsf*

COLCHESTER, New Town and The Hythe (St Stephen, St Mary Magdalen and St Leonard) *Chelmsf 21*   **R** I A HILTON   **C** H R COOPER

COLD ASH (St Mark)   *see* Hermitage *Ox*

COLD ASHBY (St Denys)   *see* Guilsborough and Hollowell and Cold Ashby etc *Pet*

COLD ASHTON (Holy Trinity)   *see* Marshfield w Cold Ashton and Tormarton etc *Bris*

COLD ASTON (St Andrew)   *see* Northleach w Hampnett and Farmington etc *Glouc*

COLD BRAYFIELD (St Mary)   *see* Lavendon w Cold Brayfield, Clifton Reynes etc *Ox*

COLD HIGHAM (St Luke)   *see* Pattishall w Cold Higham and Gayton w Tiffield *Pet*

COLD KIRBY (St Michael)   *see* Upper Ryedale *York*

COLD NORTON (St Stephen) w Stow Maries *Chelmsf 11*   **P** *Bp and Charterhouse (jt)*   **V** S E MANLEY

COLD OVERTON (St John the Baptist)   *see* Whatborough Gp *Leic*

COLD SALPERTON (All Saints)   *see* Sevenhampton w Charlton Abbots, Hawling etc *Glouc*

COLDEAN (St Mary Magdalene)   *see* Moulsecoomb *Chich*
COLDEN COMMON (Holy Trinity)   *see* Twyford and Owslebury and Morestead etc *Win*
COLDHARBOUR (Christ Church)   *see* Abinger and Coldharbour and Wotton and Holmbury St Mary *Guildf*
COLDHARBOUR (St Alban Mission Church)   *see* Mottingham St Andr w St Alban *S'wark*
COLDHURST (Holy Trinity) and Oldham St Stephen and All Martyrs *Man 16*   **P** *Patr Bd*   **V** N G SMEETON   **NSM** I C BROCKLEHURST, S M O'FLAHERTY
COLDRED (St Pancras)   *see* Bewsborough *Cant*
COLDRIDGE (St Matthew)   *see* N Creedy *Ex*
COLDWALTHAM (St Giles)   *see* Bury w Houghton and Coldwaltham and Hardham *Chich*
COLEBROOKE (St Andrew) *Ex 2*   **P** *D&C*   **V** *vacant*
COLEBY (All Saints)   *see* Graffoe Gp *Linc*
COLEFORD (Holy Trinity) w Holcombe *B & W 11*   **P** *Bp and* V *Kilmersdon (jt)*   **NSM** C R D CRIDLAND
COLEFORD (St John the Evangelist), Staunton, Newland, Redbrook and Clearwell *Glouc 1*   **P** *Bp*   **V** S BICK   **C** A W WEARMOUTH   **NSM** M M HALE
COLEHILL (St Michael and All Angels) *Sarum 9*   **P** *Governors of Wimborne Minster*   **V** S M PATTLE   **OLM** L L MCGREGOR
COLEMAN'S HATCH (Holy Trinity)   *see* Hartfield w Coleman's Hatch *Chich*
COLEORTON (St Mary the Virgin)   *see* Ashby-de-la-Zouch and Breedon on the Hill *Leic*
COLERNE (St John the Baptist) w North Wraxall *Bris 4*   **P** *New Coll and Oriel Coll Ox (alt)*   **C** J M ANDERSON-MACKENZIE, J M PHILPOTT   **NSM** A M E KEMP   **OLM** C M SOUTHGATE, G E PARKIN
COLESBOURNE (St James)   *see* Churn Valley *Glouc*
COLESHILL (All Saints)   *see* Amersham *Ox*
COLESHILL (All Saints)   *see* Gt Coxwell w Buscot, Coleshill etc *Ox*
COLESHILL (St Peter and St Paul) *Birm 9*   **P** J K Wingfield Digby Esq   **V** R N PARKER   **C** R L STEPHENS
COLEY (St John the Baptist) *Leeds 8*   **P** V Halifax   **P-in-c** J T ALLISON
COLGATE (St Saviour)   *see* Rusper w Colgate *Chich*
COLINDALE (St Matthias) *Lon 15*   **P** *Bp*   **P-in-c** J E I HAWKINS
COLKIRK (St Mary)   *see* Upper Wensum Village Gp *Nor*
COLLATON (St Mary the Virgin)   *see* Goodrington and Collaton St Mary *Ex*
COLLIER ROW (Ascension)   *see* Romford Ascension Collier Row *Chelmsf*
COLLIER ROW (Good Shepherd)   *see* Romford Gd Shep *Chelmsf*
COLLIER ROW (St James) and Havering-atte-Bower *Chelmsf 2*   **P** *CPAS and Bp (jt)*   **C** A T POULTNEY   **NSM** D J STAINER
COLLIER STREET (St Margaret)   *see* Yalding w Collier Street *Roch*
COLLIERLEY (St Thomas) w Annfield Plain *Dur 4*   **P** *Bp and The Crown (alt)*   **P-in-c** H MURRAY
COLLIERS END (St Mary)   *see* High Cross *St Alb*
COLLIERS WOOD (Christ Church)   *see* Merton Priory *S'wark*
COLLINGBOURNE DUCIS (St Andrew)   *see* Savernake *Sarum*
COLLINGBOURNE KINGSTON (St Mary)   *as above*
COLLINGHAM (All Saints)   *see* E Trent *S'well*
COLLINGHAM (St John the Baptist)   *as above*
COLLINGHAM (St Oswald) w Harewood *Leeds 23*   **P** *Earl of Harewood and G H H Wheler Esq (jt)*   **P-in-c** S EARLE
COLLINGTON (St Mary)   *see* Bredenbury *Heref*
COLLINGTREE (St Columba)   *see* Salcey *Pet*
COLLYHURST (The Saviour) *Man 4*   **P** *Bp and Trustees (jt)*   **P-in-c** C FALLONE   **OLM** M B ROGERS
COLLYWESTON (St Andrew)   *see* Ketton, Collyweston, Easton-on-the-Hill etc *Pet*
COLMWORTH (St Denys)   *see* Wilden w Colmworth and Ravensden *St Alb*
COLN ROGERS (St Andrew)   *see* Chedworth, Yanworth and Stowell, Coln Rogers etc *Glouc*
COLN ST ALDWYN (St John the Baptist)   *see* S Cotswolds *Glouc*
COLN ST DENYS (St James the Great)   *see* Chedworth, Yanworth and Stowell, Coln Rogers etc *Glouc*
COLNBROOK (St Thomas) and Datchet *Ox 12*   **P** *Bp and D&C Windsor (jt)*   **V** P J WYARD   **C** R J COSH
COLNE (Christ Church)   *see* Foulridge, Laneshawbridge and Trawden *Blackb*
COLNE (Holy Trinity) (St Bartholomew) *Blackb 6*   **P** *Bp and DBP*   **R** L E SENIOR   **NSM** C A BRAITHWAITE
COLNE (St Helen)   *see* Bluntisham cum Earith w Colne and Holywell etc *Ely*
COLNE ENGAINE (St Andrew)   *see* Halstead Area *Chelmsf*

COLNE, THE UPPER, Parishes of Great Yeldham, Little Yeldham, Stambourne, Tilbury-juxta-Clare and Toppesfield *Chelmsf 19*   **P** *Prime Min, Ld Chan, Bp, Duchy of Lancaster, and Trustees of the late Miss W M N Brett (by turn)*   **P-in-c** B C HUME
COLNEY (St Andrew)   *see* Cringleford and Colney *Nor*
COLNEY (St Peter)   *see* London Colney St Pet *St Alb*
COLNEY HEATH (St Mark) *St Alb 5*   **P** *Trustees*   **V** G P TRACEY   **NSM** J SUTTIE
COLSTERWORTH Group, The (St John the Baptist) *Linc 17*   **P** *Bp (2 turns), Mrs R S McCorquodale and J R Thorold Esq (1 turn)*   **P-in-c** E J LOMAX
COLSTON BASSETT (St John the Divine)   *see* Cropwell Bishop w Colston Bassett, Granby etc *S'well*
COLTISHALL (St John the Baptist) w Great Hautbois, Frettenham, Hainford, Horstead and Stratton Strawless *Nor 19*   **P** *D&C, Bp, K Coll Cam, and Ch Soc Trust (jt)*   **R** C J ENGELSEN   **OLM** K A DIGNUM
COLTON (Holy Trinity)   *see* Egton-cum-Newland and Lowick and Colton *Carl*
COLTON (St Andrew)   *see* Easton, Colton, Marlingford and Bawburgh *Nor*
COLTON (St Mary the Virgin)   *see* Abbots Bromley, Blithfield, Colton, Colwich etc *Lich*
COLTON (St Paul)   *see* Bolton Percy *York*
COLWALL (St Crispin's Chapel) (St James the Great) w Upper Colwall (Good Shepherd) and Coddington *Heref 5*   **P** *Bp*   **R** M J HORTON   **NSM** A C LANYON-HOGG
COLWICH (St Michael and All Angels)   *see* Abbots Bromley, Blithfield, Colton, Colwich etc *Lich*
COLWICK (St John the Baptist) *S'well 7*   **P** *DBP*   **P-in-c** A H DIGMAN
COLYFORD (St Michael)   *see* Colyton, Musbury, Southleigh and Branscombe *Ex*
COLYTON (St Andrew), Musbury, Southleigh and Branscombe *Ex 4*   **P** *D&C*   **P-in-c** H DAWSON   **C** A E FUTCHER
COMBE (St Swithin)   *see* Walbury Beacon *Ox*
COMBE DOWN (Holy Trinity) (St Andrew) w Monkton Combe and South Stoke *B & W 8*   **P** R Bath, Ox Chs Trust, and Comdr H R Salmer (jt)   **P-in-c** P H KENCHINGTON   **C** S E BUDDLE
COMBE FLOREY (St Peter and St Paul)   *see* Bishop's Lydeard w Lydeard St Lawrence etc *B & W*
COMBE HAY (not known)   *see* Bath Odd Down w Combe Hay *B & W*
COMBE LONGA (St Laurence)   *see* Stonesfield w Combe Longa *Ox*
COMBE MARTIN (St Peter ad Vincula), Berrynarbor, Lynton, Brendon, Countisbury, Parracombe, Martinhoe and Trentishoe *Ex 17*   **P** *Patr Bd*   **TR** *vacant*
COMBE PYNE (St Mary the Virgin)   *see* Axminster, Chardstock, All Saints etc *Ex*
COMBE RALEIGH (St Nicholas)   *see* Honiton, Gittisham, Combe Raleigh, Monkton etc *Ex*
COMBE ST NICHOLAS (St Nicholas)   *see* Chard St Mary w Combe St Nicholas, Wambrook etc *B & W*
COMBEINTEIGNHEAD (All Saints)   *see* Shaldon, Stokeinteignhead, Combeinteignhead etc *Ex*
COMBERFORD (St Mary and St George)   *see* Wigginton *Lich*
COMBERTON (St Mary)   *see* Lordsbridge *Ely*
COMBERTON, GREAT (St Michael)   *see* Elmley Castle w Bricklehampton and Combertons *Worc*
COMBERTON, LITTLE (St Peter)   *as above*
COMBROOK (St Mary and St Margaret)   *see* Edgehill Churches *Cov*
COMBS (St Mary) and Little Finborough *St E 6*   **P** *Bp and Pemb Coll Ox (jt)*   **P-in-c** C CHILDS   **NSM** R CORNISH
COMBWICH (St Peter)   *see* Cannington, Otterhampton, Combwich and Stockland *B & W*
COMER GARDENS (St David)   *see* Worc St Clem and Lower Broadheath *Worc*
COMMONDALE (St Peter)   *see* Danby w Castleton and Commondale *York*
COMPTON (All Saints), Hursley, and Otterbourne *Win 7*   **P** *Bp, Mrs P M A T Chamberlayne-Macdonald, and Lord Lifford (jt)*   **R** W A PRESCOTT
COMPTON (St Mary and St Nicholas)   *see* Hermitage *Ox*
COMPTON (St Mary)   *see* Octagon *Chich*
COMPTON (St Mary)   *see* Farnham *Guildf*
COMPTON (St Nicholas) w Shackleford and Peper Harow *Guildf 4*   **P** *Bp and Major J R More-Molyneux (jt)*   **P-in-c** C N BURNETT
COMPTON ABBAS (St Mary the Virgin)   *see* Shaftesbury *Sarum*
COMPTON ABDALE (St Oswald)   *see* Northleach w Hampnett and Farmington etc *Glouc*

COMPTON BASSETT (St Swithin) see Oldbury *Sarum*

COMPTON BEAUCHAMP (St Swithun) see Shrivenham and Ashbury *Ox*

COMPTON BISHOP (St Andrew) see Crook Peak *B & W*

COMPTON CHAMBERLAYNE (St Michael) see Nadder Valley *Sarum*

COMPTON DANDO (Blessed Virgin Mary) see Publow w Pensford, Compton Dando and Chelwood *B & W*

COMPTON DUNDON (St Andrew) see Somerton w Compton Dundon, the Charltons etc *B & W*

COMPTON GREENFIELD (All Saints) see Pilning w Compton Greenfield *Bris*

COMPTON MARTIN (St Michael) see Blagdon w Compton Martin and Ubley *B & W*

COMPTON PAUNCEFOOT (Blessed Virgin Mary) see Camelot Par *B & W*

COMPTON VALENCE (St Thomas à Beckett) see Dorchester and the Winterbournes *Sarum*

COMPTON, LITTLE (St Denys) see Chipping Norton *Ox*

COMPTON, NETHER (St Nicholas) see Queen Thorne *Sarum*

COMPTON, OVER (St Michael) *as above*

CONDICOTE (St Nicholas) see Stow on the Wold, Condicote and The Swells *Glouc*

CONDOVER (St Andrew and St Mary) w Frodesley, Acton Burnell and Pitchford *Heref 10*   P *Bp, Revd E W Serjeantson, and Mrs C R Colthurst (jt)*   R *G D GARRETT*
NSM *M G GILLIONS*

CONEY HILL (St Oswald) *Glouc 2*   P *The Crown*   V *vacant*

CONEY WESTON (St Mary) see Stanton, Hopton, Market Weston, Barningham etc *St E*

CONEYSTHORPE (Chapel) see The Street Par *York*

CONGERSTONE (St Mary the Virgin) see Bosworth and Sheepy Gp *Leic*

CONGHAM (St Andrew) see Ashwicken w Leziate, Bawsey etc *Nor*

CONGLETON (St James) *Ches 11*   P *Bp*   V *C J SANDERSON*

CONGLETON (St John the Evangelist) (St Peter) (St Stephen) *Ches 11*   P *Patr Bd*   TR *D TAYLOR*
TV *P M WITHINGTON*

CONGRESBURY (St Andrew) w Puxton and Hewish St Ann *B & W 10*   P *MMCET*   V *M J THOMSON*   C *J E S BILLETT*

CONINGSBY (St Michael) see Bain Valley Gp *Linc*

CONINGTON (St Mary) see Fen Drayton w Conington and Lolworth etc *Ely*

CONISBROUGH (St Peter) *Sheff 9*   P *Bp*   P-in-c *M MUGGE*

CONISCLIFFE (St Edwin) *Dur 8*   P *Bp*   V *D J RAILTON*
NSM *D V ROBINSON*

CONISHOLME (St Peter) see Somercotes and Grainthorpe w Conisholme *Linc*

CONISTON (St Andrew) and Torver *Carl 9*   P *Peache Trustees*
R *T J HARMER*

CONISTON COLD (St Peter) see Gargrave w Coniston Cold *Leeds*

CONISTONE (St Mary) see Kettlewell w Conistone, Hubberholme etc *Leeds*

CONONLEY (St John the Evangelist) w Bradley *Leeds 5*
P *Bp*   V *J C PEET*

CONSETT (Christ Church) *Dur 4*   P *Bp*   P-in-c *V SHEDDEN*

CONSTABLE LEE (St Paul) *Man 11*   P *CPAS*
NSM *J A BARRATT*

CONSTANTINE (St Constantine) *Truro 4*   P *D&C*
P-in-c *S G TURNER*   NSM *T A AXE*

COOKBURY (St John the Baptist and the Seven Maccabes) see Black Torrington, Bradford w Cookbury etc *Ex*

COOKHAMS, The (Holy Trinity) (St John the Baptist) *Ox 5*
P *Mrs E U Rogers*   V *N PLANT*   C *H CHAMBERLAIN*
OLM *D JOYNES, J E ELLINGTON*

COOKHILL (St Paul) see Inkberrow w Cookhill and Kington w Dormston *Worc*

COOKLEY (St Michael and All Angels) see Heveningham *St E*

COOKLEY (St Peter) see Kidderminster Ismere *Worc*

COOKRIDGE (Holy Trinity) *Leeds 16*   P *R Adel*
V *J F HAMILTON*

COOMBE (Christ Church) see New Malden and Coombe *S'wark*

COOMBE BISSET (St Michael and All Angels) see Chalke Valley *Sarum*

COOMBES (not known) see Lancing w Coombes *Chich*

COOPERSALE (St Alban) see Epping Distr *Chelmsf*

COPDOCK (St Peter) see Sproughton w Burstall, Copdock w Washbrook etc *St E*

COPFORD (St Michael and All Angels) see Thurstable and Winstree *Chelmsf*

COPGROVE (St Michael) see Walkingham Hill *Leeds*

COPLE (All Saints), Moggerhanger and Willington *St Alb 10*
P *Bp (2 turns), Ch Ch Ox (1 turn)*   V *F R GIBSON*

COPLOW Benefice, The *Leic 3*   P *Bp*   V *A S W BOOKER*
C *F A J SMITH*

COPMANTHORPE (St Giles) *York 1*   P *R York St Clement w St Mary Bishophill*   V *G R MUMFORD*

COPNOR (St Alban) see Portsea St Alb *Portsm*

COPNOR (St Cuthbert) see Portsea St Cuth *Portsm*

COPP (St Anne) w Inskip *Blackb 9*   P *V Garstang St Helen and St Michaels-on-Wyre*   V *A C HOWARD*

COPPENHALL (All Saints and St Paul) see Crewe All SS and St Paul w St Pet *Ches*

COPPENHALL (St Laurence) see Penkridge *Lich*

COPPENHALL (St Michael) *Ches 15*   P *Bp*   R *C H RAZZALL*

COPPULL (not known) *Blackb 4*   P *R Standish*   V *J HUDSON*

COPPULL (St John) *Blackb 4*   P *R Standish*   R *J HUDSON*

COPSTON MAGNA (St John) see Wolvey w Burton Hastings, Copston Magna etc *Cov*

COPT OAK (St Peter) see Markfield, Thornton, Bagworth and Stanton etc *Leic*

COPTHORNE (St John the Evangelist) *Chich 6*   P *Bp*
V *S G HILL*

COPYTHORNE (St Mary) *Win 11*   P *Bp Liv*   P-in-c *J R REEVE*

COQUETDALE, UPPER *Newc 6*   P *Duchy of Lanc (2 turns), Ld Chan (1 turn), and Duke of Northumberland (1 turn)*
R *M J BOAG*   NSM *S D JOYNER*   OLM *C R STACY*

CORBRIDGE (St Andrew) w Halton and Newton Hall *Newc 9*
P *D&C Carl*   V *D B HEWLETT*   NSM *J ROBSON*

CORBY (Epiphany) (St John the Baptist) *Pet 7*   P *E Brudenell Esq*   P-in-c *P W FROST*   C *A SILLEY*

CORBY (St Columba and the Northern Saints) *Pet 7*   P *Bp*
V *I A PULLINGER*   C *N J WHITE*

CORBY (St Peter and St Andrew) (Kingswood Church) *Pet 7*
P *Bp*   V *vacant*

CORBY GLEN (St John the Evangelist) *Linc 17*   P *Ld Chan (2 turns), Sir Simon Benton Jones Bt (1 turn)*
P-in-c *S L BUCKMAN*

CORELEY (St Peter) see Tenbury *Heref*

CORFE (St Nicholas) see Blackdown *B & W*

CORFE CASTLE (St Edward the Martyr), Church Knowle, Kimmeridge Steeple w Tyneham *Sarum 8*   P *Major M J A Bond, Nat Trust, and Bp (jt)*   R *I JACKSON*   NSM *S A BOND*

CORFE MULLEN (St Hubert) *Sarum 9*   P *Bp*   R *P S WALKER*
NSM *S RICHARDS*

CORHAMPTON (not known) see Meon Bridge *Portsm*

CORLEY (not known) see Fillongley and Corley *Cov*

CORNARD, GREAT (St Andrew) *St E 12*   P *Bp*   V *C J RAMSEY*

CORNARD, LITTLE (All Saints) see Bures w Assington and Lt Cornard *St E*

CORNELLY (St Cornelius) see Tregony w St Cuby and Cornelly *Truro*

CORNERSTONE TEAM, THE *Leic 4*   P *Patr Bd*
TR *J M BARRETT*   TV *R A MILES*   NSM *H M BENCE*

CORNEY (St John the Baptist) see Bootle, Corney, Whicham and Whitbeck *Carl*

CORNFORTH (Holy Trinity) and Ferryhill *Dur 5*   P *D&C (2 turns), Bp (1 turn)*   V *vacant*

CORNHILL (St Helen) w Carham *Newc 12*   P *Abp (2 turns), E M Straker-Smith Esq (1 turn)*   P-in-c *G R KELSEY*

CORNHOLME (St Michael and All Angels) see Todmorden w Cornholme and Walsden *Leeds*

CORNISH HALL END (St John the Evangelist) see Finchingfield and Cornish Hall End etc *Chelmsf*

CORNWELL (St Peter) see Chipping Norton *Ox*

CORNWOOD (St Michael and All Angels) *Ex 20*   P *Bp*
P-in-c *F G DENMAN*

CORNWORTHY (St Peter) see Totnes w Bridgetown, Berry Pomeroy etc *Ex*

CORONATION SQUARE (St Aidan) see Cheltenham St Mark *Glouc*

CORRINGHAM (St John the Evangelist) (St Mary the Virgin) and Fobbing *Chelmsf 16*   P *Bp and SMF (jt)*   R *D ROLLINS*
C *J F HUTCHERSON*

CORRINGHAM (St Lawrence) see Lea Gp *Linc*

CORSCOMBE (St Mary the Virgin) see Melbury *Sarum*

CORSE (St Margaret) see Ashleworth, Corse, Hartpury, Hasfield etc *Glouc*

CORSENSIDE (All Saints) see N Tyne and Redesdale *Newc*

CORSENSIDE (St Cuthbert) *as above*

CORSHAM, GREATER (St Bartholomew) and Lacock *Bris 4*
P *Patr Bd*   P-in-c *A R JOHNSON*   TV *A J BEAUMONT*
C *P R N HARRISON*

CORSLEY (St Margaret of Antioch) see Cley Hill Villages *Sarum*

CORSLEY (St Mary the Virgin) *as above*

CORSTON (All Saints) see Saltford w Corston and Newton St Loe *B & W*

CORSTON (All Saints) see Gt Somerford, Lt Somerford, Seagry, Corston etc *Bris*

CORTON (St Bartholomew) *see* Hopton w Corton *Nor*
CORTON (St Bartholomew) *see* Abbotsbury, Portesham and Langton Herring *Sarum*
CORTON DENHAM (St Andrew) *see* Cam Vale *B & W*
CORYTON (St Andrew) *see* Milton Abbot, Dunterton, Lamerton etc *Ex*
COSBY (St Michael and All Angels) and Whetstone *Leic 7* **P** *Bp* **V** C D ALLEN
COSELEY (Christ Church) (St Cuthbert) *Worc 10* **P** *Bp* **P-in-c** E J STANFORD
COSELEY (St Chad) *Worc 10* **P** *Bp* **V** A HOWES
COSGROVE (St Peter and St Paul) *see* Potterspury w Furtho and Yardley Gobion etc *Pet*
COSHAM (St Philip) *Portsm 6* **P** *Bp* **P-in-c** J L STRAW **Hon C** B R COOK
COSSALL (St Catherine) *see* Trowell, Awsworth and Cossall *S'well*
COSSINGTON (All Saints) *see* Sileby, Cossington and Seagrave *Leic*
COSSINGTON (Blessed Virgin Mary) *see* Woolavington w Cossington and Bawdrip *B & W*
COSTESSEY (St Edmund) *Nor 3* **P** *Gt Hosp Nor* **V** N J S PARRY
COSTESSEY, NEW (St Helen) *see* Costessey *Nor*
COSTOCK (St Giles) *see* E and W Leake, Stanford-on-Soar, Rempstone etc *S'well*
COSTON (St Andrew) *see* S Framland *Leic*
COTEBROOKE (St John and Holy Cross) *see* Tarporley *Ches*
COTEHELE HOUSE (Chapel) *see* Calstock *Truro*
COTEHILL (St John the Evangelist) *see* Scotby and Cotehill w Cumwhinton *Carl*
COTES HEATH (St James) and Standon and Swynnerton and Tittensor *Lich 13* **P** *Bp, V Eccleshall, and Simeon's Trustees (jt)* **R** S G MCKENZIE **C** J P H ROBERTS
COTESBACH (St Mary) *see* Lutterworth w Cotesbach and Bitteswell *Leic*
COTGRAVE (All Saints) *S'well 5* **P** *DBP* **R** P D S MASSEY
COTHAM (St Saviour w St Mary) and Clifton St Paul *Bris 3* **P** *Bp* **V** J R HOLROYD **NSM** V H ROYSTON
COTHELSTONE (St Thomas of Canterbury) *see* Bishop's Lydeard w Lydeard St Lawrence etc *B & W*
COTHERIDGE (St Leonard) *see* Worcs W *Worc*
COTHERSTONE (St Cuthbert) *see* Romaldkirk w Laithkirk *Leeds*
COTLEIGH (St Michael and All Angels) *see* Offwell, Northleigh, Farway, Cotleigh etc *Ex*
COTMANHAY (Christ Church) *Derby 13* **P** *Bp* **V** P J DAVEY
COTON (St Peter) *see* Lordsbridge *Ely*
COTON-IN-THE-ELMS (St Mary) *see* Seale and Lullington w Coton in the Elms *Derby*
COTSWOLDS, SOUTH Team Ministry *Glouc 7* **P** *Patr Bd* **TR** J J SWANTON **TV** A V CINNAMOND, C J SYMCOX, P J PARTINGTON **C** L C HAYLER **NSM** D HYDE, J L BROWN, T M HASTIE-SMITH
COTTENHAM (All Saints) *Ely 6* **P** *Bp* **P-in-c** K A HODGINS **C** B I BAGULEY
COTTERED (St John the Baptist) *see* Ardeley, Benington, Cottered w Throcking etc *St Alb*
COTTERIDGE (St Agnes) *Birm 4* **P** *R Kings Norton* **V** J LEWIS-GREGORY **NSM** R R COLLINS
COTTERSTOCK (St Andrew) *see* Warmington, Tansor and Cotterstock etc *Pet*
COTTESBROOKE (All Saints) *see* Guilsborough and Hollowell and Cold Ashby etc *Pet*
COTTESLOE *Ox 15* **P** *Patr Bd* **TR** P D DERBYSHIRE **TV** H C BARNES **Hon C** P LYMBERY **NSM** G M ROWELL **OLM** S TUNNICLIFFE
COTTESMORE (St Nicholas) and Burley, Clipsham, Exton, Greetham, Stretton and Thistleton *Pet 12* **P** *Bp, DBP, E R Hanbury Esq, and Sir David Davenport-Handley (jt)* **V** M J PURNELL
COTTIMORE (St John) *see* Walton-on-Thames *Guildf*
COTTINGHAM (St Mary Magdalene) *see* Gretton w Rockingham and Cottingham w E Carlton *Pet*
COTTINGHAM (St Mary) *York 14* **P** *Abp* **R** P A SMITH
COTTINGLEY (St Michael and All Angels) *Leeds 1* **P** *Bp* **V** G S HODGSON **C** H M HODGSON
COTTINGWITH, EAST (St Mary) *see* Derwent Ings *York*
COTTISFORD (St Mary the Virgin) *see* Shelswell *Ox*
COTTON (St Andrew) *see* Bacton w Wyverstone, Cotton and Old Newton etc *St E*
COTTON (St John the Baptist) *see* Kingsley and Foxt-w-Whiston and Oakamoor etc *Lich*
COTTON MILL (St Julian) *see* St Alb St Steph *St Alb*
COTTONSTONES (St Mary) *see* Ryburn *Leeds*
COUGHTON (St Peter) *see* Alcester Minster *Cov*

COULSDON (St Andrew) *S'wark 22* **P** *Bp* **P-in-c** E R FOSS
COULSDON (St John) *S'wark 22* **P** *Abp* **R** P C ROBERTS **NSM** S L THOMAS
COULSTON, EAST (St Thomas of Canterbury) *see* Bratton, Edington and Imber, Erlestoke etc *Sarum*
COUND (St Peter) *see* Wenlock *Heref*
COUNDON (St James) and Eldon *Dur 6* **P** *Bp and Prime Min (alt)* **P-in-c** G NICHOLSON
COUNTESS WEAR (St Luke) *see* Topsham and Wear *Ex*
COUNTESTHORPE (St Andrew) w Foston *Leic 7* **P** *DBP and Bp (alt)* **P-in-c** D E HEBBLEWHITE **NSM** M D GILLESPIE
COURTEENHALL (St Peter and St Paul) *see* Salcey *Pet*
COVE (St John the Baptist) (St Christopher) *Guildf 1* **P** *Bp* **TR** J H TYNDALL **TV** E T PRIOR, S J STEWART **C** G R M DICKS **NSM** M T PRIOR
COVEHITHE (St Andrew) *see* Wrentham, Covehithe w Benacre etc *St E*
COVEN (St Paul) *Lich 2* **P** *Bp* **V** M LOCKEY
COVENEY (St Peter ad Vincula) *Ely 8* **P** *Bp* **P-in-c** P TAYLOR
COVENHAM (Annunciation of the Blessed Virgin Mary) *see* Fotherby *Linc*
COVENT GARDEN (St Paul) *Lon 3* **P** *Bp* **R** S J GRIGG
COVENTRY (Holy Trinity) *Cov 2* **P** *Ld Chan* **V** D F MAYHEW **C** R BUDD
COVENTRY (St Francis of Assisi) North Radford *Cov 2* **P** *Bp* **P-in-c** E B JACKSON **C** B A ARNOLD, E K FORBES STONE
COVENTRY (St George) *Cov 2* **P** *Bp* **V** A J EVANS
COVENTRY (St John the Baptist) *Cov 2* **P** *Trustees* **R** *vacant*
COVENTRY (St Mary Magdalen) *Cov 3* **P** *Bp* **V** S BAILEY **C** D D ENGH, J GREEN
COVENTRY (St Nicholas) *see* Radford *Cov*
COVENTRY Caludon *Cov 1* **P** *Bp and Ld Chan (alt)* **TR** W M SMITH **TV** L A MUDD **C** A HOGGER-GADSBY **NSM** D R I DEKKER **Emer** A HOGGER-GADSBY
COVENTRY EAST (St Anne and All Saints) (St Margaret) (St Peter) (St Alban) *Cov 1* **P** *Patr Bd* **TV** C D HOGGER **OLM** L J CLARKE
COVENTRY Holbrooks (St Luke) *see* Holbrooks *Cov*
COVERACK (St Peter) *see* St Keverne *Truro*
COVINGHAM (St Paul) *see* Swindon Dorcan *Bris*
COVINGTON (All Saints) *see* Kym Valley *Ely*
COWARNE, LITTLE (not known) *see* Bredenbury *Heref*
COWARNE, MUCH (St Mary the Virgin) *see* Frome Valley *Heref*
COWBIT (St Mary) *Linc 19* **P** *Ld Chan and DBP (alt)* **V** *vacant*
COWCLIFFE (St Hilda) *see* Fixby and Cowcliffe *Leeds*
COWDEN (St Mary Magdalene) w Hammerwood *Chich 6* **P** *Ch Soc Trust* **P-in-c** M E TRASK
COWES (Holy Trinity) (St Mary the Virgin) *Portsm 8* **P** *Trustees and V Carisbrooke St Mary (jt)* **V** A N POPPE
COWES, EAST (St James) *see* Whippingham w E Cowes *Portsm*
COWESBY (St Michael) *York 18* **P** *Abp* **R** I D HOUGHTON **NSM** T A LEWIS
COWFOLD (St Peter) *Chich 5* **P** *Bp Lon* **P-in-c** K D LITTLEJOHN **NSM** M MILLS
COWGATE (St Peter) *Newc 4* **P** *Bp* **V** A M PATERSON **C** C M FORD
COWGILL (St John the Evangelist) *see* Dent w Cowgill *Carl*
COWICK (Holy Trinity) *see* Gt Snaith *Sheff*
COWLAM (St Mary) *see* Waggoners *York*
COWLEIGH (St Peter) *see* Malvern Link w Cowleigh *Worc*
COWLEY (St James) (St Francis) *Ox 1* **P** *Patr Bd* **TV** E K DENNO **NSM** G C F HICKSON, R W CHAND
COWLEY (St John) (St Alban) (St Bartholomew) (St Mary and St John) *Ox 1* **P** *St Steph Ho Ox* **V** P S J RITCHIE **NSM** B J WILLIAMS, M H B REES, S M ALKIRE
COWLEY (St Laurence) *Lon 24* **P** *Bp* **R** S M HARDWICKE
COWLEY (St Mary) *see* Churn Valley *Glouc*
COWLEY CHAPEL (St Antony) *see* Brampford Speke, Cadbury, Newton St Cyres etc *Ex*
COWLING (Holy Trinity) *see* Sutton w Cowling and Lothersdale *Leeds*
COWLINGE (St Margaret) *see* Bansfield *St E*
COWPEN (St Benedict) *see* Horton *Newc*
COWPLAIN (St Wilfrid) *Portsm 5* **P** *Bp* **V** I SNARES
COWTON, EAST (All Saints) *see* E Richmond *Leeds*
COWTON, SOUTH (St Luke's Pastoral Centre) *as above*
COX GREEN (Good Shepherd) *Ox 5* **P** *Bp* **P-in-c** J R HICKS
COXHEATH (Holy Trinity), East Farleigh, Hunton, Linton and West Farleigh *Roch 7* **P** *Ld Chan (1 turn), Abp, Lord Cornwallis, and D&C (1 turn)* **R** P S CALLWAY **NSM** D W JONES, E A DOYLE
COXHOE (St Mary) *see* Kelloe and Coxhoe *Dur*
COXLEY (Christ Church) w Godney, Henton and Wookey *B & W 7* **P** *Bp* **P-in-c** P I CLARKE

COXWELL, GREAT (St Giles) w Buscot, Coleshill and Eaton Hastings *Ox 25* **P** *Bp and Lord Faringdon (jt)*
P-in-c D M WILLIAMS

COXWOLD (St Michael) and Husthwaite *York 3* **P** *Abp*
V E C HASSALL **NSM** N L CHAPMAN

CRABBS CROSS (St Peter) *see* Redditch Ch the K *Worc*

CRADLEY (St James) w Mathon and Storridge *Heref 5* **P** *Bp and D&C Westmr (jt)* **R** R WARD

CRADLEY (St Peter) *see* Halas *Worc*

CRADLEY HEATH (St Luke) *see* Dudley Wood and Cradley Heath *Worc*

CRAGG VALE (St John the Baptist in the Wilderness) *see* Erringden *Leeds*

CRAKEHALL (St Gregory) *Leeds 27* **P** *Sir Henry Beresford-Peirse Bt* **P-in-c** B S DIXON **NSM** J T OLDFIELD

CRAMBE (St Michael) *see* Harton *York*

CRAMLINGTON (St Nicholas) *Newc 1* **P** *Bp*
TV S G WILKINSON **OLM** S M WARD

CRAMPMOOR (St Swithun) *see* Romsey *Win*

CRANBORNE (St Mary and St Bartholomew) w Boveridge, Edmondsham, Wimborne St Giles and Woodlands *Sarum 9*
P *Viscount Cranborne, Earl of Shaftesbury, and Mrs J E Smith (jt)*
R D J PASKINS

CRANBOURNE (St Peter) *see* Winkfield and Cranbourne *Ox*

CRANBROOK (St Dunstan) *Cant 11* **P** *Abp* **V** *vacant*

CRANFIELD (St Peter and St Paul) and Hulcote w Salford
St Alb 9 **P** *MMCET* **R** H K SYMES-THOMPSON

CRANFORD (Holy Angels) (St Dunstan) *Lon 11* **P** *R J G Berkeley Esq and Sir Hugo Huntington-Whiteley Bt (jt)*
R M J GILL

CRANFORD (St John the Baptist) w Grafton Underwood and Twywell *Pet 9* **P** *Boughton Estates, DBP, and Sir John Robinson Bt (by turn)* **R** D H P FOOT

CRANHAM (All Saints) *Chelmsf 2* **P** *St Jo Coll Ox*
NSM G K W ARBER

CRANHAM (St James the Great) *see* Painswick, Sheepscombe, Cranham, The Edge etc *Glouc*

CRANHAM PARK (St Luke) *Chelmsf 2* **P** *Bp* **V** M VICKERS
C K J BROWNING **NSM** P J WRIGHT **OLM** J A HEININK

CRANHAM PARK Moor Lane (not known) *see* Cranham Park *Chelmsf*

CRANLEIGH (St Nicolas) *Guildf 2* **P** *Bp* **R** R O WOODHAMS
NSM D C FRETT

CRANMORE, WEST (St Bartholomew) *see* Shepton Mallet w Doulting *B & W*

CRANOE (St Michael) *see* Welham, Glooston and Cranoe and Stonton Wyville *Leic*

CRANSFORD (St Peter) *see* Upper Alde *St E*

CRANSLEY (St Andrew) *see* Broughton w Loddington and Cransley etc *Pet*

CRANTOCK (St Carantoc) *see* Perranzabuloe and Crantock w Cubert *Truro*

CRANWELL (St Andrew) *see* N Lafford Gp *Linc*

CRANWICH (St Mary) *Nor 13* **P** *CPAS* **R** *vacant*

CRANWORTH (St Mary the Virgin) *see* Barnham Broom and Upper Yare *Nor*

CRASSWALL (St Mary) *see* Clodock and Longtown w Craswall, Llanveynoe etc *Heref*

CRASTER (Mission Church) *see* Embleton w Rennington and Rock *Newc*

CRATFIELD (St Mary) *see* Four Rivers *St E*

CRATHORNE (All Saints) *York 20* **P** *Lord Crathorne*
R P J SANDERS **Hon C** A J HUTCHISON **NSM** P PERCY

CRAWCROOK (Church of the Holy Spirit) *see* Greenside *Dur*

CRAWLEY (St John the Baptist) *Chich 6* **P** *Bp*
TV S J MURRAY **C** J M BALDWIN

CRAWLEY (St Mary) *see* The Downs *Win*

CRAWLEY DOWN (All Saints) *Chich 6* **P** *R Worth*
V A J HALE **NSM** J A ALDERTON

CRAWLEY, NORTH (St Firmin) *see* Sherington w Chicheley, N Crawley, Astwood etc *Ox*

CRAY (St Barnabas) *see* St Paul's Cray *St Barn Roch*

CRAY VALLEY (St Mary and St Paulinus) (St Andrew) *Roch 16*
P *Bp* **V** P F PRENTICE **C** J M WINTER

CRAY, NORTH (St James) *see* Footscray w N Cray *Roch*

CRAYFORD (St Paulinus) *Roch 15* **P** *Bp* **R** A K LANE
C J R W CROCKFORD

CRAYKE (St Cuthbert) w Brandsby and Yearsley *York 3*
P *The Crown and Abp (alt)* **R** E C HASSALL

CRAZIES HILL (Mission Room) *see* Wargrave w Knowl Hill *Ox*

CREAKE, NORTH (St Mary) and SOUTH (St Mary) w Waterden, Syderstone w Barmer and Sculthorpe *Nor 15*
P *Bp, Earl Spencer, Earl of Leicester, Guild of All So, J Labouchere Esq, Mrs M E Russell, and DBP (jt)* **R** C G WYLIE

CREATON, GREAT (St Michael and All Angels)
see Guilsborough and Hollowell and Cold Ashby etc *Pet*

CREDENHILL (St Mary) Brinsop and Wormsley, Mansel Lacy and Yazor, Kenchester, Bridge Sollers and Bishopstone
Heref 3 **P** R M Ecroyd Esq, Major D J C Davenport and Bp (3 turns), Ld Chan (1 turn) **P-in-c** R R D DAVIES-JAMES
NSM A C DEANE

CREDITON (Holy Cross) (St Lawrence) Shobrooke and Sandford w Upton Hellions *Ex 2* **P** *12 Govs of Crediton Ch*
R N GUTHRIE **NSM** P L FILLERY

CREECH ST MICHAEL (St Michael) and Ruishton w Thornfalcon *B & W 18* **P** *Bp, MMCET, and Dr W R C Batten (jt)* **V** R S HARRIS **C** J CURTIS

CREED (St Crida) *see* Probus, Ladock and Grampound w Creed and St Erme *Truro*

CREEDY, NORTH : Cheriton Fitzpaine, Woolfardisworthy, Kennerley, Washford Pyne, Puddington, Poughill, Stockleigh English, Morchard Bishop, Stockleigh Pomeroy, Down St Mary, Clannaborough, Lapford, Nymet Rowland, and Coldridge *Ex 2* **P** *Ld Chan (1 turn), Patr Bd (5 turns)*
TV L C STARRS **NSM** K J CROSS

CREEKMOOR (Christ Church) *see* N Poole Ecum Team *Sarum*

CREEKSEA (All Saints) *Chelmsf 11* **P** *Bp*
P-in-c V M WADMAN

CREETING (St Peter) *see* The Creetings and Earl Stonham w Stonham Parva *St E*

CREETING ST MARY (St Mary), Creeting St Peter and Earl Stonham w Stonham Parva *St E 1* **P** *DBP (2 turns), Pemb Coll Cam (1 turn)* **P-in-c** P J PAYNE **NSM** B J GALLAGHER

CREETON (St Peter) *see* Castle Bytham w Creeton *Linc*

CREGNEISH (St Peter) *see* Rushen *S & M*

CRESSAGE (Christ Church) *see* Wenlock *Heref*

CRESSBROOK (St John the Evangelist) *see* Tideswell *Derby*

CRESSING (All Saints) w Stisted and Bradwell-juxt-Coggeshall and Pattiswick *Chelmsf 17* **P** *Bp, Exors Mrs D E G Keen, and Abp (by turn)* **P-in-c** C M DAVEY
NSM K M KING, N F TOZER **OLM** R J BURDEN

CRESSINGHAM, GREAT (St Michael) and LITTLE (St Andrew), w Threxton *Nor 13* **P** *Bp and Sec of State for Defence*
C G FOSTER

CRESSWELL (St Bartholomew) and Lynemouth *Newc 11*
P *Bp* **V** A E SIMPSON

CRESWELL (St Mary Magdalene) *see* Elmton *Derby*

CRETINGHAM (St Peter) *see* Mid Loes *St E*

CREWE (All Saints and St Paul) (St Peter) *Ches 15* **P** *Bp*
V S J CLAPHAM **NSM** E J COLLEY

CREWE (St Andrew w St John the Baptist) *Ches 15* **P** *Bp*
NSM H RUGMAN

CREWE (St Barnabas) *Ches 15* **P** *Bp* **V** R D POWELL

CREWE GREEN (St Michael and All Angels) *see* Haslington w Crewe Green *Ches*

CREWKERNE (St Bartholomew) *see* Wulfric Benefice *B & W*

CRICH (St Mary) and South Wingfield *Derby 1* **P** *Ch Trust Fund Trust and Duke of Devonshire (jt)* **V** P D BROOKS
NSM D HIGGON

CRICK (St Margaret) and Yelvertoft w Clay Coton and Lilbourne *Pet 2* **P** *MMCET and St Jo Coll Ox (jt)*
R D M LAKE

CRICKET MALHERBIE (St Mary Magdalene) *see* Chaffcombe, Cricket Malherbie etc *B & W*

CRICKET ST THOMAS (St Thomas) *B & W 16* **P** *Bp*
V H M WILLIAMS

CRICKLADE (St Sampson) w Latton *Bris 6* **P** *D&C, Bp, and Hon P N Eliot (by turn)* **P-in-c** P J P BRADLEY
NSM S E DANBY

CRICKLEWOOD (St Gabriel) and St Michael *Lon 21* **P** *Bp*
V J E MORRIS **C** O P K ROBINSON

CRICKLEWOOD (St Peter) *Lon 15* **P** *Bp*
P-in-c K G M HILTON-TURVEY

CRIFTINS (St Matthew) w Dudleston and Welsh Frankton
Lich 17 **P** *Bp and V Ellesmere (jt)* **P-in-c** S C AIREY
OLM K E DAVIES

CRIMPLESHAM (St Mary) *see* Downham Market and Crimplesham w Stradsett *Ely*

CRINGLEFORD (St Peter) and Colney *Nor 7* **P** *Exors E H Barclay Esq and Gt Hosp Nor (alt)* **R** H D BUTCHER
C H L CRACKNELL

CROCKENHILL (All Souls) *Roch 2* **P** *Bp* **P-in-c** K R WHITE

CROCKHAM HILL (Holy Trinity) *Roch 11* **P** *J St A Warde Esq*
V S J DIGGORY

CROFT (All Saints) *see* The Wainfleet Gp *Linc*

CROFT (Christ Church) *see* Newchurch w Croft *Liv*

CROFT (St Michael and All Angels) *see* Broughton Astley and Croft w Stoney Stanton *Leic*

CROFT (St Peter) *see* E Richmond *Leeds*

CROFTON (All Saints) *Leeds 20* **P** *Duchy of Lanc*
NSM H WALKER **OLM** A JORDAN

CROFTON (Holy Rood) (St Edmund) *Portsm 2*   **P** *Bp*
C S P MARSH   **NSM** C R PRESTIDGE
CROFTON (St Paul) *Roch 16*   **P** *V Orpington*
V B A ABAYOMI-COLE
CROFTON PARK (St Hilda w St Cyprian) *S'wark 5*   **P** *V Lewisham St Mary*   **V** S G BATES
CROMER (St Peter and St Paul) *Nor 21*   **P** *CPAS*
V J R PORTER   C P D HERBERT   **OLM** J M HODGKINSON,
P E NEALE
CROMFORD (St Mary)   *see* Matlock Bath and Cromford *Derby*
CROMHALL (St Andrew), Tortworth, Tytherington, Falfield and Rockhampton *Glouc 5*   **P** *Bp, R Thornbury and Oldbury etc, Adn, and J Leigh Esq (1 turn), Earl of Ducie, Oriel Coll Ox, and MMCET (1 turn)*   **R** vacant
CROMPTON FOLD (St Saviour)   *see* E Crompton *Man*
CROMPTON, EAST (St James) *Man 15*   **P** *Bp*   **V** L CONNOLLY
OLM W H MOSTON
CROMPTON, HIGH (St Mary) and Thornham *Man 15*
P *Bp*   **V** A BUTLER   **OLM** D MORRIS
CROMWELL (St Giles)   *see* Norwell w Ossington, Cromwell etc *S'well*
CRONDALL (All Saints) and Ewshot *Guildf 3*   **P** *Bp*
V T C L HELLINGS   C E J TOMS
NSM S M R CUMMING-LATTEY
CROOK (St Catherine) *Carl 10*   **P** *CPAS*   **P-in-c** G W BRIGGS
NSM M L WOODCOCK
CROOK (St Catherine) *Dur 9*   **P** *R Brancepeth*
P-in-c V T FENTON   **NSM** L LINDSAY
CROOK PEAK *B & W 1*   **P** *R M Dodd Esq (1 turn), Ld Chan (2 turns), Bp Lon (1 turn)*   **R** vacant
CROOKES (St Thomas) *Sheff 4*   **P** *Patr Bd*   **TR** M WOODHEAD
C R GRANT
CROOKES (St Timothy) *Sheff 4*   **P** *Sheff Ch Burgesses*
V P R TOWNSEND   **NSM** J R MARSH
CROOKHAM (Christ Church) *Guildf 1*   **P** *V Crondall and Ewshot*   **V** R OLLIFF
CROOKHORN (Good Shepherd) *Portsm 5*   **P** *Simeon's Trustees*
P-in-c P D HALL   C A M WILSON, A R GOY, C SHERMAN
NSM D M YOUELL
CROPREDY (St Mary the Virgin)   *see* Shires' Edge *Ox*
CROPTHORNE (St Michael)   *see* Fladbury, Hill and Moor, Wyre Piddle etc *Worc*
CROPTON (St Gregory)   *see* Lastingham w Appleton-le-Moors, Rosedale etc *York*
CROPWELL BISHOP (St Giles) w Colston Bassett, Granby w Elton, Langar cum Barnstone and Tythby w Cropwell Butler *S'well 5*   **P** *CPAS and Bp, Ld Chan (jt)*   **R** E B GAMBLE
CROSBY (St George) (St Michael) *Linc 6*   **P** *Sir Reginald Sheffield Bt*   **V** J W THACKER
CROSBY GARRETT (St Andrew)   *see* Kirkby Stephen w Mallerstang etc *Carl*
CROSBY RAVENSWORTH (St Lawrence) *Carl 1*   **P** *DBP*
P-in-c S J FYFE
CROSBY, GREAT (All Saints)   *see* Thornton and Crosby *Liv*
CROSBY, GREAT (St Faith) and Waterloo Park St Mary the Virgin *Liv 1*   **P** *St Chad's Coll Dur and Trustees (jt)*
P-in-c S J LUCAS   C S J TIBBS   **Hon C** D A SMITH
CROSBY, GREAT (St Luke) *Liv 5*   **P** *V Sefton*   **V** P H SPIERS
C D A LOWRIE
CROSBY-ON-EDEN (St John the Evangelist)   *see* Eden, Gelt and Irthing *Carl*
CROSCOMBE (Blessed Virgin Mary)   *see* Pilton w Croscombe, N Wootton and Dinder *B & W*
CROSLAND MOOR (St Barnabas) and Linthwaite *Leeds 12*
P *Bp and R Almondbury (jt)*   **P-in-c** P M WITTS
NSM A BROXHAM, S V BROOKS
CROSLAND, SOUTH (Holy Trinity)   *see* Em TM *Leeds*
CROSS CANONBY (St John the Evangelist)   *see* Allonby, Cross Canonby and Dearham *Carl*
CROSS FELL Group, The *Carl 4*   **P** *D&C (2 turns) and DBP (1 turn)*   **P-in-c** A S PYE   **NSM** S J BAMPING
CROSS GREEN (St Saviour)   *see* Leeds Richmond Hill *Leeds*
CROSS HEATH (St Michael and All Angels) *Lich 9*   **P** *Bp*
V D J LLOYD
CROSS IN HAND (St Bartholomew)   *see* Waldron *Chich*
CROSS ROADS CUM LEES (St James)   *see* Haworth and Cross Roads cum Lees *Leeds*
CROSS TOWN (St Cross)   *see* Knutsford St Cross *Ches*
CROSSCRAKE (St Thomas) *Carl 10*   **P** *V Heversham and Milnthorpe*   **P-in-c** I J E SWIFT
CROSSENS (St John)   *see* N Meols *Liv*
CROSSFLATTS (St Aidan)   *see* Bingley All SS *Leeds*
CROSSLACON Team Ministry *Carl 5*   **P** *Patr Bd*
TR J E CURTIS   **TV** P F TURNBULL

CROSSPOOL (St Columba) *Sheff 4*   **P** *Bp*   **V** F M ECCLESTON
NSM L A FURBEY
CROSTHWAITE (St Kentigern) Keswick *Carl 6*   **P** *Bp*
V A S E PENNY
CROSTHWAITE (St Mary) Kendal *Carl 10*   **P** *DBP*
P-in-c M D WOODCOCK
CROSTON (St Michael and All Angels), Bretherton and Mawdesley w Bispham *Blackb 4*   **P** *M G Rawstorne Esq and Patr Bd (jt)*   **NSM** J H TAYLOR
CROSTWICK (St Peter)   *see* Horsham St Faith, Spixworth and Crostwick *Nor*
CROSTWIGHT (All Saints)   *see* Smallburgh w Dilham w Honing and Crostwight *Nor*
CROUCH END HILL (Christ Church)   *see* Hornsey Ch Ch *Lon*
CROUGHTON (All Saints)   *see* Aynho and Croughton w Evenley etc *Pet*
CROWAN (St Crewenna) and Treslothan *Truro 2*   **P** D L C Roberts Esq and Mrs W A Pendarves (jt)   **V** D P WHITTING
CROWBOROUGH (All Saints) *Chich 16*   **P** *Ld Chan*
C M S ASHWORTH   **NSM** J A HOBBS, R P DILLINGHAM
CROWBOROUGH (St John the Evangelist) *Chich 16*   **P** *Guild of All So*   **V** R J NORBURY
CROWCOMBE (Holy Ghost)   *see* Quantock Towers *B & W*
CROWELL (Nativity of the Blessed Virgin Mary)   *see* Chinnor, Sydenham, Aston Rowant and Crowell *Ox*
CROWFIELD (All Saints) w Stonham Aspal and Mickfield *St E 1*   **P** *DBP, Bp, and Lord de Saumarez (alt)*
P-in-c P J PAYNE   **NSM** H NORRIS
CROWHURST (St George)   *see* Catsfield and Crowhurst *Chich*
CROWHURST (St George)   *see* Oxted *S'wark*
CROWLAND (St Mary and St Bartholomew and St Guthlac) *Linc 19*   **P** *Earl of Normanton*   **P-in-c** C H BROWN
OLM M G ONGYERTH
CROWLE (St John the Baptist)   *see* Bowbrook S *Worc*
CROWLE Group, The (St Oswald) *Linc 1*   **P** *Bp (2 turns), Prime Min (1 turn)*   **V** G M LINES   **OLM** M STONIER
CROWMARSH GIFFORD (St Mary Magdalene)   *see* Wallingford *Ox*
CROWN EAST AND RUSHWICK (St Thomas)   *see* Worc Dines Green St Mich and Crown E, Rushwick *Worc*
CROWNHILL (Ascension)   *see* Plymouth Crownhill Ascension *Ex*
CROWTHORNE (St John the Baptist) *Ox 8*   **P** *Bp*
V L M CORNWELL   **NSM** D RAMSBOTTOM
CROWTON (Christ Church)   *see* Norley, Crowton and Kingsley *Ches*
CROXALL-CUM-OAKLEY (St John the Baptist)   *see* Seale and Lullington w Coton in the Elms *Derby*
CROXBY (All Saints)   *see* Swallow *Linc*
CROXDALE (St Bartholomew) and Tudhoe *Dur 6*   **P** *D&C*
P-in-c G NORMAN   C C A MITCHELL
CROXDEN (St Giles)   *see* Rocester and Croxden w Hollington *Lich*
CROXLEY GREEN (All Saints) *St Alb 4*   **P** *V Rickmansworth*
V M R MUGAN
CROXLEY GREEN (St Oswald) *St Alb 4*   **P** *Bp*
V R J RILEY-BRALEY
CROXTETH (St Paul) *Liv 8*   **P** *R W Derby and Bp (jt)*
V I G BROOKS
CROXTETH PARK (St Cuthbert) *Liv 8*   **P** *Bp*   **V** A PRINCE
CROXTON (All Saints)   *see* Thetford *Nor*
CROXTON (St James)   *see* Papworth *Ely*
CROXTON (St John the Evangelist) *Linc 8*   **P** *Ld Chan*
R vacant
CROXTON (St Paul)   *see* Ashley and Mucklestone and Broughton and Croxton *Lich*
CROXTON Group, The SOUTH (St John the Baptist) *Leic 2*
P *DBP, Ch Soc Trust, and MMCET (jt)*   **R** vacant
CROXTON KERRIAL (St Botolph and St John the Baptist)
see High Framland Par *Leic*
CROYDE (St Mary Magdalene)   *see* Georgeham *Ex*
CROYDON (All Saints)   *see* Orwell Gp *Ely*
CROYDON (Christ Church) Broad Green *S'wark 20*
P *Simeon's Trustees*   **P-in-c** J DEVADASON   **OLM** K H VEEN
CROYDON (Holy Saviour) *S'wark 21*   **P** *Bp*   **V** C J TUCKER
CROYDON (St Andrew) *S'wark 20*   **P** *Trustees*   **V** W W BELL
CROYDON (St John the Baptist) *S'wark 20*   **P** *Abp*
V C J L BOSWELL   C C J MOORE, P VOWLES
CROYDON (St Matthew) *S'wark 20*   **P** *V Croydon*
V S J D FOSTER   **NSM** R A HINDER
CROYDON (St Michael and All Angels w St James) *S'wark 20*
P *Trustees*   **V** I S BROTHWOOD
CROYDON Woodside (St Luke) *S'wark 21*   **P** *Bp*   **V** vacant
CROYDON, SOUTH (Emmanuel) *S'wark 20*   **P** *Ch Trust Fund Trust*   **V** T A MAPSTONE

CROYDON, SOUTH (St Peter) (St Augustine) *S'wark 20*
  P *V Croydon and Bp (jt)* **V** W F WARREN **NSM** L M FOX
CRUDGINGTON (St Mary Mission Church) *see* Wrockwardine
  Deanery *Lich*
CRUDWELL (All Saints) *see* Ashley, Crudwell, Hankerton and
  Oaksey *Bris*
CRUMPSALL (St Matthew w St Mary) *Man 4* **P** *Bp*
  R J M WARE
CRUMPSALL, LOWER (St Thomas) *see* Cheetham and Lower
  Crumpsall *Man*
CRUNDALE (St Mary the Blessed Virgin) *see* King's Wood *Cant*
CRUWYS MORCHARD (Holy Cross) *see* Washfield, Stoodleigh,
  Withleigh etc *Ex*
CRUX EASTON (St Michael and All Angels) *see* NW Hants *Win*
CUBBINGTON (St Mary) *Cov 11* **P** *Bp* **V** G R COLES
CUBERT (St Cubert) *see* Perranzabuloe and Crantock w Cubert
  Truro
CUBLEY (St Andrew) *see* S Dales *Derby*
CUBLINGTON (St Nicholas) *see* Cottesloe *Ox*
CUCKFIELD (Holy Trinity) *Chich 5* **P** *Bp* **V** M J MAINE
CUCKLINGTON (St Lawrence) *see* Charlton Musgrove,
  Cucklington and Stoke Trister *B & W*
CUDDESDON (All Saints) *see* Garsington, Cuddesdon and
  Horspath *Ox*
CUDDINGTON (St Mary) *Guildf 9* **P** *Bp* **V** A P CAIN
  OLM C M WHITE
CUDDINGTON (St Nicholas) *see* Haddenham w Cuddington,
  Kingsey etc *Ox*
CUDHAM (St Peter and St Paul) and Downe *Roch 16*
  P *Ch Soc Trust and Bp (jt)* **V** W J MUSSON
CUDWORTH (St John) *Leeds 18* **P** *Bp* **V** D NICHOLSON
CUDWORTH (St Michael) *see* Winsmoor *B & W*
CUFFLEY (St Andrew) *see* Northaw and Cuffley *St Alb*
CULBONE (St Beuno) *see* Oare w Culbone *B & W*
CULFORD (St Mary) *see* Lark Valley *St E*
CULGAITH (All Saints) *see* Cross Fell Gp *Carl*
CULHAM (St Paul) *see* Dorchester *Ox*
CULLERCOATS (St George) *Newc 5* **P** *Duke of Northumberland*
  V A J HUGHES **C** D J B TWOMEY
CULLERCOATS (St Paul) *see* Tynemouth Cullercoats St Paul
  Newc
CULLINGWORTH (St John the Evangelist) *see* Harden and
  Wilsden, Cullingworth and Denholme *Leeds*
CULLOMPTON (St Andrew) (Langford Chapel) *Ex 7*
  P *CPAS* **R** E Q HOBBS
CULM DAVY (St Mary's Chapel) *see* Hemyock w Culm Davy,
  Clayhidon and Culmstock *Ex*
CULMINGTON (All Saints) *see* Ludlow *Heref*
CULMSTOCK (All Saints) *see* Hemyock w Culm Davy,
  Clayhidon and Culmstock *Ex*
CULPHO (St Botolph) *see* Gt and Lt Bealings w Playford and
  Culpho *St E*
CULWORTH (St Mary the Virgin) w Sulgrave and Thorpe
  Mandeville and Chipping Warden w Edgcote and
  Moreton Pinkney *Pet 1* **P** T M Sergison-Brooke Esq, DBP,
  D L P Humfrey Esq, Ch Patr Trust, and Oriel Coll Ox (jt)
  R B D S FAIRBANK
CUMBERWORTH (St Nicholas), Denby and Denby Dale
  Leeds 13 **P** *Bp and V Penistone (jt)* **R** *vacant*
CUMDIVOCK (St John) *see* Dalston w Cumdivock, Raughton
  Head and Wreay *Carl*
CUMMERSDALE (St James) *see* Denton Holme *Carl*
CUMNOR (St Michael) *Ox 19* **P** *St Pet Coll Ox*
  V G N MAUGHAN **NSM** D WENHAM, H A AZER,
  J PRYCE-WILLIAMS
CUMREW (St Mary the Virgin) *see* Eden, Gelt and Irthing *Carl*
CUMWHINTON (St John's Hall) *see* Scotby and Cotehill w
  Cumwhinton *Carl*
CUMWHITTON (St Mary the Virgin) *see* Eden, Gelt and Irthing
  Carl
CUNDALL (St Mary and All Saints) *see* Kirby-on-the-Moor,
  Cundall w Norton-le-Clay etc *Leeds*
CURBAR (All Saints) *see* Longstone, Curbar and Stony
  Middleton *Derby*
CURBRIDGE (St John the Baptist) *see* Witney *Ox*
CURDRIDGE (St Peter) *Portsm 1* **P** *D&C Win*
  V G R MENSINGH **C** A L WEBB
CURDWORTH (St Nicholas and St Peter ad Vincula)
  (St George), Middleton and Wishaw *Birm 12* **P** *Bp*
  R J C J RAJA
CURRY MALLET (All Saints) *see* Beercrocombe w Curry Mallet,
  Hatch Beauchamp etc *B & W*
CURRY RIVEL (St Andrew) w Fivehead and Swell *B & W 14*
  P *D&C Bris (1 turn), P G H Speke Esq (2 turns)*
  P-in-c S R PATTERSON
CURRY, NORTH (St Peter and St Paul) *see* Athelney *B & W*

CURY (St Corentine) and Gunwalloe *Truro 4* **P** *Bp*
  P-in-c S O GRIFFITHS
CUSOP (St Mary) w Blakemere, Bredwardine w Brobury,
  Clifford, Dorstone, Hardwicke, Moccas and Preston-on-
  Wye *Heref 1* **P** *Bp, D&C, CPAS, MMCET, P M I S Trumper Esq,*
  S Penoyre Esq, and Mrs P Chester-Master (jt) **R** D A R SODADASI
  C C J LISVANE
CUTCOMBE (St John the Evangelist) *see* Exmoor *B & W*
CUTSDEAN (St James) *see* The Guitings, Cutsdean, Farmcote
  etc *Glouc*
CUXHAM (Holy Rood) *see* Ewelme, Brightwell Baldwin,
  Cuxham w Easington *Ox*
CUXTON (St Michael and All Angels) and Halling *Roch 6*
  P *Bp and D&C (jt)* **R** R I KNIGHT
CUXWOLD (St Nicholas) *see* Swallow *Linc*
CWM HEAD (St Michael) *see* Wistanstow *Heref*
DACRE (Holy Trinity) w Hartwith and Darley w Thornthwaite
  Leeds 25 **P** *Bp, D&C, V Masham and Healey, and Mrs K A*
  Dunbar (jt) **P-in-c** M S EVANS **NSM** A J COLLINS
DACRE (St Andrew) *Carl 4* **P** *Trustees* **V** N J H REEVES
DADLINGTON (St James) *see* Fenn Lanes Gp *Leic*
DAGENHAM (St Martin) *see* Becontree S *Chelmsf*
DAGENHAM (St Peter and St Paul) *Chelmsf 1* **P** *Ch Soc Trust*
  P-in-c J K EDWARDS
DAGLINGWORTH (Holy Rood) *see* Brimpsfield w Birdlip, Syde,
  Daglingworth etc *Glouc*
DAISY HILL (St James), Westhoughton and Wingates *Man 9*
  P *Patr Bd* **TR** C A BRACEGIRDLE **TV** G M THOMAS
  OLM V A RADFORD
DALBURY (All Saints) *see* Boylestone, Church Broughton,
  Dalbury, etc *Derby*
DALBY (St James) *see* W Coast *S & M*
DALBY (St Lawrence and Blessed Edward King) *see* Bolingbroke
  Deanery *Linc*
DALBY (St Peter) *see* Howardian Gp *York*
DALBY, GREAT (St Swithun) *see* Burrough Hill Pars *Leic*
DALBY, LITTLE (St James) *as above*
DALBY, OLD (St John the Baptist), Nether Broughton,
  Saxelbye w Shoby, Grimston and Wartnaby *Leic 2* **P** *Bp,*
  MMCET, V Rothley, and Personal Reps K J M Madocks-Wright Esq
  (jt) **V** *vacant*
DALE ABBEY (All Saints) *see* Stanton-by-Dale w Dale Abbey and
  Risley *Derby*
DALE HEAD (St James) *see* Slaidburn w Tosside *Leeds*
DALHAM (St Mary), Gazeley, Higham, Kentford and Moulton
  St E 11 **P** *Bp (2 turns), Ch Coll Cam (1 turn), C E L Philipps Esq*
  (1 turn), and D W Barclay Esq (1 turn) **V** S J MITCHELL
DALLAM (St Mark) *Liv 12* **P** *R Warrington and Bp (jt)*
  V *vacant*
DALLINGHOO (St Mary) *see* Mid Loes *St E*
DALLINGTON (St Giles) *see* Warbleton, Bodle Street Green and
  Dallington *Chich*
DALLINGTON (St Mary) *Pet 4* **P** *Earl Spencer*
  P-in-c P W BOWDEN **NSM** S M COLES
DALLOWGILL (St Peter) *see* Fountains Gp *Leeds*
DALSTON (Holy Trinity) w St Philip and Haggerston All Saints
  Lon 5 **P** *Ld Chan and Bp (alt)* **V** R M C LEIGH
DALSTON (St Mark w St Bartholomew) *Lon 5* **P** *Ch Patr*
  Trust **V** J ZVIMBA
DALSTON (St Michael) w Cumdivock, Raughton Head and
  Wreay *Carl 3* **P** *Bp, DBP, and D&C (jt)* **V** S P CARTER
DALTON (Holy Trinity) *Sheff 6* **P** *Bp* **P-in-c** S Y LEE
DALTON (St James) *see* Gilling and Kirkby Ravensworth *Leeds*
DALTON (St John the Evangelist) *see* Topcliffe, Baldersby w
  Dishforth, Dalton etc *York*
DALTON (St Michael and All Angels) *Liv 11* **P** *Bp*
  V *vacant*
DALTON HOLME (St Mary) *see* Etton w Dalton Holme *York*
DALTON LE DALE (St Andrew) and New Seaham *Dur 2* **P** *Bp*
  and D&C (alt) **V** P T HARRISON
DALTON, NORTH (All Saints) *see* Woldsburn *York*
DALTON-IN-FURNESS (St Mary) and Ireleth-with-Askam
  Carl 9 **P** *Bp* **V** A MITCHELL
DALWOOD (St Peter) *see* Kilmington, Stockland, Dalwood,
  Yarcombe etc *Ex*
DAMERHAM (St George) *see* W Downland *Sarum*
DANBURY (St John the Baptist) *Chelmsf 10* **P** *Lord Fitzwalter*
  P-in-c C A ASHLEY
DANBY (St Hilda) w Castleton and Commondale *York 21*
  P *Viscountess Downe* **V** M J HAZELTON
DANBY WISKE (not known) *see* E Richmond *Leeds*
DANE BANK (St George) *see* Denton Ch Ch *Man*
DANEHILL (All Saints) *Chich 18* **P** *Ch Soc Trust*
  V P MACBAIN
DANESMOOR (St Barnabas) *see* N Wingfield, Clay Cross and
  Pilsley *Derby*

DARBY END (St Peter) **and Netherton** *Worc 9*   **P** *Bp*
  V M RUTTER
DARBY GREEN (St Barnabas) **and Eversley** *Win 5*   **P** *Bp*
  V M W SAUNDERS   **NSM** P J SPIERS
DARENT VALLEY (St Margaret) *Roch 2*   **P** *Bp and D&C (jt)*
  V N L WILLIAMS
DARESBURY (All Saints) *Ches 4*   **P** *D G Greenhall Esq*
  V D R FELIX
DARFIELD (All Saints) *Sheff 12*   **P** *MMCET*   **R** D HILDRED
DARLASTON (All Saints) (St Lawrence) **and Moxley** *Lich 26*
  P *Patr Bd (2 turns), Prime Min (1 turn)*   **TR** E J JONES
  TV G DAVID   **OLM** A J DUCKWORTH
DARLEY (Christ Church)   *see* Dacre w Hartwith and Darley w
  Thornthwaite *Leeds*
DARLEY (St Helen), **South Darley and Winster** *Derby 7*   **P** *Bp*
  R S D MONK   **Hon C** J MARSHALL
DARLEY ABBEY (St Matthew)   *see* Allestree St Edm and Darley
  Abbey *Derby*
DARLEY, SOUTH (St Mary the Virgin)   *see* Darley, S Darley and
  Winster *Derby*
DARLINGSCOTT (St George)   *see* Tredington and Darlingscott
  Cov
DARLINGTON (Holy Trinity) *Dur 8*   **P** *Adn Dur*
  P-in-c N J W BARKER   **C** L E GOUGH
DARLINGTON (St Cuthbert) *Dur 8*   **P** *Lord Barnard*
  V R J WILLIAMSON
DARLINGTON (St Herbert) *Dur 8*   **P** *Prime Min*
  V C M BLAKESLEY
DARLINGTON (St James) *Dur 8*   **P** *The Crown*
  P-in-c K I CRAWFORD
DARLINGTON (St John) *Dur 8*   **P** *Prime Min*
  P-in-c S C WILLIAMSON   **NSM** S M PLUMMER
DARLINGTON (St Mark) **w St Paul** *Dur 8*   **P** *Bp and St Jo Coll*
  Dur   **V** P A BAKER   **NSM** C M FERGUSON
DARLINGTON (St Matthew)   *see* Heighington and Darlington
  St Matt and St Luke *Dur*
DARLINGTON St Hilda and (St Columba) *Dur 8*   **P** *Bp*
  P-in-c S C WILLIAMSON   **NSM** S BELL, S M PLUMMER
DARNALL (Church of Christ)   *see* Attercliffe and Darnall *Sheff*
DARRINGTON (St Luke and All Saints)   *see* Went Valley *Leeds*
DARSHAM (All Saints)   *see* Yoxmere *St E*
DARTFORD (Christ Church) *Roch 2*   **P** *V Dartford H Trin*
  V R J MORTIMER
DARTFORD (Holy Trinity) *Roch 2*   **P** *Bp*   **V** M J HENWOOD
DARTFORD (St Alban) *Roch 2*   **P** *V Dartford H Trin*
  P-in-c D C HELMS
DARTFORD (St Edmund the King and Martyr) *Roch 2*   **P** *Bp*
  V M J MCCARRON   **C** R C WILSON
DARTINGTON (St Mary)   *see* Totnes w Bridgetown, Berry
  Pomeroy etc *Ex*
DARTMOUTH (St Petrox) (St Saviour) **and Dittisham** *Ex 12*
  P *Sir John Seale Bt, DBP, and Bp (jt)*   **P-in-c** W P G HAZLEWOOD
  C N J DEBNEY
DARTON (All Saints) *Leeds 18*   **P** *Bp*
  P-in-c J M MACGILLIVRAY
DARWEN (St Barnabas) *Blackb 2*   **P** *Bp*   **V** L R COLLINSON
DARWEN (St Cuthbert) **w Tockholes St Stephen** *Blackb 2*
  P *Bp*   **V** *vacant*
DARWEN (St Peter) *Blackb 2*   **P** *Bp and V Blackburn (jt)*
  V F E GREEN   **C** D STEPHENSON
DARWEN, LOWER (St James) *Blackb 2*   **P** *V Blackb*
  V T J HOROBIN   **NSM** C J COUPE
DARWEN, OVER (St James) **and Hoddlesden** *Blackb 2*   **P** *Bp*
  and V Blackb (jt)   **V** T N DYER   **NSM** M E CROOK
DATCHET (St Mary the Virgin)   *see* Colnbrook and Datchet *Ox*
DATCHWORTH (All Saints)   *see* Welwyn *St Alb*
DAUBHILL (St George the Martyr)   *see* W Bolton *Man*
DAUNTSEY (St James Great)   *see* Brinkworth w Dauntsey *Bris*
DAVENHAM (St Wilfrid) *Ches 6*   **P** *Bp*   **R** R G IVESON
  NSM V G GERAERTS
DAVENTRY (Holy Cross), **Ashby St Ledgers, Braunston,**
  Catesby, Hellidon, Staverton and Welton *Pet 3*   **P** *Patr Bd*
  P-in-c M C W WEBBER   **TV** C M E T TREMTHTHANMOR,
  S R D BROWN   **Hon C** W R KILFORD
DAVIDSTOW (St David)   *see* Moorland Gp *Truro*
DAVINGTON (St Mary Magdalene)   *see* The Brents and
  Davington *Cant*
DAVYHULME (Christ Church) *Man 5*   **P** *Bp*
  P-in-c K L MARSHALL   **NSM** B R CORKE
DAVYHULME (St Mary) *Man 5*   **P** *Bp*   **V** C S FORD
  OLM S A WRIGHT
DAWLEY (Holy Trinity)   *see* Cen Telford *Lich*
DAWLEY (St Jerome)   *see* W Hayes *Lon*
DAWLISH (St Gregory), **Cofton and Starcross** *Ex 5*   **P** *D&C*
  Ex, D&C Sarum, and Earl of Devon (jt)   **C** N M HAWKINS
  Hon C C V CURD   **NSM** D CAINE

DAWLISH WARREN (Church Hall)   *see* Dawlish, Cofton and
  Starcross *Ex*
DAYBROOK (St Paul) *S'well 7*   **P** *Bp*   **V** S A BAYLIS
DAYLESFORD (St Peter)   *see* Chipping Norton *Ox*
DE BEAUVOIR TOWN (St Peter) *Lon 5*   **P** *Bp*
  V J F PORTER-PRYCE   **C** R K SPRINGER
DEAL (St Andrew) *Cant 9*   **P** *Abp*   **P-in-c** S E YOUNG
DEAL (St George the Martyr) *Cant 9*   **P** *Abp*   **V** C G SPENCER
  C B M THORPE, S PORTER
DEAL (St Leonard) (St Richard) **and Sholden w Great**
  Mongeham *Cant 9*   **P** *Abp*   **R** D W FLEWKER
  NSM P T KAVANAGH
DEAN (All Hallows)   *see* The Stodden Churches *St Alb*
DEAN (St Oswald)   *see* Clifton, Dean and Mosser *Carl*
DEAN COURT (St Andrew)   *see* Cumnor *Ox*
DEAN FOREST (Christ Church)   *see* Forest of Dean Ch Ch w
  English Bicknor *Glouc*
DEAN FOREST (St Paul)   *see* Parkend and Viney Hill *Glouc*
DEAN PRIOR (St George the Martyr)   *see* Staverton w
  Landscove, Littlehempston, Buckfastleigh and Dean
  Prior *Ex*
DEANE (All Saints)   *see* N Waltham and Steventon, Ashe and
  Deane *Win*
DEANE (St Mary the Virgin) *Man 9*   **P** *Patr Bd*   **TR** T P CLARK
  TV J G ARMSTRONG   **C** M A MURTHEN   **OLM** E B PLANT
DEANE VALE Benefice, The *B & W 19*   **P** *Bp and PCCs*
  Heathfield, Hillfarrance, and Oake (jt)   **R** A NORRIS
  C K J BRINDLE
DEANSHANGER (Holy Trinity)   *see* Passenham *Pet*
DEARHAM (St Mungo)   *see* Allonby, Cross Canonby and
  Dearham *Carl*
DEARNLEY (St Andrew), **Wardle and Smallbridge** *Man 17*
  P *Bp*   **V** S A JONES   **NSM** M S HOWARTH
DEBDEN (St Mary the Virgin)   *see* Saffron Walden and Villages
  Chelmsf
DEBENHAM (St Mary Magdalene) **and Helmingham** *St E 16*
  P *Ld Chan, Lord Henniker, MMCET, Bp, and Lord Tollemache*
  (by turn)   **P-in-c** P A W COTTON   **NSM** R J BARNES
DEDDINGTON (St Peter and St Paul) **Barford, Clifton and**
  Hempton *Ox 23*   **P** *D&C Windsor and Bp (jt)*
  V A L GOLDTHORP
DEDHAM (St Mary the Virgin) *Chelmsf 22*   **P** *Duchy of Lanc*
  and Lectureship Trustees (alt)   **V** *vacant*
DEDWORTH (All Saints) *Ox 5*   **P** *Bp*   **V** L M BROWN
DEEPCAR (St John the Evangelist) *Sheff 3*   **P** *Bp*
  P-in-c H R ISAACSON
DEEPING ST JAMES (St James) *Linc 19*   **P** *Burghley Ho*
  Preservation Trust   **V** S A PATERSON   **NSM** S M C MARSHALL
DEEPING ST NICHOLAS (St Nicholas)   *see* Spalding St Jo w
  Deeping St Nicholas *Linc*
DEEPING, WEST (St Andrew)   *see* Uffington Gp *Linc*
DEEPLISH (St Luke) **and Newbold** *Man 17*   **P** *Bp*
  V S P WATKINSON   **OLM** R K GRAY
DEERHURST (St Mary) **and Apperley w Forthampton,**
  Chaceley, Tredington, Stoke Orchard and Hardwicke
  Glouc 9   **P** *Bp, V Longdon, and J S Yorke Esq (jt)*
  P-in-c B L MESSHAM   **C** K MUNDY   **NSM** C E WHITNEY,
  D J COULTON
DEFFORD (St James) **w Besford** *Worc 4*   **P** *D&C Westmr*
  V S K RENSHAW
DEIGHTON (All Saints)   *see* Brompton w Deighton *York*
DELABOLE (St John the Evangelist)   *see* St Teath *Truro*
DELAMERE (St Peter) *Ches 6*   **P** *The Crown*   **R** E M OLLMAN
DELAVAL (Our Lady) *Newc 1*   **P** *Lord Hastings*
  V D E BOWLER   **OLM** D R ORMESHER
DEMBLEBY (St Lucia)   *see* S Lafford *Linc*
DENABY MAIN (All Saints) *Sheff 7*   **P** *Bp*   **V** R C DAVIES
DENBURY (St Mary the Virgin)   *see* Ipplepen w Torbryan,
  Denbury and Broadhempston w Woodland *Ex*
DENBY (St John the Evangelist)   *see* Cumberworth, Denby and
  Denby Dale *Leeds*
DENBY (St Mary the Virgin)   *see* Horsley and Denby *Derby*
DENBY DALE (Holy Trinity)   *see* Cumberworth, Denby and
  Denby Dale *Leeds*
DENCHWORTH (St James)   *see* Vale *Ox*
DENDRON (St Matthew)   *see* Aldingham, Dendron, Rampside
  and Urswick *Carl*
DENFORD (Holy Trinity)   *see* Thrapston, Denford and Islip *Pet*
DENGIE (St James) **w Asheldham** *Chelmsf 11*   **P** *Bp*
  R *vacant*
DENHAM (St John the Baptist)   *see* Athelington, Denham,
  Horham, Hoxne etc *St E*
DENHAM (St Mark) (St Mary the Virgin) *Ox 9*   **P** *L J Way Esq*
  R *vacant*
DENHAM (St Mary)   *see* Barrow *St E*
DENHAM, NEW (St Francis)   *see* Denham *Ox*

DENMEAD (All Saints) *Portsm 5*   **P** *Ld Chan*   **V** S M EDWARDS
   NSM A C L JOHNSON, S A OSBORNE
DENNINGTON (St Mary)   *see Upper Alde St E*
DENSHAW (Christ Church)   *see Saddleworth Man*
DENSTON (St Nicholas)   *see Bansfield St E*
DENSTONE (All Saints)   *see Alton w Bradley-le-Moors and
   Denstone etc Lich*
DENT (St Andrew) w Cowgill *Carl 10*   **P** *Bp and Sidesmen of
   Dent (alt)*   **V** P J BOYLES   **NSM** C A BROWN
DENTON (Christ Church) (St George) *Man 13*   **P** *Bp*
   P-in-c M HOWARTH   **C** A S MITCHELL, E M POPE, P R DIXON
   OLM C MASTERS
DENTON (Holy Spirit) *Newc 4*   **P** *Bp*   **V** B J STOBER
DENTON (St Andrew)   *see Harlaxton Gp Linc*
DENTON (St Helen)   *see Washburn and Mid-Wharfe Leeds*
DENTON (St Lawrence) *Man 13*   **P** *Earl of Wilton*
   P-in-c E M POPE   **C** A S MITCHELL, K V REEVES, M HOWARTH,
   P R DIXON   **OLM** S P CANT
DENTON (St Leonard) w South Heighton and Tarring Neville
   Chich 21   **P** *MMCET and Bp (alt)*   **R** P L WILSON
DENTON (St Margaret)   *see Yardley Hastings, Denton and
   Grendon etc Pet*
DENTON (St Mary Magdalene)   *see Elham w Denton and
   Wootton and Acrise Cant*
DENTON (St Mary)   *see Ditchingham, Hedenham, Broome,
   Earsham etc Nor*
DENTON HOLME (St James) *Carl 3*   **P** *Trustees*
   C J I MOORES
DENTON, NETHER (St Cuthbert)   *see Lanercost, Walton,
   Gilsland and Nether Denton Carl*
**DENVER (St Mary) and Ryston w Roxham and West Dereham
   and Bexwell** *Ely 9*   **P** *G&C Coll Cam and Bp (jt)*
   R J M T M GRUNDY
DEOPHAM (St Andrew)   *see High Oak, Hingham and Scoulton
   w Wood Rising Nor*
DEPDEN (St Mary the Virgin)   *see Chevington w Hargrave,
   Chedburgh w Depden etc St E*
DEPTFORD (St John) (Holy Trinity) (Ascension) *S'wark 2*
   P *Patr Bd*   **TR** P J FARLEY-MOORE   **TV** T A DONNELLY
DEPTFORD (St Nicholas) (St Luke) *S'wark 2*   **P** *MMCET,
   Peache Trustees, and CPAS (jt)*
   V L A J CODRINGTON-MARSHALL
DEPTFORD (St Paul) *S'wark 2*   **P** *Bp*   **R** P D BUTLER
DEPTFORD Brockley (St Peter)   *see Brockley St Pet S'wark*
DERBY (St Alkmund and St Werburgh) *Derby 9*   **P** *Simeon's
   Trustees*   **P-in-c** J A BURGESS   **C** I D MOUNTFORD
DERBY (St Andrew w St Osmund) *Derby 10*   **P** *Bp*
   P-in-c T E MORRIS
DERBY (St Anne) *Derby 9*   **P** *Bp*   **V** *vacant*
DERBY (St Augustine)   *see Walbrook Epiphany Derby*
DERBY (St Barnabas) *Derby 9*   **P** *Bp*   **V** D G HONOUR
   NSM A P GRIGGS   **OLM** W G DAY
DERBY (St Bartholomew) *Derby 10*   **P** *Bp*   **V** *vacant*
DERBY (St John the Evangelist) *Derby 9*   **P** *Bp*   **C** E J JONES
DERBY (St Luke) *Derby 9*   **P** *Bp*   **V** *vacant*
DERBY (St Mark)   *see Chaddesden St Phil w Derby St Mark
   Derby*
DERBY (St Paul) *Derby 9*   **P** *Bp*   **P-in-c** M S MITTON
DERBY (St Peter and Christ Church w Holy Trinity) *Derby 10*
   P *CPAS*   **P-in-c** P D MORRIS   **C** A K MATTHEWS
DERBY (St Thomas)   *see Walbrook Epiphany Derby*
DERBY, WEST (Good Shepherd) *Liv 8*   **P** *Bp and R W Derby (jt)*
   V A J EDWARDS   **OLM** S TRAPNELL
DERBY, WEST (St James) (St Mary) *Liv 8*   **P** *Bp and Adn Liv (jt)*
   V *vacant*
DERBY, WEST (St John) *Liv 8*   **P** *Trustees*   **V** S J P FISHER
DERBYSHIRE HILL (St Philip)   *see Parr Liv*
DEREHAM (St Nicholas) and District *Nor 17*   **P** *Ld Chan
   (2 turns), Patr Bd (1 turn)*   **TR** S M THEAKSTON
   TV A F AUBREY-JONES, G L WELLS   **C** D E TURNHAM
   NSM K G PILGRIM   **OLM** J L NURSEY
DEREHAM, WEST (St Andrew)   *see Denver and Ryston w
   Roxham and W Dereham etc Ely*
DERINGHAM BANK (Ascension) (St Thomas) *York 14*
   P *Abp*   **V** S J WHALEY
DERRINGTON (St Matthew)   *see Bradeley, Church Eaton,
   Derrington and Haughton Lich*
DERRY HILL (Christ Church)   *see Marden Vale Sarum*
**DERSINGHAM (St Nicholas), Anmer, Ingoldisthorpe and
   Shernborne** *Nor 16*   **P** *HM The Queen and Bp (alt)*
   R *vacant*
DERWENT INGS *York 2*   **P** *Abp, Lt Col J Darlington, and Sir
   Mervyn Dunnington-Jefferson Bt (jt)*   **R** I B KITCHEN
DERWENT, UPPER *Carl 6*   **P** *V Keswick St Jo (1 turn),
   V Crosthwaite (2 turns)*   **P-in-c** P H VIVASH

DERWENT, UPPER *York 19*   **P** *Viscountess Downe (1 turn),
   Sir Philip Naylor-Leyland (Bt) (1 turn), Abp (2 turns)*   **V** S G HILL
**DESBOROUGH (St Giles), Brampton Ash, Dingley and
   Braybrooke** *Pet 9*   **P** *Bp, Earl Spencer, and DBP (by turn)*
   NSM N M CLARKE
DESFORD (St Martin) and Kirby Muxloe *Leic 9*   **P** *Bp and
   Ld Chan (alt)*   **R** T L RINGLAND   **NSM** R C MARSH
DETHICK (St John the Baptist)   *see Matlock, Dethick, Lea and
   Holloway Derby*
DETLING (St Martin)   *see Boxley w Detling Cant*
DEVER, LOWER *Win 7*   **P** *Bp and D&C (jt)*   **R** M D BAILEY
   NSM J BROWN, K P KOUSSEFF
DEVER, UPPER *Win 7*   **P** *Lord Northbrook (3 turns), Bp (2 turns)*
   V S A FOSTER   **C** S J DUDDLES
DEVIZES (St John) (St Mary) *Sarum 17*   **P** *Ld Chan*
   R P RICHARDSON   **NSM** J M CLARK
DEVIZES (St Peter) *Sarum 17*   **P** *Bp*   **V** V J PERRICONE
DEVONPORT (St Bartholomew) and Ford St Mark *Ex 21*
   P *Bp and Trustees (jt)*   **P-in-c** R T SILK
DEVONPORT (St Boniface) *Ex 21*   **P** *Bp*   **V** A B SHAW
DEVONPORT (St Budeaux) *Ex 21*   **P** *V Plymouth St Andr w
   St Paul and St Geo*   **V** S J BEACH
DEVONPORT (St Thomas)   *see Plymouth St Pet and H Apostles
   Ex*
DEVONPORT St Michael (St Barnabas) *Ex 21*   **P** *Bp and
   Trustees Lord St Levan (jt)*   **V** T J BUCKLEY
DEVORAN (St John the Evangelist and St Petroc) *Truro 6*
   P *Bp*   **P-in-c** S A BONE   **C** D J F JONES   **NSM** E M SHEARD,
   S J C FLETCHER
DEWCHURCH, LITTLE (St David)   *see Heref S Wye Heref*
DEWCHURCH, MUCH (St David)   *see Wormelow Hundred
   Heref*
DEWLISH (All Saints)   *see Puddletown, Tolpuddle and Milborne
   w Dewlish Sarum*
DEWSALL (St Michael)   *see Heref S Wye Heref*
DEWSBURY (All Saints)   *see Dewsbury Leeds*
**DEWSBURY (All Saints) (St Mark) (St Matthew and St John
   the Baptist)** *Leeds 10*   **P** *Bp, Adn Pontefract, RD Dewsbury, and
   Lay Chmn Dewsbury Deanery Syn (jt)*   **TV** K ROBERTSON
   NSM A B POLLARD, H THURLOW
DEWSBURY MOOR (St John the Evangelist)   *see Dewsbury
   Leeds*
DHOON (Christ Church)   *see Maughold and S Ramsey S & M*
DIBDEN (All Saints) *Win 11*   **P** *MMCET*   **R** J CURRIN
   C P S STARK TOLLER
DIBDEN PURLIEU (St Andrew)   *see Dibden Win*
DICKER, UPPER (Holy Trinity)   *see Hellingly and Upper Dicker
   Chich*
DICKLEBURGH (All Saints) and The Pulhams *Nor 10*   **P** *Ld
   Chan (1 turn), Patr Bd (2 turns), Prime Min (1 turn)*
   R J H E ROSKELLY   **OLM** D J ADLAM, P D SCHWIER
DIDBROOK (St George)   *see Winchcombe Glouc*
DIDCOT (All Saints) *Ox 26*   **P** *BNC Ox*   **P-in-c** K M BECK
   C B M BODEKER, H R BOORMAN
DIDCOT (St Peter) *Ox 26*   **P** *Bp*   **P-in-c** H C REYNOLDS
DIDDINGTON (St Laurence)   *see The Paxtons w Diddington
   and Southoe Ely*
DIDDLEBURY (St Peter) w Munslow, Holdgate and Tugford
   Heref 11   **P** *Bp (3 turns), D&C (1 turn)*   **R** J S BEESLEY
   C M S QUAYLE
DIDLINGTON (St Michael) *Nor 13*   **P** *CPAS*
   P-in-c C P SHERLOCK
DIDMARTON (St Lawrence)   *see Boxwell, Leighterton,
   Didmarton, Oldbury etc Glouc*
DIDSBURY (St James) (Emmanuel) *Man 6*   **P** *Patr Bd*
   TR N J BUNDOCK   **TV** J B EDSON   **OLM** C K SANDIFORD
**DIDSBURY, WEST (Christ Church) and Withington
   St Christopher** *Man 6*   **P** *Trustees and Prime Min (alt)*
   R A PILKINGTON   **C** M R HEWERDINE
DIGBY GROUP, The (St Thomas of Canterbury) *Linc 14*
   P *Mrs H E Gillatt, Ld Chan, and DBP (by turn)*   **Hon**
   C D B WOODS
DIGMOOR (Christ the Servant)   *see Upholland Liv*
**DIGSWELL (St John the Evangelist) (Christ the King) and
   Panshanger** *St Alb 18*   **P** *Patr Bd*   **TV** D J CATTLE
   C R P MARSHALL   **NSM** A E COUPER
DILHAM (St Nicholas)   *see Smallburgh w Dilham w Honing
   and Crostwight Nor*
DILHORNE (All Saints)   *see Caverswall and Weston Coyney w
   Dilhorne Lich*
DILTON MARSH (Holy Trinity)   *see White Horse Sarum*
DILTON or LEIGH (Holy Saviour)   *as above*
DILWYN AND STRETFORD (St Mary the Virgin)   *see Leominster
   Heref*
DINDER (St Michael and All Angels)   *see Pilton w Croscombe,
   N Wootton and Dinder B & W*

DINEDOR (St Andrew)   *see* Heref S Wye *Heref*

DINES GREEN (St Michael)   *see* Worc Dines Green St Mich and Crown E, Rushwick *Worc*

DINGLEY (All Saints)   *see* Desborough, Brampton Ash, Dingley and Braybrooke *Pet*

DINNINGTON (St Leonard) w Laughton-en-le-Morthen and Throapham *Sheff 5*   **P** *Bp and J C Athorpe Esq (jt)*
R H A JOWETT

DINNINGTON (St Matthew)   *see* Ch the King *Newc*

DINNINGTON (St Nicholas)   *see* Merriott w Hinton, Dinnington and Lopen *B & W*

DINSDALE (St John the Baptist) w Sockburn *Dur 8*   **P** *D&C and Sherburn Hosp (alt)*   **P-in-c** A J MARTIN

DINTING VALE (Holy Trinity) *Derby 6*   **P** *Bp*   **V** I K STUBBS
NSM R F HEELEY

DINTON (St Mary)   *see* Nadder Valley *Sarum*

DINTON (St Peter and St Paul)   *see* Stone w Dinton and Hartwell *Ox*

DIPTFORD (St Mary the Virgin), North Huish, Harberton, Harbertonford, Halwell and Moreleigh *Ex 12*   **P** *Bp and D&C (jt)*   **C** C M S LUFF

DISCOED (St Michael)   *see* Presteigne w Discoed, Kinsham, Lingen and Knill *Heref*

DISEWORTH (St Michael and All Angels)   *see* Kegworth, Hathern, Long Whatton, Diseworth etc *Leic*

DISHLEY (All Saints)   *see* Thorpe Acre w Dishley *Leic*

DISLEY (St Mary the Virgin) *Ches 16*   **P** *Lord Newton*
V M J OWENS

DISS (St Mary)   *see* Diss *Nor*

DISS Team Ministry, The (St Mary) *Nor 10*   **P** *Patr Bd*
TR A C BILLETT   **TV** W N EVANS   **OLM** M D SWAYZE

DISTINGTON (Holy Spirit) *Carl 7*   **P** *Earl of Lonsdale*
P-in-c J H POWLEY   **C** H J LOWE

DITCHINGHAM (St Mary), Hedenham, Broome, Earsham, Alburgh and Denton *Nor 10*   **P** *Abp, Bp, Countess Ferrers, J M Meade Esq, and St Jo Coll Cam (jt)*   **R** C HUTTON
OLM B L CRAMP, R A KIRKPATRICK, S L CRAMP

DITCHLING (St Margaret), Streat and Westmeston *Chich 8*
P *Bp*   **R** D P WALLIS   **C** N W KINRADE

DITTERIDGE (St Christopher)   *see* Box w Hazlebury and Ditteridge *Bris*

DITTISHAM (St George)   *see* Dartmouth and Dittisham *Ex*

DITTON (St Basil and All Saints)   *see* Hough Green St Basil and All SS *Liv*

DITTON (St Michael) (St Thomas) *Liv 13*   **P** *Bp*
V L RILEY-DAWKIN   **OLM** L MOSS

DITTON (St Peter ad Vincula) *Roch 7*   **P** *Ch Trust Fund Trust*
R J R TERRANOVA

DITTON PRIORS (St John the Baptist) w Neenton, Burwarton, Cleobury North, Aston Botterell, Wheathill and Loughton and Chetton *Heref 8*   **P** *Bp, Princess Josephine zu Loewenstein, and Exors Viscount Boyne (jt)*   **R** T M MASON

DIXTON NEWTON (St Peter)   *see* Wye Reaches Gp *Heref*

DOBCROSS (Holy Trinity)   *see* Saddleworth *Man*

DOCCOMBE (Chapel)   *see* Moretonhampstead, Manaton, N Bovey and Lustleigh *Ex*

DOCK (Mission Church)   *see* Immingham Gp *Linc*

DOCKENFIELD (Church of the Good Shepherd)   *see* Rowledge and Frensham *Guildf*

DOCKING (St Mary), The Birchams, Fring, Stanhoe and Sedgeford *Nor 16*   **P** *Bp, D&C, and Mrs A J Ralli (3 turns), HM The Queen (1 turn)*   **R** *vacant*

DOCKLOW (St Bartholomew)   *see* Leominster *Heref*

DODBROOKE (St Thomas à Beckett)   *see* Kingsbridge, Dodbrooke, and W Alvington *Ex*

DODDERHILL (St Augustine)   *see* Droitwich Spa *Worc*

DODDINGHURST (All Saints) *Chelmsf 8*   **P** *Bp*
P-in-c M N JAMES   **Hon C** A V COLEMAN

DODDINGTON (All Saints)   *see* Quantock Coast *B & W*

DODDINGTON (St John the Baptist)   *see* Cleobury Mortimer w Hopton Wafers etc *Heref*

DODDINGTON (St John)   *see* Wybunbury and Audlem w Doddington *Ches*

DODDINGTON (St Mary and St Michael)   *see* Glendale Gp *Newc*

DODDINGTON (St Mary) w Benwick and Wimblington *Ely 11*
P *Bp, St Jo Coll Dur, and R Raynar Esq (jt)*   **R** *vacant*

DODDINGTON (St Peter)   *see* Skellingthorpe w Doddington *Linc*

DODDINGTON, GREAT (St Nicholas) and Wilby and Ecton *Pet 6*   **P** *Ld Chan, Exors Lt Col H C M Stockdale, and Prime Min (by turn)*   **R** *vacant*

DODDISCOMBSLEIGH (St Michael)   *see* Christow, Ashton, Bridford, Dunchideock etc *Ex*

DODFORD (Holy Trinity and St Mary) *Worc 7*   **P** *Bp*
V C A HOLZAPFEL

DODFORD (St Mary the Virgin)   *see* Weedon Bec w Everdon and Dodford *Pet*

DODLESTON (St Mary) *Ches 2*   **P** *D&C*   **R** E H CLARKE

DODWORTH (St John the Baptist) *Leeds 18*   **P** *V Silkstone*
NSM D J PERCIVAL

DOGMERSFIELD (All Saints)   *see* Hartley Wintney, Elvetham, Winchfield etc *Win*

DOGSTHORPE (Christ the Carpenter)   *see* Pet Ch Carpenter *Pet*

DOLPHINHOLME (St Mark) w Quernmore and Over Wyresdale *Blackb 11*   **P** *Bp and V Lanc (jt)*   **V** C J RIGNEY

DOLTON (St Edmund King and Martyr), Dowland, Iddesleigh, and Monkokehampton *Ex 19*   **P** *Bp and Ch Soc Trust (jt)*   **R** S Y OLDHAM   **NSM** A CONNELL, D J URSELL

DONCASTER (St George) (St Edmund's Church Centre) *Sheff 8*   **P** *Bp*   **V** D L STEVENS

DONCASTER (St Hugh of Lincoln)   *see* New Cantley *Sheff*

DONCASTER (St James) *Sheff 8*   **P** *Hyndman's Trustees*
P-in-c C J MCCARTHY

DONCASTER (St Leonard and St Jude) *Sheff 7*   **P** *The Crown*
V N J PAY

DONCASTER (St Mary) (St Paul) *Sheff 8*   **P** *Hyndman's Trustees and Bp (jt)*   **V** *vacant*

DONHEAD ST ANDREW (St Andrew)   *see* St Bartholomew *Sarum*

DONHEAD ST MARY (St Mary the Virgin) *as above*

DONINGTON (St Cuthbert)   *see* Albrighton, Boningale and Donington *Lich*

DONINGTON (St Mary and the Holy Rood)   *see* Haven Gp *Linc*

DONINGTON-ON-BAIN (St Andrew)   *see* Asterby Gp *Linc*

DONISTHORPE (St John)   *see* Woodfield *Leic*

DONNINGTON (St George) *Chich 2*   **P** *Bp*
P-in-c J P COOPER, JP COOOPER

DONNINGTON (St Mary)   *see* Redmarley D'Abitot, Bromesberrow, Pauntley etc *Glouc*

DONNINGTON WOOD (St Matthew) *Lich 21*   **P** *Bp*
P-in-c P M SMITH

DONYATT (Blessed Virgin Mary)   *see* Isle Valley *B & W*

DONYLAND, EAST (St Lawrence)   *see* Fingringhoe w E Donyland and Abberton etc *Chelmsf*

DORCHESTER (St George) (St Mary the Virgin) (St Peter, Holy Trinity and All Saints) and the Winterbournes *Sarum 1*
P *Ld Chan (1 turn), Patr Bd (4 turns)*   **TR** T M B WOODHOUSE
TV F M G HALL   **C** J E HAINE   **NSM** A R WHITING,
J LACY-SMITH, J M CULLIFORD, J SADDINGTON,
T M STEWART-SYKES

DORCHESTER (St Peter and St Paul) *Ox 20*   **P** *Patr Bd*
TR S E BOOYS   **TV** C N KING, P H CAWTHORNE
C J C ROBERTS, J MORTON   **NSM** A F ILSLEY, M J LAKEY
OLM D W HAYLETT

DORDON (St Leonard) *Birm 10*   **P** *V Polesworth*
V A SIMMONS

DORE (Christ Church) *Sheff 2*   **P** *Sir Philip Naylor-Leyland Bt*
V C L TUPLING   **NSM** A F CREASEY

DORKING (St Martin) w Ranmore *Guildf 7*   **P** *Bp*
V D J TIGHE   **NSM** D J COWAN

DORKING (St Paul) *Guildf 7*   **P** *Ch Patr Trust*
V R K F BUSHYAGER   **NSM** J C YELLAND   **OLM** J A FIRTH

DORMANSLAND (St John)   *see* Lingfield and Dormansland *S'wark*

DORMANSTOWN (All Saints)   *see* Coatham and Dormanstown *York*

DORMINGTON (St Peter)   *see* Bartestree Cross *Heref*

DORMSTON (St Nicholas)   *see* Inkberrow w Cookhill and Kington w Dormston *Worc*

DORNEY (St James the Less)   *see* Eton w Eton Wick, Boveney and Dorney *Ox*

DORRIDGE (St Philip) *Birm 6*   **P** *Bp*   **V** T D HILL-BROWN
Hon C R J HILL-BROWN

DORRINGTON (St Edward) w Leebotwood, Longnor, Stapleton, Smethcote and Woolstaston *Heref 10*   **P** *DBP and J J C Coldwell Esq (jt)*   **R** E R JESSIMAN

DORRINGTON (St James)   *see* Digby Gp *Linc*

DORSINGTON (St Peter)   *see* Vale and Cotswold Edge *Glouc*

DORSTONE (St Faith)   *see* Cusop w Blakemere, Bredwardine w Brobury etc *Heref*

DORTON (St John the Baptist)   *see* Bernwode *Ox*

DOSTHILL (St Paul) *Birm 10*   **P** *Bp*   **V** J L C SHAW

DOTTERY (St Saviour)   *see* Askerswell, Loders, Powerstock and Symondsbury *Sarum*

DOUGLAS (St George) (All Saints) *S & M*   **P** *Bp*
V A BROWN   **C** A M DI CHIARA   **OLM** S A FERRIS

DOUGLAS (St Matthew the Apostle) *S & M*   **P** *Bp*
V R L BOYLE

DOUGLAS (St Ninian) *S & M*   **P** *CPAS*   **V** J P COLDWELL

DOUGLAS (St Thomas the Apostle) *S & M*   **P** *Bp*   **V** I BRADY
NSM L BRADY

DOUGLAS-IN-PARBOLD (Christ Church)   *see* Appley Bridge and Parbold *Blackb*

DOULTING (St Aldhelm)   *see* Shepton Mallet w Doulting *B & W*

DOVE HOLES (St Paul)   *see* Peak Forest and Dove Holes *Derby*

DOVECOT (Holy Spirit) *Liv 2*   **P** *Bp*   **V** J M DUNKLING

DOVER (St Martin) *Cant 7*   **P** *CPAS*   **V** K G GARRETT   **NSM** P A GODFREY

DOVER TOWN (St Mary the Virgin) *Cant 7*   **P** *Patr Bd*   **TR** J A P WALKER   **TV** K G GARRETT   **NSM** P A GODFREY

DOVERCOURT (All Saints)   *see* Harwich Peninsula *Chelmsf*

DOVERDALE (St Mary)   *see* Ombersley w Doverdale *Worc*

DOVERIDGE (St Cuthbert)   *see* S Dales *Derby*

DOWDESWELL (St Michael)   *see* Sevenhampton w Charlton Abbots, Hawling etc *Glouc*

DOWLAND (St Peter)   *see* Dolton, Dowland, Iddesleigh etc *Ex*

DOWLES Button Oak (St Andrew)   *see* Ribbesford w Bewdley and Dowles and Wribbenhall *Worc*

DOWLISHWAKE (St Andrew)   *see* Winsmoor *B & W*

DOWN AMPNEY (All Saints)   *see* S Cotswolds *Glouc*

DOWN HATHERLEY (St Mary and Corpus Christi)   *see* Twigworth, Down Hatherley, Norton, The Leigh etc *Glouc*

DOWN ST MARY (St Mary the Virgin)   *see* N Creedy *Ex*

DOWN, East (St John the Baptist)   *see* Shirwell, Loxhore, Kentisbury, Arlington, etc *Ex*

DOWNDERRY (St Nicholas)   *see* St Germans *Truro*

DOWNE (St Mary Magdalene)   *see* Cudham and Downe *Roch*

DOWNEND (Christ Church) (Church Centre) *Bris 5*   **P** *Peache Trustees*   **V** J L VICKERY   **C** P J PETERSON   **Hon C** C J DOBSON

DOWNHAM (St Barnabas)   *see* Catford (Southend) and Downham *S'wark*

DOWNHAM (St Leonard)   *see* Chatburn and Downham *Blackb*

DOWNHAM (St Leonard)   *see* Ely *Ely*

DOWNHAM (St Luke)   *see* Catford (Southend) and Downham *S'wark*

DOWNHAM (St Margaret) w S Hanningfield and Ramsden Bellhouse *Chelmsf 10*   **P** *Bp and Reformation Ch Trust (jt)*   **V** S A ROBERTSON   **NSM** J ANDREWS, M K SEAMAN

DOWNHAM MARKET (St Edmund) and Crimplesham w Stradsett *Ely 9*   **P** *Bp*   **R** J W MATHER   **NSM** A D DAVIES

DOWNHAM, NORTH (St Mark)   *see* Catford (Southend) and Downham *S'wark*

DOWNHEAD (All Saints)   *see* Leigh upon Mendip w Stoke St Michael *B & W*

DOWNHOLME (St Michael and All Angels)   *see* Richmond w Hudswell and Downholme and Marske *Leeds*

DOWNLEY (St James the Great)   *see* High Wycombe *Ox*

DOWNS BARN and NEAT HILL (Community Church)   *see* Stantonbury and Willen *Ox*

DOWNS Benefice, The *Win 3*   **P** *Ld Chan (1 turn), Bp and Marquess Camden (1 turn)*   **R** J J MACHIN   **Hon C** D MAPES   **NSM** J A AUSSANT

DOWNSFOOT *Cant 14*   **P** *Abp and D&C (jt)*   **V** L G APPS-HUGGINS

DOWNTON (St Giles)   *see* Wigmore Abbey *Heref*

DOWNTON (St Lawrence)   *see* Forest and Avon *Sarum*

DOWSBY (St Andrew)   *see* Billingborough Gp *Linc*

DOXFORD (St Wilfrid) *Dur 1*   **P** *Bp*   **P-in-c** S R THORP

DOYNTON (Holy Trinity)   *see* Wick w Doynton and Dyrham *Bris*

DRAKES BROUGHTON (St Barnabas)   *see* Stoulton w Drake's Broughton and Pirton etc *Worc*

DRAUGHTON (St Augustine)   *see* Skipton H Trin *Leeds*

DRAUGHTON (St Catherine)   *see* Maidwell w Draughton, Lamport w Faxton *Pet*

DRAX (St Peter and St Paul)   *see* Carlton and Drax *York*

DRAYCOT *Bris 6*   **P** *Bp, D&C Sarum, and R W Neeld Esq (jt)*   **P-in-c** A J LOVE   **NSM** E M BONE

DRAYCOTE Group, The *Cov 6*   **P** *Bp (2 turns), Simeon's Trustees (1 turn), and Mrs J H Shaw-Fox (1 turn)*   **R** *vacant*

DRAYCOTT (St Mary)   *see* Wilne and Draycott w Breaston *Derby*

DRAYCOTT (St Peter)   *see* Cheddar, Draycott and Rodney Stoke *B & W*

DRAYCOTT IN THE CLAY (St Augustine)   *see* Hanbury, Newborough, Rangemore and Tutbury *Lich*

DRAYCOTT-LE-MOORS (St Margaret) w Forsbrook *Lich 6*   **P** *Bp*   **R** *vacant*

DRAYTON (St Catherine)   *see* Langport Area *B & W*

DRAYTON (St Margaret) *Nor 2*   **P** *Bp*   **R** D WELLS   **C** D E HAGAN-PALMER

DRAYTON (St Peter) Abingdon *Ox 19*   **P** *Bp*   **P-in-c** R A PETERS   **NSM** R BRUCE

DRAYTON (St Peter) Banbury   *see* Ironstone *Ox*

DRAYTON BASSETT (St Peter) *Lich 4*   **P** *Bp*   **R** J R IDDON   **NSM** R G DAVIES

DRAYTON IN HALES (St Mary) *Lich 18*   **P** *C C Corbet Esq*   **P-in-c** M P TANNER

DRAYTON PARSLOW (Holy Trinity)   *see* Newton Longville, Mursley, Swanbourne etc *Ox*

DRAYTON ST LEONARD (St Leonard and St Catherine)   *see* Dorchester *Ox*

DRAYTON, EAST (St Peter)   *see* Retford Area *S'well*

DRAYTON, LITTLE (Christ Church) *Lich 18*   **P** *V Drayton in Hales*   **P-in-c** H G SNOOK

DRAYTON, WEST (St Martin) *Lon 24*   **P** *Bp*   **V** R J BARRIE

DRAYTON, WEST (St Paul)   *see* Retford Area *S'well*

DRAYTON-BEAUCHAMP (St Mary the Virgin)   *see* Aston Clinton w Buckland and Drayton Beauchamp *Ox*

DRESDEN (Resurrection)   *see* Blurton and Dresden *Lich*

DREWSTEIGNTON (Holy Trinity)   *see* Chagford, Gidleigh, Throwleigh etc *Ex*

DRIFFIELD (St Mary)   *see* S Cotswolds *Glouc*

DRIFFIELD, GREAT (All Saints) and LITTLE (St Peter) *York 10*   **P** *Abp*   **V** A P ISON   **NSM** J A TONKIN, S P GRANT

DRIGG (St Peter)   *see* Seascale and Drigg *Carl*

DRIGHLINGTON (St Paul) *Leeds 15*   **P** *Bp*   **P-in-c** A F LAWSON   **C** D J CLARK   **NSM** B DUXBURY

DRIMPTON (St Mary)   *see* Beaminster Area *Sarum*

DRINGHOUSES (St Edward the Confessor) *York 7*   **P** *Abp*   **V** C W M BALDOCK   **NSM** L I CHESTER

DRINKSTONE (All Saints)   *see* Woolpit w Drinkstone *St E*

DROITWICH SPA (St Andrew w St Mary de Witton) (St Nicholas) (St Peter) (St Richard) *Worc 8*   **P** *Bp*   **P-in-c** N G BYARD   **TV** B J JAMESON   **C** L J HANDY   **NSM** R HOLDEN

DRONFIELD (St John the Baptist) w Holmesfield *Derby 5*   **P** *Ld Chan*   **TR** P E BOLD   **TV** R C TURNER, W R EARDLEY   **C** I WEBB

DROPMORE (St Anne)   *see* Taplow and Dropmore *Ox*

DROXFORD (St Mary and All Saints)   *see* Meon Bridge *Portsm*

DROYLSDEN (St Andrew) *Man 13*   **P** *Bp*   **P-in-c** J A HEMSWORTH   **OLM** L M COOKE

DROYLSDEN (St Martin) *Man 13*   **P** *Bp*   **P-in-c** J H FARNWORTH   **C** J A HEMSWORTH   **OLM** L M COOKE

DROYLSDEN (St Mary) (St John) *Man 13*   **P** *Bp*   **R** A M BAILIE

DRY DODDINGTON (St James)   *see* Claypole *Linc*

DRY DRAYTON (St Peter and St Paul)   *see* Lordsbridge *Ely*

DRY SANDFORD (St Helen)   *see* Wootton and Dry Sandford *Ox*

DRYBROOK (Holy Trinity), Lydbrook and Ruardean *Glouc 1*   **P** *Prime Min and Bp (alt)*   **R** N R BROMFIELD   **C** P R AVERAY

DRYPOOL (St Columba) (St John) *York 14*   **P** *Patr Bd*   **TR** P J F GOODEY   **TV** M J WESTBY   **C** A J MACPHERSON

DUCKLINGTON (St Bartholomew) *Ox 28*   **P** *DBP*   **R** *vacant*

DUCKMANTON (St Peter and St Paul)   *see* Calow and Sutton cum Duckmanton *Derby*

DUDDENHOE END (The Hamlet Church)   *see* Icknield Way Villages *Chelmsf*

DUDDESTON (St Matthew)   *see* Aston and Nechells *Birm*

DUDDINGTON (St Mary)   *see* Barrowden and Wakerley w S Luffenham etc *Pet*

DUDDON (St Peter)   *see* Tarvin *Ches*

DUDLESTON (St Mary)   *see* Criftins w Dudleston and Welsh Frankton *Lich*

DUDLEY (St Augustine) (St Barnabas) (St Francis) (St James) (St Thomas and St Luke) *Worc 9*   **P** *Patr Bd*   **TV** A ST L J WICKENS, T D ATFIELD

DUDLEY (St Edmund King and Martyr) *Worc 9*   **P** *Bp*   **V** *vacant*

DUDLEY (St John) Kate's Hill *Worc 9*   **P** *Bp*   **V** *vacant*

DUDLEY (St Paul)   *see* Weetslade *Newc*

DUDLEY WOOD (St John) and Cradley Heath *Worc 9*   **P** *Prime Min and V Darby End and Netherton (alt)*   **V** A M BAKER

DUFFIELD (St Alkmund) and Little Eaton *Derby 11*   **P** *Patr Bd*   **C** D E BARNSLEY

DUFTON (St Cuthbert)   *see* Heart of Eden *Carl*

DUKINFIELD (St John) (St Alban Mission Church) *Ches 14*   **P** *R Stockport St Mary*   **V** T J HAYES

DUKINFIELD (St Luke) *Ches 14*   **P** *Bp*   **V** *vacant*

DUKINFIELD (St Mark) *Ches 14*   **P** *Bp*   **P-in-c** A C COX   **NSM** J M DUNLOP

DULLINGHAM (St Mary)   *see* Raddesley Gp *Ely*

DULOE (St Cuby), Herodsfoot, Morval and St Pinnock *Truro 12*   **P** *Ld Chan, Ch Soc Trust, and Ball Coll Ox (by turn)*   **C** A R INGLEBY, J P W FOOT, P C BELLENES, P P C SHARP

DULVERTON (All Saints) w Brushford, Brompton Regis, Upton and Skilgate *B & W 15*   **P** *Bp, D&C, Em Coll Cam, and Keble Coll Ox (jt)*   **R** A N THOMAS

DULWICH (St Barnabas) *S'wark 9* **P** *Bp* **V** J C WATSON
C R GUNDERSON **Hon C** A G BUCKLEY, J M WHITE
DULWICH (St Clement) St Peter *S'wark 9* **P** *Bp*
V M E A COULTER
DULWICH, EAST (St John the Evangelist) *S'wark 9* **P** *Ripon*
Coll Cuddesdon **P-in-c** W M JACOB **OLM** A CLARKE
DULWICH, NORTH (St Faith) *S'wark 9* **P** *Bp*
P-in-c S J HEIGHT **NSM** C SHOWERS
DULWICH, SOUTH (St Stephen) *S'wark 9* **P** *Dulwich Coll*
V B G SCHÜNEMANN **C** R J LLOYD
DULWICH, WEST (All Saints) *S'wark 12* **P** *Bp*
V D J STEPHENSON **C** G O'NEILL **Hon C** C WILES
DULWICH, WEST (Emmanuel) *S'wark 12* **P** *Bp*
V K G A ANSAH
DUMBLETON (St Peter) *see* Winchcombe *Glouc*
DUMMER (All Saints) *see* Farleigh, Candover and Wield *Win*
DUNCHIDEOCK (St Michael and All Angels) *see* Christow,
Ashton, Bridford, Dunchideock etc *Ex*
DUNCHURCH (St Peter) *Cov 6* **P** *Bp* **V** *vacant*
DUNCTON (Holy Trinity) *Chich 10* **P** *Lord Egremont*
P-in-c R M MITCHELL
DUNDRY (St Michael) *see* Chew Magna w Dundry, Norton
Malreward etc *B & W*
DUNHAM MASSEY (St Margaret) (St Mark) (All Saints)
Ches 10 **P** J G Turnbull Esq **V** J J E SUTTON
DUNHAM, GREAT (St Andrew) and LITTLE (St Margaret),
w Great and Little Fransham *Nor 14* **P** *Hertf Coll Ox,*
Ch Soc Trust, Magd Coll Cam, and DBP (by turn)
R *vacant*
DUNHAM-ON-THE-HILL (St Luke) *see* Helsby and Dunham-
on-the-Hill *Ches*
DUNHAM-ON-TRENT (St Oswald) *see* Retford Area *S'well*
DUNHOLME (St Chad) *see* Welton and Dunholme w Scothern
Linc
DUNKERTON (All Saints) *see* Timsbury w Priston, Camerton
and Dunkerton *B & W*
DUNKESWELL (Holy Trinity) (St Nicholas), Luppitt, Sheldon
and Upottery *Ex 4* **P** *MMCET, Bp, and D&C (jt)*
P-in-c R G PECKHAM
DUNMOW, GREAT (St Mary the Virgin) and Barnston
Chelmsf 18 **P** *Ld Chan (2 turns), CPAS (1 turn)*
P-in-c R J PATTEN
DUNMOW, LITTLE (St Mary the Virgin) *see* Felsted and Lt
Dunmow *Chelmsf*
DUNNINGTON (not known) *see* Heart of England *Cov*
DUNNINGTON (St Nicholas) *see* Beeford w Frodingham and
Foston *York*
DUNNINGTON (St Nicholas) *see* Rural E York *York*
DUNS TEW (St Mary Magdalene) *see* Westcote Barton w
Steeple Barton, Duns Tew and Sandford St Martin and Over w
Nether Worton *Ox*
DUNSBY (All Saints) *see* Ringstone in Aveland Gp *Linc*
DUNSCROFT (St Edwin) *Sheff 10* **P** *Bp* **V** *vacant*
DUNSDEN (All Saints) *see* Shiplake w Dunsden and Harpsden
Ox
DUNSFOLD (St Mary and All Saints) and Hascombe *Guildf 2*
P *Bp and SMF (jt)* **P-in-c** S R WHITE
DUNSFORD (St Mary) *see* Christow, Ashton, Bridford,
Dunchideock etc *Ex*
DUNSFORTH (St Mary) *see* Aldborough w Boroughbridge and
Roecliffe *Leeds*
DUNSMORE (Chapel of the Resurrection) *see* Ellesborough,
The Kimbles and Stoke Mandeville *Ox*
DUNSOP BRIDGE (St George) *see* Slaidburn w Tosside *Leeds*
DUNSTABLE (St Augustine of Canterbury) (St Fremund the
Martyr) (St Peter) *St Alb 11* **P** *Bp* **TR** R J ANDREWS
TV L A MONEY, P M DRAPER
DUNSTALL (St Mary) *see* Barton under Needwood w Dunstall
and Tatenhill *Lich*
DUNSTER (St George), Carhampton, Withycombe w
Rodhuish, Timberscombe and Wootton Courtenay *B &*
W 15 **P** *Bp* **R** C S RALPH **NSM** J A PRICE
DUNSTON (Church House) *see* Newbold w Dunston *Derby*
DUNSTON (St Leonard) *see* Penkridge *Lich*
DUNSTON (St Nicholas) w (Christ Church) *Dur 13* **P** *Bp*
V D ATKINSON
DUNSTON (St Peter) *see* Metheringham w Blankney and
Dunston *Linc*
DUNSTON (St Remigius) *see* Stoke H Cross w Dunston,
Arminghall etc *Nor*
DUNSWELL (St Faith's Mission Church) *see* Hull St Jo Newland
York
DUNTERTON (All Saints) *see* Milton Abbot, Dunterton,
Lamerton etc *Ex*
DUNTISBOURNE ABBOTS (St Peter) *see* Brimpsfield w Birdlip,
Syde, Daglingworth etc *Glouc*

DUNTISBOURNE ROUS (St Michael and All Angels) *as above*
DUNTON (St Martin) *see* Schorne *Ox*
DUNTON (St Mary Magdalene) w Wrestlingworth and
Eyeworth *St Alb 10* **P** *Ld Chan and DBP (alt)* **R** L C DEW
DUNTON BASSETT (All Saints) *see* Upper Soar *Leic*
DUNWICH (St James) *see* Yoxmere *St E*
DURHAM (St Giles) *Dur 1* **P** *D&C* **V** A B BARTLETT
NSM A J FENTON, R A M THOMAS, R S BRIGGS
DURHAM (St Margaret of Antioch) and Neville's Cross
St John *Dur 1* **P** *D&C* **R** B T HUISH **NSM** J HIRST,
N C CHATER
DURHAM (St Nicholas) *Dur 1* **P** *CPAS* **V** J S BELLAMY
Hon C L J ELLIN **NSM** C H PATTERSON, P S JOHNSON
DURHAM (St Oswald King and Martyr) and Shincliffe *Dur 1*
P *D&C* **P-in-c** P Z KASHOURIS
DURHAM NORTH (St Cuthbert) *Dur 1* **P** *Patr Bd*
TR R W LAWRANCE **TV** C A DICK **NSM** K KITSON
DURLEIGH (St Hugh) *see* Bridgwater H Trin and Durleigh
B & W
DURLEY (Holy Cross) *Portsm 1* **P** *Ld Chan* **R** G R MENSINGH
C A L WEBB
DURNFORD (St Andrew) *see* Woodford Valley w Archers Gate
Sarum
DURRINGTON (All Saints) *see* Avon River *Sarum*
DURRINGTON (St Symphorian) *Chich 4* **P** *Bp*
P-in-c K D RICHARDS **C** B M EADON
DURSLEY (St James the Great) *Glouc 5* **P** *Bp*
P-in-c M G COZENS **C** R N KING **NSM** I N GARDNER
DURSTON (St John the Baptist) *see* Alfred Jewel *B & W*
DURWESTON (St Nicholas) *see* Pimperne, Stourpaine,
Durweston and Bryanston *Sarum*
DUSTON Team, The (St Francis) (St Luke) *Pet 4* **P** *Bp*
TR A J MARRIOTT **TV** A J DUNLOP
DUXFORD (St Peter) w St John *Ely 5* **P** *Bp*
P-in-c J H MARTIN **NSM** P M SHARKEY
DYMCHURCH (St Peter and St Paul) *see* Romney Marsh *Cant*
DYMOCK (St Mary the Virgin) *see* Redmarley D'Abitot,
Bromesberrow, Pauntley etc *Glouc*
DYRHAM (St Peter) *see* Wick w Doynton and Dyrham *Bris*
EAGLE (All Saints) *see* Swinderby *Linc*
EAKRING (St Andrew) *S'well 3* **P** *DBP* **R** *vacant*
EALING (All Saints) *Lon 22* **P** *Bp* **V** N P HENDERSON,
R E MARSZALEK
EALING (Ascension) *see* Hanger Hill Ascension and W Twyford
St Mary *Lon*
EALING (Christ the Saviour) *Lon 22* **P** *Bp* **V** A F DAVIS
C S L CUFF
EALING (St Barnabas) *Lon 22* **P** *Bp* **V** J D C DODD
EALING (St Mary) *Lon 22* **P** *Bp* **V** S D PAYNTER
NSM W M CHOW
EALING (St Paul) *Lon 22* **P** *Bp* **V** M P MELLUISH **C** C FOX,
R N THOMAS
EALING (St Peter) Mount Park *Lon 22* **P** *Bp* **V** D E NENO
NSM J O A CHOUFAR, M J JOACHIM
EALING (St Stephen) Castle Hill *Lon 22* **P** *D&C St Paul's*
V S M NEWBOLD **C** A J DAND **Hon C** C S NEWBOLD
EALING COMMON (St Matthew) *Lon 22* **P** *Bp*
V P G WATKINS
EALING, WEST (St John) w St James *Lon 22* **P** *Bp*
V P S MACKENZIE **C** A P JOHNSON, C M DUNK
EARBY (All Saints) w Kelbrook *Leeds 26* **P** *Bp* **V** H FIELDEN
EARDISLEY (St Mary Magdalene) w Bollingham, Willersley,
Brilley, Michaelchurch, Whitney, Winforton, Almeley and
Kinnersley *Heref 4* **P** *Patr Bd* **R** M J SMALL
EARL SHILTON (St Simon and St Jude) w Elmesthorpe *Leic 10*
P *Bp* **P-in-c** M R CASTLE
EARL SOHAM (St Mary) *see* Mid Loes *St E*
EARL STERNDALE (St Michael and All Angels) *see* Taddington,
Chelmorton and Monyash etc *Derby*
EARL STONHAM (St Mary) *see* The Creetings and Earl
Stonham w Stonham Parva *St E*
EARLESTOWN (St John the Baptist) *see* Newton *Liv*
EARLEY (St Bartholomew) *see* Reading St Luke w St Bart *Ox*
EARLEY (St Nicolas) *Ox 7* **P** *DBP* **V** N M WARWICK
C B A KAUTZER **NSM** E M NEWMAN
EARLEY (St Peter) *Ox 7* **P** *DBP* **V** P P HOBDAY
C H E HOBDAY
EARLEY Trinity *Ox 7* **P** *DBP* **V** J SALMON
EARLHAM (St Anne) (St Elizabeth) (St Mary) *Nor 3* **P** *Bp and*
Trustees (jt) **P-in-c** S W J WARD **C** J HEMP
OLM R M A HOUGHTON
EARLS BARTON (All Saints) *Pet 6* **P** *DBP* **P-in-c** M J HAYES
C G SHAW
EARLS COLNE (St Andrew) *see* Halstead Area *Chelmsf*
EARL'S COURT (St Cuthbert) (St Matthias) *Lon 8* **P** *Trustees*
P-in-c P A BAGOTT

EARL'S COURT (St Philip)   *see* Kensington St Mary Abbots w Ch Ch and St Phil *Lon*

EARLS CROOME (St Nicholas)   *see* Upton-on-Severn, Ripple, Earls Croome etc *Worc*

EARL'S HEATON   *see* Dewsbury *Leeds*

EARLSDON (St Barbara) *Cov 3*   **P** *Bp*   **V** T D RAISTRICK

EARLSFIELD (St Andrew) *S'wark 18*   **P** *Bp*   **V** J BROWN   **NSM** J SERTIN

EARLSFIELD (St John the Divine) *S'wark 18*   **P** *Bp*   **P-in-c** T J E MARWOOD

EARNLEY (not known) and East Wittering *Chich 2*   **P** *Bp* (2 turns), Bp Lon (1 turn)   **R** S J DAVIES

EARNSHAW BRIDGE (St John)   *see* Leyland St Jo *Blackb*

EARSDON (St Alban) and Backworth *Newc 5*   **P** *Bp*   **V** J A FRANCE   **NSM** A B BEESTON

EARSHAM (All Saints)   *see* Ditchingham, Hedenham, Broome, Earsham etc *Nor*

EARSWICK, NEW (St Andrew)   *see* Huntington *York*

EARTHAM (St Margaret)   *see* Slindon, Eartham and Madehurst *Chich*

EASBY (St Agatha) w Skeeby and Brompton on Swale and Bolton on Swale *Leeds 24*   **P** *Bp*   **V** Y S CALLAGHAN

EASEBOURNE (St Mary), Lodsworth and Selham *Chich 9*   **P** *Cowdray Trust and Rathbone Trust (jt)*   **V** D B WELSMAN   **C** D R CROOK   **NSM** A M HALLIWELL

EASINGTON (All Saints) w Liverton *York 16*   **P** *Ld Chan*   **R** *vacant*

EASINGTON (All Saints) w Skeffling, Keyingham, Ottringham, Patrington, Welwick and Winestead *York 12*   **P** *Abp and CPAS (1 turn), Ld Chan (1 turn)*   **V** C FISHER-BAILEY   **Hon C** J A SHARP

EASINGTON (St Hugh)   *see* Banbury St Hugh *Ox*

EASINGTON (St Mary) and Easington Colliery *Dur 2*   **P** *Bp*   **P-in-c** E L PARKER   **C** K E JAMIE

EASINGTON (St Peter)   *see* Ewelme, Brightwell Baldwin, Cuxham w Easington *Ox*

EASINGTON COLLIERY (The Ascension)   *see* Easington and Easington Colliery *Dur*

EASINGWOLD (St John the Baptist and All Saints) w Raskelf *York 3*   **P** *Abp*   **V** M E YOUNG   **NSM** C J TOASE

EAST   *see also under substantive place name*

EAST DEAN (All Saints), Singleton, and West Dean *Chich 3*   **P** *Bp (2 turns), D&C (1 turn)*   **P-in-c** K J BORMAN

EAST DEAN (St Simon and St Jude) w Friston and Jevington *Chich 14*   **P** *Duke of Devonshire (1 turn), D&C (2 turns)*   **R** D A BAKER

EAST DEAN (St Winifred)   *see* Lockerley and E Dean w E and W Tytherley *Win*

EAST DOWNLAND *Ox 6*   **P** *Bp and Adn (jt)*   **R** J P TOOGOOD   **C** W MCDOWELL   **NSM** D F BROWN, D J DALES

EAST HAM (St Bartholomew) (St Mary Magdalene) w Upton Park and Forest Gate (St Edmund) *Chelmsf 5*   **P** *Patr Bd*   **TV** Q B D PEPPIATT   **NSM** A R EASTER

EAST HAM (St George and St Ethelbert) *Chelmsf 5*   **P** *Bp*   **V** D T HAOKIP   **NSM** G J ANAN

EAST HAM (St Paul) *Chelmsf 5*   **P** *Ch Patr Trust*   **V** M L PLAYLE   **C** E A MATTHEWS   **NSM** A W ELEYAE

EAST LANE (St Mary)   *see* W Horsley *Guildf*

EAST MARSHLAND *Ely 14*   **P** *Bp and MMCET (1 turn), Pemb Coll Cam (2 turns), Prime Min (1 turn), and Ld Chan (1 turn)*   **V** M N DALE   **NSM** B E A PEARMAN

EAST ORCHARD (St Thomas)   *see* Shaftesbury *Sarum*

EAST WINCH (All Saints)   *see* Middlewinch *Nor*

EASTBOURNE (All Saints) *Chich 14*   **P** *Trustees*   **V** W R LOVATT   **C** D P FRASER

EASTBOURNE (All Souls) *Chich 14*   **P** *Ch Soc Trust*   **V** M D REDHOUSE   **C** J H PERCIVAL

EASTBOURNE (Christ Church) (St Philip) *Chich 14*   **P** *Bp and V Eastbourne (jt)*   **V** D G CHARLES   **C** A J RANSOM

EASTBOURNE (Holy Trinity) *Chich 14*   **P** *V Eastbourne*   **V** P J COEKIN   **C** J B P BROOK

EASTBOURNE (St Andrew) *Chich 14*   **P** *Bp*   **V** D J KING

EASTBOURNE (St Elisabeth) *Chich 14*   **P** *Bp*   **V** D J GILLARD

EASTBOURNE (St John) Meads *Chich 14*   **P** *Trustees*   **V** G M G CARPENTER   **NSM** J A PREECE

EASTBOURNE (St Mary) *Chich 14*   **P** *Bp*   **V** T O MENDEL   **C** T EZAT   **NSM** H F POWNALL

EASTBOURNE (St Michael and All Angels) Ocklynge *Chich 14*   **P** *V Eastbourne*   **V** S T MATTAPALLY

EASTBOURNE (St Saviour and St Peter) *Chich 14*   **P** *Keble Coll Ox*   **V** J T GUNN

EASTBURY (St James the Great)   *see* Lambourn Valley *Ox*

EASTCHURCH (All Saints) w Leysdown and Harty *Cant 15*   **P** *Abp and Keble Coll Ox (jt)*   **R** C J SHIPLEY

EASTCOMBE (St Augustine)   *see* Bisley, Chalford, France Lynch, and Oakridge and Bussage w Eastcombe *Glouc*

EASTCOTE (St Lawrence) *Lon 24*   **P** *Bp*   **V** C B RANKINE

EASTER, HIGH (St Mary the Virgin) and Good Easter w Margaret Roding *Chelmsf 18*   **P** *Bp Lon, Mrs H Shepherd, and D&C St Paul's (by turn)*   **P-in-c** J D GANNON

EASTERGATE (St George)   *see* Aldingbourne, Barnham and Eastergate *Chich*

EASTERN GREEN (St Andrew) *Cov 3*   **P** *R Allesley*   **P-in-c** G P SMITH   **Emer** K I MASSEY

EASTERTON (St Barnabas)   *see* The Lavingtons, Cheverells, and Easterton *Sarum*

EASTFIELD (Holy Nativity)   *see* Cayton w Eastfield *York*

EASTGATE (All Saints)   *see* Upper Weardale *Dur*

EASTHAM (St Mary the Blessed Virgin) (St Peter's Chapel) (Chapel of the Holy Spirit) *Ches 9*   **P** *D&C*   **V** E A GLOVER   **NSM** M Q COATS

EASTHAM (St Peter and St Paul)   *see* Teme Valley S *Worc*

EASTHAMPSTEAD (St Michael and St Mary Magdalene) *Ox 3*   **P** *Ch Ch Ox*   **R** G S COLE   **C** P M BESTLEY

EASTHOPE (St Peter)   *see* Wenlock *Heref*

EASTHORPE (St Mary the Virgin)   *see* Thurstable and Winstree *Chelmsf*

EASTINGTON (St Michael and All Angels), Frocester, Haresfield, Moreton Valence, Standish and Whitminster *Glouc 4*   **P** *Bp and J F Bengough Esq (1 turn), DBP and Exors Lady Mary Cooper (1 turn)*   **R** *vacant*

EASTLEACH (St Andrew)   *see* S Cotswolds *Glouc*

EASTLEIGH (All Saints) *Win 10*   **P** *Bp*   **P-in-c** I P FLETCHER   **C** J B HARVEY

EASTLEIGH Nightingale Avenue (St Francis)   *see* Eastleigh *Win*

EASTMOORS (St Mary Magdalene)   *see* Helmsley *York*

EASTNEY (St Margaret)   *see* Southsea *Portsm*

EASTNOR (St John the Baptist)   *see* Ledbury *Heref*

EASTOFT (St Bartholomew)   *see* The Marshland *Sheff*

EASTON (All Hallows) *Bris 3*   **P** *R Bris St Steph*   **P-in-c** J MUTEMWAKWENDA

EASTON (All Saints)   *see* Brandeston w Kettleburgh and Easton St *E*

EASTON (Holy Trinity w St Gabriel and St Lawrence and St Jude) *Bris 3*   **P** *Trustees*   **P-in-c** P J NOTT   **NSM** D J P MOORE

EASTON (St Mary)   *see* Itchen Valley *Win*

EASTON (St Paul)   *see* Westbury-sub Mendip w Easton *B & W*

EASTON (St Peter)   *see* E Leightonstone *Ely*

EASTON (St Peter), Colton, Marlingford and Bawburgh *Nor 17*   **P** *Bp, D&C, Adn, and Sir Edward Evans-Lombe (jt)*   **V** *vacant*

EASTON GREY (not known)   *see* Sherston Magna, Easton Grey, Luckington etc *Bris*

EASTON IN GORDANO (St George)   *see* Pill, Portbury and Easton-in-Gordano *B & W*

EASTON MAUDIT (St Peter and St Paul)   *see* Wollaston w Strixton and Bozeat etc *Pet*

EASTON NESTON (St Mary)   *see* Towcester w Caldecote and Easton Neston etc *Pet*

EASTON ON THE HILL (All Saints)   *see* Ketton, Collyweston, Easton-on-the-Hill etc *Pet*

EASTON ROYAL (Holy Trinity)   *see* Vale of Pewsey *Sarum*

EASTON, GREAT (St Andrew)   *see* Six Saints circa Holt *Leic*

EASTON, GREAT (St John and St Giles)   *see* Broxted w Chickney and Tilty etc *Chelmsf*

EASTON, LITTLE (St Mary the Virgin) *as above*

EASTRINGTON (St Michael)   *see* Howden *York*

EASTROP (St Mary) *Win 4*   **P** *CPAS*   **R** C L HAWKINS   **NSM** C E WEST

EASTRY (St Mary Blessed Virgin) and Woodnesborough *Cant 9*   **P** *Abp and Lord Northbourne (jt)*   **R** D G RIDLEY   **C** E S LANDER   **NSM** R STEVENSON

EASTTHORPE (St Paul)   *see* Mirfield *Leeds*

EASTVILLE (St Anne w St Mark and St Thomas) *Bris 3*   **P** *Bp*   **V** *vacant*

EASTWELL (St Michael)   *see* Ironstone Villages *Leic*

EASTWICK (St Botolph)   *see* High Wych and Gilston w Eastwick St *Alb*

EASTWOOD (St David) *Chelmsf 13*   **P** *Bp*   **V** P D JOYCE

EASTWOOD (St Laurence and All Saints) *Chelmsf 13*   **P** *Ld Chan*   **V** S R SPENCER   **C** E C J STOCK

EASTWOOD (St Mary) *S'well 4*   **P** *J N Plumptre Esq*   **P-in-c** D A STEVENSON   **C** A K ALLS

EATON (All Saints)   *see* Retford Area *S'well*

EATON (Christ Church) *Nor 3*   **P** *D&C*   **V** P H RICHMOND

EATON (Christ Church)   *see* Marton, Siddington w Capesthorne, and Eaton etc *Ches*

EATON (St Andrew) *Nor 3*   **P** *D&C*   **V** P R RODD

EATON (St Denys)   *see* Ironstone Villages *Leic*

EATON (St Thomas)   *see* Tarporley *Ches*

EATON BISHOP (St Michael and All Angels)   *see* Cagebrook *Heref*

EATON BRAY (St Mary the Virgin) w Edlesborough *St Alb 11*
  P *DBP*   **V** C C MCCLUSKEY
EATON HASTINGS (St Michael and All Angels)   *see* Gt Coxwell
  w Buscot, Coleshill etc *Ox*
EATON SOCON (St Mary) *St Alb 10*   **P** *E W Harper Esq*
  V T S ROBB   **C** M S NEWMAN
EATON, LITTLE (St Paul)   *see* Duffield and Lt Eaton *Derby*
EBBERSTON (St Mary)   *see* Thornton Dale w Allerston,
  Ebberston etc *York*
EBBESBOURNE WAKE (St John the Baptist)   *see* Chalke Valley
  Sarum
EBCHESTER (St Ebba) *Dur 4*   **P** *Bp*   **P-in-c** D R CLEUGH
EBERNOE (Holy Trinity)   *see* N Chapel w Ebernoe *Chich*
EBONY (St Mary the Virgin)   *see* Rother and Oxney *Cant*
EBRINGTON (St Eadburgha)   *see* Vale and Cotswold Edge
  Glouc
ECCHINSWELL (St Lawrence)   *see* Burghclere w Newtown and
  Ecchinswell w Sydmonton *Win*
ECCLES (St Mary the Virgin)   *see* Quidenham Gp *Nor*
ECCLES (St Mary the Virgin) (St Andrew) *Man 18*   **P** *Patr Bd*
  and Ld Chan (alt)   **TR** C G YOBERA   **TV** A C YOUNG,
  A-L CRITCHLOW   **NSM** M S MASEMOLA   **OLM** J J LEWIS
ECCLESALL BIERLOW (All Saints) *Sheff 2*   **P** *Dean*
  V G I WILTON
ECCLESFIELD (St Mary the Virgin) *Sheff 3*   **P** *DBF*
  V *vacant*
ECCLESHALL (Holy Trinity) *Lich 7*   **P** *Bp*   **V** J H GRAHAM
ECCLESHILL (St Luke) *Leeds 3*   **P** *V Bradf*   **V** J P HARTLEY
ECCLESTON (Christ Church)   *see* Eccleston *Liv*
ECCLESTON (St Luke) *as above*
ECCLESTON (St Mary the Virgin) *Blackb 4*   **P** *DBP*
  P-in-c A J BROWN   **NSM** A D WYNNE
ECCLESTON (St Mary the Virgin) and Pulford *Ches 2*   **P** *Duke*
  of Westmr   **R** *vacant*
ECCLESTON (St Thomas)   *see* St Helens Town Cen *Liv*
ECCLESTON PARK (St James)   *see* Eccleston *Liv*
ECCLESTON Team, The *Liv 10*   **P** *Patr Bd*   **TR** J H WELCH
  TV P W GILROY
ECKINGTON (Holy Trinity) *Worc 4*   **P** *D&C Westmr*
  V S K RENSHAW
ECKINGTON (St Peter and St Paul) and Ridgeway *Derby 3*
  P *The Crown and Patr Bd (alt)*   **R** A D WALKER
  NSM I A PRICE
ECKINGTON, UPPER (St Luke)   *see* Eckington and Ridgeway
  Derby
ECTON (St Mary Magdalene)   *see* Gt Doddington and Wilby
  and Ecton *Pet*
EDALE (Holy and Undivided Trinity) *Derby 2*   **P** *Rep*
  Landowners   **P-in-c** S H COCKSEDGE
EDBURTON (St Andrew)   *see* Poynings w Edburton,
  Newtimber and Pyecombe *Chich*
EDEN PARK (St John the Baptist)   *see* Beckenham St Jo *Roch*
EDEN, Gelt and Irthing Team Ministry, The *Carl 2*   **P** *Patr Bd*
  TR R J A TULLOCH   **TV** E A JOHNSEN   **C** T M EDWARDS
EDENBRIDGE (St Peter and St Paul) *Roch 11*   **P** *Bp*
  V S A J MITCHELL
EDENFIELD (not known)   *see* Ramsbottom and Edenfield *Man*
EDENHALL (St Cuthbert)   *see* Cross Fell Gp *Carl*
EDENHAM (St Michael) w Witham on the Hill and Swinstead
  Linc 17   **P** *Baroness Willoughby de Eresby, Ld Chan, and Bp*
  (by turn)   **V** A T HAWES   **NSM** I K WILLIAMS
EDENSOR (St Paul)   *see* Longton Hall *Lich*
EDENSOR (St Peter)   *see* Beeley and Edensor *Derby*
EDGBASTON (St Augustine) *Birm 2*   **P** *Bp*
  V M R E TOMLINSON
EDGBASTON (St Bartholomew) *Birm 2*   **P** *Sir Euan Anstruther-*
  Gough-Calthorpe Bt   **V** N J C TUCKER
EDGBASTON (St George w St Michael) (St Michael's Hall)
  Birm 2   **P** *Sir Euan Anstruther-Gough-Calthorpe Bt*
  V J M FRANCIS
EDGBASTON (St Germain) *Birm 2*   **P** *Trustees*
  V H A SCRIVEN   **C** I SMITH   **NSM** S C HAYES
EDGBASTON (St Mary and St Ambrose)   *see* Balsall Heath and
  Edgbaston SS Mary and Ambrose *Birm*
EDGCOTE (St James)   *see* Culworth w Sulgrave and Thorpe
  Mandeville etc *Pet*
EDGCOTT (St Michael)   *see* The Claydons and Swan *Ox*
EDGE HILL (St Dunstan)   *see* St Luke in the City *Liv*
EDGE HILL (St Mary)   *see* Liv All SS *Liv*
EDGE, THE (St John the Baptist)   *see* Painswick, Sheepscombe,
  Cranham, The Edge etc *Glouc*
EDGEFIELD (St Peter and St Paul)   *see* Lt Barningham, Blickling,
  Edgefield etc *Nor*
EDGEHILL CHURCHES *Cov 8*   **P** *Bp and Lord Willoughby de*
  Broke (jt)   **R** B J JACKSON   **C** R J COOKE
  NSM A J CARTWRIGHT

EDGELEY (St Mark) (St Matthew) and Cheadle Heath *Ches 18*
  P *Bp*   **V** D T BREWSTER   **NSM** J M JOHNSON
EDGESIDE (St Anne)   *see* Rossendale Middle Valley *Man*
EDGEWORTH (St Mary)   *see* Brimpsfield w Birdlip, Syde,
  Daglingworth etc *Glouc*
EDGMOND (St Peter) w Kynnersley and Preston Wealdmoors
  Lich 16   **P** *Bp, Adn Salop, Chan Lich, MMCET, and Preston Trust*
  Homes Trustees (jt)   **R** W E WARD
  NSM D N H STOKES-HARRISON
EDGTON (St Michael the Archangel)   *see* Bishop's Castle w
  Mainstone, Lydbury N etc *Heref*
EDGWARE (St Alphage)   *see* Hendon St Alphage *Lon*
EDGWARE (St Andrew) (St Margaret) (St Peter) *Lon 15*
  P *MMCET*   **TV** P E BERRY   **C** S W J REA
  NSM K CHRISTODOULOU
EDINGALE (Holy Trinity)   *see* Mease Valley *Lich*
EDINGLEY (St Giles) w Halam *S'well 3*   **P** *Bp*   **V** *vacant*
EDINGTHORPE (All Saints)   *see* N Walsham and Edingthorpe
  Nor
EDINGTON (St George)   *see* Polden Wheel *B & W*
EDINGTON (St Mary, St Katharine and All Saints)   *see* Bratton,
  Edington and Imber, Erlestoke etc *Sarum*
EDITH WESTON (St Mary)   *see* Empingham, Edith Weston,
  Lyndon, Manton etc *Pet*
EDLASTON (St James)   *see* Brailsford w Shirley, Osmaston w
  Edlaston etc *Derby*
EDLINGHAM (St John the Baptist w Bolton Chapel)
  see Whittingham and Edlingham w Bolton Chapel *Newc*
EDLINGTON (St Helen)   *see* Hemingby Gp *Linc*
EDLINGTON (St John the Baptist) and Hexthorpe *Sheff 9*
  P *Bp*   **V** S H J EDMONDS
EDMONDSHAM (St Nicholas)   *see* Cranborne w Boveridge,
  Edmondsham etc *Sarum*
EDMONTON (All Saints) (St Michael) *Lon 18*   **P** *D&C*
  St Paul's   **V** S J OWEN   **C** K M SALA
EDMONTON (St Aldhelm) *Lon 18*   **P** *V Edmonton All SS*
  V S C MADDISON
EDMONTON (St Alphege) *Lon 18*   **P** *Bp*   **V** R C KNOWLING
  C M T CHILDS
EDMONTON (St Mary w St John) (St Mary's Centre) *Lon 18*
  P *D&C St Paul's*   **V** N H ASBRIDGE   **C** M W WASWA
  NSM J A NOWAK
EDMONTON (St Peter w St Martin) *Lon 18*   **P** *Bp*
  V C D MITCHELL
EDMUNDBYERS (St Edmund)   *see* Blanchland w
  Hunstanworth and Edmundbyers etc *Newc*
EDSTASTON (St Mary the Virgin), Fauls, Prees, Tilstock and
  Whixall *Lich 22*   **P** *R Wem, R Whitchurch, and Bp (jt)*
  P-in-c J M HUNT   **C** P G WIGNALL   **OLM** S E ARMSTRONG
EDSTONE (St Michael)   *see* Kirkbymoorside w Gillamoor,
  Farndale etc *York*
EDVIN LOACH (St Mary) w Tedstone Delamere, Tedstone
  Wafer, Upper Sapey, Wolferlow and Whitbourne *Heref 2*
  P *Bp, BNC Ox, Sir Francis Winnington Bt, and D P Barneby Esq (jt)*
  P-in-c D P HOWELL
EDWALTON (Holy Rood) *S'well 5*   **P** *Exors Major R P Chaworth-*
  Musters   **P-in-c** M A FRASER   **C** I M HAMLEY
EDWARDSTONE (St Mary the Virgin)   *see* Boxford,
  Edwardstone, Groton etc *St E*
EDWINSTOWE (St Mary) *S'well 2*   **P** *Earl Manvers' Trustees*
  P-in-c A N EVANS   **C** E L HOLLIDAY   **NSM** H M ENGLISH
EDWYN RALPH (St Michael)   *see* Bredenbury *Heref*
EFFINGHAM (St Lawrence) w Little Bookham *Guildf 10*
  P *Keble Coll Ox*   **NSM** I M MCKILLOP
EFFORD (St Paul)   *see* Plymouth Em, St Paul Efford and St Aug
  Ex
EGDEAN (St Bartholomew) *Chich 10*   **P** *Bp*
  P-in-c P M GILBERT
EGERTON (St James)   *see* G7 Benefice *Cant*
EGG BUCKLAND (St Edward) *Ex 21*   **P** *Ld Chan*
  P-in-c C J ROUTLEDGE   **C** C J BUDDEN, S P RUNDELL
EGGESFORD (All Saints)   *see* Burrington, Chawleigh, Cheldon,
  Chulmleigh etc *Ex*
EGGINGTON (St Michael)   *see* Ouzel Valley *St Alb*
EGGINTON (St Wilfrid)   *see* Etwall w Egginton *Derby*
EGGLESCLIFFE (St John the Baptist) *Dur 10*   **P** *Bp*
  P-in-c S WILSON
EGGLESTON (Holy Trinity) *Dur 7*   **P** *The Crown*
  P-in-c J BARKER   **NSM** A P WALLBANK
EGHAM (St John the Baptist) *Guildf 11*   **P** *Ch Soc Trust*
  V J R WATTLEY   **C** J J RIDDLESTONE   **NSM** M J CALLAGHAN,
  T M SUDWORTH
EGHAM HYTHE (St Paul) *Guildf 11*   **P** *Bp*
  P-in-c M D A ROPER   **NSM** S M LOVEDAY   **OLM** J FRANCK
EGLETON (St Edmund)   *see* Oakham, Ashwell, Braunston,
  Brooke, Egleton etc *Pet*

EGLINGHAM (St Maurice)   see Glendale Gp Newc

EGLOSHAYLE (St Petroc)   see St Breoke and Egloshayle Truro

EGLOSKERRY (St Petrock and St Keri), North Petherwin, Tremaine, Tresmere and Trewen Truro 9   P Duchy of Cornwall and Bp (alt)   V G PENGELLY

EGMANTON (Our Lady of Egmanton) S'well 3   P SMF   V C C LEVY

EGREMONT (St Mary and St Michael) and Haile Carl 5   P Patr Bd   TR T R LEE   TV S C E CAKE   NSM M C DANKS-FLOWER, T R TAYLOR

EGTON (St Hilda)   see Middle Esk Moor York

EGTON-CUM-NEWLAND (St Mary the Virgin) and Lowick and Colton Carl 9   P Patr Bd   P-in-c B T STREETER

EIGHT ASH GREEN (All Saints)   see Fordham Chelmsf

EIGHTON BANKS (St Thomas) Dur 12   P Bp   P-in-c D M SNOWBALL   NSM N CLEE

ELBERTON (St John)   see Alveston and Littleton-on-Severn w Elberton Bris

ELBURTON (St Matthew) Ex 21   P CPAS   C T J BRASSIL   NSM A WILLIAMS

ELDENE (not known)   see Swindon Dorcan Bris

ELDERSFIELD (St John the Baptist)   see Berrow w Pendock, Eldersfield, Hollybush etc Worc

ELDON (St Mark)   see Coundon and Eldon Dur

ELDWICK (St Lawrence)   see Bingley All SS Leeds

ELFORD (St Peter)   see Mease Valley Lich

ELHAM (St Mary the Virgin) w Denton and Wootton and Acrise Cant 8   P Abp and Mert Coll Ox (jt)   V vacant

ELING (St Mary)   see Totton Win

ELING, NORTH (St Mary)   see Copythorne Win

ELKESLEY (St Giles)   see Retford Area S'well

ELKINGTON, SOUTH (All Saints)   see Louth Linc

ELKSTONE (St John the Baptist)   see Alstonfield, Butterton, Ilam etc Lich

ELKSTONE (St John the Evangelist)   see Churn Valley Glouc

ELLACOMBE (Christ Church) Ex 11   P Ch Patr Trust   P-in-c P IRETON

ELLAND (All Saints) (St Mary the Virgin) Leeds 8   P V Halifax   R D BURROWS   C M SANCHEZ RODRIGUEZ, R A CHAPMAN   OLM P E CHADWICK

ELLASTONE (St Peter)   see Alton w Bradley-le-Moors and Denstone etc Lich

ELLEL (St John the Evangelist) w Shireshead Blackb 11   P V Cockerham w Winmarleigh and Glasson   C G S PEARSON   NSM D S TATE

ELLENBROOK (St Mary's Chapel)   see Worsley Man

ELLENHALL (St Mary)   see Chebsey, Creswell, Ellenhall, Ranton etc Lich

ELLERBURN (St Hilda)   see Thornton Dale w Allerston, Ebberston etc York

ELLERBY (St James)   see Skirlaugh, Catwick, Long Riston, Rise, Swine w Ellerby York

ELLERKER (not known)   see S Cave and Ellerker w Broomfleet York

ELLESBOROUGH (St Peter and St Paul), The Kimbles and Stoke Mandeville Ox 17   P Chequers Trustees, The Hon J Hope-Morley, and D&C Linc (by turn)   R J E HENDERSON   OLM J M WALES

ELLESMERE (St Mary) Lich 17   P Bp   V P J EDGE

ELLESMERE (St Peter) Sheff 3   P Bp   P-in-c P IRESON

ELLESMERE PORT Ches 9   P Bp   R G B MCGUINNESS   C G S FOSTER   NSM G J WELCH, R G BARKER

ELLINGHAM (St Mary and All Saints)   see Hyde w Ellingham and Harbridge Win

ELLINGHAM (St Mary)   see Gillingham w Geldeston, Stockton, Ellingham etc Nor

ELLINGHAM (St Maurice) Newc 7   P D&C Dur   V B C HURST

ELLINGHAM, GREAT (St James), LITTLE (St Peter), Rockland All Saints, Rockland St Peter and Shropham w Snetterton Nor 11   P Bp, Major E H C Garnier, and CCC Cam (jt)   R M L LANGAN   NSM C M MASON

ELLINGTON (All Saints)   see E Leightonstone Ely

ELLISFIELD (St Martin)   see Farleigh, Candover and Wield Win

ELLISTOWN (St Christopher)   see Hugglescote w Donington, Ellistown and Snibston Leic

ELLOE STONE Parishes, The Linc 18   P Bp and DBP (1 turn), Ld Chan (1 turn)   OLM J E TIMINGS   OLM B A HUTCHINSON

ELLOUGHTON (St Mary) and Brough w Brantingham York 13   P Abp and D&C Dur (jt)   P-in-c M A FRYER   C J L SMITH

ELM (All Saints)   see Fen Orchards Ely

ELM (St Mary Magdalene)   see Mells w Buckland Dinham, Elm, Whatley etc B & W

ELM PARK (St Nicholas) Hornchurch Chelmsf 2   P Bp   V A J KEIGHLEY   NSM R MORTON, T C KEIGHLEY

ELMBRIDGE (St Mary)   see Elmley Lovett w Hampton Lovett and Elmbridge etc Worc

ELMDON (St Nicholas)   see Icknield Way Villages Chelmsf

ELMDON (St Nicholas) (St Stephen's Church Centre) (Valley Church Centre) Birm 11   P Ch Trust Fund Trust   R T N CROWE   C D J HUGHES

ELMERS END (St James)   see Beckenham St Jas Roch

ELMESTHORPE (St Mary)   see Earl Shilton w Elmesthorpe Leic

ELMHAM, NORTH (St Mary), Billingford, Bintree, Guist, Twyford and Worthing Nor 22   P Bp, Earl of Leicester, G&C Coll Cam, and DBP (jt)   R N C H VARNON

ELMHAM, SOUTH (St George) (St James) (St Margaret) (St Peter) (St Michael and All Angels) and Ilketshall St E 18   P Bp (3 turns), Ld Chan (1 turn), and Duke of Norfolk (1 turn)   R R H P THORNBURGH   C I B BYRNE

ELMHURST (Mission Room)   see Lich St Chad Lich

ELMLEY   see Emley Leeds

ELMLEY CASTLE (St Mary) w Bricklehampton and the Combertons Worc 4   P Bp   P-in-c R J WORSLEY

ELMLEY LOVETT (St Michael) w Hampton Lovett and Elmbridge w Rushdock Worc 8   P Bp and Ch Coll Cam (alt)   P-in-c D J ARNOLD

ELMORE (St John the Baptist)   see Hardwicke and Elmore w Longney Glouc

ELMSALL, NORTH (St Margaret)   see Badsworth Leeds

ELMSALL, SOUTH (St Mary the Virgin) Leeds 19   P Bp   V M GALLAGHER

ELMSETT (St Peter) w Aldham, Hintlesham, Chattisham and Kersey St E 3   P Bp, MMCET, and St Chad's Coll Dur (jt)   R T E FFRENCH   C J P FFRENCH

ELMSTEAD (St Anne and St Laurence) Chelmsf 22   P Jes Coll Cam   V vacant

ELMSTONE (not known)   see Canonry Cant

ELMSTONE HARDWICKE (St Mary Magdalene)   see N Cheltenham Glouc

ELMSWELL (St John the Divine) St E 10   P MMCET   R P W GOODRIDGE

ELMTON (St Peter) Derby 3   P Bp   P-in-c E KIRBY

ELSDON (St Cuthbert)   see N Tyne and Redesdale Newc

ELSECAR (Holy Trinity)   see Worsbrough w Elsecar Sheff

ELSENHAM (St Mary the Virgin)   see Henham and Elsenham w Ugley Chelmsf

ELSFIELD (St Thomas of Canterbury)   see Marston w Elsfield Ox

ELSHAM (All Saints)   see N Wolds Gp Linc

ELSING (St Mary)   see Lyng, Sparham, Elsing, Bylaugh, Bawdeswell etc Nor

ELSON (St Thomas) Portsm 3   P DBP   P-in-c K I MITCHELL   NSM M A HAY

ELSTEAD (St James) Guildf 4   P Adn Surrey   R J J PAGE   NSM P R J MUIR

ELSTED (St Paul)   see Harting w Elsted and Treyford cum Didling Chich

ELSTERNWICK (St Laurence)   see Burstwick, Burton Pidsea etc York

ELSTON (All Saints) w Elston Chapelry S'well 3   P J C S Darwin Esq   P-in-c E I MURRAY

ELSTOW (St Mary and St Helena) St Alb 9   P Patr Bd   TV S T SMITH

ELSTREE (St Nicholas) and Borehamwood St Alb 14   P Patr Bd (3 turns), Ld Chan (1 turn)   TR T G WARR   TV C M HINA, L R COLLINS

ELSWICK (St Stephen) (St Paul) Newc 4   P Ch Soc Trust and Trustees (jt)   V G R CURRY

ELSWORTH (Holy Trinity)   see Papworth Ely

ELTHAM (Holy Trinity) S'wark 3   P Bp   V B E WARD   C V J E FRANCIS-MULLINS   NSM N C WHEELER

ELTHAM (St Barnabas) S'wark 3   P Bp   V S COOK   Hon C G E STEVENSON

ELTHAM (St John the Baptist) S'wark 3   P DBP   P-in-c J F BRYSON

ELTHAM PARK (St Luke) S'wark 3   P Bp   V E J OGLESBY

ELTHAM, NEW (All Saints) S'wark 3   P Bp   V A S ROSE

ELTISLEY (St Pandionia and St John the Baptist)   see Papworth Ely

ELTON (All Saints) Ely 15   P Sir William Proby Bt   V vacant

ELTON (All Saints)   see Kirklees Valley Man

ELTON (St John) Dur 10   P St Chad Coll Dur   P-in-c P D ASHDOWN

ELTON (St Mary the Virgin)   see Wigmore Abbey Heref

ELTON (St Stephen) Man 8   P V Elton All SS   V vacant

ELTON-ON-THE-HILL (St Michael)   see Cropwell Bishop w Colston Bassett, Granby etc S'well

ELVASTON (St Bartholomew)   see Aston on Trent, Elvaston, Weston on Trent etc Derby

ELVEDEN (St Andrew and St Patrick)   see Brandon and Santon Downham w Elveden etc St E

ELVINGTON (Holy Trinity)   see Derwent Ings York

ELWICK HALL (St Peter) *see* Hart w Elwick Hall *Dur*
ELWORTH (St Peter) *Ches 11* **P** *V Sandbach* **V** D J PAGE
ELY (Holy Trinity w St Mary) (St Peter) *Ely 8* **P** *Patr Bd*
  P-in-c C M HILL   **TV** N J ANDREWS   **C** M D NEWTON
  NSM J R HICKISH
EMBERTON (All Saints) *see* Lamp *Ox*
EMBLETON (Holy Trinity) w Rennington and Rock *Newc 6*
  P *Mert Coll Ox*   **V** P D HARRATT
EMBLETON (St Cuthbert) *see* Cockermouth Area *Carl*
EMBROOK (Community of St Nicholas) *see* Wokingham
  St Paul *Ox*
EMBSAY (St Mary the Virgin) w Eastby *Leeds 26*   **P** *R Skipton*
  H Trin   **V** L M TAYLOR-KENYON
EMERY DOWN (Christ Church) *see* Lyndhurst and Emery
  Down and Minstead *Win*
EMLEY (St Michael the Archangel) *Leeds 13*   **P** *Lord Savile*
  P-in-c F J MARSH   **NSM** A P YOUNG
EMMANUEL Team Ministry, The *Leeds 6*   **P** *Patr Bd*
  TR S GOTT   **C** I D JAMIESON   **NSM** D KENT
  OLM C A SYKES
EMMAUS Parish Team, The *Leic 1*   **P** *Bp*
  P-in-c J C MCGINLEY   **C** J LINDSEY
EMMER GREEN (St Barnabas) w Caversham Park *Ox 7*   **P** *Bp*
  and Ch Ch Ox (jt)   **R** D E CHANDLER
EMNETH (St Edmund) *see* Fen Orchards *Ely*
EMPINGHAM (St Peter), Edith Weston, Lyndon, Manton,
  North Luffenham, Pilton, Preston, Ridlington, Whitwell
  and Wing *Pet 12*   **P** *Bp, Baroness Willoughby de Eresby, Sir*
  John Conant Bt, Em Coll Cam, and DBP (jt)   **R** D C NICOL
  Hon C J P TAYLOR
EMPSHOTT (Holy Rood) *see* Greatham w Empshott and
  Hawkley w Prior's Dean *Portsm*
EMSCOTE (All Saints) *see* Warwick *Cov*
EMSWORTH (St James) *see* Warblington w Emsworth *Portsm*
ENBORNE (St Michael and All Angels) *see* Walbury Beacon *Ox*
ENDCLIFFE (St Augustine) *Sheff 2*   **P** *Ch Burgesses*
  P-in-c P W BECKLEY
ENDERBY (St John the Baptist) w Lubbesthorpe and
  Thurlaston *Leic 7*   **P** *Bp and F B Drummond Esq*
  P-in-c J C TAYLOR
ENDON (St Luke) *see* Bagnall w Endon *Lich*
ENFIELD (Christ Church) Trent Park *Lon 18*   **P** *Ch Trust*
  Fund Trust   **V** R D JAMES   **C** G S BANNISTER, P HERRINGTON
ENFIELD (St Andrew) *Lon 18*   **P** *Trin Coll Cam*
  V S M GRIFFITHS
ENFIELD (St George) *Lon 18*   **P** *Bp*   **P-in-c** A T OH
ENFIELD (St James) (St Barnabas) *Lon 18*   **P** *V Enfield*
  V I M GALLAGHER   **NSM** H R GEORGE, J M FOOT
ENFIELD (St John the Baptist) *see* Clay Hill St Jo and St Luke
  Lon
ENFIELD (St Luke) *as above*
ENFIELD (St Mark) *see* Bush Hill Park St Mark *Lon*
ENFIELD (St Matthew) *see* Ponders End St Matt *Lon*
ENFIELD (St Michael and All Angels) *Lon 18*   **P** *V Enfield*
  V S M TAYLOR   **NSM** K A GOODING
ENFIELD (St Peter and St Paul) *Lon 18*   **P** *Bp*
  V J C VAUGHAN
ENFIELD (St Stephen) *see* Bush Hill Park St Steph *Lon*
ENFIELD CHASE (St Mary Magdalene) *Lon 18*   **P** *Bp*
  V G J GILES   **NSM** J W FISH, M S LUNN
ENFORD (All Saints) *see* Avon River *Sarum*
ENGLEFIELD (St Mark) *see* Theale and Englefield *Ox*
ENGLEFIELD GREEN (St Jude) *Guildf 11*   **P** *Bp*
  V M R EWBANK
ENGLISH BICKNOR (St Mary) *see* Forest of Dean Ch Ch w
  English Bicknor *Glouc*
ENGLISHCOMBE (St Peter) *see* Bath St Barn w Englishcombe
  B & W
ENMORE (St Michael) *see* Aisholt, Enmore, Goathurst, Nether
  Stowey etc *B & W*
ENMORE GREEN (St John the Evangelist) *see* Shaftesbury
  Sarum
ENNERDALE (St Mary) *see* Lamplugh w Ennerdale *Carl*
ENSBURY PARK (St Thomas) *Sarum 7*   **P** *Bp*   **V** S A EVANS
  NSM M R EVANS
ENSTONE (St Kenelm) *see* Chase *Ox*
ENVILLE (St Mary the Virgin) *see* Kinver and Enville *Lich*
EPPERSTONE (Holy Cross), Gonalston, Oxton and
  Woodborough *S'well 7*   **P** *Bp, Ld Chan, and C P L Francklin*
  Esq (by turn)   **R** A R GILES   **C** C L YARRIEN
  NSM M N TAYLOR
EPPING District (All Saints) (St John the Baptist) *Chelmsf 3*
  P *Patr Bd*   **TR** G CONNOR   **TV** B C MORRISON
  C J N A MACNEANEY
EPSOM (St Barnabas) *Guildf 9*   **P** *Bp*   **V** *vacant*

EPSOM (St Martin) (St Stephen on the Downs) *Guildf 9*
  P *Bp*   **P-in-c** N A PARISH   **B** L ALSOP
EPSOM COMMON (Christ Church) *Guildf 9*   **P** *Bp*
  V R A DONOVAN   **C** J W MCALLEN   **NSM** S A CURTIS
EPWELL (St Anne) *see* Wykeham *Ox*
EPWORTH Group, The (St Andrew) *Linc 1*   **P** *Prime Min*
  (2 turns), Ld Chan (1 turn)   **R** I R S WALKER
ERCALL, HIGH (St Michael and All Angels) *see* Wrockwardine
  Deanery *Lich*
ERDINGTON Christ the King *Birm 8*   **P** *Bp*   **V** R R SOUTER
ERDINGTON Team Ministry, The (St Barnabas) (St Chad)
  Birm 8   **P** *Patr Bd*   **TR** F C EVANS   **TV** N M A TRAYNOR
  NSM E BLAIR-CHAPPELL, J N WANYOIKE
ERIDGE GREEN (Holy Trinity) *see* Frant w Eridge *Chich*
ERISWELL (St Laurence and St Peter) *see* Mildenhall *St E*
ERITH (Christ Church) *Roch 15*   **P** *Bp*   **V** J A CONALTY
  NSM M A NORMAN
ERITH (St John the Baptist) *Roch 15*   **P** *Bp*   **V** R M RADCLIFFE
ERITH (St Paul) Northumberland Heath *Roch 15*   **P** *CPAS*
  V C BEAZLEY-LONG
ERLESTOKE (Holy Saviour) *see* Bratton, Edington and Imber,
  Erlestoke etc *Sarum*
ERMINGTON (St Peter and St Paul) and Ugborough *Ex 12*
  P *Prime Min (1 turn), Bp and Grocers' Co (3 turns)*
  C C M S LUFF
ERNESETTLE (St Aidan), Whitleigh and Honicknowle *Ex 21*
  P *Ld Chan and Bp (alt)*   **V** D R BAILEY   **NSM** D WATSON
ERPINGHAM (St Mary) w Calthorpe, Ingworth, Aldborough,
  Thurgarton and Alby w Thwaite *Nor 19*   **P** *Bp, Lord Walpole,*
  Gt Hosp Nor, Mrs S M Lilly, and DBP (by turn)
  P-in-c P R THOMAS
ERRINGDEN *Leeds 9*   **P** *Bp and V Halifax (jt)*   **V** C B REARDON
  NSM A MAUDE, M BULL
ERWARTON (St Mary the Virgin) *see* Shoreline *St E*
ERYHOLME (St Mary) *see* E Richmond *Leeds*
ESCOMB (no dedication) *Dur 6*   **P** *Bp*   **P-in-c** B E MECHANIC
  Hon C R I MECHANIC, T PITT
ESCOT (St Philip and St James) *see* Feniton and Escot *Ex*
ESCRICK (St Helen) and Stillingfleet w Naburn *York 2*
  P *Abp, D&C, and C D Forbes Adam Esq (jt)*   **R** R M KIRKMAN
  Hon C K J GARDINER
ESH (St Michael and All Angels) and Hamsteels *Dur 1*
  P *Prime Min*   **V** M J PEERS
ESHER (Christ Church) (St George) *Guildf 8*   **P** *Wadh Coll Ox*
  R S J COLLIER   **C** N W KURZ
ESHOLT (St Paul) *see* Guiseley w Esholt *Leeds*
ESK MOOR, MIDDLE *York 21*   **P** *Abp*   **V** C M HADDON-REECE
ESK, LOWER *York 21*   **P** *Abp*   **V** C AROLAN
ESKDALE (St Catherine) (St Bega's Mission), Irton,
  Muncaster and Waberthwaite *Carl 5*   **P** *Bp, Adn W*
  Cumberland, Mrs P Gordon-Duff-Pennington, and P Stanley Esq
  (jt)   **P-in-c** G M HART
ESSENDINE (St Mary the Virgin) *see* Ryhall w Essendine and
  Carlby *Pet*
ESSENDON (St Mary the Virgin) *see* Lt Berkhamsted and
  Bayford, Essendon etc *St Alb*
ESSINGTON (St John the Evangelist) *Lich 2*   **P** *Bp, R Bushbury,*
  R Wednesfield, and Simeon's Trustees (jt)   **P-in-c** S BOWIE
  Hon C W H HEATH
ESTON (Christ Church) w Normanby *York 17*   **P** *Abp*
  TR J G BLAKELEY   **NSM** T D CHARLTON
ESTOVER (Christ Church) *Ex 21*   **P** *Bp*   **C** C J ROUTLEDGE,
  S P RUNDELL
ETAL (St Mary the Virgin) *see* Ford and Etal *Newc*
ETCHILHAMPTON (St Andrew) *see* The Cannings and
  Redhorn *Sarum*
ETCHING HILL (The Holy Spirit) *see* Brereton and Rugeley
  Lich
ETCHINGHAM (Assumption and St Nicholas) *Chich 13*   **P** *Bp*
  R *vacant*
ETHERLEY (St Cuthbert) *Dur 6*   **P** *Bp*   **P-in-c** B E MECHANIC
  Hon C R I MECHANIC, T PITT
ETON (St John the Evangelist) w Eton Wick, Boveney and
  Dorney *Ox 12*   **P** *Eton Coll and Mrs J M Palmer (jt)*
  V R R STACEY
ETON WICK (St John the Baptist) *see* Eton w Eton Wick,
  Boveney and Dorney *Ox*
ETTINGSHALL (Holy Trinity) *Lich 28*   **P** *Bp*   **V** D P A FEENEY
  NSM R C GILBERT
ETTINGTON (Holy Trinity and St Thomas of Canterbury)
  see Stourdene Gp *Cov*
ETTON (St Mary) w Dalton Holme *York 8*   **P** *Lord Hotham*
  C R F PARKINSON
ETTON (St Stephen) w Helpston and Maxey *Pet 11*   **P** *Sir*
  Philip Naylor-Leyland Bt (2 turns), D&C (1 turn)   **R** *vacant*

ETWALL (St Helen) w Egginton *Derby 14* **P** *Bp, Sir Henry Every Bt, Major J W Chandos-Pole, and DBP (by turn)* **R** F B SOLMAN **NSM** F M GRANT

EUSTON (St Genevieve) *see Blackbourne St E*

EUXTON (not known) *Blackb 4* **P** *Bp* **V** W G ASHTON

EVE HILL (St James the Great) *see Dudley Worc*

EVEDON (St Mary) *see N Lafford Gp Linc*

EVENLEY (St George) *see Aynho and Croughton w Evenley etc Pet*

EVENLODE (St Edward King and Martyr) *see Broadwell, Evenlode, Oddington, Adlestrop etc Glouc*

EVENWOOD (St Paul) *Dur 7* **P** *Bp* **C** C A GIBBS

EVERCREECH (St Peter) w Chesterblade and Milton Clevedon *B & W 2* **P** *DBP* **P-in-c** R C LUNN

EVERDON (St Mary) *see Weedon Bec w Everdon and Dodford Pet*

EVERINGHAM (St Everilda) *see Holme and Seaton Ross Gp York*

EVERSDEN, GREAT (St Mary) *see Lordsbridge Ely*

EVERSDEN, LITTLE (St Helen) *as above*

EVERSHOLT (St John the Baptist) *see Woburn w Eversholt, Milton Bryan, Battlesden etc St Alb*

EVERSHOT (St Osmund) *see Melbury Sarum*

EVERSLEY (St Mary) *see Darby Green and Eversley Win*

EVERTON (Holy Trinity) *see Bawtry w Austerfield, Misson, Everton and Mattersey S'well*

EVERTON (St George) *Liv 3* **P** *Bp* **V** K E WHARTON **C** A D ROSS

EVERTON (St Mary) *see Gamlingay and Everton Ely*

EVERTON (St Mary) *see Milford Win*

EVERTON (St Peter) (St John Chrysostom) (Emmanuel) *Liv 3* **P** *Patr Bd* **R** H CORBETT **C** A L LAWLOR

EVESBATCH (St Andrew) *see Frome Valley Heref*

EVESHAM (All Saints w St Lawrence) w Norton and Lenchwick *Worc 1* **P** *Bp and D&C (jt)* **V** A SPURR

EVINGTON (St Denys) *Leic 1* **P** *Bp* **V** A J LEES-SMITH **C** E A WILSON

EVINGTON, NORTH (St Stephen) *Leic 1* **P** *Bp* **V** *vacant*

EWELL (St Francis of Assisi) Ruxley Lane *Guildf 9* **P** *Bp* **V** M L BORLEY

EWELL (St Mary the Virgin) *Guildf 9* **P** *Bp* **V** R J E DEWHURST **NSM** S P AYLING

EWELL, WEST (All Saints) *Guildf 9* **P** *Bp* **V** *vacant*

EWELME (St Mary the Virgin), Brightwell Baldwin, Cuxham w Easington *Ox 20* **P** *F D Wright Esq and Mert Coll Ox, Prime Min (alt)* **P-in-c** J P MEYER

EWERBY (St Andrew) *see Kirkby Laythorpe Linc*

EWHURST (St James the Great) *Chich 17* **P** *K Coll Cam* **R** G L WINCHESTER

EWHURST (St Peter and St Paul) *Guildf 2* **P** *Ld Chan* **R** D A MINNS **OLM** T J SELLER

EWSHOT (St Mary the Virgin) *see Crondall and Ewshot Guildf*

EWYAS HAROLD (St Michael and All Angels) w Dulas, Kenderchurch, Abbeydore, Bacton, Kentchurch, Llangua, Rowlestone, Llancillo, Walterstone, Kilpeck, St Devereux and Wormbridge *Heref 1* **P** *Bp, E Harley Esq, Mrs B Sexton, J Lucas-Scudamore Esq, Mrs M Barneby, G Clive Esq, and D&C (2 turns), Ld Chan (1 turn)* **R** A F EVANS

EXBOURNE (St Mary the Virgin) *see Okehampton, Inwardleigh, Belstone, Sourton etc Ex*

EXBURY (St Katherine) *see Beaulieu and Exbury and E Boldre Win*

EXETER (St David) (St Michael and All Angels) *Ex 3* **P** *D&C* **V** T D HONEY **C** C W DURRANT **Hon C** P A LEE

EXETER (St James) *Ex 3* **P** *D&C* **R** H H D PRYSE **C** A S DOWN

EXETER (St Leonard w Holy Trinity) *Ex 3* **P** *CPAS* **R** S N AUSTEN **C** C J KEANE, M J ROWLAND

EXETER (St Mark) (St Matthew) (St Sidwell) *Ex 3* **P** *Bp and D&C (jt)* **P-in-c** J S OLLIER **C** V RAMSEY

EXETER (St Thomas) *see Heavitree and St Mary Steps Ex*

EXETER (St Thomas the Apostle) (Emmanuel) (St Andrew) (St Philip) *Ex 3* **P** *Bp* **P-in-c** N J EDWARDS **C** W D SWEENEY **NSM** A DUNLOP

EXETER Holy Trinity *Ex 3* **P** *Bp and Ch Soc Trust (jt)* **V** J P A ELVIN

EXETER, CENTRAL (St Martin) (St Mary Arches) (St Olave) (St Pancras) (St Petrock) (St Stephen) *Ex 3* **P** *Patr Bd* **P-in-c** S R SWARBRICK

EXFORD (St Mary Magdalene) *see Exmoor B & W*

EXHALL (St Giles) *see Heart of England Cov*

EXHALL (St Giles) *Cov 5* **P** *Bp* **V** A J R GANDON

EXMINSTER (St Martin), Kenn, Kenton w Mamhead, and Powderham *Ex 5* **P** *12 Govs of Crediton Ch, D&C Sarum, SMF, Mrs M P L Bate, and Earl of Devon (jt)* **R** J D A WILLIAMS **C** M LORD-LEAR, N M HAWKINS **Hon C** P DAWKES

EXMOOR (St Luke) *B & W 15* **P** *Ld Chan (1 turn), Bp, Em Coll Cam, Peterho Cam, G A Warren Esq, and D M Warren Esq (2 turns)* **R** D A WEIR

EXMOUTH (All Saints) *see Withycombe Raleigh Ex*

EXMOUTH (Holy Trinity) *see Littleham-cum-Exmouth w Lympstone Ex*

EXMOUTH (St John in the Wilderness) *see Withycombe Raleigh Ex*

EXMOUTH (St John the Evangelist) *as above*

EXNING (St Agnes) *see Newmarket St Mary w Exning St Agnes St E*

EXNING (St Martin) (St Philip) w Landwade *St E 11* **P** *D&C Cant* **P-in-c** A G RYCRAFT **NSM** C T MCCARTY, P S GILL

EXTON (St Andrew) *see Aylesbeare, Clyst St George, Clyst St Mary etc Ex*

EXTON (St Peter and St Paul) *see Cottesmore and Burley, Clipsham, Exton etc Pet*

EXTON (St Peter and St Paul) *see Meon Bridge Portsm*

EXTON (St Peter) *see Exmoor B & W*

EXWICK (St Andrew) *Ex 3* **P** *Lord Wraxall* **P-in-c** J P BIRD

EYAM (St Lawrence) *see Baslow and Eyam Derby*

EYDON (St Nicholas) *see Aston-le-Walls, Byfield, Boddington, Eydon etc Pet*

EYE (St Matthew), Newborough and Thorney *Pet 11* **P** *Bp and Prime Min (alt)* **V** C HURST **C** S K KAYE

EYE (St Peter and St Paul) *St E 14* **P** *Bp, SMF, and Lt Comdr G C Marshall (jt)* **R** G SUMPTER

EYEWORTH (All Saints) *see Dunton w Wrestlingworth and Eyeworth St Alb*

EYKE (All Saints) *see Wilford Peninsula St E*

EYNESBURY (St Mary) *Ely 13* **P** *Bp* **C** D A NOONAN, P D ANDREWS

EYNSFORD (St Martin) w Farningham and Lullingstone *Roch 10* **P** *D&C* **R** G J OWEN **NSM** C H SALMON, M D MCGARVEY

EYNSHAM (St Leonard) and Cassington *Ox 29* **P** *Wycliffe Hall Ox and Ch Ch Ox (alt)* **V** M A C ANDREWS **C** K M COOKE **NSM** A C ATHERSTONE **OLM** R ASTON

EYPE (St Peter) *see Askerswell, Loders, Powerstock and Symondsbury Sarum*

EYRES MONSELL (St Hugh) *Leic 1* **P** *Bp* **V** I WRIGHT

EYTHORNE (St Peter and St Paul) *see Bewsborough Cant*

EYTON (All Saints) *see Leominster Heref*

EYTON (St Catherine) *see Wellington All SS w Eyton Lich*

FACCOMBE (St Barnabas) *see Hurstbourne Tarrant, Faccombe, Vernham Dean etc Win*

FACEBY (St Mary Magdalene) *see Whorlton w Carlton and Faceby York*

FACIT (St John the Evangelist) *see Whitworth w Facit Man*

FAILAND (St Bartholomew) *see Wraxall B & W*

FAILSWORTH (Holy Family) *Man 16* **P** *Prime Min and Bp (alt)* **R** A J MILLS

FAILSWORTH (St John) (St John the Evangelist) *Man 16* **P** *Bp* **R** J ELCOCK

FAIR OAK (St Thomas) *Win 10* **P** *Bp* **NSM** R G NICHOLLS

FAIRBURN (St James) *see Ledsham w Fairburn York*

FAIRFIELD (St Mark) *see Belbroughton w Fairfield and Clent Worc*

FAIRFIELD (St Peter) *Derby 4* **P** *Ch Govs* **P-in-c** C F EDWARDS

FAIRFIELD (St Thomas à Becket) *see Brookland, Fairfield, Brenzett w Snargate etc Cant*

FAIRFORD (St Mary the Virgin) *see S Cotswolds Glouc*

FAIRHAVEN (St Paul) *Blackb 10* **P** *J C Hilton Esq* **V** *vacant*

FAIRLIGHT (St Andrew) *see Fairlight and Pett Chich*

FAIRLIGHT (St Peter) *as above*

FAIRLIGHT and Pett *Chich 17* **P** *Patr Bd* **R** R D BARRON **Hon C** H E PATTEN

FAIRSEAT (Holy Innocents) *see Stansted w Fairseat and Vigo Roch*

FAIRSTEAD (St Mary) *see Witham and Villages Chelmsf*

FAIRWARP (Christ Church) *Chich 18* **P** *Bp* **P-in-c** P J BROADBENT

FAIRWEATHER GREEN (St Saviour) *Leeds 1* **P** *Bp* **V** *vacant*

FAKENHAM (St Peter and St Paul) w Alethorpe *Nor 15* **P** *Trin Coll Cam* **R** F R A MASON

FAKENHAM MAGNA (St Peter) *see Blackbourne St E*

FALCONWOOD (Bishop Ridley Church) *Roch 15* **P** *Bp* **V** *vacant*

FALDINGWORTH (All Saints) *see Middle Rasen Gp Linc*

FALFIELD (St George) *see Cromhall, Tortworth, Tytherington, Falfield etc Glouc*

FALKENHAM (St Ethelbert) *see Nacton and Levington w Bucklesham etc St E*

FALLOWFIELD (St Crispin) *see Withington St Crispin Man*

FALMER (St Laurence) *see* Stanmer w Falmer *Chich*
FALMOUTH (All Saints) *Truro 3* P *Bp* P-in-c S R F DRAKELEY
FALMOUTH (King Charles the Martyr) *Truro 3* P *Bp*
P-in-c S J TUDGEY
FALSTONE (St Peter) *see* N Tyne and Redesdale *Newc*
FAMBRIDGE, NORTH (Holy Trinity) *see* Althorne and
Latchingdon w N Fambridge *Chelmsf*
FAMBRIDGE, SOUTH (All Saints) *see* Ashingdon w S
Fambridge, Canewdon and Paglesham *Chelmsf*
FANGFOSS (St Martin) *see* Barmby Moor Gp *York*
FAR FOREST (Holy Trinity) *see* Mamble w Bayton, Rock w
Heightington etc *Worc*
FARCET (St Mary) *see* Stanground and Farcet *Ely*
FAREHAM (Holy Trinity) (St Columba) *Portsm 2* P *Bp*
P-in-c S E DAVENPORT TV R E SCHOFIELD C G P ROBERTS
NSM K F WICKERT
FAREHAM (St John the Evangelist) *Portsm 2* P *CPAS*
P-in-c B G DEANS
FAREHAM (St Peter and St Paul) *Portsm 2* P *Bp*
P-in-c R JACKSON
FAREWELL (St Bartholomew) *Lich 1* P *MMCET* V *vacant*
FARFORTH (St Peter) *see* S Ormsby Gp *Linc*
FARINGDON, GREAT (All Saints) w Little Coxwell *Ox 25*
P *Simeon's Trustees* V C J DRAPER
FARINGDON, LITTLE (St Margaret of England) *see* Shill Valley
and Broadshire
Ox
FARLAM (St Thomas à Becket) *see* Eden, Gelt and Irthing *Carl*
FARLEIGH (St Mary) *see* Warlingham w Chelsham and
Farleigh *S'wark*
FARLEIGH HUNGERFORD (St Leonard) *see* Hardington Vale
B & W
FARLEIGH WALLOP (St Andrew) *see* Farleigh, Candover and
Wield *Win*
FARLEIGH, Candover and Wield *Win 1* P *Ld Chan (1 turn),
Bp, D&C, Earl of Portsmouth, and Lord Ashburton (1 turn)*
R D M CHATTELL C S P E MOURANT
FARLEIGH, EAST (not known) *see* Coxheath, E Farleigh,
Hunton, Linton etc *Roch*
FARLEIGH, WEST (All Saints) *as above*
FARLESTHORPE (St Andrew) *see* Bilsby w Farlesthorpe *Linc*
FARLEY (All Saints) *see* Clarendon *Sarum*
FARLEY CHAMBERLAYNE (St John) *see* Michelmersh and
Awbridge and Braishfield etc *Win*
FARLEY GREEN (St Michael) *see* Shere, Albury and Chilworth
Guildf
FARLEY HILL (St John the Baptist) *St Alb 12* P *Bp*
P-in-c R P O'NEILL NSM S SMITH
FARLEY HILL (St John the Evangelist) *see* Loddon Reach *Ox*
FARLINGTON (St Andrew) (Church of the Resurrection)
Portsm 6 P *Mrs S J Wynter-Bee and Nugee Foundn (jt)*
R P D GULLY NSM A J WOOD
FARLINGTON (St Leonard) *see* Forest of Galtres *York*
FARLOW (St Giles) *see* Stottesdon w Farlow, Cleeton St Mary
etc *Heref*
FARMBOROUGH (All Saints) and Marksbury and Stanton
Prior *B & W 9* P *MMCET (3 turns), Duchy of Cornwall
(1 turn), and DBF (1 turn)* R J P KNOTT
FARMCOTE (St Faith) *see* The Guitings, Cutsdean, Farmcote
etc *Glouc*
FARMINGTON (St Peter) *see* Northleach w Hampnett and
Farmington etc *Glouc*
FARMOOR (St Mary) *see* Cumnor *Ox*
FARNBOROUGH (All Saints) *see* E Downland *Ox*
FARNBOROUGH (St Botolph) *see* Avon Dassett w Farnborough
and Fenny Compton *Cov*
FARNBOROUGH (St Giles) (St Nicholas) *Roch 16* P *Em Coll
Cam* R M J HUGHES C A M NEWMAN
FARNBOROUGH, NORTH (St Peter) (Good Shepherd) *Guildf 1*
P *Patr Bd* TR D G WILLEY TV R M BENNETTS
C A ELLIOTT, M SWIRES-HENNESSY, R M SMART
NSM R N COBBOLD
FARNBOROUGH, SOUTH (St Mark) *Guildf 1* P *Bp*
V I C HEDGES
FARNCOMBE (St John the Evangelist) *Guildf 4* P *Bp*
R J RATTUE C M A STIRLING TROY
FARNDALE (St Mary) *see* Kirkbymoorside w Gillamoor,
Farndale etc *York*
FARNDON (St Chad) and Coddington *Ches 5* P *Duke of
Westmr and D&C (jt)* V D SCURR
FARNDON (St Peter) w Thorpe, Hawton and Cotham *S'well 3*
P *Ld Chan* P-in-c W D MILNER
FARNDON, EAST (St John the Baptist) *see* Arthingworth,
Harrington w Oxendon and E Farndon *Pet*
FARNHAM (St Andrew) (St Francis) (St Mary) *Guildf 3* P *Bp*
R S A REYNOLDS

FARNHAM (St Laurence) *see* Chase *Sarum*
FARNHAM (St Mary the Virgin) *see* Stansted Mountfitchet w
Birchanger and Farnham *Chelmsf*
FARNHAM (St Mary) *see* Alde River *St E*
FARNHAM (St Oswald) *see* Walkingham Hill *Leeds*
FARNHAM COMMON (St John the Evangelist) *see* Farnham
Royal w Hedgerley *Ox*
FARNHAM ROYAL (St Mary the Virgin) w Hedgerley *Ox 12*
P *Bp and Eton Coll (jt)* R G H SAUNDERS
FARNHAM ROYAL SOUTH (St Michael) *see* Manor Park and
Whitby Road *Ox*
FARNINGHAM (St Peter and St Paul) *see* Eynsford w
Farningham and Lullingstone *Roch*
FARNLEY (All Saints) *see* Washburn and Mid-Wharfe *Leeds*
FARNLEY TYAS (St Lucias) *see* Almondbury w Farnley Tyas
Leeds
FARNLEY, NEW (St James) *see* Wortley and Farnley *Leeds*
FARNSFIELD (St Michael) *S'well 3* P *Bp* NSM M A GROVES
FARNWORTH (All Saints) (St John), Kearsley and
Stoneclough *Man 7* P *Ld Chan and Patr Bd (alt)*
TR C H PHARAOH C K E WEDGEWOOD
OLM M J WEARING
FARNWORTH (Cronton Mission) *see* E Widnes *Liv*
FARNWORTH (St George) *see* New Bury w Gt Lever *Man*
FARNWORTH (St Luke) *see* E Widnes *Liv*
FARRINGDON (All Saints) *see* Northanger *Win*
FARRINGDON (St Petrock and St Barnabas) *see* Aylesbeare,
Clyst St George, Clyst St Mary etc *Ex*
FARRINGTON GURNEY (St John the Baptist) *see* Paulton w
Farrington Gurney and High Littleton *B & W*
FARSLEY (St John the Evangelist) *Leeds 15* P V *Calverley*
V P Q TUDGE NSM L M STEVENSON TATE
FARTHINGHOE (St Michael and All Angels) *see* Aynho and
Croughton w Evenley etc *Pet*
FARTHINGSTONE (St Mary the Virgin) *see* Lambfold *Pet*
FARWAY (St Michael and All Angels) *see* Offwell, Northleigh,
Farway, Cotleigh etc *Ex*
FATFIELD (St George) *Dur 11* P *Lord Lambton*
V N J BARR-HAMILTON
FAULKBOURNE (St Germanus) *see* Witham and Villages
Chelmsf
FAULS (Holy Emmanuel) *see* Edstaston, Fauls, Prees, Tilstock
and Whixall *Lich*
FAVELL, WEST (Emmanuel) *see* Northampton Em *Pet*
FAVERSHAM (St Mary of Charity) *Cant 14* P *D&C*
P-in-c S D ROWLANDS C S R YOUNG, T J BATESON
FAWDON (St Mary the Virgin) *Newc 2* P *Bp*
P-in-c C A MACPHERSON OLM M A ATKINSON
FAWKHAM (St Mary) and Hartley *Roch 1* P *Bp and D&C (jt)*
R J A FLETCHER C M J JEMMETT
FAWLEY (All Saints) *Win 11* P *Bp* P-in-c S H HOLT
FAWLEY (St Mary the Virgin) *see* Hambleden Valley *Ox*
FAWLEY (St Mary) *see* W Downland *Ox*
FAWSLEY (St Mary the Virgin) *see* Badby w Newham and
Charwelton w Fawsley etc *Pet*
FAZAKERLEY (Emmanuel) (St Paul) *Liv 7* P *Patr Bd*
TR A J BROWN TV M A HINDLEY
FAZAKERLEY (St Nathanael) *see* Walton-on-the-Hill *Liv*
FAZELEY (St Paul) (St Barnabas) *Lich 4* P *Bp* V J R IDDON
NSM R G DAVIES
FEATHERSTONE (All Saints) (St Thomas) *Leeds 19* P *Ch Ch
Ox and Bp (jt)* V I GROSU
FECKENHAM (St John the Baptist) *see* Bowbrook N *Worc*
FEERING (All Saints) *see* Kelvedon and Feering *Chelmsf*
FELBRIDGE (St John) *S'wark 25* P *DBP* P-in-c M S FRANCIS
FELBRIGG (St Margaret) *see* Roughton and Felbrigg, Metton,
Sustead etc *Nor*
FELIXKIRK (St Felix) w Boltby *York 18* P *Abp*
V I D HOUGHTON NSM T A LEWIS
FELIXSTOWE (St John the Baptist) (St Edmund) *St E 2* P *Bp*
NSM D P WHITE
FELIXSTOWE (St Peter and St Paul) (St Andrew) (St Nicholas)
St E 2 P *Ch Trust Fund Trust* V J L ASTON
FELKIRK (St Peter) *Leeds 18* P *Bp* P-in-c M J BULLIMORE
C C J HARRISON
FELLING (Christ Church) *Dur 12* P *CPAS*
NSM T R WORSLEY
FELLISCLIFFE (Mission Church) *see* Hampsthwaite and
Killinghall and Birstwith *Leeds*
FELLSIDE TEAM, The *Blackb 9* P *Patr Bd* TR S P C COOPER
TV G WHITTAKER
FELMERSHAM (St Mary) *see* Sharnbrook, Felmersham and
Knotting w Souldrop *St Alb*
FELMINGHAM (St Andrew) *see* King's Beck *Nor*
FELPHAM (St Mary the Virgin) *Chich 1* P *D&C*
C D JARRATT

FELSHAM (St Peter)   *see* Bradfield St Clare, Bradfield St George etc *St E*

FELSTED (Holy Cross) and Little Dunmow *Chelmsf 18*
P *CPAS*   V C J TAYLOR

FELTHAM (St Dunstan) *Lon 11*   P *Bp*   V A M E DOLLERY, G M TOOGOOD

FELTHORPE (St Margaret)   *see* Horsford, Felthorpe and Hevingham *Nor*

FELTON (St Katharine and the Noble Army of Martyrs)   *see* Winford w Felton Common Hill *B & W*

FELTON (St Michael and All Angels) *Newc 6*   P *Bp*
P-in-c T J HARVEY   NSM P T ASKEW

FELTON (St Michael the Archangel)   *see* Maund Gp *Heref*

FELTWELL (St Mary)   *see* Grimshoe *Ely*

FEN AND HILL GROUP, The *Linc 13*   P *Bp, DBP, G J R Wiggins-Davies Esq, and Lt Col J L M Dymoke (jt)*   OLM K A BUSH

FEN DITTON (St Mary the Virgin) *Ely 4*   P *Bp*   R vacant

FEN DRAYTON (St Mary the Virgin) w Conington and Lolworth and Swavesey *Ely 6*   P *The Crown, Jes Coll Cam, SMF, and Ch Coll Cam (by turn)*   R J D YULE

FEN ORCHARDS, The *Ely 14*   P *Bp*   V D L MASON

FENCE-IN-PENDLE (St Anne) and Higham *Blackb 6*   P *Bp and Ld Chan (alt)*   V D J BURY

FENCOTE (St Andrew)   *see* Lower Swale *Leeds*

FENHAM (Holy Cross)   *see* Newc H Cross *Newc*

FENHAM (St James and St Basil) *Newc 4*   P *Bp*   V N P DARBY C N HESLOP   NSM B O OMOBUDE

FENISCLIFFE (St Francis) *Blackb 2*   P *Bp*   P-in-c D J ROSCOE

FENISCOWLES (Immanuel) *Blackb 2*   P V *Blackb*
P-in-c D J ROSCOE

FENITON (St Andrew) and Escot *Ex 6*   P *DBP and J M Kennaway Esq (jt)*   R vacant

FENN LANES Group, The *Leic 10*   P *Bp, D&C, and Lord O'Neill (jt)*   R L J BLAY

FENNY BENTLEY (St Edmund King and Martyr), Thorpe, Tissington, Parwich and Alsop-en-le-Dale *Derby 8*
P *Bp, D A G Shields Esq, and Sir Richard FitzHerbert Bt (jt)*
R A B LARKIN

FENNY COMPTON (St Peter and St Clare)   *see* Avon Dassett w Farnborough and Fenny Compton *Cov*

FENNY DRAYTON (St Michael and All Angels)   *see* Fenn Lanes Gp *Leic*

FENNY STRATFORD (St Martin) *Ox 14*   P *Bp*
V V J A BULLOCK   NSM I W THOMAS

FENSTANTON (St Peter and St Paul) *Ely 10*   P *Bp*
P-in-c R P MCKENZIE

FENTON (Christ Church) *Lich 12*   P *R Stoke-on-Trent*   Hon
C G C FOWELL

FEOCK (St Feock) *Truro 6*   P *Bp*   P-in-c S A BONE
C D J F JONES   NSM A L BUTCHER, E M SHEARD, S J C FLETCHER

FERNDOWN (St Mary)   *see* Hampreston *Sarum*

FERNHAM (St John the Evangelist)   *see* Shrivenham and Ashbury *Ox*

FERNHURST (St Margaret) *Chich 9*   P *Rathbone Trust Co and Cowdray Trust (jt)*   V N P HAIGH

FERNILEE (Holy Trinity)   *see* Whaley Bridge *Ches*

FERRIBY, NORTH (All Saints) *York 14*   P *CPAS*
V M C BRAILSFORD

FERRIBY, SOUTH (St Nicholas) *Linc 8*   P *Bp*   R D P ROWETT

FERRING (St Andrew) *Chich 4*   P *D&C*   V G S INGRAM
NSM J SIMPSON

FERRYBRIDGE (St Andrew) *Leeds 19*   P *D&C York*
P-in-c E M WOODCOCK   NSM S HULME

FERRYHILL (St Luke)   *see* Cornforth and Ferryhill *Dur*

FERSFIELD (St Andrew)   *see* Diss *Nor*

FETCHAM (St Mary) *Guildf 10*   P *Bp*   R A L SMITH

FEWSTON (St Michael and St Lawrence)   *see* Washburn and Mid-Wharfe *Leeds*

FIDDINGTON (St Martin)   *see* Quantock Coast *B & W*

FIELD BROUGHTON (St Peter)   *see* Cartmel Peninsula *Carl*

FIELD DALLING (St Andrew)   *see* Stiffkey and Bale *Nor*

FIFEHEAD MAGDALEN (St Mary Magdalene)   *see* Stour Vale *Sarum*

FIFEHEAD NEVILLE (All Saints)   *see* Hazelbury Bryan and the Hillside Par *Sarum*

FIFIELD (St John the Baptist)   *see* Wychwood *Ox*

FIFIELD BAVANT (St Martin)   *see* Chalke Valley *Sarum*

FIGHELDEAN (St Michael and All Angels)   *see* Avon River *Sarum*

FILBY (All Saints)   *see* S Trin Broads *Nor*

FILEY (St John) (St Oswald) *York 15*   P *PCC*
V A W ALLINGTON

FILKINS (St Peter)   *see* Shill Valley and Broadshire *Ox*

FILLEIGH (St Paul)   *see* S Molton w Nymet St George, High Bray etc *Ex*

FILLINGHAM (St Andrew)   *see* Spring Line Gp *Linc*

FILLONGLEY (St Mary and All Saints) and Corley *Cov 5*
P *Bp and Ch Soc Trust (jt)*   V I D KENNEDY

FILTON (St Gregory)   *see* Horfield St Greg *Bris*

FILTON (St Peter) *Bris 5*   P *Bp*   R E L A GREGORY
NSM M E DESMOND, S L BISHOP   OLM R CONWAY

FILWOOD PARK *Bris 1*   P *Bp and Bris Ch Trustees (jt)*
P-in-c C L GARDINER

FIMBER (St Mary)   *see* Waggoners *York*

FINBOROUGH, GREAT (St Andrew) w Onehouse, Harleston, Buxhall and Shelland *St E 6*   P *Bp*   P-in-c C CHILDS
NSM R CORNISH

FINBOROUGH, LITTLE (St Mary)   *see* Combs and Lt Finborough *St E*

FINCHAM (St Martin) *Ely 9*   P *Bp*   P-in-c B L BURTON

FINCHAMPSTEAD (St James) and California *Ox 8*   P *DBP*
R J F RAMSBOTTOM   C H V HIGGINSON, M-A B TISDALE
NSM J R EDWARDS   OLM B A BAYMAN

FINCHINGFIELD (St John the Baptist) and Cornish Hall End and Wethersfield w Shalford *Chelmsf 17*
P *Mrs E M Bishop and Bp (alt)*   P-in-c C E WILSON
NSM J E NICHOLLS

FINCHLEY (Christ Church) *Lon 14*   P *Ch Patr Trust*
V D A WALKER

FINCHLEY (Holy Trinity) *Lon 16*   P *Bp*   V vacant

FINCHLEY (St Barnabas)   *see* Woodside Park St Barn *Lon*

FINCHLEY (St Mary) *Lon 14*   P *R P A DAVISON*
C S CHRYSOSTOMOU

FINCHLEY (St Paul) (St Luke) *Lon 14*   P *Simeon Trustees and Ch Patr Trust (jt)*   V N R PYE   NSM M A CRISPIN

FINCHLEY, EAST (All Saints) *Lon 14*   P *Bp*   V C R HARDY

FINDERN (All Saints) *Derby 16*   P *Bp*   V S A STARKEY

FINDON (St John the Baptist) w Clapham and Patching *Chich 4*   P *Abp, Bp, and J E P Somerset Esq (jt)*
P-in-c H M BUQUÉ

FINDON VALLEY (All Saints) *Chich 4*   P *Bp*
Dn-in-c B A MILES

FINEDON (St Mary the Virgin) *Pet 8*   P *Bp*
P-in-c R K R COLES

FINGEST (St Bartholomew)   *see* Hambleden Valley *Ox*

FINGHALL (St Andrew)   *see* Spennithorne w Finghall and Hauxwell *Leeds*

FINGRINGHOE (St Andrew) w East Donyland and Abberton w Langenhoe *Chelmsf 24*   P *Bp (3 turns), Ld Chan (1 turn)*
P-in-c P J MCEUNE

FINHAM (St Martin in the Fields) *Cov 3*   P *Bp*   V J R G HYDE

FINMERE (St Michael)   *see* Shelswell *Ox*

FINNINGHAM (St Bartholomew)   *see* Badwell and Walsham *St E*

FINNINGLEY (Holy Trinity and St Oswald) w Auckley *Sheff 9*
P *Bp*   R N M REDEYOFF   C L TINNISWOOD

FINSBURY (St Clement) (St Barnabas) (St Matthew) *Lon 6*
P *D&C St Paul's*   V D E ALLEN

FINSBURY PARK (St Thomas) *Lon 6*   P *Abp*   V S R COLES
NSM V R ATTA-BAFFOE

FINSTALL (St Godwald)   *see* Bromsgrove *Worc*

FINSTHWAITE (St Peter)   *see* Cartmel Peninsula *Carl*

FINSTOCK (Holy Trinity)   *see* Forest Edge *Ox*

FIR VALE (St Cuthbert)   *see* Sheff St Cuth *Sheff*

FIRBANK (St John the Evangelist)   *see* Firbank, Howgill and Killington *Carl*

FIRBANK (St John the Evangelist), Howgill and Killington *Carl 10*   P *Ld Chan and V Sedbergh (alt)*
P-in-c A B MCMULLON

FIRBECK (St Martin) w Letwell *Sheff 5*   P *Bp*   R vacant

FIRLE, WEST (St Peter)   *see* Glynde, W Firle and Beddingham *Chich*

FIRSBY (St Andrew)   *see* Bolingbroke Deanery *Linc*

FIRSWOOD (St Hilda) and Gorse Hill *Man 5*   P *Prime Min*
R T R MALKIN

FISHBOURNE, NEW (St Peter and St Mary) *Chich 2*   P *Ld Chan*   R M WICKENS   C E J STONHAM

FISHBURN (St Catherine)   *see* Upper Skerne *Dur*

FISHERMEAD (Trinity Church)   *see* Woughton *Ox*

FISHERTON ANGER (St Paul) *Sarum 13*   P *Ch Patr Trust*
R C J RYALLS   NSM A ETHERIDGE

FISHLAKE (St Cuthbert) w Sykehouse and Kirk Bramwith w Fenwick and Moss *Sheff 10*   P *Duchy of Lanc (1 turn), D&C Dur (2 turns), and Bp (1 turn)*   R vacant

FISHLEY (St Mary)

FISHPOND (St John the Baptist)   *see* Golden Cap Team *Sarum*

FISHPONDS (All Saints) *Bris 3*   P *Bp*   P-in-c E A KESTEVEN

FISHPONDS (St John) *Bris 3*   P *Bp*   P-in-c R J LING
C M K MARTIN   OLM N G CALLEN

FISHPONDS (St Mary) *Bris 3*   P *Bp*   P-in-c E A KESTEVEN
NSM A THOMSON

FISHTOFT (St Guthlac) *Linc 21*   **P** *DBP*   **R** M A R COOPER

FISKERTON (St Clement)   *see* S Lawres Gp *Linc*

FITTLETON (All Saints)   *see* Avon River *Sarum*

FITTLEWORTH (St Mary the Virgin)   *see* Stopham and Fittleworth *Chich*

FITTON HILL (St Cuthbert)   *see* Bardsley *Man*

FITZ (St Peter and St Paul)   *see* Bicton, Montford w Shrawardine and Fitz *Lich*

FITZHEAD (St James)   *see* Milverton w Halse, Fitzhead and Ash Priors *B & W*

FIVE ASHES (Church of the Good Shepherd)   *see* Mayfield *Chich*

FIVE OAK GREEN (St Luke)   *see* Tudeley cum Capel w Five Oak Green *Roch*

FIVEHEAD (St Martin)   *see* Curry Rivel w Fivehead and Swell *B & W*

FIXBY (St Francis) and Cowcliffe, Huddersfield *Leeds 12*   **P** *DBP*   **P-in-c** D R WARD

FLACKWELL HEATH (Christ Church) *Ox 18*   **P** *DBP*   **V** C D BULL   **NSM** J M ROTH   **OLM** M H COURTNEY

FLADBURY (St John the Baptist), Hill and Moor, Wyre Piddle, Cropthorne and Charlton *Worc 4*   **P** *Bp and D&C (jt)*   **R** *vacant*

FLAMBOROUGH (St Oswald)   *see* Bempton w Flamborough, Reighton w Speeton *York*

FLAMSTEAD (St Leonard) and Markyate Street *St Alb 7*   **P** *Bp and Univ Coll Ox (jt)*   **V** T W SANDER

FLAUNDEN (St Mary Magdalene)   *see* Chenies and Lt Chalfont, Latimer and Flaunden *Ox*

FLAX BOURTON (St Michael and All Angels)   *see* Long Ashton w Barrow Gurney and Flax Bourton *B & W*

FLAXLEY (St Mary the Virgin)   *see* Westbury-on-Severn w Flaxley, Blaisdon etc *Glouc*

FLAXTON (St Lawrence)   *see* Harton *York*

FLEBBS   *see* Lyng, Sparham, Elsing, Bylaugh, Bawdeswell etc *Nor*

FLECKNEY (St Nicholas)   *see* Wistow *Leic*

FLECKNOE (St Mark)   *see* Leam Valley *Cov*

FLEET (All Saints) (St Philip and St James) *Guildf 1*   **P** *Bp*   **V** M W HAYTON   **NSM** J J SISTIG

FLEET (Holy Trinity)   *see* Chickerell w Fleet *Sarum*

FLEETWOOD (St Nicholas) *Blackb 12*   **P** *Bp and Meynell Trustees (jt)*   **V** P J BENFIELD

FLEETWOOD (St Peter) (St David) *Blackb 12*   **P** *Meynell Trustees*   **V** J M HALL   **C** M P MCMURRAY

FLEGG COASTAL Benefice, The: Hemsby, Winterton, East and West Somerton and Horsey *Nor 6*   **P** *Bp, D&C, SMF, and Major R A Ferrier (jt)*   **P-in-c** L S TILLETT

FLEMPTON (St Catherine of Alexandria)   *see* Lark Valley *St E*

FLETCHAMSTEAD (St James) *Cov 3*   **P** *Bp*   **V** S R BURCH   **OLM** A M RICHARDS

FLETCHING (St Mary and St Andrew) *Chich 18*   **P** *Abp*   **P-in-c** L E MURDOCH

FLETTON (St Margaret) *Ely 15*   **P** *Sir Philip Naylor-Leyland Bt*   **P-in-c** W P L GAMMON

FLIMBY (St Nicholas)   *see* Maryport, Netherton and Flimby *Carl*

FLIMWELL (St Augustine of Canterbury)   *see* Ticehurst and Flimwell *Chich*

FLINTHAM (St Augustine of Canterbury) *S'well 5*   **P** R H T *Hildyard Esq*   **P-in-c** O J LEARMONT

FLITCHAM (St Mary the Virgin)   *see* Sandringham w W Newton and Appleton etc *Nor*

FLITTON (St John the Baptist)   *see* Silsoe, Pulloxhill and Flitton *St Alb*

FLITWICK (St Andrew) (St Peter and St Paul) *St Alb 8*   **P** *DBP*   **V** L F DAVIS

FLIXBOROUGH (All Saints) w Burton upon Stather *Linc 6*   **P** *Sir Reginald Sheffield Bt*   **P-in-c** A F PLEDGER

FLIXTON (St John) *Man 5*   **P** *Bp*   **P-in-c** P THORN   **OLM** M SURREY, R W GREEN

FLIXTON (St Mary)   *see* S Elmham and Ilketshall *St E*

FLIXTON (St Michael) *Man 5*   **P** *Bp*   **NSM** A H CLEPHANE, O B MORETT

FLOCKTON (St James the Great) cum Denby Grange *Leeds 13*   **P** *R Carter's Trustees*   **P-in-c** F J MARSH   **NSM** A P YOUNG

FLOOKBURGH (St John the Baptist)   *see* Cartmel Peninsula *Carl*

FLORDON (St Michael)   *see* Mulbarton w Bracon Ash, Hethel and Flordon *Nor*

FLORE (All Saints)   *see* Heyford w Stowe Nine Churches and Flore etc *Pet*

FLOWTON (St Mary)   *see* Somersham w Flowton and Offton w Willisham *St E*

FLUSHING (St Peter)   *see* Mylor w Flushing *Truro*

FLYFORD FLAVELL (St Peter)   *see* Abberton, The Flyfords, Naunton Beauchamp etc *Worc*

FOBBING (St Michael)   *see* Corringham and Fobbing *Chelmsf*

FOLESHILL (St Laurence) *Cov 2*   **P** *Ld Chan*   **V** M R CLEVELAND

FOLESHILL (St Paul) *Cov 2*   **P** *Ld Chan*   **V** J K WOODALL

FOLEY PARK (Holy Innocents)   *see* Kidderminster St Jo and H Innocents *Worc*

FOLKE (St Lawrence)   *see* Three Valleys *Sarum*

FOLKESTONE (St Augustine) (St Mary and St Eanswythe) (St Saviour) *Cant 8*   **P** *Abp*   **V** D J ADLINGTON   **NSM** R C SIEBERT

FOLKESTONE (St John the Baptist) *Cant 8*   **P** *CPAS*   **P-in-c** S J BRADFORD   **C** B M O JONES

FOLKESTONE (St Peter) *Cant 8*   **P** *Trustees*   **V** D J ADLINGTON

FOLKESTONE Trinity Benefice, The (Holy Trinity w Christ Church) (St George) *Cant 8*   **P** *Abp and Ld Chan (alt)*   **NSM** K M MCNEICE, R O SMITH, R W BELLAMY

FOLKESWORTH (St Helen)   *see* Stilton w Denton and Caldecote etc *Ely*

FOLKINGHAM (St Andrew)   *see* S Lafford *Linc*

FOLKINGTON (St Peter ad Vincula)   *see* Alfriston w Lullington, Litlington, W Dean and Folkington *Chich*

FOLKTON (St John)   *see* Willerby w Ganton and Folkton *York*

FOLLIFOOT (St Joseph and St James)   *see* Spofforth w Kirk Deighton *Leeds*

FONTHILL BISHOP (All Saints)   *see* Nadder Valley *Sarum*

FONTHILL GIFFORD (Holy Trinity) *as above*

FONTMELL MAGNA (St Andrew)   *see* Iwerne Valley *Sarum*

FOOLOW (St Hugh)   *see* Baslow and Eyam *Derby*

FOORD (St John the Baptist)   *see* Folkestone St Jo *Cant*

FOOTSCRAY (All Saints) w North Cray *Roch 17*   **P** *Bp and Ld Chan (alt)*   **P-in-c** P G KEOWN

FORCETT (St Cuthbert) and Aldbrough and Melsonby *Leeds 24*   **P** *DBP and Univ Coll Ox (alt)*   **P-in-c** C A PELL

FORD (St Andrew)   *see* Clymping and Yapton w Ford *Chich*

FORD (St John of Jerusalem)   *see* Leominster *Heref*

FORD (St Michael and All Angels) and Etal *Newc 12*   **P** *Lord Joicey*   **R** V T DICKINSON

FORD (St Michael), Gt Wollaston and Alberbury w Cardeston *Heref 12*   **P** *Bp (3 turns), Sir Michael Leighton Bt (1 turn)*   **V** V J TAIT   **OLM** M E NEAL

FORD END (St John the Evangelist)   *see* Gt Waltham w Ford End *Chelmsf*

FORDCOMBE (St Peter)   *see* Penshurst and Fordcombe *Roch*

FORDHAM (All Saints) *Chelmsf 21*   **P** *Reformation Ch Trust, Ball Coll Ox (alt)*   **P-in-c** L J O PARKER

FORDHAM (St Peter and St Mary Magdalene)   *see* Three Rivers Gp *Ely*

FORDHOUSES (St James)   *see* Bushbury *Lich*

FORDINGBRIDGE (St Mary) and Breamore and Hale with the Charfords *Win 9*   **P** *K Coll Cam, Sir Edward Hulse Bt, and P N Hickman Esq (jt)*   **P-in-c** G J PHILBRICK   **C** R N NOEL   **NSM** N L DAVIES, S T HORNE

FORDON (St James)   *see* Burton Fleming w Fordon, Grindale etc *York*

FOREMARK (St Saviour) and Repton w Newton Solney *Derby 16*   **P** *Bp and DBP (jt)*   **V** M J FLOWERDEW   **OLM** J C SCOTT

FOREST (St Stephen)   *see* Rainow w Saltersford and Forest *Ches*

FOREST AND AVON *Sarum 10*   **P** *Patr Bd*   **TR** F H GIMSON   **TV** D G BACON   **Hon C** C W ROGERS   **NSM** V BATCHELOR

FOREST EDGE *Ox 22*   **P** *Bp, V Charlbury, and Sir Mark Norman Bt (jt)*   **V** P J MANSELL   **NSM** S C JONES

FOREST GATE (All Saints) *Chelmsf 5*   **P** *Bp*   **P-in-c** C CHIKE   **OLM** DA HOYTE, M A C MACAULEY

FOREST GATE (Emmanuel w St Peter) Upton Cross *Chelmsf 5*   **P** *Bp*   **V** C CHIKE   **C** J H JENSEN

FOREST GATE (St James)   *see* Stratford St Jo w Ch Ch *Chelmsf*

FOREST GATE (St Mark) *Chelmsf 5*   **P** *Ch Patr Trust*   **V** P J STOW

FOREST GATE (St Saviour) (St James) *Chelmsf 5*   **P** *CPAS*   **V** C A HENRY   **NSM** J V MEADWAY

FOREST GREEN (Holy Trinity)   *see* Ockley, Okewood and Forest Green *Guildf*

FOREST HILL (Christ Church) (St George) w Lower Sydenham St Michael and All Angels *S'wark 5*   **P** *Patr Bd*   **TV** J F FOLEY   **NSM** A D W DUPUY

FOREST HILL (St Augustine)   *see* Sydenham H Trin and St Aug *S'wark*

FOREST HILL (St Nicholas)   *see* Beckley, Forest Hill, Horton-cum-Studley and Stanton St John *Ox*

FOREST OF DEAN (Christ Church) w English Bicknor *Glouc 1*   **P** *The Crown (3 turns), SMF (1 turn)*   **V** A J WILLIAMS   **NSM** H RODWELL

FOREST OF DEAN (Holy Trinity)   *see* Drybrook, Lydbrook and Ruardean *Glouc*

FOREST OF GALTRES (Farlington, Marton w Moxby, Sheriff Hutton, and Sutton-on-the-Forest) *York 3*　**P** *Abp (2 turns),* *Ld Chan (1 turn)*　**V** C C ELLIS

FOREST ROW (Holy Trinity) *Chich 6*　**P** V E Grinstead　**V** A F MARTIN　**NSM** S J BALE

FOREST TOWN (St Alban) *S'well 2*　**P** *Bp*　**P-in-c** P J STEAD

FOREST-IN-TEESDALE (St Mary the Virgin)　*see* Middleton-in-Teesdale w Forest and Frith *Dur*

FORESTSIDE (Christ Church)　*see* Octagon *Chich*

FORMBY (Holy Trinity) and Altcar *Liv 5*　**P** *Bp and Trustees (jt)*　**V** M R STANFORD　**C** S THOMAS　**NSM** D C M TAYLOR

FORMBY (St Luke) *Liv 5*　**P** *Bp*　**V** H T NICOL

FORMBY (St Peter) *Liv 5*　**P** *R Walton*　**V** A E TAYLOR

FORNCETT (St Mary)　*see* Upper Tas Valley *Nor*

FORNCETT (St Peter) *as above*

FORNCETT END (St Edmund) *as above*

FORNHAM ALL SAINTS (All Saints)　*see* Lark Valley *St E*

FORNHAM ST MARTIN (St Martin) *as above*

FORRABURY (St Symphorian)　*see* Boscastle and Tintagel Gp *Truro*

FORSBROOK (St Peter)　*see* Draycott-le-Moors w Forsbrook *Lich*

FORTHAMPTON (St Mary)　*see* Deerhurst and Apperley w Forthampton etc *Glouc*

FORTON (All Saints) *Lich 16*　**P** *Bp*　**P-in-c** P W THOMAS

FORTON (St James)　*see* Ellel w Shireshead *Blackb*

FORTON (St John the Evangelist) *Portsm 3*　**P** *DBP*　**V** C J L J THOMPSON

FORTY HILL (Jesus Church) *Lon 18*　**P** *V Enfield*　**V** I H CROFTS

FOSDYKE (All Saints)　*see* Kirton in Holland w Algarkirk and Fosdyke *Linc*

FOSSE Team, The *Leic 5*　**P** *Patr Bd*　**TR** D C WHITE　**TV** L D BRABIN-SMITH, T R DAY　**C** J BULLEN　**NSM** I M HILL

FOSSE TRINITY *B & W 7*　**P** *Bp and Canon D S Salter (jt)*　**R** *vacant*

FOSTON (All Saints)　*see* Harton *York*

FOSTON (St Bartholomew)　*see* Countesthorpe w Foston *Leic*

FOSTON (St Peter)　*see* Saxonwell *Linc*

FOSTON-ON-THE-WOLDS (St Andrew)　*see* Beeford w Frodingham and Foston *York*

FOTHERBY (St Mary) *Linc 15*　**P** *Ld Chan (1 turn), DBP, MMCET and G F Sleight Esq (1 turn), and Bp (1 turn)*　**R** S A ALLISON

FOTHERINGHAY (St Mary and All Saints)　*see* Warmington, Tansor and Cotterstock etc *Pet*

FOULDEN (All Saints)　*see* Oxborough w Foulden and Caldecote *Nor*

FOULRIDGE (St Michael and All Angels), Laneshawbridge and Trawden *Blackb 6*　**P** *Bp and DBP*　**R** J W KNOTT

FOULSHAM (Holy Innocents), Guestwick, Stibbard, Themelthorpe and Wood Norton *Nor 22*　**P** *Bp, DBP, Mrs H M Cook, Lord Hastings, and B E Bulwer-Long Esq (jt)*　**P-in-c** S E KIMMIS

FOUNTAINS Group, The *Leeds 25*　**P** *D&C*　**R** C J FALKINGHAM　**Hon C** L J ASHTON

FOUR ELMS (St Paul)　*see* Hever, Four Elms and Mark Beech *Roch*

FOUR MARKS (Good Shepherd) *Win 2*　**P** *Bp*　**V** H J D WRIGHT

FOUR OAKS (All Saints) *Birm 12*　**P** *Bp*　**V** D A LEAHY　**C** J F FLITCROFT

FOUR RIVERS *St E 15*　**P** *Bp, Dr F H C Marriott, Simeon's Trustees, R C Rouse, and DBP (jt)*　**R** D P BURRELL　**NSM** R T ORAMS

FOURSTONES (St Aidan)　*see* Warden w Newbrough *Newc*

FOVANT (St George), Sutton Mandeville and Teffont Evias w Teffont Magna and Compton Chamberlayne *Sarum 11*　**P** *Reformation Ch Trust, Bp, and Ch Soc Trust (jt)*　**R** *vacant*

FOWEY (St Fimbarrus) *Truro 1*　**P** *Ch Soc Trust*　**V** P DE GREY-WARTER

FOWLMERE (St Mary), Foxton, Shepreth and Thriplow *Ely 7*　**P** *Bp*　**R** A E MELANIPHY

FOWNHOPE (St Mary) w Mordiford, Brockhampton and Fawley and Woolhope *Heref 3*　**P** *D&C (4 turns), and Major R J Hereford (1 turn)*　**R** C K W MOORE　**NSM** M M DEES

FOXCOTE (St James the Less)　*see* Peasedown St John w Wellow and Foxcote etc *B & W*

FOXDALE (St Paul)　*see* Marown, Foxdale and Baldwin *S & M*

FOXEARTH (St Peter and St Paul)　*see* N Hinckford *Chelmsf*

FOXHAM (St John the Baptist)　*see* Marden Vale *Sarum*

FOXHILL (Chapel)　*see* Frodsham *Ches*

FOXLEY (not known)　*see* Sherston Magna, Easton Grey, Luckington etc *Bris*

FOXLEY (St Thomas)　*see* Lyng, Sparham, Elsing, Bylaugh, Bawdeswell etc *Nor*

FOXT (St Mark the Evangelist)　*see* Kingsley and Foxt-w-Whiston and Oakamoor etc *Lich*

FOXTON (St Andrew) w Gumley and Laughton *Leic 3*　**P** *Bp Leic and D&C Linc (alt)*　**P-in-c** I W Y GEMMELL

FOXTON (St Laurence)　*see* Fowlmere, Foxton, Shepreth and Thriplow *Ely*

FOY (St Mary)　*see* Brampton *Heref*

FRADLEY (St Stephen)　*see* Alrewas *Lich*

FRADSWELL (St James the Less)　*see* Mid Trent *Lich*

FRAISTHORPE (St Edmund King and Martyr)　*see* Skipsea and Barmston w Fraisthorpe *York*

FRAMFIELD (St Thomas à Becket) *Chich 18*　**P** *Mrs E R Wix*　**V** C D LAWRENCE

FRAMILODE (St Peter)　*see* Frampton on Severn, Arlingham, Saul etc *Glouc*

FRAMINGHAM EARL (St Andrew)　*see* Poringland *Nor*

FRAMINGHAM PIGOT (St Andrew)　*see* Thurton *Nor*

FRAMLAND Parishes, The HIGH *Leic 2*　**P** *Duke of Rutland and Sir Lyonel Tollemache Bt (jt)*　**P-in-c** M R BASS

FRAMLAND, SOUTH *Leic 2*　**P** *Ld Chan, Duke of Rutland, Lady Gretton, and Sir Lyonel Tollemache Bt (by turn)*　**P-in-c** M W R COVINGTON

FRAMLINGHAM (St Michael) w Saxtead *St E 16*　**P** *Pemb Coll Cam*　**R** M SANDERS　**NSM** M LAMB

FRAMPTON (St Mary)　*see* Bradford Peverell, Stratton, Frampton etc *Sarum*

FRAMPTON (St Mary) (St Michael) *Linc 21*　**P** *Trustees*　**P-in-c** C W B SOWDEN

FRAMPTON COTTERELL (St Peter) and Iron Acton *Bris 5*　**P** *SMF and Ch Ch Ox (jt)*　**P-in-c** M A CLACKER　**OLM** H V SMITH

FRAMPTON MANSELL (St Luke)　*see* Kemble, Poole Keynes, Somerford Keynes etc *Glouc*

FRAMPTON ON SEVERN (St Mary), Arlingham, Saul, Fretherne and Framilode *Glouc 4*　**P** *DBP, V Standish w Haresfield etc, Brig Sir Jeffrey Darell Bt, and Bp (jt)*　**P-in-c** A E SPARGO　**NSM** M J NOAH

FRAMSDEN (St Mary)　*see* Debenham and Helmingham *St E*

FRAMWELLGATE MOOR (St Aidan)　*see* Dur N *Dur*

FRANCE LYNCH (St John the Baptist)　*see* Bisley, Chalford, France Lynch, and Oakridge and Bussage w Eastcombe *Glouc*

FRANCHE (St Barnabas)　*see* Kidderminster Ismere *Worc*

FRANKBY (St John the Divine) w Greasby St Nicholas *Ches 8*　**P** *D&C*　**V** K P OWEN　**C** P N BENTLEY

FRANKLEY (St Leonard) *Birm 4*　**P** *Bp*　**R** R H TEBBS

FRANKTON (St Nicholas)　*see* Draycote Gp *Cov*

FRANSHAM, GREAT (All Saints)　*see* Gt and Lt Dunham w Gt and Lt Fransham *Nor*

FRANSHAM, LITTLE (St Mary) *as above*

FRANT (St Alban) w Eridge *Chich 16*　**P** *Bp and Marquess of Abergavenny (jt)*　**R** J M PACKMAN　**NSM** I A TRASK

FREASLEY (St Mary)　*see* Dordon *Birm*

FRECHEVILLE (St Cyprian) *Sheff 2*　**P** *Bp*　**R** M J GILLINGHAM

FRECKENHAM (St Andrew)　*see* Mildenhall *St E*

FRECKLETON (Holy Trinity) *Blackb 10*　**P** *Bp*　**V** J E C PERCIVAL

FREEBY (St Mary)　*see* Melton Mowbray *Leic*

FREEHAY (St Chad)　*see* Cheadle w Freehay *Lich*

FREELAND (St Mary the Virgin)　*see* Hanborough and Freeland *Ox*

FREEMANTLE (Christ Church) *Win 13*　**P** *Bp*　**P-in-c** A K NUTT

FREETHORPE (All Saints)　*see* Acle and Bure to Yare *Nor*

FREISTON (St James), Butterwick w Bennington, and Leverton *Linc 21*　**P** *Ld Chan and Bp (alt)*　**P-in-c** A J HIGGINSON

FREMINGTON (St Peter), Instow and Westleigh *Ex 14*　**P** *D&C, Christie Trustees, and MMCET (jt)*　**C** K J BRIMACOMBE

FRENCHAY (St John the Baptist) and Winterbourne Down *Bris 5*　**P** *St Jo Coll Ox and SMF (jt)*　**C** M A CLACKER　**NSM** R A WARING　**OLM** H V SMITH, J M LEE

FRENSHAM (St Mary the Virgin)　*see* Rowledge and Frensham *Guildf*

FRESHFORD (St Peter) w Limpley Stoke and Hinton Charterhouse *B & W 8*　**P** *Simeon's Trustees and V Norton St Phil (jt)*　**R** *vacant*

FRESHWATER (All Saints) (St Agnes) *Portsm 8*　**P** *St Jo Coll Cam*　**R** M E C WHATSON

FRESSINGFIELD (St Peter and St Paul)　*see* Sancroft *St E*

FRESTON (St Peter)　*see* Holbrook, Stutton, Freston, Woolverstone etc *St E*

FRETHERNE (St Mary the Virgin)　*see* Frampton on Severn, Arlingham, Saul etc *Glouc*

FRETTENHAM (St Swithin)　*see* Coltishall w Gt Hautbois, Frettenham etc *Nor*

FRIAR PARK (St Francis of Assisi)　*see* W Bromwich St Fran *Lich*

FRIARMERE (St Thomas)   *see* Saddleworth *Man*

FRICKLEY (All Saints)   *see* Bilham *Sheff*

FRIDAY BRIDGE (St Mark)   *see* Fen Orchards *Ely*

FRIDAYTHORPE (St Mary)   *see* Waggoners *York*

FRIERN BARNET (All Saints) *Lon 14*   **P** *Bp*   **V** G A D PLATTEN

FRIERN BARNET (St James the Great) (St John the Evangelist) *Lon 14*   **P** *D&C St Paul's*   **R** P A WALMSLEY-MCLEOD   **C** M MIRT

FRIERN BARNET (St Peter le Poer) *Lon 14*   **P** *D&C St Paul's*   **P-in-c** M R DUCKETT

FRIESTHORPE (St Peter)   *see* Middle Rasen Gp *Linc*

FRIETH (St John the Baptist)   *see* Hambleden Valley *Ox*

FRIEZLAND (Christ Church)   *see* Saddleworth *Man*

FRILSHAM (St Frideswide)   *see* Hermitage *Ox*

FRIMLEY (St Francis) (St Peter) *Guildf 6*   **P** R Ash   **R** S G THOMAS   **C** S M BOLEN   **NSM** J M LIEVESLEY   **OLM** B M MASSEY

FRIMLEY GREEN (St Andrew) and Mytchett *Guildf 6*   **P** *Bp*   **P-in-c** P V PARKER

FRINDSBURY (All Saints) w Upnor and Chattenden *Roch 6*   **P** *Bp*   **C** S F VALLENTE-KERR

FRINGFORD (St Michael)   *see* Shelswell *Ox*

FRINSTED (St Dunstan)   *see* Tunstall and Bredgar *Cant*

FRINTON (St Mary Magdalene) (St Mary the Virgin Old Church) *Chelmsf 23*   **P** CPAS   **R** D E SMITH

FRISBY-ON-THE-WREAKE (St Thomas of Canterbury)   *see* Upper Wreake *Leic*

FRISKNEY (All Saints) *Linc 21*   **P** *Bp*   **P-in-c** F J M COTTON-BETTERIDGE

FRISTON (St Mary Magdalene)   *see* Whinlands *St E*

FRISTON (St Mary the Virgin)   *see* E Dean w Friston and Jevington *Chich*

FRITHELSTOCK (St Mary and St Gregory)   *see* Gt and Lt Torrington and Frithelstock *Ex*

FRITHVILLE (St Peter)   *see* Sibsey w Frithville *Linc*

FRITTENDEN (St Mary)   *see* Sissinghurst w Frittenden *Cant*

FRITTON (St Catherine)   *see* Hempnall *Nor*

FRITTON (St Edmund)   *see* Somerleyton, Ashby, Fritton, Herringfleet etc *Nor*

FRITWELL (St Olave)   *see* Cherwell Valley *Ox*

FRIZINGHALL (St Margaret) *Leeds 1*   **P** *Bp*   **P-in-c** M E WATSON

FRIZINGTON (St Paul)   *see* Crosslacon *Carl*

FROCESTER (St Andrew)   *see* Eastington, Frocester, Haresfield etc *Glouc*

FRODESLEY (St Mark)   *see* Condover w Frodesley, Acton Burnell etc *Heref*

FRODINGHAM (St Lawrence) and New Brumby *Linc 6*   **P** Lord St Oswald   **P-in-c** M A E ASTIN   **C** L A E COCKRAM, L GABEL   **NSM** M DUNFORD, M E C TOYNE   **OLM** G STEVENS

FRODINGHAM, NORTH (St Elgin)   *see* Beeford w Frodingham and Foston *York*

FRODSHAM (St Lawrence) *Ches 3*   **P** Ch Ch Ox   **V** M H MILLS   **NSM** K L WILLIAMSON

FROGMORE (Holy Trinity) *St Alb 5*   **P** CPAS   **V** N J WEIR   **C** N T JONES   **NSM** N A WARD

FROLESWORTH (St Nicholas)   *see* Upper Soar *Leic*

FROME (Christ Church) (St Mary) *B & W 3*   **P** *Bp*   **V** vacant

FROME (Holy Trinity) *B & W 3*   **P** *Bp*   **V** G A OWEN

FROME (St John the Baptist) *B & W 3*   **P** DBP   **V** C ALSBURY

FROME ST QUINTON (St Mary)   *see* Melbury *Sarum*

FROME VALLEY Group of Parishes, The *Heref 2*   **P** *Bp* (6 turns), MMCET (2 turns), D&C (1 turn)   **V** S BAGGS   **NSM** R P PRIEST

FROME VAUCHURCH (St Mary)   *see* Melbury *Sarum*

FROMES HILL (St Matthew)   *see* Frome Valley *Heref*

FROSTENDEN (All Saints)   *see* Wrentham, Covehithe w Benacre etc *St E*

FROSTERLEY (St Michael and All Angels)   *see* Upper Weardale *Dur*

FROXFIELD (All Saints)   *see* Whitton *Sarum*

FROXFIELD (St Peter on the Green)   *see* Steep and Froxfield w Privett *Portsm*

FROXFIELD (St Peter) *as above*

FROYLE (Assumption of the Blessed Virgin Mary)   *see* Bentley, Binsted and Froyle *Win*

FRYERNING (St Mary the Virgin)   *see* Ingatestone w Fryerning *Chelmsf*

FUGGLESTONE (St Peter)   *see* Wilton w Netherhampton and Fugglestone *Sarum*

FULBECK (St Nicholas)   *see* Caythorpe *Linc*

FULBOURN (St Vigor w All Saints) *Ely 4*   **P** St Jo Coll Cam   **R** A A GOODMAN

FULBROOK (St James the Great)   *see* Burford w Fulbrook, Taynton, Asthall etc *Ox*

FULFORD (St Oswald) *York 7*   **P** *Abp*   **V** T MCDONOUGH

FULFORD-IN-STONE (St Nicholas) w Hilderstone *Lich 13*   **P** *D&C*   **V** P D DAKIN   **NSM** C E DAKIN

FULHAM (All Saints) *Lon 9*   **P** *Bp*   **V** J P HAWES   **C** P A SEABROOK, R P WHAITE   **NSM** E MCGREGOR

FULHAM (Christ Church) *Lon 9*   **P** CPAS   **V** S C R LEES   **C** J A HARDING

FULHAM (St Alban) (St Augustine) *Lon 9*   **P** *Bp and City Corp (jt)*   **V** M HOGG

FULHAM (St Andrew) Fulham Fields *Lon 9*   **P** *Bp*   **V** G A WILKINSON   **C** L A BILINDA   **NSM** L HARVEY

FULHAM (St Dionis) Parson's Green *Lon 9*   **P** *Bp*   **V** T J STILWELL   **C** P ALLERTON

FULHAM (St Etheldreda) (St Clement) *Lon 9*   **P** *Bp*   **V** J F H HENLEY

FULHAM (St Mary) North End *Lon 9*   **P** Ch Soc Trust   **V** R W CURL

FULHAM (St Matthew) *Lon 9*   **P** Ch Patr Trust   **V** W J ROGERS   **Dss** V S PIERSON

FULHAM (St Peter) *Lon 9*   **P** *Bp*   **V** R B C STANDRING   **C** D A LEE

FULKING (Good Shepherd)   *see* Poynings w Edburton, Newtimber and Pyecombe *Chich*

FULL SUTTON (St Mary)   *see* Garrowby Hill *York*

FULLBROOK (St Gabriel)   *see* Walsall St Gabr Fulbrook *Lich*

FULLETBY (St Andrew)   *see* Hemingby Gp *Linc*

FULMER (St James)   *see* Gerrards Cross and Fulmer *Ox*

FULMODESTON (Christ Church) w Croxton *Nor 15*   **P** CCC Cam   **P-in-c** F R A MASON

FULSHAW (St Anne)   *see* Wilmslow *Ches*

FULSTOW (St Laurence)   *see* Fotherby *Linc*

FULWOOD (Christ Church) *Blackb 13*   **P** V Lanc   **V** B R MCCONKEY   **C** P MAUDSLEY

FULWOOD (Christ Church) *Sheff 4*   **P** CPAS   **V** P A WILLIAMS   **C** B C COOPER, E F Q PENNINGTON, P F SCAMMAN

FULWOOD (St Cuthbert)   *see* Preston St Cuth *Blackb*

FUNDENHALL (St Nicholas)   *see* Upper Tas Valley *Nor*

FUNTINGTON (St Mary) and West Stoke w Sennicotts *Chich 3*   **P** *Bp*   **R** C W W HOWARD

FUNTLEY (St Francis)   *see* Fareham SS Pet and Paul *Portsm*

FURNACE GREEN (St Andrew)   *see* Southgate *Chich*

FURNESS VALE (St John)   *see* Disley *Ches*

FURNEUX PELHAM (St Mary the Virgin)   *see* Albury, Braughing, Furneux Pelham, Lt Hadham etc *St Alb*

FURNHAM (Good Shepherd)   *see* Chard Gd Shep Furnham *B & W*

FURZE PLATT (St Peter) *Ox 5*   **P** *Bp*   **V** M A BALFOUR

FURZEBANK (Worship Centre)   *see* Bentley Em and Willenhall H Trin *Lich*

FURZEDOWN (St Paul) *S'wark 17*   **P** Patr Bd   **TR** R J POWELL   **TV** M S RICHEUX   **NSM** J ALLEN, J CONNELL, S E M CLARKE

FURZTON (not known)   *see* Watling Valley *Ox*

FYFIELD (St Nicholas)   *see* Upper Kennet *Sarum*

FYFIELD (St Nicholas)   *see* Appleshaw, Kimpton, Thruxton, Fyfield etc *Win*

FYFIELD (St Nicholas) w Tubney and Kingston Bagpuize *Ox 19*   **P** St Jo Coll Ox   **P-in-c** D A A PICKERING   **C** A J B SYMES

FYFIELD (St Nicholas), Moreton w Bobbingworth and Willingale w Shellow and Berners Roding *Chelmsf 3*   **P** Ld Chan, St Jo Coll Cam, MMCET, and Major G N Capel-Cure (by turn)   **P-in-c** V ROSS   **C** S E BRAZIER-GIBBS   **Hon C** A V WATSON

FYLINGDALES (St Stephen) and Hawsker cum Stainsacre *York 21*   **P** *Abp*   **V** S J SMALE

G 7 Benefice *Cant 6*   **P** *Abp, D&C, and Lord Hothfield (jt)*   **R** S M COX   **C** C T A HODGKINS, R P WELDON

GADDESBY (St Luke)   *see* S Croxton Gp *Leic*

GADDESDEN, GREAT (St John the Baptist)   *see* Gt Berkhamsted, Gt and Lt Gaddesden etc *St Alb*

GADDESDEN, LITTLE (St Peter and St Paul) *as above*

GAINFORD (St Mary) *Dur 7*   **P** Trin Coll Cam   **P-in-c** M JACQUES

GAINSBOROUGH (All Saints) (St George) and Morton *Linc 2*   **P** *Bp*   **P-in-c** M P COONEY   **C** K R DYKE, P K PAMPHILON-GREEN

GALLEY COMMON (St Peter)   *see* Hartshill and Galley Common *Cov*

GALLEYWOOD (Junior School Worship Centre)   *see* Galleywood Common *Chelmsf*

GALLEYWOOD COMMON (St Michael and All Angels) *Chelmsf 10*   **P** CPAS   **V** A T GRIFFITHS   **C** C SMITH, G E FRASER, S R GILLINGHAM

GALMINGTON (St Michael) *B & W 18*   **P** *Bp*   **V** C SNELL   **C** T L POTTAGE

GALMPTON (Chapel of The Good Shepherd)   *see* Brixham w Churston Ferrers and Kingswear *Ex*

GAMESLEY (Bishop Geoffrey Allen Church and County Centre)   *see* Charlesworth and Gamesley *Derby*

GAMLINGAY (St Mary the Virgin) and Everton *Ely 13*   **P** *Bp, Clare Coll Cam, and Down Coll Cam (by turn)*   **R** S ROTHWELL

GAMSTON (St Luke) and Bridgford *S'well 1*   **P** *DBP*   **V** M A FRASER   **C** A S G TUFNELL

GAMSTON (St Peter)   *see* Retford Area *S'well*

GANAREW (St Swithin)   *see* Wye Reaches Gp *Heref*

GANTON (St Nicholas)   *see* Willerby w Ganton and Folkton *York*

GARBOLDISHAM (St John the Baptist)   *see* Guiltcross *Nor*

GARFORD (St Luke)   *see* Marcham w Garford and Shippon *Ox*

GARFORTH (St Mary the Virgin) *Leeds 17*   **P** *DBP*   **R** G W COOPER

GARGRAVE (St Andrew) w Coniston Cold *Leeds 21*   **P** *Bp*   **V** D A HOULTON

GARRETTS GREEN (St Thomas) and Tile Cross *Birm 9*   **P** *Bp*   **V** B S CASTLE   **NSM** S J LARKIN

GARRIGILL (St John)   *see* Alston Moor *Newc*

GARROWBY HILL *York 5*   **P** *Ld Chan (1 turn), Abp, D&C, and Earl of Halifax (3 turns)*   **R** J C FINNEMORE

GARSDALE (St John the Baptist)   *see* Sedbergh, Cautley and Garsdale *Carl*

GARSDON (All Saints), Lea and Cleverton and Charlton *Bris 6*   **P** *Ch Soc Trust and Bp (jt)*   **P-in-c** S WILKINSON   **Hon C** D ORMSTON

GARSINGTON (St Mary), Cuddesdon and Horspath *Ox 20*   **P** *Ripon Coll Cuddesdon, Trin Coll Ox, and DBP (jt)*   **V** E L PENNINGTON   **NSM** M D CHAPMAN

GARSTANG (St Helen) Churchtown and St Michaels-on-Wyre *Blackb 9*   **P** *Dr I R H Jackson and R P Hornby Esq (jt)*   **V** A W WILKINSON   **NSM** C M WHALLEY

GARSTANG (St Thomas) *Blackb 9*   **P** *V Churchtown St Helen*   **V** S B GREY

GARSTON (St Michael) *Liv 4*   **P** *Trustees*   **V** R HARVEY

GARSTON, EAST (All Saints)   *see* Lambourn Valley *Ox*

GARSWOOD (St Andrew)   *see* Ashton-in-Makerfield H Trin *Liv*

GARTHORPE (St Mary)   *see* Crowle Gp *Linc*

GARTON IN HOLDERNESS (St Michael)   *see* Withernsea w Owthorne, Garton-in-Holderness etc *York*

GARTON-ON-THE-WOLDS (St Michael and All Angels)   *see* Woldsburn *York*

GARVESTON (St Margaret)   *see* Barnham Broom and Upper Yare *Nor*

GARWAY (St Michael)   *see* St Weonards *Heref*

GASTARD (St John the Baptist)   *see* Gtr Corsham and Lacock *Bris*

GATCOMBE (St Olave) *Portsm 8*   **P** *Qu Coll Ox*   **R** M C BAGG

GATE BURTON (St Helen)   *see* Lea Gp *Linc*

GATE HELMSLEY (St Mary)   *see* Harton *York*

GATEACRE (St Stephen) *Liv 4*   **P** *Bp*   **TR** P H JANVIER   **TV** J L MCKELVEY   **C** S COWAN   **NSM** K A CANTY, P J TURNER

GATELEY (St Helen)   *see* Upper Wensum Village Gp *Nor*

GATESHEAD (St Edmund's Chapel w Holy Trinity) (Venerable Bede) *Dur 12*   **P** *Bp and The Crown (alt)*   **TR** J C WILKINSON   **TV** J O M CRAIG   **NSM** A PHILLIPS

GATESHEAD (St George) *Dur 12*   **P** *Trustees*   **P-in-c** A V WEST

GATESHEAD (St Helen) *Dur 12*   **P** *Bp*   **NSM** D BROWN

GATESHEAD (St Ninian) Harlow Green   *see* Harlow Green and Lamesley *Dur*

GATESHEAD FELL (St John) *Dur 12*   **P** *Bp*   **R** A V WEST

GATESHEAD Lobley Hill (All Saints)   *see* Hillside *Dur*

GATLEY (St James) *Ches 17*   **P** *R Stockport St Thos*   **V** M D CARLISLE

GATTEN (St Paul) *Portsm 7*   **P** *Ch Patr Trust*   **V** P G ALLEN

GATTON (St Andrew)   *see* Merstham, S Merstham and Gatton *S'wark*

GAULBY (St Peter) *Leic 4*   **P** *Ch Soc Trust*   **P-in-c** B DAVIS

GAUTBY (All Saints)   *see* Bardney *Linc*

GAWBER (St Thomas) *Leeds 18*   **P** *V Darton*   **P-in-c** M S POSKITT

GAWCOTT (Holy Trinity)   *see* Lenborough *Ox*

GAWSWORTH (St James) w North Rode *Ches 13*   **P** *T R R Richards Esq and Bp (jt)*   **R** W A PWAISIHO

GAYDON (St Giles) w Chadshunt *Cov 8*   **P** *Bp*   **P-in-c** M G CADWALLADER

GAYHURST (St Peter) w Ravenstone, Stoke Goldington and Weston Underwood *Ox 16*   **P** *Bp and Lord Hesketh (jt)*   **R** C E PUMFREY

GAYTON (St Mary)   *see* Pattishall w Cold Higham and Gayton w Tiffield *Pet*

GAYTON (St Nicholas)   *see* Ashwicken w Leziate, Bawsey etc *Nor*

GAYTON (St Peter)   *see* Mid Trent *Lich*

GAYTON LE WOLD (St Peter)   *see* Asterby Gp *Linc*

GAYTON THORPE (St Mary)   *see* Ashwicken w Leziate, Bawsey etc *Nor*

GAYWOOD (St Faith) King's Lynn *Nor 20*   **P** *Patr Bd*   **TV** D R GINGRICH   **C** Z M FERGUSON

GAZELEY (All Saints)   *see* Dalham, Gazeley, Higham, Kentford and Moulton *St E*

GEDDING (St Mary the Virgin)   *see* Bradfield St Clare, Bradfield St George etc *St E*

GEDDINGTON (St Mary Magdalene) w Weekley *Pet 9*   **P** *Boughton Estates*   **P-in-c** R T PARKER-MCGEE

GEDLING (All Hallows) *S'well 7*   **P** *DBP*   **R** M J TAYLOR   **C** J E LAMB   **NSM** E C KIRK

GEDNEY Drove End (Christ Church)   *see* Long Sutton w Lutton etc *Linc*

GEDNEY HILL (Holy Trinity) (St Polycarp) *Linc 18*   **P** *Bp*   **V** R J MORRISON

GEE CROSS (Holy Trinity) (St Philip's Mission Room) *Ches 14*   **P** *V Werneth*   **V** M I BENNETT

GELDESTON (St Michael)   *see* Gillingham w Geldeston, Stockton, Ellingham etc *Nor*

GENTLESHAW (Christ Church) *Lich 1*   **P** *MMCET*   **NSM** L MCKEON

GEORGEHAM (St George) *Ex 14*   **P** *MMCET*   **R** M C NEWBON

GERMAN (St John the Baptist)   *see* W Coast *S & M*

GERMANSWEEK (St German)   *see* Okehampton, Inwardleigh, Belstone, Sourton etc *Ex*

GERMOE (St Germoe)   *see* W Kerrier *Truro*

GERRANS (St Gerran) w St Anthony-in-Roseland and Philleigh *Truro 6*   **P** *Bp and MMCET (jt)*   **P-in-c** J K EDWARDS

GERRARDS CROSS (St James) and Fulmer *Ox 9*   **P** *Bp and Simeon's Trustees (jt)*   **R** M J WILLIAMS   **C** C M LION, J R LEACH, P D MANN   **NSM** C W LINDNER, D ROWLANDSON, M R L BEEBEE

GESTINGTHORPE (St Mary)   *see* Halstead Area *Chelmsf*

GIDDING, GREAT (St Michael)   *see* N Leightonstone *Ely*

GIDDING, LITTLE (St John)   *as above*

GIDEA PARK (St Michael) *Chelmsf 2*   **P** *Bp*   **P-in-c** P R WESTON

GIDLEIGH (Holy Trinity)   *see* Chagford, Gidleigh, Throwleigh etc *Ex*

GIGGETTY LANE (The Venerable Bede)   *see* Smestow Vale *Lich*

GIGGLESWICK (St Alkelda) and Rathmell w Wigglesworth *Leeds 21*   **P** *Bp and Ch Trust Fund Trust (jt)*   **P-in-c** H A F YOUNG   **C** S C DAWSON

GILCRUX (St Mary)   *see* Aspatria w Hayton and Gilcrux *Carl*

GILDERSOME (St Peter) *Leeds 15*   **P** *V Batley*   **V** A F LAWSON   **C** D J CLARK   **NSM** B DUXBURY

GILLAMOOR (St Aidan)   *see* Kirkbymoorside w Gillamoor, Farndale etc *York*

GILLING (St Agatha) and Kirkby Ravensworth *Leeds 24*   **P** *Bp and A C P Wharton Esq (jt)*   **P-in-c** A P KIRBY   **Hon C** A GLEDHILL

GILLING EAST (Holy Cross)   *see* Ampleforth w Oswaldkirk, Gilling E etc *York*

GILLINGHAM (Holy Trinity) *Roch 3*   **P** *Bp*   **V** A RICHARDSON

GILLINGHAM (St Augustine) *Roch 3*   **P** *Bp*   **P-in-c** J P JENNINGS

GILLINGHAM (St Barnabas) *Roch 3*   **P** *Bp*   **V** *vacant*

GILLINGHAM (St Luke)   *see* New Brompton St Luke *Roch*

GILLINGHAM (St Mark) *Roch 3*   **P** *Hyndman Trustees*   **V** V M L MUTHALALY   **C** R A ENGLAND

GILLINGHAM (St Mary Magdalene) *Roch 3*   **P** *DBP*   **P-in-c** B A A LAWAL

GILLINGHAM (St Mary the Virgin) and Milton-on-Stour *Sarum 5*   **P** *Bp*   **P-in-c** J P GREENWOOD   **C** E C PEGLER   **NSM** T F HEATON

GILLINGHAM (St Mary) w Geldeston w Stockton w Ellingham St Mary and Kirby Cane *Nor 8*   **P** *Ld Chan (1 turn), Bp, MMCET and Ch Trust Fund Trust (1 turn)*   **P-in-c** J L ODDY-BATES

GILLINGHAM, SOUTH (St Matthew) *Roch 3*   **P** *Patr Bd*   **TV** G R LEWIS, P J BARNES   **NSM** E HURST   **Emer** G R LEWIS

GILMORTON (All Saints), Peatling Parva, Kimcote cum Walton, North Kilworth, South Kilworth, Misterton, Swinford, Catthorpe, Shawell and Stanford *Leic 7*   **P** *Patr Bd (5 turns), Ld Chan (1 turn)*   **P-in-c** C R OXLEY   **TV** E L DAVIES   **NSM** A J ILIFFE, J R KENNEDY

GILSLAND (St Mary Magdalene)   *see* Lanercost, Walton, Gilsland and Nether Denton *Carl*

GILSTEAD (St Wilfrid)   *see* Bingley H Trin *Leeds*
GILSTON (St Mary)   *see* High Wych and Gilston w Eastwick *St Alb*
GIMINGHAM (All Saints)   *see* Trunch Group *Nor*
GIPSY HILL (Christ Church) *S'wark 12*   **P** *CPAS*
V J E CROUCHER   **C** S J WHITTINGTON
GIPTON (Church of the Epiphany)   *see* Leeds Gipton Epiphany *Leeds*
GIRLINGTON (St Philip) *Leeds 1*   **P** *Simeon's Trustees*
V T P LEWIS
GIRTON (St Andrew) *Ely 6*   **P** *Ld Chan*   **R** M J MAXWELL
GIRTON (St Cecilia)   *see* E Trent *S'well*
GISBURN (St Mary the Virgin) *Blackb 7*   **P** *Bp*
P-in-c A H M JEREMIAH, A R HUMPHRIES
GISLEHAM (Holy Trinity)   *see* Kessingland, Gisleham and Rushmere *Nor*
GISLINGHAM (St Mary)   *see* S Hartismere *St E*
GISSING (St Mary the Virgin)   *see* Winfarthing w Shelfanger w Burston w Gissing etc *Nor*
GITTISHAM (St Michael)   *see* Honiton, Gittisham, Combe Raleigh, Monkton etc *Ex*
GIVENDALE, GREAT (St Ethelburga)   *see* Pocklington Wold *York*
GLAISDALE (St Thomas)   *see* Middle Esk Moor *York*
GLANDFORD (St Martin)   *see* Blakeney w Cley, Wiveton, Glandford etc *Nor*
GLANVILLES WOOTTON (St Mary the Virgin)   *see* Three Valleys *Sarum*
GLAPTHORN (St Leonard)   *see* Oundle w Ashton and Benefield w Glapthorn *Pet*
GLAPWELL (St Andrew)   *see* Ault Hucknall and Scarcliffe *Derby*
GLASCOTE (St George) and Stonydelph *Lich 4*   **P** *Patr Bd*
TV M J MILLS   **C** M J MALINS   **NSM** M R LE-WORTHY
OLM K R LINDSAY-SMITH, P D FAULTLESS, R J LOCKWOOD
GLASCOTE HEATH (St Peter)   *see* Glascote and Stonydelph *Lich*
GLASSHOUGHTON (St Paul)   *see* Castleford *Leeds*
GLASSON (Christ Church)   *see* Cockerham w Winmarleigh and Glasson *Blackb*
GLASTON (St Andrew)   *see* Lyddington, Bisbrooke, Caldecott, Glaston etc *Pet*
GLASTONBURY (St John the Baptist) (St Benedict) w Meare *B & W 4*   **P** *Bp*   **V** D J L MACGEOCH
C D M GREENFIELD
GLATTON (St Nicholas)   *see* Sawtry and Glatton *Ely*
GLAZEBURY (All Saints) w Hollinfare *Liv 15*   **P** *Bp and R Warrington (jt)*   **P-in-c** P J SWIFT
GLEADLESS (Christ Church) *Sheff 1*   **P** *DBP*   **TR** *vacant*
GLEADLESS VALLEY (Holy Cross) *Sheff 1*   **P** *DBP*
V D J MIDDLETON
GLEMHAM, GREAT (All Saints)   *see* Alde River *St E*
GLEMHAM, LITTLE (St Andrew) *as above*
GLEMSFORD (St Mary the Virgin), Hartest w Boxted, Somerton and Stanstead (Glem Valley United Benefice) *St E 12*   **P** *Bp, Prime Min, and Ch Soc Trust (by turn)*
R P J PRIGG
GLEN AULDYN (St Fingan)   *see* Bride, Lezayre and N Ramsey *S & M*
GLEN GROUP, The *Linc 19*   **P** *Bp*   **V** D C SWEETING
OLM P E HARDINGHAM
GLEN MAGNA (St Cuthbert) cum Stretton Magna w Carlton Curlieu and Burton Overy *Leic 4*   **P** *Bp, Dr A Llewelyn, and Sir Geoffrey Palmer Bt (jt)*   **P-in-c** K K FORD
GLENDALE Group, The *Newc 7*   **P** *Patr Bd (4 turns), Ld Chan (1 turn)*   **TR** R B S BURSTON   **TV** M J PENFOLD
GLENEAGLES *Pet 6*   **P** *Bp*   **V** M C PEREIRA
GLENFIELD (St Peter) and Newtown Linford *Leic 9*   **P** *Bp*
R *vacant*
GLENHOLT (St Anne)   *see* Bickleigh and Shaugh Prior *Ex*
GLENTHAM (St Peter)   *see* Owmby Gp *Linc*
GLENTWORTH (St Michael)   *see* Trentcliffe Gp *Linc*
GLINTON (St Benedict)   *see* Peakirk w Glinton and Northborough *Pet*
GLODWICK (St Mark w Christ Church) *Man 15*   **P** *Bp*
V G HOLLOWOOD
GLOOSTON (St John the Baptist)   *see* Welham, Glooston and Cranoe and Stonton Wyville *Leic*
GLOSSOP (All Saints) *Derby 6*   **P** *Patr Bd*   **V** I K STUBBS
OLM N W SHAW
GLOUCESTER (St Aldate)   *see* Coney Hill *Glouc*
GLOUCESTER (St Catharine) *Glouc 2*   **P** *Bp*   **V** J M ITUMU
C D WHALE
GLOUCESTER (St George) w Whaddon *Glouc 2*   **P** *Bp*
NSM B D CLIFFORD
GLOUCESTER (St James and All Saints) (Christ Church) *Glouc 2*   **P** *Bp*   **NSM** J M HOWARD, P R GIFFORD

GLOUCESTER (St Paul) and St Stephen *Glouc 2*   **P** *Bp*
V R P FITTER   **C** S A ARCHER   **NSM** J R MURPHY
GLOUCESTER CITY St Mark (St Mary de Crypt) (St John the Baptist) (St Mary de Lode) (St Nicholas) and Hempsted *Glouc 2*   **P** *D&C (1 turn), Bp (3 turns), Ld Chan (1 turn)*
R N M ARTHY
GLOUCESTER DOCKS Mariners' Church Proprietary Chapel *Glouc 2*   A M OSMOND
GLYMPTON (St Mary)   *see* Wootton w Glympton and Kiddington *Ox*
GLYNDE (St Mary), West Firle and Beddingham *Chich 21*
P *Bp and D&C Windsor (alt)*   **P-in-c** P C OWEN-JONES
GNOSALL (St Lawrence)   *see* Adbaston, High Offley, Knightley, Norbury etc *Lich*
GOADBY (St John the Baptist)   *see* Coplow *Leic*
GOADBY MARWOOD (St Denys)   *see* Ironstone Villages *Leic*
GOATHILL (St Peter)   *see* Milborne Port w Goathill etc *B & W*
GOATHLAND (St Mary)   *see* Middle Esk Moor *York*
GOATHURST (St Edward the King and Martyr)   *see* Aisholt, Enmore, Goathurst, Nether Stowey etc *B & W*
GOBOWEN (All Saints)   *see* Selattyn and Hengoed w Gobowen *Lich*
GODALMING (St Peter and St Paul) *Guildf 4*   **P** *Bp*
TR K M ROBERTS   **OLM** R HARVIE
GODINGTON (Holy Trinity)   *see* Shelswell *Ox*
GODLEY cum Newton Green (St John the Baptist) *Ches 14*
P *R Cheadle*   **V** *vacant*
GODMANCHESTER (St Mary) and Hilton *Ely 10*   **P** *D&C Westmr and Bp (jt)*   **V** D W BUSK
GODMANSTONE (Holy Trinity)   *see* Buckland Newton, Cerne Abbas, Godmanstone etc *Sarum*
GODMERSHAM (St Lawrence the Martyr)   *see* King's Wood *Cant*
GODREVY *Truro 5*   **P** *Patr Bd*   **TR** S CLIFTON
NSM P M MURLEY
GODSHILL (All Saints) *Portsm 7*   **P** *Guild of All So*
V J M RYDER
GODSHILL (St Giles)   *see* Fordingbridge and Breamore and Hale etc *Win*
GODSTONE (St Nicholas) and Blindley Heath *S'wark 25*
P *Bp and Ms C Goad (jt)*   **R** *vacant*
GOFF'S OAK (St James)   *see* Cheshunt *St Alb*
GOLBORNE (St Thomas)   *see* Lowton and Golborne *Liv*
GOLCAR (St John the Evangelist) *Leeds 12*   **P** *V Huddersfield*
P-in-c J S CURRY
GOLDEN CAP TEAM (Team Ministry) *Sarum 2*   **P** *Patr Bd*
TR S J SKINNER   **TV** J M SKINNER
GOLDENHILL (St John the Evangelist) and Tunstall *Lich 11*
P *Bp*   **V** T W J STATHER
GOLDERS GREEN (St Alban the Martyr and St Michael) *Lon 15*   **P** *Bp*   **V** R G MORTON   **C** S J DRYDEN
GOLDHANGER (St Peter)   *see* Gt Totham and Lt Totham w Goldhanger *Chelmsf*
GOLDINGTON (St Mary the Virgin) *St Alb 9*   **P** *Bp*
V R L HOWLETT   **C** B LEWIS, B W D LEWIS   **NSM** J R BUCK
GOLDS HILL (St Paul)   *see* W Bromwich St Jas w St Paul *Lich*
GOLDSBOROUGH (St Mary)   *see* Knaresborough *Leeds*
GOLDSWORTH PARK (St Andrew) *Guildf 12*   **P** *Bp*
V K E WYLES
GOLDTHORPE (St John the Evangelist and St Mary Magdalene) w Hickleton *Sheff 12*   **P** *CR (2 turns), Earl of Halifax (1 turn)*   **V** C R SCHAEFER   **Hon C** A BRISCOE
GOMERSAL (St Mary) *Leeds 7*   **P** *Bp*   **P-in-c** K NICHOLL
GONALSTON (St Laurence)   *see* Epperstone, Gonalston, Oxton and Woodborough *S'well*
GONERBY, GREAT (St Sebastian)   *see* Barrowby and Gt Gonerby *Linc*
GOOD EASTER (St Andrew)   *see* High and Gd Easter w Margaret Roding *Chelmsf*
GOODERSTONE (St George)   *see* Cockley Cley w Gooderstone *Nor*
GOODLEIGH (St Gregory)   *see* Barnstaple *Ex*
GOODMANHAM (All Saints) *York 5*   **P** *Abp*   **R** D J EVERETT
GOODMAYES (All Saints) *Chelmsf 6*   **P** *Hyndman Trustees*
V P H NYATSANZA
GOODMAYES (St Paul) *Chelmsf 6*   **P** *Bp*
P-in-c J E F BUCHAN
GOODNESTONE (Holy Cross)   *see* Canonry *Cant*
GOODNESTONE w Graveney *Cant 14*   **P** *Abp*
P-in-c J BURROWS
GOODRICH (St Giles), Marstow, Welsh Bicknor, Llangarron, Llangrove and Welsh Newton w Llanrothal *Heref 7*
P *Bp (2 turns), D&C and DBP (2 turns)*   **V** S C MONDON
NSM J STEPHENS   **OLM** P A POWDRILL
GOODRINGTON (St George) and Collaton St Mary *Ex 11*
P *Bp*   **V** *vacant*

GOODSHAW (St Mary and All Saints) and Crawshawbooth
Man 11   P *Bp and Wm Hulme Trustees (jt)*
P-in-c J S MONTGOMERY   OLM D SMITH
GOODWORTH CLATFORD (St Peter)   *see Abbotts Ann and Upper and Goodworth Clatford Win*
GOOLE (St John the Evangelist) (St Mary) (Mariners' Club and Chapel) *Sheff 10*   P *Bp*   V R S TAYLOR
C L A BATEMAN
GOOSE GREEN (St Paul) *Liv 14*   P *Bp*   P-in-c N J COOK
GOOSEY (All Saints)   *see Stanford in the Vale w Goosey and Hatford Ox*
GOOSNARGH (St Mary the Virgin)   *see Fellside Team Blackb*
GOOSTREY (St Luke) w Swettenham *Ches 11*   P V *Sandbach and MMCET (jt)*   V I GODFREY   NSM P E SOULT
GORAN HAVEN (St Just)   *see St Goran w Caerhays Truro*
GOREFIELD (St Paul)   *see Wisbech St Mary and Guyhirn w Ring's End etc Ely*
GORING (St Thomas of Canterbury) and Streatley with South
Stoke *Ox 24*   P *Ch Ch Ox and Bp (jt)*   V P H BOUGHTON
NSM E J DOWDING
GORING-BY-SEA (St Mary) (St Laurence) *Chich 20*   P *Bp*
V G J BUTLER   C S J HORTON
GORLESTON (St Andrew) *Nor 6*   P *Ch Trust Fund Trust*
C M K SIMM, N KTORIDES
GORLESTON (St Mary Magdalene) *Nor 6*   P *Bp and Ch Trust Fund Trust (jt)*   V L E RICKETTS
GORNAL (St Peter) and Sedgley *Worc 10*   P *Patr Bd*
TR S R BUCKLEY   TV A G STAND
GORNAL, LOWER (St James the Great) *Worc 10*   P *Bp*
V J W MOTT
GORSLEY (Christ Church)   *see Newent and Gorsley w Cliffords Mesne Glouc*
GORTON (Emmanuel) (St James) (St Philip) and Abbey Hey
Man 1   P *Patr Bd and Prime-Min (alt)*   TR *vacant*
GOSBECK (St Mary)   *see Coddenham w Gosbeck and Hemingstone w Henley St E*
GOSBERTON (St Peter and St Paul), Gosberton Clough and
Quadring *Linc 19*   P *Bp and D&C (jt)*   P-in-c I R WALTERS
OLM P E HARDINGHAM
GOSBERTON CLOUGH (St Gilbert and St Hugh)
see Gosberton, Gosberton Clough and Quadring Linc
GOSCOTE, EAST (St Hilda)   *see Fosse Leic*
GOSFIELD (St Catherine)   *see Halstead Area Chelmsf*
GOSFORTH (All Saints) *Newc 2*   P *Bp*   V A J SHIPTON
C S DIXON   NSM R B BIRNIE
GOSFORTH (St Hugh) *Newc 2*   P *Bp*   V *vacant*
GOSFORTH (St Mary) w Nether Wasdale and Wasdale Head
Carl 5   P *Bp, Earl of Lonsdale, V St Bees, and PCCs (jt)*
R J G RILEY   NSM L A RILEY
GOSFORTH (St Nicholas) *Newc 2*   P *Bp*   V P J CUNNINGHAM
C T D K BIRCH   NSM M C DOUGLASS
GOSFORTH VALLEY (St Andrew)   *see Dronfield w Holmesfield Derby*
GOSFORTH, NORTH (St Columba)   *see Ch the King Newc*
GOSPEL LANE (St Michael)   *see Hall Green St Mich Birm*
GOSPORT (Christ Church) *Portsm 3*   P *Bp*   V A G DAVIS
NSM P J LAMBERT
GOSPORT (Holy Trinity) *Portsm 3*   P *DBP*   V A G DAVIS
NSM P J LAMBERT
GOSSOPS GREEN (St Alban)   *see Ifield Chich*
GOTHAM (St Lawrence) *S'well 6*   P *Bp*   P-in-c R I COLEMAN
GOUDHURST (St Mary the Virgin) w Kilndown *Cant 11*
P *Abp and Prime Min (alt)*   V H E NELSON   NSM J T HUXLEY
GOULCEBY (All Saints)   *see Asterby Gp Linc*
GOXHILL (All Saints)   *see Barrow and Goxhill Linc*
GOXHILL (St Giles)   *see Aldbrough, Mappleton w Goxhill and Withernwick York*
GRADE (St Grada and the Holy Cross)   *see St Ruan w St Grade and Landewednack Truro*
GRAFFHAM (St Giles) w Woolavington *Chich 10*   P *Bp*
P-in-c M C C BARTER
GRAFFOE Group *Linc 12*   P *Ch Coll Cam, D&C and DBP, Oriel Coll Ox, and Mrs P N Fullerton (by turn)*   NSM S G WILLIAMS
GRAFHAM (All Saints)   *see E Leightonstone Ely*
GRAFHAM (St Andrew)   *see Bramley and Grafham Guildf*
GRAFTON FLYFORD (St John the Baptist)   *see Abberton, The Flyfords, Naunton Beauchamp etc Worc*
GRAFTON REGIS (St Mary)   *see Blisworth, Alderton, Grafton Regis etc Pet*
GRAFTON UNDERWOOD (St James the Apostle)   *see Cranford w Grafton Underwood and Twywell Pet*
GRAFTON, EAST (St Nicholas)   *see Savernake Sarum*
GRAIN (St James) w Stoke *Roch 6*   P *DBP*   V *vacant*
GRAINSBY (St Nicholas)   *see The North-Chapel Parishes Linc*
GRAINTHORPE (St Clement)   *see Somercotes and Grainthorpe w Conisholme Linc*

GRAMPOUND (St Nun)   *see Probus, Ladock and Grampound w Creed and St Erme Truro*
GRANBOROUGH (St John the Baptist)   *see Schorne Ox*
GRANBY (All Saints)   *see Cropwell Bishop w Colston Bassett, Granby etc S'well*
GRANDBOROUGH (St Peter)   *see Leam Valley Cov*
GRANGE (Holy Trinity)   *see Upper Derwent Carl*
GRANGE (St Andrew) *Ches 3*   P *Bp*   V W S H DOCHERTY
GRANGE FELL (not known)   *see Cartmel Peninsula Carl*
GRANGE MOOR (St Bartholomew)   *see Kirkheaton Leeds*
GRANGE PARK (St Peter) *Lon 18*   P *Bp*   V E G GREER
C A J WADSWORTH, C A STEAD
GRANGE-OVER-SANDS (St Paul)   *see Cartmel Peninsula Carl*
GRANGETOWN (St Aidan) *Dur 1*   P V *Ryhope*
V P A BOSTOCK
GRANGETOWN (St Hilda of Whitby) *York 17*   P *Abp*
V *vacant*
GRANSDEN, GREAT (St Bartholomew) and Abbotsley and
Lt Gransden and Waresley *Ely 13*   P *Pemb Coll Cam (1 turn), Clare Coll Cam (2 turns), and Ball Coll Ox (1 turn)*
P-in-c C M FURLONG
GRANSDEN, LITTLE (St Peter and St Paul)   *see Gt Gransden and Abbotsley and Lt Gransden etc Ely*
GRANTCHESTER (St Andrew and St Mary) *Ely 3*   P *CCC Cam*
V *vacant*
GRANTHAM (St Wulfram) *Linc 20*   P *Bp*   R S W CRADDUCK
C J E ROBINSON   NSM J M ROWLAND, J T FARLEY
GRANTHAM (The Epiphany) Earlesfield   *see S Grantham Linc*
GRANTHAM Harrowby w Londonthorpe *Linc 20*   P *Bp*
P-in-c C P BOLAND   C J A BELL
GRANTHAM Manthorpe *Linc 20*   P *Bp*
P-in-c S W CRADDUCK
GRANTHAM, SOUTH The Trinity (St Anne) (St John the
Evangelist) *Linc 20*   P *Bp and R Grantham (jt)*
V D SHENTON
GRAPPENHALL (St Wilfrid) *Ches 4*   P *P G Greenall Esq*
R J E PROUDFOOT
GRASBY (All Saints)   *see Caistor Gp Linc*
GRASMERE (St Oswald) *Carl 11*   P *Qu Coll Ox*
R C J BUTLAND   NSM J S M GREEN
GRASSENDALE (St Mary) *Liv 4*   P *Trustees*   V P ELLIS
NSM F C PENNIE, N ARNOLD
GRATELEY (St Leonard)   *see Portway and Danebury Win*
GRATWICH (St Mary the Virgin)   *see Uttoxeter Area Lich*
GRAVELEY (St Botolph)   *see Papworth Ely*
GRAVELEY (St Mary)   *see Stevenage St Nic and Graveley St Alb*
GRAVELLY HILL (All Saints) *Birm 8*   P *Bp*   V R J WALKER-HILL
NSM A R FRASER
GRAVENEY (All Saints)   *see Goodnestone w Graveney Cant*
GRAVENHURST, Shillington and Stondon *St Alb 8*   P *Bp*
V R C WINSLADE, S A CROFTS
GRAVESEND (Holy Family) w Ifield *Roch 4*   P *Bp and Mrs S Edmeades-Stearns (jt)*   P-in-c R A MARTIN   C K A SEGGIE
GRAVESEND (St Aidan) *Roch 4*   P *Bp*   V L NSENGA-NGOY
C K A SEGGIE   NSM J P LITTLEWOOD
GRAVESEND (St George) *Roch 4*   P *Bp*   R J C STONE
NSM H M REEVES
GRAVESEND (St Mary) *Roch 4*   P *R Gravesend*
P-in-c T OLIVER
GRAYINGHAM (St Radegunda) *Linc 8*   P *Bp*
P-in-c K E COLWELL   OLM J WILSON
GRAYRIGG (St John)   *see Beacon Carl*
GRAYS NORTH (St John the Evangelist) *Chelmsf 16*   P *Bp*
V C P RUSSELL
GRAYS THURROCK (St Peter and St Paul) *Chelmsf 16*   P *DBP*
TR D BARLOW   TV M A REYNOLDS   C R CARTWRIGHT
NSM C M WILLIAMS
GRAYSHOTT (St Luke) *Guildf 3*   P *Bp*   V C M S R THOMAS
Hon C G E KNIFTON
GRAYSWOOD (All Saints)   *see Haslemere and Grayswood Guildf*
GRAYTHWAITE (Mission Room)   *see Hawkshead and Low Wray w Sawrey and Rusland etc Carl*
GREASBROUGH (St Mary) *Sheff 6*   P *Sir Philip Naylor-Leyland Bt*   P-in-c L S WORTLEY   C A WOODING, J T BIRBECK
GREASBY (St Nicholas)   *see Frankby w Greasby Ches*
GREASLEY (St Mary) *S'well 4*   P *Bp*   V D A MARVIN
GREAT   *see also under substantive place name*
GREAT CAMBRIDGE ROAD (St John the Baptist and St James)
Lon 19   P *D&C St Paul's*   P-in-c N H ASBRIDGE
C M W WASWA
GREAT GLEN (St Cuthbert)   *see Glen Magna cum Stretton Magna etc Leic*
GREAT MOOR (St Saviour)   *see Stockport St Sav Ches*
GREATER   *see under substantive place name*
GREATFORD (St Thomas à Becket)   *see Uffington Gp Linc*

GREATHAM (not known)   *see* Amberley w N Stoke and Parham, Wiggonholt etc *Chich*
GREATHAM (St John the Baptist) *Dur 3*   **P** *Trustees*
   P-in-c P T ALLINSON
GREATHAM (St John the Baptist) w Empshott and Hawkley w Prior's Dean *Portsm 4*   **P** *DBP*   **C** R STUART-BOURNE
GREATSTONE (St Peter)   *see* Brookland, Fairfield, Brenzett w Snargate etc *Cant*
GREATWORTH (St Peter)   *see* Chenderit *Pet*
GREEN HAMMERTON (St Thomas)   *see* Gt and Lt Ouseburn w Marton cum Grafton etc *Leeds*
GREEN HEATH (St Saviour)   *see* Hednesford *Lich*
GREEN STREET GREEN (St Mary) and Pratts Bottom *Roch 16*
   P *Bp*   **V** K A CARPANI   **C** P J AVANN
GREENFIELD (St Mary)   *see* Saddleworth *Man*
GREENFIELDS (United Church)   *see* Shrewsbury St Geo w Greenfields *Lich*
GREENFORD (Holy Cross) (St Edward the Confessor) *Lon 22*
   P K Coll Cam   **R** G W MILLER
GREENFORD, NORTH (All Hallows) *Lon 22*   **P** *Bp*
   V P F HEAZELL   **Hon C** S J COLLIER
GREENGATES (St John the Evangelist) *Leeds 3*   **P** *D&C*
   V *vacant*
GREENHAM (St Mary the Virgin) *Ox 6*   **P** *Bp*
   V D L R MCLEOD   **NSM** B R JONES, J BRAMHALL
GREENHAM (St Peter)   *see* Wellington and Distr *B & W*
GREENHEAD (St Cuthbert)   *see* Haltwhistle and Greenhead *Newc*
GREENHILL (St John the Baptist) *Lon 23*   **P** *Bp, Adn, and V Harrow St Mary (jt)*   **V** B D HINGSTON   **Hon C** D P BYRNE
   NSM M MOTT
GREENHILL (St Peter) *Sheff 2*   **P** *Bp*   **P-in-c** E H STEELE
GREENHITHE (St Mary) *Roch 2*   **P** *Ch Soc Trust and Personal Reps Canon T L Livermore (jt)*   **P-in-c** A J AVERY
GREENHOW HILL (St Mary)   *see* Upper Nidderdale *Leeds*
GREENLANDS (St Anne) *Blackb 8*   **P** *Bp and V Blackpool St Steph (jt)*   **P-in-c** D A PREST
GREENLANDS (St John the Evangelist)   *see* Ipsley *Worc*
GREEN'S NORTON (St Bartholomew)   *see* Towcester w Caldecote and Easton Neston etc *Pet*
GREENSIDE (St John) *Dur 13*   **P** R Ryton w Hedgefield
   V *vacant*
GREENSTEAD (St Andrew) (St Edmund's Church Hall) (St Matthew) w Colchester St Anne *Chelmsf 21*   **P** *Patr Bd and Ld Chan (alt)*   **P-in-c** T C PLATTS
GREENSTEAD GREEN (St James Apostle)   *see* Halstead Area *Chelmsf*
GREENSTED-JUXTA-ONGAR (St Andrew) w Stanford Rivers and Stapleford Tawney w Theydon Mount *Chelmsf 3*   **P** *Bp Lon and DBP (1 turn), and Duchy of Lanc (1 turn)*   **R** *vacant*
GREENWICH (St Alfege) *S'wark 1*   **P** *The Crown*
   V C J E MOODY   **C** C L RISDON, P A MANN
   NSM S E BLACKALL, S K NSHIMYE
GREENWICH, EAST (Christ Church) (St Andrew w St Michael) (St George) *S'wark 1*   **P** *Patr Bd*   **TR** M CAVE   **TV** R L RYAN
   Hon C J P LEE   **NSM** J N PHILPOTT-HOWARD, R T YEAGER
   OLM C A FINNERTY
GREETE (St James)   *see* Tenbury *Heref*
GREETHAM (All Saints)   *see* Horncastle Gp *Linc*
GREETHAM (St Mary the Virgin)   *see* Cottesmore and Burley, Clipsham, Exton etc *Pet*
GREETLAND (St Thomas) and West Vale *Leeds 8*   **P** V Halifax
   C D BURROWS
GREETWELL (All Saints)   *see* S Lawres Gp *Linc*
GREINTON (St Michael and All Angels)   *see* Middlezoy w Othery, Moorlinch and Greinton *B & W*
GRENDON (All Saints)   *see* Baddesley Ensor w Grendon *Birm*
GRENDON (St Mary)   *see* Yardley Hastings, Denton and Grendon etc *Pet*
GRENDON BISHOP (St John the Baptist)   *see* Bredenbury *Heref*
GRENDON UNDERWOOD (St Leonard)   *see* The Claydons and Swan *Ox*
GRENOSIDE (St Mark) *Sheff 3*   **P** *Bp and V Ecclesfield (jt)*
   P-in-c S D BESSANT
GRESHAM (All Saints)   *see* Aylmerton, Runton, Beeston Regis and Gresham *Nor*
GRESLEY (St George and St Mary) *Derby 16*   **P** *Simeon's Trustees*   **V** M J FIRBANK
GRESSENHALL (Assumption of the Blessed Virgin Mary) w Longham w Wendling and Bittering Parva *Nor 14*   **P** *Ld Chan (1 turn), CPAS (2 turns)*   **P-in-c** R J MARSDEN
   NSM K D BLOGG
GRESSINGHAM (St John the Evangelist)   *see* Hornby w Claughton and Whittington etc *Blackb*
GRETTON (Christ Church)   *see* Winchcombe *Glouc*

GRETTON (St James the Great) w Rockingham and Cottingham w East Carlton *Pet 7*   **P** *Bp, Comdr L M M Saunders Watson, Sir Geoffrey Palmer Bt, and BNC Ox (jt)*
   P-in-c S J M READING
GREWELTHORPE (St James)   *see* Fountains Gp *Leeds*
GREYSTOKE (St Andrew)   *see* Greystoke w Penruddock, Mungrisdale etc *Carl*
GREYSTOKE (St Andrew) w Penruddock, Mungrisdale and Matterdale *Carl 4*   **P** *Patr Bd*   **R** W J WHITE
GREYSTONES (St Gabriel) *Sheff 2*   **P** *Dean*   **V** P W BECKLEY
GREYWELL (St Mary)   *see* N Hants Downs *Win*
GRIMEHILLS (St Mary)   *see* Darwen St Barn *Blackb*
GRIMETHORPE (St Luke) w Brierley *Leeds 18*   **P** *Bp*
   V I D MCCORMACK
GRIMLEY (St Bartholomew)   *see* Hallow and Grimley w Holt *Worc*
GRIMOLDBY (St Edith)   *see* Mid Marsh Gp *Linc*
GRIMSARGH (St Michael) *Blackb 13*   **P** R Preston
   V C E HALLIWELL
GRIMSBURY (St Leonard)   *see* Banbury St Leon *Ox*
GRIMSBY (St Augustine of Hippo) *Linc 3*   **P** TR Gt Grimsby SS Mary and Jas   **V** E J R MARTIN
GRIMSBY, GREAT (St Andrew w St Luke and All Saints) *Linc 3*
   P *Bp*   **V** E J R MARTIN
GRIMSBY, GREAT (St Mary and St James) (St Hugh) (St Mark) (St Martin) *Linc 3*   **P** *Bp*   **TR** A P DODD
   TV K L A FARRELL   **C** C M DAVIES, K A M PRICE,
   N D NAWROCKYI   **NSM** J M VASEY
GRIMSBY, LITTLE (St Edith)   *see* Fotherby *Linc*
GRIMSHOE *Ely 9*   **P** *Bp, G&C Coll Cam, and Ld Chan (by turn)*
   R J A HORAN   **C** B J ZYCH   **NSM** K R WATERS
GRIMSTEAD, EAST (Holy Trinity)   *see* Clarendon *Sarum*
GRIMSTEAD, WEST (St John) *as above*
GRIMSTON (St Botolph)   *see* Ashwicken w Leziate, Bawsey etc *Nor*
GRIMSTON (St John the Baptist)   *see* Old Dalby, Nether Broughton, Saxelbye etc *Leic*
GRIMSTON, NORTH (St Nicholas)   *see* W Buckrose *York*
GRINDALE (St Nicholas)   *see* Burton Fleming w Fordon, Grindale etc *York*
GRINDON (All Saints)   *see* Calton, Cauldon, Grindon, Waterfall etc *Lich*
GRINDON (St Oswald)   *see* Sunderland St Thos and St Oswald *Dur*
GRINGLEY-ON-THE-HILL (St Peter and St Paul)
   see Beckingham, Walkeringham, Misterton, W Stockwith, Clayworth and Gringley-on-the-Hill *S'well*
GRINSHILL (All Saints)   *see* Astley, Clive, Grinshill and Hadnall *Lich*
GRINSTEAD, EAST (St Mary the Virgin) *Chich 6*   **P** *Bp*
   V P R SEAMAN   **NSM** D W HADFIELD, J GAYFORD
GRINSTEAD, EAST (St Swithun) *Chich 6*   **P** *Bp*
   NSM G M W PARRY
GRINSTEAD, WEST (St George) *Chich 7*   **P** *Bp*
   R W E M HARRIS
GRINTON (St Andrew)   *see* Swaledale *Leeds*
GRISTHORPE (St Thomas)   *see* Filey *York*
GRISTON (St Peter and St Paul)   *see* Caston, Griston, Merton, Thompson etc *Nor*
GRITTLETON (St Mary the Virgin)   *see* By Brook *Bris*
GROBY (St Philip and St James) and Ratby *Leic 9*   **P** *Bp and Baroness Mowbray, Segrave and Stourton (jt)*   **R** P G HOOPER
   C L D CORKE   **NSM** R E COOPER
GROOMBRIDGE (St John the Evangelist)   *see* Speldhurst w Groombridge and Ashurst *Roch*
GROOMBRIDGE, NEW (St Thomas) *Chich 16*   **P** R Withyham
   P-in-c S E FRANCIS
GROSMONT (St Matthew)   *see* Middle Esk Moor *York*
GROSVENOR CHAPEL (no dedication) Chapel of Ease in the parish of Hanover Square St George w St Mark *Lon 3*
   P-in-c R M FERMER   **Hon C** S D DEWEY
GROTON (St Bartholomew)   *see* Boxford, Edwardstone, Groton etc *St E*
GROVE (St Helen)   *see* Retford Area *S'well*
GROVE (St John the Baptist)   *see* Vale *Ox*
GROVE PARK (St Augustine)   *see* Lee St Aug *S'wark*
GROVEHILL (Resurrection)   *see* Hemel Hempstead *St Alb*
GRUNDISBURGH (St Mary the Virgin)   *see* Carlford *St E*
GUARLFORD (St Mary)   *see* Powick and Guarlford and Madresfield w Newland *Worc*
GUERNSEY (Holy Trinity) *Win 14*   **P** *Trustees*   **V** J P HONOUR
GUERNSEY (St Andrew de la Pommeraye) *Win 14*   **P** *The Crown*   **R** *vacant*
GUERNSEY (St John the Evangelist) *Win 14*   **P** *Trustees*
   P-in-c L S LE VASSEUR
GUERNSEY (St Martin) *Win 14*   **P** *The Crown*   **R** M R KEIRLE
   NSM C M CLAXTON

GUERNSEY (St Matthew) *Win 14*　P *R Ste Marie du Castel*
V S J BAILEY　NSM J E C ROBILLIARD
GUERNSEY (St Michel du Valle) *Win 14*　P *The Crown*
R K C NORTHOVER　C M E J BARRETT
GUERNSEY (St Peter Port) *Win 14*　P *The Crown*
NSM G M MABIRE
GUERNSEY (St Sampson) *Win 14*　P *The Crown*
Emer T W DACK
GUERNSEY (St Stephen) *Win 14*　P *R St Peter Port*
Emer J B MOORE
GUERNSEY (Ste Marie du Castel) *Win 14*　P *The Crown*
R S J BAILEY　NSM J E C ROBILLIARD
GUERNSEY L'Islet (St Mary)　*see* Guernsey St Sampson *Win*
GUERNSEY Western Parishes (St Marguerite de la Foret)
(St Pierre du Bois) (St Philippe de Torteval) (St Saviour)
(Chapel of St Apolline) *Win 14*　TR M R CHARMLEY
NSM A DATTA, T B CHARMLEY
GUESTLING (St Laurence)　*see* Westfield and Guestling *Chich*
GUESTWICK (St Peter)　*see* Foulsham, Guestwick, Stibbard,
Themelthorpe etc *Nor*
GUILDEN MORDEN (St Mary)　*see* Shingay Gp *Ely*
GUILDEN SUTTON (St John the Baptist)　*see* Plemstall w
Guilden Sutton *Ches*
GUILDFORD (All Saints) *Guildf 5*　P *Bp*　V B A WATSON
GUILDFORD (Christ Church) (St Martha-on-the-Hill) *Guildf 5*
P *Simeon's Trustees and Duke of Northumberland (jt)*
V N J WILLIAMS　C J M HIDDEN　NSM B G MCNAIR SCOTT
GUILDFORD (Holy Spirit)　*see* Burpham *Guildf*
GUILDFORD (Holy Trinity) (St Mary the Virgin) (St Michael)
Guildf 5　P *Bp*　R R L COTTON　OLM J J HEDGECOCK,
R M PIERCE
GUILDFORD (St Luke)　*see* Burpham *Guildf*
GUILDFORD (St Nicolas) *Guildf 5*　P *Bp*　R A H NORMAN
NSM M A COOPER
GUILDFORD (St Saviour) *Guildf 5*　P *Simeon's Trustees*
R M C L NORRIS　C A C WHEELER, T J DARWENT
GUILSBOROUGH (St Ethelreda) and Hollowell and Cold
Ashby and Cottesbrooke w Great Creaton and Thornby and
Ravensthorpe and Spratton *Pet 2*　P *Bp, DBP, A R
MacDonald-Buchanan Esq, and J S McCall Esq (jt)*　R C W PECK
C J H CRAIG PECK　Hon C D L SMITH　NSM C MOSS
GUILTCROSS *Nor 11*　P *Bp, Mrs C Noel, Exors C P B Goldson, and
DBP (jt)*　P-in-c D R A SHEPPARD
GUISBOROUGH (St Nicholas) *York 16*　P *Abp*
R A PHILLIPSON
GUISELEY (St Oswald King and Martyr) w Esholt *Leeds 16*
P *Bp, Trin Coll Cam, and Mrs N A Gottlieb (jt)*　R D PICKETT
GUIST (St Andrew)　*see* N Elmham, Billingford, Bintree, Guist
etc *Nor*
GUITING POWER (St Michael)　*see* The Guitings, Cutsdean,
Farmcote etc *Glouc*
GUITINGS, Cutsdean, Farmcote, Upper and Lower Slaughter
w Eyford and Naunton, The *Glouc 8*　P *Bp, Ch Ch Ox,
Guiting Manor Amenity Trust, and F E B Witts Esq (jt)*
R K R SCOTT　NSM S M COX
GULDEFORD, EAST (St Mary)　*see* Rye *Chich*
GULVAL (St Gulval) and Madron *Truro 5*　P *Ld Chan and Bp
(jt)*　P-in-c T ST J HAWKINS　NSM P G BUTTERFIELD
GULWORTHY (St Paul)　*see* Tavistock, Gulworthy and Brent
Tor *Ex*
GUMLEY (St Helen)　*see* Foxton w Gumley and Laughton *Leic*
GUNBY (St Nicholas)　*see* Witham Gp *Linc*
GUNBY (St Peter)　*see* Burgh Gp *Linc*
GUNHOUSE (St Barnabas)　*see* Trentside E *Linc*
GUNN CHAPEL (Holy Name)　*see* Swimbridge w W Buckland
and Landkey *Ex*
GUNNERTON (St Christopher)　*see* Chollerton w Birtley and
Thockrington *Newc*
GUNNISLAKE (St Anne)　*see* Calstock *Truro*
GUNTHORPE (St John the Baptist)　*see* Lowdham w Caythorpe,
and Gunthorpe *S'well*
GUNTHORPE (St Mary)　*see* Stiffkey and Bale *Nor*
GUNTON St Peter (St Benedict) *Nor 9*　P *CPAS*　R T W RIESS
GUNWALLOE (St Winwalloe)　*see* Cury and Gunwalloe *Truro*
GURNARD (All Saints) w Cowes St Faith *Portsm 8*　P *Bp*
V A COLLINSON　NSM D M NETHERWAY
GUSSAGE (St Andrew)　*see* Sixpenny Handley w Gussage
St Andrew etc *Sarum*
GUSSAGE ALL SAINTS (All Saints)　*see* Chase *Sarum*
GUSSAGE ST MICHAEL (St Michael) *as above*
GUSTARD WOOD (St Peter)　*see* Wheathampstead *St Alb*
GUSTON (St Martin of Tours) *Cant 7*　P *Abp and D&C (jt)*
V *vacant*
GWEEK (Mission Church)　*see* Constantine *Truro*
GWENNAP (St Weneppa)　*see* St Stythians w Perranarworthal
and Gwennap *Truro*
GWINEAR (St Winnear)　*see* Godrevy *Truro*

GWITHIAN (St Gwithian) *as above*
HABBERLEY (St Mary)　*see* Minsterley, Habberley and Hope w
Shelve *Heref*
HABERGHAM (All Saints)　*see* W Burnley All SS *Blackb*
HABROUGH (St Margaret)　*see* Immingham Gp *Linc*
HABTON, GREAT (St Chad)　*see* Kirby Misperton w Normanby
and Salton *York*
HACCOMBE (St Blaise)　*see* Shaldon, Stokeinteignhead,
Combeinteignhead etc *Ex*
HACCONBY (St Andrew)　*see* Ringstone in Aveland Gp *Linc*
HACHESTON (St Andrew)　*see* Campsea Ashe w Marlesford,
Parham and Hacheston *St E*
HACKBRIDGE and Beddington Corner (All Saints) *S'wark 23*
P *Bp*　V *vacant*
HACKENTHORPE (Christ Church) *Sheff 2*　P *Bp*
V S J WILLETT　NSM A RHODES
HACKFORD (St Mary the Virgin)　*see* High Oak, Hingham and
Scoulton w Wood Rising *Nor*
HACKINGTON (St Stephen) *Cant 3*　P *Adn Cant*
P-in-c K MADDY　Hon C S C E LAIRD
HACKNESS (St Peter) w Harwood Dale *York 15*　P *Lord
Derwent*　V A J FERNELEY　NSM D MACIVER
HACKNEY (St James)　*see* Clapton St Jas *Lon*
HACKNEY (St John)　*see* St John-at-Hackney *Lon*
HACKNEY (St Luke) Homerton Terrace　*see* Homerton St Luke
Lon
HACKNEY (St Thomas)　*see* Stamford Hill St Thos *Lon*
HACKNEY MARSH (All Souls) *Lon 5*　P *Patr Bd*　TR C T MAIN
NSM T A HALEY
HACKNEY Mount Pleasant Lane (St Matthew)　*see* Upper
Clapton St Matt *Lon*
HACKNEY WICK St Mary of Eton *Lon 5*　P *Eton Coll*
V R J PRESTON
HACKNEY, OVER (Mission Room)　*see* Darley, S Darley and
Winster *Derby*
HACKNEY, SOUTH (St John of Jerusalem) (Christ Church)
Lon 5　P *Lord Amherst*　R A M W WILSON　C S A GAYLE,
S GALE
HACKNEY, SOUTH (St Michael and All Angels) London Fields
w Haggerston (St Paul) *Lon 5*　P *R S Hackney St Jo w Ch Ch*
V D GERRANS　NSM H M A ATKINSON
HACKNEY, WEST (St Paul) *Lon 5*　P *Bp*　R W D N WEIR
C G E FOUHY
HACKTHORN (St Michael and All Angels)　*see* Owmby Gp *Linc*
HADDENHAM (Holy Trinity) *Ely 8*　P *Adn Ely*
V F E G BRAMPTON　NSM J A GAGE
HADDENHAM (St Mary the Virgin) w Cuddington, Kingsey
and Aston Sandford *Ox 10*　P *D&C Roch*
P-in-c M R HODSON　C I C HERBERT　NSM J D HAWKINS
OLM P MANDER
HADDISCOE (St Mary)　*see* Raveningham Gp *Nor*
HADDLESEY (St John the Baptist)　*see* Haddlesey w Hambleton
and Birkin *York*
HADDLESEY w Hambleton and Birkin *York 4*　P *Abp and
Simeon's Trustees (jt)*　P-in-c A V BURR
HADDON (St Mary)　*see* Stilton w Denton and Caldecote etc
Ely
HADDON, EAST (St Mary the Virgin)　*see* Brington w Whilton
and Norton etc *Pet*
HADDON, OVER (St Anne)　*see* Bakewell, Ashford w Sheldon
and Rowsley *Derby*
HADDON, WEST (All Saints)　*see* Long Buckby w Watford and
W Haddon w Winwick *Pet*
HADFIELD (St Andrew) *Derby 6*　P *Bp*　V F A WALTERS
HADHAM, LITTLE (St Cecilia)　*see* Albury, Braughing, Furneux
Pelham, Lt Hadham etc *St Alb*
HADHAM, MUCH (St Andrew) *as above*
HADLEIGH (St Barnabas) *Chelmsf 13*　P *Bp*
P-in-c D R CHILDS　C G H E STOCK　NSM C ROBINSON
HADLEIGH (St James the Less) *Chelmsf 13*　P *Dr P W M
Copeman and A R C Copeman Esq (jt)*　P-in-c D R CHILDS
C G H E STOCK　NSM C ROBINSON
HADLEIGH (St Mary), Layham and Shelley *St E 3*　P *St Jo Coll
Cam and Abp (alt)*　V M C THROWER　C D E J THOMPSON
HADLEY (Holy Trinity) and Wellington Christ Church *Lich 21*
P *Bp, Adn Salop, and V Wellington All SS w Eyton*　V A P WOOD
C P H J THORNEYCROFT　NSM H PAGE
HADLEY WOOD (St Paul) Proprietary Chapel *Lon 18*
Min R MACKAY
HADLOW (St Mary) *Roch 8*　P *Exors Miss I N King*
V P J WHITE
HADLOW DOWN (St Mark)　*see* Buxted and Hadlow Down
Chich
HADNALL (St Mary Magdalene)　*see* Astley, Clive, Grinshill
and Hadnall *Lich*
HADSTOCK (St Botolph)　*see* Saffron Walden and Villages
Chelmsf

HADZOR w Oddingley (St James)   *see* Bowbrook S *Worc*
HAGBOURNE (St Andrew)   *see* The Churn *Ox*
HAGGERSTON (St Chad) *Lon 5*   **P** *The Crown*
V J J WESTCOTT
HAGLEY (St John the Baptist) *Worc 12*   **P** *Exors Viscount*
Cobham   **R** R J C NEWTON
HAGLEY, WEST (St Saviour)   *see* Hagley *Worc*
HAGNABY (St Andrew)   *see* Bolingbroke Deanery *Linc*
HAGWORTHINGHAM (Holy Trinity) *as above*
HAIGH (St David)   *see* Wigan All SS *Liv*
HAIL WESTON (St Nicholas)   *see* The Staughtons w Hail
Weston *Ely*
HAILE (not known)   *see* Egremont and Haile *Carl*
HAILES (Chapel)   *see* Winchcombe *Glouc*
HAILEY (St John the Evangelist)   *see* Witney *Ox*
HAILSHAM (St Mary) (Emmanuel) *Chich 13*   **P** *Ch Soc Trust*
V D J BOURNE   **C** J A ISAACS, S J E TOMALIN
HAINAULT (St Paul) *Chelmsf 6*   **P** *Bp*   **P-in-c** K ASHTON
NSM S M HARTLEY
HAINFORD (All Saints)   *see* Coltishall w Gt Hautbois,
Frettenham etc *Nor*
HAINTON (St Mary)   *see* Barkwith Gp *Linc*
HALA (St Paul's Centre)   *see* Scotforth *Blackb*
HALAM (St Michael)   *see* Edingley w Halam *S'well*
HALAS *Worc 9*   **P** *Patr Bd*   **TR** R S HALL   **TV** D MELVILLE,
M K LECLÉZIO   **C** S L BRUSH
HALBERTON (St Andrew)   *see* Sampford Peverell, Uplowman,
Holcombe Rogus etc *Ex*
HALDEN, HIGH (St Mary the Virgin)   *see* Bethersden w High
Halden and Woodchurch *Cant*
HALDENS (Christ the King)   *see* Digswell and Panshanger
St Alb
HALE (St David)   *see* Timperley *Ches*
HALE (St John the Evangelist)   *see* Badshot Lea and Hale *Guildf*
HALE (St Mary)   *see* S Widnes *Liv*
HALE (St Mary)   *see* Fordingbridge and Breamore and Hale etc
Win
HALE (St Peter) and Ashley *Ches 10*   **P** *V Bowdon*
V K P ADDENBROOKE   **C** P D DEAKIN, R PYE
HALE BARNS (All Saints) w Ringway *Ches 10*   **P** *Bp*
V R D CLARKE   **NSM** G C JAQUISS
HALE, GREAT (St John the Baptist)   *see* Heckington and
Helpringham Gp *Linc*
HALE, UPPER (St Mark)   *see* Badshot Lea and Hale *Guildf*
HALES (St Mary)   *see* Cheswardine, Childs Ercall, Hales,
Hinstock etc *Lich*
HALESOWEN (St John the Baptist)   *see* Halas *Worc*
HALESWORTH (St Mary)   *see* Blyth Valley *St E*
HALEWOOD (St Nicholas) (St Mary) and Hunts Cross Team,
The *Liv 4*   **P** *Patr Bd*   **TV** E J DURHAM
HALEY HILL (All Souls)   *see* Halifax *Leeds*
HALFORD (Our Blessed Lady)   *see* Stourdene Gp *Cov*
HALFORD (St Thomas) w Sidbon Carwood *Heref 10*   **P** *Bp*
and R Holden (alt)   **P-in-c** T E JESSIMAN
NSM M G WILLIAMS
HALFWAY (St Peter)   *see* W Sheppey *Cant*
HALIFAX (All Saints) *Leeds 11*   **P** *Ch Trust Fund Trust*
P-in-c S LEES
HALIFAX (Holy Trinity) (St Jude) *Leeds 11*   **P** *Bp, V Halifax,*
and trustees (jt)   **V** R J FRITH   **NSM** M RUSSELL
HALIFAX (St Anne-in-the-Grove)   *see* Southowram and
Claremount *Leeds*
HALIFAX (St Hilda) *Leeds 11*   **P** *Bp*   **C** C KAY
HALIFAX MINSTER (St John the Baptist) (All Souls) *Leeds 11*
P *The Crown*   **V** H J BARBER   **C** J J P BISH   **Hon**
C D S SIMON   **Emer** M G HUNTER
HALIFAX St Augustine (School Hall) and Mount Pellon
Leeds 11   **P** *Bp, Simeon's Trustees, and local trustees (jt)*
V J HELLEWELL   **C** L J MASLEN   **NSM** S M HEPTINSTALL
HALL GREEN (Church of the Ascension) *Birm 6*   **P** *Bp, V*
Yardley, and Vice-Chmn of PCC (jt)   **V** P R LECKEY
HALL GREEN (St Michael) *Birm 6*   **P** *Bp*   **V** *vacant*
HALL GREEN (St Peter) *Birm 6*   **P** *Bp*   **V** M W STEPHENSON
C J B FOSTER
HALL STREET (St Andrew)   *see* Stockport St Mary *Ches*
HALLAM, WEST (St Wilfred) and Mapperley w Stanley
Derby 13   **P** *Bp*   **R** G R TURNER-CALLIS
OLM I OWEN-JONES
HALLATON (St Michael and All Angels) and Allexton, w
Horninghold, Tugby, and East Norton, and Slawston *Leic 3*
P *Bp, DBP, and E Brudenell Esq (jt)*   **P-in-c** L R CURTIS
HALLING (St John the Baptist)   *see* Cuxton and Halling *Roch*
HALLINGBURY, GREAT (St Giles) (St Andrew) and LITTLE
(St Mary the Virgin) *Chelmsf 4*   **P** *Bp and Charterhouse (jt)*
P-in-c J A GREEN
HALLIWELL (St Luke)   *see* W Bolton *Man*

HALLIWELL (St Margaret)   *see* Heaton Ch Ch w Halliwell
St Marg *Man*
HALLIWELL (St Peter) (Barrow Bridge Mission) (St Andrew's
Mission Church) *Man 7*   **P** *Trustees*   **V** P D HARDINGHAM
C A W SAUNDERS, V C WHITWORTH   **NSM** C WATSON
HALLOUGHTON (St James)   *see* Thurgarton w Hoveringham
and Bleasby etc *S'well*
HALLOW (St Philip and St James) and Grimley w Holt *Worc 3*
P *Bp*   **R** R N LATHAM
HALLWOOD Ecumenical Parish (St Mark) *Ches 3*   **P** *DBP*
V L J MACINNES
HALSALL (St Cuthbert), Lydiate and Downholland *Liv 11*
P *Bp and Brig D H Blundell-Hollinshead-Blundell (jt)*
R P L ROBINSON
HALSE (Mission Church)   *see* Brackley St Pet w St Jas *Pet*
HALSE (St James the Less)   *see* Milverton w Halse, Fitzhead and
Ash Priors *B & W*
HALSETOWN (St John's in the Fields) *Truro 5*   **P** *D&C*
P-in-c A S GOUGH   **C** E V A FOOT
HALSHAM (All Saints)   *see* Burstwick, Burton Pidsea etc *York*
HALSTEAD (St Margaret)   *see* Knockholt w Halstead *Roch*
HALSTEAD AREA (St Andrew) *Chelmsf 19*   **P** *Patr Bd*
TV G W ELLIS, P R ALLEN, S E CRUSE
NSM H R MOTHERSOLE, M H M BURSELL
HALSTOCK (St Mary)   *see* Melbury *Sarum*
HALSTOW, HIGH (St Margaret) (All Hallows) and Hoo
St Mary *Roch 6*   **P** *MMCET and Ch Soc Trust (jt)*
R S G GWILT
HALSTOW, LOWER (St Margaret)   *see* The Six *Cant*
HALTER DEVIL (Mission Room)   *see* Mugginton and Kedleston
Derby
HALTON (St Mary) *Ches 3*   **P** *Bp*   **P-in-c** A MITCHELL
HALTON (St Michael and All Angels)   *see* Wendover and Halton
Ox
HALTON (St Oswald and St Cuthbert and King Alfwald)
see Corbridge w Halton and Newton Hall *Newc*
HALTON (St Wilfred)   *see* Slyne w Hest and Halton w Aughton
Blackb
HALTON (St Wilfrid)   *see* Leeds Halton St Wilfrid *Leeds*
HALTON HOLGATE (St Andrew)   *see* Bolingbroke Deanery *Linc*
HALTON QUAY (St Indract's Chapel)   *see* St Dominic,
Landulph and St Mellion w Pillaton *Truro*
HALTON WEST (Mission Church)   *see* Hellifield and Long
Preston *Leeds*
HALTON, EAST (St Peter)   *see* Immingham Gp *Linc*
HALTON, WEST (St Etheldreda)   *see* Alkborough *Linc*
HALTWHISTLE (Holy Cross) and Greenhead *Newc 10*   **P** *Bp*
V N WILSON
HALVERGATE (St Peter and St Paul)   *see* Acle and Bure to Yare
Nor
HALWELL (St Leonard)   *see* Diptford, N Huish, Harberton,
Harbertonford etc *Ex*
HALWILL (St Peter and St James)   *see* Ashwater, Halwill,
Beaworthy, Clawton etc *Ex*
HAM (All Saints)   *see* Savernake *Sarum*
HAM (St Andrew) *S'wark 15*   **P** *K Coll Cam*
V S BROCKLEHURST   **NSM** V VASETHE
HAM (St Barnabas Mission Church)   *see* Chard St Mary w
Combe St Nicholas, Wambrook etc *B & W*
HAM (St James the Less)   *see* Plymouth St Pet and H Apostles
Ex
HAM (St Richard) *S'wark 16*   **P** *Bp*   **V** P J H DUNN
HAMBLE LE RICE (St Andrew) *Win 10*   **P** *St Mary's Coll Win*
P-in-c G J WHITING   **C** R W SANDAY
HAMBLEDEN VALLEY (St Mary the Virgin) *Ox 18*   **P** *Bp,*
Viscount Hambleden, and Miss M Mackenzie (jt)
NSM S MORTON
HAMBLEDON (St Peter and St Paul) *Portsm 1*   **P** *Ld Chan*
P-in-c R I P COUTTS
HAMBLEDON (St Peter)   *see* Busbridge and Hambledon
Guildf
HAMBLETON (St Andrew)   *see* Oakham, Ashwell, Braunston,
Brooke, Egleton etc *Pet*
HAMBLETON (St Mary)   *see* Haddlesey w Hambleton and
Birkin *York*
HAMBLETON (The Blessed Virgin Mary)   *see* Waterside Par
Blackb
HAMBRIDGE (St James the Less)   *see* Isle Valley *B & W*
HAMER (All Saints) and Healey *Man 17*   **P** *Bp*   **V** I S CARTER
HAMERINGHAM (All Saints)   *see* Fen and Hill Gp *Linc*
HAMERTON (All Saints)   *see* N Leightonstone *Ely*
HAMILTON Conventional District *Leic 1*   **Min** E RAWLINGS
HAMILTON Conventional District *Leic 2*   **Min** E RAWLINGS
HAMILTON TERRACE (St Mark)   *see* St Marylebone St Mark
Hamilton Terrace *Lon*
HAMMER (St Michael)   *see* Lynchmere and Camelsdale *Chich*

HAMMERFIELD (St Francis of Assisi)   see Boxmoor St Jo St Alb
HAMMERSMITH (Holy Innocents) (St John the Evangelist)
Lon 9   P Bp   P-in-c D W G MATTHEWS   C A J ROONEY
NSM A H MEAD
HAMMERSMITH (St Luke) Lon 9   P Bp   V R M BASTABLE
HAMMERSMITH (St Matthew) Lon 9   P Trustees
V G H CHIPLIN
HAMMERSMITH (St Michael and St George)   see Shepherd's
Bush St Steph w St Thos Lon
HAMMERSMITH (St Peter) Lon 9   P Bp   V C C CLAPHAM
HAMMERSMITH (St Saviour)   see Cobbold Road St Sav w
St Mary Lon
HAMMERSMITH (St Simon) Lon 9   P Simeon's Trustees
V C J COLLINGTON
HAMMERSMITH St Paul Lon 9   P Bp   V S G DOWNHAM
C W P G LEAF   NSM V I THOMAS
HAMMERSMITH, NORTH (St Katherine) Lon 9   P Bp
P-in-c J TATE
HAMMERWICH (St John the Baptist)   see Burntwood, Chase
Terrace etc Lich
HAMMERWOOD (St Stephen)   see Cowden w Hammerwood
Chich
HAMMOON (St Paul)   see Okeford Sarum
HAMPDEN PARK (St Mary) and The Hydnye Chich 14   P Bp
P-in-c M D BLANCH   NSM J MANN
HAMPDEN, GREAT (St Mary Magdalene)   see Prestwood and
Gt Hampden Ox
HAMPDEN, LITTLE (not known)   see Gt Missenden w Ballinger
and Lt Hampden Ox
HAMPNETT (St George)   see Northleach w Hampnett and
Farmington etc Glouc
HAMPRESTON (All Saints) Sarum 9   P Patr Bd   TR S A L PIX
TV P CHABALA   NSM L F HORLOCK
HAMPSTEAD (Christ Church) Lon 16   P Trustees
V P D CONRAD   Hon C P J W BLACKBURN
HAMPSTEAD (Emmanuel) West End Lon 16   P Bp
V J G F KESTER   NSM A FRITZE-SHANKS
HAMPSTEAD (St James)   see Kilburn St Mary w All So and W
Hampstead St Jas Lon
HAMPSTEAD (St John) Lon 16   P DBP   V S R TUCKER
C D J YOUNG
HAMPSTEAD (St John) Downshire Hill Proprietary Chapel
Lon   C A PALMER   Min J G L GOULD
HAMPSTEAD (St John) Downshire Hill Proprietary Chapel
Lon 16   C A PALMER   Min J G L GOULD
HAMPSTEAD Belsize Park (St Peter)   see Belsize Park Lon
HAMPSTEAD GARDEN SUBURB (St Jude on the Hill) Lon 15
P Bp   V A R G WALKER
HAMPSTEAD NORREYS (St Mary)   see Hermitage Ox
HAMPSTEAD St Stephen w (All Hallows) Lon 16   P DBP and
D&C Cant (jt)   V D N C HOULDING
HAMPSTEAD, SOUTH (St Saviour) Lon 16   P V Hampstead
St Jo   P-in-c P S NICHOLSON   NSM M W SPEEKS
HAMPSTEAD, WEST (Holy Trinity) Lon 16   P MMCET
V A K KEIGHLEY   C K L BREUSS
HAMPSTEAD, WEST (St Cuthbert) Lon 16   P Ch Trust Fund
Trust   P-in-c D W JOHN
HAMPSTEAD, WEST (St Luke) Lon 16   P CPAS
V A C TRESIDDER   C J C TAYLOR
HAMPSTHWAITE (St Thomas à Becket) and Killinghall and
Birstwith Leeds 23   P Mrs S J Finn, Sir James Aykroyd Bt, Sir
Thomas Ingilby Bt, and Bp (jt)   V C H WILSON
HAMPTON Ely 15   P Bp   P-in-c S P KINDER
HAMPTON (All Saints) Lon 10   P Ld Chan   V G K WARDELL
HAMPTON (St Andrew)   see Herne Bay Ch Ch Cant
HAMPTON (St Andrew) w Sedgeberrow and Hinton-on-the-
Green Worc 1   P Ch Ch Ox, D&C Worc, and Laslett's Charity
(jt)   P-in-c M J G BINNEY
HAMPTON (St Mary the Virgin) Lon 10   P Ld Chan
V D N WINTERBURN
HAMPTON BISHOP (St Andrew)   see Tupsley w Hampton
Bishop Heref
HAMPTON GAY (St Giles)   see Akeman Ox
HAMPTON HILL (St James) Lon 10   P V Hampton St Mary
V P VANNOZZI   NSM J CAMMIDGE
HAMPTON LOVETT (St Mary and All Saints)   see Elmley Lovett
w Hampton Lovett and Elmbridge etc Worc
HAMPTON LUCY (St Peter ad Vincula) w Charlecote and
Loxley Cov 8   P Sir Edmund Fairfax-Lucy Bt (3 turns), Col A M
H Gregory-Hood (1 turn)   P-in-c D C JESSETT
HAMPTON POYLE (St Mary the Virgin)   see Kidlington w
Hampton Poyle Ox
HAMPTON WICK (St John the Baptist)   see Teddington St Mark
and Hampton Wick Lon
HAMPTON, GREAT AND LITTLE (St Andrew)   see Hampton w
Sedgeberrow and Hinton-on-the-Green Worc

HAMPTON-IN-ARDEN (St Mary and St Bartholomew) w
Bickenhill St Peter Birm 11   P Birm Dioc Trustees and Guild
of All So (jt)   R D C J BALLARD   NSM M A HINKS
HAMSEY (St Peter) Chich 21   P Bp   P-in-c D BASTIDE
HAMSTALL RIDWARE (St Michael and All Angels)   see The
Ridwares and Kings Bromley Lich
HAMSTEAD (St Bernard) Birm 3   P Bp   V vacant
HAMSTEAD (St Paul) Birm 3   P Bp   V M S PRASADAM
HAMSTEAD MARSHALL (St Mary)   see Walbury Beacon Ox
HAMSTERLEY (St James) and Witton-le-Wear Dur 6   P Bp
and The Crown (alt)   P-in-c B E MECHANIC   Hon
C R I MECHANIC, T PITT
HAMWORTHY (St Gabriel) (St Michael) Sarum 7   P MMCET
R S D GODDARD   C P G GODDARD
HANBOROUGH (St Peter and St Paul) and Freeland Ox 29
P St Jo Coll Ox   R D S TYLER   C S J SPANKIE
NSM P G COOKE   OLM P T BALL
HANBURY (St Mary the Virgin)   see Bowbrook N Worc
HANBURY (St Werburgh), Newborough, Rangemore and
Tutbury Lich 14   P Duchy of Lancaster (1 turn), DBP and
Lord Burton (1 turn)   P-in-c L REES   C I R WHITEHEAD
Hon C A L WHEALE
HANDBRIDGE (St Mary without the Walls)   see Ches St Mary
Ches
HANDCROSS (All Saints)   see Slaugham and Staplefield
Common Chich
HANDFORTH (St Chad) Ches 17   P R Cheadle
V S J BURMESTER   C W R MARSHALL   NSM J G KNOWLES
HANDLEY (All Saints)   see Tattenhall w Burwardsley and
Handley Ches
HANDLEY (St Mark)   see N Wingfield, Clay Cross and Pilsley
Derby
HANDSWORTH (Good News Asian Church) Proprietary
Chapel Birm   NSM J M CHAUDHARY
HANDSWORTH (Good News Asian Church) Proprietary
Chapel Birm 3   NSM J M CHAUDHARY
HANDSWORTH (St Andrew) Birm 3   P Bp
V D T MACHIRIDZA
HANDSWORTH (St James) Birm 3   P Bp   V D J P ISIORHO
HANDSWORTH (St Mary) Sheff 1   P DBP   R K H JOHNSON
HANDSWORTH (St Mary) (Epiphany) Birm 3   P Bp
R R STEPHEN
HANDSWORTH (St Michael) (St Peter) Birm 3   P Bp
V J R A SAMPSON   NSM J M CHAUDHARY
HANDSWORTH WOODHOUSE (St James)   see Woodhouse
St Jas Sheff
HANFORD (St Matthias) Lich 13   P Bp   V E W MCLEOD
C S A MORRIS
HANGER HILL (Ascension) and West Twyford Lon 22   P Bp
and DBP (jt)   V S J REED   NSM P D HARRIS
HANGER LANE (St Ann)   see S Tottenham St Ann Lon
HANGING HEATON (St Paul) Leeds 10   P R Dewsbury
P-in-c M NAYLOR
HANGLETON (St Helen) (St Richard) Chich 20   P Bp
V K G PERKINTON
HANHAM (Christ Church) (St George) Bris 5   P Bp
NSM C E EVANS, J F J GOODRIDGE
HANKERTON (Holy Cross)   see Ashley, Crudwell, Hankerton
and Oaksey Bris
HANLEY (All Saints)   see Stoke-upon-Trent Lich
HANLEY CASTLE (St Mary), Hanley Swan and Welland Worc 5
P Ld Chan and Exors Sir Berwick Lechmere Bt (alt)
NSM L D BEDFORD
HANLEY CHILD (St Michael and All Angels)   see Teme Valley S
Worc
HANLEY Holy Evangelists (St Luke) Lich 11   P Bp
TR C J BROAD   TV S A SMITH   C P D SWAN,
S L BILLINGTON, T P MERRY   OLM K E PETHERICK
HANLEY SWAN (St Gabriel)   see Hanley Castle, Hanley Swan
and Welland Worc
HANLEY WILLIAM (All Saints)   see Teme Valley S Worc
HANNAH (St Andrew) cum Hagnaby w Markby Linc 10
P Bp and Mrs A M Johnson (alt)   NSM J M MORTON
OLM R D BARRETT
HANNEY, WEST (St James the Great)   see Vale Ox
HANNINGFIELD, EAST (All Saints) Chelmsf 10   P CPAS
P-in-c L P BATSON
HANNINGFIELD, SOUTH (St Peter)   see Downham w S
Hanningfield and Ramsden Bellhouse Chelmsf
HANNINGFIELD, WEST (St Mary and St Edward) Chelmsf 10
P DBP   P-in-c S W NEED
HANNINGTON (All Saints)   see Baughurst, Ramsdell,
Wolverton w Ewhurst etc Win
HANNINGTON (St John the Baptist)   see Highworth w
Sevenhampton and Inglesham etc Bris

HANNINGTON (St Peter and St Paul)   *see* Walgrave w Hannington and Wold and Scaldwell *Pet*
HANOVER SQUARE (St George) *Lon 3*   **P** *Bp*   **R** R N S LEECE
HANSLOPE (St James the Great) w Castlethorpe *Ox 16*   **P** *Bp*
V G E ECCLESTONE
HANWELL (St Mary) (St Christopher) *Lon 22*   **P** *Bp*
R M R GRAYSHON   **C** E J MOODY   **NSM** H M V COSSTICK
HANWELL (St Mellitus w St Mark) *Lon 22*   **P** *Bp*
P-in-c M P MELLUISH
HANWELL (St Peter)   *see* Ironstone *Ox*
HANWELL (St Thomas) *Lon 22*   **P** *The Crown*
V R B CHAPMAN
HANWOOD, GREAT (St Thomas) and Longden and Annscroft w Pulverbatch *Heref 12*   **P** *J A de Grey-Warter Esq, Bp, and MMCET (jt)*   **NSM** D MOSS   **OLM** O S DAWSON-CAMPBELL
HANWORTH (All Saints) *Lon 11*   **P** *Bp*   **C** S DIDUK
HANWORTH (St Bartholomew)   *see* Roughton and Felbrigg, Metton, Sustead etc *Nor*
HANWORTH (St George) *Lon 11*   **P** *Bp*
P-in-c P S WILLIAMSON
HANWORTH (St Richard of Chichester) *Lon 11*   **P** *Bp*
V C W HOLMES   **C** S DIDUK
HAPPISBURGH (St Mary)   *see* Bacton, Happisburgh, Hempstead w Eccles etc *Nor*
HAPTON (St Margaret)   *see* Padiham w Hapton and Padiham Green *Blackb*
HAPTON (St Margaret)   *see* Upper Tas Valley *Nor*
HARBERTON (St Andrew)   *see* Diptford, N Huish, Harberton, Harbertonford etc *Ex*
HARBERTONFORD (St Peter) *as above*
HARBLEDOWN (St Michael and All Angels) *Cant 3*   **P** *Abp*
R M A MORRIS
HARBORNE (St Faith and St Laurence) *Birm 2*   **P** *Bp*
V P A WHITE
HARBORNE (St Peter) *Birm 2*   **P** *Bp*   **V** G J RICHARDSON
HARBORNE HEATH (St John the Baptist) *Birm 2*   **P** *Ch Soc Trust*   **C** A W SPENCER
HARBOROUGH MAGNA (All Saints)   *see* Revel Gp *Cov*
HARBRIDGE (All Saints)   *see* Hyde w Ellingham and Harbridge *Win*
HARBURY (All Saints) and Ladbroke *Cov 10*   **P** *Bp*
P-in-c C R GROOCOCK   **C** N J MOON
HARBY (All Saints)   *see* E Trent *S'well*
HARBY (St Mary the Virgin)   *see* Vale of Belvoir *Leic*
HARDEN (St Saviour) and Wilsden, Cullingworth and Denholme *Leeds 5*   **P** *Patr Bd*   **TR** S R EVANS
TV S MCCARTER   **NSM** E MOY
HARDENHUISH (St Nicholas)   *see* Chippenham St Paul w Hardenhuish etc *Bris*
HARDHAM (St Botolph)   *see* Bury w Houghton and Coldwaltham and Hardham *Chich*
HARDINGHAM (St George)   *see* Barnham Broom and Upper Yare *Nor*
HARDINGSTONE (St Edmund) and Piddington w Horton *Pet 4*   **P** *Bp*   **P-in-c** B J HOLLINS   **C** D L MARSH
HARDINGTON MANDEVILLE (Blessed Virgin Mary)   *see* Coker Ridge *B & W*
HARDINGTON VALE *B & W 3*   **P** *Bp and J B Owen-Jones Esq (jt)*   **R** C H WALKER   **Hon C** A M BOWERMAN
HARDLEY (St Margaret)   *see* Loddon, Sisland, Chedgrave, Hardley and Langley *Nor*
HARDRAW (St Mary and St John)   *see* Upper Wensleydale *Leeds*
HARDRES, LOWER (St Mary)   *see* Bridge *Cant*
HARDRES, UPPER (St Peter and St Paul)   *see* Chartham and Upper Hardres w Stelling *Cant*
HARDWICK (St Leonard)   *see* Mears Ashby and Hardwick and Sywell etc *Pet*
HARDWICK (St Margaret)   *see* Hempnall *Nor*
HARDWICK (St Mary)   *see* Lordsbridge *Ely*
HARDWICK, EAST (St Stephen)   *see* Carleton and E Hardwick *Leeds*
HARDWICK-CUM-TUSMORE (St Mary)   *see* Shelswell *Ox*
HARDWICKE (Holy Trinity)   *see* Cusop w Blakemere, Bredwardine w Brobury etc *Heref*
HARDWICKE (St Mary the Virgin)   *see* Schorne *Ox*
HARDWICKE (St Nicholas) and Elmore w Longney *Glouc 2*   **P** *Adn Glouc and Ld Chan (alt)*   **V** A N JAMES
NSM G R W PARFITT
HAREBY (St Peter and St Paul)   *see* Bolingbroke Deanery *Linc*
HAREFIELD (St Mary the Virgin) *Lon 24*   **P** *The Hon J E F Newdegate*   **V** W M DAVIES
HAREHILLS (St Aidan)   *see* Leeds All So and St Aid *Leeds*
HAREHILLS (St Cyprian and St James)   *see* Leeds St Cypr Harehills *Leeds*
HARESCOMBE (St John the Baptist)   *see* Painswick, Sheepscombe, Cranham, The Edge etc *Glouc*

HARESFIELD (St Peter)   *see* Eastington, Frocester, Haresfield etc *Glouc*
HAREWOOD (Methodist Chapel)   *see* Collingham w Harewood *Leeds*
HARFORD (St Petroc)   *see* Ivybridge w Harford *Ex*
HARGRAVE (All Saints)   *see* Raunds, Hargrave, Ringstead and Stanwick *Pet*
HARGRAVE (St Edmund King and Martyr)   *see* Chevington w Hargrave, Chedburgh w Depden etc *St E*
HARGRAVE (St Peter) *Ches 5*   **P** *Bp*   **P-in-c** C H DEAKIN
HARKSTEAD (St Mary)   *see* Shoreline *St E*
HARLASTON (St Matthew)   *see* Mease Valley *Lich*
HARLAXTON Group, The (St Mary and St Peter) *Linc 20*   **P** *Bp, DBP, Sir Richard Welby Bt, D&C, and Duke of Rutland (jt)*   **P-in-c** K HANSON
HARLESCOTT (Holy Spirit) (Emmanuel) *Lich 20*   **P** *Bp*   **V** M H SALMON   **C** M J HEATH
HARLESDEN (All Souls) *Lon 21*   **P** *The Crown*
V M D MOORHEAD   **NSM** V A PIMENTA
HARLESTON (St Augustine)   *see* Gt Finborough w Onehouse, Harleston, Buxhall etc *St E*
HARLESTON (St John the Baptist)   *see* Redenhall w Scole *Nor*
HARLESTONE (St Andrew)   *see* Brington w Whilton and Norton etc *Pet*
HARLEY (St Mary)   *see* Wenlock *Heref*
HARLING, EAST (St Peter and St Paul) w West, Bridgham w Roudham, Larling, Brettenham and Rushford *Nor 11*
P *Ld Chan (1 turn), DBP, Sir Robin Nugent Bt, C D F Musker Esq, Major E H C Garnier, and Exors Sir John Musker (3 turns)*
OLM C D BROWN, L J FRY
HARLINGTON (Christ Church)   *see* W Hayes *Lon*
HARLINGTON (St Mary the Virgin) *St Alb 8*   **P** *Bp*
V S J WILLIAMS
HARLINGTON (St Peter and St Paul) *Lon 24*   **P** *Bp*
R M E SMITH
HARLOW (St Mary and St Hugh w St John the Baptist) *Chelmsf 4*   **P** *Simeon's Trustees and Bp (alt)*   **V** D J WELCH
HARLOW (St Mary Magdalene) *Chelmsf 4*   **P** *V Harlow St Mary and St Hugh etc*   **P-in-c** J W E RODLEY
NSM G R NEAVE
HARLOW GREEN (St Ninian) and Lamesley *Dur 12*   **P** *Bp*   **V** M WORTHINGTON   **NSM** S J LACKENBY
HARLOW Town Centre (St Paul) w Little Parndon *Chelmsf 4*
P *Patr Bd*   **TR** M J HARRIS   **TV** S J KNIGHT   **C** D TURNER
NSM B L SURTEES   **OLM** B C AYLETT
HARLSEY (St Oswald)   *see* Osmotherley w Harlsey and Ingleby Arncliffe *York*
HARLTON (Assumption of the Blessed Virgin Mary)   *see* Lordsbridge *Ely*
HARMANSWATER (St Paul)   *see* Bracknell *Ox*
HARMONDSWORTH (St Mary the Virgin) *Lon 24*   **P** *DBP*
NSM A O CHRISTIAN-IWUAGWU
HARMSTON (All Saints)   *see* Graffoe Gp *Linc*
HARNHAM (St George) (All Saints) *Sarum 13*   **P** *Bp (1 turn), V Britford (2 turns)*   **V** R M ROBERTS   **C** H S LEPPARD
NSM J G POPPLETON
HARNHILL (St Michael and All Angels)   *see* S Cotswolds *Glouc*
HAROLD HILL (St George) *Chelmsf 2*   **P** *Bp*   **V** S C MOORE
HAROLD HILL (St Paul) *Chelmsf 2*   **P** *Bp*   **V** R D MOUL
HAROLD WOOD (St Peter) *Chelmsf 2*   **P** *New Coll Ox*
V D P BANTING   **C** J C W CROUCHER, R A HUDSON
HAROME (St Saviour)   *see* Kirkdale w Harome, Nunnington and Pockley *York*
HARPENDEN (St John the Baptist) *St Alb 7*   **P** *DBP*
V N P ANDERSON
HARPENDEN (St Nicholas) (All Saints) *St Alb 7*   **P** *Ld Chan*
R D L STAMPS   **C** L L P WILLIAMS, R M LEACH, S L SPELLER
HARPFORD (St Gregory the Great)   *see* Ottery St Mary, Alfington, W Hill, Tipton etc *Ex*
HARPHAM (St John of Beverley)   *see* The Beacon *York*
HARPLEY (St Lawrence)   *see* Ashwicken w Leziate, Bawsey etc *Nor*
HARPOLE (All Saints)   *see* Bugbrooke, Harpole, Kislingbury etc *Pet*
HARPSDEN (St Margaret)   *see* Shiplake w Dunsden and Harpsden *Ox*
HARPSWELL (St Chad)   *see* Trentcliffe Gp *Linc*
HARPTREE, EAST (St Laurence) w WEST (Blessed Virgin Mary) and Hinton Blewett *B & W 9*   **P** *Duchy of Cornwall*
NSM C R LLEWELYN-EVANS
HARPUR HILL (St James)   *see* Buxton w Burbage and King Sterndale *Derby*
HARPURHEY (Christ Church) *Man 4*   **P** *Bp and Trustees (jt)*
R M J P MCGURK   **C** J A MITSON
HARPURHEY (St Stephen)   *see* Harpurhey *Man*

HARRABY (St Elisabeth) *Carl 3*   **P** *Bp*   **V** S L WICKS
HARRIETSHAM (St John the Baptist)   *see* Len Valley *Cant*
HARRINGAY (St Paul) *Lon 19*   **P** *Bp*   **P-in-c** T D PIKE
   C P J HENDERSON   **NSM** P G ATHERTON
HARRINGTON (St Mary) *Carl 7*   **P** Mrs E H S Thornely
   P-in-c J H POWLEY   **C** H J LOWE
HARRINGTON (St Mary)   *see* S Ormsby Gp *Linc*
HARRINGTON (St Peter and St Paul)   *see* Arthingworth,
   Harrington w Oxendon and E Farndon *Pet*
HARRINGWORTH (St John the Baptist)   *see* Lyddington,
   Bisbrooke, Caldecott, Glaston etc *Pet*
HARROGATE (St Luke's Church Centre)   *see* Kirby-on-the-Moor,
   Cundall w Norton-le-Clay etc *Leeds*
HARROGATE (St Mark) *Leeds 23*   **P** Peache Trustees
   V G W DONEGAN-CROSS   **C** A PATRICK, D J WATTS
HARROGATE (St Wilfrid) *Leeds 23*   **P** *Bp*
   TR G R WADDINGTON   **TV** G NEWTON
HARROGATE, HIGH (Christ Church) *Leeds 23*   **P** *Bp*
   V vacant
HARROGATE, HIGH (St Peter) *Leeds 23*   **P** Ch Patr Trust
   Hon C T J HURREN   **NSM** R T NOLAN, S E PEARCE
HARROLD (St Peter and All Saints) and Carlton w Chellington
   St Alb 13   **P** *Bp*   **R** vacant
HARROW (Holy Trinity)   *see* Wealdstone H Trin *Lon*
HARROW (St Peter)   *see* W Harrow *Lon*
HARROW GREEN (Holy Trinity and St Augustine of Hippo)
   see Leytonstone H Trin and St Aug Harrow Green *Chelmsf*
HARROW ON THE HILL (St Mary) *Lon 23*   **P** *Bp, Adn, and Hd*
   Master Harrow Sch (jt)   **V** vacant
HARROW ROAD (Emmanuel)   *see* W Kilburn St Luke and
   Harrow Road Em *Lon*
HARROW WEALD (All Saints) *Lon 23*   **P** *Bp, Adn, V Harrow*
   St Mary, and R Bushey (jt)   **V** J J MERCER   **NSM** P M WARD
HARROW WEALD (St Michael and All Angels) *Lon 23*   **P** *Bp*
   V J STOWELL
HARROW, NORTH (St Alban) *Lon 23*   **P** *Bp*   **V** J A FOSTER
   Hon C D J TUCK
HARROW, SOUTH (St Paul) *Lon 23*   **P** R St Bride Fleet Street w
   Bridewell and Trin Gough Square   **V** I P DOWSETT
   C B R LOVELL
HARROW, WEST (St Peter) *Lon 23*   **P** *Bp and Ch Patr Trust (jt)*
   V R E A GREEN   **NSM** M S SEEVARATNAM
HARROWBARROW (All Saints)   *see* Calstock *Truro*
HARROWBY (The Ascension)   *see* Grantham, Harrowby w
   Londonthorpe *Linc*
HARROWDEN, GREAT (All Saints) w LITTLE (St Mary the
   Virgin) and Orlingbury and Isham w Pytchley *Pet 6*
   P *Bp and Sir Philip Naylor-Leyland Bt (jt)*   **R** M J IRELAND
   C Q D CHANDLER
HARSTON (All Saints) w Hauxton and Newton *Ely 5*
   P *Bp (2 turns), D&C (1 turn)*   **P-in-c** B HADFIELD
HARSTON (St Michael and All Angels)   *see* High Framland Par
   Leic
HARSWELL (St Peter)   *see* Holme and Seaton Ross Gp *York*
HART (St Mary Magdalene) w Elwick Hall *Dur 3*   **P** *Bp and*
   DBP (alt)   **P-in-c** J BURBURY
HARTBURN (All Saints)   *see* Stockton St Pet *Dur*
HARTBURN (St Andrew)   *see* Bolam w Whalton and Hartburn
   w Meldon *Newc*
HARTCLIFFE (St Andrew)   *see* Bris St Andr Hartcliffe *Bris*
HARTEST (All Saints)   *see* Glemsford, Hartest w Boxted,
   Somerton etc *St E*
HARTFIELD (St Mary) w Coleman's Hatch *Chich 16*   **P** *Bp and*
   Earl De la Warr (jt)   **R** J A C SEAR
HARTFORD (All Saints) and Houghton w Wyton *Ely 10*   **P** *Bp*
   R E B ATLING   **NSM** A O'NEILL
HARTFORD (St John the Baptist) *Ches 6*   **P** Ch Soc Trust
   V M I A SMITH   **C** C P COLLINS, J T HUGHES   **NSM** G AGAR,
   P W HIGHTON
HARTHILL (All Hallows) and Thorpe Salvin *Sheff 5*   **P** *Bp*
   P-in-c G SCHOFIELD   **Hon C** J TRICKETT
HARTING (St Mary and St Gabriel) w Elsted and Treyford cum
   Didling *Chich 9*   **P** *Bp*   **R** M P MORTON
HARTINGTON (St Giles)   *see* Taddington, Chelmorton and
   Monyash etc *Derby*
HARTISMERE, NORTH *St E 14*   **P** MMCET, K Coll Cam, Bp, and
   DBP (jt)   **R** A R WATKINS   **NSM** V A MANNING
HARTISMERE, SOUTH *St E 14*   **P** *Bp, Comdr F P Brooke-Popham,*
   MMCET, Ch Soc Trust, SMF, and Lord Henniker (jt)
   P-in-c J C LALL   **NSM** E M GOODISON
HARTLAND (St Nectan)   *see* Parkham, Alwington, Buckland
   Brewer etc *Ex*
HARTLEBURY (St James) *Worc 8*   **P** *Bp*   **P-in-c** D J ARNOLD
HARTLEPOOL (Holy Trinity) (St Mark's Centre) *Dur 3*   **P** *Bp*
   V R HALL

HARTLEPOOL (St Aidan) (St Columba) *Dur 3*   **P** *Bp*
   P-in-c L J ROGERS   **C** G M SAMPSON
HARTLEPOOL (St Hilda) *Dur 3*   **P** *Bp*   **R** vacant
HARTLEPOOL (St Luke) *Dur 3*   **P** *Bp*   **P-in-c** L BUTLER
HARTLEPOOL (St Oswald) *Dur 3*   **P** *Bp*   **V** G BUTTERY
HARTLEPOOL (St Paul) *Dur 3*   **P** *Bp*   **V** R E MASSHEDAR
HARTLEY (All Saints)   *see* Fawkham and Hartley *Roch*
HARTLEY BROOK (Mission Hall)   *see* Becontree St Mary *Chelmsf*
HARTLEY MAUDITT (St Leonard)   *see* Northanger *Win*
HARTLEY WESPALL (St Mary)   *see* Sherfield-on-Loddon and
   Stratfield Saye etc *Win*
HARTLEY WINTNEY (St John the Evangelist), Elvetham,
   Winchfield and Dogmersfield *Win 5*   **P** *Bp and Sir Euan*
   Anstruther-Gough-Calthorpe Bt (jt)   **V** M S TANNER
   NSM M J EAST
HARTLEY, NEW (St Michael and All Angels)   *see* Delaval *Newc*
HARTLIP (St Michael and All Angels)   *see* The Six *Cant*
HARTON *York 6*   **P** Abp and D&C Dur (1 turn) Abp (1 turn)
   R C L WINGFIELD
HARTON (St Peter) (St Lawrence) *Dur 15*   **P** D&C
   V vacant
HARTPLAIN (not known) *Portsm 5*   **P** DBP
   Dn-in-c K A MACFARLANE
HARTPURY (St Mary the Virgin)   *see* Ashleworth, Corse,
   Hartpury, Hasfield etc *Glouc*
HARTSHEAD (St Peter), Hightown, Roberttown and Scholes
   Leeds 7   **P** V Birstall, TR Dewsbury, and Bp (alt)
   V E C R BURGE   **NSM** S M HOLT, S P ROCHELL   **OLM** J C LEE
HARTSHILL (Holy Trinity) and Galley Common *Cov 5*   **P** Ch
   Patr Trust and Bp (jt)   **P-in-c** H D BARNES   **C** M J BRANDSMA
HARTSHILL (Holy Trinity), Penkhull and Trent Vale *Lich 12*
   P Bp and R Stoke-upon-Trent (jt)   **R** C J RUSHTON
HARTSHORNE (St Peter) and Bretby *Derby 16*   **P** Bp and
   MMCET (jt)   **C** G P RUTTER
HARTWELL (St John the Baptist)   *see* Salcey *Pet*
HARTWITH (St Jude)   *see* Dacre w Hartwith and Darley w
   Thornthwaite *Leeds*
HARTY (St Thomas Apostle)   *see* Eastchurch w Leysdown and
   Harty *Cant*
HARVINGTON (St James)   *see* Church Lench w Rous Lench and
   Abbots Morton etc *Worc*
HARWELL (St Matthew) w Chilton *Ox 26*   **P** DBP and CPAS (jt)
   R J L MOBEY   **NSM** J RADFORD   **OLM** P M ROLLS
HARWICH PENINSULA, The (St Nicholas) *Chelmsf 22*   **P** Patr
   Bd   **TR** P E MANN   **TV** R TALLOWIN
   C A L TIESEMA-SAMSOM, G D A THORBURN
   NSM S J WINNEY
HARWOOD (Christ Church) *Man 12*   **P** DBP   **V** W L OLIVER
   C J E MCKEE   **OLM** H MOLLOY
HARWOOD DALE (St Margaret)   *see* Hackness w Harwood Dale
   York
HARWOOD, GREAT (St Bartholomew) St John *Blackb 7*
   P Patr Bd   **V** C R PENFOLD   **C** J M KRAWIEC
HARWORTH (All Saints) *S'well 1*   **P** Sir John Whitaker Bt
   P-in-c L B VASEY-SAUNDERS
HASBURY (St Margaret)   *see* Halas *Worc*
HASCOMBE (St Peter)   *see* Dunsfold and Hascombe *Guildf*
HASELBECH (St Michael)   *see* Clipston w Naseby and
   Haselbech w Kelmarsh *Pet*
HASELBURY PLUCKNETT (St Michael and All Angels)
   see Wulfric Benefice *B & W*
HASELEY (St Mary)   *see* Hatton w Haseley, Rowington w
   Lowsonford etc *Cov*
HASELEY, GREAT (St Peter)   *see* Gt w Lt Milton and Gt Haseley
   Ox
HASELOR (St Mary and All Saints)   *see* Alcester Minster *Cov*
HASELTON (St Andrew)   *see* Northleach w Hampnett and
   Farmington etc *Glouc*
HASFIELD (St Mary)   *see* Ashleworth, Corse, Hartpury, Hasfield
   etc *Glouc*
HASKETON (St Andrew)   *see* Carlford *St E*
HASLAND (St Paul) *Derby 5*   **P** V Chesterfield
   R M R AINSCOUGH
HASLEMERE (St Bartholomew) (St Christopher) and
   Grayswood *Guildf 4*   **P** Ld Chan   **P-in-c** M E BOWDEN
   C C O IWUAGWU   **NSM** B A STEELE-PERKINS, C O IWUAGWU
   OLM F J GWYNN
HASLINGDEN (St James) w Grane and Stonefold *Blackb 1*
   P Bp and Hulme Trustees (jt)   **NSM** D ALLSOP
HASLINGDEN (St Peter)   *see* Laneside *Blackb*
HASLINGDEN (St Thomas)   *see* Musbury *Blackb*
HASLINGFIELD (All Saints)   *see* Lordsbridge *Ely*
HASLINGTON (St Matthew) w Crewe Green St Michael
   Ches 15   **P** Bp   **V** J L WALKER
HASSALL GREEN (St Philip)   *see* Sandbach Heath w Wheelock
   Ches

HASSINGHAM (St Mary)   *see* Burlingham St Edmund w
  Lingwood, Strumpshaw etc *Nor*

HASTINGS (Christ Church and St Andrew)   *see* Blacklands
  Hastings Ch Ch and St Andr *Chich*

HASTINGS (Emmanuel and St Mary in the Castle) *Chich* 15
  P *MMCET and Hyndman Trustees (alt)*   **V** M G LANE
  NSM R BROWNING

HASTINGS (Holy Trinity) *Chich* 15   **P** *Bp*
  P-in-c S G D LARKIN

HASTINGS (St Clement) (All Saints) *Chich* 15   **P** *Bp*
  P-in-c R L FEATHERSTONE

HASTINGS (St Peter and St Paul)   *see* Hollington St Jo *Chich*

HASWELL (St Paul), Shotton and Thornley *Dur* 2   **P** *Bp*
  P-in-c A L BROOKER   **NSM** A STAINSBY

HATCH BEAUCHAMP (St John the Baptist)   *see* Beercrocombe w
  Curry Mallet, Hatch Beauchamp etc *B & W*

HATCH END (St Anselm) *Lon* 23   **P** *Bp*   **V** C PEARCE

HATCH WARREN AND BEGGARWOOD (Immanuel) *Win* 4
  P *Bp*   **V** M E SMITH

HATCH, WEST (St Andrew)   *see* Beercrocombe w Curry Mallet,
  Hatch Beauchamp etc *B & W*

HATCHAM (St Catherine) *S'wark* 2   **P** *Haberdashers' Co*
  V S A JAMES   **NSM** J ELLIOTT

HATCHAM (St James) (St George) (St Michael) *S'wark* 2
  P *Ch Patr Soc*   **V** N D R NICHOLLS   **C** A C REES

HATCHAM PARK (All Saints) *S'wark* 2   **P** *Hyndman Trustees*
  (2 turns), Haberdashers' Co (1 turn)   **V** O J BEAMENT
  OLM J FRANCIS

HATCLIFFE (St Mary)   *see* Wolds Gateway Group *Linc*

HATFIELD (St Lawrence) *Sheff* 10   **P** *Bp*
  V E A TURNER-LOISEL   **NSM** J BARKER

HATFIELD (St Leonard)   *see* Leominster *Heref*

HATFIELD BROAD OAK (St Mary the Virgin) and Bush End
  Chelmsf 4   **P** *Bp*   **V** N A WORMELL

HATFIELD HEATH (Holy Trinity) and Sheering *Chelmsf* 4
  P *Ch Ch Ox and V Hatfield Broad Oak (alt)*   **R** *vacant*

HATFIELD HYDE (St Mary Magdalene) *St Alb* 18   **P** *Marquess*
  of Salisbury   **V** A A LAUCKNER

HATFIELD PEVEREL (St Andrew) w Ulting *Chelmsf* 24   **P** *Bp*
  V S R NORTHFIELD   **OLM** D R CLARK-MAYERS

HATHERDEN (Christ Church)   *see* Pastrow *Win*

HATHERLEIGH (St John the Baptist)   *see* Okehampton,
  Inwardleigh, Belstone, Sourton etc *Ex*

HATHERN (St Peter and St Paul)   *see* Kegworth, Hathern, Long
  Whatton, Diseworth etc *Leic*

HATHEROP (St Nicholas)   *see* S Cotswolds *Glouc*

**HATHERSAGE (St Michael and All Angels) w Bamford and
Derwent, and Grindleford** *Derby* 2   **P** *Duke of Devonshire,
Earl Temple, and A C H Barnes Esq (jt)*   **P-in-c** J A DAVIS

HATHERTON (St Saviour) *Lich* 2   **P** *A R W Littleton Esq*
  V P O HART   **C** W E HASSALL

HATTERS LANE (St Andrew)   *see* High Wycombe *Ox*

HATTERSLEY (St Barnabas) *Ches* 14   **P** *Bp*
  P-in-c L A ATKINS

HATTON (All Saints) *Derby* 14   **P** *Bp and N J M Spurrier Esq (jt)*
  P-in-c A L MARTIN

**HATTON (Holy Trinity) w Haseley, Rowington w Lowsonford
and Honiley and Wroxall** *Cov* 4   **P** *Bp*   **R** K J MOBBERLEY
  NSM S MOBBERLEY

HATTON (St Stephen)   *see* Hemingby Gp *Linc*

HAUGH (St Leonard)   *see* S Ormsby Gp *Linc*

**HAUGHLEY (St Mary the Virgin) w Wetherden and
Stowupland** *St E* 6   **P** *Ld Chan, Bp, and DBP (by turn)*
  V D J SWALES   **C** C A HOOD, M A CROSSMAN

HAUGHTON (St Anne) *Man* 13   **P** *DBP*
  P-in-c A S MITCHELL   **C** E M POPE, M HOWARTH, P R DIXON

HAUGHTON (St Chad)   *see* Whittington and W Felton w
  Haughton *Lich*

HAUGHTON (St Giles)   *see* Bradeley, Church Eaton,
  Derrington and Haughton *Lich*

HAUGHTON (St Mary the Virgin) *Man* 13   **P** *Bp*   **R** *vacant*

HAUGHTON LE SKERNE (St Andrew) *Dur* 8   **P** *Bp*
  R M R EAST   **NSM** S CHEW

HAUTBOIS, GREAT (Holy Trinity)   *see* Coltishall w Gt Hautbois,
  Frettenham etc *Nor*

HAUXTON (St Edmund)   *see* Harston w Hauxton and Newton
  Ely

HAUXWELL (St Oswald)   *see* Spennithorne w Finghall and
  Hauxwell *Leeds*

HAVANT (St Faith) *Portsm* 5   **P** *Bp*   **P-in-c** T P KENNAR

HAVEN Group, The *Linc* 21   **P** *Bp, D&C, Simeon's Trustees, and
DBP (2 tuns), Prime-Min (1 turn)*   **V** C P ROBERTSON

HAVEN, THE Conventional District *Chich* 14
  Min J B P BROOK

HAVEN, THE Conventional District *Chich* 16
  Min J B P BROOK

HAVENSTREET (St Peter) *Portsm* 7   **P** *SMF*   **NSM** V J HARDS

HAVERHILL (St Mary the Virgin) w Withersfield *St E* 8   **P** *Bp*
  V I M FINN

HAVERIGG (St Luke)   *see* Millom *Carl*

HAVERING-ATTE-BOWER (St John)   *see* Collier Row St Jas and
  Havering-atte-Bower *Chelmsf*

HAVERINGLAND (St Peter)   *see* Cawston w Booton and
  Brandiston etc *Nor*

HAVERSHAM (St Mary)   *see* Lamp *Ox*

HAVERTHWAITE (St Anne)   *see* Cartmel Peninsula *Carl*

HAWBUSH (St Mary)   *see* Brierley Hill *Worc*

HAWES (St Margaret)   *see* Upper Wensleydale *Leeds*

HAWES SIDE (St Christopher) and Marton Moss St Nicholas
  Blackb 8   **P** *Bp*   **V** G PIPER   **OLM** S TOMLINSON

HAWKCHURCH (St John the Baptist)   *see* Golden Cap Team
  Sarum

HAWKEDON (St Mary)   *see* Chevington w Hargrave,
  Chedburgh w Depden etc *St E*

HAWKESBURY (St Mary)   *see* Boxwell, Leighterton, Didmarton,
  Oldbury etc *Glouc*

HAWKHURST (St Laurance) *Cant* 11   **P** *Ch Ch Ox*
  V R G DREYER

HAWKINGE (St Luke) *Cant* 8   **P** *Abp*   **P-in-c** R P GRINSELL

HAWKLEY (St Peter and St Paul)   *see* Greatham w Empshott and
  Hawkley w Prior's Dean *Portsm*

HAWKRIDGE (St Giles)   *see* Exmoor *B & W*

HAWKSHAW (St Mary)   *see* Holcombe and Hawkshaw *Man*

**HAWKSHEAD (St Michael and All Angels) and Low Wray w
Sawrey and Rusland and Satterthwaite** *Carl* 11   **P** *Bp*
  V J S DIXON   **NSM** N F HALLAM

HAWKSWOOD (Emmanuel)   *see* Hailsham *Chich*

HAWKSWORTH (St Mary and All Saints)   *see* Whatton w
  Aslockton, Hawksworth, Scarrington etc *S'well*

HAWKSWORTH WOOD (St Mary)   *see* Abbeylands *Leeds*

HAWKWELL (Emmanuel) (St Mary the Virgin) *Chelmsf* 14
  P *CPAS*   **R** P H SMITH

HAWLEY (Holy Trinity) *Guildf* 1   **P** *Keble Coll Ox*
  V M W NEALE

HAWLEY, SOUTH (All Saints)   *see* Hawley H Trin *Guildf*

HAWLING (St Edward)   *see* Sevenhampton w Charlton Abbots,
  Hawling etc *Glouc*

HAWNBY (All Saints)   *see* Upper Ryedale *York*

**HAWORTH (St Michael and All Angels) and Cross Roads cum
Lees** *Leeds* 5   **P** *Bp, V Bradf, and Haworth Ch Lands Trust (jt)*
  R P MAYO-SMITH   **NSM** J ROBERTS, P S WILSON

HAWRIDGE (St Mary) w Cholesbury and St Leonard *Ox* 17
  P *Bp, Chpl Trust, and Neale's Charity (jt)*   **R** D J BURGESS
  NSM P C SOUNDY

HAWSKER (All Saints)   *see* Fylingdales and Hawsker cum
  Stainsacre *York*

HAWSTEAD (All Saints)   *see* St Edm Way *St E*

HAWTHORN (St Michael and All Angels) and Murton *Dur* 2
  P *D&C and I Pemberton Esq (alt)*   **R** A MILNE

HAWTON (All Saints)   *see* Farndon w Thorpe, Hawton and
  Cotham *S'well*

HAXBY (St Mary) and Wigginton *York* 7   **P** *Abp and Ld Chan
(alt)*   **R** K D JACKSON   **NSM** P A JACKSON

HAXEY (St Nicholas) *Linc* 1   **P** *Ld Chan*   **V** J N GREEN

HAY MILL (St Cyprian)   *see* Yardley St Cypr Hay Mill *Birm*

HAYDOCK (St James) *Liv* 15   **P** *R Ashton-in-Makerfield*
  V R MIDDLETON   **NSM** G J HARDMAN, I C WYNNE

HAYDOCK (St Mark) *Liv* 10   **P** *MMCET*   **V** N J HAIGH
  C I R HOPKINS, M H ROBERTS

HAYDON BRIDGE (St Cuthbert) and Beltingham w Henshaw
  Newc 10   **P** *Bp and V Haltwhistle and Greenhead (jt)*
  V B H CARTER

HAYDON WICK (St John) *Bris* 7   **P** *CPAS*   **V** R W ADAMS
  NSM S A ROBERTSON

HAYES (St Anselm) *Lon* 24   **P** *Bp*   **V** G N BORROWDALE

HAYES (St Edmund of Canterbury) *Lon* 24   **P** *Bp*
  V S M MORING

HAYES (St Mary the Virgin) *Roch* 14   **P** *D&C*   **R** N JOHN
  NSM M HALLAM

HAYES (St Mary) *Lon* 24   **P** *Keble Coll Ox*
  R P L DE S HOMEWOOD

HAYES, NORTH (St Nicholas) *Lon* 24   **P** *Bp and Keble Coll Ox
(jt)*   **V** J A EVANS

HAYES, WEST (Christ Church) (St Jerome) *Lon* 24   **P** *Bp and
Hyndman Trustees (jt)*   **V** I W JONES

HAYFIELD (St Matthew) and Chinley w Buxworth *Derby* 6
  P *Bp and Resident Freeholders (jt)*   **V** H A EDGERTON

HAYLE (St Elwyn)   *see* Godrevy *Truro*

HAYLING ISLAND (St Andrew) Eastoke *Portsm* 5   **P** *DBP*
  C T R WOOD

HAYLING, NORTH (St Peter) *Portsm* 5   **P** *DBP*   **V** *vacant*

HAYLING, SOUTH (St Mary) *Portsm* 5   **P** *DBP*   **V** *vacant*

HAYNES (Mission Room)   *see* Campton, Clophill and Haynes
St Alb
HAYNES (St Mary) *as above*
HAYTON (St James)   *see* Aspatria w Hayton and Gilcrux *Carl*
HAYTON (St Martin)   *see* Londesborough Wold *York*
HAYTON (St Mary Magdalene)   *see* Eden, Gelt and Irthing
Carl
HAYTON (St Peter)   *see* Retford Area *S'well*
HAYWARDS HEATH (Church of the Ascension) *Chich 5*   **P** *Bp*
V N TIPPLE
HAYWARDS HEATH (Church of the Presentation)   *see* Haywards
Heath St Wilfrid *Chich*
HAYWARDS HEATH (St Richard) *Chich 5*   **P** *Bp*
P-in-c D S G WEAVER   **Hon C** L D POODHUN
HAYWARDS HEATH (St Wilfrid) (Church of the Presentation)
Chich 5   **P** *Bp*   **V** R C W SMITH   **NSM** D C YOUNG,
J M ELLIOTT
HAYWOOD, GREAT (St Stephen)   *see* Abbots Bromley,
Blithfield, Colton, Colwich etc *Lich*
**HAZELBURY BRYAN (St Mary and St James) and the Hillside
Parishes** *Sarum 5*   **P** *Duke of Northumberland (2 turns), DBP, G
A L-F Pitt-Rivers Esq, Exors F N Kent Esq, and Bp (1 turn each)*
P-in-c D R R SEYMOUR   **NSM** D GINGELL
HAZELWELL (St Mary Magdalen) *Birm 5*   **P** *Bp*
V M R F SAUNDERS
HAZELWOOD (St John the Evangelist), Holbrook and Milford
Derby 11   **P** *Bp and DBP (jt)*   **V** *vacant*
HAZLEMERE (Holy Trinity) *Ox 18*   **P** *Peache Trustees*
V P C COLLIER   **C** D W E MEERING, M J MEARDON
HEACHAM (St Mary) and Snettisham *Nor 16*   **P** *Bp and CPAS
(jt)*   **R** *vacant*
HEADBOURNE WORTHY (St Swithun) *Win 7*   **P** *Univ Coll Ox
and Lord Northbrook (alt)*   **NSM** E CHASE
HEADCORN (St Peter and St Paul) and The Suttons *Cant 11*
P *Abp*   **V** F A HASKETT
**HEADINGLEY Team Ministry (St Michael and All Angels)
(St Chad)** *Leeds 16*   **P** *Patr Bd*   **TR** M A WHATMOUGH
Hon C C BARRETT   **NSM** D W PEAT, K WARD
HEADINGTON (St Andrew) *Ox 1*   **P** *Keble Coll Ox*
V D W MCFARLAND
HEADINGTON (St Mary) *Ox 1*   **P** *Bp*   **V** *vacant*
HEADINGTON QUARRY (Holy Trinity) *Ox 1*   **P** *Bp*
V T J STEAD   **C** J E DE G STICKINGS
HEADLESS CROSS (St Luke)   *see* Redditch Ch the K *Worc*
HEADLEY (All Saints) *Guildf 3*   **P** *Qu Coll Ox*
P-in-c A E BARTON   **NSM** H E KEMPSTER
HEADLEY (St Mary the Virgin) w Box Hill (St Andrew) *Guildf 9*
P *Bp*   **P-in-c** L HARKNETT
HEADLEY (St Peter)   *see* Kingsclere and Ashford Hill w
Headley *Win*
HEADON (St Peter)   *see* Retford Area *S'well*
HEADSTONE (St George) *Lon 23*   **P** *Bp*   **V** S R KEEBLE
HEAGE (St Luke)   *see* Ambergate and Heage *Derby*
HEALAUGH (St John the Baptist)   *see* Rural Ainsty *York*
HEALD GREEN (St Catherine) *Ches 17*   **P** *Bp*   **V** J F AMBROSE
HEALEY (Christ Church)   *see* Hamer and Healey *Man*
HEALEY (St John)   *see* Slaley, Healey and Whittonstall *Newc*
HEALEY (St Paul)   *see* Masham and Healey *Leeds*
HEALING (St Peter and St Paul)   *see* Wolds Gateway Group *Linc*
HEAMOOR (St Thomas)   *see* Gulval and Madron *Truro*
HEANOR (St Laurence) *Derby 12*   **P** *Wright Trustees*
V *vacant*
**HEANTON PUNCHARDON (St Augustine), Marwood and
West Down** *Ex 14*   **P** *Bp, CPAS, and St Jo Coll Cam (jt)*
R I M ROBERTSON
HEAP BRIDGE (St Thomas and St George)   *see* Heywood
St Marg and Heap Bridge *Man*
HEAPEY (St Barnabas) and Withnell *Blackb 4*   **P** *V Leyland*
V A F HOGARTH
HEAPHAM (All Saints)   *see* Lea Gp *Linc*
HEART OF EDEN *Carl 1*   **P** *Patr Bd*   **TR** S A LUNN
C J GRIFFITHS   **NSM** D J PATTIMORE, K PATTIMORE
HEART OF ENGLAND, The *Cov 7*   **P** *Bp, Peache Trustees, and
Dioc Trustees (jt)*   **R** P A WALKER   **C** D P BENSKIN,
R E WALKER   **NSM** K GRUMBALL, S M HENWOOD
HEATH (All Saints) *Derby 5*   **P** *Duke of Devonshire and Simeon's
Trustees (jt)*   **NSM** P M BAINBRIDGE
HEATH (Mission Church)   *see* Uttoxeter Area *Lich*
HEATH AND REACH (St Leonard)   *see* Ouzel Valley *St Alb*
HEATH HAYES (St John) *Lich 3*   **P** *Bp and D&C (jt)*
V D G WATKIN   **NSM** D G WATKIN, R J HEATH
HEATH TOWN (Holy Trinity) *Lich 28*   **P** *CPAS*
V R C MERRICK   **Hon C** P E V GOLDRING
HEATH, LITTLE (Christ Church) *St Alb 14*   **P** *Ch Patr Trust*
V S P REES   **C** M J GRAHAM   **NSM** R H WIKNER
HEATH, THE (not known)   *see* Ludlow *Heref*

HEATHER (St John the Baptist)   *see* Ibstock w Heather *Leic*
HEATHERLANDS (St John the Evangelist) *Sarum 7*   **P** *MMCET*
V D G M PRICE   **C** P D HOMDEN, T J FUHRI
HEATHERYCLEUGH (St Thomas)   *see* Upper Weardale *Dur*
HEATHFIELD (All Saints) *Chich 13*   **P** *Bp*   **V** D A GUEST
HEATHFIELD (St Catherine)   *see* Bovey Tracey St Jo w
Heathfield *Ex*
HEATHFIELD (St John the Baptist)   *see* Deane Vale *B & W*
HEATHFIELD (St Richard) *Chich 13*   **P** *Bp*   **P-in-c** P M JONES
HEATON (Christ Church) w Halliwell St Margaret *Man 7*
P *Patr Bd*   **V** J FRENCH
HEATON (St Barnabas) *Leeds 1*   **P** *Trustees*
P-in-c C MACLAREN   **NSM** J F BUTLER, M C FISHER
HEATON (St Gabriel)   *see* Newc St Gabr *Newc*
HEATON (St Martin) *Leeds 1*   **P** *Bp*   **P-in-c** C MACLAREN
NSM J F BUTLER
HEATON CHAPEL (St Thomas)   *see* Heatons *Man*
HEATON MERSEY (St John the Baptist) *as above*
HEATON MOOR (St Paul) *as above*
HEATON NORRIS (Christ w All Saints) *as above*
HEATON REDDISH (St Mary) *Man 2*   **P** *Trustees*
P-in-c C E LARSEN   **NSM** P P ROBINSON
HEATON, HIGH (St Francis)   *see* Newc St Fran *Newc*
HEATONS *Man 2*   **P** *Patr Bd (4 turns), Prime Min (1 turn)*
TR M H MAXWELL   **TV** D BROWNHILL, H T SCANLAN
NSM J YOUNG, O MOLUDY   **OLM** J M BUTTERWORTH
**HEAVITREE (St Michael and All Angels) (St Lawrence)
(St Loye) and St Mary Steps** *Ex 3*   **P** *Patr Bd*
TR R H S EASTOE   **TV** J F SEWARD, P R MORRELL
C P J MARCH
HEBBURN (St Cuthbert) (St Oswald) *Dur 15*   **P** *Prime Min
and TR Jarrow (alt)*   **V** A MAXWELL
HEBBURN (St John) *Dur 15*   **P** *Bp*   **P-in-c** D T OSMAN
C I M SOMASUNDRAM
HEBDEN (St Peter)   *see* Linton in Craven *Leeds*
HEBDEN BRIDGE (St James) and Heptonstall *Leeds 9*   **P** *V
Halifax*   **V** H PASK
HECK (St John the Baptist)   *see* Gt Snaith *Sheff*
HECKFIELD (St Michael)   *see* Whitewater *Win*
**HECKINGTON (St Andrew) and Helpringham Group of
Parishes, The** *Linc 14*   **P** *Bp, D&C, DBP, and the Rt Revd A C
Foottit (1 turn), Ld Chan (1 turn)*   **R** C R HARRINGTON
**HECKMONDWIKE (All Souls) (St James) (w Norristhorpe)
and Liversedge** *Leeds 7*   **P** *V Birstall*   **NSM** S M HOLT
OLM J C LEE
HEDDINGTON (St Andrew)   *see* Oldbury *Sarum*
HEDDON-ON-THE-WALL (St Andrew) *Newc 9*   **P** *Ld Chan*
P-in-c A D MCCARTAN
HEDENHAM (St Peter)   *see* Ditchingham, Hedenham, Broome,
Earsham etc *Nor*
HEDGE END (St John the Evangelist) *Win 10*   **P** *Bp*
V C M ROWBERRY   **NSM** K ROWBERRY, S E LITJENS
HEDGE END (St Luke) *Win 10*   **P** *Bp*   **P-in-c** F C GIBBS
C A M CRANE   **NSM** J WILLIAMS
HEDGE END (St Luke)   *see* Hedge End St Luke *Win*
HEDGERLEY (St Mary the Virgin)   *see* Farnham Royal w
Hedgerley *Ox*
HEDNESFORD (St Peter) *Lich 3*   **P** *Bp*   **V** P KELLY
C A C T KELLY
HEDON (St Augustine), Paull, Sproatley and Preston in
Holderness *York 12*   **P** *Abp*   **R** J J G WRIGHT
HEDSOR (St Nicholas) and Bourne End *Ox 18*   **P** *Bp*
R J V BINNS
HEDWORTH (St Nicholas)   *see* The Boldons *Dur*
HEELEY (Christ Church) *Sheff 1*   **P** *Prime Min*   **V** D W FRY
HEENE (St Botolph) *Chich 4*   **P** *D&C*   **R** *vacant*
HEIGHAM (Holy Trinity) *Nor 3*   **P** *Ch Trust Fund Trust*
R A M STRANGE   **C** W J WARREN
HEIGHAM (St Barnabas) (St Bartholomew) *Nor 3*   **P** *Bp*
V *vacant*
HEIGHAM (St Thomas) *Nor 3*   **P** *Bp*   **P-in-c** I H DYBLE
C D Z LLOYD, E C LAND
**HEIGHINGTON (St Michael) and Darlington St Matthew and
St Luke** *Dur 8*   **P** *D&C and Bp (alt)*   **V** L M SCOTT
C B A HILTON   **NSM** R A DAWSON
HEIGHTINGTON (St Giles)   *see* Mamble w Bayton, Rock w
Heightington etc *Worc*
HELHOUGHTON (All Saints)   *see* E w W Rudham, Helhoughton
etc *Nor*
HELIONS BUMPSTEAD (St Andrew)   *see* Two Rivers *Chelmsf*
HELLAND (St Helena)   *see* Blisland w Temple, St Breward and
Helland *Truro*
HELLESDON (St Mary) (St Paul and St Michael) *Nor 2*   **P** *Bp*
V A ALDER
HELLIDON (St John the Baptist)   *see* Daventry, Ashby
St Ledgers, Braunston etc *Pet*

HELLIFIELD (St Aidan) and Long Preston *Leeds 21*   **P** *Ch Ch Ox*   **V** S M STOBART

HELLINGLY (St Peter and St Paul) and Upper Dicker *Chich 13*   **P** *Abp and Bp (jt)*   **V** D M FAREY

HELMDON (St Mary Magdalene) *see Astwell Gp Pet*

HELME (Christ Church) *see Meltham Leeds*

HELMINGHAM (St Mary) *see Debenham and Helmingham St E*

HELMSLEY (All Saints) *York 19*   **P** *The Hon Jake Duncombe*   **V** T J ROBINSON   **NSM** L GROVE

HELMSLEY, UPPER (St Peter) *see Harton York*

HELPERTHORPE (St Peter) *see Weaverthorpe w Helperthorpe, Luttons Ambo etc York*

HELPRINGHAM (St Andrew) *see Heckington and Helpringham Gp Linc*

HELPSTON (St Botolph) *see Etton w Helpston and Maxey Pet*

HELSBY (St Paul) and Dunham-on-the-Hill *Ches 3*   **P** *Bp*   **V** G H GREEN

HELSINGTON (St John) *see Underbarrow w Helsington Carl*

HELSTON (St Michael) and Wendron *Truro 4*   **P** *Patr Bd*   **TR** D G MILLER   **C** J BRADBURY   **OLM** D NOAKES

HEMBLINGTON (All Saints) *see Blofield Nor*

HEMEL HEMPSTEAD (Holy Trinity) Leverstock Green *see Langelei St Alb*

HEMEL HEMPSTEAD (St Benedict) Bennetts End *as above*

HEMEL HEMPSTEAD (St Mary) *St Alb 2*   **P** *Ld Chan*   **TR** J C HILL   **TV** A S JANES, P J STEVENSON, R W GRAHAM   **NSM** L G SIMPSON-GRAY, L GEOGHEGAN, T J BARTON

HEMEL HEMPSTEAD (St Mary) Apsley End *see Langelei St Alb*

HEMINGBROUGH (St Mary the Virgin) *see Riccall, Barlby and Hemingbrough York*

HEMINGBY Group, The (St Margaret) *Linc 13*   **P** *Bp, DBP, Keble Coll Ox (2 turns), and Ld Chan (1 turn)*   **R** P J FRASER

HEMINGFORD ABBOTS (St Margaret of Antioch) *Ely 10*   **P** *Lord Hemingford*   **P-in-c** P H CUNLIFFE   **NSM** J A BOLTON

HEMINGFORD GREY (St James) *Ely 10*   **P** *CPAS*   **V** P H CUNLIFFE   **C** C E PARR, D J PARR   **NSM** J A BOLTON

HEMINGSTONE (St Gregory) *see Coddenham w Gosbeck and Hemingstone w Henley St E*

HEMINGTON (Blessed Virgin Mary) *see Hardington Vale B & W*

HEMINGTON (St Peter and St Paul) *see Barnwell, Hemington, Luddington in the Brook etc Pet*

HEMLEY (All Saints) *see Waldringfield w Hemley and Newbourn St E*

HEMLINGTON (St Timothy) *York 20*   **P** *Abp*   **V** R A DESICS

HEMPNALL (St Margaret) *Nor 5*   **P** *Ld Chan (1 turn), Patr Bd (5 turns)*   **TR** M M KINGSTON   **TV** E N BILLETT

HEMPSTEAD (All Saints) *see Barningham w Matlaske w Baconsthorpe etc Nor*

HEMPSTEAD (All Saints) *see S Gillingham Roch*

HEMPSTEAD (St Andrew) *see The Sampfords and Radwinter w Hempstead Chelmsf*

HEMPSTEAD (St Andrew) *see Bacton, Happisburgh, Hempstead w Eccles etc Nor*

HEMPSTED (St Swithun) *see Glouc City and Hempsted Glouc*

HEMPTON (Holy Trinity) and Pudding Norton *Nor 15*   **P** *The Crown*   **P-in-c** P LOCKETT

HEMPTON (St John the Evangelist) *see Deddington w Barford, Clifton and Hempton Ox*

HEMSBY (St Mary) *see Flegg Coastal Benefice Nor*

HEMSWELL (All Saints) *see Trentcliffe Gp Linc*

HEMSWORTH (St Helen) *Leeds 19*   **P** *Bp*   **R** R W HART

HEMYOCK (St Mary) w Culm Davy, Clayhidon and Culmstock *Ex 7*   **P** *DBP, SMF, and D&C (jt)*   **P-in-c** D A BURTON

HENBURY (St Mary the Virgin) *Bris 2*   **P** *Lord Middleton (1 turn), Bp (3 turns)*   **V** D P LLOYD

HENBURY (St Thomas) *see Macclesfield St Jo w Henbury Ches*

HENDON (All Saints) Childs Hill *Lon 15*   **P** *Bp*   **V** J P WAINWRIGHT

HENDON (St Alphage) *Lon 15*   **P** *Bp*   **V** H D MOORE   **C** A D GARNER

HENDON (St Ignatius) *Dur 1*   **P** *Bp*   **R** A C JONES

HENDON (St Mary) (Christ Church) *Lon 15*   **P** *Bp*   **V** T G CLEMENT   **C** D D R MASON

HENDON (St Paul) Mill Hill *Lon 15*   **P** *Bp*   **V** A J SHAW   **C** J E LOWE

HENDON, WEST (St John) *Lon 15*   **P** *Bp*   **V** J E I HAWKINS   **NSM** T J HALTON

HENDRED, EAST (St Augustine of Canterbury) *see Wantage Downs Ox*

HENDRED, WEST (Holy Trinity) *as above*

HENFIELD (St Peter) w Shermanbury and Woodmancote *Chich 8*   **P** *Bp*   **R** P S J DOICK   **C** P D O'CONNELL   **NSM** C M BENNETT

HENGROVE (Christ Church) *Bris 1*   **P** *Bp and Simeon's Trustees (alt)*   **P-in-c** J M HANCOCK

HENHAM (St Mary the Virgin) and Elsenham w Ugley *Chelmsf 20*   **P** *Ch Hosp, Ch Soc Trust, and Bp (jt)*   **V** G TOWNSEND

HENLEAZE (St Peter) *Bris 2*   **P** *Bp*   **V** C M PILGRIM   **C** I G MCCOLL

HENLEY (St Peter) *see Coddenham w Gosbeck and Hemingstone w Henley St E*

HENLEY IN ARDEN (St John the Baptist) *see Beaudesert and Henley-in-Arden w Ullenhall Cov*

HENLEY-ON-THAMES (Holy Trinity) *Ox 24*   **P** *R Rotherfield Greys St Nich*   **V** D R B CARTER

HENLEY-ON-THAMES (St Mary the Virgin) w Remenham *Ox 24*   **P** *Bp and Jes Coll Ox (jt)*   **R** M R GRIFFITHS

HENLOW (St Mary the Virgin) and Langford *St Alb 8*   **P** *Ld Chan*   **P-in-c** S A GROOM

HENNOCK (St Mary) *see Bovey Tracey SS Pet, Paul and Thos w Hennock Ex*

HENNY, GREAT (St Mary) *see N Hinckford Chelmsf*

HENSALL (St Paul) *see Gt Snaith Sheff*

HENSHAW (All Hallows) *see Haydon Bridge and Beltingham w Henshaw Newc*

HENSINGHAM (St John) (Keekle Mission) *Carl 5*   **P** *Trustees*   **V** F T PEARSON   **C** S G N WALKER

HENSTEAD (St Mary) *see Wrentham, Covehithe w Benacre etc St E*

HENSTRIDGE (St Nicholas) *see Abbas and Templecombe, Henstridge and Horsington B & W*

HENTLAND (St Dubricius) *see St Weonards Heref*

HENTON (Christ Church) *see Coxley w Godney, Henton and Wookey B & W*

HEPPLE (Christ Church) *see Upper Coquetdale Newc*

HEPTONSTALL (St Thomas Ó Becket and St Thomas the Apostle) *see Hebden Bridge and Heptonstall Leeds*

HEPWORTH (Holy Trinity) *see Upper Holme Valley Leeds*

HEPWORTH (St Peter) w Hinderclay, Wattisfield and Thelnetham *St E 9*   **P** *Bp, K Coll Cam, MMCET, and P J Holt-Wilson Esq (jt)*   **C** D H MESSER

HEREFORD (St Francis) *see Heref S Wye Heref*

HEREFORD (St Martin) *as above*

HEREFORD (St Peter w St Owen) (St James) *Heref 3*   **P** *Simeon's Trustees*   **V** P TOWNER   **C** H CLARKE   **OLM** S A ELSON

HEREFORD SOUTH WYE (St Francis) (St Martin) *Heref 3*   **P** *Patr Bd*   **P-in-c** A M DOWDESWELL   **TV** P J BROWN   **C** A L BRANSTON   **NSM** P J HOUGHTON

HEREFORD, LITTLE (St Mary Magdalene) *see Tenbury Heref*

HEREFORD, WEST Team Ministry (All Saints) (Holy Trinity) (St Barnabas Church Centre) (St Nicholas) *Heref 3*   **P** *Patr Bd (3 turns) Ld Chan (1 turn)*   **TR** R NORTH   **TV** B P CHAVE   **C** R C HULSE

HERMITAGE (Holy Trinity) *Ox 6*   **P** *Patr Bd*   **TR** R E BALL   **TV** L J HEYN   **NSM** M KIRBY

HERMITAGE (St Mary) *see Three Valleys Sarum*

HERNE (St Martin) *Cant 4*   **P** *Abp*   **V** E M RICHARDSON   **C** E R LAST

HERNE BAY (Christ Church) (St Andrew's Church and Centre) *Cant 4*   **P** *Simeon's Trustees*   **V** A W EVERETT   **C** M S H DAVEY   **NSM** S PARRETT

HERNE BAY (St Bartholomew) *see Reculver and Herne Bay St Bart and Hoath Cant*

HERNE HILL (St Paul) (St Saviour) *S'wark 9*   **P** *Bp and Simeon's Trustees (jt)*   **V** C T BARKER   **NSM** B J HUGHES, G S TAYLEUR

HERNER (Chapel) *see Barnstaple Ex*

HERNHILL (St Michael) *see Boughton under Blean w Dunkirk and Hernhill Cant*

HERODSFOOT (All Saints) *see Duloe, Herodsfoot, Morval and St Pinnock Truro*

HERONSGATE (St John the Evangelist) *see Mill End and Heronsgate w W Hyde St Alb*

HERRIARD (St Mary) *see N Hants Downs Win*

HERRINGFLEET (St Margaret) *see Somerleyton, Ashby, Fritton, Herringfleet etc Nor*

HERRINGTHORPE (St Cuthbert) *Sheff 6*   **P** *Bp*   **V** K R SKIDMORE

HERRINGTON (St Aidan), Penshaw and Shiney Row *Dur 14*   **P** *Bp and Prime Min (alt)*   **R** S W OSMAN   **C** G MACKNIGHT

HERSHAM (St Peter) *Guildf 8*   **P** *Bp*   **V** M FLETCHER   **NSM** J W ANDREW   **OLM** S H GRAY

HERSTMONCEUX (All Saints) and Wartling *Chich 13*   **P** *Bp*   **P-in-c** R J STEVEN

HERSTON (St Mark) *see Swanage and Studland Sarum*

HERTFORD (All Saints) (St Andrew) *St Alb 19*   **P** *Ld Chan (1 turn), Duchy of Lanc (2 turns), Patr Bd (1 turn)*   **TR** J M H LOVERIDGE   **TV** H A STEWART, N L SHARP, R C THOMPSON   **C** V A DEAR   **NSM** D R PEPPER, W J CHURCH

HERTINGFORDBURY (St Mary)　see Hertford St Alb
HESKETH (All Saints) w Becconsall Blackb 5　P Trustees
P-in-c N E DAVIS
HESKET-IN-THE-FOREST (St Mary the Virgin)　see Inglewood
Gp Carl
HESLERTON, WEST (All Saints)　see Buckrose Carrs York
HESLINGTON (St Paul) York 2　P Abp　V J NOBEL
HESSENFORD (St Anne)　see St Germans Truro
HESSETT (St Ethelbert)　see Rougham, Beyton w Hessett and
Rushbrooke St E
HESSLE (All Saints) York 14　P Ld Chan　V T M H BOYNS
NSM B RYAN, C R TETLEY
HESTER WAY LANE (St Silas)　see Cheltenham St Mark Glouc
HESTON (All Saints) (St Leonard) Lon 11　P Bp　V vacant
HESWALL (Church of the Good Shepherd) (St Peter) Ches 8
P W A B Davenport Esq　R M S J CANNAM　C J J WISE,
R J SHERRATT　NSM A C G LEACH
HETHE (St Edmund King and Martyr and St George)
see Shelswell Ox
HETHEL (All Saints)　see Mulbarton w Bracon Ash, Hethel and
Flordon Nor
HETHERSETT (St Remigius) w Canteloff w Little Melton and
Great Melton Nor 7　P G&C Coll Cam, E C Evans-Lombe Esq,
and Em Coll Cam (by turn)　R D A MCCLEAN
HETHERSGILL (St Mary)　see Bewcastle, Stapleton and
Kirklinton etc Carl
HETTON, SOUTH (Holy Trinity) Dur 2　P Bp　V vacant
HETTON-LYONS w Eppleton Dur 14　P Bp (1 turn), Prime Min
(2 turns)　R A ANDERSON
HEVENINGHAM (St Margaret) w Ubbeston, Huntingfield and
Cookley St E 18　P Capt the Revd J S Peel
P-in-c A B NORTON
HEVER (St Peter), Four Elms and Mark Beech Roch 11　P Bp
and C Talbot Esq (jt)　R J A WEEKS　NSM W J IZOD
HEVERSHAM (St Peter) and Milnthorpe Carl 10　P Trin Coll
Cam　P-in-c S E WILSON
HEVINGHAM (St Mary the Virgin and St Botolph)　see Horsford,
Felthorpe and Hevingham Nor
HEWELSFIELD (St Mary Magdalene)　see St Briavels w
Hewelsfield Glouc
HEWISH (Good Shepherd)　see Wulfric Benefice B & W
HEWORTH (Christ Church) York 7　P Ch Trust Fund Trust
V P DEO
HEWORTH (Holy Trinity) (St Wulstan) York 7　P Ch Trust
Fund Trust　R M B WOODMANSEY
HEWORTH (St Alban)　see Windy Nook St Alb Dur
HEWORTH (St Mary) Dur 12　P Bp　V N B WARNER
C K L BOARDMAN
HEXAGON, THE : Arnesby w Shearsby, Bruntingthorpe,
Husbands Bosworth, Mowsley and Knaptoft, and
Theddingworth Leic 7　P Bp and DBP (jt)
P-in-c A E A BICKLEY
HEXHAM (St Andrew) Newc 10　P Mercers' Co and Viscount
Allendale (alt)　R D WINTER　NSM A R CURRIE
HEXTABLE (St Peter)　see Swanley St Paul Roch
HEXTHORPE (St Jude)　see Edlington and Hexthorpe Sheff
HEXTON (St Faith)　see Barton-le-Cley w Higham Gobion and
Hexton St Alb
HEY (St John the Baptist)　see Medlock Head Man
HEYBRIDGE (St Andrew) (St George) w Langford Chelmsf 11
P D&C St Paul's and Lord Byron (alt)　V P J LOW
HEYDON (Holy Trinity)　see Icknield Way Villages Chelmsf
HEYDON (St Peter and St Paul)　see Cawston w Booton and
Brandiston etc Nor
HEYDOUR (St Michael and All Angels)　see Ancaster Wilsford
Gp Linc
HEYFORD (St Peter and St Paul) w Stowe Nine Churches and
Flore w Brockhall Pet 3　P The Revd S Hope, Ch Ch Ox, DBP
and Bp (by turn)　R S P BURROW
HEYFORD, LOWER (St Mary)　see Cherwell Valley Ox
HEYFORD, UPPER (St Mary) as above
HEYHOUSES (St Nicholas)　see W Pendleside Blackb
HEYHOUSES ON SEA (St Anne)　see St Annes St Anne Blackb
HEYSHAM (St Peter) (St Andrew) (St James) Blackb 11　P C E
C Royds Esq　R A T OSBORN
HEYSHOTT (St James)　see Cocking w W Lavington, Bepton
and Heyshott Chich
HEYSIDE (St Mark) Man 16　P Trustees　C J A READ
HEYTESBURY (St Peter and St Paul)　see Upper Wylye Valley
Sarum
HEYTHROP (St Nicholas) see Chase Ox
HEYWOOD (All Souls)　see Sudden and Heywood All So Man
HEYWOOD (St James) Man 14　P Bp　V vacant
HEYWOOD (St John) (St Luke) Man 14　P Patr Bd
V vacant

HEYWOOD (St Margaret) and Heap Bridge Man 14　P Patr
Bd　P-in-c S J BANKS　OLM I WARRINGTON
HIBALDSTOW (St Hybald)　see Scawby, Redbourne and
Hibaldstow Linc
HICKLETON (St Wilfrid)　see Goldthorpe w Hickleton Sheff
HICKLING (St Luke) w Kinoulton and Broughton Sulney
(Upper Broughton) S'well 5　P Prime Min, Qu Coll Cam, and
Bp (by turn)　P-in-c P D S MASSEY　NSM M R WOODWARD
HICKLING (St Mary)　see Ludham, Potter Heigham, Hickling
and Catfield Nor
HIGH　see also under substantive place name
HIGH CROSS (St John the Evangelist) St Alb 19　P DBP
P-in-c M B W COOK
HIGH DOWNS Cant 14　P Abp, D&C, and MMCET (jt)
V D J W LAWTON
HIGH GREEN (St Saviour)　see Mortomley St Sav High Green
Sheff
HIGH HAM (St Andrew)　see Langport Area B & W
HIGH LANE (St Thomas) Ches 16　P R Stockport
V J E PARKER
HIGH LEGH (St John)　see High Legh Ches
HIGH OAK, Hingham and Scoulton w Wood Rising Nor 7
P Patr Bd　TR C B REED
HIGHAM (St John the Evangelist)　see Fence-in-Pendle and
Higham Blackb
HIGHAM (St John the Evangelist) and Merston Roch 6
P St Jo Coll Cam　V J F SOUTHWARD
HIGHAM (St Mary), Holton St Mary, Raydon and Stratford
St Mary St E 3　P Duchy of Lanc, Reformation Ch Trust, and
Mrs S E F Holden　R R M PAUL
HIGHAM FERRERS (St Mary the Virgin) w Chelveston Pet 8
P Bp　V R B STAINER
HIGHAM GOBION (St Margaret)　see Barton-le-Cley w Higham
Gobion and Hexton St Alb
HIGHAM GREEN (St Stephen)　see Dalham, Gazeley, Higham,
Kentford and Moulton St E
HIGHAM-ON-THE-HILL (St Peter)　see Fenn Lanes Gp Leic
HIGHAMPTON (Holy Cross)　see Black Torrington, Bradford w
Cookbury etc Ex
HIGHAMS PARK (All Saints) Hale End Chelmsf 7　P Bp
V S P CLARKE
HIGHBRIDGE (St John the Evangelist) B & W 1　P Bp
V S M J CROSSMAN　C S J BALE, T NIXON
HIGHBROOK (All Saints) and West Hoathly Chich 5　P Ld
Chan　V L F WHATLEY
HIGHBURY (Christ Church) (St John) (St Saviour) Lon 6
P CPAS　V J D BREWSTER　C C A ENGA, E L CLUTTERBUCK
NSM T J I WITTER
HIGHBURY NEW PARK (St Augustine) Lon 6　P CPAS
V G A M ANSTIS
HIGHCLERE (St Michael and All Angels)　see NW Hants Win
HIGHCLIFFE (St Mark) Win 9　P Bp　V G K TAYLOR
HIGHER　see also under substantive place name
HIGHERTOWN (All Saints) and Baldhu Truro 6　P Bp and
Viscount Falmouth (alt)　P-in-c J J PUTNAM
HIGHFIELD (All Saints) Ox 1　P Bp　V J E COCKE
HIGHFIELD (St Catherine)　see New Bury w Gt Lever Man
HIGHFIELD (St Mary)　see Sheff St Mary Bramall Lane Sheff
HIGHFIELD (St Matthew) Liv 14　P Trustees　V R L PEARSON
HIGHFIELD (St Paul)　see Hemel Hempstead St Alb
HIGHGATE (All Saints) Lon 20　P Bp　P-in-c B WANDREY
C J D TRIGG　NSM J H ROGERS
HIGHGATE (St Alban the Martyr and St Patrick) Birm 1
P Keble Coll Ox　P-in-c N LO POLITO
HIGHGATE (St Augustine) Lon 20　P Bp　Hon
C W A WHITCOMBE
HIGHGATE (St Michael) Lon 20　P Bp　V J D TRIGG
C B WANDREY, J P YEATES　NSM J H ROGERS
HIGHLEY (St Mary) w Billingsley, Glazeley and Deuxhill and
Chelmarsh Heref 3　P MMCET　V M A HARRIS
NSM V R SMITH, W S RYLANCE
HIGHNAM (Holy Innocents), Lassington, Rudford,
Tibberton and Taynton Glouc 3　P D&C, T J Fenton Esq,
and A E Woolley (jt)　R vacant
HIGHTERS HEATH (Immanuel) Birm 5　P Bp
V K J R CLARKE　NSM H E GLITHERO
HIGHTOWN (All Saints)　see Castleford Leeds
HIGHTOWN (St Barnabas)　see Hartshead, Hightown,
Robertstown and Scholes Leeds
HIGHTOWN (St Stephen) Liv 5　P Bp　P-in-c S J SMITH
HIGHWEEK (All Saints) (St Mary) Ex 9　P Bp
P-in-c M D THAYER
HIGHWORTH (St Michael) w Sevenhampton and Inglesham
and Hannington Bris 7　P Bp (4 turns), Mrs M G Hussey-Freke
(1 turn)　V G D SOWDEN　C D R CAPORN　NSM T M DAY

HILBOROUGH (All Saints) w Bodney *Nor 13*   **P** *DBP*
   P-in-c C P SHERLOCK
HILDENBOROUGH (St John the Evangelist) *Roch 11*
   P *V Tonbridge*   **V** T R SAIET   **NSM** S BRAID
HILDERSHAM (Holy Trinity) *Ely 5*   **P** Trustees
   P-in-c J M NORRIS   **Hon C** J M FELLOWS   **NSM** K R BISHOP
HILDERSTONE (Christ Church)   *see* Fulford w Hilderstone
   Lich
HILFIELD (St Nicholas)   *see* Three Valleys *Sarum*
HILGAY (All Saints) *Ely 9*   **P** *Hertf Coll Ox*   **R** *vacant*
HILL (St James) *Birm 12*   **P** *Bp*   **V** A D RAMBLE
HILL (St Michael)   *see* Berkeley w Wick, Breadstone, Newport,
   Stone etc *Glouc*
HILL CROOME (St Mary)   *see* Upton-on-Severn, Ripple, Earls
   Croome etc *Worc*
HILL TOP (St James)   *see* W Bromwich St Jas w St Paul *Lich*
HILLESDEN (All Saints)   *see* Lenborough *Ox*
HILLESLEY (St Giles)   *see* Charfield and Kingswood w Wickwar
   etc *Glouc*
HILLFARRANCE (Holy Cross)   *see* Deane Vale *B & W*
HILLINGDON (All Saints) *Lon 24*   **P** *Bp*   **V** D P BANISTER
HILLINGDON (St John the Baptist) *Lon 24*   **P** *Bp*
   NSM G PINNELL
HILLINGTON (St Mary the Virgin) *Nor 16*   **P** E W Dawnay Esq
   R J B V RIVIERE
HILLMORTON (St John the Baptist) *Cov 6*   **P** *Bp*
   P-in-c M I SIMMONS   **C** S E GOLD
HILLOCK (St Andrew) and Unsworth *Man 10*   **P** *Bp, R Stand*
   All SS, and R Prestwich St Mary (jt)   **V** A WILLIAMS
   C C E GREENWOOD   **NSM** A M WHITTLEWORTH, C D BINNS
HILLSBOROUGH and Wadsley Bridge (Christ Church) *Sheff 4*
   P *Ch Patr Trust*   **P-in-c** P J GOODACRE
HILLSIDE Lobley Hill and Marley Hill *Dur 13*   **P** *Bp and Prime*
   Min (alt)   **V** R K HOPPER
HILMARTON (St Lawrence)   *see* Woodhill *Sarum*
HILPERTON MARSH (St Mary Magdalen)   *see* Canalside
   Benefice *Sarum*
HILSTON (St Margaret)   *see* Withernsea w Owthorne, Garton-
   in-Holderness etc *York*
HILTON (All Saints)   *see* Piddle Valley, Hilton, Cheselbourne etc
   Sarum
HILTON (St Mary Magdalene)   *see* Godmanchester and Hilton
   Ely
HILTON (St Peter)   *see* Stainton w Hilton *York*
HILTON w Marston-on-Dove *Derby 14*   **P** N J M Spurrier Esq
   V A G MURPHIE
HIMBLETON (St Mary Magdalene)   *see* Bowbrook S *Worc*
HIMLEY (St Michael and All Angels)   *see* Smestow Vale *Lich*
HINCASTER (Mission Room)   *see* Heversham and Milnthorpe
   Carl
HINCHLEY WOOD (St Christopher) *Guildf 8*   **P** *Bp*
   V J S KRONENBERG   **NSM** C A MULLINS
HINCKFORD, NORTH *Chelmsf 19*   **P** *Patr Bd (4 turns), Ld Chan*
   (1 turn)   **TR** M H KING   **TV** S A WOMERSLEY
HINCKLEY (Assumption of St Mary the Virgin) (St Francis)
   (St Paul) *Leic 10*   **P** *Bp*   **V** J WHITTAKER   **C** J M SURRIDGE
   NSM H J WHITTAKER, J A GIBBS
HINCKLEY (Holy Trinity) *Leic 10*   **P** *DBP*   **R** S J WEARN
HINCKLEY (St John the Evangelist) *Leic 10*   **P** *DBP*
   V G J WESTON   **C** S J COCKSEDGE
HINDERCLAY (St Mary)   *see* Hepworth, Hinderclay, Wattisfield
   and Thelnetham *St E*
HINDERWELL (St Hilda), Roxby and Staithes w Lythe,
   Ugthorpe and Sandsend *York 21*   **P** *Abp*   **R** B J PYKE
HINDHEAD (Mission Room)   *see* Churt and Hindhead *Guildf*
HINDLEY (All Saints) *Liv 14*   **P** *R Wigan*   **P-in-c** A BEAHAN
HINDLEY (St Peter) *Liv 14*   **P** *St Pet Coll Ox*
   P-in-c M J SHERWIN
HINDLEY GREEN (St John) *Liv 14*   **P** *Bp*   **V** M J SHERWIN
   C C O NICHOLSON
HINDOLVESTON (St George)   *see* Briston, Burgh Parva,
   Hindolveston etc *Nor*
HINDON (St John the Baptist)   *see* Nadder Valley *Sarum*
HINDRINGHAM (St Martin)   *see* Barney, Hindringham,
   Thursford, Great Snoring, Little Snoring and Kettlestone and
   Pensthorpe *Nor*
HINGHAM (St Andrew)   *see* High Oak, Hingham and Scoulton
   w Wood Rising *Nor*
HINKSEY, NEW (St John the Evangelist)   *see* S Hinksey *Ox*
HINKSEY, NORTH (St Lawrence)   *see* Osney *Ox*
HINKSEY, SOUTH (St Laurence) *Ox 2*   **P** *Bp*
   V J D WILKINSON
HINSTOCK (St Oswald)   *see* Cheswardine, Childs Ercall, Hales,
   Hinstock etc *Lich*
HINTLESHAM (St Nicholas)   *see* Elmsett w Aldham,
   Hintlesham, Chattisham etc *St E*

HINTON ADMIRAL (St Michael and All Angels)   *see* Bransgore
   and Hinton Admiral *Win*
HINTON AMPNER (All Saints)   *see* Upper Itchen *Win*
HINTON BLEWETT (St Margaret)   *see* E w W Harptree and
   Hinton Blewett *B & W*
HINTON CHARTERHOUSE (St John the Baptist)   *see* Freshford,
   Limpley Stoke and Hinton Charterhouse *B & W*
HINTON MARTEL (St John the Evangelist)   *see* Horton,
   Chalbury, Hinton Martel and Holt St Jas *Sarum*
HINTON PARVA (St Swithun)   *see* Lyddington and
   Wanborough and Bishopstone etc *Bris*
HINTON ST GEORGE (St George)   *see* Merriott w Hinton,
   Dinnington and Lopen *B & W*
HINTON ST MARY (St Mary)   *see* Sturminster Newton, Hinton
   St Mary and Lydlinch *Sarum*
HINTON WALDRIST (St Margaret)   *see* Cherbury w Gainfield
   Ox
HINTON-IN-THE-HEDGES (Holy Trinity)   *see* Aynho and
   Croughton w Evenley etc *Pet*
HINTON-ON-THE-GREEN (St Peter)   *see* Hampton w
   Sedgeberrow and Hinton-on-the-Green *Worc*
HINTS (St Bartholomew) *Lich 1*   **P** Personal Reps A E Jones Esq
   V *vacant*
HINXHILL (St Mary)   *see* Wye *Cant*
HINXTON (St Mary and St John) *Ely 5*   **P** *Jes Coll Cam*
   P-in-c J H MARTIN   **NSM** P M SHARKEY
HINXWORTH (St Nicholas)   *see* Ashwell w Hinxworth and
   Newnham *St Alb*
HIPSWELL (St John the Evangelist) *Leeds 24*   **P** *Bp*
   V A R M CROMARTY
HISTON (St Andrew) *Ely 6*   **P** *MMCET*
   V N J BLANDFORD-BAKER   **C** R J KELLOW
   NSM J M GLOVER, O M K COLES
HITCHAM (All Saints)   *see* Rattlesden w Thorpe Morieux,
   Brettenham etc *St E*
HITCHAM (St Mary) *Ox 12*   **P** *Eton Coll*   **V** N PLEDGER
HITCHIN (Holy Saviour) (St Faith) (St Mark) (St Mary) *St Alb 3*
   P *Patr Bd*   **TR** M A H RODEN   **TV** I C TODD,
   J F MAINWARING, M CROWLEY   **C** J C MCQUAID
   NSM F S E GIBBS
HITHER GREEN (St Swithun)   *see* Lewisham St Swithun *S'wark*
HITTISLEIGH (St Andrew)   *see* Chagford, Gidleigh, Throwleigh
   etc *Ex*
HIXON (St Peter)   *see* Mid Trent *Lich*
HOAR CROSS (Holy Angels) w Newchurch *Lich 14*   **P** *Bp and*
   Meynell Ch Trustees   **P-in-c** G P BOTT
HOARWITHY (St Catherine)   *see* St Weonards *Heref*
HOATH (Holy Cross)   *see* Reculver and Herne Bay St Bart and
   Hoath *Cant*
HOATHLY, EAST (not known)   *see* Chiddingly w E Hoathly
   Chich
HOATHLY, WEST (St Margaret)   *see* Highbrook and W Hoathly
   Chich
HOBS MOAT (St Mary) *Birm 11*   **P** *Bp*   **P-in-c** L GRANNER
HOBY (All Saints)   *see* Upper Wreake *Leic*
HOCKERILL (All Saints) *St Alb 15*   **P** *Bp Lon*
   V S D MANSFIELD   **NSM** S A TARRAN
HOCKERING (St Michael)   *see* Mattishall and the Tudd Valley
   Nor
HOCKERTON (St Nicholas)   *see* Kirklington w Hockerton
   S'well
HOCKHAM, GREAT (Holy Trinity)   *see* Caston, Griston, Merton,
   Thompson etc *Nor*
HOCKLEY (St Matthew)   *see* Wilnecote *Lich*
HOCKLEY (St Peter and St Paul) *Chelmsf 14*   **P** *Wadh Coll Ox*
   P-in-c K R HAVEY
HOCKLIFFE (St Nicholas)   *see* Ouzel Valley *St Alb*
HOCKWOLD w WILTON (St James)   *see* Grimshoe *Ely*
HOCKWORTHY (St Simon and St Jude)   *see* Sampford Peverell,
   Uplowman, Holcombe Rogus etc *Ex*
HODDESDON (St Catherine and St Paul) *St Alb 17*   **P** *Peache*
   Trustees   **V** *vacant*
HODDLESDEN (St Paul)   *see* Over Darwen St Jas and
   Hoddlesden *Blackb*
HODGE HILL (St Philip and St James) *Birm 9*   **P** *Bp*
   TR A D BARRETT   **NSM** S A NASH
HODNET (St Luke) *Lich 18*   **P** *Sir Algernon Heber-Percy KCVO*
   P-in-c E QUIREY   **Hon C** R M WILTSHIRE
HOE (St Andrew)   *see* Dereham and Distr *Nor*
HOGGESTON (Holy Cross)   *see* Schorne *Ox*
HOGHTON (Holy Trinity) *Blackb 5*   **P** *V Leyland*   **V** *vacant*
HOGNASTON (St Bartholomew)   *see* Hulland, Atlow,
   Kniveton, Bradley and Hognaston *Derby*
HOGSTHORPE (St Mary)   *see* Chapel St Leonards w
   Hogsthorpe *Linc*
HOLBEACH (All Saints) *Linc 18*   **P** *Bp*   **V** R J SEAL

HOLBECK (St Luke the Evangelist) *Leeds 15*   **P** *Bp,* **V** *Leeds St Pet, and Meynell Ch Trust (jt)*   **C** C M J MITTON   **NSM** K G ELLIOTT

HOLBETON (All Saints) *Ex 20*   **P** *The Crown*   **V** J G CRUICKSHANK   **P-in-c** A C LEGGE

HOLBORN (St Alban the Martyr) w Saffron Hill St Peter *Lon 17*   **P** *D&C St Paul's*   **V** C M SMITH   **C** G R F WILLIS   **NSM** R G CORP

HOLBORN (St George the Martyr) Queen Square (Holy Trinity) (St Bartholomew) Grays Inn Road *Lon 17*   **P** *Ch Soc Trust*   **R** J H VALENTINE

HOLBORN (St Giles-in-the-Fields)   *see* St Giles-in-the-Fields *Lon*

HOLBROOK (All Saints), Stutton, Freston, Woolverstone and Wherstead *St E 5*   **P** *Patr Bd*   **R** G P CLEMENT

HOLBROOK (St Michael)   *see* Hazelwood, Holbrook and Milford *Derby*

HOLBROOK ROAD (St Swithin)   *see* Belper *Derby*

HOLBROOKS (St Luke) *Cov 2*   **P** *Bp*   **V** C DUNKLEY

HOLBURY (Good Shepherd)   *see* Fawley *Win*

HOLCOMBE (Emmanuel) (Canon Lewis Hall) and Hawkshaw *Man 8*   **P** *R Bury St Mary and F Whowell Esq (jt)*   **R** P H SUMSION   **OLM** R W AIREY, V J D FLETCHER

HOLCOMBE (St Andrew)   *see* Coleford w Holcombe *B & W*

HOLCOMBE (St George)   *see* Dawlish, Cofton and Starcross *Ex*

HOLCOMBE BURNELL (St John the Baptist)   *see* Tedburn St Mary, Cheriton Bishop, Whitestone etc *Ex*

HOLCOMBE ROGUS (All Saints)   *see* Sampford Peverell, Uplowman, Holcombe Rogus etc *Ex*

HOLCOT (St Mary and All Saints)   *see* Brixworth w Holcot *Pet*

HOLDENHURST (St John the Evangelist) and Iford *Win 8*   **P** *Bp*   **V** A L MCPHERSON   **C** K E HICKEN   **Hon C** J NIGHTINGALE   **NSM** J M SEARE, S LEGRANT

HOLDGATE (Holy Trinity)   *see* Diddlebury w Munslow, Holdgate and Tugford *Heref*

HOLFORD (St Mary the Virgin)   *see* Quantock Coast *B & W*

HOLKHAM (St Withiburga) w Egmere w Warham, Wells-next-the-Sea and Wighton *Nor 15*   **P** *Viscount Coke (2 turns), M J Beddard Esq (2 turns), and D&C (1 turn)*   **R** *vacant*

HOLLAND FEN (All Saints)   *see* Brothertoft Gp *Linc*

HOLLAND PARK (St George the Martyr) (St John the Baptist) *Lon 12*   **P** *Trustees and Bp (jt)*   **P-in-c** J B HEARD   **C** P WOLTON

HOLLAND, GREAT (All Saints)   *see* Kirby-le-Soken w Gt Holland *Chelmsf*

HOLLAND, NEW (Christ Church)   *see* Barrow and Goxhill *Linc*

HOLLAND-ON-SEA (St Bartholomew) *Chelmsf 23*   **P** *Ch Patr Trust*   **C** D J LOWER   **OLM** S E WIGGINS

HOLLESLEY (All Saints)   *see* Wilford Peninsula *St E*

HOLLINFARE (St Helen)   *see* Glazebury w Hollinfare *Liv*

HOLLINGBOURNE (All Saints) and Hucking w Leeds and Broomfield *Cant 13*   **P** *Abp*   **V** *vacant*

HOLLINGTON (St John the Evangelist)   *see* Rocester and Croxden w Hollington *Lich*

HOLLINGTON (St John the Evangelist) (St Peter and St Paul) *Chich 15*   **P** *Ch Patr Trust*   **V** L J W DEAN   **NSM** M HINKLEY

HOLLINGTON (St Leonard) (St Anne) *Chich 15*   **P** *CPAS*   **R** D I CHARNOCK

HOLLINGWORTH (St Hilda)   *see* Milnrow *Man*

HOLLINGWORTH (St Mary) w Tintwistle *Ches 14*   **P** *Patr Bd*   **V** B A PERRIN

HOLLINWOOD (St Margaret) and Limeside *Man 16*   **P** *Bp and V Prestwich (jt)*   **V** D HAWTHORN

HOLLOWAY (Emmanuel)   *see* Tollington *Lon*

HOLLOWAY (St Mary Magdalene) (St David) *Lon 6*   **P** *Bp and V Islington St Mary (jt)*   **V** P V ZAPHIRIOU   **C** J K RUST

HOLLOWAY Hanley Road (St Saviour)   *see* Tollington *Lon*

HOLLOWAY, UPPER (St John the Evangelist) *Lon 6*   **P** *Ch Patr Trust*   **V** W K DORGU

HOLLOWAY, UPPER (St John)   *see* Upper Holloway *Lon*

HOLLOWAY, WEST (St Luke) *Lon 6*   **P** *Lon Coll Div Trustees*   **V** D W TOMLINSON   **NSM** M D E WROE

HOLLOWELL (St James)   *see* Guilsborough and Hollowell and Cold Ashby etc *Pet*

HOLLY HALL (St Augustine)   *see* Dudley *Worc*

HOLLY HILL (Church Centre)   *see* Frankley *Birm*

HOLLYBUSH (All Saints)   *see* Berrow w Pendock, Eldersfield, Hollybush etc *Worc*

HOLLYM (St Nicholas)   *see* Withernsea w Owthorne, Garton-in-Holderness etc *York*

HOLMBRIDGE (St David)   *see* Upper Holme Valley *Leeds*

HOLMBURY ST MARY (St Mary the Virgin)   *see* Abinger and Coldharbour and Wotton and Holmbury St Mary *Guildf*

HOLME (All Saints) and Seaton Ross Group, The *York 5*   **P** *St Jo Coll Cam and Ld Chan (alt)*   **R** S V COPE

HOLME (Holy Trinity)   *see* Burton and Holme *Carl*

HOLME (St Giles)   *see* Yaxley and Holme w Conington *Ely*

HOLME (St Giles)   *see* E Trent *S'well*

HOLME CULTRAM (St Cuthbert)   *see* Solway Plain *Carl*

HOLME CULTRAM (St Mary) *as above*

HOLME EDEN (St Paul) and Wetheral w Warwick *Carl 2*   **P** *D&C and DBP (jt)*   **R** D A CRAVEN

HOLME HALE (St Andrew)   *see* Necton, Holme Hale w N and S Pickenham *Nor*

HOLME PIERREPONT (St Edmund King and Martyr)   *see* Lady Bay w Holme Pierrepont and Adbolton *S'well*

HOLME RUNCTON (St James) w South Runcton and Wallington *Ely 9*   **P** *Bp*   **P-in-c** B L BURTON   **Hon C** S C MORRIS

HOLME VALLEY, The UPPER *Leeds 13*   **P** *Patr Bd*   **TR** J S ROBERTSHAW   **TV** K GRIFFIN, M D ELLERTON, N M HEATON   **NSM** A R BROOKE, S W DIXON, E BARROW   **OLM** G B BAMFORD

HOLME WOOD (St Christopher)   *see* Tong and Laisterdyke *Leeds*

HOLME, EAST (St John the Evangelist)   *see* Wareham *Sarum*

HOLME-IN-CLIVIGER (St John) w Worsthorne *Blackb 3*   **P** *Patr Bd*   **V** R K HENSHALL

HOLME-NEXT-THE-SEA (St Mary)   *see* Hunstanton St Mary w Ringstead Parva etc *Nor*

HOLME-ON-SPALDING-MOOR (All Saints)   *see* Holme and Seaton Ross Group *York*

HOLMER (St Bartholomew) (St Mary) w Huntington *Heref 3*   **P** *D&C*   **V** S M LEE

HOLMER GREEN (Christ Church)   *see* Penn Street *Ox*

HOLMES CHAPEL (St Luke)   *see* Church Hulme *Ches*

HOLMESDALE (St Philip)   *see* Dronfield w Holmesfield *Derby*

HOLMESFIELD (St Swithin) *as above*

HOLMEWOOD (St Alban Mission)   *see* Heath *Derby*

HOLMFIELD (St Andrew)   *see* Bradshaw and Holmfield *Leeds*

HOLMFIRTH (Holy Trinity)   *see* Upper Holme Valley *Leeds*

HOLMPTON (St Nicholas)   *see* Withernsea w Owthorne, Garton-in-Holderness etc *York*

HOLMSIDE (St John the Evangelist)   *see* Lanchester and Burnhope *Dur*

HOLMWOOD (St Mary Magdalene)   *see* Surrey Weald *Guildf*

HOLMWOOD, NORTH (St John the Evangelist) *Guildf 7*   **P** *Bp*   **V** S K TANSWELL

HOLNE (St Mary the Virgin)   *see* Ashburton, Bickington, Buckland in the Moor etc *Ex*

HOLNEST (Church of the Assumption)   *see* Three Valleys *Sarum*

HOLSWORTHY (St Peter and St Paul) w Hollacombe and Milton Damerel *Ex 16*   **P** *DBP and J Palmer Esq (jt)*   **P-in-c** C W PENN

HOLT (St Andrew) w High Kelling *Nor 18*   **P** *St Jo Coll Cam*   **R** H C STOKER   **C** C L ROTERS

HOLT (St James)   *see* Horton, Chalbury, Hinton Martel and Holt St Jas *Sarum*

HOLT (St Katharine)   *see* Broughton Gifford, Gt Chalfield and Holt *Sarum*

HOLT (St Martin)   *see* Hallow and Grimley w Holt *Worc*

HOLTBY (Holy Trinity)   *see* Rural E York *York*

HOLTON (St Bartholomew)   *see* Albury w Tiddington, Holton, Waterperry, Waterstock and Wheatley *Ox*

HOLTON (St Nicholas)   *see* Camelot Par *B & W*

HOLTON (St Peter)   *see* Blyth Valley *St E*

HOLTON ST MARY (St Mary)   *see* Higham, Holton St Mary, Raydon and Stratford *St E*

HOLTON-CUM-BECKERING (All Saints)   *see* Wragby Gp *Linc*

HOLTON-LE-CLAY (St Peter), Tetney and North Cotes *Linc 4*   **P** *Ld Chan, Bp, and Duchy of Lancaster (by turn)*   **V** C M WOADDEN

HOLTON-LE-MOOR (St Luke)   *see* Kelsey Gp *Linc*

HOLTSPUR (St Thomas)   *see* Beaconsfield *Ox*

HOLWELL (St Laurence)   *see* Three Valleys *Sarum*

HOLWELL (St Leonard)   *see* Ab Kettleby and Holwell w Asfordby *Leic*

HOLWELL (St Mary the Virgin)   *see* Shill Valley and Broadshire *Ox*

HOLWELL (St Peter), Ickleford and Pirton *St Alb 3*   **P** *DBP and D&C Ely (jt)*   **R** J M ROBERTSON   **NSM** M S HOLFORD

HOLWORTH (St Catherine by the Sea)   *see* Watercombe *Sarum*

HOLY ISLAND (St Mary the Virgin) *Newc 12*   **P** *Bp*   **V** P M COLLINS

HOLYBOURNE (Holy Rood)   *see* Alton *Win*

HOLYMOORSIDE (St Peter)   *see* Brampton St Thos *Derby*

HOLYSTONE (St Mary the Virgin)   *see* Upper Coquetdale *Newc*

HOLYWELL (St John the Baptist)   *see* Bluntisham cum Earith w Colne and Holywell etc *Ely*

HOLYWELL (St Mary)   *see* Seghill *Newc*

HOMERSFIELD (St Mary)　*see* S Elmham and Ilketshall *St E*

HOMERTON (Christ Church on the Mead)　*see* Hackney Marsh *Lon*

HOMERTON (St Barnabas w St Paul) *as above*

HOMERTON (St Luke) *Lon 5*　**P** *St Olave Hart Street Trustees*　**V** E BLATCHLEY

HOMINGTON (St Mary the Virgin)　*see* Chalke Valley *Sarum*

HONEYCHURCH (St Mary)　*see* Chagford, Gidleigh, Throwleigh etc *Ex*

HONICKNOWLE (St Francis)　*see* Ernesettle, Whitleigh and Honicknowle *Ex*

HONILEY (St John the Baptist)　*see* Hatton w Haseley, Rowington w Lowsonford etc *Cov*

HONING (St Peter and St Paul)　*see* Smallburgh w Dilham w Honing and Crostwight *Nor*

HONINGHAM (St Andrew) *Nor 17*　**P** *DBP*　**V** *vacant*

HONINGTON (All Saints)　*see* Shipston-on-Stour w Honington and Idlicote *Cov*

HONINGTON (All Saints)　*see* Blackbourne *St E*

HONINGTON (St Wilfred)　*see* Barkston and Hough Gp *Linc*

HONITON (St Michael) (St Paul), Gittisham, Combe Raleigh, Monkton, Awliscombe and Buckerell *Ex 4*　**P** *DBP*　**TR** S E ROBERTS　**TV** J E LANKESTER　**C** P I C BUTCHER　**Hon C** P T C MASHEDER

HONLEY (St Mary) *Leeds 6*　**P** *R Almondbury*　**V** L P BEADLE

HOO (All Hallows)　*see* High Halstow w All Hallows and Hoo St Mary *Roch*

HOO (St Andrew and St Eustachius)　*see* Mid Loes *St E*

HOO (St Werburgh) *Roch 6*　**P** *D&C*　**P-in-c** J E SMITH　**NSM** S E SMITH

HOOBROOK (St Cecilia)　*see* Kidderminster E *Worc*

HOOE (St John the Evangelist)　*see* Plymstock and Hooe *Ex*

HOOE (St Oswald) *Chich 12*　**P** *Bp*　**V** *vacant*

HOOK (St John the Evangelist)　*see* Whitewater *Win*

HOOK (St Mary the Virgin)　*see* Airmyn, Hook and Rawcliffe *Sheff*

HOOK (St Mary) w Warsash *Portsm 2*　**P** *Bp*　**P-in-c** J M TERRY, N S TERRY

HOOK COMMON (Good Shepherd)　*see* Upton-on-Severn, Ripple, Earls Croome etc *Worc*

HOOK NORTON (St Peter) w Great Rollright, Swerford and Wigginton *Ox 22*　**P** *Bp, DBP, BNC Ox, and Jes Coll Ox (jt)*　**R** J ACREMAN　**NSM** C G TURNER, W CUNNINGHAM

HOOKE (St Giles)　*see* Beaminster Area *Sarum*

HOOLE (All Saints) *Ches 2*　**P** *Simeon's Trustees*　**V** R J KIRKLAND

HOOLE (St Michael) *Blackb 5*　**P** *Reps of Mrs E A Dunne and Mrs D Downes (jt)*　**R** D A BAINES

HOOTON (St Paul) *Ches 9*　**P** *Trustees*　**V** K HOWARD

HOOTON PAGNELL (All Saints)　*see* Bilham *Sheff*

HOOTON ROBERTS (St John)　*see* Ravenfield, Hooton Roberts and Braithwell *Sheff*

HOPE (Holy Trinity)　*see* Minsterley, Habberley and Hope w Shelve *Heref*

HOPE (St James)　*see* Eccles *Man*

HOPE (St Peter), Castleton and Bradwell *Derby 2*　**P** *Bp and D&C Lich (jt)*　**V** I A DAVIS　**OLM** J E BARNES

HOPE BAGOT (St John the Baptist)　*see* Tenbury *Heref*

HOPE BOWDLER (St Andrew)　*see* Apedale Gp *Heref*

HOPE COVE (St Clements)　*see* Salcombe and Malborough w S Huish *Ex*

HOPE MANSEL (St Michael)　*see* Ariconium *Heref*

HOPESAY (St Mary the Virgin)　*see* Clun Valley *Heref*

HOPE-UNDER-DINMORE (St Mary the Virgin)　*see* Leominster *Heref*

HOPTON (All Saints)　*see* Stanton, Hopton, Market Weston, Barningham etc *St E*

HOPTON (St Peter)　*see* Mid Trent *Lich*

HOPTON CASTLE (St Edward)　*see* Middle Marches *Heref*

HOPTON w Corton *Nor 9*　**P** *Ld Chan and D&C (alt)*　**V** R A KEY

HOPTON WAFERS (St Michael and All Angels)　*see* Cleobury Mortimer w Hopton Wafers etc *Heref*

HOPTON, UPPER (St John the Evangelist)　*see* Mirfield *Leeds*

HOPWAS (St Chad)　*see* Tamworth *Lich*

HOPWOOD (St John)　*see* Heywood St Jo and St Luke *Man*

HORAM (Christ Church) (St James) *Chich 13*　**P** *Bp*　**V** P-J GUY

HORBLING (St Andrew)　*see* Billingborough Gp *Linc*

HORBURY (St Peter and St Leonard) w Horbury Bridge (St John) *Leeds 20*　**P** *Dean*　**V** B T B BELL　**C** A WENZEL

HORBURY JUNCTION (St Mary) *Leeds 20*　**P** *DBP*　**P-in-c** K R M CAMPBELL　**NSM** D M WALKER

HORDEN (St Mary) *Dur 2*　**P** *Bp*　**V** K SMITH　**C** J W LEIGH

HORDLE (All Saints) *Win 11*　**P** *Bp*　**V** P J TAYLOR　**NSM** E M BENNETT

HORDLEY (St Mary the Virgin)　*see* Baschurch and Weston Lullingfield w Hordley *Lich*

HORFIELD (Holy Trinity) *Bris 3*　**P** *Bp*　**R** J S F HADLEY　**NSM** H M BLANCHARDE　**OLM** P L HINE

HORFIELD (St Gregory) *Bris 3*　**P** *Bp*　**P-in-c** J WILSON　**OLM** P R WILLSON

HORHAM (St Mary)　*see* Athelington, Denham, Horham, Hoxne etc *St E*

HORKESLEY, GREAT (All Saints)　*see* W Bergholt and Gt Horkesley *Chelmsf*

HORKESLEY, GREAT (St John) *as above*

HORKESLEY, LITTLE (St Peter and St Paul)　*see* Wormingford, Mt Bures and Lt Horkesley *Chelmsf*

HORKSTOW (St Maurice) *Linc 8*　**P** *DBP*　**V** D P ROWETT

HORLEY (St Bartholomew) (St Francis) (St Wilfrid) *S'wark 26*　**P** *Patr Bd*　**TR** C C PRENTIS　**TV** N NGURURI　**C** D COLEMAN

HORLEY (St Etheldreda)　*see* Ironstone *Ox*

HORLEY ROW (St Wilfrid)　*see* Horley *S'wark*

HORMEAD (St Nicholas), Wyddial, Anstey, Brent Pelham and Meesden *St Alb 16*　**P** *St Jo Coll Cam, Ch Coll Cam, and Bp (by turn)*　**V** K R PEACOCK

HORN HILL (St Paul)　*see* Chalfont St Peter *Ox*

HORNBLOTTON (St Peter)　*see* Six Pilgrims *B & W*

HORNBY (St Margaret) w Claughton and Whittington w Arkholme and Gressingham *Blackb 14*　**P** *Patr Bd*　**V** M J HAMPSON

HORNBY (St Mary) *Leeds 27*　**P** *D&C York*　**P-in-c** B S DIXON　**NSM** J T OLDFIELD

HORNCASTLE Group, The (St Mary the Virgin) *Linc 13*　**P** *Bp, Baroness Willoughby de Eresby and D&C (jt)*　**R** P C PATRICK　**NSM** A C FORD, J F PARKIN　**OLM** P E SMITH

HORNCHURCH (Holy Cross) *Chelmsf 2*　**P** *Bp and New Coll Ox (alt)*　**P-in-c** J D PEARSON

HORNCHURCH (St Andrew) (St George) (St Matthew and St John) *Chelmsf 2*　**P** *New Coll Ox*　**V** B R HOBSON　**C** K A WYLIE　**OLM** S E GROOMBRIDGE

HORNCHURCH Elm Park (St Nicholas)　*see* Elm Park St Nic Hornchurch *Chelmsf*

HORNCHURCH, SOUTH (St John and St Matthew) *Chelmsf 2*　**P** *MMCET*　**V** A F BURFORD

HORNDALE (St Francis)　*see* Gt Aycliffe *Dur*

HORNDON EAST (St Francis) and West Horndon w Little Warley and Childerditch *Chelmsf 8*　**P** *Sir Antony Browne's Sch and Bp (by turn)*　**P-in-c** H A BRYAN

HORNDON ON THE HILL (St Peter and St Paul)　*see* Orsett and Bulphan and Horndon on the Hill *Chelmsf*

HORNE (St Mary)　*see* The Windmill *S'wark*

HORNING (St Benedict)　*see* Ashmanhaugh, Barton Turf etc *Nor*

HORNINGHOLD (St Peter)　*see* Hallaton and Allexton, w Horningham, Tugby etc *Leic*

HORNINGLOW (St John the Divine) *Lich 14*　**P** *Trustees*　**V** M R FREEMAN　**OLM** A J HINES

HORNINGSEA (St Peter) *Ely 4*　**P** *St Jo Coll Cam*　**V** *vacant*

HORNINGSHAM (St John the Baptist)　*see* Cley Hill Villages *Sarum*

HORNINGTOFT (St Edmund)　*see* Upper Wensum Village Gp *Nor*

HORNSEA (St Nicholas) w Atwick *York 11*　**P** *Ld Chan*　**V** P LAMB

HORNSEY (Christ Church) *Lon 20*　**P** *Bp*　**V** D O AGBELUSI

HORNSEY (Holy Innocents) *Lon 20*　**P** *Bp*　**V** T D PIKE　**C** E J LOBSINGER, P J HENDERSON　**NSM** P G ATHERTON

HORNSEY (St Mary) (St George) *Lon 20*　**P** *Bp*　**R** B BATSTONE　**C** B KERRIDGE　**NSM** P NASHASHIBI

HORNSEY RISE (St Mary) *Lon 6*　**P** *Ch Patr Trust*　**V** T L R MERCHANT　**NSM** R I MERCHANT

HORNTON (St John the Baptist)　*see* Ironstone *Ox*

HORRABRIDGE (St John the Baptist)　*see* Sampford Spiney w Horrabridge *Ex*

HORRINGER (St Leonard) *St E 13*　**P** *Bp and DBP (jt)*　**R** R J GRIFFITHS

HORSELL (St Mary the Virgin) *Guildf 12*　**P** *Bp*　**V** S E HAYES

HORSENDON (St Michael and All Angels)　*see* Risborough *Ox*

HORSEY (All Saints)　*see* Flegg Coastal Benefice *Nor*

HORSFORD (All Saints), Felthorpe and Hevingham *Nor 2*　**P** *Sir Thomas Agnew Beevor Bt and Bp (jt)*　**NSM** G G GOODMAN, P J GOODMAN

HORSFORTH (St Margaret)　*see* Abbeylands *Leeds*

HORSHAM (Holy Trinity) (St John) (St Mary the Virgin) (St Mark) *Chich 7*　**P** *Patr Bd*　**TR** G S BRIDGEWATER　**TV** D W BOUSKILL, N L LOVELESS, P L BERESFORD, R S COLDICOTT　**C** J A YOUNG　**NSM** B SINTON

HORSHAM ST FAITH (St Andrew and St Mary), Spixworth and Crostwick *Nor 2*   **P** *Bp and DBP (jt)*   **R** K A F RENGERT
HORSINGTON (All Saints)   *see* Woodhall Spa Gp *Linc*
HORSINGTON (St John the Baptist)   *see* Abbas and Templecombe, Henstridge and Horsington *B & W*
HORSLEY (Holy Trinity)   *see* N Tyne and Redesdale *Newc*
HORSLEY (St Clement) and Denby *Derby 12*   **P** *Bp and Mrs L B Palmer (jt)*   **P-in-c** A TAYLOR-COOK   **OLM** C C HOLDEN, M D JONES
HORSLEY (St Martin)   *see* Nailsworth w Shortwood, Horsley etc *Glouc*
HORSLEY HILL (St Lawrence the Martyr) South Shields *Dur 15*   **P** *D&C*   **P-in-c** D G HUNTLEY
HORSLEY WOODHOUSE (St Susanna) *Derby 12*   **P** *Bp*   **P-in-c** A TAYLOR-COOK   **OLM** M D JONES
HORSLEY, EAST (St Martin) *Guildf 10*   **P** *D&C Cant*   **R** *vacant*
HORSLEY, WEST (St Mary) *Guildf 10*   **P** *Col A R N Weston*   **R** *vacant*
HORSMONDEN (St Margaret) *Roch 8*   **P** *Bp*   **R** S G FAUCHON-JONES
HORSPATH (St Giles)   *see* Garsington, Cuddesdon and Horspath *Ox*
HORSTEAD (All Saints)   *see* Coltishall w Gt Hautbois, Frettenham etc *Nor*
HORSTED KEYNES (St Giles) *Chich 5*   **P** *Bp*   **R** J F TWISLETON   **NSM** D J HOWLAND
HORSTED PARVA (St Michael and All Angels)   *see* Lt Horsted *Chich*
HORSTED, LITTLE (St Michael and All Angels) *Chich 18*   **P** *The Rt Revd P J Ball*   **R** *vacant*
HORTON (St James the Elder)   *see* Sodbury Vale *Glouc*
HORTON (St Mary the Virgin) *Newc 1*   **P** *V Woodhorn w Newbiggin*   **NSM** J R SWINHOE
HORTON (St Michael and All Angels) and Wraysbury *Ox 12*   **P** *Major J M Halford and D&C Windsor (jt)*   **V** C T GIBSON   **C** J A D S FERNANDES
HORTON (St Peter)   *see* Isle Valley *B & W*
HORTON (St Wolfrida), Chalbury, Hinton Martel and Holt St James *Sarum 9*   **P** *DBP and Governors of Wimborne Minster (jt)*   **P-in-c** V A HERRICK   **C** B-J MARFLITT, S C ALLEN   **NSM** B GIBSON, E HARDING
HORTON, GREAT (St John the Evangelist) *Leeds 2*   **P** *V Bradf*   **V** J E BAVINGTON
HORTON, LITTLE (All Saints) (St Oswald) *Leeds 2*   **P** *Bp and J F Bardsley Esq (jt)*   **V** A S TREASURE   **C** J W HINTON   **NSM** M M MALEK, S A NEALE
HORTON-CUM-STUDLEY (St Barnabas)   *see* Beckley, Forest Hill, Horton-cum-Studley and Stanton St John *Ox*
HORTON-IN-RIBBLESDALE (St Oswald)   *see* Langcliffe w Stainforth and Horton *Leeds*
HORWICH (Holy Trinity) (St Catherine) (St Elizabeth) and Rivington *Man 9*   **P** *Patr Bd*   **TR** S FLETCHER   **TV** M C BEHRENS   **C** K E LAFFERTY   **OLM** C P TRACEY, G M SMART, T LITHERLAND
HORWOOD (St Michael)   *see* Newton Tracey, Horwood, Alverdiscott etc *Ex*
HORWOOD, GREAT (St James)   *see* Winslow w Gt Horwood and Addington *Ox*
HORWOOD, LITTLE (St Nicholas)   *see* Newton Longville, Mursley, Swanbourne etc *Ox*
HOSE (St Michael)   *see* Vale of Belvoir *Leic*
HOTHAM (St Oswald) *York 13*   **P** *Ld Chan*   **P-in-c** B WORSDALE
HOTHFIELD (St Margaret)   *see* G7 Benefice *Cant*
HOUGH GREEN (St Basil and All Saints) *Liv 13*   **P** *Bp*   **V** P W DAWKIN
HOUGHAM (All Saints)   *see* Barkston and Hough Gp *Linc*
HOUGHAM (St Laurence)   *see* Alkham w Capel le Ferne and Hougham *Cant*
HOUGH-ON-THE-HILL (All Saints)   *see* Barkston and Hough Gp *Linc*
HOUGHTON (All Saints)   *see* Broughton, Bossington, Houghton and Mottisfont *Win*
HOUGHTON (St Giles)   *see* Walsingham, Houghton and Barsham *Nor*
HOUGHTON (St John the Evangelist) (St Peter) *Carl 3*   **P** *Trustees*   **P-in-c** A P J TOWNER   **C** P M KERRY
HOUGHTON (St Martin)   *see* E w W Rudham, Helhoughton etc *Nor*
HOUGHTON (St Nicholas)   *see* Bury w Houghton and Coldwaltham and Hardham *Chich*
HOUGHTON CONQUEST (All Saints)   *see* Wilshamstead and Houghton Conquest *St Alb*
HOUGHTON LE SPRING (St Michael and All Angels) *Dur 14*   **P** *Bp*   **R** S J PINNINGTON   **C** B R TAYLOR   **NSM** M LEE

HOUGHTON REGIS (All Saints) (St Thomas) *St Alb 11*   **P** *DBP*   **P-in-c** D GALANZINO
HOUGHTON w WYTON (St Mary)   *see* Hartford and Houghton w Wyton *Ely*
HOUGHTON, GREAT (St Mary)   *see* Cogenhoe and Gt and Lt Houghton w Brafield *Pet*
HOUGHTON, LITTLE (St Mary the Blessed Virgin) *as above*
HOUGHTON, NEW (Christ Church)   *see* E Scarsdale *Derby*
HOUGHTON-ON-THE-HILL (St Catharine)   *see* Cornerstone Team *Leic*
HOUND (St Edward the Confessor) (St Mary the Virgin) *Win 10*   **P** *St Mary's Coll Win*   **P-in-c** R W SANDAY   **C** P A VARGESON
HOUNSLOW (Holy Trinity) *Lon 11*   **P** *Bp*   **P-in-c** S K WRIGHT   **NSM** N LAWRENCE
HOUNSLOW (St Paul) (Good Shepherd) *Lon 11*   **P** *Bp*   **V** E A ETHERINGTON
HOUNSLOW (St Stephen) *Lon 11*   **P** *Bp*   **V** R L RAMSDEN
HOVE (All Saints) *Chich 20*   **P** *Bp*   **NSM** K E LAWSON
HOVE (Bishop Hannington Memorial Church) (Holy Cross) *Chich 20*   **P** *Trustees*   **V** P R MOON   **C** J J MILSON, R M GRAHAM
HOVE (St Andrew Old Church) *Chich 20*   **P** *Bp*   **P-in-c** L A C MACLEAN   **C** D T HENDERSON
HOVE (St Barnabas) and St Agnes *Chich 20*   **P** *Bp and V Hove (alt)*   **V** L A C MACLEAN
HOVE (St John the Baptist) *Chich 20*   **P** *Bp*   **P-in-c** D R HOLT   **NSM** J F GREENFIELD
HOVE (St Philip)   *see* Aldrington *Chich*
HOVE EDGE (St Chad)   *see* Lightcliffe and Hove Edge *Leeds*
HOVE St Patrick *Chich 20*   **P** *Bp, V Hove, and V Brighton (jt)*   **P-in-c** T D WATSON
HOVERINGHAM (St Michael)   *see* Thurgarton w Hoveringham and Bleasby etc *S'well*
HOVETON (St John)   *see* Wroxham w Hoveton and Belaugh *Nor*
HOVETON (St Peter) *as above*
HOVINGHAM (All Saints)   *see* The Street Par *York*
HOW CAPLE (St Andrew and St Mary)   *see* Brampton *Heref*
HOWARDIAN GROUP, The *York 6*   **P** *Abp and Hon S B G Howard (jt)*   **R** C N B MORGAN
HOWDEN Team Ministry, The (St Peter) *York 13*   **P** *Abp (4 turns), Ld Chan (1 turn)*   **TR** J H LITTLE   **TV** G P THORNALLEY
HOWDEN-LE-WEAR St Mary the Virgin and Hunwick *Dur 9*   **P** *Bp and V Auckland St Andr (alt)*   **P-in-c** D L SPOKES
HOWE (St Mary the Virgin)   *see* Poringland *Nor*
HOWE BRIDGE (St Michael and All Angels)   *see* Atherton and Hindsford w Howe Bridge *Man*
HOWELL HILL (St Paul) w Burgh Heath *Guildf 9*   **P** *Bp*   **V** M J WAINWRIGHT   **C** I P HUGHES, P DEVER   **NSM** D N SENIOR, S THOMAS
HOWGILL (Holy Trinity)   *see* Firbank, Howgill and Killington *Carl*
HOWICK (St Michael and All Angels)   *see* Longhoughton w Howick *Newc*
HOWLE HILL (St John the Evangelist)   *see* Ross w Walford and Brampton Abbotts *Heref*
HOWSHAM (St John)   *see* Harton *York*
HOXNE (St Peter and St Paul)   *see* Athelington, Denham, Horham, Hoxne etc *St E*
HOXTON (Holy Trinity) (St Mary) *Lon 5*   **P** *Bp*   **V** A C NEWCOMBE
HOXTON (St Anne) (St Columba) *Lon 5*   **P** *The Crown*   **V** C M WOODS
HOXTON (St John the Baptist) w Ch Ch *Lon 5*   **P** *Haberdashers' Co and Adn (jt)*   **V** G HUNTER
HOYLAKE (Holy Trinity and St Hildeburgh) *Ches 8*   **P** *Bp*   **V** P A ROSSITER   **NSM** J C HARRISON
HOYLAND (St Peter) (St Andrew) *Sheff 11*   **P** *Bp and Sir Philip Naylor-Leyland Bt (jt)*   **V** R B PARKER
HOYLAND, HIGH (All Saints), Scissett and Clayton West *Leeds 13*   **P** *Bp*   **P-in-c** J E COUSANS   **NSM** K B CURRIE
HOYLANDSWAINE (St John the Evangelist) and Silkstone w Stainborough *Leeds 18*   **P** *Bp*   **V** M L BROWELL
HUBBERHOLME (St Michael and All Angels)   *see* Kettlewell w Conistone, Hubberholme etc *Leeds*
HUCCABY (St Raphael)   *see* Ashburton, Bickington, Buckland in the Moor etc *Ex*
HUCCLECOTE (St Philip and St James) *Glouc 2*   **P** *Bp*   **P-in-c** A J AXON
HUCKING (St Margaret)   *see* Hollingbourne and Hucking w Leeds and Broomfield *Cant*
HUCKNALL TORKARD (St Mary Magdalene) (St Peter and St Paul) (St John's Mission Church) *S'well 4*   **P** *Bp*   **TR** K HERROD   **TV** J L STEPHENS, L V NICOLLS   **C** J S PACEY   **NSM** C E TYACK

HUDDERSFIELD (Holy Trinity) *Leeds 12*   **P** *Simeon's Trustees*
V M R WILKINS   **NSM** R C SWINDELL

HUDDERSFIELD (St Francis) Fixby   *see Fixby and Cowcliffe*
Leeds

HUDDERSFIELD (St Hilda) Cowcliffe *as above*

HUDDERSFIELD (St John the Evangelist)   *see Birkby and*
Woodhouse Leeds

HUDDERSFIELD (St Peter) *Leeds 12*   **P** *DBP*   **V** S A MOOR
C S C CROOK

HUDDERSFIELD All Saints (St Thomas) *Leeds 12*   **P** *DBP*
V L A PINFIELD

HUDDERSFIELD Emmanuel   *see Em TM Leeds*

HUDDERSFIELD, NORTH (St Cuthbert)   *see Birkby and*
Birchencliffe Leeds

HUDDINGTON (St James)   *see Bowbrook S Worc*

HUDSWELL (St Michael and All Angels)   *see Richmond w*
Hudswell and Downholme and Marske Leeds

HUGGATE (St Mary)   *see Pocklington Wold York*

HUGGLESCOTE (St John the Baptist) w Donington, Ellistown
and Snibston *Leic 8*   **P** *Bp*   **TR** O S WOOLCOCK
NSM P ASHBY

HUGHENDEN (St Michael) *Ox 18*   **P** *DBP*   **V** S N CRONK
NSM H E PETERS

HUGHLEY (St John the Baptist)   *see Wenlock Heref*

HUISH (St James the Less)   *see Shebbear, Buckland Filleigh,*
Sheepwash etc Ex

HUISH (St Nicholas)   *see Vale of Pewsey Sarum*

HUISH CHAMPFLOWER (St Peter)   *see Wiveliscombe and the*
Hills B & W

HUISH EPISCOPI (Blessed Virgin Mary)   *see Langport Area*
B & W

HUISH, SOUTH (Holy Trinity)   *see Salcombe and Malborough w*
S Huish Ex

HULCOTE (St Nicholas)   *see Cranfield and Hulcote w Salford*
St Alb

HULCOTT (All Saints)

HULL (Ascension)   *see Derringham Bank York*

HULL (Holy Apostles)   *see Kingston upon Hull H Trin York*

HULL (Most Holy and Undivided Trinity) *as above*

HULL (St Aidan) Southcoates   *see Kingston upon Hull St Aid*
Southcoates York

HULL (St Alban)   *see Kingston upon Hull St Alb York*

HULL (St Cuthbert) *York 14*   **P** *Abp*   **V** J C COWAN

HULL (St John the Baptist)   *see Newington w Hull St Andr*
York

HULL (St John) Newland *York 14*   **P** *Abp*   **V** M TINKER
C L J MCMUNN

HULL (St Martin) w The Transfiguration *York 14*   **P** *Abp*
V S R J ELLIOTT

HULL (St Mary the Virgin) Lowgate   *see Kingston upon Hull*
St Mary York

HULL (St Mary) Sculcoates *York 14*   **P** *V Sculcoates*
P-in-c M G CROOK

HULL (St Nicholas)   *see Kingston upon Hull St Nic York*

HULL (St Paul)   *see Sculcoates York*

HULL (St Stephen) *as above*

HULL (St Thomas)   *see Derringham Bank York*

HULL, NORTH (St Michael and All Angels) *York 14*   **P** *Abp*
V D A WALKER   **NSM** A RICHARDS

HULLAND (Christ Church), Atlow, Kniveton, Bradley and
Hognaston *Derby 8*   **P** *Patr Bd*   **R** P L MICHELL

HULLAVINGTON (St Mary Magdalene), Norton and Stanton
St Quintin *Bris 6*   **P** *Bp, Eton Coll, and R W Neeld Esq (jt)*
P-in-c C P BRYAN   **Hon C** M M MASLEN   **OLM** S E HARVEY

HULLBRIDGE (St Thomas of Canterbury)   *see Rettendon and*
Hullbridge Chelmsf

HULME (Ascension) *Man 3*   **P** *Trustees*   **P-in-c** F SHER

HULME WALFIELD (St Michael)   *see Marton, Siddington w*
Capesthorne, and Eaton etc Ches

HULTON, LITTLE (St John the Baptist)   *see Walkden and Lt*
Hulton Man

HULTON, OVER (St Andrew)   *see Deane Man*

HUMBER (St Mary the Virgin)   *see Leominster Heref*

HUMBERSTON (St Peter) *Linc 4*   **P** *Bp*   **OLM** P R SALMON

HUMBERSTONE (St Mary)   *see Ascension TM Leic*

HUMBLE, WEST (St Michael)   *see Leatherhead and Mickleham*
Guildf

HUMBLETON (St Peter)   *see Burstwick, Burton Pidsea etc York*

HUMPHREY PARK (St Clement)   *see Urmston Man*

HUMSHAUGH (St Peter) w Simonburn and Wark *Newc 8*
P *Bp*   **R** *vacant*

HUNCOAT (St Augustine)   *see Accrington St Jo w Huncoat*
Blackb

HUNCOTE (St James the Greater)   *see Narborough and*
Huncote Leic

HUNDLEBY (St Mary)   *see Bolingbroke Deanery Linc*

HUNDON (All Saints)   *see Stourhead St E*

HUNDRED RIVER and Wainford *St E 18*   **P** *DBP, Shadingfield*
Property Ltd, Bp, F D L Barnes Esq, Miss to Seafarers,
Magd Coll Cam, and Ch Soc Trust (jt)   **R** P J NELSON
NSM J M LOFTUS

HUNGARTON (St John the Baptist)   *see Coplow Leic*

HUNGERFORD (St Lawrence) and Denford *Ox 6*   **P** *D&C*
Windsor   **V** *vacant*

HUNMANBY (All Saints) w Muston *York 15*   **P** *MMCET*
V *vacant*

HUNNINGHAM (St Margaret) *Cov 10*   **P** *Ld Chan*
V *vacant*

HUNSDON (St Dunstan) (St Francis) w Widford and
Wareside *St Alb 19*   **P** *DBP*   **R** M P DUNSTAN

HUNSINGORE (St John the Baptist)   *see Lower Nidderdale*
Leeds

HUNSLET (St Mary the Virgin) w Cross Green *Leeds 15*
P *Keble Coll Ox, Bp and TR Leeds City (jt)*   **C** A C N BUCKLEY

HUNSTANTON (St Edmund) w Ringstead *Nor 16*   **P** *H Le*
Strange Esq   **V** J S BLOOMFIELD

HUNSTANTON (St Mary) w Ringstead Parva, Holme-next-
the-Sea, Thornham, Brancaster, Burnham Deepdale and
Titchwell *Nor 16*   **P** *Bp, Exors of the late H le Strange Esq, and*
Exors of the late H S N Simms-Adams Esq (jt)
P-in-c S M BOWDEN-PICKSTOCK   **NSM** A J MONRO

HUNSTANWORTH (St James)   *see Blanchland w*
Hunstanworth and Edmundbyers etc Newc

HUNSTON (St Leodegar)   *see N Mundham w Hunston and*
Merston Chich

HUNSTON (St Michael)   *see Badwell and Walsham St E*

HUNTINGDON (All Saints w St John the Baptist) (St Mary) w
St Benedict and the Stukeleys *Ely 10*   **P** *Bp (2 turns), Ld*
Chan (1 turn), SMF (1 turn)   **V** A J MILTON

HUNTINGDON (St Barnabas) and the Riptons *Ely 10*   **P** *Lord*
de Ramsey, D&C, and Bp (jt)   **R** R H MASKELL

HUNTINGFIELD (St Mary)   *see Heveningham St E*

HUNTINGTON (All Saints) *York 7*   **P** *D&C*
R I G BIRKINSHAW   **C** P G CARMAN

HUNTINGTON (St Luke) *Ches 2*   **P** *Bp*
P-in-c S T PENDLEBURY   **C** C J S BLUNT

HUNTINGTON (St Mary Magdalene)   *see Holmer w*
Huntington Heref

HUNTINGTON (St Thomas à Becket)   *see Kington w*
Huntington, Old Radnor, Kinnerton etc Heref

HUNTINGTON (St Thomas)   *see Cannock and Huntington*
Lich

HUNTLEY (St John the Baptist) and Longhope, Churcham
and Bulley *Glouc 3*   **P** *Bp and D&C (jt)*   **P-in-c** C STERRY
C D A GILL

HUNTON (St James)   *see Upper Dever Win*

HUNTON (St Mary)   *see Coxheath, E Farleigh, Hunton, Linton*
etc Roch

HUNTS CROSS (St Hilda)   *see Halewood and Hunts Cross Liv*

HUNTSHAM (All Saints)   *see Bampton, Morebath, Clayhanger,*
Petton etc Ex

HUNTSHAW (St Mary Magdalene)   *see Newton Tracey,*
Horwood, Alverdiscott etc Ex

HUNTSPILL (St Peter and All Hallows) *B & W 1*   **P** *Ball Coll Ox*
P-in-c T NIXON   **C** S M J CROSSMAN

HUNWICK (St Paul)   *see Howden-le-Wear and Hunwick Dur*

HUNWORTH (St Lawrence)   *see Brinton, Briningham,*
Hunworth, Stody etc Nor

HURDSFIELD (Holy Trinity) *Ches 13*   **P** *Hyndman Trustees*
V *vacant*

HURLEY (Resurrection)   *see Baxterley w Hurley and Wood End*
and Merevale etc Birm

HURLEY (St Mary the Virgin)   *see Burchetts Green Ox*

HURSLEY (All Saints)   *see Compton, Hursley, and Otterbourne*
Win

HURST (St John the Evangelist) *Man 13*   **P** *The Crown*
P-in-c E J DEVALL

HURST (St Nicholas)   *see Ruscombe and Twyford w Hurst Ox*

HURST GREEN (Holy Trinity) *Chich 13*   **P** *Bp*   **V** *vacant*

HURST GREEN (St John the Evangelist)   *see Oxted S'wark*

HURST GREEN (St John the Evangelist) and Mitton *Blackb 7*
P *Bp and J E R Aspinall Esq (jt)*   **V** G F MACK

HURSTBOURNE PRIORS (St Andrew), Longparish, St Mary
Bourne and Woodcott *Win 6*   **P** *Bp and J C Woodcock Esq (jt)*
V C L MARSHALL   **NSM** D M MARSDEN, R J SUTCLIFFE,
T E HEMMING

HURSTBOURNE TARRANT (St Peter) and Faccombe and
Vernham Dean and Linkenholt *Win 3*   **P** *Bp*
P-in-c D J KEIGHLEY

HURSTPIERPOINT (Holy Trinity) (St George) *Chich 8*
P *Hurstpierpoint Coll*   **P-in-c** J E WILLIS   **C** W KEMP
NSM D M BEER

HURSTWOOD, HIGH (Holy Trinity) *Chich* 18   P *Abp*
  P-in-c D A TIDSWELL
HURWORTH (All Saints) *Dur* 8   P *Ch Soc Trust*
  P-in-c A J MARTIN
HUSBANDS BOSWORTH (All Saints)   *see* Hexagon *Leic*
HUSBORNE CRAWLEY (St Mary Magdalene or St James)
  see Aspley Guise w Husborne Crawley and Ridgmont *St Alb*
HUSTHWAITE (St Nicholas)   *see* Coxwold and Husthwaite *York*
HUTHWAITE (All Saints) *S'well* 4   P *V* Sutton-in-Ashfield
  V C A K MAIDEN
HUTTOFT (St Margaret)   *see* Sutton, Huttoft and Anderby *Linc*
HUTTON (All Saints) (St Peter) *Chelmsf* 8   P *D&C St Paul's*
  NSM A BAXTER
HUTTON (Blessed Virgin Mary) and Locking *B & W* 10
  P *DBP and MMCET (jt)*   **R** A L LEE
HUTTON BUSCEL (St Matthew)   *see* Upper Derwent *York*
HUTTON CRANSWICK (St Peter) w Skerne, Watton and
  Beswick *York* 10   P *Abp*   **P-in-c** B J LEES   **NSM** H J BOON
HUTTON HENRY (St Francis)   *see* Wheatley Hill and Wingate w
  Hutton Henry *Dur*
HUTTON MAGNA (St Mary)   *see* Barningham w Hutton
  Magna and Wycliffe *Leeds*
HUTTON ROOF (St John the Divine)   *see* Kirkby Lonsdale *Carl*
HUTTON, OLD (St John the Baptist) and New Hutton
  (St Stephen) *Carl* 10   P *V Kendal*   **P-in-c** A WHITTAKER
  NSM M MAIDEN
HUTTON-IN-THE-FOREST (St James)   *see* Inglewood Gp *Carl*
HUTTON-LE-HOLE (St Chad)   *see* Lastingham w Appleton-le-
  Moors, Rosedale etc *York*
HUTTONS AMBO (St Margaret)   *see* Howardian Gp *York*
HUXHAM (St Mary the Virgin)   *see* Brampford Speke, Cadbury,
  Newton St Cyres etc *Ex*
HUXLEY (St Andrew)   *see* Hargrave *Ches*
HUYTON (St George)   *see* 4Saints Team *Liv*
HUYTON (St Michael) *Liv* 2   P *Earl of Derby*   **V** J A STANLEY
HUYTON QUARRY (St Gabriel) *Liv* 2   P *V Huyton St Mich*
  V M K ROGERS
HYDE (Holy Ascension)   *see* Hyde w Ellingham and Harbridge
  Win
HYDE (Holy Ascension) w Ellingham and Harbridge *Win* 9
  P *Earl of Normanton and Keble Coll Ox (jt)*
  P-in-c I S WHITHAM
HYDE (St George) *Ches* 14   P *R Stockport St Mary*
  V J C PARKER
HYDE (St Thomas) *Ches* 14   P *Bp*   **P-in-c** P J HIBBERT
HYDE HEATH (Mission Church)   *see* Lt Missenden *Ox*
HYDE, WEST (St Thomas of Canterbury)   *see* Mill End and
  Heronsgate w W Hyde *St Alb*
HYDNEYE (St Peter)   *see* Hampden Park and The Hydnye *Chich*
HYKEHAM (All Saints) (St Hugh) (St Michael and All Angels)
  Linc 12   P *Ld Chan and Bp (alt)*   **R** P G COLLINS
  NSM G F REID
HYLTON, SOUTH (St Mary) *Dur* 1   P *Bp*   **V** *vacant*
HYSON GREEN (St Stephen) and Forest Fields *S'well* 9
  P *CPAS*   **V** C R BURROWS   **NSM** D WATKINSON
HYSSINGTON (St Etheldreda)   *see* Churchstoke w Hyssington
  and Sarn *Heref*
HYTHE (St John the Baptist) *Win* 11   P *Bp*   **P-in-c** J ELVIDGE
HYTHE (St Leonard) (St Michael and All Angels) *Cant* 8
  P *R Saltwood*   **P-in-c** A J SWEENEY
HYTHE Butts Ash (St Anne)   *see* Hythe *Win*
IBBERTON (St Eustace)   *see* Hazelbury Bryan and the Hillside
  Par *Sarum*
IBSTOCK (St Denys) w Heather *Leic* 8   P *Bp and MMCET (jt)*
  P-in-c P L BAILEY
IBSTONE (St Nicholas)   *see* Stokenchurch and Ibstone *Ox*
ICKBURGH (St Peter) w Langford *Nor* 13   P *Bp*   **R** *vacant*
ICKENHAM (St Giles) *Lon* 24   P *Eton Coll*   **R** F A DAVIES
ICKFORD (St Nicholas)   *see* Worminghall w Ickford, Oakley
  and Shabbington *Ox*
ICKHAM (St John the Evangelist)   *see* Littlebourne and Ickham
  w Wickhambreaux etc *Cant*
ICKLEFORD (St Katherine)   *see* Holwell, Ickleford and Pirton
  St Alb
ICKLESHAM (St Nicolas)   *see* Winchelsea and Icklesham *Chich*
ICKLETON (St Mary Magdalene) *Ely* 5   P *Ld Chan*
  P-in-c J H MARTIN   **NSM** P M SHARKEY
ICKLINGHAM (All Saints w St James)   *see* Mildenhall *St E*
ICKNIELD *Ox* 20   P *Ld Chan (1 turn), Ch Ch Ox (1 turn), Bp and
  Earl of Macclesfield (1 turn)*   **R** C I EVANS
  NSM A M PATERSON, L AUSTIN
ICKNIELD WAY VILLAGES *Chelmsf* 20   P *Patr Bd*
  R A COLEBROOKE
ICOMB (St Mary)   *see* Broadwell, Evenlode, Oddington,
  Adlestrop etc *Glouc*
IDBURY (St Nicholas)   *see* Wychwood *Ox*

IDDESLEIGH (St James)   *see* Dolton, Dowland, Iddesleigh
  etc *Ex*
IDE (St Ida)   *see* Alphington, Shillingford St George and
  Ide *Ex*
IDE HILL (St Mary the Virgin)   *see* Sundridge w Ide Hill and Toys
  Hill *Roch*
IDEFORD (St Mary the Virgin)   *see* Teignmouth, Ideford w
  Luton, Ashcombe etc *Ex*
IDEN (All Saints)   *see* Rye *Chich*
IDLE (Holy Trinity) *Leeds* 3   P *V Calverley*   **P-in-c** R P GAMBLE
  C N J TAYLOR
IDLICOTE (St James the Great)   *see* Shipston-on-Stour w
  Honington and Idlicote *Cov*
IDRIDGEHAY (St James)   *see* Wirksworth *Derby*
IDSWORTH (St Hubert)   *see* Blendworth w Chalton w Idsworth
  Portsm
IFFLEY (St Mary the Virgin) *Ox* 1   P *Ch Ch Ox*
  V A R MCKEARNEY   **C** S E NORTHALL   **NSM** W C BEAVER
IFIELD (St Margaret) *Chich* 6   P *Bp*   **TR** S F E NEWHAM
  TV A M ALEXANDER   **C** J GATER   **NSM** D M GOODWIN,
  G M BURGESS
IFIELD (St Margaret)   *see* Gravesend H Family w Ifield *Roch*
IFORD (St Nicholas) w Kingston and Rodmell and Southease
  Chich 21   P *Bp and Gorham Trustees (jt)*   **V** G M DAW
  NSM M C BROWN, M E SITWELL
IFORD (St Saviour)   *see* Holdenhurst and Iford *Win*
IGHTFIELD (St John the Baptist)   *see* Adderley, Ash, Calverhall,
  Ightfield etc *Lich*
IGHTHAM (St Peter) *Roch* 10   P *C B Winnifrith Esq*
  R T R HATWELL
IKEN (St Botolph)   *see* Wilford Peninsula *St E*
ILAM (Holy Cross)   *see* Alstonfield, Butterton, Ilam etc *Lich*
ILCHESTER (St Mary Major) w Northover, Limington,
  Yeovilton and Podimore *B & W* 5   P *Bp Lon (7 turns),*
  Bp (1 turn), and Wadh Coll Ox (1 turn)   **P-in-c** B S FAULKNER
ILDERTON (St Michael)   *see* Glendale Gp *Newc*
ILFORD, GREAT (St Alban) *Chelmsf* 6   P *Bp*   **V** S HALSTEAD
ILFORD, GREAT (St Andrew) *Chelmsf* 6   P *Bp*   **V** M SEGAL
  NSM S H STERRY
ILFORD, GREAT (St John the Evangelist) *Chelmsf* 6   P *Bp*
  V *vacant*
ILFORD, GREAT (St Luke) *Chelmsf* 6   P *Bp*   **V** J BROWN
ILFORD, GREAT (St Margaret of Antioch) (St Clement)
  Chelmsf 6   P *Patr Bd*   **V** S G PUGH
ILFORD, GREAT (St Mary the Virgin) *Chelmsf* 6   P *V Gt Ilford*
  V G E J P JONES
ILFORD, LITTLE (St Barnabas) *Chelmsf* 5   P *Bp*
  V J A RAMSAY
ILFORD, LITTLE (St Michael and All Angels) *Chelmsf* 5
  P *Hertf Coll Ox*   **R** B J LEWIS   **C** N P MORROW
ILFRACOMBE (Holy Trinity) (St Peter), Lee, Woolacombe,
  Bittadon and Mortehoe *Ex* 14   P *Patr Bd*
  P-in-c R D HARRIS   **TV** G A B KING-SMITH
  NSM J W ROLES, L WALTERS
ILFRACOMBE (St Philip and St James) *Ex* 14   P *Ch Trust Fund*
  Trust   **R** M H W ROGERS
ILKESTON (Holy Trinity) *Derby* 13   P *Bp*   **P-in-c** R A JUPP
  Hon C P R S BOLTON
ILKESTON (St John the Evangelist) *Derby* 13   P *V Ilkeston*
  St Mary   **P-in-c** W P WATERS   **NSM** C J GRAHAM
ILKESTON (St Mary the Virgin) *Derby* 13   P *Bp*
  V M D PETITT
ILKETSHALL ST ANDREW (St Andrew)   *see* Hundred River and
  Wainford *St E*
ILKETSHALL ST JOHN (St John the Baptist)   *see* S Elmham and
  Ilketshall *St E*
ILKETSHALL ST LAWRENCE (St Lawrence) *as above*
ILKETSHALL ST MARGARET (St Margaret) *as above*
ILKLEY (All Saints) *Leeds* 4   P *Hyndman Trustees*
  V P J BATEMAN   **C** S PROUDLOVE   **NSM** M P REID,
  R F WATSON
ILKLEY (St Margaret) *Leeds* 4   P *CR*   **V** P C GRAY
  C C P PHILLIPS
ILLOGAN (St Illogan)   *see* St Illogan *Truro*
ILLSTON (St Michael and All Angels)   *see* Gaulby *Leic*
ILMER (St Peter)   *see* Risborough *Ox*
ILMINGTON (St Mary) and Stretton-on-Fosse and Ditchford
  w Preston-on-Stour w Whitchurch and Atherstone-on-
  Stour *Cov* 9   P *Bp, MMCET, and Ms C A Alston-Roberts-West*
  (jt)   **P-in-c** C C GOBLE   **Hon C** S A EDMONDS
ILMINSTER (Blessed Virgin Mary) and Whitelackington
  B & W 16   P *Bp*   **V** N A DONE   **NSM** V M HOARE
ILSINGTON (St Michael) *Ex* 8   P *D&C Windsor*
  P-in-c D R HARRIS
ILSLEY, EAST (St Mary)   *see* Hermitage *Ox*
ILSLEY, WEST (All Saints)   *see* E Downland *Ox*

ILTON (St Peter)   *see* Isle Valley *B & W*

IMMINGHAM Group, The (St Andrew) *Linc 4*   **P** *Bp and DBP*
C J DONN

IMPINGTON (St Andrew) *Ely 6*   **P** *Adn Ely*
P-in-c N J BLANDFORD-BAKER   **C** R J KELLOW
NSM J M GLOVER, O M K COLES

INCE IN MAKERFIELD (Christ Church)   *see* Wigan All SS *Liv*

INCE IN MAKERFIELD (St Mary) *as above*

INDIAN QUEEN (St Francis)   *see* St Enoder *Truro*

INGATESTONE (St Edmund and St Mary) w Fryerning
Chelmsf 8   **P** *Bp and Wadh Coll Ox (jt)*   **V** P SHERRING
C A D FINN   **NSM** C A PARKES

INGESTRE (St Mary the Virgin)   *see* Stafford St Jo and Tixall w
Ingestre *Lich*

INGHAM (All Saints)   *see* Spring Line Gp *Linc*

INGHAM (Holy Trinity)   *see* Stalham, E Ruston, Brunstead,
Sutton and Ingham *Nor*

INGHAM (St Bartholomew)   *see* Blackbourne *St E*

INGLEBY ARNCLIFFE (All Saints)   *see* Osmotherley w Harlsey
and Ingleby Arncliffe *York*

INGLEBY BARWICK (St Francis) *York 20*   **P** *Abp*
V J C ROUNDTREE   **C** C E REID   **NSM** D J SLADDEN

INGLEBY GREENHOW (St Andrew), Bilsdale Priory and
Kildale w Kirkby-in-Cleveland *York 20*   **P** *Abp, Adn
Cleveland, Bp Whitby, Viscount De L'Isle, R G Beckett Esq, and
A H W Sutcliffe Esq (jt)*   **V** M A HEADING

INGLETON (St John the Evangelist) *Dur 8*   **P** *Lord Barnard*
P-in-c K STEVENTON

INGLETON (St Mary the Virgin)   *see* Bentham, Burton-in-
Lonsdale, Chapel-le-Dale etc *Leeds*

INGLEWOOD Group, The *Carl 4*   **P** *Bp, D&C, CCC Ox, and E
P Ecroyd Esq (jt)*   **R** P J DORLING

INGOL (St Margaret) *Blackb 13*   **P** *Bp*   **V** N F E STARKEY

INGOLDMELLS (St Peter and St Paul)   *see* Skegness Gp *Linc*

INGOLDSBY (St Bartholomew)   *see* N Beltisloe Gp *Linc*

INGRAM (St Michael)   *see* Glendale Gp *Newc*

INGRAVE (St Nicholas) (St Stephen) *Chelmsf 8*   **P** *Bp and
Ch Patr Trust (jt)*   **V** P S HAMILTON

INGRAVE (St Stephen) Conventional District *Chelmsf 8*
NSM J A SEDANO

INGROW (St John the Evangelist) with Hainworth *Leeds 5*
P *Bp*   **V** C H KIRKE

INGS (St Anne)   *see* Staveley, Ings and Kentmere *Carl*

INGWORTH (St Lawrence)   *see* Erpingham w Calthorpe,
Ingworth, Aldborough etc *Nor*

INHAM NOOK (St Barnabas)   *see* Chilwell *S'well*

INKBERROW (St Peter)   *see* Inkberrow w Cookhill and Kington
w Dormston *Worc*

INKBERROW (St Peter) w Cookhill and Kington w Dormston
Worc 1   **P** *Bp*   **NSM** D HAYWARD-WRIGHT

INKERSALL (St Columba)   *see* Staveley and Barrow Hill *Derby*

INKPEN (St Michael)   *see* Walbury Beacon *Ox*

INSKIP (St Peter)   *see* Copp w Inskip *Blackb*

INSTOW (All Saints Chapel)   *see* Fremington, Instow and
Westleigh *Ex*

INSTOW (St John the Baptist) *as above*

INTAKE (All Saints)   *see* Wheatley Hills w Intake *Sheff*

INTWOOD (All Saints)   *see* Swardeston w E Carleton, Intwood,
Keswick etc *Nor*

INWARDLEIGH (St Petroc)   *see* Okehampton, Inwardleigh,
Belstone, Sourton etc *Ex*

INWORTH (All Saints)   *see* Thurstable and Winstree *Chelmsf*

IPING (St Mary)   *see* Stedham w Iping *Chich*

IPPLEPEN (St Andrew) w Torbryan, Denbury and
Broadhempston w Woodland *Ex 9*   **P** *PM (1 turn) and D&C
Windsor and SMF (jt)*   **R** P M ASHMAN

IPSDEN (St Mary the Virgin)   *see* Langtree *Ox*

IPSLEY (St Peter) *Worc 7*   **P** *Patr Bd*   **TR** G E P NATHANIEL
TV R W HARDING   **C** G R NOYES   **NSM** I D EVANS

IPSTONES (St Leonard) w Berkhamsytch and Onecote w
Bradnop *Lich 6*   **P** *Bp and R Leek and Meerbrook (jt)*
V M J EVANS

IPSWICH (All Hallows) *St E 4*   **P** *Bp*   **P-in-c** A J OAKEY-JONES

IPSWICH (All Saints)   *see* Triangle, St Matt and All SS *St E*

IPSWICH (St Andrew) *St E 4*   **P** *Bp*   **P-in-c** M N PRENTICE

IPSWICH (St Augustine of Hippo) *St E 4*   **P** *Bp*
V T GOLDING   **NSM** I G DANIELS

IPSWICH (St Bartholomew) *St E 4*   **P** *Bp*   **V** P J CARTER

IPSWICH (St Helen) (Holy Trinity) (St Clement w St Luke)
St E 4   **P** *Ch Patr Trust*   **P-in-c** T ROUT

IPSWICH (St John the Baptist) *St E 4*   **P** *Simeon's Trustees*
P-in-c M N PRENTICE

IPSWICH (St Margaret) *St E 4*   **P** *Simeon's Trustees*
V D CUTTS

IPSWICH (St Mary at Stoke) (St Peter) (St Francis) (St Clare's
Church Centre) *St E 4*   **P** *Bp*   **TR** R C HINSLEY

TV A L CHESWORTH, M S G MORGAN

IPSWICH (St Mary at the Elms) *St E 4*   **P** *Guild of All So*
P-in-c J A THACKRAY

IPSWICH (St Mary-le-Tower) (St Nicholas) *St E 4*   **P** *Bp (3
turns), Ch Patr Trust (1 turn)*   **V** C A G JENKIN

IPSWICH (St Matthew)   *see* Triangle, St Matt and All SS *St E*

IPSWICH (St Thomas) *St E 4*   **P** *Bp*   **V** *vacant*

IRBY (St Chad's Mission Church)   *see* Thurstaston *Ches*

IRBY ON HUMBER (St Andrew)   *see* Wolds Gateway Group *Linc*

IRBY-IN-THE-MARSH (All Saints)   *see* Burgh Gp *Linc*

IRCHESTER (St Katharine) *Pet 8*   **P** *Bp*   **V** *vacant*

IRELAND WOOD (St Paul) *Leeds 16*   **P** *R Adel*
P-in-c I J WHITE   **NSM** I H JOHNSTON, L E LUDKIN

IRLAM (St John the Baptist) *Man 18*   **P** *Trustees*
V J E WARHURST   **OLM** J DODD

IRNHAM (St Andrew)   *see* Corby Glen *Linc*

IRON ACTON (St James the Less)   *see* Frampton Cotterell and
Iron Acton *Bris*

IRONBRIDGE (St Luke)   *see* Coalbrookdale, Iron-Bridge and
Lt Wenlock *Heref*

IRONSTONE VILLAGES Family of Churches, The *Leic 2*
P *Lady Gretton, Ld Chan, Duke of Rutland, Bp, and Sir Lyonel
Tollemache Bt (by turn)*   **R** B A STARK

IRONSTONE : Drayton, Hanwell, Horley, Hornton,
Shenington w Alkerton, and Wroxton w Balscote *Ox 23*
P *Ld Chan (1 turn), Bp, Earl De la Warr, and DBP (1 turn)*
R J READER   **C** H R B WHITE

IRONVILLE (Christ Church)   *see* Riddings and Ironville *Derby*

IRSTEAD (St Michael)   *see* Ashmanhaugh, Barton Turf etc *Nor*

IRTHINGTON (St Kentigern)   *see* Eden, Gelt and Irthing *Carl*

IRTHLINGBOROUGH (St Peter), Great Addington, Little
Addington and Woodford *Pet 8*   **P** *Bp, Sir Philip Naylor-
Leyland Bt, and DBP (jt)*   **R** J T P HALL   **C** E R BOND
NSM P M TATE

IRTON (St Paul)   *see* Eskdale, Irton, Muncaster and
Waberthwaite *Carl*

ISFIELD (St Margaret) *Chich 18*   **P** *Abp*   **R** *vacant*

ISHAM (St Peter)   *see* Gt w Lt Harrowden and Orlingbury and
Isham etc *Pet*

ISLE ABBOTTS (Blessed Virgin Mary)   *see* Isle Valley *B & W*

ISLE BREWERS (All Saints) *as above*

ISLE OF DOGS (Christ Church and St John) (St Luke) *Lon 7*
P *Bp*   **V** T F PYKE   **C** E J DIX, U A CHINDABATA

ISLE VALLEY *B & W 16*   **P** *Bp, D&C Bris, and Dr W P Palmer (jt)*
NSM M E CRANSTON, T J GIBSON

ISLEHAM (St Andrew)   *see* Three Rivers Gp *Ely*

ISLES OF SCILLY : St Mary's, St Agnes, St Martin's, Bryher
and Tresco *Truro 6*   **P** *Duchy of Cornwall*   **C** E MARTIN
Hon **C** P A PRINCE

ISLEWORTH (All Saints) *Lon 11*   **P** *D&C Windsor*
NSM V LUCKETT

ISLEWORTH (St Francis of Assisi) *Lon 11*   **P** *Bp*   **V** *vacant*

ISLEWORTH (St John the Baptist) (St Mary the Virgin) *Lon 11*
P *Bp and V Isleworth All SS (jt)*   **V** T A GILLUM
C D S MACLURE   Hon **C** J K KAOMA

ISLEWORTH (St Luke)   *see* Spring Grove St Mary *Lon*

ISLEWORTH (St Mary) Osterley Road *as above*

ISLEY WALTON (All Saints)   *see* Ashby-de-la-Zouch and Breedon
on the Hill *Leic*

ISLINGTON (St James the Apostle) (St Peter) *Lon 6*   **P** *Bp*
V A J BURNISTON

ISLINGTON (St Jude and St Paul)   *see* Mildmay Grove St Jude
and St Paul *Lon*

ISLINGTON (St Mary Magdalene)   *see* Holloway St Mary Magd
Lon

ISLINGTON (St Mary) *Lon 6*   **P** *CPAS*   **V** S J HARVEY
C G NAYLOR

ISLIP (St Nicholas)   *see* Ray Valley *Ox*

ISLIP (St Nicholas)   *see* Thrapston, Denford and Islip *Pet*

ISTEAD RISE (St Barnabas) *Roch 4*   **P** *Bp*   **V** A K VAUGHAN

ITCHEN ABBAS (St John the Baptist)   *see* Itchen Valley *Win*

ITCHEN VALLEY, The *Win 1*   **P** *Ld Chan*   **R** A J DENNISS
C R S FARDELL   **NSM** A M PEASE

ITCHEN, UPPER *Win 1*   **P** *Prime Min (2 turns), D&C (1 turn)*
R G P BOWKETT   **NSM** C M E STRUDWICK

ITCHENOR, WEST (St Nicholas)   *see* W Wittering and Birdham
w Itchenor *Chich*

ITCHINGFIELD (St Nicholas) w Slinfold *Chich 6*   **P** *Bp*
P-in-c S J HALL

ITTERINGHAM   *see* Lt Barningham, Blickling, Edgefield etc *Nor*

IVEGILL (Christ Church)   *see* Inglewood Gp *Carl*

IVER (St Peter) *Ox 12*   **P** *Trustees*   **V** R H GOODING

IVER HEATH (St Margaret) *Ox 12*   **P** *Trustees*
R A S MONTGOMERIE

IVINGHOE (St Mary the Virgin) w Pitstone and Slapton and
Marsworth *Ox 15*   **P** *Bp and Ch Ch Ox (jt)*   **V** A P MANNING

IVINGTON (St John)   *see* Leominster *Heref*
IVYBRIDGE (St John the Evangelist) w Harford *Ex* 20   **P** *Bp*
   V C H OSBORNE
IVYCHURCH (St George)   *see* Romney Marsh *Cant*
IWADE (All Saints)   *see* The Six *Cant*
IWERNE COURTNEY (St Mary)   *see* Iwerne Valley *Sarum*
IWERNE MINSTER (St Mary) *as above*
IWERNE VALLEY *Sarum* 7   **P** *D&C Windsor, DBP, G A L F Pitt-
   Rivers Esq, and A C L Sturge Esq (jt)*   **Hon C** J E WARING
   NSM J H SIMMONS
IXWORTH (St Mary)   *see* Blackbourne *St E*
IXWORTH THORPE (All Saints) *as above*
JACKFIELD (St Mary)   *see* Broseley w Benthall, Jackfield,
   Linley etc *Heref*
JACOBSTOW (St James)   *see* Week St Mary Circle of Par *Truro*
JACOBSTOWE (St James)   *see* Okehampton, Inwardleigh,
   Belstone, Sourton etc *Ex*
JARROW (St John the Baptist) (St Mark) (St Paul) (St Peter)
   Dur 15   **P** *Bp*   **P-in-c** G H MAUDE   **C** E H CAMPBELL
JARROW GRANGE (Christ Church) *Dur* 15   **P** *Lord
   Northbourne*   **P-in-c** D T OSMAN
JARVIS BROOK (St Michael and All Angels) *Chich* 16   **P** *Bp*
   V A W WEAVER
JERSEY (All Saints) *Win* 15   **P** *R St Helier, Bp, and The Crown (by
   turn)*   **V** D G GRANTHAM, P46026J SEQUESTRATORS
   NSM J A DAVY
JERSEY (Holy Trinity) *Win* 15   **P** *The Crown*
   R G J HOUGHTON
JERSEY (St Andrew) *Win* 15   **P** *Dean of Jersey*   **V** M S TAYLOR
JERSEY (St Brelade) (Communicare Chapel) (St Aubin)
   Win 15   **P** *The Crown*   **R** M F W BOND
JERSEY (St Clement) *Win* 15   **P** *The Crown*   **R** D M SHAW
   NSM M J DRYDEN, T LE COUTEUR
JERSEY (St Helier) *Win* 15   **P** *The Crown*   **R** F KEY
   C C JERVIS   **NSM** A D WILLIAMS
JERSEY (St John) *Win* 15   **P** *The Crown*   **R** A J THEWLIS
JERSEY (St Lawrence) *Win* 15   **P** *The Crown*   **R** P J WARREN
JERSEY (St Luke) St James *Win* 15   **P** *Bp and The Crown (alt)*
   V N B P BARRY
JERSEY (St Mark) *Win* 15   **P** *Bp*   **V** M P L SHEA
JERSEY (St Martin) *Win* 15   **P** *The Crown*   **R** G L BAUDAINS
JERSEY (St Mary) *Win* 15   **P** *The Crown*   **Hon C** B ROSTILL
JERSEY (St Ouen) (St George) *Win* 15   **P** *The Crown*
   R I PALLENT
JERSEY (St Paul) Proprietary Chapel *Win* 15   **Min** P J BROOKS
JERSEY (St Peter) *Win* 15   **P** *The Crown*   **R** *vacant*
JERSEY (St Saviour) *Win* 15   **P** *The Crown*   **R** *vacant*
JERSEY (St Simon) *Win* 15   **P** *R St Helier, Bp, and The Crown
   (by turn)*   **V** D G GRANTHAM   **NSM** J A DAVY
JERSEY DE GROUVILLE (St Martin) (St Peter la Roque) *Win* 15
   P *The Crown*   **R** M L LANGE-SMITH   **NSM** R C DUPRÉ
JERSEY Gouray (St Martin) *Win* 15   **P** *Bp and The Crown (alt)*
   V G R P ASHENDEN, P46007R SEQUESTRATORS
JERSEY Greve d'Azette (St Nicholas)   *see* Jersey St Clem *Win*
JERSEY Millbrook (St Matthew) *Win* 15   **P** *The Crown*
   V P J WARREN
JESMOND (Clayton Memorial Church) *Newc* 2   **P** *Trustees*
   V D R J HOLLOWAY   **C** J J S PRYKE   **Hon C** A F MUNDEN
JESMOND (Holy Trinity) *Newc* 2   **P** *Trustees*   **V** M WROE
   C T SANDERSON   **NSM** J B CARR
JESMOND (St George)   *see* Newc St Geo and St Hilda *Newc*
JESMOND (St Hilda) *as above*
JEVINGTON (St Andrew)   *see* E Dean w Friston and Jevington
   Chich
JOYDENS WOOD (St Barnabas) *Roch* 17   **P** *Bp*
   V R E L HARDING
JURBY (St Patrick)   *see* Andreas, Ballaugh, Jurby and Sulby
   S & M
KATE'S HILL (St John)   *see* Dudley St Jo *Worc*
KEA (All Hallows) (Old Church) *Truro* 6   **P** *V St Clement*
   P-in-c M C BAKER   **C** J L HILLS
KEAL, EAST (St Helen)   *see* Bolingbroke Deanery *Linc*
KEAL, WEST (St Helen) *as above*
KEARSLEY (St Stephen)   *see* Farnworth, Kearsley and
   Stoneclough *Man*
KEASDEN (St Matthew)   *see* Clapham-with-Keasden and
   Austwick *Leeds*
KEDINGTON (St Peter and St Paul)   *see* Stourhead *St E*
KEEDWELL HILL (Ascension)   *see* Long Ashton w Barrow
   Gurney and Flax Bourton *B & W*
KEELBY (St Bartholomew)   *see* Wolds Gateway Group *Linc*
KEELE (St John the Baptist) *Lich* 9   **P** *T H G Howard-Sneyd Esq*
   V P C JONES
KEEVIL (St Leonard)   *see* Trowbridge St Jas and Keevil *Sarum*
KEGWORTH (St Andrew), Hathern, Long Whatton,
   Diseworth, Belton and Osgathorpe *Leic* 6   **P** *Patr Bd*
   TV T E EDMONDS   **NSM** L A BUTLER

KEIGHLEY (All Saints) *Leeds* 5   **P** *Bp and R Keighley St Andr*
   P-in-c J L PRITCHARD   **Hon C** M S FOY
KEIGHLEY (St Andrew) *Leeds* 5   **P** *Bp*   **TR** *vacant*
KEINTON MANDEVILLE (St Mary Magdalene)   *see* Wheathill
   Priory Gp *B & W*
KELBROOK (St Mary)   *see* Earby w Kelbrook *Leeds*
KELBY (St Andrew)   *see* Ancaster Wilsford Gp *Linc*
KELHAM (St Wilfrid)   *see* Averham w Kelham *S'well*
KELLET, NETHER (St Mark)   *see* Bolton-le-Sands *Blackb*
KELLET, OVER (St Cuthbert) *Blackb* 14   **P** *Reformation Ch Trust*
   V K CLAPHAM
KELLING (St Mary)   *see* Weybourne Gp *Nor*
KELLINGTON (St Edmund)   *see* Knottingley and Kellington w
   Whitley *Leeds*
KELLOE (St Helen) and Coxhoe *Dur* 5   **P** *Bp*   **P-in-c** D J BELL
KELLS (St Peter) *Carl* 5   **P** *Bp*   **P-in-c** S G SANDHAM
   NSM A J BANKS
KELLY (St Mary the Virgin)   *see* Lifton, Broadwoodwidger,
   Stowford etc *Ex*
KELMARSH (St Denys)   *see* Clipston w Naseby and Haselbech w
   Kelmarsh *Pet*
KELSALE (St Peter)   *see* Saxmundham w Kelsale cum Carlton
   St E
KELSALL (St Philip) *Ches* 2   **P** *V Tarvin*   **V** P J MACKRIELL
KELSEY Group, The *Linc* 7   **P** *Bp (3 turns), J M B Young Esq
   and S B Young Esq (1 turn)*   **P-in-c** G SPENCER
KELSEY, NORTH (All Hallows)   *see* Kelsey Gp *Linc*
KELSEY, SOUTH (St Mary) *as above*
KELSHALL (St Faith)   *see* Therfield w Kelshall *St Alb*
KELSTERN (St Faith)   *see* Binbrook Gp *Linc*
KELSTON (St Nicholas)   *see* Bath Weston St Jo w Kelston
   B & W
KELVEDON (St Mary the Virgin) and Feering *Chelmsf* 24
   P *Bp*   **P-in-c** S F GARWOOD
KELVEDON HATCH (St Nicholas)   *see* Bentley Common,
   Kelvedon Hatch and Navestock *Chelmsf*
KEMBERTON (St Andrew)   *see* Beckbury, Badger, Kemberton,
   Ryton, Stockton etc *Lich*
KEMBLE (All Saints), Poole Keynes, Somerford Keynes w
   Sharncote, Coates, Rodmarton and Sapperton w Frampton
   Mansell *Glouc* 7   **P** *Bp, Lord Bathurst, Mrs L R Rank, Guild of
   All So, and DBP (2 turns), Duchy of Lanc (1 turn)*   **R** T G KEMP
   NSM D R E AUSTIN
KEMERTON (St Nicholas)   *see* Ashchurch and Kemerton
   Glouc
KEMP TOWN (St Mary) *Chich* 19   **P** *Bp, Mrs R A Hinton, A C R
   Elliott Esq, T J Elliott Esq, and the Revd Canon D H McKittrick (jt)*
   P-in-c A J WOODWARD
KEMPLEY (St Edward)   *see* Redmarley D'Abitot, Bromesberrow,
   Pauntley etc *Glouc*
KEMPSEY (St Mary the Virgin) and Severn Stoke w Croome
   d'Abitot *Worc* 5   **P** *D&C and Croome Estate Trustees (alt)*
   R M BADGER   **C** P M SARGENT
KEMPSFORD (St Mary)   *see* S Cotswolds *Glouc*
KEMPSHOTT (St Mark) *Win* 4   **P** *Bp*   **V** K J TAYLOR
KEMPSTON (All Saints) *St Alb* 9   **P** *Bp*   **V** S L HUCKLE
KEMPSTON (Transfiguration) *St Alb* 9   **P** *Bp*
   V L A HUMPHREYS   **C** V E O'NEILL
KEMSING (St Mary the Virgin) w Woodlands *Roch* 10   **P** *DBP*
   P-in-c J R OAKLEY
KENARDINGTON (St Mary)   *see* Saxon Shoreline *Cant*
KENCHESTER (St Michael)   *see* Credenhill w Brinsop and
   Wormsley etc *Heref*
KENCOT (St George)   *see* Shill Valley and Broadshire *Ox*
KENDAL (Holy Trinity) (All Hallows Chapel) *Carl* 10   **P** *Trin
   Coll Cam*   **P-in-c** R J SANER-HAIGH   **C** J HURST
   NSM G SKILLING, P A HENDERSON, P SMITH
KENDAL (St George)   *see* Beacon *Carl*
KENDAL (St Thomas) *Carl* 10   **P** *CPAS*   **P-in-c** G W BRIGGS
   NSM M L WOODCOCK, S R WEATHERILL
KENDRAY (St Andrew) *Sheff* 12   **P** *V Ardsley*
   V P C W JACKSON
KENILWORTH (St John) *Cov* 4   **P** *Simeon's Trustees*
   V A M ATTWOOD
KENILWORTH (St Nicholas) (St Barnabas) *Cov* 4   **P** *Ld Chan*
   V *vacant*
KENLEY (All Saints) *S'wark* 22   **P** *Abp*   **P-in-c** C G THOMSON
   NSM E J GOODRIDGE
KENLEY (St John the Baptist)   *see* Wenlock *Heref*
KENN (St Andrew)   *see* Exminster, Kenn, Kenton w Mamhead,
   and Powderham *Ex*
KENN (St John the Evangelist)   *see* Yatton Moor *B & W*
KENNERLEIGH (St John the Baptist)   *see* N Creedy *Ex*
KENNET, EAST (Christ Church)   *see* Upper Kennet *Sarum*
KENNETT (St Nicholas)   *see* Three Rivers Gp *Ely*
KENNINGHALL (St Mary)   *see* Guiltcross *Nor*

KENNINGTON (St John the Divine w St James the Apostle)
S'wark 11   **P** *Ripon Coll Cuddesdon and Bp (jt)*
V M WILLIAMS   **Hon C** E L WAKEHAM
KENNINGTON (St Mark) *S'wark 11*   **P** *Abp*   **V** S H COULSON
KENNINGTON (St Mary) *Cant 6*   **P** *Abp*   **P-in-c** R D KING
NSM P J NEWELL
KENNINGTON (St Swithun)   *see Radley, Sunningwell and
Kennington Ox*
KENNINGTON CROSS (St Anselm)   *see N Lambeth S'wark*
KENNINGTON PARK (St Agnes) *S'wark 10*   **P** *Trustees*
V P G ENSOR
KENSAL GREEN (St John) *Lon 2*   **P** *Bp*   **V** D M ACKERMAN
KENSAL RISE (St Mark) *Lon 21*   **P** *Bp and Trustees (jt)*
V O H D RYDER
KENSAL RISE (St Martin) *Lon 21*   **P** *Bp and Trustees (jt)*
V G P NOYCE   **Hon C** E J BARRATT
KENSAL TOWN (St Thomas) (St Andrew) (St Philip) *Lon 12*
P *Hyndman Trustees*   **V** M A MILLER   **C** A N TRIGLE
KENSALL TOWN ST THOMAS *Lon 12*   **I** *vacant*
KENSINGTON (St Barnabas) *Lon 12*   **P** *V Kensington St Mary
Abbots w St Geo and Ch Ch*   **V** T M HUMPHREY
KENSINGTON (St Clement)   *see Notting Dale St Clem w
St Mark and St Jas Lon*
KENSINGTON (St George)   *see Holland Park Lon*
KENSINGTON (St Helen) (Holy Trinity) *Lon 12*   **P** *Bp*
V S R DIVALL   **C** A D A FRANCE-WILLIAMS
KENSINGTON (St Luke)   *see S Kensington St Luke Lon*
KENSINGTON (St Mary Abbots) (Christ Church) (St Philip)
Lon 12   **P** *Bp*   **V** G W CRAIG   **C** D C WALSH, J L WELSH,
M R O'DONOGHUE   **NSM** I AJIBADE, J M HEDLEY, L A PERRY
KENSINGTON, SOUTH (Holy Trinity w All Saints) *Lon 3*
P *D&C Westmr*   **P-in-c** E M V RUSSELL   **NSM** P KETTLE
KENSINGTON, SOUTH (St Stephen) *Lon 12*   **P** *Guild of All So*
V R F BUSHAU
KENSINGTON, SOUTH St Luke *Lon 8*   **P** *Ch Patr Trust*
V A N BEAVIS
KENSINGTON, WEST (St Andrew)   *see Fulham St Andr Lon*
KENSINGTON, WEST (St Mary)   *see Fulham St Mary N End Lon*
KENSWORTH (St Mary the Virgin), Studham and Whipsnade
St Alb 11   **P** *Ld Chan and D&C St Paul's (alt)*
V N Y LENTHALL
KENTCHURCH (St Mary)   *see Ewyas Harold w Dulas,
Kenderchurch etc Heref*
KENTFORD (St Mary)   *see Dalham, Gazeley, Higham, Kentford
and Moulton St E*
KENTISBEARE (St Mary)   *see Willand, Uffculme, Kentisbeare
etc Ex*
KENTISBURY (St Thomas)   *see Shirwell, Loxhore, Kentisbury,
Arlington, etc Ex*
KENTISH TOWN (St Benet and All Saints) *Lon 17*   **P** *Prime
Min and D&C St Paul's (alt)*   **P-in-c** P B ANTHONY
KENTISH TOWN (St Martin) (St Andrew) *Lon 17*   **P** *Exors
Dame Jewell Magnus-Allcroft*   **V** C J BRICE
KENTISH TOWN (St Silas) and (Holy Trinity) w St Barnabas
Lon 17   **P** *Bp and D&C St Paul's (jt)*   **V** G C ROWLANDS
KENTMERE (St Cuthbert)   *see Staveley, Ings and Kentmere Carl*
KENTON (All Saints)   *see Exminster, Kenn, Kenton w
Mamhead, and Powderham Ex*
KENTON (All Saints)   *see Debenham and Helmingham St E*
KENTON (Ascension) *Newc 2*   **P** *Bp*   **P-in-c** L CHAPMAN
NSM S RENDALL
KENTON (St Mary the Virgin) *Lon 23*   **P** *Bp*   **V** E J LEWIS
KENTON, SOUTH (Annunciation) *Lon 21*   **P** *Bp*
NSM T P GODDARD
KENWYN (St Keyne) w St Allen *Truro 6*   **P** *Bp*
P-in-c C P PARSONS   **OLM** R W HUMPHRIES
KERESLEY (St Thomas) and Coundon *Cov 2*   **P** *Bp*
V M NORRIS
KERESLEY END (Church of the Ascension)   *see Keresley and
Coundon Cov*
KERRIDGE (Holy Trinity)   *see Bollington Ches*
KERRIER, WEST *Truro 4*   **P** *Bp and Prime Min (alt)*
V P C JOHNSON
KERSAL MOOR (St Paul) *Man 20*   **P** *Trustees*   **R** L K BATTYE
OLM M J DYSON
KERSAL, LOWER (St Aidan)   *see Salford All SS Man*
KERSEY (St Mary)   *see Elmsett w Aldham, Hintlesham,
Chattisham etc St E*
KERSWELL GREEN (St John the Baptist)   *see Kempsey and
Severn Stoke w Croome d'Abitot Worc*
KESGRAVE (All Saints) *St E 4*   **P** *Bp*   **V** R SPITTLE
C C L LING   **NSM** C J NUNN
KESSINGLAND (St Edmund), Gisleham and Rushmere *Nor 9*
P *Ld Chan (1 turns) and Bp (2 turns)*   **R** J B WYER
KESTON (not known) (St Audrey) *Roch 14*   **P** *D&C*
R C F MORRISON

KESWICK (All Saints)   *see Swardeston w E Carleton, Intwood,
Keswick etc Nor*
KESWICK (St John) *Carl 6*   **P** *Trustees*   **NSM** H J MARSHALL
KESWICK, EAST (St Mary Magdalene)   *see Bardsey Leeds*
KETLEY (St Mary the Virgin)   *see Cen Telford Lich*
KETTERING (All Saints) *Pet 9*   **P** *SMF*   **P-in-c** A R G DUTTON
KETTERING (Christ the King) *Pet 9*   **P** *R Barton Seagrave w
Warkton*   **V** R J BEWLEY   **C** E R JEANS, J F ALDWINCKLE
KETTERING (St Andrew) *Pet 9*   **P** *Bp*   **V** N R WILLS   **Hon
C** P A M GOMPERTZ   **NSM** H M GOMPERTZ
KETTERING (St Mary the Virgin) (St John the Evangelist) *Pet 9*
P *SMF*   **P-in-c** J E MOWBRAY
KETTERING (St Peter and St Paul) (St Michael and All Angels)
Pet 9   **P** *Comdr L M M Saunders Watson*   **NSM** J S SMITH,
L S MCCORMACK
KETTERINGHAM (St Peter)   *see Swardeston w E Carleton,
Intwood, Keswick etc Nor*
KETTLEBROOK (St Andrew)   *see Tamworth Lich*
KETTLEBURGH (St Andrew)   *see Brandeston w Kettleburgh and
Easton St E*
KETTLESTONE (All Saints)   *see Barney, Hindringham,
Thursford, Great Snoring, Little Snoring and Kettlestone and
Pensthorpe Nor*
KETTLETHORPE (St Peter and St Paul)   *see Saxilby Gp Linc*
**KETTLEWELL (St Mary) w Conistone, Hubberholme and
Arncliff w Halton Gill** *Leeds 26*   **P** *Bp, Mrs J E Wright, and
W R G Bell Esq (jt)*   **C** F JENKINS
**KETTON (St Mary the Virgin), Collyweston, Easton-on-the-
Hill, Tinwell and Wittering** *Pet 12*   **P** *Burghley Ho
Preservation Trust, Bp, and Ld Chan (by turn)*
P-in-c A D RAYMENT   **C** J J S MCGARRIGLE, P J DAVIES
Hon C J M SAUNDERS   **NSM** K VOTH HARMAN
KEW (St Anne) *S'wark 16*   **P** *The Crown*   **V** N J WORN
KEW (St Francis of Assisi) *Liv 9*   **P** *Bp, Adn Warrington, and
V Southport All SS and All So (jt)*   **V** A P J GALBRAITH
KEW (St Philip and All Saints) (St Luke) *S'wark 16*   **P** *Bp*
V P W HART
KEWSTOKE (St Paul)   *see Milton and Kewstoke B & W*
KEYINGHAM (St Nicholas)   *see Easington w Skeffling,
Keyingham, Ottringham etc York*
KEYMER (St Cosmas and St Damian)   *see Clayton w Keymer
Chich*
KEYMER (St Francis of Assisi) *as above*
KEYNSHAM (St Francis) (St John the Baptist) *B & W 9*
P *Patr Bd*   **TR** S A M'CAW   **TV** A D JUDGE, M R BURKE
C D M CALVERLEY, I D ROUSELL
KEYSOE (St Mary the Virgin)   *see Bolnhurst w Keysoe St Alb*
KEYSTON (St John the Baptist)   *see W Leightonstone Ely*
**KEYWORTH (St Mary Magdalene) and Stanton-on-the-Wolds
and Bunny w Bradmore** *S'well 5*   **P** *Bp and Ld Chan (alt)*
R J F WELLINGTON
**KIBWORTH (St Wilfrid) and Smeeton Westerby and
Saddington** *Leic 4*   **P** *Mert Coll Ox and Bp (jt)*
P-in-c L FREMMER
KIDBROOKE (St James) *S'wark 1*   **P** *Patr Bd*   **R** K W HITCH
KIDBROOKE (St Nicholas) *S'wark 1*   **P** *Bp and Simeon's Trustees
(jt)*   **V** T M LINKENS   **NSM** P FRANKLIN
KIDDERMINSTER (St John the Baptist) (Holy Innocents)
Worc 11   **P** *Patr Bd*   **TR** T J WILLIAMS   **TV** D GEORGE
KIDDERMINSTER (St Mary and All Saints) Ismere *Worc 11*
P *Patr Bd*   **TV** J H H ASHTON, N R TAYLOR, R A LAWLEY
NSM A VACCARO
KIDDERMINSTER EAST (St George) (St Chad) *Worc 11*
P *Ld Chan (1 turn), Patr Bd (2 turns)*   **TR** H A BURTON
TV R J LEGGE   **C** R L AKERS
KIDDINGTON (St Nicholas)   *see Wootton w Glympton and
Kiddington Ox*
KIDLINGTON (St Mary the Virgin) w Hampton Poyle *Ox 2*
P *Patr Bd*   **TR** F M-L SCROGGIE   **TV** M J DAVIS
NSM W H WHYTE
KIDLINGTON, SOUTH (St John the Baptist)   *see Kidlington w
Hampton Poyle Ox*
KIDMORE END (St John the Baptist)   *see Rotherfield Peppard
and Kidmore End etc Ox*
KIDSGROVE (St Thomas) *Lich 9*   **P** *MMCET*   **V** I BAKER
C M A J WILSON
KILBURN (Mission Room)   *see Horsley and Denby Derby*
KILBURN (St Augustine) (St John) *Lon 2*   **P** *SMF*
V C J AMOS   **NSM** S G BROWN
KILBURN (St Mary)   *see Thirkleby w Kilburn and Bagby York*
**KILBURN Priory Road (St Mary) w All Souls and W
Hampstead St James** *Lon 16*   **P** *Bp, Ch Patr Trust, and trustees
(jt)*   **V** A D FORESHEW-CAIN   **NSM** M-E B R BRAGG,
R HUTCHISON
KILBURN, WEST (St Luke) and Harrow Road Emmanuel *Lon 2*
P *CPAS and Hyndman Trustees (jt)*   **V** A G THOM

C C D LANDAU, J F BARRY **NSM** B A ENWUCHOLA
KILBY (St Mary Magdalene) *see* Wistow *Leic*
KILDALE (St Cuthbert) *see* Ingleby Greenhow, Bilsdale Priory etc *York*
KILDWICK (St Andrew) *Leeds 5* **P** Ch Ch Ox **V** R A R FIGG
KILHAM (All Saints) *see* Rudston w Boynton, Carnaby and Kilham *York*
KILKHAMPTON (St James the Great) w Morwenstow *Truro 8*
P *DBP and Bp (jt)* **NSM** R WARD-SMITH
KILLAMARSH (St Giles) and Renishaw *Derby 3* **P** *Prime Min*
R H GUEST
KILLERTON (Holy Evangelist) *see* Broadclyst, Clyst Honiton, Pinhoe, Rockbeare etc *Ex*
KILLINGHALL (St Thomas the Apostle) *see* Hampsthwaite and Killinghall and Birstwith *Leeds*
KILLINGHOLME, NORTH (St Denys) *see* Immingham Gp *Linc*
KILLINGTON (All Saints) *see* Firbank, Howgill and Killington *Carl*
KILLINGWORTH (St John) *Newc 1* **P** V Longbenton St Bart
V D M GRAY **NSM** AH MEIGHEN
KILMERSDON (St Peter and St Paul) w Babington *B & W 11*
P *Lord Hylton* **R** *vacant*
KILMESTON (St Andrew) *see* Upper Itchen *Win*
KILMINGTON (St Giles) *see* Kilmington, Stockland, Dalwood, Yarcombe etc *Ex*
KILMINGTON (St Giles), Stockland, Dalwood, Yarcombe and Shute *Ex 4* **P** *Bp and D&C (2 turns), Prime Min (1 turn)*
P-in-c S A HOLLOWAY **NSM** L A MILLS
KILMINGTON (St Mary the Virgin) *see* Upper Stour *Sarum*
KILNDOWN (Christ Church) *see* Goudhurst w Kilndown *Cant*
KILNGREEN (Diggle Mission Church) *see* Saddleworth *Man*
KILNHURST (St Thomas) *Sheff 12* **P** Ld Chan
V A R BREWERTON **C** N D R ROBSON
KILNWICK (All Saints) *see* Woldsburn *York*
KILPECK (St Mary and St David) *see* Ewyas Harold w Dulas, Kenderchurch etc *Heref*
KILSBY (St Faith) *see* Barby w Kilsby *Pet*
KILVE (Blessed Virgin Mary) *see* Quantock Coast *B & W*
KILVERSTONE (St Andrew) *see* Thetford *Nor*
KILVINGTON (St Mary) *S'well 3* **P** E G Staunton Esq
P-in-c E I MURRAY
KILVINGTON, SOUTH (St Wilfrid) *see* Thirsk *York*
KILWORTH, NORTH (St Andrew) *see* Gilmorton, Peatling Parva, Kimcote etc *Leic*
KILWORTH, SOUTH (St Nicholas) *as above*
KIMBERLEY (Holy Trinity) and Nuthall *S'well 8* **P** Bp
R B M HOLBROOK
KIMBERLEY (St Peter) *see* Barnham Broom and Upper Yare *Nor*
KIMBERWORTH (St Thomas) (St Mark) and Kimberworth Park *Sheff 6* **P** Bp **P-in-c** A WOODING **C** J T BIRBECK, L S WORTLEY
KIMBERWORTH PARK (St John) *see* Kimberworth and Kimberworth Park *Sheff*
KIMBLE, GREAT (St Nicholas) *see* Ellesborough, The Kimbles and Stoke Mandeville *Ox*
KIMBLE, LITTLE (All Saints) *as above*
KIMBLESWORTH (St Philip and St James) *see* Dur N *Dur*
KIMBOLTON (St Andrew) *see* Kym Valley *Ely*
KIMCOTE (All Saints) *see* Gilmorton, Peatling Parva, Kimcote etc *Leic*
KIMMERIDGE (St Nicholas of Myra) *see* Corfe Castle, Church Knowle, Kimmeridge etc *Sarum*
KIMPTON (St Peter and St Paul) *see* Appleshaw, Kimpton, Thruxton, Fyfield etc *Win*
KIMPTON (St Peter and St Paul) w Ayot St Lawrence *St Alb 7*
P Bp **P-in-c** B J EVANS-HILLS
KINETON (St Peter) *see* Edgehill Churches *Cov*
KING CROSS (St Paul) *Leeds 11* **P** Bp **V** K J BARNARD
KING STERNDALE (Christ Church) *see* Buxton w Burbage and King Sterndale *Derby*
KINGHAM (St Andrew) *see* Chipping Norton *Ox*
KINGMOOR (St Peter) *see* Houghton *Carl*
KING'S BECK *Nor 12* **P** Bp, D&C, P H C Barber Esq, and J T D Shaw Esq (jt) **P-in-c** K R DALLY
KINGS BROMLEY (All Saints) *see* The Ridwares and Kings Bromley *Lich*
KING'S CAPLE (St John the Baptist) *see* Wormelow Hundred *Heref*
KING'S CLIFFE (All Saints), Bulwick and Blatherwycke and Laxton *Pet 10* **P** Bp, G T G Conant Esq, and F and A George Ltd (jt) **R** P J DAVIES **NSM** K VOTH HARMAN
KINGS HEATH (All Saints) *Birm 5* **P** V Moseley St Mary
V Q D WARBRICK **C** D THOMPSON
KINGS HEATH (Church on the Heath) *Pet 4* **P** Bp
V R A WOODS

KING'S HILL (St Andrew) *see* Wednesbury St Bart *Lich*
KINGS LANGLEY (All Saints) *see* Langelei *St Alb*
KING'S LYNN (All Saints) *see* S Lynn *Nor*
KING'S LYNN (St John the Evangelist) *Nor 20* **P** Bp
P-in-c R J ROGERS
KING'S LYNN (St Margaret) (St Edmund) w St Nicholas
Nor 20 **P** D&C **R** C J IVORY **C** L M BAKER, R J ROGERS
KING'S NORTON (St John the Baptist) *see* Gaulby *Leic*
KINGS NORTON (St Nicolas) *Birm 4* **P** Patr Bd **TR** vacant
KING'S PYON (St Mary the Virgin) *see* Canon Pyon w King's Pyon, Birley and Wellington *Heref*
KINGS RIPTON (St Peter) *see* Huntingdon St Barn and the Riptons *Ely*
KING'S STANLEY (St George) *see* The Stanleys w Selsley *Glouc*
KING'S SUTTON (St Peter and St Paul) and Newbottle and Charlton *Pet 1* **P** SMF and Lady Townsend (jt)
V M R H BELLAMY
KING'S WALDEN (St Mary) and Offley w Lilley *St Alb 3*
P Sir Thomas Pilkington Bt (2 turns), St Jo Coll Cam (1 turn), D K C Salusbury-Hughes Esq and Mrs P A L McGrath (2 turns)
V T J BELL
KING'S WOOD *Cant 2* **P** Abp and J S Wheeler Esq (jt)
R P R RATCLIFF **C** S A STARKINGS
KING'S WORTHY (St Mary) (St Mary's Chapel) *Win 7*
P Univ Coll Ox and Lord Northbrook (alt) **R** E CHASE
KINGSBRIDGE (St Edmund the King and Martyr), Dodbrooke, and West Alvington *Ex 13* **P** Bp Ex and D&C
Sarum (jt) **R** J M TAYLOR **C** D H T BOND
KINGSBURY (Holy Innocents) *Lon 21* **P** D&C St Paul's
V N C WOODWARD **NSM** S HAMEEM
KINGSBURY (St Andrew) *Lon 21* **P** The Crown **V** J RENDELL
KINGSBURY (St Peter and St Paul) *Birm 10* **P** Bp
P-in-c J C WHITE
KINGSBURY EPISCOPI (St Martin) *see* Martock w Kingsbury Episcopi and Ash *B & W*
KINGSCLERE (St Mary) and Ashford Hill w Headley *Win 6*
P Bp **V** vacant
KINGSCOTE (St John the Baptist) *see* Nailsworth w Shortwood, Horsley etc *Glouc*
KINGSDON (All Saints) *see* Somerton w Compton Dundon, the Charltons etc *B & W*
KINGSDOWN (St Edmund the King and Martyr) *Roch 10*
P D&C **R** vacant
KINGSDOWN (St John the Evangelist) *see* Ringwould w Kingsdown and Ripple etc *Cant*
KINGSDOWN and Creekside *Cant 14* **P** Ld Chan (1 turn), Abp, Adn Cant, D&C, and MMCET (1 turn) **V** S H LILLICRAP
C J P HUGGINS **NSM** R A BIRCH
KINGSEY (St Nicholas) *see* Haddenham w Cuddington, Kingsey etc *Ox*
KINGSHURST (St Barnabas) *Birm 9* **P** Bp **V** F J JOHNSON
KINGSKERSWELL (St Mary) w Coffinswell *Ex 9* **P** V
St Marychurch **V** J F LEONARD
KINGSLAND (St Michael and All Angels) w Eardisland, Aymestrey and Leinthall Earles *Heref 6* **P** DBP (2 turns), Ld Chan (1 turn) **P-in-c** J M READ
KINGSLEY (All Saints) *see* Northanger *Win*
KINGSLEY (St John the Evangelist) *see* Norley, Crowton and Kingsley *Ches*
KINGSLEY (St Werburgh) and Foxt-w-Whiston and Oakamoor w Cotton *Lich 6* **P** R Cheadle w Freehay and Mrs N A Faulkner (jt) **C** C M RICHARDSON
KINGSNORTH (St Michael and All Angels) and Shadoxhurst
Cant 6 **P** Abp **R** vacant
KINGSNYMPTON (St James) *see* S Molton w Nymet St George, High Bray etc *Ex*
KINGSTAG (not known) *see* Spire Hill *Sarum*
KINGSTANDING (St Luke) *Birm 3* **P** Bp **V** B A I SMART
KINGSTANDING (St Mark) *Birm 3* **P** Bp **V** P CALVERT
KINGSTEIGNTON (St Michael) and Teigngrace *Ex 9* **P** Bp
V M P SMITH **NSM** S J GILL
KINGSTHORPE (St John the Baptist) (St David) (St Mark)
Pet 4 **P** Patr Bd **TR** L J BUTLER **TV** E M REW
C K M HUTCHINS, R M HETHERINGTON
KINGSTON (All Saints and St Andrew) *see* Papworth *Ely*
KINGSTON (All Saints) (St John the Evangelist) (St John the Baptist) *S'wark 15* **P** Patr Bd **TR** J P WILKES
TV A R BECK, V A MAUNDER **NSM** A J WILLIAMS, D BELL, S A CRAGG
KINGSTON (St Giles) *see* Barham Downs *Cant*
KINGSTON (St James)
KINGSTON (St James)
KINGSTON (St James), Langton Matravers and Worth Matravers *Sarum 8* **P** Bp, D E Scott Esq, and R Swanage and Studland (jt) **P-in-c** G E BURRETT

KINGSTON (St Pancras)   *see* Iford w Kingston and Rodmell and Southease *Chich*

KINGSTON (St Winifred) and Ratcliffe-on-Soar *S'well 6*
   P *D&C*   **P-in-c** R I COLEMAN

KINGSTON BAGPUIZE (St John the Baptist) w Southmoor
   see Fyfield w Tubney and Kingston Bagpuize *Ox*

KINGSTON BUCI (St Giles)   *see* Old Shoreham and Kingston Buci *Chich*

KINGSTON BUCI (St Julian) *as above*

KINGSTON DEVERILL (St Mary)   *see* Cley Hill Villages *Sarum*

KINGSTON HILL (St Paul) *S'wark 15*   **P** *DBP*
   V S C COUPLAND   **C** S P PLUMB   **NSM** F M M DE QUIDT

KINGSTON LACY (St Stephen)   *see* Bridge Par *Sarum*

KINGSTON LISLE (St John the Baptist)   *see* Ridgeway *Ox*

KINGSTON PARK (not known) *Newc 2*   **P** *Bp*   **V** R C MILLS

KINGSTON SEYMOUR (All Saints)   *see* Yatton Moor *B & W*

KINGSTON ST MARY (The Blessed Virgin Mary)   *see* W Monkton w Kingston St Mary, Broomfield etc *B & W*

KINGSTON UPON HULL (Most Holy and Undivided Trinity) *York 14*   **P** *CPAS*   **V** N D BARNES   **C** M R WOODCOCK
   NSM I M WILSON

KINGSTON UPON HULL (St Aidan) Southcoates *York 14*
   P *Simeon's Trustees*   **V** R P PHILLIPS   **C** A ORAM

KINGSTON UPON HULL (St Alban) *York 14*   **P** *Abp*
   V D JAGO

KINGSTON UPON HULL (St Cuthbert)   *see* Hull St Cuth *York*

KINGSTON UPON HULL (St Martin)   *see* Hull St Martin w Transfiguration *York*

KINGSTON UPON HULL (St Mary the Virgin) *York 14*
   P *Abp*   **P-in-c** P A BURKITT

KINGSTON UPON HULL (St Nicholas) *York 14*   **P** *Abp*
   V P COPLEY

KINGSTON UPON THAMES (All Saints)   *see* Kingston *S'wark*

KINGSTON UPON THAMES (St John the Evangelist) *as above*

KINGSTON UPON THAMES (St Luke) *S'wark 15*   **P** *Bp*
   V M G HISLOP

KINGSTON VALE (St John the Baptist)   *see* Kingston *S'wark*

KINGSTONE (St John and All Saints)   *see* Winsmoor *B & W*

KINGSTONE (St John the Baptist)   *see* Uttoxeter Area *Lich*

KINGSTONE (St Michael and All Angels)   *see* Cagebrook *Heref*

KINGSWEAR (St Thomas of Canterbury)   *see* Brixham w Churston Ferrers and Kingswear *Ex*

KINGSWINFORD (St Mary) *Worc 10*   **P** *Patr Bd*
   P-in-c G KENDALL   **NSM** J E ARNOLD

KINGSWOOD (Church of the Ascension) (Holy Trinity) *Bris 5*
   P *Patr Bd*   **TV** A J MASON   **NSM** C E EVANS,
   J F J GOODRIDGE

KINGSWOOD (St Andrew) *S'wark 26*   **P** *Bp and R&S Ch Trust
(jt)*   **P-in-c** C A COLTON   **NSM** A G F BOWYER

KINGSWOOD (St Mary the Virgin)   *see* Charfield and Kingswood w Wickwar etc *Glouc*

KINGSWOOD, LOWER (Wisdom of God)   *see* Kingswood *S'wark*

KINGTON (St James)   *see* Inkberrow w Cookhill and Kington w Dormston *Worc*

KINGTON (St Mary) w Huntington, Old Radnor, Kinnerton and Titley *Heref 4*   **P** *Patr Bd*   **NSM** P J BUCKINGHAM

KINGTON LANGLEY (St Peter)   *see* Draycot *Bris*

KINGTON MAGNA (All Saints)   *see* Stour Vale *Sarum*

KINGTON ST MICHAEL (St Michael) *Bris 4*   **P** *Patr Bd*
   OLM D J KILMISTER

KINGTON, WEST (St Mary the Virgin)   *see* By Brook *Bris*

KINGWESTON (All Saints)   *see* Wheathill Priory Gp *B & W*

KINLET (St John the Baptist)   *see* Cleobury Mortimer w Hopton Wafers etc *Heref*

KINNERLEY (St Mary) w Melverley and Knockin w Maesbrook
Lich 19   **P** W H C Montgomery Esq, Sir Brooke Boothby Bt, and
Viscount Boyne (jt)   **P-in-c** H M MORBY   **C** M A SMITH
   OLM P L WEST

KINNERSLEY (St James)   *see* Eardisley w Bollingham, Willersley, Brilley etc *Heref*

KINNERTON (St Mary the Virgin)   *see* Kington w Huntington, Old Radnor, Kinnerton etc *Heref*

KINNERTON, HIGHER (All Saints)   *see* Dodleston *Ches*

KINNINVIE (Mission Room)   *see* Barnard Castle w Whorlton *Dur*

KINOULTON (St Luke)   *see* Hickling w Kinoulton and Broughton Sulney *S'well*

KINSBOURNE GREEN (St Mary)   *see* Harpenden St Nic *St Alb*

KINSHAM (All Saints)   *see* Presteigne w Discoed, Kinsham, Lingen and Knill *Heref*

KINSLEY (Resurrection) w Wragby *Leeds 19*   **P** *Bp and Lord
St Oswald (jt)*   **V** J HADJIOANNOU

KINSON (St Andrew) (St Philip) and West Howe *Sarum 7*
   P *Patr Bd*   **TR** L SHIRVILL   **TV** C A BROOKS

KINTBURY (St Mary the Virgin)   *see* Walbury Beacon *Ox*

KINVER (St Peter) and Enville *Lich 24*   **P** *Bp, Mrs A D Williams,
and DBP (jt)*   **R** K J STANTON   **C** M W SOAR

KINWARTON (St Mary the Virgin)   *see* Alcester Minster *Cov*

KIPPAX (St Mary the Virgin) w Allerton Bywater *Leeds 17*
   P *Bp*   **P-in-c** R E HAYES   **TV** D M FLYNN   **C** V MASTERS

KIPPINGTON (St Mary) *Roch 9*   **P** *DBP*   **V** D B KITLEY

KIRBY BEDON (St Andrew)   *see* Rockland St Mary w Hellington, Bramerton etc *Nor*

KIRBY BELLARS (St Peter)   *see* Upper Wreake *Leic*

KIRBY CANE (All Saints)   *see* Gillingham w Geldeston, Stockton, Ellingham etc *Nor*

KIRBY GRINDALYTHE (St Andrew)   *see* Weaverthorpe w Helperthorpe, Luttons Ambo etc *York*

KIRBY MISPERTON (St Laurence) w Normanby and Salton
York 19   **P** *Lady Clarissa Collin, Abp, and St Jo Coll Cam
(by turn)*   **V** S R GAMBLE   **C** M BROSNAN

KIRBY MUXLOE (St Bartholomew)   *see* Desford and Kirby Muxloe *Leic*

KIRBY SIGSTON (St Lawrence)   *see* Northallerton w Kirby Sigston *York*

KIRBY UNDERDALE (All Saints)   *see* Garrowby Hill *York*

KIRBY WISKE (St John the Baptist)   *see* Lower Swale *Leeds*

KIRBY, WEST (St Andrew) *Ches 8*   **P** *D&C*   **V** P WALSH

KIRBY, WEST (St Bridget) *Ches 8*   **P** *D&C*   **R** J G BLEAZARD
   NSM D K CHESTER

KIRBY-LE-SOKEN (St Michael) w Great Holland *Chelmsf 23*
   P *Bp and CPAS (jt)*   **R** M D J HOLDAWAY

**KIRBY-ON-THE-MOOR (All Saints), Cundall w Norton-le-Clay
and Skelton-cum-Newby** *Leeds 25*   **P** *Bp, Sir Arthur Collins,
and R E J Compton Esq (jt)*   **P-in-c** A J ASKEW

KIRDFORD (St John the Baptist) *Chich 10*   **P** *Lord Egremont*
   P-in-c P R REDPARTH

KIRK ANDREAS (St Andrew)   *see* Andreas, Ballaugh, Jurby and Sulby *S & M*

KIRK BRAMWITH (St Mary)   *see* Fishlake w Sykehouse and Kirk Bramwith etc *Sheff*

KIRK CHRIST RUSHEN (Holy Trinity)   *see* Rushen *S & M*

KIRK DEIGHTON (All Saints)   *see* Spofforth w Kirk Deighton *Leeds*

KIRK ELLA (St Andrew) and Willerby *York 14*   **P** *D&C*
   R J S JUCKES

KIRK HALLAM (All Saints) *Derby 13*   **P** *Bp*   **P-in-c** C FRENCH
   C C A VICENCIO PRIOR

KIRK HAMMERTON (St John the Baptist)   *see* Lower Nidderdale *Leeds*

KIRK IRETON (Holy Trinity)   *see* Wirksworth *Derby*

KIRK LANGLEY (St Michael) *Derby 11*   **P** *G Meynell Esq and J M
Clark-Maxwell Esq (alt)*   **P-in-c** A P HARPER

KIRK MAROWN (St Runius)   *see* Marown, Foxdale and Baldwin *S & M*

KIRK MAUGHOLD (St Maughold)   *see* Maughold and S Ramsey *S & M*

KIRK ONCHAN (St Peter)   *see* Onchan, Lonan and Laxey *S & M*

KIRK PATRICK (Holy Trinity)   *see* W Coast *S & M*

KIRK SANDALL and Edenthorpe (Good Shepherd) *Sheff 8*
   P *Ld Chan*   **R** M E GREGORY

KIRK SMEATON (St Peter)   *see* Went Valley *Leeds*

KIRKANDREWS ON EDEN (St Mary)   *see* Barony of Burgh *Carl*

KIRKANDREWS ON ESK (St Andrew)   *see* Arthuret w Kirkandrews-on-Esk and Nicholforest *Carl*

KIRKBAMPTON (St Peter)   *see* Barony of Burgh *Carl*

KIRKBRIDE (St Bride)   *see* Bowness-on-Solway, Kirkbride and Newton Arlosh *Carl*

KIRKBRIDE (St Bridget)   *see* Bride, Lezayre and N Ramsey *S & M*

KIRKBURN (St Mary)   *see* Woldsburn *York*

KIRKBURTON (All Hallows) *Leeds 13*   **P** *Bp*
   OLM R A CHAMBERS

KIRKBY (St Andrew)   *see* Kelsey Gp *Linc*

KIRKBY (St Chad) (St Mark) (St Martin) (St Andrew) *Liv 7*
   P *Patr Bd*   **TR** J D FAGAN   **TV** P C WETHERELL, P F SMYTH

KIRKBY FLEETHAM (St Mary)   *see* Lower Swale *Leeds*

KIRKBY GREEN (Holy Cross)   *see* Digby Gp *Linc*

KIRKBY IN ASHFIELD (St Thomas) *S'well 4*   **P** *Bp*
   V N A POPHAM   **NSM** K CHARLES

KIRKBY IN ASHFIELD (St Wilfrid) *S'well 4*   **P** *Bp*
   P-in-c N A POPHAM

KIRKBY IRELETH (St Cuthbert) *Carl 9*   **P** *D&C York*
   V *vacant*

KIRKBY KNOWLE (St Wilfrid) *York 18*   **P** *Abp*
   V I D HOUGHTON   **NSM** T A LEWIS

KIRKBY KNOWLE (St Wilfrid)   *see* Kirkby Knowle *York*

KIRKBY LAYTHORPE (St Denys) *Linc 14*   **P** *Bp and DBP (alt)*
   OLM V GREENE

KIRKBY LONSDALE (St Mary the Virgin) Team Ministry
Carl 10   **P** *Patr Bd*   **TR** R J SNOW   **NSM** A E PETTIFOR,
D A PRESTON

KIRKBY MALHAM (St Michael the Archangel)   *see* Kirkby-in-Malhamdale *Leeds*

KIRKBY MALLORY (All Saints)   *see* Newbold de Verdun, Barlestone and Kirkby Mallory *Leic*

KIRKBY MALZEARD (St Andrew)   *see* Fountains Gp *Leeds*

KIRKBY OVERBLOW (All Saints)   *see* Lower Wharfedale *Leeds*

KIRKBY RAVENSWORTH (St Peter and St Felix)   *see* Gilling and Kirkby Ravensworth *Leeds*

KIRKBY STEPHEN (not known) w Mallerstang and Crosby Garrett w Soulby *Carl 1*   **P** *Bp, Earl of Lonsdale, and Lord Hothfield (jt)*   **P-in-c** A PARKINSON   **NSM** J WRIGHT

KIRKBY THORE (St Michael) w Temple Sowerby and Newbiggin *Carl 1*   **P** *Lord Hothfield (3 turns), Major and Mrs Sawrey-Cookson (1 turn)*   **P-in-c** S A LUNN   **NSM** D J PATTIMORE, K PATTIMORE

KIRKBY UNDERWOOD (St Mary and All Saints)   *see* Ringstone in Aveland Gp *Linc*

KIRKBY, SOUTH (All Saints) *Leeds 19*   **P** *Guild of All So*   **V** T H KAYE

KIRKBY-IN-CLEVELAND (St Augustine)   *see* Ingleby Greenhow, Bilsdale Priory etc *York*

KIRKBY-IN-MALHAMDALE (St Michael the Archangel) *Leeds 21*   **P** D&C   **V** M I JACKSON

KIRKBYMOORSIDE (All Saints) w Gillamoor, Farndale, Bransdale and Edstone *York 19*   **P** *Lady Clarissa Collin and Abp (jt)*   **V** M BROSNAN

KIRKBY-ON-BAIN (St Mary)   *see* Bain Valley Gp *Linc*

KIRKDALE (St Athanaseus with St Mary) *Liv 3*   **P** *Simeon's Trustees*   **C** P A LEEMAN

KIRKDALE (St Gregory) w Harome, Nunnington and Pockley *York 19*   **P** *Abp, Adn Cleveland, and Lady Clarissa Collin (2 turns), Ox Univ (1 turn)*   **V** A C DE SMET   **NSM** S J BINKS

KIRKDALE (St Lawrence) *Liv 3*   **P** CPAS   **V** M J GRIFFIN

KIRKDALE (St Paul)   *see* Kirkdale St Lawr *Liv*

KIRKHAM (St Michael) *Blackb 10*   **P** *Ch Ch Ox*   **V** R W BUNDAY   **NSM** J L ATKINSON, K THORN

KIRKHARLE (St Wilfrid)   *see* Kirkwhelpington, Kirkharle, Kirkheaton and Cambo *Newc*

KIRKHAUGH (Holy Paraclete)   *see* Alston Moor *Newc*

KIRKHEATON (St Bartholomew)   *see* Kirkwhelpington, Kirkharle, Kirkheaton and Cambo *Newc*

KIRKHEATON (St John the Baptist) *Leeds 6*   **P** *Ch Trust Fund Trust*   **R** R J STEEL   **C** J C WHITNEY

KIRKHOLT (St Thomas) *Man 17*   **P** *Bp*   **P-in-c** A E BRYAN

KIRKLAND (Mission Church)   *see* Lamplugh w Ennerdale *Carl*

KIRKLAND (St Lawrence)   *see* Cross Fell Gp *Carl*

KIRKLEATHAM (St Cuthbert) (St Hilda) *York 16*   **P** *Abp*   **V** *vacant*

KIRKLEES VALLEY *Man 8*   **P** *R Bury St Mary*   **V** S D J COOK

KIRKLEVINGTON (St Martin and St Hilary) w Picton, and High and Low Worsall *York 20*   **P** *Abp (3 turns), V Northallerton w Kirby Sigston (1 turn)*   **V** P J SANDERS   **Hon C** A J HUTCHINSON   **NSM** P PERCY

KIRKLEY (St Peter and St John) *Nor 9*   **P** *Bp and DBP (jt)*   **R** A P WHITE

KIRKLINGTON (St Michael) w Burneston and Wath and Pickhill *Leeds 27*   **P** *Ch Soc Trust, Mrs M St B Anderson, G W Prior-Wandesforde Esq, and DBP (jt)*   **R** *vacant*

KIRKLINGTON (St Swithin) w Hockerton *S'well 3*   **P** *Bp*   **V** *vacant*

KIRKLINTON (St Cuthbert)   *see* Bewcastle, Stapleton and Kirklinton etc *Carl*

KIRKNEWTON (St Gregory)   *see* Glendale Gp *Newc*

KIRKOSWALD (St Oswald), Renwick w Croglin, Great Salkeld and Lazonby *Carl 4*   **P** *Bp*   **R** D M FOWLER

KIRKSTALL (St Stephen)   *see* Abbeylands *Leeds*

KIRKSTEAD (St Leonard)   *see* Woodhall Spa Gp *Linc*

KIRKTHORPE (St Peter)   *see* Warmfield *Leeds*

KIRKWHELPINGTON (St Bartholomew) w Kirkharle and Kirkheaton, and Cambo *Newc 11*   **P** *Ld Chan (2 turns), J P P Anderson Esq (1 turn), and Bp (1 turn)*   **NSM** F H DOWER

KIRMINGTON (St Helen)   *see* Brocklesby Park *Linc*

KIRMOND-LE-MIRE (St Martin)   *see* Walesby *Linc*

KIRSTEAD (St Margaret)   *see* Brooke, Kirstead, Mundham w Seething and Thwaite *Nor*

KIRTLING (All Saints) *Ely 4*   **P** *Mrs D A Bowlby and Countess Ellesmere (alt)*   **V** *vacant*

KIRTLINGTON (St Mary the Virgin)   *see* Akeman *Ox*

KIRTON (Holy Trinity) *S'well 3*   **P** SMF   **R** C C LEVY

KIRTON (St Mary and St Martin)   *see* Nacton and Levington w Bucklesham etc *St E*

KIRTON HOLME (Christ Church)   *see* Brothertoft Gp *Linc*

KIRTON IN HOLLAND (St Peter and St Paul)   *see* Kirton in Holland w Algarkirk and Fosdyke *Linc*

KIRTON IN HOLLAND (St Peter and St Paul) w Algarkirk and Fosdyke *Linc 21*   **P** *Bp and Mercers' Co (1 turn), Prime Min (1 turn)*   **V** *vacant*

KIRTON IN LINDSEY (St Andrew) w Manton *Linc 8*   **P** *Bp*   **P-in-c** K E COLWELL   **OLM** J WILSON

KISLINGBURY (St Luke)   *see* Bugbrooke, Harpole, Kislingbury etc *Pet*

KITT GREEN (St Francis of Assisi)   *see* Pemberton St Fran Kitt Green *Liv*

KITTISFORD (St Nicholas)   *see* Wellington and Distr *B & W*

KNAITH (St Mary)   *see* Lea Gp *Linc*

KNAPHILL (Holy Trinity) w Brookwood *Guildf 12*   **P** CPAS   **V** N D GREW   **C** C N LANGRY   **OLM** J LEVETT

KNAPTON (St Peter)   *see* Trunch Group *Nor*

KNAPWELL (All Saints)   *see* Papworth *Ely*

KNARESBOROUGH (Holy Trinity) (St John the Baptist) *Leeds 23*   **P** *Bp and Earl of Harewood (jt)*   **TR** G A F HINCHCLIFFE   **Hon C** A G PEARSE

KNARESDALE (St Jude)   *see* Alston Moor *Newc*

KNEBWORTH (St Martin) (St Mary the Virgin and St Thomas of Canterbury) *St Alb 20*   **P** *Hon D A Fromanteel*   **R** J T PYE

KNEESALL w Laxton and Wellow *S'well 3*   **P** *DBP and Bp (jt)*   **P-in-c** C C LEVY

KNEETON (St Helen)   *see* E Bridgford and Kneeton *S'well*

KNIGHTLEY (Christ Church)   *see* Adbaston, High Offley, Knightley, Norbury etc *Lich*

KNIGHTON (St Guthlac) Conventional District *Leic 1*   **NSM** R J BONNEY

KNIGHTON (St Guthlac) Conventional District *Leic 2*   **NSM** R J BONNEY

KNIGHTON (St Mary Magdalene) *Leic 1*   **P** *Bp*   **V** K R MAGEE   **C** N G O BULLEN

KNIGHTON, WEST (St Peter)   *see* Watercombe *Sarum*

KNIGHTON-ON-TEME (St Michael and All Angels)   *see* Teme Valley N *Worc*

KNIGHT'S ENHAM (St Michael and All Angels) (St Paul's Church Centre) *Win 3*   **P** *Bp*   **V** A W H ASHDOWN

KNIGHTSBRIDGE (St Paul) Wilton Place   *see* Wilton Place St Paul *Lon*

KNILL (St Michael and All Angels)   *see* Presteigne w Discoed, Kinsham, Lingen and Knill *Heref*

KNIPTON (All Saints)   *see* High Framland Par *Leic*

KNIVETON (St Michael and All Angels)   *see* Hulland, Atlow, Kniveton, Bradley and Hognaston *Derby*

KNOCKHOLT (St Katharine) w Halstead *Roch 9*   **P** D&C   **R** J P BENSON

KNOCKIN (St Mary)   *see* Kinnerley w Melverley and Knockin w Maesbrook *Lich*

KNODISHALL (St Lawrence)   *see* Whinlands *St E*

KNOOK (St Margaret)   *see* Upper Wylye Valley *Sarum*

KNOSSINGTON (St Peter)   *see* Whatborough Gp *Leic*

KNOTTINGLEY (St Botolph) and Kellington w Whitley *Leeds 19*   **P** *Patr Bd*   **TR** C A FLATTERS   **NSM** M J MARSH

KNOTTY ASH (St John) *Liv 2*   **P** *R W Derby*   **V** E R DORAN

KNOWBURY (St Paul)   *see* Ludlow *Heref*

KNOWL HILL (St Peter)   *see* Wargrave w Knowl Hill *Ox*

KNOWLE (Holy Nativity) *Bris 1*   **P** *Bp*   **P-in-c** C D KINCH

KNOWLE (St Barnabas)   *see* Filwood Park *Bris*

KNOWLE (St John the Baptist) (St Lawrence and St Anne) *Birm 11*   **P** *Bp*   **V** M J PARKER   **C** D M EDGERTON, R J TRETHEWEY   **NSM** S C ASHTON

KNOWLE (St John)   *see* Budleigh Salterton, E Budleigh w Bicton etc *Ex*

KNOWLE (St Martin) *Bris 1*   **P** *Bp*   **NSM** A D EVERITT

KNOWSLEY (St Mary)   *see* 4Saints Team *Liv*

KNOWSTONE (St Peter)   *see* Bishopsnympton, Rose Ash, Mariansleigh etc *Ex*

KNOYLE, EAST (St Mary the Virgin)   *see* St Bartholomew *Sarum*

KNOYLE, WEST (St Mary the Virgin)   *see* Mere w W Knoyle and Maiden Bradley *Sarum*

KNUTSFORD (St Cross) Cross Town *Ches 12*   **P** *Mrs J Singer*   **NSM** P M COPE

KNUTSFORD (St John the Baptist) and Toft *Ches 12*   **P** *Bp (2 turns), Mrs L M Anderson (1 turn)*   **V** N T ATKINSON   **C** D G H YOUNG

KNUTTON (St Mary) *Lich 9*   **P** *Sir Beville Stanier Bt and T H G Howard-Sneyd Esq (alt)*   **P-in-c** L M A TIDESWELL

KNUZDEN (St Oswald) *Blackb 2*   **P** *Bp*   **V** M A MORRIS

KNYPERSLEY (St John the Evangelist)   *see* Biddulph Moor and Knypersley *Lich*

KYM VALLEY, The *Ely 10*   **P** *Patr Bd*   **R** S J BOWRING   **NSM** L N BLAND

KYME, NORTH (St Luke)   *see* Carr Dyke Gp *Linc*

KYME, SOUTH (St Mary and All Saints) *as above*

KYNNERSLEY (St Chad)   *see* Edgmond w Kynnersley and Preston Wealdmoors *Lich*

KYRE WYARD (St Mary)   *see* Teme Valley S *Worc*

LACEBY (St Margaret)   *see* Wolds Gateway Group *Linc*

LACEY GREEN (St John the Evangelist)   *see* Risborough *Ox*

LACH DENNIS (All Saints)   *see* Lostock Gralam *Ches*

LACHE (St Mark) cum Saltney *Ches 2*   P *Bp*
V H E A JOHNSTON   C G KENNAUGH, J R PHILLIPS
NSM W A E STEADMAN

LACKFORD (St Lawrence)   *see* Lark Valley *St E*

LACOCK (St Cyriac)   *see* Gtr Corsham and Lacock *Bris*

LADBROKE (All Saints)   *see* Harbury and Ladbroke *Cov*

LADBROKE GROVE (St Michael and All Angels)   *see* Notting Hill
St Mich and Ch Ch *Lon*

LADDINGFORD (St Mary)   *see* Yalding w Collier Street *Roch*

LADOCK (St Ladoca)   *see* Probus, Ladock and Grampound w
Creed and St Erme *Truro*

LADY BAY (All Hallows) w Holme Pierrepont and Adbolton
S'well 6   P *Bp and DBP (jt)*   V M N RODEL

LADYBARN (St Chad) *Man 6*   P *Bp*   P-in-c E J DAVIES

LADYBROOK (St Mary the Virgin)   *see* Mansfield St Jo w
St Mary *S'well*

LADYWOOD (St John the Evangelist) (St Peter) *Birm 1*
P *Trustees*   V I HARPER   NSM W HAMILTON

LAFFORD Group, The North *Linc 14*   P *Bp and DBP (jt)*
R C PENNOCK   NSM L M HUNTER, N R PANTING
OLM G MACHELL

LAFFORD, SOUTH *Linc 14*   P *G Heathcote Esq, Bp, J Wilson Esq,
D&C, DBP, N Playne Esq, Sir Bruno Welby Bt, and Lady
Willoughby de Eresby (by turn)*   R N J MUNDAY

LAINDON (St Nicholas) w Dunton *Chelmsf 12*   P *Bp*
P-in-c A A PETRINE

LAIRA (St Mary the Virgin)   *see* Sutton-on-Plym, Plymouth
St Simon and St Mary *Ex*

LAISTERDYKE (St Mary)   *see* Tong and Laisterdyke *Leeds*

LAITHKIRK (not known)   *see* Romaldkirk w Laithkirk *Leeds*

LAKE (Good Shepherd) *Portsm 7*   P *Bp*   V *vacant*

LAKENHAM (St Alban)   *see* Nor Lakenham St Alb and St Mark
Nor

LAKENHAM (St John the Baptist and All Saints)   *see* Nor
Lakenham St Jo and All SS and Tuckswood *Nor*

LAKENHAM (St Mark)   *see* Nor Lakenham St Alb and St Mark
Nor

LAKENHEATH (St Mary)   *see* Brandon and Santon Downham w
Elveden etc *St E*

LALEHAM (All Saints) *Lon 13*   P *Earl of Lucan*   V A SAVILLE
C C K CONN   I C SMAILES

LAMARSH (Holy Innocents)   *see* N Hinckford *Chelmsf*

LAMBERHURST (St Mary) and Matfield *Roch 8*   P *D&C and
V Brenchley (jt)*   NSM R J BISHOP

LAMBETH (St John the Evangelist)   *see* Waterloo St Jo w St Andr
S'wark

LAMBETH, NORTH (St Anselm) (St Mary's Mission) (St Peter)
S'wark 11   P *The Crown (1 turn), Patr Bd (2 turns)*
TR A R AAGAARD   TV A M KENNEDY   Hon C R F VICKERY
NSM B S ALAGOA, M A K HILBORN

LAMBETH, SOUTH (St Anne and All Saints) *S'wark 11*
P *Abp and Bp*   P-in-c F C DYER

LAMBETH, SOUTH (St Stephen) *S'wark 11*   P *CPAS*
V W A WILSON

LAMBFOLD Benefice, The *Pet 5*   P *Bp, Hertf Coll Ox,
Sons of Clergy Corp, and S R de C Grant-Rennick Esq (alt)*
R C J M OLEY

LAMBLEY (Holy Trinity) *S'well 7*   P *Revd W J Gull*
P-in-c M J TAYLOR

LAMBLEY (St Mary and St Patrick)   *see* Alston Moor *Newc*

LAMBOURN VALLEY, The (St Michael and All Angels) *Ox 6*
P *Bp and Ch Ch Ox (jt)*   V M C CAWTE

LAMBOURNE (St Mary and All Saints) w Abridge and
Stapleford Abbotts *Chelmsf 3*   P *CCC Cam and Ld Chan (alt)*
P-in-c R K GAYLER

LAMBROOK, EAST (St James)   *see* S Petherton w The
Seavingtons and The Lambrooks *B & W*

LAMERTON (St Peter)   *see* Milton Abbot, Dunterton, Lamerton
etc *Ex*

LAMESLEY (St Andrew)   *see* Harlow Green and Lamesley *Dur*

LAMMAS (St Andrew)   *see* Bure Valley *Nor*

LAMORBEY (Holy Redeemer) *Roch 17*   P *Bp*
P-in-c C A TERRY

LAMORBEY (Holy Trinity) *Roch 17*   P *Mrs H K L Whittow*
V P A WELLS

LAMORRAN (St Moran)   *see* Tresillian and Lamorran w
Merther *Truro*

LAMP *Ox 16*   P *CPAS*   R R A CADDELL   OLM H J LOWNDES

LAMPLUGH (St Michael) w Ennerdale *Carl 5*   P *Trustees*
R *vacant*

LAMPORT (All Saints)   *see* Maidwell w Draughton, Lamport w
Faxton *Pet*

LAMYATT (St Mary and St John)   *see* Bruton and Distr *B & W*

LANCASTER (Christ Church) (Christ Church Worship Centre)
Blackb 11   P *V Lanc and Trustees (alt)*   V P S HUDD
C S M SEED

LANCASTER (St Chad)   *see* Skerton St Chad *Blackb*

LANCASTER (St Mary) w St John and St Anne *Blackb 11*
P *Trustees*   V C W NEWLANDS   NSM J NOVELL

LANCASTER (St Paul)   *see* Scotforth *Blackb*

LANCASTER (St Thomas) *Blackb 11*   P *CPAS*
V J L SCAMMAN   C C A ABBOTT   NSM H C SCAMMAN

LANCHESTER (All Saints) and Burnhope *Dur 4*   P *Ld Chan
(2 turns), Prime Min (1 turn)*   V R KALUS   C A MILLER

LANCING (St James the Less) w Coombes *Chich 4*   P *Bp Lon*
P-in-c S J DATE

LANCING (St Michael and All Angels) *Chich 4*   P *Bp*
V B G CARTER

LANDBEACH (All Saints) *Ely 6*   P *CCC Cam*
P-in-c D J CHAMBERLIN   C P H BUTLER
NSM D M BAGULEY, S BRADFORD

LANDCROSS (Holy Trinity)   *see* Bideford, Northam, Westward
Ho!, Appledore etc *Ex*

LANDEWEDNACK (St Wynwallow)   *see* St Ruan w St Grade and
Landewednack *Truro*

LANDFORD (St Andrew)   *see* Forest and Avon *Sarum*

LANDKEY (St Paul)   *see* Swimbridge w W Buckland and
Landkey *Ex*

LANDRAKE (St Michael) w St Erney and Botus Fleming
Truro 11   P *Bp and MMCET (jt)*   P-in-c A BUTLER

LANDSCOVE (St Matthew)   *see* Staverton w Landscove,
Littlehempston, Buckfastleigh and Dean Prior *Ex*

LANDULPH (St Leonard and St Dilpe)   *see* St Dominic,
Landulph and St Mellion w Pillaton *Truro*

LANDYWOOD (St Andrew)   *see* Gt Wyrley *Lich*

LANE END (Holy Trinity) w Cadmore End *Ox 18*   P *Bp*
V R H JENNINGS

LANEAST (St Sidwell and St Gulvat)   *see* Moorland Gp *Truro*

LANEHAM (St Peter)   *see* Retford Area *S'well*

LANERCOST (St Mary Magdalene), Walton, Gilsland and
Nether Denton *Carl 2*   P *Bp, Adn, and the Hon P C W Howard
(jt)*   R R D ALLON-SMITH   NSM A GRAY

LANESIDE (St Peter) *Blackb 1*   P *V Haslingden St Jas*
V S C BROWN   NSM D ALLSOP

LANGAR (St Andrew)   *see* Cropwell Bishop w Colston Bassett,
Granby etc *S'well*

LANGCLIFFE (St John the Evangelist) w Stainforth and
Horton-in-Ribblesdale *Leeds 21*   P *Bp, Adn Craven, W R G
Bell Esq, N Caton Esq, and Churchwardens of Horton-in-
Ribblesdale (jt)*   P-in-c S C DAWSON

LANGDALE (Holy Trinity)   *see* Loughrigg *Carl*

LANGDALE END (St Peter)   *see* Upper Derwent *York*

LANGDALE, LITTLE (Mission Chapel)   *see* Loughrigg *Carl*

LANGDON HILLS (St Mary and All Saints) *Chelmsf 12*
P *D&C St Paul's*   R C E HOPKINSON   C J F PATCHING,
M P PETITT

LANGDON, EAST (St Augustine)   *see* St Margarets-at-Cliffe w
Westcliffe etc *Cant*

LANGDON, WEST (St Mary the Virgin) *as above*

LANGELEI *St Alb 2*   P *Patr Bd*   TR D M LAWSON
TV E M HOOD, L J WILSON

LANGFORD (Blessed Virgin Mary)   *see* Churchill and Langford
B & W

LANGFORD (St Andrew)   *see* Henlow and Langford *St Alb*

LANGFORD (St Bartholomew)   *see* E Trent *S'well*

LANGFORD (St Giles)   *see* Heybridge w Langford *Chelmsf*

LANGFORD (St Matthew)   *see* Shill Valley and Broadshire *Ox*

LANGFORD BUDVILLE (St Peter)   *see* Wellington and Distr
B & W

LANGFORD, LITTLE (St Nicholas of Mira)   *see* Lower Wylye and
Till Valley *Sarum*

LANGHAM (St Mary the Virgin)   *see* Badwell and Walsham *St E*

LANGHAM (St Mary the Virgin) w Boxted *Chelmsf 21*   P *Bp
and Duchy of Lanc (alt)*   P-in-c A J ELMES

LANGHAM (St Peter and St Paul)   *see* Oakham, Ashwell,
Braunston, Brooke, Egleton etc *Pet*

LANGHAM EPISCOPI (St Andrew and St Mary)   *see* Stiffkey and
Bale *Nor*

LANGHAM PLACE (All Souls) *Lon 4*   P *The Crown*
R H PALMER   C D M WELLS, L A IJAZ, M B JACKSON,
P NICHOLAS, R I TICE, S R C NICHOLS
Hon C M J H MEYNELL

LANGHO BILLINGTON (St Leonard) *Blackb 7*   P *V Blackb*
V A A MALCOLM   Hon C M J DUERDEN

LANGLEY (All Saints and Martyrs) *Man 14*   P *Patr Bd*
V P H MILLER   Hon C S D MORGAN   OLM P E JONES

LANGLEY (St Francis)   *see* Fawley *Win*

LANGLEY (St John the Evangelist)   *see* Clavering w Langley,
Arkesden etc *Chelmsf*

LANGLEY (St John)   *see* Oldbury, Langley and Londonderry
Birm

LANGLEY (St Mary the Virgin)   *see* Arden Valley *Cov*

LANGLEY (St Mary)   *see* Otham w Langley *Cant*
LANGLEY (St Michael)   *see* Loddon, Sisland, Chedgrave, Hardley and Langley *Nor*
LANGLEY BURRELL (St Peter)   *see* Chippenham St Paul w Hardenhuish etc *Bris*
LANGLEY GREEN (St Leonard)   *see* Ifield *Chich*
LANGLEY MARISH (St Mary the Virgin) *Ox 12*   **P** *Patr Bd*   **TR** R J GRAYSON   **TV** B H RUSSELL, C R HARTLEY
LANGLEY MARSH (St Luke's Mission Church)   *see* Wiveliscombe and the Hills *B & W*
LANGLEY MILL (St Andrew) and Aldercar *Derby 12*   **P** *V Heanor*   **V** vacant
LANGLEY PARK (All Saints) *Dur 1*   **P** *Prime Min*   **V** M J PEERS
LANGLEY PARK (St Peter's Church Hall)   *see* Beckenham St Barn *Roch*
LANGLEYBURY (St Paul) *St Alb 6*   **P** D W A Loyd Esq   **V** Y R PENTELOW
LANGNEY (St Richard of Chichester) *Chich 14*   **P** *Bp*   **NSM** M F WOODWARD
LANGOLD (St Luke)   *see* Carlton-in-Lindrick and Langold w Oldcotes *S'well*
LANGPORT Area Churches, The *B & W 5*   **P** *Patr Bd*   **C** J PITMAN, R J TWITTY   **NSM** J M CUMMINGS
LANGRICK (St Margaret of Scotland)   *see* Brothertoft Gp *Linc*
LANGRIDGE (St Mary Magdalene)   *see* Bath Weston All SS w N Stoke and Langridge *B & W*
LANGRISH (St John the Evangelist) *Portsm 4*   **P** *Bp*   **V** J BALL
LANGSTONE (St Nicholas)   *see* Havant *Portsm*
LANGTOFT (St Michael)   *see* Ness Gp *Linc*
LANGTOFT (St Peter) w Foxholes, Butterwick, Cottam and Thwing *York 10*   **P** *Abp and Keble Coll Ox (2 turns), Ld Chan (1 turn)*   **V** A P ISON   **NSM** J A TONKIN, S P GRANT
LANGTON (St Andrew)   *see* W Buckrose *York*
LANGTON (St Margaret)   *see* Woodhall Spa Gp *Linc*
LANGTON (St Peter) *as above*
LANGTON BY PARTNEY (St Peter and St Paul)   *see* Bolingbroke Deanery *Linc*
LANGTON GREEN (All Saints) *Roch 12*   **P** *R Speldhurst*   **V** M J GENTRY
LANGTON HERRING (St Peter)   *see* Abbotsbury, Portesham and Langton Herring *Sarum*
LANGTON LONG (All Saints)   *see* Blandford Forum and Langton Long *Sarum*
LANGTON MATRAVERS (St George)   *see* Kingston, Langton Matravers and Worth Matravers *Sarum*
LANGTON ON SWALE (St Wilfrid)   *see* Lower Swale *Leeds*
LANGTON, GREAT (St Wilfrid) *as above*
LANGTON-BY-WRAGBY (St Giles)   *see* Wragby Gp *Linc*
LANGTONS and Shangton, The *Leic 3*   **P** *Bp, E Brudenell Esq, and MMCET (jt)*   **P-in-c** J E GASPER
LANGTREE *Ox 24*   **P** *Patr Bd*   **TR** K G DAVIES   **TV** L J SMITH   **NSM** A M LINTON, C L ALCOCK, D J F ADDISON
LANGTREE (All Saints)   *see* Shebbear, Buckland Filleigh, Sheepwash etc *Ex*
LANGWATHBY (St Peter)   *see* Cross Fell Gp *Carl*
LANGWITH, UPPER (Holy Cross)   *see* E Scarsdale *Derby*
LANGWORTH (St Hugh)   *see* Barlings *Linc*
LANHYDROCK (St Hydrock)   *see* Bodmin w Lanhydrock and Lanivet *Truro*
LANIVET (St Ia) *as above*
LANLIVERY (St Brevita) *Truro 10*   **P** *Bp (1 turn), Adn Bodmin (1 turn), and DBP (2 turns)*   **V** vacant
LANNER (Christ Church)   *see* Redruth w Lanner and Treleigh *Truro*
LANREATH (St Marnarck), Pelynt and Bradoc *Truro 12*   **P** A D G Fortescue Esq, J B Kitson Esq, and H M Parker Esq (jt)   **P-in-c** M E ELLIOTT
LANSALLOS (St Ildierna) *Truro 12*   **P** *DBP and W Gundry-Mills Esq (alt)*   **P-in-c** M E ELLIOTT
LANTEGLOS BY CAMELFORD (St Julitta) w Advent *Truro 10*   **P** *Duchy of Cornwall*   **R** vacant
LANTEGLOS BY FOWEY (St Wyllow) *Truro 12*   **P** *D&C*   **P-in-c** M E ELLIOTT
LAPAL (St Peter)   *see* Halas *Worc*
LAPFORD (St Thomas of Canterbury)   *see* N Creedy *Ex*
LAPLEY (All Saints)   *see* Watershed *Lich*
LAPWORTH (St Mary the Virgin) *Birm 6*   **P** *Mert Coll Ox*   **R** P H GERARD
LARK VALLEY Benefice, The *St E 13*   **P** R W Gough Esq (1 turn), Bp (2 turns)   **P-in-c** M N HAWORTH   **Hon C** T L JONES   **NSM** J C MANN
LARKFIELD (Holy Trinity) *Roch 7*   **P** *DBP*   **V** D J WALKER
LARLING (St Ethelbert)   *see* E w W Harling, Bridgham w Roudham, Larling etc *Nor*

LASBOROUGH (St Mary)   *see* Boxwell, Leighterton, Didmarton, Oldbury etc *Glouc*
LASHAM (St Mary)   *see* Bentworth, Lasham, Medstead and Shalden *Win*
LASHBROOK (Mission Room)   *see* Shiplake w Dunsden and Harpsden *Ox*
LASTINGHAM (St Mary) w Appleton-le-Moors, Rosedale and Cropton *York 19*   **P** *Abp (2 turns), Ld Chan (1 turn)*   **V** vacant
LATCHFORD (Christ Church) *Ches 4*   **P** *R Grappenhall*   **V** J L GOODE   **NSM** T HODSON
LATCHFORD (St James) (St Hilda) *Ches 4*   **P** *R Grappenhall*   **P-in-c** J L GOODE
LATCHINGDON (Christ Church)   *see* Althorne and Latchingdon w N Fambridge *Chelmsf*
LATHBURY (All Saints)   *see* Newport Pagnell w Lathbury and Moulsoe *Ox*
LATHOM PARK (St John)   *see* Ormskirk *Liv*
LATIMER (St Mary Magdalene)   *see* Chenies and Lt Chalfont, Latimer and Flaunden *Ox*
LATTON (St John the Baptist)   *see* Cricklade w Latton *Bris*
LAUGHTON (All Saints)   *see* Trentcliffe Gp *Linc*
LAUGHTON (All Saints) w Ripe and Chalvington *Chich 21*   **P** *Bp (2 turns), Hertf Coll Ox (1 turn)*   **P-in-c** D M B MATHERS
LAUGHTON (St Luke)   *see* Foxton w Gumley and Laughton *Leic*
LAUGHTON-EN-LE-MORTHEN (All Saints)   *see* Dinnington w Laughton and Throapham *Sheff*
LAUNCELLS (St Andrew and St Swithin)   *see* Stratton and Launcells *Truro*
LAUNCESTON (St Mary Magdalene) (St Thomas the Apostle) (St Stephen) *Truro 9*   **P** *Patr Bd*   **TR** J EVERITT   **NSM** M C WILLIAMSON
LAUNTON (Assumption of the Blessed Virgin Mary)   *see* Bicester w Bucknell, Caversfield and Launton *Ox*
LAVANT (St Mary) (St Nicholas) *Chich 2*   **P** *Earl of March and Kinrara*   **R** J S RADCLIFFE
LAVENDER HILL (The Ascension) and Battersea St Philip w St Bartholomew *S'wark 14*   **P** *Bp and Keble Coll Ox (jt)*   **V** I C YOUNG
LAVENDON (St Michael) w Cold Brayfield, Clifton Reynes and Newton Blossomville *Ox 16*   **P** T V Sutthery Esq, The Revd S F Hamill-Stewart, Exors M E Farrer Esq, and Bp (jt)   **R** C E PUMFREY
LAVENHAM (St Peter and St Paul)   *see* Lavenham w Preston *St E*
LAVENHAM (St Peter and St Paul) w Preston *St E 10*   **P** *G&C Coll Cam, and Em Coll Cam (by turn)*   **R** S G F EARL   **C** M J WOODROW
LAVER, HIGH (All Saints) w Magdalen Laver and Little Laver and Matching *Chelmsf 3*   **P** *Bp*   **P-in-c** G A ANDERSON
LAVER, LITTLE (St Mary the Virgin)   *see* High Laver w Magdalen Laver and Lt Laver etc *Chelmsf*
LAVERSTOCK (St Andrew)   *see* Salisbury St Mark and Laverstock *Sarum*
LAVERSTOKE (St Mary)   *see* Overton w Laverstoke and Freefolk *Win*
LAVERTON (Blessed Virgin Mary)   *see* Hardington Vale *B & W*
LAVINGTONS, Cheverells, and Easterton, The *Sarum 17*   **P** *Bp and Ch Ch Ox (jt)*   **R** J M CAMPBELL
LAWFORD (St Mary) *Chelmsf 22*   **P** *St Jo Coll Cam*   **P-in-c** S A HERON   **NSM** P W MANN
LAWHITTON (St Michael)   *see* Three Rivers *Truro*
LAWLEY (St John the Evangelist)   *see* Cen Telford *Lich*
LAWRENCE WESTON (St Peter) and Avonmouth *Bris 2*   **P** *Bp*   **P-in-c** A J MURRAY
LAWRES Group, The SOUTH *Linc 5*   **P** *D&C Linc, D&C Pet, and Mercers' Co (jt)*   **R** D P GREEN   **C** C W HEWITT   **OLM** C BASON, S K BRADLEY
LAWSHALL (All Saints)   *see* St Edm Way *St E*
LAWTON (All Saints)   *see* Church Lawton *Ches*
LAWTON MOOR (St Michael and All Angels) *Man 6*   **P** *Bp*   **V** vacant
LAXEY (Christ Church)   *see* Onchan, Lonan and Laxey *S & M*
LAXFIELD (All Saints)   *see* Four Rivers *St E*
LAXTON (All Saints)   *see* King's Cliffe, Bulwick and Blatherwycke etc *Pet*
LAXTON (St Michael)   *see* Kneesall w Laxton and Wellow *S'well*
LAXTON (St Peter)   *see* Howden *York*
LAYER BRETON (St Mary the Virgin)   *see* Thurstable and Winstree *Chelmsf*
LAYER MARNEY (St Mary the Virgin) *as above*
LAYER-DE-LA-HAYE (St John the Baptist) *as above*
LAYHAM (St Andrew)   *see* Hadleigh, Layham and Shelley *St E*
LAYTON (St Mark) and Staining St Luke *Blackb 8*   **P** *CPAS*   **V** P A LILLICRAP

LAYTON, EAST (Christ Church)   *see* Forcett and Aldbrough and Melsonby *Leeds*

LAZONBY (St Nicholas)   *see* Kirkoswald, Renwick w Croglin, Gt Salkeld etc *Carl*

LEA (St Christopher) (St Barnabas) *Blackb 13*   **P** *Bp*
V P G HAMBORG

LEA (St Giles)   *see* Garsdon, Lea and Cleverton and Charlton *Bris*

LEA CROSS (St Anne)   *see* Pontesbury I and II *Heref*

LEA Group, The (St Helen) *Linc 2*   **P** *DBP, Bp, and Exors Lt Col J E W G Sandars (1 turn), Ld Chan (1 turn)*   **R** P WAIN
NSM L Y LUCAS   **OLM** D J COTTON

LEA HALL (St Richard) *Birm 9*   **P** *Bp*   **V** P M BRACHER

LEA MARSTON (St John the Baptist)   *see* The Whitacres, Lea Marston, and Shustoke *Birm*

LEA, THE (St John the Baptist)   *see* Ariconium *Heref*

LEADEN RODING (St Michael)   *see* S Rodings *Chelmsf*

LEADENHAM (St Swithin) *Linc 22*   **P** P R Reeve *Esq*
R A S J HEALY

LEADGATE (St Ives) *Dur 4*   **P** *Bp*   **P-in-c** D R CLEUGH

LEAFIELD (St Michael and All Angels)   *see* Forest Edge *Ox*

LEAGRAVE (St Luke) *St Alb 12*   **P** *Bp*
V G K N SENTAMU BAVERSTOCK   **NSM** L A JONES

LEAKE (St Mary) w Over and Nether Silton and Kepwick *York 18*   **P** *Abp*   **V** I D HOUGHTON   **NSM** T A LEWIS

LEAKE, EAST (St Mary), WEST (St Helena), Stanford-on-Soar, Rempstone and Costock *S'well 6*   **P** *Bp, DBP, Lord Belper, and SS Coll Cam (jt)*   **P-in-c** T J PARKER
NSM P A EDWARDS

LEAKE, OLD (St Mary) w Wrangle *Linc 21*   **P** *Bp and DBP (alt)*
P-in-c F J M COTTON-BETTERIDGE

LEALHOLM (St James's Chapel)   *see* Middle Esk Moor *York*

LEAM LANE (St Andrew) *Dur 12*   **P** *Bp*   **V** A RAINE

LEAM VALLEY *Cov 6*   **P** *Bp (2 turns), Mrs H M O Lodder (1 turn)*
P-in-c J CLOSE

LEAMINGTON HASTINGS (All Saints)   *see* Leam Valley *Cov*

LEAMINGTON PRIORS (All Saints) *Cov 11*   **P** *Bp*
V C H WILSON   **NSM** A MORRIS

LEAMINGTON PRIORS (St Mary) *Cov 11*   **P** Ch Patr Trust
V C KNIGHT

LEAMINGTON PRIORS (St Paul) *Cov 11*   **P** Ch Patr Trust
V J N JEE   **C** E L WOOLF

LEAMINGTON SPA (Holy Trinity) *Cov 11*   **P** *Bp and M Heber-Percy Esq (jt)*   **V** C H WILSON   **C** C GALE   **NSM** A MORRIS, F A SMITH

LEAMINGTON, SOUTH (St John the Baptist) *Cov 11*   **P** *Bp*
V D W LAWSON

LEAMORE (St Aidan)   *see* Blakenall Heath *Lich*

LEASINGHAM (St Andrew)   *see* N Lafford Gp *Linc*

LEASOWE (St Chad) *Ches 7*   **P** *Bp*   **P-in-c** A P WATTS

LEATHERHEAD (All Saints) (St Mary and St Nicholas) and Mickleham *Guildf 10*   **P** *Bp Guildf and D&C Roch (jt)*
R G D OSBORNE   **Hon C** M E RABY

LEATHLEY (St Oswald)   *see* Washburn and Mid-Wharfe *Leeds*

LEATON (Holy Trinity) and Albrighton w Battlefield *Lich 20*
P Mrs J M Jagger   **P-in-c** M TOOP   **Hon C** R M PARSONS

LEAVELAND (St Laurence)   *see* Downsfoot *Cant*

LEAVENHEATH (St Matthew)   *see* Stoke by Nayland w Leavenheath and Polstead *St E*

LEAVENING (not known)   *see* W Buckrose *York*

LEAVESDEN (All Saints) *St Alb 6*   **P** *Bp*   **V** E B GREEN
C R J KOZAK

LECHLADE (St Lawrence)   *see* S Cotswolds *Glouc*

LECK (St Peter)   *see* E Lonsdale *Blackb*

LECKFORD (St Nicholas)   *see* Test Valley *Win*

LECKHAMPSTEAD (Assumption of the Blessed Virgin Mary)   *see* N Buckingham *Ox*

LECKHAMPSTEAD (St James)   *see* W Downland *Ox*

LECKHAMPTON (St Christopher)   *see* S Cheltenham *Glouc*

LECKHAMPTON (St Peter)   *as above*

LECKHAMPTON (St Philip and St James) *as above*

LECONFIELD (St Catherine)   *see* Lockington and Lund and Scorborough w Leconfield *York*

LEDBURY Team Ministry, The (St Michael and All Angels) (St Katherine's Chapel) *Heref 5*   **P** Patr Bd   **TV** H J MAYELL
C A M HODDER, W F SIMMONDS   **NSM** E C REED, E N SEABRIGHT, J A RHODES, J G WATKINS
OLM J L SCHOLEFIELD

LEDGEMOOR (Mission Room)   *see* Canon Pyon w King's Pyon, Birley and Wellington *Heref*

LEDSHAM (All Saints) w Fairburn *York 4*   **P** Lady Elizabeth Hastings Estate Charity   **P-in-c** A D ROBINSON

LEDSTON LUCK (Mission Church)   *see* Ledsham w Fairburn *York*

LEE (Good Shepherd) (St Peter) *S'wark 4*   **P** R Lee St Marg
V B C SHEPHERD

LEE (St Augustine) Grove Park *S'wark 4*   **P** *Bp*
V G A BERRIMAN

LEE (St Margaret) *S'wark 4*   **P** Ld Chan   **R** A RACE
NSM J K BURKITT-GRAY

LEE (St Matthew)   *see* Ilfracombe, Lee, Woolacombe, Bittadon etc *Ex*

LEE (St Mildred) Burnt Ash Hill *S'wark 4*   **P** *Bp*
V T W C LAKE   **NSM** M BARBER

LEE (St Oswald)   *see* St Oswald in Lee w Bingfield *Newc*

LEE BROCKHURST (St Peter) *Lich 22*   **P** Lord Barnard
P-in-c N P HERON   **NSM** T D SMITH

LEE, THE (St John the Baptist) *Ox 17*   **P** *Bp*   **V** D J BURGESS

LEEBOTWOOD (St Mary)   *see* Dorrington w Leebotwood, Longnor, Stapleton etc *Heref*

LEEDS (All Hallows) *Leeds 16*   **P** *Bp and DBP (jt)*   **Hon C** D H RANDOLPH-HORN

LEEDS (All Saints) w Osmondthorpe *Leeds 17*   **P** *Bp*
V vacant

LEEDS (All Souls) (St Aidan) *Leeds 14*   **P** Patr Bd
NSM C T RAWLINS, D ZANKER, G W W TURNBULL

LEEDS (Parish Church)   *see* Leeds City *Leeds*

LEEDS (St Cyprian and St James) Harehills *Leeds 14*   **P** *Bp*
P-in-c A S KASIBANTE

LEEDS (St Edmund King and Martyr)   *see* Roundhay St Edm *Leeds*

LEEDS (St George) *Leeds 16*   **P** Simeon's Trustees
TR J J CLARK   **TV** J R SEABOURNE   **C** M J HARLOW   **Hon C** J H WALKER

LEEDS (St Nicholas)   *see* Hollingbourne and Hucking w Leeds and Broomfield *Cant*

LEEDS (St Paul)   *see* Ireland Wood *Leeds*

LEEDS (St Saviour)   *see* Leeds Richmond Hill *Leeds*

LEEDS (St Wilfrid) *Leeds 14*   **P** *Bp*   **NSM** T J BUCKINGHAM

LEEDS Belle Isle (St John and St Barnabas) *Leeds 15*   **P** *Bp*
P-in-c A C N BUCKLEY

LEEDS CITY (St Peter) (Holy Trinity) *Leeds 14*   **P** DBP
C H J SMITH   **NSM** S J ROBINSON

LEEDS Gipton (Church of the Epiphany) *Leeds 14*   **P** *Bp*
P-in-c K A FITZSIMONS

LEEDS Halton (St Wilfrid) *Leeds 17*   **P** *Bp*   **V** vacant

LEEDS Richmond Hill (St Saviour) *Leeds 14*   **P** *Bp and Keble Coll Ox (jt)*   **V** vacant

LEEDSTOWN (St James's Mission Church)   *see* Crowan and Treslothan *Truro*

LEEK (All Saints) (St Edward the Confessor) (St John the Evangelist) (St Luke) (St Paul) and Meerbrook *Lich 8*
P Patr Bd   **TR** N R IRONS

LEEK WOOTTON (All Saints) *Cov 4*   **P** Lord Leigh
P-in-c J E PERRYMAN

LEEMING (St John the Baptist)   *see* Bedale and Leeming and Thornton Watlass *Leeds*

LEEMING BAR (St Augustine) *as above*

LEE-ON-THE-SOLENT (St Faith) *Portsm 3*   **P** *Bp*
P-in-c P M CHAMBERLAIN   **NSM** B T WILLIAMS, S E DENT

LEES HILL (Mission Hall)   *see* Lanercost, Walton, Gilsland and Nether Denton *Carl*

LEESFIELD (St Thomas) *Man 15*   **P** *Bp*   **V** E J DISLEY
NSM D J HALFORD

LEESFIELD Knoll's Lane (St Agnes)   *see* Leesfield *Man*

LEGBOURNE (All Saints) and Wold Marsh *Linc 15*
P Ld Chan (1 turn), Bp, Exors Viscountess Chaplin, Ch Trust Fund Trust, D&C, and DBP (1 turn), Duchy of Lanc (1 turn)
P-in-c L E TURNER

LEGH, HIGH *Ches 12*   **P** R H Cornwall-Legh Esq   **V** vacant

LEGSBY (St Thomas) *Linc 7*   **P** *Bp*   **P-in-c** S W JOHNSON

LEICESTER (Holy Apostles) (St Oswald) *Leic 1*   **P** DBP and Ridley Hall Cam (jt)   **P-in-c** P R BERRY   **NSM** A R LEIGHTON

LEICESTER (Holy Spirit) (St Andrew) (St Nicholas) *Leic 1*
P *Bp*   **NSM** H F FADRIQUELA

LEICESTER (Holy Trinity w St John the Divine) *Leic 1*
P Peache Trustees   **V** J C MCGINLEY   **C** E A SUTHERLAND, J LINDSEY   **NSM** S J HILL

LEICESTER (Martyrs) *Leic 1*   **P** *Bp*   **V** R V WORSFOLD
C S M ROWBORY   **NSM** S LEIGHTON

LEICESTER (St Aidan) *Leic 1*   **P** *Bp*   **V** S LUMBY

LEICESTER (St Alban)   *see* Leic Resurr *Leic*

LEICESTER (St Anne) (St Paul) w St Augustine *Leic 1*   **P** *Bp*
V S P J BURNHAM

LEICESTER (St Chad) *Leic 1*   **P** *Bp*   **P-in-c** M J COURT
C C M KING

LEICESTER (St James the Greater) *Leic 1*   **P** *Bp*
V G RICHERBY   **NSM** J M SHARP

LEICESTER (St Mary de Castro) *Leic 1*   **P** *Bp*
P-in-c D MAUDLIN   **NSM** S P WARD

LEICESTER (St Philip) *Leic 1*   **P** Adn Leic, V Evington, V Leic H Trin, G A Cooling Esq, and A S Price Esq (jt)   **V** vacant

LEICESTER (St Stephen)   *see* N Evington *Leic*
LEICESTER (St Theodore of Canterbury) *Leic 1*   **P** *Bp*
P-in-c E T SKINNER
LEICESTER FOREST EAST (St Andrew) *Leic 9*   **P** *Bp*
R A HUMPHREY
LEICESTER Presentation of Christ (St Barnabas) (St Peter)
Leic 1   **P** *Bp*   **TR** *vacant*
LEICESTER Resurrection (St Alban) *Leic 1*   **P** *Bp*
P-in-c P CLEMENT   **C** S GEORGE, S M STEVENS
LEICESTER St Christopher *Leic 1*   **P** *MMCET*   **V** A M ROCHE
LEICESTER, The Abbey (St Margaret and All Saints) *Leic 1*
P *Bp*   **TR** *vacant*
LEIGH (All Saints' Mission)   *see* Bedford Leigh *Man*
LEIGH (All Saints)   *see* Ashton Keynes, Leigh and Minety *Bris*
LEIGH (All Saints)   *see* Uttoxeter Area *Lich*
LEIGH (St Andrew)   *see* Three Valleys *Sarum*
LEIGH (St Bartholomew) *S'wark 26*   **P** *N J Charrington Esq*
P-in-c J M A WILLANS
LEIGH (St Catherine)   *see* Twigworth, Down Hatherley,
Norton, The Leigh etc *Glouc*
LEIGH (St Clement) *Chelmsf 13*   **P** *Bp*   **P-in-c** C R HILLMAN
C L A TAYLOR   **NSM** CE SANDOVER
LEIGH (St Edburga)   *see* Worcs W *Worc*
LEIGH (St Mary the Virgin) *Man 19*   **P** *Bp*   **V** K D CRINKS
LEIGH (St Mary) *Roch 11*   **P** *Ch Trust Fund Trust*
V L W G KEVIS
LEIGH PARK (St Francis) *Portsm 5*   **P** *Bp*   **V** J G P JEFFERY
LEIGH UPON MENDIP (St Giles) w Stoke St Michael *B & W 3*
P *DBP and V Doulting (jt)*   **P-in-c** A E DICKSON
LEIGH WOODS (St Mary the Virgin)   *see* Abbots Leigh w Leigh
Woods *Bris*
LEIGH, NORTH (St Mary) *Ox 28*   **P** *Ld Chan*   **V** S T KIRBY
C M I G DIXON   **NSM** N K PIKE
LEIGH, SOUTH (St James the Great)   *see* Cogges and S Leigh
Ox
LEIGH, WEST (St Alban) *Portsm 5*   **P** *Bp*   **P-in-c** K B GREEN
LEIGHLAND (St Giles)   *see* Old Cleeve, Leighland and
Treborough *B & W*
LEIGH-ON-SEA (St Aidan) the Fairway *Chelmsf 13*   **P** *Bp*
V G M TARRY   **NSM** S K POSS
LEIGH-ON-SEA (St James) *Chelmsf 13*   **P** *Bp*
V W G BULLOCH
LEIGH-ON-SEA (St Margaret of Antioch) *Chelmsf 13*   **P** *Bp*
V I G BOOTH
LEIGHS, GREAT (St Mary the Virgin) and LITTLE (St John) and
Little Waltham *Chelmsf 9*   **P** *Linc Coll Ox, Reformation Ch
Trust, and Ex Coll Ox (jt)*   **P-in-c** C J BROWN
OLM R F BRAISBY, S SYKES
LEIGHTERTON (St Andrew)   *see* Boxwell, Leighterton,
Didmarton, Oldbury etc *Glouc*
LEIGHTON (St Mary)   *see* Wrockwardine Deanery *Lich*
LEIGHTON BROMSWOLD (St Mary)   *see* W Leightonstone *Ely*
LEIGHTON BUZZARD (All Saints)   *see* Ouzel Valley *St Alb*
LEIGHTON-CUM-MINSHULL VERNON (St Peter) and
Warmingham *Ches 15*   **P** *Bp and J C Crewe Esq (jt)*
V P F DE J GOGGIN
LEIGHTONSTONE, EAST *Ely 10*   **P** *Bp (2 turns), Peterho Cam
(1 turn)*   **C** J V TAYLOR, S J BOWRING
LEIGHTONSTONE, NORTH *Ely 10*   **P** *Patr Bd*   **R** M P JEPP
LEIGHTONSTONE, WEST *Ely 10*   **P** *Bp and Sir Philip Naylor-
Leyland Bt (jt)*   **P-in-c** B A STEWART
LEINTHALL EARLES (St Andrew)   *see* Kingsland w Eardisland,
Aymestrey etc *Heref*
LEINTHALL STARKES (St Mary Magdalene)   *see* Wigmore Abbey
Heref
LEINTWARDINE (St Andrew) Adforton *as above*
LEINTWARDINE (St Mary Magdalene) *as above*
LEIRE (St Peter)   *see* Upper Soar *Leic*
LEISTON (St Margaret) *St E 17*   **P** *Ch Hosp*
P-in-c M PHILLIPS-LAST   **NSM** R ELLIS
LELANT (St Uny)   *see* Carbis Bay w Lelant *Truro*
LEMINGTON, LOWER (St Leonard)   *see* Moreton-in-Marsh w
Batsford, Todenham etc *Glouc*
LEMSFORD (St John the Evangelist)   *see* Bp's Hatfield, Lemsford
and N Mymms *St Alb*
LEN VALLEY, The *Cant 13*   **P** *Abp, All So Coll Ox, Viscount
Chilston, and Lord Cornwallis (jt)*   **P-in-c** R F VENN
NSM M E HART
LENBOROUGH *Ox 11*   **P** *Ch Ch Ox, Cam Univ, and New Coll Ox
(2 turns), Ld Chan (1 turn)*   **V** R M ROBERTS   **NSM** K M PECK
LENHAM (St Mary)   *see* Len Valley *Cant*
LENTON (Holy Trinity) (Priory Church of St Anthony) *S'well 9*
P *CPAS*   **V** M R SMITH
LENTON (St Peter)   *see* N Beltisloe Gp *Linc*
LENTON ABBEY (St Barnabas) *S'well 9*   **P** *CPAS*
P-in-c A R HOWE   **C** L P B O'BOYLE

LEOMINSTER (St Peter and St Paul) *Heref 6*   **P** *Patr Bd*
TR M J KNEEN   **TV** M BURNS, S B THOMSON   **C** K A CLARKE
NSM E M G BROWN, W DUMMERT   **OLM** C P REES, P C REES,
P SMITH
LEONARD STANLEY (St Swithun)   *see* The Stanleys w Selsley
Glouc
LEPTON (St John the Evangelist) *Leeds 6*   **P** *R Kirkheaton*
P-in-c A J RAGGETT
LESBURY (St Mary) w Alnmouth *Newc 6*   **P** *Dioc Soc*
V I D MACKARILL
LESNEWTH (St Michael and All Angels)   *see* Boscastle and
Tintagel Gp *Truro*
LESSINGHAM (All Saints)   *see* Bacton, Happisburgh,
Hempstead w Eccles etc *Nor*
LETCHWORTH (St Mary the Virgin) (St Michael) *St Alb 3*
P *Guild of All So*   **R** P BENNETT
LETCHWORTH (St Paul) w Willian *St Alb 3*   **P** *Bp*
V S Q MOORE   **C** G M FOSTER, M L MOORE
NSM A J FERRIS, M P DACK
LETCOMBE BASSETT (St Michael and All Angels)   *see* Ridgeway
Ox
LETCOMBE REGIS (St Andrew) *as above*
LETHERINGHAM (St Mary)   *see* Mid Loes *St E*
LETHERINGSETT (St Andrew)   *see* Blakeney w Cley, Wiveton,
Glandford etc *Nor*
LETTON (St John the Baptist) w Staunton, Byford, Mansel
Gamage and Monnington *Heref 4*   **P** *Sir John Cotterell Bt
(2 turns), Exors Mrs Dew (1 turn), Ch Ch Ox (3 turns), and
DBP (1 turn)*   **R** *vacant*
LETWELL (St Peter)   *see* Firbeck w Letwell *Sheff*
LEUSDON (St John the Baptist)   *see* Ashburton, Bickington,
Buckland in the Moor etc *Ex*
LEVEDALE (Mission Church)   *see* Penkridge *Lich*
LEVEN (Holy Trinity)   *see* Brandesburton and Leven *York*
LEVENS (St John the Evangelist) *Carl 10*   **P** *Trustees*
P-in-c R J CROSSLEY   **NSM** A MILLER
LEVENSHULME (St Andrew) (St Mark) (St Peter) *Man 2*   **P** *Bp
and Trustees (jt)*   **R** C E THROUP   **C** D GILL   **OLM** F G KERR
LEVER BRIDGE (St Stephen and All Martyrs)   *see* Leverhulme
Man
LEVER, GREAT (St Michael w St Bartholomew)   *see* New Bury w
Gt Lever *Man*
LEVER, LITTLE (St Matthew) *Man 7*   **P** *V Bolton-le-Moors St Pet*
V J WISEMAN   **NSM** I C ANTHONY
LEVERHULME *Man 12*   **P** *Prime Min*   **TR** S EDWARDS
TV S WHITING   **OLM** S P MCGREGOR
LEVERINGTON (St Leonard), Newton and Tydd St Giles *Ely 14*
P *Bp*   **R** S K GARDNER
LEVERTON (St Helena)   *see* Freiston, Butterwick w Bennington,
and Leverton *Linc*
LEVERTON, NORTH (St Martin)   *see* Retford Area *S'well*
LEVERTON, SOUTH (All Saints) *as above*
LEVINGTON (St Peter)   *see* Nacton and Levington w
Bucklesham etc *St E*
LEVISHAM (St John the Baptist)   *see* Pickering w Lockton and
Levisham *York*
LEWANNICK (St Martin)   *see* Three Rivers *Truro*
LEWES (St Anne) (St Michael) (St Thomas at Cliffe) w All
Saints *Chich 21*   **P** *Bp and SMF (1 turn), Ld Chan (1 turn)*
R R A MOATT   **Hon C** D N A BROAD   **NSM** J A EGAR,
P D YATES, S A WILKINSON
LEWES (St John sub Castro) and South Malling *Chich 21*
P *Bp and MMCET (jt)*   **P-in-c** S J DAUGHTERY
LEWES (St Mary)   *see* Lewes St Anne and St Mich and St Thos
etc *Chich*
LEWISHAM (St Mary) *S'wark 4*   **P** *Earl of Dartmouth*
V S P HALL   **C** D M A EVANS   **Hon C** R C PEERS
LEWISHAM (St Stephen) and St Mark *S'wark 4*   **P** *Keble Coll
Ox*   **P-in-c** P P CORBETT   **Hon C** F D GARDOM
NSM P J HUDSON
LEWISHAM (St Swithun) Hither Green *S'wark 4*   **P** *V
Lewisham St Mary*   **P-in-c** J L KUSTNER
LEWKNOR (St Margaret)   *see* Thame *Ox*
LEWSEY (St Hugh)   *see* Luton Lewsey St Hugh *St Alb*
LEWTRENCHARD (St Peter)   *see* Lifton, Broadwoodwidger,
Stowford etc *Ex*
LEXDEN (St Leonard) *Chelmsf 21*   **P** *Bp*   **P-in-c** T A J WYNNE
C D T ARMSTRONG
LEXHAM, EAST (St Andrew)   *see* Litcham w Kempston, E and
W Lexham, Mileham etc *Nor*
LEXHAM, WEST (St Nicholas) *as above*
LEYBOURNE (St Peter and St Paul) *Roch 7*   **P** *Major Sir David
Hawley Bt*   **R** M A J BUCHAN
LEYBURN (St Matthew) w Bellerby *Leeds 27*   **P** *Lord Bolton
and Mrs M E Scragg (alt)*   **P-in-c** C M A HEPPER
C R D C LAWTON

LEYFIELDS (St Francis)   *see* Tamworth *Lich*

LEYLAND (St Ambrose) *Blackb 5*   **P** *V Leyland*
  V D J E CLARKE   **NSM** C D F CROMBIE, G E ASHWORTH

LEYLAND (St Andrew) *Blackb 5*   **P** *CPAS*   **V** D R A GIBB
  C J J GWYN-THOMAS, M L SIMPSON

LEYLAND (St James) *Blackb 5*   **P** *Sir Henry Farington Bt*
  P-in-c M A M WOLVERSON   **NSM** T J SWINDELLS

LEYLAND (St John) *Blackb 5*   **P** *V Leyland St Andr and CPAS (jt)*
  V A MCHAFFIE   **NSM** B J WILSON

LEYTON (All Saints) *Chelmsf 7*   **P** *V St Mary's Leyton*
  V M I HOLMDEN

LEYTON (Christ Church) *Chelmsf 7*   **P** *Ch Trust Fund Trust*
  V M E BURKILL   **C** N A ALGEO

LEYTON (Emmanuel) *Chelmsf 7*   **P** *Bp*   **V** A ADEMOLA

LEYTON (St Catherine) (St Paul) *Chelmsf 7*   **P** *V Leyton St Mary w St Edw*   **V** J W B WADDELL

LEYTON (St Mary w St Edward) and St Luke *Chelmsf 7*
  P *Simeon's Trustees*   **V** C M RABLEN   **NSM** H GILBERT

**LEYTONSTONE (Holy Trinity and St Augustine of Hippo)
Harrow Green** *Chelmsf 7*   **P** *Bp*   **P-in-c** N-A WALSH
  C B D DEUCHAR DE MELLO

LEYTONSTONE (St Andrew) *Chelmsf 7*   **P** *Bp*
  P-in-c N R DUNN

LEYTONSTONE (St John the Baptist) *Chelmsf 7*   **P** *Bp*
  V D R BRITTON

LEYTONSTONE (St Margaret w St Columba) *Chelmsf 7*
  P *Bp*   **P-in-c** N-A WALSH

LEZANT (St Briochus)   *see* Three Rivers *Truro*

LEZAYRE (Holy Trinity)   *see* Bride, Lezayre and N Ramsey *S & M*

LICHBOROUGH (St Martin)   *see* Lambfold *Pet*

LICHFIELD (Christ Church) *Lich 1*   **P** *Bp*
  P-in-c J L WATERFIELD

LICHFIELD (St Chad) *Lich 1*   **P** *D&C*   **R** P R CLARK
  C J P J PENDUCK

LICHFIELD (St John's Hospital) Proprietary Chapel *Lich 1*
  P *Bp*   **Master** A A GORHAM

LICHFIELD (St Michael) (St Mary) and Wall St John *Lich 1*
  P *D&C*   **R** S N H BAKER   **C** L K COLLINS   **NSM** D YOUNGS, R L C BULL

LICKEY, THE (Holy Trinity) *Birm 4*   **P** *V Bromsgrove*
  V M E BRIGHTON

LIDEN (St Timothy)   *see* Swindon Dorcan *Bris*

LIDGATE (St Mary)   *see* Bansfield *St E*

LIDGET GREEN (St Wilfrid)   *see* Bradf St Wilfrid w St Columba *Leeds*

**LIFTON (St Mary), Broadwoodwidger, Stowford,
Lewtrenchard, Thrushelton and Kelly w Bradstone** *Ex 22*
  P *Bp, Mrs A M Baring-Gould Almond, W F Kelly Esq, and J B Wollocombe Esq (jt)*   **P-in-c** T R DEACON

LIGHTBOWNE (St Luke) *Man 4*   **P** *D&C*   **P-in-c** P A STAMP

LIGHTCLIFFE (St Matthew) and Hove Edge *Leeds 8*   **P** *Bp and V Halifax (jt)*   **V** K M BUCK

LIGHTHORNE (St Laurence) *Cov 8*   **P** *Lady Willoughby de Broke*   **R** J D PARKER

LIGHTWATER (All Saints) *Guildf 6*   **P** *Ld Chan and Bp (alt)*
  V M G WALLACE   **OLM** R D BROWNING, R KIDD

LILBOURNE (All Saints)   *see* Crick and Yelvertoft w Clay Coton and Lilbourne *Pet*

LILLESHALL (St Michael and All Angels) and Muxton *Lich 16*
  P *Bp*   **V** M W LEFROY   **C** R J CRESSWELL   **OLM** J EVANS

LILLEY (St Peter)   *see* King's Walden and Offley w Lilley *St Alb*

LILLINGSTONE DAYRELL (St Nicholas)   *see* N Buckingham *Ox*

LILLINGSTONE LOVELL (Assumption of the Blessed Virgin Mary) *as above*

LILLINGTON (St Martin)   *see* Sherborne w Castleton, Lillington and Longburton *Sarum*

LILLINGTON (St Mary Magdalene) and Old Milverton *Cov 11*
  P *Bp*   **V** C GALE   **NSM** N J NIXON, S FAIRHURST

LILLIPUT (Holy Angels) *Sarum 7*   **P** *Bp*   **V** C M LANGFORD
  C C M COUZENS

LIMBER, GREAT (St Peter)   *see* Brocklesby Park *Linc*

LIMEHOUSE (St Anne) (St Peter) *Lon 7*   **P** *BNC Ox*
  R R A BRAY   **C** A J LATIMER, M C C NODDER

LIMESIDE (St Chad)   *see* Hollinwood and Limeside *Man*

LIMINGTON (The Blessed Virgin Mary)   *see* Ilchester w Northover, Limington, Yeovilton etc *B & W*

LIMPENHOE (St Botolph)   *see* Acle and Bure to Yare *Nor*

LIMPLEY STOKE (St Mary)   *see* Freshford, Limpley Stoke and Hinton Charterhouse *B & W*

LIMPSFIELD (St Peter) (St Andrew) and Tatsfield *S'wark 25*
  P *Bp*   **TR** J F PERCIVAL   **TV** E L ELLIS   **C** M J DRUMMOND
  NSM G P SOUTH, W M HARVEY

LINBY (St Michael) w Papplewick *S'well 4*   **P** *T W A Cundy Esq*
  R K H TURNER

LINCH (St Luke)   *see* Lynch w Iping Marsh and Milland *Chich*

LINCHMERE (St Peter)   *see* Lynchmere and Camelsdale *Chich*

LINCOLN (All Saints) *Linc 11*   **P** *Bp*   **P-in-c** D EDGAR   **Hon**
  C R G WILKINSON

LINCOLN (St Botolph by Bargate) *Linc 11*   **P** *Bp*
  P-in-c J S CULLIMORE   **Hon C** N BURGESS   **NSM** J L HART

LINCOLN (St Faith) (St Martin) (St Peter-at-Arches) *Linc 11*
  P *Bp*   **V** J A WEARING   **Hon C** N BURGESS

LINCOLN (St George) Swallowbeck *Linc 11*   **P** *Bp and V Skellingthorpe (jt)*   **V** I G SILK   **C** J N GANDON, S A BIRD
  NSM D L FREEMAN

LINCOLN (St Giles) *Linc 11*   **P** *Bp*   **V** N J BUCK

LINCOLN (St John the Baptist) (St John the Evangelist)
  Linc 11   **P** *Bp*   **V** S A HOY   **C** P J WHITE

**LINCOLN (St Mary Magdalene w St Paul in the Bail)
(St Michael on the Mount)** *Linc 11*   **P** *Bp, D&C, and Adn Linc (jt)*   **V** M A WHITEHEAD

LINCOLN (St Mary-le-Wigford) (St Benedict) (St Mark)
  Linc 11   **P** *Bp*   **P-in-c** J S CULLIMORE   **Hon C** N BURGESS
  NSM J L HART

LINCOLN (St Nicholas) (St John) Newport *Linc 11*   **P** *Bp and D&C (alt)*   **V** H W F JONES   **C** J C WATT

LINCOLN (St Peter in Eastgate) *Linc 11*   **P** *Bp*
  V E M C BOWES-SMITH   **C** S J DURANT

LINCOLN (St Peter-at-Gowts) (St Andrew) *Linc 11*   **P** *Bp*
  P-in-c J S CULLIMORE   **Hon C** N BURGESS   **NSM** J L HART

LINCOLN (St Swithin) *Linc 11*   **P** *Bp*   **P-in-c** J A PRESTWOOD
  Hon C N BURGESS

LINDAL AND MARTON (St Peter)   *see* Pennington and Lindal w Marton and Bardsea *Carl*

LINDALE (St Paul)   *see* Cartmel Peninsula *Carl*

LINDFIELD (All Saints) *Chich 5*   **P** *Ch Soc Trust*   **V** D J CLARKE
  C H E BOURNE, S C SILK

LINDLEY (St Stephen) *Leeds 12*   **P** *V Huddersfield*
  V R N FIRTH

LINDOW (St John) *Ches 12*   **P** *Bp*   **V** S R GALES

LINDRIDGE (St Lawrence)   *see* Teme Valley N *Worc*

LINDSELL (St Mary the Virgin)   *see* Stebbing and Lindsell w Gt and Lt Saling *Chelmsf*

LINDSEY (St Peter)   *see* Bildeston w Wattisham and Lindsey, Whatfield etc *St E*

LINFORD (St Francis)   *see* E and W Tilbury and Linford *Chelmsf*

LINFORD, GREAT (St Andrew)   *see* Stantonbury and Willen *Ox*

LINFORD, LITTLE (St Leonard)   *see* Lamp *Ox*

LINGDALE (Mission Room)   *see* Boosbeck and Lingdale *York*

LINGEN (St Michael and All Angels)   *see* Presteigne w Discoed, Kinsham, Lingen and Knill *Heref*

LINGFIELD (St Peter and St Paul) and Dormansland *S'wark 25*
  P *Bp*   **V** K J PERCIVAL   **NSM** E RANDALL, J A ATTWOOD, N K HINTON

LINGWOOD (St Peter)   *see* Burlingham St Edmund w Lingwood, Strumpshaw etc *Nor*

LINKENHOLT (St Peter)   *see* Hurstbourne Tarrant, Faccombe, Vernham Dean etc *Win*

LINKINHORNE (St Mellor) *Truro 12*   **P** *DBP*
  P-in-c A W STEPHENS

LINSLADE (St Barnabas)   *see* Ouzel Valley *St Alb*

LINSLADE (St Mary) *as above*

LINSTEAD PARVA (St Margaret)   *see* Blyth Valley *St E*

LINTHORPE (St Barnabas) *York 17*   **P** *Abp*   **V** E WILSON
  C M D STRAND, T STEPHENS

LINTHWAITE (Christ Church)   *see* Crosland Moor and Linthwaite *Leeds*

LINTON (Christ Church)   *see* Walton-on-Trent w Croxall, Rosliston etc *Derby*

LINTON (St Mary the Virgin)   *see* Ariconium *Heref*

LINTON (St Mary) *Ely 5*   **P** *Patr Bd*   **TV** J M NORRIS,
  M A GUITE

LINTON (St Nicholas)   *see* Coxheath, E Farleigh, Hunton, Linton etc *Roch*

LINTON IN CRAVEN (St Michael) *Leeds 26*   **P** *D&C*
  R D MACHA   **C** F JENKINS

LINWOOD (St Cornelius) *Linc 7*   **P** *MMCET*
  P-in-c S W JOHNSON

LIPHOOK (Church Centre)   *see* Bramshott and Liphook *Portsm*

LISCARD (St Thomas) *Ches 7*   **P** *Bp*   **V** R T NELSON

LISCARD Resurrection (St Mary w St Columba) *Ches 7*   **P** *Bp*
  V A J MANNINGS

LISKEARD (St Martin) and St Keyne *Truro 12*   **P** *Simeon's Trustees*   **P-in-c** A R INGLEBY   **C** M A J DAVIES

LISS (St Mary) (St Peter) (St Saviour) *Portsm 4*   **P** *Bp*
  R C D WILLIAMS   **C** M TARIQ

LISSET (St James of Compostella)   *see* Beeford w Frodingham and Foston *York*

LISSINGTON (St John the Baptist) *Linc 7*   **P** *D&C York*
  P-in-c S W JOHNSON

LISSINGTON (St John the Baptist)   *see* Lissington *Linc*
LISTON (not known)   *see* N Hinckford *Chelmsf*
LITCHAM (All Saints) w Kempston, East and West Lexham,
Mileham, Beeston-next-Mileham, Stanfield, Tittleshall
and Godwick *Nor 14*   **P** *Bp, Earl of Leic, Ch Soc Tr, DBP,*
Mrs E M Olesen, and N W D Foster Esq (jt)   **R** *vacant*
LITCHFIELD (St James the Less)   *see* Whitchurch w Tufton and
Litchfield *Win*
LITHERLAND (St Andrew)   *see* Bootle *Liv*
LITHERLAND (St John and St James)   *see* Orrell Hey St Jo and
St Jas *Liv*
LITHERLAND (St Paul) Hatton Hill *Liv 1*   **P** *Bp*
V J W WHITLEY
LITHERLAND (St Philip) *Liv 1*   **P** *Trustees*
P-in-c C L DAWSON   **NSM** A J FINCH
LITLINGTON (St Catherine)   *see* Shingay Gp *Ely*
LITLINGTON (St Michael the Archangel)   *see* Alfriston w
Lullington, Litlington, W Dean and Folkington *Chich*
LITTLE   *see also under substantive place name*
LITTLE BIRCH (St Mary)   *see* Wormelow Hundred *Heref*
LITTLE VENICE (St Mary) (St Saviour) *Lon 2*   **P** *Bp*
V G S BRADLEY
LITTLEBOROUGH (Holy Trinity) *Man 17*   **P** *Bp, TR Rochdale,*
and D&C (jt)   **V** I BULLOCK   **Dss** K J OLIVER
LITTLEBOURNE (St Vincent) and Ickham w Wickhambreaux
and Stodmarsh *Cant 1*   **P** *Abp, D&C, Ch Trust Fund Trust,*
and Adn Cant (jt)   **P-in-c** J W LLOYD   **C** C M WILKINSON
LITTLEBURY (Holy Trinity)   *see* Saffron Walden and Villages
Chelmsf
LITTLEBURY GREEN (St Peter) *as above*
LITTLEDEAN (St Ethelbert)   *see* Cinderford w Littledean *Glouc*
LITTLEHAM (St Margaret) w Lympstone *Ex 1*   **P** *Patr Bd*
TR J B B HUTCHINGS   **TV** B H CAMBRIDGE
NSM L A HOLMAN, M E DOUGLAS, S HUMPHRIES
LITTLEHAM (St Swithin)   *see* Bideford, Northam, Westward
Ho!, Appledore etc *Ex*
LITTLEHAMPTON (St James) (St Mary) and Wick *Chich 1*
P *Bp*   **TR** R J CASWELL   **TV** S R MERRIMAN
NSM P P SEDLMAYR
LITTLEHEMPSTON (St John the Baptist)   *see* Staverton w
Landscove, Littlehempston, Buckfastleigh and Dean
Prior *Ex*
LITTLEMOOR (St Francis of Assisi)   *see* Preston w Sutton Poyntz,
Littlemoor etc *Sarum*
LITTLEMORE (St Mary the Virgin and St Nicholas) *Ox 1*
P *Or Coll Ox*   **P-in-c** M C M ARMITSTEAD   **C** T R ALBINSON
NSM T J MORGAN
LITTLEOVER (St Peter) *Derby 10*   **P** PCC   **V** A C M DRING
C A J RACE
LITTLEPORT (St George) *Ely 8*   **P** *Bp*   **V** J H ROBSON
LITTLETON (St Catherine of Alexandria)   *see* The Downs *Win*
LITTLETON (St Mary Magdalene)   *see* Shepperton and Littleton
Lon
LITTLETON DREW (All Saints)   *see* By Brook *Bris*
LITTLETON, HIGH (Holy Trinity)   *see* Paulton w Farrington
Gurney and High Littleton *B & W*
LITTLETON, NORTH (St Nicholas)   *see* Cleeve Prior and The
Littletons *Worc*
LITTLETON, SOUTH (St Michael the Archangel) *as above*
LITTLETON, WEST (St James)   *see* Marshfield w Cold Ashton
and Tormarton etc *Bris*
LITTLETON-ON-SEVERN (St Mary of Malmesbury)
see Alveston and Littleton-on-Severn w Elberton *Bris*
LITTLEWICK (St John the Evangelist)   *see* Burchetts Green *Ox*
LITTLEWORTH (Holy Ascension)   *see* Cherbury w Gainfield *Ox*
LITTON (Christ Church)   *see* Tideswell *Derby*
LITTON (St Mary the Virgin)   *see* Chewton Mendip w Ston
Easton, Litton etc *B & W*
LITTON CHENEY (St Mary)   *see* Bride Valley *Sarum*
LIVERMERE, GREAT (St Peter)   *see* Blackbourne *St E*
LIVERPOOL (All Souls) Springwood *Liv 4*   **P** *The Crown*
V P ELLIS   **NSM** F C PENNIE
LIVERPOOL (Christ Church) Norris Green *Liv 8*   **P** *Bp*
V H A EDWARDS   **C** A R MAYNARD
LIVERPOOL (Our Lady and St Nicholas) *Liv 3*   **P** *Sir William*
Gladstone Bt   **R** C A PAILING   **C** D J BAVERSTOCK
NSM M A MONTROSE
LIVERPOOL (St Anne)   *see* Stanley w Stoneycroft St Paul *Liv*
LIVERPOOL (St Christopher) Norris Green *Liv 8*   **P** *Bp*
V P H BURMAN   **NSM** B A SMITH
LIVERPOOL (St James in the City) *Liv 6*   **P** *Bp*   **V** N R SHORT
C J PADFIELD
LIVERPOOL (St Luke in the City) (St Bride w St Saviour)
(St Michael in the City) (St Stephen w St Catherine) *Liv 6*
P *Patr Bd*   **TR** G C ELSMORE   **TV** M WATERS   **C** R V STOCK
NSM S DOYLE

LIVERPOOL (St Philip w St David)   *see* Liv All SS *Liv*
LIVERPOOL All Saints (St Mary) (St John the Divine)
(St Philip w St David) *Liv 3*   **P** *Patr Bd*   **V** M D COATES
C L PASTERFIELD, P SALTMARSH, R M SHEEHAN
NSM A MURRAY, I D CASSIDY
LIVERPOOL Stoneycroft (St Paul)   *see* Stanley w Stoneycroft
St Paul *Liv*
LIVERSEDGE (Christ Church)   *see* Heckmondwike (w
Norristhorpe) and Liversedge *Leeds*
LIVERTON (St Michael)   *see* Easington w Liverton *York*
LIVERTON MINES (St Hilda) *as above*
LIVESEY (St Andrew) *Blackb 2*   **P** *Trustees*
V J P MILTON-THOMPSON
LLANDINABO (St Junabius)   *see* Wormelow Hundred *Heref*
LLANFAIR WATERDINE (St Mary)   *see* Middle Marches *Heref*
LLANGARRON (St Deinst)   *see* Goodrich, Marstow, Welsh
Bicknor, Llangarron etc *Heref*
LLANGROVE (Christ Church) *as above*
LLANGUA (St James)   *see* Ewyas Harold w Dulas, Kenderchurch
etc *Heref*
LLANVEYNOE (St Beuno and St Peter)   *see* Clodock and
Longtown w Craswall, Llanveynoe etc *Heref*
LLANWARNE (Christ Church)   *see* Wormelow Hundred *Heref*
LLANYBLODWEL (St Michael), Llanymynech, Morton and
Trefonen *Lich 19*   **P** *Ld Chan (1 turn), Bp and Earl of Powis*
(2 turns)   **R** K R TRIMBY
LLANYMYNECH (St Agatha)   *see* Llanyblodwel, Llanymynech,
Morton and Trefonen *Lich*
LOCKERLEY (St John) and East Dean w East and West
Tytherley *Win 12*   **P** *DBP (1 turn), H B G Dalgety Esq (2 turns)*
V J M PITKIN
LOCKING (St Augustine)   *see* Hutton and Locking *B & W*
LOCKINGE (All Saints)   *see* Wantage Downs *Ox*
LOCKINGE, WEST (All Souls) *as above*
LOCKINGTON (St Mary) and Lund and Scorborough w
Leconfield *York 8*   **P** *Abp*   **R** E M MARSHMAN
LOCKINGTON (St Nicholas)   *see* Castle Donington and
Lockington cum Hemington *Leic*
LOCKS HEATH (St John the Baptist) *Portsm 2*   **P** *Bp*
V C E SUGDEN
LOCKTON (St Giles)   *see* Pickering w Lockton and Levisham
York
LODDINGTON (St Leonard)   *see* Broughton w Loddington and
Cransley etc *Pet*
LODDINGTON (St Michael and All Angels) *Leic 2*   **P** *Bp*
P-in-c A J CHRISTIAN
LODDISWELL (St Michael and All Angels)   *see* Thurlestone, S
Milton, Churchstow etc *Ex*
LODDON (Holy Trinity), Sisland, Chedgrave, Hardley and
Langley *Nor 8*   **P** *Bp, E G Gilbert Esq, Gt Hosp, and Sir*
Christopher Beauchamp Bt (jt)   **V** D C OWEN
C J L ODDY-BATES   **NSM** R M SEEL   **OLM** A M BALL,
J C HAYLOCK, R M HOFFMANN
LODDON REACH *Ox 7*   **P** *Patr Bd*   **TV** P WILLIS
C P T JARVIS   **NSM** C A SPENCE, C J LESLIE
LODE (St James)   *see* Anglesey Gp *Ely*
LODERS (St Mary Magdalene)   *see* Askerswell, Loders,
Powerstock and Symondsbury *Sarum*
LODGE MOOR (St Luke) *Sheff 4*   **P** *CPAS*   **V** C H STEBBING
LODSWORTH (St Peter)   *see* Easebourne, Lodsworth and
Selham *Chich*
LOFTHOUSE (Christ Church)   *see* Rothwell, Lofthouse, Methley
etc *Leeds*
LOFTUS-IN-CLEVELAND (St Leonard) and Carlin How w
Skinningrove *York 16*   **P** *Ld Chan (2 turns), Abp (1 turn)*
R A GAUNT
LOLWORTH (All Saints)   *see* Fen Drayton w Conington and
Lolworth etc *Ely*
LONAN (All Saints)   *see* Onchan, Lonan and Laxey *S & M*
LONDESBOROUGH (All Saints)   *see* Londesborough Wold *York*
LONDESBOROUGH WOLD *York 5*   **P** *Abp (1 turn), Abp and*
Mrs P R Rowlands (1 turn)   **R** G HOLLINGSWORTH
LONDON CITY CHURCHES:
All Hallows Berkynchirche-by-the-Tower w St Dunstan-in-
the-East *Lon 1*   **P** *Abp*   **V** B M D OLIVIER
Hon C G R DE MELLO   **NSM** S C A ACLAND
Emer S D HAINES
Great St Bartholomew, Smithfield *Lon 1*   **P** *D&C Westmr*
R M R DUDLEY   **Hon C** M G C YOUNG, P M FREEMAN
St Andrew-by-the-Wardrobe w St Ann, Blackfriars *Lon 1*
P *PCC and Mercers' Co (jt)*   **P-in-c** L J MILLER
Hon C E R NORMAN
St Botolph Aldgate w Holy Trinity Minories *Lon 1*   **P** *Bp*
V L J JØRGENSEN   **C** A E J RICHARDSON   **NSM** J PEIRCE
St Botolph without Bishopsgate *Lon 1*   **P** *D&C St Paul's*
Hon C H J M TURNER

St Bride Fleet Street w Bridewell and Trinity Gough Square *Lon 1*   **P** *D&C Westmr*   **R** A J JOYCE   **NSM** J R LAKE
St Clement Eastcheap w St Martin Orgar *Lon 1*   **P** *D&C St Paul's*   **P-in-c** O C M ROSS
St Edmund the King and St Mary Woolnoth w St Nicholas Acons, All Hallows Lombard Street, St Benet Gracechurch, St Leonard Eastcheap, St Dionis Backchurch and St Mary Woolchurch Haw *Lon 1*   **P** *The Crown (3 turns), D&C Cant (1 turn), Bp (1 turn), and Abp (1 turn)*   **P-in-c** W J H CROSSLEY
St Giles Cripplegate w St Bartholomew Moor Lane and St Alphage London Wall and St Luke Old Street w St Mary Charterhouse and St Paul Clerkenwell *Lon 1*   **P** *D&C St Paul's*   **R** K M RUMENS
St Helen, Bishopsgate w St Andrew Undershaft and St Ethelburga, Bishopsgate and St Martin Outwich and St Mary Axe *Lon 1*   **P** *Merchant Taylors' Co*   **R** W T TAYLOR C A GLYN, A JONES, A SACH, C D FISHLOCK, C W D SKRINE, J J CHILD, J O ROACH, M C BANKS, M J FULLER
St James Garlickhythe w St Michael Queenhithe and Holy Trinity-the-Less *Lon 1*   **P** *D&C St Paul's*   **Hon C** E R NORMAN
St Magnus the Martyr w St Margaret New Fish Street and St Michael Crooked Lane *Lon 1*   **P** *DBP*   **R** J P WARNER
St Margaret Lothbury and St Stephen Coleman Street w St Christopher-le-Stocks, St Bartholomew-by-the-Exchange, St Olave Old Jewry, St Martin Pomeroy, St Mildred Poultry and St Mary Colechurch *Lon 1*   **P** *Simeon's Trustees*   **R** W J H CROSSLEY   **NSM** M FOX, T BUCHANAN
St Mary at Hill w St Andrew Hubbard, St George Botolph Lane and St Botolph by Billingsgate *Lon 1*   **P** *Ball Coll Ox (2 turns), PCC (1 turn), and Abp (1 turn)*   **P-in-c** R J HUDSON-WILKIN
St Mary le Bow w St Pancras Soper Lane, All Hallows Honey Lane, All Hallows Bread Street, St John the Evangelist Watling Street, St Augustine w St Faith under St Paul's and St Mildred Bread Street w St Margaret Moyses *Lon 1*   **P** *Grocers' Co (1 turn), Abp (2 turns)*   **R** G R BUSH
St Michael Cornhill w St Peter le Poer and St Benet Fink *Lon 1*   **P** *Drapers' Co*   **R** S G PLATTEN   **NSM** H V THOMAS
St Olave Hart Street w All Hallows Staining and St Catherine Coleman *Lon 1*   **P** *Trustees*   **R** O C M ROSS   **NSM** N J L MOTTERSHEAD, S BAXTER
St Peter Cornhill *Lon 1*   **P** *City Corp*   **R** W T TAYLOR
St Sepulchre w Christ Church Greyfriars and St Leonard Foster Lane *Lon 1*   **P** *St Jo Coll Ox*   **P-in-c** D L INGALL
St Stephen Walbrook and St Swithun London Stone w St Benet Sherehog and St Mary Bothaw w St Laurence Pountney *Lon 1*   **P** *Grocers' Co and Magd Coll Cam (alt)*   **P-in-c** J A H EVENS   **C** S A MUGGERIDGE
St Vedast w St Michael-le-Querne, St Matthew Friday Street, St Peter Cheap, St Alban Wood Street, St Olave Silver Street, St Michael Wood Street, St Mary Staining, St Anne and St Agnes and St John Zachary Gresham Street *Lon 1*   **P** *D&C St Paul's*   **R** *vacant*
LONDON COLNEY (St Peter) *St Alb 5*   **P** *Bp*   **V** L FAWNS   **NSM** P S GREEN
LONDON DOCKS (St Peter) w Wapping St John *Lon 7*   **P** *Bp*   **R** T E JONES   **Hon C** R S LADDS
LONDON GUILD CHURCHES:
All Hallows London Wall *Lon 1*   **P** *Ld Chan*   **V** G B HEWITT   **NSM** C J ROSE, M C DONEY
St Andrew Holborn *Lon 1*   **P** *Bp*   **V** *vacant*
St Benet Paul's Wharf *Lon 1*   **P** *Bp*   **V** *vacant*
St Botolph without Aldersgate *Lon 1*   **P** *Bp*   **P-in-c** S M C DOWDY   **C** P B BRENTFORD
St Dunstan in the West *Lon 1*   **P** *Abp*   **V** *vacant*
St Katharine Cree *Lon 1*   **P** *Bp*   **P-in-c** O C M ROSS
St Lawrence Jewry *Lon 1*   **P** *City Corp*   **V** D W PARROTT
St Margaret Pattens *Lon 1*   **P** *Ld Chan*   **P-in-c** O C M ROSS   **NSM** A J KEEP
St Martin Ludgate *Lon 1*   **P** *D&C St Paul's*   **P-in-c** R HAWES
St Mary Abchurch *Lon 1*   **P** *CCC Cam*   **V** *vacant*
St Mary Aldermary *Lon 1*   **P** *The Crown and Ld Chan (alt)*   **Emer** J R MOTHERSOLE
St Michael Paternoster Royal *Lon 1*   **P** *Bp*   **Hon C** K PETERS
LONDONDERRY (St Mark)   *see* Oldbury, Langley and Londonderry *Birm*
LONDONTHORPE (St John the Baptist)   *see* Grantham, Harrowby w Londonthorpe *Linc*
LONG ASHTON (All Saints) w Barrow Gurney and Flax Bourton *B & W 12*   **P** *Bp and Lady Virginia Gibbs (jt)*   **R** A SARGENT   **NSM** R Q GREATREX
LONG BENNINGTON (St Swithin)   *see* Saxonwell *Linc*
LONG BENTON (St Bartholomew) *Newc 3*   **P** *Ball Coll Ox*   **V** M P LEE

LONG BENTON (St Mary Magdalene) *Newc 3*   **P** *Ball Coll Ox*   **V** P A CRAIGHEAD
LONG BREDY (St Peter)   *see* Bride Valley *Sarum*
LONG BUCKBY (St Lawrence) w Watford and West Haddon w Winwick *Pet 2*   **P** *Bp and DBP (1 turn), Ld Chan (1 turn)*   **V** G I COLLINGRIDGE   **NSM** T JORDAN
LONG CLAWSON (St Remigius)   *see* Vale of Belvoir *Leic*
LONG COMPTON (St Peter and St Paul)   *see* S Warks Seven Gp *Cov*
LONG CRENDON (St Mary the Virgin) w Chearsley and Nether Winchendon *Ox 10*   **P** *Bp and R V Spencer-Bernard Esq (jt)*   **V** *vacant*
LONG DITTON (St Mary) *Guildf 8*   **P** *Bp S'wark*   **C** K SATKUNANAYAGAM
LONG EATON (St John) *Derby 13*   **P** *Bp*   **V** P T WALLER
LONG EATON (St Laurence) *Derby 13*   **P** *Bp*   **V** R A JUPP   **Hon C** P R S BOLTON
LONG HANBOROUGH (Christ Church)   *see* Hanborough and Freeland *Ox*
LONG ITCHINGTON (Holy Trinity) and Marton *Cov 10*   **P** *Bp*   **OLM** D J FORSTER
LONG LANE (Christ Church)   *see* Boylestone, Church Broughton, Dalbury, etc *Derby*
LONG MARSTON (All Saints)   *see* N Ainsty *York*
LONG MARTON (St Margaret and St James)   *see* Heart of Eden *Carl*
LONG MELFORD (Holy Trinity)   *see* Chadbrook *St E*
LONG MELFORD (St Catherine) *as above*
LONG NEWNTON (Holy Trinity)   *see* Tetbury, Beverston, Long Newnton etc *Glouc*
LONG PRESTON (St Mary the Virgin)   *see* Hellifield and Long Preston *Leeds*
LONG RISTON (St Margaret)   *see* Skirlaugh, Catwick, Long Riston, Rise, Swine w Ellerby *York*
LONG STANTON (All Saints) w St Michael *Ely 6*   **P** *Magd Coll Cam and Bp (alt)*   **P-in-c** J ANDERSON
LONG STANTON (St Michael and All Angels)   *see* Wenlock *Heref*
LONG SUTTON (All Saints)   *see* N Hants Downs *Win*
LONG SUTTON (Holy Trinity)   *see* Langport Area *B & W*
LONG SUTTON (St Mary) w Lutton and Gedney Drove End, Dawsmere *Linc 18*   **P** *Prime Min, Bp, and Ld Chan (by turn)*   **V** J P E SIBLEY   **OLM** H M DEAN
LONG WHATTON (All Saints)   *see* Kegworth, Hathern, Long Whatton, Diseworth etc *Leic*
LONG WITTENHAM (St Mary the Virgin)   *see* Dorchester *Ox*
LONGBOROUGH (St James)   *see* Moreton-in-Marsh w Batsford, Todenham etc *Glouc*
LONGBRIDGE (St John the Baptist) *Birm 4*   **P** *Bp*   **V** C J CHANDY
LONGBRIDGE DEVERILL (St Peter and St Paul)   *see* Cley Hill Villages *Sarum*
LONGBURTON (St James)   *see* Sherborne w Castleton, Lillington and Longburton *Sarum*
LONGCOT (St Mary the Virgin)   *see* Shrivenham and Ashbury *Ox*
LONGDEN (St Ruthen)   *see* Gt Hanwood and Longden and Annscroft etc *Heref*
LONGDON (St James) *Lich 1*   **P** *Bp*   **P-in-c** J L WATERFIELD
LONGDON (St Mary), Castlemorton, Bushley, Queenhill w Holdfast *Worc 5*   **P** *Bp, D&C Westmr, and Soc of the Faith (jt)*   **V** C A MOSS
LONGDON-UPON-TERN (St Bartholomew)   *see* Wrockwardine Deanery *Lich*
LONGFIELD (Mission Room) (St Mary Magdalene) *Roch 1*   **P** *Ld Chan*   **P-in-c** D L TURNER
LONGFLEET (St Mary) *Sarum 7*   **P** *MMCET*   **V** A N PERRY   **C** J M TOMKINS, M A HAY
LONGFORD (St Chad)   *see* Boylestone, Church Broughton, Dalbury, etc *Derby*
LONGFORD (St Thomas) *Cov 2*   **P** *Bp*   **V** A D COLEMAN
LONGFRAMLINGTON (St Mary the Virgin) w Brinkburn *Newc 6*   **P** *Bp*   **P-in-c** T J HARVEY
LONGHAM (St Andrew and St Peter)   *see* Gressenhall w Longham w Wendling etc *Nor*
LONGHILL (St Margaret)   *see* Sutton St Mich *York*
LONGHIRST (St John the Evangelist)   *see* Bothal and Pegswood w Longhirst *Newc*
LONGHOPE (All Saints)   *see* Huntley and Longhope, Churcham and Bulley *Glouc*
LONGHORSLEY (St Helen) *Newc 11*   **P** *Ld Chan*   **P-in-c** P S MCCONNELL
LONGHOUGHTON (St Peter and St Paul) (including Boulmer) w Howick *Newc 6*   **P** *Duke of Northumberland and Bp (alt)*   **V** I D MACKARILL
LONGLEVENS (Holy Trinity)   *see* Wotton St Mary *Glouc*

LONGNEWTON (St Mary)   see Preston-on-Tees and Longnewton *Dur*
LONGNEY (St Lawrence)   see Hardwicke and Elmore w Longney *Glouc*
LONGNOR (St Bartholomew), Quarnford and Sheen *Lich 5*   **P** *Bp, V Alstonfield, and DBP (jt)*   **V** J O FORRESTER
LONGNOR (St Mary)   see Dorrington w Leebotwood, Longnor, Stapleton etc *Heref*
LONGPARISH (St Nicholas)   see Hurstbourne Priors, Longparish etc *Win*
LONGRIDGE (St Lawrence) (St Paul) *Blackb 13*   **P** *Trustees*   **V** D L ANDERSON
LONGSIGHT (St Agnes)   see Birch-in-Rusholme St Agnes w Longsight St Jo etc *Man*
LONGSIGHT (St Luke) *Man 1*   **P** *D&C and Trustees (jt)*   **R** E O ADOYO
LONGSLEDDALE (St Mary)   see Beacon *Carl*
LONGSOLE (Mission Room)   see Barming *Roch*
LONGSTOCK (St Mary)   see Test Valley *Win*
LONGSTONE (St Giles), Curbar and Stony Middleton *Derby 2*   **P** *V Bakewell etc and R Hathersage etc (jt)*   **V** J S CROFT   **NSM** L E ELLSWORTH
LONGSTOWE (St Mary)   see Papworth *Ely*
LONGTHORPE (St Botolph) *Pet 11*   **P** *Sir Philip Naylor-Leyland Bt*   **P-in-c** W S CROFT   **C** M R ALBERT   **NSM** J A C WIEGMAN
LONGTON (St Andrew) *Blackb 5*   **P** *A F Rawstorne Esq*   **V** A PARKINSON
LONGTON (St James and St John) *Lich 12*   **P** *Bp*   **P-in-c** P W BENNETT
LONGTON (St Mary and St Chad) *Lich 12*   **P** *Bp*   **V** K A PALMER
LONGTON HALL *Lich 12*   **P** *Prime Min*   **P-in-c** J ALESSI
LONGTON, NEW (All Saints) *Blackb 5*   **P** *Bp*   **V** D M ROGERS
LONGWELL GREEN (All Saints) *Bris 5*   **P** *Bp*   **P-in-c** A J M SPEAR   **OLM** S P BRITTON
LONGWOOD (St Mark) *Leeds 12*   **P** *V Huddersfield*   **P-in-c** J S CURRY
LONGWORTH (St Mary)   see Cherbury w Gainfield *Ox*
LONSDALE, EAST *Blackb 14*   **P** *Patr Bd*   **P-in-c** M H CANNON   **Hon C** R HANNAFORD
LOOE, WEST (St Nicholas)   see St Martin w Looe *Truro*
LOOSE (All Saints) *Cant 12*   **P** *Abp*   **V** S A PRICE   **NSM** C H THOM
LOPEN (All Saints)   see Merriott w Hinton, Dinnington and Lopen *B & W*
LOPHAM NORTH (St Nicholas)   see Diss *Nor*
LOPHAM SOUTH (St Andrew) *as above*
LOPPINGTON (St Michael and All Angels) w Newtown *Lich 22*   **P** *Bp and R Wem (jt)*   **P-in-c** A J B CLAYTON   **OLM** A EVANS
LORDSBRIDGE Team, The *Ely 1*   **P** *Ld Chan (1 turn), Patr Bd (2 turns)*   **TR** M P M BOOKER   **TV** A M MYERS, R GILBERT   **Hon C** G CHATFIELD   **NSM** C I A FRASER, C M REDSELL, J E E POLKINHORN, M J REISS
LORTON (St Cuthbert) and Loweswater w Buttermere *Carl 6*   **P** *Bp and Earl of Lonsdale (alt)*   **P-in-c** S HUGHES
LOSCOE (St Luke) *Derby 12*   **P** *Bp*   **P-in-c** A TAYLOR-COOK   **OLM** M D JONES
LOSTOCK (St Thomas and St John) *Man 9*   **P** *Bp and TR Deane St Mary the Virgin (jt)*   **V** *vacant*
LOSTOCK GRALAM (St John the Evangelist) *Ches 6*   **P** *V Witton*   **P-in-c** J B HARRIS
LOSTOCK HALL (St James) and Farington Moss *Blackb 5*   **P** *Bp and V Penwortham (jt)*   **V** M RIMMER
LOSTWITHIEL (St Bartholomew), St Winnow w St Nectan's Chapel, St Veep and Boconnoc *Truro 10*   **P** *D&C and A D G Fortescue Esq (jt)*   **R** *vacant*
LOTHERSDALE (Christ Church)   see Sutton w Cowling and Lothersdale *Leeds*
LOTHERTON (St James)   see Aberford w Micklefield *York*
LOTTISHAM (The Blessed Virgin Mary)   see Baltonsborough w Butleigh, W Bradley etc *B & W*
LOUDWATER (St Peter) *Ox 10*   **P** *MMCET*   **V** T G BUTLIN
LOUGHBOROUGH (All Saints) w Holy Trinity *Leic 6*   **P** *Bp and Em Coll Cam (jt)*   **R** W M DALRYMPLE
LOUGHBOROUGH (Emmanuel) *Leic 6*   **P** *Bp and Em Coll Cam (jt)*   **P-in-c** M J BROADLEY   **C** A J HUMM
LOUGHBOROUGH (Good Shepherd) *Leic 6*   **P** *Bp*   **NSM** R J WHITLEY
LOUGHRIGG Team Ministry, The *Carl 11*   **P** *Patr Bd*   **NSM** G G WRIGLEY, N F HALLAM
LOUGHTON (All Saints)   see Watling Valley *Ox*
LOUGHTON (not known)   see Ditton Priors w Neenton, Burwarton etc *Heref*

LOUGHTON (St John the Baptist) (St Gabriel) (St Nicholas) *Chelmsf 3*   **P** *W W Maitland Esq*   **C** R J FISHER
LOUGHTON (St Mary the Virgin) *Chelmsf 3*   **P** *Bp*   **V** M C MACDONALD   **NSM** S D POLLARD
LOUGHTON (St Michael and All Angels) *Chelmsf 3*   **P** *Bp*   **V** N M COULTHARD   **OLM** LA SMART
LOUND (St John the Baptist)   see Somerleyton, Ashby, Fritton, Herringfleet etc *Nor*
LOUNDSLEY GREEN (Church of the Ascension) *Derby 5*   **P** *Bp*   **P-in-c** P J GREEN
LOUTH (Holy Trinity Church Centre) (St James) (St Michael) *Linc 15*   **P** *Patr Bd*   **P-in-c** N J W BROWN   **TV** C A HAWKINS, L E TURNER   **C** K L TOOGOOD, M M HARBAGE   **OLM** R W MANSFIELD
LOVERSALL (St Katherine)   see Wadworth w Loversall *Sheff*
LOVINGTON (St Thomas à Becket)   see Six Pilgrims *B & W*
LOW   see also under substantive place name
LOW FELL (St Helen)   see Gateshead St Helen *Dur*
LOW HAM (Chapel)   see Langport Area *B & W*
LOW HILL (Good Shepherd)   see Bushbury *Lich*
LOW MOOR (Holy Trinity) and Oakenshaw *Leeds 2*   **P** *Bp and V Bradf (jt)*   **V** I R JENNINGS   **Hon C** D P ELLIS
LOWDHAM (St Mary the Virgin) w Caythorpe, and Gunthorpe *S'well 7*   **P** *Bp*   **V** C A TAINTON
LOWER   see also under substantive place name
LOWESBY (All Saints)   see Whatborough Gp *Leic*
LOWESTOFT (Christ Church) *Nor 9*   **P** *CPAS*   **V** M C PAYNE
LOWESTOFT (Good Shepherd)   see Lowestoft St Marg *Nor*
LOWESTOFT (St Andrew) *Nor 9*   **P** *Ch Patr Tr*   **V** D ROGERS
LOWESTOFT (St Margaret) *Nor 9*   **P** *Bp, Adn Norfolk, and DBP (jt)*   **R** M J ASQUITH
LOWESWATER (St Bartholomew)   see Lorton and Loweswater w Buttermere *Carl*
LOWICK (St John the Baptist) and Kyloe w Ancroft *Newc 12*   **P** *D&C (2 turns), Bp (1 turn)*   **V** V T DICKINSON
LOWICK (St Luke)   see Egton-cum-Newland and Lowick and Colton *Carl*
LOWICK (St Peter)   see Brigstock w Stanion and Lowick and Sudborough *Pet*
LOWSONFORD (St Luke)   see Hatton w Haseley, Rowington w Lowsonford etc *Cov*
LOWTHER (St Michael) and Askham and Clifton and Brougham *Carl 1*   **P** *Earl of Lonsdale*   **P-in-c** A MAGUIRE
LOWTHORPE (St Martin)   see The Beacon *York*
LOWTON (St Luke) (St Mary) and Golborne *Liv 15*   **P** *Patr Bd*   **TR** J R STOTT   **TV** J W REED
LOXBEARE (St Michael and All Angels)   see Washfield, Stoodleigh, Withleigh etc *Ex*
LOXHORE (St Michael and All Angels)   see Shirwell, Loxhore, Kentisbury, Arlington, etc *Ex*
LOXLEY (St Nicholas)   see Hampton Lucy w Charlecote and Loxley *Cov*
LOXTON (St Andrew)   see Crook Peak *B & W*
LOXWOOD (St John the Baptist)   see Alfold and Loxwood *Guildf*
LOZELLS (St Paul and St Silas) *Birm 3*   **P** *Aston Patr Trust*   **P-in-c** L C WRIGHT
LUBENHAM (All Saints)   see Market Harborough and The Transfiguration etc *Leic*
LUCCOMBE (The Blessed Virgin Mary)   see Porlock and Porlock Weir w Stoke Pero etc *B & W*
LUCKER (St Hilda)   see Belford and Lucker *Newc*
LUCKINGTON (St Mary)   see Sherston Magna, Easton Grey, Luckington etc *Bris*
LUDBOROUGH (St Mary)   see Fotherby *Linc*
LUDDENDEN (St Mary) w Luddenden Foot *Leeds 9*   **P** *Bp and V Halifax (alt)*   **P-in-c** I SPARKS
LUDDESDOWN (St Peter and St Paul)   see Cobham w Luddesdowne and Dode *Roch*
LUDDINGTON (All Saints)   see Stratford-upon-Avon, Luddington etc *Cov*
LUDDINGTON (St Margaret)   see Barnwell, Hemington, Luddington in the Brook etc *Pet*
LUDDINGTON (St Oswald)   see Crowle Gp *Linc*
LUDFORD (St Giles)   see Ludlow *Heref*
LUDFORD MAGNA (St Mary)   see Binbrook Gp *Linc*
LUDGERSHALL (St Mary the Virgin)   see Bernwode *Ox*
LUDGERSHALL (St James) and Faberstown *Sarum 14*   **P** *DBP*   **V** C M A MAXIM
LUDGVAN (St Ludgvan and St Paul), Marazion, St Hilary and Perranuthnoe *Truro 5*   **P** *D&C, Lord St Levan, and H M Parker Esq (jt)*   **R** N G MARNS   **NSM** A HENRY HOLLAND
LUDHAM (St Catherine), Potter Heigham, Hickling and Catfield *Nor 12*   **P** *Bp and G M H Mills Esq (jt)*   **V** J M STRIDE
LUDLOW Team Minstry, The (St John) (St Laurence) *Heref 11*   **P** *Patr Bd*   **TV** K I PRICE

LUFFENHAM, NORTH (St John the Baptist)   *see* Empingham, Edith Weston, Lyndon, Manton etc *Pet*

LUFFENHAM, SOUTH (St Mary the Virgin)   *see* Barrowden and Wakerley w S Luffenham etc *Pet*

LUFTON (St Peter and St Paul)   *see* Odcombe, Brympton, Lufton and Montacute *B & W*

LUGWARDINE (St Peter)   *see* Bartestree Cross *Heref*

LULLINGSTONE (St Botolph)   *see* Eynsford w Farningham and Lullingstone *Roch*

LULLINGTON (All Saints)   *see* Beckington w Standerwick, Berkley, Rodden etc *B & W*

LULLINGTON (All Saints)   *see* Seale and Lullington w Coton in the Elms *Derby*

LULLINGTON (Good Shepherd)   *see* Alfriston w Lullington, Litlington, W Dean and Folkington *Chich*

LULWORTHS, (St Andrew) (Holy Trinity) Winfrith Newburgh and Chaldon, The *Sarum 8*   **P** *Bp (3 turns), Col Sir Joseph Weld (1 turn)*   **P-in-c** N J COLEMAN

LUMLEY (Christ Church) *Dur 11*   **P** *Bp*   **P-in-c** R A COLLINS

LUND (All Saints)   *see* Lockington and Lund and Scorborough w Leconfield *York*

LUND (St John the Evangelist) *Blackb 10*   **P** *Ch Ch Ox*
V J L BANNISTER

LUNDWOOD (St Mary Magdalene) *Leeds 18*   **P** *Bp*
NSM S A OAKLEY

LUPPITT (St Mary)   *see* Dunkeswell, Luppitt, Sheldon and Upottery *Ex*

LUPSET (St George) *Leeds 20*   **P** *Bp*   **P-in-c** M C CRABTREE

LUPTON (All Saints)   *see* Kirkby Lonsdale *Carl*

LURGASHALL (St Lawrence) *Chich 10*   **P** *Lord Egremont*
P-in-c C P R HAYES

LUSBY (St Peter)   *see* Bolingbroke Deanery *Linc*

LUSTLEIGH (St John the Baptist)   *see* Moretonhampstead, Manaton, N Bovey and Lustleigh *Ex*

LUTON (All Saints) (St Peter) *St Alb 12*   **P** *Bp*
P-in-c D W KESTERTON

LUTON (Christ Church) *Roch 5*   **P** *R Chatham*   **R** D J SUTTON

LUTON (Holy Cross)   *see* Marsh Farm *St Alb*

LUTON (St Andrew) *St Alb 12*   **P** *Bp*   **V** G A FINLAYSON

LUTON (St Anne) (St Christopher) **Round Green** *St Alb 12*
P *Bp, V Luton St Mary, and Peache Trustees*   **V** P C BUDGELL

LUTON (St Francis) *St Alb 12*   **P** *Peache Trustees, Bp, and V Luton (jt)*   **V** *vacant*

LUTON (St John)   *see* Teignmouth, Ideford w Luton, Ashcombe etc *Ex*

LUTON (St Mary) *St Alb 12*   **P** *Peache Trustees*   **V** M C JONES
NSM C A MOSS

LUTON (St Matthew) **High Town** *St Alb 12*   **P** *Ch Patr Trust*
V M J PRITCHARD

LUTON (St Paul) *St Alb 12*   **P** *Peache Trustees*   **V** A SELLERS

LUTON (St Saviour) *St Alb 12*   **P** *Bp*   **P-in-c** Y M SMEJKAL
NSM D C ANDERSON

LUTON Lewsey (St Hugh) *St Alb 12*   **P** *Bp*   **V** J PIENAAR
C N S WALSH

LUTON Limbury (St Augustine of Canterbury) *St Alb 12*
P *Bp*   **V** J MACKENZIE   **C** E J YOUNG

LUTTERWORTH (St Mary) **w Cotesbach and Bitteswell** *Leic 7*
P *Prime Min (3 turns), Ld Chan (1 turn), and Ch Hosp (1 turn)*
P-in-c C A M STYLES

LUTTON (St Nicholas)   *see* Long Sutton w Lutton etc *Linc*

LUTTON (St Peter)   *see* Barnwell, Hemington, Luddington in the Brook etc *Pet*

LUTTONS AMBO (St Mary)   *see* Weaverthorpe w Helperthorpe, Luttons Ambo etc *York*

LUXBOROUGH (Blessed Virgin Mary)   *see* Exmoor *B & W*

LUXULYAN (St Cyrus and St Julietta) *Truro 1*   **P** *Bp (1 turn), Adn Cornwall (1 turn), and DBP (2 turns)*   **V** *vacant*

LYDBROOK (Holy Jesus)   *see* Drybrook, Lydbrook and Ruardean *Glouc*

LYDBURY NORTH (St Michael and All Angels)   *see* Bishop's Castle w Mainstone, Lydbury N etc *Heref*

LYDD (All Saints)   *see* Brookland, Fairfield, Brenzett w Snargate etc *Cant*

LYDDEN (St Mary the Virgin)   *see* Temple Ewell w Lydden *Cant*

LYDDINGTON (All Saints) **and Wanborough and Bishopstone w Hinton Parva** *Bris 7*   **P** *Bp and Ld Chan (alt)*
P-in-c W A O'CONNELL

LYDDINGTON (St Andrew), **Bisbrooke, Caldecott, Glaston, Harringworth, Seaton and Stoke Dry** *Pet 12*   **P** *Bp, G T G Conant Esq, Exors R E M Elborne Esq, Burghley Ho Preservation Trust, and Peterho Cam (jt)*   **V** J E BAXTER

LYDEARD ST LAWRENCE (St Lawrence)   *see* Bishop's Lydeard w Lydeard St Lawrence etc *B & W*

LYDFORD (St Petrock)   *see* Okehampton, Inwardleigh, Belstone, Sourton etc *Ex*

LYDFORD ON FOSSE (St Peter)   *see* Wheathill Priory Gp *B & W*

LYDGATE (St Anne)   *see* Saddleworth *Man*

LYDHAM (Holy Trinity)   *see* Wentnor w Ratlinghope, Myndtown, Norbury etc *Heref*

LYDIARD MILLICENT (All Saints)   *see* W Swindon and the Lydiards *Bris*

LYDIARD TREGOZE (St Mary) *as above*

LYDIATE (St Thomas)   *see* Halsall, Lydiate and Downholland *Liv*

LYDLINCH (St Thomas à Beckett)   *see* Sturminster Newton, Hinton St Mary and Lydlinch *Sarum*

LYDNEY (St Mary the Virgin) *Glouc 1*   **P** *Ld Chan*
P-in-c S L FENBY

LYE, THE (Christchurch) **and Stambermill** *Worc 12*   **P** *Bp and CPAS (alt)*   **P-in-c** S M FALSHAW   **C** T R H FISH
NSM C A KENT

LYFORD (St Mary)   *see* Cherbury w Gainfield *Ox*

LYME REGIS (St Michael the Archangel)   *see* Golden Cap Team *Sarum*

LYMINGE (St Mary and St Ethelburga) **w Paddlesworth and Stanford w Postling and Radegund** *Cant 8*   **P** *Abp*
R P N ASHMAN   **OLM** S G DOUGAL

LYMINGTON (St Thomas the Apostle) (All Saints) *Win 11*
P *Bp*   **V** P B C SALISBURY   **C** E F J MULLINER

LYMINSTER (St Mary Magdalene) *Chich 1*   **P** *Eton Coll on nomination of BNC Ox*   **P-in-c** J C QUIGLEY

LYMM (St Mary the Virgin) *Ches 4*   **P** *Bp*   **R** K MAUDSLEY

LYMPNE (St Stephen) **and Saltwood** *Cant 8*   **P** *Abp*
R N J COOPER   **NSM** P F HILL

LYMPSHAM (St Christopher)   *see* Brent Knoll, E Brent and Lympsham *B & W*

LYMPSTONE (Nativity of the Blessed Virgin Mary)
see Littleham-cum-Exmouth w Lympstone *Ex*

LYNCH (St Luke) **w Iping Marsh and Milland** *Chich 9*
P *Rathbone Trust Co, Cowdray Trust and Bp (jt)*
R P A BANCROFT

LYNCHMERE (St Peter) **and Camelsdale** *Chich 9*   **P** *Prime Min*
P-in-c D B WELSMAN, D TALKS

LYNDHURST (St Michael) **and Emery Down and Minstead**
Win 11   **P** *Bp and P J P Green Esq (jt)*   **V** J H BRUCE

LYNDON (St Martin)   *see* Empingham, Edith Weston, Lyndon, Manton etc *Pet*

LYNEAL (St John the Evangelist)   *see* Petton w Cockshutt, Welshampton and Lyneal etc *Lich*

LYNEHAM (St Michael) **w Bradenstoke** *Sarum 16*   **P** *Ld Chan*
P-in-c R G SELBY-BOOTHROYD   **C** E R H ABBOTT

LYNEMOUTH (St Aidan)   *see* Cresswell and Lynemouth *Newc*

LYNESACK (St John the Evangelist) *Dur 7*   **P** *Bp*
C C A GIBBS

LYNG (St Bartholomew)   *see* Athelney *B & W*

LYNG (St Margaret), **Sparham, Elsing, Bylaugh, Bawdeswell and Foxley** *Nor 22*   **P** *DBP, Sir Edward Evans-Lombe, and Bp (by turn)*   **P-in-c** L C PAGE

LYNGFORD (St Peter)   *see* Taunton Lyngford *B & W*

LYNN, SOUTH (All Saints) *Nor 20*   **P** *Bp*   **R** A R LING
OLM P J NORWOOD

LYNN, WEST (St Peter)   *see* Clenchwarton and W Lynn *Ely*

LYONS (St Michael and All Angels)   *see* Hetton-Lyons w Eppleton *Dur*

LYONSDOWN (Holy Trinity) *St Alb 14*   **P** *Ch Patr Trust*
V C W G DOBBIE

LYONSHALL (St Michael and All Angels)   *see* Pembridge w Moor Court, Shobdon, Staunton etc *Heref*

LYTCHETTS, The (not known) (St Mary the Virgin) **and Upton**
Sarum 7   **P** *Patr Bd*   **TR** J H T DE GARIS   **TV** A G S MEPHAM
NSM J A ALEXANDER   **OLM** H D PAGE-CLARK

LYTHAM (St Cuthbert) *Blackb 10*   **P** *DBP*   **V** *vacant*

LYTHAM (St John the Divine) *Blackb 10*   **P** *J C Hilton Esq*
P-in-c A R WOOD

LYTHAM ST ANNE (St Margaret of Antioch)   *see* St Annes St Marg *Blackb*

LYTHAM ST ANNE (St Thomas)   *see* St Annes St Thos *Blackb*

LYTHAM ST ANNES (St Paul)   *see* Fairhaven *Blackb*

LYTHE (St Oswald)   *see* Hinderwell, Roxby and Staithes etc *York*

MABE (St Laudus) *Truro 3*   **P** *Bp*   **P-in-c** S SMITH

MABLETHORPE (St Mary) **w Trusthorpe** *Linc 10*   **P** *Bp Lon (2 turns), Bp Linc (1 turn)*   **R** P J LILEY   **Hon C** C H LILLEY
OLM J TOMPKINS

MACCLESFIELD (Holy Trinity)   *see* Hurdsfield *Ches*

MACCLESFIELD (St John the Evangelist) **w Henbury** *Ches 13*
P *Bp*   **V** T ROBINSON   **NSM** N G ROBINSON

MACCLESFIELD (St Paul) *Ches 13*   **P** *Bp*   **V** *vacant*

MACCLESFIELD Team Parish, The (All Saints) (Christ Church) (St Michael and All Angels) (St Peter) (St Barnabas) *Ches 13*
P *Patr Bd*   **TV** D L MOCK   **NSM** D W L WIGHTMAN,
R WARDLE

MACKWORTH (All Saints) *Derby 11*　**P** *J M Clark-Maxwell Esq*
P-in-c A P HARPER
MACKWORTH (St Francis) *Derby 9*　**P** *Bp*　**V** *vacant*
MADEHURST (St Mary Magdalene)　*see* Slindon, Eartham and
Madehurst *Chich*
MADELEY (All Saints) *Lich 9*　**P** *J C Crewe Esq*
V P T CHANTRY　**NSM** G A BAILEY
MADELEY (St Michael) *Heref 13*　**P** *Patr Bd*
P-in-c A H WALDEN, L N CRONIN　**C** G D PHILLIPS
NSM R FREEMAN
MADINGLEY (St Mary Magdalene) *Ely 6*　**P** *Bp*
P-in-c M J MAXWELL
MADLEY (Nativity of the Blessed Virgin Mary) w Tyberton,
Peterchurch, Vowchurch and Turnastone *Heref 1*
P *Bp and D&C (jt)*　**R** S D LOCKETT　**NSM** J M DINNEN
MADRESFIELD (St Mary)　*see* Powick and Guarlford and
Madresfield w Newland *Worc*
MADRON (St Maddern)　*see* Gulval and Madron *Truro*
MAER (St Peter)　*see* Chapel Chorlton, Maer and Whitmore
Lich
MAESBROOK (St John)　*see* Kinnerley w Melverley and
Knockin w Maesbrook *Lich*
MAESBURY (St John the Baptist) *Lich 19*　**P** *Bp*
P-in-c H M MORBY
MAGDALEN LAVER (St Mary Magdalen)　*see* High Laver w
Magdalen Laver and Lt Laver etc *Chelmsf*
MAGHULL (St Andrew) (St James) (St Peter) and Melling
Liv 11　**P** *Patr Bd*　**TR** N A WELLS　**TV** M S FOLLIN, S JONES
C A J BAKER　**NSM** G ARDERN
MAIDEN BRADLEY (All Saints)　*see* Mere w W Knoyle and
Maiden Bradley *Sarum*
MAIDEN NEWTON (St Mary)　*see* Melbury *Sarum*
MAIDENHEAD (St Andrew and St Mary Magdalene) *Ox 5*
P *Peache Trustees*　**V** W M C STILEMAN　**C** D A ATALLAH,
S ALLBERRY, S P W BREWSTER　**Emer** R P TAYLOR
MAIDENHEAD (St Luke) *Ox 5*　**P** *Bp*　**V** S M LYNCH
C N A HULKS　**NSM** T J ROBINSON
MAIDFORD (St Peter and St Paul)　*see* Lambfold *Pet*
MAIDS MORETON (St Edmund)　*see* N Buckingham *Ox*
MAIDSTONE (All Saints) (St Philip) w St Stephen Tovil
Cant 12　**P** *Abp*　**P-in-c** I R PARRISH
MAIDSTONE (St Faith) *Cant 12*　**P** *Abp*　**P-in-c** A J HOUSTON
MAIDSTONE (St Luke the Evangelist) *Cant 12*　**P** *Trustees*
V C H KEY
MAIDSTONE (St Martin) *Cant 12*　**P** *Abp*
P-in-c J H ADDISON
MAIDSTONE (St Michael and All Angels) *Cant 12*　**P** *Abp*
C P A ROWE
MAIDSTONE (St Paul) *Cant 12*　**P** *Abp*　**P-in-c** A W SEWELL
C M A PAVEY
MAIDSTONE Barming Heath (St Andrew)　*see* Barming Heath
Cant
MAIDWELL (St Mary) w Draughton and Lamport w Faxton
Pet 2　**P** *Bp (3 turns), Sir Ian Isham Bt (1 turn)*
P-in-c M Y GARBUTT　**C** J V J G WATSON
MAINSTONE (St John the Baptist)　*see* Bishop's Castle w
Mainstone, Lydbury N etc *Heref*
MAISEMORE (St Giles)　*see* Ashleworth, Corse, Hartpury,
Hasfield etc *Glouc*
MAKER (St Mary and St Julian) w Rame *Truro 11*　**P** *The
Crown and Earl of Mount Edgcumbe (jt)*　**P-in-c** M B BROWN
MALBOROUGH (All Saints)　*see* Salcombe and Malborough w
S Huish *Ex*
MALDEN (St James) *S'wark 15*　**P** *Bp*
V L M M FERNANDEZ-VICENTE　**OLM** C PIGGOTT
MALDEN (St John) *S'wark 15*　**P** *Mert Coll Ox*　**V** K W SCOTT
MALDEN, NEW (Christ Church) (St John the Divine) and
Coombe *S'wark 15*　**P** *CPAS*　**P-in-c** S J KUHRT
C H M DURANT-STEVENSEN　**NSM** C G LUCAS
MALDON (All Saints w St Peter) *Chelmsf 11*　**P** *Bp*
V S CARTER
MALDON (St Mary) w Mundon *Chelmsf 11*　**P** *D&C Westmr*
OLM J F DICKENS
MALEW (St Lupus) (St Mark) and Santan *S & M*　**P** *The
Crown*　**V** J MCGOWAN
MALIN BRIDGE (St Polycarp) *Sheff 4*　**P** *Bp*　**V** G L KALSI
NSM C L CHAPMAN
MALINSLEE (St Leonard)　*see* Cen Telford *Lich*
MALLERSTANG (St Mary)　*see* Kirkby Stephen w Mallerstang
etc *Carl*
MALLING, EAST (St James), Wateringbury and Teston *Roch 7*
P *D&C and Peache Trustees (jt)*　**V** J D BROWN
NSM A M SEARLE, P R RINK
MALLING, SOUTH (St Michael the Archangel)　*see* Lewes St Jo
sub Castro and S Malling *Chich*

MALLING, WEST (St Mary) w Offham *Roch 7*　**P** *Ld Chan and
DBP (alt)*　**P-in-c** D R J GREEN　**C** M MONTGOMERY
MALMESBURY (St Peter and St Paul) w Westport and
Brokenborough *Bris 6*　**P** *Ch Trust Fund Trust*
P-in-c N J ARCHER　**C** J E MONAGHAN
NSM H A MONAGHAN, M CHURCHER　**OLM** L M SULLIVAN
MALPAS (St Andrew)　*see* St Clement *Truro*
MALPAS (St Oswald) and Threapwood and Bickerton *Ches 5*
P *Patr Bd*　**R** I A DAVENPORT
MALTBY (St Bartholomew) (Ascension) (Venerable Bede)
Sheff 5　**P** *Bp*　**TR** *vacant*
MALTON (St Michael) and Old Malton *York 6*　**P** *Sir Philip
Naylor-Leyland Bt*　**V** P C ROBINSON　**C** A D BOWDEN,
G W DIGGINS
MALTON, OLD (St Mary the Virgin)　*see* Malton and Old
Malton *York*
MALVERN (Holy Trinity) (St James) *Worc 2*　**P** *Bp and D&C
Westmr (jt)*　**V** W D NICHOL　**C** E L GOLDBY
NSM A C LANYON-HOGG, R HERBERT
MALVERN (St Andrew)　*see* Malvern Chase *Worc*
MALVERN CHASE *Worc 2*　**P** *Patr Bd*　**TV** L SPARKES
MALVERN LINK (Church of the Ascension) (St Matthias) w
Cowleigh *Worc 2*　**P** *Trustees of late Else Countess Beauchamp*
V P J KNIGHT　**NSM** M J NOBLES
MALVERN, GREAT (Christchurch) *Worc 2*　**P** *Bp*
V R G JONES　**Hon C** H F GODDARD
MALVERN, GREAT (St Mary and St Michael) *Worc 2*　**P** *Bp*
V M J A BARR　**NSM** A J GRAY, M E BARR
MALVERN, LITTLE (St Giles) *Worc 2*　**P** *Exors T M Berington Esq*
V E G KNOWLES
MALVERN, WEST (St James)　*see* Malvern H Trin and St Jas *Worc*
MAMBLE (St John the Baptist) w Bayton, Rock w
Heightington w Far Forest *Worc 4*　**P** *Ld Chan and R
Ribbesford w Bewdley etc (alt)*　**V** J G CRUICKSHANK
MAMHEAD (St Thomas the Apostle)　*see* Exminster, Kenn,
Kenton w Mamhead, and Powderham *Ex*
MANACCAN (St Manaccus and St Dunstan)　*see* Meneage *Truro*
MANATON (St Winifred)　*see* Moretonhampstead, Manaton,
N Bovey and Lustleigh *Ex*
MANBY (St Mary)　*see* Mid Marsh Gp *Linc*
MANCETTER (St Peter) *Cov 5*　**P** *Ch Patr Trust*
P-in-c A A TOOBY
MANCHESTER (Apostles) w Miles Platting *Man 1*　**P** *DBP*
P-in-c E L TRIMBLE
MANCHESTER (Church of the Resurrection)　*see* Manchester Gd
Shep and St Barn *Man*
MANCHESTER (St Ann) *Man 3*　**P** *Bp*　**R** J N ASHWORTH
C P R HORLOCK
MANCHESTER (St John Chrysostom) Victoria Park *Man 1*
P *Bp*　**R** I D GOMERSALL　**Hon C** K A C WASEY
OLM C N HARTLEY
MANCHESTER Clayton (St Cross w St Paul) *Man 1*　**P** *Bp*
R L T YOUNG
MANCHESTER Good Shepherd (St Barnabas) (Church of the
Resurrection) *Man 1*　**P** *Prime Min and Trustees (alt)*
R A S JONES
MANEA (St Nicholas)　*see* Christchurch and Manea and
Welney *Ely*
MANEY (St Peter) *Birm 12*　**P** *Bp*　**V** M I RHODES
C P MORTON
MANFIELD (All Saints)　*see* E Richmond *Leeds*
MANGOTSFIELD (St James) *Bris 5*　**P** *Peache Trustees*
V T M TAYLOR
MANNINGFORD BRUCE (St Peter)　*see* Vale of Pewsey *Sarum*
MANNINGHAM (St Paul and St Jude) *Leeds 1*　**P** *Bp, V Bradf
St Pet, Adn Bradf, Community of the Resurr Mirfield, and
Ch Patr Trust (jt)*　**V** A T HELM　**C** S M JENNINGS
MANNINGS HEATH (Church of the Good Shepherd)
see Nuthurst and Mannings Heath *Chich*
MANOR PARK (St Barnabas)　*see* Lt Ilford St Barn *Chelmsf*
MANOR PARK (St John the Baptist) and Whitby Road *Ox 12*
P *Eton Coll*　**V** G V R HOWARD
MANOR PARK (St Mary the Virgin)　*see* Lt Ilford St Mich
Chelmsf
MANOR PARK (St Michael and All Angels) *as above*
MANOR PARK (William Temple)　*see* Sheff Manor *Sheff*
MANSEL LACY (St Michael)　*see* Credenhill w Brinsop and
Wormsley etc *Heref*
MANSERGH (St Peter)　*see* Kirkby Lonsdale *Carl*
MANSFIELD (St Augustine) and Pleasley Hill St Barnabas
S'well 2　**P** *Bp*　**V** C J PHILLIPS
MANSFIELD (St John the Evangelist) (St Mary) *S'well 2*
P *Bp*　**V** J M A ADAMS　**C** J L SHARPE
MANSFIELD (St Lawrence) *S'well 2*　**P** *Bp*　**P-in-c** P BENTLEY,
P J STEAD

MANSFIELD (St Mark) *S'well 2*   **P** *Bp*   **V** D J FUDGER
C K O HEBDEN
MANSFIELD (St Peter and St Paul) *S'well 2*   **P** *Bp*
V D J FUDGER   **C** K O HEBDEN
MANSFIELD Oak Tree Lane *S'well 2*   **P** *DBP*   **P-in-c** P J STEAD
MANSFIELD WOODHOUSE (St Edmund King and Martyr)
S'well 2   **P** *Bp*   **V** R A SCRIVENER
MANSTON (St Catherine)   *see* St Laur in Thanet *Cant*
MANSTON (St James) *Leeds 17*   **P** *R Barwick in Elmet*
P-in-c C A JAMES   **C** S C FEASTER
MANSTON (St Nicholas)   *see* Okeford *Sarum*
MANTHORPE (St John the Evangelist)   *see* Grantham,
Manthorpe *Linc*
MANTON (St Mary the Virgin)   *see* Empingham, Edith Weston,
Lyndon, Manton etc *Pet*
MANUDEN (St Mary the Virgin)   *see* Clavering w Langley,
Arkesden etc *Chelmsf*
MAPERTON (St Peter and St Paul)   *see* Camelot Par *B & W*
MAPLEBECK (St Radegund) *S'well 3*   **P** *Sir Philip Naylor-
Leyland Bt*   **V** *vacant*
MAPLEDURHAM (St Margaret)   *see* Caversham Thameside and
Mapledurham *Ox*
MAPLEDURWELL (St Mary)   *see* N Hants Downs *Win*
MAPLESTEAD, GREAT (St Giles)   *see* Halstead Area *Chelmsf*
MAPLESTEAD, LITTLE (St John) *as above*
MAPPERLEY (Holy Trinity)   *see* W Hallam and Mapperley w
Stanley *Derby*
MAPPLEBOROUGH GREEN (Holy Ascension)   *see* Arden
Marches *Cov*
MAPPLETON (All Saints)   *see* Aldbrough, Mappleton w Goxhill
and Withernwick *York*
MAPPOWDER (St Peter and St Paul)   *see* Hazelbury Bryan and
the Hillside Par *Sarum*
MARAZION (All Saints)   *see* Ludgvan, Marazion, St Hilary and
Perranuthnoe *Truro*
MARBURY (St Michael) w Tushingham and Whitewell *Ches 5*
P *MMCET and Bp (jt)*   **R** *vacant*
MARCH (St John) (St Mary) (St Peter) (St Wendreda) *Ely 11*
P *Patr Bd*   **TR** A J SMITH   **TV** C B STOCKING
MARCHAM (All Saints) w Garford and Shippon *Ox 19*
P *Bp and Ch Ch Ox (jt)*   **V** R G ZAIR
MARCHINGTON (St Peter)   *see* Uttoxeter Area *Lich*
MARCHINGTON WOODLANDS (St John) *as above*
MARCHWOOD (St John) *Win 11*   **P** *Bp*
P-in-c S A HONES
MARCLE, LITTLE (St Michael and All Angels)   *see* Ledbury *Heref*
MARCLE, MUCH (St Bartholomew) *as above*
MARDEN (All Saints)   *see* The Cannings and Redhorn *Sarum*
MARDEN (St Hilda) w Preston Grange *Newc 5*   **P** *Bp*
V P S BAGSHAW
MARDEN (St Mary the Virgin)   *see* Maund Gp *Heref*
MARDEN (St Michael and All Angels) *Cant 11*   **P** *Abp*
V A A DUGUID   **C** S R SIVYER
MARDEN ASH (St James)   *see* High Ongar w Norton
Mandeville *Chelmsf*
MARDEN VALE *Sarum 16*   **P** *Prime Min and Patr Bd (alt)*
TR R A KENWAY   **TV** E A MASSEY
MARDEN, EAST (St Peter)   *see* Octagon *Chich*
MARDEN, NORTH (St Mary) *as above*
MARDYKE Team, The *Chelmsf 16*   **P** *Patr Bd*
TR A T FRANKLAND   **TV** A J HUDSON, P D RABIN
C A C UZOIGWE   **NSM** D F BATES
MAREHAM ON THE HILL (All Saints)   *see* Fen and Hill Gp *Linc*
MAREHAM-LE-FEN (St Helen) *as above*
MARESFIELD (St Bartholomew) *Chich 18*   **P** *Ch Trust Fund
Trust*   **R** N S CORNELL   **NSM** P C INGRAM
MARFLEET (St Giles) (St George) (St Hilda) (St Philip) *York 14*
P *Patr Bd*   **TR** D A ROGERS   **TV** R J W LONG
MARGARET MARSH (St Margaret)   *see* Shaftesbury *Sarum*
MARGARET RODING (St Margaret)   *see* High and Gd Easter w
Margaret Roding *Chelmsf*
MARGARET STREET (All Saints)   *see* St Marylebone All SS *Lon*
**MARGARETTING (St Margaret) w Mountnessing and
Buttsbury** *Chelmsf 8*   **P** *Bp*   **P-in-c** P SHERRING
C A D FINN   **NSM** C A PARKES
MARGATE (All Saints) *Cant 5*   **P** *Abp*   **P-in-c** D L YELDHAM
C D L CAWLEY
MARGATE (Holy Trinity) *Cant 5*   **P** *Ch Patr Trust*
V J S RICHARDSON
MARGATE (St John the Baptist in Thanet) *Cant 5*   **P** *Abp*
P-in-c D L YELDHAM
MARGATE (St Paul)   *see* Cliftonville *Cant*
MARGATE (St Philip) Northdown Park *Cant 5*   **P** *Ch Patr
Trust*   **V** S GAY
MARHAM (Holy Trinity) *Ely 9*   **P** *St Jo Coll Cam*
P-in-c B L BURTON

MARHAMCHURCH (St Marwenne)   *see* Bude Haven and
Marhamchurch *Truro*
MARHOLM (St Mary the Virgin)   *see* Castor w Upton and
Stibbington and Water Newton, Marholm and Sutton *Pet*
MARIANSLEIGH (St Mary)   *see* Bishopsnympton, Rose Ash,
Mariansleigh etc *Ex*
MARISHES, THE (St Francis)   *see* Pickering w Lockton and
Levisham *York*
MARK (Holy Cross) w Allerton *B & W 1*   **P** *Bp and D&C (jt)*
P-in-c T NIXON   **Emer** P A KINGDOM, R W NEILL
MARK BEECH (Holy Trinity)   *see* Hever, Four Elms and Mark
Beech *Roch*
MARK CROSS (St Mark)   *see* Rotherfield w Mark Cross *Chich*
MARKBY (St Peter)   *see* Hannah cum Hagnaby w Markby *Linc*
MARKET BOSWORTH (St Peter)   *see* Bosworth and Sheepy Gp
Leic
MARKET DEEPING (St Guthlac) *Linc 19*   **P** *Ld Chan*
R P BRENT   **C** N A KNOX
MARKET DRAYTON (St Mary)   *see* Drayton in Hales *Lich*
**MARKET HARBOROUGH (St Dionysius) (The Transfiguration)
- Little Bowden w Lubenham and Great Bowden** *Leic 3*
P *Patr Bd*   **TR** R H G BRAND   **TV** A QUIGLEY,
J D G SHAKESPEARE   **C** J L LEWIS   **NSM** S M COOPER
MARKET LAVINGTON (St Mary of the Assumption)   *see* The
Lavingtons, Cheverells, and Easterton *Sarum*
MARKET OVERTON (St Peter and St Paul)   *see* Oakham,
Ashwell, Braunston, Brooke, Egleton etc *Pet*
MARKET RASEN (St Thomas the Apostle) *Linc 7*   **P** *Ld Chan*
P-in-c S W JOHNSON
MARKET WEIGHTON (All Saints) *York 5*   **P** *Abp*
V D J EVERETT   **NSM** S H PULKO
MARKET WESTON (St Mary)   *see* Stanton, Hopton, Market
Weston, Barningham etc *St E*
**MARKFIELD (St Michael), Thornton, Bagworth and Stanton
under Bardon, and Copt Oak** *Leic 9*   **P** *MMCET*
R S J NICHOLLS
MARKHAM CLINTON (All Saints)   *see* Tuxford w Weston,
Markham Clinton etc *S'well*
MARKHAM, EAST (St John the Baptist)   *see* Retford Area *S'well*
MARKINGTON (St Michael)   *see* Bishop Thornton, Burnt Yates,
Markington etc *Leeds*
MARKS GATE (St Mark) Chadwell Heath *Chelmsf 1*   **P** *Bp*
V *vacant*
MARKS TEY (St Andrew) and Aldham *Chelmsf 21*   **P** *CPAS
and MMCET (jt)*   **P-in-c** I M SCOTT-THOMPSON
MARKSBURY (St Peter)   *see* Farmborough, Marksbury and
Stanton Prior *B & W*
MARKYATE STREET (St John the Baptist)   *see* Flamstead and
Markyate Street *St Alb*
MARLBOROUGH (St Mary the Virgin) *Sarum 18*   **P** *Patr Bd*
TR A G STUDDERT-KENNEDY   **TV** M F KEEN
C J H BLOKLAND   **OLM** D P MAURICE
MARLBROOK (St Luke)   *see* Bromsgrove *Worc*
MARLDON (St John the Baptist)   *see* Totnes w Bridgetown,
Berry Pomeroy etc *Ex*
MARLESFORD (St Andrew)   *see* Campsea Ashe w Marlesford,
Parham and Hacheston *St E*
MARLEY HILL (St Cuthbert)   *see* Hillside *Dur*
MARLINGFORD (Assumption of the Blessed Virgin Mary)
see Easton, Colton, Marlingford and Bawburgh *Nor*
MARLOW BOTTOM (St Mary the Virgin)   *see* Gt Marlow w
Marlow Bottom, Lt Marlow and Bisham *Ox*
**MARLOW, GREAT (All Saints) w Marlow Bottom, Little
Marlow and Bisham** *Ox 18*   **P** *Patr Bd*   **TR** D T BULL
TV G H L WATTS, S A L WATTS, S FITZGERALD   **C** W J BULL
NSM G L C SMITH
MARLOW, LITTLE (St John the Baptist)   *see* Gt Marlow w
Marlow Bottom, Lt Marlow and Bisham *Ox*
MARLPIT HILL (St Paulinus)   *see* Edenbridge *Roch*
MARLPOOL (All Saints) *Derby 12*   **P** *V Heanor*   **V** K PADLEY
C J M LYON
MARLSTON (St Mary)   *see* Bucklebury w Marlston *Ox*
MARNHULL (St Gregory) *Sarum 5*   **P** *DBF*   **V** *vacant*
**MAROWN (Old Parish Church) (St Runius), Foxdale and
Baldwin** *S & M*   **P** *The Crown*   **V** J A WARD
C I M SKIDMORE
MARPLE (All Saints) *Ches 16*   **P** *R Stockport St Mary*
V I R PARKINSON   **C** D R CURRIE, G J ROBINSON
NSM B J LOWE, C M BLODWELL, L S CURRIE
MARPLE, LOW (St Martin) *Ches 16*   **P** *Keble Coll Ox*
V E P MCKENNA   **NSM** A HYDE
MARR (St Helen)   *see* Bilham *Sheff*
MARSDEN (St Bartholomew) *Leeds 12*   **P** *R Almondbury*
V *vacant*
**MARSDEN, GREAT (St John's Church Centre) w Nelson
St Philip** *Blackb 6*   **P** *Prime Min and Bp (alt)*   **V** L A HILLIARD

MARSDEN, LITTLE (St Paul) w Nelson St Mary and Nelson St Bede *Blackb 6* **P** *Bp* **V** *vacant*
MARSH (St George) *see* Lancaster St Mary w St John and St Anne *Blackb*
MARSH BALDON (St Peter) *see* Dorchester *Ox*
MARSH FARM (Holy Cross) *St Alb 12* **P** *Bp*
 P-in-c D C BERESFORD
MARSH GIBBON (St Mary the Virgin) *see* The Claydons and Swan *Ox*
MARSH GREEN (St Barnabas) *Liv 14* **P** *Bp, Duke of Sutherland, and V Pemberton (jt)* **V** D A HAYES
MARSHALSWICK (St Mary) *see* St Alb St Mary Marshalswick *St Alb*
MARSHAM (All Saints) *see* Bure Valley *Nor*
MARSHCHAPEL (St Mary the Virgin) *see* The North-Chapel Parishes *Linc*
MARSHFIELD (St Mary the Virgin) w Cold Ashton and Tormarton w West Littleton *Bris 4* **P** *New Coll Ox and Bp (alt)* **P-in-c** S A V WHEELER **C** V J WHIFFIN
MARSHLAND, The *Sheff 10* **P** *Ld Chan and Bp (alt)* **NSM** K W SARGEANTSON
MARSHWOOD (St Mary) *see* Golden Cap Team *Sarum*
MARSKE (St Edmund King and Martyr) *see* Richmond w Hudswell and Downholme and Marske *Leeds*
MARSKE IN CLEVELAND (St Mark) *York 16* **P** *Trustees* **V** D TEMBEY
MARSKE, NEW (St Thomas) *York 16* **P** *Abp* **V** A M F REED
MARSTON (St Leonard) *see* Stafford St Mary and Marston *Lich*
MARSTON (St Mary) *see* Barkston and Hough Gp *Linc*
MARSTON (St Nicholas) w Elsfield *Ox 1* **P** *Bp and D&C (jt)* **V** A R PRICE **C** R M GLENNY **NSM** A J PRICE
MARSTON BIGOT (St Leonard) *see* Nunney and Witham Friary, Marston Bigot etc *B & W*
MARSTON GREEN (St Leonard) *Birm 9* **P** *Birm Dioc Trustees* **V** P A HARRISON
MARSTON MAGNA (Blessed Virgin Mary) *see* Chilton Cantelo, Ashington, Mudford, Rimpton etc *B & W*
MARSTON MEYSEY (St James) *see* S Cotswolds *Glouc*
MARSTON MONTGOMERY (St Giles) *see* S Dales *Derby*
MARSTON MORTEYNE (St Mary the Virgin) w Lidlington *St Alb 9* **P** *Bp and (St Jo Coll Cam (alt)* **P-in-c** G A WEBB
MARSTON ON DOVE (St Mary) *see* Hilton w Marston-on-Dove *Derby*
MARSTON SICCA (St James the Great) *see* Quinton, Welford, Weston and Marston Sicca *Glouc*
MARSTON ST LAWRENCE (St Lawrence) *see* Chenderit *Pet*
MARSTON TRUSSELL (St Nicholas) *see* Welford w Sibbertoft and Marston Trussell *Pet*
MARSTON, NEW (St Michael and All Angels) *Ox 1* **P** *Bp* **V** E B BARDWELL
MARSTON, NORTH (Assumption of the Blessed Virgin Mary) *see* Schorne *Ox*
MARSTON, SOUTH (St Mary Magdalene) *see* Stratton St Margaret w S Marston etc *Bris*
MARSTOW (St Matthew) *see* Goodrich, Marstow, Welsh Bicknor, Llangarron etc *Heref*
MARSWORTH (All Saints) *see* Ivinghoe w Pitstone and Slapton and Marsworth *Ox*
MARTHAM (St Mary) and Repps w Bastwick, Thurne and Clippesby *Nor 6* **P** *Bp, D&C, DBP and K Edw VI Gr Sch (jt)* **P-in-c** K J RAYNER **NSM** S H MITCHELL
MARTIN (All Saints) *see* W Downland *Sarum*
MARTIN (Holy Trinity) *see* Carr Dyke Gp *Linc*
MARTIN (St Michael) *see* Horncastle Gp *Linc*
MARTIN HUSSINGTREE (St Michael) *see* Salwarpe and Hindlip w Martin Hussingtree *Worc*
MARTINDALE (Old Church) *see* Barton, Pooley Bridge, Martindale etc *Carl*
MARTINDALE (St Peter) *as above*
MARTLESHAM (St Mary the Virgin) w Brightwell *St E 2* **P** *Bp* **NSM** M RITTMAN
MARTLESHAM HEATH (St Michael and All Angels) *see* Martlesham w Brightwell *St E*
MARTLEY (St Peter) *see* Worcs W *Worc*
MARTOCK (All Saints) w Kingsbury Episcopi and Ash *B & W 5* **P** *Bp and D&C (jt)* **V** D R GENT **NSM** M I MACCORMACK
MARTON (Room) *see* Middleton, Newton and Sinnington *York*
MARTON (St Esprit) *see* Long Itchington and Marton *Cov*
MARTON (St James), Siddington w Capesthorne, and Eaton w Hulme Walfield *Ches 11* **P** *Bp and Sir W A B Davenport (jt)* **V** I M ARCH
MARTON (St Margaret of Antioch) *see* Lea Gp *Linc*
MARTON (St Mary) *see* Forest of Galtres *York*
MARTON (St Paul) *Blackb 8* **P** *V Poulton-le-Fylde* **V** C J WREN **C** K A WREN **NSM** C M MORTON

MARTON CUM GRAFTON (Christ Church) *see* Gt and Lt Ouseburn w Marton cum Grafton etc *Leeds*
MARTON IN CRAVEN (St Peter) *see* Broughton, Marton and Thornton *Leeds*
MARTON-IN-CHIRBURY (St Mark) *see* Chirbury, Marton, Middleton and Trelystan etc *Heref*
MARTON-IN-CLEVELAND (St Cuthbert) *York 17* **P** *Abp* **V** A J GRANT **C** B J NORTON
MARTYR WORTHY (St Swithun) *see* Itchen Valley *Win*
MARWOOD (St Michael and All Angels) *see* Heanton Punchardon, Marwood and W Down *Ex*
MARY TAVY (St Mary) *see* Peter Tavy and Mary Tavy *Ex*
MARYFIELD (St Philip and St James) *see* Antony w Sheviock and Torpoint *Truro*
MARYLEBONE ROAD (St Marylebone) *see* St Marylebone w H Trin *Lon*
MARYPORT (St Mary) (Christ Church), Netherton and Flimby *Carl 7* **P** *Patr Bd* **TV** S M MCKENDREY **C** N G PENNINGTON
MARYSTOWE (St Mary the Virgin) *see* Milton Abbot, Dunterton, Lamerton etc *Ex*
MASBROUGH (St Paul) *Sheff 6* **P** *Bp and Ld Chan (alt)* **V** *vacant*
MASHAM (St Mary the Virgin) and Healey *Leeds 25* **P** *Trin Coll Cam* **V** D J CLEEVES **C** N J MORGAN **NSM** M A WARNER, M SAUNDERS
MASSINGHAM, GREAT (St Mary) *see* Ashwicken w Leziate, Bawsey etc *Nor*
MASSINGHAM, LITTLE (St Andrew) *as above*
MATCHBOROUGH (Christ Church) *see* Ipsley *Worc*
MATCHING (St Mary) *see* High Laver w Magdalen Laver and Lt Laver etc *Chelmsf*
MATCHING GREEN (St Edmund) *as above*
MATFEN (Holy Trinity) *see* Stamfordham w Matfen *Newc*
MATFIELD (St Luke) *see* Lamberhurst and Matfield *Roch*
MATHON (St John the Baptist) *see* Cradley w Mathon and Storridge *Heref*
MATLASKE (St Peter) *see* Barningham w Matlaske w Baconsthorpe etc *Nor*
MATLOCK (St Giles) (St John the Baptist), Dethick, Lea and Holloway *Derby 7* **P** *Bp and DBF (jt)* **R** B M CROWTHER-ALWYN
MATLOCK BANK (All Saints) and Tansley *Derby 7* **P** *Bp* **V** R B READE **C** D J BATTISON
MATLOCK BATH (Holy Trinity) and Cromford *Derby 7* **P** *Ch Trust Fund Trust* **P-in-c** P N W GRAYSHON
MATSON (St Katharine) *Glouc 2* **P** *D&C* **P-in-c** F B QUIST
MATTERDALE (not known) *see* Greystoke w Penruddock, Mungrisdale etc *Carl*
MATTERSEY (All Saints) *see* Bawtry w Austerfield, Misson, Everton and Mattersey *S'well*
MATTINGLEY (not known) *see* Whitewater *Win*
MATTISHALL (All Saints) and the Tudd Valley *Nor 17* **P** *Bp, G&C Coll Cam, DBP, and J V Berney Esq (jt)* **R** M A MCCAGHREY **OLM** S E THURGILL
MATTISHALL BURGH (St Peter) *see* Mattishall and the Tudd Valley *Nor*
MAUGHOLD (St Maughold) and South Ramsey *S & M* **P** *The Crown* **V** C I LOWDON
MAULDEN (St Mary) *St Alb 8* **P** *Bp* **R** L KLIMAS
MAUNBY (St Michael) *see* Lower Swale *Leeds*
MAUND Group of Parishes *Heref 3* **P** *Bp (2 turns), D&C (1 turn)* **R** H M SHORT
MAUTBY (St Peter and St Paul) *see* S Trin Broads *Nor*
MAVESYN RIDWARE (St Nicholas) *see* The Ridwares and Kings Bromley *Lich*
MAVIS ENDERBY (St Michael) *see* Bolingbroke Deanery *Linc*
MAWDESLEY (St Peter) *see* Croston, Bretherton and Mawdesley w Bispham *Blackb*
MAWNAN (St Mawnan) (St Michael) *Truro 3* **P** *Bp* **P-in-c** S G TURNER
MAXEY (St Peter) *see* Etton w Helpston and Maxey *Pet*
MAXSTOKE (St Michael and All Angels) *Birm 9* **P** *Lord Leigh* **V** R N PARKER **C** R L STEPHENS
MAY HILL (All Saints) *see* Huntley and Longhope, Churcham and Bulley *Glouc*
MAYBRIDGE (St Richard) *Chich 4* **P** *Bp* **V** *vacant*
MAYBUSH (St Peter) and Southampton St Jude *Win 13* **P** *Bp* **V** R A HEMMINGS **C** D G OADES
MAYBUSH Redbridge (All Saints) *see* Maybush and Southampton St Jude *Win*
MAYFAIR (Christ Church) extra-parochial place *Lon 3* **C** A S B CARTER, M RILEY **NSM** M BEEBY, P ALLCOCK
MAYFIELD (St Dunstan) *Chich 16* **P** *Keble Coll Ox* **V** N J PRIOR **Hon C** J P CAPERON

MAYFIELD (St John the Baptist) *see* Alton w Bradley-le-Moors and Denstone etc *Lich*
MAYFORD (Emmanuel) *see* Woking St Jo *Guildf*
MAYLAND (St Barnabas) (St Barnabas Family Centre) *Chelmsf 11* **P** *Bp* **P-in-c** B C R JOHNSON
MEANWOOD (Holy Trinity) *Leeds 16* **P** *Bp* **NSM** M J BRADLEY
MEARE (Blessed Virgin Mary and All Saints) *see* Glastonbury w Meare *B & W*
MEARS ASHBY (All Saints) and Hardwick and Sywell w Overstone *Pet 6* **P** *Duchy of Cornwall (2 turns), Bracegirdle Trustees (1 turn), and Mrs C K Edmiston (1 turn)* **P-in-c** D C BEET
MEASE VALLEY *Lich 4* **P** *Bp, Exors Major F C Pipe-Wolferstan, and Mrs E V G Inge-Innes-Lillingston (jt)* **R** G J THOMPSON **NSM** D BURGESS **OLM** C S TYLER
MEASHAM (St Laurence) *see* Woodfield *Leic*
MEAVY (St Peter) *see* Yelverton, Meavy, Sheepstor and Walkhampton *Ex*
MEDBOURNE (St Giles) *see* Six Saints circa Holt *Leic*
MEDLOCK HEAD *Man 15* **P** *Prime Min (2 turns), Patr Bd (1 turn)* **TR** R W HAWKINS **TV** P M S MONK **C** S C NOLAN **NSM** P A ROBINSON
MEDMENHAM (St Peter and St Paul) *see* Hambleden Valley *Ox*
MEDOMSLEY (St Mary Magdalene) *Dur 4* **P** *Bp* **P-in-c** D R CLEUGH
MEDSTEAD (St Andrew) *see* Bentworth, Lasham, Medstead and Shalden *Win*
MEERBROOK (St Matthew) *see* Leek and Meerbrook *Lich*
MEESDEN (St Mary) *see* Hormead, Wyddial, Anstey, Brent Pelham etc *St Alb*
MEETH (St Michael and All Angels) *see* Okehampton, Inwardleigh, Belstone, Sourton etc *Ex*
MEIR (Holy Trinity) *Lich 6* **P** *Bp* **P-in-c** P W BENNETT
MEIR HEATH (St Francis of Assisi) and Normacot *Lich 12* **P** *Bp and DBP (jt)* **V** D W MCHARDY
MEIR PARK (St Clare) *see* Meir Heath and Normacot *Lich*
MELBECKS (Holy Trinity) *see* Swaledale *Leeds*
MELBOURN (All Saints) *Ely 7* **P** *D&C* **NSM** M L PRICE
MELBOURNE (St Michael), Ticknall, Smisby and Stanton by Bridge *Derby 15* **P** *Bp* **V** M POWELL **C** A A PLUMMER
MELBURY (St Mary the Virgin) (St Osmund) *Sarum 3* **P** *Patr Bd* **TV** D P HARKNETT, L J WILCOCK
MELBURY ABBAS (St Thomas) *see* Shaftesbury *Sarum*
MELBURY BUBB (St Mary the Virgin) *see* Melbury *Sarum*
MELBURY OSMUND (St Osmund) *as above*
MELCHBOURNE (St Mary Magdalene) *see* The Stodden Churches *St Alb*
MELCOMBE HORSEY (St Andrew) *see* Piddle Valley, Hilton, Cheselbourne etc *Sarum*
MELDON (St John the Evangelist) *see* Bolam w Whalton and Hartburn w Meldon *Newc*
MELDRETH (Holy Trinity) *Ely 7* **P** *D&C* **NSM** M L PRICE
MELKSHAM (St Barnabas) (St Michael and All Angels) *Sarum 15* **P** *DBP* **TR** B D BLACKFORD **TV** A SOWTON **NSM** H BEGLEY
MELKSHAM FOREST (St Andrew) *see* Melksham *Sarum*
MELLING (St Thomas) *see* Maghull and Melling *Liv*
MELLING (St Wilfrid) *see* E Lonsdale *Blackb*
MELLIS (St Mary the Virgin) *see* S Hartismere *St E*
MELLOR (St Mary) *see* Balderstone, Mellor and Samlesbury *Blackb*
MELLS (St Andrew) w Buckland Dinham, Elm, Whatley, Vobster and Chantry *B & W 3* **P** *DBP (2 turns), Bp (1 turns)* **NSM** B L DAVIES
MELMERBY (St John the Baptist) *see* Cross Fell Gp *Carl*
MELPLASH (Christ Church) *see* Beaminster Area *Sarum*
MELSONBY (St James the Great) *see* Forcett and Aldbrough and Melsonby *Leeds*
MELTHAM (St Bartholomew) *see* Meltham *Leeds*
MELTHAM Christ the King (St Bartholomew) (St James) *Leeds 6* **P** *Simeon's Trustees, R Almondbury w Farnley Tyas, and Bp (jt)* **V** M E READ **C** C SMITH **NSM** D SHIELDS, P ROLLS **OLM** J F RADCLIFFE
MELTHAM MILLS (St James) *see* Meltham *Leeds*
MELTON (St Andrew) and Ufford *St E 7* **P** *D&C Ely (3 turns), and T R E Blois-Brooke Esq (1 turn)* **R** P G HAMBLING
MELTON CONSTABLE (St Peter) *see* Briston, Burgh Parva, Hindolveston etc *Nor*
MELTON MOWBRAY (St Mary) *Leic 2* **P** *Patr Bd* **TR** K P ASHBY **C** C M CUMMING
MELTON ROSS (Ascension) *see* Brocklesby Park *Linc*
MELTON, GREAT (All Saints) *see* Hethersett w Canteloff w Lt and Gt Melton *Nor*
MELTON, HIGH (St James) *see* Barnburgh w Melton on the Hill etc *Sheff*

MELTON, LITTLE (All Saints) *see* Hethersett w Canteloff w Lt and Gt Melton *Nor*
MELVERLEY (St Peter) *see* Kinnerley w Melverley and Knockin w Maesbrook *Lich*
MEMBURY (St John the Baptist) *see* Axminster, Chardstock, All Saints etc *Ex*
MENDHAM (All Saints) *see* Sancroft *St E*
MENDLESHAM (St Mary) *St E 6* **P** *SMF* **V** P T GRAY
MENEAGE (St Anthony) (St Martin) (St Mawgan) *Truro 4* **P** *Ld Chan and Bp (alt)* **R** L A WALKER **C** H J ASTON
MENHENIOT (St Lalluwy and St Antoninus) *Truro 12* **P** *Ex Coll Ox* **P-in-c** M A J DAVIES
MENSTON (St John the Divine) w Woodhead *Leeds 4* **P** *Bp* **V** R J YEOMAN
MENTMORE (St Mary the Virgin) *see* Cottesloe *Ox*
MEOLE BRACE (Holy Trinity) *Lich 20* **P** *J K Bather Esq* **V** P J CANSDALE **C** D C BRUCE, P J HUBBARD **NSM** C RUXTON, V PITT
MEOLS, GREAT (St John the Baptist) *Ches 8* **P** *Bp* **V** G A ROSSITER
MEOLS, NORTH Team Ministry, The (St Cuthbert) *Liv 9* **P** *Patr Bd* **TR** P C GREEN **C** S T MARSHALL
MEON BRIDGE *Portsm 1* **P** *Bp* **R** A W FORREST
MEON, EAST (All Saints) *Portsm 4* **P** *Ld Chan* **V** J BALL
MEON, WEST (St John the Evangelist) and Warnford *Portsm 4* **P** *Bp and DBP (alt)* **P-in-c** L C STOCK **C** J BALL
MEONSTOKE (St Andrew) *see* Meon Bridge *Portsm*
MEOPHAM (St John the Baptist) w Nurstead *Roch 1* **P** *D&C and Mrs S Edmeades-Stearns (jt)* **P-in-c** A E DAVIE **NSM** C D FORMAN
MEPAL (St Mary) *see* Witcham w Mepal *Ely*
MEPPERSHALL (St Mary the Virgin) and Shefford *St Alb 8* **P** *Bp and St Jo Coll Cam (alt)* **V** V M GOODMAN
MERE (St Michael the Archangel) w West Knoyle and Maiden Bradley *Sarum 12* **P** *Bp* **P-in-c** C A WILSON-BARKER
MERESIDE (St Wilfrid) *see* Blackpool St Wilfrid *Blackb*
MEREVALE (St Mary the Virgin) *see* Baxterley w Hurley and Wood End and Merevale etc *Birm*
MEREWORTH (St Lawrence) w West Peckham *Roch 7* **P** *Viscount Falmouth and D&C (alt)* **P-in-c** P M DICKIN **C** M MONTGOMERY
MERIDEN (St Laurence) *Cov 4* **P** *Chapter Cov Cathl* **NSM** L J EDWARDS
MERRINGTON (St John the Evangelist) *Dur 6* **P** *D&C* **P-in-c** G NORMAN
MERRIOTT (All Saints) w Hinton, Dinnington and Lopen *B & W 14* **P** *D&C Bris (2 turns), Bp (1 turn)* **R** J R HICKS **C** R B HICKS
MERROW (St John the Evangelist) *Guildf 5* **P** *Earl of Onslow* **R** C J LUCKRAFT **C** J A DRAKE-SMITH **NSM** D H VERSCHOYLE
MERRY HILL (St Joseph of Arimathea) *see* Penn Fields *Lich*
MERRYMEET (St Mary) *see* Menheniot *Truro*
MERSEA, WEST (St Peter and St Pau) w East (St Edmund), Peldon, Great and Little Wigborough *Chelmsf 24* **P** *Prime Min (1 turn), Patr Bd (2 turns)* **R** S C NORTON **NSM** J R PANTRY
MERSHAM (St John the Baptist) *see* A20 Benefice *Cant*
MERSTHAM (St Katharine) (Epiphany), South Merstham and Gatton *S'wark 26* **P** *Patr Bd* **P-in-c** P M PULLINGER **TV** B B M BROWN **OLM** V J WILLIAMS
MERSTHAM, SOUTH (All Saints) *see* Merstham, S Merstham and Gatton *S'wark*
MERTON (All Saints) *see* Shebbear, Buckland Filleigh, Sheepwash etc *Ex*
MERTON (St James) *S'wark 13* **P** *Bp and V Merton St Mary (jt)* **V** *vacant*
MERTON (St John the Divine) *see* Merton Priory *S'wark*
MERTON (St Mary) *S'wark 13* **P** *Bp* **V** J A HAYWARD
MERTON (St Peter) *see* Caston, Griston, Merton, Thompson etc *Nor*
MERTON (St Swithun) *see* Ray Valley *Ox*
MERTON PRIORY *S'wark 13* **P** *Patr Bd* **TR** C J I PALMER **C** K A TUCKETT
MESHAW (St John) *see* Burrington, Chawleigh, Cheldon, Chulmleigh etc *Ex*
MESSING (All Saints) *see* Thurstable and Winstree *Chelmsf*
MESSINGHAM (Holy Trinity) *Linc 6* **P** *Bp* **V** D J SWANNACK
MESTY CROFT (St Luke) *see* Wednesbury St Paul Wood Green *Lich*
METFIELD (St John the Baptist) *see* Sancroft *St E*
METHERINGHAM (St Wilfred) w Blankney and Dunston *Linc 12* **P** *Bp (2 turns), Br Field Products Ltd (1 turn)* **V** A T COATES **C** J S PARKIN

METHLEY (St Oswald)   *see* Rothwell, Lofthouse, Methley etc *Leeds*

METHWOLD (St George)   *see* Grimshoe *Ely*

METTINGHAM (All Saints)   *see* Bungay *St E*

METTON (St Andrew)   *see* Roughton and Felbrigg, Metton, Sustead etc *Nor*

MEVAGISSEY (St Peter)   *see* St Mewan w Mevagissey and St Ewe *Truro*

MEXBOROUGH (St John the Baptist) *Sheff 12*   **P** *Adn York*   **V** D R WISE

MEYSEY HAMPTON (St Mary)   *see* S Cotswolds *Glouc*

MICHAEL (St Michael and All Angels)   *see* W Coast *S & M*

MICHAELCHURCH ESCLEY (St Michael)   *see* Clodock and Longtown w Craswall, Llanveynoe etc *Heref*

MICHELDEVER (St Mary)   *see* Upper Dever *Win*

MICHELMERSH (Our Lady) and Awbridge and Braishfield and Farley Chamberlayne and Timsbury *Win 12*   **P** *Bp*   **R** S C PITTIS

MICKLEFIELD (St Mary the Virgin)   *see* Aberford w Micklefield *York*

MICKLEGATE (Holy Trinity)   *see* York H Trin Micklegate *York*

MICKLEHAM (St Michael)   *see* Leatherhead and Mickleham *Guildf*

MICKLEHURST (All Saints Institute) *Ches 14*   **P** *Bp*   **V** *vacant*

MICKLEOVER (All Saints) (St John) *Derby 10*   **P** *Bp and MMCET (jt)*   **V** P F WALLEY   **NSM** M P STAUNTON   **OLM** A G ROWLANDS, I D GODLINGTON, P M PRITCHARD

MICKLETON (St Lawrence)   *see* Vale and Cotswold Edge *Glouc*

MICKLEY (St George)   *see* Bywell and Mickley *Newc*

MICKLEY (St John the Evangelist)   *see* Fountains Gp *Leeds*

MID ELLOE Group, The *Linc 18*   **P** *V Holbeach and DBP (1 turn), Prime Min (1 turn)*   **R** A S MASON   **NSM** E D CRUST

MID LOES *St E 16*   **P** *Ld Chan (1 turn), MMCET, CPAS, Bp, and Wadh Coll Ox (1 turn)*   **R** S F BRIAN

MID MARSH Group, The *Linc 15*   **P** *A M D Hall Esq, Bp, D&C, and Lady Mowbray (by turn)*   **R** C M TURNER   **OLM** J R SELFE, L W CARROLL

MID TRENT *Lich 10*   **P** *Patr Bd*   **TR** P S DANIEL   **TV** S J ABRAM

MIDDLE   *see also under substantive place name*

MIDDLE MARCHES Benefice, The *Heref 9*   **P** *Earl of Powis, J Coltman-Rogers Esq, Grocers' Co (1 turn), Mrs E B Rocke, Sir Huw Ripley Bt, P J H Barnes Esq (1 turn)*   **V** *vacant*

MIDDLE RASEN Group, The *Linc 7*   **P** *Bp, Charterhouse, and DBP (jt)*   **R** *vacant*

MIDDLEHAM (St Mary and St Alkelda) w Coverdale and East Witton and Thornton Steward *Leeds 27*   **P** *Bp, R Craven-Smith-Milnes Esq, and W R Burdon Esq (jt)*   **Emer** K COUCHMAN

MIDDLESBROUGH (All Saints) *York 17*   **P** *Abp*   **V** G HOLLAND

MIDDLESBROUGH (Ascension) *York 17*   **P** *Abp*   **V** D G HODGSON   **NSM** R A BROWN

MIDDLESBROUGH (St Agnes) *York 17*   **P** *Abp*   **P-in-c** A M GRANGE   **NSM** M EDWARDS

MIDDLESBROUGH (St Columba w St Paul) *York 17*   **P** *Abp*   **V** S COOPER   **NSM** P M KRONBERGS

MIDDLESBROUGH (St John the Evangelist) *York 17*   **P** *Abp*   **V** S COOPER

MIDDLESBROUGH (St Martin of Tours) (St Cuthbert) *York 17*   **P** *Abp*   **V** D C KING

MIDDLESBROUGH (St Oswald) (St Chad) *York 17*   **P** *Abp*   **V** S RICHARDSON

MIDDLESBROUGH (St Thomas) *York 17*   **P** *Abp*   **V** T M LEATHLEY

MIDDLESMOOR (St Chad)   *see* Upper Nidderdale *Leeds*

MIDDLESTOWN (St Luke) *Leeds 20*   **P** *R Thornhill*   **V** *vacant*

MIDDLETON (All Saints)   *see* N Hinckford *Chelmsf*

MIDDLETON (Holy Ghost)   *see* Kirkby Lonsdale *Carl*

MIDDLETON (Holy Trinity)   *see* Ludlow *Heref*

MIDDLETON (Holy Trinity)   *see* Yoxmere *St E*

MIDDLETON (St Andrew), Newton and Sinnington *York 19*   **P** *Abp (2 turns), Simeon's Trustees (1 turn)*   **R** S R GAMBLE

MIDDLETON (St John the Baptist)   *see* Curdworth, Middleton and Wishaw *Birm*

MIDDLETON (St Leonard) (St Margaret) and Thornham *Man 14*   **P** *Bp*   **R** M R SHORT   **OLM** D E BROOKS, P J DEMAIN, S L SPENCER

MIDDLETON (St Mary the Virgin) (St Cross) *Leeds 15*   **P** *V Rothwell and DBP (jt)*   **V** A T C MYERS

MIDDLETON (St Mary)   *see* Middlewinch *Nor*

MIDDLETON (St Michael and All Angels)   *see* Youlgreave, Middleton, Stanton-in-Peak etc *Derby*

MIDDLETON (St Nicholas) *Chich 1*   **P** *D&C*   **V** W T MARSTON

MIDDLETON CHENEY (All Saints)   *see* Chenderit *Pet*

MIDDLETON JUNCTION (St Gabriel) *Man 14*   **P** *Bp*   **V** *vacant*

MIDDLETON ON LEVEN (St Cuthbert)   *see* Rudby in Cleveland w Middleton *York*

MIDDLETON ST GEORGE (St George) (St Laurence) *Dur 8*   **P** *Bp*   **P-in-c** C M BLAKESLEY   **NSM** S E BRUCE

MIDDLETON STONEY (All Saints)   *see* Akeman *Ox*

MIDDLETON TYAS (St Michael and All Angels)   *see* E Richmond *Leeds*

MIDDLETON-BY-WIRKSWORTH (Holy Trinity)   *see* Wirksworth *Derby*

MIDDLETON-IN-CHIRBY (Holy Trinity)   *see* Chirbury, Marton, Middleton and Trelystan etc *Heref*

MIDDLETON-IN-TEESDALE (St Mary the Virgin) w Forest and Frith *Dur 7*   **P** *Lord Barnard and The Crown (alt)*   **P-in-c** J BARKER   **NSM** A P WALLBANK

MIDDLETON-ON-THE-WOLDS (St Andrew)   *see* Woldsburn *York*

MIDDLEWICH (St Michael and All Angels) w Byley *Ches 6*   **P** *Bp*   **V** S M DREW   **NSM** C M HUGHES, E WOODE, L V REED

MIDDLEWINCH *Nor 20*   **P** *Ld Chan (2 turns), Bp and W O Lancaster Esq (1 turn), Ms E J C Bostock and Ms C M Mackay (1 turn)*   **R** R MUBARAK

MIDDLEZOY (Holy Cross) w Othery, Moorlinch and Greinton *B & W 4*   **P** *Bp*   **R** J K L POWELL

MIDGHAM (St Matthew)   *see* Aldermaston and Woolhampton *Ox*

MIDHURST (St Mary Magdalene and St Denis) *Chich 9*   **P** *Rathbone Trust Co and Cowdray Trust (jt)*   **V** D A WILLIS

MIDSOMER NORTON (St John the Baptist) w Clandown *B & W 11*   **P** *Ch Ch Ox*   **V** C G CHIPLIN

MILBER (St Luke) *Ex 9*   **P** *Bp*   **V** J E POTTER

MILBORNE (St Andrew)   *see* Puddletown, Tolpuddle and Milborne w Dewlish *Sarum*

MILBORNE PORT (St John the Evangelist) w Goathill and Charlton Horethorne w Stowell *B & W 2*   **P** *Bp and J K Wingfield Digby Esq (jt)*   **V** S J GODFREY

MILBORNE WICK (Mission Church)   *see* Milborne Port w Goathill etc *B & W*

MILBOURNE (Holy Saviour)   *see* Ponteland *Newc*

MILBURN (St Cuthbert)   *see* Heart of Eden *Carl*

MILCOMBE (St Laurence)   *see* Bloxham w Milcombe and S Newington *Ox*

MILDEN (St Peter)   *see* Monks Eleigh w Chelsworth and Brent Eleigh etc *St E*

MILDENHALL (St John the Baptist)   *see* Marlborough *Sarum*

MILDENHALL (St Mary) *St E 11*   **P** *Patr Bd (2 turns), Bp (1 turn)*   **P-in-c** S J MITCHELL   **C** R I S RYCRAFT, S BARTON, S M LEATHLEY

MILDMAY GROVE (St Jude and St Paul) *Lon 6*   **P** *CPAS*   **V** J A OMOYAJOWO

MILE CROSS (St Catherine) *Nor 2*   **P** *Dr J P English, Canon G F Bridger, the Revd K W Habershon, and the Revd H Palmer (jt)*   **V** P D MACKAY   **OLM** R E LAMBERT

MILE OAK (The Good Shepherd)   *see* Portslade St Nic and St Andr and Mile Oak *Chich*

MILEHAM (St John the Baptist)   *see* Litcham w Kempston, E and W Lexham, Mileham etc *Nor*

MILES PLATTING (St Cuthbert)   *see* Man Apostles w Miles Platting *Man*

MILFORD (Holy Trinity)   *see* Hazelwood, Holbrook and Milford *Derby*

MILFORD (St John the Evangelist) *Guildf 4*   **P** *V Witley*   **V** C G POTTER   **OLM** D P HEWSON

MILFORD, SOUTH (St Mary the Virgin)   *see* Monk Fryston and S Milford *York*

MILFORD-ON-SEA (All Saints) *Win 11*   **P** *Bp*   **V** D J FURNESS

MILL END (St Peter) and Heronsgate w West Hyde *St Alb 4*   **P** *Bp and V Rickmansworth*   **V** S G CUTMORE   **C** J O NYAONGO

MILL HILL (John Keble Church) *Lon 15*   **P** *Bp*   **C** S P YOUNG

MILL HILL (St Michael and All Angels) *Lon 15*   **P** *Bp*   **P-in-c** S P YOUNG

MILL HILL (St Paul)   *see* Hendon St Paul Mill Hill *Lon*

MILLAND (St Luke)   *see* Lynch w Iping Marsh and Milland *Chich*

MILLBROOK (All Saints)   *see* St John w Millbrook *Truro*

MILLBROOK (Christ the King)   *see* Kettering Ch the King *Pet*

MILLBROOK (Holy Trinity) *Win 13*   **P** *Bp*   **P-in-c** W F P PERRY

MILLBROOK (St James) *Ches 14*   **P** *Bp, V Stalybridge St Paul, and Mrs E Bissill (jt)*   **V** *vacant*

MILLBROOK (St Michael and All Angels) *see* Ampthill w Millbrook and Steppingley *St Alb*

MILLERS DALE (St Anne) *see* Tideswell *Derby*

MILLFIELD (St Mark) and Pallion St Luke *Dur 1* **P** *Bp* **V** A J HAMPTON

MILLFIELD (St Mary) *Dur 1* **P** *The Crown* **V** B SKELTON **NSM** D RAINE

MILLHOUSES (Holy Trinity) *see* Abbeydale and Millhouses *Sheff*

MILLHOUSES (St Oswald) *see* Sheff St Pet and St Oswald *Sheff*

MILLINGTON (St Margaret) *see* Pocklington Wold *York*

MILLOM (Holy Trinity) (St George) *Carl 9* **P** *Bp and Trustees (jt)* **P-in-c** C R SHAW **NSM** C CARTER

MILNROW (St James) *Man 17* **P** *TR Rochdale* **V** R R USHER **NSM** S E WARD

MILNSHAW (St Mary Magdalen) *see* Accrington St Andr, St Mary and St Pet *Blackb*

MILNTHORPE (St Thomas) *see* Heversham and Milnthorpe *Carl*

MILSON (St George) *see* Cleobury Mortimer w Hopton Wafers etc *Heref*

MILSTEAD (St Mary and the Holy Cross) *see* Tunstall and Bredgar *Cant*

MILSTON (St Mary) *see* Avon River *Sarum*

MILTON (All Saints) *Ely 6* **P** K *Coll Cam* **R** D J CHAMBERLIN **NSM** D M BAGULEY, S BRADFORD

MILTON (St Blaise) *see* Steventon w Milton *Ox*

MILTON (St James) (St Andrew's Church Centre) (St Patrick) *Portsm 6* **P** *V Portsea St Mary* **P-in-c** P R ARMSTEAD **C** P M AMEY

MILTON (St John the Evangelist) *see* Adderbury w Milton *Ox*

MILTON (St Mary Magdalene) *Win 9* **P** *V Milford* **R** A H BAILEY

MILTON (St Peter) w St Jude and Kewstoke *B & W 10* **P** *Ld Chan* **V** G P EALES **NSM** G PUTNAM

MILTON (St Philip and St James) *Lich 8* **P** *Bp* **V** B E STATHAM

MILTON (St Simon and St Jude) *see* Gillingham and Milton-on-Stour *Sarum*

MILTON ABBAS (St James the Great) *see* Winterborne Valley and Milton Abbas *Sarum*

MILTON ABBOT (St Constantine), Dunterton, Lamerton, Sydenham Damerel, Marystowe and Coryton *Ex 22* **P** *Bp, Bedford Estates, J W Tremayne Esq, Mrs E J Bullock, P T L Newman Esq (jt)* **P-in-c** A J ATKINS

MILTON BRYAN (St Peter) *see* Woburn w Eversholt, Milton Bryan, Battlesden etc *St Alb*

MILTON CLEVEDON (St James) *see* Evercreech w Chesterblade and Milton Clevedon *B & W*

MILTON COMBE (Holy Spirit) *see* Buckland Monachorum *Ex*

MILTON ERNEST (All Saints), Pavenham and Thurleigh *St Alb 13* **P** *Bp (2 turns), Lord Luke (1 turn)* **P-in-c** P R KAY

MILTON KEYNES (Christ the Cornerstone) *Ox 14* **P** *Bp* **V** E LOZADA-UZURIAGA **C** T NORWOOD **NSM** K STRAUGHAN, P OXLEY

MILTON KEYNES VILLAGE (All Saints) *see* Walton Milton Keynes *Ox*

MILTON LILBOURNE (St Peter) *see* Vale of Pewsey *Sarum*

MILTON MALSOR (Holy Cross) *see* Blisworth, Alderton, Grafton Regis etc *Pet*

MILTON NEXT GRAVESEND (Christ Church) *Roch 4* **P** *Bp* **V** S C BREWER **C** K A SEGGIE **Hon C** A P WIBROE

MILTON NEXT GRAVESEND (St Peter and St Paul) w Denton *Roch 4* **P** *Bp* **R** G V HERBERT

MILTON NEXT SITTINGBOURNE (Holy Trinity) *Cant 15* **P** *D&C* **P-in-c** G M A ROGERS **C** L M JONES

MILTON REGIS (Holy Trinity) *see* Milton next Sittingbourne *Cant*

MILTON, GREAT (St Mary the Virgin) w Little (St James) and Great Haseley *Ox 20* **P** *Bp and D&C Windsor (jt)* **R** *vacant*

MILTON, SOUTH (All Saints) *see* Thurlestone, S Milton, Churchstow etc *Ex*

MILTON-UNDER-WYCHWOOD (St Simon and St Jude) *see* Wychwood *Ox*

MILVERTON (St Michael) w Halse, Fitzhead and Ash Priors *B & W 19* **P** *Bp, Adn, R Wiveliscombe and the Hills, and MMCET (jt)* **R** H L STAINER

MILVERTON, NEW (St Mark) *Cov 11* **P** *CPAS* **V** P MANUEL **NSM** S W HOOD

MILVERTON, OLD (St James) *see* Lillington and Old Milverton *Cov*

MILWICH (All Saints) *see* Mid Trent *Lich*

MIMMS *see also* MYMMS

MIMMS, SOUTH (Christ Church) *Lon 14* **P** *Ch Patr Trust* **V** N T W TAYLOR **C** J E JAMES

MINCHINHAMPTON (Holy Trinity) w Box and Amberley *Glouc 4* **P** *Bp and DBP (jt)* **R** H M BAILEY **Hon C** B C ATKINSON **NSM** S F EMERY

MINEHEAD (St Andrew) (St Michael) (St Peter) *B & W 15* **P** *Lt Col G W F Luttrell and Bp (jt)* **V** S J ROBINSON **NSM** C M MACDONALD

MINETY (St Leonard) *see* Ashton Keynes, Leigh and Minety *Bris*

MININGSBY WITH EAST KIRKBY (St Nicholas) *see* Bolingbroke Deanery *Linc*

MINLEY (St Andrew) *Guildf 1* **P** *Bp* **V** M W NEALE

MINSKIP (Mission Room) *see* Aldborough w Boroughbridge and Roecliffe *Leeds*

MINSTEAD (All Saints) *see* Lyndhurst and Emery Down and Minstead *Win*

MINSTER (St Mary the Virgin) *see* Wantsum Gp *Cant*

MINSTER (St Merteriana) *see* Boscastle and Tintagel Gp *Truro*

MINSTER IN SHEPPEY (St Mary and St Sexburga) *see* W Sheppey *Cant*

MINSTER LOVELL (St Kenelm) *Ox 28* **P** *Eton Coll and Ch Ch Ox (jt)* **P-in-c** P M CLIFFORD

MINSTERLEY (Holy Trinity), Habberley and Hope w Shelve *Heref 12* **P** *Bp (3 turns), DBP (3 turns), New Coll Ox (2 turns), J J C Coldwell Esq (1 turn)* **NSM** C A CHADWICK

MINSTERWORTH (St Peter) *see* Westbury-on-Severn w Flaxley, Blaisdon etc *Glouc*

MINTERNE MAGNA (St Andrew) *see* Buckland Newton, Cerne Abbas, Godmanstone etc *Sarum*

MINTING (St Andrew) *see* Bardney *Linc*

MIREHOUSE (St Andrew) *Carl 5* **P** *Bp* **P-in-c** C N CASEY

MIRFIELD (St Mary) *Leeds 10* **P** *Bp* **V** H C BAKER **NSM** H C BUTLER

MISERDEN (St Andrew) *see* Brimpsfield w Birdlip, Syde, Daglingworth etc *Glouc*

MISSENDEN, GREAT (St Peter and St Paul) w Ballinger and Little Hampden *Ox 17* **P** *Bp* **V** R E HARPER **NSM** C BAILEY

MISSENDEN, LITTLE (St John the Baptist) *Ox 17* **P** *Earl Howe* **P-in-c** J V SIMPSON

MISSION (St John the Baptist) *see* Bawtry w Austerfield, Misson, Everton and Mattersey *S'well*

MISTERTON (All Saints) *see* Beckingham, Walkeringham, Misterton, W Stockwith, Clayworth and Gringley-on-the-Hill *S'well*

MISTERTON (St Leonard) *see* Wulfric Benefice *B & W*

MISTERTON (St Leonard) *see* Gilmorton, Peatling Parva, Kimcote etc *Leic*

MISTLEY (St Mary and St Michael) w Manningtree and Bradfield *Chelmsf 22* **P** *DBP and Bp (jt)* **P-in-c** C A HILLS **NSM** J R BRIEN **OLM** C F SCARGILL

MITCHAM (Ascension) Pollards Hill *S'wark 13* **P** *Bp* **V** J M THOMAS **NSM** J E ROBERTS

MITCHAM (St Barnabas) *S'wark 13* **P** *Bp* **V** J G CAVALCANTI **C** S DAWSON **Hon C** T PAYNE

MITCHAM (St Mark) *S'wark 13* **P** *Bp* **V** N J STONE

MITCHAM (St Olave) *S'wark 13* **P** *The Crown* **P-in-c** R J WRIGHT

MITCHAM (St Peter and St Paul) *S'wark 13* **P** *Keble Coll Ox* **V** D M B PENNELLS **NSM** M J COCKFIELD

MITCHELDEAN (St Michael and All Angels) *see* Abenhall w Mitcheldean *Glouc*

MITFORD (St Mary Magdalene) and Hebron *Newc 11* **P** *Ld Chan and the Revd B W J Mitford (alt)* **P-in-c** J J L DOBSON **OLM** J ROWLEY

MIXBURY (All Saints) *see* Shelswell *Ox*

MIXENDEN (Holy Nativity) and Illingworth *Leeds 11* **P** *Bp and V Halifax (jt)* **V** R SUTHERLAND

MOBBERLEY (St Wilfrid) *Ches 12* **P** *Bp* **R** I BLAY

MOCCAS (St Michael and All Angels) *see* Cusop w Blakemere, Bredwardine w Brobury etc *Heref*

MODBURY (St George), Bigbury, Ringmore, Kingston, Aveton Gifford, and East Allington *Ex 13* **P** *Bp Ex, D&C Ex, DBP, MMCET, and P K M Ramm Esq* **R** N A BARKER

MODDERSHALL (All Saints) *see* Stone Ch Ch and Oulton *Lich*

MOGGERHANGER (St John the Evangelist) *see* Cople, Moggerhanger and Willington *St Alb*

MOLASH (St Peter) *see* King's Wood *Cant*

MOLDGREEN (Christ Church) and Rawthorpe St James *Leeds 6* **P** *R Kirkheaton and DBP (jt)* **P-in-c** H D ATKINSON

MOLESCROFT (St Leonard) *see* Beverley Minster *York*

MOLESEY, EAST (St Mary) (St Paul) *Guildf 8* **P** *Bp* **P-in-c** B C HUNT **C** R G LLOYD **NSM** L K KAYE-BESLEY

MOLESEY, WEST (St Peter) *Guildf 8* **P** *Canon W K Perry-Gore* **V** P A TAILBY

MOLESWORTH (St Peter) *see* W Leightonstone *Ely*

MOLLAND (St Mary)   *see* Bishopsnympton, Rose Ash, Mariansleigh etc *Ex*

MOLLINGTON (All Saints)   *see* Shires' Edge *Ox*

MOLTON, NORTH (All Saints)   *see* S Molton w Nymet St George, High Bray etc *Ex*

MOLTON, SOUTH (St Mary Magdalene) w Nymet St George, High Bray, Charles, Filleigh, East Buckland, Warkleigh w Satterleigh, Chittlehamholt, Kingsnympton, North Molton w Twitchen and Chittlehampton *Ex 18*   **P** *DBP*
P-in-c F M GRANDEY   **C** D P BAKER   **NSM** C M G POUNCEY, L P FLATT

MONEWDEN (St Mary)   *see* Mid Loes *St E*

MONGEHAM, GREAT (St Martin)   *see* Deal St Leon w St Rich and Sholden etc *Cant*

MONK BRETTON (St Paul) *Leeds 18*   **P** *V Royston*
OLM J M CROSSLAND

MONK FRYSTON (St Wilfrid of Ripon) and South Milford *York 4*   **P** *Ld Chan and Abp (alt)*   **R** J C HETHERINGTON
C D JOHNSON

MONK SHERBORNE (All Saints)   *see* The Sherbornes w Pamber *Win*

MONK SOHAM (St Peter)   *see* Four Rivers *St E*

MONKEN HADLEY (St Mary the Virgin) *Lon 14*   **P** *Bp*
R T RENZ

MONKHOPTON (St Peter)   *see* Upton Cressett w Monk Hopton *Heref*

MONKLAND (All Saints)   *see* Leominster *Heref*

MONKLEIGH (St George)   *see* Bideford, Northam, Westward Ho!, Appledore etc *Ex*

MONKLEIGH (St Mary)   *see* Bideford, Northam, Westward Ho!, Appledore etc *Ex*

MONKMOOR (St Peter)   *see* Shrewsbury H Cross *Lich*

MONKOKEHAMPTON (All Saints)   *see* Dolton, Dowland, Iddesleigh etc *Ex*

MONKS ELEIGH (St Peter) w Chelsworth and Brent Eleigh w Milden and Kettlebaston *St E 10*   **P** *Bp, Guild of All So, Ld Chan (2 turns), and M J Hawkins Esq*   **P-in-c** C MANSELL
NSM J WRIGHT

MONKS HORTON (St Peter)   *see* A20 Benefice *Cant*

MONKS KIRBY (St Edith)   *see* Revel Gp *Cov*

MONKS RISBOROUGH (St Dunstan)   *see* Risborough *Ox*

MONKSEATON (St Mary) *Newc 5*   **P** *Bp*   **V** P J KNIBBS
NSM P M MORAN

MONKSEATON (St Peter) *Newc 5*   **P** *Bp*   **V** *vacant*

MONKSILVER (All Saints)   *see* Quantock Towers *B & W*

MONKTON (St Mary Magdalene)   *see* Wantsum Gp *Cant*

MONKTON COMBE (St Michael)   *see* Combe Down w Monkton Combe and S Stoke *B & W*

MONKTON FARLEIGH (St Peter)   *see* N Bradford on Avon and Villages *Sarum*

MONKTON WYLD (St Andrew)   *see* Golden Cap Team *Sarum*

MONKTON, WEST (St Augustine) w Kingston St Mary, Broomfield and Cheddon Fitzpaine *B & W 18*   **P** *Bp and D&C (jt)*   **C** A J WOODWARD

MONKWEARMOUTH (All Saints) (St Andrew) (St Peter) *Dur 1*
P *Bp*   **TR** R G E BRADSHAW   **TV** A M WATSON
C P W D CHILD   **OLM** P G A SMITHSON

MONKWOOD (Mission Church)   *see* Bishop's Sutton and Ropley and W Tisted *Win*

MONNINGTON-ON-WYE (St Mary)   *see* Letton w Staunton, Byford, Mansel Gamage etc *Heref*

MONTACUTE (St Catherine of Alexandria)   *see* Odcombe, Brympton, Lufton and Montacute *B & W*

MONTFORD (St Chad)   *see* Bicton, Montford w Shrawardine and Fitz *Lich*

MONTON (St Paul)   *see* Eccles *Man*

MONXTON (St Mary)   *see* Portway and Danebury *Win*

MONYASH (St Leonard)   *see* Taddington, Chelmorton and Monyash etc *Derby*

MOOR (St Thomas)   *see* Fladbury, Hill and Moor, Wyre Piddle etc *Worc*

MOOR ALLERTON (St John the Evangelist) (St Stephen) and Shadwell Team Ministry *Leeds 14*   **P** *Patr Bd*
TR C P DOBBIN   **TV** D L M YOUNG, S V KAYE
NSM D L LOFTHOUSE

MOOR GRANGE (St Andrew)   *see* Abbeylands *Leeds*

MOOR MONKTON (All Saints)   *see* Rural Ainsty *York*

MOORCOURT (St Mary)   *see* Pembridge w Moor Court, Shobdon, Staunton etc *Heref*

MOORDOWN (St John the Baptist) *Win 8*   **P** *Bp*
V S W MILLER   **C** J M SHARP   **NSM** J L WILLIAMS

MOORE MILNER (Church Institute)   *see* Daresbury *Ches*

MOORENDS (St Wilfrith) *Sheff 10*   **P** *Bp*   **P-in-c** N J PAY

MOORHOUSE (Chantry Chapel)   *see* Kneesall w Laxton and Wellow *S'well*

MOORHOUSES (St Lawrence)   *see* Fen and Hill Gp *Linc*

MOORLAND Group, The *Truro 9*   **P** *Duchy of Cornwall (1 turn), Bp, D&C, and SMF (1 turn)*   **R** D A ROBERTS

MOORLINCH (Blessed Virgin Mary)   *see* Middlezoy w Othery, Moorlinch and Greinton *B & W*

MOORSHOLM (St Mary) *York 21*   **P** *Abp*   **V** M J HAZELTON

MOORSIDE (St Thomas)   *see* Oldham Moorside *Man*

MOORTOWN (St Stephen)   *see* Moor Allerton and Shadwell *Leeds*

MORBORNE (All Saints)   *see* Stilton w Denton and Caldecote etc *Ely*

MORCHARD BISHOP (St Mary)   *see* N Creedy *Ex*

MORCOTT (St Mary the Virgin)   *see* Barrowden and Wakerley w S Luffenham etc *Pet*

MORDEN (St Lawrence) (St George) (St Martin) (Emmanuel Church Hall) *S'wark 13*   **P** *Patr Bd*   **TR** D R HEATH-WHYTE
TV D M RUDDICK, D R H MCGOWAN, L J WELLS   **Hon C** P S OMUKU

MORDEN (St Mary)   *see* Red Post *Sarum*

MORDIFORD (Holy Rood)   *see* Fownhope w Mordiford, Brockhampton etc *Heref*

MORE (St Peter)   *see* Wentnor w Ratlinghope, Myndtown, Norbury etc *Heref*

MOREBATH (St George)   *see* Bampton, Morebath, Clayhanger, Petton etc *Ex*

MORECAMBE (Holy Trinity)   *see* Poulton-le-Sands w Morecambe St Laur *Blackb*

MORECAMBE (St Barnabas) *Blackb 11*   **P** *R Poulton-le-Sands*
V T H DAVIS

MORECAMBE (St Christopher)   *see* Bare *Blackb*

MORECAMBE (St James)   *see* Heysham *Blackb*

MORECAMBE (St John)   *see* Sandylands *Blackb*

MORECAMBE (St Peter)   *see* Heysham *Blackb*

MORECAMBE (The Ascension)   *see* Torrisholme *Blackb*

MORELEIGH (All Saints)   *see* Diptford, N Huish, Harberton, Harbertonford etc *Ex*

MORESBY (St Bridget) *Carl 5*   **P** *Earl of Lonsdale*   **R** *vacant*

MORESTEAD (not known)   *see* Twyford and Owslebury and Morestead etc *Win*

MORETON (Christ Church) *Ches 8*   **P** *Simeon's Trustees*
R G J COUSINS   **NSM** D A STOTT

MORETON (St Mary)   *see* Fyfield, Moreton w Bobbingworth etc *Chelmsf*

MORETON (St Mary)   *see* Adbaston, High Offley, Knightley, Norbury etc *Lich*

MORETON (St Nicholas), Woodsford and Crossways w Tincleton *Sarum 1*   **P** *R Frampton-Hobb Esq*   **R** J A BIRDSEYE

MORETON CORBET (St Bartholomew) *Lich 22*   **P** *C C Corbet Esq*   **R** *vacant*

MORETON HALL (Christ Church)   *see* Bury St Edmunds Ch Ch *St E*

MORETON MORRELL (Holy Cross)   *see* Newbold Pacey w Moreton Morrell *Cov*

MORETON PINKNEY (St Mary the Virgin)   *see* Culworth w Sulgrave and Thorpe Mandeville etc *Pet*

MORETON SAY (St Margaret of Antioch)   *see* Adderley, Ash, Calverhall, Ightfield etc *Lich*

MORETON VALENCE (St Stephen)   *see* Eastington, Frocester, Haresfield etc *Glouc*

MORETON, NORTH (All Saints)   *see* The Churn *Ox*

MORETON, SOUTH (St John the Baptist) *as above*

MORETONHAMPSTEAD (St Andrew), Manaton, North Bovey and Lustleigh *Ex 8*   **P** *Bp and DBP (jt)*
R S G FRANKLIN

MORETON-IN-MARSH (St David) w Batsford, Todenham, Lower Lemington and Longborough w Sezincote *Glouc 8*
P *Bp and Lord Dulverton (1 turn), and Bp, Lord Dulverton, Lord Leigh, and Mrs S Peake (1 turn)*   **R** S M WOOKEY
C B J P THOMPSON   **NSM** J POUT

MORETON-ON-LUGG (St Andrew)   *see* Pipe-cum-Lyde and Moreton-on-Lugg *Heref*

MORGAN'S VALE (St Birinus)   *see* Forest and Avon *Sarum*

MORLAND (St Lawrence), Thrimby, Gt Strickland and Cliburn *Carl 1*   **P** *Lord Hothfield and D&C (jt)*
P-in-c S J FYFE   **NSM** K M BUTTERFIELD

MORLEY (St Botolph)   *see* High Oak, Hingham and Scoulton w Wood Rising *Nor*

MORLEY (St Matthew) and Smalley *Derby 12*   **P** *Bp*
V L SHEMILT

MORLEY (St Peter)   *see* High Oak, Hingham and Scoulton w Wood Rising *Nor*

MORLEY (St Peter) (St Paul) *Leeds 15*   **P** *Patr Bd*
TV M J GODFREY   **OLM** K M DAVIS

MORNINGTHORPE (St John the Baptist)   *see* Hempnall *Nor*

MORPETH (St Aidan) (St James) (St Mary the Virgin) *Newc 11*
P *Bp*   **R** S J H WHITE   **C** E ROOKWOOD (NEE TASH)

MORRIS GREEN (St Bede)   *see* Bolton St Bede *Man*

MORSTON (All Saints)　　*see* Stiffkey and Bale *Nor*

MORTEHOE (St Mary Magdalene)　　*see* Ilfracombe, Lee, Woolacombe, Bittadon etc *Ex*

MORTIMER COMMON (St John)　　*see* Stratfield Mortimer and Mortimer W End etc *Ox*

MORTIMER WEST END (St Saviour)　*as above*

MORTLAKE (St Mary) w East Sheen *S'wark 16*　　**P** *Patr Bd*
TR A L NICKSON　　**TV** S G LEE　　**C** T P CARSON　　**Hon C** P D KING

MORTOMLEY (St Saviour) High Green *Sheff 3*　　**P** *Bp*
V S D BESSANT

MORTON (Holy Cross) and Stonebroom w Shirland *Derby 1*
　P *Bp, St Jo Coll Cam, Adn Chesterfield, and trustees (by turn)*
R M I JACQUES　　**NSM** C D WOOD, J A EPTON, J A S WOOD

MORTON (St Denis)　　*see* Rolleston w Fiskerton, Morton and Upton *S'well*

MORTON (St John the Baptist)　　*see* Ringstone in Aveland Gp *Linc*

MORTON (St Luke) *Leeds 5*　　**P** *Bp*　　**P-in-c** M C CANSDALE
NSM J RAMSDEN

MORTON (St Paul)　　*see* Gainsborough and Morton *Linc*

MORTON (St Philip and St James)　　*see* Llanyblodwel, Llanymynech, Morton and Trefonen *Lich*

MORTON BAGOT (Holy Trinity)　　*see* Arden Marches *Cov*

MORTON, EAST　　*see* Morton St Luke *Leeds*

MORVAH (St Bridget of Sweden)　　*see* Pendeen w Morvah *Truro*

MORVAL (St Wenna)　　*see* Duloe, Herodsfoot, Morval and St Pinnock *Truro*

MORVILLE (St Gregory) w Aston Eyre *Heref 8*　　**P** *DBP*
V S H CAWDELL　　**Hon C** H J PATTERSON

MORWENSTOW (St John the Baptist)　　*see* Kilkhampton w Morwenstow *Truro*

MOSBOROUGH (St Mark) *Sheff 1*　　**P** *Bp*　　**V** S T STEWART

MOSELEY (St Agnes) *Birm 5*　　**P** *V Moseley St Mary*
V P H ANSELL

MOSELEY (St Anne) (St Mary) *Birm 5*　　**P** *Bp*　　**C** H S WHITE
NSM F J BERRY

MOSLEY COMMON (St John)　　*see* Astley, Tyldesley and Mosley Common *Man*

MOSS BANK (Mission Church)　　*see* Carr Mill *Liv*

MOSS SIDE (Christ Church) *Man 3*　　**P** *Trustees*
R S D A KILLWICK

MOSSER (St Michael's Chapel)　　*see* Clifton, Dean and Mosser *Carl*

MOSSER (St Philip)　*as above*

MOSSLEY (Holy Trinity)　　*see* Congleton *Ches*

MOSSLEY (St George) *Man 13*　　**P** *R Ashton-under-Lyne St Mich*
OLM P PHILLIPS

MOSSLEY ESTATE (St Thomas Church)　　*see* Bloxwich *Lich*

MOSSLEY HILL (St Barnabas) (St Matthew and St James) *Liv 4*
　P *Patr Bd*　　**TV** A KENNEDY　　**NSM** W H ADDY

MOSSWOOD (St Barnabas)　　*see* Cannock and Huntington *Lich*

MOSTERTON (St Mary)　　*see* Beaminster Area *Sarum*

MOSTON (St Chad) *Man 4*　　**P** *Bp*　　**P-in-c** K S REEVES
OLM I L SMITH

MOSTON (St John) Ashley Lane *Man 4*　　**P** *Bp*
P-in-c K S REEVES　　**OLM** I L SMITH

MOSTON (St Luke)　　*see* Lightbowne *Man*

MOSTON (St Mary) *Man 4*　　**P** *D&C*
P-in-c M R M CALLADINE

MOTCOMBE (St Mary)　　*see* Shaftesbury *Sarum*

MOTSPUR PARK (Holy Cross) *S'wark 13*　　**P** *Bp*　　**V** R S TAYLOR

MOTTINGHAM (St Andrew) (St Alban Mission Church)
S'wark 3　　**P** *Bp*　　**R** I M WELCH

MOTTINGHAM (St Edward the Confessor) *S'wark 3*　　**P** *Bp*
V M J JACKSON　　**NSM** S J CHARLES

MOTTISFONT (St Andrew)　　*see* Broughton, Bossington, Houghton and Mottisfont *Win*

MOTTISTONE (St Peter and St Paul)　　*see* Brighstone and Brooke w Mottistone *Portsm*

MOTTRAM IN LONGDENDALE (St Michael) *Ches 14*　　**P** *Bp*
V J HALSTEAD　　**C** A W KNIGHT

MOULSECOOMB (St Andrew) *Chich 19*　　**P** *Bp*
P-in-C J C WALL　　**TV** B GRAY-HAMMOND　　**C** A E WHALLEY
NSM J W M COLLINS

MOULSFORD (St John the Baptist)　　*see* Cholsey and Moulsford *Ox*

MOULSHAM (St John the Evangelist) *Chelmsf 10*　　**P** *Dean*
P-in-c C SMITH　　**C** A T GRIFFITHS, S R GILLINGHAM

MOULSHAM (St Luke) *Chelmsf 10*　　**P** *Bp*　　**V** C SMITH
C A T GRIFFITHS, S R GILLINGHAM

MOULSOE (The Assumption of the Blessed Virgin Mary)
see Newport Pagnell w Lathbury and Moulsoe *Ox*

MOULTON (Mission Church)　　*see* E Richmond *Leeds*

MOULTON (St Peter and St Paul) *Pet 4*　　**P** *Ch Soc Trust*
V A T J BYFIELD　　**C** R J BURBIDGE

MOULTON (St Peter)　　*see* Dalham, Gazeley, Higham, Kentford and Moulton *St E*

MOULTON (St Stephen the Martyr) *Ches 6*　　**P** *R Davenham*
P-in-c G R KEGG　　**NSM** G KEGG

MOULTON, GREAT (St Michael)　　*see* Bunwell, Carleton Rode, Tibenham, Gt Moulton etc *Nor*

MOUNT BURES (St John)　　*see* Wormingford, Mt Bures and Lt Horkesley *Chelmsf*

MOUNT HAWKE (St John the Baptist)　　*see* St Agnes and Mount Hawke w Mithian *Truro*

MOUNT PELLON (Christ Church)　　*see* Halifax St Aug and Mount Pellon *Leeds*

MOUNTFIELD (All Saints)　　*see* Brightling, Mountfield and Netherfield *Chich*

MOUNTNESSING (St Giles)　　*see* Margaretting w Mountnessing and Buttsbury *Chelmsf*

MOUNTSORREL (Christ Church) (St Peter) *Leic 6*　　**P** *CPAS*
and Bp　　**P-in-c** C E RESCH

MOW COP (St Luke's Mission Church)　　*see* Odd Rode *Ches*

MOW COP (St Thomas) *Lich 11*　　**P** *Prime Min*
P-in-c G C HUBBARD

MOWSLEY (St Nicholas)　　*see* Hexagon *Leic*

MOXLEY (All Saints)　　*see* Darlaston and Moxley *Lich*

MUCH　　*see also under substantive place name*

MUCH BIRCH (St Mary and St Thomas à Becket)
see Wormelow Hundred *Heref*

MUCHELNEY (St Peter and St Paul)　　*see* Langport Area *B & W*

MUCKLESTONE (St Mary)　　*see* Ashley and Mucklestone and Broughton and Croxton *Lich*

MUDEFORD (All Saints) *Win 9*　　**P** *Bp*　　**V** H M GRIFFISS

MUDFORD (Blessed Virgin Mary)　　*see* Chilton Cantelo, Ashington, Mudford, Rimpton etc *B & W*

MUGGINTON (All Saints) and Kedleston *Derby 11*
　P *Major J W Chandos-Pole*　　**P-in-c** A P HARPER

MUGGLESWICK (All Saints)　　*see* Blanchland w Hunstanworth and Edmundbyers etc *Newc*

MUKER (St Mary)　　*see* Swaledale *Leeds*

MULBARTON (St Mary Magdalene) w Bracon Ash, Hethel and Flordon *Nor 7*　　**P** R T Berney Esq *(1 turn), Mrs R M Watkinson (2 turns), DBP (1 turn), and Ld Chan (1 turn)*
R A D MILLER

MULLION (St Mellanus) *Truro 4*　　**P** *Bp*　　**P-in-c** S O GRIFFITHS

MUMBY (St Thomas of Canterbury)　　*see* Willoughby *Linc*

MUNCASTER (St Michael)　　*see* Eskdale, Irton, Muncaster and Waberthwaite *Carl*

MUNDEN, LITTLE (All Saints)　　*see* Standon and The Mundens w Sacombe *St Alb*

MUNDESLEY (All Saints)　　*see* Trunch Group *Nor*

MUNDFORD (St Leonard) w Lynford *Nor 13*　　**P** *Ch Patr Trust*
R *vacant*

MUNDHAM (St Peter)　　*see* Brooke, Kirstead, Mundham w Seething and Thwaite *Nor*

MUNDHAM, NORTH (St Stephen) w Hunston and Merston
Chich 2　　**P** *St Jo Coll Cam*　　**P-in-c** J A T RUSSELL

MUNGRISDALE (St Kentigern)　　*see* Greystoke w Penruddock, Mungrisdale etc *Carl*

MUNSLEY (St Bartholomew)　　*see* Ledbury *Heref*

MUNSLOW (St Michael)　　*see* Diddlebury w Munslow, Holdgate and Tugford *Heref*

MUNSTER SQUARE (Christ Church) (St Mary Magdalene)
Lon 17　　**P** *Bp*　　**V** M R POOLE

MURCOTT (Mission Room)　　*see* Ray Valley *Ox*

MURSLEY (St Mary the Virgin)　　*see* Newton Longville, Mursley, Swanbourne etc *Ox*

MURSTON (All Saints) w Bapchild and Tonge *Cant 15*　　**P** *Abp and St Jo Coll Cam (jt)*　　**P-in-c** G M A ROGERS　　**C** L M JONES

MURTON (Holy Trinity)　　*see* Hawthorn and Murton *Dur*

MURTON (St James)　　*see* Osbaldwick w Murton *York*

MURTON (St John the Baptist)　　*see* Heart of Eden *Carl*

MUSBURY (St Michael)　　*see* Colyton, Musbury, Southleigh and Branscombe *Ex*

MUSBURY (St Thomas) *Blackb 1*　　**P** *The Crown*
NSM D ALLSOP, J A BALKWELL

MUSGRAVE (St Theobald)　　*see* Brough w Stainmore, Musgrave and Warcop *Carl*

MUSKHAM, NORTH (St Wilfrid) and SOUTH (St Wilfrid)
S'well 3　　**P** *Ld Chan*　　**NSM** C WALL

MUSTON (All Saints)　　*see* Hunmanby w Muston *York*

MUSTON (St John the Baptist)　　*see* Vale of Belvoir *Leic*

MUSWELL HILL (St James) (St Matthew) *Lon 20*　　**P** *Bp and CPAS (jt)*　　**V** C M GREEN　　**C** G J DALY, J SALLADIN, M I JOHN
NSM H C HENDRY

MUTFORD (St Andrew)　　*see* Carlton Colville and Mutford *Nor*

MUXTON (St John the Evangelist)   see Lilleshall and Muxton
Lich
MYDDELTON SQUARE (St Mark)   see Clerkenwell St Mark Lon
MYDDLE (St Peter) Lich 22   P Bp   P-in-c A J B CLAYTON
OLM A EVANS
MYLAND (St Michael)   see Colchester St Mich Myland Chelmsf
MYLOR (St Mylor) w Flushing Truro 3   P Bp
P-in-c J A JAMES   NSM A J STEVENSON
MYLOR BRIDGE (All Saints)   see Mylor w Flushing Truro
MYMMS   see also MIMMS
MYMMS, NORTH (St Mary)   see Bp's Hatfield, Lemsford and
N Mymms St Alb
MYMMS, SOUTH (King Charles the Martyr)   see Potters Bar K
Chas St Alb
MYMMS, SOUTH (St Giles) and Ridge St Alb 14   P DBP
NSM K L TURNER
MYNDTOWN (St John the Baptist)   see Wentnor w
Ratlinghope, Myndtown, Norbury etc Heref
MYTHOLMROYD (St Michael)   see Erringden Leeds
MYTON ON SWALE (St Mary)   see Brafferton w Pilmoor,
Myton-on-Swale etc York
NABURN (St Matthew)   see Escrick and Stillingfleet w
Naburn York
NACKINGTON (St Mary)   see Bridge Cant
NACTON (St Martin) and Levington w Bucklesham and
Foxhall w Kirton and Falkenham St E 2   P Ld Chan and
DBP (alt)   NSM H STALKER
NADDER VALLEY Sarum 11   P Patr Bd (4 turns), Ld Chan
(1 turn)   TR G SOUTHGATE   TV A STALEY, J D TAILBY
C M H G HAYTER   Dss A R SYMES
NAFFERTON (All Saints) w Wansford York 10   P Abp
P-in-c B J LEES
NAILSEA (Christ Church) w Tickenham B & W 12   P CPAS
(3 turns), Ld Chan (1 turn)   R A R G ROAKE
NAILSEA (Holy Trinity) B & W 12   P MMCET   R C J TRICKEY
C J E PENNINGTON, J S TILLEY   NSM T S DEAN
NAILSTONE (All Saints) and Carlton w Shackerstone Leic 10
P The Crown and DBP (alt)   C J G HARGREAVES
NAILSWORTH (St George) w Shortwood, Horsley and
Newington Bapath w Kingscote Glouc 4   P Bp
V M R G SMITH   NSM S C SOBCZAK
NANPANTAN (St Mary in Charnwood) Leic 6   P Bp and Em
Coll Cam (jt)   V S E FIELD   C L N COLLEY
NANPEAN (St George)   see St Stephen in Brannel Truro
NANSTALLON (St Stephen's Mission Room)   see Bodmin w
Lanhydrock and Lanivet Truro
NANTWICH (St Mary) Ches 15   P Q H Crewe Esq and
J C Crewe Esq (jt)   R B F WILSON   C K DAVID
NSM S T SNELLING
NAPTON-ON-THE-HILL (St Lawrence), Lower Shuckburgh
and Stockton Cov 10   P Ld Chan (2 turns), Sir Rupert
Shuckburgh Bt (1 turn), and New Coll Ox (2 turns)
C G S ROBERTS, R D CLUCAS
NAR VALLEY, The Nor 13   P Bp (1 turn), Earl of Leicester, H C
Birkbeck Esq, and Bp (1 turn)   R S R NAIRN
NSM R G HOWELLS
NARBOROUGH (All Saints)   see Nar Valley Nor
NARBOROUGH (All Saints) and Huncote Leic 7   P SMF
R A J HAWKER
NARFORD (St Mary)   see Nar Valley Nor
NASEBY (All Saints)   see Clipston w Naseby and Haselbech w
Kelmarsh Pet
NASH (All Saints)   see Buckingham Ox
NASH (St John the Baptist)   see Tenbury Heref
NASSINGTON (St Mary the Virgin and All Saints), Apethorpe,
Thornhaugh and Wansford, Woodnewton and Yarwell
(The Watersmete Benefice) Pet 10   P Bp and Personal Reps
Lord Brassey of Apethorpe (jt)   V M R MATTHEWS
NATELY SCURES (St Swithun)   see N Hants Downs Win
NATLAND (St Mark) Carl 10   P V Kendal H Trin
P-in-c A WHITTAKER   NSM M MASHITER, M P JAYNE
NAUGHTON (St Mary)   see Bildeston w Wattisham and
Lindsey, Whatfield etc St E
NAUNTON (St Andrew)   see The Guitings, Cutsdean, Farmcote
etc Glouc
NAUNTON BEAUCHAMP (St Bartholomew)   see Abberton, The
Flyfords, Naunton Beauchamp etc Worc
NAVENBY (St Peter)   see Graffoe Gp Linc
NAVESTOCK (St Thomas)   see Bentley Common, Kelvedon
Hatch and Navestock Chelmsf
NAYLAND (St James) w Wiston St E 3   P Ld Chan (2 turns) and
DBP (1 turn)   V vacant
NAZEING (All Saints) (St Giles) Chelmsf 4   P Ld Chan
P-in-c H E-A GHEORGHIU GOULD
NEASDEN (St Catherine w St Paul) Lon 21   P Bp and D&C
St Paul's (jt)   V R W HARRISON

NEATISHEAD (St Peter)   see Ashmanhaugh, Barton Turf etc Nor
NECTON (All Saints), Holme Hale w Pickenham, North and
South Nor 13   P Major-Gen R S Broke, Ch Soc Trust, MMCET
and S Pickenham Estate Co Ltd (jt)   R S L THORP
NEDGING (St Mary)   see Bildeston w Wattisham and Lindsey,
Whatfield etc St E
NEEDHAM (St Peter)   see Redenhall w Scole Nor
NEEDHAM MARKET (St John the Baptist) w Badley St E 1
P PCC   P-in-c D R WILLIAMS
NEEN SAVAGE (St Mary)   see Cleobury Mortimer w Hopton
Wafers etc Heref
NEEN SOLLARS (All Saints) as above
NEENTON (All Saints)   see Ditton Priors w Neenton, Burwarton
etc Heref
NEITHROP (St Paul)   see Banbury St Paul Ox
NELSON (St Bede)   see Lt Marsden w Nelson St Mary and
Nelson St Bede Blackb
NELSON (St Mary) as above
NELSON (St Paul) as above
NEMPNETT THRUBWELL (Blessed Virgin Mary)   see Chew Stoke
w Nempnett Thrubwell B & W
NENTHEAD (St John)   see Alston Moor Newc
NESS Group, The Linc 19   P Ld Chan (1 turn), Bp and DBP
(2 turns)   V J M BEADLE   OLM M J HOWARD
NESS, GREAT (St Andrew)   see Ruyton XI Towns w Gt and
Lt Ness Lich
NESS, LITTLE (St Martin) as above
NESTON (St Mary and St Helen) Ches 9   P D&C
V A D H DAWSON   NSM J CALVERT
NESTON (St Phillip and St James)   see Gtr Corsham and Lacock
Bris
NESTON, LITTLE (St Michael and All Angels)   see Neston Ches
NETHER   see under substantive place name
NETHERAVON (All Saints)   see Avon River Sarum
NETHERBURY (St Mary)   see Beaminster Area Sarum
NETHEREXE (St John the Baptist)   see Brampford Speke,
Cadbury, Newton St Cyres etc Ex
NETHERFIELD (St George) S'well 7   P DBP   R vacant
NETHERFIELD (St John the Baptist)   see Brightling, Mountfield
and Netherfield Chich
NETHERHAMPTON (St Katherine)   see Wilton w
Netherhampton and Fugglestone Sarum
NETHERLEY (Christ Church)   see Gateacre Liv
NETHERSEAL (St Peter)   see Seale and Lullington w Coton in
the Elms Derby
NETHERTHONG (All Saints)   see Upper Holme Valley Leeds
NETHERTHORPE (St Stephen)   see Sheffield Vine Sheff
NETHERTON (All Souls)   see Maryport, Netherton and Flimby
Carl
NETHERTON (St Andrew)   see Middlestown Leeds
NETHERTON (St Andrew)   see Darby End and Netherton Worc
NETHERTON (St Oswald) Liv 1   P Bp, Patr Bd
TR D H STATTER   TV S M ELLIOTT
NETLEY MARSH (St Matthew)   see Totton Win
NETTLEBED (St Bartholomew) w Bix, Highmoor, Pishill and
Rotherfield Greys Ox 24   P DBP, Earl of Macclesfield, Ch Patr
Trust, and Trin Coll Ox (jt)   R B J BAILEY
NSM A C WILLIAMS
NETTLECOMBE (Blessed Virgin Mary)   see Quantock Towers
B & W
NETTLEDEN (St Lawrence)   see Gt Berkhamsted, Gt and
Lt Gaddesden etc St Alb
NETTLEHAM (All Saints) Linc 5   P Bp   V R H CROSSLAND
NSM C A ZOTOV, R O THORNTON
NETTLESTEAD (St Mary the Virgin)   see E Peckham and
Nettlestead Roch
NETTLESTEAD (St Mary)   see Gt and Lt Blakenham w Baylham
and Nettlestead St E
NETTLETON (St John the Baptist)   see Swallow Linc
NETTLETON (St Mary)   see By Brook Bris
NEVENDON (St Peter)   see Pitsea w Nevendon Chelmsf
NEVILLE'S CROSS (St John)   see Dur St Marg and Neville's Cross
St Jo Dur
NEW   see also under substantive place name
NEW BOROUGH and Leigh (St John the Evangelist) Sarum 9
P Ch Soc Trust   V P H BRECKWOLDT   C B H DYSON
NEW BUILDINGS (Beacon Church)   see Crediton, Shobrooke
and Sandford etc Ex
NEW FERRY (St Mark) Ches 8   P R Bebington
V A Q GREENHOUGH   NSM A D DRURY
NEW HAW (All Saints) Guildf 11   P Bp   P-in-c F E SIMON
OLM M OLIVER
NEW MILL (Christ Church)   see Upper Holme Valley Leeds
NEW MILLS (St George) Derby 6   P V Glossop   V J C BAINES
NSM J M OVERTON, N M PEPPER

NEWARK-UPON-TRENT (St Mary Magdalene) (Christ Church) (St Leonard) w Coddington S'well 3   P The Crown
P-in-c S F MORRIS   **TV** D E ANDERTON, S J TREDWELL
NSM P R SMITH
NEWBALD (St Nicholas) York 13   **P** Abp   **P-in-c** M R BUSHBY
NEWBIGGIN (St Edmund)   see Kirkby Thore w Temple Sowerby and Newbiggin Carl
NEWBIGGIN HALL (St Wilfrid) Newc 4   **P** Bp   **V** S L MILLER
NEWBIGGIN-BY-THE-SEA (St Bartholomew)   see Woodhorn w Newbiggin Newc
NEWBOLD (St John the Evangelist) w Dunston Derby 5
P R Chesterfield   **V** vacant
NEWBOLD (St Peter)   see Deeplish and Newbold Man
NEWBOLD DE VERDUN (St James), Barlestone and Kirkby Mallory Leic 10   **P** Bp and Trin Coll Ox (jt)
R T H C MEYRICK   **NSM** J A DOWNS
NEWBOLD ON AVON (St Botolph) Cov 6   **P** H A F W Boughton Leigh Esq   **V** P M WILKINSON
NEWBOLD ON STOUR (St David)   see Stourdene Gp Cov
NEWBOLD PACEY (St George) w Moreton Morrell Cov 8
P Qu Coll Ox and Lt Col J E Little (alt)   **V** J D PARKER
NEWBOROUGH (All Saints)   see Hanbury, Newborough, Rangemore and Tutbury Lich
NEWBOROUGH (St Bartholomew)   see Eye, Newborough and Thorney Pet
NEWBOTTLE (St James)   see King's Sutton and Newbottle and Charlton Pet
NEWBOTTLE (St Matthew) Dur 14   **P** Bp   **V** E WILKINSON
NEWBOURNE (St Mary)   see Waldringfield w Hemley and Newbourn St E
NEWBROUGH (St Peter)   see Warden w Newbrough Newc
NEWBURGH (Christ Church) w Westhead Liv 11   **P** Bp
and V Ormskirk (jt)   **V** G A MILFORD   **OLM** C DRAPER, J SEPHTON
NEWBURN (St Michael and All Angels) Newc 4   **P** MMCET
V R J FILLINGHAM   **OLM** M P LEDGER
NEWBURY (St George) (St John the Evangelist) Ox 6   **P** Bp
V P H COWAN   **C** D K M DAVISON   **NSM** T WINROW
NEWBURY (St Nicolas and St Mary Speenhamland) Ox 6
P Bp   **R** W D HUNTER SMART   **C** W J BRIGGS
NSM M H YATES, M YATES
NEWBY (St Mark) York 15   **P** Abp   **V** M J LEIGH
NSM D MACIVER
NEWCASTLE (Christ Church) (St Ann) Newc 2   **P** Bp
P-in-c A W MARKS   **C** A D O'GRADY
NEWCASTLE (St Andrew) (St Luke) Newc 2   **P** Bp and V Newcastle (jt)   **P-in-c** G EVANS   **NSM** R C I WARD
NEWCASTLE (St John the Evangelist)   see Clun Valley Heref
NEWCASTLE (St Philip) and St Augustine and (St Matthew w St Mary) Newc 4   **P** Bp   **V** R G S DEADMAN
NEWCASTLE UNDER LYME (St George) Lich 9   **P** R Newcastle w Butterton   **V** M F BALL
NEWCASTLE UNDER LYME (St Giles) w Butterton Lich 9
P Simeon's Trustees   **R** R F DABORN   **NSM** P NISBECK
OLM J WARHAM, M A TAYLOR
NEWCASTLE UNDER LYME (St Paul) Lich 9   **P** Trustees
V D J LLOYD
NEWCASTLE UPON TYNE (Holy Cross) Newc 4   **P** Bp
V G WORT   **C** J MOONEY
NEWCASTLE UPON TYNE (St Barnabas and St Jude) Newc 2
P V Jesmond Clayton Memorial and CPAS (alt)   **P-in-c** M WROE
C T SANDERSON
NEWCASTLE UPON TYNE (St Francis) High Heaton Newc 3
P Bp   **V** vacant
NEWCASTLE UPON TYNE (St Gabriel) Heaton Newc 3   **P** Bp
V J H LAWSON   **C** A J KENNEDY
NEWCASTLE UPON TYNE (St George) (St Hilda) Newc 2
P Bp   **V** N A CHAMBERLAIN   **NSM** P H PEARSON
OLM C M CROMPTON
NEWCASTLE UPON TYNE (St John the Baptist) Newc 2   **P** V Newc   **P-in-c** N A V BUXTON
NEWCASTLE UPON TYNE (St Thomas) Proprietary Chapel Newc []C M LACK   **NSM** J SKINNER
NEWCASTLE UPON TYNE (St Thomas) Proprietary Chapel Newc 2[]C M LACK   **NSM** J SKINNER
NEWCHAPEL (St James the Apostle) Lich 11   **P** CPAS
V W E SLATER
NEWCHURCH (All Saints) Portsm 7   **P** Bp
V J F O'SHAUGHNESSY
NEWCHURCH (not known) w Croft Liv 15   **P** Bp
R C I JONES   **OLM** B ALLDRED
NEWCHURCH (St Nicholas w St John)   see Rossendale Middle Valley Man
NEWCHURCH (St Peter and St Paul)   see Romney Marsh Cant
NEWDIGATE (St Peter)   see Surrey Weald Guildf

NEWENDEN (St Peter)   see Rother and Oxney Cant
NEWENT (St Mary the Virgin) and Gorsley w Cliffords Mesne
Glouc 3   **P** Bp   **R** S I V MASON   **NSM** R G CHIVERS
NEWHALL (St John) Derby 16   **P** Bp   **P-in-c** J L WHITEHEAD
NEWHAVEN (St Michael) Chich 21   **P** Ch Patr Trust
R M M MILLER
NEWHEY (St Thomas) Man 17   **P** Bp   **NSM** S E WARD
NEWICK (St Mary) Chich 18   **P** Ch Soc Trust   **R** vacant
NEWINGTON (St Christopher)   see St Laur in Thanet Cant
NEWINGTON (St Giles)   see Dorchester Ox
NEWINGTON (St John the Baptist) w Hull St Andrew York 14
P Abp and V Hull H Trin (jt)   **V** T A COTSON
NSM L A ROBINSON
NEWINGTON (St Mary the Virgin)   see The Six Cant
NEWINGTON (St Mary) S'wark 10   **P** Bp   **P-in-c** G A FRASER
Hon C M E TODD
NEWINGTON (St Nicholas)   see Cheriton w Newington Cant
NEWINGTON (St Paul) S'wark 10   **P** Bp
P-in-c K L HACKER HUGHES
NEWINGTON, SOUTH (St Peter ad Vincula)   see Bloxham w Milcombe and S Newington Ox
NEWLAND (All Saints)   see Coleford, Staunton, Newland, Redbrook etc Glouc
NEWLAND (St John)   see Hull St Jo Newland York
NEWLAND (St Lawrence)   see Bradwell on Sea and St Lawrence Chelmsf
NEWLANDS (not known)   see Upper Derwent Carl
NEWLAY LANE (St Margaret's Church Hall)   see Bramley Leeds
NEWLYN (St Newlyn) Truro 5   **P** Bp   **P-in-c** H L SAMSON
NEWLYN (St Peter) Truro 5   **P** Bp   **P-in-c** K R OWEN
C A M YATES, S YATES
NEWMARKET (All Saints) St E 11   **P** Bp   **V** M E OSBORNE
NSM S P SHAW
NEWMARKET (St Mary the Virgin) w Exning St Agnes St E 11
P Bp and DBP (alt)   **R** J C HARDY
NEWNHAM (St Mark)   see Cambridge St Mark Ely
NEWNHAM (St Michael and All Angels)   see Badby w Newham and Charwelton w Fawsley etc Pet
NEWNHAM (St Nicholas)   see N Hants Downs Win
NEWNHAM (St Peter) w Awre and Blakeney Glouc 1
P Haberdashers' Co and Bp (alt)   **V** R W JAMES
NEWNHAM (St Vincent)   see Ashwell w Hinxworth and Newnham St Alb
NEWNTON, NORTH (St James)   see Vale of Pewsey Sarum
NEWPORT (St John the Baptist) Portsm 8   **P** Ch Patr Trust
V K P ARKELL   **NSM** J K HALLAM
NEWPORT (St John the Baptist)   see Barnstaple Ex
NEWPORT (St Mary the Virgin) w Widdington, Quendon and Rickling Chelmsf 21   **P** Bp and DBP (jt)   **V** N R MCLEOD
NEWPORT (St Nicholas) w Longford, and Chetwynd Lich 16
P Bp   **V** S MITCHELL
NEWPORT (St Stephen)   see Howden York
NEWPORT (St Thomas) Portsm 8   **P** Bp   **V** K P ARKELL
NSM J K HALLAM
NEWPORT PAGNELL (St Luke) w Lathbury and Moulsoe Ox 16
P Bp, Ch Ch Ox, and Lord Carrington (jt)   **R** N A P EVANS
NSM K BROWNE   **OLM** G M BELL
NEWQUAY (St Michael) Truro 7   **P** Bp   **NSM** P J KNEEBONE
NEWSHAM (St Bede) Newc 1   **P** Bp   **V** R J PRINGLE
NEWSHOLME (St John)   see Oakworth Leeds
NEWSOME (St John the Evangelist)   see Em TM Leeds
NEWTIMBER (St John the Evangelist)   see Poynings w Edburton, Newtimber and Pyecombe Chich
NEWTON (Good Shepherd)   see Clifton w Newton and Brownsover Cov
NEWTON (Mission Church)   see Embleton w Rennington and Rock Newc
NEWTON (St Botolph)   see S Lafford Linc
NEWTON (St John the Baptist)   see Clodock and Longtown w Craswall, Llanveynoe etc Heref
NEWTON (St Margaret)   see Harston w Hauxton and Newton Ely
NEWTON (St Mary) w Flowery Field Ches 14   **P** V Mottram
V A C WOODCOCK   **NSM** C W VINEY
NEWTON (St Michael and All Angels) Ches 8   **P** R W Kirby St Bridget   **V** C J COVERLEY
NEWTON (St Oswald)   see Gt Ayton w Easby and Newton under Roseberry York
NEWTON (St Petrock)   see Shebbear, Buckland Filleigh, Sheepwash etc Ex
NEWTON ABBOT (St Paul)   see Wolborough and Ogwell Ex
NEWTON ARLOSH (St John the Evangelist)   see Bowness-on-Solway, Kirkbride and Newton Arlosh Carl
NEWTON AYCLIFFE (St Clare)   see Gt Aycliffe Dur
NEWTON BLOSSOMVILLE (St Nicolas)   see Lavendon w Cold Brayfield, Clifton Reynes etc Ox

NEWTON BROMSWOLD (St Peter)   *see* Rushden St Mary w Newton Bromswold *Pet*

NEWTON BY TOFT (St Michael)   *see* Middle Rasen Gp *Linc*

NEWTON FERRERS (Holy Cross) w Revelstoke *Ex 20*   **P** *Bp and Comdr P E Yonge*   **P-in-c** A C LEGGE

NEWTON FLOTMAN (St Mary the Virgin), Swainsthorpe, Tasburgh, Tharston, Saxlingham Nethergate and Shotesham *Nor 5*   **P** *Patr Bd*   **TR** S A GAZE   **TV** D M DAVIDSON   **C** M J E HARTLEY

NEWTON GREEN (All Saints)   *see* Boxford, Edwardstone, Groton etc *St E*

NEWTON HALL (All Saints)   *see* Dur N *Dur*

NEWTON HARCOURT (St Luke)   *see* Wistow *Leic*

NEWTON HEATH (All Saints) *Man 4*   **P** *Prime Min and D&C (alt)*   **R** A P WICKENS   **OLM** I L SMITH

NEWTON IN MAKERFIELD (Emmanuel)   *see* Newton *Liv*

NEWTON IN MAKERFIELD (St Peter) *as above*

NEWTON IN THE ISLE (St James)   *see* Leverington, Newton and Tydd St Giles *Ely*

NEWTON LONGVILLE (St Faith), Mursley, Swanbourne, Little Horwood and Drayton Parslow *Ox 15*   **P** *New Coll Ox, Ch Soc Trust, Lord Cottesloe, Ch Patr Trust, and MMCET (jt)*   **V** S G FAULKS   **Hon C** J M SAUNDERS   **OLM** J K BROWN

NEWTON ON OUSE (All Saints)   *see* Skelton w Shipton and Newton on Ouse *York*

NEWTON POPPLEFORD (St Luke)   *see* Ottery St Mary, Alfington, W Hill, Tipton etc *Ex*

NEWTON PURCELL (St Michael)   *see* Shelswell *Ox*

NEWTON REGIS (St Mary)   *see* N Warks *Birm*

NEWTON REIGNY (St John)   *see* Penrith w Newton Reigny and Plumpton Wall *Carl*

NEWTON SOLNEY (St Mary the Virgin)   *see* Foremark and Repton w Newton Solney *Derby*

NEWTON ST CYRES (St Cyr and St Julitta)   *see* Brampford Speke, Cadbury, Newton St Cyres etc *Ex*

NEWTON ST LOE (Holy Trinity)   *see* Saltford w Corston and Newton St Loe *B & W*

NEWTON Team, The (Emmanuel) (St Peter) *Liv 15*   **P** *Patr Bd*   **TR** J M MATTHEWS   **TV** C J STAFFORD, V E HUGHES   **NSM** C A CLOSE

NEWTON TONY (St Andrew)   *see* Bourne Valley *Sarum*

NEWTON TRACEY (St Thomas à Becket), Horwood, Alverdiscott, Huntshaw, Yarnscombe, Tawstock, Atherington, High Bickington, Roborough, St Giles in the Wood and Beaford *Ex 19*   **P** *Ld Chan (1 turn), Patr Bd (3 turns)*   **TV** M J CLARK   **C** K L CROSS

NEWTON VALENCE (St Mary)   *see* Northanger *Win*

NEWTON, NORTH (St Peter)   *see* Alfred Jewel *B & W*

NEWTON, OLD (St Mary)   *see* Bacton w Wyverstone, Cotton and Old Newton etc *St E*

NEWTON, SOUTH (St Andrew)   *see* Lower Wylye and Till Valley *Sarum*

NEWTON, WEST (St Matthew)   *see* Solway Plain *Carl*

NEWTON, WEST (St Peter and St Paul)   *see* Sandringham w W Newton and Appleton etc *Nor*

NEWTON-BY-CASTLE-ACRE (All Saints)   *see* Nar Valley *Nor*

NEWTON-IN-WIRRAL (St Michael and All Angels)   *see* Newton *Ches*

NEWTON-LE-WILLOWS (All Saints)   *see* Newton *Liv*

NEWTON-ON-RAWCLIFFE (St John)   *see* Middleton, Newton and Sinnington *York*

NEWTON-ON-TRENT (St Peter)   *see* Saxilby Gp *Linc*

NEWTOWN (Holy Spirit)   *see* Calbourne w Newtown *Portsm*

NEWTOWN (Holy Trinity)   *see* Soberton w Newtown *Portsm*

NEWTOWN (King Charles the Martyr)   *see* Loppington w Newtown *Lich*

NEWTOWN (St George)   *see* Birm St Geo *Birm*

NEWTOWN (St Mark) *Liv 14*   **P** *Bp, Duke of Sutherland, and V Pemberton (jt)*   **P-in-c** W J GIBBONS   **OLM** E TAULTY, M JENNINGS, S Y FULFORD

NEWTOWN (St Mary the Virgin and St John the Baptist)   *see* Burghclere w Newtown and Ecchinswell w Sydmonton *Win*

NEWTOWN (St Paul)   *see* Longnor, Quarnford and Sheen *Lich*

NEWTOWN LINFORD (All Saints)   *see* Glenfield and Newtown Linford *Leic*

NIBLEY, NORTH (St Martin)   *see* Tyndale *Glouc*

NICHOLFOREST (St Nicholas)   *see* Arthuret w Kirkandrews-on-Esk and Nicholforest *Carl*

NIDD (St Paul and St Margaret) *Leeds 23*   **P** *Viscount Mountgarret and R Knaresborough (alt)*   **V** *vacant*

NIDDERDALE, LOWER *Leeds 25*   **P** *Trustees K Bell Esq, DBP, and C J Dent Esq (jt)*   **R** M P SPURGEON

NIDDERDALE, UPPER *Leeds 25*   **P** *D&C and V Masham and Healey (jt)*   **V** D C HALL

NINEBANKS (St Mark)   *see* Allendale w Whitfield *Newc*

NINEFIELDS (St Lawrence School Worship Centre)   *see* Waltham H Cross *Chelmsf*

NINFIELD (St Mary the Virgin) *Chich 12*   **P** *D&C Cant*   **R** *vacant*

NITON (St John the Baptist) *Portsm 7*   **P** *Qu Coll Ox*   **P-in-c** N J PORTER

NOAK HILL (St Thomas)   *see* Harold Hill St Paul *Chelmsf*

NOCTON (All Saints)   *see* Branston w Nocton and Potterhanworth *Linc*

NOEL PARK (St Mark) *Lon 19*   **P** *Bp*   **P-in-c** S P J CLARK

NOKE (St Giles)   *see* Ray Valley *Ox*

NONINGTON (St Mary the Virgin)   *see* Aylesham w Adisham and Nonington *Cant*

NORBITON (St Peter) *S'wark 15*   **P** *V Kingston All SS*   **V** P A HOLMES

NORBURY (All Saints)   *see* Wentnor w Ratlinghope, Myndtown, Norbury etc *Heref*

NORBURY (St Mary and St Barlok) w Snelston *Derby 8*   **P** *Mrs M F Stanton, L A Clowes Esq, and V Ashbourne (by turn)*   **P-in-c** G P POND   **NSM** P A SHORT

NORBURY (St Oswald) *S'wark 21*   **P** *Bp*   **V** A BRUNT

NORBURY (St Peter)   *see* Adbaston, High Offley, Knightley, Norbury etc *Lich*

NORBURY (St Philip) *S'wark 21*   **P** *Bp*   **P-in-c** Y FRANCIS

NORBURY (St Stephen) and Thornton Heath *S'wark 21*   **P** *Bp*   **P-in-c** G P THOMPSON   **OLM** J B FORBES

NORBURY (St Thomas) *Ches 16*   **P** *Lord Newton*   **V** R H LAWRY   **C** R H GREEN

NORDEN (St Paul) w Ashworth and Bamford *Man 17*   **P** *Bp*   **NSM** J M WATSON

NORFOLK PARK (St Leonard)   *see* Arbourthorne and Norfolk Park *Sheff*

NORHAM (St Cuthbert) and Duddo *Newc 12*   **P** *D&C (1 turn), D&C Dur (2 turns)*   **V** G R KELSEY

NORK (St Paul) *Guildf 9*   **P** *The Crown*   **P-in-c** J S CRESSWELL

NORLAND (St Luke)   *see* Ryburn *Leeds*

NORLANDS (St James)   *see* Notting Dale St Clem w St Mark and St Jas *Lon*

NORLEY (St John the Evangelist), Crowton and Kingsley *Ches 3*   **P** *Bp, V Frodsham, and V Weaverham (jt)*   **V** P RUGEN   **NSM** H MERRINGTON

NORMACOT (Holy Evangelists)   *see* Meir Heath and Normacot *Lich*

NORMANBY (St Andrew)   *see* Kirby Misperton w Normanby and Salton *York*

NORMANBY (St George)   *see* Eston w Normanby *York*

NORMANBY-LE-WOLD (St Peter)   *see* Walesby *Linc*

NORMANTON (All Saints) *Leeds 20*   **P** *Trin Coll Cam*   **V** A MURRAY   **C** P J MARIES

NORMANTON (St Giles) *Derby 10*   **P** *CPAS*   **V** N A A BARBER   **C** D A TODD

NORMANTON, SOUTH (St Michael) *Derby 1*   **P** *MMCET*   **R** S M POTTER

NORMANTON-LE-HEATH (Holy Trinity)   *see* Woodfield *Leic*

NORMANTON-ON-SOAR (St James)   *see* Sutton Bonington w Normanton-on-Soar *S'well*

NORMANTON-ON-TRENT (St Matthew)   *see* Tuxford w Weston, Markham Clinton etc *S'well*

NORRIS BANK (St Martin)   *see* Heatons *Man*

NORRIS GREEN (St Christopher)   *see* Liv St Chris Norris Green *Liv*

NORRISTHORPE (All Souls)   *see* Heckmondwike (w Norristhorpe) and Liversedge *Leeds*

NORTH   *see also under substantive place name*

NORTH BLACKWATER *Chelmsf 24*   **P** *Patr Bd*   **V** G B T BAYLISS   **OLM** C GORRINGE, D CORLEY

NORTH CAVE (All Saints) w Cliffe *York 13*   **P** *C H J Carver Esq*   **P-in-c** B WORSDALE

NORTH CHAPEL (St Michael) w Ebernoe *Chich 10*   **P** *Lord Egremont*   **P-in-c** P R HAYES

NORTH CORNWALL Cluster of Churches *Truro 10*   **P** *Bp and DBP (jt)*   **P-in-c** E J WILD   **NSM** A D E LEWIS, J POLLINGER

NORTH COVE (St Botolph)   *see* Worlingham w Barnby and N Cove *St E*

NORTH END (Ascension)   *see* Portsea Ascension *Portsm*

NORTH END (Chapel of Ease)   *see* Burton Dassett *Cov*

NORTH END (St Francis)   *see* Portsea N End St Mark *Portsm*

NORTH END (St Mark) *as above*

NORTH END (St Nicholas) *as above*

NORTH HAMPSHIRE DOWNS Benefice, The *Win 5*   **P** *Bp, Qu Coll Ox, St Jo Coll Ox, N McNair Scott Esq, and J L Jervoise Esq (jt)*   **R** P W DYSON   **C** A L BROWN   **NSM** J E LEESE, K O'LOUGHLIN, L D POWER, L J SCARD

NORTH HILL (St Torney)   *see* Three Rivers *Truro*

NORTH SHIELDS (St Augustine) (Christ Church) *Newc 2*   **P** *Patr Bd*   **TR** A D KIRKWOOD   **C** Y GREENER   **NSM** K COCKBURN

NORTH SHIELDS (St Augustine) (Christ Church) *Newc 5*
  P *Patr Bd*   **TR** A D KIRKWOOD   **C** Y GREENER
  NSM K COCKBURN
NORTH WEALD BASSETT (St Andrew) *Chelmsf 3*   **P** *Bp*
  P-in-c J W E RODLEY
NORTH WEST HAMPSHIRE Benefice, The *Win 6*   **P** *Bp and*
  Earl of Carnarvon (jt)   **R** C DALE   **NSM** A C PETTS
NORTHALLERTON (All Saints) w Kirby Sigston *York 18*
  P *D&C Dur*   **V** F R MAYER-JONES
NORTHAM (St Margaret)   *see* Bideford, Northam,
  Westward Ho!, Appledore etc *Ex*
NORTHAMPTON (All Saints w St Katharine) (St Peter) *Pet 4*
  P *Bp and R Foundn of St Kath (jt)*   **P-in-c** D B MCCONKEY
NORTHAMPTON (Christ Church) *Pet 4*   **P** *Bp*
  P-in-c D J WISEMAN   **NSM** A M MARCH
NORTHAMPTON (Emmanuel) *Pet 4*   **P** *DBP*
  TR M A H JOHNSON   **C** H DU G SPENCELEY
NORTHAMPTON (Holy Sepulchre w St Andrew and
  St Lawrence) *Pet 4*   **P** *Bp*   **V** M W J HILLS
  NSM A M MARCH
NORTHAMPTON (Holy Trinity) (St Paul) *Pet 4*   **P** *Bp*
  V A C MCGOWAN   **C** G BROOKS   **NSM** A M MARCH
NORTHAMPTON (St Alban the Martyr) (Glorious Ascension)
  Pet 4   **P** *Bp*   **V** J A EVANS
NORTHAMPTON (St Benedict) *Pet 4*   **P** *Bp*   **V** *vacant*
NORTHAMPTON (St David)   *see* Kingsthorpe *Pet*
NORTHAMPTON (St Giles) *Pet 4*   **P** *Simeon's Trustees*
  V S A KELLY   **C** D M REES-JONES, J J DADE
NORTHAMPTON (St James) *Pet 4*   **P** *Bp*
  P-in-c P W BOWDEN   **NSM** S M COLES
NORTHAMPTON (St Mary the Virgin) *Pet 4*   **P** *Bp*
  V I S HOLDSWORTH
NORTHAMPTON (St Matthew) *Pet 4*   **P** *DBP*
  V N M SETTERFIELD
NORTHAMPTON (St Michael and All Angels w St Edmund)
  Pet 4   **P** *Bp*   **V** M W J HILLS   **NSM** A M MARCH,
  P D MUNCH
NORTHANGER Benefice, The *Win 2*   **P** *Bp (1 turn), D&C*
  (1 turn), Bp, Earl of Selborne and Sir James Scott Bt (1 turn)
  R A J PEARS   **Hon C** R A EWBANK   **NSM** L A LEON
NORTHAW (St Thomas of Canterbury) and Cuffley *St Alb 17*
  P *Mrs S Peasley*   **V** R S PHILLIPS
NORTHBOROUGH (St Andrew)   *see* Peakirk w Glinton and
  Northborough *Pet*
NORTHBOURNE (St Augustine)   *see* Eastry and
  Woodnesborough *Cant*
NORTH-CHAPEL Parishes, The *Linc 4*   **P** *The Revd J M Ashley,*
  Mrs M F Davis, R H C Haigh Esq, and Trustees (1 turn), and Duchy
  of Lanc (1 turn)   **R** R K EMM
NORTHCHURCH (St Mary) and Wigginton *St Alb 1*   **P** *Duchy*
  of Cornwall and Bp (alt)   **R** J A GORDON
  NSM M J EGGLETON
NORTHDOWN PARK (St Philip)   *see* Margate St Phil *Cant*
NORTHENDEN (St Wilfrid) *Man 6*   **P** *Bp*   **R** G S FORSTER
NORTHFIELD (St Laurence) *Birm 4*   **P** *Keble Coll Ox*
  R C A E LAWRENCE   **NSM** D PYCOCK
NORTHFLEET (All Saints)   *see* Perry Street *Roch*
NORTHFLEET (St Botolph) and Rosherville *Roch 4*   **P** *Patr Bd*
  and Prime Min (alt)   **TR** L P SMITH   **TV** K J CABLE
  C M J PAYNE
NORTHGATE (St Elizabeth)   *see* Crawley *Chich*
NORTHIAM (St Mary) *Chich 17*   **P** *MMCET*   **R** R H WHITE
NORTHILL (St Mary the Virgin)   *see* Caldecote, Northill and Old
  Warden *St Alb*
NORTHINGTON (St John the Evangelist)   *see* Farleigh,
  Candover and Wield *Win*
NORTHLEACH (St Peter and St Paul) w Hampnett and
  Farmington, Cold Aston w Notgrove and Turkdean, and
  Compton Abdale w Haselton *Glouc 8*   **P** *Bp (2 turns), Ld*
  Chan (1 turn)   **P-in-c** D S FORD   **Hon**
  C S J GOUNDREY-SMITH
NORTHLEIGH (St Giles)   *see* Offwell, Northleigh, Farway,
  Cotleigh etc *Ex*
NORTHLEW (St Thomas of Canterbury)   *see* Okehampton,
  Inwardleigh, Belstone, Sourton etc *Ex*
NORTHMOOR (St Denys)   *see* Lower Windrush *Ox*
NORTHMOOR GREEN (St Peter and St John)   *see* Alfred Jewel *B*
  & W
NORTHOLT (St Joseph the Worker) (St Hugh) West End
  Lon 22   **P** *DBP*   **V** S C BENFORD   **C** S F METRY
NORTHOLT (St Mary) (St Richard) *Lon 22*   **P** *BNC Ox*
  R C D HILL
NORTHOLT PARK (St Barnabas) *Lon 22*   **P** *Bp*
  V E A J CARGILL THOMPSON
NORTHORPE (St John the Baptist)   *see* Scotton w Northorpe
  Linc

NORTHOWRAM (St Matthew) *Leeds 8*   **P** *Bp*   **V** *vacant*
NORTHREPPS (St Mary)   *see* Poppyland *Nor*
NORTHUMBERLAND HEATH (St Paul)   *see* Erith St Paul *Roch*
NORTHWICH St Luke (Holy Trinity) *Ches 6*   **P** *Bp*
  V C S SEDDON
NORTHWOLD (St Andrew)   *see* Grimshoe *Ely*
NORTHWOOD (Emmanuel) *Lon 23*   **P** *Ch Trust Fund Trust*
  V D M TALBOT   **C** H M WILKINSON, J ROTH, J W D DOUGLAS
NORTHWOOD (Holy Trinity) *Lon 23*   **P** *Trustees*
  V R C BARTLETT   **C** P J H GODDEN   **NSM** A CLARRIDGE
NORTHWOOD (Holy Trinity)   *see* Hanley H Ev *Lich*
NORTHWOOD (St John the Baptist) *Portsm 8*   **P** *Bp*
  R A COLLINSON   **NSM** D M NETHERWAY
NORTHWOOD GREEN (Mission Church)   *see* Westbury-on-
  Severn w Flaxley, Blaisdon etc *Glouc*
NORTHWOOD HILLS (St Edmund the King) *Lon 23*   **P** *Bp*
  V P R BARNES
NORTHWOOD Pinner Road (St Edmund the King)
  see Northwood Hills St Edm *Lon*
NORTON (All Saints)   *see* Hullavington, Norton and Stanton
  St Quintin *Bris*
NORTON (All Saints)   *see* Brington w Whilton and Norton etc
  Pet
NORTON (St Andrew)   *see* Pakenham w Norton and Tostock
  St E
NORTON (St Berteline and St Christopher) *Ches 3*   **P** *DBP*
  V *vacant*
NORTON (St Egwin)   *see* Evesham w Norton and Lenchwick
  Worc
NORTON (St George) (St Nicholas) *St Alb 3*   **P** *Bp*
  V D V COLLINS   **C** N J EVERETT
NORTON (St James) *Sheff 2*   **P** *CCC Cam*   **R** G B WHITE
NORTON (St James)   *see* Stoulton w Drake's Broughton and
  Pirton etc *Worc*
NORTON (St Mary the Virgin) *Dur 10*   **P** *Bp*
  P-in-c M E ANDERSON   **NSM** C WALTON, P J JOHNSON
NORTON (St Mary)   *see* Twigworth, Down Hatherley, Norton,
  The Leigh etc *Glouc*
NORTON (St Michael and All Angels) *Dur 10*   **P** *V Norton*
  St Mary   **P-in-c** M E ANDERSON   **NSM** C WALTON,
  P J JOHNSON
NORTON (St Michael and All Angels)   *see* Stourbridge St Mich
  Norton *Worc*
NORTON (St Peter)   *see* Norton juxta Malton *York*
NORTON BAVANT (All Saints)   *see* Upper Wylye Valley *Sarum*
NORTON BRIDGE (St Luke)   *see* Chebsey, Creswell, Ellenhall,
  Ranton etc *Lich*
NORTON CANES (St James) *Lich 3*   **P** *Bp*   **R** N L HIBBINS
NORTON CANON (St Nicholas)   *see* Weobley w Sarnesfield
  and Norton Canon *Heref*
NORTON CUCKNEY (St Mary) *S'well 1*   **P** *Lady Alexandra*
  Cavendish Bentinck   **P-in-c** S A CASH
  C L H DE ANDRADE LIMA
NORTON DISNEY (St Peter)   *see* Bassingham Gp *Linc*
NORTON FITZWARREN (All Saints)   *see* Staplegrove w Norton
  Fitzwarren *B & W*
NORTON IN HALES (St Chad)   *see* Woore and Norton in Hales
  Lich
NORTON IN THE MOORS (St Bartholomew) *Lich 8*
  P *Walsingham Coll Trust Assn*   **R** S J LORD
NORTON JUXTA MALTON (St Peter) *York 6*   **P** *Abp*
  V R A HIRST
NORTON JUXTA TWYCROSS (Holy Trinity)   *see* Woodfield *Leic*
NORTON LEES (St Paul) *Sheff 2*   **P** R *Norton*   **V** P M BROWN
NORTON LINDSEY (Holy Trinity)   *see* Arden Valley *Cov*
NORTON MALREWARD (Holy Trinity)   *see* Chew Magna w
  Dundry, Norton Malreward etc *B & W*
NORTON MANDEVILLE (All Saints)   *see* High Ongar w Norton
  Mandeville *Chelmsf*
NORTON ST PHILIP (St Philip and St James)   *see* Hardington
  Vale *B & W*
NORTON SUB HAMDON (Blessed Virgin Mary) w West
  Chinnock, Chiselborough and Middle Chinnock *B & W 7*
  P *Bp*   **P-in-c** P J THOMAS   **NSM** G J W EDMUNDS
NORTON SUBCOURSE (St Mary)   *see* Raveningham Gp *Nor*
NORTON WOODSEATS (St Chad)   *see* Woodseats St Chad
  Sheff
NORTON, EAST (All Saints)   *see* Hallaton and Allexton, w
  Horninghold, Tugby etc *Leic*
NORTON, OVER (St James)   *see* Chipping Norton *Ox*
NORWELL (St Laurence) w Ossington, Cromwell, Caunton,
  and Sutton w Carlton on Trent *S'well 3*   **P** *Bp and SMF (jt)*
  V *vacant*
NORWICH (Christ Church)   *see* Eaton Ch Ch *Nor*
NORWICH (Christ Church)   *see* New Catton Ch Ch *Nor*
NORWICH (Holy Trinity)   *see* Heigham H Trin *Nor*

NORWICH (St Andrew) *Nor 1*   **P** *PCC*   **P-in-c** M J YOUNG
NORWICH (St Andrew)   *see Eaton St Andr Nor*
NORWICH (St Anne)   *see Earlham Nor*
NORWICH (St Barnabas)   *see Heigham St Barn w St Bart Nor*
NORWICH (St Catherine)   *see Mile Cross Nor*
NORWICH (St Elizabeth)   *see Earlham Nor*
NORWICH (St Francis)   *see Nor Heartsease St Fran Nor*
NORWICH (St George) Colegate *Nor 1*   **P** *D&C*
   P-in-c P MCFADYEN   **NSM** M J MCFADYEN
NORWICH (St George) Tombland *Nor 1*   **P** *Bp*
   P-in-c J C MINNS
NORWICH (St Giles) *Nor 1*   **P** *Ld Chan and Bp (alt)*
   V D T THORNTON
NORWICH (St Helen) *Nor 1*   **P** *Gt Hosp Nor*   **V** B R OAKE
NORWICH (St John the Baptist) Timberhill w Norwich
   St Julian *Nor 1*   **P** *Bp, Guild of All So, and D&C (jt)*
   R C D WOOD
NORWICH (St Julian)   *see Nor St Jo w St Julian Nor*
NORWICH (St Luke)   *see New Catton St Luke w St Aug Nor*
NORWICH (St Mary in the Marsh) *Nor 1*   **P** *D&C*
   P-in-c A W BRYANT
NORWICH (St Mary Magdalene) w St James *Nor 2*   **P** *D&C*
   V M R PALMER   **OLM** J SPENCER
NORWICH (St Mary)   *see Earlham Nor*
NORWICH (St Matthew)   *see Thorpe St Matt Nor*
NORWICH (St Michael)   *see Bowthorpe Nor*
NORWICH (St Peter Mancroft) (St John Maddermarket) *Nor 1*
   P *PCC*   **R** *vacant*
NORWICH (St Stephen) *Nor 1*   **P** *D&C*   **P-in-c** M M LIGHT
   OLM M C A HUTTON
NORWICH (St Thomas)   *see Heigham St Thos Nor*
NORWICH Heartsease (St Francis) *Nor 1*   **P** *Bp*
   P-in-c P L HOWARD
NORWICH Lakenham (St Alban) (St Mark) *Nor 1*   **P** *D&C*
   V S E WEST-LINDELL   **C** D Z LLOYD, I H DYBLE
NORWICH, Lakenham (St John the Baptist and All Saints) and
   Tuckswood St Paul *Nor 1*   **P** *Bp and D&C (jt)*   **V** P J FOX
   NSM C J A BELCHER, R J RAYNER
NORWOOD (St Leonard)   *see Sheff St Leon Norwood Sheff*
NORWOOD (St Mary the Virgin) *Lon 22*   **P** *SMF*
   R J M PAYNE
NORWOOD, SOUTH (Holy Innocents) *S'wark 21*   **P** *Bp*
   P-in-c R F HUNTE   **NSM** D L THOMPSON, S E WHEELER-KILEY
NORWOOD, SOUTH (St Alban the Martyr) *S'wark 21*
   P *Bp*   **V** R T LAWSON
NORWOOD, SOUTH (St Mark) *S'wark 21*   **P** *Bp*
   P-in-c R F HUNTE   **NSM** S E WHEELER-KILEY
NORWOOD, UPPER (All Saints) *S'wark 21*   **P** *V Croydon*
   V L S A MARSH
NORWOOD, UPPER (St John) *S'wark 21*   **P** *Bp*
   P-in-c J A PRITCHARD
NORWOOD, WEST (St Luke) *S'wark 12*   **P** *Abp*
   V D R DAVIS
NOTGROVE (St Bartholomew)   *see Northleach w Hampnett*
   and Farmington etc Glouc
NOTTING DALE (St Clement) (St Mark) and Norlands
   St James *Lon 12*   **P** *Bp*   **V** A N EVERETT   **C** M M CLARKE
   Hon C R G THOMPSON   **NSM** M F A AYO
NOTTING HILL (All Saints) (St Columb) *Lon 12*   **P** *SMF*
   V J K BROWNSELL
NOTTING HILL (St John) *Lon 12*   **P** *Bp*   **V** W H TAYLOR
   Hon C L R GALON   **NSM** R HAWES
NOTTING HILL (St Michael and All Angels) (Christ Church)
   (St Francis) *Lon 12*   **P** *Trustees*   **V** A B ANDREWS
NOTTING HILL (St Peter) *Lon 12*   **P** *Bp*   **V** M K HARGREAVES
   NSM A MAY
NOTTINGHAM (All Saints) (St Mary the Virgin) (St Peter and
   St James) *S'well 9*   **P** *Bp*   **R** C D HARRISON   **C** R H DAVEY
NOTTINGHAM (St Andrew) *S'well 9*   **P** *Peache Trustees*
   V C E GOODE
NOTTINGHAM (St Ann w Emmanuel) *S'well 9*   **P** *Trustees*
   V K S F ROOMS   **C** N J FENTON, N J HILL
NOTTINGHAM (St George w St John the Baptist) *S'well 9*
   P *Bp*   **P-in-c** C S RUSHFORTH
NOTTINGHAM (St Jude) *S'well 7*   **P** *CPAS*   **V** J C ALLISTER
   C B T CLAYTON
NOTTINGHAM (St Nicholas) *S'well 9*   **P** *CPAS*
   R S D SILVESTER   **C** J G TATUM   **NSM** I B PAUL
NOTTINGHAM (St Saviour) *S'well 9*   **P** *CPAS*   **V** *vacant*
NOTTINGHAM (St Stephen)   *see Hyson Green and Forest*
   Fields S'well
NOWTON (St Peter)   *see St Edm Way St E*
NUFFIELD (Holy Trinity) *Ox 24*   **P** *MMCET*   **P-in-c** B J BAILEY
NUN MONKTON (St Mary)   *see Lower Nidderdale Leeds*
NUNBURNHOLME (St James)   *see Pocklington Wold York*
NUNEATON (St Mary) *Cov 5*   **P** *V Nuneaton*   **V** M LIDDELL
   C T G WINTLE

NUNEATON (St Nicolas) *Cov 5*   **P** *The Crown*
   V K A BETTERIDGE
NUNHEAD (St Antony) (St Silas) *S'wark 8*   **P** *Bp*
   P-in-c D J OGUNYEMI
NUNNEY (All Saints) and Witham Friary, Marston Bigot,
   Wanstrow and Cloford *B & W 3*   **P** *Bp, SMF, and C N Clarke*
   Esq and Duke of Somerset (jt)   **P-in-c** A E DICKSON
NUNNINGTON (All Saints)   *see Kirkdale w Harome,*
   Nunnington and Pockley York
NUNTHORPE (St Mary the Virgin) (St Mary's Church Hall)
   York 20   **P** *Abp*   **P-in-c** L J BIGGS   **NSM** J M COOK
NUNTON (St Andrew)   *see Chalke Valley Sarum*
NURSLING (St Boniface) and Rownhams *Win 12*   **P** *Bp*
   R J T WILLIAMS
NURSTEAD (St Mildred)   *see Meopham w Nurstead Roch*
NUTBOURNE (St Wilfrid)   *see Chidham Chich*
NUTFIELD (St Peter and St Paul)   *see Bletchingley and Nutfield*
   S'wark
NUTFIELD, SOUTH (Christ Church) *S'wark 25*   **P** *Ch Patr Trust*
   V A J WAY
NUTHALL (St Patrick)   *see Kimberley and Nuthall S'well*
NUTHURST (St Andrew) and Mannings Heath *Chich 7*
   P *Bp Lon*   **R** I C HUTCHINSON CERVANTES   **NSM** B P NEW
NUTHURST (St Thomas)   *see Packwood w Hockley Heath Birm*
NUTLEY (St James the Less) *Chich 18*   **P** *R Maresfield*
   V N S CORNELL   **NSM** P C INGRAM
NYMET (St George)   *see S Molton w Nymet St George, High*
   Bray etc Ex
NYMET ROWLAND (St Bartholomew)   *see N Creedy Ex*
NYMPSFIELD (St Bartholomew)   *see Uley w Owlpen and*
   Nympsfield Glouc
NYNEHEAD (All Saints)   *see Wellington and Distr B & W*
OADBY (St Paul) (St Peter) *Leic 4*   **P** *Bp*   **TR** M F RUSK
   TV S A BAILEY   **C** G F GAMBLE
OAKAMOOR (Holy Trinity)   *see Kingsley and Foxt-w-Whiston*
   and Oakamoor etc Lich
OAKDALE (St George)   *see N Poole Ecum Team Sarum*
OAKE (St Bartholomew)   *see Deane Vale B & W*
OAKENGATES (Holy Trinity) and Wrockwardine Wood *Lich 21*
   P *Bp*   **R** *vacant*
OAKENSHAW CUM WOODLANDS (St Andrew)   *see Low Moor*
   and Oakenshaw Leeds
OAKFORD (St Peter)   *see Washfield, Stoodleigh, Withleigh*
   etc Ex
OAKHAM (All Saints), Ashwell, Braunston, Brooke, Egleton,
   Hambleton, Langham, Market Overton, Teigh and
   Whissendine *Pet 12*   **P** *Patr Bd*   **TR** L T FRANCIS-DEHQANI
   TV J E TEBBY, J L HUTCHINSON   **C** D J COAD
   NSM H A CROWTHER
OAKHANGER (St Luke's Mission Church)   *see Alsager Ch Ch*
   Ches
OAKHANGER (St Mary Magdalene)   *see Northanger Win*
OAKHILL (All Saints)   *see Ashwick w Oakhill and Binegar*
   B & W
OAKINGTON (St Andrew) *Ely 6*   **P** *Qu Coll Cam*
   V J C ALEXANDER
OAKLEY (St Leonard) w Wootton St Lawrence *Win 4*   **P** *Qu*
   Coll Ox and D&C (alt)   **R** C J M VAUGHAN
   NSM C A VAUGHAN
OAKLEY (St Mary)   *see Worminghall w Ickford, Oakley and*
   Shabbington Ox
OAKLEY (St Mary)   *see Bromham w Oakley and Stagsden St Alb*
OAKLEY (St Nicholas)   *see N Hartismere St E*
OAKLEY, GREAT (All Saints) w Wix and Wrabness *Chelmsf 22*
   P *Ld Chan, Ch Patr Trust, and St Jo Coll Cam (by turn)*
   R *vacant*
OAKLEY, GREAT (St Michael) and LITTLE (St Peter) *Pet 7*
   P *H W G de Capell Brooke Esq and Boughton Estates Ltd (alt)*
   V *vacant*
OAKRIDGE (St Bartholomew)   *see Bisley, Chalford, France*
   Lynch, and Oakridge and Bussage w Eastcombe Glouc
OAKS IN CHARNWOOD (St James the Greater)   *see Shepshed*
   and Oaks in Charnwood Leic
OAKSEY (All Saints)   *see Ashley, Crudwell, Hankerton and*
   Oaksey Bris
OAKWOOD (no dedication) *Derby 9*   **P** *Bp and MMCET (jt)*
   V *vacant*
OAKWOOD (St Thomas) *Lon 18*   **P** *Bp*   **V** C J P HOBBS
   C B C G VANE   **Hon C** M A PICKLES
OAKWORTH (Christ Church) *Leeds 5*   **P** *Bp*   **V** J ROGERS
   NSM B G PARTRIDGE
OARE (Blessed Virgin Mary) w Culbone *B & W 15*   **P** *Bp*
   P-in-c C D BURKE
OARE (Holy Trinity)   *see Vale of Pewsey Sarum*
OARE (St Bartholomew)   *see E Downland Ox*
OATLANDS (St Mary) *Guildf 8*   **P** *Bp*   **V** S BRUNN
   OLM L BOWDEN

OBORNE (St Cuthbert)   *see* Queen Thorne *Sarum*
OCCOLD (St Michael)   *see* Eye *St E*
OCKBROOK (All Saints) *Derby 13*   **P** *Lt Col T H Pares*
V T M SUMPTER   **NSM** A J MACGREGOR
OCKENDON, NORTH (St Mary Magdalene) *Chelmsf 2*   **P** *Bp*
P-in-c M K SPARROW
OCKER HILL (St Mark) *Lich 26*   **P** *Bp*   **V** A J GWILLIM
OCKFORD RIDGE (St Mark)   *see* Godalming *Guildf*
OCKHAM (All Saints) w Hatchford and Downside *Guildf 10*
P *Bp*   **R** *vacant*
OCKLEY (St Margaret), Okewood and Forest Green *Guildf 7*
P *Bp and J P M H Evelyn Esq (alt)*
P-in-c N A KNIGHTS JOHNSON   **OLM** J MARSH
OCLE PYCHARD (St James the Great)   *see* Frome Valley
Heref
OCTAGON *Chich 3*   **P** *Bp, Bp Lon,and Stansted Park Foundation
(jt)*   **V** J D STRAIN
ODCOMBE (St Peter and St Paul), Brympton, Lufton and
Montacute *B & W 6*   **P** *Ch Ch Ox (4 turns), C E B Clive-
Ponsonby-Fane Esq (1 turn)*   **R** *vacant*
ODD RODE (All Saints) *Ches 11*   **P** *R Astbury*
R P S ATKINSON   **NSM** B R MOSS
ODDINGTON (Holy Ascension)   *see* Broadwell, Evenlode,
Oddington, Adlestrop etc *Glouc*
ODDINGTON (St Andrew)   *see* Ray Valley *Ox*
ODDINGTON (St Nicholas)   *see* Broadwell, Evenlode,
Oddington, Adlestrop etc *Glouc*
ODELL (All Saints) *St Alb 13*   **P** *Lord Luke*   **R** *vacant*
ODIHAM (All Saints)   *see* N Hants Downs *Win*
ODSTOCK (St Mary)   *see* Chalke Valley *Sarum*
OFFCHURCH (St Gregory) *Cov 10*   **P** *Bp*   **V** *vacant*
OFFENHAM (St Mary and St Milburgh)   *see* Badsey w
Aldington and Offenham and Bretforton *Worc*
OFFERTON (St Alban) (St John) and Stockport St Thomas
Ches 18   **P** *Bp*   **V** A S LYTHALL   **NSM** G M SELLORS,
J E MAYO-LYTHALL, J OWENS
OFFHAM (Old St Peter)   *see* Hamsey *Chich*
OFFHAM (St Michael)   *see* W Malling w Offham *Roch*
OFFLEY (St Mary Magdalene)   *see* King's Walden and Offley w
Lilley *St Alb*
OFFLEY, HIGH (St Mary the Virgin)   *see* Adbaston, High Offley,
Knightley, Norbury etc *Lich*
OFFORD D'ARCY w OFFORD CLUNY (All Saints)   *see* Buckden w
the Offords *Ely*
OFFTON (St Mary)   *see* Somersham w Flowton and Offton w
Willisham *St E*
OFFWELL (St Mary the Virgin), Northleigh, Farway, Cotleigh
and Widworthy *Ex 4*   **P** *Trustees, R T Marker Esq, Cotleigh
PCC, and Bp (jt)*   **P-in-c** P S C WALKER
OGBOURNE (St Andrew)   *see* Ridgeway *Sarum*
OGBOURNE (St George) *as above*
OGLEY HAY (St James) *Lich 1*   **P** *Bp*   **V** D BISHOP
OGWELL (St Bartholomew)   *see* Wolborough and Ogwell *Ex*
OKEFORD Benefice, The *Sarum 6*   **P** *G A L-F Pitt-Rivers Esq and
DBP (alt)*   **C** D R R SEYMOUR, W T RIDDING
OKEFORD FITZPAINE (St Andrew)   *see* Okeford *Sarum*
OKEHAMPTON (All Saints) (St James), Inwardleigh, Belstone,
Sourton, Bridestowe, Bratton Clovelly, Germansweek,
Lydford, Hatherleigh, Northlew w Ashbury, Exbourne,
Meeth and Jacobstowe *Ex 10*   **P** *Patr Bd (5 turns), Duchy of
Cornwall (1 turn)*   **TR** S W COOK   **TV** A J BROOK,
R P HANSFORD   **C** R A F BACHE
OKEWOOD (St John the Baptist)   *see* Ockley, Okewood and
Forest Green *Guildf*
OLD   *see also under substantive place name*
OLD FORD (St Paul) (St Mark) *Lon 7*   **P** *Hyndman Trustees and
CPAS (jt)*   **V** J C HUGHESDON   **NSM** A I KEECH
OLD HEATH (St Barnabas)   *see* Colchester St Barn *Chelmsf*
OLD HILL (Holy Trinity) *Worc 9*   **P** *Ch Soc Trust*
V N S GOWERS
OLD KIRK BRADDAN (St Brendan)   *see* Braddan *S & M*
OLD LANE (Mission Church)   *see* Bloxwich *Lich*
OLDBERROW (St Mary)   *see* Arden Marches *Cov*
OLDBURY *Sarum 16*   **P** *Bp, CPAS, Marquess of Lansdowne,
and C E R Money-Kyrle Esq (jt)*   **R** P A BROMILEY
OLDBURY (Christ Church), Langley, and Londonderry *Birm 7*
P *Prime Min (1 turn), Bp (3 turns)*   **V** N P PELLING
OLDBURY (St Nicholas)   *see* Bridgnorth, Tasley, Astley Abbotts,
etc *Heref*
OLDBURY-ON-SEVERN (St Arilda)   *see* Thornbury and
Oldbury-on-Severn w Shepperdine *Glouc*
OLDCOTES (St Mark's Mission Church)   *see* Carlton-in-
Lindrick and Langold w Oldcotes *S'well*
OLDHAM (St Barnabas)   *see* Medlock Head *Man*
OLDHAM (St James) (St Ambrose) *Man 15*   **P** *Bp and R
Prestwich (jt)*   **V** P PLUMPTON

OLDHAM (St Mary w St Peter) *Man 16*   **P** *Patr Bd*
V D J PALMER   **OLM** J M HURLSTON
OLDHAM (St Paul) and Werneth *Man 16*   **P** *Bp*
V N J ANDREWES   **C** J E PITMAN   **Hon C** D J QUARMBY
OLDHAM (St Stephen and All Martyrs)   *see* Coldhurst and
Oldham St Steph *Man*
OLDHAM Moorside (St Thomas) *Man 15*   **P** *Trustees*
P-in-c B M MITCHELL
OLDHURST (St Peter)   *see* Somersham w Pidley and Oldhurst
and Woodhurst *Ely*
OLDLAND (St Anne) *Bris 5*   **P** *Bp*   **V** A J M SPEAR
C G J WATERS
OLDRIDGE (St Thomas)   *see* Tedburn St Mary, Cheriton
Bishop, Whitestone etc *Ex*
OLDSWINFORD (St Mary)   *see* Old Swinford Stourbridge
Worc
OLIVER'S BATTERY (St Mark)   *see* Stanmore *Win*
OLLERTON (St Giles) (St Paulinus) w Boughton *S'well 3*
P *Ld Chan and Bp (alt)*   **P-in-c** Z BURTON   **NSM** C A DUNK
OLNEY (St Peter and St Paul) *Ox 16*   **P** *Bp*   **R** C WOOD
NSM C P MANSFIELD
OLTON (St Margaret) *Birm 11*   **P** *Bp and V Bickenhill (jt)*
NSM D A CHEETHAM, S M CHANDLER
OLVESTON (St Mary the Virgin)   *see* Almondsbury and
Olveston *Bris*
OMBERSLEY (St Andrew) w Doverdale *Worc 8*   **P** *Bp and
Lord Sandys (alt)*   **P-in-c** D J ARNOLD
ONCHAN (St Peter), Lonan and Laxey *S & M*   **P** *The Crown*
TR C B BURGESS   **TV** J DUDLEY   **OLM** J E GUILFORD
ONECOTE (St Luke)   *see* Ipstones w Berkhamsytch and
Onecote w Bradnop *Lich*
ONEHOUSE (St John the Baptist)   *see* Gt Finborough w
Onehouse, Harleston, Buxhall etc *St E*
ONGAR, HIGH (St Mary the Virgin) w Norton Mandeville
Chelmsf 3   **P** *Ch Soc Trust*   **P-in-c** M J PETERS
C J R KNOWLES   **NSM** A G FAIRBAIRN
ONIBURY (St Michael and All Angels)   *see* Ludlow *Heref*
ONSLOW SQUARE (Holy Trinity) St Paul and South
Kensington St Augustine *Lon 8*   **P** *Bp, MMCET, and Keble
Coll Ox (jt)*   **V** N G P GUMBEL   **C** A S GORDON, D G WALKER,
E R J HODGES, J DAVIES, M F J RUOFF, M P LAYZELL, N K LEE,
P J P WYNTER, P W COWLEY, R WALL, S FOSTER, T FLINT,
W R VAN DER HART   **Hon C** J A K MILLAR   **NSM** S COLMAN,
T C JACKSON
ONSLOW SQUARE (St Paul)   *see* Onslow Square and S
Kensington St Aug *Lon*
OPENSHAW (St Barnabas)   *see* Manchester Gd Shep and
St Barn *Man*
OPENSHAW, HIGHER (St Clement) *Man 1*   **P** *Trustees*
P-in-c P G JUMP
OPENWOODGATE (St Mark)   *see* Belper *Derby*
ORBY (All Saints)   *see* Burgh Gp *Linc*
ORCHARD PORTMAN (St Michael)   *see* Beercrocombe w Curry
Mallet, Hatch Beauchamp etc *B & W*
ORCHARD WAY (St Barnabas)   *see* Cheltenham St Mark *Glouc*
ORCHARDLEIGH (Blessed Virgin Mary)   *see* Beckington w
Standerwick, Berkley, Rodden etc *B & W*
ORCOP (St John the Baptist)   *see* St Weonards *Heref*
ORDSALL (All Hallows)   *see* Retford Area *S'well*
ORDSALL (St Clement) and Salford Quays *Man 20*   **P** *Bp*
P-in-c S KEARNEY
ORE (Christ Church) *Chich 15*   **P** *Simeon's Trustees*
V L C J DUCKETT
ORE (St Helen) (St Barnabas) *Chich 15*   **P** *Simeon's Trustees*
P-in-c P PARKS   **C** A M HAWKINS
ORESTON (Church of the Good Shepherd)   *see* Plymstock and
Hooe *Ex*
ORFORD (St Andrew) *Liv 12*   **P** *Bp*   **V** M RAYNOR
ORFORD (St Bartholomew)   *see* Wilford Peninsula *St E*
ORFORD (St Margaret) *Liv 12*   **P** *Bp*   **V** S W BOYD
ORLESTONE (St Mary)   *see* Saxon Shoreline *Cant*
ORLETON (St George)   *see* Leominster *Heref*
ORLINGBURY (St Mary)   *see* Gt w Lt Harrowden and
Orlingbury and Isham etc *Pet*
ORMESBY (St Cuthbert) *York 17*   **P** *Abp*   **V** J S CROFT
ORMESBY ST MARGARET (St Margaret) w Scratby, Ormesby
St Michael and Rollesby *Nor 6*   **P** *Bp, D&C, DBP and
R J H Tacon Esq (jt)*   **V** M L BISHOP
ORMESBY ST MICHAEL (St Michael)   *see* Ormesby St Marg w
Scratby, Ormesby St Mich etc *Nor*
ORMESBY, NORTH (Holy Trinity) *York 17*   **P** *Abp*
V D P BLACK   **NSM** C SUNLEY
ORMSBY Group, The South (St Leonard) *Linc 9*   **P** *A J
Massingham-Mundy Esq, Sir Thomas Ingilby Bt, Mert Coll Ox, Bp,
and DBP (jt)*   **P-in-c** C HILLIAM
NSM T M I M MCLAUGHLIN
ORMSGILL (St Francis)   *see* N Barrow *Carl*

ORMSIDE (St James)   *see* Heart of Eden *Carl*
ORMSKIRK (St Peter and St Paul) *Liv 11*   **P** *Earl of Derby*
   V C H JONES   **NSM** S E HAYNES   **OLM** L CAMP
ORPINGTON (All Saints) *Roch 16*   **P** *D&C*   **V** B E MCHENRY
   C C M KNIGHT-SCOTT   **NSM** J DRIVER
ORPINGTON (Christ Church) *Roch 16*   **P** *Ch Trust Fund Trust,*
   Bp, and V Orpington (jt)   **V** J P COLWILL   **C** D C MONEME
ORRELL (St Luke) *Liv 14*   **P** *Bp*   **V** P G WHITTINGTON
ORRELL HEY (St John and St James) *Liv 1*   **P** *CPAS*
   P-in-c C L DAWSON
ORSETT (St Giles and All Saints) and Bulphan and Horndon
   on the Hill *Chelmsf 16*   **P** *Bp and D&C St Paul's (jt)*
   NSM S R BLAKE
ORSTON (St Mary)   *see* Whatton w Aslockton, Hawksworth,
   Scarrington etc *S'well*
ORTON (All Saints) and Tebay w Ravenstonedale and
   Newbiggin-on-Lune *Carl 1*   **P** *Bp and Ravenstonedale*
   Trustees (1 turn), Resident Landowners (1 turn)   **P-in-c** B LOCK
   NSM S E WARD
ORTON GOLDHAY (St John)   *see* The Ortons *Ely*
ORTON GOLDHAY (St John) Conventional District *Ely 13*
   Min S C GOWER
ORTON LONGUEVILLE (Holy Trinity)   *see* The Ortons *Ely*
ORTON MALBORNE (not known) *as above*
ORTON WATERVILLE (St Mary) *as above*
ORTON, GREAT (St Giles)   *see* Barony of Burgh *Carl*
ORTON-ON-THE-HILL (St Edith of Polesworth)   *see* Bosworth
   and Sheepy Gp *Leic*
ORTONS, The (Holy Trinity) (St Mary) (St John) (not known)
   Ely 15   **P** *Bp and Pemb Coll Cam (jt)*   **V** D C R MCFADYEN
   C R A WINFREY, S P BRIDGES
ORWELL Group, The (St Andrew) *Ely 7*   **P** *Bp, DBP, and Trin*
   Coll Cam (jt)   **R** F A COUCH
OSBALDWICK (St Thomas) w Murton *York 2*   **P** *Abp*
   V A CLEMENTS
OSBOURNBY (St Peter and St Paul)   *see* S Lafford *Linc*
OSENEY CRESCENT (St Luke) *Lon 17*   **P** *Bp*   **V** J MARCH
   C J M FINCH
OSGATHORPE (St Mary the Virgin)   *see* Kegworth, Hathern,
   Long Whatton, Diseworth etc *Leic*
OSMASTON (St Martin)   *see* Brailsford w Shirley, Osmaston w
   Edlaston etc *Derby*
OSMINGTON (St Osmond)   *see* Preston w Sutton Poyntz,
   Littlemoor etc *Sarum*
OSMONDTHORPE (St Philip)   *see* Leeds All SS w
   Osmondthorpe *Leeds*
OSMOTHERLEY (St Peter) w Harlsey and Ingleby Arncliffe
   York 18   **P** J N Barnard Esq (1 turn), Ld Chan (2 turns)*
   V I D HOUGHTON   **NSM** T A LEWIS
OSMOTHERLY (St John)   *see* Ulverston St Mary w H Trin *Carl*
OSNEY (St Frideswide) *Ox 2*   **P** *Bp and Ch Ch Ox (jt)*
   R C M SYKES   **C** S A CROWTHER   **NSM** J M BROWN,
   J MOFFETT-LEVY, M E HENIG
OSPRINGE (St Peter and St Paul) *Cant 14*   **P** *St Jo Coll Cam*
   P-in-c S D ROWLANDS   **C** T J BATESON
OSSETT (Holy and Undivided Trinity) and Gawthorpe
   Leeds 20   **P** *Bp and R Dewsbury (jt)*   **OLM** A SHACKLETON
OSSETT, SOUTH (Christ Church) *Leeds 20*   **P** *Bp*
   V D J ROBERTSON   **C** D HORSFALL
OSSINGTON (Holy Rood)   *see* Norwell w Ossington, Cromwell
   etc *S'well*
OSWALDKIRK (St Oswald)   *see* Ampleforth w Oswaldkirk,
   Gilling E etc *York*
OSWALDTWISTLE (Immanuel) (All Saints) (St Paul) *Blackb 1*
   P *Bp, DBP, R Church Kirk, The Ven C W D Carroll, G F Garnett*
   Esq, and PCCs (jt)   **V** J S HOLLAND   **NSM** C F COLTON,
   C GARNER
OSWESTRY (Holy Trinity) *Lich 19*   **P** *Bp*   **V** P T DARLINGTON
   C S J NICHOLSON
OSWESTRY (St Oswald) *Lich 19*   **P** *Earl of Powis*
   V S G THORBURN   **C** M E GRACE
OTFORD (St Bartholomew) *Roch 10*   **P** *D&C Westmr*
   V R M WORSSAM
OTHAM (St Nicholas) w Langley *Cant 13*   **P** *Abp and CPAS (jt)*
   P-in-c S P HUGHES
OTHERY (St Michael)   *see* Middlezoy w Othery, Moorlinch and
   Greinton *B & W*
OTLEY (All Saints) *Leeds 16*   **P** *Bp*   **V** G C BUTTANSHAW
OTLEY (St Mary)   *see* Carlford *St E*
OTTERBOURNE (St Matthew)   *see* Compton, Hursley, and
   Otterbourne *Win*
OTTERBURN (St John the Evangelist)   *see* N Tyne and Redesdale
   Newc
OTTERFORD (St Leonard)   *see* Blackdown *B & W*
OTTERHAM (St Denis)   *see* Boscastle and Tintagel Gp *Truro*
OTTERINGTON, NORTH (St Michael and All Angels)   *see* The
   Thorntons and The Otteringtons *York*

OTTERINGTON, SOUTH (St Andrew) *as above*
OTTERSHAW (Christ Church) *Guildf 11*   **P** *Bp*
   V S C FACCINI   **OLM** J A M VICKERS
OTTERTON (St Michael)   *see* Budleigh Salterton, E Budleigh w
   Bicton etc *Ex*
OTTERY ST MARY (St Mary the Virgin), Alfington, West Hill,
   Tipton St John, Venn Ottery, Newton Poppleford, Harpford
   and Colaton Raleigh *Ex 6*   **P** *Patr Bd*   **P-in-c** S J A WESTON
   TV C E EDMONDS, M WARD   **C** L C MCGOVERN   **Hon**
   C A E H TURNER, J G PANGBOURNE   **NSM** M G DICK,
   R J ALLEN
OTTRINGHAM (St Wilfrid)   *see* Easington w Skeffling,
   Keyingham, Ottringham etc *York*
OUGHTIBRIDGE (Ascension) *Sheff 3*   **P** *V Wadsley*
   V J F E MANN
OUGHTRINGTON (St Peter) and Warburton *Ches 10*   **P** *Bp*
   and Viscount Ashbrook (jt)   **R** E M BURGESS   **NSM** T R LEGGE
OULTON (St John the Evangelist)   *see* Stone Ch Ch and Oulton
   Lich
OULTON (St John)   *see* Rothwell, Lofthouse, Methley etc *Leeds*
OULTON (St Michael) *Nor 9*   **P** *Ch Soc Trust*
   R A R PRITCHARD   **P-in-c** A M BEANE
   NSM C S PRITCHARD
OULTON (St Peter and St Paul)   *see* Lt Barningham, Blickling,
   Edgefield etc *Nor*
OULTON BROAD (St Mark) (St Luke the Evangelist) *Nor 9*
   P *Simeon's Trustees*   **V** I R BENTLEY   **C** S E QUANTRILL
   NSM G POWELL   **OLM** J M FOWLER, M A BARNES, M E ZIPFEL
OUNDLE (St Peter) w Ashton and Benefield w Glapthorn
   Pet 10   **P** *Bp and Mrs G S Watts-Russell (jt)*   **R** S J WEBSTER
   C J M BALL, L DAVIES
OUSBY (St Luke)   *see* Cross Fell Gp *Carl*
OUSDEN (St Peter)   *see* Bansfield *St E*
OUSEBURN, GREAT (St Mary) and LITTLE (Holy Trinity) w
   Marton cum Grafton and Whixley w Green Hammerton
   Leeds 25   **P** *Bp, R Knaresborough and DBP (3 turns), St Jo Coll*
   Cam (1 turn)   **V** M C PARKIN   **NSM** J ROPER
OUT RAWCLIFFE (St John the Evangelist)   *see* Waterside Par
   Blackb
OUTLANE (St Mary Magdalene)   *see* Stainland w Outlane
   Leeds
OUTWELL (St Clement) *Ely 14*   **P** *Bp*   **P-in-c** M P SKILLINGS
OUTWOOD (St John the Baptist)   *see* The Windmill *S'wark*
OUTWOOD (St Mary Magdalene) *Leeds 20*   **P** *V Stanley*
   V J W BUTTERWORTH
OUTWOOD COMMON (St John the Divine)   *see* Billericay and
   Lt Burstead *Chelmsf*
OUZEL VALLEY, The *St Alb 11*   **P** *Patr Bd*   **TR** G FELLOWS
   TV B J MINTON, N MCGEENEY, P K NIEMIEC   **OLM** W JONES
OVAL WAY (All Saints)   *see* Chalfont St Peter *Ox*
OVENDEN (St George) *Leeds 11*   **P** *V Halifax*   **V** G M BARLEY
   NSM G ROPER, P A PICKARD
OVENDEN (St John the Evangelist)   *see* Bradshaw and
   Holmfield *Leeds*
OVER   *see also under substantive place name*
OVER (St Chad) *Ches 6*   **P** *Bp*   **C** H R L ROULSTON
OVER (St John the Evangelist) *Ches 6*   **P** *Lord Delamere and*
   W R Cullimore Esq (jt)   **V** G T CROWDER
OVER (St Mary) *Ely 6*   **P** *Trin Coll Cam*   **P-in-c** J ANDERSON
OVER WALLOP (St Peter)   *see* Portway and Danebury *Win*
OVERBURY (St Faith) w Teddington, Alstone and Little
   Washbourne w Beckford and Ashton under Hill *Worc 4*
   P *D&C and MMCET (jt)*   **P-in-c** M T C BAYNES, R J WORSLEY
   C S K RENSHAW
OVERSEAL (St Matthew)   *see* Seale and Lullington w Coton in
   the Elms *Derby*
OVERSTONE (St Nicholas)   *see* Mears Ashby and Hardwick and
   Sywell etc *Pet*
OVERSTRAND (St Martin)   *see* Poppyland *Nor*
OVERTON (St Helen) *Blackb 11*   **P** *V Lanc*
   P-in-c H G THOMAS
OVERTON (St Mary) w Laverstoke and Freefolk *Win 6*
   P *Bp*   **P-in-c** I K SMALE
OVERTON (St Michael and All Angels)   *see* Upper Kennet *Sarum*
OVING (All Saints)   *see* Schorne *Ox*
OVING (St Andrew)   *see* Tangmere and Oving *Chich*
OVINGDEAN (St Wulfran) *Chich 19*   **P** *SMF*
   P-in-c P G WOLFENDEN
OVINGHAM (St Mary the Virgin) *Newc 9*   **P** *Bp*
   P-in-c E LEWIS
OVINGTON (St John the Evangelist)   *see* Watton *Nor*
OVINGTON (St Mary)   *see* N Hinckford *Chelmsf*
OVINGTON (St Peter)   *see* Arle Valley *Win*
OWERMOIGNE (St Michael)   *see* Watercombe *Sarum*
OWERSBY, NORTH (St Martin)   *see* Kelsey Gp *Linc*
OWLERTON (St John the Baptist) *Sheff 4*   **P** *Ch Patr Trust*
   V N A DAWSON   **NSM** R W YOUNG

OWLPEN (Holy Cross)   *see* Uley w Owlpen and Nympsfield *Glouc*

OWLSMOOR (St George) *Ox 8*   **P** *Bp*   **V** *vacant*

OWLSWICK (Chapel)   *see* Risborough *Ox*

OWMBY Group, The (St Peter and St Paul) *Linc 5*   **P** *Duchy of Lanc, Bp and D&C, Bp and Mrs S Hutton, and C W A Cracroft-Eley (by turn)*   **R** A P SMITH   **OLM** J M HEPBURN, S DEACON, S E TURNBULL

OWSLEBURY (St Andrew)   *see* Twyford and Owslebury and Morestead etc *Win*

OWSTON (All Saints) *Sheff 7*   **P** *DBP*   **P-in-c** A B WALTON

OWSTON (St Andrew)   *see* Whatborough Gp *Leic*

OWSTON (St Martin) *Linc 1*   **P** *The Crown*   **V** J N GREEN

OWTHORNE (St Matthew)   *see* Withernsea w Owthorne, Garton-in-Holderness etc *York*

OWTHORPE (St Margaret) *S'well 5*   **P** *Trustees Sir Rupert Bromley Bt*   **P-in-c** P D S MASSEY

OWTON MANOR (St James) *Dur 3*   **P** *Bp*   **V** S J LOCKE

OXBOROUGH (St John the Evangelist) w Foulden and Caldecote *Nor 13*   **P** *G&C Coll Cam*   **P-in-c** C P SHERLOCK

OXCLOSE (not known) *Dur 11*   **P** *R Washington, TR Usworth, and V Fatfield (jt)*   **P-in-c** S M ASTON

OXENDON (St Helen)   *see* Arthingworth, Harrington w Oxendon and E Farndon *Pet*

OXENHALL (St Anne)   *see* Redmarley D'Abitot, Bromesberrow, Pauntley etc *Glouc*

OXENHOPE (St Mary the Virgin) *Leeds 5*   **P** *Bp*   **P-in-c** N C J WRIGHT   **NSM** J ROBERTS

OXENTON (St John the Baptist)   *see* Bishop's Cleeve and Woolstone w Gotherington etc *Glouc*

OXFORD (St Aldate) *Ox 2*   **P** *Simeon's Trustees*   **R** C S G CLEVERLY   **C** K V SEAGRAVE, M BRICKMAN, P J ATKINSON, S C R PONSONBY, W R DONALDSON   **NSM** C HOFREITER

OXFORD (St Andrew) *Ox 2*   **P** *Trustees*   **V** A R WINGFIELD DIGBY   **C** P M WHITE, S J POTTER   **NSM** E J PITKETHLY, J M VAUGHAN, R M CUNNINGHAM

OXFORD (St Barnabas and St Paul) (St Thomas the Martyr) *Ox 2*   **P** *Keble Coll Ox and Ch Ch Ox (jt)*   **V** J W BESWICK   **Hon C** R A H GREANY   **NSM** J M HANKS

OXFORD (St Clement) *Ox 1*   **P** *Ox Ch Trust*   **R** R E GIBSON

OXFORD (St Ebbe w Holy Trinity and St Peter-le-Bailey) *Ox 2*   **P** *Ox Ch Trust*   **R** V E ROBERTS   **C** A W GIBBS, D G REID, J J G FLETCHER, P D L WILKINSON   **NSM** J C POOLE

OXFORD (St Frideswide)   *see* Osney *Ox*

OXFORD (St Giles) St Philip and St James (St Margaret) *Ox 2*   **P** *St Jo Coll Ox*   **V** A W H BUNCH   **Hon C** G SIMPSON, J N A BRADBURY

OXFORD (St Mary Magdalen) *Ox 2*   **P** *Ch Ch Ox*   **V** P J GROVES   **C** D KEECH, J A MERCER   **NSM** J JONG

OXFORD (St Mary the Virgin) (St Cross or Holywell) (St Peter in the East) *Ox 2*   **P** *Or Coll Ox and Mert Coll Ox (jt)*   **V** B W MOUNTFORD   **C** A E RAMSEY

OXFORD (St Matthew) *Ox 2*   **P** *Ox Ch Trust*   **R** S J HELLYER   **NSM** J SHERWOOD, M J RAYNER

OXFORD (St Michael at the North Gate w St Martin and All Saints) *Ox 2*   **P** *Linc Coll Ox*   **V** R A WILKES

OXFORD Canning Crescent (St Luke)   *see* Ox St Matt *Ox*

OXHEY (All Saints) *St Alb 6*   **P** *Bp*   **V** P M WISE   **C** R R TURNER

OXHEY (St Matthew) *St Alb 6*   **P** *DBP*   **V** D M SHEPHERD

OXHILL (St Lawrence)   *see* Tysoe w Oxhill and Whatcote *Cov*

OXLEY (Epiphany) and Wednesfield St Gregory *Lich 29*   **P** *Bp*   **V** *vacant*

OXNEAD (St Michael & all Angels)   *see* Bure Valley *Nor*

OXSHOTT (St Andrew) *Guildf 10*   **P** *Bp*   **V** J P CRESSWELL   **OLM** M L L HAWRISH

OXTED (St Mary) *S'wark 25*   **P** *Bp*   **TR** A P RUMSEY   **TV** A ELTRINGHAM   **C** P BROOKS   **OLM** D C WEIGHTMAN

OXTON (St Peter and St Paul)   *see* Epperstone, Gonalston, Oxton and Woodborough *S'well*

OXTON (St Saviour) *Ches 1*   **P** *DBP*   **V** J KENNEDY   **C** G V LAUTENBACH

PACKINGTON (Holy Rood)   *see* Woodfield *Leic*

PACKWOOD (St Giles) w Hockley Heath *Birm 6*   **P** *Bp and M R Parkes Esq (alt)*   **V** M CATLEY

PADBURY (St Mary the Virgin)   *see* Lenborough *Ox*

PADDINGTON (St James) *Lon 2*   **P** *Bp*   **V** P R THOMAS   **C** O J DOBSON

PADDINGTON (St John the Evangelist) (St Michael and All Angels) *Lon 2*   **P** *DBP*   **V** S D MASON   **C** A GARCIA FUERTE, R J A SIMS-WILLIAMS   **NSM** M LEGG

PADDINGTON (St Mary Magdalene) (St Peter) *Lon 2*   **P** *Keble Coll Ox and Ch Patr Trust*   **V** R H EVERETT   **NSM** F W WARD, R RAJ-SINGH

PADDINGTON (St Saviour)   *see* Lt Venice *Lon*

PADDINGTON (St Stephen w St Luke) *Lon 2*   **P** *Bp*   **V** J R ALLCOCK   **C** W P H COLERIDGE   **NSM** M J LEE

PADDINGTON GREEN (St Mary)   *see* Lt Venice *Lon*

PADDLESWORTH (St Oswald)   *see* Lyminge w Paddlesworth, Stanford w Postling etc *Cant*

PADDOCK WOOD (St Andrew) *Roch 8*   **P** *D&C Cant*   **V** B T KNAPP   **C** R E BROWNING

PADGATE (Christ Church)   *see* Warrington E *Liv*

PADIHAM (St Leonard) w Hapton and Padiham Green *Blackb 3*   **P** *Bp*   **V** M A JONES   **C** M G PRINT

PADSTOW (St Petroc) *Truro 7*   **P** *P J N Prideaux-Brune Esq*   **V** C M MALKINSON

PADWORTH (St John the Baptist)   *see* Stratfield Mortimer and Mortimer W End etc *Ox*

PAGANHILL (Holy Spirit)   *see* Stroud Team *Glouc*

PAGHAM (St Thomas à Becket) *Chich 1*   **P** *Abp*   **V** M F EMINSON

PAGLESHAM (St Peter)   *see* Ashingdon w S Fambridge, Canewdon and Paglesham *Chelmsf*

PAIGNTON (Christ Church) and Preston St Paul *Ex 11*   **P** *Bp and Peache Trustees (jt)*   **V** D W WITCHELL

PAIGNTON (St John the Baptist) (St Andrew) (St Boniface) *Ex 11*   **P** *DBP*   **V** R J CARLTON   **C** G DEIGHTON

PAILTON (St Denis)   *see* Revel Gp *Cov*

PAINSWICK (St Mary the Virgin), Sheepscombe, Cranham, The Edge, Pitchcombe, Harescombe and Brookthorpe *Glouc 4*   **P** *Bp, D&C, Mrs N Owen (1 turn), and Ld Chan (1 turn)*   **V** M S HOLLOWAY   **NSM** A J P LEACH   **OLM** D W NEWELL

PAKEFIELD (All Saints and St Margaret) *Nor 9*   **P** *Ch Patr Trust*   **R** R J K BAKER   **C** M A CAPRON

PAKENHAM (St Mary) w Norton and Tostock *St E 9*   **P** *Bp and Peterho Cam (jt)*   **P-in-c** K A VALENTINE

PALGRAVE (St Peter)   *see* N Hartismere *St E*

PALMARSH (Holy Cross)   *see* Hythe *Cant*

PALMERS GREEN (St John the Evangelist) *Lon 18*   **P** *V Southgate Ch Ch*   **V** S LEADER

PAMBER (St Mary and St John the Baptist)   *see* The Sherbornes w Pamber *Win*

PAMPISFORD (St John the Baptist) *Ely 5*   **P** *Mrs B A Killander*   **NSM** C S WILSON

PANFIELD (St Mary the Virgin) and Rayne *Chelmsf 17*   **P** *Bp and DBP (alt)*   **C** E J BENDREY   **NSM** J E NICHOLLS

PANGBOURNE (St James the Less) w Tidmarsh and Sulham *Ox 4*   **P** *Bp, Ch Soc Trust, and Mrs I E Moon (jt)*   **R** H C W PARBURY   **NSM** A T BOND

PANNAL (St Robert of Knaresborough) w Beckwithshaw *Leeds 23*   **P** *Bp and Peache Trustees (jt)*   **V** J SMITH

PAPPLEWICK (St James)   *see* Linby w Papplewick *S'well*

PAPWORTH (St Peter) *Ely 1*   **P** *Patr Bd*   **TR** N A DI CASTIGLIONE   **TV** S M DAY   **NSM** A N M CLARKE, N H A PEARSON, P GILDERSLEVE

PAR (St Mary the Virgin) (Good Shepherd) *Truro 1*   **P** *The Crown*   **P-in-c** P A SPREADBRIDGE

PARHAM (St Mary the Virgin)   *see* Campsea Ashe w Marlesford, Parham and Hacheston *St E*

PARHAM (St Peter)   *see* Amberley w N Stoke and Parham, Wiggonholt etc *Chich*

PARK BARN (St Clare)   *see* Westborough *Guildf*

PARKEND (St Paul) and Viney Hill *Glouc 1*   **P** *Bp and Univ Coll Ox (jt)*   **V** A BRUNT

PARKFIELD (Holy Trinity)   *see* Rhodes and Parkfield *Man*

PARKGATE (St Thomas)   *see* Neston *Ches*

PARKHAM (St James), Alwington, Buckland Brewer, Hartland, Welcombe, Clovelly, Woolfardisworthy West, Bucks Mills and Lundy *Ex 15*   **P** *Patr Bd (4 turns), The Crown (1 turn)*   **TV** W M MITCHELL   **NSM** K L C BEER

PARKSTONE (Good Shepherd)   *see* Heatherlands St Jo *Sarum*

PARKSTONE (St John the Evangelist)   *as above*

PARKSTONE (St Luke) *Sarum 7*   **P** *Ch Trust Fund Trust*   **V** C M STRAIN   **C** K ROGERS

PARKSTONE (St Peter) and St Osmund w Branksea St Mary *Sarum 7*   **P** *Patr Bd*   **R** M M CAMP   **C** S BEDBOROUGH   **NSM** D J NEWMAN, H S WRIGHT   **OLM** P E SOUTHGATE   **Dss** D J NEWMAN

PARKWOOD (Christ Church) Conventional District *Cant 15*   **Min** A J HOUSTON

PARKWOOD (St Paul)   *see* S Gillingham *Roch*

PARLAUNT ROAD (Christ the Worker)   *see* Langley Marish *Ox*

PARLEY, WEST (All Saints) (St Mark) *Sarum 9*   **P** *P E E Prideaux-Brune Esq*   **R** E C BOOTH

PARNDON, GREAT (St Mary) *Chelmsf 4*   **P** *Bp*   **V** *vacant*

PARNDON, LITTLE (St Mary)   *see* Harlow Town Cen w Lt Parndon *Chelmsf*

PARR (St Peter) (St Paul) (St Philip) (Holy Trinity) *Liv 10*   **P** *Patr Bd*   **TR** J L ROBERTS   **TV** C DORAN   **OLM** A KIRKHAM, H MCCANN, M E TAYLOR

PARR MOUNT (Holy Trinity)   *see* Parr *Liv*
PARSON CROSS (St Cecilia)   *see* Sheff St Cecilia Parson Cross *Sheff*
PARSON'S GREEN (St Dionis)   *see* Fulham St Dionis *Lon*
PARTINGTON (St Mary) and Carrington *Ches 10*   **P** *Bp and V Bowdon (alt)*   **V** P H GEDDES
PARTNEY (St Nicholas)   *see* Bolingbroke Deanery *Linc*
PARTRIDGE GREEN (St Michael and All Angels)   *see* W Grinstead *Chich*
PARWICH (St Peter)   *see* Fenny Bentley, Thorpe, Tissington, Parwich etc *Derby*
PASSENHAM (St Guthlac) *Pet 5*   **P** MMCET   **R** C J MURRAY
PASTON (All Saints) *Pet 11*   **P** *Bp*   **R** M S BRIDGEN
PASTON (St Margaret)   *see* Trunch Group *Nor*
PASTROW *Win 3*   **P** *Bp, Qu Coll Ox, and St Mary's Coll Win (jt)*   **P-in-c** A P RANDLE-BISSELL   **NSM** V E GAGEN
PATCHAM (All Saints) *Chich 19*   **P** MMCET   **V** A L FLOWERDAY   **C** A M BOUSFIELD, B W SEAR   **NSM** M PHILIP
PATCHING (St John the Divine)   *see* Findon w Clapham and Patching *Chich*
PATCHWAY (St Chad) *Bris 5*   **P** *Trustees*   **P-in-c** H K JAMESON
PATELEY BRIDGE (St Cuthbert)   *see* Upper Nidderdale *Leeds*
PATRICK BROMPTON (St Patrick) and Hunton *Leeds 27*   **P** *Bp*   **P-in-c** B S DIXON   **NSM** J T OLDFIELD
PATRICROFT (Christ Church)   *see* Eccles *Man*
PATRINGTON (St Patrick)   *see* Easington w Skeffling, Keyingham, Ottringham etc *York*
PATRIXBOURNE (St Mary)   *see* Bridge *Cant*
PATTERDALE (St Patrick) *Carl 4*   **P** *Bp and the Hon J N Lowther (jt)*   **V** T G WILCOCK
PATTINGHAM (St Chad) w Patshull *Lich 24*   **P** *Bp and M Kwiatkowska Esq (jt)*   **V** M P HOBBS
PATTISHALL (Holy Cross) w Cold Higham and Gayton w Tiffield *Pet 5*   **P** *Bp, SS Coll Cam, and SMF (jt)*   **P-in-c** M REYNOLDS
PAUL (St Pol de Lion) *Truro 5*   **P** *Ld Chan*   **P-in-c** A M YATES   **C** K R OWEN, S YATES
PAULERSPURY (St James the Apostle)   *see* Silverstone and Abthorpe w Slapton etc *Pet*
PAULL (St Andrew and St Mary)   *see* Hedon, Paull, Sproatley and Preston *York*
PAULSGROVE (St Michael and All Angels) *Portsm 6*   **P** *Bp*   **V** I NEWTON   **C** P J O'MAOIL MHEANA
PAULTON (Holy Trinity) w Farrington Gurney and High Littleton *B & W 11*   **P** *Bp and Hyndman Trustees (jt)*   **V** J G EDWARDS   **NSM** C E HUSBAND
PAUNTLEY (St John the Evangelist)   *see* Redmarley D'Abitot, Bromesberrow, Pauntley etc *Glouc*
PAVENHAM (St Peter)   *see* Milton Ernest, Pavenham and Thurleigh *St Alb*
PAWLETT (St John the Baptist)   *see* Puriton and Pawlett *B & W*
PAXFORD (Mission Church)   *see* Vale and Cotswold Edge *Glouc*
PAXTONS, The (Holy Trinity) (St James) w Diddington and Southoe *Ely 13*   **P** *D&C Linc (2 turns), E G W Thornhill Esq and Mert Coll Ox (1 turn each)*   **V** A S REED
PAYHEMBURY (St Mary the Virgin)   *see* Broadhembury, Payhembury and Plymtree *Ex*
PEACEHAVEN (Ascension) and Telscombe Cliffs w Piddinghoe and Telscombe Village *Chich 21*   **P** *Bp and Gorham Trustees (jt)*   **C** C R GORING
PEAK DALE (Holy Trinity)   *see* Tideswell *Derby*
PEAK FOREST (Charles the King and Martyr) and Dove Holes *Derby 4*   **P** *Bp and Duke of Devonshire (jt)*   **P-in-c** C F EDWARDS   **OLM** M WASHBROOK
PEAKIRK (St Pega) w Glinton and Northborough *Pet 11*   **P** *D&C*   **P-in-c** H P GEISOW
PEAR TREE (Jesus Chapel)   *see* Southampton St Mary Extra *Win*
PEASEDOWN ST JOHN (St John the Baptist) w Wellow and Foxcote w Shoscombe *B & W 11*   **P** *Bp*   **V** M G STREET   **C** T Y BENYON   **Hon C** R P FOTHERGILL
PEASEMORE (St Barnabas)   *see* E Downland *Ox*
PEASENHALL (St Michael)   *see* Yoxmere *St E*
PEASLAKE (St Mark)   *see* Shere, Albury and Chilworth *Guildf*
PEASMARSH (St Michael)   *see* Shalford *Guildf*
PEASMARSH (St Peter and St Paul)   *see* Brede w Udimore and Beckley and Peasmarsh *Chich*
PEATLING MAGNA (All Saints)   *see* Willoughby Waterleys, Peatling Magna etc *Leic*
PEATLING PARVA (St Andrew)   *see* Gilmorton, Peatling Parva, Kimcote etc *Leic*
PEBMARSH (St John the Baptist)   *see* Halstead Area *Chelmsf*
PEBWORTH (St Peter)   *see* Vale and Cotswold Edge *Glouc*
PECKHAM (All Saints) Blenheim Grove *S'wark 8*   **P** *Ch Trust Fund Trust*   **V** J M MORTIMER   **C** J C DAWKINS

PECKHAM (St John w St Andrew) *S'wark 8*   **P** *Bp*   **P-in-c** P A PACKER
PECKHAM (St Mary Magdalene) (St Paul) *S'wark 8*   **P** *Ch Patr Soc*   **V** O A ADAMS   **NSM** A O ADETAYO
PECKHAM (St Saviour) *S'wark 9*   **P** *Bp*   **V** P E COLLIER
PECKHAM, EAST (Holy Trinity) and Nettlestead *Roch 8*   **P** *St Pet Coll Ox and D&C Cant (jt)*   **R** A H CARR   **NSM** S M MORRELL
PECKHAM, WEST (St Dunstan)   *see* Mereworth w W Peckham *Roch*
PECKLETON (St Mary Magdalene) *Leic 9*   **P** *Ld Chan*   **R** P G HOOPER
PEDMORE (St Peter) *Worc 12*   **P** *Oldswinford Hosp*   **R** *vacant*
PEEL (St Paul)   *see* Walkden and Lt Hulton *Man*
PEEL GREEN (St Michael and All Angels)   *see* Barton w Peel Green *Man*
PEGSWOOD (St Margaret)   *see* Bothal and Pegswood w Longhirst *Newc*
PELDON (St Mary)   *see* W w E Mersea, Peldon, Gt and Lt Wigborough *Chelmsf*
PELSALL (St Michael and All Angels) *Lich 25*   **P** *Bp*   **V** C A ST A RAMSAY   **C** D P S BABBINGTON   **NSM** A M MORRIS
PELTON (Holy Trinity) and West Pelton *Dur 11*   **P** *Bp*   **V** J LINTERN
PELTON, WEST (St Paul)   *see* Pelton and W Pelton *Dur*
PELYNT (St Nun)   *see* Lanreath, Pelynt and Bradoc *Truro*
PEMBERTON (St Francis of Assisi) Kitt Green *Liv 14*   **P** *R Wigan and Bp (jt)*   **V** D A HAYES
PEMBERTON (St John) *Liv 14*   **P** *R Wigan*   **V** P G ANDERSON
PEMBRIDGE (St Mary the Virgin) w Moor Court, Shobdon, Staunton-on-Arrow, Byton and Lyonshall *Heref 4*   **P** *Ld Chan (1 turn), Patr Bd (4 turns)*   **R** B M JACOBS
PEMBURY (St Peter) *Roch 8*   **P** *Ch Ch Ox*   **V** D L ROBERTSON   **NSM** C E WALSHAW, H A HUGHES
PEN SELWOOD (St Michael) *B & W 2*   **P** *Bp*   **R** N C M FEAVER
PENCOMBE (St John)   *see* Bredenbury *Heref*
PENCOYD (St Denys)   *see* St Weonards *Heref*
PENCOYS (St Andrew)   *see* Redruth w Lanner and Treleigh *Truro*
PENDEEN (St John the Baptist) w Morvah *Truro 5*   **P** *R A H Aitken Esq and C W M Aitken Esq (jt)*   **V** *vacant*
PENDEFORD (St Paul)   *see* Tettenhall Regis *Lich*
PENDLEBURY (St Augustine)   *see* Swinton and Pendlebury *Man*
PENDLEBURY (St John) *Man 20*   **P** *Trustees*   **OLM** J BRANDRETH, V TYLDESLEY
PENDLESIDE, WEST *Blackb 7*   **P** *Bp and J E R Aspinall (jt)*   **V** R J CARMYLLIE   **NSM** J E HOLT
PENDLETON (All Saints)   *see* W Pendleside *Blackb*
PENDLETON (St Thomas)   *see* Salford All SS *Man*
PENDLETON Claremont (Holy Angels) *as above*
PENDOCK CROSS (Holy Redeemer)   *see* Berrow w Pendock, Eldersfield, Hollybush etc *Worc*
PENDOMER (St Roch)   *see* Coker Ridge *B & W*
PENGE (Christ Church w Holy Trinity)   *see* Anerley *Roch*
PENGE (St John the Evangelist) *Roch 13*   **P** *Simeon's Trustees*   **P-in-c** M D FITTER   **C** NJG POOLE
PENGE (St Paul)   *see* Anerley *Roch*
PENGE LANE (Holy Trinity) *Roch 13*   **P** *Bp*   **V** N G READ   **C** A J D BOND   **NSM** M A WILKINSON
PENHILL *Leeds 27*   **P** *Trin Coll Cam and Lord Bolton (jt)*   **R** L PURVIS-LEE   **NSM** P S YEADON
PENHILL (St Peter) *Bris 7*   **P** *Bp*   **NSM** E P MUKHOLI
PENHURST (St Michael the Archangel)   *see* Ashburnham w Penhurst *Chich*
PENISTONE (St John the Baptist) and Thurlstone *Sheff 11*   **P** *Bp*   **TR** D J HOPKIN   **C** N MARCHANT   **OLM** A P PARR
PENKETH (St Paul)   *see* Warrington *N Liv*
PENKEVIL (St Michael)   *see* St Michael Penkevil *Truro*
PENKHULL (St Thomas)   *see* Hartshill, Penkhull and Trent Vale *Lich*
PENKRIDGE Team, The (St Michael and All Angels) *Lich 2*   **P** *Patr Bd*   **TR** G H YERBURY   **C** C L SHAW   **OLM** V E D HOWARTH
PENN (Holy Trinity) and Tylers Green *Ox 9*   **P** *Earl Howe*   **V** M D BISSET   **C** G SUMMERS
PENN (St Bartholomew) (St Anne) *Lich 24*   **P** *Bp*   **V** B N WHITMORE   **C** I A KEMP
PENN FIELDS St Philip (St Aidan) *Lich 24*   **P** *Ch Trust Fund Trust*   **V** J S OAKLEY   **C** C N RUDD, G D REGAN   **NSM** J DALE, R E CARTER
PENN STREET (Holy Trinity) *Ox 9*   **P** *Earl Howe*   **V** P M SIMMONS
PENNARD, EAST (All Saints)   *see* Fosse Trinity *B & W*

PENNARD, WEST (St Nicholas)   *see* Baltonsborough w
Butleigh, W Bradley etc *B & W*
PENNINGTON (Christ Church) *Man 19*   **P** *Trustees*
V A J BUTTERWORTH   **C** E J WHITE, L H LEE
PENNINGTON (St Mark) *Win 11*   **P** *V Milford*
P-in-c A B RUSSELL   **NSM** E A ELLIOTT
PENNINGTON (St Michael and the Holy Angels) and Lindal w
Marton and Bardsea *Carl 9*   **P** *Bp and DBP (jt)*
P-in-c G A TUBBS
PENNY LANE (St Barnabas)   *see* Mossley Hill *Liv*
PENNYCROSS (St Pancras) *Ex 21*   **P** *CPAS*
P-in-c J J MARLOW   **C** W E BRAY
PENNYWELL (St Thomas)   *see* Sunderland St Thos and
St Oswald *Dur*
PENPONDS (Holy Trinity) *Truro 2*   **P** *The Crown*   **V** *vacant*
PENRITH (Christ Church) (St Andrew) w Newton Reigny and
Plumpton Wall *Carl 4*   **P** *Bp*   **TR** D G SARGENT
C A M E OSMASTON, R L STAVERT
PENRUDDOCK (All Saints)   *see* Greystoke w Penruddock,
Mungrisdale etc *Carl*
PENSAX (St James the Great)   *see* Teme Valley N *Worc*
PENSBY (St Michael and All Angels)   *see* Barnston *Ches*
PENSHAW (All Saints)   *see* Herrington, Penshaw and Shiney
Row *Dur*
PENSHURST (St John the Baptist) and Fordcombe *Roch 12*
P *Viscount De L'Isle*   **R** T E HOLME
PENSILVA (St John)   *see* St Ive and Pensilva w Quethiock *Truro*
PENSNETT (St Mark) *Worc 10*   **P** *Bp*   **P-in-c** S J OLIVER
PENTEWAN (All Saints)   *see* St Austell *Truro*
PENTLOW (St George and St Gregory)   *see* N Hinckford
Chelmsf
PENTNEY (St Mary Magdalene)   *see* Nar Valley *Nor*
PENTON MEWSEY (Holy Trinity)   *see* Pastrow *Win*
PENTONVILLE (St Silas w All Saints) (St James) *Lon 6*   **P** *Bp*
V R A WAKELING
PENTRICH (St Matthew)   *see* Swanwick and Pentrich *Derby*
PENTRIDGE (St Rumbold)   *see* Sixpenny Handley w Gussage
St Andrew etc *Sarum*
PENWERRIS (St Michael and All Angels) (Holy Spirit) *Truro 3*
P *V St Gluvias*   **P-in-c** M T MESLEY
PENWORTHAM (St Leonard) *Blackb 5*   **P** *Bp*
V J N MANSFIELD   **NSM** S J BAINES
PENWORTHAM (St Mary) *Blackb 5*   **P** *Miss A M Rawstorne*
V C J NELSON   **C** R H CROWE
PENZANCE (St Mary) (St Paul) (St John the Baptist) *Truro 5*
P *Bp*   **TR** S YATES   **C** A M YATES, K R OWEN
PEOPLETON (St Nicholas) and White Ladies Aston w
Churchill and Spetchley and Upton Snodsbury and
Broughton Hackett *Worc 4*   **P** *Bp, Croom Estate Trustees, and
Major R J G Berkley (1 turn), and Ld Chan (1 turn)*
NSM N S MURRAY-PETERS
PEOVER, OVER (St Lawrence) w Lower Peover (St Oswald)
Ches 12   **P** *DBP and Man Univ (jt)*   **V** P J LLOYD
PEPER HAROW (St Nicholas)   *see* Compton w Shackleford and
Peper Harow *Guildf*
PEPLOW (The Epiphany)   *see* Hodnet *Lich*
PERIVALE (St Nicholas) *Lon 22*   **P** *Trustees*
P-in-c V A AITKEN
PERLETHORPE (St John the Evangelist) *S'well 2*   **P** *Earl
Manvers' Trustees*   **P-in-c** A N EVANS   **C** E L HOLLIDAY
NSM H M ENGLISH
PERRANARWORTHAL (St Piran)   *see* St Stythians w
Perranarworthal and Gwennap *Truro*
PERRANPORTH (St Michael's Mission Church)
see Perranzabuloe and Crantock w Cubert *Truro*
PERRANUTHNOE (St Michael and St Piran)   *see* Ludgvan,
Marazion, St Hilary and Perranuthnoe *Truro*
PERRANZABULOE (St Piran) and Crantock w Cubert *Truro 7*
P *Patr Bd*   **V** *vacant*
PERROTT, NORTH (St Martin)   *see* Wulfric Benefice *B & W*
PERROTT, SOUTH (St Mary)   *see* Beaminster Area *Sarum*
PERRY BARR (St John the Evangelist) *Birm 3*   **P** *Bp and trustees
(jt)*   **V** B SCOTT
PERRY BEECHES (St Matthew) *Birm 3*   **P** *St Martin's Trustees*
V A J A ROMANIS
PERRY COMMON (St Martin)   *see* Erdington Ch the K *Birm*
PERRY GREEN (St Thomas)   *see* Albury, Braughing, Furneux
Pelham, Lt Hadham etc *St Alb*
PERRY HILL (St George)   *see* Forest Hill w Lower Sydenham
S'wark
PERRY STREET (All Saints) *Roch 4*   **P** *Bp*   **P-in-c** L P SMITH
C K J CABLE, M J PAYNE
PERSHORE (Holy Cross) w Pinvin, Wick and Birlingham
Worc 4   **P** *Patr Bd*   **P-in-c** C A LORDING   **NSM** A ORGAN
PERTENHALL (St Peter)   *see* The Stodden Churches *St Alb*

PETER TAVY (St Peter) and Mary Tavy *Ex 22*   **P** *Guild of All So*
R J C HIGMAN
PETERBOROUGH (All Saints) *Pet 11*   **P** *Bp*
P-in-c G S ROBERTS   **C** B J B KIM
PETERBOROUGH (Christ the Carpenter) *Pet 11*   **P** *Bp*
V N E FRY
PETERBOROUGH (Holy Spirit) Bretton *Pet 11*   **P** *Bp*
P-in-c W S CROFT   **NSM** J A C WIEGMAN
PETERBOROUGH (St John the Baptist) (Mission Church)
Pet 11   **P** *Bp*   **V** I C BLACK   **NSM** R DEANS
PETERBOROUGH (St Jude) *Pet 11*   **P** *Bp*   **V** G J KEATING
PETERBOROUGH (St Mark) and St Barnabas *Pet 11*   **P** *Bp*
P-in-c A C HOLDSTOCK   **C** K C FEAR
PETERBOROUGH (St Mary) Boongate *Pet 11*   **P** *D&C*
V M P J MOORE   **C** C KUTIWULU
PETERBOROUGH (St Paul) *Pet 11*   **P** *Bp*
P-in-c R F WATKINSON
PETERCHURCH (St Peter)   *see* Madley w Tyberton, Peterchurch,
Vowchurch etc *Heref*
PETERLEE (St Cuthbert) *Dur 2*   **P** *Bp*   **V** E E JONES
C A M RICHARDSON, T WALL
PETERSFIELD (St Peter) *Portsm 4*   **P** *Bp*   **V** W P M HUGHES
PETERSHAM (All Saints) (St Peter) *S'wark 16*   **P** *Bp*
V T J E MARWOOD
PETERSMARLAND (St Peter)   *see* Shebbear, Buckland Filleigh,
Sheepwash etc *Ex*
PETERSTOW (St Peter)   *see* Brampton *Heref*
PETHAM (All Saints)   *see* Wye *Cant*
PETHERTON, NORTH (St Mary the Virgin)   *see* Alfred Jewel
B & W
PETHERTON, SOUTH (St Peter and St Paul) w The
Seavingtons and The Lambrooks *B & W 14*   **P** *Bp and D&C
(jt)*   **R** T HANDY
PETHERWIN, NORTH (St Paternus)   *see* Egloskerry, N
Petherwin, Tremaine, Tresmere etc *Truro*
PETHERWIN, SOUTH (St Paternus)   *see* Three Rivers *Truro*
PETROCKSTOWE (St Petrock)   *see* Shebbear, Buckland Filleigh,
Sheepwash etc *Ex*
PETT (St Mary and St Peter)   *see* Fairlight and Pett *Chich*
PETT LEVEL (St Nicholas) *as above*
PETTAUGH (St Catherine)   *see* Debenham and Helmingham
St E
PETTISTREE (St Peter and St Paul)   *see* Wickham Market w
Pettistree *St E*
PETTON (not known) w Cockshutt, Welshampton and Lyneal
w Colemere *Lich 17*   **P** *Bp and R K Mainwaring Esq (jt)*
P-in-c S D HARROP
PETTON (St Petrock)   *see* Bampton, Morebath, Clayhanger,
Petton etc *Ex*
PETTS WOOD (St Francis) *Roch 16*   **P** *Bp*   **V** R D LANE
PETWORTH (St Mary) *Chich 10*   **P** *Lord Egremont*
P-in-c P M GILBERT
PEVENSEY (St Nicolas) (St Wilfrid) *Chich 14*   **P** *Bp*
V *vacant*
PEWSEY (St John the Baptist)   *see* Vale of Pewsey *Sarum*
PHEASEY (St Chad) *Lich 25*   **P** *DBP*   **P-in-c** J R BARNETT
PHILADELPHIA (St Thomas) Extra-Parochial Place *Sheff 4*
C D J BROWN, M J RUTTER, P FINDLEY, T P BASSFORD
PHILLACK (St Felicitas)   *see* Godrevy *Truro*
PHILLEIGH (St Philleigh)   *see* Gerrans w St Anthony-in-
Roseland and Philleigh *Truro*
PICCADILLY (St James)   *see* Westmr St Jas *Lon*
PICKENHAM, NORTH (St Andrew)   *see* Necton, Holme Hale w
N and S Pickenham *Nor*
PICKENHAM, SOUTH (All Saints) *as above*
PICKERING (St Peter and St Paul) w Lockton and Levisham
York 19   **P** *Abp*   **V** A M PRITCHETT   **C** C N JOHNSON
PICKHILL (All Saints)   *see* Kirklington w Burneston and Wath
and Pickhill *Leeds*
PICKWELL (All Saints)   *see* Burrough Hill Pars *Leic*
PICKWORTH (All Saints)   *see* Gt and Lt Casterton w Pickworth
and Tickencote *Pet*
PICKWORTH (St Andrew)   *see* S Lafford *Linc*
PIDDINGHOE (St John)   *see* Peacehaven and Telscombe Cliffs
w Piddinghoe etc *Chich*
PIDDINGTON (St John the Baptist)   *see* Hardingstone and
Piddington w Horton *Pet*
PIDDINGTON (St Nicholas)   *see* Ray Valley *Ox*
PIDDLE VALLEY, Hilton, Cheselbourne and Melcombe
Horsey, The *Sarum 1*   **P** *Bp, Eton Coll, G A L-F Pitt-Rivers Esq,
D&C Sarum, and D&C Win (by turn)*   **V** *vacant*
PIDDLE, NORTH (St Michael)   *see* Abberton, The Flyfords,
Naunton Beauchamp etc *Worc*
PIDDLEHINTON (St Mary the Virgin)   *see* Piddle Valley, Hilton,
Cheselbourne etc *Sarum*

PIDDLETRENTHIDE (All Saints) *as above*
PIDLEY CUM FENTON (All Saints)   *see* Somersham w Pidley and Oldhurst and Woodhurst *Ely*
PIERCEBRIDGE (St Mary)   *see* Coniscliffe *Dur*
PILHAM (All Saints)   *see* Lea Gp *Linc*
PILL (Christ Church), Portbury and Easton-in-Gordano *B & W 12*   **P** *Bp*   **V** R H M LEGG
PILLATON (St Modwen)   *see* Penkridge *Lich*
PILLATON (St Odulph)   *see* St Dominic, Landulph and St Mellion w Pillaton *Truro*
PILLERTON HERSEY (St Mary)   *see* Stourdene Gp *Cov*
PILLEY (Mission Church)   *see* Tankersley, Thurgoland and Wortley *Sheff*
PILLEY (St Nicholas)   *see* Boldre w S Baddesley *Win*
PILLING (St John the Baptist)   *see* Stalmine w Pilling *Blackb*
PILNING (St Peter) w Compton Greenfield *Bris 2*   **P** *Bp*
C P W ROWE
PILSLEY (St Mary the Virgin)   *see* N Wingfield, Clay Cross and Pilsley *Derby*
PILTON (All Saints)   *see* Aldwincle, Clopton, Pilton, Stoke Doyle etc *Pet*
PILTON (St John the Baptist) w Croscombe, North Wootton and Dinder *B & W 7*   **P** *Bp and Peache Trustees (jt)*
P-in-c C J BUTLER   **NSM** E BRIGHTWELL
PILTON (St Mary the Virgin)   *see* Barnstaple *Ex*
PILTON (St Nicholas)   *see* Empingham, Edith Weston, Lyndon, Manton etc *Pet*
PIMLICO (St Barnabas) *Lon 3*   **P** *Bp*   **V** *vacant*
PIMLICO (St Gabriel) *Lon 3*   **P** *Bp*   **V** O C G HIGGS
C L R CLARK
PIMLICO (St Mary) Bourne Street *Lon 3*   **P** *Trustees*
NSM S N LEAMY
PIMLICO (St Peter) w Westminster Christ Church *Lon 3*
P *Bp*   **V** R J WILLIAMSON   **C** J M KHOVACS
PIMLICO (St Saviour) *Lon 3*   **P** *Bp*   **V** M J CATTERICK
PIMLICO Bourne Street (St Mary)   *see* Pimlico St Mary Bourne Street *Lon*
PIMPERNE (St Peter), Stourpaine, Durweston and Bryanston *Sarum 6*   **P** *DBP (2 turns), D&C (1 turn)*   **R** S P COULTER
NSM J W WHITTLE
PINCHBECK (St Mary)   *see* Glen Gp *Linc*
PINCHBECK, WEST (St Bartholomew) *as above*
PINHOE (Hall)   *see* Broadclyst, Clyst Honiton, Pinhoe, Rockbeare etc *Ex*
PINHOE (St Michael and All Angels) *as above*
PINNER (St Anselm)   *see* Hatch End St Anselm *Lon*
PINNER (St John the Baptist) *Lon 23*   **P** *V Harrow*
V P C HULLYER   **C** O AYODEJI   **NSM** A J SMITH
PINNER VIEW (St George)   *see* Headstone St Geo *Lon*
PINVIN (St Nicholas)   *see* Pershore w Pinvin, Wick and Birlingham *Worc*
PINXTON (St Helen) (Church Hall) *Derby 1*   **P** *Bp*
C G MANLEY   **OLM** P F GOODCHILD
PIPE-CUM-LYDE (St Peter) and Moreton-on-Lugg *Heref 3*
P *Bp, Soc of the Faith, and D&C (by turn)*
P-in-c P A LITTLEWOOD   **NSM** E S V VERWEY
PIRBRIGHT (St Michael and All Angels) *Guildf 12*   **P** *Ld Chan*
P-in-c C MUSSER   **OLM** G WILLIAMSON
PIRTON (St Mary)   *see* Holwell, Ickleford and Pirton *St Alb*
PIRTON (St Peter)   *see* Stoulton w Drake's Broughton and Pirton etc *Worc*
PISHILL (not known)   *see* Nettlebed w Bix, Highmoor, Pishill etc *Ox*
PITCHCOMBE (St John the Baptist)   *see* Painswick, Sheepscombe, Cranham, The Edge etc *Glouc*
PITCHFORD (St Michael and All Angels)   *see* Condover w Frodesley, Acton Burnell etc *Heref*
PITCOMBE (St Leonard)   *see* Bruton and Distr *B & W*
PITMINSTER (St Mary and St Andrew)   *see* Blackdown *B & W*
PITNEY (St John the Baptist)   *see* Langport Area *B & W*
PITSEA (St Gabriel) w Nevendon *Chelmsf 12*   **P** *Bp*
R S A LAW
PITSFORD (All Saints) w Boughton *Pet 2*   **P** *Bp*   **R** S TROTT
PITSMOOR (Christ Church) *Sheff 3*   **P** *Ch Patr Trust*
V P IRESON   **C** H L HALL
PITTINGTON (St Laurence)   *see* Belmont and Pittington *Dur*
PITTON (St Peter)   *see* Clarendon *Sarum*
PIXHAM (St Mary the Virgin)   *see* Dorking w Ranmore *Guildf*
PIXLEY (St Andrew)   *see* Ledbury *Heref*
PLAISTOW (Holy Trinity)   *see* Kirdford *Chich*
PLAISTOW (St Martin) (St Mary) (St Philip and St James) and North Canning Town *Chelmsf 5*   **P** *Patr Bd*
TR M R THOMAS   **C** F G WAKELING   **Hon C** P B KENNEDY
NSM C T OLADUJI
PLAISTOW (St Mary) *Roch 14*   **P** *Bp*   **V** A KEELER
C R M PEET

PLAITFORD (St Peter)   *see* Forest and Avon *Sarum*
PLAS NEWTON (St Michael) *Ches 2*   **P** *Simeon's Trustees*
V R D PETERS
PLATT (St Mary the Virgin) *Roch 10*   **P** *Bp*   **V** E M R WALKER
PLATT BRIDGE (St Nathaniel) *Liv 14*   **P** *Bp*
P-in-c L MCGREGOR
PLAXTOL (not known)   *see* Shipbourne w Plaxtol *Roch*
PLAYDEN (St Michael)   *see* Rye *Chich*
PLAYFORD (St Mary)   *see* Gt and Lt Bealings w Playford and Culpho *St E*
PLEASLEY (St Michael)   *see* E Scarsdale *Derby*
PLEASLEY HILL (St Barnabas)   *see* Mansfield St Aug and Pleasley Hill *S'well*
PLEASLEY VALE (St Chad)   *see* Mansfield Woodhouse *S'well*
PLEMSTALL (St Peter) w Guilden Sutton *Ches 2*
P *Capt P Egerton Warburton*   **V** M HART   **NSM** B A KING
PLESHEY (Holy Trinity) *Chelmsf 9*   **P** *Bp*   **V** *vacant*
PLUCKLEY (St Nicholas)   *see* G7 Benefice *Cant*
PLUMPTON (All Saints) (St Michael and All Angels) w East Chiltington cum Novington *Chich 21*   **P** *Ld Chan*
R G D BROSTER
PLUMPTON WALL (St John the Evangelist)   *see* Penrith w Newton Reigny and Plumpton Wall *Carl*
PLUMSTEAD (All Saints) Shooters Hill *S'wark 6*   **P** *CPAS*
V *vacant*
PLUMSTEAD (Ascension)   *see* Plumstead Common *S'wark*
PLUMSTEAD (St John the Baptist) w St James and St Paul *S'wark 6*   **P** *Simeon's Trustees and CPAS (alt)*   **V** P J ROGERS
PLUMSTEAD (St Mark and St Margaret)   *see* Plumstead Common *S'wark*
PLUMSTEAD (St Michael)   *see* Barningham w Matlaske w Baconsthorpe etc *Nor*
PLUMSTEAD (St Nicholas) *S'wark 6*   **P** *V Plumstead St Mark w St Marg*   **V** A G STEVENS
PLUMSTEAD COMMON *S'wark 6*   **P** *Bp and DBP (jt)*
V C R WELHAM   **C** B T ASMELASH
PLUMSTEAD, GREAT (St Mary) and LITTLE (St Gervase and Protase) w Thorpe End and Witton *Nor 4*   **P** *Bp and D&C (jt)*   **P-in-c** D J PLATTIN
PLUMTREE (St Mary) *S'well 5*   **P** *DBP*   **R** T H KIRKMAN
PLUNGAR (St Helen)   *see* Vale of Belvoir *Leic*
PLYMOUTH (Emmanuel), St Paul Efford and St Augustine *Ex 21*   **P** *Patr Bd*   **TR** K F FREEMAN
PLYMOUTH (St Andrew) and St Paul Stonehouse *Ex 21*
P *Patr Bd*   **TR** J M DENT   **TV** L P T SIM   **C** L BRASCHI
PLYMOUTH (St Gabriel) Peverell *Ex 21*   **P** *Bp*
P-in-c K F HAYDON   **C** T P JORDAN   **NSM** A OVERTON
PLYMOUTH (St John the Evangelist)   *see* Sutton-on-Plym, Plymouth St Simon and St Mary *Ex*
PLYMOUTH (St Jude) *Ex 21*   **P** *Trustees*   **P-in-c** T SMITH
PLYMOUTH (St Matthias)   *see* Charles w Plymouth St Matthias *Ex*
PLYMOUTH (St Pancras)   *see* Pennycross *Ex*
PLYMOUTH (St Peter) and the Holy Apostles *Ex 21*
P *Bp and Keble Coll Ox (jt)*   **P-in-c** D C WAY
PLYMOUTH (St Simon)   *see* Sutton-on-Plym, Plymouth St Simon and St Mary *Ex*
PLYMOUTH Crownhill (Ascension) *Ex 21*   **P** *Bp*
P-in-c T THORP   **C** C J ROUTLEDGE, E M A BURKE,
S P RUNDELL
PLYMPTON (St Mary the Blessed Virgin) *Ex 21*   **P** *Bp*
C R W BECK   **NSM** M BRIMICOMBE
PLYMPTON (St Maurice) *Ex 21*   **P** *D&C Windsor*   **R** *vacant*
PLYMSTOCK (St Mary and All Saints) and Hooe *Ex 21*
P *Patr Bd*   **P-in-c** S M PAYNE   **TV** D APPLEBY
NSM J APPLEBY, M P HINKS
PLYMTREE (St John the Baptist)   *see* Broadhembury, Payhembury and Plymtree *Ex*
POCKLEY (St John the Baptist)   *see* Kirkdale w Harome, Nunnington and Pockley *York*
POCKLINGTON (All Saints)   *see* Pocklington Wold *York*
POCKLINGTON WOLD *York 5*   **P** *Abp*   **R** G HOLLINGSWORTH
PODIMORE (St Peter)   *see* Ilchester w Northover, Limington, Yeovilton etc *B & W*
PODINGTON (St Mary the Virgin)   *see* Wymington w Podington *St Alb*
POINT CLEAR (Mission)   *see* St Osyth and Great Bentley *Chelmsf*
POINTON (Christ Church)   *see* Billingborough Gp *Linc*
POKESDOWN (All Saints) *Win 8*   **P** *V Christchurch*
P-in-c M R POWIS
POKESDOWN (St James) *Win 8*   **P** *Bp*   **P-in-c** J PARES
POLDEN WHEEL, The *B & W 4*   **P** *Bp*   **NSM** A C HUNT,
S C PARSONS
POLEBROOK (All Saints)   *see* Barnwell, Hemington, Luddington in the Brook etc *Pet*

POLEGATE (St John) *Chich 14* **P** *Bp* **V** C G SPINKS
NSM R A HERKES
POLESWORTH (St Editha) *Birm 10* **P** *Ld Chan* **V** P A WELLS
POLING (St Nicholas) *Chich 1* **P** *Bp* **P-in-c** M M SLATTERY
POLLINGTON (St John the Baptist) *see Gt Snaith Sheff*
POLRUAN (St Saviour) *see Lanteglos by Fowey Truro*
POLSTEAD (St Mary) *see Stoke by Nayland w Leavenheath and Polstead St E*
POLTIMORE (St Mary the Virgin) *see Brampford Speke, Cadbury, Newton St Cyres etc Ex*
PONDERS END (St Matthew) *Lon 18* **P** *V Enfield*
P-in-c R C KNOWLING **C** M T CHILDS
PONDERSBRIDGE (St Thomas) *see Whittlesey, Pondersbridge and Coates Ely*
PONSANOOTH (St Michael and All Angels) *see Mabe Truro*
PONSBOURNE (St Mary) *see Lt Berkhamsted and Bayford, Essendon etc St Alb*
PONSONBY (not known) *see Beckermet St Jo and St Bridget w Ponsonby Carl*
PONTEFRACT (All Saints) *Leeds 19* **P** *Bp*
P-in-c V IWANUSCHAK **NSM** K B WARRENER, W D PHILLIPS
OLM H MERRICK
PONTEFRACT (St Giles) (St Mary) *Leeds 19* **P** *Bp*
V R G COOPER **C** G R CAVIESES ARAYA **NSM** M J TAYLOR
PONTELAND (St Mary the Virgin) *Newc 4* **P** *Mert Coll Ox*
V P BARHAM **NSM** C L BROWN
PONTESBURY First and Second Portions (St George) *Heref 12*
P *St Chad's Coll Dur* **P-in-c** M A JONES **C** M LAMBOURNE
NSM C WRIGHT, S M SMALL
PONTON, GREAT (Holy Cross) *see Colsterworth Gp Linc*
PONTON, LITTLE (St Guthlac) *as above*
POOL (St Wilfrid) *see Lower Wharfedale Leeds*
POOLBROOK (St Andrew) *see Malvern Chase Worc*
POOLE (St James w St Paul) *Sarum 7* **P** *Ch Soc Trust*
R L J HOLT **C** C M HARWOOD
POOLE KEYNES (St Michael and All Angels) *see Kemble, Poole Keynes, Somerford Keynes etc Glouc*
POOLE, NORTH Ecumenical Team *Sarum 7* **P** *Bp*
TV J E AUDIBERT **C** M A MAK
POOLEY BRIDGE (St Paul) *see Barton, Pooley Bridge, Martindale etc Carl*
POORTON, NORTH (St Mary Magdalene) *see Askerswell, Loders, Powerstock and Symondsbury Sarum*
POPLAR (All Saints) *Lon 7* **P** *Patr Bd* **TV** J A C HODGES
C S S MCCALLA **NSM** J C SHELDON, T J DUNCAN
POPLEY w Limes Park and Rooksdown (St Gabriel) *Win 4*
P *Bp* **V** A BOTHAM
POPPLETON, NETHER (St Everilda) w Upper (All Saints) *York 1*
P *Abp* **V** J C E SYLVESTER **NSM** M C S FOSSETT
POPPYLAND *Nor 21* **P** *Duchy of Lancaster (2 turns), DBP, MMCET, and Bp (4 turns)* **R** *vacant*
PORCHESTER (St James) *S'well 7* **P** *Bp* **V** P A WILLIAMS
PORINGLAND (All Saints) *Nor 8* **P** *Bp, BNC Ox, J D Alston Esq, and G H Hastings Esq (3 turns) and DBP (1 turn)*
R R H PARSONAGE **OLM** D J DRIVER
PORKELLIS (St Christopher) *see Helston and Wendron Truro*
PORLOCK (St Dubricius) and Porlock Weir w Stoke Pero, Selworthy and Luccombe *B & W 15* **P** *Ld Chan*
R W H M LEMMEY **NSM** S R B HUMPHREYS
PORLOCK WEIR (St Nicholas) *see Porlock and Porlock Weir w Stoke Pero etc B & W*
PORT ERIN (St Catherine) *see Rushen S & M*
PORT ST MARY (St Mary) *as above*
PORTBURY (Blessed Virgin Mary) *see Pill, Portbury and Easton-in-Gordano B & W*
PORTCHESTER (St Mary) *Portsm 2* **P** *J R Thistlethwaite Esq*
P-in-c I MEREDITH **C** M A WILLIAMS
PORTESHAM (St Peter) *see Abbotsbury, Portesham and Langton Herring Sarum*
PORTHILL (St Andrew)
PORTHLEVEN (St Bartholomew) *see W Kerrier Truro*
PORTHPEAN (St Levan) *see St Austell Truro*
PORTISHEAD (St Peter) *B & W 12* **P** *Patr Bd*
TV C A J UDSON, T E HODGETT
PORTLAND Team Minstry (All Saints) (St Andrew) (St John)
Sarum 4 **P** *Patr Bd* **TR** T F GOMM **TV** J K MENZIES
C M S PHILLIPS
PORTLEMOUTH, EAST (St Winwaloe Onocaus) *see Stokenham, Slapton, Charleton w Buckland etc Ex*
PORTLOE (All Saints) *see Veryan w Ruan Lanihorne Truro*
PORTMAN SQUARE (St Paul) *see Langham Place All So Lon*
PORTON (St Nicholas) *see Bourne Valley Sarum*
PORTREATH (St Mary) *see St Illogan Truro*
PORTSDOWN (Christ Church) *Portsm 5* **P** *Simeon's Trustees*
V A M WILSON **C** C SHERMAN, P D HALL
NSM S G PHILLIPS

PORTSEA (All Saints) *Portsm 6* **P** *V Portsea St Mary and Bp (jt)*
V M F PYE
PORTSEA (St Alban) *Portsm 6* **P** *Bp* **V** *vacant*
PORTSEA (St Cuthbert) *Portsm 6* **P** *Bp* **V** D M POWER
NSM C G GULLY, J POWER, K E MARLOW
PORTSEA (St George) *Portsm 6* **P** *Bp* **P-in-c** B J DAVIES
PORTSEA (St Mary) (St Faith and St Barnabas) (St Wilfrid)
Portsm 6 **P** *Win Coll* **V** R C WHITE
C C E HETHERINGTON, J D F M CHESTERFIELD-TERRY
NSM B J O'SULLIVAN, S K WHITELOCK
PORTSEA (St Saviour) *Portsm 6* **P** *Bp* **V** *vacant*
PORTSEA (The Ascension) *Portsm 6* **P** *Bp* **V** *vacant*
PORTSEA North End (St Mark) *Portsm 6* **P** *DBP*
TV C E KEAY **NSM** L C DENNESS, R E WEEKS
PORTSLADE (St Nicolas) (St Andrew) and Mile Oak *Chich 20*
P *Bp* **P-in-c** A J PERRY **C** A G BIRKS **NSM** P G PANNETT
PORTSWOOD (Christ Church) *Win 13* **P** *Bp*
P-in-c M J ARCHER **C** N J HOPKINS **NSM** E J ROBERTS, F M TYSON
PORTSWOOD (St Denys) *Win 13* **P** *Bp* **P-in-c** K J RANDALL
PORTWAY AND DANEBURY Benefice, The *Win 3* **P** *Patr Bd*
TR P M GILKS **TV** V A COLE
POSBURY (St Francis Proprietary Chapel) *see Crediton, Shobrooke and Sandford etc Ex*
POSLINGFORD (St Mary) *see Stour Valley St E*
POSTBRIDGE (St Gabriel) *see Ashburton, Bickington, Buckland in the Moor etc Ex*
POSTLING (St Mary and St Radegund) *see Lyminge w Paddlesworth, Stanford w Postling etc Cant*
POSTWICK (All Saints) *see Brundall w Braydeston and Postwick Nor*
POTT SHRIGLEY (St Christopher) *Ches 13* **P** *MMCET*
V *vacant*
POTTEN END (Holy Trinity) *see Gt Berkhamsted, Gt and Lt Gaddesden etc St Alb*
POTTER HEIGHAM (St Nicholas) *see Ludham, Potter Heigham, Hickling and Catfield Nor*
POTTERHANWORTH (St Andrew) *see Branston w Nocton and Potterhanworth Linc*
POTTERNE (St Mary the Virgin) w Worton and Marston
Sarum 17 **P** *Bp* **V** D J HOWARD
POTTERNEWTON (St Martin) *Leeds 14* **P** *Trustees*
NSM S J DE GAY
POTTERS BAR (King Charles the Martyr) *St Alb 14* **P** *Bp Lon*
V M J BURNS
POTTERS BAR (St Mary and All Saints) *St Alb 14* **P** *Bp Lon*
V P J BEVAN
POTTERS GREEN (St Philip Deacon) *Cov 1* **P** *Ld Chan*
P-in-c M L EAMAN
POTTERS MARSTON (St Mary) *see Barwell w Potters Marston and Stapleton Leic*
POTTERSPURY (St Nicholas) w Furtho and Yardley Gobion w Cosgrove and Wicken *Pet 5* **P** *D&C, Jes Coll Ox, and Soc Merchant Venturers Bris (jt)* **P-in-c** D C WHITTAKER
POTTO (St Mary) *see Whorlton w Carlton and Faceby York*
POTTON (St Mary the Virgin) w Sutton and Cockayne Hatley
St Alb 10 **P** *The Crown (3 turns), St Jo Coll Ox (1 turn)*
R G SMITH
POUGHILL (St Michael and All Angels) *see N Creedy Ex*
POUGHILL (St Olaf King and Martyr) *Truro 8* **P** *Ch Soc Trust*
V P A WHYBROW
POULNER (St John) *see Ringwood Win*
POULSHOT (St Peter) *see Seend, Bulkington and Poulshot Sarum*
POULTON (St Michael and All Angels) *see S Cotswolds Glouc*
POULTON CARLETON (St Chad) and Singleton *Blackb 12*
P *DBP and Exors R Dumbreck Esq (jt)* **V** M P KEIGHLEY
C C A LEITCH
POULTON LANCELYN (Holy Trinity) *Ches 8* **P** *R Bebington*
V R K WILES
POULTON-LE-FYLDE (St Chad) *see Poulton Carleton and Singleton Blackb*
POULTON-LE-SANDS (Holy Trinity) w Morecambe
St Laurence *Blackb 11* **P** *V Lanc* **R** M R PEATMAN
POUND HILL (St Barnabas) *see Worth, Pound Hill and Maidenbower Chich*
POUNDSBRIDGE (Chapel) *see Penshurst and Fordcombe Roch*
POUNDSTOCK (St Winwaloe) *see Week St Mary Circle of Par Truro*
POWDERHAM (St Clement Bishop and Martyr) *see Exminster, Kenn, Kenton w Mamhead, and Powderham Ex*
POWERSTOCK (St Mary the Virgin) *see Askerswell, Loders, Powerstock and Symondsbury Sarum*
POWICK (St Peter) and Guarlford and Madresfield w Newland *Worc 2* **P** *Bp, Lady Rosalind Morrison, and Croome Estate Trustees (jt)* **R** S E IRWIN

POYNINGS (Holy Trinity) w Edburton, Newtimber and Pyecombe *Chich 8* **P** *Ld Chan (1 turn), Bp and Abp (1 turn)*
P-in-c C M CURRER
POYNTINGTON (All Saints) *see Queen Thorne Sarum*
POYNTON (St George) *Ches 17* **P** *Bp* **V** R I MCLAREN
C A S LIVINGSTON **NSM** C J BUCKLEY, L P CUMMINS
POYNTON, HIGHER (St Martin) *see Poynton Ches*
PRADOE (extra-parochial place) *Lich 19* **Hon**
C A C NETHERWOOD
PRATTS BOTTOM (All Souls) *see Green Street Green and Pratts Bottom Roch*
PREES (St Chad) *see Edstaston, Fauls, Prees, Tilstock and Whixall Lich*
PREESALL (St Oswald) *see Waterside Par Blackb*
PRENTON (St Stephen) *Ches 1* **P** *Bp* **V** E W LAUTENBACH
C H E BUCKLEY
PRENTON DELL (St Alban) *see Prenton Ches*
PRESCOT (St Mary) St Paul *Liv 2* **P** *K Coll Cam*
V J A TAYLOR
PRESHUTE (St George) *see Marlborough Sarum*
PRESTBURY (St Mary) *see N Cheltenham Glouc*
PRESTBURY (St Nicolas) *as above*
PRESTBURY (St Peter) *Ches 13* **P** *Ms C J C B Legh*
V P J M ANGIER **NSM** A S RAVENSCROFT, S H CALLIS
PRESTEIGNE (St Andrew) w Discoed, Kinsham, Lingen and Knill *Heref 4* **P** *Patr Bd* **R** S HOLLINGHURST
NSM D VENABLES
PRESTON (All Saints) *see Hedon, Paull, Sproatley and Preston York*
PRESTON (All Saints) *Blackb 13* **P** *Trustees*
V D P AP G MEIRION-JONES **C** M J AYERS
PRESTON (All Saints) *see S Cerney w Cerney Wick, Siddington and Preston Glouc*
PRESTON (Church of the Ascension) *Lon 21* **P** *Bp*
V O J FIELD **NSM** G E BEVAN
PRESTON (Emmanuel) *Blackb 13* **P** *R Preston*
V P G HAMBORG
PRESTON (Good Shepherd) *see Brighton Gd Shep Preston Chich*
PRESTON (St Andrew) w Sutton Poyntz, Littlemoor, and Osmington w Poxwell *Sarum 4* **P** *Patr Bd* **TR** T R WEST
TV L S DOBBINS **NSM** B E J ELLIS
PRESTON (St Cuthbert) *Blackb 13* **P** *Bp* **V** E P BOSSWARD
PRESTON (St John the Baptist) *see Redmarley D'Abitot, Bromesberrow, Pauntley etc Glouc*
PRESTON (St John) (St George the Martyr) (Christ the King Chapel) *Blackb 13* **P** *DBP* **R** T W LIPSCOMB
PRESTON (St John) w Brighton St Augustine and St Saviour *Chich 19* **P** *Bp* **V** A V BOWMAN
PRESTON (St Martin) *see St Paul's Walden St Alb*
PRESTON (St Mary the Virgin) *see Lavenham w Preston St E*
PRESTON (St Matthias) *see Brighton St Matthias Chich*
PRESTON (St Mildred) *see Canonry Cant*
PRESTON (St Oswald) St Jude *Blackb 13* **P** *Bp, Simeon's Trustees, and R Preston St Jo and St Geo (jt)* **P-in-c** G W NELSON
PRESTON (St Paul) *see Paignton Ch Ch and Preston St Paul Ex*
PRESTON (St Peter and St Paul) *see Empingham, Edith Weston, Lyndon, Manton etc Pet*
PRESTON (St Stephen) *Blackb 13* **P** *Bp* **V** M COOK
PRESTON Acregate Lane (Mission) *see Preston Risen Lord Blackb*
PRESTON BAGOT (All Saints) *see Claverdon w Preston Bagot Cov*
PRESTON BISSET (St John the Baptist) *see The Claydons and Swan Ox*
PRESTON CAPES (St Peter and St Paul) *see Badby w Newham and Charwelton w Fawsley etc Pet*
PRESTON ON STOUR (St Mary) *see Ilmington w Stretton-on-Fosse etc Cov*
PRESTON PATRICK (St Patrick) *see Kirkby Lonsdale Carl*
PRESTON PLUCKNETT (St James the Great) (St Peter) *B & W 6* **P** *Bp (2 turns), Mrs S W Rawlins (1 turn)* **V** A PERRIS
C A D HANDCOCK, D M KEEN
PRESTON The Risen Lord (St Matthew) (St Hilda) (St James's church hall) *Blackb 13* **P** *Patr Bd* **P-in-c** P R NUNN
C K BHATTI
PRESTON UNDER SCARR (St Margaret) *see Penhill Leeds*
PRESTON WEALDMOORS (St Lawrence) *see Edgmond w Kynnersley and Preston Wealdmoors Lich*
PRESTON WYNNE (Holy Trinity) *see Maund Gp Heref*
PRESTON, EAST (St Mary) w Kingston *Chich 1* **P** *D&C*
V J H LYON
PRESTON, WEST *Blackb 13* **P** *Patr Bd* **P-in-c** D J RADCLIFFE
C J D G NASH
PRESTON-NEXT-FAVERSHAM (St Catherine) *Cant 14*
P *Abp* **V** S C WILSON

PRESTON-ON-TEES (All Saints) and Longnewton *Dur 10*
P *Bp* **P-in-c** J C LAMBERT
PRESTON-ON-WYE (St Lawrence) *see Cusop w Blakemere, Bredwardine w Brobury etc Heref*
PRESTONVILLE (St Luke) *Chich 19* **P** *CPAS* **V** M B POOLE
PRESTWICH (St Gabriel) *Man 10* **P** *Bp* **P-in-c** S S WILLIAMS
NSM M TRIVASSE
PRESTWICH (St Hilda) *Man 10* **P** *Trustees* **V** *vacant*
PRESTWICH (St Margaret) (St George) *Man 10* **P** *R Prestwich St Mary* **C** S S WILLIAMS
PRESTWICH (St Mary the Virgin) *Man 10* **P** *Trustees*
P-in-c C G WEDGE **C** S S WILLIAMS
PRESTWOLD (St Andrew) *see Wymeswold and Prestwold w Hoton Leic*
PRESTWOOD (Holy Trinity) and Great Hampden *Ox 17*
P *Bp and Hon I H Hope-Morley (jt)*
R D J O KEARLEY-HEYWOOD **Hon** C E T B A DERLÉN
PRIDDY (St Lawrence) *B & W 1* **P** *Bp*
V P M HOLLINGSWORTH
PRIESTWOOD (St Andrew) *see Bracknell Ox*
PRIMROSE HILL (Holy Trinity) *see Lydney Glouc*
PRIMROSE HILL (St Mary the Virgin) w Avenue Road (St Paul) *Lon 16* **P** *Trustees* **V** M J BROWN **C** T I MILLER
NSM M J WAKEFIELD
PRINCE'S PARK (Christ the King) *Roch 5* **P** *Bp*
P-in-c D E D'SOUZA
PRINCES RISBOROUGH (St Mary) *see Risborough Ox*
PRIOR'S DEAN (not known) *see Greatham w Empshott and Hawkley w Prior's Dean Portsm*
PRIORS HARDWICK (St Mary the Virgin) w Priors Marston and Wormleighton *Cov 10* **P** *Earl Spencer* **C** G S ROBERTS, R D CLUCAS
PRIORS LEE (St Peter) and St Georges' *Lich 21* **P** *Bp and V Shifnal (jt)* **C** K S EVANS, T S CARTER **Hon**
C R B BALKWILL
PRIORS MARSTON (St Leonard) *see Priors Hardwick, Priors Marston and Wormleighton Cov*
PRISTON (St Luke) *see Timsbury w Priston, Camerton and Dunkerton B & W*
PRITTLEWELL (St Luke) *Chelmsf 15* **P** *Bp* **V** J T MCCLUSKEY
PRITTLEWELL (St Mary the Virgin) *Chelmsf 15* **P** *Bp*
V *vacant*
PRITTLEWELL (St Peter) w Westcliff St Cedd and the Saints of Essex *Chelmsf 15* **P** *Bp* **OLM** D R PIERCE
PRITTLEWELL (St Stephen) *Chelmsf 15* **P** *Bp*
P-in-c C S BALDWIN
PROBUS (St Probus and St Grace), Ladock and Grampound w Creed and St Erme *Truro 6* **P** *DBP* **TR** A J WADE
TV E E GOLDSMITH **C** M E RICHARDS
PRUDHOE (St Mary Magdalene) *Newc 9* **P** *Dioc Soc*
V C H HOPE
PSALTER LANE (St Andrew) *Sheff 2* **P** *Trustees* **V** *vacant*
PUBLOW (All Saints) w Pensford, Compton Dando and Chelwood *B & W 9* **P** *Bp* **R** *vacant*
PUCKINGTON (St Andrew) *see Winsmoor B & W*
PUCKLECHURCH (St Thomas à Becket) and Abson *Bris 5*
P *D&C* **V** S K YOUNG
PUDDINGTON (St Thomas à Becket) *see N Creedy Ex*
PUDDLETOWN (St Mary the Virgin), Tolpuddle and Milborne w Dewlish *Sarum 1* **P** *Bp, Ch Ch Ox, Viscount Rothermere, and trustees (jt)* **R** S C HILLMAN
PUDLESTON (St Peter) *see Leominster Heref*
PUDSEY (St James the Great) *see Woodhall Leeds*
PUDSEY (St Lawrence and St Paul) *Leeds 15* **P** *Bp and V Calverley (jt)* **V** P N AYERS **C** B T RANDALL
PULBOROUGH (St Mary) *Chich 11* **P** *Lord Egremont*
R P B WELCH
PULFORD (St Mary the Virgin) *see Eccleston and Pulford Ches*
PULHAM (St Thomas à Beckett) *see Three Valleys Sarum*
PULHAM MARKET (St Mary Magdalene) *see Dickleburgh and The Pulhams Nor*
PULHAM ST MARY (St Mary the Virgin) *as above*
PULLOXHILL (St James the Apostle) *see Silsoe, Pulloxhill and Flitton St Alb*
PULVERBATCH (St Edith) *see Gt Hanwood and Longden and Annscroft etc Heref*
PUNCKNOWLE (St Mary the Blessed Virgin) *see Bride Valley Sarum*
PURBROOK (St John the Baptist) *Portsm 5* **P** *Bp*
P-in-c C SHERMAN **C** A M WILSON, P D HALL
NSM J A JONES
PUREWELL (St John) *see Christchurch Win*
PURITON (St Michael and All Angels) and Pawlett *B & W 13*
P *Ld Chan (1 turn), D&C Windsor (2 turns)*
P-in-c D GODDARD **NSM** R A SELLERS
PURLEIGH (All Saints) *Chelmsf 11* **P** *Oriel Coll Ox*
V *vacant*

PURLEY (Christ Church) *S'wark 22*   P *Bp*   V C R TREFUSIS
Hon C S P STOCKS   OLM S P BISHOP
PURLEY (St Barnabas) *S'wark 22*   P *Bp*
P-in-c C G THOMSON   NSM E J GOODRIDGE
PURLEY (St Mark) Woodcote *S'wark 22*   P *Bp*
P-in-c F M WEAVER   NSM L ABRAMS
PURLEY (St Mary the Virgin) *Ox 4*   P *Ld Chan*
R D J ARCHER   OLM A MACKIE
PURLEY (St Swithun) *S'wark 22*   P *Bp*   P-in-c F M WEAVER
PURLWELL (St Andrew)   *see* Batley All SS and Purlwell *Leeds*
PURSE CAUNDLE (St Peter)   *see* Spire Hill *Sarum*
PURTON (St John)   *see* Sharpness, Purton, Brookend and Slimbridge *Glouc*
PURTON (St Mary) *Bris 7*   P *Bp*   V I D TWEEDIE-SMITH
OLM J M WELLS
PUSEY (All Saints)   *see* Cherbury w Gainfield *Ox*
PUTLEY (not known)   *see* Ledbury *Heref*
PUTNEY (St Margaret) *S'wark 18*   P *Bp*   V A BRODIE
PUTNEY (St Mary) (All Saints) *S'wark 18*   P *Patr Bd*
TR A B NEWBY   TV C D EYDEN   C L J FAWCETT
PUTNEY, EAST (St Stephen)   *see* Wandsworth St Mich w St Steph *S'wark*
PUTTENHAM (St John the Baptist)   *see* Seale, Puttenham and Wanborough *Guildf*
PYECOMBE (Transfiguration)   *see* Poynings w Edburton, Newtimber and Pyecombe *Chich*
PYLLE (St Thomas à Becket)   *see* Fosse Trinity *B & W*
PYPE HAYES (St Mary the Virgin)   *see* Erdington *Birm*
PYRFORD (Church of the Good Shepherd)   *see* Wisley w Pyrford *Guildf*
PYRFORD (St Nicholas) *as above*
PYRTON (St Mary)   *see* Icknield *Ox*
PYTCHLEY (All Saints)   *see* Gt w Lt Harrowden and Orlingbury and Isham etc *Pet*
PYWORTHY (St Swithun), Pancrasweek and Bridgerule *Ex 16*
P *DBP*   R *vacant*
QUADRING (St Margaret)   *see* Gosberton, Gosberton Clough and Quadring *Linc*
QUAINTON (Holy Cross and St Mary)   *see* Schorne *Ox*
QUANTOCK COAST Benefice, The *B & W 17*   P *Bp, DBP, Eton Coll, and Lady Gass (jt)*   R N MORGAN   Hon C A F TATHAM
NSM S L CAMPBELL
QUANTOCK TOWERS, The *B & W 17*   P *Bp, D&C Windsor, and D&C Wells (jt)*   Hon C B R G FLENLEY   NSM J G ROSE
QUANTOXHEAD, EAST (Blessed Virgin Mary)   *see* Quantock Coast *B & W*
QUANTOXHEAD, WEST (St Ethelreda) *as above*
QUARLEY (St Michael and All Angels)   *see* Portway and Danebury *Win*
QUARNDON (St Paul) *Derby 11*   P *Exors Viscount Scarsdale*
P-in-c W F BATES   NSM J M NEEDLE
QUARNFORD (St Paul)   *see* Longnor, Quarnford and Sheen *Lich*
QUARRENDON ESTATE (St Peter)   *see* Aylesbury *Ox*
QUARRINGTON (St Botolph) w Old Sleaford *Linc 14*
P *Bp*   R *vacant*
QUATFORD (St Mary Magdalene)   *see* Bridgnorth, Tasley, Astley Abbotts, etc *Heref*
QUATT (St Andrew)   *see* Alveley and Quatt *Heref*
QUEDGELEY (St James) *Glouc 2*   P *Bp*   V J F WARD
QUEEN CAMEL (St Barnabas)   *see* Cam Vale *B & W*
QUEEN CHARLTON (St Margaret)   *see* Keynsham *B & W*
QUEEN THORNE *Sarum 3*   P *Bp, The Revd J M P Goodden, J K Wingfield Digby Esq, and MMCET (jt)*   R V J ENEVER
C R E WYLD
QUEENBOROUGH (Holy Trinity)   *see* W Sheppey *Cant*
QUEENHILL (St Nicholas)   *see* Longdon, Castlemorton, Bushley, Queenhill etc *Worc*
QUEEN'S GATE (St Augustine)   *see* Onslow Square and S Kensington St Aug *Lon*
QUEENSBURY (All Saints) *Lon 23*   P *The Crown*   V K N BLAKE
QUEENSBURY (Holy Trinity) *Leeds 2*   P *Bp*
P-in-c S E W SHRINE
QUENDON (St Simon and St Jude)   *see* Newport w Widdington, Quendon and Rickling *Chelmsf*
QUENIBOROUGH (St Mary)   *see* Fosse *Leic*
QUENINGTON (St Swithun)   *see* S Cotswolds *Glouc*
QUERNMORE (St Peter)   *see* Dolphinholme w Quernmore and Over Wyresdale *Blackb*
QUETHIOCK (St Hugh)   *see* St Ive and Pensilva w Quethiock *Truro*
QUIDENHAM Group, The (St Andrew) *Nor 11*   P *Ld Chan (1 turn), Bp, Sir Thomas Beevor Bt, Major E H C Garnier, Trustees, and New Buckenham PCC (3 turns)*   P-in-c S M WRIGHT
QUINTON (St Swithun), Welford, Weston and Marston Sicca *Glouc 8*   P *Bp, D&C Worc, and DBP (jt)*   V *vacant*

QUINTON and PRESTON DEANERY (St John the Baptist)
see Wootton w Quinton and Preston Deanery *Pet*
QUINTON ROAD WEST (St Boniface) *Birm 2*   P *Bp*
V R P YATES   NSM J KNOX
QUINTON, THE (Christ Church) *Birm 2*   P *Bp*   R J A ARNOLD
C M J SIMPSON   NSM A P WELLS
QUORN (St Bartholomew)   *see* Quorndon *Leic*
QUORNDON (St Bartholomew) *Leic 6*   P *Bp*
V D H BOWLER
QUY (St Mary)   *see* Anglesey Gp *Ely*
RACKENFORD (All Saints)   *see* Washfield, Stoodleigh, Withleigh etc *Ex*
RACKHEATH (Holy Trinity) and Salhouse *Nor 4*   P *Bp*
P-in-c S R DUTTON
RACTON (St Peter)   *see* Octagon *Chich*
RADBOURNE (St Andrew)   *see* Boylestone, Church Broughton, Dalbury, etc *Derby*
RADCLIFFE (St Andrew) Black Lane *Man 10*   P *R Radcliffe St Mary*   V *vacant*
RADCLIFFE (St Mary) (St Thomas and St John) (St Philip Mission Church) *Man 10*   P *Patr Bd*   TV C T HAYDEN
NSM E A BINNS
RADCLIFFE-ON-TRENT (St Mary) and Shelford *S'well 5*
P *DBP and Ld Chan (alt)*   V G E ANDERSON
RADCLIVE (St John the Evangelist)   *see* Buckingham *Ox*
RADDESLEY Group of Parishes, The *Ely 4*   P E H Vestey Esq, Mrs B O Killander, Mrs B A Taylor, Duke of Sutherland, Exors C Thomas (5 turns), St Jo Coll Cam (1 turn)*   R *vacant*
RADDINGTON (St Michael)   *see* Wiveliscombe and the Hills *B & W*
RADFORD (All Souls) (St Peter) *S'well 9*   P *Bp*   Hon
C M T PHILLIPS   NSM K D BURTON
RADFORD (St Nicholas) *Cov 2*   P *Bp*   V *vacant*
RADFORD SEMELE (St Nicholas) *Cov 10*   P *Bp*
P-in-c M C GREEN   C V J BISIKER
RADFORD, NORTH (St Francis of Assisi)   *see* Cov St Fran N Radford *Cov*
RADIPOLE (Emmanuel) (St Adhelm) (St Ann) and Melcombe Regis *Sarum 4*   P *Patr Bd*   TV P J SALMON, T J GREENSLADE
C D NEWMAN   NSM G A HEBBERN, P E LEGG
RADLETT (Christ Church)   *see* Aldenham, Radlett and Shenley *St Alb*
RADLETT (St John) *as above*
RADLEY (St James the Great), Sunningwell and Kennington *Ox 19*   P *Bp, DBP, and Radley Coll (jt)*   R P J MCKELLEN
C A K MATHEW   OLM G J BECKETT
RADNAGE (St Mary)   *see* W Wycombe w Bledlow Ridge, Bradenham and Radnage *Ox*
RADNOR, OLD (St Stephen)   *see* Kington w Huntington, Old Radnor, Kinnerton etc *Heref*
RADSTOCK (St Nicholas) w Writhlington *B & W 11*
P *Bp*   R *vacant*
RADSTONE (St Lawrence)   *see* Astwell Gp *Pet*
RADWAY (St Peter)   *see* Edgehill Churches *Cov*
RADWELL (All Saints)   *see* Stotfold and Radwell *St Alb*
RADWINTER (St Mary the Virgin)   *see* The Sampfords and Radwinter w Hempstead *Chelmsf*
RAGDALE (All Saints)   *see* Upper Wreake *Leic*
RAINBOW HILL (St Barnabas)   *see* Worc St Barn w Ch Ch *Worc*
RAINFORD (All Saints) *Liv 11*   P V *Prescot*   V J E HEIGHTON
RAINHAM (St Helen and St Giles) w Wennington *Chelmsf 2*
P *MMCET*   R H PRADELLA
RAINHAM (St Margaret) *Roch 3*   P *Bp*   V J HENNING
C J M HARRATT, M L SIMMS
RAINHILL (St Ann) *Liv 10*   P *Trustees*   V A R CONANT
C A J H LEATHERBARROW
RAINOW (Holy Trinity) w Saltersford and Forest *Ches 13*
P *Bp*   V S D RATHBONE
RAINTON (not known)   *see* Topcliffe, Baldersby w Dishforth, Dalton etc *York*
RAINTON, EAST (St Cuthbert) *Dur 14*   P *D&C*
P-in-c M L BECK
RAINTON, WEST (St Mary) *Dur 14*   P *Bp*   P-in-c M L BECK
RAINWORTH (St Simon and St Jude)   *see* Blidworth w Rainworth *S'well*
RAITHBY (Holy Trinity)   *see* Bolingbroke Deanery *Linc*
RAITHBY (St Peter)   *see* Legbourne and Wold Marsh *Linc*
RAME (St Germanus)   *see* Maker w Rame *Truro*
RAMPISHAM (St Michael and All Angels)   *see* Melbury *Sarum*
RAMPSIDE (St Michael)   *see* Aldingham, Dendron, Rampside and Urswick *Carl*
RAMPTON (All Saints) *Ely 6*   P *Bp*   P-in-c K A HODGINS
RAMPTON (All Saints)   *see* Retford Area *S'well*
RAMSBOTTOM (St Andrew) (St John) (St Paul) and Edenfield *Man 8*   P *Patr Bd (3 turns), Prime Min (1 turn)*   TR A J LINDOP
C S P OPENSHAW

RAMSBURY (Holy Cross)   *see* Whitton *Sarum*
RAMSDELL (Christ Church)   *see* Baughurst, Ramsdell, Wolverton w Ewhurst etc *Win*
RAMSDEN (St James)   *see* Forest Edge *Ox*
RAMSDEN BELLHOUSE (St Mary the Virgin)   *see* Downham w S Hanningfield and Ramsden Bellhouse *Chelmsf*
RAMSDEN HEATH (St John) *as above*
RAMSEY (St Michael)   *see* Harwich Peninsula *Chelmsf*
RAMSEY ST MARY'S (St Mary)   *see* The Ramseys and Upwood *Ely*
RAMSEY, NORTH (St Olave)   *see* Bride, Lezayre and N Ramsey *S & M*
RAMSEY, SOUTH (St Paul)   *see* Maughold and S Ramsey *S & M*
RAMSEYS (St Thomas à Becket) (St Mary) and Upwood, The   *Ely 12*   **P** *Lord De Ramsey and Bp (jt)*   **R** R A DARMODY
RAMSGATE (Christ Church) *Cant 5*   **P** *Ch Patr Trust*   **V** P F TIZZARD
RAMSGATE (Holy Trinity) (St George) *Cant 5*   **P** *Abp*   **R** P A ADAMS
RAMSGATE (St Luke) *Cant 5*   **P** *CPAS*   **V** P R WORLEDGE
RAMSGATE (St Mark) *Cant 5*   **P** *CPAS*   **V** *vacant*
RAMSGILL (St Mary)   *see* Upper Nidderdale *Leeds*
RAMSHOLT (All Saints)   *see* Wilford Peninsula *St E*
RANBY (St German)   *see* Asterby Gp *Linc*
RANBY (St Martin)   *see* Retford Area *S'well*
RAND (St Oswald)   *see* Wragby Gp *Linc*
RANDWICK (St John the Baptist)   *see* Stroud Team *Glouc*
RANGEMORE (All Saints)   *see* Hanbury, Newborough, Rangemore and Tutbury *Lich*
RANGEWORTHY (Holy Trinity)   *see* Charfield and Kingswood w Wickwar etc *Glouc*
RANMOOR (St John the Evangelist) *Sheff 4*   **P** *Trustees*   **V** N BOWLER   **NSM** A M LAUENER
RANMORE (St Barnabas)   *see* Dorking w Ranmore *Guildf*
RANSKILL (St Barnabas)   *see* Blyth and Scrooby w Ranskill *S'well*
RANTON (All Saints)   *see* Chebsey, Creswell, Ellenhall, Ranton etc *Lich*
RANWORTH (St Helen)   *see* Broadside *Nor*
RASEN DRAX, MIDDLE (St Peter and St Paul)   *see* Middle Rasen Gp *Linc*
RASEN, WEST (All Saints) *as above*
RASKELF (St Mary)   *see* Easingwold w Raskelf *York*
RASTRICK (St John the Divine) (St Matthew) *Leeds 8*   **P** *Bp and V Halifax (jt)*   **V** M RUSSELL   **NSM** R S HANNAM
RATBY (St Philip and St James)   *see* Groby and Ratby *Leic*
RATCLIFFE CULEY (All Saints)   *see* Bosworth and Sheepy Gp *Leic*
RATCLIFFE ON THE WREAKE (St Botolph)   *see* Fosse *Leic*
RATCLIFFE-ON-SOAR (Holy Trinity)   *see* Kingston and Ratcliffe-on-Soar *S'well*
RATHMELL (Holy Trinity)   *see* Giggleswick and Rathmell w Wigglesworth *Leeds*
RATLEY (St Peter at Vincula)   *see* Edgehill Churches *Cov*
RATLINGHOPE (St Margaret)   *see* Wentnor w Ratlinghope, Myndtown, Norbury etc *Heref*
RATTERY (Blessed Virgin Mary)   *see* S Brent and Rattery *Ex*
RATTLESDEN (St Nicholas) w Thorpe Morieux, Brettenham and Hitcham *St E 10*   **P** *Bp (3 turns), Ld Chan (1 turn)*   **R** C M S ROBINSON
RAUCEBY (St Peter)   *see* Ancaster Wilsford Gp *Linc*
RAUGHTON HEAD (All Saints)   *see* Dalston w Cumdivock, Raughton Head and Wreay *Carl*
RAUNDS (St Peter), Hargrave, Ringstead and Stanwick *Pet 8*   **P** *Ld Chan (1 turn), Bp and L G Stopford-Sackville Esq (2 turns)*   **R** S M BELL
RAVENDALE, EAST (St Martin)   *see* Waltham Gp *Linc*
RAVENFIELD (St James), Hooton Roberts and Braithwell *Sheff 6*   **P** *Bp and Sir Philip Naylor-Leyland Bt (jt)*   **P-in-c** J E BOLTON
RAVENGLASS (Mission Room)   *see* Eskdale, Irton, Muncaster and Waberthwaite *Carl*
RAVENHEAD (St John the Evangelist)   *see* Eccleston *Liv*
RAVENINGHAM Group, The (St Andrew) *Nor 8*   **P** *Bp, Adn Nor, Sir Nicholas Bacon Bt, Major C A Boycott, D&C, K Coll Cam, and DBP (jt)*   **R** N J WILL   **Hon C** A M R HOUSMAN
RAVENSCAR (St Hilda) and Staintondale *York 15*   **P** *Abp*   **V** A J FERNELEY   **NSM** D C PYNN, D MACIVER
RAVENSDEN (All Saints)   *see* Wilden w Colmworth and Ravensden *St Alb*
RAVENSHEAD (St Peter) *S'well 4*   **P** *Bp*   **V** C J RATTENBERRY   **NSM** L M RAYNOR
RAVENSTHORPE (St Denys)   *see* Guilsborough and Hollowell and Cold Ashby etc *Pet*
RAVENSTHORPE (St Saviour) and Thornhill Lees w Savile Town *Leeds 10*   **P** *Bp and V Mirfield (jt)*   **P-in-c** P W ATKINSON

RAVENSTONE (All Saints)   *see* Gayhurst w Ravenstone, Stoke Goldington etc *Ox*
RAVENSTONE (St Michael and All Angels)   *see* Coalville w Bardon Hill and Ravenstone *Leic*
RAVENSTONEDALE (St Oswald)   *see* Orton and Tebay w Ravenstonedale etc *Carl*
RAWCLIFFE (St James)   *see* Airmyn, Hook and Rawcliffe *Sheff*
RAWCLIFFE (St Mark)   *see* Clifton *York*
RAWDON (St Peter) *Leeds 16*   **P** *Trustees*   **V** M G R D SMITH
RAWMARSH (St Mary the Virgin) w Parkgate *Sheff 6*   **P** *Ld Chan*   **R** J T BIRBECK   **C** A WOODING, L S WORTLEY
RAWMARSH (St Nicolas)   *see* Ryecroft St Nic *Sheff*
RAWNSLEY (St Michael)   *see* Hednesford *Lich*
RAWRETH (St Nicholas) *Chelmsf 14*   **P** *Pemb Coll Cam*   **P-in-c** R W JORDAN   **Hon C** E A JORDAN
RAWTENSTALL (St Mary) *Man 11*   **P** *CPAS*   **V** *vacant*
RAWTHORPE (St James)   *see* Moldgreen and Rawthorpe *Leeds*
RAY VALLEY, The *Ox 21*   **P** *Canon E G A W Page-Turner, Ex Coll Ox, and Piddington PCC (1 Turn), D&C Westmr, Qu Coll Ox, and Walsingham Coll (1 turn)*   **C** S V MELLOR-SMITH   **Hon C** L R THIRTLE   **OLM** L HOLMES
RAYDON (St Mary)   *see* Higham, Holton St Mary, Raydon and Stratford *St E*
RAYLEIGH (Holy Trinity) (St Michael) *Chelmsf 14*   **P** *Patr Bd*   **TR** M J LODGE   **TV** N E ROWAN   **C** T M MARLOW   **NSM** T J NUTTER
RAYNE (All Saints)   *see* Panfield and Rayne *Chelmsf*
RAYNES PARK (St Saviour) and South Wimbledon All Saints *S'wark 13*   **P** *Bp*   **V** M O BLACKMAN   **NSM** C W NOKE
RAYNHAM, EAST (St Mary)   *see* E w W Rudham, Helhoughton etc *Nor*
RAYNHAM, SOUTH (St Martin) *as above*
REACH (St Ethelreda and the Holy Trinity)   *see* Burwell w Reach *Ely*
READ (St John the Evangelist) and Simonstone St Peter *Blackb 7*   **P** *V Whalley*   **P-in-c** R D FIELDING
READ IN WHALLEY (St John the Evangelist)   *see* Read and Simonstone *Blackb*
READING (Christ Church) *Ox 7*   **P** *Bp*   **V** P A DAY   **C** E C RATCLIFFE
READING (Holy Trinity) *Ox 7*   **P** *SMF*   **P-in-c** N J CHEESEMAN   **C** R J SIMMONDS
READING (St Agnes w St Paul) (St Barnabas) *Ox 7*   **P** *Bp*   **R** R V ORR   **C** L J COLLYER, P J CUTHBERT
READING (St Giles w St Saviour) *Ox 7*   **P** *Bp*   **R** D A HARRIS   **C** S J MCNALLY-CROSS
READING (St John the Evangelist and St Stephen) *Ox 7*   **P** *Simeon's Trustees*   **V** V L GARDNER
READING (St Laurence) *Ox 7*   **P** *Bp*   **V** C I RUSSELL   **C** D C PICKERSGILL
READING (St Luke) (St Bartholomew) *Ox 7*   **P** *Bp and V Reading St Giles (alt)*   **V** G FANCOURT   **C** R CHRISTOPHER   **NSM** C F BLACKMAN
READING (St Mark) (All Saints) *Ox 7*   **P** *Bp*   **V** N J CHEESEMAN
READING (St Mary the Virgin) *Ox 7*   **P** *Bp*   **P-in-c** S J PULLIN   **NSM** S A PULLIN
READING (St Matthew) *Ox 7*   **P** *Bp*   **V** M P DOLPHIN   **C** C J A MORGAN
READING Greyfriars (St James) *Ox 7*   **P** *Ch Trust Fund Trust*   **C** J K ATKINS
READING STREET (St Andrew) *Cant 5*   **P** *Abp*   **V** P MUSINDI
REAPSMOOR (St John)   *see* Longnor, Quarnford and Sheen *Lich*
REARSBY (St Michael and All Angels)   *see* Fosse *Leic*
RECULVER (St Mary the Virgin), St Bartholomew Herne Bay and Holy Cross Hoath *Cant 4*   **P** *Abp*   **P-in-c** S J MARTIN   **OLM** J L HADLOW
RED POST *Sarum 6*   **P** *Mrs V M Chattey, H W Plunkett-Ernle-Erle-Drax Esq, and Bp (by turn)*   **V** J C E POTTINGER
REDBOURN (St Mary) *St Alb 7*   **P** *Earl of Verulam*   **V** W J M GIBBS
REDBROOK (St Saviour)   *see* Coleford, Staunton, Newland, Redbrook etc *Glouc*
REDCAR (St Peter) *York 16*   **P** *Trustees*   **V** R E HARRISON   **C** N A PENN-ALLISON
REDCLIFFE BAY (St Nicholas)   *see* Portishead *B & W*
REDCLIFFE WAY (St Mary the Virgin)   *see* Bris St Mary Redcliffe w Temple etc *Bris*
REDDISH (St Elisabeth) *Man 2*   **P** *Bp*   **P-in-c** A M STANTON   **C** P A KING
REDDISH (St Mary)   *see* Heaton Reddish *Man*
REDDISH, NORTH (St Agnes) *Man 2*   **P** *The Crown*   **P-in-c** C E LARSEN
REDDITCH (St Stephen)   *see* Redditch H Trin *Worc*

REDDITCH Christ the King *Worc 7*   **P** *Patr Bd*
TR M F BARTLETT   **TV** G T READING
REDDITCH Holy Trinity *Worc 7*   **P** *Patr Bd*   **TR** R M CLARK
TV P J IRVING, P LAWLOR, R M JOHNSON   **NSM** A C DAVIES
REDE (All Saints)   *see* Chevington w Hargrave, Chedburgh w
Depden etc *St E*
REDENHALL (Assumption of the Blessed Virgin Mary) w
Scole *Nor 10*   **P** *Bp, Ex Coll Ox, MMCET, Adn Norfolk, and*
Sir Rupert Mann (jt)   **R** N O TUFFNELL   **OLM** S F AUCKLAND
REDGRAVE cum Botesdale St Mary w Rickinghall *St E 14*
P P J H Wilson Esq   **R** C R NORBURN
REDHILL (Christ Church)   *see* Wrington w Butcombe and
Burrington *B & W*
REDHILL (Holy Trinity) *S'wark 26*   **P** *Simeon's Trustees*
V M J HOUGH   **C** A N APPADOO, S L ALEXANDER
REDHILL (St John the Evangelist) (Meadvale Hall) *S'wark 26*
P *Bp*   **V** vacant
REDHILL (St Matthew) *S'wark 26*   **P** *Bp*   **V** A T CUNNINGTON
OLM C R W WEBB
REDISHAM (St Peter)   *see* Hundred River and Wainford *St E*
REDLAND (not known) *Bris 3*   **P** *Ch Trust Fund Trust*
V R P SYMMONS   **C** L M NAGEL   **OLM** S A TRUSCOTT
REDLINGFIELD (St Andrew)   *see* Athelington, Denham,
Horham, Hoxne etc *St E*
REDLYNCH (St Mary)   *see* Forest and Avon *Sarum*
REDLYNCH (St Peter)   *see* Bruton and Distr *B & W*
REDMARLEY D'ABITOT (St Bartholomew), Bromesberrow,
Pauntley, Upleadon, Oxenhall, Dymock, Donnington,
Kempley and Preston *Glouc 3*   **P** *Pemb Coll Ox, Bp, R D*
Marcon Esq, and Miss C Daniel (jt)   **R** A D LOMAS
C L S BLOOM   **NSM** J M BOND   **OLM** V G CHESTER
REDMILE (St Peter)   *see* Vale of Belvoir *Leic*
REDMIRE (St Mary)   *see* Penhill *Leeds*
REDNAL (St Stephen the Martyr) *Birm 4*   **P** *Bp*
V M F SIBANDA   **NSM** S J JONES
REDRUTH (St Andrew) (St Euny) w Lanner and Treleigh
Truro 2   **P** *DBP*   **TR** C J B BUSH   **TV** S A HARRISON
C A BROWN
REED (St Mary)   *see* Barkway, Reed and Buckland w Barley
St Alb
REEDHAM (St John the Baptist)   *see* Acle and Bure to
Yare *Nor*
REEPHAM (St Mary) and Hackford w Whitwell and Kerdiston,
Thurning w Wood Dalling and Salle *Nor 22*   **P** *Bp, CCC*
Cam, Pemb Coll Cam, Trin Coll Cam, and Ch Soc Trust (jt)
R M H DEAN   **NSM** T C P DEAN
REEPHAM (St Peter and St Paul)   *see* S Lawres Gp *Linc*
REGENT'S PARK (St Mark) *Lon 16*   **P** *D&C St Paul's*
V W D F GULLIFORD   **C** M GREBE
REGIL (St James Mission Church)   *see* Winford w Felton
Common Hill *B & W*
REIGATE (St Luke) *S'wark 26*   **P** *Bp*   **P-in-c** A C COLPUS
NSM M T Z MUTIKANI
REIGATE (St Mark) *S'wark 26*   **P** *Bp*   **V** M P COLTON
NSM S M WEAKLEY
REIGATE (St Mary Magdalene) *S'wark 26*   **P** *Trustees*
V P J ANDREW   **C** H J FRASER   **Hon C** M J H FOX
NSM D G O ROBINSON
REIGATE (St Philip) *S'wark 26*   **P** *Bp*   **P-in-c** J A PENN
REIGATE HEATH (not known)   *see* Reigate St Mary *S'wark*
REIGHTON (St Peter)   *see* Bempton w Flamborough, Reighton
w Speeton *York*
REKENDYKE (St Jude) *Dur 15*   **P** *The Crown and D&C*
P-in-c P M BULLOCK
REMENHAM (St Nicholas)   *see* Henley w Remenham *Ox*
REMPSTONE (All Saints)   *see* E and W Leake, Stanford-on-Soar,
Rempstone etc *S'well*
RENDCOMB (St Peter)   *see* Churn Valley *Glouc*
RENDHAM (St Michael)   *see* Upper Alde *St E*
RENDLESHAM (St Gregory the Great)   *see* Wilford Peninsula
St E
RENHOLD (All Saints) *St Alb 9*   **P** *MMCET*
P-in-c A S BURROW
RENISHAW (St Matthew)   *see* Killamarsh and Renishaw *Derby*
RENNINGTON (All Saints)   *see* Embleton w Rennington and
Rock *Newc*
RENWICK (All Saints)   *see* Kirkoswald, Renwick w Croglin,
Gt Salkeld etc *Carl*
REPPS (St Peter)   *see* Martham and Repps w Bastwick, Thurne
etc *Nor*
REPTON (St Wystan)   *see* Foremark and Repton w Newton
Solney *Derby*
RESTON, NORTH (St Edith)   *see* Legbourne and Wold Marsh
Linc
RETFORD AREA Team Ministry, The (St Michael the
Archangel) (St Saviour) (St Swithin) *S'well 1*   **P** *Patr Bd*

TR A C ST J WALKER   **TV** J M JESSON, M J CANTRILL,
M R VASEY-SAUNDERS, S CADDY   **C** G A L HADLEY
NSM I CARTER
RETTENDON (All Saints) and Hullbridge *Chelmsf 14*   **P** *Ld*
Chan and Bp (alt)   **P-in-c** B C WALLACE   **NSM** S ADAMS
REVEL GROUP, The *Cov 6*   **P** *Bp, Trin Coll Cam, and*
H A F W Boughton-Leigh Esq (2 turns), Ld Chan (1 turn)
R J A FOX
REVELSTOKE (St Peter)   *see* Newton Ferrers w Revelstoke *Ex*
REVESBY (St Lawrence)   *see* Fen and Hill Gp *Linc*
REWE (St Mary the Virgin)   *see* Brampford Speke, Cadbury,
Newton St Cyres etc *Ex*
REYDON (St Margaret)   *see* Sole Bay *St E*
REYMERSTON (St Peter)   *see* Barnham Broom and Upper Yare
Nor
RHODES (All Saints) (St Thomas) *Man 14*   **P** *R Middleton*
V vacant
RHODES and Parkfield *Man 14*   **P** *Patr Bd*   **V** M Z WALL
RHYDYCROESAU (Christ Church) *Lich 19*   **P** *Bp*
R S G THORBURN
RIBBESFORD (St Leonard) w Bewdley and Dowles and
Wribbenhall *Worc 11*   **P** *E J Winnington-Ingram Esq and R*
Kidderminster (alt)   **R** K N JAMES   **NSM** C L ALLEN
RIBBLETON (St Mary Magdalene) (St Anne's Church Centre)
(Ascension) *Blackb 13*   **P** *Bp, DBP, K Simpson Esq, D V*
Johnson Esq, and the Ven K Gibbons (jt)   **R** K J FENTON
RIBBY CUM WREA (St Nicholas) and Weeton St Michael
Blackb 10   **P** *V Kirkham*   **V** R W MARKS
RIBCHESTER (St Wilfred) w Stidd *Blackb 13*   **P** *Bp*
R G K HENWOOD   **NSM** A B JEPSON
RIBSTON, LITTLE (St Helen)   *see* Spofforth w Kirk Deighton
Leeds
RIBY (St Edmund)   *see* Wolds Gateway Group *Linc*
RICCALL (St Mary), Barlby and Hemingbrough *York 2*
P *Abp*   **V** F LOFTUS
RICHARDS CASTLE (All Saints)   *see* Ludlow *Heref*
RICHINGS PARK (St Leonard)   *see* Iver *Ox*
RICHMOND (Holy Trinity and Christ Church) *S'wark 16*
P *CPAS*   **V** T H PATTERSON   **C** A C WEBB
RICHMOND (St Luke)   *see* Kew St Phil and All SS w St Luke
S'wark
RICHMOND (St Mary Magdalene) (St Matthias) (St John the
Divine) *S'wark 16*   **P** *K Coll Cam*   **TR** R J TITLEY
TV D A GARDINER, N T SUMMERS   **NSM** A R SYKES
RICHMOND (St Mary w Holy Trinity) w Hudswell and
Downholme and Marske *Leeds 24*   **P** *Bp*   **R** J R CHAMBERS
RICHMOND HILL (St Saviour)   *see* Leeds Richmond Hill *Leeds*
RICHMOND, EAST *Leeds 24*   **P** *Patr Bd*   **P-in-c** J M LANE
TV D T LEWIS   **Hon C** S J GOLDING
RICKERSCOTE (St Peter) *Lich 10*   **P** *Bp and V Stafford St Paul*
(jt)   **P-in-c** D C BAKER
RICKLING (All Saints)   *see* Newport w Widdington, Quendon
and Rickling *Chelmsf*
RICKMANSWORTH (St Mary the Virgin) *St Alb 4*   **P** *Bp*
V D J SNOWBALL
RIDDINGS (Holy Spirit)   *see* Bottesford w Ashby *Linc*
RIDDINGS (St James) and Ironville *Derby 1*   **P** *Wright Trustees*
and V Alfreton (jt)   **P-in-c** F J C MERCURIO
NSM J OK PENFOLD
RIDDLESDEN (St Mary the Virgin) *Leeds 5*   **P** *Bp*
P-in-c M C CANSDALE   **NSM** J RAMSDEN
RIDDLESDOWN (St James) *S'wark 22*   **P** *Bp*   **V** C F SPURWAY
RIDDLESWORTH (St Peter)   *see* Guiltcross *Nor*
RIDGE (St Margaret)   *see* S Mymms and Ridge *St Alb*
RIDGEWAY *Ox 27*   **P** *DBP, CCC Ox, and Qu Coll Ox (jt)*
R L A HILL
RIDGEWAY *Sarum 18*   **P** *D&C Windsor and O H Langton Esq (jt)*
R R R POWELL
RIDGEWAY (St John the Evangelist)   *see* Eckington and
Ridgeway *Derby*
RIDGEWELL (St Laurence)   *see* Two Rivers *Chelmsf*
RIDGMONT (All Saints)   *see* Aspley Guise w Husborne Crawley
and Ridgmont *St Alb*
RIDING MILL (St James) *Newc 9*   **P** *Viscount Allendale*
V vacant
RIDLEY (St Peter) *Roch 1*   **P** *J R A B Scott Esq*   **P-in-c** R OATES
NSM E M ROBERTSON
RIDLINGTON (St Mary Magdalene and St Andrew)
see Empingham, Edith Weston, Lyndon, Manton etc *Pet*
RIDLINGTON (St Peter)   *see* Bacton, Happisburgh, Hempstead
w Eccles etc *Nor*
RIDWARES and Kings Bromley, The *Lich 1*   **P** *Bp, Lord Leigh,*
and D&C (jt)   **R** T J LEYLAND   **NSM** D J SHERIDAN
RIEVAULX (St Mary)   *see* Helmsley *York*
RIGSBY (St James)   *see* Alford w Rigsby *Linc*
RIGTON, NORTH (St John)   *see* Lower Wharfedale *Leeds*

RILLINGTON (St Andrew)   *see* Buckrose Carrs *York*

RIMPTON (Blessed Virgin Mary)   *see* Chilton Cantelo, Ashington, Mudford, Rimpton etc *B & W*

RINGLAND (St Peter)   *see* Wensum Benefice *Nor*

RINGMER (St Mary the Virgin) *Chich 21*   **P** *Abp*
V E M WOODGATE

RINGMORE (All Hallows)   *see* Modbury, Bigbury, Ringmore etc *Ex*

RINGSFIELD (All Saints)   *see* Hundred River and Wainford *St E*

RINGSHALL (St Catherine) w Battisford, Barking w Darmsden and Great Bricett *St E 1*   **P** *Bp, Ch Patr Trust, and J C W de la Bere Esq (jt)*   **R** *vacant*

RINGSTEAD (Nativity of the Blessed Virgin Mary)   *see* Raunds, Hargrave, Ringstead and Stanwick *Pet*

RINGSTEAD (St Andrew)   *see* Hunstanton St Edm w Ringstead *Nor*

RINGSTONE IN AVELAND Group, The *Linc 17*   **P** *Bp (2 turns), Baroness Willoughby de Eresby and Charterhouse (1 turn)*
P-in-c L PUGH   **OLM** L BATTY

RINGWAY Hale Barns (All Saints)   *see* Hale Barns w Ringway *Ches*

RINGWOOD (St Peter and St Paul) *Win 9*   **P** *K Coll Cam*
P-in-c D K MIELL   **C** L W CAMPBELL

RINGWOULD (St Nicholas) w Kingsdown and Ripple w Sutton by Dover *Cant 9*   **P** *Abp, Ch Patr Trust, and S R Monins Esq (jt)*   **R** C M SIGRIST

RIPE (St John the Baptist)   *see* Laughton w Ripe and Chalvington *Chich*

RIPLEY (All Saints) *Derby 12*   **P** *Wright Trustees*
V J M WIGRAM   **OLM** M BROOKES

RIPLEY (All Saints)   *see* Bishop Thornton, Burnt Yates, Markington etc *Leeds*

RIPLEY (St Mary) *Guildf 12*   **P** *Bp*   **V** C J ELSON

RIPON (Holy Trinity) *Leeds 25*   **P** *Simeon's Trustees*
V C BUTLER   **C** M J BRADFORD   **NSM** J A MONTGOMERY, J S RUTTER, W H GOWING

RIPPINGALE (St Andrew)   *see* Ringstone in Aveland Gp *Linc*

RIPPLE (St Mary the Virgin)   *see* Ringwould w Kingsdown and Ripple etc *Cant*

RIPPLE (St Mary)   *see* Upton-on-Severn, Ripple, Earls Croome etc *Worc*

RIPPONDEN (St Bartholomew) *Leeds 11*   **P** *Bp and V Halifax (jt)*   **V** C J BALL   **NSM** C A HIRST

RISBOROUGH *Ox 10*   **P** *Ld Chan (2 turns), Patr Bd (1 turn)*
TR D G WILLIAMS   **TV** A F BUNDOCK, J A TOMKINS
C D E BEESLEY   **NSM** J M LOCKE

RISBY (St Giles)   *see* Barrow *St E*

RISE (All Saints)   *see* Skirlaugh, Catwick, Long Riston, Rise, Swine w Ellerby *York*

RISE PARK   *see* Bestwood Park w Rise Park *S'well*

RISEHOLME (St Mary)   *see* Nettleham *Linc*

RISELEY (All Saints) w Bletsoe *St Alb 13*   **P** *MMCET*
V M T BAILEY

RISHTON (St Peter and St Paul) *Blackb 7*   **P** *Trustees*
V M WOODS   **NSM** P G HUNT

RISHWORTH (St John)   *see* Ripponden *Leeds*

RISLEY (All Saints)   *see* Stanton-by-Dale w Dale Abbey and Risley *Derby*

RISSINGTON, GREAT (St John the Baptist)   *see* Bourton-on-the-Water w Clapton etc *Glouc*

RISSINGTON, LITTLE (St Peter) *as above*

RIVENHALL (St Mary the Virgin and All Saints)   *see* Witham and Villages *Chelmsf*

RIVER (St Peter and St Paul) *Cant 7*   **P** *Abp*
P-in-c A J BAWTREE

RIVERHEAD (St Mary) w Dunton Green *Roch 9*   **P** *R Sevenoaks and Bp (jt)*   **V** M A BOOTH

RIVERS Team Ministry, The *Sheff 6*   **P** *Patr Bd*   **TR** D M BENT
TV M BAKER   **C** H M BENT   **NSM** P L BARRINGER

RIVERSMEET Benefice, The *St Alb 10*   **P** *Prime Min, Trin Coll Cam (2 turns), and Ball Coll Ox (by turn)*   **R** M E MARSHALL

RIVINGTON (not known)   *see* Horwich and Rivington *Man*

ROADE (St Mary the Virgin)   *see* Salcey *Pet*

ROADWATER (St Luke)   *see* Old Cleeve, Leighland and Treborough *B & W*

ROBERTSBRIDGE (Mission Room)   *see* Salehurst *Chich*

ROBERTTOWN (All Saints)   *see* Hartshead, Hightown, Roberttown and Scholes *Leeds*

ROBOROUGH (St Peter)   *see* Newton Tracey, Horwood, Alverdiscott etc *Ex*

ROBY (St Bartholomew) *Liv 2*   **P** *Bp*   **V** T C GILL

ROCESTER (St Michael) and Croxden w Hollington *Lich 15*
P *Bp and Trustees (jt)*   **P-in-c** S H VAZ

ROCHDALE (St Chad) St Edmund (St John the Divine) (St Mary) *Man 17*   **P** *Bp*   **R** J M COLEMAN
NSM S A TAUSON

ROCHE (St Gomonda of the Rock) *Truro 1*   **P** *Bp and DBP (jt)*
P-in-c R M MURFITT

ROCHESTER (St Justus) *Roch 5*   **P** *Bp*   **V** H M BURN
C A S LEONARD

ROCHESTER (St Margaret) (St Peter's Parish Centre) *Roch 5*
P *Bp and D&C (jt)*   **V** J A LOVE   **NSM** P M ALEXANDER

ROCHFORD (St Andrew) and Sutton w Shopland *Chelmsf 14*
P *Bp and SMF (jt)*   **P-in-c** A J HURD

ROCHFORD (St Michael)   *see* Teme Valley S *Worc*

ROCK (St Peter and St Paul)   *see* Mamble w Bayton, Rock w Heightington etc *Worc*

ROCK (St Philip and St James)   *see* Embleton w Rennington and Rock *Newc*

ROCK FERRY (St Peter) *Ches 1*   **P** *Bp*   **V** C R SLATER
NSM J LEAL

ROCKBEARE (St Mary w St Andrew)   *see* Broadclyst, Clyst Honiton, Pinhoe, Rockbeare etc *Ex*

ROCKBOURNE (St Andrew)   *see* W Downland *Sarum*

ROCKCLIFFE (St Mary the Virgin) and Blackford *Carl 2*
P *D&C*   **P-in-c** J J VAN DEN BERG

ROCKHAMPTON (St Oswald)   *see* Cromhall, Tortworth, Tytherington, Falfield etc *Glouc*

ROCKINGHAM (St Leonard)   *see* Gretton w Rockingham and Cottingham w E Carlton *Pet*

ROCKLAND (All Saints)   *see* Gt and Lt Ellingham, Rockland and Shropham etc *Nor*

ROCKLAND (St Peter) *as above*

ROCKLAND ST MARY (St Mary) with Hellington, Bramerton, Surlingham, Claxton, Carleton St Peter and Kirby Bedon w Whitlingham *Nor 8*   **P** *Bp, Adn Nor, MMCET, and BNC Ox (jt)*
R C D ELLIS, J B SHAW   **OLM** M ANSELL

RODBOROUGH (St Mary Magdalene) *Glouc 4*   **P** *Bp*
P-in-c M M LUDLOW   **NSM** B P LUDLOW

RODBOURNE (Holy Rood)   *see* Gt Somerford, Lt Somerford, Seagry, Corston etc *Bris*

RODBOURNE CHENEY (St Mary) *Bris 7*   **P** *CPAS*
R N D J LINES   **OLM** C COOMBS

RODDEN (All Saints)   *see* Beckington w Standerwick, Berkley, Rodden etc *B & W*

RODE (St Lawrence)   *see* Hardington Vale *B & W*

RODE HEATH (Good Shepherd)   *see* Odd Rode *Ches*

RODE, NORTH (St Michael)   *see* Gawsworth w North Rode *Ches*

RODHUISH (St Bartholomew)   *see* Dunster, Carhampton, Withycombe w Rodhuish etc *B & W*

RODING, HIGH (All Saints)   *see* Gt Canfield w High Roding and Aythorpe Roding *Chelmsf*

RODINGS, SOUTH *Chelmsf 18*   **P** *Ld Chan, Bp, and Viscount Gough (by turn)*   **P-in-c** C R DUXBURY

RODINGTON (St George)   *see* Wrockwardine Deanery *Lich*

RODLEY (Ecumenical Centre)   *see* Bramley *Leeds*

RODLEY (Mission Church)   *see* Westbury-on-Severn w Flaxley, Blaisdon etc *Glouc*

RODMELL (St Peter)   *see* Iford w Kingston and Rodmell and Southease *Chich*

RODMERSHAM (St Nicholas)   *see* Tunstall and Bredgar *Cant*

RODNEY STOKE (St Leonard)   *see* Cheddar, Draycott and Rodney Stoke *B & W*

ROEHAMPTON (Holy Trinity) *S'wark 18*   **P** *Bp*
V J A MCKINNEY

ROFFEY (All Saints)   *see* Roughey *Chich*

ROGATE (St Bartholomew) w Terwick and Trotton w Chithurst *Chich 9*   **P** *Ld Chan*   **R** E M DOYLE

ROGERS LANE (St Andrew's Chapel)   *see* Stoke Poges *Ox*

ROLLESBY (St George)   *see* Ormesby St Marg w Scratby, Ormesby St Mich etc *Nor*

ROLLESTON (Holy Trinity) w Fiskerton, Morton and Upton *S'well 3*   **P** *Ld Chan*   **V** *vacant*

ROLLESTON (St John the Baptist)   *see* Coplow *Leic*

ROLLESTON (St Mary) *Lich 14*   **P** *MMCET*
R I R WHITEHEAD   **C** L REES   **Hon C** A L WHEALE

ROLLRIGHT, GREAT (St Andrew)   *see* Hook Norton w Gt Rollright, Swerford etc *Ox*

ROLLRIGHT, LITTLE (St Phillip)   *see* Chipping Norton *Ox*

ROLVENDEN (St Mary the Virgin)   *see* Rother and Oxney *Cant*

ROMALDKIRK (St Romald) w Laithkirk *Leeds 24*   **P** *Bp and Earl of Strathmore's Trustees (alt)*   **P-in-c** J BARKER

ROMANBY (St James)   *see* Northallerton w Kirby Sigston *York*

ROMFORD (Ascension) Collier Row *Chelmsf 2*   **P** *Trustees*
P-in-c B M HULL   **Hon C** S J MAYES

ROMFORD (Good Shepherd) Collier Row *Chelmsf 2*   **P** *CPAS*
V D H HAGUE   **C** D SCOTT, T D SCOTT   **Hon C** K S TURNER

ROMFORD (St Alban) *Chelmsf 2*   **P** *Bp*   **V** R S P HINGLEY

ROMFORD (St Andrew) (St Agnes) *Chelmsf 2*   **P** *New Coll Ox*
P-in-c L E DOSE   **NSM** M WILLIAMS

ROMFORD (St Augustine) Rush Green   *see* Rush Green *Chelmsf*
ROMFORD (St Edward the Confessor) *Chelmsf 2*   **P** *New Coll Ox*   **V** M A POWER
ROMILEY (St Chad) *Ches 16*   **P** *R Stockport St Mary*   **V** R L PENNYSTAN   **C** J M LINDSAY-SCOTT
ROMNEY MARSH, The *Cant 10*   **P** *Abp*   **P-in-c** J V COLEMAN
ROMNEY, NEW (St Nicholas)   *see* Romney Marsh *Cant*
ROMNEY, OLD (St Clement) *as above*
ROMSEY (St Mary and St Ethelflaeda) *Win 12*   **P** *Bp*   **V** T C K SLEDGE   **C** D S POTTERTON   **NSM** B G TAPHOUSE, D F WILLIAMS
ROMSLEY (Mission Room)   *see* Halas *Worc*
ROMSLEY (St Kenelm) *as above*
ROOKERY, THE (St Saviour)   *see* Mow Cop *Lich*
ROOS (All Saints)   *see* Withernsea w Owthorne, Garton-in-Holderness etc *York*
ROOSE (St Perran)   *see* S Barrow *Carl*
ROPLEY (St Peter)   *see* Bishop's Sutton and Ropley and W Tisted *Win*
ROPSLEY (St Peter)   *see* N Beltisloe Gp *Linc*
ROSE ASH (St Peter)   *see* Bishopsnympton, Rose Ash, Mariansleigh etc *Ex*
ROSEDALE (St Lawrence)   *see* Lastingham w Appleton-le-Moors, Rosedale etc *York*
ROSHERVILLE (St Mark)   *see* Northfleet and Rosherville *Roch*
ROSLEY (Holy Trinity)   *see* Westward, Rosley-w-Woodside and Welton *Carl*
ROSLISTON (St Mary)   *see* Seale and Lullington w Coton in the Elms *Derby*
ROSS (St Mary the Virgin) w Walford and Brampton Abbotts *Heref 7*   **P** *Bp (4 turns), Ld Chan (1 turn)*   **R** S J JONES   **C** N J D ADLEY   **NSM** L A S MATHEW
ROSSENDALE (St Anne) (St Nicholas w St John) Middle Valley *Man 11*   **P** *Patr Bd*   **TR** R BEVAN
ROSSINGTON (St Michael) *Sheff 9*   **P** *Bp*   **R** N R RAO
ROSSINGTON, NEW (St Luke) *Sheff 9*   **P** *Bp*   **V** *vacant*
ROSTHERNE (St Mary) w Bollington *Ches 12*   **P** C L S *Cornwall-Legh Esq*   **V** P J ROBINSON
ROTHBURY (All Saints)   *see* Upper Coquetdale *Newc*
ROTHER and Oxney *Cant 10*   **P** *Abp*   **C** E K G HARROP, J R DARKINS, P L M FOGDEN   **NSM** J A SHAW, M ROYLANCE   **C** J W DRAPER
ROTHERBY (All Saints)   *see* Upper Wreake *Leic*
ROTHERFIELD (St Denys) w Mark Cross *Chich 16*   **P** *Bp, Adn Lewes and Hastings, and Ch Patr Trust (jt)*   **R** N F MASON
ROTHERFIELD GREYS (Holy Trinity)   *see* Henley H Trin *Ox*
ROTHERFIELD GREYS (St Nicholas)   *see* Nettlebed w Bix, Highmoor, Pishill etc *Ox*
ROTHERFIELD PEPPARD (All Hallows) and Kidmore End and Sonning Common *Ox 24*   **P** *Bp and Jes Coll Ox (jt)*   **R** G D FOULIS BROWN   **NSM** S E C COOPER
ROTHERHAM (All Saints) *Sheff 6*   **P** *Bp*   **V** D C BLISS
ROTHERHITHE (Holy Trinity) *S'wark 7*   **P** *R Rotherhithe St Mary*   **V** A M DOYLE
ROTHERHITHE (St Katharine)   *see* Bermondsey St Kath w St Bart *S'wark*
ROTHERHITHE (St Mary) w All Saints *S'wark 7*   **P** *Clare Coll Cam*   **R** M R NICHOLLS
ROTHERSTHORPE (St Peter and St Paul)   *see* Bugbrooke, Harpole, Kislingbury etc *Pet*
ROTHERWICK (not known)   *see* Whitewater *Win*
ROTHLEY (St Mary the Virgin and St John the Baptist) *Leic 5*   **P** MMCET   **V** R M GLADSTONE   **C** J J BAILEY
ROTHWELL (Holy Trinity) w Orton and Rushton w Glendon and Pipewell *Pet 9*   **P** *Hosp of Jes (1 turn), Bp (2 turns), J Hipwell Esq (1 turn), and Mert Coll Ox (1 turn)*   **P-in-c** J R WESTWOOD
ROTHWELL (Holy Trinity), Lofthouse, Methley w Mickletown and Oulton w Woodlesford Team Ministry, The *Leeds 17*   **P** *Duchy of Lancaster (1 turn), Patr Bd (3 turns)*   **TR** J M TRIGG   **TV** A L RHODES, S A HANCOX   **C** S S MCMAIN
ROTHWELL (St Mary the Virgin)   *see* Swallow *Linc*
ROTTINGDEAN (St Margaret) *Chich 19*   **P** *Bp*   **V** M P MORGAN
ROUGH CLOSE (St Matthew)   *see* Meir Heath and Normacot *Lich*
ROUGH COMMON (St Gabriel)   *see* Harbledown *Cant*
ROUGH HAY (St Christopher)   *see* Darlaston and Moxley *Lich*
ROUGH HILLS (St Martin) *Lich 28*   **P** *Bp*   **P-in-c** S W POWELL   **NSM** A H HUTCHINSON
ROUGHAM (St Mary), Beyton w Hessett and Rushbrooke *St E 10*   **P** *Bp, MMCET (2 turns), and Ld Chan*   **R** N CUTLER
ROUGHAM (St Mary), Weasenham and Wellingham *Nor 20*   **P** *Bp, Earl of Leicester, and T F North Esq (jt)*   **R** H E BERRY
ROUGHEY or Roffey (All Saints) *Chich 7*   **P** *Bp*   **P-in-c** R J STAGG

ROUGHTON (St Margaret)   *see* Bain Valley Gp *Linc*
ROUGHTON (St Mary) and Felbrigg, Metton, Sustead, Bessingham and Gunton w Hanworth *Nor 21*   **P** *Bp and Exors G Whately Esq (jt)*   **NSM** P J CHAPMAN
ROUGHTOWN (St John the Baptist) *Man 13*   **P** *Bp*   **P-in-c** C NIGHTINGALE   **OLM** D BRADWELL
ROUNDHAY (St Edmund King and Martyr) *Leeds 14*   **P** *Bp*   **V** D G PATON-WILLIAMS
ROUNDHAY (St John the Evangelist) *Leeds 14*   **P** *DBF*   **P-in-c** C H CHEESEMAN
ROUNDS GREEN (St James) *Birm 7*   **P** *V Langley*   **P-in-c** M J SERMON
ROUNDSHAW (St Paul)   *see* S Beddington and Roundshaw *S'wark*
ROUNTON, WEST (St Oswald) and East (St Laurence) w Welbury *York 18*   **P** *Ld Chan*   **R** J M E COOPER
ROUS LENCH (St Peter)   *see* Church Lench w Rous Lench and Abbots Morton etc *Worc*
ROUSHAM (St Leonard and St James) *Ox 21*   **P** C *Cottrell-Dormer Esq*   **P-in-c** R C SMAIL
ROUTH (All Saints) *York 8*   **P** *Ch Soc Trust and Reformation Ch Trust (jt)*   **P-in-c** J J FLETCHER
ROWBERROW (St Michael and All Angels)   *see* Axbridge w Shipham and Rowberrow *B & W*
ROWDE (St Matthew) and Bromham *Sarum 17*   **P** *DBP and J A L Spicer Esq (jt)*   **P-in-c** J N REES   **NSM** A E WINTOUR
ROWINGTON (St Laurence)   *see* Hatton w Haseley, Rowington w Lowsonford etc *Cov*
ROWLANDS CASTLE (St John the Baptist) *Portsm 5*   **P** *Bp*   **P-in-c** T M FILTNESS
ROWLANDS GILL (St Barnabas)   *see* High Spen and Rowlands Gill *Dur*
ROWLEDGE (St James) and Frensham *Guildf 3*   **P** *Adn Surrey and Ld Chan (alt)*   **NSM** J L WALKER, S J CRABTREE
ROWLESTONE (St Peter)   *see* Ewyas Harold w Dulas, Kenderchurch etc *Heref*
ROWLEY (St Peter) w Skidby *York 8*   **P** *Abp and N A C Hildyard Esq (jt)*   **P-in-c** R E YOUNG   **NSM** R K NEWTON
ROWLEY REGIS (St Giles) *Birm 7*   **P** *Ld Chan*   **V** I R SHELTON
ROWNER (St Mary the Virgin) *Portsm 3*   **P** *R J F Prideaux-Brune Esq*   **R** J W DRAPER
ROWNHAMS (St John the Evangelist)   *see* Nursling and Rownhams *Win*
ROWSLEY (St Katherine)   *see* Bakewell, Ashford w Sheldon and Rowsley *Derby*
ROWSTON (St Clement)   *see* Digby Gp *Linc*
ROWTON (All Hallows)   *see* Wrockwardine Deanery *Lich*
ROXBOURNE (St Andrew) *Lon 23*   **P** *Bp*   **V** L P NORTH
ROXBY (St Mary)   *see* Winterton Gp *Linc*
ROXBY (St Nicholas)   *see* Hinderwell, Roxby and Staithes etc *York*
ROXETH (Christ Church) *Lon 23*   **P** *Bp and Ch Patr Trust (jt)*   **V** *vacant*
ROXTON (St Mary Magdalene)   *see* Riversmeet *St Alb*
ROXWELL (St Michael and All Angels) *Chelmsf 9*   **P** *New Coll Ox*   **P-in-c** J JONES   **NSM** S E IVES
ROYAL WOOTTON BASSETT (St Bartholomew and All Saints) *Sarum 16*   **P** *DBP*   **V** V E BURROWS   **Hon C** B W HORLOCK
ROYDON (All Saints)   *see* Ashwicken w Leziate, Bawsey etc *Nor*
ROYDON (St Peter) *Chelmsf 4*   **P** *Earl Cowley*   **P-in-c** S J KNIGHT
ROYDON (St Remigius)   *see* Diss *Nor*
ROYSTON (St John the Baptist) *Leeds 18*   **P** *Bp*   **V** M J BULLIMORE   **C** C J HARRISON
ROYSTON (St John the Baptist) *St Alb 16*   **P** *Bp*   **V** H A HUNTLEY   **NSM** J H FIDLER
ROYTON (St Anne) Longsight *Man 16*   **P** *Bp*   **P-in-c** J A READ   **NSM** M R YOUNG
ROYTON (St Paul) and Shaw *Man 16*   **P** *R Prestwich St Mary*   **V** P B MCEVITT
RUAN LANIHORNE (St Rumon)   *see* Veryan w Ruan Lanihorne *Truro*
RUAN MINOR (St Rumon)   *see* St Ruan w St Grade and Landewednack *Truro*
RUARDEAN (St John the Baptist)   *see* Drybrook, Lydbrook and Ruardean *Glouc*
RUBERY (St Chad) *Birm 4*   **P** *The Crown*   **P-in-c** C E TURNER
RUCKINGE (St Mary Magdalene)   *see* Saxon Shoreline *Cant*
RUCKLAND (St Olave)   *see* S Ormsby Gp *Linc*
RUDBY IN CLEVELAND (All Saints) w Middleton *York 20*   **P** *Abp*   **V** P J SANDERS   **Hon C** A J HUTCHINSON   **NSM** P PERCY
RUDDINGTON (St Peter) *S'well 6*   **P** *Simeon's Trustees*   **V** A D BUCHANAN
RUDFORD (St Mary the Virgin)   *see* Highnam, Lassington, Rudford, Tibberton etc *Glouc*

RUDGWICK (Holy Trinity) *Chich 7*   **P** *Ld Chan*   **V** M P J KING

RUDHAM, EAST and WEST (St Mary), Helhoughton,
Houghton-next-Harpley, The Raynhams, Tatterford,
and Tattersett *Nor 15*   **P** *Bp, The Most Revd G D Hand,
Marquess of Cholmondeley, and Marquess Townshend (jt)*
R E L BUNDOCK   **C** A M THOMSON

RUDHEATH (Licensed Room)   *see* Witton *Ches*

RUDSTON (All Saints) w Boynton, Carnaby and Kilham *York 9*
P *Ld Chan (1 turn), Abp (3 turns)*   **V** G J OWEN

RUFFORD (St Mary the Virgin) and Tarleton *Blackb 5*   **P** *Bp
and St Pet Coll Ox (jt)*   **R** N E DAVIS

RUFFORTH (All Saints)   *see* N Ainsty *York*

RUGBY (St Andrew) *Cov 6*   **P** *Bp*   **R** I J NAY
NSM P J PRIVETT, R C ROGERS

RUGBY (St George) *Cov 6*   **P** *Bp*   **V** H G IREDALE

RUGBY WEST (St Matthew and St Oswald) *Cov 6*   **P** *Dioc
Trustees and Ch Trust Fund Trust (jt)*   **V** H M MEARS,
O H J MEARS   **C** C C HIGGINS, E V HIGGINS

RUGELEY (St Augustine)   *see* Brereton and Rugeley *Lich*

RUGELEY (The Good Shepherd) *as above*

RUISHTON (St George)   *see* Creech St Michael and Ruishton w
Thornfalcon *B & W*

RUISLIP (St Martin) *Lon 24*   **P** *D&C Windsor*   **V** S EVANS
C J M NOBLE   **NSM** D M GREEN, M A BEDFORD

RUISLIP (St Mary) *Lon 24*   **P** *Bp*   **V** N G T WHEELER

RUISLIP MANOR (St Paul) *Lon 24*   **P** *Bp*   **V** J E MANLEY
NSM J BEVIS-KNOWLES

RUMBURGH (St Michael and All Angels and St Felix)   *see* S
Elmham and Ilketshall *St E*

RUNCORN (All Saints) (Holy Trinity) *Ches 3*   **P** *Bp and Ch Ch
Ox (jt)*   **V** *vacant*

RUNCORN (St John the Evangelist) Weston *Ches 3*   **P** *Bp*
V V B GISBY

RUNCORN (St Michael and All Angels) *Ches 3*   **P** *Bp*
V V L SCHOFIELD   **NSM** H BROWNE

RUNCTON HOLME (St James)   *see* Holme Runcton w S
Runcton and Wallington *Ely*

RUNCTON, NORTH (All Saints)   *see* Middlewinch *Nor*

RUNCTON, SOUTH (St Andrew)   *see* Holme Runcton w S
Runcton and Wallington *Ely*

RUNHALL (All Saints)   *see* Barnham Broom and Upper
Yare *Nor*

RUNHAM (St Peter and St Paul)   *see* S Trin Broads *Nor*

RUNNINGTON (St Peter and St Paul)   *see* Wellington and
Distr *B & W*

RUNTON (Holy Trinity)   *see* Aylmerton, Runton, Beeston Regis
and Gresham *Nor*

RUNTON, EAST (St Andrew) *as above*

RUNWELL (St Mary)   *see* Wickford and Runwell *Chelmsf*

RURAL East York *York 2*   **P** *Abp*   **R** N W R BIRD
C D M COYNE   **NSM** T A JOYCE

RUSCOMBE (St James the Great) and Twyford w Hurst *Ox 8*
P *Bp*   **V** S C HOWARD   **Hon C** C SMITH, G F THEOBALD
NSM G W PUGH

RUSH GREEN (St Augustine) Romford *Chelmsf 2*   **P** *Bp*
V M D HOWSE

RUSHALL (Christ the King) (St Michael the Archangel)
Lich 25   **P** *Sir Andrew Buchanan Bt and H C S Buchanan Esq (jt)*
V C R SUCH

RUSHALL (St Mary)   *see* Dickleburgh and The Pulhams *Nor*

RUSHALL (St Matthew)   *see* Vale of Pewsey *Sarum*

RUSHBROOKE (St Nicholas)   *see* Rougham, Beyton w Hessett
and Rushbrooke *St E*

RUSHBURY (St Peter)   *see* Apedale Gp *Heref*

RUSHDEN (St Mary)   *see* Clothall, Rushden, Sandon,
Wallington and Weston *St Alb*

RUSHDEN (St Mary) w Newton Bromswold *Pet 8*   **P** *CPAS*
R S K PRIOR   **C** M T TAYLOR, N D BRADY

RUSHDEN (St Peter) *Pet 8*   **P** *CPAS*   **V** R A HAWKINS

RUSHEN Christ Church (Holy Trinity) *S & M*   **P** *The Crown*
V J A T HEATON

RUSHEY MEAD (St Theodore of Canterbury)   *see* Leic
St Theodore *Leic*

RUSHFORD (St John the Evangelist)   *see* E w W Harling,
Bridgham w Roudham, Larling etc *Nor*

RUSHLAKE GREEN (Little St Mary)   *see* Warbleton, Bodle Street
Green and Dallington *Chich*

RUSHMERE (St Andrew) *St E 4*   **P** *Bp*   **V** B WAKELING

RUSHMERE (St Michael)   *see* Kessingland, Gisleham and
Rushmere *Nor*

RUSHOCK (St Michael)   *see* Elmley Lovett w Hampton Lovett
and Elmbridge etc *Worc*

RUSHOLME (Holy Trinity) *Man 3*   **P** *CPAS*   **R** S L JAMES
C J BRETT, M R GLEW, P M MATHOLE   **NSM** P J GASKELL

RUSHTON (All Saints)   *see* Rothwell w Orton, Rushton w
Glendon and Pipewell *Pet*

RUSKIN PARK (St Saviour)   *see* Herne Hill *S'wark*

RUSKINGTON (All Saints)   *see* N Lafford Gp *Linc*

RUSLAND (St Paul)   *see* Hawkshead and Low Wray w Sawrey
and Rusland etc *Carl*

RUSPER (St Mary Magdalene) w Colgate *Chich 7*   **P** *P H
Calvert Esq and Bp (alt)*   **R** N A FLINT

RUSTHALL (St Paul) (St Paul's Mission Church) *Roch 12*
P *R Speldhurst*   **V** R E N WILLIAMS

RUSTINGTON (St Peter and St Paul) *Chich 1*   **P** *Bp*
V Z E ALLEN   **C** C E KEYTE

RUSTON PARVA (St Nicholas)   *see* The Beacon *York*

RUSWARP (St Bartholomew)   *see* Whitby w Ruswarp *York*

RUYTON XI TOWNS (St John the Baptist) w Great Ness and
Little Ness *Lich 17*   **P** *Bp and Guild of All So (jt) and Ld Chan
(alt)*   **P-in-c** L R BURNS   **OLM** J M BAKER

RYAL (All Saints)   *see* Stamfordham w Matfen *Newc*

RYARSH (St Martin)   *see* Birling, Addington, Ryarsh and
Trottiscliffe *Roch*

RYBURGH, GREAT (St Andrew)   *see* Upper Wensum Village Gp
Nor

RYBURN Benefice, The (Cottonstones, Norland and Sowerby)
Leeds 9   **P** *Bp and DBP (jt)*   **V** J ROBERTS   **C** I SPARKS
NSM L ENNIS

RYDAL (St Mary) *Carl 11*   **P** *Bp*   **V** C J BUTLAND
NSM J S M GREEN

RYDE (All Saints) *Portsm 7*   **P** *Bp*   **P-in-c** G E MORRIS
C P J ISAAC

RYDE (St James) Proprietary Chapel *Portsm 7*
C-in-c J H A LEGGETT

RYDE (St John the Baptist) Oakfield and Holy Trinity *Portsm 7*
P *Bp and V St Helens (jt)*   **P-in-c** S A THEOBALD

RYE (St Mary the Virgin) *Chich 17*   **P** *Patr Bd*   **TR** D R FROST
NSM G R ATFIELD, T F MUNRO

RYE HARBOUR (Holy Spirit)   *see* Rye *Chich*

RYE PARK (St Cuthbert) *St Alb 17*   **P** *DBP*   **V** J A EVANS
NSM A JACKSON

RYECROFT (St Nicolas) Rawmarsh *Sheff 6*   **P** *Bp*
P-in-c S Y LEE

RYEDALE, UPPER *York 19*   **P** *Abp and the Hon Jake Duncombe (jt)*
R T J ROBINSON   **NSM** L GROVE

RYHALL (St John the Evangelist) w Essendine and Carlby
Pet 12   **P** *Burghley Ho Preservation Trust*   **V** P J MCKEE

RYHILL (St James) *Leeds 20*   **P** *Bp*   **NSM** M E REED

RYHOPE (St Paul) *Dur 1*   **P** *Bp*   **V** D E CHADWICK

RYLSTONE (St Peter)   *see* Burnsall w Rylstone *Leeds*

RYME INTRINSECA (St Hypolytus)   *see* Three Valleys *Sarum*

RYSTON (St Michael)   *see* Denver and Ryston w Roxham and
W Dereham etc *Ely*

RYTHER (All Saints)   *see* Cawood w Ryther and Wistow *York*

RYTON (Holy Cross) *Dur 13*   **P** *Bp*   **R** T L JAMIESON

RYTON (Mission Chapel)   *see* Condover w Frodesley, Acton
Burnell etc *Heref*

RYTON (St Andrew)   *see* Beckbury, Badger, Kemberton, Ryton,
Stockton etc *Lich*

RYTON ON DUNSMORE (St Leonard)   *see* Baginton w
Bubbenhall and Ryton-on-Dunsmore *Cov*

SACOMBE (St Catherine)   *see* Standon and The Mundens w
Sacombe *St Alb*

SADBERGE (St Andrew) *Dur 8*   **P** *Bp*   **R** M R EAST
NSM S CHEW

SADDINGTON (St Helen)   *see* Kibworth and Smeeton
Westerby and Saddington *Leic*

SADDLEWORTH (St Chad) *Man 15*   **P** *Patr Bd*
TR C N R HALLIDAY   **TV** J R ROSEDALE   **NSM** J CALOW,
M C DONMALL

SAFFRON WALDEN (St Mary) and Villages *Chelmsf 20*
P *Ld Chan (1 turn), Patr Bd (2 turns)*   **TR** D R TOMLINSON
TV H M DAVEY, J D A PARSONS, R D SPENCER   **C** L J SMITH
NSM A P WANT, J C TOMLINSON, P W L GRIFFITHS,
T K HARDINGHAM

SAHAM TONEY (St George)   *see* Ashill, Carbrooke, Ovington
and Saham Toney *Nor*

ST AGNES (St Agnes)   *see* Is of Scilly *Truro*

ST AGNES (St Agnes) and Mount Hawke w Mithian *Truro 6*
P *Bp and D&C (alt)*   **C** D J WILLOUGHBY

ST ALBANS (Christ Church) *St Alb 5*   **P** *Trustees*
V J M FOLLETT   **NSM** P N BODDAM-WHETHAM

ST ALBANS (St Luke) *St Alb 5*   **P** *DBP*   **V** M A SLATER
NSM R C GOATLY

ST ALBANS (St Mary) Marshalswick *St Alb 5*   **P** *Bp*
V G W HOLMES

ST ALBANS (St Michael) *St Alb 5*   **P** *Earl of Verulam*
V K P J PADLEY   **NSM** J A HAYTON

ST ALBANS (St Paul) *St Alb 5*   **P** *V St Alb St Pet*   **V** A R HURLE
C J P FARAGHER   **Hon C** G M ABBOTT   **NSM** L M HURLE

ST ALBANS (St Peter) *St Alb 5*   **P** *The Crown*   **C** J C PERRIS

ST ALBANS (St Saviour) *St Alb 5*   **P** *Bp*   **V** P R WADSWORTH   **NSM** A N FERRAR

ST ALBANS (St Stephen) *St Alb 5*   **P** J N W Dudley Esq   **V** D RIDGEWAY   **NSM** C BAYNES, P J MADGWICK

ST ALLEN (St Alleyne)   *see* Kenwyn w St Allen *Truro*

ST ANNES-ON-THE-SEA (St Anne) Heyhouses *Blackb 10*   **P** J C Hilton Esq   **V** A D LYON

ST ANNES-ON-THE-SEA (St Margaret of Antioch) *Blackb 10*   **P** *Bp*   **V** A R HODGSON

ST ANNES-ON-THE-SEA (St Thomas) *Blackb 10*   **P** J C Hilton Esq   **V** C M SCARGILL

ST ANTHONY-IN-MENEAGE (St Anthony)   *see* Meneage *Truro*

ST AUSTELL (Holy Trinity) *Truro 1*   **P** *The Crown*   **V** M D MARSHALL

ST BARTHOLOMEW *Sarum 11*   **P** Ch Ch Ox, New Coll Ox, and DBP (by turn)   **R** R WARHURST   **C** A E GOODALL

ST BEES (St Mary and St Bega) *Carl 5*   **P** Trustees   **V** vacant

ST BLAZEY (St Blaise) *Truro 1*   **P** *Bp*   **V** vacant

ST BREOKE (St Breoke) and Egloshayle in Wadebridge *Truro 10*   **P** *Bp and DBP (jt)*   **R** J O HEREWARD

ST BREWARD (St Breward)   *see* Blisland w Temple, St Breward and Helland *Truro*

ST BRIAVELS (St Mary the Virgin) w Hewelsfield *Glouc 1*   **P** *D&C Heref*   **P-in-c** D O TREHARNE   **C** R C SIMPSON

ST BURYAN (St Buriana), St Levan and Sennen *Truro 5*   **P** *Duchy of Cornwall*   **P-in-c** V S BENHAM

ST CLEER (St Clarus) *Truro 12*   **P** Ld Chan   **V** vacant

ST CLEMENT (St Clement) *Truro 6*   **P** *Bp*   **V** D J WILLOUGHBY

ST CLETHER (St Clederus)   *see* Moorland Gp *Truro*

ST COLAN (St Colan)   *see* St Columb Minor and St Colan *Truro*

ST COLUMB MAJOR (St Columba) *Truro 7*   **P** *Bp*   **P-in-c** E B PRUEN

ST COLUMB MINOR (St Columba) and St Colan *Truro 7*   **P** *Bp*   **P-in-c** C C MCQUILLEN-WRIGHT

ST DENNIS (St Denys) *Truro 1*   **P** *Bp*   **P-in-c** K P ARTHUR

ST DEVEREUX (St Dubricius)   *see* Ewyas Harold w Dulas, Kenderchurch etc *Heref*

ST DOMINIC (St Dominica), Landulph and St Mellion w Pillaton *Truro 11*   **P** *D&C and Trustees Major J Coryton, Duchy of Cornwall, and SMF (by turn)*   **P-in-c** C M PAINTER

ST EDMUND WAY *St E 10*   **P** *Bp, Mrs J Oakes, and Lord de Saumarez*   **R** J E BUCKLES

ST ENDELLION (St Endelienta)   *see* N Cornwall Cluster *Truro*

ST ENODER (St Enoder) *Truro 7*   **P** *Bp*   **P-in-c** H L SAMSON

ST ENODOC (St Enodoc)   *see* N Cornwall Cluster *Truro*

ST ERME (St Hermes)   *see* Probus, Ladock and Grampound w Creed and St Erme *Truro*

ST ERNEY (St Erney)   *see* Landrake w St Erney and Botus Fleming *Truro*

ST ERTH (St Erth)   *see* Godrevy *Truro*

ST ERVAN (St Ervan)   *see* St Mawgan w St Ervan and St Eval *Truro*

ST EVAL (St Uvelas) *as above*

ST EWE (All Saints)   *see* St Mewan w Mevagissey and St Ewe *Truro*

ST GENNYS (St Gennys)   *see* Week St Mary Circle of Par *Truro*

ST GEORGE-IN-THE-EAST (St Mary) *Lon 7*   **P** *Bp*   **V** P MCGEARY

ST GEORGE-IN-THE-EAST w St Paul *Lon 7*   **P** *Bp*   **P-in-c** A W M RITCHIE   **Hon C** T CLAPTON

ST GEORGES (St George)   *see* Priors Lee and St Georges' *Lich*

ST GERMANS (St Germans of Auxerre) *Truro 11*   **P** *D&C Windsor*   **V** M E GOODLAND   **C** A BUTLER   **NSM** G H EVE

ST GILES IN THE WOOD (St Giles)   *see* Newton Tracey, Horwood, Alverdiscott etc *Ex*

ST GILES-IN-THE-FIELDS *Lon 3*   **P** *Bp*   **R** A C CARR

ST GILES-IN-THE-HEATH (St Giles)   *see* Boyton, N Tamerton, Werrington etc *Truro*

ST GLUVIAS (St Gluvias) *Truro 3*   **P** *Bp*   **V** S F WALES

ST GORAN (St Goranus) w Caerhays *Truro 1*   **P** *Bp*   **P-in-c** C D NEWELL

ST HELENS (St Helen) (St Catherine by the Green) *Portsm 7*   **P** *Bp*   **P-in-c** R W WYNFORD-HARRIS

ST HELENS Town Centre (St Helen) (Barton Street Mission) (St Andrew) (St Mark) (St Thomas) *Liv 10*   **P** *Patr Bd*   **TR** D D EASTWOOD   **NSM** H WOOD

ST HELIER (St Peter) (Bishop Andrewes Church) *S'wark 23*   **P** *Bp*   **V** H WONG   **C** K J LEWIS   **NSM** A E DOERR

ST HILARY (St Hilary)   *see* Ludgvan, Marazion, St Hilary and Perranuthnoe *Truro*

ST ILLOGAN (St Illogan) *Truro 2*   **P** *Ch Soc Trust*   **R** S P ROBINSON   **NSM** M CARVETH

ST IPPOLYTS (St Ippolyts) w Great and Little Wymondley *St Alb 3*   **P** *Bp and MMCET (jt)*   **R** A E J POLLINGTON

ST ISSEY (St Issey)   *see* St Merryn and St Issey w St Petroc Minor *Truro*

ST IVE (St Ive) and Pensilva w Quethiock *Truro 12*   **P** *Bp (1 turn), The Crown (2 turns)*   **P-in-c** M A J DAVIES

ST IVES (All Saints) *Ely 12*   **P** *Guild of All So*   **V** J M AMEY

ST IVES (St Ia the Virgin) *Truro 5*   **P** V Lelant   **P-in-c** A S GOUGH

ST JOHN (St John the Baptist) w Millbrook *Truro 11*   **P** *Bp and Col Sir John Carew-Pole Bt (alt)*   **P-in-c** M B BROWN

ST JOHN IN BEDWARDINE (St John the Baptist) *Worc 3*   **P** *D&C*   **P-in-c** C J STUART   **C** S L COTTRILL

ST JOHN IN WEARDALE (St John the Baptist)   *see* Upper Weardale *Dur*

ST JOHN LEE (St John of Beverley) *Newc 10*   **P** *Viscount Allendale*   **R** J J T THOMPSON   **OLM** S J PENN

ST JOHN ON BETHNAL GREEN *Lon 7*   **P** *Patr Bd*   **TR** A J E GREEN   **NSM** C B HALL, J M HUTCHINSON, R R R O'CALLAGHAN

ST JOHN-AT-HACKNEY *Lon 5*   **P** *Bp, Adn, and Lord Amherst of Hackney (jt)*   **C** S MAKIN   **NSM** S C EJIAKU

ST JOHN'S WOOD (St John) *Lon 4*   **P** *Bp*   **V** A K BERGQUIST   **C** J C TAYLER

ST JOHN'S-IN-THE-VALE (St John), St Mary's Threlkeld and Wythburn *Carl 6*   **P** *Bp, Adn, V Crosthwaite, and Earl of Lonsdale (jt)*   **R** P F BARNES

ST JULIOT (St Julitta)   *see* Boscastle and Tintagel Gp *Truro*

ST JUST IN PENWITH (St Just) *Truro 5*   **P** Ld Chan   **V** vacant

ST JUST-IN-ROSELAND (St Just) and St Mawes *Truro 6*   **P** A M J Galsworthy Esq   **P-in-c** K J BOULTON   **C** A J COOPER

ST KEVERNE (St Keverne) *Truro 4*   **P** CPAS   **P-in-c** P R SHARPE   **NSM** D A MACKRILL

ST KEW (St James the Great)   *see* N Cornwall Cluster *Truro*

ST KEYNE (St Keyna)   *see* Liskeard and St Keyne *Truro*

ST LAURENCE in the Isle of Thanet (St Laurence) *Cant 5*   **P** *Patr Bd*   **P-in-c** I A JACOBSON   **TV** O I AOKO   **NSM** K I R COX

ST LAWRENCE (Old Church) (St Lawrence) *Portsm 7*   **P** *Bp*   **P-in-c** N J PORTER

ST LEONARD (St Leonard)   *see* Hawridge w Cholesbury and St Leonard *Ox*

ST LEONARDS (Christ Church and St Mary Magdalen) St Peter and St Paul *Chich 15*   **P** *Bp and SMF (jt)*   **R** L T IRVINE-CAPEL   **C** S W GILBERT   **NSM** R G RALPH

ST LEONARDS and St Ives (All Saints) *Win 9*   **P** *Bp*   **V** J MORTON

ST LEONARDS, UPPER (St John the Evangelist) *Chich 15*   **P** Trustees   **R** D R HILL   **NSM** J N HARTMAN, J M MURRILLS

ST LEONARDS-ON-SEA (St Leonard) (St Ethelburga) *Chich 15*   **P** Hyndman Trustees   **R** P T MEAD   **Hon C** E V WHEELER, W D BOULTON

ST LEONARDS-ON-SEA (St Matthew)   *see* Silverhill St Matt *Chich*

ST LEVAN (St Levan)   *see* St Buryan, St Levan and Sennen *Truro*

ST MABYN (St Mabena)   *see* St Tudy w St Mabyn and Michaelstow *Truro*

ST MARGARET'S (St Margaret)   *see* Clodock and Longtown w Craswall, Llanveynoe etc *Heref*

ST MARGARETS-AT-CLIFFE (St Margaret of Antioch) w Westcliffe and East Langdon w West Langdon *Cant 7*   **P** Abp   **P-in-c** D E FAWCETT

ST MARGARET'S-ON-THAMES (All Souls) *Lon 11*   **P** *Bp*   **V** R S FRANK   **C** J B Q CARR

ST MARTHA-ON-THE-HILL (St Martha)   *see* Guildf Ch Ch w St Martha-on-the-Hill *Guildf*

ST MARTIN (St Martin) w Looe St Nicholas *Truro 12*   **P** *Bp and Revd W M M Picken (jt)*   **P-in-c** P P C SHARP   **C** J P W FOOT

ST MARTIN-IN-MENEAGE (St Martin)   *see* Meneage *Truro*

ST MARTIN-IN-THE-FIELDS *Lon 3*   **P** *Bp*   **V** S M B WELLS   **C** A J M MCKAY, J A H EVENS, K HEDDERLY, R A CARTER   **Hon C** D R JACKSON   **NSM** P F HULLAH, W H MORRIS

ST MARTIN'S (St Martin)   *see* Is of Scilly *Truro*

ST MARTINS (St Martin) and Weston Rhyn *Lich 19*   **P** *Bp (2 turns), Bp and Lord Trevor (1 turn)*   **V** S J JERMY

ST MARY BOURNE (St Peter)   *see* Hurstbourne Priors, Longparish etc *Win*

ST MARY LE STRAND w St Clement Danes *Lon 3*   **P** Ld Chan and Burley Ho Preservation Trust (alt)   **P-in-c** P A E CHESTER

ST MARY-AT-LATTON Harlow *Chelmsf 4*   **P** J L H Arkwright Esq   **V** L S HURRY   **C** T A SHARP

ST MARYCHURCH (St Mary the Virgin) *Ex 11*   **P** *D&C*   **P-in-c** R A P WARD

ST MARY-IN-THE-MARSH (St Mary the Virgin)   *see* Romney Marsh *Cant*

ST MARYLEBONE (All Saints) *Lon 4*   **P** *Bp*   **V** L A MOSES   **C** M N R BOWIE

ST MARYLEBONE (All Souls)   *see* Langham Place All So *Lon*
ST MARYLEBONE (Annunciation) Bryanston Street *Lon 4*
   P *Bp*   **P-in-c** G C BEAUCHAMP   **NSM** S-H CHOI
ST MARYLEBONE (St Cyprian) *Lon 4*   **P** *Bp*
   P-in-c G C BEAUCHAMP   **NSM** J BROWNING, S J STOKES
ST MARYLEBONE (St Mark w St Luke)   *see* Bryanston Square
   St Mary w St Marylebone St Mark *Lon*
ST MARYLEBONE (St Mark) Hamilton Terrace *Lon 4*   **P** *The*
   Crown   **V** A S G PLATTEN
ST MARYLEBONE (St Marylebone) (Holy Trinity) *Lon 4*
   P *The Crown*   **R** S J EVANS   **C** A S WALKER, E C THORNLEY
   NSM R C D MACKENNA
ST MARYLEBONE (St Paul) *Lon 4*   **P** *Prime Min*
   R C A E DOWDING   **NSM** D HORE, M J REDMAN
ST MARYLEBONE (St Peter)   *see* Langham Place All So *Lon*
ST MARY'S (St Mary)   *see* Is of Scilly *Truro*
ST MARY'S BAY (All Saints)   *see* Romney Marsh *Cant*
ST MAWES (St Mawes)   *see* St Just-in-Roseland and St Mawes
   Truro
ST MAWGAN (St Mawgan) w St Ervan and St Eval *Truro 7*
   P *D&C and Bp (alt)*   **P-in-c** E B PRUEN
ST MAWGAN-IN-MENEAGE (St Mawgan)   *see* Meneage *Truro*
ST MELLION (St Melanus)   *see* St Dominic, Landulph and
   St Mellion w Pillaton *Truro*
ST MERRYN (St Merryn) and St Issey w St Petroc Minor
   Truro 7   **P** *Bp and Keble Coll Ox (jt)*   **R** J M WILKINSON
ST MEWAN (St Mewan) w Mevagissey and St Ewe *Truro 1*
   P *Bp, DBP, Penrice Ho (St Austell) Ltd, and A M J Galsworthy Esq*
   (jt)   **R** M L BARRETT   **NSM** R H GRIGG
ST MICHAEL PENKEVIL (St Michael) *Truro 6*   **P** *Viscount*
   Falmouth   **P-in-c** L M BARLEY
ST MICHAEL ROCK (St Michael)   *see* N Cornwall Cluster *Truro*
ST MICHAELCHURCH (St Michael)   *see* Alfred Jewel *B & W*
ST MICHAELS-ON-WYRE (St Michael)   *see* Garstang St Helen
   and St Michaels-on-Wyre *Blackb*
ST MINVER (St Menefreda)   *see* N Cornwall Cluster *Truro*
ST NECTAN (St Nectan)   *see* Lostwithiel, St Winnow w
   St Nectan's Chpl etc *Truro*
ST NEOTS (St Mary) *Ely 13*   **P** P W Rowley Esq
   P-in-c P D ANDREWS   **C** D A NOONAN, E J WHALLEY,
   H L TAME
ST NEWLYN EAST (St Newlina)   *see* Newlyn St Newlyn *Truro*
ST NICHOLAS AT WADE (St Nicholas)   *see* Wantsum Gp *Cant*
ST OSWALD IN LEE w Bingfield (St Mary) *Newc 8*   **P** *Bp*
   P-in-c C F BULL
ST OSYTH (St Peter and St Paul) and Great Bentley *Chelmsf 23*
   P *Bp*   **V** S E A MILES   **NSM** E HOWSON
ST PANCRAS (Holy Cross) (St Jude) (St Peter) *Lon 17*   **P** *Bp*
   P-in-c C W CAWRSE
ST PANCRAS (Holy Trinity)   *see* Kentish Town St Silas and H Trin
   w St Barn *Lon*
ST PANCRAS (Old Church) *Lon 17*   **P** *Patr Bd*   **TR** J I ELSTON
   TV D R P WORTON   **C** O R H PETTER   **NSM** S J ATKINSON
ST PANCRAS (St Pancras) (St James) (Christ Church) *Lon 17*
   P *D&C St Paul's*   **V** A H STEVENS
ST PAUL'S CRAY (St Barnabas) *Roch 16*   **P** *CPAS*
   V N G COLEMAN   **Hon C** J E RAWLING
ST PAUL'S WALDEN (All Saints) *St Alb 3*   **P** *D&C St Paul's*
   P-in-c M A H RODEN   **NSM** E BUNKER
ST PETER in the Isle of Thanet (St Peter the Apostle) *Cant 5*
   P *Abp*   **V** A M FREED
ST PETROC MINOR (St Petroc)   *see* St Merryn and St Issey w
   St Petroc Minor *Truro*
ST PINNOCK (St Pinnock)   *see* Duloe, Herodsfoot, Morval and
   St Pinnock *Truro*
ST RUAN w St Grade and Landewednack *Truro 4*   **P** *CPAS and*
   A F Vyvyan-Robinson Esq (jt)   **P-in-c** P R SHARPE
   NSM D A MACKRILL
ST SAMPSON (St Sampson) *Truro 1*   **P** *Bp*
   P-in-c P DE GREY-WARTER
ST STEPHEN IN BRANNEL (not known) *Truro 1*   **P** *Capt J D G*
   Fortescue   **P-in-c** E J WESTERMANN-CHILDS
ST STEPHENS (St Stephen)   *see* Saltash *Truro*
ST STYTHIANS w Perranarworthal and Gwennap *Truro 2*
   P *Viscount Falmouth (2 turns), D&C (1 turn)*   **P-in-c** S A BONE
   C D J F JONES   **NSM** A L BUTCHER, E M SHEARD,
   S J C FLETCHER
ST TEATH (St Teatha) *Truro 10*   **P** *Bp*   **V** *vacant*
ST TUDY (St Tudy) w St Mabyn and Michaelstow *Truro 10*
   P *Ch Ch Ox, Viscount Falmouth, and Duchy of Cornwall (by turn)*
   C D J ELKINGTON
ST VEEP (St Cyricius)   *see* Lostwithiel, St Winnow w St Nectan's
   Chpl etc *Truro*
ST WENN (St Wenna) and Withiel *Truro 7*   **P** *Bp and DBP*
   NSM E C DEELEY

ST WEONARDS (St Weonard) *Heref 7*   **P** *Bp, D&C, and*
   MMCET (jt)   **C** F J PULLEN
ST WINNOW (St Winnow)   *see* Lostwithiel, St Winnow w
   St Nectan's Chpl etc *Truro****
SALCEY Benefice, The *Pet 5*   **P** *Ld Chan and Bp (1 turn),*
   N C Phipps Walker Esq and H C Wake Esq (1 turn)
   V M J BURTON
SALCOMBE (Holy Trinity) and Malborough w South Huish
   Ex 13   **P** *Keble Coll Ox and D&C Sarum (jt)*   **V** D A FRENCH
   Hon C E F CULLY   **NSM** S J BALL
SALCOMBE REGIS (St Mary and St Peter)   *see* Sidmouth,
   Woolbrook, Salcombe Regis, Sidbury etc *Ex*
SALCOTT VIRLEY (St Mary the Virgin)   *see* N Blackwater *Chelmsf*
SALE (St Anne) (St Francis's Church Hall) *Ches 10*   **P** *DBP*
   V J R HEATON
SALE (St Paul) *Ches 10*   **P** *Trustees*   **V** B E SHARP
SALEBY (St Margaret) w Beesby and Maltby *Linc 10*   **P** *Bp*
   and DBP (jt)   **NSM** J M MORTON   **OLM** R D BARRETT
SALEHURST (St Mary) *Chich 13*   **P** *Bp*   **V** *vacant*
SALESBURY (St Peter) *Blackb 7*   **P** *V Blackb*   **V** M J DUERDEN
   NSM A A MALCOLM
SALFORD (Sacred Trinity) (St Philip) *Man 20*   **P** *D&C Man*
   and Sir Josslyn Gore-Booth Bt (jt)   **P-in-c** A I SALMON
   C H D THOMAS   **NSM** R C CRAVEN
SALFORD (St Mary)   *see* Chipping Norton *Ox*
SALFORD (St Mary)   *see* Cranfield and Hulcote w Salford
   St Alb
SALFORD (St Paul w Christ Church) *Man 20*   **P** *The Crown*
   and Trustees (alt)   **R** D S C WYATT
SALFORD All Saints *Man 20*   **P** *Patr Bd*   **TR** D J A BURTON
   TV I C J GORTON   **C** C D HEWITT, L K MAGUIRE
   OLM J I WHITTINGHAM
SALFORD PRIORS (St Matthew)   *see* Heart of England *Cov*
SALFORDS (Christ the King) *S'wark 26*   **P** *Bp*   **V** S G L WOOD
   NSM D ROSS, M WOOD
SALHOUSE (All Saints)   *see* Rackheath and Salhouse *Nor*
SALING, GREAT (St James)   *see* Stebbing and Lindsell w Gt and
   Lt Saling *Chelmsf*
SALING, LITTLE (St Peter and St Paul) *as above*
SALISBURY (St Francis) and St Lawrence Stratford sub Castle
   Sarum 13   **P** *Bp (3 turns), D&C (1 turn)*   **V** P F D TAYLOR
   C P A OSTLI-EAST, T G MANN, T P COOPEY   **Hon C** P A JOYCE
SALISBURY (St Mark) and Laverstock *Sarum 13*   **P** *D&C and*
   Bp (alt)   **V** J FINDLAY   **C** M C EARWICKER   **OLM** J P OFFER
SALISBURY (St Martin) *Sarum 13*   **P** *Bp*   **P-in-c** D B FISHER
   Hon C B DUNCAN
SALISBURY (St Thomas and St Edmund) *Sarum 13*   **P** *Bp and*
   D&C (alt)   **R** D J J R LINAKER   **C** D O THORNTON
   NSM C ALLEN, J PLOWS, W COOPER
SALISBURY PLAIN *Sarum 14*   **P** *Ld Chan (1 turn), Bp (2 turns),*
   D&C (1 turn)   **V** E J RANCE   **NSM** D A WALTERS
SALKELD, GREAT (St Cuthbert)   *see* Kirkoswald, Renwick w
   Croglin, Gt Salkeld etc *Carl*
SALLE (St Peter and St Paul)   *see* Reepham, Hackford w
   Whitwell, Kerdiston etc *Nor*
SALT (St James the Great)   *see* Mid Trent *Lich*
SALTASH (St Nicholas and St Faith) *Truro 11*   **P** *Patr Bd*
   TR A BUTLER   **TV** J M LOBB   **C** J C JUKES, M E GOODLAND
   NSM D BURROWS, P M SELLIX
SALTBURN-BY-THE-SEA (Emmanuel) *York 16*   **P** *Abp, Adn*
   Cleveland, Marquis of Zetland, Mrs M Brignall, and Mrs S L Vernon
   (jt)   **V** A M F REED   **C** A C YOUNG, J L SMITH
SALTBY (St Peter)   *see* High Framland Par *Leic*
SALTDEAN (St Nicholas) *Chich 19*   **P** *Bp*   **V** *vacant*
SALTER STREET (St Patrick) and Shirley *Birm 6*   **P** *Patr Bd*
   TR P D LAW-JONES   **TV** J A HUMPHRIES   **Hon**
   C W E G CARTER
SALTERHEBBLE (All Saints)   *see* Halifax All SS *Leeds*
SALTERSFORD (St John the Baptist)   *see* Rainow w Saltersford
   and Forest *Ches*
SALTFLEETBY (St Peter) *Linc 15*   **P** *Or Coll Ox, Bp, and MMCET*
   (jt)   **V** C M TURNER
SALTFORD (Blessed Virgin Mary) w Corston and Newton
   St Loe *B & W 9*   **P** *DBP (2 turns), Duchy of Cornwall (1 turn)*
   R D M WILSHERE
SALTHOUSE (St Nicholas)   *see* Weybourne Gp *Nor*
SALTLEY (St Saviour) and Washwood Heath *Birm 13*
   P *Bp and Trustees (jt)*   **V** A THOMPSON
SALTNEY FERRY (St Matthew)   *see* Lache cum Saltney *Ches*
SALTON (St John of Beverley)   *see* Kirby Misperton w
   Normanby and Salton *York*
SALTWOOD (St Peter and St Paul)   *see* Lympne and Saltwood
   Cant
SALWARPE (St Michael) and Hindlip w Martin Hussingtree
   Worc 8   **P** *Bp, D&C, and Exors Lady Hindlip (by turn)*
   P-in-c N G BYARD   **C** B J JAMESON

SALWAY ASH (Holy Trinity)   *see* Beaminster Area *Sarum*

SAMBOURNE (Mission Church)   *see* Alcester Minster *Cov*

SAMBROOK (St Luke)   *see* Cheswardine, Childs Ercall, Hales, Hinstock etc *Lich*

SAMLESBURY (St Leonard the Less)   *see* Balderstone, Mellor and Samlesbury *Blackb*

SAMPFORD ARUNDEL (Holy Cross)   *see* Wellington and Distr *B & W*

SAMPFORD BRETT (St George)   *see* Quantock Towers *B & W*

SAMPFORD COURTENAY (St Andrew)   *see* Chagford, Gidleigh, Throwleigh etc *Ex*

SAMPFORD PEVERELL (St John the Baptist), Uplowman, Holcombe Rogus, Hockworthy, Burlescombe and Halberton w Ash Thomas *Ex 7*   **P** *Patr Bd*   **TR** R S J BLADE   **NSM** G LEWRY

SAMPFORD SPINEY (St Mary) w Horrabridge *Ex 22*   **P** *D&C Windsor*   **C** E P PARKES

SAMPFORD, GREAT (St Michael)   *see* The Sampfords and Radwinter w Hempstead *Chelmsf*

SAMPFORD, LITTLE (St Mary) *as above*

SAMPFORDS, The (St Michael) (St Mary) and Radwinter with Hempstead *Chelmsf 20*   **P** *Guild of All So, New Coll Ox, and Keble Coll Ox (jt)*   **P-in-c** P G TARRIS

SANCREED (St Creden) *Truro 5*   **P** *D&C*   **V** *vacant*

SANCROFT *St E 15*   **P** *Bp, Ch Soc Trust, Em Coll Cam, and SMF (jt)*   **R** S A LOXTON   **C** C R BLADEN   **NSM** P A SCHWIER

SANCTON (All Saints) *York 5*   **P** *Abp*   **V** D J EVERETT

SAND HILL (Church of the Good Shepherd)   *see* N Farnborough *Guildf*

SAND HUTTON (St Mary)   *see* Harton *York*

SANDAL (St Catherine) *Leeds 20*   **P** *V Sandal Magna*   **NSM** D DODGSON

SANDAL MAGNA (St Helen) *Leeds 20*   **P** *Peache Trustees*   **V** R G MARTIN

SANDBACH (St Mary) *Ches 11*   **P** *DBP*   **V** T SHEPHERD

SANDBACH HEATH (St John the Evangelist) w Wheelock *Ches 11*   **P** *V Sandbach*   **V** G K STANNING   **C** L S CULLENS

SANDBANKS (St Nicolas)   *see* Canford Cliffs and Sandbanks *Sarum*

SANDERSTEAD (All Saints) (St Antony) (St Edmund the King and Martyr) (St Mary) *S'wark 22*   **P** *Bp*   **P-in-c** M R GREENFIELD   **TV** G G COHEN, S F ATKINSON-JONES   **NSM** J C GROOMBRIDGE

SANDFORD (All Saints)   *see* Winscombe and Sandford *B & W*

SANDFORD (St Martin)   *see* Wareham *Sarum*

SANDFORD (St Swithin)   *see* Crediton, Shobrooke and Sandford etc *Ex*

SANDFORD ORCAS (St Nicholas)   *see* Queen Thorne *Sarum*

SANDFORD ST MARTIN (St Martin)   *see* Westcote Barton w Steeple Barton, Duns Tew and Sandford St Martin and Over w Nether Worton *Ox*

SANDFORD-ON-THAMES (St Andrew) *Ox 1*   **P** *DBP*   **P-in-c** R C MORGAN

SANDGATE (St Paul)   *see* Folkestone Trin *Cant*

SANDHURST (Mission Church)   *see* Benenden and Sandhurst *Cant*

SANDHURST (St Lawrence)   *see* Twigworth, Down Hatherley, Norton, The Leigh etc *Glouc*

SANDHURST (St Michael and All Angels) *Ox 8*   **P** *Bp*   **R** J A CASTLE

SANDHURST (St Nicholas)   *see* Benenden and Sandhurst *Cant*

SANDHURST, LOWER (St Mary)   *see* Sandhurst *Ox*

SANDHUTTON (St Leonard)   *see* Thirsk *York*

SANDIACRE (St Giles) *Derby 13*   **P** *Ld Chan*   **R** O TRELENBERG   **NSM** K W G JOHNSON

SANDIWAY (St John the Evangelist) *Ches 6*   **P** *Bp*   **V** R J HUGHES

SANDLEHEATH (St Aldhelm)   *see* Fordingbridge and Breamore and Hale etc *Win*

SANDON (All Saints)   *see* Mid Trent *Lich*

SANDON (All Saints)   *see* Clothall, Rushden, Sandon, Wallington and Weston *St Alb*

SANDON (St Andrew) *Chelmsf 10*   **P** *Qu Coll Cam*   **P-in-c** T G A BROWN

SANDOWN (Christ Church) *Portsm 7*   **P** *Ch Patr Trust*   **NSM** T B RICHARDS

SANDOWN, LOWER (St John the Evangelist) *Portsm 7*   **P** *Bp*   **NSM** T B RICHARDS

SANDRIDGE (St Leonard) *St Alb 7*   **P** *Earl Spencer*   **V** E L COLEY   **NSM** P G CRUMPLER

SANDRINGHAM (St Mary Magdalene) w West Newton and Appleton, Wolferton w Babingley and Flitcham *Nor 16*   **P** *The Crown*   **R** J B V RIVIERE

SANDS (Church of the Good Shepherd)   *see* Seale, Puttenham and Wanborough *Guildf*

SANDS (St Mary and St George)   *see* High Wycombe *Ox*

SANDSEND (St Mary)   *see* Hinderwell, Roxby and Staithes etc *York*

SANDWELL (St Philip)   *see* W Bromwich St Phil *Lich*

SANDWICH (St Clement) and Worth *Cant 9*   **P** *Abp and Adn Cant (jt)*   **R** J M A ROBERTS   **NSM** R A BENDALL   **OLM** H T PASHLEY

SANDY (St Swithun) *St Alb 10*   **P** *Lord Pym*   **R** P H DAVIES   **C** D J GRAY

SANDY LANE (St Mary and St Nicholas)   *see* Rowde and Bromham *Sarum*

SANDYLANDS (St John) *Blackb 11*   **P** *Bp*   **V** L MACLUSKIE   **C** L S MOFFATT

SANKEY, GREAT (St Mary)   *see* Warrington W *Liv*

SANTON DOWNHAM (St Mary the Virgin)   *see* Brandon and Santon Downham w Elveden etc *St E*

SAPCOTE (All Saints) and Sharnford w Wigston Parva *Leic 10*   **P** *Ld Chan and DBP (alt)*   **R** M J NORMAN

SAPEY, UPPER (St Michael)   *see* Edvin Loach w Tedstone Delamere etc *Heref*

SAPPERTON (St Kenelm)   *see* Kemble, Poole Keynes, Somerford Keynes etc *Glouc*

SAPPERTON (St Nicholas)   *see* N Beltisloe Gp *Linc*

SARISBURY (St Paul) *Portsm 2*   **P** *V Titchfield*   **V** A J MATHESON

SARK (St Peter) *Win 14*   **P** *Le Seigneur de Sercq*   **NSM** J A DALLEN

SARN (Holy Trinity)   *see* Churchstoke w Hyssington and Sarn *Heref*

SARNESFIELD (St Mary)   *see* Weobley w Sarnesfield and Norton Canon *Heref*

SARRATT (Holy Cross) and Chipperfield *St Alb 4*   **P** *Churchwardens and DBP (jt)*   **R** M M DU SAIRE

SATLEY (St Cuthbert), Stanley and Tow Law *Dur 9*   **P** *Bp, Ld Chan, and R Brancepeth (by turn)*   **P-in-c** J P L WHALLEY   **Hon C** G H LAWES

SATTERTHWAITE (All Saints)   *see* Hawkshead and Low Wray w Sawrey and Rusland etc *Carl*

SAUGHALL, GREAT (All Saints) *Ches 9*   **P** *Bp*   **P-in-c** D R NUGENT   **NSM** H M PANG

SAUL (St James the Great)   *see* Frampton on Severn, Arlingham, Saul etc *Glouc*

SAUNDERTON (St Mary and St Nicholas)   *see* Risborough *Ox*

SAUNTON (St Anne)   *see* Braunton *Ex*

SAUSTHORPE (St Andrew)   *see* Bolingbroke Deanery *Linc*

SAVERNAKE (St Katharine) *Sarum 19*   **P** *Patr Bd*   **TR** M T MCHUGH   **TV** J REID   **NSM** A J DEBOO, R A GRIST

SAW MILLS (St Mary)   *see* Ambergate and Heage *Derby*

SAWBRIDGEWORTH (Great St Mary) *St Alb 15*   **P** *Bp*   **V** F M ARNOLD

SAWLEY (All Saints) (St Mary) *Derby 13*   **P** *D&C Lich*   **R** A J STREET   **NSM** J H HENDERSON SMITH

SAWLEY (St Michael)   *see* Fountains Gp *Leeds*

SAWREY (St Peter)   *see* Hawkshead and Low Wray w Sawrey and Rusland etc *Carl*

SAWSTON (St Mary) *Ely 5*   **P** *SMF*   **P-in-c** A C PARTRIDGE

SAWTRY (All Saints) and Glatton *Ely 15*   **P** *Duke of Devonshire*   **R** R C WARD   **NSM** I R FALVEY

SAXBY (St Helen)   *see* Owmby Gp *Linc*

SAXBY ALL SAINTS (All Saints) *Linc 8*   **P** *F C H H Barton Esq*   **R** D P ROWETT

SAXELBYE (St Peter)   *see* Old Dalby, Nether Broughton, Saxelbye etc *Leic*

SAXHAM, GREAT (St Andrew)   *see* Barrow *St E*

SAXHAM, LITTLE (St Nicholas) *as above*

SAXILBY Group, The (St Botolph) *Linc 2*   **P** *Bp and DBP (jt)*   **NSM** S PROSSER   **OLM** J A VICKERS

SAXLINGHAM (St Margaret)   *see* Stiffkey and Bale *Nor*

SAXLINGHAM NETHERGATE (St Mary)   *see* Newton Flotman, Swainsthorpe, Tasburgh, etc *Nor*

SAXMUNDHAM (St John the Baptist) w Kelsale cum Carlton *St E 17*   **P** *Patr Bd*   **R** A J WOLTON

SAXON SHORELINE, The *Cant 10*   **P** *Abp and Ld Chan (alt)*   **R** T R WHATELEY   **C** M P JONES

SAXONWELL *Linc 22*   **P** *Duchy of Lanc (2 turns), Ld Chan (1 turn)*   **P-in-c** H G ORRIDGE

SAXTEAD (All Saints)   *see* Framlingham w Saxtead *St E*

SAXTHORPE (St Andrew)   *see* Lt Barningham, Blickling, Edgefield etc *Nor*

SAXTON (All Saints)   *see* Sherburn in Elmet w Saxton *York*

SAYERS COMMON (Christ Church)   *see* Albourne w Sayers Common and Twineham *Chich*

SCACKLETON (St George the Martyr)   *see* The Street Par *York*

SCALBY (St Laurence) *York 15*   **P** *Abp*   **V** A J FERNELEY   **NSM** D C PYNN, D MACIVER

SCALDWELL (St Peter and St Paul)   *see* Walgrave w Hannington and Wold and Scaldwell *Pet*

SCALEBY (All Saints) *see* Eden, Gelt and Irthing *Carl*
SCALFORD (St Egelwin) *see* Ironstone Villages *Leic*
SCAMMONDEN, WEST (St Bartholomew) *see* Barkisland w
   W Scammonden *Leeds*
SCAMPSTON (St Martin) *see* Buckrose Carrs *York*
SCAMPTON (St John the Baptist) *see* Spring Line Gp *Linc*
SCARBOROUGH (St Columba) *York 15*   **P** *Abp*
   P-in-c S R DRURY
SCARBOROUGH (St James w Holy Trinity) *York 15*   **P** *Abp and*
   CPAS (jt)   **P-in-c** P W WHITE   **NSM** L M HOLLIS
SCARBOROUGH (St Luke) *York 15*   **P** *Abp*   **V** A J FERNELEY
   NSM D C PYNN, D MACIVER
SCARBOROUGH (St Martin) *York 15*   **P** *Trustees*
   V D M DIXON   **C** A C WOGAN   **NSM** R G C COSTIN
SCARBOROUGH (St Mary) w Christ Church and (Holy
   Apostles) *York 15*   **P** *Abp*   **V** M P DUNNING
   C C N MINETT STEVENS
SCARBOROUGH (St Saviour w All Saints) *York 15*   **P** *Abp*
   V D M DIXON
SCARCLIFFE (St Leonard) *see* Ault Hucknall and Scarcliffe
   Derby
SCARISBRICK (St Mark) (Good Shepherd) *Liv 11*   **P** *V*
   Ormskirk   **P-in-c** E HEANEY
SCARLE, NORTH (All Saints) *see* Swinderby *Linc*
SCARLE, SOUTH (St Helena) *see* E Trent *S'well*
SCARNING (St Peter and St Paul) *see* Dereham and Distr *Nor*
SCARRINGTON (St John of Beverley) *see* Whatton w
   Aslockton, Hawksworth, Scarrington etc *S'well*
SCARSDALE, EAST *Derby 3*   **P** *Patr Bd*   **TR** J E DRAYCOTT
   TV K T BRADLEY   **OLM** J A PALMER
SCARTHO (St Giles) St Matthew *Linc 3*   **P** *Jes Coll Ox*
   R *vacant*
SCAWBY (St Hybald), Redbourne and Hibaldstow *Linc 8*
   P T M S Nelthorpe Esq (2 turns), Bp (1 turn), and Duke of St Alb
   (1 turn)   **P-in-c** D J EAMES
SCAWTHORPE (St Luke) *see* Doncaster St Leon and St Jude
   Sheff
SCAWTON (St Mary) *see* Upper Ryedale *York*
SCAYNES HILL (St Augustine) *Chich 5*   **P** *Bp*   **V** L H BARNETT
SCHOLES (St Philip and St James) *see* Hartshead, Hightown,
   Roberttown and Scholes *Leeds*
SCHOLES (St Philip) *see* Barwick in Elmet *Leeds*
SCHORNE *Ox 13*   **P** *Patr Bd (2 turns), Ld Chan (1 turn)*
   TR D J MEAKIN   **TV** V M CRUDDAS   **C** R A LIGHTBOWN
   OLM J BAYLY
SCISSETT (St Augustine) *see* High Hoyland, Scissett and
   Clayton W *Leeds*
SCOFTON (St John the Evangelist) *see* Retford Area *S'well*
SCOLE (St Andrew) *see* Redenhall w Scole *Nor*
SCOPWICK (Holy Cross) *see* Digby Gp *Linc*
SCORBOROUGH (St Leonard) *see* Lockington and Lund and
   Scorborough w Leconfield *York*
SCORTON (St Peter) and Barnacre All Saints and Calder Vale
   St John the Evangelist *Blackb 9*   **P** *Bp, V Lanc St Mary w St Jo*
   and St Anne, and Mrs V O Shepherd-Cross (jt)   **V** A M MÜLLER
SCOT WILLOUGHBY (St Andrew) *see* S Lafford *Linc*
SCOTBY (All Saints) and Cotehill w Cumwhinton *Carl 2*
   P *Trustees (2 turns), Prime Min (1 turn)*   **V** I S LAWRENCE
SCOTFORTH (St Paul) *Blackb 11*   **P** *The Rt Revd J Nicholls*
   V M A GISBOURNE   **C** S T WILKINSON
SCOTHERN (St Germain) *see* Welton and Dunholme w
   Scothern *Linc*
SCOTSWOOD (St Margaret) *see* Benwell and Scotswood *Newc*
SCOTTER (St Peter) w East Ferry *Linc 6*   **P** *Bp*
   P-in-c D J SWANNACK
SCOTTON (St Genewys) w Northorpe *Linc 6*   **P** *Ld Chan*
   P-in-c D J SWANNACK   **OLM** D L LANGFORD, W KEAST
SCOTTON (St Thomas) *see* Walkingham Hill *Leeds*
SCOTTOW (All Saints) *see* Worstead, Westwick, Sloley,
   Swanton Abbot etc *Nor*
SCOULTON (Holy Trinity) *see* High Oak, Hingham and
   Scoulton w Wood Rising *Nor*
SCRAMBLESBY (St Martin) *see* Asterby Gp *Linc*
SCRAPTOFT (All Saints) *Leic 1*   **P** *Bp, Dr M J A Sharp, and DBP*
   (jt)   **V** M J COURT
SCRAYINGHAM (St Peter and St Paul) *see* Stamford Bridge Gp
   York
SCREDINGTON (St Andrew) *see* Heckington and
   Helpringham Gp *Linc*
SCREMBY (St Peter and St Paul) *see* Bolingbroke Deanery *Linc*
SCREMERSTON (St Peter) *Newc 12*   **P** *Bp*   **P-in-c** M S KNOX
   NSM A M PETERS-WOTHERSPOON
SCREVETON (St Wilfrid) *see* Car Colston w Screveton *S'well*
SCRIVELSBY (St Benedict) *see* Fen and Hill Gp *Linc*
SCROOBY (St Wilfrid) *see* Blyth and Scrooby w Ranskill *S'well*
SCROPTON (St Paul) *see* S Dales *Derby*

SCRUTON (St Radegund) *see* Lower Swale *Leeds*
SCULCOATES (St Mary) *see* Hull St Mary Sculcoates *York*
SCULCOATES (St Paul) (St Stephen) *York 14*   **P** *Abp and*
   V Hull H Trin (1 turn), Ld Chan (1 turn)   **P-in-c** M G CROOK
SCULTHORPE (St Mary and All Saints) *see* N and S Creake w
   Waterden, Syderstone etc *Nor*
SCUNTHORPE (All Saints) *see* Brumby *Linc*
SCUNTHORPE (The Resurrection) *see* Trentside E *Linc*
SEA MILLS (St Edyth) *Bris 2*   **P** *Bp*   **V** D A IZZARD
SEA PALLING (St Margaret) *see* Bacton, Happisburgh,
   Hempstead w Eccles etc *Nor*
SEA VIEW (St Peter) *Portsm 7*   **P** *Bp*
   P-in-c R W WYNFORD-HARRIS
SEABOROUGH (St John) *see* Beaminster Area *Sarum*
SEABROOK (Mission Hall) *see* Cheriton w Newington *Cant*
SEACOMBE (St Paul) w Poulton *Ches 7*   **P** *Bp and trustees (jt)*
   V P T COOPER
SEACROFT (St James) (Church of the Ascension) (St Richard)
   (St Luke) (St Paul) *Leeds 17*   **P** *DBF*   **TR** M P BENWELL
   TV C BANDAWE, F J HARRISON-SMITH
SEAFORD (St Leonard) w Sutton *Chich 21*   **P** *Ld Chan*
   V P J OWEN   **C** C RUDGE, P A LUCAS
SEAGRAVE (All Saints) *see* Sileby, Cossington and Seagrave *Leic*
SEAGRY (St Mary the Virgin) *see* Gt Somerford, Lt Somerford,
   Seagry, Corston etc *Bris*
SEAHAM (St Mary the Virgin) *Dur 2*   **P** *Bp*   **V** *vacant*
SEAHAM HARBOUR (St John) and Dawdon *Dur 2*   **P** *Bp*
   V P TWISLETON
SEAHAM, NEW (Christ Church) *see* Dalton le Dale and New
   Seaham *Dur*
SEAL (St Lawrence) *Roch 9*   **P** *Bp*   **V** E C KITCHENER
SEAL (St Peter and St Paul) *Roch 9*   **P** *DBP*   **V** J A LE BAS
SEALE (St Lawrence), Puttenham and Wanborough *Guildf 4*
   P *Adn Surrey, C R I Perkins Esq, and Ld Chan (by turn)*
   P-in-c A G HARBIDGE   **C** D J ORME
SEALE (St Peter) (St Matthew) and Lullington w Coton in the
   Elms *Derby 16*   **P** *Bp, R D Nielson Esq, and C W Worthington*
   Esq (jt)   **R** M A YATES
SEAMER (St Martin) w East Ayton *York 15*   **P** *Abp*
   V A J MORELAND
SEAMER IN CLEVELAND (St Martin) *see* Stokesley w Seamer
   York
SEARBY (St Nicholas) *see* Caistor Gp *Linc*
SEASALTER (St Alpheg) *see* Whitstable *Cant*
SEASCALE (St Cuthbert) and Drigg *Carl 5*   **P** *DBP*
   P-in-c L D GRAY
SEATHWAITE (Holy Trinity) *see* Broughton and Duddon
   Carl
SEATON (All Hallows) *see* Lyddington, Bisbrooke, Caldecott,
   Glaston etc *Pet*
SEATON (St Gregory) and Beer *Ex 4*   **P** *Lord Clinton and*
   D&C (jt)   **V** J C TREW   **NSM** A M STUCKEY
SEATON (St Paul) *see* Camerton, Seaton and W Seaton *Carl*
SEATON CAREW (Holy Trinity) *Dur 3*   **P** *Bp*
   P-in-c P T ALLINSON
SEATON HIRST (St John) (St Andrew) *Newc 11*   **P** *Bp*
   R D P PALMER
SEATON ROSS (St Edmund) *see* Holme and Seaton Ross Gp
   York
SEATON SLUICE (St Paul) *see* Delaval *Newc*
SEATON, WEST (Holy Trinity) *see* Camerton, Seaton and W
   Seaton *Carl*
SEAVINGTON (St Michael and St Mary) *see* S Petherton w
   The Seavingtons and The Lambrooks *B & W*
SEBERGHAM (St Mary) *see* Caldbeck, Castle Sowerby and
   Sebergham *Carl*
SECKINGTON (All Saints) *see* N Warks *Birm*
SEDBERGH (St Andrew), Cautley and Garsdale *Carl 10*
   P *Trin Coll Cam*   **V** A B MCMULLON
SEDGEBERROW (St Mary the Virgin) *see* Hampton w
   Sedgeberrow and Hinton-on-the-Green *Worc*
SEDGEBROOK (St Lawrence) *see* Saxonwell *Linc*
SEDGEFIELD (St Edmund) *see* Upper Skerne *Dur*
SEDGEHILL (St Katherine) *see* St Bartholomew *Sarum*
SEDGLEY (All Saints) *see* Gornal and Sedgley *Worc*
SEDGLEY (St Mary the Virgin) *Worc 10*   **P** *Bp and V Sedgley All*
   SS (jt)   **P-in-c** E J STANFORD, S R BUCKLEY
   NSM T WESTWOOD
SEDLESCOMBE (St John the Baptist) w Whatlington *Chich 12*
   P *Ld Chan and Bp (alt)*   **P-in-c** K A MEPHAM
SEEND (Holy Cross), Bulkington and Poulshot *Sarum 17*
   P *D&C (2 turns), Bp (1 turn)*   **P-in-c** M A ALLCHIN
SEER GREEN (Holy Trinity) *see* Chalfont St Giles, Seer Green
   and Jordans *Ox*
SEETHING (St Margaret) *see* Brooke, Kirstead, Mundham w
   Seething and Thwaite *Nor*

SEFTON (St Helen) *Liv 5*   **P** *Bp*   **C** N C MILFORD
SEFTON PARK (Christ Church)   *see* Toxteth Park Ch Ch and
St Mich w St Andr *Liv*
SEGHILL (Holy Trinity) *Newc 1*   **P** *The Crown*
V P G J HUGHES
SEIGHFORD (St Chad)   *see* Chebsey, Creswell, Ellenhall,
Ranton etc *Lich*
SELATTYN (St Mary) and Hengoed w Gobowen *Lich 19*
P *Bp and Mrs A F Hamilton-Hill (jt)*   **P-in-c** A R BAILEY
SELBORNE (St Mary)   *see* Northanger *Win*
SELBY (St James the Apostle) *York 4*   **P** *Simeon's Trustees*
V C J REID   **Hon C** D M REID
SELBY ABBEY (St Mary and St Germain) (St Richard) *York 4*
P *Abp*   **V** J C WEETMAN   **C** M G WEAVER, N B WOODHALL
NSM J S WATSON, N B WOODHALL
SELHAM (St James)   *see* Easebourne, Lodsworth and Selham
Chich
SELLACK (St Tysilio)   *see* Wormelow Hundred *Heref*
SELLINDGE (St Mary the Virgin)   *see* A20 Benefice *Cant*
SELLING (St Mary the Virgin)   *see* Downsfoot *Cant*
SELLY OAK (St Mary) *Birm 2*   **P** *Bp*   **V** J D R COX
NSM D J PARKER, J M ADAMS
SELLY PARK (Christ Church) *Birm 5*   **P** *Trustees*
V G P LANHAM   **C** M C GIBBINS
SELLY PARK (St Stephen) (St Wulstan) *Birm 5*   **P** *Trustees*
V C B HOBBS   **C** A P MARTIN
SELMESTON (St Mary)   *see* Arlington, Berwick, Selmeston w
Alciston etc *Chich*
SELSDON (St Francis) Conventional District *S'wark 19*
NSM A ONYEKWELU   **Min** P C WYATT
SELSDON (St John) (St Francis) *S'wark 19*   **P** *Bp*
R J J E ROWLEY
SELSEY (St Peter) *Chich 2*   **P** *Bp*   **R** A E WILKES
SELSIDE (St Thomas)   *see* Beacon *Carl*
SELSLEY (All Saints)   *see* The Stanleys w Selsley *Glouc*
SELSTON (St Helen) *S'well 4*   **P** *Wright Trustees*
V M F SHOULER   **C** A W MUNNS
SELWORTHY (All Saints)   *see* Porlock and Porlock Weir w Stoke
Pero etc *B & W*
SELWORTHY (Lynch Chapel) *as above*
SEMER (All Saints)   *see* Bildeston w Wattisham and Lindsey,
Whatfield etc *St E*
SEMINGTON (St George)   *see* Canalside Benefice *Sarum*
SEMLEY (St Leonard)   *see* St Bartholomew *Sarum*
SEMPRINGHAM (St Andrew)   *see* Billingborough Gp *Linc*
SEND (St Mary the Virgin) *Guildf 12*   **P** *Bp*   **P-in-c** A J SHUTT
SENNEN (St Sennen)   *see* St Buryan, St Levan and Sennen
Truro
SENNICOTTS (St Mary)   *see* Funtington and W Stoke w
Sennicotts *Chich*
SESSAY (St Cuthbert) *York 18*   **P** *Viscountess Downe*
R N J CARNALL   **Hon C** M I KIMBALL
SETCHEY (St Mary)   *see* Middlewinch *Nor*
SETTLE (Holy Ascension) *Leeds 21*   **P** *Trustees*
P-in-c H A F YOUNG   **C** S C DAWSON
SETTRINGTON (All Saints)   *see* W Buckrose *York*
SEVENHAMPTON (St Andrew) w Charlton Abbots, Hawling
and Whittington, Dowdeswell and Andoversford w The
Shiptons and Cold Salperton, and Withington *Glouc 8*
P *Bp, MMCET, T W Bailey Esq, E M Bailey Esq, and Mrs J A*
Stringer (1 turn); Bp, MMCET, and Mrs L E Evans (1 turn)
P-in-c C A RANDALL
SEVENHAMPTON (St James)   *see* Highworth w Sevenhampton
and Inglesham etc *Bris*
SEVENOAKS (St John the Baptist) *Roch 9*   **P** *Guild of All So*
V R D E JONES   **C** M J ROBINSON
SEVENOAKS (St Luke) *Roch 9*   **P** *Bp*   **V** M R GRIFFIN
NSM A C BOURNE
SEVENOAKS (St Nicholas) *Roch 9*   **P** *Trustees*
R A M MACLEAY   **C** A A FEARNLEY, G J MCGRATH, T J NASH
Hon C N N HENSHAW
SEVENOAKS WEALD (St George) *Roch 9*   **P** *R Sevenoaks*
V A H CARR
SEVERN STOKE (St Dennis)   *see* Kempsey and Severn Stoke w
Croome d'Abitot *Worc*
SEVINGTON (St Mary)   *see* Willesborough w Sevington
Cant
SEWARDS END (St James)   *see* Saffron Walden and Villages
Chelmsf
SEWERBY (St John)   *see* Bridlington H Trin and Sewerby w
Marton *York*
SEWSTERN (Holy Trinity)   *see* S Framland *Leic*
SHABBINGTON (St Mary Magdalene)   *see* Worminghall w
Ickford, Oakley and Shabbington *Ox*
SHACKERSTONE (St Peter)   *see* Nailstone and Carlton w
Shackerstone *Leic*

SHACKLEFORD (St Mary the Virgin)   *see* Compton w
Shackleford and Peper Harow *Guildf*
SHADFORTH (St Cuthbert)   *see* Shadforth and Sherburn *Dur*
SHADFORTH (St Cuthbert) and Sherburn *Dur 1*   **P** *D&C*
P-in-c A B BARTLETT   **NSM** A J FENTON, R S BRIGGS
SHADINGFIELD (St John the Baptist)   *see* Hundred River and
Wainford *St E*
SHADOXHURST (St Peter and St Paul)   *see* Kingsnorth and
Shadoxhurst *Cant*
SHADWELL (St Paul)   *see* Moor Allerton and Shadwell *Leeds*
SHADWELL (St Paul) w Ratcliffe St James *Lon 7*   **P** *Bp*
C A M LILLEY, C I ROGERS   **Hon C** R Q EDWARDS
SHAFTESBURY (St James) (St Peter) *Sarum 5*   **P** *Patr Bd*
TR H E DAWES   **TV** S P CHAMBERS   **NSM** C J CROSSLEY
SHALBOURNE (St Michael and All Angels)   *see* Savernake *Sarum*
SHALDEN (St Peter and St Paul)   *see* Bentworth, Lasham,
Medstead and Shalden *Win*
SHALDON (St Nicholas) (St Peter), Stokeinteignhead,
Combeinteignhead and Haccombe *Ex 9*   **P** *SMF and Col*
G P Arnold (jt)   **R** A M CHURCH
SHALFLEET (St Michael the Archangel) *Portsm 8*   **P** *Ld Chan*
V D J BEVINGTON
SHALFORD (St Andrew)   *see* Finchingfield and Cornish Hall
End etc *Chelmsf*
SHALFORD (St Mary the Virgin) *Guildf 5*   **P** *Ld Chan*
V J J CRUSE
SHALSTONE (St Edward the Confessor)   *see* W Buckingham *Ox*
SHAMLEY GREEN (Christ Church) *Guildf 2*   **P** *Bp*
V S J DAVIES
SHANGTON (St Nicholas)   *see* The Langtons and Shangton
Leic
SHANKLIN (St Blasius) *Portsm 7*   **P** *Bp*   **R** *vacant*
SHANKLIN (St Paul)   *see* Gatten St Paul *Portsm*
SHANKLIN (St Saviour on the Cliff) *Portsm 7*   **P** *Bp*
V *vacant*
SHAP (St Michael) w Swindale and Bampton w Mardale
Carl 1   **P** *Earl of Lonsdale*   **P-in-c** B LOCK   **NSM** S E WARD
SHAPWICK (St Bartholomew)   *see* Bridge Par *Sarum*
SHAPWICK (The Blessed Virgin Mary)   *see* Polden Wheel *B & W*
SHARD END (All Saints) *Birm 9*   **P** *Keble Coll Ox*
V A J CLUCAS
SHARDLOW (St James)   *see* Aston on Trent, Elvaston, Weston
on Trent etc *Derby*
SHARESHILL (St Luke and St Mary the Virgin) *Lich 2*
P *Bp*   **P-in-c** S BOWIE   **OLM** N E BELLAMY
SHARLSTON (St Luke) *Leeds 20*   **P** *Bp*   **V** *vacant*
SHARNBROOK (St Peter), Felmersham and Knotting w
Souldrop *St Alb 13*   **P** *Bp*   **R** *vacant*
SHARNFORD (St Helen)   *see* Sapcote and Sharnford w
Wigston Parva *Leic*
SHARPNESS (St Andrew), Purton, Brookend and Slimbridge
Glouc 5   **P** *Magd Coll Ox and Bp (alt)*   **R** W J BOON
NSM G M TUCKER
SHARRINGTON (All Saints)   *see* Stiffkey and Bale *Nor*
SHAUGH PRIOR (St Edward)   *see* Bickleigh and Shaugh Prior *Ex*
SHAVINGTON (St Mark)   *see* Weston *Ches*
SHAW (Christchurch)   *see* Atworth w Shaw and Whitley
Sarum
SHAW (Holy Trinity)   *see* W Swindon and the Lydiards *Bris*
SHAW (Holy Trinity)   *see* Royton St Paul and Shaw *Man*
SHAW (St Mary) cum Donnington *Ox 6*   **P** *DBP*
R M WOOD
SHAWBURY (St Mary the Virgin) *Lich 22*   **P** *C C Corbet Esq*
V *vacant*
SHAWELL (All Saints)   *see* Gilmorton, Peatling Parva, Kimcote
etc *Leic*
SHEARSBY (St Mary Magdalene)   *see* Hexagon *Leic*
SHEBBEAR (St Michael), Buckland Filleigh, Sheepwash,
Langtree, Newton St Petrock, Petrockstowe,
Petersmarland, Merton and Huish *Ex 19*   **P** *Ld Chan*
(1 turn), Patr Bd (2 turns)   **TR** M J WARREN   **TV** S METZ
SHEDFIELD (St John the Baptist) and Wickham *Portsm 1*
P *DBP and Sir Richard Rashleigh Bt (jt)*   **Hon C** J MONTAGUE
NSM B R MCHUGH, L B CAMERON
SHEEN (St Luke)   *see* Longnor, Quarnford and Sheen *Lich*
SHEEN, EAST (All Saints)   *see* Mortlake w E Sheen *S'wark*
SHEEN, EAST (Christ Church) *as above*
SHEEPSTOR (St Leonard)   *see* Yelverton, Meavy, Sheepstor and
Walkhampton *Ex*
SHEEPWASH (St Lawrence)   *see* Shebbear, Buckland Filleigh,
Sheepwash etc *Ex*
SHEEPY (All Saints)   *see* Bosworth and Sheepy Gp *Leic*
SHEERING (St Mary the Virgin)   *see* Hatfield Heath and
Sheering *Chelmsf*
SHEERNESS (Holy Trinity w St Paul)   *see* W Sheppey *Cant*
SHEERWATER (St Michael and All Angels)   *see* Woodham *Guildf*

SHEET (St Mary Magdalene) *Portsm 4*　**P** *Bp*
V R G SAUNDERS　**C** M D CROSS　**NSM** A J MARSH,
P W MICKLETHWAITE
SHEFFIELD (St Aidan w St Luke)　*see* Sheff Manor *Sheff*
SHEFFIELD (St Andrew)　*see* Psalter Lane St Andr *Sheff*
SHEFFIELD (St Catherine of Siena) Richmond Road *Sheff 1*
　P *The Crown*　**V** P A KNOWLES
SHEFFIELD (St Cecilia) Parson Cross *Sheff 3*　**P** *Bp*
　V K RYDER-WEST
SHEFFIELD (St Cuthbert) *Sheff 3*　**P** *Ch Burgesses*
　NSM M R SUTTON
SHEFFIELD (St John the Evangelist) *Sheff 1*　**P** *Ch Burgesses*
　P-in-c C C FFRENCH-HODGES
SHEFFIELD (St Leonard) Norwood *Sheff 3*　**P** *Bp*
　P-in-c K RYDER-WEST　**NSM** J H DALEY
SHEFFIELD (St Mark) Broomhill *Sheff 4*　**P** *Ch Burgesses*
　V S HAMMERSLEY　**NSM** S E RUSH
SHEFFIELD (St Mary) Bramall Lane *Sheff 2*　**P** *Ch Burgesses*
　and Dean (alt)　**V** J C SULLIVAN　**NSM** G C D DUNCAN,
　K E CRIBB
SHEFFIELD (St Matthew) Carver Street *Sheff 2*　**P** *Bp and Sheff*
　Ch Burgess Trust (jt)　**P-in-c** G L NAYLOR
SHEFFIELD (St Oswald) St Peter *Sheff 2*　**P** *Ch Burgesses*
　V A NASCIMENTO COOK
SHEFFIELD (St Paul) Wordsworth Avenue *Sheff 3*　**P** *DBP*
　P-in-c K J CROOKES　**NSM** D J KERSHAW
SHEFFIELD MANOR (St Swithun) *Sheff 1*　**P** *Patr Bd*
　TR J UPTON　**C** S G CHAPMAN　**NSM** K COLLEY
SHEFFIELD PARK (St John the Evangelist)　*see* Sheff St Jo *Sheff*
SHEFFIELD The Vine *Sheff 4*　**P** *Ch Burgesses and Ch Patr Trust*
　(jt)　**V** P J BATCHFORD　**NSM** L C BOLSTER
SHEFFORD (St Michael)　*see* Meppershall and Shefford *St Alb*
SHEFFORD, GREAT (St Mary)　*see* W Downland *Ox*
SHEINTON (St Peter and St Paul)　*see* Wenlock *Heref*
SHELDON (St Giles) *Birm 9*　**P** J K Wingfield Digby Esq
　P-in-c B S CASTLE　**NSM** A E LAVIN
SHELDON (St James the Greater)　*see* Dunkeswell, Luppitt,
　Sheldon and Upottery *Ex*
SHELDON (St Michael and All Angels)　*see* Bakewell, Ashford w
　Sheldon and Rowsley *Derby*
SHELDWICH (St James)　*see* Downsfoot *Cant*
SHELF (St Michael and All Angels) w Buttershaw St Aidan
　Leeds 2　**P** *Bp*　**TR** M I GASKELL　**TV** A J GREIFF
　C T J-L GUILLEMIN
SHELFANGER (All Saints)　*see* Winfarthing w Shelfanger w
　Burston w Gissing etc *Nor*
SHELFIELD (St Mark) and High Heath *Lich 25*　**P** R Walsall
　V R J FARMER　**NSM** A J MCCOSH, C SILVESTER
SHELFORD (St Peter and St Paul)　*see* Radcliffe-on-Trent and
　Shelford *S'well*
SHELFORD, GREAT (St Mary) *Ely 5*　**P** *Bp*　**P-in-c** S J TALBOTT
　C M E CAMERON
SHELFORD, LITTLE (All Saints) *Ely 5*　**P** *Bp*　**R** S J SCOTT
　C S C R TOMKINS
SHELLAND (King Charles the Martyr)　*see* Gt Finborough w
　Onehouse, Harleston, Buxhall etc *St E*
SHELLEY (All Saints)　*see* Hadleigh, Layham and Shelley *St E*
SHELLEY (Emmanuel) and Shepley *Leeds 13*　**P** V Kirkburton
　P-in-c J R JONES　**C** K I FREEMAN　**OLM** J M CRAVEN
SHELLEY (St Peter)　*see* Chipping Ongar w Shelley *Chelmsf*
SHELLINGFORD (St Faith)　*see* Uffington, Shellingford,
　Woolstone and Baulking *Ox*
SHELSLEY BEAUCHAMP (All Saints)　*see* Worcs W *Worc*
SHELSLEY WALSH (St Andrew) *as above*
SHELSWELL *Ox 21*　**P** Ld Chan (1 turn) and Ch Ch Ox, CCC Ox,
　Baroness von Maltzahn, and R J Vallings Esq (1 turn)
　NSM W MUNCEY
SHELTON (Christ Church) and Oxon *Lich 20*　**P** V Shrewsbury
　St Chad w St Mary　**P-in-c** D O'BRIEN
SHELTON (St Mark)　*see* Hanley H Ev *Lich*
SHELTON (St Mary and All Saints) *S'well 3*　**P** *Bp*
　P-in-c E I MURRAY
SHELTON (St Mary)　*see* Hempnall *Nor*
SHELTON (St Mary)　*see* The Stodden Churches *St Alb*
SHELVE (All Saints)　*see* Minsterley, Habberley and Hope w
　Shelve *Heref*
SHENFIELD (St Mary the Virgin) *Chelmsf 8*　**P** Personal Reps R
　H Courage　**R** D G THOMAS　**NSM** E A LOCKHART
SHENINGTON (Holy Trinity)　*see* Ironstone *Ox*
SHENLEY (St Mary)　*see* Watling Valley *Ox*
SHENLEY GREEN (St David) *Birm 4*　**P** *Bp*　**V** *vacant*
SHENSTONE (St John the Baptist) and Stonnall *Lich 1*
　P MMCET　**V** E A CHAMBERLAIN
SHENTON (St John the Evangelist)　*see* Bosworth and Sheepy
　Gp *Leic*
SHEPHERD'S BUSH (St Luke) Uxbridge Road　*see* Hammersmith
　St Luke *Lon*

SHEPHERD'S BUSH (St Michael and St George) (St Stephen)
　(St Thomas) *Lon 9*　**P** *Bp*　**V** R W MAYO　**C** P J HOYLE
　NSM J A COWLEY
SHEPLEY (St Paul)　*see* Shelley and Shepley *Leeds*
SHEPPERDINE (Chapel)　*see* Thornbury and Oldbury-on-
　Severn w Shepperdine *Glouc*
SHEPPERTON (St Nicholas) and Littleton *Lon 13*　**P** Bp and
　C W L Barratt Esq (jt)　**R** C J SWIFT　**C** T M ROSE
　NSM P BARRIE
SHEPPEY, WEST *Cant 15*　**P** Abp and Ch Patr Trust (jt)
　V T P HALL　**C** J M MCLAREN, P A KITE, P A RUSH
SHEPRETH (All Saints)　*see* Fowlmere, Foxton, Shepreth and
　Thriplow *Ely*
SHEPSHED (St Botolph) and Oaks in Charnwood *Leic 6*
　P DBP and Lord Crawshaw (jt)　**V** C M HEBDEN
　C E T W BAMPTON　**NSM** J A BIRD
SHEPTON BEAUCHAMP (St Michael)　*see* Winsmoor *B & W*
SHEPTON MALLET (St Peter and St Paul) w Doulting *B & W 7*
　P Duchy of Cornwall and Bp (alt)　**P-in-c** J HUNTER DUNN
　C R A PRIESTLEY
SHEPTON MONTAGUE (St Peter)　*see* Bruton and Distr *B & W*
SHERBORNE (Abbey Church of St Mary) (All Souls)
　(St Paul) w Castleton, Lillington and Longburton *Sarum 3*
　P J K Wingfield Digby Esq　**V** E J WOODS　**C** D R TREGALE,
　J E TREGALE, R C J R MARTIN, R M WYLD　**NSM** J M CRAW,
　L A MCCREADIE, R N F COLLINS
SHERBORNE (St Mary Magdalene), Windrush, the
　Barringtons and Aldsworth *Glouc 8*　**P** C T R Wingfield Esq,
　Ch Ch Ox, and DBP (by turn)　**P-in-c** N FISHER　**Hon**
　C S J GOUNDREY-SMITH
SHERBORNES (St Andrew) (Vyne Chapel) w Pamber, The
　Win 4　**P** Bp and Qu Coll Ox (jt)　**R** J N HAMILTON
SHERBOURNE (All Saints)　*see* Barford w Wasperton and
　Sherbourne *Cov*
SHERBURN (St Hilda)　*see* Buckrose Carrs *York*
SHERBURN (St Mary)　*see* Shadforth and Sherburn *Dur*
SHERBURN IN ELMET (All Saints) w Saxton *York 4*　**P** Abp
　V C WILTON　**C** M J OTTER　**NSM** D T HAYES
SHERE (St James), Albury and Chilworth *Guildf 2*　**P** Bp, Mrs
　H Bray, Duke of Northumberland, W F P Hugonin Esq, and the
　Hon M W Ridley (jt)　**R** N J WHITEHEAD　**C** A M PEARSON,
　S M SOKOLOWSKI　**NSM** J A POTTER, S F HUTTON
　OLM D I OAKDEN
SHEREFORD (St Nicholas)　*see* Upper Wensum Village Gp *Nor*
SHERFIELD ENGLISH (St Leonard)　*see* E w W Wellow and
　Sherfield English *Win*
SHERFIELD-ON-LODDON (St Leonard) and Stratfield Saye w
　Hartley Wespall w Stratfield Turgis and Bramley *Win 5*
　P Bp, Duke of Wellington, D&C Windsor, and Qu Coll Ox (jt)
　NSM J R LENTON
SHERFORD (St Martin)　*see* Stokenham, Slapton, Charleton w
　Buckland etc *Ex*
SHERIFF HUTTON (St Helen and the Holy Cross)　*see* Forest of
　Galtres *York*
SHERIFFHALES (St Mary)　*see* Shifnal and Sheriffhales *Lich*
SHERINGHAM (St Peter) *Nor 21*　**P** *Bp*　**V** C J HEYCOCKS
SHERINGHAM, UPPER (All Saints)　*see* Weybourne Gp *Nor*
SHERINGTON (St Laud) w Chicheley, North Crawley,
　Astwood and Hardmead *Ox 16*　**P** Bp (2 turns), MMCET
　(1 turn), and Major J G B Chester (1 turn)　**OLM** P F FIELDING
SHERMANBURY (St Giles)　*see* Henfield w Shermanbury and
　Woodmancote *Chich*
SHERRARDS GREEN (St Mary the Virgin)
SHERRINGTON (St Cosmo and St Damian)　*see* Upper Wylye
　Valley *Sarum*
SHERSTON MAGNA (Holy Cross), Easton Grey, Luckington,
　Alderton and Foxley w Bremilham *Bris 6*　**P** D&C, Bp, Adn
　Malmesbury and Lord Lilford (jt)　**P-in-c** C P BRYAN　**Hon**
　C M M MASLEN　**OLM** S E HARVEY
SHERWOOD (St Martin) *S'well 8*　**P** *Bp*　**V** S J GRIFFITHS
　NSM J E WALKER
SHEVINGTON (St Anne) *Blackb 4*　**P** R Standish
　V P I DENNISON　**C** D I GERRARD
SHEVIOCK (Blessed Virgin Mary)　*see* Antony w Sheviock and
　Torpoint *Truro*
SHIFFORD (St Mary)　*see* Bampton w Clanfield *Ox*
SHIFNAL (St Andrew) and Sheriffhales *Lich 16*　**P** Bp and
　R I Legge Esq (jt)　**V** C D C THORPE　**C** C CHESHIRE
　OLM S A DAY
SHILBOTTLE (St James) *Newc 6*　**P** Dioc Soc
　P-in-c M J GILLHAM　**OLM** P E RENNISON
SHILBOTTLE (St James)　*see* Shilbottle *Newc*
SHILDON (St John) *Dur 6*　**P** *Bp*　**P-in-c** D R TOMLINSON
SHILL VALLEY and Broadshire *Ox 28*　**P** J Heyworth Esq,
　Mrs P Allen, and Ch Ch Ox (1 turn), Ch Soc Tr, F R Goodenough
　Esq, and D F Goodenough Esq (1 turn)　**R** H C MACINNES
　C D R SPENCE　**NSM** A E MCGRATH, K H ROSS, K H YOUNG

SHILLINGFORD (St George)   *see* Alphington, Shillingford
St George and Ide *Ex*
SHILLINGSTONE (Holy Rood)   *see* Okeford *Sarum*
SHILLINGTON (All Saints)   *see* Gravenhurst, Shillington and
Stondon *St Alb*
SHILTON (Holy Rood)   *see* Shill Valley and Broadshire *Ox*
SHILTON (St Andrew)   *see* Ansty and Shilton *Cov*
SHIMPLINGTHORNE (St George)   *see* Chadbrook *St E*
SHINCLIFFE (St Mary the Virgin)   *see* Dur St Oswald and
Shincliffe *Dur*
SHINEY ROW (St Oswald)   *see* Herrington, Penshaw and
Shiney Row *Dur*
SHINFIELD (St Mary)   *see* Loddon Reach *Ox*
SHINGAY Group of Parishes, The *Ely 7*   **P** *Bp, Mrs E E Sclater,*
Ch Patr Trust, Down Coll Cam, New Coll Ox, and Jes Coll Cam (jt)
R S F C WILLIAMS
SHIPBOURNE (St Giles) w Plaxtol *Roch 10*   **P** *Bp and Sir*
Edward Cazalet   **R** A D PROCTER
SHIPDHAM (All Saints)   *see* Dereham and Distr *Nor*
SHIPHAM (St Leonard)   *see* Axbridge w Shipham and
Rowberrow *B & W*
SHIPHAY COLLATON (St John the Baptist) *Ex 11*   **P** *Bp*
V C E DEACON
SHIPLAKE (St Peter and St Paul) w Dunsden and Harpsden
Ox 24   **P** *All So Coll Ox, D&C Windsor, and DBP (jt)*
R P E BRADISH
SHIPLEY (St Mary the Virgin) *Chich 7*   **P** *C R Burrell Esq*
P-in-c P A SINTON
SHIPLEY (St Paul) *Leeds 1*   **P** *Simeon's Trustees*   **V** S HOPE
NSM H LEALMAN
SHIPLEY (St Peter) *Leeds 1*   **P** *V Shipley St Paul*   **V** J C RAINER
C J BACON   **NSM** M S BERNARD
SHIPPON (St Mary Magdalene)   *see* Marcham w Garford and
Shippon *Ox*
SHIPSTON-ON-STOUR (St Edmund) w Honington and
Idlicote *Cov 9*   **P** *Jes Coll Ox, D&C Worc, Bp (jt)*
R A M COLEBY   **C** S BOURNE   **NSM** J TUCKER
SHIPTON (Holy Evangelist)   *see* Skelton w Shipton and Newton
on Ouse *York*
SHIPTON (St James)   *see* Wenlock *Heref*
SHIPTON BELLINGER (St Peter)   *see* Appleshaw, Kimpton,
Thruxton, Fyfield etc *Win*
SHIPTON GORGE (St Martin)   *see* Bride Valley *Sarum*
SHIPTON MOYNE (St John the Baptist)   *see* Tetbury, Beverston,
Long Newnton etc *Glouc*
SHIPTON OLIFFE (St Oswald)   *see* Sevenhampton w Charlton
Abbots, Hawling etc *Glouc*
SHIPTON ON CHERWELL (Holy Cross)   *see* Blenheim *Ox*
SHIPTONTHORPE (All Saints)   *see* Londesborough Wold *York*
SHIPTON-UNDER-WYCHWOOD (St Mary)   *see* Wychwood *Ox*
SHIREBROOK (Holy Trinity)   *see* E Scarsdale *Derby*
SHIREGREEN (St James and St Christopher) *Sheff 3*
P *Bp and Dean (alt)*   **P-in-c** D F DEAN-REVILL
NSM D J KERSHAW
SHIREHAMPTON (St Mary) *Bris 2*   **P** *Bp*   **NSM** I A BAILEY
SHIREMOOR (St Mark) *Newc 5*   **P** *Bp*   **V** A G CURTIS
SHIREOAKS (St Luke)   *see* Worksop Ch Ch and Shireoaks
S'well
SHIRES' EDGE *Ox 23*   **P** *Bp*   **V** H A CAMPBELL
OLM L M ALCOCK
SHIRLAND (St Leonard)   *see* Morton and Stonebroom w
Shirland *Derby*
SHIRLEY (St George) *S'wark 19*   **P** *Bp*   **P-in-c** B HENGIST
Hon C H A FIFE   **NSM** A M S DOVEY
SHIRLEY (St James the Great)   *see* Salter Street and Shirley *Birm*
SHIRLEY (St James) (St John) *Win 13*   **P** *Ch Patr Trust*
P-in-c D A CLARK   **C** A V POWIS   **NSM** L PHILLIPS
SHIRLEY (St John the Divine)   *see* Salter Street and Shirley *Birm*
SHIRLEY (St John) *S'wark 19*   **P** *Bp*   **V** S J KNOWERS
NSM A M S DOVEY
SHIRLEY (St Michael)   *see* Brailsford w Shirley, Osmaston w
Edlaston etc *Derby*
SHIRWELL (St Peter), Loxhore, Kentisbury, Arlington, East
Down, Bratton Fleming, Challacombe and Stoke Rivers
Ex 17   **P** *Patr Bd*   **TR** R E AUSTIN
SHOBDON (St John the Evangelist)   *see* Pembridge w Moor
Court, Shobdon, Staunton etc *Heref*
SHOBROOKE (St Swithin)   *see* Crediton, Shobrooke and
Sandford etc *Ex*
SHOCKLACH (St Edith)   *see* Tilston and Shocklach *Ches*
SHOEBURY, NORTH (St Mary the Virgin) *Chelmsf 15*   **P** *Ld*
Chan   **V** *vacant*
SHOEBURY, SOUTH (St Andrew) (St Peter) *Chelmsf 15*
P *Hyndman Trustees*   **R** L M WILLIAMS
SHOLDEN (St Nicholas)   *see* Deal St Leon w St Rich and
Sholden etc *Cant*

SHOLING (St Francis of Assisi) (St Mary) *Win 13*   **P** *Bp*
V G K BAKKER   **C** J A OLIVER   **NSM** J J BAKKER
SHOOTERS HILL (All Saints)   *see* Plumstead All SS *S'wark*
SHOOTERS HILL (Christ Church) *S'wark 6*   **P** *Bp*
V A R M VAN DEN HOF
SHORE (St Barnabas)   *see* Littleborough *Man*
SHOREDITCH (All Saints) Haggerston Road   *see* Dalston H Trin
w St Phil and Haggerston All SS *Lon*
SHOREDITCH (St Anne) Hoxton Street   *see* Hoxton St Anne w
St Columba *Lon*
SHOREDITCH (St Leonard) w St Michael *Lon 5*   **P** *Bp and*
Adn (jt)   **V** P R TURP
SHOREHAM (St Peter and St Paul) *Roch 10*   **P** *D&C Westmr*
V D E REES
SHOREHAM BEACH (The Good Shepherd)   *see* New Shoreham
and Shoreham Beach *Chich*
SHOREHAM, NEW (St Mary de Haura) and Shoreham Beach
Chich 20   **P** *Bp*   **V** A E WAIZENEKER   **C** H A ROSE
Hon C T S STRATFORD   **NSM** J-J S AIDLEY
SHOREHAM, OLD (St Nicolas) and Kingston Buci *Chich 20*
P *Bp and Lord Egremont (jt)*   **NSM** B A WILSON
SHORELINE Benefice, The *St E 5*   **P** *Ld Chan (1 turn), Bp*
(3 turns)   **R** L OOSTERHOF
SHORNE (St Peter and St Paul) *Roch 4*   **P** *D&C*
V G J ACKERLEY
SHORT HEATH (Holy Trinity)   *see* Bentley Em and Willenhall
H Trin *Lich*
SHORT HEATH (St Margaret)   *see* Erdington Ch the K *Birm*
SHORTHAMPTON (All Saints)   *see* Charlbury w Shorthampton
Ox
SHORTLANDS (St Mary) *Roch 13*   **P** *Bp*   **V** M A H FINCH
NSM J E PETERS, R W FINCH
SHORWELL (St Peter) w Kingston *Portsm 8*   **P** *Bp*
P-in-c H L O'SULLIVAN
SHOTESHAM (All Saints w St Mary)   *see* Newton Flotman,
Swainsthorpe, Tasburgh, etc *Nor*
SHOTLEY (St John) *Newc 9*   **P** *Lord Crewe's Trustees*
NSM D J WOOD
SHOTLEY (St Mary)   *see* Shoreline *St E*
SHOTTERMILL (St Stephen) *Guildf 4*   **P** *Adn Surrey*
V D R P WIGNALL   **C** C F SHEPHERD
SHOTTERY (St Andrew) *Cov 8*   **P** *Bp*   **V** J R WARREN
C K DYER   **NSM** P EDMONDSON
SHOTTESBROOKE (St John the Baptist)   *see* White Waltham w
Shottesbrooke *Ox*
SHOTTESWELL (St Lawrence)   *see* Edgehill Churches *Cov*
SHOTTISHAM (St Margaret)   *see* Wilford Peninsula *St E*
SHOTTLE (St Lawrence)   *see* Hazelwood, Holbrook and Milford
Derby
SHOTTON (St Saviour)   *see* Haswell, Shotton and Thornley *Dur*
SHOTWICK (St Michael)   *see* Burton and Shotwick *Ches*
SHOULDHAM (All Saints) *Ely 9*   **P** *Bp*   **P-in-c** B L BURTON
SHOULDHAM THORPE (St Mary) *Ely 9*   **P** *Bp*
P-in-c B L BURTON
SHRAWARDINE (St Mary)   *see* Bicton, Montford w Shrawardine
and Fitz *Lich*
SHRAWLEY (St Mary), Witley, Astley and Abberley *Worc 13*
P *Bp and Guild of All So (jt)*   **P-in-c** E G WHITTAKER
C M TURNER
SHRED (Mission Church)   *see* Slaithwaite w E Scammonden
Leeds
SHREWSBURY (All Saints and St Michael) *Lich 20*   **P** *Bp*
P-in-c M FISH
SHREWSBURY (Christ Church)   *see* Shelton and Oxon *Lich*
SHREWSBURY (Holy Cross) (St Peter) *Lich 20*   **P** *Bp*
V P G FIRMIN
SHREWSBURY (Holy Trinity) (St Julian) *Lich 20*   **P** *Bp and*
Ch Patr Trust (jt)   **V** *vacant*
SHREWSBURY (St Chad) St Mary (St Alkmund) *Lich 20*   **P** *Bp*
V M W A CHADWICK   **NSM** A C RYLANDS
SHREWSBURY (St George of Cappadocia) w Greenfields
United Church *Lich 20*   **P** *V Shrewsbury St Chad*
V M MCBRIDE   **C** L DAVIDSON
SHREWSBURY (St Giles) w Sutton and Atcham *Lich 20*   **P** *Bp*
and R L Burton Esq (jt)   **R** A R KNIGHT
SHRIVENHAM (St Andrew) and Ashbury *Ox 25*   **P** *Ld Chan*
V R M A HANCOCK   **NSM** N FERGUSSON
SHROPHAM (St Peter)   *see* Gt and Lt Ellingham, Rockland and
Shropham etc *Nor*
SHRUB END (All Saints) (St Cedd) *Chelmsf 21*   **P** *Bp*
V N A W DAVIS
SHUCKBURGH, LOWER (St John the Baptist)   *see* Napton-on-
the-Hill, Lower Shuckburgh etc *Cov*
SHURDINGTON (St Paul)   *see* Badgeworth, Shurdington and
Witcombe w Bentham *Glouc*

SHUSTOKE (St Cuthbert)　*see* The Whitacres, Lea Marston, and Shustoke *Birm*
SHUTE (St Michael)　*see* Kilmington, Stockland, Dalwood, Yarcombe etc *Ex*
SHUTFORD (St Martin)　*see* Wykeham *Ox*
SHUTTINGTON (St Matthew)　*see* N Warks *Birm*
SHUTTLEWORTH (St John)　*see* Ramsbottom and Edenfield *Man*
SIBBERTOFT (St Helen)　*see* Welford w Sibbertoft and Marston Trussell *Pet*
SIBERTSWOLD (St Andrew)　*see* Bewsborough *Cant*
SIBFORD (Holy Trinity)　*see* Wykeham *Ox*
SIBLE HEDINGHAM (St Peter) w Castle Hedingham *Chelmsf 19*　**P** *Bp, and Hon T R Lindsay (alt)*　**NSM** E G PAXTON
SIBSEY (St Margaret) w Frithville *Linc 21*　**P** *Ld Chan*　**V** R E TAYLOR　**OLM** M L HOULDERSHAW
SIBSON (St Botolph)　*see* Bosworth and Sheepy Gp *Leic*
SIBTHORPE (St Peter) *S'well 3*　**P** *Bp*　**P-in-c** E I MURRAY
SIBTON (St Peter)　*see* Yoxmere *St E*
SICKLINGHALL (St Peter)　*see* Lower Wharfedale *Leeds*
SIDBURY (St Giles and St Peter)　*see* Sidmouth, Woolbrook, Salcombe Regis, Sidbury etc *Ex*
SIDCUP (Christ Church) Longland *Roch 17*　**P** *Ch Trust Fund Trust*　**V** T J PARSONS
SIDCUP (St Andrew) *Roch 17*　**P** *Bp*　**V** R C A HANKEY
SIDCUP (St John the Evangelist) *Roch 17*　**P** *D&C*　**V** S SEALY　**NSM** S A NIECHCIAL
SIDDAL (St Mark) *Leeds 11*　**P** *Ch Trust Fund Trust*　**P-in-c** H J BARBER
SIDDINGTON (All Saints)　*see* Marton, Siddington w Capesthorne, and Eaton etc *Ches*
SIDDINGTON (St Peter)　*see* S Cerney w Cerney Wick, Siddington and Preston *Glouc*
SIDESTRAND (St Michael)　*see* Poppyland *Nor*
SIDFORD (St Peter)　*see* Sidmouth, Woolbrook, Salcombe Regis, Sidbury etc *Ex*
SIDLESHAM (St Mary Our Lady) *Chich 2*　**P** *Bp*　**P-in-c** S GUISE
SIDLEY (All Saints) *Chich 12*　**P** *R Bexhill*　**P-in-c** M J BAILEY　**NSM** M P TURNBULL
SIDLOW BRIDGE (Emmanuel) *S'wark 26*　**P** *DBP*　**R** *vacant*
SIDMOUTH (St Nicholas w St Giles), Woolbrook, Salcombe Regis, Sidbury w Sidford, and All Saints Sidmouth *Ex 6*　**P** *Patr Bd*　**TR** P J BOURNE　**TV** R D TRUMPER, S M M WILLIAMS　**C** M H BARRETT
SIGGLESTHORNE (St Lawrence) w Nunkeeling and Bewholme *York 11*　**P** *Prime Min*　**R** *vacant*
SILCHESTER (St Mary)　*see* Tadley w Pamber Heath and Silchester *Win*
SILCHESTER COMMON (Mission Church)　*as above*
SILEBY (St Mary), Cossington and Seagrave *Leic 5*　**P** *Patr Bd*　**R** R C J HOPKINS　**C** T G HUTCHINGS
SILK WILLOUGHBY (St Denis) *Linc 14*　**P** *Sir Lyonel Tollemache Bt*　**R** *vacant*
SILKSTONE (All Saints)　*see* Hoylandswaine and Silkstone w Stainborough *Leeds*
SILKSTONE COMMON (Mission Room)　*as above*
SILKSWORTH (St Matthew) *Dur 1*　**P** *Bp*　**V** D TOLHURST
SILLOTH (Christ Church)　*see* Solway Plain *Carl*
SILSDEN (St James) *Leeds 5*　**P** *Bp, Adn Craven, and Trustees (jt)*　**V** D J GRIFFITHS　**C** S A GRIFFITHS　**NSM** P SMITH
SILSOE (St James), Pulloxhill and Flitton *St Alb 8*　**P** *Ball Coll Ox and Bp (alt)*　**V** D B BELL
SILTON (St Nicholas) *Sarum 5*　**P** *DBP*　**R** *vacant*
SILTON, NETHER (All Saints)　*see* Leake w Over and Nether Silton and Kepwick *York*
SILTON, OVER (St Mary)　*as above*
SILVER END (St Francis)　*see* Witham and Villages *Chelmsf*
SILVERDALE (St John) *Blackb 14*　**P** *V Warton*　**P-in-c** P K WARREN
SILVERDALE (St Luke) *Lich 9*　**P** *T H G Howard-Sneyd Esq*　**V** P C JONES
SILVERHILL (St Matthew) *Chich 15*　**P** *Simeon's Trustees*　**R** M S COE　**C** M D WILLIAMS
SILVERSTONE (St Michael) and Abthorpe w Slapton and Whittlebury and Paulerspury *Pet 5*　**P** *T L Langton-Lockton Esq, Leeson's Trustees, and New Coll Ox (3 turns), Prime Min (2 turns)*　**R** P D MCLEOD　**NSM** G C BUCKLE
SILVERTON (St Mary), Butterleigh, Bickleigh and Cadeleigh *Ex 7*　**P** *Bp and Sir Rivers Carew Bt*　**R** A H MACDONALD　**NSM** C JENKINS, R L MAUDSLEY, T M THOMPSON
SILVINGTON (St Michael)　*see* Stottesdon w Farlow, Cleeton St Mary etc *Heref*
SIMONBURN (St Mungo)　*see* Humshaugh w Simonburn and Wark *Newc*

SIMONSTONE (St Peter)　*see* Read and Simonstone *Blackb*
SIMPSON (St Thomas)　*see* Woughton *Ox*
SINFIN (St Stephen) *Derby 10*　**P** *CPAS*　**P-in-c** N H ELLIOTT
SINFIN MOOR (not known) *Derby 10*　**P** *Bp*　**V** *vacant*
SINGLETON (Blessed Virgin Mary)　*see* E Dean, Singleton, and W Dean *Chich*
SINGLETON (St Anne)　*see* Poulton Carleton and Singleton *Blackb*
SINNINGTON (All Saints)　*see* Middleton, Newton and Sinnington *York*
SISLAND (St Mary)　*see* Loddon, Sisland, Chedgrave, Hardley and Langley *Nor*
SISSINGHURST (Holy Trinity) w Frittenden *Cant 11*　**P** *CPAS*　**R** D F OLNEY
SITHNEY (St Sithney)　*see* W Kerrier *Truro*
SITTINGBOURNE (Holy Trinity) (St Mary) (St Michael) w Bobbing *Cant 15*　**P** *Patr Bd*　**TR** M J RESCH　**TV** J L PETTIT　**C** A H L PETTIT　**NSM** E B RESCH　**OLM** S M SAMSON
SIX HILLS (Mission)　*see* Old Dalby, Nether Broughton, Saxelbye etc *Leic*
SIX MILE BOTTOM (St George)　*see* Lt Wilbraham *Ely*
SIX PILGRIMS, The *B & W 2*　**P** *Ch Soc Trust, D&C, DBF, and Bp (by turn)*　**R** *vacant*
SIX SAINTS circa Holt: Bringhurst, Great Easton, Medbourne cum Holt, Stockerston and Blaston *Leic 3*　**P** *D&C Pet and Adn Leic (2 turns), St Jo Coll Cam (1 turn)*　**R** S J BISHOP
SIX, The *Cant 15*　**P** *Abp, D&C, and Adn Maidstone (jt)*　**V** J M STANIFORTH　**C** M P HAM, S P PLUMB　**NSM** S P PLUMB
SIXHILLS (All Saints)　*see* Barkwith Gp *Linc*
SIXPENNY HANDLEY (St Mary) w Gussage St Andrew and Pentridge *Sarum 6*　**P** *D&C Windsor and DBP (alt)*　**P-in-c** M R B DURRANT　**C** M J FOSTER　**NSM** P A SKINNER　**OLM** P H SKINNER
SKEEBY (St Agatha's District Church)　*see* Easby w Skeeby and Brompton on Swale etc *Leeds*
SKEFFINGTON (St Thomas à Beckett)　*see* Coplow *Leic*
SKEFFLING (St Helen)　*see* Easington w Skeffling, Keyingham, Ottringham etc *York*
SKEGBY (St Andrew) w Teversal *S'well 4*　**P** *DBP and Ld Chan (alt)*　**R** R KELLETT　**C** C M BYROM　**NSM** A DEMPSTER
SKEGNESS Group, The (St Clement) (St Matthew) *Linc 10*　**P** *Bp and DBP (2 turns), and Ld Chan (1 turn)*　**OLM** C ANDERSON
SKELBROOKE (St Michael and All Angels)　*see* Adwick-le-Street w Skelbrooke *Sheff*
SKELLINGTHORPE (St Lawrence) w Doddington *Linc 12*　**P** *MMCET*　**R** R G BILLINGHURST　**OLM** F CLARKE
SKELLOW (St Michael and All Angels)　*see* Owston *Sheff*
SKELMANTHORPE (St Aidan) *Leeds 13*　**P-in-c** P D REYNOLDS
SKELMERSDALE (St Paul) *Liv 11*　**P** *V Ormskirk*　**P-in-c** C B SPITTLE　**C** T MCLOUGHLIN　**OLM** C JACKSON
SKELMERSGH (St John the Baptist)　*see* Beacon *Carl*
SKELTON (All Saints) w Upleatham *York 16*　**P** *Abp*　**R** V E M-B HAYNES
SKELTON (St Giles) w Shipton and Newton on Ouse *York 3*　**P** *Abp*　**P-in-c** M H WAINWRIGHT　**NSM** A T LINDLEY
SKELTON (St Michael)　*see* Inglewood Gp *Carl*
SKELTON-CUM-NEWBY (St Helen's Old Church)　*see* Kirby-on-the-Moor, Cundall w Norton-le-Clay etc *Leeds*
SKENDLEBY (St Peter and St Paul)　*see* Bolingbroke Deanery *Linc*
SKERNE (St Leonard)　*see* Hutton Cranswick w Skerne, Watton and Beswick *York*
SKERNE, UPPER *Dur 5*　**P** *Ld Chan (1 turn), Patr Bd (2 turns)*　**TR** M G T GOBBETT　**TV** M THOMPSON
SKERTON (St Chad) *Blackb 11*　**P** *Bp*　**V** N J HEALE
SKERTON (St Luke) *Blackb 11*　**P** *Trustees*　**V** T STOTT
SKEYTON (All Saints)　*see* King's Beck *Nor*
SKIDBY (St Michael)　*see* Rowley w Skidby *York*
SKILGATE (St John the Baptist)　*see* Dulverton w Brushford, Brompton Regis etc *B & W*
SKILLINGTON (St James)　*see* Colsterworth Gp *Linc*
SKIPSEA (All Saints) and Barmston w Fraisthorpe *York 9*　**P** *Abp and The Hon S E Cunliffe-Lister (jt)*　**V** *vacant*
SKIPTON (Christ Church) w Carleton St Mary *Leeds 26*　**P** *Ch Ch Ox and R Skipton H Trin (jt)*　**NSM** V A LOWE
SKIPTON (Holy Trinity) *Leeds 26*　**P** *Ch Ch Ox*　**R** V N JAMES　**C** H J HOULTON
SKIPTON ON SWALE (St John)　*see* Topcliffe, Baldersby w Dishforth, Dalton etc *York*
SKIPWITH (St Helen)　*see* Bubwith w Skipwith *York*
SKIRBECK (Holy Trinity) *Linc 21*　**P** *Trustees*　**C** P J SLATER
SKIRBECK (St Nicholas) *Linc 21*　**P** *DBP*　**R** P V NOBLE

SKIRBECK QUARTER (St Thomas)   *see* Boston *Linc*

SKIRLAUGH (St Augustine), Catwick, Long Riston, Rise, Swine w Ellerby *York 11* **P** *Abp, Abp and Baroness de Stempel, and Ld Chan (by turn)* **V** A C SIMPSON **NSM** M M DESBOROUGH

SKIRPENBECK (St Mary) *see* Garrowby Hill *York*

SKIRWITH (St John the Evangelist) *see* Cross Fell Gp *Carl*

SLAD (Holy Trinity) *see* Stroud Team *Glouc*

SLADE GREEN (St Augustine) *Roch 15* **P** *Bp* **V** A J TARPER

SLAIDBURN (St Andrew) w Tosside *Leeds 21* **P** *Bp and Ch Soc Trust (jt)* **R** G DARBY

SLAITHWAITE (St James) w East Scammonden *Leeds 12* **P** *V Huddersfield* **V** C R TOWNSEND

SLALEY (St Mary the Virgin), Healey and Whittonstall *Newc 9* **P** *Bp, V Bywell St Pet, and D&C (jt)* **V** H SAVAGE

SLAPTON (Holy Cross) *see* Ivinghoe w Pitstone and Slapton and Marsworth *Ox*

SLAPTON (St Botolph) *see* Silverstone and Abthorpe w Slapton etc *Pet*

SLAPTON (St James the Great) *see* Stokenham, Slapton, Charleton w Buckland etc *Ex*

SLAUGHAM (St Mary) and Staplefield Common *Chich 5* **P** *Mrs D M Irwin-Clark* **R** G D SIMMONS **Hon C** K W HABERSHON **NSM** C D SUTTON

SLAUGHTER, LOWER (St Mary) *see* The Guitings, Cutsdean, Farmcote etc *Glouc*

SLAUGHTER, UPPER (St Peter) *as above*

SLAUGHTERFORD (St Nicholas) *see* By Brook *Bris*

SLAWSTON (All Saints) *see* Hallaton and Allexton, w Horninghold, Tugby etc *Leic*

SLEAFORD (St Denys) *Linc 14* **P** *Bp* **V** P A JOHNSON **C** R ANGELICI

SLEEKBURN (St John) *see* Cambois and Sleekburn *Newc*

SLEIGHTS (St John) *see* Lower Esk *York*

SLIMBRIDGE (St John the Evangelist) *see* Sharpness, Purton, Brookend and Slimbridge *Glouc*

SLINDON (St Chad) *see* Eccleshall *Lich*

SLINDON (St Mary), Eartham and Madehurst *Chich 1* **P** *Bp, D&C, and Mrs J Izard (jt)* **R** vacant

SLINFOLD (St Peter) *see* Itchingfield w Slinfold *Chich*

SLINGSBY (All Saints) *see* The Street Par *York*

SLIPTON (St John the Baptist) *Pet 9* **P** *L G Stopford Sackville Esq* **P-in-c** D H P FOOT

SLITTING MILL (St John the Baptist) *see* Brereton and Rugeley *Lich*

SLOANE STREET (Holy Trinity) *see* Upper Chelsea H Trin and St Sav *Lon*

SLOLEY (St Bartholomew) *see* Worstead, Westwick, Sloley, Swanton Abbot etc *Nor*

SLOUGH (St Paul) (Christ Church) *Ox 12* **P** *Trustees* **V** M C COTTERELL

SLYNE W HEST (St Luke) and Halton St Wilfrid w Aughton St Saviour *Blackb 14* **P** *Bp and Exors R T Sanderson (jt)* **R** P A BICKNELL **NSM** H L LEATHARD

SMALL HEATH (All Saints) *Birm 13* **P** *Patr Bd* **V** O J COSS **C** A J R MURLEY

SMALLBURGH (St Peter) w Dilham w Honing and Crostwight *Nor 12* **P** *Bp, T R Cubitt Esq, and J C Wickman Esq (jt)* **R** vacant

SMALLEY (St John the Baptist) *see* Morley and Smalley *Derby*

SMALLFIELD (Church Room) *see* The Windmill *S'wark*

SMALLHYTHE (St John the Baptist) *see* Tenterden and Smallhythe *Cant*

SMALLTHORNE (St Saviour) *Lich 11* **P** *R Norton in the Moors* **C** A C SWIFT

SMALLWOOD (St John the Baptist) *see* Astbury and Smallwood *Ches*

SMARDEN (St Michael) *see* Biddenden and Smarden *Cant*

SMEATON, GREAT (St Eloy) *see* E Richmond *Leeds*

SMEETH (St Mary) *see* A20 Benefice *Cant*

SMEETON WESTERBY (Christ Church) *see* Kibworth and Smeeton Westerby and Saddington *Leic*

SMESTOW VALE TEAM *Lich 24* **P** *Patr Bd* **TR** A P BROWN **TV** C A HOST, J M HARTWELL **OLM** R A M COOK

SMETHCOTT (St Michael) *see* Dorrington w Leebotwood, Longnor, Stapleton etc *Heref*

SMETHWICK (Old Church) *Birm 7* **P** *Dorothy Parkes Trustees* **V** D BUCKLEY

SMETHWICK (Resurrection) (St Stephen and St Michael) *Birm 7* **P** *Bp* **V** D R GOULD **NSM** N M ROSS

SMETHWICK (St Matthew w St Chad) *Birm 7* **P** *Bp and V Smethwick (alt)* **P-in-c** L M ARLIDGE

SMISBY (St James) *see* Melbourne, Ticknall, Smisby and Stanton *Derby*

SMITHILLS HALL (Chapel) *see* Halliwell St Pet *Man*

SMORRALL LANE (St Andrew) *see* Bedworth *Cov*

SNAILWELL (St Peter) *see* Three Rivers Gp *Ely*

SNAINTON (St Stephen) *see* Upper Derwent *York*

SNAITH (St Laurence Priory) *see* Gt Snaith *Sheff*

SNAITH, GREAT (Holy Trinity) (St John the Baptist) (St Paul) *Sheff 10* **P** *Bp* **TR** E E M ROBERTSHAW **NSM** P W HIBBS

SNAPE (St John the Baptist) *see* Alde River *St E*

SNAPE CASTLE (Chapel of St Mary) *see* W Tanfield and Well w Snape and N Stainley *Leeds*

SNARESTONE (St Bartholomew) *see* Woodfield *Leic*

SNARGATE (St Dunstan) *see* Brookland, Fairfield, Brenzett w Snargate etc *Cant*

SNEAD (St Mary the Virgin) *see* Wentnor w Ratlinghope, Myndtown, Norbury etc *Heref*

SNEATON (St Hilda) *see* Lower Esk *York*

SNEINTON (St Christopher) w St Philip *S'well 9* **P** *CPAS and Trustees (alt)* **P-in-c** N J HILL

SNEINTON (St Cyprian) *S'well 9* **P** *Bp* **P-in-c** A L WAUDE

SNEINTON (St Stephen) w St Matthias *S'well 9* **P** *Bp and SMF (jt)* **P-in-c** C S RUSHFORTH

SNELLAND (All Saints) *see* Wragby Gp *Linc*

SNELSTON (St Peter) *see* Norbury w Snelston *Derby*

SNEYD (Holy Trinity) *Lich 11* **P** *Bp* **V** B L WILLIAMS

SNEYD GREEN (St Andrew) *Lich 11* **P** *Bp* **V** G R DAVIES

SNIBSTON (St Mary) *see* Hugglescote w Donington, Ellistown and Snibston *Leic*

SNITTERBY (St Nicholas) *see* Bishop Norton, Waddingham and Snitterby *Linc*

SNITTERFIELD (St James the Great) *see* Arden Valley *Cov*

SNODLAND (All Saints) (Christ Church) *Roch 1* **P** *Bp and CPAS (jt)* **R** H P C BROADBENT **C** M E YOUNG **NSM** S M BROOKS

SNORING, GREAT (St Mary) *see* Barney, Hindringham, Thursford, Great Snoring, Little Snoring and Kettlestone and Pensthorpe *Nor*

SNORING, LITTLE (St Andrew) *as above*

SNOWSHILL (St Barnabas) *see* Winchcombe *Glouc*

SOAR, UPPER *Leic 7* **P** *Prime Min (1 turn), Mrs A M Finn, Adn Loughb, and Ball Coll Ox (1 turn)* **R** C M BRENNAND

SOBERTON (St Peter) w Newtown *Portsm 1* **P** *Bp* **P-in-c** S K BEAVIS

SOCKBURN (All Saints) *see* Dinsdale w Sockburn *Dur*

SODBURY VALE Benefice, The *Glouc 5* **P** *D&C Worc, Duke of Beaufort, and CPAS (jt)* **NSM** P T FEWINGS, Y R BRAE

SODBURY, LITTLE (St Adeline) *see* Sodbury Vale *Glouc*

SODBURY, OLD (St John the Baptist) *as above*

SOHAM (St Andrew) and Wicken *Ely 4* **P** *Pemb Coll Cam (1 turn), Pemb Coll Cam and Ch Patr Trust (jt) (1 turn)* **V** vacant

SOHO (St Anne) (St Thomas) (St Peter) *Lon 3* **P** *R Westmr St Jas* **P-in-c** R S F BUCKLEY

SOLE BAY *St E 18* **P** *Patr Bd* **TR** S J PITCHER **TV** R HENDERSON

SOLIHULL (Catherine de Barnes) (St Alphege) (St Helen) (St Michael) *Birm 11* **P** *Patr Bd* **TR** J E B KENCHINGTON **TV** H T GREENHAM, S H MARSHALL **NSM** R J MURRAY

SOLLERS HOPE (St Michael) *see* Brampton *Heref*

SOLWAY PLAIN *Carl 7* **P** *Patr Bd* **TR** B ROTHWELL **NSM** M I STUDHOLME

SOMERBY (All Saints) *see* Burrough Hill Pars *Leic*

SOMERBY (St Margaret) *see* N Wolds Gp *Linc*

SOMERBY, OLD (St Mary Magdalene) *see* N Beltisloe Gp *Linc*

SOMERCOTES (St Thomas) *Derby 1* **P** *Bp* **V** vacant

SOMERCOTES and Grainthorpe w Conisholme *Linc 15* **P** *Duchy of Lanc (2 turns), Magd Coll Cam and Bp (1 turn)* **R** S A ALLISON

SOMERCOTES, NORTH (St Mary) *see* Somercotes and Grainthorpe w Conisholme *Linc*

SOMERFORD (All Saints) *see* Astbury and Smallwood *Ches*

SOMERFORD KEYNES (All Saints) *see* Kemble, Poole Keynes, Somerford Keynes etc *Glouc*

SOMERFORD, GREAT (St Peter and St Paul), Little Somerford, Seagry and Corston w Rodbourne *Bris 6* **P** *Bp, MMCET, and Ex Coll Ox (jt) (3 turns), Ld Chan (2 turns)* **P-in-c** S WILKINSON **C** J E MONAGHAN, N J ARCHER **Hon C** D ORMSTON **NSM** H A MONAGHAN

SOMERFORD, LITTLE (St John the Baptist) *see* Gt Somerford, Lt Somerford, Seagry, Corston etc *Bris*

SOMERLEYTON (St Mary), Ashby, Fritton, Herringfleet, Blundeston and Lound *Nor 9* **P** *Lord Somerleyton and SMF (jt)* **P-in-c** D BODDY

SOMERS TOWN (St Mary the Virgin) *see* Old St Pancras *Lon*

SOMERSAL HERBERT (St Peter) *see* S Dales *Derby*

SOMERSBY (St Margaret) *see* S Ormsby Gp *Linc*

SOMERSHAM (St John the Baptist) w Pidley and Oldhurst and Wooodhurst *Ely 12* **P** *Bp* **V** S F SIMPSON **Hon C** F J KILNER

SOMERSHAM (St Mary) w Flowton and Offton w Willisham
St E 1   **P** *Bp and MMCET (jt)*   **R** *vacant*
SOMERTON (St James)   *see Cherwell Valley Ox*
SOMERTON (St Margaret)   *see Glemsford, Hartest w Boxted,*
Somerton etc *St E*
SOMERTON (St Michael and All Angels) w Compton
Dundon, the Charltons and Kingsdon *B & W 5*   **P** *Bp Lon*
(1 turn), Bp (2 turns), and DBP (1 turn)   **P-in-c** A J SYMONDS
C C J HOPKINS
SOMERTON, WEST (St Mary)   *see Flegg Coastal Benefice Nor*
SOMPTING (St Mary the Virgin) (St Peter) *Chich 4*   **P** *OStJ*
V E K HOWARD
SONNING (St Andrew) (St Patrick) *Ox 8*   **P** *Bp*
V J A F TAYLOR   **C** A J WATERS
SONNING COMMON (Christ the King)   *see Rotherfield*
Peppard and Kidmore End etc *Ox*
SOOKHOLME (St Augustine)   *see Warsop S'well*
SOPLEY (St Michael and All Angels)   *see Burton and Sopley Win*
SOPWORTH (St Mary the Virgin)   *see Boxwell, Leighterton,*
Didmarton, Oldbury etc *Glouc*
SOTHERTON (St Andrew)   *see Sole Bay St E*
SOTWELL (St James)   *see Wallingford Ox*
SOUDLEY (St Michael)   *see Cinderford w Littledean Glouc*
SOULBURY (All Saints)   *see Cottesloe Ox*
SOULDERN (Annunciation of the Blessed Virgin Mary)
see Cherwell Valley Ox
SOULDROP (All Saints)   *see Sharnbrook, Felmersham and*
Knotting w Souldrop *St Alb*
SOUNDWELL (St Stephen) *Bris 5*   **P** *Bp*   **NSM** A J G COOPER,
E A PERRY   **OLM** J C CHARD, J M WILTSHIRE
SOURTON (St Thomas of Canterbury)   *see Okehampton,*
Inwardleigh, Belstone, Sourton etc *Ex*
SOUTH   *see also under substantive place name*
SOUTH BANK (St John) *York 17*   **P** *Abp*   **V** T M LEATHLEY
SOUTH CAVE (All Saints) and Ellerker w Broomfleet *York 13*
P *CPAS and D&C Dur (jt)*   **V** M J PROCTOR   **C** L A KENNY
NSM P R DRAPER
SOUTH COVE (St Lawrence)   *see Sole Bay St E*
SOUTH DALES, The *Derby 14*   **P** *Bp and Duke of Devonshire (jt)*
R J J VICKERSTAFF   **NSM** J M LEGH, P R JONES
SOUTH HILL (St Sampson) w Callington *Truro 11*   **P** *PCC*
P-in-c A W STEPHENS
SOUTH MOOR (St George)   *see Stanley and S Moor Dur*
SOUTH PARK (St Luke)   *see Reigate St Luke S'wark*
SOUTH POOL (St Nicholas and St Cyriac)   *see Stokenham,*
Slapton, Charleton w Buckland etc *Ex*
SOUTH SHIELDS (All Saints) (St Mary w St Martin) *Dur 15*
P *Patr Bd*   **TR** M P THOMPSON
SOUTH SHIELDS (St Hilda) w St Thomas *Dur 15*   **P** *D&C*
P-in-c C J FULLER
SOUTH SHIELDS (St Lawrence the Martyr)   *see Horsley Hill*
St Lawr *Dur*
SOUTH SHIELDS (St Simon) *Dur 15*   **P** *The Crown*
P-in-c E H CAMPBELL
SOUTH SHIELDS St Aidan (St Stephen) The Lawe *Dur 15*
P *Bp and D&C*   **P-in-c** P M BULLOCK
SOUTH SHORE (Holy Trinity) *Blackb 8*   **P** J C Hilton Esq
V T CHARNOCK   **NSM** A R BEVERLEY
SOUTH SHORE (St Peter) *Blackb 8*   **P** *Bp*   **V** T CHARNOCK
NSM A R BEVERLEY
SOUTH TRINITY BROADS Benefice, The: Filby, Thrigby,
Mautby, Stokesby, Runham and Burgh w Billockby *Nor 6*
P *Bp, Adn Nor, DBP, Mrs Z K Cognetti, R T Daniel Esq, and I*
F M Lucas Esq (jt)   **R** G R STEEL
SOUTH WARWICKSHIRE SEVEN Group, The *Cov 9*   **P** *Bp,*
Mert Coll Ox, Ch Ch Ox, and Trin Coll Ox (jt)   **R** S P ALLEN
Hon C G EVANS
SOUTHACRE (St George)   *see Nar Valley Nor*
SOUTHALL (Christ the Redeemer) *Lon 22*   **P** *Bp*
V N J ORCHARD   **NSM** W MASIH
SOUTHALL (Emmanuel) *Lon 22*   **P** *Bp and Ch Patr Trust (jt)*
V W E GILL
SOUTHALL (Holy Trinity) *Lon 22*   **P** *Ch Patr Trust*
V M F BOLLEY   **NSM** Y KHUSHI
SOUTHALL (St George) *Lon 22*   **P** *D&C St Paul's*
V C RAMSAY   **C** D JEWSON
SOUTHALL GREEN (St John) *Lon 22*   **P** *Ch Patr Trust*
V A L POULSON   **C** M A FINLAY   **Hon C** D J C BOOKLESS
SOUTHAM (Ascension)   *see Bishop's Cleeve and Woolstone w*
Gotherington etc *Glouc*
SOUTHAM (St James) *Cov 10*   **P** *The Crown*
P-in-c J E ARMSTRONG
SOUTHAMPTON (Christ Church) Portswood   *see Portswood*
Ch Ch *Win*
SOUTHAMPTON (St Alban the Martyr)   *see Swaythling Win*
SOUTHAMPTON (St Barnabas) *Win 13*   **P** *Bp*   **V** B J FRY

SOUTHAMPTON (St Denys) Portswood   *see Portswood*
St Denys *Win*
SOUTHAMPTON (St Jude)   *see Maybush and Southampton*
St Jude *Win*
SOUTHAMPTON (St Mark) *Win 13*   **P** *Ch Patr Trust*
V *vacant*
SOUTHAMPTON (St Mary Extra) *Win 13*   **P** *Bp*
P-in-c M J A NEWTON
SOUTHAMPTON City Centre (St Mary) (St Michael) *Win 13*
P *Bp*   **TR** J E DAVIES   **TV** D G DEBOYS   **C** P S HAUGHTON
NSM P R HAND
SOUTHAMPTON Lord's Hill and Lord's Wood *Win 13*   **P** *Bp*
V *vacant*
SOUTHAMPTON Thornhill (St Christopher) *Win 13*   **P** *Bp*
P-in-c D W JENNINGS   **C** N P HUTCHINSON
SOUTHBERGH (St Andrew)   *see Barnham Broom and Upper*
Yare *Nor*
SOUTHBOROUGH (St Peter) (Christ Church) (St Matthew)
and Bidborough *Roch 12*   **P** *Patr Bd*   **TR** G E HOVENDEN
TV C B WICKS, S A HILLS   **C** M S A BARKER, N T GRIFFITHS
SOUTHBOROUGH (St Thomas) *Roch 12*   **P** *Bp*   **V** *vacant*
SOUTHBOURNE (All Saints)   *see Pokesdown All SS Win*
SOUTHBOURNE (St Christopher) *Win 8*   **P** *Bp*
P-in-c A L MCPHERSON   **NSM** N S LEGRAND
SOUTHBOURNE (St John the Evangelist) w West Thorney
Chich 3   **P** *MMCET*   **NSM** S FLASHMAN
SOUTHBOURNE (St Katharine) (St Nicholas) *Win 8*
P *Bp*   **V** *vacant*
SOUTHBROOM (St James) *Sarum 17*   **P** *D&C*
NSM S A IBBETSON
SOUTHCHURCH (Christ Church) *Chelmsf 15*   **P** *Bp*
V S N ROSCOE
SOUTHCHURCH (Holy Trinity) *Chelmsf 15*   **P** *Abp Cant*
P-in-c T R LILLEY
SOUTHCOURT (Good Shepherd) *Ox 10*   **P** *Ch Patr Trust*
V *vacant*
SOUTHEA (Emmanuel)   *see Wisbech St Mary and Guyhirn w*
Ring's End etc *Ely*
SOUTHEASE (St Peter)   *see Iford w Kingston and Rodmell and*
Southease *Chich*
SOUTHEND (St John the Baptist) (St Mark) (All Saints)
(St Alban) *Chelmsf 15*   **P** *Patr Bd*   **TR** S M BURDETT
TV P A ROBERTS, W N PAXTON   **NSM** P E OWEN
OLM D J BOOTH
SOUTHEND (St Peter)   *see Bradfield and Stanford Dingley Ox*
SOUTHEND-ON-SEA (St Saviour) Westcliff *Chelmsf 15*
P *Bp, Adn Southend, and Churchwardens (jt)*   **V** L R MULLEN
OLM C L PALMER
SOUTHERY (St Mary) *Ely 9*   **P** *Guild of All So*   **R** *vacant*
SOUTHFIELDS (St Barnabas) *S'wark 18*   **P** *Bp*   **V** I S TATTUM
NSM J G BOYCE
SOUTHFIELDS (St Michael and All Angels)   *see Wandsworth*
St Mich w St Steph *S'wark*
SOUTHFLEET (St Nicholas) *Roch 4*   **P** *CPAS*
R D W J HOUSTON
SOUTHGATE (Christ Church) *Lon 18*   **P** *V Edmonton All SS*
V C LIMBERT   **NSM** H H MIALL
SOUTHGATE (St Andrew) *Lon 18*   **P** *Bp*   **V** E N TURNER
SOUTHGATE (St Mary) *Chich 6*   **P** *Patr Bd*   **TR** T J WILSON
TV H W SCHNAAR, R E POOLE, R J EDWARDS   **C** P J STEPHENS
NSM G D M RICHARDS, N B JONES
SOUTHGATE, NEW (St Paul) *Lon 14*   **P** *V Southgate Ch Ch*
V M J S MCAULAY
SOUTHILL (All Saints)   *see Clifton and Southill St Alb*
SOUTHLAKE (St James) *Ox 7*   **P** *DBP*   **V** N D JACKSON
SOUTHLEIGH (St Lawrence)   *see Colyton, Musbury,*
Southleigh and Branscombe *Ex*
SOUTHMEAD (St Stephen) *Bris 2*   **P** *Bp*   **P-in-c** T M LORD
SOUTHMINSTER (St Leonard) and Steeple *Chelmsf 11*
P *Govs Charterhouse and Lord Fitzwalter (jt)*
P-in-c P E C BEGLEY
SOUTHOE (St Leonard)   *see The Paxtons w Diddington and*
Southoe *Ely*
SOUTHOVER (St John the Baptist) *Chich 21*   **P** *CPAS*
R S J DAUGHTERY   **NSM** H L F GARRATT, J L BAMBER
SOUTHOWRAM (St Anne-in-the-Grove) and Claremont
Leeds 11   **P** *V Halifax*   **V** G S JAMIESON
NSM E S KILPATRICK
SOUTHPORT (All Saints) *Liv 9*   **P** *Trustees*   **V** *vacant*
SOUTHPORT (Christ Church) *Liv 9*   **P** *Trustees*   **V** S T REID
NSM R MILTON
SOUTHPORT (Emmanuel) *Liv 9*   **P** *PCC*   **P-in-c** I C COWELL
C N STOTHERS
SOUTHPORT (Holy Trinity) *Liv 9*   **P** *Trustees*   **V** R G GARNER
NSM J E MORGAN

SOUTHPORT (St Luke) *Liv 9*   **P** *V Southport H Trin*
P-in-c P HUTCHINS
SOUTHPORT (St Philip) (St Paul) *Liv 9*   **P** *V Southport Ch Ch and Trustees (jt)*   **C** R J GIBBS
SOUTHPORT (St Simon and St Jude) All Souls *Liv 9*
P *Trustees*   **P-in-c** D G WHITEHOUSE
SOUTHPORT, KEW (St Francis of Assisi)   *see Kew Liv*
SOUTHREPPS (St James)   *see Poppyland Nor*
SOUTHREY (St John the Divine)   *see Bardney Linc*
SOUTHROP (St Peter)   *see S Cotswolds Glouc*
SOUTHSEA (Holy Spirit) *Portsm 6*   **P** *Bp*   **P-in-c** P M AMEY
C P R ARMSTEAD
SOUTHSEA (St Jude) *Portsm 6*   **P** *Trustees*   **V** M I DUFF
SOUTHSEA (St Luke) (St Peter) *Portsm 6*   **P** *Bp and Ch Patr Trust (jt)*   **P-in-c** A-M MCCABE
SOUTHSEA (St Margaret of Scotland) *Portsm 6*   **P** *Bp*
V *vacant*
SOUTHSEA (St Simon) *Portsm 6*   **P** *Ch Patr Trust*   **V** *vacant*
SOUTHTOWN (St Mary)   *see Gt Yarmouth Nor*
SOUTHWARK (Christ Church) *S'wark 10*   **P** *Marshall's Charity*
R J COORE
SOUTHWARK (Holy Trinity w St Matthew) *S'wark 10*   **P** *Bp*
R N A MCKINNON
SOUTHWARK (St George the Martyr) (St Alphege) (St Jude)
S'wark 10   **P** *Lon Corp (1 turn), Ld Chan (4 turns), Walsingham Coll Trust Assn (1 turn)*   **P-in-c** J M W SEDGWICK   **Hon**
C F Y-C HUNG   **OLM** D PAPE
SOUTHWATER (Holy Innocents) *Chich 7*   **P** *V Horsham*
V K F GODFREY
SOUTHWAY (Holy Spirit) *Ex 21*   **P** *Ld Chan*   **C** D B M GILL
SOUTHWELL (Holy Trinity) *S'well 3*   **P** *CPAS*   **V** A W PORTER
SOUTHWELL (St Andrew)   *see Portland Sarum*
SOUTHWICK (Holy Trinity)   *see N Wearside Dur*
SOUTHWICK (St James) w Boarhunt *Portsm 1*   **P** *R Thistlewayte Esq*   **P-in-c** R L GREEN
SOUTHWICK (St Mary the Virgin)   *see Warmington, Tansor and Cotterstock etc Pet*
SOUTHWICK (St Michael and All Angels) (St Peter) *Chich 20*
P *Bp and Ld Chan (alt)*   **R** J D S FRENCH
SOUTHWICK (St Thomas)   *see N Bradley, Southwick, Heywood and Steeple Ashton Sarum*
SOUTHWOLD (St Edmund King and Martyr)   *see Sole Bay St E*
SOWERBY (St Mary)   *see Ryburn Leeds*
SOWERBY (St Oswald) *York 18*   **P** *Abp*   **V** N J CARNALL
C D E GAMBLE   **Hon C** M I KIMBALL
SOWERBY (St Peter)   *see Ryburn Leeds*
SOWERBY BRIDGE (Christ Church) *Leeds 11*   **P** *V Halifax*
V A DICK
SOWTON (St Michael and All Angels)   *see Broadclyst, Clyst Honiton, Pinhoe, Rockbeare etc Ex*
SPALDING (St John the Baptist) w Deeping St Nicholas
Linc 19   **P** *Bp*   **V** *vacant*
SPALDING (St Mary and St Nicolas) *Linc 19*   **P** *Feoffees*
V J D BENNETT   **C** M CHESHER   **NSM** A WORKMAN
SPALDING (St Paul) *Linc 19*   **P** *Bp and V Spalding (jt)*
P-in-c J D BENNETT   **C** M CHESHER   **NSM** A WORKMAN
SPALDWICK (St James)   *see E Leightonstone Ely*
SPARHAM (St Mary)   *see Lyng, Sparham, Elsing, Bylaugh, Bawdeswell etc Nor*
SPARKBROOK (Christ Church) *Birm 13*   **P** *Aston Trustees*
P-in-c R J SUDWORTH
SPARKBROOK (St Agatha) w Balsall Heath St Barnabas *Birm 1*
P *Bp*   **V** *vacant*
SPARKBROOK (St Agatha) w Balsall Heath St Barnabas
Birm 13   **P** *Bp*   **V** *vacant*
SPARKFORD (St Mary Magdalene)   *see Cam Vale B & W*
SPARKHILL (St John the Evangelist) *Birm 13*   **P** *Dioc Trustees and Aston Trustees (alt)*   **V** J A SELF   **NSM** G MORSE
SPARKWELL (All Saints) *Ex 20*   **P** *D&C Windsor*
V F G DENMAN
SPARROW HALL (St George)   *see Fazakerley Em Liv*
SPARSHOLT (Holy Cross)   *see Ridgeway Ox*
SPARSHOLT (St Stephen)   *see The Downs Win*
SPAXTON (St Margaret)   *see Aisholt, Enmore, Goathurst, Nether Stowey etc B & W*
SPEEN (St Mary the Virgin)   *see Newbury St Nic and Speen Ox*
SPEETON (St Leonard)   *see Bempton w Flamborough, Reighton w Speeton York*
SPEKE (St Aidan) (All Saints) *Liv 4*   **P** *Bp*   **TV** G PINNINGTON
C K R MILLER
SPELDHURST (St Mary the Virgin) w Groombridge and Ashurst *Roch 12*   **P** *DBP*   **R** D P WREN
SPELSBURY (All Saints)   *see Chase Ox*
SPEN, HIGH (St Patrick) and Rowlands Gill *Dur 13*   **P** *Bp*
V J W BARRON   **NSM** M MACKAY

SPENCERS WOOD (St Michael and All Angels)   *see Loddon Reach Ox*
SPENNITHORNE (St Michael) w Finghall and Hauxwell
Leeds 27   **P** *R J Dalton Esq and M C A Wyvill Esq (alt)*
P-in-c B S DIXON   **NSM** J T OLDFIELD
SPENNYMOOR (St Paul) and Whitworth *Dur 6*   **P** *D&C*
V M P TARLING   **C** L M MOSS
SPETISBURY (St John the Baptist) w Charlton Marshall and Blandford St Mary *Sarum 6*   **P** *Worc Coll Ox (1 turn), Bp (2 turns)*   **P-in-c** A J H EDWARDS
SPEXHALL (St Peter)   *see Blyth Valley St E*
SPILSBY (St James)   *see Bolingbroke Deanery Linc*
SPIRE HILL *Sarum 5*   **P** *Bp, CCC Cam, and Mrs J C M Langmead (jt)*   **R** W T RIDDING   **C** L A ANNESLEY-GAMESTER
SPITAL (St Agnes)   *see New Windsor Ox*
SPITAL (St Leonard's Mission Room)   *see Chesterfield St Mary and All SS Derby*
SPITALFIELDS (Christ Church w All Saints) *Lon 7*   **P** *MMCET*
R A RIDER   **C** D J WOLF, P R WILLIAMS
SPITTAL (St John) *Newc 12*   **P** *Bp and Mercers' Co (alt)*
P-in-c M S KNOX   **NSM** A M PETERS-WOTHERSPOON
SPIXWORTH (St Peter)   *see Horsham St Faith, Spixworth and Crostwick Nor*
SPOFFORTH (All Saints) w Kirk Deighton *Leeds 23*   **P** *Bp*
P-in-c S EARLE
SPONDON (St Werburgh) *Derby 9*   **P** *Mrs L B Palmer*
V J F HOLLYWELL   **NSM** E S BERRY
SPOTLAND (St Clement) and Oakenrod *Man 17*   **P** *Bp*
V K L SMEETON   **C** D OWEN   **NSM** S BARRON
SPRATTON (St Andrew)   *see Guilsborough and Hollowell and Cold Ashby etc Pet*
SPREYTON (St Michael)   *see Chagford, Gidleigh, Throwleigh etc Ex*
SPRIDLINGTON (St Hilary)   *see Owmby Gp Linc*
SPRING GROVE (St Mary) *Lon 11*   **P** *Ch Patr Trust*
V R C HOAD   **Hon C** M A WARMAN
SPRING LINE Group, The *Linc 5*   **P** *Lady Monson, Ball Coll Ox, J M Wright Esq, Bp, and DBP (jt)*   **R** A P SMITH
OLM J M HEPBURN, S DEACON, W G WILLIAMS
SPRING PARK (All Saints) *S'wark 19*   **P** *Bp*   **V** Y V CLARKE
SPRINGFIELD (All Saints) *Chelmsf 9*   **P** *Air Cdre N S Paynter*
P-in-c S M M ISKANDER
SPRINGFIELD (Holy Trinity) *Chelmsf 9*   **P** *Simeon's Trustees*
V K A RODDY   **C** S J HULL
SPRINGFIELD (St Christopher) *Birm 13*   **P** *Trustees*
V D J CUNDILL, T THOMAS   **C** R S ALLEN
SPRINGFIELD, EAST (Church of Our Saviour) (not known)
Chelmsf 9   **P** *Bp*   **P-in-c** A MACKENZIE
NSM M C HEWSON
SPRINGFIELD, NORTH (St Augustine of Canterbury)
Chelmsf 9   **P** *Bp*   **P-in-c** J V ANDERSON   **C** L P BATSON
SPRINGFIELDS (St Stephen)   *see Wolverhampton St Steph Lich*
SPRINGTHORPE (St George and St Laurence)   *see Lea Gp Linc*
SPRINGWOOD (All Souls)   *see Liv All So Springwood Liv*
SPROATLEY (St Swithin)   *see Hedon, Paull, Sproatley and Preston York*
SPROTBROUGH (St Mary the Virgin) *Sheff 7*   **P** *Bp*
R B A J BARRACLOUGH
SPROUGHTON (All Saints) w Burstall, Copdock w Washbrook and Belstead and Bentley w Tattingstone *St E 5*   **P** *Patr Bd*
R A D SHANNON
SPROWSTON (St Cuthbert) (St Mary and St Margaret) w Beeston *Nor 2*   **P** *D&C*   **R** S C STOKES   **C** D AKRILL
NSM H M WRIGHT, M A HIDER
SPROXTON (St Bartholomew)   *see High Framland Par Leic*
SPROXTON (St Chad)   *see Helmsley York*
SQUIRRELS HEATH (All Saints) *Chelmsf 2*   **P** *Bp*
V C W WRAGG
STADHAMPTON (St John the Baptist)   *see Dorchester Ox*
STAFFHURST WOOD (St Silvan)   *see Limpsfield and Tatsfield S'wark*
STAFFORD (St Bertelin) and Whitgreave St John *Lich 10*
P *Bp and Earl of Harrowby (jt)*   **V** J E EVANS
STAFFORD (St Chad) *Lich 10*   **P** *Bp*   **V** R J S GRIGSON
NSM J J DAVIS
STAFFORD (St John the Baptist) and Tixall w Ingestre *Lich 10*
P *Bp and Earl of Shrewsbury and Talbot (jt)*   **V** A G STONE
C R M RICHARDS
STAFFORD (St Mary) and Marston *Lich 10*   **P** *Bp and Earl of Harrowby (jt)*   **V** R J S GRIGSON   **NSM** J J DAVIS
STAFFORD (St Paul) (St Thomas and St Andrew) *Lich 10*
P *V Castle Ch and Hyndman Trustees (jt)*   **V** M G STRANG
STAFFORD, WEST (St Andrew)   *see Dorchester and the Winterbournes Sarum*

STAGSDEN (St Leonard)   *see* Bromham w Oakley and Stagsden *St Alb*

STAGSHAW CHAPEL (St Aidan)   *see* St John Lee *Newc*

STAINBY (St Peter)   *see* Witham Gp *Linc*

STAINCLIFFE (Christ Church) and Carlinghow *Leeds* 10
  P *V Brownhill and V Batley (jt)*   **Hon C** M G INMAN

STAINCROSS (St John the Evangelist) *Leeds* 18   **P** *Bp*
  V J K BUTTERWORTH   **NSM** M SCHOLEY
  OLM J M CROSSLAND

STAINDROP (St Mary) *Dur* 7   **P** *Lord Barnard*
  P-in-c K STEVENTON

STAINES (Christ Church) (St Mary) (St Peter) *Lon* 13
  P *Bp and Ld Chan (alt)*   **P-in-c** M BURLEY   **C** P JENNER
  NSM S P WOOD

STAINFIELD (St Andrew)   *see* Bardney *Linc*

STAINFORTH (St Mary) *Sheff* 10   **P** *Bp*   **P-in-c** J FRANKLIN

STAINFORTH (St Peter)   *see* Langcliffe w Stainforth and Horton *Leeds*

STAINING (St Luke Mission Church)   *see* Layton and Staining *Blackb*

STAINLAND (St Andrew) w Outlane *Leeds* 8   **P** *V Halifax*
  V R A CHAPMAN   **C** D BURROWS

STAINLEY, NORTH (St Mary the Virgin)   *see* W Tanfield and Well w Snape and N Stainley *Leeds*

STAINLEY, SOUTH (St Wilfrid)   *see* Bishop Thornton, Burnt Yates, Markington etc *Leeds*

STAINMORE (St Stephen)   *see* Brough w Stainmore, Musgrave and Warcop *Carl*

STAINTON (St Peter w St Paul) w Hilton *York* 20   **P** *Abp (2 turns), DBP (1 turn)*   **V** V G HATTON   **NSM** W A DEWING

STAINTON (St Winifred)   *see* Tickhill w Stainton *Sheff*

STAINTON BY LANGWORTH (St John the Baptist)   *see* Barlings *Linc*

STAINTON LE VALE (St Andrew)   *see* Walesby *Linc*

STAINTONDALE (St John the Baptist)   *see* Ravenscar and Staintondale *York*

STAITHES (St Peter)   *see* Hinderwell, Roxby and Staithes etc *York*

STAKEFORD (Holy Family)   *see* Choppington *Newc*

STALBRIDGE (St Mary)   *see* Spire Hill *Sarum*

STALHAM (St Mary), East Ruston, Brunstead, Sutton and Ingham *Nor* 12   **P** *Bp, DBP and Mrs S F Baker (jt)*
  R S P LAWRENCE   **C** M T M MCPHEE

STALLING BUSK (St Matthew)   *see* Upper Wensleydale *Leeds*

STALLINGBOROUGH (St Peter and St Paul)   *see* Immingham Gp *Linc*

STALMINE (St James) w Pilling St John the Baptist *Blackb* 9
  P *Bp, V Lanc St Mary, Mrs C B Mason-Hornby, and H D H Elletson Esq (jt)*   **V** A J SHAW   **NSM** D A DICKINSON
  OLM J M KIRKHAM

STALYBRIDGE (Holy Trinity and Christ Church) *Ches* 14
  P *Trustees*   **V** T R PARKER   **C** L S BRIGGS

STALYBRIDGE (St George) *Man* 13   **P** *Lord Deramore and R Ashton-under-Lyne St Mich (jt)*   **P-in-c** P BRIERLEY

STALYBRIDGE (St Paul) *Ches* 14   **P** *Trustees*   **V** *vacant*

STAMBOURNE (St Peter and St Thomas Becket)   *see* Upper Colne *Chelmsf*

STAMBRIDGE (St Mary and All Saints) *Chelmsf* 14   **P** *Ld Chan (1 turn), Charterhouse (3 turns)*   **R** *vacant*

STAMFORD (All Saints) w St John the Baptist *Linc* 16   **P** *Ld Chan and Burghley Ho Preservation Trust (alt)*   **V** M WARRICK
  C A P BEESLEY, N A MANN   **Hon C** D M BOND
  NSM H B BRANDON

STAMFORD (Christ Church) *Linc* 16   **P** *Bp*   **V** N J BATES

STAMFORD (St George) (St Paul) *Linc* 16   **P** *Burghley Ho Preservation Trust*   **R** M A N TAYLOR   **C** E WARD

STAMFORD (St Mary) (St Martin) *Linc* 16   **P** *Burghley Ho Preservation Trust*   **P-in-c** G A COOPER

STAMFORD BRIDGE Group of Parishes, The (St John the Baptist) *York* 5   **P** *Lord Egremont (2 turns), Prime Min (1 turn)*
  R A F WAKEFIELD   **T** G T WAKEFIELD, M H ELLISON

STAMFORD HILL (St Bartholomew) *Lon* 5   **P** *The Crown*
  V C L CARD-REYNOLDS

STAMFORD HILL (St Thomas) *Lon* 5   **P** *R Hackney*
  V W G CAMPBELL-TAYLOR   **NSM** G STEVENSON,
  M F E STEWART

STAMFORDHAM (St Mary the Virgin) w Matfen *Newc* 9
  P *Ld Chan*   **P-in-c** R L SQUIRES

STANBRIDGE (St John the Baptist)   *see* Totternhoe, Stanbridge and Tilsworth *St Alb*

STANBURY (Mission Church)   *see* Haworth and Cross Roads cum Lees *Leeds*

STAND (All Saints) *Man* 10   **P** *Earl of Wilton*   **R** A J HARDY
  C D A WILLIAMS   **NSM** A M WHITTLEWORTH, C D BINNS

STANDISH (St Nicholas)   *see* Eastington, Frocester, Haresfield etc *Glouc*

STANDISH (St Wilfrid) *Blackb* 4   **P** *Bp*   **R** A HOLLIDAY
  C T J G BRAMPTON

STANDLAKE (St Giles)   *see* Lower Windrush *Ox*

STANDON (All Saints)   *see* Cotes Heath and Standon and Swynnerton etc *Lich*

STANDON (St Mary) and The Mundens w Sacombe *St Alb* 15
  P *Ch Trust Fund Trust, K Coll Cam, and R Abel-Smith Esq (1 turn), Ch Trust Fund Trust (1 turn)*   **R** A COMFORT

STANFIELD (St Margaret)   *see* Litcham w Kempston, E and W Lexham, Mileham etc *Nor*

STANFORD (All Saints) *Nor* 13   **P** *Bp*   **V** *vacant*

STANFORD (All Saints)   *see* Lyminge w Paddlesworth, Stanford w Postling etc *Cant*

STANFORD (St Nicholas)   *see* Gilmorton, Peatling Parva, Kimcote etc *Leic*

STANFORD BISHOP (St James)   *see* Frome Valley *Heref*

STANFORD DINGLEY (St Denys)   *see* Bradfield and Stanford Dingley *Ox*

STANFORD IN THE VALE (St Denys) w Goosey and Hatford
  Ox 25   **P** *D&C Westmr (3 turns), Simeon's Trustees (2 turns)*
  V P A EDDY

STANFORD RIVERS (St Margaret)   *see* Greensted-juxta-Ongar w Stanford Rivers etc *Chelmsf*

STANFORD-LE-HOPE (St Margaret) w Mucking *Chelmsf* 16
  P *MMCET*   **R** J A K GUEST   **C** J G M POYNTZ

STANFORD-ON-SOAR (St John the Baptist)   *see* E and W Leake, Stanford-on-Soar, Rempstone etc *S'well*

STANFORD-ON-TEME (St Mary)   *see* Teme Valley S *Worc*

STANGROUND (St John the Baptist) (St Michael and All Angels) and Farcet *Ely* 15   **P** *Em Coll Cam*   **V** A R SHORTER
  C S A DAWKINS

STANHOPE (St Thomas)   *see* Upper Weardale *Dur*

STANION (St Peter)   *see* Brigstock w Stanion and Lowick and Sudborough *Pet*

STANLEY (All Saints)   *see* W Hallam and Mapperley w Stanley *Derby*

STANLEY (St Andrew)   *as above*

STANLEY (St Andrew) and South Moor *Dur* 4   **P** *Bp (3 turns) and Prime Min (1 turn)*   **V** A JOHNSTON   **NSM** A E DART

STANLEY (St Anne) w Stoneycroft St Paul *Liv* 8   **P** *V W Derby St Mary and St Chad's Coll Dur (jt)*   **V** E L WILLIAMS
  Hon C C WARRILOW

STANLEY (St Thomas)   *see* Satley, Stanley and Tow Law *Dur*

STANLEY PONTLARGE (Chapel)   *see* Winchcombe *Glouc*

STANLEY St Peter *Leeds* 20   **P** *Dean*   **V** W E HENDERSON
  NSM D TEECE, J KILSBY

STANLEYS w Selsey, The *Glouc* 4   **P** *Bp and Jes Coll Cam (jt)*
  V M M LUDLOW   **NSM** B P LUDLOW

STANMER w Falmer *Chich* 19   **P** *Bp*   **P-in-c** C R LAWLOR

STANMORE (St Luke) *Win* 7   **P** *M R GARDNER*

STANMORE, GREAT (St John the Evangelist) *Lon* 23
  P *R O Bernays Esq*   **R** I M STONE   **NSM** DR NORRIS

STANMORE, LITTLE (St Lawrence) *Lon* 23   **P** *Bp*
  R P M REECE

STANNINGFIELD (St Nicholas)   *see* St Edm Way *St E*

STANNINGLEY (St Thomas) *Leeds* 15   **P** *V Leeds St Pet*
  R R I M COUTTS

STANNINGTON (Christ Church) *Sheff* 4   **P** *Bp*
  P-in-c T J FLETCHER

STANNINGTON (St Mary the Virgin) *Newc* 11   **P** *Bp*
  P-in-c C R PICKFORD

STANSFIELD (All Saints)   *see* Bansfield *St E*

STANSTEAD (St James)   *see* Glemsford, Hartest w Boxted, Somerton etc *St E*

STANSTEAD ABBOTS (St Andrew)   *see* Gt Amwell w St Margaret's and Stanstead Abbots *St Alb*

STANSTEAD ST MARGARET (St Mary the Virgin)   *as above*

STANSTED (St Mary) w Fairseat and Vigo *Roch* 10
  P *Bp*   **R** C J L NOBLE

STANSTED MOUNTFITCHET (St John) w Birchanger and Farnham *Chelmsf* 18   **P** *Bp, New Coll Ox, and Mrs L A Murphy (jt)*   **R** P J WILKIN

STANTON (All Saints), Hopton, Market Weston, Barningham and Coney Weston *St E* 9   **P** *Ld Chan (2 turns) and Bp (1 turn)*
  R D H MESSER   **C** S D COBURN

STANTON (St Gabriel)   *see* Golden Cap Team *Sarum*

STANTON (St Mary and All Saints)   *see* Markfield, Thornton, Bagworth and Stanton etc *Leic*

STANTON (St Mary)   *see* Alton w Bradley-le-Moors and Denstone etc *Lich*

STANTON (St Michael and All Angels)   *see* Winchcombe *Glouc*

STANTON BY BRIDGE (St Michael)   *see* Melbourne, Ticknall, Smisby and Stanton *Derby*

STANTON DREW (St Mary)   *see* Chew Magna w Dundry, Norton Malreward etc *B & W*

STANTON FITZWARREN (St Leonard)   *see* Stratton St Margaret w S Marston etc *Bris*

STANTON HARCOURT (St Michael)   *see* Lower Windrush *Ox*

STANTON HILL (All Saints)   *see* Skegby w Teversal *S'well*

STANTON LACY (St Peter)   *see* Ludlow *Heref*

STANTON ON HINE HEATH (St Andrew) *Lich 22*   **P** *Sir Beville Stanier Bt*   **V** *vacant*

STANTON PRIOR (St Lawrence)   *see* Farmborough, Marksbury and Stanton Prior *B & W*

STANTON ST BERNARD (All Saints)   *see* Vale of Pewsey *Sarum*

STANTON ST JOHN (St John the Baptist)   *see* Beckley, Forest Hill, Horton-cum-Studley and Stanton St John *Ox*

STANTON ST QUINTIN (St Giles)   *see* Hullavington, Norton and Stanton St Quintin *Bris*

STANTONBURY (Christ Church) and Willen *Ox 14*   **P** *Patr Bd*   **TR** P A SMITH   **TV** A R B JOWITT

STANTON-BY-DALE (St Michael and All Angels) w Dale Abbey and Risley *Derby 13*   **P** *Bp*   **R** G A LUCAS   **C** J R BELL

STANTON-IN-PEAK (Holy Trinity)   *see* Youlgreave, Middleton, Stanton-in-Peak etc *Derby*

STANTON-ON-THE-WOLDS (All Saints)   *see* Keyworth and Stanton-on-the-Wolds and Bunny etc *S'well*

STANWAY (St Albright) (St Andrew) *Chelmsf 21*   **P** *Magd Coll Ox*   **P-in-c** A C BUSHELL

STANWAY (St Peter)   *see* Winchcombe *Glouc*

STANWELL (St Mary the Virgin) *Lon 13*   **P** *Ld Chan*   **V** *vacant*

STANWICK (St Laurence)   *see* Raunds, Hargrave, Ringstead and Stanwick *Pet*

STANWIX (St Michael) *Carl 3*   **P** *Bp*   **V** N D BEER   **C** C J HARDING

STAPEHILL (All Saints)   *see* Hampreston *Sarum*

STAPENHILL (Immanuel) *Derby 16*   **P** *Ch Soc Trust*   **V** *vacant*

STAPENHILL (St Peter) w Cauldwell *Derby 16*   **P** *Ch Soc Trust*   **V** M ANDREYEV

STAPLE (St James)   *see* Eastry and Woodnesborough *Cant*

STAPLE FITZPAINE (St Peter)   *see* Beercrocombe w Curry Mallet, Hatch Beauchamp etc *B & W*

STAPLE TYE (St James) *Chelmsf 4*   **P** *Bp*   **V** *vacant*

STAPLECROSS (St Mark)   *see* Ewhurst *Chich*

STAPLEFIELD COMMON (St Mark)   *see* Slaugham and Staplefield Common *Chich*

STAPLEFORD (All Saints)   *see* Bassingham Gp *Linc*

STAPLEFORD (St Andrew) *Ely 5*   **P** *D&C*   **V** *vacant*

STAPLEFORD (St Helen) (St Luke) *S'well 8*   **P** *CPAS*   **V** P A HUXTABLE

STAPLEFORD (St Mary)   *see* Lower Wylye and Till Valley *Sarum*

STAPLEFORD (St Mary)   *see* Bramfield, Stapleford, Waterford etc *St Alb*

STAPLEFORD ABBOTTS (St Mary)   *see* Lambourne w Abridge and Stapleford Abbotts *Chelmsf*

STAPLEFORD TAWNEY (St Mary the Virgin)   *see* Greensted-juxta-Ongar w Stanford Rivers etc *Chelmsf*

STAPLEGROVE (St John the Evangelist) w Norton Fitzwarren *B & W 18*   **P** *Bp and MMCET (jt)*   **R** M S KIVETT

STAPLEHURST (All Saints) *Cant 11*   **P** *St Jo Coll Cam*   **R** S TETZLAFF

STAPLETON (Holy Trinity) *Bris 3*   **P** *Bp*   **NSM** R A WARING

STAPLETON (St John)   *see* Dorrington w Leebotwood, Longnor, Stapleton etc *Heref*

STAPLETON (St Martin)   *see* Barwell w Potters Marston and Stapleton *Leic*

STAPLETON (St Mary)   *see* Bewcastle, Stapleton and Kirklinton etc *Carl*

STARBECK (St Andrew) *Leeds 23*   **P** *V Harrogate Ch Ch*   **V** F S K WAINAINA

STARCROSS (St Paul)   *see* Dawlish, Cofton and Starcross *Ex*

STARSTON (St Margaret)   *see* Dickleburgh and The Pulhams *Nor*

STARTFORTH (Holy Trinity) and Bowes and Rokeby w Brignall *Leeds 24*   **P** *Ld Chan (1 turn), Bp, Earl of Lonsdale and Lords of the Manor of Bowes (2 turns)*   **P-in-c** J BARKER

STATFOLD (St Matthew)   *see* Mease Valley *Lich*

STATHERN (St Guthlac)   *see* Vale of Belvoir *Leic*

STAUGHTONS, The (St Andrew) (All Saints) w Hail Weston *Ely 13*   **P** *Mert Coll Ox, St Jo Coll Ox, and CCC Ox (by turn)*   **V** J I CLARKE

STAUNTON (All Saints)   *see* Coleford, Staunton, Newland, Redbrook etc *Glouc*

STAUNTON (St James)   *see* Ashleworth, Corse, Hartpury, Hasfield etc *Glouc*

STAUNTON (St Mary) w Flawborough *S'well 3*   **P** E G *Staunton Esq*   **P-in-c** E I MURRAY

STAUNTON-ON-ARROW (St Peter)   *see* Pembridge w Moor Court, Shobdon, Staunton etc *Heref*

STAUNTON-ON-WYE (St Mary the Virgin)   *see* Letton w Staunton, Byford, Mansel Gamage etc *Heref*

STAVELEY (All Saints)   *see* Walkingham Hill *Leeds*

STAVELEY (St James), Ings and Kentmere *Carl 11*   **P** *V Kendal H Trin*   **P-in-c** S H P THOMPSON

STAVELEY (St John the Baptist) and Barrow Hill *Derby 3*   **P** *Bp, Adn Chesterfield, and Duke of Devonshire (jt)*   **TR** S F JONES   **TV** A P ARNOLD

STAVELEY IN CARTMEL (St Mary)   *see* Cartmel Peninsula *Carl*

STAVERTON (St Catherine)   *see* Twigworth, Down Hatherley, Norton, The Leigh etc *Glouc*

STAVERTON (St Mary the Virgin)   *see* Daventry, Ashby St Ledgers, Braunston etc *Pet*

STAVERTON (St Paul de Leon) w Landscove, Littlehempston, Buckfastleigh and Dean Prior *Ex 12*   **P** *Bp, D&C, DBP (jt)*   **R** T H F BENSON

STAWELL (St Francis)   *see* Middlezoy w Othery, Moorlinch and Greinton *B & W*

STAWLEY (St Michael and All Angels)   *see* Wellington and Distr *B & W*

STEANE (St Peter)   *see* Aynho and Croughton w Evenley etc *Pet*

STEART BAY (St Andrew)   *see* Cannington, Otterhampton, Combwich and Stockland *B & W*

STEBBING (St Mary the Virgin) and Lindsell w Great and Little (Bardfield) Saling *Chelmsf 18*   **P** *Bp*   **P-in-c** T E GOODBODY   **NSM** C M HAWKES   **OLM** M H PELLY

STECHFORD (All Saints) (St Andrew) *Birm 13*   **P** *St Pet Coll Ox*   **V** G S GAKURU

STEDHAM (St James) w Iping *Chich 9*   **P** *Bp*   **R** *vacant*

STEEP (All Saints) and Froxfield w Privett *Portsm 4*   **P** *Ld Chan and Magd Coll Cam (alt)*   **V** J E OWEN   **NSM** C J PRIOR-JONES, J S E FARRELL

STEEPING, GREAT (All Saints)   *see* Bolingbroke Deanery *Linc*

STEEPING, LITTLE (St Andrew)   *as above*

STEEPLE (St Lawrence and All Saints)   *see* Southminster and Steeple *Chelmsf*

STEEPLE (St Michael and All Angels)   *see* Corfe Castle, Church Knowle, Kimmeridge etc *Sarum*

STEEPLE ASHTON (St Mary the Virgin)   *see* N Bradley, Southwick, Heywood and Steeple Ashton *Sarum*

STEEPLE ASTON (St Peter and St Paul) w North Aston and Tackley *Ox 29*   **P** *BNC Ox, St Jo Coll Ox, and J D Taylor Esq (jt)*   **R** E M GREEN

STEEPLE BARTON (St Mary)   *see* Westcote Barton w Steeple Barton, Duns Tew and Sandford St Martin and Over w Nether Worton *Ox*

STEEPLE BUMPSTEAD (St Mary)   *see* Two Rivers *Chelmsf*

STEEPLE CLAYDON (St Michael)   *see* The Claydons and Swan *Ox*

STEEPLE LANGFORD (All Saints)   *see* Lower Wylye and Till Valley *Sarum*

STEEPLE MORDEN (St Peter and St Paul)   *see* Shingay Gp *Ely*

STEETLY (All Saints)   *see* Whitwell *Derby*

STEETON (St Stephen) *Leeds 5*   **P** *V Kildwick*   **P-in-c** J A SAVAGE   **NSM** F M GRASHAM

STELLA (St Cuthbert)   *see* Blaydon and Swalwell *Dur*

STELLING (St Mary)   *see* Chartham and Upper Hardres w Stelling *Cant*

STENIGOT (St Nicholas)   *see* Asterby Gp *Linc*

STEPNEY (St Dunstan and All Saints) *Lon 7*   **P** *Bp*   **R** T F CRITCHLOW   **NSM** C L J MORGAN

STEPPINGLEY (St Lawrence)   *see* Ampthill w Millbrook and Steppingley *St Alb*

STERNFIELD (St Mary Magdalene)   *see* Alde River *St E*

STERT (St James)   *see* The Cannings and Redhorn *Sarum*

STETCHWORTH (St Peter)   *see* Raddesley Gp *Ely*

STEVENAGE (All Saints) Pin Green *St Alb 20*   **P** *Bp*   **V** P E SEYMOUR   **NSM** E W FAURE WALKER

STEVENAGE (Holy Trinity) (Christ the King) *St Alb 20*   **P** *Bp*   **V** V C ORAM   **NSM** A J THOMAS

STEVENAGE (St Andrew and St George) *St Alb 20*   **P** *Bp*   **P-in-c** C E BUNCE   **NSM** J A PAGE

STEVENAGE (St Hugh) (St John) Chells *St Alb 20*   **P** *Bp*   **V** C K PERERA

STEVENAGE (St Mary) Shephall w Aston *St Alb 20*   **P** *Bp*   **V** V A HATHAWAY

STEVENAGE (St Nicholas) and Graveley *St Alb 20*   **P** *Bp*   **P-in-c** D M BROWN   **C** D J FREYHAN

STEVENAGE (St Peter) Broadwater *St Alb 20*   **P** *Bp*   **V** T E HORLOCK   **C** C R SHARPLES

STEVENTON (St Michael and All Angels) w Milton *Ox 19*   **P** *Ch Ch Ox and D&C Westmr (jt)*   **R** *vacant*

STEVENTON (St Nicholas)   *see* N Waltham and Steventon, Ashe and Deane *Win*

STEVINGTON (Church Room) (St Mary the Virgin) *St Alb 13*
P *Bp*   **V** *vacant*

STEWKLEY (St Michael and All Angels)   *see* Cottesloe *Ox*

STEWTON (St Andrew)   *see* Louth *Linc*

STEYNING (St Andrew) *Chich 11*   **P** *Bp*   **V** N C ROBERTS
NSM R W TOOVEY

STIBBARD (All Saints)   *see* Foulsham, Guestwick, Stibbard,
Themelthorpe etc *Nor*

STIBBINGTON (St John the Baptist)   *see* Castor w Upton and
Stibbington and Water Newton, Marholm and Sutton *Pet*

STICKER (St Mark's Mission Church)   *see* St Mewan w
Mevagissey and St Ewe *Truro*

STICKFORD (St Helen)   *see* Bolingbroke Deanery *Linc*

STICKLEPATH (St Mary)   *see* Okehampton, Inwardleigh,
Belstone, Sourton etc *Ex*

STICKLEPATH (St Paul)   *see* Barnstaple *Ex*

STICKNEY (St Luke)   *see* Bolingbroke Deanery *Linc*

STIDD (St Saviour)   *see* Ribchester w Stidd *Blackb*

STIFFKEY (St John and St Mary) and Bale *Nor 18*   **P** *MMCET,
Bp, DBP, Keble Coll Ox, and Sir Euan Hamilton Anstruther-Gough-
Calthorpe Bt (jt)*   **R** I C WHITTLE

STIFFORD (St Cedd) (St Mary) *Chelmsf 16*   **P** *Bp*
R A R B HIGGS

STILLINGFLEET (St Helen)   *see* Escrick and Stillingfleet w
Naburn *York*

STILLINGTON (St Nicholas)   *see* Forest of Galtres *York*

STILTON (St Mary Magdalene) w Denton and Caldecote
and Folkesworth w Morborne and Haddon *Ely 15*
P *MMCET and Bp, Ld Chan (alt)*   **R** *vacant*

STINCHCOMBE (St Cyr)   *see* Cam w Stinchcombe *Glouc*

STINSFORD (St Michael)   *see* Charminster and Stinsford *Sarum*

STIRCHLEY (All Saints)   *see* Cen Telford *Lich*

STIRCHLEY (Ascension) *Birm 5*   **P** R Kings Norton
P-in-c J E M HOUGHTON

STISTED (All Saints)   *see* Cressing w Stisted and Bradwell etc
Chelmsf

STITHIANS (St Stythians)   *see* St Stythians w Perranarworthal
and Gwennap *Truro*

STIXWOULD (St Peter)   *see* Woodhall Spa Gp *Linc*

STOAK (St Lawrence)   *see* Ellesmere Port *Ches*

STOCK (St Barnabas)   *see* Spire Hill *Sarum*

STOCK HARVARD (All Saints) *Chelmsf 10*   **P** *Guild of All So*
P-in-c S W NEED

STOCKBRIDGE (Old St Peter)   *see* Test Valley *Win*

STOCKBRIDGE (St Peter) *as above*

STOCKBRIDGE VILLAGE (St Jude)   *see* 4Saints Team *Liv*

STOCKBURY (St Mary Magdalene)   *see* The Six *Cant*

STOCKCROSS (St John)   *see* E Downland *Ox*

STOCKERSTON (St Peter)   *see* Six Saints circa Holt *Leic*

STOCKING FARM (St Luke) and Beaumont Leys *Leic 1*
P *Bp*   **V** S R DELAFORCE

STOCKING PELHAM (St Mary)   *see* Albury, Braughing, Furneux
Pelham, Lt Hadham etc *St Alb*

STOCKINGFORD (St Paul) *Cov 5*   **P** V Nuneaton
V K I MASSEY

STOCKLAND (St Mary Magdalene)   *see* Cannington,
Otterhampton, Combwich and Stockland *B & W*

STOCKLAND (St Michael and All Angels)   *see* Kilmington,
Stockland, Dalwood, Yarcombe etc *Ex*

STOCKLAND GREEN (St Mark) *Birm 8*   **P** The Crown
P-in-c R J WALKER-HILL

STOCKLEIGH ENGLISH (St Mary the Virgin)   *see* N Creedy *Ex*

STOCKLEIGH POMEROY (St Mary the Virgin) *as above*

STOCKLINCH (St Mary Magdalene)   *see* Winsmoor *B & W*

STOCKPORT (St George) *Ches 18*   **P** *Trustees*   **V** E C HALL
C C B MOORE   **Hon C** S B WOODHEAD

STOCKPORT (St Mark)   *see* Edgeley and Cheadle Heath *Ches*

STOCKPORT (St Mary) *Ches 18*   **P** G&C Coll Cam
R R P SCOONES

STOCKPORT (St Matthew)   *see* Edgeley and Cheadle Heath
Ches

STOCKPORT (St Peter) *Ches 18*   **P** Ch Union   **R** *vacant*

STOCKPORT (St Saviour) *Ches 18*   **P** *Trustees*
V D V COOKSON

STOCKSBRIDGE (St Matthias) *Sheff 3*   **P** *Bp*   **V** *vacant*

STOCKSFIELD (St John)   *see* Bywell and Mickley *Newc*

STOCKTON (St Andrew)   *see* Teme Valley N *Worc*

STOCKTON (St Chad) *Dur 10*   **P** *Bp*   **V** *vacant*

STOCKTON (St Chad)   *see* Beckbury, Badger, Kemberton,
Ryton, Stockton etc *Lich*

STOCKTON (St John the Baptist)   *see* Lower Wylye and Till
Valley *Sarum*

STOCKTON (St Michael and All Angels)   *see* Napton-on-the-
Hill, Lower Shuckburgh etc *Cov*

STOCKTON (St Michael and All Angels)   *see* Gillingham w
Geldeston, Stockton, Ellingham etc *Nor*

STOCKTON Country Parish *Dur 10*   **P** *Bp, Ld Chan, Prime Min,
and D&C (by turn)*   **P** R D M BROOKE

STOCKTON HEATH (St Thomas) *Ches 4*   **P** P G Greenall Esq
V M L RIDLEY   **NSM** L E J CHUMBLEY

STOCKTON ON TEES (Holy Trinity) (St Mark) *Dur 10*   **P** *Bp*
P-in-c P S D NEVILLE

STOCKTON ON TEES (St James) *Dur 10*   **P** *Bp*
P-in-c D J BELL   **C** D C PIERCE

STOCKTON-ON-TEES (St Chad)   *see* Stockton St Chad *Dur*

STOCKTON-ON-TEES (St John the Baptist) *Dur 10*   **P** *Bp*
P-in-c D J BELL   **C** D C PIERCE

STOCKTON-ON-TEES (St Paul) *Dur 10*   **P** The Crown
V *vacant*

STOCKTON-ON-TEES (St Peter) *Dur 10*   **P** *Bp*
V P D ASHDOWN

STOCKTON-ON-TEES (St Thomas) *Dur 10*   **P** *Bp*
P-in-c A J FARISH   **C** M G MILLER

STOCKTON-ON-THE-FOREST (Holy Trinity)   *see* Rural E York
York

STOCKWELL (St Andrew) (St Michael) *S'wark 11*   **P** *Bp*
V N C WHITTLE   **NSM** O O OGBEDE   **OLM** I A BOWMAN

STOCKWITH, EAST (St Peter)   *see* Trentcliffe Gp *Linc*

STOCKWITH, WEST (St Mary the Virgin)   *see* Beckingham,
Walkeringham, Misterton, W Stockwith, Clayworth and
Gringley-on-the-Hill *S'well*

STOCKWOOD (Christ the Servant)   *see* Bris Ch the Servant
Stockwood *Bris*

STODDEN Churches, The *St Alb 13*   **P** MMCET and DBP (alt)
P-in-c S C HOLROYD

STODMARSH (St Mary)   *see* Littlebourne and Ickham w
Wickhambreaux etc *Cant*

STODY (St Mary)   *see* Brinton, Briningham, Hunworth, Stody
etc *Nor*

STOGUMBER (Blessed Virgin Mary)   *see* Quantock Towers
B & W

STOGURSEY (St Andrew)   *see* Quantock Coast *B & W*

STOKE (St Mary and St Andrew)   *see* Colsterworth Gp *Linc*

STOKE (St Michael)   *see* Coventry Caludon *Cov*

STOKE (St Peter and St Paul)   *see* Grain w Stoke *Roch*

STOKE ABBOTT (St Mary)   *see* Beaminster Area *Sarum*

STOKE ALBANY (St Botolph) w Wilbarston and Ashley w
Weston-by-Welland and Sutton Bassett *Pet 7*   **P** Comdr
L M M Saunders-Watson (2 turns), Bp (1 turn), DBP (1 turn)
P-in-c S L HUGHES

STOKE ASH (All Saints)   *see* S Hartismere *St E*

STOKE BARDOLPH (St Luke)   *see* Burton Joyce w Bulcote and
Stoke Bardolph *S'well*

STOKE BISHOP (St Mary Magdalene) *Bris 2*   **P** *Bp*
V M D INESON   **NSM** E G INESON, J HARRIS
OLM A K CATTELL, H J TRAPNELL, M J HALL

STOKE BLISS (St Peter)   *see* Teme Valley N *Worc*

STOKE BRUERNE (St Mary the Virgin)   *see* Blisworth, Alderton,
Grafton Regis etc *Pet*

STOKE BY CLARE (St John the Baptist)   *see* Stour Valley *St E*

STOKE BY NAYLAND (St Mary) w Leavenheath and Polstead
St E 3   **P** Mrs S E F Holden and St Jo Coll Ox (alt)
NSM J A D SEPHTON, V ARMSTRONG

STOKE CANON (St Mary Magdalene)   *see* Brampford Speke,
Cadbury, Newton St Cyres etc *Ex*

STOKE CHARITY (St Mary and St Michael)   *see* Upper Dever
Win

STOKE CLIMSLAND (not known) *Truro 12*   **P** Bp and Duchy of
Cornwall (alt)   **P-in-c** A W STEPHENS

STOKE D'ABERNON (St Mary the Virgin)   *see* Cobham and
Stoke D'Abernon *Guildf*

STOKE DAMEREL (St Andrew w St Luke) and Devonport
St Aubyn *Ex 21*   **P** Trustees Lord St Levan (2 turns), Prime Min
(1 turn)   **R** *vacant*

STOKE DOYLE (St Rumbold)   *see* Aldwincle, Clopton, Pilton,
Stoke Doyle etc *Pet*

STOKE DRY (St Andrew)   *see* Lyddington, Bisbrooke, Caldecott,
Glaston etc *Pet*

STOKE EDITH (St Mary)   *see* Ledbury *Heref*

STOKE FLEMING (St Peter), Blackawton and Strete *Ex 13*
P Bp and DBP (jt)   **V** *vacant*

STOKE GABRIEL (St Gabriel)   *see* Totnes w Bridgetown, Berry
Pomeroy etc *Ex*

STOKE GIFFORD (St Michael) *Bris 5*   **P** *Bp*   **TR** S JONES
TV P F HINCKLEY   **C** K E JONES   **Hon C** I J TOMKINS
NSM J C BRADLEY

STOKE GOLDING (St Margaret)   *see* Fenn Lanes Gp *Leic*

STOKE GOLDINGTON (St Peter)   *see* Gayhurst w Ravenstone,
Stoke Goldington etc *Ox*

STOKE HAMMOND (St Luke)   *see* Brickhills and Stoke
Hammond *Ox*

STOKE HEATH (St Alban)   *see* Cov E *Cov*
STOKE HILL (St Peter) *Guildf 5*   **P** *Bp*   **V** K L ROSSLYN-SMITH
STOKE HOLY CROSS (Holy Cross) w Dunston, Arminghall
  and Caistor St Edmunds w Markshall *Nor 8*   **P** *D&C and*
  Mrs D Pott (jt)   **R** R J BAKER
STOKE LACY (St Peter and St Paul)   *see* Bromyard and Stoke
  Lacy *Heref*
STOKE LYNE (St Peter)   *see* Shelswell *Ox*
STOKE MANDEVILLE (St Mary the Virgin)   *see* Ellesborough,
  The Kimbles and Stoke Mandeville *Ox*
STOKE NEWINGTON (St Andrew) *Lon 5*   **P** *Bp*   **V** vacant
STOKE NEWINGTON (St John the Evangelist)   *see* Brownswood
  Park *Lon*
STOKE NEWINGTON (St Mary) (Old Parish Church) *Lon 5*
  P *Bp*   **R** H M BAKER   **C** M W WALL
STOKE NEWINGTON (St Olave) *Lon 5*   **P** *Ld Chan*
  V V A ROBERTS
STOKE NEWINGTON COMMON (St Michael and All Angels)
  Lon 5   **P** *Bp*   **V** J B LAWSON
STOKE NEWINGTON St Faith (St Matthias) and All Saints
  Lon 5   **P** *City Corp*   **V** D J LAMBERT
STOKE ORCHARD (St James the Great)   *see* Deerhurst and
  Apperley w Forthampton etc *Glouc*
STOKE PARK (St Peter)   *see* Ipswich St Mary at Stoke w St Pet
  and St Fran *St E*
STOKE PERO (not known)   *see* Porlock and Porlock Weir w
  Stoke Pero etc *B & W*
STOKE POGES (St Giles) *Ox 12*   **P** *Ch Ch Ox*
  V H N L LATHAM   **NSM** A M PARRY
STOKE PRIOR (St Luke)   *see* Leominster *Heref*
STOKE PRIOR (St Michael), Wychbold and Upton Warren
  Worc 8   **P** *Bp and D&C (alt)*   **P-in-c** V W BEYNON
  NSM A D MORRIS, G P CRELLIN
STOKE RIVERS (St Bartholomew)   *see* Shirwell, Loxhore,
  Kentisbury, Arlington, etc *Ex*
STOKE ROW (St John the Evangelist)   *see* Langtree *Ox*
STOKE ST GREGORY (St Gregory)   *see* Athelney *B & W*
STOKE ST MARY (St Mary)   *see* Beercrocombe w Curry Mallet,
  Hatch Beauchamp etc *B & W*
STOKE ST MICHAEL (St Michael)   *see* Leigh upon Mendip w
  Stoke St Michael *B & W*
STOKE ST MILBOROUGH (St Milburgha)   *see* Ludlow *Heref*
STOKE SUB HAMDON (Blessed Virgin Mary) (All Saints
  Mission Church) *B & W 5*   **P** *Ch Patr Trust*
  P-in-c P J THOMAS
STOKE TALMAGE (St Mary Magdalene)   *see* Thame *Ox*
STOKE TRISTER (St Andrew)   *see* Charlton Musgrove,
  Cucklington and Stoke Trister *B & W*
STOKE UPON TERN (St Peter)   *see* Cheswardine, Childs Ercall,
  Hales, Hinstock etc *Lich*
STOKE, EAST (St Oswald) w Syerston *S'well 3*   **P** *Bp*
  P-in-c E I MURRAY
STOKE, NORTH (St Martin)   *see* Bath Weston All SS w N Stoke
  and Langridge *B & W*
STOKE, NORTH (St Mary the Virgin)   *see* Langtree *Ox*
STOKE, SOUTH (St Andrew)   *see* Goring and Streatley w S Stoke
  Ox
STOKE, SOUTH (St James the Great)   *see* Combe Down w
  Monkton Combe and S Stoke *B & W*
STOKE, SOUTH (St Leonard)   *see* Arundel w Tortington and
  S Stoke *Chich*
STOKE, WEST (St Andrew)   *see* Funtington and W Stoke w
  Sennicotts *Chich*
STOKEHAM (St Peter)   *see* Retford Area *S'well*
STOKEINTEIGNHEAD (St Andrew)   *see* Shaldon,
  Stokeinteignhead, Combeinteignhead etc *Ex*
STOKENCHURCH (St Peter and St Paul) and Ibstone *Ox 18*
  P *Bp*   **P-in-c** R A FRANCE
STOKE-NEXT-GUILDFORD (St John the Evangelist) *Guildf 5*
  P *Simeon's Trustees*   **R** M C WOODWARD   **C** K THOMAS
STOKENHAM (St Michael and All Angels), Slapton, Charleton
  w Buckland-Tout-Saints, East Portlemouth, South Pool, and
  Chivelstone *Ex 13*   **P** *Prime Min (1 turn), Bp, DBP, Sir Neil*
  Jephcott Bt, and Ms S Tyler (1 turn), and Ld Chan (1 turn)
  NSM M NORTH
STOKESAY (St Christopher) (St John the Baptist) *Heref 10*
  P *T P D La Touche Esq*   **P-in-c** T E JESSIMAN
  NSM M G WILLIAMS
STOKESBY (St Andrew)   *see* S Trin Broads *Nor*
STOKESLEY (St Peter and St Paul) w Seamer *York 20*   **P** *Abp*
  R A P HUTCHINSON   **C** S E STRAND   **NSM** G MCCLEAVE
STOKE-UPON-TRENT (St Peter-ad-Vincula) (St Paul) *Lich 12*
  P *Bp*   **TR** D P LINGWOOD   **TV** G E EZE   **C** V L FLANAGAN
  OLM H W DUROSE
STOLFORD (St Peter)   *see* Quantock Coast *B & W*

STON EASTON (Blessed Virgin Mary)   *see* Chewton Mendip w
  Ston Easton, Litton etc *B & W*
STONDON (All Saints)   *see* Gravenhurst, Shillington and
  Stondon *St Alb*
STONDON MASSEY (St Peter and St Paul)   *see* Blackmore and
  Stondon Massey *Chelmsf*
STONE (All Saints)   *see* Berkeley w Wick, Breadstone, Newport,
  Stone etc *Glouc*
STONE (Christ Church) and Oulton-with-Moddershall *Lich 13*
  P *Simeon's Trustees*   **V** P H C KINGMAN
STONE (St John the Baptist) w Dinton and Hartwell *Ox 10*
  P *Bp and Grocers' Co (jt)*   **P-in-c** P G RICH
STONE (St Mary the Virgin)   *see* Kidderminster E *Worc*
STONE (St Michael and St Wulfad) w Aston (St Saviour)
  Lich 13   **P** *Bp*   **R** I R CARDINAL   **NSM** J G COTTERILL
STONE CROSS (St Luke) w Langney, North *Chich 14*
  P *Bp*   **V** J D VINE   **C** T HOCKLEY
STONE near Dartford (St Mary) *Roch 2*   **P** *Bp*   **R** K W CLARK
STONE QUARRY (St Luke)   *see* E Grinstead St Swithun *Chich*
STONEBRIDGE (St Michael and All Angels) *Lon 21*   **P** *Bp*
  V R HERBERT
STONEBROOM (St Peter)   *see* Morton and Stonebroom w
  Shirland *Derby*
STONEGATE (St Peter) *Chich 16*   **P** *E J B Hardcastle Esq and Mrs*
  C J J Reid (jt)   **P-in-c** J R JAMES
STONEGRAVE (Holy Trinity)   *see* Ampleforth w Oswaldkirk,
  Gilling E etc *York*
STONEHAM, NORTH (St Nicholas) (All Saints) and Bassett
  Win 10   **P** R H W *Fleming Esq*   **NSM** R PRIETO-DURAN
STONEHAM, SOUTH (St Mary)   *see* Swaythling *Win*
STONEHOUSE (St Cyr) *Glouc 4*   **P** *The Crown*
  P-in-c C S MINCHIN
STONE-IN-OXNEY (St Mary the Virgin)   *see* Rother and Oxney
  Cant
STONELEIGH (St John the Baptist) *Guildf 9*   **P** *Bp*
  V L M HELLMUTH
STONELEIGH (St Mary the Virgin) w Ashow *Cov 4*   **P** *Lord*
  Leigh and Bp (jt)   **P-in-c** S L GOBLE
STONESBY (St Peter)   *see* Ironstone Villages *Leic*
STONESFIELD (St James the Great) w Combe Longa *Ox 29*
  P *Duke of Marlborough*   **P-in-c** A R TURNER
STONEY MIDDLETON (St Martin)   *see* Longstone, Curbar and
  Stony Middleton *Derby*
STONEY STANTON (St Michael)   *see* Broughton Astley and
  Croft w Stoney Stanton *Leic*
STONEYCROFT (All Saints) *Liv 8*   **P** *Bp*   **V** R W WILLIAMS
  C A COOPER   **NSM** S-A MASON
STONHAM ASPAL (St Mary and St Lambert)   *see* Crowfield w
  Stonham Aspal and Mickfield *St E*
STONNALL (St Peter)   *see* Shenstone and Stonnall *Lich*
STONTON WYVILLE (St Denys)   *see* Welham, Glooston and
  Cranoe and Stonton Wyville *Leic*
STONY STRATFORD (St Mary and St Giles) w Calverton *Ox 14*
  P *Bp and DBP (jt)*   **R** R NORTHING   **C** B G DRURY
STONYDELPH (St Martin in the Delph)   *see* Glascote and
  Stonydelph *Lich*
STOODLEIGH (St Margaret)   *see* Washfield, Stoodleigh,
  Withleigh etc *Ex*
STOPHAM (St Mary the Virgin) and Fittleworth *Chich 10*
  P *D&C and Col Sir Brian Barttelot Bt (jt)*   **R** vacant
STOPSLEY (St Thomas) *St Alb 12*   **P** *Bp*   **V** D G ALEXANDER
STORRIDGE (St John the Baptist)   *see* Cradley w Mathon and
  Storridge *Heref*
STORRINGTON (St Mary) *Chich 11*   **P** *Keble Coll Ox*
  R K A WINDSLOW   **C** C P SPENCER   **Hon C** C A HADLEY
  NSM A R ROSS
STOTFOLD (St Mary the Virgin) and Radwell *St Alb 3*
  P *Bp*   **V** W T BRITT
STOTTESDON (St Mary) w Farlow, Cleeton St Mary,
  Silvington, Sidbury and Middleton Scriven *Heref 8*
  P *Bp*   **P-in-c** M H DABORN
STOUGHTON (Emmanuel) *Guildf 5*   **P** *Simeon's Trustees*
  V F SCAMMELL   **C** S CHATTEN   **OLM** R P F MASTERS
STOUGHTON (St Mary)   *see* Octagon *Chich*
STOULTON (St Edmund) w Drake's Broughton and Pirton
  and Norton *Worc 4*   **P** *Croome Estate Trustees, D&C, and Bp*
  (jt)   **R** D G SLOGGETT
STOUR PROVOST (St Michael and All Angels)   *see* Stour Vale
  Sarum
STOUR ROW (All Saints) *as above*
STOUR VALE *Sarum 5*   **P** *Bp*   **V** A HAGENBUCH
STOUR VALLEY, The *St E 8*   **P** *DBP, Jes Coll Cam, Lady Loch, and*
  Duchy of Lanc (by turn)   **R** S MITCHELL
STOUR, EAST (Christ Church)   *see* Stour Vale *Sarum*
STOUR, UPPER *Sarum 12*   **P** H C *Hoare Esq (1 turn), Bp (2 turns),*
  and Bourton Chpl Trustees (1 turn)   **R** vacant

STOUR, WEST (St Mary)   *see* Stour Vale *Sarum*
STOURBRIDGE (St Michael and All Angels) Norton *Worc 12*
P *Bp*   P-in-c N G KALENIUK
STOURBRIDGE (St Thomas) *Worc 12*   P *Bp*   V A K SILLIS
P-in-c A K SILLIS
STOURDENE Group, The *Cov 9*   P *SMF, Bp, Major and Mrs
J E Shirley, Miss M L P Shirley, P E Shirley Esq, Ch Ch Ox,
Jes Coll Ox, and Mr and Mrs G Howell*   R C M VICKERS
C A J MASSEY   NSM J HORTON
STOURHEAD *St E 8*   P E H Vestey Esq, St Chad's Coll Dur,
Ridley Hall Cam, and Walsingham Coll Trust (jt)*   V D HOLLIS
STOURPAINE (Holy Trinity)   *see* Pimperne, Stourpaine,
Durweston and Bryanston *Sarum*
STOURPORT-ON-SEVERN (St Michael and All Angels) and
Wilden *Worc 13*   P *Earl Baldwin of Bewdley and V
Kidderminster St Mary and All SS (jt)*   V I E MCINTYRE
STOURTON (St Peter)   *see* Upper Stour *Sarum*
STOURTON CAUNDLE (St Peter)   *see* Spire Hill *Sarum*
STOVEN (St Margaret)   *see* Hundred River and Wainford *St E*
STOW BARDOLPH (Holy Trinity)   *see* Wimbotsham w Stow
Bardolph and Stow Bridge etc *Ely*
STOW BEDON (St Botolph)   *see* Caston, Griston, Merton,
Thompson etc *Nor*
STOW BRIDGE Mission (St Peter)   *see* Wimbotsham w Stow
Bardolph and Stow Bridge etc *Ely*
STOW Group, The (St Mary the Virgin) *Linc 2*   P *Bp and DBP
(jt)*   OLM J A VICKERS, P I ROSE
STOW LONGA (St Botolph)   *see* Kym Valley *Ely*
STOW MARIES (St Mary and St Margaret)   *see* Cold Norton w
Stow Maries *Chelmsf*
STOW ON THE WOLD (St Edward), Condicote and The Swells
Glouc 8   P *DBP and Ch Ch Ox (jt)*   R M P SHORT
C J A GOODWIN
STOW, WEST (St Mary)   *see* Lark Valley *St E*
STOWE (Assumption of St Mary the Virgin) *Ox 11*   P *Stowe
Sch*   P-in-c S A SAMPSON
STOWE (St Michael and All Angels)   *see* Middle Marches *Heref*
STOWE BY CHARTLEY (St John the Baptist)   *see* Mid Trent *Lich*
STOWE NINE CHURCHES (St Michael)   *see* Heyford w Stowe
Nine Churches and Flore etc *Pet*
STOWE, UPPER (St James) *as above*
STOWELL (St Leonard)   *see* Chedworth, Yanworth and Stowell,
Coln Rogers etc *Glouc*
STOWELL (St Mary Magdalene)   *see* Milborne Port w Goathill
etc *B & W*
STOWEY (St Nicholas and Blessed Virgin Mary)   *see* Clutton w
Cameley, Bishop Sutton and Stowey *B & W*
STOWEY, NETHER (Blessed Virgin Mary)   *see* Aisholt, Enmore,
Goathurst, Nether Stowey etc *B & W*
STOWEY, OVER (St Peter and St Paul) *as above*
STOWFORD (St John the Baptist)   *see* Lifton,
Broadwoodwidger, Stowford etc *Ex*
STOWLANGTOFT (St George)   *see* Badwell and Walsham *St E*
STOWMARKET (St Peter and St Mary) *St E 6*   P *Ch Patr Trust*
V M W EDEN   NSM R M STRETCH
STOWTING (St Mary the Virgin)   *see* A20 Benefice *Cant*
STOWUPLAND (Holy Trinity)   *see* Haughley w Wetherden and
Stowupland *St E*
STRADBROKE (All Saints)   *see* Sancroft *St E*
STRADISHALL (St Margaret)   *see* Bansfield *St E*
STRADSETT (St Mary)   *see* Downham Market and
Crimplesham w Stradsett *Ely*
STRAGGLETHORPE (St Michael)   *see* Brant Broughton and
Beckingham *Linc*
STRAITS, The (St Andrew)   *see* Gornal and Sedgley *Worc*
STRAMSHALL (St Michael and All Angels)   *see* Uttoxeter Area
Lich
STRANTON (All Saints) *Dur 3*   P St Jo Coll Dur
P-in-c N R SHAVE   C N J MOORE   NSM A J CRAIG, S C JAY
STRATFIELD MORTIMER (St Mary) and Mortimer West End w
Padworth *Ox 4*   P *Eton Coll, Ld Chan, and Englefield Estate
Trust Corp (by turn)*   V P CHAPLIN
STRATFIELD SAYE (St Mary)   *see* Sherfield-on-Loddon and
Stratfield Saye etc *Win*
STRATFORD (St John the Evangelist w Christ Church)
Chelmsf 5   P V W Ham   V D A RICHARDS
C A-M MCTIGHE
STRATFORD (St Paul) and St James *Chelmsf 5*   P *Ch Patr
Trust*   P-in-c J S FRASER   C A-M MCTIGHE
Hon C D M WEBB   NSM J V MEADWAY
OLM I B ANDERSON, M G P BENNETT
STRATFORD ST MARY (St Mary)   *see* Higham, Holton St Mary,
Raydon and Stratford *St E*
STRATFORD SUB CASTLE (St Lawrence)   *see* Salisbury St Fran
and Stratford sub Castle *Sarum*

STRATFORD-UPON-AVON (Holy Trinity), Luddington and
Clifford Chambers *Cov 8*   P *Bp*   R P J TAYLOR
C S D BATE   NSM N M CHATTERTON
STRATTON (St Andrew) and Launcells *Truro 8*   P *Duchy of
Cornwall and CPAS (alt)*   P-in-c D K BARNES   C A J HARDY
STRATTON (St Mary the Virgin)   *see* Bradford Peverell, Stratton,
Frampton etc *Sarum*
STRATTON (St Mary) (St Michael) and Wacton *Nor 5*
P *G&C Coll Cam, DBP, and New Coll Ox (by turn)*
R H Y WILCOX   OLM E R SPRY, G M OSBORNE
STRATTON (St Peter)   *see* Churn Valley *Glouc*
STRATTON AUDLEY (St Mary and St Edburga)   *see* Shelswell *Ox*
STRATTON ON THE FOSSE (St Vigor)   *see* Chilcompton w
Downside and Stratton on the Fosse *B & W*
STRATTON ST MARGARET (St Margaret) w South Marston
and Stanton Fitzwarren *Bris 7*   P *Patr Bd*
P-in-c V R FLEMING   C H C BABER
STRATTON STRAWLESS (St Margaret)   *see* Coltishall w Gt
Hautbois, Frettenham etc *Nor*
STRATTON, EAST (All Saints)   *see* Upper Dever *Win*
STRATTON, UPPER (St Philip) *Bris 7*   P *Bp*
NSM E P MUKHOLI
STREAT (not known)   *see* Ditchling, Streat and Westmeston
Chich
STREATHAM (Christ Church) *S'wark 12*   P *Bp and R Streatham
St Leon (jt)*   V S TRICKLEBANK
STREATHAM (Immanuel) (St Andrew) *S'wark 12*   P *Bp,
Hyndman Trustees, and R Streatham St Leon (jt)*
V E M SHEARCROFT
STREATHAM (St Leonard) *S'wark 12*   P *Bp*   R A J HODGSON
C J B REY
STREATHAM (St Peter) *S'wark 12*   P St Steph Ho Ox
V P D ANDREWS
STREATHAM HILL (St Margaret the Queen) *S'wark 12*
P *Bp*   P-in-c D J STEPHENSON   C G S A POWELL
STREATHAM PARK (St Alban)   *see* Furzedown *S'wark*
STREATHAM VALE (Holy Redeemer) *S'wark 12*   P CPAS
V I H GILMOUR
STREATHAM, WEST (St James)   *see* Furzedown *S'wark*
STREATLEY (St Margaret) *St Alb 12*   P *Bp*   V S P WOOD
STREATLEY (St Mary)   *see* Goring and Streatley w S Stoke *Ox*
STREET (Holy Trinity) (Mission Church) w Walton *B & W 4*
P *DBP*   R S A WALKER   C D M GREENFIELD
Hon C D N HATREY
STREET Parishes, The *York 6*   P *Patr Bd*   R M E ALLWOOD
STREETLY (All Saints) *Lich 25*   P *Bp*   V A F WALKER
OLM J W BLUNT
STRELLEY (All Saints)   *see* Bilborough and Strelley *S'well*
STRENSALL (St Mary the Virgin) *York 3*   P *Abp*
V M HARRISON   C R P SUEKARRAN
STRETE (St Michael)   *see* Stoke Fleming, Blackawton and Strete
Ex
STRETFORD (All Saints) *Man 5*   P *Bp*   R *vacant*
STRETFORD (St Matthew) *Man 5*   P *D&C*
P-in-c K L BURGESS   NSM S W SCHOFIELD
STRETHALL (St Mary the Virgin)   *see* Icknield Way Villages
Chelmsf
STRETHAM (St James)   *see* Ely *Ely*
STRETTON (St John)   *see* Penkridge *Lich*
STRETTON (St Mary) w Claymills *Lich 14*   P *Baroness Gretton*
V K A THOMAS   NSM D V WARNER
STRETTON (St Matthew) and Appleton Thorn *Ches 4*
P *Mrs P F du Bois Grantham and Dr S P L du Bois Davidson (jt)*
V A D J JEWELL
STRETTON (St Nicholas)   *see* Cottesmore and Burley,
Clipsham, Exton etc *Pet*
STRETTON GRANDISON (St Lawrence)   *see* Ledbury *Heref*
STRETTON ON DUNSMORE (All Saints)   *see* Draycote Gp *Cov*
STRETTON ON DUNSMORE (Mission Church) *as above*
STRETTON ON FOSSE (St Peter)   *see* Ilmington w Stretton-on-
Fosse etc *Cov*
STRETTON PARVA (St John the Baptist)   *see* Gaulby *Leic*
STRETTON SUGWAS (St Mary Magdalene) *Heref 3*   P *DBP*
P-in-c P A LITTLEWOOD   NSM E S V VERWEY
STRETTON, LITTLE (All Saints)   *see* Church Stretton *Heref*
STRICKLAND, GREAT (St Barnabas)   *see* Morland, Thrimby,
Gt Strickland and Cliburn *Carl*
STRINES (St Paul)   *see* Marple All SS *Ches*
STRINGSTON (St Mary the Virgin)   *see* Quantock Coast *B & W*
STRIXTON (St Romwald)   *see* Wollaston w Strixton and Bozeat
etc *Pet*
STROOD (St Francis) *Roch 6*   P *Bp*   V S L COPESTAKE
STROOD (St Nicholas) w St Mary *Roch 6*   P *Bp and D&C (jt)*
V D W GREEN   C L J POWELL
STROUD (Holy Trinity)   *see* Stroud Team *Glouc*
STROUD (Mission Church)   *see* Steep and Froxfield w Privett
Portsm

STROUD (St Alban Mission Church) *see* Stroud Team *Glouc*
STROUD GREEN (Holy Trinity) *Lon 20* **P** *Bp*
V P J HENDERSON **C** T D PIKE **NSM** P G ATHERTON
STROUD Team Ministry, The (St Laurence) (Holy Trinity)
(St Alban Mission Church) *Glouc 4* **P** *Patr Bd*
TR M S KING **TV** B WOOLLASTON, P F QUINNELL,
S G HOWELL **C** J G CLARK **NSM** M J PAGE
STROXTON (All Saints) *see* Harlaxton Gp *Linc*
STRUBBY (St Oswald) *see* Legbourne and Wold Marsh *Linc*
STRUMPSHAW (St Peter) *see* Burlingham St Edmund w
Lingwood, Strumpshaw etc *Nor*
STUBBINGS (St James the Less) *see* Burchetts Green *Ox*
STUBBINS (St Philip) *see* Ramsbottom and Edenfield *Man*
STUBBS CROSS (St Francis) *see* Kingsnorth and Shadoxhurst
Cant
STUBSHAW CROSS (St Luke) *see* Ashton-in-Makerfield St Thos
Liv
STUBTON (St Martin) *see* Claypole *Linc*
STUDHAM (St Mary the Virgin) *see* Kensworth, Studham and
Whipsnade *St Alb*
STUDLAND (St Nicholas) *see* Swanage and Studland *Sarum*
STUDLEY (Nativity of the Blessed Virgin Mary) *see* Arden
Marches *Cov*
STUDLEY (St John the Evangelist) *Sarum 15* **P** *R Trowbridge*
St Jas **V** S F DEACON **NSM** E A GIFFORD
STUKELEY, GREAT (St Bartholomew) *see* Huntingdon All SS w
St Jo St Mary etc *Ely*
STUKELEY, LITTLE (St Martin) *as above*
STUNTNEY (Holy Cross) *see* Ely *Ely*
STURMER (St Mary) *see* Two Rivers *Chelmsf*
STURMINSTER MARSHALL (St Mary) *see* Bridge Par *Sarum*
STURMINSTER NEWTON (St Mary), Hinton St Mary and
Lydlinch *Sarum 5* **P** *Col J L Yeatman (1 turn), G A L-F Pitt-*
Rivers Esq (3 turns), V Iwerne Valley (1 turn) **V** D R R SEYMOUR
NSM L M S COOK
STURRY (St Nicholas) w Fordwich and Westbere w Hersden
Cant 3 **P** *Abp, Ld Chan, and St Aug Foundn Cant (by turn)*
R P A CORNISH
STURTON (St Hugh) *see* Stow Gp *Linc*
STURTON, GREAT (All Saints) *see* Hemingby Gp *Linc*
STURTON-LE-STEEPLE (St Peter and St Paul) *see* Retford Area
S'well
STUSTON (All Saints) *see* N Hartismere *St E*
STUTTON (St Peter) *see* Holbrook, Stutton, Freston,
Woolverstone etc *St E*
STYVECHALE (St James) *Cov 3* **P** *Col A M H Gregory-Hood*
V J M MAYNARD **OLM** A PRETT, C M NEWBORN
SUCKLEY (St John the Baptist) *see* Worcs W *Worc*
SUDBOROUGH (All Saints) *see* Brigstock w Stanion and Lowick
and Sudborough *Pet*
SUDBOURNE (All Saints) *see* Wilford Peninsula *St E*
SUDBROOKE (St Edward) *see* Barlings *Linc*
SUDBURY (All Saints) *see* S Dales *Derby*
SUDBURY (All Saints) w Ballingdon and Brundon *St E 12*
P *Simeon's Trustees* **P-in-c** S D GILL **NSM** J M RIDLEY
SUDBURY (St Andrew) *Lon 21* **P** *Bp* **V** G S THOMAS
SUDBURY (St Gregory) St Peter and Chilton *St E 12*
P *Bp (3 turns), Ch Soc Trust (1 turn)* **NSM** H M MITCHELL
SUDDEN (St Aidan) and Heywood All Souls *Man 14*
P *Patr Bd* **P-in-c** M A READ **OLM** I TAYLOR
SUDELEY MANOR (St Mary) *see* Winchcombe *Glouc*
SUFFIELD (St Margaret) *see* King's Beck *Nor*
SUFFIELD PARK (St Martin) *see* Cromer *Nor*
SUGLEY (Holy Saviour) *Newc 4* **P** *Bp* **V** A J FORD
SULBY (St Stephen's Chapel) *see* Andreas, Ballaugh, Jurby and
Sulby *S & M*
SULGRAVE (St James the Less) *see* Culworth w Sulgrave and
Thorpe Mandeville etc *Pet*
SULHAM (St Nicholas) *see* Pangbourne w Tidmarsh and
Sulham *Ox*
SULHAMSTEAD ABBOTS (St Mary) and Bannister w Ufton
Nervet *Ox 4* **P** *Qu Coll Ox and Or Coll Ox (alt)*
P-in-c W H N WATTS
SULLINGTON (St Mary) and Thakeham w Warminghurst
Chich 11 **P** *Bp and DBP (alt)* **R** D K SPENCER
SUMMERFIELD (Christ Church) (Cavendish Road Hall) *Birm 2*
P *R Birm St Martin w Bordesley* **V** P D SAINSBURY
SUMMERSDALE (St Michael) *see* Chich St Paul and
Westhampnett *Chich*
SUMMERSTOWN (St Mary) *S'wark 17* **P** *Ch Soc Trust*
V R J RYAN
SUMMERTOWN (St Michael and All Angels) *Ox 2* **P** *St Jo*
Coll Ox **V** G R KNIGHT **C** S M STAYTE
NSM C BANNISTER-PARKER, W L A PRYOR
SUNBURY, UPPER (St Saviour) *Lon 13* **P** *V Sunbury*
V R CROSS **C** C M A CLARKE

SUNBURY-ON-THAMES (St Mary) *Lon 13* **P** *D&C St Paul's*
Emer S P THOMPSON
SUNDERLAND (St Bede) Town End Farm *see* N Wearside *Dur*
SUNDERLAND (St Chad) *Dur 1* **P** *Bp* **V** J D CHADD
NSM P THOMPSON
SUNDERLAND (St Cuthbert) Red House *see* N Wearside *Dur*
SUNDERLAND (St Ignatius) *see* Hendon *Dur*
SUNDERLAND (St Mary the Virgin) (St Peter) *Dur 1* **P** *Bp*
P-in-c K J BAGNALL
SUNDERLAND (St Thomas) (St Oswald) *Dur 1* **P** *Bp*
V *vacant*
SUNDERLAND MINSTER (St Michael and All Angels and
St Benedict Biscop) Extra-Parochial Place *Dur 1*
Can Provost S J BAMBER **C** F M COLLIN **Hon C** C S HOWSON
Min A C DOWSETT
SUNDERLAND POINT (Mission Church) *see* Overton *Blackb*
SUNDERLAND, NORTH (St Paul) *Newc 7* **P** *Lord Crewe's*
Trustees **V** J R GLOVER
SUNDON (St Mary) *St Alb 12* **P** *Bp* **P-in-c** Y M SMEJKAL
SUNDRIDGE (St Mary) w Ide Hill and Toys Hill *Roch 9*
P *Abp* **R** P E DAVIES **NSM** A M BOYLE, L LEITHEAD
SUNNINGDALE (Holy Trinity) *Ox 3* **P** *Bp* **V** H D UFFINDELL
C S M COOKE
SUNNINGHILL (St Michael and All Angels) and South Ascot
Ox 3 **P** *St Jo Coll Cam* **V** S A JOHNSON
NSM T L WILLIAMS **OLM** J M JONES
SUNNINGWELL (St Leonard) *see* Radley, Sunningwell and
Kennington *Ox*
SUNNYSIDE (St Barnabas) *see* E Grinstead St Swithun *Chich*
SUNNYSIDE (St Michael and All Angels) w Bourne End
St Alb 1 **P** *CPAS* **V** D J ABBOTT **NSM** R CLARKSON
SURBITON (St Andrew) (St Mark) *S'wark 15* **P** *Bp*
V R S STANIER **C** L SELMAN
SURBITON HILL (Christ Church) *S'wark 15* **P** *Ch Soc Trust and*
Trustees (jt) **V** J D BIRCHALL **C** J B ERLEBACH, S D SWINNEY
SURFLEET (St Laurence) *see* Glen Gp *Linc*
SURLINGHAM (St Mary) *see* Rockland St Mary w Hellington,
Bramerton etc *Nor*
SURREY WEALD *Guildf 7* **P** *Patr Bd (1 turn), Ld Chan (2 turns)*
TR A D J COE **TV** B STEADMAN-ALLEN
NSM E R RICHARDSON, N E COE
SUSTEAD (St Peter and St Paul) *see* Roughton and Felbrigg,
Metton, Sustead etc *Nor*
SUTTERTON (St Mary) *see* Haven Gp *Linc*
SUTTON (All Saints) *see* Potton w Sutton and Cockayne Hatley
St Alb
SUTTON (All Saints) *see* Wilford Peninsula *St E*
SUTTON (Christ Church) (St Barnabas) (St Nicholas)
S'wark 23 **P** *Patr Bd* **TR** J MIDDLEMISS **C** C SCHNYDER,
S F SEWELL **NSM** B FRASER
SUTTON (St Andrew) *Ely 8* **P** *D&C* **P-in-c** M HANCOCK
SUTTON (St Barnabas' Mission Church) *see* Macclesfield Team
Ches
SUTTON (St Clement), Huttoft and Anderby *Linc 10*
P *Bp (2 turns), Magd Coll Cam (1 turn)* **R** P J LILEY
Hon C C H LILLEY **OLM** J TOMPKINS
SUTTON (St James) *York 14* **P** *Abp* **V** D J CLUNE
SUTTON (St James), Wincle, Wildboarclough and Bosley
Ches 13 **P** *Patr Bd* **V** J E HARRIES
SUTTON (St John the Baptist) *see* Barlavington, Burton w
Coates, Sutton and Bignor *Chich*
SUTTON (St Mary) *see* Calow and Sutton cum Duckmanton
Derby
SUTTON (St Michael and All Angels) *see* Castor w Upton and
Stibbington and Water Newton, Marholm and Sutton *Pet*
SUTTON (St Michael) *see* Stalham, E Ruston, Brunstead,
Sutton and Ingham *Nor*
SUTTON (St Nicholas) (All Saints) (St Michael and All Angels)
Liv 10 **P** *Patr Bd* **TR** A J BRUCE **TV** M J TAYLOR
C D S LANGDON-GRIFFITHS
SUTTON (St Thomas) w Cowling and Lothersdale *Leeds 5*
P *Ch Ch Ox and Bp (jt)* **V** H M COLLINGS **NSM** T CALOW
SUTTON BASSETT (All Saints) *see* Stoke Albany w Wilbarston
and Ashley etc *Pet*
SUTTON BENGER (All Saints) *see* Draycot *Bris*
SUTTON BINGHAM (All Saints) *see* Coker Ridge *B & W*
SUTTON BONINGTON (St Michael) (St Anne) w Normanton-
on-Soar *S'well 6* **P** *Bp* **P-in-c** M J BROCK
NSM K CHARLES
SUTTON BRIDGE (St Matthew) and Tydd St Mary *Linc 18*
P *Bp and Ld Chan (alt)* **V** D A OXTOBY
SUTTON BY DOVER (St Peter and St Paul) *see* Ringwould w
Kingsdown and Ripple etc *Cant*
SUTTON CHENEY (St James) *see* Bosworth and Sheepy Gp *Leic*
SUTTON COLDFIELD (Holy Trinity) *Birm 12* **P** *Bp*
R W J ROUTH

SUTTON COLDFIELD (St Chad) *Birm 12*   P *Bp*
 V J NICHOLAS
SUTTON COLDFIELD (St Columba) *Birm 12*   P *Bp*
 V R P TUCKER
SUTTON COURTENAY (All Saints) w Appleford *Ox 19*
    P *D&C Windsor*   P-in-c H G KENDRICK   NSM T W HEWES
SUTTON GREEN (All Souls)   *see* Woking St Pet *Guildf*
SUTTON HILL (Pastoral Centre)   *see* Madeley *Heref*
SUTTON IN ASHFIELD (St Mary Magdalene) *S'well 4*
    P *Bp*   V D W JAMES   C M C A'HERNE-SMITH
SUTTON IN ASHFIELD St Michael and All Angels *S'well 4*
    P *Bp*   V vacant
SUTTON IN HOLDERNESS (St Michael) *York 14*   P *Abp*
 V M A JEAVONS   C P A WICK   NSM H M HOTCHIN
SUTTON LE MARSH (St Clement)   *see* Sutton, Huttoft and
    Anderby *Linc*
SUTTON MADDOCK (St Mary)   *see* Beckbury, Badger,
    Kemberton, Ryton, Stockton etc *Lich*
SUTTON MANDEVILLE (All Saints)   *see* Nadder Valley *Sarum*
SUTTON MONTIS (Holy Trinity)   *see* Cam Vale *B & W*
SUTTON ON DERWENT (St Michael)   *see* Derwent Ings *York*
SUTTON ON THE FOREST (All Hallows)   *see* Forest of Galtres
    York
SUTTON ON THE HILL (St Michael)   *see* Boylestone, Church
    Broughton, Dalbury, etc *Derby*
SUTTON PARK (St Andrew) *York 14*   P *Abp*   V vacant
SUTTON ST EDMUND (St Edmund King and Martyr)
    see Sutton St James and Sutton St Edmund *Linc*
SUTTON ST JAMES (St James) and Sutton St Edmund *Linc 18*
    P *V Long Sutton w Lutton etc*   V vacant
SUTTON ST MICHAEL (St Michael)   *see* Maund Gp *Heref*
SUTTON ST NICHOLAS (St Nicholas)   *as above*
SUTTON UNDER BRAILES (St Thomas à Becket) *Cov 9*
    P *Bp*   R N J MORGAN   NSM J W ROLFE
SUTTON VALENCE (St Mary the Virgin)   *see* Headcorn and The
    Suttons *Cant*
SUTTON VENY (St John the Evangelist)   *see* Upper Wylye Valley
    Sarum
SUTTON WALDRON (St Bartholomew)   *see* Iwerne Valley
    Sarum
SUTTON, EAST (St Peter and St Paul)   *see* Headcorn and The
    Suttons *Cant*
SUTTON, GREAT (St John the Evangelist) *Ches 9*
    P *V Eastham*   V A J DUTTON
SUTTON-CUM-LOUND (St Bartholomew)   *see* Retford Area
    S'well
SUTTON-ON-PLYM (St John the Evangelist), Plymouth
    St Simon and St Mary Laira *Ex 21*   P *Bp, St Simon Trustees,*
    and Keble Coll Ox (jt)   P-in-c K F HAYDON   C T P JORDAN
    NSM A OVERTON
SUTTON-ON-TRENT (All Saints)   *see* Norwell w Ossington,
    Cromwell etc *S'well*
SWABY (St Nicholas)   *see* Legbourne and Wold Marsh *Linc*
SWADLINCOTE (Emmanuel) *Derby 16*   P *V Gresley*
    P-in-c G P RUTTER
SWAFFHAM (St Peter and St Paul) and Sporle *Nor 13*
    P *Bp (2 turns), DBP (1 turn)*   V T S LAWES
    NSM H B DE LYON
SWAFFHAM BULBECK (St Mary)   *see* Anglesey Gp *Ely*
SWAFFHAM PRIOR (St Mary) *as above*
SWAFIELD (St Nicholas)   *see* Trunch Group *Nor*
SWAINSTHORPE (St Peter)   *see* Newton Flotman,
    Swainsthorpe, Tasburgh, etc *Nor*
SWAINSWICK (Blessed Virgin Mary)   *see* Bath St Sav w
    Swainswick and Woolley *B & W*
SWALCLIFFE (St Peter and St Paul)   *see* Wykeham *Ox*
SWALE, LOWER *Leeds 27*   P *D&C York, Duke of*
    Northumberland, and Bp (jt)   R C TODD   NSM M TONGE
SWALECLIFFE (St John the Baptist)   *see* Whitstable *Cant*
SWALEDALE *Leeds 24*   P *Bp*   V C J HEWLETT
SWALLOW (Holy Trinity) *Linc 7*   P *J R Thorold Esq, DBP, Bp,*
    and Earl of Yarborough (by turn)   R vacant
SWALLOWBECK (St George)   *see* Linc St Geo Swallowbeck
    Linc
SWALLOWCLIFFE (St Peter)   *see* Nadder Valley *Sarum*
SWALLOWFIELD (All Saints)   *see* Loddon Reach *Ox*
SWALWELL (Holy Trinity)   *see* Blaydon and Swalwell *Dur*
SWANAGE (All Saints) (St Mary the Virgin) and Studland
    Sarum 8   P *Patr Bd*   TR J S WOOD   TV A J CORKE
    NSM S A BOND   OLM A C HIGGINS
SWANBOURNE (St Swithun)   *see* Newton Longville, Mursley,
    Swanbourne etc *Ox*
SWANLAND (St Barnabas) *York 14*   P *CPAS*   V F R SCOTT
    NSM D KITCHING
SWANLEY (St Mary) *Roch 2*   P *Guild of All So*
    V D C BATLEY-GLADDEN

SWANLEY (St Paul) *Roch 2*   P *Merchant Taylors' Co*
    P-in-c R C SAMMÉ
SWANMORE (St Barnabas) *Portsm 1*   P *DBP*   V C L TOWNS
SWANMORE (St Michael and All Angels) *Portsm 7*   P *SMF*
    P-in-c G E MORRIS   C P J ISAAC
SWANNINGTON (St George)   *see* Whitwick, Thringstone and
    Swannington *Leic*
SWANNINGTON (St Margaret)   *see* Wensum Benefice *Nor*
SWANSCOMBE (St Peter and St Paul) *Roch 4*   P *DBP*
    P-in-c M T HURLEY
SWANTON ABBOT (St Michael)   *see* Worstead, Westwick,
    Sloley, Swanton Abbot etc *Nor*
SWANTON MORLEY (All Saints)   *see* Dereham and Distr *Nor*
SWANTON NOVERS (St Edmund)   *see* Brinton, Briningham,
    Hunworth, Stody etc *Nor*
SWANWICK (St Andrew) and Pentrich *Derby 1*   P *Wright*
    Trustees and Duke of Devonshire (alt)   V vacant
SWARBY (St Mary and All Saints)   *see* S Lafford *Linc*
SWARCLIFFE (St Luke)   *see* Seacroft *Leeds*
SWARDESTON (St Mary the Virgin) w East Carleton,
    Intwood, Keswick and Ketteringham *Nor 7*   P *Bp, DBP,*
    and Miss M B Unthank (jt)   R P D BURR
SWARKESTONE (St James)   *see* Aston on Trent, Elvaston,
    Weston on Trent etc *Derby*
SWATON (St Michael)   *see* Heckington and Helpringham Gp
    Linc
SWAVESEY (St Andrew)   *see* Fen Drayton w Conington and
    Lolworth etc *Ely*
SWAY (St Luke) *Win 11*   P *Bp*   V J PAWSON
    NSM R D C ELLIOTT
SWAYFIELD (St Nicholas)   *see* Corby Glen *Linc*
SWAYTHLING (St Mary) (St Alban the Martyr) *Win 13*
    P *Bp and TR Southn City Cen (jt)*   V P M DOCKREE
SWEFFLING (St Mary)   *see* Upper Alde *St E*
SWELL (St Catherine)   *see* Curry Rivel w Fivehead and Swell
    B & W
SWELL, LOWER (St Mary)   *see* Stow on the Wold, Condicote
    and The Swells *Glouc*
SWELL, UPPER (St Mary) *as above*
SWEPSTONE (St Peter)   *see* Woodfield *Leic*
SWERFORD (St Mary)   *see* Hook Norton w Gt Rollright,
    Swerford etc *Ox*
SWETTENHAM (St Peter)   *see* Goostrey w Swettenham *Ches*
SWILLAND (St Mary)   *see* Carlford *St E*
SWILLINGTON (St Mary) *Leeds 17*   P *Bp*   P-in-c R E HAYES
SWIMBRIDGE (St James the Apostle) w West Buckland and
    Landkey *Ex 17*   P *Bp and Trustees Earl Fortescue (jt)*
    P-in-c S O'ROURKE   NSM G F SQUIRE
SWINBROOK (St Mary)   *see* Burford w Fulbrook, Taynton,
    Asthall etc *Ox*
SWINDERBY (All Saints) *Linc 12*   P *Bp, Ld Chan, E M K Kirk*
    Esq, and D&C (by turn)   NSM J T ROOKE   OLM P W WALKER
SWINDON (All Saints) (St Barnabas) *Bris 7*   P *Bp*
    P-in-c H L GIBBONS   C A M OVERTON-BENGE
SWINDON (Christ Church) (St Mary) *Bris 7*   P *Ld Chan*
    V S M STEVENETTE   NSM N E MCKEMEY
    OLM D A HARDWICK
SWINDON (St Andrew) (St John the Baptist) *Bris 7*   P *Ld*
    Chan   P-in-c L E FLETCHER   NSM T M MICHAUX
SWINDON (St Augustine) *Bris 7*   P *Bp*   P-in-c H L GIBBONS
    C A M OVERTON-BENGE
SWINDON (St John the Evangelist)   *see* Smestow Vale *Lich*
SWINDON (St Lawrence)   *see* N Cheltenham *Glouc*
SWINDON (St Peter)   *see* Penhill *Bris*
SWINDON Dorcan *Bris 7*   P *Bp*   P-in-c T A WIGLEY
    OLM S F FISHER
SWINDON New Town (St Mark) (St Adhelm) (St Luke)
    (St Saviour) *Bris 7*   P *Patr Bd*   P-in-c D L BRACEY
SWINDON, NORTH (St Andrew) *Bris 7*   P *Bp*
    P-in-c C J BASTON   Hon C A E FAULKNER   NSM P C ASHBY,
    R E COOK
SWINDON, WEST and the Lydiards *Bris 7*   P *Bp*
    TV C D DEVERELL, T V ROBERTS   NSM P F ROBERTS
SWINE (St Mary)   *see* Skirlaugh, Catwick, Long Riston, Rise,
    Swine w Ellerby *York*
SWINEFLEET (St Margaret)   *see* The Marshland *Sheff*
SWINESHEAD (St Mary)   *see* Haven Gp *Linc*
SWINESHEAD (St Nicholas)   *see* The Stodden Churches *St Alb*
SWINFORD (All Saints)   *see* Gilmorton, Peatling Parva, Kimcote
    etc *Leic*
SWINFORD, OLD Stourbridge (St Mary) *Worc 12*   P *Bp*
    P-in-c S M AGNEW
SWINHOPE (St Helen)   *see* Binbrook Gp *Linc*
SWINNOW (Christ the Saviour)   *see* Stanningley St Thos *Leeds*
SWINSTEAD (St Mary)   *see* Edenham w Witham on the Hill
    and Swinstead *Linc*

SWINTON (Holy Rood) *Man 18* **P** *TR Swinton and Pendlebury*
P-in-c D E FAIR **C** G TURNER
SWINTON (St Margaret) *Sheff 12* **P** *Sir Philip Naylor-Leyland
Bt* **V** C J BARLEY **C** C BRADING
SWINTON (St Peter) and Pendlebury *Man 18* **P** *Patr Bd*
TR J P SHEEHY
SWISS COTTAGE (Holy Trinity) *see* W Hampstead Trin *Lon*
SWITHLAND (St Leonard) *see* Woodhouse, Woodhouse Eaves
and Swithland *Leic*
SWYNCOMBE (St Botolph) *see* Icknield *Ox*
SWYNNERTON (St Mary) *see* Cotes Heath and Standon and
Swynnerton etc *Lich*
SWYRE (Holy Trinity) *see* Bride Valley *Sarum*
SYDE (St Mary) *see* Brimpsfield w Birdlip, Syde, Daglingworth
etc *Glouc*
SYDENHAM (All Saints) *S'wark 5* **P** *V Sydenham St Bart*
P-in-c P H SMITH
SYDENHAM (Holy Trinity) (St Augustine) *S'wark 5* **P** *Bp and
Simeon's Trustees (jt)* **NSM** M BROOKS
SYDENHAM (St Bartholomew) *S'wark 5* **P** *Earl of Dartmouth*
V M J KINGSTON **C** S P A EDMONDS
SYDENHAM (St Mary) *see* Chinnor, Sydenham, Aston Rowant
and Crowell *Ox*
SYDENHAM (St Philip) *S'wark 5* **P** *V Sydenham St Bart*
V P W TIERNAN
SYDENHAM DAMEREL (St Mary) *see* Milton Abbot,
Dunterton, Lamerton etc *Ex*
SYDENHAM, LOWER (St Michael and All Angels) *see* Forest Hill
w Lower Sydenham *S'wark*
SYDERSTONE (St Mary) *see* N and S Creake w Waterden,
Syderstone etc *Nor*
SYDLING ST NICHOLAS (St Nicholas) *see* Bradford Peverell,
Stratton, Frampton etc *Sarum*
SYERSTON (All Saints) *see* E Stoke w Syerston *S'well*
SYKEHOUSE (Holy Trinity) *see* Fishlake w Sykehouse and Kirk
Bramwith etc *Sheff*
SYLEHAM (St Mary) *see* Athelington, Denham, Horham,
Hoxne etc *St E*
SYMONDS GREEN (Christ the King) *see* Stevenage H Trin
St Alb
SYMONDSBURY (St John the Baptist) *see* Askerswell, Loders,
Powerstock and Symondsbury *Sarum*
SYRESHAM (St James) *see* Astwell Gp *Pet*
SYSONBY (St Leonard) *see* Melton Mowbray *Leic*
SYSTON (St Anne) *see* Warmley, Syston and Bitton *Bris*
SYSTON (St Mary) *see* Barkston and Hough Gp *Linc*
SYSTON (St Peter and St Paul) *see* Fosse *Leic*
SYWELL (St Peter and St Paul) *see* Mears Ashby and Hardwick
and Sywell etc *Pet*
TABLEY, OVER (St Paul) *Ches 12* **P** *Bp* **V** *vacant*
TACKLEY (St Nicholas) *see* Steeple Aston w N Aston and
Tackley *Ox*
TACOLNESTON (All Saints) *see* Upper Tas Valley *Nor*
TADCASTER (St Mary the Virgin) *York 1* **P** *J Fielden Esq and
T E Fielden Esq (1 turn), Abp (1 turn)* **V** S SHERIFF
C J M DOYLE-BRETT
**TADDINGTON (St Michael), Chelmorton and Monyash,
Hartington, Biggin and Earl Sterndale** *Derby 4* **P** *Duke of
Devonshire and V Bakewell (jt)* **V** R J BENSON
NSM J S FOUNTAIN
TADDIPORT (St Mary Magdalene) *see* Gt and Lt Torrington
and Frithelstock *Ex*
**TADLEY (St Mary) (St Peter) (St Paul) w Pamber Heath and
Silchester** *Win 4* **P** *Bp and Duke of Wellington (jt)*
R R J ST C HARLOW **Hon C** K V BATT **NSM** J R PENN
TADLEY (St Paul) *see* Tadley w Pamber Heath and Silchester
Win
TADLEY (St Peter) *as above*
TADLEY, NORTH (St Mary) *as above*
TADLOW (St Giles) *see* Shingay Gp *Ely*
TADMARTON (St Nicholas) *see* Wykeham *Ox*
TADWORTH (Good Shepherd) *S'wark 26* **P** *V Kingswood
St Andr* **V** M W ELFRED **NSM** F A HENDRY
OLM A S BLAIN
TAKELEY (Holy Trinity) w Little Canfield *Chelmsf 18* **P** *Bp and
Ch Coll Cam* **P-in-c** R J BURLES **C** K A LEPLEY
TALATON (St James the Apostle) *see* Whimple, Talaton and
Clyst St Lawr *Ex*
TALBOT VILLAGE (St Mark) *Sarum 7* **P** *Trustees*
V R A HIGGINS **C** A J HUMPHREYS
TALKE O' THE HILL (St Martin) *see* Alsagers Bank, Audley and
Talke *Lich*
TALKIN (not known) *see* Eden, Gelt and Irthing *Carl*
TALLAND (St Tallan) *Truro 12* **P** *DBP and W Gundry-Mills Esq
(alt)* **P-in-c** M E ELLIOTT
TALLINGTON (St Lawrence) *see* Uffington Gp *Linc*

TAMERTON FOLIOT (St Mary) *Ex 21* **P** *Ld Chan*
P-in-c D B M GILL
TAMERTON, NORTH (St Denis) *see* Boyton, N Tamerton,
Werrington etc *Truro*
TAMWORTH (St Editha) *Lich 4* **P** *Bp* **V** A W GORDON
C V M C VAN DEN BERGH
TANDRIDGE (St Peter) *see* Oxted *S'wark*
**TANFIELD (St Margaret of Antioch) w Burnopfield and
Dipton** *Dur 4* **P** *Bp* **V** A P MILLER
**TANFIELD, WEST (St Nicholas) and Well w Snape and North
Stainley** *Leeds 25* **P** *Bp and Mrs M E Bourne-Arton (alt)*
R *vacant*
TANGLEY (St Thomas of Canterbury) *see* Pastrow *Win*
TANGMERE (St Andrew) and Oving *Chich 2* **P** *Bp and
Duke of Richmond (jt)* **R** *vacant*
TANHOUSE The Oaks (Conventional District) *Liv 11*
C A KAZICH **Min** W D PETTY
TANKERSLEY (St Peter), Thurgoland and Wortley *Sheff 11*
P *Dowager Countess of Wharncliffe, Sir Philip Naylor-Leyland Bt,
and V Silkstone (jt)* **R** K J E HALE
TANNINGTON (St Ethelbert) *see* Four Rivers *St E*
TANSLEY (Holy Trinity) *see* Matlock Bank and Tansley *Derby*
TANSOR (St Mary) *see* Warmington, Tansor and Cotterstock
etc *Pet*
TANWORTH (St Mary Magdalene) *Birm 6* **P** *F D Muntz Esq*
V P E F CUDBY
TAPLOW (St Nicolas) and Dropmore *Ox 12* **P** *Eton Coll and
DBP (jt)* **V** *vacant*
TARDEBIGGE (St Bartholomew) *Worc 7* **P** *Earl of Plymouth*
V R M CLARK
TARLETON (Holy Trinity) *see* Rufford and Tarleton *Blackb*
TARPORLEY (St Helen) *Ches 5* **P** *Bp (4 turns), D&C (1 turn),
and Sir John Grey Regerton Bt (1 turn)* **R** G J A WATMORE
TARRANT GUNVILLE (St Mary) *see* Chase *Sarum*
TARRANT HINTON (St Mary) *as above*
TARRANT KEYNSTON (All Saints) *as above*
TARRANT MONKTON (All Saints) *as above*
TARRANT RUSHTON (St Mary) *as above*
TARRING NEVILLE (St Mary) *see* Denton w S Heighton and
Tarring Neville *Chich*
TARRING, WEST (St Andrew) *Chich 4* **P** *Abp*
P-in-c K D RICHARDS **C** M J LYON **NSM** G T SPENCER
TARRINGTON (St Philip and St James) *see* Ledbury *Heref*
TARVIN (St Andrew) *Ches 2* **P** *Bp* **V** A L D FRIEND
TASBURGH (St Mary) *see* Newton Flotman, Swainsthorpe,
Tasburgh, etc *Nor*
TASLEY (St Peter and St Paul) *see* Bridgnorth, Tasley, Astley
Abbotts, etc *Heref*
TATENHILL (St Michael and All Angels) *see* Barton under
Needwood w Dunstall and Tatenhill *Lich*
TATHAM (St James the Less) *see* E Lonsdale *Blackb*
TATHAM FELLS (Good Shepherd) *as above*
TATHWELL (St Vedast) *see* Legbourne and Wold Marsh *Linc*
TATSFIELD (St Mary) *see* Limpsfield and Tatsfield *S'wark*
TATTENHALL (St Alban) w Burwardsley and Handley *Ches 5*
P *Bp, Miss N C Barbour, and D&C (jt)* **R** L MUTETE
TATTENHAM CORNER (St Mark) *Guildf 9* **P** *Bp*
V D C WILLIAMSON
TATTENHOE (St Giles) *see* Watling Valley *Ox*
TATTERFORD (St Margaret) *see* E w W Rudham, Helhoughton
etc *Nor*
TATTERSETT (All Saints and St Andrew) *as above*
TATTERSHALL (Holy Trinity) *see* Bain Valley Gp *Linc*
TATTINGSTONE (St Mary) *see* Sproughton w Burstall,
Copdock w Washbrook etc *St E*
TATWORTH (St John the Evangelist) *see* Chaffcombe, Cricket
Malherbie etc *B & W*
TAUNTON (All Saints) *B & W 18* **P** *Bp* **V** D C W FAYLE
TAUNTON (Holy Trinity) *B & W 18* **P** *Bp* **V** J B V LAURENCE
TAUNTON (St Andrew) *B & W 18* **P** *Bp* **V** R P LODGE
TAUNTON (St James) *B & W 18* **P** *Simeon's Trustees*
V T R N JONES
TAUNTON (St Mary Magdalene) (St John the Evangelist)
B & W 18 **P** *Bp and Ch Patr Trust (jt)* **V** R G CORKE
Hon C D E CAVAGHAN, J R EASTELL **NSM** S E MURRAY
TAUNTON (St Peter) *Lyngford* *B & W 18* **P** *Bp* **V** D TURLEY
TAVERHAM (St Edmund) *Nor 2* **P** *Bp* **R** P SEABROOK
C D E HAGAN-PALMER **NSM** P CHARLESWORTH
TAVISTOCK (St Eustachius), Gulworthy and Brent Tor *Ex 22*
P *Bp* **V** C G HARDWICK **NSM** M J LOADER
TAWSTOCK (St Peter) *see* Newton Tracey, Horwood,
Alverdiscott etc *Ex*
TAWTON, NORTH (St Peter) *see* Chagford, Gidleigh,
Throwleigh etc *Ex*
TAWTON, SOUTH (St Andrew) *as above*
TAYNTON (St John the Evangelist) *see* Burford w Fulbrook,
Taynton, Asthall etc *Ox*

TAYNTON (St Laurence)   *see* Highnam, Lassington, Rudford, Tibberton etc *Glouc*

TEALBY (All Saints)   *see* Walesby *Linc*

TEBAY (St James)   *see* Orton and Tebay w Ravenstonedale etc *Carl*

TEDBURN ST MARY (St Mary), Cheriton Bishop, Whitestone w Oldridge and Holcombe Burnell *Ex 5*   **P** *Bp, DBP, and Em Coll Cam (jt)*   **V** M R WOOD

TEDDINGTON (St Mark) and Hampton Wick *Lon 11*   **P** *Bp*   **P-in-c** K A WELLMAN   **C** J P SALES

TEDDINGTON (St Mary) (St Alban the Martyr) *Lon 10*   **P** *Bp*   **V** J B MOFFATT   **C** G R THOMAS   **NSM** M E HAWES

TEDDINGTON (St Nicholas)   *see* Overbury w Teddington, Alstone etc *Worc*

TEDDINGTON (St Peter and St Paul) and Fulwell St Michael and St George *Lon 10*   **P** *Bp*   **V** J W KNILL-JONES   **C** E J KENDALL

TEDSTONE DELAMERE (St James)   *see* Edvin Loach w Tedstone Delamere etc *Heref*

TEFFONT EVIAS (St Michael)   *see* Nadder Valley *Sarum*

TEFFONT MAGNA (St Edward)   *as above*

TEIGH (Holy Trinity)   *see* Oakham, Ashwell, Braunston, Brooke, Egleton etc *Pet*

TEIGNGRACE (St Peter and St Paul)   *see* Kingsteignton and Teigngrace *Ex*

TEIGNMOUTH (St James) (St Michael the Archangel), Ideford w Luton, Ashcombe and Bishopsteignton *Ex 5*   **P** *Patr Bd*   **TR** R D WITHNELL   **TV** S P WEST   **NSM** V ATKINSON

TELFORD PARK (St Stephen) (St Thomas) *S'wark 12*   **P** *V Streatham and CPAS (jt)*   **P-in-c** M L GORDON

TELFORD, CENTRAL (Christ the King)   *see* Cen Telford *Lich*

TELFORD, CENTRAL : Dawley, Lawley, Malinslee, Stirchley, Brookside and Hollinswood *Lich 21*   **P** *Patr Bd (3 turns), The Crown (1 turn)*   **TR** T STOREY   **TV** G N CROWE, J E HOLMES, L R PLUMMER   **C** L R HARPER

TELLISFORD (All Saints)   *see* Hardington Vale *B & W*

TELSCOMBE (St Laurence)   *see* Peacehaven and Telscombe Cliffs w Piddinghoe etc *Chich*

TEME VALLEY NORTH : Knighton-on-Teme, Lindridge, Pensax, Menith Wood, and Stockton *Worc 13*   **P** *Bp and D&C (alt)*   **P-in-c** E G WHITTAKER   **NSM** S JONES

TEME VALLEY SOUTH : Eastham, Rochford, Stoke Bliss, Hanley Child, Hanley William, Kyre Wyard and Stanford-on-Teme *Worc 13*   **P** *Ld Chan, Bp, and Mrs M M Miles (by turn)*   **P-in-c** R M BARLOW

TEMPLE (St Catherine)   *see* Blisland w Temple, St Breward and Helland *Truro*

TEMPLE BALSALL (St Mary) *Birm 11*   **P** *Lady Leveson Hosp*   **V** K A M LLOYD ROBERTS

TEMPLE BRUER (St John the Baptist)   *see* Graffoe Gp *Linc*

TEMPLE CLOUD (St Barnabas)   *see* Clutton w Cameley, Bishop Sutton and Stowey *B & W*

TEMPLE EWELL (St Peter and St Paul) w Lydden *Cant 7*   **P** *Abp*   **R** P CHRISTIAN

TEMPLE GRAFTON (St Andrew)   *see* Heart of England *Cov*

TEMPLE GUITING (St Mary)   *see* The Guitings, Cutsdean, Farmcote etc *Glouc*

TEMPLE HIRST (St John the Baptist)   *see* Haddlesey w Hambleton and Birkin *York*

TEMPLE NORMANTON (St James the Apostle) *Derby 5*   **P** *Bp*   **V** M R AINSCOUGH

TEMPLE SOWERBY (St James)   *see* Kirkby Thore w Temple Sowerby and Newbiggin *Carl*

TEMPLECOMBE (Blessed Virgin Mary)   *see* Abbas and Templecombe, Henstridge and Horsington *B & W*

TEMPLETON (St Margaret)   *see* Washfield, Stoodleigh, Withleigh etc *Ex*

TEMPSFORD (St Peter)   *see* Riversmeet *St Alb*

TEN MILE BANK (St Mark)   *see* Hilgay *Ely*

TENBURY Team Minstry, The (St Mary) (St Michael and All Angels) *Heref 11*   **P** *Patr Bd*   **TV** S E HARRIS   **NSM** S FOSTER

TENDRING (St Edmund King and Martyr) and Little Bentley w Beaufort cum Moze *Chelmsf 22*   **P** *Em Coll Cam, DBP, and Ball Coll Ox (by turn)*   **R** *vacant*

TENTERDEN (St Mildred) (St Michael and All Angels) and Smallhythe *Cant 10*   **P** *Abp and D&C (jt)*   **V** L J HAMMOND   **C** E K G HARROP, J R DARKINS, P L M FOGDEN   **NSM** J A SHAW, M ROYLANCE

TERLING (All Saints)   *see* Witham and Villages *Chelmsf*

TERRIERS (St Francis) *Ox 18*   **P** *V High Wycombe*   **V** A W DICKINSON

TERRINGTON (All Saints)   *see* Howardian Gp *York*

TERRINGTON ST CLEMENT (St Clement) *Ely 14*   **P** *The Crown*   **V** R J SLIPPER   **C** W D MARTIN

TERRINGTON ST JOHN (St John)   *see* E Marshland *Ely*

TERWICK (St Peter)   *see* Rogate w Terwick and Trotton w Chithurst *Chich*

TEST VALLEY Benefice, The *Win 12*   **P** *Bp and St Jo Coll Ox (jt)*   **R** J WATKINS

TESTON (St Peter and St Paul)   *see* E Malling, Wateringbury and Teston *Roch*

TESTWOOD (St Winfrid)   *see* Totton *Win*

TETBURY (St Mary the Virgin and St Mary Magdalen), Beverston, Long Newnton and Shipton Moyne *Glouc 7*   **P** *DBP, R Boggis-Rolfe Esq, and Mrs J C B Joynson (4 turns), Prime Min (1 turn)*   **R** V J HUGHES   **C** K HARTSHORNE

TETCOTT (Holy Cross)   *see* Ashwater, Halwill, Beaworthy, Clawton etc *Ex*

TETFORD (St Mary)   *see* S Ormsby Gp *Linc*

TETNEY (St Peter and St Paul)   *see* Holton-le-Clay, Tetney and N Cotes *Linc*

TETSWORTH (St Giles)   *see* Thame *Ox*

TETTENHALL REGIS (St Michael and All Angels) *Lich 24*   **P** *Patr Bd*   **TR** R M REEVE   **TV** J M PERRY, S A DOUGLAS   **C** D ANDERTON   **NSM** A ROBERTS

TETTENHALL WOOD (Christ Church) and Perton *Lich 24*   **P** *Patr Bd*   **TR** P C WOOTTON   **TV** J M CODY   **OLM** C A HARLEY

TEVERSAL (St Katherine)   *see* Skegby w Teversal *S'well*

TEVERSHAM (All Saints) *Ely 4*   **P** *Bp*   **R** *vacant*

TEW, GREAT (St Michael and All Angels) w Little (St John the Evangelist) and Heythrop *Ox 22*   **P** *Bp and J M Johnston Esq (jt)*   **V** V J THOMAS

TEWIN (St Peter)   *see* Welwyn *St Alb*

TEWKESBURY (Holy Trinity) *Glouc 9*   **P** *Ch Soc Trust*   **V** S M M WALKER

TEWKESBURY (St Mary the Virgin) w Walton Cardiff and Twyning *Glouc 9*   **P** *Ld Chan (2 turns) and Ch Ch Ox (1 turn)*   **V** P R WILLIAMS   **C** B L MESSHAM, W A RUFFLE   **NSM** C E WHITNEY, D J COULTON

TEY, GREAT (St Barnabas) and LITTLE (St James the Less) w Wakes Colne and Chappel *Chelmsf 19*   **P** *Bp, DBP, PCC Chappel and Ch Patr Trust (jt)*   **R** J RICHARDSON

THAKEHAM (St Mary)   *see* Sullington and Thakeham w Warminghurst *Chich*

THAME (St Mary the Virgin) (Barley Hill Church) *Ox 20*   **P** *Patr Bd*   **TR** A W GARRATT   **TV** R B CROSS   **C** E J RACKLYEFT   **Hon C** J H FIELDSEND, R COPPING, S H BAYNES   **NSM** G C CHOLDCROFT, G P WATERSON

THAMES DITTON (St Nicholas) *Guildf 8*   **P** *K Coll Cam*   **V** A C COWIE

THAMES VIEW (Christ Church)   *see* Barking *Chelmsf*

THAMESMEAD (Church of the Cross) (St Paul's Ecumenical Centre) (William Temple) *S'wark 6*   **P** *Bp*   **TR** H P EGGLESTON   **TV** J E G MACY, V J YEADON

THANET (St Andrew)   *see* Reading Street *Cant*

THANET (St Peter the Apostle)   *see* St Peter-in-Thanet *Cant*

THANINGTON (St Nicholas) (St Faith's Mission Church) *Cant 3*   **P** *Abp*   **V** *vacant*

THARSTON (St Mary)   *see* Newton Flotman, Swainsthorpe, Tasburgh, etc *Nor*

THATCHAM (St Mary) *Ox 6*   **P** *Patr Bd*   **TR** M D BENNET   **TV** P A JONES   **C** A J GILL   **NSM** B HARLAND   **OLM** M E FISHMAN

THATTO HEATH (St Matthew)   *see* Eccleston *Liv*

THAXTED (St John the Baptist, Our Lady and St Laurence) *Chelmsf 20*   **P** *Bp*   **NSM** D C BROWN

THE   *see under substantive place name*

THEALE (Christ Church)   *see* Wedmore w Theale and Blackford *B & W*

THEALE (Holy Trinity) and Englefield *Ox 4*   **P** *Magd Coll Ox and Englefield Estate Trust (jt)*   **P-in-c** A J TEMPLEMAN   **Hon C** N W WYNNE-JONES, P M TEMPLEMAN

THEBERTON (St Peter)   *see* Yoxmere *St E*

THEDDINGWORTH (All Saints)   *see* Hexagon *Leic*

THEDDLETHORPE (St Helen) *Linc 15*   **P** *Baroness Willoughby de Eresby (2 turns), Bp (1 turn)*   **R** C M TURNER

THELBRIDGE (St David)   *see* Burrington, Chawleigh, Cheldon, Chulmleigh etc *Ex*

THELNETHAM (St Nicholas)   *see* Hepworth, Hinderclay, Wattisfield and Thelnetham *St E*

THELVETON (St Andrew)   *see* Dickleburgh and The Pulhams *Nor*

THELWALL (All Saints) *Ches 4*   **P** *Keble Coll Ox*   **V** D J BLACK

THEMELTHORPE (St Andrew)   *see* Foulsham, Guestwick, Stibbard, Themelthorpe etc *Nor*

THENFORD (St Mary the Virgin)   *see* Chenderit *Pet*

THERFIELD (St Mary the Virgin) w Kelshall *St Alb 16*   **P** *Ld Chan and D&C St Paul's (alt)*   **R** R M MORGAN

THETFORD (St Cuthbert) St Peter *Nor 11*   **P** *Patr Bd*
TR R M BAKER   **TV** H L JARY, R A HEYWOOD
THETFORD, LITTLE (St George)   *see Ely Ely*
THEYDON BOIS (St Mary) and Theydon Garnon *Chelmsf 3*
P *Bp*   **V** S P WALKER   **C** J E FRY
THEYDON GARNON (All Saints)   *see Theydon Bois and Theydon Garnon Chelmsf*
THEYDON MOUNT (St Michael)   *see Greensted-juxta-Ongar w Stanford Rivers etc Chelmsf*
THIMBLEBY (St Margaret)   *see Horncastle Gp Linc*
THIRKLEBY (All Saints) w Kilburn and Bagby *York 18*
P *Abp*   **V** N J CARNALL   **Hon C** M I KIMBALL
THIRSK (St Mary) *York 18*   **P** *Abp*   **R** R F ROWLING
THISTLETON (St Nicholas)   *see Cottesmore and Burley, Clipsham, Exton etc Pet*
THIXENDALE (St Mary)   *see Waggoners York*
THOCKRINGTON (St Aidan)   *see Chollerton w Birtley and Thockrington Newc*
THOMPSON (St Martin)   *see Caston, Griston, Merton, Thompson etc Nor*
THORESBY, NORTH (St Helen)   *see The North-Chapel Parishes Linc*
THORESBY, SOUTH (St Andrew)   *see Legbourne and Wold Marsh Linc*
THORESWAY (St Mary)   *see Swallow Linc*
THORGANBY (All Saints)   *see Binbrook Gp Linc*
THORGANBY (St Helen)   *see Derwent Ings York*
THORINGTON (St Peter)   *see Blyth Valley St E*
THORLEY (St James the Great) *St Alb 15*   **P** *Bp*   **R** C M ORME
THORLEY (St Swithun) *Portsm 8*   **P** *Bp*   **V** *vacant*
THORMANBY (St Mary Magdalene)   *see Brafferton w Pilmoor, Myton-on-Swale etc York*
THORNABY, NORTH (St Luke) (St Paul) *York 17*   **P** *Abp*
V H C HOPKINS   **NSM** N PETTY
THORNABY, SOUTH (St Mark) (St Peter ad Vincula) *York 17*
P *Abp*   **V** M L CATHERALL
THORNAGE (All Saints)   *see Brinton, Briningham, Hunworth, Stody etc Nor*
THORNBOROUGH (St Mary)   *see Buckingham Ox*
THORNBURY (St Anna)   *see Bredenbury Heref*
THORNBURY (St Margaret) *Leeds 3*   **P** *Vs Bradf, Calverley, and Laisterdyke (jt)*   **P-in-c** N CLEWS
THORNBURY (St Mary) (St Paul) and Oldbury-on-Severn w Shepperdine *Glouc 5*   **P** *Ch Ch Ox*   **V** J K VAN DER LELY
C M B COTTRELL   **NSM** T F KEATES
THORNBURY (St Peter)   *see Black Torrington, Bradford w Cookbury etc Ex*
THORNBY (St Helen)   *see Guilsborough and Hollowell and Cold Ashby etc Pet*
THORNCOMBE (The Blessed Virgin Mary)   *see Chaffcombe, Cricket Malherbie etc B & W*
THORNDON (All Saints)   *see S Hartismere St E*
THORNE (St Nicholas) *Sheff 10*   **P** *Bp*   **V** D A GREEN
THORNE COFFIN (St Andrew)   *see Tintinhull w Chilthorne Domer, Yeovil Marsh etc B & W*
THORNE ST MARGARET (St Margaret)   *see Wellington and Distr B & W*
THORNER (St Peter) *Leeds 17*   **P** *Earl of Mexborough*
P-in-c A J NICHOLSON   **NSM** A B HAIGH
THORNES (St James) w Christ Church *Leeds 20*   **P** *DBP*
P-in-c M C CRABTREE   **NSM** J M VILES
THORNEY (St Helen)   *see E Trent S'well*
THORNEY HILL (All Saints)   *see Bransgore and Hinton Admiral Win*
THORNEY, WEST (St Nicholas)   *see Southbourne w W Thorney Chich*
THORNEYBURN (St Aidan)   *see N Tyne and Redesdale Newc*
THORNFALCON (Holy Cross)   *see Creech St Michael and Ruishton w Thornfalcon B & W*
THORNFORD (St Mary Magdalene)   *see Three Valleys Sarum*
THORNGUMBALD (St Mary)   *see Burstwick, Burton Pidsea etc York*
THORNHAM (St James)   *see High Crompton and Thornham Man*
THORNHAM (All Saints)   *see Hunstanton St Mary w Ringstead Parva etc Nor*
THORNHAM (St John)   *see Middleton and Thornham Man*
THORNHAM MAGNA (St Mary Magdalene)   *see S Hartismere St E*
THORNHAM PARVA (St Mary) *as above*
THORNHAUGH (St Andrew)   *see Nassington, Apethorpe, Thornhaugh etc Pet*
THORNHILL (Mission Church)   *see Beckermet St Jo and St Bridget w Ponsonby Carl*
THORNHILL (St Christopher)   *see Southampton Thornhill St Chris Win*

THORNHILL (St Michael and All Angels) and Whitley Lower
Leeds 10   **P** *Lord Savile*   **P-in-c** S C CLARKE
THORNHILL LEES (Holy Innocents w St Mary)
see Ravensthorpe and Thornhill Lees w Savile Town Leeds
THORNLEY (St Bartholomew)   *see Wolsingham and Thornley Dur*
THORNTHWAITE (St Mary the Virgin)   *see Upper Derwent Carl*
THORNTHWAITE (St Saviour)   *see Dacre w Hartwith and Darley w Thornthwaite Leeds*
THORNTON (St Frideswyde) and Crosby All Saints *Liv 5*
P *V Sefton, Bp, V St Luke, and CPAS (jt)*   **V** K ROGERS
THORNTON (St James) *Leeds 1*   **P** *V Bradf*   **V** C H GWINNETT
NSM G HARDISTY
THORNTON (St Michael)   *see Barmby Moor Gp York*
THORNTON (St Peter)   *see Markfield, Thornton, Bagworth and Stanton etc Leic*
THORNTON (St Wilfrid)   *see Horncastle Gp Linc*
THORNTON CURTIS (St Lawrence)   *see Ulceby Gp Linc*
THORNTON DALE (All Saints) w Allerston, Ebberston, Ellerburn and Wilton *York 19*   **P** *A R Dudley-Smith Esq (1 turn), Abp (3 turns)*   **R** J M WHITE
THORNTON HEATH (St Jude w St Aidan) *S'wark 21*
P *Bp*   **V** N K NTEGE
THORNTON HEATH (St Paul) *S'wark 21*   **P** *The Crown*
V *vacant*
THORNTON HOUGH (All Saints) *Ches 9*   **P** *Simeon's Trustees*
V D J HOWARD
THORNTON IN CRAVEN (St Mary)   *see Broughton, Marton and Thornton Leeds*
THORNTON LE FEN (St Peter)   *see Brothertoft Gp Linc*
THORNTON LE STREET (St Leonard)   *see The Thorntons and The Otteringtons York*
THORNTON RUST (Mission Room)   *see Penhill Leeds*
THORNTON STEWARD (St Oswald)   *see Middleham w Coverdale and E Witton etc Leeds*
THORNTON WATLASS (St Mary the Virgin)   *see Bedale and Leeming and Thornton Watlass Leeds*
THORNTON, LITTLE (St John) *Blackb 12*   **P** *Bp*
V P R F CLEMENCE
THORNTON-IN-LONSDALE (St Oswald)   *see Bentham, Burton-in-Lonsdale, Chapel-le-Dale etc Leeds*
THORNTON-LE-FYLDE (Christ Church) *Blackb 12*   **P** *Trustees*
V *vacant*
THORNTON-LE-MOOR (All Saints)   *see Kelsey Gp Linc*
THORNTON-LE-MOORS (St Mary) w Ince and Elton *Ches 3*
P *Bp*   **V** R ACKROYD
THORNTONS and The Otteringtons, The *York 18*   **P** *Ch Ch Ox, Linc Coll Ox, and Abp (by turn)*   **R** S D RUDKIN
THOROTON (St Helena)   *see Whatton w Aslockton, Hawksworth, Scarrington etc S'well*
THORP ARCH (All Saints)   *see Bramham York*
THORPE (St Andrew) (Good Shepherd) *Nor 1*   **P** *Trustees W J Birkbeck Esq*   **C** D R SMITH
THORPE (St Laurence)   *see Farndon w Thorpe, Hawton and Cotham S'well*
THORPE (St Leonard)   *see Fenny Bentley, Thorpe, Tissington, Parwich etc Derby*
THORPE (St Mary) *Guildf 11*   **P** *Keble Coll Ox*   **V** D S MILES
THORPE (St Matthew) *Nor 1*   **P** *R Thorpe St Andr*
C H C RENGERT
THORPE (St Peter)   *see The Wainfleet Gp Linc*
THORPE ABBOTS (All Saints)   *see Redenhall w Scole Nor*
THORPE ACHURCH (St John the Baptist)   *see Aldwincle, Clopton, Pilton, Stoke Doyle etc Pet*
THORPE ACRE w Dishley (All Saints) *Leic 6*   **P** *Bp*
V K A ELLIOTT
THORPE ARNOLD (St Mary the Virgin)   *see Melton Mowbray Leic*
THORPE AUDIN (Mission Room)   *see Woolley Leeds*
THORPE BASSETT (All Saints)   *see Buckrose Carrs York*
THORPE BAY (St Augustine) *Chelmsf 15*   **P** *The Crown*
V J COLLIS   **C** J R ALLAN
THORPE CONSTANTINE (St Constantine)   *see Mease Valley Lich*
THORPE EDGE (St John the Divine) *Leeds 3*   **P** *Vs Bradf, Calverley, and Idle (jt)*   **V** *vacant*
THORPE END (St David)   *see Gt and Lt Plumstead w Thorpe End and Witton Nor*
THORPE EPISCOPI (St Andrew)   *see Thorpe St Andr Nor*
THORPE HESLEY (Holy Trinity) *Sheff 6*   **P** *Sir Philip Naylor-Leyland Bt*   **V** L BROADHEAD
THORPE LANGTON (St Leonard)   *see The Langtons and Shangton Leic*
THORPE MALSOR (All Saints)   *see Broughton w Loddington and Cransley etc Pet*
THORPE MANDEVILLE (St John the Baptist)   *see Culworth w Sulgrave and Thorpe Mandeville etc Pet*

THORPE MARKET (St Margaret)   *see* Poppyland *Nor*

THORPE MORIEUX (St Mary the Virgin)   *see* Rattlesden w Thorpe Morieux, Brettenham etc *St E*

THORPE SALVIN (St Peter)   *see* Harthill and Thorpe Salvin *Sheff*

THORPE SATCHVILLE (St Michael and All Angels)   *see* S Croxton Gp *Leic*

THORPE WILLOUGHBY (St Francis of Assisi)   *see* Brayton *York*

THORPE-LE-SOKEN (St Michael) *Chelmsf 23*   **P** *Bp*
  P-in-c J C DOWDING

THORPE-NEXT-HADDISCOE (St Matthias)   *see* Raveningham Gp *Nor*

THORPE-ON-THE-HILL (St Michael)   *see* Swinderby *Linc*

THORRINGTON (St Mary Magdalene)   *see* Alresford and Frating w Thorrington *Chelmsf*

THORVERTON (St Thomas of Canterbury)   *see* Brampford Speke, Cadbury, Newton St Cyres etc *Ex*

THRANDESTON (St Margaret)   *see* N Hartismere *St E*

THRAPSTON (St James), Denford and Islip *Pet 10*   **P** *Ld Chan* (2 turns), L G Stopford-Sackville Esq (1 turn)   **R** *vacant*

THREAPWOOD (St John)   *see* Malpas and Threapwood and Bickerton *Ches*

THRECKINGHAM (St Peter)   *see* S Lafford *Linc*

THREE LEGGED CROSS (All Saints)   *see* Verwood *Sarum*

THREE RIVERS Group, The *Ely 4*   **P** *Jes Coll Cam and Mrs D A Crawley (2 turns), Ld Chan (1 turn)*   **R** M G BANYARD
  NSM P M DEBENHAM, S P POTTS

THREE RIVERS, The *Truro 9*   **P** *Ld Chan (1 turn), Ox Univ, Bp, and DBP (1 turn)*   **P-in-c** A E BROWN   **NSM** H J WEST

THREE VALLEYS, The *Sarum 3*   **P** *Patr Bd*   **TR** A J D GILBERT
  TV J R F KIRLEW   **NSM** A M BUDGELL, M ANDERSON

THRELKELD (St Mary)   *see* St John's-in-the-Vale, Threlkeld and Wythburn *Carl*

THREXTON (All Saints)   *see* Gt and Lt Cressingham w Threxton *Nor*

THRIGBY (St Mary)   *see* S Trin Broads *Nor*

THRIMBY (St Mary)   *see* Morland, Thrimby, Gt Strickland and Cliburn *Carl*

THRINGSTONE (St Andrew)   *see* Whitwick, Thringstone and Swannington *Leic*

THRIPLOW (St George)   *see* Fowlmere, Foxton, Shepreth and Thriplow *Ely*

THROCKING (Holy Trinity)   *see* Ardeley, Benington, Cottered w Throcking etc *St Alb*

THROCKLEY (St Mary the Virgin)   *see* Newburn *Newc*

THROCKMORTON (Chapelry)   *see* Abberton, The Flyfords, Naunton Beauchamp etc *Worc*

THROOP (St Paul) *Win 8*   **P** *Ch Soc Trust*   **P-in-c** R K MODY

THROPTON (St Andrew)   *see* Upper Coquetdale *Newc*

THROWLEIGH (St Mary the Virgin)   *see* Chagford, Gidleigh, Throwleigh etc *Ex*

THRUMPTON (All Saints) *S'well 6*   **P** *Mrs M Gottlieb*
  P-in-c R I COLEMAN

THRUSHELTON (St George)   *see* Lifton, Broadwoodwidger, Stowford etc *Ex*

THRUSSINGTON (Holy Trinity)   *see* Fosse *Leic*

THRUXTON (St Bartholomew)   *see* Cagebrook *Heref*

THRUXTON (St Peter and St Paul)   *see* Appleshaw, Kimpton, Thruxton, Fyfield etc *Win*

THRYBERGH (St Leonard) *Sheff 6*   **P** *Mrs P N Fullerton*
  P-in-c D WARD

THUNDERSLEY (St Michael and All Angels) (St Peter)
  Chelmsf 13   **P** *Bp*   **R** M E STURROCK

THUNDERSLEY, NEW (St George) *Chelmsf 13*   **P** *Bp*
  V A J ROSE

THUNDRIDGE (St Mary) *St Alb 19*   **P** *Bp*
  P-in-c M B W COOK

THURCASTON (All Saints)   *see* Anstey and Thurcaston w Cropston *Leic*

THURCROFT (St Simon and St Jude) *Sheff 5*   **P** *Bp*
  V *vacant*

THURGARTON (St Peter) w Hoveringham and Bleasby w Halloughton *S'well 3*   **P** *Ld Chan and Trin Coll Cam (alt)*
  P-in-c P W WHITE

THURGOLAND (Holy Trinity)   *see* Tankersley, Thurgoland and Wortley *Sheff*

THURLASTON (All Saints)   *see* Enderby w Lubbesthorpe and Thurlaston *Leic*

THURLASTON (St Edmund)   *see* Dunchurch *Cov*

THURLBY (St Firmin)   *see* Ness Gp *Linc*

THURLBY (St Germain)   *see* Bassingham Gp *Linc*

THURLEIGH (St Peter)   *see* Milton Ernest, Pavenham and Thurleigh *St Alb*

THURLESTONE (All Saints), South Milton, Churchstow, Woodleigh and Loddiswell *Ex 13*   **P** *Bp Ex, D&C Ex, D&C Sarum, and MMCET (jt)*   **R** D G HARTLEY

THURLOW, GREAT (All Saints)   *see* Stourhead *St E*

THURLOW, LITTLE (St Peter) *as above*

THURLOXTON (St Giles)   *see* Alfred Jewel *B & W*

THURLTON (All Saints)   *see* Raveningham Gp *Nor*

THURMASTON (St Michael and All Angels)   *see* Fosse *Leic*

THURNBY (St Luke)   *see* Cornerstone Team *Leic*

THURNBY LODGE (Christ Church)   *see* Ascension TM *Leic*

THURNE (St Edmund)   *see* Martham and Repps w Bastwick, Thurne etc *Nor*

THURNHAM (St Mary the Virgin)   *see* Bearsted w Thurnham *Cant*

THURNING (St Andrew)   *see* Reepham, Hackford w Whitwell, Kerdiston etc *Nor*

THURNING (St James the Great)   *see* Barnwell, Hemington, Luddington in the Brook etc *Pet*

THURNSCOE (St Helen) (St Hilda) *Sheff 12*   **P** *Bp and Sir Philip Naylor-Leyland Bt (jt)*   **R** *vacant*

THURROCK, LITTLE (St John the Evangelist)   *see* Grays North *Chelmsf*

THURROCK, LITTLE (St Mary the Virgin)   *see* Grays Thurrock *Chelmsf*

THURROCK, WEST (Church Centre) *as above*

THURSBY (St Andrew) *Carl 3*   **P** *D&C*   **P-in-c** G P RAVALDE

THURSFORD (St Andrew)   *see* Barney, Hindringham, Thursford, Great Snoring, Little Snoring and Kettlestone and Pensthorpe *Nor*

THURSLEY (St Michael and All Angels) *Guildf 4*   **P** *V Witley*
  V J J PAGE   **NSM** P R J MUIR

THURSTASTON (St Bartholomew) *Ches 8*   **P** *D&C*
  R E J TURNER

THURSTON (St Peter)   *see* Gt Barton and Thurston *St E*

THURSTONLAND (St Thomas)   *see* Upper Holme Valley *Leeds*

THURTON (St Ethelbert) w Ashby St Mary, Bergh Apton w Yelverton and Framingham Pigot *Nor 8*   **P** *Bp and Major J H Thursby, Bp and MMCET, and Ld Chan (by turn)*
  R *vacant*

THUXTON (St Paul)   *see* Barnham Broom and Upper Yare *Nor*

THWAITE (All Saints)   *see* Erpingham w Calthorpe, Ingworth, Aldborough etc *Nor*

THWAITE (St Mary)   *see* Brooke, Kirstead, Mundham w Seething and Thwaite *Nor*

THWAITES (St Anne)   *see* Millom *Carl*

THWAITES BROW (St Barnabas) *Leeds 5*   **P** *DBP*
  P-in-c J L PRITCHARD

THWING (All Saints)   *see* Langtoft w Foxholes, Butterwick, Cottam etc *York*

TIBBERTON (All Saints) w Bolas Magna and Waters Upton
  Lich 16   **P** *R Edgmond w Kynnersley etc, MMCET, and A B Davies Esq (jt)*   **P-in-c** W E WARD
  NSM D N H STOKES-HARRISON

TIBBERTON (Holy Trinity)   *see* Highnam, Lassington, Rudford, Tibberton etc *Glouc*

TIBBERTON (St Peter ad Vincula)   *see* Bowbrook S *Worc*

TIBENHAM (All Saints)   *see* Bunwell, Carleton Rode, Tibenham, Gt Moulton etc *Nor*

TIBSHELF (St John the Baptist)   *see* Blackwell w Tibshelf *Derby*

TICEHURST (St Mary) and Flimwell *Chich 16*   **P** *Bp, J A Sellick Esq, and K M H Millar Esq (jt)*   **V** T J MILLS

TICHBORNE (St Andrew)   *see* Upper Itchen *Win*

TICHMARSH (St Mary the Virgin)   *see* Aldwincle, Clopton, Pilton, Stoke Doyle etc *Pet*

TICKENCOTE (St Peter)   *see* Gt and Lt Casterton w Pickworth and Tickencote *Pet*

TICKENHAM (St Quiricus and St Julietta)   *see* Nailsea Ch Ch w Tickenham *B & W*

TICKHILL (St Mary) w Stainton *Sheff 9*   **P** *Bp*   **V** C J BETSON

TICKNALL (St George)   *see* Melbourne, Ticknall, Smisby and Stanton *Derby*

TICKTON (St Paul)   *see* Beverley Minster *York*

TIDCOMBE (St Michael)   *see* Savernake *Sarum*

TIDDINGTON   *see* Albury w Tiddington, Holton, Waterperry, Waterstock and Wheatley *Ox*

TIDDINGTON (St Peter)   *see* Alveston *Cov*

TIDEBROOK (St John the Baptist) *Chich 16*   **P** *V Wadhurst and V Mayfield (alt)*   **V** J R JAMES

TIDEFORD (St Luke)   *see* St Germans *Truro*

TIDENHAM (St Mary) w Beachley and Lancaut *Glouc 1*
  P *Bp*   **V** D O TREHARNE

TIDENHAM CHASE (St Michael and All Angels)   *see* Tidenham w Beachley and Lancaut *Glouc*

TIDESWELL (St John the Baptist) *Derby 4*   **P** *D&C Lich*
  V S I D WHITE   **C** S M IVES-SMITH   **NSM** A M WHITE

TIDMARSH (St Laurence)   *see* Pangbourne w Tidmarsh and Sulham *Ox*

TIDMINGTON (not known)   *see* Shipston-on-Stour w Honington and Idlicote *Cov*

TIDWORTH (Holy Trinity) *Sarum 14*   **P** *Ld Chan*
  P-in-c A S M COPELAND

TIFFIELD (St John the Baptist)　see Pattishall w Cold Higham and Gayton w Tiffield *Pet*
TILBROOK (All Saints)　see Kym Valley *Ely*
TILBURY DOCKS (St John the Baptist) *Chelmsf 16*　P *Bp*　V T M CODLING
TILBURY, EAST (St Katherine) and West Tilbury and Linford *Chelmsf 16*　P *Ld Chan*　P-in-c P L ROBINSON
TILBURY-JUXTA-CLARE (St Margaret)　see Upper Colne *Chelmsf*
TILE CROSS (St Peter)　see Garretts Green and Tile Cross *Birm*
TILE HILL (St Oswald) *Cov 3*　P *Bp*　V N W M LEGGETT
TILEHURST (St Catherine of Siena) and Calcot *Ox 7*　P *Magd Coll Ox*　V D R SMITH　OLM L D COLAM
TILEHURST (St George) (St Mary Magdalen) *Ox 7*　P *Bp*　V A J CARLILL
TILEHURST (St Michael) *Ox 7*　P *Magd Coll Ox*　R J A ROGERS
TILFORD (All Saints)　see The Bourne and Tilford *Guildf*
TILGATE (Holy Trinity)　see Southgate *Chich*
TILLINGHAM (St Nicholas) *Chelmsf 11*　P *D&C St Paul's*　V vacant
TILLINGTON (All Hallows) *Chich 10*　P *Lord Egremont*　P-in-c R M MITCHELL
TILMANSTONE (St Andrew)　see Eastry and Woodnesborough *Cant*
TILNEY ALL SAINTS (All Saints)　see E Marshland *Ely*
TILNEY ST LAWRENCE (St Lawrence) *as above*
TILSTOCK (Christ Church)　see Edstaston, Fauls, Prees, Tilstock and Whixall *Lich*
TILSTON (St Mary) and Shocklach *Ches 5*　P *Bp*　R J E STEPHENSON　NSM D R BLACK
TILSTONE FEARNALL (St Jude)　see Bunbury and Tilstone Fearnall *Ches*
TILSWORTH (All Saints)　see Totternhoe, Stanbridge and Tilsworth *St Alb*
TILTON ON THE HILL (St Peter)　see Whatborough Gp *Leic*
TILTY (St Mary the Virgin)　see Broxted w Chickney and Tilty etc *Chelmsf*
TIMBERHILL (St John the Baptist)　see Nor St Jo w St Julian *Nor*
TIMBERLAND (St Andrew)　see Carr Dyke Gp *Linc*
TIMBERSCOMBE (St Petroc)　see Dunster, Carhampton, Withycombe w Rodhuish etc *B & W*
TIMPERLEY (Christ Church) (Holy Cross) *Ches 10*　P *Trustees*　V J W BRIDGMAN　C J C BRIDGMAN
TIMSBURY (Blessed Virgin Mary) w Priston, Camerton and Dunkerton *B & W 11*　P *Bp, Ball Coll Ox, and R W Lovegrove Esq (jt)*　P-in-c M A BLEWETT　NSM G RIPLEY
TIMSBURY (St Andrew)　see Michelmersh and Awbridge and Braishfield etc *Win*
TIMWORTH (St Andrew)　see Lark Valley *St E*
TINCLETON (St John the Evangelist)　see Moreton, Woodsford and Crossways w Tincleton *Sarum*
TINGEWICK (St Mary Magdalene)　see W Buckingham *Ox*
TINGRITH (St Nicholas)　see Westoning w Tingrith *St Alb*
TINSLEY (St Lawrence)　see Rivers Team *Sheff*
TINTAGEL (St Materiana)　see Boscastle and Tintagel Gp *Truro*
TINTINHULL (St Margaret) w Chilthorne Domer, Yeovil Marsh and Thorne Coffin *B & W 6*　P *Guild of All So*　P-in-c P M DOWN　NSM A J YOUNG
TINTWISTLE (Christ Church)　see Hollingworth w Tintwistle *Ches*
TINWELL (All Saints)　see Ketton, Collyweston, Easton-on-the-Hill etc *Pet*
TIPTOE (St Andrew)　see Hordle *Win*
TIPTON (St John the Evangelist) *Lich 26*　P V W Bromwich *St Jas*　V S B SAYER
TIPTON (St John)　see Ottery St Mary, Alfington, W Hill, Tipton etc *Ex*
TIPTON (St Mark)　see Ocker Hill *Lich*
TIPTON (St Martin) (St Paul) *Lich 26*　P MMCET　V vacant
TIPTON (St Matthew) *Lich 26*　P *Simeon's Trustees*　V A C BOWER
TIPTREE (St Luke)　see Thurstable and Winstree *Chelmsf*
TIRLEY (St Michael)　see Ashleworth, Corse, Hartpury, Hasfield etc *Glouc*
TISBURY (St John the Baptist)　see Nadder Valley *Sarum*
TISMANS COMMON (St John the Baptist)　see Rudgwick *Chich*
TISSINGTON (St Mary)　see Fenny Bentley, Thorpe, Tissington, Parwich etc *Derby*
TISTED, EAST w Colemore (St James)　see Northanger *Win*
TISTED, WEST (St Mary Magdalene)　see Bishop's Sutton and Ropley and W Tisted *Win*
TITCHFIELD (St Peter) *Portsm 2*　P *D&C Win*　P-in-c S ALLMAN　NSM J A TREVITHICK
TITCHWELL (St Mary)　see Hunstanton St Mary w Ringstead Parva etc *Nor*

TITLEY (St Peter)　see Kington w Huntington, Old Radnor, Kinnerton etc *Heref*
TITTENSOR (St Luke)　see Cotes Heath and Standon and Swynnerton etc *Lich*
TITTLESHALL (St Mary)　see Litcham w Kempston, E and W Lexham, Mileham etc *Nor*
TIVERTON (St Andrew) *Ex 7*　P *Bp*　P-in-c R J GORDON　C A P SHEATH
TIVERTON (St George) (St Paul) *Ex 7*　P *MMCET and Peache Trustees (jt)*　C S J DURRANT　NSM D A LYDDON
TIVERTON (St Peter) and Chevithorne w Cove *Ex 7*　P *Peache Trustees (3 turns), Ld Chan (1 turn)*　R R J GORDON　C S K JEFFS
TIVETSHALL (St Mary and St Margaret)　see Winfarthing w Shelfanger w Burston w Gissing etc *Nor*
TIVIDALE (St Michael the Archangel) (Holy Cross) (St Augustine) *Lich 26*　P *Bp*　V M M ENNIS　C K D CYRUS
TIVINGTON (St Leonard)　see Porlock and Porlock Weir w Stoke Pero etc *B & W*
TIXALL (St John the Baptist)　see Stafford St Jo and Tixall w Ingestre *Lich*
TIXOVER (St Luke)　see Barrowden and Wakerley w S Luffenham etc *Pet*
TOCKENHAM (St Giles)　see Woodhill *Sarum*
TOCKHOLES (St Stephen)　see Darwen St Cuth w Tockholes St Steph *Blackb*
TOCKWITH (Epiphany)　see N Ainsty *York*
TODBER (St Andrew)　see Stour Vale *Sarum*
TODDINGTON (St Andrew)　see Winchcombe *Glouc*
TODDINGTON (St George of England) and Chalgrave *St Alb 11*　P *Bp and DBP (jt)*　R A E CRAWFORD
TODENHAM (St Thomas of Canterbury)　see Moreton-in-Marsh w Batsford, Todenham etc *Glouc*
TODMORDEN (St Mary) (Christ Church) w Cornholme and Walsden *Leeds 9*　P *DBP and Bp (jt)*　V O R PAGE　C J KERSHAW　NSM G L PAGE, J L FLOOD, N K WHITE
TODWICK (St Peter and St Paul) *Sheff 5*　P *Bp*　P-in-c V C CAMBER
TOFT (St Andrew)　see Lordsbridge *Ely*
TOFT (St John the Evangelist)　see Knutsford St Jo and Toft *Ches*
TOFT MONKS (St Margaret)　see Raveningham Gp *Nor*
TOFTREES (All Saints) *Nor 15*　P *Marquess Townshend*　V vacant
TOFTS, WEST and Buckenham Parva *Nor 13*　P *Guild of All So*　R vacant
TOKYNGTON (St Michael) *Lon 21*　P *Bp*　V H L YOUNG
TOLLADINE (Christ Church)　see Worc St Barn w Ch Ch *Worc*
TOLLAND (St John the Baptist)　see Wiveliscombe and the Hills *B & W*
TOLLARD ROYAL (St Peter ad Vincula)　see Chase *Sarum*
TOLLER FRATRUM (St Basil)　see Melbury *Sarum*
TOLLER LANE St Chad *Leeds 1*　P *Keble Coll Ox*　V S R CROWE
TOLLER PORCORUM (St Andrew)　see Beaminster Area *Sarum*
TOLLERTON (St Michael)　see Alne *York*
TOLLERTON (St Peter) *S'well 5*　P *Ld Chan*　R vacant
TOLLESBURY (St Mary)　see N Blackwater *Chelmsf*
TOLLESHUNT D'ARCY (St Nicholas) *as above*
TOLLESHUNT MAJOR (St Nicholas) *as above*
TOLLINGTON (St Mark) *Lon 6*　P *Patr Bd*　TR D R BIRD　TV S E HAIGH　C S E HAIGH
TOLPUDDLE (St John the Evangelist)　see Puddletown, Tolpuddle and Milborne w Dewlish *Sarum*
TOLWORTH (Emmanuel)　see Surbiton Hill Ch Ch *S'wark*
TOLWORTH (St George), Hook and Surbiton *S'wark 15*　P *Prime Min (1 turn), Patr Bd (2 turns)*　TR vacant
TONBRIDGE (St Peter and St Paul) (St Andrew) (St Philip) (St Saviour) *Roch 11*　P *Mabledon Trust*　V M E BROWN　C A L HAMMILL, S P M COUPER
TONBRIDGE (St Stephen) (St Eanswythe Mission Church) *Roch 11*　P *CPAS*　V M BARKER　NSM J E PERKINS, S B PERKINS
TONG (St Bartholomew) *Lich 16*　P *Bp*　P-in-c C D C THORPE　C C CHESHIRE
TONG (St James) and Laisterdyke *Leeds 3*　P *Simeon's Trustees and CR (jt)*　C D J MUGHAL, J P HUSTWICK
TONGE (St Giles)　see Murston w Bapchild and Tonge *Cant*
TONGE (St Michael) w Alkrington *Man 14*　P *R Middleton St Leon*　V vacant
TONGE MOOR (St Augustine) (St Aidan) *Man 12*　P *Keble Coll Ox*　V D A DAVIES
TONGHAM (St Paul) *Guildf 1*　P *Adn Surrey*　V C F HOLT
TOOT BALDON (St Lawrence)　see Dorchester *Ox*
TOOTING (All Saints) *S'wark 17*　P *Bp*　V S D METZNER　OLM G R WALLER

TOOTING GRAVENEY (St Nicholas) *S'wark 17* **P** *MMCET*
R C J DAVIS

TOOTING, UPPER (Holy Trinity) (St Augustine) *S'wark 17*
P *Bp and R Streatham St Leon (jt)* **V** A P DAVEY
C S J LIEBERT

TOP VALLEY (St Philip) *see* Bestwood St Matt w St Phil *S'well*

**TOPCLIFFE (St Columba), Baldersby w Dishforth, Dalton and
Skipton on Swale** *York 18* **P** *Abp, Viscountess Downe, and
D&C (jt)* **V** S JUKES

TOPCROFT (St Margaret) *see* Hempnall *Nor*

TOPPESFIELD (St Margaret) *see* Upper Colne *Chelmsf*

TOPSHAM (St Margaret) *see* Topsham and Wear *Ex*

TOPSHAM (St Margaret) and Wear *Ex 3* **P** *D&C*
V L S GRACE **Hon C** M D A WILLIAMS **NSM** J J HORWOOD

TORBRYAN (Holy Trinity) *see* Ipplepen w Torbryan, Denbury
and Broadhempston w Woodland *Ex*

TORKSEY (St Peter) *see* Stow Gp *Linc*

TORMARTON (St Mary Magdalene) *see* Marshfield w Cold
Ashton and Tormarton etc *Bris*

TORPOINT (St James) *see* Antony w Sheviock and Torpoint
Truro

TORQUAY (St John) *Ex 11* **P** *Bp* **V** *vacant*

TORQUAY (St Luke) *Ex 11* **P** *D&C* **P-in-c** H C JEVONS

TORQUAY (St Martin) Barton *Ex 11* **P** *V St Marychurch*
V G CHAPMAN

TORQUAY (St Matthias) (St Mark) (Holy Trinity) *Ex 11*
P *Ch Patr Trust, Bp and Torwood Trustees (jt)*
P-in-c J A BECKETT **NSM** P BARTON

TORRE (All Saints) *Ex 11* **P** *Bp* **NSM** P D EVANS

TORRINGTON, EAST (St Michael) *see* Barkwith Gp *Linc*

**TORRINGTON, GREAT (St Michael), Little Torrington and
Frithelstock** *Ex 19* **P** *Ch Ch Ox (8 turns), Lord Clinton (1 turn),
Prayer Book Soc (1 turn)* **V** *vacant*

TORRINGTON, LITTLE (St Giles) *see* Gt and Lt Torrington and
Frithelstock *Ex*

TORRISHOLME (Ascension) *Blackb 11* **P** *Bp* **V** C G HOLDEN

TORTWORTH (St Leonard) *see* Cromhall, Tortworth,
Tytherington, Falfield etc *Glouc*

TORVER (St Luke) *see* Coniston and Torver *Carl*

TOSELAND (St Michael) *see* Papworth *Ely*

TOSSIDE (St Bartholomew) *see* Slaidburn w Tosside *Leeds*

TOSTOCK (St Andrew) *see* Pakenham w Norton and Tostock
St E

TOTHAM, GREAT (St Peter) and Little Totham w Goldhanger
Chelmsf 24 **P** *Bp and Ld Chan (alt)* **R** J PEARCE
OLM S M GODSMARK

TOTHAM, LITTLE (All Saints) *see* Gt Totham and Lt Totham w
Goldhanger *Chelmsf*

TOTLAND BAY (Christ Church) *Portsm 8* **P** *Ch Patr Trust*
NSM J R COOK

TOTLEY (All Saints) *Sheff 2* **P** *Bp* **V** R P OAKLEY

**TOTNES (St Mary) w Bridgetown, Berry Pomeroy,
Dartington, Maarldon, Ashprington, Cornworthy and
Stoke Gabriel** *Ex 12* **P** *Patr Bd* **TR** J C OULD
TV D A PARSONS **NSM** A D SUMNER, J H FROST

TOTON (St Peter) *S'well 9* **P** *CPAS* **V** C D BOURNE
C D A LORD

TOTTENHAM (All Hallows) *Lon 19* **P** *D&C St Paul's*
V R B PEARSON

TOTTENHAM (Holy Trinity) *Lon 19* **P** *Bp* **V** O A FAGBEMI
C A D WILLIAMS

TOTTENHAM (St Bartholomew) *see* Stamford Hill St Bart *Lon*

TOTTENHAM (St Benet Fink) *Lon 19* **P** *D&C St Paul's*
P-in-c J A H HILL **NSM** M G BURRIDGE

TOTTENHAM (St Cuthbert) *see* Chitts Hill St Cuth *Lon*

TOTTENHAM (St Mary the Virgin) *Lon 19* **P** *Bp*
V S J MORRIS

TOTTENHAM (St Paul) *Lon 19* **P** *V Tottenham All Hallows*
V R J WILKINSON

TOTTENHAM (St Philip the Apostle) *Lon 19* **P** *Bp*
P-in-c J A H HILL **NSM** M G BURRIDGE

TOTTENHAM, SOUTH (St Ann) *Lon 19* **P** *D&C St Paul's*
V J M WOOD **C** C R LACEY **Emer** R W GOODHEW

TOTTENHILL (St Botolph) w Wormegay *Ely 9* **P** *Bp*
P-in-c B L BURTON **Hon C** S C MORRIS

TOTTERIDGE (St Andrew) *St Alb 14* **P** *R Hatfield*
P-in-c T P SEAGO

TOTTERNHOE (St Giles), Stanbridge and Tilsworth *St Alb 11*
P *Bp* **V** H E GARDNER

TOTTINGTON (St Ann) *Man 8* **P** *R Bury St Mary*
V H W BEARN

TOTTON *Win 11* **P** *Bp* **TR** C D STEED **TV** J R REEVE,
S M MARCHANT

TOW LAW (St Philip and St James) *see* Satley, Stanley and Tow
Law *Dur*

**TOWCESTER (St Lawrence) w Caldecote and Easton
Neston and Greens Norton and Bradden (The Tove
Benefice)** *Pet 5* **P** *Prime Min (1 turn), Bp, Lord Hesketh,
and J E Grant-Ives Esq (1 turn)* **V** B L M PHILLIPS
C E W PELLY, P E CHALLEN

TOWEDNACK (St Tewinock) *Truro 5* **P** *Bp*
P-in-c E V A FOOT

TOWER CHAPEL (St Nicholas) *see* Whitehaven *Carl*

TOWERSEY (St Catherine) *see* Thame *Ox*

TOWNEND (St Paul) *see* Morley *Leeds*

TOWNSTAL (St Clement) *see* Dartmouth and Dittisham *Ex*

TOXTETH (St Bede) (St Clement) *Liv 6* **P** *Simeon's Trustees*
V E JONES

TOXTETH (St Margaret) *Liv 6* **P** *St Chad's Coll Dur*
P-in-c R G LEWIS

TOXTETH (St Philemon) (St Gabriel) St Cleopas *Liv 6* **P** *Patr
Bd* **TR** B R ELFICK **TV** D G GAVIN **C** D L GRIFFITH-JONES
OLM P R A BRIDSON

**TOXTETH PARK (Christ Church) (St Michael-in-the-Hamlet)
(St Andrew)** *Liv 6* **P** *Simeon's Trustees and Trustees (jt)*
V D A PARRY

TOXTETH PARK (St Agnes and St Pancras) *Liv 6* **P** *St Chad's
Coll Dur* **V** J C D COOK

TOYNTON ALL SAINTS (All Saints) *see* Bolingbroke Deanery
Linc

TOYNTON ST PETER (St Peter) *as above*

TOYNTON, HIGH (St John the Baptist) *see* Horncastle Gp
Linc

TOYS HILL (Hall) *see* Hever, Four Elms and Mark Beech *Roch*

TRAFALGAR SQUARE (St Martin-in-the-Fields) *see* St Martin-in-
the-Fields *Lon*

TRAFFORD, OLD (St Bride) *Man 5* **P** *Trustees*
P-in-c P J MATTHEWS **OLM** O H SAMUEL, V M ECCLES

TRAFFORD, OLD (St Hilda) *see* Firswood and Gorse Hill *Man*

TRAFFORD, OLD (St John the Evangelist) *Man 5* **P** *The
Crown* **P-in-c** J D HUGHES **NSM** P M SCOTT

TRANMERE (St Catherine) *Ches 1* **P** *R Bebington*
V J R TERRY **NSM** D S MARSHALL

TRANMERE (St Paul w St Luke) *Ches 1* **P** *Bp* **V** *vacant*

TRAWDEN (St Mary the Virgin) *see* Foulridge, Laneshawbridge
and Trawden *Blackb*

TREALES (Christ Church) *see* Wesham and Treales *Blackb*

TREBOROUGH (St Peter) *see* Old Cleeve, Leighland and
Treborough *B & W*

TREDINGTON (St Gregory) and Darlingscott *Cov 9*
P *Jes Coll Ox* **P-in-c** C GOBLE **Hon C** S A EDMONDS

TREDINGTON (St John the Baptist) *see* Deerhurst and
Apperley w Forthampton etc *Glouc*

TREETON (St Helen) *see* Rivers Team *Sheff*

TREFONEN (All Saints) *see* Llanyblodwel, Llanymynech,
Morton and Trefonen *Lich*

TREGADILLET (St Mary's Mission) *see* Launceston *Truro*

TREGONY (not known) w St Cuby and Cornelly *Truro 6*
P *Bp* **P-in-c** E L WATSON

TREKNOW (Holy Family) *see* Boscastle and Tintagel Gp *Truro*

TRELEIGH (St Stephen) *see* Redruth w Lanner and Treleigh
Truro

TRELYSTAN (St Mary the Virgin) *see* Chirbury, Marton,
Middleton and Trelystan etc *Heref*

TREMAINE (St Winwalo) *see* Egloskerry, N Petherwin,
Tremaine, Tresmere etc *Truro*

TRENEGLOS (St Gregory) *see* Week St Mary Circle of Par *Truro*

TRENT (St Andrew) *see* Queen Thorne *Sarum*

TRENT VALE (St John the Evangelist) *see* Hartshill, Penkhull
and Trent Vale *Lich*

TRENT, EAST Group of Parishes, The *S'well 3* **P** *Bp, Ld Chan,
D&C Pet, and Keble Coll Ox (by turn)* **V** *vacant*

TRENTCLIFFE Group, The *Linc 2* **P** *Bp, Meynell Ch Trustees,
Ch Soc Trust, and MMCET (1 turn), Ld Chan (1 turn)*
V M BRISCOE **NSM** C A SULLY

TRENTHAM (St Mary and All Saints) *Lich 13* **P** *CPAS*
V E W MCLEOD **C** A P MORGAN, S A MORRIS

TRENTSIDE EAST *Linc 6* **P** *Bp Linc (2 turns), Bp Lon (1 turn)*
R *vacant*

TRESCO (St Nicholas) *see* Is of Scilly *Truro*

TRESHAM (not known) *see* Tyndale *Glouc*

TRESILLIAN (Holy Trinity) and Lamorran w Merther *Truro 6*
P *Viscount Falmouth* **P-in-c** L M BARLEY

TRESLOTHAN (St John the Evangelist) *see* Crowan and
Treslothan *Truro*

TRESMERE (St Nicholas) *see* Egloskerry, N Petherwin,
Tremaine, Tresmere etc *Truro*

TRESWELL (St John the Baptist) *see* Retford Area *S'well*

TRETHEVY (St Piran) *see* Boscastle and Tintagel Gp *Truro*

TRETIRE (St Mary) *see* St Weonards *Heref*

TREVALGA (St Petroc) *see* Boscastle and Tintagel Gp *Truro*

TREVENSON (St Illogan)   *see* St Illogan *Truro*
TREVERBYN (St Peter) *Truro 1*   **P** *The Crown*   **V** *vacant*
TREVONE (St Saviour)   *see* Padstow *Truro*
TREWEN (St Michael)   *see* Egloskerry, N Petherwin, Tremaine, Tresmere etc *Truro*
TREYFORD CUM DIDLING (St Andrew)   *see* Harting w Elsted and Treyford cum Didling *Chich*
TRIANGLE (All Saints) (St Matthew) (Community Centre) Ipswich *St E 4*   **P** *Bp and Ld Chan (alt)*   **R** N S ATKINS   **C** D F MORRISON, T J TATE   **NSM** R H BEST
TRIMDON (St Mary Magdalene)   *see* Upper Skerne *Dur*
TRIMINGHAM (St John the Baptist)   *see* Poppyland *Nor*
TRIMLEY (St Martin)   *see* Walton and Trimley *St E*
TRIMLEY (St Mary the Virgin)   *as above*
TRIMPLEY (Holy Trinity)   *see* Kidderminster Ismere *Worc*
TRING (St Martha) (St Peter and St Paul) (St Mary) *St Alb 1* **P** *Bp*   **TR** H BELLIS   **C** G J WHITE   **NSM** D F JAQUET, J C BANISTER
TROSTON (St Mary the Virgin)   *see* Blackbourne *St E*
TROTTISCLIFFE (St Peter and St Paul)   *see* Birling, Addington, Ryarsh and Trottiscliffe *Roch*
TROTTON (St George)   *see* Rogate w Terwick and Trotton w Chithurst *Chich*
TROUTBECK (Jesus Church)   *see* Windermere St Mary and Troutbeck *Carl*
TROWBRIDGE (Holy Trinity)   *see* Trowbridge St Thos and W Ashton *Sarum*
TROWBRIDGE (St James) and Keevil *Sarum 15*   **P** *Ch Patr Trust and D&C (jt)*   **R** R G THOMAS
TROWBRIDGE (St Thomas) and West Ashton *Sarum 15* **P** *CPAS*   **V** J A COUTTS
TROWELL (St Helen)   *see* Trowell, Awsworth and Cossall *S'well*
TROWELL (St Helen), Awsworth and Cossall *S'well 8*   **P** *Bp and Lord Middleton (jt)*   **R** A M LORD   **NSM** B D BROWN, P C WHITEHEAD
TROWSE (St Andrew) *Nor 1*   **P** *D&C*   **P-in-c** J B SCOTT **NSM** R R BRABY
TRULL (All Saints) w Angersleigh *B & W 18*   **P** *DBP and M V Spurway Esq (jt)*   **R** A YOUINGS   **C** M W CLOSE
TRUMPINGTON (St Mary and St Michael) *Ely 3*   **P** *Trin Coll Cam*   **V** A J CHRICH   **C** S C ATKINS   **NSM** S M HARRIS
TRUNCH GROUP, The (St Botolph) *Nor 21*   **P** *Duchy of Lancaster (3 turns), Bp, Adn, DBP, and Peterho Cam (1 turn)* **R** A E JONES   **C** P A BAGGALEY
TRURO (St Mary's Cathedral and Parish Church) *Truro 6* **P** *The Crown*   **C** L M BARLEY, M J HORTON   **Hon C** A G BASHFORTH
TRURO St Paul (St George the Martyr) (St John the Evangelist) *Truro 6*   **P** *Prime Min (1 turn), Bp and V Kenwyn St Cuby (1 turn)*   **V** C D EPPS
TRUSHAM (St Michael and All Angels)   *see* Chudleigh w Chudleigh Knighton and Trusham *Ex*
TRUSLEY (All Saints)   *see* Boylestone, Church Broughton, Dalbury, etc *Derby*
TRUSTHORPE (St Peter)   *see* Mablethorpe w Trusthorpe *Linc*
TRYSULL (All Saints)   *see* Smestow Vale *Lich*
TUBNEY (St Lawrence)   *see* Fyfield w Tubney and Kingston Bagpuize *Ox*
TUCKHILL (Holy Innocents)   *see* Claverley w Tuckhill *Heref*
TUCKSWOOD (St Paul)   *see* Nor Lakenham St Jo and All SS and Tuckswood *Nor*
TUDDENHAM (St Martin)   *see* Westerfield and Tuddenham w Witnesham *St E*
TUDDENHAM (St Mary)   *see* Mildenhall *St E*
TUDDENHAM, EAST (All Saints)   *see* Mattishall and the Tudd Valley *Nor*
TUDDENHAM, NORTH (St Mary the Virgin) *as above*
TUDELEY (All Saints) cum Capel w Five Oak Green *Roch 8* **P** *Bp*   **P-in-c** J G A IVE   **C** P F IVE
TUDHOE (St David)   *see* Croxdale and Tudhoe *Dur*
TUDHOE GRANGE (St Andrew) *Dur 6*   **P** *Bp* **P-in-c** J LIVESLEY
TUEBROOK (St John)   *see* W Derby St Jo *Liv*
TUFFLEY (St Barnabas) *Glouc 2*   **P** *Bp*   **V** J D FAULL
TUFNELL PARK (St George and All Saints) *Lon 6*   **P** *Trustees and CPAS (jt)*   **V** M L TOOGOOD
TUFTON (St Mary)   *see* Whitchurch w Tufton and Litchfield *Win*
TUGBY (St Thomas à Becket)   *see* Hallaton and Allexton, w Horninghold, Tugby etc *Leic*
TUGFORD (St Catherine)   *see* Diddlebury w Munslow, Holdgate and Tugford *Heref*
TULSE HILL (Holy Trinity and St Matthias) *S'wark 12* **P** *Simeon's Trustees and Peache Trustees (jt)*   **V** R P DORMANDY **C** S JAMES   **NSM** W W SHARPE

TUNBRIDGE WELLS (Holy Trinity w Christ Church) *Roch 12* **P** *Mabledon Trust and CPAS (jt)*   **V** H M FLINT
TUNBRIDGE WELLS (King Charles the Martyr) *Roch 12* **P** *Trustees*   **V** R E AVERY   **NSM** S M PARTRIDGE
TUNBRIDGE WELLS (St Barnabas) *Roch 12*   **P** *Guild of All So* **P-in-c** J F CASTER
TUNBRIDGE WELLS (St James) *Roch 12*   **P** *Ch Trust Fund Trust* **V** J P STEWART   **C** W J MAURITZ
TUNBRIDGE WELLS (St John) *Roch 12*   **P** *CPAS and V Tunbridge Wells H Trin (jt)*   **V** G R WALTER   **C** R W FARR **NSM** C E SANDOM, S D BOON
TUNBRIDGE WELLS (St Luke) *Roch 12*   **P** *Five Trustees* **V** C M GLASS GOWER
TUNBRIDGE WELLS (St Mark) Broadwater Down *Roch 12* **P** *Bp*   **V** P T SANLON
TUNBRIDGE WELLS (St Peter) Windmill Fields *Roch 12* **P** *Trustees and CPAS (jt)*   **V** M P WARREN   **C** J R READ
TUNBRIDGE WELLS (St Philip) *Roch 12*   **P** *Ch Trust Fund Trust* **V** B S SENIOR
TUNSTALL (All Saints)   *see* Withernsea w Owthorne, Garton-in-Holderness etc *York*
TUNSTALL (Christ Church)   *see* Goldenhill and Tunstall *Lich*
TUNSTALL (Holy Trinity)   *see* Catterick *Leeds*
TUNSTALL (St John the Baptist)   *see* E Lonsdale *Blackb*
TUNSTALL (St John the Baptist) and Bredgar *Cant 15* **P** *Abp, D&C, O P Doubleday Esq, S G McCandlish Esq, Lady Kingsdown, and J Nightingale Esq (jt)*   **NSM** K D JACOBS, M N H BOND
TUNSTALL (St Michael and All Angels)   *see* Wilford Peninsula *St E*
TUNSTEAD (Holy Trinity)   *see* Bacup and Stacksteads *Man*
TUNSTEAD (St Mary) w Sco' Ruston *Nor 12*   **P** *Bp* **P-in-c** A R LONG
TUNWORTH (All Saints)   *see* N Hants Downs *Win*
TUPSLEY (St Paul) w Hampton Bishop *Heref 3*   **P** *Bp* **V** N P ARMSTRONG   **C** A J WILLIAMS, M J INGLIS
TUPTON (St John)   *see* N Wingfield, Clay Cross and Pilsley *Derby*
TUR LANGTON (St Andrew)   *see* The Langtons and Shangton *Leic*
TURKDEAN (All Saints)   *see* Northleach w Hampnett and Farmington etc *Glouc*
TURNASTONE (St Mary Magdalene)   *see* Madley w Tyberton, Peterchurch, Vowchurch etc *Heref*
TURNDITCH (All Saints)   *see* Belper Ch Ch w Turnditch *Derby*
TURNERS HILL (St Leonard) *Chich 6*   **P** *Bp* **P-in-c** D A TICKNER
TURNFORD (St Clement)   *see* Cheshunt *St Alb*
TURNHAM GREEN (Christ Church) *Lon 11*   **P** *Bp*   **V** R J MOY **C** K L SHREEVES, M TUFNELL, N L MOY
TURNWORTH (St Mary)   *see* Winterborne Valley and Milton Abbas *Sarum*
TURTON MOORLAND MINISTRY (St Anne) (St James) *Man 12* **P** *Patr Bd*   **TR** S D PARSONS   **TV** K B LUND **NSM** J H M AINSWORTH   **OLM** A J HESLOP, A M BULCOCK, C D JAMIESON, S FOSTER
TURVEY (All Saints) *St Alb 13*   **P** *Mrs P K C Hanbury* **R** *vacant*
TURVILLE (St Mary)   *see* Hambleden Valley *Ox*
TURWESTON (Assumption of the Blessed Virgin Mary) *see* W Buckingham *Ox*
TUSHINGHAM (St Chad)   *see* Marbury w Tushingham and Whitewell *Ches*
TUTBURY (St Mary the Virgin)   *see* Hanbury, Newborough, Rangemore and Tutbury *Lich*
TUTSHILL (St Luke)   *see* Tidenham w Beachley and Lancaut *Glouc*
TUTTINGTON (St Peter and St Paul)   *see* King's Beck *Nor*
TUXFORD (St Nicholas) w Weston, Markham Clinton, Normanton upon Trent and Marnham *S'well 3*   **P** *Bp and Ld Chan (alt)*   **V** G P PRICE
TWEEDMOUTH (St Bartholomew) *Newc 12*   **P** *D&C Dur* **P-in-c** M S KNOX   **NSM** A M PETERS-WOTHERSPOON
TWICKENHAM (All Hallows) *Lon 10*   **P** *D&C St Paul's* **V** K D BELL   **NSM** A J WILLIAMS
TWICKENHAM (All Saints) *Lon 10*   **P** *Bp*   **V** A J LANE
TWICKENHAM (St Mary the Virgin) *Lon 10*   **P** *D&C Windsor* **V** R J H WILLIAMS   **C** P J ASHWIN-SIEJKOWSKI
TWICKENHAM COMMON (Holy Trinity) *Lon 10*   **P** *Bp* **V** T M GARRETT   **Hon C** N R GARRETT
TWICKENHAM, EAST (St Stephen) (St Paul) *Lon 10*   **P** *CPAS* **V** J P B BARNES   **C** A G D WATKINS, A X CACOURIS, S M ARNOLD
TWIGWORTH (St Matthew), Down Hatherley, Norton, The Leigh, Evington, Sandhurst and Staverton w Boddington *Glouc 3*   **P** *Ld Chan (1 turn), Bp Glouc and D&C Bris (1 turn)* **V** S J SKEPPER

TWINEHAM (St Peter)   *see* Albourne w Sayers Common and Twineham *Chich*

TWINSTEAD (St John the Evangelist)   *see* N Hinckford *Chelmsf*

TWITCHEN (St Peter)   *see* S Molton w Nymet St George, High Bray etc *Ex*

TWO GATES (St Peter)   *see* Wilnecote *Lich*

TWO MILE ASH (not known)   *see* Watling Valley *Ox*

TWO MILE HILL (St Michael) *Bris 3*   **P** *Prime Min*
P-in-c R J LING   **C** M K MARTIN   **OLM** N G CALLEN

TWO RIVERS, The *Chelmsf 19*   **P** *Duchy of Lancaster (1 turn), Bp and DBP (1 turn), Ld Chan (1 turn)*   **R** J D LOWE

TWYCROSS (St James)   *see* Bosworth and Sheepy Gp *Leic*

TWYFORD (Assumption of the Blessed Virgin Mary)   *see* The Claydons and Swan *Ox*

TWYFORD (St Andrew)   *see* Aston on Trent, Elvaston, Weston on Trent etc *Derby*

TWYFORD (St Andrew)   *see* S Croxton Gp *Leic*

TWYFORD (St Mary the Virgin)   *see* Ruscombe and Twyford w Hurst *Ox*

TWYFORD (St Mary) and Owslebury and Morestead and Colden Common *Win 7*   **P** *Bp and Em Coll Cam (jt)*
V J P WATTS

TWYFORD (St Nicholas)   *see* N Elmham, Billingford, Bintree, Guist etc *Nor*

TWYNING (St Mary Magdalene)   *see* Tewkesbury w Walton Cardiff and Twyning *Glouc*

TWYWELL (St Nicholas)   *see* Cranford w Grafton Underwood and Twywell *Pet*

TYBERTON (St Mary)   *see* Madley w Tyberton, Peterchurch, Vowchurch etc *Heref*

TYDD ST GILES (St Giles)   *see* Leverington, Newton and Tydd St Giles *Ely*

TYDD ST MARY (St Mary)   *see* Sutton Bridge and Tydd St Mary *Linc*

TYE GREEN (St Barnabas)   *see* Cressing w Stisted and Bradwell etc *Chelmsf*

TYE GREEN (St Stephen) w St Andrew Netteswell *Chelmsf 4*
P J L H Arkwright Esq   **P-in-c** C E A GUEST   **C** R J ATTEW
NSM S M FERNANDES

TYLDESLEY (St George)   *see* Astley, Tyldesley and Mosley Common *Man*

TYLERS GREEN (St Margaret)   *see* Penn and Tylers Green *Ox*

TYLER'S HILL (St George)   *see* Gt Chesham *Ox*

TYNDALE *Glouc 5*   **P** *Ch Ch Ox and Bp (jt)*   **V** R H AXFORD
NSM C R AXFORD

TYNE, NORTH and Redesdale Team *Newc 4*   **P** *Patr Bd*
TR S M RAMSARAN   **TV** P J MANDER   **NSM** S H M CAMERON
OLM R VIRDEN

TYNEMOUTH (St John Percy) *Newc 5*   **P** *Dioc Soc*
P-in-c H B GILL   **Hon C** P INGHAM

TYNEMOUTH Balkwell (St Peter)   *see* Balkwell *Newc*

TYNEMOUTH Cullercoats (St Paul) *Newc 5*   **P** *Dioc Soc*
V G F GILCHRIST

TYNEMOUTH PRIORY (Holy Saviour) *Newc 5*   **P** *Dioc Soc*
NSM D A ROBINSON

TYNINGS LANE (St Mary's Mission Church)   *see* Aldridge *Lich*

TYRINGHAM (St Peter)   *see* Lamp *Ox*

TYRLEY (Mission Room)   *see* Drayton in Hales *Lich*

TYSELEY (St Edmund) *Birm 13*   **P** *The Crown*   **V** S R SIMCOX

TYSOE (Assumption of the Blessed Virgin Mary) w Oxhill and Whatcote *Cov 9*   **P** *Marquess of Northampton and DBP (jt)*
P-in-c N J MORGAN   **Hon C** M J LEATON

TYTHBY (Holy Trinity)   *see* Cropwell Bishop w Colston Bassett, Granby etc *S'well*

TYTHERINGTON (St James)   *see* Cromhall, Tortworth, Tytherington, Falfield etc *Glouc*

TYTHERINGTON (St James)   *see* Upper Wylye Valley *Sarum*

TYTHERLEY, EAST (St Peter)   *see* Lockerley and E Dean w E and W Tytherley *Win*

TYTHERLEY, WEST (St Peter) *as above*

TYTHERTON KELLAWAYS (St Giles)   *see* Draycot *Bris*

TYTHERTON LUCAS (St Nicholas)   *see* Chippenham St Andr w Tytherton Lucas *Bris*

TYWARDREATH (St Andrew) w Tregaminion *Truro 1*
P *DBP*   **V** *vacant*

UBLEY (St Bartholomew)   *see* Blagdon w Compton Martin and Ubley *B & W*

UCKFIELD (Holy Cross) (St Saviour) *Chich 18*   **P** *Abp*
C C S MITCHELL

UDIMORE (St Mary)   *see* Brede w Udimore and Beckley and Peasmarsh *Chich*

UFFCULME (St Mary the Virgin)   *see* Willand, Uffculme, Kentisbeare etc *Ex*

UFFINGTON (Holy Trinity)   *see* Wrockwardine Deanery *Lich*

UFFINGTON (St Mary), Shellingford, Woolstone and Baulking *Ox 25*   **P** *Bp (2 turns), J J Twynam Esq (1 turn)*
R J H GOULSTON

UFFINGTON Group, The (St Michael and All Angels) *Linc 16*
P *Ld Chan (2 turns), Bp (2 turns), D&C (1 turn)*
R C R KENNEDY   **C** M S THOMSON

UFFORD (Assumption of the Blessed Virgin Mary)   *see* Melton and Ufford *St E*

UFTON (St Michael and All Angels) *Cov 10*   **P** *Bp*
P-in-c J E ARMSTRONG

UGBOROUGH (St Peter)   *see* Ermington and Ugborough *Ex*

UGGESHALL (St Mary)   *see* Sole Bay *St E*

UGGLEBARNBY (All Saints)   *see* Lower Esk *York*

UGLEY (St Peter)   *see* Henham and Elsenham w Ugley *Chelmsf*

UGTHORPE (Christ Church)   *see* Hinderwell, Roxby and Staithes etc *York*

ULCEBY (All Saints)   *see* Willoughby *Linc*

ULCEBY Group, The (St Nicholas) *Linc 8*   **P** *Ld Chan*
V *vacant*

ULCOMBE (All Saints)   *see* Len Valley *Cant*

ULEY (St Giles) w Owlpen and Nympsfield *Glouc 5*   **P** *Ld Chan*   **P-in-c** D E CROOK

ULGHAM (St John the Baptist) *Newc 11*   **P** *Bp*
Emer H M BARTON

ULLENHALL (St Mary the Virgin)   *see* Beaudesert and Henley-in-Arden w Ullenhall *Cov*

ULLEY (Holy Trinity)   *see* Aston cum Aughton w Swallownest and Ulley *Sheff*

ULLINGSWICK (St Luke)   *see* Bredenbury *Heref*

ULPHA (St John)   *see* Broughton and Duddon *Carl*

ULROME (St Andrew)   *see* Bessingby *York*

ULTING (All Saints)   *see* Hatfield Peverel w Ulting *Chelmsf*

ULVERSTON (St Mary w Holy Trinity) (St Jude) *Carl 9*
P *Peache Trustees*   **R** A C BING   **C** M P KEDDILTY

UMBERLEIGH (Church of the Good Shepherd)   *see* S Molton w Nymet St George, High Bray etc *Ex*

UNDERBARROW (All Saints) w Helsington *Carl 10*   **P** *V Kendal H Trin*   **P-in-c** B J CROWE

UNDERRIVER (St Margaret) *Roch 9*   **P** *Bp*   **V** E C KITCHENER

UNDERSKIDDAW (Parish Room)   *see* Crosthwaite Keswick *Carl*

UNDERWOOD (St Michael and All Angels)   *see* Brinsley w Underwood *S'well*

UNSTONE (St Mary)   *see* Dronfield w Holmesfield *Derby*

UP HATHERLEY (St Philip and St James) *Glouc 6*   **P** *Soc of the Faith*   **V** V R DUNSTAN-MEADOWS

UP NATELY (St Stephen)   *see* N Hants Downs *Win*

UP WALTHAM (St Mary the Virgin)   *see* UPWALTHAM *Chich*

UPAVON (St Mary the Virgin)   *see* Vale of Pewsey *Sarum*

UPCHURCH (St Mary the Virgin)   *see* The Six *Cant*

UPHAM (All Saints) (Blessed Mary of Upham) *Portsm 1*
P *Ld Chan*   **R** J C HUNT   **NSM** J BELOE

UPHILL (St Barnabas Mission Church)   *see* Weston-super-Mare St Nic w St Barn *B & W*

UPHILL (St Nicholas) *as above*

UPHOLLAND (St Thomas the Martyr) *Liv 11*   **P** *Patr Bd*
P-in-c H C HANKE   **TV** D M HARRISON

UPLANDS (All Saints)   *see* Stroud Team *Glouc*

UPLEADON (St Mary the Virgin)   *see* Redmarley D'Abitot, Bromesberrow, Pauntley etc *Glouc*

UPLOWMAN (St Peter)   *see* Sampford Peverell, Uplowman, Holcombe Rogus etc *Ex*

UPLYME (St Peter and St Paul) w Axmouth *Ex 4*   **P** *CPAS and Hyndman Trustees (jt)*   **P-in-c** C M WOOLVEN

UPMINSTER (St Laurence) *Chelmsf 2*   **P** *W R Holden Esq*
R S M RUDGE

UPNOR (St Philip and St James)   *see* Frindsbury w Upnor and Chattenden *Roch*

UPOTTERY (St Mary the Virgin)   *see* Dunkeswell, Luppitt, Sheldon and Upottery *Ex*

UPPER   *see also under substantive place name*

UPPER KENNET *Sarum 18*   **P** *Bp*   **R** M T SHEPHERDSON

UPPER TAS VALLEY *Nor 7*   **P** *Bp, Keble Coll Ox, Ch Coll Cam, and MMCET (by turn)*   **P-in-c** S COOKE

UPPERBY (St John the Baptist) *Carl 3*   **P** *D&C*   **R** T J HYSLOP
C C G Y HYSLOP

UPPERBY (St John the Baptist)   *see* Upperby *Carl*

UPPERTHONG (St John the Evangelist)   *see* Upper Holme Valley *Leeds*

UPPINGHAM (St Peter and St Paul) w Ayston and Belton w Wardley *Pet 12*   **P** *Bp*   **R** R D WATTS   **C** O L WILLIAMS

UPPINGTON (Holy Trinity)   *see* Wrockwardine Deanery *Lich*

UPSHIRE (St Thomas)   *see* Waltham H Cross *Chelmsf*

UPTON (All Saints)   *see* Lea Gp *Linc*

UPTON (Holy Ascension) *Ches 2*   **P** *Duke of Westmr*
V P D SAYLE

UPTON (St Dunstan)   *see* The Lytchetts and Upton *Sarum*

UPTON (St James)   *see* Dulverton w Brushford, Brompton Regis etc *B & W*

UPTON (St John the Baptist)   *see* Castor w Upton and Stibbington and Water Newton, Marholm and Sutton *Pet*
UPTON (St Laurence)   *see* Upton cum Chalvey *Ox*
UPTON (St Margaret)   *see* N Leightonstone *Ely*
UPTON (St Margaret)   *see* Broadside *Nor*
UPTON (St Mary Magdalene) *Ex 11*   **P** *Simeon's Trustees and Ch Patr Trust (alt)*   **P-in-c** M R SEARLE   **NSM** J H GARNER
UPTON (St Mary the Virgin)   *see* The Churn *Ox*
UPTON (St Mary) *Ches 8*   **P** *Simeon's Trustees*   **V** G J SKINNER   **C** N J EASTWOOD
UPTON (St Peter and St Paul)   *see* Rolleston w Fiskerton, Morton and Upton *S'well*
UPTON BISHOP (St John the Baptist)   *see* Ariconium *Heref*
UPTON CRESSETT w Monk Hopton *Heref 8*   **P** *DBP and Miss E A Bird (alt)*   **Hon C** H J PATTERSON
UPTON CROSS (St Paul)   *see* Linkinhorne *Truro*
UPTON CUM CHALVEY (St Mary) *Ox 12*   **P** *Bp*   **TR** A S ALLEN   **TV** A C STEWART   **NSM** L R HILLIER
UPTON GREY (St Mary)   *see* N Hants Downs *Win*
UPTON HELLIONS (St Mary the Virgin)   *see* Crediton, Shobrooke and Sandford etc *Ex*
UPTON LOVELL (St Augustine of Canterbury)   *see* Upper Wylye Valley *Sarum*
UPTON MAGNA (St Lucia)   *see* Wrockwardine Deanery *Lich*
UPTON NOBLE (St Mary Magdalene)   *see* Bruton and Distr *B & W*
UPTON PARK (St Alban)   *see* E Ham w Upton Park and Forest Gate *Chelmsf*
UPTON PRIORY (Church of the Resurrection) *Ches 13*   **P** *Bp*   **NSM** S H CALLIS
UPTON PYNE (Our Lady)   *see* Brampford Speke, Cadbury, Newton St Cyres etc *Ex*
UPTON SCUDAMORE (St Mary the Virgin)   *see* Warminster St Denys and Upton Scudamore *Sarum*
UPTON SNODSBURY (St Kenelm)   *see* Peopleton and White Ladies Aston w Churchill etc *Worc*
UPTON ST LEONARDS (St Leonard) *Glouc 2*   **P** *Bp*   **P-in-c** C J BIRKETT
UPTON WARREN (St Michael)   *see* Stoke Prior, Wychbold and Upton Warren *Worc*
UPTON-ON-SEVERN (St Peter and St Paul), Ripple, Earls Croome w Hill Croome and Strensham *Worc 5*   **P** *Bp (2 turns), Mrs A J Hyde-Smith and Mrs A L Wynne (1 turn)*   **NSM** G R MOORE
UPWALTHAM (St Mary the Virgin) *Chich 10*   **P** *Lord Egremont*   **P-in-c** R M MITCHELL
UPWELL (St Peter) *Ely 14*   **P** *R T Townley Esq*   **P-in-c** M P SKILLINGS
UPWELL CHRISTCHURCH (Christ Church)   *see* Christchurch and Manea and Welney *Ely*
UPWEY (St Laurence)   *see* Bincombe w Broadwey, Upwey and Buckland Ripers *Sarum*
UPWOOD (St Peter)   *see* The Ramseys and Upwood *Ely*
URCHFONT (St Michael and All Angels)   *see* The Cannings and Redhorn *Sarum*
URMSTON (St Clement) *Man 5*   **P** *Bp*   **P-in-c** K L MARSHALL   **NSM** B R CORKE   **OLM** C A BAILEY
URSWICK (St Mary the Virgin and St Michael)   *see* Aldingham, Dendron, Rampside and Urswick *Carl*
USHAW MOOR (St Luke)   *see* Brandon and Ushaw Moor *Dur*
USSELBY (St Margaret)   *see* Kelsey Gp *Linc*
USWORTH (Holy Trinity) (St Michael and All Angels) *Dur 11*   **P** *Bp*   **R** J WING
UTKINTON (St Paul)   *see* Tarporley *Ches*
UTLEY (St Mark) *Leeds 5*   **P** *Bp and R Keighley St Andr (jt)*   **V** D WALMSLEY   **C** T A RAISTRICK   **NSM** J LONG, J M INESON
UTTERBY (St Andrew)   *see* Fotherby *Linc*
UTTOXETER AREA (St Mary the Virgin) *Lich 15*   **P** *Patr Bd*   **TV** J C CANT, S WILLETTS   **OLM** C H BROWN, C W DALE, I M SMITH, J S LANDER
UXBRIDGE (St Andrew) (St Margaret) (St Peter) *Lon 24*   **P** *Bp*   **TR** A F SHEARD   **TV** C W BOWMAN   **C** A J LEWIS, J A HUGHMAN   **Hon C** T D ATKINS   **NSM** J JENKINS
VALE *Ox 27*   **P** *Bp, D&C Windsor, and Worc Coll Ox (jt)*   **V** W J N DURANT   **NSM** G R MOODY, P D B GOODING
VALE and Cotswold Edge *Glouc 8*   **P** *Patr Bd (3 turns) and Ld Chan (1 turn)*   **TR** S C BISHOP   **TV** D J FORMAN, D L DELAP   **NSM** C M WOODRUFF
VALE OF BELVOIR Parishes *Leic 2*   **P** *Patr Bd (2 turns), Ld Chan (1 turn)*   **TV** D C PAYNE
VALE OF PEWSEY *Sarum 19*   **P** *Patr Bd*   **TR** D F LARKEY   **TV** J C TOTNEY, M J WINDSOR   **OLM** G E R OSBORNE
VALLEY END (St Saviour)   *see* Chobham w Valley End *Guildf*
VALLEY PARK (St Francis) *Win 10*   **P** *Bp*   **V** P F HUTCHINSON
VANGE (St Chad) *Chelmsf 12*   **P** *MMCET*   **R** D A O IBIAYO

VAUXHALL (St Peter)   *see* N Lambeth *S'wark*
VENN OTTERY (St Gregory)   *see* Ottery St Mary, Alfington, W Hill, Tipton etc *Ex*
VENTNOR (Holy Trinity) *Portsm 7*   **P** *Bp*   **V** H E WRIGHT
VENTNOR (St Alban)   *see* Godshill *Portsm*
VENTNOR (St Catherine) *Portsm 7*   **P** *Ch Patr Trust*   **V** H E WRIGHT
VERNHAM DEAN (St Mary the Virgin)   *see* Hurstbourne Tarrant, Faccombe, Vernham Dean etc *Win*
VERWOOD (St Michael and All Angels) *Sarum 9*   **P** *Bp*   **V** A J M SINCLAIR   **NSM** P E MILES, W S FRENCH   **OLM** N F MOULAND
VERYAN (St Symphorian) w Ruan Lanihorne *Truro 6*   **P** *D&C and DBP (jt)*   **P-in-c** D G ROBINS
VICTORIA DOCKS (Ascension) *Chelmsf 5*   **P** *Bp*   **V** D V CHESNEY
VICTORIA DOCKS (St Luke) *Chelmsf 5*   **P** *Ld Chan*   **V** D P WADE   **Hon C** P E EJINKONYE   **NSM** I E C CHUKUKA
VICTORIA PARK (St Chrysostom)   *see* Man Victoria Park *Man*
VICTORIA PARK (St Mark)   *see* Old Ford St Paul and St Mark *Lon*
VIGO (Village Hall)   *see* Stansted w Fairseat and Vigo *Roch*
VINEY HILL (All Saints)   *see* Parkend and Viney Hill *Glouc*
VIRGINIA WATER (Christ Church) *Guildf 11*   **P** *Simeon's Trustees*   **V** S R SIZER   **C** S P WILLETTS   **NSM** W C BISSETT
VIRGINSTOW (St Bridget)   *see* Boyton, N Tamerton, Werrington etc *Truro*
VOWCHURCH (St Bartholomew)   *see* Madley w Tyberton, Peterchurch, Vowchurch etc *Heref*
WABERTHWAITE (St John)   *see* Eskdale, Irton, Muncaster and Waberthwaite *Carl*
WACTON (All Saints)   *see* Stratton St Mary w Stratton St Michael etc *Nor*
WADDESDON (St Michael and All Angels)   *see* Schorne *Ox*
WADDINGHAM (St Mary and St Peter)   *see* Bishop Norton, Waddingham and Snitterby *Linc*
WADDINGTON (St Helen) *Blackb 7*   **P** *E C Parker Esq*   **V** J R BROCKLEHURST   **Hon C** G F MACK
WADDINGTON (St Michael) *Linc 12*   **P** *Linc Coll Ox*   **R** A R BARBER
WADDON (St George)   *see* Croydon St Jo *S'wark*
WADENHOE (St Michael and All Angels)   *see* Aldwincle, Clopton, Pilton, Stoke Doyle etc *Pet*
WADHURST (St Peter and St Paul) *Chich 16*   **P** *J M Hardcastle Esq and M R Toynbee Esq (jt)*   **V** J R JAMES
WADSLEY (no dedication) *Sheff 4*   **P** *Ch Patr Trust*   **V** *vacant*
WADWORTH (St John the Baptist) w Loversall *Sheff 9*   **P** *V Doncaster and DBP (jt)*   **P-in-c** A PRICE
WAGGONERS *York 10*   **P** *Abp and Sir Tatton Sykes Bt, and Ld Chan (alt)*   **P-in-c** D E FLETCHER
WAINCLIFFE (St David)   *see* Beeston *Leeds*
WAINFLEET (All Saints)   *see* The Wainfleet Gp *Linc*
WAINFLEET (St Mary)   *as above*
WAINFLEET (St Michael)   *as above*
WAINFLEET Group, The, (All Saints) (St Mary) (St Michael) *Linc 10*   **P** *Ld Chan, Bp and T E Pitts Esq (alt)*   **R** G MORGAN
WAKEFIELD (St Andrew and St Mary) (St Swithun) *Leeds 20*   **P** *Peache Trustees*   **V** *vacant*
WAKEFIELD (St John the Baptist) *Leeds 20*   **P** *Dean*   **V** S J BUCHANAN   **NSM** P ELLIS
WAKEFIELD (St Michael the Archangel)   *see* Westgate Common *Leeds*
WAKERING, GREAT (St Nicholas) w Foulness *Chelmsf 15*   **P** *Bp*   **P-in-c** A J HURD
WAKERING, LITTLE (St Mary the Virgin)   *see* Barling w Lt Wakering *Chelmsf*
WAKES COLNE (All Saints)   *see* Gt and Lt Tey w Wakes Colne and Chappel *Chelmsf*
WALBERSWICK (St Andrew)   *see* Sole Bay *St E*
WALBERTON (St Mary) w Binsted *Chich 18*   **P** *Bp*   **V** T J C WARD
WALBROOK Epiphany *Derby 10*   **P** *Patr Bd*   **TR** A J WARD   **TV** S J CARTWRIGHT   **C** P J DOUGLAS   **NSM** A S KAY
WALBURY BEACON Benefice, The *Ox 6*   **P** *Bp, D&C Windsor, DBP, and H M Henderson Esq (jt)*   **R** R V C LEWIS   **NSM** C F ROBINSON, M J G COOKSON, S M WEBSTER
WALCOT (St Nicholas)   *see* S Lafford *Linc*
WALCOTT (All Saints)   *see* Bacton, Happisburgh, Hempstead w Eccles etc *Nor*
WALCOTT (St Oswald)   *see* Carr Dyke Gp *Linc*
WALDEN, LITTLE (St John)   *see* Saffron Walden and Villages *Chelmsf*
WALDERSLADE (St William)   *see* S Chatham H Trin *Roch*
WALDINGFIELD, GREAT (St Lawrence)   *see* Acton w Gt Waldingfield *St E*

WALDINGFIELD, LITTLE (St Lawrence) *see* Boxford,
Edwardstone, Groton etc *St E*
WALDITCH (St Mary) *see* Bridport *Sarum*
WALDRINGFIELD (All Saints) w Hemley and Newbourn *St E 2*
  P *The Revd Canon T Waller and the Revd A H N Waller, Ld Chan,
  and Mrs S E F Holden (by turn)* **R** *vacant*
WALDRON (All Saints) *Chich 13* **P** *Ex Coll Ox*
  P-in-c G M PITCHER
WALES (St John the Baptist) *Sheff 5* **P** *Bp* **V** G SCHOFIELD
WALESBY (St Edmund) *S'well 3* **P** *DBP* **V** C C LEVY
WALESBY (St Mary and All Saints) *Linc 7* **P** *Bp, DBP, and
  C Drakes Esq (jt)* **R** J H P CARR **OLM** E TURNER
WALFORD (St Michael and All Angels) *see* Ross w Walford and
  Brampton Abbotts *Heref*
WALGRAVE (St Peter) w Hannington and Wold and Scaldwell
  Pet 2 **P** *Bp (2 turns), BNC Ox (1 turn)* **P-in-c** K A I JONGMAN
WALHAM GREEN (St John) (St James) *Lon 9* **P** *Bp*
  V M W OSBORNE
WALKDEN (St Paul) and Little Hulton *Man 18* **P** *Patr Bd*
  TR A R GARNER **TV** G F PAGE **C** T C R THOMAS
WALKER (Christ Church) *Newc 3* **P** *Bp* **V** T FOREMAN
WALKERGATE (St Oswald) *see* Byker St Mark and Walkergate
  St Oswald *Newc*
WALKERINGHAM (St Mary Magdalene) *see* Beckingham,
  Walkeringham, Misterton, W Stockwith, Clayworth and
  Gringley-on-the-Hill *S'well*
WALKERN (St Mary the Virgin) *see* Ardeley, Benington,
  Cottered w Throcking etc *St Alb*
WALKHAMPTON (St Mary the Virgin) *see* Yelverton, Meavy,
  Sheepstor and Walkhampton *Ex*
WALKINGHAM HILL *Leeds 23* **P** *Bp, DBP, R Knaresborough,
  MMCET, and Major Sir Arthur Collins (jt)*
  R C A CAMPLING-DENTON
WALKINGTON (All Hallows) *York 8* **P** *Abp*
  P-in-c R E YOUNG
WALKLEY (St Mary) *Sheff 4* **P** *Bp* **V** M A FITZGERALD
WALL (St George) *see* St Oswald in Lee w Bingfield *Newc*
WALL (St John the Baptist) *see* Lich St Mich w St Mary and
  Wall *Lich*
WALLASEY (St Hilary) *Ches 7* **P** *Bp* **R** A W WARD
  C C L PIPER
WALLASEY (St Nicholas) All Saints *Ches 7* **P** *Bp and DBP (jt)*
  V J J STAPLES
WALLINGFORD (St Mary le More w All Hallows) (St Leonard)
  Ox 26 **P** *Bp* **TR** D RICE **Hon C** J K SPENCE
WALLINGTON (Holy Trinity) *S'wark 23* **P** *Ch Soc Trust*
  V S D COE **C** A D WENHAM
WALLINGTON (Springfield Church) Extra-Parochial Place
  S'wark 23 **Min** W COOKSON
WALLINGTON (St Mary) *see* Clothall, Rushden, Sandon,
  Wallington and Weston *St Alb*
WALLINGTON (St Michael and All Angels) *see* S Beddington
  and Roundshaw *S'wark*
WALLINGTON (St Patrick) *S'wark 23* **P** *Ch Soc Trust*
  V D M KING
WALLISDOWN (St Saviour) *see* Talbot Village *Sarum*
WALLOP, NETHER (St Andrew) *see* Portway and Danebury
  Win
WALLSEND (St John the Evangelist) *Newc 5* **P** *Bp*
  P-in-c A R S FALUDY **NSM** F G CHARLTON
WALLSEND (St Peter) (St Luke) *Newc 5* **P** *Bp*
  R D J SUDRON
WALMER (St Mary) (St Saviour) (Blessed Virgin Mary) *Cant 9*
  P *Abp* **V** S W COOPER **C** C G MACLEAN
WALMERSLEY ROAD (Christ Church) (St John w St Mark)
  Man 8 **P** *R Bury St Mary and trustees (jt)* **V** D J THOMPSON
  C G BARNETT **OLM** P SANDERSON
WALMGATE (St Denys) *see* York St Denys *York*
WALMLEY (St John the Evangelist) *Birm 12* **P** *Trustees*
  V P S DOEL **C** A J EVANS
WALMSLEY (Christ Church) *see* Turton Moorland *Man*
WALNEY ISLAND (St Mary the Virgin) *Carl 8* **P** *V Dalton-in-
  Furness* **V** A G BATCHELOR
WALPOLE (St Mary the Virgin) *see* Blyth Valley *St E*
**WALPOLE ST PETER (St Peter and St Paul) w Walpole
  St Andrew** *Ely 14* **P** *The Crown and DBP (alt)* **R** *vacant*
WALSALL (Annunciation of Our Lady) *see* Walsall St Gabr
  Fulbrook *Lich*
WALSALL (St Andrew) *Lich 25* **P** *Bp* **V** I M TEMPLETON
WALSALL (St Gabriel) Fulbrook *Lich 25* **P** *Bp*
  V R M MCINTYRE **C** S P OAKES
WALSALL (St Luke) *Lich 25* **P** *Bp* **V** M R KINDER
  C E J REYNOLDS
WALSALL (St Martin) *Lich 25* **P** *Bp* **V** S C BICKERSTETH
  NSM P E BALL

WALSALL (St Matthew) *Lich 25* **P** *Patr Bd*
  P-in-c J W TROOD **C** G S EVANS, M ARNOLD **Hon**
  C G A FISHER
WALSALL (St Michael and All Angels) *see* Caldmore w Palfrey
  Lich
WALSALL (St Peter) *Lich 25* **P** *R Walsall*
  P-in-c A G BURNAGE
WALSALL St Paul *Lich 25* **P** *R Walsall* **V** M R KINDER
  C E J REYNOLDS, G S EVANS
WALSALL THE PLECK (St John) and Bescot *Lich 25* **P** *V
  Walsall* **V** G S EVANS **C** M R KINDER, Y J BECKETT
WALSALL WOOD (St John) *Lich 25* **P** *R Walsall*
  V N J CARTER
WALSDEN (St Peter) *see* Todmorden w Cornholme and
  Walsden *Leeds*
WALSGRAVE ON SOWE (St Mary) *Cov 1* **P** *Ld Chan*
  V M TYLER **NSM** F E TYLER
WALSHAM LE WILLOWS (St Mary) *see* Badwell and Walsham
  St E
WALSHAM, NORTH (St Nicholas) and Edingthorpe *Nor 12*
  P *Bp (3 turns), Duchy of Lancaster (1 turn)* **V** P CUBITT
  NSM S M GUNNER **OLM** N J M PATERSON
WALSHAM, SOUTH (St Mary) *see* Broadside *Nor*
WALSHAW (Christ Church) *Man 8* **P** *Simeon's Trustees*
  V *vacant*
**WALSINGHAM (St Mary and All Saints) (St Peter), Houghton
  and Barsham** *Nor 15* **P** *J Gurney Esq and Capt J D A Keith (jt)*
  V A M MITCHAM
WALSOKEN (All Saints) *Ely 14* **P** *DBP* **R** A R LANDALL
WALTERSTONE (St Mary) *see* Ewyas Harold w Dulas,
  Kenderchurch etc *Heref*
WALTHAM (Holy Cross) *Chelmsf 3* **P** *Patr Bd* **TR** P H SMITH
  TV G F HOPKINS, K F WOOLMER **NSM** J M SMITH, T I SCOTT
WALTHAM CROSS (Christ Church) *see* Cheshunt *St Alb*
WALTHAM Group, The (All Saints) (St Matthew) *Linc 4*
  P *Parkinson Settled Estates and Bp (1 turn), Prime Min (1 turn),
  Ld Chan (1 turn)* **R** K A BOHAN **NSM** A HUNDLEBY,
  C E BUTLER
WALTHAM ON THE WOLDS (St Mary Magdalene)
  see Ironstone Villages *Leic*
WALTHAM ST LAWRENCE (St Lawrence) *Ox 5* **P** *Lord
  Braybrooke* **P-in-c** P B WATTS
WALTHAM, GREAT (St Mary and St Lawrence) w Ford End
  Chelmsf 9 **P** *Trin Coll Ox* **P-in-c** C J BROWN
  OLM R F BRAISBY, S SYKES
WALTHAM, LITTLE (St Martin) *see* Gt and Lt Leighs and Lt
  Waltham *Chelmsf*
WALTHAM, NEW (St Matthew) *see* Waltham Gp *Linc*
**WALTHAM, NORTH (St Michael) and Steventon, Ashe and
  Deane** *Win 6* **P** *DBP* **P-in-c** I K SMALE **NSM** J FOSTER
WALTHAMSTOW (St Andrew) *Chelmsf 7* **P** *Bp*
  P-in-c S G O O OLUKANMI
WALTHAMSTOW (St Barnabas and St James the Great)
  Chelmsf 7 **P** *Bp* **V** S M P SAXBY
  C L E CROMPTON-THOMAS
WALTHAMSTOW (St Gabriel) St Luke (St Mary) (St Stephen)
  Chelmsf 7 **P** *Patr Bd* **TR** V C CONANT
  TV J F SHOESMITH, N J ANSTEY **C** J V MOWBRAY,
  P M NGUGI, Y LEE
WALTHAMSTOW (St John) *Chelmsf 7* **P** *TR Walthamstow*
  V K J C BUSH
WALTHAMSTOW (St Michael and All Angels) *Chelmsf 7*
  P *Bp* **V** A W M SUMMERS
WALTHAMSTOW (St Peter-in-the-Forest) *Chelmsf 7*
  P *Bp* **V** P K TRATHEN
WALTHAMSTOW (St Saviour) *Chelmsf 7* **P** *Bp*
  V S R S TELEN
WALTON (Holy Trinity) *Ox 10* **P** *Ch Patr Trust*
  V A K E BLYTH **C** R M PHILLIPS
WALTON (Holy Trinity) *see* Street w Walton *B & W*
WALTON (not known) *see* Gilmorton, Peatling Parva, Kimcote
  etc *Leic*
WALTON (St John the Evangelist) *Ches 4* **P** *P G Greenall Esq*
  V *vacant*
WALTON (St John) *Derby 5* **P** *Bp* **V** B G MAGORRIAN
  C D P MOUNCER **NSM** R SMITH
WALTON (St John) *see* Walton St Jo *Derby*
WALTON (St Mary) *see* Lanercost, Walton, Gilsland and
  Nether Denton *Carl*
WALTON (St Mary) (St Philip) and Trimley *St E 2*
  P *Patr Bd (2 turns), Ld Chan (1 turn)* **P-in-c** C A ALLEN
  TV M G KICHENSIDE, V J WHITE **NSM** W P SMITH
WALTON (St Paul) *see* Sandal St Helen *Leeds*
WALTON (St Peter) *see* Bramham *York*
WALTON (St Thomas) *see* Baswich *Lich*

WALTON BRECK (Christ Church) (Holy Trinity) *Liv 3*
  P *Simeon's Trustees*   **P-in-c** K BOLTON   **C** D J POLLOCK
WALTON CLEVEDON (St Mary)   *see* E Clevedon w Clapton in Gordano etc *B & W*
WALTON D'EIVILLE (St James) *Cov 8*   **P** *Sir Richard Hamilton Bt*   **R** C E MIER
WALTON IN GORDANO (St Paul)   *see* E Clevedon w Clapton in Gordano etc *B & W*
WALTON LE SOKEN (All Saints) (St George) *Chelmsf 23*
  P *Bp*   **NSM** L M PORTER
WALTON LE WOLDS (St Mary)   *see* Barrow upon Soar w Walton le Wolds *Leic*
WALTON Milton Keynes *Ox 14*   **P** *DBP*   **R** M J TRENDALL
WALTON ON THE HILL (St John) *Liv 7*   **P** *Bp, Adn, and R Walton (jt)*   **P-in-c** E F LOUDON   **C** F E MYATT
WALTON ON THE HILL (St Luke) *Liv 7*   **P** *Bp*
  P-in-c E F LOUDON   **C** C E A ERVING
WALTON STREET (St Saviour)   *see* Upper Chelsea H Trin and St Sav *Lon*
WALTON, EAST (St Mary)   *see* Ashwicken w Leziate, Bawsey etc *Nor*
WALTON, HIGHER (All Saints) *Blackb 5*   **P** *V Blackb*
  V S J HUNT
WALTON, WEST (St Mary) *Ely 14*   **P** *Ld Chan*   **R** *vacant*
WALTON-LE-DALE (St Leonard) *Blackb 5*   **P** *V Blackb St Mary and St Paul*   **P-in-c** S JOHNSON   **NSM** N J PROCTER
WALTON-ON-THAMES (St Mary) *Guildf 8*   **P** *Bp*
  C C D OWEN   **OLM** J A RICHARDSON
WALTON-ON-THE-HILL (St Mary) (St Aidan) *Liv 5*   **P** *Bp*
  TR T M LATHAM   **TV** S W C GOUGH   **NSM** J A FLOOD
WALTON-ON-THE-HILL (St Peter) *Guildf 9*   **P** *Bp*   **R** *vacant*
WALTON-ON-TRENT (St Lawrence) w Croxall, Rosliston w Linton and Castle Gresley *Derby 16*   **P** *Bp and R D Nielson Esq (jt)*   **C** M A YATES
WALWORTH (St Christopher) *S'wark 10*   **P** *Bp and Pemb Coll Miss*   **V** D J J EVANS   **C** M E MOUK
WALWORTH (St John w the Lady Margaret) *S'wark 10*
  P *Bp*   **V** J F WALKER   **Hon C** G S ASKEY   **NSM** O S CROWN
WALWORTH (St Peter) *S'wark 10*   **P** *Bp*
  R A D P MOUGHTIN-MUMBY   **Hon C** S MOUGHTIN-MUMBY
  NSM A J WILD
WAMBROOK (Blessed Virgin Mary)   *see* Chard St Mary w Combe St Nicholas, Wambrook etc *B & W*
WANBOROUGH (St Andrew)   *see* Lyddington and Wanborough and Bishopstone etc *Bris*
WANBOROUGH (St Bartholomew)   *see* Seale, Puttenham and Wanborough *Guildf*
WANDSWORTH (All Saints) (Holy Trinity) *S'wark 18*   **P** *Ch Soc Trust*   **V** G S PRIOR   **C** G D CUSHING
WANDSWORTH (St Anne) (St Faith) *S'wark 18*   **P** *Bp*
  V G P JEANES
WANDSWORTH (St Michael and All Angels) (St Stephen) *S'wark 18*   **P** *CPAS and Ch Soc Trust (jt)*   **V** S MELLUISH
  C R BOOTHROYD   **NSM** P M TAYLOR
WANDSWORTH (St Paul) Wimbledon Park *S'wark 18*
  P *Bp*   **V** H D TÖLLER   **Hon C** E M TÖLLER
  NSM N VON FRAUNHOFER
WANDSWORTH COMMON (St Mary Magdalene) *S'wark 17*
  P *Bp*   **V** N J PEACOCK   **NSM** S D JACKSON
WANDSWORTH COMMON (St Michael)   *see* Battersea St Mich *S'wark*
WANGFORD (St Peter)   *see* Sole Bay *St E*
WANLIP (Our Lady and St Nicholas)   *see* Birstall and Wanlip *Leic*
WANSFORD (St Mary the Virgin)   *see* Nassington, Apethorpe, Thornhaugh etc *Pet*
WANSFORD (St Mary)   *see* Nafferton w Wansford *York*
WANSTEAD (Holy Trinity) Hermon Hill *Chelmsf 6*   **P** *Bp*
  V R E HAMPSON
WANSTEAD (St Mary) (Christ Church) *Chelmsf 6*   **P** *Bp*
  R E HORWELL   **C** C J WUTSCHER   **NSM** R J WYBER
WANSTROW (Blessed Virgin Mary)   *see* Nunney and Witham Friary, Marston Bigot etc *B & W*
WANTAGE (St Peter and St Paul) *Ox 27*   **P** *D&C Windsor*
  V J L SALTER   **NSM** M V BERRETT
WANTAGE DOWNS *Ox 27*   **P** *Bp, CCC Ox, and C L Loyd Esq (jt)*
  R E A M BIRCH   **NSM** D J PAGE
WANTISDEN (St John the Baptist)   *see* Wilford Peninsula *St E*
WANTSUM Group, The *Cant 5*   **P** *Abp*   **V** A R BRADDY
  C J M ROSENTHAL
WAPLEY (St Peter)   *see* Yate *Bris*
WAPPENBURY (St John the Baptist) w Weston under Wetherley *Cov 10*   **P** *Bp*   **V** *vacant*
WAPPENHAM (St Mary the Virgin)   *see* Astwell Gp *Pet*
WARBLETON (St Mary), Bodle Street Green and Dallington *Chich 13*   **P** *Bp and The Revd E S Haviland (jt)*   **R** M A LLOYD

WARBLINGTON (St Thomas à Becket) w Emsworth *Portsm 5*
  P *Bp and J H Norris Esq (alt)*   **R** S P SAYERS   **C** D A DRAISEY
  NSM J E PRICE
WARBOROUGH (St Lawrence) *Ox 20*   **P** *CCC Ox*
  V S E BOOYS
WARBOYS (St Mary Magdalene) w Broughton and Bury w Wistow *Ely 12*   **P** *Bp and Ch Soc Trust (jt)*
  R G A DAWSON-JONES   **NSM** J TIPLADY
WARBSTOW (St Werburgh)   *see* Week St Mary Circle of Par *Truro*
WARBURTON (St Werburgh)   *see* Oughtrington and Warburton *Ches*
WARCOP (St Columba)   *see* Brough w Stainmore, Musgrave and Warcop *Carl*
WARD END Holy Trinity (St Margaret) w Bordesley Green *Birm 13*   **P** *Prime Min (1 turn), Bp and Aston Patr Trust (1 turn)*
  V P H SMITH   **C** S K BARTER   **NSM** E R KING
WARDEN (St Michael and All Angels) w Newbrough *Newc 10*
  P *Bp*   **V** J J T THOMPSON   **OLM** S J PENN
WARDEN, OLD (St Leonard)   *see* Caldecote, Northill and Old Warden *St Alb*
WARDINGTON (St Mary Magdalene)   *see* Shires' Edge *Ox*
WARDLEWORTH (St Mary w St James)   *see* Rochdale *Man*
WARDLOW (Good Shepherd)   *see* Longstone, Curbar and Stony Middleton *Derby*
WARE (Christ Church) *St Alb 19*   **P** *CPAS*   **V** J L W HOOKWAY
  C K A MURPHY   **NSM** L MOSS
WARE (St Mary the Virgin) *St Alb 19*   **P** *Trin Coll Cam*
  V D PEEL
WAREHAM (Lady St Mary) (St Martin) *Sarum 8*   **P** *Patr Bd*
  TR S F EVERETT   **TV** J MAW   **NSM** B BARRETT, M YOUNG
WAREHORNE (St Matthew)   *see* Saxon Shoreline *Cant*
WARESIDE (Holy Trinity)   *see* Hunsdon w Widford and Wareside *St Alb*
WARESLEY (St James)   *see* Gt Gransden and Abbotsley and Lt Gransden etc *Ely*
WARFIELD (St Michael the Archangel) (All Saints) (St Peter) *Ox 3*   **P** *DBP*   **P-in-c** M GRIFFITHS   **C** J A TAFT,
  P M COLLINS
WARGRAVE (St Mary the Virgin) w Knowl Hill *Ox 8*   **P** *Lord Remnant*   **V** J R M COOK   **C** J C DRAKE
WARHAM (All Saints)   *see* Holkham w Egmere w Warham, Wells and Wighton *Nor*
WARK (St Michael)   *see* Humshaugh w Simonburn and Wark *Newc*
WARKLEIGH (St John)   *see* S Molton w Nymet St George, High Bray etc *Ex*
WARKTON (St Edmund King and Martyr)   *see* Barton Seagrave w Warkton *Pet*
WARKWORTH (St Lawrence) and Acklington *Newc 6*
  P *Bp and Duke of Northumberland (alt)*   **V** M L DENT
  NSM C A SHIELD, M E HOBROUGH
WARKWORTH (St Mary the Virgin)   *see* Chenderit *Pet*
WARLEGGAN (St Bartholomew)   *see* St Neot and Warleggan w Cardynham *Truro*
WARLEY (Christ Church) and Gt Warley St Mary *Chelmsf 8*
  P *Bp and Hon G C D Jeffreys (jt)*   **P-in-c** R P BINKS
  C A W MCCONNAUGHIE
WARLEY (St John the Evangelist) *Leeds 11*   **P** *V Halifax*
  C C KAY   **NSM** J S BRADBERRY
WARLEY WOODS (St Hilda) *Birm 7*   **P** *Bp*   **V** P R G HINTON
  C M J HOPKINS
WARLEY, GREAT (St Mary the Virgin)   *see* Warley Ch Ch and Gt Warley St Mary *Chelmsf*
WARLEY, LITTLE (St Peter)   *see* E and W Horndon w Lt Warley and Childerditch *Chelmsf*
WARLINGHAM (All Saints) w Chelsham and Farleigh *S'wark 24*   **P** *Patr Bd*   **TR** J A BLUNDEN
  TV M K EDMONDS
WARMFIELD (St Peter) *Leeds 20*   **P** *Oley Trustees Clare Coll Cam*   **V** *vacant*
WARMINGHAM (St Leonard)   *see* Leighton-cum-Minshull Vernon and Warmingham *Ches*
WARMINGTON (St Mary the Blessed Virgin), Tansor and Cotterstock and Fotheringhay and Southwick *Pet 10*
  P *Bp and D&C Linc (alt)*   **V** *vacant*
WARMINGTON (St Michael)   *see* Edgehill Churches *Cov*
WARMINSTER (Christ Church) *Sarum 12*   **P** *R Warminster St Denys etc*   **P-in-c** P W HUNTER   **NSM** A J EDWARDS,
  M R COLLINS
WARMINSTER (St Denys) and Upton Scudamore *Sarum 12*
  P *Bp and Qu Coll Ox (jt)*   **P-in-c** J T M DESROSIERS
  NSM C J OWEN
WARMLEY (St Barnabas), Syston and Bitton *Bris 5*   **P** *Bp*
  R J C E ANDREW   **Hon C** J E NORMAN   **NSM** C A COSTER
  OLM R A HUMPHREY

WARMSWORTH (St Peter) *Sheff 9*   **P** *Bp*   **R** I SMITH
WARMWELL (Holy Trinity)   *see* Watercombe *Sarum*
WARNBOROUGH, SOUTH (St Andrew)   *see* N Hants Downs *Win*
WARNDON (St Nicholas) *Worc 6*   **P** *Bp*   **C** D M COOKSEY
  NSM S E POLLARD
WARNDON (St Wulstan)   *see* Worc St Wulstan *Worc*
WARNERS END (St Alban)   *see* Hemel Hempstead *St Alb*
WARNFORD (Our Lady)   *see* W Meon and Warnford *Portsm*
WARNHAM (St Margaret) *Chich 7*   **P** J C Lucas Esq
  NSM R A CATTELL
WARREN PARK (St Clare) *Portsm 5*   **P** *Bp*   **V** J G P JEFFERY
WARREN ROW (St Paul)   *see* Wargrave w Knowl Hill *Ox*
WARRINGTON (Holy Trinity) (St Ann) *Liv 12*   **P** R Warrington
  and Simeon's Trustees (jt)   **OLM** C E BATEY, P LOVATT
WARRINGTON (St Barnabas) Bank Quay *Liv 12*   **P** R
  Warrington and Bp (jt)   **V** K L F TIMMIS
WARRINGTON (St Elphin) (St John) *Liv 12*   **P** Lord Lilford
  R P D WILSON
WARRINGTON EAST (Christ Church) (Transfiguration)
  (Resurrection) (Ascension) *Liv 12*   **P** *Patr Bd*
  TR D L WILLIAMS   **TV** L A MONTGOMERY, N G SHAW
  NSM A A C FAIRCLOUGH
WARRINGTON WEST *Liv 12*   **P** *Patr Bd*   **TR** S J BAKER
  TV J C TEAR, M X THORPE, S F PEPPIATT
WARSLOW (St Lawrence)   *see* Alstonfield, Butterton, Ilam etc
  Lich
WARSOP (St Peter and St Paul) *S'well 2*   **P** *Trustees*
  R A FLETCHER   **C** B E RIENSTRA
WARTHILL (St Mary)   *see* Rural E York *York*
WARTLING (St Mary Magdalene)   *see* Herstmonceux and
  Wartling *Chich*
WARTNABY (St Michael)   *see* Old Dalby, Nether Broughton,
  Saxelbye etc *Leic*
WARTON (Holy Trinity)   *see* N Warks *Birm*
WARTON (St Oswald or Holy Trinity) w Yealand Conyers
  Blackb 14   **P** *Bp*   **V** D M PORTER
WARTON (St Paul) *Blackb 10*   **P** Ch Ch Ox
  P-in-c M L HARTLEY   **C** P J SANDERSON
WARWICK (St Leonard)   *see* Holme Eden and Wetheral w
  Warwick *Carl*
WARWICK SQUARE (St Gabriel)   *see* Pimlico St Gabr *Lon*
WARWICK Team, The New (St Mary) (St Nicholas) (St Paul)
  Cov 11   **P** Ld Chan and Patr Bd (alt)   **TR** V S ROBERTS
  TV J HEARN, L J DUCKERS
WARWICKSHIRE, NORTH All Souls *Birm 10*   **P** Ld Chan (1
  turn), V Polesworth, Birm Dioc Trustees and Mrs E V G Inge-Innes
  Lillington (1 turn)   **R** S J BANKS
WASDALE HEAD (not known)   *see* Gosforth w Nether Wasdale
  and Wasdale Head *Carl*
WASDALE, NETHER (St Michael) *as above*
WASH COMMON (St George)
WASHBOURNE, GREAT (St Mary)   *see* Winchcombe *Glouc*
WASHBURN and Mid-Wharfe *Leeds 23*   **P** *Bp*, G N le G Horton-
  Fawkes Esq, Lt Col H V Dawson and C Wyvill Esq (jt)
  R G F SHIELD
WASHFIELD (St Mary the Virgin), Stoodleigh, Withleigh,
  Calverleigh, Oakford, Templeton, Loxbeare, Rackenford,
  and Cruwys Morchard *Ex 7*   **P** *Patr Bd*
  NSM J C W ROBERTS
WASHFORD (St Mary)   *see* Old Cleeve, Leighland and
  Treborough *B & W*
WASHFORD PYNE (St Peter)   *see* N Creedy *Ex*
WASHINGBOROUGH (St John) w Heighington and Canwick
  Linc 12   **P** DBP and Mercers' Co (jt)   **R** G C GOALBY
  NSM R E TREVELYAN
WASHINGTON (Holy Trinity) *Dur 11*   **P** *Bp*   **R** D C GLOVER
  C T I BRAZIER   **NSM** T M LAYBOURNE
WASHINGTON (St Mary)   *see* Ashington, Washington and
  Wiston w Buncton *Chich*
WASHWOOD HEATH (St Mark)   *see* Saltley and Washwood
  Heath *Birm*
WASING (St Nicholas)   *see* Aldermaston and Woolhampton *Ox*
WASKERLEY (St Andrew)   *see* Blanchland w Hunstanworth and
  Edmundbyers etc *Newc*
WASPERTON (St John the Baptist)   *see* Barford w Wasperton
  and Sherbourne *Cov*
WASS (St Thomas)   *see* Coxwold and Husthwaite *York*
WATCHET (St Decuman) (Holy Cross Chapel) and Williton
  B & W 17   **P** *Bp*   **V** C F GILBERT   **C** F M B GUTTRIDGE
WATCHFIELD (St Thomas's Chapel)   *see* Shrivenham and
  Ashbury *Ox*
WATER EATON (St Frideswide) *Ox 14*   **P** *Bp*
  NSM E L BREUILLY
WATER NEWTON (St Remigius)   *see* Castor w Upton and
  Stibbington and Water Newton, Marholm and Sutton *Pet*

WATER ORTON (St Peter and St Paul) *Birm 9*   **P** *Patr Bd*
  V P B TULLETT
WATER STRATFORD (St Giles)   *see* W Buckingham *Ox*
WATERBEACH (St John) *Ely 6*   **P** *Bp*   **P-in-c** D J CHAMBERLIN
  C P H BUTLER   **NSM** D M BAGULEY, P M THORN,
  S BRADFORD
WATERCOMBE *Sarum 1*   **P** M Cree Esq (1 turn), MMCET (2
  turns), and Sir Robert Williams Bt (1 turn)   **R** D J A DOBLE
  NSM W P A BUSH
WATERDEN (All Saints)   *see* N and S Creake w Waterden,
  Syderstone etc *Nor*
WATERFALL (St James and St Bartholomew)   *see* Calton,
  Cauldon, Grindon, Waterfall etc *Lich*
WATERFORD (St Michael and All Angels)   *see* Bramfield,
  Stapleford, Waterford etc *St Alb*
WATERHEAD (Holy Trinity)   *see* Medlock Head *Man*
WATERHOUSES (St Paul) *Dur 1*   **P** R Brancepeth Esq
  V M J PEERS
WATERINGBURY (St John the Baptist)   *see* E Malling,
  Wateringbury and Teston *Roch*
WATERLOO (Christ Church) St John *Liv 1*   **P** Trustees and
  Simeon's Trustees (jt)   **V** G J CUFF
WATERLOO (St John the Evangelist) (St Andrew) *S'wark 11*
  P Abp and CPAS (jt)   **V** G W GODDARD   **C** J E RISBRIDGER
  Hon **C** R M LAMPARD   **NSM** G S N KAZIRO   **OLM** D PAPE
WATERLOO PARK (St Mary the Virgin)   *see* Gt Crosby St Faith
  and Waterloo Park St Mary *Liv*
WATERLOOVILLE (St George the Martyr) *Portsm 5*
  P *Bp*   **V** M J SHEFFIELD
WATERMOOR (Holy Trinity)   *see* Cirencester *Glouc*
WATERPERRY (St Mary the Virgin)   *see* Albury w Tiddington,
  Holton, Waterperry, Waterstock and Wheatley *Ox*
WATERS UPTON (St Michael)   *see* Tibberton w Bolas Magna
  and Waters Upton *Lich*
WATERSHED *Lich 2*   **P** Keble Coll Ox and Earl of Bradford
  Trustees (jt)   **R** R E DALE   **NSM** A J HACK
WATERSIDE PARISHES of Hambleton, Out Rawcliffe and
  Preesall *Blackb 9*   **P** *Bp*, V Kirkham, and V Garstang St Helen
  etc (jt)   **V** A J SHAW   **NSM** D BANKS   **OLM** J A SQUIRES,
  J M KIRKHAM
WATERSTOCK (St Leonard)   *see* Albury w Tiddington, Holton,
  Waterperry, Waterstock and Wheatley *Ox*
WATFORD (Christ Church) (St Mark) *St Alb 6*   **P** *Bp*, V
  Watford, and Churchwardens (jt)   **V** J D CAMPBELL
WATFORD (St Andrew) *St Alb 6*   **P** Bp and Churchwardens (jt)
  V I C PANKHURST
WATFORD (St John) *St Alb 6*   **P** *Bp*   **V** D E STEVENSON
WATFORD (St Luke) *St Alb 6*   **P** Bp, Adn St Alb, V Watford, and
  Ch Trust Fund Trust (jt)   **V** D J MIDDLEBROOK   **C** C R JONES
WATFORD (St Mary) *St Alb 6*   **P** Ch Trust Fund Trust
  V A W RINDL   **C** L ROLLS
WATFORD (St Michael and All Angels) *St Alb 6*   **P** *Bp*
  V G R CALVERT
WATFORD (St Peter and St Paul)   *see* Long Buckby w Watford
  and W Haddon w Winwick *Pet*
WATFORD (St Peter) *St Alb 6*   **P** *Bp*   **V** C P COTTEE
  NSM A D T GORTON, A P PRIOR, M PILAVACHI
WATH (St Mary)   *see* Kirklington w Burneston and Wath and
  Pickhill *Leeds*
WATH-UPON-DEARNE (All Saints) *Sheff 12*   **P** Ch Ch Ox
  V S E HOBLEY   **NSM** M C BURN
WATLING VALLEY, Milton Keynes (not known) *Ox 14*
  P *Patr Bd*   **TR** M J MORRIS   **OLM** T HADDEN
WATLINGTON (St Leonard)   *see* Icknield *Ox*
WATLINGTON (St Peter and St Paul) *Ely 9*   **P** *Bp*
  P-in-c B L BURTON   **Hon C** S C MORRIS
WATTISFIELD (St Margaret)   *see* Hepworth, Hinderclay,
  Wattisfield and Thelnetham *St E*
WATTON (St Mary) *Nor 13*   **P** Ld Chan   **V** G FOSTER
  C D HAMILTON-GREY
WATTON (St Mary)   *see* Hutton Cranswick w Skerne, Watton
  and Beswick *York*
WATTON AT STONE (St Mary and St Andrew)   *see* Bramfield,
  Stapleford, Waterford etc *St Alb*
WAVENDON (Assumption of the Blessed Virgin Mary)
  see Walton Milton Keynes *Ox*
WAVERTON (Christ Church)   *see* Solway Plain *Carl*
WAVERTON (St Peter) w Aldford and Bruera *Ches 5*
  P Bp, D&C, and Duke of Westmr (jt)   **R** J T P BEAUCHAMP
WAVERTREE (Holy Trinity) *Liv 6*   **P** *Bp*   **R** J EASTWOOD
  NSM J PHILLIPS
WAVERTREE (St Bridget) (St Thomas) *Liv 6*   **P** Simeon's
  Trustees and R Wavertree H Trin (jt)   **P-in-c** W J SANDERS
WAVERTREE (St Mary) *Liv 6*   **P** *Bp*   **R** J P ASQUITH
WAWNE (St Peter) *York 14*   **P** *Abp*   **V** *vacant*

WAXHAM, GREAT (St John)   *see* Bacton, Happisburgh, Hempstead w Eccles etc *Nor*
WAYFORD (St Michael and All Angels)   *see* Wulfric Benefice *B & W*
WEALD (St George)   *see* Sevenoaks Weald *Roch*
WEALD, SOUTH (St Peter) *Chelmsf 8*   **P** *Bp*   **V** *vacant*
WEALDSTONE (Holy Trinity) *Lon 23*   **P** *Bp*   **V** T M MALONEY   **C** K T K KERR   **NSM** F E MALONEY
WEARDALE, UPPER *Dur 9*   **P** *Bp (5 turns), Duchy of Lancaster (1 turn), and Ld Chan (1 turn)*   **R** S E KENT
WEARE (St Gregory)   *see* Crook Peak *B & W*
WEARE GIFFARD (Holy Trinity)   *see* Bideford, Northam, Westward Ho!, Appledore etc *Ex*
WEARSIDE, NORTH *Dur 1*   **P** *Patr Bd*   **TR** S W ELSTOB   **TV** H T REYNOLDS, J A BRADSHAW
WEASENHAM (All Saints)   *see* Rougham, Weasenham and Wellingham *Nor*
WEASENHAM (St Peter) *as above*
WEASTE (St Luke w All Saints)   *see* Salford All SS *Man*
WEAVERHAM (St Mary the Virgin) *Ches 6*   **P** *Bp*   **V** A BROWN   **C** J BROWN
WEAVERTHORPE (St Andrew) w Helperthorpe, Luttons Ambo and Kirby Grindalythe w Wharram *York 6*   **P** *Abp and D&C (jt)*   **P-in-c** A D BOWDEN
WEBHEATH (St Philip)   *see* Redditch H Trin *Worc*
WEDDINGTON (St James) and Caldecote *Cov 5*   **P** *Bp*   **P-in-c** K A BETTERIDGE
WEDMORE (St Mary) w Theale and Blackford *B & W 1*   **P** *Bp*   **V** R W NEILL   **NSM** J E HAWES, P A KINGDOM
WEDNESBURY (St Bartholomew) *Lich 26*   **P** *Bp*   **V** T R VASBY-BURNIE   **C** S P SKIDMORE
WEDNESBURY (St James and St John) *Lich 26*   **P** *Trustees*   **P-in-c** M M ENNIS
WEDNESBURY (St Paul) Wood Green *Lich 26*   **P** *Bp*   **V** D C NJUGUNA
WEDNESFIELD (St Thomas) (St Augustine and St Chad) (St Alban) *Lich 29*   **P** *Patr Bd*   **TR** N E WATSON   **TV** S M LEACH   **C** V J TOBIN
WEEDON (School Chapel)   *see* Schorne *Ox*
WEEDON BEC (St Peter and St Paul) w Everdon and Dodford *Pet 3*   **P** *Bp*   **P-in-c** J F A M KNIGHT
WEEDON LOIS (St Mary and St Peter)   *see* Astwell Gp *Pet*
WEEFORD (St Mary the Virgin)   *see* Whittington w Weeford *Lich*
WEEK ST MARY Circle of Parishes (St Mary the Virgin) *Truro 8*   **P** *Bp, Walsingham Coll, Guild of All So, SS Coll Cam, and Earl of St Germains (jt)*   **R** A M WINDROSS
WEEKLEY (St Mary the Virgin)   *see* Geddington w Weekley *Pet*
WEELEY (St Andrew) and Little Clacton *Chelmsf 23*   **P** *Bp and BNC Ox (alt)*   **R** D M NEWMAN
WEETHLEY (St James)   *see* Alcester Minster *Cov*
WEETING (St Mary)   *see* Grimshoe *Ely*
WEETON (St Barnabas)   *see* Lower Wharfedale *Leeds*
WEETON (St Michael)   *see* Ribby cum Wrea and Weeton *Blackb*
WEETSLADE (St Paul) *Newc 1*   **P** *Bp*   **V** A MAUGHAN
WELBORNE (All Saints)   *see* Mattishall and the Tudd Valley *Nor*
WELBOURN (St Chad) *Linc 22*   **P** *Hyndman Trustees*   **R** A S J HEALY
WELBURN (St John the Evangelist)   *see* Howardian Gp *York*
WELBURY (St Leonard)   *see* Rounton w Welbury *York*
WELBY (St Bartholomew)   *see* Ancaster Wilsford Gp *Linc*
WELBY (St Bartholomew)   *see* Melton Mowbray *Leic*
WELCOMBE (St Nectan)   *see* Parkham, Alwington, Buckland Brewer etc *Ex*
WELDON (St Mary the Virgin) w Deene *Pet 7*   **P** *DBP and E Brudenell Esq (jt)*   **P-in-c** K M TAYLOR
WELFORD (St Gregory)   *see* W Downland *Ox*
WELFORD (St Mary the Virgin) w Sibbertoft and Marston Trussell *Pet 2*   **P** *Bp*   **P-in-c** J E DONALDSON
WELFORD (St Peter)   *see* Quinton, Welford, Weston and Marston Sicca *Glouc*
WELHAM (St Andrew), Glooston and Cranoe and Stonton Wyville *Leic 3*   **P** *Bp, E Brudenell Esq, and MMCET (jt)*   **P-in-c** J E GASPER
WELL (St Margaret) *Linc 10*   **P** *Bp*   **NSM** J M MORTON   **OLM** R D BARRETT
WELL (St Michael)   *see* W Tanfield and Well w Snape and N Stainley *Leeds*
WELL HILL (Mission)   *see* Chelsfield *Roch*
WELLAND (St James)   *see* Hanley Castle, Hanley Swan and Welland *Worc*
WELLESBOURNE (St Peter) *Cov 8*   **P** *Ld Chan*   **V** C E MIER   **NSM** W E BIDDINGTON
WELLING (St John the Evangelist) *Roch 15*   **P** *Bp*   **V** A J D FOOT   **C** S K BROADIE

WELLING (St Mary the Virgin) *S'wark 6*   **P** *Bp*   **V** K E ASTON   **NSM** S E GREENWOOD
WELLINGBOROUGH (All Hallows) *Pet 6*   **P** *Exors Major E C S Byng-Maddick*   **P-in-c** A J LYNETT   **NSM** G ALDERSON
WELLINGBOROUGH (All Saints) *Pet 6*   **P** *V Wellingborough*   **V** A M LYNETT   **NSM** G ALDERSON
WELLINGBOROUGH (St Andrew) *Pet 6*   **P** *Bp*   **P-in-c** M S COTTON
WELLINGBOROUGH (St Barnabas) *Pet 6*   **P** *Bp*   **P-in-c** C A OSTLER   **C** R RAILTON
WELLINGBOROUGH (St Mark) *Pet 6*   **P** *Bp*   **V** A CUTHBERTSON
WELLINGBOROUGH (St Mary the Virgin) *Pet 6*   **P** *Guild of All So*   **V** R J T FARMER
WELLINGHAM (St Andrew)   *see* Rougham, Weasenham and Wellingham *Nor*
WELLINGORE (All Saints)   *see* Graffoe Gp *Linc*
WELLINGTON (All Saints) (St John the Baptist) and District *B & W 16*   **P** *Patr Bd*   **TR** T L V TREANOR   **TV** A G ELLACOTT, S N PAINTING   **C** M H PERRY   **NSM** M C HEARL
WELLINGTON (All Saints) w Eyton (St Catherine) *Lich 21*   **P** *Ch Trust Fund Trust*   **V** M C IRELAND   **C** D N ASH, J W R GRICE   **Hon C** M A SMALLMAN   **NSM** R A KIRBY
WELLINGTON (Christ Church)   *see* Hadley and Wellington Ch Ch *Lich*
WELLINGTON HEATH (Christ Church)   *see* Ledbury *Heref*
WELLOW (St Julian the Hospitaller)   *see* Peasedown St John w Wellow and Foxcote etc *B & W*
WELLOW (St Swithin)   *see* Kneesall w Laxton and Wellow *S'well*
WELLOW, EAST w WEST (St Margaret) and Sherfield English *Win 12*   **P** *Bp and CPAS (jt)*   **V** C F PETTET
WELLS (St Cuthbert) w Wookey Hole *B & W 7*   **P** *D&C*   **V** A Q H WHEELER   **NSM** J A COLE
WELLS (St Thomas) w Horrington *B & W 7*   **P** *D&C*   **P-in-c** T C OSMOND   **NSM** C M COWLIN, N T FRIDD
WELLS-NEXT-THE-SEA (St Nicholas)   *see* Holkham w Egmere w Warham, Wells and Wighton *Nor*
WELNEY (St Mary)   *see* Christchurch and Manea and Welney *Ely*
WELSH FRANKTON (St Andrew)   *see* Criftins w Dudleston and Welsh Frankton *Lich*
WELSH NEWTON (St Mary the Virgin)   *see* Goodrich, Marstow, Welsh Bicknor, Llangarron etc *Heref*
WELSHAMPTON (St Michael)   *see* Petton w Cockshutt, Welshampton and Lyneal etc *Lich*
WELSHPOOL (St Mary) and Castle Caereinion *St As 8*   **R** S G WILLSON
WELTON (St Helen) w Melton *York 14*   **P** *DBP*   **V** E E BIELBY   **NSM** A A V SCHRIMSHAW
WELTON (St James)   *see* Westward, Rosley-w-Woodside and Welton *Carl*
WELTON (St Martin)   *see* Daventry, Ashby St Ledgers, Braunston etc *Pet*
WELTON (St Mary) and Dunholme w Scothern *Linc 5*   **P** *Bp and DBP (jt)*   **V** A S WATSON   **NSM** P J IEVINS   **OLM** C A JONES
WELTON-LE-MARSH (St Martin)   *see* Burgh Gp *Linc*
WELTON-LE-WOLD (St Martin)   *see* Louth *Linc*
WELWICK (St Mary)   *see* Easington w Skeffling, Keyingham, Ottringham etc *York*
WELWYN GARDEN CITY (St Francis of Assisi) *St Alb 18*   **P** *Bp*   **V** J E FENNELL   **C** J M YOUNG
WELWYN Team Ministry, The (St Mary the Virgin) (St Michael) *St Alb 18*   **P** *Patr Bd*   **TR** D L MUNCHIN   **TV** S L UNDERWOOD   **C** L J C DALLAS
WEM (St Peter and St Paul) *Lich 22*   **P** *Lord Barnard*   **P-in-c** N P HERON   **NSM** T D SMITH
WEMBDON (St George) *B & W 13*   **P** *Ch Soc Trust*   **V** C D E MOLL
WEMBLEY (St Augustine)   *see* Wembley Park *Lon*
WEMBLEY (St John the Evangelist) *Lon 21*   **P** *Ch Patr Trust*   **V** F ADU-BOACHIE   **NSM** U P HARRY
WEMBLEY PARK (St Augustine) *Lon 21*   **P** *Bp*   **V** H M ASKWITH
WEMBLEY, NORTH (St Cuthbert) *Lon 21*   **P** *Bp*   **V** S R MORRIS
WEMBURY (St Werburgh) *Ex 20*   **P** *D&C Windsor*   **P-in-c** M L KIRKBRIDE   **C** V R YOUNG
WEMBWORTHY (St Michael)   *see* Burrington, Chawleigh, Cheldon, Chulmleigh etc *Ex*
WENDENS AMBO (St Mary the Virgin)   *see* Saffron Walden and Villages *Chelmsf*
WENDLEBURY (St Giles)   *see* Akeman *Ox*
WENDLING (St Peter and St Paul)   *see* Gressenhall w Longham w Wendling etc *Nor*

WENDOVER (St Mary)   *see* Wendover and Halton *Ox*
WENDOVER (St Mary) (St Agnes's Chapel) and Halton *Ox 17*
  P *Ld Chan*   **R** M C DEARNLEY   **NSM** M D HUNT
WENDRON (St Wendron)   *see* Helston and Wendron *Truro*
WENDY (All Saints)   *see* Shingay Gp *Ely*
WENHAM, GREAT (St John)   *see* Capel St Mary w Lt and Gt
  Wenham *St E*
WENHASTON (St Peter)   *see* Blyth Valley *St E*
WENLOCK *Heref 10*   **P** *Patr Bd*   **TR** M C STAFFORD
  NSM J A CUMBERLAND
WENLOCK, LITTLE (St Lawrence)   *see* Coalbrookdale, Iron-
  Bridge and Lt Wenlock *Heref*
WENLOCK, MUCH (Holy Trinity)   *see* Wenlock *Heref*
WENNINGTON (St Mary and St Peter)   *see* Rainham w
  Wennington *Chelmsf*
WENSLEYDALE, UPPER *Leeds 27*   **P** *Bp, R Penhill, G L Metcalfe,*
  and E A Cherniavsky (jt)   **V** A B CHAPMAN
WENSUM Benefice, The *Nor 22*   **P** *New Coll Ox, Margaret Lady*
  Prince-Smith, Bp, and D&C (jt)   **R** *vacant*
WENSUM VILLAGE Group, UPPER *Nor 15*   **P** *Marquess*
  Townshend, the Revd C S P Douglas Lane, Ch Coll Cam, and
  DBP (jt)   **R** R D STAPLEFORD
WENT VALLEY *Leeds 19*   **P** *Bp, Earl of Rosse, and Sir Philip*
  Naylor-Leyland Bt (jt)   **V** A T JUDD
WENTBRIDGE (St John)   *see* Went Valley *Leeds*
WENTNOR (St Michael and All Angels) w Ratlinghope,
  Myndtown, Norbury, More, Lydham and Snead *Heref 9*
  P *Ch Ch Ox (4 turns) and J J C Coldwell Esq (1 turn)*
  R N F M MORRIS
WENTWORTH (Harley Mission Church) (Holy Trinity) *Sheff 12*
  P *Sir Philip Naylor-Leyland Bt*   **P-in-c** J C BARNES
WENTWORTH (St Peter)   *see* Witchford w Wentworth *Ely*
WEOBLEY (St Peter and St Paul) w Sarnesfield and Norton
  Canon *Heref 4*   **P** *Bp (2 turns), R A Marshall Esq (1 turn)*
  V S A J SEMPLE   **C** C J JOHNSON
WEOLEY CASTLE (St Gabriel) *Birm 2*   **P** *Bp*   **V** *vacant*
WEREHAM (St Margaret) *Ely 9*   **P** *Bp*   **P-in-c** B L BURTON
WERNETH (St Paul) *Ches 16*   **P** *DBP*   **V** L BOYLE
  NSM W S ATKINSON
WERRINGTON (St John the Baptist w Emmanuel) *Pet 11*
  P *Bp*   **V** G H ROGERS   **C** S FEAR
WERRINGTON (St Martin of Tours)   *see* Boyton, N Tamerton,
  Werrington etc *Truro*
WERRINGTON (St Philip) and Wetley Rocks *Lich 6*
  P *Bp and V Caverswall and Weston Coyney w Dilhorne (jt)*
  V S E GOODWIN   **C** D EDGE   **OLM** I T COPELAND,
  S J PARKER
WESHAM (Christ Church) and Treales *Blackb 10*   **P** *V*
  Kirkham   **V** J D JONES
WESSINGTON (Christ Church)   *see* Ashover and Brackenfield w
  Wessington *Derby*
WEST   *see also under substantive place name*
WEST BAY (St John)   *see* Bridport *Sarum*
WEST COAST *S & M*   **V** N P GODFREY
  NSM E D MARCHMENT, J E HAMER
WEST DEAN (All Saints)   *see* Alfriston w Lullington, Litlington,
  W Dean and Folkington *Chich*
WEST DEAN (St Andrew)   *see* E Dean, Singleton, and W Dean
  Chich
WEST DEAN (St Mary)   *see* Clarendon *Sarum*
WEST DOWN (St Calixtus)   *see* Heanton Punchardon,
  Marwood and W Down *Ex*
WEST DOWNLAND *Ox 6*   **P** *Bp, Sir Philip Wroughton, and D&C*
  Westmr (jt)   **R** J P TOWNEND   **NSM** M A HARWOOD
WEST END (Holy Trinity)   *see* Bisley and W End *Guildf*
WEST END (St George)   *see* Esher *Guildf*
WEST END (St James) *Win 10*   **P** *Bp*   **P-in-c** T G WHARTON
  NSM L S GALVIN
WEST FELTON (St Michael)   *see* Whittington and W Felton w
  Haughton *Lich*
WEST GREEN (Christ Church w St Peter) *Lon 19*   **P** *Bp*
  V *vacant*
WEST GREEN (St Peter)   *see* Crawley *Chich*
WEST HAM (All Saints) *Chelmsf 5*   **P** *The Crown*   **V** S R KIRBY
  NSM S M CHANDLER
WEST HAM (St Matthew) *Chelmsf 5*   **P** CPAS
  P-in-c D A RICHARDS   **C** C C ASINUGO
WEST HAM (St Matthew)   *see* W Ham St Matt *Chelmsf*
WEST HEATH (St Anne) *Birm 4*   **P** *Bp*   **V** S C L DIMES
WEST HILL (St Michael the Archangel)   *see* Ottery St Mary,
  Alfington, W Hill, Tipton etc *Ex*
WEST MOORS (St Mary the Virgin) *Sarum 9*   **P** *Bp*
  V A J W ROWLAND   **NSM** L MORRIS
WEST ORCHARD (St Luke)   *see* Shaftesbury *Sarum*
WEST ROW (St Peter)   *see* Mildenhall *St E*
WEST WOODHAY (St Laurence)   *see* Walbury Beacon *Ox*

WESTACRE (All Saints)   *see* Nar Valley *Nor*
WESTBERE (All Saints)   *see* Sturry w Fordwich and Westbere w
  Hersden *Cant*
WESTBOROUGH (All Saints)   *see* Claypole *Linc*
WESTBOROUGH (St Clare) (St Francis) *Guildf 5*   **P** *Bp*
  TR S M HODGES   **TV** S POWNALL
WESTBOURNE (Christ Church) Chapel *Win 8*
  Min N R T HISCOCKS
WESTBOURNE (St John the Baptist) *Chich 3*   **P** *Bp*
  R F A WRIGHT
WESTBROOK (All Saints)   *see* Margate All SS *Cant*
WESTBROOK (St James)   *see* Warrington W *Liv*
WESTBROOK (St Philip) *as above*
WESTBURY (All Saints)   *see* White Horse *Sarum*
WESTBURY (St Augustine)   *see* W Buckingham *Ox*
WESTBURY (St Mary), Worthen and Yockleton *Heref 12*
  P *Bp (2 turns), New Coll Ox (1 turn)*   **R** J P ROWE
WESTBURY PARK (St Alban)   *see* Westbury-on-Trym St Alb *Bris*
WESTBURY SUB MENDIP (St Lawrence) w Easton *B & W 1*
  P *Bp*   **V** P M HOLLINGSWORTH
WESTBURY-ON-SEVERN (St Peter and St Paul) w Flaxley,
  Blaisdon and Minsterworth *Glouc 3*   **P** *Bp, D&C Heref, and*
  Sir Thomas Crawley-Boevey Bt (jt)   **P-in-c** S C TAYLOR
  C C STERRY, D A GILL
WESTBURY-ON-TRYM (Holy Trinity) *Bris 2*   **P** SMF
  V A H HART
WESTBURY-ON-TRYM (St Alban) *Bris 2*   **P** *Bp*
  V E L LANGLEY   **OLM** J M DOYLE
WESTCLIFF (Church of Reconciliation)   *see* Brumby *Linc*
WESTCLIFF (St Andrew) *Chelmsf 15*   **P** *Bp*   **V** *vacant*
WESTCLIFF (St Cedd and the Saints of Essex)   *see* Prittlewell
  St Pet w Westcliff St Cedd *Chelmsf*
WESTCLIFF (St Michael and All Angels) *Chelmsf 15*   **P** *Bp*
  P-in-c T LOH
WESTCLIFF (St Saviour)   *see* Southend St Sav Westcliff
  Chelmsf
WESTCLIFFE (St Peter)   *see* St Margarets-at-Cliffe w Westcliffe
  etc *Cant*
WESTCOMBE PARK (St George)   *see* E Greenwich *S'wark*
WESTCOTE (St Mary the Virgin)   *see* Broadwell, Evenlode,
  Oddington, Adlestrop etc *Glouc*
WESTCOTE BARTON (St Edward the Confessor) w Steeple
  Barton, Duns Tew and Sandford St Martin and Over w
  Nether Worton *Ox 29*   **P** *Bp, DBP, Duke of Marlborough, Exors*
  Mrs S C Rittson-Thomas, P J Schuster, and D C C Webb Esq (jt)
  R G R ARTHUR
WESTCOTT (Holy Trinity) *Guildf 7*   **P** *Bp*   **P-in-c** A C JONAS
WESTCOTT (St Mary)   *see* Schorne *Ox*
WESTDENE (The Ascension)   *see* Patcham *Chich*
WESTERDALE (Christ Church) *York 21*   **P** *Abp*
  V M J HAZELTON
WESTERFIELD (St Mary Magdalene) and Tuddenham w
  Witnesham *St E 4*   **P** *Bp, Peterho Cam, and DBP (alt)*
  NSM A W FORSDIKE, C A FORSDIKE
WESTERHAM (St Mary the Virgin) *Roch 9*   **P** J St A Warde Esq
  V K P BARNARD
WESTERLEIGH (St James the Great)   *see* Yate *Bris*
WESTERN DOWNLAND *Sarum 11*   **P** *Hyndman Trustees,*
  A N Hanbury Esq, and W J Purvis Esq (jt)   **R** L M PLAYER
WESTFIELD (St Andrew)   *see* Barnham Broom and Upper Yare
  Nor
WESTFIELD (St John the Baptist) and Guestling *Chich 17*
  P *Bp and DBP (jt)*   **V** R MULFORD   **NSM** J C COLLINS
WESTFIELD (St Mark)   *see* Woking St Pet *Guildf*
WESTFIELD (St Mary) *Carl 7*   **P** *Bp*   **V** S G AXTELL
WESTFIELD (St Peter) *B & W 11*   **P** *Bp*   **V** *vacant*
WESTGATE (St Andrew)   *see* Upper Weardale *Dur*
WESTGATE (St James) *Cant 5*   **P** *Abp*   **V** S G RAE
WESTGATE (St Martin of Tours)   *see* Torrisholme *Blackb*
WESTGATE COMMON (St Michael the Archangel) *Leeds 20*
  P *V Alverthorpe*   **P-in-c** G A SYKES
WESTGATE-ON-SEA (St Saviour) *Cant 5*   **P** *Abp*   **C** B E WAY
WESTHALL (St Andrew)   *see* Hundred River and Wainford *St E*
WESTHAM (St Mary the Virgin) *Chich 14*   **P** *Duke of*
  Devonshire   **P-in-c** C A CLARK
WESTHAMPNETT (St Peter)   *see* Chich St Paul and
  Westhampnett *Chich*
WESTHEAD (St James)   *see* Newburgh w Westhead *Liv*
WESTHIDE (St Bartholomew)   *see* Bartestree Cross *Heref*
WESTHOPE (Mission Room)   *see* Canon Pyon w King's Pyon,
  Birley and Wellington *Heref*
WESTHORPE (St Margaret)   *see* Badwell and Walsham *St E*
WESTHOUGHTON (St Bartholomew)   *see* Daisy Hill,
  Westhoughton and Wingates *Man*
WESTLANDS (St Andrew) *Lich 9*   **P** *Simeon's Trustees*
  V J A DAWSWELL   **C** L SIU

WESTLEIGH (St Paul) *Man 19*   **P** *V Leigh St Mary*
P-in-c J M COOPER
WESTLEIGH (St Peter) *Man 19*   **P** *Bp, Dioc Chan, and V Leigh
St Mary (jt)*   **V** J M COOPER
WESTLEIGH (St Peter)   *see* Fremington, Instow and Westleigh
Ex
WESTLETON (St Peter)   *see* Yoxmere *St E*
WESTLEY (St Mary)   *see* Horringer *St E*
WESTLEY WATERLESS (St Mary the less)   *see* Raddesley Gp *Ely*
WESTMESTON (St Martin)   *see* Ditchling, Streat and
Westmeston *Chich*
WESTMILL (St Mary the Virgin)   *see* Aspenden, Buntingford
and Westmill *St Alb*
WESTMINSTER (St James the Less) *Lon 3*   **P** *D&C Westmr*
V E A GODDARD   **Hon C** A J GODDARD
WESTMINSTER (St James) Piccadilly *Lon 3*   **P** *Bp (2 turns),
Ld Chan (1 turn)*   **R** L C WINKETT   **C** J L MEADER
NSM H W J VALENTINE, I P KHOVACS
WESTMINSTER (St Mary le Strand)   *see* St Mary le Strand w
St Clem Danes *Lon*
WESTMINSTER (St Matthew) *Lon 3*   **P** *D&C Westmr*
V P A E CHESTER   **NSM** P L HANAWAY
WESTMINSTER (St Michael)   *see* Ches Square St Mich w St Phil
Lon
WESTMINSTER (St Saviour)   *see* Pimlico St Sav *Lon*
WESTMINSTER (St Stephen) w St John *Lon 3*   **P** *The Crown*
V G M BUCKLE   **C** C V DUCE   **NSM** J M HICKS
WESTMINSTER Hanover Square (St George)   *see* Hanover
Square St Geo *Lon*
WESTOE, SOUTH (St Michael and All Angels) *Dur 15*
P *Bp*   **V** P J A KENNEDY
WESTON (All Saints) *Ches 15*   **P** *Bp*   **V** M J LEYDEN
WESTON (All Saints) *Guildf 8*   **P** *Bp*   **V** P T JOHNSON
WESTON (All Saints)   *see* Bath Weston All SS w N Stoke and
Langridge *B & W*
WESTON (All Saints)   *see* Quinton, Welford, Weston and
Marston Sicca *Glouc*
WESTON (All Saints)   *see* Washburn and Mid-Wharfe *Leeds*
WESTON (All Saints)   *see* Tuxford w Weston, Markham Clinton
etc *S'well*
WESTON (Emmanuel)   *see* Bath Weston St Jo w Kelston
B & W
WESTON (Holy Trinity) *Win 13*   **P** *Bp*   **P-in-c** D MEDWAY
WESTON (Holy Trinity)   *see* Clothall, Rushden, Sandon,
Wallington and Weston *St Alb*
WESTON (St John the Evangelist)   *see* Bath Weston St Jo w
Kelston *B & W*
WESTON (St John the Evangelist)   *see* Runcorn St Jo Weston
Ches
WESTON (St Mary)   *see* Cowbit *Linc*
WESTON (St Peter)   *see* Hundred River and Wainford *St E*
WESTON BAMPFYLDE (Holy Cross)   *see* Cam Vale *B & W*
WESTON BEGGARD (St John the Baptist)   *see* Bartestree Cross
Heref
WESTON BY WELLAND (St Mary)   *see* Stoke Albany w
Wilbarston and Ashley etc *Pet*
WESTON COLVILLE (St Mary)   *see* Balsham, Weston Colville,
W Wickham etc *Ely*
WESTON COYNEY (St Andrew)   *see* Caverswall and Weston
Coyney w Dilhorne *Lich*
WESTON FAVELL (St Peter) *Pet 4*   **P** *DBP*   **R** D G KIRBY
C A L TWIGG
WESTON HILLS (St John the Evangelist)   *see* Cowbit *Linc*
WESTON IN GORDANO (St Peter and St Paul)   *see* E Clevedon
w Clapton in Gordano etc *B & W*
WESTON LONGVILLE (All Saints)   *see* Wensum Benefice *Nor*
WESTON LULLINGFIELD (Holy Trinity)   *see* Baschurch and
Weston Lullingfield w Hordley *Lich*
WESTON MILL (St Philip) *Ex 21*   **P** *Bp*   **V** *vacant*
WESTON ON TRENT (St Mary the Virgin)   *see* Aston on Trent,
Elvaston, Weston on Trent etc *Derby*
WESTON PATRICK (St Margaret)   *see* N Hants Downs *Win*
WESTON RHYN (St John)   *see* St Martins and Weston Rhyn *Lich*
WESTON SUPER MARE (All Saints) and St Saviour *B & W 10*
P *Bp*   **P-in-c** A K W HUGHES   **NSM** S A BOYD
WESTON SUPER MARE (Christ Church) (Emmanuel) *B & W 10*
P *Trustees*   **V** T G E WEBBER   **C** R A CLARK
WESTON SUPER MARE (St John the Baptist) *B & W 10*
P *Bp and Trustees (jt)*   **R** R J TAYLOR   **NSM** J A BIRKETT
WESTON TURVILLE (St Mary the Virgin) *Ox 17*   **P** *All So Coll
Ox*   **R** D N WALES   **C** S P Z SMITH   **NSM** S E FELLOWS
WESTON UNDER REDCASTLE (St Luke) *Lich 22*   **P** *Sir
Algernon Heber-Percy KCVO*   **V** *vacant*
WESTON UNDER WETHERLEY (St Michael)   *see* Wappenbury w
Weston under Wetherley *Cov*

WESTON UNDERWOOD (St Laurence)   *see* Gayhurst w
Ravenstone, Stoke Goldington etc *Ox*
WESTON UPON TRENT (St Andrew)   *see* Mid Trent *Lich*
WESTON ZOYLAND (Blessed Virgin Mary) w Chedzoy *B &
W 13*   **P** *Bp*   **V** C D KEYS
WESTON, OLD (St Swithun)   *see* W Leightonstone *Ely*
WESTON, SOUTH (St Lawrence)   *see* Thame *Ox*
WESTONING (St Mary Magdalene) w Tingrith *St Alb 8*
P *Ld Chan*   **V** N L WASHINGTON
WESTON-ON-THE-GREEN (St Mary)   *see* Akeman *Ox*
WESTON-SUB-EDGE (St Lawrence)   *see* Vale and Cotswold
Edge *Glouc*
WESTON-SUPER-MARE (St Andrew) Bournville *B & W 10*
P *Bp*   **P-in-c** T J ERRIDGE
WESTON-SUPER-MARE (St Nicholas) (St Barnabas) *B & W 10*
P *Patr Bd*   **R** M K MADELEY
WESTON-SUPER-MARE (St Paul) *B & W 10*   **P** *Bp*
V A M ALDEN   **C** A K WOLTON
WESTON-UNDER-LIZARD (St Andrew)   *see* Watershed *Lich*
WESTON-UNDER-PENYARD (St Lawrence)   *see* Ariconium
Heref
WESTOW (St Mary)   *see* W Buckrose *York*
WESTWARD (St Hilda), Rosley-with-Woodside and Welton
Carl 3   **P** *D&C*   **P-in-c** N L ROBINSON   **NSM** E REID
WESTWARD HO! (Holy Trinity)   *see* Bideford, Northam,
Westward Ho!, Appledore etc *Ex*
WESTWAY (St Katherine)   *see* N Hammersmith St Kath *Lon*
WESTWELL (St Mary)   *see* G7 Benefice *Cant*
WESTWELL (St Mary)   *see* Shill Valley and Broadshire *Ox*
WESTWICK (St Botolph)   *see* Worstead, Westwick, Sloley,
Swanton Abbot etc *Nor*
WESTWOOD (St John the Baptist) *Cov 3*   **P** *Bp*
P-in-c D G HAMMOND   **C** G I IRVINE, J A IRVINE
NSM A M HOWARTH, C R HOWARTH
WESTWOOD (St Mary the Virgin)   *see* Bradford on Avon H
Trin, Westwood and Wingfield *Sarum*
WESTWOOD (St Mary) Jacksdale   *see* Selston *S'well*
WESTWOOD, LOW (Christ Church)   *see* Ebchester *Dur*
WETHERAL (Holy Trinity and St Constantine)   *see* Holme Eden
and Wetheral w Warwick *Carl*
WETHERBY (St James) *Leeds 23*   **P** *Bp*   **P-in-c** B A GIBLIN
C T J LAUNDON
WETHERDEN (St Mary the Virgin)   *see* Haughley w Wetherden
and Stowupland *St E*
WETHERINGSETT (All Saints)   *see* S Hartismere *St E*
WETHERSFIELD (St Mary Magdalene)   *see* Finchingfield and
Cornish Hall End etc *Chelmsf*
WETLEY ROCKS (St John the Baptist)   *see* Werrington and
Wetley Rocks *Lich*
WETTENHALL (St David)   *see* Acton and Worleston, Church
Minshull etc *Ches*
WETTON (St Margaret)   *see* Alstonfield, Butterton, Ilam etc
Lich
WETWANG (St Nicholas)   *see* Waggoners *York*
WEXHAM (St Mary) *Ox 12*   **P** *Ld Chan*   **P-in-c** M KENT
**WEYBOURNE (All Saints), Upper Sheringham, Kelling,
Salthouse, Bodham and East and West Beckham (The
Weybourne Group)** *Nor 18*   **P** *Bp (2 turns), Sir Charles
Mott-Radclyffe (1 turn), D&C (1 turn), and Lord Walpole (1 turn)*
R P G BLAMIRE   **OLM** F A CLARKE
WEYBREAD (St Andrew)   *see* Sancroft *St E*
WEYBRIDGE (St James) *Guildf 8*   **P** *Ld Chan*
R B D PROTHERO   **C** T L RICKETTS
WEYHILL (St Michael and All Angels)   *see* Pastrow *Win*
WEYMOUTH (Holy Trinity) (St Nicholas) *Sarum 4*   **P** *Bp*
V R H FRANKLIN   **C** P ELLIOTT   **OLM** A DUNN
WEYMOUTH (St Edmund)   *see* Wyke Regis *Sarum*
WEYMOUTH (St John)   *see* Radipole and Melcombe Regis
Sarum
WEYMOUTH (St Mary) *as above*
WEYMOUTH (St Paul) *Sarum 4*   **P** *Bp*   **V** R M HARPER
WHADDON (St Margaret)   *see* Glouc St Geo w Whaddon *Glouc*
WHADDON (St Mary the Virgin)   *see* Canalside Benefice *Sarum*
WHADDON (St Mary) *Ely 7*   **P** *D&C Windsor*   **V** C J YANDELL
WHADDON (St Mary)   *see* Buckingham *Ox*
WHADDON (St Mary)   *see* Clarendon *Sarum*
WHALEY BRIDGE (St James) *Ches 16*   **P** *Bp and Bp Derby (alt)*
P-in-c M A JONES
WHALEY THORNS (St Luke)   *see* E Scarsdale *Derby*
WHALLEY (St Mary and All Saints)   *see* W Pendleside *Blackb*
**WHALLEY RANGE (St Edmund) and Moss Side St James w
St Clement** *Man 3*   **P** *Bp and Simeon's Trustees (jt)*
R A W HARDY   **C** F SHER, N R ELLIOTT
WHALLEY RANGE (St Margaret) *Man 3*   **P** *Trustees*
P-in-c R G BOULTER

WHALTON (St Mary Magdalene) *see* Bolam w Whalton and Hartburn w Meldon *Newc*

WHAPLODE DROVE (St John the Baptist) *Linc 18* **P** *Feoffees* **V** R J MORRISON

WHARFEDALE, LOWER *Leeds 23* **P** *Bp, V Otley, and W G C Sheepshanks Esq (jt)* **R** S W LEWIS **NSM** R E WILSON, R HUDSPETH

WHARRAM (St Mary) *see* Weaverthorpe w Helperthorpe, Luttons Ambo etc *York*

WHARTON (Christ Church) *Ches 6* **P** R Davenham **V** T D HANSON **C** M W GUEST

WHATBOROUGH Group of Parishes, The *Leic 3* **P** *Bp* **V** J D CURTIS

WHATCOTE (St Peter) *see* Tysoe w Oxhill and Whatcote *Cov*

WHATFIELD (St Margaret) *see* Bildeston w Wattisham and Lindsey, Whatfield etc *St E*

WHATLEY (St George) *see* Mells w Buckland Dinham, Elm, Whatley etc *B & W*

WHATLINGTON (St Mary Magdalene) *see* Sedlescombe w Whatlington *Chich*

WHATTON (St John of Beverley) w Aslockton, Hawksworth, Scarrington, Orston and Thoroton *S'well 5* **P** *Trustees* **V** B A WOOD

WHEATACRE (All Saints) *see* Raveningham Gp *Nor*

WHEATCROFT (St Michael and All Angels) *see* Scarborough St Martin *York*

WHEATFIELD (St Andrew) *see* Thame *Ox*

WHEATHAMPSTEAD (St Helen) *St Alb 7* **P** *Bp* **R** R M BANHAM

WHEATHILL (Holy Trinity) *see* Ditton Priors w Neenton, Burwarton etc *Heref*

WHEATHILL PRIORY Group of Parishes, The *B & W 2* **P** *Ch Soc Trust and J H Cordle Esq (1 turn), A J Whitehead Esq (2 turns), Bp (1 turn), and Mrs E J Burden (1 turn)* **R** *vacant*

WHEATLEY (St Mary the Virgin) *see* Albury w Tiddington, Holton, Waterperry, Waterstock and Wheatley *Ox*

WHEATLEY (St Mary) *see* Doncaster St Mary and St Paul *Sheff*

WHEATLEY HILL (All Saints) and Wingate w Hutton Henry *Dur 2* **P** *Bp* **P-in-c** F J GRIEVE

WHEATLEY HILLS (St Aidan) w Intake *Sheff 8* **P** *Bp* **V** D J GOSS

WHEATLEY PARK (St Paul) *see* Doncaster St Mary and St Paul *Sheff*

WHEATLEY, NORTH (St Peter and St Paul) *see* Retford Area *S'well*

WHEATON ASTON (St Mary) *see* Watershed *Lich*

WHEELOCK (Christ Church) *see* Sandbach Heath w Wheelock *Ches*

WHELDRAKE (St Helen) *see* Derwent Ings *York*

WHELFORD (St Anne) *see* S Cotswolds *Glouc*

WHELLEY (St Stephen) *see* Wigan All SS *Liv*

WHELNETHAM, GREAT (St Thomas à Becket) *see* St Edm Way *St E*

WHELNETHAM, LITTLE (St Mary) *see* Bradfield St Clare, Bradfield St George etc *St E*

WHEPSTEAD (St Petronilla) *see* Horringer *St E*

WHERSTEAD (St Mary) *see* Holbrook, Stutton, Freston, Woolverstone etc *St E*

WHERWELL (St Peter and Holy Cross) *see* The Downs *Win*

WHETSTONE (St John the Apostle) *Lon 14* **P** *Bp* **P-in-c** C KENT

WHETSTONE (St Peter) *see* Cosby and Whetstone *Leic*

WHICHAM (St Mary) *see* Bootle, Corney, Whicham and Whitbeck *Carl*

WHICHFORD (St Michael) *see* S Warks Seven Gp *Cov*

WHICKHAM (St Mary the Virgin) *Dur 13* **P** *Ld Chan* **R** B J ABBOTT

WHILTON (St Andrew) *see* Brington w Whilton and Norton etc *Pet*

WHIMPLE (St Mary), Talaton and Clyst St Lawrence *Ex 6* **P** *DBP, D&C and MMCET (jt)* **P-in-c** C E MARTIN **NSM** S WALKER

WHINBURGH (St Mary) *see* Barnham Broom and Upper Yare *Nor*

WHINLANDS Benefice, The *St E 17* **P** *Mrs A C V Wentworth, Ch Patr Trust, and Ch Soc Trust (by turn)* **P-in-c** P M LOWTHER **NSM** S E HART

WHINMOOR (St Paul) *see* Seacroft *Leeds*

WHINNEY HILL (St Peter) *see* Thrybergh *Sheff*

WHIPPINGHAM (St Mildred) w East Cowes *Portsm 8* **P** *Ld Chan* **P-in-c** A M KERR **C** V M BROWN

WHIPSNADE (St Mary Magdalene) *see* Kensworth, Studham and Whipsnade *St Alb*

WHIPTON (St Boniface) *Ex 3* **P** *Bp* **P-in-c** J W BYATT

WHISSENDINE (St Andrew) *see* Oakham, Ashwell, Braunston, Brooke, Egleton etc *Pet*

WHISSONSETT (St Mary) *see* Upper Wensum Village Gp *Nor*

WHISTON (St Mary Magdalene) *Sheff 6* **P** *Bp* **R** D E CRAIG-WILD

WHISTON (St Mary the Virgin) *see* Yardley Hastings, Denton and Grendon etc *Pet*

WHISTON (St Mildred) *see* Kingsley and Foxt-w-Whiston and Oakamoor etc *Lich*

WHISTON (St Nicholas) *Liv 2* **P** *V Prescot* **V** A J TELFER

WHITACRE, NETHER (St Giles) *see* The Whitacres, Lea Marston, and Shustoke *Birm*

WHITACRE, OVER (St Leonard) *as above*

WHITACRES, Lea Marston, and Shustoke, The *Birm 9* **P** *J K Wingfield Digby Esq (1 turn), Bp (2 turns), and Ld Chan (1 turn)* **R** *vacant*

WHITBECK (St Mary) *see* Bootle, Corney, Whicham and Whitbeck *Carl*

WHITBOURNE (St John the Baptist) *see* Edvin Loach w Tedstone Delamere etc *Heref*

WHITBURN (no dedication) *Dur 1* **P** *Bp* **R** *vacant*

WHITBY (St Hilda) (St John) (St Mary) w Ruswarp *York 21* **P** *Abp* **C** M JACKSON

WHITBY (St Thomas) *see* Ellesmere Port *Ches*

WHITCHURCH (All Hallows) w Tufton and Litchfield *Win 6* **P** *Bp* **V** K J INGLIS **Hon C** M R CHRISTIAN

WHITCHURCH (St Alkmund) *Lich 22* **P** *Bp* **R** J M HUNT **C** R A CLARKSON **OLM** S E ARMSTRONG

WHITCHURCH (St Andrew) *Ex 22* **P** *Bp* **P-in-c** S A BRASSIL **NSM** M L DONNE

WHITCHURCH (St Augustine) *Bris 1* **P** *Bp* **V** N J HAY **C** H L JOHNSON

WHITCHURCH (St Dubricius) *see* Wye Reaches Gp *Heref*

WHITCHURCH (St John the Evangelist) *see* Schorne *Ox*

WHITCHURCH (St Mary the Virgin) *see* Ilmington w Stretton-on-Fosse etc *Cov*

WHITCHURCH (St Mary the Virgin) *see* Langtree *Ox*

WHITCHURCH (St Nicholas) *Bris 1* **P** *Bp* **V** J M HANCOCK

WHITCHURCH CANONICORUM (St Candida and Holy Cross) *see* Golden Cap Team *Sarum*

WHITCHURCH HILL (St John the Baptist) *see* Langtree *Ox*

WHITE COLNE (St Andrew) *see* Halstead Area *Chelmsf*

WHITE HORSE, The *Sarum 12* **P** *Bp* **TV** S R JARVIS **C** S S MILES

WHITE LADIES ASTON (St John) *see* Peopleton and White Ladies Aston w Churchill etc *Worc*

WHITE NOTLEY (St Etheldreda) *see* Witham and Villages *Chelmsf*

WHITE RODING (St Martin) *see* S Rodings *Chelmsf*

WHITE WALTHAM (St Mary the Virgin) w Shottesbrooke *Ox 5* **P** *Sir John Smith* **P-in-c** D N ANDREW

WHITECHAPEL (St James) *see* Fellside Team *Blackb*

WHITEFRIARS (no dedication) Rushden *Pet 8* **P** *CPAS* **V** C A YOUNGMAN

WHITEGATE (St Mary) w Little Budworth *Ches 6* **P** *Bp, Lord Delamere and W R Cullimore Esq (alt)* **V** C W HUMPHRIES

WHITEHALL (St Ambrose) *see* E Bris St Ambrose and St Leon *Bris*

WHITEHALL PARK (St Andrew) *Lon 6* **P** *Ch Patr Trust* **V** S R CLARKE

WHITEHAVEN (St James) *Carl 5* **P** *Patr Bd* **P-in-c** R JACKSON

WHITEHAWK (St Cuthman) *Chich 19* **P** *Bp* **P-in-c** R M COATES **NSM** D R S PORTER

WHITEHILLS (St Mark) *see* Kingsthorpe *Pet*

WHITELACKINGTON (Blessed Virgin Mary) *see* Ilminster and Whitelackington *B & W*

WHITELEAS (St Mary w St Martin) *see* S Shields All SS *Dur*

WHITELEY Conventional District *Portsm 2* **C-in-c** P J MILLS **Min** A J MATHESON

WHITEPARISH (All Saints) *see* Clarendon *Sarum*

WHITESHILL (St Paul) *see* Stroud Team *Glouc*

WHITESTAUNTON (St Andrew) *see* Chard St Mary w Combe St Nicholas, Wambrook etc *B & W*

WHITESTONE (St Catherine) *see* Tedburn St Mary, Cheriton Bishop, Whitestone etc *Ex*

WHITESTONE (St John the Evangelist) *as above*

WHITEWATER Benefice, The *Win 5* **P** *Bp and New Coll Ox (alt)* **P-in-c** M E DE QUIDT

WHITEWELL (St Mary) *see* Marbury w Tushingham and Whitewell *Ches*

WHITEWELL (St Michael) *see* Chipping and Whitewell *Blackb*

WHITFIELD (Holy Trinity) *see* Allendale w Whitfield *Newc*

WHITFIELD (St James) (St Luke) *Derby 6* **P** *Bp* **V** A D HARGREAVES **C** D B LEATHERS

WHITFIELD (St John the Evangelist) *see* Astwell Gp *Pet*

WHITFIELD (St John) *see* Allendale w Whitfield *Newc*

WHITFIELD (St Peter) *see* Bewsborough *Cant*

WHITFORD (St Mary at the Cross) *see* Kilmington, Stockland, Dalwood, Yarcombe etc *Ex*

WHITGIFT (St Mary Magdalene) *see* The Marshland *Sheff*

WHITGREAVE (St John the Evangelist) *see* Stafford St Bertelin and Whitgreave St Jo *Lich*

WHITKIRK (St Mary) *Leeds 17* **P** *Meynell Trustees* **P-in-c** M PEAT

WHITLEIGH (St Chad) *see* Ernesettle, Whitleigh and Honicknowle *Ex*

WHITLEY (Christ Church) *see* Reading Ch Ch *Ox*

WHITLEY (St Helen) *Newc 10* **P** *Bp* **V** A J PATTERSON

WHITLEY (St James) *Cov 1* **P** *Bp* **C** G HEIGHTON

WHITLEY BRIDGE (All Saints) *see* Knottingley and Kellington w Whitley *Leeds*

WHITLEY LOWER (St Mary and St Michael) *see* Thornhill and Whitley Lower *Leeds*

WHITMINSTER (St Andrew) *see* Eastington, Frocester, Haresfield etc *Glouc*

WHITMORE (St Mary and All Saints) *see* Chapel Chorlton, Maer and Whitmore *Lich*

WHITNASH (St Margaret) *Cov 11* **P** *Lord Leigh* **R** R W S SUFFERN **C** P I A HOWELL

WHITNEY (St Peter and St Paul) *see* Eardisley w Bollingham, Willersley, Brilley etc *Heref*

WHITSBURY (St Leonard) *see* W Downland *Sarum*

WHITSTABLE (All Saints) (St Alphage) (St Andrew) (St Peter) *Cant 4* **P** *DBP* **TR** S J CONEYS **TV** D VAN K VANNERLEY, R C WEBBLEY, S C TILLOTSON **C** F R M WUYTS

WHITSTONE (St Anne) *see* Week St Mary Circle of Par *Truro*

WHITTINGHAM (St Bartholomew) and Edlingham w Bolton Chapel *Newc 6* **P** *D&C Carl and D&C Dur (alt)* **V** *vacant*

WHITTINGTON (Christ Church) *see* Wretton w Stoke Ferry and Whittington *Ely*

WHITTINGTON (St Bartholomew) *Derby 5* **P** *Bp* **R** J E MORRIS **OLM** J QUICK

WHITTINGTON (St Bartholomew) *see* Sevenhampton w Charlton Abbots, Hawling etc *Glouc*

WHITTINGTON (St John the Baptist) and West Felton w Haughton *Lich 19* **P** *Bp and Mrs A F Hamilton-Hill (jt)* **R** S E BURTON

WHITTINGTON (St Michael the Archangel) *see* Hornby w Claughton and Whittington etc *Blackb*

WHITTINGTON (St Philip and St James) *see* Worc SE *Worc*

WHITTINGTON, NEW (St Barnabas) *see* Whittington *Derby*

WHITTLEBURY (St Mary) *see* Silverstone and Abthorpe w Slapton etc *Pet*

WHITTLE-LE-WOODS (St John the Evangelist) *Blackb 4* **P** *V Leyland* **V** P R M VENABLES **C** A S MEESON

WHITTLESEY (St Andrew) (St Mary), Pondersbridge and Coates *Ely 11* **P** *Ld Chan (2 turns), Patr Bd (1 turn)* **TR** N A WHITEHOUSE **TV** G STEVENS

WHITTLESFORD (St Mary and St Andrew) *Ely 5* **P** *Jes Coll Cam* **NSM** C S WILSON

WHITTON *Sarum 18* **P** *Patr Bd* **TR** S A WEEDEN **TV** C A MARCUS, S E RODD

WHITTON (St Augustine of Canterbury) *Lon 10* **P** *Bp* **V** S M CAPLE

WHITTON (St John the Baptist) *see* Alkborough *Linc*

WHITTON (St Mary and St Botolph) and Thurleston w Akenham *St E 4* **P** *Bp (2 turns), Exors G K Drury Esq (1 turn)* **R** A S DOTCHIN

WHITTON (St Mary) *see* Tenbury *Heref*

WHITTON (St Philip and St James) *Lon 10* **P** *V Twickenham St Mary* **V** D M CLOAKE

WHITTONSTALL (St Philip and St James) *see* Slaley, Healey and Whittonstall *Newc*

WHITWELL (St John the Evangelist) *see* Harton *York*

WHITWELL (St Lawrence) *Derby 3* **P** *Bp* **P-in-c** E KIRBY

WHITWELL (St Mary and St Rhadegunde) *Portsm 7* **P** *Bp* **P-in-c** N J PORTER

WHITWELL (St Michael and All Angels) *see* Reepham, Hackford w Whitwell, Kerdiston etc *Nor*

WHITWELL (St Michael and All Angels) *see* Empingham, Edith Weston, Lyndon, Manton etc *Pet*

WHITWICK (St John the Baptist), Thringstone and Swannington *Leic 8* **P** *Duchy of Lanc (2 turns), Bp (1 turn)* **R** A J BURGESS

WHITWOOD (All Saints) *see* Castleford *Leeds*

WHITWORTH (not known) *see* Spennymoor and Whitworth *Dur*

WHITWORTH (St Bartholomew) w Facit *Man 11* **P** *Bp and Keble Coll Ox (jt)* **V** L E M WOODALL **NSM** S SHEPHERD

WHIXALL (St Mary) *see* Edstaston, Fauls, Prees, Tilstock and Whixall *Lich*

WHIXLEY (Ascension) *see* Gt and Lt Ouseburn w Marton cum Grafton etc *Leeds*

WHORLTON (Holy Cross Old Church) w Carlton and Faceby *York 20* **P** *Mrs A P F Kynge* **V** L M SHIPP

WHORLTON (St John the Evangelist) *Newc 4* **P** *Bp* **V** J M GRIEVE

WHORLTON (St Mary) *see* Barnard Castle w Whorlton *Dur*

WHYKE (St George) w Rumboldswhyke St Mary and Portfield All Saints *Chich 2* **P** *Bp* **R** T L PESKETT **Hon C** J RHODES-WRIGLEY

WHYTELEAFE (St Luke) *see* Caterham *S'wark*

WIBSEY (St Paul) *Leeds 2* **P** *Bp* **P-in-c** T J-L GUILLEMIN

WIBTOFT (Assumption of Our Lady) *see* Upper Soar *Leic*

WICHENFORD (St Lawrence) *see* Worcs W *Worc*

WICK (All Saints) *see* Littlehampton and Wick *Chich*

WICK (St Bartholomew) w Doynton and Dyrham *Bris 5* **P** *Simeon's Trustees, Ld Chan, and M H W Blaythwayt Esq (by turn)* **P-in-c** T J K BELL

WICK (St Mary) *see* Pershore w Pinvin, Wick and Birlingham *Worc*

WICK ST LAWRENCE (St Lawrence) *see* Worle *B & W*

WICKEN (St John the Evangelist) *see* Potterspury w Furtho and Yardley Gobion etc *Pet*

WICKEN (St Laurence) *see* Soham and Wicken *Ely*

WICKEN BONHUNT (St Margaret) *see* Clavering w Langley, Arkesden etc *Chelmsf*

WICKENBY (St Peter and St Lawrence) *see* Wragby Gp *Linc*

WICKERSLEY (St Alban) *Sheff 6* **P** *DBP* **R** P J HUGHES

WICKFORD (St Andrew) (St Catherine) and Runwell *Chelmsf 12* **P** *Patr Bd* **TR** J FREEMAN **TV** J H DELFGOU, N CHUMU MUTUKU **C** M J SIMPKINS, S M MANN **NSM** S J WISE

WICKHAM (St Nicholas) *see* Shedfield and Wickham *Portsm*

WICKHAM (St Swithun) *see* W Downland *Ox*

WICKHAM BISHOPS (St Bartholomew) w Little Braxted *Chelmsf 24* **P** *Bp (3 turns), CCC Cam (1 turn)* **P-in-c** J H LE SÈVE **OLM** D R CLARK-MAYERS

WICKHAM MARKET (All Saints) w Pettistree *St E 16* **P** *Ch Trust Fund Trust and Ld Chan (alt)* **V** J F ELDRIDGE

WICKHAM SKEITH (St Andrew) *see* Bacton w Wyverstone, Cotton and Old Newton etc *St E*

WICKHAM ST PAUL (St Paul and All Saints) *see* N Hinckford *Chelmsf*

WICKHAM, EAST (St Michael the Archangel) *S'wark 6* **P** *D&C* **V** P ORGAN **NSM** M W SMITH

WICKHAM, WEST (St Francis) (St Mary of Nazareth) *S'wark 19* **P** *Bp* **P-in-c** H M O'SULLIVAN **NSM** R T FORD

WICKHAM, WEST (St John) *S'wark 19* **P** *Bp* **V** J J H WARD **NSM** R T FORD

WICKHAM, WEST (St Mary) *see* Balsham, Weston Colville, W Wickham etc *Ely*

WICKHAMBREAUX (St Andrew) *see* Littlebourne and Ickham w Wickhambreaux etc *Cant*

WICKHAMBROOK (All Saints) *see* Bansfield *St E*

WICKHAMFORD (St John the Baptist) *see* Broadway w Wickhamford *Worc*

WICKHAMPTON (St Andrew) *see* Acle and Bure to Yare *Nor*

WICKLEWOOD (All Saints) *see* High Oak, Hingham and Scoulton w Wood Rising *Nor*

WICKMERE (St Andrew) *see* Lt Barningham, Blickling, Edgefield etc *Nor*

WICKWAR (Holy Trinity) *see* Charfield and Kingswood w Wickwar etc *Glouc*

WIDDINGTON (St Mary) *see* Newport w Widdington, Quendon and Rickling *Chelmsf*

WIDDRINGTON (Holy Trinity) *Newc 11* **P** *Bp* **V** *vacant*

WIDECOMBE-IN-THE-MOOR (St Pancras) *see* Ashburton, Bickington, Buckland in the Moor etc *Ex*

WIDEMOUTH BAY (Our Lady and St Anne) *see* Week St Mary Circle of Par *Truro*

WIDFORD (St John the Baptist) *see* Hunsdon w Widford and Wareside *St Alb*

WIDFORD (St Mary) (Holy Spirit) *Chelmsf 10* **P** *CPAS* **P-in-c** S R GILLINGHAM **C** A T GRIFFITHS, C SMITH

WIDFORD (St Oswald) *see* Burford w Fulbrook, Taynton, Asthall etc *Ox*

WIDMER END (Good Shepherd) *see* Hazlemere *Ox*

WIDMERPOOL (St Peter) *see* Willoughby-on-the-Wolds w Wysall and Widmerpool *S'well*

WIDNES, EAST (St Ambrose) (St John) (St Luke) (Cronton Mission) *Liv 13* **P** *Patr Bd* **TR** H C BLACKBURN **TV** L C MCIVER **C** L LEATHERBARROW

WIDNES, SOUTH (St Mary) (St Paul) *Liv 13* **P** *Patr Bd* **TR** J M COLLIER **TV** J DUFF **C** G S SHARPLES

WIDWORTHY (St Cuthbert) *see* Offwell, Northleigh, Farway, Cotleigh etc *Ex*

WIELD (St James) *see* Farleigh, Candover and Wield *Win*

WIGAN (All Saints) (St Andrew) (St Anne) (St Catharine) (St George) (St John the Baptist) (St Michael and All Angels) (St Stephen) *Liv 14*   **P** *Patr Bd*
TV S G PRITCHARD, S HIGGINSON, S NICHOLSON, W J J MATTHEWS   **OLM** M L PERRIN

WIGAN (St James) (St Thomas) *Liv 14*   **P** *R Wigan and Bp (jt)*
P-in-c N J COOK

WIGBOROUGH, GREAT (St Stephen) *see* W w E Mersea, Peldon, Gt and Lt Wigborough *Chelmsf*

WIGBOROUGH, LITTLE (St Nicholas) *as above*

WIGGATON (St Edward the Confessor) *see* Ottery St Mary, Alfington, W Hill, Tipton etc *Ex*

WIGGENHALL ST GERMANS (St Mary the Virgin)
see E Marshland *Ely*

WIGGENHALL ST MARY (St Mary Magdalene) *as above*

WIGGINTON (St Bartholomew) *see* Northchurch and Wigginton *St Alb*

WIGGINTON (St Giles) *see* Hook Norton w Gt Rollright, Swerford etc *Ox*

WIGGINTON (St Leonard) (St James) *Lich 4*   **P** *V Tamworth*
V D A DYSON   **NSM** R DAVIES   **OLM** V B MORRIS

WIGGINTON (St Nicholas) *see* Haxby and Wigginton *York*

WIGGONHOLT (not known) *see* Amberley w N Stoke and Parham, Wiggonholt etc *Chich*

WIGHILL (All Saints) *see* Rural Ainsty *York*

WIGHTON (All Saints) *see* Holkham w Egmere w Warham, Wells and Wighton *Nor*

WIGMORE (St James the Apostle) *see* Wigmore Abbey *Heref*

WIGMORE ABBEY *Heref 6*   **P** *Trustees*   **R** M D CATLING

WIGSTON (All Saints) (St Wistan) (St Thomas) *Leic 4*
P *Haberdashers' Co*   **V** T THURSTON-SMITH   **C** P DAY

WIGSTON (St Wistan) *see* Wigston *Leic*

WIGSTON MAGNA (All Saints) *as above*

WIGSTON PARVA (St Mary the Virgin) *see* Sapcote and Sharnford w Wigston Parva *Leic*

WIGSTON, SOUTH (St Thomas) *see* Wigston *Leic*

WIGTOFT (St Peter and St Paul) *see* Haven Gp *Linc*

WIGTON (St Mary) *Carl 3*   **P** *Bp*   **V** G P RAVALDE

WILBARSTON (All Saints) *see* Stoke Albany w Wilbarston and Ashley etc *Pet*

WILBERFOSS (St John the Baptist) w Kexby *York 5*   **P** *Viscount de Vesci and Lord Egremont (alt)*

WILBRAHAM, GREAT (St Nicholas) *Ely 4*   **P** *DBP*
V A A GOODMAN

WILBRAHAM, LITTLE (St John) *Ely 4*   **P** *CCC Cam*
R A A GOODMAN

WILBURTON (St Peter) *Ely 8*   **P** *Adn Ely*   **V** F E G BRAMPTON
NSM J A GAGE

WILBURY (St Thomas) *St Alb 3*   **P** *Bp*   **V** B E C PATE

WILBY (All Saints) *see* Quidenham Gp *Nor*

WILBY (St Mary the Virgin) *see* Gt Doddington and Wilby and Ecton *Pet*

WILBY (St Mary) *see* Four Rivers *St E*

WILCOT (Holy Cross) *see* Vale of Pewsey *Sarum*

WILCOTE (St Peter) *see* Forest Edge *Ox*

WILDBOARCLOUGH (St Saviour) *see* Sutton, Wincle, Wildboarclough and Bosley *Ches*

WILDEN (All Saints) *see* Stourport and Wilden *Worc*

WILDEN (St Nicholas) w Colmworth and Ravensden *St Alb 13*
P *Ld Chan, Bp, and DBP (by turn)*   **R** *vacant*

WILFORD (St Wilfrid) *S'well 6*   **P** *Lt Col Peter Clifton*
R P E MARSH   **C** A M COLLINS

WILFORD HILL (St Paul) *S'well 6*   **P** *DBP*   **V** C J HODDER

WILFORD PENINSULA, The *St E 7*   **P** *Patr Bd*
TR D J MURDOCH   **TV** J M ANDREWS, J P LEAVER, R M HATCHETT

WILKSBY (All Saints) *see* Fen and Hill Gp *Linc*

WILLAND (St Mary the Virgin) *see* Willand, Uffculme, Kentisbeare etc *Ex*

WILLAND (St Mary the Virgin), Uffculme, Kentisbeare and Blackborough *Ex 7*   **P** *Bp, CPAS, and H Chandler Esq (jt)*
P-in-c S G G TALBOT   **C** S C GARNER

WILLASTON (Christ Church) *Ches 9*   **P** *DBF*
P-in-c S W BAZELY   **NSM** L R BANNON

WILLASTON (St Luke) *see* Wistaston *Ches*

WILLEN (St Mary Magdalene) *see* Stantonbury and Willen *Ox*

WILLENHALL (St Anne) *Lich 29*   **P** *Mrs L Grant-Wilson*
V G A WELSBY

WILLENHALL (St Giles) *Lich 29*   **P** *Trustees*   **V** G A WELSBY

WILLENHALL (St John the Divine) *Cov 1*   **P** *V Cov H Trin*
C G HEIGHTON

WILLENHALL (St Stephen) *Lich 29*   **P** *Bp*   **V** G E T BENNETT
OLM M P BATCHELOR

WILLERBY (St Luke) *see* Kirk Ella and Willerby *York*

WILLERBY (St Peter) w Ganton and Folkton *York 15*   **P** N H T Wrigley Esq, MMCET, and the Revd C G Day (by turn)
P-in-c K G F HOLDING

WILLERSEY (St Peter) *see* Vale and Cotswold Edge *Glouc*

WILLESBOROUGH (St Mary the Virgin) w Sevington *Cant 6*
P *D&C and Ch Soc Trust (jt)*   **R** J C N MACKENZIE
NSM D C STAMPER

WILLESBOROUGH, SOUTH (St Barnabas) *see* Willesborough w Sevington *Cant*

WILLESDEN (St Mark) *see* Kensal Rise St Mark *Lon*

WILLESDEN (St Martin) *see* Kensal Rise St Martin *Lon*

WILLESDEN (St Mary) *Lon 21*   **P** *D&C St Paul's*   **V** *vacant*

WILLESDEN (St Matthew) *Lon 21*   **P** *Bp*   **V** A J TEATHER

WILLESDEN GREEN (St Andrew) (St Francis of Assisi) *Lon 21*
P *Bp*   **V** C P M PATTERSON

WILLEY (St Leonard) *see* Revel Gp *Cov*

WILLIAN (All Saints) *see* Letchworth St Paul w Willian *St Alb*

WILLINGALE (St Christopher) *see* Fyfield, Moreton w Bobbingworth etc *Chelmsf*

WILLINGDON (St Mary the Virgin) *Chich 14*   **P** *D&C*
P-in-c K R C AGNEW   **NSM** C I WOODWARD

WILLINGHAM (St Mary and All Saints) *Ely 6*   **P** *Bp*
P-in-c L S LIVERSIDGE

WILLINGHAM BY STOW (St Helen) *see* Stow Gp *Linc*

WILLINGHAM, NORTH (St Thomas) *see* Walesby *Linc*

WILLINGHAM, SOUTH (St Martin) *see* Barkwith Gp *Linc*

WILLINGTON (St Lawrence) *see* Cople, Moggerhanger and Willington *St Alb*

WILLINGTON (St Michael) *Derby 16*   **P** *CPAS*   **V** S A STARKEY

WILLINGTON (St Stephen) and Sunnybrow *Dur 9*   **P** *R Brancepeth*   **P-in-c** D L SPOKES

WILLINGTON QUAY (St Paul) *see* Willington *Newc*

WILLINGTON Team, The (Good Shepherd) (St Mary the Virgin) (St Paul) *Newc 5*   **P** *Prime Min*   **TR** S MCCORMACK
C E C DUFF

WILLISHAM (St Mary) *see* Somersham w Flowton and Offton w Willisham *St E*

WILLITON (St Peter) *see* Watchet and Williton *B & W*

WILLOUGHBY (St Helen) *Linc 10*   **P** *Baroness Willoughby de Eresby, Ball Coll Ox, and Bp (jt)*   **C** R E CARROLL
NSM J M MORTON   **OLM** R D BARRETT

WILLOUGHBY (St Nicholas) *see* Leam Valley *Cov*

WILLOUGHBY WATERLEYS (St Mary), Peatling Magna and Ashby Magna *Leic 7*   **P** *Bp*   **R** *vacant*

WILLOUGHBY-ON-THE-WOLDS (St Mary and All Saints) w Wysall and Widmerpool *S'well 5*   **P** *MMCET*
V S D HIPPISLEY-COX

WILLOUGHTON (St Andrew) *see* Trentcliffe Gp *Linc*

WILMCOTE (St Andrew) *see* Aston Cantlow and Wilmcote w Billesley *Cov*

WILMINGTON (St Mary and St Peter) *see* Arlington, Berwick, Selmeston w Alciston etc *Chich*

WILMINGTON (St Michael) *Roch 2*   **P** *D&C*   **V** R ARDING
Hon C P J IVESON

WILMSLOW (St Bartholomew) *Ches 12*   **P** *Bp*   **R** P A SMITH
C L C RHODES, M M SMITH   **NSM** R A YATES

WILNE (St Chad) and Draycott w Breaston *Derby 13*   **P** *Bp*
R C J SMEDLEY   **NSM** G W DUNDAS, M C PRZESLAWSKI

WILNECOTE (Holy Trinity) *Lich 4*   **P** *V Tamworth*
V O HARRISON   **OLM** C J ROBINSON

WILSDEN (St Matthew) *see* Harden and Wilsden, Cullingworth and Denholme *Leeds*

WILSFORD (St Mary) *see* Ancaster Wilsford Gp *Linc*

WILSFORD (St Michael) *see* Woodford Valley w Archers Gate *Sarum*

WILSFORD (St Nicholas) *see* The Cannings and Redhorn *Sarum*

WILSHAMSTEAD (All Saints) and Houghton Conquest *St Alb 9*   **P** *St Jo Coll Cam and Bp (alt)*   **V** S J TOZE

WILSHAW (St Mary) *see* Meltham *Leeds*

WILSILL (St Michael and All Angels) *see* Upper Nidderdale *Leeds*

WILSTHORPE (St Faith) *see* Uffington Gp *Linc*

WILSTONE (St Cross) *see* Tring *St Alb*

WILTON (St Cuthbert) *York 16*   **P** *Abp*   **V** *vacant*

WILTON (St George) *B & W 18*   **P** *Mrs E C Cutbush*
V G H J CLAPHAM

WILTON (St George) *see* Thornton Dale w Allerston, Ebberston etc *York*

WILTON (St Mary and St Nicholas) w Netherhampton and Fugglestone *Sarum 11*   **P** *Earl of Pembroke*   **R** M R WOOD
NSM S M WOOD

WILTON PLACE (St Paul) *Lon 3*   **P** *Bp*   **V** A G GYLE
C A L SLOANE   **Hon C** N S MERCER

WIMBISH (All Saints) *see* Saffron Walden and Villages *Chelmsf*

WIMBLEDON (Emmanuel) Ridgway Proprietary Chapel *S'wark 12*   **C** J ADAMS   **NSM** R DRYER, R J COEKIN
Min R A R WEEKES

WIMBLEDON (Emmanuel) Ridgway Proprietary Chapel
S'wark 13   **C** J ADAMS   **NSM** R DRYER, R J COEKIN
Min R A R WEEKES
WIMBLEDON (St Luke)   *see* Wimbledon Park St Luke *S'wark*
WIMBLEDON (St Mary) (St Matthew) (St Mark) (St John the
Baptist) *S'wark 13*   **P** *Patr Bd*   **TR** M E BIDE
TV C B GARDNER, H C ORCHARD   **C** B W RICKARDS,
C R GRIFFITHS   **NSM** A M BUDDEN
WIMBLEDON PARK (St Luke) *S'wark 13*   **P** *Simeon's Trustees*
V R J R PAICE   **C** A P O'BRIEN
WIMBLEDON PARK (St Paul)   *see* Wandsworth St Paul *S'wark*
WIMBLEDON, SOUTH (All Saints)   *see* Raynes Park St Sav and S
Wimbledon All SS *S'wark*
WIMBLEDON, SOUTH (Holy Trinity and St Peter)   *see* Merton
Priory *S'wark*
WIMBLEDON, SOUTH (St Andrew) *S'wark 13*   **P** *Bp*
V A D WAKEFIELD
WIMBLEDON, WEST (Christ Church) *S'wark 13*   **P** *TR*
Wimbledon   **V** R P LANE
WIMBLINGTON (St Peter)   *see* Doddington w Benwick and
Wimblington *Ely*
WIMBORNE (St John the Evangelist)   *see* New Borough and
Leigh *Sarum*
WIMBORNE MINSTER (St Cuthberga) *Sarum 9*   **P** *Governors
of Wimborne Minster*   **R** V A HERRICK   **C** B-J MARFLITT,
S C ALLEN   **Hon C** L J FARMER   **NSM** B GIBSON, E HARDING
WIMBORNE ST GILES (St Giles)   *see* Cranborne w Boveridge,
Edmondsham etc *Sarum*
WIMBOTSHAM (St Mary) w Stow Bardolph and Stow Bridge
w Nordelph *Ely 9*   **P** *Bp*   **P-in-c** K BURNETT-HALL
WIMPOLE (St Andrew)   *see* Orwell Gp *Ely*
WINCANTON (St Peter and St Paul) *B & W 2*   **P** *D&C*
R N C M FEAVER
WINCH, WEST (St Mary)   *see* Middlewinch *Nor*
WINCHCOMBE (St Peter) *Glouc 9*   **P** *Patr Bd*   **TV** J A HOOK,
J A NEWCOMBE   **C** J R PICKERSGILL   **NSM** N A CARTER
WINCHELSEA (St Thomas) (St Richard) and Icklesham
Chich 17   **P** *Bp and Guild of All So (jt)*   **R** R L WHITEHEAD
Hon C H M MOSELEY
WINCHENDON, NETHER (St Nicholas)   *see* Long Crendon w
Chearsley and Nether Winchendon *Ox*
WINCHENDON, OVER (St Mary Magdalene)   *see* Schorne *Ox*
WINCHESTER (All Saints)   *see* E Win *Win*
WINCHESTER (Christ Church) *Win 7*   **P** *Simeon's Trustees*
C A R SMITH, T GLEGHORN   **NSM** B R WAKELIN
WINCHESTER (Holy Trinity) *Win 7*   **P** *Bp*   **R** M F JONES
WINCHESTER (St Barnabas) *Win 7*   **P** *Bp*
P-in-c E P A DINES
WINCHESTER (St Bartholomew) (St Lawrence) (St Swithun-
upon-Kingsgate) *Win 7*   **P** *Ld Chan*   **R** C J BANNISTER
C S L GOODSON   **NSM** A GOULDING
WINCHESTER (St Cross Hospital w St Faith) *Win 7*
P *Bp*   **P-in-c** P A KENNEDY
WINCHESTER (St Luke)   *see* Stanmore *Win*
WINCHESTER St Matthew (St Paul's Mission Church) *Win 7*
P *Bp*   **R** N P SEAL   **C** A R A GRANT   **NSM** M C COPPING,
N W BIRKETT
WINCHESTER, EAST *Win 7*   **P** *Bp and Ld Chan (alt)*
R P A KENNEDY   **NSM** C M SMITH, M T SCRIVENER
WINCHFIELD (St Mary the Virgin)   *see* Hartley Wintney,
Elvetham, Winchfield etc *Win*
WINCHMORE HILL (Holy Trinity) *Lon 18*   **P** *V Winchmore Hill
St Paul*   **P-in-c** R D E BOLTON
WINCHMORE HILL (St Paul) *Lon 18*   **P** *V Edmonton*
V W J ADAM   **C** S P L COLEMAN   **NSM** L A YATES
WINCLE (St Michael)   *see* Sutton, Wincle, Wildboarclough and
Bosley *Ches*
WINCOBANK (St Thomas)   *see* Brightside w Wincobank
Sheff
WINDERMERE (St Martin) and St John *Carl 11*   **P** *Bp and
Trustees (jt)*   **R** J J RICHARDS
WINDERMERE (St Mary) Applethwaite and Troutbeck *Carl 11*
P *Bp*   **V** D M B WILMOT
WINDHILL (Christ Church) *Leeds 1*   **P** *Bp*
P-in-c M E WATSON
WINDLESHAM (St John the Baptist) *Guildf 6*   **P** *Ld Chan*
R J HILLMAN
WINDMILL, The *S'wark 25*   **P** *Ld Chan (1 turn), Bp (2 turns)*
R N J CALVER
WINDRUSH (St Peter)   *see* Sherborne, Windrush, the
Barringtons etc *Glouc*
WINDRUSH, LOWER *Ox 28*   **P** *Bp, DBP, St Jo Coll Ox, D&C Ex,
and B Babington-Smith Esq (jt)*   **R** A C M TWEEDY
WINDSOR, NEW (Holy Trinity) (St John the Baptist w All
Saints) *Ox 5*   **P** *Ld Chan*   **TR** A L SWIFT   **P-in-c** R WEBB
C K M HARRISON   **Hon C** D I DADSWELL   **NSM** M K BIRD
OLM J M QUICK

WINDSOR, OLD (St Peter and St Andrew) (St Luke's Mission
Room) *Ox 5*   **P** *Ld Chan*   **V** A S M SHOKRALLA
WINDY NOOK (St Alban) *Dur 12*   **P** *V Heworth St Mary*
V C L CULLINGWORTH   **NSM** K COULSON
WINESTEAD (St German)   *see* Easington w Skeffling,
Keyingham, Ottringham etc *York*
WINFARTHING (St Mary) w Shelfanger w Burston w Gissing
and Tivetshall *Nor 10*   **P** *Ld Chan, Bp, and DBP (jt), Hertf Coll
Ox (alt)*   **R** D F MILLS
WINFORD (Blessed Virgin Mary and St Peter) w Felton
Common Hill *B & W 9*   **P** *Worc Coll Ox and Mrs H D Pullman
(jt)*   **P-in-c** P STEPHENS
WINFORTON (St Michael and All Angels)   *see* Eardisley w
Bollingham, Willersley, Brilley etc *Heref*
WINFRITH NEWBURGH (St Christopher)   *see* The Lulworths,
Winfrith Newburgh and Chaldon *Sarum*
WING (St Peter and St Paul)   *see* Empingham, Edith Weston,
Lyndon, Manton etc *Pet*
WING w Grove (All Saints)   *see* Cottesloe *Ox*
WINGATE GRANGE (Holy Trinity)   *see* Wheatley Hill and
Wingate w Hutton Henry *Dur*
WINGATES (St John the Evangelist)   *see* Daisy Hill,
Westhoughton and Wingates *Man*
WINGERWORTH (All Saints) *Derby 5*   **P** *Bp*   **R** J D POSTON
OLM J A WILLIS
WINGFIELD (St Andrew)   *see* Athelington, Denham, Horham,
Hoxne etc *St E*
WINGFIELD (St Mary)   *see* Bradford on Avon H Trin, Westwood
and Wingfield *Sarum*
WINGFIELD, NORTH (St Lawrence), Clay Cross and Pilsley
Derby 5   **P** *Bp*   **TR** C COOPER   **TV** K E HAMBLIN,
R A K LAW   **C** J E FRYMANN, M H BOWN, R G LAWRENCE
WINGFIELD, SOUTH (All Saints)   *see* Crich and S Wingfield
Derby
WINGHAM (St Mary the Virgin)   *see* Canonry *Cant*
WINGRAVE (St Peter and St Paul)   *see* Cottesloe *Ox*
WINKBURN (St John of Jerusalem) *S'well 3*   **P** *Bp*   **V** *vacant*
WINKFIELD (St Mary the Virgin) and Cranbourne *Ox 3*
P *Bp*   **V** *vacant*
WINKLEBURY (Good Shepherd) and Worting *Win 4*
P *MMCET*   **R** J A K WIGMORE
WINKLEIGH (All Saints) *Ex 19*   **P** *D&C*   **V** P J NORMAN
WINKSLEY (St Cuthbert and St Oswald)   *see* Fountains Gp *Leeds*
WINLATON (St Paul) *Dur 13*   **P** *Bp*   **R** T E GLOVER
WINMARLEIGH (St Luke)   *see* Cockerham w Winmarleigh and
Glasson *Blackb*
WINNERSH (St Mary the Virgin) *Ox 8*   **P** *Bp*   **R** S DENYER
WINSCOMBE (St James) and Sandford *B & W 10*   **P** *D&C*
P-in-c L D A AVERY
WINSFORD (St Mary Magdalene)   *see* Exmoor *B & W*
WINSHAM (St Stephen)   *see* Chaffcombe, Cricket Malherbie
etc *B & W*
WINSHILL (St Mark) *Derby 16*   **P** *Lady H M Gretton and
Baroness Gretton (jt)*   **V** *vacant*
WINSLEY (St Nicholas)   *see* N Bradford on Avon and Villages
Sarum
WINSLOW (St Laurence) w Great Horwood and Addington
Ox 13   **P** *Ld Chan (3 turns), New Coll Ox (2 turns), and DBP
(1 turn)*   **R** *vacant*
WINSMOOR *B & W 14*   **P** *Bp, D&C, CR, and P G H Speke Esq (jt)*
V G A WADE   **NSM** D B FYFE
WINSON (St Michael)   *see* S Cotswolds *Glouc*
WINSTER (Holy Trinity) *Carl 10*   **P** *V Kendal H Trin*
P-in-c M D WOODCOCK
WINSTER (St John the Baptist)   *see* Darley, S Darley and Winster
Derby
WINSTON (St Andrew) *Dur 7*   **P** *Bp*   **P-in-c** M JACQUES
WINSTON (St Andrew)   *see* Debenham and Helmingham *St E*
WINSTONE (St Bartholomew)   *see* Brimpsfield w Birdlip, Syde,
Daglingworth etc *Glouc*
WINTERBORNE CLENSTON (St Nicholas)   *see* Winterborne
Valley and Milton Abbas *Sarum*
WINTERBORNE HOUGHTON (St Andrew) *as above*
WINTERBORNE KINGSTON (St Nicholas)   *see* Red Post *Sarum*
WINTERBORNE STICKLAND (St Mary)   *see* Winterborne Valley
and Milton Abbas *Sarum*
WINTERBORNE VALLEY and Milton Abbas, The *Sarum 6*
P *Bp (3 turns) and P D H Chichester Esq (1 turn)*
P-in-c A J RYAN   **NSM** C M CHICHESTER
WINTERBORNE WHITECHURCH (St Mary)   *see* Winterborne
Valley and Milton Abbas *Sarum*
WINTERBOURNE (St James)   *see* E Downland *Ox*
WINTERBOURNE (St Michael the Archangel) *Bris 5*
P *St Jo Coll Ox*   **P-in-c** M A CLACKER   **OLM** H V SMITH
WINTERBOURNE ABBAS (St Mary)   *see* Dorchester and the
Winterbournes *Sarum*

WINTERBOURNE BASSETT (St Katharine)   *see* Upper Kennet *Sarum*
WINTERBOURNE DOWN (All Saints)   *see* Frenchay and Winterbourne Down *Bris*
WINTERBOURNE EARLS (St Michael and All Angels)   *see* Bourne Valley *Sarum*
WINTERBOURNE GUNNER (St Mary) *as above*
WINTERBOURNE MONKTON (St Mary Magdalene)   *see* Upper Kennet *Sarum*
WINTERBOURNE MONKTON (St Simon and St Jude)   *see* Dorchester and the Winterbournes *Sarum*
WINTERBOURNE ST MARTIN (St Martin) *as above*
WINTERBOURNE STEEPLETON (St Michael) *as above*
WINTERBOURNE STOKE (St Peter)   *see* Lower Wylye and Till Valley *Sarum*
WINTERBOURNE ZELSTONE (St Mary)   *see* Red Post *Sarum*
WINTERINGHAM (All Saints)   *see* Winterton Gp *Linc*
WINTERSLOW (All Saints)   *see* Clarendon *Sarum*
WINTERSLOW (St John) *as above*
WINTERTON (Holy Trinity and All Saints)   *see* Flegg Coastal Benefice *Nor*
WINTERTON Group, The (All Saints) *Linc 6*   **P** *Bp, Lord St Oswald, Exors Capt J G G P Elwes, and Em Coll Cam (jt)*   **V** A C NUNN   **NSM** P A COOKE   **OLM** J J WHITEHEAD
WINTHORPE (All Saints)   *see* E Trent *S'well*
WINTHORPE (St Mary)   *see* Skegness Gp *Linc*
WINTON (St Mary Magdalene) *Man 18*   **P** *Trustees*   **P-in-c** I A HALL
WINWICK (All Saints)   *see* N Leightonstone *Ely*
WINWICK (St Michael and All Angels)   *see* Long Buckby w Watford and W Haddon w Winwick *Pet*
WINWICK (St Oswald) *Liv 15*   **P** *Bp*   **R** J L STEVENTON   **NSM** H GREENHALGH
WIRKSWORTH (St Mary) *Derby 7*   **P** *Bp*   **TR** D C TRUBY   **TV** K K WERNER   **C** J E TURVILLE   **NSM** K J ORFORD
WISBECH (St Augustine) *Ely 14*   **P** *Bp*   **P-in-c** N K GARDNER
WISBECH (St Peter and St Paul) *Ely 14*   **P** *Bp*   **P-in-c** P J WEST   **C** N K GARDNER
WISBECH ST MARY (St Mary) and Guyhirn w Ring's End and Gorefield and Southea w Murrow and Parson Drove *Ely 14*   **P** *Bp*   **V** M L BRADBURY   **NSM** J E REES, R D PARKINSON
WISBOROUGH GREEN (St Peter ad Vincula) *Chich 10*   **P** *Bp Lon*   **P-in-c** C R JENKINS
WISHAW (St Chad)   *see* Curdworth, Middleton and Wishaw *Birm*
WISHFORD, GREAT (St Giles)   *see* Lower Wylye and Till Valley *Sarum*
WISLEY (not known) w Pyrford *Guildf 12*   **P** *Bp*   **R** N J AIKEN   **C** J D LAMONT   **OLM** C D GIBSON
WISSETT (St Andrew)   *see* Blyth Valley *St E*
WISSINGTON (St Mary the Virgin)   *see* Nayland w Wiston *St E*
WISTANSTOW (Holy Trinity) *Heref 10*   **P** *Bp*   **P-in-c** T E JESSIMAN
WISTASTON (St Mary) *Ches 15*   **P** *Trustees*   **R** M F TURNBULL   **NSM** K H SAMBROOK
WISTOW (All Saints)   *see* Cawood w Ryther and Wistow *York*
WISTOW (St John the Baptist)   *see* Warboys w Broughton and Bury w Wistow *Ely*
WISTOW (St Wistan) *Leic 4*   **P** *Bp and The Hon Ann Brooks (jt)*   **V** P J O'REILLY   **C** S D MATTHEWS
WITCHAM (St Martin) w Mepal *Ely 8*   **P** *D&C*   **P-in-c** M HANCOCK
WITCHAMPTON (St Mary and St Cuthberga and All Saints), Stanbridge and Long Crichel w Moor Crichel *Sarum 9*   **P** *DBP*   **P-in-c** V A HERRICK   **C** B-J MARFLITT, S C ALLEN   **NSM** B GIBSON, E HARDING
WITCHFORD (St Andrew) w Wentworth *Ely 8*   **P** *D&C*   **P-in-c** F E G BRAMPTON   **NSM** J A GAGE, T M DIXON
WITCHINGHAM GREAT (St Mary)   *see* Wensum Benefice *Nor*
WITCOMBE, GREAT (St Mary)   *see* Badgeworth, Shurdington and Witcombe w Bentham *Glouc*
WITHAM (St Nicolas)   *see* Witham and Villages *Chelmsf*
WITHAM (St Nicolas) and Villages *Chelmsf 24*   **P** *Patr Bd*   **TR** S N LODGE   **TV** P S G WATKIN, R J KEAN   **C** A JEEWAN   **NSM** S M MALAM
WITHAM FRIARY (Blessed Virgin Mary and St John the Baptist and All Saints)   *see* Nunney and Witham Friary, Marston Bigot etc *B & W*
WITHAM Group, The *Linc 17*   **P** *Sir Lyonel Tollemache Bt, J R Thorold Esq, and Bp (jt)*   **R** *vacant*
WITHAM, NORTH (St Mary)   *see* Witham Gp *Linc*
WITHAM, SOUTH (St John the Baptist) *as above*
WITHAM-ON-THE-HILL (St Andrew)   *see* Edenham w Witham on the Hill and Swinstead *Linc*
WITHCALL (St Martin)   *see* Legbourne and Wold Marsh *Linc*

WITHERIDGE (St John the Baptist)   *see* Burrington, Chawleigh, Cheldon, Chulmleigh etc *Ex*
WITHERLEY (St Peter)   *see* Fenn Lanes Gp *Leic*
WITHERNSEA (St Nicholas) w Owthorne, Garton-in-Holderness w Grimston, Hilston, Hollym, Holmpton, Roos and Tunstall *York 12*   **P** *Abp, SMF, and Ld Chan (by turn)*   **V** *vacant*
WITHERNWICK (St Alban)   *see* Aldbrough, Mappleton w Goxhill and Withernwick *York*
WITHERSDALE (St Mary Magdalene)   *see* Sancroft *St E*
WITHERSFIELD (St Mary the Virgin)   *see* Haverhill w Withersfield *St E*
WITHERSLACK (St Paul) *Carl 10*   **P** *DBP*   **P-in-c** M D WOODCOCK
WITHIEL (St Clement)   *see* St Wenn and Withiel *Truro*
WITHIEL FLOREY (St Mary Magdalene)   *see* Dulverton w Brushford, Brompton Regis etc *B & W*
WITHINGTON (St Christopher)   *see* W Didsbury and Withington St Chris *Man*
WITHINGTON (St Crispin) *Man 3*   **P** *Bp*   **P-in-c** P C S DAVIES
WITHINGTON (St John the Baptist)   *see* Wrockwardine Deanery *Lich*
WITHINGTON (St Michael and All Angels)   *see* Sevenhampton w Charlton Abbots, Hawling etc *Glouc*
WITHINGTON (St Paul) *Man 6*   **P** *Trustees*   **R** G R RAINES   **OLM** R A W SMITH
WITHINGTON (St Peter)   *see* Bartestree Cross *Heref*
WITHLEIGH (St Catherine)   *see* Washfield, Stoodleigh, Withleigh etc *Ex*
WITHNELL (St Paul)   *see* Heapey and Withnell *Blackb*
WITHYBROOK (All Saints)   *see* Wolvey w Burton Hastings, Copston Magna etc *Cov*
WITHYCOMBE (St Nicholas)   *see* Dunster, Carhampton, Withycombe w Rodhuish etc *B & W*
WITHYCOMBE RALEIGH (St John the Evangelist) (St John in the Wilderness) (All Saints) *Ex 1*   **P** *Patr Bd*   **TR** R SELLERS   **TV** S J HOYLE
WITHYHAM (St John the Evangelist)   *see* Crowborough St Jo *Chich*
WITHYHAM (St Michael and All Angels) *Chich 16*   **P** *Earl De la Warr*   **R** *vacant*
WITHYPOOL (St Andrew)   *see* Exmoor *B & W*
WITHYWOOD (shared church) *Bris 1*   **P** *Bp*   **P-in-c** D A J MADDOX
WITLEY (All Saints) *Guildf 4*   **P** *Bp*   **V** J E VLACH
WITLEY, GREAT (St Michael)   *see* Shrawley, Witley, Astley and Abberley *Worc*
WITLEY, LITTLE (St Michael) *as above*
WITNESHAM (St Mary)   *see* Westerfield and Tuddenham w Witnesham *St E*
WITNEY (St Mary the Virgin) (Holy Trinity) *Ox 28*   **P** *Patr Bd*   **TR** T C WRIGHT   **TV** N O TRAYNOR   **C** A J P BLAINE, J HANCE   **Hon C** S J WRIGHT   **NSM** J R COLLICUTT MCGRATH   **OLM** C TITCOMB
WITTENHAM, LITTLE (St Peter)   *see* Dorchester *Ox*
WITTERING (All Saints)   *see* Ketton, Collyweston, Easton-on-the-Hill etc *Pet*
WITTERING, EAST (St Anne)   *see* Earnley and E Wittering *Chich*
WITTERING, WEST (St Peter and St Paul) and Birdham w Itchenor *Chich 2*   **P** *Bp*   **R** J R SWINDELLS   **Hon C** C J HANKINS   **NSM** B F HOLBEN, J M MOULD, S J MANOUCH
WITTERSHAM (St John the Baptist)   *see* Rother and Oxney *Cant*
WITTON (St Helen) *Ches 6*   **P** *Bp*   **V** A A HARRIS   **NSM** S J MILLINCHIP
WITTON (St Margaret)   *see* Bacton, Happisburgh, Hempstead w Eccles etc *Nor*
WITTON (St Margaret)   *see* Gt and Lt Plumstead w Thorpe End and Witton *Nor*
WITTON GILBERT (St Michael and All Angels)   *see* Dur N *Dur*
WITTON LE WEAR (St Philip and St James)   *see* Hamsterley and Witton-le-Wear *Dur*
WITTON PARK (St Paul) *Dur 6*   **P** *Bp*   **P-in-c** B E MECHANIC   **Hon C** R I MECHANIC, T PITT
WITTON, NETHER (St Giles) *Newc 11*   **P** *Ld Chan*   **V** M A G BRYCE   **NSM** F J SAMPLE
WITTON, WEST (St Bartholomew)   *see* Penhill *Leeds*
WIVELISCOMBE (St Andrew) and the Hills *B & W 19*   **P** *Bp and A H Trollope-Bellew Esq (4 turns), Ld Chan (1 turn)*   **R** D C R WIDDOWS
WIVELSFIELD (St Peter and St John the Baptist) *Chich 5*   **P** *DBP*   **V** C R BREEDS
WIVENHOE (St Mary) *Chelmsf 21*   **P** *Bp*   **R** E B E LAMMENS
WIVETON (St Mary)   *see* Blakeney w Cley, Wiveton, Glandford etc *Nor*

WIX (St Mary the Virgin)   *see* Gt Oakley w Wix and Wrabness *Chelmsf*

WIXFORD (St Milburga)   *see* Heart of England *Cov*

WIXOE (St Leonard)   *see* Stour Valley *St E*

WOBURN (St Mary) w Eversholt, Milton Bryan, Battlesden and Pottesgrove *St Alb 8*   **P** *Bedf Estates Trustees*
V S W NUTH

WOBURN SANDS (St Michael) *St Alb 8*   **P** *Bp*
V C L D BEALES   **NSM** N J PARKINSON

WOKING (Christ Church) *Guildf 12*   **P** *Ridley Hall Cam*
V P J HARWOOD   **C** A K REID   **NSM** M S SMITH,
P A SIMPSON

WOKING (St John the Baptist) *Guildf 12*   **P** *V Woking St Pet*
V T A CANNON   **C** P J MATTHEW   **OLM** R G BENNETT

WOKING (St Mary of Bethany) *Guildf 12*   **P** *V Woking Ch Ch*
V S R BEAK   **C** B PIMENTEL, Z L PIMENTEL

WOKING (St Paul) *Guildf 12*   **P** *Ridley Hall Cam*
P-in-c J L BLAIR   **C** C J BLAIR

WOKING (St Peter) *Guildf 12*   **P** *Patr Bd*
P-in-c J M G THOMAS

WOKINGHAM (All Saints) *Ox 8*   **P** *Bp*   **R** D P HODGSON
C A C HARWOOD, M R JOHNSON   **NSM** H J CHARLTON

WOKINGHAM (St Paul) *Ox 8*   **P** *DBP*   **R** R J LAMEY
C P S KING   **NSM** J H A HATTAWAY, R G HOLMES

WOKINGHAM (St Sebastian) *Ox 8*   **P** *Bp*   **V** A P MARSDEN
NSM E C FUDGE, R I SEYMOUR

WOLBOROUGH (St Mary) and Ogwell *Ex 9*   **P** *Earl of Devon and Bp (jt)*   **R** *vacant*

WOLD (St Andrew)   *see* Walgrave w Hannington and Wold and Scaldwell *Pet*

WOLD NEWTON (All Saints)   *see* Binbrook Gp *Linc*

WOLD NEWTON (All Saints)   *see* Burton Fleming w Fordon, Grindale etc *York*

WOLDINGHAM (St Agatha)   *see* Caterham *S'wark*

WOLDINGHAM (St Paul) *as above*

WOLDS GATEWAY Group, The *Linc 4*   **P** *DBP, Bp, Earl of Yarborough, J E Spilman Esq and Ridley Hall Cam (jt)*
V P T STEVENS   **C** J M GLOSSOP   **OLM** J M GLOSSOP

WOLDS, NORTH Group *Linc 8*   **P** *Bp, DBP, and D&C (jt)*
V *vacant*

WOLDSBURN *York 10*   **P** *Abp, St Jo Coll Ox, and A J Page Esq (1 turn), and Ld Chan (1 turn)*   **P-in-c** D E FLETCHER
NSM R D WAITE

WOLFERTON (St Peter)   *see* Sandringham w W Newton and Appleton etc *Nor*

WOLFORD (St Michael)   *see* S Warks Seven Gp *Cov*

WOLLASTON (St James) *Worc 12*   **P** *Bp*
P-in-c N G KALENIUK   **Hon C** D M FARMER

WOLLASTON (St Mary) w Strixton and Bozeat and Easton Maudit *Pet 6*   **P** *Bp and Marquess of Northn (jt)*
V A I MORTON   **C** W N D TRENHOLME

WOLLASTON, GREAT (St John the Baptist)   *see* Ford, Gt Wollaston and Alberbury w Cardeston *Heref*

WOLLATON (St Leonard) *S'well 8*   **P** *Lord Middleton*
R T J PULLEN

WOLLATON PARK (St Mary) *S'well 9*   **P** *CPAS*   **V** J H CURRAN
C T C DEVAS

WOLLESCOTE (St Andrew) *Worc 12*   **P** *Bp*   **V** *vacant*

WOLSINGHAM (St Mary and St Stephen) and Thornley *Dur 9*
P *Bp*   **P-in-c** J P L WHALLEY

WOLSTANTON (St Margaret) *Lich 9*   **P** *Bp*   **V** *vacant*

WOLSTON (St Margaret) and Church Lawford *Cov 6*   **P** *DBP (2 turns), Bp (1 turn)*   **V** K J FLANAGAN   **Hon C** P A H SIMMONDS

WOLVERCOTE (St Peter) and Wytham *Ox 2*   **P** *Ch Ch Ox and Mert Coll Ox (jt)*   **Hon C** J M CONEY   **NSM** R J C GILBERT, V P BRIDGES

WOLVERHAMPTON (St Andrew) *Lich 28*   **P** *Bp*
P-in-c P S ROBERTSON

WOLVERHAMPTON (St Jude) *Lich 28*   **P** *CPAS*
V P S ROBERTSON   **OLM** I J SAUNDERS

WOLVERHAMPTON (St Luke) Blakenhall *Lich 28*   **P** *Trustees*
V R J ESPIN-BRADLEY

WOLVERHAMPTON (St Martin)   *see* Rough Hills *Lich*

WOLVERHAMPTON (St Matthew) *Lich 28*   **P** *Baldwin Pugh Trustees*   **V** M HIRD

WOLVERHAMPTON (St Stephen) *Lich 28*   **P** *Bp*
P-in-c S W POWELL

WOLVERHAMPTON Pond Lane (Mission Hall) *see* Wolverhampton St Luke *Lich*

WOLVERHAMPTON, CENTRAL (All Saints) (St Chad and St John) (St John in the Square) (St Peter) *Lich 28*   **P** *Patr Bd*   **TR** D W WRIGHT   **TV** S SCHOFIELD   **C** J S E WILLIAMS, S J WATSON   **OLM** E W BROOKES

WOLVERLEY (St John the Baptist)   *see* Kidderminster Ismere *Worc*

WOLVERTON (Holy Trinity) (St George the Martyr) *Ox 14*
P *Bp*   **R** G S BARROW-JONES   **C** A E KEMBER

WOLVERTON (St Catherine)   *see* Baughurst, Ramsdell, Wolverton w Ewhurst etc *Win*

WOLVERTON (St Mary the Virgin)   *see* Arden Valley *Cov*

WOLVEY (St John the Baptist) w Burton Hastings, Copston Magna and Withybrook *Cov 5*   **P** *Bp*   **V** *vacant*

WOMBOURNE (St Benedict)   *see* Smestow Vale *Lich*

WOMBRIDGE (St Mary and St Leonard) *Lich 21*   **P** *W J Charlton Meyrick Esq*   **P-in-c** K S EVANS

WOMBWELL (St Mary) (St George) *Sheff 12*   **P** *Trin Coll Cam*
R *vacant*

WOMERSLEY (St Martin) *Leeds 19*   **P** *Earl of Rosse*
V A C MARTLEW

WONERSH (St John the Baptist) w Blackheath *Guildf 2*
P *Selw Coll Cam*   **V** D M SELLIN   **NSM** D PETERS
OLM E A TILLEY, J M COOKE, K N BATESON

WONSTON (Holy Trinity)   *see* Upper Dever *Win*

WONSTON, SOUTH (St Margaret)   *see* Lower Dever *Win*

WOOBURN (St Paul) *Ox 18*   **P** *Bp*   **V** M J WALLINGTON

WOOD DALLING (St Andrew)   *see* Reepham, Hackford w Whitwell, Kerdiston etc *Nor*

WOOD DITTON (St Mary) w Saxon Street *Ely 4*   **P** *Duke of Sutherland*   **V** *vacant*

WOOD END (St Chad) *Cov 1*   **P** *Ld Chan*   **V** A J FISHER

WOOD END (St Michael and All Angels)   *see* Baxterley w Hurley and Wood End and Merevale etc *Birm*

WOOD GREEN (St Michael) w Bounds Green (St Gabriel) (St Michael-at-Bowes) *Lon 19*   **P** *Patr Bd*   **TR** C W COPPEN
NSM B MAHILUM

WOOD GREEN (St Paul)   *see* Wednesbury St Paul Wood Green *Lich*

WOOD NORTON (All Saints)   *see* Foulsham, Guestwick, Stibbard, Themelthorpe etc *Nor*

WOOD STREET (St Alban)   *see* Worplesdon *Guildf*

WOODBASTWICK (St Fabian and St Sebastian)   *see* Broadside *Nor*

WOODBOROUGH (St Mary Magdalene)   *see* Vale of Pewsey *Sarum*

WOODBOROUGH (St Swithun)   *see* Epperstone, Gonalston, Oxton and Woodborough *S'well*

WOODBRIDGE (St John the Evangelist) and Bredfield *St E 7*
P *Ch Patr Trust (3 turns), and Ld Chan (1 turn)*   **V** C E HOWARD
NSM M M E ROBERTS

WOODBRIDGE (St Mary the Virgin) *St E 7*   **P** *Bp*
R K S MCCORMACK   **NSM** M J HARE

WOODBURY (Holy Cross)   *see* Axminster, Chardstock, All Saints etc *Ex*

WOODBURY (St Swithun)   *see* Aylesbeare, Clyst St George, Clyst St Mary etc *Ex*

WOODBURY SALTERTON (Holy Trinity) *as above*

WOODCHESTER (St Mary) and Brimscombe *Glouc 4*
P *Simeon's Trustees*   **P-in-c** P A FRANCIS

WOODCHURCH (All Saints)   *see* Bethersden w High Halden and Woodchurch *Cant*

WOODCHURCH (Holy Cross) *Ches 1*   **P** *DBP*   **R** M A DAVIS
C J R ARNOLD

WOODCOTE (St Leonard)   *see* Langtree *Ox*

WOODCOTE (St Mark)   *see* Purley St Mark *S'wark*

WOODCOTT (St James)   *see* Hurstbourne Priors, Longparish etc *Win*

WOODDITTON (St Mary)   *see* Wood Ditton w Saxon Street *Ely*

WOODEATON (Holy Rood)   *see* Ray Valley *Ox*

WOODFIELD Team Benefice, The *Leic 8*   **P** *Patr Bd (6 turns), Prime Min (1 turn), Ld Chan (1 turn)*   **TR** V M ELPHICK
TV S F BRADLEY   **C** L J COX   **NSM** L S BIRTWISTLE

WOODFORD (Christ Church) *Ches 12*   **P** *W A B Davenport Esq*
V D J T RUSSELL

WOODFORD (St Barnabas) *Chelmsf 6*   **P** *Bp*   **V** W OBEDOZA

WOODFORD (St Mary the Virgin)   *see* Irthlingborough, Gt Addington, Lt Addington etc *Pet*

WOODFORD (St Mary w St Philip and St James) *Chelmsf 6*
P *Bp*   **R** I D TARRANT   **C** S BEURKLIAN-CARTER

WOODFORD BRIDGE (St Paul) *Chelmsf 6*   **P** *R Woodford*
V O FRANKLIN

WOODFORD HALSE (St Mary the Virgin)   *see* Aston-le-Walls, Byfield, Boddington, Eydon etc *Pet*

WOODFORD VALLEY (All Saints) w Archers Gate *Sarum 14*
P *Bp*   **V** M J M PERRY   **NSM** J M NAISH, P M POWELL

WOODFORD WELLS (All Saints) (St Andrew) *Chelmsf 6*
P *Trustees*   **V** P G HARCOURT   **C** J E TALBOT, S MARSHALL
NSM D J BLACKLEDGE, M D PORTER   **OLM** D MARTIN

WOODFORD, SOUTH (Holy Trinity)   *see* Wanstead H Trin Hermon Hill *Chelmsf*

WOODGATE VALLEY (St Francis)   *see* Bartley Green *Birm*

WOODGREEN (St Boniface)   *see* Fordingbridge and Breamore and Hale etc *Win*

WOODHALL (St James the Great) *Leeds 3* **P** *Bp*
P-in-c N CLEWS
WOODHALL SPA Group *Linc 13* **P** *Bp and DBP (jt)*
R R J E MAJOR
WOODHAM (All Saints) *Guildf 12* **P** *Bp* **V** I W FORBES
WOODHAM (St Elizabeth of Hungary) *see Gt Aycliffe Dur*
WOODHAM FERRERS (St Mary) and Bicknacre *Chelmsf 10*
P *Lord Fitzwalter* **P-in-c** C M BALL **C** M J MARSHALL
NSM J S RICHARDS
WOODHAM FERRERS, SOUTH (Holy Trinity) (St Mary)
Chelmsf 10 **P** *Bp* **V** C M BALL **C** M J MARSHALL
NSM J S RICHARDS
WOODHAM MORTIMER (St Margaret) w Hazeleigh
Chelmsf 11 **P** *Bp* **R** *vacant*
WOODHAM WALTER (St Michael) *Chelmsf 11* **P** *Ch Soc Trust*
R *vacant*
WOODHAY, EAST (St Martin) *see NW Hants Win*
WOODHILL *Sarum 16* **P** *Ld Chan, DBP, and Prime Min (by*
turns) **P-in-c** E R H ABBOTT **NSM** R G SELBY-BOOTHROYD
WOODHORN w Newbiggin *Newc 11* **P** *Bp* **V** P M SINCLAIR
NSM J A ANDERSON **OLM** F WALTON
WOODHOUSE (Christ Church) *see Birkby and Woodhouse*
Leeds
WOODHOUSE (St James) *Sheff 1* **P** *Bp* **V** D R GOUGH
WOODHOUSE (St Mary in the Elms), Woodhouse Eaves and
Swithland *Leic 6* **P** *Ld Chan and DBP (alt)*
R L C TEMPERLEY-BARNES
WOODHOUSE EAVES (St Paul) *see Woodhouse, Woodhouse*
Eaves and Swithland Leic
WOODHOUSE PARK (Wm Temple Church) *see Wythenshawe*
Man
WOODHOUSE St Mark and Wrangthorn *Leeds 16* **P** *DBP*
P-in-c J R SEABOURNE
WOODHOUSES (not known) *see Bardsley Man*
WOODHURST (St John the Baptist) *see Somersham w Pidley*
and Oldhurst and Woodhurst Ely
WOODINGDEAN (Holy Cross) *Chich 19* **P** *Bp* **V** *vacant*
WOODKIRK (St Mary) *see W Ardsley Leeds*
WOODLAND (St John the Baptist) *see Ipplepen w Torbryan,*
Denbury and Broadhempston w Woodland Ex
WOODLAND (St John the Evangelist) *see Broughton and*
Duddon Carl
WOODLAND (St Mary) *see Lynesack Dur*
WOODLANDS (All Saints) *Sheff 7* **P** *Bp* **V** S J GARDNER
C S A BECK
WOODLANDS (Ascension) *see Cranborne w Boveridge,*
Edmondsham etc Sarum
WOODLANDS (St Katherine) *B & W 3* **P** *DBP*
V C ALSBURY
WOODLANDS (St Mary) *see Kemsing w Woodlands Roch*
WOODLEIGH (St Mary the Virgin) *see Thurlestone, S Milton,*
Churchstow etc Ex
WOODLEY (St John the Evangelist) *Ox 7* **P** *DBP*
V E MARQUEZ **C** S C RIORDAN **OLM** J LEWIS
WOODMANCOTE (Mission Church) *see Westbourne Chich*
WOODMANCOTE (St James) *see Upper Dever Win*
WOODMANCOTE (St Mark) *see Dursley Glouc*
WOODMANCOTE (St Peter) *see Henfield w Shermanbury and*
Woodmancote Chich
WOODMANSEY (St Peter) *see Beverley Minster York*
WOODMANSTERNE (St Peter) *S'wark 26* **P** *Ld Chan*
R D J L MCHARDIE **NSM** A H BARRON
WOODNESBOROUGH (St Mary the Blessed Virgin) *see Eastry*
and Woodnesborough Cant
WOODNEWTON (St Mary) *see Nassington, Apethorpe,*
Thornhaugh etc Pet
WOODPLUMPTON (St Anne) *Blackb 9* **P** *V St Michael's-on-*
Wyre **V** *vacant*
WOODRISING (St Nicholas) *see High Oak, Hingham and*
Scoulton w Wood Rising Nor
WOODSEATS (St Chad) *Sheff 2* **P** *Bp* **V** T K HOLE
C D J BELL
WOODSETTS (St George) *Sheff 5* **P** *Bp* **V** *vacant*
WOODSFORD (St John the Baptist) *see Moreton, Woodsford*
and Crossways w Tincleton Sarum
WOODSIDE (All Saints) *see Lymington Win*
WOODSIDE (St Andrew) *St Alb 12* **P** *D&C St Paul's*
P-in-c C A PULLINGER
WOODSIDE (St James) *Leeds 16* **P** *Bp* **P-in-c** R J DIMERY
C N W LATTIMER **NSM** B M HAWKINS
WOODSIDE (St Luke) *see Croydon Woodside S'wark*
WOODSIDE PARK (St Barnabas) *Lon 14* **P** *Ch Patr Trust*
V H D KENDAL **C** C S BROOKES, D BROWN, H L SHANNON,
M PAVLOU
WOODSTOCK (St Mary Magdalene) *see Blenheim Ox*
WOODSTON (St Augustine of Canterbury) (Mission Church)
Ely 15 **P** *Bp* **R** W P L GAMMON

WOODTHORPE (St Mark) *S'well 7* **P** *Bp* **C** M D JOHNSON
WOODTON (All Saints) *see Hempnall Nor*
WOOKEY (St Matthew) *see Coxley w Godney, Henton and*
Wookey B & W
WOOKEY HOLE (St Mary Magdalene) *see Wells St Cuth w*
Wookey Hole B & W
WOOL (Holy Rood) and East Stoke *Sarum 8* **P** *Bp (3 turns),*
Keble Coll Ox (1 turn) **R** R C FLOATE
WOOLACOMBE (St Sabinus) *see Ilfracombe, Lee,*
Woolacombe, Bittadon etc Ex
WOOLASTON (St Andrew) w Alvington and Aylburton
Glouc 1 **P** *DBP and Ld Chan (by turn)* **P-in-c** S L FENBY
NSM A JONES
WOOLAVINGTON (Blessed Virgin Mary) w Cossington and
Bawdrip *B & W 13* **P** *D&C Windsor and J A Church Esq (alt)*
R K J WRIGHT
WOOLBEDING (All Hallows) *Chich 9* **P** *Rathbone Trust Co and*
Cowdray Trust (jt) **R** D A WILLIS
WOOLBROOK (St Francis of Assisi) *see Sidmouth, Woolbrook,*
Salcombe Regis, Sidbury etc Ex
WOOLER (St Mary) *see Glendale Gp Newc*
WOOLFARDISWORTHY (Holy Trinity) *see Parkham, Alwington,*
Buckland Brewer etc Ex
WOOLFARDISWORTHY EAST (St Mary) *see N Creedy Ex*
WOOLFOLD (St James) *see Kirklees Valley Man*
WOOLHAMPTON (St Peter) *see Aldermaston and*
Woolhampton Ox
WOOLHOPE (St George) *see Fownhope w Mordiford,*
Brockhampton etc Heref
WOOLLAND (not known) *see Hazelbury Bryan and the*
Hillside Par Sarum
WOOLLEY (All Saints) *see Bath St Sav w Swainswick and*
Woolley B & W
WOOLLEY (St Peter) *Leeds 20* **P** *Bp* **P-in-c** S P KELLY
WOOLPIT (Blessed Virgin Mary) w Drinkstone *St E 10*
P *Bp and A Harvie-Clark Esq (alt)* **R** M R FARRELL
WOOLSTASTON (St Michael and All Angels) *see Dorrington w*
Leebotwood, Longnor, Stapleton etc Heref
WOOLSTHORPE (St James) *see Harlaxton Gp Linc*
WOOLSTON (Church of the Ascension) *see Warrington E Liv*
WOOLSTON (St Mark) *Win 13* **P** *Bp* **V** M J A NEWTON
WOOLSTONE (All Saints) *see Uffington, Shellingford,*
Woolstone and Baulking Ox
WOOLSTONE (Holy Trinity) *see Woughton Ox*
WOOLSTONE (St Martin) *see Bishop's Cleeve and Woolstone*
w Gotherington etc Glouc
WOOLTON HILL (St Thomas) *see NW Hants Win*
WOOLTON, MUCH (St Peter) *Liv 4* **P** *Bp* **R** C J CROOKS
C R J A GEDGE, S J DORAGH
WOOLVERSTONE (St Michael) *see Holbrook, Stutton, Freston,*
Woolverstone etc St E
WOOLWICH (St Mary Magdelene and St Andrew)
(St Michael and All Angels) *S'wark 1* **P** *Bp and Keble Coll Ox*
(jt) **R** J VAN DER VALK
WOOLWICH (St Thomas) *see Charlton S'wark*
WOOLWICH, NORTH (St John) w Silvertown *Chelmsf 5*
P *Bp and Lon Corp (alt)* **P-in-c** S J P CROOS
WOORE (St Leonard) and Norton in Hales *Lich 18* **P** *Bp and*
CPAS (jt) **P-in-c** D G ALCOCK
WOOSEHILL (Community Church) *see Winnersh Ox*
WOOTTON (St Andrew) *see Ulceby Gp Linc*
WOOTTON (St Edmund) *Portsm 8* **P** *DBP* **R** *vacant*
WOOTTON (St George the Martyr) w Quinton and Preston
Deanery *Pet 4* **P** *Ex Coll Ox and Bp (alt)*
P-in-c L A JEFFREYS
WOOTTON (St Martin) *see Elham w Denton and Wootton*
and Acrise Cant
WOOTTON (St Mary the Virgin) *St Alb 9* **P** *MMCET*
V P M ACKROYD **C** L C DURANT
WOOTTON (St Mary) w Glympton and Kiddington *Ox 29*
P *New Coll Ox (2 turns), Bp (1 turn), and Exors E W Towler Esq*
(1 turn) **P-in-c** E E S JONES
WOOTTON (St Peter) and Dry Sandford *Ox 19* **P** *Bp and*
Ox Churches Trust (jt) **P-in-c** J A WILLIAMS **C** P N TOVEY
Hon C T R PERRY **NSM** J R WILLIAMS
WOOTTON BASSETT (St Bartholomew and All Saints)
see R Wootton Bassett Sarum
WOOTTON BRIDGE (St Mark) *see Wootton Portsm*
WOOTTON COURTENAY (All Saints) *see Dunster,*
Carhampton, Withycombe w Rodhuish etc B & W
WOOTTON FITZPAINE (not known) *see Golden Cap Team*
Sarum
WOOTTON RIVERS (St Andrew) *see Vale of Pewsey Sarum*
WOOTTON ST LAWRENCE (St Lawrence) *see Oakley w*
Wootton St Lawrence Win
WOOTTON WAWEN (St Peter) *Cov 7* **P** *K Coll Cam*
V *vacant*

WOOTTON, NORTH (All Saints) w SOUTH (St Mary) *Nor 20*
P *Ld Chan and G Howard Esq (alt)*   R J A NASH
C G P WILKINS   OLM L ASHBY
WOOTTON, NORTH (St Peter)   *see* Pilton w Croscombe,
N Wootton and Dinder *B & W*
WORCESTER (All Saints)   *see* Worc St Nic and All SS w St Helen
Worc
WORCESTER (St Barnabas) (Christ Church) *Worc 6*   P *Bp*
TR J A WATSON   C P E JONES
WORCESTER (St Clement) and Lower Broadheath *Worc 3*
P *Bp and D&C (jt)*   C C J STUART
WORCESTER (St George w St Mary Magdalene) *Worc 6*
P *Bp and V Claines (alt)*   P-in-c J C MUSSON
NSM D P DAVIES
WORCESTER (St John in Bedwardine)   *see* St Jo in Bedwardine
Worc
WORCESTER (St Martin in the Cornmarket)   *see* Worc St Martin
w St Swithun and St Paul *Worc*
**WORCESTER (St Martin in the Cornmarket) w St Swithun
and St Paul** *Worc 6*   P *Patr Bd*   V *vacant*
WORCESTER (St Nicholas)   *see* Warndon St Nic *Worc*
WORCESTER (St Wulstan) *Worc 6*   P *Bp*   V C L THOMAS
**WORCESTER Dines Green (St Michael), and Crown East,
Rushwick** *Worc 3*   P *Bp and D&C (jt)*   V R CHARLES
P-in-c P J BRADFORD   C A M POTTER
WORCESTER PARK (Christ Church w St Philip) *S'wark 23*
P R *Cheam*   V S A NADARAJAH   NSM C A ROWLES
**WORCESTER SOUTH EAST (St Martin w St Peter) (St Mark in
the Cherry Orchard) (Holy Trinity w St Matthew)** *Worc 6*
P *Patr Bd*   TR K A BOYCE   TV C E GRIFFITHS, G S DAVIS
C H CHARLTON   NSM A M WHERRY, N W DAW
WORCESTER St Nicholas (All Saints) (St Helen) *Worc 6*
P *Patr Bd*   V R W JOHNSON   C O T GALLACHER
WORCESTERSHIRE WEST RURAL TEAM Ministry, The *Worc 3*
P *Patr Bd (2 turns), Prime Min (1 turn)*   TR D R SHERWIN
TV A M POTTER   C R W TWEEDY   Hon C J G SUMNER
NSM J M WHITTAKER
WORDSLEY (Holy Trinity) *Worc 10*   P *Patr Bd*   TR C S JONES
C R L ROWSON   NSM G HODGSON
WORFIELD (St Peter) *Heref 8*   P *Trustees of the late J R S
Greenshields Esq*   P-in-c J H STOKES
WORKINGTON (St John) *Carl 7*   P R *Workington*
NSM M T STILWELL
WORKINGTON (St Michael) *Carl 7*   P *Mrs E H S Thornely*
R B ROWE
WORKSOP (Christ Church) and Shireoaks *S'well 1*
P *Bp and CPAS (jt)*   V M C ALVEY
WORKSOP (St Anne) *S'well 1*   P *Bp*   P-in-c S A CASH
C L H DE ANDRADE LIMA
WORKSOP (St John the Evangelist) *S'well 1*   P *CPAS*
P-in-c T C STANFORD
WORKSOP (St Paul) *S'well 1*   P *Bp*   P-in-c N SPICER
WORKSOP PRIORY (St Mary and St Cuthbert) *S'well 1*
P *St Steph Ho Ox*   V N SPICER   C S PARKER
WORLABY (St Clement) *Linc 8*   P *DBP*   V G O MITCHELL
WORLDHAM, EAST (St Mary the Virgin)   *see* Northanger *Win*
WORLDHAM, WEST (St Nicholas) *as above*
WORLE (St Martin) (St Mark's Church Centre) *B & W 10*
P *Ld Chan*   TR P R LARCOMBE   TV A L FARMER, C G ELMS,
E C AMYES   NSM G C BUNCE
WORLESTON (St Oswald)   *see* Acton and Worleston, Church
Minshull etc *Ches*
WORLINGHAM (All Saints) w Barnby and North Cove *St E 18*
P *Ld Chan*   P-in-c S M ELLIS
WORLINGTON (All Saints)   *see* Mildenhall *St E*
WORLINGTON, EAST (St Mary)   *see* Burrington, Chawleigh,
Cheldon, Chulmleigh etc *Ex*
WORLINGTON, WEST (St Mary) *as above*
WORLINGWORTH (St Mary)   *see* Four Rivers *St E*
WORMBRIDGE (St Peter)   *see* Ewyas Harold w Dulas,
Kenderchurch etc *Heref*
WORMEGAY (St Michael and All Angels and Holy Cross)
see Tottenhill w Wormegay *Ely*
WORMELOW HUNDRED *Heref 7*   P *A W Twiston-Davies Esq
(1 turn), Bp (3 turns), and Ld Chan (1 turn)*   R M JOHNSON
WORMHILL (St Margaret)   *see* Tideswell *Derby*
**WORMINGFORD (St Andrew), Mount Bures and Little
Horkesley** *Chelmsf 21*   P *Exors J J Tufnell Esq, G Reynolds Esq,
and Keble Coll Ox (jt)*   P-in-c J CHANDLER
**WORMINGHALL (St Peter and St Paul) w Ickford, Oakley and
Shabbington** *Ox 10*   P *Bp and Guild of All So (jt)*
R D R KABOLEH
WORMINGTON (St Katharine)   *see* Winchcombe *Glouc*
WORMLEIGHTON (St Peter)   *see* Priors Hardwick, Priors
Marston and Wormleighton *Cov*
WORMLEY (Church Room)   *see* Broxbourne w Wormley
St Alb

WORMLEY (St Laurence) *as above*
WORMSHILL (St Giles)   *see* Tunstall and Bredgar *Cant*
WORPLESDON (St Mary the Virgin) *Guildf 5*   P *Eton Coll*
R H M GREAR   NSM A PAYNE, T J WEIL   OLM A J WELCH
WORSALL, HIGH AND LOW (All Saints)   *see* Kirklevington w
Picton, and High and Low Worsall *York*
WORSBROUGH (St Mary) w Elsecar *Sheff 11*   P *DBP and
Sir Philip Naylor-Leyland Bt (alt)*   V A EARL
WORSBROUGH (St Thomas)   *see* Worsbrough Common w
Worsbrough St Thos *Sheff*
**WORSBROUGH COMMON (St Luke) w Worsbrough
St Thomas and St James** *Sheff 11*   P *Bp (2 turns), Prime Min
(1 turn)*   V T C KEIGHTLEY
WORSLEY (St Mark) *Man 18*   P *Bp*   TR G TURNER
TV K HOPWOOD OWEN   NSM D E FAIR   OLM D HAWKINS
WORSLEY MESNES (not known)   *see* Wigan St Jas w St Thos
Liv
**WORSTEAD (St Mary), Westwick, Sloley, Swanton Abbot
and Scottow** *Nor 12*   P *DBP, J T D Shaw Esq, D&C, and
Bp (by turn)*   R A R LONG
WORSTHORNE (St John the Evangelist)   *see* Holme-in-Cliviger
w Worsthorne *Blackb*
WORTH (St Nicholas), Pound Hill and Maidenbower *Chich 6*
P *DBP*   R A J BALL   C J N GRANT, S BURSTON
WORTH (St Peter and St Paul)   *see* Sandwich and Worth
Cant
WORTH MATRAVERS (St Aldhelm)   *see* Kingston, Langton
Matravers and Worth Matravers *Sarum*
WORTH MATRAVERS (St Nicholas) *as above*
WORTHAM (St Mary the Virgin)   *see* N Hartismere *St E*
WORTHEN (All Saints)   *see* Westbury, Worthen and Yockleton
Heref
WORTHING (Holy Trinity) (Christ Church) *Chich 4*   P R
Broadwater, Bp and Bp Horsham, Ch Soc Trust, and CPAS (jt)
P-in-c M J LUFF
WORTHING (St Andrew) *Chich 4*   P *Keble Coll Ox*
V *vacant*
WORTHING (St George) (Emmanuel) *Chich 4*   P *Ch Soc Trust*
V B R PENFOLD
WORTHING (St Margaret)   *see* N Elmham, Billingford, Bintree,
Guist etc *Nor*
WORTHING (St Matthew) *Chich 4*   P R *Broadwater, Bp and
Bp Horsham, Ch Soc Trust, and CPAS (jt)*   V E J CHITHAM
C S STEVENS   NSM M E PARISH
WORTHING, WEST (St John the Divine) *Chich 4*   P *Bp*
V J K T ELDRIDGE   C P S EDELL
WORTHINGTON (St Matthew)   *see* Ashby-de-la-Zouch and
Breedon on the Hill *Leic*
WORTING (St Thomas of Canterbury)   *see* Winklebury and
Worting *Win*
WORTLEY (St John the Evangelist) and Farnley *Leeds 15*
P *Bp and Trustees (jt)*   R K A P DOWLING
WORTLEY (St Leonard)   *see* Tankersley, Thurgoland and
Wortley *Sheff*
WORTON (Christ Church)   *see* Potterne w Worton and Marston
Sarum
WORTON, NETHER (St James)   *see* Westcote Barton w Steeple
Barton, Duns Tew and Sandford St Martin and Over w
Nether Worton *Ox*
WORTON, OVER (Holy Trinity) *as above*
WOTTON (St John the Evangelist)   *see* Abinger and
Coldharbour and Wotton and Holmbury St Mary *Guildf*
WOTTON ST MARY WITHOUT (Holy Trinity) *Glouc 2*   P *Bp*
V G A GIBBENS   C A BLAND
WOTTON UNDERWOOD (All Saints)   *see* Bernwode *Ox*
WOUGHTON *Ox 14*   P *Bp*   OLM P NORRIS
WOUGHTON-ON-THE-GREEN (St Mary)   *see* Woughton *Ox*
WOULDHAM (All Saints)   *see* Burham and Wouldham *Roch*
WRABNESS (All Saints)   *see* Gt Oakley w Wix and Wrabness
Chelmsf
WRAGBY (St Michael and Our Lady)   *see* Kinsley w Wragby
Leeds
WRAGBY Group, The (All Saints) *Linc 13*   P *Bp, MMCET, and
DBP (jt)*   R M N HOLDEN
WRAMPLINGHAM (St Peter and St Paul)   *see* Barnham Broom
and Upper Yare *Nor*
WRANGLE (St Mary and St Nicholas)   *see* Old Leake w Wrangle
Linc
WRANGTHORN (St Augustine of Hippo)   *see* Woodhouse and
Wrangthorn *Leeds*
WRATTING, GREAT (St Mary)   *see* Stourhead *St E*
WRATTING, LITTLE (St Mary) *as above*
WRATTING, WEST (St Andrew)   *see* Balsham, Weston Colville,
W Wickham etc *Ely*
WRAWBY (St Mary the Virgin)   *see* Brigg, Wrawby and Cadney
cum Howsham *Linc*

WRAXALL (All Saints) *B & W 12* **P** *Trustees*
P-in-c F M BINDING **NSM** F A TRICKEY
WRAXALL (St Mary) *see* Melbury *Sarum*
WRAXALL, NORTH (St James) *see* Colerne w N Wraxall *Bris*
WRAXALL, SOUTH (St James) *see* N Bradford on Avon and Villages *Sarum*
WRAY (Holy Trinity) *see* E Lonsdale *Blackb*
WRAYSBURY (St Andrew) *see* Horton and Wraysbury *Ox*
WREAKE, UPPER *Leic 2* **P** *Bp and DBP (jt)* **V** *vacant*
WREAY (St Mary) *see* Dalston w Cumdivock, Raughton Head and Wreay *Carl*
WRECCLESHAM (St Peter) *Guildf 3* **P** *Bp* **V** A E GELL
NSM S J CAVALIER
WRENBURY (St Margaret) *see* Baddiley and Wrenbury w Burleydam *Ches*
WRENINGHAM (All Saints) *see* Upper Tas Valley *Nor*
WRENTHAM (St Nicholas), Covehithe w Benacre, Henstead w Hulver and Frostenden *St E 18* **P** *Susan Lady Gooch*
V L J PAYNE
WRENTHORPE (St Anne) *Leeds 20* **P** *Bp* **P-in-c** R HARRIS
WRESSLE (St John of Beverly) *see* Howden *York*
WRESTLINGWORTH (St Peter) *see* Dunton w Wrestlingworth and Eyeworth *St Alb*
WRETHAM (St Ethelbert) *see* Thetford *Nor*
WRETTON (All Saints) w Stoke Ferry and Whittington *Ely 9*
P *Ld Chan and Ch Patr Trust (alt)* **V** *vacant*
WRIBBENHALL (All Saints) *see* Ribbesford w Bewdley and Dowles and Wribbenhall *Worc*
WRIGHTINGTON (St James the Great) *Blackb 4* **P** *Bp*
V P MASON
WRINGTON (All Saints) w Butcombe and Burrington *B & W 10* **P** *Patr Bd* **R** N R MADDOCK
NSM A M HEMMING
WRITTLE (All Saints) w Highwood *Chelmsf 9* **P** *New Coll Ox*
P-in-c J JONES **NSM** S E IVES
WROCKWARDINE WOOD (Holy Trinity) *see* Oakengates and Wrockwardine Wood *Lich*
WROCKWARDINE, The Deanery of (St Peter) *Lich 23*
P *Patr Bd* **TR** D F CHANTREY **NSM** G PHILLIPS, P A SHAW
WROOT (St Pancras) *see* Epworth Gp *Linc*
WROSE (St Cuthbert) *Leeds 3* **P** *The Crown* **Hon**
C P B STOODLEY
WROTHAM (St George) *Roch 10* **P** *D&C* **R** E M A WRIGHT
WROUGHTON (St John the Baptist and St Helen) *Bris 7*
P *Bp* **V** M A JOHNSON **C** N J SUCH **OLM** B M ABREY
WROXALL (St John the Evangelist) *Portsm 7* **P** *Bp*
P-in-c K R ADLAM
WROXETER (St Mary) *see* Wrockwardine Deanery *Lich*
WROXHAM (St Mary) w Hoveton St John w Hoveton St Peter and Belaugh *Nor 12* **P** *Bp* **R** E A JUMP
WROXTON (All Saints) *see* Ironstone *Ox*
WULFRIC Benefice, The *B & W 14* **P** *Ld Chan (4 turns), Bp and H W F Hoskyns Esq (1 turn)* **R** S M HUNTLEY **C** J R MORRIS
WYBERTON (St Leodegar) *Linc 21* **P** *DBP*
P-in-c C W B SOWDEN
WYBUNBURY (St Chad) and Audlem w Doddington *Ches 15*
P *Bp and Lady Rona Delves Broughton (jt)* **V** H F CHANTRY
WYCH, HIGH (St James) and Gilston w Eastwick *St Alb 15*
P *V Sawbridgeworth (2 turns), P T S Bowlby Esq (1 turn)*
R A J GILES
WYCHBOLD (St Mary de Wyche) *see* Stoke Prior, Wychbold and Upton Warren *Worc*
WYCHE (All Saints) *see* Malvern Chase *Worc*
WYCHNOR (St Leonard) *Lich 1* **P** *Personal Reps W H Harrison Esq* **V** J W ALLAN **NSM** E A WALL
WYCHWOOD *Ox 22* **P** *Bp* **V** K E STACEY
OLM A T HARTLEY
WYCK RISSINGTON (St Laurence) *see* Bourton-on-the-Water w Clapton etc *Glouc*
WYCLIFFE (St Mary) *see* Barningham w Hutton Magna and Wycliffe *Leeds*
WYCOMBE AND CHADWELL (St Mary) *see* Ironstone Villages *Leic*
WYCOMBE LANE (St Mary) *see* Wooburn *Ox*
WYCOMBE MARSH (St Anne and St Peter) *see* High Wycombe *Ox*
WYCOMBE, HIGH (All Saints) (St Andrew) (St Anne and St Peter) (Christ the Servant King) (St James) (St Mary and St George) *Ox 18* **P** *Patr Bd* **TR** H W ELLIS **TV** A FINCH, S A WHITMORE, S P DUST **C** L H CAMPOS DE SANTANA
NSM P VINEY **OLM** J LOCK, M A JACKSON, R M WOOSTER, V INCH
WYCOMBE, WEST (St Laurence) (St Paul) w Bledlow Ridge, Bradenham and Radnage *Ox 18* **P** *Bp, DBP, Peache Trustees, and Sir Francis Dashwood Bt (jt)* **R** N J LACEY
NSM L J RICHARDSON, V J BEAUMONT

WYDDIAL (St Giles) *see* Hormead, Wyddial, Anstey, Brent Pelham etc *St Alb*
WYE (St Gregory and St Martin) *Cant 2* **P** *Abp* **V** R HOLY
C L M LAWRENCE **OLM** L A CROSS
WYE REACHES Group, The *Heref 7* **P** *Bp (5 turns), Ld Chan (1 turn)* **V** K V CECIL **NSM** R J STEPHENS
OLM P A POWDRILL
WYESHAM (St James) *see* Wye Reaches Gp *Heref*
WYFORDBY (St Mary) *see* S Framland *Leic*
WYKE (Holy Trinity) *see* Bruton and Distr *B & W*
WYKE (St Mark) *Guildf 5* **P** *Bp* **V** A R M CRAVEN
WYKE (St Mary the Virgin) *Leeds 2* **P** *Bp* **V** E W A CRAGG
Hon C M R M LYONS
WYKE REGIS (All Saints) (St Edmund) *Sarum 4* **P** *D&C*
R D J SMITH **C** R J BUTCHER **NSM** B A PORT, E W D TILDESLEY
WYKEHAM (All Saints) *see* Upper Derwent *York*
WYKEHAM : Broughton w North Newington, Epwell w Sibford, Shutford, Swalcliffe, and Tadmarton *Ox 23*
P *New Coll, Worc Coll, and Lord Saye and Sele (jt)*
R R L HAWKES **NSM** E A HAWKES, J H TATTERSALL
WYKEN (Church of Risen Christ) *see* Coventry Caludon *Cov*
WYKEN (Holy Cross) *as above*
WYKEN (St Mary Magdalene) *as above*
WYLAM (St Oswin) *Newc 9* **P** *Bp* **P-in-c** R H MCLEAN
WYLDE GREEN (Emmanuel) *Birm 12* **P** *Bp*
P-in-c R M SHEPPARD **C** J J BRIDGE
WYLYE (St Mary the Virgin) *see* Lower Wylye and Till Valley *Sarum*
WYLYE AND TILL VALLEY, LOWER *Sarum 14* **P** *Patr Bd*
TV H R L BONSEY, V M GARRARD
WYLYE VALLEY TEAM, UPPER *Sarum 12* **P** *Patr Bd (5 turns), Ld Chan (1 turn)* **NSM** J E SHAW **OLM** A E BENNETT-SHAW, D M HAMMOND
WYMERING (St Peter and St Paul) *Portsm 6* **P** *Nugee Foundn*
P-in-c J L STRAW **Hon C** B R COOK
WYMESWOLD (St Mary) and Prestwold w Hoton *Leic 6*
P *S J Packe-Drury-Lowe Esq and Bp (by turn)* **C** E J YORK
NSM S J RICHARDSON
WYMINGTON (St Lawrence) w Podington *St Alb 13*
P *R M Orlebar Esq (1 turn), DBP (3 turns)* **R** *vacant*
WYMONDHAM (St Mary and St Thomas) *Nor 7* **P** *Bp*
V C J DAVIES **C** C P RELF-PENNINGTON **NSM** A K SLATER
WYMONDHAM (St Peter) *see* S Framland *Leic*
WYMONDLEY, GREAT (St Mary the Virgin) *see* St Ippolyts w Gt and Lt Wymondley *St Alb*
WYMONDLEY, LITTLE (St Mary the Virgin) *as above*
WYMYNSWOLD (St Margaret) *see* Barham Downs *Cant*
WYRE PIDDLE (St Anne) *see* Fladbury, Hill and Moor, Wyre Piddle etc *Worc*
WYRESDALE, OVER (Christ Church) *see* Dolphinholme w Quernmore and Over Wyresdale *Blackb*
WYRLEY, GREAT (St Mark) *Lich 3* **P** *R Cannock* **V** G HORNER
C R A WESTWOOD **OLM** M J PRICE
WYSALL (Holy Trinity) *see* Willoughby-on-the-Wolds w Wysall and Widmerpool *S'well*
WYTHALL (St Mary) *Birm 6* **P** *R Kings Norton* **V** R A BURLEY
C M E PARTON
WYTHAM (All Saints) *see* Wolvercote and Wytham *Ox*
WYTHBURN (not known) *see* St John's-in-the-Vale, Threlkeld and Wythburn *Carl*
WYTHENSHAWE (St Francis of Assisi) (St Luke) (St Martin) (St Richard of Chichester) (William Temple Church) *Man 6*
P *Patr Bd* **TR** S M EDWARDS **TV** M J APPLEBY
C A A DICKSON **OLM** G R MILLER
WYTHENSHAWE Lawton Moor (St Michael and All Angels) *see* Lawton Moor *Man*
WYTHER (Venerable Bede) *Leeds 15* **P** *Bp*
P-in-c A J PEARSON
WYTHOP (St Margaret) *see* Cockermouth Area *Carl*
WYVERSTONE (St George) *see* Bacton w Wyverstone, Cotton and Old Newton etc *St E*
WYVILLE (St Catherine) *see* Harlaxton Gp *Linc*
YAFFORTH (All Saints) *see* Lower Swale *Leeds*
YALDING (St Peter and St Paul) w Collier Street *Roch 8*
P *Ld Chan* **V** P J FILMER
YANWORTH (St Michael) *see* Chedworth, Yanworth and Stowell, Coln Rogers etc *Glouc*
YAPHAM (St Martin) *see* Barmby Moor Gp *York*
YAPTON (St Mary) *see* Clymping and Yapton w Ford *Chich*
YARCOMBE (St John the Baptist) *see* Kilmington, Stockland, Dalwood, Yarcombe etc *Ex*
YARDLEY (St Cyprian) Hay Mill *Birm 13* **P** *Bp*
P-in-c R ANETTS
YARDLEY (St Edburgha) *Birm 13* **P** *St Pet Coll Ox*
V W J SANDS

YARDLEY GOBION (St Leonard)   *see* Potterspury w Furtho and Yardley Gobion etc *Pet*

YARDLEY HASTINGS (St Andrew), Denton and Grendon w Castle Ashby and Whiston *Pet 6*   **P** *Marquess of Northampton and Bp (alt)*   **R** P YORK

YARDLEY WOOD (Christ Church) *Birm 5*   **P** *Bp*
  V L M GASTON   **Hon C** D G JONES

YARDLEY, SOUTH (St Michael and All Angels) *Birm 13*
  P *Bp*   **P-in-c** R ANETTS

YARKHILL (St John the Baptist)   *see* Ledbury *Heref*

YARLINGTON (Blessed Virgin Mary)   *see* Camelot Par *B & W*

YARM (St Mary Magdalene) *York 20*   **P** *Abp*   **R** W J FORD

YARMOUTH (St James) *Portsm 8*   **P** *Keble Coll Ox*
  R M E C WHATSON

YARMOUTH, GREAT (St John) (St Nicholas) (St Paul) (St Luke) (St Mary) *Nor 6*   **P** *Patr Bd*   **TR** C L TERRY
  TV J SANDER-HEYS, C G W V BOLTON-DEBBAGE
  OLM F W CLIFF, S R ANDREWS

YARNFIELD (Mission Room St Barnabas)   *see* Cotes Heath and Standon and Swynnerton etc *Lich*

YARNSCOMBE (St Andrew)   *see* Newton Tracey, Horwood, Alverdiscott etc *Ex*

YARNTON (St Bartholomew)   *see* Blenheim *Ox*

YARWELL (St Mary Magdalene)   *see* Nassington, Apethorpe, Thornhaugh etc *Pet*

YATE (St Mary) *Bris 5*   **P** *Bp*   **TR** I M WALLACE
  TV I P MACFARLANE   **C** B M CHARLES

YATELEY (St Peter) *Win 5*   **P** *Bp*   **R** A C EDMUNDS
  C M J GRIFFITHS, S E YETMAN

YATESBURY (All Saints)   *see* Oldbury *Sarum*

YATTENDON (St Peter and St Paul)   *see* Hermitage *Ox*

YATTON (All Saints)   *see* Ledbury *Heref*

YATTON KEYNELL (St Margaret)   *see* By Brook *Bris*

YATTON MOOR (St Mary the Virgin) *B & W 12*   **P** *DBF*
  TR T C N SCOTT   **TV** D B HARREX   **Hon C** J L W WILLIAMS

YAVERLAND (St John the Baptist)   *see* Brading w Yaverland *Portsm*

YAXHAM (St Peter)   *see* Mattishall and the Tudd Valley *Nor*

YAXLEY (St Mary the Virgin)   *see* S Hartismere *St E*

YAXLEY (St Peter) and Holme w Conington *Ely 15*   **P** *Ld Chan (2 turns), J H B Heathcote Esq (1 turn)*   **V** J A RANDALL
  C M J T FULLER

YEADON (St John the Evangelist) *Leeds 16*   **P** *Bp and R Guiseley w Esholt (jt)*   **V** R M WALKER   **C** B L SPROATS

YEALAND CONYERS (St John the Evangelist)   *see* Warton St Oswald w Yealand Conyers *Blackb*

YEALMPTON (St Bartholomew) and Brixton *Ex 20*   **P** *D&C Windsor and Bp (jt)*   **P-in-c** O MURPHY

YEARSLEY (Holy Trinity)   *see* Crayke w Brandsby and Yearsley *York*

YEAVELEY (Holy Trinity)   *see* Brailsford w Shirley, Osmaston w Edlaston etc *Derby*

YEDINGHAM (St John the Baptist)   *see* Buckrose Carrs *York*

YELDEN (St Mary)   *see* The Stodden Churches *St Alb*

YELDHAM, GREAT (St Andrew)   *see* Upper Colne *Chelmsf*

YELDHAM, LITTLE (St John the Baptist)   *as above*

YELFORD (St Nicholas and St Swithin)   *see* Lower Windrush *Ox*

YELLING (Holy Cross)   *see* Papworth *Ely*

YELVERTOFT (All Saints)   *see* Crick and Yelvertoft w Clay Coton and Lilbourne *Pet*

YELVERTON (St Mary)   *see* Thurton *Nor*

YELVERTON (St Paul), Meavy, Sheepstor and Walkhampton *Ex 22*   **P** *Ld Chan (1 turn), Patr Bd (2 turns)*   **P-in-c** N S SHUTT
  C E P PARKES, G R SHIRLEY   **NSM** M SALMON

YEOFORD CHAPEL (Holy Trinity)   *see* Crediton, Shobrooke and Sandford etc *Ex*

YEOVIL (Holy Trinity) w Barwick *B & W 6*   **P** *Ms Y L Bennett and Ms R S Mullen (1 turn), The Crown (3 turns)*
  R G M HOCKEY

YEOVIL (St Andrew) (St John the Baptist) w Kingston Pitney *B & W 6*   **P** *DBP*   **R** J DUDLEY-SMITH   **C** T D PUTT

YEOVIL (St Michael and All Angels) *B & W 6*   **P** *Bp*
  P-in-c D R ANDERSON

YEOVIL (St Peter)   *see* Preston Plucknett *B & W*

YEOVIL MARSH (All Saints)   *see* Tintinhull w Chilthorne Domer, Yeovil Marsh etc *B & W*

YETMINSTER (St Andrew)   *see* Three Valleys *Sarum*

YIEWSLEY (St Matthew) *Lon 24*   **P** *V Hillingdon*
  V R C YOUNG

YOCKLETON (Holy Trinity)   *see* Westbury, Worthen and Yockleton *Heref*

YORK (All Saints) North Street *York 7*   **P** *D&C*   **V** *vacant*

YORK (All Saints) Pavement w St Crux and St Michael Spurriergate *York 7*   **P** *Abp*   **P-in-c** E J NATTRASS
  C S D EARIS   **Hon C** P A W JONES   **NSM** D C E SIMPSON

YORK (Holy Redeemer)   *see* Acomb H Redeemer *York*

YORK (Holy Trinity) Micklegate *York 7*   **P** *D&C*
  P-in-c E J NATTRASS   **C** E C ROBINSON

YORK (James the Deacon)   *see* Acomb Moor *York*

YORK (St Barnabas) *York 7*   **P** *CPAS*   **P-in-c** U L SIMPSON
  Hon C R W SIMPSON

YORK (St Chad) *York 7*   **P** *Abp*   **V** *vacant*

YORK (St Clement w St Mary) Bishophill *York 7*   **P** *Abp and D&C (jt)*   **R** A STOKER   **NSM** D H EFIRD, G J PETERS

YORK (St Denys) *York 7*   **P** *Abp*   **P-in-c** E J NATTRASS
  C S D EARIS   **Hon C** P A W JONES   **NSM** D C E SIMPSON

YORK (St Helen) Stonegate w (St Martin) Coney Street *York 7*
  P *Abp*   **P-in-c** E J NATTRASS   **C** S D EARIS   **Hon C** P A W JONES   **NSM** D C E SIMPSON

YORK (St Hilda) *York 7*   **P** *Abp*   **V** *vacant*

YORK (St Lawrence w St Nicholas) *York 7*   **P** *D&C*
  P-in-c E J NATTRASS

YORK (St Luke) *York 7*   **P** *Abp*   **NSM** M E CARRINGTON, T M GANT

YORK (St Michael-le-Belfrey) (St Cuthbert) *York 7*   **P** *Abp*
  V M J PORTER   **C** B DOOLAN, G C DOWNES
  NSM C N SELVARATNAM, E A RANSFORD, W J ROBERTS

YORK (St Olave w St Giles) *York 7*   **P** *Abp*
  P-in-c E J NATTRASS   **C** S D EARIS   **Hon C** P A W JONES
  NSM D C E SIMPSON

YORK (St Paul) Holgate Road *York 7*   **P** *CPAS*   **R** J M A LEE

YORK (St Stephen)   *see* Acomb St Steph and St Aid *York*

YORK (St Thomas w St Maurice) *York 7*   **P** *Abp*
  P-in-c A J RYCROFT

YORK Acomb (St Aidan)   *see* Acomb St Steph and St Aid *York*

YOULGREAVE (All Saints), Middleton, Stanton-in-Peak and Birchover *Derby 2*   **P** *Duke of Devonshire and N B B Davie-Thornhill Esq (jt)*   **V** G C GRIFFITHS

YOXALL (St Peter) *Lich 1*   **P** *Bp*   **P-in-c** M H HAWKSWORTH
  OLM M BINSLEY

YOXFORD (St Peter)   *see* Yoxmere *St E*

YOXMERE Benefice, The *St E 17*   **P** *Prime Min (1 turn), Ch Patr Trust, Lady Penelope Gilbey, Shadingfield Property, J K A Brooke Esq, CPAS, and Bp (2 turns)*   **V** C H REDGRAVE
  C S R BATES

ZEAL MONACHORUM (St Peter) *Ex 2*   **P** *DBP*   **R** *vacant*

ZEALS (St Martin)   *see* Upper Stour *Sarum*

ZENNOR (St Senera) *Truro 5*   **P** *Bp*   **P-in-c** E V A FOOT

WELSH BENEFICES AND CHURCHES

An index of benefices of the Church in Wales (shown in bold type), together with entries for churches and other licensed places of worship. Where the church name is the same as the benefice (or the first place name in the benefice), the church entry is omitted. Church dedications are indicated in brackets.

The benefice entry gives the full legal name, followed by the diocese, its deanery number (p. 1045), and the name(s) and appointment(s) of the clergy serving there. The following are the main abbreviations used; for others see the full list of abbreviations.

C	Curate	P-in-c	Priest-in-charge
C-in-c	Curate-in-charge	Par Dn	Parish Deacon
Hon C	Honorary Curate	R	Rector
Hon Par Dn	Honorary Parish Deacon	TR	Team Rector
I	Incumbent	TV	Team Vicar
NSM	Non-stipendiary Minister	V	Vicar

ABBEY CWMHIR (St Mary the Virgin)   see Lower Ithon Valley S & B

ABERAERON (Holy Trinity)   see Henfynyw w Aberaeron and Llanddewi Aberarth etc St D

ABERAMAN (St Margaret) and Abercwmboi w Cwmaman Llan 8   **V** vacant

ABERAVON (St Mary) (Holy Trinity) (St Agnes) Llan 5   **TR** N CAHILL   **TV** B T RABJOHNS   **C** R G AP ROBERT   **NSM** J A SLENNETT

ABERBARGOED (St Peter)   see Bedwellty and New Tredegar Mon

ABERCANAID (St Peter)   see Merthyr Tydfil St Dav and Abercanaid Llan

ABERCRAF (St David)   see Cwmtawe Uchaf S & B

ABERCWMBOI   see Aberaman and Abercwmboi w Cwmaman Llan

ABERCYNON (St Donat) (St Gwynno) Llan 8   **P-in-c** S A ROGERS

ABERDARE (St Fagan) Llan 8   **V** R A GREEN

ABERDARE (St John the Baptist) (St Elvan) (St Matthew) (St John the Evangelist) Llan 8   **V** R E DAVIES

ABERDARON (St Hywyn)   see Bro Enlli Ban

ABERDYFI (St Peter)   see Bro Ystumanner Ban

ABEREDW (St Cewydd)   see Erwood Gp w Painscastle Gp S & B

ABERERCH (St Cawrdaf)   see Bro'r Holl Saint Ban

ABERFFRAW (St Beuno)   see Bro Cadwaladr Ban

ABERGAVENNY (Holy Trinity) (Christ Church) Mon 1   **P-in-c** M SOADY

ABERGAVENNY (St Mary) (Christchurch) w Llanwenarth Citra Mon 1   **V** M SOADY   **Par Dn** S K GILLARD-FAULKNER

ABERGELE (St David) (St Michael) and St George St As 5   **V** K A JOHNSON

ABERGORLECH (St David)   see Cynwyl Gaeo w Llansawel and Talley etc St D

ABERGWILI (St David)   see Carmarthen St Pet and Abergwili etc St D

ABERGWYNGREGYN (St Bodfan)   see Dwylan Ban

ABERGYNOLWYN   see Bro Ystumanner Ban

ABERHAFESP (St Gwynog)   see Llanllwchaiarn and Newtown w Aberhafesp St As

ABERKENFIG (St John)   see Llansantffraid, Bettws and Aberkenfig Llan

ABERNANT (St Lucia) St D 10   **P-in-c** J GAINER

ABERNANT (St Matthew)   see Aberdare Llan

ABERPERGWM (St Cadoc)   see Vale of Neath Llan

ABERPORTH (St Cynwyl) w Blaenporth w Betws Ifan St D 5   **V** vacant

ABERTILLERY (St Michael) w Cwmtillery w Llanhilleth w Six Bells Mon 8   **P-in-c** W J RITCHIE   **Hon C** M PARKER

ABERTYSSWG (St Paul)   see Rhymney Mon

ABERYSKIR (St Mary and St Cynidr)   see Dan yr Eppynt S & B

ABERYSTWYTH (St Michael) (Holy Trinity) (St Mary) (St Anne) St D 9   **P-in-c** M A FARAH   **TV** A F HERRICK, I J GIRLING   **C** J-D LAURENCE   **NSM** D C JONES

AFAN VALE   see Glyncorrwg and the Upper Afan Valley etc Llan

ALLTMAWR (St Mauritius)   see Buallt S & B

ALLTWEN (St John the Baptist)   see Cilybebyll Llan

AMBLESTON (St Mary)   see Spittal w Trefgarn and Ambleston w St Dogwells St D

AMLWCH (St Eleth) (St Gwenllwyfo) (St Eilian) (St Tyfrydog) Ban 7   **R** vacant

AMMANFORD (All Saints)   see Betws w Ammanford St D

AMMANFORD (St Michael) as above

AMROTH (St Elidyr)   see St Issell's and Amroth w Crunwere and Marros St D

ANGLE (St Mary)   see Monkton St D

ARTHOG (St Catherine)   see Bro Cymer Ban

BAGILLT (St Mary) St As 4   **P-in-c** B HARVEY   **NSM** J M GEARY

BAGLAN (St Catherine) (St Baglan) Llan 5   **P-in-c** S JENKYNS   **C** E JENKYNS

BALA (Christ Church) St As 13   **R** E ATACK

BANGOR   see Bro Deiniol Ban

BANGOR MONACHORUM (St Dunawd), Worthenbury and Marchwiel St As 10   **R** S M HUYTON

BANGOR TEIFI (St David)   see Llandysul w Bangor Teifi and Llanfairollwyn etc St D

BARGOED (St Gwladys) and Deri w Brithdir Llan 9   **P-in-c** J M WIDDESS

BARMOUTH   see Llanaber w Caerdeon Ban

BARRY (All Saints) (St John w St Baruc) Llan 3   **P-in-c** K W LAKE   **C** E L REES

BARRY (St Paul)   see Merthyr Dyfan Llan

BASSALEG (St Basil) Mon 5   **TR** C M L STONE   **NSM** E E KERL, H I PREST, R P MULCAHY

BEACONS, The S & B 3   **P-in-c** K RICHARDS   **C** A N JEVONS

BEAUFORT (St David)   see Upper Ebbw Valleys Mon

BEAUMARIS (St Mary and St Nicholas) (St Catherine) (St Seiriol) (St Cawrdaf) (St Michael) w Llanddona and Llaniestyn Ban 6   **R** N FAIRLAMB

BEDDGELERT (St Mary)   see Bro Moelwyn Ban

BEDWAS (St Barrwg) w Machen w Michaelston-y-Fedw w Rudry Mon 5   **R** P D CROCKER   **C** R C STEVENS   **NSM** M MOORE

BEDWELLTY (St Sannan) and New Tredegar Mon 6   **V** R C DYMOND   **C** L K PHILBRICK   **NSM** B JONES

BEGELLY (St Mary) w Ludchurch and East Williamston St D 3   **NSM** R LEWIS

BEGUILDY (St Michael and All Angels) (St Peter) and Heyope and Llangynllo and Bleddfa S & B 5   **P-in-c** J HANNA

BENLLECH (St Andrew)   see Bro Tysilio Ban

BERRIEW (St Beuno) St As 8   **V** P J PIKE   **NSM** E C YATES

BERSHAM (St Mary)   see Wrexham St As

BETTISFIELD (St John the Baptist)   see Hanmer, Bronington, Bettisfield and Penley St As

BETTWS   see Dan yr Eppynt S & B

BETTWS (St David) Mon 7   **P-in-c** H J DAVIES

BETTWS (St David)   see Llansantffraid, Bettws and Aberkenfig Llan

BETTWS CHAPEL   see Llantilio Pertholey w Bettws Chpl etc Mon

BETTWS DISSERTH (St Mary)   see Colwyn S & B

BETTWS NEWYDD (not known)   see Raglan Gp Mon

BETWS (Holy Trinity)   see Glasbury and Llowes w Clyro and Betws S & B

BETWS (St David) w Ammanford St D 12   **V** vacant

BETWS BLEDRWS (St Bledrws or St Michael)   see Lampeter w Maestir and Silian and Llangybi and Betws Bledrws St D

BETWS CEDEWAIN (St Beuno) and Tregynon and Llanwyddelan St As 6   **V** vacant

BETWS GARMON (St Garmon)   see Llanbeblig w Caernarfon and Betws Garmon etc Ban

BETWS GWERFUL GOCH (St Mary) w Llangwm w Llawrybetws St As 13   **P-in-c** S J ROBERTS

BETWS LEUCU (St Lucia)   see Llanddewi Brefi and Llangeitho St D

BETWS-Y-COED (St Mary) and Capel Curig w Penmachno w Dolwyddelan *Ban 2* **P-in-c** S ELLIOTT

BETWS-YN-RHOS (St Michael) *see* Petryal and Betws yn Rhos *St As*

BEULAH *see* Blaenau Irfon *S & B*

BIRCHGROVE (St John) *see* Llansamlet *S & B*

BISHOPSTON (St Teilo) *S & B 8* **V** A J PEARCE

BISHTON (St Cadwaladr) *see* Magor *Mon*

BISTRE (Emmanuel) (All Saints) (St Cecilia) *St As 11* **V** M J BATCHELOR **NSM** S BAIRD

BLACKWOOD (St Margaret) w Fleur-de-Lis *Mon 6* **Hon C** T MORGAN

BLAENAU FFESTINIOG (St David) *see* Bro Moelwyn *Ban*

BLAENAU IRFON *S & B 2* **C** P M E B BERESFORD-WEBB

BLAENAVON (St Peter) w Capel Newydd *Mon 8* **V** J S BRAY **C** R W NOY

BLAENGWRACH (St Mary) *see* Vale of Neath *Llan*

BLAENPENNAL (St David) *see* Tregaron Gp *St D*

BLAENPORTH (St David) *see* Aberporth w Blaenporth w Betws Ifan *St D*

BLAENWYSG *S & B 1* **V** M P WILDING

BLAINA (St Peter) *see* Upper Ebbw Valleys *Mon*

BLEDDFA (St Mary Magdalene) *see* Beguildy and Heyope and Llangynllo and Bleddfa *S & B*

BLETHERSTON (St Mary) *see* Llawhaden w Bletherston and Uzmaston *St D*

BODEDERN (St Edern) *see* Bro Cwyfan *Ban*

BODELWYDDAN (St Margaret) *see* Rhuddlan and Bodelwyddan *St As*

BODEWRYD (St Mary) *see* Bro Padrig *Ban*

BODFARI (St Stephen) *see* Caerwys and Bodfari *St As*

BODWROG (St Twrog) *see* Bro Cyngar *Ban*

BONTDDU *see* Llanaber w Caerdeon *Ban*

BONVILSTON (St Mary) *see* St Nicholas w Bonvilston and St George-super-Ely *Llan*

BONYMAEN (St Margaret) *see* Glantawe *S & B*

BORTH (St Matthew) and Eglwys-fach and Llangynfelyn *St D 9* **V** vacant

BOSHERSTON (St Michael) *see* Monkton *St D*

BOTWNNOG (St Beuno) *see* Bro Madryn *Ban*

BOUGHROOD (St Cynog) *see* Llandefalle and Llyswen w Boughrood etc *S & B*

BRACKLA (St Mary) *see* Coity, Nolton and Brackla w Coychurch *Llan*

BRAWDY (St David) *see* Dewisland *St D*

BRECHFA (St Teilo) and Llanfihangel Rhos-y-corn *St D 13* **P-in-c** L CHAMBERS

BRECON (Cathedral of St John the Evangelist) *S & B 1* **V** vacant

BRECON (St David) w Llanspyddid and Llanilltyd *S & B 1* **V** T J WILLIAMS

BRECON (St Mary) *S & B 1* **P-in-c** S E GRIFFITH **NSM** J M DAY

BRIDELL (St David) *see* Cilgerran w Bridell and Llantwyd and Eglwyswrw *St D*

BRIDGEND (St Illtud) *see* Newcastle *Llan*

BRIDGEND (St Mary) *see* Coity, Nolton and Brackla w Coychurch *Llan*

BRIGHTON, NEW (St James) *see* Mold *St As*

BRITHDIR (St David) *see* Bargoed and Deri w Brithdir *Llan*

BRITHDIR (St Mary) *see* Llanrhaeadr ym Mochnant etc *St As*

BRO ARDUDWY *Ban 8* **R** B BAILEY **C** M J BEECROFT

BRO ARWYSTLI *Ban 9* **V** L B COWAN **C** E A VARLEY

BRO CADWALADR *Ban 4* **V** E C WILLIAMS **NSM** E R ROBERTS

BRO CWYFAN *Ban 3* **R** N A RIDINGS

BRO CYBI *Ban 3* **V** K S ELLIS **C** J R BAILEY

BRO CYFEILIOG A MAWDDWY *Ban 10* **P-in-c** K A ROGERS, R P BARNES **C** D J J A F MCCLEAN **NSM** P N WARD

BRO CYMER *Ban 12* **R** T R WEBB **NSM** R L FORD

BRO CYNGAR *Ban 4* **R** S R LEYLAND

BRO DEINIOL *Ban 5* **TR** vacant

BRO DWYNWEN *Ban 6* **C** E ROBERTS **Hon C** L J FRANCIS

BRO ENLLI *Ban 11* **C** A JONES, H A BRYANT, N E STARKEY

BRO ERYRI *Ban 1* **V** C S B ROBERTS **C** R W TOWNSEND

BRO FAUMA *see* Cilcain, Gwernaffield, Llanferres etc *St As*

BRO MADRYN *Ban 11* **V** R S WOOD

BRO MOELWYN *Ban 8* **R** D L R BROWNRIDGE

BRO OGWEN (Christ Church) *Ban 5* **V** J G MATTHEWS **NSM** C E MCCREA

BRO PADRIG *Ban 7* **R** T J JONES

BRO TYSILIO *Ban 6* **V** A WILLIAMS **Hon C** G T JONES **NSM** T AP SION

BRO YSTUMANNER *Ban 12* **V** R A VROOM **C** J FLETCHER **NSM** C C TEN WOLDE

BRONINGTON (Holy Trinity) *see* Hanmer, Bronington, Bettisfield and Penley *St As*

BRONLLYS (St Mary) *see* Talgarth w Bronllys w Llanfilo *S & B*

BRONWYDD (St Celynnin) *see* Llanpumsaint w Llanllawddog *St D*

BRO'R HOLL SAINT *Ban 11* **V** D J WILLIAMS **TV** K V WILLIAMS

BROUGHTON (St Mary) *see* Hawarden *St As*

BROUGHTON (St Paul) w Berse and Southsea *St As 9* **V** J G AYLWARD

BRYMBO (St Mary) w Bwlchgwyn *St As 9* **V** P POWELL

BRYN (St Tydfil) *see* Llangynwyd w Maesteg *Llan*

BRYNAMAN (St Catherine) w Cwmllynfell *St D 12* **V** A TEALE

BRYNCETHIN *see* Llansantffraid, Bettws and Aberkenfig *Llan*

BRYNCOEDIFOR (St Paul) *see* Bro Cymer *Ban*

BRYNCROES (St Mary) *see* Bro Madryn *Ban*

BRYNEGLWYS (St Tysilio) *see* Llandegla and Bryneglwys *St As*

BRYNFORD (St Michael) *see* Gorsedd w Brynford, Ysgeifiog and Whitford *St As*

BRYNGWRAN *see* Bro Cwyfan *Ban*

BRYNGWYN (St Michael) *see* Erwood Gp w Painscastle Gp *S & B*

BRYNGWYN (St Peter) *see* Raglan Gp *Mon*

BRYNMAWR (St Mary the Virgin) *S & B 3* **V** P M WINCHESTER

BRYNNA *see* Llanharan w Peterston-super-Montem *Llan*

BRYNYMAEN (Christ Church) *see* Colwyn Bay w Brynymaen *St As*

BUALLT (St Mary) *S & B 2* **V** N HOOK

BUCKHOLT (St John the Baptist) *see* Monmouth w Overmonnow etc *Mon*

BUCKLEY (St Matthew) (Good Shepherd) *St As 11* **P-in-c** N A KELLY

BUILTH WELLS (St Mary) *see* Buallt *S & B*

BULWARK (St Christopher) *see* Chepstow *Mon*

BURRY PORT (St Mary) and Pwll *St D 11* **P-in-c** M R P WHEATLEY

BURTON (St Mary) and Rosemarket *St D 4* **R** vacant

BUTE TOWN (St Aidan) *see* Pontlottyn w Fochriw *Llan*

BUTTINGTON (All Saints) *see* Guilsfield w Buttington and Pool Quay *St As*

BWLCH (All Saints) *see* Llyn Safaddan *S & B*

BWLCHGWYN (Christ Church) *see* Brymbo w Bwlchgwyn *St As*

BWLCHYCIBAU (Christ Church) *see* Llanfyllin, Bwlchycibau and Llanwddyn *St As*

BYLCHAU (St Thomas) *see* Henllan and Llannefydd and Bylchau *St As*

CADOXTON-JUXTA-BARRY (St Cadoc) (St Mary) *Llan 3* **R** B ANDREWS **C** C C SEATON

CADOXTON-JUXTA-NEATH (St Catwg) and Tonna *Llan 6* **P-in-c** A J M MEREDITH

CAERAU (St Cynfelin) *see* Glyncorrwg and the Upper Afan Valley etc *Llan*

CAERAU w Ely (St David) (St Timothy) *Llan 2* **V** J L SMITH **NSM** C J LEE

CAERDEON (St Philip) *see* Llanaber w Caerdeon *Ban*

CAEREITHIN (St Teilo) *S & B 10* **V** P F M GALLAGHER

CAERFALLWCH (St Paul) *see* Halkyn w Caerfallwch w Rhesycae *St As*

CAERGEILIOG *see* Bro Cwyfan *Ban*

CAERGYBI *see* Bro Cybi *Ban*

CAERHUN (St Mary) and Llangelynnin and Llanbedr-y-Cennin *Ban 2* **V** T BONNET

CAERLEON (St Cadoc) and Llanfrechfa Group, The *Mon 7* **V** P A COCHRANE **C** R M REARDON **NSM** E HILLS

CAERNARFON (Feed My Lambs) *see* Llanbeblig w Caernarfon and Betws Garmon etc *Ban*

CAERNARFON (St Mary) *as above*

CAERPHILLY (St Andrew) *see* Eglwysilan and Caerphilly *Llan*

CAERPHILLY (St Catherine) *as above*

CAERPHILLY (St Martin) *as above*

CAERWENT (St Stephen and St Tathan) *see* Wentwood *Mon*

CAERWYS (St Michael) and Bodfari *St As 2* **R** J D P LOMAS

CALDICOT (St Mary) *Mon 3* **P-in-c** D RICHARDS **C** D C BOUTFLOWER **NSM** H J DAVIES

CALLWEN (St John the Baptist) *see* Cwmtawe Uchaf *S & B*

CAMROSE (St Ishmael) *St D 1* **V** vacant

CANTON (St Catherine) *Llan 1* **V** vacant

CANTON (St John) *Llan 1* **R** vacant

CANTON Cardiff (St Luke) *Llan 1* **TR** M R PREECE **TV** R O'HARE

CANTREF (St Mary) *see* The Beacons *S & B*

CAPEL (Dewi Sant) *see* Llansadwrn w Llanwrda and Manordeilo *St D*

CAPEL BANGOR (St David) *see* Llanbadarn Fawr and Elerch and Penrhyncoch etc *St D*

CAPEL COELBREN (Capel Coelbren) *see* Cwmtawe Uchaf *S & B*

CAPEL COLMAN (St Colman)   *see* Maenordeifi Gp *St D*

CAPEL CYNON (St Cynon)   *see* Llanarth and Capel Cynon w Talgarreg etc *St D*

CAPEL DEWI (St David)   *see* Llanfihangel-ar-arth w Capel Dewi *St D*

CAPEL GARMON   *see* Llanrwst, Llanddoged w Capel Garmon etc *St As*

CAPEL IFAN (St John the Baptist)   *see* Gwendraeth Fawr *St D*

CAPEL LLANILLTERNE (St Ellteyrn)   *see* Pentyrch w Capel Llanillterne *Llan*

CAPEL MAIR   *see* Llangeler w Pen-Boyr *St D*

CAPEL NEWYDD (St Paul)   *see* Blaenavon w Capel Newydd *Mon*

CAPEL TYGWYDD   *see* Maenordeifi Gp *St D*

CAPEL Y GROES   *see* Carmarthen St Pet and Abergwili etc *St D*

CAPEL-Y-FFIN (St Mary)   *see* Hay w Llanigon and Capel-y-Ffin *S & B*

CARDIFF (Christ Church) Roath Park *Llan 1*
P-in-c T O HUGHES   **NSM** K MIDDLETON

CARDIFF (Dewi Sant) *Llan 1*   **V** D C LLOYD
NSM R W LINECAR

CARDIFF (St Andrew and St Teilo)   *see* Cathays *Llan*

CARDIFF (St German) (St Saviour) *Llan 1*   **V** D J ATKINS

CARDIFF (St Luke)   *see* Canton Cardiff *Llan*

CARDIFF (St Mary) (St Dyfrig and St Samson) *Llan 1*
V G J FRANCIS   **C** D T MORRIS

CARDIFF (St Michael and All Angels)   *see* Cathays *Llan*

CARDIFF City Parish (St John the Baptist) *Llan 1*
P-in-c S C ROWLAND JONES   **NSM** R W LINECAR

CARDIGAN (St Mary) w Mwnt and Y Ferwig w Llangoedmor
St D 5   **V** J S BENNETT   **NSM** A G KENT

CAREW (St Mary) and Cosheston and Nash and Redberth
St D 3   **P-in-c** C M T WOOD

CARMARTHEN (St Peter) (St John the Evangelist) and Abergwili and Capel y Groes *St D 10*
P-in-c L L RICHARDSON   **C** B S READ   **NSM** H M OWEN, J M BRITTON

CARMARTHEN St David (Christ Church) *St D 10*
V P H B THOMAS   **NSM** D A RICHARDS

CARMEL (Eglwys Fair)   *see* Catheiniog *St D*

CARNHEDRYN   *see* Dewisland *St D*

CARNO (St John)   *see* Bro Arwystli *Ban*

CARROG (St Ffraid)   *see* Corwen w Llangar w Glyndyfrdwy etc *St As*

CASCOB (St Michael)   *see* E Radnor *S & B*

CASTELLAN   *see* Maenordeifi Gp *St D*

CASTLE BYTHE   *see* Letterston w Llanfair Nant-y-Gof etc *St D*

CASTLE CAEREINION (St Garmon)   *see* Welshpool and Castle Caereinion *St As*

CATHAYS (St Andrew and St Teilo) (St Michael and All Angels) *Llan 1*   **P-in-c** C R DOWNS   **C** M J UNDERDOWN

CATHEDINE (St Michael)   *see* Llyn Safaddan *S & B*

CATHEINIOG *St D 13*   **P-in-c** S E JONES   **C** S MILNE
NSM V A HOPE-BELL

CEFN (St Mary)   *see* Trefnant w Tremeirchion w Cefn *St As*

CEFN COED (St John the Baptist) w Vaynor *S & B 1*
V *vacant*

CEFN FOREST (St Thomas)   *see* Blackwood w Fleur-de-Lis *Mon*

CEFNLLYS (St Michael)   *see* Llandrindod w Cefnllys and Disserth *S & B*

CELLAN (All Saints)   *see* Llanddewi Brefi and Llangeitho *St D*

CEMAES   *see* Bro Padrig *Ban*

CEMAIS (St Tydecho)   *see* Bro Cyfeiliog a Mawddwy *Ban*

CENARTH (St Llawddog)   *see* Newcastle Emlyn and Llandyfriog etc *St D*

CERRIGYDRUDION (St Mary Magdalene) w Llanfihangel Glyn Myfyr w Ysbyty Ifan and Pentrefoelas *St As 13*
V *vacant*

CHEPSTOW (St Mary) *Mon 3*   **V** C J BLANCHARD

CHERITON   *see* Monkton *St D*

CHERITON (St Cadoc)   *see* Llangennith w Llanmadoc and Cheriton *S & B*

CHIRK (St Mary) *St As 10*   **V** M J G WILKINSON

CILCAIN (St Mary), Gwernaffield, Llanferres, Rhyd-y-mwyn and Nannerch *St As 12*   **R** A W A COPPING

CILCENNIN (Holy Trinity)   *see* Llanfihangel Ystrad and Cilcennin w Trefilan etc *St D*

CILFYNYDD (St Luke)   *see* Pontypridd St Matt and Cilfynydd w Llanwynno *Llan*

CILGERRAN (St Llawddog) w Bridell and Llantwyd and Eglwyswrw *St D 5*   **P-in-c** P G B RATCLIFFE

CILIAU AERON (St Michael)   *see* Llanerch Aeron w Ciliau Aeron and Dihewyd etc *St D*

CILYBEBYLL (St John the Evangelist) *Llan 6*   **R** H M O'SHEA

CIL-Y-CWM (St Michael) and Ystrad-ffin w Rhandirmwyn Llanfair-ar-y-Bryn *St D 14*   **NSM** E A MCKNIGHT

CLOCAENOG (St Foddhyd) and Gyffylliog *St As 3*
P-in-c R W CARTER

CLUNDERWEN (St David)   *see* Whitland w Cyffig and Henllan Amgoed etc *St D*

CLYDACH (St Mary) (St Michael) *S & B 7*   **NSM** D J LEWIS

CLYDACH VALE (St Thomas)   *see* Tonypandy w Clydach Vale w Williamstown *Llan*

CLYDAU (St Clydai)   *see* Crymych Gp *St D*

CLYNNOG FAWR (St Beuno)   *see* Uwch Gwyrfai Beuno Sant *Ban*

CLYRO (St Michael and All Angels)   *see* Glasbury and Llowes w Clyro and Betws *S & B*

CLYTHA   *see* Llanddewi Rhydderch w Llangattock-juxta-Usk etc *Mon*

COCKETT (St Peter)   *see* Swansea St Pet *S & B*

COEDKERNEW   *see* Marshfield w St Bride's Wentloog *Mon*

COEDYPAEN (Christchurch)   *see* Usk Min Area *Mon*

COETMOR (Christ Church)   *see* Bro Ogwen *Ban*

COITY (St Mary), Nolton and Brackla w Coychurch *Llan 4*
R M KOMOR   **C** P P SMITH   **NSM** J SHAW

COLVA (St David)   *see* New Radnor and Llanfihangel Nantmelan etc *S & B*

COLWINSTON (St Michael), Llandow and Llysworney *Llan 7*
P-in-c A M KETTLE

COLWYN *S & B 2*   **V** *vacant*

COLWYN (St John the Baptist) and Llanelian *St As 5*
R D Q BELLAMY   **NSM** G COOPER

COLWYN BAY (St Paul) (St David) w Brynymaen *St As 5*
V C R OWEN

COMINS COCH   *see* Llanbadarn Fawr and Elerch and Penrhyncoch etc *St D*

CONNAH'S QUAY (St Mark) (St David's Mission Church)
St As 11   **V** R F DENNIS

CONWY (St Mary and All Saints) w Gyffin *Ban 2*   **V** *vacant*

CORRIS (Holy Trinity)   *see* Bro Cyfeiliog a Mawddwy *Ban*

CORWEN (St Mael and St Sulien) w Llangar w Glyndyfrdwy w Llansantffraid Glyn Dyfrdwy w Gwyddelwern *St As 13*
V M K SNELLGROVE

COSHESTON (St Michael)   *see* Carew and Cosheston and Nash and Redberth *St D*

COWBRIDGE (Holy Cross) *Llan 7*   **TV** E F DOWLAND-OWEN
NSM D R BOULT

COYCHURCH (St Crallo)   *see* Coity, Nolton and Brackla w Coychurch *Llan*

CRAI (St Ilid)   *see* Blaenwysg *S & B*

CREGRINA (St David)   *see* Colwyn *S & B*

CRIBYN (St Silin)   *see* Llanfihangel Ystrad and Cilcennin w Trefilan etc *St D*

CRICCIETH (St Catherine)   *see* Bro'r Holl Saint *Ban*

CRICKADARN (St Mary)   *see* Erwood Gp w Painscastle Gp *S & B*

CRICKHOWELL (St Edmund) w Cwmdu and Tretower *S & B 3*
V B LETSON

CRIGGION (St Michael)   *see* Llandysilio and Penrhos and Llandrinio etc *St As*

CRINDAU (All Saints)   *see* Newport All SS *Mon*

CRINOW (St Teilo)   *see* Narberth w Mounton w Robeston Wathen etc *St D*

CROESCEILIOG (St Mary)   *see* Cwmbran *Mon*

CROSS HANDS (St Anne)   *see* Gors-las *St D*

CROSS INN (Holy Trinity)   *see* Llanllwchaearn and Llanina *St D*

CROSS KEYS (St Catherine)   *see* Lower Islwyn *Mon*

CROSSGATES   *see* Lower Ithon Valley *S & B*

CRUGYBYDDAR (St Peter)   *see* Beguildy and Heyope and Llangynllo and Bleddfa *S & B*

CRYMYCH Group, The *St D 1*   **P-in-c** J H L COPUS

CRYNANT (St Margaret)   *see* Dulais Valley *Llan*

CWM (St Mael and St Sulien)   *see* Dyserth and Trelawnyd and Cwm *St As*

CWM (St Paul)   *see* Upper Ebbw Valleys *Mon*

CWMAFAN (St Michael) *Llan 5*   **P-in-c** E JENKYNS
C S JENKYNS

CWMAMAN (Christ Church) *St D 12*   **V** A J MAUNDER

CWMAMAN (St Joseph)   *see* Aberaman and Abercwmboi w Cwmaman *Llan*

CWMANN (St James)   *see* Pencarreg and Llanycrwys *St D*

CWMAVON (St Michael)   *see* Cwmafan *Llan*

CWMBACH (St Mary Magdalene) *Llan 8*
P-in-c C B W SMITH

CWMBACH LLECHRYD (St John the Divine)   *see* Upper Wye *S & B*

CWMBRAN (St Gabriel) *Mon 8*   **TR** M J PHILLIPS
Hon C R LANGTON   **NSM** F M A EVANS

CWMCARN (St John the Evangelist)   *see* Lower Islwyn *Mon*

CWMCARVAN (St Clement)   *see* Rockfield and Dingestow Gp *Mon*

CWM-COCH (St Mark)   *see* Llandybie *St D*
CWMDARE (St Luke)   *see* Aberdare St Fagan *Llan*
CWMDDAUDDWR (St Bride)   *see* Gwastedyn *S & B*
CWMDDAUDDWR (St Winifred)   *as above*
CWMDU (St Michael the Archangel)   *see* Crickhowell w Cwmdu and Tretower *S & B*
CWMDUAD (St Alban)   *see* Cynwyl Elfed w Newchurch and Trelech a'r Betws *St D*
CWMFFRWD (St Anne)   *see* Llangunnor w Cwmffrwd *St D*
CWMLLYNFELL (St Margaret)   *see* Brynaman w Cwmllynfell *St D*
CWMPARC (St George)   *see* Pen Rhondda Fawr *Llan*
CWMTAWE UCHAF *S & B 7*   **V** *vacant*
CWMTILLERY (St Paul)   *see* Abertillery w Cwmtillery w Llanhilleth etc *Mon*
CWMYOY (St Martin)   *see* Llanfihangel Crucorney w Oldcastle etc *Mon*
CWRT-HENRI (St Mary)   *see* Catheiniog *St D*
CYDWELI (St Mary) (St Teilo) and Llandyfaelog *St D 11*   **V** *vacant*
CYFFIG (St Cyffig)   *see* Whitland w Cyffig and Henllan Amgoed etc *St D*
CYMAU (All Saints)   *see* Llanfynydd *St As*
CYMMER (St John the Evangelist)   *see* Porth Newydd *Llan*
CYNCOED (All Saints) (St Edeyrn) *Mon 5*
   TR C M LAWSON-JONES   A V TEMPLE-WILLIAMS, S G CARBY   **C** P W GODSELL   **NSM** A B PARKES
CYNWYL ELFED (St Cynwyl) w Newchurch and Trelech a'r Betws *St D 10*   **C** J C ROLLINSON
CYNWYL GAEO (St Cynwyl) w Llansawel and Talley and Abergorlech *St D 14*   **NSM** D A WILSON
DAFEN (St Michael and All Angels) and Felinfoel *St D 11*
   P-in-c D H E MOSFORD   **C** E L WHITTICK
DALE (St James) and St Brides w Marloes and Hasguard w St Ishmael's *St D 4*   **P-in-c** A P JOHNSON
DAN YR EPPYNT *S & B 1*   **V** C A OWEN
DAROWEN (St Tudur)   *see* Bro Cyfeiliog a Mawddwy *Ban*
DEFYNNOG (St Cynog)   *see* Blaenwysg *S & B*
DEGANWY (All Saints)   *see* Rhos-Cystennin *St As*
DENBIGH (St Mary) (St Marcella) *St As 2*   **R** *vacant*
DENIO (St Peter)   *see* Bro'r Holl Saint *Ban*
DERI (St Peter)   *see* Bargoed and Deri w Brithdir *Llan*
DEVAUDEN (St James)   *see* Itton and St Arvans w Penterry and Kilgwrrwg w Devauden *Mon*
DEWISLAND (Cathedral of St David and St Andrew) *St D 2*
   TR D J R LEAN   **TV** A T FURSE, D P DAVIES   **NSM** M I PLANT
DIHEWYD (St Vitalis)   *see* Llanerch Aeron w Ciliau Aeron and Dihewyd etc *St D*
DINAS (Misson) w Penygraig *Llan 11*   **V** C R LEWIS-JENKINS
DINAS (St Brynach)   *see* Newport w Cilgwyn and Dinas w Llanllawer etc *St D*
DINGESTOW (St Dingad)   *see* Rockfield and Dingestow Gp *Mon*
DINHAM   *see* Wentwood *Mon*
DINMAEL (St Catherine)   *see* Betws Gwerful Goch w Llangwm w Llawrybetws *St As*
DISSERTH (St Cewydd)   *see* Llandrindod w Cefnllys and Disserth *S & B*
DOLBENMAEN (St Mary)   *see* Bro'r Holl Saint *Ban*
DOLFOR (St Paul)   *see* Kerry, Llanmerewig, Dolfor and Mochdre *Llan*
DOLGARROG (St Mary)   *see* Caerhun and Llangelynnin and Llanbedr-y-Cennin *Ban*
DOLGELLAU (St Mary)   *see* Bro Cymer *Ban*
DOLWYDDELAN (St Gwyddelan)   *see* Betws-y-Coed and Capel Curig w Penmachno etc *Ban*
DOWLAIS (All Saints) (Christ Church) and Penydarren *Llan 9*   **R** K J HARMAN
DULAIS VALLEY *Llan 6*   **V** *vacant*
DWYGYFYLCHI (St David)   *see* Dwylan *Ban*
DWYGYFYLCHI (St Gwynin)   *as above*
DWYGYFYLCHI (St Seiriol)   *as above*
DWYLAN *Ban 2*   **V** J E BROWN   **C** S BLAGDEN
DYFFRYN   *see* Bro Ardudwy *Ban*
DYFFRYN (St Matthew) *Llan 6*   **V** S J BODYCOMBE
DYFFRYN HONDDU (St Cynog)   *see* Dan yr Eppynt *S & B*
DYSERTH (St Bridget) (St Michael) (St Mael and St Sulien) and Trelawnyd and Cwm *St As 1*   **V** R W ROWLAND
EBBW VALE (Christchurch)   *see* Upper Ebbw Valleys *Mon*
EDERN (St Edern)   *see* Bro Madryn *Ban*
EFENECHTYD (St Michael)   *see* Llanfair DC, Derwen, Llanelidan and Efenechtyd *St As*
EGLWYS FAIR A CURIG *St D 10*   *vacant*
EGLWYS FAIR GLYN-TAF   *see* Whitland w Cyffig and Henllan Amgoed etc *St D*
EGLWYS GYMYN (St Margaret)   *see* Lampeter Velfrey and Llanddewi Velfrey etc *St D*

EGLWYS NEWYDD (St Michael)   *see* Grwp Bro Ystwyth a Mynach *St D*
EGLWYS OEN DUW   *see* Blaenau Irfon *S & B*
EGLWYSFACH   *see* Llanrwst, Llanddoged w Capel Garmon etc *St As*
EGLWYS-FACH (St Michael)   *see* Borth and Eglwys-fach and Llangynfelyn *St D*
EGLWYSILAN (St Ilan) and Caerphilly *Llan 9*
   TR M GREENAWAY-ROBBINS   **C** G J COOMBES, S A PRATTEN
EGLWYSRHOS (St Eleri and St Mary)   *see* Rhos-Cystennin *St As*
EGLWYSWRW (St Cristiolus)   *see* Cilgerran w Bridell and Llantwyd and Eglwyswrw *St D*
ELERCH (St Peter)   *see* Llanbadarn Fawr and Elerch and Penrhyncoch etc *St D*
ELY (St David)   *see* Caerau w Ely *Llan*
ELY (St Timothy)   *as above*
ERBISTOCK (St Hilary)   *see* Overton and Erbistock *St As*
ERWOOD Group w The Painscastle Group, The *S & B 2*
   P-in-c B L T GRIFFITH
ESCLUSHAM (Holy Trinity)   *see* Wrexham *St As*
ESGAIRGEILIOG   *see* Bro Cyfeiliog a Mawddwy *Ban*
EVANCOYD (St Peter)   *see* New Radnor and Llanfihangel Nantmelan etc *S & B*
EWENNY (St Michael) w St Brides Major *Llan 4*
   P-in-c P G MORRIS   **NSM** M J SPENCE
EYTON (St Deiniol)   *see* Bangor Monachorum, Worthenbury and Marchwiel *St As*
FAIRBOURNE (St Cynon)   *see* Bro Cymer *Ban*
FAIRHILL   *see* Cwmbran *Mon*
FAIRWATER (St Peter) *Llan 2*   **V** C P SUTTON
FAWR   *see* Llandeilo Fawr and Taliaris *St D*
FELINDRE (St Barnabas)   *see* Llangeler w Pen-Boyr *St D*
FELIN-FOEL (Holy Trinity)   *see* Dafen and Felinfoel *St D*
FELIN-GWM (St John)   *see* Llanegwad w Llanfihangel Uwch Gwili *St D*
FERNDALE (St Dunstan)   *see* Rhondda Fach Uchaf *Llan*
FERRYSIDE (St Thomas)   *see* St Ishmael's w Llan-saint and Ferryside *St D*
FFESTINIOG (St Michael)   *see* Bro Moelwyn *Ban*
FFYNNONGROYW (All Saints)   *see* Llanasa and Ffynnongroew *St As*
FISHGUARD (St Mary) w Llanychar and Pontfaen w Morfil and Llanychlwydog *St D 2*   **V** C C BROWN
   NSM J M ANNIS
FLEMINGSTON (St Michael)   *see* Cowbridge *Llan*
FLEUR-DE-LIS (St David)   *see* Blackwood w Fleur-de-Lis *Mon*
FLINT (St Mary) (St Thomas) *St As 4*   **R** B HARVEY
   NSM J M GEARY
FOCHRIW (St Mary and St Andrew)   *see* Pontlottyn w Fochriw *Llan*
FORD (St Margaret)   *see* Nolton w Roch and St Lawrence w Ford etc *St D*
FORDEN (St Michael)   *see* Montgomery and Forden and Llandyssil *St As*
FREYSTROP (St Justinian)   *see* Llangwm w Freystrop and Johnston *St D*
FRON (Mission Church)   *see* Berriew *St As*
FRONCYSYLLTE (St David)   *see* Chirk *St As*
FRONGOCH   *see* Bala *St As*
GABALFA (St Mark) *Llan 1*   **V** R M CAPPER   **C** J B GRIFFITHS
GAERWEN   *see* Bro Cadwaladr *Ban*
GARTHBEIBIO (St Tydecho), Llanerfel and Llangadfan *St As 7*   **V** *vacant*
GARTHELI (St Gartheli)   *see* Llanddewi Brefi and Llangeitho *St D*
GELLIGAER (St Catwg) (St Margaret) *Llan 9*
   P-in-c G C POWELL
GILESTON (St Giles)   *see* Llantwit Major *Llan*
GILFACH GOCH (St Barnabas)   *see* Tonyrefail w Gilfach Goch *Llan*
GILVACH (St Margaret)   *see* Gelligaer *Llan*
GLADWESTRY (St Mary)   *see* New Radnor and Llanfihangel Nantmelan etc *S & B*
GLAIS (St Paul)   *see* Llansamlet *S & B*
GLAN ELY (Resurrection) *Llan 2*   **P-in-c** J GOULD
GLANGRWYNEY (Mission Church)   *see* Vale of Gwrynne *S & B*
GLANOGWEN (Christ Church)   *see* Bro Ogwen *Ban*
GLANTAWE (St Margaret) (St Peter) *S & B 11*
   V C P G DICKSON
GLASBURY (St Peter) (All Saints) and Llowes w Clyro and Betws *S & B 4*   **V** D E THOMAS
GLASCOED (St Michael)   *see* Mamhilad w Monkswood and Glascoed Chapel *Mon*
GLASCOMBE (St David)   *see* Colwyn *S & B*
GLYN   *see* Brecon St David w Llanspyddid and Llanilltyd *S & B*
GLYNCORRWG (St John the Baptist) and the Upper Afan Valley w Caerau St Cynfelyn *Llan 5*   **P-in-c** B J REANEY

GLYNDYFRDWY (St Thomas)   *see* Corwen w Llangar w Glyndyfrdwy etc *St As*
GLYNTAFF (St Mary), Rhydfelin and the Craig *Llan 10*
   V M D GABLE   **NSM** W A DAVID
GOETRE (St Peter) w Llanover *Mon 4*   **R** *vacant*
GOLDCLIFFE (St Mary Magdalen)   *see* Magor *Mon*
GOODWICK (St Peter)   *see* Llanwnda, Goodwick w Manorowen and Llanstinan *St D*
GORSEDD (St Paul) w Brynford, Ysgeifiog and Whitford
   St As 4   **Par Dn** S M MORIARTY
GORSEINON (St Catherine) *S & B 9*   **V** M L COX
   C A MORGAN
GORS-LAS (St Lleian) *St D 12*   **NSM** J B JONES
GOVILON (Christchurch) w Llanfoist w Llanelen *Mon 1*
   P-in-c C R WALTERS
GOWER, SOUTH WEST *S & B 8*   **R** *vacant*
GOWERTON (St John the Evangelist) *S & B 9*   **V** I K REES
   NSM H REES
GRAIG (St John)   *see* Glyntaff, Rhydfelin and the Graig *Llan*
GRANDSTON (St Catherine)   *see* Llanrhian and Mathry w Grandstone etc *St D*
GRANGETOWN (St Paul) *Llan 1*   **V** G J FRANCIS
GRESFORD (All Saints)   *see* Holt and Gresford *St As*
GRIFFITHSTOWN (St Hilda)   *see* Panteg and Griffithstown *Mon*
GROESWEN (St David)   *see* Pentyrch w Capel Llanilllterne *Llan*
GRONANT (St Winifred)   *see* Llanasa and Ffynnongroew *St As*
GROSMONT (St Nicholas) and Skenfrith and Llangattock Lingoed and Llanfair Chapel *Mon 1*   **P-in-c** J PROSSER
   NSM A M H HARTER
GRWP BRO YSTWYTH A MYNACH: Llanfihangel-y-Creuddyn w Llanafan-y-Trawscoed w Llanwnnws w Ysbyty Ystwyth w Ysbyty Cynfyn w Lantrisant w Eglwys Newydd *St D 9*
   P-in-c E M LE GRICE   **NSM** R G MORRIS
GUILSFIELD (St Aelhaiarn) w Buttington and Pool Quay
   St As 8   **V** C L RHODES
GUMFRESTON (St Lawrence)   *see* Tenby *St D*
GWAENYSGOR   *see* Meliden and Gwaenysgor *St As*
GWASTEDYN *S & B 5*   **P-in-c** G D WATHAN
GWEHELOG   *see* Usk Min Area *Mon*
GWENDDWR (St Dubricius)   *see* Erwood Gp w Painscastle Gp *S & B*
GWENDRAETH FAWR *St D 11*   **P-in-c** M C CHARLES
GWENLLI (St Mark)   *see* Llanarth and Capel Cynon w Talgarreg etc *St D*
GWERNAFFIELD (Holy Trinity)   *see* Cilcain, Gwernaffield, Llanferres etc *St As*
GWERNESNEY (St Michael)   *see* Usk Min Area *Mon*
GWERNFFRWD (St David)   *see* Llanrhidian w Llanyrnewydd *S & B*
GWERSYLLT (Holy Trinity) *St As 9*   **V** P R-M DE G GOWER
GWRYNNE   *see* Vale of Gwrynne *S & B*
GWYDDELWERN (St Beuno)   *see* Corwen w Llangar w Glyndyfrdwy etc *St As*
GWYNFE (All Saints)   *see* Llangadog and Gwynfe w Llanddeusant *St D*
GWYTHERIN (St Winifred)   *see* Petryal and Betws yn Rhos *St As*
GYFFIN (St Benedict)   *see* Conwy w Gyffin *Ban*
GYFFYLLIOG (St Mary)   *see* Clocaenog and Gyffylliog *St As*
HAFOD (St John)   *see* Cen Swansea *S & B*
HAKIN (St Mary)   *see* Hubberston and Herbrandston *St D*
HALKYN (St Mary the Virgin) w Caerfallwch w Rhesycae
   St As 4   **P-in-c** H N BURGESS
HANMER (St Chad), Bronington, Bettisfield and Penley
   St As 10   **V** C HUGHES
HARLECH (St Tanwg)   *see* Bro Ardudwy *Ban*
HAROLDSTON ST ISSELLS (St Issell)   *see* Haverfordwest *St D*
HAROLDSTON WEST (St Madog)   *see* Walton W w Talbenny and Haroldston W *St D*
HAVERFORDWEST (St Martin) (St Mary) *St D 4*
   P-in-c N CALE   **C** J M ZIPPERLEN   **NSM** B H ROBERTS,
   H CALE
HAWARDEN (St Deiniol) (Holy Spirit) *St As 11*
   TR D T B LEWIS   **TV** D B EVANS   **C** A E M EVANS
   NSM L E COOKE
HAY (St Mary) (St John) w Llanigon and Capel-y-Ffin *S & B 4*
   V R D WILLIAMS
HAYSCASTLE (St Mary)   *see* Nolton w Roch and St Lawrence w Ford etc *St D*
HENDY (St David)   *see* Llangennech and Hendy and Llwynhendy *St D*
HENEGLWYS (St Llwydian)   *see* Bro Cyngar *Ban*
HENFYNYW (St David) w Aberaeron and Llanddewi Aberarth w Llanbadarn Trefeglwys *St D 7*   **V** J P LEWIS
   C M S ANSELL
HENLLAN (St Sadwrn) and Llannefydd and Bylchau *St As 2*
   P-in-c V E LEWIS   **Hon C** R J PEARCE

HENLLYS (St Peter)   *see* Cwmbran *Mon*
HENRY'S MOAT (St Bernard)   *see* W Preseli Gp *St D*
HEOL-Y-CYW (St Paul)   *see* Llanilid w Pencoed *Llan*
HERBRANDSTON (St Mary)   *see* Hubberston and Herbrandston *St D*
HEYOPE (St David)   *see* Beguildy and Heyope and Llangynllo and Bleddfa *S & B*
HIGH CROSS (St Anne)   *see* Bassaleg *Mon*
HIRWAUN (St Lleurwg) (St Winifred) *Llan 8*   **P-in-c** C J REES
HOLT (St Chad) and Gresford *St As 9*   **V** J T HUGHES
HOLY ISLAND   *see* Bro Cybi *Ban*
HOLYHEAD *as above*
HOLYWELL (St James) (Holy Trinity) (St Peter) *St As 4*
   V A W COLEMAN
HOPE (St Cynfarch) *St As 11*   **R** A R PAWLEY
HOWEY (St David)   *see* Llandrindod w Cefnllys and Disserth *S & B*
HUBBERSTON (St David) (Holy Spirit) and Herbrandston
   St D 4   **I** A P BOOKLESS   **C** J P MAYNARD   **NSM** J R CECIL
HUNDLETON (St David)   *see* Monkton *St D*
ILSTON (St Illtyd)   *see* Three Cliffs *S & B*
IRFON VALLEY *S & B 2*   **C** P M E B BERESFORD-WEBB
ISLWYN   *see* Lower Islwyn *Mon*
ISYCOED (St Paul)   *see* Llay, Rossett and Isycoed *St As*
ITHON VALLEY, LOWER *S & B 5*   **C** A PERRIN
ITHON VALLEY, UPPER *S & B 5*   **C** A PERRIN
ITTON (St Deiniol) and St Arvans w Penterry and Kilgwrrwg w Devauden *Mon 3*   **V** M J GOLLOP   **NSM** M E ZORAB
JEFFREYSTON (St Jeffrey) w Reynoldston and Loveston and Martletwy w Lawrenny and Yerbeston *St D 3*
   P-in-c P BOYLE   **NSM** R C LEWIS
JOHNSTON (St Peter)   *see* Llangwm w Freystrop and Johnston *St D*
JORDANSTON (St Cawrda)   *see* Llanrhian and Mathry w Grandstone etc *St D*
KEMEYS COMMANDER (All Saints)   *see* Raglan Gp *Mon*
KENFIG   *see* Pyle w Kenfig *Llan*
KENFIG HILL (St Theodore) *Llan 5*   **P-in-c** J R H DURLEY
KERRY (St Michael), Llanmerewig, Dolfor and Mochdre
   St As 6   **V** A O MAYES
KILGETTY   *see* Begelly w Ludchurch and E Williamston *St D*
KILGWRRWG (Holy Cross)   *see* Itton and St Arvans w Penterry and Kilgwrrwg w Devauden *Mon*
KILLAY (St Hilary) (St Martin) *S & B 6*   **V** *vacant*
KILVEY (All Saints)   *see* Swansea St Thos and Kilvey *S & B*
KNELSTON   *see* SW Gower *S & B*
KNIGHTON (St Edward)   *see* E Radnor *S & B*
LALESTON (St David) and Merthyr Mawr w Penyfai *Llan 4*
   NSM J M LEWIS
LAMPETER (St Peter) w Maestir and Silian and Llangybi and Betws Bledrws *St D 8*   **NSM** J C M KIMBER
LAMPETER VELFREY (St Peter) and Llanddewi Velfrey and Eglwys Gymyn *St D 3*   **V** *vacant*
LAMPHEY (St Faith and St Tyfei)   *see* Monkton *St D*
LANDORE w Treboeth *S & B 10*   **V** D JONES
LANGSTONE (not known)   *see* Magor *Mon*
LAUGHARNE (St Martin) and Llansadwrnen and Pendine and Llanmiloe *St D 3*   **P-in-c** C M BROWNE
LAWRENNY (St Caradog)   *see* Jeffreyston w Reynoldston and Loveston etc *St D*
LECKWITH   *see* Penarth and Llandough *Llan*
LETTERSTON (St Giles) w Llanfair Nant-y-Gof and Puncheston w Little Newcastle and Castle Bythe *St D 2*
   NSM P G S ROGERS, R DAVIES
LISVANE (St Denys) *Llan 1*   **V** C E BURR
LISWERRY   *see* Newport St Andr *Mon*
LITTLE NEWCASTLE (St Peter)   *see* Letterston w Llanfair Nant-y-Gof etc *St D*
LLANABER (St Mary) (St John) (St David) w Caerdeon *Ban 8*
   R K G HORSWELL   **NSM** L R BAILY
LLANAELHAEARN (St Aelhaiarn)   *see* Uwch Gwyrfai Beuno Sant *Ban*
LLANAFAN FAWR (St Afan)   *see* Upper Wye *S & B*
LLANAFAN-Y-TRAWSCOED (St Afan)   *see* Grwp Bro Ystwyth a Mynach *St D*
LLANALLGO (St Gallo)   *see* Llaneugrad w Llanallgo and Penrhosllugwy etc *Ban*
LLANANNO (St Anno)   *see* Upper Ithon Valley *S & B*
LLANARMON (St Garmon)   *see* Bro'r Holl Saint *Ban*
LLANARMON DYFFRYN CEIRIOG (St Garmon)
   see Llansantffraid Glyn Ceiriog and Llanarmon etc *St As*
LLANARMON MYNYD (St Garmon)   *see* Llanrhaeadr ym Mochnant etc *St As*
LLANARMON YN IAL (St Garmon)   *see* Llanbedr DC, Llangynhafal, Llanychan etc. *St As*

LLANARTH (St David) (St Teilo) and Capel Cynon w
Talgarreg and (St Mark) *St D 7* V C L BOLTON
LLANARTHNE (St David) and Llanddarog *St D 10*
P-in-c B D WITT
LLANASA (St Asaph and St Cyndeyrn) (St Winifred) and
Ffynnongroew *St As 1* V *vacant*
LLANBABO (St Pabo) *see* Bro Cwyfan *Ban*
LLANBADARN FAWR (St Padarn) *see* Lower Ithon Valley
S & B
LLANBADARN FAWR (St Padarn) and Elerch and
Penrhyncoch and Capel Bangor *St D 9* P-in-c A G LOAT
C L L DAFIS NSM H R EVANS
LLANBADARN FYNYDD (St Padarn) *see* Upper Ithon Valley
S & B
LLANBADARN ODWYN (St Padarn) *see* Llanddewi Brefi and
Llangeitho *St D*
LLANBADARN TREFEGLWYS (St Padarn) *see* Henfynyw w
Aberaeron and Llanddewi Aberarth etc *St D*
LLANBADARN-Y-GARREG (St Padarn) *see* Erwood Gp w
Painscastle Gp *S & B*
LLANBADOC (St Madog) *see* Usk Min Area *Mon*
LLANBADRIG (St Padrig) *see* Bro Padrig *Ban*
LLANBEBLIG (St Peblig) w Caernarfon and Betws Garmon w
Waunfawr *Ban 1* TR R F DONALDSON
LLANBEDER (St Peter) *see* Bro Ardudwy *Ban*
LLANBEDR DYFFRYN CLWYD (St Peter), Llangynhafal,
Llanychan and Llanynys and Llanarman yn Ial *St As 3*
R P V F CHEW C D G GOSLING
LLANBEDR PAINSCASTLE (St Peter) *see* Erwood Gp w
Painscastle Gp *S & B*
LLANBEDR PONT STEFFAN *see* Lampeter w Maestir and Silian
and Llangybi and Betws Bledrws *St D*
LLANBEDR YSTRAD YW (St Peter) *see* Vale of Gwrynne *S & B*
LLANBEDRGOCH (St Peter) *see* Bro Tysilio *Ban*
LLANBEDROG (St Pedrog) *see* Bro Enlli *Ban*
LLANBEDR-Y-CENNIN (St Peter) *see* Caerhun and
Llangelynnin and Llanbedr-y-Cennin *Ban*
LLANBERIS (St Padarn) *see* Bro Eryri *Ban*
LLANBERIS (St Peris) *as above*
LLANBISTER (St Cynllo) *see* Upper Ithon Valley *S & B*
LLANBLETHIAN (St Blethian) *see* Cowbridge *Llan*
LLANBOIDY (St Brynach) *see* Meidrim and Llanboidy and
Merthyr *St D*
LLANBRYN-MAIR (St Mary) *see* Bro Cyfeiliog a Mawddwy *Ban*
LLANCARFAN (St Cadoc) *see* Penmark w Llancarfan w
Llantrithyd *Llan*
LLANDAFF (Cathedral of St Peter and St Paul w St Dyfrig,
St Teilo and St Euddogwy) *Llan 2* V G H CAPON
LLANDAFF NORTH (All Saints) *see* Whitchurch *Llan*
LLANDANWG *see* Bro Ardudwy *Ban*
LLANDAVENNY *see* Wentwood *Mon*
LLANDDAROG (St Twrog) *see* Llanarthne and Llanddarog *St D*
LLANDDEINIOL (St Deiniol) *see* Llansantffraed w Llanrhystud
and Llanddeiniol *St D*
LLANDDEINIOLEN (St Deiniol) *see* Bro Eryri *Ban*
LLANDDEW (St David) *S & B 1* V *vacant*
LLANDDEWI *see* Blaenau Irfon *S & B*
LLANDDEWI (St David) *see* SW Gower *S & B*
LLANDDEWI ABERARTH (St David) *see* Henfynyw w Aberaeron
and Llanddewi Aberarth etc *St D*
LLANDDEWI BREFI (St David) and Llangeitho *St D 8*
P-in-c W D JONES
LLANDDEWI FACH (St David) *see* Erwood Gp w Painscastle Gp
S & B
LLANDDEWI RHONDDA (St David) *see* Pwllgwaun and
Llanddewi Rhondda *Llan*
LLANDDEWI RHYDDERCH (St David) w Llangattock-juxta-
Usk and Llanarth w Clytha and Llansantffraed *Mon 1*
P-in-c J HUMPHRIES
LLANDDEWI VELFREY (St David) *see* Lampeter Velfrey and
Llanddewi Velfrey etc *St D*
LLANDDEWI YSTRADENNI (St David) *see* Upper Ithon Valley
S & B
LLANDDEWI'R CWM (St David) *see* Buallt *S & B*
LLANDDOGET (St Doged) *see* Llanrwst, Llanddoged w Capel
Garmon etc *St As*
LLANDDONA (St Dona) *see* Beaumaris w Llanddona *Ban*
LLANDDOWROR (St Teilo) *see* St Clears w Llangynin and
Llanddowror etc *St D*
LLANDDULAS (St Cynfryd) and Llysfaen *St As 5*
R M C JAMES
LLANDDWYWE (St Ddwywe) *see* Bro Ardudwy *Ban*
LLANDECWYN (St Tecwyn) *as above*
LLANDEFAELOG-FACH (St Maelog) *see* Dan yr Eppynt *S & B*
LLANDEFALLE (St Matthew) and Llyswen w Boughrood and
Llanstephen w Talachddu *S & B 4* R I P CHARLESWORTH

LLANDEGFAN (St Tegfan) *see* Bro Tysilio *Ban*
LLANDEGLA (St Tecla) and Bryneglwys *St As 13*
R R H GRIFFITHS
LLANDEGLEY (St Tecla) *see* Lower Ithon Valley *S & B*
LLANDEGVETH (St Tegfeth) *see* Caerleon and Llanfrechfa *Mon*
LLANDEILO *see* W Preseli Gp *St D*
LLANDEILO ABERCYWYN *see* Llansteffan and Llan-y-bri etc
St D
LLANDEILO FAWR (St Teilo) and Taliaris *St D 13*
V M S SADLER
LLANDEILO GRABAN (St Teilo) *see* Erwood Gp w Painscastle
Gp *S & B*
LLANDEILO TAL-Y-BONT (St Teilo) (St Michael) *S & B 9*
C E BRAMLEY
LLANDENNY (St John the Apostle) *see* Raglan Gp *Mon*
LLANDEUSSANT (St Simon and St Jude) *see* Llangadog and
Gwynfe w Llanddeusant *St D*
LLANDEVAUD (St Peter) *see* Wentwood *Mon*
LLANDEWI FACH *see* Caerleon and Llanfrechfa *Mon*
LLANDEWI SKIRRID (St David) *see* Llantilio Pertholey w Bettws
Chpl etc *Mon*
LLANDILO'R FAN (St Teilo) *see* Blaenwysg *S & B*
LLANDINAM (St Llonio) *see* Bro Arwystli *Ban*
LLANDINGAT (St Dingad) w Myddfai *St D 14* V I H AVESON
LLANDINORWIG (Christ Church) *see* Bro Eryri *Ban*
LLANDOGO (St Oudoceus) w Whitebrook Chapel and
Tintern Parva *Mon 2* NSM N HILL OLM J F AVERY,
R A DAGGER
LLANDOUGH (St Dochdwy) *see* Penarth and Llandough *Llan*
LLANDOUGH (St Dochwy) *see* Cowbridge *Llan*
LLANDOVERY *see* Llandingat w Myddfai *St D*
LLANDOW (Holy Trinity) *see* Colwinston, Llandow and
Llysworney *Llan*
LLANDRE (St Michael) *see* Llanfihangel Genau'r Glyn and
Llangorwen *St D*
LLANDRILLO-YN-EDEIRNION (St Trilio) and Llandderfel
St As 13 V S J ROBERTS
LLANDRILLO-YN-RHOS (St Trillo) (St George) *St As 5*
V D JACKS
LLANDRINDOD (Holy Trinity) (Old Parish Church) w Cefnllys
and Disserth *S & B 5* R J S PENBERTHY NSM A TWEED
LLANDRINIO (St Trinio, St Peter and St Paul) *see* Llandysilio
and Penrhos and Llandrinio etc *St As*
LLANDRYGARN (St Trygarn) *see* Bro Cyngar *Ban*
LLANDUDNO (St Tudno) (Holy Trinity) *Ban 2* R J E NICE
LLANDUDWEN (St Tudwen) *see* Bro Madryn *Ban*
LLANDULAIS IN TIR ABAD (St David) *see* Blaenau Irfon *S & B*
LLANDWROG (St Twrog) *see* Uwch Gwyrfai Beuno Sant *Ban*
LLANDYBIE (St Tybie) *St D 12* V E A HOWELLS
LLANDYFAELOG (St Maelog) *see* Cydweli and Llandyfaelog
St D
LLANDYFAN (Church) *see* Llandybie *St D*
LLANDYFODWG (St Tyfodwg) and Cwm Ogwr *Llan 4*
P-in-c J J JENKINS
LLANDYFRIOG (St Tyfriog) *see* Newcastle Emlyn and
Llandyfriog etc *St D*
LLANDYFRYDOG (St Tyfrydog) *see* Amlwch *Ban*
LLANDYGAI (St Ann) *see* Bro Ogwen *Ban*
LLANDYGAI (St Tegai) *as above*
LLANDYGWYDD (St Tygwydd) *see* Maenordeifi Gp *St D*
LLANDYRNOG (St Tyrnog) (St Cwyfan) and Llangwyfan
St As 2 R *vacant*
LLANDYRY (Church) *see* Pen-bre *St D*
LLANDYSILIO (St Tysilio) *see* Bro Tysilio *Ban*
LLANDYSILIO (St Tysilio) *see* Whitland w Cyffig and Henllan
Amgoed etc *St D*
LLANDYSILIO (St Tysilio) (St Mary) and Penrhos and
Llandrinio w Criggion *St As 8* R *vacant*
LLANDYSILIOGOGO (St Tysilio) *see* Llangrannog w
Llandysiliogogo w Penbryn *St D*
LLANDYSSIL (St Tyssil) *see* Montgomery and Forden and
Llandyssil *St As*
LLANDYSUL (St Tysul) w Bangor Teifi and Llanfairollwyn w
Llangynllo *St D 6* P-in-c G M REID
LLANEDEYRN (All Saints) *see* Cyncoed *Mon*
LLANEDI (St Edith) w Tycroes and Saron *St D 12* V *vacant*
LLANEDWEN (St Edwen) *see* Bro Dwynwen *Ban*
LLANEGRYN (St Mary and St Egryn) *see* Bro Ystumanner *Ban*
LLANEGWAD (St Egwad) w Llanfihangel Uwch Gwili *St D 13*
V R J PATTINSON
LLANEILIAN (St Eilian) *see* Amlwch *Ban*
LLANELEN (St Helen) *see* Govilon w Llanfoist w Llanelen *Mon*
LLANELIAN (St Elian) *see* Colwyn and Llanelian *St As*
LLANELIDAN (St Elidan) *see* Llanfair DC, Derwen, Llanelidan
and Efenechtyd *St As*
LLANELLI (St Elli) *S & B 3* C C J BEVAN

LLANELLI (St Elli) (St Peter) *St D 11*   **NSM** G PAYNE, P C A MANSEL LEWIS

LLANELLTUD (St Illtyd)   *see* Bro Cymer *Ban*

LLANELWEDD (St Matthew)   *see* Colwyn *S & B*

LLANENDDWYN (St Enddwyn)   *see* Bro Ardudwy *Ban*

LLANENGAN (St Engan)   *see* Bro Enlli *Ban*

LLANERCH AERON (St Non) w Ciliau Aeron and Dihewyd and Mydroilyn *St D 7*   **P-in-c** R H E DAVIES

LLANERFYL (St Erfyl)   *see* Garthbeibio, Llanerfel and Llangadfan *St As*

LLANEUGRAD (St Eugrad) w Llanallgo and Penrhosllugwy w Llanfihangel Tre'r Beirdd *Ban 7*   **P-in-c** J K WILSON

LLANFABON (St Mabon)   *see* Treharris, Trelewis, Bedlinog and Llanfabon *Llan*

LLANFACHRAETH (St Machraeth)   *see* Bro Cwyfan *Ban*

LLANFACHRETH (St Machreth)   *see* Bro Cymer *Ban*

LLANFAELOG (St Maelog)   *see* Bro Cwyfan *Ban*

LLANFAELRHYS (St Maelrhys)   *see* Bro Enlli *Ban*

LLANFAES   *see* Brecon St David w Llanspyddid and Llanilltyd *S & B*

LLANFAETHLU (St Maethlu)   *see* Bro Padrig *Ban*

LLANFAIR (St Mary)   *see* Grosmont and Skenfrith and Llangattock etc *Mon*

LLANFAIR (St Mary)   *see* Llandingat w Myddfai *St D*

LLANFAIR CAEREINION (St Mary), Llanllugan and Manafon *St As 7*   **NSM** M E DUNN

LLANFAIR CLYDOGAU (St Mary)   *see* Llanddewi Brefi and Llangeitho *St D*

LLANFAIR DISCOED (St Mary)   *see* Wentwood *Mon*

LLANFAIR DYFFRYN CLWYD (St Cynfarch and St Mary) and Derwen and Llanelidan and Efenechtyd *St As 3*   **P-in-c** R W CARTER

LLANFAIR KILGEDDIN   *see* Raglan Gp *Mon*

LLANFAIR MATHAFARN EITHAF (St Mary)   *see* Bro Tysilio *Ban*

LLANFAIR NANT-GWYN (St Mary)   *see* Maenordeifi Gp *St D*

LLANFAIR NANT-Y-GOF (St Mary)   *see* Letterston w Llanfair Nant-y-Gof etc *St D*

LLANFAIR TALHAEARN (St Mary)   *see* Petryal and Betws yn Rhos *St As*

LLANFAIR-AR-Y-BRYN (St Mary)   *see* Cil-y-Cwm and Ystrad-ffin w Rhandir-mwyn etc *St D*

LLANFAIRFECHAN (Christ Church)   *see* Dwylan *Ban*

LLANFAIR-IS-GAER (St Mary) (Old Parish Church) *Ban 1*   I *vacant*

LLANFAIR-JUXTA-HARLECH (St Mary)   *see* Bro Ardudwy *Ban*

LLANFAIRPWLLGWYNGYLLGOGERYCHWYRNDROBWLL-LLANTISILIOGOGOGOCH (St Mary)   *see* Bro Dwynwen *Ban*

LLANFAIR-YNG-NGHORNWY (St Mary)   *see* Bro Padrig *Ban*

LLANFAIR-YN-NEUBWLL   *see* Bro Cwyfan *Ban*

LLANFAIR-YN-Y-CWMWD (St Mary)   *see* Bro Dwynwen *Ban*

LLANFALLTEG w Castell Dwyran *St D 15*   **V** *vacant*

LLANFAREDD (St Mary)   *see* Colwyn *S & B*

LLANFECHAIN (St Garmon)   *see* Llansantffraid-ym-Mechain and Llanfechain *St As*

LLANFECHAN (St Afan)   *see* Irfon Valley *S & B*

LLANFECHELL (St Mechell)   *see* Bro Padrig *Ban*

LLANFERRES (St Berres)   *see* Cilcain, Gwernaffield, Llanferres etc *St As*

LLANFEUGAN (St Meugan)   *see* The Beacons *S & B*

LLANFFINAN (St Ffinan)   *see* Bro Cadwaladr *Ban*

LLANFFLEWIN (St Fflewin)   *see* Bro Padrig *Ban*

LLANFIHANGEL ABERCYWYN (St Michael)   *see* St Clears w Llangynin and Llanddowror etc *St D*

LLANFIHANGEL ABERGWESSIN   *see* Blaenau Irfon *S & B*

LLANFIHANGEL ABERYTHYCH (St Michael)   *see* Catheiniog *St D*

LLANFIHANGEL BRYNPABUAN (St Michael and All Angels)   *see* Upper Wye *S & B*

LLANFIHANGEL CILFARGEN   *see* Catheiniog *St D*

LLANFIHANGEL CRUCORNEY (St Michael) w Oldcastle and Cwmyoy and Llanthony *Mon 1*   **P-in-c** D J YOUNG   **Hon Par Dn** D A LEE

LLANFIHANGEL FECHAN (St Michael)   *see* Dan yr Eppynt *S & B*

LLANFIHANGEL GENAU'R GLYN (St Michael) and Llangorwen *St D 9*   **P-in-c** P O JONES

LLANFIHANGEL GLYN MYFYR (St Michael)   *see* Cerrigydrudion w Llanfihangel Glyn Myfyr etc *St As*

LLANFIHANGEL GOBION (St Michael)   *see* Raglan Gp *Mon*

LLANFIHANGEL HELYGEN (St Michael)   *see* Upper Wye *S & B*

LLANFIHANGEL LLEDROD (St Michael)   *see* Llanilar w Rhostie and Llangwyryfon etc *St D*

LLANFIHANGEL NANTBRAN (St Michael)   *see* Dan yr Eppynt *S & B*

LLANFIHANGEL NANTMELAN (St Michael)   *see* New Radnor and Llanfihangel Nantmelan etc *S & B*

LLANFIHANGEL PENBEDW   *see* Maenordeifi Gp *St D*

LLANFIHANGEL PONTYMOILE (St Michael)   *see* Panteg and Griffithstown *Mon*

LLANFIHANGEL RHOS-Y-CORN (St Michael)   *see* Brechfa and Llanfihangel Rhos-y-corn *St D*

LLANFIHANGEL RHYDITHON (St Michael)   *see* Lower Ithon Valley *S & B*

LLANFIHANGEL ROGIET   *see* Caldicot *Mon*

LLANFIHANGEL TALYLLYN (St Michael)   *see* Llyn Safaddan *S & B*

LLANFIHANGEL TRE'R BEIRDD (St Mihangel)   *see* Llaneugrad w Llanallgo and Penrhosllugwy etc *Ban*

LLANFIHANGEL YNG NGHWYNFA (St Michael) and Llwydiarth *St As 7*   **V** *vacant*

LLANFIHANGEL YSGEIFIOG (St Michael)   *see* Bro Cadwaladr *Ban*

LLANFIHANGEL YSTRAD (St Michael) and Cilcennin w Trefilan and Nantcwnlle *St D 7*   **P-in-c** M A R HILL

LLANFIHANGEL-AR-ARTH (St Michael) w Capel Dewi *St D 6*   **V** B D TIMOTHY

LLANFIHANGEL-TOR-Y-MYNYDD (St Michael)   *see* Llanishen w Trellech Grange and Llanfihangel etc *Mon*

LLANFIHANGEL-UWCH-GWILI (St Michael)   *see* Llanegwad w Llanfihangel Uwch Gwili *St D*

LLANFIHANGEL-Y-CREUDDYN (St Michael)   *see* Grwp Bro Ystwyth a Mynach *St D*

LLANFIHANGEL-YN-NHYWYN   *see* Bro Cwyfan *Ban*

LLANFIHANGEL-Y-PENNANT (St Michael)   *see* Bro Ystumanner *Ban*

LLANFIHANGEL-YSTERN-LLEWERN (St Michael)   *see* Rockfield and Dingestow Gp *Mon*

LLANFIHANGEL-Y-TRAETHAU (St Michael)   *see* Bro Ardudwy *Ban*

LLANFILO (St Bilo)   *see* Talgarth w Bronllys w Llanfilo *S & B*

LLANFOIST (St Ffwyst)   *see* Govilon w Llanfoist w Llanelen *Mon*

LLANFRECHFA (All Saints)   *see* Caerleon and Llanfrechfa *Mon*

LLANFRYNACH (St Brynach)   *see* Cowbridge *Llan*

LLANFRYNACH (St Brynach)   *see* The Beacons *S & B*

LLANFWROG (St Mwrog and St Mary)   *see* Ruthin w Llanrhydd and Llanfwrog *St As*

LLANFYLLIN (St Myllin), Bwlchycibau and Llanwddyn *St As 7*   **R** H J MORRIS   **NSM** J P SKIPPER

LLANFYNYDD (St Egwad)   *see* Catheiniog *St D*

LLANFYNYDD (St Michael) (All Saints) *St As 11*   **R** *vacant*

LLANFYRNACH (St Brynach)   *see* Crymych Gp *St D*

LLANGADFAN (St Cadfan)   *see* Garthbeibio, Llanerfel and Llangadfan *St As*

LLANGADOG (St Cadog) and Gwynfe w Llanddeusant *St D 13*   **V** K M D COTTAM

LLANGADWALADR (St Cadwaladr)   *see* Bro Cadwaladr *Ban*

LLANGADWALADR (St Cadwaladr)   *see* Llansilin w Llangadwaladr and Llangedwyn *St As*

LLANGAFFO (St Caffo)   *see* Bro Cadwaladr *Ban*

LLANGAIN (St Cain)   *see* Llan-llwch w Llangain and Llangynog *St D*

LLANGAMMARCH (St Cadmarch)   *see* Irfon Valley *S & B*

LLAN-GAN   *see* Whitland w Cyffig and Henllan Amgoed etc *St D*

LLANGAN (St Canna) and St Mary Hill *Llan 7*   **R** *vacant*

LLANGANTEN (St Cannen)   *see* Irfon Valley *S & B*

LLANGAR (St John the Evangelist)   *see* Corwen w Llangar w Glyndyfrdwy etc *St As*

LLANGASTY TALYLLYN (St Gastyn)   *see* Llyn Safaddan *S & B*

LLANGATHEN (St Cathen)   *see* Catheiniog *St D*

LLANGATTOCK (St Cattwg) and Llangyndir *S & B 3*   **R** *vacant*

LLANGATTOCK LINGOED (St Cadoc)   *see* Grosmont and Skenfrith and Llangattock etc *Mon*

LLANGATTOCK-JUXTA-USK (St Cadoc)   *see* Llanddewi Rhydderch w Llangattock-juxta-Usk etc *Mon*

LLANGATTOCK-VIBON-AVEL (St Cadoc)   *see* Rockfield and Dingestow Gp *Mon*

LLANGEDWYN (St Cedwyn)   *see* Llansilin w Llangadwaladr and Llangedwyn *St As*

LLANGEFNI (St Cyngar)   *see* Bro Cyngar *Ban*

LLANGEINOR (St Ceinor) and the Garw Valley *Llan 4*   **P-in-c** R T PITMAN

LLANGEINWEN (St Ceinwen)   *see* Bro Dwynwen *Ban*

LLANGEITHO (St Ceitho)   *see* Llanddewi Brefi and Llangeitho *St D*

LLANGELER (St Celer) w Pen-Boyr *St D 6*   **V** J N GILLIBRAND

LLANGELYNIN (St Celynnin)   *see* Caerhun and Llangelynnin and Llanbedr-y-Cennin *Ban*

LLANGELYNNIN (St Celynin)   *see* Bro Cymer *Ban*

LLANGENNECH (St Gwynog) and Hendy and Llwynhendy *St D 11*   **P-in-c** J K PLESSIS

LLANSANTFFRAID GLYN CEIRIOG (St Ffraid) and Llanarmon Dyffryn Ceiriog and Pontfadog *St As* 10
P-in-c J E T YENDALL

LLANSANTFFRAID, Bettws and Aberkenfig *Llan* 4
P-in-c S C PARE

LLANSANTFFRAID-YM-MECHAIN (St Ffraid) and Llanfechain *St As* 7 **V** *vacant*

LLANSANTFFRAID GLYN DYFRDWY (St Ffraid) *see* Corwen w Llangar w Glyndyfrdwy etc *St As*

LLANSAWEL (St Mary), Briton Ferry *Llan* 6 **V** *vacant*

LLANSAWEL (St Sawyl) *see* Cynwyl Gaeo w Llansawel and Talley etc *St D*

LLANSILIN (St Silin) w Llangadwaladr and Llangedwyn
St As 7 **P-in-c** R M HUGHES

LLANSOY (St Tysoi) *see* Llanishen w Trellech Grange and Llanfihangel etc *Mon*

LLANSPYDDID (St Cattwg) *see* Brecon St David w Llanspyddid and Llanilltyd *S & B*

LLANSTADWEL (St Tudwal) *St D* 4 **P-in-c** A M CHADWICK
NSM J L HANCOCK, S M BESSANT

LLANSTEFFAN (St Ystyffan) and Llan-y-bri and Llandeilo Abercywyn *St D* 10 **V** *vacant*

LLANSTEPHEN (St Steffan) *see* Llandefalle and Llyswen w Boughrood etc *S & B*

LLANTARNAM (St Michael) *see* Cwmbran *Mon*

LLANTHETTY (St Tetti) *see* The Beacons *S & B*

LLANTHONY (St David) *see* Llanfihangel Crucorney w Oldcastle etc *Mon*

LLANTILIO CROSSENNY (St Teilo) and Penrhos w Llanvetherine and Llanvapley *Mon* 1 **P-in-c** C H A PRINCE

LLANTILIO PERTHOLEY (St Teilo) w Bettws Chapel and Llanddewi Skirrid *Mon* 1 **P-in-c** J F GRAY
NSM J L HUGHES

LLANTRISANT (Church) *see* Grwp Bro Ystwyth a Mynach *St D*

LLANTRISANT (St Afran, St Ieuan and St Sanan) *see* Bro Cwyfan *Ban*

LLANTRISANT (St Illtyd, St Gwynno and St Dyfodwg) (St Michael) (St David) *Llan* 10 **V** V L PARKINSON

LLANTRISANT (St Peter, St Paul and St John) *see* Usk Min Area *Mon*

LLANTRITHYD (St Illtyd) *see* Penmark w Llancarfan w Llantrithyd *Llan*

LLANTWIT FARDRE (St Illtyd) *Llan* 10 **V** P M N GULLIDGE
NSM K G SIMPSON

LLANTWIT MAJOR (St Illtud) *Llan* 7 **TR** H BUTLER
TV A M BEER **C** R V SIMPSON

LLANTYSILIO (St Tysilio) *see* Llangollen w Trevor and Llantysilio *St As*

LLANULID (St Ilid) *see* Blaenwysg *S & B*

LLANVACHES (St Dyfrig) *see* Wentwood *Mon*

LLANVAPLEY (St Mable) *see* Llantilio Crossenny w Penrhos, Llanvetherine etc *Mon*

LLANVETHERINE (St James the Elder) *as above*

LLANWDDYN (St Wyddyn) *see* Llanfyllin, Bwlchycibau and Llanwddyn *St As*

LLANWELLWYFO (St Gwenllwyfo) *see* Amlwch *Ban*

LLANWENARTH CITRA (St Peter) *see* Abergavenny St Mary w Llanwenarth Citra *Mon*

LLANWENOG (St Gwenog) *see* Llanybydder and Llanwenog w Llanllwni etc *St D*

LLANWERN (St Mary) *see* Magor *Mon*

LLANWINIO (St Gwynio) *see* Crymych Gp *St D*

LLANWNDA (St Gwyndaf) *see* Uwch Gwyrfai Beuno Sant *Ban*

LLANWNDA (St Gwyndaf) and Goodwick (St Peter) w Manorowen and Llanstinan *St D* 2 **V** *vacant*

LLANWNNEN (St Lucia) *see* Llanybydder and Llanwenog w Llanllwni etc *St D*

LLANWNNOG (St Gwynog) *see* Bro Arwystli *Ban*

LLANWNNWS (St Gwnnws) *see* Llanilar w Rhostie and Llangwyryfon etc *St D*

LLANWRDA (St Cwrdaf) *see* Llansadwrn w Llanwrda and Manordeilo *St D*

LLANWRIN (St Ust and St Dyfrig) *see* Bro Cyfeiliog a Mawddwy *Ban*

LLANWRTHWL (St Gwrthwl) *see* Gwastedyn *S & B*

LLANWRTYD (St David) *see* Blaenau Irfon *S & B*

LLANWRTYD WELLS (St James) *as above*

LLANWYDDELAN (St Gwyddelan) *see* Betws Cedewain and Tregynon and Llanwyddelan *St As*

LLANWYNNO (Christ Church) *see* Pontypridd St Matt and Cilfynydd w Llanwynno *Llan*

LLANWYNNO (St Gwynno) *as above*

LLANYBYDDER (St Peter) and Llanwenog w Llanllwni and Llanwnnen *St D* 8 **P-in-c** S BALE

LLANYCHAEARN (St Llwchaiarn) *see* Aberystwyth *St D*

LLANYCHAN (St Hychan) *see* Llanbedr DC, Llangynhafal, Llanychan etc. *St As*

LLANYCHAR (St David) *see* Fishguard w Llanychar and Pontfaen w Morfil etc *St D*

LLANYCHLWYDOG *as above*

LLANYCRWYS (St David) *see* Pencarreg and Llanycrwys *St D*

LLANYNGHENEDL VALLEY (St Michael) *see* Bro Cwyfan *Ban*

LLANYNYS *see* Buallt *S & B*

LLANYNYS (St Saeran) *see* Llanbedr DC, Llangynhafal, Llanychan etc. *St As*

LLANYRE *see* Upper Wye *S & B*

LLANYRNEWYDD (St Gwynour) *see* Llanrhidian w Llanyrnewydd *S & B*

LLANYSTYMDWY (St John the Baptist) *see* Bro'r Holl Saint *Ban*

LLANYWERN (St Mary the Virgin) *see* Llyn Safaddan *S & B*

LLAWHADEN (St Aidan), w Bletherston and Uzmaston *St D* 1
V P H DAVIES

LLAWRYBETWS (St James) *see* Betws Gwerful Goch w Llangwm w Llawrybetws *St As*

LLAY (St Martin), Rossett and Isycoed *St As* 9 **V** P A WALKER
C S B ERLANDSON

LLECHRYD (St Tydfil) *see* Maenordeifi Gp *St D*

LLECHYLCHED (Holy Trinity) *see* Bro Cwyfan *Ban*

LLISWERRY *see* Newport St Andr *Mon*

LLOWES (St Meilig) *see* Glasbury and Llowes w Clyro and Betws *S & B*

LLWYDCOED (St James) *see* Aberdare St Fagan *Llan*

LLWYDIARTH (St Mary) *see* Llanfihangel yng Nghwynfa and Llwydiarth *St As*

LLWYNDERW (Holy Cross) (Clyne Chapel) *S & B* 6
NSM C A DAVIES

LLWYNGWRIL *see* Bro Cymer *Ban*

LLWYNHENDY (St David) *see* Llangennech and Hendy and Llwynhendy *St D*

LLWYNYPIA *see* Pont Rhondda *Llan*

LLYN SAFADDAN *S & B* 4 **P-in-c** K RICHARDS **C** A N JEVONS

LLYSFAEN (St Cynfran) *see* Llanddulas and Llysfaen *St As*

LLYSWEN (St Gwendoline) *see* Llandefalle and Llyswen w Boughrood etc *S & B*

LLYSWORNEY (St Tydfil) *see* Colwinston, Llandow and Llysworney *Llan*

LLYS-Y-FRAN (St Meilyr) *see* W Preseli Gp *St D*

LLYWEL (St David) *see* Blaenwysg *S & B*

LOUGHOR (St Michael) (St David) *S & B* 9
P-in-c I DREW-JONES

LOVESTON (St Leonard) *see* Jeffreyston w Reynoldston and Loveston etc *St D*

LOWER ISLWYN *Mon* 6 **V** M J JEFFORD **C** M H EVANS
NSM D G BATE, L B GRIFFITHS, M REDWOOD, V I HODGES

LUDCHURCH (St Elidyr) *see* Begelly w Ludchurch and E Williamston *St D*

MACHEN (St John the Baptist) *see* Bedwas w Machen w Michaelston-y-Fedw w Rudry *Mon*

MACHEN (St Michael) *as above*

MACHYNLLETH (St Peter) *see* Bro Cyfeiliog a Mawddwy *Ban*

MAENCLOCHOG (St Mary) *see* W Preseli Gp *St D*

MAENORDEIFI Group, The (St David) *St D* 5 **R** *vacant*

MAENTWROG (St Twrog) *see* Bro Moelwyn *Ban*

MAESGLAS and Duffryn *Mon* 7 **P-in-c** L C HALL

MAESMYNIS AND LLANYNYS (St David) *see* Buallt *S & B*

MAESTEG (St David) *see* Llangynwyd w Maesteg *Llan*

MAESTEG (St Michael) *as above*

MAESTEILO (St John) *see* Llandeilo Fawr and Taliaris *St D*

MAESTIR (St Mary) *see* Lampeter w Maestir and Silian and Llangybi and Betws Bledrws *St D*

MAGOR (St Mary) *Mon* 3 **TR** J D HARRIS **TV** C L JONES
NSM A R DAVIES, A S LITTLER, L BATT

MAINDEE NEWPORT (St John the Evangelist) (St Mary) *Mon* 7
V D NEALE **NSM** C H HOCKEY, J K BEARDMORE

MALLYWD (St Tydecho) *see* Bro Cyfeiliog a Mawddwy *Ban*

MALPAS (St Mary) *Mon* 7 **V** D G PARFITT **NSM** J A SIMS

MAMHILAD (St Illtud) w Monkswood and Glascoed Chapel *Mon* 4 **R** J A COLLIER

MANAFON (St Michael) *see* Llanfair Caereinion, Llanllugan and Manafon *St As*

MANORBIER (St James) and St Florence *St D* 3
P-in-c A GRACE

MANORDEILO (St Paul) *see* Llansadwrn w Llanwrda and Manordeilo *St D*

MANOROWEN (St Mary) *see* Llanwnda, Goodwick w Manorowen and Llanstinan *St D*

MANSELTON (St Michael and All Angels) and Cwmbwrla *S & B* 10 **V** J B DAVIES

MARCHWIEL (St Marcella) *see* Bangor Monachorum, Worthenbury and Marchwiel *St As*

MARCROSS (Holy Trinity) *see* Llantwit Major *Llan*

MARGAM (St Mary) (St David) *Llan 5*   **V** *vacant*
MARLOES (St Peter)   *see* Dale and St Brides w Marloes and Hasguard w St Ishmael's *St D*
MARROS (St Lawrence)   *see* St Issell's and Amroth w Crunwere and Marros *St D*
MARSHFIELD (St Mary) w St Bride's Wentloog *Mon 5*
P-in-c D E COLLINGBOURNE, S L COLLINGBOURNE
MATHERN (St Tewdric) *Mon 3*   **V** J E L WHITE
MATHRY (Holy Martyrs)   *see* Llanrhian and Mathry w Grandstone etc *St D*
MATTHEWSTOWN (All Saints)   *see* Penrhiwceiber, Matthewstown and Ynysboeth *Llan*
MAUDLAM (St Mary Magdalene)   *see* Pyle w Kenfig *Llan*
MEIDRIM (St David) and Llanboidy and Merthyr *St D 10*
V J GAINER
MEIFOD (St Tysilio and St Mary) w Llangynyw w Pont Robert w Pont Dolanog *St As 7*   **P-in-c** J E JAMES
MELIDEN (St Melyd) (St Mary Magdalene) and Gwaenysgor
St As 1   **V** J C HARVEY
MENAI BRIDGE (St Mary)   *see* Bro Tysilio *Ban*
MERTHYR (St Martin)   *see* Meidrim and Llanboidy and Merthyr *St D*
MERTHYR CYNOG (St Cynog)   *see* Dan yr Eppynt *S & B*
MERTHYR DYFAN (St Dyfan and St Teilo) *Llan 3*
R R C PARRISH
MERTHYR MAWR (St Teilo)   *see* Laleston and Merthyr Mawr w Penyfai *Llan*
MERTHYR TYDFIL (Christ Church) (St Luke) *Llan 9*
P-in-c M PERRY
MERTHYR TYDFIL (St David) (St Tydfil's Well) and Abercanaid *Llan 9*   **P-in-c** M N PREVETT   **T H R** ST J BATES
MERTHYR VALE (St Mary and Holy Innocents)   *see* Troedyrhiw w Merthyr Vale *Llan*
MICHAELSTON-LE-PIT (St Michael and All Angels)
see St Andrews Major w Michaelston-le-Pit *Llan*
MICHAELSTON-SUPER-AVON   *see* Cwmafan *Llan*
MICHAELSTON-Y-FEDW (St Michael)   *see* Bedwas w Machen w Michaelston-y-Fedw w Rudry *Mon*
MICHEL TROY (St Michael)   *see* Monmouth w Overmonnow etc *Mon*
MILFORD HAVEN (St Katherine) (St Peter) *St D 4*
V H A M WILLIAMS
MINERA (St Mary) (St Tudfil) w Coedpoeth *St As 9*
V J P HARRIS
MINWEAR (St Womar)   *see* Jeffreyston w Reynoldston and Loveston etc *St D*
MOCHDRE (All Saints)   *see* Kerry, Llanmerewig, Dolfor and Mochdre *St As*
MOLD (St Mary) *St As 12*   **V** *vacant*
MONINGTON (St Nicholas)   *see* St Dogmael's and Monington and Nevern etc *St D*
MONKNASH (St Mary)   *see* Llantwit Major *Llan*
MONKSWOOD (St Matthew)   *see* Mamhilad w Monkswood and Glascoed Chapel *Mon*
MONKTON (St Nicholas and St John) *St D 3*   **TR** W P NASH
TV G P HOWELL, R JONES
MONMOUTH (St Mary the Virgin) w Overmonnow w Wonastow w Michel Troy *Mon 2*   **V** D J MCGLADDERY
C C M HAYNES   **NSM** J M BONE
MONTGOMERY (St Nicholas) and Forden and Llandyssil
St As 8   **R** T E BENNETT
MORFIL   *see* Fishguard w Llanychar and Pontfaen w Morfil etc *St D*
MORRISTON (St David) *S & B 7*   **V** H M LERVY
MOSTYN (Christ Church) *St As 4*   **V** *vacant*
MOUNTAIN ASH (St Margaret) and Miskin *Llan 8*
V M K JONES
MOUNTON   *see* Narberth w Mounton w Robeston Wathen etc *St D*
MOUNTON (St Andoenus)   *see* Mathern *Mon*
MWNT (Holy Cross)   *see* Cardigan w Mwnt and Y Ferwig w Llangoedmor *St D*
MYDDFAI (St Michael)   *see* Llandingat w Myddfai *St D*
MYDROILYN (Holy Trinity)   *see* Llanerch Aeron w Ciliau Aeron and Dihewyd etc *St D*
MYNACHLOGDDU (St Dogmael)   *see* Crymych Gp *St D*
MYNYDD ISA   *see* Bistre *St As*
MYNYDDISLWYN (St Tudor) *Mon 6*   **P-in-c** M OWEN
C V J BUTLER
NANNERCH (St Michael)   *see* Cilcain, Gwernaffield, Llanferres etc *St As*
NANTGLYN (St James)   *see* Llanrhaeadr-yng-Nghinmeirch and Prion w Nantglyn *St As*
NANTMEL (St Cynllo)   *see* Gwastedyn *S & B*
NANTYGLO (Holy Trinity and St Anne)   *see* Upper Ebbw Valleys *Mon*

NARBERTH (St Andrew) w Mounton w Robeston Wathen and Crinow and Minwear w Templeton *St D 3*   **R** *vacant*
NASH (St Mary)   *see* Magor *Mon*
NASH (St Mary)   *see* Carew and Cosheston and Nash and Redberth *St D*
NEATH (St Thomas) (St David) (St Catherine) (St Peter and St Paul) *Llan 6*   **TR** S J RYAN   **TV** L E NEWMAN
C E M REES, W C TAYLER
NEBO (Dewi Sant)   *see* Llansantffraed w Llanrhystud and Llanddeiniol *St D*
NEFYN (St David)   *see* Bro Madryn *Ban*
NELSON (St John the Baptist)   *see* Treharris, Trelewis, Bedlinog and Llanfabon *Llan*
NERCWYS (St Mary)   *see* Treuddyn w Nercwys *St As*
NEVERN (St Brynach)   *see* St Dogmael's and Monington and Nevern etc *St D*
NEW HEDGES (St Anne)   *see* Tenby *St D*
NEW MOAT (St Nicholas)   *see* W Preseli Gp *St D*
NEW RADNOR (St Mary) and Llanfihangel Nantmelan and Evancoyd w Gladwestry and Colva *S & B 5*   **R** M T BEATON
NEW TREDEGAR (St Dingat)   *see* Bedwellty and New Tredegar *Mon*
NEWBOROUGH (St Peter)   *see* Bro Dwynwen *Ban*
NEWBRIDGE (St Paul)   *see* Lower Islwyn *Mon*
NEWBRIDGE (St Peter)   *as above*
NEWBRIDGE-ON-WYE (All Saints)   *see* Upper Wye *S & B*
NEWCASTLE (St Illtud) *Llan 4*   **V** D E C LLOYD
NEWCASTLE EMLYN (Holy Trinity) and Llandyfriog and Troedyraur and Cenarth and Henllan *St D 6*
V D J L ROBERTS   **C** V R SAYER
NEWCHURCH (St Mary)   *see* Erwood Gp w Painscastle Gp *S & B*
NEWCHURCH (St Mary)   *see* Cynwyl Elfed w Newchurch and Trelech a'r Betws *St D*
NEWCHURCH (St Michael)   *as above*
NEWCHURCH (St Peter)   *see* Wentwood *Mon*
NEWCHURCH (St Peter)   *see* Cynwyl Elfed w Newchurch and Trelech a'r Betws *St D*
NEWMARKET   *see* Dyserth and Trelawnyd and Cwm *St As*
NEWPORT (All Saints) *Mon 7*   **P-in-c** C WATKINS
NEWPORT (Cathedral of St Woolos) (St Martin) (St Mark)
Mon 7   **V** L TONGE
NEWPORT (St Andrew) (St Philip) *Mon 7*
P-in-c H C P M HALL
NEWPORT (St John Baptist) *Mon 7*   **V** *vacant*
NEWPORT (St John the Evangelist)   *see* Maindee Newport *Mon*
NEWPORT (St Mark)   *see* Newport St Woolos w St Mark *Mon*
NEWPORT (St Mary)   *see* Maindee Newport *Mon*
NEWPORT (St Mary) w Cilgwyn and Dinas w Llanllawer and Moylgrove and Meline *St D 5*   **V** N A LLEWELLYN
NEWPORT (St Stephen) and Holy Trinity *Mon 7*
V E L MATHIAS-JONES
NEWPORT (St Teilo) *Mon 7*   **P-in-c** T H J PALMER
NEWPORT Christ Church *Mon 7*   **P-in-c** M R JARMAN
NEWPORT St Julian (St Julius and St Aaron) *Mon 7*
P-in-c D C MATTHEWS
NEWPORT St Paul *Mon 7*   **P-in-c** J S J GROVES   **C** J A HENLEY
NEWQUAY (St Llwchaiarn)   *see* Llanllwchaearn and Llanina *St D*
NEWTON (St Peter) *S & B 6*   **V** G E BENNETT
NEWTON NOTTAGE (St John the Baptist) (All Saints) (St David) *Llan 5*   **R** P R MASSON   **NSM** C VAUGHAN
NEYLAND (St Clement)   *see* Llanstadwel *St D*
NICHOLASTON (St Nicholas)   *see* Three Cliffs *S & B*
NOLTON (St Madog) w Roch and St Lawrence w Ford and Hayscastle *St D 4*   **R** M H ROWLANDS
NOLTON (St Mary)   *see* Coity, Nolton and Brackla w Coychurch *Llan*
NORTHOP (St Eurgain and St Peter) (St Mary) *St As 12*
V R J HAINSWORTH
NORTON (Mission Church)   *see* Oystermouth *S & B*
NORTON (St Andrew)   *see* E Radnor *S & B*
NOTTAGE (St David)   *see* Newton Nottage *Llan*
OGMORE VALE (St David)   *see* Llandyfodwg and Cwm Ogwr *Llan*
OVERMONNOW (St Thomas)   *see* Monmouth w Overmonnow etc *Mon*
OVERTON (St Mary the Virgin) and Erbistock *St As 10*
P-in-c D F CHILD
OXWICH (St Illtyd)   *see* SW Gower *S & B*
OYSTERMOUTH (All Saints) *S & B 6*   **V** K EVANS
PAINSCASTLE (St Peter)   *see* Erwood Gp w Painscastle Gp *S & B*
PANTEG (St Mary) and Griffithstown *Mon 8*
R P A GOLLEDGE   **NSM** N J TAYLOR
PANTYFFRID (Mission Church)   *see* Berriew *St As*
PATRICIO (St Issui the Martyr)   *see* Vale of Gwrynne *S & B*

PEMBROKE (St Mary)   *see* Monkton *St D*
PEMBROKE DOCK (St John) (St Patrick) (St Teilo) *St D 3*
 P-in-c N R SKIPWORTH   **C** C A MANSELL   **NSM** M A EVANS
PEN RHONDDA FAWR *Llan 11*   **P-in-c** P A LEYSHON
PENALLT (Old Church)   *see* Trellech and Penallt *Mon*
PENALLY (St Nicholas)   *see* Tenby *St D*
PENARTH (All Saints) (St Peter) *Llan 3*   **V** P A COX
 C S BIRDSALL
PENARTH (St Augustine) (Holy Nativity) and Llandough
 Llan 3   **NSM** R M GRIFFITHS
PEN-BOYR (St Llawddog)   *see* Llangeler w Pen-Boyr *St D*
PEN-BRE (St Illtud) *St D 11*   **V** D G DAVIES
PENBRYN (St Michael)   *see* Llangrannog w Llandysiliogogo w
 Penbryn *St D*
PENCADER (St Mary)   *see* Llanfihangel-ar-arth w Capel Dewi
 St D
PENCARREG (St Patrick) and Llanycrwys *St D 8*
 V W A STRANGE
PENCLAWDD   *see* Llanrhidian w Llanyrnewydd *S & B*
PENCOED (St David)   *see* Llanilid w Pencoed *Llan*
PENCOED (St Paul) *as above*
PENDERYN MELLTE (St Cynog) *S & B 1*   **R** vacant
PENDINE (St Margaret)   *see* Laugharne and Llansadwrnen and
 Pendine and Llanmiloe *St D*
PENDOYLAN (St Cadoc) w Welsh St Donats *Llan 7*
 P-in-c M J WILLIAMS
PENEGOES (St Cadfarch)   *see* Bro Cyfeiliog a Mawddwy *Ban*
PENHOW (St John the Baptist)   *see* Wentwood *Mon*
PENISARWAEN (St Helen)   *see* Bro Eryri *Ban*
PENLEY (St Mary Magdalene)   *see* Hanmer, Bronington,
 Bettisfield and Penley *St As*
PENLLECH   *see* Bro Madryn *Ban*
PENLLERGAER (St David) *S & B 9*   **V** F A BAYES
PENLLWYN (St Mary the Virgin)   *see* Mynyddislwyn *Mon*
PENLLYN (Chapel of Ease)   *see* Cowbridge *Llan*
PENMACHNO (St Tudclud)   *see* Betws-y-Coed and Capel Curig
 w Penmachno etc *Ban*
PENMAEN (St David)   *see* Mynyddislwyn *Mon*
PENMAEN (St John the Baptist)   *see* Three Cliffs *S & B*
PENMAENMAWR   *see* Dwylan *Ban*
PENMARK (St Mary) w Llancarfan w Llantrithyd *Llan 3*
 P-in-c D G BELCHER
PENNANT (St Thomas)   *see* Llanrhaeadr ym Mochnant etc
 St As
PENNANT MELANGELL (St Melangel) *as above*
PENNARD (St Mary)   *see* Three Cliffs *S & B*
PENPONT (no dedication)   *see* Dan yr Eppynt *S & B*
PENRHIWCEIBER (St Winifred), Matthewstown and
 Ynysboeth *Llan 8*   **V** A K HOLMES
PENRHOS (Holy Trinity)   *see* Llandysilio and Penrhos and
 Llandrinio etc *St As*
PENRHOS (St Cadoc)   *see* Llantilio Crossenny w Penrhos,
 Llanvetherine etc *Mon*
PENRHOSLLUGWY (St Michael)   *see* Llaneugrad w Llanallgo
 and Penrhosllugwy etc *Ban*
PENRHYDD   *see* Maenordeifi Gp *St D*
PENRHYNCOCH (St John)   *see* Llanbadarn Fawr and Elerch and
 Penrhyncoch etc *St D*
PENRHYNDEUDRAETH (Holy Trinity)   *see* Bro Moelwyn *Ban*
PENRHYNSIDE BAY (St David)   *see* Rhos-Cystennin *St As*
PENRHYS (no dedication)   *see* Rhondda Fach Uchaf *Llan*
PENRICE (St Andrew)   *see* SW Gower *S & B*
PENSARN (St David)   *see* Abergele and St George *St As*
PENSTROWED (St Gwrhai)   *see* Bro Arwystli *Ban*
PENTERRY (St Mary)   *see* Itton and St Arvans w Penterry and
 Kilgwrrwg w Devauden *Mon*
PENTIR (St Cedol)   *see* Bro Ogwen *Ban*
PENTRAETH (St Mary)   *see* Bro Tysilio *Ban*
PENTRE (St Peter)   *see* Ystradyfodwg *Llan*
PENTRECHWYTH (St Peter)   *see* Glantawe *S & B*
PENTWYN (St David)   *see* Cyncoed *Mon*
PENTYRCH (St Cadwg) w Capel Llanillterne *Llan 2*
 V S M JOHN
PENYBONTFAWR   *see* Llanrhaeadr ym Mochnant etc *St As*
PENYCAE (St Thomas)   *see* Rhosllanerchrugog and Penycae
 St As
PENYCLAWDD (St Martin)   *see* Rockfield and Dingestow Gp
 Mon
PENYFAI (All Saints)   *see* Laleston and Merthyr Mawr w Penyfai
 Llan
PENYFFORDD (Emmanuel)   *see* Hope *St As*
PENYGRAIG (St Barnabas)   *see* Dinas w Penygraig *Llan*
PENYWAUN (St Winifred)   *see* Hirwaun *Llan*
PETERSTON-SUPER-ELY (St Peter) w St Brides-super-Ely *Llan 7*
 R M J DAVIES

PETERSTON-SUPER-MONTEM (St Peter)   *see* Llanharan w
 Peterston-super-Montem *Llan*
PETRYAL and Betws yn Rhos *St As 5*   **R** S J ROGERS
 C L G BADGER-WATTS
PILLETH (Our Lady of Pilleth)   *see* E Radnor *S & B*
PISTYLL (St Beuno)   *see* Bro Madryn *Ban*
PONT AMAN (St Thomas)   *see* Betws w Ammanford *St D*
PONT DOLANOG (St John the Evangelist)   *see* Meifod w
 Llangynyw w Pont Robert w Pont Dolanog *St As*
PONT RHONDDA *Llan 11*   **V** P S GALE
PONT ROBERT (St John the Evangelist)   *see* Meifod w
 Llangynyw w Pont Robert w Pont Dolanog *St As*
PONTARDAWE (St Peter)   *see* Llangiwg *S & B*
PONTARDDULAIS   *see* Llandeilo Tal-y-bont *S & B*
PONTARFYNACH   *see* Grwp Bro Ystwyth a Mynach *St D*
PONTARGOTHI (Holy Trinity)   *see* Llanegwad w Llanfihangel
 Uwch Gwili *St D*
PONTBLYDDYN (Christ Church) *St As 12*   **V** vacant
PONTERWYD   *see* Grwp Bro Ystwyth a Mynach *St D*
PONTFADOG (St John)   *see* Llansantffraid Glyn Ceirog and
 Llanarmon etc *St As*
PONTFAEN (St Brynach)   *see* Fishguard w Llanychar and
 Pontfaen w Morfil etc *St D*
PONT-IETS (St Mary)   *see* Gwendraeth Fawr *St D*
PONTLLANFRAITH (St Augustine)   *see* Mynyddislwyn *Mon*
PONTLLIW (St Anne)   *see* Penllergaer *S & B*
PONTLOTTYN (St Tyfaelog) (St Aidan) w Fochriw *Llan 9*
 P-in-c R A D LINDSAY
PONTNEATHVAUGHAN (St John)   *see* Penderyn Mellte
 S & B
PONTNEWYDD (Holy Trinity) *Mon 8*   **P-in-c** V L ASHLEY
 NSM S M HOBBS   **OLM** D L THOMAS
 Par Dn H D THOMAS
PONTPRENNAU (no dedication)   *see* Cyncoed *Mon*
PONTRHYDFENDIGAID (St David)   *see* Tregaron Gp *St D*
PONTROBIN (St John) *St As 11*   **C** B P JONES
PONTSIAN (St John)   *see* Llandysul w Bangor Teifi and
 Llanfairollwyn etc *St D*
PONTYATES (St Mary)   *see* Gwendraeth Fawr *St D*
PONTYBEREM (St John) *as above*
PONTYCLUN (St Paul) w Talygarn *Llan 7*   **P-in-c** S M REES
PONTYCYMMER (St David)   *see* Llangeinor and the Garw
 Valley *Llan*
PONTYMISTER (St Margaret)   *see* Lower Islwyn *Mon*
PONTYPOOL (St Matthew) *Mon 8*   **R** B R PIPPEN
 TV M C WARREN
PONTYPRIDD (St Catherine) *Llan 10*   **V** P A LEWIS
PONTYPRIDD St Matthew and Cilfynydd w Llanwynno
 Llan 10   **V** vacant
POOL QUAY (St John the Evangelist)   *see* Guilsfield w
 Buttington and Pool Quay *St As*
PORT EYNON (St Cattwg)   *see* SW Gower *S & B*
PORT TALBOT (St Agnes)   *see* Aberavon *Llan*
PORT TALBOT (St David)   *see* Margam *Llan*
PORT TALBOT (St Theodore) (St Peter) *Llan 5*
 V M WILLIAMS
PORTH NEWYDD *Llan 11*   **P-in-c** J M THOMAS
PORTHCAWL (All Saints)   *see* Newton Nottage *Llan*
PORTHKERRY (St Curig) and Rhoose *Llan 3*
 P-in-c M A PRINCE
PORTHMADOG (St John)   *see* Bro'r Holl Saint *Ban*
PORTMADOC (St Cyngar) *as above*
PORTSKEWETT (St Mary)   *see* Caldicot *Mon*
PRENDERGAST (St David) w Rudbaxton *St D 1*
 R G D GWYTHER
PRESELI, WEST *St D 1*   **V** R J DAVIES
PRESTATYN (Christ Church) (Church of Holy Spirit) *St As 1*
 V D N ASH
PRINCES GATE (St Catherine)   *see* Lampeter Velfrey and
 Llanddewi Velfrey etc *St D*
PUNCHESTON (St Mary)   *see* Letterston w Llanfair Nant-y-Gof
 etc *St D*
PUNCHSTON   *see* Fishguard w Llanychar and Pontfaen w
 Morfil etc *St D*
PWLL (Holy Trinity)   *see* Burry Port and Pwll *St D*
PWLLCROCHAN   *see* Monkton *St D*
PWLLGWAUN and Llanddewi Rhondda *Llan 10*   **V** vacant
PWLLHELI   *see* Bro'r Holl Saint *Ban*
PYLE (St James) (St Mary Magdalene) w Kenfig *Llan 5*
 V D A WALKER
QUAR, THE (St Tydfil's Well)   *see* Merthyr Tydfil St Dav and
 Abercanaid *Llan*
QUEENSFERRY (St Andrew)   *see* Shotton *St As*
RADNOR (St Mary)   *see* New Radnor and Llanfihangel
 Nantmelan etc *S & B*

RADNOR, EAST *S & B 5*   **V** M L COPE
RADYR (St John the Baptist) (Christ Church) *Llan 2*
   R J WIGLEY
RAGLAN GROUP (St Cadoc) *Mon 4*   **R** T G CLEMENT
REDBERTH (Church)   *see* Carew and Cosheston and Nash and
   Redberth *St D*
REDWICK (St Thomas)   *see* Magor *Mon*
RESOLVEN (St David)   *see* Vale of Neath *Llan*
REYNOLDSTON (St George)   *see* SW Gower *S & B*
REYNOLDSTON (St James)   *see* Jeffreyston w Reynoldston and
   Loveston etc *St D*
RHANDIRMWYN (St Barnabas)   *see* Cil-y-Cwm and Ystrad-ffin
   w Rhandir-mwyn etc *St D*
RHAYADER (St Clement)   *see* Gwastedyn *S & B*
RHESYCAE (Christ Church)   *see* Halkyn w Caerfallwch w
   Rhesycae *St As*
RHEWL (Church)   *see* Llanbedr DC, Llangynhafal, Llanychan
   etc. *St As*
RHIWLAS (Mission Church)   *see* Llansilin w Llangadwaladr and
   Llangedwyn *St As*
RHONDDA FACH UCHAF *Llan 11*   **P-in-c** D M JONES
RHOOSE (St Peter)   *see* Porthkerry and Rhoose *Llan*
RHOS (St James)   *see* Llangeler w Pen-Boyr *St D*
RHOSBEIRIO   *see* Bro Padrig *Ban*
RHOSCOLYN   *see* Bro Cybi *Ban*
RHOS-CYSTENNIN *St As 5*   **TR** N W CARTER
   TV G CHIGUMIRA, P R WALKER
RHOSDDU   *see* Wrexham *St As*
RHOSESEMOR   *see* Halkyn w Caerfallwch w Rhesycae *St As*
RHOSILI (St Mary the Virgin)   *see* SW Gower *S & B*
RHOSLLANNERCHRUGOG (St David) (St Mary) and Penycae
   St As 10   **V** J A CARTER   **NSM** P J CAREY
RHOSTIE   *see* Llanilar w Rhostie and Llangwyryfon etc *St D*
RHOSYMEDRE (St John the Evangelist)   *see* Ruabon and
   Rhosymedre *St As*
RHUDDLAN (St Mary) and Bodelwyddan *St As 1*   **V** C I DAY
RHULEN (St David)   *see* Colwyn *S & B*
RHYDYBRIW (Capel Rhydybriw)   *see* Blaenwysg *S & B*
RHYDYFELIN (St Luke)   *see* Glyntaff, Rhydfelin and the Graig
   Llan
RHYD-Y-MWYN (St John the Evangelist)   *see* Cilcain,
   Gwernaffield, Llanferres etc *St As*
RHYL (Holy Trinity) (St Thomas) (St John) (St Ann) *St As 1*
   V A S GRIMWOOD   **C** G R MANSFIELD, S F WALKER
RHYMNEY (St David) *Mon 6*   **P-in-c** R A D LINDSAY
RISCA (St Mary)   *see* Lower Islwyn *Mon*
ROATH (St German)   *see* Cardiff St German w St Sav *Llan*
ROATH (St Margaret) (St Anne) (St Edward) *Llan 1*   **V** S LISK
   NSM J R JENKINS
ROATH (St Martin) *Llan 1*   **V** I D HAMER   **NSM** T G WATKIN
ROATH (St Saviour)   *see* Cardiff St German w St Sav *Llan*
ROATH PARK (Christ Church)   *see* Cardiff Ch Ch Roath Park
   Llan
ROBESTON WATHEN (Church)   *see* Narberth w Mounton w
   Robeston Wathen etc *St D*
ROBESTON WEST (St Andrew)   *see* Walwyn's Castle and
   Robeston W *St D*
ROCH (St Mary)   *see* Nolton w Roch and St Lawrence w Ford
   etc *St D*
**ROCKFIELD (St Cenedlon) w St Maughans w Llangattock-
   vibon-Avel w Llanfihangel-ystern-Llewern w Dingestow w
   Llangovan and Penyclawdd w Tregaer w Cwmcarvan** *Mon 2*
   V S L GUEST
ROGERSTONE (St John the Baptist)   *see* Bassaleg *Mon*
ROGIET (St Mary)   *see* Caldicot *Mon*
ROSEMARKET (St Ishmael)   *see* Burton and Rosemarket *St D*
ROSSETT (Christ Church)   *see* LLay, Rossett and Isycoed
   St As
RUABON (St Mary) (All Saints) and Rhosymedre *St As 10*
   V K J TILTMAN   **NSM** P M OWENS
RUDBAXTON (St Michael)   *see* Prendergast w Rudbaxton
   St D
RUDRY (St James)   *see* Bedwas w Machen w Michaelston-y-
   Fedw w Rudry *Mon*
RUMNEY (St Augustine) *Mon 5*   **V** J R CONNELL
RUTHIN (St Peter) w Llanrhydd and Llanfwrog *St As 3*
   R J S EVANS
**ST ANDREWS MAJOR (St Andrew) (St Peter) w Michaelston-
   le-Pit** *Llan 3*   **P-in-c** A P JAMES   **C** J R ORMROD
ST ASAPH (Cathedral of St Asaph and St Cyndeyrn) *St As 1*
   TR N H WILLIAMS
ST ATHAN (St Tathan)   *see* Llantwit Major *Llan*
ST BRIDES (St Bridget)   *see* Dale and St Brides w Marloes and
   Hasguard w St Ishmael's *St D*
ST BRIDES MAJOR (St Bridget)   *see* Ewenny w St Brides Major
   Llan

ST BRIDES MINOR (St Bride)   *see* Llansantffraid, Bettws and
   Aberkenfig *Llan*
ST BRIDES NETHERWENT (St Bridget)   *see* Wentwood *Mon*
ST BRIDE'S WENTLOOG   *see* Marshfield w St Bride's Wentloog
   Mon
ST BRIDES-SUPER-ELY (St Bride)   *see* Peterston-super-Ely w
   St Brides-super-Ely *Llan*
**ST CLEARS (St Mary Magdalene) w Llangynin and
   Llanddowror and Llanfihangel Abercywyn** *St D 10*
   V *vacant*
ST DAVIDS (Cathedral of St David and St Andrew)
   see Dewisland *St D*
**ST DOGMAEL'S (St Thomas) and Monington and Nevern and
   Y Beifil West** *St D 5*   **V** *vacant*
ST DOGWELLS (St Dogfael)   *see* Spittal w Trefgarn and
   Ambleston w St Dogwells *St D*
ST DONATS (St Donat)   *see* Llantwit Major *Llan*
ST EDREN'S   *see* Llanrhian and Mathry w Grandstone etc *St D*
ST ELVIS   *see* Dewisland *St D*
ST FAGANS (St Mary) and Michaelston-super-Ely *Llan 2*
   P-in-c F A JACKSON
ST FLORENCE (St Florentius)   *see* Manorbier and St Florence
   St D
ST GEORGE (St George)   *see* Abergele and St George *St As*
ST GEORGE-SUPER-ELY (St George)   *see* St Nicholas w
   Bonvilston and St George-super-Ely *Llan*
ST HARMON (St Garmon)   *see* Gwastedyn *S & B*
ST HILARY (St Hilary)   *see* Cowbridge *Llan*
ST ISHMAEL'S (St Ishmael)   *see* Dale and St Brides w Marloes
   and Hasguard w St Ishmael's *St D*
ST ISHMAEL'S (St Ishmael) w Llan-saint and Ferryside *St D 11*
   P-in-c S H WIGHT   **NSM** D H JENKINS
ST ISSELL'S (St Issell) and Amroth w Crunwere and Marros
   St D 3   **P-in-c** M L OSBORNE
ST LAWRENCE (St Lawrence)   *see* Nolton w Roch and
   St Lawrence w Ford etc *St D*
ST LYTHANS (St Bleiddian)   *see* Wenvoe and St Lythans *Llan*
ST MARY CHURCH (St Mary)   *see* Cowbridge *Llan*
ST MARY HILL (St Mary)   *see* Llangan and St Mary Hill *Llan*
ST MAUGHEN'S (St Meugan)   *see* Rockfield and Dingestow Gp
   Mon
ST MELLONS (St Mellon) (Resurrection) *Mon 5*   **V** D KELLEN
ST NICHOLAS (St Nicholas)   *see* Llanrhian and Mathry w
   Grandstone etc *St D*
**ST NICHOLAS (St Nicholas) w Bonvilston and St George-
   super-Ely** *Llan 7*   **P-in-c** M J DAVIES
ST PETROX (St Pedrog)   *see* Monkton *St D*
ST PIERRE (St Peter)   *see* Mathern *Mon*
ST THOMAS   *see* Haverfordwest *St D*
ST TWYNNELLS (St Gwynog)   *see* Monkton *St D*
SANDFIELDS   *see* Aberavon *Llan*
SANDYCROFT (Holy Spirit)   *see* Hawarden *St As*
SANDYCROFT (St Francis) *as above*
SARON (St David)   *see* Llanedi w Tycroes and Saron *St D*
SAUNDERSFOOT   *see* St Issell's and Amroth w Crunwere and
   Marros *St D*
SEALAND (St Barth)   *see* Hawarden *St As*
SEBASTOPOL (St Oswald)   *see* Panteg and Griffithstown *Mon*
SENGHENYDD (St Peter)   *see* Eglwysilan and Caerphilly *Llan*
SEVEN SISTERS (St David)   *see* Dulais Valley *Llan*
SEVEN SISTERS (St Mary) *as above*
SHIRENEWTON (St Thomas à Becket)   *see* Mathern *Mon*
SHOTTON (St Ethelwold) *St As 11*   **V** S D GREEN
SILIAN (St Sulien)   *see* Lampeter w Maestir and Silian and
   Llangybi and Betws Bledrws *St D*
SINAN (All Saints)   *see* Trefnant w Tremeirchion w Cefn *St As*
SIX BELLS (St John)   *see* Abertillery w Cwmtillery w Llanhilleth
   etc *Mon*
SKENFRITH (St Bride)   *see* Grosmont and Skenfrith and
   Llangattock etc *Mon*
SKETTY (St Paul) (Holy Trinity) *S & B 6*   **C** A JONES
SKEWEN (St John) (St Mary) *Llan 6*   **P-in-c** C W COLES
SOLVA (St Aidan)   *see* Dewisland *St D*
SOUTHERNDOWN (All Saints)   *see* Ewenny w St Brides Major
   Llan
SOUTHSEA (All Saints)   *see* Broughton w Berse and Southsea
   St As
SPITTAL (St Mary) w Trefgarn and Ambleston w St Dogwells
   St D 1   **V** D R REES
STACKPOLE ELIDOR (St James and St Elidyr) *as above*
STEYNTON (St Cewydd and St Peter) *St D 4*
   NSM D G DAVIES
STRATA FLORIDA (St Mary)   *see* Tregaron Gp *St D*
SULLY (St John the Baptist) *Llan 3*   **P-in-c** J R ORMROD
SWANSEA (St Barnabas) *S & B 11*   **V** *vacant*
SWANSEA (St Gabriel) *S & B 11*   **V** D M GRIFFITHS

SWANSEA (St James) *S & B 11*   **V** H M WILLIAMS
SWANSEA (St Luke)   *see* Manselton and Cwmbwrla *S & B*
SWANSEA (St Peter) *S & B 10*   **V** A F PYE
SWANSEA (St Thomas) (St Stephen) and Kilvey *S & B 11*
  P-in-c S L BUNTING
SWANSEA St Jude (St Nicholas-on-the-Hill) *S & B 11*
  V vacant
SWANSEA, CENTRAL (St Mary) (Holy Trinity) (Christ Church)
  (St John) *S & B 11*   **TR** S M GRIFFITHS   **TV** S M KNIGHT
  NSM J T ANTHONY
TAI'RGWAITH (St David)   *see* Cwmaman *St D*
TALACHDDU (St Mary)   *see* Llandefalle and Llyswen w
  Boughrood etc *S & B*
TALBENNY (St Mary)   *see* Walton W w Talbenny and
  Haroldston W *St D*
TALGARREG (St David)   *see* Llanarth and Capel Cynon w
  Talgarreg etc *St D*
TALGARTH (St Gwendoline) w Bronllys w Llanfilo *S & B 4*
  V R T EDWARDS   **NSM** L R EVANS
TALIARIS (Holy Trinity)   *see* Llandeilo Fawr and Taliaris *St D*
TALLEY (St Michael)   *see* Cynwyl Gaeo w Llansawel and Talley
  etc *St D*
TALYBONT (St Cross)   *see* Bro Ogwen *Ban*
TALYBONT (St David)   *see* Llanfihangel Genau'r Glyn and
  Llangorwen *St D*
TALYGARN (St Anne)   *see* Pontyclun w Talygarn *Llan*
TAL-Y-LLYN (St David)   *see* Bro Ystumanner *Ban*
TEMPLETON (St John)   *see* Narberth w Mounton w Robeston
  Wathen etc *St D*
TENBY (St Mary) (St Julian's Chapel) *St D 3*   **TR** A J DAVIES,
  A J GRACE   **TV** R N WAINWRIGHT   **NSM** J W MORGAN
THREE CLIFFS *S & B 8*   **V** P BROOKS
TINTERN (St Michael)   *see* Llandogo w Whitebrook Chpl and
  Tintern Parva *Mon*
TON PENTRE   *see* Ystradyfodwg *Llan*
TONDU (St John)   *see* Llansantffraid, Bettws and Aberkenfig
  Llan
TONGWYNLAIS (St Michael) (St James) *Llan 2*
  P-in-c Z E KING
TONMAWR (St Teilo)   *see* Neath *Llan*
TONNA (St Anne)   *see* Cadoxton-juxta-Neath and Tonna
  Llan
TONYPANDY (St Andrew) w Clydach Vale w Williamstown
  Llan 11   **V** vacant
TONYREFAIL (St David) (St Alban) w Gilfach Goch *Llan 11*
  V R E MOVERLEY
TON-YR-YWEN (School)   *see* Llanishen *Llan*
TOWNHILL   *see* Swansea St Jude w St Nic *S & B*
TOWYN (St Mary) *St As 1*   **P-in-c** C M FEAK
TRAEAN-GLAS (St Mary)   *see* Blaenwysg *S & B*
TRALLWNG (St David)   *see* Dan yr Eppynt *S & B*
TRAWSFYNYDD (St Madryn)   *see* Bro Moelwyn *Ban*
TREALAW (All Saints)   *see* Pont Rhondda *Llan*
TREBANOS (St Michael)   *see* Clydach *S & B*
TREBOETH (St Mary)   *see* Landore w Treboeth *S & B*
TREDEGAR (St George) (St James) *Mon 6*   **V** J G DAVIS
  C H-M DE GRUCHY   **NSM** E JONES
TREFDRAETH (Eglwys Crist y Brenin)   *see* Bro Cadwaladr *Ban*
TREFDRAETH (St Beuno) *as above*
TREFEGLWYS (St Michael)   *see* Bro Arwystli *Ban*
TREFGARN (St Michael)   *see* Spittal w Trefgarn and Ambleston
  w St Dogwells *St D*
TREFILAN (St Hilary)   *see* Llanfihangel Ystrad and Cilcennin w
  Trefilan etc *St D*
TREFLYS (St Michael)   *see* Bro'r Holl Saint *Ban*
TREFNANT (Holy Trinity) w Tremeirchion w Cefn *St As 2*
  R C E MANSLEY
TREFRIW (St Mary)   *see* Caerhun and Llangelynnin and
  Llanbedr-y-Cennin *Ban*
TREGAEAN (St Caian)   *see* Bro Cyngar *Ban*
TREGAER (St Mary)   *see* Rockfield and Dingestow Gp *Mon*
TREGARON GROUP (St Caron) *St D 8*   **V** P W DAVIES
TREGARTH (St Mair)   *see* Bro Ogwen *Ban*
TRE-GROES (St Ffraid)   *see* Llandysul w Bangor Teifi and
  Llanfairollwyn etc *St D*
TREGYNON (St Cynon)   *see* Betws Cedewain and Tregynon
  and Llanwyddelan *St As*
TREHARRIS (St Matthias), Trelewis, Bedlinog and Llanfabon
  Llan 9   **P-in-c** M GIBBON
TREHERBERT (St Mary Communion Centre)   *see* Pen Rhondda
  Fawr *Llan*
TRELAWNYD (St Michael)   *see* Dyserth and Trelawnyd and
  Cwm *St As*
TRE-LECH A'R BETWS (St Teilo)   *see* Cynwyl Elfed w Newchurch
  and Trelech a'r Betws *St D*
TRELLECH (St Nicholas) and Penallt *Mon 2*   **V** S J HOWELLS
  NSM D A PRIME, K R PRIME

TRELLECH GRANGE (not known)   *see* Llanishen w Trellech
  Grange and Llanfihangel etc *Mon*
TREMEIRCHION (Corpus Christi)   *see* Trefnant w Tremeirchion
  w Cefn *St As*
TREMORFA (St Philip) Conventional District *Llan 1*
  P-in-c R M CAPPER
TREORCHY (St Matthew)   *see* Pen Rhondda Fawr *Llan*
TRETHOMAS (St Thomas)   *see* Bedwas w Machen w
  Michaelston-y-Fedw w Rudry *Mon*
TRETOWER (St John the Evangelist)   *see* Crickhowell w Cwmdu
  and Tretower *S & B*
TREUDDYN (St Mary) w Nercwys *St As 12*
  P-in-c C M POOLMAN
TREVETHIN (St Cadoc)   *see* Pontypool *Mon*
TREVETHIN (St John the Divine) *as above*
TREVOR (Church)   *see* Llangollen w Trevor and Llantysilio
  St As
TREWALCHMAI (St Morhaiarn)   *see* Bro Cyngar *Ban*
TRISANT *St D 11*   **TR** M A ROWLANDS
TROEDRHIWGARTH (St Mary the Virgin) *Llan 4*
  V C T REANEY
TROED-YR-AUR (St Michael)   *see* Newcastle Emlyn and
  Llandyfriog etc *St D*
TROEDYRHIW (St John) w Merthyr Vale *Llan 9*   **V** S J BARNES
TROSTEY (St David)   *see* Raglan Gp *Mon*
TUDWEILIOG (St Cwyfan)   *see* Bro Madryn *Ban*
TUMBLE (Dewi Sant)   *see* Trisant *St D*
TY SIGN (St David)   *see* Lower Islwyn *Mon*
TYCOCH (All Souls) *S & B 6*   **V** P J GWYNN
TYCROES (St Edmund)   *see* Llanedi w Tycroes and Saron *St D*
TYLORSTOWN (Holy Trinity)   *see* Rhondda Fach Uchaf *Llan*
TYWYN (St Cadfan)   *see* Bro Ystumanner *Ban*
UNDY (St Mary)   *see* Magor *Mon*
UPPER EBBW VALLEYS *Mon 8*   **TR** N C PERRY
  TV G J WAGGETT   **C** W J LAMBERT   **NSM** C I LEWIS,
  C MORGAN, P V GRIFFITHS
UPPER WYE, The *S & B 2*   **V** vacant
USK (St Mary) Ministry Area *Mon 4*   **V** K J HASLER
  Hon C G W OPPERMAN   **NSM** P E LOVE
UWCH GWYRFAI Beuno Sant *Ban 1*   **V** J L JONES
UZMASTON (St Ismael)   *see* Llawhaden w Bletherston and
  Uzmaston *St D*
VALE OF GWRYNNE, The *S & B 3*   **C** C P BOWLER
VALE OF NEATH *Llan 6*   **V** A J DAVIES
VAYNOR (St Gwynno)   *see* Cefn Coed w Vaynor *S & B*
WALTON EAST (St Mary)   *see* Wiston w Walton E and
  Clarbeston *St D*
WALTON WEST (All Saints) w Talbenny and Haroldston
  West *St D 4*   **P-in-c** D C HOARE
WALWYN'S CASTLE (St James the Great) and Robeston
  West *St D 4*   **P-in-c** R M M JOHNSON
WATERSTON   *see* Llanstadwel *St D*
WAUNARLLWYDD (St Barnabas) *S & B 9*   **V** I DAVIES
  NSM J WAGSTAFF
WAUNFELIN (St John the Divine)   *see* Pontypool *Mon*
WELSH ST DONATS (St Donat)   *see* Pendoylan w Welsh
  St Donats *Llan*
WELSHPOOL (St Mary) AND CASTLE CAEREINION *St As 8*
  R S G WILLSON
WENTWOOD *Mon 3*   **P-in-c** W C INGLE-GILLIS
  NSM E N M DAVIES, J S WATERS
WENVOE (St Mary) and St Lythans *Llan 3*
  P-in-c J R ORMROD
WHITCHURCH (St David)   *see* Dewisland *St D*
WHITCHURCH (St Mary) (St Thomas) (All Saints) *Llan 2*
  TR J H L ROWLANDS   **TV** A M FLIPSE, P A MORTIMER
  C J S WRIGHT   **Hon C** H G LEWIS
WHITFORD (St Mary and St Beuno)   *see* Gorsedd w Brynford,
  Ysgeifiog and Whitford *St As*
WHITLAND (St Mary) w Cyffig and Henllan Amgoed and
  Llan-gan w Llandysilio and Clunderwen *St D 3*
  V K G TAYLOR
WHITTON (St David)   *see* E Radnor *S & B*
WICK (St James)   *see* Llantwit Major *Llan*
WILCRICK (St Mary)   *see* Magor *Mon*
WILLIAMSTON, EAST (Church)   *see* Begelly w Ludchurch and
  E Williamston *St D*
WILLIAMSTOWN (St Illtud)   *see* Tonypandy w Clydach Vale w
  Williamstown *Llan*
WISTON (St Mary Magdalene) w Walton East and Clarbeston
  St D 1   **V** vacant
WOLVESNEWTON (St Thomas à Becket)   *see* Usk Min Area *Mon*
WONASTOW (St Wonnow)   *see* Monmouth w Overmonnow
  etc *Mon*
WORTHENBURY (St Deiniol)   *see* Bangor Monachorum,
  Worthenbury and Marchwiel *St As*

WREXHAM (St Giles's Parish Church) (St Mark) (St Mary) (All Saints) (St Margaret) (St James) (St John) *St As 14*
  TV J P SMITH, S ERRINGTON   **C** P K BETTINSON
WYNDHAM (St David)   *see* Llandyfodwg and Cwm Ogwr *Llan*
Y FERWIG (St Pedrog)   *see* Cardigan w Mwnt and Y Ferwig w Llangoedmor *St D*
YERBESTON   *see* Jeffreyston w Reynoldston and Loveston etc *St D*
YNYSBOETH   *see* Penrhiwceiber, Matthewstown and Ynysboeth *Llan*
YNYSCYNON (St Cynon)   *see* Pont Rhondda *Llan*
YNYSDDU (St Theodore)   *see* Mynyddislwyn *Mon*
YNYSHIR (St Anne) *Llan 11*   **V** G P BIGMORE
YSBYTY CYNFYN (St John the Baptist)   *see* Grwp Bro Ystwyth a Mynach *St D*
YSBYTY IFAN (St John the Baptist)   *see* Cerrigydrudion w Llanfihangel Glyn Myfyr etc *St As*

YSBYTY YSTWYTH (St John the Baptist)   *see* Grwp Bro Ystwyth a Mynach *St D*
YSFA (St Mark)   *see* Gwastedyn *S & B*
YSGEIFIOG (St Mary)   *see* Gorsedd w Brynford, Ysgeifiog and Whitford *St As*
YSTALYFERA (St David) *S & B 7*   **V** T J HEWITT
YSTRAD MEURIG (St John the Baptist)   *see* Tregaron Gp *St D*
YSTRAD MYNACH (Holy Trinity) w Llanbradach *Llan 9*
  V S P KIRK
YSTRAD RHONDDA (St Stephen)   *see* Pont Rhondda *Llan*
YSTRAD ROAD (St Illtyd)   *see* Swansea St Pet *S & B*
YSTRADFELLTE (St Mary)   *see* Penderyn Mellte *S & B*
YSTRAD-FFIN (St Paulinus)   *see* Cil-y-Cwm and Ystrad-ffin w Rhandir-mwyn etc *St D*
YSTRADGYNLAIS (St Cynog) *S & B 7*   **R** D ROBERTS
YSTRADOWEN (St Owain)   *see* Cowbridge *Llan*
YSTRADYFODWG (St John the Baptist) *Llan 11*
  V H H ENGLAND-SIMON

SCOTTISH INCUMBENCIES

An index of incumbencies of the Scottish Episcopal Church. The incumbency entry gives the full legal name, followed by the diocese and the name(s) and appointment(s) of the clergy serving there. Church dedications are indicated in brackets. The following are the main abbreviations used; for others see the full list of abbreviations.

C	Curate	**NSM**	Non-stipendiary Minister
Dss	Deaconess	**P-in-c**	Priest-in-charge
Hon C	Honorary Curate	**R**	Rector

ABERCHIRDER (St Marnan) *Mor*   **NSM** N C MILNE
ABERDEEN (St Clement) *Ab*   **P-in-c** K D GORDON
    NSM N O EGBE
ABERDEEN (St Devenick)   *see* Bieldside *Ab*
ABERDEEN (St James) *Ab*   **P-in-c** R A HINES   **NSM** M JASON,
    R B EDWARDS
ABERDEEN (St John the Evangelist) *Ab*   **R** I M POOBALAN
ABERDEEN (St Margaret of Scotland) *Ab*   **R** A E NIMMO
    Hon C D H WRIGHT
ABERDEEN (St Mary) *Ab*   **R** J MERRICK   **C** J M HOBBS
ABERDEEN (St Ninian) *Ab*   **P-in-c** J B LYON
ABERDEEN (St Peter) *Ab*   **P-in-c** I M POOBALAN
    C M H RICHARDSON
ABERDOUR (St Columba) - West Fife Team Ministry *St And*
    NSM M A STIRZAKER
ABERFOYLE (St Mary) *St And*   **R** R W GROSSE
ABERLOUR (St Margaret of Scotland) *Mor*   **R** C G KETLEY
ABOYNE (St Peter) *Ab*   **P-in-c** V R HANCOCK
ALEXANDRIA (St Mungo) *Glas*   **R** K L MACAULAY
ALFORD (St Andrew) *Ab*   **P-in-c** A L JAMES
ALLOA (St John the Evangelist) *St And*   **NSM** E FORGAN
ALYTH (St Ninian) *St And*   **R** K W RATHBAND
    Hon C J I CAMERON   **NSM** D A CAMERON
ANNAN (St John the Evangelist) *Glas*
    P-in-c M P CALLAGHAN   **NSM** J B M MACLEOD
APPIN   *see* Portnacrois *Arg*
APPIN   *see* W Highland Region *Arg*
ARDBRECKNISH (St James) *Arg*   **R** N MCNELLY
ARDCHATTAN (Holy Spirit) *Arg*   **R** N MCNELLY
ARDROSSAN (St Andrew) *Glas*   **R** M SOFIELD
    NSM A MONTGOMERIE
ARPAFEELIE (St John the Evangelist) *Mor*   **R** M O LANGILLE
ARRAN, ISLE OF *Arg*   **P-in-c** S P M MACKENZIE
AUCHENBLAE   *see* Drumtochty *Bre*
AUCHINDOIR (St Mary) *Ab*   **R** J B WALKER
    NSM D ATKINSON
AYR (Holy Trinity) *Glas*   **R** A R BALDOCK   **C** N COX
BAILLIESTON (St John)   *see* Glas E End *Glas*
BALERNO (St Mungo) *Edin*   **R** M J H ROUND
BALLATER (St Kentigern) *Ab*   **P-in-c** V R HANCOCK
BANCHORY (St Ternan) *Ab*   **R** L K EUNSON
    C D GREENWOOD
BANFF (St Andrew) *Ab*   **P-in-c** J M PAISEY
BATHGATE (St Columba) *Edin*   **R** C A BARCLAY
BEARSDEN (All Saints) w Milngavie *Glas*   **TR** K H FREEMAN
BELLS WYND   *see* Douglas *Glas*
BIELDSIDE (St Devenick) *Ab*   **R** P R WATSON
    Dss J E MACCORMACK
BIRNAM   *see* Dunkeld *St And*
BISHOPBRIGGS (St James-the-Less) *Glas*   **R** S A MARSH
BLAIR ATHOLL   *see* Kilmaveonaig *St And*
BLAIRGOWRIE (St Catherine) *St And*   **R** K W RATHBAND
    NSM D A CAMERON
BRECHIN (St Andrew) *Bre*   **R** D C MUMFORD
BRIDGE OF ALLAN (St Saviour) *St And*   **R** D M IND
BRIDGE OF WEIR (St Mary) *Glas*   **R** D C GIFFORD
    C H GONZALEZ PENA
BRIDGEND   *see* Islay *Arg*
BROUGHTY FERRY (St Mary) *Bre*   **R** F W BRIDGER
    C H R BRIDGER
BUCKIE (All Saints) *Ab*   **P-in-c** J M PAISEY
BUCKSBURN (St Machar) *Ab*   **P-in-c** D HEDDLE
BUCKSTONE (St Fillan)   *see* Edin St Fillan *Edin*
BURNSIDE   *see* Moffat *Glas*
BURNTISLAND (St Serf) - West Fife Team Ministry *St And*
    P-in-c D L NORBY   **NSM** M A STIRZAKER
BURRAVOE (St Colman) *Ab*   **NSM** E H MCNAB
CALLANDER (St Andrew) *St And*   **R** R W GROSSE
CAMBUSLANG (St Cuthbert) *Glas*   **P-in-c** D JASPER

CARNOUSTIE (Holy Rood) *Bre*   **Hon C** J B HARDIE
CASTLE DOUGLAS (St Ninian) *Glas*   **R** D W BAYNE
CATHEDRAL OF THE ISLES   *see* Cumbrae (or Millport) *Arg*
CHALLOCH (All Saints) *Glas*   **P-in-c** M R B HILLS
CHAPELHILL   *see* Cruden Bay *Ab*
CLARKSTON (St Aidan) *Glas*   **R** N H TAYLOR
CLERMISTON   *see* Edin Clermiston *Em Edin*
COLDSTREAM (St Mary and All Souls) *Edin*   **R** J B SMITH
    Hon C J L EVANS
COLINTON   *see* Edin St Cuth *Edin*
COMRIE (St Serf) *St And*   **R** P LEWER ALLEN
COUPAR ANGUS (St Anne) *St And*   **R** K W RATHBAND
    NSM D A CAMERON
COURTHILL Chapel   *see* Kishorn *Mor*
CRAIGHALL   *see* Ellon *Ab*
CRIEFF (St Columba) *St And*   **R** P LEWER ALLEN
CROACHY   *see* Strathnairn St Paul *Mor*
CROMARTY (St Regulus) *Mor*   **R** M O LANGILLE
CRUDEN BAY (St James the Less) *Ab*   **R** A M TUCKER
    NSM G P WHALLEY
CUMBERNAULD (Holy Name) *Glas*   **R** B A OGUGUO
CUMINESTOWN (St Luke) *Ab*   **P-in-c** P G D JONES
CUMINESTOWN (St Luke)   *see* Cen Buchan *Ab*
CUPAR (St James the Great) *St And*   **R** A HASELHURST
    Hon C D O'CONNOR, J B BLACK
DALBEATTIE (Christ Church) *Glas*   **Hon C** R W STEPHENS
    NSM B M SCOTT
DALKEITH (St Mary) *Edin*   **R** P S HARRIS   **NSM** E S JONES,
    J O GODFREY, M E JONES
DALMAHOY (St Mary) *Edin*   **R** D L COLLINGWOOD
DALRY (St Peter) *Glas*   **R** M SOFIELD
DENNISTOUN (St Kentigern)   *see* Glas E End *Glas*
DINGWALL (St James the Great) *Mor*   **P-in-c** I N PALLETT
    NSM R FLOCKHART, V C SAUNDERS
DOLLAR (St James the Great) *St And*   **R** A R FREARSON
DOUNE (St Modoc) *St And*   **R** A M PEDEN
DOWNFIELD (St Luke)   *see* Dundee St Luke *Bre*
DRUMLITHIE (St John the Baptist) *Bre*   **R** M J R TURNER
DRUMTOCHTY (St Palladius) *Bre*   **R** M J R TURNER
DUFFTOWN (St Michael and All Angels) *Mor*   **R** C G KETLEY
DUMBARTON (St Augustine) *Glas*   **R** K L MACAULAY
DUMFRIES (St John the Evangelist) *Glas*   **R** S R PAISLEY
    Hon C A M SHUKMAN, G J SIMMONS, G M WARWICK,
    S P BALLARD   **NSM** J M G CLARK-MAXWELL
DUNBAR (St Anne) *Edin*   **R** A J BAIN
DUNBLANE (St Mary) *St And*   **R** N GREEN
DUNDEE (Cathedral of St Paul) *Bre*   **C** T A DOWLING
DUNDEE (St Luke) *Bre*   **P-in-c** K J DIXON
DUNDEE (St Margaret) *Bre*   **Hon C** A WALLER
DUNDEE (St Mary Magdalene) *Bre*   **R** D SHEPHERD
DUNDEE (St Ninian) *Bre*   **P-in-c** E M LAMONT
DUNDEE (St Salvador) *Bre*   **R** C H CLAPSON
    Hon C G M GREIG
DUNFERMLINE (Holy Trinity) - West Fife Team Ministry
    St And   **R** A J COZENS   **Hon C** R K KENNEDY
DUNKELD (St Mary) w Birnam *St And*   **R** D F BROOKE
    P-in-c S R BOARDMAN   **NSM** I ATKINSON
DUNOON (Holy Trinity) *Arg*   **P-in-c** A C SWIFT
    C E GARMAN
DUNS (Christ Church) *Edin*   **P-in-c** K G WEBB
DUROR (St Adamnan)   *see* W Highland Region *Arg*
EAST END   *see* Glas E End *Glas*
EAST KILBRIDE (St Mark) *Glas*   **R** P G M FLETCHER
EASTGATE (St Peter)   *see* Peebles *Edin*
EASTRIGGS (St John the Evangelist) *Glas*
    P-in-c M P CALLAGHAN   **NSM** J B M MACLEOD
EDINBURGH (Cathedral of St Mary) *Edin*   **R** G J T FORBES
    NSM G P FOSTER
EDINBURGH (Christ Church) *Edin*   **R** S E MACDONALD
    C M M RODE, N S RODE

EDINBURGH (Emmanuel) *Edin*   **R** T J HARKIN
EDINBURGH (Good Shepherd) *Edin*   **R** D J B FOSTEKEW
  C N MOLL, R A ADDIS   **NSM** B M JOHNSON
EDINBURGH (Holy Cross) *Edin*   **R** W D KORNAHRENS
EDINBURGH (Old St Paul) *Edin*   **R** I J PATON
  C K S M REYNOLDS   **Hon C** C S DAVIES-COLE, M C REED
  NSM C NAISMITH
EDINBURGH (St Barnabas) *Edin*   **P-in-c** P D DIXON
  NSM A C ANDERSON
EDINBURGH (St Columba) *Edin*   **TV** J S RICHARDSON,
  R O GOULD   **C** A C W WAGSTAFF
EDINBURGH (St Cuthbert) *Edin*   **R** M I HOUSTON
  C S SHAW
EDINBURGH (St David of Scotland) *Edin*   **R** R GREEN
EDINBURGH (St James the Less) *Edin*   **R** S I BUTLER
  NSM J L MACLAREN, J P MITCHELL, M S NORTHCOTT
EDINBURGH (St John the Evangelist) *Edin*
  R M DUENZKOFER   **C** D COOPER, D REID, S M HOLMES
  NSM C A HUME, F E ALEXANDER, P J BRAND, S KILBEY
EDINBURGH (St Margaret of Scotland) *Edin*
  P-in-c M C REED
EDINBURGH (St Mark) *Edin*   **R** S B MARRIAGE
EDINBURGH (St Martin of Tours) *Edin*   **R** J A CONWAY
  NSM D J WARNES
EDINBURGH (St Michael and All Saints) *Edin*
  R M D ROBSON   **C** J B PENMAN
EDINBURGH (St Ninian) *Edin*   **R** F S BURBERRY
EDINBURGH (St Paul and St George) *Edin*   **R** D G RICHARDS
  C J E M GREEN, J E MCK GREEN, R J CORNFIELD
EDINBURGH (St Peter) *Edin*   **R** F W TOMLINSON
  NSM R T HALLIDAY
EDINBURGH (St Philip and St James) *Edin*
  R T N RONGONG
EDINBURGH (St Salvador) *Edin*   **P-in-c** N MOLL
EDINBURGH (St Thomas) Private Chapel *Edin*
  I D W MCCARTHY
EDINBURGH (St Vincent) Private Chapel *Edin*
  P-in-c A M MACLEAN   **C** W L F MOUNSEY
ELGIN (Holy Trinity) w Lossiemouth (St Margaret) *Mor*
  R C G KETLEY   **NSM** J SCLATER
ELLON (St Mary on the Rock) *Ab*   **R** A M TUCKER
  NSM C A FOX, G P WHALLEY
EORROPAIDH (St Moluag) *Arg*   **P-in-c** T TAGGART
  NSM C P A LOCKHART
ERSKINE   *see* Renfrew *Glas*
EYEMOUTH (St Ebba) *Edin*   **NSM** F D J SMOUT
FALKIRK (Christ Church) *Edin*   **R** R INNES
  Hon C T NJUGUNA
FASQUE (St Andrew) *Bre*   **R** M J R TURNER
FETTERCAIRN   *see* Fasque *Bre*
FOCHABERS Gordon Chapel *Mor*   **C** F A FORSHAW
FORFAR (St John the Evangelist) *St And*   **R** D A CAMERON
FORRES (St John the Evangelist) *Mor*   **P-in-c** C J PIPER
FORT WILLIAM (St Andrew) *Arg*   **R** G A GUINNESS
FORTROSE (St Andrew) *Mor*   **R** M O LANGILLE
FRASERBURGH (St Peter) *Ab*   **P-in-c** K E SUCKLING
GALASHIELS (St Peter) *Edin*   **R** D I MCCOSH
GALLOWGATE   *see* Aberdeen St Marg *Ab*
GIRVAN (St John) *Glas*   **R** A R BALDOCK   **C** N COX
GLASGOW (All Saints) *Glas*   **R** S M P MAITLAND
GLASGOW (Cathedral of St Mary the Virgin) *Glas*
  R K HOLDSWORTH   **NSM** C A MCKILLOP
GLASGOW (Holy Cross) *Glas*   **NSM** D D KEEBLE
GLASGOW (St Bride) *Glas*   **Hon C** K FRANCIS
  NSM I T DRAPER
GLASGOW (St Margaret) *Glas*   **R** S ROBERTSON
  C M S MCTERNAN
GLASGOW (St Matthew) *Glas*   **P-in-c** D K WOSTENHOLM
GLASGOW (St Ninian) *Glas*   **R** P ROMANO
GLASGOW East End (St John) (St Kentigern) (St Serf) *Glas*
  NSM L A IRELAND
GLENCARSE (All Saints) *Bre*   **R** K A REID
GLENROTHES (St Luke the Evangelist) - Central Fife
  Team Ministry *St And*   **C** G F DILLON, M A DINELEY,
  MA DINELEY
GLENURQUHART (St Ninian) *Mor*   **P-in-c** C MYLNE
GOUROCK (St Bartholomew) *Glas*   **P-in-c** A R SHERIDAN
GOVAN   *see* Glas St Gabr *Glas*
GRANTOWN-ON-SPEY (St Columba) *Mor*
  Hon C R J GILLINGS
GREENOCK (St John the Evangelist) *Glas*   **R** A R SHERIDAN
  NSM E A O'RYAN
GRETNA (All Saints) *Glas*   **P-in-c** M P CALLAGHAN
  NSM J B M MACLEOD
GREYFRIARS   *see* Kirkcudbright *Glas*

GRULINE (St Columba)   *see* W Highland Region *Arg*
HADDINGTON (Holy Trinity) *Edin*   **R** A C DYER
  NSM J WOOD
HAMILTON (St Mary the Virgin) *Glas*   **R** I D BARCROFT
HARRIS, ISLE OF   *see* Leverburgh *Arg*
HARRIS, ISLE OF (Christ Church) *Arg*   **P-in-c** J D L DAVIES
HAY DRIVE   *see* Edin St Andr and St Aid *Edin*
HELENSBURGH (St Michael and All Angels) *Glas*
  P-in-c D A COOK
HILLINGTON (Good Shepherd)   *see* Glas Gd Shep and
  Ascension *Glas*
HUNTLY (Christ Church) *Mor*   **NSM** N C MILNE
HYNDLAND (St Bride)   *see* Glas St Bride *Glas*
INNERLEITHEN (St Andrew) *Edin*   **R** M J W BENTON-EVANS
  NSM C B AITCHISON, C CHAPLIN
INSCH (St Drostan) *Ab*   **R** J DUTHIE
INVERARAY (All Saints) *Arg*   **P-in-c** S P M MACKENZIE
INVERBERVIE (St David of Scotland) *Bre*   **R** S J FERGUSON
INVERGOWRIE (All Souls) *Bre*   **P-in-c** A W CUMMINS
INVERKEITHING (St Peter) - West Fife Team Ministry *St And*
  NSM M A STIRZAKER
INVERNESS (St John the Evangelist) *Mor*   **P-in-c** J CUTHBERT
INVERNESS (St Michael and All Angels) *Mor*
  P-in-c J CUTHBERT   **Hon C** G H STRANRAER-MULL
INVERURIE (St Mary) *Ab*   **R** J B WALKER   **NSM** D ATKINSON
IONA (St Columba) *Arg*   **NSM** J WATSON
ISLE OF HARRIS   *see* Harris Ch *Arg*
JEDBURGH (St John the Evangelist) *Edin*   **R** D J DALGLISH
  Hon C W J GROVER
JOHNSTONE (St John) *Glas*   **P-in-c** D M ORR   **C** P J SMITH
JORDANHILL (All Saints)   *see* Glas All SS *Glas*
KELSO (St Andrew) *Edin*   **R** R D KING   **Hon C** J L EVANS
KEMNAY (St Anne) *Ab*   **P-in-c** J B WALKER
  NSM D ATKINSON
KENTALLEN (St Moluag)   *see* W Highland Region *Arg*
KESSOCK-TORE   *see* Arpafeelie *Mor*
KILMACOLM (St Fillan) *Glas*   **R** D C GIFFORD
  C H GONZALEZ PENA
KILMARTIN (St Columba) *Arg*   **P-in-c** S P M MACKENZIE
KILMAVEONAIG (St Adamnan) *St And*   **R** E M J M BAKER
KINCARDINE O'NEIL (Christ Church) *Ab*   **R** L K EUNSON
  C D GREENWOOD
KINGHORN (St Mary and St Leonard) *St And*   **R** C N FRASER
KINLOCH RANNOCH (All Saints) *St And*   **R** E M J M BAKER
KINLOCHLEVEN (St Paul)   *see* W Highland Region *Arg*
KINROSS (St Paul) *St And*   **R** D G MACKENZIE MILLS
KIRKCALDY (St Peter) *St And*   **R** C N FRASER
KIRKWALL (St Olaf) *Ab*   **P-in-c** D DAWSON
KIRRIEMUIR (St Mary) *St And*   **P-in-c** R P HARLEY
KISHORN Chapel *Mor*   **NSM** H S WIDDOWS
KNIGHTSWOOD (Holy Cross)   *see* Glas H Cross *Glas*
LADYBANK (St Mary) *St And*   **R** A HASELHURST
LADYCROFT   *see* Balerno *Edin*
LARGS (St Columba) *Glas*   **R** G B FYFE   **C** J E P CURRALL
LASSWADE (St Leonard) *Edin*   **R** P S HARRIS
  NSM E S JONES, J O GODFREY, M E JONES
LAURENCEKIRK (St Laurence) *Bre*   **R** M J R TURNER
LEITH (St James the Less)   *see* Edin St Jas *Edin*
LENZIE (St Cyprian) *Glas*   **R** L S IRELAND   **C** M E JAMIESON
LERWICK (St Magnus) *Ab*   **R** N A BRICE   **NSM** E H MCNAB
LEVEN (St Margaret) - Central Fife Team Ministry *St And*
  C G F DILLON, M A DINELEY, MA DINELEY
LEWIS, ISLE OF   *see* Stornoway *Arg*
LINLITHGOW (St Peter) *Edin*   **R** C A BARCLAY
LOCHEARNHEAD (St Angus) *St And*   **R** P LEWER ALLEN
LOCHEE (St Margaret)   *see* Dundee St Marg *Bre*
LOCHGELLY (St Finnian) - Central Fife Team Ministry *St And*
  C G F DILLON, M A DINELEY, MA DINELEY
LOCHGILPHEAD (Christ Church) *Arg*
  P-in-c S P M MACKENZIE
LOCKERBIE (All Saints) *Glas*   **P-in-c** M P CALLAGHAN
  NSM J B M MACLEOD
LONGSIDE (St John)   *see* Cen Buchan *Ab*
LOSSIEMOUTH (St Margaret)   *see* Elgin w Lossiemouth *Mor*
MARYGATE   *see* Pittenweem *St And*
MASTRICK (St Clement)   *see* Aberdeen St Clem *Ab*
MAYBOLE (St Oswald) *Glas*   **R** A R BALDOCK   **C** N COX
MELROSE (Holy Trinity) *Edin*   **R** P V P BLACKLEDGE
  NSM D W WOOD
MILLPORT   *see* Cumbrae (or Millport) *Arg*
MILNGAVIE (St Andrew)   *see* Bearsden w Milngavie *Glas*
MOFFAT (St John the Evangelist) *Glas*
  P-in-c M P CALLAGHAN   **NSM** J B M MACLEOD
MONIFIETH (Holy Trinity) *Bre*   **P-in-c** K G G GIBSON
  NSM W J MCAUSLAND

MONKLANDS   *see* Airdrie *Glas*
MONKSTOWN   *see* Ladybank *St And*
MONTROSE (St Mary and St Peter) *Bre*   **R** S J FERGUSON
MORNINGSIDE (Christ Church)   *see* Edin Ch Ch *Edin*
MOTHERWELL (Holy Trinity) *Glas*   **P-in-c** A WYLIE
MULL, ISLE OF   *see* Gruline *Arg*
MULL, ISLE OF   *see* Lochbuie *Arg*
MULL, ISLE OF   *see* W Highland Region *Arg*
MURRAYFIELD (Good Shepherd)   *see* Edin Gd Shep *Edin*
NAIRN (St Columba) *Mor*   **R** A J SIMPSON
NEW GALLOWAY (St Margaret of Scotland) *Glas*
  P-in-c J R REPATH
NEW PITSLIGO (St John the Evangelist)   *see* Cen Buchan *Ab*
NEWLANDS (St Margaret)   *see* Glas St Marg *Glas*
NEWPORT-ON-TAY (St Mary) *St And*   **R** D B H HERBERT
NEWTON STEWART   *see* Challoch *Glas*
NORTH BALLACHULISH   *see* Onich *Arg*
NORTH MEARNS   *see* Stonehaven *Bre*
OBAN (Cathedral of St John) *Arg*   **Hon C** I E WALTER
OLD DEER (St Drostan)   *see* Cen Buchan *Ab*
OLDMELDRUM (St Matthew) *Ab*   **P-in-c** R SPENCER
OXGANGS (St Hilda)   *see* Edin St Hilda *Edin*
PAISLEY (Holy Trinity) *Glas*   **R** T D WILSON
PAISLEY (St Barnabas) *Glas*   **R** T D WILSON
PEEBLES (St Peter) *Edin*   **R** M J W BENTON-EVANS
  NSM C B AITCHISON, C CHAPLIN
PENICUIK (St James the Less) *Edin*   **R** L M DOWNS
  NSM N F SUTTLE, T A BRAMLEY
PERTH (Cathedral of St Ninian) *St And*   **NSM** R F SAUNDERS
PERTH (St John the Baptist) *St And*   **R** G S TAYLOR
PETERHEAD (St Peter) *Ab*   **R** R N O'SULLIVAN
PILTON (St David)   *see* Edin St Dav *Edin*
PITLOCHRY (Holy Trinity) *St And*   **R** E M J M BAKER
POLLOCKSHIELDS (St Ninian)   *see* Glas St Ninian *Glas*
POLTALLOCH   *see* Kilmartin *Arg*
POOLEWE (St Maelrubha) *Mor*   **NSM** H S WIDDOWS
PORT GLASGOW (St Mary the Virgin) *Glas*   **R** D C GIFFORD
  C H GONZALEZ PENA
PORTNACROIS (Holy Cross)   *see* W Highland Region *Arg*
PORTPATRICK (St Ninian) *Glas*   **P-in-c** M R B HILLS
PORTREE (St Columba) *Arg*   **C** R BUNGARD
PORTSOY (St John the Baptist) *Ab*   **P-in-c** J M PAISEY
POSSILPARK (St Matthew)   *see* Glas St Matt *Glas*
PRESTWICK (St Ninian) *Glas*   **R** H J ROSS
RENFREW (St Margaret) w Erskine *Glas*   **P-in-c** D M ORR
  C P J SMITH
ROSLIN (Collegiate Church of St Matthew) *Edin*
  P-in-c J E ROULSTON

ROTHESAY (St Paul) *Arg*   **P-in-c** A C SWIFT   **C** E GARMAN
ROTHIEMURCHUS (St John the Baptist) *Mor*
  Hon C R J GILLINGS   **NSM** J M JONES
ST ANDREWS (All Saints) *St And*   **C** M-L MOFFETT
  Hon C D W DAY, G D WHITE, G J M SAUNDERS,
  M C ALDCROFT   **NSM** I M MICHAEL
ST ANDREWS (St Andrew) *St And*   **R** T A HART   **C** D M HALL
  NSM D A BEADLE, R T EVANS
SANDYLOAN   *see* Gullane *Edin*
SELKIRK (St John the Evangelist) *Edin*   **Hon C** D D SCEATS
SHETTLESTON (St Serf)   *see* Glas E End *Glas*
SKYE, ISLE OF   *see* Portree *Arg*
**SOUTH QUEENSFERRY (Priory Church St Mary of
  Mount Carmel)** *Edin*   **P-in-c** T J HARKIN
  NSM I MACROBERT
STANLEY (St Columba) *St And*   **P-in-c** S R BOARDMAN
  NSM R F SAUNDERS
STORNOWAY (St Peter) *Arg*   **P-in-c** T TAGGART
STRANRAER (St John the Evangelist) *Glas*
  P-in-c M R B HILLS, N E H NEWTON
STRATHNAIRN (St Paul) *Mor*   **P-in-c** K B COLLINS,
  R F BURKITT
STRATHPEFFER (St Anne) *Mor*   **P-in-c** I N PALLETT
  NSM R FLOCKHART, V C SAUNDERS
STRATHTAY (St Andrew) *St And*   **R** D F BROOKE,
  E M J M BAKER
STRICHEN (All Saints)   *see* Cen Buchan *Ab*
TAIN (St Andrew) *Mor*   **P-in-c** C P MAYO
TARFSIDE (St Drostan) *Bre*   **R** D C MUMFORD
  NSM J NELSON
TEINDHILLGREEN   *see* Duns *Edin*
THURSO (St Peter and Holy Rood) *Mor*   **P-in-c** W G KNOTT
  Hon C F E DAVIES
TOFTS   *see* Dalry *Glas*
TORRY   *see* Aberdeen St Pet *Ab*
TROON (St Ninian) *Glas*   **R** T C O MONTGOMERY
TURRIFF (St Congan) *Ab*   **P-in-c** S C PALMER
UDDINGSTON (St Andrew) *Glas*   **P-in-c** D JASPER
WEST HIGHLAND Region *Arg*   **C** D DAVIDSON
WEST LINTON (St Mungo) *Edin*   **NSM** T A BRAMLEY
WESTGATE   *see* Dunbar *Edin*
WESTHILL (Trinity) *Ab*   **R** I J FERGUSON
WHITING BAY   *see* Is of Arran *Arg*
WICK (St John the Evangelist) *Mor*   **R** W G KNOTT
  Hon C F E DAVIES
WISHAW (St Andrew) *Glas*   **P-in-c** A WYLIE
WOODHEAD OF FETTERLETTER   *see* Fyvie *Ab*
YELL   *see* Burravoe *Ab*

An index of benefices of the Church of Ireland (shown in bold type), together with entries for churches and other licensed places of worship. Where the church name is the same as that of the benefice (or the first place name in the benefice), the church entry is omitted. Church dedications are indicated in brackets.

The benefice entry gives the full legal name, together with the diocese and the name(s) and appointment(s) of clergy serving there. The following are the main abbreviations used; for others see the full list of abbreviations.

Bp's C	Bishop's Curate	**Hon C**	Honorary Curate
C	Curate	**I**	Incumbent (includes Rector or Vicar)
C-in-c	Curate-in-charge	**NSM**	Non-stipendiary Minister
		P-in-c	Priest-in-charge

AASLEAGH (St John the Baptist)   *see* Tuam w Cong and Aasleagh *T, K & A*

ABBEYLEIX (St Michael and All Angels) w Ballyroan, Ballinakill, Killermogh, Aughmacart, Durrow and Attanagh *C & O*   **I** P A HARVEY   **NSM** A WALLACE

ABBEYSTREWRY (no dedication) w Creagh, Tullagh, Castlehaven and Caheragh *C, C & R*   **I** J K ARDIS

ABINGDON (no dedication)   *see* Killaloe w Stradbally *L & K*

ACHILL (Holy Trinity)   *see* Aughaval w Achill, Knappagh, Dugort etc *T, K & A*

ACTON (no dedication) and Drumbanagher *Arm* **Bp's C** D W R DUNN

ADARE (St Nicholas) and Kilmallock w Kilpeacon, Croom, Kilflynn, Kilfinane, Knockaney, Bruff and Caherconlish *L & K*   **I** E P BEASLEY

AGHABOG (no dedication)   *see* Ematris w Rockcorry, Aghabog and Aughnamullan *Clogh*

AGHADE (All Saints)   *see* Fenagh w Myshall, Aghade and Ardoyne *C & O*

AGHADOE   *see* Killarney w Aghadoe and Muckross *L & K*

AGHADOWEY (St Guaire) w Kilrea *D & R* **I** L D A CRAWFORD-MCCAFFERTY

AGHADOWN (Church Cross)   *see* Ballydehob w Aghadown *C, C & R*

AGHADOWN (St Matthew) *as above*

AGHALEE (Holy Trinity) *D & D*   **I** R C MCCARTNEY

AGHALURCHER (no dedication) w Tattykeeran, Cooneen and Mullaghfad *Clogh*   **I** J M MCCLENAGHAN

AGHANAGH (no dedication)   *see* Boyle and Elphin w Aghanagh, Kilbryan etc *K, E & A*

AGHANCON (no dedication)   *see* Shinrone w Aghancon etc *L & K*

AGHANLOO (St Lugha)   *see* Tamlaghtard w Aghanloo *D & R*

AGHAVEA (no dedication) *Clogh*   **I** G MCMURRAY

AGHAVILLY (St Mary)   *see* Tynan w Middletown and Aghavilly *Arm*

AGHAVOE (no dedication)   *see* Rathdowney w Castlefleming, Donaghmore etc *C & O*

AGHER (no dedication)   *see* Dunboyne and Rathmolyon *M & K*

AGHERTON (St John the Baptist) *Conn*   **I** S A FIELDING

AGHOLD (no dedication)   *see* Tullow w Shillelagh, Aghold and Mullinacuff *C & O*

AGHOUR (St Lachtan)   *see* Kilkenny w Aghour and Kilmanagh *C & O*

AHASCRAGH   *see* Aughrim w Ballinasloe etc *L & K*

AHERLA   *see* Moviddy Union *C, C & R*

AHOGHILL (St Colmanell) w Portglenone *Conn*   **I** G MILLAR

ALDERGROVE   *see* Killead w Gartree *Conn*

ALMORITIA (St Nicholas)   *see* Mullingar, Portnashangan, Moyliscar, Kilbixy etc *M & K*

ALTEDESERT (no dedication)   *see* Kildress w Altedesert *Arm*

ANNACLONE (Christ Church)   *see* Magherally w Annaclone *D & D*

ANNADUFF (St Ann)   *see* Kiltoghart w Drumshambo, Annaduff and Kilronan *K, E & A*

ANNAGH (St Andrew) w Drumaloor, Cloverhill and Drumlane *K, E & A*   **C** T J WOODS

ANNAGHMORE (St Francis) *Arm*   **I** D S MCVEIGH

ANNAHILT (Ascension) w Magherahamlet *D & D* **I** J R HOWARD

ANNESTOWN   *see* Waterford w Killea, Drumcannon and Dunhill *C & O*

ANTRIM (All Saints) *Conn*   **I** S R MCBRIDE

ANTRIM (St Patrick)   *see* Connor w Antrim St Patr *Conn*

ARBOE (no dedication)   *see* Ballinderry, Tamlaght and Arboe *Arm*

ARDAGH (St Patrick) w Tashinny, Shrule and Kilcommick *K, E & A*   **Bp's C** A W KINGSTON

ARDAMINE (St John the Evangelist) w Kiltennel, Glascarrig, Kilnamanagh, Kilmuckridge and Monamolin *C & O* **I** R J GRAY

ARDARA (St Connall) w Glencolumbkille, Inniskeel, Glenties and Lettermacaward *D & R*   **I** J DEANE **NSM** M C CLASSON

ARDCARNE (no dedication)   *see* Boyle and Elphin w Aghanagh, Kilbryan etc *K, E & A*

ARDCLINIS (St Mary) and Tickmacrevan w Layde and Cushendun *Conn*   **P-in-c** H A MACARTHUR

ARDCOLM (no dedication)   *see* Wexford and Kilscoran Union *C & O*

ARDEE (St Mary)   *see* Drogheda w Ardee, Collon and Termonfeckin *Arm*

ARDGLASS (St Nicholas)   *see* Lecale Gp *D & D*

ARDKEEN (Christ Church)   *see* Ballyhalbert w Ardkeen *D & D*

ARDMORE (St Paul)   *see* Youghal Union *C, C & R*

ARDNAGEEHY (no dedication)   *see* Fermoy Union *C, C & R*

ARDOYNE (Holy Trinity)   *see* Fenagh w Myshall, Aghade and Ardoyne *C & O*

ARDOYNE (Immanuel)   *see* Belfast H Trin and St Silas *Conn*

ARDQUIN (no dedication)   *see* Ballyphilip w Ardquin *D & D*

ARDRAHAN   *see* Aughrim w Ballinasloe etc *L & K*

ARDSTRAW (St Eugene) w Baronscourt, Badoney Lower and Badoney Upper and Greenan *D & R*   **I** I E DINSMORE

ARDTREA (St Andrew) w Desertcreat *Arm*   **I** D J BELL

ARKLOW (St Saviour) w Inch and Kilbride *D & G* **I** N J W SHERWOOD

ARMAGH (St Mark) *Arm*   **I** M T KINGSTON

ARMAGHBREAGUE (no dedication)   *see* Keady w Armaghbreague and Derrynoose *Arm*

ARMOY (St Patrick) w Loughguile and Drumtullagh *Conn* **I** C R A EASTON   **NSM** D J STEELE, G H NEVIN

ARVAGH (no dedication) w Carrigallen, Gowna and Columbkille *K, E & A*   **P-in-c** H R HICKS

ASHFIELD (no dedication)   *see* Drumgoon *K, E & A*

ASKEATON (St Mary)   *see* Rathkeale w Askeaton, Kilcornan and Kilnaughtin *L & K*

ATHBOY (St James)   *see* Trim and Athboy Gp *M & K*

ATHLONE (St Mary) w Benown, Kiltoom and Forgney *M & K* **I** G T DOYLE

ATHY (St Michael) w Kilberry, Fontstown and Kilkea *D & G* **I** O M R DONOHOE

AUGHANUNSHIN   *see* Conwal Union w Gartan *D & R*

AUGHAVAL (no dedication) w Achill, Knappagh, Dugort, Castlebar and Turlough *T, K & A*   **I** V H ROGERS

AUGHAVAS (no dedication)   *see* Mohill w Farnaught, Aughavas, Oughteragh etc *K, E & A*

AUGHMACART (St Tighernagh)   *see* Abbeyleix w Ballyroan etc *C & O*

AUGHNACLIFFE   *see* Arvagh w Carrigallen, Gowna and Columbkille *K, E & A*

AUGHNACLOY   *see* Carnteel and Crilly *Arm*

AUGHNAMULLAN (Christ Church)   *see* Ematris w Rockcorry, Aghabog and Aughnamullan *Clogh*

AUGHRIM (St John the Evangelist)   *see* Castlemacadam w Ballinaclash, Aughrim etc *D & G*

BADONEY LOWER (St Patrick)   *see* Ardstraw w Baronscourt, Badoney Lower etc *D & R*

BADONEY UPPER (St Aichen) *as above*

BAGENALSTOWN   *see* Dunleckney w Nurney, Lorum and Kiltennel *C & O*

BAILIEBOROUGH (no dedication) w Knockbride, Shercock and Mullagh *K, E & A*   **I** F E J RANKIN   **C** I HORNER

BALBRIGGAN (St George)   *see* Holmpatrick w Balbriggan and Kenure *D & G*

BALGRIFFIN (St Doulagh)   *see* Malahide w Balgriffin *D & G*

BALLAGHTOBIN (no dedication)   *see* Kells Gp *C & O*

BALLEE (no dedication)   *see* Bright w Ballee and Killough *D & D*

BALLIGAN   *see* Ballywalter w Inishargie *D & D*

BALLINA   *see* Killala w Dunfeeny, Crossmolina, Kilmoremoy etc *T, K & A*

BALLINACLASH (no dedication)   *see* Castlemacadam w Ballinaclash, Aughrim etc *D & G*

BALLINADEE (no dedication)   *see* Bandon Union *C, C & R*

BALLINAFAD   *see* Boyle and Elphin w Aghanagh, Kilbryan etc *K, E & A*

BALLINAKILL (All Saints)   *see* Abbeyleix w Ballyroan etc *C & O*

BALLINALEA   *see* Mostrim w Granard, Clonbroney, Killoe etc *K, E & A*

BALLINALECK   *see* Cleenish w Mullaghdun *Clogh*

BALLINAMALLARD   *see* Magheracross *Clogh*

BALLINAMORE   *see* Mohill w Farnaught, Aughavas, Oughteragh etc *K, E & A*

BALLINASLOE (St John the Evangelist)   *see* Aughrim w Ballinasloe etc *L & K*

BALLINATONE   *see* Castlemacadam w Ballinaclash, Aughrim etc *D & G*

BALLINDERRY (no dedication) *Conn*   **I** T CLELAND

BALLINDERRY (St John), Tamlaght and Arboe *Arm*
   I W B PAINE

BALLINEEN   *see* Kinneigh Union *C, C & R*

BALLINGARRY (no dedication)   *see* Cloughjordan w Borrisokane etc *L & K*

BALLINLOUGH   *see* Roscommon w Donamon, Rathcline, Kilkeevin etc *K, E & A*

BALLINROBE (St Mary)   *see* Tuam w Cong and Aasleagh *T, K & A*

BALLINTEMPLE (no dedication)   *see* Kilmore w Ballintemple *K, E & A*

BALLINTEMPLE (St Mary)   *see* Cashel w Magorban, Tipperary, Clonbeg etc *C & O*

BALLINTOGHER   *see* Taunagh w Kilmactranny, Ballysumaghan etc *K, E & A*

BALLINTOY (no dedication) w Rathlin and Dunseverick *Conn*
   I P M BARTON

BALLINTUBBERT (St Brigid)   *see* Stradbally w Ballintubbert, Coraclone etc *C & O*

BALLISODARE (Holy Trinity) w Collooney and Emlaghfad *T, K & A*   **I** A W PULLEN

BALLIVOR   *see* Trim and Athboy Gp *M & K*

BALLNACARGY   *see* Mullingar, Portnashangan, Moyliscar, Kilbixy etc *M & K*

BALLYBAY (Christ Church) w Mucknoe and Clontibret *Clogh*
   I N D S PHAIR

BALLYBEEN (St Mary) *D & D*   **I** J M HARVEY
   NSM N GORDON

BALLYBRACK (St Matthias)   *see* Killiney Ballybrack *D & G*

BALLYBUNNION   *see* Tralee w Kilmoyley, Ballymacelligott etc *L & K*

BALLYCANEW (no dedication)   *see* Gorey w Kilnahue, Leskinfere and Ballycanew *C & O*

BALLYCARNEY (no dedication)   *see* Ferns w Kilbride, Toombe, Kilcormack etc *C & O*

BALLYCARRY   *see* Kilroot and Templecorran *Conn*

BALLYCASTLE (Holy Trinity)   *see* Ramoan w Ballycastle and Culfeightrin *Conn*

BALLYCLARE   *see* Ballynure and Ballyeaston *Conn*

BALLYCLOG (St Patrick)   *see* Brackaville w Donaghendry and Ballyclog *Arm*

BALLYCLUG (St Patrick)   *see* Ballymena w Ballyclug *Conn*

BALLYCOMMON   *see* Geashill w Killeigh and Ballycommon *M & K*

BALLYCONNELL   *see* Kildallon and Swanlinbar *K, E & A*

BALLYCOTTON   *see* Youghal Union *C, C & R*

BALLYCULTER (Christ Church)   *see* Lecale Gp *D & D*

BALLYDEHOB (St Matthias) w Aghadown *C, C & R*
   I S T MCCANN

BALLYEASTON (St John the Evangelist)   *see* Ballynure and Ballyeaston *Conn*

BALLYEGLISH (St Matthias)   *see* Desertlyn w Ballyeglish *Arm*

BALLYFIN (no dedication)   *see* Maryborough w Dysart Enos and Ballyfin *C & O*

BALLYGAWLEY (no dedication)   *see* Errigle Keerogue w Ballygawley and Killeshil *Arm*

BALLYHAISE   *see* Drung w Castleterra, Larah and Lavey etc *K, E & A*

BALLYHALBERT (St Andrew) w Ardkeen *D & D*
   I J J HEMPHILL

BALLYHOLME (St Columbanus) *D & D*   **I** S E DOOGAN
   C A J MORRISON

BALLYHOOLEY (no dedication)   *see* Fermoy Union *C, C & R*

BALLYJAMESDUFF (no dedication)   *see* Kildrumferton w Ballymachugh and Ballyjamesduff *K, E & A*

BALLYKELLY   *see* Tamlaghtfinlagan w Myroe *D & R*

BALLYLESSON   *see* Drumbo *D & D*

BALLYMACARRETT (St Patrick) (St Christopher) (St Martin)
   D & D   **I** J J CUNNINGHAM   **NSM** I M FRAZER

BALLYMACASH (St Mark) *Conn*   **I** W G IRWIN
   NSM K W GAMBLE

BALLYMACELLIGOTT (no dedication)   *see* Tralee w Kilmoyley, Ballymacelligott etc *L & K*

BALLYMACHUGH (St Paul)   *see* Kildrumferton w Ballymachugh and Ballyjamesduff *K, E & A*

BALLYMACKEY (St Michael)   *see* Nenagh *L & K*

BALLYMACORMACK (no dedication)   *see* Templemichael w Clongish, Clooncumber etc *K, E & A*

BALLYMAGLASSON   *see* Dunboyne and Rathmolyon *M & K*

BALLYMAHON   *see* Ardagh w Tashinny, Shrule and Kilcommick *K, E & A*

BALLYMARTLE (no dedication)   *see* Kinsale Union *C, C & R*

BALLYMASCANLAN (St Mary) w Creggan and Rathcor *Arm*
   NSM R W R MOORE

BALLYMENA (St Patrick) w Ballyclug *Conn*   **I** S G E LLOYD
   C I B JAMIESON, J MCCLURE

BALLYMONEY   *see* Kinneigh Union *C, C & R*

BALLYMONEY (St Patrick) w Finvoy and Rasharkin *Conn*
   I A J SWEENEY   **NSM** B M HOWE

BALLYMORE   *see* Clondehorkey w Cashel *D & R*

BALLYMORE (St Mark) *Arm*   **I** T S FORSTER   **C** G B SPENCE

BALLYMORE EUSTACE (St John)   *see* Blessington w Kilbride, Ballymore Eustace etc *D & G*

BALLYMOTE   *see* Ballisodare w Collooney and Emlaghfad *T, K & A*

BALLYMOYER (St Luke)   *see* Newtownhamilton w Ballymoyer and Belleck *Arm*

BALLYNAFEIGH (St Jude) *D & D*   **I** N JARDINE

BALLYNAHINCH   *see* Magheradroll *D & D*

BALLYNAKILL (St Thomas)   *see* Omey w Ballynakill, Errislannan and Roundstone *T, K & A*

BALLYNASCREEN   *see* Kilcronaghan w Draperstown and Sixtowns *D & R*

BALLYNURE (Ascension)   *see* Baltinglass w Ballynure etc *C & O*

BALLYNURE (Christ Church) and Ballyeaston *Conn*
   I R M MCCONNELL

BALLYRASHANE (St John the Baptist) w Kildollagh *Conn*
   I A E ADAMS

BALLYROAN (no dedication)   *see* Abbeyleix w Ballyroan etc *C & O*

BALLYSALLY (St Andrew)   *see* Coleraine *Conn*

BALLYSCULLION (no dedication)   *see* Drummaul w Duneane and Ballyscullion *Conn*

BALLYSCULLION (St Tida) *D & R*   **P-in-c** E R LAVERY

BALLYSEEDY (no dedication)   *see* Tralee w Kilmoyley, Ballymacelligott etc *L & K*

BALLYSHANNON   *see* Kilbarron w Rossnowlagh and Drumholm *D & R*

BALLYSILLAN   *see* Belfast St Mark *Conn*

BALLYSUMAGHAN (no dedication)   *see* Taunagh w Kilmactranny, Ballysumaghan etc *K, E & A*

BALLYWALTER (Holy Trinity) w Inishargie *D & D*   **I** S C BELL

BALLYWARD   *see* Drumgath w Drumgooland and Clonduff *D & D*

BALLYWILLAN (Holy Trinity) *Conn*   **I** P K MCDOWELL
   NSM R J SIMPSON

BALRATHBOYNE   *see* Kells Union *M & K*

BALTEAGH (St Canice) w Carrick *D & R*   **I** D H J FERRY

BALTIMORE   *see* Abbeystrewry Union *C, C & R*

BALTINGLASS (St Mary) w Ballynure, Stratford-on-Slaney and Rathvilly *C & O*   **I** M J WHALE

BANAGHER (St Moresuis)   *see* Cumber Lower w Banagher *D & R*

BANAGHER (St Paul)   *see* Clonfert Gp *L & K*

BANBRIDGE   *see* Seapatrick *D & D*

BANDON (St Peter) w Rathclaren, Innishannon, Ballinadee and Brinny *C, C & R*   **I** D F A MACCARTHY   **C** D WHITE
   NSM E C M FERGUSON

BANGOR (St Columbanus)   *see* Ballyholme *D & D*

BANGOR (St Comgall) *D & D*   **I** N H PARKER

BANGOR ABBEY (Bangor Abbey) *D & D*   **I** R NESBITT
   C A P CAMPBELL, J W CHESHIRE

BANGOR Primacy (Christ Church) *D & D*
   Bp's C F G RUTLEDGE

BANNOW (no dedication)   *see* Taghmon w Horetown and Bannow *C & O*

BANTRY   *see* Kilmocomogue *C, C & R*

BARONSCOURT (no dedication)   *see* Ardstraw w Baronscourt, Badoney Lower etc *D & R*

BARR (no dedication)   *see* Donacavey w Barr *Clogh*

BEARA (St Peter)   *see* Kilmocomogue *C, C & R*

BECTIVE   *see* Trim and Athboy Gp *M & K*

BELFAST (All Saints) *Conn*   I T S JOHNSTON

BELFAST (Cathedral of St Anne) *Conn*   I J O MANN
   NSM J M ELSDON

BELFAST (Holy Trinity) (St Silas) *Conn*   I R M M CREIGHTON

BELFAST (St Aidan) *Conn*   **P-in-c** R MOORE

BELFAST (St Andrew) *Conn*   **NSM** S K HOUSTON

BELFAST (St Bartholomew) *Conn*   I T K D GRAHAM

BELFAST (St Brendan) *D & D*   **P-in-c** I M CRUICKSHANK
   C J HARRIS

BELFAST (St Christopher)   *see* Ballymacarrett *D & D*

BELFAST (St Donard) *D & D*   I K H HIGGINS
   NSM S P HOOPER

BELFAST (St George) *Conn*   I B STEWART

BELFAST (St Jude)   *see* Ballynafeigh St Jude *D & D*

BELFAST (St Katharine) *Conn*   I W J TAGGART

BELFAST (St Mark) *Conn*   I R H MOORE

BELFAST (St Martin)   *see* Ballymacarrett *D & D*

BELFAST (St Mary Magdalene) *Conn*   **NSM** R E COTTER

BELFAST (St Mary) (Holy Redeemer) *Conn*
   P-in-c R H MOORE

BELFAST (St Matthew) *Conn*   I T MCROBERTS

BELFAST (St Nicholas) *Conn*   I E HANNA

BELFAST (St Patrick)   *see* Ballymacarrett *D & D*

BELFAST (St Peter) (St James) *Conn*   I C B LACEY

BELFAST (St Simon) (St Philip) *Conn*   **P-in-c** R MOORE

BELFAST (St Thomas) *Conn*   I P JACK

BELFAST Malone (St John) *Conn*   I R W JONES   C R SMYTH

BELFAST Titanic Quarter *D & D*   **Bp's C** C I BENNETT

BELFAST Upper Falls (St John the Baptist) *Conn*
   NSM M A REID

BELLAGHY   *see* Ballyscullion *D & R*

BELLEEK (no dedication)   *see* Garrison w Slavin and Belleek *Clogh*

BELLEEK (St Luke)   *see* Newtownhamilton w Ballymoyer and Belleck *Arm*

BELLERENA   *see* Tamlaghtard w Aghanloo *D & R*

BELMONT (St Peter)   *see* Londonderry Ch Ch, Culmore, Muff and Belmont *D & R*

BELTURBET   *see* Annagh w Drumaloor, Cloverhill and Drumlane *K, E & A*

BELVOIR (Transfiguration) *D & D*   I T KEIGHTLEY
   C A A MCCARTNEY, J MOULD

BENOWN (no dedication)   *see* Athlone w Benown, Kiltoom and Forgney *M & K*

BILBOA (no dedication)   *see* Castlecomer w Colliery Ch, Mothel and Bilboa *C & O*

BILLIS (no dedication)   *see* Lurgan w Billis, Killinkere and Munterconnaught *K, E & A*

BILLY (no dedication) w Derrykeighan *Conn*
   I J R ANDERSON

BIRR (St Brendan) w Eglish, Lorrha, Dorrha and Lockeen *L & K*   I R W CARNEY   **NSM** R M GILL

BLACKLION   *see* Killinagh w Kiltyclogher and Innismagrath *K, E & A*

BLACKROCK (All Saints)   *see* Stillorgan w Blackrock *D & G*

BLACKROCK (St Michael)   *see* Douglas Union w Frankfield *C, C & R*

BLARNEY   *see* Carrigrohane Union *C, C & R*

BLESSINGTON (St Mary) w Kilbride, Ballymore Eustace and Holywood *D & G*   I L W RUDDOCK

BOHO (no dedication)   *see* Devenish w Boho *Clogh*

BOOTERSTOWN (St Philip and St James)   *see* Dublin Booterstown *D & G*

BORNACOOLA   *see* Templemichael w Clongish, Clooncumber etc *K, E & A*

BORRIS Clonagoose   *see* Leighlin w Grange Sylvae, Shankill etc *C & O*

BORRIS Littleton   *see* Kilcooley w Littleon, Crohane and Fertagh *C & O*

BORRIS-IN-OSSORY (no dedication)   *see* Clonenagh w Offerlane, Borris-in-Ossory etc *C & O*

BORRISNAFARNEY (no dedication)   *see* Cloughjordan w Borrisokane etc *L & K*

BORRISOKANE (no dedication) *as above*

BOURNEY (St Burchin)   *see* Roscrea w Kyle, Bourney and Corbally *L & K*

BOVEVAGH (St Eugenius)   *see* Dungiven w Bovevagh *D & R*

BOYLE (no dedication) and Elphin w Aghanagh, Kilbryan, Ardcarne and Croghan *K, E & A*   I R S J BOURKE

BRACKAVILLE (Holy Trinity) w Donaghendry and Ballyclog *Arm*   I A RAWDING

BRANTRY (Holy Trinity)   *see* Caledon w Brantry *Arm*

BRAY (Christ Church) *D & G*   I B T STANLEY

BRIGOWN (St George)   *see* Fermoy Union *C, C & R*

BRINNY (no dedication)   *see* Bandon Union *C, C & R*

BROOKEBOROUGH   *see* Aghavea *Clogh*

BROOMHEDGE (St Matthew) *Conn*   I P J GALBRAITH

BROUGHSHANE   *see* Skerry w Rathcavan and Newtowncrommelin *Conn*

BRYANSFORD   *see* Castlewellan w Kilcoo *D & D*

BUNBEG   *see* Gweedore, Carrickfin and Templecrone *D & R*

BUNCLODY (St Mary) w Kildavin, Clonegal and Kilrush *C & O*   I M R N STEVENSON

BUNCRANA   *see* Fahan Lower and Upper *D & R*

BUNDORAN   *see* Cloonclare w Killasnett, Lurganboy and Drumlease *K, E & A*

BUSH   *see* Ballymascanlan w Creggan and Rathcor *Arm*

BUSHMILLS   *see* Dunluce *Conn*

CAHERAGH (St Mary)   *see* Abbeystrewry Union *C, C & R*

CAHERCONLISH (St Ailbe)   *see* Adare and Kilmallock w Kilpeacon, Croom etc *L & K*

CAHIR (St Paul)   *see* Clonmel w Innislounagh, Tullaghmelan etc *C & O*

CAIRNCASTLE (St Patrick)   *see* Kilwaughter w Cairncastle and Craigy Hill *Conn*

CALARY (no dedication)   *see* Newcastle w Newtownmountkennedy and Calary *D & G*

CALRY (no dedication) *K, E & A*   I P H BAMBER

CAMLOUGH (Christ the Redeemer) w Mullaglass *Arm*
   C W J MCCRACKEN

CAMP   *see* Dingle w Killiney and Kilgobbin *L & K*

CAMUS-JUXTA-BANN (St Mary) *D & R*   I M P ROEMMELE

CAMUS-JUXTA-MOURNE (Christ Church) *D & R*
   C M R W LENNOX

CAPPAGH (St Eugene) w Lislimnaghan *D & R*   I D J QUINN

CAPPOQUIN (St Anne)   *see* Lismore w Cappoquin, Kilwatermoy, Dungarvan etc *C & O*

CARBURY (no dedication)   *see* Clonsast w Rathangan, Thomastown etc *M & K*

CARLOW (St Mary) w Urglin and Staplestown *C & O*
   I O H WILLIAMS

CARNALEA (St Gall) *D & D*   I M A PARKER

CARNALWAY (St Patrick)   *see* Newbridge w Carnalway and Kilcullen *M & K*

CARNDONAGH   *see* Moville w Greencastle, Donagh, Cloncha etc *D & R*

CARNEW (All Saints)   *see* Crosspatrick Gp *C & O*

CARNLOUGH   *see* Ardclinis and Tickmacrevan w Layde and Cushendun *Conn*

CARNMONEY (Holy Evangelists) *Conn*   I M A MALCOLM
   NSM C R HARVEY

CARNTEEL (St James) and Crilly *Arm*   I E R G WEST

CARRICK (no dedication)   *see* Balteagh w Carrick *D & R*

CARRICKFERGUS (St Nicholas) *Conn*   I G T W DAVISON
   C C C W JONES

CARRICKFIN (St Andrew)   *see* Gweedore, Carrickfin and Templecrone *D & R*

CARRICKMACROSS (St Fin Barre) w Magheracloone *Clogh*
   NSM M B PRINGLE

CARRICK-ON-SHANNON   *see* Kiltoghart w Drumshambo, Annaduff and Kilronan *K, E & A*

CARRIGALINE (St Mary) w Killanully and Monkstown *C, C & R*   I E M E MURRAY   **NSM** A M MURPHY, H E A MINION

CARRIGALLEN (no dedication)   *see* Arvagh w Carrigallen, Gowna and Columbkille *K, E & A*

CARRIGANS   *see* Taughboyne, Craigadooish, Newtowncunningham etc *D & R*

CARRIGART   *see* Mevagh w Glenalla *D & R*

CARRIGROHANE (St Peter) w Garrycloyne, Inniscarra and Magourney *C, C & R*   I I R JONAS   C R J FERRIS

CARRIGTWOHILL (St David)   *see* Rathcooney Union *C, C & R*

CARROWDORE (Christ Church) w Millisle *D & D*
   I C A J DAVIS

CARRYDUFF (St Ignatius)   *see* Killaney w Carryduff *D & D*

CASHEL (Cathedral of St John the Baptist) w Magorban, Tipperary, Clonbeg and Ballintemple *C & O*   I G G FIELD

CASHEL (no dedication)   *see* Clonderhorkey w Cashel *D & R*

CASTLEARCHDALE (St Patrick)   *see* Derryvullen N w Castlearchdale *Clogh*

CASTLEBAR (Christ Church)   *see* Aughaval w Achill, Knappagh, Dugort etc *T, K & A*

CASTLEBLAYNEY   *see* Ballybay w Mucknoe and Clontibret *Clogh*

CASTLECOMER (St Mary) w the Colliery Church, Mothel and Bilboa *C & O*   **I** P BURKE

CASTLECONNELL   *see* Killaloe w Stradbally *L & K*

CASTLECONNOR (no dedication)   *see* Killala w Dunfeeny, Crossmolina, Kilmoremoy etc *T, K & A*

CASTLEDAWSON (Christ Church) *D & R*   **I** C R J WELSH

CASTLEDERG   *see* Derg w Termonamongan *D & R*

CASTLEDERMOT (St James)   *see* Narraghmore and Timolin w Castledermot etc *D & G*

CASTLEFLEMING (no dedication)   *see* Rathdowney w Castlefleming, Donaghmore etc *C & O*

CASTLEGREGORY   *see* Dingle w Killiney and Kilgobbin *L & K*

CASTLEHAVEN (no dedication)   *see* Abbeystrewry Union *C, C & R*

CASTLEKNOCK (St Brigid) and Mulhuddart w Clonsilla *D & G*   **I** W P HOUSTON   **C** E T GRIFFIN

CASTLELOST   *see* Mullingar, Portnashangan, Moyliscar, Kilbixy etc *M & K*

CASTLEMACADAM (Holy Trinity) w Ballinaclash, Aughrim and Macreddin *D & G*   **I** G W BUTLER

CASTLEMAINE   *see* Kilcolman w Kiltallagh, Killorglin, Knockane etc *L & K*

CASTLEMARTYR (St Anne)   *see* Youghal Union *C, C & R*

CASTLEPOLLARD (St Michael) and Oldcastle w Loughcrew, Mount Nugent, Mayne and Drumcree *M & K*   **I** D G O'CATHAIN

CASTLEREA   *see* Roscommon w Donamon, Rathcline, Kilkeevin etc *K, E & A*

CASTLERICKARD   *see* Dunboyne and Rathmolyon *M & K*

CASTLEROCK (Christ Church) w Dunboe and Fermoyle *D & R*   **I** D M MATCHETT   **NSM** A QUIGLEY

CASTLETERRA (no dedication)   *see* Drung w Castleterra, Larah and Lavey etc *K, E & A*

CASTLETOWN   *see* Killeshin w Cloydagh and Killabban *C & O*

CASTLETOWN   *see* Rathkeale w Askeaton, Kilcornan and Kilnaughtin *L & K*

CASTLETOWN   *see* Kells Union *M & K*

CASTLETOWNBERE (St Peter)   *see* Kilmocomogue *C, C & R*

CASTLETOWNROCHE (no dedication)   *see* Mallow Union *C, C & R*

CASTLETOWNSEND   *see* Abbeystrewry Union *C, C & R*

CASTLEVENTRY (no dedication)   *see* Ross Union *C, C & R*

CASTLEWELLAN (St Paul) w Kilcoo *D & D*   **I** B S CADDEN

CAVAN   *see* Urney w Denn and Derryheen *K, E & A*

CELBRIDGE (Christ Church) w Straffan and Newcastle-Lyons *D & G*   **I** S M NEILL

CHAPELIZOD (St Laurence)   *see* Dublin Crumlin w Chapelizod *D & G*

CHARLEMONT (no dedication)   *see* Moy w Charlemont *Arm*

CLABBY (St Margaret)   *see* Tempo and Clabby *Clogh*

CLANABOGAN (no dedication)   *see* Edenderry w Clanabogan *D & R*

CLARE (no dedication)   *see* Loughgilly w Clare *Arm*

CLAUDY   *see* Cumber Upper w Learmount *D & R*

CLEENISH (no dedication) w Mullaghdun *Clogh*   **I** G P BRIDLE

CLIFDEN   *see* Omey w Ballynakill, Errislannan and Roundstone *T, K & A*

CLOGH (Holy Trinity)   *see* Aghadrumsee w Clogh and Drumsnatt *Clogh*

CLOGHER (Cathedral of St Macartan) w Errigal Portclare *Clogh*   **I** N H L REGAN

CLOGHERNY (St Patrick) w Seskinore and Drumnakilly *Arm*   **R** A J HEBER

CLONAGOOSE (St Moling)   *see* Leighlin w Grange Sylvae, Shankill etc *C & O*

CLONAKILTY   *see* Kilgariffe Union *C, C & R*

CLONALLON (no dedication) and Warrenpoint w Kilbroney *D & D*   **I** C J MCCORMACK

CLONARD   *see* Mullingar, Portnashangan, Moyliscar, Kilbixy etc *M & K*

CLONASLEE   *see* Mountmellick w Coolbanagher, Rosenallis etc *M & K*

CLONBEG (St Sedna)   *see* Cashel w Magorban, Tipperary, Clonbeg etc *C & O*

CLONBRONEY (St John)   *see* Mostrim w Granard, Clonbroney, Killoe etc *K, E & A*

CLONBULLOGUE   *see* Clonsast w Rathangan, Thomastown etc *M & K*

CLONCHA (no dedication)   *see* Moville w Greencastle, Donagh, Cloncha etc *D & R*

CLONDALKIN (St John) w Rathcoole *D & G*   **I** A J RUFLI   **NSM** A A SHINE, O BOOTHMAN

CLONDEHORKEY (St John) w Cashel *D & R*   **I** C D PIERCE

CLONDEVADDOCK (Christ the Redeemer) w Portsalon and Leatbeg *D & R*   **P-in-c** D P HOEY

CLONDUFF (St John)   *see* Drumgath w Drumgooland and Clonduff *D & D*

CLONE (St Paul)   *see* Enniscorthy w Clone, Clonmore, Monart etc *C & O*

CLONEGAL (no dedication)   *see* Bunclody w Kildavin, Clonegal and Kilrush *C & O*

CLONEGAM (Holy Trinity)   *see* Fiddown w Clonegam, Guilcagh and Kilmeaden *C & O*

CLONENAGH (no dedication) w Offerlane, Borris-in-Ossory, Seirkieran and Roskelton *C & O*   **I** I P POULTON

CLONES (St Tighernach) w Killeevan *Clogh*   **I** H STEED

CLONEYHURKE (no dedication)   *see* Portarlington w Cloneyhurke, Lea etc *M & K*

CLONFADFORAN   *see* Tullamore w Durrow, Newtownfertullagh, Rahan etc *M & K*

CLONFEACLE (St Patrick) w Derrygortreavy *Arm*   **I** J R MCLOUGHLIN

CLONGISH (St Paul)   *see* Templemichael w Clongish, Clooncumber etc *K, E & A*

CLONLARA   *see* Killaloe w Stradbally *L & K*

CLONLEIGH (St Lugadius)   *see* Raphoe w Raymochy and Clonleigh *D & R*

CLONMACNOISE (St Kieran)   *see* Clara w Liss, Moate and Clonmacnoise *M & K*

CLONMEL (St Mary) w Innislounagh, Tullaghmelan, Fethard, Kilvemnon and Cahir *C & O*   **I** B Y FRYDAY   **C** A E CARTER

CLONMELLON   *see* Trim and Athboy Gp *M & K*

CLONMORE (St John)   *see* Enniscorthy w Clone, Clonmore, Monart etc *C & O*

CLONMORE (St John)   *see* Kiltegan w Hacketstown, Clonmore and Moyne *C & O*

CLONOE (St Michael)   *see* Tullaniskin w Clonoe *Arm*

CLONSAST (no dedication) w Rathangan, Thomastown, Monasteroris, Carbury and Rahan *M & K*   **I** L E A PEILOW   **C** M O'KELLY

CLONSILLA (St Mary)   *see* Castleknock and Mulhuddart w Clonsilla *D & G*

CLONTARF   *see* Dublin Clontarf *D & G*

CLONTIBRET (St Colman)   *see* Ballybay w Mucknoe and Clontibret *Clogh*

CLONTUSKERT (St Matthew)   *see* Aughrim w Ballinasloe etc *L & K*

CLOONCLARE (no dedication) w Killasnett, Lurganboy and Drumlease *K, E & A*   **P-in-c** B M MCCARTHY

CLOONCUMBER (no dedication)   *see* Templemichael w Clongish, Clooncumber etc *K, E & A*

CLOONEY (All Saints) w Strathfoyle *D & R*   **I** D R MCBETH   **NSM** M T E PEOPLES

CLOUGH   *see* Craigs w Dunaghy and Killagan *Conn*

CLOUGHFERN (Ascension) *Conn*   **I** D LOCKHART   **C** A E STEWART

CLOUGHMILLS   *see* Craigs w Dunaghy and Killagan *Conn*

CLOVERHILL (St John)   *see* Annagh w Drumaloor, Cloverhill and Drumlane *K, E & A*

CLOYDAGH (no dedication)   *see* Killeshin w Cloydagh and Killabban *C & O*

CLOYNE (Cathedral of St Colman) w Inch, Corkbeg, Midleton and Gurranekennefeake *C, C & R*   **I** A G MARLEY

COACHFORD   *see* Carrigrohane Union *C, C & R*

COALISLAND   *see* Brackaville w Donaghendry and Ballyclog *Arm*

COBH   *see* Clonmel Union *C, C & R*

COLAGHTY   *see* Lack *Clogh*

COLEBROOK   *see* Aghalurcher w Tattykeeran, Cooneen etc *Clogh*

COLERAINE   *see* Killowen *D & R*

COLERAINE (St Patrick) *Conn*   **I** R COOKE

COLIN (St Andrew)   *see* Derriaghy w Colin *Conn*

COLLIERY CHURCH, THE   *see* Castlecomer w Colliery Ch, Mothel and Bilboa *C & O*

COLLON (no dedication)   *see* Drogheda w Ardee, Collon and Termonfeckin *Arm*

COLLOONEY (St Paul)   *see* Ballisodare w Collooney and Emlaghfad *T, K & A*

COLPE (St Columba)   *see* Julianstown and Colpe w Drogheda and Duleek *M & K*

COLUMBKILLE (St Thomas)   *see* Arvagh w Carrigallen, Gowna and Columbkille *K, E & A*

COMBER (St Mary) *D & D*   **I** J P O BARRY   **NSM** W M N JAMISON

COMERAGH   *see* Lismore w Cappoquin, Kilwatermoy, Dungarvan etc *C & O*

CONARY (St Bartholomew)   *see* Dunganstown w Redcross and Conary *D & G*
CONG (St Mary)   *see* Tuam w Cong and Aasleagh *T, K & A*
CONNOR (St Saviour) w Antrim St Patrick *Conn*
    I I W MAGOWAN
CONVOY (St Ninian) w Monellan and Donaghmore *D & R*
    I W T LONG
CONWAL (no dedication) w Aughanunshin and Gartan *D & R*   **I** W C S WRIGHT
COOKSTOWN   *see* Derryloran *Arm*
COOLBANAGHER (St John)   *see* Mountmellick w Coolbanagher, Rosenallis etc *M & K*
COOLCARRIGAN (no dedication)   *see* Clane w Donadea and Coolcarrigan *M & K*
COOLKELLURE (St Edmund)   *see* Fanlobbus Union *C, C & R*
COOLOCK (St John)   *see* Raheny w Coolock *D & G*
COONEEN (no dedication)   *see* Aghalurcher w Tattykeeran, Cooneen etc *Clogh*
COOTEHILL   *see* Drumgoon *K, E & A*
CORACLONE (St Peter)   *see* Stradbally w Ballintubbert, Coraclone etc *C & O*
CORBALLY (Christ Church)   *see* Roscrea w Kyle, Bourney and Corbally *L & K*
CORK (Cathedral of St Fin Barre) (St Nicholas) *C, C & R*
    I N K DUNNE   **NSM** E W HUNTER
CORK (St Ann) Shandon w St Mary *C, C & R*
    P-in-c S L MARRY
CORKBEG (St Michael and All Angels)   *see* Cloyne Union *C, C & R*
CORRAWALLEN (no dedication)   *see* Kildallon and Swanlinbar *K, E & A*
COURTMACSHERRY (St John the Evangelist)   *see* Kilgariffe Union *C, C & R*
CRAIGADOOISH (no dedication)   *see* Taughboyne, Craigadooish, Newtowncunningham etc *D & R*
CRAIGAVAD   *see* Glencraig *D & D*
CRAIGAVON (St Saviour)   *see* Ardmore w Craigavon *D & D*
CRAIGS (no dedication) w Dunaghy and Killagan *Conn*
    I W R G WILLANS   **NSM** T S KELLY
CRAIGY HILL (All Saints)   *see* Kilwaughter w Cairncastle and Craigy Hill *Conn*
CREAGH   *see* Abbeystrewry Union *C, C & R*
CREAGH   *see* Aughrim w Ballinasloe etc *L & K*
CRECORA   *see* Adare and Kilmallock w Kilpeacon, Croom etc *L & K*
CREGAGH (St Finnian) *D & D*   **I** J D M PIERCE   **C** C DARLING
CREGGAN (no dedication)   *see* Ballymascanlan w Creggan and Rathcor *Arm*
CRILLY (St George)   *see* Carnteel and Crilly *Arm*
CRINKEN (St James) *D & G*   **I** T D STEVENSON
CROGHAN (Holy Trinity)   *see* Boyle and Elphin w Aghanagh, Kilbryan etc *K, E & A*
CROHANE (no dedication)   *see* Kilcooley w Littleon, Crohane and Fertagh *C & O*
CROM (Holy Trinity)   *see* Kinawley w H Trin *K, E & A*
CROOKHAVEN (St Brendan)   *see* Kilmoe Union *C, C & R*
CROOM (no dedication)   *see* Adare and Kilmallock w Kilpeacon, Croom etc *L & K*
CROSSGAR   *see* Kilmore and Inch *D & D*
CROSSHAVEN   *see* Templebreedy w Tracton and Nohoval *C, C & R*
CROSSMOLINA (no dedication)   *see* Killala w Dunfeeny, Crossmolina, Kilmoremoy etc *T, K & A*
CROSSPATRICK Group (no dedication) w Kilcommon, Kilpipe, Preban and Carnew, The *C & O*   **I** R K ELMES
CRUMLIN   *see* Dublin Crumlin w Chapelizod *D & G*
CRUMLIN (St John)   *see* Glenavy w Tunny and Crumlin *Conn*
CRUMLIN ROAD   *see* Belfast St Mary w H Redeemer *Conn*
CULDAFF (no dedication)   *see* Moville w Greencastle, Donagh, Cloncha etc *D & R*
CULFEIGHTRIN (no dedication)   *see* Ramoan w Ballycastle and Culfeightrin *Conn*
CULLYBACKEY   *see* Craigs w Dunaghy and Killagan *Conn*
CULMORE (Holy Trinity)   *see* Londonderry Ch Ch, Culmore, Muff and Belmont *D & R*
CUMBER UPPER (no dedication) w Learmount *D & R*
    I J R D SLATER
CURRAGH (Garrison Church of St Paul)   *see* Kildare w Kilmeague and Curragh *M & K*
CUSHENDALL   *see* Ardclinis and Tickmacrevan w Layde and Cushendun *Conn*
CUSHENDUN (no dedication) *as above*
DALKEY (St Patrick) *D & G*   **I** B J HAYES
DARTREY   *see* Ematris w Rockcorry, Aghabog and Aughnamullan *Clogh*

DELGANY (Christ Church) *D & G*   **I** N J W WAUGH
    NSM H E A LEW
DENN (no dedication)   *see* Urney w Denn and Derryheen *K, E & A*
DERG (no dedication) w Termonamongan *D & R*
    I P A FERGUSON   **C** N QUINN
DERNAKESH (Chapel of Ease)   *see* Drumgoon *K, E & A*
DERRALOSSARY   *see* Rathdrum w Glenealy, Derralossary and Laragh *D & G*
DERRIAGHY (Christ Church) w Colin *Conn*   **I** J C BUDD
DERRYBRUSK (St Michael)   *see* Maguiresbridge w Derrybrusk *Clogh*
DERRYGONNELLY   *see* Inishmacsaint *Clogh*
DERRYGORTREAVY (St Columba)   *see* Clonfeacle w Derrygortreavy *Arm*
DERRYHEEN (no dedication)   *see* Urney w Denn and Derryheen *K, E & A*
DERRYKIGHAN (St Colman)   *see* Billy w Derrykeighan *Conn*
DERRYLANE (no dedication)   *see* Killeshandra w Killegar and Derrylane *K, E & A*
DERRYLIN   *see* Kinawley w H Trin *K, E & A*
DERRYLORAN (St Luran) *Arm*   **I** R J N PORTEUS
    NSM W J A DAWSON
DERRYNOOSE (St John)   *see* Keady w Armaghbreague and Derrynoose *Arm*
DERRYVOLGIE (St Columba) *Conn*   **I** R S MCELHINNEY
DERRYVULLEN SOUTH (St Tighernach) w Garvary *Clogh*
    I J W STEWART
DERVOCK   *see* Billy w Derrykeighan *Conn*
DESERTCREAT (no dedication)   *see* Ardtrea w Desertcreat *Arm*
DESERTLYN (St John) w Ballyeglish *Arm*   **I** A N STRINGER
DESERTMARTIN (St Conghall) w Termoneeny *D & R*
    I M P DORNAN
DESERTOGHILL (no dedication)   *see* Errigal w Garvagh *D & R*
DESERTSERGES (no dedication)   *see* Kinneigh Union *C, C & R*
DEVENISH (St Molaise) w Boho *Clogh*   **Bp's C** S C AJUKA
DIAMOND (St Paul)   *see* Tartaraghan w Diamond *Arm*
DOAGH   *see* Kilbride *Conn*
DOLLINGSTOWN (St Saviour)   *see* Magheralin w Dollingstown *D & D*
DONABATE (St Patrick)   *see* Swords w Donabate and Kilsallaghan *D & G*
DONADEA (St Peter)   *see* Clane w Donadea and Coolcarrigan *M & K*
DONAGH (no dedication)   *see* Moville w Greencastle, Donagh, Cloncha etc *D & R*
DONAGH (St Salvator) w Tyholland and Errigal Truagh *Clogh*
    NSM E G MCM THOMPSON
DONAGHADEE (no dedication) *D & D*   **R** I R GAMBLE
DONAGHCLONEY (St Patrick) w Waringstown *D & D*
    I B R MARTIN   **C** A THOMPSON
DONAGHEADY (St James) *D & R*   **I** R P STOCKITT
DONAGHENDRY (St Patrick)   *see* Brackaville w Donaghendry and Ballyclog *Arm*
DONAGHMORE (no dedication)   *see* Rathdowney w Castlefleming, Donaghmore etc *C & O*
DONAGHMORE (St Bartholomew)   *see* Aghaderg w Donaghmore and Scarva *D & D*
DONAGHMORE (St Michael) w Upper Donaghmore *Arm*
    I P A THOMPSON
DONAGHMORE (St Patrick)   *see* Convoy w Monellan and Donaghmore *D & R*
DONAGHMORE, UPPER (St Patrick)   *see* Donaghmore w Upper Donaghmore *Arm*
DONAGHPATRICK (St Patrick)   *see* Kells Union *M & K*
DONAMON (no dedication)   *see* Roscommon w Donamon, Rathcline, Kilkeevin etc *K, E & A*
DONANAUGHTA (St John the Baptist)   *see* Clonfert Gp *L & K*
DONARD (no dedication)   *see* Donoughmore and Donard w Dunlavin *D & G*
DONEGAL (no dedication) w Killymard, Lough Eske and Laghey *D & R*   **I** D I HUSS
DONEGORE (St John)   *see* Templepatrick w Donegore *Conn*
DONEMANA   *see* Donagheady *D & R*
DONERAILE (St Mary)   *see* Mallow Union *C, C & R*
DONNYBROOK (St Mary)   *see* Dublin Irishtown w Donnybrook *D & G*
DORRHA (no dedication)   *see* Birr w Lorrha, Dorrha and Lockeen *L & K*
DOUGLAS (St Luke) w Blackrock, Frankfield and Marmullane *C, C & R*   **I** A M WILKINSON   **C** D G D BOWLES
    NSM P T HANNA
DOWN (St Margaret) w Hollymount *D & D*   **I** S S BURNS
DOWNPATRICK   *see* Down Cathl *D & D*
DRAPERSTOWN (St Columb)   *see* Kilcronaghan w Draperstown and Sixtowns *D & R*

DREW MEMORIAL   *see* Belfast St Simon w St Phil *Conn*
DRIMOLEAGUE (St Matthew)   *see* Fanlobbus Union *C, C & R*
DRINAGH (Christ Church) *as above*
DROGHEDA (St Mary)   *see* Julianstown and Colpe w Drogheda and Duleek *M & K*
DROGHEDA (St Peter) w Ardee, Collon and Termonfeckin
Arm   **I** M GRAHAM   **NSM** J MOORE
DROMAHAIR   *see* Cloonclare w Killasnett, Lurganboy and Drumlease *K, E & A*
DROMARD (Christ Church)   *see* Skreen w Kilmacshalgan and Dromard *T, K & A*
DROMOD (St Michael and All Angels)   *see* Kenmare w Sneem, Waterville etc *L & K*
DROMORE (Cathedral of Christ the Redeemer) *D & D*
I B T KERR   **NSM** T J MCKEOWN
DROMORE (Holy Trinity) *Clogh*   **I** W J BOYD
DRUM (no dedication)   *see* Currin w Drum and Newbliss *Clogh*
DRUMACHOSE (Christ Church) *D & R*   **I** S MCVEIGH
DRUMALOOR (St Andrew)   *see* Annagh w Drumaloor, Cloverhill and Drumlane *K, E & A*
DRUMANY (Christ Church)   *see* Kinawley w H Trin *K, E & A*
DRUMBANAGHER (St Mary)   *see* Acton and Drumbanagher *Arm*
DRUMBEG (St Patrick) *D & D*   **I** W S NIXON
DRUMBO (Holy Trinity) *D & D*   **I** R C NEILL
DRUMCANNON (Christ Church)   *see* Waterford w Killea, Drumcannon and Dunhill *C & O*
DRUMCAR   *see* Kilsaran w Drumcar, Dunleer and Dunany *Arm*
DRUMCLAMPH (no dedication) w Lower Langfield and Upper Langfield *D & R*   **I** R G KEOGH
DRUMCLIFFE (St Columba) w Kilrush, Kilfenora, Kilfarboy, Kilnasoolagh, Shannon and Kilferagh *L & K*   **I** R C HANNA
NSM P E MCKEE HANNA
DRUMCLIFFE (St Columba) w Lissadell and Munninane *K, E & A*   **I** I J HANNA
DRUMCONDRA   *see* Dublin Drumcondra w N Strand *D & G*
DRUMCONRATH (St Peter)   *see* Kingscourt w Syddan *M & K*
DRUMCREE (Ascension) *Arm*   **I** G F GALWAY
DRUMCREE (St John)   *see* Castlepollard and Oldcastle w Loughcrew etc *M & K*
DRUMGATH (St John) w Drumgooland and Clonduff *D & D*
I G W MACARTNEY
DRUMGLASS (St Anne) w Moygashel *Arm*   **I** A J FORSTER
C P B JONES   **NSM** M E M STEVENSON
DRUMGOOLAND (no dedication)   *see* Drumgath w Drumgooland and Clonduff *D & D*
DRUMHOLM (no dedication)   *see* Kilbarron w Rossnowlagh and Drumholm *D & R*
DRUMINISKILL (Chapel of Ease)   *see* Killesher *K, E & A*
DRUMKEERAN   *see* Killinagh w Kiltyclogher and Innismagrath *K, E & A*
DRUMKEERAN (no dedication) w Templecarne and Muckross *Clogh*   **P-in-c** C T PRINGLE
DRUMLANE (no dedication)   *see* Annagh w Drumaloor, Cloverhill and Drumlane *K, E & A*
DRUMLEASE (no dedication)   *see* Cloonclare w Killasnett, Lurganboy and Drumlease *K, E & A*
DRUMMAUL (St Brigid) w Duneane and Ballyscullion *Conn*   **I** D P KERR
DRUMMULLY (no dedication)   *see* Galloon w Drummully and Sallaghy *Clogh*
DRUMNAKILLY (Holy Trinity)   *see* Clogherny w Seskinore and Drumnakilly *Arm*
DRUMQUIN   *see* Drumclamph w Lower and Upper Langfield *D & R*
DRUMRAGH (St Columba) w Mountfield *D & R*
I B I LINTON   **C** L A CAPPER, R J ROBINSON
DRUMREILLY (no dedication)   *see* Mohill w Farnaught, Aughavas, Oughteragh etc *K, E & A*
DRUMSHAMBO (St John)   *see* Kiltoghart w Drumshambo, Annaduff and Kilronan *K, E & A*
DRUMSNATT (St Molua)   *see* Aghadrumsee w Clogh and Drumsnatt *Clogh*
DRUMTALLAGH (no dedication)   *see* Armoy w Loughguile and Drumtullagh *Conn*
DUBLIN (Christ Church Cathedral) Group: (St Andrew) (St Werburgh) (St Michan) and Grangegorman *D & G*
V D A PIERPOINT   **C** A SINES   **NSM** R W LAWSON
DUBLIN (Irish Church Missions) and St Thomas *D & G*
E J COULTER
DUBLIN (St Ann) (St Stephen) *D & G*   **I** D I GILLESPIE
NSM M J O'CONNOR
DUBLIN (St Bartholomew) w Leeson Park *D & G*
I A W MCCROSKERY

DUBLIN (St Catherine and St James) (St Audoen) *D & G*
I M D GARDNER   **C** C S COONEY   **NSM** C E BAKER, M WALLER
DUBLIN (St George and St Thomas) *D & G*
Bp's **C** O C ULOGWARA
DUBLIN (Zion Church) *D & G*   **I** S A FARRELL
DUBLIN Booterstown (St Philip and St James) *D & G*
I G V WHARTON   **NSM** S S HARRIS
DUBLIN Clontarf (St John the Baptist) *D & G*
I E C L ROBINSON
DUBLIN Crumlin (St Mary) w Chapelizod *D & G*
I R E JACKSON
DUBLIN Drumcondra (no dedication) w North Strand *D & G*
I R H BYRNE
DUBLIN Irishtown (St Matthew) w Donnybrook *D & G*
Bp's **C** J B MARCHANT
DUBLIN Mount Merrion (St Thomas) *D & G*
I G V WHARTON
DUBLIN Rathfarnham (no dedication) *D & G*   **I** A GALLIGAN
C R J O'KELLY
DUBLIN Rathmines (Holy Trinity) w Harold's Cross *D & G*
I N G MCENDOO   **TV** R D JONES
DUBLIN Sandford (no dedication) w Milltown *D & G*
I S O GYLES   **NSM** A M O'FARRELL
DUBLIN Sandymount (St John the Evangelist) *D & G*
P-in-c P A BARLOW
DUBLIN Santry (St Pappan) w Glasnevin and Finglas *D & G*
I D W OXLEY
DUBLIN Whitechurch (no dedication) *D & G*
I A H N MCKINLEY   **NSM** P COMERFORD
DUGORT (St Thomas)   *see* Aughaval w Achill, Knappagh, Dugort etc *T, K & A*
DULEEK   *see* Julianstown and Colpe w Drogheda and Duleek *M & K*
DUN LAOGHAIRE (Christ Church) *D & G*
I A BJÖRK OLAFSDOTTIR
DUNAGHY (St James)   *see* Craigs w Dunaghy and Killagan *Conn*
DUNANY   *see* Kilsaran w Drumcar, Dunleer and Dunany *Arm*
DUNBOE (St Paul)   *see* Castlerock w Dunboe and Fermoyle *D & R*
DUNBOYNE (St Peter and St Paul) w Rathmolyon, Dunshaughlin, Maynooth, Agher and Rathcore *M & K*
I J H AITON   **C** C A MCCONAGHIE   **NSM** A V STEWART
DUNDALK (St Nicholas) w Heynestown *Arm*
NSM R W R MOORE
DUNDELA (St Mark) *D & D*   **I** A T W DORRIAN
C L M GIBSON
DUNDONALD (St Elizabeth) *D & D*   **I** T G ANDERSON
C P C BOURKE
DUNDRUM   *see* Cashel w Magorban, Tipperary, Clonbeg etc *C & O*
DUNDRUM (St Donard)   *see* Kilmegan w Maghera *D & D*
DUNEANE (no dedication)   *see* Drummaul w Duneane and Ballyscullion *Conn*
DUNFANAGHY (Holy Trinity), Raymunterdoney and Tullaghbegley *D & R*   **I** D A MACDONNELL
DUNFEENY (no dedication)   *see* Killala w Dunfeeny, Crossmolina, Kilmoremoy etc *T, K & A*
DUNGANNON   *see* Drumglass w Moygashel *Arm*
DUNGANSTOWN (St Kevin) w Redcross and Conary *D & G*
I J R HEANEY
DUNGARVAN (St Mary)   *see* Lismore w Cappoquin, Kilwatermoy, Dungarvan etc *C & O*
DUNGIVEN (no dedication) w Bovevagh *D & R*
I M W J LONEY
DUNGLOE   *see* Gweedore, Carrickfin and Templecrone *D & R*
DUNHILL (St John the Baptist)   *see* Waterford w Killea, Drumcannon and Dunhill *C & O*
DUNKERRIN (no dedication)   *see* Shinrone w Aghancon etc *L & K*
DUNLAVIN (St Nicholas)   *see* Donoughmore and Donard w Dunlavin *D & G*
DUNLECKNEY (St Mary) w Nurney, Lorum and Kiltennel *C & O*   **I** K M RONNÉ   **NSM** H M OXLEY
DUNLEER (no dedication)   *see* Kilsaran w Drumcar, Dunleer and Dunany *Arm*
DUNLUCE (St John the Baptist) *Conn*   **I** G E GRAHAM
DUNMANWAY   *see* Fanlobbus Union *C, C & R*
DUNMORE EAST   *see* Waterford w Killea, Drumcannon and Dunhill *C & O*
DUNMURRY (St Colman) *Conn*   **I** A R MCLAUGHLIN
DUNNALONG (St John)   *see* Leckpatrick w Dunnalong *D & R*
DUNSEVERICK (no dedication)   *see* Ballintoy w Rathlin and Dunseverick *Conn*
DUNSFORD (St Mary)   *see* Lecale Gp *D & D*

DUNSHAUGHLIN (St Seachnal)   *see* Dunboyne and
Rathmolyon *M & K*
DURROW (St Columba)   *see* Tullamore w Durrow,
Newtownfertullagh, Rahan etc *M & K*
DURROW (St Fintan)   *see* Abbeyleix w Ballyroan etc *C & O*
DURRUS (St James the Apostle)   *see* Kilmocomogue *C, C & R*
DYSART ENOS (Holy Trinity)   *see* Maryborough w Dysart Enos
and Ballyfin *C & O*
EASKEY (St Anne)   *see* Killala w Dunfeeny, Crossmolina,
Kilmoremoy etc *T, K & A*
EDENDERRY   *see* Clonsast w Rathangan, Thomastown etc
M & K
EDENDERRY (no dedication) w Clanabogan *D & R*
I R W CLARKE
EDGEWORTHSTOWN   *see* Mostrim w Granard, Clonbroney,
Killoe etc *K, E & A*
EGLANTINE (All Saints) *Conn*   I J W KERNOHAN
EGLINTON   *see* Faughanvale *D & R*
EGLISH (Holy Trinity) w Killylea *Arm*   I F W ATKINS
ELPHIN (no dedication)   *see* Boyle and Elphin w Aghanagh,
Kilbryan etc *K, E & A*
**EMATRIS (St John the Evangelist) w Rockcorry, Aghabog and
Aughnamullan** *Clogh*   **NSM** D G BEATTIE
EMLAGHFAD (no dedication)   *see* Ballisodare w Collooney and
Emlaghfad *T, K & A*
ENNIS   *see* Drumcliffe w Kilnasoolagh *L & K*
**ENNISCORTHY (St Mary) w Clone, Clonmore, Monart and
Templescobin** *C & O*   **NSM** R J STOTESBURY
ENNISKEEN   *see* Kingscourt w Syddan *M & K*
ENNISKERRY   *see* Powerscourt w Kilbride *D & G*
ENNISKILLEN   *see* Rossorry *Clogh*
ENNISKILLEN (Cathedral of St Macartin) *Clogh*   I K R J HALL
C O M G DOWNEY, R W CLEMENTS
ENNISNAG (St Peter)   *see* Kells Gp *C & O*
ERRIGAL (St Paul) w Garvagh *D & R*   I K P WHITTAKER
ERRIGAL PORTCLARE (no dedication)   *see* Clogh w Errigal
Portclare *Clogh*
ERRIGAL TRUAGH (St Muadhan)   *see* Donagh w Tyholland and
Errigal Truagh *Clogh*
ERRISLANNNAN (no dedication)   *see* Omey w Ballynakill,
Errislannan and Roundstone *T, K & A*
ESKRAHOOLE (no dedication)   *see* Augher w Newtownsaville
and Eskrahoole *Clogh*
EYRECOURT   *see* Clonfert Gp *L & K*
FAHAN LOWER (Christ Church) and UPPER (St Mura) *D & R*
NSM J H MCGAFFIN
FALLS, LOWER (St Luke)   *see* Belfast St Steph w St Luke *Conn*
FALLS, UPPER   *see* Belfast Upper Falls *Conn*
**FANLOBBUS (St Mary) w Drimoleague, Drinagh and
Coolkellure** *C, C & R*   I C P JEFFERS
FARNAUGHT (no dedication)   *see* Mohill w Farnaught,
Aughavas, Oughteragh etc *K, E & A*
FAUGHANVALE (St Canice) *D & R*   **NSM** B J HASSAN
FENAGH (All Saints) w Myshall, Aghade and Ardoyne *C & O*
I L D D SCOTT
**FERMOY (Christ Church) w Ballyhooley, Knockmourne,
Ardnageehy and Brigown** *C, C & R*   I E V CREMIN
NSM W H HILL
FERMOYLE (no dedication)   *see* Castlerock w Dunboe and
Fermoyle *D & R*
**FERNS (Cathedral of St Edan) w Kilbride, Toombe,
Kilcormack and Ballycarney** *C & O*   I P G MOONEY
NSM I F DUNGAN
FERRY, EAST   *see* Cloyne Union *C, C & R*
FERTAGH (no dedication)   *see* Kilcooley w Littleon, Crohane
and Fertagh *C & O*
FETHARD (Holy Trinity)   *see* Clonmel w Innislounagh,
Tullaghmelan etc *C & O*
FETHARD (St Mogue)   *see* New w Old Ross, Whitechurch,
Fethard etc *C & O*
**FIDDOWN (no dedication) w Clonegam, Guilcagh and
Kilmeaden** *C & O*   **P-in-c** M E JEFFERS
FINAGHY (St Polycarp) *Conn*   I A L STEWART
FINGLAS (St Canice)   *see* Dublin Santry w Glasnevin and
Finglas *D & G*
FINNER (Christ Church)   *see* Killinagh w Kiltyclogher and
Innismagrath *K, E & A*
FINTONA   *see* Donacavey w Barr *Clogh*
FINVOY (no dedication)   *see* Ballymoney w Finvoy and
Rasharkin *Conn*
FIVEMILETOWN (St John) *Clogh*   I T K HANLON
FLORENCECOURT   *see* Killesher *K, E & A*
FONTSTOWN (St John the Evangelist)   *see* Athy w Kilberry,
Fontstown and Kilkea *D & G*
FORGNEY (St Munis)   *see* Athlone w Benown, Kiltoom and
Forgney *M & K*

FOUNTAINS   *see* Lismore w Cappoquin, Kilwatermoy,
Dungarvan etc *C & O*
FOXFORD   *see* Straid *T, K & A*
FOYNES   *see* Rathkeale w Askeaton, Kilcornan and
Kilnaughtin *L & K*
FRANKFIELD (Holy Trinity)   *see* Douglas Union w Frankfield
C, C & R
FRENCH CHURCH   *see* Portarlington w Cloneyhurke, Lea etc
M & K
FRENCHPARK   *see* Roscommon w Donamon, Rathcline,
Kilkeevin etc *K, E & A*
GALLOON (St Comgall) w Drummully and Sallaghy *Clogh*
I A D C KERR
GALWAY (St Nicholas) w Kilcummin *T, K & A*
I G L HASTINGS   C J M GODFREY
GARRISON (no dedication) w Slavin and Belleek *Clogh*
I C N NJOKU
GARRYCLOYNE (no dedication)   *see* Carrigrohane Union
C, C & R
GARTAN (St Columba)   *see* Conwal Union w Gartan *D & R*
GARTREE (no dedication)   *see* Killead w Gartree *Conn*
GARVAGH   *see* Errigal w Garvagh *D & R*
GARVAGHY (no dedication)   *see* Dromara w Garvaghy *D & D*
GARVARY (Holy Trinity)   *see* Derryvullen S w Garvary *Clogh*
GEASHILL (St Mary) w Killeigh and Ballycommon *M & K*
P-in-c D HUTTON-BURY
GILFORD   *see* Tullylish *D & D*
GILFORD (St Paul) *D & D*   I D I CADDOO
GILNAHIRK (St Dorothea) *D & D*   I N D J KIRKPATRICK
NSM M S WALSHE
GLANDORE   *see* Ross Union *C, C & R*
GLANMIRE (St Mary and All Saints)   *see* Rathcooney Union
C, C & R
GLASCARRIG (no dedication)   *see* Ardamine w Kiltennel,
Glascarrig etc *C & O*
GLASLOUGH   *see* Donagh w Tyholland and Errigal Truagh
Clogh
GLASNEVIN (St Mobhi)   *see* Dublin Santry w Glasnevin and
Finglas *D & G*
GLENAGEARY (St Paul) *D & G*   I G G DOWD
GLENALLA (St Columbkille)   *see* Mevagh w Glenalla *D & R*
GLENARM   *see* Ardclinis and Tickmacrevan w Layde and
Cushendun *Conn*
GLENAVY (St Aidan) w Tunny and Crumlin *Conn*
I J E C RUTTER
GLENBEIGH (St John)   *see* Kilcolman w Kiltallagh, Killorglin,
Knockane etc *L & K*
GLENCAIRN   *see* Belfast St Andr *Conn*
GLENCAR   *see* Cloonclare w Killasnett, Lurganboy and
Drumlease *K, E & A*
GLENCOLUMBKILLE (St Columba)   *see* Ardara w
Glencolumbkille, Inniskeel etc *D & R*
GLENCRAIG (Holy Trinity) *D & D*   I S K C RICHARDSON
NSM B W PARKER
GLENDERMOTT (no dedication) *D & R*   I F D CREIGHTON
NSM W A BURNS
GLENEALY (no dedication)   *see* Rathdrum w Glenealy,
Derralossary and Laragh *D & G*
GLENOE   *see* Glynn w Raloo *Conn*
GLENTIES (no dedication)   *see* Ardara w Glencolumbkille,
Inniskeel etc *D & R*
GLENVILLE   *see* Fermoy Union *C, C & R*
GLYNN (St John) w Raloo *Conn*   I S B FORDE
GORESBRIDGE   *see* Leighlin w Grange Sylvae, Shankill etc
C & O
**GOREY (Christ Church) w Kilnahue, Leskinfere and
Ballycanew** *C & O*   I M J J HAYDEN
NSM C CASSERLY-FARRAR
GORTIN   *see* Ardstraw w Baronscourt, Badoney Lower etc
D & R
GOWNA (no dedication)   *see* Arvagh w Carrigallen, Gowna
and Columbkille *K, E & A*
GRACEFIELD (no dedication)   *see* Woodschapel w Gracefield
Arm
GRANARD (St Patrick)   *see* Mostrim w Granard, Clonbroney,
Killoe etc *K, E & A*
GRANGE (St Aidan)   *see* Loughgall w Grange *Arm*
GRANGE SYLVAE (St George)   *see* Leighlin w Grange Sylvae,
Shankill etc *C & O*
GRANGEGORMAN (All Saints)   *see* Dublin Ch Ch Cathl Gp
D & G
GREENAN (no dedication)   *see* Ardstraw w Baronscourt,
Badoney Lower etc *D & R*
GREENCASTLE (St Finian)   *see* Moville w Greencastle, Donagh,
Cloncha etc *D & R*
GREENISLAND (Holy Name) *Conn*   I P LYONS

GREY ABBEY (St Saviour) w Kircubbin *D & D* I G WITHERS

GREYSTONES (St Patrick) *D & G* I D S MUNGAVIN
C A T BREEN

GROOMSPORT (no dedication) *D & D* I D J M POLLOCK

GUILCAGH (St John the Evangelist)   *see* Fiddown w Clonegam, Guilcagh and Kilmeaden *C & O*

GURRANEKENNEFEAKE (no dedication)   *see* Cloyne Union *C, C & R*

GWEEDORE (St Patrick), Carrickfin and Templecrone *D & R* P-in-c T D ALLEN

HACKETSTOWN (St John the Baptist)   *see* Kiltegan w Hacketstown, Clonmore and Moyne *C & O*

HAROLD'S CROSS (no dedication)   *see* Dublin Rathmines w Harold's Cross *D & G*

HELEN'S BAY (St John the Baptist) *D & D* I T C KINAHAN

HEYNESTOWN (St Paul)   *see* Dundalk w Heynestown *Arm*

HIGHFIELD   *see* Belfast Whiterock *Conn*

HILLSBOROUGH (St Malachi) *D & D* I B A FOLLIS
C D MARTIN

HILLTOWN   *see* Drumgath w Drumgooland and Clonduff *D & D*

HOLLYFORT   *see* Gorey w Kilnahue, Leskinfere and Ballycanew *C & O*

HOLLYMOUNT (no dedication)   *see* Down H Trin w Hollymount *D & D*

HOLMPATRICK (St Patrick) w Balbriggan and Kenure *D & G* Bp's C A KELLY

HOLYCROSS   *see* Templemore w Thurles and Kilfithmone *C & O*

HOLYWOOD (St Kevin)   *see* Blessington w Kilbride, Ballymore Eustace etc *D & G*

HOLYWOOD (St Philip and St James) *D & D* C G N HAUGH

HORETOWN (St James)   *see* Taghmon w Horetown and Bannow *C & O*

HORSELEAP   *see* Clara w Liss, Moate and Clonmacnoise *M & K*

HOWTH (St Mary) *D & G* I W K M BREW

INCH   *see* Cloyne Union *C, C & R*

INCH (no dedication)   *see* Kilmore and Inch *D & D*

INCH (no dedication)   *see* Arklow w Inch and Kilbride *D & G*

INISHARGIE (St Andrew)   *see* Ballywalter w Inishargie *D & D*

INISTIOGE (St Mary)   *see* Kells Gp *C & O*

INNISCALTRA (St Caimin)   *see* Killaloe w Stradbally *L & K*

INNISCARRA (no dedication)   *see* Carrigrohane Union *C, C & R*

INNISHANNON (Christ Church)   *see* Bandon Union *C, C & R*

INNISKEEL (no dedication)   *see* Ardara w Glencolumbkille, Inniskeel etc *D & R*

INNISLOUNAGH (St Patrick)   *see* Clonmel w Innislounagh, Tullaghmelan etc *C & O*

INNISMAGRATH (no dedication)   *see* Killinagh w Kiltyclogher and Innismagrath *K, E & A*

INVER   *see* Larne and Inver *Conn*

INVER (St John the Evangelist) w Mountcharles, Killaghtee and Killybegs *D & R* I R J WEST

IRISHTOWN   *see* Dublin Irishtown w Donnybrook *D & G*

IRVINESTOWN   *see* Derryvullen N w Castlearchdale *Clogh*

ISLANDMAGEE (St John)   *see* Whitehead and Islandmagee *Conn*

JOANMOUNT   *see* Belfast H Trin and St Silas *Conn*

JOHNSTOWN   *see* Kilcooley w Littleon, Crohane and Fertagh *C & O*

JORDANSTOWN (St Patrick) *Conn* I N P BAYLOR
C J D CAMPBELL-SMYTH NSM C B DIXON

JULIANSTOWN (St Mary) and Colpe w Drogheda and Duleek *M & K* I P M RUTHERFORD NSM T HOLMES

KELLS (St Columba) w Balrathboyne, Moynalty, Donaghpatrick and Castletown *M & K* I W A SEALE

KELLS (St Mary) w Ballaghtobin, Kilmoganny, Ennisnag, Inistioge and Kilfane *C & O* I M HILLIARD

KENAGH   *see* Ardagh w Tashinny, Shrule and Kilcommick *K, E & A*

KENMARE (St Patrick) w Sneem, Dromod and Valentia *L & K* P-in-c M R CAVANAGH

KENTSTOWN (St Mary)   *see* Navan w Kentstown, Tara, Slane, Painestown etc *M & K*

KENURE (no dedication)   *see* Holmpatrick w Balbriggan and Kenure *D & G*

KESH   *see* Magheraculmoney *Clogh*

KILBARRON (St Anne) w Rossnowlagh and Drumholm *D & R* I B R RUSSELL

KILBERRY (no dedication)   *see* Athy w Kilberry, Fontstown and Kilkea *D & G*

KILBIXY (St Bigseach)   *see* Mullingar, Portnashangan, Moyliscar, Kilbixy etc *M & K*

KILBONANE (St Mark)   *see* Moviddy Union *C, C & R*

KILBRIDE (Holy Trinity)   *see* Ferns w Kilbride, Toombe, Kilcormack etc *C & O*

KILBRIDE (no dedication)   *see* Blessington w Kilbride, Ballymore Eustace etc *D & G*

KILBRIDE (St Bride) *Conn* I P REDFERN

KILBRIDE (St Brigid)   *see* Arklow w Inch and Kilbride *D & G*

KILBRIDE BRAY (no dedication)   *see* Powerscourt w Kilbride *D & G*

KILBRONEY (no dedication)   *see* Clonallon and Warrenpoint w Kilbroney *D & D*

KILBRYAN (no dedication)   *see* Boyle and Elphin w Aghanagh, Kilbryan etc *K, E & A*

KILCLEAGH   *see* Clara w Liss, Moate and Clonmacnoise *M & K*

KILCLIEF (no dedication)   *see* Lecale Gp *D & D*

KILCLUNEY (St John)   *see* Mullabrack w Markethill and Kilcluney *Arm*

KILCOCK   *see* Dunboyne and Rathmolyon *M & K*

KILCOLMAN (no dedication) w Kiltallagh, Killorglin, Knockane and Glenbeigh *L & K* C J C STEPHENS

KILCOMMICK (no dedication)   *see* Ardagh w Tashinny, Shrule and Kilcommick *K, E & A*

KILCOMMON (no dedication)   *see* Crosspatrick Gp *C & O*

KILCOO (no dedication)   *see* Castlewellan w Kilcoo *D & D*

KILCOOLEY (no dedication) w Littleton, Crohane and Fertagh *C & O* I V R A FITZPATRICK

KILCOOLEY (St Columba)   *see* Bangor Abbey *D & D*

KILCORMACK (St Cormac)   *see* Ferns w Kilbride, Toombe, Kilcormack etc *C & O*

KILCORNAN (no dedication)   *see* Rathkeale w Askeaton, Kilcornan and Kilnaughtin *L & K*

KILCROHANE   *see* Kenmare w Sneem, Waterville etc *L & K*

KILCRONAGHAN (no dedication) w Draperstown and Sixtowns *D & R* I C M HAYES

KILCULLEN (St John)   *see* Newbridge w Carnalway and Kilcullen *M & K*

KILCUMMIN (no dedication)   *see* Galway w Kilcummin *T, K & A*

KILDALLON (no dedication) w Newtowngore and Corrawallen and Swanlinbar w Kinawley, Templeport and Tomregan *K, E & A* Bp's C J WOODS

KILDARTON (no dedication)   *see* Lisnadill w Kildarton *Arm*

KILDAVIN (St Paul)   *see* Bunclody w Kildavin, Clonegal and Kilrush *C & O*

KILDOLLAGH (St Paul)   *see* Ballyrashane w Kildollagh *Conn*

KILDRESS (St Patrick) w Altedesert *Arm* I B J A CRUISE

KILDRUMFERTON (St Patrick) w Ballymachugh and Ballyjamesduff *K, E & A* Bp's C C SNELL

KILFANE (no dedication)   *see* Kells Gp *C & O*

KILFARBOY (Christ Church)   *see* Drumcliffe w Kilnasoolagh *L & K*

KILFAUGHNABEG (Christ Church)   *see* Ross Union *C, C & R*

KILFENORA (Cathedral of St Fachan)   *see* Drumcliffe w Kilnasoolagh *L & K*

KILFERAGH (no dedication) *as above*

KILFINANE (St Andrew)   *see* Adare and Kilmallock w Kilpeacon, Croom etc *L & K*

KILFITHMONE (no dedication)   *see* Templemore w Thurles and Kilfithmone *C & O*

KILFLYNN (no dedication)   *see* Adare and Kilmallock w Kilpeacon, Croom etc *L & K*

KILGARIFFE (no dedication) w Kilmalooda, Kilnagross, Timoleague and Courtmacsherry *C, C & R* I D J OWEN

KILGLASS (no dedication)   *see* Killala w Dunfeeny, Crossmolina, Kilmoremoy etc *T, K & A*

KILGLASS (St Anne)   *see* Mostrim w Granard, Clonbroney, Killoe etc *K, E & A*

KILGOBBIN (no dedication)   *see* Dingle w Killiney and Kilgobbin *L & K*

KILHORNE   *see* Annalong *D & D*

KILKEA (no dedication)   *see* Athy w Kilberry, Fontstown and Kilkea *D & G*

KILKEE   *see* Drumcliffe w Kilnasoolagh *L & K*

KILKEEL (Christ Church) *D & D* I K D MCGRATH
NSM S J K TEGGARTY

KILKEEVIN (Holy Trinity)   *see* Roscommon w Donamon, Rathcline, Kilkeevin etc *K, E & A*

KILKENNY (Cathedral of St Canice) (St John), Aghour and Kilmanagh *C & O* I K M POULTON, V S T IRVINE

KILKENNY WEST   *see* Athlone w Benown, Kiltoom and Forgney *M & K*

KILL (no dedication) *D & G* I A YOUNG

KILL (St John)   *see* Naas w Kill and Rathmore *M & K*

KILL O' THE GRANGE   *see* Kill *D & G*

KILLABBAN (no dedication)   *see* Killeshin w Cloydagh and Killabban *C & O*

KILLADEAS (Priory Church)   *see* Trory w Killadeas *Clogh*

KILLAGAN (no dedication)   *see* Craigs w Dunaghy and Killagan *Conn*

KILLAGHTEE (St Peter)   *see* Inver w Mountcharles, Killaghtee and Killybegs *D & R*
KILLALA (Cathedral of St Patrick) w Dunfeeny, Crossmolina, Kilmoremoy, Castleconnor, Easkey and Kilglass *T, K & A* Bp's **C** N J O'RAW
KILLALLON (St John)   *see* Trim and Athboy Gp *M & K*
KILLALOE (Cathedral of St Flannan) w Stradbally, Clonlara, Mountshannon, Abingdon and Tuomgraney *L & K*   **I** G A PAULSEN   **NSM** L J GREEN
KILLANEY (St Andrew) w Carryduff *D & D*   **I** S H LOWRY
KILLANNE (St Anne) w Killegney, Rossdroit and Templeshanbo *C & O*   **I** R J HARMSWORTH
KILLANULLY   *see* Carrigaline Union *C, C & R*
KILLARGUE (no dedication)   *see* Killinagh w Kiltyclogher and Innismagrath *K, E & A*
KILLARNEY (St Mary) w Aghadoe and Muckross *L & K* **P-in-c** S J LUMBY
KILLASHEE (St Paul)   *see* Templemichael w Clongish, Clooncumber etc *K, E & A*
KILLASNETT (no dedication)   *see* Cloonclare w Killasnett, Lurganboy and Drumlease *K, E & A*
KILLCONNELL   *see* Aughrim w Ballinasloe etc *L & K*
KILLEA (St Andrew)   *see* Waterford w Killea, Drumcannon and Dunhill *C & O*
KILLEA (St Fiach)   *see* Taughboyne, Craigadooish, Newtowncunningham etc *D & R*
KILLEAD (St Catherine) w Gartree *Conn*   **I** W J C ORR
KILLEDMOND   *see* Dunleckney w Nurney, Lorum and Kiltennel *C & O*
KILLEEVAN (no dedication)   *see* Clones w Killeevan *Clogh*
KILLEGAR (no dedication)   *see* Killeshandra w Killegar and Derrylane *K, E & A*
KILLEGNEY (no dedication)   *see* Killanne w Killegney, Rossdroit and Templeshanbo *C & O*
KILLEIGH (no dedication)   *see* Geashill w Killeigh and Ballycommon *M & K*
KILLELAGH (no dedication)   *see* Maghera w Killelagh *D & R*
KILLENAULE (no dedication)   *see* Kilcooley w Littleon, Crohane and Fertagh *C & O*
KILLERMOGH (no dedication)   *see* Abbeyleix w Ballyroan etc *C & O*
KILLERY   *see* Taunagh w Kilmactranny, Ballysumaghan etc *K, E & A*
KILLESHANDRA (no dedication) w Killegar and Derrylane *K, E & A*   **I** A N CALVIN
KILLESHER (St John) *K, E & A*   **I** I J RUITERS
KILLESHERDONEY (St Mark)   *see* Drumgoon *K, E & A*
KILLESHIL (St Paul)   *see* Errigle Keerogue w Ballygawley and Killeshil *Arm*
KILLESHIN (no dedication) w Cloydagh and Killabban *C & O*   **I** P TARLETON
KILLESK (All Saints)   *see* New w Old Ross, Whitechurch, Fethard etc *C & O*
KILLETER   *see* Derg w Termonamongan *D & R*
KILLINCHY (no dedication) w Kilmood and Tullynakill *D & D*   **I** S T R GAMBLE
KILLINEY (Holy Trinity) *D & G*   **I** N J SLOANE
KILLINEY (St Brendan)   *see* Dingle w Killiney and Kilgobbin *L & K*
KILLINEY Ballybrack (St Matthias) *D & G*   **I** W P OLHAUSEN   **NSM** N STRATFORD
KILLINICK (no dedication)   *see* Wexford and Kilscoran Union *C & O*
KILLINKERE (no dedication)   *see* Lurgan w Billis, Killinkere and Munterconnaught *K, E & A*
KILLISKEY (no dedication)   *see* Wicklow w Killiskey *D & G*
KILLODIERNAN (no dedication)   *see* Nenagh *L & K*
KILLOE (St Catherine)   *see* Mostrim w Granard, Clonbroney, Killoe etc *K, E & A*
KILLORAN (no dedication)   *see* Tubbercurry w Killoran *T, K & A*
KILLORGLIN (no dedication)   *see* Kilcolman w Kiltallagh, Killorglin, Knockane etc *L & K*
KILLOUGH (St Anne)   *see* Bright w Ballee and Killough *D & D*
KILLOUGHTER (no dedication)   *see* Drung w Castleterra, Larah and Lavey etc *K, E & A*
KILLOUGHY   *see* Tullamore w Durrow, Newtownfertullagh, Rahan etc *M & K*
KILLOWEN   *see* Kinneigh Union *C, C & R*
KILLOWEN (St John) *D & R*   **I** D M COLLINS   **NSM** W J HOLMES
KILLSALLAGHAN (St David)   *see* Swords w Donabate and Kilsallaghan *D & G*
KILLUCAN (St Etchen)   *see* Mullingar, Portnashangan, Moyliscar, Kilbixy etc *M & K*
KILLURIN (no dedication)   *see* Wexford and Kilscoran Union *C & O*

KILLYBEGS (no dedication)   *see* Inver w Mountcharles, Killaghtee and Killybegs *D & R*
KILLYGARVAN (St Columb)   *see* Tullyaughnish w Kilmacrennan and Killygarvan *D & R*
KILLYLEA (St Mark)   *see* Eglish w Killylea *Arm*
KILLYMAN (St Andrew) *Arm*   **I** S R T BOYD
KILLYMARD (no dedication)   *see* Donegal w Killymard, Lough Eske and Laghey *D & R*
KILMACABEA (no dedication)   *see* Ross Union *C, C & R*
KILMACDUAGH (no dedication)   *see* Aughrim w Ballinasloe etc *L & K*
KILMACRENNAN (St Finnian and St Mark)   *see* Tullyaughnish w Kilmacrennan and Killygarvan *D & R*
KILMACSHALGAN (St Mary)   *see* Skreen w Kilmacshalgan and Dromard *T, K & A*
KILMACTHOMAS (no dedication)   *see* Lismore w Cappoquin, Kilwatermoy, Dungarvan etc *C & O*
KILMACTRANNY (no dedication)   *see* Taunagh w Kilmactranny, Ballysumaghan etc *K, E & A*
KILMAINHAMWOOD   *see* Kingscourt w Syddan *M & K*
KILMAKEE (St Hilda) *Conn*   **I** D H BOYLAND
KILMALLOCK (St Peter and St Paul)   *see* Adare and Kilmallock w Kilpeacon, Croom etc *L & K*
KILMALOODA (All Saints)   *see* Kilgariffe Union *C, C & R*
KILMANAGH (no dedication)   *see* Kilkenny w Aghour and Kilmanagh *C & O*
KILMEADEN (St Mary)   *see* Fiddown w Clonegam, Guilcagh and Kilmeaden *C & O*
KILMEAGUE (no dedication)   *see* Kildare w Kilmeague and Curragh *M & K*
KILMEEN (Christ Church)   *see* Kinneigh Union *C, C & R*
KILMEGAN (no dedication) w Maghera *D & D*   **I** C J CARSON
KILMOCOMOGUE (St Brendan the Navigator) w Castletownbere and Durrus *C, C & R*   **I** P M WILLOUGHBY   **NSM** A M SKUSE
KILMOE (no dedication) w Teampol-na-mbocht, Schull and Crookhaven *C, C & R*   **I** T R LESTER
KILMOGANNY (St Matthew)   *see* Kells Gp *C & O*
KILMOOD (St Mary)   *see* Killinchy w Kilmood and Tullynakill *D & D*
KILMORE (Christ Church) and Inch *D & D*   **I** W R S SMYTH
KILMORE (no dedication)   *see* Monaghan w Tydavnet and Kilmore *Clogh*
KILMORE (no dedication)   *see* Kiltoghart w Drumshambo, Annaduff and Kilronan *K, E & A*
KILMOREMOY (St Michael)   *see* Killala w Dunfeeny, Crossmolina, Kilmoremoy etc *T, K & A*
KILMOYLEY   *see* Tralee w Kilmoyley, Ballymacelligott etc *L & K*
KILMUCKRIDGE (no dedication)   *see* Ardamine w Kiltennel, Glascarrig etc *C & O*
KILMURRY (St Andrew)   *see* Moviddy Union *C, C & R*
KILNAGROSS (no dedication)   *see* Kilgariffe Union *C, C & R*
KILNAHUE (St John the Evangelist)   *see* Gorey w Kilnahue, Leskinfere and Ballycanew *C & O*
KILNALECK   *see* Kildrumferton w Ballymachugh and Ballyjamesduff *K, E & A*
KILNAMANAGH (St John)   *see* Ardamine w Kiltennel, Glascarrig etc *C & O*
KILNASOOLAGH (no dedication)   *see* Drumcliffe w Kilnasoolagh *L & K*
KILNAUGHTIN (St Brendan)   *see* Rathkeale w Askeaton, Kilcornan and Kilnaughtin *L & K*
KILPEACON (St Beacon)   *see* Adare and Kilmallock w Kilpeacon, Croom etc *L & K*
KILPIPE (no dedication)   *see* Crosspatrick Gp *C & O*
KILREA (St Patrick)   *see* Aghadowey w Kilrea *D & R*
KILRONAN (St Thomas)   *see* Kiltoghart w Drumshambo, Annaduff and Kilronan *K, E & A*
KILROOT (St Colman) and Templecorran *Conn*   **I** M J MCCANN
KILROSSANTY (no dedication)   *see* Lismore w Cappoquin, Kilwatermoy, Dungarvan etc *C & O*
KILRUSH   *see* Drumcliffe w Kilnasoolagh *L & K*
KILRUSH (St Brigid)   *see* Bunclody w Kildavin, Clonegal and Kilrush *C & O*
KILSARAN (St Mary) w Drumcar, Dunleer and Dunany *Arm*   **I** M GRAHAM
KILSCORAN (no dedication)   *see* Wexford and Kilscoran Union *C & O*
KILSKEERY (no dedication) w Trillick *Clogh*   **I** R C LOGUE
KILTALLAGH (St Carthage)   *see* Kilcolman w Kiltallagh, Killorglin, Knockane etc *L & K*
KILTEEVOGUE (St John)   *see* Stranorlar w Meenglas and Kilteevogue *D & R*
KILTEGAN (St Peter) w Hacketstown, Clonmore and Moyne *C & O*   **I** S E B DURAND

MAGUIRESBRIDGE (Christ Church) w Derrybrusk *Clogh*
  I D SKUCE
MALAHIDE (St Andrew) w Balgriffin *D & G*   I N E C GAMBLE
  NSM K H SHERWOOD
MALIN   *see* Moville w Greencastle, Donagh, Cloncha etc *D & R*
MALLOW (St James) w Doneraile and Castletownroche
  C, C & R   I E E M LYNCH
MALLUSK (St Brigid) *Conn*   I W A BOYCE
MALONE   *see* Belfast Malone St Jo *Conn*
MALONE, UPPER   *see* Belfast Upper Malone (Epiphany) *Conn*
MANORCUNNINGHAM   *see* Raphoe w Raymochy and
  Clonleigh *D & R*
MANORHAMILTON   *see* Cloonclare w Killasnett, Lurganboy
  and Drumlease *K, E & A*
MARKETHILL (no dedication)   *see* Mullabrack w Markethill and
  Kilcluney *Arm*
MARMULLANE (St Mary)   *see* Douglas Union w Frankfield
  C, C & R
MARYBOROUGH (St Peter) w Dysart Enos and Ballyfin *C & O*
  I B J G O'ROURKE
MAYNE   *see* Castlepollard and Oldcastle w Loughcrew etc
  M & K
MAYNOOTH (St Mary)   *see* Dunboyne and Rathmolyon *M & K*
MAYO (no dedication)   *see* Killeshin w Cloydagh and
  Killabban *C & O*
MEALIFFE   *see* Templemore w Thurles and Kilfithmone *C & O*
MEENGLASS (Ascension)   *see* Stranorlar w Meenglas and
  Kilteevogue *D & R*
MIDDLE CHURCH (no dedication)   *see* Ballinderry *Conn*
MIDDLETOWN (St John)   *see* Tynan w Middletown and
  Aghavilly *Arm*
MIDLETON (St John the Baptist)   *see* Cloyne Union *C, C & R*
MILLISLE (St Patrick)   *see* Carrowdore w Millisle *D & D*
MILLTOWN   *see* Kilcolman w Kiltallagh, Killorglin, Knockane
  etc *L & K*
MILLTOWN (St Andrew) *Arm*   I M H T MILLIKEN
MILLTOWN (St Philip)   *see* Dublin Sandford w Milltown *D & G*
MILLTOWN MALBAY   *see* Drumcliffe w Kilnasoolagh *L & K*
MITCHELSTOWN   *see* Fermoy Union *C, C & R*
MOATE (St Mary)   *see* Clara w Liss, Moate and Clonmacnoise
  M & K
MOHILL (St Mary) w Farnaught, Aughavas, Oughteragh,
  Kiltubride and Drumreilly *K, E & A*   C L M FROST
MOIRA (St John) *D & D*   I J M MEGARRELL
MONAGHAN (St Patrick) w Tydavnet and Kilmore *Clogh*
  I I T H BERRY
MONAMOLIN (St Molig)   *see* Ardamine w Kiltennel,
  Glascarrig etc *C & O*
MONART (St Peter)   *see* Enniscorthy w Clone, Clonmore,
  Monart etc *C & O*
MONASTEREVAN (St John the Evangelist)   *see* Portarlington w
  Cloneyhurke, Lea etc *M & K*
MONASTERORIS (no dedication)   *see* Clonsast w Rathangan,
  Thomastown etc *M & K*
MONELLAN (St Anne)   *see* Convoy w Monellan and
  Donaghmore *D & R*
MONEYMORE   *see* Desertlyn w Ballyeglish *Arm*
MONEYREAGH (no dedication)   *see* Orangefield w
  Moneyreagh *D & D*
MONKSTOWN (Good Shepherd) *Conn*   **P-in-c** A MOORE
MONKSTOWN (no dedication) *D & G*   **NSM** Y A GINNELLY
MONKSTOWN (St John)   *see* Carrigaline Union *C, C & R*
MOSSLEY (Holy Spirit) *Conn*   I N R CUTCLIFFE
MOSTRIM (St John) w Granard, Clonbroney, Killoe,
  Rathaspeck and Streete *K, E & A*   **P-in-c** J M CATTERALL
MOTHEL (no dedication)   *see* Castlecomer w Colliery Ch,
  Mothel and Bilboa *C & O*
MOUNT MERRION (Pentecost) *D & D*   I A P GREEN
  P-in-c D A MCCLAY
MOUNT MERRION (St Thomas)   *see* Dublin Mt Merrion *D & G*
MOUNT NUGENT (St Bride)   *see* Castlepollard and Oldcastle w
  Loughcrew etc *M & K*
MOUNTCHARLES (Christ Church)   *see* Inver w Mountcharles,
  Killaghtee and Killybegs *D & R*
MOUNTFIELD (no dedication)   *see* Drumragh w Mountfield
  D & R
MOUNTRATH   *see* Clonenagh w Offerlane, Borris-in-Ossory
  etc *C & O*
MOUNTSHANNON   *see* Killaloe w Stradbally *L & K*
MOVIDDY (no dedication), Kilbonane, Kilmurry,
  Templemartin and Macroom *C, C & R*   **NSM** P J GEARY
MOVILLA (no dedication) *D & D*   I A N PEEK
MOY (St James) w Charlemont *Arm*   I A W A MAYES
MOYBOLOGUE   *see* Kingscourt w Syddan *M & K*
MOYDOW (no dedication)   *see* Ardagh w Tashinny, Shrule and
  Kilcommick *K, E & A*

MOYGASHEL (no dedication)   *see* Drumglass w Moygashel *Arm*
MOYGLARE (All Saints)   *see* Dunboyne and Rathmolyon *M & K*
MOYLISCAR   *see* Mullingar, Portnashangan, Moyliscar, Kilbixy
  etc *M & K*
MOYNALTY (St Mary)   *see* Kells Union *M & K*
MOYNE (St John)   *see* Kiltegan w Hacketstown, Clonmore and
  Moyne *C & O*
MOYNTAGHS   *see* Ardmore w Craigavon *D & D*
MOYRUS   *see* Omey w Ballynakill, Errislannan and
  Roundstone *T, K & A*
MUCKAMORE (St Jude) (St Matthias) *Conn*   I W J C ORR
MUCKNOE (St Maeldoid)   *see* Ballybay w Mucknoe and
  Clontibret *Clogh*
MUCKROSS (Holy Trinity)   *see* Killarney w Aghadoe and
  Muckross *L & K*
MUCKROSS (St John)   *see* Drumkeeran w Templecarne and
  Muckross *Clogh*
MUFF (no dedication)   *see* Londonderry Ch Ch, Culmore, Muff
  and Belmont *D & R*
MULHUDDART (St Thomas)   *see* Castleknock and Mulhuddart
  w Clonsilla *D & G*
MULLABRACK (no dedication) w Markethill and Kilcluney
  Arm   I N J HUGHES
MULLAGH (no dedication)   *see* Bailieborough w Knockbride,
  Shercock and Mullagh *K, E & A*
MULLAGHDUN (no dedication)   *see* Cleenish w Mullaghdun
  Clogh
MULLAGHFAD (All Saints)   *see* Aghalurcher w Tattykeeran,
  Cooneen etc *Clogh*
MULLAGLASS (St Luke)   *see* Camlough w Mullaglass *Arm*
MULLAVILLY (no dedication) *Arm*   I D E CAIRNS
MULLINACUFF (no dedication)   *see* Tullow w Shillelagh,
  Aghold and Mullinacuff *C & O*
MULLINGAR (All Saints) w Portnashangan, Moyliscar, Kilbixy,
  Almoritia, Killucan, Clonard and Castlelost *M & K*
  I M A GRAHAM   **NSM** H M SCULLY
MULRANKIN (St David)   *see* Wexford and Kilscoran Union
  C & O
MUNNINANE (St Kevin)   *see* Drumcliffe w Lissadell and
  Munninane *K, E & A*
MUNTERCONNAUGHT (no dedication)   *see* Lurgan w Billis,
  Killinkere and Munterconnaught *K, E & A*
MURRAGH (no dedication)   *see* Kinneigh Union *C, C & R*
MYROE (St John)   *see* Tamlaghtfinlagan w Myroe *D & R*
MYROSS   *see* Ross Union *C, C & R*
MYSHALL (Christ the Redeemer)   *see* Fenagh w Myshall,
  Aghade and Ardoyne *C & O*
NAAS (St David) w Kill and Rathmore *M & K*   I P G HEAK
NARRAGHMORE (Holy Saviour) and Timolin w Castledermot
  and Kinneagh *D & G*   **NSM** T ALCOCK
NAVAN (St Mary) w Kentstown, Tara, Slane, Painestown and
  Stackallen *M & K*   I J D M CLARKE
NENAGH (St Mary) w Ballymackey, Templederry and
  Killodiernan *L & K*   **NSM** P E MCKEE HANNA
NEWBLISS (no dedication)   *see* Currin w Drum and Newbliss
  Clogh
NEWCASTLE (no dedication) w Newtownmountkennedy
  and Calary *D & G*   I W L BENNETT
NEWCASTLE (St John) *D & D*   I I M ELLIS
NEWCASTLE-LYONS (no dedication)   *see* Celbridge w Straffan
  and Newcastle-Lyons *D & G*
NEWCESTOWN   *see* Kinneigh Union *C, C & R*
NEWMARKET-ON-FERGUS   *see* Drumcliffe w Kilnasoolagh
  L & K
NEWRY (St Mary) (St Patrick) *D & D*   I K E SUTTON
NEWTOWNARDS (St Mark) *D & D*   I C J MATCHETT
NEWTOWNBARRY   *see* Bunclody w Kildavin, Clonegal and
  Kilrush *C & O*
NEWTOWNBUTLER   *see* Galloon w Drummully and Sallaghy
  Clogh
NEWTOWNCROMMELIN (no dedication)   *see* Skerry w
  Rathcavan and Newtowncrommelin *Conn*
NEWTOWNCUNNINGHAM (All Saints)   *see* Taughboyne,
  Craigadooish, Newtowncunningham etc *D & R*
NEWTOWNFERTULLAGH   *see* Tullamore w Durrow,
  Newtownfertullagh, Rahan etc *M & K*
NEWTOWNFORBES   *see* Templemichael w Clongish,
  Clooncumber etc *K, E & A*
NEWTOWNGORE (no dedication)   *see* Kildallon and
  Swanlinbar *K, E & A*
NEWTOWNMOUNTKENNEDY (St Matthew)   *see* Newcastle w
  Newtownmountkennedy and Calary *D & G*
NEWTOWNSAVILLE (no dedication)   *see* Augher w
  Newtownsaville and Eskrahoole *Clogh*
NEWTOWNSTEWART   *see* Ardstraw w Baronscourt, Badoney
  Lower etc *D & R*

NOHOVAL (no dedication) *see* Templebreedy w Tracton and Nohoval *C, C & R*

NURNEY (no dedication) *see* Portarlington w Cloneyhurke, Lea etc *M & K*

NURNEY (St John) *see* Dunleckney w Nurney, Lorum and Kiltennel *C & O*

OFFERLANE (no dedication) *see* Clonenagh w Offerlane, Borris-in-Ossory etc *C & O*

OLD LEIGHLIN *see* Leighlin w Grange Sylvae, Shankill etc *C & O*

OLDCASTLE (St Bride) *see* Castlepollard and Oldcastle w Loughcrew etc *M & K*

OMAGH *see* Drumragh w Mountfield *D & R*

OMEY (Christ Church) w Ballynakill, Errislannan and Roundstone *T, K & A*   **P-in-c** S G EVANS

ORANGEFIELD (St John the Evangelist) w Moneyreagh *D & D*   **I** R R WILSON   **NSM** R A B MOLLAN

OSSORY *see* Kilcooley w Littleon, Crohane and Fertagh *C & O*

OUGHTERAGH (no dedication) *see* Mohill w Farnaught, Aughavas, Oughteragh etc *K, E & A*

OUGHTERARD *see* Galway w Kilcummin *T, K & A*

PACKANE *see* Nenagh *L & K*

PAINESTOWN *see* Navan w Kentstown, Tara, Slane, Painestown etc *M & K*

PALLASKENRY *see* Rathkeale w Askeaton, Kilcornan and Kilnaughtin *L & K*

PASSAGE WEST *see* Douglas Union w Frankfield *C, C & R*

PAULSTOWN *see* Leighlin w Grange Sylvae, Shankill etc *C & O*

PETTIGO *see* Drumkeeran w Templecarne and Muckross *Clogh*

PILTOWN *see* Fiddown w Clonegam, Guilcagh and Kilmeaden *C & O*

PORT LAOIS *see* Maryborough w Dysart Enos and Ballyfin *C & O*

PORTADOWN (St Columba) *Arm*   **I** W M ADAIR

PORTADOWN (St Mark) *Arm*   **C** K W MARSHALL   **NSM** A MCWILLIAMS

PORTAFERRY *see* Ballyphilip w Ardquin *D & D*

PORTARLINGTON (St Paul) w Cloneyhurke, Lea, Monasterevin, Nurney and Rathdaire *M & K*   **I** L T C STEVENSON

PORTGLENONE (no dedication) *see* Ahoghill w Portglenone *Conn*

PORTLAOISE *see* Maryborough w Dysart Enos and Ballyfin *C & O*

PORTLAW *see* Fiddown w Clonegam, Guilcagh and Kilmeaden *C & O*

PORTNASHANGAN *see* Mullingar, Portnashangan, Moyliscar, Kilbixy etc *M & K*

PORTRUSH *see* Ballywillan *Conn*

PORTSALON (All Saints) *see* Clondevaddock w Portsalon and Leatbeg *D & R*

PORTSTEWART *see* Agherton *Conn*

PORTUMNA (Christ Church) *see* Clonfert Gp *L & K*

POWERSCOURT (St Patrick) w Kilbride *D & G*   **I** R B ROUNTREE   **NSM** R I T LILBURN

PREBAN (St John) *see* Crosspatrick Gp *C & O*

RAHAN *see* Clonsast w Rathangan, Thomastown etc *M & K*

RAHAN (St Carthach) *see* Tullamore w Durrow, Newtownfertullagh, Rahan etc *M & K*

RAHENY (All Saints) w Coolock *D & G*   **I** N MCCAUSLAND

RALOO (no dedication) *see* Glynn w Raloo *Conn*

RAMELTON *see* Tullyaughnish w Kilmacrennan and Killygarvan *D & R*

RAMOAN (St James) w Ballycastle and Culfeightrin *Conn*   **I** D E FERGUSON

RANDALSTOWN *see* Drummaul w Duneane and Ballyscullion *Conn*

RAPHOE (Cathedral of St Eunan) w Raymochy and Clonleigh *D & R*   **I** K A L BARRETT

RASHARKIN (St Andrew) *see* Ballymoney w Finvoy and Rasharkin *Conn*

RATHANGAN (no dedication) *see* Clonsast w Rathangan, Thomastown etc *M & K*

RATHASPECK (St Thomas) *see* Mostrim w Granard, Clonbroney, Killoe etc *K, E & A*

RATHBARRON *see* Tubbercurry w Killoran *T, K & A*

RATHCAVAN (no dedication) *see* Skerry w Rathcavan and Newtowncrommelin *Conn*

RATHCLAREN (Holy Trinity) *see* Bandon Union *C, C & R*

RATHCLINE (no dedication) *see* Roscommon w Donamon, Rathcline, Kilkeevin etc *K, E & A*

RATHCOOLE (no dedication) *see* Clondalkin w Rathcoole *D & G*

RATHCOOLE (St Comgall) *Conn*   **P-in-c** J M NIBLOCK

RATHCOONEY (St Mary and All Saints) w Little Island and Carrigtwohill *C, C & R*   **I** B M O'REILLY

RATHCOR (no dedication) *see* Ballymascanlan w Creggan and Rathcor *Arm*

RATHCORE (St Ultan) *see* Dunboyne and Rathmolyon *M & K*

RATHDAIRE (Ascension) *see* Portarlington w Cloneyhurke, Lea etc *M & K*

RATHDOWNEY (no dedication) w Castlefleming, Donaghmore, Rathsaran and Aghavoe *C & O*   **I** R D SEYMOUR-WHITELEY

RATHDRUM (St Saviour) w Glenealy, Derralossary and Laragh *D & G*   **I** B M O'REILLY

RATHFARNHAM *see* Dublin Rathfarnham *D & G*

RATHFRILAND *see* Drumgath w Drumgooland and Clonduff *D & D*

RATHGAR *see* Dublin Zion Ch *D & G*

RATHKEALE (Holy Trinity) w Askeaton, Foynes, Kilcornan and Kilnaughtin *L & K*   **P-in-c** K B DE S SCOTT

RATHLIN (St Thomas) *see* Ballintoy w Rathlin and Dunseverick *Conn*

RATHMICHAEL (no dedication) *D & G*   **I** F C APPELBE

RATHMINES *see* Dublin Rathmines w Harold's Cross *D & G*

RATHMOLYON (St Michael and All Angels) *see* Dunboyne and Rathmolyon *M & K*

RATHMORE (St Columbkille) *see* Naas w Kill and Rathmore *M & K*

RATHMULLAN *see* Tullyaughnish w Kilmacrennan and Killygarvan *D & R*

RATHOWEN *see* Mostrim w Granard, Clonbroney, Killoe etc *K, E & A*

RATHSARAN (no dedication) *see* Rathdowney w Castlefleming, Donaghmore etc *C & O*

RATHVILLY (St Mary) *see* Baltinglass w Ballynure etc *C & O*

RAYMOCHY (no dedication) *see* Raphoe w Raymochy and Clonleigh *D & R*

RAYMUNTERDONEY (St Paul) *see* Dunfanaghy, Raymunterdoney and Tullaghbegley *D & R*

REDCROSS (Holy Trinity) *see* Dunganstown w Redcross and Conary *D & G*

REDHILLS *see* Drung w Castleterra, Larah and Lavey etc *K, E & A*

RICHHILL (St Matthew) *Arm*   **I** D SOMERVILLE

RIVERSTOWN *see* Taunagh w Kilmactranny, Ballysumaghan etc *K, E & A*

ROCHFORT BRIDGE *see* Mullingar, Portnashangan, Moyliscar, Kilbixy etc *M & K*

ROCKCORRY (no dedication) *see* Ematris w Rockcorry, Aghabog and Aughnamullan *Clogh*

ROSCOMMON (St Colman) w Donamon, Rathcline, Kilkeevin, Kiltullagh and Tybohine *K, E & A*   **C** A P DONALDSON

ROSCREA (St Cronan) w Kyle, Bourney and Corbally *L & K*   **I** J A GALBRAITH

ROSENALLIS (St Brigid) *see* Mountmellick w Coolbanagher, Rosenallis etc *M & K*

ROSKELTON (no dedication) *see* Clonenagh w Offerlane, Borris-in-Ossory etc *C & O*

ROSS (Cathedral of St Fachtna) w Kilmacabea, Myross, Kilfaughnabeg and Castleventry *C, C & R*   **I** C L PETERS

ROSS, NEW (St Mary) w OLD (St Mary), Whitechurch, Fethard, Killesk and Tintern *C & O*   **P-in-c** M SYKES

ROSSCARBERY *see* Ross Union *C, C & R*

ROSSDROIT (St Peter) *see* Killanne w Killegney, Rossdroit and Templeshanbo *C & O*

ROSSES POINT (no dedication) *see* Sligo w Knocknarea and Rosses Pt *K, E & A*

ROSSINVER (no dedication) *see* Killinagh w Kiltyclogher and Innismagrath *K, E & A*

ROSSMIRE *see* Lismore w Cappoquin, Kilwatermoy, Dungarvan etc *C & O*

ROSSNAKILL *see* Clondevaddock w Portsalon and Leatbeg *D & R*

ROSSNOWLAGH (St John) *see* Kilbarron w Rossnowlagh and Drumholm *D & R*

ROSSORRY (no dedication) *Clogh*   **I** I W ELLIS   **NSM** F I NIXON

ROSTREVOR *see* Clonallon and Warrenpoint w Kilbroney *D & D*

ROUNDSTONE (no dedication) *see* Omey w Ballynakill, Errislannan and Roundstone *T, K & A*

RUNCURRAN *see* Kinsale Union *C, C & R*

RUSHBROOKE (Christ Church) *see* Clonmel Union *C, C & R*

RUTLAND *see* Carlow w Urglin and Staplestown *C & O*

RYNAGH *see* Clonfert Gp *L & K*

SAINTFIELD (no dedication) *D & D*   **I** C J POLLOCK

SALLAGHY (no dedication) *see* Galloon w Drummully and Sallaghy *Clogh*

SANDFORD *see* Dublin Sandford w Milltown *D & G*

TRACTON   *see* Templebreedy w Tracton and Nohoval *C, C & R*

TRALEE (St John the Evangelist) w Kilmoyley, Ballymacelligott, Ballyseedy, Listowel and Ballybunnion *L & K*   I S M WATTERSON

TRAMORE   *see* Waterford w Killea, Drumcannon and Dunhill *C & O*

TRILLICK (Christ Church)   *see* Kilskeery w Trillick *Clogh*

TRIM (Cathedral of St Patrick) and Athboy Group, The *M & K*   I P D BOGLE

TRORY (St Michael) w Killadeas *Clogh*   I G M S WATSON

TUAM (Cathedral of St Mary) w Cong and Aasleagh *T, K & A*   I A J GRIMASON   C M S RYAN

TUAMGRANEY (St Cronan)   *see* Killaloe w Stradbally *L & K*

TUBBERCURRY (St George) w Killoran *T, K & A* P-in-c F D SWANN

TUBRID   *see* Drumkeeran w Templecarne and Muckross *Clogh*

TULLAGH (no dedication)   *see* Abbeystrewry Union *C, C & R*

TULLAGHBEGLEY (St Ann)   *see* Dunfanaghy, Raymunterdoney and Tullaghbegley *D & R*

TULLAGHMELAN (no dedication)   *see* Clonmel w Innislounagh, Tullaghmelan etc *C & O*

TULLAMORE (St Catherine) w Durrow, Newtownfertullagh, Rahan, Tyrellspass and Killoughy *M & K*   I I G DELAMERE

TULLANISKIN (Holy Trinity) w Clonoe *Arm*   C W ANDERSON

TULLOW (no dedication) *D & G*   I L J TANNER

TULLOW (St Columba) w Shillelagh, Aghold and Mullinacuff *C & O*   I A D H ORR

TULLYAUGHNISH (St Paul) w Kilmacrennan and Killygarvan *D & R*   I H GILMORE

TULLYNAKILL (no dedication)   *see* Killinchy w Kilmood and Tullynakill *D & D*

TUNNY (St Andrew)   *see* Glenavy w Tunny and Crumlin *Conn*

TURLOUGH (no dedication)   *see* Aughaval w Achill, Knappagh, Dugort etc *T, K & A*

TYBOHINE (no dedication)   *see* Roscommon w Donamon, Rathcline, Kilkeevin etc *K, E & A*

TYDAVNET (St Davnet)   *see* Monaghan w Tydavnet and Kilmore *Clogh*

TYHOLLAND (St Sillian)   *see* Donagh w Tyholland and Errigal Truagh *Clogh*

TYNAN (St Vindic) w Middletown and Aghavilly *Arm* I M H HAGAN

TYRELLA (St John)   *see* Rathmullan w Tyrella *D & D*

TYRELLSPASS (St Sinian)   *see* Tullamore w Durrow, Newtownfertullagh, Rahan etc *M & K*

UPPER DONAGHMORE (St Patrick)   *see* Donaghmore w Upper Donaghmore *Arm*

URGLIN (no dedication)   *see* Carlow w Urglin and Staplestown *C & O*

URNEY (Christ Church) w Sion Mills *D & R* I M G GREENSTREET

URNEY (no dedication) w Denn and Derryheen *K, E & A* I M R LIDWILL

VALENTIA (St John the Baptist)   *see* Kenmare w Sneem, Waterville etc *L & K*

VIRGINIA   *see* Lurgan w Billis, Killinkere and Munterconnaught *K, E & A*

WARINGSTOWN (Holy Trinity)   *see* Donaghcloney w Waringstown *D & D*

WARRENPOINT (no dedication)   *see* Clonallon and Warrenpoint w Kilbroney *D & D*

WATERFORD (Christ Church Cathedral) w Killea, Drumcannon and Dunhill *C & O*   I M P JANSSON C J M WALLACE

WATERVILLE   *see* Kenmare w Sneem, Waterville etc *L & K*

WESTPORT   *see* Aughaval w Achill, Knappagh, Dugort etc *T, K & A*

WEXFORD (St Iberius) and Kilscoran Union *C & O* I A MINION   C N J HALFORD   NSM P A NEILAND

WHITECHURCH   *see* Dublin Whitechurch *D & G*

WHITECHURCH (no dedication)   *see* New w Old Ross, Whitechurch, Fethard etc *C & O*

WHITEGATE   *see* Cloyne Union *C, C & R*

WHITEHEAD (St Patrick) and Islandmagee *Conn* I M F TAYLOR

WHITEHOUSE (St John) *Conn*   I E O'BRIEN

WHITEROCK   *see* Belfast Whiterock *Conn*

WICKLOW (no dedication) w Killiskey *D & G* P-in-c J A H KINKEAD   NSM K RUE

WILLOWFIELD (no dedication) *D & D*   I D A MCCLAY C W N DONOGHUE

WOODBURN (Holy Trinity) *Conn*   I T A G MCCANN

WOODLAWN (no dedication)   *see* Aughrim w Ballinasloe etc *L & K*

WOODSCHAPEL (St John) w Gracefield *Arm*   I E R MURRAY

ZION   *see* Dublin Zion Ch *D & G*

THE DIOCESE IN EUROPE

Diocesan Office, 14 Tufton Street, London SW1P 3QZ
T: (020) 7898 1155   F: 7898 1166
E: bron.panter@churchofengland.org
W: www.europe.anglican.org

ARCHDEACONS
1. Eastern   C H WILLIAMS
2. France   I F NAYLOR
3. Gibraltar   G S JOHNSTON
4. Italy and Malta   J BOARDMAN
5. North West Europe   *vacant*
6. Germany and Northern Europe   C H WILLIAMS
7. Switzerland   P M POTTER

Further information may be obtained from the appropriate archdeacon (the archdeaconry number is given after the name of each country), and a detailed leaflet is obtainable from the diocesan office. Mission to Seafarers chaplaincies are listed separately at the end of the section.

Andorra 3
vacant

Armenia 1
YEREVAN   *vacant*

Austria 1
VIENNA (Christ Church)   Chapl P M S CURRAN,
Asst Chapl J BARKER, C M WALTNER

Belgium 5
ANTWERP (St Boniface)   Chapl A R WAGSTAFF
BRUSSELS (Pro-Cathedral of the Holy Trinity)
Assoc Chapl J A WILKINSON
CHARLEROI   *vacant*
GHENT (St John)   P-in-c S MURRAY
KNOKKE (St George)   P-in-c S MURRAY
LEUVEN   P-in-c J D MCDONALD
LIÈGE   P-in-c P M YIEND
MONS   Served by Sen CF UK Support Unit Supreme
Headquarters Allied Powers Europe
OSTEND   P-in-c A U NWAEKWE
TERVUREN   Chapl S J TYNDALL, Asst Chapl N J GREGORY
YPRES (St George)   P-in-c B M LLEWELLYN

Bosnia and Herzegovina 1
SARAJEVO (St Anthony)   *vacant*

Bulgaria 1
Served from Bucharest (Romania)

Croatia 1
Served from Vienna (Austria)

Czech Republic 1
PRAGUE   P-in-c W J YATES

Denmark 6
COPENHAGEN (St Alban) w Aarhus   Chapl D M MCCALLIG

Estonia 6
TALLINN (St Timothy and St Titus)   P-in-c G P PIIR

Finland 6
HELSINKI w Kerava, Kuopio, Mikkeli, Oulu, Pori,
Tampere, Turku and White Nile   Chapl T MÄKIPÄÄ,
Asst Chapl D L OLIVER, C A M Y MANGA

France 2
AIX-EN-PROVENCE   *see* Marseille w Aix-en-Provence
AMBERNAC   *see* Poitou-Charentes
AQUITAINE (Bertric Burée, Bordeaux, Limeuil, Monteton,
Périgueux-Chancelade, Sorges, Ste Nathalène and
Doudrac)   Chapl P D VROLIJK, Asst Chapl G L STRACHAN,
B A BEARCROFT, C E A MORRIS, C L SULLIVAN
ARRAS   P-in-c D M R FLACH
BARBÉZIEUX ST HILAIRE   *see* Poitou-Charentes
BEAULIEU-SUR-MER (St Michael)   P-in-c A W INGHAM
BORDEAUX   *see* Aquitaine
BOULOGNE-SUR-MER   *see* Pas de Calais
BRITTANY (Ploërmel, Huelgoat and Rostrene)
P-in-c F M TRETHEWEY
CAEN   *see* Paris St George
CAHORS   *see* Midi-Pyrénés and Aude
CALAIS   *see* Pas de Calais
CANNES (Holy Trinity)   Chapl G P WILLIAMS
CAYLUS   *see* Midi-Pyrénés and Aude
CHANTILLY (St Peter)   Chapl N J CLARKE
CHEF BOUTONNE   *see* Poitou-Charentes
CIVRAY   *see* Poitou-Charentes
DINARD (St Bartholomew)   P-in-c G J RANDALL
FONTAINEBLEAU   *vacant*
GIF SUR YVETTE   *see* Versailles
GRATOT HOMÉEL (Christ Church)   *see* La Manche
GRENOBLE   Chapl R HURLEY
HESDIN   *see* Pas de Calais
HUELGOAT   *see* Brittany
JARNAC   *see* Poitou-Charentes
LA MANCHE w Gratot Hommëel and Virey   *vacant*
LA ROCHEFOUCAULD   *see* Poitou-Charentes
LE GARD   P-in-c S LOWE
LILLE (Christ Church)   P-in-c D M R FLACH
LIMEUIL   *see* Aquitaine
LORGUES w Fayence   P-in-c W P MASSEY
LYON   Chapl B L HARDING
MAGNÉ   *see* Poitou-Charentes
MAISONS-LAFFITTE (Holy Trinity)   Chapl O L ERIKSSON
MARSEILLE (All Saints) w Aix-en-Provence   *vacant*
MENTON (St John)   P-in-c D A HART
MIDI-PYRÉNÉS and Aude (Cahors, Caylus, Tarn, Toulouse
and Valence d'Agen)   Chapl A R HAWKEN,
Asst Chapl A H JEWISS, M J HUTCHINSON, NSM P J D S SCOTT
MONTETON   *see* Aquitaine
NANTES   *see* Vendée
NICE (Holy Trinity) w Vence   Chapl P J E JACKSON
NORD PAS DE CALAIS (Boulogne-sur-Mer, Calais and
Hesdin)   *vacant*
PARIS (St George)   Chapl M H HARRISON, Asst Chapl A J BIGG
PARIS (St Michael)   Chapl A M LAMB
PARTHENAY   *see* Poitou-Charentes
PAU (St Andrew)   *vacant*
PÉRIGUEUX-CHANCELADE   *see* Aquitaine
PLOËRMEL   *see* Brittany
POITOU-CHARENTES (Christ the Good Shepherd) w
Ambernac, Barbézieux St Hilaire, Chef Boutonne, Civray,
Jarnac, La Rochefoucauld, Magné, Parthenay, St Jean
d'Angély, Verteuil and Villejésus   Chapl H L DOOR

PORT GRIMAUD   *see* St Raphaël
ROSTRENEN   *see* Brittany
ST JEAN D'ANGÉLY   *see* Poitou-Charentes
ST RAPHAËL (St John the Evangelist) w Port Grimaud
   P-in-c K M BRETEL
STE NATHALÈNE   *see* Aquitaine
SORGES   *see* Aquitaine
STRASBOURG   *vacant*
TARN   *see* Midi-Pyrénés and Aude
TOULOUSE   *see* Midi-Pyrénés and Aude
VALENCE D'AGEN   *see* Midi-Pyrénés and Aude
VENCE (St Hugh)   *see* Nice w Vence
VENDÉE (Puy de Serre, La Chapelle Archard and La Chapelle Palluau)   **P-in-c** C E SACKLEY
VERNET-LES-BAINS (St George)   **P-in-c** D T PHILLIPS
VERSAILLES (St Mark)   **Asst Chapl** E O LABOUREL
VERTEUIL   *see* Poitou-Charentes
VILLEJESUS   *see* Poitou-Charentes
VIREY   *see* La Manche

Georgia 1
TBILISI   *vacant*

Germany 6
BERLIN (St George)   **Chapl** C W JAGE-BOWLER,
   Asst Chapl I K E AHRENS
BONN w Cologne   **Asst Chapl** R A GARDINER
DRESDEN   *see* Berlin
DÜSSELDORF (Christ Church)   **Chapl** S J WALTON
FREIBURG-IM-BREISGAU   *vacant*
HAMBURG (St Thomas à Becket)   **Asst Chapl** E G ANDERS
HEIDELBERG   **P-in-c** E R KOEPPING
LEIPZIG   **Chapl** G M REAKES-WILLIAMS
STUTTGART   **P-in-c** K R DIMMICK

Gibraltar 3
GIBRALTAR (Cathedral of the Holy Trinity)
   Chapl J A B PADDOCK (Dean)

Greece 1
ATHENS, GREATER   **Sen Chapl** M M BRADSHAW,
   Asst Chapl P C LAMBERT, **C** A R LANE
CORFU (Holy Trinity)   **P-in-c** J J WILSON

Hungary 1
BUDAPEST   **P-in-c** F M HEGEDUS

Italy 4
AVIANO   *see* Venice
BARI   *see* Naples
BOLOGNA   *see* Florence
BORDIGHERA   *vacant*
CADENABBIA   *see* Milan
CAPRI   *see* Naples
FLORENCE (St Mark) w Siena (St Peter) and Bologna
   Chapl W B LISTER
GENOVA (The Holy Ghost)   *vacant*
MACERATA   *see* Rome
MILAN (All Saints)   **Chapl** V L SIMS
NAPLES (Christ Church) w Sorrento, Capri and Bari
   Chapl J R BACKHOUSE
PADOVA   **P-in-c** J BOARDMAN
PALERMO (Holy Cross)   *see* Sicily
ROME (All Saints) w Macerata   **Chapl** J BOARDMAN,
   C M E STYLES, D L ENGLISH
SICILY   *vacant*
SIENA   *see* Florence
SORRENTO   *see* Naples
TAORMINA (St George)   *see* Sicily
TRIESTE   *see* Venice
VARESE   Served from Lugano (Switzerland)
VENICE (St George) w Trieste   **P-in-c** H LEVETT
VINCENZA   Served by US Army Base

Latvia 6
RIGA (St Saviour)   **Chapl** J JERUMA-GRINBERGA

Luxembourg 5
LUXEMBOURG   **Chapl** C D LYON, **Asst Chapl** A J MARKEY

Malta and Gozo 4
VALLETTA (Pro-Cathedral of St Paul) w Sliema (Holy Trinity)
   Sen Chapl S H M GODFREY

Monaco 2
MONTE CARLO (St Paul)   **Chapl** W RAYMOND

Morocco 3
CASABLANCA (St John the Evangelist)
   P-in-c M S EL KISS MIHANNY
TANGIER (St Andrew)   *vacant*

The Netherlands 5
AMSTERDAM (Christ Church) w
   Heiloo   **Asst Chapl** F C BLIGHT, J A S HILL, **C** E FLORENTINUS
ARNHEM (St Willibrord)   *vacant*
EINDHOVEN   **Chapl** F P NOORDANUS
HAARLEM   **Chapl** D D S DE VERNY
HAGUE, THE (St John and St Philip)   **Chapl** A J GREADY,
   C J-L J SERGENT
NIJMEGEN   *vacant*
ROTTERDAM (St Mary)   **Chapl** S D HAZLETT,
   C A ROBINSON-MULLER
TWENTE (St Mary)   **P-in-c** A T M TOLLEFSEN VAN DER LANS
UTRECHT (Holy Trinity) w Zwolle   **Chapl** D G PHILLIPS,
   C C A NICHOLLS, **Hon Asst Chapl** S W VAN LEER
VOORSCHOTEN   **Chapl** R J CREW
ZWOLLE   *see* Utrecht

Norway 6
OSLO (St Edmund) w Bergen, Trondheim, Stavanger,
   Drammen, Moss, Sandefjord, Tromsö and Kristiansand
   Sen Chapl B K RUSSELL, **Asst Chapl** P R HOGARTH,
   NSM M N STRØMMEN

Poland 1
WARSAW w Gdansk   **P-in-c** D V A BROWN

Portugal 3
ALGARVE (St Vincent)   *vacant*
ALMANCIL   *see* Algarve
ESTORIL   *see* Lisbon
GORJÕES   *see* Algarve
LISBON (St George) w Estoril (St Paul)   *vacant*
MADEIRA (Holy Trinity)   **Chapl** J W BLAIR
PORTO (or OPORTO) (St James)   **Chapl** R J BATES
PRAIA DA LUZ   *see* Algarve
TAVIRA   *see* Algarve

Romania 1
BUCHAREST (The Resurrection)   *vacant*

Russian Federation 1
MOSCOW (St Andrew) w Vladivostock
   Chapl C A FAIRCLOUGH
ST PETERSBURG   *vacant*

Serbia 1
BELGRADE   **Chapl** J R FOX

Slovakia
Served from Vienna (Austria)

Slovenia
Served from Vienna (Austria)

Spain 3
ALCOCEBRE   *see* Costa Azahar

ALBOX   *see* Costa Almeria and Costa Calida
ALHAURÍN EL GRANDE   *see* Costa del Sol East
ALMUÑÉCAR   *see* Nerja and Almuñécar
BARCELONA (St George)   Chapl J B CHAPMAN
BENALMADENA COSTA   *see* Costa del Sol East
CALA D'OR   *see* Palma de Mallorca
CALAHONDA   *see* Costa del Sol East
CALPE   *see* Costa Blanca
CAMPOVERDE   *see* Torrevieja
COIN   *see* Costa del Sol East
COSTA ALMERIA   P-in-c P M WILLIAMS,
   Asst Chapl A W BENNETT
COSTA AZAHAR   *vacant*
COSTA BLANCA   Sen Chapl Q M RONCHETTI, **Chapl** S FOSTER
COSTA BRAVA   P-in-c A C JENKINS
COSTA CALIDA   *see* Costa Almeria
COSTA DEL SOL EAST   Chapl A E LEWIS
COSTA DEL SOL WEST   P-in-c A A LOW
COSTACABANA   *see* Costa Almeria and Costa Calida
DENIA   *see* Costa Blanca
EL CAMPELLO   *see* Costa Blanca
FORMENTERA   *see* Ibiza
FUENGIROLA (St Andrew)   *see* Costa del Sol East
FUERTEVENTURA   *see* Lanzarote
GANDIA   *see* Costa Blanca
IBIZA   P-in-c P E PIMENTEL
JÁVEA   *see* Costa Blanca
LA MANGA   *see* Torrevieja
LA MARINA   *see* Torrevieja
LA PALMA   *see* Puerto de la Cruz
LA SIESTA   *see* Torrevieja
LAGO JARDIN   *see* Torrevieja
LANZAROTE   *vacant*
LAS PALMAS (Holy Trinity)   P-in-c B M W STARES
LOS BALCONES   *see* Torrevieja
LOS GIGANTES   *see* Tenerife Sur
MADRID (St George)   Chapl P W ORMROD, **C** N C THOMAS,
   M J D PHIPPS
MÁLAGA (St George)   Chapl M E DOLAN,
   Asst Chapl D CAGE
MALLORCA   *see* Palma de Mallorca
MENORCA   P-in-c P STRUDWICK
MOJÁCAR   *see* Costa Almeria
NAZARET   *see* Lanzarote
NERJA and Almuñécar   *vacant*
PALMA DE MALLORCA (St Philip and St James)
   Chapl D J WALLER, **Asst Chapl** N L STIMPSON
PLAYA BLANCA   *see* Lanzarote
PLAYA DE LAS AMERICAS   *see* Tenerife Sur
PLAYA DEL INGLES   *see* Las Palmas
PUERTO DE LA CRUZ Tenerife (All Saints)
   C J K ELLIOTT DE RIVEROL
PUERTO DEL CARMEN   *see* Lanzarote
PUERTO POLLENSA   *see* Palma de Mallorca
PUERTO SOLLER   *see* Palma de Mallorca
ROQUETAS DE MAR   *see* Costa Almeria and Costa Calida
SAN PEDRO   *see* Costa del Sol West
SAN RAFAEL   *see* Ibiza

SANTA EULALIA   *see* Ibiza
SOTOGRANDE   *see* Costa del Sol West
TENERIFE SUR (St Eugenio)   *vacant*
TORREVIEJA   P-in-c R A SEABROOK
VINAROS   *see* Costa Azahar

Sweden 6

**GOTHENBURG (St Andrew) w Halmstad, Jönköping and
   Uddevalla   P-in-c** B P MOSS
**STOCKHOLM (St Peter and St Sigfrid) w Gävle and Västerås
   Chapl** N S HOWE

Switzerland 7

ANZERE   *see* Montreux
BADEN   *see* Zürich
BASLE   Chapl H C JONES, **Asst Chapl** R B HILLIARD,
   NSM A L LOWEN
BERNE (St Ursula)   Chapl P M POTTER,
   Asst Chapl L D BISIG
CHÂTEAU D'OEX   *see* Vevey
GENEVA (Holy Trinity)   Chapl A R GORDON
GSTAAD   *see* Montreux
LA CÔTE   P-in-c C J COOKE, **Asst Chapl** J CHAMBEYRON
LAUSANNE (Christ Church) w Neuchâtel   P-in-c A KELHAM
LUGANO (St Edward the Confessor)   *vacant*
MONTHEY   *see* Montreux
**MONTREUX (St John) w Anzere, Gstaad and Monthey
   P-in-c** D P DALZELL
NEUCHÂTEL   *see* Lausanne
ST GALLEN   *see* Zürich
VEVEY (All Saints) w Château d'Oex   Chapl C J ATKINSON
VILLARS   *see* Montreux
ZUG   *see* Zürich
ZÜRICH (St Andrew) w Baden, St Gallen and Zug   *vacant*

Turkey 1

ANKARA (St Nicholas)   Hon C E E AHMADINIA
**ISTANBUL (Christ Church) (Chapel of St Helena) w
   Moda (All Saints)   Chapl** I W L SHERWOOD,
   Asst Chapl R WILKINSON
**IZMIR (SMYRNA) (St John the Evangelist) w Bornova
   (St Mary Magdalene)   Chapl** R W EVANS

Turkmenistan 1

Served from Moscow (Russian Federation)

Ukraine 1

KIEV (Christ Church)   *vacant*

Uzbekistan 1

Served from Moscow (Russian Federation)

MISSION TO SEAFARERS CHAPLAINCIES

Belgium 5
ANTWERP   *Lay Chapl*
GHENT   Chapl S MURRAY

France 2
DUNKERQUE   Chapl B P HUMPHRIES

The Netherlands 5
ROTTERDAM and Schiedam   Chapl S D HAZLETT
VLISSINGEN   Chapl R ROBINSON

CHAPLAINS TO HER MAJESTY'S SERVICES

ROYAL NAVY

Chaplain of the Fleet and Archdeacon for the Royal Navy
Director General Naval Chaplaincy Service
The Ven J GREEN CB
Royal Naval Chaplaincy Service, Mail Point 1–2, Leach Building, Whale Island, Portsmouth PO2 8BY
T: (023) 9262 5055   F: 9262 5134

Chaplains RN

M D ALLSOPP
P R ANDREW
O J BALOGUN
R W BARBER
N A BEARDSLEY
S A R BEVERIDGE
J M BRIDGES
B R CLARKE
A S CORNESS
M L EVANS
J S FRANCIS
P F GARVIE

M F GODFREY
M J GOUGH
S P HALLAM
M J HILLS
G E D HITCHINS
M H JACKSON
T M ST J JAMES
N J KELLY
A J F MANSFIELD
J C MONEY
S J MORGAN
P J PYE

S P RASON
K A ROBUS
D J SIMPSON
P SLATER
S P SPRINGETT
J H TABOR
M WAGSTAFF
A A WEBBER
I J WHEATLEY
D V WYLIE

ARMY

Chaplain-General HM Land Forces
The Revd J Wodehouse
(The present Chaplain General is a Baptist Minister)
Archdeacon for the Army
The Ven P A EAGLES
*Ministry of Defence, Chaplains (Army), Army Headquarters, Blenheim Building,
Ground Floor Zone 1, Marlborough Lines, Monxton Road, Andover SP11 8HT*
M: 07766-762326

Chaplains to the Forces

D J ADAMS
G D ALLEN
P B ARCHIBALD
D G BAILEY
F A BAILLIE
K G BARRY
H W BEARN
W C BEAVER
S K BEAVIS
C D BELL
A S F BENNETT
H D BISHOP
S F BLOXAM-ROSE
P R BOSHER
J R G BRADBURY
C S T BRODDLE
P G BURROWS
D M BUXTON
P J CABLE
J W CALDWELL
R CAVAGAN
M CHESTER
J S CLARKE
P T CLEMETT
T A R COLE
M S R COLES
I R COLSON
D P CONNING
S COOK
A J COOPER
D P CREES

P J S CROCKETT
A I DALTON
A C DEEGAN
R J DOWNES
S J H DUNWOODY
P A EAGLES
D A EATON
B ELLIOTT
A EVANS
H D EVANS
M R EWBANK
S J FARMER
A J FELTHAM-WHITE
B G FLUX
P T FRANCIS
S A FRANKLIN
L F GANDIYA
C A GILLHAM
G C GOALBY
S H M GODFREY
E G A GORRINGE
J R B GOUGH
B Z GREEN
R T GREY
C J GROOCOCK
R A B HALL
A B HARDING
D A G HATHAWAY
R HAYES
D R HILL
L T J HILLARY

T R C HINEY
D HITCHCOCK
C H HOPE
P C HULLYER
G J HUMPHRYES
P J HUNT
A F JESSON
W H G JOHNSTONE
M F JONES
M V JONES
G M W KEITH
C D KINCH
P W S KING
N P KINSELLA
J M KNIGHT
C M LANGSTON
A M LATIFA
E R LAVERY
S H LODWICK
T J MATHEWS
D MCALISTER
S T J MCCAULAY
J A MCWHIRTER
K D MENTZEL
P J MILLS
J S MOESEL
D T MORGAN
N F M MORRIS
N P NICHOLSON
T R PLACE
R PLUCK

S S PRATT
I M R PRICE
R M PRIEST
S V PRINS
M O PRITCHARD
K PUNSHON
S A RICHARDS
L L RICHARDSON
R J RICHARDSON
A ROACHE
J S ROBERTSHAW
I C ROGERS
P W RUSHTON
A T J SALTER
G J SCOTT
R M SHEPPARD
J W SHEWAN

G C SMITH
M SOADY
M W SPEEKS
P H STARNES
A C STEELE
T M SUMPTER
P H SUMSION
O SWAN
M P TANNER
S B THATCHER
J A THOMPSON-VEAR
M-A B TISDALE
N S TODD
C A TOME DA SILVA
A J TOTTEN
K S TROMANS

T VAUGHAN
D E VINCE
J L VINCENT
M J VOLLAND
M P WADSWORTH
D O WALL
N J WALL
D C WEAVER
J P L WHALLEY
P C WHITEHEAD
A W WILKINSON
J S WILLIAMS
A C WILSON
S G WILSON
F J L WINFIELD
W WORLEY

ROYAL AIR FORCE

Chaplain-in-Chief and Archdeacon for the RAF
The Ven R J PENTLAND QHC
Chaplaincy Services, Valiant Block, HQ Air Command, RAF High Wycombe HP14 4UE
T: (01494) 496800   F: 496343

Chaplains RAF

J M AMEY
J M ANNIS
M A J BUCHAN
D M BUXTON
R L CANNON
K S CAPELIN-JONES
J P M CHAFFEY
A J CHAPMAN
M F CHATFIELD
R P CLEMENT
D M CLOAKE
M A COHEN
N L COOK
A L DYER
A J EARL
M J ELLIOTT
J R ELLIS
G D FIRTH
R V HAKE

D V R HARVEY
A D HEWETT
J A HOBSON
J M S HOLLAND
R J ISHERWOOD
W J IZOD
I A JONES
R JONES
M P D KENNARD
P S KNIGHT
S P LAMOND
C D LAWRENCE
N W M LEGGETT
G L LEGOOD
C A MITCHELL
D J NORFIELD
C J O'DELL
D T OSBORN
R G PECKHAM

M PERRY
L S PULLAN
S J RADLEY
P A RENNIE
D RICHARDSON
W J SCOTT
S J SHAW
M D SHELDON
A J STARK-ORDISH
M STEVENS
P L SWEETING
A W WAKEHAM-DAWSON
I S WARD
G WILLIAMS
E R WILLS
G E WITHERS
T WRIGHT
E L WYNN

PRISON CHAPLAINS

HM PRISON SERVICE
(England and Wales)

Chaplain General to HM Prisons
The Ven W A NOBLETT
Anglican Adviser Canon M L KAVANAGH

Chaplaincy HQ, Post Point 3.08, 3rd Floor Red Zone, Clive House, 70 Petty France, London SW1H 9HD
T: 03000-475186   F: 476822/3

Prisons

Acklington   M D TETLEY
Altcourse   K A CANTY
Ashfield   E A PERRY
Askham Grange   R A CLEGG
Bedford   S C GRENHAM-THOMPSON
Belmarsh   T G JACQUET
Birmingham   P GILLON
Bristol   D J H POWE
Brixton   P T J CHADDER
Bronzefield   B E DAVIS
Buckley Hall   R W A REECE
Bullingdon   A J FORAN
Bure   A V HEDGES
Cardiff   M C JOHN
Channings Wood   N R MARTIN
Chelmsford   J S RIDGE
Coldingley   I G THOMPSON
Cookham Wood   A Y BENNETT
Dartmoor   L H COOPER
Doncaster   G A O JESSON
Dorchester   R A BETTS, E W D TILDESLEY
Downview   W M HARVEY
Drake Hall   F V G BALLENTYNE
Eastwood Park   L G HEWISH, A J WILLIAMS
Elmley   J K M NJOROGE
Erlestoke   S G ASCOUGH, S A IBBETSON, P THOMPSON
Exeter   M D MILLER
Featherstone   D S FARLEY
Ford   A C OEHRING
Frankland   P G E TYLER
Full Sutton   A ATKINSON
Garth   D W GOODWIN, G C TURNER
Gartree   I L JOHNSON
Gloucester   C RAWLINSON
Grendon and Spring Hill   M B WHITAKER
Guys Marsh   P C BROWNE
Haverigg   G JONES, R P SPRATT
Hewell   M A SCHUTTE
Highpoint (north)   E R BELL, J K B FOWLER
Highpoint (south)   A L FOWLER
Hollesley Bay   J T PERRY, M R RENNARD
Holloway   K WILKIN
Holme House   K M BROOKE, A V DOUGLAS, J N GREENWOOD
Hull   N J WHETTON
Huntercombe   I D THACKER

Isis   S A SIMPSON
Isle of Wight   J A SWAINE
Kennet   A PIERCE-JONES
Kirkham   B J MAYNE, D NOBLET
Lewes   D E KENDRICK
Leyhill   C F TODD
Lincoln   A J ROBERTS
Lindholme   S E WALSH
Littlehey   D J KINDER, T MCFADDEN
Lowdham Grange   J M SAVAGE
Maidstone   A M FRANCIS
Manchester   J E CALLADINE, H R F MARTIN
Moorland   S E WALSH
Mount, The   P J ABREY
New Hall   C J TRUMAN
Norwich   O O SOTONWA
Nottingham   S NTOYIMONDO, M TYACK
Oakwood   D C WELLER
Onley   G R HOCKEN
Parc (Bridgend)   D C TILT
Pentonville   R A D STURT
Peterborough   R B THOMPSON, J A C WIEGMAN
Preston   B A EATON
Ranby   D K BEEDON
Risley   N D HAWLEY, L J SWEET
Rye Hill   N I JONES
Send   L J MASON
Stafford   J D BIRD, C M RICHARDSON
Standford Hill   S H DUNN
Stocken   S NTOYIMONDO
Styal   Y L YATES
Swaleside   E A COX
Swansea   N R SANDFORD
Swinfen Hall   M J NEWSOME, R C PAYNE
Thameside   D HARTLEY
Verne, The   G A HEBBERN
Wandsworth   T A BRYAN, R D S SANDERS
Warren Hill   J T PERRY
Wayland   I COOPER
Wealstun   K F A GABBADON
Whatton   J C HONOUR
Winchester   M E BRAIN
Wolds, The   B WORSDALE
Woodhill   A P HODGETTS
Wymott   C D F CROMBIE, P N TYERS

Young Offender Institutions

Aylesbury   S C LUCAS
Feltham   M J BOYES, A R J COOPER, P FOSTER
Glen Parva   T S WRIGHT
Lancaster Farms   D NOBLET

Portland   D J B HAZLEHURST
Rochester   G L BURN, B N B MUSINDI
Stoke Heath   S J MORRIS
Thorn Cross   M P MARTIN, S G VERHEY
Wetherby   D E HERTH, A R ROWE

Immigration Centres

Colnbrook   J W GEEN

Haslar   N G STARTIN

CHANNEL ISLANDS PRISON SERVICE

Guernsey   J E D LUFF, K C NORTHOVER

SCOTTISH PRISON SERVICE

Polmont   S C BONNEY

NORTHERN IRELAND PRISON SERVICE

Maghaberry   J R HOWARD

HOSPITAL CHAPLAINS

An index of whole-time and part-time hospital chaplains

Hospital and Health Care Chaplaincy
Church House, Great Smith Street, London SW1P 3AZ
Tel (020) 7898 1895

ABERDEEN ROYAL INFIRMARY   *see* Grampian Univ Hosp NHS Trust
ADELAIDE AND MEATH Dublin   T ALCOCK, M A J WILSON
AIREDALE NHS FOUNDATION TRUST   D J GRIFFITHS, J P SMITH, R L MULLIGAN
ALDER HEY Liverpool   *see* R Liverpool Children's NHS Trust
ANDOVER DISTRICT COMMUNITY HEALTH CARE NHS TRUST   D F KING
ANDOVER WAR MEMORIAL NHS TRUST   *see* Andover District Community Health Care NHS Trust
ARMAGH AND DUNGANNON HEALTH AND SOCIAL SERVICES TRUST   C W M ROLSTON
ARTHUR RANK HOUSE BROOKFIELDS Hospital Cambridge   K C MORRISON
BARKING, HAVERING AND REDBRIDGE UNIVERSITY HOSPITALS NHS TRUST   P J WRIGHT, T COLEMAN
BARNET AND CHASE FARM HOSPITALS NHS TRUST   T M BARON, T R BONIWELL
BARNET, ENFIELD AND HARINGEY MENTAL HEALTH TRUST   T M BARON
BARNSLEY HOSPITAL NHS FOUNDATION TRUST   P D NEEDHAM
BASILDON AND THURROCK UNIVERSITY HOSPITALS NHS FOUNDATION TRUST   L G PEALL
BATH AND WEST COMMUNITY NHS TRUST   M JOYCE
BEDFORD HOSPITAL NHS TRUST   N A MCINTOSH
BELFAST HEALTH AND SOCIAL CARE TRUST   D G BEATTIE, D W GAMBLE
BETHLEM AND MAUDSLEY NHS TRUST London   *see* S Lon and Maudsley NHS Foundn Trust
BIRMINGHAM CHILDREN'S HOSPITAL NHS TRUST   P NASH, E BLAIR-CHAPPELL, M A ROBINSON, N E BALL, R J HILL-BROWN
BIRMINGHAM SPECIALIST COMMUNITY HEALTH NHS TRUST   L M MORRIS
BIRMINGHAM WOMEN'S NHS FOUNDATION TRUST   D G JONES, E L WYNN
BLACKPOOL, FYLDE AND WYRE HOSPITALS NHS TRUST   C G LORD
BOLTON HOSPITALS NHS TRUST   C D BINNS, S FOSTER
BRADFORD HOSPITALS NHS TRUST   J N FIELDER
BRIDGWATER   D GODDARD
BRIGHTON AND SUSSEX UNIVERSITY HOSPITALS NHS TRUST   P R WELLS
BUCKINGHAMSHIRE HOSPITALS NHS TRUST   D R ELLIOTT
BURTON HOSPITALS NHS FOUNDATION TRUST   A C THORP, G J CROSSLEY, H J BAKER
CALDERDALE AND HUDDERSFIELD NHS FOUNDATION TRUST   G SPENCER, M D ELLERTON
CAMBRIDGE UNIVERSITY HOSPITALS NHS FOUNDATION TRUST   D P FORD, S D GRIFFITHS
CAMBRIDGESHIRE AND PETERBOROUGH NHS FOUNDATION TRUST   J P NICHOLSON
CAMDEN AND ISLINGTON NHS FOUNDATION TRUST   N P MORROW
CARDIFF AND VALE NHS TRUST   E J BURKE
CARDIFF AND VALE UNIVERSITY LOCAL HEALTH BOARD   P DAVIES
CARDIFF COMMUNITY HEALTHCARE NHS TRUST   J H L ROWLANDS
CENTRAL LONDON COMMUNITY HEALTHCARE NHS TRUST   M L T MCGONIGLE
CENTRAL MANCHESTER/MANCHESTER CHILDREN'S UNIVERSITY HOSPITAL NHS TRUST   J S A LAW
CENTRAL MIDDLESEX NHS TRUST   M D MOORHEAD
CHELSEA AND WESTMINSTER HOSPITAL NHS FOUNDATION TRUST   C BEARDSLEY
CHESHIRE AND WIRRAL PARTNERSHIPS NHS TRUST   D R NUGENT, A SCAIFE, G L HODKINSON
CHRISTIE HOSPITAL NHS TRUST Manchester   A R BRADLEY, K L DUNN

CITY HOSPITALS SUNDERLAND NHS FOUNDATION TRUST   O R OMOLE, P H WEBB
COLCHESTER HOSPITAL UNIVERSITY NHS FOUNDATION TRUST   H A N PLATTS, M W THOMPSON
COMMUNITY HEALTH SHEFFIELD NHS TRUST   *see* Sheff Care Trust
CORK UNIVERSITY   D R NUZUM
CORNWALL PARTNERSHIP NHS TRUST   C D NEWELL, E C DEELEY
COUNTESS OF CHESTER HOSPITAL NHS FOUNDATION TRUST   E M GARDNER, G M HIBBERT
COUNTY DURHAM AND DARLINGTON NHS FOUNDATION TRUST   K S TROMANS, T P GIBBONS
DARTFORD AND GRAVESHAM NHS TRUST   M H KELLY
DERBY HOSPITALS NHS FOUNDATION TRUST   S C NEAL, D W ASHTON, M HARGREAVES
DONCASTER AND BASSETLAW HOSPITALS NHS FOUNDATION TRUST   C S W VAN D'ARQUE, J L MCKENNA
DONCASTER AND SOUTH HUMBER HEALTHCARE NHS TRUST   *see* Rotherham, Doncaster and S Humber NHS Trust
DORCHESTER HOSPITALS   *see* Dorset Co Hosp NHS Foundn Trust
DORSET COUNTY HOSPITAL NHS FOUNDATION TRUST   R A BETTS, R MARTIN, R C J R MARTIN
DORSET HEALTH CARE NHS TRUST   *see* Dorset HealthCare University NHS Foundn Trust
DORSET HEALTHCARE UNIVERSITY NHS FOUNDATION TRUST   M G OATES
DUMFRIES AND GALLOWAY PRIMARY CARE HEALTH NHS TRUST   *see* NHS Dumfries and Galloway
DUMFRIES AND GALLOWAY ROYAL INFIRMARY   *see* NHS Dumfries and Galloway
EALING HOSPITAL NHS TRUST   E J WALLER, M K DAVIDGE-SMITH, Y KHUSHI
EAST AND NORTH HERTFORDSHIRE NHS TRUST   J E HATTON
EAST CHESHIRE NHS TRUST   J BUCKLEY
EAST HAMPSHIRE PRIMARY CARE TRUST   C R PRESTIDGE
EAST KENT HOSPITALS NHS TRUST   M P M STEWART, P F HILL
EAST LANCASHIRE HOSPITALS NHS TRUST   A S HORSFALL
EAST LONDON NHS FOUNDATION TRUST   N J COPSEY
EAST SUFFOLK LOCAL HEALTH SERVICES NHS TRUST   *see* Local Health Partnerships NHS Trust
EAST SURREY HOSPITAL AND COMMUNITY HEALTHCARE NHS TRUST   *see* Surrey and Sussex Healthcare NHS Trust
EAST SURREY PRIORITY CARE NHS TRUST   N J COPSEY
EAST SUSSEX HEALTHCARE NHS TRUST   F M BALDWIN
EAST SUSSEX HOSPITALS NHS TRUST   G J A COOK
ENFIELD PRIMARY CARE TRUST   T M BARON
EPSOM AND ST HELIER UNIVERSITY HOSPITALS NHS TRUST   S F SEWELL, S J ELLISON
ESSEX RIVERS HEALTHCARE NHS TRUST   *see* Colchester Hosp Univ NHS Foundn Trust
EVELINA CHILDREN'S   *see* Guy's and St Thomas' NHS Foundation Trust
FORTH VALLEY NHS TRUST   T NJUGUNA
FRIMLEY HEALTH NHS FOUNDATION TRUST   E J TOMS
FRIMLEY PARK HOSPITAL NHS FOUNDATION TRUST   B D BURBIDGE, J J SISTIG
GATESHEAD HEALTH NHS TRUST   J R PERRY
GEORGE ELIOT HOSPITAL NHS TRUST Nuneaton   M J HAMMOND, R J WITCOMBE
GLOUCESTERSHIRE HOSPITALS NHS FOUNDATION TRUST   W B IRVINE, W B M DOWIE
GOOD HOPE HOSPITAL NHS TRUST Sutton Coldfield   A T BALL
GRAMPIAN HEALTHCARE NHS TRUST   *see* NHS Grampian
GRAMPIAN UNIVERSITY HOSPITAL NHS TRUST   N C MILNE
GREAT ORMOND STREET HOSPITAL FOR CHILDREN NHS FOUNDATION TRUST   D A MOORE BROOKS, J D LINTHICUM, P J SHERRINGTON
GREAT WESTERN HOSPITALS NHS FOUNDATION TRUST   A GOSDEN

GREATER MANCHESTER WEST MENTAL HEALTH NHS FOUNDATION TRUST   B S GASKELL, D R SUTTON, J S A LAW

GUY'S AND ST THOMAS' NHS FOUNDATION TRUST London   C B HALL, M A K HILBORN, S M TAYLOR, W W SHARPE, R A SHAW

GWENT HEALTHCARE NHS TRUST   A W TYLER, D C ROBERTS, M J MARSDEN

HAMPSHIRE HOSPITALS NHS FOUNDATION TRUST   A D WATTS

HARROGATE AND DISTRICT NHS FOUNDATION TRUST   T P PARKER

HEART OF ENGLAND NHS FOUNDATION TRUST   L M BUSFIELD, M MACLACHLAN

HEATHERWOOD AND WEXHAM PARK HOSPITALS NHS FOUNDATION TRUST   C E L SMITH, S M VAN BEVEREN

HEREFORD HOSPITALS NHS TRUST   L C RHODES

HERTFORDSHIRE PARTNERSHIP NHS FOUNDATION TRUST   R J S ALLEN, V M HARVEY

HEXHAM GENERAL   A J PATTERSON

HINCHINGBROOKE HEALTH CARE NHS TRUST   C M FURLONG, P M DUFFETT-SMITH, S GRIFFITH, S A WATTS

HOPE, SALFORD ROYAL AND LADYWELL HOSPITALS Manchester   see Salford R NHS Foundn Trust

HULL AND EAST YORKSHIRE HOSPITALS NHS TRUST   A M LAIRD, C R TETLEY, J A SHARP

HUMBER MENTAL HEALTH TEACHING NHS TRUST   E ROSE

HYWEL DDA HEALTH BOARD   E HOWELLS

IMPERIAL COLLEGE HEALTHCARE NHS TRUST   J G S MORGAN, R RATCLIFFE

INVICTA COMMUNITY CARE NHS TRUST   S A J MITCHELL

ISLE OF WIGHT NHS PRIMARY CARE TRUST   D M NETHERWAY, J K HALLAM, K S BURKE

JAMES PAGET HEALTHCARE NHS TRUST   M E ZIPFEL

JERSEY GROUP   M TURNER

KENT AND MEDWAY NHS AND SOCIAL CARE PARTNERSHIP TRUST   M CLEEVE, R A BIERBAUM

KENT AND SUSSEX WEALD NHS TRUST   see Maidstone and Tunbridge Wells NHS Trust

KETTERING GENERAL HOSPITAL NHS TRUST   R G BROWN

KING EDWARD VII Midhurst   D B WELSMAN

KING'S COLLEGE HOSPITAL NHS FOUNDATION TRUST   L SEEAR, B RHODES, K PARKES, S NJOKA, T J MERCER

KNEESWORTH HOUSE Royston   N TAYLOR

LEEDS AND YORK PARTNERSHIP NHS FOUNDATION TRUST   B M KIMARU, M I KIMBALL

LEEDS TEACHING HOSPITALS NHS TRUST   A CLAYTON, C J SWIFT

LEICESTERSHIRE PARTNERSHIP NHS TRUST   T H GIRLING

LEIGHTON Crewe   see Mid Cheshire Hosps Trust

LEWISHAM AND GREENWICH NHS TRUST   E A NEWMAN, R EMMANUEL, W J DAVID

LEWISHAM HEALTHCARE NHS TRUST   M J HANCOCK

LINCOLN DISTRICT HEALTH SERVICES NHS TRUST AND LINCOLN HOSPITALS NHS TRUST   W G WILLIAMS

LINCOLNSHIRE PARTNERSHIP NHS FOUNDATION TRUST   A M PAVEY

LITTLEHAMPTON   see Worthing Priority Care NHS Trust

LITTLEMORE Oxford   see Ox Health NHS Foundn Trust

LOCAL HEALTH PARTNERSHIPS NHS TRUST Suffolk   G T MELVIN

LOTHIAN UNIVERSITY HOSPITALS NHS TRUST   C T UPTON

LUTON AND DUNSTABLE HOSPITAL NHS FOUNDATION TRUST   M A TREMBATH

MAIDSTONE AND TUNBRIDGE WELLS NHS TRUST   N J MITRA

MAUDSLEY London   E DAWSON

MAYDAY HEALTHCARE NHS TRUST Thornton Heath   H A FIFE

MEDWAY NHS FOUNDATION TRUST   D V GOWER, S C SPENCER

MERSEY CARE NHS TRUST   C J MOON, J P RAFFAY

MID CHESHIRE HOSPITALS TRUST   C J SANDERSON, D MARSH

MID STAFFORDSHIRE NHS FOUNDATION TRUST   M J COULTER

MID YORKSHIRE HOSPITALS NHS TRUST   R J BAILES, S HULME

MID-ESSEX HOSPITAL SERVICES NHS TRUST   J SHEFFIELD

MOORFIELDS EYE HOSPITAL NHS TRUST   D E ALLEN

MORAY Hospitals   A L WILLIS

MORECAMBE BAY HOSPITALS NHS TRUST   see Univ Hosps of Morecambe Bay NHS Trust

NEWCASTLE UPON TYNE HOSPITALS NHS FOUNDATION TRUST   K J FRANCIS, M J SHIPTON

NEWHAM PRIMARY CARE TRUST   N J COPSEY

NEWHAM UNIVERSITY HOSPITAL NHS TRUST   T N ALEXANDER-WATTS

NHS DUMFRIES AND GALLOWAY   S R PAISLEY

NHS GRAMPIAN   J DUTHIE, N C MILNE

NHS TAYSIDE   D SHEPHERD

NORFOLK AND NORWICH UNIVERSITY HOSPITAL NHS TRUST   J M STEWART, A V WOODROW, E S LANGAN, J L NURSEY, S L GREEN

NORFOLK COMMUNITY HEALTH AND CARE NHS TRUST   E H GARRARD

NORFOLK PRIMARY CARE TRUST   M J MCFADYEN, P A ATKINSON

NORTH BRISTOL NHS TRUST   A J PARKER, A M BUCKNALL, N A HECTOR, S J ORAM, A R GOOD

NORTH CUMBRIA UNIVERSITY HOSPITALS NHS TRUST   A M ROBERTS, M C DANKS-FLOWER, S C E CAKE

NORTH EAST LONDON NHS FOUNDATION TRUST   A F RABLEN, G F JENKINS

NORTH GLAMORGAN NHS TRUST   E A POWELL

NORTH KENT HEALTH CARE NHS TRUST   see Thames Gateway NHS Trust

NORTH MIDDLESEX HOSPITAL NHS TRUST   B D FENTON, P C ATHERTON

NORTH STAFFORDSHIRE COMBINED HEALTHCARE NHS TRUST   L P LUCKING

NORTH SURREY PRIMARY CARE TRUST   J C L RUNNACLES, J M ALLFORD

NORTH TEES AND HARTLEPOOL NHS TRUST   R J COOPER

NORTH WARWICKSHIRE NHS TRUST   S P MOULT

NORTH WEST WALES NHS TRUST   R H GRIFFITHS, W ROBERTS

NORTHAMPTON GENERAL HOSPITAL NHS TRUST   G A SARMEZEY

NORTHAMPTONSHIRE COUNTY GENERAL LUNATIC ASYLUM   see St Andr Hosp Northn

NORTHAMPTONSHIRE HEALTHCARE NHS TRUST   R J T FARMER

NORTHERN DEVON HEALTHCARE NHS TRUST   J A CARTWRIGHT, K E W MATHERS

NORTHERN LINCOLNSHIRE AND GOOLE HOSPITALS NHS TRUST   A I MCCORMICK, C M J THODY

NORTHUMBERLAND HEALTH AUTHORITY   see Northumbria Healthcare NHS Foundn Trust

NORTHUMBERLAND MENTAL HEALTH NHS TRUST   S D MASON

NORTHUMBERLAND, TYNE AND WEAR NHS FOUNDATION TRUST   C J WORSFOLD

NORTHUMBRIA HEALTHCARE NHS FOUNDATION TRUST   J WAIYAKI, J L J COOPER, K L JONES

NORWICH COMMUNITY HEALTH PARTNERSHIP NHS TRUST   see Norfolk Primary Care Trust

NORWICH PRIMARY CARE TRUST   see Norfolk Primary Care Trust

NORWICH The Great Hospital (Almshouses)   B R OAKE

NOTTINGHAM UNIVERSITY HOSPITAL NHS TRUST City Hospital Campus   A DE C LADD, P KEY

NOTTINGHAM UNIVERSITY HOSPITAL NHS TRUST Queen's Medical Centre Campus   A M BROOKS, C T DOLBY, G SPENCER, J HEMSTOCK

NOTTINGHAMSHIRE HEALTHCARE NHS TRUST   T W POWNALL-JONES

OSWESTRY ORTHOPAEDIC   see Robert Jones/Agnes Hunt Orthopaedic NHS Trust

OXFORD HEALTH NHS FOUNDATION TRUST   G P HARRISON

OXFORD UNIVERSITY HOSPITALS NHS TRUST   J RADFORD, J E COCKE, M J WHIPP, P F SUTTON

OXFORDSHIRE AND BUCKINGHAMSHIRE MENTAL HEALTH PARTNERSHIP NHS TRUST   S L BUSHELL

OXFORDSHIRE MENTAL HEALTHCARE NHS TRUST   see Ox Health NHS Foundn Trust

PAPWORTH HOSPITAL NHS FOUNDATION TRUST   G R ROWLANDS

PATHFINDER MENTAL HEALTH SERVICES NHS TRUST   see SW Lon and St George's Mental Health NHS Trust

PEACE HOSPICE Watford   M J CARTER

PENNINE ACUTE HOSPITALS NHS TRUST, THE   P E JONES, S A TAUSON

PETERBOROUGH AND STAMFORD HOSPITALS NHS FOUNDATION TRUST   J J PRICE, M B JONES

PETERBOROUGH HOSPITALS NHS TRUST   R E HIGGINS

PLYMOUTH HOSPITALS NHS TRUST   J M COLLIS, S J T PEARCE

POOLE HOSPITAL NHS TRUST   I R PEARCE, E J LLOYD

PORTSMOUTH HOSPITALS NHS TRUST   J S E FARRELL, R E SCHOFIELD, B R SMITH, J POWER, M J A LINDSAY

PRINCESS ALEXANDRA HOSPITAL NHS TRUST Harlow   C OKEKE, T R WEEKS

PRINCESS ELIZABETH Guernsey   L S LE VASSEUR

PRIORY Birmingham   J A GRIFFIN

PROSPECT PARK Reading   R S WADEY

QUEEN ELIZABETH HOSPITAL KING'S LYNN NHS FOUNDATION TRUST   J M THOMSON, P S HOLLINS

RAIGMORE HOSPITAL NHS TRUST Inverness   A A SINCLAIR

RIBCHESTER   A D HINDLEY
RICHMOND AND TWICKENHAM PRIMARY CARE TRUST
   J W KNILL-JONES
ROBERT JONES/AGNES HUNT ORTHOPAEDIC HOSPITAL NHS
   TRUST Oswestry   A R BAILEY
ROTHERHAM NHS FOUNDATION TRUST   H FERGUSON-STUART
ROTHERHAM GENERAL HOSPITALS NHS TRUST   J E ASHTON
ROTHERHAM, DONCASTER AND SOUTH HUMBER MENTAL
   HEALTH NHS TRUST   J E BAKER
ROYAL BERKSHIRE NHS FOUNDATION TRUST   L D COLAM,
   R J SIMMONDS
ROYAL BOLTON HOSPITAL NHS FOUNDATION TRUST
   B S GASKELL
ROYAL BOURNEMOUTH AND CHRISTCHURCH HOSPITALS
   NHS TRUST   A SESSFORD, A M NEWTON
ROYAL BROMPTON AND HAREFIELD NHS TRUST   N K LEE,
   R G THOMPSON, T HANDLEY MACMATH
ROYAL CORNWALL HOSPITALS TRUST   J K P S ROBERTSHAW
ROYAL DEVON AND EXETER NHS FOUNDATION TRUST
   S R SWARBRICK
ROYAL FREE HAMPSTEAD NHS TRUST   see R Free London
   NHS Foundn Trust
ROYAL FREE LONDON NHS FOUNDATION TRUST
   D W RUSHTON, P D CONRAD, R H MITCHELL
ROYAL GROUP OF HOSPITALS AND DENTAL HOSPITALS
   HEALTH AND SOCIAL SERVICES TRUST Belfast   A MALLON
ROYAL LIVERPOOL AND BROADGREEN UNIVERSITY
   HOSPITALS NHS TRUST   C J PETER, G A PERERA
ROYAL LIVERPOOL CHILDREN'S NHS TRUST   D J WILLIAMS
ROYAL MARSDEN NHS FOUNDATION TRUST London
   and Surrey   A BURGESS, A E DOERR, A J MCCULLOCH,
   D F G BUTLIN
ROYAL NATIONAL ORTHOPAEDIC HOSPITAL NHS TRUST
   W A BROOKER
ROYAL SURREY COUNTY HOSPITAL NHS TRUST
   J S MCARTHUR-EDWARDS, D N HOBDEN
ROYAL UNITED HOSPITAL BATH NHS TRUST   A J DAVIES
ROYAL VICTORIA Belfast   see R Gp of Hosps Health and Soc
   Services Trust
ROYAL VICTORIA INFIRMARY AND ASSOCIATED HOSPITALS
   NHS TRUST Newcastle   see Newcastle upon Tyne Hosps NHS
   Foundn Trust
ROYAL WOLVERHAMPTON HOSPITALS NHS TRUST   N P ELY,
   S PETTY, C W FULLARD, J A LEACH
SALFORD ROYAL NHS FOUNDATION TRUST   A J HESLOP,
   J I WHITTINGHAM, J L HOOD, L H LEE
SALISBURY NHS FOUNDATION TRUST   F E CANHAM,
   K S M STEPHENS, A R SYMES
SANDWELL AND WEST BIRMINGHAM HOSPITALS NHS TRUST
   D H GARNER
SANDWELL MENTAL HEALTH NHS AND SOCIAL CARE TRUST
   A E HANNY, E C LOUIS
SEVENOAKS   see Invicta Community Care NHS Trust
SHEFFIELD CARE TRUST   S H ROSS
SHEFFIELD CHILDREN'S NHS FOUNDATION TRUST
   G J HUTCHISON
SHEFFIELD TEACHING HOSPITALS NHS FOUNDATION TRUST
   M J NEWITT, G L WILTON, J H DALEY, J J PERKINS, K G LOWE,
   M J KERRY, M R COBB
SHERWOOD FOREST HOSPITALS NHS TRUST   R A E LAMBERT
SHREWSBURY AND TELFORD NHS TRUST   M G WILLIAMS,
   M I FEARNSIDE, P HRYZIUK
SOMERSET PARTNERSHIP NHS FOUNDATION TRUST
   B E PRIORY, E J ROTHWELL, H P SHARP
SOUTH DEVON HEALTHCARE NHS FOUNDATION TRUST
   A D SUMNER, J H GARNER
SOUTH DOWNS HEALTH NHS TRUST   D L I PERKS
SOUTH ESSEX MENTAL HEALTH AND COMMUNITY CARE
   NHS TRUST   J H DELFGOU
SOUTH LONDON AND MAUDSLEY NHS FOUNDATION TRUST
   I N FISHWICK
SOUTH LONDON HEALTHCARE NHS TRUST   G M HESKINS,
   D COUTTS
SOUTH MANCHESTER UNIVERSITY HOSPITALS NHS TRUST
   see Univ Hosp of S Man NHS Foundn Trust
SOUTH SHIELDS GENERAL   see S Tyneside Healthcare Trust
SOUTH STAFFORDSHIRE HEALTHCARE NHS TRUST
   K A SHAW
SOUTH TEES HOSPITALS NHS TRUST   A M GRANGE,
   M EDWARDS
SOUTH TYNESIDE HEALTHCARE TRUST   P R BEALING
SOUTH WARWICKSHIRE GENERAL HOSPITALS NHS TRUST
   F E TYLER, H F COCKELL
SOUTH WEST DORSET PRIMARY CARE TRUST   E J WOODS
SOUTH WEST LONDON AND ST GEORGE'S MENTAL HEALTH
   NHS TRUST   A R BECK, C CARSON

SOUTH WEST YORKSHIRE PARTNERSHIP NHS FOUNDATION
   TRUST   B M KIMARU, C M GARTLAND
SOUTHAMPTON UNIVERSITY HOSPITALS NHS TRUST
   see Univ Hosp Southn NHS Foundn Trust
SOUTHEND HEALTH CARE NHS TRUST   G L CROOK
SOUTHERN DERBYSHIRE ACUTE HOSPITALS NHS TRUST
   see Derby Hosps NHS Foundn Trust
SOUTHERN HEALTH NHS FOUNDATION TRUST
   N P FENNEMORE
ST ANDREW'S HEALTHCARE Birmingham, Essex,
   Northampton, Nottinghamshire   R M HETHERINGTON,
   C D WOOD, M J MARSHALL, P R EVANS
ST ANDREW'S Northampton   N PURVEY-TYRER
ST GEORGE'S AND COTTAGE Morpeth   see Northd Mental
   Health NHS Trust
ST GEORGE'S HEALTHCARE NHS TRUST London
   R B REYNOLDS, R W WALL
ST HELENS AND KNOWSLEY HOSPITALS NHS TRUST
   P TAYLOR
ST MARTIN'S Bath   see Bath and West Community
   NHS Trust
ST MARY'S HOSPITAL NHS TRUST Newport (Isle of Wight)
   see Isle of Wight NHS Primary Care Trust
ST PETER'S HOSPITAL NHS TRUST Chertsey   see N Surrey
   Primary Care Trust
STATES OF GUERNSEY BOARD OF HEALTH   J LE BILLON,
   J E D LUFF
STOCKPORT NHS TRUST   B J LOWE
SUFFOLK COASTAL PRIMARY CARE TRUST   N J WINTER
SURREY AND BORDERS PARTNERSHIP NHS TRUST
   N J COPSEY, S H BULL
SURREY AND SUSSEX HEALTHCARE NHS TRUST
   D G O ROBINSON, F G LEHANEY, J M GLASSPOOL
SUSSEX PARTNERSHIP NHS FOUNDATION TRUST   G REEVES,
   G S JOHNSON
SWANSEA NHS TRUST   D M GRIFFITHS, N R GRIFFIN,
   P J GWYNN
TAMESIDE AND GLOSSOP ACUTE SERVICES NHS TRUST
   J HILDITCH
TAUNTON AND SOMERSET NHS TRUST   J P LAWRENCE
TEES AND NORTH EAST YORKSHIRE NHS TRUST   P L WALKER
TEES, ESK AND WEAR VALLEY NHS TRUST   C JAY
THAMES GATEWAY NHS TRUST   P R BECKINSALE
THORNBURY Hospital   G E FOOKS
TRAFFORD HEALTHCARE NHS TRUST   C J BROWN
TRINITY Retford (Almshouses)   R C LEWIS
UNITED BRISTOL HEALTHCARE NHS TRUST   see Univ Hosps
   Bris NHS Foundn Trust
UNITED LINCOLNSHIRE HOSPITALS NHS TRUST   A AMELIA,
   B A HUTCHINSON, B M S CHAMBERS, C M BONNEYWELL,
   J C B PEMBERTON, J M ROWLAND
UNIVERSITY COLLEGE LONDON HOSPITALS NHS
   FOUNDATION TRUST   J E CANDY, P M FREEMAN
UNIVERSITY HOSPITAL BIRMINGHAM NHS FOUNDATION
   TRUST   R M WHARTON
UNIVERSITY HOSPITAL OF NORTH STAFFORDSHIRE NHS
   TRUST   J M AUSTERBERRY, L B VARQUEZ
UNIVERSITY HOSPITAL OF SOUTH MANCHESTER NHS
   FOUNDATION TRUST   L E J LEAVER, P BUTLER
UNIVERSITY HOSPITAL SOUTHAMPTON NHS FOUNDATION
   TRUST   J V PERCIVAL, K A MACKINNON, P A BOGGUST,
   S M PITKIN
UNIVERSITY HOSPITALS BRISTOL NHS FOUNDATION TRUST
   J E NORMAN, M A SNOOK
UNIVERSITY HOSPITALS COVENTRY AND WARWICKSHIRE
   NHS TRUST   E JONES, H PRIESTNER, S F BETTERIDGE
UNIVERSITY HOSPITALS OF LEICESTER NHS TRUST
   G ANGELL, I P BRENNAND, J WOOD
UNIVERSITY HOSPITALS OF MORECAMBE BAY NHS TRUST
   E A A NORTHEY, I J J DEWAR, J L TYRER
VICTORIA Blackpool   see Blackpool, Fylde and Wyre Hosps
   NHS Trust
WALSALL HOSPITALS NHS TRUST   A E COLES, D J SUNLEY
WANDSWORTH HEALTH AUTHORITY MENTAL HEALTH
   UNIT   see SW Lon and St George's Mental Health
   NHS Trust
WARRINGTON AND HALTON HOSPITALS NHS FOUNDATION
   TRUST   J E DUFFIELD, P J TURNER
WARRINGTON COMMUNITY HEALTH CARE NHS TRUST
   P LOVATT
WATERFORD REGIONAL   J E CROWLEY
WELLHOUSE NHS TRUST   see Barnet and Chase Farm Hosps
   NHS Trust
WEST HERTFORDSHIRE HOSPITALS NHS TRUST
   D H LOVERIDGE, G O OCHOLA
WEST LONDON MENTAL HEALTH NHS TRUST   S J HORNER

WEST MIDDLESEX UNIVERSITY HOSPITAL NHS TRUST
  M W SSERUNKUMA
WEST SUFFOLK HOSPITALS NHS TRUST   L DAWSON,
  D WEBB
WESTERN SUSSEX HOSPITALS NHS FOUNDATION TRUST
  J V EMERSON, R E BENNETT
WESTON AREA HEALTH NHS TRUST   D L GRACE
WEXHAM PARK Slough   *see* Heatherwood & Wexham Park
  Hosps NHS Foundn Trust
WHITCHURCH Cardiff   *see* Cardiff Community Healthcare
  NHS Trust
WHITTINGTON HOSPITAL NHS TRUST   E C M K JONES
WILTSHIRE AND SWINDON HEALTHCARE NHS TRUST
  J A COUTTS, P F YACOMENI

WORCESTERSHIRE ACUTE HOSPITALS NHS TRUST   D P RYAN,
  G E HEWLETT
WORCESTERSHIRE COMMUNITY AND MENTAL HEALTH
  TRUST, The   L L BURN, M E BARR
WORCESTERSHIRE PRIMARY CARE TRUST   S ROSENTHAL
WORTHING PRIORITY CARE NHS TRUST   R J CASWELL
WRIGHTINGTON WIGAN AND LEIGH NHS TRUST
  A J EDWARDS, C JACKSON, J VOST, M THOMPSON
YEOVIL DISTRICT HOSPITAL NHS FOUNDATION TRUST
  J M CUMMINGS, S A SMITH
YORK HOSPITALS NHS FOUNDATION TRUST
  A C BORTHWICK, A C ROWLEY
YORK TEACHING HOSPITAL NHS FOUNDATION TRUST
  L M HOLLIS, C J HAYES, M C DOE

HOSPICE CHAPLAINS

ACORNS Wolverhampton   P H SMITH
BLUEBELL WOOD CHILDREN'S Sheffield   S E RUSH
BOLTON   M O BRACKLEY
CHESTNUT TREE HOUSE Arundel   S J GURR
CHILDREN'S SOUTH WEST Fremington   G C PHILLIPS
COMPTON Wolverhampton   E I ANDERTON
CRANSLEY   L S MCCORMACK
DOUGLAS MACMILLAN Blurton   S GOODWIN
DOVE HOUSE Hull   R A LENS VAN RIJN
DR KERSHAW'S Oldham   M HOWARTH
EAST CHESHIRE   N JONES
EXETER HOSPISCARE   D J WALFORD
FARLEIGH Chelmsford   L ASHDOWN
FLORENCE NIGHTINGALE Stoke Mandeville   C E HOUGH
GARDEN HOUSE Letchworth   M L MOORE
HEART OF KENT   D F G BUTLIN
ISLE OF MAN   L BRADY
JERSEY   G J HOUGHTON
KATHARINE HOUSE Banbury   J P JONES
KATHARINE HOUSE Stafford   P J GRAYSMITH
KEMP Kidderminster   S FOSTER
KIRKWOOD Huddersfield   M E WOOD
LECKHAMPTON COURT   R C PESTELL
LOROS   B DAVIES
MARIE CURIE Glasgow   R F JONES
MARY ANN EVANS Nuneaton   G HANCOCK
MYTON HAMLET Warwick   W S GRAHAM
NAOMI HOUSE Sutton Scotney   A EDMEADS
NORFOLK, THE Snettisham   S M MARTIN
NORTH DEVON   B P LUCK
OAKHAVEN TRUST   J E L ALEXANDER
OVERGATE Elland   D BURROWS
PHYLLIS TUCKWELL Farnham   J L WALKER
PRIMROSE Bromsgrove   D R L WHITE
PRINCESS OF WALES Pontefract   S J HOTCHEN
RICHARD HOUSE   T N ALEXANDER-WATTS
ROWANS, THE Purbrook   C G GULLY

ROWCROFT Torquay   G STILL
ST ANDREW'S Grimsby   D M MCCORMICK
ST ANN'S Manchester   J F AMBROSE
ST BARNABAS HOUSE Worthing   S J GURR
ST CLARE Hastingwood   M WILLIAMS
ST COLUMBA'S Edinburgh   M S PATERSON
ST GEMMA'S Moortown   D L LOFTHOUSE
ST HELENA Colchester   G M MOORE
ST JOHN'S Wirral   P B PRITCHARD
ST JOSEPH'S Hackney   S M HARTLEY
ST LEONARD'S York   C W M BALDOCK
ST LUKE'S CHESHIRE Winsford   R J GATES
ST LUKE'S Plymouth   T A SMITH
ST LUKE'S Sheffield   G L WILTON
ST MARGARET'S Taunton   A E FULTON
ST MARY'S Birmingham   S G BARNDEN
ST MICHAEL'S Harrogate (Crimple House)   C HENSON
ST MICHAEL'S Hereford   J GROVES
ST MICHAEL'S St Leonards-on-Sea   G L DRIVER
ST NICHOLAS' Bury St Edmunds   S M NUTT
ST OSWALD'S Newcastle upon Tyne   C L BROWN
ST PETER AND ST JAMES North Chailey   S C M MCLARNON
ST RICHARD'S Worcester   S ROSENTHAL
ST WILFRID'S Chichester   B M WATERS
SAM BEARE Weybridge   B D PROTHERO
SEVERN Shrewsbury   E C PHILLIPS
SHAKESPEARE Stratford-upon-Avon   H W TURNER
SPRINGHILL Rochdale   A L OXBORROW
STRATHCARRON Denny   S M COATES
SUE RYDER Nettlebed   C A SMITH
SUSSEX BEACON Brighton   J K T ELDRIDGE
THORPE HALL Peterborough   P D STELL
TYNEDALE Hexham   J L JACKSON
WAKEFIELD   A D WOOD
WHEATFIELDS Leeds   D A BUCK
WILLEN Milton Keynes   S W BARNES
WOKING   P J HARWOOD

EDUCATIONAL CHAPLAINS

UNIVERSITIES

ABERDEEN D HEDDLE
ABERTAY D SHEPHERD
ABERYSTWYTH S R BELL
ANGLIA RUSKIN A D CANT, N S COOPER
ASTON N M SHEPHARD
BATH A V I BERNERS-WILSON, B F CHAPMAN
BEDFORDSHIRE A F M GOODMAN
BIRMINGHAM C J SHELLEY
BOLTON O MOLUDY
BOURNEMOUTH B MERRINGTON
BRADFORD S J C CORLEY, S VERNON-YORKE
BRIGHTON C R LAWLOR
BRISTOL E G A DAVIS
BRUNEL *Uxbridge Campus* S A HITCHINER
CAMBRIDGE
 Christ's M S SMITH
 Churchill J RAWLINSON
 Clare G J SEACH
 Corpus Christi J A D BUXTON
 Downing K J EYEONS
 Emmanuel A J ROSS
 Fitzwilliam J M MUNNS
 Girton A M GUITE
 Gonville and Caius C J-B HAMMOND, D H JONES
 Jesus N J WIDDOWS
 King's A C R HAMMOND
 Magdalene S BARRINGTON-WARD
 Newnham H D SHILSON-THOMAS
 Peterhouse G J W DUMBRECK
 Queens' T C HARLING
 Robinson M E DAWN
 Selwyn H D SHILSON-THOMAS
 St Catharine D A NEAUM
 St John's E ADEKUNLE
 Trinity P A DOMINIAK, R E GREENE, K L ROSS
 Trinity Hall S J PLANT
 University Staff P J HAYLER
CARDIFF D K SHEEN
CARDIFF METROPOLITAN P K FITZPATRICK
CENTRAL LANCASHIRE A CLITHEROW
CHESTER E M BURGESS, R J E CLACK, I M DELINGER, P J JENNER, G D THOMAS
COVENTRY R A DEEDES
CRANFIELD H K SYMES-THOMPSON
CUMBRIA M P FIRTH, A J LOGAN
DE MONTFORT H A SURRIDGE
DERBY A P DICKENS
DUBLIN CITY J B MARCHANT
DUNDEE A WALLER
DURHAM
 Hatfield A BASH
 St Chad's A P WILSON
 St Hild and St Bede T M FERGUSON
 St Mary's J L MOBERLY
 University H F CLEUGH
EAST ANGLIA D T THORNTON
EAST LONDON J A RAMSAY
EDINBURGH F S BURBERRY, H A HARRIS, I J PATON
EDINBURGH NAPIER M F CHATTERLEY
ESSEX J M MURPHY
EXETER C M MASON
GLASGOW K FRANCIS
GLOUCESTERSHIRE B W GOODWIN
GREENWICH S-A APOKIS, S E BLACKALL, S COOK
HERIOT-WATT M J H ROUND
HUDDERSFIELD A J RAGGETT
HULL J C COWAN
KEELE S J COUVELA
KENT S-A APOKIS, S C E LAIRD
KINGSTON D BUCKLEY
LANCASTER K J HUGGETT
LEEDS M A J WARD
LEICESTER S A FOSTER, J C MICKLETHWAITE
LIVERPOOL R G LEWIS
LIVERPOOL JOHN MOORES R G LEWIS

LONDON
 Central Chaplaincies A W WILLSON
 Goldsmiths' College A C REES
 Imperial College of Science, Technology and Medicine A W WILLSON
 King's K G RIGLIN, J E SPECK, S F STAVROU
 London School of Economics and Political Science J A WALTERS
 Queen Mary and Westfield N J GOULDING, J E PETERSEN
 Royal Free and University College Medical School P A TURNER
 Royal Holloway and Bedford New C F IRVINE
 Royal Veterinary College P A TURNER
 University C E BRADLEY
LONDON METROPOLITAN C J F BARBER
LOUGHBOROUGH J O AJAEFOBI, C D TAYLOR
MANCHESTER T E BIDDINGTON, J M PRESTWOOD
MANCHESTER METROPOLITAN T E BIDDINGTON, J M PRESTWOOD
NEWCASTLE C M LACK
NORTHAMPTON S N MOUSIR-HARRISON
NORTHUMBRIA AT NEWCASTLE A P BOWSHER
NOTTINGHAM J W BENTHAM, M R SMITH
NOTTINGHAM TRENT R H DAVEY, J S PADDISON
OXFORD
 All Souls J H DRURY
 Balliol B R L KINSEY
 Brasenose D KEECH
 Christ Church C J Y HAYNS
 Exeter A M ALLEN
 Hertford G F HUGHES
 Jesus M I J DAFFERN
 Lady Margaret Hall A G DOIG
 Lincoln M K MARSHALL
 Magdalen S M ALKIRE
 Merton S M JONES, J A MERCER, M STAFFORD
 New E D LONGFELLOW
 Oriel R B TOBIN
 Pembroke A R TEAL
 Queen's D D INMAN
 St Edmund Hall W R DONALDSON
 St Hilda's B W MOUNTFORD
 St Hugh's S C HENSON
 St John's E C MACFARLANE
 St Peter's E J PITKETHLY
 Trinity E M PERCY
 University A F GREGORY
 Worcester J A ARNOLD
PORTSMOUTH A S MARSHALL
READING M D LAYNESMITH
ROEHAMPTON D J ESHUN
ROYAL NORTHERN COLLEGE OF MUSIC T E BIDDINGTON, J M PRESTWOOD
SALFORD K A C WASEY
SHEFFIELD J M S CLINES, A J COLLEDGE
SHEFFIELD HALLAM I MAHER
ST MARK AND ST JOHN N P GRIFFIN
ST MELLITUS *College* P J SWITHINBANK
STAFFORDSHIRE M WILLIAMS
STIRLING D M IND
SUNDERLAND C S HOWSON
SURREY A S BISHOP
SUSSEX C F P MCDERMOTT
TEESSIDE T STEPHENS
UNIVERSITY OF THE ARTS *Chelsea College of Art and Design* J HOGAN
UNIVERSITY OF THE ARTS *London* M W J DEAN, W A WHITCOMBE
WALES
 Swansea N JOHN
 Trinity St David A B BARTON
WARWICK K E PEARSON
WEST LONDON D M AYRES
WINCHESTER C A DAY, P M WADDELL
WORCESTER F H HAWORTH
YORK R C WILLIAMS

COLLEGES OF HIGHER EDUCATION

GUILDFORD   M C WOODWARD
HARPER ADAMS UNIVERSITY COLLEGE *Newport*
  W E WARD

ROYAL NAVAL *Greenwich*   S E BLACKALL, P A MANN
SANDWELL *West Bromwich*   J A LEACH, K S NJENGA
TRINITY AND ALL SAINTS COLLEGE *Leeds*   R G BOULTER

COLLEGES OF FURTHER EDUCATION

DUCHY COLLEGE *Stoke Climsland*   A W STEPHENS
GOWER COLLEGE SWANSEA   A MORGAN
LEICESTER   J M SHARP
NORTH NOTTINGHAMSHIRE   K BOTTLEY

ROYAL ACADEMY OF MUSIC   E C THORNLEY
SUFFOLK NEW   T ROUT
TRINITY AND ALL SAINTS COLLEGE *Leeds*   R G BOULTER

SIXTH-FORM COLLEGES

FARNBOROUGH   R M BENNETTS
ST VINCENT *Gosport*   C J L J THOMPSON

STRODE'S *Egham*   T M SUDWORTH

SCHOOLS

ABBOTS BROMLEY   G P BOTT
ABINGDON   P D B GOODING, S M STEER
ADCOTE *Shrewsbury*   L R BURNS
ALDENHAM *Hertfordshire*   S J CHAPMAN
ALL SAINTS' ACADEMY *Cheltenham*   K J SAMUEL
ALL SAINTS ACADEMY *Dunstable*   A C COLES
ALL SAINTS' CHURCH OF ENGLAND PRIMARY *Peterborough*
  M C FLAHERTY
ALL SAINTS COLLEGE *Newcastle upon Tyne*   J M GRIEVE
ALLEYN'S *Dulwich*   A G BUCKLEY
ALTON   H J BENNET, W MATTHEWS
ARCHBISHOP SENTAMU ACADEMY *Hull*   A RICHARDS
ARCHBISHOP'S *Canterbury*   K MADDY
ARDINGLY COLLEGE *Haywards Heath*   D L LAWRENCE-MARCH
ARK ALL SAINTS ACADEMY *Camberwell*   J G A ROBERTS
ASHRIDGE BUSINESS SCHOOL   L GEOGHEGAN
BABLAKE *Coventry*   J-S SLAVIC
BACON'S COLLEGE *Rotherhithe*   R J HALL
BANCROFT'S *Woodford Green*   I MOORE
BARNARD CASTLE   D R MOORE
BATH SPA   J P KNOTT
BEDFORD   A S ATKINS
BEESTON *Norfolk*   M L BANKS
BENENDEN *Kent*   C J HUXLEY
BENNETT MEMORIAL DIOCESAN *Tunbridge Wells*   R A KNAPP
BERKHAMSTED *Herts*   J E MARKBY
BISHOP BELL *Eastbourne*   D J GARRATT
BISHOP BURTON COLLEGE OF AGRICULTURE *York*
  R F PARKINSON
BISHOP GROSSETESTE *Lincoln*   P G GREEN, M J S JACKSON
BISHOP HENDERSON *Taunton*   J A JEFFERY
BISHOP LUFFA *Chichester*   P M GILBERT
BISHOP OF LLANDAFF HIGH   G W RAYNER-WILLIAMS
BISHOP STOPFORD *Kettering*   H M JEFFERY
BISHOP WAND *Sunbury-on-Thames*   S E LEESON
BISHOP WORDSWORTH *Salisbury*   J A BERSWEDEN
BISHOPS' COLLEGE *Gloucester*   C J H BLOCKLEY
BLACKHEATH BLUECOAT CHURCH OF ENGLAND   E A NEWMAN
BLOXHAM   G G MOATE, M G PRICE
BLUE COAT *Liverpool*   J EASTWOOD
BLUNDELL'S *Tiverton*   T C HUNT
BRADFIELD COLLEGE *Berkshire*   S J N GRAY
BRADFORD ACADEMY   R I TAYLOR
BRENTWOOD *Essex*   A W MCCONNAUGHIE
BRIGHTON COLLEGE   R P S EASTON
BROMSGROVE   P S J HEDWORTH
BRYANSTON *Dorset*   A M J HAVILAND
BUCKINGHAMSHIRE NEW   A W DICKINSON
CANFORD *Wimborne*   P A JACK
CANTERBURY CHRIST CHURCH   S-A APOKIS, J T LAW,
  D A STROUD
CHARTERHOUSE *Godalming*   C A CASE, S J HARKER
CHATHAM AND CLARENDON GRAMMAR SCHOOL
  FEDERATION   S C THOMAS
CHELTENHAM COLLEGE   A J DUNNING, A F G SAMUEL,
  K J SAMUEL
CHELTENHAM LADIES' COLLEGE   C A MCCLURE, H R WOOD
CHICHESTER   J W DANE, K J ROBINSON
CHIGWELL *Essex*   S N PAUL
CHRIST'S COLLEGE *Brecon*   R M LLEWELLYN

CHRIST'S HOSPITAL *Horsham*   S GOLDING
CHRIST'S *Richmond*   S L WILLOUGHBY
CITY OF BATH   A R HAWKINS
CITY OF LONDON FREEMEN'S *Ashtead*   J R L PRIOR
CLIFTON COLLEGE *Bristol*   P M HANSELL
COTHILL HOUSE *Abingdon*   T R PERRY
COVENTRY BLUE COAT CHURCH OF ENGLAND   P J MESSAM
CRANLEIGH PREPARATORY *Surrey*   N H GREEN
CRANLEIGH *Surrey*   T M P LEWIS
CULFORD *Bury St Edmunds*   S C BATTERSBY
DAGENHAM PARK CHURCH OF ENGLAND   Y A GOOLJARY
DAUNTSEY'S *Devizes*   D R JOHNSON
DAVID YOUNG COMMUNITY ACADEMY *Leeds*   J C MILNES
DEAN CLOSE *Cheltenham*   E L TALBOT
DENSTONE COLLEGE *Uttoxeter*   R C M JARVIS
DERBY HIGH   R J A BARRETT
DOWNE HOUSE *Berkshire*   A D TAYLOR
DUKE OF YORK'S ROYAL MILITARY *Dover*   N L COOK
DULWICH COLLEGE   J M WHITE
DULWICH PREPARATORY *Cranbrook*   D F P RUTHERFORD
DURHAM   P J BENTHAM, S A MCMURTARY
DURHAM HIGH   B P S VALLIS
EASTBOURNE COLLEGE   C K MACDONALD
ELIZABETH COLLEGE *Guernsey*   R G HARNISH
ELLESMERE COLLEGE *Shropshire*   P J GRATION
EMANUEL *Wandsworth*   P M HUNT
ENTERPRISE SOUTH LIVERPOOL ACADEMY   A J COLMER
EPSOM COLLEGE   P THOMPSON
ETON COLLEGE *Berkshire*   R E R DEMERY, P A HESS, C M JONES,
  K H WILKINSON
FARNBOROUGH COLLEGE OF TECHNOLOGY   G P H NEWTON
FELSTED *Essex*   N J LITTLE
FETTES COLLEGE *Edinburgh*   A CLARK
GLENALMOND COLLEGE   G W DOVE
GLENDALOUGH, EAST   S M ZIETSMAN
GODOLPHIN *Salisbury*   S M WOOD
GORDON'S *Woking*   D H ROBINSON
GREIG CITY ACADEMY   P J HENDERSON
GRESHAM'S *Holt*   B R ROBERTS
GREYCOAT HOSPITAL   G D SWINTON
GRYPHON *Sherborne*   D R TREGALE
HABERDASHERS' ASKE'S *Elstree*   M BRANDON
HABERDASHERS' MONMOUTH SCHOOL FOR GIRLS
  C M HAYNES
HAILEYBURY COLLEGE *Hertfordshire*   C R BRIGGS
HARROW   J E POWER, N TIVEY
HARTFORD CHURCH OF ENGLAND HIGH   P W HIGHTON
HEATHFIELD *Ascot*   T F TREGUNNO
HEREFORD CATHEDRAL   P A ROW
HIGHGATE *London*   P J J KNIGHT, N H LAMB, R S S WEIR
HURSTPIERPOINT COLLEGE *Hassocks*   J J N SYKES
IAN RAMSEY *Stockton*   P J JOHNSON
IMMANUEL COLLEGE CHURCH OF ENGLAND *Bradford*
  S P HACKING
KENT COLLEGE *Pembury*   H J MATTHEWS
KILKENNY COLLEGE   S D GREEN
KIMBOLTON *Cambridgeshire*   L N BLAND
KING EDWARD VI *Southampton*   J G POPPLETON
KING EDWARD'S *Bath*   C L O'NEILL
KING EDWARD'S *Birmingham*   D H RAYNOR

KING EDWARD'S *Witley*   D C STANDEN
KING HENRY VIII *Coventry*   A HOGGER-GADSBY
KING WILLIAM'S COLLEGE *Isle of Man*   E J SCOTT
KINGHAM HILL *Oxfordshire*   A M SAVAGE
KING'S *Bruton*   N H WILSON-BROWN
KING'S COLLEGE *Cambridge*   A C R HAMMOND
KING'S COLLEGE SCHOOL *Wimbledon*   J W CROSSLEY
KING'S COLLEGE *Taunton*   M A SMITH
KING'S *Dublin*   P R CAMPION
KING'S ELY   R A LANE
KING'S *Rochester*   S J PADFIELD
KING'S *Tynemouth*   C J CLINCH
KING'S *Wolverhampton*   H L DUCKETT, K A DUCKETT
KING'S *Worcester*   M R DORSETT
KING'S, THE *Canterbury*   C F ARVIDSSON, M C ROBBINS
KING'S, THE *Peterborough*   M C FLAHERTY
KIRKLEY HALL   M A G BRYCE
LADY MARGARET *Fulham*   C S NEWBOLD
LANCING COLLEGE   R K HARRISON
LICHFIELD CATHEDRAL   A M STEAD
LIVERPOOL HOPE   S SHAKESPEARE, I C STUART
LLANDAFF CATHEDRAL   P S O'HARE
LLANDOVERY COLLEGE   R A STIDOLPH
MAGDALEN COLLEGE SCHOOL *Oxford*   T H N KUIN LAWTON
MAIDWELL HALL   J V J G WATSON
MALCOLM ARNOLD ACADEMY *Northampton*   C E NANCARROW
MALVERN COLLEGE   A P LAW
MALVERN ST JAMES GIRLS' SCHOOL   K TAPLIN
MANOR *York*   M A HAND
MARLBOROUGH COLLEGE   D CAMPBELL
MERCHANT TAYLORS' *Crosby*   D A SMITH
MERCHANT TAYLORS' *Northwood*   D M BOND
MILL HILL *London*   R J WARDEN
MILLFIELD *Somerset*   P C A HARBRIDGE
MILTON ABBEY *Dorset*   J H DAVIS
MINSTER *Southwell*   M ASKEY
MONKTON COMBE *Bath*   A G P HUTCHINSON
MONMOUTH   D J MCGLADDERY
MORETON HALL   A B STRATFORD
N LINCS Coll   D EDGAR
NATIONAL CHURCH OF ENGLAND ACADEMY *Hucknall*
   L V NICOLLS
NORTH EAST LONDON   S P J CLARK
NORTH WARWICKSHIRE AND HINCKLEY   N S DUNLOP
NORTHBOURNE PARK *Deal*   D N J HALE
NORTHUMBERLAND   D P PALMER
NORWICH   C J CHILD
OAKHAM   A C V ALDOUS
OLD SWINFORD HOSPITAL *Stourbridge*   M W SOAR
OSWESTRY   A D CRANSTON
OUNDLE *Peterborough*   B J CUNNINGHAM, A M SEARLE
PANGBOURNE COLLEGE *Berkshire*   N G T JEFFERS
PETER SYMONDS COLLEGE *Winchester*   N P SEAL
PETERBOROUGH   I C WATTS
PIPERS CORNER   M S GURR
PITSFORD *Northamptonshire*   S TROTT
POCKLINGTON *York*   J GOODAIR, W J ROBERTS
PORTSMOUTH GRAMMAR   A K BURTT
PRESTFELDE *Shrewsbury*   P J HUBBARD
QUEEN ANNE'S *Caversham*   R A ROSS
QUEEN MARGARET'S *York*   R L OWEN
QUEEN MARY'S *Baldersby Park*   G J A WRIGHT
RADLEY COLLEGE *Oxfordshire*   T J E FERNYHOUGH, D WILSON
RANBY HOUSE *Retford*   P FINLINSON
RAVENSCLIFFE HIGH *Halifax*   A MAUDE
REED'S *Cobham*   A C WINTER
RENDCOMB COLLEGE *Cirencester*   R J EDY
REPTON *Derby*   A J M WATKINSON
RIDDLESWORTH HALL *Norwich*   K A HAWKES
RISHWORTH *Ripponden*   J S BRADBERRY
ROEDEAN *Brighton*   G N RAINEY
ROSSALL *Fleetwood*   E VAN BLERK
ROSSHALL ACADEMY *Glasgow*   J F LYON
ROYAL ALEXANDRA AND ALBERT *Reigate*   P JOHNSTONE
ROYAL COLLEGE OF ART   A W WILLSON
ROYAL MASONIC FOR GIRLS *Rickmansworth*   J S QUILL
ROYAL RUSSELL *Croydon*   H L KIRK
ROYAL WOLVERHAMPTON   R MAXFIELD
RUGBY   R M HORNER
SALFORD CITY ACADEMY   A E KAY
SALISBURY CATHEDRAL   J A TAYLOR
SEAFORD COLLEGE *Petworth*   M C C BARTER
SEDBERGH   P L SWEETING
SEVENOAKS   N N HENSHAW
SHERBORNE   L R F COLLINS, N J MERCER
SHERBORNE Girls   R T AYERS-HARRIS

SHIPLAKE *Henley-on-Thames*   S M COUSINS
SHREWSBURY   G W DOBBIE
SIR ROBERT WOODARD ACADEMY *Lancing*   H J HUGHES
SOLIHULL   A C HUTCHINSON
SOMERSET COLLEGE OF ARTS AND TECHNOLOGY
   P J HUGHES
ST ALBANS   C D PINES
ST ALBAN'S ACADEMY *Highgate, Birmingham*   N LO POLITO
ST ALBANS HIGH SCHOOL FOR GIRLS   D C FITZGERALD CLARK
ST ANDREW'S CHURCH OF ENGLAND HIGH *Croydon*
   W W BELL
ST ANTONY'S LEWESTON *Sherborne*   E J WOODS
ST AUGUSTINE ACADEMY *Maidstone*   K GRANT
ST BEDE'S *Cambridge*   A N M CLARKE
ST BEDE'S ECUMENICAL *Reigate*   J A PENN
ST BEDE'S INTER-CHURCH SECONDARY *Cambridge*
   H J CROMPTON-BATTERSBY
ST CATHERINE'S *Bramley*   B G MCNAIR SCOTT
ST CECILIA'S WANDSWORTH CHURCH OF ENGLAND   P A KURK
ST DAVID'S COLLEGE *Llandudno*   T R HALL
ST EDMUND'S *Canterbury*   M S BENNETT
ST EDWARD'S *Oxford*   E C KERR
St Gabr Coll *Camberwell*   E L WAKEHAM
ST GEORGE'S *Ascot*   J J SISTIG
ST GEORGE'S *Blackpool*   H S HOUSTON
ST GEORGE'S *Gravesend*   T OLIVER
ST HELEN'S AND ST KATHARINE'S *Abingdon*   C E WINDLE
ST HELEN'S *Northwood*   M J WALKER
ST JOHN'S *Leatherhead*   C M S MOLONEY, S E WOOD-ROE
ST JOSEPH'S *Wrexham*   M K R STALLARD
ST LAWRENCE COLLEGE *Ramsgate*   P R RUSSELL
ST MARGARET'S CHURCH OF ENGLAND HIGH *Aigburth,*
   Liverpool   K L MILLER
ST MARK'S CHURCH OF ENGLAND ACADEMY *Mitcham*
   R A BURGE-THOMAS
ST MARY MAGDALENE ACADEMY *London*   A I KEECH
ST MARYLEBONE CHURCH OF ENGLAND   E C THORNLEY
ST MARY'S *Calne*   J M BEACH, P M O GILES
ST MARY'S HALL *Brighton*   D J BIGGS, A H MANSON-BRAILSFORD
ST MARY'S *Shaftesbury*   L J LANE
ST MARY'S *Westbrook*   B D R WOOD
ST MICHAEL'S *Otford*   D E REES
ST OLAVE'S GRAMMAR *Orpington*   A D MCCLELLAN
ST PAUL'S *Barnes*   P L F ALLSOP
ST PAUL'S GIRLS' *Hammersmith*   V L BARON
ST PETER'S ACADEMY *Stoke-on-Trent*   V L FLANAGAN
ST PETER'S *Cambridge*   C N TWEDDELL
ST PETER'S COLLEGIATE *Wolverhampton*   P J L CODY
ST PETER'S *York*   D A JONES
ST SAVIOUR'S AND ST OLAVE'S *Newington*   I E VIBERT
ST SWITHUN'S *Winchester*   K M DYKES
STAMFORD   M A S GOODMAN
STOCKPORT GRAMMAR   L E J LEAVER
STOWE *Buckingham*   C M B HUXTABLE, S A SAMPSON
TAUNTON   M P R DIETZ
TAVERHAM HALL *Norwich*   R W B MASSINGBERD-MUNDY
TELFORD *City Tech Coll*   B T SWYNNERTON
TONBRIDGE   D A PETERS
TRENT COLLEGE *Nottingham*   B C RANDALL
TRINITY *Carlisle*   C J KENNEDY
TRINITY *Lewisham*   J A DONNELLY
TRINITY *Teignmouth*   J E ROSS-MCNAIRN
TUDOR HALL *Banbury*   J F JACKSON
TWYFORD CHURCH OF ENGLAND HIGH *Acton*   J SEYMOUR
ULSTER   J E G BACH
UPPINGHAM *Leicestershire*   J B J SAUNDERS
WARMINSTER   D A PRESCOTT
WARWICK   A W GOUGH
WELLINGBOROUGH   M J WALKER
WELLINGTON ACADEMY *Ludgershall*   A S M COPELAND
WELLINGTON COLLEGE *Berkshire*   T W G NOVIS
WELLINGTON *Somerset*   J P HELLIER
WELLS CATHEDRAL   J M HULME
WESTMINSTER   G J WILLIAMS
WESTMINSTER CITY   G D SWINTON
WESTONBIRT   H A MONAGHAN
WILSON'S HOSPITAL *Multyfarnham*   H M SCULLY
WINCHESTER COLLEGE   S A THORN
WOODBRIDGE   I A WILSON
WORKSOP COLLEGE *Nottinghamshire*   P FINLINSON
WORTH   A J BALL
WREKIN COLLEGE *Telford*   M J HORTON
WYCLIFFE COLLEGE *Gloucestershire*   J M MCHALE
WYCOMBE ABBEY *High Wycombe*   J F CHAFFEY
WYMONDHAM COLLEGE   I JONES
YORK ST JOHN   L NJENGA, A C ROWLEY

THEOLOGICAL COLLEGES AND COURSES

This index includes the name of the principal or warden and the names of staff members who are Anglican clergy and whose appointments are at least half-time.

Theological Colleges

Church of Ireland Theological College
Braemor Park, Dublin 14, Republic of Ireland
T: (00353) (1) 492 3506   F: 492 3082
E: admin@theologicalinstitute.ie
PRIN M J ELLIOTT TUTORS/LECTS P G MCGLINCHEY,
P COMERFORD, J K MCWHIRTER

College of the Resurrection
Stocks Bank Road, Mirfield WF14 0BW
T: (01924) 490441   F: 492738
E: lgordon-taylor@mirfield.org.uk
PRIN P G ALLAN CR TUTOR/LECT B N GORDON-TAYLOR,
J E COOPER, R F PAILING

Cranmer Hall
St John's College, 3 South Bailey, Durham DH1 3RJ
T: 0191–334 3894   F: 334 3501
E: enquiries@cranmerhall.com
PRIN S D WILKINSON[1] WARDEN M S A TANNER
DIR MISS AND PIONEER MIN M J VOLLAND
DIR MINL PRACTICE D J GOODHEW TUTORS P J REGAN,
H M THORP

Oak Hill College
Chase Side, London N14 4PS
T: (020) 8449 0467   E: reception@oakhill.ac.uk
PRIN M J OVEY   VICE-PRIN *vacant*
TUTORS/LECTS R J PORTER, M T SLEEMAN, M J LACY,
K BIRKETT, M A PICKLES

The Queen's Foundation
Somerset Road, Edgbaston, Birmingham B15 2QH
T: 0121–454 1527   F: 454 8171   E: enquire@queens.ac.uk
PRIN D J P HEWLETT   DIR OF READER TRAINING P M SHELTON
TUTOR/LECT M R EAREY, R G GASTON, R J SUDWORTH

Ridley Hall
Ridley Hall Road, Cambridge CB3 9HG
T: (01223) 746580   F: 746581   E: ridleypa@hermes.cam.ac.uk
PRIN A R NORMAN   VICE-PRIN M B THOMPSON
DIR STUDIES R A HIGGINSON TUTORS/LECTS P P JENSON,
P D A WESTON, J E KEILLER, D E MALE, A C WALTON,
A F CHATFIELD, A L ALDRIDGE, R W MCDONALD, C J WRIGHT

Ripon College
Cuddesdon, Oxford OX44 9EX
T: (01865) 877400   F: 875431   E: enquiries@rcc.ac.uk
PRIN THE RT REVD H I J SOUTHERN   VICE-PRIN M D CHAPMAN
TUTORS/LECTS J R BAUN, G D BAYLISS,
J R COLLICUTT MCGRATH, D S HEYWOOD, P N TOVEY,
M J LAKEY

St John's College
Chilwell Lane, Bramcote, Nottingham NG9 3DS
T: 0115–925 1114   F: 943 6438
E: enquiries@stjohns-nottm.ac.uk
PRIN D H K HILBORN DIR OF MIN AND FORMATION N M LADD
TUTORS/LECTS T D HULL, A R ANGEL, M N RODEL,
J M CORCORAN

St Michael's College
54 Cardiff Road, Llandaff, Cardiff CF5 2YJ
T: (029) 2056 3379   E: info@stmichaels.ac.uk
PRIN *vacant* DEAN MIN DEVELOPMENT S P ADAMS
DEAN CHAPL STUDIES A J TODD   TUTOR W C INGLE-GILLIS

St Stephen's House
16 Marston Street, Oxford OX4 1JX
T: (01865) 613500   F: 613513   E: enquiries@ssho.ox.ac.uk
PRIN R WARD   VICE-PRIN H WORSLEY TUTORS A K M ADAM,
L M GARDNER, D WENHAM

Sarum College
19 The Close, Salisbury SP1 2EE
T: (01722) 424820   E: courses@sarum.ac.uk
PRIN J W WOODWARD   DIR MIN P BURDEN
DIR LITURGY AND WORSHIP J H S STEVEN

Scottish Episcopal Institute
21 Grosvenor Crescent, Edinburgh EH12 5EE
T: 0131–225 6357   E: institute@scotland.anglican.org
PRIN A L TOMLINSON TUTORS N H TAYLOR, M J FULLER

Trinity College
Stoke Hill, Bristol BS9 1JP
T: 0117–968 2803   F: 968 7470   E: principal@trinity-bris.ac.uk
PRIN E G INESON   DIR PART-TIME COURSES S E GENT
TUTORS/LECTS N A D SCOTLAND, J L NOLLAND, P J ROBERTS,
H J WORSLEY

Westcott House
Jesus Lane, Cambridge CB5 8BP
T: (01223) 741000   E: info@westcott.cam.ac.uk
PRIN C M CHIVERS VICE-PRIN W R S LAMB
TUTORS A M BARRETT, S J T GATENBY, V E RAYMER

Wycliffe Hall
54 Banbury Road, Oxford OX2 6PW
T: (01865) 274200   F: 274215   E: enquiries@wycliffe.ox.ac.uk
PRIN M F LLOYD   VICE-PRIN S D N VIBERT
TUTORS J R WILLIAMS, E A HOARE, A C ATHERSTONE,
J E ROBSON

Regional Courses

All Saints Centre for Mission and Ministry
Aiken Hall, University of Chester, Crab Lane,
Warrington WA2 0BD
T: (01925) 534373   E: info@allsaintscentre.org
PRIN THE VEN J APPLEGATE   VICE-PRIN L P LONGDEN

Eastern Region Ministry Course
Westcott House, Jesus Lane, Cambridge CB5 8BP
T: (01223) 366378   E: secretary@ermc.cam.ac.uk
PRIN *vacant*   DIR PRACTICAL TH E ROTHWELL

Lancashire and Cumbria Theological Partnership
Church House, West Walls, Carlisle CA3 8UE
T: (01228) 815405   F: 815400   E: admin@lctp.co.uk
PRIN *vacant*   VICE-PRIN R A LATHAM

Lincoln School of Theology
Edward King House, Minster Yard, Lincoln LN2 1PU
T: (01522) 504050   E: sally.myers@lincoln.anglican.org
PRIN S A MYERS

Lindisfarne Regional Training Partnership
Church House, St John's Terrace, North Shields, NE29 6HS
T: 0191–270 4144   E: enquiries@lindisfarnertp.org
PRIN C ROWLING   DIR STUDIES D J BRYAN   DIR IME R L
SIMPSON DEVELOPING DISCIPLESHIP E J SCOTT
TUTOR M L BECK

Oxford Ministry Course
Ripon College, Cuddesdon, Oxford OX44 9EX
T: (01865) 874404   F: 875431
E: enquiries@ripon-cuddesdon.ac.uk
DEAN T J N NAISH

The Queen's Foundation (Course)
Somerset Road, Edgbaston, Birmingham B15 2QH
T: 0121–454 1527   F: 454 8171   E: enquire@queens.ac.uk
PRIN D J P HEWLETT TUTOR/LECT M R EAREY, R G GASTON

---

[1]   Dr Wilkinson is a Methodist.

St Mellitus College
St Jude's Church, 24 Collingham Road, London SW5 0LX
T: (020) 7052 0573   E: info@stmellitus.org
DEAN A N EMERTON ASST-DEAN L HARVEY
TUTORS S W DOHERTY, R I MERCHANT, J HARDING, L A YATES,
D J LAZENBY, C R WALSH

The South East Institute for Theological Education
Room Hf17, Hepworth Building,
Canterbury Christ Church University,
North Holmes Road, Canterbury CT1 1QU
T: (01227) 471120   E: administrator@seite.co.uk
PRIN A P R GREGORY TUTORS S P STOCKS, C M HERBERT

South West Ministry Training Course
Suite 1.3, Renslade House, Bonhay Road, Exeter EX4 3AY
T: (01392) 272544   E: admin@swmtc.org.uk
PRIN C SOUTHGATE[2] TUTORS S SHEPPARD, L LARKIN,
E P PARKES   DIR READER TR AND LAY EDUCN T J GIBSON

West of England Ministerial Training Course
12 College Green, Gloucester GL1 2LX
T: (01452) 874969   E: office@wemtc.org.uk
DIR STUDIES J P WILLIAMS

Yorkshire Ministry Course
Mirfield Centre, Stocks Bank Road, Mirfield WF14 0BW
T: (01924) 481925   F: 481922   E: office@ymc.org.uk
PRIN M T POWLEY   DIR PAST STUDIES T S EVANS
TUTOR S C SPENCER

Ordained Local Ministry Schemes

Guildford Diocesan Ministry Course
Diocesan House, Quarry Street, Guildford GU1 3XG
T: (01483) 790319   E: steve.summers@cofeguildford.org.uk
PRIN S B SUMMERS

Lichfield OLM Scheme
St Mary's House, The Close, Lichfield WS13 7LD
T: (01543) 306220   E: angela.bruno@lichfield.anglican.org
PRIN vacant

Oxford OLM Scheme
Diocesan Church House, North Hinksey Lane,
Oxford OX2 0NB
T: (01865) 208282
E: keith.beech-gruneberg@oxford.anglican.org
PRIN K BEECH-GRÜNEBERG

---

[2]   Dr Southgate is a lay person.

BISHOPS OF ANGLICAN DIOCESES OVERSEAS

AUSTRALIA

PROVINCE OF NEW SOUTH WALES

Armidale
Richard (Rick) Lewers
PO Box 198, Armidale NSW 2350, Australia
T: (0061) (2) 6772 4491
F: (0061) (2) 6772 9261
E: office@armidaleanglicandiocese.com

Bathurst
Ian Palmer
PO Box 23, Bathurst NSW 2795, Australia
T: (0061) (2) 6331 1722
F: (0061) (2) 6332 2772
E: registrar@bathurstanglican.org.au

Canberra and Goulburn
Stuart Peter Robinson
GPO Box 1981, Canberra ACT 2601, Australia
T: (0061) (2) 6248 0811
F: (0061) (2) 6247 6829
E: stuart.robinson@anglicancg.org.au

(Assistant)
Matt Brain
GPO Box 8605, Wagga Wagga NSW 2650, Australia
T/F: (0061) (2) 6926 4226
E: matt.brain@anglicancg.org.au

(Assistant)
Trevor William Edwards
28 McBryde Crescent, Wanniassa ACT 2903, Australia
T: (0061) (2) 6232 3610
F: (0061) (2) 6232 3650
E: trevor.edwards@anglicancg.org.au

(Assistant)
Stephen Pickard
c/o GPO Box 1981, Canberra ACT, Australia
E: s.k.pickard@gmail.com

Grafton
Sarah Macneil
The Bishop's Registry, PO Box 4, Grafton NSW 2460, Australia
T: (0061) (2) 6643 4122
F: (0061) (2) 6643 1814
E: admin@graftondiocese.org.au

Newcastle
Greg Thompson
The Bishop's Registry, PO Box 817, Newcastle NSW 2300, Australia
T: (0061) (2) 4926 3733
F: (0061) (2) 4936 1968
E: info@newcastleanglican.org.au

(Assistant)
Peter Derrick James Stuart
PO Box 817, Newcastle NSW 2300, Australia
T: (0061) (2) 4926 3733
F: (0061) (2) 4926 1968
E: bishoppeter@newcastleanglican.org.au

Riverina
Rob Gillion
PO Box 10, Narrandera NSW 2700, Australia
T: (0061) (2) 6959 1648
F: (0061) (2) 6959 2903
E: rivdio@bigpond.com

Sydney (Archbishop and Metropolitan)
Glenn Davies
PO Box Q190, QVB Post Office, Sydney NSW 1230, Australia
T: (0061) (2) 9265 1555
F: (0061) (2) 9261 1170
E: registry@sydney.anglican.asn.au

(Liverpool)
Peter Lin
address as above
T: (0061) (2) 9265 1530
F: (0061) (2) 9261 1543

(North Sydney)
Chris Edwards
address as above
T: (0061) (2) 9265 1533
F: (0061) (2) 9265 1543

(South Sydney)
Robert Charles Forsyth
address as above
T: (0061) (2) 9265 1501
F: (0061) (2) 9265 1543
E: robforsyth@sydney.anglican.asn.au

(Western Sydney, *formerly* Parramatta)
Ivan Yin Lee
PO Box 129, Parramatta NSW 2124, Australia 2124
T: (0061) (2) 9265 1574
F: (0061) (2) 9689 3636
E: ilee@sydney.anglican.asn.au

(Wollongong)
Peter L Hayward
74 Church Street, Wollongong NSW 2500, Australia
T: (0061) (2) 4201 1800
F: (0061) (2) 4228 4296
E: phaywood@wollongong.anglican.asn.au

PROVINCE OF QUEENSLAND

Brisbane (Archbishop and Metropolitan)
Phillip John Aspinall
PO Box 421, Brisbane QLD 4001, Australia
T: (0061) (7) 3835 2222
F: (0061) (7) 3831 1170
E: archbishop@anglicansq.org.au

(Northern Region)
Jonathan Charles Holland
address as above
T: (0061) (7) 3835 2213
F: (0061) (7) 3832 5030
E: jholland@anglicanchurchsq.org.au

(Southern Region)
Alison Taylor
address as above
T: (0061) (7) 3835 2213
F: (0061) (7) 3832 5030
E: amtaylor@anglicanbrisbane.org.au

(Western Region)
Cameron Venables
PO Box 2600, Toowoomba QLD 4350, Australia
T: (0061) (7) 4639 1875
F: (0061) (7) 4632 6882
E: cveneables@anglicanchurchsq.org.au

North Queensland
William James (Bill) Ray
PO Box 1244, Townsville QLD 4810, Australia
T: (0061) (7) 4771 4175
F: (0061) (7) 4721 1756
E: bishopnq@anglicannq.org

Northern Territory, The
Gregory Anderson
PO Box 2950, Darwin NT 0801, Australia
T: (0061) (8) 8941 7440
F: (0061) (8) 8941 7446
E: bishop@ntanglican.org.au

Rockhampton
David Robinson
PO Box 710, Rockhampton QLD 4702, Australia
T/F: (0061) (7) 4927 3188
E: bishop@anglicanrock.org.au

PROVINCE OF SOUTH AUSTRALIA

Adelaide (Archbishop and Metropolitan)
Jeffrey William Driver
18 King William Road, North Adelaide SA 5006, Australia
T: (0061) (8) 8305 9350
F: (0061) (8) 8305 9399
E: archbishop@adelaide.anglican.com.au

(Assistant)
Timothy Harris
address as above
T: (0061) (8) 8305 9350
E: tharris@adelaide.anglican.com.au

(Assistant)
Christopher McLeod
PO Box 70, Brighton SA 5048, Australia
E: cmcleod203@gmail.com

The Murray
John Ford
PO Box 394, Murray Bridge SA 5253, Australia
T: (0061) (8) 8532 2270
F: (0061) (8) 8532 5760
E: registry@murray.anglican.org

Willochra
John Stead
PO Box 96, Gladstone SA 5473, Australia
T: (0061) (8) 8662 2249
F: (0061) (8) 8662 2027
E: registry@diowillochra.org.au

PROVINCE OF VICTORIA

Ballarat | Garry John Weatherill
PO Box 89, Ballarat Vic 3350, Australia
T: (0061) (3) 5331 1183
F: (0061) (3) 5333 2982
E: secretary@ballaratanglican.org.au

Bendigo | Andrew William Curnow AM
PO Box 2, Bendigo Vic 3552, Australia
T: (0061) (3) 5443 4711
F: (0061) (3) 5441 2173
E: registry@bendigoanglican.org.au

Gippsland | Kay Goldsworthy
PO Box 928, Sale Vic 3853, Australia
T: (0061) (3) 5144 2044
F: (0061) (3) 5144 7183
E: registryoffice@gippsanglican.org.au

Melbourne
(Archbishop
and Primate) | Philip Leslie Freier
The Anglican Centre, 209 Flinders Lane,
Melbourne Vic 3000, Australia
T: (0061) (3) 9653 4220
F: (0061) (3) 9653 4268
E: archbishopsoffice
reception@melbourneanglican.org.au

(Eastern
Region) | Genieve Blackwell
address, T and F as above
E: gblackwell@melbourneanglican.org.au

(North-
western
Region) | Philip James Huggins
address, T and F as above
E: bishopphiliphuggins@melbourne
anglican.org.au

(Southern
Region) | Paul Raymond White
address, T and F as above
E: sthregbishop@melbourneanglican.org.au

Wangaratta | Anthony John Parkes AM
Bishop's Registry, PO Box 457,
Wangaratta Vic 3676, Australia
T: (0061) (3) 5721 3484
F: (0061) (3) 5722 1427
E: registry@wangarattaanglican.org.au

PROVINCE OF WESTERN AUSTRALIA

Bunbury | Allan Bowers Ewing
Bishopscourt, PO Box 15,
Bunbury WA 6231, Australia
T: (0061) (8) 9721 2100
F: (0061) (8) 9791 2300
E: secretary@bunbury.org.au

North West
Australia | Gary Nelson
PO Box 2783, Geraldton WA 6531, Australia
T: (0061) (8) 9921 7277
F: (0061) (8) 9964 2220
E: reception@anglicandnwa.org

Perth
(Archbishop
and
Metropolitan) | Roger Adrian Herft AM
GPO Box W2067, Perth WA 6001, Australia
T: (0061) (8) 9325 7455
F: (0061) (8) 9221 4118
E: diocese@perth.anglican.org

(Assistant) | Kate Wilmot
address, T and F as above
E: kwilmot@perth.anglican.org

(Asistant) | Tom Wilmot
address, T and F as above
E: twilmot@perth.anglican.org

EXTRA-PROVINCIAL DIOCESES

Defence Force
(and Bishop
Assistant to
the Primate) | Ian Lambert
Department of Defence,
DSG-Duntroon ACT 2600, Australia
T: (0061) (2) 9265 9935
F: (0061) (2) 9265 9959
E: ian.lambert1@defence.gov.au

Tasmania | John Douglas Harrower OAM
GPO Box 748, Hobart TAS 7001, Australia
T: (0061) (3) 6220 2015
F: (0061) (3) 6223 8968
E: bishop@anglicantas.org.au

BRAZIL

Amazon | Saulo Maurício de Barros
Av. Sezerdelo Correia, 514 – Batista Campos,
Belem, 66025–240, Brazil
T/F: (0055) (91) 3241 9720
E: saulomauricio@gmail.com

Brasília | Maurício José Araújo de Andrade
EQS 309–310, sala 1 – Asa Sul,
Caixa Postal 093, Brasília, 70359–970, Brazil
T: (0055) (61) 3443 4305
F: (0055) (61) 3443 4337
E: mandrade@ieab.org.br

Curitiba | Naudal Alves Gomes
Rua Sete de Setembro, 3927 – Centro,
Curitiba, 80250–010, Brazil
T: (0055) (41) 3232 0917
E: naudal@yahoo.com.br

Pelotas | Renato da Cruz Raatz
Rua Felix da Cunha, 425 – Centro, Caixa
Postal 791, Pelotas, 96001–970, Brazil
T/F: (0055) (53) 3302 8618
E: renato.raatz@terra.com.br

Recife | João Câncio Peixoto
Rua Alfredo de Medeiros, 60 – Espinheiro,
Recife, 52021–030, Brazil
T: (0055) (81) 3421 1684
E: joao.peixoto1@uol.com.br

Rio de Janeiro | Filadelfo Oliveira Neto
Rua Fonseca Guimarães, 12 Sta.Teresa, Rio de
Janeiro, 20240–260, Brazil
T: (0055) (21) 2220 2148
F: (0055) (21) 2252 9686
E: oliveira.ieab@org.br

São Paulo | Flávio Borges Irala
Rua Borges Lagoa 172 – Vila Clementino,
São Paulo, 04038–030, Brazil
T: (0055) (11) 5549 9086
F: (0055) (11) 5083 2619
E: flavioirala@ieab.org

South Western
Brazil (Primate) | Francisco de Assis da Silva
Av. Rio Branco, 880 / Sub-solo – Centro,
Caixa Postal 116, Santa Maria, 97010–970,
Brazil
T/F: (0055) (55) 3223 4328
E: fassis@ieab.org.br

Southern Brazil | Humberto Maiztegui
Av. Ludolfo Boehl, 278 – Baairro,
Teresópolis, Porto Alegre, 91720–150,
Brazil
T/F: (0055) (51) 3318 6199
E: bispohumberto@ieab.org.br

BURMA *see* MYANMAR

BURUNDI

Bujumbura | Eraste Bigirimana
BP 1300, Bujumbura, Burundi
T: (00257) (22) 249 104
E: bigirimanaeraste@yahoo.fr

Buye | Sixbert Macumi
BP 94, Ngozi, Burundi
T: (00257) (22) 302 210
F: (00257) (22) 302 317
E: buyedioc@yahoo.fr

Gitega | Jean W Nduwayo
BP 23, Gitega, Burundi
T: (00257) (22) 402 247
E: eab.gitega@cbinf.com

Makamba | Martin Blaise Nyaboho
BP 96, Makamba, Burundi
T: (00257) (22) 508 080
E: eabdiocmak@yahoo.fr

Matana
(Archbishop) | Bernard Ntahoturi
BP 447, Bujumbura, Burundi
T: (00257) (76) 924 595
F: (00257) (22) 229 129
E: ntahober@yahoo.co.uk

Muyinga	Paisible Ndacayisaba BP 55, Muyinga, Burundi T: (00257) (79) 700 043 E: ndacp@yahoo.com
Rumonge	Pedaculi Birakengana T: (00257) (79) 970 926 E: birakepeda@yahoo.fr

CANADA

Primate of Canada	Fred J Hiltz 80 Hayden Street, Toronto ON M4Y 3G2, Canada T: (001) (416) 924 9192 F: (001) (416) 924 0211 E: primate@national.anglican.ca

PROVINCE OF BRITISH COLUMBIA AND YUKON

British Columbia	Logan McMenamie 900 Vancouver Street, Victoria BC V8V 3V7, Canada T: (001) (250) 386 7781 F: (001) (250) 386 4013 E: bishop@bc.anglican.ca
Caledonia	William (Bill) J Anderson 201–4716 Lazelle Avenue, Terrace BC V8G 1T2, Canada T: (001) (250) 635 6016 F: (001) (250) 635 6026 E: bishopbill@telus.net
Anglican Parishes of the Central Interior	Barbara J Andrews 360 Nicola Street, Kamloops BC V2C 2P5, Canada T: (001) (778) 471 5573 F: (001) (778) 471 5586 E: apcibishop@shaw.ca
Kootenay (Archbishop and Metropolitan)	John E Privett 201–380 Leathead Road, Kelowna BC V1X 2H8, Canada T: (001) (778) 478 8310 F: (001) (778) 478 8314 E: bishop@kootenay.info
New Westminster	Melissa Skelton 580, 401 West Georgia Street, Vancouver BC V6B 5A1, Canada T: (001) (604) 684 6306 F: (001) (604) 684 7017 E: bishop@vancouver.anglican.ca
Yukon	Larry D Robertson PO Box 31136, Whitehorse YT Y1A 3T3, Canada T: (001) (867) 667 7746 F: (001) (867) 667 6125 E: synodoffice@klondiker.com

PROVINCE OF CANADA

Central Newfoundland	F David Torraville 34 Fraser Road, Gander NL A1V 2E8, Canada T: (001) (709) 256 2372 F: (001) (709) 256 2396 E: bishopcentral@nfld.net
Eastern Newfoundland and Labrador	Geoffrey Peddle 19 King's Bridge Road, St John's NL A1C 3K4, Canada T: (001) (709) 576 6697 F: (001) (709) 576 7122 E: geoffpeddle48@gmail.com
Fredericton	David Edwards 115 Church Street, Fredericton NB E3B 4C8, Canada T: (001) (506) 459 1801 F: (001) (506) 460 0520 E: edwardsdavid300@gmail.com
Montreal	Mary Irwin-Gibson 1444 Union Avenue, Montreal QC H3A 2B8, Canada T: (001) (514) 843 9443 F: (001) (514) 843 3221 E: bishops.office@montreal.anglican.org

Nova Scotia and Prince Edward Island	Ronald W Cutler 1340 Martello Street, Halifax NS B3H 2Z1 Canada T: (001) (902) 420 0717 F: (001) (902) 425 0717 E: rcutler@nspeidiocese.ca
Quebec	Dennis P Drainville 31 rue des Jardins, Quebec QC G1R 4L6, Canada T: (001) (418) 692 3858 F: (001) (418) 692 3876 E: bishopqc@quebec.anglican.ca
Western Newfoundland (Archbishop and Metropolitan)	Percy D Coffin 25 Main Street, Corner Brook NF A2H 1C2, Canada T: (001) (705) 363 6021 F: (001) (709) 639 1636 E: bishop_dsown@nf.aibn.com

PROVINCE OF ONTARIO

Algoma	Stephen G W Andrews, PO Box 1168, Sault Ste Marie ON P6A 5N7 Canada T: (001) (705) 256 5061 F: (001) (705) 946 1860 E: bishop@dioceseofalgoma.com
Huron	Robert (Bob) F Bennett, 190 Queens Avenue, London ON N6A 6H7, Canada T: (001) (519) 434 6893 F: (001) (519) 673 4151 E: bishops@huron.anglican.org
Moosonee (Moosonee Mission Area)	Colin R Johnson 135 Adelaide Street East, Toronto ON M5C 1L8, Canada T: (001) (416) 363 6021 F: (001) (416) 363 3683 E: cjohnson@toronto.anglican.ca
Niagara	Michael A Bird Cathedral Place, 252 James Street North, Hamilton ON L8R 2L3, Canada T: (001) (905) 527 1316 F: (001) (905) 527 1281 E: bishop@niagara.anglican.ca
Ontario	Michael D Oulton 90 Johnson Street, Kingston ON K7L 1X7, Canada T: (001) (613) 544 4774 F: (001) (613) 547 3745 E: moulton@ontario.anglican.ca
Ottawa	John H Chapman 71 Bronson Avenue, Ottawa ON K1R 6G6, Canada T: (001) (613) 233 7741 F: (001) (613) 521 6613 E: bishopsoffice@ottawa.anglican.ca
Toronto (Archbishop and Metropolitan)	Colin R Johnson 135 Adelaide Street East, Toronto ON M5C 1L8, Canada T: (001) (416) 363 6021 F: (001) (416) 363 3683 E: cjohnson@toronto.anglican.ca
(Trent-Durham)	Linda C Nicholls 965 Dundas Street West, Suite 207, Whitby ON L1P 1G8, Canada T: (001) (905) 668 1558 F: (001) (905) 668 8216 E: lnicholls@toronto.anglican.ca
(York- Credit Valley)	M Philip Poole 135 Adelaide Street East Toronto ON M5C 1L8, Canada T: (001) (416) 363 6021 F: (001) (416) 363 3683 E: ppoole@toronto.anglican.ca
(York- Scarborough)	Patrick T Yu 135 Adelaide Street East, Scarborough ON M5C 1L8, Canada T: (001) (416) 363 6021 F: (001) (416) 363 3683 E: pyu@toronto.anglican.ca

(York-Simcoe)   Peter D Fenty
                  PO Box 233, King City ON L7B 1A5,
                  Canada
                  T: (001) (905) 833 8327
                  F: (001) (905) 833 8329
                  E: pfenty@torontoanglican.ca

PROVINCE OF RUPERT'S LAND

The Arctic   David Parsons
                  PO Box 190, 4910 51st Street
                  Yellowknife NT X1A 2N2, Canada
                  T: (001) (867) 873 5432
                  F: (001) (867) 837 8478
                  E: arctic@arcticnet.org

(Suffragan)   Darren McCartney
                  PO Box 5, Iqaluit, NU X0A 0H0, Canada
                  T: (001) (867) 873 5432
                  F: (001) (867) 873 8478
                  E: darren@artic.net.org

Athabasca   Fraser W Lawton
                  Box 6868, Peace River AB T8S 1S6,
                  Canada
                  T: (001) (780) 624 2767
                  F: (001) (780) 624 2365
                  E: bpath@telusplanet.net

Brandon   *Vacant*
                  PO Box 21009, WEPO,
                  Brandon MB R7B 3W8, Canada
                  T: (001) (204) 727 7550
                  F: (001) (204) 727 4135
                  E: diobran@mymts.net

Calgary   Gregory K Kerr-Wilson
                  180–1209 59th Avenue SE
                  Calgary AB T2H 2P6, Canada
                  T: (001) (403) 243 3673
                  F: (001) (403) 243 2182
                  E: gkerrwilson@calgary.anglican.ca

Edmonton   Jane Alexander
                  10035 103rd Street NW,
                  Edmonton AB T5J 0X5, Canada
                  T: (001) (780) 439 7344
                  F: (001) (780) 962 2103
                  E: bishop@edmonton.anglican.ca

Keewatin   *Diocese exists but has no parishes under its
                  jurisdicvtion*

Mishamikoweesh   Lydia Mamakwa
(Indigenous   PO Box 65
Spiritual   Kingfisher Lake ON P0V 1Z0, Canada
Ministry of)   T: (001) (807) 532 2085
                  F: (001) (807) 532 2344
                  E: lydiam@kingfisherlake.ca

Qu'Appelle   Robert Hardwick
                  1501 College Avenue, Regina SK S4P 1B8,
                  Canada
                  T: (001) (306) 522 1608
                  F: (001) (306) 352 6808
                  E: bishoprob@sasktel.net

Rupert's Land   Donald D Phillips
                  935 Nesbitt Bay, Winnipeg MB R3T 1W6,
                  Canada
                  T: (001) (204) 992 4212
                  F: (001) (204) 992 4219
                  E: bishop@rupertsland.ca

Saskatchewan   Michael W Hawkins
                  1308 Fifth Avenue East,
                  Prince Albert SK S6V 2H7, Canada
                  T: (001) (306) 763 2455
                  F: (001) (306) 764 5172
                  E: bishopmichael@sasktel.net

Saskatoon   David M Irving
                  1403 9th Avenue N, Saskatoon SK S7K 3S5,
                  Canada
                  T: (001) (306) 244 5651
                  F: (001) (306) 933 4606
                  E: bishopdavid@sasktel.net

CENTRAL AFRICA

Botswana   Metlhayothlhe Rawlings Belemi
                  PO Box 679, Gaborone, Botswana
                  T: (00267) 395 3779
                  F: (00267) 391 3015
                  E: angli_diocese@info.bw

Central Zambia   Derek Gary Kamukwamba
                  PO Box 70172, Ndola, Zambia
                  T: (00260) (2) 612 431
                  M: (00260) 977 899 530
                  F: (00260) (2) 615 954
                  E: adcznla@zamnet.zm

Central   Ishmael Mukuwanda
Zimbabwe   PO Box 25, Gweru, Zimbabwe
                  T: (00263) (54) 221 030
                  F: (00263) (54) 221 097
                  E: diocent@telconet.co.zw

Eastern Zambia   William J Muchombo
                  PO Box 510154, Chipata, Zambia
                  T/F: (00260) (62) 221 294
                  E: dioeastzm@zamnet.zm

Harare   Chad Nicholas Gandiya
                  9 Monmouth Road,
                  Avondale, Harare, Zimbabwe
                  T: (00263) (4) 308 042
                  M: (00265) 772 133 608
                  E: chandgandiya@gmail.com

Lake Malawi   Francis Kaulanda
                  PO Box 30349, Lilongwe 3, Malawi
                  T: (00265) (1) 797 858
                  F: (00265) 797 548
                  E: franciskaulanda@yahoo.com

Luapula   Robert Mumbi
                  PO Box 70210, Mansa, Luapula, Zambia
                  T: (00260) (2) 821 680
                  E: diopula@zamtel.zm

Lusaka   David Njovu
                  Bishop's Lodge, PO Box 30183
                  Lusaka, Zambia
                  T/F: (00260) (1) 254 515
                  F: (00260) (1) 252 379
                  E: davidnjovu1961@zamnet.zm
                  or davidnjovu1961@gmail.com

Manicaland   Erick Ruwona
                  115 Herbert Chitepo Road
                  Mutare, Zimbabwe
                  T: (00263) (20) 68418
                  M: (00263) 772 131 288

Masvingo   Godfrey Tawonezvi
                  PO 1421, Masvingo, Zambia
                  T: (00263) (39) 362 536
                  E: bishopgodfreytawonezvi@gmail.com

Matabeleland   Cleophas Lunga
                  PO Box 2422, Bulawayo, Zimbabwe
                  T: (00263) (9) 61370
                  F: (00263) (9) 68353
                  E: clunga@aol.com

Northern   Fanuel E C Magangani
Malawi   PO Box 120, Mzuzu, Malawi
                  T: (00265) (1) 312 858
                  F: (00265) (1) 310 802
                  E: magangani@sdnp.org.mw

Northern   Albert C Chama
Zambia   PO Box 20798, Kitwe, Zambia
(Archbishop)   T: (00260) (2) 223 264
                  M: (00265) 999 545 609
                  F: (00260) (2) 224 778
                  E: chama_albert@yahoo.ca

Southern   Alinafe Kalemba
Malawi   PO Box 30220, Chichiri, Blantyre, 3, Malawi
                  T: (00265) (1) 841 218
                  M: (00265) 772 131 288
                  F: (00265) (1) 841 235
                  E: dean@sdnp.org.mw

Upper Shire   Brighton Vitta Masala
                  Private Bag 1, Chilema, Zomba, Malawi
                  T/F: (00265) (1) 539 203
                  M: (00265) 999 545 609
                  E: malasab@yahoo.co.uk

CENTRAL AMERICA

Costa Rica   Hector Monterroso
Apartado 2773-1000 San José, Costa Rica
T: (00506) 225 0209 *or* 253 0790
F: (00506) 253 8331
E: iarca@me.com

El Salvador   Jan David Alvarado Melgar
47 Avenida Sur, 723 Col Flor Blanca,
Apt Postal (01), 274 San Salvador, El Salvador
T: (00503) 2 223 2252
F: (00503) 2 223 7952
E: anglican.es@gmail.com

Guatemala   Armando Roman Guerra-Soria
Apartado 58A, Avenida La Castellana 40-06,
Guatemala City, Zona 8, Guatemala
T: (00502) 2472 0852
F: (00502) 2472 0764
E: ageposcopal@yahoo.com

Nicaragua   Sturdie Wyman Downs
(Primate)   Apartado 1207, Managua, Nicaragua
T: (00505) (2) 222 5174
F: (00505) (2) 254 5248
E: secretaria_diocesana@hotmail.com

Panama   Julio Murray
Box R, Balboa, Republic of Panama
T: (00507) 212 0062
F: (00507) 262 2097
E: bpmurray@hotmail.com

CEYLON (SRI LANKA)

Colombo   Dhiloraj R Canagasabey
368/3A Bauddhaloka Mawatha,
Colombo 7, Sri Lanka
T: (0094) (1) 684810
F: (0094) (1) 684811
E: anglican@sltnet.lk

Kurunagala   *Vacant*
Bishop's House, 31 Kandy Road
Kurunegala, Sri Lanka
T: (0094) (37) 222 2191
F: (0094) (37) 222 6806
E: bishopkg@sltnet.lk

CONGO (formerly ZAÏRE)

Aru   Georges Titre Ande
PO Box 226 Arua, Uganda
T: (00243) (81) 039 3071
E: revdande@yahoo.co.uk

Boga   William Bahemuka Mugenyi
PO Box 25586, Kampala, Uganda
T: (00243) (99) 066 8639
E: mugenyiwilliam@yahoo.com

Bukavu   Sylvestre Bahati Bali-Busane
Av Mgr Ndahura, No. Q/Nyalukemba,
C/Ibanda, CAC-Bukavu, BP 2876,
Bukavu, DR Congo *or* PO Box 134,
Cyangugu, Rwanda
M: (00243) (99) 401 3647
E: bhati_bali@yahoo.fr

Kasais   Marcel Kapinga Kayibabu wa Ilunga
PO Box 16482, Kinshasa 1, DR Congo
T: (00243) (99) 357 0080
E: anglicanekasai@yahoo.fr

Katanga   Corneille Kasima Muno
(*formerly* Shaba)   1309 Chaussee do Kasenga, Bel-Air,
Lubumbashi, PO Box 22037, Kitwe, Zambia
T/F: (00243) (81) 475 6075
E: kasimammuno@yahoo.fr

Kindu   Zacharie Masimango Katanda
PO Box 5, Gisenyi, Rwanda
T: (243) (99) 891 6258
M: (243) (813) 286 255
E: angkindu@yahoo.fr
or angkindu@antenna.nl

Kinshasa   Henri Isingoma Kahwa
(Archbishop)   11 Av Basalakal, Quartier Immocongo
Commune de Kalamu, Kinshasa 1, PO Box
16482, DR Congo
T: (00243) (99) 333 30908
E: peac_isingoma@yahoo.fr

(Assistant)   Jean Molanga Botola
EAC-Kinshasa, BP 16482, Kinshasa 1,
DR Congo
T: (00243) (99) 471 3802
E: molanga2k@yahoo.co.uk

Kisangani   Lambert Funga Botolome
Av. Bowane, No. 10, Quartier des Musiciens,
C/Makiso, PO Box 86, Kisangani, DR Congo
or PO Box 25586, Kampala, Uganda
M: (00243) (99) 7 25 2868
E: lambertfunga@hotmail.com

Nord Kivu   Adolph Muihindo Isesomo
PO Box 322, Burtembo, DR Congo *or*
PO Box 25586, Kampala, Uganda
T: (00243) (99) 854 8601
E: revd_isesomo@yahoo.fr

HONG KONG

Eastern   Timothy Kwok
Kowloon   Diocesan Office,
4/F Holy Trinity Bradbury Centre,
139 Ma Tau Chung Road,
Kowloon, Hong Kong, China
T: (00852) 2713 9983
F: (00852) 2711 1609
E: ekoffice@ekhkskh.org.hk

Hong Kong   Paul Kwong
Island   71 Bonham Road, Hong Kong, China
(Archbishop)   T: (00852) 2526 5366
F: (00852) 2525 3344
E: do.dhk@hkskh.org

Western   Andrew Chan
Kowloon   Diocesan Office, 11 Pak Po Street,
Mongkok, Kowloon, Hong Kong, China
T: (00852) 2783 0811
F: (00852) 2783 0799
E: dwk@hkskh.org

INDIAN OCEAN

Antananarivo   Samoela Jaona Ranarivelo
Evêché Anglican,
Lot VK57 ter, Ambohimanoro,
101 Antananarivo, Madagascar
T: (00261) (20) 222 0827
F: (00261) (20) 226 1331
E: eemdanta@yahoo.com

(Assistant)   Todd McGregor
address as above
E: revmctodd@yahoo.vcom

Antsiranana   Theophile Botomazava
Evêché Anglican, BP 278, 4 Rue Grandidier,
201 Antsiranana, Madagascar
T: (00261) (20) 822 277

Fianarantsoa   Gilbert Rateloson Rakotondravelo
Évêché du diocese Fianarantsoa, BP 1418,
301 Fianarantsoa, Madagascar
T: (00261) (20) 755 1583

Mahajanga   Jean-Claude Andrianjafimanana
Evêché Anglican, BP 570, 401 Mahajanga,
Madagascar
E: andrianjajc@yahoo.fr

Mauritius   Ian Gerald James Ernest
(Archbishop)   Bishop's House, Nallatamby Road, Phoenix,
Mauritius
T: (00230) 686 5158
F: (00230) 697 1096
E: dioang@intnet.mu

Seychelles   James Richard Wong Yin Song
Bishop's House, PO Box 44, Victoria, Mahe,
Seychelles
T: (00248) 321 977
F: (00248) 323 879
E: angdio@seychelles.net

Toamasina   Jean Paul Solo
Evêché Anglican
Lot VK57 ter, Ambohimanoro,
101 Antananarivo, Madagascar
T: (00261) (20) 533 1663
F: (00261) (20) 533 1689
E: eemtoam@wanadoo.mg

Toliara   *new diocese – awaiting details*

JAPAN

Chubu
Peter Ichiro Shibusawa
28–1 Meigetsu-cho, 2-chome,
Showa-ku, Nagoya 466–0034, Japan
T: (0081) (52) 858 1007
F: (0081) (52) 858 1008
E: office.chubu@nskk.org

Hokkaido
(Primate)
Nathaniel Makoto Uematsu
Kita 15 jo, Nishi 5–20,
Kita-ku, Sapporo 001–0015, Japan
T: (0081) (11) 717 8181
F: (0081) (11) 736 8377
E: hokkaido@nskk.org

Kita Kanto
Zerubbabel Katsuichi Hirota
2–172 Sakuragi-cho, Omiya-ku,
Saitama-shi 331–0852, Japan
T: (0081) (48) 642 2680
F: (0081) (48) 648 0358
E: kitakanto@nskk.org

Kobe
Andrew Yutaka Nakamura, 5–11–1
Yamatedori, Chuo-ku, Kobe-shi 650–0011,
Japan
T: (0081) (78) 351 5469
F: (0081) (78) 382 1095
E: aao52850@syd.odn.ne.jp

Kyoto
Stephen Takashi Kochi
380 Okakuencho, Shimotachiuri-agaru,
Karasumadori, Kamigyo-ku, Kyoto 602–8011,
Japan
T: (0081) (75) 431 7204
F: (0081) (75) 441 4238
E: nskk-kyoto@kyp.biglobe.ne.jp

Kyushu
Luke Ken-ichi Muto
2–9–22 Kusakae, Chuo-ku,
Fukuoka 810–0045, Japan
T: (0081) (92) 771 2050
F: (0081) (92) 771 9857
E: d-kyushu@ymt.bbiq.jp

Okinawa
David Eisho Uehara
3–5–5 Meada, Urasoe-shi,
Okinawa 910–2102, Japan
T: (0081) (98) 942 1101
F: (0081) (98) 942 1102
E: office.okinawa@nskk.org

Osaka
Andrew Haruhisa Iso
2–1–8 Matsuzaki-cho, Abeno-ku,
Osaka 545–0053, Japan
T: (0081) (6) 6621 2179
F: (0081) (6) 6621 3097
E: office.osaka@nskk.org

Tohoku
John Hiromichi Kato
2–13–15 Kokobun-cho, Aoba-ku,
Sendai 980–0803, Japan
T: (0081) (22) 223 2349
F: (0081) (22) 223 2387
E: se.tohoku@nskk.org

Tokyo
Andrew Yoshimichi Ohata
3–6–18 Shiba Koen, Minato-ku,
Tokyo 105–0011, Japan
T: (0081) (3) 3433 0987
F: (0081) (3) 3433 8678
E: general-sec.tko@nskk.org

Yokohama
Laurence Yutaka Minabe
14–57 Mitsuzawa Shimo-cho,
Kanagawa-ku, Yokohama 221–0852, Japan
T: (0081) (45) 321 4988
F: (0081) (45) 321 4978
E: yokohama.kyouku@nskk.org

JERUSALEM AND THE MIDDLE EAST

Cyprus and
the Gulf
(Bishop in)
Michael Augustine Owen Lewis
PO Box 22075, 1517 Nicosia, Cyprus
T: (00357) (22) 671220
F: (00357) (22) 674553
E: bishop@spidernet.com.cy

Egypt with
North Africa
and the Horn
of Africa
(Bishop in)
(Primate)
Mouneer Hanna Anis
Diocesan Office, PO Box 87,
Zamalek Distribution, 11211, Cairo, Egypt
T: (0020) (2) 738 0829
F: (0020) (2) 735 8941
E: bishopmouneer@gmail.com

(Suffragan)
(Horn of
Africa)
Grant Lemarquand
address etc as above

Iran (Bishop in)
Azad Marshall
St Thomas Center, Raiwind Road,
PO Box 688, Lahore, Punjab, 54000, Pakistan
T: (0092) (42) 542 0452
E: bishop@saintthomascenter.org

Jerusalem
(Bishop in)
(Archbishop)
Suheil Dawani
St George's Close, PO Box 9122,
20 Nablus Rd, Jerusalem 91 191, Israel
T: (00972) (2) 627 1670
F: (00972) (2) 627 3847
E: bishop@j-diocese.com

KENYA

All Saints
Cathedral
(Primate)
Eliud Wabukala
PO Box 40502, 00100 Nairobi, Kenya
T: (00254) (20) 714 755
F: (00254) (20) 718 442/714 750
E: archoffice@ackenya.org

Bondo
Johannes Otieno Angela
PO Box 240, 40601 Bondo, Kenya
M: (00254) 0705 213964
E: bishopjohannes@gmail.com

Bungoma
George Wafula Mechumo
PO Box 2392, 50200 Bungoma, Kenya
T/F: (00254) (337) 30481
M: (00254) 0726 400718
E: georgemechumo@yahoo.com

Butere
Timothy Wambunya
PO Box 54, 50101 Butere, Kenya
T: (00254) (20) 244 7585
F: (00254) 206 2785
E: buterediocese@gmail.com

Eldoret
Christopher K Ruto
PO Box 3404, 30100 Eldoret, Kenya
T: (00254) (53) 206 2785
M: (00254) 0710 577545
E: ackeldoret@africaonline.co.ke

Embu
David Muriithi Ireri
PO Box 189, Embu, Kenya
T: (00254) (68) 30614
M: (00254) 0728 787403
F: (00254) (68) 30468
E: ackembu@yahoo.com

Kajiado
Gadiel Katanga Lenini
PO Box 203, 01100 Kajiado, Kenya
T: (00254) (203) 513 911
M: (00254) 9716 392564
E: ackajiado@gmail.com

Katakwa
Zakayo Iteba Epusi
PO Box 68, 50244 Amagoro, Kenya
T: (00254) (55) 54079
E: itebazake@gmail.com

Kericho
Jackson Ole Sapit
PO Box 181, 20200 Kericho, Kenya
M: (00254) 0717 267442
E: ackkcodioc@yahoo.com

Kirinyaga
Joseph Kibuchua
PO Box 95, 10304 Kutus, Kenya
T: (00254) (020) 212 4416
F: (00254) (163) 44020
E: info@ackirinyaga.org

Kitale
Stephen Kewasis Nyorsok
PO Box 4176, 30200 Kitale, Kenya
T: (00254) (020) 202 8911
E: ack.ktl@gmail.com

Kitui
Josephat Mule
PO Box 1054, 90200 Kitui, Kenya
T: (00254) 04444
E: ac.kitui09@yahoo.com

Machakos	Joseph Mutungi PO Box 282, 90100 Machakos, Kenya T: (00254) (044) 21379 M: (00254) 0704 521061 F: (00254) (044) 20178 E: ackmachakos@swiftkenya.com
Makueni	Joseph Kanuku PO Box 532, 90300 Makueni, Kenya M: (00254) 0733 757767 E: ackmakueni@gmail.com
Malindi	Lawrence Dena E: dena_larry@yahoo.com
Maralal	Jacob A Lesuuda PO Box 42, 20600 Marala, Kenya E: bishopjlesuuda@gmail.com
Marsabit	Robert Martin PO Box 51, 60500 Marsabit, Kenya *or* c/o MAF Kenya, PO Box 21223, 00505 Nairobi, Kenya M: (00254) 0720 006693 E: ackbishopmarsabit@gmail.com
Maseno North	Simon Mutingole Oketch PO Box 416, 50100 Kakemega, Kenya T/F: (00254) (056) 30729 E: ackmnorth@jambo.co.ke
Maseno South	Francis Mwayi Abiero PO Box 114, 40100 Kisumu, Kenya T: (00254) (057) 202 5148 M: (00254) 0733 709378 F: (00254) (35) 21009 E: bpfabiero@yahoo.com
Maseno West	Joseph Otieno Wasonga PO Box 793, 40600 Siaya, Kenya M: (00254) 0722 280648 E: bishopjoseph@gmail.com
Mbeere	Moses Masambe Nthuka PO Box 122, 60104 Siakago, Kenya E: bishopmbeere@gmail.com
Meru	Charles Ndiga Mwendwa PO Box 427, 60200 Meru, Kenya M: (00254) 0721 270460 E: ackdmeru@yahoo.com
Mombasa	Julius Robert Katoi Kalu PO Box 80072, 80100 Mombasa, Kenya T: (00254) (41) 233 1365 E: kalunangombo@yahoo.co.uk
Mt Kenya Central	Isaac Maina Ng'ang'a PO Box 121, 10200 Murang'a, Kenya T: (00254) (60) 203 560 E: ackmkcentral@wananchi.com
(Assistant)	Allan Waithaka *address etc as above*
Mt Kenya South	Timothy Ranji PO Box 886, 00900 Kiambu, Kenya T: (00254) (66) 22521 E: info@ack.mtkenya.org
Mt Kenya West	Joseph M Kagunda PO Box 229, 10100 Nyeri, Kenya T: (00254) (61) 203 2281 E: ackmtkwest@wananchi.com
Mumias	Beneah Justin Okumu Salalah PO Box 213, 50102 Mumias, Kenya T: (00254) (020) 244 2846 E: ackmumiasdiocese@yahoo.com
Murang's South	Julius Karanu PO Box 414, 01020 Kenol, Murang'a, Kenya M: (00254) 0737 436466 E: ackmurangasouth@gmail.com
Nairobi	Joel Wawerua PO Box 72846, 00200 Nairobi, Kenya T: (00254) (020) 444 0524 F: (00254) (2) 226 259 E: acknairobi@swiftkenya.com
Nakuru	Jospeh Muchai PO Box 56, (Moi Road), 20100 Nakuru, Kenya T: (00254) (051) 221 2155 F: (00254) (051) 221 2437 E: acknkudioc@net2000ke.com
(Suffragan)	Musa Kamuren (Baringo Mission Area)
Nambale	Robert Magina PO Box 4, 50409 Nambale, Kenya T: (00254) (065) 24040 E: magina12@yahoo.co.uk

Nyahururu	Stephen Kabora PO Box 926, 20300 Nyahururu, Kenya T: (00254) (065) 203 2179 E: nyahudc@gmail.com
Southern Nyanza	James Kenneth Ochiel PO Box 65, 40300 Homa Bay, Kenya T: (00254) (059) 22054 M: (00254) 0721 794968 E: acksnyanza@swiftkenya.com
Taita Taveta	Samson Mwakitawa Mwaluda PO Box 75, 80300 Voi, Kenya T: (00254) (043) 203 0096 E: acktaita@ackeenya.org
Thika	Julius Wanyoike PO Box 214, 01000 Thika, Kenya T: (00254) (067) 31654 F: (00254) (067) 31544 E: info@ackthikadiocese.org

KOREA

(Primate and Bishop of Seoul)	Paul Keun Sang Kim 15 sejong-daero 21-gil, Jung-gu, Seoul 100–120, Republic of Korea T: (0082) (2) 735 6157 F: (0082) (2) 723 2640 E: paulkim7@hitel.net
Daejeon	Moses Nakjun Yoo 53 Dongseo-daero 1466 beon-gil, Jung-gu, Daejeon 310-823, Republic of Korea
Pusan	Onesimus Dongsin Park 5–1 Daecheongro 99 beon-gil, Jung-gu, Busan 600-092, Republicm of Korea T: (0082) (51) 463 5742 F: (0082) (51) 463 5957 E: onesimus63@hanmail.net

MELANESIA

Banks and Torres	Alfred Patteson Worek T: (00678) 38520 E: dobtbishop@gmail.com
Central Melanesia (Archbishop)	David Vunagi Church of Melanesia, PO Box 19, Honiara, Solomon Islands T: (00677) 26101 F: (00677) 21098 E: dvunagi@comphq.org.sb
Central Solomons	Ben Seka Church of Melanesia, PO Box 52, Tulagi, CIP, Solomon Islands T: (00677) 32006 F: (00677) 32113 E: bishopseka@gmail.com
Guadalcanal	Nathan Tome PO Box 19, Honiara, Solomon Islands T: (00677) 23337 E: ntome4080@gmail.com
Hanuato'o	Alfred Karibongi PO Box 20, Kira Kira, Makira Province, Solomon Islands T: (00677) 50012 E: bishophanuatoo@solomon.com.sb
Malaita	Samuel Sahu Bishop's House, PO Box 7, Auki Malaita, Solomon Islands T: (00677) 745 8686 E: sam.malaita@gmail.com
Temotu	George Angus Takeli Bishop's House, Lluesalo, Lata, Santa Cruz, Temotu Province, Solomon Islands T: (00677) 53080 E: peace.gtakeli@gmail.com
Vanuatu	James Marvin Ligo Bishop's House, PO Box 238, Luganville, Santo, Vanuatu T: (00678) 37065 *or* 36631 F: (00678) 36631 E: dovbishop@vanatu.com.vu

Ysabel
Richard Naramana
PO Box 6, Buala, Jejevo,
Ysabel Province, Solomon Islands
T: (00677) 35124
E: episcopal@solomon.com.sb

MEXICO

Cuernavaca
Enrique Treviño Cruz
Calle Minerva No 1, Col. Delicas,
CP 62330 Cuernavaca, Morelos, Mexico
T: (0052) (777) 315 2870 or 322 2259
E: diocesisdecuernavaca@hotmail.com

Mexico
Carlos Touché Porter
Ave San Jerónimo 117, Col. San Ángel,
Delegación Álvaro Obregón, 01000, Mexico
T: (0052) (55) 5616 3193
F: (0052) (55) 5616 2205
E: diomex@@axtel.net

Northern
Mexico
(Archbishop)
Francisco Manuel Moreno
Acatlán 102 Ote,
Col. Mitras Centro CP 64460,
Monterrey NL, Mexico
T: (0052) (81) 8333 0992
F: (0052) (81) 8348 7362
E: primado@mexico-anglican.org

Southeastern
Mexico
Benito Juárez-Martínez
Avenida de Las Américas #73, Col. Aguacatal
91130 Xalapa, Veracruz, Mexico
T: (0052) (228) 814 6951
F: (0052) (228) 814 4387
E: obispobenito.49@gmail.com

Western
Mexico
Lino Rodríguez-Amaro
Torres Quintero # 15, Col. Seattle, 45150
Zapopan, Jalisco, Mexico
T: (0052) (33) 3560 4726
F: (0052) (33) 3616 4726
E: obispolino@hotmail.com

MYANMAR (BURMA)

Hpa-an
Saw Stylo
Bishop Kone: Ward 4, Hpa-an, Kayin State,
Myanmar
T: (0095) (58) 21696
F: (0095) (1) 77512

Mandalay
David Nyi Nyi Naing
Bishopscourt, 22 Pinya Road, Mandalay,
Myanmar
T: (0095) (2) 34110
E: davidnaing@gmail.com

Mytikyina
John Zau Li
147 Thankin Net Pe Road, Thinda Quarters,
Myitkyina, Kachin State, Myanmar
T: (0095) (74) 23104
E: john.zauli@gmail.com

Sittwe
James Min Dein
May Yu Street, Sittwe, Rakhine State,
Myanmar
T: (0095) (43) 53622

Toungoo
Saw (John) Wilme
Diocesan Office, Nat-shin-Naung Street,
Ward 20, Toungoo, Myanmar
T: (0095) (54) 23159
E: bishopwilme@gmail.com

Yangon
(Archbishop)
Stephen Than Myint Oo
PO Box 11191,
140 Pyidaungsu-Yeiktha Rd, Dagon, Yangon,
Myanmar
T: (0095) (1) 395 279
F: (0095) (1) 395 314
E: stephentan777@gmail.com

(Assistant)
Samuel Htang Oak
44 Bishop Home, Pyay Road, Yangon,
Myanmar
T: (0095) (1) 372 300
E: sthangoak40@gmail.com

NEW ZEALAND
(AOTEAROA, NEW ZEALAND AND POLYNESIA)

(Primate/
Archbishop
and Bishop of
Aotearoa and
te Tairawhiti)
William Brown Turei
PO Box 568, Gisborne 4040, New Zealand
T: (0064) (6) 868 7028
F: (0064) (6) 867 8859
E: bishop@tairawhiti.org.nz

(Primate/
Archbishop
and Bishop of
Polynesia)
Winston Halapua
Bishop's House, Disraeli Road, Suva
Fiji Islands
T: (0067) (9) 330 4716
F: (0067) (9) 330 2152
E: bishoppolynesia@connect.com.fj

(Primate/
Archbishop
and Bishop of
Taranaki)
Philip Richardson
PO Box 547, New Plymouth 4621,
New Zealand
T: (0064) (6) 759 1178
F: (0064) (6) 759 1180
E: bishop@taranakianglican.org.nz

(Bishop of
Te Manawa
O Te Wheke)
Ngarahu Katene
42B Carter Drive, Rotorua 3040, New Zealand
T (0064) (7) 348 3015
F: (0064) (7) 345 7800
E: bishop@motw.org.nz

(Bishop of Te
Tai Tokerau)
Te Kitohi Wiremu Pikaahu
PO Box 59103, Mangere Bridge,
Auckland 2151, New Zealand
T: (0064) (9) 275 7520
E: tkwp@xtra.co.nz

(Bishop of Te
Upoko O
Te Ika)
Muru Walters
14 Amesbury Drive, Churton Park,
Wellington 6037, New Zealand
T: (0064) (4) 478 3549
F: (0064) (4) 472 8863
E: muru.walters@xtra.co.nz

(Bishop of Te
Waipounamu)
Te Kitohi Wiremu Pikaahu
PO Box 10086, Phillipstown,
Christchurch 8145, New Zealand
T: (0064) (3) 389 1683
F: (0064) (3) 389 0912

Auckland
Ross Graham Bay
PO Box 37242, Parnell,
Auckland 1151, New Zealand
T: (0064) (9) 302 7201
F: (0064) (9) 302 7217
E: bishop@auckanglican.org.nz

(Assistant)
James Andrew White
address etc as above
E: jwhite@auckanglican.org.nz

Christchurch
Victoria Matthews
PO Box 4438, Christchurch 8140,
New Zealand
T: (0064) (3) 348 6960
F: (0064) (3) 348 2373
E: bishop@anglicanlife.org.nz

Dunedin
Kelvin Peter Wright
PO Box 13170, Green Island, Dunedin 9052,
New Zealand
T: (0064) (3) 488 0820
F: (0064) (3) 488 2038
E: kelvin@calledsouth.org.nz

Nelson
Victor Richard Ellena
PO Box 100, Nelson 7040, New Zealand
T: (0064) (3) 548 3124
F: (0064) (3) 548 2125
E: bprichard@nelsonanglican.org.nz

Waiapu
Andrew Hedge
PO Box 227, Napier 4140, New Zealand
T: (0064) (6) 835 8230
F: (0064) (6) 835 0680
E: bishop@waiapu.com

Waikato
Helen-Ann Hartley
PO Box 21, Hamilton 3240, New Zealand
T: (0064) (7) 857 0020
F: (0064) (7) 836 9975
E: bishopspa@waikatoanglican.org.nz

Taranaki
Philip Richardson
PO Box 547, Taranaki Mail Centre,
New Plymouth, 4340, New Zealand
T: (0064) (6) 759 1178
F: (0064) (6) 759 1180
E: bishop@taranakianglican.org.nz

Wellington	Justin Charles Hopkins Duckworth PO Box 12046, Wellington 6144, New Zealand T: (0064) (4) 472 1057 E: justin@www.wn.ang.org.nz

NIGERIA

PROVINCE OF ABA

Arochukwu- Ohafia	Johnson Chibueze Onuoha Bishopscourt, PO Box 193, Arochukwa, Abia State, Nigeria M: (00234) (802) 538 6407 E: aroohafia@anglican.ng.org
Ikwuano	Chigozirim U Onyegbule Bishopscourt, PO Box 5, Ahaba-Oloko, Abia State, Nigeria M: (00234) (803) 085 9319 E: ikwuano@anglican-nig.org
Isiala Ngwa	Owen Nwankujuobi Azubuike Bishopscourt, St George's Cathedral Compound, PNB 2033, Mbawsi, Abia State, Nigeria M: (00234) (805) 467 0528 E: bpowenazubuike@yahoo.com
Isiala Ngwa South	Isaac Nwaobia St Peter's Cathedral Compound, PO Box 15, Owerrinta, Abia State, Nigeria M: (00234) (803) 711 9317 E: isialangwasouth@anglican-nig.org
Isuikwuato (Missionary diocese)	Manasses Chijiokem Okere Bishopscourt, PO Box 350, Ovim, Abia State, Nigeria M: (00234) (803) 338 6221 E: isuikwuato@anglican-nig.org
Ukwa	Samuel Kelechi Eze PO Box 20468, Aba, Abia State, Nigeria M: (00234) (803) 789 2431 E: kelerem53787@yahoo.com
Umuahia (Archbishop)	Ikechi Nwachukwu Nwosu St Stephen's Cathedral Church Compound, PO Box 96, Umuahia, Abia State, Nigeria T: (00234) (88) 221 037 F: (00234) (803) 549 9066 E: ik_nwosu01@yahoo.com

PROVINCE OF ABUJA

Abuja (Archbishop and Primate)	Nicholas D Okoh Episcopal House, 24 Douala Street, Wuse District, Zone 5, PO Box 212, Abuja, ADCP Garki, Nigeria T: (00234) (56) 580 682 E: nickorogodo@yahoo.com
Bida	Jonah G Kolo Bishop's House, St John's Mission Compound, PO Box 14, Bida, Nigeria T: (00234) (66) 461 694 E: bida@anglican-nig.org
Gboko	Emmanuel Nyitsse
Gwagwalada	Moses Tabwaye Diocesan Headquarters, Secretariat Road, PO Box 287, Gwagwalada, Abuja, Nigeria T: (00234) (9) 882 2083 E: anggwag@skannet.com.ng
Idah	Joseph N Musa Bishopscourt, PO Box 25, Idah, Kogi State, Nigeria E: idah@anglican-nig.org
Kafanchan	Marcus M Dogo PO Box 29, Kafanchan, Kaduna State, Nigeria T: (00234) (61) 20 634
Kubwa	Duke Timothy Akamisoko Bishop's House, PO Box 67, Kubwa, Abuja FCT, Nigeria M: (00234) (803) 451 9437 E: dukesoko@yahoo.com
Kwoi	Paul Samuel Zamani Bishop's Residence, Cathedral Compound, Samban Gide, PO Box 173, Kwoi, Kaduna State, Nigeria M: (00234) (80) 651 8160 E: paulzamani@yahoo.com

Lafia	Miller Kangdim Maza PO Box 560, Lafia, Nasarawa State, Nigeria M: (00234) (803) 973 5973 E: anglicandioceseoflafia@yahoo.com
Makurdi	Nathaniel N Inyom Bishopscourt, PO Box 1, Makurdi, Benue State, Nigeria T: (00234) (44) 533 349 F: (00234) (803) 614 5319 E: makurdi@anglican.skannet.com.ng
Otukpo	David K Bello Bishopscourt, PO Box 360, Otukpo, Benue State, Nigeria M: (00234) (803) 309 1778 E: bishopdkbello@yahoo.com
Zaki-Biam	Benjamin A Vager Bishopscourt, PO Box 600, Yam Market Road, Zaki-Biam, Benue State, Nigeria M: (00234) (803) 676 0018 E: rubavia@yahoo.com
Zonkwa (Missionary diocese)	Jacob W Kwashi Bishop's Residence, PO Box 26, Zonkwa, Kaduna State, Nigeria M: (00234) (803) 311 0252 E: zonkwa@anglican-nig.org

PROVINCE OF BENDEL

Akoko Edo	Jolly Oyekpen Bishopscourt, PO Box 10, Igarra, Edo State, Nigeria M: (00234) (803) 470 5941 E: venjollye@yahoo.com
Asaba	Justus Nnaemeka Mogekwu Bishopscourt, PO Box 216, Cable Point, Asaba, Delta State, Nigeria M: (00234) (802) 819 2980 E: justusmogekwu@yahoo.com
Benin	Peter O J Imasuen Bishopscourt, PO Box 82, Benin City, Edo State, Nigeria T: (00234) (52) 250 552
Esan (Archbishop)	Friday John Imaekhai Bishopscourt, Ojoelen, PO Box 921, Ekpoma, Edo State, Nigeria T: (00234) (55) 981 079 E: bishopimaekhai@hotmail.com
Etsako	Jacob O B Bada Bishopscourt, PO Box 11, Jattu, Auchi, Edo State, Nigeria
Ikka	Peter Onekpe St John's Cathedral, PO Box 1063, Agbor, Delta State, Nigeria T: (00234) (55) 250 14
Ndokwa	David Obiosa Bishopscourt, 151 Old Sapele Road, Obiaruka, Delta State, Nigeria M: (00234) (803) 776 9464 E: dfao1963@yahoo.com
Oleh	John Usiwoma Aruakpor Bishopscourt, PO Box 8, Oleh, Delta State, Nigeria T: (00234) (53) 701 062 F: (00234) (802) 307 4008 E: angoleh2000@yahoo.com
Sabongidda-Ora	John Akao Bishopscourt, PO Box 13, Sabongidda-Ora, Edo State, Nigeria T: (00234) (57) 54 132 F: (00234) (806) 087 7137 E: akaojohn@yahoo.com
Sapele	Blessing Erifeta Bishopscourt, PO Box 52, Sapele, Delta State, Nigeria M: (00234) (803) 662 4282 E: dioceseofsapele@yahoo.com
Ughelli	Cyril Odutemu Bishopscourt, Ovurodawanre, PO Box 760, Ughelli, Delta State, Nigeria T: (00234) (53) 600 403 F: (00234) (803) 530 7114 E: ughellianglican@yahoo.com

Warri | Christian Esezi Ideh
Bishopscourt, 17 Mabiaku Rd, GRA,
PO Box 4571, Warn, Delta State, Nigeria
T: (00234) (53) 255 857
F: (00234) (805) 102 2680
E: angdioceseofwarri@yahoo.com

Western Izon
(Missionary
diocese) | Benjamin Edafe Emamezi
Bishopscourt, PO Box 5, Patani,
Delta State, Nigeria
M: (00234) (822) 05 6228
E: anglizon@yahoo.co.uk

PROVINCE OF ENUGU

Abakaliki | Monday C Nkwoagu
All Saints' Cathedral, PO Box 112, Abakaliki,
Ebonyi State, Nigeria
T: (00234) (43) 220 762
E: abakaliki@anglican-nig.org

Afikpo | Paul A Udogu
Bishop's House, Uwana, PO Box 699, Afikpo,
Ebonyi State, Nigeria
E: udogupaul@yahoo.com

Awgu-Aninri | Emmanuel Ugwu
Bishopscourt,
PO Box 305, Awgu, Enugu State, Nigeria
M: (00234) (803) 334 9360
E: afamnonye@yahoo.com

Eha-Amufu | Daniel Olinya
St Andrew's Cathedral, Bishopscourt,
PO Box 85
Eh-Amufu, Enugu State, Nigeria
M: (00234) (803) 089 2131
E: dankol@yahoo.com

Ikwo | Kenneth Ifemene
Bishop's Residence, Agubia Ikwo, PO Box 998,
Abakaliki, Ebonyi State, Nigeria
M: (00234) (805) 853 4849
E: bishopikwoanglican.@yahoo.com

Ngbo | Christian I Ebisike
Bishop's House, PO Box 93, Abakaliki, Ebonyi
State, Nigeria
M: (00234) (806) 779 4899
E: vendchris@yahoo.com

Nike | Evans Jonathan Ibeagha
Bishopscourt, Trans-Ekulu, PO Box 2416,
Enugu, Enugu State, Nigeria
M: (00234) (803) 324 1387
E: pnibeagha@yahoo.com

Nsukka | Aloysius Agbo
St Cypran's Compound, PO Box 516, Nsukka,
Enugu State, Nigeria
M: (00234) (803) 932 7840
E: nsukka@anglican-nig.org

Oji River | Amos Amankechinelo Madu
(Archbishop) PO Box 123 Oji River,
Enugu State, Nigeria
M: (00234) (803) 670 4888
E: amosmadu@yahoo.com

Udi | Chjioke Augustine Aneke
Bishopscourt, PO Box 30,
Udi, Enugu State, Nigeria
M: (00234) (806) 908 9690
E: bchijiokeudi@yahoo.com

PROVINCE OF IBADAN

Ajayi Crowther | Olugbenga Oduntan
Bishopscourt, Iseyin, PO Box 430, Iseyin,
Oyo State, Nigeria
M: (00234) (803) 719 8182
E: ajayicrowtherdiocese@yahoo.com

Ekiti Kwara | Andrew Ajayi
M: (00234) (803) 470 3522
E: andajayi@yahoo.com

Ibadan
(Archbishop) | Joseph O Akinfenwa
PO Box 3075, Mapo,
Ibadan, Nigeria
T: (00234) (2) 810 1400
F: (00234) (2) 810 1413
E: ibadan@anglican.skannet.com.ng

Ibadan North | Dr Segun Okubadejo
Bishopscourt, Moyede, PO
Box 28961, Agodi, Ibadan, Nigeria
T: (00234) (2) 810 7482
E: angibn@skannet.com

Ibadan South | Jacob Ademola Ajetunmobi
Bishopscourt, PO Box 166, St David's
Compound, Kudeti, Ibadan, Nigeria
T/F: (00234) (2) 231 9141
E: jacajet@skannet.com.ng

Ife | Oluwole Odubogun
Bishopscourt, PO Box 312, Ife, Osun State,
Nigeria
T: (00234) (36) 230 046
E: rantiodubogun@yahoo.com

Ife East | Oluseyi Oyelade
Bishop's House, PMB 505, Modakeke-Ife,
Osun State, Nigeria
M: (00234) (802) 322 4962
E: seyioyelade@yahoo.com

Ijesa North East | Joseph Alaba Olusola
PO Box 40, Ipetu, Ijesa, Ogun State, Nigeria
M: (00234) (803) 942 8275
E: bpjafsola@gmail.com

Ijesha North | Isaac Oluyamo
Bishopscourt, PO Box 4, Ijebu-Jesa, Osun
State, Nigeria
M: (00234) (802) 344 0333

Ilesa | Samuel Olubayu Sowale
Diocesan Headquarters, Muroko Road, PO
Box 237, Ilesa, Osun State, Nigeria
T: (00234) (36) 460 138
E: ilesha@anglican-nig.org

Ilesa South West | Samuel Egbebunmi
Bishopscourt, Cathedral of the Holy Trinity,
Imo Ilesa, Osun State, Nigeria
M: (00234) (803) 307 1876
E: segbebunmi@yahoo.com

Ogbomosho
(Missionary
diocese) | Dr Matthew Osunade
Bishopscourt, St David's Anglican Cathedral
PO Box 1909, Ogbomoso, Osun State, Nigeria
M: (00234) (805) 593 6164
E: maaosunade@yahoo.com

Oke-Ogun | Solomon Amusan
Bishopscourt, PO Box 30, Saki, Oyo State,
Nigeria
M: (00234) (802) 323 3365
E: solomonamusan@yahoo.com

Oke-Osun | Abraham Akinlalu
Bishopscourt, PO Box 251, Gbongan, Osun
State, Nigeria
M: (00234) (803) 771 7194
E: abrahamakinlalu@yahoo.com

Osun | James Afolabi Popoola
PO Box 285, Osogbo, Osun State, Nigeria
T: (00234) (35) 240 325
F: (00234) (803) 356 1628
E: folapool@yahoo.com

Osun North East | Humphery B Olumakaiye
Bishopscourt, PO Box 32, Otan Ayegbaju,
Osun State, Nigeria
M: (00234) (803) 388 2678
E: bamisebi2002@yahoo.co.uk

Oyo | Jacob Ola Fasipe
Bishopscourt, PO Box 23, Oyo, Oyo State,
Nigeria
T: (00234) (38) 240 225
F: (00234) (803) 857 2120
E: oyo@anglican-nig.org

PROVINCE OF JOS

Bauchi | Musa Tula
Bishop's House, 2 Hospital Rd, PO Box 2450,
Bauchi, Nigeria
T: (00234) (77) 546 460
E: bauchi@anglican-nig.org

Bukuru | Jwan Zhumbes
Bishopscourt, Citrus Estate Sabon Bariki, PO
Box 605, Plateau State, Nigeria

Damaturu | Abiodun Ogunyemi
PO Box 312, Damaturu, Yobe State, Nigeria
T: (00234) (74) 522 142
E: damaturu@anglican-nig.org

Gombe	Henry C Ndukuba Cathedral Church of St Peter, PO Box 39, Gombe, Nigeria T: (00234) (72) 221 212 F: (00234) (72) 221 141 E: gombe@anglican-nig.org
Jalingo	Timothy Yahaya PO Box 4, Magami, Jalingo, Taraba State, Nigeria M: (00234) (806) 594 4694 E: timothyyahaya@yahoo.com
Jos (Archbishop)	Benjamin A Kwashi Bishopscourt, PO Box 6283, Jos, 930001, Plateau State, Nigeria T: (00234) (73) 612 2215 E: benkwashi@gmail.com
Langtang	Stanley Fube 87 Solomon Lar Road, PO Box 38, Langtang, Plateau State, Nigeria M: (00234) (803) 605 8767 E: stanleyfube@gmail.com
Maiduguri	Emmanuel Kana Mani Bishopscourt, PO Box 1693, Maiduguri, Borno State, Nigeria T/F: (00234) (76) 234 010 E: bishope-45@yahoo.com
Pankshin	Olumuyiwa Ajayi Diocesan Secretariat, PO Box 24, Pankshin, Plateau State, Nigeria M: (00234) (803) 344 7318 E: olumijayi@yahoo.com
Yola	Markus A Ibrahim PO Box 601, Yola Adamawa State, Nigeria T: (00234) (75) 624 303 F: (00234) (803) 045 7576 E: marcusibrahim2002@yahoo.com

PROVINCE OF KADUNA

Bari	Idris Zubairu Bishopscourt, Gidan Mato Bari, Kano State, Nigeria M: (00234) (808) 559 7183
Dutse	Yesufu Ibrahim Lumu PO Box 67, Yadi, Dutse, Jigawa State, Nigeria T: (00234) (64) 721 379 E: dutse@anglican-nig.org
Gusau	John Garba PO Box 64, Gusau, Zamfara State, Nigeria T: (00234) (63) 204 747 E: gusau@anglican.skannet.com
Ikara	Yusuf Ishaya Janfalan Bishopscourt, PO Box 23, Ikara, Kaduna State, Nigeria M: (00234) (803) 679 3865 E: ikara@anglican-nig.org
Kaduna	*Vacant* PO Box 72, Kaduna, Nigeria T: (00234) (62) 240 085 F: (00234) (62) 244 408
Kano	Zakka Lalle Nyam Bishopscourt, PO Box 362, Kano, Nigeria T/F: (00234) (64) 647 816 E: kano@anglican.skannet.com.ng
Katsina	Jonathan Sani Bamaiyi Bishop's Lodge, PO Box 904, Katsina, Nigeria T: (00234) (65) 432 718 M: (00234) (803) 601 5584 E: bpjonathanbamaiyi@yahoo.co.uk
Kebbi (Archbishop)	Edmund E Akanya Bishop's Residence, PO Box 701, Birnin Kebbi, Kebbi State, Nigeria T: (00234) (68) 321 179 F: (00234) (803) 586 1060 E: eekanya@yahoo.com
Sokoto	Augustine Omole Bishop's Lodge, 68 Shuni Road, PO Box 3489, Sokoto, Nigeria T: (00234) (60) 234 639 F: (00234) (803) 542 3765 E: akin_sok@yahoo.com

Wusasa	Ali Buba Lamido PO Box 28, Wusasa, Zaria, Kaduna State, Nigeria T: (00234) (69) 334 594 F: (00234) 727 2504 E: lamido2sl@aol.co.uk
Zaria	Cornelius Salifu Bello Bishopscourt, PO Box 507, Zaria, Kaduna State, Nigeria M: (00234) (802) 708 9555 E: cssbello@hotmail.com

PROVINCE OF KWARA

Igbomina (Archbishop)	Michael Akinyemi, Bishopscourt, PO Box 102, Oro, Kwara State, Nigeria M: (00234) (803) 669 1940 E: oluakinyemi2000@yahoo.com
Igbomina West	James Olaoti Akinola Bishop's House, PO Box 32, Oke Osin, Kwara State, Nigeria M: (00234) (803) 392 3720 E: olaotimuyiwa@yahoo.com
Jebba	Timothy Adewole Bishopscourt, PO Box 2, Jebba, Kwara State, Nigeria M: (00234) (803) 572 5298 E: bishopadewole@yahoo.com
Kwara	Olusegun Adeyemi Bishopscourt, Fate Rd, PO Box 1884, Ilorin, Kwara State, Nigeria T: (00234) (31) 220 879 F: (00234) (803) 325 8068 E: bishopolusegun@yahoo.com
New Busa	Israel Amoo Bishopscourt, PO Box 208, New Busa, Niger State, Nigeria M: (00234) (803) 677 3839 E: bishopamoo@yahoo.com
Offa	Akintunde Popoola Bishop's House, 78–80 Ibrahim Rd, PO Box 21, Offa, Kwara State, Nigeria M: (00234) (805) 925 0011 E: tpopoola@anglican-nig.org
Omu-Aran	Philip Adeyemo Bishop's House, PO Box 244, Omu-Aran, Kwara State, Nigeria M: (00234) (806) 592 4891 E: rtrevadeyemo@yahoo.com

PROVINCE OF LAGOS

Awori	Johnson Akinwamide Atere Bishopscourt, PO Box 10, Ota, Ogun State, Nigeria M: (00234) (803) 553 7284 E: dioceseofawori@yahoo.com
Badagry (Missionary diocese)	Joseph Babatunde Adeyemi Bishopscourt, PO Box 7, Badagry, Lagos State, Nigeria T: (00234) (1) 773 5546 M: (00234) (803) 306 4601 E: badagry@anglican-nig.org
Egba	Emmanuel O Adekunle, Bishopscourt, Cathedral of St Peter, PO Box 46, Ile-oluji, Ondo State, Nigeria E: egba@anglican-nig.org *or* mowadayo@yahoo.com
Egba West	Samuel Ajani Bishopscourt, Oke-Ata Housing Estate, PO Box 6204, Sapon, Abeokuta, Nigeria M: (00234) (805) 518 4822 E: samuelajani@yahoo.com
Ifo	Nathaniel Oladejo Ogundipe Bishopscourt, Trinity House KM1, Ibogun Rd, PO Box 104, Ifo, Ogun State, Nigeria M: (00234) (802) 778 4377 E: dioceseofifo@gmail.com
Ijebu	Ezekiel Ayodele Awosoga Bishopscourt, Ejinrin Rd, PO Box 112, Ijebu-Ode, Nigeria T: (00234) (37) 432 886 E: ijebu@anglican-nig.org *or* bishop@ang-ijebudiocese.com

Ijebu North	Solomon Kuponu Bishopscourt, Oke-Sopen, Ijebu-Igbo, Ogun State, Nigeria M: (00234) (803) 741 9372 E: dioceseofijebunorth@yahoo.com
Lagos (Archbishop)	Ephraim Adebola Ademowo 29 Marina, PO Box 13, Lagos, Nigeria T: (00234) (1) 263 6026 F: (00234) (803) 403 1358 E: adebolaademowo@dioceseoflagos.org
Lagos Mainland	Adebayo Akinde Bishop's House, PO Box 849, Ebute, Lagos, Nigeria T: (00234) (703) 390 5522 F: (00234) (803) 403 1358 E: adakinde@gmail.com
Lagos West	James O Odedeji Vining House, 3rd Floor, Archbishop Vining Memorial Cathedral, Oba Akinjobi Road, GRA Ikeja, Nigeria T: (00234) (1) 493 7333 F: (00234) (2) 493 7337 E: dioceseoflagoswest@yahoo.com
Remo	Michael O Fape Bishopscourt, Ewusi Street, PO Box 522, Sagamu, Ogun State, Nigeria T: (00234) (37) 640 598 F: (00234) (803) 726 7949 E: remo@anglican-nig.org
Yewa	Michael Adebayo Oluwarohunbi Bishopscourt, PO Box 484, Ilaro, Ogun State, Nigeria T: (00234) (39) 440 695

PROVINCE OF LOKOJA

Doko	Uriah Nadakolo Kolo PO Box 1513, Bida, Niger State, Nigeria M: (00234) (803) 590 6327 E: uriahkolo@gmail.com
Ijuma	Ezekiel Ikupolati Bishopscourt, PO Box 90, Iyara-Ijumi Kogi State, Nigeria M: (00234) (807) 500 8780 E: efikupolati@yahoo.com
Kabba	Steven Akobe Bishopscourt, Obara Way, PO Box 62, Kabba, Kogi State, Nigeria T: (00234) (58) 300 633 F: (00234) (803) 471 4759
Kontagora	Jonah Ibrahim Bishop's House, GPA PO Box 1, Kontagora, Niger State, Nigeria M: (00234) (803) 625 2032 E: jonahibrahim@yahoo.co.uk
Kutigi	Jeremiah Ndana Kolo Bishop's House, St John's Mission Compound, PO Box 14, Bida, Nigeria M: (00234) (803) 625 2032 E: bishopkolo@yahoo.com
Lokoja (Archbishop)	Emmanuel Sokowamju Egbunu Bishopscourt, PO Box 11, Bethany, Lokoja, Koji State, Nigeria T: (00234) (58) 220 588 E: emmanuelegbunu@yahoo.co.uk
Minna	Daniel Abu Yisa Bishopscourt, Dutsen Kura, PO Box 2469, Minna, Nigeria M: (00234) (803) 588 6552 E: danyisa2007@yahoo.com
Ogori-Magongo	Festus Davies Bishop's House, St Peter's Cathedral Ogori, Kogi State, Nigeria M: (00234) (803) 451 0378 E: fessyoladiran@yahoo.com
Okene	Emmanuel Bayo Ajulo Bishopscourt, PO Box 43, Okene, Kogi State, Nigeria M: (00234) (803) 700 0016 E: okenediocese@yahoo.com

PROVINCE OF THE NIGER

Aguata (Archbishop)	Christian Ogochukwo Efobi Bishopscourt, PO Box 1128, Ekwulobia, Anambra State, Nigeria M: (00234) (803) 750 1077 E: christianefobi@yahoo.com
Amichi	Ephraim Ikeakor Bishopscourt, PO Box 13, Amichi, Anambra State, Nigeria M: (00234) (803) 317 0916 E: eoikeakor@yahoo.com
Awka	Alexander Ibezim Bishopscourt, PO Box 130, Awka, Anambra State, Nigeria T: (00234) (48) 550 058 E: chioma1560@aol.com
Enugu	Dr Emmanuel O Chukwuma Bishop's House, PO Box 418, Enugu, Enugu State, Nigeria T: (00234) (42) 453 804 F: (00234) (42) 259 808 E: enugu@anglican-nig.org
Ihiala	Ralph Okafor Bishopscourt, St Silas Cathedral, PO Box 11, Ihiala, Anambra State, Nigeria M: (00234) (803) 711 2408 E: raphoka@yahoo.com
Mbamili	Henry Okeke Bishopscourt, PO Box 2653, Onitsha, Anambra State, Nigeria M: (00234) (803) 644 9780 E: bishopokeke@yahoo.com
Niger West	Johnson Ekwe Bishop's House, Anambra, Anaambra State, Nigeria M: (00234) (803) 384 3339
Nnewi	Godwin Izundu Nmezinwa Okpala Bishopscourt, PO Box 2630, Uruagu-Nnewi, Anambra State, Nigeria T: (00234) (803) 348 5714 F: (00234) (803) (46) 462 676 E: okpalagodwin@yahoo.co.uk
Ogbaru	Samuel Ezeofor Bishopscourt, PO Box 46, Atani, Anambra State, Nigeria E: ezechukwunyere@yahoo.com
On the Niger	Owen Chidozie Nwokolo Bishopscourt, Ozala Rd, Onitsha, Anambra State, Nigeria M: (00234) (803) 726 0548 E: owenelsie@yahoo.com

PROVINCE OF NIGER DELTA

Aba	Ugochukwa Ezuoke Bishopscourt, 70–72 St Michael's Rd, PO Box 212, Aba, Abia State, Nigeria T: (00234) (82) 227 666 E: aba@anglican-nig.org
Aba Ngwa North	Nathan C Kanu Bishopscourt, All Saints Cathedral, Abayi- Umuocham 1610165, Owerri Road, PO Box 43, Aba, Abia State, Nigeria M: (00234) (803) 822 4623 E: odinathnfe@sbcglobal.net
Ahoada	Clement Nathan Ekpeye Bishopscourt, St Paul's Cathedral, PO Box 4, Ahoada East L.G.A., Rivers State, Nigeria T: (00234) (806) 356 624 E: ahoada@anglican-nig.org
Calabar	Tunde Adeleye Bishopscourt, PO Box 74, Calabar, Cross River State, Nigeria T: (00234) (87) 232 812 F: (00234) (88) 220 835 E: calabar@anglican-nig.org
Enugu North	Sosthenes Eze Bishopscourt, St Mary's Cathedral, Ngwo- Enugu, Nigeria M: (00234) (803) 870 9362 E: bishopsieze@yahoo.com

Etche   Precious Nwala
                      Bishopscourt, PO Box 89, Okehi, Etche, Rivers
                      State, Nigeria
                      M: (00234) (807) 525 2842
                      E: etchediocese@anglican.com
                      or precious_model5@yahoo.com

Evo   Innocent U Ordu, Bishopscourt
                      PO Box 3576, Port Harcourt, Rivers State,
                      Nigeria
                      M: (00234) (803) 715 2706
                      E: innocent-ordu@yahoo.com

Ikwerre   Blessing Chinyere Enyindah
                      Bishopscourt, St Peter's Cathedral, PO Box
                      14229, Port Harcourt, Rivers State, Nigeria
                      M: (00234) (802) 321 2824
                      E: blessingenyindah@yahoo.com

Niger Delta   Ralph Ebirien
                      PO Box 115, Port Harcourt, Rivers State,
                      Nigeria
                      M: (00234) (708) 427 9095
                      E: revpalph_ebirien@yahoo.com

Niger Delta   Ignatius C O Kattey
North   PO Box 53, Diobu, Port Harcourt, Rivers State,
(Archbishop)   Nigeria
                      M: (00234) (803) 309 4331
                      E: bishopicokattey@yahoo.com

Niger Delta   Emmanuel O Oko-Jaja
West   Bishopscourt, PO Box 10, Yenagoa, Bayelsa
                      State, Nigeria
                      M: (00234) (803) 870 2099
                      E: niger-delta-west@anglican-nig.org

Northern Izon   Fred Nyanabo
                      Bishopscourt, PO Box 705, Yenagoa, Bayelsa
                      State, Nigeria
                      M: (00234) (803) 316 0938
                      E: fred_nyanabo@yahoo.co.uk

Ogbia   James Oruwori
                      Bishop's House, 10 Queens Street, Ogbia
                      Town, Bayelsea State, Nigeria
                      M: (00234) (803) 73 4746
                      E: jaoruwori@yahoo.com

Ogoni   Solomon S Gberegbara
(Missionary   Bishopscourt, PO Box 73, Bori-Ogoni,
diocese)   Rivers State, Nigeria
                      M: (00234) (803) 339 2545
                      E: ogoni@anglican-nig.org

Okrika   Tubokosemie Abere
                      Bishopscourt, PO Box 11, Okrika, Rivers State,
                      Nigeria
                      M: (00234) (803) 312 5226
                      E: dioceseofokrika@yahoo.com

Uyo   Prince Asukwo Antail
                      Bishopscourt, PO Box 70, Uyo, Akwa Ibom
                      State, Nigeria
                      M: (00234) (802) 916 2305
                      E: uyo@anglican-nig.org

PROVINCE OF ONDO

Akoko   Gabriel Akinbiyi
                      PO Box 572, Ikare-Akoko, Ondo State, Nigeria
                      T: (00234) (31) 801 011
                      E: bishopgabrielakinbiyi@yahoo.com

Akure   Simeon O Borokini
                      Bishopscourt, PO Box 1622, Akure, Ondo
                      State, Nigeria
                      T/F: (00234) (34) 241 572

Diocese on the   Joshua Ogunele
Coast   Bishopscourt, Ikoya Road, PMB 3,
(formerly   Ilutitun-Osooro, Ondo State, Nigeria
Ikale-Ilaje)   M: (00234) (803) 467 1879
                      E: joshuaonthecoast@yahoo.ca

Ekiti   Samuel Abe
(Archbishop)   Bishopscourt, PO Box 12,
                      Okesa Street, Ado-Ekiti, Ekiti State, Nigeria
                      T: (00234) (30) 250 305
                      E: adedayoekiti@yahoo.com

Ekiti Oke   Isaac O Olubowale
                      Bishopscourt, PO Box 207, Usi-Ekiti, Ekiti
                      State, Nigeria
                      M: (00234) (803) 600 9582
                      E: ekitioke@anglican-nig.org

Ekiti West   Samuel O Oke
                      Bishop's Residence, 6 Ifaki Street, PO Box 477,
                      Ijero-Ekiti, Nigeria
                      T: (00234) (30) 850 314
                      E: ekitiwest@anglican-nig.org

Idoani   Ezekiel Dahunsi
                      Bishopscourt, PO Box 100 Idoani, Ondo State,
                      Nigeria
                      M: (00234) (803) 384 4029
                      E: bolaezek@yahoo.com

Ilaje   Fredrick Idowu Olugbemi
                      Bishopscourt, PO Box 146, Igbokoda, Ondo
                      State, Nigeria
                      M: (00234) (806) 624 8662
                      E: forogbemi@yahoo.com

Ile-Oluji   Samson Adekunle
                      Bishopscourt, Cathedral of St Peter, PO Box
                      46, Ile-Oluji, Ondo State, Nigeria
                      M: (00234) (803) 454 1236
                      E: adkulesamson86@yahoo.co.uk

Irele-Eseodo   Felix O Akinbuluma
                      Bishopscourt, Sabomi Road, Ode Irele,
                      Ondo State, Nigeria
                      M: (00234) (805) 671 2653
                      E: felixgoke@yahoo.com

Ondo   George L Lasebikan
(Archbishop)   Bishopscourt, College Rd,
                      PO Box 265, Ondo, Nigeria
                      T: (00234) (34) 610 718
                      F: (00234) (803) 472 1813
                      E: ondoanglican@yahoo.co.uk

Owo   James Adedayo Oladunjoye
                      Bishopscourt, PO Box 472, Owo, Ondo State,
                      Nigeria
                      T: (00234) (51) 241 463
                      F: (00234) (803) 475 4291
                      E: bishopoladunjoye@yahoo.co.uk

PROVINCE OF OWERRI

Egbu   Geoffrey E Okorafor
                      All Saints' Cathedral, PO Box 1967, Owerri,
                      Imo State, Nigeria
                      T: (00234) (83) 231 797
                      E: egbu@anglican-nig.org

Ideato   Caleb A Maduomo
                      Bishopscourt, PO Box 2,
                      Ndizuogu, Imo State, Nigeria
                      M: (00234) (803) 745 4503
                      E: bpomacal@hotmail.com

Ikeduru   Emmanuel C Maduwike
                      Bishop's House, PO Box 56, Atta, Imo State,
                      Nigeria
                      M: (00234) (803) 704 4686
                      E: emmamaduwike@yahoo.com

Mbaise   Chamberlain Chinedu Ogunedo
                      Bishopscourt, PO Box 10, Ife, Ezinihitte
                      Mbaise, Imo State, Nigeria
                      M: (00234) (803) 336 9836
                      E: ogunedochi@yahoo.com

Ohaji-Egbema   Chidi Collins Oparaojiaku
                      Bishop's House, PO Box 8026, New Owerri,
                      Imo State, Nigeria
                      M: (00234) (803) 312 1063
                      E: chidioparachiaku@yahoo.com

Okigwe   Edward Osuegbu
                      Bishopscourt, PO Box 156, Okigwe, Imo State,
                      Nigeria
                      M: (00234) (803) 724 6374
                      E: edchuc@justice.com

Okigwe North   Godson Udochukwu Ukanwa
                      PO Box 127, Anara, Imo State, Nigeria
                      M: (00234) (803) 672 4314
                      E: venukanwa@yahoo.com

Okigwe South   David Onuoha
                      Bishopscourt, Ezeoke Nsu, PO Box 235, Nsu,
                      Ehime Mbano LGA, Imo State, Nigeria
                      E: okisouth@yahoo.com

On the Lake   Chijioke Oti
                      Bishopscourt, PO Box 36, Oguta, Imo State,
                      Nigeria
                      M: (00234) (802) 788 8738
                      E: chijiokeoti72@yahoo.com

Orlu
(Archbishop)
Bennett C I Okoro
Bishopscourt, PO Box 260,
Nkwerre, Imo State, Nigeria
T: (00234) (82) 440 538
F: (00234) (803) 671 1271
E: anglicannaorlu@yahoo.com

Oru
Geoffrey Chukwunenye
PO Box 91, Mgbidi, Imo State, Nigeria
M: (00234) (803) 308 1270
E: geoinlagos@yahoo.com

Owerri
Dr Cyril Chukwunonyerem Okorocha
Bishop's Bourne, PMB 1063, Owerri,
Imo State, Nigeria
T: (00234) (83) 230 784
F: (00234) (803) 338 9344
E: owerri_anglican@yahoo.com

PAPUA NEW GUINEA

Archbishop of
Papua New
Guinea
Clyde Igara
E: clydemigara@gmail.com

Aipo Rongo
Nathan Ingen
PO Box 893, Mount Hagen,
Western Highlands Province, Papua New
Guinea
T: (00675) 542 1131
F: (00675) 542 1181
E: bishopnathan2@gmail.com

(Suffragan)
Denys Ririka
PO Box 1178, Goroka, Eastern Highlands
Province, Papua New Guinea
E: acpngair@global.net.pg

Dogura
Tennyson Bogar
PO Box 19, Dogura, MBP, Papua New Guinea
T: (00675) 641 1530
F: (00675) 641 1129
E: tennysonbogar.tb@gmail.com

New Guinea
Islands, The
Allan Migi
Bishop's House, PO Box 806,
Kimbe, Papua New Guinea
T/F: (00675) 983 5120
E: simon.kamong@gmail.com

Popondota
Lindsley Ihove
Anglican Diocese of Popondota, PO Box 26,
Popondetta, Oro Province, Papua New
Guinea
T: (00675) 329 7194
F: (00675) 329 7476
E: bplindsleyihove@gmail.com

Port Moresby
Denny Bray Guka
PO Box 6491, Boroko, NCD
Port Moresby, Papua New Guinea
T: (00675) 323 2489
F: (00675) 323 2493
E: dennyguka@gmail.com

THE PHILIPPINES

Prime Bishop
Renato Mag-Gay Abibico
275 E Rodriguez Sr Avenue
1102 Quezon City, Philippines
T: (0063) (2) 722 8481
F: (0063) (2) 721 1923
E: reneabibico@yahoo.com

Central
Philippines
Dixie Copanut Taclobao
281 E Rodriguez Sr. Avenue, 1102 Quezon
City, Philippines
T: (0063) (2) 412 8561
F: (0063) (2) 724 2143
E: central@i-next.net

Davao
Jonathan Labasan Casimina
Km 3 MacArthur Highway, Matina,
8000 Davao City, Philippines
T: (0063) (82) 299 1511
F: (0063) (82) 296 9629
E: episcopaldioceseofdavao@yahoo.com

North Central
Philippines
Joel Atiwag Pachao
358 Magsaysay Avenue,
2600 Baguio City, Philippines
T: (0063) (74) 443 7705
F: (0063) (74) 442 2432
E: edncp@digitelone.com

Northern Luzon
Vacant
Bulanao, 3800 Tabuk,
Kalinga, Philippines

Northern
Philippines
Brent Harry W Alawas
Diocesan Center, Bontoc,
2616 Mountain Province, Philippines
T: (0063) (74) 602 1026
F: (0063) (74) 462 4099
E: ednpvic@hotmail.com

Santiago
Alexander A Wandag Sr
Maharlika Highway, 3311 Divisoria, Santiago
City, Isabela, Philippines
T: (0063) (78) 682 3756
F: (0063) (78) 682 1256
E: alexwandageds@yahoo.com

Southern
Philippines
Danilo Labacanacruz Bustamente
186 Sinsuat Avenue, Rosario Heights,
9600 Cotabato City, Philippines
T: (0063) (64) 421 2960
F: (0063) (64) 421 1703
E: edsp_ecp@yahoo.com

RWANDA

Butare
Nathan Gasatura
BP 255, Butare, Rwanda
T: (00250) 30 710
F: (00250) 30 504
E: nathan.gasatura@gmail.com

Byumba
Emmanuel Ngendahayo
BP 17, Byumba, Rwanda
T/F: (00250) 64242
E: engendahayo@ymail.com

Cyangugu
Nathan Amooti Rusengo
PO Box 52, Cyangugu, Rwanda
T: (00250) 788 409 061
E: nathanamooti@gmail.com

Gahini
Alexis Bilindabagabo
BP 22, Kigali, Rwanda
T: (00250) 67 422
F: (00250) 77 831
E: abilindabagabo@gmail.com

Gasabo
(Archbishop)
Onesphore Rwaje
PO Box 22487, Kigali, Rwanda
F: (00250) 64 242
E: onesphorerwaje@yahoo.fr

Kibungo
Emmanuel Ntazinda
EER Kibungo Diocese,
BP 719, Kibungo, Rwanda
T/F: (00250) 566 194
E: emmanuelntazinda@ymail.com

Kigali
Louis Muvunyi
EER/DK, BP 61, Kigali, Rwanda
T: (00250) 576 340
F: (00250) 573 213
E: louismuvunyi@hotmail.com

Kigeme
Augustin Mvunabandi
BP 67, Gikongoro, Rwanda
T: (00250) 535 086
E: dkigemeear@yahoo.fr

Kivu
Augustin Ahimana
BP 166 Gisenyi
T: (00250) 788 350 119
E: aamurekezi@gmail.com

Shyira
Laurent Mbanda
EER Shyira Diocese, BP 52, Ruhengeri,
Rwanda
T: (00250) 466 02
F: (00250) 546 449
E: mbandalaurent@yahoo.com

Shyogwe
Jéred Kalimba
BP 27, Gitarama, Rwanda
T: (00250) 62 372
F: (00250) 62 460
E: kalimbaj60@yahoo.fr

SOUTH EAST ASIA

Kuching
(Primate)
Datuk Bolly Anak Lapok
Bishop's House, PO Box 347,
93704 Kuching, Sarawak, Malaysia
T: (0060) (82) 240 187
F: (0060) (82) 426 488
E: bpofkuching@gmail.com

(Assistant) Aeries Sumping Jingan
PO Box 347, 93704 Kuching, Sarawak,
Malaysia
T: (0060) (82) 429 755
F: (0060) (82) 426 488
E: aersumjin@gmail.com

(Assistant) Solomon Cheong Sung Voon
St Columba's Church, PO Box 233,
98007 Miri, Sarawak, Malaysia
T: (0060) (85) 417 284
F: (0060) (85) 435 370
E: solomon.cheong@gmail.com

Sabah Melter Jiki Tais
PO Box 10811, 88809 Kota Kinabalu, Sabah,
Malaysia
T: (0060) (88) 245 846
F: (0060) (88) 261 422
E: uskupmjtais@gmail.com

(Assistant) John Yeo, 201, Jalan Dunlop, 91000 Tawau,
Malaysia
E: ad.johnyeo@gmail.com

Singapore Rennis Ponniah
St Andrew's Village No 1, Francis Thomas
Drive, #01–01, Singapore 359340, Republic
of Singapore
T: (0065) (62) 887 585
F: (0065) (62) 885 574
E: rennis@anglican.org.sg

(Assistant) Low Jee King
address as above
T: (0065) (62) 885 944
F: (0064) (62) 885 574
E: lowjeeking@gmail.com

(Assistant) Kuan Kim Seng
Chapel of the Resurrection, No. 1 Francis
Thomas Drive, #2–17, Singapore 359340,
Republic of Singapore
T: (0065) (62) 888 944
F: (0065) (62) 885 574
E: kuanks@cor.org.sg

West Malaysia Datuk Ng Moon Hing
No.16 Jalan Pudu Lama, 50200 Kuala
Lumpur, Malaysia
T: (0060) (3) 2031 3213
F: (0060) (3) 2031 3225
E: canonmoon@gmail.com

(Assistant) Jason Selvaraj
Christ Church, 48, Jalan Gereja, 75000
Melaka, Malaysia
T/F: (0060) (62) 848 804
E: jasondaphne101@gmail.com

Auckland Charles K Samuel
St George's Church, 1 Lebuh Farquhar,
10200 Penang, Malaysia
T: (0060) (64) 261 2739
F: (0060) (6) 4264 2292

SOUTHERN AFRICA

Angola Andre Soares
(Missionary Av. Lenini, Travessa D. Antonia Saldanha
diocese) N. 134, CP10 341, Luanda, Angola
T: (00244) (2) 395 792
F: (00244) (2) 396 794
E: anglicana@ebonet.net

Cape Town Thabo Makgoba
(Primate) 20 Bishopscourt Drive, Bishopscourt,
Claremont, Cape Town, 7708 South Africa
T: (0027) (21) 763 1300
F: (0027) (21) 797 4193
E: archpa@anglicanchurchsa.org.za

(Table Bay) Garth Counsell
PO Box 1932, Cape Town, 8000 South Africa
T/F: (0027) (21) 469 3773
E: bishop.suffragan@ctdiocese.oorg.za

Christ the King Peter John Lee
PO Box 1653, Rosettenville, Gauteng,
2130 South Africa
T: (0027) (11) 435 0097
F: (0027) (11) 435 2868
E: bishop@ctkdiocese.co.za

Diocese of the Dintoe Letloenyane
Free State PO Box 411, Bloemfontein, 9300 South Africa
T: (0027) (51) 447 6053
F: (0027) (51) 447 5874
E: bishopdintoe@dsc.co.za

False Bay Margaret Brenda Vertue
PO Box 2804, Somerset West, 7129
South Africa
T: (0027) (21) 852 5243
F: (0027) (21) 852 9430
E: bishopm@falsebaydiocese.org.za

George Brian Melvyn Marajh
PO Box 227, George, Cape Province,
6530 South Africa
T/F: (0027) (44) 873 5680
E: bishopbrian@george.diocese.co.za

Grahamstown Ebenezer St Mark Ntlali
PO Box 181, Grahamstown, Eastern Cape,
6140 South Africa
T: (0027) (46) 636 1996
F: (0027) (46) 622 5231
E: bishop@grahamstowndiocese.org.za

Highveld Charles May
PO Box 17462, Benoni West, Gauteng,
1503 South Africa
T: (0027) (11) 422 2231
F: (0027) (11) 420 1336
E: diohveld@iafrica.com

Johannesburg Stephen Mosimanegape Moreo
PO Box 39, Westhoven, Gauteng,
2142 South Africa
T: (0027) (11) 375 2700
F: (0027) (11) 486 1015
E: steve.moreo@anglicanjoburg.org.za

Kimberley Oswald Peter Patrick Swartz
and Kuruman PO Box 45, Kimberley, 8300 South Africa
T: (0027) (53) 833 2433
F: (0027) (53) 831 2730
E: oppswartz@onetel.com

Lebombo Carlos Simao Matsinhe
CP 120, Maputo, Mozambique
T: (00258) (1) 404 885
F: (00258) (1) 401 093
E: carlosmatsinhe@rocketmail.com

Lesotho Adam Andrease Mallane Taaso
PO Box 87, Maseru 100, Lesotho
T: (00266) (22) 311 974
F: (00266) (22) 310 161
E: dioceselesotho@ecoweb.co.ls

Matlosane Stephen Molopi Diseko
PO Box 11417, Klerksdorp, 2570 South Africa
T: (0027) (18) 464 2260
F: (0027) (18) 462 4939
E: bishopstephen@diocesematlosane.co.za

Mbashe Elliot Sebenzile Williams
PO Box 1184, Butterworth, 4960 South Africa
T: (0027) (47) 491 8127
F: (0027) (43) 491 9218
E: dioceseofmbhashe@telkomsa.net

Mpumalanga Daniel Malasela Kgomosotho
PO Box 4327, White River, 1240 South Africa
T: (0027) (13) 751 1960
F: (0027) (13) 751 3638
E: bishopdan@telkomsa.net

Mthatha Sitembele Tobela Mzamane
PO Box 25, Umtata, Transkei,
5100 South Africa
T: (0027) (47) 532 4450
F: (0027) (47) 532 4191
E: anglicbspmthatha@intekom.co.za

Namibia *Vacant*
PO Box 57, Windhoek 9000, Namibia
T: (00264) (61) 238 920
F: (00264) (61) 225 903
E: bishop@anglicanchurchnamibia.com

Natal Ruben Phillip
PO Box 47439, Greyville, Durban,
4023 South Africa
T: (0027) (31) 308 9302
F: (0027) (31) 308 9316
E: bishop@dionatal.org.za

(North-West) | Tsietse Edward Seleoane
PO Box 463, Ladysmith, 3370 South Africa
T: (0027) (36) 631 4650
F: (0027) (86) 637 4949
E: bishopseleoane@dionatal.org.za

(South) | Hummingfield Charles Nkosinathi
Ndwandwe
PO Box 889, Pietermaritzburg, 3200 South
Africa
T: (0027) (33) 394 1560
F: (0027) (33) 394 8785
E: bishopndwandwe@dionatal.org.za

Niassa | Mark van Koevering
CP 264, Lichinga, Niassa, Mozambique
T/F: (00258) (27) 12 0735
E: bishop.niassa@gmail.com

(Suffragan) | Manuel Ernesto
address as above
T: (00258) (27) 121 377
E: mernesto.diocese.niassa@gmail.com

Port Elizabeth | Nceba Bethlehem Nopece
PO Box 7109, Newton Park, 6055 South Africa
T: (0027) (41) 365 1387
F: (0027) (41) 365 2049
E: bpsec@pediocese.org.za

Pretoria | Johannes Thomas Seoka
PO Box 1032, Pretoria, 0001 South Africa
T: (0027) (12) 322 2218
F: (0027) (12) 322 9411
E: ptabish@dioceseofpretoria.org

Saldanha Bay | Raphael Bernard Viburt Hess
PO Box 420, Malmesbury, 7299 South Africa
T: (0027) (22) 487 3885
F: (0027) (22) 487 3886
E: bishop@dioceseofsaldanhabay.org.za

St Helena | Richard David Fenwick
PO Box 62, Isle of St Helena, South Atlantic
Ocean
T: (00290) 4471
F: (00290) 4728
E: richard.d.fenwick@googlemail.com

St Mark
the Evangelist | Martin Andre Breytenbach
PO Box 643, Polokwane, 0700 South
Africa
T: (0027) (15) 297 3297
F: (0027) (15) 297 0408
E: martin@stmark.org.za

Swaziland | Ellinah Ntfombi Wamukoya
Bishop's House, Muir Street, Mbabane,
Swaziland
T: (00268) 404 3624
F: (00268) 404 6759
E: bishopen@safricaonline.co

Ukhahlamba | Mazwi Ernest Tisani
PO Box 1673, Queenstown, Eastern Cape,
5320 South Africa
T: (0027) (45) 838 3261
F: (0027) (51) 838 2874
E: bishopmazwi@mweb.co.za

Umzimvubu | Mlibo Mteteleli Ngewu
PO Box 644, Kokstad, 4700 South Africa
T/F: (0027) (39) 727 4117
E: mzimvubu@futurenet.co.za

Zululand | Dino Gabriel
PO Box 147, Eshowe,
Zululand, 3815 South Africa
T/F: (0027) (354) 742047
E: bishopdino@netactive.co.za

SOUTH AMERICA

Argentina | Gregory Venables
25 de Mayo 282, Capital Federal,
Buenos Aires 1001, Argentina
T: (0054) (11) 4342 4618
F: (0054) (11) 4784 1277
E: bishopdonp@etactive.co.za

Bolivia | Raphael Samuel
Iglesia Anglicana Episcopal de Bolivia, Casilla
848, Cochabamba, Bolivia
T/F: (00591) (4) 440 1168
E: raaphaelsamuel@gmail.com

Chile
(Presiding
Bishop) | Héctor Zavala Muñoz
Casilla 50675, Correo Central, Santiago,
Chile
T: (0056) (2) 638 3009 *or* 639 1509
F: (0056) (2) 639 4581
E: tzavala@iach.cl

(Suffragan) | Abelino Manuel Apeleo
Pasaje Viña Poniente 4593, Puente Alto,
Santiago, Chile
T/F: (0056) (2) 638 3009
E: aapeleo@gmail.com

Northern
Argentina | Nicholas James Quested Drayson
Iglesia Anglicana, Casilla 187, Salta 4400,
Argentina
T: (0054) (387) 431 1718
F: (0054) (371) 142 0100
E: nicobispo@gmail.com

Paraguay | Peter John Henry Bartlett
Iglesia Anglicana de Paraguaya,
Casilla de Correo 1124, Asunción, Paraguay
T: (00595) (21) 200 933
F: (00595) (21) 214 328
E: peterparaguay@gmail.com

Peru | Harold William Godfrey
Calle Doña María 141, Los Rosales, Surco,
Lima 33, Peru
T: (0051) (1) 449 0600
E: hwgodfrey@gmail.com

(Suffragan) | Juan Carlos Revilla Liendo
address, etc as above
E: jucareli1208@hotmail.es

(Suffragan) | Jorge Luis Aguilar Ocampo
address, etc as above
E: cocosac59@hotmail.com

(Suffragan) | Eulogio Alejandro Mesco Turpo
Residencial Monte Bello D4, Cerro Colorado,
Arequipa, Peru
E: alejandromesco@hotmail.com

Uruguay | Michael Pollesel
Reconquista 522, Montevideo 11000, Uruguay
T: (00598) (2) 915 9627
F: (00598) (2) 916 2519
E: iglesiaau@gmail.com

(Suffragan) | Gilberto Obdulio Porcal Martinez
address etc as above
E: gilbertoporcal@hotmail.cm

SUDAN

A number of new dioceses have been created in the Church of the Province of Sudan. At the time of going to press, some details were unavailable, and so this list is incomplete.

Akot | Isaac Dhieu Ater
T: (00211) 928 122 065
E: bishop@akot.anglican.org

Athooch | Moses Anur Ayom
T: (00211) 956 602 346
E: mosesanurayom@yahoo.com

Aweil | Abraham Yel Nhial
T: (00211) 955 621 584
E: bishop@aweil.anglican.org

Awerial | David Akau Kuol
T: (00211) 955 526 396
E: bishop.awerial@yirol.anglican.org

Bor | Ruben Akurdid
T: (00211) 955 309 767
E: bishop.akurdid@gmail.com

Cueibet | Elijah Matueny
T: (00211) 921 192 138
E: bishop@cueibet.anglican.org

Duk | Daniel Deng Abot
T: (00211) 955 523 896
E: danieldengabot@gmail.com

El-Obeid | Ismail Gabriel Abudigin
T: (00211) 967 247 262
E: bishop@elobeid.anglican.org

Ezo | John Zawo
T: (00211) 954 745 046
E: bishop@ezo.anglican.org

Ibba	Wilson Elisa Kamani T: (00211) 956 438 805 E: bishop@ibba.anglican.org
Juba (Archbishop)	Daniel Deng Bul Yak PO Box 110, Juba, South Sudan T: (00211) 912 299 275 E: archbishop@sudan.anglican.org
(Assistant)	Fraser Yugu Elias T: (00211) 956 143 577 E: ass.bishop@juba.anglican.org
Kadugli and Nuba Mountains	Andudu Adam Einail T: (00211) 912 230 250 E: bishop@kadugli.anglican.org
Kajo-Keji	Anthony Poggo T: (00211) 956 697 429 E: bishopkk@gmail.com
Khartoum	Ezekiel Kondo PO Box 65, Omdurman, 35 Khartoum, Sudan T: (00249) 912 359 768 E: bishop@khartoum.anglican.org
Kongor	Gabriel Thuch Agot E: gabrielthuchagot@yahoo.com
Lainya	Elioba Lako Obede T: (00211) 956 009 774 E: bishop@lainya.anglican.org
Lomega	Paul Yugusuk T: (00211) 955 681 468 E: lomegarea@yahoo.com
Lui	Stephen Dokolo Ismael T: (00211) 917 704 534 E: bishop@lui.anglican.org
Malakal	Hilary Garang PO Box 114, Malakal, South Sudan T: (00211) 913 333 333 E: bishop@malakal.anglican.org
Malek	Peter Joh Abraham Mayom T: (00211) 977 435 602 E: johabraham@yahoo.com
Malek Rup	Peter Marial Agok T: (00211) 955 263 347
Maridi	Justin Badi Arama T: (00211) 927 012 719 E: ecsmaridi@hotmail.com
Mundri	Bismark Monday Avokaya T: (00211) 927 602 751 E: bishop@mundri.anglican.org
Nzara	Samuel Enosa Peni T: (00211) 955 511 555 E: bishop@nzara.anglican.org
Olo	Tandema Obede T: (00211) 928 403 619 E: bishopolo65@gmail.com
Pacong	Joseph Maker Atot T: (00211) 929 154 246 E: ecs.pacongdiocese@yahoo.com
Port Sudan	Abdu Elnur Kodi T: (00249) 927 246 576 E: durukaa@live.com
Rejaf	Enoch Tombe T: (00211) 955 673 779 E: bishop@rejaf.anglican.org
Renk	Joseph Garang Atem T: (00211) 912 197 051 E: josephatem@gmail.com
Rokon	Francis Loyo T: (00211) 928 122 065 E: bployo@yahoo.co.uk
Rumbek	Alapayo Manyang Kuctiel T: (00211) 955 288 730 E: bishop@rumbek.anglican.org
Terekeka	Paul Modi Farjala T: (00211) 954 125 968 E: bishop@terekaka.anglican.org
Torit	Bernard Oringa Balmoi T: (00211) 955 210 268 E: bishop@torit.anglican.org
Twic East	Ezekiel Diing T: (00211) 955 099 182 E: bishop@twiceast.anglican.org

Wad Medani	Samaan Farjalla T: (00249) 929 587 98
Wau	Moses Deng Bol T: (00211) 926 954 187 E: bishop@wau.anglican.org
Wondurba	Matthew Taban Peter T: (00211) 911 225 000 E: bplmatthewpeter@gmail.com
Yambio	Peter Munde Yacoub T: (00211) 955 805 007 E: yambio2002@yahoo.com
Yei	Hilary Luate Adeba PO Box 588, Arua, Uganda T: (00256) (756) 561 175 E: hill_shepherd@yahoo.com
Yeri	John Abraham Nyari T: (00211) 923 149 110 E: yeridioceses@gmail.com
Yirol	Simon Adut Yuang T: (00211) 927 277 975 E: ecsyiroldiocese@yahoo.com

TANZANIA

Central Tanganyika	Dickson Chilongani Makay House, PO Box 15, Dodoma, Tanzania T: (00255) (26) 232 1714 F: (00255) (26) 232 4518 E: chilongani@anglican.or.tz
Dar-es-Salaam	Valentino Mokiwa PO Box 25016, Dar-es-Salaam, Tanzania T: (00255) (22) 286 4426 F: (00225) (22) 286 5840 E: mokiwa_valentine@hotmail.com
Kagera	Aaron Kijanjali PO Box 18, Ngara, Tanzania T: (00255) (28) 222 3624 F: (00255) (28) 222 2518 E: dkagera@gmail.com
Kibondo	*awaiting details* PO Box 15, Kibondo, Kigoma, Tanzania
Kiteto	Isaiah Chambala PO Box 74, Kibaya, Tanzania T: (00255) (27) 255 2106 E: bishopofkiteto@yahoo.com
Kondoa	Given Gaula PO Box 7, Kondoa, Tanzania T: (00255) (26) 236 0312 F: (00255) (26) 236 0304 *or* 0324 E: givenmgaula@gmail.comz
Lake Rukwa	Mathayo Kasagara PO Box 19, Mpanda, Tanzania E: kasagarajr@gmail.com
Lweru	Jackton Yeremiah Lugumira PO Box 12, Muleba, Tanzania T: (00255) (713) 274 085 E: jact@bukobaonline.com
Mara	*Vacant* PO Box 131, Musoma, Tanzania T: (00255) (28) 262 2376 F: (00255) (28) 262 2414 E: omindo@anglican.or.tz
Masasi	James Almasi Private Bag, PO Masasi, Mtwara Region, Tanzania T: (00255) (23) 251 0016 F: (00255) (23) 251 0351 E: jamesalmasi@yahoo.com
Morogoro	Godfrey Sehaba PO Box 320, Morogoro, Tanzania T/F: (00255) (23) 260 4602 E: bishopgsehaba@yahoo.com
Mount Kilimanjaro	Stanley Elilekia Hotay PO Box 1057, Arusha, Tanzania T: (00255) (27) 254 8396 F: (00255) (27) 254 4187 E: hotaystanley@yahoo.com
Mpwapwa (Archbishop)	Jacob Erasto Chimeledya PO Box 2, Mpwapwa, Tanzania T: (00255) (26) 232 0017 *or* 0825 F: (00255) (26) 232 0063 E: jacobchimeledya@hotmail.com

Newala	Oscar Mnung'a PO Box 92, Newala, Tanzania E: rtrevonewala@gmail.com
Rift Valley	John Daudi Lupaa PO Box 16, Manyoni, Tanzania T: (00255) (26) 254 0013 F: (00255) (26) 250 3014 E: act-drv@maf.or.tz
Ruaha	Joseph Mgomi Box 1028, Iringa, Tanzania T: (00255) (26) 270 1211 F: (00225) (26) 270 2479 E: actruaha@gmail.com
Ruvuma	*Vacant* PO Box 1357, Songea, Ruvuma, Tanzania T: (00255) (25) 260 0090 F: (00255) (25) 260 2987
Shinyanga	*Vacant* PO Box 421, Shinyanga, Tanzania T: (00255) (28) 276 3584
Southern Highlands	John Mwela PO Box 198, Mbeya, Tanzania T: (00255) (25) 250 0216 E: mwelajohn@yahoo.co.uk
South-West Tanganyika	Matthew Mhagama Bishop's House, PO Box 32, Njombe, Tanzania T: (00255) (26) 278 2010 F: (00255) (26) 278 2403 E: dswt@africaonline.co.tz
Tabora	Elias Chakupewa PO Box 1408, Tabora, Tanzania T: (00255) (26) 260 4124 F: (00255) (26) 260 4899 E: chakupewalucy@yahoo.com
Tanga	Maimbo Mndolwa PO Box 35, Korogwe, Tanga, Tanzania T: (00255) (27) 264 0522 F: (00255) (27) 264 0631 E: imba612@yahoo.com
Victoria Nyanza	Boniface Kwangu PO Box 278, Mwanza, Tanzania T: (00255) (28) 250 0627 F: (00255) (28) 250 0676 E: bandmkwangu@yahoo.co.uk
Western Tanganyika	Sadock Makaya PO Box 13, Kasulu, Tanzania T: (00255) (28) 281 0321 F: (00255) (28) 281 0706 E: smakaya1@yahoo.co.uk
Zanzibar	Michael Hafidh PO Box 5, Mkunazini, Zanzibar, Tanzania T: (00255) (24) 223 5348 F: (00255) (24) 223 6772 E: mhhafidh@gmail.com

UGANDA

Ankole	Sheldon Frederick Mwesigwa PO Box 14, Mbarara, Ankole, Uganda T: (00256) 787 084 301 E: smwesigwafred@gmail.com
Bukedi	Samuel Egesa PO Box 170, Tororo, Uganda T: (00256) 772 542 164 E: bukedidiocese@yahoo.com
Bunyoro-Kitara	Nathan Kyamanywa PO Box 20, Hoima, Uganda M: (00256) 776 648 232 E: nathan.kyamanywa@gmail.com
Busoga	Michael Kyomya PO Box 1658, Jinja, Uganda M: (00256) 752 649 102 F: (00256) 43 20 547 E: busogadiocese@gmail.com
Central Buganda	Jackson Matovu PO Box 1200, Kinoni-Gomba, Mpigi, Uganda T: (00256) 772 475 640 F: (00256) 772 242 742 E: mapetoruvusi@yahoo.com
East Ruwenzori	Edward Bamucwanira PO Box 1439, Kamwenge T: (00256) 772 906 236 E: edward_bamu@yahoo.com
Kampala (Archbishop)	Stanley Ntagali PO Box 335, Kampala, Uganda T: (00256) (414) 279 218 F: (00256) (414) 251 925 E: abpcou@gmail.com
(Assistant)	Hannington Mutebi PO Box 335, Kampala, Uganda T/F: (00256) (414) 342 601 E: mutebihanning@yahoo.com
Karamoja	Joseph Abura PO Box 44, Moroto, Uganda T: (00256) 782 658 502 E: loukomoru@gmail.com
Kigezi	George Bagamuhunda PO Box 3, Kabale, Uganda T: (00256) 772 450 019 E: bishopkigezi@infocom.co.ug
Kinkizi	Dan Zoreka PO Box 77, Kanungu, Uganda M: (00256) 772 507 163 E: zorekadan@yahoo.com
Kitgum	Stanley Ntagali PO Box 187, Kitgum, Uganda M: (00256) 772 959 924 E: abpcou@gmail.com
Kumi	Thomas Edison Irigei PO Box 18, Kumi, Uganda M: (00256) 772 659 460 E: kumimothersunion@yahoo.com
Lango	John Charles Odurkami PO Box 6, Lira, Uganda M: (00256) 772 614 000 E: bishoplango@yahoo.com
Luwero	Eridard Kironde Nsubuga PO Box 125, Luwero, Uganda M: (00256) 772 349 669 E: eridard.nsubuga@gmail.com
Madi and West Nile	Joel Obetia PO Box 370, Arua, Uganda M: (00256) 752 625 414 E: jobetia@yahoo.com
Masindi-Kitara	George Kasangaki PO Box 515, Masindi, Uganda T: (00256) 772 618 822 E: georgewakasa@gmail.com
Mbale	Patrick Gidudu Bishop's House, PO Box 473, Mbale, Uganda M: (00256) 782 625 619 E: mbalediocese7@rocketmail.com
Mityana	Stephen Samuel Kaziimba PO Box 102, Mityana, Uganda T: (00256) 772 512 175 E: skaziimba@yahoo.com
Muhabura	Cranmer Mugisha PO Box 22, Kisoro, Uganda T: (00256) 712 195 891 E: cranhopmu@yahoo.co.uk
Mukono	William James Ssebaggala PO Box 39, Mukono, Uganda M: (00256) 712 860 742 E: jamesebagala@yahoo.co.uk
Namirembe	Wilberforce Kityo Luwalira PO Box 14297, Kampala, Uganda T: (00256) 712 942 161 E: omulabirizi@gmail.com
Nebbi	Alphonse Watho-kudi PO Box 27, Nebbi, Uganda T: (00256) 772 650 032 E: bpalphonse@ekk.org
North Ankole	Steephen Namanya c/o PO Box 1, Rusher-Kiruhura, Uganda T: (00256) 772 622 116 E: nadrushere@yahoo.com
North Karamoja	James Nasak PO Box 26, Kotido, Uganda T: (00256) 772 660 228 E: jn.nasak@gmail.com

North Kigezi	Patrick Tugume-Tusingwire PO Box 23, Rukungiri, Uganda T: (00256) 777 912 010 E: earfchairman@yahoo.com
North Mbale	Samuel Gidudu PO Box 23577, Mbale, Uganda T: (00256) 782 853 094 E: revsamgidudu@yahoo.com
Northern Uganda	Johnson Gakumba PO Box 232, Gulu, Uganda M: (00256) 772 601 421 E: johnson.gakumba@gmail.com
Ruwenzori	Reuben Kisembo PO Box 37, Fort Portal, Uganda T: (00256) 772 838 193 E: reubenkisembo@gmail.com
Sebei	Paul Kiptoo Masaba PO Box 23, Kapchorwa, Uganda T: (00256) 772 312 502 E: repkmasaba@yahoo.com
Soroti	Charles George Erwau PO Box 107, Soroti, Uganda T: (00256) 772 5656 607 E: georgeerwau@yahoo.com
South Ankole	Nathan Ahimbisibwe PO Box 39, Ntungamo T: (00256) 772 660 636 E: revnathan2000@yahoo.com
South Rwenzori	Jackson T Nzerebende PO Box 42, Kasese, Uganda T: (00256) 772 713 736 F: (00256) (483) 44450 E: srdiocese@gmail.com
West Ankole	Yonah Katoneene PO Box 140, Bushenyi, Uganda T: (00256) 752 377 192 E: yona.katoneene@yahoo.com
West Buganda	Jackson Matovu PO Box 242, Masaka, Uganda T: (00256) 772475 640 E: mapetoruvusi@yahoo.com

UNITED STATES OF AMERICA

The roman numerals indicate to which of the nine provinces of ECUSA the diocese belongs.

Presiding Bishop	Michael Bruce Curry Episcopal Church Center, 815 Second Avenue, New York NY 10017, USA T: (001) (212) 716 6000 E: pboffice@episcopalchurch.org
(Office of Pastoral Development)	F Clayton Matthews 2857 Trent Road, New Bern NC 28562, USA T: (001) (252) 635 5004 F: (001) (804) 635 5006 E: cmatthews@episcopalchurch.org
(Bishop Suffragan for Armed Services and Federal Ministries)	James B Magness 3504 Woodley Road NW, Washington DC 20016 T: (001) (646) 434 0295 E: jmagness@episcopalchurch.org
Alabama (IV)	John McKee Sloan 521 North 20th Street, Birmingham AL 35203–2611, USA T: (001) (205) 715 2060 F: (001) (205) 715 2066 E: ksloan@dioala.org
Alaska (VIII)	Mark Lattime 1205 Denali Way, Fairbanks AK 99701–41, USA T: (001) (907) 452 3040 F: (001) (907) 456 6552 E: mlattime@gci.net
Albany (II)	William Howard Love 580 Burton Road, Greenwich NY 12834, USA T: (001) (518) 692 3350 F: (001) (518) 692 3352 E: via www.albanyepiscopaldiocese.org

Arizona (VIII)	Kirk Stevan Smith 114 West Roosevelt Street, Phoenix AZ 85003–1406, USA T: (001) (602) 254 0976 F: (001) (602) 495 6603 E: bishop@azdiocese.org
Arkansas (VII)	Larry R Benfield 310 West 17th Street, Little Rock AR 72216–4668, USA T: (001) (501) 372 2168 F: (001) (501) 372 2147 E: bishopbenfield@mac.com
Atlanta (IV)	Robert Wright 2744 Peachtree Road, Atlanta GA 30305, USA T: (001) (404) 601 5320 F: (001) (404) 601 5330 E: bishopwright@episcopalatlanta.org
(Assistant)	Keith Bernard Whitmore address etc as above E: bishopkeith@episcopalatlanta.org
Bethlehem (III)	Sean Rowe 333 Wyandotte Street, Bethlehem PA 18015–1527, USA T: (001) (610) 691 5655 or 691 5656 F: (001) (610) 691 1682 E: seanrowe@diobeth.org
California (VIII)	Marc Handley Andrus 1055 Taylor Street, San Francisco CA 94108, USA T: (001) (415) 673 5015 F: (001) (415) 673 9268 E: bishopmarc@diocal.org
Central Ecuador (IX)	Victor Scantlebury Calle Hernando Sarmiento N 39–54 y Portete, Sector El Batán, Quito, Ecuador T: (002) 254 1735
Central Florida (IV)	Gregory O Brewer Diocesan Office, 1017 E Robinson Street, Orlando FL 32801, USA T: (001) (407) 423 3567 F: (001) (407) 872 0006 E: bpbrewer@cfdiocese.org
Central Gulf Coast (IV)	James Russell Kendrick 201 N Baylen Street, Pensacola FL 32502, USA T: (001) (850) 434 7337 F: (001) (850) 434 8577 E: bishopkendrick@diocgc.org
Central New York (II)	Gladstone Bailey 'Skip' Adams 1020 7th North Street, Liverpool NY 13088, USA T: (001) (315) 474 6596 F: (001) (315) 478 1632 E: bishop@cnyepiscopal.org
Central Pennsylvania (III)	Audrey Scanlan 101 Pine Street, Harrisburg, PA 17101, USA T: (001) (717) 236 5959 F: (001) (717) 236 6448 E: ascanlan@diocesecpa.org
Chicago (V)	Jeffrey Dean Lee 65 East Huron Street, Chicago IL 60611, USA T: (001) (312) 751 4200 or 751 4217 F: (001) (312) 787 4534 E: bishop@episcopalchicago.org
(Assisting)	C Christopher Epting address etc as above E: cepting@aol.com
Colombia (IX)	Francisco Jose Duque-Gómez Cra 6 No 49–85 Piso 2, Bogotá DC, Colombia T: (0057) (1) 288 3187 or 288 3167 F: (0057) (1) 288 3248 E: obispoduque@hotmail.com
Colorado (VI)	Robert John O'Neill 1300 Washington Street, Denver CO 80203, USA T: (001) (303) 837 1173 F: (001) (303) 837 1311 E: bishoponeill@coloradodiocese.org

Connecticut (I)	Ian Theodore Douglas 290 Pratt Street, Meriden CT 06450–2295, USA T: (001) (203) 639 3501 F: (001) (203) 235 1008 E: itdouglas@episcopalct.org
(Suffragan)	Laura Ahrens *address etc as above* E: lahrens@episcopalct.org
Dallas (VII)	George Sumner 1630 North Garrett Avenue, Dallas TX 75206, USA T: (001) (214) 826 8310 F: (001) (214) 826 5968 E: gsumner@edod.org
(Suffragan)	Paul E Lambert *address etc as above* E: plambert@edod.org
Delaware (III)	Wayne Parker Wright 913 Wilson Road, Wilmington DE 19803–4012, USA T: (001) (302) 256 0374 F: (001) (302) 543 8084 E: bishop@dioceseofdelaware.net
Dominican Republic (IX)	Julio Cesar Holguin Apartado 764, Calle Santiago No 114, Gazcue, Santo Domingo, Dominican Republic T: (001) (809) 686 7493 F: (001) (809) 686 6364 E: iglepidom@codetel.net.do
East Carolina (IV)	Robert Stuart Skirving 705 Doctors Drive, Kinston, NC 27803, USA T: (001) (252) 522 0885 F: (001) (252) 523 5272 E: rskirving@diocese-eastcarolina.org
East Tennessee (IV)	George Dibrell Young III 814 Episcopal School Way, Knoxville TN 37932, USA T: (001) (865) 966 2110 F: (001) (865) 966 2535 E: gyoung@dioet.org
Eastern Michigan (V)	(Steven) Todd Ousley 924 North Niagara Street, Saginaw MI 48602, USA T: (001) (989) 752 6020 F: (001) (989) 752 6120 E: tousely@eastmich.org
Eastern Oregon (VIII)	Bavi Edna 'Nedi' Rivera 1104 Church Street, Cove OR 97824, USA T: (001) (541) 568 4514 F: (001) (541) 568 5000 E: nrivera@episdioeo.org
Easton (III)	Henry Nutt Parsley 314 North Street, Easton MD 21601–3684, USA T: (001) (410) 822 1919 F: (001) (410) 763 8259 E: hparsley@dioceseofeaston.org
Eau Claire (V)	William Jay Lambert 510 South Farwell Street, Eau Claire WI 54701, USA T: (001) (715) 835 3331 F: (001) (715) 835 9212 E: bishop1075@icloud.com
El Camino Real (VIII)	Mary Gray-Reeves 154 Central Avenue, Salinas CA 93901, USA T: (001) (831) 394 4465 F: (001) (831) 394 7133 E: info@realepiscopal.org
Europe, Convocation of American Churches in (VII)	Pierre Welté Whalon American Cathedral of the Holy Trinity, 23 avenue George V, F-75008 Paris, France T: (0033) (1) 53 23 84 06 F: (0033) (1) 49 52 96 85 E: bishop@tec-europe.org
Florida (IV)	Samuel Johnson Howard 325 Market Street, Jacksonville FL 32202–2796, USA T: (001) (904) 356 1328 F: (001) (904) 355 1934 E: jhoward@diocesefl.org
Fond du Lac (V)	Matthew Alan Gunter 1051 North Lynndale Drive, Suite 1B, Appleton WI 54914–3094, USA T: (001) (920) 830 8866 F: (001) (920) 830 8761 E: mgunter@diofdl.org
Fort Worth (VII)	James Scott Mayer 4301 Meadowbank Drive, Fort Worth TX 76103, USA T: (001) (817) 534 1900 F: (001) (817) 534 1904 E: contact@edfw.org
Georgia (IV)	Scott Anson Benhase 611 East Bay Street, Savannah GA 31401– 1296, USA T: (001) (912) 236 4279 F: (001) (912) 236 2007 E: contact@edfw.org
Haiti (II)	Jean Zache Duracin BP 1309, Port-au-Prince, Haiti T: (00509) 257 1624 E: epihaiti@egliseepiscopaldhaiti.org
Hawaii (VIII)	Robert LeRoy Fitzpatrick 229 Queen Emma Square, Honolulu HI 96813-2304, USA T: (001) (808) 536 7776 F: (001) (808) 538 7194 E: rlfitzpatrick@episcopalhawaii.org
Honduras (IX)	Lloyd Emmanuel Allen 23 Ave C. 21 St Colony Trejo, San Pedro Sula, Honduras 21105, Central America T: (00504) 566 6155 *or* 556 6268 F: (00504) 556 6467 E: Honduras@anglicano.hh@yahoo.com
Idaho (VIII)	Brian James Thom 1858 Judith Lane, Boise ID 83705, USA T: (001) (208) 345 4440 F: (001) (208) 345 9735 E: bthom@idahodiocese.org
Indianapolis (V)	Catherine Elizabeth Maples Waynick 1100 West 42nd Street, Indianapolis IN 46208, USA T: (001) (317) 926 5454 F: (001) (317) 926 5456 E: bishop@indydio.org
Iowa (VI)	Alan Scarfe 225 37th Street, Des Moines IA 50312–4399, USA T: (001) (515) 277 6165 F: (001) (515) 277 0273 E: ascarfe@iowaepiscopal.org
Kansas (VII)	Dean Elliott Wolfe 833–35 SW Polk Street, Topeka KS 66612–1688, USA T: (001) (785) 235 9255 F: (001) (785) 235 2449 E: dwolfe@episcopal-ks.org
Kentucky (IV)	Terry Allen White 425 South 2nd Street, Louisville KY 40202, USA T: (001) (502) 584 7148 F: (001) (502) 587 8123 E: bishopwhite@episcopalky.org
Lexington (IV)	Douglas Hahn 203 East 4th Street, Lexington KY 40586–1515, USA T: (001) (859) 252 6527 F: (001) (859) 231 9077 E: dhahn@.diolex.org
Litoral Diocese of Ecuador (IX)	Alfredo Ulloa Morante España Box 0901–5250, Calle Amarilis Fuentes 603 entre Avenida Trujillo y Calle 'D', Barrio Centenario, Guayaquil, Ecuador T: (00593) (4) 244 6699 F: (00593) (4) 244 3088 E: info@litoralepiscopal.org@hotmail.com
Long Island (II)	Laurence C Provenzano 36 Cathedral Avenue, Garden City NY 11530, USA T: (001) (516) 248 4800 F: (001) (516) 248 1616 E: lprovenzano@dioceseli.org

Los Angeles (VIII)	Joseph Jon Bruno 840 Echo Park Avenue, Los Angeles CA 90026, USA T: (001) (213) 482 2040 ext 236 F: (001) (213) 482 5304 E: bishop@ladiocese.org	Nebraska (VIII)	J Scott Barker 109 North 18th Street, Omaha NE 68102–4903, USA T: (001) (402) 341 5373 F: (001) (402) 341 8683 E: sbarker@episcopal-ne.org
(Suffragans)	Diane M Jardine Bruce *address etc as above* E: djbsuffragan@ladiocese.org Mary Douglas Glasspool *address etc as above* E: mdgsuffragan@ladiocese.org	Nevada (VIII)	Dan Thomas Edwards 9480 S. Eastern Avenue, Suite 236 Las Vegas NV 89123–8037, USA T: (001) (702) 737 9190 F: (001) (702) 737 6488 E: dan@episcopalnevada.org
Louisiana (IV)	Morris K Thompson 1623 7th Street, New Orleans LA 7011501 T: (001) (504) 895 6634 F: (001) (504) 895 6637 E: mthompson@edola.org	New Hampshire (I)	A Robert Hirschfield 63 Green Street, Concord, NH 03301, USA T: (001) (603) 224 1914 F: (001) (603) 225 7884 E: arh@nhepiscopal.org
Maine (I)	Stephen Taylor Lane Loring House, 143 State Street, Portland ME 04101–3799, USA T: (001) (207) 772 1953 F: (001) (207) 773 0095 E: slane@episcopalmaine.org	New Jersey (II)	William H Stokes 808 West State Street, Trenton NJ 08618–5326, USA T: (001) (609) 394 5281 F: (001) (609) 394 9546 E: wstokes@dioceseofnj.org
Maryland (III)	Eugene Taylor Sutton 4 East University Parkway, Baltimore MD 21218, USA T: (001) (410) 467 1399 F: (001) (410) 554 6387 E: esutton@eepiscopalmaryland.org	New York (II)	Andrew M L Dietsche Synod House, 1047 Amsterdam Avenue, New York NY 10025, USA T: (001) (212) 316 7400 F: (001) (212) 316 7405 E: *via website* www.dioceseny.org
(Assistant)	Chilton R Knudsen *address etc as above* E: cknudsen@episcopalmaryland.org	(Suffragan)	Allen K Shin *address etc as above*
Massachusetts (I)	Alan M Gates 138 Tremont Street, Boston MA 02111–1318, USA T: (001) (617) 482 5800 F: (001) (617) 482 8431 E: dianep@diomass.org	Newark (II)	Mark Beckwith 31 Mulberry Street, Newark NJ 07102, USA T: (001) (973) 430 9900 F: (001) (973) 622 3503 E: mbeckwith@dioceseofnewark.org
(Suffragan)	Gayle Elizabeth Harris *address etc as above* E: msearle@diomass.org	North Carolina (IV)	*Vacant* 200 West Morgan Street, Suite 300, Raleigh, NC 27601, USA T: (001) (919) 834 7474 F: (001) (919) 834 7546 E: margo.acomb@episdionc.org
Michigan (V)	Wendell Nathaniel Gibbs 4800 Woodward Avenue, Detroit MI 48201, USA T: (001) (313) 832 4400 F: (001) (313) 831 0259 E: bishop@edomi.org	(Suffragan)	Anne Elliott Hodges-Copple 301 North Elm Street, Suite 308-C, Greensboro NC 27401, USA T: (001) (336) 273 5770 F: (001) (336) 273 9253 E: bishopanne@episdionc.org
Milwaukee (V)	Steven Andrew Miller 804 East Juneau Street, Milwaukee WI 53202–2798, USA T: (001) (414) 272 3028 E: bishop11@diomil.org	North Dakota (VI)	Michael Gene Smith 3600 25th Street South, Fargo ND 58104–6861, USA T: (001) (701) 235 6688 F: (001) (701) 232 3077 E: BpNoDak@aol.com
Minnesota (VI)	Brian N Prior 1730 Clifton Place, Suite 201, Minneapolis MN 55403–3242, USA T: (001) (612) 871 5311 F: (001) (612) 871 0552 E: brianp@episcopalmn.org	Northern California (VIII)	Barry Leigh Beisner 350 University Avenue, Suite 280, Sacramento CA 95816, USA T: (001) (916) 442 6918 F: (001) (916) 442 6927 E: barry@norcalepiscopal.org
Mississippi (IV)	Brian Seage 118 N Congress Street, Jackson MS 39225–3107, USA T: (001) (601) 948 5954 F: (001) (601) 354 3401 E: brseage@dioms.org	Northern Indiana (V)	Edward Stuart Little II 117 North Lafayette Boulevard, South Bend IN 46601, USA T: (001) (574) 233 6489 F: (001) (574) 287 7914 E: bishop@ednin.org
Missouri (V)	George Wayne Smith 1210 Locust Street, St Louis MO 63103, USA T: (001) (314) 231 1220 F: (001) (314) 231 3373 E: bishop@diocesemo.org	Northern Michigan (V)	Rayford J Ray 131 East Ridge Street, Marquette MI 49855, USA T: (001) (906) 228 7160 F: (001) (906) 228 7171 E: rayfordray@upepiscopal.org
Montana (VI)	Charles Franklin Brookhart, Jr 515 North Park Avenue, Helena MT 59601–8135, USA T: (001) (406) 422 2230 F: (001) (406) 442 2238 E: cfbmt@qwestoffice.net	Northwest Texas (VII)	James Scott Mayer 1802 Broadway, Lubbock TX 79401, USA T: (001) (806) 763 1370 F: (001) (804) 472 0641 E: bishopmayer@nwtdiocese.org
Navajoland Area Mission (VIII)	David Earle Bailey 1127 Mission Avenue, Farmington, NM 87499–0720, USA T: (001) (505) 327 7549 F: (001) (505) 327 6904 E: *via* www.episcopal-navajoland.org	Northwestern Pennsylvania (III)	Sean W Rowe 145 West 6th Street, Erie PA 16501, USA T: (001) (814) 456 4203 *or* (800) 643 2351 F: (001) (814) 454 8703 E: seanrowe@dionwpa.org

Ohio (V)
Mark Hollingsworth Jr
2230 Euclid Avenue,
Cleveland OH 44115–2499, USA
T: (001) (216) 771 4815
F: (001) (216) 623 0735
E: mh@dohio.org

(Assisting)
Wiliam D Persell
Arthur B Williams
address etc as above

Oklahoma (VII)
Edward Joseph Konieczny
924 North Robinson,
Oklahoma City OK 73102, USA
T: (001) (405) 232 4820
F: (001) (405) 232 4912
E: bishoped@epiok.org

Olympia (VIII)
Gregory H Rickel
1551 10th Avenue E, Seattle WA 98102,
USA
T: (001) (206) 325 4200
F: (001) (206) 325 4631
E: grickel@ecww.org

Oregon (VIII)
Michael J Hanley
11800 SW Military Lane, Portland OR 97219,
USA
T: (001) (503) 636 5613
F: (001) (503) 636 5616
E: bishop@episcopaldioceseoregon.org

Pennsylvania (III)
Clifton Daniel III
3717 Chestnut Street, Suite 300
Philadelphia PA 19104, USA
T: (001) (215) 627 6434
F: (001) (267) 900 2928
E: cdaniel@diopa.org

(Assisting)
Rodney R Michel
address etc as above
E: rodneym@diopa.org

Edward L Lee
address etc as above
E: bpedwardlee@yahoo.com

Pittsburgh (III)
Dorsey W M McConnell
325 Oliver Avenue, Suite 300, Pittsburgh
PA 15222–2403, USA
T: (001) (412) 721 0853
F: (001) (412) 232 6408
E: dmcconnell@episcopalpgh.org

Puerto Rico
Wilfredo Ramos Orench
Carr. 848 Km. 1.1 Bo, St Just,
Trujillo Alto 00978, Puerto Rico
T: (001) (787) 761 9800
F: (001) (787) 761 0320
E: iep@episcopalpr.org

Rhode Island (I)
W Nicholas Knisely
275 North Main Street,
Providence RI 02903–1298, USA
T: (001) (401) 274 4500
F: (001) (401) 331 9430
E: nicholas@episcopalri.org

Rio Grande (VII)
Michael Louis Vono
6400 Coors Boulevard North West,
Albuquerque NM 87107–4811, USA
T: (001) (505) 881 0636
F: (001) (505) 883 9048
E: bp.michael@dioceserg.org

Rochester (II)
Prince G Singh
935 East Avenue, Rochester NY 14607,
USA
T: (001) (585) 473 2977
F: (001) (585) 473 3195
E: prince@episcopaldioceseofrochester.org

San Diego (VIII)
James Robert Mathes
2083 Sunset Cliffs Boulevard, San Diego
CA 92107, USA
T: (001) (619) 291 5947
F: (001) (619) 291 8362
E: bishopmathes@edsd.org

San Joaquin (VIII)
David C Rice
1528 Oakdale Road, Modesto CA 95355,
USA
T: (001) (559) 576 0104
F: (001) (559) 576 0114
E: bishop@diosanjoaquin.org

South Carolina (IV)
Charles vonRosenberg
98 Wentworth Street, Charleston SC
29413, USA
T: (001) (843) 259 2016
F: (001) (843) 723 7628
E: bishop@episcopalchurchsc.org

South Dakota (VI)
John Thomas Tarrant
500 South Main Avenue,
Sioux Falls SD 57104–6814, USA
T: (001) (605) 338 9751
F: (001) (605) 336 6243
E: bishop.diocese@midconetwork.com

Southeast Florida (IV)
Peter Eaton
525 North East 15th Street,
Miami FL 33132, USA
T: (001) (305) 373 0881
F: (001) (305) 375 8054
E: info@diosef.org

Southern Ohio (V)
Thomas Edward Breidenthal
412 Sycamore Street,
Cincinnati OH 45202–4179, USA
T: (001) (513) 421 0311
F: (001) (513) 421 0315
E: tbreidenthal@diosohio.org

Southern Virginia (III)
Herman 'Holly' Hollerith
11827 Canon Boulevard, Suite 101,
Newport News VA 23606, USA
T: (001) (757) 423 8287
F: (001) (757) 440 5354
E: bishop@diosova.org

Southwest Florida (IV)
Dabney T Smith
8005 25th Street East, Parrish FL
34219–9405, USA
T: (001) (941) 556 0315
F: (001) (941) 556 0321
E: dsmith@episcopalswfla.org

(Assisting)
J Michael Garrison
Barry R Howe

Southwestern Virginia (III)
Mark Allen Bourlakas
1002 First Street, Roanoke VA 24016,
USA
T: (001) (757) 423 8287
F: (001) (757) 440 5354
E: bishopmark@dioswva.org

Spokane (VIII)
James Edward Waggoner
245 East 13th Avenue, Spokane
WA 99202–1114, USA
T: (001) (509) 624 3191
F: (001) (509) 747 0049
E: jimw@spokanediocese.org

Springfield (VIII)
Daniel Hayden Martins
821 South 2nd Street, Springfield
IL 62704–2694, USA
T: (001) (217) 525 1876
F: (001) (217) 525 1877
E: bishop@episcopalspringfield.org

Taiwan (VIII)
David Jung-Hsin Lai
Hangzhou South Rd, Taipei City 105,
Taiwan, Republic of China
T: (00886) (2) 2341 1265
F: (00886) (2) 2396 2014
E: skh.tpe@msa.hinet.net

Tennessee (IV)
John Crawford Bauerschmidt
3700 Woodmont Boulevard
Nashville TN 37215, USA
T: (001) (615) 251 3322
F: (001) (615) 251 8010
E: info@edtn.org

Texas (VII)
Charles Andrew Doyle
1225 Texas Avenue, Houston TX 77002, USA
T: (001) (713) 520 6444
E: adoyle@epicenter.org

(Suffragans)
Dena A Harrison
address etc as above
E: dharrison@epicenter.org
Jeff W Fisher
address etc as above

Upper South Carolina (IV)
W Andrew Waldo
1115 Marion Street, Columbia SC 29201, USA
T: (001) (803) 771 7800
F: (001) (803) 799 5119
E: bishopwaldo@edusc.org

Utah (VIII)
Scott B Hayashi
75 South 200 East Street, PO Box 3090,
Salt Lake City UT 84110–2147, USA
T: (001) (801) 322 4131
F: (001) (801) 322 5096
E: shayashi@episcopal-ut.org

Venezuela (IX)
Orlando Guerrero
Colinas de Bello Monte Avenida Caroni,
Caracas, Venezuela
T: (0058) (212) 751 3046
F: (0058) (212) 751 3180
E: obispoguerrero@iglesianglicanavzla.org

Vermont (I)
Thomas Clark Ely
5 Rock Point Road,
Burlington VT 05401–2735, USA
T: (001) (802) 863 3431
F: (001) (802) 860 1562
E: tely@dioceseofvermont.org

Virgin Islands (II)
Edward Ambrose Gumbs
13 Commandant Gade Charlotte Amaille, St
Thomas VI 00801, USA
T: (001) (340) 776 1797
F: (001) (809) 777 8485
E: bpambrosegumbs@yahoo.com

Virginia (III)
Shannon Sherwood Johnston
110 West Franklin Street,
Richmond VA 23220, USA
T: (001) (804) 643 8451
F: (001) (804) 644 6928
E: sjohnston@thediocese.net

(Suffragan)
Susan Ellyn Goff
address etc as above
E: sgoff@thediocese.net

(Assistant)
Edwin F 'Ted' Gulick
115 East Fairfax Street, Falls Church VA 22046
T: (001) 703 241 0441
E: tgulick@thediocese.net

Washington (III)
Mariann Edgar Budde
Mount St Alban, Washington DC
20016–5094, USA
T: (001) (202) 537 6555
F: (001) (202) 364 6605
E: mebudde@edow.org

West Missouri (VII)
Martin S Field
420 West 14th Street, Kansas City
MO 64105, USA
T: (001) (816) 471 6161
F: (001) (816) 471 0379
E: bishopfield@diowestmo.org

West Tennessee (IV)
Don Edward Johnson
692 Poplar Avenue,
Memphis TN 38105, USA
T: (001) (901) 526 0023
F: (001) (901) 526 1555
E: bishopjohnston@episwtn.org

West Texas (VII)
Gary Richard Lillibridge
111 Torcido Drive, San Antonio TX 78209,
USA
T: (001) (210) 824 5387
F: (001) (210) 824 2164
E: gary.lillibridge@dwtx.org

(Coadjutor)
David Reed
address etc as above
E: david.reed@dwtx.org

West Virginia (III)
William Michie Klusmeyer
1608 Virginia Street East, Charleston
WV 25361–5400, USA
T: (001) (304) 344 3597
F: (001) (304) 343 3295
E: mklusmeyer@wvdiocese.org

Western Kansas (VII)
Michael P Milliken
1 North Main Street, Suite 502, Hutchinson
KS 67502, USA
T: (001) (620) 669 —6
F: (001) (620) 669 9783
E: tec.wks2011@gmail.com

Western Louisiana (VII)
Jacob W Owensby
335 Main Street, Pineville LA
71360, USA
T: (001) (318) 442 1304
F: (001) (318) 442 8712
E: bishopjake@diocesewla.org

Western Massachusetts (I)
Douglas John Fisher
37 Chestnut Street,
Springfield MA 01103, USA
T: (001) (413) 737 4786
F: (001) (413) 746 9873
E: communications@diocesewma.org

Western Michigan (V)
Robert R Gepert
Episcopal Center, 5355 Burdick
Street, Suite 1, Kalamazoo MI 49007, USA
T: (001) (296) 381 2710
E: diowestmi@edwm.org
or edwmorg@edwm.org

Western New York (II)
William Franklin
1064 Brighton Road, Tonawanda
NY 14150, USA
T: (001) (716) 881 0660
F: (001) (716) 881 1724
E: rwfranklin@episcopalwny.org

Western North Carolina (IV)
Granville Porter Taylor
900B Center Park Drive, Asheville
NC 28805, USA
T: (001) (828) 225 6656
F: (001) (828) 225 6657
E: bishop@diocesewnc.org

Wyoming (VI)
John S Smylie
123 South Durbin Street,
Casper WY 82601, USA
T: (001) (307) 265 5200
E: bishopsmylie@wyoming.diocese.org

WEST AFRICA

Accra
Daniel S M Torto
Bishopscourt, PO Box 8, Accra, Ghana
T: (00233) 302 662 292
E: dantorto@yahoo.com

Asante Mampong
Cyril K Ben-Smith
Anglican Diocese of Asante Mampong,
Mampong, Ashanti Region, Ghana
M: (00233) 2477 4308
E: bishop.mampong@yahoo.co.uk

Bo
Emmanuel Josie Samuel Tucker
PO Box 21, Bo, Southern Province, Sierra
Leone
T: (00232) (32) 648
M: (00232) (76) 677 862
F: (00233) (32) 605
E: bomission@justice.com
or ejstucker@gmail.com

Cameroon
Thomas-Babyngton Elango Dibo
BP 15705, New Bell, Duala, Cameroon
T: (00237) 755 58276
E: revdivbo2@yahoo.com

Cape Coast
Victor R Atta-Baffoe
Bishopscourt, PO Box A233,
Adisadel Estates, Cape Coast, Ghana
T: (00233) (33) 21 23 502
M: (00233) 2065 2319
F: (00233) (42) 32 637
E: victorattabaffoe@yahoo.com

Dunkwa-on-Offin
Edmund K Dawson-Ahmoah
PO Box DW 42, Dunkwa-on-Offin, Ghana
M: (00233) (24) 464 4764
E: papacy11@yahoo.co.uk

Freetown
Thomas Arnold Ikunika Wilson
Bishop's Court, PO Box 537,
Freetown, Sierra Leone
M: (00232) (22) 251 307

The Gambia
Vacant
Bishopscourt, PO Box 51,
Banjul, The Gambia
T: (00220) 228 405

Guinea
Jacques Boston
BP 187, Conakry, Guinea
M: (00224) 635 879 38
E: bostonjacques@yahoo.com

Ho
Matthias K Mededues-Badohu
Bishopslodge, PO Box MA 300, Ho, Volta
Region, Ghana
T: (00233) 3620 26644 *or* 26806
M: (00233) 208 162 246
E: matthoda@ucomgh.com
or matthiaskwab@googlemail.com

Koforidua	Francis B Quashie PO Box 980, Koforidua, Ghana T: (00233) 3420 22 329 F: (00233) 3420 22 060 E: fbquashie@yahoo.com
Kumasi	Daniel Yinka Sarfo Bishop's House, PO Box 144, Kumasi, Ghana T/F: (00233) (51) 24 117 M: (00233) 277 890 411 E: anglicandioceseofkumasi@yahoo.com *or* dysarfo2000@yahoo.co.uk
Liberia	Jonathan B B Hart PO Box 10–0277, 1000 Monrovia 10, Liberia T: (00231) 224 760 M: (00231) 651 6343 F: (00231) 227 519 E: jbbhart@yahoo.com *or* bishopec112@yahoo.com
Sekondi	John Kwamina Otoo PO Box 85, Sekondi, Ghana T: (00233) 3120 46832 M: (00233) 208 200887 E: angdiosek@yahoo.com
Sunyani	Festus Yeboah-Asuamah PO Box 23, Sunyani, Ghana T: (00233) (61) 23213 M: (00233) 208 121 670 F: (00233) (61) 712300 E: fyasuamah@yahoo.com
Tamale	Jacob Kofi Ayeebo PO Box 110, Tamale, Ghana T: (00233) 3720 26639 M: (00233) 243 419 864 F: (00233)3729 22906 E: bishopea2000@yahoo.com
Wiawso	Abraham Kobina Ackah PO Box 4, Sefwi, Wiawso, Ghana M: (00233) 274 005 952 E: bishopackah@yahoo.com

WEST INDIES

Barbados (Archbishop)	John Walder Dunlop Holder Mandeville House, Henry's Lane, Collymore Rock, St Michael, Barbados T: (001246) 426 2761 F: (001246) 426 0871 E: jwdh@sunbeach.net
Belize	Philip S Wright Diocesan Office, 2 Rectory Lane, PO Box 535, Belize City, Belize T: (00501) 227 3029 F: (00501) 227 6898 E: bzediocese@btl.net
Guyana	*Vacant* Diocesan Office, 49 Barrack Street, PO Box 10949, Georgetown, Guyana T: (00592) 226 3862 F: (00592) 226 6091 E: dioofguy@networksgy.com
Jamaica and the Cayman Islands	Howard Gregory 2 Caledonia Avenue, Kingston, Jamaica T: (001876) 920 2712 F: (001876) 960 1774 E: hkagregory@hotmail.com
(Kingston)	Robert McLean Thompson 3 Dyke Street, Kingston, Jamaica T: (001876) 924 9044 F: (001876) 948 5362 E: bishop.kingston@anglican.diocese.com
(Mandeville)	*Vacant* 8 Morningside Drive, PO Box 346, Montego Bay, Jamaica T: (001876) 625 6817 F: (001876) 625 6819
(Montego Bay)	Leon Paul Golding 8 Cliveden Avenue, Kingston, Jamaica T: (001876) 920 2712
North Eastern Caribbean and Aruba	Leroy Errol Brooks Bishop's Lodge, Redcliffe Street, PO Box 23, St John's, Antigua T: (001264) 462 0151 F: (001264) 462 2090 E: brookx@dioceseofneca@hotmail.com
Trinidad and	Claud Berkley All Saints Rectory, Newtown, Port of Spain, Trinidad T: (001868) 622 7387 F: (001868) 628 1319 E: claberk@yahoo.com
Windward Islands	Calvert Leopold Friday Diocesan Pastoral Centre, Montrose, PO Box 502, St Vincent and the Grenadines T: (001784) 456 1895 F: (001784) 456 2591 E: diocesewi@vincysurf.com

EXTRA-PROVINCIAL DIOCESES

Bermuda	Nicholas B B Dill Diocesan Office, PO Box HM 769, Hamilton HM CX, Bermuda T: (001441) 292 6987 F: (001441) 292 5421 E: bishop@anglican.bm
§ Cuba	Maria Griselda Delgado del Carpio Calle 6 No 273, Vedado Plaza, Ciudad de La Habana, CP 10400, Cuba T: (0053) (7) 833 5760 E: griselda@enet.cu
(Suffragan)	Ulises Prendes Calle Escario No. 459, entre 3 y 4, Santiago de Cuba, CP 90100, Cuba T: (0053) (2) 262 7815 E: bpulises@enet.cu
Falkland Islands	William Nigel Stock Lambeth Palace, London SE1 7JU, United Kingdom E: nigelstock@lambethpalace.org
Lusitanian Church (Canterbury)	José Jorge Tavares de Pína Cabral Diocesan Centre, Rua Afonso de Albuquerque, No. 86, 4430–003 Vila Nova de Gaia, Portugal T: (00351) (22) 375 4018 F: (00351) (22) 375 2016 E: bispopinacabral@igreja-lusitana.org
Spanish Reformed Episcopal Church (Canterbury)	Carlos López Lozano Calle Beneficencia 18, 28004 Madrid, Spain T: (0034) (91) 445 2560 F: (0034) (91) 594 4572 E: eclesiae@arrakis.es

§ Under a Metropolitan Council of the Primate of Canada, the Archbishop of the West Indies and the President-Bishop of the Episcopal Church's Province IX.

BISHOPS OF CHURCHES WHERE ANGLICANS HAVE UNITED WITH CHRISTIANS OF OTHER TRADITIONS

NORTH INDIA

Agra
Prem Prakash Habil
Bishop's House, 4/116-B Church Road,
Civil Lines, Agra 282 002, Uttar Pradesh, India
T: (0091) (562) 285 4845
M: (0091) (9412) 722501
F: (0092) (562) 252 0074
E: doacni@gmail.com *or*
bishopofagra@gmail.com

Amritsar
(Moderator)
Pradeep Kumar Samantaroy
26 R B Prakash Chand Road, opp Police
Ground,
Amritsar, Punjab, 143 001, India
T/F: (0091) (183) 222 2910
M: (0091) (9815) 462121
E: bunu13@rediffmail.com

Andaman and
Nicobar
Islands
Christopher Paul
Cathedral Church Compound, MUS, Car
Nicobar 744301, India *or* PO Box 19,
Port Blair, Andaman and Nicobar Islands,
744 101, India
T/F: (0091) (3192) 231 362
M: (0091) (9476) 016029
E: cniportblair@yahoo.co.in

Barrackpore
(Moderator's
Episcopal
Commissary)
P P Marandih
Bishop's Lodge, 86 Middle Road, Barrackpore,
Kolkata, West Bengal, 700120, India
T: (0091) (33) 2593 1852
F: (0091) (33) 2592 0147

Bhopal
Robert Ali
Masihi Kanya Hr Sec School Campus,
9 Boundary Road, Indore, Madhya Pradesh,
452 001, India
T: (0091) (731) 249 2789
M: (0091) (099) 2518 6636
E: revrobertali@gmail.com
or bhopal_diocese@yahoo.com

Chandigarh
Younas Massey
Bishop's House, Mission Compound,
Brown Road, Ludhiana,
Punjab, 141 001, India
T/F: (0091) (161) 222 5707
M: (0091) (9915) 641109
E: massey.younas@yahoo.in
or bishopdoc2000@yahoo.com

Chhattisgarh
(Moderator's
Episcopal
Commissary)
Probal K Dutta
Opp Raj Bhavan, Gate No 1, Civil Lines,
Raipur, Chhattisgarh, 492 001, India
T: (0091) (771) 221 0015
F: (0091) (812) 001 8000
E: probal_dutta@yahoo.com

Chotanagpur
B B Baskey
Bishop's Lodge, PO Box 1, Church Road,
Ranchi, Bihar, 834 001, India
T: (0091) (651) 235 0281
M: (0091) (9470) 193053
F: (0091) (651) 235 1184
E: rch_cndta@sancharnet.in *or*
chotanagpurdiocese@gmail.com

Cuttack
(Moderator's
Episcopal
Commissary)
Sukant Das
Bishop's House, Mission Road,
Cuttack, Orissa, 753 001, India
T: (0091) (671) 230 0102
M: (0091) (986) 192 4474
E: bishopsamsondas@gmail.com

Delhi
(Moderator's
Episcopal
Commissary)
Warris Masih
Bishop's House, 1 Church Lane,
off North Avenue,
New Delhi, 110 001, India
T: 0091) (11) 2371 7471 *or* (0091) (10) 103 520
M: (0091) (9911) 287611
F: (0091) (11) 2335 8006
E: warrisk.masih@yahoo.in *or*
wkmasih@yahoo.co.in

Durgapur
Probal Kanto Dutta
St Michael's Church Compound, Aldrin Path,
Bidhan Nagar, Dugapur, West Bengal,
713 212, India
T: (0091) (343) 253 4552
F: (0091) (343) 253 6220
E: probal_dutta@yahoo.com

Eastern Himalaya
Episcopal
Commissary)
Samuel Lepcha
CNI Diocesan Centre, Gandhi Road, PO Box 4,
Darjeeling, West Bengal, 734 101, India
M: (0091) (9832) 094806
E: revds127@yahoo.com *or*
easternhimalaya2010@yahoo.co.in

Gujarat
Silvans S Christian
Bishop's House, IP Mission Compound,
Ellisbridge,
Ahmedabad, Gujarat, 380 006, India
T/F: (0091) (79) 2656 1950
M: (0091) (7405) 227 086
E: gujdio@yahoo.co.in
or christiansilvans@yahoo.com

Jabalpur
Prem Chand Singh
Bishop's House, 2131 Napier Town,
Jabalpur, Madhya Pradesh, 482 001, India
T: (0091) (761) 2622 109
E: bishoppcsingh@yahoo.co.in

Kolhapur
Bathuel Ramchandra Tiwade
Bishop's House, EP School Compound,
Kolhapur, Maharashtra, 416 001, India
T/F: (0091) (231) 2654 832
M: (0091) (9422) 414 057
E: bishopofkolhapur@rediffmail.com
or kdcdbss@yahoo.com

Kolkata
Ashoke Biwas
Bishop's House, 51 Chowringhee Road,
Calcutta, West Bengal, 700 071, India
T: (0091) (33) 6534 7770
M: (0091) (9478) 456981
F: (0091) (33) 2822 6340
E: ashokebiswas@vsnl.net

Lucknow
P P Habil
Bishop's House, 25/11 Mahatma Gandhi
Marg, Allahabad, Uttar Pradesh, 211 001,
India
T: (0091) (532) 242 7053
or (0091) (532) 2427 052
M: (0091) (9451) 089682

Marathwada
M U Kasab
Bungalow 28/A, Mission Compound,
Cantonment, Aurangabad, Maharashtra,
431 002, India
T/F: (0091) (240) 237 3136
M: (0091) (9764) 822 888
E: revmukasab@yahoo.co.in
or bishopofmarathwada@rediffmail.com

Mumbai
Prakash Dinkar Patole
19 Hazarimal Somani Marg Fort,
Mumbai, 400 001, India
T: (0091) (22) 2207 3904
M: (0091) (9833) 480 299
F: (0091) (22) 2206 0248
E: cnibombaydiocese@yahoo.com
or bishopprakashpatole@gmail.com

Nagpur
Paul Dupare
Cathedral House, opp Indian Coffee House,
Sadar, Nagpur, Maharashtra, 440 001, India
T/F: (0091) (712) 2553 351
M: (0091) (9823) 354614
E: nagpurdiocese@rediffmail.com

Nasik
Pradip Lemuel Kamble
Bishop's House, 1 Outram Road, Tarakur,
Ahmednagar, Maharashtra, 414 001, India
T: (0091) (241) 241 1806
M: (0091) (9225) 321 691
F: (0091) (241) 242 2314
E: bishopofnasik@rediffmail.com

North East India
Michael Herenz
Bishop's Kuti, Shillong,
Meghalaya, 793 001, India
T: (0091) (364) 222 3155
E: bishopnei15@hotmail.com

Patna
Philip Phembuar Marandih
Bishop's House, Christ Church Compound,
Bhagalpur, Bihar, 812 001, India
T: (0091) (641) 240 0033 or 230 0714
M: (0091) (943) 1213 138
E: cnipatna@rediffmail.com

Phulbani
Bijay Kumar Nayak
Bishop's House, Mission Compound,
Gudripori, Gudaigiri, Phulbani, Kandhamal,
Orissa, 762 100, India
T: (0091) (684) 7260569
M: (0091) (9437) 965389
E: bp.bkn@rediffmail.com

Pune
A B Rathod
1A General Bhagat Marg (Steveley Road),
Red Bungalow, Pune, Maharashtra, 411 001,
India
T: (0091) (202) 633 4374
E: rev.andrewrathod@gmail.com
or punediocese@yahoo.com

Rajasthan
Warris Masih
2/10 CNI Social Centre,
Civil Lines, opp Bus Stand, Jaipur Rd, Ajmer,
305 001, India
T: (0091) (145) 2420 633
M: (0091) (8003) 602 000
F: (0091) (145) 262 1627
E: warrisk.masih@yahoo.in
or wkmasih@yahoo.co.in

Sambalpur
Pinuel Dip
Bishop's House, Mission Compound,
Bolangir, Orissa, 767 001, India
T/F: (0091) (665) 2230 625
M: (0091) (9438) 336 476
E: pinuel_dip@rediffmail.com

SOUTH INDIA

Cochin
(formerly
North Kerala)
Baker Ninan Fenn
CSI Diocesan Office, PO Box 104, Shoranur,
Kerala State, 679 121, India
T: (0091) (466) 222 4454
F: (0091) (466) 222 2545
E: revdbnfeen@gmail.com

Coimbatore
(Bishop in)
Timothy Ravinder
Diocesan House, 256 Race Course Road,
Coimbatore, Tamil Nadu, 641018, India
T: (0091) (422) 222 3605
F: (0091) (442) 222 3369
E: csi.bpcbe@gmail.com

Dornakal
(Bishop in)
Vadapalli Prasada Rao
Diocesan Office, Epiphany Cathedral
Compound, Dornakal, Telangana, 506 381,
India
T: (0091) (8719) 227 752 or
(0091) (8719) 227 535
E: bshvadapallidornakal@hotmail.com

East Kerala
(Bishop in)
K G Daniel
CSI Diocesan Office, Melukavumattom,
Kottayam,
Kerala State, 686 652, India
T/F: (0091) (482) 291 044
E: bishopkgdaniel@rediffmail.com

Jaffna
Daniel S Thiagarajah
Bishop's Office in Colombo,
36 5/2 Sinsapa Road, Colombo, Sri Lanka
T: (0094) (21) 225 0827
F: (0094) (11) 258 2015
E: dsthiagarajah@yahoo.com

Kanyakumari
(Bishop in)
G Devakadasham
CSI Diocesan Office, 71A Dennis Street,
Nagercoil, Tamil Nadu, 629 001, India
T: (0094) (21) 225 0827
F: (0094) (11) 258 2015
E: csikkd@vsnl.in

Karimnagar
(Bishop in)
K Reuben Mark
CSI Diocesan Office, 2–8–95 CVRN Road,
PO Box 40, Mukarampura Post, Karimnagar,
Telangana, 505 001, India
T: (0091) (878) 226 2229
F; (0091) (878) 226 2972
E: reubenmark@hotmail.com

Karnataka
Central
(Bishop in)
Prasanna Kumar Samuel
CSI Diocesan Office, 20 Third Cross,
CSI Compound, Bangalore, Karnataka,
560 027, India
T: (0091) (80) 222 3766
E: revdpksamuel@gmail.com

Karnataka
North
(Bishop in)
Ravikumar j Niranjan
CSI Diocesan Office, All Saints Church
Compound, Dharwad, Karnataka, 580 008,
India
T: (0091) (836) 244 7733
F: (0091) (836) 274 5461
E: haradoni.rn@gmail.com

Karnataka
South
(Bishop in)
Mohan Manoraj
CSI Diocesan Office, Balmatta, Mangalore,
Karnataka, 575 001, India
T: (0091) (824) 243 2657
F: (0091) (824) 243 2363
E: mohhanrraj@gmailc.om

Kollam
Kottarakara
Vacant (contact A Dharmaraj Rasalm,
Moderator's Commissary) (formerly within
South Kerala) Diocesan Office, N H 208,
Chinnakada, Kollam, Kerala State, 691 001,
India

Krishna-
Godavari
(Moderator)
G Dyvasirvadam
CSI Diocesan Office, CSI TA Bass Complex,
Gopala Reddy Road, Governorpet,
Vijayawada, 520 002, Andhra Pradesh, India
T/F: (0091) (8662) 573 673
E: bishopkrishna@yahoo.com

Madhya
Kerala
(Deputy
Moderator)
Thomas K Oommen
CSI Bishop's Office, Cathedral Road,
Kottayam, Kerala State, 686 018, India
T/F: (0091) (481) 2566 536
E: csimkdbishopsoffice@gmail.com

Madras
Vacant (contact G Dvyasirvadam,
Moderator/Bishop-in-charge)
Diocesan Office, PO Box 4914, 226 Cathedral
Road, Chennai, Tamil Nadu, 600 086,
India
T: (0091) (4428) 113 929
F: (0091 (4428) 110 608
E: csinkd@md5.vsnl.net

Madurai-
Ramnad
(Bishop in)
M Joseph
'Rev. Grub's Garden', CSI Diocesan Office,
5 Bhulabai Desai Rd,
Chockikulam, Madurai District,
Tamil Nadu, 625 002, India
T: (0091) (452) 233 8222
F: (0091) (452) 233 9888
E: bishopmjoseph@gmail.com

Malabar
(formerly within
North Kerala)
Vacant (contact Baker Ninan Finn,
Moderator's Commissary)
CSI Diocesan Office, Bank Road, Calicut,
Kerala, 673 001, India

Medak
Vacant (contact G Dyvasirvadam,
Moderator/Bishop-in-charge)
Diocesan Office, 10–3–165, Church House,
Golden Jubilee Bhavan, Old Lancer Lane,
Secunderabad, Telangana, 500 025, India
T: (0091) (40) 2783 3151
F: (0091) (40) 2784 4215

Nandyal
E Pushpalalitha
CSI Diocesan Office, Nandyal RS, Kurnool
District, Andhra Pradesh, 518 502, India
T: (0091) (8514) 222 477
E: rt.rev.pushpalalitha@gmail.com

Rayalaseema
(Bishop in)
B D Prasada Rao
CSI Diocesan Office, R S Road, Kadapa,
Andhra Pradesh, 515 401, India
T: (0091) (866) 232 5320
F: (0091) (856) 227 5200
E: lbd_prasad@yahoo.co.in

South Kerala (Bishop *in*)	A Dharmaraj Rasalam CSI Diocesan Office, LMS Compound, Trivandrum, Kerala State, 695 033 India T: (0091) (471) 231 5490 F: (0091) (471) 231 6439 E: bishoprasalam@yahoo.com	Faisalabad	John Samuel Bishop's House, PO Box 27, Mission Road, Gojra, Distt Toba Tek Sing, Faisalabad, Pakistan T: (0092) (46) 351 4689 M: (0092) 300 655 0074 E: jsamuel@brain.net.pk
Thoothukudi-Nazareth (Moderator's Commissary)	Jesu Sagayam Diocesan Office, Caldwell Hr Sec School Campus, Beach Road, Thoothukudi, Tamil Nadu, 628 001, India T: (0091) (462) 257 8744 F: (0091) (431) 257 4525 E: sagayam08@rediffmail.com	Hyderabad	Kaleem John 27 Liaquat Road, Civil Lines, Hyderabad, Sind, 71000, Pakistan T: (0092) (51) 289 0420 M: (0092) 301 244 5690 E: kaleemjohn@aol.com
Tirunelveli (Bishop *in*)	J J Chirstdoss CSI Diocesan Office, PO Box 118, 16 North High Ground Road, Tirunelveli, Tamil Nadu, 627 002, India T: (431) 227 0172 F: (431) 241 8485 E: bishopcsitirunelveli@gmail.com	Karachi	Sadiq Daniel Holy Trinity Cathedral, Fatima Jinnah Rd, Karachi 75530, Pakistan T: (0092) (21) 521 6843 M: (0092) 301 822 2003 E: sadiqdaniel@hotmail.com
Trichy-Tanjore (Bishop *in*)	G P Vasanthakumar CSI Diocesan Office, Allithurai Road, Puthur, Tiruchirapalli, Tamil Nadu, 620 017, India T: (0091) (431) 277 0172 F: (0091) (431) 241 8485 E: csittd@rediffmail.com	Lahore	Irfan Jamil Bishopsbourne, Cathedral Close, The Mall, Lahore, 54000, Pakistan T: (0092) (42) 723 3560 M: (0092) 333 475 6730 F: (0092) (42) 722 1270 E: bishop_Lahore@hotmail.com
Vellore (Bishop *in*)	A Rajavelu CSI Diocesan Office, 3/1, Anna Salai, Vellore, 632 001, India T: (0091) (416) 2232 160 F: (0091) (416) 2223 835 E: bishoprajavelu@gmail.com	Multan	Leo Rodrick Paul 113 Qasim Road, PO Box 204, Multan Cantt, Pakistan T: (0092) (61) 458 3694 M: (0092) 300 630 2101 E: bishop_mdcop@bain.net.pk

BANGLADESH

Dhaka (Moderator)	Paul S Sarker Church of Bangladesh, 54/1 Barobag, Mirpur 2, Dhaka 1216, Bangladesh T: (00880) (2) 902 5876 F: (00880) (2) 805 3729 E: cobsynod@churchofbangladesh.org	Peshawar	Humphrey Sarfaraz Peters Diocesan Centre, 1 Sir Syed Road, Peshawar, NWFP 2500, Pakistan T: (0092) (91) 527 9094 M: (0092) 300 858 0325 F: (0092) (91) 527 7499 E: bishopdop@hotmail.com
Kushtia	Samuel S Mankhin 94 NS Road, Thanapara, Kushtia, Bangladesh T/F: (00880) (71) 54618 E: bishop_mankin@yahoo.com	Raiwind (Moderator)	Samuel Robert Azariah 17 Warris Road, PO Box 2319, Lahore 54000, Pakistan T: (0092) (42) 758 8950 F: (0092) (42) 757 7255 M: (0092) 300 841 7982 E: sammyazariah@yahoo.com

PAKISTAN

The Arabian Gulf (Bishop *for*) (Area Bishop within the Diocese of Cyprus)	Azad Marshall PO Box 688, Lahore, Punjab, 54660 Pakistan T: (0092) (42) 542 0452 E: bishop@saintthomascenter.org	Sialkot	Alwin Samuel Lal Kothi, Barah Patthar, Sialkot 2, Punjab, Pakistan T: (0092) (43) 226 4895 M: (0092) 305 730 2201 F: (0092) (43) 226 4828 E: chs_sialkot@yahoo.com

PROVINCIAL OFFICES

From which further information may be sought.

Anglican Communion Office   St Andrew's House, 16 Tavistock Crescent, Westbourne Park, London W11 1AP, UK
   T: (020) 7313 3900   F: (020) 7313 3999   E: aco@anglicancommunion.org

Australia   Suite 4, Level 5, 189 Kent Street, Sydney NSW 2000, Australia
   T: (0061) (2) 8267 2700   F: (0061) (2) 8267 2727   E: gsoffice@anglican.org.au

Bangladesh   Church of Bangladesh, 54/1 Barobag, Mirpur 2, Dhaka 1100, Bangladesh
   T: (00880) (2) 902 5876   F: (00880) (2) 805 3729   E: cobsynod@churchofbangladesh.org

Brazil   Praça Olavo Bilac 63, Campos Elíseos, CEP 01201–050, São Paulo, Brazil
   T/F: (0055) (11) 3667 8161   E: acavalcante@ieab.org.br

Burundi   BP 2098, Bujumbura, Burundi
   T: (00257) 22 224 839   E: peab@cbinf.com

Canada   80 Hayden Street, Toronto ON M4Y 3G2, Canada
   T: (001) (416) 924 9192   F: (001) (416) 968 7983   E: mthompson@national.anglican.ca

Central Africa   Central Africa PO Box 22317, Kitwe, Zambia   T: (00260) (2) 223 264   F: (00260) (2) 224 778

Central America   Apartado 1207, Managua, Nicaragua
   T: (00505) (2) 222 5174   F: (00505) 222 452 48   E: secretaria_diocesana@hotmail.com

Ceylon   Bishop's House, 368/3A Bauddhaloka Mawatha, Colombo 7, Sri Lanka
   T: (0094) (1) 684810   F: (0094) (1) 684811   E: sec.diocese.tr@gmail.com

Congo   11 Av Basalakala, Commune de Kalamu, Kinshasa 1, DR Congo
   T: (00243) (99) 541 2138   E: anglican.congo@yahoo.com

England   Church House, Great Smith Street, London SW1P 3NZ, UK
   T: (020) 7898 1000   E: enquiry@churchofengland.org

Hong Kong   16/F Tung Wai Commercial Building, 109–111 Gloucester Road, Wanchai, Hong Kong SAR
   T: (00852) 2526 5355   F: (00852) 2521 2199   E: office1@hkskh.org

Indian Ocean   Diocesan Church House, 37th St Paul Rd, Vacoas, Mauritius
   T: (00230) 686 5158   E: indian.ocean.psec@gmail.com

Ireland   Church of Ireland House, Church Avenue, Rathmines, Dublin 6, DO6 CF67, Republic of Ireland
   T: (00353) (1) 4978 422   F: (00353) (1) 49 8 821   E: office@rcbdub.org

Japan   65–3 Yarai-cho, Shinjuku-ku, Tokyo 162–0805, Japan
   T: (0081) (35) 228 3171   F: (0081) (3) 5228 3175   E: province@nskk.org

Jerusalem and the Middle East   2 Grigori Afxentiou, Nicosia 1515, PO Box 22075, Cyprus
   E: georgia@spidernet.com.cy

Kenya   PO Box 40502, 00100 Nairobi, Kenya
   T: (00254) (20) 714 755   F: (00254) (2) 718 442   E: archoffice@ackenya.org

Korea   15 Sejong-daero 21-gil, Jung-gu, Seoul 100–120, Korea
   T: (0082) (2) 738 8952   F: (0082) (2) 737 4210   E: anglicankorea@gmail.com

Melanesia   Provincial Headquarters, PO Box 19, Honiara, Solomon Islands
   T: (0067) 20470   E: hauriasi_A@comphq.org.sb

Mexico   Acatlán 102 Oriente, Col Mitras Centro, Monterrey, Nuevo Leon, 64460, Mexico
   T: (0052) (81) 8333 0992   F: (0052) (81) 8348 7362   E: awalls@mexico-anglican.org

Myanmar (Burma)   PO Box 11191, 140 Pyidaungsu Yeiktha Road, Dagon, Yangon, Myanmar
   T: (0095) (1) 395 279   F: (0095) (1) 39 5350   E: markmgdoe@gmail.com

New Zealand (Aotearoa, New Zealand and Polynesia)   PO Box 87188, Meadowbank, Auckland 1742, New Zealand
   T: (0064) (9) 521 4439   E: gensec@anglicanchurch.org.nz

Nigeria   24 Douala Street, Wuse Zone 5, Abuja, Nigeria
   T: (00234) (95) 236 950   E: communicator1@anglican-nig.org

North India   CNI, 16 Pandit Pant Marg, New Delhi 110001, India
   T: (0091) (11) 4231 4000   E: alwanmasih@cnisynod.org

Pakistan   St John's Cathedral, 1 Sir Syed Road, Peshawar Cantt 2500, Pakistan
   T: (0092) (91) 527 8643   E: kanwal4454@gmail.com

Papua New Guinea   Box 673, Lae 411, Morobe Province, Papua New Guinea
   T: (00675) 472 4111   F: (00675) 472 1852   E: schicki@acpng.org.pg

Philippines   PO Box 10321, Broadway Centrum, 1112 Quezon City, Philippines
   F: (0063) (2) 721 1923   E: flaw997@gmail.com

Rwanda   BP 2487, Kigali, Rwanda
   F: (00250) 516 162   E: frkaremera@yahoo.co.uk

Scotland   21 Grosvenor Crescent, Edinburgh EH12 5EE, UK
   T: (0131) 255 6357   F: (0131) 346 7247   E: *via website* www.scotland.anglican.org

South East Asia   c/o Mr Leonard David Shim, Messrs. Reddi & Co. Advocates, REDDI Building, No. 393,
   Jalan Datuk Abang Abdul Rahim, 93450 Kuching, Sarawak, Malaysia
   T: (0060) (82) 484 466   F: (0060) (82) 484 477   E: leonardshin@reddi.com.my

South India   CSI Centre, 5 Whites Road, Royapettah, Chennai 600 041, India
   T: (0091) (44) 2852 1566   F: (0091) (44) 2852 3528   E: synodcsi@gmail.com

Southern Africa   20 Bishopscourt Drive, Bishopscourt, Claremont, 7708 South Africa
   T: (0027) (21) 763 1300   F: (0027) (21) 797 1329   E: peo@anglicanchurchsa.org.za

South America   Cro. Gral. Belgrano 946, Hurlingham, Buenos Aires 1686, Argentina
   T: (0053) (114) 452 7555   E: danielgenovesi@gmail.com

Sudan   PO Box 110, Juba, South Sudan
   E: provincialsecretary@sudan.anglican.org

Tanzania   PO Box 899, Dodoma, Tanzania
   T: (00255) (26) 232 4574   F: (00255) (26) 232 4565   E: chinyongole@anglican.or.tz

Uganda   PO Box 14123, Kampala, Uganda
   F: (00256) (414) 251 925   E: COUOffice@gmail.com

USA   Episcopal Church Center, 815 Second Avenue, New York NY 10017, USA
   T: (001) (212) 716 6000   F: (001) (212) 490 3298   E: *via website* www.episcopalchurch.org

Wales   39 Cathedral Road, Cardiff CF11 9XF, UK
   T: (029) 2034 8200   E: *via website* wwwchurchinwales.org.uk

West Africa   PO Box Lt 226, Lartebiokorshie, Accra, Ghana
   T: (00233) (302) 257 370   E: cpwa2014@gmail.com *or* morkeiwuley@gmail.com

West Indies   Provincial Secretariat, Bamford House, Society Hill, St John, Barbados, West Indies
   T: (001) (246) 423 0842   F: (001) (246) 423 0855   E: cpwi@caribsurf.com

DIRECTORIES OF THE ANGLICAN PROVINCES

Many provinces in the Anglican Communion now maintain online directories of their clergy. The website addresses given below are for the home pages of the provinces concerned. From the home page, follow links either to the online church or clergy directory, or to the pages for individual dioceses and, where available, to the information for individual parishes. The 'Member Churches' web page on the Anglican Communion website (http://www.anglicancommunion.org/structures/member-churches.aspx) also lists information about Anglican provinces (bishops, provincial secretary, provincial treasurer), and gives links to online provincial information where this is available.

Where a province is known to publish a printed directory, details are given below. For the provinces not listed here, information should be sought from the provincial secretary or from dioceses.

Australia   www.anglican.org.au

Burundi   www.anglican.burundi.org

Canada   www.anglican.ca; *Anglican Church Directory*, published annually by Anglican Book Centre/Augsberg Fortress Canada, Box 9940, Kitchener ON N2G 4Y4, Canada T: (001) (800) 265 6397 Online shop: store.afcanada.com

Congo   www.anglican.congo.org

Hong Kong   www.hkskh.org

Ireland   www.ireland.anglican.org

Japan   www.nskk.org; *Seikokai Yearbook*, published annually (in Japanese) by Nippon Sei Ko Kai Provincial Office, 65 Yarai-cho, Shinijuku, Tokyo 162–0805, Japan T: (0081) (3) 5228 3175 E: province@nskk.org

Jerusalem and the Middle East   *A Provincial Directory*, published by Provincial Office, Box 1248, 20 Nablus Road, Jerusalem 91 191, Israel T: (00972) (2) 627 1670

Kenya   www.ackenya.org

Melanesia   www.acom.org.sb

New Zealand   www.anglican.org.nz; *Clerical Directory*, published annually by General Synod Office, PO Box 87188, Meadowbank, Auckland 1742, New Zealand T: (0064) (9) 521 4439 E: gensec@anglicanchurch.org.nz

Nigeria   www.anglican-nig.org

North India   www.cnisynod.org

Philippines   www.episcopalchurchphilippines.com

Rwanda   www.ear-acr.org

Scotland   www.scotland.anglican.org

South India   www.csisynod.com

Southern Africa   www.anglicanchurchsa.org

Sudan   www.sudan.anglican.org

Tanzania   www.anglican.or.tz

Uganda   www.churchofuganda.org

United States of America   www.episcopalchurch.org; *Episcopal Clerical Directory*, published every two years by Church Publishing Incorporated, 19 East 34th Street, New York 10016, USA T: (001) (800) 672 1789 Online shop: www.churchpublishing.org

Extra-provincial Dioceses

Cuba   www.cuba.anglican.org

Bermuda   www.anglican.bm

Lusitanian Church   www.igreja-lusitana.org

Reformed Episcopal Church of Spain   www.anglicanos.org

Close links with many overseas provinces are maintained by the following missionary organizations:

Church Mission Society Watlington Road, Oxford OX4 6BZ T: (01865) 787400 F: (01865) 776375 E: info@cms-uk.org

Crosslinks (formerly the Bible Churchmen's Missionary Society) 251 Lewisham Way, London SE4 1XF
T: (020) 8691 6111 F: (020) 8694 8023 E: *via website* www.crosslinks.org (link to Headquarters staff at the foot of the Contact page)

Mission to Seafarers (formerly The Missions to Seamen) St Michael Paternoster Royal, College Hill, London EC4R 2RL
T: (020) 7248 5202 E: *via website* www.missiontoseafarers.org

Mothers' Union Mary Sumner House, 24 Tufton Street, London SW1P 3RB T: (020) 7222 5533 F: (020) 7227 9397
E: *via website* www.mothersunion.org

Society for Promoting Christian Knowledge 36 Causton Street, London SW1P 4ST T: (020) 7592 3900
F: (020) 7592 3939 E: spckww@spck.org.uk

South American Mission Society *now merged with* **Church Mission Society** *(see above)*

Us. (formerly United Society for the Propagation of the Gospel) Harling House, 47–51 Great Suffolk Street,
London SE1 4YB T: (020) 7921 2200 E: info@weareUs.org.uk

ABRAMS, Leonard. **d** 14. NSM Purley St Mark *S'wark* from 14.
ASKEY, Thomas Cyril. b 29. **d** 73. rtd 81.
AYOK-LOEWENBERG, Joseph. b 60. **d** 88.
BAKER, Mrs Julie Ann Louise. b 77. **d** 06. PV Llan Cathl 09-13.
BARRETT, Mrs Alexandra Mary. b 75. **d** 03. USA from 14.
BEDFORD, Mrs Linda. b 43. **d** 07. NSM Hanley Castle, Hanley Swan and Welland *Worc* from 06.
BENSON, Gareth Neil. b 47. **d** 81. rtd 12.
BLANCHFLOWER, Mrs Rachel Elizabeth. b 80. **d** 15. C Chesterton Gd Shep *Ely* from 15.
BRECH, Miss Suzy Zelda. b 73. **d** 09. NSM Battersea St Mich *S'wark* 09-12.
BRENDON-COOK, John Lyndon. b 37. **d** 81. rtd 98; PtO *Truro* from 98.
BROMAGE, Kenneth Charles. b 51. **d** 90. rtd 11.
BROTHERTON, Michael. b 56. **d** 81. rtd 11.
BROWN, Kenneth Arthur Charles. b 27. **d** 84. OLM Ingoldsby *Linc* 84-97.
CHAMBERS, Robert Anthony. b 46. **d** 05. OLM Kirkburton *Leeds* from 14.
CHISLETT, David Norman Hilton. b 61. **d** 02. TV Eston w Normanby *York* 05-09.
CLARK, Frederick Albert George. b 15. **d** 67. PtO *Glouc* 85-97.
CLIFFORD, Erin Chrisanne. b 77. **d** 08. USA from 13.
COLES, Mrs Olivia Mary Kana. b 64. **d** 15. NSM Histon *Ely* from 15; NSM Impington *Ely* from 15.
COLLINS, Margaret Ruth. **d** 14. NSM Warminster Ch Ch *Sarum* from 14.
COOPER, Donna. **d** 14. C Edin St Jo from 14.
CORDINER, Alan Dobson. b 61. **d** 92. P-in-c Bootle, Corney, Whicham and Whitbeck *Carl* 98-05.
COULTON, David Stephen. b 41. **d** 67. rtd 04.
COUTTS, Ian Alexander. b 56. **d** 89. PtO *Ox* from 03.
DALEY, David Michael. b 50. **d** 92. rtd 14.
DARLISON, Geoffrey Stuart. b 49. **d** 91. rtd 14; P-in-c Greengates *Leeds* 14; P-in-c Thorpe Edge *Leeds* 14.
DAVIES, Miss Caroline Elizabeth. b 82. **d** 15.
DAWSON, Frederick William. b 44. **d** 69. rtd 14.
DILLON, Gerard Francis. **d** 14. C Glenrothes *St And* from 14; C Leven *St And* from 14; C Lochgelly *St And* from 14.
DONAGHY, Paul Robert Blount. b 56. **d** 00. OLM Goldsworth Park *Guildf* 00-14.
DOWNS, Miss Geinor. b 47. **d** 87. Chapl Sandwell and W Birm Hosps NHS Trust 02-06.
DRYER, Richard. **d** 14. NSM Wimbledon Em Ridgway Prop Chpl *S'wark* from 14.
DUFF, Andrew John. b 57. **d** 92. rtd 12.
EDEN, Henry. b 36. **d** 87. PtO *St E* from 01; PtO *Ely* from 03.
EMBLIN, Canon Richard John. b 48. **d** 86. rtd 13.
EVANS, Miss Daphne Gillian. b 41. **d** 87. rtd 88.
EVANS, Robert Arnold Hughes. b 90. **d** 15. C Cambridge St Andr Less *Ely* from 15.
FAIRHURST, Susan. **d** 14. NSM Lillington and Old Milverton *Cov* from 14.
FRAMPTON, Mrs Ruth. b 57. **d** 15.
FRANK, Penelope Edith. b 45. **d** 99. rtd 06.
FROGGATT, Mrs Elaine Muriel. b 43. **d** 00. rtd 10.
FRY, Michael John. b 59. **d** 86. C Dovecot *Liv* 89-91.
GALLAGHER, Robert. b 43. **d** 67. rtd 13.
GANGA, Jeremy Franklin. b 62. **d** 95. Progr Dir Angl Inst for Sch Leadership from 10.
GARDHAM, Mrs Linda Elizabeth. b 49. **d** 05. rtd 13.
GARVIE, Mrs Anna-Lisa Karen. b 48. **d** 96. Chapl NHS Borders 12-13.
GILCHRIST, Mrs Alison Roxanne. b 62. **d** 04. V Bassendean and Dioc Evang Enabler Perth Australia from 12.
GINEVER, Paul Michael John. b 49. **d** 72. C Halesowen *Worc* 80; rtd 14.
GRAHAM, Mrs Susan Lochrie. b 46. **d** 90. NSM Combe Martin, Berrynarbor, Lynton, Brendon etc *Ex* 08-11.
GREENISH, Brian Vivian Isitt. b 20. **d** 89. PtO *St Alb* 91-08.
GREGORY, Mrs Sally Ann. b 65. **d** 15.
GRIER, Ms Sally Jane. b 60. **d** 15.
GRIEVES, David James. b 59. **d** 15.
GRIFFITH, Justin David. b 48. **d** 06. New Zealand from 14.
GRIFFITHS, Dorothy Anastasia de Jaegher. **d** 14. NSM Cheltenham St Mary w St Matt and St Luke *Glouc* from 14.
GUY, Kate Anne. b 26. **d** 88. PtO *Linc* 96-02.

HALE, Mrs Margaret McLeish (Greta). b 37. **d** 95. NSM Coleford, Staunton, Newland, Redbrook etc *Glouc* from 06.
HALFORD, David John. b 47. **d** 96. NSM Leesfield *Man* from 12.
HALL, Andrew John. **d** 14. C Cheltenham St Mary w St Matt and St Luke *Glouc* from 14.
HALL, Diana Mary. **d** 14. C St Andrews St Andr *St And* from 14.
HANMER, Sister Phoebe Margaret. b 31. **d** 96. PtO *Birm* from 04.
HARGER, Robin Charles Nicholas. b 49. **d** 81. rtd 12.
HARTLAND, Michael. b 58. **d** 08. PtO *S'wark* 10-11.
HARTLEY, Graeme William. b 68. **d** 07. Sherborne w Castleton, Lillington and Longburton *Sarum* 07.
HASLAM, Andrew James. b 57. **d** 83. V Birkenhead Ch Ch *Ches* 05-13.
HAWES, Mrs Joy Elizabeth. b 58. **d** 15. NSM Wedmore w Theale and Blackford *B & W* from 15.
HAYTER, Mark Harrison George. b 49. **d** 12. C Nadder Valley *Sarum* from 14.
HEARN, Stephen Isaac Raphael. b 79. **d** 09. Fell and Chapl Ex Coll Ox 11-13.
HERBERT, Malcolm Francis. b 53. **d** 77. rtd 13.
HIGGS, Mrs Karen Elizabeth. b 66. **d** 15.
HINE, Keith Ernest. b 50. **d** 89. rtd 14.
HOCKRIDGE, Joan. b 25. **d** 87. PtO *Lon* 95-00.
HODGE, Nigel John. b 61. **d** 85. LtO *Mon* from 99.
HOLMES, Trevor. **d** 13. NSM Julianstown and Colpe w Drogheda and Duleek *M & K* from 13.
HONNOR, Jonathan Michael Bellamy. b 62. **d** 00. P-in-c Aylesham w Adisham and Nonington *Cant* 12-13.
HOWARD, Martin John Aidan. b 68. **d** 97. TV Hampreston *Sarum* 06-08.
HUBBARD, Haynes Quinton. b 68. **d** 96. Canada from 12.
HUGHES, Albert William. b 48. **d** 92. rtd 13.
HUGHES, Canon Philip. b 47. **d** 81. R Llanberis, Llanrug and Llandinorwig *Ban* 03; rtd 12; PtO *Ban* from 12.
HUNT, Ms Rosalind Edna Mary. b 55. **d** 88. PtO *Man* from 05.
BOURNE, Mrs Janet. **d** 15. C Shipston-on-Stour w Honington and Idlicote *Cov* from 15.
ILIFFE, Mrs Felicity Mary. b 57. **d** 09. C Ledbury *Heref* 09-13.
INGERSLEV, Peter John. b 48. **d** 15.
JACKSON, Miss Freda. b 41. **d** 92. rtd 12; PtO *Man* from 12.
JACKSON, Ms Gillian Rosemary. b 52. **d** 04. Bp's Exec Asst *Leic* 08-10.
JAY, Mrs Sarah Clare. b 52. **d** 12. NSM Stranton *Dur* from 12.
JONES, Elizabeth. **d** 14. NSM Bulkington *Cov* from 14; Chapl Univ Hosps Cov and Warks NHS Trust from 14.
JONES, Sharon. b 74. **d** 07. P-in-c New Springs and Whelley *Liv* 11-13.
JOYCE, Kingsley Reginald. b 49. **d** 73. Chapl Naples w Sorrento, Capri and Bari *Eur* 08-13.
KAMBLE-HANSELL, Anupama. b 76. **d** 02. C Bure Valley *Nor* 11-13.
KAVANAGH, John Paul. b 63. **d** 94. R Forest Lake Australia 98; Chapl Dub Inst of Tech 11; Australia from 12.
KELLY, Brian Eugene. b 56. **d** 90. PtO *Cant* from 06.
KEMP, Ms Audrey. b 26. **d** 87. rtd 88.
KILBOURN-MACKIE, Canon Mary Elizabeth. b 26. **d** 77. PtO *Sarum* and *B & W* from 01.
KITELEY, Robert John. b 51. **d** 83. rtd 14.
KNIGHT, Miss Beth Marie. b 80. **d** 15.
LAKE, Jeffrey Ronald. b 70. **d** 15. NSM St Bride Fleet Street w Bridewell etc *Lon* from 15.
LAMB, Bruce. b 47. **d** 73. rtd 14.
LANDMANN, Ulrike Helene Kathryn. b 57. **d** 06. PtO *Birm* 10-13.
LANGMAN, Barry Edward. b 46. **d** 90. rtd 08.
LAYBOURNE, Mrs Teresa Margaret. b 52. **d** 12. NSM Washington *Dur* from 12.
LEYSHON, Simon. b 63. **d** 89. Chapl Lord Wandsworth Coll Hook 02-13.
LILES, Malcolm David. b 48. **d** 71. rtd 14.
LITTLE, Herbert Edwin Samuel. b 21. **d** 80. rtd 88.
McELWEE, Rachel. b 49. **d** 10. USA from 13.
McKINTY, Norman Alexander (Fionn). b 63. **d** 99. TV Portland *Sarum* 10-13.
MANN, Terence John. b 47. **d** 94. rtd 12.
MANNERS, Jennifer Helen Edith. b 50. **d** 06. OLM Bearsted w Thurnham *Cant* 06-13.
MARKEY, Andrew John. b 73. **d** 02. Chapl Luxembourg *Eur* from 12.
MARSDEN, Andrew Robert. b 49. **d** 72. rtd 13.

MARSHALL, Ms Karen Lesley. b 59. **d** 07. P-in-c Urmston *Man* from 14; P-in-c Davyhulme Ch Ch *Man* from 14.

MARTIN, Steven. b 50. **d** 08. Malvern St Andr and Malvern Wells and Wyche *Worc* 08; rtd 15.

MEIER, Paul. b 64. **d** 98. P-in-c Horsmonden *Roch* 10-13.

MIALL, Peter Brian. b 30. **d** 89. PtO *Sheff* from 98.

MILLS, Pamela Ann. b 44. **d** 97. rtd 11.

MITCHELL, Elizabeth Edgar. **d** 14. C S Cheltenham *Glouc* from 14.

MOFFITT, Mrs Vivien Louisa. b 37. **d** 91. rtd 01.

MORETON, Rupert Robert James. b 66. **d** 92. Finland from 13.

MORGAN, Glyn. b 21. **d** 76. PtO *Pet* 00-11.

MORTON, Michelle. b 67. **d** 02. P-in-c Stewkley w Soulbury and Drayton Parslow *Ox* 05-09.

MOSS, David. b 60. **d** 15. NSM Gt Hanwood and Longden and Annscroft etc *Heref* from 15.

MOSSLEY, Iain Stephen. b 72. **d** 98. P-in-c Ashton-upon-Mersey St Martin *Ches* 13.

MUNDY, Kay. **d** 14. C Deerhurst and Apperley w Forthampton etc *Glouc* from 14.

NAUDÉ, John Donald. b 62. **d** 97. V Crookhorn *Portsm* 06-12.

NEWLING, Scott John. b 77. **d** 08. PtO *Ely* from 12.

NEWNES, Steven William. **d** 14. C Brockworth *Glouc* from 14.

NORTH, Adam. b 81. **d** 15.

O'CONNELL, Miss Mary Joy. b 49. **d** 87. C Cinderhill *S'well* 94; rtd 14.

O'KELLY, Martin. **d** 11. C Clonsast w Rathangan, Thomastown etc *M & K* from 11.

OSBORNE, Norma. b 36. **d** 97. NSM Wandsworth St Mich w St Steph *S'wark* 06-07.

OWENS, Stephen Graham Frank. b 49. **d** 75. rtd 14.

PARKER, Stephen George. b 65. **d** 98. Hd Postgraduate Studies in Educn Worc Univ 08-12.

PARSONS, Roger John. b 37. **d** 65. TV E Dereham and Scarning *Nor* 89.

PATERSON, David. b 33. **d** 58. rtd 04; PtO *Ox* from 05.

PATON, Preb John David Marshall. b 47. **d** 83. rtd 12.

PAULUS, Garrett Keith. b 76. **d** 05. USA from 11.

PEMBERTON FORD, Carrie Mary. b 55. **d** 87. Development Officer Cam Cen for Applied Research in Human Trafficking from 08.

PENN, Jane Rachel. b 45. **d** 10. NSM Tadley w Pamber Heath and Silchester *Win* from 13.

PERRINS, Mrs Lesley. b 53. **d** 93. NSM Haxby w Wigginton *York* 94-00; Asst Chapl York Health Services NHS Trust 99-00.

PESTELL, Miss Josephine Frances. b 72. **d** 15.

PHILLIPS, Andrew Graham. b 58. **d** 87. rtd 12.

PHILLIPS, Mrs Brenda. b 41. **d** 04. rtd 11; PtO *Sarum* from 11.

PIERCE, Robert John. b 77. **d** 15.

PLATT, Anthea Kate Helen. b 71. **d** 08. C Thorley *St Alb* 08-14.

PRESTON, Michael Christopher. b 47. **d** 78. rtd 14.

PROSSER, Richard Hugh Keble. b 31. **d** 57. rtd 00; PtO *Sarum* from 02.

RABY, Mrs Caroline Jean. b 58. **d** 15.

RANSLEY, Steven Edward. b 82. **d** 15.

RAVEN, Tony. b 39. **d** 97. rtd 05.

REEVES, Michael Richard Ewert. b 74. **d** 02. Th Adv UCCF 05-12.

RICHARDS, Brian William. b 45. **d** 03. rtd 14.

RICHARDS, Llewelyn. b 15. **d** 75. rtd 85.

RIDGEWELL, Miss Mary Jean. b 54. **d** 91. rtd 12; PtO *Sarum* from 12.

ROBERTS, John Charles. b 50. **d** 73. LtO *Bris* 93-95.

ROBERTSON, Canon John Charles. b 61. **d** 90. Dir Ecum Miss *Ox* from 12.

RODWELL, Mrs Jacqueline Margaret. b 59. **d** 04. NSM Cheltenham Em w St Steph *Glouc* 08-09.

ROGERS, Richard Jonathan. b 64. **d** 96. PtO *B & W* 00-06.

SALMON, William John. b 50. **d** 79. Chapl HM Pris Belmarsh 04-07.

SEARS, Michael Antony. b 50. **d** 80. R Wroxham w Hoveton and Belaugh *Nor* 07-13.

SIMPSON, Herbert. b 20. **d** 82. NSM Barrow St Aid *Carl* 82; rtd 90.

SIVILL, David. **d** 14. OLM Atherton and Hindsford w Howe Bridge *Man* from 14.

SLACK, Michael. b 53. **d** 76. TR Cullercoats St Geo *Newc* 98-05.

SLATER, Victoria Ruth. b 59. **d** 89. Research and Development Officer Ox Cen for Ecclesiology and Practical Th 09-13.

SMITH, Mark Graham. b 63. **d** 90. V Scotforth *Blackb* 03-10; Dioc World Development Adv *Blackb* 00-10.

STIBBE, Mark William Godfrey. b 60. **d** 86. Ldr Father's Ho Trust 09-12.

STRUTT, Preb Susan. b 45. **d** 90. rtd 14.

SULLIVAN, Mrs Charlotte Lucy. b 66. **d** 15. C Aquitaine *Eur* from 15.

SULLIVAN, Mrs Linda Mary. b 45. **d** 14. OLM Malmesbury w Westport and Brokenborough etc *Bris* from 14.

TAME, Mrs Helene Louise. b 63. **d** 15. C St Neots *Ely* from 15.

THÖRNQVIST, Miss Karin Elisabet. b 41. **p** 84. Gen Preacher *Linc* from 07.

TODD, Jeremy Stephen Bevan. b 69. **d** 97. PtO *S'wark* 07-13.

TOMLINSON, Helen. b 53. **d** 07. NSM Blackley St Paul *Man* from 12.

TOMPKINS, Peter Michael. b 58. **d** 96. P-in-c Brough w Stainmore, Musgrave and Warcop *Carl* 11-13.

TUGWELL, Elizabeth Ann. b 36. **d** 94. rtd 10.

TURNER, Kevin Louis Sinclair. b 60. **d** 00. Evang Adv Croydon Area Miss Team *S'wark* 05-08.

TURNER, Tina. b 60. **d** 02. TV Warlingham w Chelsham and Farleigh *S'wark* 06-08.

UNDERDOWN, Margaret Jean (Meg). b 49. **d** 08. C Cathays *Llan* from 13.

VAUGHAN, Craig. **d** 12. NSM Newton Nottage *Llan* from 12.

WADSWORTH, Roy. b 37. **d** 89. NSM Alne *York* from 89; rtd 02.

WAIYAKI, Canon Jennie. b 34. **d** 92. Chapl Northumbria Healthcare NHS Foundn Trust from 97.

WAKERELL, Richard Hinton. b 55. **d** 84. V Rickerscote *Lich* 93.

WALKER, Paul Gary. b 59. **d** 84. V Wrose *Bradf* 97-13.

WALKER, Simon Patrick. b 71. **d** 97. PtO *B & W* from 11.

WALLACE, James Stephen. b 60. **d** 98. USPG Sri Lanka 02-08.

WALLER, Canon Derek James Keith. b 54. **d** 91. CMS S Sudan from 14.

WALTNER, Moise (Mike). b 75. **d** 15. C Vienna *Eur* from 15.

WANLISS, Hector. b 62. **d** 88. CF 99-11.

WARDMAN, Canon Carol Joy. b 56. **d** 94. Bps' Adv for Ch and Soc Ch in Wales from 11; Metrop Can Llan Cathl from 15.

WATSON, Mrs Gillian Edith. b 49. **d** 09. rtd 14.

WEEDING, Paul Stephen. b 62. **d** 90. Asst Chapl Qu Medical Cen Nottm Univ Hosp NHS Trust 03-10.

WELSFORD, Oliver Lewis. b 89. **d** 15.

WHEELER, Ms Pamela. b 48. **d** 15.

WILLIAMS, Philip James. b 52. **d** 76. rtd 14.

WILLIAMS, Samuel Patrick Sutherland. b 86. **d** 15.

WILSON, Kenneth. b 59. **d** 89. PtO *Lich* 00-08.

WILSON, Paul Thomas Wardley. b 43. **d** 70. Chief Exec Carr-Gomm Soc 88-10.

WORRALL, Peter Henry. b 62. **d** 95. TV Redditch H Trin *Worc* 07-12.

YATES, Francis Edmund. b 49. **d** 95. rtd 12.

ZAIDI-CROSSE, Philip Kenneth. b 63. **d** 05. NSM Erdington *Birm* 05-12.

CLERGY WHO HAVE DIED SINCE THE LAST EDITION

A list of clergy who have died since 12 August 2013, when the compilation of the 2014–2015 edition was completed. The month and year of death (if known) are recorded with each entry.

ABBEY, Anthony James. 04/14
ABBOTT, Barry Ingle. 07/14
ACKROYD, John Michael Calvert. 12/14
ADAMS, John Christopher Ronald. 01/14
ADAMSON, Paul. 03/14
ADDISON, Philip Ives. 02/15
AFFLECK, John. 11/13
AGNEW, Kenneth David. 02/14
AINSLEY, Anthony Dixon. 02/15
AINSLEY, Peter Dixon. 07/14
ALEXANDER, Douglas Keith. 10/14
ALFORD, Rosalie Grace. 09/13
ALLEN, John Catling. 03/15
AMOR, Peter David Card. 06/15
ANDERSON, David. 12/14
ANDREW, Frank. 05/15
ANDREW, John Gerald Barton. 10/14
ANDREWES UTHWATT, Henry. 01/14
ANDREWS, Anthony Frederick. 02/14
ANGEL, Robin Alan. 12/13
ANTHAPURUSHA, Paul Andrew. 06/14
APTHORP, Arthur Norman. 11/13
✠ARDEN, Donald Seymour. 07/14
ARMSTEAD, Geoffrey Malcolm. 01/14
ASHLING, Raymond Charles. 06/14
ATKINS, Timothy Samuel. 09/14
AXTELL, Ronald Arthur John. 01/14
BACK, Christopher George. 05/14
BAGLEY, Roy Victor. 01/14
BAILEY, Edward Ian. 04/15
BAIRD, Robert Douglas. 07/14
BAKER, John Albert. 11/13
✠BAKER, John Austin. 06/14
BALCH, John Robin. 03/15
BAMFORD, Marion. 04/14
BANFIELD, David John. 10/14
BANKS, Aleck George. 12/13
BARBER, Michael. 05/14
BARKER, Brian Wallwork. 03/15
BARKER, John Stuart. 08/15
BARKER, William Edward. 09/14
BARNARD, Leslie William. 07/15
BARRACLOUGH, Dennis. 04/14
BARRODALE, George Bryan. 09/14
BARTLE, Reginald Stephen. 11/13
BARTLES-SMITH, Douglas Leslie. 06/14
BARTLETT, Michael George. 03/14
BARTON, Margaret Anne. 09/13
BARTON, Samuel David. 05/14
BASON, Brian Vaudrey. 12/13
BASSETT, John Edmund. 12/14
BATEMAN, Kenneth William. 01/14
BATES, Derek Alvin. 04/15
BATY, Edward. 08/14
BAYLY, Samuel Niall Maurice. 10/13
BECKETT, George. 02/14
BECKETT, Stanley. 12/13
BEDFORD, Richard Derek Warner. 09/13
BEECH, Derek Charles. 05/14
BEETY, Arthur Edward. 01/13
BELLAMY, Robert John. 11/14
BENNELL, Richard. 11/13
BENNETT, Arthur Harling. 10/14
BENNETT, Doreen. 06/14
BENNETT, Edwin James. 01/15
BENNETT, Joyce Mary. 07/15
BETTS, George William John. 03/15
BILLINGTON, Charles Alfred. 12/14
BIRT, Malcolm Douglas. 02/14
BIRT, Patrick. 03/14
BLACKBURN, Frederick John Barrie. 05/14
BLACKMAN, John Franklyn. 07/14

BLAKE, Patrick John. 04/15
BOIT, Mervyn Hays. 10/13
BOND, Arthur Edward Stephen. 11/13
✠BONE, John Frank Ewan. 07/14
BOOTES, Michael Charles Edward. 09/14
BOWERING, John Anthony (Tony). 12/14
BOWERING, Michael Ernest. 04/15
BOWERS, Peter William Albert. 12/14
BRACE, Stuart. 05/14
BRANCHE, Brian Maurice. 12/13
BRASSELL, Kenneth William. 01/14
BREWSTER, Susan Jacqueline. 06/15
✠BRIDGES, Dewi Morris. 05/15
BRIDGES, Peter Sydney Godfrey. 01/15
BRIGHAM, John Keith. 04/14
BRITTENDEN, Gerald James Scott. 10/14
BRODRIBB, Carolyn Ann. 11/13
BROOM, Jacqueline Anne. 06/15
BROOMFIELD, David John. 10/14
BROWN, Arthur Basil Etheredge. 01/15
BROWN, Christopher Francis. 10/14
BROWN, Geoffrey Harold. 05/15
BROWN, John. 03/15
BROWN, John Dixon. 05/14
BROWNLESS, Philip Paul Stanley. 09/14
BROXTON, Alan. 04/14
BRUCE, John. 09/13
BRYAN, Philip Richard. 09/14
BRYN-THOMAS, John. 11/14
BUCKLEY, Robert William. 05/14
BUDDEN, Clive John. 12/14
BUFFREY, Samuel John Thomas. 01/15
BUNTING, Jeremy John. 05/15
BURGESS, Patricia Jean. 03/14
BURKE, Charles Michael. 11/13
BURMAN, Thomas George. 10/13
BURNHAM, Frank Leslie. 02/15
BURRELL, Godfrey John. 05/15
✠BURROWS, Simon Hedley. 08/15
BUTLER, Henry. 01/14
BUTLER, Ian Malcolm. 10/14
BUTLER, Michael John. 11/14
BUTLER, Robert Clifford. 04/14
BUTLER-SMITH, Basil George (Bob). 10/13
CALDECOURT, Frances Ann. 10/13
CALDER, Roger Paul. 05/15
CALDICOTT, Anthony. 06/15
CAMERON, Donald Eric Nelson. 12/14
CANHAM, Robert Edwin Francis. 10/14
CANHAM, William Alexander. 01/15
CANNER, Peter George. 11/13
CANNING, Graham Gordon Blakeman. 01/15
CANTI, Shirley Christine. 06/14
CARE, Charles Richard. 03/14
CAREW, Bryan Andrew. 06/14
CARNE, Norman David John. 08/13
CARSON, Ernest. 02/14
CARSON, Gerald James Alexander. 07/14
CARTER, Dudley Herbert. 10/13
CARTER, Joy. 10/14
CASIOT, David John. 01/14
CASON, Ronald Arthur. 04/15
CASSIDY, Joseph Patrick. 03/15
CASSWELL, Peter Joyce. 08/14
CASTLETON, David Miles. 06/14
CATCHPOLE, Guy St George. 02/14
CHADWICK, Peter MacKenzie. 02/15
CHADWICK, Roger Vernon. 07/15
CHADWICK, William Owen. 07/15

CHAMBERLAIN, Eric Edward. 04/14
CHAMBERLAIN, Frederick George. 10/14
CHAPMAN, Margaret. 08/13
CHAPMAN, Raymond. 11/13
CHARRINGTON, Nicholas John. 01/15
CHATFIELD, Thomas William. 01/14
CHEESEMAN, Kenneth Raymond. 01/15
CHEEVERS, George Alexander. 08/14
CHERRY, Malcolm Stephen. 07/15
CHESTERTON, Robert Eric. 08/13
CHESWORTH, Stanley Herbert James. 02/15
CHEUNG, Anita Yen. 09/13
CHISHOLM, Samuel James. 09/13
CHITTY, William Paul Thomas. 12/13
CHURCHMAN, David Ernest Donald. 03/14
CLARK, Arthur. 11/14
CLARKE, Frank. 01/14
CLARKE, Richard Leon. 04/15
CLAYTON, Sydney Cecil Leigh. 03/15
CLEAVER, Gerald. 03/15
CLEMENT, Barbara Winifred. 03/14
CLEMENTS, Edwin George. 02/14
COCHRANE, Roy Alan. 03/15
COLE, Charles Vincent. 04/14
COLEMAN, Terence Norman. 08/14
CONNELL, Heather Josephine. 09/14
CONNER, Charles Borthwick. 05/15
CONSTANTINE, Elaine Muriel. 06/14
CONWAY-LEE, Stanley. 04/14
COOMBE, John Morrell (Brother Martin). 05/14
COOPER, Jack. 01/14
COOPER, Joseph Trevor. 11/14
COPLEY, Colin. 01/15
CORNECK, Warrington Graham. 03/15
COSBY, Ingirid St Clair. 08/14
COTTER, James England. 04/14
COUNSELL, Michael John Radford. 07/15
COURTAULD, Augustine Christopher Caradoc. 01/14
COURTNEY, Michael Monlas. 03/15
COWLING, Douglas Anderson. 01/15
COWMEADOW, Derek Lowe. 01/15
CRAVEN, Allan. 03/15
CRAWFORD, Robin. 01/14
CRAWLEY, John Lloyd Rochfort. 02/15
CRIPPS, Keith Richard John. 02/15
CROOKS, Eric. 01/14
CROSS, Michael Harry. 11/13
CROW, Arthur. 07/14
CULBERTSON, Eric Malcolm. 11/13
CUNNINGHAM, Arthur. 01/14
CURRY, David John. 12/14
DABBS, Norman Arthur. 01/15
DACK, Paul Marven. 08/13
DALY, Dorothy Isabel. 06/15
DARBY, Anthony Ernest. 03/15
DARROCH, Ronald Humphrey. 01/15
DAVID, Michael Anthony Louis. 08/15
DAVIDSON, William Watkins. 05/15
DAVIES, Carol Ann. 03/14
DAVIES, David Barry Grenville. 02/15
DAVIES, John Edwards Gurnos. 02/15
DAVIS, Ronald Frank. 04/14
DAVISON, William. 06/14
DAVOLL, Ivan John (Snowy). 03/14
DAY, Charles George. 08/14
DAY, John Cuthbert. 04/15
DEARDEN, James Varley. 10/14
DEBNEY, Wilfred Murray. 12/14

DEEDES, Arthur Colin Bouverie. 10/13
DELANY, Michael Edward. 08/13
DELL, Murray John. 04/15
DENNETT, John Edward. 12/14
DICKSON, Brian John. 11/14
DIXON, Francesca Dorothy. 06/14
DIXON, Sheila. 01/14
✠DOCKER, Ivor Colin. 11/14
DODD, Alan Henry. 03/15
DOMMETT, Richard Radmore. 01/15
DRAKE, Frances Maud. 01/15
DUNCAN, John. 01/15
DUNN, David. 05/15
DURNELL, John. 08/14
DYKE, George Edward. 12/13
DYSON, Frank. 03/15
EARLE, John Nicholas Francis. 01/14
EDMUNDS, Eric John. 01/15
EDWARDS, Graham Arthur. 09/14
EDWARDS, Henry St John. 04/14
EFEMEY, Raymond Frederick. 01/15
ELLACOTT, David Alfred. 03/14
ELLIOT, William. 06/15
EVANS, Ernest Maurice. 11/13
EVANS, Frederick James Stephens.
03/14
EVANS, Geoffrey Bainbridge. 04/15
EVANS, Kenneth Roy. 07/15
EVANS-PUGHE, Thomas Goronwy.
02/15
EVERETT, David Gordon. 01/15
EVERETT, John Wilfred. 04/14
EWBANK, Walter Frederick. 03/14
EYERS, Frederick Thomas Laurence.
01/15
FARRANT, Jonathan. 06/14
FAULDS, John Parker. 10/14
FEIT, Michael John. 09/14
FENNELL, John Michael Rivers. 06/15
FENTON, Ian Christopher Stuart. 08/13
FENWICK, Jeffrey Robert. 09/14
FIELD, Geoffrey Alder. 02/14
FINLAY, Christopher John. 12/14
FINNEY, Fred. 09/14
FINNEY, John Thomas. 07/15
FIRMIN, Dorrie Eleanor Frances. 03/15
FISHER, Adrian Charles Proctor. 04/14
FISHER, Roy Percy. 07/14
FISHER, Thomas Andrew. 09/14
FITCH, John Ambrose. 04/15
FLATHER, Peter George. 04/15
FLETCHER, Colin John. 11/13
FLYNN, Alexander Victor George. 09/14
FORDHAM, June Erica. 04/14
FOREMAN, Joseph Arthur. 04/14
FOREMAN, Roy Geoffrey Victor. 02/15
FORMAN, Diana Blanche Grant. 08/13
FOSTER, Ronald George. 09/13
FOSTER, Steven. 01/15
FOX, Herbert Frederick. 02/15
FRANCE, Malcolm Norris. 07/14
FRANCIS, Claude Vernon Eastwood.
10/13
FRASER, Leslie. 05/15
FREEMAN, Alan John Samuel. 07/15
FREEMAN, Philip Michael. 11/14
FRENCH, Basil Charles Elwell. 09/14
FREWIN, William Charles. 10/13
FRIEND, Frederick James. 05/14
FROWLEY, Peter Austin. 05/15
FRY, James Reinhold. 12/13
GAFVERT, Dan. 06/15
GALILEE, George David Surtees. 01/15
GALLOWAY, Charles Bertram. 09/13
GAMESTER, Sidney Peter. 04/14
GARDINER, Brian John. 11/14
GARLAND, Peter Stephen John. 05/15
GARSIDE, Howard. 08/13
GIBSON, Garry Stuart. 08/14
GIBSON, Raymond Frank. 12/13
GIBSON, Robert Swinton. 02/15
GIDDENS, Leslie Vernon. 06/14
GILBERT, Sidney Horace. 10/13
GILDING, James Peter. 06/14
GILLETT, Vincent. 01/14
GILLHESPEY, Clive. 06/15

GIRLING, Francis Richard (Vincent).
02/14
✠GITARI, David Mukuba. 09/13
GODFREY, John Frederick. 05/14
GOLDING, Piers Edwin Hugh. 12/14
GOODALL, Malcolm. 01/15
GOODE, Anthony Thomas Ryall. 02/14
GOODFIELD, Dudley Francis. 04/15
GOODMAN, John. 05/15
GOULD, Douglas Walter. 04/14
GOUPILLON, Jane Elizabeth. 01/14
GOW, Peter Draffin. 07/14
GRACE, Kenneth. 08/13
GRACE, Richard Maurice. 10/13
GRACIE, Anthony Johnstone. 01/15
GRAHAM, John Galbraith. 11/13
GRANT, Alistair Sims. 03/14
GRANT, Geoffrey. 06/15
GRAY, Donald Cecil. 02/14
GRAY, Percy. 05/14
GREEN, Maurice Paul. 09/13
GREENFIELD, Norman John Charles.
02/15
GREENWOOD, Gordon Edwin. 12/14
GREETHAM, William Frederick. 02/14
GRIFFIN, Kenneth Francis. 05/15
GRIFFITH, Brian Vann. 06/14
GRIFFITH, Donald Bennet. 01/14
GRIFFITH, Peter Malcolm. 09/13
GRUNDY, Jocelyn Pratchitt. 09/14
GUMMER, Dudley Harrison. 10/14
HABERMEHL, Kenneth Charles. 03/14
HADDLETON, Peter Gordon. 11/13
HAGGAR, Keith Ivan. 05/15
✠HALL, Albert Peter. 12/13
HALL, Arthur John. 01/14
HALLING, William Laurence. 03/15
HAMBLEN, John William Frederick.
06/15
HAMILTON, James. 11/14
HAMMON, David Edward. 06/14
HANCOCK, Barbara. 10/13
HANDFORD, John Richard. 12/14
HARDING, John William Christopher.
01/15
HARDING, Sylvia. 08/14
HARDWICK, Dennis Egerton. 08/14
HARDY, Michael John. 01/14
✠HARE DUKE, Michael Geoffrey. 12/14
HAREWOOD, John Rupert. 08/14
HARLOW, Derrick Peter. 11/13
HARRIES, Henry Rayner Mackintosh.
08/14
HARRINGTON, William Harry. 06/14
HARRIS, Leslie Gerald Conley Eyre.
09/14
HARRIS-DOUGLAS, John Douglas.
07/15
HARRISON, Bernard Charles. 05/15
HARRISON, Herbert Gerald. 11/14
HARRISON, William Roy. 07/15
HARTE, Frederick George. 03/15
HAWKINS, Francis John. 01/15
HAWTHORN, Thomas Russell. 12/14
HAZELTON, John. 07/14
HAZELDINE, Basil William. 09/14
HEARD, Charles. 09/13
HEASLIP, William John (Jack). 02/15
HEDGES, Leslie Norman. 06/14
HELFT, Gunter. 06/15
HENDERSON, Euan Russell Milne.
07/14
✠HENLEY, Michael Harry George.
03/14
HEPWORTH, Michael Edward. 05/15
HERITAGE, Barry. 01/15
HESELWOOD, Hilda. 08/13
HEWETT, Maurice Gordon. 07/15
HIBBERT, Charles Dennis. 02/14
HICKS, Francis Fuller. 11/14
HICKS, Stuart Knox. 08/14
HIGGINS, John. 03/15
HILL, James Arthur. 01/14
HILL, John Michael. 05/15
HINDLEY, Thomas Richard. 04/14
HINGE, David Gerald Francis. 03/15

HODGSON, Christopher. 12/13
HODGSON, Roger Vaughan. 11/13
HODGSON, Vernon Charles. 03/14
HODSON, William. 10/13
HOGAN, John James. 12/13
HOLLIS, Christopher Barnsley. 02/14
HOLMES, Theodore John. 02/15
HOOPER, William Gilbert. 10/13
HOPCRAFT, Jonathan Richard. 11/13
HORE, Michael John. 02/14
HORNER, Philip David Forster. 02/14
HORTON, Christopher Peter. 02/14
HOSKIN, Eric James. 05/14
HOW, John Maxloe. 06/15
HOWARD, John Alexander. 02/14
HOWELL, Walter Ernest. 03/15
HOWES, Michael John Norton. 05/15
HUBBARD, Elisabeth Ann. 05/15
HUDSON, Clive. 06/14
HUGHES, Gwyndaf Morris. 04/14
HUGHES, John Mark David. 06/14
HUGHES, Leonard Mordecai. 04/14
HUMPHREYS, James Graham. 09/14
HUSSEY, Martin John. 10/14
HUTCHINSON, David Bamford. 03/14
HYDE, Edgar Bonsor. 12/14
INGHAM, Dawn. 02/15
INGRAM, Joanna Mary. 01/15
INMAN, Martin. 12/14
ISAAC, Edward Henry. 08/14
IVES, Raymond Charles. 07/15
JACKSON, Kenneth William. 03/14
JACKSON, Peter Lewis. 09/14
JACOBSON, Norman. 11/14
JAGGS, Michael Richard Moore. 01/15
JAMES, Derek George. 12/14
JAMES, John Morgan. 09/14
JAMES, Michael John. 07/14
JAMES, Sarah Alison Livingston. 12/14
JAMESON, David Kingsbury. 05/15
JAMESON, Geoffrey Vaughan. 11/14
JENKINS, David Thomas Ivor. 09/14
JENKINS, John Raymond. 01/14
JENKINS, Robert Francis. 12/13
JENNINGS, Mervyn. 08/14
JOHN, Elwyn Crebey. 08/13
JOHNSON, Donald Arnold. 02/14
JOHNSON, Gordon Edward. 08/14
JOHNSON, Graham. 03/15
JOHNSON, Graham James. 10/13
JOHNSON, Robin Edward Hobbs. 03/15
JOHNSON, Solomon Tilewa. 01/14
JONES, Clifford Albert. 05/15
JONES, David James Hammond. 06/15
JONES, Emile Conrad Modupe Kojo.
07/15
JONES, Frederick John. 01/15
JONES, Gordon Michael Campbell.
12/14
JONES, Harold Desmond. 12/13
JONES, Keith Bythell. 04/15
JONES, Raymond Blake. 10/14
JONES, Thomas Percy Norman
Devonshire. 02/15
JOWITT, John Frederick Benson. 01/15
JUPE, Derek Robert. 03/15
KEARNS, Mary Leah. 01/15
✠KELSHAW, Terence. 07/15
KEMP, Geoffrey Bernard. 10/14
KENCH, Michael John Phillip. 07/14
KENDAL, Stephen. 01/15
KER, Desmond Agar-Ellis. 08/14
KIDD, Carol Ivy. 06/14
KIDD, John Alan. 06/14
KIGHTLEY, David John. 12/13
KILNER, James Martin. 10/13
KIME, Thomas Frederick. 08/13
KIRK, Peter Fenwick. 07/15
KIRKHAM, Clifford Gerald Frank. 09/14
KITTS, Joseph. 08/13
KNELL, Raymond John. 03/15
KNOWLES-BROWN, John Henry. 03/14
KNUCKEY, William Thomas. 02/14
KRONENBERG, Selwyn Thomas Denzil.
04/15
LAKE, Wynne Vaughan. 01/15

LANCASTER, Susan Louise. 07/14
LANDEN, Edgar Sydney. 08/13
LANE, Christopher George. 09/13
LAPHAM, Fred. 12/14
LAST, Norman Percy George. 12/14
LATHAM, John Westwood. 05/15
LAURIE, James Andrew Stewart. 06/14
LAWRENSON, Michael. 02/15
LAWTON, David Andrew. 02/15
LAYBOURNE, Michael Frederick. 07/15
LAYCOCK, Lawrence. 06/15
LEANING, David. 07/15
LEDGER, James Henry. 08/14
LEE, Colin John Willmot. 01/14
LEEMING, John Maurice. 12/13
LEESON, David Harry Stanley. 05/15
LEIGH-HUNT, Edward Christopher. 02/14
LEVERTON, Peter James Austin. 02/14
LEVICK, Brian William. 04/14
LEWERS, Benjamin Hugh. 03/15
LEWIS, Frederick Norman. 02/14
LEWIS, William George Melville. 07/14
LINDSAY, Richard John Alan. 03/15
LINDSAY-PARKINSON, Michael. 01/15
LINGARD, Keith Patrick. 09/14
LINTON, Alan Ross. 02/15
LINTON, Joseph Edmund. 11/13
LITTLER, Keith Trevor. 06/15
LLOYD, David John Silk. 05/15
LLOYD, John Francis. 10/14
LLOYD, Peter John. 06/14
LLOYD, Robert James Clifford. 08/13
LOBANOV-ROSTOVSKY, Andrew Russell. 12/13
LOCKHART, Patricia May. 11/14
LOFTHOUSE, Alexander Francis Joseph. 02/14
LOVELESS, Christopher Hugh. 07/15
LOVELESS, William Harry. 05/15
LOXLEY, Deirdre Phyllis. 08/14
LOXLEY, Ronald Alan Keith. 07/15
LUGG, Stuart John. 02/14
LUSBY, Dennis John. 11/14
✠LUXMOORE, Christopher Charles. 02/14
McCABE, William Alexander Beck. 05/15
McCOULL, Denis Cecil. 10/13
McDERMID, Norman George Lloyd Roberts. 09/14
McDERMOTT, John Michael. 08/14
MACFARLANE, William Angus. 11/14
McGEE, Stuart Irwin. 10/13
McGONIGLE, Thomas. 10/13
McGRANAGHAN, Patrick Joseph Colum. 05/14
McGREGOR, Alistair Darrant. 05/15
McGUIRE, Alec John. 04/15
McKENNA, Dermot William. 04/14
MacKENZIE, Lawrence Duncan. 10/15
McKITTRICK, Noel Thomas Llewellyn. 02/14
McLEAN-REID, Robert. 06/15
McNEILE, Donald Hugh. 01/15
MACOURT, William Albany. 07/14
MacPHEE, Roger Hunter. 01/15
MACPHERSON, John. 04/15
MacWILLIAM, Alexander Gordon. 10/14
MAKAMBWE, Francis James. 10/14
MALCOLM, Edward. 11/13
MANN, Ralph Norman. 04/14
MANSBRIDGE, Michael Winstanley. 01/14
MARCHANT, Ronald Albert. 04/15
MARKEY, Michael John. 05/14
MARKS, Anthony Wendt. 12/14
MARSDEN, John Robert. 09/14
MARSHALL, John Douglas. 07/14
MARSHALL, Peter John. 06/15
MARSHALL, Richard Albert. 07/14
MARTIN, John Pringle. 09/13
MASON, Alan Hambleton. 08/13
MASON, Geoffrey Charles. 02/14
MATHER, Stephen Albert. 09/13

MATTEN, Derek Norman William. 01/15
MATTHEWS, Peter Henry. 05/14
MATTHEWS, William Andrew. 11/13
MAYES, Anthony Bernard Duncan. 10/14
✠MEARS, John Cledan. 07/14
MEIRION-JONES, Huw Geraint (Gary). 05/14
MERCER, John James Glendinning. 04/15
METCALF, Robert Laurence. 12/14
MILES, Malcolm Robert. 11/14
MILES, Robert William. 02/14
MILLER, Anthony Talbot. 06/14
MILLER, Rosslyn Leslie. 02/14
MILLS, Ian Anderson. 02/14
MILLS, John Kettlewell. 09/13
MINTY, Kenneth Desmond. 12/14
MOCKFORD, John Frederick. 01/14
MOGFORD, Stanley Howard. 09/13
MOON, Thomas Arnold. 03/15
MOORE, Leonard Richard. 01/15
MORETON, Michael Joseph. 09/14
MORGAN, Beryl. 06/14
MORGAN, John Geoffrey Basil. 10/14
MORGAN, John Roland. 08/14
MORGAN, Michael. 01/15
MORLEY, Athelstan John. 02/15
MORLEY, Peter. 12/14
MORRIS, Alan Ralph Oakden. 03/14
MORRIS, Elizabeth Mary. 05/14
MORRIS, Ian Henry. 01/14
MORRIS, Robin Edward. 04/15
MORT, Margaret Marion. 09/14
MORTIMER, William Raymond. 01/15
MOTHERSDALE, Paul John. 01/14
MURPHY, John Gervase Maurice Walker (Gerry). 01/14
MURRAY, Ian William. 08/14
MUSGRAVE, James Robert Lord. 02/15
MUSTON, David Alan. 08/14
MYCOCK, Geoffrey John Arthur. 12/14
MYLNE, Denis Colin. 02/15
MYNETT, John Alan. 05/15
NASH, William Henry. 11/14
NELSON, Michael. 04/14
NEWTON, Gerald Blamire. 04/15
NICHOLAS, Maurice Lloyd. 11/14
NICHOLLS, Michael Stanley. 05/14
NICHOLS, Raymond Maurice. 12/14
NINIS, Richard Betts. 10/14
NORTH, Barry Albert. 07/15
NUNN, Richard Ernest. 02/14
NUTTALL, George Herman. 12/14
O'BEIRNE, Peter Donald Moray. 08/14
OCKWELL, Herbert Grant. 12/13
O'CONNOR, Alfred Stanley. 01/15
OLDROYD, Colin Mitchell. 02/15
OLIVER, John Andrew George. 02/15
ONIONS, Martin Giles. 05/15
OSBORNE, Alexander Deas. 10/13
OSMAN, Ernest. 07/15
OUTHWAITE, Stephen Anthony (Tony). 07/15
OVERTON, Thomas Vincent Edersheim. 03/14
OVERY, Arthur William. 03/14
OWEN, Derek Malden. 07/14
PACEY, Michael John. 04/15
PAGE, John Laurance Howard. 09/14
PAGE, Richard Dennis. 12/13
PALMER, Francis Harvey. 01/14
PALMER FINCH, Barry Marshall. 07/14
PANNETT, Philip Anthony. 02/15
PARKER, Ramon Lewis (Brother Raphael). 09/14
PARSONS, Desmond John. 01/14
PARSONS, Mary Elizabeth. 03/15
PARTINGTON, Fred. 03/14
PARTRIDGE, Margaret Edith. 09/14
PATIENT, Terence Ian. 02/15
PATSTON, Raymond Sidney Richard. 03/15
PATTERSON, Charles David Gilliat. 07/15

PAYNE, Cyril Gordon. 12/14
PAYNE, David James. 03/14
PAYNE, James John Henry. 12/13
PAYNE, John Percival. 06/14
PEARCE, Gerald Nettleton. 03/15
PEEL, John Bruce. 04/14
PEEL, Jonathan Sidney. 12/14
PEEL, Michael Jerome. 05/14
PEET, Derek Edwin. 12/13
PENGELLEY, Peter John. 12/14
PERRY, Michael Charles. 01/15
PHARAOH, Douglas William. 03/15
PHELPS, Ian James. 07/14
PHILLIPS, Geoffrey John. 09/14
PHILLIPS, Percy Graham. 01/15
PHILLIPS, Stephen. 01/15
PICKARD, William Priestley. 06/15
PICKTHORN, Charles Howard. 03/14
POMFRET, Albert. 09/14
POPE, David Allan. 12/14
POSTLES, Donald. 12/13
POTTER, Richard Antony. 05/15
POW, Joyce. 01/15
POWELL, Eric Michael. 07/14
POWNE, Peter Rebbeck Lamb. 11/13
PREECE, Joseph. 10/14
PRESTON, William. 01/14
PRICE, John Francis. 03/14
PRIDAY, Gerald Nelson. 12/13
PRIESTNALL, Reginald Hayward. 07/14
PRINGLE, Janyce Mary. 04/14
PRIOR, John Miskin. 04/14
PROBETS, Desmond. 04/14
PROCTER, Robert Hendy. 03/15
PRYTHERCH, David. 06/14
PUGH, William Bryan (Brian). 02/15
PUMPHREY, Norman John Albert. 01/14
PURCHAS, Catherine Patience Ann. 11/13
PYATT, Noel Watson. 04/15
PYBURN, Alan. 04/14
PYM, Gordon Sydney. 05/14
RANSON, Terence William James. 03/14
RAPLEY, Frederick Arthur. 01/15
RASON, Frederick George. 02/15
RATINGS, John William. 11/14
RAWLINS, Geoffrey Ernest Francis. 03/14
RAYNER, Richard Noel. 09/13
REDMAN, Arthur Thomas. 10/13
REED, Geoffrey Martin. 08/14
REES, David Frederick. 06/14
REES, David Philip Dunn Hugh. 01/15
RENSHAW, Anthony. 04/14
REVELEY, Valerie Mary. 03/14
RHYS, David Edwin. 02/14
RICHARDSON, Charles Leslie Joseph. 11/14
RICHARDSON, David Gwynne. 08/14
RICHARDSON, John Peter. 03/14
RIDDLE, Kenneth Wilkinson. 09/13
RIDGE, Haydn Stanley. 03/14
RILEY, Peter Arthur. 07/14
RIMMER, Peter Anthony. 01/15
ROBERTS, Colin Edward. 07/15
ROBERTS, Henry Edward (Ted). 06/15
ROBERTSON, Priscilla Biddulph. 06/15
ROBINSON, Bryan. 02/14
ROBINSON, Ian Cameron. 03/15
ROGERS, Angela. 08/14
ROLSTON, John Ormsby. 09/14
RONE, James. 01/14
ROPER, Timothy Hamilton. 06/14
ROSE, Barry Ernest. 09/13
ROSE, John David. 08/13
ROWDON, John Michael Hooker. 01/14
ROWE, Andrew Gidleigh Bruce. 11/14
ROWE, Stanley Hamilton. 01/15
ROWLAND, Charles Louis Gordon (Tim). 07/14
ROWLAND, Eric Edward James. 01/15
SADDINGTON, Peter David. 10/13
ST JOHN-CHANNELL, Michael Alister Morrell. 02/14

SALONIA, Ivan. 11/13
SAMPFORD, John Alfred. 10/13
SAMUELS, Peter. 04/15
SANSOME, Geoffrey Hubert. 10/13
SARGENT, John Philip Hugh. 11/14
✠SATTERTHWAITE, John Richard.
05/14
SAWARD, Michael John. 02/15
SCHARF, Ulrich Eduard Erich Julian.
01/15
SCHOFIELD, David. 08/14
✠SCOTT, Colin John Fraser. 04/14
✠SCOTT-JOYNT, Michael Charles.
09/14
SCUFFHAM, Frank Leslie. 10/13
SELWOOD, Eveline Mary. 04/14
SENIOR, John Peter. 07/15
SHAPLAND, David Edward. 02/14
SHARPE, Mary Primrose. 02/14
SHAW, Alison Ruth. 01/15
SHAW, Norman. 01/14
SHAW, Roderick Kenneth. 09/14
SHEARING, Michael James. 12/14
SHEEN, Victor Alfred. 04/14
SHEPHERD, Michael John. 04/15
SHIRESS, David Henry Faithfull. 12/13
SHORROCK, John Musgrave. 10/13
SHORT, John Sinclair. 02/14
SHORTT, Noel Christopher. 01/15
SHRIVES, Austen Geoffrey. 10/14
SIDAWAY, Geoffrey Harold. 04/14
SILLIS, Graham William. 06/15
SIMPSON, Godfrey Lionel. 09/14
SINCLAIR, Robert Michael. 05/15
SINGLETON, Editha Mary. 03/14
SKELTON, Pamela Dora. 12/14
SKINNER, Peter William. 06/14
SMART, Beryl. 08/13
SMART, Clifford Edward James. 07/14
SMETHURST, Leslie Beckett. 05/15
SMITH, Anthony Michael Percival.
09/13
SMITH, Clarice Mary. 04/14
SMITH, Donald John. 08/14
SMITH, Elizabeth Ann. 09/13
SMITH, Jeffery Donald Morris. 08/13
SMITH, Norman George. 08/14
SMITH, Ralston Antonio. 10/14
SMITH, Raymond Horace David. 10/13
SMITH, Richard Geoffrey. 02/15
SMITH, Ronald Deric. 04/15
SMITH, Vernon Hemingway. 01/15
SNEATH, Sidney Dennis. 08/13
SPARKES, Donald James Henry. 04/15
SPENDLOVE, Lindsay Kate. 11/14
SPOTTISWOODE, Anthony Derek.
02/14
SPRATT, Laurence Herbert. 07/15
STACEY, Helen Norman. 11/13
STANBRIDGE, Leslie Cyril. 03/15
STARKEY, John Douglas. 02/15
STAUNTON, Richard Steedman. 06/15
STEELE, Charles Edward Ernest. 03/15
STEPHENS, Grahame Frank Henry.
04/14
STEVENS, Cyril David Richard. 06/14
STEVENS, Frederick Crichton. 01/15
STEWART, John Roberton. 12/13
STEWART, William. 02/15
STINSON, William Gordon. 06/14
STONE, Carol Ann. 12/14
STOREY, William Leslie Maurice. 11/13
STRATFORD, Ralph Montgomery.
08/14

STROUD, Ernest Charles Frederick.
06/14
STUBBINGS, Frank Edward. 03/14
STURMAN, Robert George. 10/14
STUTZ, Clifford Peter. 12/14
SULLY, Martin John. 12/13
SUTHERLAND, Graham Russell. 07/14
SUTTON, Ronald. 11/13
SWEETMAN, Denis Harold. 05/14
SWINNERTON, Ernest George Francis.
09/14
✠SYKES, Stephen Whitefield. 09/14
SYKES, William George David. 01/15
SYMES, Percy Peter. 03/14
TABERN, James. 09/13
TAMS, Gordon Thomas Carl. 03/14
TAYLOR, Edward Frank. 03/14
TAYLOR, Godfrey Alan. 10/14
TAYLOR, Jan William Karel. 01/15
TAYLOR, Peter. 02/15
TAYLOR, Stella Isabelle. 04/14
TESTER, Clarence Albert. 10/13
THAME, Margaret Eve. 01/15
THEODOSIUS, Richard Francis. 08/13
THOMAS, Austin George. 12/14
THOMAS, Cheeramattathu John. 07/15
THOMAS, Geoffrey Charles. 06/14
THOMAS, Hugh. 03/14
THOMAS, Theodore Eilir. 06/14
THOMPSON, Donald Frazer. 12/14
THOMPSON, James. 01/15
THOMPSON, Kenneth. 11/13
THOMPSON, Timothy. 08/14
THOMSON, Clarke Edward Leighton.
04/14
THOMSON, Peter Malcolm. 08/13
THORBURN, Peter Hugh. 05/15
THORN, Robert Anthony D'Venning.
04/14
THORNLEY, Geoffrey Pearson. 06/14
THURMER, John Alfred. 01/15
THURSTON, Ian Charles. 04/14
TINGLE, Michael Barton. 10/14
TOOLEY, Geoffrey Arnold. 02/14
TOOVEY, Kenneth Frank. 06/14
TORODE, Brian Edward. 03/14
TOWERS, Terence John. 01/14
TRAVIS, Jean Kathleen. 02/14
TREADGOLD, John David. 02/15
TREASURE, Ronald Charles. 07/14
TREVOR-MORGAN, Basil Henry. 11/14
TRIMBY, George Henry. 05/14
TUBBS, Margaret Amy. 03/15
TUCKER, Harold George. 02/15
TURNBULL, William George. 12/14
TURNER, Mark Richard
Haythornthwaite. 04/15
TURNHAM ELVINS, Mark Anthony
Lawrence. 05/14
UPCOTT, Derek Jarvis. 10/14
USHER-WILSON, Lucian Neville. 02/14
VANDYCK, Salli Diane Seymour. 08/13
VARNEY, Donald James. 12/14
VAUGHAN, Gloria Ann. 03/14
VERE HODGE, Francis. 12/13
VINCENT, William Alfred Leslie. 01/14
VINCER, Michael. 01/14
VIPOND, John. 10/13
VIRTUE, Thomas James. 05/14
✠VOCKLER, John Charles (Brother
John-Charles). 02/14
VORLEY, Kenneth Arthur. 12/14
WAINWRIGHT, Joseph Allan. 12/14
WAKEHAM, Geoffrey. 01/14

WALFORD, David Sanderson. 07/14
WALKER, Brian Cecil. 01/15
WALKER, John Cameron. 11/14
WALKER, Martin Frank. 08/13
WALLER, John Pretyman. 12/13
WALLIS, Peter. 08/14
WARBURTON, Piers Eliot de Dutton.
06/15
WARD, Kenneth Arthur. 11/13
WARDLE-HARPUR, James. 01/14
WARNER, James Morley. 01/14
WARNES, Warren Hugh. 03/15
WARREN, Christopher Pelham. 04/14
WATKINS, Christine Dorothy (Sue).
08/14
WATSON, John Francis Wentworth.
06/14
WATSON, John Harold. 03/14
WAYTE, Christopher John. 11/13
WEBB, David William. 01/15
WEBB, Gregory John. 08/15
WEBLEY, Robin Bowen. 07/15
WEDDERSPOON, Alexander Gillan.
06/14
WEDGWOOD, George Peter. 06/14
WELLS, Charles Francis. 10/13
WEST, Clive. 08/14
WHALES, Jeremy Michael. 11/14
WHATMORE, Michael John. 12/14
WHEATON, Ralph Ernest. 03/15
WHEBLE, Eric Clement. 01/14
WHETTEM, John Curtiss. 03/14
WHITAKER, David Arthur Edward.
06/14
WHITE, Alan Albert. 06/15
WHITE, Derek James. 04/14
WHITE, Ruth Anna. 10/14
WHITEHEAD, Burton Jones. 09/13
WHITFIELD, Charles. 08/14
WHITLEY, John Duncan Rooke. 05/14
WHITTOME, Donald Marshall. 01/15
WICKENS, John Philip. 08/14
WIDDOWSON, Ian Roy. 02/15
WIGGINTON, Peter Walpole. 01/15
WILKINSON, Kevin Harold. 04/15
WILKINSON, Roger. 09/14
WILLIAMS, Arthur Edwin. 05/14
WILLIAMS, Elfed Owain. 02/14
WILLIAMS, Geoffrey Thomas. 11/13
WILLIAMS, Henry Leslie. 09/13
WILLIAMS, Robert Edward. 07/14
WILLIAMSON, Edward McDonald.
02/14
WILLIS, Thomas Charles. 01/14
WILSON, Mark John Crichton. 10/13
WILSON, Quentin Harcourt. 02/15
WINDMILL, Roy Stanley. 01/15
WITHERS, Michael Selby. 09/13
WITHERS GREEN, Timothy. 11/13
WOLLASTON, Barbara Kathleen. 02/15
WOOD, David Arthur. 01/14
WOOD, Edward Francis. 01/15
✠WOOD, Stanley Mark. 09/14
WOODHEAD, Christopher Godfrey.
01/15
WORSFOLD, John. 03/14
WORTHINGTON, George. 03/14
WRENBURY. 09/14
WRIGHT, Frederick John. 03/14
WRIGHT, Robert Charles. 06/14
WRIGHT, Robert Doogan. 03/15
✠WRIGHT, Royston Clifford. 02/14
YOUNG, Peter John. 06/14
YULE, Robert White. 04/14

MAPS

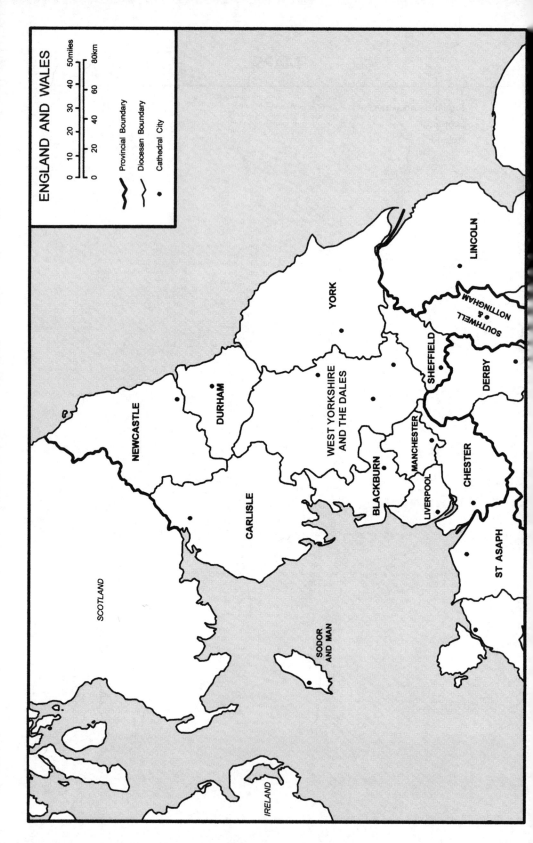

ENGLAND AND WALES

50miles
80km

Provincial Boundary
Diocesan Boundary
Cathedral City

SCOTLAND

NEWCASTLE

DURHAM

CARLISLE

YORK

WEST YORKSHIRE
AND THE DALES

BLACKBURN

MANCHESTER

LIVERPOOL

CHESTER

SHEFFIELD

LINCOLN

SOUTHWELL
&
NOTTINGHAM

DERBY

ST ASAPH

SODOR
AND MAN

IRELAND

NORWICH

ST EDMUNDSBURY AND IPSWICH

CANTERBURY

CHELMSFORD

ROCHESTER

ELY

CHICHESTER

ST ALBANS

LONDON

SOUTHWARK

GUILDFORD

PETERBOROUGH

WINCHESTER

LEICESTER

OXFORD

PORTSMOUTH

COVENTRY

BIRMINGHAM

GLOUCESTER

BRISTOL

SALISBURY

LICHFIELD

WORCESTER

HEREFORD

BATH AND WELLS

The Channel Islands are annexed to the Diocese of Winchester

MONMOUTH

SWANSEA AND BRECON

LLANDAFF

BANGOR

EXETER

ST DAVIDS

TRURO

The Isles of Scilly are included in the Diocese of Truro

SCOTLAND

| 0 | 10 | 20 | 30 | 40 | 50miles |
| 0 | 20 | 40 | 60 | 80km |

∿∿ Provincial Boundary

⌇ Diocesan Boundary

● Location of Cathedral

ABERDEEN
AND
ORKNEY

ABERDEEN
AND
ORKNEY

*SHETLAND
ISLANDS*

MORAY,

ROSS

AND

CAITHNESS

Inverness

ABERDEEN

AND

ORKNEY

Aberdeen ●

ARGYLL

AND

THE ISLES

● Oban

ST ANDREWS,

DUNKELD

AND

DUNBLANE

BRECHIN

● Dundee

Perth ●

Glasgow ●

Edinburgh ●

GLASGOW

AND

GALLOWAY

EDINBURGH

IRELAND

ENGLAND

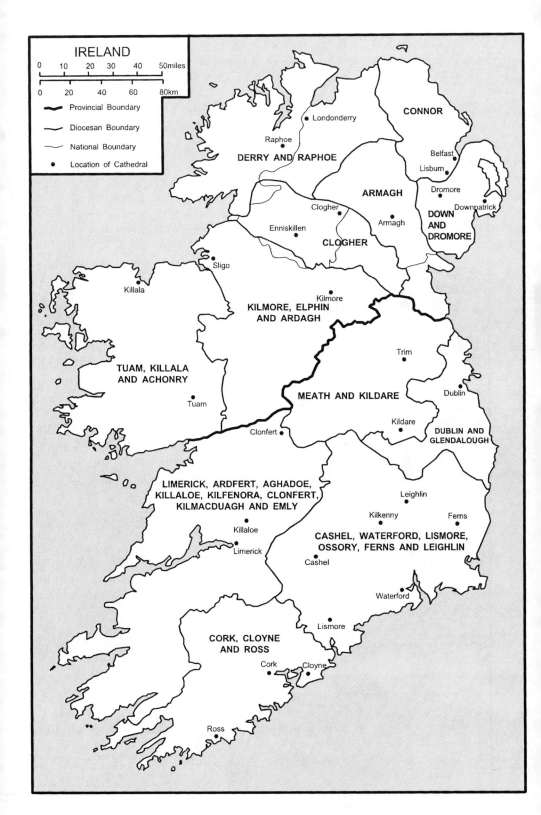

IRELAND

0 10 20 30 40 50miles

0 20 40 60 80km

━━━ Provincial Boundary

──── Diocesan Boundary

─── National Boundary

• Location of Cathedral

CONNOR

• Londonderry

Raphoe

DERRY AND RAPHOE

Belfast

Lisburn

ARMAGH

Dromore

Downpatrick

Clogher

Armagh

DOWN AND DROMORE

Enniskillen

CLOGHER

Sligo

Killala

Kilmore

KILMORE, ELPHIN AND ARDAGH

Trim

TUAM, KILLALA AND ACHONRY

Tuam

MEATH AND KILDARE

Dublin

Clonfert

Kildare

DUBLIN AND GLENDALOUGH

LIMERICK, ARDFERT, AGHADOE, KILLALOE, KILFENORA, CLONFERT, KILMACDUAGH AND EMLY

Leighlin

Kilkenny

Ferns

Killaloe

CASHEL, WATERFORD, LISMORE, OSSORY, FERNS AND LEIGHLIN

Limerick

Cashel

Waterford

Lismore

CORK, CLOYNE AND ROSS

Cork Cloyne

Ross